STRONG'S EXHAUSTIVE CONCORDANCE

HANDY EDITION

JAMES STRONG

GUARDIAN PRESS
Grand Rapids, Michigan 49509

 Published 1976.
Printed in the United States of America.

ISBN 0-89086-027-0

PUBLISHER'S PREFACE

STRONG'S IS THE STANDARD *Strong's Exhaustive Concordance,* first published in 1894, is without a doubt the most thorough word index ever to be published on any version of the English Bible. It has the distinction of being the only concordance listing practically every occurrence of every word in the King James (Authorized) Version of the Bible. In its original form *Strong's Exhaustive Concordance* was composed of five distinct sections: (1) the Main Concordance, unexcelled for completeness and usefulness, since it permits the reader to locate any verse in the Bible by looking up a key word in that verse; (2) the Appendix, which lists every occurrence of forty-seven words too common to be helpful in locating a verse of Scripture; (3) the Comparative Concordance, which shows the word changes made in the English Revised Version of 1881 and the American Standard Version of 1901 (these versions are rarely used today); (4) the Hebrew-Chaldee Dictionary, which is tied to the Main Concordance by a number code, listing every Hebrew and Chaldee word in the original Old Testament in its root form; and (5) the Greek Dictionary, which utilizes the same number code, listing every Greek word in the original New Testament in its root form. As valuable as each of these sections is, only the Main Concordance is used by most people who own *Strong's Exhaustive Concordance.*

All of the above-mentioned sections combine to make *Strong's Exhaustive Concordance* the largest work of its kind. But its largeness makes it too unwieldy and too expensive for most Bible readers. And yet there is a feature that makes *Strong's Exhaustive Concordance* justly famous and useful to many people, and that is its *Main Concordance.* The Main Concordance by itself fulfills James Strong's original goal: to compile an entirely new concordance that would be a permanent standard reference tool noted for *completeness, simplicity,* and *accuracy.* For the first time in its history, *Strong's Exhaustive Concordance,* has been made into "a concordance for the people" in this new *Handy Edition.*

STRONG'S — NOW IN AN UNCOMPLICATED EDITION The need for a handy, yet exhaustive, concordance has been expressed by many people for a number of years. Guardian Press determined to fulfill this need by publishing *Strong's Exhaustive Concordance* in an *economical* edition that everyone can afford, and in an *uncomplicated* form that anyone can use and enjoy. This purpose has been achieved in a remarkable way: by eliminating those sections that are rarely used by most Bible readers, *Strong's* has been changed from a gigantic (and somewhat complex) index into a handy reference tool. By publishing just the Main Concordance in this *Handy Edition,* Guardian Press has produced the most complete and easy-to-use concordance available for today's Bible reader. One may carry this handy concordance to Bible studies for quick reference or pack it in one's suitcase when traveling.

STRONG'S IS EASY TO USE *Strong's Exhaustive Concordance: Handy Edition* is unrivalled as the most complete of all the so-called "complete" or "unabridged" concordances. Every word is listed in alphabetical order just as it is spelled in the King James Version. In seeking to locate a verse quickly, follow this simple procedure. Choose an important or key word in that verse that you remember. Suppose, for example, your verse includes the word *walk.* Under the heading *walk* all the verses that include that word are listed in exact Biblical order according to book, chapter, and verse. Each reference is given as an extract, so that the most distinctive words that precede and follow the key word in its context are there to help you quickly find the verse. The key word is always abbreviated by its initial letter. Suppose your verse containing *walk* is Leviticus 26:3. This is how the reference extract reads: "If ye *w.* in my statutes, and keep. . . ." Also, at the boldface heading there are cross references to *walked, walkest, walketh,* and *walking.* These may be consulted should the verse in question prove to contain a different form of the same verb. If you are not able to locate your verse with the first key word, then try another word in the verse.

STUDY HINTS There are some basic rules of research that will greatly help you to get the most good out of *Strong's Exhaustive Concordance: Handy Edition*. As you become more familiar with God's Word and gain more proficiency in your study of the Bible, these will become almost second nature to you. *First,* choose the most distinctive and unusual word in the verse that you can remember. Let us take as an example the popular memory verse, "For God so loved the world, that He gave his only begotten Son, that whosoever believeth in him should not perish, but have everlasting life" (John 3:16). The most unusual words in this verse are "begotten", "everlasting", "perish", "whosoever", "only", and "life", in that order. Therefore, these words will be the ones most likely to help you locate the verse. *Secondly,* try to recall the historical setting of the verse you seek. (1) Is it from the Old Testament or the New Testament? (2) Is it history, law, poetry, wisdom literature, or prophecy? (3) Who is the speaker or narrator? (4) Does it speak of Christ's Person and Work in terms of the future or as accomplished fact? All such questions will help you to limit your research to only those references to the books, chapters, and verses of Scripture in which you are likely to find the verse you are seeking. *Thirdly,* use *Strong's* to locate other occurrences of a word as it appears in various contexts throughout the Bible. This will help you to gain insights into a word's true meaning and proper interpretation. A companion volume that will help you trace basic *ideas* through the Bible (when you want to study the synonyms of a word or an entire subject that embraces it) is *Nave's Topical Bible: Original Edition with Index.* Should the depth of your study consistently demand that you know which of the Hebrew and Greek words of the original Scriptures is behind a given word in the King James Version (and other English versions as well), then it will be time to invest in the original edition of *Strong's Exhaustive Concordance,* since it contains a number code and two special Hebrew-Chaldee and Greek dictionaries for this purpose. But for most of your Bible study needs, this *Strong's Exhaustive Concordance: Handy Edition* will prove to be a faithful companion.

THE COMPILER James Strong (1822-1894) was an American Biblical linguist of the first rank. He wrote numerous books on the Biblical languages and other Biblical subjects, and taught Hebrew and Greek at Drew Theological Seminary for twenty-five years. He also collaborated with John M'Clintock in the editing of the monumental *Cyclopaedia of Biblical, Theological, and Ecclesiastical Literature* (10 vols. plus 2 vols. of supplement, 1867-1887). James Strong's best and most widely used work is, by far, his *Exhaustive Concordance of the Bible,* which was completed and copyrighted in 1890 and issued in 1894, the year of his death.

ABBREVIATIONS OF THE NAMES OF THE BOOKS OF THE BIBLE

Ge = Genesis
Ex = Exodus
Le = Leviticus
Nu = Numbers
De = Deuteronomy
Jos = Joshua
J'g = Judges
Ru = Ruth
1Sa = I Samuel
2Sa = II Samuel
1Ki = I Kings
2Ki = II Kings
1Ch = I Chronicles
2Ch = II Chronicles
Ezr = Ezra
Ne = Nehemiah
Es = Esther

Job = Job
Ps = Psalms
Pr = Proverbs
Ec = Ecclesiastes
Ca = Canticles
Isa = Isaiah
Jer = Jeremiah
La = Lamentations
Eze = Ezekiel
Da = Daniel
Ho = Hosea
Joe = Joel
Am = Amos
Ob = Obadiah
Jon = Jonah
Mic = Micah
Na = Nahum

Hab = Habakkuk
Zep = Zephaniah
Hag = Haggai
Zec = Zechariah
Mal = Malachi
M't = Matthew
M'r = Mark
Lu = Luke
Joh = John
Ac = Acts
Ro = Romans
1Co = I Corinthians
2Co = II Corinthians
Ga = Galatians
Eph = Ephesians
Ph'p = Philippians
Col = Colossians

1Th = I Thessalonians
2Th = II Thessalonians
1Ti = I Timothy
2Ti = II Timothy
Tit = Titus
Ph'm = Philemon
Heb = Hebrews
Jas = James
1Pe = I Peter
2Pe = II Peter
1Jo = I John
2Jo = II John
3Jo = III John
Jude = Jude
Re = Revelation

MAIN CONCORDANCE.

A.

Aaron (*a'-ur-un*) See also AARONITES; AARON'S.
Ex 4:14 Is not A· the Levite thy brother?
27 the Lord said to A·, Go into the
28 Moses told A· all the words of the
29 Moses and A· went and gathered
30 A· spake all the words which the
5: 1 afterward Moses and A· went in,
4 Wherefore do ye, Moses and A·, let
20 they met Moses and A., who stood
6:13 Lord spake unto Moses and unto A·,
20 and she bare him A· and Moses:
23 A· took him Elisheba, daughter of
26 These are that A· and Moses, to
27 these are that Moses and A·.
7: 1 and A· thy brother shall be thy
2 and A· thy brother shall speak
6 Moses and A· did as the Lord
7 and A· fourscore and three years
8 Lord spake unto Moses and unto A·,
9 then thou shalt say unto A·, Take
10 And Moses and A· went in unto
10 and A· cast down his rod before
19 Lord spake unto Moses, Say unto A·,
20 Moses and A· did so, as the Lord
8: 5 Say unto A·, Stretch forth thine
6 A· stretched out his hand over the
8 Pharaoh called for Moses and A·,
12 Moses and A· went out from
16 Say unto A·, Stretch out thy rod,
17 for A· stretched out his hand with
25 Pharaoh called for Moses and for A·,
9: 8 Lord said unto Moses and unto A·,
27 sent, and called for Moses and A·,
10: 3 Moses and A· came in unto
8 Moses and A· were brought again
16 Pharaoh called for Moses and A· in
11:10 Moses and A· did all these wonders
12: 1 the Lord spake unto Moses and A·
28 Lord had commanded Moses and A·,
31 he called for Moses and A· by night,
43 the Lord said unto Moses and A·,
50 the Lord commanded Moses and A·,
15:20 the prophetess, the sister of A·,
16: 2 murmured against Moses and A·
6 Moses and A· said unto all the
9 Moses spake unto A·, Say unto all
10 as A· spake unto the whole
33 Moses said unto A·, Take a pot,
34 so A· laid it up before the
17:10 and Moses, A·, and Hur went up
12 and A· and Hur stayed up his
18:12 and A· came, and all the elders of
19:24 thou shalt come up, thou, and A·
24: 1 up unto the Lord thou and A·,
9 Then went up Moses, and A·,
14 and, behold, A· and Hur are with
27:21 A· and his sons shall order it from
28: 1 take thou unto thee A· thy
1 in the priest's office, even A·,
2 shalt make holy garments for A·
4 shall make holy garments for A·
12 and A· shall bear their names
29 A· shall bear the names of the
30 and A· shall bear the judgment of
35 And it shall be upon A· to minister
38 that A· may bear the iniquity of
41 thou shalt put them upon A· thy
43 they shall be upon A·, and upon
29: 4 A· and his sons thou shalt bring
5 and put upon A· the coat, and the
9 shalt gird them with girdles, A·
9 thou shalt consecrate A· and his
10, 15, 19 A· and his sons shall put their
20 upon the tip of the right ear of A·,
21 and sprinkle it upon A·, and upon
24 shalt put all in the hands of A·,
27 even of that which is for A·, and
29 the holy garments of A· shall be
32 A· and his sons shall eat the flesh
35 thus shalt thou do unto A·, and to
44 I will sanctify also both A· and
30: 7 A· shall burn thereon sweet
8 when A· lighteth the lamps at even,
10 A· shall make an atonement upon
19 For A· and his sons shall wash
30 thou shalt anoint A· and his sons,
31:10 and the holy garments for A· the
32: 1 themselves together unto A·, and
2 A· said unto them, Break off the
3 and brought them unto A·.
5 when A· saw it he built an altar
5 A· made proclamation, and said,
21 Moses said unto A·, What did this
Ex 32:22 A· said, Let not the anger of my
25 (for A· had made them naked unto
35 they made the calf, which A· made.
34:30 when A· and all the children of
31 A· and all the rulers of the
35:19 the holy garments for A·, the
38:21 by the hand of Ithamar, son to A·
39: 1 made the holy garments for A·;
27 fine linen of woven work for A·,
41 and the holy garments for A· the
40:12 thou shalt bring A· and his sons
13 thou shalt put upon A· the holy
31 Moses and A· and his sons washed
Le 1: 7 the sons of A· the priest shall put
3:13 the sons of A· shall sprinkle the
6: 9 Command A· and his sons, saying,
14 the sons of A· shall offer it before
16 the remainder thereof shall A·
18 males among the children of A·
20 This is the offering of A· and of
25 Speak unto A· and to his sons,
7:10 and dry, shall all the sons of A·
33 He among the sons of A·, that
34 and have given them unto A· the
35 the portion of the anointing of A·,
8: 2 Take A· and his sons with him,
6 Moses brought A· and his sons,
14, 18 A· and his sons laid their hands
22 the ram of consecration: and A·
30 and sprinkled it upon A·, and
30 sanctified A·, and his garments,
31 Moses said unto A·, and to his
31 as I commanded, saying, A· and
36 So A· and his sons did all things
9: 1 the eighth day, that Moses called A·
2 he said unto A·, Take thee a young
7 Moses said unto A·, Go into the
8 A· therefore went unto the altar,
9 the sons of A· brought the blood
21 And the right shoulder A· waved
22 A· lifted up his right hand toward
23 Moses and A· went into the
10: 1 Nadab and Abihu, the sons of A·,
3 Moses said unto A·, This is it that
3 And A· held his peace.
4 the sons of Uzziel the uncle of A·,
6 Moses said unto A· and unto
8 the Lord spake unto A·, saying,
12 Moses spake unto A· and unto
16 the sons of A· which were left
19 A· said unto Moses, Behold, this
11: 1 Lord spake unto Moses and to A·,
13: 1 the Lord spake unto Moses and A·,
2 then he shall be brought unto A·
14:33 Lord spake unto Moses and unto A·,
15: 1 Lord spake unto Moses and to A·,
16: 1 the death of the two sons of A·,
2 Speak unto A· thy brother, that
3 Thus shall A· come into the holy
6 A· shall offer his bullock of the sin
8 A· shall cast lots upon the two goats
9 A· shall bring the goat upon which
11 A· shall bring the bullock of the sin
21 A· shall lay both his hands upon the
23 A· shall come into the tabernacle
17: 2 Speak unto A·, and unto his sons,
21: 1 unto the priests the sons of A·, and
17 Speak unto A·, saying, Whosoever
21 hath a blemish of the seed of A· the
24 Moses told it unto A·, and to his
22: 2 Speak unto A· and to his sons, that
4 What man soever of the seed of A·
18 Speak unto A·, and to his sons, and
24: 3 Shall A· order it from the evening
Nu 1: 3 thou and A· shall number them by
17 Moses and A· took these men which
44 which Moses and A· numbered, and
2: 1 Lord spake unto Moses and unto A·,
3: 1 also are the generations of A· and
2, 3 are the names of the sons of A·
4 the priest's office in the sight of A·
6 and present them before A· the
9 thou shalt give the Levites unto A·
10 thou shalt appoint A· and his sons
32 Eleazar the son of A· the priest
38 shall be Moses, and A· and his sons
39 which Moses and A· numbered at
48 is to be redeemed, unto A· and to
51 that were redeemed unto A· and to
4: 1 Lord spake unto Moses and unto A·,
5 when the camp setteth forward, A·
15 when A· and his sons have made an
16 the office of Eleazar the son of A·
17 Lord spake unto Moses and unto A·,
19 A· and his sons shall go in, and
Nu 4:27 At the appointment of A· and his
28, 33 hand of Ithamar the son of A·
34 Moses and A· and the chief of the
37 which Moses and A· did number
41 whom Moses and A· did number
45 whom Moses and A· numbered
46 whom Moses and A· and the chief
6:23 Speak unto A· and unto his sons,
7: 8 the hand of Ithamar the son of A·
8: 2 Speak unto A·, and say unto him,
3 A· did so; he lighted the lamps
11 A· shall offer the Levites before the
13 shalt set the Levites before A·, and
19 given the Levites as a gift to A· and
20 And Moses, and A·, and all the
21 and A· offered them as an offering
21 A· made an atonement for them
22 of the congregation before A·, and
9: 6 came before Moses and before A·
10: 8 the sons of A·, the priests, shall
12: 1 And Miriam and A· spake against
4 suddenly unto Moses, and unto A·,
5 and called A· and Miriam:
10 and A· looked upon Miriam, and,
11 A· said unto Moses, Alas, my lord,
13:26 and came to Moses, and to A·, and
14: 2 against Moses and against A·: and
5 Moses and A· fell on their faces
26 Lord spake unto Moses and unto A·,
15:33 brought him unto Moses and A·,
16: 3 against Moses and against A·, and
11 and what is A·, that ye murmur
16 thou, and they, and A·, to morrow:
17 and A·, each of you his censer.
18 congregation with Moses and A·.
20 Lord spake unto Moses and unto A·,
37 Speak unto Eleazar the son of A·
40 which is not of the seed of A·, come
41, 42 against Moses and against A·,
43 And Moses and A· came before the
46 Moses said unto A·, Take a censer
47 A· took as Moses commanded, and
50 A· returned unto Moses unto the
17: 6 the rod of A· was among their rods.
8 the rod of A· for the house of Levi
18: 1 the Lord said unto A·, Thou and
8 the Lord spake unto A·, Behold, I
20 the Lord spake unto A·, Thou
28 the Lord's heave offering to A· the
19: 1 Lord spake unto Moses and unto A·,
20: 2 against Moses and against A·.
6 And Moses and A· went from the
8 thou and A· thy brother, and speak
10 And Moses and A· gathered the
12, 23 Lord spake unto Moses and A·,
24 A· shall be gathered unto his people
25 Take A· and Eleazar his son, and
26 strip A· of his garments, and put
26 and A· shall be gathered unto his
28 Moses stripped A· of his garments
28 and A· died there in the top of the
29 congregation saw that A· was dead,
29 they mourned for A· thirty days
25: 7 the son of Eleazar, the son of A· the
11 the son of A· the priest, hath turned
26: 1 and unto Eleazar the son of A· the
9 and against A· in the company of
59 and she bare unto Amram A· and
60 And unto A· was born Nadab and
64 a man of them whom Moses and A·
27:13 as A· thy brother was gathered.
33: 1 under the hand of Moses and A·.
38 A· the priest went up into mount
39 A· was a hundred and twenty and
De 9:20 Lord was very angry with A· to
20 and I prayed for A· also the
10: 6 there A· died, and there he was
32:50 as A· thy brother died in mount
Jos 21: 4 and the children of A· the priest,
10 Which the children of A·, being of
13 Thus they gave to the children of A·
19 All the cities of the children of A·,
24: 5 I sent Moses also and A·, and I
33 And Eleazar the son of A· died;
J'g 20:28 the son of A·, stood before it in
1Sa 12: 6 Lord that advanced Moses and A·,
8 then the Lord sent Moses and A·,
1Ch 6: 3 the children of Amram; A·, and
3 The sons also of A·; Nadab and
49 But A· and his sons offered upon
50 these are the sons of A·; Eleazar
54 of the sons of A·, of the families of
57 And to the sons of A· they gave the
15: 4 David assembled the children of A·,
23:13 of Amram; A· and Moses: and A·

1Ch 23:28 office was to wait on the sons of *A*·
32 and the charge of the sons of *A*·
24: 1 are the divisions of the sons of *A*·.
1 The sons of *A*·; Nadab and
19 to their manner, under *A*· their
31 their brethren the sons of *A*· in the
2Ch 13: 9 the sons of *A*·, and the Levites, and
10 unto the Lord, are the sons of *A*·,
26:18 but to the priests the sons of *A*·,
29:21 the priests the sons of *A*· to offer
31:19 Also of the sons of *A*· the priests,
35:14 because the priests the sons of *A*·
14 and for the priests the sons of *A*·.
Ezr 7: 5 Eleazar, the son of *A*· the chief
Ne 10:38 the priest the son of *A*· shall be
12:47 them unto the children of *A*·.
Ps 77:20 flock by the hand of Moses and *A*·.
99: 6 Moses and *A*· among his priests,
105:26 He sent Moses his servant; and *A*·
106:16 Moses also in the camp, and *A*·
115:10 O house of *A*·, trust in the Lord:
12 he will bless the house of *A*·.
118: 3 Let the house of *A*· now say, that
135:19 bless the Lord, O house of *A*·;
Mic 6: 4 I sent before thee Moses, *A*·, and
Lu 1: 5 wife was of the daughters of *A*·,
Ac 7:40 Saying unto *A*·, Make us gods to
Heb 5: 4 that is called of God, as was *A*·.
7:11 not be called after the order of *A*·?

Aaronites (*a'-ur-un-ites*)
1Ch 12:27 Jehoiada was the leader of the *A*·,
27:17 the son of Kemuel: of the *A*·,

Aaron's (*a'-ur-uns*)
Ex 6:25 Eleazar *A*· son took him one of the
7:12 but *A*· rod swallowed up their rods.
28: 1 Eleazar and Ithamar, *A*· sons.
3 that they may make *A*· garments
30 and they shall be upon *A*· heart,
38 And it shall be upon *A*· forehead
40 for *A*· sons thou shalt make coats,
29:26 of the ram of *A*· consecration,
28 it shall be *A*· and his sons' by a
Le 1: 5 the priests, *A*· sons, shall bring
8 the priests, *A*· sons, shall lay the
11 the priests, *A*· sons, shall sprinkle
2: 2 he shall bring it to *A*· sons the
3, 10 of the meat offering shall be *A*·
3: 2 *A*· sons the priests shall sprinkle
5 *A*· sons shall burn it on the altar
8 *A*· sons shall sprinkle the blood
7:31 but the breast shall be *A*· and his
8:12 the anointing oil upon *A*· head,
13 Moses brought *A*· sons, and put
23 put it upon the tip of *A*· right ear,
24 he brought *A*· sons, and Moses
27 he put all upon *A*· hands, and
9:12, 18 and *A*· sons presented unto him
24: 9 it shall be *A*· and his sons'; and
Nu 17: 3 thou shalt write *A*· name upon
10 Bring *A*· rod again before the
Ps 133: 2 upon the beard, even *A*· beard:
Heb 9: 4 pot that had manna, and *A*· rod

Abaddon (*ab-ad'-dun*)
Re 9:11 name in the Hebrew tongue is *A*·,

Abagtha (*ab-ag'-thah*)
Es 1:10 Bigtha, and *A*·, Zethar, and Carcas,

Abana (*ab-ay'-nah*)
2Ki 5:12 Are not *A*· and Pharpar, rivers of

Abarim (*ab'-ar-im*) See also IJE-ABARIM.
Nu 27:12 Get thee up into this mount *A*·,
33:47 pitched in the mountains of *A*·,
48 departed from the mountains of *A*·,
De 32:49 get thee up into this mountain *A*·,

abase See also ABASED; ABASING.
Job 40:11 every one that is proud, and *a*·
Isa 31: 4 nor *a*· himself for the noise of
Eze 21:26 is low, and *a*· him that is high.
Da 4:37 that walk in pride he is able to *a*·.

abased
M't 23:12 shall exalt himself shall be *a*·;
Lu 14:11 that exalteth himself shall be *a*·:
18:14 that exalteth himself shall be *a*·;
Ph'p 4:12 I know both how to be *a*·, and I

abasing
2Co 11: 7 *a*· myself that ye might be exalted,

abated
Ge 8: 3 and fifty days the waters were *a*·.
8 him to see if the waters were *a*·
11 nor knew that the waters were *a*·
Le 27:18 shall be *a*· from thy estimation
De 34: 7 not dim, nor his natural force *a*·.
J'g 8: 3 their anger was *a*· towards him

Abba (*ab'-bah*)
M'r 14:36 And he said, *A*·, Father, all things
Ro 8:15 of adoption, whereby we cry, *A*·,
Ga 4: 6 into your hearts, crying, *A*·, Father.

Abbas See BARABBAS.

Abda (*ab'-dah*)
1Ki 4: 6 and Adoniram the son of *A*·
Ne 11:17 and *A*· the son of Shammua,

Abdeel (*ab'-de-el*)
Jer 36:26 and Shelemiah the son of *A*·, to

Abdi (*ab'-di*)
1Ch 6:44 the son of Kishi, the son of *A*·,
2Ch 29:12 Kish the son of *A*·, and Azariah
Ezr 10:26 and Jehiel, and *A*·, and Jeremoth,

Abdiel (*ab'-de-el*)
1Ch 5:15 Ahi the son of *A*·, the son of Guni,

Abdon (*ab'-dun*)
Jos 21:30 Mishal with her suburbs, *A*· with
J'g 12:13 And after him *A*· the son of
15 And *A*· the son of Hillel the
1Ch 6:74 Moshal with her suburbs, and *A*·
8:23 Eliel and *A*·, and Zichri, and
30 his firstborn son *A*·, and Zur, and
9:36 *A*·, then Zur, and Kish, and Baal,
2Ch 34:20 and *A*· the son of Micah, and

Abed-nego (*ab-ed'-ne-go*)
Da 1: 7 Meshach; and to Azariah, of *A*·.
2:49 Shadrach, Meshach, and *A*·, over
3:12, 13, 14, 16, 19, 20, 22, 23, 26, 26, 28,
29, 30 Shadrach, Meshach, and *A*·

Abel (*a'-bel*) See also ABEL-BETH-MAACHAH; ABEL-MAIM; ABEL-MEHOLAH; ABEL-MIZRAIM; ABEL-SHITTIM.
Ge 4: 2 bare his brother *A*·. And *A*· was
4 And *A*·, he also brought of the
4 the Lord had respect unto *A*· and
8 Cain talked with *A*· his brother:
8 that Cain rose up against *A*· his
9 Lord said unto Cain, Where is *A*·
25 me another seed instead of *A*·,
1Sa 6:18 even unto the great stone of *A*·,
2Sa 20:14 all the tribes of Israel unto *A*·,
15 they came and besieged him in *A*·
18 They shall surely ask counsel at *A*·:
M't 23:35 from the blood of righteous *A*· unto
Lu 11:51 From the blood of *A*· unto the
Heb 11: 4 By faith *A*· offered unto God a more
12:24 better things than that of *A*·.

Abel-beth-maachah (*a''-bel-beth-ma'-a-kah*)
1Ki 15:20 and smote Ijon, and Dan, and *A*·,
2Ki 15:29 and took Ijon, and *A*·, and

Abel-maim (*a''-bel-ma'-im*)
2Ch 16: 4 they smote Ijon, and Dan, and *A*·,

Abel-meholah (*a''-bel-me-ho'-lah*) See also MEHOLATHITE.
J'g 7:22 and to the border of *A*·, unto
1Ki 4:12 from Beth-shean to *A*·, even unto
19:16 Elisha the son of Shaphat of *A*·

Abel-mizraim (*a''-bel-miz'-ra-im*)
Ge 50:11 the name of it was called *A*·, which

Abel-shittim (*a''-bel-shit'-tim*)
Nu 33:49 from Beth-jesimoth even unto *A*·

Abez (*a'-bez*)
Jos 19:20 And Rabbith, and Kishion, and *A*·,

abhor See also ABHORRED; ABHORREST; ABHORRETH; ABHORRING.
Le 26:11 and my soul shall not *a*· you.
15 if your soul *a*· my judgments, so
30 your idols, and my soul shall *a*· you.
44 neither will I *a*· them, to destroy
De 7:26 thou shalt utterly *a*· it; for it is a
23: 7 Thou shalt not *a*· an Edomite;
7 thou shalt not *a*· an Egyptian;
1Sa 27:12 his people Israel utterly to *a*· him
Job 9:31 and mine own clothes shall *a*· me.
30:10 They *a*· me, they flee far from me,
42: 6 Wherefore I *a*· myself, and repent
Ps 5: 6 the Lord will *a*· the bloody and
119:163 I hate and *a*· lying: but thy
Pr 24:24 the people curse, nations shall *a*·
Jer 14:21 Do not *a*· us, for thy name's sake,
Am 5:10 and they *a*· him that speaketh
6: 8 I *a*· the excellency of Jacob, and
Mic 3: 9 Israel, that *a*· judgment, and
Ro 12: 9 *A*· that which is evil; cleave to

abhorred
Ex 5:21 ye have made our savour to be *a*·
Le 20:23 things, and therefore I *a*· them.
26:43 because their soul *a*· my statutes.
De 32:19 when the Lord saw it, he *a*· them,
1Sa 2:17 men *a*· the offering of the Lord.
2Sa 16:21 shall hear that thou art *a*· of thy
1Ki 11:25 and he *a*· Israel, and reigned
Job 19:19 All my inward friends *a*· me:
Ps 22:24 he hath not despised nor *a*· the
78:59 was wroth, and greatly *a*· Israel:
89:38 thou hast cast off and *a*·, thou
106:40 that he *a*· his own inheritance.
Pro 22:14 he that is *a*· of the Lord shall fall
La 2: 7 he hath *a*· his sanctuary, he hath
Eze 16:25 hast made thy beauty to be *a*·,
Zec 11: 8 and their soul also *a*· me.

abhorrest
Isa 7:16 the land that thou *a*· shall be
Ro 2:22 that *a*· idols, dost thou commit

abhorreth
Job 33:20 So that his life *a*· bread, and
Ps 10: 3 the covetous, whom the Lord *a*·.
36: 4 that is not good; he *a*· not evil.
107:18 Their soul *a*· all manner of meat;
Isa 49: 7 to him whom the nation *a*·, to a

abhorring
Isa 66:24 they shall be an *a*· unto all flesh.

Abi (*a'-bi*) See also ABI-ALBON; ABI-EZER.
2Ki 18: 2 His mother's name also was *A*·,

Abia (*ab-i'-ah*) See also ABIAH; ABIJAH; ABIJAM.
1Ch 3:10 *A*· his son, Asa his son,
M't 1: 7 Roboam begat *A*·; and *A*· begat
Lu 1: 5 Zacharias, of the course of *A*·:

Abiah (*ab-i'-ah*) See also ABIA.
1Sa 8: 2 and the name of his second, *A*·:
1Ch 2:24 *A*· Hezron's wife bare him Ashur
6:28 the firstborn Vashni, and *A*·.
7: 8 Jerimoth, and *A*·, and Anathoth,

Abi-albon (*ab''-i-al'-bun*)
2Sa 23:31 *A*· the Arbathite, Azmaveth the

Abiasaph (*ab-i'-as-af*) See also EBI-ASAPH.
Ex 6:24 Assir, and Elkanah, and *A*·:

Abiathar (*ab-i'-uth-ur*) See also ABIATHAR'S.
1Sa 22:20 son of Ahitub, named *A*·, escaped,
21 And *A*· shewed David that Saul had
22 David said unto *A*·, I knew it that
23: 6 when *A*· the son of Ahimelech fled
9 and he said to *A*· the priest, Bring
30: 7 And David said to *A*· the priest,
7 And *A*· brought thither the ephod
2Sa 8:17 and Ahimelech the son of *A*·, were
15:24 *A*· went up, until all the people
27 and Jonathan the son of *A*·.
29 Zadok therefore and *A*· carried the
35 not there with thee Zadok and *A*·
35 thou shalt tell it to Zadok and *A*·
17:15 said Hushai unto Zadok and to *A*·
19:11 king David sent to Zadok and to *A*·
20:25 and Zadok and *A*· were the priests:
1Ki 1: 7 the son of Zeruiah, and with *A*·
19 sons of the king, and *A*· the priest,
25 the captains of the host, and *A*· the
42 Jonathan the son of *A*· the priest
2:22 for him, and for *A*· the priest,
26 unto *A*· the priest said the king,
27 Solomon thrust out *A*· from being
35 did the king put in the room of *A*·.
4: 4 and Zadok and *A*· were the priests:
1Ch 15:11 And David called for Zadok and *A*·
18:16 and Abimelech the son of *A*·, were
24: 6 priest, and Ahimelech the son of *A*·,
27:34 the son of Benaiah, and *A*·:
M'r 2:26 in the days of *A*· the high priest,

Abiathar's (*ab-i'-uth-urs*)
2Sa 15:36 Zadok's son, and Jonathan *A*·

Abib (*a'-bib*) See also TAL-ABIB.
Ex 13: 4 day came ye out in the month *A*·.
23:15 time appointed of the month *A*·;
34:18 in the time of the month *A*·: for in
18 the month *A*· thou camest out from
De 16: 1 Observe the month of *A*·, and keep
1 in the month of *A*· the Lord thy God

Abida (*ab'-id-ah*) See also ABIDAH.
1Ch 1:33 and Epher, and Henoch, and *A*·,

Abidah (*ab'-id-ah*) See also ABIDA.
Gen 25: 4 and Hanoch, and *A*·, and Eldaah.

Abidan (*ab'-id-an*)
Nu 1:11 Of Benjamin; *A*· the son of Gideoni.
2:22 of the sons of Benjamin shall be *A*·
7:60 On the ninth day *A*· the son of
65 offering of *A*· the son of Gideoni.
10:24 of the children Benjamin was *A*·

abide See also ABIDETH; ABIDING; ABODE.
Ge 19: 2 we will *a*· in the street all night.
22: 5 *A*· ye here with the ass;
24:55 Let the damsel *a*· with us a few
29:19 *a*· with me.
44:33 let thy servant *a*· instead of the lad
Ex 16:29 *a*· ye every man in his place,
Le 8:35 Therefore shall ye *a*· at the door of
19:13 shall not *a*· with thee all night
Nu 22: 5 they *a*· over against me:
31:19 *a*· without the camp seven days:
23 Every thing that may *a*· the fire,
35:25 he shall *a*· in it unto the death of
De 3:19 *a*· in your cities which I have
Jos 18: 5 Judah shall *a*· in their coast on
5 Joseph shall *a*· in their coasts on
Ru 2: 8 *a*· here fast by my maidens:
1Sa 1:22 and there *a*· for ever.
5: 7 God of Israel shall not *a*· with us:
19: 2 and *a*· in a secret place, and hide
22: 5 *A*· not in the hold;
23 *A*· thou with me, fear not:
30:21 whom they had made also to *a*· at
2Sa 11:11 the ark, and Israel, and Judah, *a*·
15:19 return to thy place, and *a*· with
16:18 with him will I *a*·.
1Ki 8:13 a settled place for thee to *a*· in
2Ch 25:19 *a*· now at home;
32:10 ye *a*· in the siege in Jerusalem?
Job 24:13 nor *a*· in the paths thereof.
38:40 and *a*· in the covert to lie in wait?
39: 9 to serve thee, or *a*· by thy crib?
Ps 15: 1 who shall *a*· in thy tabernacle?
61: 4 I will *a*· in thy tabernacle
7 He shall *a*· before God for ever:
91: 1 shall *a*· under the shadow
Pr 7:11 her feet *a*· not in her house:
19:23 he that hath it shall *a*· satisfied;
Ec 8:15 shall *a*· with him of his labour
Jer 10:10 the nations shall not be able to *a*·
42:10 If ye will still *a*· in this land,
49:18 no man shall *a*· there,
33 there shall no man *a*· there,
50:40 so shall no man *a*· there,
Ho 3: 3 Thou shalt *a*· for me many days;
4 children of Israel shall *a*· many
11: 6 the sword shall *a*· on his cities,
Joe 2:11 and who can *a*· it?
Mic 5: 4 and they shall *a*·:
Na 1: 6 who can *a*· in the fierceness of his
Mal 3: 2 may *a*· the day of his coming?
M't 10:11 and there *a*· till ye go thence.
M'r 6:10 *a*· till ye depart from that place.
Lu 9: 4 there *a*·, and thence depart.
19: 5 for to-day I must *a*· at thy house.
24:29 constrained him, saying, *A*· with
Joh 12:46 believeth on me should not *a*· in
14:16 that he may *a*· with you for ever;
15: 4 *A*· in me, and I in you.

Joh 15:4 except it a· in the vine;
4 no more can ye, except ye a· in me.
6 If a man a· not in me, he is cast
7 If ye a· in me, and my words a· in
10 ye shall a· in my love;
10 and a· in his love.
Ac 15:34 it pleased Silas to a· there still.
16:15 come into my house, and a· there.
20:23 and afflictions a· me.
27:31 Except these a· in the ship,
Ro 11:23 if they a· not still in unbelief,
1Co 3:14 any man's work a· which he hath
7: 8 if they a· even as I.
20 every man a· in the same calling
24 every man,....therein a· with God.
40 she is happier if she so a·,
16: 6 And it may be that I will a·, yea,
Ph'p 1:24 to a· in the flesh is more needful
25 know that I shall a· and continue
1Ti 1: 3 to a· still at Ephesus,
1Jo 2:24 Let that therefore a· in you,
27 ye shall a· in him.
28 little children, a· in him;

abideth
Nu 31:23 all that a· not the fire ye shall
2Sa 16: 3 he a· at Jerusalem:
Job 39:28 She dwelleth and a· on the rock,
Ps 49:12 man being in honour a· not:
55:19 even he that a· of old.
119:90 established the earth, and it a·.
125: 1 cannot be removed, but a· for ever.
Pr 15:31 reproof of life a· among the wise.
Ec 1: 4 the earth a· for ever.
Jer 21: 9 He that a· in this city shall die
Joh 3:36 the wrath of God a· on him.
8:35 the servant a· not in the house for
35 but the Son a· ever.
12:24 ground and die, it a· alone:
34 of the law that Christ a· for ever:
15: 5 He that a· in me, and I in him,
1Co 13:13 now a· faith, hope, charity,
2Ti 2:13 he a· faithful: he cannot deny
Heb 7: 3 a· a priest continually.
1Pe 1:23 which liveth and a· for ever.
1Jo 2: 6 He that saith he a· in him
10 a· in the light,
14 the word of God a· in you,
17 doeth the will of God a· for ever.
27 received of him a· in you,
3: 6 Whosoever a· in him sinneth not:
14 He that loveth not his brother a· in
24 hereby we know that he a· in us,
2Jo 1: 9 a· not in the doctrine of Christ,
9 He that a· in the doctrine

abiding
Nu 24: 2 he saw Israel a· in his tents
J'g 16: 9 a· with her in the chamber.
12 a· in the chamber.
1Sa 26:19 driven me out this day from a·
1Ch 29:15 there is none a·.
Lu 2: 8 shepherds a· in the field,
Joh 5:38 ye have not his word a· in you:
Ac 16:12 were in that city a· certain days.
1Jo 3:15 no murderer hath eternal life a·

Abiel (a'-be-el)
1Sa 9: 1 name was Kish, the son of A·,
14:51 father of Abner was the son of A·.
1Ch 11:32 Hurai of the brooks of Gaash, A·.

Abiezer[1] **[Abi-ezer**[2] **in J'g 6:34; 8:2; 1Ch 11:28]** (ab-e-e'-zur) See also ABI-EZRITE; JEEZER.
Jos 17: 2 for the children of A·[1], and for the
J'g 6:34 and A·[2] was gathered after him.
8: 2 better than the vintage of A·[2]?
2Sa 23:27 A·[1] the Anethothite, Mebunnai the
1Ch 7:18 Hammoleketh bare Ishod, and A·[1],
11:28 Ikkesh the Tekoite, A·[2] the Antothite
27:12 captain for the ninth month was A·[1]

Abi-ezrite (ab-e-ez'-rite) See also ABI-EZRITES.
J'g 6:11 that pertained unto Joash the A·.

Abi-ezrites (ab-e-ez'-rites)
J'g 6:24 it is yet in Ophrah of the A·.
8:32 his father, in Ophrah of the A·.

Abigail (ab'-e-gul)
1Sa 25: 3 Nabal: and the name of his wife A·:
14 But one of the young men told A·,
18 Then A· made haste, and took two
23 when A· saw David, she hasted,
32 David said to A·, Blessed be the Lord
36 And A· came to Nabal; and, behold,
39 David sent and communed with A·,
40 servants of David were come to A·
42 And A· hasted, and arose, and rode
27: 3 A· the Carmelitess, Nabal's wife.
30: 5 A· the wife of Nabal the Carmelite.
2Sa 2: 2 and A· Nabal's wife the Carmelite.
3: 3 A· the wife of Nabal the Carmelite;
17:25 in to A· the daughter of Nahash,
1Ch 2:16 Whose sisters were Zeruiah, and A·.
17 and A· bare Amasa: and the father
3: 1 the second Daniel, of A· the

Abihail (ab-e-ha'-il)
Nu 3:35 of Merari was Zuriel the son of A·:
1Ch 2:29 name of the wife of Abishur was A·,
5:14 These are the children of A· the son
2Ch 11:18 and A· the daughter of Eliab the
Es 2:15 the daughter of A· the uncle of
9:29 Esther the queen, the daughter of A·,

Abihu (a-bi'-hew)
Ex 6:23 and she bare him Nadab and A·,
24: 1 thou, and Aaron, Nadab, and A·,
9 Moses, and Aaron, Nadab, and A·,
28: 1 office, even Aaron, Nadab and A·,
Le 10: 1 Nadab and A·, the sons of Aaron,
Nu 3: 2 Nadab the firstborn, and A·,
4 Nadab and A· died before the Lord,
26:60 unto Aaron was born Nadab, and A·,
61 And Nadab and A· died, when they
1Ch 6: 3 sons also of Aaron; Nadab, and A·,
24: 1 The sons of Aaron; Nadab, and A·,
2 But Nadab and A· died before their

Abihud (a-bi'-hud)
1Ch 8: 3 Addar, and Gera, and A·,

Abijah (a-bi'-jah) See also ABIA; ABIJAM.
1Ki 14: 1 At that time A· the son of Jeroboam
1Ch 24:10 seventh to Hakkoz, the eighth to A·,
2Ch 11:20 which bare him A·, and Attai, and
22 Rehoboam made A· the son of
12:16 and A· his son reigned in his stead.
13: 1 year of king Jeroboam began A· to
2 was war between A· and Jeroboam.
3 And A· set the battle in array with
4 A· stood up upon mount Zemaraim,
15 Jeroboam and all Israel before A·
17 And A· and his people slew them
19 And A· pursued after Jeroboam,
20 strength again in the days of A·:
21 But A· waxed mighty, and married
22 rest of the acts of A·, and his ways,
14: 1 So A· slept with his fathers,
29: 1 And his mother's name was A·,
Ne 10: 7 Meshullam, A·, Mijamin,
12: 4 Iddo, Ginnetho, A·,
17 Of A·, Zichri; of Miniamin, of

Abijam (a-bi'-jum) See also ABIJAH.
1Ki 14:31 And A· his son reigned in his stead.
15: 1 reigned A· over Judah.
7 the rest of the acts of A·, and all
7 was war between A· and Jeroboam.
8 And A· slept with his fathers; and

Abilene (ab-i-le'-ne)
Lu 3: 1 Lysanias the tetrarch of A·,

ability
Le 27: 8 according to his a· that vowed
Ezr 2:69 They gave after their a·
Ne 5: 8 We after our a· have redeemed
Da 1: 4 such as had a· in them
M't 25:15 according to his several a·;
Ac 11:29 every man according to his a·,
1Pe 4:11 as of the a· which God giveth;

Abimael (a-bim'-ah-el)
Ge 10:28 And Obal, and A·, and Sheba,
1Ch 1:22 And Ebal, and A·, and Sheba,

Abimelech (a-bim'-e-lek) See also ABIMELECH'S; AHIMELECH.
Ge 20: 2 and A· king of Gerar sent, and took
3 But God came to A· in a dream
4 But A· had not come near her:
8 A· rose early in the morning,
9 Then A· called Abraham, and said
10 A· said unto Abraham, What sawest
14 And A· took sheep, and oxen, and
15 A· said, Behold, my land is before
17 and God healed A·, and his wife,
18 all the wombs of the house of A·,
21:22 that A· and Phichol the chief captain
25 And Abraham reproved A· because
26 A· said, I wot not who hath done
27 and oxen, and gave them unto A·;
29 A· said unto Abraham, What mean
32 then A· rose up, and Phichol the
26: 1 And Isaac went unto A· king of the
8 A· king of the Philistines looked
9 And A· called Isaac, and said,
10 A· said, What is this thou hast done
11 A· charged all his people, saying,
16 And A· said unto Isaac, Go from us;
26 Then A· went to him from Gerar,
J'g 8:31 a son, whose name he called A·.
9: 1 And A· the son of Jerubbaal went
3 their hearts inclined to follow A·;
4 A· hired vain and light persons,
6 and went, and made A· king,
16 in that ye have made A· king,
18 made A·, the son of his maidservant,
19 then rejoice ye in A·, and let him
20 But if not, let fire come out from A·,
20 the house of Millo, and devour A·.
21 and dwelt there, for fear of A· his
22 When A· had reigned three years
23 God sent an evil spirit between A·
23 dealt treacherously with A·:
24 A· their brother, which slew them;
25 way by them: and it was told A·.
27 did eat and drink, and cursed A·.
28 Who is A·, and who is Shechem,
29 my hand! then would I remove A·.
29 he said to A·, Increase thine army,
31 he sent messengers unto A· privily,
34 And A· rose up, and all the people
35 And A· rose up, and the people that
38 Who is A·, that we should serve him?
39 of Shechem, and fought with A·.
40 A· chased him, and he fled before
41 And A· dwelt at Arumah: and Zebul
42 out into the field; and they told A·.
44 A·, and the company that was with
45 And A· fought against the city all
47 And it was told A·, that all the men
48 A· gat him up to mount Zalmon,
48 and A· took an axe in his hand,
49 and followed A·, and put them to the
50 went A· to Thebez, and encamped
52 And A· came unto the tower,
55 men of Israel saw that A· was dead,
56 God rendered the wickedness of A·,
10: 1 after A· there arose to defend Israel
2Sa 11:21 smote A· the son of Jerubbesheth?
1Ch 18:16 and A· the son of Abiathar,
Ps 34:*title* changed his behaviour before A·;

Abimelech's (a-bim'-e-leks)
Ge 21:25 A· servants had violently taken
J'g 9:53 a piece of a millstone upon A· head,

Abinadab (a-bin'-ah-dab)
1Sa 7: 1 and brought it into the house of A·
16: 8 Jesse called A·, and made him pass
17:13 and next unto him A·, and the third
31: 2 Philistines slew Jonathan, and A·,
2Sa 6: 3 brought it out of the house of A·
3 the sons of A·, drave the new cart.
4 brought it out of the house of A·
1Ki 4:11 son of A·, in all the region of Dor;
1Ch 2:13 begat his firstborn Eliab, and A· the
8:33, 9:39 and Malchishua, and A·,
10: 2 Philistines slew Jonathan, and A·,
13: 7 in a new cart out of the house of A·:

Abinoam (a-bin'-o-am)
J'g 4: 6 sent and called Barak the son of A·
12 that Barak the son of A· was gone
5: 1 Deborah and Barak the son of A·
12 thy captivity captive, thou son of A·.

Abiram (a-bi'-rum)
Nu 16: 1 Dathan and A·, the sons of Eliab,
12 Moses sent to call Dathan and A·,
24 tabernacle of Korah, Dathan, and A·.
25 up and went unto Dathan and A·;
27 tabernacle of Korah, Dathan, and A·,
27 Dathan and A· came out, and stood
26: 9 Eliab; Nemuel, and Dathan, and A·.
9 Dathan and A·, which were famous
De 11: 6 what he did unto Dathan and A·,
1Ki 16:34 he laid the foundations thereof in A·
Ps 106:17 and covered the company of A·.

Abishag (ab'-e-shag)
1Ki 1: 3 and found A· a Shunammite,
15 and A· the Shunammite ministered
2:17 give me A· the Shunammite to wife.
21 she said, Let A· the Shunammite be
22 dost thou ask A· the Shunammite

Abishai (ab'-e-shahee)
1Sa 26: 6 and to A· the son of Zeruiah,
6 A· said, I will go down with thee.
7 So David and A· came to the people
8 said A· to David, God hath delivered
9 David said to A·, Destroy him not:
2Sa 2:18 sons of Zeruiah there, Joab, and A·,
24 also and A· pursued after Abner:
3:30 Joab and A· his brother slew Abner,
10:10 he delivered into the hand of A·
14 then fled they also before A·,
16: 9 Then said A· the son of Zeruiah unto
11 David said to A·, and to all his
18: 2 a third part under the hand of A·
5 the king commanded Joab and A·
12 hearing the king charged thee and A·
19:21 But A· the son of Zeruiah answered
20: 6 David said to A·, Now shall Sheba
10 So Joab and A· his brother pursued
21:17 A· the son of Zeruiah succoured him,
23:18 And A·, the brother of Joab, the son
1Ch 2:16 the sons of Zeruiah; A·, and Joab,
11:20 A· the brother of Joab, he was chief
18:12 A· the son of Zeruiah slew of the
19:11 he delivered unto the hand of A·
15 likewise fled before A· his brother,

Abishalom (a-bish'-ah-lum) See also ABSALOM.
1Ki 15: 2, 10 Maachah, the daughter of A·.

Abishua (a-bish'-u-ah)
1Ch 6: 4 begat Phinehas, Phinehas begat A·,
5 A· begat Bukki, and Bukki begat
50 Phinehas his son, A· his son,
8: 4 And A·, and Naaman, and Ahoah,
Ezr 7: 5 The son of A·, the son of Phinehas,

Abishur (ab'-e-shur)
1Ch 2:28 the sons of Shammai; Nadab and A·
29 name of the wife of A· was Abihail,

Abital (ab'-e-tal)
2Sa 3: 4 the fifth, Shephatiah the son of A·;
1Ch 3: 3 The fifth, Shephatiah of A·:

Abitub (ab'-e-tub)
1Ch 8:11 of Hushim he begat A·, and Elpaal.

Abiud (a-bi'-ud)
M't 1:13 Zorobabel begat A·; and A· begat

abjects
Ps 35:15 a· gathered themselves together

able See also BLAMEABLE; CHANGEABLE; CHARGEABLE; COMFORTABLE; COMPARABLE; CONFORMABLE; CORRUPTIBLE; DAMNABLE; DECEIVABLENESS; DELECTABLE; DESIRABLE; DETESTABLE; DURABLE; ENABLED; FAVOURABLE; FORCIBLE; HONOURABLE; INCORRUPTIBLE; INCREDIBLE; INCURABLE; INEXCUSABLE; INFALLIBLE; LAMENTABLE; MISERABLE; MOVEABLE; PEACEABLE; POSSIBLE; PROFITABLE; QUENCHABLE; REBUKABLE; REPROVABLE; REASONABLE; SATIABLE; SEARCHABLE; VARIABLENESS.
Ge 13: 6 the land was not a· to bear them,
15: 5 if thou be a· to number them:
33:14 and the children be a· to endure,
Ex 10: 5 one cannot be a· to see the earth:
18:18 thou art not a· to perform it
21 provide out of all the people a·
23 then thou shalt be a· to endure,
25 Moses chose a· men out of all
40:35 Moses was not a· to enter into the
Le 5: 7 be not a· to bring a lamb,
11 he be not a·
12: 8 be not a· to bring a lamb,
14:22 such as he is a· to get;

Le 31 such as he is a' to get, the one for
32 whose hand is not a' to get that
25:26 himself be a' to redeem it;
28 if he be not a' to restore it 4672,
49 he be a', he may redeem himself.
Nu 1: 3 all that are a' to go forth to war
20, 22, 24, 26, 28, 30, 32, 34, 36, 38, 40,
42, 45 all that were a' to go forth to war
11:14 I am not a' to bear all this people
13:30 we are well a' to overcome it.
31 not a' to go up against the people;
14:16 the Lord was not a' to bring this
22:11 I shall be a' to overcome them,
37 am I not a' indeed to promote thee
26: 2 all that are a' to go to war
De 1: 9 am not a' to bear you myself alone:
7:24 no man be a' to stand before thee,
9:28 Lord was not a' to bring them
11:25 no man be a' to stand before you:
14:24 thou art not a' to carry it;
16:17 man shall give as he is a', 4979,
Jos 1: 5 There shall not any man be a' to
14:12 I shall be a' to drive them out,
23: 9 hath been a' to stand before you
J'g 8: 3 what was I a' to do
1Sa 6:20 Who is a' to stand before this holy
17: 9 If he be a' to fight with me,
33 Thou art not a' to go against this
1Ki 3: 9 a' to judge this thy so great people?
9:21 children of Israel also were not a'
2Ki 3:21 all that were a' to put on armour,
18:23 thou be a' on thy part to set riders
29 he shall not be a' to deliver you
1Ch 5:18 men a' to bear buckler and sword,
9:13 a' men for the work of the service
26: 8 a' men for strength for the service,
29:14 that we should be a' to offer
2Ch 2: 6 is a' to build him an house,
7: 7 a' to receive the burnt offerings,
20: 6 that none is a' to withstand thee?
37 they were not a' to go to Tarshish.
25: 5 choice men, a' to go forth to war,
9 Lord is a' to give thee much more
32:13 any ways a' to deliver their lands
14 your God should be a' to deliver
15 was a' to deliver his people
Ezr 10:13 we are not a' to stand without,
Ne 4:10 we are not a' to build the wall.
Job 41:10 who then is a' to stand before me?
Ps 18:38 that they were not a' to rise:
21:11 they are not a' to perform.
36:12 shall not be a' to rise.
40:12 I am not a' to look up;
Pro 27: 4 who is a' to stand before envy?
Ec 8:17 yet shall he not be a' to find it.
Isa 36: 8 thou be a' on thy part to set riders
14 he shall not be a' to deliver you.
47:11 thou shalt not be a' to put it off:
12 if so be thou shalt be a' to profit,
Jer 10:10 the nations shall not be a' to abide
11:11 they shall not be a' to escape;
49:10 he shall not be a' to hide himself:
La 1:14 I am not a' to rise up.
Eze 7:19 their gold shall not be a' to deliver
33:12 shall the righteous be a' to live
46: 5 as he shall be a' to give,
11 the lambs as he is a' to give,
Da 2:26 Art thou a' to make known unto
3:17 God whom we serve is a' to deliver
4:18 not a' to make known unto me the
18 but thou art a'; for the spirit of
37 walk in pride he is a' to abase.
6:20 a' to deliver thee from the lions?
Am 7:10 land is not a' to bear all his words.
Zep 1:18 nor their gold shall be a' to deliver
M't 3: 9 God is a' of these stones to raise
9:28 Believe ye that I am a' to do this?
10:28 but are not a' to kill the soul:
28 fear him which is a' to destroy
19:12 He that is a' to receive it, let him
20:22 Are ye a' to drink of the cup that I
22 They say unto him, We are a'.
22:46 no man was a' to answer him
26:61 am a' to destroy the temple of God,
M'r 4:33 as they were a' to hear
Lu 1:20 shalt be dumb, and not a' to speak,
3: 8 God is a' of these stones to raise
12:26 ye then be not a' to do that thing
13:24 to enter in, and shall not be a'.
14:29 is not a' to finish it, all that behold
30 began to build, and was not a' to
31 whether he be a' with ten
21:15 not be a' to gainsay nor resist.
Joh 10:29 no man is a' to pluck them out of
21: 6 now they were not a' to draw it
Ac 6:10 were not a' to resist the wisdom
15:10 neither our fathers nor we were a'
20:32 the word of his grace, which is a'
25: 5 which among you are a', go down
Ro 4:21 what he had promised, he was a'
8:39 shall be a' to separate us from the
11:23 God is a' to graff them in again.
14: 4 for God is a' to make him stand.
15:14 a' also to admonish one another.
1Co 3: 2 hitherto ye were not a' to bear it,
2 neither yet now are ye a'.
6: 5 not one that shall be a' to judge
10:13 to be tempted above that ye are a';
13 that ye may be a' to bear it.
2Co 1: 4 may be a' to comfort them which
3: 6 hath made us a' ministers of the
9: 8 God is a' to make all grace abound
Eph 3:18 a' to comprehend with all saints
20 Now unto him that is a' to do
6:11 that ye may be a' to stand against
13 that ye may be a' to withstand in
Eph 6:16 ye shall be a' to quench all the
Ph'p 3:21 he is a' even to subdue all things
2Ti 1:12 persuaded that he is a' to keep
2: 2 shall be a' to teach others also.
3: 7 never a' to come to the knowledge
15 scriptures, which are a' to make
Tit 1: 9 he may be a' by sound doctrine
Heb 2:18 he is a' to succour them that are
5: 7 was a' to save him from death,
7:25 Wherefore he is a' also to save
11:19 that God was a' to raise him up,
Jas 1:21 which is a' to save your souls.
3: 2 a' also to bridle the whole body.
4:12 lawgiver, who is a' to save and to
2Pe 1:15 ye may be a' after my decease to
Jude 24 Now unto him that is a' to keep
Re 5: 3 was a' to open the book, neither
6:17 who shall be a' to stand?
13: 4 who is a' to make war with him?
15: 8 was a' to enter into the temple,

ably See ABOMINABLY; BLAMEABLY.

Abner (*ab'-nur*) See also ABNER'S.
1Sa 14:50 of the captain of his host was A',
51 Ner the father of A' was the son of
17:55 said unto A', the captain of the host,
55 A', whose son is this youth?
55 A' said, As thy soul liveth, O king,
57 A' took him, and brought him
20:25 and Jonathan arose, and A' sat by
26: 5 and A' the son of Ner, the captain
7 A' and the people lay round about
14 David cried to the people, and to A'
14 saying, Answerest thou not, A'?
14 A' answered and said, Who art thou
15 David said to A', Art not thou a
2Sa 2: 8 A' the son of Ner, captain of Saul's
12 A' the son of Ner, and the servants
14 A' said to Joab, Let the young men
17 A' was beaten, and the men of Israel,
19 And Asahel pursued after A'; and
19 nor to the left from following A'.
20 A' looked behind him, and said,
21 And A' said to him, Turn thee aside
22 A' said again to Asahel, Turn thee
23 A' with the hinder end of the spear
24 also and Abishai pursued after A':
25 themselves together after A',
26 Then A' called to Joab, and said,
29 A' and his men walked all that
30 Joab returned from following A':
3: 6 that A' made himself strong for the
7 Ishbosheth said to A', Wherefore
8 Then was A' very wroth for the
9 So do God to A', and more also,
11 And he could not answer A' a word
12 And A' sent messengers to David
16 Then said A' unto him, Go, return.
17 And A' had communication with
19 And A' also spake in the ears of
19 A' went also to speak in the ears of
20 So A' came to David to Hebron,
20 David made A' and the men that
21 A' said unto David, I will arise and
21 David sent A' away; and he went in
22 A' was not with David in Hebron;
23 A' the son of Ner came to the king,
24 behold, A' came unto thee; why is
25 Thou knowest A' the son of Ner,
26 he sent messengers after A', which
27 when A' was returned to Hebron,
28 for ever from the blood of A' the
30 and Abishai his brother slew A',
31 sackcloth, and mourn before A'.
32 And they buried A' in Hebron: and
32 voice, and wept at the grave of A';
33 the king lamented over A', and said,
33 Died A' as a fool dieth?
37 that it was not of the king to slay A'
4: 1 Saul's son heard that A' was dead
12 and buried it in the sepulchre of A'
1Ki 2: 5 unto A' the son of Ner, and unto
32 to wit, A' the son of Ner, captain of
1Ch 26:28 Saul the son of Kish, and A' the son
27:21 of Benjamin, Jaasiel the son of A':

Abner's (*ab'-nurs*)
2Sa 2:31 of Benjamin, and of A' men, so that

aboard
Ac 21: 2 we went a', and set forth.

abode See also ABODEST.
Ge 29:14 a' with him the space of a month,
49:24 But his bow a' in strength, and
Ex 24:16 glory of the Lord a' upon mount
40:35 because the cloud a' thereon,
Nu 9:17 the place where the cloud a', there
18 as long as the cloud a' upon the
20 a' in their tents, and according
21 when the cloud a' from even
22 the children of Israel a' in their
11:35 unto Hazeroth; and a' at
20: 1 and the people a' in Kadesh;
22: 8 princes of Moab a' with Balaam.
25: 1 And Israel a' in Shittim, and the
De 1:46 So ye a' in Kadesh many days,
46 according unto the days that ye a'
3:29 So we a' in the valley over against
9: 9 then I a' in the mount forty days
Jos 2:22 and a' there three days, until the
5: 8 they a' in their places in the camp,
8: 9 and a' between Beth-el and Ai,
J'g 5:17 Gilead a' beyond Jordan:
17 and a' in his breaches.
11:17 and Israel a' in Kadesh.
19: 4 and he a' with him three days:
20:47 a' in the rock Rimmon four months.
J'g 21: 2 and a' there till even before God,
1Sa 1:23 the woman a', and gave her son
7: 2 while the ark a' in Kirjath-jearim,
13:16 a' in Gibeah of Benjamin:
22: 6 Saul a' in Gibeah under a tree
23:14 David a' in the wilderness
18 and David a' in the wood,
25 and a' in the wilderness of Maon.
25:13 two hundred a' by the stuff.
26: 3 David a' in the wilderness, and he
30:10 for two hundred a' behind, which
2Sa 1: 1 David had a' two days in Ziklag;
11:12 Uriah a' in Jerusalem that day,
15: 8 while I a' in Geshur in Syria,
1Ki 17:19 him up into a loft, where he a',
2Ki 19:27 I know thy a', and thy going out,
Ezr 8:15 there a' we in tents three days:
32 came to Jerusalem, and a' there
Isa 37:28 I know thy a', and thy going out,
Jer 38:28 So Jeremiah a' in the court of the
M't 17:22 while they a' in Galilee, Jesus
Lu 1:56 a' with her about three months,
8:27 a' in any house, but in the tombs,
21:37 he went out, and a' in the mount
Joh 1:32 like a dove, and it a' upon him.
39 saw where he dwelt, and a' with
4:40 he a' there two days.
7: 9 he a' still in Galilee.
8:44 a' not in the truth, because there
10:40 and there he a'.
11: 6 a' two days still in the same place
14:23 and make our a' with him.
Ac 1:13 where a' both Peter, and James,
12:19 Judæa to Cæsarea, and there a'.
14: 3 Long time therefore a' they
28 a' long time with the disciples.
17:14 Silas and Timotheus a' there still.
18: 3 he a' with them, and wrought:
20: 3 And there a' three months.
6 where we a' seven days.
21: 7 saluted the brethren, and a' with
8 one of the seven, and a' with him.
Ga 1:18 see Peter, and a' with him fifteen
2Ti 4:20 Erastus a' at Corinth:

abodest
J'g 5:16 a' thou among the sheepfolds, to

abolish See also ABOLISHED.
Isa 2:18 the idols he shall utterly a'.

abolished
Isa 51: 6 my righteousness shall not be a'.
Eze 6: 6 and your works may be a'.
2Co 3:13 to the end of that which is a':
Eph 2:15 Having a' in his flesh the enmity,
2Ti 1:10 Christ, who hath a' death,

abominable
Le 7:21 or any a' unclean thing,
11:43 ye shall not make yourselves a'
18:30 not any one of these a' customs,
19: 7 it is a'; it shall not be accepted.
20:25 ye shall not make your souls a'
De 14: 3 Thou shalt not eat any a' thing.
1Ch 21: 6 the king's word was a' to Joab.
2Ch 15: 8 put away the a' idols out of all
Job 15:16 How much more a' and filthy is
Ps 14: 1 they have done a' works,
53: 1 and have done a' iniquity:
Isa 14:19 thy grave like an a' branch,
65: 4 of a' things is in their vessels;
Jer 16:18 detestable and a' things.
44: 4 do not this a' thing that I hate.
Eze 4:14 neither came there a' flesh into
8:10 and a' beasts, and all the idols
16:52 thou hast committed more a' than
Mic 6:10 the scant measure that is a'?
Na 3: 6 I will cast a' filth upon thee,
Tit 1:16 him, being a', and disobedient,
1Pe 4: 3 banquetings, and a' idolatries:
Re 21: 8 unbelieving, and the a', and

abominably
1Ki 21:26 he did very a' in following idols,

abomination See also ABOMINATIONS.
Ge 43:32 is an a' unto the Egyptians.
46:34 every shepherd is an a' unto the
Ex 8:26, 26 the a' of the Egyptians
Le 7:18 it shall be an a',
11:10 they shall be an a' unto you:
11 be even an a' unto you;
11 ye shall have their carcases in a'.
12 that shall be an a'
13 shall have in a' among the fowls;
13 they are an a':
20 an a' unto you.
23 four feet, shall be an a' unto you.
41 the earth shall be an a';
42 shall not eat; for they are an a'.
18:22 with womankind: it is a'.
20:13 of them have committed an a':
De 7:25 for it is an a' to the Lord thy God.
26 shalt thou bring an a' into thine
12:31 for every a' to the Lord, which he
13:14 such a' is wrought among you;
17: 1 an a' unto the Lord
4 such a' is wrought in Israel;
18:12 these things are an a' unto the
22: 5 all that do so are an a' unto the
23:18 both these are an a' unto the Lord
24: 4 that is a' before the Lord:
25:16 unrighteously, are an a' unto
27:15 molten image, an a' unto
1Sa 13: 4 Israel also was had in a'
1Ki 11: 5 the a' of the Ammonites.
7 the a' of Moab,
7 the a' of the children of Ammon.

2Ki 23:13 the a· of the Zidonians, and for
13 Chemosh the a· of the Moabites,
13 Milcom the a· of the children
Ps 88: 8 thou hast made me an a· unto
Pro 3:32 the froward is a· to the Lord:
6:16 seven are an a· unto him:
8: 7 and wickedness is an a· to my lips.
11: 1 false balance is a· to the Lord:
20 are of a froward heart are a· to
12:22 Lying lips are a· to the Lord:
13:19 it is a· to fools to depart from evil.
15: 8 wicked is an a· to the Lord:
9 way of the wicked is an a· unto the
26 thoughts of the wicked are an a· to
16: 5 proud in heart is an a· to
12 a· to kings to commit wickedness:
17:15 both are a· to the Lord.
20:10 both of them are alike a· to the
23 Divers weights are an a· unto
21:27 sacrifice of the wicked is a·:
24: 9 and the scorner is an a· to men.
28: 9 even his prayer shall be a·.
29:27 An unjust man is an a· to the just:
27 is upright in the way is a· to the
Isa 1:13 incense is an a· unto me;
41:24 an a· is he that chooseth you.
44:19 make the residue thereof an a·?
66:17 eating swine's flesh, and the a·,
Jer 2: 7 made mine heritage an a·.
6:15 when they had committed a·?
8:12 when they had committed a·?
32:35 do this a·, to cause Judah to sin.
Eze 16:50 were haughty, and committed a·
18:12 the idols, hath committed a·,
22:11 a· with his neighbour's wife;
33:26 ye work a·, and ye defile every
Da 11:31 place the a· that maketh desolate.
12:11 the a· that maketh desolate set up,
Mal 2:11 and an a· is committed in Israel
M't 24:15 see the a· of desolation,
M'r 13:14 shall see the a· of desolation,
Lu 16:15 is a· in the sight of God.
Re 21:27 worketh a·, or maketh a lie:

abominations
Le 18:26 not commit any of these a·;
27 all these a· have the men of the
29 shall commit any of these a·,
De 18: 9 after the a· of these nations.
12 and because of these a· the Lord
20:18 you not to do after all their a·,
29:17 have seen their a·, and their idols,
32:16 a· provoked they him to anger.
1Ki 14:24 all the a· of the nations
2Ki 16: 3 according to the a· of the heathen,
21: 2 after the a· of the heathen,
11 Judah hath done these a·,
23:24 the a· that were spied in the land
2Ch 28: 3 after the a· of the heathen
33: 2 like unto the a· of the heathen,
34:33 Josiah took away all the a· out of
36: 8 and his a· which he did,
14 after all the a· of the heathen;
Ezr 9: 1 according to their a·,
11 with their a·, which have filled
14 the people of these a·?
Pro 26:25 for there are seven a· in his heart.
Isa 66: 3 their soul delighteth in their a·.
Jer 4: 1 put away thine a· out of my sight,
7:10 delivered to do all these a·?
30 have set their a· in the house
13:27 whoredom, and thine a· on the
32:34 they set their a· in the house,
44:22 a· which ye have committed;
Eze 5: 9 the like, because of all thine a·.
11 and with all thine a·, therefore
6: 9 have committed in all their a·.
11 Alas for all the evil a· of the house
7: 3 recompense upon thee all thine a·.
4 a· shall be in the midst of thee:
8 recompense thee for all thine a·.
9 according to thy ways and thine a·
20 made the images of their a·
8: 6 a· that the house of Israel
6, 13, 15 thou shalt see greater a·
9 wicked a· that they do here.
17 Judah that they commit the a·
9: 4 that cry for all the a· that be done
11:18 all the a· thereof from thence.
21 detestable things and their a·,
12:16 may declare all their a· among the
14: 6 faces from all your a·.
16: 2 cause Jerusalem to know her a·,
22 in all thine a· and thy whoredoms
36 with all the idols of thy a·,
43 lewdness above all thine a·.
47 nor done after their a·:
51 thou hast multiplied thine a· more
51 in all thine a· which thou hast done.
58 borne thy lewdness and thine a·,
18:13 hath done all these a·;
24 doeth according to all the a·
20: 4 cause them to know the a· of their
7 Cast ye away every man the a· of
8 cast away the a· of their eyes,
30 commit ye whoredom after their a·?
22: 2 thou shalt shew her all her a·.
23:36 declare unto them their a·;
33:29 desolate because of all their a·
36:31 iniquities and for your a·.
43: 8 defiled my holy name by their a·
44: 6 suffice you of all your a·,
7 because of all your a·.
13 bear their shame, and their a·
Da 9:27 the overspreading of a· he shall
Ho 9:10 a· were according as they loved.
Zec 9: 7 and his a· from between his teeth:

Re 17: 4 full of a· and filthiness of
5 mother of harlots and a· of the

abound See also ABOUNDED; ABOUNDETH; ABOUNDING.
Pro 28:20 A faithful man shall a· with
M't 24:12 because iniquity shall a·,
Ro 5:20 the offence might a·. But where
20 grace did much more a·:
6: 1 that grace may a·?
15:13 that ye may a· in hope, through
2Co 1: 5 sufferings of Christ a· in us, so our
8: 7 as ye a· in every thing, in faith,
7 that ye a· in this grace also.
9: 8 to make all grace a· toward you:
8 may a· to every good work:
Ph'p 1: 9 that your love may a· yet more
4:12 and I know how to a·:
12 both to a· and to suffer need.
17 that may a· to your account.
18 I have all and a·:
1Th 3:12 make you to increase and a· in
4: 1 so ye would a· more and more.
2Pe 1: 8 if these things be in you, and a·,

abounded
Ro 3: 7 hath more a· through my lie unto
5:15 hath a· unto many.
20 But where sin a·, grace did much
2Co 8: 2 a· unto the riches of their liberality
Eph 1: 8 Wherein he hath a· toward us in

aboundeth
Pro 29:22 a furious man a· in transgression.
2Co 1: 5 consolation also a· by Christ.
2Th 1: 3 all toward each other a·;

abounding
Pro 8:24 no fountains a· with water.
1Co 15:58 always a· in the work of the Lord,
Col 2: 7 a· therein with thanksgiving.

about^ See also THEREABOUT; WHEREABOUT.
Ge 23:17 were in all the borders round a·,
35: 5 the cities that were round a· them,
37: 7 round a·, and made obeisance
38:24 came to pass a· three months after
39:11 it came to pass a· this time,
41:25 shewed Pharaoh what he is a· to
28 What God is a· to do he sheweth
42 and put a gold chain a· his neck;
48 which was round a· every city,
42:24 he turned himself a· from them,
46:34 servants' trade hath been a·
Ex 7:24 the Egyptians digged round a·
9:18 to-morrow a· this time I will cause
13:18 God led the people a·, through
16:13 the morning the dew lay round a·
19:12 bounds unto the people round a·,
23 Set bounds a· the mount, and
25:11 a crown of gold round a·.
24 thereto a crown of gold round a·.
25 border of an hand breadth round a·,
25 to the border thereof round a·.
27:17 All the pillars round a· the court
28:32 a binding of woven work round a·
33 round a· the hem thereof; and bells
33 of gold between them round a·:
34 upon the hem of the robe round a·.
29:16 sprinkle it round a· upon the altar.
20 the blood upon the altar round a·.
30: 3 the sides thereof round a·,
3 unto it a crown of gold round a·.
32:28 fell of the people that day a· three
37: 2 a crown of gold to it round a·.
11 thereunto a crown of gold round a·.
12 border of an handbreadth round a·;
12 for the border thereof round a·.
26 the sides thereof round a·,
26 unto it a crown of gold round a·.
38:16 the hangings of the court round a·
20 and of the court round a·,
31 the sockets of the court round a·,
31 all the pins of the court round a·.
39:23 with a band round a· the hole,
25 a· between the pomegranates;
26 round a· the hem of the robe
40: 8 shalt set up the court round a·,
33 he reared up the court round a· the
Le 1: 5 sprinkle the blood round a· upon
11 sprinkle his blood round a· upon
3: 2 the blood upon the altar round a·.
8 sprinkle the blood thereof round a·
13 thereof upon the altar round a·.
6: 5 Or all that a· which he hath sworn
7: 2 sprinkle round a· upon the altar.
8:15 horns of the altar round a· with
19, 24 blood upon the altar round a·.
9:12 sprinkled round a· upon the altar.
18 sprinkled upon the altar round a·
14:41 to be scraped within round a·,
16:18 the horns of the altar round a·.
25:31 which have no wall round a· them
44 the heathen that are round a· you;
Nu 1:50 encamp round a· the tabernacle.
53 the Levites shall pitch round a·
2: 2 far off a· the tabernacle of the
3:26 by the altar round a·,
37 the pillars of the court round a·,
4: 4 tabernacle of the congregation, a·
14 wherewith they minister a·
26 altar round a·, and their cords,
32 the pillars of the court round a·,
11: 8 people went a·, and gathered it,
24 set them round a· the tabernacle.
31 the other side, round a· the camp.
32 for themselves round a· the camp.
16:24 up from a· the tabernacle of Korah,
34 Israel that were round a· them fled

Nu 16:49 that died a· the matter of Korah.
22: 4 lick up all that are round a· us,
32:33 the cities of the country round a·.
34:12 with the coasts thereof round a·.
35: 2 suburbs for the cities round a·
4 a thousand cubits round a·.
De 6:14 the people which are round a· you;
12:10 rest from all your enemies round a·,
13: 7 the people which are round a· you,
17:14 as all the nations that are a· me;
21: 2 round a· him that is slain:
25:19 rest from all thine enemies round a·,
31:21 imagination which they go a·,
32:10 he led him a·, he instructed him,
Jos 2: 5 to pass a· the time of shutting of
3: 4 you and it, a· two thousand
4:13 A· forty thousand prepared for
6: 3 ye men of war, and go round a·
11 compassed the city, going a· it
15 they rose early a· the dawning of
7: 3 let a· two or three thousand men
4 up thither of the people a· three
5 men of Ai smote of them a· thirty
8:12 he took a· five thousand men, and
10:13 not to go down a· a whole day.
11: 6 to-morrow a· this time will I
15:12 of the children of Judah round a·
16: 6 the border went a· eastward unto
18:20 by the coasts thereof round a·,
19: 8 a· these cities to Baalath-beer,
21:11 the suburbs thereof round a· it.
42 with their suburbs round a· them:
44 the Lord gave them rest round a·,
23: 1 from all their enemies round a·,
J'g 2:12 the people that were round a· them,
14 hands of their enemies round a·,
3:29 they slew of Moab at that time a·
7:21 every man in his place round a·
8:10 with them, a· fifteen thousand men,
26 chains that were a· their camels'
9:49 of Shechem died also, a· a thousand
16:27 upon the roof a· three thousand
17: 2 silver that were taken from thee, a·
19:22 Belial, beset the house round a·,
20: 5 beset the house round a· upon me
29 set liers in wait round a· Gibeah.
31 in the field, a· thirty men of Israel.
39 the men of Israel a· thirty persons:
43 Benjamites round a·, and chased
Ru 1: 4 and they dwelled there a· ten years.
19 all the city was moved a· them,
2:17 and it was a· an ephah of barley.
1Sa 1:20 the time was come a· after Hannah
4: 2 in the field a· four thousand men.
20 And a· the time of her death
5: 8 of the God of Israel be carried a·,
8 ark of the God of Israel a· thither.
9 after they had carried it a·,
10 brought a· the ark of the God of
9:13 a· this time ye shall find him.
16 To morrow a· this time I will send
22 which were a· thirty persons.
26 to pass a· the spring of the day,
13:15 present with him, a· six hundred
14: 2 with him were a· six hundred
14 was a· twenty men, within as it
21 from the country round a·,
15:12 set him up a place, and is gone a·,
27 as Samuel turned a· to go away,
17:42 when the Philistine looked a·,
20:12 a· to morrow any time, or the
21: 5 kept from us a· these three days,
22: 2 with him a· four hundred men.
6 servants were standing a· him;)
7 his servants that stood a· him,
17 the footmen that stood a· him,
23:13 David and his men, which were a·
26 his men round a· to take them.
25:13 there went up after David a· four
38 a· ten days after, that the Lord
26: 5 the people pitched round a· him.
7 Abner and the people lay round a·,
31: 9 land of the Philistines round a·,
2Sa 3:12 to bring a· all Israel unto thee.
4: 5 and came a· the heat of the day to
5: 9 David built round a· from Millo
7: 1 Lord had given him rest round a·
14:20 To fetch a· this form of speech
18:15 compassed a· and smote Absalom,
20:26 Jairite was a chief ruler a· David.
22: 6 sorrows of hell compassed me a·;
12 made darkness pavilions round a·
24: 6 to Dan-jaan, and a· to Zidon,
1Ki 2: 5 his girdle that was a· his loins,
15 howbeit the kingdom is turned a·,
3: 1 the wall of Jerusalem round a·.
4:24 had peace on all sides round a·
31 fame was in all nations round a·.
5: 3 for the wars which were a· him
6: 5 built chambers round a·, against
5 the walls of the house round a·,
5 he made chambers round a·:
6 he made narrowed rests round a·,
29 the walls of the house round a·
7:12 the great court round a· was with
15 did compass either of them a·.
18 two rows round a· upon the one
20 two hundred in rows round a·
23 it was round all a·,
23 cubits did compass it round a·.
24 under the brim of it round a·
24 compassing the sea round a·:
36 and additions round a·.
8:14 And the king turned his face a·,
18:32 he made a trench a· the altar,
35 the water ran round a· the altar:

1Ki 19: 2 of them by to morrow a· this time.
20: 6 unto thee to morrow a· this time,
22: 6 prophets together, a· four hundred
36 throughout the host a· the going
2Ki 1: 8 with a girdle of leather a· his loins.
3:25 the slingers went a· it, and smote
4:16 A· this season, according to the
6:14 and compassed the city a·.
17 chariots of fire round a· Elisha.
7: 1 To morrow a· this time shall a
18 shall be to morrow a· this time in
8:21 which compassed him a·.
11: 7 the house of the Lord a· the king.
8 shall compass the king round a·,
11 in his hand, round a· the king,
17:15 heathen that were round a· them,
23: 5 in the places round a· Jerusalem;
25: 1 built forts against it round a·.
4 were against the city round a·:)
10 the walls of Jerusalem round a·.
17 upon the chapiter round a·,
1Ch 4:33 villages that were round a· the
6:55 the suburbs thereof round a· it.
9:27 lodged round a· the house of God,
10: 9 land of the Philistines round a·,
11: 8 he built the city round a·,
8 even from Millo round a·:
15:22 he instructed a· the song, because
18:17 the sons of David were chief a· the
22: 9 from all his enemies round a·:
28:12 of all the chambers round a·,
2Ch 2: 9 house which I am a· to build shall
4: 2 cubits did compass it round a·.
3 which did compass it round a·:
3 compassing the sea round a·.
13:13 caused an ambushment to come a·
14: 7 make a· them walls, and towers,
14 smote all the cities round a· Gerar;
15:15 the Lord gave them rest round a·.
17: 9 went a· throughout all the cities
10 lands that were round a· Judah,
18:31 they compassed a· him to fight:
34 a· the time of the sun going down
20:30 God gave him rest round a·.
23: 2 And they went a· in Judah,
7 shall compass the king round a·
10 the temple, by the king round a·
26: 6 built cities a· Ashdod, and
33:14 compassed a· Ophel, and raised it
34: 6 with their mattocks round a·.
Ezr 1: 6 that were a· them strengthened
10:15 Tikvah were employed a· this
Ne 5:17 among the heathen that are a· us.
6:16 all the heathen that were a· us
12:28 plain country round a· Jerusalem,
29 had builded them villages round a·
13:21 them, Why lodge ye a· the wall?
Job 1: 5 of their feasting were gone a·,
10 a· him, and a· his house, and a·
8:17 roots are wrapped a· the heap,
10: 8 fashioned me together round a·;
11:18 yea, thou shalt dig a· thee, and
16:13 archers compass me round a·,
19:12 encamp round a· my tabernacle.
20:23 When he is a· to fill his belly, God
22:10 Therefore snares are round a·
29: 5 when my children were a· me;
30:18 bindeth me a· as the collar of my
37:12 turned round a· by his counsels:
40:22 of the brook compass him a·.
41:14 his teeth are terrible round a·.
Ps 3: 6 themselves against me round a·.
7: 7 of the people compass thee a·:
17: 9 enemies, who compass me a·.
18: 5 sorrows of hell compassed me a·:
11 his pavilion round a· him were
27: 6 above mine enemies round a· me:
32: 7 shalt compass me a· with songs
10 mercy shall compass him a·.
34: 7 encampeth round a· them that
40:12 compassed me a·: mine iniquities
44:13 derision to them that are round a·
48:12 Walk a· Zion, and go round
12 Zion, and round a· her:
49: 5 of my heels shall compass me a·?
50: 3 very tempestuous round a· him.
55:10 Day and night they go a· it upon
59: 6, 14 like a dog, and go round a· the city.
73: 6 pride compasseth them a· as a
76:11 let all that be round a· him bring
78:28 round a· their habitations.
79: 3 like water round a· Jerusalem;
4 to them that are round a· us.
88:17 They came round a· me daily like
17 they compassed me a· together.
89: 7 reverence of all them that are a·
8 to thy faithfulness round a· thee?
97: 2 and darkness are round a· him:
3 burneth up his enemies round a·.
109: 3 They compassed me a· also with
118:10 All nations compassed me a·:
11 me a·; yea, they compassed me a·:
12 They compassed me a· like bees;
125: 2 As the mountains are round a·
2 so the Lord is round a· his people
128: 3 olive plants round a· thy table.
139:11 the night shall be light a· me.
140: 9 of those that compass me a·,
142: 7 righteous shall compass me a·;
Pr 1: 9 thy head, and chains a· thy neck.
3: 3 bind them a· thy neck; write
6:21 thine heart, and tie them a· thy
20:19 He that goeth a· as a talebearer
Ec 1: 6 and turneth a· unto the north;
6 it whirleth a· continually,
2:20 I went a· to cause my heart

Ec 12: 5 the mourners go a· the streets:
Ca 3: 2 I will rise now, and go a· the city
3 The watchmen that go a· the city
7 threescore valiant men are a· it,
5: 7 watchmen that went a· the city
7: 2 heap of wheat set a· with lilies.
Isa 3:18 tinkling ornaments a· their feet,
15: 8 cry is gone round a· the borders of
23:16 Take an harp, go a· the city,
26:20 and shut thy doors a· thee: hide
28:27 neither is a cart wheel turned a·
29: 3 will camp against thee round a·,
42:25 it hath set him on fire round a·,
49:18 Lift up thine eyes round a·,
50:11 compass yourselves a· with sparks:
60: 4 Lift up thine eyes round a·, and
Jer 1:15 all the walls thereof round a·,
2:36 Why gaddest thou a· so much
4:17 are they against her round a·;
6: 3 their tents against her round a·;
12: 9 birds round a· are against her;
14:18 the prophet and the priest go a·
17:26 from the places a· Jerusalem,
21:14 shall devour all things round a· it.
25: 9 all these nations round a·,
31:22 How long wilt thou go a·,
39 and shall compass a· to Goath.
32:44, 33:13 in the places a· Jerusalem,
41:14 cast a· and returned, and went
46: 5 fear was round a·, saith the Lord.
14 sword shall devour round a· thee.
48:17 ye that are a· him, bemoan him;
39 a dismaying to all them a· him.
49: 5 from all those that be a· thee;
50:14 in array against Babylon round a·:
15 Shout against her round a·:
29 camp against it round a·;
32 it shall devour all round a· him.
51: 2 they shall be against her round a·.
52: 4 built forts against it round a·.
7 were by the city round a·:)
14 the walls of Jerusalem round a·.
22 upon the chapiters round a·,
23 were an hundred round a·.
La 1:17 his adversaries should be round a·
2: 3 fire, which devoureth round a·.
22 solemn day my terrors round a·,
3: 7 hath hedged me a·, that I cannot
Eze 1: 4 a brightness was a· it,
18 rings were full of eyes round a·
27 as the appearance of fire round a·
27 it had brightness round a·.
28 of the brightness round a·.
4: 2 battering rams against it round a·.
5: 2 and smite a· it with a knife:
5, 6 countries that are round a· her.
7, 7 nations that are round a· you;
12 fall by the sword round a· thee;
14, 15 nations that are round a· thee,
6: 5 scatter your bones round a· your
13 among their idols round a· their
8:10 pourtrayed upon the wall round a·.
16 were a· five and twenty men, with
10:12 full of eyes round a·, even the
11:12 the heathen that are round a· you.
12:14 all that are a· him to help him,
16:10 I girded thee a· with fine linen,
37 I will even gather them round a·
57 and all that are round a· her,
57 which despise thee round a·.
23:24 and shield and helmet round a·:
27:11 were upon thy walls round a·,
11 shields upon thy walls round a·;
28:24 all that are round a· them,
26 despise them round a· them;
31: 4 rivers running round a· his plants.
32:22 his graves are a· him:
23 her company is round a· her grave:
24 her multitude round a· her grave,
25, 26 her graves are round a· him:
34:26 places round a· my hill a blessing;
36: 4 of the heathen that are round a·;
7 Surely the heathen that are a· you,
36 heathen that are left round a· you
37: 2 me to pass by them round a·:
40: 5 the outside of the house round a·,
14 unto the post of the court round a·
16 posts within the gate round a·,
16 windows were round a· inward:
17 made for the court round a·:
25 in the arches thereof round a·,
29 round a·: it was fifty cubits long,
30 the arches round a· were five and
33 in the arches thereof round a·: it
36 the windows to it round a·:
43 hand broad, fastened round a·:
41: 5 round a· the house on every side.
6 for the side chambers round a·,
7 a winding a· still upward to the
7 the winding a· of the house went
7 still upward round a· the house:
8 the height of the house round a·:
10 twenty cubits round a· the house
11 five cubits round a·.
12 five cubits thick round a·,
16 galleries round a· on their three
16 cieled with wood round a·,
17 by all the wall round a·
19 through all the house round a·.
42:15 and measured it round a·.
16, 17 the measuring reed round a·.
19 He turned a· to the west side, and
20 had a wall round a·, five hundred
43:12 limit thereof round a· shall be
13 the edge thereof round a· shall be
17 border a· it shall be half a cubit;

Eze 43:17 bottom thereof shall be a cubit a·;
20 and upon the border round a·:
45: 1 in all the borders thereof round a·.
2 in breadth, square round a·;
2 and fifty cubits round a·
46:23 a row of building round a· in them,
23 round a· them four,
23 under the rows round a·.
47: 2 led me a· the way without unto
48:35 was round a· eighteen thousand
Da 5: 7 have a chain of gold a· his neck,
16 a chain of gold a· thy neck,
29 put a chain of gold a· his neck,
31 kingdom, being a· threescore and
9:16 a reproach to all that are a· us.
21 me a· the time of the evening
Ho 7: 2 own doings have beset them a·;
11:12 Ephraim compassed me a· with
Joe 3:11 yourselves together round a·:
12 to judge all the heathen round a·.
Am 3:11 even round a· the land;
Jon 2: 3 the floods compassed me a·: all
5 The waters compassed me a·, even
5 the depth closed me round a·, the
5 weeds were wrapped a· my head.
6 with her bars was a· me for
Na 3: 8 that had the waters round a· it,
Hab 1: 4 the wicked doth compass a· the
Zec 2: 5 unto her a wall of fire round a·,
7: 7 cities thereof round a· her,
9: 8 And I will encamp a· mine house
12: 2 unto all the people round a·,
6 devour all the people round a·,
14:14 wealth of all the heathen round a·
M't 1:11 a· the time they were carried
3: 4 girdle a· his loins;
5 all the region round a· Jordan,
4:23 And Jesus went a· all Galilee,
8:18 Jesus saw great multitudes a·
9:22 Jesus turned him a·, and when
35 Jesus went a· all the cities and
14:21 were a· five thousand men,
35 all that country round a·, and
18: 6 millstone were hanged a· his neck,
20: 3 he went out a· the third hour,
5 Again he went out a· the sixth and
6 And a· the eleventh hour he went
9 were hired a· the eleventh hour,
21:33 hedged it round a·, and digged
27:46 And a· the ninth hour Jesus cried
M'r 1: 6 girdle of a skin a· his loins;
28 all the region round a· Galilee.
2: 2 not so much as a· the door:
3: 5 when he had looked round a· on
8 and they a· Tyre and Sidon,
32 And the multitude sat a· him,
34 And he looked round a· on them
34 on them which sat a· him,
4:10 they that were a· him
5:13 they were a· two thousand;) and
30 turned him a· in the press, and
32 he looked round a· to see her
6: 6 he went round a· the villages,
36 into the country round a·, and into
44 were a· five thousand men.
48 a· the fourth watch of the night
55 that whole region round a·,
55 carry a· in beds those that were
8: 9 had eaten were a· four thousand:
33 But when he had turned a· and
9: 8 when they had looked round a·,
14 he saw a great multitude a· them,
42 millstone were hanged a· his neck,
10:23 Jesus looked round a·, and saith
11:11 and when he had looked round a·
12: 1 and set an hedge a· it,
14:51 cloth cast a· his naked body;
15:17 thorns, and put it a· his head
Lu 1:56 And Mary abode with her a· three
65 on all that dwelt round a· them:
2: 9 glory of the Lord shone round a·
37 she was a widow of a· fourscore
49 be a· my Father's business?
3: 3 into all the country a· Jordan,
23 began to be a· thirty years of age,
4:14 through all the region round a·.
37 place of the country round a·.
6:10 looking round a· upon them all,
7: 9 at him, and turned him a·,
17 all the region round a·.
8:37 country of the Gadarenes round a·
42 a· twelve years of age, and she lay
9:12 and country round a·, and lodge,
14 were a· five thousand men.
28 a· an eight days after these,
10:40 Martha was cumbered a· much
41 and troubled a· many things:
12:35 Let your loins be girded a·, and
13: 8 till I shall dig a· it, and dung it:
17: 2 hanged a· his neck, and he cast
19:43 shall cast a trench a· thee, and
22:41 withdrawn from them a· a stone's
49 When they which were a· him
59 a· the space of one hour after
23:44 And it was a· the sixth hour, and
24:13 Jerusalem a· threescore furlongs.
Joh 1:39 for it was a· the tenth hour.
3:25 and the Jews a· purifying.
4: 6 well: and it was a· the sixth hour.
6:10 in number a· five thousand.
19 rowed a· five and twenty or thirty
7:14 a· the midst of the feast Jesus
19 Why go ye a· to kill me?
20 who goeth a· to kill thee?
10:24 came the Jews round a· him,
11:18 a· fifteen furlongs off:

Joh 11:44 face was bound a' with a napkin.
19:14 and a' the sixth hour:
39 a' an hundred pound weight.
20: 7 the napkin, that was a' his head,
21:20 Then Peter, turning a', seeth the
Ac 1:15 together were a' an hundred and
2:10 of Libya a' Cyrene,
41 them a' three thousand souls.
3: 3 seeing Peter and John a' to go
4: 4 of the men was a' five thousand.
5: 7 a' the space of three hours after,
16 cities round a' unto Jerusalem,
36 men, a' four hundred, joined
9: 3 there shined round a' him a light
29 they went a' to slay him.
10: 3 a' the ninth hour of the day,
9 to pray a' the sixth hour:
38 went a' doing good, and healing
11:19 persecution that arose a' Stephen
12: 1 Now a' that time Herod the king
8 Cast thy garment a' thee, and
13:11 went a' seeking some to lead him
18 a' the time of forty years suffered
20 a' the space of four hundred and
14: 6 the region that lieth round a':
20 the disciples stood round a' him,
15: 2 the apostles and elders a' this
18:14 when Paul was now a' to open his
19: 7 all the men were a' twelve.
23 no small stir a' that way.
34 a' the space of two hours cried
20: 3 as he was a' to sail into Syria,
21:31 And as they went a' to kill him,
22: 6 a' noon, suddenly there shone
6 light round a' me.
24: 6 Who also hath gone a' to profane
25: 7 from Jerusalem stood round a',
15 A' whom, when I was at
24 a' whom all the multitude of the
26:13 shining round a' me and them
21 and went a' to kill me.
27:27 Adria, a' midnight the shipmen
30 the shipmen were a' to flee out
Ro 4:19 when he was a' an hundred years
10: 3 and going a' to establish their
15:19 from Jerusalem, and round a'
1Co 9: 5 power to lead a' a sister, a wife,
13 which minister a' holy things live
2Co 4:10 Always bearing a' in the body
Eph 4:14 and carried a' with every wind of
6:14 having your loins girt a' with
1Ti 5:13 wandering a' from house to
6: 4 doting a' questions and strifes of
2Ti 2:14 that they strive not a' words to no
Tit 3: 9 strivings a' the law; for they are
Heb 8: 5 he was a' to make the tabernacle:
9: 4 overlaid round a' with gold,
11:30 after they were compassed a'
37 they wandered a' in sheepskins
12: 1 we also are compassed a' with so
13: 9 Be not carried a' with divers and
Jas 3: 3 and we turn a' their whole body.
4 yet are they turned a' with a very
1Pe 5: 8 walketh a', seeking whom he may
Jude 1: 7 Gomorrha, and the cities a' them
9 disputed a' the body of Moses,
12 carried a' of winds; trees whose
Re 1:13 girt a' the paps with a golden
4: 3 a rainbow round a' the throne,
4 And round a' the throne were four
6 and round a' the throne, were four
8 six wings a' him;
5:11 angels round a' the throne and
7:11 all the angels stood round a' the
8: 1 a' the space of half an hour.
10: 4 their voices, I was a' to write:
16:21 every stone a' the weight of a
20: 9 the camp of the saints a',

above
Ge 1: 7 which were a' the firmament:
20 a' the earth in the open
3:14 cursed a' all cattle, and a' every
6:16 in a cubit shalt thou finish it a';
7:17 and it was lift up a' the earth.
27:39 and of the dew of heaven from a';
28:13 Lord stood a' it, and said, I am
48:22 one portion a' thy brethren, which
49:25 with blessings of heaven a',
26 prevailed a' the blessings of my
Ex 18:11 dealt proudly he was a' them.
19: 5 treasure unto me a' all people:
20: 4 of any thing that is in heaven a',
25:21 the mercy seat a' upon the ark;
22 with thee from a' the mercy seat,
26:14 a covering a' of badgers' skins.
24 be coupled together a' the head
28:27, 28 a' the curious girdle of the
29:13 and the caul that is a' the liver,
22 and the caul a' the liver, and the
30:14 from twenty years old and a',
36:19 covering of badgers' skins a' that.
39:20 a' the curious girdle of the ephod.
21 it might be a' the curious girdle
40:19 covering of the tent a' upon it;
20 the mercy seat a' upon the ark:
Le 3: 4 and the caul a' the liver, with
10 flanks, and the caul a' the liver,
15 and the caul a' the liver, with
4: 9 flanks, and the caul a' the liver,
7: 4 and the caul that is a' the liver,
8:16 inwards, and the caul a' the liver,
25 and the caul a' the liver, and the
9:10 a' the liver of the sin offering,
19 kidneys, and the caul a' the liver:
11:21 which have legs a' their feet,
27: 7 from sixty years old and a';
Nu 3:49 of them that were over and a'
4:25 is a' upon it, and the hanging for
12: 3 Moses was very meek, a' all the
16: 3 lift ye up yourselves a' the
De 4:39 he is God in heaven a',
5: 8 that is in heaven a', or that is in
7: 6 a' all people that are upon the face
14 Thou shalt be blessed a' all people:
10:15 even you a' all people, as it is this
14: 2 a' all the nations that are upon
17:20 his heart be not lifted up a' his
25: 3 and beat him a' these with many
26:19 high a' all nations which he hath
28: 1 set thee on high a' all nations of
13 thou shalt be a' only,
43 is within thee shall get up a' thee
30: 5 and multiply thee a' thy fathers.
Jos 2:11 he is God in heaven a',
3:13 waters that come down from a';
16 waters which came down from a'
J'g 5:24 Blessed a' women shall Jael the
24 blessed shall she be a' women in
1Sa 2:29 and honourest thy sons a' me, to
2Sa 22:17 He sent from a', he took me;
49 hast lifted me up on high a' them
1Ki 7: 3 covered with cedar a' upon the
11 And a' were costly stones,
20 had pomegranates also a',
25 the sea was set a' upon them,
29 there was a base a':
31 within the chapiter and a' was a
8: 7 and the staves thereof a'.
23 no God like thee, in heaven a',
14: 9 But hast done evil a' all that were
22 they had committed, a' all that
16:30 in the sight of the Lord a' all that
2Ki 21:11 hath done wickedly a' all that the
25:28 set his throne a' the throne of
1Ch 5: 2 Judah prevailed a' his brethren,
16:25 he also is to be feared a' all gods.
23:27 from twenty years old and a':
27: 6 a' the thirty: and in his course
29: 3 house of my God, over and a' all
11 and thou art exalted as head a' all.
2Ch 2: 5 for great is our God a' all gods.
4: 4 the sea was set a' upon them,
5: 8 the staves thereof a'.
11:21 daughter of Absalom a' all his
25: 5 from twenty years old and a',
34: 4 images, that were on high a'
Ne 3:28 From a' the horse gate repaired
7: 2 man, and feared God a' many.
8: 5 (for he was a' all the people;) and
9: 5 which is exalted a' all blessing
12:37 of the wall, a' the house of David,
39 And from a' the gate of Ephraim,
39 a' the old gate, and a' the fish
Es 2:17 king loved Esther a' all the women,
3: 1 and set his seat a' all the princes
Job 3: 4 let not God regard it from a',
18:16 and a' shall his branch be cut off.
28:18 the price of wisdom is a' rubies.
31: 2 portion of God is there from a'?
28 denied the God that is a'.
Ps 8: 1 hast set thy glory a' the heavens.
10: 5 judgments are far a' out of his
18:16 He sent from a', he took me, he
48 yea, thou liftest me up a' those
27: 6 lifted up a' mine enemies round
45: 7 the oil of gladness a' thy fellows.
50: 4 call to the heavens from a',
57: 5 exalted, O God, a' the heavens;
5, 11 let thy glory be a' all the earth.
11 exalted, O God, a' the heavens:
78:23 commanded the clouds from a',
95: 3 God, and a great king a' all gods.
96: 4 praised: he is to be feared a' all
97: 9 Lord, art high a' all the earth:
9 thou art exalted far a' all gods.
99: 2 and he is high a' all the people.
103:11 as the heaven is high a' the earth,
104: 6 the water stood a' the mountains.
108: 4 thy mercy is great a' the heavens:
5 exalted, O God, a' the heavens:
5 and thy glory a' all the earth;
113: 4 the Lord is high a' all nations,
4 and his glory a' the heavens.
119:127 commandments a' gold; yea, a'
135: 5 and that our Lord is a' all gods.
136: 6 stretched out the earth a' the
137: 6 prefer not Jerusalem a' my chief
138: 2 magnified thy word a' all thy
144: 7 Send thine hand from a'; rid me,
148: 4 ye waters that be a' the heavens
13 glory is a' the earth and heaven.
Pr 8:28 established the clouds a':
15:24 The way of life is a' to the wise,
31:10 for her price is far a' rubies
Ec 2: 7 and small cattle a' all that were
3:19 a man hath no preeminence a' a
Isa 2: 2 and shall be exalted a' the hills;
6: 2 A' it stood the seraphims:
7:11 or in the height a'.
14:13 a' the stars of God:
14 I will ascend a' the heights of the
45: 8 Drop down, ye heavens, from a',
Jer 4:28 the heavens a' be black:
15: 8 increased to me a' the sand of the
17: 9 The heart is deceitful a' all things,
31:37 If heaven a' can be measured,
35: 4 was a' the chamber of Maaseiah
52:32 set his throne a' the throne of the
La 1:13 From a' hath he sent fire into my
Eze 1:22 stretched forth over their heads a'.
26 And a' the firmament that was
26 appearance of a man a' upon it.
Eze 10: 1 firmament that was a' the head
19 God of Israel was over them a'.
11:22 God of Israel was over them a'.
16:43 a' all thine abominations.
29:15 itself any more a' the nations: for
31: 5 his height was exalted a' all the
37: 8 the skin covered them a':
41:17 To that a' the door, even unto the
20 From the ground unto a' the door
Da 6: 3 Daniel was preferred a' the
11: 5 and he shall be strong a' him, and
36 and magnify himself a' every god,
37 for he shall magnify himself a' all.
Am 2: 9 I destroyed his fruit from a',
Mic 4: 1 and it shall be exalted a' the hills;
Na 3:16 merchants a' the stars of heaven:
M't 10:24 The disciple is not a' his master,
24 nor the servant a' his lord.
Lu 3:20 Added yet this a' all, that he
6:40 The disciple is not a' his master:
13: 2 sinners a' all the Galilæans,
4 they were sinners a' all men that
Joh 3:31 cometh from a' is a' all:
31 cometh from heaven is a' all.
6:13 which remained over and a'
8:23 are from beneath; I am from a':
19:11 except it were given thee from a':
Ac 2:19 I will shew wonders in heaven a',
4:22 the man was a' forty years old,
26:13 a' the brightness of the sun,
Ro 10: 6 is, to bring Christ down from a':)
14: 5 one day a' another:
1Co 4: 6 not to think of men a' that which
10:13 to be tempted a' that ye are able;
15: 6 seen of a' five hundred brethren
2Co 1: 8 out of measure, a' strength,
12: 2 a' fourteen years ago (whether in
6 a' that which he seeth me to be,
7 I should be exalted a' measure
7 should be exalted a' measure.
Ga 1:14 Jews' religion a' many my equals
4:26 Jerusalem which is a' is free,
Eph 1:21 Far a' all principality, and power,
3:20 exceeding abundantly a' all that
4: 6 who is a' all, and through all,
10 ascended up far a' all heavens,
6:16 A' all, taking the shield of faith,
Ph'p 2: 9 a name which is a' every name:
Col 3: 1 seek those things which are a',
2 Set your affections on things a',
14 a' all these things put on charity,
2Th 2: 4 a' all that is called God,
Ph'm 16 Not now as a servant, but a' a
Heb 1: 9 the oil of gladness a' thy fellows.
10: 8 A' when he said, Sacrifice and
Jas 1:17 every perfect gift is from a',
3:15 descendeth not from a', but is
17 the wisdom that is from a' is first
5:12 But a' all things, my brethren,
1Pe 4: 8 a' all things have fervent charity
3Jo 2 I wish a' all things that thou

Abraham (*a'-bra-ham*) See also ABRAHAM'S; ABRAM.
Ge 17: 5 but thy name shall be A';
9 God said unto A', Thou shalt keep
15 God said unto A', As for Sarai thy
17 A' fell upon his face, and laughed,
18 A' said unto God, Oh that Ishmael
22 and God went up from A'.
23 And A' took Ishmael his son, and
24 A' was ninety years old and nine,
26 selfsame day was A' circumcised,
18: 6 A' hastened into the tent unto
7 A' ran unto the herd, and fetcht
11 A' and Sarah were old and well
13 the Lord said unto A', Wherefore
16 A' went with them to bring them
17 Shall I hide from A' that thing
18 Seeing that A' shall surely become
19 that the Lord may bring upon A'
22 but A' stood yet before the Lord.
23 A' drew near, and said, Wilt thou
27 A' answered and said, Behold now,
33 as he had left communing with A':
33 and A' returned unto his place.
19:27 A' gat up early in the morning to
29 God remembered A', and sent Lot
20: 1 A' journeyed from thence toward
2 A' said of Sarah his wife, She is my
9 Abimelech called A', and said unto
10 Abimelech said unto A', What
11 A' said, Because I thought, surely
14 gave them unto A', and restored
17 So A' prayed unto God: and God
21: 2 and bare A' a son in his old age,
3 A' called the name of his son that
4 A' circumcised his son Isaac
5 A' was an hundred years old, when
7 Who would have said unto A', that
8 A' made a great feast the same day
9 which she had born unto A',
10 she said unto A', Cast out this
12 God said unto A', Let it not be
14 A' rose up early in the morning,
22 captain of his host spake unto A',
24 And A' said, I will swear.
25 A' reproved Abimelech because of a
27 A' took sheep and oxen, and gave
28 A' set seven ewe lambs of the flock
29 Abimelech said unto A', What mean
33 A' planted a grove in Beer-sheba,
34 A' sojourned in the Philistines' land
22: 1 that God did tempt A', and said
1 unto him, A': and he said, Behold,
3 A' rose up early in the morning,
4 day A' lifted up his eyes, and saw

Ge 22: 5 A' said unto his young men, Abide
6 A' took the wood of the burnt
7 Isaac spake unto A' his father, and
8 A' said, My son, God will provide
9 A' built an altar there, and laid the
10 A' stretched forth his hand, and
11 him out of heaven, and said, A', A':
13 A' lifted up his eyes, and looked,
13 A' went and took the ram, and
14 A' called the name of that place
15 the angel of the Lord called unto A'
19 So A' returned unto his young men,
19 and A' dwelt at Beer-sheba.
20 it was told A', saying, Behold,
23: 2 and A' came to mourn for Sarah,
3 A' stood up from before his dead,
5 the children of Heth answered A',
7 A' stood up, and bowed himself to
10 Ephron the Hittite answered A'
12 A' bowed down himself before the
14 Ephron answered A', saying unto
16 And A' hearkened unto Ephron;
16 A' weighed to Ephron the silver,
18 Unto A' for a possession in the
19 after this, A' buried Sarah his wife
20 made sure into A' for a possession
24: 1 A' was old, and well stricken in age:
1 Lord had blessed A' in all things.
2 A' said unto his eldest servant of
6 A' said unto him, Beware thou that
9 put his hand under the thigh of A'
12 O Lord God of my master A', I pray
12 shew kindness unto my master A'
27 be the Lord God of my master A',
42 said, O Lord God of my master A',
48 the Lord God of my master A',
25: 1 Then again A' took a wife, and her
5 A' gave all that he had unto Isaac
6 concubines, which A' had, A' gave
8 Then A' gave up the ghost, and died
10 The field which A' purchased of the
10 there was A' buried, and Sarah his
11 the death of A', that God blessed
12 Sarah's handmaid, bare unto A':
19 A' begat Isaac:
26: 1 famine that was in the days of A'.
3 the oath which I sware unto A'
5 Because that A' obeyed my voice,
15 had digged in the days of A'
18 they had digged in the days of A'
18 stopped them after the death of A':
24 and said, I am the God of A' thy
28: 4 And give thee the blessing of A',
4 a stranger, which God gave unto A'.
13 I am the Lord God of A' thy father,
31:42 the God of my father, the God of A',
53 The God of A', and the God of Nahor,
32: 9 Jacob said, O God of my father A',
35:12 the land which I gave A' and Isaac,
27 which is Hebron, where A' and
48:15 before whom my fathers A' and
16 and the name of my fathers A' and
49:30 which A' bought with the field of
31 There they buried A' and Sarah his
50:13 which A' bought with the field for a
24 unto the land which he sware to A',
Ex 2:24 remembered his covenant with A',
3: 6 the God of thy father, the God of A',
15 God of your fathers, the God of A',
16 God of A', of Isaac, and of Jacob,
4: 5 God of their fathers, the God of A',
6: 3 I appeared unto A', unto Isaac, and
8 which I did sware to give it to A',
32:13 Remember A', Isaac, and Israel,
33: 1 the land which I sware unto A',
Le 26:42 also my convenant with A' will I
Nu 32:11 see the land which I sware unto A',
De 1: 8 Lord sware unto your fathers, A',
6:10 he sware unto thy fathers, to A',
9: 5 Lord sware unto thy fathers, A',
27 Remember thy servants, A', Isaac,
29:13 hath sworn unto thy fathers, to A',
30:20 Lord sware unto thy fathers, to A',
34: 4 is the land which I sware unto A',
Jos 24: 2 even Terah, the father of A',
3 I took your father A' from the
1Ki 18:36 came near, and said, Lord God of A',
2Ki 13:23 because of his covenant with A',
1Ch 1:27 Abram; the same is A'.
28 The sons of A'; Isaac, and Ishmael.
34 And A' begat Isaac. The sons of
16:16 covenant which he made with A',
29:18 O Lord God of A', Isaac, and of
2Ch 20: 7 and gavest it to the seed of A'
30: 6 again unto the Lord God of A',
Ne 9: 7 and gavest him the name of A';
Ps 47: 9 even the people of the God of A':
105: 6 O ye seed of A' his servant,
9 Which covenant he made with A',
42 his holy promise, and A'
Isa 29:22 saith the Lord, who redeemed A',
41: 8 the seed of A' my friend.
51: 2 Look unto A' your father, and unto
63:16 though A' be ignorant of us,
Jer 33:26 to be rulers over the seed of A',
Eze 33:24 A' was one, and he inherited the
Mic 7:20 truth to Jacob, and the mercy to A',
M't 1: 1 the son of David, the son of A'.
2 A' begat Isaac; and Isaac begat
17 the generations from A' to David
3: 9 We have A' to our father:
9 to raise up children unto A'.
8:11 shall sit down with A',
22:32 I am the God of A', and the God of
M'r 12:26 I am the God of A',
Lu 1:55 As he spake to our fathers, to A'.
Lu 1:73 he sware to our father A',
3: 8 We have A' to our father:
8 to raise up children unto A'.
34 which was the son of A',
13:16 this woman, being a daughter of A',
28 when ye shall see A', and Isaac,
16:23 and seeth A' afar off,
24 Father A', have mercy on me,
25 But A' said, Son, remember that
29 A' saith unto him, They have Moses
30 Nay, father A': but if one went
19: 9 forsomuch as he also is a son of A'.
Lu 20:37 he calleth the Lord the God of A',
Joh 8:39 answered and said unto him, A' is
39 ye would do the works of A'.
40 this did not A'.
52 A' is dead, and the prophets;
53 Art thou greater than our father A'
56 A' rejoiced to see my day:
57 and hast thou seen A'?
58 Before A' was, I am.
Ac 3:13 The God of A', and of Isaac,
25 saying unto A', And in thy seed
7: 2 appeared unto our father A',
8 circumcision: and so A' begat
16 the sepulchre that A' bought
17 which God had sworn to A',
32 God of thy fathers, the God of A',
13:26 children of the stock of A',
Ro 4: 1 A' our father, as pertaining
2 if A' were justified by works,
3 A' believed God, and it was counted
9 faith was reckoned to A' for
12 that faith of our father A',
13 not to A', or to his seed, through
16 which is of the faith of A';
9: 7 because they are the seed of A',
11: 1 of the seed of A', of the tribe of
2Co 11:22 Are they the seed of A'? so am I.
Ga 3: 6 Even as A' believed God,
7 are the children of A'.
8 preached before the gospel unto A',
9 blessed with faithful A'.
14 the blessing of A' might come
16 to A' and his seed were the
18 God gave it to A' by promise.
4:22 A' had two sons, the one by
Heb 2:16 but he took on him the seed of A'.
6:13 when God made promise to A',
7: 1 A' returning from the slaughter
2 To whom also A' gave a tenth
4 A' gave the tenth of the spoils.
5 they come out of the loins of A':
6 received tithes of A',
9 payed tithes in A'.
11: 8 By faith A', when he was called to
17 By faith A', when he was tried,
Jas 2:21 Was not A' our father justified by
23 A' believed God, and it was imputed
1Pe 3: 6 Sara obeyed A', calling him lord:

Abraham's (*a'-bra-hams*)
Ge 17:23 every male among the men of A'
20:18 because of Sarah A' wife.
21:11 thing was very grievous in A' sight
22:23 eight Milcah did bear to Nahor, A'
24:15 son of Milcah, the wife of Nahor, A'
34 And he said, I am A' servant.
52 when A' servant heard their words,
59 and her nurse, and A' servant, and
25: 7 these are the days of the years of A'
12 are the generations of Ishmael, A'
19 are the generations of Isaac, A'
26:24 multiply thy seed for my servant A'
28: 9 the daughter of Ishmael A'
1Ch 1:32 the sons of Keturah, A' concubine:
Lu 16:22 carried by the angels into A' bosom:
Joh 8:33 We be A' seed, and were never in
37 I know that ye are A' seed;
39 If ye were A' children, ye would do
Ga 3:29 then are ye A' seed, and heirs

Abram (*a'-brum*) See also ABRAHAM; ABRAM'S.
Ge 11:26 lived seventy years, and begat A',
27 Terah begat A', Nahor, and Haran;
29 And A' and Nahor took them wives:
31 And Terah took A' his son, and Lot
12: 1 the Lord had said unto A', Get thee
4 So A' departed, as the Lord had
4 A' was seventy and five years old
5 A' took Sarai his wife, and Lot
6 A' passed through the land unto
7 Lord appeared unto A', and said,
9 A' journeyed, going on still toward
10 and A' went down into Egypt to
14 when A' was come into Egypt, the
16 And he entreated A' well for her
18 Pharaoh called A', and said, What
13: 1 A' went up out of Egypt, he, and
2 And A' was very rich in cattle,
4 and there A' called on the name of
5 Lot also, which went with A', had
8 A' said unto Lot, Let there be no
12 A' dwelled in the land of Canaan,
14 the Lord said unto A', after that
18 Then A' removed his tent, and
14:13 one that had escaped, and told A'
13 and these were confederate with A'.
14 when A' heard that his brother was
19 Blessed be A' of the most high God,
21 the king of Sodom said unto A',
22 A' said to the king of Sodom,
23 thou shouldest say, I have made A'
15: 1 the word of the Lord came unto A'
1 in a vision, saying, Fear not, A':
2 A' said, Lord God, what wilt thou
3 A' said, Behold, to me thou hast
Ge 15:11 came down upon the carcasses, A'
12 a deep sleep fell upon A';
13 he said unto A', Know of a surety
18 the Lord made a covenant with A',
16: 2 Sarai said unto A', Behold now, the
2 And A' hearkened to the voice of
3 after A' had dwelt ten years in the
3 and gave her to her husband A'
5 Sarai said unto A', My wrong be
6 A' said unto Sarai, Behold, thy
15 Hagar bare A' a son: and A' called
16 A' was fourscore and six years old,
16 when Hagar bare Ishmael to A'.
17: 1 when A' was ninety years old and
1 the Lord appeared to A',
3 A' fell on his face: and God talked
5 thy name any more be called A',
1Ch 1:27 A'; the same is Abraham.
Ne 9: 7 Lord the God, who didst choose A',

Abram's (*a'-brums*)
Ge 11:29 the name of A' wife was Sarai;
31 his daughter in law, his son A' wife;
12:17 because of Sarai, A' wife.
13: 7 a strife between the herdmen of A'
14:12 they took Lot, A' brother's son,
16: 1 Now Sarai, A' wife, bare him no
3 And Sarai, A' wife, took Hagar her

abroad
Ge 10:18 of the Canaanites spread a'.
11: 4 lest we be scattered a' upon the
8 the Lord scattered them a' from
9 did the Lord scatter them a'
15: 5 he brought him forth a', and
19:17 had brought them forth a',
28:14 and thou shalt spread a' to the
Ex 5:12 So the people were scattered a'
9:29 I will spread a' my hands unto
33 from Pharaoh, and spread a' his
12:46 carry forth aught of the flesh a'
21:19 walk a' upon his staff,
40:19 And he spread a' the tent over
Le 13: 7 But if the scab spread much a' in
12 And if a leprosy break out a' in
22 And if it spread much a' in the
27 if it be spread much a' in the
14: 8 tarry a' out of his tent seven days.
18: 9 at home, or born a',
Nu 11:32 they spread them all a' for
De 23:10 then shall he go a' out of the
12 whither thou shalt go forth a':
13 when thou wilt ease thyself a',
24:11 Thou shalt stand a', and the
11 shall bring out the pledge a'
32:11 spreadeth a' her wings, taketh
J'g 12: 9 daughters, whom he sent a',
9 took in thirty daughters from a'
1Sa 9:26 he and Samuel, a'.
30:16 they were spread a' upon all the
2Sa 22:43 did spread them a'.
1Ki 2:42 and walkest a' any whither,
2Ki 4: 3 vessels a' of all thy neighbours,
1Ch 13: 2 a' unto our brethren everywhere,
14:13 themselves a' in the valley.
2Ch 26: 8 Uzziah: and his name spread a'
15 his name spread far a';
29:16 it out a' into the brook Kidron.
31: 5 as the commandment came a',
Ne 1: 8 I will scatter you a' among the
Es 1:17 deed of the queen shall come a'
3: 8 is a certain people scattered a'
Job 4:11 lion's whelps are scattered a'.
15:23 wandereth a' for bread, saying,
40:11 Cast a' the rage of thy wrath:
Ps 41: 6 when he goeth a', he telleth it.
77:17 thine arrows also went a'.
Pr 5:16 thy fountains be dispersed a',
Isa 24: 1 a' the inhabitants thereof.
28:25 doth he not cast a' the fitches,
44:24 spreadeth a' the earth by myself;
Jer 6:11 pour it out upon the children a',
La 1:20 a' the sword bereaveth, at home
Eze 34:21 till ye have scattered them a';
Zec 1:17 prosperity shall yet be spread a';
2: 6 spread you a' as the four winds
M't 9:26 went a' into all that land.
31 a' his fame in all that country.
36 scattered a', as sheep having no
12:30 not with me scattereth a'.
26:31 the flock shall be scattered a'.
M'r 1:28 fame spread a' throughout all
45 blaze a' the matter, insomuch that
4:22 but that it should come a'.
6:14 (for his name was spread a':)
Lu 1:65 these sayings were noised a'
2:17 made known a' the saying
5:15 more went there a fame a' of him:
8:17 be known and come a'.
Joh 11:52 of God that were scattered a'.
21:23 went this saying a' among the
Ac 2: 6 when this was noised a',
8: 1 all scattered a' throughout the
4 they that were scattered a' went
11:19 scattered a' upon the persecution
Ro 5: 5 love of God is shed a' in our hearts
16:19 your obedience is come a' unto all
2Co 9: 9 He hath dispersed a'; he hath
1Th 1: 8 faith to God-ward is spread a':
Jas 1: 1 tribes which are scattered a'.

Absalom (*ab'-sal-um*) See also ABISHALOM; ABSALOM'S.
2Sa 3: 3 the third, A' the son of Maacah
13: 1 that A' the son of David had a fair
20 And A' her brother said unto her,
22 And A' spake unto his brother
22 Amnon neither good nor bad: for A'

2Sa 13:23 A' had sheepshearers in Baal-hazor,
23 and A' invited all the king's
24 And A' came to the king, and said,
25 the king said to A', Nay, my son,
26 Then said A', If not, I pray thee,
27 A' pressed him, that he let Amnon
28 Now A' had commanded his
29 And the servants of A' did unto
29 Amnon as A' had commanded.
30 A' hath slain all the king's sons,
32 by the appointment of A' this hath
34 But A' fled. And the young man
37 But A' fled, and went to Talmai,
38 So A' fled, and went to Geshur,
39 David longed to go forth unto A':
14: 1 that the king's heart was toward A'.
21 bring the young man A' again.
23 went to Geshur, and brought A' to
24 So A' returned to his own house,
25 much praised as A' for his beauty:
27 unto A' there were born three sons,
28 A' dwelt two full years in Jerusalem,
29 A' sent for Joab, to have sent him
31 Then Joab arose, and came to A'
32 A' answered Joab, Behold, I sent
33 when he had called for A', he came
33 the king: and the king kissed A'.
15: 1 that A' prepared him chariots and
2 And A' rose up early, and stood
2 then A' called unto him, and said,
3 A' said unto him, See, thy matters
4 A' said moreover, Oh that I were
6 on this manner did A' to all Israel
6 so A' stole the hearts of the men of
7 A' said unto the king, I pray thee,
10 But A' sent spies throughout all the
10 ye shall say, A' reigneth in Hebron.
11 And with A' went two hundred men
12 A' sent for Ahithophel the Gilonite,
12 people increased continually with A'
13 of the men of Israel are after A'.
14 for we shall not else escape from A':
31 is among the conspirators with A'.
34 say unto A', I will be thy servant,
37 came into the city, and A' came into
16: 8 the kingdom into the hand of A'
15 And A', and all the people the men
16 David's friend, was come unto A',
16 Hushai said unto A', God save the
17 A' said to Hushai, Is this thy
18 Hushai said unto A', Nay; but whom
20 said A' to Ahithophel, Give counsel
21 Ahithophel said unto A', Go in unto
22 So they spread A' a tent upon the
22 and A' went in unto his father's
23 both with David and with A'.
17: 1 Ahithophel said unto A', Let me
4 And the saying pleased A' well,
5 Then said A', Call now Hushai
6 When Hushai was come to A', A'
7 Hushai said unto A', The counsel
9 among the people that follow A'.
14 A' and all the men of Israel said,
14 the Lord might bring evil upon A'.
15 and thus did Ahithophel counsel A'
18 a lad saw them, and told A':
24 And A' passed over Jordan, he and
25 A' made Amasa captain of the host
26 Israel and A' pitched in the land of
18: 5 with the young man, even with A'.
5 the captains charge concerning A'.
9 and A' met the servants of David.
9 And A' rode upon a mule,
10 Behold, I saw A' hanged in an oak.
12 that none touch the young man A'.
14 them through the heart of A',
15 about and smote A', and slew him.
17 they took A', and cast him into a
18 Now, A' in his life time had taken
29 said, Is the young man A' safe?
32 Cushi, Is the young man A' safe?
33 O my son A', my son, my son A'!
33 died for thee, O A', my son, my son!
19: 1 king weepeth and mourneth for A'.
4 with a loud voice, O my son A',
4 O A', my son, my son!
6 I perceive, that if A' had lived,
9 now he is fled out of the land for A'.
10 And A', whom we anointed over us,
20: 6 do us more harm than did A':
1Ki 1: 6 and his mother bare him after A'.
2: 7 I fled because of A' thy brother.
28 though he turned not after A'.
1Ch 3: 2 The third, A' the son of Maachah
2Ch 11:20 took Maachah the daughter of A';
21 loved Maachah the daughter of A'
Ps 3:*title* Psalm of David, when he fled from A'

Absalom's (*ab'-sal-ums*)
2Sa 13: 4 I love Tamar, my brother A' sister,
20 desolate in her brother A' house.
14:30 And A' servants set the field on fire.
17:20 A' servants came to the woman
18:18 it is called unto this day, A' place.

absence
Lu 22: 6 in the a' of the multitude.
Ph'p 2:12 now much more in my a',

absent
Ge 31:49 when we are a' one from another.
1Co 5: 3 For I verily, as a' in body, but
2Co 5: 6 we are a' from the Lord:
8 rather to be a' from the body,
9 that, whether present or a',
10: 1 being a' am bold toward you:
11 by letters when we are a', such
13: 2 a' now I write to them
2Co 13:10 write these things being a',
Ph'p 1:27 come and see you, or else be a',
Col 2: 5 though I be a' in the flesh,

abstain
Ac 15:20 they a' from pollutions of idols,
29 ye a' from meats offered to idols,
1Th 4: 3 that ye should a' from fornication:
5:22 A' from all appearance of evil.
1Ti 4: 3 commanding to a' from meats,
1Pe 2: 11 a' from fleshly lusts, which war

abstinence
Ac 27:21 after long a' Paul stood forth in

abundance
De 28:47 for the a' of all things;
33:19 they shall suck of the a' of the
1Sa 1:16 out of the a' of my complaint
2Sa 12:30 the spoil of the city in great a'.
1Ki 1:19 and fat cattle and sheep in a',
25 fat cattle and sheep in a',
10:10 came no more such a' of spices
27 as the sycomore trees .... for a'.
18:41 there is a sound of a' of rain.
1Ch 22: 3 David prepared iron in a' for the
3 brass in a' without weight;
4 Also cedar trees in a':
14 iron without weight; for it is in a':
15 workmen with thee in a',
29: 2 marble stones in a'.
21 sacrifices in a' for all Israel:
2Ch 1:15 as the sycomore trees .... for a'.
2: 9 to prepare me timber in a':
4:18 vessels in great a':
9: 1 spices, and gold in a',
9 of spices great a', and precious
27 as the sycomore trees .... in a'.
11:23 gave them victual in a'.
14:15 sheep and camels in a',
15: 9 fell to him out of Israel in a',
17: 5 he had riches and honour in a'.
18: 1 had riches and honour in a',
2 killed sheep and oxen for him in a',
20:25 found among them in a' both riches
24:11 gathered money in a'.
29:35 the burnt offerings were in a',
31: 5 children of Israel brought in a'
32: 5 made darts and shields in a'.
29 flocks and herds in a':
Ne 9:25 fruit trees in a':
Es 1: 7 royal wine in a', according to the
Job 22:11 and a' of waters cover thee.
36:31 he giveth meat in a'.
38:34 that a' of waters may cover
Ps 37:11 delight themselves in the a' of
52: 7 trusted in the a' of his riches,
72: 7 a' of peace so long as the moon
105:30 land brought forth frogs in a',
Ec 5:10 he that loveth a' with increase:
12 but the a' of the rich will not
Isa 7:22 for the a' of milk that they shall
15: 7 the a' they have gotten,
47: 9 great a' of thine enchantments.
60: 5 a' of the sea shall be converted
66:11 with the a' of her glory.
Jer 33: 6 reveal unto them the a' of peace
Eze 16:49 and a' of idleness was in her
26:10 By reason of the a' of his horses
Zec 14:14 silver, and apparel, in great a'.
M't 12:34 out of the a' of the heart the
13:12 and he shall have more a':
25:29 and he shall have a':
M'r 12:44 did cast in of their a';
Lu 6:45 of the a' of the heart his mouth
12:15 consisteth not in the a' of the
21: 4 these have of their a' cast in unto
Ro 5:17 they which receive a' of grace
2Co 8: 2 the a' of their joy and their deep
14 your a' may be a supply for their
14 that their a' also may be a supply
20 blame us in this a' which is
12: 7 through the a' of the revelations,
Re 18: 3 the a' of her delicacies.

abundant
Ex 34: 6 and a' in goodness and truth,
Isa 56:12 much more a'.
Jer 51:13 many waters, a' in treasures,
1Co 12:23 we bestow more a' honour;
23 have more a' comeliness.
24 given more a' honour
2Co 4:15 that the a' grace might through
7:15 his inward affection is more a'
9:12 is a' also by many thanksgivings
11:23 in labours more a', in stripes
Ph'p 1:26 may be more a' in Jesus Christ
1Ti 1:14 of our Lord was exceeding a'
1Pe 1: 3 according to his a' mercy hath

abundantly
Ge 1:20 Let the waters bring forth a'
21 the waters brought forth a',
8:17 they may breed a' in the earth,
9: 7 bring forth a' in the earth, and
Ex 1: 7 fruitful, and increased a', and
8: 3 river shall bring forth frogs a',
Nu 20:11 the water came out a',
1Ch 12:40 oxen, and sheep a': for there
22: 5 David prepared a' before his
8 Thou hast shed blood a',
2Ch 31: 5 all things brought they in a'.
Job 12: 6 whose hand God bringeth a'.
33:28 distil upon man a'.
Ps 36: 8 They shall be a' satisfied with
65:10 waterest the ridges thereof a':
132:15 I will a' bless her provision:
145: 7 They shall a' utter the memory
Ca 5: 1 drink, yea, drink a', O beloved.
Isa 15: 3 every one shall howl, weeping a'.
35: 2 it shall blossom a', and rejoice
55: 7 for he will a' pardon.
Jo 10:10 might have it more a'.
1Co 15:10 I laboured more a' than they all:
2Co 1:12 and more a' to you-ward.
2: 4 I have more a' unto you.
10:15 according to our rule a',
12:15 the more a' I love you, the less I
Eph 3:20 able to do exceeding a' above
1Th 2:17 endeavoured the more a' to see
Tit 3: 6 Which he shed on us a' through
Heb 6:17 willing more a' to shew unto the
2Pe 1:11 shall be ministered unto you a'

abuse See also ABUSED; ABUSING.
1Sa 31: 4 thrust me through, and a' me.
1Ch 10: 4 these uncircumcised come and a'
1Co 9:18 I a' not my power in the gospel.

abused
J'g 19:25 they knew her, and a' her

abusers
1Co 6: 9 a' of themselves with mankind,

abusing
1Co 7:31 that use this world, as not a' it:

Accad (*ak'-kad*)
Ge 10:10 Babel, and Erech, and A', and

accept See also ACCEPTED; ACCEPTEST; ACCEPTETH; ACCEPTING.
Ge 32:20 peradventure he will a' of me.
Ex 22:11 the owner of it shall a' thereof,
Le 26:41 they then a' of the punishment
43 they shall a' of the punishment
De 33:11 a' the work of his hands:
1Sa 26:19 me, let him a' an offering:
2Sa 24:23 The Lord thy God a' thee.
Job 13: 8 Will ye a' his person? will ye
10 if ye do secretly a' persons.
32:21 Let me not, I pray you, a' any
42: 8 for him will I a':
Ps 20: 3 a' thy burnt sacrifice;
82: 2 a' the persons of the wicked?
119:108 A', I beseech thee, the freewill
Pr 18: 5 to a' the person of the wicked,
Jer 14:10 the Lord doth not a' them;
12 I will not a' them:
Eze 20:40 there will I a' them, and there will
41 will a' you with your sweet savour,
43:27 I will a' you, saith the Lord God.
Am 5:22 meat offerings, I will not a' them;
Mal 1: 8 pleased with thee, or a' thy
10 neither will I a' an offering at
13 should I a' this of your hand?
Ac 24: 3 We a' it always, and in all places,

acceptable
Le 22:20 it shall not be a' for you.
De 33:24 let him be a' to his brethren,
Ps 19:14 be a' in thy sight, O Lord,
69:13 is unto thee, O Lord, in an a' time:
Pr 10:32 of the righteous know what is a':
21: 3 justice and judgment is more a'
Ec 12:10 preacher sought to find out a'
Isa 49: 8 In an a' time have I heard thee,
58: 5 a fast, and an a' day to the Lord?
61: 2 proclaim the a' year of the Lord,
Jer 6:20 your burnt offerings are not a',
Da 4:27 O king, let my counsel be a' unto
Lu 4:19 To preach the a' year of the Lord.
Ro 12: 1 living sacrifice, holy, a' unto God,
2 and a', and perfect, will of God.
14:18 a' to God, and approved of men.
15:16 up of the Gentiles might be a',
Eph 5:10 Proving what is a' unto the Lord.
Ph'p 4:18 a sweet smell, a sacrifice a',
1Ti 2: 3 this is good and a' in the sight of
5: 4 good and a' before God.
1Pe 2: 5 a' to God by Jesus Christ.
20 this is a' with God.

acceptably
Heb 12:28 serve God a' with reverence and

acceptance
Isa 60: 7 come up with a' on mine altar,

acceptation
1Ti 1:15 worthy of all a', that
4: 9 saying and worthy of all a'.

accepted
Ge 4: 7 doest well, shalt thou not be a'?
19:21 I have a' thee concerning this
Ex 28:38 they may be a' before the Lord.
Le 1: 4 and it shall be a' for him to make
7:18 the third day, it shall not be a',
10:19 been a' in the sight of the Lord?
19: 7 is abominable; it shall not be a'.
22:21 shall be perfect to be a';
23 for a vow it shall not be a'.
25 they shall not be a' for you.
27 it shall be a' for an offering made
23:11 before the Lord, to be a' for you:
1Sa 18: 5 and he was a' in the sight of all
25:35 and have a' thy person.
Es 10: 3 and a' of the multitude of his
Job 42: 9 the Lord also a' Job.
Isa 56: 7 their sacrifices shall be a' upon
Jer 37:20 let my supplication .... be a'
42: 2 Let .... our supplication be a'
Lu 4:24 No prophet is a' in his own
Ac 10:35 worketh righteousness, is a'
Ro 15:31 may be a' of the saints;
2Co 5: 9 we may be a' of him.
6: 2 I have heard thee in a time a',
2 behold, now is the a' time;
8:12 it is a' according to that a man
17 For indeed he a' the exhortation;

2Co 11: 4 gospel, which ye have not *a*˙,
Eph 1: 6 wherein he hath made us *a*˙ in

acceptest
Lu 20:21 neither *a*˙ thou the person of any,

accepteth
Job 34:19 him that *a*˙ not the persons of
Ec 9: 7 God now *a*˙ thy works.
Ho 8:13 the Lord *a*˙ them not;
Ga 2: 6 God *a*˙ no man's person:)

accepting
Heb 11:35 were tortured, not *a*˙ deliverance;

access
Ro 5: 2 we have *a*˙ by faith into this grace
Eph 2:18 we both have *a*˙ by one Spirit
3:12 *a*˙ with confidence by the faith of

Accho (*ak'-ko*)
J'g 1:31 drive out the inhabitants of *A*˙,

accompanied
Ac 10:23 brethren from Joppa *a*˙ him.
11:12 these six brethren *a*˙ me,
20: 4 *a*˙ him into Asia Sopater of Berea;
38 And they *a*˙ him unto the ship.

accompany See also ACCOMPANIED; ACCOMPANYING.
Heb 6: 9 things that *a*˙ salvation,

accompanying
2Sa 6: 4 *a*˙ the ark of God:

accomplish See also ACCOMPLISHED, ACCOMPLISHING.
Le 22:21 to *a*˙ his vow,
1Ki 5: 9 and thou shalt *a*˙ my desire,
Job 14: 6 till he shall *a*˙, as an hireling,
Ps 64: 6 they *a*˙ a diligent search:
Isa 55:11 it shall *a*˙ that which I please,
Jer 44:25 ye will surely *a*˙ your vows,
Eze 6:12 thus will I *a*˙ my fury upon them
7: 8 and *a*˙ mine anger upon thee:
13:15 Thus will I *a*˙ my wrath upon the
20: 8, 21 to *a*˙ my anger against them
Da 9: 2 that he would *a*˙ seventy years in
Lu 9:31 which he should *a*˙ at Jerusalem.

accomplished
2Ch 36:22 word of the Lord . . . might be *a*˙,
Es 2:12 days of their purifications *a*˙,
Job 15:32 It shall be *a*˙ before his time,
Pr 13:19 The desire *a*˙ is sweet to the soul:
Isa 40: 2 her warfare is *a*˙, that her
Jer 25:12 when seventy years are *a*˙, that I
34 and of your dispersions are *a*˙;
29:10 after seventy years be *a*˙ at
39:16 and they shall be *a*˙ in that
La 4:11 The Lord hath *a*˙ his fury;
22 punishment of thine iniquity is *a*˙,
Eze 4: 6 And when thou hast *a*˙ them,
5:13 Thus shall mine anger be *a*˙,
13 when I have *a*˙ my fury in them.
Da 11:36 till the indignation be *a*˙:
12: 7 and when he shall have *a*˙ to
Lu 1:23 days of his ministration were *a*˙,
2: 6 the days were *a*˙ that she should
21 eight days were *a*˙
22 when the days . . . . were *a*˙,
12:50 straitened till it be *a*˙!
18:31 the Son of man shall be *a*˙.
22:37 must yet be *a*˙ in me,
Joh 19:28 all things were now *a*˙,
Ac 21: 5 when we had *a*˙ those days,
1Pe 5: 9 are *a*˙ in your brethren

accomplishing
Heb 9: 6 *a*˙ the service of God.

accomplishment
Ac 21:26 the *a*˙ of the days of purification,

accord See also ACCORDING.
Le 25: 5 which groweth of its own *a*˙
Jos 9: 2 and with Israel, with one *a*˙.
Ac 1:14 continued with one *a*˙ in prayer
2: 1 were all with one *a*˙ in one place.
46 daily with one *a*˙ in the temple,
4:24 up their voice to God with one *a*˙,
5:12 they were all with one *a*˙ in
7:57 and ran upon him with one *a*˙,
8: 6 the people with one *a*˙ gave heed
12:10 opened to them of his own *a*˙:
20 but they came with one *a*˙ to him,
15:25 being assembled with one *a*˙, to
18:12 made insurrection with one *a*˙
19:29 rushed with one *a*˙ into the
2Co 8:17 of his own *a*˙ he went unto you.
Ph'p 2: 2 love, being of one *a*˙, of one mind.

according^
Ge 18:10 return unto thee *a*˙ to the time
25:13 by their names, *a*˙ to their
16 twelve princes *a*˙ to their nations.
27: 8 *a*˙ to that which I command thee.
30:34 I would it might be *a*˙ to thy word.
33:14 *a*˙ as the cattle that goeth before
34:12 and I will give *a*˙ as ye shall say
36:40 the dukes that came of Esau, *a*˙
43 *a*˙ to their habitations in the land
39:17 she spake unto him *a*˙ to these
40: 5 each man *a*˙ to the interpretation
41:11 we dreamed each man *a*˙ to the
12 to each man *a*˙ to his dream he
40 *a*˙ unto thy word shall all my
54 dearth began to come, *a*˙ as
43: 7 we told him *a*˙ to the tenor of
33 before him, the firstborn *a*˙ to his
33 and the youngest *a*˙ to his youth:
44: 2 he did *a*˙ to the word that Joseph
7 thy servants should do *a*˙ to this
10 let it be *a*˙ unto your words:

Ge 45:21 *a*˙ to the commandment of
47:12 with bread, *a*˙ to their families.
49:28 every one *a*˙ to his blessing he
50: 6 and bury thy father, *a*˙ as he
12 sons did unto him *a*˙ as he
Ex 6:16 the sons of Levi *a*˙ to their
17 Libni, and Shimi, *a*˙ to their
19 are the families of Levi *a*˙ to
25 of the fathers of the Levites *a*˙
8:10 Be it *a*˙ to thy word: that thou
13 the Lord did *a*˙ to the word of
31 *a*˙ to the word of Moses; and he
12: 3 every man a lamb, *a*˙ to the
4 take it *a*˙ to the number of
4 every man *a*˙ to his eating shall
21 a lamb *a*˙ to your families, and
25 the Lord will give you, *a*˙ as he
35 Israel did *a*˙ to the word of
16:16 every man *a*˙ to his eating,
16 every man, *a*˙ to the number of
18, 21 every man *a*˙ to his eating.
17: 1 *a*˙ to the commandment of the
21:22 *a*˙ as the woman's husband will
31 *a*˙ to this judgment shall it be
22:17 he shall pay money *a*˙ to the
24: 4 twelve pillars, *a*˙ to the twelve tribes
25: 9 *A*˙ to all that I shew thee, after
35 *a*˙ to the six branches that
26:30 *a*˙ to the fashion thereof which
28: 8 the same, *a*˙ to the work
10 the rest on the other stone, *a*˙ to
21 *a*˙ to their names, like the
21 with his name shall they be *a*˙ to
29:35 *a*˙ to all things which I have
41 do thereto *a*˙ to the meat offering
41 and *a*˙ to the drink offering
30:37 not make to yourselves *a*˙ to the
31:11 *a*˙ to all that I have commanded
32:28 the children of Levi did *a*˙ to
36: 1 *a*˙ to all that the Lord had
37:21 *a*˙ to the six branches going out
29 *a*˙ to the work of the apothecary.
38:21 as it was counted, *a*˙ to the
39: 5 the same, *a*˙ to the work thereof;
14 the stones were *a*˙ to the names
14 twelve, *a*˙ to their names, like the
14 every one with his name, *a*˙ to the
32 did *a*˙ to all that the Lord
42 *A*˙ to all that the Lord
40:16 Thus did Moses: *a*˙ to all that
Le 4: 3 do sin *a*˙ to the sin of the people;
35 *a*˙ to the offerings made by fire
5:10 burnt offering, *a*˙ to the manner:
12 *a*˙ to the offerings made by fire
9:16 offered it *a*˙ to the manner.
10: 7 did *a*˙ to the word of Moses.
12: 2 *a*˙ to the days of the separation
25:15 *A*˙ to the number of years after
15 *a*˙ unto the number of years of
16 *A*˙ to the multitude of years
16 *a*˙ to the fewness of years thou
16 *a*˙ to the number of the years of
50 price of his sale shall be *a*˙ unto
50 *a*˙ to the time of an hired servant
51 *a*˙ unto them he shall give again
52 *a*˙ unto his years shall he give
26:21 more plagues upon you *a*˙ to
27: 8 *a*˙ to his ability that vowed
16 thy estimation shall be *a*˙ to the
17 year of jubile, *a*˙ to thy
18 *a*˙ to the years that remain,
25 estimations shall be *a*˙ to the
27 then he shall redeem it *a*˙ to
27 then it shall be sold *a*˙ to thy
Nu 1: 18, 20, 22, 24, 26, 28, 30, 32, 34, 36, 38,
40, 42 *a*˙ to the number of the names,
54 *a*˙ to all that the Lord commanded
2:10 the camp of Reuben *a*˙ to their
18 the camp of Ephraim *a*˙ to their
34 *a*˙ to all that the Lord commanded
34 after their families, *a*˙ to the
3:16 Moses numbered them *a*˙ to the
20 families of the Levites *a*˙ to the
22, 34 *a*˙ to the number of all the
51 Aaron and to his sons, *a*˙ to the
4:31 *a*˙ to all their service in the
33 families of the sons of Merari, *a*˙
37 *a*˙ to the commandment of the
41 number *a*˙ to the commandment
45 Moses and Aaron numbered *a*˙ to
49 *A*˙ to the commandment of the
49 Moses, every one *a*˙ to his service,
49 and *a*˙ to his burden: thus were
6:21 *a*˙ to the vow which he vowed,
7: 5 every man *a*˙ to his service.
7 *a*˙ to their service:
8 *a*˙ unto their service,
8: 4 *a*˙ unto the pattern which the
20 *a*˙ unto all that the Lord
9: 3 *a*˙ to all the rites of it, and *a*˙ to
5 *a*˙ to all that the Lord commanded
12 *a*˙ to all the ordinances of the
14 unto the Lord; *a*˙ to the
14 and *a*˙ to the manner thereof,
20 *a*˙ to the commandment of the
20 and *a*˙ to the commandment of
10:13 their journey *a*˙ to the
14 camp of the children of Judah *a*˙
18 camp of Reuben set forward *a*˙
22 of Ephraim set forward *a*˙ to
28 of the children of Israel *a*˙ to
14:17 be great, *a*˙ as thou hast spoken,
19 this people *a*˙ unto the greatness
20 I have pardoned *a*˙ to thy word:
29 all that were numbered of you, *a*˙
15:12 *A*˙ to the number that ye shall

Nu 15:12 to every one *a*˙ to their number.
24 *a*˙ to the manner, and one kid of
17: 2 a rod *a*˙ to the house of their
2 of all their princes *a*˙ to the house
6 for each prince one, *a*˙ to their
18:16 redeem, *a*˙ to thine estimation,
23:23 *a*˙ to this time it shall be said
24: 2 saw Israel abiding in his tents *a*˙
26:18 children of Gad *a*˙ to those that
22 families of Judah *a*˙ to those
25 families of Issachar *a*˙ to those
27 of the Zebulunites *a*˙ to those
37 of the sons of Ephraim *a*˙ to
43 of the Shuhamites, *a*˙ to those
47 of the sons of Asher *a*˙ to those
50 the families of Naphtali *a*˙ to
53 *a*˙ to the number of names.
54 be given *a*˙ to those that were
55 *a*˙ to the names of the tribes of their
56 *A*˙ to the lot shall...possession
29: 6 *a*˙ unto their manner, for a sweet
18 shall be *a*˙ to their number, after
21, 24 *a*˙ to their number, after the
27 shall be *a*˙ to their number, after
30 *a*˙ to their number, after the
33 shall be *a*˙ to their number, after
37 *a*˙ to their number, after the
40 *a*˙ to all that the Lord commanded
30: 2 do *a*˙ to all that proceedeth out of
33: 2 Moses wrote their goings out *a*˙ to
2 these are their journeys *a*˙ to
54 *a*˙ to the tribes of your fathers ye
34:14 children of Reuben *a*˙ to the house
14 children of Gad *a*˙ to the house
35: 8 the Levites *a*˙ to his inheritance
24 the revenger of blood *a*˙ to these
36: 5 children of Israel *a*˙ to the word
De 1: 3 *a*˙ unto all that the Lord had
30 *a*˙ to all that he did for you in
41 *a*˙ to all that the Lord our God
46 *a*˙ unto the days that ye abode
3:24 *a*˙ to thy works, and *a*˙ to thy
4:34 *a*˙ to all that the Lord your God
9:10 *a*˙ to all the words, which the Lord
10: 4 *a*˙ to the first writing, the ten
9 his inheritance, *a*˙ as the Lord thy
10 *a*˙ to the first time, forty days
12:15 *a*˙ to the blessing of the Lord thy
16:10 *a*˙ as the Lord thy God hath
17 *a*˙ to the blessing of the Lord thy
17:10 shalt do *a*˙ to the sentence,
10 observe to do *a*˙ to all that they
11 *A*˙ to the sentence of the law
11 and *a*˙ to the judgment which
18:16 *A*˙ to all that thou desiredst of the
23:23 *a*˙ as thou hast vowed unto the
24: 8 *a*˙ to all that the priests the
25: 2 *a*˙ to his fault, by a certain
26:13 *a*˙ to all thy commandments
14 and have done *a*˙ to all that thou
29:21 *a*˙ to all the curses of the
30: 2 *a*˙ to all that I command thee this
31: 5 *a*˙ unto all the commandments
32: 8 *a*˙ to the number of the children
34: 5 Moab, *a*˙ to the word of the Lord.
Jos 1: 7 observe to do *a*˙ to all the law,
8 thou mayest observe to do *a*˙ to
17 *A*˙ as we hearkened unto Moses
2:21 *A*˙ unto your words, so be it.
4: 5 *a*˙ unto the number of the tribes
8 *a*˙ to the number of the tribes of
10 *a*˙ to all that Moses commanded
7:14 be brought *a*˙ to your tribes:
14 shall come *a*˙ to the families
8: 8 *a*˙ to the commandment of the
27 *a*˙ unto the word of the Lord
34 *a*˙ to all that is written in the
10:32, 35, 37 *a*˙ to all that he had done
11:23 *a*˙ to all that the Lord said unto
23 inheritance unto Israel *a*˙ to their
12: 7 Israel for a possession *a*˙ to their
13:15 children of Reuben inheritance *a*˙
24 even unto the children of Gad *a*˙
15:12 children of Judah round about *a*˙
13 *a*˙ to the commandment of the
20 tribe of the children of Judah *a*˙
16: 5 children of Ephraim *a*˙ to their
17: 4 *a*˙ to the commandment of the
18: 4 *a*˙ to the inheritance of them;
10 the children of Israel *a*˙ to their
11 came up *a*˙ to their families:
20 round about, *a*˙ to their families.
21, 28 children of Benjamin *a*˙ to
19: 1, 8 children of Simeon *a*˙ to their
10, 16 children of Zebulun *a*˙ to their
17, 23 the children of Issachar *a*˙ to
24, 31 children of Asher *a*˙ to their
32, 39 the children of Naphtali *a*˙ to
40, 48 the children of Dan *a*˙ to their
50 *A*˙ to the word of the Lord they
21:33 All the cities of the Gershonites *a*˙
44 *a*˙ to all that he sware unto their
22: 9 *a*˙ to the word of the Lord by the
24: 5 *a*˙ to that which I did among
J'g 8:35 *a*˙ to all the goodness which he
9:16 done unto him *a*˙ to the deserving
11:10 if we do not so *a*˙ to thy words.
36 to me *a*˙ to that which hath
39 who did with her *a*˙ to his vow
20:10 *a*˙ to all the folly that they have
21:23 wives, *a*˙ to their number, of them
Ru 3: 6 did *a*˙ to all that her mother in law
1Sa 2:35 that shall do *a*˙ to that which is in
6: 4 *a*˙ to the number of the lords of
18 *a*˙ to the number of all the cities
8: 8 *A*˙ to all the works which they

1Sa 13: 8 a' to the set time that Samuel had
14: 7 behold, I am with thee a' to thy
17: 23 spake a' to the same words:
23:20 come down a' to all the desire of
25: 9 they spake to Nabal a' to all those
30 a' to all the good that he hath
2Sa 3:39 reward the doer of evil a' to his
7:17 A' to all these words, and a' to all
21 sake, and a' to thine own heart,
22 a' to all that we have heard with
9:11 A' to all that my lord the king
14:20 a' to the wisdom of an angel of
22:21 the Lord rewarded me a' to my
21 a' to the cleanness of my hands
25 Lord hath recompensed me a' to
25 a' to my cleanness in his eye sight.
24:19 David, a' to the saying of Gad,
1Ki 2: 6 Do therefore a' to thy wisdom,
3: 6 a' as he walked before thee in
12 Behold, I have done a' to thy
4:28 every man a' to his charge.
5: 6 give hire for thy servants a' to all
10 cedar trees and fir trees a' to all
6: 3 a' to the breadth of the house;
38 and a' to all the fashion of it.
7: 9 a' to the measures of hewed
36 a' to the proportion of every one,
8:32 give him a' to his righteousness.
39 give to every man a' to his ways,
43 and do a' to all that the stranger
56 rest unto his people Israel, a' to
9: 4 a' to all that I have commanded
11 with gold, a' to all his desire,)
11:37 and thou shalt reign a' to all that
12:24 returned to depart, a' to the word
13: 5 out from the altar, a' to the sign
26 slain him, a' to the word of the
14:18 a' to the word of the Lord, which
24 they did a' to all the abominations
15:29 destroyed him, a' unto the
16:12 Baasha, a' to the word of the Lord,
34 Segub, a' to the word of the Lord,
17: 1 a' to my word.
5 did a' unto the word of the Lord:
15 a' to the saying of Elijah:
16 oil fail, a' to the word of the Lord,
18:31 a' to the number of the tribes of
20: 4 O king, a' to thy saying, I am thine,
21:26 following idols, a' to all things as
22:38 a' unto the word of the Lord
53 a' to all that his father had done.
2Ki 1:17 he died a' to the word of the Lord
2:22 a' to the saying of Elisha
4:16 About this season, a' to the time
17 unto her, a' to the time of life.
44 left thereof, a' to the word of the
5:14 a' to the saying of the man of God:
6:18 with blindness a' to the word of
7:16 barley for a shekel, a' to the word
9:26 ground, a' to the word of the Lord.
10:17 destroyed him, a' to the saying of
30 a' to all that was in mine heart,
11: 9 did a' to all things that Jehoiada
14: 3 he did a' to all things as Joash
6 a' unto that which is written in the
25 a' to the word of the Lord God of
15: 3 a' to all that his father Amaziah
34 a' to all that his father Uzziah
16: 3 fire, a' to the abominations of the
10 a' to all the workmanship thereof.
11 altar a' to all that king Ahaz had
16 the priest, a' to all that king Ahaz
17:13 a' to all the law which I
18: 3 a' to all that David his father did.
21: 8 they will observe to do a' to all
8 a' to all the law that my servant
22:13 to do a' unto all that which is
23:16 polluted it, a' to the word of the
19 a' to all the acts that he had done
25 might, a' to all the law of Moses;
32 a' to all that his fathers had done.
35 to give the money a' to the
35 of every one a' to his taxation, to
37 a' to all that his fathers had done.
24: 2 destroy it, a' to the word of the
3 Manasseh, a' to all that he did;
9 sight of the Lord, a' to all that
19 a' to all that Jehoiakim had done.
1Ch 6:19 the families of the Levites a' to
32 waited on their office a' to their
49 a' to all that Moses the servant of
9: 9 brethren, a' to their generations,
11: 3 a' to the word of the Lord by
10 a' to the word of the Lord
12:23 of Saul to him, a' to the word of
15:15 a' to the word of the Lord.
16:40 a' to all that is written in the law
17:15 A' to all these words, and a' to all
17 regarded me a' to the estate of a
19 a' to thine own heart, hast thou
20 a' to all that we have heard with
23:11 reckoning, a' to their father's
31 a' to the order commanded unto
24: 3 a' to their offices in their service.
4 sons of Ithamar a' to the house
19 a' to their manner, under Aaron,
25: 1 the number of the workmen a' to
2 prophesied a' to the order of the
6 a' to the king's order to Asaph,
26:13 a' to the house of their fathers.
31 a' to the generations of his fathers.
28:15 a' to the use of every candlestick.
2Ch 3: 4 length of it was a' to the breadth
8 the length whereof was a' to the
4: 7 gold a' to their form,
6:23 giving him a' to his righteousness.

2Ch 6:30 render unto every man a' unto all
33 a' to all that the stranger calleth to
7:17 and do a' to all that I have
18 a' as I have covenanted with
8:13 offering a' to the commandment
14 a' to the order of David his
17:14 numbers of them a' to the house
23: 8 a' to all things that Jehoiada the
24: 6 a' to the commandment of Moses
25: 5 a' to the houses of their fathers,
26: 4 sight of the Lord, a' to all that
11 a' to the number of their account
27: 2 a' to all that his father Uzziah
29: 2 a' to all that David his father
15 came, a' to the commandment of
25 a' to the commandment of David,
30: 6 and Judah, and a' to the
16 a' to the law of Moses the man of
19 he be not cleansed a' to the
31: 2 every man a' to his service,
16 their service in their charges a'
32:25 rendered not again a' to the
33: 8 a' to the whole law and the
34:32 did a' to the covenant of God,
35: 4 a' to the writing of David king of
4 and a' to the writing of Solomon
5 the holy place a' to the divisions
6 may do a' to the word of the Lord
10 a' to the king's commandment.
13 with fire a' to the ordinance:
15 a' to the commandment of David,
16 a' to the commandment of king
26 a' to that which was written in the
Ezr 3: 4 a' to the custom, as the duty of
7 a' to the grant that they had of
6: 9 a' to the appointment of the
13 a' to that which Darius the king
14 a' to the commandment of the
14 and a' to the commandment of
17 twelve he goats, a' to the number
7: 6 a' to the hand of the Lord his God
9 to Jerusalem, a' to the good hand
14 a' to the law of thy God which is in
9: 1 doing a' to their abominations,
10: 3 a' to the counsel of my Lord, and
3 and let it be done a' to the law.
5 do a' to this word. And they sware,
8 come within three days, a' to the
Ne 2: 8 a' to the good hand of my God
5:12 should do a' to this promise.
13 people did a' to this promise.
19 a' to all that I have done for this
6: 6 be their king, a' to these words.
7 reported to the king a' to these
14 a' to these their works, and on
8:18 a solemn assembly, a' unto the
9:27 a' to thy manifold mercies thou
28 didst thou deliver them a' to thy
12:24, 45 a' to the commandment of
13:22 and spare me a' to the greatness
24 but a' to the language of each
Es 1: 7 royal wine in abundance, a' to the
8 the drinking was a' to the law;
8 that they should do a' to every
15 we do unto the queen Vashti a'
21 did a' to the word of Memucan:
22 into every province a' to the writing
22 should be published a' to the
2:12 she had been twelve months, a' to
18 and gave gifts, a' to the state of
3:12 and there was written a' to all
12 every people of every province a'
4:16 king, which is not a' to the law:
17 and did a' to all that Esther had
8: 9 written a' to all that Mordecai
9 unto every province a' to the
9 Jews a' to their writing, and a' to
9:13 to do to morrow also a' unto this
27 a' to their writing, and a' to their
31 a' as Mordecai the Jew and
Job 1: 5 offered burnt offerings a' to the
20:18 a' to his substance shall the
33: 6 I am a' to thy wish in God's
34:11 every man to find a' to his ways.
33 Should it be a' to thy mind? he
36:27 they pour down rain a' to the
42: 9 and did a' as the Lord commanded
Ps 7: 8 a' to my righteousness, and [a'] to
17 I will praise the Lord a' to his
18:20 The Lord rewarded me a' to my
20 a' to the cleanness of my hands
24 hath the Lord recompensed me a'
24 a' to the cleanness of my hands
20: 4 Grant thee a' to thine own heart,
25: 7 a' to thy mercy remember thou
28: 4 them a' to their deeds, and a' to
33:22 upon us, a' as we hope in thee.
35:24 Judge me, O Lord my God, a' to thy
48:10 A' to thy name, O God, so is thy
51: 1 Have mercy upon me, O God, a' to
1 a' unto the multitude of thy
62:12 renderest to every man a' to his
69:16 turn unto me a' to the multitude
74: 5 A man was famous a' as he had
78:72 So he fed them a' to the integrity
79:11 a' to the greatness of thy power
90:11 even a' to thy fear, so is thy
15 a' to the days wherein thou hast
103:10 rewarded us a' to our iniquities.
106:45 and repented a' to the multitude
109:26 O Lord my God: O save me a' to
119: 9 taking heed thereto a' to thy word.
25 quicken thou me a' to thy word.
28 strengthen thou me a' unto thy
41 even thy salvation, a' to thy word.
58 merciful unto me a' to thy word.

Ps 119:65 O Lord, a' unto thy word.
76 be for my comfort, a' to thy word
91 this day a' to thine ordinances:
107 quicken me, O Lord, a' unto thy
116 Uphold me a' unto thy word, that
124 Deal with thy servant a' unto
149 hear my voice a' unto thy
149 quicken me a' to thy judgment.
154 and deliver me: quicken me a' to
156 quicken me a' to thy judgments.
159 quicken me, O Lord, a' to thy
169 me understanding a' to thy word.
150: 2 praise him a' to his excellent
Pr 12: 8 shall be commended a' to his
24:12 render to every man a' to his
29 I will render to the man a' to
26: 4 Answer not a fool a' to his folly,
5 Answer a fool a' to his folly, lest
Ec 1: 6 and the wind returneth again a'
8:14 a' to the work of the wicked;
14 a' to the work of the righteous:
Isa 8:20 if they speak not a' to this word,
9: 3 they joy before thee a' to the joy
10:26 a' to the slaughter of Midian at
21:16 Within a year, a' to the years of
23:15 forgotten seventy years, a' to the
27: 7 or is he slain a' to the slaughter of
44:13 the figure of a man, a' to the
59:18 A' to their deeds, accordingly he
63: 7 a' to all that the Lord hath
7 he hath bestowed on them a' to
7 and a' to the multitude of his
Jer 2:28 for a' to the number of thy cities
3:15 And I will give you pastors a' to
11: 4 and do them, a' to all which I
13 For a' to the number of thy cities
13 and a' to the number of the
13: 2 girdle a' to the word of the Lord,
17:10 a' to his ways, and a' to the fruit
21: 2 the Lord will deal with us a' to
14 But I will punish you a' to the
25:14 recompense them a' to their
14 a' to the works of their own hands.
26:20 against this land a' to all the
27:12 to Zedekiah king of Judah a' to
31:32 Not a' to the covenant that I made
32: 8 a' to the word of the Lord, and
11 both that which was sealed a' to
19 to give every one a' to his ways,
19 and a' to the fruit of his doings:
35:10 and done a' to all that Jonadab
18 and done a' unto all that he hath
36: 8 did a' to all that Jeremiah the
38:27 a' to all these words that the king
40: 3 Lord hath brought it, and done a'
42: 4 a' to your words;
5 if we do not even a' to all things
20 and a' unto all that the Lord our
50:21 do a' to all that I have commanded
29 recompense her a' to her work;
29 a' to all that she hath done, do
52: 2 a' to all that Jehoiakim had done.
La 3:32 compassion a' to the multitude
64 a' to the work of their hands.
Eze 4: 4 a' to the number of the days
5 their iniquity, a' to the number of
9 make thee bread thereof, a' to the
5: 7 have done a' to the judgments
7: 3 and will judge thee a' to thy ways,
8 I will judge thee a' to thy ways,
9 I will recompense thee a' to thy
27 and a' to their deserts will I judge
8: 4 a' to the vision that I saw in the
14: 4 that cometh a' to the multitude
18:24 committeth iniquity, and doeth a'
30 every one a' to his ways, saith the
20:44 not a' to your wicked ways,
44 nor a' to your corrupt doings,
23:24 judge thee a' to their judgments.
24:14 a' to thy ways, and
14 a' to thy doings,
24 a' to all that he hath done shall
25:14 in Edom a' to mine anger and
14 a' to my fury;
35:11 do a' to thine anger, and
11 a' to thine envy
36:19 a' to their way and
19 a' to their doings I judged them.
39:24 A' to their uncleanness and
24 a' to their transgressions
40:24 and the arches thereof a' to these
28 measured the south gate a' to
29 and the arches thereof, a' to these
32 and he measured the gate a' to
33 the arches thereof, were a' to
35 the north gate, and measured it a'
42:11 both a' to their fashions, and
11 a' to their doors.
12 a' to the doors of the chambers
43: 3 a' to the appearance of the vision
3 even a' to the vision that I saw
44:24 judge it a' to my judgments:
45: 8 give to the house of Israel a' to
25 a' to the sin offering,
25 a' to the burnt offering,
25 and a' to the meat offering,
25 and a' to the oil.
46: 7 for the lambs a' as his hand shall
47:10 their fish shall be a' to their kinds,
12 bring forth new fruit a' to his
13 ye shall inherit the land a' to the
21 divide this land unto you a' to the
Da 4: 8 whose name was Belteshazzar, a'
35 and he doeth a' to his will in the
6: 8 a' to the law of the Medes and
12 is true, a' to the law of the Medes

Da 8: 4 but he did a' to his will, and
9:16 O Lord, a' to all thy righteousness,
11: 3 with great dominion, and do a'
4 to his posterity, nor a' to his
16 shall do a' to his own will, and
36 And the king shall do a' to his
Ho 3: 1 a' to the love of the Lord
9:10 their abominations were a' as
10: 1 a' to the multitude of his fruit he
1 a' to the goodness of his land
12: 2 a' to his ways; a' to his doings
13: 2 and idols a' to their own
6 A' to their pasture, so were they
Jon 3: 3 a' to the word of the Lord.
Mic 7:15 A' to the days of thy coming out
Hab 3: 9 made quite naked, a' to the
Hag 2: 5 A' to the word that I covenanted
Zec 1: 6 a' to our ways, and a' to our
5: 3 cut off as on this side a' to it;
3 cut off as on that side a' to it.
Mal 2: 9 a' as ye have not kept my ways,
M't 2:16 a' to the time which he had
9:29 A' to your faith be it unto you.
16:27 he shall reward every man a' to
25:15 to every man a' to his several
M'r 7: 5 Why walk not thy disciples a' to
Lu 1: 9 A' to the custom of the priest's
38 be it unto me a' to thy word.
2:22 a' to the law of Moses were
24 a' to that which is said in the law
29 in peace, a' to thy word:
39 a' to the law of the Lord,
5:14 and offer for thy cleansing, a' as
12:47 neither did a' to his will,
23:56 a' to the commandment.
Joh 7:24 Judge not a' to the appearance,
18:31 judge him a' to your law.
Ac 2:30 a' to the flesh, he would raise up
4:35 unto every man a' as he had need.
7:44 should make it a' to the fashion
11:29 every man a' to his ability,
13:23 a' to his promise raised unto
22: 3 taught a' to the perfect manner
12 a devout man a' to the law,
24: 6 would have judged a' to our law.
Ro 1: 3 of the seed of David a' to the flesh;
4 a' to the spirit of holiness,
2: 2 the judgment of God is a' to truth
6 to every man a' to his deeds:
16 a' to my gospel.
4:18 a' to that which was spoken, So
8:27 a' to the will of God.
28 a' to his purpose.
9: 3 my kinsmen a' to the flesh:
11 a' to election might stand, not of
10: 2 have a zeal of God, but not a' to
11: 5 a' to the election of grace.
8 (A' as it is written, God hath given
12: 3 a' as God hath dealt to every
6 differing a' to the grace
6 a' to the proportion of faith;
15: 5 a' to Christ Jesus:
16:25 a' to my gospel,
25 a' to the revelation of the mystery,
26 a' to the commandment of the
1Co 1:31 a' as it is written, He that glorieth,
3: 8 a' to his own labour.
10 A' to the grace of God which is
15: 3 died for our sins a' to the
4 a' to the scriptures:
2Co 1:17 do I purpose a' to the flesh,
4:13 a' as it is written, I believed,
5:10 a' to that he hath done,
8:12 a' to that a man hath and not a'
9: 7 a' as he purposeth in his heart,
10: 2 as if we walked a' to the flesh.
13 but a' to the measure of the rule
15 a' to our rule abundantly,
11:15 and shall be a' to their works.
13:10 a' to the power which the Lord
Ga 1: 4 a' to the will of God and our Father:
2:14 a' to the truth of the gospel,
3:29 heirs a' to the promise.
6:16 And as many as walk a' to this
Eph 1: 4 A' as he hath chosen us in him
5 a' to the good pleasure of his will,
7 a' to the riches of his grace;
9 a' to his good pleasure
11 a' to the purpose of him who
19 a' to the working of his mighty
2: 2 a' to the course of this world,
2 a' to the prince of the power
3: 7 a' to the gift of the grace of God
11 A' to the eternal purpose which he
16 a' to the riches of his glory,
20 a' to the power that worketh in us,
4: 7 grace a' to the measure of the
16 a' to the effectual working
22 a' to the deceitful lusts;
6: 5 a' to the flesh, with fear and
Ph'p 1:20 A' to my earnest expectation and
3:21 a' to the working whereby he is
4:19 a' to his riches in glory by Christ
Col 1:11 a' to his glorious power,
25 a' to the dispensation of God
29 striving a' to his working,
3:22 obey in all thing your masters a'
2Th 1:12 a' to the grace of our God
1Ti 1:11 A' to the glorious gospel of the
18 a' to the prophecies which went
6: 3 which is a' to godliness;
2Ti 1: 1 a' to the promise of life
8 a' to the power of God;
9 not a' to our works, but a' to his
2: 8 a' to my gospel:
4:14 Lord reward him a' to his works:
Tit 1: 1 a' to the faith of God's elect,
3 a' to the commandment of God
3: 5 but a' to his mercy he saved us,
7 a' to the hope of eternal life.
Heb 2: 4 a' to his own will?
7: 5 tithes of the people a' to the law,
8: 4 offer gifts a' to the law:
5 a' to the pattern shewed to thee
9 Not a' to the covenant that I made
9:19 a' to the law, he took the blood
Jas 2: 8 fulfil the royal law a' to the
1Pe 1: 2 Elect a' to the foreknowledge of
3 a' to his abundant mercy hath
14 not fashioning yourselves a' to
17 judgeth a' to every man's work,
3: 7 a' to knowledge, giving honour
4: 6 judged a' to men in the flesh,
6 but live a' to God in the spirit.
19 that suffer a' to the will of God
2Pe 1: 3 A' as his divine power hath given
2:22 a' to the true proverb, The dog is
3:13 a' to his promise, look for new
15 a' to the wisdom given unto him
1Jo 5:14 if we ask any thing a' to his will,
Re 2:23 a' to your works.
18: 6 double a' to her works:
20:12, 13 a' to their works.
21:17 a' to the measure of a man, that
22:12 to give every man a' as his work

accordingly
Isa 59:18 a' he will repay, fury to his

account See also ACCOUNTED; ACCOUNTING; ACCOUNTS.
2Ki 12: 4 of every one that passeth the a',
1Ch 27:24 was the number put in the a' of
2Ch 26:11 number of their a' by the hand
Job 33:13 he giveth not a' of any of his
Ps 144: 3 son of man, that thou makest a'
Ec 7:27 one by one, to find out the a':
M't 12:36 they shall give a' thereof in the
18:23 would take a' of his servants.
Lu 16: 2 give an a' of thy stewardship;
Ac 19:40 whereby we may give an a' of this
Ro 14:12 every one of us shall give a' of
1Co 4: 1 Let a man so a' of us, as of the
Ph'p 4:17 fruit that may abound to your a'.
Ph'm 18 put that on mine a';
Heb 13:17 as they that must give a',
1Pe 4: 5 shall give a' to him that is ready
2Pe 3:15 And a' that the longsuffering

accounted
De 2:11 Which also were a' giants, as the
20 (That also was a' a land of giants:
1Ki 10:21 it was nothing a' of in the days
2Ch 9:20 of silver; it was not any thing a'
Ps 22:30 it shall be a' to the Lord for a
Isa 2:22 wherein is he to be a' of?
M'r 10:42 they which are a' to rule over
Lu 20:35 which shall be a' worthy to
21:36 that ye may be a' worthy to
22:24 which of them should be a' the
Ro 8:36 we are a' as sheep for the
Ga 3: 6 it was a' to him for righteousness.

accounting
Heb 11:19 A' that God was able to raise

accounts
Da 6: 2 that the princes might give a'

accursed
De 21:23 he that is hanged is a' of God;)
Jos 6:17 the city shall be a',
18 keep yourselves from the a'
18 lest ye make yourselves a',
18 when ye take of the a' thing, and
7: 1 a trespass in the a' thing:
1 took of the a' thing:
11 have even taken of the a' thing,
12 because they were a':
12 except ye destroy the a' from
13 an a' thing in the midst of thee,
13 until ye take away the a' thing
15 taken with the a' thing shall be
22:20 commit a trespass in the a' thing,
1Ch 2: 7 who transgressed in the thing a'.
Isa 65:20 an hundred years old shall be a'.
Ro 9: 3 that myself were a' from Christ
1Co 12: 3 calleth Jesus a': and that no man
Ga 1: 8 preached unto you, let him be a'.
9 have received, let him be a'

accusation
Ezr 4: 6 wrote they unto him an a' against
M't 27:37 over his head his a' written,
M'r 15:26 his a' was written over,
Lu 6: 7 might find an a' against him.
19: 8 thing from any man by false a',
Joh 18:29 What a' bring ye against this
Ac 25:18 they brought none a' of such
1Ti 5:19 receive not an a', but before two
2Pe 2:11 bring not railing a' against them
Jude 9 a railing a', but said, The Lord

accuse See also ACCUSED; ACCUSETH; ACCUSING.
Pr 30:10 A' not a servant unto his master,
M't 12:10 that they might a' him.
M'r 3: 2 sabbath day; that they might a'
Lu 3:14 neither a' any falsely; and be
11:54 his mouth, that they might a'
23: 2 they began to a' him,
14 whereof ye a' him:
Joh 5:45 Do not think that I will a' you to
8: 6 that they might have to a' him.
Ac 24: 2 Tertullus began to a' him,
8 these things, whereof we a' him.
13 whereof they now a' me.
25: 5 go down with me, and a' this man,
Ac 25:11 whereof these a' me, no man may
28:19 ought to a' my nation of.
1Pe 3:16 ashamed that falsely a' your

accused
Da 3: 8 Chaldeans came near, and a'
6:24 those men which had a'
M't 27:12 he was a' of the chief priests
M'r 15: 3 the chief priests a' him of many
Lu 16: 1 the same was a' unto him that he
23:10 scribes stood and vehemently a'
Ac 22:30 wherefore he was a' of the Jews,
23:28 the cause wherefore they a' him,
29 be a' of questions of their law,
25:16 before that he which is a' have
26: 2 things whereof I am a' of the
7 king Agrippa, I am a' of the Jews.
Tit 1: 6 children not a' of riot, or
Re 12:10 which a' them before our God

accuser See also ACCUSERS.
Re 12:10 for the a' of our brethren is cast

accusers
Joh 8:10 where are those thine a'?
Ac 23:30 gave commandment to his a'
35 when thine a' are also come.
24: 8 Commanding his a' to come unto
25:16 have the a' face to face,
18 when the a' stood up,
2Ti 3: 3 trucebreakers, false a',
Tit 2: 3 not false a', not given to much

accuseth
Joh 5:45 there is one that a' you, even

accusing
Ro 2:15 their thoughts the mean while a'

accustomed See also UNACCUSTOMED.
Jer 13:23 that are a' to do evil.

Aceldama (*as-el'-dam-ah*)
Ac 1:19 A', that is to say, The field of

Achaia (*ak-ah'-yah*)
Ac 18:12 Gallio was the deputy of A',
27 to pass into A', the brethren wrote,
19:21 passed through Macedonia and A',
Ro 15:26 them of Macedonia and A' to make
16: 5 who is the firstfruits of A' unto
1Co 16:15 firstfruits of A', and that they have
2Co 1: 1 saints which are in all A':
9: 2 A' was ready a year ago;
11:10 of boasting in the regions of A'.
1Th 1: 7 that believe in Macedonia and A'.
8 not only in Macedonia and A', but

Achaicus (*ak-ah'-yah-cus*)
1Co 16:17 Fortunatus and A':
subscr. Stephanas, and Fortunatus, and A'.

Achan (*a'-kan*) See also ACHAR.
Jos 7: 1 for A', the son of Carmi, the son
18 his household man by man; and A',
19 And Joshua said unto A', My son,
20 And A' answered Joshua, and said,
24 and all Israel with him, took A'
22:20 Did not A' the son of Zerah

Achar (*a'-kar*) See also ACHAN.
1Ch 2: 7 And the sons of Carmi; A', the

Achaz (*a'-kaz*) See also AHAZ.
M't 1: 9 Joatham begat A';
9 and A' begat Ezekias;

Achbor (*ak'-bor*)
Ge 36:38 and Baal-hanan the son of A'
39 Baal-hanan the son of A' died,
2Ki 22:12 And A' the son of Michaiah, and
14 and A', and Shaphan, and Asahiah,
1Ch 1:49 Baal-hanan the son of A' reigned
Jer 26:22 namely, Elnathan the son of A',
36:12 Elnathan the son of A', and

Achim (*a'-kim*)
M't 1:14 and Sadoc begat A';
14 and A' begat Eliud;

Achish (*a'-kish*)
1Sa 21:10 and went to A' the king of Gath.
11 the servants of A' said unto him,
12 was sore afraid of A' the king
14 Then said A' unto his servants,
27: 2 unto A', the son of Maoch, king
3 David dwelt with A' at Gath,
5 David said unto A', If I have
6 A' gave him Ziklag that day:
9 and returned, and came to A'.
10 A' said, Whither have ye made
12 A' believed David, saying, He hath
28: 1 A' said unto David, Know thou
2 David said to A', Surely thou shalt
2 A' said to David, Therefore will I
29: 2 passed on in the rereward with A'.
3 A' said unto the princes of the
6 A' called David, and said unto him,
8 David said unto A', But what have I
9 A' answered and said to David,
1Ki 2:39 servants of Shimei ran away unto A'
40 and went to Gath to A' to seek his

Achmetha (*ak'-meth-ah*)
Ezr 6: 2 And there was found at A', in the

Achor (*a'-kor*)
Jos 7:24 them unto the valley of A'.
26 was called, The valley of A', unto
15: 7 toward Debir from the valley of A',
Isa 65:10 and the valley of A' a place for the
Ho 2:15 and the valley of A' for a door of

Achsa (*ak'-sah*) See also ACHSAH.
1Ch 2:49 the daughter of Caleb was A'.

Achsah (*ak'-sah*) See also ACHSA.
Jos 15:16 him will I give A' my daughter
17 and he gave him A' his daughter

J'g 1:12 and taketh it, to him will I give *A'*
13 took it: and he gave him *A'* his

Achshaph (*ak'-shaf*)
Jos 11: 1 of Shimron, and to the king of *A'*,
12:20 the king of *A'*, one;
19:25 and Hali, and Beten, and *A'*,

Achzib (*ak'-zib*) See also CHEZIB.
Jos 15:44 Keilah, and *A'*, and Mereshah;
19:29 at the sea from the coast to *A'*:
J'g 1:31 nor of *A'*, nor of Helbah,
Mic 1:14 the houses of *A'* shall be a lie

acknowledge See also ACKNOWLEDGED; ACKNOWLEDGETH; ACKNOWLEDGING.
De 21:17 he shall *a'* the son of the hated
33: 9 neither did he *a'* his brethren,
Ps 51: 3 I *a'* my transgressions:
Pr 3: 6 In all thy ways *a'* him,
Isa 33:13 ye that are near, *a'* my might.
61: 9 all that see them shall *a'* them,
63:16 Israel *a'* us not:
Jer 3:13 Only *a'* thine iniquity,
14:20 We *a'*, O Lord, our wickedness,
24: 5 so will I *a'* them that are carried
Da 11:39 a strange god, whom he shall *a'*
Ho 5:15 till they *a'* their offence,
1Co 14:37 let him *a'* that the things that I
16:18 therefore *a'* ye them that are such.
2Co 1:13 than what ye read or *a'*;
13 ye shall *a'* even to the end;

acknowledged
Ge 38:26 And Judah *a'* them,
Ps 32: 5 I *a'* my sin unto thee, and mine
2Co 1:14 ye have *a'* us in part,

acknowledgeth
1Joh 2:23 he that *a'* the Son hath the Father

acknowledging
2Ti 2:25 repentance to the *a'* of the truth;
Tit 1: 1 and the *a'* of the truth which is
Ph'm 6 by the *a'* of every good thing

acknowledgment
Col 2: 2 to the *a'* of the mystery of God,

acquaint See also ACQUAINTED; ACQUAINTING.
Job 22:21 *A'* now thyself with him,

acquaintance
2Ki 12: 5 it to them, every man of his *a'*:
7 receive no more money of your *a'*,
Job 19:13 and mine *a'* are verily estranged
42:11 all they that had been of his *a'*
Ps 31:11 a fear to mine *a'*:
55:13 my guide, and mine *a'*.
88: 8 Thou hast put away mine *a'*
18 mine *a'* into darkness.
Lu 2:44 among their kinsfolk and *a'*.
23:49 all his *a'*, and the women that
Ac 24:23 he should forbid none of his *a'*

acquainted
Ps 139: 3 and art *a'* with all my ways.
Isa 53: 3 man of sorrows, and *a'* with grief:

acquainting
Ec 2: 3 *a'* mine heart with wisdom;

acquit
Job 10:14 thou wilt not *a'* me from mine
Na 1: 3 will not at all *a'* the wicked:

Acrabbim See MAALEH-ACRABBIM.

acre See also ACRES.
1Sa 14:14 as it were an half *a'* of land,

acres
Isa 5:10 ten *a'* of vineyard shall yield

act See also ACTS; EXACT.
Isa 28:21 to pass his *a'*, his strange *a'*.
59: 6 *a'* of violence is in their hands.
Joh 8: 4 taken in adultery, in the very *a'*.

actions See also EXACTIONS.
1Sa 2: 3 by him *a'* are weighed.

activity
Ge 47: 6 if thou knowest any men of *a'*

acts
De 11: 3 his *a'*, which he did in the midst
7 seen all the great *a'* of the Lord
J'g 5:11 the righteous *a'* of the Lord,
11 even the righteous *a'*
1Sa 12: 7 all the righteous *a'* of the Lord,
2Sa 23:20 who had done many *a'*, he slew
1Ki 10: 6 heard in mine own land of thy *a'*
11:41 the rest of the *a'* of Solomon,
41 in the book of the *a'* of Solomon?
14:19 the rest of the *a'* of Jeroboam, how
29 the rest of the *a'* of Rehoboam, and
15: 7 the rest of the *a'* of Abijam, and
23 rest of all the *a'* of Asa, and all his
31 the rest of the *a'* of Nadab, and all
16: 5 the rest of the *a'* of Baasha, and
14 the rest of the *a'* of Elah, and all
20 the rest of the *a'* of Zimri, and his
27 the rest of the *a'* of Omri which he
22:39 the rest of the *a'* of Ahab, and all
45 the rest of the *a'* of Jehoshaphat,
2Ki 1:18 the rest of the *a'* of Ahaziah which
8:23 the rest of the *a'* of Joram,
10:34 the rest of the *a* of Jehu, and all
12:19 the rest of the *a'* of Joash, and all
13: 8 the rest of the *a'* of Jehoahaz,
12 the rest of the *a'* of Joash,
14:15 the rest of the *a'* of Jehoash which
18 the rest of the *a'* of Amaziah,
28 the rest of the *a'* of Jeroboam, and
15: 6 the rest of the *a'* of Azariah,
11 the rest of the *a'* of Zachariah,
15 the rest of the *a'* of Shallum, and
2Ki 15:21 the rest of the *a'* of Menahem,
26 the rest of the *a'* of Pekahiah,
31 the rest of the *a'* of Pekah,
36 the rest of the *a'* of Jotham,
16:19 the rest of the *a'* of Ahaz
20:20 the rest of the *a'* of Hezekiah, and
21:17 the rest of the *a'* of Manasseh, and
25 the rest of the *a'* of Amon which
23:19 *a'* that he had done in Beth-el.
28 the rest of the *a'* of Josiah, and all
24: 5 the rest of the *a'* of Jehoiakim,
1Ch 11:22 who had done many *a'*;
29:29 Now the *a'* of David the king, first
2Ch 9: 5 in mine own land of thine *a'*, and
29 the rest of the *a'* of Solomon,
12:15 Now the *a'* of Rehoboam, first and
13:22 the rest of the *a'* of Abijah, and
16:11 behold, the *a'* of Asa, first and last,
20:34 the rest of the *a'* of Jehoshaphat,
25:26 the rest of the *a'* of Amaziah, first
26:22 the rest of the *a'* of Uzziah,
27: 7 the rest of the *a'* of Jotham, and
28:26 Now the rest of his *a'* and of all his
32:32 the rest of the *a'* of Hezekiah, and
33:18 the rest of the *a'* of Manasseh, and
35:26 the rest of the *a'* of Josiah, and his
36: 8 the rest of the *a'* of Jehoiakim,
Es 10: 2 all the *a'* of his power and of his
Ps 103: 7 his *a'* unto the children of Israel.
106: 2 Who can utter the mighty *a'* of
145: 4 and shall declare thy mighty *a'*.
6 the might of thy terrible *a'*:
12 to the sons of men his mighty *a'*,
150: 2 Praise him for his mighty *a'*:

Adadah (*ad'-ad-ah*)
Jos 15:22 Kinah, and Dimonah, and *A'*,

Adah (*a'-dah*)
Ge 4:19 the name of the one was *A'*,
20 and *A'* bare Jabal: he was the
23 *A'* and Zillah, Hear my voice;
36: 2 *A'* the daughter of Elon the
4 And *A'* bare to Esau Eliphaz;
10 Eliphaz the son of *A'* the wife of
12 these were the sons of *A'* Esau's
16 Edom: these were the sons of *A'*.

Adaiah (*ad-a-i'-yah*)
2Ki 22: 1 was Jedidah, the daughter of *A'*
1Ch 6:41 the son of Zerah, the son of *A'*,
8:21 *A'*, and Beraiah, and Shimrath,
9:12 and *A'* the son of Jeroham, the
2Ch 23: 1 and Maaseiah the son of *A'*, and
Ezr 10:29 Malluch, and *A'*, Jashub, and
39 and Nathan, and *A'*,
Ne 11: 5 the son of Hazaiah, the son of *A'*,
12 and *A'* the son of Jeroham, the son

Adalia (*ad-al-i'-yah*)
Es 9: 8 Poratha, and *A'*, and Aridatha,

Adam (*ad'-um*) See also ADAM'S.
Ge 2:19 brought them unto *A'* to see what
19 whatsoever *A'* called every living
20 *A'* gave names to all cattle,
20 but for *A'* there was not found an
21 a deep sleep to fall upon *A'*,
23 *A'* said, This is now bone of my
3: 8 *A'* and his wife hid themselves
9 And the Lord God called unto *A'*,
17 And unto *A'* he said, Because
20 *A'* called his wife's name Eve;
21 Unto *A'* also and to his wife did the
4: 1 And *A'* knew Eve his wife;
25 *A'* knew his wife again;
5: 1 the book of the generations of *A'*.
2 called their name *A'*, in the day
3 *A'* lived an hundred and thirty years,
4 And the days of *A'* after he had
5 the days that *A'* lived
De 32: 8 when he separated the sons *A'*,
Jos 3:16 very far from the city *A'*,
1Ch 1: 1 *A'*, Sheth, Enosh,
Job 31:33 I covered my transgressions as *A'*,
Lu 3:38 which was the son of *A'*,
Ro 5:14 death reigned from *A'* to Moses,
1Co 15:22 as in *A'* all die, even so in Christ
45 The first man *A'* was made a
45 the last *A'* was made
1Ti 2:13 For *A'* was first formed,
14 And *A'* was not deceived,
Jude 14 Enoch also, the seventh from *A'*,

Adamah (*ad'-am-ah*)
Jos 19:36 And *A'*, and Ramah, and Hazor,

adamant
Eze 3: 9 As an *a'* harder than flint
Zec 7:12 made their hearts as an *a'* stone,

adamant-stone See ADAMANT and STONE.

Adami (*ad'-am-i*)
Jos 19:33 from Allon to Zaanannim, and *A'*,

Adam's (*ad'-ums*)
Ro 5:14 similitude of *A'* transgression,

Adan See NEBUZAR-ADAN.

Adar (*a'-dar*) See also ADDAR; ATAROTH-ADAR.
Jos 15: 3 and went up to *A'*, and fetched a
Ezr 6:15 on the third day of the month *A'*,
Es 3: 7 twelfth month, that is, the month *A'*.
13 which is the month *A'*,
8:12 month, which is the month *A'*.
9: 1 that is the month *A'*,
15 fourteenth day also of the month *A'*,
17 thirteenth day of the month *A'*;
19, 21 fourteenth day of the month *A'*,

Adbeel (*ad'-be-el*)
Ge 25:13 and Kedar, and *A'*, and Mibsam,
1Ch 1:29 then Kedar, and *A'*, and Mibsam,

add See also ADDED; ADDETH.
Ge 30:24 Lord shall *a'* to me another son.
Le 5:16 shall *a'* the fifth part thereto, and
6: 5 shall *a'* the fifth part more thereto,
27:13 then he shall *a'* a fifth part
15, 19 then he shall *a'* the fifth part
27 and shall *a'* a fifth part
31 he shall *a'* thereto the fifth part
Nu 5: 7 *a'* unto it the fifth part thereof,
35: 6 to them ye shall *a'* forty and two
De 4: 2 Ye shall not *a'* unto the word
12:32 thou shalt not *a'* thereto, nor
19: 9 then shalt thou *a'* three cities
29:19 to *a'* drunkenness to thirst:
2Sa 24: 3 Now the Lord thy God *a'* unto the
1Ki 12:11 I will *a'* to your yoke:
14 heavy, and I will *a'* to your yoke:
2Ki 20: 6 And I will *a'* unto thy days fifteen
1Ch 22:14 thou mayest *a'* thereto.
2Ch 10:14 I will *a'* thereto: my father
28:13 ye intend to *a'* more to our sins
Ps 69:27 *A'* iniquity unto their iniquity:
Pr 3: 2 peace, shall they *a'* to thee.
30: 6 *A'* thou not unto his words, lest he
Isa 29: 1 *a'* ye year to year;
30: 1 that they may *a'* sin to sin:
38: 5 I will *a'* unto thy days fifteen
M't 6:27 can *a'* one cubit unto his stature?
Lu 12:25 can *a'* to his stature one cubit?
Ph'p 1:16 to *a'* affliction to my bonds:
2Pe 1: 5 *a'* to your faith virtue;
Re 22:18 If any man shall *a'* unto these,
18 God shall *a'* unto him the

Addan (*ad'-dan*)
Ezr 2:59 Tel-harsa, Cherub, *A'*, and Immer:

Addar (*ad'-dar*) See also ADAR; ATAROTH-ADDAR; HAZAR-ADDAR.
1Ch 8: 3 And the sons of Bela were, *A'*, and

added
De 5:22 great voice: and he *a'* no more.
1Sa 12:19 we have *a'* unto all our sins this
Jer 36:32 there were *a'* besides unto them
45: 3 Lord hath *a'* grief to my sorrow;
Da 4:36 excellent majesty was *a'* unto me.
M't 6:33 these things shall be *a'* unto you.
Lu 3:20 *A'* yet this above all, that he shut
12:31 these things shall be *a'* unto you.
19:11 he *a'* and spake a parable,
Ac 2:41 there were *a'* unto them about
47 And the Lord *a'* to the church
5:14 believers were the more *a'* to the
11:24 much people was *a'* unto the Lord.
Ga 2: 6 in conference *a'* nothing to me:
3:19 was *a'* because of transgressions,

adder See also ADDERS'.
Ge 49:17 serpent by the way, an *a'* in the
Ps 58: 4 the deaf *a'* that stoppeth her ear;
91:13 shalt tread upon the lion and *a'*:
Pr 23:32 a serpent, and stingeth like an *a'*.

adders'
Ps 140: 3 *a'* poison is under their lips.

addeth
Job 34:37 he *a'* rebellion unto his sin,
Pr 10:22 he *a'* no sorrow with it.
16:23 *a'* learning to his lips.
Ga 3:15 no man disannulleth, or *a'*

Addi (*ad'-di*)
Lu 3:28 which was the son of *A'*, which

addicted
1Co 16:15 they have *a'* themselves to the

addition See also ADDITIONS.
1Ki 7:30 at the side of every *a'*.

additions
1Ki 7:29 certain *a'* made of thin work.
36 and *a'* round about.

Addon (*ad'-don*)
Ne 7:61 Tel-haresha, Cherub, *A'*, and

Ader (*a'-dur*)
1Ch 8:15 And Zebadiah, and Arad, and *A'*,

Adiel (*a'-de-el*)
1Ch 4:36 and Asaiah, and *A'*, and Jesimiel,
9:12 and Maasiai the son of *A'*,
27:25 was Azmaveth the son of *A'*:

Adin (*a'-din*)
Ezr 2:15 The children of *A'*, four hundred
8: 6 Of the sons also of *A'*; Ebed the
Ne 7:20 The children of *A'*, six hundred
10:16 Adonijah, Bigvai, *A'*,

Adina (*ad'-in-ah*)
1Ch 11:42 *A'* the son of Shiza the Reubenite,

Adino (*ad'-in-o*)
2Sa 23: 8 the same was *A'* the Eznite: he

Adithaim (*ad-ith-a'-im*)
Jos 15:36 Sharaim, and *A'*, and Gederah,

adjure See also ADJURED.
1Ki 22:16 How many times shall I *a'* thee
2Ch 18:15 How many times shall I *a'* thee
M't 26:63 I *a'* thee by the living God,
M'r 5: 7 I *a'* thee by God, that thou
Ac 19:13 We *a'* you by Jesus whom Paul

adjured
Jos 6:26 Joshua *a'* them at that time,
1Sa 14:24 for Saul had *a'* the people,

Adlai (*ad'-la-i*)
1Ch 27:29 was Shaphat the son of *A'*:

Admah (*ad'-mah*)
Ge 10:19 Sodom, and Gomorrah, and *A*'.
14: 2 of Gomorrah, Shinab king of *A*',
8 of Gomorrah, and the king of *A*',
De 29:23 *A*', and Zeboim, which the Lord
Ho 11: 8 how shall I make thee as *A*'?
Admatha (*ad'-math-ah*)
Es 1:14 Shethar, *A*', Tarshish, Meres,
administered
2Co 8:19 which is *a*' by us to the glory of
20 abundance which is *a*' by us:
administration See also ADMINISTRATIONS.
2Co 9:12 For the *a*' of this service
administrations
1Co 12: 5 are differences of *a*', but the
admiration
Jude 16 having men's persons in *a*'
Re 17: 6 her, I wondered with great *a*'.
admired
2Th 1: 10 to be *a*' in all them that believe
admonish See also ADMONISHED; ADMONISHING.
Ro 15:14 able also to *a*' one another.
1Th 5:12 over you in the Lord, and *a*' you;
2Th 3:15 but *a*' him as a brother.
admonished
Ec 4:13 who will no more be *a*'.
12:12 by these, my son, be *a*':
Jer 42:19 know certainly that I have *a*'
Ac 27: 9 already past, Paul *a*' them,
Heb 8: 5 as Moses was *a*' of God when
admonishing
Col 3:16 *a*' one another in psalms and
admonition
1Co 10:11 they are written for our *a*',
Eph 6: 4 the nurture and *a*' of the Lord.
Tit 3:10 after the first and second *a*' reject;
Adna (*ad'-nah*) See also ADNAH.
Ezr 10:30 *A*', and Chelal, Benaiah, Maaseiah,
Ne 12:15 Of Harim, *A*'; of Meraioth,
Adnah (*ad'-nah*) See also ADNA.
1Ch 12:20 fell to him of Manasseh, *A*',
2Ch 17:14 *A*' the chief, and with him mighty
ado
M'r 5:39 Why make ye this *a*', and weep?
Adoni See ADONI-BEZEK; ADONI-ZEDEK.
Adoni-bezek (*ad''-on-i-be'-zek*)
J'g 1: 5 And they found *A*' in Bezek:
6 *A*' fled; and they pursued after him,
7 *A*' said, Threescore and ten kings,
Adonijah (*ad-on-i'-jah*) See also TOB-ADONIJAH.
2Sa 3: 4 the fourth, *A*' the son of Haggith;
1Ki 1: 5 *A*' the son of Haggith exalted
7 and they following *A*' helped him.
8 belonged to David, were not with *A*'
9 And *A*' slew sheep and oxen and
11 Hast thou not heard that *A*' the son
13 why then doth *A*' reign?
18 And now, behold, *A*' reigneth;
24 hast thou said, *A*' shall reign after
25 and say, God save king *A*'.
41 And *A*' and all the guests that were
42 and *A*' said unto him, Come in;
43 Jonathan answered and said to *A*',
49 guests that were with *A*' were afraid,
50 *A*' feared because of Solomon,
51 Behold, *A*' feareth king Solomon:
2:13 And *A*' the son of Haggith came to
19 to speak unto him for *A*'.
21 the Shunammite be given to *A*'
22 ask Abishag the Shunammite for *A*'?
23 if *A*' have not spoken this word
24 *A*' shall be put to death this day.
28 for Joab had turned after *A*',
1Ch 3: 2 the fourth, *A*' the son of Haggith:
2Ch 17: 8 Jehonathan, and *A*', and Tobijah,
Ne 10:16 *A*', Bigvai, Adin,
Adonikam (*ad-on-i'-kam*)
Ezr 2:13 The children of *A*', six hundred
8:13 And of the last sons of *A*', whose
Ne 7:18 The children of *A*', six hundred
Adoniram (*ad-on-i'-ram*). See also ADORAM.
1Ki 4: 6 *A*' the son of Abda was over the
5:14 and *A*' was over the levy.
Adoni-zedec (*ad''-on-i-ze'-dek*)
Jos 10: 1 when *A*' king of Jerusalem had
3 *A*' king of Jerusalem sent unto
adoption
Ro 8:15 ye have received the Spirit of *a*',
23 waiting for the *a*', to wit, the
9: 4 to whom pertaineth the *a*', and
Ga 4: 5 we might receive the *a*' of sons.
Eph 1: 5 unto the *a*' of children by Jesus
Adoraim (*ad-o-ra'-im*)
2Ch 11: 9 And *A*', and Lachish, and Azekah,
Adoram (*ad-o'-ram*). See also ADONIRAM.
2Sa 20:24 And *A*' was over the tribute:
1Ki 12:18 Then king Rehoboam sent *A*',
adorn See also ADORNED; ADORNETH; ADORNING.
1Ti 2: 9 that women *a*' themselves in
Tit 2:10 they may *a*' the doctrine of God
adorned
Jer 31: 4 thou shalt again be *a*' with thy
Lu 21: 5 how it was *a*' with goodly stones
1Pe 3: 5 *a*' themselves, being in subjection
Re 21: 2 as a bride *a*' for her husband.
adorneth
Isa 61:10 a bride *a*' herself with her jewels.
adorning
1Pe 3: 3 *a*' let it not be that outward *a*'
Adrammelech (*a-dram'-mel-ek*)
2Ki 17:31 burnt their children in fire to *A*'
19:37 *A*' and Sharezer his sons smote
Isa 37:38 *A*' and Sharezer his sons smote
Adramyttium (*a-dram-mit'-te-um*)
Ac 27: 2 entering into a ship of *A*',
Adria (*a'-dre-ah*)
Ac 27:27 driven up and down in *A*',
Adriel (*a'-dre-el*)
1Sa 18:19 that she was given unto *A*' the
2Sa 21: 8 whom she brought up for *A*' the
Adullam (*a-dul'-lam*) See also ADULLAMITE.
Jos 12:15 of Libnah, one; the king of *A*',
15:35 Jarmuth, and *A*', Socoh, and
1Sa 22: 1 and escaped to the cave *A*': and
2Sa 23:13 harvest time unto the cave of *A*':
1Ch 11:15 rock to David, into the cave of *A*';
2Ch 11: 7 And Beth-zur, and Shoco, and *A*',
Ne 11:30 Zanoah, *A*', and in their villages,
Mic 1:15 he shall come unto *A*' the glory
Adullamite (*a-dul'-lam-ite*)
Ge 38: 1 turned in to a certain *A*', whose
12 he and his friend Hirah the *A*'.
20 by the hand of his friend the *A*',
adulterer See also ADULTERERS.
Le 20:10 the *a*' and the adulteress shall
Job 24:15 the eye also of the *a*' waiteth for
Isa 57: 3 the seed of the *a*'
adulterers
Ps 50:18 hast been partaker with *a*'.
Jer 9: 2 they be all *a*',
23:10 the land is full of *a*';
Ho 7: 4 They are all *a*',
Mal 3: 5 the sorcerers, and against the *a*',
Lu 18:11 extortioners, unjust, *a*',
1Co 6: 9 nor idolaters, nor *a*',
Heb 13: 4 whoremongers and *a*' God will
Jas 4: 4 Ye *a*' and adulteresses,
adulteress See also ADULTERESSES.
Le 20:10 adulterer and the *a*' shall surely
Pr 6:26 and the *a*' will hunt for the
Ho 3: 1 beloved of her friend, yet an *a*',
Ro 7: 3 she shall be called an *a*':
3 so that she is no *a*',
adulteresses
Eze 23:45 after the manner of *a*',
45 because they are *a*',
Jas 4: 4 Ye adulterers and *a*',
adulteries
Jer 13:27 I have seen thine *a*',
Eze 23:43 her that was old in *a*',
Ho 2: 2 out of her sight, and her *a*'
M't 15:19 murders, *a*', fornications,
M'r 7:21 evil thoughts, *a*', fornications,
adulterous
Pr 30:20 such is the way of an *a*' woman;
M't 12:39 An evil and *a*' generation seeketh
16: 4 A wicked and *a*' generation
M'r 8:38 in this *a*' and sinful generation;
adultery See also ADULTERIES.
Ex 20:14 Thou shalt not commit *a*'.
Le 20:10 the man that committeth *a*'
10 he that committeth *a*'
De 5:18 Neither shalt thou commit *a*'.
Pr 6:32 committeth *a*' with a woman
Jer 3: 8 backsliding Israel committed *a*'
9 and committed *a*' with stones
5: 7 they then committed *a*', and
7: 9 ye steal, murder, and commit *a*',
23:14 they commit *a*', and walk in lies:
29:23 in Israel, and have committed *a*'
Eze 16:32 a wife that committeth *a*',
23:37 they have committed *a*', and blood
37 their idols have they committed *a*',
Ho 4: 2 stealing, and committing *a*',
13 your spouses shall commit *a*'.
14 when they commit *a*':
M't 5:27 Thou shalt not commit *a*':
28 hath committed *a*' with her
32 causeth her to commit *a*':
32 that is divorced committeth *a*'.
19: 9 marry another, committeth *a*':
9 is put away doth commit *a*'.
18 Thou shalt not commit *a*',
M'r 10:11 committeth *a*' against her.
12 to another, she committeth *a*'.
19 Do not commit *a*',
Lu 16:18 marrieth another, committeth *a*':
18 from her husband committeth *a*'.
18:20 Do not commit *a*', Do not kill,
Joh 8: 3 unto him a woman taken in *a*';
4 was taken in *a*', in the very act.
Ro 2:22 should not commit *a*',
22 dost thou commit *a*'?
13: 9 Thou shalt not commit *a*', Thou
Ga 5:19 *A*', fornication, uncleanness,
Jas 2:11 Do not commit *a*', said also
11 Now if thou commit no *a*',
2Pe 2:14 Having eyes full of *a*',
Re 2:22 and them that commit *a*' with her
Adummim (*a-dum'-mim*)
Jos 15: 7 that is before the going up to *A*',
18:17 over against the going up of *A*',
advanced
1Sa 12: 6 Lord that *a*' Moses and Aaron,
Es 3: 1 and *a*' him, and set his seat above
5:11 he had *a*' him above the princes
10: 2 whereunto the king *a*' him,
advantage See also ADVANTAGED; ADVANTAGETH.
Job 35: 3 thou saidst, What *a*' will it be
Ro 3: 1 What *a*' then hath the Jew?
2Co 2:11 Lest Satan should get an *a*' of us:
Jude 16 in admiration because of *a*'.
advantaged
Lu 9:25 For what is a man *a*',
advantageth
1Co 15:32 what *a*' it me, if the dead rise
adventure See also ADVENTURED; PERADVENTURE.
De 28:56 would not *a*' to set the sole of her
Ac 19:31 not *a*' himself into the theatre.
adventured
J'g 9:17 fought for you, and *a*' his life far,
adversaries
Ex 23:22 and an adversary unto thine *a*'.
De 32:27 *a*' should behave themselves
43 render vengeance to his *a*',
Jos 5:13 Art thou for us, or for our *a*'?
1Sa 2:10 *a*' of the Lord shall be broken to
2Sa 19:22 should this day be *a*' unto me?
Ezr 4: 1 the *a*' of Judah and Benjamin
Ne 4:11 And our *a*' said, They shall not
Ps 38:20 render evil for good are mine *a*';
69:19 mine *a*' are all before thee.
71:13 *a*' to my soul;
81:14 turned my hand against their *a*'.
89:42 hast set the right hand of his *a*';
109: 4 For my love they are my *a*':
20 the reward of mine *a*'
29 Let mine *a*' be clothed with
Isa 1:24 I will ease me of mine *a*',
9:11 shall set up the *a*' of Rezin against
11:13 and the *a*' of Judah shall be cut
59:18 he will repay, fury to his *a*',
63:18 our *a*' have trodden down thy
64: 2 make thy name known to thine *a*',
Jer 30:16 devoured; and all thine *a*',
46:10 avenge him of his *a*':
50: 7 and their *a*' said, We offend not,
La 1: 5 Her *a*' are the chief,
7 the *a*' saw her, and did mock
17 his *a*' should be round about him:
2:17 set up the horn of thine *a*'.
Mic 5: 9 lifted up upon thine *a*',
Na 1: 2 Lord will take vengeance on his *a*',
Lu 13:17 all his *a*' were ashamed:
21:15 which all your *a*' shall not be able
1Co 16: 9 unto me, and there are many *a*'.
Ph'p 1:28 in nothing terrified by your *a*':
Heb 10:27 which shall devour the *a*'.
adversary See also ADVERSARIES.
Ex 23:22 and an *a*' unto thine adversaries.
Nu 22:22 stood in the way for an *a*' against
1Sa 1: 6 her *a*' also provoked her sore,
29: 4 lest in the battle he be an *a*'
1Ki 5: 4 is neither *a*' nor evil occurrent.
11:14 the Lord stirred up an *a*' unto
23 God stirred him up another *a*',
25 he was an *a*' to Israel all the days
Es 7: 6 The *a*' and enemy is this wicked
Job 31:35 mine *a*' had written a book.
Ps 74:10 how long shall the *a*' reproach?
Isa 50: 8 who is mine *a*'?
La 1:10 The *a*' hath spread out his hand
2: 4 with his right hand as an *a*',
4:12 have believed that the *a*' and the
Am 3:11 An *a*' there shall be even round
M't 5:25 Agree with thine *a*' quickly,
25 at any time the *a*' deliver
Lu 12:58 with thine *a*' to the magistrate,
18: 3 saying, Avenge me of mine *a*'.
1Ti 5:14 give none occasion to the *a*'
1Pe 5: 8 because your *a*' the devil,
adversities
1Sa 10:19 saved you out of all your *a*'
Ps 31: 7 hast known my soul in *a*';
adversity See also ADVERSITIES.
2Sa 4: 9 redeemed my soul out of all *a*',
2Ch 15: 6 God did vex them with all *a*'.
Ps 10: 6 I shall never be in *a*'.
35:15 But in mine *a*' they rejoiced,
94:13 give him rest from the days of *a*',
Pr 17:17 a brother is born for *a*'.
24:10 If thou faint in the day of *a*',
Ec 7:14 in the day of *a*' consider:
Isa 30:20 the Lord give you the bread of *a*',
Heb 13: 3 and them which suffer *a*',
advertise
Nu 24:14 I will *a*' thee what this people
Ru 4: 4 And I thought to *a*' thee,
advice
J'g 19:30 consider of it, take *a*', and speak
20: 7 give here your *a*' and counsel.
1Sa 25:33 blessed be thy *a*', and blessed be
2Sa 19:43 that our *a*' should not be first had
2Ch 10: 9 What *a*' give ye that we may
14 answered them after the *a*' of
25:17 Amaziah king of Judah took *a*',
Pr 20:18 and with good *a*' make war.
2Co 8:10 herein I give my *a*': for this is
advise See also ADVISED.
2Sa 24:13 *a*', and see what answer I shall
1Ki 12: 6 How do ye *a*' that I may answer
1Ch 21:12 *a*' thyself what word I shall
advised
Pr 13:10 with the well *a*' is wisdom.
Ac 27:12 the more part *a*' to depart
advisement
1Ch 12:19 the Philistines upon *a*' sent him

advocate
1Jo 2: 1 a· with the Father, Jesus Christ
a-dying See DYING.
Æneas (e'-ne-as)
Ac 9:33 found a certain man named Æ·,
34 And Peter said unto him, Æ·,
Ænon (e'-non)
Joh 3:23 baptizing in Æ· near to Salim,
afar ^
Ge 22: 4 Abraham.... saw the place a· off.
37:18 when they saw him a· off,
Ex 2: 4 his sister stood a· off,
20:18 they removed, and stood a· off.
21 the people stood a· off, and Moses
24: 1 worship ye a· off.
Ex 33: 7 pitched it without the camp, a· off
Nu 9:10 in a journey a· off,
1Sa 26:13 Stood on the top of a hill a· off;
2Ki 2: 7 went, and stood to view a· off:
Ezr 3:13 the noise was heard a· off.
Ne 12:43 Jerusalem was heard even a· off.
Job 2:12 they lifted up their eyes a· off,
36: 3 I will fetch my knowledge from a·,
25 man may behold it a· off.
39:25 and he smelleth the battle a· off,
29 her eyes behold a· off.
Ps 10: 1 Why standest thou a· off, O Lord?
38:11 my kinsmen stand a· off.
65: 5 them that are a· off upon the sea:
138: 6 the proud he knoweth a· off.
139: 2 understandest my thought a· off.
Pr 31:14 she bringeth her food from a·.
Isa 23: 7 her own feet shall carry her a· off
59:14 justice standeth a· off:
66:19 isles a· off, that have not heard
Jer 23:23 saith the Lord, and not a God a·
30:10 I will save thee from a·,
31:10 declare it in the isles a· off,
46:27 I will save thee from a· off,
51:50 remember the Lord a· off,
Mic 4: 3 rebuke strong nations a· off;
M't 26:58 Peter followed him a· off
27:55 women were there beholding a·
M'r 5: 6 when he saw Jesus a· off,
11:13 seeing a fig tree a· off
14:54 Peter followed him a· off,
15:40 women looking on a· off:
Lu 16:23 and seeth Abraham a· off,
17:12 lepers, which stood a· off:
18:13 the publican, standing a· off,
22:54 Peter followed a· off.
23:49 stood a· off, beholding these
Ac 2:39 and to all that are a· off,
Eph 2:17 peace to you which were a· off,
Heb 11:13 but having seen them a· off,
2Pe 1: 9 is blind, and cannot see a· off,
Re 18:10 Standing a· off for the fear of her
15 shall stand a· off for the fear of
17 as many as trade by sea, stood a·
affairs
1Ch 26:32 pertaining to God, and a· of the
Ps 112: 5 he will guide his a·
Da 2:49 the a· of the province of Babylon:
3:12 whom thou hast set over the a· of
Eph 6:21 also may know my a·,
22 ye might know our a·,
Ph'p 1:27 I may hear of your a·, that ye
2Ti 2: 4 entangleth himself with the a· of
affect See also AFFECTED; AFFECTETH.
Ga 4:17 They zealously a· you, but not
17 that ye might a· them.
affected
Ac 14: 2 and made their minds evil a·
Ga 4:18 be zealously a· always in a good
affecteth
La 3:51 Mine eye a· mine heart
affection See also AFFECTIONED; AFFECTIONS.
1Ch 29: 3 because I have set my a· to the
Ro 1:31 without natural a·, implacable,
2Co 7:15 his inward a· is more abundant
Col 3: 2 Set your a· on things above,
5 uncleanness, inordinate a·,
2Ti 3: 3 Without natural a·, trucebreakers,
affectionately
1Th 2: 8 So being a· desirous of you, we
affectioned
Ro 12:10 Be kindly a· one to another
affections
Ro 1:26 God gave them up unto vile a·:
Ga 5:24 crucified the flesh with the a·
affinity
1Ki 3: 1 Solomon made a· with Pharaoh
2Ch 18: 1 and joined a· with Ahab.
Ezr 9:14 and join in a· with the people
affirm See also AFFIRMED.
Ro 3: 8 and as some a· that we say,)
1Ti 1: 7 they say, nor whereof they a·.
Tit 3: 8 I will that thou a· constantly,
affirmed
Lu 22:59 another confidently a·, saying,
Ac 12:15 she constantly a· that it was even
25:19 whom Paul a· to be alive.
afflict See also AFFLICTED; AFFLICTEST.
Ge 15:13 they shall a· them four hundred
31:50 If thou shalt a· my daughters,
Ex 1:11 over them taskmasters to a· them
22:22 Ye shall not a· any widow,
23 If thou a· them in any wise,
Le 16:29 ye shall a· your souls,
31 you, and ye shall a· your souls,
Le 23:27 ye shall a· your souls, and offer an
32 ye shall a· your souls: in the ninth
Nu 24:24 shall a· Asshur, and shall a· Eber,
29: 7 and ye shall a· your souls:
30:13 every binding oath to a· the soul,
J'g 16: 5 that we may bind him to a· him:
6 thou mightest be bound to a· thee.
19 and she began to a· him,
2Sa 7:10 shall the children of wickedness a·
1Ki 11:39 I will for this a· the seed of David,
2Ch 6:26 when thou dost a· them;
Ezr 8:21 a· ourselves before our God,
Job 37:23 plenty of justice: he will not a·.
Ps 44: 2 how thou didst a· the people,
55:19 God shall hear, and a· them,
89:22 nor the son of wickedness a· him.
94: 5 and a· thine heritage.
143:12 destroy all them that a· my soul:
Isa 9: 1 afterward did more grievously a·
51:23 into the hand of them that a·
58: 5 a day for a man to a· his soul?
64:12 hold thy peace, and a· us very sore?
Jer 31:28 down, and to destroy, and to a·;
La 3:33 For he doth not a· willingly
Am 5:12 they a· the just, they take a bribe,
6:14 and they shall a· you
Na 1:12 I will a· thee no more.
Zep 3:19 I will undo all that a· thee:
afflicted ^
Ex 1:12 But the more they a· them, the
Le 23:29 shall not be a· in that same day,
Nu 11:11 Wherefore hast thou a· thy
De 26: 6 evil entreated us, and a· us,
Ru 1:21 the Almighty hath a· me?
2Sa 22:28 the a· people thou wilt save:
1Ki 2:26 thou hast been a· in all
26 wherein my father was a·.
2Ki 17:20 all the seed of Israel, and a· them,
Job 6:14 To him that is a· pity should be
30:11 he hath loosed my cord, and a·
34:28 and he heareth the cry of the a·.
Ps 18:27 thou wilt save the a· people;
22:24 abhorred the affliction of the a·;
25:16 me; for I am desolate and a·.
82: 3 do justice to the a· and needy.
88: 7 hast a· me with all thy waves.
15 I am a· and ready to die from my
90:15 thou hast a· us,
102:*title* A prayer of the a·, when he
107:17 because of their iniquities, are a·.
116:10 I was greatly a·:
119:67 Before I was a· I went astray:
71 good for me that I have been a·;
75 thou in faithfulness hast a· me.
107 I am a· very much:
129: 1, 2 Many a time have they a· me
140:12 maintain the cause of the a·, and
Pr 15:15 All the days of the a· are evil:
22:22 neither oppress the a· in the gate:
26:28 hateth those that are a· by it;
31: 5 the judgment of any of the a·.
Isa 9: 1 lightly a· the land of Zebulun,
49:13 and will have mercy upon his a·.
51:21 Therefore hear now this, thou a·,
53: 4 smitten of God, and a·.
7 He was oppressed, and he was a·,
58: 3 wherefore have we a· our soul,
10 satisfy the a· soul;
60:14 The sons also of them that a· thee
63: 9 In all their affliction he was a·,
La 1: 4 priests sigh, her virgins are a·,
5 for the Lord hath a· her for the
12 wherewith the Lord hath a· me
Mic 4: 6 her that I have a·;
Na 1:12 Though I have a· thee,
Zep 3:12 of thee an a· and poor people,
M't 24: 9 they deliver you up to be a·,
2Co 1: 6 And whether we be a·,
1Ti 5:10 if she have relieved the a·,
Heb 11:37 being destitute, a·, tormented;
Jas 4: 9 Be a·, and mourn, and weep:
5:13 Is any among you a·?
afflictest
1Ki 8:35 their sin, when thou a· them:
affliction See also AFFLICTIONS.
Ge 16:11 the Lord hath heard thy a·.
29:32 the Lord hath looked upon my a·;
31:42 God hath seen mine a·
41:52 in the land of my a·.
Ex 3: 7 surely seen the a· of my people
17 bring you up out of the a· of Egypt
4:31 he had looked upon their a·,
De 16: 3 the bread of a·;
26: 7 and looked on our a·,
1Sa 1:11 look on the a· of thine handmaid,
2Sa 16:12 the Lord will look on mine a·,
1Ki 22:27 feed him with bread of a·
27 and with water of a·,
2Ki 14:26 the Lord saw the a· of Israel,
2Ch 18:26 feed him with bread of a·
26 and with water of a·,
20: 9 and cry unto thee in our a·,
33:12 when he was in a·, he besought
Ne 1: 3 in great a· and reproach:
9: 9 didst see the a· of our fathers
Job 5: 6 a· cometh not forth of the dust,
10:15 see thou mine a·;
30:16 days of a· have taken hold upon
27 the days of a· prevented me.
36: 8 in cords of a·;
15 He delivereth the poor in his a·,
21 hast thou chosen rather than a·.
Ps 22:24 the a· of the afflicted;
25:18 Look upon mine a· and my pain;
44:24 our a· and our oppression?
Ps 66:11 thou laidst a· upon our loins.
88: 9 eye mourneth by reason of a·:
106:44 he regarded their a·,
107:10 bound in a· and iron;
39 through oppression, a·, and
41 he the poor on high from a·,
119:50 my comfort in my a·:
92 then have perished in mine a·.
153 Consider mine a·,
Isa 30:20 water of a·, yet shall not
48:10 in the furnace of a·.
63: 9 In all their a· he was afflicted,
Jer 4:15 a· from mount Ephraim.
15:11 of evil and in the time of a·.
16:19 my refuge in the day of a·,
30:15 Why criest thou for thine a·?
48:16 and his a· hasteth fast.
La 1: 3 gone into captivity because of a·,
7 remembered in the days of her a·
9 O Lord, behold my a·:
3: 1 I am the man that hath seen a·
19 Remembering mine a· and my
Ho 5:15 in their a· they will seek me early.
Am 6: 6 not grieved for the a· of Joseph.
Ob 13 not have looked on their a·
Jon 2: 2 reason of mine a· unto the Lord,
Na 1: 9 a· shall not rise up the second time.
Hab 3: 7 I saw the tents of Cushan in a·:
Zec 1:15 they helped forward the a·.
8:10 out or came in because of the a·:
10:11 pass through the sea with a·,
M'r 4:17 when a· or persecution ariseth
13:19 in those days shall be a·,
Ac 7:11 Egypt and Chanaan, and great a·:
34 I have seen the a· of my people
2Co 2: 4 out of much a· and anguish of
4:17 light a·, which is but for a moment,
8: 2 How that in a great trial of a·
Ph'p 1:16 to add a· to my bonds:
4:14 ye did communicate with my a·.
1Th 1: 6 the word in much a·,
3: 7 our a· and distress by your faith:
Heb 11:25 Choosing rather to suffer a· with
Jas 1:27 and widows in their a·,
5:10 an example of suffering a·, and
afflictions
Ps 34:19 Many are the a· of the righteous:
132: 1 remember David, and all his a·:
Ac 7:10 delivered him out of all his a·,
20:23 bonds and a· abide me.
2Co 6: 4 in a·, in necessities, in distresses,
Col 1:24 which is behind of the a· of Christ
1Th 3: 3 man should be moved by these a·:
2Ti 1: 8 partaker of the a· of the gospel
3:11 Persecutions, a·, which came
4: 5 a·, do the work of an evangelist,
Heb 10:32 endured a great fight of a·;
33 both by reproaches and a·;
1Pe 5: 9 the same a· are accomplished
affording
Ps 144:13 That our garners may be full, a·
affright See also AFFRIGHTED.
2Ch 32:18 to a· them, and to trouble them;
affrighted
De 7:21 Thou shalt not be a· at them:
Job 18:20 that went before were a·.
39:22 He mocketh at fear, and is not a·;
Isa 21: 4 fearfulness a· me:
Jer 51:32 and the men of war are a·.
M'r 16: 5 white garment; and they were a·.
6 And he saith unto them, Be not a·:
Lu 24:37 But they were terrified and a·,
Re 11:13 remnant were a·, and gave glory
a-fishing See FISHING.
afoot
M'r 6:33 ran a· thither out of all cities,
Ac 20:13 minding himself to go a·.
afore See also AFOREHAND; AFORETIME; BEFORE.
2Ki 20: 4 came to pass, a· Isaiah was gone
Ps 129: 6 which withereth a· it groweth up:
Isa 18: 5 a· the harvest, when the bud is
Eze 33:22 a· he that was escaped came;
Ro 1: 2 had promised a· by his prophets
9:23 he had a· prepared unto glory,
Eph 3: 3 (as I wrote a· in few words,
aforehand
M'r 14: 8 she is come a· to anoint my body
aforetime
Ne 13: 5 a· they laid the meat offerings,
Job 17: 6 a· I was as a tabret.
Isa 52: 4 My people went down a· into
Jer 30:20 Their children also shall be as a·,
Da 6:10 his God, as he did a·.
Joh 9:13 him that a· was blind.
Ro 15: 4 things were written a· were
afraid
Ge 3:10 I was a·, because I was naked;
18:15 I laughed not; for she was a·.
20: 8 and the men were sore a·.
28:17 And he was a·, and said,
31:31 Because I was a·: for I said,
32: 7 Then Jacob was greatly a· and
42:28 failed them, and they were a·,
35 bundles of money, they were a·.
43:18 And the men were a·, because
Ex 3: 6 he was a· to look upon God.
14:10 and they were sore a·: and the
15:14 people shall hear, and be a·:
34:30 they were a· to come nigh him.
Le 26: 6 none shall make you a·:
Nu 12: 8 then were ye not a· to speak
22: 3 Moab was sore a· of the people,

De 1:17 ye shall not be a· of the face of man;
29 Dread not, neither be a· of them.
2: 4 and they shall be a· of you:
5: 5 ye were a· by reason of the fire,
7:18 Thou shalt not be a· of them: but
19 all the people of whom thou art a·.
9:19 For I was a· of the anger and hot
18:22 thou shalt not be a· of him.
20: 1 be not a· of them: for the Lord
28:10 and they shall be a· of thee.
60 of Egypt, which thou wast a· of;
31: 6 fear not, nor be a· of them:
Jos 1: 9 not a·, neither be thou dismayed
9:24 we were sore a· of our lives
11: 6 Be not a· because of them:
J'g 7: 3 Whosoever is fearful and a·,
Ru 3: 8 that the man was a·, and turned
1Sa 4: 7 And the Philistines were a·, for
7: 7 they were a· of the Philistines.
17:11 were dismayed, and greatly a·.
24 fled from him, and were sore a·.
18:12 And Saul was a· of David,
15 very wisely, he was a· of him.
29 Saul was yet the more a· of David:
21: 1 Ahimelech was a· at the meeting
12 was sore a· of Achish the king of
23: 3 we be a· here in Judah:
28: 5 he was a·, and his heart
13 the king said unto her, Be not a·:
20 was sore a·, because of the words
31: 4 would not: for he was sore a·.
2Sa 1:14 How wast thou not a· to stretch
6: 9 David was a· of the Lord that day,
14:15 the people have made me a·:
17: 2 and will make him a·:
22: 5 of ungodly men made me a·;
46 they shall be a· out of their close
1Ki 1:49 that were with Adonijah were a·,
2Ki 1:15 down with him: be not a· of him.
10: 4 But they were exceedingly a·,
19: 6 Be not a· of the words which thou
25:26 they were a· of the Chaldees.
1Ch 10: 4 would not; for he was sore a·.
13:12 David was a· of God that day,
21:30 he was a· because of the sword
2Ch 20:15 Be not a· nor dismayed by reason
32: 7 be not a· nor dismayed for the
Ne 2: 2 Then I was very sore a·,
4:14 Be not ye a· of them:
6: 9 they all made us a·, saying,
13 was he hired, that I should be a·,
Es 7: 6 Haman was a· before the king
Job 3:25 which I was a· of is come unto me.
5:21 shalt thou be a· of destruction
22 neither shalt thou be a· of the
6:21 see my casting down, and are a·.
9:28 I am a· of all my sorrows, I
11:19 none shall make thee a·;
13:11 not his excellency make you a·?
21 let not thy dread make me a·.
15:24 anguish shall make him a·;
18:11 Terrors shall make him a· on every
19:29 Be ye a· of the sword:
21: 6 when I remember I am a·,
23:15 when I consider, I am a· of him.
32: 6 wherefore I was a·, and durst
33: 7 my terror shall not make thee a·,
39:20 Canst thou make him a· as a
41:25 the mighty are a·:
Ps 3: 6 I will not be a· of ten thousands
18: 4 floods of ungodly men made me a·.
45 shall fade away, and be a·
27: 1 of whom shall I be a·?
49:16 Be not thou a· when one is made
56: 3 time I am a·, I will trust in thee.
11 not be a· what man can do unto me.
65: 8 in the uttermost parts are a· at
77:16 they were a·: the depths also
83:15 make them a· with thy storm.
91: 5 Thou shalt not be a· for the
112: 7 He shall not be a· of evil tidings:
8 is established, he shall not be a·,
119:120 I am a· of thy judgments.
Pr 3:24 thou shalt not be a·:
25 Be not a· of sudden fear,
31:21 She is not a· of the snow for her
Ec 12: 5 they shall be a· of that which is
Isa 8:12 fear ye their fear, nor be a·.
10:24 be not a· of the Assyrian:
29 Ramah is a·; Gibeah of Saul is
12: 2 I will trust, and not be a·:
13: 8 And they shall be a·: pangs and
17: 2 none shall make them a·.
19:16 and it shall be a· and fear because
17 mention thereof shall be a· in
20: 5 they shall be a· and ashamed
31: 4 he will not be a· of their voice,
9 princes shall be a· of the ensign.
33:14 The sinners in Zion are a·;
37: 6 Be not a· of the words
40: 9 lift it up, be not a·;
41: 5 the ends of the earth were a·,
44: 8 Fear ye not, neither be a·:
51: 7 neither be ye a· of their revilings.
12 that thou shouldest be a· of a man
57:11 of whom hast thou been a· or
Jer 1: 8 Be not a· of their faces:
2:12 be horribly a·, be ye very desolate,
10: 5 Be not a· of them; for they cannot
26:21 he was a·, and fled, and went into
30:10 none shall make him a·.
36:16 heard all the words, they were a·
24 Yet they were not a·,
38:19 I am a· of the Jews
39:17 of the men of whom thou art a·.
41:18 a· of them, because of Ishmael

Jer 42:11 Be not a· of the king of Babylon,
11 of whom ye are a·;
11 be not a· of him, saith the Lord
16 the famine, whereof ye were a·,
46:27 and none shall make him a·.
Eze 2: 6 son of man, be not a· of them,
6 neither be a· of their words,
6 be not a· of their words,
27:35 their kings shall be sore a·,
30: 9 make the careless Ethiopians a·,
32:10 their kings shall be horribly a·
34:28 none shall make them a·.
39:26 none made them a·.
Da 4: 5 I saw a dream which made me a·,
8:17 when he came, I was a·,
Joe 2:22 Be not a·, ye beasts of the field:
Am 3: 6 the people not be a·?
Jon 1: 5 Then the mariners were a·,
10 Then were the men exceedingly a·,
Mic 4: 4 none shall make them a·:
7:17 they shall be a· of the Lord
Na 2:11 none made them a·?
Hab 2:17 beasts, which made them a·,
3: 2 heard thy speech, and was a·:
Zep 3:13 none shall make them a·.
Mal 2: 5 was a· before my name.
M't 2:22 he was a· to go thither:
14:27 it is I; be not a·.
30 the wind boisterous, he was a·;
17: 6 fell on their face, and were sore a·.
7 Arise, and be not a·.
25:25 And I was a·, and went and hid
28:10 Be not a·: go tell my brethren
M'r 5:15 his right mind: and they were a·.
36 Be not a·, only believe.
6:50 it is I; be not a·.
9: 6 to say; for they were sore a·.
32 and were a· to ask him.
10:32 and as they followed, they were a·.
16: 8 any man; for they were a·.
Lu 2: 9 and they were sore a·.
8:25 And they being a· wondered,
35 and they were a·.
12: 4 Be not a· of them that kill the body,
24: 5 as they were a·, and bowed down
Joh 6:19 unto the ship: and they were a·.
20 It is I; be not a·.
14:27 be troubled, neither let it be a·.
19: 8 he was the more a·;
Ac 9:26 but they were all a· of him,
10: 4 looked on him, he was a·,
18: 9 Be not a·, but speak, and hold
22: 9 saw indeed the light, and were a·;
29 and the chief captain also was a·,
Ro 13: 3 Wilt thou then not be a· of the
4 if thou do that which is evil, be a·;
Ga 4:11 I am a· of you, lest I have bestowed
Heb 11:23 and they were not a· of the king's
1Pe 3: 6 are not a· with any amazement.
14 and be not a· of their terror,
2Pe 2:10 they are not a· to speak evil of

afresh
Heb 6: 6 to themselves the Son of God a·,

after^ See also AFTERNOON; AFTERWARD; HEREAFTER.
Ge 1:11 fruit tree yielding fruit a· his kind,
12 herb yielding seed a· his kind,
12 seed was in itself, a· his kind;
21 abundantly, a· their kind,
21 and every winged fowl a· his kind:
24 the living creature a· his kind,
24 the beast of the earth a· his kind:
25 a· his kind, and cattle a· their kind,
25 creepeth upon the earth a· his kind:
4:17 a· the name of his son, Enoch.
5: 3 his own likeness, a· his image;
4 a· he had begotten Seth
7 a· he begat Enos
10 a· he begat Cainan
13 a· he begat Mahalaleel
16 a· he begat Jared
19 a· he begat Enoch eight hundred
22 a· he begat Methuselah
26 a· he begat Lamech
30 a· he begat Noah
6: 4 also a· that, when the sons of God
20 fowls a· their kind, and of cattle a· their
20 creeping thing of the earth a· his kind,
7:10 it came to pass a· seven days,
14 beast a· his kind,
14 and all the cattle a· their kind,
14 a· his kind, and every fowl a· his kind,
8: 3 a· the end of the hundred and
19 creepeth upon the earth, a· their kinds.
9: 9 with your seed a· you;
28 Noah lived a· the flood three
10: 1 unto them were born sons a· the flood
5 one a· his tongue, a· their families,
20, 31 a· their families, a· their tongues,
31 in their lands, a· their nations.
32 sons of Noah, a· their generations,
32 divided in the earth a· the flood.
11:10 Arphaxad two years a· the flood:
11 Shem lived a· he begat Arphaxad
13 Arphaxad lived a· he begat Salah
15 Salah lived a· he begat Eber
17 Eber lived a· he begat Peleg
19 Peleg lived a· he begat Reu
21 Reu lived a· he begat Serug
23 Serug lived a· he begat Nahor
25 Nahor lived a· he begat Terah
13:14 a· that Lot was separated from
14:17 a· his return from the slaughter
15: 1 A· these things the word of the
16: 3 a· Abraham had dwelt ten years

Ge 16:13 here looked a· him that seeth me?
17: 7 me and thee and thy seed a· thee
7 God unto thee, and to the seed a·
8 to thy seed a· thee,
9 thy seed a· thee in their generations.
10 between me and you and thy seed a·
19 with his seed a· him.
18: 5 a· that ye shall pass on:
12 A· I am waxed old shall I have
19 children and his household a· him,
19: 6 shut the door a· him,
22: 1, 20 it came to pass a· these things,
23:19 And a· this, Abraham buried Sarah
24:55 the least ten; a· that she shall go.
67 Isaac was comforted a· his mother's
25:11 it came to pass a· the death of
26 And a· that came his brother out,
26:18 the Philistines had stopped them a·
18 he called their names a· the names
31:23 pursued a· him seven days'
30 thou sore longedst a· thy father's
36 thou hast so hotly pursued a· me?
32:29 that thou dost ask a· my name?
33: 2 Leah and her children a·,
7 a· came Joseph near and Rachel,
35: 5 did not pursue a· the sons of Jacob.
12 thy seed a· thee will I give the land.
36:40 to their families, a· their places,
37:17 Joseph went a· his brethren,
38:24 about three months a·, that it
39: 7 it came to pass a· these things,
19 A· this manner did thy servant
40: 1 it came to pass a· these things,
13 cup into his hand, a· the former
41: 3 seven other kine came up a· them
6 the east wind sprung up a· them.
19 seven other kine came up a· them,
23 the east wind, sprung up a· them:
27 came up a· them are seven years;
30 shall arise a· them seven years of
44: 4 Up, follow a· the men;
45:15 a· that his brethren talked with him,
23 And to his father he sent a· this
48: 1 it came to pass a· these things,
4 give this land to thy seed a· thee
6 which thou begettest a· them.
6 shall be called a· the name of
50:14 a· he had buried his father.
Ex 3:20 and a· that he will let you go.
5:19 in evil case, a· it was said,
7:25 seven days were fulfilled, a· that
10:14 neither a· them shall be such.
11: 8 and a· that I will go out.
14: 4 that he shall follow a· them;
8 he pursued a· the children of Israel:
9 the Egyptians pursued a· them,
10 the Egyptians marched a· them;
23 went in a· them to the midst of the
28 that came into the sea a· them;
15:20 all the women went out a· her with
16: 1 a· their departing out of the land
17: 1 from the wilderness of Sin, a·
18: 2 a· he had sent her back,
21: 9 shall deal with her a· the manner
23: 2 to decline a· many to wrest
24 nor serve them, nor do a· their
25:40 a· their pattern, which was
28:15 a· the work of the ephod thou
43 his seed a· him.
29:29 Aaron shall be his sons' a· him.
30:12 sum of the children of Israel a·
13 half a shekel a· the shekel of the
24 five hundred shekels, a· the shekel
25 compound a· the art of the
32 ye make any other like it, a·
35 a confection a· the art of the
32: 4 with a graving tool, a· he had
33: 8 looked a· Moses, until he was gone
34:15 they go a whoring a· their gods,
16 go a whoring a· their gods, and
16 make thy sons go a whoring a·
27 for a· the tenor of these words I
37:19 Three bowls made a· the fashion
38:24 thirty shekels, a· the shekel of the
25 fifteen shekels, a· the shekel of the
26 a· the shekel of the sanctuary,
Le 5:15 a· the shekel of the sanctuary,
11:14 vulture, and the kite a· his kind;
15 Every raven a· his kind;
16 cuckow, and the hawk a· his kind,
19 the stork, the heron a· her kind,
22 a· his kind, and the bald locust a· his
22 a· his kind, and the grasshopper a· his
29 mouse, and the tortoise a· his kind,
13: 7 a· that he hath been seen of the
35 in the skin a· his cleansing;
55 a· that it is washed:
56 somewhat dark a· the washing of
14: 8 a· that he shall come into the camp,
43 a· that he hath taken away the
43 and a· he hath scraped the house,
43 and a· it is plaistered;
48 a· the house was plaistered:
15:28 and a· that she shall be clean.
16: 1 a· the death of the two sons of
17: 7 a· whom they have gone a whoring.
18: 3 A· the doings of the land of Egypt,
3 a· the doings of the land of Canaan,
19:31 neither seek a· wizards, to be
20: 5 all that go a whoring a· him, to
6 a·...familiar spirits, and a· wizards,
6 to go a whoring a· them,
23:15 from the morrow a· the sabbath,
16 unto the morrow a· the seventh
25:15 number of years a· the jubile
29 within a whole year a· it is sold;

Le 25:46 inheritance for your children a· you,
48 A· that he is sold he may be
26:33 will draw out a sword a· you:
27: 3 a· the shekel of the sanctuary.
18 if he sanctify his field a· the jubile,
Nu 1: 1 a· they were come out of the
2 a· their families, by the house of
18 their pedigrees a· their families,
20 their generations, a· their families,
22 a· their families, by the house of
24 of Gad, by their generations, a·
26 of Judah, by their generations, a·
28 Issachar, by their generations, a·
30 Zebulun, by their generations, a·
32 a· their families, by the house of
34 Manasseh, by their generations, a·
36 Benjamin, by their generations, a·
38 of Dan, by their generations, a·
40 of Asher, by their generations, a·
42 throughout their generations, a·
47 Levites a· the tribe of their fathers
2:34 every one a· their families,
3:15 the children of Levi a· the house
47 a· the shekel of the sanctuary
50 threescore and five shekels, a·
4: 2 a· their families, by the house of
15 a· that, the sons of Kohath shall
29 number them a· their families,
34 a· their families, and a· the house
44 a· their families, were three
46 a· their families, and a· the house
6:19 a· the hair of his separation is
20 and a· that the Nazarite may drink
21 so he must do a· the law of his
7:13 bowl of seventy shekels, a· the shekel
19 a· the shekel of the sanctuary;
25, 31, 37, 43, 49, 55, 61, 67, 73, 79 of
seventy shekels, a· the shekel of
85 four hundred shekels, a· the shekel
86 ten shekels apiece, a· the shekel
88 a· that it was anointed.
8:15 And a· that shall the Levites go
22 And a· that went the Levites in
9: 1 a· they were come out of the land
17 a· that the children of Israel
12:14 and a that let her be received in
13:25 searching of the land a· forty
14:34 A· the number of the days in
15:13 do these things a· this manner,
39 seek not a· your own heart and
39 and your own eyes, a· which
16:29 visited a· the visitation of all men;
18:16 a· the shekel of the sanctuary,
25: 8 he went a· the man of Israel
13 shall have it, and his seed a· him,
26: 1 it came to pass a· the plague,
12 sons of Simeon a· their families:
15 The children of Gad a· their
20 sons of Judah a· their families
23 Of the sons of Issachar a· their
26 sons of Zebulun a· their families:
28 sons of Joseph a· their families
35 are the sons of Ephraim a· their
37 These are the sons of Joseph a· their
38 The sons of Benjamin a· their
41 are the sons of Benjamin a· their
42 These are the sons of Dan a· their
42 These are the families of Dan a· their
44 Of the children of Asher a· their
48 sons of Naphtali a· their families:
57 numbered of the Levites a· their
27:21 for him a· the judgment of Urim
28:24 A· this manner ye shall offer
26 offering unto the Lord, a· your
29:18, 21, 24, 27, 30, 33, 37 number, a· the
30:15 make them void a· that he hath
32:15 if ye turn away from a· him,
42 thereof, and called it Nobah, a· his
33: 3 on the morrow a· the passover
38 a· the children of Israel were
35:28 a· the death of the high priest
De 1: 4 A· he had slain Sihon the king of
8 to their seed a· them.
3:11 the breadth of it, a· the cubit of
14 and called them a· his own name,
4:37 therefore he chose their seed a·
40 with thy children a· thee,
45 a· they came forth out
46 a· they were come forth out
6:14 Ye shall not go a· other gods,
8:19 and walk a· other gods, and serve
9: 4 a· that the Lord thy God hath
10:15 he chose their seed a· them,
11: 4 as they pursued a· you,
28 to go a· other gods, which ye
12: 8 Ye shall not do a· all the things
15, 20, 21 thy soul lusteth a·,
25 with thy children a· thee, when
28 with thee, and with thy children a·
30 following them, a· that they be
30 thou enquire not a· their gods,
13: 2 Let us go a· other gods,
4 Ye shall walk a· the Lord your God,
14:13 kite, and the vulture a· his kind,
14 And every raven a· his kind,
15 cuckow, and the hawk a· his kind,
18 stork, and the heron a· her kind,
14:26 whatsoever thy soul lusteth a·,
16:13 a· that thou hast gathered in thy
18: 9 learn to do a· the abominations
20:18 That they teach you not to do a·
21:13 a· that thou shalt go in unto her,
22: 2 thee until thy brother seek a· it,
24: 4 a· that she is defiled;
9 a· that ye were come forth out
28:14 to go a· other gods to serve them.
De 29:22 that shall rise up a· you,
31:16 go a whoring a· the gods of the
27 how much more a· my death?
29 I know that a· my death ye will
Jos 1: 1 Now a· the death of Moses
2: 5 pursue a· them quickly;
7 the men pursued a· them the way
7 as soon as they which pursued a·
3: 2 came to pass a· three days,
3 remove from your place, and go a·
5: 4 a· they came out of Egypt.
12 a· they had eaten of the old corn
6: 9 and the rereward came a· the ark,
13 but the rereward came a· the ark of
15 compassed the city a· the same
7:25 burned them with fire, a· they
8: 6 (For they will come out a· us)
16 called together to pursue a· them:
16 and they pursued a· Joshua,
17 that went not out a· Israel: and
17 left the city open, and pursued a·
9:16 a· they had made a league with
10:14 no day like that before it or a· it,
19 stay ye not, but pursue a· your
13:23 of the children of Reuben a· their
28 of the children of Gad a· their
19:47 called Leshem, Dan, a· the name
20: 5 the avenger of blood pursue a· him,
22:27 and you, and our generations a· us,
23: 1 it came to pass a long time a·
24: 6 Egyptians pursued a· your fathers
20 consume you, a· that he hath done
29 it came to pass a· these things,
J'g 1: 1 Now a· the death of Joshua
6 fled: and they pursued a· him,
2:10 arose another generation a· them,
17 went a whoring a· other gods,
3:22 the haft also went in a· the blade;
28 he said unto them, Follow a· me:
28 they went down a· him,
31 And a· him was Shamgar the son
4:14 ten thousand men a· him.
16 Barak pursued a· the chariots,
16 and a· the host,
5:14 a· thee, Benjamin, among thy
6:34 Abi-ezer was gathered a· him.
35 who also was gathered a· him:
7:23 pursued a· the Midianites.
8: 5 I am pursuing a· Zebah and
12 pursued a· them, and took the two
27 went thither a whoring a· it:
33 went a whoring a· Baalim,
10: 1 a· Abimelech there arose to defend
3 a· him arose Jair, a Gileadite,
12: 8 a· him Ibzan of Beth-lehem judged
11 a· him Elon, a Zebulonite,
13 a· him Abdon the son of Hillel,
13:11 Manoah arose, and went a· his wife,
18 Why askest thou thus a· my
14: 8 a· a time he returned to take her,
15: 1 it came to pass within a while a·,
7 and a· that I will cease.
16:22 to grow again a· he was shaven.
18: 7 a· the manner of the Zidonians,
29 the name of the city Dan, a· the
19: 3 her husband arose, and went a· her,
20:45 pursued hard a· them unto Gidom,
Ru 1:15 return thou a· thy sister in law.
16 or to return from following a· thee:
2: 2 glean ears of corn a· him in whose
3 gleaned in the field a· the reapers:
7 let me glean and gather a· the
9 they do reap, and go thou a· them:
2:18 to her that she had reserved a· she
4: 4 I am a· thee. And he said, I will
1Sa 1: 9 a· they had eaten in Shiloh,
9 and a· they had drunk.
20 a· Hannah had conceived, that
5: 9 a· they had carried it about,
6:12 the lords of the Philistines went a·
7: 2 house of Israel lamented a· the
8: 3 but turned aside a· lucre,
10: 5 A· that thou shalt come to the hill
11: 5 Saul came a· the herd out of the
7 Whosoever cometh not forth a· Saul
7 and a· Samuel,
12:21 for then should ye go a· vain things,
13: 4 called together a· Saul to Gilgal.
14 the Lord hath sought him a man a·
14:12 armourbearer, Come up a· me:
13 his armourbearer a· him:
13 his armourbearer slew a· him.
22 they also followed hard a· them
36 Let us go down a· the Philistines
37 Shall I go down a· the Philistines?
15:31 So Samuel turned again a· Saul;
17:27 answered him a· this manner,
30 and spake a· the same manner:
30 him again a· the former manner.
35 I went out a· him, and smote him,
53 returned from chasing a· the
18:30 a· they went forth,
20:37, 38 Jonathan cried a· the lad,
22:20 Abiathar, escaped, and fled a·
23:25 he pursued a· David in the
28 Saul returned from pursuing a·
24: 8 out of the cave, and cried a· Saul,
14 A· whom is the king of Israel come
14 a· whom dost thou pursue?
14 a· a dead dog, a· a flea.
21 not cut off my seed a· me,
25:13 there went up a· David
19 behold, I come a· you.
38 about ten days a·, that the Lord
42 damsels of hers that went a· her;
42 she went a· the messengers of
1Sa 26: 3 Saul came a· him into the
18 my lord thus pursue a· his servant?
30: 8 Shall I pursue a· this troop?
2Sa 1: 1 Now it came to pass a· the death
6 horsemen followed hard a· him.
10 he could not live a· that he was
2: 1 it came to pass a· this,
19 Asahel pursued a· Abner;
24 Joab also and Abishai pursued a·
25 gathered themselves together a·
28 pursued a· Israel no more,
3:26 he sent messengers a· Abner,
5:13 a· he was come from Hebron:
7:12 I will set up thy seed a· thee,
8: 1 a· this it came to pass,
10: 1 it came to pass a· this,
11: 1 a· the year was expired, at the
3 And David sent and enquired a·
12:28 city, and it be called a· my name.
13: 1 it came to pass a· this,
17 bolt the door a· her.
18 bolted the door a· her.
23 a· two full years, that Absalom
14:26 head at two hundred shekels a·
15: 1 it came to pass a· this,
15: 7 it came to pass a· forty years,
13 the men of Israel are a· Absalom.
16 and all his household a· him.
17 went forth, and all the people a·
18 six hundred men which came a·
17: 1 I will arise and pursue a· David
6 saying, Ahithophel hath spoken a·
6 shall we do a· his saying? if not;
21 it came to pass, a· they were
18:16 returned from pursuing a· Israel:
18 and he called the pillar a· his own
22 let me, I pray thee, also run a·
20: 2 of Israel went up from a· David,
6 pursue a· him, lest he get him
7 there went out a· him Joab's men,
7 of Jerusalem, to pursue a· Sheba
10 Abishai his brother pursued a·
11 he that is for David, let him go a·
13 went on a· Joab, to pursue a· Sheba
14 together, and went also a· him.
21: 1 three years, year a· year;
14 a· that God was intreated for the
18 it came to pass a· this,
23: 4 of the earth by clear shining a· rain.
9 And a· him was Eleazar the son
10 the people returned a· him only to
11 And a· him was Shammah
24:10 David's heart smote him a· that
1Ki 1: 6 his mother bare him a· Absalom.
13 Solomon thy son shall reign a· me,
14 I also will come in a· thee,
17 Solomon thy son shall reign a· me,
20 throne of my lord the king a· him.
24 Adonijah shall reign a· me,
27 the throne of my lord the king a·
30 shall reign a· me, and he shall sit
35 Then ye shall come up a· him,
40 all the people came up a· him,
2:28 for Joab had turned a· Adonijah,
28 though he turned not a· Absalom.
3:12 neither a· thee shall any arise like
18 And it came to pass the third day a·
6: 1 a· the children of Israel were
7:11 costly stones, a· the measures of
31 the mouth thereof was round a·
37 A· this manner he made the ten
9:21 Their children that were left a·
11: 2 turn away your heart a· their gods:
4 his wives turned away his heart a·
5 Solomon went a· Ashtoreth
5 a· Milcom the abomination of the
6 went not fully a· the Lord,
10 he should not go a· other gods:
15 a· he had smitten every male in
12:14 spake to them a· the counsel of
13:14 went a· the man of God,
23 a· he had eaten bread, and a· he
31 it came to pass, a· he had buried
33 A· this thing Jeroboam returned not
15: 4 to set up his son a· him, and to
16:24 a· the name of Shemer, owner of
17: 7 a· a while, that the brook dried
13 a· make for thee and for thy son.
17 it came to pass a· these things,
18: 1 a· many days, that the word of the
19:11 and a· the wind an earthquake;
12 And a· the earthquake a fire;
12 and a· the fire a still small voice.
20 he left the oxen, and ran a· Elijah,
21 Then he arose, and went a· Elijah,
20:15 a· them he numbered all the people,
21: 1 it came to pass a· these things,
2Ki 1: 1 against Israel a· the death of Ahab.
5:20 as the Lord liveth, I will run a· him,
21 So Gehazi followed a· Naaman.
21 Naaman saw him running a· him,
6:24 it came to pass a· this,
7:14 king sent a· the host of the Syrians,
15 they went a· them unto Jordan:
8: 2 a· the saying of the man of God:
9:25 I and thou rode together a· Ahab
27 Jehu followed a· him,
10:29 Jehu departed not from a· them,
14:17 Joash king of Judah lived a· the
19 they sent a· him to Lachish,
22 a· that the king slept with his
17:15 and went a· the heathen
33 a· the manner of the nations
34 they do a· the former manners:
34 do they a· their statutes, or a· their
34 or a· the law and commandment

2Ki 17:40 they did a' their former manner.
18: 5 so that a' him was none like him
21: 2 a' the abominations of the heathen,
23: 3 to walk a' the Lord,
25 neither a' him arose there any like
25: 5 the Chaldees pursued a' the king,
1Ch 2:24 And a' that Hezron was dead
5: 1 not to be reckoned a' the birthright.
25 went a whoring a' the gods
6:31 in the house of the Lord, a' that
7: 4 generations, a' the house of their
9 number of them, a' their genealogy
8: 8 a' he had sent them away;
9:25 in their villages, were to come a'
10: 2 hard a' Saul, and a' his sons;
11:12 And a' him was Eleazar the son
14:14 said unto him, Go not up a' them;
15:13 sought him not a' the due order.
17:11 I will raise up thy seed a' thee,
18: 1 Now a' this it came to pass,
19: 1 Now it came to pass a' this,
20: 1 a' the year was expired,
4 it came to pass a' this, that there
23:24 sons of Levi a' the house of their
24:30 Levites a' the house of their fathers.
27: 1 of Israel a' their number, to wit,
7 Zebadiah his son a' him:
34 And a' Ahithophel was Jehoiada
28: 8 inheritance for your children a' you
29:14 able to offer so willingly a' this sort?
21 Lord, on the morrow a' that day,
2Ch 1:12 there any a' thee have the like.
2:17 a' the numbering wherewith
3: 3 length by cubits a' the first measure
4:20 burn a' the manner before the
8: 8 who were left a' them in the land,
13 Even a' a certain rate every day,
10: 5 again unto me a' three days.
14 answered them a' the advice of
11:16 And a' them out of all the tribes
20 And a' her he took Maachah
13: 9 priests a' the manner of the nations
19 Abijah pursued a' Jeroboam,
18: 2 a' certain years he went down to
19 one spake saying a' this manner,
19 another saying a' that manner.
20: 1 It came to pass a' this also,
35 And a' this did Jehoshaphat
21:18 And a' all this the Lord smote him,
19 a' the end of two years, his
22: 4 his counsellors a' the death of his
5 He walked also a' their counsel,
23:21 a' that they had slain Athaliah
24: 4 it came to pass a' this,
17 Now a' the death of Jehoiada
25:14 it came to pass, a' that Amaziah
15 sought a' the gods of the people,
20 they sought a' the gods of Edom.
25 lived a' the death of Joash son of
27 a' the time that Amaziah did
27 sent to Lachish a' him, and slew
26: 2 a' that the king slept with his
17 Azariah the priest went in a' him,
28: 3 a' the abominations of the
30:16 a' their manner, according to the
31: 2 a' their courses, every man
32: 1 A' these things, and the
9 A' this did Sennacherib king of
33:14 Now a' this he built a wall
34: 3 he began to seek a' the God of
21 to do a' all that is written in this
31 to walk a' the Lord,
35: 4 a' your courses, according to the
5 a' the division of the families of
20 A' all this, when Josiah had
36:14 transgressed very much a' all the
Ezr 2:61 Gileadite, and was called a' their
69 They gave a' their ability unto
3:10 praise the Lord, a' the ordinance
5: 4 a' this manner, What are the
12 a' that our fathers had provoked
7: 1 Now a' these things,
18 that do a' the will of your God.
25 And thou, Ezra, a' the wisdom of
9:10 what shall we say a' this?
13 And a' all that is come upon us
10:16 chief of the fathers, a' the house of
Ne 3:16 A' him repaired Nehemiah
17 A' him repaired the Levites,
18 A' him repaired their brethren,
20 A' him Baruch the son of Zabbai
21 A' him repaired Meremoth
22 And a' him repaired the priests,
23 A' him repaired Benjamin
23 A' him repaired Azariah
24 A' him repaired Binnui
25 A' him Pedaiah the son of Parosh.
27 A' them the Tekoites repaired
29 A' them repaired Zadok
29 A' him repaired also Shemaiah
30 A' him repaired Hananiah
30 A' him repaired Meshullam
31 A' him repaired Malchiah
4:13 I even set the people a' their
5: 8 We a' our ability, have redeemed
6: 4 sent unto me four times a' this
4 and I answered them a' the same
7:63 and was called a' their name.
9:28 But a' they had rest, they did
10:34 a' the houses of our fathers,
11: 8 And a' him Gabbai, Sallai,
12:32 a' them went Hoshaiah,
38 went over against them, and I a'
13: 6 and a' certain days obtained I
19 not be opened till a' the sabbath:
Es 1:22 to every people a' their language,

Es 2: 1 A' these things, when the wrath
12 a' that she had been twelve
3: 1 A' these things did king Ahasuerus
12 to every people a' their language;
8: 9 thereof, and unto every people a'
9:26 they called these days Purim a'
Job 3: 1 A' this opened Job his mouth,
10: 6 thou enquirest a' mine iniquity,
18:20 come a' him shall be astonied
19:26 though a' my skin worms destroy
21: 3 and a' that I have spoken, mock on.
21 in his house a' him,
33 and every man shall draw a' him,
29:22 A' my words they spake not again;
30: 5 (they cried a' them
5 as a' a thief;)
31: 7 mine heart walked a' mine eyes,
37: 4 A' it a voice roareth:
39: 8 he searcheth a' every green thing.
10 will he harrow the valleys a' thee?
41:32 He maketh a path to shine a' him;
42: 7 a' the Lord had spoken these words
16 A' this lived Job an hundred and
Ps 4: 2 love vanity, and seek a' leasing?
10: 4 will not seek a' God: God is not
16: 4 shall be multiplied that hasten a'
27: 4 that will I seek a'; that I may
28: 4 give them a' the work of their
35: 4 put to shame that seek a' my
38:12 They also that seek a' my life
40:14 that seek a' my soul to destroy it;
42: 1 As the hart panteth a' the water
1 so panteth my soul a' thee, O God.
49:11 they call their lands a' their own
17 his glory shall not descend a' him.
51 (*title*) a' he had gone in to Bath-sheba.
54: 3 and oppressors seek a' my soul:
63: 8 My soul followeth hard a' thee:
68:25 players on instruments followed a';
70: 2 confounded that seek a' my soul:
78:34 returned and enquired early a'
86:14 violent men have sought a' my
103:10 not dealt with us a' our sins; nor
104:21 The young lions roar a' their prey,
110: 4 Thou art a priest for ever a' the
119:40 I have longed a' thy precepts:
88 Quicken me a' thy lovingkindness;
150 nigh that follow a' mischief:
143: 6 my soul thirsteth a' thee, as a
144:12 as corner stones, polished a' the
Pr 2: 3 if thou criest a' knowledge, and
6:25 a' her beauty in thine heart;
7:22 He goeth a' her straightway,
15: 9 he loveth him that followeth a'
20: 7 his children are blessed a' him.
25 and a' vows to make enquiry.
21:21 that followeth a' righteousness
28:19 he that followeth a' vain persons
Ec 1:11 come with those that shall come a'.
2:12 man do that cometh a' the king?
18 unto the man that shall be a' me.
3:22 bring him to see what shall be a'
4:16 also that come a' shall not rejoice
6:12 who can tell a man what shall be a'
7:14 that man should find nothing a'
9: 3 and a' that they go to the dead.
10:14 what shall be a' him,
11: 1 thou shalt find it a' many days.
12: 2 nor the clouds return a' the rain:
Ca 1: 4 Draw me, we will run a' thee:
Isa 1:23 and followeth a' rewards:
5:17 lambs feed a' their manner, and
10:24 against thee, a' the manner of
26 so shall he lift it up a' the manner
11: 3 not judge a' the sight of his eyes,
3 neither reprove a' the hearing of
23:15, 17 a' the end of seventy years
24:22 and a' many days shall they be
43:10 formed, neither shall there be a'
44:13 maketh it a' the figure of a man,
45:14 they shall come a' thee;
49:20 a' thou hast lost the other, shall
51: 1 ye that follow a' righteousness,
65: 2 a' their own thoughts;
Jer 2: 2 when thou wentest a' me in the
5 have walked a' vanity,
8 walked a' things that do not profit.
23 I have not gone a' Baalim?
25 and a' them will I go.
3: 7 a' she had done all these things,
17 a' the imagination of their evil
5: 8 morning: every one neighed a'
7: 6 neither walk a' other gods to
9 a' other gods whom ye know not;
8: 2 a' whom they have walked,
9:14 have walked a' the imagination
14 of their own heart, and a' Baalim,
16 I will send a sword a' them,
22 as the handful a' the harvestman,
11:10 they went a' other gods to serve
12: 6 have called a multitude a' thee:
15 a' that I have plucked them out
13: 6 a' many days, that the Lord said
9 A' this manner will I mar the
10 walk a' other gods, to serve them,
16:11 have walked a' other gods,
12 a' the imagination of his evil heart,
16 a' will I send for many hunters,
18:12 we will walk a' our own devices,
23:17 every one that walketh a' the
24: 1 a' that Nebuchadrezzar king of
25: 6 go not a' other gods to serve them,
26 of Sheshach shall drink a' them.
28:12 a' that Hananiah the prophet had
29: 2 (A' that Jeconiah the king,
10 a' seventy years be accomplished

Jer 30:17 Zion, whom no man seeketh a'.
18 palace shall remain a' the manner
31:19 a' that I was turned, I repented;
19 and a' that I was instructed,
33 A' those days, saith the Lord.
32:18 into the bosom of their children a'
39 of their children a' them:
34: 8 a' that the king Zedekiah had
35:15 go not a' other gods to serve them,
36:27 a' that the king had burned the
39: 5 the Chaldeans' army pursued a'
40: 1 a' that Nebuzar-adan the captain
41: 4 day a' he had slain Gedaliah, and
16 a' that he had slain Gedaliah
42: 7 a' ten days, that the word of the
16 shall follow close a' you
49:37 I will send the sword a' them,
50:21 waste and utterly destroy a' them,
51:46 and a' that in another year shall
52: 8 the Chaldeans pursued a' the king,
Eze 5: 2, 12 I will draw out a sword a' them.
6: 9 which go a whoring a' their idols:
7:27 I will do unto them a' their way,
9: 5 Go ye a' him through the city,
11:12 a' the manners of the heathen
21 whose heart walketh a' the heart
12:14 I will draw out the sword a' them.
16:23 came to pass a' all thy wickedness,
47 walked a' [*] their ways, nor done a'
20:16 for their heart went a' their idols.
24 eyes were a' their fathers' idols.
30 a' the manner of your fathers?
30 whoredom a' their abominations?
23:15 a' the manner of the Babylonians
30 thou hast gone a whoring a' the
45 shall judge them a' the manner of
45 and a' the manner of women that
48 may be taught not to do a' your
29:16 when they shall look a' them:
33:20 I will judge you every one a' his
31 heart goeth a' their covetousness.
34: 6 none did search or seek a' them.
36:11 I will settle you a' your old estates,
38: 8 A' many days thou shalt be
39:14 a' the end of seven months shall
26 A' that they have borne their
40: 1 fourteenth year a' that the city was
1 the arches thereof were a' the
22 a' the measure of the gate that
24 A' that he brought me toward
41: 5 A' he measured the wall of the
43:13 a' the cubits: The cubit is a cubit
44:10 astray away from me a' their
26 And a' he is cleansed,
45:11 the measure thereof shall be a'
46:12 a' his going forth one shall shut
17 a' it shall return to the prince:
19 A' he brought me through the
48:31 be a' the names of the tribes of
Da 2:39 And a' thee shall arise another
3:29 no other God that can deliver a'
4:26 a' that thou shalt have known
7: 6 A' this I beheld, and lo another,
7 A' this I saw in the night visions,
24 and another shall rise a' them;
8: 1 a' that which appeared unto me at
9:26 And a' threescore and two weeks
11:13 come a' certain years
18 A' this shall he turn his face unto
23 And a' the league made with him
Ho 2: 5 I will go a' my lovers,
7 And she shall follow a' her lovers,
13 she went a' her lovers,
5: 8 a' thee, O Benjamin.
11 walked a' the commandment.
6: 2 A' two days will he revive us: in
7: 4 who ceaseth from raising a' he
11:10 They shall walk a' the Lord:
12: 1 and followeth a' the east wind:
Joe 2: 2 neither shall be any more a' it,
Am 2: 4 a' the which their fathers have
7 pant a' the dust of the earth on
4: 4 and your tithes a' three years:
10 pestilence a' the manner of Egypt:
7: 1 growth a' the king's mowings.
Zec 2: 8 A' the glory hath he sent me unto
6: 6 the white go forth a' them;
7:14 the land was desolate a' them,
M't 1:12 a' they were brought to Babylon,
3:11 but he that cometh a' me
5: 6 they which do hunger and thirst a'
28 looketh on a woman to lust a' her
6: 9 A' this manner therefore pray ye:
32 a' all these things do the Gentiles
10:38 and followeth a' me, is not worthy
12:39 generation seeketh a' a sign;
15:12 were offended, a' they heard this
23 for she crieth a' us.
16: 4 generation seeketh a' a sign;
24 If any man will come a' me,
17: 1 a' six days Jesus taketh Peter,
18:32 lord, a' that he had called him,
23: 3 but do not ye a' their works:
24:29 Immediately a' the tribulation
25:19 A' a long time the lord of those
26: 2 Ye know that a' two days is the
32 But a' I am risen again, I will go
73 And a' a while came unto him
27:31 a' that they had mocked him,
53 of the graves a' his resurrection,
63 A' three days I will rise again.
M'r 1: 7 cometh one mightier than I a' me,
14 a' that John was put in prison,
17 Come ye a' me,
20 and went a' him.
36 that were with him followed a'

M'r 2: 1 into Capernaum a' some days;
4:28 a' that the full corn in the ear.
8:12 Why doth this generation seek a'
25 A' that he put his hands again
31 and a' three days rise again.
34 Whosoever will come a' me,
9: 2 a' six days Jesus taketh with him
12:34 no man a' that durst ask him
13:24 a' that tribulation, the sun shall
14: 1 A' two days was the feast of the
28 But a' that I am risen,
70 And a little a', they that stood by
16:12 A' that he appeared in another
14 not them which had seen him a'
19 a' the Lord had spoken unto them,
Lu 1:24 And a' those days his wife
59 a' the name of his father.
2:27 a' the custom of the law,
42 a' the custom of the feast.
46 a' three days they found him in
5:27 a' these things he went forth,
6: 1 second sabbath a' the first, that
7:11 it came to pass the day a',
9:23 If any man will come a' me,
28 an eight days a' these sayings,
10: 1 A' these things the Lord
12: 4 a' that have no more that they
5 which a' he hath killed hath power
30 the nations of the world seek a':
13: 9 a' that thou shalt cut it
14:27 and come a' me, cannot be my
29 a' he hath laid the foundation,
15: 4 and go a' that which is lost, until
13 not many days a' the younger
17:23 or, see there: go not a' them,
19:14 and sent a messsage a' him,
20:40 And a' that they durst not ask
21: 8 go ye not therefore a' them.
26 and for looking a' those things
22:20 also the cup a' supper,
58 a' a little while another saw him,
59 about the space of one hour a'
23:26 that he might bear it a' Jesus.
55 followed a', and beheld the
Joh 1:15 He that cometh a' me is preferred
27 He it is, who coming a' me is
30 A' me cometh a man which is
35 the next day a', John stood,
2: 6 a' the manner of the purifying
12 A' this he went down to
3:22 A' these things came Jesus and
4:43 Now a' two days he departed
5: 1 A' this there was a feast of the
4 first a' the troubling of the water
6: 1 A' these things Jesus went over
23 a' that the Lord had given thanks:)
7: 1 A' these things Jesus walked in
8:15 Ye judge a' the flesh; I judge no
11: 7 a' that saith he to his disciples,
11 and a' that he saith unto them,
12:19 the world is gone a' him.
13: 5 A' that he poureth water into a
12 So a' he had washed their feet,
27 a' the sop Satan entered into him.
19:28 a' this, Jesus knowing that all
38 a' this Joseph of Arimathæa,
20:26 a' eight days again his disciples
21: 1 A' these things Jesus shewed
14 a' that he was risen from the dead.
Ac 1: 2 a' that he through the Holy Ghost
3 a' his passion by many infallible
8 receive power, a' that the Holy
3:24 those that follow a', as many
5: 4 and a' it was sold, was it not in
7 three hours a', when his wife, not
37 A' this man rose up Judas of
37 drew away much people a' him:
7: 5 and to his seed a' him,
7 and a' that shall they come forth,
36 a' that he had shewed wonders
45 our fathers that came a' brought
9:23 a' that many days were fulfilled,
10:24 And the morrow a' they entered
37 a' the baptism which John
41 a' he rose from the dead.
12: 4 intending a' Easter to bring him
13:15 And a' the reading of the law
20 And a' that he gave unto them
22 a man a' mine own heart,
25 there cometh one a' me,
36 For David, a' he had served his
14:24 a' they had passed throughout
15: 1 a' the manner of Moses, ye cannot
13 And a' they had held their peace,
16 A' this I will return, and will
17 men might seek after the Lord,
23 they wrote letters by them a' this
33 a' they had tarried there a space,
36 And some days a' Paul said unto
16: 7 A' they were come to Mysia,
10 And a' he had seen the vision,
17:27 if haply they might feel a' him,
18: 1 A' these things Paul departed
18 And Paul a' this tarried there yet
23 a' he had spent some time there,
19: 4 which should come a' him,
21 A' these things were ended,
21 A' I have been there, I must also
20: 1 And a' the uproar was ceased,
6 a' the days of unleavened bread,
18 a' what manner I have been with
29 a' my departing shall grievous
30 to draw away disciples a' them.
21: 1 it came to pass, that a' we were
15 And a' those days we took up our
21 neither to walk a' the customs.

Ac 21:36 multitude of the people followed a',
22:29 a' he knew that he was a Roman,
23: 3 to judge me a' the law, and
25 a letter a' this manner:
24: 1 a' five days Ananias the high
10 Then Paul, a' that the governor
14 a' the way which they call heresy,
17 a' many years I came to bring
24 And a' certain days, when Felix
27 a' two years Porcius Festus came
25: 1 a' three days he ascended from
13 a' certain days king Agrippa and
26 thee, O king Agrippa, that, a'
26: 5 that a' the most straitest sect of
27:14 not long a' there arose against it
21 a' long abstinence Paul stood
28: 6 a' they had looked a great while,
11 a' three months we departed
13 a' one day the south wind blew,
17 a' three days Paul called the chief
25 a' that Paul had spoken one word,
Ro 2: 5 a' thy hardness and impenitent
3:11 none that seeketh a' God.
5:14 had not sinned a' the similitude
6:19 I speak a' the manner of men
7:22 I delight in the law of God a' the
8: 1 walk not a' the flesh, but a'
4 walk not a' the flesh, but a'
5 that are a' the flesh do mind the
5 that are a' the Spirit the things of
12 not to the flesh, to live a' the flesh.
13 if ye live a' the flesh, ye shall die:
9:30 followed not a' righteousness,
31 which followed a' the law of
10:20 unto them that asked not a' me.
14:19 therefore follow a' the things
1Co 1:21 for a' that in the wisdom of God
22 and the Greeks seek a' wisdom:
26 wise men a' the flesh,
7: 7 one a' this manner, and another a'
40 so abide, a' my judgment:
10: 6 we should not lust a' evil things,
18 Behold Israel a' the flesh:
11:25 A' the same manner also he
12:28 a' that miracles, then gifts
14: 1 Follow a' charity, and desire
15: 6 A' that, he was seen of above five
7 A' that, he was seen of James;
32 If a' the manner of men I have
2Co 5:16 know we no man a' the flesh: yea,
16 we have known Christ a' the flesh,
7: 9 made sorry a' a godly manner,
11 ye sorrowed a' a godly sort,
9:14 long a' you for the exceeding
10: 3 we do not war a' the flesh:
7 a' the outward appearance?
11:17 I speak it not a' the Lord,
18 that many glory a' the flesh,
Ga 1:11 which was preached of me is not a'
18 Then a' three years I went up to
2: 1 fourteen years a' I went up
14 a' the manner of the Gentiles,
3:15 I speak a' the manner of men;
17 thirty years a', cannot disannul,
25 But a' that faith is come, we are
4: 9 now, a' that ye have known God,
23 was born a' the flesh;
29 he that was born a' the flesh
29 persecuted him that was born a'
Eph 1:11 all things a' the counsel of his own
13 also trusted, a' that ye heard the
13 whom also a' that ye believed, ye
15 a' I heard of your faith in the
4:24 a' God is created in righteousness
Ph'p 1: 8 how greatly I long a' you all
2:26 For he longed a' you all,
3:12 I follow a', if that I may
Col 2: 8 a' the tradition of men,
8 a' the rudiments of the world,
8 and not a' Christ.
22 a' the commandments and
3:10 a' the image of him that created
1Th 2: 2 a' that we had suffered before,
2Th 2: 9 whose coming is a' the working
3: 6 and not a' the tradition
1Ti 5:15 already turned aside a' Satan.
24 some men they follow a'.
6:10 while some coveted a', they have
11 follow a' righteousness, godliness,
2Ti 4: 3 but a' their own lusts
Tit 1: 1 the truth which is a' godliness;
4 own son a' the common faith:
3: 4 a' that the kindness and love of
10 a' the first and second admonition
Heb 3: 5 which were to be spoken a';
4: 7 a' so long a time;
11 a' the same example of unbelief.
5: 6 a' the order of Melchisedec.
10 an high priest a' the order of
6:15 a' he had patiently endured, he
20 a' the order of Melchisedec.
7: 2 a' that also king of Salem,
11 rise a' the order of Melchisedec,
11 be called a' the order of Aaron?
15 a' the similitude of Melchisedec
16 not a' the law of a carnal
16 but a' the power of an
17 a' the order of Melchisedec.
21 a' the order of Melchisedec:)
8:10 a' those days, saith the Lord;
9: 3 And a' the second veil,
17 a testament is of force a' men
27 but a' this the judgment:
10:12 a' he had offered one sacrifice
15 for a' that he had said before,
16 a' those days, saith the Lord,

Heb 10:26 a' that we have received the
32 a' ye were illuminated, ye endured
36 a' ye have done the will of God,
11: 8 which he should a' receive
30 Jericho fell down, a' they were
12:10 chastened us a' their own
Jas 3: 9 a' the similitude of God.
1Pe 3: 5 a' this manner in the old time
5:10 by Christ Jesus, a' that ye have
2Pe 1:15 ye may be able a' my decease
2: 6 that a' should live ungodly;
10 that walk a' the flesh in
21 a' they have known it, to turn
3: 3 walking a' their own lusts,
2Jo 6 we walk a' his commandments.
3Jo 6 forward on their journey a' a
Jude 7 and going a' strange flesh,
11 and ran greedily a' the error of
16 complainers, walking a' their
18 who should walk a' their own
Re 4: 1 A' this I looked, and, behold,
7: 1 a' these things I saw four angels
9 A' this I beheld, and, lo,
11:11 And a' three days and an half
12:15 as a flood a' the woman,
13: 3 the world wondered a' the beast.
15: 5 And a' that I looked,
18: 1 a' these things I saw another angel
14 the fruits that thy soul lusted a'
19: 1 a' these things I heard a great
20: 3 a' that he must be loosed

afternoon
J'g 19: 8 they tarried until a', and

afterward See also AFTERWARDS.
Ge 10:18 and a' were the families of the
15:14 a' shall they come out with
32:20 and a' I will see his face;
38:30 And a' came out his brother,
Ex 5: 1 a' Moses and Aaron went in, and
34:32 a' all the children of Israel
Le 14:19 a' he shall kill the burnt offering:
36 a' the priest shall go in to see
16:26 a' come into the camp.
28 a' he shall come into the camp.
22: 7 and shall a' eat of the holy things;
Nu 5:26 a' shall cause the woman to drink
12:16 a' the people removed from
19: 7 a' he shall come into the camp,
31: 2 a' shalt thou be gathered unto thy
24 a' ye shall come into the camp.
32:22 a' ye shall return, and be guiltless
De 17: 7 a' the hands of all the people.
24:21 thou shalt not glean it a':
Jos 2:16 and a' may ye go your way.
8:34 a' he read all the words of the
10:26 a' Joshua smote them, and
24: 5 and a' I brought you out.
J'g 1: 9 a' the children of Judah went down
7:11 a' shall thine hands be strengthened
16: 4 came to pass a', that he loved
19: 5 and a' go your way.
1Sa 24: 5 a', that David's heart smote
8 David also arose a', and went
2Sa 3:28 a' when David heard it, he said,
1Ch 2:21 a' Hezron went in to the daughter
2Ch 35:14 a' they made ready for themselves,
Ezr 3: 5 a' offered the continual burnt
Ne 6:10 A' I came unto the house of
Ps 73:24 and a' receive me to glory.
Isa 1:26 a' thou shalt be called,
9: 1 a' did more grievously afflict
Jer 21: 7 a', saith the Lord, I will
34:11 a' they turned, and caused
46:26 a' it shall be inhabited,
49: 6 a' I will bring again the
Eze 41: 1 A' he brought me to the temple,
43: 1 A' he brought me to the gate,
47: 1 A' he brought me again unto the
5 A' he measured a thousand;
Da 8:27 a' I rose up, and did the king's
Ho 3: 5 A' shall the children of Israel
Joe 2:28 come to pass a', that I will
Mat 4: 2 he was a' an hungred.
21:29 but a' he repented, and went.
32 ye had seen it, repented not a',
25:11 A' came also the other virgins,
M'r 4:17 a', when affliction or persecution
16:14 A' he appeared unto the eleven
Lu 4: 2 they were ended, he a' hungered.
8: 1 it came to pass a', that he went
17: 8 a' thou shalt eat and drink?
18: 4 but a' he said within himself,
Joh 5:14 A' Jesus findeth him in the
Ac 13:21 And a' they desired a king:
1Co 15:23 a' they that are Christ's at his
46 a' that which is spiritual.
Heb 4: 8 would he not a' have spoken
12:11 a' it yieldeth the peaceable fruit
17 ye know how that a', when he
Jude 5 a' destroyed them that believed

afterwards See also AFTERWARD.
Ge 30:21 And a' she bare a daughter,
Ex 11: 1 a' he will let you go hence:
De 13: 9 and a' the hand of all the people.
1Sa 9:13 a' they eat that be bidden.
Job 18: 2 and a' we will speak.
Pr 20:17 a' his mouth shall be filled with
24:27 a' build thine house.
28:23 rebuketh a man a' shall find
29:11 a wise man keepeth it in till a'.
Eze 11:24 A' the spirit took me up, and
Joh 13:36 but thou shalt follow me a'.
Ga 1:21 A' I came into the regions of
3:23 which should a' be revealed.

Agabus (*ag'-ab-us*)
Ac 11:28 one of them named *A'*.
21:10 a certain prophet, named *A'*.

Agag (*a'-gag*) See also AGAGITE.
Nu 24: 7 his king shall be higher than *A'*,
1Sa 15: 8 took *A'* the king of the Amalekites
9 But Saul and the people spared *A'*,
20 have brought *A'* the king of Amalek,
32 Bring ye hither to me *A'* the king
32 And *A'* came unto him delicately.
32 *A'* said, Surely the bitterness of
33 And Samuel hewed *A'* in pieces

Agagite (*ag'-ag-ite*)
Es 3: 1, 10 the son of Hammedatha the *A'*,
8: 3 away the mischief of Haman the *A'*,
5 the son of Hammedatha the *A'*,
9:24 the son of Hammedatha the *A'*,

again
Ge 4: 2 And she *a'* bare his brother Abel.
25 And Adam knew his wife *a'*:
8:10 *a'* he sent forth the dove out of
12 returned not *a'* unto him
21 I will not *a'* curse the ground
21 neither will I *a'* smite any more
14:16 brought *a'* his brother Lot, and
15:16 they shall come hither *a'*:
18:29 And he spake unto him yet *a'*,
19: 9 And they said *a'*, This one fellow
22: 5 and worship, and come *a'* to you.
24: 5 bring thy son *a'* unto the land
6, 8 bring not my son thither *a'*.
25: 1 Then *a'* Abraham took a wife,
26:18 Isaac digged *a'* the wells of water,
28:15 will bring thee *a'* into this land;
21 I come *a'* to my father's house in
29: 3 put the stone *a'* upon the well's
33, 34, 35 conceived *a'*, and bare a
30: 7 conceived *a'*, and bare Jacob a
19 conceived *a'*, and bare Jacob the
31 I will *a'* feed and keep thy flock.
35: 9 And God appeared unto Jacob *a'*,
37:14 and bring me word *a'*.
22 to deliver him to his father *a'*.
38: 4 conceived *a'*, and bare a son; and
5 *a'* conceived, and bare a son; and
26 he knew her *a'* no more.
40:21 butler unto his butlership *a'*;
42:24 and returned to them *a'*, and
37 I will bring him to thee *a'*.
43: 2 Go *a'*, buy us a little food.
12 the money that was brought *a'*
12 carry it *a'* in your hand;
13 and arise, go *a'* unto the man:
21 we have brought it *a'* in our hand.
44: 8 money....we brought *a'* unto thee
25 Go *a'*, and buy us a little food.
46: 4 I will also surely bring thee up *a'*:
48:21 and bring you *a'* unto the land of
50: 5 bury my father, and I will come *a'*.
Ex 4: 7 Put thine hand into thy bosom *a'*.
7 he put his hand into his bosom *a'*;
7 it was turned *a'* as his other flesh.
10: 8 Moses and Aaron were brought *a'*
29 I will see thy face *a'* no more.
14:13 ye shall see them *a'* no more
26 may come *a'* upon the Egyptians,
15:19 the Lord brought *a'* the waters
21:19 If he rise *a'*, and walk abroad
23: 4 thou shalt surely bring it back *a'*.
24:14 until we come *a'* unto you:
33:11 And he turned *a'* into the camp:
34:35 Moses put the vail upon his face *a'*,
Le 13: 6 look on him *a'* the seventh day:
7 he shall be seen of the priest *a'*:
16 if the raw flesh turn *a'*,
14:39 shall come *a'* the seventh day,
43 if the plague come *a'*, and break
20: 2 *A'*, thou shalt say to the children
24:20 so shall it be done to him *a'*.
25:48 may be redeemed *a'*; one of his
51 he shall give *a'* the price of his
52 his years shall he give him *a'*
26:26 shall deliver you your bread *a'*
Nu 11: 4 the children of Israel also wept *a'*,
12:14 after that let her be received in *a'*.
17:10 Bring Aaron's rod *a'* before the
22: 8 and I will bring you word *a'*, as
15 And Balak sent yet *a'* princes,
25 and he smote her *a'*.
34 thee, I will get me back *a'*.
23:16 Go *a'* unto Balak, and say thus.
32:15 he will yet *a'* leave them in the
33: 7 and turned *a'* unto Pi-hahiroth,
35:32 come *a'* to dwell in the land,
De 1:22 bring us word *a'* by what way
25 and brought us word *a'*, and said,
5:30 Get you into your tents *a'*.
13:16 for ever; it shall not be built *a'*.
15: 3 thou mayest exact it *a'*: but that
18:16 Let me not hear *a'* the voice of
22: 1 shalt in any case bring them *a'*
2 thou shalt restore it to him *a'*.
4 surely help to lift them up *a'*.
23:11 he shall come into the camp *a'*.
24: 4 not take her *a'* to be his wife,
13 shalt deliver him the pledge *a'*
19 thou shalt not go *a'* to fetch it: it
20 shalt not go over the boughs *a'*:
28:68 shall bring thee into Egypt *a'*
68 Thou shalt see it no more *a'*: and
30: 9 will *a'* rejoice over thee for good,
33:11 hate him, that they rise not *a'*.
Jos 5: 2 and circumcise *a'* the children of
8:21 then they turned *a'*, and slew the
14: 7 I brought him word *a'* as it was
Jos 18: 4 and they shall come *a'* to me.
8 describe it, and come *a'* to me,
9 came *a'* to Joshua to the host of
22:28 that we may say *a'*, Behold the
32 and brought them word *a'*.
J'g 3:12 the children of Israel did evil *a'*
19 turned *a'* from the quarries
4: 1 the children of Israel *a'* did evil
20 *A'* he said unto her, Stand in the
6:18 I will tarry until thou come *a'*.
8: 9 When I come *a'* in peace, I will
33 the children of Israel turned *a'*.
9:37 And Gaal spake *a'* and said,
10: 6 the children of Israel did evil *a'*
11: 8 we turn *a'* to thee now, that thou
9 If ye bring me home *a'* to fight
13 restore those lands *a'* peaceably.
14 Jephthah sent messengers *a'*
13: 1 the children of Israel did evil *a'*
8 thou didst send come *a'* unto us,
9 the angel of God came *a'* unto the
15:19 he had drunk, his spirit came *a'*,
16:22 hair of his head began to grow *a'*
19: 3 unto her, and to bring her *a'*,
7 therefore he lodged there *a'*.
20:22 and set their battle *a'* in array in
23 Shall I go up *a'* to battle
25 ground of the children of Israel *a'*
28 Shall I yet *a'* go out to battle
41 the men of Israel turned *a'*, the
48 the men of Israel turned *a'*
21:14 Benjamin came *a'* at that time;
Ru 1:11 Naomi said, Turn *a'*, my
12 Turn *a'*, my daughters, go your
14 lifted up their voice, and wept *a'*:
21 Lord hath brought me home *a'*
4: 3 Naomi, that is come *a'* out of the
1Sa 3: 5 I called not; lie down *a'*.
6 the Lord called yet *a'*, Samuel.
6 I called not, my son; lie down *a'*.
8 And the Lord called Samuel *a'* the
21 the Lord appeared *a'* in Shiloh:
4: 5 so that the earth rang *a'*.
5: 3 and set him in his place *a'*.
11 and let it go *a'* to his own place,
6:21 Philistines have brought *a'* the ark
9: 8 the servant answered Saul *a'*,
15:25, 30 and turn *a'* with me, that
31 So Samuel turned *a'* after Saul;
16:10 *A'*, Jesse made seven of his sons
17:30 the people answered him *a'* after
19: 8 And there was war *a'*: and David
15 Saul sent the messengers *a'* to
21 And Saul sent messengers *a'*
20:17 Jonathan caused David to swear *a'*,
23: 4 David enquired of the Lord yet *a'*.
23 and come ye *a'* to me with the
25:12 turned their way, and went *a'*,
27: 4 he sought no more *a'* for him.
29: 4 that he may go *a'* to his place
30:12 when...his spirit came *a'* to him:
2Sa 1: 9 He said unto me *a'*, Stand, I pray
2:22 And Abner said *a'* to Asahel,
3:11 not answer Abner a word *a'*,
26 Abner, which brought him *a'*
34 all the people wept *a'* over him.
5:22 the Philistines came up yet *a'*.
6: 1 *A'*, David gathered together all
12:23 can I bring him back *a'*?
14:13 the king doth not fetch home *a'*
14 which cannot be gathered up *a'*;
21 bring the young man Absalom *a'*.
29 when he sent *a'* the second time,
15: 8 Lord shall bring me *a'* indeed to
25 he will bring me *a'*, and shew me
29 Abiathar carried the ark of God *a'*
16:19 And *a'*, whom should I serve?
18:22 Then said Ahimaaz.... yet *a'* to
19:24 until the day he came *a'* in peace.
30 my lord the king is come *a'* in
37 servant, I pray thee, turn back *a'*,
20:10 struck him not *a'*, and he died.
21:15 Philistines had yet war *a'* with
18 was *a'* a battle with the Philistines
19 there was *a'* a battle in Gob with
22:38 not *a'* until I had consumed
24: 1 And *a'* the anger of the Lord was
1Ki 1:45 so that the city rang *a'*. This is
2:30 Benaiah brought the king word *a'*,
41 Jerusalem to Gath, and was come *a'*.
8:33 shall turn *a'* to thee, and confess
34 and bring them *a'* unto the land
12: 5 for three days, then come *a'* to me.
12 Come to me *a'* the third day.
20 that Jeroboam was come *a'*,
21 to bring the kingdom *a'* to
27 this people turn *a'* unto their lord
27 go *a'* to Rehoboam king of Judah.
13: 4 he could not pull it in *a'* to him.
6 my hand may be restored me *a'*.
6 king's hand was restored him *a'*,
9 nor turn *a'* by the same way that
17 nor turn *a'* to go by the way that
33 but made *a'*... priests of the high
17:21 this child's soul come into him *a'*.
22 soul of the child came into him *a'*,
18:37 hast turned their heart back *a'*.
43 And he said, Go *a'* seven times.
19: 6 and drink, and laid him down *a'*.
7 the angel of the Lord came *a'* the
20 Go back *a'*: for what have I done
20: 5 the messengers came *a'*, and said,
9 departed, and brought him word *a'*.
2Ki 1: 6 turn *a'* unto the king that sent you,
11 *A'* also he sent unto him another
13 sent *a'* a captain of the third fifty
2Ki 2:18 when they came *a'* to him, (for he
4:22 to the man of God, and come *a'*.
29 salute thee, answer him not *a'*:
31 Wherefore he went *a'* to meet
38 Elisha came *a'* to Gilgal:
43 He said *a'*, Give the people,
5:10 thy flesh shall come *a'* to thee,
14 his flesh came *a'* like unto the flesh
26 when the man turned *a'* from his
7: 8 came *a'*, and entered into another
9:18 he cometh not *a'*.
20 even unto them, and cometh not *a'*:
36 Wherefore they came *a'*, and told
13:25 the son of Jehoahaz took *a'*
19: 9 sent messengers *a'* unto Hezekiah,
30 shall yet *a'* take root downward,
20: 5 Turn again, and tell Hezekiah the
21: 3 For he built up *a'* the high places
22: 9 and brought the king word *a'*,
20 they brought the king word *a'*.
24: 7 the king of Egypt came not *a'* any
1Ch 13: 3 bring *a'* the ark of our God to us:
14:13 Philistines yet *a'* spread
14 Therefore David enquired *a'* of
20: 5 was war *a'* with the Philistines;
6 yet *a'* there was war at Gath,
21:12 what word I shall bring *a'* to him
27 put his sword *a'* into the sheath
2Ch 6:25 bring them *a'* unto the land which
10: 5 Come *a'* unto me after three days.
12 Come *a'* to me on the third day.
11: 1 bring the kingdom *a'* to Rehoboam.
12:11 brought them *a'* into the guard
13:20 did Jeroboam recover strength *a'*
18:18 *A'* he said, Therefore hear the
32 turned back *a'* from pursuing
19: 4 he went out *a'* through the people
20:27 to go *a'* to Jerusalem with joy;
24:11 carried it to his place *a'*.
19 to bring them *a'* unto the Lord;
25:10 out of Ephraim, to go home *a'*:
28:11 and deliver the captives *a'*,
30: 6 *a'* unto the Lord God of Abraham,
9 if ye turn *a'* unto the Lord,
9 they shall come *a'* into this land:
32:25 Hezekiah rendered not *a'*
33: 3 For he built *a'* the high places
13 *a'* to Jerusalem into his kingdom.
34:16 brought the king word back *a'*,
28 So they brought the king word *a'*.
Ezr 2: 1 *a'* unto Jerusalem and Judah,
4:13 the walls set up *a'*, then will they
16 if this city be builded *a'*, and the
6: 5 and brought *a'* unto the temple
21 Israel, which were come *a'* out of
9:14 we *a'* break thy commandments,
Ne 7: 6 *a'* to Jerusalem and to Judah,
8:17 *a'* out of the captivity made booths,
9:28 they did evil *a'* before thee:
29 that thou mightest bring them *a'*
13: 9 brought I *a'* the vessels of the
21 if ye do so *a'*, I will lay hands on
Es 4:10 *A'* Esther spake unto Hatach,
6:12 Mordecai came *a'* to the king's
7: 2 the king said *a'* unto Esther on
8: 3 Esther spake yet *a'* before the
Job 2: 1 *A'* there was a day when the sons
6:29 not be iniquity; yea, return *a'*,
10: 9 wilt thou bring me into dust *a'*?
16 and *a'* thou shewest thyself
12:14 down, and it cannot be built *a'*:
23 nations, and straiteneth them *a'*.
14: 7 cut down, that it will sprout *a'*,
14 If a man die, shall he live *a'*? all
20:15 and he shall vomit them up *a'*:
29:22 After my words they spake not *a'*;
34:15 man shall turn *a'* unto dust.
Ps 18:37 neither did I turn *a'* till they were
37:21 payeth not *a'*: but the righteous
60: 1 O turn thyself to us *a'*.
68:22 I will bring *a'* from Bashan,
22 I will bring my people *a'*
71:20 shalt quicken me *a'*, and shalt
20 bring me up *a'* from the depths
78:39 passeth away, and cometh not *a'*.
80: 3 Turn us *a'*, O God, and cause thy
7 Turn us *a'*, O God of hosts,
19 Turn us *a'*, O Lord God of hosts,
85: 6 Wilt thou not revive us *a'*:
8 let them not turn *a'* to folly.
104: 9 turn not *a'* to cover the earth.
107:26 they go down *a'* to the depths:
39 *A'*, they are minished and brought
126: 1 the Lord turned *a'* the captivity
4 Turn *a'* our captivity, O Lord,
6 shall doubtless come *a'* with
140:10 pits, that they rise not up *a'*.
Pr 2:19 that go unto her return *a'*,
3:28 thy neighbour, Go, and come *a'*,
19:17 he hath given will he pay him *a'*.
19 yet thou must do it *a'*.
24 much as bring it to his mouth *a'*.
23:35 I awake? I will seek it yet *a'*.
24:16 seven times, and riseth up *a'*:
26:15 grieveth him to bring it *a'* to his
Ec 1: 6 the wind returneth *a'* according
7 thither they return *a'*.
3:20 the dust, and all turn to dust *a'*.
4: 4 *A'*, I considered all travail, and
11 *A'*, if two lie together, then they
8:14 *a'*, there be wicked men, to whom
Isa 7:10 the Lord spake *a'* unto Ahaz,
8: 5 The Lord spake also unto me *a'*,
10:20 shall no more *a'* stay upon him
11:11 the Lord shall set his hand *a'*
24:20 it shall fall, and not rise *a'*.

Isa 37:31 a' take root downward, and
38: 8 I will bring a' the shadow of the
46: 8 it a' to mind, O ye transgressors.
49: 5 to bring Jacob a' to him,
20 shall say a' in thine ears, The
51:22 thou shalt no more drink it a':
52: 8 the Lord shall bring a' Zion.
Jer 3: 1 man's, shall he return unto her a'
1 yet return a' to me, saith the Lord.
12:15 will bring them a', every man to
15:19 return, then will I bring thee a',
16:15 I will bring them a' into their land
18: 4 so he made it a' another vessel,
19:11 that cannot be made whole a':
23: 3 will bring them a' to their folds;
24: 4 A' the word of the Lord came
6 I will bring them a' to this land:
25: 5 Turn ye a' now every one from
27:16 be brought a' from Babylon:
28: 3 a' into this place all the vessels
4 will bring a' to this place Jeconiah
6 bring a' the vessels of the Lord's
29:14 I will bring you a' into the place
30: 3 bring a' the captivity of my people
18 I will bring a' the captivity of
31: 4 A' I will build thee, and thoushalt
4 thou shalt a' be adorned with thy
16 they shall come a' from the land
17 that thy children shall come a' to
21 turn a', O virgin of Israel, turn a'
23 I shall bring a' their captivity;
32:15 vineyards shall be possessed a'
37 will bring them a' unto this place,
33:10 A' there shall be heard in this
12 A' in this place, which is desolate
13 of Judah, shall the flocks pass a'
36:28 Take thee a' another roll,
37: 8 the Chaldeans shall come a', and
41:16 whom he had brought a' from
46:16 let us go a' to our own people,
48:47 bring a' the captivity of Moab
49: 6 I will bring a' the captivity of the
39 will bring a' the captivity of Elam,
50:19 And I will bring Israel a' to his
La 3:40 our ways, and turn a' to the Lord.
Eze 3:20 A', When a righteous man doth
4: 6 lie a' on thy right side, and thou
5: 4 take of them a', and cast them
7: 7 sounding a' of the mountains.
8: 6 turn thee yet a', and thou shalt
13 Turn thee yet a', and thou shalt
15 O son of man? turn thee yet a',
12:26 A' the word of the Lord came to
14:12 word of the Lord came a' to me,
16: 1 A' the word of the Lord came
53 I shall bring a' their captivity,
53 then will I bring a' the captivity
18: 1 word of the Lord came unto me a',
27 A', when the wicked man turneth
21: 8 A' the word of the Lord came
18 word of the Lord came unto me a',
23: 1 word of the Lord came a' unto me,
24: 1 A' in the ninth year, in the tenth
25: 1 The word of the Lord came a'
26:21 shalt thou never be found a',
27: 1 The word of the Lord came a'
28: 1 The word of the Lord came a'
20 A' the word of the Lord came
29:14 bring a' the captivity of Egypt,
30: 1 the word of the Lord came a' unto
33: 1 A' the word of the Lord came
14 A', when I say unto the wicked,
15 restore the pledge, give a' that he
34: 4 neither have ye brought a'
16 bring a' that which was driven
37: 4 A' he said unto me, Prophesy
15 The word of the Lord came a'
39:25 bring a' the captivity of Jacob,
27 When I have brought them a'
47: 1 Afterward he brought me a' unto
4, 4 A' he measured a thousand,
Da 2: 7 They answered a' and said,
9:25 the street shall be built a', and
10:18 there came a' and touched me
Ho 1: 6 And she conceived a', and bare a
Joe 3: 1 bring a' the captivity of Judah,
Am 7: 8 not a' pass by them any more:
13 prophesy not a' any more at
8: 2 not a' pass by them any more.
14 shall fall, and never rise up a'.
9:14 And I will bring a' the captivity
Jon 2: 4 look a' toward thy holy temple.
Mic 7:19 He will turn a', he will have
Zep 3:20 At that time will I bring you a',
Hag 2:20 a' the word of the Lord came
Zec 2: 1 I lifted up mine eyes a', and
12 and shall choose Jerusalem a'.
4: 1 that talked with me came a',
12 answered a', and said unto him,
8: 1 A' the word of the Lord of hosts
15 a' have I thought in these days
10: 6 will bring them a' to place them;
9 with their children, and turn a'.
10 bring them a' also out of the land
12: 6 be inhabited a' in her own place,
Mal 2:13 And this have ye done a',
M't 2: 8 bring me word a', that I may
4: 7 It is written a', Thou shalt not
8 A', the devil taketh him up
5:33 A', ye have heard that it hath been
7: 2 it shall be measured to you a'.
6 and turn a' and rend you.
11: 4 and shew John a' those things
13:44 A', the kingdom of heaven
45, 47 A', the kingdom of heaven
16:21 and be raised a' the third day.

M't 17: 9 until the son of man be risen a'
23 third day he shall be raised a'.
18:19 A' I say unto you, That if two of
19:24 And a' I say unto you, It is easier
20: 5 A' he went out about the sixth
19 the third day he shall rise a'.
21:36 A', he sent other servants more
22: 1 spake unto them a' by parables,
4 A', he sent forth other servants,
26:32 after I am risen a' I will go
42 He went away a' the second time,
43 came and found them asleep a':
44 went away a', and prayed the
52 Put up a' thy sword into his place,
72 And a' he denied with an oath,
27: 3 brought a' the thirty pieces of
50 Jesus, when he had cried a' with
63 After three days I will rise a'.
M'r 2: 1 a' he entered into Capernaum
13 he went forth a' by the seaside;
3: 1 he entered a' into the synagogue;
20 the multitude cometh together a',
4: 1 began a' to teach by the sea side:
5:21 when Jesus was passed over a' by
7:31 a', departing from the coasts of
8:13 entering into the ship a' departed
25 he put his hands a' upon his eyes,
31 after three days rise a'.
10: 1 resort unto him a'; and, as he
1 was wont, he taught them a'.
10 his disciples asked him a' of the
24 But Jesus answereth a', and saith
32 he took a' the twelve, and began
34 the third day he shall rise a'.
11:27 And they come a' to Jerusalem:
12: 4 and a' he sent unto them another
5 And a' he sent another; and him
13:16 is in the field not turn back a'
14:39 a' he went away, and prayed,
40 he found them asleep a',
61 A' the high priest asked him,
69 a maid saw him a', and began to
70 he denied it a'. And a little after,
70 they that stood by said a' to Peter,
15: 4 And Pilate asked him a', saying,
12 Pilate answered and said a' unto
13 And they cried out a', Crucify him.
Lu 2:34 and rising a' of many in Israel;
45 turned back a' to Jerusalem,
4:20 he gave it a' to the minister, and
6:30 thy goods ask them not a'.
34 to sinners, to receive as much a'.
35 lend, hoping for nothing a'; and
38 measured to you a'.
8:37 the ship, and returned back a'.
55 her spirit came a', and she arose
9: 8 of the old prophets was risen a'.
19 one of the old prophets is risen a'.
39 him that he foameth a',
42 delivered him a' to his father.
10: 6 if not, it shall turn to you a'.
17 the seventy returned a' with joy,
35 when I come a', I will repay thee.
13:20 And a' he said, Whereunto shall
14: 6 could not answer him a' to these
12 lest they also bid thee a', and a
15:24 my son was dead, and is alive a';
32 brother was dead, and is alive a';
17: 4 turn a' to thee, saying, I repent:
18:33 the third day he shall rise a'.
20:11 a' he sent another servant:
12 And a' he sent a third: and
23:11 robe, and sent him a' to Pilate.
20 willing to release Jesus, spake a'
24: 7 crucified, and the third day rise a'.
Joh 1:35 A' the next day after John stood,
3: 3 Except a man be born a', he
7 Ye must be born a'.
4: 3 and departed a' into Galilee.
13 of this water shall thirst a':
46 Jesus came a' into Cana of Galilee,
54 This is a' the second miracle that
6:15 he departed a' into a mountain
39 should raise it up a' at the last
8: 2 he came a' into the temple,
8 a' he stooped down, and wrote
12 Then spake Jesus a' unto them,
21 Then said Jesus a' unto them, I go
9:15 Then a' the Pharisees also asked
17 They say unto the blind man a'.
24 Then a' called they the man
26 said they to him a', What did he
27 wherefore would you hear it a'?
10: 7 Then said Jesus unto them a',
17 my life, that I might take it a'.
18 and I have power to take it a'.
19 a division therefore a' among the
31 the Jews took up stones a' to stone
39 Therefore they sought a' to take
40 And went away a' beyond Jordan
11: 7 Let us go into Judæa a'.
8 and goest thou thither a'?
23 unto her, Thy brother shall rise a'.
24 I know that he shall rise a' in the
38 a' groaning in himself
12:22 a' Andrew and Philip tell Jesus.
28 and will glorify it a'.
39 because that Esaias said a',
13:12 and was set down a', he said
14: 3 I will come a', and receive you
28 I go away, and come a' unto you.
16:16 and a', a little while, and ye shall
17, 19 and a', a little while, and
22 but I will see you a',
28 a', I leave the world, and go to the
18: 7 Then asked he them a', Whom

Joh 18:27 Peter then denied a':
33 into the judgment hall a',
38 he went out a' unto the Jews,
40 Then cried they all a', saying,
19: 4 Pilate therefore went forth a',
9 went a' into the judgment hall,
37 And a' another scripture saith,
20: 9 he must rise a' from the dead.
10 the disciples went away a' unto
21 said Jesus to them a',
26 And after eight days a' his disciples
21: 1 Jesus shewed himself a' to the
16 He saith to him a' the second time,
Ac 1: 6 this time restore a' the kingdom
7:26 would have set them at one a',
39 their hearts turned back a' into
10:15 the voice spake unto him a' the
16 the vessel was received up a' into
11: 9 voice answered me a' from
10 all were drawn up a' into heaven.
13:33 he hath raised up Jesus a';
37 he, whom God raised a', saw no
14:21 they returned a' to Lystra,
15:16 will build a' the tabernacle
16 I will build a' the ruins thereof,
36 us go a' and visit our brethren
17: 3 suffered, and risen a' from the
32 will hear thee a' of this matter.
18:21 I will return a' unto you,
20:11 was come up a', and had broken
21: 6 and they returned home a'.
22:17 I was come a' to Jerusalem,
27:28 sounded a', and found it fifteen
Ro 4:25 raised a' for our justification.
8:15 the spirit of bondage a' to fear;
34 yea rather, that is risen a',
10: 7 bring up Christ a' from the dead.)
11:23 is able to graff them in a'.
35 shall be recompensed unto him a'?
15:10 a' he saith, Rejoice, ye Gentiles,
11 a', Praise the Lord, all ye Gentiles;
12 And a', Esaias saith,
1Co 3:20 And a', The Lord knoweth the
7: 5 and come together a', that Satan
12:21 nor a' the head to the feet, I have
15: 4 rose a' the third day according
2Co 1:16 and to come a' out of Macedonia
2: 1 not come a' to you in heaviness.
3: 1 begin a' to commend ourselves?
5:12 we commend not ourselves a' unto
15 which died for them, and rose a'.
10: 7 let him of himself think this a',
11:16 say a', Let no man think me a fool;
12:19 A', think ye that we excuse
21 And lest, when I come a',
13: 2 come a', I will not spare:
Ga 1: 9 so say I now a', if any man preach
17 returned a' unto Damascus.
2: 1 went up a' to Jerusalem
18 For if I build a' the things which I
4: 9 how turn ye a' to the weak
9 ye desire a' to be in bondage?
19 of whom I travail in birth a'
5: 1 not entangled a' with the yoke of
3 For I testify a' to every man
Ph'p 1:26 by my coming to you a'.
2:28 when ye see him a', ye may rejoice,
4: 4 and a' I say, Rejoice.
10 care of me hath flourished a';
16 ye sent once and a' unto my
1Th 2:18 even I Paul, once and a';
3: 9 can we render to God a' for you,
4:14 Jesus died and rose a', even so
Tit 2: 9 in all things; not answering a';
Ph'm 12 Whom I have sent a': thou
Heb 1: 5 And a', I will be to him a Father,
6 And a', when he bringeth in the
2:13 And a', I will put my trust in him.
13 And a', Behold I and the children
4: 5 in this place a', If they shall enter
7 A', he limiteth a certain day,
5:12 ye have need that one teach you a'
6: 1 not laying a' the foundation of
6 to renew them a' unto repentance;
10: 3 there is a remembrance a' made
30 And a', The Lord shall judge his
11:35 their dead raised to life a':
13:20 that brought a' from the dead
Jas 5:18 he prayed a', and the heaven gave
1Pe 1: 3 which hath begotten us a' unto
23 Being born a', not of corruptible
2:23 he was reviled, reviled not a';
2Pe 2:20 they are a' entangled therein, and
22 dog is turned to his own vomit a';
1Jo 2: 8 A', a new commandment I write
Re 10: 8 from heaven spake unto me a',
11 prophesy a' before many peoples,
19: 3 a' they said, Alleluia.
20: 5 the rest of the dead lived not a'

against^
Ge 4: 8 Cain rose up a' Abel his brother,
14:15 And he divided himself a' them,
15:10 laid each piece one a' another:
16:12 his hand will be a' every man,
12 and every man's hand a' him;
20: 6 withheld thee from sinning a' me:
21:16 sat her down over a' him a good
16 she sat over a' him, and lifted up
30: 2 anger was kindled a' Rachel: and
32:25 that he prevailed not a' him,
34:30 gather themselves together a' me,
37:18 unto them, they conspired a' him
39: 9 this great wickedness, and sin a' God?
40: 2 Pharaoh was wroth a' two of his
2 a' the chief...butlers, and a' the chief"
41:36 a' the seven years of famine, which

Ge 42:22 you, saying, Do not sin a' the child;
36 away: all these things are a' me.
43:18 he may seek occasion a' us, and
25 ready the present a' Joseph came
44:18 let not thine anger burn a' thy servant
50:20 ye thought evil a' me: but God
Ex 1:10 unto our enemies, and fight a' us,
4:14 of the Lord was kindled a' Moses,
7:15 stand by the river's brink a' he
8:12 he had brought a' Pharaoh.
10:16 a' the Lord your God, and a' you.
11: 7 But a' any of the children of Israel
7 move his tongue, a' man or beast:
12:12 and a' all the gods of Egypt
14: 2 the sea, over a' Baal-zephon:
5 servants was turned a' the people,
25 Lord fighteth for them a' the Egyptians.
27 the Egyptians fled a' it;
15: 7 them that rose up a' thee:
24 the people murmured a' Moses,
16: 2 Israel murmured a' Moses and
7 your murmurings a' the Lord;
7 are we, that you murmur a' us?
8 which ye murmur a' him:
8 are not a' us, but a' the Lord.
17: 3 the people murmured a' Moses,
19:11 be ready a' the third day: for the
15 the people, Be ready a' the third day:
20:16 bear false witness a' thy neighbour.
23:29 beast of the field multiply a' thee.
33 land, lest they make thee sin a'
25:27 Over a' the border shall the rings
37 they may give light over a'
26:17 set in order one a' another: thus
35 the candlestick over a' the table
28:27 a' the other coupling thereof
32:10 my wrath may wax hot a' them,
11 thy wrath wax hot a' thy people,
12 and repent of this evil a' thy
33 Whosoever hath sinned a' me,
37:14 Over a' the border were the rings,
39:20 a' the other coupling thereof,
40:24 congregation, over a' the table,
Le 4: 2 sin through ignorance a' any of
2 not to be done, and shall do a'
13 have done somewhat a' any of
14 which they have sinned a' it, is
22 somewhat through ignorance a'
27 a' any of the commandments
5:19 certainly trespassed a' the Lord.
6: 2 commit a trespass a' the Lord,
17:10 blood; I will even set my face a'
19:16 a' the blood of thy neighbour:
18 nor bear any grudge a' the
20: 3 I will set my face a' that man,
5 a' that man, and a' his family,
6 even set my face a' that soul,
26:17 set my face a' you, and ye shall
40 trespass which they trespassed a'
Nu 5: 6 to do a trespass a' the Lord, and
7 give it unto him a' whom he
12 and commit a trespass a' him,
13 and there be no witness a' her,
27 done trespass a' her husband,
8: 2 lamps shall give light over a'
3 therefore over a'...candlestick,
10: 9 to war in your land a' the enemy
21 did set up the tabernacle a' they
11:18 Sanctify yourselves a' to morrow,
33 Lord was kindled a' the people,
12: 1 Miriam and Aaron spake a' Moses
8 not afraid to speak a' my servant
13:31 be not able to go up a' the people;
14: 2 Israel murmured a' Moses and a'
9 Only rebel not ye a' the Lord,
27 congregation, which murmur a'
27 Israel, which they murmur a' me.
29 upward, which have murmured a'
35 gathered together a' me: in this
36 congregation to murmur a' him,
16: 3 gathered themselves together a'
3 Moses and a' Aaron, and said
11 company are gathered together a'
11 what is Aaron, that ye murmur a'
19 the congregation a' them unto
38 these sinners a' their own souls,
41 children of Israel murmured a'
41 Moses, and a' Aaron, saying,
42 gathered a' Moses and a' Aaron,
17: 5 whereby they murmur a' you.
10 be kept for a token a' the rebels;
20: 2 together a' Moses and a' Aaron.
18 lest I come out a' thee with the
20 Edom came out a' him
24 rebelled a' my word at the water
21: 1 then he fought a' Israel, and took
5 spake a' God, and a' Moses,
7 spoken a' the Lord, and a' thee;
23 out a' Israel into the wilderness:
23 to Jahaz, and fought a' Israel.
26 who had fought a' the former king
33 the king of Bashan went out a'
22: 5 they abide over a' me:
22 in the way for an adversary a' him.
25 crushed Balaam's foot a' the wall:
34 thou stoodest in the way a' me:
23:23 there is no enchantment a' Jacob,
23 is there any divination a' Israel:
24:10 And Balak's anger was kindled a'
25: 3 of the Lord was kindled a' Israel.
4 before the Lord a' the sun,
26: 9 who strove a' Moses and a' Aaron
9 when they strove a' the Lord:
27: 3 a' the Lord in the company
14 ye rebelled a' my commandment
30: 9 bound their souls, shall stand a'
Nu 31: 3 and let them go a' the Midianites,
7 they warred a' the Midianites, as
16 to commit trespass a' the Lord in
32:13 Lord's anger was kindled a' Israel,
23 ye have sinned a' the Lord: and
35:30 one witness shall not testify a'
De 1: 1 in the plain over a' the Red sea,
26 rebelled a' the commandment of
41 We have sinned a' the Lord, we
43 a' the commandment of the Lord,
44 came out a' you, and chased you,
2:15 the hand of the Lord was a' them,
19 over a' the children of Ammon,
32 Sihon came out a' us, he and all
3: 1 king of Bashan came out a' us,
29 in the valley over a' Beth-peor.
4:26 earth to witness a' you this day,
46 in the valley over a' Beth-peor,
5:20 shalt thou bear false witness a'
6:15 Lord thy God be kindled a' thee,
7: 4 anger of the Lord be kindled a'
8:19 I testify a' you this day that ye
9: 7 have been rebellious a' the Lord.
16 behold, ye had sinned a' the Lord
19 wherewith the Lord was wroth a'
23 rebelled a' the commandment of
24 ye have been rebellious a' the Lord
11:17 Lord's wrath be kindled a' you,
30 in the champaign over a' Gilgal,
15: 9 eye be evil a' thy poor brother,
9 and he cry unto the Lord a' thee,
19:11 rise up a' him, and smite him
15 One witness shall not rise up a'
16 a false witness rise up a' any man
16 testify a' him that which is wrong;
18 testified falsely a' his brother;
20: 1 to battle a' thine enemies, and
3 approach this day unto battle a'
4 to fight for you a' your enemies,
10 a city to fight a' it, then proclaim
12 but will make war a' thee, then
18 ye sin a' the Lord your God.
19 a long time, in making war a' it
19 thereof by forcing an ax a' them:
20 shalt build bulwarks a' the city
21:10 forth to war a' thine enemies,
22:14 give occasions of speech a' her,
17 given occasions of speech a' her,
26 a man riseth a' his neighbour,
23: 4 they hired a' thee Balaam
9 host goeth forth a' thine enemies,
24:15 lest he cry a' thee unto the Lord,
28: 7 enemies that rise up a' thee to
7 shall come out a' thee one way,
25 shalt go out one way a' them,
48 the Lord shall send a' thee, in
49 Lord shall bring a nation a' thee
29: 7 the king of Bashan, came out a'
20 jealousy shall smoke a' that man,
27 anger of the Lord was kindled a'
30:19 and earth to record this day a'
31:17 my anger shall be kindled a' them
19 a witness for me a' the children
21 this song shall testify a' them as
26 may be there for a witness a' thee.
27 have been rebellious a' the Lord;
28 and earth to record a' them.
32:49 of Moab that is over a' Jericho;
51 Because ye trespassed a' me
33:11 the loins of them that rise a' him,
34: 1 Pisgah that is over a' Jericho.
6 of Moab, over a' Beth-peor:
Jos 1:18 doth rebel a' thy commandment,
3:16 passed over right a' Jericho.
5:13 stood a man over a' him with his
7: 1 anger of the Lord was kindled a'
13 Sanctify yourselves a' to morrow:
20 I have sinned a' the Lord God
8: 3 the people of war, to go up a' Ai:
4 ye shall lie in wait a' the city, even
5 when they come out a' us,
14 men of the city went out a' Israel
14 that there were liers in ambush a'
22 issued out of the city a' them;
33 over a'...Gerizim,...over a'...Ebal;
9: 1 over a' Lebanon,
18 the congregation murmured a'
10: 5 before Gibeon, and made war a' it.
6 are gathered together a' us.
21 none moved his tongue a' any of
25 to all your enemies a' whom ye
29 him, unto Libnah, and fought a'
31, 34 encamped a' it, and fought
31, 34 encamped...and fought a' it;
36 unto Hebron; and they fought a'
38 him, to Debir; and fought a' it:
11: 5 of Merom, to fight a' Israel.
7 people of war with him, a' them
20 should come a' Israel in battle,
18:17 a' the going up of Adummim,
18 over a' Arabah northward,
19:47 Dan went up to fight a' Leshem,
22:11 over a' the land of Canaan,
12 at Shiloh, to go up to war a' them.
16 committed a' the God of Israel,
16 might rebel this day a' the Lord?
18 seeing ye rebel to day a' the Lord,
19 not a' the Lord, nor rebel a' us,
22 or if in transgression a' the Lord,
29 God forbid that we should rebel a'
31 this trespass a' the Lord:
33 intend to go up a' them in battle,
23:16 anger of the Lord be kindled a'
24: 9 Moab, arose and warred a' Israel,
11 the men of Jericho fought a' you,
22 Ye are witnesses a' yourselves
J'g 1: 1 a' the Canaanites first, to fight a'
3 we may fight a' the Canaanites;
5 in Bezek: and they fought a' him,
8 Judah had fought a' Jerusalem,
9 down to fight a' the Canaanites,
10 And Judah went a' the Canaanites
11 thence he went a' the inhabitants
22 they also went up a' Beth-el:
2:14 anger of the Lord was hot a' Israel,
15 the hand of the Lord was a' them
20 anger of the Lord was hot a' Israel;
3: 8 anger of the Lord was hot a' Israel,
10 prevailed a' Chushan-rishathaim.
12 Eglon the king of Moab a' Israel,
4:24 and prevailed a' Jabin the king
5:14 there a root of them a' Amalek;
20 in their courses fought a' Sisera.
23 to the help of the Lord a' the
6: 2 the hand of Midian prevailed a'
3 east, even they came up a' them;
4 And they encamped a' them, and
31 Joash said unto all that stood a'
32 Let Baal plead a' him, because he
39 Let not thine anger be hot a' me,
7: 2 Israel vaunt themselves a' me,
22 the Lord set every man's sword a'
24 Come down a' the Midianites,
9:18 risen up a' my father's house
31 behold, they fortify the city a'
33 people that is with him come out a'
34 they laid wait a' Shechem in four
43 he rose up a' them, and smote
45 Abimelech fought a' the city all
50 encamped a' Thebez, and took it.
52 unto the tower, and fought a' it,
10: 7 anger of the Lord was hot a' Israel,
9 passed over Jordan to fight also a'
9 and a' Benjamin, and a' the house
10 Lord, saying, We have sinned a'
18 will begin to fight a' the children
11: 4 children of Ammon made war a'
5 of Ammon made war a' Israel,
8 fight a' the children of Ammon,
9 again to fight a' the children
12 come a' me to fight in my land?
20 pitched in Jahaz, and fought a'
25 a' Israel, or did he ever fight a'
27 I have not sinned a' thee,
27 thou doest me wrong to war a' me:
32 children of Ammon to fight a' them;
12: 3 over a' the children of Ammon,
3 unto me this day, to fight a' me?
14: 4 that he sought an occasion a' the
5 a young lion roared a' him.
15:10 Why are ye come up a' us? And
14 the Philistines shouted a' him:
16: 5 what means we may prevail a'
18: 9 Arise, that we may go up a' them:
19: 2 a' him, and went away from him
10 a' Jebus, which is Jerusalem;
20: 5 the men of Gibeah rose a' me,
9 Gibeah; we will go up by lot a' it;
11 Israel were gathered a' the city,
14 to battle a' the children of Israel.
18 shall go up first to the battle a'
19 in the morning, and encamped a'
20 went out to battle a' Benjamin;
20 array to fight a' them at Gibeah.
23 battle a' the children of Benjamin
23 And the Lord said, Go up a' him.)
24 Israel came near a' the children
25 Benjamin went forth a' them
28 I yet again go out to battle a'
30 Israel went up a' the children of
30 put themselves in array a' Gibeah,
31 Benjamin went out a' the people
34 came a' Gibeah ten thousand
43 a' Gibeah toward the sunrising.
Ru 1:13 hand of the Lord is gone out a' me.
21 the Lord hath testified a' me,
1Sa 2:25 If one man sin a' another, the
25 but if a man sin a' the Lord, who
3:12 In that day I will perform a' Eli
4: 1 Israel went out a' the Philistines
2 put themselves in array a' Israel:
7: 6 We have sinned a' the Lord.
7 the Philistines went up a' Israel.
10 Philistines drew near to battle a'
13 the hand of the Lord was a' the
9:14 Samuel came out a' them,
11: 1 came up, and encamped a'
12: 3 witness a' me before the Lord,
5 The Lord is witness a' you, and
9 and they fought a' them.
12 of the children of Ammon came a'
14 not rebel a' the commandment
15 but rebel a' the commandment
15 the hand of the Lord be a' you,
15 as it was a' your fathers.
23 that I should sin a' the Lord in
14: 5 northward over a' Michmash,
5 southward over a' Gibeah.
20 every man's sword was a' his
33 Behold, the people sin a' the Lord,
34 sin not a' the Lord in eating with
47 and fought a' all his enemies on
47 a' Moab, and a' the children of
47 a' Edom, and a' the kings of Zobah,
47 and a' the Philistines:
52 war a' the Philistines all the days
15: 7 Shur, that is over a' Egypt.
18 the Amalekites, and fight a' them
17: 2 battle in array a' the Philistines.
9 if I prevail a' him, and kill him,
21 army a' army.
28 Eliab's anger was kindled a' David,

1Sa 17:33 not able to go a· this Philistine
35 when he arose a· me, I caught him
55 Saul saw David go forth a· the
18:21 of the Philistines may be a· him.
19: 4 the king sin a· his servant, a· David;
4 because he hath not sinned a· thee,
5 wilt thou sin a· innocent blood,
20:30 Then Saul's anger was kindled a·
22: 8 all of you have conspired a· me,
8 son hath stirred up my servant a·
13 Why have ye conspired a· me,
13 that he should rise up a· me, to
23: 1 the Philistines fight a· Keilah,
3 come to Keilah a· the armies of
9 secretly practised mischief a·
28 pursuing after David, and went a·
24: 6 to stretch forth mine hand a· him,
7 suffered them not to rise a· Saul.
10 not put forth mine hand a· my
11 I have not sinned a· thee; yet thou
25:17 evil is determined a· our master,
17 and a· all his household: for he is
20 his men came down a· her;
22, 34 light any that pisseth a·
26: 9 stretch forth his hand a· the Lord's
11 I should stretch forth mine hand a·
19 Lord have stirred thee up a· me,
23 not stretch forth mine hand a· the
27:10 David said, A· the south of Judah,
10 a· the south of the Jerahmeelites,
10 and a· the south of the Kenites.
28:15 the Philistines make war a· me,
29: 8 I may not go fight a· the enemies
30:23 delivered...company that came a·
31: 1 the Philistines fought a· Israel:
3 And the battle went sore a· Saul,
2Sa 1:16 thy mouth hath testified a· thee,
3: 8 Am I a dog's head, which a· Judah
5:23 come upon them over a· the
6: 7 the Lord was kindled a· Uzzah;
8:10 he had fought a· Hadadezer,
10: 9 the front of the battle was a· him
9 put them in array a· the Syrians:
10 in array a· the children of Ammon.
13 unto the battle a· the Syrians:
17 set themselves in array a· David,
11:23 Surely the men prevailed a· us,
25 make thy battle more strong a·
12: 5 anger was greatly kindled a·
11 I will raise up evil a· thee out of
13 I have sinned a· the Lord. And
26 Joab fought a· Rabbah of the
27 I have fought a· Rabbah, and have
28 encamp a· the city, and take it:
29 and fought a· it, and took it.
14: 7 family is risen a· thine handmaid,
13 thought such a thing a· the people
16:13 on the hill's side over a· him,
17:21 Ahithophel counselled a· you.
18: 6 people went out into the field a·
12 I not put forth mine hand a· the
13 should have wrought falsehood a·
13 wouldest have set thyself a·
28 lifted up their hand a· my lord
31 this day of all them that rose up a·
32 all that rise a· thee to do thee hurt,
20:15 they cast up a bank a· the city,
21 hath lifted up his hand a· the king,
21: 5 and that devised a· us that we
15 and fought a· the Philistines: and
22:40 rose up a· me hast thou subdued
49 also... above them that rose up a·
23: 8 lift up his spear a· eight hundred,
18 up his spear a· three hundred,
24: 1 anger of the Lord was kindled a·
1 he moved David a· them to say,
4 the king's word prevailed a· Joab,
4 and a· the captains of the host.
17 thine hand, I pray thee, be a· me,
17 and a· my father's house.
1Ki 2:23 have not spoken this word a· his
6: 5 a· the wall of the house he built
5 a· the walls of the house round
10 And then he built chambers a· all
7: 4 light was a· light in three ranks.
5 light was a· light in three
20 over a· the belly which was by
39 eastward over a· the south.
8:31 any man trespass a· his neighbour,
33 because they have sinned a· thee,
35 rain, because they have sinned a·
44 go out to battle a· their enemy,
46 If they sin a· thee, (for there is no
50 people that have sinned a· thee,
50 they have transgressed a· thee,
11:26, 27 he lifted up his hand a· the king.
12:19 So Israel rebelled a· the house of
21 to fight a· the house of Israel, to
24 nor fight a· your brethren the
13: 2 And he cried a· the altar in the
4 of God, which had cried a· the
4 hand, which he put forth a· him,
32 cried by the word of the Lord a·
32 and a· all the houses of the high
14:10 Jeroboam him that pisseth a·
25 of Egypt came up a· Jerusalem:
15:17 king of Israel went up a· Judah,
20 of the hosts which he had a·
27 of Issachar, conspired a· him;
16: 1 Jehu the son of Hanani a· Baasha,
7 the word of the Lord a· Baasha,
7 and a· his house, even for all
9 his chariots, conspired a· him,
11 a· a wall, neither of his kinsfolks,
12 which he spake a· Baasha by Jehu
15 were encamped a· Gibbethon,

1Ki 16:22 prevailed a· the people that
20: 1 besieged Samaria, and warred a·
12 themselves in array a· the city.
22 king of Syria will come up a· thee.
23 let us fight a· them in the plain,
25 we will fight a· them in the plain,
26 up to Aphek, to fight a· Israel.
27 all present, and went a· them:
29 they pitched one over a· the other
21:10 before him, to bear witness a· him,
13 men of Belial witnessed a· him,
13 even a· Naboth, in the presence
21 off from Ahab him that pisseth a·
22: 6 I go a· Ramoth-gilead to battle,
15 shall we go a· Ramoth-gilead
32 they turned aside to fight a· him:
35 stayed up in his chariot a· the
2Ki 1: 1 Then Moab rebelled a· Israel
3: 5 king of Moab rebelled a· the king
7 king of Moab hath rebelled a· me:
7 wilt thou go with me a· Moab
21 the kings were come up to fight a·
27 was great indignation a· Israel:
5: 7 how he seeketh a quarrel a· me.
6: 8 king of Syria warred a· Israel,
7: 6 king of Israel hath hired a· us
8:28 the war a· Hazael king of Syria
29 Ramah, when he fought a· Hazael
9: 8 from Ahab him that pisseth a·
14 son of Nimshi conspired a· Joram.
21 they went out a· Jehu, and met
10: 9 I conspired a· my master, and
12:17 went up, and fought a· Gath, and
13: 3 anger of the Lord was kindled a·
12 his might wherewith he fought a·
14:19 they made a conspiracy a· him
15:10 the son of Jabesh conspired a·
19 Pul the king of Assyria came a·
25 conspired a· him, and smote him
30 son of Elah made a conspiracy a·
37 the Lord began to send a· Judah
16: 7 king of Israel, which rise up a·
9 of Assyria went up a· Damascus
11 made it a· king Ahaz came from
17: 3 A· him came up Shalmaneser
7 children of Israel had sinned a·
9 things that were not right a·
13 testified a· Israel, and a· Judah,
15 which he testified a· them; and
18: 7 rebelled a· the king of Assyria,
9 of Assyria came up a· Samaria,
13 come up a· all the fenced cities
17 with a great host a· Jerusalem.
20 trust, that thou rebellest a· me?
25 come up without the Lord a· this
25 Go up a· this land, and destroy it.
19: 8 of Assyria warring a· Libnah:
9 he is come out to fight a· thee:
20 a· Sennacherib king of Assyria I
22 and a· whom hast thou exalted
22 even a· the Holy One of Israel.
27 coming in, and thy rage a· me.
28 thy rage a· me and thy tumult
32 with shield, nor cast a bank a·
21:23 servants of Amon conspired a·
24 that had conspired a· king Amon;
22:13 wrath of the Lord that is kindled a·
17 my wrath shall be kindled a· this
19 what I spake a· this place,
19 and a· the inhabitants thereof,
23:17 hast done a· the altar of Beth-el.
26 his anger was kindled a· Judah,
29 went up a· the king of Assyria
29 the king Josiah went a· him;
24: 1 he turned and rebelled a· him.
2 sent a· him bands of the Chaldees,
2 sent them a· Judah to destroy it,
10 king of Babylon came a·
11 came a· the city, and his servants
20 Zedekiah rebelled a· the king of
25: 1 and all his host, a· Jerusalem,
1 a· it; and they built forts a· it
4 the Chaldees were a· the city
1Ch 5:11 children of Gad dwelt over a·
20 And they were helped a· them,
25 transgressed a· the God of their
8:32 in Jerusalem, over a· them.
9:38 brethren at Jerusalem, over a·
10: 1 the Philistines fought a· Israel;
3 And the battle went sore a· Saul,
13 which he committed a· the Lord,
13 even a· the word of the Lord,
11:11 up his spear a· three hundred
20 up his spear a· three hundred,
12:19 came with the Philistines a· Saul
21 they helped David a· the band
13:10 anger of the Lord was kindled a·
14: 8 heard of it, and went out a· them.
10 Shall I go up a· the Philistines?
14 them over a· the mulberry trees.
18:10 he had fought a· Hadarezer,
19:10 the battle was set a· him before
10 put them in array a· the Syrians.
11 set themselves in array a· the
17 set the battle in array a· them.
17 the battle in array a· the Syrians,
21: 1 And Satan stood up a· Israel,
4 the king's word prevailed a· Joab.
24:31 cast lots over a· their brethren
31 over a· their younger brethren.
25: 8 they cast lots, ward a· ward,
26:12 having wards one a· another,
16 ward a· ward.
27:24 there fell wrath for it a· Israel;
2Ch 4:10 east end, over a· the south.
6:22 if a man sin a· his neighbour, and

2Ch 6:24 because they have sinned a· thee;
26 rain, because they have sinned a·
34 go out to war a· their enemies
36 If they sin a· thee, (for there is no
39 people which have sinned a· thee.
8: 3 Hamath-zobah, and prevailed a·
9:29 of Iddo the seer a· Jeroboam
10:19 Israel rebelled a· the house of
11: 1 were warriors, to fight a· Israel,
4 shall not go up, nor fight a· your
4 returned from going a· Jeroboam.
12: 2 Shishak king of Egypt came up a·
2 they had transgressed a· the Lord,
9 Shishak king of Egypt came up a·
13: 3 also set the battle in array a· him
6 up, and hath rebelled a· his lord.
7 have strengthened themselves a·
12 sounding trumpets to cry alarm a·
12 fight ye not a· the Lord God
14: 9 there came out a· them Zerah
10 Then Asa went out a· him,
11 thy name we go a· this multitude.
11 God; let not man prevail a· thee.
16: 1 king of Israel came up a· Judah,
4 captains of his armies a· the cities
17: 1 strengthened himself a· Israel.
10 made no war a· Jehoshaphat.
18:22 Lord hath spoken evil a· thee.
34 up in his chariot a· the Syrians
19:10 they trespass not a· the Lord,
20: 1 came a· Jehoshaphat to battle.
2 cometh a great multitude a· thee
12 we have no might a· this great
12 company that cometh a· us;
16 To morrow go ye down a· them:
17 to morrow go out a· them:
22 ambushments a· the children of
22 Seir, which were come a· Judah;
23 a· the inhabitants of mount Seir,
29 the Lord fought a· the enemies
37 prophesied a· Jehoshaphat,
21:16 the Lord stirred up a· Jehoram
22: 5 king of Israel to war a· Hazael
7 went out with Jehoram a· Jehu
24:19 the Lord; and they testified a·
21 conspired a· him, and stoned him
23 the host of Syria came up a· him·
24 executed judgment a· Joash.
25 own servants conspired a· him
26 are they that conspired a· him;
25:10 anger was greatly kindled a·
15 anger of the Lord was kindled a·
27 they made a conspiracy a· him
26: 6 and warred a· the Philistines,
7 God helped him a· the Philistines,
7 and a· the Arabians that dwelt
13 to help the king a· the enemy.
16 transgressed a· the Lord his God,
27: 5 the Ammonites, and prevailed a·
28:10 you, sins a· the Lord your God?
12 stood up a· them that came from
13 we have offended a· the Lord
13 great, and there is fierce wrath a·
19 and transgressed sore a· the Lord.
22 trespass yet more a· the Lord:
30: 7 trespassed a· the Lord God of
32: 1 into Judah, and encamped a· the
2 purposed to fight a· Jerusalem,
9 he himself laid siege a· Lachish,
16 his servants spake yet more a· the
16 God, and a· his servant Hezekiah.
17 Lord God of Israel, and to speak a
19 a· the God of Jerusalem,
19 as a· the gods of the people
33:24 And his servants conspired a· him,
25 that had conspired a· king Amon;
34:27 when thou heardest his words a·
27 and a· the inhabitants thereof,
35:20 king of Egypt came up to fight a·
20 and Josiah went out a· him.
21 I come not a· thee this day, but
21 a· the house wherewith I have
36: 6 A· him came up Nebuchadnezzar
13 rebelled a· king Nebuchadnezzar,
16 the wrath of the Lord arose a· his
Ezr 4: 5 And hired counsellors a· them,
6 a· the inhabitants of Judah
8 wrote a letter a· Jerusalem unto
19 made insurrection a· kings,
7:23 should there be wrath a· the realm
8:22 help us a· the enemy in the way:
22 wrath is a· all them that forsake
10: 2 We have trespassed a· our God,
Ne 1: 6 which we have sinned a· thee:
7 have dealt very corruptly a· thee,
2:19 will ye rebel a· the king?
3:10 even over a· his house.
16 over a· the sepulchres of David,
19 a· the going up to the armoury
23 Benjamin and Hashub over a·
25 over a· the turning of the wall,
26 a· the water gate toward the east,
27 over a· the great tower that lieth
28 every one over a· his house.
29 Zadok the son of Immer over a·
31 over a· the gate Miphkad,
4: 8 fight a· Jerusalem, and to hinder it.
9 a watch a· them day and night,
5: 1 wives a· their brethren the Jews.
7 I set a great assembly a· them.
6:12 pronounced this prophecy a· me:
7: 3 every one to be over a· his house.
9:10 that they dealt proudly a·
26 disobedient, and rebelled a· thee,
26 prophets which testified a· them
29 And testifiedst a· them, that thou

Ne 9:29 commandments, but sinned *a'* thy
30 testifiedst *a'* them by thy spirit in
34 wherewith thou didst testify *a'*
12: 9 were over *a'* them in the watches.
24 brethren over *a'* them, to praise
24 ward over *a'* ward.
37 fountain gate, which was over *a'*
38 that gave thanks went over *a'*
13: 2 but hired Balaam *a'* them, that
15 sabbath day: and I testified *a'*
21 Then I testified *a'* them, and said
27 transgress *a'* our God in marrying
Es 2: 1 and what was decreed *a'* her.
3:14 they should be ready *a'* that day.
5: 1 over *a'* the king's house:
1 over *a'* the gate of the house.
9 full of indignation *a'* Mordecai.
6:13 thou shalt not prevail *a'* him, but
7: 7 determined *a'* him by the king.
8: 3 that he had devised *a'* the Jews.
13 Jews should be ready *a'* that day
9:24 devised *a'* the Jews to destroy
25 which he devised *a'* the Jews,
Job 2: 3 although thou movedst me *a'* him,
6: 4 do set themselves in array *a'* me.
7:20 why hast thou set me as a mark *a'*
8: 4 If thy children have sinned *a'* him,
9: 4 hath hardened himself *a'* him,
10:17 renewest thy witnesses *a'* me,
17 changes and war are *a'* me.
11: 5 speak, and open his lips *a'* thee;
13:26 thou writest bitter things *a'* me,
14:20 Thou prevailest for ever *a'* him,
15: 6 yea, thine own lips testify *a'* thee.
13 that thou turnest thy spirit *a'* God,
24 they shall prevail *a'* him, as a king
25 he stretcheth out his hand *a'* God,
25 strengtheneth himself *a'* the
16: 4 I could heap up words *a'* you, and
8 wrinkles, which is a witness *a'* me.
10 gathered themselves together *a'*
17: 8 innocent shall stir up himself *a'*
18: 9 the robber shall prevail *a'* him.
19: 5 ye will magnify yourselves *a'*
5 and plead *a'* me my reproach:
11 hath also kindled his wrath *a'* me,
12 and raise up their way *a'* me, and
18 I arose, and they spake *a'* me.
19 they whom I loved are turned *a'* me.
20:27 and the earth shall rise up *a'* him.
21:27 ye wrongfully imagine *a'* me.
23: 6 *a'* me with his great power?
24:13 They are of those that rebel *a'* the
27: 7 riseth up *a'* me as the unrighteous.
30:12 they raise up *a'* me the ways of
21 thou opposest thyself *a'* me.
31:21 up my hand *a'* the fatherless,
38 If my land cry *a'* me, or that the
32: 2 *a'* Job was his wrath kindled,
3 Also *a'* his three friends was his
14 hath not directed his words *a'* me:
33:10 he findeth occasions *a'* me,
13 Why dost thou strive *a'* him?
34: 6 Should I lie *a'* my right? my
29 done *a'* a nation, or *a'* a man only:
37 and multiplieth his words *a'* God.
35: 6 sinnest, what doest thou *a'* him?
38:23 reserved *a'* the time of trouble,
23 *a'* the day of battle and war?
39:16 She is hardened *a'* her young
23 The quiver rattleth *a'* him, the
42: 7 My wrath is kindled *a'* thee, and *a'*
Ps 2: 2 counsel together, *a'* the Lord,
2 and *a'* his anointed, saying,
3: 6 have set themselves *a'* me round
5:10 for they have rebelled *a'* thee.
7:13 he ordaineth his arrows *a'* the
10: 8 his eyes are privily set *a'* the poor.
13: 4 say, I have prevailed *a'* him;
15: 3 up a reproach *a'* his neighbour.
5 taketh reward *a'* the innocent.
17: 7 from those that rise up *a'* them.
18:39 under me those that rose up *a'* me.
48 rise up *a'* me: thou hast delivered
21:11 For they intended evil *a'* thee:
12 thine arrows upon thy strings *a'*
27: 3 host should encamp *a'* me, my
3 though war should rise *a'* me, in
12 false witnesses are risen up *a'* me,
31:13 they took counsel together *a'* me,
18 proudly and contemptuously *a'*
34:16 the Lord is *a'* them that do evil,
35: 1 fight *a'* them that fight *a'* me.
3 way *a'* them that persecute me:
15 gathered themselves together *a'*
20 devise deceitful matters *a'* them
21 mouth wide *a'* me, and said, Aha,
26 that magnify themselves *a'* me.
36:11 Let not the foot of pride come *a'*
37: 1 envious *a'* the workers of iniquity.
12 The wicked plotteth *a'* the just,
38:16 they magnify themselves *a'*
41: 4 my soul; for I have sinned *a'* thee.
7 hate me whisper together *a'* me:
7 *a'* me do they devise my hurt.
9 bread, hath lifted up his heel *a'* me.
43: 1 plead my cause *a'* an ungodly
44: 5 tread them under that rise up *a'*
50: 7 O Israel, and I will testify *a'* thee:
20 Thou sittest and speakest *a'* thy
51: 4 *A'* thee, thee only, have I sinned,
53: 5 the bones of him that encampeth *a'*
54: 3 strangers are risen up *a'* me,
55:12 that did magnify himself *a'* me;
18 peace from the battle that was *a'*
20 his hands *a'* such as be at peace

Ps 56: 2 for they be many that fight *a'* me,
5 their thoughts are *a'* me for evil.
59: 1 me from them that rise up *a'* me.
3 the mighty are gathered *a'* me;
62: 3 ye imagine mischief *a'* a man?
65: 3 Iniquities prevail *a'* me: as for
69:12 that sit in the gate speak *a'* me;
71:10 mine enemies speak *a'* me;
73: 9 set their mouth *a'* the heavens,
15 I should offend *a'* the generation
74: 1 smoke *a'* the sheep of thy pasture?
23 tumult of those that rise up *a'*
78:17 *a'* him by provoking the most High
19 Yea, they spake *a'* God; and said,
21 so a fire was kindled *a'* Jacob,
21 and anger also came up *a'* Israel;
79: 8 O remember not *a'* us former
80: 4 be angry *a'* the prayer of thy
81:14 my hand *a'* their adversaries.
83: 3 have taken crafty counsel *a'* thy
3 consulted *a'* thy hidden ones.
5 they are confederate *a'* thee:
86:14 O God, the proud are risen *a'* me,
91:12 lest thou dash thy foot *a'* a stone.
92:11 the wicked that rise up *a'* me.
94:16 rise up for me *a'* the evildoers?
16 or who will stand up for me *a'* the
21 *a'* the soul of the righteous,
102: 8 are mad *a'* me are sworn *a'* me
105:28 and they rebelled not *a'* his word.
106:26 he lifted up his hand *a'* them,
40 the Lord kindled *a'* his people,
107:11 they rebelled *a'* the words of God,
109: 2 the deceitful are opened *a'* me:
2 *a'* me with a lying tongue.
3 and fought *a'* me without a cause.
20 them that speak evil *a'* my soul.
119:11 heart, that I might not sin *a'* thee.
23 also did sit and speak *a'* me:
69 proud have forged a lie *a'* me:
124: 2 our side, when men rose up *a'* us:
3 when their wrath was kindled *a'* us.
129: 2 yet they have not prevailed *a'* me.
137: 9 thy little ones *a'* the stones.
138: 7 stretch forth thine hand *a'* the
139:20 they speak *a'* thee wickedly,
21 I grieved with those that rise up *a'*
Pr 3:29 Devise not evil *a'* thy neighbour,
8:36 sinneth *a'* me wrongeth his own
14:35 his wrath is *a'* him that causeth
17:11 messenger shall be sent *a'* him.
19: 3 his heart fretteth *a'* the Lord.
20: 2 to anger sinneth *a'* his own soul.
21:30 nor understanding nor counsel *a'*
31 the horse is prepared *a'* the day
24: 1 Be not thou envious *a'* evil men,
15 *a'* the dwelling of the righteous;
28 Be not a witness *a'* thy neighbour
25:18 false witness *a'* his neighbour
Ec 4:12 And if one prevail *a'* him, two
7:14 God also hath set the one over *a'*
8:11 sentence *a'* an evil work is not
9:14 great king *a'* it, and besieged it,
14 and built great bulwarks *a'* it:
10: 4 spirit of the ruler rise up *a'* thee,
Isa 1: 2 and they have rebelled *a'* me.
2: 4 nation shall not lift up sword *a'*
3: 5 shall behave himself proudly *a'*
5 and the base *a'* the honourable.
8 and their doings are *a'* the Lord,
9 countenance doth witness *a'* them;
5:25 the Lord kindled *a'* his people,
25 stretched forth his hand *a'* them,
30 roar *a'* them like the roaring of
7: 1 toward Jerusalem to war *a'* it,
1 but could not prevail *a'* it.
5 have taken evil counsel *a'*
6 Let us go up *a'* Judah, and vex it,
9:11 the adversaries of Rezin *a'* him,
21 they together shall be *a'* Judah.
10: 6 send him *a'* an hypocritical nation,
6 and *a'* the people of my wrath
15 Shall the ax boast itself *a'* him
15 shall the saw magnify itself *a'*
15 if the rod should shake itself *a'*
24 and shall lift up his staff *a'* thee,
32 shake his hand *a'* the mount of
13:17 I will stir up the Medes *a'* them,
14: 4 proverb *a'* the king of Babylon,
8 no feller is come up *a'* us.
22 For I will rise up *a'* them,
19: 2 I will set the Egyptians *a'* the
2 fight every one *a'* his brother,
2 every one *a'* his neighbour; city *a'*
2 city, and kingdom *a'* kingdom.
17 which he hath determined *a'* it.
20: 1 fought *a'* Ashdod, and took it;
23: 8 hath taken this counsel *a'* Tyre,
11 *a'* the merchant city, to destroy
25: 4 terrible ones is as a storm *a'* the
27: 4 set the briers and thorns *a'* me in
29: 3 I will camp *a'* thee round about,
3 lay siege *a'* thee with a mount,
3 and I will raise forts *a'* thee.
7 of all the nations that fight *a'*
7 fight *a'* her and her munition,
8 be, that fight *a'* mount Zion.
31: 2 arise *a'* the house of the evildoers,
2 and *a'* the help of them that work
4 shepherds is called forth *a'* him.
32: 6 and to utter error *a'* the Lord, to
36: 1 *a'* all the defenced cities of Judah,
5 trust, that thou rebellest *a'* me?
10 Lord *a'* this land to destroy it?
10 Go up *a'* this land, and destroy it.
37: 8 king of Assyria warring *a'* Libnah:

Isa 37:21 *a'* Sennacherib king of Assyria:
23 *a'* whom hast thou exalted thy
23 even *a'* the Holy One of Israel.
28 thy coming in, and thy rage *a'* me.
29 Because thy rage *a'* me, and thy
33 with shields, nor cast a bank *a'* it.
41:11 incensed *a'* thee shall be ashamed
12 war *a'* thee shall be as nothing,
42:13 he shall prevail *a'* his enemies.
24 Lord, he *a'* whom we have sinned?
43:27 teachers have transgressed *a'* me.
45:24 incensed *a'* him shall be ashamed.
54:15 *a'* thee shall fall for thy sake.
17 is formed *a'* thee shall prosper;
17 every tongue that shall rise *a'* thee
57: 4 *A'* whom do ye sport yourselves?
4 *a'* whom make ye a wide mouth,
59:12 and our sins testify *a'* us: for
13 and lying *a'* the Lord,
19 shall lift up a standard *a'* him.
63:10 enemy, and he fought *a'* them.
66:24 transgressed *a'* me: for their
Jer 1:15 and *a'* all the walls thereof round
15 and *a'* all the cities of Judah.
16 my judgments *a'* them touching
18 brasen walls *a'* the whole land,
18 *a'* the kings of Judah,
18 *a'* the princes
18 *a'* the priests thereof, and *a'* the
19 And they shall fight *a'* thee; but
19 not prevail *a'* thee; for I am with
2: 8 pastors also trangressed *a'* me,
29 ye all have transgressed *a'* me,
3:13 thou hast transgressed *a'* the Lord
25 have sinned *a'* the Lord our God,
4:12 also will I give sentence *a'* them.
16 *a'* Jerusalem, that watchers come
16 their voice *a'* the cities of Judah.
17 field, are they *a'* her round about;
17 she hath been rebellious *a'* me,
5:11 dealt very treacherously *a'* me,
6: 3 pitch their tents *a'* her
4 Prepare ye war *a'* her; arise,
6 and cast a mount *a'* Jerusalem:
23 set in array as men for war *a'* thee.
8:14 drink, because we have sinned *a'*
18 I would comfort myself *a'* sorrow,
11:17 hath pronounced evil *a'* thee,
17 they have done *a'* themselves
19 they had devised devices *a'* me,
12: 8 it crieth out *a'* me: therefore
9 the birds round about are *a'* her;
14 Lord *a'* all mine evil neighbours,
13:14 I will dash them one *a'* another,
14: 7 though our iniquities testify *a'* us,
7 are many; we have sinned *a'* thee.
20 for we have sinned *a'* thee.
15: 6 will I stretch out my hand *a'* thee,
8 brought upon them *a'* the mother
20 and they shall fight *a'* thee,
20 they shall not prevail *a'* thee:
16:10 pronounced all this great evil *a'*
10 committed *a'* the Lord our God?
18: 8 If that nation, *a'* whom I have
11 *a'* you, and devise a device *a'* you:
18 let us devise devices *a'* Jeremiah:
23 all their counsel *a'* me to slay me:
19:15 evil that I have pronounced *a'* it,
20:10 and we shall prevail *a'* him,
21: 2 king of Babylon maketh war *a'*
4 fight *a'* the king of Babylon, and *a'*
5 myself will fight *a'* you with an
10 I have set my face *a'* this city for
13 I am *a'* thee, O inhabitant of the
13 Who shall come down *a'* us? or
22: 7 I will prepare destroyers *a'* thee,
23: 2 saith the Lord God of Israel *a'* the
30 *a'* the prophets, saith the Lord.
31 Behold, I am *a'* the prophets, saith
32 *a'* them that prophesy false
25: 9 my servant, and will bring them *a'*
9 and *a'* the inhabitants thereof,
9 *a'* all these nations round about,
13 which I have pronounced *a'* it,
13 Jeremiah hath prophesied *a'* all
30 prophesy thou *a'* them all these
30 *a'* all the inhabitants of the earth.
26: 9 were gathered *a'* Jeremiah
11 to die; for he hath prophesied *a'*
12 sent me to prophesy *a'* this house
12 and *a'* this city all the words that
13 that he hath pronounced *a'* you.
19 he had pronounced *a'* them?
19 we procure great evil *a'* our souls.
20 *a'* this city and *a'* this land
27:13 Lord hath spoken *a'* the nation
28: 8 *a'* many countries,
8 and *a'* great kingdoms,
16 hast taught rebellion *a'* the Lord.
29:32 taught rebellion *a'* the Lord.
31:20 since I spake *a'* him, I do
39 over *a'* it upon the hill Gareb,
32:24 of the Chaldeans, that fight *a'* it,
29 Chaldeans, that fight *a'* this city,
33: 8 whereby they have sinned *a'* me;
8 they have transgressed *a'* me.
34: 1, 7 fought *a'* Jerusalem, and *a'* all
7 *a'* Lachish, and *a'* Azekah: for
22 they shall fight *a'* it, and take it,
35:17 that I have pronounced *a'* them:
36: 2 have spoken unto thee *a'* Israel,
2 *a'* Judah, and *a'* all the nations,
7 the Lord hath pronounced *a'* this
31 that I have pronounced *a'* them;
37: 8 come again, and fight *a'* this
10 of the Chaldeans that fight *a'* you,

Jer 37:18 have I offended a' thee, or a' thy
18 or a' this people, that ye have put
19 Babylon shall not come a' you,
19 nor a' this land?
38: 5 he that can do any thing a' you.
22 on, and have prevailed a' thee:
39: 1 and all his army a' Jerusalem,
40: 3 because ye have sinned a' the Lord,
43: 3 son of Neriah setteth thee on a' us,
44: 7 this great evil a' your souls,
11 I will set my face a' you for evil,
23 because ye have sinned a' the Lord,
29 my words shall surely stand a' you
46: 1 the prophet a' the Gentiles;
2 A' Egypt,
2 a' the army of
12 hath stumbled a' the mighty,
22 army, and come a' her with axes,
47: 1 the prophet a' the Philistines,
7 charge a' Ashkelon, and a' the
48: 1 A' Moab thus saith the Lord of
2 they have devised evil a' it;
26, 42 magnified himself a' the Lord
49:14 ye together, and come a' her,
19 a' the habitation of the strong:
20 Lord, that he hath taken a' Edom;
20 hath purposed a' the inhabitants
30 hath taken counsel a' you,
30 hath conceived a purpose a' you.
34 Jeremiah the prophet a' Elam
50: 1 that the Lord spake a' Babylon
1 and a' the land of the Chaldeans
3 there cometh up a nation a' her,
7 they have sinned a' the Lord,
9 come up a' Babylon an assembly
9 set themselves in array a' her;
14 in array a' Babylon round about:
14 for she hath sinned a' the Lord.
15 Shout a' her round about: she
21 Go up a' the land of Merathaim,
21 even a' it,
21 and a' the inhabitants
24 thou hast striven a' the Lord.
26 a' her from the utmost border,
29 together the archers a' Babylon:
29 bend the bow, camp a' it round
29 proud a' the Lord, a' the Holy One
31 I am a' thee, O thou most proud,
42 a' thee, O daughter of Babylon.
45 that he hath taken a' Babylon;
45 a' the land of the Chaldeans:
51: 1 raise up a' Babylon,
1 and a' them
1 midst of them that rise up a' me,
2 they shall be a' her round about.
3 A' him that bendeth let the
3 a' him that lifteth himself up
5 sin a' the Holy One of Israel.
11 for his device is a' Babylon, to
12 a' the inhabitants of Babylon.
14 they shall lift up a shout a' thee.
25 a' thee, O destroying mountain,
27 prepare the nations a' her,
27 call together a' her the kingdoms
27 appoint a captain a' her; cause
28 Prepare a' her the nations with
29 of the Lord shall be performed a'
46 violence in the land, ruler a' ruler.
60 that are written a' Babylon.
62 thou hast spoken a' this place,
52: 3 that Zedekiah rebelled a' the king
4 a' Jerusalem, and pitched a' it,
4 and built forts a' it round about.
La 1:13 and it prevaileth a' them:
15 an assembly a' me to crush my
18 rebelled a' his commandment:
2: 3 burned a' Jacob like a flaming
16 opened their mouth a' thee:
3: 3 Surely a' me is he turned; he
3 turneth his hand a' me all the
5 He hath builded a' me, and
46 have opened their mouths a' us.
60 all their imaginations a' me.
61 all their imaginations a' me;
62 lips of those that rose up a' me,
62 their device a' me all the day.
5:22 us; thou art very wroth a' us.
Eze 1:20 were lifted up over a' them:
21 were lifted up over a' them:
2: 3 nation that hath rebelled a' me:
3 fathers have transgressed a' me,
3: 8 thy face strong a' their faces,
8 forehead strong a' their foreheads.
13 noise of the wheels over a' them,
4: 2 lay siege a' it, and build a fort
2 a' it, and cast a mount a' it;
2 set the camp also a' it, and set
2 battering rams a' it round
3 and set thy face a' it, and it shall
3 and thou shalt lay siege a' it.
7 and thou shalt prophesy a' it.
5: 8 Behold, I, even I, am a' thee, and
6: 2 of Israel, and prophesy a' them,
11: 4 prophesy a' them, prophesy, O
13: 2 prophesy a' the prophets of Israel
8 I am a' you, saith the Lord God.
17 a' the daughters of thy people,
17 and prophesy thou a' them,
20 Behold, I am a' your pillows,
14:13 land sinneth a' me by trespassing
15: 7 And I will set my face a' them;
7 Lord, when I set my face a' them.
16:37 gather them round about a' thee,
40 also bring up a company a' thee,
44 shall use this proverb a' thee,
17:15 But he rebelled a' him in sending

Eze 17:20 that he hath trespassed a' me.
19: 8 Then the nations set a' him on
20: 8 they rebelled a' me, and would
8 accomplish my anger a' them in
13 the house of Israel rebelled a' me
21 the children rebelled a' me:
21 to accomplish my anger a' them
27 have committed a trespass a' me.
38 and them that transgress a'
46 and prophesy a' the forest of the
21: 2 places, and prophesy a' the land
3 Lord; Behold, I am a' thee, and
4 a' all flesh from the south to
15 of the sword a' all their gates,
22 battering rams a' the gates,
31 I will blow a' thee in the fire of
22: 3 idols a' herself to defile herself,
23:22 I will raise up thy lovers a' thee,
22 bring them a' thee on every side;
24 shall come a' thee with chariots,
24 of people, which shall set a' thee
25 And I will set my jealousy a' thee,
24: 2 set himself a' Jerusalem this
25: 2 set thy face a' the Ammonites,
2 and prophesy a' them;
3 thou saidst, Aha, a' my sanctuary,
3 a' the land of Israel, when it was
3 a' the house of Judah, when they
6 all thy despite a' the land of Israel;
12 Edom hath dealt a' the house of
26: 2 Tyrus hath said a' Jerusalem,
3 Behold, I am a' thee, O Tyrus,
3 many nations to come up a' thee,
8 and he shall make a fort a' thee,
8 a mount a' thee, and lift up the
8 buckler a' thee.
9 set engines of war a' thy walls,
27:30 their voice to be heard a' thee,
28: 7 draw their swords a' the beauty of
21 set thy face a' Zidon,
21 and prophesy a' it,
22 Behold, I am a' thee, O Zidon;
29: 2 set thy face a' Pharaoh king of
2 prophesy a' him, and a' all Egypt:
3 I am a' thee, Pharaoh king of
10 therefore I am a' thee,
10 and a' thy rivers,
18 to serve a great service a' Tyrus:
18 service that he had served a' it:
20 labour wherewith he served a' it,
30:22 I am a' Pharaoh king of Egypt,
33:30 of thy people still are talking a'
34: 2 prophesy a' the shepherds of
10 I am a' the shepherds; and I will
35: 2 set thy face a' mount Seir,
2 and prophesy a' it,
3 O mount Seir, I am a' thee,
3 stretch out mine hand a' thee,
11 used out of thy hatred a' them;
12 spoken a' the mountains of Israel,
13 mouth ye have boasted a' me,
13 have multiplied your words a' me:
36: 2 the enemy hath said a' you,
5 a' the residue of the heathen,
5 and a' all Idumea,
38: 2 set thy face a' Gog, the land of
2 and Tubal, and prophesy a'
3 I am a' thee, O Gog, the chief
8 many people, a' the mountains
16 come up a' my people of Israel,
16 I will bring thee a' my land,
17 that I would bring thee a' them?
18 shall come a' the land of Israel,
21 sword a' him throughout all my
21 man's sword shall be a' his brother.
22 will plead a' him with pestilence
39: 1 thou son of man, prophesy a' Gog,
1 the Lord God; Behold, I am a' thee,
23 because they trespassed a' me,
26 they have trespassed a' me,
40:13 and twenty cubits, door a' door.
18 of the gates over a' the length
23 over a' the gate toward the north.
41:15 over a' the separate place which
16 over a' the door, ceiled with wood
42: 1 was over a' the separate place,
3 Over a' the twenty cubits which
3 court, and over a' the pavement
7 without over a' the chambers,
10 over a' the separate place,
10 and over a' the building.
44:12 I lifted up mine hand a' them,
45: 6 over a' the oblation of the holy
7 over a' one of the portions,
46: 9 but shall go forth over a' it.
47:20 a man come over a' Hamath.
48:13 over a' the border of the priests
15 a' five and twenty thousand,
18 in length over a' the oblation
18 it shall be over a' the oblation
21 a' the five and twenty
21 a' the five and twenty
21 over a' the portions for the prince:
Da 3:19 visage was changed a' Shadrach,
29 a' the God of Shadrach, Meshach,
5: 5 over a' the candlestick upon the
6 his knees smote one a' another.
23 up thyself a' the Lord of heaven;
6: 4 occasion a' Daniel concerning
5 find any occasion a' this Daniel,
5 find it a' him concerning the law
7:21 with the saints, and prevailed a'
25 great words a' the most High,
8: 7 he was moved with choler a' him,
12 given him a' the daily sacrifice
25 stand up a' the Prince of princes;

Da 9: 7 that they have trespassed a' thee.
8 because we have sinned a'
9 though we have rebelled a' him:
11 because we have sinned a' him.
12 which he spake a' us,
12 and a' our judges
11: 2 stir up all a' the realm of Grecia.
7 and shall deal a' them, and shall
14 stand up a' the king of the south:
16 cometh a' him shall do according
24 forecast his devices a' the strong
25 his courage a' the king of the south
25 they shall forecast devices a' him.
28 shall be a' the holy covenant;
30 of Chittim shall come a' him:
30 indignation a' the holy covenant:
32 do wickedly a' the covenant shall
36 marvellous things a' the God
40 come a' him like a whirlwind,
Ho 4: 7 increased, so they sinned a' me:
5: 7 dealt treacherously a' the Lord:
6: 7 they dealt treacherously a' me.
7:13 they have transgressed a' me:
13 yet they have spoken lies a' me.
14 and wine, and they rebel a' me.
15 do they imagine mischief a' me.
8: 1 an eagle a' the house of the Lord
1 covenant, and trespassed a' my law.
5 mine anger is kindled a' them:
10: 9 Gibeah a' the children of iniquity
10 people shall be gathered a' them,
13:16 for she hath rebelled a' her God:
Joe 3:19 violence a' the children of Judah,
Am 1: 8 I will turn mine hand a' Ekron:
3: 1 that the Lord hath spoken a' you,
1 a' the whole family which I
5: 1 up a' you, even a lamentation,
9 strengtheneth the spoiled a' the
9 shall come a' the fortress.
6:14 a' you a nation, O house of Israel,
7: 9 will rise a' the house of Jeroboam
10 Amos hath conspired a' thee in
16 sayest, Prophesy not a' Israel,
16 drop not thy word a' the house of
Ob 1 and let us rise up a' her in battle.
7 thee, and prevailed a' thee;
10 For thy violence a' thy brother
Jon 1: 2 that great city, and cry a' it;
13 and was tempestuous a' them.
Mic 1: 2 Lord God be witness a' you,
2: 3 a' this family do I devise an evil,
4 shall one take up a parable a' you,
3: 5 they even prepare war a' him.
4: 3 shall not lift up a sword a' nation,
11 nations are gathered a' thee,
5: 1 troops: he hath laid siege a' us:
5 raise a' him seven shepherds,
6: 3 have I wearied thee? testify a' me.
7: 6 daughter riseth up a' her mother,
6 in law a' her mother in law:
8 Rejoice not a' me, O mine enemy:
9 the Lord, because I have sinned a'
Na 1: 9 do ye imagine a' the Lord?
11 that imagineth evil a' the Lord,
2: 4 one a' another in the broad ways:
13 I am a' thee, saith the Lord of
3: 5 Behold, I am a' thee, saith the
Hab 2: 6 parable a' him,
6 and a taunting proverb a'
10 and hast sinned a' thy soul.
3: 8 the Lord displeased a' the rivers?
8 was thine anger a' the rivers?
8 was thy wrath a' the sea,
Zep 1:16 a' the fenced cities,
16 and a' the high towers.
17 they have sinned a' the Lord:
2: 5 the word of the Lord is a' you;
8 themselves a' their border.
10 themselves a' the people
13 stretch out his hand a' the north,
3:11 thou hast transgressed a' me:
Zec 1:12 a' which thou hast had indignation
7:10 evil a' his brother in your heart.
8:10 men every one a' his neighbour.
17 in your hearts a' his neighbour;
9:13 O Zion, a' thy sons, O Greece,
10: 3 was kindled a' the shepherds,
12: 2 both a' Judah
2 and a' Jerusalem.
3 earth be gathered together a' it.
7 magnify themselves a' Judah.
9 nations that come a' Jerusalem.
13: 7 Awake, O sword, a' my shepherd,
7 and a' the man that is my fellow,
14: 2 nations a' Jerusalem to battle;
3 forth, and fight a' those nations,
12 that have fought a' Jerusalem;
13 up a' the hand of his neighbour.
16 of all the nations which came a'
Mal 1: 4 The people a' whom the Lord
2:10 every man a' his brother,
14 a' whom thou hast dealt
15 a' the wife of his youth.
3: 5 a swift witness a' the sorcerers,
5 and a' the adulterers,
5 and a' false swearers,
5 and a' those that oppress
13 words have been stout a' me,
13 have we spoken so much a' thee?
M't 4: 6 thou dash thy foot a' a stone.
5:11 all manner of evil a' you falsely,
23 thy brother hath aught a' thee;
10: 1 them power a' unclean spirits,
18 a' them and the Gentiles.
21 shall rise up a' their parents,
35 a man at variance a' his father,

M't 10:35 and the daughter *a·* her mother,
35 daughter in law *a·* her mother in
12:14 held a council *a·* him,
25 kingdom divided *a·* itself,
25 city or house divided *a·* itself,
26 he is divided *a·* himself;
30 He that is not with me is *a·* me;
31 the blasphemy *a·* the Holy Ghost
32 a word *a·* the Son of man,
32 speaketh *a·* the Holy Ghost,
16:18 gates of hell shall not prevail *a·* it.
18:15 thy brother shall trespass *a·* thee,
21 how oft shall my brother sin *a·* me,
20:11 murmured *a·* the goodman of the
24 indignation *a·* the two brethren.
21: 2 Go into the village over *a·* you,
23:13 the kingdom of heaven *a·* men:
24: 7 nation shall rise *a·* nation,
7 and kingdom *a·* kingdom:
26:55 are ye come out as *a·* a thief
59 sought false witness *a·* Jesus,
62 is it which these witness *a·* thee?
27: 1 took counsel *a·* Jesus to put him
13 many things they witness *a·* thee?
61 sitting over *a·* the sepulchre.
M'r 3: 6 counsel with the Herodians *a·* him,
24 kingdom be divided *a·* itself,
25 a house be divided *a·* itself,
26 if Satan rise up *a·* himself,
29 shall blaspheme *a·* the Holy Ghost
6:11 feet for a testimony *a·* them.
19 Herodias had a quarrel *a·* him,
9:40 he that is not *a·* us is on our part
10:11 committeth adultery *a·* her.
11: 2 way into the village over *a·* you:
25 if ye have aught *a·* any:
12:12 had spoken the parable *a·* them:
41 Jesus sat over *a·* the treasury,
13: 3 mount of Olives over *a·* the temple,
8 nation shall rise *a·* nation,
8 and kingdom *a·* kingdom:
9 sake, for a testimony *a·* them.
12 children shall rise up *a·* their
14: 5 they murmured *a·* her.
48 Are ye come out, as *a·* a thief,
55 sought for witness *a·* Jesus to put
56 bare false witness *a·* him,
57 and bare false witness *a·* him,
60 is it which these witness *a·* thee?
15: 4 many things they witness *a·* thee.
39 which stood over *a·* him,
Lu 2:34 which shall be spoken *a·*;
4:11 thou dash thy foot *a·* a stone.
5:30 murmured *a·* his disciples,
6: 7 might find an accusation *a·* him.
49 *a·* which the stream did beat
7:30 counsel of God *a·* themselves,
8:26 Gadarenes, which is over *a·* Galilee.
9: 5 your feet for a testimony *a·* them.
50 he that is not *a·* us is for us.
10:11 on us, we do wipe off *a·* you:
11:17 Every kingdom divided *a·* itself,
17 a house divided *a·* a house,
18 Satan also be divided *a·* himself,
23 he that is not with me is *a·* me:
12:10 speak a word *a·* the Son of man,
10 blasphemeth *a·* the Holy Ghost,
52 three *a·* two, and two *a·* three.
53 *a·* the son,
53 and the son *a·* the father;
53 the mother *a·* the daughter,
53 and the daughter *a·* the mother;
53 mother in law *a·* her daughter in
53 daughter in law *a·* her mother in
14:31 to make war *a·* another king,
31 to meet him that cometh *a·* him
15:18, 21 I have sinned *a·* heaven,
17: 3 If thy brother trespass *a·* thee,
4 if he trespass *a·* thee seven times
19:30 Go ye into the village over *a·* you;
20:19 had spoken this parable *a·* them.
21:10 Nation shall rise *a·* nation,
10 and kingdom *a·* kingdom:
22:52 Be ye come out, as *a·* a thief,
53 ye stretched forth no hands *a·* me:
65 blasphemously spake they *a·* him.
Joh 12: 7 *a·* the day of my burying has she
13:18 lifted up his heel *a·* me.
29 we have need of *a·* the feast;
18:29 accusation bring ye *a·* this man?
19:11 no power at all *a·* me,
12 himself a king speaketh *a·* Cæsar.
Ac 4:14 they could say nothing *a·* it.
26 gathered together *a·* the Lord,
26 and *a·* his Christ.
27 a truth *a·* thy holy child Jesus,
5:39 ye be found even to fight *a·* God.
6: 1 of the Grecians *a·* the Hebrews,
11 blasphemous words *a·* Moses,
11 and *a·* God.
13 *a·* this holy place,
8: 1 persecution *a·* the church
9: 1 *a·* the disciples of the Lord,
5 for thee to kick *a·* the pricks.
29 and disputed *a·* the Grecians:
13:45 spake *a·* those things which
50 raised persecution *a·* Paul
51 dust of their feet *a·* them,
14: 2 evil affected *a·* the brethren.
16:22 rose up together *a·* them:
18:12 insurrection with one accord *a·*
19:16 and prevailed *a·* them,
36 these things cannot be spoken *a·*,
38 have a matter *a·* any man,
20:15 came the next day over *a·* Chios;
21:28 every where *a·* the people,

Ac 22:24 wherefore they cried so *a·* him.
23: 9 to him, let us not fight *a·* God.
30 what they had *a·* him.
24: 1 informed the governor *a·* Paul.
19 if they had aught *a·* me.
25: 2 informed him *a·* Paul,
3 desired favour *a·* him,
7 grievous complaints *a·* Paul,
8 neither *a·* the law of the Jews,
8 neither *a·* the temple,
8 nor yet *a·* Cæsar,
15 to have judgment *a·* him.
16 concerning the crime laid *a·* him.
18 *A·* whom, when the accusers
19 certain questions *a·* him of their
27 the crimes laid *a·* him.
26:10 to death, I gave my voice *a·* them.
11 being exceedingly mad *a·* them,
14 hard for thee to kick *a·* the pricks.
27: 7 scarce were come over *a·* Cnidus,
7 under Crete, over *a·* Salmone;
14 arose *a·* it a tempestuous wind,
28:17 committed nothing *a·* the people,
19 when the Jews spake *a·* it,
22 every where it is spoken *a·*.
Ro 1:18 from heaven *a·* all ungodliness
26 into that which is *a·* nature:
2: 2 *a·* them which commit such
5 wrath *a·* the day of wrath
4:18 Who *a·* hope believed in hope,
7:23 warring *a·* the law of my mind,
8: 7 carnal mind is enmity *a·* God:
31 God be for us, who can be *a·* us?
9:20 who art thou that repliest *a·* God?
11: 2 to God *a·* Israel, saying,
18 Boast not *a·* the branches.
1Co 4: 6 puffed up for one *a·* another.
6: 1 having a matter *a·* another,
18 sinneth *a·* his own body.
8:12 ye sin so *a·* the brethren,
12 ye sin *a·* Christ.
9:17 if *a·* my will, a dispensation
2Co 10: 2 I think to be bold *a·* some,
5 itself *a·* the knowledge of God,
13: 8 we can do nothing *a·* the truth,
Ga 3:21 law then *a·* the promises of God?
5:17 the flesh lusteth *a·* the Spirit,
17 and the Spirit *a·* the flesh:
23 *a·* such there is no law.
Eph 6:11 able to stand *a·* the wiles of the
12 we wrestle not *a·* flesh and blood,
12 but *a·* principalities, *a·* powers,
12 *a·* the rulers of the darkness of
12 *a·* spiritual wickedness in high
Col 2:14 ordinances that was *a·* us,
3:13 if any man have a quarrel *a·* any:
19 be not bitter *a·* them.
1Ti 5:11 *a·* Christ, they will marry;
19 *A·* an elder receive not an
6:19 a good foundation *a·* the time to
2Ti 1:12 committed unto him *a·* that day.
Heb 12: 3 contradiction of sinners *a·* himself,
4 unto blood, striving *a·* sin.
Jas 2:13 and mercy rejoiceth *a·* judgment
3:14 and lie not *a·* the truth.
5: 9 Grudge not one *a·* another,
1Pe 2:11 which war *a·* the soul;
12 they speak *a·* you as evildoers,
3:12 the Lord is *a·* them that do evil.
2Pe 2:11 accusation *a·* them before the
3: 7 reserved unto fire *a·* the day of
3Jo 10 *a·* us with malicious words:
Jude 9 bring *a·* him a railing accusation,
15 ungodly sinners have spoken *a·*
Re 2: 4 I have somewhat *a·* thee,
14 I have a few things *a·* thee,
16 will fight *a·* them with the sword
20 I have a few things *a·* thee,
11: 7 shall make war *a·* them,
12: 7 his angels fought *a·* the dragon;
13: 6 his mouth in blasphemy *a·* God,
19:19 war *a·* him that sat on the horse,
19 and *a·* his army.

Agar (*a'-gar*) See also HAGAR.
Ga 4:24 gendereth to bondage, which is *A·*.
25 For this *A·* is mount Sinai

agate See also AGATES.
Ex 28:19 the third row a ligure, an *a·*, and
39:12 And the third row a ligure, an *a·*,
Eze 27:16 fine linen, and coral, and *a·*.

agates
Isa 54:12 I will make thy windows of *a·*,

age^ See also AGED; AGES.
Ge 15:15 shalt be buried in a good old *a·*.
18:11 well stricken in *a·*; and it ceased
21: 2 bare Abraham a son in his old *a·*,
7 have born him a son in his old *a·*.
24: 1 was old, and well stricken in *a·*:
25: 8 Abraham...died in a good old *a·*,
37: 3 he was the son of his old *a·*:
44:20 child of his old *a·*, a little one;
47:28 whole *a·* of Jacob was an hundred
48:10 the eyes of Israel were dim for *a·*,
Nu 8:25 And from the *a·* of fifty years
Jos 23: 1 waxed old and stricken in *a·*.
2 I am old and stricken in *a·*:
J'g 8:32 Gideon...died in a good old *a·*,
Ru 4:15 and a nourisher of thine old *a·*:
1Sa 2:33 shall die in the flower of their *a·*.
1Ki 14: 4 eyes were set by reason of his *a·*.
15:23 in the time of his old *a·* he was
1Ch 23: 3 from the *a·* of thirty years and
24 from the *a·* of twenty years and
29:28 died in a good old *a·*, full of days,

2Ch 36:17 or him that stooped for *a·*:
Job 5:26 come to thy grave in a full *a·*,
8: 8 I pray thee, of the former *a·*,
11:17 And thine *a·* shall be clearer
30: 2 in whom old *a·* was perished?
Ps 39: 5 mine *a·* is as nothing before thee:
71: 9 me not off in the time of old *a·*;
92:14 still bring forth fruit in old *a·*;
Isa 38:12 Mine *a·* is departed, and is
46: 4 even to your old *a·* I am he;
Zec 8: 4 his staff in his hand for very *a·*.
M'r 5:42 she was of the *a·* of twelve years.
Lu 1:36 also conceived a son in her old *a·*:
2:36 was of a great *a·*, and had lived
3:23 about thirty years of *a·*, being (as
Joh 9:21 we know not: he is of *a·*:
23 said his parents, He is of *a·*;
1Co 7:36 she pass the flower of her *a·*,
Heb 5:14 to them that are of full *a·*,
11:11 when she was past *a·*, because she

aged
2Sa 19:32 Barzillai was a very *a·* man,
Job 12:20 away the understanding of the *a·*.
15:10 the grayheaded and very *a·* men,
29: 8 and the *a·* arose, and stood up.
32: 9 neither do the *a·* understand
Jer 6:11 *a·* with him that is full of days.
Tit 2: 2 That the *a·* men be sober, grave,
3 The *a·* women likewise, that they
Ph'm 9 being such an one as Paul the *a·*,

Agee (*ag'-ee*)
2Sa 23:11 him was Shammah the son of *A·*

ages
Eph 2: 7 That in the *a·* to come he might
3: 5 Which in other *a·* was not made
21 throughout all *a·*, world without
Col 1:26 hid from *a·* and from generations

ago See also AGONE.
1Sa 9:20 asses that were lost three days *a·*,
2Ki 19:25 Hast thou not heard long *a·* how
Ezr 5:11 was builded these many years *a·*,
Isa 22:11 unto him that fashioned it long *a·*.
37:26 Hast thou not heard long *a·*,
M't 11:21 repented long *a·* in sackcloth
M'r 9:21 How long is it *a·* since this came
Lu 10:13 they had a great while *a·*
Ac 10:30 And Cornelius said, Four days *a·*
15: 7 how that a good while *a·* God made
2Co 8:10 also to be forward a year *a·*.
9: 2 that Achaia was ready a year *a·*;
12: 2 in Christ above fourteen years *a·*,

agone See also AGO.
1Sa 30:13 because three days *a·* I fell sick.

agony
Lu 22:44 being in an *a·* he prayed more

agree See also AGREED; AGREETH.
M't 5:25 *A·* with thine adversary quickly,
18:19 That if two of you shall *a·* on
20:13 didst not thou *a·* with me for a
M'r 14:59 neither so did their witness *a·*
Ac 15:15 *a·* the words of the prophets;
1Jo 5: 8 blood: and these three *a·* in one.
Re 17:17 fulfil his will, and to *a·*,

agreed
Am 3: 3 walk together, except they be *a·*?
M't 20: 2 And when he had *a·* with the
M'r 14:56 their witness *a·* not together.
Joh 9:22 for the Jews had *a·* already,
Ac 5: 9 How is it that ye have *a·* together
40 And to him they *a·*:
23:20 The Jews have *a·* to desire thee
28:25 they *a·* not among themselves,

agreement
2Ki 18:31 an *a·* with me by a present,
Isa 28:15 with hell are we at *a·*;
18 and your *a·* with hell shall not
36:16 Assyria, Make an *a·* with me by
Da 11: 6 king of the north to make an *a·*:
2Co 6:16 what *a·* hath the temple of God

agreeth
M'r 14:70 and thy speech *a·* thereto.
Lu 5:36 *a·* not with the old.

Agrippa (*ag-rip'-pah*)
Ac 25:13 king *A·* and Bernice came
22 Then *A·* said unto Festus,
23 when *A·* was come,
24 And Festus said, King *A·*,
26 specially before thee, O king *A·*, that
26: 1 Then *A·* said unto Paul,
2 I think myself happy, king *A·*,
7 For which hope's sake, king *A·*,
19 Whereupon, O king *A·*,
27 King *A·*, believest thou the prophets?
28 Then *A·* said unto Paul,
32 Then said *A·* unto Festus,

aground
Ac 27:41 they ran the ship *a·*;

ague
Le 26:16 consumption, and the burning *a·*,

Agur (*a'-gur*)
Pr 30: 1 The words of *A·* the son of Jakeh,

ah See also AHA.
Ps 35:25 *A·*, so would we have it: let them
Isa 1: 4 *A·* sinful nation, a people laden
24 *A·*, I will ease me of mine
Jer 1: 6 Then said I, *A·*, Lord God! behold,
4:10 *A·*, Lord God! surely thou hast
14:13 *A·*, Lord God! behold, the prophets
22:18 *A·* my brother! or, *A·* sister!
18 saying, *A·* Lord! or *A·* his glory!

Jer 32:17 A' Lord God! behold, thou hast
34: 5 will lament thee, saying, A' lord!
Eze 4:14 Then said I, A' Lord God!
9: 8 cried, and said, A' Lord God!
11:13 and said, A' Lord God!
20:49 Then said I, A' Lord God!
21:15 a'! it is made bright,
M'r 15:29 A', thou that destroyest the

aha See also AH.
Ps 35:21 said, A', a', our eye hath seen it.
40:15 that say unto me, A', a'.
70: 3 of their shame that say, A', a'.
Isa 44:16 saith, A', I am warm,
Eze 25: 3 Because thou saidst, A', against
26: 2 A', she is broken that was the gates
36: 2 enemy hath said against you, A',

Ahab (a'-hab) See also AHAB'S.
1Ki 16:28 and A' his son reigned in his stead.
29 began A' the son of Omri to reign
29 and A' the son of Omri reigned
30 A' the son of Omri did evil
33 A' made a grove; and A' did more
17: 1 said unto A', As the Lord God of
18: 1 Go, shew thyself unto A'; and I will
2 Elijah went to shew himself unto A'.
3 A' called Obadiah, which was the
5 A' said unto Obadiah, Go into the
6 A' went one way by himself, and
9 thy servant into the hand of A',
12 and so when I come and tell A',
16 So Obadiah went to meet A', and
16 and A' went to meet Elijah.
17 it came to pass, when A' saw Elijah,
17 that A' said unto him, Art thou he
20 So A' sent unto all the children of
41 Elijah said unto A', Get thee up, eat
42 So A' went up to eat and to drink.
44 And he said, Go up, say unto A',
45 And A' rode, and went to Jezreel
46 and ran before A' to the entrance
19: 1 A' told Jezebel all that Elijah had
20: 2 sent messengers to A' king of Israel
13 there came a prophet unto A',
14 A' said, By whom? And he said,
34 Then said A', I will send thee away
21: 1 the palace of A' king of Samaria.
2 A' spake unto Naboth, saying,
3 Naboth said to A', The Lord forbid
4 A' came into his house heavy and
15 Jezebel said to A', Arise, take
16 A' heard that Naboth was dead,
16 that A' rose up
18 go down to meet A' king of Israel,
20 A' said to Elijah, Hast thou found
21 and will cut off from A' him
24 Him that dieth of A' in the city
25 But there was none like unto A',
27 to pass, when A' heard those words,
29 Seest thou how A' humbleth himself
22:20 Lord said, Who shall persuade A',
39 Now the rest of the acts of A',
40 So A' slept with his fathers;
41 the fourth year of A' king of Israel.
49 said Ahaziah the son of A' unto
51 Ahaziah the son of A' began to reign
2Ki 1: 1 against Israel after the death of A'.
3: 1 Jehoram the son of A' began to reign
5 it came to pass, when A' was dead,
8:16 the fifth year of Joram the son of A'
18 as did the house of A';
18 for the daughter of A' was his wife:
25 twelfth year of Joram the son of A'
27 walked in the way of the house of A',
27 as did the house of A': for he was
27 the son in law of the house of A'.
28 he went with Joram the son of A'
29 see Joram the son of A' in Jezreel,
9: 7 thou shalt smite the house of A'
8 the whole house of A' shall perish:
8 and I will cut off from A' him
9 I will make the house of A' like the
25 I and thou rode together after A'
29 year of Joram the son of A'
10: 1 A' had seventy sons in Samaria.
10 spake concerning the house of A':
11 all that remained of the house of A'
17 he slew all that remained unto A'
18 unto them, A' served Baal a little;
30 and hast done unto the house of A'
21: 3 and made a grove, as did A'
13 and the plummet of the house of A':
2Ch 18: 1 and joined affinity with A'.
2 certain years he went down to A'
2 A' killed sheep and oxen for him
3 A' king of Israel said unto
19 Who shall entice A' king of Israel,
21: 6 like as did the house of A':
6 he had the daughter of A' to wife:
13 to the whoredoms of the house of A',
22: 3 in the ways of the house of A':
4 of the Lord like the house of A':
5 went with Jehoram the son of A'
6 down to see Jehoram the son of A'
7 anointed to cut off the house of A'.
8 judgment upon the house of A',
Jer 29:21 of A' the son of Kolaiah, and of
22 make thee like Zedekiah and like A',
Mic 6:16 all the works of the house of A',

Ahab's (a'-habs)
1Ki 21: 8 So she wrote letters in A' name,
2Ki 10: 1 them that brought up A' children,

Aharah (a-har'-ah) See also AHER; AHIRAM; EHI.
1Ch 8: 1 the second, and A' the third,

Aharhel (a-har'-hel)
1Ch 4: 8 families of A' the son of Harum,

Ahasai (a-ha'-sa-i)
Ne 11:13 the son Azareel, the son of A',

Ahasbai (a-has'-ba-i)
2Sa 23:34 Eliphalet the son of A', the son of

Ahasuerus (a-has-u-e'-rus) See also AHASUERUS'.
Ezr 4: 6 in the reign of A', in the beginning
Es 1: 1 in the days of A',
1 (this is A' which reigned from India
2 when the king A' sat on the throne
9 house which belonged to king A'.
10 in the presence of A' the king,
15 the commandment of the king A'
16 in all the provinces of the king A'.
17 The king A' commanded Vashti
19 Vashti come no more before king A';
2: 1 the wrath of king A' was appeased,
12 turn was come to go in to king A',
16 So Esther was taken unto king A'
21 sought to lay hand on the king A'.
3: 1 After these things did king A'
6 throughout the whole kingdom of A',
7 in the twelfth year of king A', they
8 Haman said unto king A', There
12 in the name of king A' was it
6: 2 sought to lay hand on the king A'.
7: 5 Then the king A' answered and
8: 1 On that day did the king A' give
7 Then the king A' said unto Esther
12 day in all the provinces of king A',
9: 2 all the provinces of the king A',
20 the provinces of the king A', both
30 of the kingdom of A', with words
10: 1 the king A' laid a tribute upon the
3 the Jew was next unto king A',
Da 9: 1 first year of Darius the son of A',

Ahasuerus' (a-has-u-e'-rus)
Es 8:10 he wrote in the king A' name,

Ahava (a-ha'-vah) See also IVA.
Ezr 8:15 the river that runneth to A';
21 a fast there, at the river of A',
31 we departed from the river of A'

Ahaz (a'-haz) See also ACHAZ.
2Ki 15:38 A' his son reigned in his stead.
16: 1 A' the son of Jotham king of Judah
2 Twenty years old was A' when he
5 they besieged A', but could not
7 So A' sent messengers to
8 A' took the silver and gold that was
10 king A' went to Damascus to meet
10 king A' sent to Urijah the priest
11 king A' had sent from Damascus:
11 priest made it against king A' came
15 king A' commanded Urijah the
16 to all that king A' commanded.
17 A' cut off the borders of the bases,
19 rest of the acts of A' which he did,
20 A' slept with his fathers, and was
17: 1 In the twelfth year of A' king of
18: 1 of A' king of Judah began to reign.
20:11 it had gone down in the dial of A'.
23:12 the top of the upper chamber of A',
1Ch 3:13 A' his son, Hezekiah his son,
8:35 and Melech, and Tarea, and A'.
36 And A' begat Jehoiadah; and
9:41 and Melech, and Tahrea, and A'.
42 And A' begat Jarah; and Jarah
2Ch 27: 9 A' his son reigned in his stead.
28: 1 A' was twenty years old when he
16 At that time did king A' send unto
19 brought Judah low because of A'
21 A' took away a portion out of the
22 against the Lord: this is that king A'
24 A' gathered together the vessels of
27 And A' slept with his fathers, and
29:19 all the vessels, which king A' in his
Isa 1: 1 in the days of Uzziah, Jotham, A',
7: 1 the days of A' the son of Jotham,
3 Go forth now to meet A', thou,
10 the Lord spake again unto A',
12 But A' said, I will not ask,
14:28 that king A' died was this burden.
38: 8 is gone down in the sun dial of A',
Ho 1: 1 A', and Hezekiah, kings of Judah,
Mic 1: 1 in the days of Jotham, A', and

Ahaziah (a-haz-i'-ah) See also AZARIAH; JEHOAHAZ.
1Ki 22:40 A' his son reigned in his stead.
49 Then said A' the son of Ahab unto
51 A' the son of Ahab began to reign
2Ki 1: 2 And A' fell down through a lattice
18 rest of the acts of A' which he did,
8:24 and A' his son reigned in his stead.
25 did A' the son of Jehoram king of
26 Two and twenty years old was A'
29 A' the son of Jehoram king of Judah
9:16 A' king of Judah was come down
21 and A' king of Judah went out,
23 his hands, and fled, and said to A',
23 There is treachery, O A'.
27 when A' king of Judah saw this,
29 began A' to reign over Judah.
10:13 Jehu met with the brethren of A'
13 answered, We are the brethren of A';
11: 1 the mother of A' saw that her son
2 daughter of king Joram, sister of A',
2 took Joash the son of A',
12:18 and A', his fathers, kings of Judah,
13: 1 twentieth year of Joash the son of A'
14:13 the son of Jehoash the son of A',
1Ch 3:11 Joram his son, A' his son, Joash
2Ch 20:35 join himself with A' king of Israel,
37 thou hast joined thyself with A',
22: 1 made A' his youngest son king in
1 So A' the son of Jehoram king of
2 Forty and two years old was A'
7 the destruction of A' was of God
8 and the sons of the brethren of A',
8 that ministered to A',
9 he sought A': and they caught him,
9 So the house of A' had no power
10 Athaliah the mother of A' saw that
11 the king, took Joash the son of A',
11 (for she was the sister of A',) hid

Ahban (ah'-ban)
1Ch 2:29 and she bare him A', and Molid.

Aher (a'-hur) See also AHARAH.
1Ch 7:12 Ir, and Hushim, the sons of A'.

Ahi (a'-hi).
1Ch 5:15 A' the son of Abdiel, the son of
7:34 A', and Rohgah, Jehubbah, and

Ahiah (a-hi'-ah) See also AHIJAH.
1Sa 14: 3 And A', the son of Ahitub,
18 Saul said unto A', Bring hither the
1Ki 4: 3 Elihoreph and A', the sons of
1Ch 8: 7 And Naaman, and A', and Gera,

Ahiam (a-hi'-am)
2Sa 23:33 Shammah the Hararite, A' the
1Ch 11:35 A' the son of Sacar the Hararite,

Ahian (a-hi'-an)
1Ch 7:19 the sons of Shemidah were, A',

Ahiezer (a-hi-e'-zer)
Nu 1:12 A' the son of Ammishaddai.
2:25 of the children of Dan shall be A'
7:66 On the tenth day A' the son of
71 this was the offering of A' the son
10:25 over his host was A' the son of
1Ch 12: 3 The chief was A', then Joash, the

Ahihud (a-hi'-hud)
Nu 34:27 of Ashar, A' the son of Shelomi.
1Ch 8: 7 them, and begat Uzza, and A'.

Ahijah (a-hi'-jah) See also AHIAH; AHIMELECH.
1Ki 11:29 A' the Shilonite found him in
30 A' caught the new garment that
12:15 which the Lord spake by A' the
14: 2 there is A' the prophet, which told
4 and came to the house of A'.
4 But A' could not see; for his eyes
5 the Lord said unto A', Behold, the
6 when A' heard the sound of her feet,
18 spake by the hand of his servant A'
15:27 Baasha the son of A', of the house
29 which he spake by his servant A'
33 began Baasha the son of A' to reign
21:22 the house of Baasha the son of A',
2Ki 9: 9 the house of Baasha the son of A':
1Ch 2:25 Bunah, and Oren, and Ozem, and A'.
11:36 Hepher the Mecherathite, A' the
26:20 A' was over the treasures of the
2Ch 9:29 and in the prophecy of A' the
10:15 by the hand of A' the Shilonite to
Ne 10:26 And A', Hanan, Anan,

Ahikam (a-hi'-kam)
2Ki 22:12 Hilkiah the priest, and A' the son
14 So Hilkiah the priest, and A', and
25:22 he made Gedaliah the son of A',
2Ch 34:20 king commanded Hilkiah, and A'
Jer 26:24 the hand of A' the son of Shaphan
39:14 him unto Gedaliah the son of A'
40: 5 back also to Gedaliah the son of A'
6 Jeremiah unto Gedaliah the son of A'
7 Gedaliah the son of A' governor
9 the son of A' the son of Shaphan
11 over them Gedaliah the son of A'
14 the son of A' believed them not.
16 the son of A' said unto Johanan the
41: 1 came unto Gedaliah the son of A'
2 and smote Gedaliah the son of A'
6 Come to Gedaliah the son of A'.
10 committed to Gedaliah the son of A':
16, 18 had slain Gedaliah the son of A',
43: 6 left with Gedaliah the son of A'

Ahilud (a-hi'-lud)
2Sa 8:16 Jehoshaphat the son of A' was
20:24 Jehoshaphat the son of A' was
1Ki 4: 3 Jehoshaphat the son of A', the
12 Baana the son of A'; to him
1Ch 18:15 Jehoshaphat the son of A', recorder.

Ahimaaz (a-him'-a-az)
1Sa 14:50 was Ahinoam, the daughter of A':
2Sa 15:27 A' thy son, and Jonathan the son
36 A' Zadok's son, and Jonathan
17:17 Jonathan and A' stayed by
20 Where is A' and Jonathan?
18:19 Then said A' the son of Zadok, Let
22 Then said A' the son of Zadok yet
23 A' ran by the way of the plain,
27 foremost is like the running of A'
28 A' called, and said unto the king,
29 A' answered, When Joab sent the
1Ki 4:15 A' was in Naphtali; he also took
1Ch 6: 8 begat Zadok, and Zadok begat A',
9 A' begat Azariah, and Azariah
53 Zadok his son, A' his son.

Ahiman (a-hi'-man)
Nu 13:22 where A', Sheshai, and Talmai,
Jos 15:14 A', and Talmai, the children of
J'g 1:10 they slew Sheshai, and A', and
1Ch 9:17 Talmon, and A', and their brethren:

Ahimelech (*a-him'-el-ek*) See also AHIMELECH'S; ABIMELECH; AHIAH.
1Sa 21: 1 came David to Nob to *A*· the priest:
1 *A*· was afraid at the meeting of
2 David said unto *A*· the priest, The
8 David said unto *A*·, And is there
22: 9 coming to Nob, to *A*· the son of
11 Then the king sent to call *A*· the
14 Then *A*· answered the king, and
16 king said, Thou shalt surely die, *A*·,
20 one of the sons of *A*· the son of
23: 6 when Abiathar the son of *A*· fled
26: 6 answered David and said to *A*·
2Sa 8:17 Ahitub, and *A*·, the son of Abiathar,
1Ch 24: 3 and *A*· of the sons of Ithamar,
6 *A*· the son of Abiathar, and before
31 David the king, and Zadok, and *A*·,
Ps 52:*title* David is come to the house of *A*·.

Ahimelech's (*a-him'-el-eks*)
1Sa 30:7 to Abiathar the priest, *A*· son,

Ahimoth (*a-hi'-moth*)
1Ch 6:25 sons of Elkanah; Amasai, and *A*·.

Ahinadab (*a-hin'-ad-ab*)
1Ki 4:14 *A*· the son of Iddo had Mahanaim:

Ahinoam (*a-hin'-o-am*)
1Sa 14:50 the name of Saul's wife was *A*·,
25:43 David also took *A*· of Jezreel;
27: 3 *A*· the Jezreelitess, and Abigail
30: 5 two wives were taken captives, *A*·
2Sa 2: 2 *A*· the Jezreelitess, and Abigail
3: 2 his firstborn was Amnon, of *A*·
1Ch 3: 1 the firstborn Amnon, of *A*· the

Ahio (*a-hi'-o*)
2Sa 6: 3 and Uzzah and *A*·, the sons of
4 and *A*· went before the ark.
1Ch 8:14 And *A*·, Shashak, and Jeremoth,
31 And Gedor, and *A*·, and Zacher.
9:37 And Gedor, and *A*·, and Zechariah,
13: 7 and Uzzah and *A*· drave the cart.

Ahira (*a-hi'-rah*)
Nu 1:15 Of Naphtali; *A*· the son of Enan.
2:29 Naphtali shall be *A*· the son of Enan.
7:78 the twelfth day *A*· the son of Enan,
83 this was the offering of *A*· the son
10:27 of the children of Naphtali was *A*·

Ahiram (*a-hi'-rum*) See also AHARAH; AHIRAMITES.
Nu 26:38 *A*·, the family of the Ahiramites:

Ahiramites (*a-hi'-rum-ites*)
Nu 26:38 of Ahiram, the family of the *A*·:

Ahisamach (*a-his'-am-ak*)
Ex 31: 6 with him Aholiab, the son of *A*·,
35:34 both he, and Aholiab, the son of *A*·,
38:23 with him was Aholiab, son of *A*·,

Ahishahar (*a-hish'-a-har*)
1Ch 7:10 Zethan, and Tharshish, and *A*·.

Ahishar (*a-hi'-shar*)
1Ki 4: 6 And *A*· was over the household:

Ahithophel (*a-hith'-o-fel*)
2Sa 15:12 Absalom sent for *A*· the Gilonite,
31 *A*· is among the conspirators with
31 the counsel of *A*· into foolishness.
34 for me defeat the counsel of *A*·.
16:15 to Jerusalem, and *A*· with him.
20 said Absalom to *A*·, Give counsel
21 *A*· said unto Absalom, Go in unto
23 counsel of *A*·, which he counselled
23 so was all the counsel of *A*·
17: 1 *A*· said unto Absalom, Let me now
6 *A*· hath spoken after this manner:
7 The counsel that *A*· hath given is
14 is better than the counsel of *A*·.
14 to defeat the good counsel of *A*·,
15 Thus and thus did *A*· counsel
21 hath *A*· counselled against you.
23 when *A*· saw that his counsel was
23:34 Eliam the son of *A*· the Gilonite,
1Ch 27:33 *A*· was the king's counsellor:
34 after *A*· was Jehoida the son of

Ahitub (*a-hi'-tub*)
1Sa 14: 3 Ahiah, the son of *A*·, I-chabod's
22: 9 to Ahimelech the son of *A*·.
11 the son of *A*·, and all his father's
12 Saul said, Hear now, thou son of *A*·.
20 the sons of Ahimelech the son of *A*·,
2Sa 8:17 Zadok the son of *A*·, and Ahimelech
1Ch 6: 7 Amariah, and Amariah begat *A*·,
8 And *A*· begat Zadok, and Zadok
11 Amariah, and Amariah begat *A*·,
12 *A*· begat Zadok, and Zadok begat
52 Amariah his son, *A*· his son,
9:11 *A*·, the ruler of the house of God;
18:16 And Zadok the son of *A*·, and
Ezr 7: 2 the son of Zadok, the son of *A*·,
Ne 11:11 the son of *A*·, was the ruler of the

Ahlab (*ah'-lab*)
J'g 1:31 of Zidon, nor of *A*·, nor of Achzib,

Ahlai (*ah'-lahee*)
1Ch 2:31 And the children of Sheshan; *A*·.
11:41 the Hittite, Zabad the son of *A*·,

Ahoah (*a-ho'-ah*) See also AHOHITE.
1Ch 8: 4 Abishua, and Naaman, and *A*·,

Ahohite (*a-ho'-hite*)
2Sa 23: 9 Eleazar the son of Dodo the *A*·
28 Zalmon the *A*·, Maharai the
1Ch 11:12 Eleazar the son of Dodo, the *A*·,
29 the Hushathite, Ilai the *A*·,
27: 4 the second month was Dodai an *A*·,

Aholah (*a-ho'-lah*)
Eze 23: 4 names of them were *A*· the elder,
4 were their names; Samaria is *A*·,
5 *A*· played the harlot when she was
36 Son of man, wilt thou judge *A*·
44 so went they in unto *A*· and unto

Aholiab (*a-ho'-lee-ab*)
Ex 31: 6 behold, I have given with him *A*·,
35:34 he may teach, both he, and *A*·,
36: 1 Then wrought Bezaleel and *A*·,
2 And Moses called Bezaleel and *A*·,
38:23 And with him was *A*·, son of

Aholibah (*a-hol'-ib-ah*)
Eze 23: 4 the elder, and *A*· her sister:
4 is Aholah, and Jerusalem *A*·.
11 when her sister *A*· saw this, she
22 Therefore, O *A*·, thus saith the Lord
36 wilt thou judge Aholah and *A*·?
44 and unto *A*·, the lewd women.

Aholibamah (*a-hol''-ib-a'-mah*)
Ge 36: 2 and *A*· the daughter of Anah
5 And *A*· bare Jeush, and Jaalam,
14 these were the sons of *A*·, the
18 are the sons of *A*· Esau's wife:
18 were the dukes that came of *A*·
25 and *A*· the daughter of Anah.
41 Duke *A*·, duke Elah, duke Pinon,
1Ch 1:52 Duke *A*·, duke Elah, duke Pinon,

Ahumai (*a-hoo'-mahee*)
1Ch 4: 2 and Jahath begat *A*·, and Lahad.

Ahuzam (*a-hoo'-zam*)
1Ch 4: 6 And Naarah bare him *A*·, and

Ahuzzath (*a-huz'-zath*)
Ge 26:26 *A*· one of his friends, and Phichol

Ai (*a'-i*) See also AIATH; AIJA; HAI.
Jos 7: 2 sent men from Jericho to *A*·,
2 the men went up and viewed *A*·.
3 thousand men go up and smite *A*·;
4 and they fled before the men of *A*·.
5 men of *A*· smote of them about
8: 1 and arise, go up to *A*·:
1 given into thy hand the king of *A*·,
2 thou shalt do to *A*· and her king
3 people of war, to go up against *A*·:
9 and abode between Beth-el and *A*·,
9 on the west side of *A*·: but Joshua
10 of Israel, before the people to *A*·.
11 pitched on the north side of *A*·:
11 was a valley between them and *A*·.
12 between Beth-el and *A*·, on the
14 when the king of *A*· saw it, that
16 the people that were in *A*· were
17 there was not a man left in *A*· or
18 that is in thy hand toward *A*·;
20 the men of *A*· looked behind them,
21 again, and slew the men of *A*·.
23 And the king of *A*· they took alive,
24 slaying all the inhabitants of *A*· in
24 all the Israelites returned unto *A*·,
25 thousand, even all the men of *A*·.
26 destroyed all the inhabitants of *A*·.
28 And Joshua burnt *A*·, and made it
29 the king of *A*· he hanged on a tree
9: 3 had done unto Jericho and to *A*·,
10: 1 heard how Joshua had taken *A*·,
1 her king, so he had done to *A*· and
2 because it was greater than *A*·,
12: 9 king of *A*·, which is beside Beth-el,
Ezr 2:28 The men of Beth-el and *A*·,
Ne 7:32 The men of Beth-el and *A*·,
Jer 49: 3 Howl, O Heshbon, for *A*· is spoiled:

Aiah (*a-i'-ah*) See also AJAH.
2Sa 3: 7 was Rizpah, the daughter of *A*·:
21: 8 sons of Rizpah the daughter of *A*·,
10 Rizpah the daughter of *A*· took
11 daughter of *A*·, the concubine of
1Ch 1:40 the sons of Zibeon; *A*·, and Anah.

Aiath (*a-i'-ath*) See also AI.
Isa 10:28 He is come to *A*·, he is passed to

aided
J'g 9:24 which *a*· him in the killing

Aija (*a-i'-jah*) See also AI.
Ne 11:31 Geba dwelt at Michmash, and *A*·,

Aijalon (*a-ij'-el-on*) See also AJALON.
Jos 21:24 *A*· with her suburbs, Gath-rimmon
J'g 1:35 would dwell in mount Heres in *A*·,
12:12 was buried in *A*· in the country of
1Sa 14:31 that day from Michmash to *A*·:
1Ch 6:69 And *A*· with her suburbs, and
8:13 the fathers of the inhabitants of *A*·,
2Ch 11:10 And Zorah, and *A*·, and Hebron,

Aijeleth (*a-ij'-el-eth*)
Ps 22:*title* chief Musician upon *A*· Shahar,

ailed
Ps 114: 5 What *a*· thee, O thou sea, that

aileth
Ge 21:17 said unto her, What *a*· thee, Hagar?
J'g 18:23 said unto Micah, What *a*· thee,
24 ye say unto me, What *a*· thee?
1Sa 11: 5 What *a*· the people that they weep?
2Sa 14: 5 king said unto her, What *a*· thee?
2Ki 6:28 king said unto her, What *a*· thee
Isa 22: 1 What *a*· thee now, that thou art

Ain (*a'-in*) See also EN.
Nu 34:11 to Riblah, on the east side of *A*·;
Jos 15:32 *A*·, and Rimmon: all the cities are
19: 7 *A*·, Remmon, and Ether, and
21:16 *A*· with her suburbs, and Juttah
1Ch 4:32 their villages were, Etam, and *A*·,

air
Ge 1:26, 28 the fowl of the *a*·, and over
30 every fowl of the *a*·, and to every
2:19 the field, and every fowl of the *a*·;
20 gave names...to the fowl of the *a*·,
6: 7 fowls of the *a*·; for it repenteth me
7: 3 Of fowls also of the *a*· by sevens,
9: 2 upon every fowl of the *a*·,
De 4:17 winged fowl that flieth in the *a*·,
28:26 all fowls of the *a*·, and unto the
1Sa 17:44 thy flesh unto the fowls of the *a*·,
46 carcases...unto the fowls of the *a*·,
2Sa 21:10 the birds of the *a*· to rest on them
1Ki 14:11 shall the fowls of the *a*· eat:
16: 4 shall the fowls of the *a*· eat.
21:24 field shall the fowls of the *a*· eat.
Job 12: 7 fowls of the *a*·, and they shall tell
28:21 kept close from the fowls of the *a*·.
41:16 no *a*· can come between them.
Ps 8: 8 The fowl of the *a*·, and the fish of
Pr 30:19 The way of an eagle in the *a*·;
Ec 10:20 bird of the *a*· shall carry the voice.
M't 6:26 Behold the fowls of the *a*·:
8:20 the birds of the *a*· have nests;
13:32 birds of the *a*· come and lodge in
M'r 4: 4 the fowls of the *a*· came and
32 fowls of the *a*· may lodge under
Lu 8: 5 the fowls of the *a*· devoured it.
9:58 and birds of the *a*· have nests;
13:19 the fowls of the *a*· lodged in the
Ac 10:12 things, and fowls of the *a*·.
11: 6 and fowls of the *a*·,
22:23 clothes, and threw dust into the *a*·,
1Co 9:26 not as one that beateth the *a*·:
14: 9 for ye shall speak into the *a*·.
Eph 2: 2 prince of the power of the *a*·,
1Th 4:17 to meet the Lord in the *a*·: and
Re 9: 2 the sun and the *a*· were darkened
16:17 poured out his vial into the *a*·;

Ajah (*a'-jah*) See also AIAH.
Ge 36:24 children of Zibeon; both *A*·, and

Ajalon (*aj'-a-lon*) See also AIJALON.
Jos 10:12 thou, Moon, in the valley of *A*·.
19:42 Shaalabbin, and *A*·, and Jethlah,
2Ch 28:18 had taken Beth-shemesh, and *A*·,

Akan (*a'-kan*) See also JAAKAN; JAKAN.
Ge 36:27 Bilhan, and Zaavan, and *A*·.

Akkub (*ak'-kub*)
1Ch 3:24 Pelaiah, and *A*·, and Johanan,
9:17 Shallum, and *A*·, and Talmon,
Ezr 2:42 of Talmon, the children of *A*·, the
45 of Hagabah, the children of *A*·,
Ne 7:45 the children of *A*·, the children of
8: 7 Sherebiah, Jamin, *A*·, Shabbethai,
11:19 Moreover the porters, *A*·, Talmon,
12:25 Talmon, *A*·, were porters keeping

Akrabbim (*ac-rab'-bim*) See also MAALEH-ACRABBIM.
Nu 34: 4 from the south to the ascent of *A*·,
J'g 1:36 from the going up to *A*·, from the

Al See AL-TASCHITH.

alabaster
M't 26: 7 having an *a*· box of very precious
M'r 14: 3 having an *a*· box of ointment
Lu 7:37 brought an *a*· box of ointment,

alabaster-box See ALABASTER and BOX.

Alameth (*al'-am-eth*)
1Ch 7: 8 and Abiah, and Anathoth, and *A*·.

Alammelech (*a-lam'-mel-ek*)
Jos 19:26 *A*·, and Amad, and Mishael;

Alamoth (*al'-am-oth*)
1Ch 15:20 with psalteries on *A*·;
Ps 46:*title* A Song upon *A*·.

alarm
Nu 10: 5 When ye blow an *a*·, then the
6 When ye blow an *a*· the second
6 they shall blow an *a*· for their
7 blow, ye shall not sound an *a*·.
9 blow an *a*· with the trumpets;
2Ch 13:12 with sounding trumpets to cry *a*·
Jer 4:19 sound of the trumpet, the *a*· of war.
49: 2 I will cause an *a*· of war to be heard
Joe 2: 1 sound an *a*· in my holy mountain:
Zep 1:16 A day of the trumpet and *a*·

alas
Nu 12:11 Aaron said unto Moses, *A*·, my,
24:23 *A*·, who shall live when God doeth
Jos 7: 7 Joshua said, *A*·, O Lord
J'g 6:22 Gideon said, *A*·, O Lord God!
11:35 *A*·, my daughter! thou hast
1Ki 13:30 mourned over him, saying, *A*·, my
2Ki 3:10 the king of Israel said, *A*·!
6: 5 *A*·, master! for it was borrowed.
15 *A*·, my master! how shall we do?
Jer 30: 7 *A*·! for that day is great,
Eze 6:11 *A*· for all the evil abominations
Joe 1:15 *A*· for the day! for the day of the
Am 5:16 say in all the highways, *A*·! *a*·!
Re 18:10 *A*· *a*·, that great city Babylon,
16 *A*·, *a*· that great city, that was
19 *A*·, *a*· that great city, wherein

albeit
Eze 13: 7 Lord saith it; *a*· I have not spoken?
Ph'm 19 *a*· I do not say to thee how thou

Albon See ABI-ALBON.

Alemeth (*al-e'-meth*)
1Ch 6:60 and *A*· with her suburbs, and
8:36 Jehoadah begat *A*·, and Azmaveth,
9:42 Jarah begat *A*·, and Azmaveth,

Alexander (*al-ex-an'-dur*)
M'r 15:21 the father of A' and Rufus,
Ac 4: 6 John, and A', and as many as were
19:33 they drew A' out of the multitude,
33 A' beckoned with the hand,
1Ti 1:20 Of whom is Hymenæus and A';
2Ti 4:14 A' the coppersmith did me much

Alexandria (*al-ex-an'-dree-ah*) See also ALEXANDRIANS.
Ac 18:24 Apollos, born at A', an eloquent
27: 6 a ship of A' sailing into Italy;
28:11 we departed in a ship of A',

Alexandrians (*al-ex-an'-dree-uns*)
Ac 6: 9 A', and of them of Cilicia and of

algum (*al'-gum*) See also ALMUG.
2Ch 2: 8 and a' trees, out of Lebanon:
9:10 a' trees and precious stones.
11 king made of the a' trees terraces

algum-trees See ALGUM and TREES.

Aliah (*a-li'-ah*) See also ALVAH.
1Ch 1:51 were; duke Timnah, duke A',

Alian (*a-li'-un*) See also ALVAN.
1Ch 1:40 of Shobal; A', and Manahath,

alien See also ALIENS.
Ex 18: 3 I have been an a' in a strange
De 14:21 thou mayest sell it unto an a':
Job 19:15 I am an a' in their sight.
Ps 69: 8 an a' unto my mother's children.
Isa 61: 5 the a' shall be your ploughmen

alienate See also ALIENATED.
Eze 48:14 nor a' the first fruits of the land:

alienated
Eze 23:17 and her mind was a' from them.
18 then my mind was a' from her,
18 like as my mind was a' from her
22 whom thy mind is a', and I will
28 them from whom thy mind is a':
Eph 4:18 being a' from the life of God
Col 1:21 that were sometime a' and enemies

aliens
La 5: 2 our houses to a'.
Eph 2:12 being a' from the commonwealth
Heb 11:34 to flight the armies of the a'.

alike
De 12:22 the clean shall eat of them a'.
15:22 the clean person shall eat it a',
1Sa 30:24 they shall part a'.
Job 21:26 They shall lie down a' in the dust.
Ps 33:15 He fashioneth their hearts a';
139:12 darkness and the light are both a'
Pr 20:10 both of them are a' abomination
27:15 and a contentious woman are a'.
Ec 9: 2 All things come a' to all:
11: 6 whether they both shall be a' good.
Ro 14: 5 another esteemeth every day a'.

alive See also QUICK.
Ge 6:19 to keep them a' with thee;
20 come unto thee, to keep them a'.
7: 3 to keep seed a' upon the face of
23 and Noah only remained a', and
12:12 but they will save thee a'.
43: 7 Is your father yet a'?
27 of whom ye spake? Is he yet a'?
28 he is yet a'.
45:26 told him, saying, Joseph is yet a',
28 Joseph my son is yet a':
46:30 because thou art yet a'.
50:20 to save much people a'.
Ex 1:17 but saved the men children a'.
18 have saved the men children a'?
22 every daughter ye shall save a'.
4:18 see whether they be yet a'.
22: 4 be certainly found in his hand a',
Le 10:16 sons of Aaron which were left a',
14: 4 cleansed two birds a' and clean,
16:10 be presented a' before the Lord,
26:36 And upon them that are left a'
Nu 16:33 went down a' into the pit, and the
21:35 until there was none left him a':
22:33 I had slain thee, and saved her a'.
31:15 Have ye saved all the women a'?
18 keep a' for yourselves.
De 4: 4 a' every one of you this day.
5: 3 who are all of us here a' this day.
6:24 that he might preserve us a',
20:16 save a' nothing that breatheth:
31:27 while I am yet a' with you this
32:39 I kill, and I make a'; I wound,
Jos 2:13 And that ye will save a' my father,
6:25 Joshua saved Rahab the harlot a',
8:23 the king of Ai they took a',
14:10 the Lord hath kept me a',
J'g 8:19 if ye had saved them a', I would
21:14 which they had saved a' of the
1Sa 2: 6 The Lord killeth, and maketh a':
15: 8 Agag the king of the Amalekites a',
27: 9 left neither man nor woman a',
11 saved neither man nor woman a',
2Sa 8: 2 with one full line to keep a'.
12:18 while the child was yet a',
21 weep for the child, while it was a';
22 While the child was yet a', I fasted
18:14 while he was yet a' in the midst of
1Ki 18: 5 to save the horses and mules a',
20:18 come out for peace, take them a';
18 be come out for war, take them a'.
32 said, Is he yet a'? he is my brother.
21:15 for Naboth is not a', but dead.
2Ki 5: 7 Am I God, to kill and to make a',
7: 4 if they save us a', we shall live;
12 catch them a', and get into the

2Ki 10:14 he said, Take them a'.
14 And they took them a',
2Ch 25:12 other ten thousand left a'
Ps 22:29 none can keep a' his own soul.
30: 3 thou hast kept me a',
33:19 and to keep them a' in famine.
41: 2 will preserve him, and keep him a':
Pr 1:12 swallow them up a' as the grave;
Ec 4: 2 than the living which are yet a'.
Jer 49:11 I will preserve them a';
Eze 7:13 although they were yet a':
13:18 save the souls a' that come unto
19 save the souls a' that should not
18:27 he shall save his soul a'.
Da 5:19 whom he would he kept a';
M't 27:63 said, while he was yet a', After
M'r 16:11 when they had heard that he was a',
Lu 15:24 my son was dead, and is a' again;
32 brother was dead, and is a' again;
24:23 angels, which said that he was a'.
Ac 1: 3 he shewed himself a' after his
9:41 and widows, presented her a'.
20:12 they brought the young man a',
25:19 whom Paul affirmed to be a'.
Ro 6:11 dead indeed unto sin, but a' unto
13 as those that are a' from the dead,
7: 9 I was a' without the law once:
1Co 15:22 so in Christ shall all be made a'.
1Th 4:15 we which are a' and remain
17 are a' and remain shall be caught
Re 1:18 behold, I am a' for evermore,
2: 8 which was dead, and is a';
19:20 both were cast a' into a lake of fire

all^ See also ALBEIT; ALMIGHTY; ALMOST; ALREADY; ALTOGETHER; ALTHOUGH; ALWAY.
Ge 1:26 the cattle, and over a' the earth,
29 is upon the face of a' the earth,
2: 1 finished, and a' the host of them.
2 the seventh day from a' his work
3 rested from a' his work which God
20 a' cattle, and to the fowl of the air,
3:14 thou art cursed above a' cattle,
14 thou eat a' the days of thy life:
17 eat of it a' the days of thy life;
20 she was the mother of a' living.
4:21 a' such as handle the harp and
5: 5 a' the days that Adam lived were
8 a' the days of Seth were
11 a' the days of Enos were
14 a' the days of Cainan were
17 a' the days of Mahalaleel were
20 a' the days of Jared were
23 a' the days of Enoch were
27 a' the days of Methuselah were
31 a' the days of Lamech were
6: 2 wives of a' which they chose.
12 for a' flesh had corrupted his way
13 of a' flesh is come before me;
17 upon the earth, to destroy a' flesh,
19 of a' flesh, two of every sort shalt
21 unto thee of a' food that is eaten,
22 according to a' that God
7: 1 Come thou and a' thy house into
3 keep seed alive upon the face of a'
5 Noah did according unto a' that
11 the same day were a' the fountains
14 and a' the cattle after their kind,
15 the ark, two and two of a' flesh,
16 in male and female of a' flesh,
19 a' the high hills, that were under
21 And a' flesh died that moved upon
22 A' in whose nostrils was the
22 of a' that was in the dry land, died.
8: 1 and a' the cattle that was with him
17 of a' flesh, both of fowl, and of
9: 2 fowl of the air, upon a' that moveth
2 and upon a' the fishes of the sea;
3 herb have I given you a' things.
10 from a' that go out of the ark, to
11 neither shall a' flesh be cut off any
15 you and every living creature of a'
15 become a flood to destroy a' flesh.
16 and every living creature of a' flesh
17 between me and a' flesh that is
29 a' the days of Noah were
10:21 Unto Shem also, the father of a'
29 a' these were the sons of Joktan.
11: 6 and they have a' one language;
8 upon the face of a' the earth:
9 the language of a' the earth:
9 upon the face of a' the earth.
12: 3 in thee shall a' families of the
20 and his wife, and a' that he had.
13:10 beheld a' the plain of Jordan, that
11 chose him a' the plain of Jordan;
15 a' the land which thou seest, to
14: 3 A' these were joined together in
7 and smote a' the country of the
11 they took a' the goods of Sodom
11 and a' their victuals, and went
16 he brought back a' the goods,
20 And he gave him tithes of a'.
15:10 And he took unto him a' these,
17:23 and a' that were born in his house,
23 a' that were bought with his money,
27 And a' the men of his house, born
18:18 and all the nations of the earth
25 Shall not the Judge of a' the earth
26 then I will spare a' the place for
28 wilt thou destroy a' the city for
19: 2 tarry a' night, and wash your feet,
2 we will abide in the street a' night.
4 a' the people from every quarter:
17 neither stay thou in a' the plain;
25 a' the plain, and a' the inhabitants
28 Gomorrah, and toward a' the land

Ge 19:31 after the manner of a' the earth:
20: 7 die, thou, and a' that are thine.
8 called a' his servants, and told a'
16 a' that are with thee, and with a'
18 closed up a' the wombs of the
21: 6 so that a' that hear will laugh
12 a' that Sarah hath said unto thee,
24:54 with him, and tarried a' night;
66 Isaac a' things that he had done.
25: 4 A' these were the children of
5 gave a' that he had unto Isaac.
18 died in the presence of a' his
25 a' over like an hairy garment;
26: 3 seed, I will give a' these countries,
4 unto thy seed a' these countries;
4 a' the nations of the earth be
11 Abimelech charged a' his people,
15 For a' the wells which his father's
27:33 I have eaten of a' before thou
37 and a' his brethren have I given
28:11 tarried there a' night, because
14 in thy seed shall a' the families
15 and will keep thee in a' places
22 a' that thou shalt give me I will
29: 3 thither were a' the flocks gathered:
8 until a' the flocks be gathered
13 he told Laban a' these things.
22 Laban gathered together a' the
30:32 I will pass through a' thy flock
32 from thence a' the speckled and
32 and a' the brown cattle among
35 and a' the she goats that were
35 some white in it, and a' the brown
40 a' the brown in the flock of Laban;
31: 1 away a' that was our father's;
1 father's hath he gotten a' this glory.
6 know that with a' my power I have
8 then a' the cattle bare speckled:
8 bare a' the cattle ringstraked.
12 eyes, and see, a' the rams which
12 I have seen a' that Laban doeth
16 For a' the riches which God hath
18 carried away a' his cattle, and a'
21 So he fled with a' that he had; and
34 And Laban searched a' the tent,
37 Whereas thou hast searched a' my
37 what hast thou found of a' thy
43 and a' that thou seest is mine.
54 tarried a' night in the mount.
32:10 of the least of a' the mercies,
10 of a' the truth, which thou hast
19 third, and a' that followed
33: 8 What meanest thou by a' this
13 them one day, a' the flock will die.
34:19 was more honorable than a' the
24 hearkened a' that went out of
25 city boldly, and slew a' the males.
29 a' their wealth, and a' their little
29 and spoiled even a' that was in the
35: 2 and to a' that were with him,
4 unto Jacob a' the strange gods
4 and a' their earrings which were
6 Beth-el, he and a' the people that
36: 6 and a' the persons of his house,
6 a' his beasts, and a' his substance,
37: 3 loved Joseph more than a' his
4 him more than a' his brethren,
35 a' his sons and a' his daughters
39: 3 made a' that he did to prosper
4 and a' that he had he put into his
5 and over a' that he had, that the
5 blessing of the Lord was upon a'
6 he left a' that he had in Joseph's
8 and he hath committed a' that he
22 to Joseph's hand a' the prisoners
40:17 uppermost basket there was of a'
20 that he made a feast unto a' his
41: 8 he sent and called for a' the
8 and a' the wise men thereof: and
19 I never saw in a' the land of Egypt
29 throughout a' the land of Egypt:
30 a' the plenty shall be forgotten
35 let them gather a' the food of
37 and in the eyes of a' his servants.
39 as God hath shewed thee a' this,
40 word shall a' my people be ruled:
41 I have set thee over a' the land
43 ruler over a' the land of Egypt.
44 his hand or foot in a' the land
45 out over a' the land of Egypt.
46 throughout a' the land of Egypt.
48 And he gathered up a' the food of
51 hath made me forget a' my toil,
51 and a' my father's house.
54 dearth was in a' lands; but in a'
55 a' the land of Egypt was famished,
55 said unto a' the Egyptians, Go
56 was over a' the face of the earth:
56 Joseph opened a' the storehouses,
57 a' countries came into Egypt to
57 famine was so sore in a' lands.
42: 6 he it was that sold to a' the people
11 We are a' one man's sons; we are
17 And he put them a' together into
29 told him a' that befell unto them;
36 a' these things are against me.
45: 1 not refrain himself before a' them
8 Pharaoh, and lord of a' his house,
8 throughout a' the land of Egypt.
9 hath made me lord of a' Egypt:
10 thy herds, and a' that thou hast:
11 a' that thou hast, come to poverty.
13 tell my father of a' my glory in
13 Egypt, and of a' that ye have seen;
15 kissed a' his brethren, and wept
20 the good of a' the land of Egypt

Ge 45:22 To *a'* of them he gave each man
26 governor over *a'* the land of Egypt.
27 told him *a'* the words of Joseph,
46: 1 And Israel took his journey with *a'*
6 Jacob, and *a'* his seed with him:
7 *a'* his seed brought he with him
15 *a'* the souls of his sons and his
22 Jacob: *a'* the souls were fourteen.
25 Jacob: *a'* the souls were seven.
26 *A'* the souls that came with Jacob
26 *a'* the souls were threescore and
27 *a'* the souls of the house of Jacob,
32 their herds, and *a'* that they have.
47: 1 *a'* that they have, are come out of
12 and *a'* his father's household, with
13 there was no bread in *a'* the land;
13 *a'* the land of Canaan fainted
14 Joseph gathered up *a'* the money
15 *a'* the Egyptians came unto Joseph,
17 for *a'* their cattle for that year.
20 Joseph bought *a'* the land of Egypt
48:15 God which fed me *a'* my life long
16 which redeemed me from *a'* evil,
49:28 *A'* these are the twelve tribes of
50: 7 with him went up *a'* the servants
7 *a'* the elders of the land of Egypt,
8 *a'* the house of Joseph, and his
14 *a'* that went up with him to bury
15 *a'* the evil which we did unto him.
Ex 1: 6 and *a'* his brethren, and *a'* that
14 *a'* manner of service in the field: *a'*
22 And Pharaoh charged *a'* his people,
3:15 my memorial unto *a'* generations.
4:21 *a'* those wonders before Pharaoh,
28 Moses told Aaron *a'* the words of
28 him, and *a'* the signs which he had
29 gathered together *a'* the elders
30 Aaron spake *a'* the words which
5:12 throughout *a'* the land of Egypt
23 hast thou delivered thy people at *a'*
6:29 of Egypt *a'* that I say unto thee.
7: 2 speak *a'* that I command thee:
19 ponds, and upon *a'* their pools of
19 throughout *a'* the land of Egypt,
20 *a'* the waters that were in the
21 throughout *a'* the land of Egypt.
24 And *a'* the Egyptians digged round
8: 2 smite *a'* thy borders with frogs:
4 people, and upon *a'* thy servants.
24 and into *a'* the land of Egypt:
9: 4 nothing die of *a'* that is the
6 morrow, and *a'* the cattle of Egypt
9 small dust in *a'* the land of Egypt,
9 throughout *a'* the land of Egypt.
11 and upon *a'* the Egyptians.
14 *a'* my plagues upon thine heart,
14 is none like me in *a'* the earth.
16 declared throughout *a'* the earth.
19 and *a'* that thou hast in the field;
25 throughout *a'* the land of Egypt
25 *a'* that was in the field, both man
10: 6 and the houses of *a'* thy servants,
6 houses of *a'* the Egyptians;
12 even *a'* that the hail hath left.
13 land *a'* that day,
13 and *a'* that night;
14 went up over *a'* the land of Egypt,
14 rested in *a'* the coasts of Egypt:
15 of the land, and *a'* the fruit of the
15 through *a'* the land of Egypt.
19 locust in *a'* the coasts of Egypt.
22 darkness in *a'* the land of Egypt
23 *a'* the children of Israel had light
11: 5 And *a'* the firstborn in the land
5 and *a'* the firstborn of beasts.
6 throughout *a'* the land of Egypt,
8 *a'* these thy servants shall come
8 and *a'* the people that follow thee:
10 *a'* these wonders before Pharaoh:
12: 3 Speak ye unto *a'* the congregation
9 nor sodden at *a'* with water, but
12 smite *a'* the firstborn in the land
12 against *a'* the gods of Egypt I will
20 in *a'* your habitations shall ye eat
21 Then Moses called for *a'* the elders
29 the Lord smote *a'* the firstborn
29 and *a'* the firstborn of cattle.
30 *a'* his servants,
30 and *a'* the Egyptians;
41 *a'* the hosts of the Lord went out
42 observed of *a'* the children of
47 *A'* the congregation of Israel shall
48 to the Lord, let *a'* his males be
50 Thus did *a'* the children of Israel;
13: 2 Sanctify unto me *a'* the firstborn,
12 Lord *a'* that openeth the matrix,
13 and *a'* the firstborn of man among
15 that the Lord slew *a'* the firstborn
15 sacrifice to the Lord *a'* that
15 but *a'* the firstborn of my children
14: 7 chosen chariots, and *a'* the chariots
9 *a'* the horses and chariots of
17 honour upon Pharaoh, and upon *a'*
20 not near the other *a'* the night.
21 to go back by a strong east wind *a'*
23 the sea, even *a'* Pharaoh's horses,
28 and *a'* the host of Pharaoh that
15:15 *a'* the inhabitants of Canaan shall
20 hand; and *a'* the women went out
26 keep *a'* his statutes, I will put none
16: 1 *a'* the congregation of the children
6 said unto *a'* the children of Israel,
9 *a'* the congregation of the children
22 *a'* the rulers of the congregation
17: 1 *a'* the congregation of the children
18: 1 heard of *a'* that God had done

Ex 18: 8 *a'* that the Lord had done unto
8 for Israel's sake, and *a'* the travail
9 *a'* the goodness which the Lord
11 the Lord is greater than *a'* gods:
12 *a'* the elders of Israel, to eat
14 saw *a'* that he did to the people,
14 alone, and *a'* the people stand
21 provide out of *a'* the people able
22 let them judge the people at *a'*
23 and *a'* this people shall also go
24 and did *a'* that he had said.
25 chose able men out of *a'* Israel,
26 judged the people at *a'* seasons:
19: 5 treasure unto me above *a'* people:
5 for *a'* the earth is mine:
7 before their faces *a'* these words
8 *a'* the people answered together,
8 *A'* that the Lord hath spoken we
11 in the sight of *a'* the people upon
16 so that *a'* the people that was in
20: 1 And God spake *a'* these words,
9 shalt thou labour, and do *a'* thy
11 and earth, the sea, and *a'* that in
18 *a'* the people saw the thunderings,
24 in *a'* places where I record my
22: 9 For *a'* manner of trespass,
23 and they cry at *a'* unto me, I will
26 If thou at *a'* take thy neighbour's
23:13 in *a'* things that I have said unto
17 *a'* thy males shall appear before
22 his voice, and do *a'* that I speak;
27 will destroy *a'* the people to whom
27 and I will make *a'* thine enemies
24: 3 *a'* the words of the Lord,
3 and *a'* the judgments:
3 *a'* the people answered with one
3 *A'* the words which the Lord hath
4 Moses wrote *a'* the words of the
7 *A'* that the Lord hath said will we
8 you concerning *a'* these words.
25: 9 *a'* that I shew thee, after the
9 the pattern of *a'* the instruments
22 of *a'* things which I will give thee
36 *a'* it shall be one beaten work of
39 he make it, with *a'* these vessels.
26: 8 shall be *a'* of one measure.
17 *a'* the boards of the tabernacle.
27: 3 *a'* the vessels thereof thou shalt
17 *A'* the pillars round about the
19 *A'* the vessels of the tabernacle
19 in *a'* the service thereof,
19 and *a'* the pins thereof,
19 and *a'* the pins of the court,
28: 3 unto *a'* that are wise hearted,
31 the robe of the ephod *a'* of blue.
29:12 pour *a'* the blood beside the
13 take *a'* the fat that covereth the
24 put *a'* in the hands of Aaron,
35 *a'* things which I have commanded
30:27 *a'* his vessels, and the candlestick
28 burnt offering with *a'* his vessels,
31: 3 and in *a'* manner of workmanship,
5 *a'* manner of workmanship.
6 hearts of *a'* that are wise hearted
6 *a'* that I have commanded thee;
7 *a'* the furniture of the tabernacle,
8 candlestick with *a'* his furniture,
9 offering with *a'* his furniture,
11 *a'* that I have commanded thee
32: 3 And *a'* the people brake off the
13 *a'* this land that I have spoken of
26 *a'* the sons of Levi gathered
33: 8 that *a'* the people rose up, and
10 *a'* the people saw the cloudy
10 and *a'* the people rose up and
16 and thy people, from *a'* the people
19 *a'* my goodness pass before thee,
34: 3 be seen throughout *a'* the mount;
10 *a'* thy people I will do marvels,
10 have not been done in *a'* the earth,
10 *a'* the people among which thou
19 *A'* that openeth the matrix is mine;
20 *A'* the firstborn of thy sons thou
23 *a'* your men-children appear
30 *a'* the children of Israel saw Moses,
31 Aaron and *a'* the rulers of the
32 *a'* the children of Israel came nigh:
32 commandment *a'* that the Lord
35: 1 *a'* the congregation of the children
4 spake unto *a'* the congregation
10 *a'* that the Lord hath commanded;
13 *a'* his vessels, and the shewbread,
16 *a'* his vessels, the laver and his foot,
20 *a'* the congregation of the children
21 for *a'* his service, and for the holy
22 and tablets, *a'* jewels of gold:
25 And *a'* the women that were wise
26 *a'* the women whose heart stirred
29 them willing to bring for *a'* manner
31 in *a'* manner of workmanship;
35 to work *a'* manner of work, of the
36: 1 *a'* manner of work for the service
1 according to *a'* that the Lord had
3 *a'* the offering, which the children
4 *a'* the wise men,
4 *a'* the work of the sanctuary,
7 sufficient for *a'* the work to make
9 the curtains were *a'* of one size.
22 *a'* the boards of the tabernacle.
37:22 *a'* of it was one beaten work of
24 it, and *a'* the vessels thereof.
38: 3 made *a'* the vessels of the altar,
3 *a'* the vessels thereof made he of
16 *A'* the hangings of the court round
17 *a'* the pillars of the court were
20 *a'* the pins of the tabernacle,

Ex 38:22 *a'* that the Lord commanded
24 *A'* the gold that was occupied
24 for the work in *a'*
30 and *a'* the vessels of the altar,
31 and *a'* the pins of the tabernacle,
31 and *a'* the pins of the court
39:22 ephod of woven work, *a'* of blue.
32 was *a'* the work of the tabernacle
32 according to *a'* that the Lord
33 *a'* his furniture, his taches, his
36 and *a'* the vessels thereof, and the
37 *a'* the vessels thereof, and the oil
39 his staves, and *a'* his vessels,
40 *a'* the vessels of the service of the
42 to *a'* that the Lord commanded
42 of Israel made *a'* the work.
43 Moses did look upon *a'* the work.
40: 9 and *a'* that is therein, and shalt
9 it, and *a'* the vessels thereof:
10 burnt offering, and *a'* his vessels,
16 *a'* that the Lord commanded him,
36 Israel went onward in *a'* their
38 the sight of *a'* the house of Israel,
38 throughout *a'* their journeys.
Le 1: 9 priest shall burn *a'* on the altar,
13 priest shall bring it *a'*, and burn
2: 2 with *a'* the frankincense thereof;
13 with *a'* thine offerings thou shalt
16 with *a'* the frankincense thereof:
3: 3 and *a'* the fat that is upon the
9 the inwards, and *a'* the fat that is
14 *a'* the fat that is upon the inwards,
16 savour: *a'* the fat is the Lord's.
17 *a'* your dwellings, that ye eat
4: 7 pour *a'* the blood of the bullock
8 take off from it *a'* the fat of the
8 *a'* the fat that is upon the inwards,
11 and *a'* his flesh, with his head,
18 pour out *a'* the blood at the bottom
19 take *a'* his fat from him, and burn
26 he shall burn *a'* his fat upon the
30 pour out *a'* the blood thereof at
31 shall take away *a'* the fat thereof,
35 *a'* the fat thereof, as the fat of the
6: 3 in any of *a'* these that a man doeth.
5 Or *a'* that about which he hath
7 anything of *a'* that he hath done
9 upon the altar *a'* night unto the
15 *a'* the frankincense which is upon
18 *A'* the males among the children
29 *A'* the males among the priests
7: 3 shall offer of it *a'* the fat thereof;
9 And *a'* the meat offering that is
9 and *a'* that is dressed in the
10 oil, and dry, shall *a'* the sons of
18 eaten at *a'* on the third day, it
19 *a'* that be clean shall eat thereof.
8: 3 gather thou *a'* the congregation
10 *a'* that was therein, and sanctified
11 anointed the altar and *a'* his vessels.
16 he took *a'* the fat that was upon
25 *a'* the fat that was upon the
27 put *a'* upon Aaron's hands, and
36 sons did *a'* things which the Lord
9: 5 *a'* the congregation drew near
23 Lord appeared unto *a'* the people.
24 when *a'* the people saw, they
10: 3 and before *a'* the people I will be
6 wrath come upon *a'* the people:
11 children of Israel *a'* the statutes
11: 2 eat among *a'* the beasts that are
9 ye eat of *a'* that are in the waters:
10 *a'* that have not fins and scales in
10 of *a'* that move in the waters,
20 *A'* fowls that creep,
20 going upon *a'* four,
21 thing, that goeth upon *a'* four,
23 *a'* other flying creeping things,
27 among *a'* manner of beasts
27 that go on *a'* four,
31 unclean to you among *a'* that
34 Of *a'* meat which may be eaten,
34 and *a'* drink that may be drunk
42 whatsoever goeth upon *a'* four,
42 feet among *a'* creeping things
13:12 leprosy cover *a'* the skin of him
13 leprosy have covered *a'* his flesh,
46 *A'* the days wherein the plague
14: 8 clothes, and shave off *a'* his hair,
9 *a'* his hair off his head and his
9 even *a'* his hair he shall shave off:
36 *a'* that is in that house be not
45 and *a'* the morter of the house;
46 *a'* the while that it is shut up shall
54 law for *a'* manner of plague of
15:16 wash *a'* his flesh in water, and be
24 And if any man lie with her at *a'*,
24 *a'* the bed whereon he lieth shall
25 of her separation; *a'* the days of
26 whereon she lieth *a'* the days of
16: 2 not at *a'* times into the holy place
16 transgressions in *a'* their sins:
17 for *a'* the congregation of Israel.
21 *a'* the iniquities of the children
21 *a'* their transgressions in *a'* their
22 bear upon him *a'* their iniquities
29 no work at *a'*, whether it be one
30 be clean from *a'* your sins before
33 *a'* the people of the congregation.
34 for *a'* their sins once a year.
17: 2 and unto *a'* the children of Israel,
14 For it is the life of *a'* flesh; the
14 life of *a'* flesh is the blood thereof:
18:24 in *a'* these the nations are defiled
27 (For *a'* these abominations have
19: 2 Speak unto *a'* the congregation of

Le 19: 7 it be eaten at a' on the third day,
13 thee a' night until the morning.
20 not at a' redeemed, nor freedom
23 have planted a' manner of trees
24 a' the fruit thereof shall be holy
37 observe a' my statutes,
37 and a' my judgments,
20: 5 family, and will cut him off, and a'
22 keep a' my statutes,
22 and a' my judgments,
23 for they committed a' these things,
21:24 and unto a' the children of Israel.
22: 3 a' your seed among your
18 and unto a' the children of Israel,
18 for a' his vows,
18 and for a' his freewill offerings,
23: 3 of the Lord in a' your dwellings.
14 generations in a' your dwellings.
21 in a' your dwellings throughout
31 generations in a' your dwellings.
38 beside a' your vows,
38 beside a' your freewill offerings,
42 a' that are Israelites born shall
24:14 a' that heard him lay their hands
14 let a' the congregation stone him.
16 a' the congregation shall certainly
25: 7 a' the increase thereof be meat.
9 sound throughout a' your land.
10 liberty throughout a' the land
10 unto a' the inhabitants thereof:
24 in a' the land of your possession
26:14 not do a' these commandments;
15 will not do a' my commandments.
18 yet for a' this hearken unto me,
27 not for a' this hearken unto me,
44 yet for a' that, when they be in
27: 9 a' that any man giveth of such
10 shall at a' change beast for beast,
13 But if he will at a' redeem it,
25 a' thy estimations shall be
28 unto the Lord of a' that he hath,
30 a' the tithe of the land, whether of
31 at a' redeem ought of his tithes,
33 and if he change it at a', then
Nu 1: 2 ye the sum of a' the congregation
3 a' that are able to go forth to war
18 assembled a' the congregation
20, 22, 24, 26, 28, 30, 32, 34, 36, 38, 40,
42 a' that were able to go forth to war;
45 were a' those that were numbered
45 a' that were able to go forth to war
46 Even a' they that were numbered
50 over a' the vessels thereof,
50 and over a' things
50 tabernacle, and a' the vessels
54 did according to a' that the Lord
2: 9, 16 A' that were numbered in the
24 A' that were numbered of the
31 A' they that were numbered in the
32 a' those that were numbered of the
34 to a' that the Lord commanded
3: 8 they shall keep a' the instruments
12 of a' the firstborn that openeth the
13 Because a' the firstborn are mine;
13 I smote a' the firstborn in the land
13 unto me a' the firstborn in Israel,
22 to the number of a' the males,
26 the cords of it for a' the service
28 number of a' the males, from a
31 hanging, and a' the service thereof.
34 to the number of a' the males,
36 a' the vessels thereof,
36 and a' that serveth thereto,
39 A' that were numbered of the
39 a' the males from a month old and
40 Number a' the firstborn of the
41 a' the firstborn among the children
41 a' the firstlings among the cattle
42 a' the firstborn among the children
43 And a' the firstborn males by the
45 Levites instead of a' the firstborn
4: 3 a' that enter into the host, to do
9 snuffdishes, and a' the oil vessels
10 put it and a' the vessels thereof
12 a' the instruments of ministry,
14 a' the vessels thereof, wherewith
14 basons, a' the vessels of the altar;
15 a' the vessels of the sanctuary,
16 the oversight of a' the tabernacle,
16 and of a' that therein is,
23 a' that enter in to perform the
26 a' the instruments of their
26 and a' that is made for them:
27 a' the service of the sons of the
27 in a' their burdens,
27 and in a' their service: and ye
27 them in charge a' their burdens.
31 according to a' their service in the
32 with a' their instruments,
32 and with a' their service:
33 according to a' their service,
37, 41 a' that might do service in the
46 A' those that were numbered of
5: 9 offering of a' the holy things of the
30 shall execute upon her a' this law.
6: 4 A' the days of his separation
5 A' the days of the vow of his
6 A' the days that he separateth
8 A' the days of his separation he is
7: 1 a' the instruments thereof,
1 both the altar and a' the vessels
85 a' the silver vessels weighed
86 a' the gold of the spoons was
87 A' the oxen for the burnt offering
88 A' the oxen for the sacrifice of
8: 7 and let them shave a' their flesh,

Nu 8:16 of the firstborn of a' the children
17 For a' the firstborn of the children
18 Levites for a' the firstborn of the
20 Aaron, and a' the congregation
20 unto a' that the Lord commanded
9: 3 appointed season: according to a'
3 according to a' the ceremonies
5 to a' that the Lord commanded
12 according to a' the ordinances of
10: 3 a' the assembly shall assemble
25 was the rereward of a' the camps
11: 6 nothing at a', beside this manna,
11 burden of a' this people upon me?
12 Have I conceived a' this people?
13 flesh to give unto a' this people?
14 able to bear a' this people alone,
22 a' the fish of the sea be gathered
29 would God that a' the Lord's
32 the people stood up a' that day,
32 and a' that night,
32 and a' the next day,
32 they spread them a' abroad
12: 3 above a' the men which were upon
7 who is faithful in a' mine house.
13: 3 a' those men were heads of the
26 Aaron, and to a' the congregation
26 and unto a' the congregation,
32 a' the people that we saw in it are
14: 1 a' the congregation lifted up their
2 a' the children of Israel murmured
5 their faces before a' the assembly
7 spake unto a' the company of the
10 a' the congregation bade stone
10 before a' the children of Israel.
11 me, for a' the signs which I have
15 kill a' this people as one man,
21 a' the earth shall be filled with
22 Because a' those men which have
35 do it unto a' this evil congregation
36 a' the congregation to murmur
39 these sayings unto a' the children
15:13 A' that are born of the country
23 a' that the Lord hath commanded
24 a' the congregation shall offer one
25 atonement for a' the congregation
26 be forgiven a' the congregation
26 a' the people were in ignorance.
33 and unto a' the congregation.
35 a' the congregation shall stone him
36 a' the congregation brought him
39 remember a' the commandments
40 do a' my commandments, and be
16: 3 a' the congregation are holy,
5 Korah and unto a' his company,
6 censers, Korah, and a' his company;
10 a' thy brethren the sons of Levi
11 and a' thy company are gathered
16 Be thou and a' thy company before
19 gathered a' the congregation
19 appeared unto a' the congregation.
22 the God of the spirits of a' flesh,
22 wroth with a' the congregation?
26 ye be consumed in a' their sins.
28 Lord hath sent me to do a' these
29 die the common death of a' men,
29 after the visitation of a' men;
30 a' that appertained unto them,
31 an end of speaking a' these words,
32 them up, and their houses, and a'
32 unto Korah, and a' their goods.
33 a' that appertained to them, went
34 a' Israel that were round about
41 a' the congregation of the children
17: 2 their fathers, of a' their princes
9 a' the rods from before the Lord
9 unto a' the children of Israel:
18: 3 the charge of a' the tabernacle:
4 for a' the service of the tabernacle:
8 offerings of a' the hallowed
11 with a' the wave offerings of the
12 A' the best of the oil,
12 and a' the best of the wine,
15 openeth the matrix in a' flesh,
19 A' the heave offerings of the holy
21 a' the tenth in Israel for an
28 offering unto the Lord of a' your
29 Out of a' your gifts ye shall offer
29 offering of the Lord, of a' the best
19:14 a' that come into the tent,
14 and a' that is in the tent,
18 the tent, and upon a' the vessels,
20:14 Thou knowest a' the travel that
27 in the sight of a' the congregation.
29 when a' the congregation saw that
29 for Aaron thirty days, even a' the
21:23 Sihon gathered a' his people
25 And Israel took a' these cities:
25 in a' the cities of the Amorites,
25 in Heshbon, and in a'
26 taken a' his land out of his hand,
33 he, and a' his people, to the battle
34 into thy hand, and a' his people,
35 and his sons, and a' his people,
22: 2 the son of Zippor saw a' that Israel
4 this company lick up a' that are
38 any power at a' to say any thing?
23: 6 sacrifice, he, and a' the princes
13 of them, and shalt not see them a':
25 Neither curse them at a',
25 nor bless them at a'.
26 A' that the Lord speaketh, that I
24:17 destroy a' the children of Sheth.
25: 4 Take a' the heads of the people,
6 Moses, and in the sight of a' the
26: 2 sum of a' the congregation of the
2 a' that are able to go to war in

Nu 26:43 A' the families of the Shuahmites,
62 a' males from a month old and
27: 2 princes and a' the congregation,
16 the God of the spirits of a' flesh,
19 and before a' the congregation;
20 upon him, that a' the congregation
21 and a' the children of Israel with
21 even a' the congregation.
22 and before a' the congregation:
29:40 to a' that the Lord commanded
30: 4 her: then a' her vows shall stand,
6 if she had at a' an husband,
11 then a' her vows shall stand,
14 establisheth a' her vows,
14 or a' her bonds,
31: 4 throughout a' the tribes of Israel,
7 and they slew a' the males.
9 a' the women of Midian captives,
9 a' their cattle,
9 and a' their flocks,
9 and a' their goods.
10 And they burnt a' their cities
10 a' their goodly castles, with fire.
11 took a' the spoil,
11 and a' the prey, both of men and
13 a' the princes of the congregation,
15 Have ye saved a' the women alive?
18 a' the women children, that have
20 And purify a' your raiment,
20 and a' that is made of skins,
20 and a' work of goats' hair,
20 and a' things made of wood.
23 a' that abideth not the fire ye shall
27 and between a' the congregation:
30 flocks, of a' manner of beasts,
35 and two thousand persons in a',
51 of them, even a' wrought jewels.
52 a' the gold of the offering that they
32:13 forty years, until a' the generation,
15 and ye shall destroy a' this people.
21 go a' of you armed over Jordan
26 a' our cattle, shall be there in the
33: 3 in the sight of a' the Egyptians.
4 Egyptians buried a' their firstborn,
52 shall drive out a' the inhabitants
52 and destroy a' their pictures, and
52 destroy a' their molten images,
52 pluck down a' their high places:
35: 3 their goods, and for a' their beasts.
7 a' the cities which ye shall give to
29 generations in a' your dwellings.
De 1: 1 a' Israel on this side Jordan
3 unto a' that the Lord had given
7 unto a' the places nigh thereunto,
18 a' the things which ye should do.
19 a' that great and terrible
30 to a' that he did for you in Egypt
31 son, in a' the way that ye went,
41 to a' that the Lord our God
2: 7 thee in a' the works of thy hand:
14 until a' the generation of the men
16 when a' the men of war were
32 a' his people, to fight at Jahaz.
33 and his sons, and a' his people.
34 we took a' his cities at that time,
36 Lord our God delivered a' unto us:
3: 1 he and a' his people, to battle at
2 and a' his people, and his land,
3 king of Bashan, and a' his people:
4 we took a' his cities at that time,
4 a' the region of Argob, the kingdom
5 A' these cities were fenced with
7 But a' the cattle, and the spoil of
10 A' the cities of the plain,
10 and a' Gilead, and a' Bashan,
13 the rest of Gilead, and a' Bashan,
13 a' the region of Argob,
13 with a' Bashan,
14 Manasseh took a' the country of
18 a' that are meet for the war.
21 a' that the Lord your God hath
21 the Lord do unto a' the kingdoms
4: 3 a' the men that followed Baal-peor,
6 which shall hear a' these statutes,
7 in a' things that we call upon him
8 so righteous as a' this law,
9 thy heart a' the days of thy life:
10 may learn to fear me a' the days
19 even a' the host of heaven,
19 God hath divided unto a' nations
29 with a' thy heart
29 and with a' thy soul.
30 and a' these things are come upon
34 according to a' that the Lord
49 a' the plain on this side Jordan
5: 1 Moses called a' Israel, and said
3 are a' of us here alive this day.
13 shalt labour, and do a' thy work:
22 a' your assembly in the mount
23 even a' the heads of your tribes,
26 For who is there of a' flesh, that
27 hear a' that the Lord our God
27 unto us a' that the Lord our God
28 said a' that they have spoken.
29 a' my commandments always,
31 unto thee a' the commandments,
33 walk in a' the ways which the
6: 2 thy God, to keep a' his statutes
2 son's son, a' the days of thy life;
5 Lord thy God with a' thine heart,
5 and with a' thy soul,
5 and with a' thy might.
11 And houses full of a' good things,
19 To cast out a' thine enemies from
22 and upon a' his household,
24 commanded us to do a' these

De 6:25 to do a' these commandments
7: 6 above a' people that are upon the
7 for ye were the fewest of a' people:
14 shalt be blessed above a' people:
15 take away from thee a' sickness,
15 upon a' them that hate thee.
16 consume a' the people which the
18 unto Pharaoh, and unto a' Egypt;
19 God do unto a' the people of whom
8: 1 A' the commandments which I
2 remember all the way which the
13 multiplied, and a' that thou hast
19 do at a' forget the Lord thy God,
9:10 according to a' the words,
18 of a' your sins which ye sinned,
10:12 thy God, to walk in a' his ways,
12 Lord thy God with a' thy heart
12 and with a' thy soul,
14 earth also, with a' that therein is.
15 even you above a' people, as it is
11: 3 of Egypt, and unto a' his land;
6 and a' the substance that was in
6 in the midst of a' Israel:
7 seen a' the great acts of the Lord
8 ye keep a' the commandments
13 to serve him with a' your heart
13 and with a' your soul,
22 keep a' these commandments
22 your God, to walk in a' his ways,
23 Lord drive out a' these nations
25 you upon a' the land that ye shall
32 to do a' the statutes and judgments
12: 1 a' the days that ye live upon the
2 shall utterly destroy a' the places,
5 shall choose out of a' your tribes
7 in a' that ye put your hand unto,
8 a' the things that we do here this
10 you rest from a' your enemies
11 ye bring a' that I command you;
11 a' your choice vows which ye vow
14 shalt do a' that I command thee.
15 kill and eat flesh in a' thy gates,
18 before the Lord thy God in a'
28 Observe and hear a' these words
13: 3 God with a' your heart
3 and with a' your soul.
9 the hand of a' the people.
11 a' Israel shall hear, and fear,
15 it utterly, and a' that is therein,
16 gather a' the spoil of it into the
16 the city, and a' the spoil thereof
18 to keep a' his commandments
14: 2 above a' the nations that are
9 eat of a' that are in the waters:
9 a' that have fins and scales shall
11 Of a' clean birds ye shall eat.
20 But of a' clean fowls ye may eat.
22 tithe a' the increase of thy seed,
28 bring forth a' the tithe of thine
29 bless thee in a' the work of thine
15: 5 to do a' these commandments
10 God shall bless thee in a' thy works,
10 in a' that thou puttest thine hand
18 bless thee in a' that thou doest.
19 A' the firstling males that come
16: 3 of Egypt a' the days of thy life.
4 seen with thee in a' thy coast
4 remain a' night until the morning.
15 bless thee in a' thine increase,
15 and in a' the works of thine hands,
16 shall a' thy males appear before
18 thou make thee in a' thy gates,
17: 7 the hands of a' the people.
10 according to a' that they inform
13 And a' the people shall hear, and
14 a' the nations that are about me;
19 read therein a' the days of his life:
19 to keep a' the words of this law
18: 1 Levites, and a' the tribe of Levi,
5 chosen him out of a' thy tribes,
6 any of thy gates out of a' Israel,
6 come with a' the desire of his mind
7 as a' his brethren the Levites do,
12 For a' that do these things are
16 a' that thou desiredst of the Lord
18 them a' that I shall command him.
19: 8 a' the land which he promised
9 keep a' these commandments to
20:11 a' the people that is found therein
14 a' that is in the city,
14 even a' the spoil thereof,
15 shalt thou do unto a' the cities
18 to do after a' their abominations,
21: 6 And a' the elders of that city,
14 shalt not sell her at a' for money,
17 double portion of a' that he hath.
21 And a' the men of his city shall
21 a' Israel shall hear, and fear.
23 remain a' night upon the tree,
22: 3 a' lost thing of thy brother's,
5 for a' that do so are abomination
19, 29 not put her away a' his days.
23: 6 prosperity a' thy days forever.
20 God may bless thee in a' that
24: 8 to a' that the priests the Levites
19 God may bless thee in a' the work
25:16 a' that do such things,
16 and a' that do unrighteously,
18 of thee, even a' that were feeble
19 from a' thine enemies round about,
26: 2 the first of a' the fruit of the earth,
12 a' the tithes of thine increase
13 to a' thy commandments which
14 a' that thou hast commanded me.
16 and do them with a' thine heart.
16 and with a' thy soul.

De 26:18 keep a' his commandments;
19 a' nations which he hath made,
27: 1 Keep a' the commandments which
3 upon them a' the words of this law,
8 the stones a' the words of this law
9 the Levites spake unto a' Israel,
14 and say unto a' the men of Israel
15 And a' the people shall answer
16, 17, 18, 19, 20, 21, 22, 23, 24, 25 And
a' the people shall say, Amen.
26 confirmeth not a' the words of
26 a' the people shall say, Amen.
28: 1 and to do a' his commandments
1 high above a' nations of the earth:
2 a' these blessings shall come on
8 in a' that thou settest thine hand
10 a' people of the earth shall see
12 bless a' the work of thine hand:
15 to do a' his commandments
15 a' these curses shall come upon
20 vexation, and rebuke, in a' that
25 into a' the kingdoms of the earth.
26 shall be meat unto a' fowls of the
32 longing for them a' the day long:
33 a' thy labours, shall a nation which
37 among a' nations whither the Lord
40 olive trees throughout a' thy coasts,
42 A' thy trees and fruit of thy land
45 a' these curses shall come upon
47 for the abundance of a' things;
48 nakedness, and in want of a' things:
52 shall besiege thee in a' thy gates,
52 trustedst, throughout a' thy land:
52 shall besiege thee in a' thy gates,
52 throughout a' thy land, which the
55 shall distress thee in a' thy gates.
57 for want of a' things secretly in
58 to do a' the words of this law
60 upon thee a' the diseases of Egypt,
64 shall scatter thee among a' people,
29: 2 And Moses called unto a' Israel,
2 Ye have seen a' that the Lord did
2 and unto a' his servants,
2 and unto a' his land;
9 ye may prosper in a' that ye do.
10 a' of you before the Lord your
10 officers, with a' the men of Israel,
20 a' the curses that are written in
21 evil out of a' the tribes of Israel,
21 a' the curses of the covenant that
24 Even a' nations shall say,
27 to bring upon it a' the curses that
29 may do a' the words of this law.
30: 1 when a' these things are come
1 to mind among a' the nations,
2 according to a' that I command
2 with a' thine heart,
2 and with a' thy soul;
3 gather thee from a' the nations,
6 Lord thy God with a' thine heart,
6 and with a' thy soul, that thou
7 God will put a' these curses upon
8 and do a' his commandments
10 turn unto the Lord thy God with a'
10 thine heart, and with a' thy soul.
31: 1 spake these words unto a' Israel,
5 unto a' the commandments which
7 sight of a' Israel, Be strong and
9 and unto a' the elders of Israel.
11 When a' Israel is come to appear
11 thou shalt read this law before a'
12 to do a' the words of this law:
18 a' the evils which they shall have
28 unto me a' the elders of your tribes,
30 in the ears of a' the congregation
32: 4 for a' his ways are judgment:
27 and the Lord hath not done a' this.
44 spake a' the words of this song,
45 a' these words to a' Israel:
46 hearts unto a' the words which I
46 to do, a' the words of this law.
33: 3 a' his saints are in thy hand:
12 shall cover him a' the day long,
34: 1 shewed him a' the land of Gilead,
2 And a' Naphtali, and the land of
2 Manasseh, and a' the land of Judah,
11 In a' the signs and the wonders,
11 to a' his servants,
11 and to a' his land,
12 And in a' that mighty hand,
12 and in a' the great terror
12 shewed in the sight of a' Israel.
Jos 1: 2 Jordan, thou, and a' this people,
4 a' the land of the Hittites, and
5 before thee a' the days of thy life:
7 do according to a' the law, which
8 according to a' that is written
14 a' the mighty men of valour, and
16 A' that thou commandest us we
17 hearkened unto Moses in a' things,
18 words in a' that thou commandest
2: 3 come to search out a' the country.
9 that a' the inhabitants of the land
13 my sisters, and a' that they have,
18 and a' thy father's household,
22 throughout a' the way, but found
23 told him a' things that befell them:
24 into our hands a' the land;
24 a' the inhabitants of the country
3: 1 he and a' the children of Israel,
7 thee in the sight of a' Israel,
11 covenant of the Lord of a' the earth
13 the Lord, the Lord of a' the earth,
15 a' his banks a' the time
17 and a' the Israelites passed over
17 a' the people were passed clean

Jos 4: 1 when a' the people were clean
10 according to a' that Moses
11 when a' the people were clean
14 Joshua in the sight of a' Israel;
14 Moses, a' the days of his life.
18 and flowed over a' his banks, as
24 That a' the people of the earth
5: 1 when a' the kings of the Amorites,
1 a' the kings of the Canaanites,
4 A' the people that came out of
4 males, even a' the men of war,
5 Now a' the people that came out
5 but a' the people that were born
6 years in the wilderness, till a' the
8 done circumcising a' the people,
6: 3 compass the city, a' ye men of war,
5 trumpet, a' the people shall shout
17 even it, and a' that are therein,
17 a' that are with her in the house,
19 But a' the silver, and gold, and
21 destroyed a' that was in the city,
22 the woman, and a' that she hath,
23 her brethren, and a' that she had;
23 brought out a' her kindred, and
24 with fire, and a' that was therein:
25 and a' that she had; and she
27 noised throughout a' the country.
7: 3 Let not a' the people go up; but
3 make not a' the people to labour
7 thou at a' brought this people over
9 a' the inhabitants of the land
15 with fire, he and a' that he hath:
23 and unto a' the children of Israel
24 Joshua, and a' Israel with him,
24 and his tent, and a' that he had:
25 a' Israel stoned him with stones,
8: 1 take a' the people of war with thee,
3 arose, and a' the people of war,
4 from the city, but be ye a' ready:
5 and a' the people that are with me,
11 And a' the people, even the people
13 even a' the host that was on the
14 to battle, he and a' his people,
15 And Joshua and a' Israel made as
16 And a' the people that were in Ai
21 when Joshua and a' Israel saw
24 slaying a' the inhabitants of Ai
24 a' fallen on the edge of the sword,
24 a' the Israelites returned unto Ai,
25 that a' that fell that day, both of
25 even a' the men of Ai.
26 destroyed a' the inhabitants of Ai.
33 And a' Israel, and their elders,
34 he read a' the words of the law,
34 a' that is written in the book of the
35 word of a' that Moses commanded,
35 a' the congregation of Israel,
9: 1 when a' the kings which were on
1 a' the coasts of the great sea over
5 a' the bread of their provision
9 of him, and a' that he did in Egypt,
10 a' that he did to the two kings of
11 our elders and a' the inhabitants
18 And a' the congregation murmured
21 of water unto a' the congregation;
24 Moses to give you a' the land,
24 a' the inhabitants of the land from
10: 2 a' the men thereof were mighty.
5 they and a' their hosts, and
6 for a' the kings of the Amorites
7 a' the people of war with him,
7 and a' the mighty men
9 and went up from Gilgal a' night.
15 returned, and a' Israel with him,
21 a' the people returned to the camp
24 called for a' the men of Israel,
25 the Lord do to a' your enemies
28 them, and a' the souls that
29 from Makkedah, and a' Israel
30 and a' the souls that were therein;
31 Libnah, and a' Israel with him,
32 and a' the souls that were therein,
32 according to a' that he had done
34 unto Eglon, and a' Israel with him;
35 and a' the souls that were therein,
35 according to a' that he had done
36 from Eglon, and a' Israel with him;
37 thereof, and a' the cities thereof,
37 and a' the souls that were therein;
37 according to a' that he had done
37 it utterly, and a' the souls
38 and a' Israel with him, to Debir;
39 thereof, and a' the cities thereof;
39 a' the souls that were therein;
40 So Joshua smote a' the country of
40 of the springs, and a' their kings:
40 utterly destroyed a' that breathed,
41 and a' the country of Goshen,
42 And a' these kings and their land
43 returned, and a' Israel with him,
11: 4 they and a' their hosts with them,
5 a' these kings were met together,
6 time will I deliver them up a' slain
7 and a' the people of war with him,
10 the head of a' those kingdoms.
11 a' the souls that were therein with
12 And a' the cities of those kings,
12 and a' the kings
14 And a' the spoil of these cities,
15 of a' that the Lord commanded
16 So Joshua took a' that land,
16 and a' the south country,
16 and a' the land of Goshen,
17 under Mount Hermon: and a'
18 a long time with a' those kings.
19 Gibeon: a' other they took in battle.

Jos 11:21 from a' the mountains of Judah,
21 a' the mountains of Israel:
23 a' that the Lord said unto Moses;
12: 1 Hermon, and a' the plain on the
5 and in a' Bashan, unto the border
24 one: a' the kings thirty and one.
13: 2 a' the borders of the Philistines,
2 and a' Geshuri,
4 a' the land of the Canaanites,
5 and a' Lebanon, toward the
6 A' the inhabitants of the hill
6 and a' the Sidonians, then will I
9 a' the plain of Medeba unto Dibon;
10 And a' the cities of Sihon king of
11 a' mount Hermon,
11 and a' Bashan unto Salcah;
12 A' the kingdom of Og in Bashan,
16 river, and a' the plain by Medeba;
17 a' her cities that are in the plain;
21 And a' the cities of the plain,
21 and a' the kingdom of Sihon
25 Jazer, and a' the cities of Gilead,
30 from Mahanaim, a' Bashan,
30 a' the kingdom of Og king of
30 a' the towns of Jair, which are in
15:32 and Rimmon: a' the cities are
46 a' that lay near Ashdod, with their
16: 9 a' the cities with their villages.
17:16 for us: and a' the Canaanites
19: 8 a' the villages that were round
20: 9 appointed for a' the children of
21:19 A' the cities of the children of
26 A' the cities were ten with their
33 A' the cities of the Gershonites
39 her suburbs; four cities in a'.
40 So a' the cities for the children of
41 A' the cities of the Levites within
42 them: thus were a' these cities.
43 Lord gave unto Israel a' the land.
44 according to a' that he sware unto
44 not a man of a' their enemies
44 Lord delivered a' their enemies
45 house of Israel; a' came to pass.
22: 2 a' that Moses the servant of the
2 in a' that I commanded you:
5 Lord your God, and to walk in a'
5 a' your heart and with a' your soul.
14 a' the tribes of Israel;
20 wrath fell on a' the congregation
23: 1 unto Israel from a' their enemies
2 And Joshua called for a' Israel,
3 seen a' that the Lord your God
3 done unto a' these nations because
4 a' the nations that I have cut off,
6 do a' that is written in the book of
14 I am going the way of a' the earth:
14 know in a' your hearts
14 and in a' your souls, that
14 hath failed of a' the good things
14 concerning you; a' are come to
15 a' good things are come upon you,
15 Lord bring upon you a' evil things,
24: 1 Joshua gathered a' the tribes of
2 Joshua said unto a' the people,
3 throughout a' the land of Canaan,
17 and preserved us in a' the way
17 among a' the people through whom
18 out from before us a' the people,
27 Joshua said unto a' the people,
27 unto us; for it hath heard a' the
31 Israel served the Lord a' the days
31 and a' the days of the elders that
31 known a' the works of the Lord,
J'g 1:25 let go the man and a' his family.
2: 4 unto a' the children of Israel,
7 people served the Lord a' the days
7 and a' the days of the elders that
7 seen a' the great works of the Lord,
10 a' that generation were gathered
18 hand of their enemies a' the days
3: 1 not known a' the wars of Canaan;
3 and a' the Canaanites, and the
19 And a' that stood by him went out
29 ten thousand men, a' lusty,
29 a' men of valour; and there
4:13 gathered together a' his chariots,
13 a' the people that were with him,
15 and a' his chariots,
15 and a' his host, with the
16 a' the host of Sisera fell upon the
5:31 let a' thine enemies perish, O Lord:
6: 9 out of the hand of a' that oppressed
13 why then is a' this befallen us?
13 and where be a' his
31 unto a' that stood against him, Will
33 Then a' the Midianites and the
35 throughout a' Manasseh;
37 and it be dry upon a' the earth
39 upon a' the ground let there be dew.
40 there was dew on a' the ground.
7: 1 who is Gideon, and a' the people
6 but a' the rest of the people bowed
7 let a' the other people go every
8 he sent a' the rest of Israel every
12 and the Amalekites and a' the
14 hath God delivered Midian, and a'
18 a trumpet, I and a' that are with
18 also on every side of a' the camp,
21 and a' the host ran, and cried, and
22 fellow, even throughout a' the host:
23 of Asher, and out of a' Manasseh,
24 messengers throughout a' mount
24 a' the men of Ephraim gathered
8:10 a' that were left of a' the hosts of
12 and discomfited a' the host.
27 Ophrah: and a' Israel went thither

J'g 8:34 out of the hands of a' their enemies
35 according to a' the goodness which
9: 1 with them, and with a' the family
2 pray you, in the ears of a' the men
2 that a' the sons of Jerubbaal,
3 the ears of a' the men of Shechem
3 a' these words: and their hearts
6 a' the men of Shechem gathered
6 and a' the house of Millo, and went,
14 said a' the trees unto the bramble,
25 they robbed a' that came along
34 rose up, and a' the people that
44 companies ran upon a' the people
45 fought against the city a' that day;
46 when a' the men of the tower of
47 a' the men of the tower of Shechem
48 he and a' the people that were
49 a' the people likewise cut down
49 a' the men of the tower of Shechem
51 thither fled a' the men and women,
51 and a' they of the city,
53 Abimelech's head, and a' to brake
57 a' the evil of the men of Shechem
10: 8 a' the children of Israel
18 over a' the inhabitants of Gilead.
11: 8 be our head over a' the inhabitants
11 Jephthah uttered a' his words,
20 but Sihon gathered a' his people
21 delivered Sihon and a' his people
21 so Israel possessed a' the land of
22 possessed a' the coasts of the
26 in a' the cities that be along by the
12: 4 Jephthah gathered together a' the
13:13 Of a' that I said unto the woman
14 a' that I commanded her let her
23 have shewed us a' these things,
14: 3 brethren, or among a' my people,
16: 2 wait for him a' night in the gate of
2 were quiet a' the night, saying,
3 went away with them, bar and a',
17 that he told her a' his heart, and
18 that he had told her a' his heart,
18 he hath shewed me a' his heart.
27 a' the lords of the Philistines were
30 bowed himself with a' his might;
30 fell upon the lords, and upon a'
31 his brethren and a' the house of
18: 1 that day a' their inheritance had
31 a' the time that the house of God
19: 6 tarry a' night, and let thine heart
9 I pray you tarry a' night:
13 to lodge a' night, in Gibeah, or in
20 howsoever let a' thy wants lie
25 a' the night until the morning:
29 sent her into a' the coasts of Israel.
30 that a' that saw it said, There was
20: 1 a' the children of Israel went out,
2 And the chief of a' the people,
2 even of a' the tribes of Israel,
6 sent her throughout a' the country
7 ye are a' children of Israel; give
8 a' the people arose as one man,
10 men of an hundred throughout a'
10 according to a' the folly that they
11 a' the men of Israel were gathered
12 through a' the tribe of Benjamin,
16 Among a' this people there were
17 sword: a' these were men of war.
25 men; a' these drew the sword.
26 Then a' the children of Israel,
26 and a' the people, went up,
33 And a' the men of Israel rose up
34 chosen men out of a' Israel, and
35 a' these drew the sword.
37 smote a' the city with the edge of
44 men; a' these were men of valour.
46 a' which fell that day of Benjamin
46 drew the sword; a' these were men
48 and a' that came to hand: also
48 they set on fire a' the cities that
21: 5 among a' the tribes of Israel,
Ru 1:19 that a' the city was moved about
2:11 fully been shewed me, a' that thou
21 they have ended a' my harvest.
3: 5 A' that thou sayest unto me I will
6 a' that her mother in law bade her.
11 do to thee a' that thou requirest:
11 for a' the city of my people doth
16 my daughter? And she told her a'
4: 7 confirm a' things; a man plucked
9 the elders, and unto a' the people,
9 this day, that I have bought a'
9 and a' that was Chilion's
11 a' the people that were in the gate,
1Sa 1: 4 Peninnah his wife, and to a' her
11 give him unto the Lord a' the days
21 man Elkanah, and a' his house,
2:14 a' that the fleshhook brought up
14 So they did in Shiloh unto a'
22 heard a' that his sons did
22 unto a' Israel;
23 evil dealings by a' this people.
28 choose him out of a' the tribes of
28 give unto the house of thy father a'
29 fat with the chiefest of a' the
2:32 a' the wealth which God shall give
33 grieve thine heart: and a' the
3:12 will perform against Eli a' things
17 hide anything from me of a' the
20 And a' Israel from Dan even to
4: 1 word of Samuel came to a' Israel.
5 into the camp, a' Israel shouted
8 that smote the Egyptians with a'
13 into the city, and told it, a' the city
5: 8 a' the lords of the Philistines unto
11 gathered together a' the lords of

1Sa 5:11 destruction throughout a' the city;
6: 4 for one plague was on you a', and
18 according to the number of a' the
7: 2 a' the house of Israel lamented
3 Samuel spake unto a' the house of
3 unto the Lord with a' your hearts,
5 Gather a' Israel to Mizpeh, and I
13 against the Philistines a' the days
15 Samuel judged Israel a' the days
16 judged Israel in a' those places.
8: 4 a' the elders of Israel gathered
5 to judge us like a' the nations.
7 of the people in a' that they say
8 According to a' the works which
10 Samuel told a' the words of the Lord
20 we also may be like a' the nations;
21 And Samuel heard a' the words of
9: 6 a' that he saith cometh surely to
19 tell thee a' that is in thine heart.
20 on whom is a' the desire of Israel?
20 and on a' thy father's house?
21 least of a' the families of the tribe
10: 9 a' those signs came to pass that
11 when a' that knew him beforetime
18 Egyptians, and out of the hand of a'
19 saved you out of a' your adversities
20 had caused a' the tribes of Israel
24 And Samuel said to a' the people,
24 none like him among a' the people?
24 a' the people shouted, and said,
25 Samuel sent a' the people away,
11: 1 a' the men of Jabesh said unto
2 may thrust out a' your right eyes,
2 lay it for a reproach upon a' Israel.
3 send messengers unto a' the coasts
4 a' the people lifted up their voices,
7 throughout a' the coasts of Israel
10 a' that seemeth good unto you.
15 And a' the people went to Gilgal;
15 and a' the men of Israel rejoiced
12: 1 Samuel said unto a' Israel, Behold,
1 voice in a' that ye said unto me,
7 a' the righteous acts of the Lord,
18 a' the people greatly feared the
19 a' the people said unto Samuel,
19 added unto a' our sins this evil,
20 done a' this wickedness: yet turn
20 serve the Lord with a' your heart;
24 him in truth with a' your heart.
13: 4 And a' Israel heard say that Saul
7 and a' the people followed him
19 throughout a' the land of Israel:
20 a' the Israelites went down to the
14: 7 Do a' that is in thine heart: turn
15 the host, in the field; and among a'
20 Saul and a' the people that were
22 Likewise a' the men of Israel
25 And a' they of the land came to a
38 hither, a' the chief of the people:
39 a' the people that answered him.
40 unto a' Israel, Be ye on one side,
47 fought against a' his enemies on
52 against the Philistines a' the days
15: 3 and utterly destroy a' that they
6 to a' the children of Israel,
8 destroyed a' the people with the
9 the lambs, and a' that was good.
11 he cried unto the Lord a' night.
16:11 Jesse, Are here a' thy children?
17:11 and a' Israel heard those words of
19 and a' the men of Israel, were
24 And a' the men of Israel, when
46 a' the earth may know that there
47 And a' this assembly shall know
18: 5 in the sight of a' the people,
6 came out of a' cities of Israel,
14 behaved himself wisely in a' his
16 a' Israel and Judah loved David,
22 hath delight in thee and a' his
30 himself more wisely than a'
19: 1 to Jonathan his son, and to a'
5 a great salvation for a' Israel:
7 and Jonathan shewed him a' those
18 told him a' that Saul had done to
24 lay down naked a' that day
24 and a' that night.
20: 6 If thy father at a' miss me, then
6 sacrifice there for a' the family.
22: 1 and a' his father's house heard it,
4 with him a' the while that David
6 in his hand, and a' his servants
7 make you a' captains of thousands,
8 That a' of you have conspired
11 Ahitub, and a' his father's house,
11 they came a' of them to the king.
14 so faithful among a' thy servants
15 nor to a' the house of my father:
15 servant knew nothing of a' this,
16 thou, and a' thy father's house.
22 the death of a' the persons of
23: 8 called a' the people together to war,
20 according to a' the desire of thy
23 knowledge of a' the lurking places
23 a' the thousands of Judah.
24: 2 three thousand chosen men out of a'
25: 1 a' the Israelites were gathered
6 peace be unto a' that thou hast.
7 them, a' the while they were in
9 Nabal according to a' those words
12 again, and came and told him a'
16 by night and day, a' the while
17 against our master, and against a'
21 have I kept a' that this fellow
21 was missed of a' that pertained
22 if I leave of a' that pertain to him
28 not been found in thee a' thy days.

1Sa 25:30 according to a· the good that he
26:12 for they were a· asleep; because
24 deliver me out of a· tribulation.
27:11 manner a· the while he dwelleth
28: 3 dead, and a· Israel had lamented
4 and Saul gathered a· Israel
20 a· along on the earth,
20 eaten no bread a· the day,
20 nor a· the night.
29: 1 gathered together a· their armies
30: 6 soul of a· the people was grieved,
8 them, and without fail recover a·.
16 spread abroad upon a· the earth,
16 dancing, because of a· the great
18 recovered a· that the Amalekites
19 taken to them: David recovered a·.
20 And David took a· the flocks and
22 answered a· the wicked men and
31 in Hebron, and to a· the places
31: 6 armourbearer, and a· his men,
12 A· the valiant men arose,
12 and went a· night, and
2Sa 1:11 them; and likewise a· the men that
2: 9 Benjamin, and over a· Israel.
28 and a· the people stood still, and
29 and his men walked a· that night
29 and went through a· Bithron,
30 gathered a· the people together,
32 Joab and his men went a· night,
3:12 be with thee, to bring about a·
18 out of the hand of a· their enemies.
19 of David in Hebron a· that seemed
21 will gather a· Israel unto my lord
21 over a· that thine heart desireth.
23 Joab and a· the host that was with
25 and to know a· that thou doest.
29 and on a· his father's house;
31 and to a· the people that were
32 of Abner; and a· the people wept.
34 a· the people wept again over him.
35 when a· the people came to cause
36 a· the people took notice of it,
36 whatsoever the king did pleased a·
37 For a· the people and a· Israel
4: 1 and a· the Israelites were troubled.
7 away through the plain a· night.
9 my soul out of a· adversity,
5: 1 came a· the tribes of Israel to
3 So a· the elders of Israel came to
5 years over a· Israel and Judah.
17 a· the Philistines came up to seek
6: 1 a· the chosen men of Israel,
2 arose, and went with a· the people
5 and a· the house of Israel played
5 on a· manner of instruments made
11 Obed-edom, and a· his household.
12 Obed-edom, and a· that pertaineth
14 before the Lord with a· his might;
15 a· the house of Israel brought up
19 And he dealt among a· the people,
19 So a· the people departed every
21 and before a· his house, to appoint
7: 1 round about from a· his enemies;
3 Go, do a· that is in thine heart;
7 a· the places wherein I have walked
7 with a· the children of Israel
9 a· thine enemies out of thy sight,
11 to rest from a· thine enemies.
17 According to a· these words, and
21 thou done a· these great things,
22 God beside thee, according to a·
8: 4 houghed a· the chariot horses,
9 smitten a· the host of Hadadezer,
11 of a· nations which he subdued;
14 throughout a· Edom put he
14 garrisons, and a· they of Edom
15 And David reigned over a· Israel;
15 and justice unto a· his people.
9: 7 a· the land of Saul thy father;
9 a· that pertained to Saul
9 and to a· his house.
11 According to a· that my lord the
12 And a· that dwelt in the house of
10: 7 and a· the host of the mighty men.
9 of a· the choice men of Israel,
17 he gathered a· Israel together,
19 a· the kings that were servants to
11: 1 and his servants with him, and a·
9 with a· the servants of his lord,
18 a· the things concerning the war;
22 shewed David a· that Joab had
12:12 I will do this thing before a· Israel,
16 and lay a· night upon the earth.
29 And David gathered a· the people
31 unto a· the cities of the children of
31 David and a· the people returned
13: 9 said, Have out a· men from me.
21 king David heard of a· these things,
23 Absalom invited a· the king's sons.
25 Nay, my son, let us not a· now go,
27 and a· the king's sons go with him.
29 Then a· the king's sons arose,
30 hath slain a· the king's sons,
31 a· his servants stood by with their
32 they have slain a· the young men
33 that a· the king's sons are dead:
36 and a· his servants wept very sore.
14:19 hand of Joab with thee in a· this?
19 put a· these words in the mouth
20 to know a· things that are in the
25 But in a· Israel there was none to
15: 6 manner did Absalom to a· Israel
10 sent spies throughout a· the tribes
14 David said unto a· his servants
16 went forth, and a· his household
17 forth, and a· the people after him,

2Sa 15:18 a· his servants passed on beside
18 and a· the Cherethites,
18 and a· the Pelethites,
18 and a· the Gittites, six hundred
22 passed over, and a· his men,
22 and a· the little ones
23 a· the country wept with a loud
23 a· the people passed over: the king
23 a· the people passed over, toward
24 Zadok also, and a· the Levites
24 a· the people had done passing out
30 went barefoot: and a· the people
16: 4 thine are a· that pertained unto
6 and at a· the servants
6 of king David: and a· the people
6 and a· the mighty men
8 a· the blood of the house of Saul,
11 to Abishai, and to a· his servants,
14 the king, and a· the people that
15 and a· the people the men
18 and a· the men of Israel, choose,
21 a· Israel shall hear that thou art
21 then shall the hands of a· that
22 concubines in the sight of a· Israel.
23 so was a· the counsel of Ahithophel
17: 2 a· the people that are with him
3 bring back a· the people unto thee:
3 thou seekest is as if a· returned:
3 so a· the people shall be in peace.
4 pleased Absalom well, and a· the
10 a· Israel knoweth that thy father
11 a· Israel be generally gathered
12 of a· the men that are with him
13 a· Israel bring ropes to that city,
14 and a· the men of Israel said,
16 swallowed up, and a· the people
22 arose, and a· the people that were
24 Jordan, he and a· the men of Israel
18: 4 by the gate side, and a· the people
5 And a· the people heard when
5 king gave a· the captains charge
8 scattered over the face of a· the
17 a· Israel fled every one to his tent.
28 and said unto the king, A· is well.
31 avenged thee this day of a· them
32 a· that rise against thee to do
19: 2 into mourning unto a· the people:
5 day the faces of a· thy servants,
6 had lived, and a· we had died
7 worse unto thee than a· the evil
8 unto a· the people, saying, Behold,
8 a· the people came before the king:
9 a· the people were at strife
9 throughout a· the tribes of Israel,
11 the speech of a· Israel is come
14 the heart of a· the men of Judah,
14 Return thou, and a· thy servants.
20 the first this day of a· the house
28 For a· of my father's house were
30 Yea, let him take a·, forasmuch
39 a· the people went over Jordan.
40 and a· the people of Judah
41 behold, a· the men of Israel came to
41 and a· David's men with him,
42 a· the men of Judah answered
42 we eaten at a· of the king's cost?
20: 7 and a· the mighty men:
12 saw that a· the people stood still,
13 a· the people went on after Joab,
14 through a· the tribes of Israel
14 and to Beth-maachah, and a· the
15 a· the people that were with Joab
22 woman went unto a· the people in
23 was over a· the host of Israel:
21: 9 and they fell a· seven together,
14 his father: and they performed a·
22: 1 out of the hand of a· his enemies,
23 a· his judgments were before me:
31 Lord is tried: he is a buckler to a·
23: 5 ordered in a· things, and sure:
5 a· my salvation, and a· my desire,
6 a· of them as thorns thrust away,
39 Hittite: thirty and seven in a·.
24: 2 now through a· the tribes of Israel,
7 and to a· the cities of the Hivites,
8 they had gone through a· the land,
23 A· these things did Araunah, as a
1Ki 1: 3 damsel throughout a· the coasts
9 a· his brethren the king's sons,
9 a· the men of Judah the king's
19 hath called a· the sons of the king,
20 the eyes of a· Israel are upon thee,
25 called a· the king's sons, and the
29 redeemed my soul out of a· distress,
39 and a· the people said, God save
40 a· the people came up after him,
41, 49 a· the guests that were with
2: 2 I go the way of a· the earth: be
3 prosper in a· that thou doest,
4 in truth with a· their heart
4 and with a· their soul,
15 that a· Israel set their faces on me,
26 thou hast been afflicted in a·
44 a· the wickedness which thine
3:13 kings like unto thee a· thy days.
15 made a feast to a· his servants.
28 a· Israel heard of the judgment
4: 1 Solomon was king over a· Israel.
7 had twelve officers over a· Israel,
10 Sochoh, and a· the land of Hepher:
11 Abinadab, in a· the region of Dor;
12 Taanach and Megiddo, and a·
21 Solomon reigned over a· kingdoms
21 Solomon a· the days of his life.
24 a· the region on this side the river,
24 a· the kings on this side the river:

1Ki 4:24 peace on a· sides round about him.
25 Beer-sheba, a· the days of Solomon.
27 for king Solomon, and for a·
30 excelled the wisdom of a· the
30 and a· the wisdom of Egypt.
31 For he was wiser than a· men;
31 was in a· nations round about.
34 of a· people to hear the wisdom
34 Solomon, from a· kings of the earth,
5: 6 servants according to a· that thou
8 I will do a· thy desire concerning
10 trees according to a· his desire.
13 raised a levy out of a· Israel;
6:10 chambers against a· the house,
12 and keep a· my commandments
18 a· was cedar; there was no stone
22 with gold, until he had finished a·
29 carved a· the walls of the house
38 house finished throughout a· the
38 according to a· the fashion of it.
7: 1 thirteen years, and he finished a·
5 a· the doors and posts were square,
9 A· these were of costly stones,
14 cunning to work a· works in brass.
14 Solomon, and wrought a· his work.
23 round a· about, and his height
25 a· their hinder parts were
33 and their spokes, were a· molten.
37 a· of them had one casting, one
40 made an end of doing a· the work
45 and a· these vessels, which Hiram
47 left a· the vessels unweighed,
48 made a· the vessels that pertained
51 a· the work that king Solomon
8: 1 of Israel, and a· the heads of the
2 a· the men of Israel assembled
3 And a· the elders of Israel came,
4 a· the holy vessels that were in the
5 And king Solomon, and a·
14 and blessed a· the congregation
14 (and a· the congregation of Israel
16 I chose no city out of a· the tribes
22 of a· the congregation of Israel,
23 before thee with a· their heart:
38 any man, or by a· thy people Israel,
39 hearts of a· the children of men;)
40 thee a· the days that they live
43 according to a· that the stranger
43 that a· people of the earth may
48 unto thee with a· their heart,
48 and with a· their soul, in the land
50 sinned against thee, and a· their
52 unto them in a· that they call
53 them from among a· the people of
54 had made an end of praying a·
55 a· the congregation of Israel
56 people Israel, according to a· that
56 hath not failed one word of a·
58 unto him, to walk in a· his ways,
59 of his people Israel at a· times,
60 That a· the people of the earth
62 the king, and a· Israel with him,
63 king and a· the children of Israel
65 held a feast, and a· Israel with him,
66 a· the goodness that the Lord had
9: 1 and a· Solomon's desire which he
4 to do according to a· that I have
6 at a· turn from following me,
7 and a byword among a· people:
9 brought upon them a· this evil.
11 gold, according to a· his desire,)
19 a· the cities of store that Solomon
19 and in a· the land of his dominion.
20 And a· the people that were left
10: 2 him of a· that was in her heart.
3 Solomon told her a· her questions:
4 had seen a· Solomon's wisdom,
13 the queen of Sheba a· her desire,
15 and of a· the kings of Arabia,
21 a· king Solomon's drinking vessels
21 a· the vessels of the house
23 exceeded a· the kings of the earth
24 a· the earth sought to Solomon,
29 so for a· the kings of the Hittites,
11: 8 did he for a· his strange wives,
13 will not rend away a· the kingdom;
16 did Joab remain there with a·
25 to Israel a· the days of Solomon,
28 a· the charge of the house of
32 out of a· the tribes of Israel:)
34 prince a· the days of his life
37 to a· that thy soul desireth,
38 hearken unto a· that I command
41 acts of Solomon, and a· that he did,
42 reigned in Jerusalem over a· Israel
12: 1 for a· Israel were come to Shechem
3 and a· the congregation of Israel
12 Jeroboam and a· the people came
16 when a· Israel saw that the king
18 a· Israel stoned him with stones,
20 a· Israel heard that Jeroboam was
20 and made him king over a· Israel:
21 assembled a· the house of Judah,
23 and unto a· the house of Judah
13:11 came and told him a· the works
32 altar in Beth-el, and against a· the
14: 8 who followed me with a· his heart,
9 evil above a· that were before thee:
10 away dung, till it be a· gone.
13 a· Israel shall mourn for him,
18 buried him; and a· Israel mourned
21 out of a· the tribes of Israel.
22 a· that their fathers had done.
24 according to a· the abominations
26 house; he even took away a·:
26 he took away a· the shields of gold

1Ki 14:29 Rehoboam, and a· that he did,
30 Rehoboam and Jeroboam a·
15: 3 walked in a· the sins of his father,
5 commanded him a· the days of his
6 Jeroboam a· the days of his life.
7 acts of Abijam, and a· that he did,
12 a· the idols that his fathers
14 perfect with the Lord a· his days.
16 Asa and Baasha king of Israel a·
18 Asa took a· the silver and the gold
20 and a· Cinneroth,
20 with a· the land of Naphtali.
22 made a proclamation throughout a·
23 The rest of a· the acts of Asa,
23 and a· his might,
23 and a· that he did, and the cities
27 a· Israel laid siege to Gibbethon.
29 smote a· the house of Jeroboam;
31 acts of Nadab, and a· that he did,
32 Asa and Baasha king of Israel a·
33 son of Ahijah to reign over a· Israel
16: 7 for a· the evil that he did in the
11 he slew a· the house of Baasha:
12 destroy a· the house of Baasha,
13 For a· the sins of Baasha, and the
14 the acts of Elah, and a· that he did,
16 wherefore a· Israel made Omri,
17 and a· Israel with him, and they
25 did worse than a· that were before
26 walked in a· the way of Jeroboam
30 of the Lord above a· that were
33 Lord God of Israel to anger than a·
18: 5 land, unto a· fountains of water,
5 and unto a· brooks: peradventure
5 mules alive, that we lose not a·
19 gather to me a· Israel unto mount
20 Ahab sent unto a· the children of
21 Elijah came unto a· the people,
24 by fire, let him be God. And a·
30 And Elijah said unto a· the people,
30 a· the people came near unto him.
36 done a· these things at thy word.
39 And when a· the people saw it,
19: 1 Ahab told Jezebel a· that Elijah
1 how he had slain a· the prophets
18 a· the knees which have not bowed
20: 1 king of Syria gathered a· his host
4 thy saying, I am thine, and a· that
7 king of Israel called a· the elders
8 And a· the elders
8 and a· the people said,
9 A· that thou didst send for thy
10 for handfuls for a· the people that
13 thou seen a· this great multitude?
15 he numbered a· the people,
15 even a· the children of Israel, being
27 numbered, and were a· present,
28 I deliver a· this great multitude
21:26 in following idols, according to a·
22:10, 12 a· the prophets prophesied
17 a· Israel scattered upon the hills,
19 sitting on his throne, and a· the
22 in the mouth of a· his prophets.
23 a· these thy prophets, and the Lord
28 said, If thou return at a· in peace,
39 acts of Ahab, and a· that he did,
39 and a· the cities that he built,
43 in a· the ways of Asa his father;
53 Lord God of Israel, according to a·
2Ki 3: 6 time, and numbered a· Israel.
19 every good tree, and stop a· wells
21 And when a· the Moabites heard
21 a· that were able to put on armour,
25 they stopped a· the wells of water,
25 and felled a· the good trees:
4: 3 abroad of a· thy neighbours,
4 shalt pour into a· those vessels,
13 careful for us with a· this care;
5:12 better than a· the waters of
15 to the man of God, he and a· his
15 there is no God in a· the earth,
21 to meet him, and said, Is a· well?
22 A· is well. My master hath sent
6:24 king of Syria gathered a· his host,
7:13 are as a· the multitude of Israel
13 behold, I say, they are even as a·
15 lo, a· the way was full of garments
8: 4 a· the great things that Elisha
6 Restore a· that was hers,
6 and a· the fruits of the field
21 Zair, and a· the chariots with him:
23 acts of Joram, and a· that he did,
9: 5 Jehu said, Unto which of a· of us?
7 of a· the servants of the Lord,
11 one said unto him, Is a· well?
14 Ramoth-gilead, he and a· Israel,
10: 5 will do a· that thou shalt bid us;
9 to a· the people, Ye be righteous:
11 Jehu slew a· that remained of the
11 in Jezreel, and a· his great men,
17 slew a· that remained unto Ahab
18 gathered a· the people together,
19 unto me a· the prophets of Baal,
19 a· his servants, and a· his priests:
21 And Jehu sent through a· Israel:
21 and a· the worshippers of Baal
22 vestments for a· the worshippers
30 to a· that was in mine heart, thy
31 with a· his heart: for he departed
32 them in a· the coasts of Israel;
33 eastward, a· the land of Gilead,
34 acts of Jehu, and a· that he did,
34 and a· his might,
11: 1 arose and destroyed a· the seed
7 a· you that go forth on the sabbath,
9 a· things that Jehoiada the priest

2Ki 11:14, 18, 19, 20 a· the people of the land
12: 2 the sight of the Lord a· his days
4 A· the money of the dedicated
4 a· the money that cometh into any
9 put therein a· the money
12 of the house of the Lord, and for a·
18 Jehoash king of Judah took a· the
18 a· the gold that was found in the
19 acts of Joash, and a· that he did,
13: 3 the son of Hazael, a· their days.
8 of the acts of Jehoahaz, and a·
11 he departed not from a· the sins of
12 acts of Joash, and a· that he did,
22 Israel a· the days of Jehoahaz.
14: 3 according to a· things as Joash
14 he took a· the gold and silver,
14 and a· the vessels that were found
21 And a· the people of Judah took
24 he departed not from a· the sins
28 acts of Jeroboam, and a· that he
15: 3 a· that his father Amaziah had
6 acts of Azariah, and a· that he did,
16 smote Tiphsah, and a· that were
16 him, therefore he smote it; and a·
18 he departed not a· his days from
20 of a· the mighty men of wealth,
21 acts of Menahem, and a· that he
26 of Pekahiah, and a· that he did,
29 Gilead, and Galilee, a· the land of
31 of the acts of Pekah, and a· that
34 according to a· that his father
36 acts of Jotham, and a· that he did,
16:10 according to a· the workmanship
11 according to a· that king Ahaz
15 of a· the people of the land,
15 a· the blood of the burnt offering,
15 a· the blood of the sacrifice: and
16 to a· that king Ahaz commanded.
17: 5 came up throughout a· the land,
9 them high places in a· their cities,
11 incense in a· the high places,
13 by a· the prophets,
13 and by a· the seers, saying,
13 to a· the law which I commanded
16 a· the commandments of the Lord
16 worshipped a· the host of heaven,
20 Lord rejected a· the seed of Israel,
22 of Israel walked in a· the sins
23 by a· his servants the prophets.
39 deliver you out of the hand of a·
18: 3 to a· that David his father did.
5 was none like him among a· the
12 his covenant, and a· that Moses
13 up against a· the fenced cities
15 gave him a· the silver that was
21 king of Egypt unto a· that trust on
33 delivered at a· his land out of
35 a· the gods of the countries,
19: 4 thy God will hear a· the words
11 of Assyria have done to a· lands,
15 thou alone, of a· the kingdoms
19 of his hand, that a· the kingdoms
24 sole of my feet have I dried up a·
35 behold, they were a· dead corpses.
20:13 a· the house of his precious things,
13 a· the house of his armour,
13 a· that was found in his treasures:
13 nor in a· his dominion, that
15 A· the things that are in mine
17 days come, that a· that is in thine
20 acts of Hezekiah, and a· his might,
21: 3 of Israel; and worshipped a· the
5 altars for a· the host of heaven
7 which I have chosen out of a·
8 observe to do according to a· that
8 a· the law that my servant Moses
11 above a· that the Amorites
14 and a spoil to a· their enemies;
17 the acts of Manasseh, and a· that
21 a· the way that his father walked
24 of the land slew a· them that had
22: 2 in a· the way of David his father,
13 me, and for the people, and for a·
13 a· that which is written concerning
16 thereof, even a· the words
17 me to anger with a· the works of
20 shall not see a· the evil which I
23: 1 unto him a· the elders of Judah
2 and a· the men of Judah
2 a· the inhabitants of Jerusalem
2 the prophets, and a· the people,
2 their ears a· the words of the book
3 and his statutes with a· their heart
3 and a· their soul,
3 a· the people stood to the covenant.
4 a· the vessels that were made for
4 and for a· the host of heaven:
5 and to a· the host of heaven.
8 a· the priests out of the cities
19 And a· the houses also of the high
19 according to a· the acts that he had
20 he slew a· the priests of the high
21 king commanded a· the people,
22 a· the days of the kings of Israel,
24 and a· the abominations that were
25 to the Lord with a· his heart,
25 and with a· his soul,
25 and with a· his might,
25 according to a· the law of Moses;
26 a· the provocations that Manasseh
28 the acts of Josiah, and a· that he
32 to a· that his fathers had done.
37 sight of the Lord, according to a·
24: 3 sins of Manasseh, according to a·
5 of Jehoiakim, and a· that he did,
7 a· that pertained to the king of

2Ki 24:9 sight of the Lord, according to a·
13 carried out thence a· the treasures
13 cut in pieces a· the vessels of gold
14 he carried away a· Jerusalem,
14 a· the princes, and a· the mighty
14 a· the craftsmen and smiths:
16 And a· the men of might, even
16 a· that were strong and apt for war,
19 according to a· that Jehoiakim
25: 1 and a· his host, against Jerusalem,
4 and a· the men of war fled by night
5 and a· his army were scattered
9 and a· the houses of Jerusalem,
10 And a· the army of the Chaldees,
14 a· the vessels of brass wherewith
16 a· these vessels was without weight.
17 upon the chapiter round about, a·
23 when a· the captains of the armies,
26 a· the people, both small and great,
29 continually before him, a· the days
30 every day, a· the days of his life.
1Ch 1:23 A· these were the sons of Joktan.
33 A· these are the sons of Keturah.
2: 4 A· the sons of Judah were five.
6 and Dara: five of them in a·.
23 A· these belonged to the sons of
3: 9 These were a· the sons of David,
4:27 did a· their family multiply, like
33 a· their villages that were round
5:10 a· the east land of Gilead.
16 and in a· the suburbs of Sharon,
17 A· these were reckoned by
20 and a· that were with them: for
6:48 appointed unto a· manner of
49 a· the work of the place most holy,
49 to a· that Moses the servant of God
60 A· their cities throughout their
7: 3 five: a· of them chief men.
5 brethren among a· the families
5 of might, reckoned in a· by their
8 A· these are the sons of Becher.
11 A· these the sons of Jediael, by
40 A· these were the children of Asher,
8:38 A· these were the sons of Azel.
40 A· these are the sons of Benjamin.
9: 1 So a· Israel were reckoned by
9 A· these men were chief of the
22 A· these which were chosen to be
29 a· the instruments of the sanctuary,
10: 6 and a· his house died together.
7 a· the men of Israel that were in
11 And when a· Jabesh-gilead
11 heard a· that the Philistines had
12 They arose, a· the valiant men,
11: 1 Then a· Israel gathered themselves
3 a· the elders of Israel to the king
4 and a· Israel went to Jerusalem,
10 him in his kingdom, and with a·
12:15 when it had overflown a· his
15 put to flight a· them of the valleys,
21 they were a· mighty men of valour,
32 and a· their brethren were at their
33 war, with a· instruments of war,
37 tribe of Manasseh, with a· manner
38 A· these men of war, that could
38 make David king over a· Israel:
38 a· the rest also of Israel were of
13: 2 unto a· the congregation of Israel,
2 that are left in a· the land of Israel,
4 And a· the congregation said that
4 right in the eyes of a· the people.
5 David gathered a· Israel together,
6 And David went up, and a· Israel,
8 and a· Israel played before God
8 with a· their might, and with
14 house of Obed-edom, and a· that he
14: 8 David was anointed king over a·
8 a· the Philistines went up to seek
17 of David went out into a· lands;
17 the fear of him upon a· nations.
15: 3 David gathered a· Israel together
27 and a· the Levites that bare the ark,
28 Thus a· Israel brought up the ark
16: 9 talk ye of a· his wondrous works.
14 his judgments are in a· the earth.
23 Sing unto the Lord, a· the earth;
24 works among a· nations.
25 also is to be feared above a· gods.
26 a· the gods of the people are idols:
30 Fear before him, a· the earth:
32 fields rejoice, and a· that is therein.
36 And a· the people said, Amen, and
40 according to a· that is written in
43 And a· the people departed every
17: 2 David, Do a· that is in thine heart;
6 I have walked with a· Israel, spake
8 a· thine enemies from before thee,
10 I will subdue a· thine enemies.
15 According to a· these words, and
15 according to a· this vision, so did
19 thine own heart, hast thou done a·
19 known a· these great things.
20 God beside thee, according to a·
18: 4 houghed a· the chariot horses,
9 David had smitten a· the host of
10 him a· manner of vessels of gold
11 he brought from a· these nations;
13 a· the Edomites became David's
14 So David reigned over a· Israel,
14 and justice among a· his people.
19: 8 and a· the host of the mighty men.
10 chose out of a· the choice of Israel,
17 told David; and he gathered a·
20: 3 so dealt David with a· the cities of
3 And David and a· the people
21: 3 they not a· my lord's servants?

1Ch 21: 4 and went throughout *a'* Israel, and
5 people unto David. And *a'* they of
12 throughout *a'* the coasts of Israel.
23 for the meat offering; I give it *a'*.
22: 5 of glory throughout *a'* countries:
9 rest from *a'* his enemies round
15 and *a'* manner of cunning men for
17 also commanded *a'* the princes
23: 2 together *a'* the princes of Israel,
29 for *a'* manner of measure and size;
31 And to offer *a'* burnt sacrifices
25: 5 *A'* these were the sons of Heman
6 *A'* these were under the hands of
7 in the songs of the Lord, even *a'*
26: 8 *A'* these of the sons of Obed-edom:
11 *a'* the sons and brethren of Hosah
26 and his brethren were over *a'* the
28 And *a'* that Samuel the seer, and
30 in *a'* the business of the Lord, and
27: 1 *a'* the months of the year, of
3 the chief of *a'* the captains of the
31 *A'* these were the rulers of the
28: 1 assembled *a'* the princes of Israel,
1 the stewards over *a'* the substance
1 and with *a'* the valiant men, unto
4 of Israel chose me before *a'* the
4 to make me king over *a'* Israel:
5 And of *a'* my sons, (for the Lord
8 sight of *a'* Israel the congregation
8 seek for *a'* the commandments of
9 mind: for the Lord searcheth *a'*
9 understandeth *a'* the imaginations
12 of *a'* that he had by the spirit,
12 of *a'* the chambers round about,
13 for *a'* the work of the service of the
13 for *a'* the vessels of service in the
14 of gold, for *a'* instruments
14 of *a'* manner of service;
14 *a'* instruments of silver by weight,
14 *a'* instruments of every kind of
19 *A'* this, said David, the Lord made
19 upon me, even *a'* the works of this
20 thou hast finished *a'* the work
21 they shall be with thee for *a'* the
21 for *a'* manner of workmanship
21 and *a'* the people will be wholly
29: 1 king said unto *a'* the congregation,
2 I have prepared with *a'* my might
2 and *a'* manner of precious stones,
3 of my God, over and above *a'* that
5 for *a'* manner of work to be made
10 Lord before *a'* the congregation:
11 *a'* that is in the heaven and in the
11 thou art exalted as head above *a'*.
12 of thee, and thou reignest over *a'*;
12 great, and to give strength unto *a'*.
14 for *a'* things come of thee, and of
15 sojourners, as were *a'* our fathers:
16 *a'* this store that we have prepared
16 of thine hand, and is *a'* thine own.
17 willingly offered *a'* these things:
19 statutes, and to do *a'* these things,
20 David said to *a'* the congregation,
20 *a'* the congregation blessed the
21 in abundance for *a'* Israel:
23 and *a'* Israel obeyed him.
24 *a'* the princes, and the mighty men,
24 *a'* the sons likewise of king David,
25 exceedingly in the sight of *a'* Israel,
26 son of Jesse reigned over *a'* Israel.
30 With *a'* his reign and his might,
30 *a'* the kingdoms of the countries.
2Ch 1: 2 spake unto *a'* Israel, to the captains
2 and to every governor in *a'* Israel,
3 and *a'* the congregation with him,
17 out horses for *a'* the kings of the
2: 5 for great is our God above *a'* gods.
17 Solomon numbered *a'* the strangers
4: 4 and *a'* their hinder parts were
16 *a'* their instruments, did Huram
18 Solomon made *a'* these vessels in
19 Solomon made *a'* the vessels that
5: 1 *a'* the work that Solomon made
1 *a'* the things that David his father
1 and *a'* the instruments, put he
2 elders of Israel, and *a'* the heads
3 *a'* the men of Israel assembled
4 And *a'* the elders of Israel came;
5 *a'* the holy vessels that were in
6 Solomon, and *a'* the congregation
11 (for *a'* the priests that were present
12 *a'* of them of Asaph, of Heman, of
6: 3 *a'* the congregation of Israel stood.
5 among *a'* the tribes of Israel to
12 of the Lord in the presence of *a'*
13 before *a'* the congregation of Israel,
14 that walk before thee with *a'*
29 or of *a'* thy people Israel, when
30 man according unto *a'* his ways,
33 to *a'* that the stranger calleth to
33 that *a'* people of the earth may
38 return to thee with *a'* their heart
38 *a'* their soul in the land of their
7: 3 when *a'* the children of Israel saw
4 the king and *a'* the people offered
5 the king and *a'* the people dedicated
6 before them, and *a'* Israel stood.
8 seven days, and *a'* Israel with him,
11 *a'* that came into Solomon's heart
17 *a'* that I have commanded thee,
20 and a byword among *a'* nations.
22 he brought *a'* this evil upon them.
8: 4 *a'* the store cities, which he built
6 *a'* the store cities that Solomon
6 *a'* the chariot cities, and the cities
6 *a'* that Solomon desired to build

2Ch 8: 6 *a'* the land of his dominion.
7 As for *a'* the people that were left
16 Now *a'* the work of Solomon was
9: 1 him of *a'* that was in her heart.
2 Solomon told her *a'* her questions:
12 the queen of Sheba *a'* her desire,
14 And *a'* the kings of Arabia and
20 *a'* the drinking vessels of king
20 *a'* the vessels of the house of the
22 Solomon passed *a'* the kings of
23 *a'* the kings of the earth sought
26 he reigned over *a'* the kings from
28 out of Egypt, and out of *a'* lands.
30 Jerusalem over *a'* Israel forty years.
10: 1 *a'* Israel come to make him king.
3 and *a'* Israel came and spake to
12 *a'* the people came to Rehoboam
16 when *a'* Israel saw that the king
11: 3 and to *a'* Israel in Judah and
13 the Levites that were in *a'* Israel
13 to him out of *a'* their coasts.
16 them out of *a'* the tribes of Israel
21 of Absalom above *a'* his wives
23 and dispersed of *a'* his children
23 throughout *a'* the countries of
12: 9 he took *a'*: he carried away also
13 chosen out of *a'* the tribes of Israel,
13: 4 me, thou Jeroboam, and *a'* Israel;
15 smote Jeroboam and *a'* Israel
14: 5 away out of *a'* the cities of Judah
8 *a'* these were mighty men of
14 *a'* the cities round about Gerar;
14 and they spoiled *a'* the cities;
15: 2 Asa, and *a'* Judah and Benjamin;
5 were upon *a'* the inhabitants
6 did vex them with *a'* adversity.
8 *a'* the land of Judah and Benjamin,
9 gathered *a'* Judah and Benjamin,
12 their fathers with *a'* their heart
12 and with *a'* their soul;
15 And *a'* Judah rejoiced at the oath:
15 sworn with *a'* their heart, and
17 of Asa was perfect *a'* his days.
16: 6 Then Asa the king took *a'* Judah;
17: 2 in *a'* the fenced cities of Judah,
5 *a'* Judah brought to Jehoshaphat
9 throughout *a'* the cities of Judah,
10 Lord fell upon *a'* the kingdoms
19 fenced cities throughout *a'* Judah.
18: 9 *a'* the prophets prophesied before
11 *a'* the prophets prophesied so,
16 I did see *a'* Israel scattered upon
18 sitting upon his throne, and *a'* the
21 in the mouth of *a'* his prophets.
27 And he said, Hearken, *a'* ye people.
19: 5 judges in the land throughout *a'*
11 you in *a'* the matters of the Lord;
11 house of Judah, for *a'* the king's
20: 3 a fast throughout *a'* Judah.
4 Lord: even out of *a'* the cities of
13 *a'* Judah stood before the Lord,
15 he said, Hearken ye, *a'* Judah,
18 his face to the ground: and *a'*
29 of God was on *a'* the kingdoms,
21: 2 *a'* these were the sons of
4 slew *a'* his brethren with the sword,
9 and *a'* his chariots with him:
14 and thy wives, and *a'* thy goods:
17 away *a'* the substance that was
18 after *a'* this the Lord smote him
22: 1 to the camp had slain *a'* the eldest.
9 sought the Lord with *a'* his heart.
10 destroyed *a'* the seed royal of the
23: 2 Levites out of *a'* the cities of Judah,
3 And *a'* the congregation made a
5 *a'* the people shall be in the courts
6 *a'* the people shall keep the watch
8 and *a'* Judah did according to
8 *a'* things that Jehoiada the priest
10 he set *a'* the people, every man
13 *a'* the people of the land rejoiced,
16 between *a'* the people, and between
17 *a'* the people went to the house of
20 people, and *a'* the people of the
21 *a'* the people of the land rejoiced:
24: 2 the Lord *a'* the days of Jehoiada
5 gather of *a'* Israel money to repair
7 the house of God; and also *a'* the
10 And *a'* the princes
10 and *a'* the people rejoiced,
14 continually *a'* the days of Jehoiada.
23 destroyed *a'* the princes of the
23 sent *a'* the spoil of them unto the
25: 5 of their fathers, throughout *a'*
7 not with Israel, to wit, with *a'* the
12 the rock, that they *a'* were broken
24 he took *a'* the gold and the silver,
24 and *a'* the vessels that were found
26: 1 *a'* the people of Judah took Uzziah,
4 according to *a'* that his father
14 prepared for them throughout *a'*
20 *a'* the priests, looked upon him,
27: 2 sight of the Lord, according to *a'*
7 acts of Jotham, and *a'* his wars,
28: 6 which were *a'* valiant men;
14 princes and *a'* the congregation.
15 clothed *a'* that were naked among
15 carried *a'* the feeble of them upon
23 the ruin of him, and of *a'* Israel.
26 rest of his acts and of *a'* his ways,
29: 2 according to *a'* that David his
16 brought out *a'* the uncleanness
18 cleansed *a'* the house of the Lord,
18 offering, with *a'* the vessels thereof.
18 table, with *a'* the vessels thereof.
19 Moreover *a'* the vessels, which

2Ch 29:24 make an atonement for *a'* Israel:
24 should be made for *a'* Israel.
28 *a'* the congregation worshipped,
28 *a'* this continued until the burnt
29 and *a'* that were present with him
32 *a'* these were for a burnt offering
34 not flay *a'* the burnt offerings:
36 rejoiced, and *a'* the people,
30: 1 sent to *a'* Israel and Judah, and
2 counsel, and his princes, and *a'*
4 the king and *a'* the congregation.
5 proclamation throughout *a'* Israel,
6 his princes throughout *a'* Israel
14 *a'* the altars for incense took they
22 spake comfortably unto *a'* the
25 And *a'* the congregation of Judah,
25 Levites, and *a'* the congregation
31: 1 Now when *a'* this was finished,
1 *a'* Israel that were present went
1 out of *a'* Judah and Benjamin,
1 they had utterly destroyed them *a'*.
1 *a'* the children of Israel returned,
5 and of *a'* the increase of the field;
5 tithe of *a'* things brought they in
18 genealogy of *a'* their little ones,
18 through *a'* the congregation:
19 to *a'* the males among the priests,
19 and to *a'* that were reckoned by
20 did Hezekiah throughout *a'* Judah,
21 he did it with *a'* his heart, and
32: 4 people together, who stopped *a'*
5 built up *a'* the wall that was broken,
7 for *a'* the multitude that is with
9 Lachish, and *a'* his power with
9 king of Judah, and unto *a'* Judah
13 and my fathers have done unto *a'*
14 among *a'* the gods of those nations
21 off *a'* the mighty men of valour,
22 and from the hand of *a'* other,
23 magnified in the sight of *a'* nations
27 for *a'* manner of pleasant jewels;
28 and stalls for *a'* manner of beasts,
30 Hezekiah prospered in *a'* his works.
31 know *a'* that was in his heart.
33 *a'* Judah and the inhabitants of
33: 3 worshipped *a'* the host of heaven,
5 altars for *a'* the host of heaven in
7 before *a'* the tribes of Israel,
8 *a'* that I have commanded them,
14 captains of war in *a'* the fenced
15 and *a'* the altars that he had built
19 intreated of him, and *a'* his sins,
22 unto *a'* the carved images,
25 the people of the land slew *a'* them
34: 7 and cut down *a'* the idols
7 throughout *a'* the land of Israel,
9 and of *a'* the remnant of Israel,
9 and of *a'* Judah and Benjamin;
12 *a'* that could skill of instruments
13 of *a'* that wrought the work
16 *A'* that was committed to thy
21 *a'* that is written in this book.
24 even *a'* the curses that are written
25 with *a'* the works of their hands;
28 eyes see *a'* the evil that I will
29 gathered together *a'* the elders
30 and *a'* the men of Judah, and the
30 and the Levites, and *a'* the people,
30 he read in their ears *a'* the words
31 his statutes, with *a'* his heart,
31 and with *a'* his soul, to perform
32 *a'* that were present in Jerusalem
33 took away *a'* the abominations
33 out of *a'* the countries
33 *a'* that were present in Israel
33 And *a'* his days they departed not
35: 3 the Levites that taught *a'* Israel,
7 *a'* for the passover offerings,
7 for *a'* that were present,
13 them speedily among *a'* the people.
16 So *a'* the service of the Lord was
18 neither did *a'* the kings of Israel
18 the priests, and the Levites, and *a'*
20 After *a'* this, when Josiah had
24 *a'* Judah and Jerusalem mourned
25 lamented for Josiah: and *a'* the
36:14 Moreover *a'* the chief of the priests,
14 much after *a'* the abominations of
17 for age: he gave them *a'* into
18 *a'* the vessels of the house of God,
18 *a'* these he brought to Babylon.
19 *a'* the palaces thereof with fire,
19 destroyed *a'* the goodly vessels
22 throughout *a'* his kingdom,
23 *A'* the kingdoms of the earth hath
23 there among you of *a'* his people?
Ezra 1: 1 throughout *a'* his kingdom, and
2 hath given me *a'* the kingdoms
3 among you of *a'* his people? his
5 with *a'* them whose spirit God had
6 *a'* they that were about them
6 things, beside *a'* that was willingly
11 *A'* the vessels of gold and of silver
11 *A'* these did Sheshbazzar bring up
2:42 in *a'* an hundred thirty and nine.
58 *A'* the Nethinims, and the children
70 cities, and *a'* Israel in their cities.
3: 5 new moons, and of *a'* the set feasts
8 and *a'* they that were come out
11 *a'* the people shouted with a great
4: 5 their purpose, *a'* the days of Cyrus
20 which have ruled over *a'* countries
5: 7 Unto Darius the king, *a'* peace.
6:12 destroy *a'* kings and people,
17 for a sin offering for *a'* Israel,
20 Levites were purified together, *a'*

Ezr 6:20 and killed the passover for a'
21 again out of captivity, and a' such
7: 6 king granted him a' his request,
13 that a' they of the people of Israel
16 a' the silver and gold that thou
16 find in a' the province of Babylon,
21 decree to a' the treasurers which
25 which may judge a' the people
25 river, a' such as know the laws
28 before a' the king's mighty princes.
8:20 a' of them were expressed by
21 for our little ones, and for a' our
22 hand of our God is upon a' them
22 power and his wrath is against a'
25 lords, and a' Israel there present,
34 a' the weight was written at that
35 twelve bullocks for a' Israel,
35 a' this was a burnt offering unto
9:13 And after a' that is come upon us
10: 3 our God to put away a' the wives,
5 and a' Israel, to swear that they
7 a' the children of the captivity,
8 a' his substance should be
9 a' the men of Judah and Benjamin
9 a' the people sat in the street of
12 a' the congregation answered and
14 rulers of a' the congregation stand,
14 and let a' them which have
16 and a' of them by their names,
17 made an end with a' the men that
44 A' these had taken strange wives:
Ne 4: 6 a' the wall was joined together
8 And conspired a' of them together
12 From a' places whence ye shall
15 we returned a' of us to the wall,
16 were behind a' the house of Judah.
5:13 a' the congregation said, Amen,
16 and a' my servants were gathered
18 ten days store of a' sorts of wine:
18 for a' this required not I the bread
19 my God, for good, according to a'
6: 9 For they a' made us afraid, saying,
16 when a' our enemies heard thereof,
16 a' the heathen that were about us
7:60 A' the Nethinims, and the children
73 and a' Israel, dwelt in their cities;
8: 1 a' the people gathered themselves
2 and a' that could hear with
3 ears of a' the people were attentive
5 book in the sight of a' the people;
5 (for he was above a' the people;)
5 it, a' the people stood up:
6 And a' the people answered, Amen,
9 taught the people, said unto a' the
9 For a' the people wept, when they
11 the Levites stilled a' the people,
12 And a' the people went their way
13 the chief of the fathers of a'
15 and proclaim in a' their cities, and
17 And a' the congregation of them
9: 2 separated themselves from a'
5 name, which is exalted above a'
6 the heaven of heavens, with a'
6 and a' things that are therein,
6 the seas, and a' that is therein,
6 preservest them a'; and the host
10 wonders upon Pharaoh, and on a'
10 and on a' the people of his land:
25 possessed houses full of a' goods,
32 covenant and mercy, let not a'
32 our fathers, and on a' thy people,
33 Howbeit thou art just in a' that is
38 of a' this we make a sure covenant,
10:28 and a' they that had separated
29 a' the commandments of the Lord
33 and for a' the work of the house
35 and the firstfruits of a' fruit
35 of a' trees, year by year,
37 and the fruit of a' manner of trees,
37 tithes in a' the cities of our tillage.
11: 2 the people blessed a' the men,
6 A' the sons of Perez that dwelt at
18 A' the Levites in the holy city
20 were in a' the cities of Judah,
24 at the king's hand in a' matters
12:27 the Levites out of a' their places,
47 a' Israel in the days of Zerubbabel,
13: 3 Israel a' the mixed multitude.
6 a' this time was not I at Jerusalem:
8 I cast forth a' the household stuff
12 brought a' Judah the tithe of the
15 grapes, and figs, and a' manner of
16 and a' manner of ware, and sold
18 a' this evil upon us, and upon this
20 sellers of a' kind of ware lodged
26 God made him king over a' Israel:
27 unto you to do a' this great evil,
30 cleansed I them from a' strangers,
Es 1: 3 made a feast unto a' his princes
5 feast unto a' the people that were
8 had appointed to a' the officers
13 the king's manner toward a' that
16 but also to a' the princes,
16 and to a' the people that are
16 in a' the provinces of the king
17 queen shall come abroad unto a'
18 and Media say this day unto a'
20 throughout a' his empire,
20 a' the wives shall give to their
22 into a' the king's provinces,
2: 3 appoint officers in a' the provinces
3 together a' the fair young virgins
15 in the sight of a' them that looked
17 loved Esther above a' the women,
17 in his sight more than a' the
18 a great feast unto a' his princes

Es 3: 1 set his seat above a' the princes
2 a' the king's servants, that were in
6 sought to destroy a' the Jews that
8 the people in a' the provinces of
8 laws are diverse from a' people;
12 a' that Haman had commanded
13 posts into a' the king's provinces,
13 and to cause to perish, a' Jews,
14 was published unto a' people, that
4: 1 Mordecai perceived a' that was
7 told him of a' that had happened
11 A' the king's servants, and the
13 house, more than a' the Jews.
16 a' the Jews that are present in
17 a' that Esther had commanded
5:11 a' the things wherein the king had
13 Yet a' this availeth me nothing,
14 wife and a' his friends unto him,
6:10 fail of a' that thou hast spoken.
13 told Zeresh his wife and a' his
8: 5 are in a' the king's provinces:
9 to a' that Mordecai commanded
11 perish, a' the power of the people
12 Upon one day in a' the provinces
13 was published unto a' people,
9: 2 throughout a' the provinces of the
2 the fear of them fell upon a' people.
3 And a' the rulers of the provinces,
4 throughout a' the provinces:
5 the Jews smote a' their enemies
20 things, and sent letters unto a'
20 Jews that were in a' the provinces
24 enemy of a' the Jews, had devised
26 for a' the words of this letter,
27 upon a' such as joined themselves
29 the Jew, wrote with a' authority,
30 sent the letters unto a' the Jews,
10: 2 And a' the acts of his power and of
3 and speaking peace to a' his seed.
Job 1: 3 greatest of a' the men of the east.
5 according to the number of them a':
10 a' that he hath on every side?
11 and touch a' that he hath, and he
12 a' that he hath is in thy power;
22 In a' this Job sinned not,
2: 4 yea, a' that a man hath will he give
10 In a' this did not Job sin with his
11 three friends heard of a' this evil
4:14 which made a' my bones to shake.
8:13 the paths of a' that forget God;
9:28 I am afraid of a' my sorrows,
12: 9 Who knoweth not in a' these that
10 and the breath of a' mankind.
13: 1 Lo, mine eye hath seen a' this,
4 ye are a' physicians of no value.
27 narrowly unto a' my paths;
14:14 a' the days of my appointed time
15:20 travaileth with pain a' his days,
16: 2 miserable comforters are ye a'.
7 made desolate a' my company.
17: 7 dim by reason of sorrow, and a' my
10 But as for you a', do ye return,
19:19 A' my inward friends abhorred me:
20:26 A' darkness shall be hid in his
24:24 taken out of the way as a' other,
27: 3 A' the while my breath is in me,
12 a' ye yourselves have seen it;
28: 3 and searcheth out a' perfection:
21 it is hid from the eyes of a' living,
29:19 dew lay a' night upon my branch.
30:23 the house appointed for a' living.
31: 4 my ways, and count a' my steps?
12 would root out a' mine increase.
33: 1 and hearken to a' my words.
11 in the stocks, he marketh a' my
29 Lo, a' these things worketh God
34:15 A' flesh shall perish together,
19 they a' are the work of his hands.
21 of man, and he seeth a' his goings.
36:19 gold, nor a' the forces of strength.
37: 7 every man; that a' men may know
38: 7 a' the sons of God shouted for joy?
18 earth? declare if thou knowest it a'.
40:20 a' the beasts of the field play.
41:34 He beholdeth a' high things:
34 over a' the children of pride.
42:11 there unto him a' his brethren,
11 and a' his sisters,
11 and a' they that had been of
11 and comforted him over a' the evil
15 in a' the land were no women
Ps 2:12 Blessed are a' they that put their
3: 7 thou hast smitten a' mine enemies
5: 5 thou hatest a' workers of iniquity.
11 let a' those that put their trust in
6: 6 a' the night make I my bed to
7 old because of a' mine enemies.
8 from me, a' ye workers of iniquity;
10 Let a' mine enemies be ashamed
7: 1 from a' them that persecute me,
8: 1 is thy name in a' the earth!
6 hast put a' things under his feet:
7 A' sheep and oxen, yea, and the
9 is thy name in a' the earth!
9: 1 forth a' thy marvellous works.
14 that I may shew forth a' thy praise
17 and a' the nations that forget God.
10: 4 God is not in a' his thoughts.
5 as for a' his enemies, he puffeth
12: 3 Lord shall cut off a' flattering lips,
14: 3 They are a' gone aside,
3 they are a' together become
4 Have a' the workers of iniquity
16: 3 in whom is a' my delight.
18:title from the hand of a' his enemies,
22 a' his judgments were before me,

Ps 18:30 he is a buckler to a' those that
19: 4 is gone out through a' the earth,
20: 3 Remember a' thy offerings, and
4 heart, and fulfil a' thy counsel.
20: 5 the Lord fulfil a' thy petitions.
21: 8 shall find out a' thine enemies:
22: 7 A' they that see me laugh me to
14 out like water, and a' my bones,
17 I may tell a' my bones: they look
23 praise him; a' ye the seed of Jacob,
23 fear him, a' ye the seed of Israel.
27 A' the ends of the world shall
27 and a' the kindreds of the nations
29 A' they that be fat upon earth
29 a' they that go down to the dust
23: 6 mercy shall follow me a' the days
25: 5 on thee do I wait a' the day.
10 A' the paths of the Lord are mercy
18 and my pain; and forgive a' my
22 O God, out of a' his troubles.
26: 7 and tell of a' thy wondrous works.
27: 4 in the house of the Lord a' the days
31:11 reproach among a' mine enemies,
23 O love the Lord, a' ye his saints:
24 heart, a' ye that hope in the Lord.
32: 3 through my roaring a' the day long.
11 a' ye that are upright in heart.
33: 4 Lord is right; and a' his works
6 a' the host of them by the breath
8 Let a' the earth fear the Lord:
8 let a' the inhabitants of the world
11 of his heart to a' generations.
13 from heaven; he beholdeth a' the
14 a' the inhabitants of the earth.
15 hearts alike; he considereth a'
34: 1 I will bless the Lord at a' times:
4 delivered me from a' my fears.
6 saved him out of a' his troubles.
17 them out of a' their troubles.
19 Lord delivereth him out of them a'.
20 He keepeth a' his bones: not one
35:10 A' my bones shall say, Lord, who
28 and of thy praise a' the day long.
38: 6 I go mourning a' the day long.
9 Lord, a' my desire is before thee;
12 imagine deceits a' the day long.
39: 8 me from a' my transgressions:
12 a sojourner, as a' my fathers
40:16 Let a' those that seek thee rejoice
41: 3 make a' his bed in his sickness.
7 A' that hate me whisper together
42: 7 a' thy waves and thy billows are
44: 8 In God we boast a' the day long,
17 A' this is come upon us; yet have
22 sake are we killed a' the day long;
45: 8 A' thy garments smell of myrrh,
13 The king's daughter is a' glorious
16 make princes in a' the earth.
17 thy name to be remembered in a'
47: 1 O clap your hands, a' ye people;
2 is a great King over a' the earth.
7 God is the King of a' the earth:
49: 1 Hear this, a' ye people;
1 give ear, a' ye inhabitants
11 dwelling places to a' generations;
50:11 a' the fowls of the mountains:
51: 9 from my sins, and blot out a' mine
52: 4 Thou lovest a' devouring words,
54: 7 delivered me out of a' trouble:
56: 5 a' their thoughts are against me
57: 2 that performeth a' things for me.
5, 11 glory be above a' the earth.
59: 5 awake to visit a' the heathen:
8 have a' the heathen in derision.
62: 3 ye shall be slain a' of you: as a
8 Trust in him at a' times;
64: 8 a' that see them shall flee away.
9 And a' men shall fear, and shall
10 a' the upright in heart shall glory.
65: 2 unto thee shall a' flesh come.
5 of a' the ends of the earth, and
66: 1 noise unto God, a' ye lands:
4 A' the earth shall worship thee,
16 Come and hear, a' ye that fear God,
67: 2 saving health among a' nations.
3, 5 let a' the people praise thee.
7 and a' the ends of the earth shall
69:19 adversaries are a' before thee.
70: 4 Let a' those that seek thee rejoice
71: 8 praise and with thy honour a' the
15 salvation a' the day; for I know
24 righteousness a' the day long:
72: 5 throughout a' generations.
11 a' kings shall fall down before
11 a' nations shall serve him.
17 in him: a' nations shall call
73:14 For a' the day long have I been
27 thou hast destroyed a' them that
28 that I may declare a' thy works.
74: 3 even a' that the enemy hath done
8 burned up a' the synagogues of God
17 set a' the borders of the earth:
75: 3 a' the inhabitants thereof are
8 a' the wicked of the earth shall
10 A' the horns of the wicked also
76: 9 to save a' the meek of the earth.
11 your God: let a' that be round
77:12 I will meditate also of a' thy work,
78:14 a' the night with a light of fire.
32 For a' this they sinned still, and
38 and did not stir up a' his wrath.
51 smote a' the firstborn in Egypt;
79:13 forth thy praise to a' generations.
80:12 so that a' they which pass by the
82: 5 a' the foundations of the earth are
6 a' of you are children of the most

Ps 82: 8 for thou shalt inherit a' nations.
83:11 a' their princes as Zebah, and as
18 art the most high over a' the
85: 2 thou hast covered a' their sin.
3 hast taken away a' thy wrath:
86: 5 unto a' them that call upon thee.
9 A' nations whom thou hast made
12 Lord my God, with a' my heart:
87: 2 than a' the dwellings of Jacob.
7 be there: a' my springs are in thee.
88: 7 afflicted me with a' thy waves.
89: 1 thy faithfulness to a' generations.
4 up thy throne to a' generations.
7 of a' them that are about him.
16 name shall they rejoice a' the day:
40 hast broken down a' his hedges;
41 A' that pass by the way spoil him:
42 made a' his enemies to rejoice.
47 hast thou made a' men in vain?
50 reproach of a' the mighty people;
90: 1 dwelling place in a' generations.
9 a' our days are passed away in
14 rejoice and be glad a' our days.
92: 7 when a' the workers of iniquity do
9 a' the workers of iniquity shall be
94: 4 and a' the workers of iniquity boast
15 a' the upright in heart shall follow
95: 3 and a great King above a' gods.
96: 1 sing unto the Lord, a' the earth.
3 his wonders among a' people.
4 he is to be feared above a' gods.
5 a' the gods of the nations are idols:
9 fear before him, a' the earth.
12 be joyful, and a' that is therein:
12 a' the trees of the wood rejoice
97: 6 and a' the people see his glory.
7 a' they that serve graven images,
7 of idols: worship him, a' ye gods.
9 art high above a' the earth:
9 thou art exalted far above a' gods.
98: 3 a' the ends of the earth have seen
4 noise unto the Lord, a' the earth:
99: 2 and he is high above a' the people.
100: 1 noise unto the Lord, a' ye lands.
5 truth endureth to a' generations.
101: 8 destroy a' the wicked of the land;
8 that I may cut off a' wicked doers
102: 8 enemies reproach me a' the day;
12 remembrance unto a' generations.
15 a' the kings of the earth thy
24 are throughout a' generations.
26 but thou shalt endure: yea, a' of
103: 1 a' that is within me, bless his holy
2 and forget not a' his benefits:
3 Who forgiveth a' thine iniquities;
3 who healeth a' thy diseases;
6 judgment for a' that are oppressed.
19 and his kingdom ruleth over a'.
21 Bless ye the Lord, a' ye his hosts;
22 Bless the Lord, a' his works
22 in a' places of his dominion:
104:20 wherein a' the beasts of the forest
24 in wisdom hast thou made them a':
27 These wait a' upon thee; that
105: 2 talk ye of a' his wondrous works.
21 of his house, and ruler of a' his
31 flies, and lice in a' their coasts.
35 eat up a' the herbs in their land,
36 also a' the firstborn in their land,
36 the chief of a' their strength.
106: 2 who can shew forth a' his praise?
3 doeth righteousness at a' times.
31 unto a' generations for evermore.
46 a' those that carried them
48 and let a' the people say, Amen.
107:18 abhorreth a' manner of meat;
42 a' iniquity shall stop her mouth.
108: 5 and thy glory above a' the earth;
109:11 extortioner catch a' that he hath;
111: 2 Lord are great, sought out of a'
7 a' his commandments are sure.
10 a good understanding have a'
113: 4 The Lord is high above a' nations,
116:11 said in my haste, A' men are liars.
12 unto the Lord for a' his benefits
14 in the presence of a' his people.
18 the Lord now in the presence of a'
117: 1 O praise the Lord, a' ye nations:
1 praise him, a' ye people.
118:10 A' nations compassed me about:
119: 6 unto a' thy commandments.
13 With my lips have I declared a'
14 as much as in a' riches.
20 unto thy judgments at a' times.
63 of a' them that fear thee, and of
86 A' thy commandments are faithful:
90 faithfulness is unto a' generations:
91 for a' are thy servants.
97 it is my meditation a' the day.
99 than a' my teachers: for thy
118 trodden down a' them that err
119 a' the wicked of the earth like
128 I esteem a' thy precepts
128 concerning a' things to be right;
151 a' thy commandments are truth.
168 for a' my ways are before thee.
172 for a' thy commandments are
121: 7 shall preserve thee from a' evil:
128: 5 Jerusalem a' the days of thy life.
129: 5 Let them a' be confounded and
130: 8 Israel from a' his iniquities.
132: 1 David, and a' his afflictions:
134: 1 Lord, a' ye servants of the Lord,
135: 5 that our Lord is above a' gods.
6 in the seas, and a' deep places.
9 Pharaoh, and upon a' his servants.

Ps 135:11 and a' the kingdoms of Canaan:
13 O Lord, throughout a' generations.
136:25 Who giveth food to a' flesh: for
138: 4 A' the kings of the earth shall
139: 3 art acquainted with a' my ways.
16 book a' my members were written,
143: 5 the days of old; I meditate on a'
12 destroy a' them that afflict my soul:
144:13 garners may be full, affording a'
145: 9 The Lord is good to a': and his
9 mercies are over a' his works.
10 A' thy works shall praise thee, O
13 throughout a' generations.
14 The Lord upholdeth a' that fall,
14 raiseth up a' those that be bowed
15 The eyes of a' wait upon thee; and
17 Lord is righteous in a' his ways,
17 and holy in a' his works.
18 The Lord is nigh unto a' them that
18 to a' that call upon him in truth.
20 preserveth a' them that love him:
20 but a' the wicked will he destroy.
21 and let a' flesh bless his holy name
146: 6 earth, the sea, and a' that therein
10 God, O Zion, unto a' generations.
147: 4 of the stars; he calleth them a'
148: 2 Praise ye him, a' his angels:
2 praise ye him, a' his hosts.
3 praise him, a' ye stars of light.
9 Mountains, and a' hills;
9 fruitful trees, and a' cedars:
10 Beasts, and a' cattle; creeping
11 Kings of the earth, and a' people;
11 princes, and a' judges of the earth:
14 the praise of a' his saints; even of
149: 9 written: this honour have a'
Pr 1:13 shall find a' precious substance,
14 us; let us a' have one purse:
25 have set at nought a' my counsel,
30 of my counsel: they despised a'
3: 5 in the Lord with a' thine heart;
6 In a' thy ways acknowledge him,
9 and with the firstfruits of a'
15 precious than rubies: and a' the
17 ways of pleasantness, and a' her
4: 7 a' thy getting get understanding.
22 find them, and health to a' their
23 Keep thy heart with a' diligence;
26 of thy feet, and let a' thy ways be
5:14 I was almost in a' evil in the midst
21 and he pondereth a' his goings.
6:31 shall give a' the substance of his
8: 8 A' the words of my mouth are in
9 a' plain to him that understandeth,
11 than rubies; and a' the things
16 and nobles, even a' the judges of
36 a' they that hate me love death.
10:12 strifes: but love covereth a' sins.
14:23 In a' labour there is profit: but
15:15 A' the days of the afflicted are
16: 2 A' the ways of a man are clean in
4 hath made a' things for himself:
11 a' the weights of the bag are his
17:17 A friend loveth at a' times, and a
18: 1 intermeddleth with a' wisdom.
19: 7 A' the brethren of the poor do hate
20: 8 away a' evil with his eyes.
27 candle of the Lord, searching a'
21:26 He coveteth greedily a' the day
22: 2 the Lord is the maker of them a'.
23:17 fear of the Lord a' the day long.
24: 4 a' precious and pleasant riches.
31 it was a' grown over with thorns,
26:10 great God that formed a' things
28: 5 the Lord understand a' things
29:11 A fool uttereth a' his mind: but a
12 to lies, a' his servants are wicked.
30:4 established a' the ends of the earth?
27 king, yet go they forth a' of them
31: 8 for the dumb in the cause of a'
12 and not evil a' the days of her life.
21 a' her household are clothed with
29 but thou excellest them a'.
Ec 1: 2 vanity of vanities; a' is vanity.
3 What profit hath a man of a' his
7 A' the rivers run into the sea;
8 A' things are full of labour; man
13 by wisdom concerning a' things
14 I have seen a' the works that are
14 a' is vanity and vexation of spirit.
16 a' they that have been before me
2: 3 heaven a' the days of their life.
5 trees in them of a' kind of fruits:
7 a' that were in Jerusalem before
8 instruments, and that of a' sorts.
9 increased more than a' that were
10 my heart rejoiced in a' my labour:
10 was my portion of a' my labour.
11 Then I looked on a' the works that
11 a' was vanity and vexation of
14 one event happeneth to them a'.
16 days to come shall a' be forgotten.
17 me: for a' is vanity and vexation
18 I hated a' my labour which I had
19 he have rule over a' my labour
20 to despair of a' the labour which
22 what hath man of a' his labour,
23 For a' his days are sorrows, and
3:13 enjoy the good of a' his labour,
19 yea, they have a' one breath; so
19 above a beast: for a' is vanity.
20 A' go unto one place;
20 a' are of the dust,
20 and a' turn to dust again.
4: 1 and considered a' the oppressions
4 Again, I considered a' travail, and

Ec 4: 8 is there no end of a' his labour;
15 a' the living which walk under the
16 There is no end of a' the people,
16 of a' that have been before them:
5: 9 the profit of the earth is for a':
16 that in a' points as he came, so
17 A' his days also he eateth in
18 to enjoy the good of a' his labour
18 the sun a' the days of his life,
6: 2 for his soul of a' that he desireth,
6 no good: do not a' go to one place?
7 A' the labour of man is for his
12 a' the days of his vain life which
7: 2 for that is the end of a' men;
15 A' things have I seen in the days
18 God shall come forth of them a'.
21 heed unto a' words that are spoken;
23 A' this have I proved by wisdom:
28 among a' those have I not found.
8: 9 A' this have I seen, and applied
17 Then I beheld a' the work of God,
9: 1 a' this I considered in my heart
1 even to declare a' this,
1 or hatred by a' that is before them.
2 A' things come alike to a': there
3 This is an evil among a' things
3 that there is one event unto a':
4 joined to a' the living there is hope:
9 wife whom thou lovest a' the days
9 a' the days of thy vanity: for that
11 and chance happeneth to them a'.
10:19 but money answereth a' things.
11: 5 the works of God who maketh a'.
8 many years, and rejoice in them a';
8 many. A' that cometh is vanity.
9 that for a' these things God will
12: 8 saith the preacher; a' is vanity.
Ca 1:13 unto me; he shall lie a' night
3: 6 with a' powders of the merchant?
8 They a' hold swords, being expert
4: 4 bucklers, a' shields of mighty men.
7 Thou art a' fair, my love; there is
10 thine ointments than a' spices!
14 with a' trees of frankincense;
14 aloes, with a' the chief spices:
7:13 are a' manner of pleasant fruits,
8: 7 a' the substance of his house for
Isa 1:25 away thy dross, and take away a'
2: 2 the hills; and a' nations shall flow
13 upon a' the cedars of Lebanon,
13 and upon a' the oaks of Bashan,
2:14 And upon a' the high mountains,
14 upon a' the hills that are lifted up
16 And upon a' the ships of Tarshish,
16 and upon a' pleasant pictures.
4: 5 upon a' the glory shall be a defence.
5:25 For a' this his anger is not turned
28 are sharp, and a' their bows bent,
7:19 come, and shall rest a' of them in
19 of the rocks, and upon a' thorns,
19 and upon a' bushes.
24 a' the land shall become briers
25 And on a' hills that shall be digged
8: 7 king of Assyria, and a' his glory:
7 come up over a' his channels,
7 and go over a' his banks:
9 give ear, a' ye of far countries:
12 confederacy, to a' them to whom
9: 9 And a' the people shall know,
12 with open mouth. For a' this
17 speaketh folly. For a' this his
21 Judah. For a' this his anger is
10: 4 For a' this his anger is not turned
14 that are left, have I gathered a'
23 in the midst of a' the land.
11: 9 destroy in a' my holy mountain:
12: 5 this is known in a' the earth.
13: 7 Therefore shall a' hands be faint,
14: 9 even a' the chief ones of the earth;
9 thrones a' the kings of the nations.
10 A' they shall speak and say unto
18 A' the kings of the nations,
18 even a' of them, lie in glory,
26 stretched out upon a' the nations.
15: 2 on a' their heads shall be baldness,
16:14 be contemned, with a' that great
18: 3 A' ye inhabitants of the world,
6 a' the beasts of the earth shall
19: 8 shall mourn, and a' they that cast
10 a' that make sluices and ponds for
21: 9 is fallen; and a' the graven images
16 and a' the glory of Kedar shall fail:
22: 3 A' thy rulers are fled together,
3 a' that are found in thee are
24 him a' the glory of his father's
24 and the issue, a' vessels of small
24 the vessels of cups, even to a' the
23: 9 to stain the pride of a' glory,
9 a' the honourable of the earth.
17 with a' the kingdoms of the world
24: 7 a' the merryhearted do sigh.
11 a' joy is darkened, the mirth of
25: 6 hosts make unto a' people a feast
7 covering cast over a' people,
7 vail that is spread over a' nations.
8 wipe away tears from off a' faces;
8 shall he take away from off a'
26:12 hast wrought a' our works in us.
14 made a' their memory to perish.
15 far unto a' the ends of the earth.
27: 9 a' the fruit to take away his sin;
9 maketh a' the stones of the altar
28: 8 For a' tables are full of vomit and
24 the plowman plow a' day to sow?
29: 7 of a' the nations that fight against
7 even a' that fight against her and

Isa 29: 8 so shall the multitude of *a·* the
11 *a·* is become unto you as the words
20 *a·* that watch for iniquity are cut
30:18 blessed are *a·* they that wait for
31: 3 fall down, and they *a·* shall fail
32:13 upon *a·* the houses of joy in the
20 are ye that sow beside *a·* waters,
34: 1 let the earth hear, and *a·* that is
1 and *a·* things that come forth of it.
2 of the Lord is upon *a·* nations,
2 and his fury upon *a·* their armies:
4 And *a·* the host of heaven shall be
4 and *a·* their host shall fall down,
12 *a·* her princes shall be nothing.
36: 1 Assyria came up against *a·* the
6 of Egypt to *a·* that trust in him.
20 among *a·* the gods of these lands,
37:11 *A·* lands by destroying them
16 of *a·* the kingdoms of the earth:
17 hear *a·* the words of Sennacherib,
18 have laid waste *a·* the nations,
20 that *a·* the kingdoms of the earth
25 *a·* the rivers of the besieged places.
36 behold, they were *a·* dead corpses.
38:13 so will he break *a·* my bones:
15 *a·* my years in the bitterness of my
16 men live, and in *a·* these things
17 cast *a·* my sins behind thy back.
20 *a·* the days of our life in the house
39: 2 and *a·* the house of his armour,
2 *a·* that was found in his treasures:
2 nor in *a·* his dominion, that
4 *A·* that is in mine house have they
6 that *a·* that is in thine house,
40: 2 Lord's hand double for *a·* her sins.
5 the Lord shall be revealed, and *a·*
6 *A·* flesh is grass,
6 and *a·* the goodliness thereof
17 *A·* nations before him are as
26 he calleth them *a·* by names by
41:11 *a·* they that were incensed against
29 they are *a·* vanity; their works
42:10 to the sea, and *a·* that is therein;
15 and hills, and dry up *a·*
22 they are *a·* of them snared in holes,
43: 9 Let *a·* the nations be gathered
14 have brought down *a·* their nobles,
44: 9 graven image are *a·* of them vanity;
11 *a·* his fellows shall be ashamed:
11 of men: let them *a·* be gathered
24 the Lord that maketh *a·* things;
28 my shepherd, and shall perform *a·*
45: 7 I the Lord do *a·* these things.
12 *a·* their host have I commanded.
13 and I will direct *a·* his ways:
16 *a·* of them: they shall go to
22 ye saved, *a·* the ends of the earth:
24 *a·* that are incensed against him
25 shall *a·* seed of Israel be justified,
46: 3 *a·* the remnant of the house of
10 and I will do *a·* my pleasure:
48: 6 Thou hast heard, see *a·* this;
14 *A·* ye, assemble yourselves, and
49: 9 pastures shall be in *a·* high places.
11 I will make *a·* my mountains a
18 *a·* these gather themselves
18 surely clothe thee with them *a·*.
26 *a·* flesh shall know that I the Lord
50: 2 Is my hand shortened at *a·*, that
9 *a·* shall wax old as a garment;
11 Behold, *a·* ye that kindle a fire,
51: 3 Zion: he will comfort *a·* her
18 to guide her among *a·* the sons
20 fainted, they lie at the head of *a·* the
52:10 bare his holy arm in the eyes of *a·*
10 *a·* the ends of the earth shall see
53: 6 *A·* we like sheep have gone astray;
6 laid on him the iniquity of us *a·*.
54:12 *a·* thy borders of pleasant stones.
13 *a·* thy children shall be taught of
55:12 *a·* the trees of the field shall clap
56: 7 an house of prayer for *a·* people.
9 *A·* ye beasts of the field, come to
9 yea, *a·* ye beasts in the forest.
10 they are *a·* ignorant,
10 they are *a·* dumb dogs,
11 they *a·* look to their own way,
57:13 wind shall carry them *a·* away;
58: 3 pleasure, and exact *a·* your labours.
59:11 We roar *a·* like bears, and mourn
60: 4 eyes round about, and see: *a·* they
6 *a·* they from Sheba shall come:
7 *A·* the flocks of Kedar shall be
14 and *a·* they that despised thee
21 people also shall be *a·* righteous:
61: 2 our God; to comfort *a·* that mourn;
9 *a·* that see them shall acknowledge
11 spring forth before *a·* the nations.
62: 2 and *a·* kings thy glory:
63: 3 and I will stain *a·* my raiment.
7 according to *a·* that the Lord
9 In *a·* their affliction he was afflicted,
9 carried them *a·* the days of old.
64: 6 we are *a·* as an unclean thing,
6 and *a·* our righteousnesses
6 are as filthy rags; and we *a·* do
8 we *a·* are the work of thy hand.
9 beseech thee, we are *a·* thy people.
11 and *a·* our pleasant things are laid
65: 2 spread out my hands *a·* the day
5 a fire that burneth *a·* the day.
8 that I may not destroy them *a·*.
25 destroy in *a·* my holy mountain,
66: 2 For *a·* those things hath mine
2 *a·* those things have been, saith
10 glad with her, *a·* ye that love her:

Isa 66:10 with her, *a·* ye that mourn for her:
16 will the Lord plead with *a·* flesh:
18 gather *a·* nations and tongues;
20 *a·* your brethren for an offering
20 out of *a·* nations upon horses,
23 to another, shall *a·* flesh come
24 shall be an abhorring unto *a·* flesh.
Jer 1: 7 go to *a·* that I shall send thee,
14 upon *a·* the inhabitants of the land.
15 I will call *a·* the families of the
15 against *a·* the walls thereof round
15 and against *a·* the cities of Judah.
16 touching *a·* their wickedness,
17 unto them *a·* that I command thee:
2: 3 *a·* that devour him shall offend;
4 the Lord, O house of Jacob, and *a·*
24 *a·* they that seek her will not
29 ye *a·* have transgressed against
34 secret search, but upon *a·* these.
3: 7 after she had done *a·* these things,
8 when for *a·* the causes whereby
10 *a·* this her treacherous sister Judah
17 *a·* the nations shall be gathered
4:24 and *a·* the hills moved lightly.
25 *a·* the birds of the heavens were
:26 and *a·* the cities thereof
5:16 sepulchre, they are *a·* mighty men.
19 our God *a·* these things unto us?
6:15 nay, they were not at *a·* ashamed,
28 They are *a·* grievous revolters,
28 and iron; they are *a·* corrupters.
7: 2 word of the Lord, *a·* ye of Judah,
10 to do *a·* these abominations?
13 ye have done *a·* these works,
15 I have cast out *a·* your brethren,
23 walk ye in *a·* the ways that I have
25 even sent unto you *a·* my servants
27 speak *a·* these words unto them;
8: 2 and *a·* the host of heaven, whom
3 rather than life by *a·* the residue
3 which remain in *a·* the places
12 they were not at *a·* ashamed,
16 the land, and *a·* that is in it; the
9: 2 for they be *a·* adulterers, an
25 I will punish *a·* them which are
26 *a·* that are in the utmost corners,
26 for *a·* these nations are
26 and *a·* the house of Israel are
10: 7 *a·* the wise men of the nations,
7 and in *a·* their kingdoms, there is
9 are *a·* the work of cunning men.
16 for he is the former of *a·* things;
20 and *a·* my cords are broken:
21 *a·* their flocks shall be scattered.
11: 4 do them, according to *a·* which I
6 Proclaim *a·* these words in the
8 them *a·* the words of this covenant,
12 at *a·* in the time of their trouble.
12: 1 wherefore are *a·* they happy that
9 assemble *a·* the beasts of the field,
12 are come upon *a·* high places
14 against *a·* mine evil neighbours,
13:13 *a·* the inhabitants of this land,
13 *a·* the inhabitants of Jerusalem,
19 be carried away captive *a·* of it,
14:22 for thou hast made *a·* these things.
15: 4 to be removed into *a·* kingdoms of
13 and that for *a·* thy sins,
13 even in *a·* thy borders.
16:10 shew this people *a·* these words,
10 *a·* this great evil against us?
15 from *a·* the lands whither he had
17 mine eyes are upon *a·* their ways:
17: 3 and *a·* thy treasures to the spoil,
3 for sin, throughout *a·* thy borders.
9 heart is deceitful above *a·* things,
13 *a·* that forsake thee shall be
19 and in *a·* the gates of Jerusalem;
20 kings of Judah, and *a·* Judah,
20 *a·* the inhabitants of Jerusalem,
18:23 thou knowest *a·* their counsel
19: 8 because of *a·* the plagues thereof.
13 place of Tophet, because of *a·* the
13 incense unto *a·* the host of heaven,
14 house; and said to *a·* the people,
15 and upon *a·* her towns
15 *a·* the evil that I have pronounced
20: 4 to thyself, and to *a·* thy friends:
4 give *a·* Judah into the hand of the
5 deliver *a·* the strength of this city,
5 and *a·* the labours thereof,
5 and *a·* the precious things thereof,
5 *a·* the treasures of the kings of
6 *a·* that dwell in thine house shall
6 and *a·* thy friends, to whom thou
10 *A·* my familiars watched for my
21: 2 us according to *a·* his wondrous
14 devour *a·* things round about it.
22:20 for *a·* thy lovers are destroyed.
22 wind shall eat up *a·* thy pastors,
22 confounded for *a·* thy wickedness.
23: 3 the remnant of my flock out of *a·*
8 and from *a·* countries whither I
9 *a·* my bones shake; I am like a
14 are *a·* of them unto me as Sodom,
15 gone forth into *a·* the land.
32 shall not profit this people at *a·*,
24: 9 removed into *a·* the kingdoms of
9 *a·* places whither I shall
25: 1 Jeremiah concerning *a·* the people
2 spake unto *a·* the people of Judah,
2 *a·* the inhabitants of Jerusalem,
4 you *a·* his servants the prophets,
9 take *a·* the families of the north,
9 *a·* these nations round about,
13 that land *a·* my words which I

Jer 25:13 even *a·* that is written in this book,
13 prophesied against *a·* the nations.
15 this fury at my hand, and cause *a·*
17 and made *a·* the nations to drink,
19 and his princes, and *a·* his people;
20 And *a·* the mingled people,
20 and *a·* the kings of the land of Uz,
20 and *a·* the kings of the land of the
22 And *a·* the kings of Tyrus,
22 and *a·* the kings of Zidon,
23 Buz, and *a·* that are in the utmost
24 And *a·* the kings of Arabia,
24 and *a·* the kings of the
25 And *a·* the kings of Zimri,
25 and *a·* the kings of Elam,
25 and *a·* the kings of the Medes,
26 And *a·* the kings of the north, far
26 and *a·* the kingdoms of the world,
29 upon *a·* the inhabitants of the
30 thou against them *a·* these words,
30 *a·* the inhabitants of the earth.
31 he will plead with *a·* flesh; he will
26: 2 speak unto *a·* the cities of Judah,
2 *a·* the words that I command thee
6 to *a·* the nations of the earth.
7 and *a·* the people heard Jeremiah
8 *a·* that the Lord had commanded
8 him to speak unto *a·* the people,
8 prophets and *a·* the people took
9 And *a·* the people were gathered
11 and to *a·* the people, saying, This
12 spake Jeremiah unto *a·* the princes
12 and to *a·* the people,
12 *a·* the words that ye have heard.
15 speak *a·* these words in your ears.
16 the princes and *a·* the people unto
17 elders of the land, and spake to *a·*
18 to *a·* the people of Judah, saying,
19 king of Judah and *a·* Judah
19 put him at *a·* to death?
20 to *a·* the words of Jeremiah:
21 the king, with *a·* his mighty men,
21 and *a·* the princes, heard his
27: 6 given *a·* these lands into the hand
12 king of Judah according to *a·*
16 the priests and to *a·* this people,
20 and *a·* the nobles of Judah and
28: 1 the priests and of *a·* the people,
3 *a·* the vessels of the Lord's house,
4 with *a·* the captives of Judah, that
5 in the presence of *a·* the people
6 vessels of the Lord's house, and *a·*
7 and in the ears of *a·* the people;
11 in the presence of *a·* the people,
11 from the neck of *a·* nations within
14 upon the neck of *a·* these nations,
29: 1 and to *a·* the people whom
4 *a·* that are carried away captives,
13 search for me with *a·* your heart.
14 will gather you from *a·* the nations,
14 from *a·* the places whither I have
16 *a·* the people that dwelleth in this,
18 to *a·* the kingdoms of the earth,
18 among *a·* the nations whither I
20 *a·* ye of the captivity, whom I have
22 curse by *a·* the captivity of Judah
25 in thy name unto *a·* the people
25 the priest, and to *a·* the priests,
31 to *a·* them of the captivity, saying,
30: 2 Write thee *a·* the words that I have
6 *a·* faces are turned into paleness?
11 I make a full end of *a·* nations
14 *A·* thy lovers have forgotten thee;
16 Therefore *a·* they that devour thee
16 *a·* thine adversaries, every one
16 and *a·* that prey upon thee will I
20 will punish *a·* that oppress them.
31: 1 God of *a·* the families of Israel,
12 shall not sorrow any more at *a·*.
24 in *a·* the cities thereof together,
34 for they shall *a·* know me, from
37 I will also cast off *a·* the seed of
37 Israel for *a·* that they have done,
40 *a·* the fields unto the brook of
32:12 before *a·* the Jews that sat in the
19 upon *a·* the ways of the sons of men:
23 of *a·* that thou commandest
23 caused *a·* this evil to come upon
27 I am the Lord, the God of *a·* flesh:
32 *a·* the evil of the children of Israel
37 gather them out of *a·* countries,
42 brought *a·* this great evil upon this
42 upon them *a·* the good that I
33: 5 and for *a·* whose wickedness I
8 cleanse them from *a·* their iniquity,
8 I will pardon *a·* their iniquities,
9 before *a·* the nations of the earth,
9 which shall hear *a·* the good that
9 tremble for *a·* the goodness
9 *a·* the prosperity that I procure
12 and in *a·* the cities thereof, shall
34: 1 king of Babylon, and *a·* his army,
1 and *a·* the kingdoms of the earth
1 and *a·* the people, fought against
1 and against *a·* the cities thereof,
6 the prophet spake *a·* these words
7 against *a·* the cities of Judah that
8 a covenant with *a·* the people
10 Now when *a·* the princes,
10 *a·* the people, which had entered
17 be removed into *a·* the kingdoms
34:19 and *a·* the people of the land,
35: 3 *a·* his sons, and the whole house
7 *a·* your days ye shall dwell in tents;
8 in *a·* that he hath charged us,
8 no wine *a·* our days, we, our wives,

Jer 35:10 according to *a'* that Jonadab our
15 *a'* my servants the prophets,
17 bring upon Judah and upon *a'* the
17 Jerusalem *a'* the evil that I have
18 and kept *a'* his precepts,
18 and done according unto *a'*
36: 2 and write therein *a'* the words
2 and against *a'* the nations,
3 of Judah will hear *a'* the evil
4 from the mouth of Jeremiah *a'* the
6 read them in the ears of *a'* Judah
8 son of Neriah did according to *a'*
9 to *a'* the people in Jerusalem,
9 *a'* the people that came from the
10 house, in the ears of *a'* the people.
11 the book *a'* the words of the Lord,
12 and, lo, *a'* the princes sat there,
12 of Hananiah, and *a'* the princes.
13 declared unto them *a'* the words
14 Therefore *a'* the princes sent Jehudi
16 when they had heard *a'* the words,
16 surely tell the king of *a'* these words.
17 didst thou write *a'* these words
18 He pronounced *a'* these words
20 *a'* the words in the ears of the king.
21 and in the ears of *a'* the princes
23 until *a'* the roll was consumed in
24 servants that heard *a'* these words.
28 and write in it *a'* the former words
31 the men of Judah, *a'* the evil that
32 mouth of Jeremiah *a'* the words
37:21 *a'* the bread in the city was spent.
38: 1 had spoken unto *a'* the people,
4 and the hands of *a'* the people,
9 *a'* that they have done to Jeremiah
22 *a'* the women that are left in the
23 they shall bring out *a'* thy wives
27 came *a'* the princes unto Jeremiah,
27 according to *a'* these words that
39: 3 And *a'* the princes of the king
3 with *a'* the residue of the princes
4 saw them, and *a'* the men of war,
6 king of Babylon slew *a'* the nobles
13 *a'* the king of Babylon's princes;
40: 1 among *a'* that were carried away
4 behold, *a'* the land is before thee:
7 when *a'* the captains of the forces
11 *a'* the Jews that were in Moab,
11 and that were in *a'* the countries,
12 Even *a'* the Jews returned
12 out of *a'* places whither they
13 son of Kareah, and *a'* the captains
15 *a'* the Jews which are gathered
41: 3 Ishmael also slew *a'* the Jews that
6 to meet them, weeping *a'* along
9 had cast *a'* the dead bodies
10 *a'* the residue of the people
10 and *a'* the people that remained
11 and *a'* the captains of the forces
11 heard of *a'* the evil that Ishmael
12 Then they took *a'* the men,
13 *a'* the people which were with
13 son of Kareah, and *a'* the captains
14 So *a'* the people that Ishmael had
16 son of Kareah, and *a'* the captains
16 him, *a'* the remnant of the people
42: 1 Then *a'* the captains of the forces,
1 and *a'* the people from the least
2 thy God, even for *a'* this remnant;
5 if we do not even according to *a'*
8 and *a'* the captains of the forces
8 and *a'* the people from the least
17 So shall it be with *a'* the men
20 according unto *a'* that the Lord
43: 1 end of speaking unto *a'* the people
1 *a'* the words of the Lord their God,
1 him to them, even *a'* these words,
2 and *a'* the proud men, saying unto
4 *a'* the captains of the forces,
4 and *a'* the people, obeyed not
5 son of Kareah, and *a'* the captains
5 took *a'* the remnant of Judah,
5 were returned from *a'* nations,
44: 1 concerning *a'* the Jews which dwell
2 *a'* the evil that I have brought
2 and upon *a'* the cities of Judah;
4 you *a'* my servants the prophets,
8 a curse and a reproach among *a'*
11 for evil, and to cut off *a'* Judah.
12 and they shall *a'* be consumed,
15 *a'* the men which knew that their
15 other gods, and *a'* the women
15 great multitude, even *a'* the people
18 we have wanted *a'* things,
20 Jeremiah said unto *a'* the people,
20 to the women, and to *a'* the people
24 Jeremiah said unto *a'* the people,
24 *a'* the women, Hear the word
24 of the Lord, *a'* Judah that are in
26 *a'* Judah that dwell in the land of
26 in *a'* the land of Egypt, saying,
27 and *a'* the men of Judah that are
28 and *a'* the remnant of Judah,
45: 5 I will bring evil upon *a'* flesh,
5 unto thee for a prey in *a'* places
46:25 and *a'* them that trust in him:
28 make a full end of *a'* the nations
47: 2 the land, and *a'* that is therein;
2 and *a'* the inhabitants of the land
4 cometh to spoil *a'* the Philistines,
48:17 *A'* ye that are about him,
17 bemoan him; and *a'* ye that know
24 *a'* the cities of the land of Moab,
31 and I will cry out for *a'* Moab;
37 *a'* the hands shall be cuttings,
38 upon *a'* the housetops of Moab,

Jer 48:39 and a dismaying to *a'* them about
49: 5 from *a'* those that be about thee;
13 and *a'* the cities thereof shall be
17 shall hiss at *a'* the plagues thereof.
26 *a'* the men of war shall be cut off
29 *a'* their vessels, and their camels;
32 I will scatter into *a'* winds them
32 their calamity from *a'* sides
36 them toward *a'* those winds;
50: 7 *A'* that found them have devoured
10 *a'* that spoil her shall be satisfied,
13 be astonished, and hiss at *a'* her
14 *a'* ye that bend the bow, shoot at
21 *a'* that I have commanded thee.
27 Slay *a'* her bullocks; let them go
29 the archers against Babylon: *a'* ye
29 according to *a'* that she hath done,
30 *a'* her men of war shall be cut off
32 shall devour *a'* round about him.
33 and *a'* that took them captives
37 and upon *a'* the mingled people
51: 3 young men; destroy ye utterly *a'*
7 that made *a'* the earth drunken:
19 for he is the former of *a'* things:
24 to *a'* the inhabitants of Chaldea
24 *a'* their evil that they have done
25 which destroyest *a'* the earth:
28 and *a'* the rulers thereof,
28 and *a'* the land of his dominion.
47 *a'* her slain shall fall in the midst
48 and *a'* that is therein, shall sing
49 shall fall the slain of *a'* the earth.
52 through *a'* her land the wounded
60 a book *a'* the evil that should come
60 *a'* these words that are written
61 and shalt read *a'* these words;
52: 2 of the Lord, according to *a'* that
4 *a'* his army, against Jerusalem,
7 up, and *a'* the men of war fled,
8 *a'* his army was scattered from
10 slew also *a'* the princes of Judah
13 and *a'* the houses of Jerusalem,
13 *a'* the houses of the great men,
14 And *a'* the army of the Chaldeans,
14 down *a'* the walls of Jerusalem
17 carried *a'* the brass . . . to Babylon.
18 the bowls, and the spoons, and *a'*
20 the brass of *a'* these vessels was
22 chapiters round about, *a'* of brass.
23 *a'* the pomegranates upon the
30 *a'* the persons were four thousand
33 before him *a'* the days of his life.
34 until the day of his death, *a'* the
La 1: 2 among *a'* her lovers she hath none
2 *a'* her friends have dealt
3 *a'* her persecutors overtook her
4 *a'* her gates are desolate; her
6 daughter of Zion *a'* her beauty is
7 *a'* her pleasant things that she had
8 *a'* that honoured her despise her,
10 hath spread out his hand upon *a'*
11 *A'* her people sigh, they seek bread;
12 to you, *a'* ye that pass by? behold,
13 me desolate and faint *a'* the day.
15 trodden under foot *a'* my mighty
18 hear, I pray you, *a'* people,
21 *a'* mine enemies have heard of my
22 *a'* their wickedness come before
22 thou hast done unto me for *a'* my
2: 2 The Lord hath swallowed up *a'*
3 fierce anger *a'* the horn of Israel:
4 and slew *a'* that were pleasant to
5 hath swallowed up *a'* her palaces:
15 *A'* that pass by clap their hands at
16 *A'* thine enemies have opened their
3: 3 he turneth his hand against me *a'*
14 I was a derision to *a'* my people;
14 and their song *a'* the day.
34 feet *a'* the prisoners of the earth,
46 *A'* our enemies have opened their
60 Thou hast seen *a'* their vengeance
60, 61 *a'* their imaginations against
62 device against me *a'* the day.
4:12 and *a'* the inhabitants of the world,
Eze 3: 7 *a'* the house of Israel are impudent
10 *a'* my words that I shall speak
5: 4 forth into *a'* the house of Israel.
9 because of *a'* thine abominations.
10 will I scatter into *a'* the winds.
11 with *a'* thy detestable things,
11 and with *a'* thine abominations,
12 third part into *a'* the winds,
14 in the sight of *a'* that pass by.
6: 6 In *a'* your dwellingplaces the
9 in *a'* their abominations.
11 Alas for *a'* the evil abominations
13 in *a'* the tops of the mountains,
13 sweet savour to *a'* their idols.
14 in *a'* their habitations: and they
7: 3 upon thee *a'* thine abominations.
8 and will recompense thee for *a'*
12 wrath is upon *a'* the multitude
14 trumpet, even to make *a'* ready;
14 battle: for my wrath is upon *a'*
16 *a'* of them mourning, every one
17 *A'* hands shall be feeble,
17 and *a'* knees shall be weak
18 shame shall be upon *a'* faces,
18 and baldness upon *a'* their heads.
8:10 *a'* the idols of the house of Israel,
9: 4 cry for *a'* the abominations that
8 destroy *a'* the residue of Israel
11:15 and *a'* the house of Israel wholly,
18 shall take away *a'* the detestable
18 and *a'* the abominations thereof
25 *a'* the things that the Lord had

Eze 12:10 and *a'* the house of Israel that
14 toward every wind *a'* that are
14 to help him, and *a'* his bands;
16 may declare *a'* their abominations
19 be desolate from *a'* that is therein,
19 of *a'* them that dwell therein.
13:18 that sew pillows to *a'* armholes,
14: 3 face: should I be enquired of at *a'*
6 faces from *a'* your abominations.
11 polluted any more with *a'* their
22 concerning *a'* that I have brought
23 cause *a'* that I have done in it,
16: 4 thou wast not salted at *a'*,
4 nor swaddled at *a'*.
22 And in *a'* thine abominations and
23 to pass after *a'* thy wickedness,
30 seeing thou doest *a'* these things,
33 They give gifts to *a'* whores: but
33 givest thy gifts to *a'* thy lovers,
36 *a'* the idols of thy abominations,
37 I will gather *a'* thy lovers, with
37 and *a'* them that thou hast loved,
37 with *a'* them that thou hast hated;
37 they may see *a'* thy nakedness.
43 hast fretted me in *a'* these things;
43 above *a'* thine abominations.
47 more than they in *a'* thy ways.
51 in *a'* thine abominations which
54 *a'* that thou hast done, in that thou
57 and *a'* that are round about her,
63 toward thee for *a'* that thou
17: 9 in *a'* the leaves of her spring,
18 and hath done *a'* these things, he
21 And *a'* his fugitives
21 with *a'* his bands shall fall by the
21 be scattered toward *a'* winds:
23 shall dwell *a'* fowl of every wing;
24 And *a'* the trees of the field shall
18: 4 Behold, *a'* souls are mine; as the
13 not live: he hath done *a'* these
14 that seeth *a'* his father's sins which
19 kept *a'* my statutes, and hath
21 will turn from *a'* his sins that he
21 and keep *a'* my statutes, and do
22 *A'* his transgressions that he
23 at *a'* that the wicked should die?
24 according to *a'* the abominations
24 *A'* his righteousness that he hath
28 and turneth away from *a'*
30 from *a'* your transgressions;
31 from you *a'* your transgressions,
20: 6, 15 which is the glory of *a'* lands:
26 to pass through the fire *a'* that
28 high hill, and *a'* the thick trees,
31 pollute yourselves with *a'* your
32 into your mind shall not be at *a'*,
40 there shall *a'* the house of Israel,
40 *a'* of them in the land, serve me:
40 oblations, with *a'* your holy things.
43 your ways, and *a'* your doings,
43 for *a'* your evils that ye have
47 and *a'* faces from the south to the
48 *a'* flesh shall see that I the Lord
21: 4 *a'* flesh from the south to the north:
5 That *a'* flesh may know that I
7 melt, and *a'* hands shall be feeble,
7 faint, and *a'* knees shall be weak
12 be upon *a'* the princes of Israel:
15 the sword against *a'* their gates,
24 so that in *a'* your doings your sins
22: 2 shalt shew her *a'* her abominations.
4 and a mocking to *a'* countries.
18 Israel is to me become dross: *a'*
19 Because ye are *a'* become dross,
23: 6 *a'* of them desirable young men,
7 *a'* them that were the chosen men
7 with *a'* on whom she doted:
7 with *a'* their idols she defiled
12 *a'* of them desirable young men.
15 *a'* of them princes to look to, after
23 and *a'* the Chaldeans, Pekod, and
23 and *a'* the Assyrians with them:
23 *a'* of them desirable young men,
23 *a'* of them riding upon horses.
29 shall take away *a'* thy labour,
48 that *a'* women may be taught
24:24 *a'* that he hath done shall ye do:
25: 6 *a'* thy despite against the land of
8 Judah is like unto *a'* the heathen;
26:11 shall he tread down *a'* thy streets:
16 Then *a'* the princes of the sea shall
17 terror to be on *a'* that haunt it!
27: 5 made *a'* thy ship boards of fir trees
9 *a'* the ships of the sea with their
12 of the multitude of *a'* kind of riches;
18 for the multitude of *a'* riches; in
21 Arabia, and *a'* the princes of Kedar,
22 of *a'* spices, and with *a'* precious
24 merchants in *a'* sorts of things,
27 and *a'* thy men of war,
27 and in *a'* thy company
29 And *a'* that handle the oar,
29 the mariners, and *a'* the pilots
34 and *a'* thy company in the midst
35 *A'* the inhabitants of the isles
28:18 earth in the sight of *a'* them that
19 *A'* they that know thee among the
24 of *a'* that are round about them,
26 judgments upon *a'* those that
29: 2 against him, and against *a'* Egypt:
4 and *a'* the fish of thy rivers shall
5 wilderness, thee and *a'* the fish
6 And *a'* the inhabitants of Egypt
7 break, and rend *a'* their shoulder:
30: 5 Lydia, and *a'* the mingled people,
8 *a'* her helpers shall be destroyed.

Eze 30:12 land waste, and a' that is therein,
31: 4 unto a' the trees of the field.
5 his height was exalted above a' the
6 A' the fowls of heaven made their
6 a' the beasts of the field bring
6 his shadow dwelt a' great nations.
9 so that a' the trees of Eden,
12 in a' the valleys his branches are
12 broken by a' the rivers of the land;
12 a' the people of the earth are gone
13 a' the fowls of the heaven remain,
13 and a' the beasts of the field shall
14 To the end that none of a' the trees
14 a' that drink water: for
14 they are a' delivered unto death,
15 a' the trees of the field fainted for
16 and a' the trees of Eden,
16 a' that drink water, shall be
18 is Pharaoh and a' his multitude,
32: 4 cause a' the fowls of the heaven
8 A' the bright lights of heaven
12 terrible of the nations, a' of them:
12 and a' the multitude thereof
13 destroy also a' the beasts thereof
15 smite a' them that dwell therein,
16 Egypt, and for a' her multitude,
20 draw her and a' her multitudes.
22 is there and a' her company:
22 a' of them slain, fallen by the
23 round about her grave: a' of them
24 Elam and a' her multitude round
24 her grave, a' of them slain, fallen
25 the slain with a' her multitude:
25 are round about him: a' of them
26 Tubal, and a' her multitude:
26 a' of them uncircumcised, slain
29 her kings, and a' her princes,
30 princes of the north, a' of them,
30 and a' the Zidonians, which are
31 comforted over a' his multitude,
31 Pharaoh and a' his army slain by
32 Pharaoh and a' his multitude,
33:13 iniquity, a' his righteousnesses
29 land most desolate because of a'
34: 5 meat to a' the beasts of the field,
6 through a' the mountains,
6 was scattered upon a' the face
12 and will deliver them out of a'
13 and in a' the inhabited places of
21 and pushed a' the diseased with
35: 8 and in a' thy rivers, shall they fall
12 I have heard a' thy blasphemies
36: 5 and against a' Idumea, which have
5 with the joy of a' their heart,
10 multiply men upon you, a' the
10 Israel, even a' of it: and the cities
24 gather you out of a' countries,
25 from a' your filthiness,
25 and from a' your idols,
29 you from a' your uncleannesses:
33 you from a' your iniquities
34 in the sight of a' that passed by.
37:16 of Ephraim, and for a' the house
22 one king shall be king to them a':
22 two kingdoms any more at a':
23 out of a' their dwellingplaces,
24 they a' shall have one shepherd:
38: 4 thee forth, and a' thine army,
4 a' of them clothed
4 with a' sorts of armour,
4 a' of them handling swords:
5 a' of them with shield and helmet:
6 Gomer, and a' his bands;
6 north quarters, and a' his bands:
7 prepare for thyself, thou, and a'
8 they shall dwell safely a' of them.
9 thou, and a' thy bands, and many
11 a' of them dwelling without walls,
13 Tarshish, with a' the young lions
15 a' of them riding upon horses,
20 and a' creeping things that creep
20 a' the men that are upon the face
21 him throughout a' my mountains,
39: 4 mountains of Israel, thou, and a'
11 bury Gog and a' his multitude:
13 Yea, a' the people of the land shall
18 a' of them fatlings of Bashan.
20 men, and with a' men of war,
21 and a' the heathen shall see my
23 so fell they a' by the sword.
26 and a' their trespasses whereby
40: 4 upon a' that I shall shew thee;
4 declare a' that thou seest to the
41:17 and by a' the wall round about
19 it was made through a' the house
42:11 and a' their goings out were both
43:11 ashamed of a' that they have done,
11 and a' the forms thereof,
11 and a' the ordinances thereof,
11 and a' the forms thereof,
11 and a' the laws thereof:
11 and a' the ordinances thereof,
44: 5 hear with thine ears a' that I say
5 concerning a' the ordinances of
5 a' the laws thereof; and mark well
6 suffice you of a' your abominations,
7 because of a' your abominations.
14 for a' the service thereof, and
14 for a' that shall be done therein.
24 my statutes in a' mine assemblies;
30 And the first of a' the firstfruits
30 of a' things, and
30 of every oblation of a', of every sort
45: 1 a' the borders thereof round about.
16 A' the people of the land shall give
17 a' solemnities of the house of Israel:

Eze 45:22 and for a' the people of the land
47:12 shall grow a' trees for meat,
48:13 a' the length shall be five and
19 it out of a' the tribes of Israel.
20 A' the oblation shall be five and
Da 1: 4 skilful in a' wisdom, and cunning
15 fatter in flesh than a' the children
17 knowledge and skill in a' learning
17 understanding in a' visions and
19 among them a' was found none like
20 And in a' matters of wisdom and
20 them ten times better than a'
20 astrologers that were in a' his
2:12 a' the wise men of Babylon.
38 made thee ruler over them a'.
39 shall bear rule over a' the earth.
40 in pieces and subdueth a' things:
40 and as iron that breaketh a' these,
44 and consume a' these kingdoms,
48 over a' the wise men of Babylon.
3: 2, 3 a' the rulers of the provinces,
5 dulcimer, and a' kinds of musick,
7 a' the people heard the sound of
7 and a' kinds of musick, a' the
10 and a' kinds of musick, shall fall
15 psaltery, and dulcimer, and a'
4: 1 a' people, nations, and languages,
1 that dwell in a' the earth;
6 in a' the wise men of Babylon
11 thereof to the end of a' the earth:
12 and in it was meat for a':
12 a' flesh was fed of it.
18 forasmuch as a' the wise men
20 the sight thereof to a' the earth;
21 much, and in it was meat for a';
28 A' this came upon the king
35 And a' the inhabitants of the earth
37 a' whose works are truth,
5: 8 came in a' the king's wise men:
19 a' people, nations, and languages,
22 though thou knewest a' this;
23 and whose are a' thy ways,
6: 7 A' the presidents of the kingdom,
24 and brake a' their bones in pieces
25 a' people, nations, and languages,
25 that dwell in a' the earth;
7: 7 it was diverse from a' the beasts
14 a' people, nations, and languages,
16 and asked him the truth of a' this.
19 was diverse from a' the others,
23 shall be diverse from a' kingdoms,
27 a' dominions shall serve and obey
9: 6 and to a' the people of the land.
7 and unto a' Israel, that are near,
7 a' the countries whither thou hast
11 a' Israel have transgressed thy law,
13 Moses, a' this evil is come upon us:
14 God is righteous in a' his works
16 according to a' thy righteousness,
16 a reproach to a' that are about us.
10: 3 did I anoint myself at a',
11: 2 shall be far richer than they a':
2 up a' against the realm of Grecia.
37 he shall magnify himself above a'.
43 a' the precious things of Egypt:
12: 7 a' these things shall be finished.
Ho 2:11 also cause a' her mirth to cease,
11 sabbaths, and a' her solemn feasts.
5: 2 I have been a rebuker of them a'.
7: 2 I remember a' their wickedness:
4 They are a' adulterers, as an oven
6 their baker sleepeth a' the night;
7 They are a' hot as an oven,
7 a' their kings are fallen: there is
10 Lord their God, nor seek him for a'
9: 4 a' that eat thereof shall be polluted:
8 is a snare of a fowler in a' his
15 A' their wickedness is in Gilgal:
15 a' their princes are revolters.
10:14 a' thy fortresses shall be spoiled,
11: 7 most High, none at a' would exalt
12: 8 in a' my labours they shall find
13: 2 a' of it the work of the craftsmen:
10 that may save thee in a' thy cities?
15 the treasure of a' pleasant vessels.
14: 2 Take away a' iniquity, and receive
Joe 1: 2 ear, a' ye inhabitants of the land.
5 and howl, a' ye drinkers of wine,
12 even a' the trees of the field,
13 come, lie a' night in sackcloth,
14 and a' the inhabitants of the land
19 the flame hath burned a' the trees
2: 1 let a' the inhabitants of the land
6 a' faces shall gather blackness.
12 ye even to me with a' your heart,
28 pour out my spirit upon a' flesh;
3: 2 I will also gather a' nations,
4 and a' the coasts of Palestine?
9 let a' the men of war draw near;
11 and come, a' ye heathen, and
12 judge a' the heathen round about.
18 a' the rivers of Judah shall flow
Am 1:11 the sword, and did cast off a' pity,
2: 3 and will slay a' the princes thereof
3: 2 of a' the families of the earth:
2 punish you for a' your iniquities.
5 and have taken nothing at a'?
4: 6 you cleanness of teeth in a' your
6 want of bread in a' your places:
5:16 Wailing shall be in a' streets;
16 they shall say in a' the highways,
17 in a' vineyards shall be wailing:
6: 8 up the city with a' that is therein.
7:10 land is not able to bear a' his
8:10 a' your songs into lamentation;
10 bring up sackcloth upon a' loins,

Am 9: 1 cut them in the head, a' of them;
5 a' that dwell therein shall mourn:
9 house of Israel among a' nations,
10 A' the sinners of my people shall
12 and of a' the heathen, which are
13 wine, and a' the hills shall melt.
Ob 7 A' the men of thy confederacy have
15 Lord is near upon a' the heathen:
16 a' the heathen drink continually,
Jon 2: 3 a' thy billows and thy waves
Mic 1: 2 Hear, a' ye people; hearken,
2 O earth, and a' that therein is:
5 transgression of Jacob is a' this,
7 And a' the graven images thereof
7 and a' the hires thereof shall be
7 and a' the idols thereof will I lay
10 it not at Gath, weep ye not at a':
2:12 assemble, O Jacob, a' of thee;
3: 7 yea, they shall a' cover their lips;
9 judgment, and pervert a' equity.
4: 5 a' people will walk every one in the
5: 9 and a' thine enemies shall be cut
11 throw down a' thy strong holds:
6:16 are kept, and a' the works of the
7: 2 among men: they a' lie in wait
16 be confounded at a' their might:
19 cast a' their sins into the depths
Na 1: 3 will not at a' acquit the wicked:
4 maketh it dry, and drieth up a'
5 world, and a' that dwell therein.
2: 9 out of a' the pleasant furniture.
10 pain is in a' loins,
10 faces of them a' gather blackness.
3: 1 city! it is a' full of lies and
7 that a' they that look upon thee
10 pieces at the top of a' the streets:
10 and a' her great men were bound
12 A' thy strongholds shall be like fig
19 a' that hear the bruit of thee shall
Hab 1: 9 They shall come a' for violence:
15 take up a' of them with the angle,
2: 5 gathereth unto him a' nations,
5 and heapeth unto him a' people:
6 Shall not a' these take up a parable
8 a' the remnant of the people shall
8, 17 city, and of a' that dwell therein.
19 no breath at a' in the midst of it.
20 let a' the earth keep silence
Zep 1: 2 a' things from off the land,
4 hand upon Judah, and upon a'
8 and a' such as are clothed with
9 will I punish a' those that leap on
11 a' the merchant people are cut
11 down; a' they that bear
18 a speedy riddance of a' them that
2: 3 the Lord, a' ye meek of the earth,
11 famish a' the gods of the earth;
11 one from his place, even a' the
14 in the midst of her, a' the beasts
3: 7 and corrupted a' their doings.
8 even a' my fierce anger:
8 for a' the earth shall be devoured
9 that they may a' call upon the name
11 not be ashamed for a' thy doings,
14 glad and rejoice with a' the heart,
19 time I will undo a' that afflict thee:
20 name and a praise among a' people
Hag 1:11 upon a' the labour of the hands.
12 with a' the remnant of the people,
14 the spirit of a' the remnant of the
2: 4 strong, a' ye people of the land,
7 And I will shake a' nations,
7 and the desire of a' nations
17 hail in a' the labours of your hands;
Zec 2:13 Be silent, O a' flesh, before the
4: 2 and behold a candlestick a' of gold,
5: 6 resemblance through a' the earth.
6: 5 before the Lord of a' the earth.
7: 5 unto a' the people of the land,
5 years, did ye at a' fast unto me,
14 a' the nations whom they knew
8:10 for I set a' men every one against
12 of this people to possess a'
17 for a' these are things that I hate,
23 take hold out of a' languages of
9: 1 of man, as of a' the tribes of Israel,
10:11 a' the deeps of the river shall dry
11:10 I had made with a' the people.
12: 2 of trembling unto a' the people
3 a burdensome stone for a' people:
3 a' that burden themselves with it
3 though a' the people of the earth
6 devour a' the people round about,
9 destroy a' the nations that come
14 A' the families that remain, every
13: 8 that in a' the land, saith the Lord,
14: 2 a' nations against Jerusalem to
5 come, and a' the saints with thee.
9 shall be king over a' the earth:
10 A' the land shall be turned as a
12 the Lord will smite a' the people
14 and the wealth of a' the heathen
15 a' the beasts that shall be in these
16 that is left of a' the nations which
17 will not come up of a' the families
19 and the punishment of a' nations
21 the Lord of hosts: and a' they that
Mal 2: 9 and base before a' the people,
10 Have we not a' one father? hath
3:10 a' the tithes into the storehouse,
12 a' nations shall call you blessed:
4: 1 and a' the proud, yea,
1 and a' that do wickedly,
4 unto him in Horeb for a' Israel,
M't 1:17 a' the generations from Abraham
22 Now a' this was done, that it

M't 2: 3 and a' Jerusalem with him.
4 had gathered a' the chief priests
16 and slew a' the children that were
16 and in a' the coasts thereof,
3: 5 to him Jerusalem, and a' Judæa,
5 a' the region round about Jordan,
15 us to fulfil a' righteousness.
4: 8 and sheweth him a' the kingdoms
9 A' these things will I give thee,
23 Jesus went about a' Galilee,
23 healing a' manner of sickness
23 and a' manner of disease
24 fame went throughout a' Syria:
24 brought unto him a' sick people
5:11 say a' manner of evil against you
15 giveth light unto a' that are in
18 till a' be fulfilled.
34 Swear not at a'; neither by
6:29 Solomon in a' his glory was not
32 (For after a' these things do the
32 ye have need of a' these things.
33 a' these things shall be added
7:12 Therefore a' things whatsoever
8:16 and healed a' that were sick:
9:26 went abroad into a' that land.
31 his fame in a' that country.
35 Jesus went about a' the cities
10: 1 and to heal a' manner of sickness,
1 and a' manner of disease.
22 ye shall be hated of a' men for my
30 of your head are a' numbered.
11:13 For a' the prophets and the law
27 A' things are delivered unto me
28 Come unto me, a' ye that labour
12:15 and he healed them a';
23 And a' the people were amazed,
31 A' manner of sin and blasphemy
13:32 indeed is the least of a' seeds:
34 A' these things spake Jesus
41 out of his kingdom a' things that
44 and selleth a' that he hath,
46 went and sold a' that he had,
51 ye understood a' these things?
56 sisters, are they not a' with us?
56 hath this man a' these things?
14:20 And they did a' eat, and were filled:
35 they sent out into a' that country
35 and brought unto him a' that
15:37 And they did a' eat, and were
17:11 first come, and restore a' things.
18:25 and a' that he had, and payment
26 with me, and I will pay thee a'.
29 with me, and I will pay thee a'.
31 unto their lord a' that was done.
32 I forgave thee a' that debt,
34 till he should pay a' that was due
19:11 A' men cannot receive this saying,
20 A' these things have I kept from
26 with God a' things are possible.
27 we have forsaken a', and followed
20: 6 Why stand ye here a' the day idle?
21: 4 A' this was done, that it might
10 a' the city was moved, saying,
12 and cast out a' them that sold
22 a' things, whatsoever ye shall ask
26 for a' hold John as a prophet.
37 of a' he sent unto them his son,
22: 4 and a' things are ready:
10 and gathered together a' as many
27 And last of a' the woman died
28 for they a' had her.
37 the Lord thy God with a' thy heart,
37 and with a' thy soul,
37 and with a' thy mind.
40 a' the law and the prophets.
23: 3 A' therefore whatsoever they bid
5 But a' their works they do for to
8 and a' ye are brethren.
20 and by a' things thereon.
27 and of a' uncleanness.
35 may come a' the righteous blood
36 A' these things shall come upon
24: 2 See ye not a' these things?
6 for a' these things must come to
8 A' these are the beginning of
9 ye shall be hated of a' nations for
14 in a' the world for a witness
14 unto a' nations; and then
30 then shall a' the tribes of the
33 when ye shall see a' these things,
34 till a' these things be fulfilled.
39 flood came, and took them a' away;
47 make him ruler over a' his goods.
25: 5 they a' slumbered and slept.
7 Then a' those virgins arose,
31 and a' the holy angels with him,
32 him shall be gathered a' nations:
26: 1 Jesus had finished a' these
27 saying, Drink ye a' of it;
31 A' ye shall be offended because of
33 Though a' men shall be offended
35 Likewise also said a' the disciples.
52 for a' they that take the sword
56 But a' this was done.
56 Then a' the disciples forsook him,
59 and a' the council, sought false
70 But he denied before them a',
27: 1 morning was come, a' the chief,
22 They a' say unto him, Let him be
25 Then answered a' the people,
45 there was darkness over a' the land
28: 9 Jesus met them, saying, A' hail.
11 unto the chief priests a' the things
18 A' power is given unto me in
19 and teach a' nations, baptising
20 to observe a' things whatsoever

M'r 1: 5 out unto him a' the land of Judæa,
5 and were a' baptized of him
27 And they were a' amazed,
28 throughout a' the region round
32 brought unto him a' that were
33 a' the city was gathered together
37 A' men seek for thee.
39 synagogues throughout a' Galilee,
2:12 went forth before them a';
12 that they were a' amazed,
13 and a' the multitude resorted
3:28 A' sins shall be forgiven unto
4:11 a' these things are done in
13 then will ye know a' parables?
31 is less than a' the seeds that be in
32 becometh greater than a' herbs,
34 expounded a' things to his disciples.
5:12 And a' the devils besought him,
20 and a' men did marvel.
26 and had spent a' that she had,
33 and told him a' the truth.
40 when he had put them a' out,
6:30 and told him a' things, both
33 ran afoot thither out of a' cities,
39 to make a' sit down by companies
41 fishes divided he among them a'.
42 And they did a' eat,
50 For they a' saw him, and were
7: 3 and a' the Jews, except they wash
14 when he had called a' the people
19 purging a' meats?
23 A' these evil things come from
37 He hath done a' things well:
9:12 and restoreth a' things;
15 And straightway a' the people,
23 a' things are possible to him that
35 the same shall be last of a',
35 and servant of a'.
10:20 a' these have I observed from my
27 with God a' things are possible.
28 Lo, we have left a', and have
44 chiefest, shall be servant of a'.
11:11 looked round about upon a' things,
17 of a' nations the house of prayer?
18 a' the people were astonished at
32 for a' men counted John, that he
12:22 last of a' the woman died also.
28 is the first commandment of a'?
29 The first of a' the commandments
30 Lord thy God with a' thy heart,
30 and with a' thy soul,
30 and with a' thy mind,
30 and with a' thy strength:
33 to love him with a' the heart,
33 and with a' the understanding,
33 and with a' the soul,
33 and with a' the strength,
33 more than a' whole burnt offerings
43 hath cast more in, than a' they
44 For a' they did cast in of their
44 did cast in a' that she had,
44 even a' her living.
13: 4 a' these things shall be fulfilled?
10 be published among a' nations.
13 hated of a' men for my name's sake:
23 I have foretold you a' things.
30 till a' these things be done.
37 I say unto a', Watch.
14:23 and they a' drank of it.
27 A' ye shall be offended because of
29 Although a' shall be offended,
31 Likewise also said they a'.
36 a' things are possible unto thee;
50 And they a' forsook him, and fled.
53 were assembled a' the chief priests
55 a' the council sought for witness
64 a' condemned him to be guilty of
16:15 Go ye into a' the world,

Lu 1: 3 perfect understanding of a' things
6 walking in a' the commandments
48 from henceforth a' generations
63 And they marvelled a'.
65 a' that dwelt round about them:
65 and a' these sayings were noised
65 a' the hill country of Judæa.
66 And a' they that heard them
71 from the hand of a' that hate us;
75 before him, a' the days of our life.
2: 1 that a' the world should be taxed.
3 And a' went to be taxed,
10 which shall be to a' people.
18 a' they that heard it wondered
19 But Mary kept a' these things,
20 praising God for a' the things
31 before the face of a' people;
38 a' them that looked for redemption
39 they had performed a' things
47 a' that heard him were astonished
51 kept a' these sayings in her heart.
3: 3 into a' the country about Jordan,
6 And a' flesh shall see the salvation
15 and a' men mused in their hearts
16 answered, saying unto them a',
19 a' the evils which Herod had done,
20 Added yet this above a',
21 when a' the people were baptized,
4: 5 him a' the kingdoms of the world
6 A' this power will I give thee,
7 worship me, a' shall be thine.
13 had ended a' the temptation,
14 fame of him through a' the region
15 being glorified of a'.
20 a' them that were in the synagogue
22 And a' bare him witness,
25 famine was throughout a' the land;
28 And a' they in the synagogue,
4:36 And they were a' amazed,
40 a' they that had any sick
5: 5 we have toiled a' the night,
9 and a' that were with him,
11 they forsook a', and followed him.
26 a' amazed, and they glorified God,
28 left a', rose up, and followed him.
6:10 looking round about upon them a',
12 continued a' night in prayer to
17 people out of a' Judæa
19 and healed them a'.
26 a' men shall speak well of you!
7: 1 when he had ended a' his sayings
16 there came a fear on a':
17 went forth throughout a' Judæa,
17 a' the region round about.
18 shewed him of a' these things.
29 and a' the people that heard him,
35 wisdom is justified of a' her
8:40 for they were a' waiting for him.
43 a' her living upon physicians
45 When a' denied, Peter and they
47 declared unto him before a' the
52 And a' wept and bewailed her:
54 And he put them a' out, and took
9: 1 and authority over a' devils,
7 heard of a' that was done by him:
10 told him a' that they had done.
13 buy meat for a' this people.
15 did so, and made them a' sit down.
17 and were a' filled:
23 he said to them a', If any man will
43 a' amazed at the mighty power of
43 wondered every one at a' things,
48 for he that is least among you a',
10:19 over a' the power of the enemy:
22 A' things are delivered to me of
27 Lord thy God with a' thy heart,
27 and with a' thy soul,
27 and with a' thy strength,
27 and with a' thy mind;
11:22 taketh from him a' his armour
41 a' things are clean unto you.
42 rue and a' manner of herbs,
50 That the blood of a' the prophets,
12: 1 to say unto his disciples first of a',
7 hairs of your head are a'
18 there will I bestow a' my fruits
27 Solomon in a' his glory was not
30 For a' these things do the nations
31 and a' these things shall be added
41 this parable unto us, or even to a'?
44 make him ruler over a' that he
13: 2 sinners above a' the Galilæans,
3 ye shall a' likewise perish.
4 sinners above a' men
5 ye shall a' likewise perish.
17 a' his adversaries were ashamed:
17 and a' the people rejoiced
17 for a' the glorious things
27 from me, a' ye workers of iniquity.
28 a' the prophets, in the kingdom
14:17 for a' things are now ready.
18 And they a' with one consent
29 a' that behold it begin to mock him,
33 that forsaketh not a' that he hath,
15: 1 a' the publicans and sinners
13 younger son gathered a' together,
14 And when he had spent a',
31 and a' that I have is thine.
16:14 covetous, heard a' these things:
26 And beside a' this, between us
17:10 ye shall have done a' those things
27 flood came, and destroyed them a'.
29 heaven, and destroyed them a'.
18:12 I give tithes of a' that I possess.
21 A' these have I kept from my
22 sell a' that thou hast,
28 we have left a', and followed thee
31 and a' things that are written
43 a' the people, when they saw it,
19: 7 they saw it, they a' murmured,
37 loud voice for a' the mighty works
48 a' the people were very attentive
20: 6 a' the people will stone us:
32 Last of a' the woman died also.
38 for a' live unto him.
40 not ask him any question at a'.
45 in the audience of a' the people
21: 3 cast in more than they a':
4 a' these have of their abundance
4 cast in a' the living that she had.
12 before a' these, they shall lay their
15 which a' your adversaries shall
17 hated of a' men for my name's sake:
22 that a' things which are written
24 led away captive into a' nations:
29 Behold the fig tree, and a' the trees;
32 not pass away, till a' be fulfilled.
35 on a' them that dwell on the face
36 to escape a' these things
38 And a' the people came early
22:70 Then said they a', Art thou then
23: 5 teaching throughout a' Jewry,
18 they cried out a' at once, saying,
44 darkness over a' the earth until
48 a' the people that came together
49 And a' his acquaintance,
24: 9 told a' these things unto the eleven,
9 and to a' the rest.
14 talked together of a' these things
19 before God and a' the people:
21 beside a' this, to day is the third
25 a' that the prophets have spoken:
27 at Moses and a' the prophets,
27 unto them in a' the scriptures

Lu 24:44 that *a*' things must be fulfilled,
47 *a*' nations, beginning at
Joh 1: 3 *A*' things were made by him;
7 *a*' men through him might believe.
16 of his fulness have *a*' we received,
2:15 drove them *a*' out of the temple,
24 because he knew *a*' men,
3:26 and *a*' men come to him.
31 cometh from above is above *a*':
31 cometh from heaven is above *a*'.
35 given *a*' things into his hand.
4:25 is come, he will tell us *a*' things.
29 told me *a*' things that ever I did:
39 He told me *a*' that ever I did.
45 seen *a*' the things that he did
5:20 and sheweth him *a*' things
22 committed *a*' judgment unto the
23 *a*' men should honour the Son,
28 *a*' that are in the graves shall
6:37 *A*' that the Father giveth me shall
39 of *a*' which he hath given me
45 they shall be *a*' taught of God.
7:21 done one work, and ye *a*' marvel.
8: 2 and *a*' the people came unto him;
10: 8 *A*' that ever came before me
29 gave them me, is greater than *a*';
41 but *a*' things that John spake
11:48 alone, *a*' men will believe on him:
49 unto them, Ye know nothing at *a*',
12:32 will draw *a*' men unto me.
13: 3 the Father had given *a*' things
10 ye are clean, but not *a*'.
11 Ye are not *a*' clean.
18 I speak not of you *a*':
35 By this shall *a*' men know
14:26 shall teach you *a*' things, and bring
26 *a*' things to your remembrance,
15:15 for *a*' things that I have heard
21 *a*' these things will they do unto
16:13 he will guide you into *a*' truth:
15 *A*' things that the Father hath are
30 that thou knowest *a*' things,
17: 2 given him power over *a*' flesh,
7 known that *a*' things whatsoever
10 And *a*' mine are thine,
21 That they *a*' may be one;
18: 4 *a*' things that should come upon
38 I find in him no fault at *a*'.
40 Then cried they *a*' again, saying,
19:11 have no power at *a*' against me,
28 *a*' things were now accomplished.
21:11 and for *a*' there were so many,
17 Lord, thou knowest *a*' things;
Ac 1: 1 of *a*' that Jesus began both to do
8 and in *a*' Judæa, and in Samaria,
14 These *a*' continued with one accord
18 and *a*' his bowels gushed out.
19 it was known unto *a*' the dwellers
21 companied with us *a*' the time
24 knowest the hearts of *a*' men,
2: 1 *a*' with one accord in one place.
2 filled *a*' the house where they were
4 were *a*' filled with the Holy Ghost,
7 And they were *a*' amazed
7 *a*' these which speak Galilæans?
12 And they were *a*' amazed,
14 *a*' ye that dwell at Jerusalem,
17 out of my Spirit upon *a*' flesh:
32 whereof we *a*' are witnesses.
36 Therefore let *a*' the house of Israel
39 and to *a*' that are afar off,
44 *a*' that believed were together,
44 and had *a*' things common;
45 and parted them to *a*' men,
47 having favour with *a*' the people.
3: 9 *a*' the people saw him walking
11 *a*' the people ran together
16 in the presence of you *a*'.
18 by the mouth of *a*' his prophets,
21 times of restitution of *a*' things,
21 the mouth of *a*' his holy prophets
22 *a*' things whatsoever he shall say
24 and *a*' the prophets from Samuel
25 shall *a*' the kindreds of the earth
4:10 Be it known unto you *a*',
10 and to *a*' the people of Israel,
16 to *a*' them that dwell in Jerusalem:
18 not to speak at *a*' nor teach in the
21 for *a*' men glorified God for that
23 reported *a*' that the chief priests
24 the sea, and *a*' that in them is:
29 with *a*' boldness they may speak
31 were *a*' filled with the Holy Ghost,
32 they had *a*' things common.
33 great grace was upon them *a*'.
5: 5 and great fear came on *a*'
11 And great fear came upon *a*'
12 *a*' with one accord in Solomon's
17 and *a*' they that were with him,
20 *a*' the words of this life.
21 *a*' the senate of the children of
23 found we shut with *a*' safety,
34 in reputation among *a*' the people,
36 and *a*', as many as obeyed him,
37 *a*', even as many as obeyed him,
6:15 *a*' that sat in the council, looking
7:10 delivered him out of *a*' his
10 governor over Egypt and *a*'
11 a dearth over *a*' the land of Egypt
14 and *a*' his kindred, threescore
22 in *a*' the wisdom of the Egyptians,
50 my hands made *a*' these things?
8: 1 and they were *a*' scattered abroad
10 To whom they *a*' gave heed,
27 had the charge of *a*' her treasure,
37 thou believest with *a*' thine heart,

Ac 8:40 he preached in *a*' the cities,
9:14 to bind *a*' that call on thy name.
21 *a*' that heard him were amazed,
26 but they were *a*' afraid of him,
31 churches rest throughout *a*' Judæa
32 passed throughout *a*' quarters,
35 And *a*' that dwelt at Lydda
39 and *a*' the widows stood by him
40 But Peter put them *a*' forth,
42 was known throughout *a*' Joppa;
10: 2 feared God with *a*' his house,
8 declared *a*' these things unto them,
12 *a*' manner of fourfooted beasts of
22 among *a*' the nation of the Jews,
33 Now therefore are we *a*' here
33 *a*' things that are commanded thee
36 (he is Lord of *a*':)
37 published throughout *a*' Judæa,
38 *a*' that were oppressed of the devil
39 witnesses of *a*' things which he did
41 Not to *a*' the people, but unto
43 him give *a*' the prophets witness,
44 the Holy Ghost fell on *a*' them
11:10 *a*' were drawn up again into
14 thou and *a*' thy house shall be
23 and exhorted them *a*', that with
28 dearth throughout *a*' the world:
12:11 *a*' the expectation of the people
13:10 full of *a*' subtilty and *a*' mischief,
10 thou enemy of *a*' righteousness,
22 which shall fulfil *a*' my will.
24 repentance to *a*' the people of
29 fulfilled *a*' that was written of him,
39 And by him *a*' that believe
39 are justified from *a*' things,
49 throughout *a*' the region.
14:15 and *a*' things that are therein:
16 in times past suffered *a*' nations
27 *a*' that God had done with them,
15: 3 great joy unto *a*' the brethren.
4 declared *a*' things that God had
12 Then *a*' the multitude kept silence,
17 *a*' the Gentiles, upon whom my name
17 who doeth *a*' these things.
18 Known unto God are *a*' his works
16: 3 *a*' that his father was a Greek.
26 *a*' the doors were opened, and
28 Do thyself no harm: for we are *a*'
32 to *a*' that were in his house.
33 baptized, he and *a*' his, straightway.
34 believing in God with *a*' his house.
17: 5 and set *a*' the city on an uproar,
7 *a*' do contrary to the decrees of
11 the word with *a*' readiness
15 to come to him with *a*' speed,
21 *a*' the Athenians and strangers
22 *a*' things ye are too superstitious.
24 the world and *a*' things therein,
25 to *a*' life, and breath, and *a*' things;
26 of one blood *a*' nations of men
26 dwell on *a*' the face of the earth,
30 commandeth *a*' men every where
31 hath given assurance unto *a*' men,
18: 2 Claudius had commanded *a*' Jews
8 believed on the Lord with *a*' his
17 *a*' the Greeks took Sosthenes,
21 must by *a*' means keep this feast
23 over *a*' the country of Galatia
23 strengthening *a*' the disciples.
19: 7 And *a*' the men were about twelve.
10 that *a*' they which dwelt in Asia
17 this was known to *a*' the Jews
17 and fear fell on them *a*',
19 and burned them before *a*' men:
26 almost throughout *a*' Asia,
27 whom *a*' Asia and the world
34 *a*' with one voice about the space
20:18 I have been with you at *a*' seasons,
19 with *a*' humility of mind,
25 I know that ye *a*', among whom
26 pure from the blood of *a*' men.
27 *a*' the counsel of God.
28 and to *a*' the flock, over the which
32 *a*' them which are sanctified.
35 I have shewed you *a*' things,
36 and prayed with them *a*'.
37 And they *a*' wept sore,
38 Sorrowing most of *a*' for the words
21: 5 they *a*' brought us on our way,
18 and *a*' the elders were present.
20 and they are *a*' zealous of the law:
21 that thou teachest *a*' the Jews
24 *a*' may know that those things,
27 stirred up *a*' the people, and laid
28 that teacheth *a*' men every where
30 And *a*' the city was moved,
31 *a*' Jerusalem was in an uproar.
22: 3 as ye *a*' are this day.
5 and *a*' the estate of the elders:
10 it shall be told thee of *a*' things
12 having a good report of *a*' the Jews
15 shalt be his witness unto *a*' men
30 and *a*' their council to appear,
23: 1 I have lived in *a*' good conscience
24: 3 always, and in *a*' places,
3 most noble Felix, with *a*'
5 of sedition among *a*' the Jews
8 take knowledge of *a*' these things,
14 believing *a*' things which are
25: 8 have I offended any thing at *a*'.
24 King Agrippa, and *a*' men which
24 whom *a*' the multitude of the Jews
26: 2 touching *a*' the things whereof
3 to be expert in *a*' customs
4 know *a*' the Jews;
14 we were *a*' fallen to the earth,

Ac 26:20 throughout *a*' the coasts of Judæa,
29 but also *a*' that hear me this day,
27:20 *a*' hope that we should be saved
24 God hath given thee *a*' them
33 besought them *a*' to take meat,
35 in presence of them *a*':
36 Then were they *a*' of good cheer,
37 we were in *a*' in the ship
44 they escaped *a*' safe to land.
28:30 and received *a*' that came in unto,
31 with *a*' confidence, no man
Ro 1: 5 to the faith among *a*' nations, for
7 To *a*' that be in Rome,
8 through Jesus Christ for you *a*',
18 against *a*' ungodliness and
29 filled with *a*' unrighteousness,
3: 9 that they are *a*' under sin;
12 They are *a*' gone out of the way,
19 *a*' the world may become guilty
22 by faith of Jesus Christ unto *a*'
22 and upon *a*' them that believe
23 For *a*' have sinned, and come short
4:11 might be the father of *a*' them that
16 might be sure to *a*' the seed;
16 who is the father of us *a*',
5:12 and so death passed upon *a*' men,
12 for that *a*' have sinned:
18 upon *a*' men to condemnation;
18 upon *a*' men unto justification of
7: 8 in me *a*' manner of concupiscence.
8:28 *a*' things work together for good
32 delivered him up for us *a*',
32 also freely give us *a*' things?
36 we are killed *a*' the day long;
37 Nay, in *a*' these things we are
9: 5 who is over *a*', God blessed for ever.
6 For they are not *a*' Israel,
7 of Abraham, are they *a*' children:
17 declared throughout *a*' the earth.
10:12 same Lord over *a*' is rich
12 unto *a*' that call upon him
16 they have not *a*' obeyed the gospel.
18 their sound went into *a*' the earth,
21 *A*' day long I have stretched forth
11:26 And so *a*' Israel shall be saved:
32 concluded them *a*' in unbelief,
32 that he might have mercy upon *a*'.
36 and to him, are *a*' things:
12: 4 and *a*' members have not the
17 honest in the sight of *a*' men.
18 live peaceably with *a*' men.
13: 7 Render therefore to *a*' their dues:
14: 2 that he may eat *a*' things:
10 for we shall *a*' stand before the
20 *A*' things indeed are pure;
15:11 Praise the Lord, *a*' ye Gentiles;
11 and laud him, *a*' ye people.
13 fill you with *a*' joy and peace in
14 filled with *a*' knowledge,
33 the God of peace be with you *a*'.
16: 4 but also *a*' the churches of the
15 and *a*' the saints which are with
19 is come abroad unto *a*' men.
24 be with you *a*'. Amen.
26 made known to *a*' nations
1Co 1: 2 with *a*' that in every place call
5 in *a*' utterance,
5 and in *a*' knowledge;
10 that ye *a*' speak the same thing,
2:10 the Spirit searcheth *a*' things,
15 is spiritual judgeth *a*' things,
3:21 For *a*' things are yours;
22 or things to come; *a*' are yours;
4:13 the offscouring of *a*' things unto
6:12 *A*' things are lawful unto me,
12 but *a*' things are not expedient:
12 *a*' things are lawful for me,
7: 7 For I would that *a*' men were
17 And so ordain I in *a*' churches.
8: 1 know that we *a*' have knowledge,
6 of whom are *a*' things, and we in
6 by whom are *a*' things, and we by
9:12 but suffer *a*' things, lest we should
19 though I be free from *a*' men, yet
19 have I made myself servant unto *a*'
22 I am made *a*' things to *a*' men,
22 that I might by *a*' means save
24 run in a race run *a*', but one
25 is temperate in *a*' things.
10: 1 how that *a*' our fathers were
1 and *a*' passed through the sea;
2 And were *a*' baptized unto Moses
3 And did *a*' eat the same
4 And did *a*' drink the same
11 Now *a*' these things happened
17 for we are *a*' partakers of that one
23 *A*' things are lawful for me,
23 but *a*' things are not expedient:
23 *a*' things are lawful for me,
23 but *a*' things edify not.
31 do *a*' to the glory of God.
33 I please *a*' men in *a*' things,
11: 2 that ye remember me in *a*' things,
5 even *a*' one as if she were shaven.
12 but *a*' things of God.
18 For first of *a*' when ye come
12: 6 same God which worketh *a*' in *a*'.
11 But *a*' these worketh that one
12 and *a*' the members of that one
13 are we *a*' baptized into one
13 and have been *a*' made to drink
19 And if they were *a*' one member,
26 *a*' the members suffer with it;
26 *a*' the members rejoice with it.
29 Are *a*' apostles? are *a*' prophets?
29 are *a*' teachers? are *a*' workers

1Co 12:30 Have a' the gifts of healing?
30 do a' speak with tongues?
30 do a' interpret?
13: 2 and understand a' mysteries,
2 and a' knowledge;
2 and though I have a' faith,
3 though I bestow a' my goods to
7 Beareth a' things, believeth a'
7 hopeth a' things, endureth a'
14: 5 I would that ye a' spake with
18 with tongues more than ye a':
21 yet for a' that will they not hear
23 and a' speak with tongues,
24 But if a' prophesy, and there come
24 convinced of a', he is judged of a':
26 Let a' things be done unto
31 For ye may a' prophesy one by one,
31 that a' may learn,
31 and a' may be comforted.
33 as in a' churches of the saints.
40 Let a' things be done decently and
15: 3 delivered unto you first of a'
7 then of a' the apostles.
8 And last of a' he was seen of me
10 more abundantly than they a':
19 we are of a' men most miserable.
22 For as in Adam a' die,
22 in Christ shall a' be made alive.
24 he shall have put down a' rule
24 and a' authority and power.
25 till he hath put a' enemies under
27 hath put a' things under his feet.
27 But when he saith a' things
27 which did put a' things under him.
28 And when a' things shall be
28 him that put a' things under him,
28 that God may be a' in a'.
29 dead, if the dead rise not at a'?
39 A' flesh is not the same flesh:
51 We shall not a' sleep,
51 but we shall a' be changed,
16:12 was not at a' to come at this time;
14 Let a' your things be done with
20 A' the brethren greet you.
24 My love be with you a' in Christ
2Co 1: 1 with a' the saints which are
1 which are in a' Achaia:
3 the God of a' comfort;
4 in a' our tribulation,
20 For a' the promises of God in
2: 3 having confidence in you a',
3 that my joy is the joy of you a'.
5 I may not overcharge you a'.
9 ye be obedient in a' things.
3: 2 known and read of a' men:
18 But we a', with open face
4:15 For a' things are for your sakes,
5:10 For we must a' appear before
14 if one died for a',
14 then were a' dead:
15 And that he died for a',
17 behold, a' things are become new.
18 And a' things are of God,
6: 4 But in a' things approving
10 and yet possessing a' things.
7: 1 from a' filthiness of the flesh
4 joyful in a' our tribulation.
11 In a' things ye have approved
13 was refreshed by you a'.
14 but as we spake a' things to you
15 the obedience of you a',
16 confidence in you in a' things.
8: 7 and in a' diligence,
18 throughout a' the churches;
9: 8 God is able to make a' grace
8 always having a' sufficiency in
8 a' things, may abound to every
11 in everything to a' bountifulness,
9:13 unto them, and unto a' men;
10: 6 to revenge a' disobedience,
11: 6 manifest among you in a' things.
9 and in a' things I have kept
28 the care of a' the churches.
12:12 among you in a' patience,
19 but we do a' things, dearly
13: 2 and to a' other, that, if I come
13 A' the saints salute you.
14 Ghost, be with you a'. Amen.
Ga 1: 2 And a' the brethren which are with
2:14 said unto Peter before them a',
3: 8 In thee shall a' nations be blessed.
10 in a' things which are written
22 hath concluded a' under sin,
26 For ye are a' the children of God
28 for ye are a' one in Christ Jesus.
4: 1 though he be lord of a';
12 ye have not injured me at a'.
26 which is the mother of us a'.
5:14 For a' the law is fulfilled in one
6: 6 that teacheth in a' good things.
10 let us do good unto a' men,
Eph 1: 3 hath blessed us with a' spiritual
8 abounded toward us in a' wisdom
10 gather together in one a' things
11 who worketh a' things
15 and love unto a' the saints,
21 Far above a' principality,
22 put a' things under his feet,
22 to be the head over a' things
23 of him that filleth a' in a'.
2: 3 Among whom also we a' had our
21 In whom a' the building
3: 8 less than the least of a' saints,
9 and to make a' men see
9 created a' things by Jesus Christ:
18 to comprehend with a' saints

Eph 3:19 with a' the fulness of God.
20 above a' that we ask or think,
21 throughout a' ages, world without
4: 2 With a' lowliness and meekness,
6 and Father of a', who is above a',
6 and through a', and in you a'.
10 up far above a' heavens,
10 that he might fill a' things.
13 Till we a' come in the unity of
15 grow up into him in a' things,
19 to work a' uncleanliness with
31 Let a' bitterness, and wrath,
31 put away from you, with a' malice:
5: 3 and a' uncleanness,
9 of the spirit is in a' goodness
13 a' things that are reproved
20 always for a' things unto God
6:13 having done a', to stand.
16 Above a', taking the shield of
16 to quench a' the fiery darts
18 Praying always with a' prayer
18 with a' perseverance and
18 supplication for a' saints;
21 make known to you a' things:
24 Grace be with a' them that love
Ph'l 1: 1 to a' the saints in Christ Jesus,
4 you a' making request with joy,
7 to think this of you a',
7 ye a' are partakers of my grace.
8 I long after you a' in the bowels
9 and in a' judgment;
13 in a' the palace,
13 and in a' other places,
20 with a' boldness, as always,
25 with you a' for your furtherance
2:14 Do a' things without murmurings
17 and rejoice with you a'.
21 For a' seek their own,
26 he longed after you a',
29 with a' gladness; and hold such in
3: 8 I count a' things but loss
8 suffered the loss of a' things,
21 to subdue a' things unto himself.
4: 5 be known unto a' men.
7 passeth a' understanding,
12 everywhere and in a' things I am
13 I can do a' things through Christ
18 But I have a', and abound:
19 shall supply a' your need
22 A' the saints salute you,
23 Christ be with you a'. Amen.
Col 1: 4 which ye have to a' the saints,
6 as it is in a' the world;
9 knowledge of his will in a' wisdom
10 unto a' pleasing, being fruitful in
11 Strengthened with a' might,
11 unto a' patience and
16 by him were a' things created,
16 a' things were created by him,
17 he is before a' things,
17 and by him a' things consist.
18 that in a' things he might have
19 in him should a' fulness dwell;
20 to reconcile a' things unto himself;
28 teaching every man in a' wisdom;
2: 2 and unto a' riches of the full
3 are hid a' the treasures of wisdom
9 dwelleth a' the fulness of the
10 the head of a' principality
13 forgiven you a' trespasses;
19 from which a' the body
22 Which a' are to perish with the
3: 8 put off a' these; anger, wrath,
11 but Christ is a', and in a'.
14 And above a' these things
16 dwell in you richly in a' wisdom;
17 do a' in the name of the Lord
20 obey your parents in a' things:
22 obey in a' things your masters
4: 7 A' my state shall Tychicus declare
9 make known unto you a' things
12 complete in a' the will of God.
1Th 1: 2 to God always for you a',
7 ensamples to a' that believe
2:15 and are contrary to a' men:
3: 7 in a' our affliction
9 for a' the joy wherewith we joy
12 and toward a' men,
13 Jesus Christ with a' his saints.
4: 6 is the avenger of a' such,
10 ye do it toward a' the brethren
10 which are in a' Macedonia:
5: 5 Ye are a' the children of light,
14 be patient toward a' men.
15 among yourselves, and to a' men.
21 Prove a' things; hold fast that
22 Abstain from a' appearance of
26 Greet a' the brethren with an holy
27 be read unto a' the holy brethren.
2Th 1: 3 charity of every one of you a'
4 faith in a' your persecutions
10 admired in a' them that believe
11 and fulfil a' the good pleasure
2: 4 above a' that is called God,
9 with a' power and signs
10 And with a' deceivableness
12 That they a' might be damned
3: 2 for a' men have not faith.
11 disorderly, working not at a', but
16 you peace always by a' means.
16 The Lord be with you a'.
18 Christ be with you a'. Amen.
1Ti 1:15 worthy of a' acceptation,
16 shew forth a' longsuffering,
2: 1 that, first of a', supplications,
1 be made for a' men;

1Ti 2: 2 for a' that are in authority;
2 peaceable life in a' godliness
4 Who will have a' men to be saved,
6 gave himself a ransom for a',
11 in silence with a' subjection.
3: 4 in subjection with a' gravity;
11 faithful in a' things.
4: 8 is profitable unto a' things,
9 worthy of a' acceptation.
10 who is the Saviour of a' men,
15 thy profiting may appear to a'.
5: 2 younger as sisters, with a' purity.
20 rebuke before a', that others also
6: 1 masters worthy of a' honour,
10 money is the root of a' evil:
13 who quickeneth a' things,
17 richly a' things to enjoy;
2Ti 1:15 a' they which are in Asia be
2: 7 thee understanding in a' things.
10 I endure a' things for the elect's
24 but be gentle unto a' men,
3: 9 shall be manifest unto a' men,
11 out of them a' the Lord delivered
12 Yea, and a' that will live godly
16 A' scripture is given by
17 furnished unto a' good works.
4: 2 exhort with a' longsuffering
5 watch thou in a' things,
8 but unto a' them also that love
16 but a' men forsook me:
17 and that a' the Gentiles might
21 and a' the brethren.
Tit 1:15 Unto the pure a' things are pure:
2: 7 In a' things shewing thyself
9 to please them well in a' things;
10 shewing a' good fidelity;
10 of God our Saviour in a' things.
11 hath appeared to a' men,
14 might redeem us from a' iniquity,
15 rebuke with a' authority.
3: 2 shewing a' meekness unto a' men.
15 A' that are with me salute thee.
15 Grace be with you a'.
Ph'm 5 and toward a' saints;
Heb 1: 2 appointed heir of a' things,
3 upholding a' things by the word
6 And let a' the angels of God
11 and they a' shall wax old
14 Are they not a' ministering spirits,
2: 8 hast put a' things in subjection
8 he put a' in subjection under him,
8 not yet a' things put under him.
10 for whom are a' things,
10 and by whom are a' things,
11 sanctified are a' of one:
15 a' their lifetime subject to bondage.
17 in a' things it behoved him
3: 2 Moses was faithful in a' his house.
4 but he that built a' things is God.
5 verily was faithful in a' his house,
16 not a' that came out of Egypt
4: 4 the seventh day from a' his works.
13 but a' things are naked
15 was in a' points tempted
5: 9 unto a' them that obey him;
6:16 is to them an end of a' strife.
7: 2 gave a tenth part of a';
7 And without a' contradiction
8: 5 a' things according to the pattern
11 for a' shall know me,
9: 3 which is called the Holiest of a';
8 that the way into the holiest of a'
17 it is of no strength at a' while the
19 every precept to a' the people
19 both the book, and a' the people,
21 and a' the vessels of the ministry.
22 almost a' things are by the law
10:10 body of Jesus Christ once for a'.
11:13 These a' died in faith, not having
39 these a', having obtained a good
12: 8 whereof a' are partakers,
14 Follow peace with a' men,
23 to God the Judge of a',
13: 4 marriage is honourable in a',
18 a' things willing to live honestly.
24 Salute a' them that have the rule
24 and a' the saints.
25 Grace be with you a'. Amen.
Jas 1: 2 count it a' joy when ye fall
5 that giveth to a' men liberally,
8 unstable in a' his ways.
21 lay apart a' filthiness
2:10 he is guilty of a'.
3: 2 in many things we offend a'.
4:16 a' such rejoicing is evil.
5:12 above a' things, my brethren,
1Pe 1:15 holy in a' manner of conversation;
24 For a' flesh is as grass,
24 and a' the glory of man
2: 1 laying aside a' malice, and a' guile,
1 and a' evil speakings,
17 Honour a' men. Love the
18 masters with a' fear;
3: 8 be ye a' of one mind,
4: 7 the end of a' things is at hand:
8 a' things have fervent charity
11 God in a' things may be glorified
5: 5 a' of you be subject one to another,
7 Casting a' your care upon him;
10 But the God of a' grace,
14 Peace be with you a' that are in
2Pe 1: 3 a' things that pertain unto life
5 giving a' diligence, add to your
3: 4 a' things continue as they were
9 that a' should come to repentance.
11 a' these things shall be dissolved,

2Pe 3:16 As also in a' his epistles,
1Jo 1: 5 and in him is no darkness at a'.
7 cleanseth us from a' sin.
9 us from a' unrighteousness.
2:16 For a' that is in the world,
19 that they were not a' of us.
20 and ye know a' things.
27 teacheth you of a' things,
3:20 and knoweth a' things.
5:17 A' unrighteousness is sin:
2Jo 1 a' they that have known the truth;
3Jo 2 I wish above a' things that thou
12 hath good report of a' men,
Jude 3 when I gave a' diligence
15 judgment upon a',
15 and to convince a'
15 of a' their ungodly deeds
15 and of a' their hard speeches
Re 1: 2 and of a' things that he saw.
7 a' kindreds of the earth shall wail
2:23 and a' the churches shall know
3:10 shall come upon a' the world,
4:11 for thou hast created a' things,
5: 6 sent forth into a' the earth.
13 sea, and a' that are in them,
7: 4 of a' the tribes of the children of
9 of a' nations, and kindreds,
11 a' the angels stood round about
17 away a' tears from their eyes.
8: 3 with the prayers of a' saints
7 and a' green grass was burnt up.
11: 6 smite the earth with a' plagues,
12: 5 rule a' nations with a rod of iron:
13: 3 a' the world wondered after the
7 over a' kindreds, and tongues,
8 And a' that dwell upon the earth
12 a' the power of the first beast
16 causeth a', both small and great,
14: 8 because she made a' nations drink
15: 4 for a' nations shall come and
18: 3 a' nations have drunk of the wine
12 and a' thyine wood,
12 a' manner vessels of ivory,
12 and a' manner vessels of most
14 and a' things which were dainty
14 shalt find them no more at a'.
17 shipmaster, and a' the company
19 rich a' that had ships in the sea
21 and shall be found no more at a'.
22 shall be heard no more at a'
22 shall be heard no more at a'
23 shall shine no more at a' in thee;
23 shall be heard no more at a' in
23 sorceries were a' nations deceived.
24 a' that were slain upon the earth.
19: 5 Praise our God, a' ye his servants,
17 saying to a' the fowls that fly in
18 flesh of a' men, both free and bond,
21 a' the fowls were filled with their
21: 4 God shall wipe away a' tears
5 Behold, I make a' things new.
7 shall inherit a' things;
8 and a' liars, shall have their part
19 with a' manner of precious stones.
25 shall not be shut at a' by day:
22:21 Lord Jesus Christ be with you a'.

allege See ALLEGING.

alleging
Ac 17: 3 Opening and a', that Christ

allegory
Ga 4:24 Which things are an a': for these

Alleluia (*al-le-loo'-yah*)
Re 19: 1 people in heaven, saying, A';
3 they said, A'. And her
4 the throne, saying, Amen; A'.
6 mighty thunderings, saying, A':

allied
Ne 13: 4 the priest, ... was a' unto Tobiah:

Allon (*al'-lon*) See also ALLON-BACHUTH; ELON.
Jos 19:33 Heleph, from A' to Zaanannim,
1Ch 4:37 the son of Shiphi, the son of A',

Allon-bachuth (*al''-lon-bak'-ooth*)
Ge 35: 8 and the name of it was called A'.

allow See also ALLOWED; ALLOWETH; ALLOWING; DISALLOW.
Lu 11:48 ye a' the deeds of your fathers:
Ac 24:15 which they themselves also a',
Ro 7:15 that which I do I a' not:

allowance
2Ki 25:30 And his a' was a continual a'

allowed See also DISALLOWED.
1Th 2: 4 But as we were a' of God to be

alloweth
Ro 14:22 in that thing which he a'.

all-to (J'g 9:53) See ALL.

allure
Ho 2:14 I will a' her, and bring her into
2Pe 2:18 a' through the lusts of the flesh,

Almighty
Ge 17: 1 said unto him, I am the A' God;
28: 3 And God A' bless thee,
35:11 God said unto him, I am God A':
43:14 God A' give you mercy
48: 3 God A' appeared unto me at Luz
49:25 and by the A', who shall bless thee
Ex 6: 3 by the name of God A',
Nu 24: 4, 16 which saw the vision of the A',
Ru 1:20 A' hath dealt very bitterly with me.
21 and the A' hath afflicted me?
Job 5:17 not thou the chastening of the A':
6: 4 arrows of the A' are within me,
14 he forsaketh the fear of the A'.
8: 3 doth the A' pervert justice?
5 make thy supplication to the A';
11: 7 find out the A' unto perfection?
13: 3 Surely I would speak to the A',
15:25 himself against the A'.
21:15 What is the A', that we should
20 shall drink of the wrath of the A'.
22: 3 Is it any pleasure to the A',
17 what can the A' do for them?
23 If thou return to the A',
25 the A' shall be thy defence,
26 have thy delight in the A',
23:16 and the A' troubleth me:
24: 1 times are not hidden from the A',
27: 2 the A', who hath vexed my soul;
10 Will he delight himself in the A'?
11 with the A' will I not conceal.
13 they shall receive of the A'.
29: 5 When the A' was yet with me,
31: 2 inheritance of the A' from on high?
35 that the A' would answer me,
32: 8 inspiration of the A' giveth them
33: 4 breath of the A' hath given me life.
34:10 and from the A', that he should
12 will the A' pervert judgment.
35:13 neither will the A' regard it.
37:23 the A', we cannot find him out:
40: 2 he that contendeth with the A'
Ps 68:14 When the A' scattered kings
91: 1 under the shadow of the A'.
Isa 13: 6 as a destruction from the A'.
Eze 1:24 as the voice of the A',
10: 5 the A' God when he speaketh.
Joe 1:15 as a destruction from the A'
2Co 6:18 saith the Lord A'.
Re 1: 8 and which is to come, the A'.
4: 8 Holy, holy, holy, Lord God A',
11:17 O Lord God A', which art, and wast,
15: 3 thy works, Lord God A';
16: 7 Lord God A', true and righteous
14 that great day of God A'.
19:15 and wrath of A' God.
21:22 the Lord God A' and the Lamb are

Almodad (*al-mo'-dad*)
Ge 10:26 Joktan begat A', and Sheleph,
1Ch 1:20 Joktan begat A', and Sheleph,

Almon (*al'-mon*) See also ALMON-DIBLATHAIM.
Jos 21:18 A' with her suburbs; four cities.

almond See also ALMONDS.
Ec 12: 5 the a' tree shall flourish,
Jer 1:11 I see a rod of an a' tree.

Almon-diblathaim (*al''-mon-dib-lath-a'-im*)
Nu 33:46 Dibon-gad, and encamped in A'.
47 And they removed from A', and

almonds
Ge 43:11 myrrh, nuts, and a':
Ex 25:33 Three bowls made like unto a',
33 bowls made like a'
34 four bowls made like unto a',
37:19 made after the fashion of a'
19 three bowls made like a'
20 four bowls made like a',
Nu 17: 8 blossoms, and yielded a'.

almond-tree See ALMOND and TREE.

almost
Ex 17: 4 they be a' ready to stone me.
Ps 73: 2 as for me my feet were a' gone;
94:17 my soul had a' dwelt in silence.
119:87 had a' consumed me upon earth;
Pr 5:14 I was a' in all evil
Ac 13:44 came a' the whole city together
19:26 but a' throughout all Asia,
21:27 the seven days were a' ended,
26:28 A' thou persuadest me to be
29 a', and altogether such as I
Heb 9:22 And a' all things are by the law

alms See also ALMSDEEDS.
M't 6: 1 do not your a' before men,
2 when thou doest thine a',
3 when thou doest a', let not
4 That thine a' may be in secret:
Lu 11:41 give a' of such things as ye have;
12:33 Sell that ye have, and give a';
Ac 3: 2 to ask a' of them that entered
3 into the temple asked an a'.
10 it was he which sat for a'
10: 2 gave much a' to the people,
4 prayers and thine a' are come up
31 thine a' are had in remembrance
24:17 I came to bring a' to my nation,

almsdeeds
Ac 9:36 full of good works and a' which

almug (*al'-mug*) See also ALGUM.
1Ki 10:11 great plenty of a' trees,
12 king made of the a' trees pillars
12 there came no such a' trees,

almug-trees See ALMUG and TREES.

aloes
Nu 24: 6 as the trees of lign a' which the
Ps 45: 8 garments smell of myrrh, and a',
Pr 7:17 perfumed my bed with myrrh, a',
Ca 4:14 and a', with all the chief spices:
Joh 19:39 brought a mixture of myrrh and a',

alone^A
Ge 2:18 good that the man should be a';
32:24 And Jacob was left a'; and there
42:38 brother is dead, and he is left a':
44:20 brother is dead, and he a' is left
Ex 14:12 thee in Egypt, saying, Let us a',
18:14 why sittest thou thyself a',
18 art not able to perform it thyself a'.
24: 2 And Moses a' shall come near the
32:10 Now therefore let me a',
Le 13:46 shall dwell a'; without the camp
Nu 11:14 able to bear all this people a',
17 that thou bear it not thyself a',
23: 9 the people shall dwell a',
De 1: 9 not able to bear you myself a':
12 How can I myself a' bear your
9:14 me a', that I may destroy them,
32:12 the Lord a' did lead him,
33:28 Israel then shall dwell in safety a':
Jos 22:20 man perished not a' in his iniquity.
J'g 3:20 which he had for himself a'.
11:37 let me a' two months,
1Sa 21: 1 Why art thou a', and no man with
2Sa 16:11 let him a', and let him curse;
18:24 and behold a man running a'.
25 And the king said, If he be a',
26 Behold another man running a'.
1Ki 11:29 and they two were a' in the field:
2Ki 4:27 Let her a'; for her soul is vexed
19:15 thou art the God, even thou a', of
23:18 And he said, Let him a';
18 So they let his bones a',
1Ch 29: 1 my son, whom a' God hath chosen,
Ezr 6: 7 the work of this house of God a';
Ne 9: 6 Thou, even thou, art Lord a';
Es 3: 6 scorn to lay hands on Mordecai a';
Job 1:15, 16, 17, 19 am escaped a' to tell thee.
7:16 let me a'; for my days are vanity.
19 let me a' till I swallow down my
9: 8 a' spreadeth out the heavens,
10:20 let me a', that I may take comfort
13:13 Hold your peace, let me a', that I
15:19 whom a' the earth was given,
31:17 have eaten my morsel myself a',
Ps 83:18 thou, whose name a' is Jehovah,
102: 7 as a sparrow a' upon the housetop.
136: 4 him who a' doeth great wonders:
Pr 9:12 scornest, thou a' shalt bear it.
Ec 4: 8 There is one a', and there is not a
10 him that is a' when he falleth;
11 but how can one be warm a'?
Isa 2:11, 17 Lord a' shall be exalted in that
5: 8 placed a' in the midst of the earth!
14:31 none shall be a' in his appointed
37:16 thou art the God, even thou a',
44:24 stretcheth forth the heavens a';
49:21 Behold, I was left a'; these, where
51: 2 I called him a', and blessed him,
63: 3 I have trodden the winepress a';
Jer 15:17 I sat a' because of thy hand:
49:31 which dwell a'.
La 3:28 He sitteth a' and keepeth silence,
Da 10: 7 And I Daniel a' saw the vision:
8 Therefore I was left a', and saw
Ho 4:17 is joined to idols: let him a'.
8: 9 a wild ass a' by himself:
M't 4: 4 shall not live by bread a',
14:23 he was there a'.
15:14 Let them a': they be blind leaders
18:15 between thee and him a':
M'r 1:24 Saying, Let us a'; what have we
4:10 And when he was a',
34 and when they were a',
6:47 and he a' on the land.
14: 6 Let her a'; why trouble ye her?
15:36 saying, Let a'; let us see whether
Lu 4: 4 not live by bread a', but by every
34 Saying, Let us a'; what have we
5:21 Who can forgive sins, but God a'?
6: 4 but for the priests a'?
9:18 as he was a' praying,
36 Jesus was found a'.
10:40 hath left me to serve a'?
13: 8 Lord, let it a' this year also,
Joh 6:15 into a mountain himself a'.
22 his disciples were gone away a';
8: 9 and Jesus was left a',
16 for I am not a', but I and the
29 the Father hath not left me a';
11:48 If we let him thus a', all men will
12: 7 Then said Jesus, Let her a':
24 and die, it abideth a':
16:32 and shall leave me a':
32 and yet I am not a', because the
17:20 pray I for these a', but for
Ac 5:38 from these men, and let them a':
19:26 not a' at Ephesus, but almost
Ro 4:23 for his sake a', that it was
11: 3 and I am left a', and they seek
Gal 6: 4 have rejoicing in himself a',
1Th 3: 1 to be left at Athens a';
Heb 9: 7 went the high priest a' once every
Jas 2:17 not works, is dead, being a'.

along
Ex 2: 5 walked a' by the river's side;
9:23 the fire ran a' upon the ground;
Nu 21:22 will go a' by the king's high way,
34: 3 wilderness of Zin a' by the coast
De 2:27 I will go a' by the highway,
Jos 10:10 and chased them a' the way
15: 3 and passed a' to Zin,
3 and passed a' to Hezron,
6 a' by the north of Beth-arabah
10 a' unto the side of mount Jearim,
11 and passed a' to mount Baalah,
16: 2 and passeth a' unto the borders
17: 7 border went a' on the right hand
18:18 And passed a' toward the side to
19 And the border passed a' to the
19:13 And from thence passeth on a' the
J'g 7:12 of the east lay a' in the valley

J'g 7:13 it, that the tent lay *a*'.
9:25 robbed all that came *a*' that way
37 *a*' by the plain of Meonenim.
11:18 went *a*' through the wilderness,
26 cities that be *a*' by the coasts of
20:37 liers in wait drew themselves *a*',
1Sa 6:12 went *a*' the highway, lowing as
28:20 Saul fell straightway all *a*'
2Sa 3:16 went with her *a*' weeping
16:13 Shimei went *a*' on the hill's side
2Ki 11:11 *a*' by the altar and the temple.
2Ch 23:10 *a*' by the altar and the temple,
Jer 41: 6 weeping all *a*' as he went:

aloof
Ps 38:11 friends stand *a*' from my sore;

Aloth (*a'-loth*) See also BEALOTH.
1Ki 4:16 Hushai was in Asher and in *A*':

aloud
Gen 45: 2 And he wept *a*':
1Ki 18:27 Cry *a*': for he is a god;
28 they cried *a*', and cut
Ezr 3:12 many shouted *a*' for joy:
Job 19: 7 I cry *a*', but there is no
Ps 51:14 my tongue shall sing *a*' of thy
55:17 will I pray, and cry *a*': and he
59:16 yea, I will sing *a*' of thy mercy
81: 1 Sing *a*' unto God our strength:
132:16 her saints shall shout *a*' for joy.
149: 5 let them sing *a*' upon their beds.
Isa 24:14 they shall cry *a*' from the sea.
54: 1 break forth into singing and cry *a*',
58: 1 Cry *a*', spare not, lift up thy voice
Da 3: 4 Then an herald cried *a*', To you
4:14 He cried *a*', and said thus, Hew
5: 7 The king cried *a*' to bring in the
Ho 5: 8 cry *a*' at Beth-aven,
Mic 4: 9 thou cry out *a*'? is there no king
M'r 15: 8 the multitude crying *a*' began to

Alpha (*al'-fah*)
Re 1: 8 I am *A*' and Omega, the
11 I am *A*' and Omega, the first and
21: 6 I am *A*' and Omega, the beginning
22:13 I am *A*' and Omega, the beginning

Alphæus (*al-fe'-us*) See also CLEOPAS.
M't 10: 3 James the son of *A*',
M'r 2:14 Levi the son of *A*' sitting
3:18 James the son of *A*',
Lu 6:15 James the son of *A*',
Ac 1:13 James the son of *A*',

Alpheus See ALPHAEUS.

already^
2Ch 28:13 offended against the Lord *a*',
Ne 5: 5 are brought unto bondage *a*',
Ec 1:10 it hath been *a*' of old time,
2:12 even that which hath been *a*' done.
3:15 which is to be hath *a*' been;
4: 2 the dead which are *a*' dead,
6:10 which hath been is named *a*',
Mal 2: 2 I have cursed them *a*', because
M't 5:28 committed adultery with her *a*'
17:12 Elias is come *a*', and they knew
M'r 15:44 marvelled if he were *a*' dead:
Lu 12:49 what will I, if it be *a*' kindled?
Joh 3:18 believeth not is condemned *a*',
4:35 they are white *a*' to harvest.
9:22 for the Jews have agreed *a*',
27 I have told you *a*', and ye did not
11:17 had lain in the grave four days *a*',
19:33 saw that he was dead *a*',
Ac 11:11 were three men *a*' come unto the
27: 9 because the fast was now *a*' past,
1Co 5: 3 have judged *a*', as though I were
2Co 12:21 many which have sinned *a*',
Ph'p 3:12 Not as though I had *a*' attained,
12 either were *a*' perfect:
16 whereto we have *a*' attained, let
2Th 2: 7 mystery of iniquity doth *a*' work:
1Ti 5:15 For some are *a*' turned aside
2Ti 2:18 that the resurrection is past *a*';
1Jo 4: 3 even now *a*' is it in the world.
Re 2:25 that which ye have *a*' hold fast

also^
Ge 1:16 rule the night: he made the stars *a*'.
2: 9 life *a*' in the midst of the garden,
3: 6 *a*' unto her husband with her;
18 Thorns *a*' and thistles shall it
21 Unto Adam *a*' and to his wife did
22 and take *a*' of the tree of life, and
4: 4 he *a*' brought of the firstlings of
22 Zillah, she *a*' bare Tubal-cain, an
26 to him also there was born a son;
6: 3 for that he *a*' is flesh:
4 the earth in those days; and *a*'
11 The earth *a*' was corrupt before
7: 3 Of fowls *a*' of the air by sevens,
8: 2 The fountains *a*' of the deep and
8 *A*' he sent forth a dove from him,
10:21 Unto Shem *a*', the father of all
12:15 The princes *a*' of Pharaoh saw
13: 5 And Lot *a*', which went with
16 shall thy seed *a*' be numbered.
14: 7 and *a*' the Amorites, that dwelt in
16 *a*' brought again his brother Lot,
16 and the women *a*', and the people.
15:14 *a*' that nation, whom they shall
16:13 Have I *a*' here looked after him
17:16 and give thee a son *a*' of her:
18:12 pleasure, my lord being old *a*'?
23 thou *a*' destroy the righteous
24 wilt thou *a*' destroy and not spare
19:21 thee concerning this thing *a*',
34 make him drink wine this night *a*';
35 father drink wine that night *a*':

Ge 20: 4 thou slay *a*' a righteous nation?
24:53 he gave *a*' to her brother and to
26:21 well, and strove for that *a*':
27:31 he *a*' had made savoury meat,
34 Bless me, even me *a*', O my father.
38 *a*', O my father. And Esau lifted
45 deprived *a*' of you both in one?
29:27 and we will give thee this *a*' for
28 Rachel his daughter to wife *a*'.
30 And he went in *a*' unto Rachel,
30 *a*' Rachel more than Leah, and
33 therefore given me this son *a*':
30: 3 that I may *a*' have children by
6 God hath judged me, and hath *a*'
15 away my son's mandrakes *a*'?
30 I provide for mine own house *a*'?
31:15 sold us, and hath quite devoured *a*'
32: 6 Esau, and *a*' he cometh to meet
18 lord Esau: and, behold, *a*' he is
33: 7 Leah *a*' with her children came
35:17 thou shalt have this son *a*'.
38:10 Lord: wherefore he slew him *a*'.
11 Lest peradventure he die *a*', as his
22 find her; and *a*' the men of the
24 hath played the harlot; and *a*',
40:15 land of the Hebrews: and here *a*'
16 unto Joseph, I *a*' was in my dream,
42:22 behold, *a*' his blood is required.
43: 8 both we, and thou, and *a*' our
13 Take *a*' your brother, and arise,
44: 9 die, and we *a*' will be my lord's
10 Now *a*' let it be according unto
16 he *a*' with whom the cup is found.
29 And if ye take this *a*' from me,
45:20 *A*' regard not your stuff; for the
46: 4 will *a*' surely bring thee up again:
34 until now, both we, and *a*' our
47: 3 both we, and *a*' our fathers.
18 lord *a*' hath our herds of cattle;
48:11 God hath shewed me *a* thy seed.
19 he *a*' shall become a people,
19 and he *a*' shall be great:
50:18 his brethren *a*' went and fell down
23 the children *a*' of Machir the son
Ex 1:10 they join *a*' unto our enemies,
2:19 and *a*' drew water enough for us,
3: 9 I have *a*' seen the oppression
4: 9 not believe *a*' these two signs,
14 And *a*', behold, he cometh forth
6: 4 I have *a*' established my covenant
5 I have *a*' heard the groaning of
7:11 Pharaoh *a*' called the wise men
11 Egypt, they *a*' did in like manner
23 did he set his heart to this *a*'.
8:32 hardened his heart at this time *a*',
10:24 let your little ones *a*' go with you.
25 Thou must give us *a*' sacrifices
26 Our cattle *a*' shall go with us:
12:32 *A*' take your flocks and your
32 and be gone; and bless me *a*'.
38 multitude went up *a*' with them;
15: 4 *a*' are drowned in the Red sea.
19:22 And let the priests *a*' which come
21: 6 shall *a*' bring him to the door,
29 owner *a*' shall be put to death.
35 the dead ox *a*' shall divide.
23: 9 *A*' thou shalt not oppress a
24:11 *a*' they saw God, and eat and
25:23 Thou shalt *a*' make a table of
29:15 Thou shalt *a*' take one ram; and
22 *A*' thou shalt take of the ram the
44 sanctify *a*' both Aaron and his
30:18 shalt *a*' make a laver of brass,
18 foot *a*' of brass, to wash withal:
23 thou *a*' unto thee principal spices,
31:13 Speak thou *a*' unto the children
33:12 thou hast *a*' found grace in my
17 I will do this thing *a*' that thou
35:14 The candlestick *a*' for the light,
37:12 *A*' he made thereunto a border
26 *a*' he made unto it a crown of
Le 5: 2 he *a*' shall be unclean, and
7:16 *a*' the remainder of it shall be
8: 8 *a*' he put in the breastplate the
9 *a*' upon the mitre, even upon his
9: 4 *A*' a bullock and a ram for peace
18 He slew *a*' the bullock and the ram
11:29 These *a*' shall be unclean unto
40 he *a*' that beareth the carcase of
13:18 The flesh *a*', in which, even in
38 If a man *a*' or a woman have in
47 The garment *a*' that the plague
14: 9 *a*' he shall wash his flesh in water,
15:18 The woman *a*' with whom man
20 every thing *a*' that she sitteth upon
18:19 *A*' thou shalt not approach unto
28 That the land spue not you out *a*'.
20:13 If a man *a*' lie with mankind, as
27 A man *a*' or woman that hath a
22:12 priest's daughter *a*' be married
23:27 *A*' on the tenth day of this seventh
39 *A*' in the fifteenth day of the
26:16 I *a*' will do this unto you; I will
22 I will *a*' send wild beasts among
24 Then will I *a*' walk contrary
28 contrary unto you *a*' in fury;
40 that *a*' they have walked contrary
41 that I *a*' have walked contrary
42 my covenant with Jacob, and *a*'
42 my covenant with Isaac, and *a*'
43 The land *a*' shall be left of them,
Nu 3: 1 These *a*' are generations of
4:22 Take *a*' the sum of the sons of
6:17 shall offer *a*' his meat offering,
9: 2 Let the children of Israel *a*' keep
10:10 *A*' in the day of your gladness,

Nu 11: 4 children of Israel *a*' wept again,
10 Moses *a*' was displeased.
12: 2 hath he not spoken *a*' by us?
15:15 *a*' for the stranger that sojourneth
16:10 and seek ye the priesthood *a*'?
17 thou *a*', and Aaron, each of you
34 Lest the earth swallow us up *a*'.
18: 2 brethren *a*' of the tribe of Levi,
3 neither they, nor ye *a*', die.
8 I *a*' have given thee the charge
28 ye *a*' shall offer an heave offering
20:11 drank, and their beasts *a*'.
22:19 tarry ye *a*' here this night,
33 surely now *a*' I had slain thee,
24:12 Spake I not *a*' to thy messengers
18 Seir *a*' shall be a possession for
24 and he *a*' shall perish for ever.
25 and Balak *a*' went his way.
27:13 thou *a*' shall be gathered unto
28:26 *A*' in the day of the firstfruits,
30: 3 If a woman *a*' vow a vow unto
31: 8 Balaam *a*' the son of Beor they
33: 4 *a*' the Lord executed judgments.
35: 2 give *a*' unto the Levites suburbs
De 1:37 *A*' the Lord was angry with me
2: 6 ye shall *a*' buy water of them
11 Which *a*' were accounted giants,
12 Horims *a*' dwelt in Seir beforetime:
20 (That *a*' was accounted a land of
3: 3 delivered into our hands Og *a*',
17 The plain *a*', and Jordan, and
20 until they *a*' possess the land
7:13 multiply thee: he will *a*' bless
8: 5 shalt *a*' consider in thine heart,
9: 8 *A*' in Horeb ye provoked the
19 hearkened unto me at that time *a*'.
20 I prayed for Aaron *a*' the same
10:10 hearkened unto me at that time *a*'
14 God, the earth *a*', with all that
15:17 And *a*' unto thy maidservant
18: 4 The firstfruit *a*' of thy corn,
20: 6 let him *a*' go and return unto
23:12 Thou shalt have a place *a*'
26:13 *a*' have given them unto the
28:51 which *a*' shall not leave thee
61 *A*' every sickness, and every
29:15 *a*' with him that is not here with
31: 2 and come in: *a*' the Lord hath
32:24 I will *a*' send the teeth of beasts
25 the suckling *a*' with the man of
33:28 *a*' his heavens shall drop down
Jos 1:15 they *a*' have possessed the land
2:12 ye will *a*' shew kindness unto my
7:11 they have *a*' transgressed my
11 have *a*' stolen, and dissembled *a*',
10:30 And the Lord delivered it *a*',
39 as he had done *a*' to Libnah,
13: 3 the Ekronites; *a*' the Avites:
22 Balaam *a*' the son of Beor,
15:19 south land; give me *a*' springs of
17: 1 There was *a*' a lot for the tribe
2 There was *a*' a lot for the rest
9 the coast of Manasseh *a*' was on
19:30 Ummah *a*', and Aphek, and Rehob:
20: 1 The Lord *a*' spake unto Joshua,
22: 7 them away *a*' unto the tents,
24: 5 I sent Moses *a*' and Aaron,
18 will we *a*' serve the Lord;
J'g 1:15 give me *a*' springs of water.
18 *A*' Judah took Gaza with the
22 they *a*' went up against Beth-el:
2: 3 I *a*' said, I will not drive them
10 And *a*' all that generation were
21 I *a*' will not henceforth drive out
3:22 the haft *a*' went in after the blade;
31 and he *a*' delivered Israel.
5: 4 the clouds *a*' dropped water.
15 even Issachar, and *a*' Barak:
6:35 who *a*' was gathered after him:
7:18 the trumpets *a*' on every side of
8: 9 he spake *a*' unto the men of Penuel,
22 and thy son, and thy son's son *a*':
31 she *a*' bare him a son, whose name
9: 2 remember *a*' that I am your bone
19 and let him *a*' rejoice in you:
49 of the tower of Shechem died *a*',
10: 9 passed over Jordan to fight *a*'
10 our God, and *a*' served Baalim.
12 The Zidonians *a*', and the
15: 5 and *a*' the standing corn, with
17: 2 and spakest of *a*' in mine ears,
19:10 his concubine *a*' was with him.
16 which was *a*' of mount Ephraim;
19 is bread and wine *a*' for me,
20:48 *a*' they set on fire all the cities
Ru 1: 5 Mahlon and Chilion died *a*' both
12 to night, and should *a*' bear sons;
17 and more *a*', if ought but death
2:16 let fall *a*' some of the handfuls
21 He said unto me *a*', Thou shalt
3:15 *A*' he said, Bring the vail that
4: 5 thou must buy it *a*' of Ruth the
1Sa 1: 6 adversary *a*' provoked her sore,
28 *a*' I have lent him to the Lord;
2:15 *A*' before they burnt the fat,
26 with the Lord, and *a*' with men.
3:12 I begin, I will *a*' make an end.
17 and more *a*', if thou hide
4:17 been *a*' a great slaughter among
17 two sons *a*', Hophni and Phinehas,
8: 8 other goods, so do they *a*' unto thee.
20 we *a*' may be like all the nations;
10:11, 12 Is Saul *a*' among the prophets?
26 And Saul *a*' went to Gibeah;
12:14 *a*' the king that reigneth over you
13: 4 Israel *a*' was had in abomination

1Sa 14:15 they a' trembled, and the earth
21 a' turned to be with the Israelites
22 they a' followed hard after them
44 answered, God do so and more a':
15: 1 Samuel a' said unto Saul,
23 a' rejected thee from being king.
29 a' the Strength of Israel will not
17:38 a' he armed him with a coat of
18: 5 and a' in the sight of Saul's
19:11 Saul a' sent messengers unto
20 of Saul, and they a' prophesied.
21 third time, and they prophesied a'.
22 Then went he a' to Ramah,
23 the Spirit of God was upon him a',
24 And he stripped off his clothes a',
24 say, Is Saul a' among the prophets?
20:15 But a' thou shalt not cut off thy
22:17 their hand a' is with David,
23:17 that a' Saul my father knoweth.
25 Saul a' and his men went to seek
24: 8 David a' arose afterward, and went
25:13 David a' girded on his sword:
22 more a' do God unto the enemies
43 David a' took Ahinoam of Jezreel;
26:25 things, and a' shalt still prevail.
28:19 the Lord will a' deliver Israel
19 thy sons be with me: the Lord a'
22 hearken thou a' unto the voice of
30:21 a' to abide at the brook Besor:
2Sa 1: 4 many of the people a' are fallen
4 and Jonathan his son are dead a'.
18 (A' he bade them teach the
2: 2 up thither, and his two wives a',
6 I a' will requite you this kindness,
7 and a' the house of Judah have
24 Joab a' and Abishai pursued
3: 9 So do God to Abner, and more a',
12 a', Make thy league with me, and,
19 Abner a' spake in the ears of
19 a' to speak in the ears of David
35 So do God to me, and more a', if I
4: 2 (for Beeroth a' was reckoned to
5: 2 A' in time past, when Saul was
15 Ibhar a', and Elishua, and
18 The Philistines a' came and
7:11 A' the Lord telleth thee that he
19 spoken a' of thy servant's house
8: 3 David smote also Hadadezer,
11 Which a' king David did dedicate
10:14 then fled they a' before Abishai,
11:12 to Uriah, Tarry here to day a',
17 and Uriah the Hittite died a'.
21, 24 Uriah the Hittite is dead a'.
12:13 The Lord a' hath put away thy sin;
14 the child a' that is born unto thee
13:36 king a' and all his servants wept
14: 7 and we will destroy the heir a':
15:19 Wherefore goest thou a' with us?
19 art a stranger, and a' an exile.
21 even there a' will thy servant be.
23 the king a' himself passed over
24 lo Zadok a', and all the Levites
27 king said a' unto Zadok the priest,
34 hitherto, so will I now also be
17: 5 Call now Hushai the Archite a',
10 he a' that is valiant, whose heart
18: 2 surely go forth with you myself a'.
22 I pray thee, a' run after Cushi.
26 said, He a' bringeth tidings.
19:13 God do so to me, and more a',
40 and a' half the people of Israel.
43 we have a' more right in David
20:14 together, and went a' after him.
26 Ira a' the Jairite was a chief ruler
21:20 and he also was born to the giant.
22:10 He bowed the heavens a', and came
20 brought me forth a' into a large
24 I was a' upright before him, and
36 Thou hast a' given me the shield
41 Thou hast a' given me the necks
44 a' hast delivered me from the
49 thou a' hast lifted me up on high
23:20 he went down a' and slew a lion
1Ki 1: 6 and he a' was a very goodly man;
14 I a' will come in after thee, and
22 Nathan the prophet a' came in.
33 The king a' said unto them, Take
46 a' Solomon sitteth on the throne
48 And a' thus said the king, Blessed
2: 5 Moreover thou knowest a' what
22 ask for him the kingdom a';
23 God do so to me, and more a',
3:13 I have a' given thee that which
18 that this woman was delivered a':
4:13 to him a' pertained the region of
15 he a' took Basmath the daughter
28 Barley a' and straw for the horses
33 he spake a' of beasts, and of fowl,
6:22 a' the whole altar that was by the
32 two doors a' were of olive tree;
33 So a' made he for the door of the
7: 2 built a' the house of the forest
8 Solomon made a' an house for
20 two pillars had pomegranates a'
31 and a' upon the mouth of it were
8:24 thou spakest a' with thy mouth,
9:21 the children of Israel a' were not
10:11 And the navy a' of Hiram, that
12 house, harps a' and psalteries
12:14 a' chastised you with whips,
13: 5 altar a' was rent, and the ashes
11 them they told a' to their father.
18 I am a prophet a' as thou art;
24 the lion a' stood by the carcase.
14:23 they a' built them high places,
24 were a' sodomites in the land:

1Ki 15:13 And a' Maachah his mother,
16: 7 a' by the hand of the prophet
16 and hath a' slain the king:
17:20 Lord my God, hast thou a' brought
18:35 he filled the trench a' with water.
19: 2 the gods do to me, and more a',
20: 3 thy wives a' and thy children,
10 more a', if the dust of Samaria
21:19 killed, and a' taken possession?
23 And of Jezebel a' spake the Lord,
22:22 persuade him, and prevail a':
2Ki 1:11 Again a' he sent unto him
2:13 He took up a' the mantle of Elijah
14 and when he a' had smitten the
3:18 the Moabites a' into your hand.
5: 1 was a' a mighty man in valour,
6:31 God do so and more a' to me, if
7: 4 if we sit still here, we die a'.
8 and carried thence a', and went
8: 1 and it shall a' come upon the land
9:27 Smite him a' in the chariot.
10: 2 a fenced city a', and armour;
5 was over the city, the elders a',
11:17 between the king a' and the
13: 6 and there remained the grove a'
16:14 he brought a' the brasen altar,
17:19 A' Judah kept not the
18: 2 His mother's name a' was Abi,
21:11 made Judah a' to sin with idols:
22:19 a' have heard thee, saith the Lord.
23: 5 them a' that burned incense unto
19 the houses a' of the high places
27 remove Judah a' out of my sight,
24: 4 And a' for the innocent blood
1Ch 1:14 The Jebusite a', and the Amorite,
21 Hadoram a', and Uzal, and
51 Hadad died a'. And the dukes of
2: 9 The sons a' of Hezron, that were
26 Jerahmeel had a' another wife,
49 She bare a' Shaaph the father of
3: 6 Ibhar a', and Elishama, and
18 Malchiram a', and Pedaiah, and
6: 3 The sons a' of Aaron; Nadab,
48 Their brethren a' the Levites
67 gave a' Gezer with her suburbs,
79 Kedemoth a' with her suburbs,
7:10 The sons a' of Jediael; Bilhan:
12 Shuppim a', and Huppim,
25 Rephah was his son, a' Resheph,
28 Shechem a' and the towns thereof,
8:13 Beriah a', and Shemia, who were
18 Ishmerai a', and Jezliah, and
32 these a' dwelt with their brethren
9:29 Some of them a' were appointed
38 they a' dwelt with their brethren
10:13 and a' for asking counsel of one
11:10 These a' are the chief of the
22 a' he went down and slew a lion
26 A' the valiant men of the armies
12:38 and all the rest a' of Israel were
13: 2 and with them a' to the priests
15:27 David a' had upon him an ephod
16: 6 Benaiah a' and Jahaziel the
30 the world a' shall be stable, that
38 Obed-edom a' the son of Jeduthun
17: 9 A' I will ordain a place for my
17 a' spoken of thy servant's house
18: 4 David a' houghed all the chariot
11 Them a' king David dedicated
20: 2 brought a' exceeding much spoil
6 he a' was the son of the giant.
21:23 lo, I give thee the oxen a' for
22: 4 A' cedar trees in abundance:
14 a' and stone have I prepared;
17 David a' commanded all the
23:26 And a' unto the Levites; they
24:30 The sons a' of Mushi; Mahli,
26: 6 A' unto Shemaiah his son were
10 A' Hosah, of the children of
27: 4 course was Mikloth a' the ruler:
30 Over the camels a' was Obil
32 A' Jonathan David's uncle was a
28:13 A' for the courses of the priests
14 silver a' for all instruments of
15 and a' for the lamps thereof,
17 A' pure gold for the fleshhooks,
21 a' the princes and all the people
29: 9 David the king a' rejoiced with
17 I know a', my God, that thou
2Ch 2: 8 Send me a' cedar trees, fir trees,
14 a' to grave any manner of graving,
3: 7 He overlaid a' the house,
12 the other wing was five cubits a',
15 A' he made before the house
4: 2 A' he made a molten sea of ten
6 He made a' ten lavers, and put
8 He made a' ten tables, and placed
14 He made a' bases, and lavers
16 The pots a', and the shovels,
19 the golden altar a', and the tables
5: 6 A' king Solomon, and a' the
12 A' the Levites which were the
7: 6 the Levites a' with instruments
8 A' at the same time Solomon
8: 5 A' he built Beth-horon the upper,
14 the porters a' by their courses at
9: 4 cupbearers a', and their apparel;
10 And the servants a' of Huram,
12: 5 a' left you in the hand of Shishak.
9 he carried away a' the shields of
12 and a' in Judah things went well.
13: 2 mother's name a' was Michaiah
3 Jeroboam a' set the battle in
11 the shewbread a' set they in order
14: 5 A' he took away out of all the
15 They smote a' the tents of cattle,

2Ch 15:16 And a' concerning Maachah the
17: 7 A' in the third year of his reign
11 A' some of the Philistines
18:21 him, and thou shalt a' prevail:
19:11 a' the Levites shall be officers
20: 1 It came to pass after this a',
21: 4 divers a' of the princes of Israel.
10 The same time a' did Libnah
13 and a' hast slain thy brethren of
17 king's house, and his sons a',
22: 2 mother's name a' was Athaliah
3 He a' walked in the ways of the
5 He walked a' after their counsel,
23:13 and sounded with trumpets, a'
18 A' Jehoiada appointed the offices
24: 1 his mother's name a' was Zibiah
7 and a' all the dedicated things
12 a' such as wrought iron and brass
20 the Lord, he hath a' forsaken you.
25: 6 a' an hundred thousand mighty
24 the hostages a', and returned to
26: 3 mother's name a' was Jecoliah
10 A' he built towers in the desert,
10 husbandmen a', and vine
20 yea, himself hasted a' to go out,
27: 1 mother's name a' was Jerushah.
5 He fought a' with the king of the
28: 2 a' molten images for Baalim.
4 sacrificed a' and burnt incense
5 he was a' delivered into the hand
8 and took a' away much spoil
18 Philistines a' had invaded the cities
18 Gimzo a' and the villages thereof:
29: 7 A' they have shut up the doors of
22 they killed a' the lambs, and they
27 Lord began a' with the trumpets,
35 a' the burnt offerings were in
30: 1 a' to Ephraim and Manasseh,
12 A' in Judah the hand of God was
31: 1 in Ephraim a' and Manasseh,
3 He appointed a' the king's portion
6 a' brought in the tithe of oxen and
19 A' of the sons of Aaron the priests,
32: 5 A' he strengthened himself, and
17 He wrote a' letters to rail on the
28 a' for the increase of corn, and
30 This same Hezekiah a' stopped
33: 4 A' he built altars in the house of
6 a' he observed times, and used
19 His prayer a', and how God was
34:13 A' they were over the bearers of
27 I have even heard thee a', saith
35: 9 Conaniah a', and Shemaiah and
36: 7 Nebuchadnezzar a' carried off the
13 And he a' rebelled against king
22 all his kingdom, and put it a' in
Ezr 1: 1 and put it a' in writing, saying,
7 A' Cyrus the king brought forth
3: 4 They kept a' the feast of the
7 gave money a' unto the masons,
4:20 mighty kings a' over Jerusalem,
5:10 We asked their names a', to
14 the vessels a' of gold and silver
6: 5 And a' let the golden and silver
11 A' I have made a decree, that
7:19 The vessels a' that are given thee
24 A' we certify you, that touching
8: 6 Of the sons a' of Adin; Ebed the
14 Of the sons a' of Bigvai; Uthai,
16 a' for Joiarib, and for Elnathan,
20 A' of the Nethinims, whom
27 A' twenty basons of gold, of a
28 Lord; the vessels are holy a';
35 A' the children of those that had
10: 4 we a' will be with thee: be of
23 A' of the Levites; Jozabad, and
24 Of the singers a'; Eliashib: and
28 Of the sons a' of Bebai;
Ne 1: 3 wall of Jerusalem a' is broken down,
2: 6 me, (the queen a' sitting by him,)
18 as a' the king's words that he had
3: 3 sons of Hassenaah build, who a'
8 unto him a' repaired Hananiah
29 After him repaired a' Shemaiah
5: 3 Some a' there were that said, We
4 There were a' that said, We have
9 A' I said, It is not good that ye do:
11 a' the hundredth part of the money,
13 A' I shook my lap, and said, So
16 Yea, a' I continued in the work
18 a' fowls were prepared for me,
6: 7 And thou hast a' appointed
19 A' they reported his good deeds
7:61 And... went up a' from Tel-melah,
8: 7 A' Jeshua, and Bani, and Sherebiah,
18 A' day by day, from the first day
9:13 down a' upon mount Sinai,
20 Thou gavest a' thy good spirit to
23 Their children a' multipliedst
37 a' they have dominion over our
10:32 A' we made ordinances for us,
36 A' the firstborn of our sons, and of
11: 1 the rest of the people a' cast lots,
15 A' of the Levites: Shemaiah the
22 The overseer a' of the Levites at
31 The children a' of Benjamin from
12: 9 A' Bakbukiah and Unni, their
10 Joiakim a' begat Eliashib, and
22 a' the priests, to the reign of
29 A' from the house of Gilgal, and
43 A' that day they offered great
43 a' and the children rejoiced:
13:15 as a' wine, grapes, and figs, and
16 There dwelt men of Tyre a' therein,
22 O my God, concerning this a',
23 a' saw I Jews that had married

Es 1: 9 A' Vashti the queen made a feast
16 wrong to the king only, but a'
2: 8 brought a' unto the king's house,
3:11 given to thee, the people a', to do
4: 8 A' he gave him a copy of the
16 I a' and my maidens will fast
5:12 am I invited unto her a' with
7: 8 Will he force the queen a' before
9 Behold a', the gallows fifty cubits
8: 8 Write ye a' for the Jews, as it
9:13 to do to morrow a' according unto
15 together on the fourteenth day a'
Job 1: 3 a' was seven thousand sheep,
6 and Satan came a' among them.
16 speaking, there came a' another,
17 came a' another, and said, The
18 came a' another and said, Thy
2: 1 Satan came a' among them to
5:25 Thou shalt know a' that thy seed
7: 1 a' like the days of an hireling?
9:11 he passeth on a', but I perceive
20 am perfect, it shall a' prove me
11:11 vain men: he seeth wickedness a';
19 A' thou shalt lie down, and none
12:15 a' he sendeth them out, and they
13: 2 know, the same do I know a':
16 He a' shall be my salvation: for an
27 puttest my feet a' in the stocks,
14: 2 he fleeth a' as a shadow, and
16: 4 I a' could speak as ye do: if your
12 he hath a' taken me by my neck,
17 in mine hands: a' my prayer
19 A' now, behold, my witness is in
17: 6 He hath made me a' a byword of
7 Mine eye a' is dim by reason of
9 The righteous a' shall hold on his
19:11 He hath a' kindled his wrath
20: 9 The eye a' which saw him shall
22:28 Thou shalt a' decree a thing, and
24:15 The eye a' of the adulterer waiteth
22 He draweth a' the mighty with his
30:11 they have a' let loose the bridle
31 My harp a' is turned to mourning,
31:28 This a' were an iniquity to be
32: 3 A' against his three friends was
10 me; I a' will shew mine opinion.
17 said, I will answer a' my part,
17 I a' will shew mine opinion.
33: 6 I a' am formed out of the clay.
19 He is chastened a' with pain upon
36: 1 Elihu a' proceeded, and said,
10 openeth a' their ear to discipline,
29 A' can any understand the
33 the cattle concerning the vapour.
37: 1 At this a' my heart trembleth,
11 A' by watering he wearieth the
39:30 young ones a' suck up blood:
40: 8 Wilt thou a' disannul my
14 Then will I a' confess unto thee
42: 9 them: the Lord a' accepted Job.
10 a' the Lord gave Job twice as
11 every man a' gave him a piece of
13 He had a' seven sons and three
Ps 1: 3 his leaf a' shall not wither; and
5:11 let them a' that love thy name
6: 3 My soul is a' sore vexed: but thou,
7:13 He hath a' prepared for him the
9: 9 The Lord a' will be a refuge for the
16: 7 a' instruct me in the night
9 my flesh a' shall rest in hope.
18: 7 the foundations a' of the hills
9 He bowed the heavens a', and came
13 Lord a' thundered in the heavens,
19 me forth a' into a large place;
23 I was a' upright before him, and I
35 Thou hast a' given me the shield
40 Thou hast a' given me the necks of
19:10 sweeter a' than honey and the
13 a' from presumptuous sins;
26: 1 I have trusted a' in the Lord;
27: 7 have mercy a' upon me, and
28: 9 feed them a', and lift them up for
29: 6 maketh them a' to skip like a calf;
35: 3 Draw out a' the spear, and stop
37: 4 Delight thyself a' in the Lord; and
5 unto the Lord; trust a' in him;
38:10 mine eyes, it a' is gone from me.
12 They a' that seek after my life
20 They a' that render evil for good
40: 2 me up a' out of an horrible pit, out
45:10 forget a' thine own people, and
52: 6 The righteous a' shall see, and
55:10 mischief a' and sorrow are in the
60: 7 Ephraim a' is the strength of mine
62:12 A' unto thee, O Lord, belongeth
65: 8 They a' that dwell in the
13 the valleys a' are covered over
13 they shout for joy, they a' sing.
68: 1 let them a' that hate him flee
8 the heavens a' dropped at the
18 yea, for the rebellious a', that the
69:11 made sackcloth a' my garment;
21 They gave me a' gall for my meat;
31 This a' shall please the Lord
36 The seed a' of his servants shall
71:18 a' when I am old and greyheaded,
19 Thy righteousness a', O God, is
22 I will a' praise thee with the
24 My tongue a' shall talk of thy
72: 8 have dominion a' from sea to sea,
12 the poor a', and him that hath no
15 prayer a' shall be made for him
74:16 day is thine, the night a' is thine:
75:10 horns of the wicked a' will I cut
76: 2 In Salem a' is his tabernacle,
77:12 I will meditate a' of all thy work,
Ps 77:16 the depths a' were troubled.
17 thine arrows a' went abroad.
78:14 In the daytime a' he led them
16 brought streams a' out of the rock,
20 bread a'? can he provide flesh for
21 anger a' came up against Israel;
27 rained flesh a' upon them as dust,
46 He gave a' their increase unto the
48 gave up their cattle a' to the hail,
55 cast out the heathen a' before them,
62 his people over a' unto the sword;
70 He chose David a' his servant,
81:16 He should have fed them a' with the
83: 8 Assur a' is joined with them:
84: 6 the rain a' filleth the pools.
89: 5 faithfulness a' in the congregation
11 heavens are thine, the earth a' is
21 mine arm a' shall strengthen him.
25 I will set his hand a' in the sea,
27 A' I will make him my firstborn,
29 His seed a' will I make to endure
43 Thou hast a' turned the edge of
92:11 Mine eye a' shall see my desire
95: 4 the strength of the hills is his a'.
96:10 the world a' shall be established
99: 4 king's strength a' loveth judgment;
105:23 Israel a' came into Egypt;
33 smote their vines a' and their
36 He smote a' all the firstborn in
37 forth a' with silver and gold:
106: 9 He rebuked the Red sea a', and it
16 They envied Moses a' in the camp,
27 their seed a' among the nations,
28 joined themselves a' unto Baal-peor,
32 him a' at the waters of strife,
42 Their enemies a' oppressed them,
46 He made them a' to be pitied of
107:32 exalt him a' in the congregation
38 He blesseth them a', so that they
108: 8 Ephraim a' is the strength of mine
109: 3 compassed me about a' with words
10 seek their bread a' out of their
25 I became a' a reproach unto them:
119: 3 They a' do no iniquity: They
23 Princes a' did sit and speak
24 Thy testimonies a' are my delight
41 Let thy mercies come a' unto me,
46 thy testimonies a' before kings,
48 My hands a' will I lift up unto
132:12 a' sit upon thy throne for evermore.
16 I will a' clothe her priests with
139:17 How precious a' are thy thoughts
141: 5 a' shall be in their calamities.
145:19 he a' will hear their cry, and will
148: 6 He hath a' stablished them for
14 He a' exalteth the horn of his
Pr 1:26 I a' will laugh at your calamity;
4: 4 He taught me a', and said unto
9: 2 she hath a' furnished her
11:25 shall be watered a' himself.
17:26 A' to punish the just is not good,
18: 3 cometh, then cometh a' contempt,
9 He a' that is slothful in his work
19: 2 A', that the soul be without
21:13 his ears at the cry of the poor, he a'
23:23 and sell it not; a' wisdom,
28 She a' lieth in wait as for a prey,
24:23 These things a' belong to the wise.
25: 1 These are a' proverbs of Solomon,
26: 4 according to his folly, lest thou a'
28:16 wanteth understanding is a' a
30:31 A greyhound: an he goat a';
31:15 She riseth a' while it is yet night,
28 her husband a', and he praiseth
Ec 1: 5 The sun a' ariseth, and the sun
17 that this a' is vexation of spirit.
2: 1 and, behold, this a' is vanity.
7 a' I had great possessions of great
8 gathered me a' silver and gold,
9 a' my wisdom remained with me.
14 perceived a' that one event
15 in my heart, that this a' is vanity.
19 under the sun. This is a' vanity.
21 This a' is vanity and a great evil.
23 rest in the night. This is a' vanity.
24 This a' I saw, that it was from the
26 This a' is vanity and vexation of
3:11 a' he hath set the world in their
13 a' that every man should eat and
4: 4 This is a' vanity and vexation of
8 a' vanity, yea, it is a sore travail
14 a' he that is born in his kingdom
16 they a' that come after shall not
16 Surely this a' is vanity and vexation
5: 7 there are a' divers vanities:
10 with increase: this is a' vanity.
16 And this a' is a sore evil, that in
17 his days a' he eateth in darkness,
19 a' to whom God hath given riches
6: 3 and a' that he have no burial;
9 this is a' vanity and vexation
7: 6 of the fool: this a' is vanity.
14 God a' hath set the one over
18 a' from this withdraw not thine
21 A' take no heed unto all words
22 a' thine own heart knoweth that
8:10 had so done: this is a' vanity.
14 I said that this a' is vanity.
16 (for a' there is that neither day
9: 3 a' the heart of the sons of men is
6 A' their love, and their hatred,
12 For man a' knoweth not his time:
13 wisdom have I seen a' under the
10: 3 Yea a', when he that is a fool
14 A fool a' is full of words: a man
11: 2 portion to seven, and a' to eight;
Ec 12: 5 A' when they shall be afraid of
Ca. 1:16 my beloved, yea, pleasant: a'
7: 8 of the boughs thereof: now a'
Isa 2: 7 Their land a' is full of silver and
7 their land is a' full of horses,
8 Their land a' is full of idols;
5: 2 of it, and a' made a winepress
6 I will a' command the clouds
6: 1 I saw a' the Lord sitting upon
8 A' I heard the voice of the Lord,
7:13 but will ye weary my God a'?
20 and it shall a' consume the beard.
8: 5 Lord spake a' unto me again,
11: 6 The wolf a' shall dwell with the
13 The envy a' of Ephraim shall
12: 2 he a' is become my salvation.
13: 3 I have a' called my mighty ones
16 Their children a' shall be dashed
18 bows a' shall dash the young
14:10 Art thou a' become weak as we?
13 I will sit a' upon the mount of
23 I will a' make it a possession for
17: 3 The fortress a' shall cease from
19: 8 The fishers a' shall mourn, and
13 Noph are deceived; they have a'
21:12 morning cometh, and a' the night:
22: 9 Ye have seen a' the breaches of
11 a' a ditch between the two walls
23:12 there a' shalt thou have no rest.
24: 5 The earth a' is defiled under the
26:12 for thou a' hast wrought all our
21 earth a' shall disclose her blood,
28: 7 they a' have erred through wine,
17 Judgment a' will I lay to the line,
29 a' cometh forth from the Lord
29:19 The meek a' shall increase their
24 They a' that erred in spirit shall
30: 5 but a shame, and a' a reproach.
22 defile a' the covering of thy graven
31: 2 Yet he a' is wise, and will bring
5 defending a' he will deliver it;
32: 4 The heart a' of the rash shall
7 instruments a' of the churl are evil:
33: 2 salvation a' in the time of trouble.
34: 3 Their slain a' shall be cast out,
11 the owl a' and the raven shall
14 beasts of the desert shall a' meet
14 the screech owl a' shall rest there,
15 shall the vultures a' be gathered,
38:22 Hezekiah a' had said, What is the
40:24 and he shall a' blow upon them,
44:19 a' I have baked bread upon the
45:16 be ashamed, and a' confounded,
46:11 I will a' bring it to pass;
11 have purposed it, I will a' do it.
48:12 I am the first, I a' am the last.
13 Mine hand a' hath laid the
19 Thy seed a' had been as the sand,
21 clave the rock a', and the waters
49: 6 I will a' give thee for a light to
7 arise, princes a' shall worship,
56: 6 A' the sons of the stranger, that
57: 8 Behind the doors a' and the posts
15 with him a' that is of a contrite
18 I will lead him a', and restore
60:14 sons a' of them that afflicted thee
16 Thou shalt a' suck the milk of
17 I will a' make thy officers peace,
21 people a' shall be all righteous:
62: 3 Thou shalt a' be a crown of glory
66: 4 I a' will choose their delusions,
21 I will a' take of them for priests
Jer 1: 3 came a' in the days of Jehoiakim
2: 8 pastors a' transgressed against me,
16 A' the children of Noph and
33 a' taught the wicked ones thy
34 A' in thy skirts is found the blood
36 a' shalt be ashamed of Egypt,
3: 6 Lord said a' unto me in the days
8 but went and played the harlot a'.
4:12 now a' will I give sentence against
6:14 healed a' the hurt of the daughter
17 A' I set watchmen over you,
7:27 thou shalt a' call unto them;
9:16 scatter them a' among the heathen.
10: 5 a' is it in them to do good.
13:23 then may ye a' do good, that are
14: 5 the hind a' calved in the field,
16: 1 word of the Lord came a' unto me,
8 shalt not a' go into the house of
19: 5 They have built a' the high places
20: 1 who was a' chief governor in the
23:14 I have seen a' in the prophets of
14 strengthen a' the hands of evildoers,
25:14 serve themselves of them a':
26:20 was a' a man that prophesied
27: 6 the field have I given him a' to
12 a' to Zedekiah king of Judah
16 A' I spake to the priests and to
28:14 him the beasts of the field a'.
29:24 Thus shalt thou a' speak to
30:19 I will a' glorify them, and they
20 children a' shall be as aforetime,
31:36 the seed of Israel a' shall cease
37 a' cast off all the seed of Israel
33:21 may a' my covenant be broken
36: 6 and a' thou shalt read them in the
39: 6 a' the king of Babylon slew all
40: 5 Go back a' to Gedaliah the son
41: 3 Ishmael a' slew all the Jews that
43:13 He shall break a' the images of
46:21 A' her hired men are in the midst
21 for they a' are turned back,
48: 2 A' thou shalt be cut down, O
7 treasures, thou shalt a' be taken:
8 the valley a' shall perish, and the

Jer 48:26 Moab a' shall wallow in his vomit,
26 and he a' shall be in derision.
34 for the waters a' of Nimrim shall
49:17 A' Edom shall be a desolation:
50:24 for thee, and thou art a' taken,
24 thou art found, and a' caught,
51:22 With thee a' will I break in
23 I will a' break in pieces with
52:10 slew a' all the princes of Judah
17 A' the pillars of brass that were
18 the caldrons a', and the shovels,
22 The second pillar a' and the
25 took a' out of the city an eunuch,
La 2: 9 her prophets a' find no vision
3: 8 A' when I cry and shout, he
16 He hath a' broken my teeth with
4:21 cup a' shall pass through unto
Eze 1: 5 A' out of the midst thereof came
10 four a' had the face of an eagle.
3:13 I heard a' the noise of the wings
21 a' thou hast delivered thy soul.
4: 1 Thou a', son of man, take thee a
2 set the camp a' against it,
4 Lie thou a' upon thy left side,
9 Take thou a' unto thee wheat,
11 shalt drink a' water by measure,
5: 3 Thou shalt a' take thereof a few
11 therefore will I a' diminish
7: 2 A', thou son of man, thus saith
18 They shall a' gird themselves
22 My face will I turn a' from them,
24 will a' make the pomp of the strong
8:13 He said a' unto me, Turn thee yet
18 Therefore will I a' deal in fury:
9: 1 He cried a' in mine ears with a
10 And as for me a', mine eye shall
10:16 the same wheel a' turned not from
17 these lifted up themselves a':
19 the wheels a' were beside them,
12: 1 word of the Lord a' came unto me
13 My net a' will I spread upon him,
13:21 Your kerchiefs a' will I tear,
16:10 I clothed thee a' with broidered
11 I decked thee a' with ornaments,
17 Thou hast a' taken thy fair jewels
19 My meat a' which I gave thee,
24 That thou hast a' built unto thee
26 hast a' committed fornication
28 Thou hast played the whore a'
39 will a' give thee into their hand,
39 shall strip thee a' of thy clothes,
40 They shall a' bring up a company
41 and thou a' shalt give no hire
43 therefore I a' will recompense
52 Thou a', which hast judged thy
52 yea, be thou confounded a',
17: 5 He took a' of the seed of the land,
7 There was a' another great eagle
13 a' taken the mighty of the land:
22 I will a' take of the highest branch
18: 4 so a' the soul of the son is mine:
19: 4 The nations a' heard of him;
20:15 Yet a' I lifted up my hand unto
23 unto them a' in the wilderness,
25 I gave them a' statutes that were
28 a' they made their sweet savour,
39 hereafter a', if ye will not hearken
21: 9 is sharpened, and a' furbished:
17 will a' smite mine hands together,
19 A', thou son of man, appoint thee
23:26 a' strip thee out of thy clothes,
35 bear thou a' thy lewdness and
37 and have a' caused their sons,
24: 3 set it on, and a' pour water
5 of the flock, and burn a' the
15 A' the word of the Lord came
25 A', thou son of man, shall it not
25:13 I will a' stretch out mine hand
26: 4 I will a' scrape her dust from her,
27:19 Dan a' and Javan going to and fro
30: 6 They a' that uphold Egypt shall
10 a' make the multitude of Egypt
13 I will a' destroy the idols, and I
18 At Tehaphnehes a' the day shall
31:17 They a' went down into hell
32: 6 a' water with thy blood the land
9 I will a' vex the hearts of many
13 I will destroy a' all the beasts
17 came to pass a' in the twelfth year,
33:30 A', thou son of man, the children
36: 1 A', thou son of man, prophesy
26 A new heart a' will I give you,
29 I will a' save you from all your
33 a' cause you to dwell in the cities,
37:24 shall a' walk in my judgments,
27 tabernacle a' shall be with them:
38:10 It shall a' come to pass, that at
39:16 And a' the name of the city shall
40: 8 measured a' the porch of the gate
12 The space a' before the little
14 He made a' posts of threescore
42 a' they laid the instruments
41: 8 I saw a' the height of the house
14 A' the breadth of the face of the
43:21 take the bullock a' of the sin
25 shall a' prepare a young bullock,
44:30 shall a' give unto the priest the
45: 5 shall a' the Levites, the ministers
47:20 side a' shall be the great sea
Da 6:22 and a' before thee, O king, have I
7: 6 the beast had a' four heads;
8:25 And through his policy a' he shall
25 shall a' stand up against the Prince
10: 6 His body a' was like the beryl,
11: 1 A' I in the first year of Darius
8 a' carry captives into Egypt

Da 11:14 a' the robbers of thy people shall
17 He shall a' set his face to enter
22 be broken, yea, a' the prince of
41 enter a' into the glorious land,
42 stretch forth his hand a' upon
Ho 2:11 will a' cause all her mirth to cease.
3: 3 man: so will I a' be for thee.
4: 3 sea a' shall be taken away.
5 and the prophet a' shall fall with
6 hast rejected knowledge, I will a'
6 law of thy God, I will a' forget thy
5: 5 Judah a' shall fall with them.
6:11 A', O Judah, he hath set an harvest
7:11 Ephraim a' is like a silly dove
8: 6 For from Israel was it a': the
9:12 yea, woe a' to them when I
10: 6 shall be a' carried unto Assyria
8 The high places a' of Aven, the sin
11: 3 I taught Ephraim a' to go,
12: 2 hath a' a controversy with Judah,
10 have a' spoken by the prophets,
Joe 1:12 tree, the palm tree a', and
20 The beasts of the field cry a'
2:12 Therefore a' now, saith the Lord,
29 And a' upon the servants and
3: 2 I will a' gather all nations, and will
6 The children a' of Judah and the
16 Lord a' shall roar out of Zion,
Am 1: 5 break a' the bar of Damascus,
2:10 A' I brought you up from the land
3:14 I will a' visit the altars of Beth-el:
4: 6 And I a' have given you cleanness
7 And a' I have withholden the rain
7: 6 This a' shall not be, saith the Lord
12 A' Amaziah said unto Amos,
9:14 they shall a' make gardens, and
Jon 4:11 and their left hand; and a' much
Mic 3: 3 Who a' eat the flesh of my people,
4:11 a' many nations are gathered
5:13 graven images a' will I cut off,
6:13 Therefore a' will I make thee sick
7:12 In that day a' he shall come even
Na 3:10 children a' were dashed in pieces
11 Thou a' shalt be drunken: thou
11 thou a' shalt seek strength
Hab 1: 8 Their horses a' are swifter than
2: 5 Yea a', because he transgresseth
15 him, and makest him drunken a',
16 shame for glory: drink thou a',
Zep 1: 4 I will a' stretch out mine hand
9 In the same day a' will I punish
13 they shall a' build houses, but
2:12 Ye Ethiopians a', ye shall be
3:12 I will a' leave in the midst of
Zec 3: 7 thou shalt a' judge my house,
7 and shalt a' keep my courts,
4: 9 his hands shall a' finish it; and
8: 6 should it a' be marvellous in mine
21 the Lord of hosts: I will go a'.
9: 2 Hamath a' shall border thereby;
5 Gaza a' shall see it, and be very
11 As for thee a', by the blood of thy
10:10 bring them again a' out of the
11: 8 Three shepherds a' I cut off in
8 lothed them, and their soul a'
12: 7 The Lord a' shall save the tents of
13: 2 and a' I will cause the prophets
14:14 Judah a' shall fight at Jerusalem;
Mal 1:13 Ye said a', Behold, what a
2: 9 Therefore have I a' made you
M't 2: 8 I may come and worship him a'.
3:10 And now a' the ax is laid unto
5:39 cheek, turn to him the other a'.
40 thy coat, let him have thy cloke a'.
6:14 heavenly Father will a' forgive you:
21 is, there will your heart be a'.
10: 4 Iscariot, who a' betrayed him.
32 will I confess a' before my Father
33 him will I a' deny before my Father
12:45 be a' unto this wicked generation.
13:22 He a' that received seed among
23 which a' beareth fruit, and
26 fruit, then appeared the tares a'.
29 ye root up a' the wheat with them.
15: 3 Why do ye a' transgress the
16 ye a' yet without understanding?
16: 1 a' with the Sadducees came,
18 And I say a' unto thee, That thou
17:12 Likewise shall a' the Son of man
18:33 not thou a' have had compassion
35 shall my heavenly Father do a'
19: 3 The Pharisees a' came unto him,
28 ye a' shall sit upon twelve thrones,
20: 4 Go ye a' into the vineyard, and
7 them, Go ye a' into the vineyard;
21:21 but a' if ye shall say unto this
24 I a' will ask you one thing,
22:26 Likewise the second a', and the
27 And last of all the woman died a'.
23:26 outside of them may be clean a'.
28 Even so ye a' outwardly appear
24:27 a' the coming of the Son of man
37 days of Noe were, so shall a' the
39 all away; so shall a' the coming
44 Therefore be ye a' ready: for in
25:11 Afterward came a' the other
17 two, he a' gained other two.
22 He a' that had received two
41 Then shall he say a' unto them
44 Then shall they a' answer him,
26:13 there shall a' this, that this
35 Likewise a' said all the disciples.
69 Thou a' wast with Jesus of Galilee.
71 This fellow was a' with Jesus of
73 Surely thou a' art one of them;
27:44 The thieves a', which were

M't 27:57 a' himself was Jesus' disciple:
M'r 1:19 who a' were in the ship mending
38 towns, that I may preach there a':
2:15 publicans and sinners sat a'
21 No man a' seweth a piece of new
26 and gave a' to them which were
28 of man is Lord a' of the sabbath.
3:19 Iscariot, which a' betrayed him:
4:36 And there were a' with him other
5:16 and a' concerning the swine.
7:18 ye so without understanding a'?
8: 7 to set them a' before them.
34 unto him with his disciples a',
38 of him a' shall the Son of man be
11:25 that your Father a' which is in
29 I will a' ask of you one question,
12: 6 he sent him a' last unto them,
22 last of all the woman died a'.
14: 9 this a' that she hath done shall
31 anywise. Likewise a' said they all.
67 a' wast with Jesus of Nazareth.
15:31 Likewise a' the chief priests
40 There were a' women looking on
41 (Who a', when he was in Galilee,
43 which a' waited for the kingdom of
Lu 1: 3 It seemed good to me a', having
35 therefore a' that holy thing which
36 thy cousin Elizabeth, she hath a'
2: 4 And Joseph a' went up from
35 pierce through thy own soul a',)
3: 9 And now a' the axe is laid unto
12 Then came a' publicans to be
4:23 do a' here in thy country.
41 And devils a' came out of many,
43 kingdom of God to other cities a':
5:10 And so was a' James, and John,
36 he spake a' a parable unto them;
39 No man a' having drunk old wine
6: 4 gave a' to them that were with
5 the Son of man is Lord a' of the
6 a' on another sabbath, that he
13 whom a' he named apostles;
14 Simon, (whom he a' named Peter,)
16 Iscariot, which a' was the traitor.
29 on the one cheek offer a' the other;
29 cloke forbid not to take thy coat a'.
31 to you, do ye a' to them likewise.
32 sinners a' love those that love
33 for sinners a' do even the same.
34 for sinners a' lend to sinners,
36 as your Father a' is merciful.
7: 8 I a' am a man set under authority,
49 Who is this that forgiveth sins a'?
8:36 They a' which saw it told them
9:61 another a' said, Lord, I will follow
10: 1 Lord appointed other seventy a',
39 Mary, which a' sat at Jesus' feet,
11: 1 as John a' taught his disciples.
4 for we a' forgive every one that is
18 If Satan a' be divided against
30 so shall a' the Son of man be to
34 thy whole body a' is full of light;
34 thy body a' is full of darkness.
40 make that which is within a'.
45 saying thou reproachest us a'?
46 Woe unto you a', ye lawyers!
49 a' said the wisdom of God, I will
12: 8 A' I say unto you, Whosoever
8 Son of man a' confess before the
34 is, there will your heart be a'.
40 Be ye therefore ready a': for the
54 And he said a' to the people,
13: 6 He spake a' this parable;
8 Lord, let it alone this year a',
14:12 said he a' to him that bade him,
12 lest they a' bid thee again,
26 and his own life a', he cannot be
16: 1 he said a' unto his disciples,
10 is least is faithful a' in much:
10 in the least is unjust a' in much.
14 And the Pharisees a', who were
22 the rich man a' died, and was
28 lest they a' come into this place
17:24 a' the Son of man be in his day.
26 a' in the days of the Son of man.
28 a' as it was in the days of Lot;
18:15 a' infants, that he would touch
19: 9 as he a' is a son of Abraham.
19 to him, Be thou a' over five cities.
20: 3 I will a' ask you one thing;
11 they beat him a', and entreated
12 a third: and they wounded him a',
31 and in like manner the seven a':
32 Last of all the woman died a'.
21: 2 a' a certain poor widow casting
22:20 Likewise a' the cup after supper,
24 there was a' a strife among them,
39 and his disciples a' followed
56 said, This man was a' with him.
58 Thou art a' of them. And Peter
59 truth this fellow a' was with him:
68 And if I a' ask you, ye will not
23: 7 who himself a' was at Jerusalem
27 of women, which a' bewailed and
32 And there were a' two other,
35 the rulers a' with them derided
36 And the soldiers a' mocked him,
38 a superscription a' was written
51 a' himself waited for the
55 And the women a', which came
24:22 certain women a' of our company
23 had a' seen a vision of angels,
Joh 3:23 John a' was baptizing in Ænon
5:18 said a' that God was his Father,
19 soever he doeth, these a' doeth
27 authority to execute judgment a',

Joh 6:24 disciples, they a· took shipping,
36 That ye a· have seen me, and
67 the twelve, Will ye a· go away?
7: 3 disciples a· may see the works
10 then went he a· up unto the feast,
47 the Pharisees, Are ye a· deceived?
52 Art thou a· of Galilee?
8:17 It is a· written in your law, that
19 should have known my Father a·.
9:15 again the Pharisees a· asked him
27 will ye a· be his disciples?
40 said unto him, Are we blind a·?
10:16 this fold: them a· I must bring,
11:16 Let us a· go, that we may die
33 a· weeping which came with her,
52 that a· he should gather together
12: 9 that they might see Lazarus a·,
10 that they might put Lazarus a·
18 this cause the people a· met him,
26 I am, there shall a· my servant be:
42 the chief rulers a· many believed
13: 9 but a· my hands and my head.
14 ye a· ought to wash one another's
32 God shall a· glorify him in himself,
34 that ye a· love one another.
14: 1 ye believe in God, believe a· in me.
3 where I am, there ye may be a·.
7 should have known my Father a·:
12 the works that I do shall he do a·;
19 because I live, ye shall live a·.
15:20 me, they will a· persecute you;
20 saying, they will keep yours a·.
23 hateth me hateth my Father a·.
27 And ye a· shall bear witness,
17: 1 that thy Son a· may glorify thee:
18 have I a· sent them into the world.
19 that they a· might be sanctified
20 for these alone, but for them a·
21 that they a· may be one in us:
24 Father, I will that they a·, whom
18: 5 And Judas a·, which betrayed him,
17 Art not thou a· one of this man's
25 not thou a· one of his disciples?
19:23 soldier a part; and a· his coat:
39 And there came a· Nicodemus,
20: 8 Then went in a· that other disciple
21: 3 say unto him, We a· go with thee.
20 a· leaned on his breast at supper,
25 a· many other things which Jesus
Ac 1: 3 To whom a· he shewed himself
11 Which a· said, Ye men of Galilee,
2:22 midst of you, as ye yourselves a·
26 moreover a· my flesh shall rest
3:17 ye did it, as did a· your rulers.
5: 2 part of the price, his wife a· being
16 There came a· a multitude out of
32 and so is a· the Holy Ghost,
37 he a· perished; and all, even as
7:45 Which a· our fathers that came
8:13 Then Simon himself believed a·:
19 Give me a· this power,
9:32 he came down a· to the saints
10:26 I myself a· am a man.
45 a· was poured out the gift of the
11: 1 had a· received the word of God.
18 God a· to the Gentiles granted
30 Which a· they did, and sent it to
12: 3 proceeded further to take Peter a·.
13: 5 had a· John to their minister.
9 Then Saul, (who a· is called Paul,)
22 to whom a· he gave testimony,
33 again; as it is a· written in the
35 he saith a· in another psalm,
14: 5 a· of the Jews with their rulers,
15 We a· are men of like passions
15:27 shall a· tell you the same things
32 Judas and Silas, being prophets a·
35 Paul a· and Barnabas continued
35 of the Lord, with many others a·.
17: 6 upside down are come hither a·;
12 a· of honourable women which
13 at Berea, they came thither a·,
28 as certain a· of your own poets
28 For we are a· his offspring.
19:17 to all the Jews and Greeks a·
19 them a· which used curious arts
21 been there, I must a· see Rome.
27 a· that the temple of the great
20:30 A· of your own selves shall men
21:13 a· to die at Jerusalem for the
16 with us a· certain of the disciples
24 thou thyself a· walkest orderly,
28 brought Greeks a· into the temple,
22: 5 As a· the high priest doth bear
5 from whom a· I received letters
20 was shed, I a· was standing
29 the chief captain a· was afraid,
23:11 must thou bear witness a· at Rome.
30 his accusers a· to say before thee
33 presented Paul a· before him.
35 when thine accusers are a· come.
24: 6 a· hath gone about to profane
9 And the Jews a· assented, saying
15 which they themselves a· allow,
26 hoped a· that money
25:22 I would a· hear the man myself.
24 both at Jerusalem, and a· here,
26:10 Which thing I a· did in Jerusalem:
26 before whom a· I speak freely:
29 but a· all that hear me this day,
27:10 lading and ship, but a· of our lives.
12 part advised to depart thence a·,
36 and they a· took some meat.
28: 9 So when this was done, others a·,
10 a· honoured us with many honours;
Ro 1:13 have some fruit among you a·,
Ro 1:16 Jew first, and a· to the Greek.
24 a· gave them up to uncleanness
27 And likewise a· the men, leaving
2: 9 Jew first, and a· of the Gentile;
10 good, to the Jew first, and a·
12 law shall a· perish without law:
15 conscience a· bearing witness,
3: 7 yet am I a· judged as a sinner?
29 of the Jews only? is he not a· of
29 Yes, of the Gentiles a·:
4: 6 David a· describeth the blessedness
9 or upon the uncircumcision a·?
11 might be imputed unto them a·:
12 who a· walk in the steps of that
16 to that a· which is of the faith of
21 he was able a· to perform.
24 But for us a·, to whom it shall be
5: 3 but we glory in tribulations a·:
11 we a· joy in God through our Lord
15 the offence, so a· is the free gift.
6: 4 a· should walk in newness of life.
5 we shall be a· in the likeness of
8 believe that we shall a· live with
11 reckon ye a· yourselves to be dead
7: 4 ye a· are become dead to the law
8:11 shall a· quicken your mortal bodies
17 that we may be a· glorified
21 creature itself a· shall be delivered
23 not only they, but ourselves a·,
26 Spirit a· helpeth our infirmities:
29 foreknow, he a· did predestinate
30 he did predestinate, them he a·
30 he called, them he a· justified:
30 he justified, them he a· glorified.
34 who a· maketh intercession for us.
9: 1 a· bearing me witness in the Holy
10 but when Rebecca a· had
24 Jews only, but a· of the Gentiles?
25 As he saith a· in Osee, I will call
27 Esaias a· crieth concerning Israel,
11: 1 For I a· am an Israelite, of the
5 present time a· there is a remnant
16 be holy, the lump is a· holy:
21 heed lest he a· spare not thee.
22 otherwise thou a· shalt be cut off.
31 so have these a· now not believed,
13: 5 wrath, but a· for conscience sake.
6 for this cause pay ye tribute a·:
15: 7 receive ye one another, as Christ a·
14 I myself a· am persuaded of you,
14 that ye a· are full of goodness,
14 able a· to admonish one another.
22 a· I have been much hindered
27 their duty is a· to minister unto
16: 2 of many, and of myself a·.
4 a· all the churches of the Gentiles.
1Co 1: 8 Who shall a· confirm you unto
16 And I baptized a· the household
2:13 Which things a· we speak, not in
4: 8 that we a· might reign with you.
5:12 what have I to do to judge them a·
6:14 and will a· raise up us by his own
7: 3 a· the wife unto the husband.
4 a· the husband hath not power of
22 likewise a· he that is called,
34 difference a· between a wife and a
40 I think a· that I have the Spirit
9: 8 saith not the law the same a·?
10: 6 evil things, as they a· lusted.
9 as some of them a· tempted,
10 as some of them a· murmured,
13 the temptation a· make a way to
11: 1 even as I a· am of Christ.
6 not covered, let her a· be shorn:
12 so is the man a· by the woman;
19 must be a· heresies among you,
23 the Lord that which a· I delivered
25 same manner a· he took the cup,
12:12 are one body: so a· is Christ.
13:12 I know even as a· I am known.
14:15 pray with the understanding a·:
15 sing with the understanding a·.
19 my voice I might teach others a·,
34 under obedience, as a· saith the
15: 1 which a· ye have received,
2 By which a· ye are saved, if ye
3 of all that which I a· received,
8 he was seen of me a·,
14 vain, and your faith is a· vain.
18 they a· which are fallen asleep
21 a· the resurrection of the dead.
28 shall the Son a· himself be subject
40 There are a· celestial bodies,
42 a· is the resurrection of the dead.
48 such are they a· that are earthy:
48 such are they a· that are heavenly.
49 a· bear the image of the heavenly,
16: 4 And if it be meet that I go a·,
10 the work of the Lord, as I a· do.
2Co 1: 5 consolation a· aboundeth by Christ.
6 sufferings which we a· suffer:
7 shall ye be a· of the consolation.
11 Ye a· helping together by prayer
14 As a· ye have acknowledged us in
14 even as ye a· are ours in the day
22 Who hath a· sealed us, and given
2: 9 For to this end a· did I write,
10 ye forgive any thing, I forgive a·:
3: 6 Who a· hath made us able
4:10 that the life a· of Jesus might be
11 for Jesus' sake, that the life a·
13 we a· believe, and therefore speak;
14 raise up us a· by Jesus, and shall
5: 5 who a· hath given unto us the
11 and I trust a· are made manifest
6: 1 beseech ye a· that ye receive not
2Co 6:13 my children,) be ye a· enlarged.
8: 6 so he would a· finish in you
6 the same grace a·.
7 see that ye abound in this grace a·.
10 but a· to be forward a year ago.
11 so there may be a performance a·
14 abundance a· may be a supply for
19 a· chosen of the churches to travel
21 Lord, but a· in the sight of men.
9: 6 sparingly shall reap a· sparingly;
6 shall reap a· bountifully.
12 abundant a· by many thanksgivings
10:11 such will we be a· in deed when
14 as far as to you a· in preaching
11:15 his ministers a· be transformed as
18 after the flesh, I will glory a·.
21 speak foolishly,) I am bold a·.
13: 4 For we a· are weak in him, but we
9 and this a· we wish, even your
Ga 2: 1 and took Titus with me a·.
10 which I a· was forward to do.
13 Barnabas a· was carried away
17 we ourselves a· are found sinners.
5:21 as I have a· told you in time past,
25 Spirit, let us a· walk in the Spirit.
6: 1 thyself, lest thou a· be tempted.
7 man soweth, that shall he a· reap.
Eph 1:11 In whom a· we have obtained an
13 In whom ye a· trusted, after that
13 in whom a· after that ye believed,
15 I a·, after I heard of your faith
21 but a· in that which is to come:
2: 3 a· we all had our conversation
22 In whom ye a· are builded together
4: 9 but that he a· descended first into
10 is the same a· that ascended
5: 2 in love, as Christ a· hath loved us,
25 love your wives, even as Christ a·
6: 9 that your Master a· is in heaven;
21 that ye a· may know my affairs,
Ph'p 1:15 strife; and some a· of good will:
20 now a· Christ shall be magnified
29 but a· to suffer for his sake;
2: 4 man a· on the things of others.
5 you, which was a· in Christ Jesus:
9 God a· hath highly exalted him,
18 For the same cause a· do ye joy,
19 that I a· may be of good comfort,
27 not on him only, but on me a·,
3: 4 though I might a· have confidence
12 for which a· I am apprehended
20 whence a· we look for the Saviour,
4: 3 I intreat thee a·, true yokefellow,
3 with Clement a·, and with other
10 wherein ye were a· careful, but
15 Now ye Philippians know a·,
Col 1: 6 forth fruit, as it doth a· in you,
7 As ye a· learned of Epaphras our
8 Who a· declared unto us your love
9 For this cause we a·, since the day
29 Whereunto I a· labour, striving
2:11 In whom a· ye are circumcised
12 with him in baptism, wherein a·
3: 4 ye a· appear with him in glory.
7 the which ye a· walked some time,
8 But now ye a· put off all these;
13 Christ forgave you, so a· do ye.
15 which a· ye are called in one body;
4: 3 Withal praying a· for us, that God
3 of Christ, for which I am a·
16 that it be read a· in the church
1Th 1: 5 a· in power, and in the Holy Ghost,
8 but a· in every place your faith to
2: 8 of God only, but a· our own souls,
10 Ye are witnesses, and God a·,
13 For this cause a· thank we God
13 which effectually worketh a· in
14 for ye a· have suffered like things
3: 6 to see us, as we a· to see you:
4: 6 as we a· have forewarned you and
8 a· given unto us his holy Spirit.
14 so them a· which sleep in Jesus
5:11 edify one another, even as a· ye do.
24 that calleth you, who a· will do it.
2Th 1: 5 of God, for which ye a· suffer:
11 Wherefore a· we pray always for
1Ti 2: 9 In like manner a·, that women
3:10 And let these a· first be proved;
5:13 but tattlers a· and busybodies,
20 before all, that others a· may fear.
25 Likewise a· the good works of
6:12 life, whereunto thou art a· called,
2Ti 1: 5 I am persuaded that in thee a·.
12 cause I a· suffer these things:
2: 2 shall be able to teach others a·.
5 if a man a· strive for masteries,
10 they may a· obtain the salvation
11 with him, we shall a· live with him:
12 suffer, we shall a· reign with him:
12 we deny him, he a· will deny us:
20 but a· of wood and of earth;
22 Flee a· youthful lusts: but follow
3: 1 This know a·, that in the last days
8 so do these a· resist the truth:
9 manifest unto all men, as theirs a·
4: 8 them a· that love his appearing.
15 Of whom be thou ware a·; for he
Ph'm 21 thou wilt a· do more than I say.
22 withal prepare me a· a lodging:
Heb 1: 2 by whom a· he made the worlds;
2: 4 God a· bearing them witness,
14 he a· himself likewise took part
3: 2 as a· Moses was faithful in all his
4:10 he a· hath ceased from his own
5: 2 he himself a· is compassed with
3 for the people, so a· for himself.

Heb 5: 5 So a· Christ glorified not himself
6 As he saith a· in another place,
7: 2 a· Abraham gave a tenth part of
2 and after that a· King of Salem,
9 Levi a·, who receiveth tithes,
12 necessity a change a· of the law.
25 Wherefore he is able a· to save
8: 3 this man have somewhat a· to offer.
6 by how much a· he is the mediator
9: 1 first covenant had a· ordinances
16 there must a· of necessity be the
10:15 the Holy Ghost a· is a witness
11:11 Through faith a· Sara herself
19 from whence a· he received him
32 of David a·, and Samuel, and of
12: 1 seeing we a· are compassed about
26 not the earth only, but a· heaven.
13: 3 being yourselves a· in the body.
12 Wherefore Jesus a·, that he might
Jas 1:11 so a· shall the rich man fade away
2: 2 in a· a poor man in vile raiment;
19 the devils a· believe, and tremble.
25 Likewise a· was not Rahab the
26 faith without works is dead a·.
3: 2 able a· to bridle the whole body.
4 Behold a· the ships, which though
5: 8 Be ye a· patient; stablish your
1Pet 2: 5 Ye a·, as lively stones, are built up
6 Wherefore a· it is contained in
8 whereunto a· they were appointed.
18 and gentle, but a· to the froward.
21 because Christ a· suffered for us,
3: 1 they a· may without the word
5 in the old time the holy women a·,
18 For Christ a· hath once suffered
19 By which a· he went and preached
21 even baptism doth a· now save us
4: 6 preached a· to them that are dead,
13 may be glad a· with exceeding joy.
5: 1 I exhort, who am a· an elder, and
1 and a· a partaker of the glory
2Pet 1:19 We have a· a more sure word of
2: 1 But there were false prophets a·
3:10 the earth a· and the works that
15 brother Paul a· according to the
16 As a· in all his epistles, speaking
16 as they do a· the other scriptures,
17 things before, beware lest ye a·
1Jo 1: 3 that ye a· may have fellowship
2: 2 a· for the sins of the whole world.
6 ought himself a· so to walk,
23 the Son hath the Father a·.
24 ye a· shall continue in the Son,
3: 4 sin transgresseth a· the law:
4:11 we ought a· to love one another
21 loveth God love his brother a·.
5: 1 him a· that is begotten of him.
2Jo 1 but a· all they that have known the
3Jo 12 and we a· bear record; and ye
Jude 8 Likewise a· these filthy dreamers
14 And Enoch a·, the seventh from
Re 1: 7 him, and they a· which pierced
9 I John, who a· am your brother,
2: 6 the Nicolaitanes, which I a· hate.
15 So hast thou a· them that hold
3:10 I a· will keep thee from the hour
21 even as I a· overcame, and am set
6:11 fellowservants a· and their
11: 8 where a· our Lord was crucified.
14:17 he a· having a sharp sickle.

altar See also ALTARS.
Ge 8:20 Noah builded an a· unto the Lord
20 offered burnt offerings on the a·.
12: 7 there builded he an a·
8 there he builded an a·
13: 4 Unto the place of the a·,
18 built there an a· unto the Lord.
22: 9 Abraham built an a· there,
9 laid him on the a·
26:25 he builded an a· there,
33:20 And he erected there an a·,
35: 1 make there an a· unto God,
3 I will make there an a·
7 he built there an a·,
Ex 17:15 And Moses built an a·,
20:24 An a· of earth thou shalt make
25 if thou wilt make me an a· of stone,
26 go up by steps unto mine a·,
21:14 thou shalt take him from mine a·,
24: 4 builded an a· under the hill,
6 the blood he sprinkled on the a·.
27: 1 thou shalt make an a·
1 the a· shall be foursquare:
5 compass of the a· beneath, that
5 may be even to the midst of the a·.
6 thou shalt make staves for the a·,
7 be upon the two sides of the a·,
28:43 when they come near unto the a·
29:12 put it upon the horns of the a·
12 beside the bottom of the a·.
13 burn them upon the a·.
16 sprinkle it round about upon the a·.
18 burn the whole ram upon the a·:
20 sprinkle the blood upon the a·
21 the blood that is upon the a·,
25 burn them upon the a·
36 thou shalt cleanse the a·,
37 an atonement for the a·, and
37 and it shall be an a· most holy:
37 toucheth the a· shall be holy.
38 thou shalt offer upon the a·;
44 the congregation, and the a·:
30: 1 thou shalt make an a· to burn
18 the congregation and the a·,
20 when they come near to the a·

Ex 30:27 and the a· of incense,
28 the a· of burnt offering
31: 8 the a· of incense,
9 the a· of burnt offering
32: 5 he built an a· before it;
35:15 the incense a·, and his staves,
16 The a· of burnt offering,
37:25 he made the incense a·
38: 1 he made the a· of burnt offering
3 he made all the vessels of the a·,
4 he made for the a· a brasen grate
7 the rings on the sides of the a·,
7 made the a· hollow with boards.
30 and the brasen a·,
30 all the vessels of the a·,
39:38 the golden a·, and the anointing
39 The brasen a·, and his grate
40: 5 thou shalt set the a· of gold
6 the a· of the burnt offering
7 of the congregation and the a·,
10 shalt anoint the a· of the burnt
10 all his vessels, and sanctify the a·:
10 and it shall be an a· most holy.
26 he put the golden a· in the tent
29 he put the a· of burnt offering
30 tent of the congregation and the a·,
32 they came near unto the a·,
33 about the tabernacle and the a·,
Le 1: 5 blood round about upon the a·
7 shall put fire upon the a·,
8 the fire which is upon the a·:
9 the priest shall burn all on the a·,
11 kill it on the side of the a·
11 blood round about upon the a·.
12 the fire which is upon the a·:
13 burn it upon the a·:
15 the priest shall bring it unto the a·,
15 burn it on the a·; and the blood
15 wrung out at the side of the a·:
16 cast it beside the a·
17 the priest shall burn it upon the a·,
2: 2 burn the memorial of it upon the a·,
8 he shall bring it unto the a·.
9 shall burn it upon the a·:
12 shall not be burnt on the a·
3: 2 shall sprinkle the blood upon the a·
5 shall burn it on the a·
8 round about upon the a·.
11 the priest shall burn it upon the a·:
13 upon the a· round about.
16 priest shall burn them upon the a·.
4: 7 blood upon the horns of the a·
7 the bullock at the bottom of the a·
10 shall burn them upon the a·
18 blood upon the horns of the a·
18 the blood at the bottom of the a·
19 burn it upon the a·.
25 it upon the horns of the a·
25 blood at the bottom of the a·
26 burn all his fat upon the a·,
30 it upon the horns of the a·
30 thereof at the bottom of the a·.
31 shall burn it upon the a·
34 it upon the horns of the a·
34 thereof at the bottom of the a·:
35 shall burn them upon the a·,
5: 9 upon the side of the a·;
9 out at the bottom of the a·:
12 burn it on the a·,
6: 9 the burning upon the a·
9 the fire of the a· shall be burning
10 with the burnt offering on the a·,
10 and he shall put them beside the a·.
12 the fire upon the a· shall be
13 shall ever be burning upon the a·;
14 before the Lord, before the a·.
15 shall burn it upon the a·
7: 2 sprinkle round about upon the a·.
5 priest shall burn them upon the a·
31 shall burn the fat upon the a·:
8:11 he sprinkled thereof upon the a·
11 and anointed the a· and all
15 put it upon the horns of the a·
15 and purified the a·, and poured
15 blood at the bottom of the a·,
16 Moses burnt it upon the a·.
19 sprinkled the blood upon the a·
21 burnt the whole ram upon the a·:
24 sprinkled the blood upon the a·
28 burnt them on the a·
30 the blood which was upon the a·,
9: 7 Go unto the a·,
8 Aaron therefore went unto the a·,
9 put it upon the horns of the a·,
9 the blood at the bottom of the a·:
10 he burnt upon the a·;
12 sprinkled round about upon the a·.
13 and he burnt them upon the a·.
14 the burnt offering on the a·.
17 burnt it upon the a·,
18 which he sprinkled upon the a·
20 he burnt the fat upon the a·
24 upon the a· the burnt offering
10:12 eat it without leaven beside the a·:
14:20 the meat offering upon the a·:
16:12 burning coals of fire from off the a·
18 he shall go out unto the a·
18 put it upon the horns of the a·
20 the a·, he shall bring the live goat:
25 shall he burn upon the a·.
33 of the congregation, and for the a·,
17: 6 sprinkle the blood upon the a·
11 to you upon the a·
21:23 nor come nigh unto the a·,
22:22 offering by fire of them upon the a·
Nu 3:26 by the a· round about,

Nu 4:11 golden a· they shall spread a cloth
13 take away the ashes from the a·,
14 all the vessels of the a·;
26 by the a· round about,
5:25 offer it upon the a·:
26 and burn it upon the a·,
7: 1 both the a· and all the vessels
10 offered for dedicating of the a·
10 offered their offering before the a·.
11 for the dedicating of the a·.
84 This was the dedication of the a·,
88 the dedication of the a·, after that
16:38, 39 plates for a covering of the a·:
46 put fire therein from off the a·,
18: 3 vessels of the sanctuary and the a·,
5 the charge of the a·:
7 for everything of the a·,
17 sprinkle their blood upon the a·,
23: 2 on every a· a bullock and a ram.
4 upon every a· a bullock and a ram.
14 a bullock and a ram on every a·.
30 a bullock and a ram on every a·.
De 12:27 upon the a· of the Lord thy God:
27 shall be poured out upon the a·
16:21 trees near unto the a· of the Lord
26: 4 set it down before the a·
27: 5 shalt thou build an a·
5 an a· of stones:
6 build the a· of the Lord thy God
33:10 burnt sacrifice upon thine a·.
Jos. 8:30 Then Joshua built an a·
31 an a· of whole stones,
9:27 and for the a· of the Lord,
22:10 there an a· by Jordan, a great a·
11 have built an a· over against
16 in that ye have builded you an a·,
19 in building you an a·
19 beside the a· of the Lord
23 That we have built us an a·
26 prepare to build us an a·,
28 Behold the pattern of the a· of
29 to build an a· for burnt offerings,
29 beside the a· of the Lord
34 called the a· Ed:
J'g 6:24 Then Gideon built an a· there
25 throw down the a· of Baal
26 and build an a· unto the Lord
28 the a· of Baal was cast down,
28 offered upon the a· that was built
30 he hath cast down the a· of Baal,
31 because one hath cast down his a·.
32 because he hath thrown down his a·.
13:20 toward heaven from off the a·,
20 in the flame of the a·.
21: 4 built there an a·,
1 Sa 2:28 to offer upon mine a·,
33 I shall not cut off from mine a·,
7:17 and there he built an a·
14:35 And Saul built an a·
35 the same was the first a·
2Sa 24:18 rear an a· unto the Lord
21 to build an a· unto the Lord,
25 David built there an a·
1Ki 1:50 caught hold on the horns of the a·.
51 on the horns of the a·, saying, Let
53 they brought him down from the a·.
2:28 caught hold on the horns of the a·.
29 behold, he is by the a·.
3: 4 did Solomon offer upon that a·.
6:20 and so covered the a·
22 also the whole a·
7:48 the a· of gold, and the table of gold,
8:22 Solomon stood before the a· of the
31 the oath come before thine a·
54 he arose from before the a·
64 the brasen a· that was before the
9:25 upon the a· which he built
25 he burnt incense upon the a· that
12:32 he offered upon the a·.
33 So he offered upon the a· which he
33 he offered upon the a·, and burnt
13: 1 Jeroboam stood by the a·
2 he cried against the a· in the word
2 and said, O a·, a·,
3 the a· shall be rent,
4 which had cried against the a· in
4 he put forth his hand from the a·,
5 the a· also was rent, and
5 the ashes poured out from the a·,
32 against the a· in Beth-el,
16:32 he reared up an a· for Baal
18:26 they leaped upon the a·
30 he repaired the a· of the Lord
32 And with the stones he built an a·
32 he made a trench about the a·,
35 the water ran round about the a·;
2Ki 11:11 by the a· and the temple.
12: 9 set it beside the a·,
16:10 saw an a· that was at Damascus:
10 the fashion of the a·,
11 And Urijah the priest built an a·
12 the king saw the a·: and
12 the king approached to the a·,
13 his peace offerings, upon the a·.
14 he brought also the brasen a·,
14 from between the a·
14 put it on the north side of the a·.
15 Upon the great a· burn
15 and the brasen a· shall be for me
18:22 Ye shall worship before this a·
23: 9 came not up to the a· of the Lord
15 the a· that was at Beth-el,
15 both that a· and the high place
16 burned them upon the a·,
17 hast done against the a· of Beth-el.
1Ch 6:49 and his sons offered upon the a·

1Ch 6:49 and on the a' of incense,
16:40 upon the a' of the burnt offering
21:18 set up an a' unto the Lord
22 that I may build an a'
26 built there an a' unto the Lord
26 fire upon the a' of burnt offering.
29 and the a' of the burnt offering,
22: 1 this is the a' of the burnt offering
28:18 And for the a' of incense
2Ch 1: 5 the brasen a', that Bezaleel
6 went up thither to the brasen a'
4: 1 Moreover he made an a' of brass,
19 the golden a' also,
5:12 stood at the east end of the a',
6:12 he stood before the a' of the Lord
22 and the oath come before thine a'
7: 7 brasen a' which Solomon had made
9 kept the dedication of the a' seven
8:12 on the a' of the Lord,
15: 8 renewed the a' of the Lord,
23:10 along by the a' and the temple,
26:16 incense upon the a' of incense.
19 from beside the incense a'.
29:18 the a' of burnt offering,
19 they are before the a' of the Lord.
21 to offer them on the a' of the Lord.
22 sprinkled it on the a':
22 upon the a': they killed also the
22 sprinkled the blood upon the a'.
24 their blood upon the a',
27 the burnt offering upon the a'.
32:12 Ye shall worship before one a',
33:16 he repaired the a' of the Lord,
35:16 to offer burnt offerings upon the a'
Ezr 3: 2 builded the a' of the God of Israel,
3 they set the a' upon his bases;
7:17 and offer them upon the a'
Ne 10:34 to burn upon the a' of the Lord
Ps 26: 6 so will I compass thine a',
43: 4 Then will I go unto the a' of God,
51:19 they offer bullocks upon thine a'.
118:27 unto the horns of the a'.
Isa 6: 6 with the tongs from off the a':
19:19 in that day shall there be an a'
27: 9 maketh all the stones of the a'
36: 7 Ye shall worship before this a'?
56: 7 accepted upon mine a';
60: 7 with acceptance on mine a',
La 2: 7 The Lord hath cast off his a',
Eze 8: 5 at the gate of the a' this image
16 between the porch and the a',
9: 2 stood beside the brasen a'.
40:46 the keepers of the charge of the a':
47 the a' that was before the house.
41:22 The a' of wood was three cubits
43:13 measures of the a' after the cubits:
13 the higher place of the a'.
15 So the a' shall be four cubits;
15 and from the a' and upward
16 And the a' shall be twelve cubits
18 are the ordinances of the a'
22 they shall cleanse the a',
26 Seven days shall they purge the a'
27 your burnt offerings upon the a',
45:19 four corners of the settle of the a',
47: 1 at the south side of the a'.
Joel 1:13 howl, ye ministers of the a':
2:17 weep between the porch and the a',
Am 2: 8 laid to pledge by every a',
3:14 the horns of the a' shall be cut off,
9: 1 the Lord standing upon the a':
Zec 9:15 as the corners of the a'.
14:20 be like the bowls before the a'.
Mal 1: 7 offer polluted bread upon mine a';
10 do ye kindle fire on mine a' for
2:13 covering the a' of the Lord with
M't 5:23 bring thy gift to the a',
24 thy gift before the a',
23:18 shall swear by the a',
19 the gift, or the a'
20 shall swear by the a',
35 the temple and the a'.
Lu 1:11 of the a' of incense.
11:51 between the a' and the temple:
Ac 17:23 I found an a' with this inscription,
1Co 9:13 and they which wait at the a'
13 partakers with the a'?
10:18 partakers of the a'?
Heb 7:13 no man gave attendance at the a'.
13:10 We have an a', whereof
Jas 2:21 offered Isaac his son upon the a'?
Re 6: 9 under the a' the souls
8: 3 stood at the a', having a golden
3 of all saints upon the golden a'
5 filled it with fire of the a',
9:13 horns of the golden a'
11: 1 the temple of God, and the a',
14:18 another angel came out from the a',
16: 7 I heard another out of the a' say,

altars
Ex 34:13 But ye shall destroy their a',
Nu 3:31 the candlestick, and the a',
23: 1 Build me here seven a',
4 I have prepared seven a',
14 and built seven a',
29 Build me here seven a', and prepare
De 7: 5 ye shall destroy their a',
12: 3 ye shall overthrow their a',
J'g 2: 2 ye shall throw down their a':
1Ki 19:10, 14 thrown down thine a',
2Ki 11:18 his a' and his images
18 the priest of Baal before the a'.
18:22 whose a' Hezekiah hath taken
21: 3 he reared up a' for Baal,
4 he built a' in the house of the Lord,
5 built a' for all the host of heaven
2Ki 23:12 the a' that were on the top
12 the a' which Manasseh had made
20 that were there upon the a'.
2Ch 14: 3 he took away the a' of the strange
23:17 brake his a' and his images
17 the priest of Baal before the a'.
28:24 a' in every corner of Jerusalem.
30:14 they arose and took away the a'
14 the a' for incense took they away,
31: 1 the a' out of all Judah
32:12 away his high places and his a',
33: 3 he reared up a' for Baalim,
4 Also he built a' in the house
5 built a' for all the host of heaven
15 all the a' that he had built
34: 4 they brake down the a' of Baalim
5 bones of the priests upon their a',
7 when he had broken down the a'
Ps 84: 3 even thine a', O Lord of hosts,
Isa 17: 8 he shall not look to the a',
36: 7 whose a' Hezekiah hath taken
65: 3 burneth incense upon a' of brick;
Jer 11:13 set up a' to that shameful thing,
13 even a' to burn incense unto Baal.
17: 1 upon the horns of your a';
2 their children remember their a'
Eze 6: 4 your a' shall be desolate,
5 your bones round about your a'.
6 that your a' may be laid waste
13 round about their a',
Ho 8:11 Ephraim hath made many a' to sin,
11 a' shall be unto him to sin.
10: 1 he hath increased the a';
2 he shall break down their a',
8 shall come up on their a';
12:11 their a' are as heaps
Am 3:14 I will also visit the a' of Beth-el:
Ro 11: 3 and digged down thine a';

Al-taschith (*al-tas'-kith*)
Ps 57:*title* To the chief Musician, A',
58:*title* chief Musician, A', Michtam of
59:*title* A', Michtam of David; when Saul
75:*title* Musician, A', A Psalm or Song

alter See also ALTERED; ALTERETH.
Le 27:10 He shall not a' it, nor change it,
Ezr 6:11 that whosoever shall a' this word,
12 that shall put to their hand to a'
Ps 89:34 covenant will I not break, nor a'

altered
Es 1:19 it be not a', That Vashti come
Lu 9:29 of his countenance was a',

altereth
Da 6: 8, 12 and Persians, which a' not.

although
Ex 13:17 a' that was near; for God said,
Jos 22:17 a' there was a plague in the
2Sa 23: 5 A' my house be not so with God;
5 a' he make it not to grow.
1Ki 20: 5 A' I have sent unto thee, saying,
Es 7: 4 held my tongue, a' the enemy
Job 2: 3 integrity, a' thou movedst me
5: 6 A' affliction cometh not forth
35:14 A' thou sayest thou shalt
Jer 31:32 a' I was an husband unto them,
Eze 7:13 is sold, a' they were yet alive:
11:16 A' I have cast them far off
16 and a' I have scattered them
Hab 3:17 A' the fig tree shall not blossom,
M'r 14:29 A' all shall be offended,
Heb 4: 3 a' the works were finished

all-to (J'g 9:53) See ALL; ALTOGETHER.

altogether ^
Ge 18:21 whether they have done a'
Ex 11: 1 thrust you out hence a'.
19:18 And mount Sinai was a' on a
Nu 16:13 make thyself a' a prince over us?
23:11 behold, thou hast blest them a'.
24:10 behold, thou hast a' blessed them
30:14 her husband a' hold his peace
De 16:20 which is a' just shalt thou follow,
2Ch 12:12 he would not destroy him a':
Es 4:14 For if thou a' holdest thy peace
Job 13: 5 O that ye would a' hold your
27:12 why then are ye thus a' vain?
Ps 19: 9 are true and righteous a'.
39: 5 every man at his best state is a'
50:21 thoughtest that I was a' such an
53: 3 they are a' become filthy:
62: 9 they are a' lighter than vanity.
139: 4 lo, O Lord, thou knowest it a'.
Isa 10: 8 Are not my princes a' kings?
Jer 5: 5 these have a' broken the yoke,
10: 8 they are a' brutish and foolish:
15:18 wilt thou be a' unto me as a
30:11 not leave thee a' unpunished.
49:12 that shall a' go unpunished?
Joh 9:34 Thou wast a' born in sins,
Ac 26:29 both almost, and a' such as
1Co 5:10 Yet not a' with the fornicators
9:10 Or saith he it a' for our sakes?

Alush (*a'-lush*)
Nu 33:13 Dophkah, and encamped in A'.
14 removed from A', and encamped

Alvah (*al'-vah*) See also ALIAH.
Ge 36:40 names; duke Timnah, duke A',

Alvan (*al'-van*) See also ALIAN.
Ge 36:23 children of Shobal were these; A',

alway See also ALWAYS.
Ex 25:30 the table shewbread before me a'.
Nu 9:16 So it was a': the cloud covered it
De 11: 1 his commandments, a'.
28:33 oppressed and crushed a':
2Sa 9:10 shall eat bread a' at my table.
1Ki 11:36 have a light a' before me
2Ki 8:19 to give him a' a light,
Job 7:16 I would not live a':
Ps 9:18 needy shall not a' be forgotten:
119:112 heart to perform thy statutes a',
Pr 28:14 Happy is the man that feareth a':
M't 28:20 I am with you a', even unto
Joh 7: 6 but your time is a' ready.
Ac 10: 2 the people, and prayed to God a'.
Ro 11:10 bow down their back a'.
2Co 4:11 we which live are a' delivered
6:10 As sorrowful, yet a' rejoicing;
Ph'p 4: 4 Rejoice in the Lord a':
Col 4: 6 Let your speech be a' with grace,
1Th 2:16 to fill up their sins a':
2Th 2:13 bound to give thanks a' to God
Tit 1:12 The Cretians are a' liars,
Heb 3:10 They do a' err in their heart:

always See also ALWAY.
Ge 6: 3 My spirit shall not a' strive with
Ex 27:20 to cause the lamp to burn a'.
28:38 it shall be a' upon his forehead,
De 5:29 all my commandments a',
6:24 for our good a',
11:12 the Lord thy God are a' upon it,
14:23 to fear the Lord thy God a'.
1Ch 16:15 Be ye mindful a' of his covenant;
2Ch 18: 7 good unto me, but a' evil:
Job 27:10 will he a' call upon God?
32: 9 Great men are not a' wise:
Ps 10: 5 His ways are a' grievous;
16: 8 I have set the Lord a' before me:
103: 9 He will not a' chide:
Pr 5:19 be thou ravished a' with her love.
8:30 rejoicing a' before him;
Ec 9: 8 Let thy garments be a' white;
Isa 57:16 neither will I be a' wroth:
Jer 20:17 her womb to be a' great with me.
Eze 38: 8 which have been a' waste:
M't 18:10 their angels do a' behold the
26:11 ye have the poor a' with you;
11 but me ye have not a'.
M'k 5: 5 a', night and day, he was in the
14: 7 ye have the poor with you a',
7 but me ye have not a'.
Lu 18: 1 that men ought a' to pray,
21:36 pray a', that ye may be
Joh 8:29 I do a' those things that please
11:42 I knew that thou hearest me a':
12: 8 the poor a' ye have with you;
8 but me ye have not a'.
18:20 whither the Jews a' resort;
Ac 2:25 I foresaw the Lord a' before
7:51 ye do a' resist the Holy Ghost:
24: 3 We accept it a', and in all places,
16 a' a conscience void of offence
Ro 1: 9 mention of you a' in my prayers;
1Co 1: 4 thank my God a' on your behalf,
15:58 a' abounding in the work of the
2Co 2:14 a' causeth us to triumph in Christ,
4:10 A' bearing about in the body
5: 6 Therefore we are a' confident,
9: 8 that ye, a' having all sufficiency
Ga 4:18 affected a' in a good thing,
Eph 5:20 Giving thanks a' for all things
6:18 Praying a' with all
Ph'p 1: 4 A' in every prayer of mine for you
20 with all boldness, as a', so now
2:12 my beloved, as ye have a' obeyed,
Col 1: 3 praying a' for you,
4:12 a' labouring fervently for you
1Th 1: 2 We give thanks to God a' for you
3: 6 have good remembrance of us a',
2Th 1: 3 bound to thank God a' for you,
11 Wherefore also we pray a' for you,
3:16 you peace a' by all means.
Ph'm 4 mention of thee a' in my prayers,
Heb 9: 6 went a' into the first tabernacle,
1Pe 3:15 be ready a' to give an answer
2Pe 1:12 a' in remembrance of these things.
15 these things a' in remembrance.

am ^
Ge 4: 9 A' I my brother's keeper?
15: 1 Fear not, Abram: I a' thy shield,
7 I a' the Lord that brought thee
17: 1 unto him, I a' the Almighty God;
18:12 herself, saying, After I a' waxed
13 surety bear a child, which a' old?
27 speak unto the Lord, which a' but
22: 1 and he said, Behold, here I a'.
7 and he said, Here a' I, my son.
11 Abraham: and he said, Here a' I.
23: 4 I a' a stranger and a sojourner
24:24 I a' the daughter of Bethuel the
34 he said, I a' Abraham's servant.
25:22 said, If it be so, why a' I thus?
30 for I a' faint: therefore was his
32 Behold, I a' at the point to die:
26:24 I a' the God of Abraham thy father:
24 I a' with thee, and will bless thee,
27: 1 said unto him, Behold, here a' I.
2 Behold now, I a' old, I know not
11 hairy man, and I a' a smooth man:
18 Here a' I; who art thou, my son?
19 his father, I a' Esau thy firstborn;
24 son Esau? And he said, I a'.
32 I a' thy son, thy firstborn Esau.
46 said to Isaac, I a' weary of my life,
28:13 said, I a' the Lord God of Abraham
15 And, behold, I a' with thee,
30: 2 and he said, A' I in God's stead,
13 And Leah said, Happy a' I,
31:11 Jacob: and I said, Here a' I.
13 I a' the God of Beth-el, where thou

Ge 32:10 I a' not worthy of the least of all
10 and now I a' become two bands.
35:11 unto him, I a' God Almighty:
37:13 And he said to him, Here a' I.
38:25 whose these are, a' I with child:
41:44 I a' Pharaoh, and without thee
43:14 bereaved of my children, I a'
45: 3 said unto his brethren, I a' Joseph;
4 he said, I a' Joseph your brother,
46: 2 Jacob: and he said, Here a' I.
3 I a' God, the God of thy father:
49:29 a' to be gathered unto my people:
50:19 for a' I in the place of God?
Ex 3: 4 Moses. And he said, Here a' I.
6 he said, I a' the God of thy father,
8 I a' come down to deliver them
11 Who a' I, that I should go unto
14 said unto Moses, I A' that I A':
14 Israel, I A' hath sent me unto you.
19 I a' sure that the king of Egypt
4:10 O Lord, I a' not eloquent,
10 but I a' slow of speech, and of a
6: 2 and said unto him, I a' the Lord:
6 children of Israel, I a' the Lord,
7 know that I a' the Lord your God,
8 you for a heritage: I a' the Lord.
12 me, who a' of uncircumcised lips?
29 unto Moses, saying, I a' the Lord:
30 Behold, I a' of uncircumcised lips,
7: 5 shall know that I a' the Lord,
17 shalt know that I a' the Lord:
8:22 I a' the Lord in the midst of the
9:29 As soon as I a' gone out of the city,
10: 2 know how that I a' the Lord.
12:12 execute judgment: I a' the Lord.
14: 4 may know that I a' the Lord.
18 that I a' the Lord, when I have
15:26 for I a' the Lord that healeth thee.
16:12 know that I a' the Lord your God.
18: 6 I thy father in law Jethro a' come
20: 2 I a' the Lord thy God, which have
5 for I the Lord thy God a' a jealous
22:27 that I will hear; for I a' gracious.
29:46 they shall know that I a' the Lord
46 dwell among them: I a' the Lord
31:13 a' the Lord that doth sanctify you.
Le 8:35 die not: for so I a' commanded.
10:13 by fire: for so I a' commanded.
11:44 For I a' the Lord your God:
44 and ye shall be holy; for I a' holy:
45 For I a' the Lord that bringeth you
45 therefore be holy, for I a' holy.
18: 2 unto them, I a' the Lord your God.
4 therein: I a' the Lord your God.
5 shall live in them: I a' the Lord.
6 their nakedness: I a' the Lord.
21 the name of thy God: I a' the Lord.
30 therein: I a' the Lord your God.
19: 2 for I the Lord your God a' holy.
3 sabbaths: I a' the Lord your God.
4 gods: I a' the Lord your God.
10 stranger: I a' the Lord your God.
12 the name of thy God: I a' the Lord.
14 shalt fear thy God: I a' the Lord.
16 of thy neighbour: I a' the Lord.
25 thereof: I a' the Lord your God.
30 my sanctuary: I a' the Lord.
31 by them: I a' the Lord your God.
32 and fear thy God: I a' the Lord.
34 of Egypt: I a' the Lord your God.
36 I a' the Lord your God, which
37 and do them: I a' the Lord.
20: 7 be ye holy: for I a' the Lord
8 I a' the Lord which sanctify you.
24 I a' the Lord your God, which have
26 for I the Lord a' holy, and have
21: 8 Lord, which sanctify you, a' holy.
12 God is upon him: I a' the Lord.
22: 2 they hallow unto me: I a' the Lord.
3 off from my presence: I a' the Lord.
8 himself therewith: I a' the Lord.
30 until the morrow: I a' the Lord.
31 and do them: I a' the Lord.
32 of Israel: I a' the Lord which
33 to be your God: I a' the Lord.
23:22 stranger: I a' the Lord your God.
43 Egypt: I a' the Lord your God.
24:22 country: for I a' the Lord your God.
25:17 thy God: for I a' the Lord your God.
38 I a' the Lord your God, which
55 Egypt: I am the Lord your God.
26: 1 unto it: for I a' the Lord your God.
2 my sanctuary: I a' the Lord.
13 I a' the Lord your God, which
44 them: for I a' the Lord their God.
45 might be their God: I a' the Lord.
Nu 3:13 mine shall they be: I a' the Lord.
41 Levites for me (I a' the Lord)
45 Levites shall be mine: I a' the Lord.
10:10 God: I a' the Lord your God.
11:14 I a' not able to bear all this people
21 The people among whom I a',
15:41 I a' the Lord your God, which
41 God: I a' the Lord your God.
18:20 I a' thy part and thine inheritance
22:30 A' not I thine ass, upon which thou
37 a' I not able indeed to promote
38 Lo, I a' come unto thee: have I now
De 1: 9 I a' not able to bear you myself
42 fight; for I a' not among you;
5: 6 I a' the Lord thy God, which
9 the Lord thy God a' a jealous God,
26: 3 that I a' come unto the country
29: 6 know that I a' the Lord your God.
31: 2 I a' an hundred and twenty years
27 while I a' yet alive with you this

De 32:39 even I, a' he, and there is no god
Jos 5:14 the host of the Lord a' I now come.
14:10 I a' this day fourscore and five
11 As yet I a' as strong this day as I
17:14 inherit, seeing I a' a great people,
23: 2 I a' old and stricken in age:
14 this day I a' going the way of all
J'g 4:19 little water to drink; for I a' thirsty.
6:10 unto you, I a' the Lord your God;
15 and I a' the least in my father's
8: 5 and I a' pursuing after Zebah
9: 2 I a' your bone and your flesh.
13:11 the woman? And he said, I a'.
17: 9 I a' a Levite of Beth-lehem-judah,
18: 4 hired me, and I a' his priest.
19:18 Ephraim; from thence a' I:
18 but I a' now going to the house
Ru 1:12 for I a' too old to have an husband.
2:10 of me, seeing I a' a stranger?
3: 9 answered, I a' Ruth thine handmaid:
12 true that I a' thy near kinsman:
4: 4 beside thee; and I a' after thee.
1Sa 1: 8 a' not I better to thee than ten sons?
15 I a' a woman of a sorrowful spirit:
26 I a' the woman that stood by thee
3: 4 and he answered, Here a' I.
5 and said, Here a' I; for thou
6, 8 went to Eli, and said, Here a' I;
16 son. And he answered, Here a' I.
4:16 Eli, I a' he that came out of the
9:19 Saul, and said, I a' the seer:
21 answered and said, A' not I
12: 2 and I a' old and grayheaded;
3 Behold, here I a': witness against
14: 7 I a' with thee according to thy
16: 2 I a' come to sacrifice to the Lord.
5 Peaceably: I a' come to sacrifice
17: 8 a' not I a Philistine, and ye
43 said unto David, A' I a dog,
58 I a' the son of thy servant Jesse
18:18 David said unto Saul, Who a' I?
23 that I a' a poor man, and
22:12 he answered, Here I a', my lord.
28:15 answered, I a' sore distressed;
30:13 said, I a' a young man of Egypt,
2Sa 1: 3 the camp of Israel a' I escaped.
7 me. And I answered, Here a' I.
8 him, I a' an Amalekite.
13 I a' the son of a stranger, an
26 I a' distressed for thee, my brother
2:20 Asahel? And he answered, I a'.
3: 8 A' I a dog's head, which against
39 And I a' this day weak, though
7:18 he said, Who a' I, O Lord God?
9: 8 upon such a dead dog as I a'?
11: 5 David, and said, I a' with child.
14: 5 she answered, I a' indeed a widow
15 that I a' come to speak of this
32 Wherefore a' I come from Geshur?
15:26 behold, here a' I, let him do to me
19:20 I a' come the first this day of all
22 do not I know that I a' this day
35 I a' this day fourscore years old:
20:17 And he answered, I a' he. Then
19 I a' one of them that are peaceable
24:14 I a' in a great strait: let us fall
1Ki 3: 7 and I a' but a little child: I know
8:20 and I a' risen up in the room of
13:14 from Judah? And he said, I a'.
18 I a' a prophet also as thou art;
31 when I a' dead, then bury me in
14: 6 for I a' sent to thee with heavy
17:12 I a' gathering two sticks, that I
18: 8 And he answered him, I a':
12 as soon as I a' gone from thee,
36 and that I a' thy servant, and that
19: 4 for I a' not better than my fathers.
10 and I, even I only, a' left; and
14 I only, a' left; and they seek my
20: 4 saying, I a' thine, and all that I
13 thou shalt know that I a' the Lord.
28 ye shall know that I a' the Lord
22: 4 I a' as thou art, my people as thy
34 of the host; for I a' wounded.
2Ki 2:10 see me when I a' taken from thee,
3: 7 I a' as thou art, my people as thy
5: 7 A' I God, to kill and to make alive,
16: 7 I a' thy servant and thy son: come
18:25 A' I now come up without the Lord
19:23 I a' come up to the height of the
21:12 I a' bringing such evil upon
1Ch 17:16 Who a' I, O Lord God, and what is
21:13 I a' in a great strait: let me fall
29:14 But who a' I, and what is my people,
2Ch 2: 6 who a' I then, that I should build
9 the house which I a' about to build
6:10 for I a' risen up in the room of
10 a' set on the throne of Israel,
18: 3 I a' as thou art, and my people as
33 of the host; for I a' wounded.
35:23 me away; for I a' sore wounded.
Ezr 9: 6 God, I a' ashamed and blush to lift
Ne 6: 3 I a' doing a great work, so that I
11 there, that, being as I a', would
Es 5:12 to morrow a' I invited unto her
Job 1:15 and I only a' escaped alone to tell
16 consumed them; and I only a'
17 the sword; and I only a' escaped
19 are dead; and I only a' escaped
7: 3 So a' I made to possess months of
4 and I a' full of tossings to and fro
8 eyes are upon me, and I a' not.
12 A' I a sea, or a whale, that thou
20 so that I a' a burden to myself?
9:20 if I say, I a' perfect, it shall
28 I a' afraid of all my sorrows, I know

Job 9:32 For he is not a man, as I a', that I
10: 7 Thou knowest that I a' not wicked:
15 I a' full of confusion: therefore
11: 4 doctrine is pure, and I a' clean in
12: 3 I a' not inferior to you: yea, who 1961
4 I a' as one mocked of his neighbour,
13: 2 also: I a' not inferior unto you.
16: 6 though I forbear, what a' I eased?
19: 7 cry out of wrong, but I a' not heard:
10 and I a' gone: and mine hope hath
15 I a' an alien in their sight
20 and I a' escaped with the skin of
21: 6 I remember I a' afraid, and
23:15 Therefore a' I troubled at his
15 I consider, I a' afraid of him.
30: 9 And now a' I their song,
9 yea, I a' their byword.
19 and I a' become like dust and ashes.
29 I a' a brother to dragons, and a
32: 6 said, I a' young, and ye are very
18 For I a' full of matter, the spirit
33: 6 Behold, I a' according to thy wish
6 I also a' formed out of the clay.
9 I a' clean without transgression,
9 I a' innocent; neither is there
34: 5 For Job hath said, I a' righteous:
40: 4 Behold, I a' vile; what shall I
Ps 6: 2 for I a' weak: O Lord, heal me;
6 I a' weary with my groaning;
13: 4 trouble me rejoice when I a' moved.
17: 3 I a' purposed that my mouth shall
22: 2 the night season, and a' not silent.
6 But I a' a worm, and no man;
14 I a' poured out like water, and all
25:16 for I am desolate and afflicted.
28: 7 trusted in him, and I a' helped:
31: 9 O Lord, for I am in trouble:
12 I a' forgotten as a dead man out
12 I a' like a broken vessel.
22 I a' cut off from before thine eyes:
35: 3 say unto my soul, I a' thy salvation.
37:25 I have been young, and now a' old;
38: 6 I a' troubled;
6 I a' bowed down greatly;
8 I a' feeble and sore broken:
17 For I a' ready to halt, and my
39: 4 that I may know how frail I a'.
10 I a' consumed by the blow of thine
39:12 for I a' a stranger with thee,
40:12 so that I a' not able to look up;
17 But I a' poor and needy:
46:10 Be still, and know that I a' God:
50: 7 I a' God, even thy God.
52: 8 But I a' like a green olive tree
56: 3 What time I a' afraid, I will trust
69: 2 I a' come into deep waters, where
3 I a' weary of my crying:
8 I a' become a stranger unto my
17 I a' in trouble: hear me speedily.
20 and I a' full of heaviness:
29 But I a' poor and sorrowful:
70: 5 But I a' poor and needy;
71: 7 I a' as a wonder unto many;
18 when I a' old and grayheaded,
73:23 Nevertheless I a' continually with
77: 4 I a' so troubled that I cannot
81:10 I a' the Lord thy God which
86: 1 hear me: for I a' poor and needy.
2 Preserve my soul; for I am holy:
88: 4 I a' counted with them that go
4 I a' as a man that hath no strength:
8 I a' shut up, and I cannot come
15 I a' afflicted and ready to die from
15 I suffer thy terrors I a' distracted.
102: 2 in the day when I a' in trouble;
6 I a' like a pelican of the wilderness:
6 a' like an owl of the desert.
7 I watch, and a' as a sparrow alone
11 and I a' withered like grass.
109:22 For I a' poor and needy,
23 I a' gone like the shadow when
23 I a' tossed up and down as the
116:16 truly I a' thy servant;
16 I a' thy servant,
119:19 I a' a stranger in the earth:
63 I a' a companion of all them
83 I a' become like a bottle in the
94 I a' thine, save me; for I have
107 I a' afflicted very much: quicken
120 fear of thee; and I a' afraid of
125 I a' thy servant; give me
141 I a' small and despised: yet do
120: 7 I a' for peace: but when I speak,
139:14 I a' fearfully and wonderfully
18 I awake, I a' still with thee.
142: 6 for I a' brought very low:
143:12 for I a' thy servant.
Pr 8:14 I a' understanding;
20: 9 I a' pure from my sin?
26:19 and saith, A' not I in sport?
30: 2 I a' more brutish than any man,
Ec 1:16 Lo, I a' come to great estate,
Ca 1: 5 I a' black, but comely, O ye
6 not upon me, because I a' black,
2: 1 I a' the rose of Sharon, and the
5 for I a' sick of love.
16 My beloved is mine, and I a' his:
5: 1 I a' come into my garden, my
8 ye tell him, that I a' sick of love.
6: 3 I a' my beloved's, and my beloved
7:10 I a' my beloved's, and his desire
8:10 I a' a wall, and my breasts like
Isa 1:11 I a' full of the burnt offerings of
14 I a' weary to bear them.
6: 5 Woe is me! for I a' undone;
5 because I a' a man of unclean

Isa 6: 8 Then said I, Here a· I; send me.
10:13 by my wisdom; for I a· prudent:
19:11 I a· the son of the wise, the son
21: 8 and I a· set in my ward whole
29:12 and he saith, I a· not learned.
33:24 inhabitant shall not say, I a· sick:
36:10 a· I now come up without the
37:24 of my chariots a· I come up
38:10 I a· deprived of the residue of my
14 O Lord, I a· oppressed; undertake
41: 4 the first, and with the last; I a· he.
10 Fear thou not; for I a· with thee:
10 be not dismayed; for I a· thy God:
42: 8 I a· the Lord; that is my name:
43: 3 For I a· the Lord thy God, the
5 Fear not; for I a· with thee:
10 and understand that I a· he:
11 I, even I, a· the Lord;
12 saith the Lord, that I a· God.
13 Yea, before the day was I a· he;
15 I a· the Lord, your Holy One,
25 I, even I, a· he that blotteth out
44: 5 One shall say, I a the Lord's;
6 I a· the first,
6 and I a· the last;
16 and saith, Aha, I a· warm,
24 I a· the Lord that maketh all
45: 3 a· the God of Israel.
5, 6, I a· the Lord, and there is
18 I a· the Lord; and there is none
22 I a· God, and there is none else.
46: 4 and even to your old age I a· he;
9 I a· God, and there is none else;
9 I a· God, and there is none like me,
47: 8 that sayest in thine heart, I a·.
10 I a·, and none else beside me,
48:12 I a· he; I a· the first,
12 I also a· the last.
16 the time that it was, there a· I:
17 I a· the Lord thy God which
49:21 lost my children, and a· desolate,
23 thou shalt know that I a· the Lord:
26 that I the Lord a· thy Saviour
51:12 even I, a· he that comforteth you:
15 But I a· the Lord thy God,
52: 6 in that day that I a· he that doth
56: 3 Behold, I a· a dry tree.
58: 9 and he shall say, Here I a·.
60:16 that I the Lord a· thy Saviour
65: 1 I a· sought of them that asked
1 I a· found of them that sought
5 for I a· holier than thou.
Jer 1: 6 I cannot speak: for I a· a child.
7 Say not, I a· a child:
8 I a· with thee to deliver thee,
19 I a· with thee, saith the Lord,
2:23 canst thou say, I a· not polluted,
35 sayest, Because I a· innocent,
3:12 for I a· merciful, saith the Lord,
14 for I a· married unto you:
4:19 I a· pained at my very heart;
6:11 I a· full of the fury of the Lord;
11 I a· weary with holding in:
8:21 daughter of my people a· I hurt;
21 I a· black; astonishment hath
9:24 that I a· the Lord which exercise
15: 6 I a· weary with repenting.
16 for I a· called by thy name,
20 I a· with thee to save thee and to
20: 7 I a· in derision daily, every one
21:13 I a· against thee, O inhabitant of
23: 9 I a· like a drunken man, and like
23 A· I a God at hand, saith the Lord,
30, 31 I a· against the prophets, saith
32 I a· against them that prophesy
24: 7 to know me, that I a· the Lord;
26:14 behold, I a· in your hand:
29:23 and a· a witness, saith the Lord.
30:11 For I a· with thee, saith the Lord,
31: 9 for I a· a father to Israel,
32:27 I a· the Lord, the God of all flesh:
36: 5 Baruch, saying, I a· shut up;
38:19 I a· afraid of the Jews that are
42:11 for I a· with you to save you,
46:28 for I a· with thee; for I will make
51:35 Behold, I a· against thee, O
La 1:11 for I a· become vile.
14 I a· not able to rise up.
20 I a· in distress: my bowels are
3: 1 I a· the man that hath seen
54 mine head; then I said, I a· cut off.
63 sitting down and rising up; I a·
Eze 5: 8 Behold, I, even I, a· against thee,
6: 7, 14 shall know that I a· the Lord.
10, 13 shall know that I a· the Lord,
7: 4 ye shall know that I a· the Lord.
9 ye shall know that I a· the Lord
27 they shall know that I a· the Lord.
11:10, 12 shall know that I a· the Lord.
12:11 I a· your sign: like as I have done,
15, 16, 20 shall know that I a· the Lord.
25 for I a· the Lord: I will speak,
13: 8 I a· against you, saith the Lord
9, 14 shall know that I a· the Lord
20 Behold, I a· against your pillows,
21, 23 shall know that I a· the Lord.
14: 8 ye shall know that I a· the Lord.
15: 7 ye shall know that I a· the Lord,
16:62 thou shalt know that I a· the Lord:
63 when I a· pacified toward thee
20: 5, 7 I a· the Lord your God.
12 I a· the Lord that sanctify them.
19 I a· the Lord your God; walk in
20 know that I a· the Lord your God.
26, 38, 42, 44 know that I a· the Lord,
21: 3 I a· against thee, and will draw

Eze 22:16 thou shalt know that I a· the Lord.
26 and I a· profaned among them.
23:49 shall know that I a· the Lord God.
24:24 shall know that I a· the Lord God.
27 they shall know that I a· the Lord.
25: 5 ye shall know that I a· the Lord.
7 thou shalt know that I a· the Lord.
11 they shall know that I a· the Lord.
17 shall know that I a· the Lord, when
26: 3 Behold, I a· against thee, O Tyrus,
6 they shall know that I a· the Lord.
27: 3 hast said, I a· of perfect beauty.
28: 2 thou hast said, I a· a God,
9 I a· God? but thou shalt be a man,
22 Behold, I a· against thee, O Zidon;
22 that I a· the Lord, when I shall have
23 shall know that I a· the Lord.
24 shall know that I a· the Lord God.
26 know that I a· the Lord their God.
29: 3 Behold, I a· against thee, Pharaoh
6 shall know that I a· the Lord,
9 they shall know that I a· the Lord:
10 Behold, therefore I a· against thee,
16 shall know that I a· the Lord God.
21 they shall know that I a· the Lord.
30: 8, 19 shall know that I a· the Lord.
22 Behold, I a· against Pharaoh
25, 26 shall know that I a· the Lord.
32:15 shall they know that I a· the Lord.
33:29 shall they know that I a· the Lord,
34:10 I a· against the shepherds; and I
27 they shall know that I a· the Lord,
30 I the Lord their God a· with them,
31 I a· your God, saith the Lord God.
35: 3 I a· against thee, and I will stretch
4 thou shalt know that I a· the Lord.
9 ye shall know that I a· the Lord.
12 shalt know that I a· the Lord,
15 they shall know that I a· the Lord.
36: 9 For, behold, I a· for you, and I will
11 ye shall know that I a· the Lord.
23 shall know that I a· the Lord,
38 they shall know that I a· the Lord.
37: 6 ye shall know that I a· the Lord.
13 know that I a· the Lord, when
38: 3 I a· against thee, O Gog, the chief
23 they shall know that I a· the Lord.
39: 1 I a· against thee, O Gog, the chief
6 they shall know that I a· the Lord.
7 shall know that I a· the Lord,
22 Israel shall know that I a· the
27 and a· sanctified in them in the
28 shall they know that I a· the Lord,
44:28 I a· their inheritance: and ye shall
28 no possession in Israel: I a· their
Da 9:22 O Daniel, I a· now come forth to
23 and I a· come to shew thee; for
10:11 stand upright: for unto thee a· I
12 thy words were heard, and I a· come
14 Now I a· come to make thee
20 of Persia; and when I a· gone
Ho 2: 2 neither a· I her husband: let her
11: 9 for I a· God, and not man; the
12: 8 Yet I a· become rich, I have found
9 And I that a· the Lord thy God
13: 4 Yet I a· the Lord thy God from the
14: 8 I a· like a green fir tree. From me
Joe 2:27 know that I a· in the midst of Israel,
27 and that I a· the Lord your God,
3:10 let the weak say, I a· strong.
17 ye know that I a· the Lord your
Am 2:13 Behold, I a· pressed under you,
Jon 1: 9 I a· an Hebrew; and I fear the
2: 4 I a· cast out of thy sight; yet I will
Mic 3: 8 But truly I a· full of power by the
7: 1 for I a· as when they have gathered
Na 2:13 Behold, I a· against thee, saith the
3: 5 Behold, I a· against thee, saith the
Hab 2: 1 what I shall answer when I a· *
Zep 2:15 I a·, and there is none beside me:
Hag 1:13 saying, I a· with you, saith the
2: 4 for I a· with you, saith the Lord of
Zec 1:14 I a· jealous for Jerusalem and for
15 And I a· very sore displeased with
16 I a· returned to Jerusalem with
8: 3 I a· returned unto Zion, and will
10: 6 for I a· the Lord their God, and
11: 5 for I a· rich: and their own
13: 5 I a· no prophet,
5 I a· an husbandman;
Mal 1:14 for I a· a great king, saith
3: 6 For I a· the Lord, I change not;
M't 3:11 whose shoes I a· not worthy to
17 my beloved Son, in whom I a· well
5:17 Think not that I a· come to
17 I a· not come to destroy, but to
8: 8 I a· not worthy
9 For I a· a man under authority,
9:13 a· not come to call the righteous,
28 Believe ye that I a· able to do this?
10:34 Think not that I a· come to send
35 For I a· come to set a man at
11:29 for I a· meek and lowly in heart:
15:24 a· not sent but unto the lost sheep
16:13 that I the Son of man a·?
15 But whom say ye that I a·
17: 5 my beloved Son, in whom I a· well
18:20 there a· I in the midst of them.
20:15 Is thine eye evil, because I a· good?
22, 23 with the baptism that I a·
22:32 I a· the God of Abraham, and the
24: 5 saying, I a· Christ; and shall
26:32 But after I a· risen again, I will go
61 I a· able to destroy the temple of
27:24 I a· innocent of the blood of this
43 for he said, I am the Son of God.

M't 28:20 and, lo, I a· with you alway, even
M'r 1: 7 whose shoes I a· not worthy to
11 Son, in whom I a· well pleased.
8:27 Whom do men say that I a·?
29 But whom say ye that I a·? And
10:38 baptism that I a· baptized with?
39 baptism that I a· baptized withal
12:26 I a· the God of Abraham, and the
13: 6 in my name, saying, I a· Christ;
14:28 But after that I a· risen, I will go
62 And Jesus said, I a·: and ye shall
Lu 1:18 for I a· an old man, and my wife
19 I a· Gabriel, that stand in the
19 and a· sent to speak unto thee,
3:16 whose shoes I a· not worthy to
22 Son, in thee I a· well pleased.
4:43 other cities also: for therefore a·
5: 8 for I a· a sinful man, O Lord.
7: 6 for I a· not worthy that thou
8 For I also a· a man set under
9:18 Whom say the people that I a·?
20 But whom say ye that I a·? Peter
12:49 I a· come to send fire on the earth;
50 and how a· I straitened till it
51 Suppose ye that I a· come to give
15:19 And a· no more worthy to be called
21 in thy sight, and a· no more worthy
16: 3 I cannot dig; to beg I a· ashamed.
4 I a· resolved what to do,
4 that, when I a· put
24 cool my tongue; for I a· tormented
18:11 that I a· not as other men are,
21: 8 saying, I a· Christ; and the time
22:27 I a· among you as he that serveth.
33 Lord, I a· ready to go with thee,
58 And Peter said, Man, I a· not.
70 he said unto them, Ye say that I a·.
Joh 1:20 but confessed, I a· not the Christ.
21 And he saith, I a· not. Art thou that
23 I a· the voice of one crying in the
27 whose shoe's latchet I a· not
31 therefore a· I come baptizing
3:28 I a· not the Christ,
28 but that I a· sent
4: 9 me, which a· a woman of Samaria?
26 I that speak to thee a· he.
5: 7 but while I a· coming, another
43 I a· come in my father's name, and
6:35 said unto them, I a· the bread of
41 I a· the bread which came down
48 I a· that bread of life.
51 I a· the living bread which came
7:28 and ye know whence I a·:
28 and I a· not come
29 But I know him: for I a· from him,
33 Yet a little while a· I with you,
34, 36 where I a·, thither ye cannot
8:12 I a· the light of the world: he that
16 for I a· not alone, but I and the
18 I a· one that bear witness of myself,
23 I a· from above: ye are of this
23 I a· not of this world.
24 believe not that I a· he, ye shall
28 ye know that I a· he, and that I do
58 Before Abraham was, I a·.
9: 5 As long as I a· in the world,
5 I a· the light of the world.
9 He is like him: but he said, I a· he.
39 For judgment I a· come into this
10: 7 I a· the door of the sheep.
9 I a· the door: by me if any man
10 a· come that they might have life,
11 I a· the good shepherd: the good
14 I a· the good shepherd, and know
14 and a· known of mine.
36 because I said, I a· the Son of God?
11:15 And I a· glad for your sakes that I
25 I a· the resurrection, and the life:
12:26 and where I a·, there shall also my
46 I a· come a light into the world,
13:13 and ye say well: for so I a·.
19 ye may believe that I a· he.
33 yet a little while I a· with you.
14: 3 that where I a·, there ye may be
6 I a· the way, the truth, the life:
10 that I a· in the Father, and the
11 Believe me that I a· in the Father,
20 that I a· in my Father, and ye in
15: 1 I a· the true vine, and my Father
5 I a· the vine, ye are the branches:
16:28 the Father, and a· come into the
32 and yet I a· not alone, because
17:10 mine; and I a· glorified in them.
11 now I a· no more in the world
14, 16 even as I a· not of the world.
24 be with me where I a·; that they
18: 5 Jesus saith unto them, I a· he.
6 he said unto them, I a· he, they
8 I have told you that I a· he: if
17 man's disciples? He saith, I a· not.
25 He denied it, and said, I a· not.
35 A· I a Jew? Thine own nation
37 Thou sayest that I a· a king.
19:21 but that he said, I a· King of the
20:17 for I a· not yet ascended to my
Ac 7:32 I a· the God of thy fathers, the
34 and a· come down to deliver them.
9: 5 I a· Jesus whom thou persecutest:
10 he said, Behold, I a· here, Lord.
10:21 Behold, I a· he whom ye seek:
26 Stand up; I myself also a· a man.
13:25 Whom think ye that I a·?
25 I a· not he. But, behold, there
25 his feet I a· not worthy to loose.
18: 6 I a· clean: from henceforth I will
10 For I a· with thee, and no man

Ac 20:26 that I *a'* pure from the blood of
21:13 for I *a'* ready not to be bound only,
39 But Paul said, I *a'* a man which
39 which *a'* a Jew of Tarsus,
22: 3 I *a'* verily a man which...a Jew
3 which *a'* a Jew, born in Tarsus,
8 I *a'* Jesus of Nazareth, whom thou
23: 6 Men and brethren, I *a'* a Pharisee,
6 of the dead I *a'* called in question.
24:21 I *a'* called in question by you this
26: 2 whereof I *a'* accused of the Jews.
6 And now I stand and *a'* judged
7 sake, king Agrippa, I *a'* accused
15 I *a'* Jesus whom thou persecutest.
25 I *a'* not mad, most noble Festus;
26 for I *a'* persuaded that none of
29 altogether such as I *a'*, except
27:23 the angel of God, whose I *a'*,
28:20 for the hope of Israel I *a'* bound
Ro 1:14 I *a'* debtor both to the Greeks,
15 I *a'* ready to preach the gospel
16 For I *a'* not ashamed of the
3: 7 yet *a'* I also judged as a sinner?
7:14 but I *a'* carnal, sold under sin.
24 O wretched man that I *a'*! who
8:38 For I *a'* persuaded, that neither
11: 1 For I also *a'* an Israelite, of the
3 and I *a'* left alone, and they seek my
13 inasmuch as I *a'* the apostle of
14:14 and *a'* persuaded by the Lord
15:14 I myself also *a'* persuaded of you,
29 And I *a'* sure that, when I come
16:19 *a'* glad therefore on your behalf:
1Co 1:12 one of you saith, I *a'* of Paul;
3: 4 For while one saith, I *a'* of Paul;
4 and another, I *a'* of Apollos;
4: 4 yet *a'* I not hereby justified: but
9: 1 *A'* I not an apostle?
1 *a'* I not free? have I not seen
2 yet doubtless I *a'* to you: for the
22 I *a'* made all things to all men,
10:30 by grace be a partaker, why *a'* I
11: 1 of me, even as I also *a'* of Christ.
12:15 Because I *a'* not the hand,
15 I *a'* not of the body;
16 Because I *a'* not the eye,
16 I *a'* not of the body;
13: 1 I *a'* become as sounding brass,
2 have not charity, I *a'* nothing.
12 I know even as also I *a'* known.
15: 9 For I *a'* the least of the apostles,
9 that *a'* not meet
10 the grace of God I *a'* what I *a'*:
16:17 I *a'* glad of the coming of
2Co 7: 4 I *a'* filled with comfort,
4 I *a'* exceeding joyful
14 to him of you, I *a'* not ashamed;
10: 1 who in presence *a'* base among
1 being absent *a'* bold toward you:
2 may not be bold when I *a'* present
11: 2 For I *a'* jealous over you with
21 (I speak foolishly,) I *a'* bold also.
22 Are they Hebrews? so *a'* I.
22 Are they Israelites? so *a'* I.
22 they the seed of Abraham? so *a'* I.
23 (I speak as a fool) I *a'* more;
29 I *a'* not weak? who is offended,
12:10 for when I *a'* weak,
10 then *a'* I strong.
11 I *a'* become a fool in glorying;
11 for in nothing *a'* I behind the very
14 the third time I *a'* ready to come
13: 1 is the third time I *a'* coming to you
Ga 2:19 For I through the law *a'* dead
20 I *a'* crucified with Christ:
4:11 I *a'* afraid of you, lest I have
12 be as I *a'*; for I *a'* as ye are;
16 *A'* I therefore become your enemy,
18 and not only when I *a'* present
Eph 3: 8 who *a'* less than the least of all
6:20 For which I *a'* an ambassador
Ph'p 1:17 that I *a'* set for the defence
23 For I *a'* in a strait betwixt two,
3:12 *a'* apprehended of Christ Jesus.
4:11 in whatsoever state I *a'*,
12 and in all things I *a'* instructed
18 I *a'* full, having received of
Col 1:23 I Paul *a'* made a minister;
25 I *a'* made a minister, according
2: 5 flesh, yet *a'* I with you in the
4: 3 for which I *a'* also in bonds:
1Ti 1:15 to save sinners; of whom I *a'*
2: 7 Whereunto I *a'* ordained a
2Ti 1: 5 and I *a'* persuaded that in thee
11 Whereunto I *a'* appointed a
12 nevertheless I *a'* not ashamed:
12 and *a'* persuaded that he is able
4: 6 For I *a'* now ready to be offered,
1Pe 1:16 Be ye holy; for I *a'* holy.
5: 1 I exhort, who *a'* also an elder,
2Pe 1:13 so long as I *a'* in this tabernacle,
17 son in whom I *a'* well pleased.
Re 1: 8 I *a'* Alpha and Omega, the
9 I John, who also *a'* your brother,
11 I *a'* Alpha and Omega, the first
17 not; I *a'* the first and the last:
18 I *a'* he that liveth, and was dead;
18 I *a'* alive for evermore, Amen;
2:23 know that I *a'* he which searcheth
3:17 Because thou sayest, I *a'* rich,
21 and *a'* set down with my Father
18: 7 and *a'* no widow, and shall see
19:10 I *a'* thy fellow servant, and of thy
21: 6 I *a'* Alpha and Omega, the
22: 9 for I *a'* thy fellowservant, and of
13 I *a'* Alpha and Omega, the
Re 22:16 I *a'* the root and the offspring

Amad (*a'-mad*)
Jos 19:26 and *A'*, and Misheal;

Amal (*a'-mal*)
1Ch 7:35 and Imna, and Shelesh, and *A'*.

Amalek (*am'-al-ek*) See also AMALEKITE.
Ge 36:12 and she bare to Eliphaz *A'*:
16 Korah, duke Gatam, and duke *A'*:
Ex 17: 8 Then came *A'*, and fought with
9 men, and go out, fight with *A'*:
10 said to him, and fought with *A'*:
11 let down his hand, *A'* prevailed.
13 And Joshua discomfited *A'* and
14 put out the remembrance of *A'*
16 the Lord will have war with *A'*
Nu 24:20 And when he looked on *A'*, he
20 *A'* was the first of the nations;
De 25:17 Remember what *A'* did unto thee
19 blot out the remembrance of *A'*
J'g 3:13 the children of Ammon and *A'*,
5:14 there a root of them against *A'*;
1Sa 15: 2 that which *A'* did to Israel, how
3 Now go, and smite *A'*, and utterly
5 And Saul came to a city of *A'*, and
20 have brought Agag the king of *A'*,
28:18 his fierce wrath upon *A'*,
2Sa 8:12 and of *A'*, and of the spoil of
1Ch 1:36 Gatam, Kenaz, and Timna, and *A'*.
18:11 the Philistines, and from *A'*.
Ps 83: 7 Gebal, and Ammon, and *A'*;

Amalekite (*am'-al-ek-ite*) See also AMALEKITES.
1Sa 30:13 man of Egypt, servant to an *A'*;
2Sa 1: 8 And I answered him, I am an *A'*.
13 am the son of a stranger, an *A'*.

Amalekites (*am'-al-ek-ites*)
Ge 14: 7 smote all the country of the *A'*,
Nu 13:29 *A'* dwell in the land of the south:
14:25 (Now the *A'* and the Canaanites
43 For the *A'* and the Canaanites
45 Then the *A'* came down, and the
J'g 6: 3 *A'*, and the children of the east
33 all the Midianites and the *A'* and
7:12 *A'*, and all the children of the east
10:12 The Zidonians also, and the *A'*,
12:15 Ephraim, in the mount of the *A'*.
1Sa 14:48 an host, and smote the *A'*, and
15: 6 get you down from among the *A'*,
6 departed from among the *A'*.
7 Saul smote the *A'* from Havilah
8 he took Agag the king of the *A'*
15 have brought them from the *A'*:
18 utterly destroy the sinners the *A'*,
20 have utterly destroyed the *A'*.
32 to me Agag the king of the *A'*.
27: 8 and the Gezerites, and the *A'*:
30: 1 that the *A'* had invaded the south,
18 all that the *A'* had carried away:
2Sa 1: 1 from the slaughter of the *A'*, and
1Ch 4:43 And they smote the rest of the *A'*

Amam (*a'-mam*)
Jos 15:26 *A'*, and Shema, and Moladah.

Amana (*am-a'-nah*)
Ca 4: 8 look from the top of *A'*,

Amariah (*am-a-ri'-ah*)
1Ch 6: 7 Meraioth begat *A'*,
7 and *A'* begat Ahitub,
11 Azariah begat *A'*,
11 and *A'* begat Ahitub,
52 Meraioth his son, *A'* his son,
23:19 Jeriah the first, *A'* the second,
24:23 *A'* the second, Jahaziel the third,
2Ch 19:11 *A'* the chief priest is over you
31:15 Shemaiah, *A'*, and Shecaniah,
Ezr 7: 3 The son of *A'*, the son of Azariah,
10:42 Shallum, *A'*, and Joseph.
Ne 10: 3 Pashur, *A'*, Malchijah,
11: 4 son of *A'*, the son of Shephatiah,
12: 2 *A'*, Malluch, Hattush,
13 of *A'*, Jehohanan;
Zep 1: 1 the son of *A'*, the son of Hizkiah,

Amasa (*am'-a-sah*)
2Sa 17:25 Absalom made *A'* captain of the
25 which *A'* was a man's son,
19:13 And say ye to *A'*, Art thou not
20: 4 Then said the king to *A'*,
5 So *A'* went to assemble the men
8 which is in Gibeon, *A'* went before
9 And Joab said to *A'*, Art thou
9 And Joab took *A'* by the beard
10 But *A'* took no heed to the sword
12 And *A'* wallowed in blood in the
12 he removed *A'* out of the highway
1Ki 2: 5 and unto *A'* the son of Jether,
32 and *A'* the son of Jether, captain
1Ch 2:17 And Abigail bare *A'*:
17 and the father of *A'* was Jether
2Ch 28:12 and *A'* the son of Hadlai, stood up

Amasai (*am'-as-ahee*)
1Ch 6:25 of Elkanah; *A'*, and Ahimoth.
35 the son of Mahath, the son of *A'*,
12:18 Then the spirit came upon *A'*,
15:24 Nathaneel, and *A'*, and Zechariah,
2Ch 29:12 Levites arose, Mahath the son of *A'*,

Amashai (*am'-ash-ahee*)
Ne 11:13 and *A'* the son of Azareel,

Amasiah (*am-a-si'-ah*)
2Ch 17:16 next him was *A'* the son of Zichri,

amazed
Ex 15:15 the dukes of Edom shall be *a'*;
J'g 20:41 the men of Benjamin were *a'*:
Job 32:15 They were *a'*, they answered no
Isa 13: 8 they shall be *a'* one at another;
Eze 32:10 will make many people *a'* at thee,
M't 12:23 all the people were *a'*,
19:25 they were exceedingly *a'*,
M'r 1:27 And they were all *a'*,
2:12 insomuch that they were all *a'*,
6:51 they were sore *a'* in themselves,
9:15 they beheld him, were greatly *a'*,
10:32 and they were *a'*;
14:33 began to be sore *a'*,
16: 8 for they trembled and were *a'*:
Lu 2:48 they saw him, they were *a'*:
4:36 And they were all *a'*,
5:26 And they were all *a'*,
9:43 *a'* at the mighty power of God.
Ac 2: 7 they were all *a'* and marvelled,
12 were all *a'*, and were in doubt,
9:21 all that heard him were *a'*.

amazement
Ac 3:10 filled with wonder and *a'*
1Pe 3: 6 and are not afraid with any *a'*.

Amaziah (*am-a-zi'-ah*)
2Ki 12:21 *A'* his son reigned in his stead.
13:12 wherewith he fought against *A'*
14: 1 reigned *A'* the son of Joash
8 *A'* sent messengers to Jehoash,
9 the king of Israel sent to *A'*
11 *A'* would not hear. Therefore
11 he and *A'* king of Judah looked
13 Jehoash king of Israel took *A'*
15 and how he fought with *A'* king of
17 *A'* the son of Joash king of Judah
18 the rest of the acts of *A'*,
21 him king instead of his father *A'*.
23 In the fifteenth year of *A'* the son
15: 1 Azariah son of *A'* king of Judah
3 to all that his father *A'* had done;
1Ch 3:12 *A'* his son, Azariah his son,
4:34 Jamlech, and Joshah the son of *A'*,
6:45 son of Hashabiah, the son of *A'*,
2Ch 24:27 *A'* his son reigned in his stead.
25: 1 *A'* was twenty and five years old
5 *A'* gathered Judah together,
9 *A'* said to the man of God,
10 Then *A'* separated them, to wit,
11 *A'* strengthened himself, and led
13 of the army which *A'* sent back,
14 *A'* was come from the slaughter
15 of the Lord was kindled against *A'*,
17 *A'* king of Judah took advice,
18 Joash king of Judah sent to *A'*
20 But *A'* would not hear; for it came
21 both he and *A'* king of Judah,
23 Joash the king of Israel took *A'*,
25 *A'* the son of Joash king of Judah
26 the rest of the acts of *A'*,
27 the time that *A'* did turn away
26: 1 king in the room of his father *A'*
4 to all that his father *A'* did.
Am 7:10 *A'* the priest of Beth-el sent to
12 *A'* said unto Amos, O thou seer,
14 answered Amos, and said to *A'*,

ambassador See also AMBASSADORS.
Pr 13:17 but a faithful *a'* is health.
Jer 49:14 an *a'* is sent unto the heathen,
Ob 1 an *a'* is sent among the heathen,
Eph 6:20 For which I am an *a'* in bonds:

ambassadors
Jos 9: 4 and made as if they had been *a'*,
2Ch 32:31 in the business of the *a'* of the
35:21 he sent *a'* to him,
Isa 18: 2 That sendeth *a'* by the sea,
30: 4 and his *a'* came to Hanes.
33: 7 the *a'* of peace shall weep bitterly.
Eze 17:15 in sending his *a'* into Egypt,
2Co 5:20 we are *a'* for Christ,

ambassage
Lu 14:32 he sendeth an *a'*,

amber
Eze 1: 4 as the colour of *a'*,
27 I saw as the colour of *a'*,
8: 2 as the colour of *a'*.

ambush See also AMBUSHES; AMBUSHMENT.
Jos 8: 2 lay thee an *a'* for the city
7 ye shall rise up from the *a'*,
9 they went to lie in *a'*,
12 set them to lie in *a'* between
14 liers in *a'* against him
19 And the *a'* arose quickly
21 saw that the *a'* had taken the city,

ambushes
Jer 51:12 up the watchmen, prepare the *a'*:

ambushment See also AMBUSHMENTS.
2Ch 13:13 Jeroboam caused an *a'*
13 and the *a'* was behind them.

ambushments
2Ch 20:22 the Lord set *a'*

Amen
Nu 5:22 And the woman shall say, *A'*, *a'*.
De 27:15, 16 people shall answer and say, *A'*.
17, 18, 19, 20, 21, 22, 23, 24, 25, 26 And
all the people shall say, *A'*.
1Ki 1:36 answered the king, and said, *A'*:
1Ch 16:36 And all the people said, *A'*,
Ne 5:13 all the congregation said, *A'*,
8: 6 the people answered, *A'*, *A'*,
Ps 41:13 to everlasting. *A'*, and *A'*.
72:19 filled with his glory; *A'*, and *A'*.
89:52 for evermore. *A'*, and *A'*.
106:48 *A'*. Praise ye the Lord.
Jer 28: 6 the prophet Jeremiah said, *A'*:
M't 6:13 and the glory, for ever. *A'*.

M't 28:20 unto the end of the world. *A*.
M'k 16:20 the word with signs following. *A*.
Lu 24:53 praising and blessing God. *A*.
Joh 21:25 books that should be written. *A*.
Ro 1:25 Creator, who is blessed for ever. *A*.
9: 5 over all, God blessed for ever. *A*.
11:36 to whom be glory for ever. *A*.
15:33 God of peace be with you all. *A*.
16:20 Jesus Christ be with you. *A*.
24 Jesus Christ be with you all. *A*.
27 through Jesus Christ for ever. *A*.
1Co 14:16 unlearned say *A* at thy giving of
16:24 with you all in Christ Jesus. *A*.
2Co 1:20 yea, and in him *A*, unto the glory
13:14 Holy Ghost, be with you all. *A*.
Ga 1: 5 be glory for ever and ever. *A*.
6:18 Christ be with your spirit. *A*.
Eph 3:21 all ages, world without end. *A*.
6:24 Jesus Christ in sincerity. *A*.
Ph'p 4:20 be glory for ever and ever. *A*.
23 Jesus Christ be with you all. *A*.
Col 4:18 my bonds. Grace be with you. *A*.
1Th 5:28 of... Christ be with you. *A*.
2Th 3:18 of...Christ be with you all. *A*.
1Ti 1:17 and glory for ever and ever. *A*.
6:16 honour and power everlasting. *A*.
21 Grace be with thee. *A*.
2Ti 4:18 be glory for ever and ever. *A*.
22 Grace be with you. *A*.
Tit 3:15 Grace be with you all. *A*.
Ph'm 25 Christ be with your spirit. *A*.
Heb 13:21 be glory for ever and ever. *A*.
25 Grace be with you all. *A*.
1Pe 4:11 dominion for ever and ever. *A*.
5:11 dominion for ever and ever. *A*.
14 all that are in Christ Jesus. *A*.
2Pe 3:18 glory both now and for ever. *A*.
1Jo 5:21 keep yourselves from idols. *A*.
2Jo 13 of thy elect sister greet thee. *A*.
Jude 25 and power, both now and ever. *A*.
Re 1: 6 dominion for ever and ever. *A*.
7 wail because of him. Even so, *A*.
18 I am alive for evermore, *A*;
3:14 These things saith the *A*,
5:14 And the four beasts said, *A*.
7:12 Saying, *A*: Blessing, and glory,
12 unto our God for ever and ever. *A*.
19: 4 Sat on the throne, saying, *A*;
22:20 *A*. Even so, come, Lord Jesus.
21 Jesus Christ be with you all. *A*.

amend See also AMENDS.
2Ch 34:10 to repair and *a* the house:
Jer 7: 3 *A* your ways and your doings,
5 if ye throughly *a* your ways
26:13 *a* your ways and your doings,
35:15 and *a* your doings,
Joh 4:52 hour when he began to *a*.

amends
Le 5:16 he shall make *a* for the harm

amerce
De 22:19 shall *a* him in an hundred shekels,

amethyst
Ex 28:19 a ligure, an agate, and an *a*.
39:12 a ligure, an agate, and an *a*.
Re 21:20 a jacinth; the twelfth, an *a*.

Ami (*a'-mi*)
Ezr 2:57 of Zebaim, the children of *A*.

amiable
Ps 84: 1 How *a* are thy tabernacles,

Aminadab (*a-min'-a-dab*) See also AMMINADAB.
M't 1: 4 Aram begat *A*;
4 and *A* begat Naasson;
Lu 3:33 Which was the son of *A*,

amiss
2Ch 6:37 We have sinned, we have done *a*,
Da 3:29 speak anything *a* against the God
Lu 23:41 this man hath done nothing *a*.
Jas 4: 3 receive not, because ye ask *a*,

Amittai (*a-mit'-tahee*)
2Ki 14:25 Jonah, the son of *A*, the prophet,
Jon 1: 1 came unto Jonah the son of *A*,

Ammah (*am'-mah*) See also METHEG-AMMAH.
2Sa 2:24 they were come to the hill of *A*,

Ammi (*am'-mi*) See also AMMI-NADIB; BEN-AMMI; LO-AMMI.
Ho 2: 1 Say ye unto your brethren, *A*;

Ammiel (*am'-me-el*) See also ELIAM.
Nu 13:12 of Dan, *A* the son of Gemalli.
2Sa 9: 4, 5 house of Machir, the son of *A*,
17:27 Machir the son of *A* of Lo-debar,
1Ch 3: 5 Bath-shua the daughter of *A*:
26: 5 *A* the sixth, Issachar the seventh,

Ammihud (*am-mi'-hud*)
Nu 1:10 Elishama the son of *A*:
2:18 shall be Elishama the son of *A*.
7:48 seventh day Elishama the son of *A*,
53 offering of Elishama the son of *A*.
10:22 host was Elishama the son of *A*.
34:20 Simeon, Shemuel the son of *A*.
28 Pedahel the son of *A*.
2Sa 13:37 went to Talmai, the son of *A*.
1Ch 7:26 Laadan his son, *A* his son,
9: 4 Uthai the son of *A*, the son of

Amminadab (*am-min'-a-dab*) See also AMINADAB; AMMI-NADIB.
Ex 6:23 Elisheba, daughter of *A*, sister
Nu 1: 7 Nahshon the son of *A*.
2: 3 Nahshon the son of *A* shall be
7:12 the son of *A*, of the tribe of Judah
Nu 7:17 offering of Nahshon the son of *A*.
10:14 his host was Nahshon the son of *A*.
Ru 4:19 begat Ram, and Ram begat *A*,
20 *A* begat Nahshon, and Nahshon
1Ch 2:10 Ram begat *A*;
10 and *A* begat Nahshon,
6:22 *A* his son, Korah his son,
15:10 *A* the chief, and his brethren
11 Shemaiah, and Eliel, and *A*,

Ammi-nadib (*am-min'-a-dib*) See also AMMINADAB.
Ca 6:12 made me like the chariots of *A*.

Ammishaddai (*am-mi-shad'-dahee*)
Nu 1:12 Of Dan; Ahiezer the son of *A*.
2:25 shall be Ahiezer the son of *A*.
7:66 tenth day Ahiezer the son of *A*,
71 offering of Ahiezer the son of *A*.
10:25 host was Ahiezer the son of *A*.

Ammizabad (*am-miz'-a-bad*)
1Ch 27: 6 in his course was *A* his son.

Ammon (*am'-mon*) See also AMMONITE.
Ge 19:38 the children of *A* unto this day.
Nu 21:24 even unto the children of *A*:
24 of the children of *A* was strong.
De 2:19 over against the children of *A*,
19 the children of *A* any possession;
37 of the children of *A* thou camest
3:11 in Rabbath of the children of *A*?
16 is the border of the children of *A*;
Jos 12: 2 the border of the children of *A*;
13:10 the border of the children of *A*;
25 half the land of the children of *A*,
J'g 3:13 unto him the children of *A*
10: 6 and the gods of the children of *A*,
7 into the hands of the children of *A*.
9 children of *A* passed over Jordan
11 Amorites, from the children of *A*,
17 the children of *A* were gathered
18 to fight against the children of *A*?
11: 4 children of *A* made against Israel.
5 when the children of *A* made war
6 we may fight with the children of *A*.
8, 9 against the children of *A*,
12 king of the children of *A*, saying,
13 king of the children of *A* answered
14 unto the king of the children of *A*:
15 nor the land of the children of *A*:
27 of Israel and the children of *A*.
28 the king of the children of *A*
29 passed over unto the children of *A*.
30 children of *A* into mine hands,
31 in peace from the children of *A*,
32 passed over unto the children of *A*
33 the children of *A* were subdued
36 enemies, even of the children of *A*.
12: 1 against the children of *A*,
2 great strife with the children of *A*;
3 over against the children of *A*,
1Sa 12:12 the king of the children of *A*
14:47 against the children of *A*,
2Sa 8:12 of Moab, and of the children of *A*,
10: 1 the king of the children of *A* died,
2 into the land of the children of *A*.
3 the princes of the children of *A*
6 when the children of *A* saw that
6 the children of *A* sent and hired
8 And the children of *A* came out,
10 array against the children of *A*.
11 if the children of *A* be too strong
14 when the children of *A* saw that
14 returned from the children of *A*,
19 feared to help the children of *A*.
11: 1 they destroy the children of *A*,
12: 9 with the sword of the children of *A*.
26 of *A*, and took the royal city.
31 all the cities of the children of *A*.
17:27 of Rabbah of the children of *A*,
1Ki 11: 7 abomination of the children of *A*.
33 the god of the children of *A*,
2Ki 23:13 abomination of the children of *A*,
24: 2 and bands of the children of *A*,
1Ch 18:11 and from the children of *A*.
19: 1 the king of the children of *A* died,
2 into the land of the children of *A*
3 princes of the children of *A* said
6 of *A* saw that they had made
6 of *A* sent a thousand talents of
7 of *A* gathered themselves together
9 of *A* came out, and put the battle
11 array against the children of *A*.
12 of *A* be too strong for thee, then
15 of *A* saw that the Syrians were
19 the Syrians help the children of *A*
20: 1 of *A*, and came and besieged
3 all the cities of the children of *A*.
2Ch 20: 1 of *A*, and with them other beside
10 the children of *A* and Moab,
22 against the children of *A*,
23 children of *A* and Moab stood up
27: 5 of *A* gave him the same year an
5 So much did the children of *A* pay
Ne 13:23 married wives of Ashdod, of *A*,
Ps 83: 7 Gebal, and *A*, and Amalek;
Isa 11:14 the children of *A* shall obey them.
Jer 9:26 of *A*, and Moab, and all that are
25:21 and Moab, and the children of *A*,
49: 6 the captivity of the children of *A*,
Da 11:41 and the chief of the children of *A*.
Am 1:13 transgressions of the children of *A*,
Zep 2: 8 the revilings of the children of *A*,
9 of *A* as Gomorrah, even the

Ammonite (*am'-mon-ite*) See also AMMONITES; AMMONITESS.
De 23: 3 An *A* or Moabite shall not enter
1Sa 11: 1 the *A* came up, and encamped
2 Nahash the *A* answered them,
2Sa 23:37 Zelek the *A*, Naharai the
1Ch 11:39 Zelek the *A*, Naharai the
Ne 2:10 and Tobiah the servant, the *A*,
19 the *A*, and Geshem the Arabian,
4: 3 Now Tobiah the *A* was by him,
13: 1 the *A* and the Moabite should not

Ammonites (*am'-mon-ites*)
De 2:20 the *A* call them Zamzummims;
1Sa 11:11 slew the *A* until the heat of the
1Ki 11: 1 women of the Moabites, *A*,
5 Milcom the abomination of the *A*.
2Ch 20: 1 and with them other beside the *A*,
26: 8 the *A* gave gifts to Uzziah:
27: 5 fought also with the king of the *A*,
Ezr 9: 1 the Perizzites, the Jebusites, the *A*,
Ne 4: 7 and the Arabians, and the *A*,
Jer 27: 3 to the king of the *A*, and to the
40:11 among the *A*, and in Edom,
14 Baalis the king of the *A* hath
41:10 departed to go over to the *A*.
15 eight men, and went to the *A*.
49: 1 Concerning the *A*, thus saith
2 to be heard in Rabbah of the *A*;
Eze 21:20 come to Rabbath of the *A*,
28 concerning the *A*, and
25: 2 set thy face against the *A*,
3 unto the *A*, Hear the word
5 *A* a couchingplace for flocks
10 men of the east with the *A*,
10 *A* may not be remembered

Ammonitess (*am'-mon-i-tess*)
1Ki 14:21 mother's name was Naamah an *A*.
31 was Naamah an *A*. And Abijam
2Ch 12:13 mother's name was Naamah an *A*.
24:26 Zabad the son of Shimeath, an *A*,

Amnon (*am'-non*) See also AMNON'S.
2Sa 3: 2 his firstborn was *A*, of Ahinoam
13: 1 and *A* the son of David loved her.
2 *A* was so vexed, that he fell sick
2 *A* thought it hard for him to do
3 But *A* had a friend whose name
4 *A* said unto him, I love Tamar,
6 So *A* lay down, and made himself
6 *A* said unto the king, I pray thee,
9 *A* said, Have out all men from me.
10 *A* said unto Tamar, Bring the
10 them into the chamber to *A*
15 Then *A* hated her exceedingly;
15 *A* said unto her, Arise, be gone.
20 Hath *A* thy brother been with thee?
22 Absalom spake unto his brother *A*
22 for Absalom hated *A*, because he
26 I pray thee, Let my brother *A* go
27 he let *A* and all the king's sons go
28 and when I say unto you, Smite *A*;
29 did unto *A* as Absalom had
32 for *A* only is dead: for by the
33 *A* only is dead. But Absalom fled.
39 he was comforted concerning *A*,
1Ch 3: 1 the firstborn *A*, of Ahinoam
4:20 the sons of Shimon were, *A*, and

Amnon's (*am'-nons*)
2Sa 13: 7 Go now to thy brother *A* house
8 So Tamar went to her brother *A*
28 when *A* heart is merry with

Amok (*a'-mok*)
Ne 12: 7 Sallu, *A*, Hilkiah, Jedaiah.
20 Of Sallai, Kallai: of *A*, Eber;

Amon (*a'-mon*)
1Ki 22:26 and carry him back unto *A* the
2Ki 21:18 and *A* his son reigned in his stead.
19 *A* was twenty and two years old
23 the servants of *A* conspired against
24 that had conspired against king *A*;
25 the rest of the acts of *A* which he
1Ch 3:14 *A* his son, Josiah his son.
2Ch 18:25 carry him back to *A* the governor
33:20 and *A* his son reigned in his stead.
21 *A* was two and twenty years old
22 *A* sacrificed unto all the carved
23 but *A* trespassed more and more.
25 that had conspired against king *A*
Ne 7:59 of Zebaim, the children of *A*.
Jer 1: 2 in the days of Josiah the son of *A*
25: 3 year of Josiah the son of *A*
Zep 1: 1 the son of *A*, king of Judah.
M't 1:10 Manasses begat *A*;
10 and *A* begat Josias;

among^ See also AMONGST.
Ge 17:10 child *a* you shall be circumcised.
12 shall be circumcised *a* you, every
23 every male child *a* the men of
23: 6 thou art a mighty prince *a* us:
10 Ephron dwelt *a* the children of
24: 3 daughters of the Canaanites, *a*
30:32 all the brown cattle *a* the sheep,
32 spotted and speckled *a* the goats:
30:33 that is not speckled and spotted *a*
33 and brown *a* the sheep, that shall
35 and all the brown *a* the sheep,
41 that they might conceive *a* the rods.
34:22 if every male *a* us be circumcised,
30 me to stink *a* the inhabitants of
30 *a* the Canaanites and the
35: 2 strange gods that are *a* you,
36:30 Hori, *a* their dukes in the land
40:20 chief baker *a* his servants.
42: 5 of Israel came to buy corn *a* those
47: 6 knowest any men of activity *a* them.
Ex 2: 5 when she saw the ark *a* the flags,
7: 5 the children of Israel from *a* them.

Ex 9:20 the word of the Lord a' the servants
12:31 get you forth from a' my people,
49 stranger that sojourneth a' you.
13: 2 whatsoever openeth the womb a'
13 and all the firstborn of man a' thy
15:11 Who is like unto thee, O Lord, a'
17: 7 Is the Lord a' us,
25: 8 that I may dwell a' them.
28: 1 him, from a' the children of Israel,
29:45 I will dwell a' the children of Israel,
46 that I may dwell a' them:
30:12 that there be no plague a' them,
13 a' them that are numbered,
14 Every one that passeth a' them
31:14 shall be cut off from a' his people.
32:25 them naked unto their shame a'
34: 9 let my Lord, I pray thee, go a' us;
10 the people a' which thou art
19 and every firstling a' thy cattle,
35: 5 Take ye from a' you an offering
10 And every wise hearted a' you shall
36: 8 a' them that wrought the work
Le 6:18 the males a' the children of Aaron
29 the males a' the priests shall eat
7: 6 Every male a' the priests shall eat
33 He a' the sons of Aaron, that
34 by a statute for ever from a' the
11: 2 which ye shall eat a' all the beasts
3 and cheweth the cud, a' the beasts,
13 have in abomination a' the fowls;
27 goeth upon his paws, a' all manner
29 shall be unclean unto you a' the
31 unclean to you a' all that creep:
42 or whatsoever hath more feet a'
15:31 defile my tabernacle that is a'
16:16 that remaineth a' them in the
29 a stranger that sojourneth a' you:
17: 4 that man shall be cut off from a'
8 strangers which sojourn a' you,
9 that man shall be cut off from a'
10 strangers that sojourn a' you,
10 cut him off from a' his people.
12 stranger that sojourneth a' you
13 the strangers that sojourn a' you,
18:26 stranger that sojourneth a' you:
29 cut off from a' their people.
19: 8 that soul shall be cut off from a'
16 go up and down as a talebearer a'
34 be unto you as one born a' you,
20: 3 will cut him off from a' his people;
5 cut him off,...from a' their people.
6 cut him off from a' his people.
14 there be no wickedness a' you.
18 be cut off from a' their people.
21: 1 defiled for the dead a' his people:
4 being a chief man a' his people, to
10 the high priest a' his brethren,
15 he profane his seed a' his people:
22: 3 all your seed a' your generations,
32 hallowed a' the children of Israel:
23:29 shall be cut off from a' his people.
30 will I destroy from a' his people.
24:10 went out a' the children of Israel:
25:33 possession a' the children of
45 strangers that do sojourn a' you,
26:11 set my tabernacle a' you:
12 I will walk a' you,
22 send wild beasts a' you, which
25 I will send the pestilence a' you;
33 I will scatter you a' the heathen,
38 And ye shall perish a' the heathen,
Nu 1:47 were not numbered a' them.
49 them a' the children of Israel:
2:33 numbered a' the children of Israel;
3:12 from a' the children of Israel
12 that openeth the matrix a'
41 firstborn a' the children of Israel;
41 the firstlings a' the cattle of the
45 a' the children of Israel, and the
4: 2 from a' the sons of Levi,
18 Kohathites from a' the Levites:
5:21 a curse and an oath a' thy people,
27 a curse a' her people.
8: 6, 14, 16, 19 a' the children of Israel,
19 no plague a' the children of Israel,
9: 7 appointed season a' the children
13 soul shall be cut off from a' his
14 if a stranger shall sojourn a' you,
11: 1 the fire of the Lord burnt a' them,
3 because the fire of the Lord burnt a'
4 mixt multitude that was a' them
20 the Lord which is a' you,
21 The people, a' whom I am,
12: 6 If there be a prophet a' you, I the
13: 2 send a man, every one a ruler a'
14:11 which I have shewed a' them?
13 this people in thy might from a'
14 thou Lord art a' this people,
42 the Lord is not a' you;
15:14 whosoever be a' you in your
23 Moses, and henceforward a' your
26 stranger that sojourneth a' them;
29 is born a' the children of Israel,
29 stranger that sojourneth a' them.
30 cut off from a' his people.
16: 3 and the Lord is a' them:
21 Separate yourselves from a' this
33 perished from a' the congregation.
45 you up from a' this congregation,
47 plague was begun a' the people:
17: 6 rod of Aaron was a' their rods.
18: 6 from a' the children of Israel:
20 neither shalt thou have any part a'
20 inheritance a' the children of Israel.
23 that a' the children of Israel
24 A' the children of Israel they

Nu 19:10 stranger that sojourneth a' them.
20 shall be cut off from a' the
21: 6 sent fiery serpents a' the people,
23: 9 not be reckoned a' the nations.
23:21 and the shout of a king is a' them.
25: 7 rose up from a' the congregation,
11 was zealous for my sake a' them,
14 a chief house a' the Simeonites.
26:62 numbered a' the children of Israel,
62 them a' the children of Israel.
64 But a' these there was not a man
27: 4 done away from a' his family,
4 a' the brethren of our father.
7 an inheritance a' their father's
31:16 was a plague a' the congregation
17 kill every male a' the little ones,
32:30 they shall have possessions a' you
33: 4 the Lord had smitten a' them:
54 by lot for an inheritance a' your
35: 6 And a' the cities which ye shall
15 and for the sojourner a' them:
34 dwell a' the children of Israel.
De 1:13 understanding, and known a'
15 tens, and officers a' your tribes.
42 I am not a' you;
2:14 wasted out from a' the host,
15 to destroy them from a' the host,
16 and dead from a' the people,
4: 3 destroyed them from a' you.
27 shall scatter you a' the nations,
27 left few in number a' the heathen,
6:15 a jealous God a' you)
7:14 male or female barren a' you,
14 or a' your cattle.
20 God will send the hornet a' them,
21 the Lord thy God is a' you,
13: 1 If there arise a' you a prophet,
11 such wickedness as this is a' you.
13 Belial, are gone out from a' you,
14 abomination is wrought a' you;
14: 6 cheweth the cud a' the beasts,
15: 4 there shall be no poor a' you;
7 If there be a' you a poor man of
16:11 and the widow, that are a' you,
17: 2 If there be found a' you,
7 put the evil away from a' you.
15 one from a' thy brethren
18: 2 no inheritance a' their brethren:
10 not be found a' you any one
18 a Prophet from a' their brethren,
19:19 put the evil away from a' you.
20 no more any such evil a' you.
21: 9 of innocent blood from a' you,
11 seest a' the captives a beautiful
21 thou put evil away from a' you;
22:21 thou put evil away from a' you.
24 put away evil from a' you.
23:10 If there be a' you any man, that
16 dwell with thee, even a' you,
24: 7 put evil away from a' you.
26:11 the stranger that is a' you.
28:37 a' all nations whither the Lord
54 the man that is tender a' you,
56 tender and delicate woman a' you,
64 the Lord shall scatter thee a' all
65 a' these nations shalt thou find no
29:17 and gold, which were a' them:)
18 Lest there should be a' you man,
18 a' you a root that beareth gall
30: 1 them to mind a' all the nations,
31:16 whither they go to be a' them,
17 because our God is not a' us?
32:26 of them to cease from a' men:
34 and sealed up a' my treasures?
46 the words which I testify a' you
51 a' the children of Israel
Jos 3: 5 the Lord will do wonders a' you.
10 the living God is a' you,
4: 6 That this may be a sign a' you,
7:11 put it even a' their own stuff.
12 destroy the accursed from a' you.
13 the accursed thing from a' you.
21 When I saw a' the spoils a goodly
8: 9 lodged that night a' the people.
33 as he that was born a' them;
35 that were conversant a' them.
9: 7 Peradventure ye dwell a' us;
16 and that they dwelt a' them.
22 when ye dwell a' us?
10: 1 inhabitants of Gibeon....were a'
13:13 the Maachathites dwell a' the
22 slay with the sword a' them that
14: 3 he gave none inheritance a' them.
15 Arba was a great man a' the
15:13 a part a' the children of Judah,
16: 9 the children of Ephraim were a'
10 the Canaanites dwell a' the
17: 4 an inheritance a' our brethren.
4 an inheritance a' the brethren
6 had an inheritance a' his sons:
9 cities of Ephraim are a' the cities
18: 2 remained a' the children of Israel
4 a' you three men of each tribe:
7 the Levites have no part a' you;
19:49 Joshua the son of Nun a' them:
20: 4 a place, that he may dwell a' them.
9 stranger that sojourneth a' them,
22: 7 gave Joshua a' their brethren
14 their fathers a' the thousands of
19 take possession a' us:
31 perceive that the Lord is a' us,
23: 7 ye come not a' these nations,
7 remain a' you; neither make
12 even these that remain a' you,
24: 5 that which I did a' them:
17 and a' all the people through

Jos 24:23 strange gods which are a' you,
J'g 1:16 went and dwelt a' the people.
29 Canaanites dwelt in Gezer a' them.
30 the Canaanites dwelt a' them,
32 Asherites dwelt a' the Canaanites,
33 Naphtali....dwelt a' the Canaanites,
3: 5 children of Israel dwelt a' the
5: 8 seen a' forty thousand in Israel?
9 offered themselves willingly a'
13 over the nobles a' the people:
14 after thee, Benjamin, a' thy people;
16 abodest thou a' the sheepfolds,
10:16 away the strange gods from a'
12: 4 Ephraim a' the Ephraimites,
4 and a' the Manassites.
14: 3 a' the daughters of thy brethren,
3 or a' all my people, that thou
18: 1 unto them a' the tribes of Israel.
25 Let not thy voice be heard a' us,
20:12 is this that is done a' you?
16 A' all this people there were
21: 5 there a' all the tribes of Israel
12 a' the inhabitants of Jabesh-gilead
Ru 2: 7 gather after the reapers a' the
15 Let her glean even a' the sheaves,
4:10 not cut off from a' his brethren,
1Sa 2: 8 to set them a' princes, and to
4: 3 when it cometh a' us, it may
17 a great slaughter a' the people,
6: 6 had wrought wonderfully a' them,
7: 3 Ashtaroth from a' you,
9: 2 was not a' the children of Israel
22 place a' them that were bidden,
10:10 and he prophesied a' them.
11 he prophesied a' the prophets,
23 when he stood a' the people,
14:15 a' all the people: the garrison,
30 much greater slaughter a' the
34 Saul said, Disperse yourselves a'
39 a' all the people that answered
15: 6 down from a' the Amalekites,
6 departed from a' the Amalekites.
33 thy mother be childless a' women.
16: 1 have provided me a king a' his sons.
17:12 man went a' men for an old man
19:24 Is Saul also a' the prophets?
22:14 a' all thy servants as David,
31: 9 the house of their idols, and a'
2Sa 6:19 And he dealt a' all the people,
19 even a' the whole multitude
15:31 Ahithophel is a' the conspirators
16:20 Give counsel a' you what we
17: 9 There is a slaughter a' the people
19:28 didst thou set thy servant a' them
22:50 unto thee, O Lord, a' the heathen.
23: 8 chief a' the captains; the same
18 of Zeruiah, was chief a' three.
18 and had the name a' three.
22 had the name a' three mighty men.
1Ki 3:13 a' the kings like unto thee all thy
5: 6 there is not a' us any that can
6:13 I will dwell a' the children of
7:51 put a' the treasures of the house
8:53 them from a' all the people of
9: 7 and a byword a' all people:
11:20 a' the sons of Pharaoh.
14: 7 I exalted thee from a' the people,
21: 9 a fast, and set Naboth on high a'
12 Naboth on high a' the people.
2Ki 4:13 I dwell a' mine own people.
9: 2 arise up from a' his brethren,
11: 2 stole him from a' the king's sons
17:25, 26 the Lord sent lions a' them,
18: 5 after him was none like him a' all
35 a' all the gods of the countries,
20:15 there is nothing a' my treasures
23: 9 bread a' their brethren.
1Ch 4:23 and those that dwelt a' plants
7: 5 their brethren a' all the families
11:20 and had a name a' the three.
24 the name a' the three mighties.
25 he was honourable a' the thirty,
12: 1 and they were a' the mighty men,
4 the Gibeonite, a mighty man a'
16: 8 known his deeds a' the people.
24 Declare his glory a' the heathen;
24 marvellous works a' all nations.
31 men say a' the nations, The Lord
18:14 judgment and justice a' all his
21: 6 Benjamin counted he not a' them:
23: 6 into courses a' the sons of Levi,
24: 4 A' the sons of Eleazar there were
4 eight a' the sons of Ithamar
26:12 A' these were the divisions of
12 even a' the chief men, having
19 divisions of the porters a' the
19 of Kore, and a' the sons of Merari.
30 were officers a' them of Israel on
31 A' the Hebronites was Jerijah
31 even a' the Hebronites, according
31 were found a' them mighty men
27: 6 who was mighty a' the thirty,
28: 4 a' the sons of my father he liked
2Ch 5: 1 put he a' the treasures of the
6: 5 I chose no city a' all the tribes
7:13 I send pestilence a' my people;
20 and a byword a' all nations.
11:22 to be ruler a' his brethren:
20:25 they found a' them in abundance
22:11 stole him from a' the king's sons
24:16 buried him in the city of David a'
23 all the princes of the people from a'
26: 6 Ashdod, and a' the Philistines.
28:15 clothed all that were naked a'
31:19 to all the males a' the priests,
19 reckoned by genealogies a' the

2Ch 32:14 Who was there *a*· all the gods of
33:11 took Manasseh *a*· the thorns,
19 they are written *a*· the sayings
35:13 divided them speedily *a*· all the
36:23 is there *a*· you of all his people?
Ezr 1: 3 is there *a*· you of all his people?
2:62 *a*· those that were reckoned
65 *a*· them two hundred singing
10:18 And *a*· the sons of the priests
Ne 1: 8 scatter you abroad *a*· the nations:
4:11 we come in the midst *a*· them,
5:17 unto us from *a*· the heathen that
6: 6 It is reported *a*· the heathen,
7:64 *a*· those that were reckoned by
9:17 thy wonders thou didst *a*· them;
10:34 we cast the lots *a*· the priests,
11:17 the second *a*· his brethren,
13:26 yet *a*· many nations was there no
Es 1:19 and let it be written *a*· the laws of
3: 8 scattered abroad and dispersed *a*·
4: 3 was great mourning *a*· the Jews,
9:21 To stablish this *a*· them,
28 should not fail from *a*· the Jews,
10: 3 great *a*· the Jews, and accepted
Job 1: 6 Satan came also *a*· them.
2: 1 came also *a*· them to present
8 he sat down *a*· the ashes.
15:19 no stranger passed *a*· them.
17:10 cannot find one wise man *a*· you.
18:19 neither have son nor nephew *a*·
28:10 He cutteth out rivers *a*· the rocks;
30: 5 driven forth from *a*· men,
7 *A*· the bushes they brayed;
33:23 one *a*· a thousand, to shew unto
34: 4 know *a*· ourselves what is good.
37 he clappeth his hands *a*· us,
36:14 and their life is *a*· the unclean.
39:25 He saith *a*· the trumpets, Ha, Ha;
41: 6 part him *a*· the merchants?
42:15 inheritance *a*· their brethren.
Ps 9:11 declare *a*· the people his doings.
12: 1 fail from *a*· the children of men.
18:49 unto thee, O Lord, *a*· the heathen,
21:10 seed from *a*· the children of men.
22:18 They part my garments *a*· them,
28 he is the governor *a*· the nations.
31:11 a reproach *a*· all mine enemies,
11 especially *a*· my neighbours,
35:18 I will praise thee *a*· much people.
44:11 hast scattered us *a*· the heathen.
14 makest us a byword *a*· the heathen,
14 shaking of the head *a*· the people.
45: 9 were *a*· thy honourable women:
12 even the rich *a*· the people shall
46:10 I will be exalted *a*· the heathen,
55:15 in their dwellings, and *a*· them.
57: 4 My soul is *a*· lions: and I lie
4 even *a*· them that are set on fire,
9 praise thee, O Lord, *a*· the people:
9 will sing unto thee *a*· the nations.
67: 2 thy saving health *a*· all nations.
68:13 though ye have lien *a*· the pots,
17 the Lord is *a*· them, as in Sinai,
18 the Lord God might dwell *a*· them.
25 *a*· them were the damsels
74: 9 neither is their *a*· us any that
77:14 declared thy strength *a*· the people.
78:45 sent divers sorts of flies *a*· them,
49 by sending evil angels *a*· them.
60 the tent which he placed *a*· men;
79:10 let him be known *a*· the heathen
80: 6 our enemies laugh *a*· themselves.
82: 1 mighty; he judgeth *a*· the gods.
86: 8 *A*· the gods there is none like
88: 5 Free *a*· the dead, like the slain
89: 6 who *a*· the sons of the mighty can
94: 8 ye brutish *a*· the people: and ye
96: 3 Declare his glory *a*· the heathen,
3 his wonders *a*· all people.
10 Say *a*· the heathen that the Lord
99: 6 Moses and Aaron *a*· his priests,
6 and Samuel *a*· them that call
104:10 valleys, which run *a*· the hills.
12 which sing *a*· the branches.
105: 1 known his deeds *a*· the people.
27 they shewed his signs *a*· them,
37 one feeble person *a*· their tribes.
106:27 their seed also *a*· the nations,
35 were mingled *a*· the heathen,
47 and gather us from *a*· the heathen,
108: 3 praise thee, O Lord, *a*· the people:
3 praises unto thee *a*· the nations.
109:30 yea, I will praise him *a*· the
110: 6 He shall judge *a*· the heathen,
126: 2 then said they *a*· the heathen,
136:11 brought out Israel from *a*· them:
Pr 1:14 Cast in thy lot *a*· us; let us all
6:19 that soweth discord *a*· brethren.
7: 7 And beheld *a*· the simple ones,
7 I discerned *a*· the youths, a young
14: 9 *a*· the righteous there is favour.
15:31 reproof of life abideth *a*· the wise.
17: 2 of the inheritance *a*· the brethren.
23:20 Be not *a*· winebibbers; *a*· riotous
28 the transgressors *a*· men.
27:22 a mortar *a*· wheat with a pestle,
30:14 earth, and the needy from *a*· men.
30 lion which is strongest *a*· beasts,
31:23 sitteth *a*· the elders of the land.
Ec 6: 1 sun, and it is common *a*· men:
7:28 one man *a*· a thousand have I
28 but a woman *a*· all those have I
9: 3 This is an evil *a*· all things that
17 cry of him that ruleth *a*· fools.
Ca 1: 8 O thou fairest *a*· women, go thy
2: 2 As the lily *a*· thorns,

Ca 2: 2 so is my love *a*· the daughters.
3 As the apple tree *a*· the trees of
3 so is my beloved *a*· the sons. I sat
16 am his: he feedeth *a*· the lilies.
4: 2 twins, and none is barren *a*· them.
5 are twins, which feed *a*· the lilies.
5: 9 O thou fairest *a*· women? what is
10 the chiefest *a*· ten thousand.
6: 1 O thou fairest *a*· women?
3 is mine: he feedeth *a*· the lilies.
6 and there is not one barren *a*· them.
Isa 2: 4 he shall judge *a*· the nations,
4: 3 written *a*· the living in Jerusalem:
5:27 be weary nor stumble *a*· them;
8:15 many *a*· them shall stumble,
16 the testimony, seal the law *a*·
10:16 send *a*· his fat ones leanness;
12: 4 declare his doings *a*· the people,
24:13 midst of the land *a*· the people,
29:14 to do a marvellous work *a*· this
19 and the poor *a*· men shall rejoice
33:14 Who *a*· us shall dwell with the
14 *a*· us shall dwell with everlasting
36:20 Who are they *a*· all the gods of these
39: 4 there is nothing *a*· my treasures
41:28 even *a*· them, and there was no
42:23 Who *a*· you will give ear to this?
43: 9 who *a*· them can declare this,
12 there was no strange god *a*· you:
44: 4 shall spring up as *a*· the grass,
14 himself *a*· the trees of the forest:
48:14 which *a*· them hath declared these
50:10 Who is *a*· you that feareth the
51:18 none to guide her *a*· all the sons
57: 6 *A*· the smooth stones of the stream
61: 9 shall be known *a*· the Gentiles,
9 and their offspring *a*· the people:
65: 4 Which remain *a*· the graves,
66:19 And I will set a sign *a*· them,
19 declare my glory *a*· the Gentiles.
Jer 3:19 shall I put thee *a*· the children,
4: 3 ground, and sow not *a*· thorns.
5:26 For *a*· my people are found
6:15 they shall fall *a*· them that fall:
18 O congregation, what is *a*· them.
27 for a tower and a fortress *a*· my
8:12 *a*· them that fall: in the time of
17 send serpents, cockatrices, *a*· you,
9:16 scatter them also *a*· the heathen,
10: 7 *a*· all the wise men of the nations,
11: 9 conspiracy is found *a*· the men
9 *a*· the inhabitants of Jerusalem.
12:14 the house of Judah from *a*· them.
14:22 *a*· the vanities of the Gentiles
18:13 Ask ye now *a*· the heathen,
24:10 and the pestilence, *a*· them, till
25:16 sword that I will send *a*· them.
27 sword which I will send *a*· you.
29:18 *a*· all the nations whither I have
32 a man to dwell *a*· this people;
31: 7 shout *a*· the chief of the nations:
32:20 this day, and in Israel, and *a*·
37: 4 Jeremiah came in and went out *a*·
10 remained but wounded men *a*·
39:14 so he dwelt *a*· the people.
40: 1 bound in chains *a*· all that were
5 dwell with him *a*· the people:
6 dwelt with him *a*· the people that
11 *a*· the Ammonites, and in Edom,
41: 8 But ten men were found *a*· them
8 slew them not *a*· their brethren.
44: 8 a reproach *a*· all the nations of
46:18 as Tabor is *a*· the mountains,
48:27 was he found *a*· thieves?
49:15 small *a*· the heathen,
15 and despised *a*· men.
50: 2 Declare ye *a*· the nations,
23 a desolation *a*· the nations!
46 is moved, and the cry is heard *a*·
51:27 blow the trumpet *a*· the nations,
41 Babylon become an astonishment *a*·
La 1: 1 she that was great *a*· the nations,
1 and princess *a*· the provinces,
2 *a*· all her lovers she hath none to
3 she dwelleth *a*· the heathen,
17 as a menstruous woman *a*· them.
2: 9 her princes are *a*· the Gentiles:
4:15 wandered, they said *a*· the heathen,
20 we shall live *a*· the heathen.
Eze 1: 1 as I was *a*· the captives by the
13 and down *a*· the living creatures;
2: 5 hath been a prophet *a*· them.
6 and thou dost dwell *a*· scorpions:
3:15 astonished *a*· them seven days.
25 thou shalt not go out *a*· them:
4:13 eat their defiled bread *a*· the
5:14 and a reproach *a*· the nations
6: 8 escape the sword *a*· the nations,
9 shall remember me *a*· the nations
13 slain men shall be *a*· their idols
9: 2 one man *a*· them was clothed
11: 1 *a*· whom I saw Jaazaniah the
9 will execute judgments *a*· you.
16 cast them far off *a*· the heathen,
16 scattered them *a*· the countries,
12:10 house of Israel that are *a*· them.
12 the prince that is *a*· them
15 I shall scatter them *a*· the nations,
16 their abominations *a*· the heathen
13:19 will ye pollute me *a*· my people
15: 2 which is *a*· the trees of the forest?
6 As the vine tree *a*· the trees of the
16:14 renown went forth *a*· the heathen
18:18 which is not good *a*· his people,
19: 2 lioness: she lay down *a*· lions,
2 her whelps *a*· young lions.

Eze 19: 6 he went up and down *a*· the lions,
11 exalted *a*· the thick branches,
20: 9 heathen, *a*· whom they were,
23 would scatter them *a*· the heathen,
38 purge out from *a*· you the rebels,
22:15 scatter thee *a*· the heathen,
26 sabbaths, I am profaned *a*· them.
30 And I sought for a man *a*· them,
23:10 she became famous *a*· women;
25:10 may not be remembered *a*·
27:24 of cedar, *a*· thy merchandise.
36 The merchants *a*· the people
28:19 they that know thee *a*· the people
25 house of Israel from the people *a*·
29:12 her cities *a*· the cities that are
12 the Egyptians *a*· the nations,
30:23, 26 the Egyptians *a*· the nations
26 disperse them *a*· the countries;
31: 3, 10 his top was *a*· the thick boughs,
14 their top *a*· the thick boughs,
18 glory and in greatness *a*· the trees
32: 9 bring thy destruction *a*· the nations,
21 The strong *a*· the mighty shall
33: 6 take any person from *a*· them,
33 that a prophet hath been *a*· them.
34:12 the day that he is *a*· his sheep
24 servant David a prince *a*· them
35:11 will make myself known *a*· them,
36:19 I scattered them *a*· the heathen,
21 Israel had profaned *a*· the heathen,
22 ye have profaned *a*· the heathen,
23 great name, which was profaned *a*·
24 take you from *a*· the heathen,
30 reproach of famine *a*· the heathen.
37:21 the children of Israel from *a*· the
39: 6 a fire on Magog, and *a*· them
21 I will set my glory *a*· the heathen,
28 them to be led into captivity *a*·
40:46 *a*· the sons of Levi, which come
44: 9 stranger that is *a*· the children
47:22 strangers that sojourn *a*· you,
22 which shall beget children *a*· you:
22 country *a*· the children of Israel;
22 with you *a*· the tribes of Israel.
Da 1: 6 Now *a*· these were of the children
19 and *a*· them all was found none
4:35 in the army of heaven, and *a*·
7: 8 there came up *a*· them another
11:24 shall scatter *a*· them the prey,
33 that understand *a*· the people
Ho 5: 9 *a*· the tribes of Israel have I made
7: 7 there is none *a*· them that
8 hath mixed himself *a*· the people;
8: 8 up: now shall they be *a*·
10 they have hired *a*· the nations,
9:17 shall be wanderers *a*· the nations.
10:14 shall a tumult arise *a*· thy people,
13:15 he be fruitful *a*· his brethren,
Joe 2:17 should they say *a*· the people,
19 you a reproach *a*· the heathen;
25 great army which I sent *a*·
3: 2 scattered *a*· the nations, and parted
9 Proclaim ye this *a*· the Gentiles;
Am 1: 1 Amos, who was *a*· the herdmen
2:16 that is courageous *a*· the mighty
4:10 I have sent *a*· you the pestilence
9: 9 the house of Israel *a*· all nations,
Ob 1 is sent *a*· the heathen,
2 made thee small *a*· the heathen:
4 thou set thy nest *a*· the stars,
Mic 3:11 Is not the Lord *a*· us? none
4: 3 he shall judge *a*· many people,
5: 2 Ephratah, though thou be little *a*·
8 Jacob shall be *a*· the Gentiles
8 people as a lion *a*· the beasts
8 young lion *a*· the flocks of sheep:
7: 2 and there is none upright *a*· men:
Na 3: 8 that was situate *a*· the rivers,
Hab 1: 5 Behold ye *a*· the heathen, and
Zep 3:20 praise *a*· all people of the earth,
Hag 2: 3 Who is left *a*· you that saw this
5 so my spirit remaineth *a*· you:
Zec 1: 8 and he stood *a*· the myrtle trees
10 man that stood *a*· the myrtle trees
11 Lord that stood *a*· the myrtle trees,
3: 7 give the places *a*· these that
7:14 a whirlwind *a*· all the nations
8:13 ye were a curse *a*· the heathen,
10: 9 And I will sow them *a*· the people:
12: 6 like an hearth of fire *a*· the wood,
8 and he that is feeble *a*· them at that
14:13 from the Lord shall be *a*· them;
Mal 1:10 Who is there even *a*· you that
11 shall be great *a*· the Gentiles;
11 name shall be great *a*· the heathen,
14 name is dreadful *a*· the heathen.
M't 2: 6 not the least *a*· the princes of
4:23 manner of disease *a*· the people.
9:35 and every disease *a*· the people.
11:11 *A*· them that are born of women
12:11 What man shall there be *a*· you,
13: 7 and some fell *a*· thorns; and the
22 that received seed *a*· the thorns
25 sowed tares *a*· the wheat,
32 it is the greatest *a*· herbs,
49 the wicked from *a*· the just,
16: 7 they reasoned *a*· themselves,
8 why reason ye *a*· yourselves,
20:26 But it shall not be so *a*· you:
26 whosoever will be great *a*· you,
27 whosoever will be chief *a*· you,
21:38 they said *a*· themselves, This is
23:11 But he that is greatest *a*· you shall
26: 5 there be an uproar *a*· the people.
27:35 parted my garments *a*· them,
56 *A*· which was Mary Magdalene,

M't 28:15 reported a' the Jews until this day
M'r 1:27 they questioned a' themselves,
4: 7 some fell a' thorns, and the thorns
18 they which are sown a' thorns;
5: 3 had his dwelling a' the tombs;
6: 4 own country, and a' his own kin,
41 two fishes divided he a' them all.
8:16 they reasoned a' themselves,
19 the five loaves a' five thousand,
20 when the seven a' four thousand,
9:33 that ye disputed a' yourselves
34 they had disputed a' themselves,
10:26 saying a' themselves, Who then
43 so shall it not be a' you:
43 whosoever will be great a' you,
12: 7 husbandmen said a' themselves,
13:10 first be published a' all nations.
15:31 said a' themselves with the
40 a' whom was Mary Magdelene,
16: 3 they said a' themselves, Who
Lu 1: 1 are most surely believed a' us,
25 take away my reproach a' men.
28 thee: blessed art thou a' women.
42 Blessed art thou a' women,
2:44 a' their kinsfolk and acquaintance.
4:36 amazed and spake a' themselves,
7:16 a great prophet is risen up a' us;
28 A' those that are born of women
8: 7 some fell a' thorns: and
14 that which fell a' thorns are they,
9:46 there arose a reasoning a' them,
48 that is least a' you all, the same
10: 3 forth as lambs a' wolves.
30 and fell a' thieves, which stripped
36 unto him that fell a' the thieves?
16:15 which is highly esteemed a' men
19: 2 was the chief a' the publicans,
39 the Pharisees from a' the multitude
20:14 him they reasoned a' themselves
22:17 this, and divide it a' yourselves:
23 began to enquire a' themselves,
24 was also a strife a' them,
26 he that is greatest a' you,
27 a' you as he that serveth.
37 reckoned a' the transgressors:
55 together, Peter sat down a' them.
24: 5 seek ye the living a' the dead?
47 in his name a' all nations,
Joh 1:14 was made flesh, and dwelt a'
26 there standeth one a' you,
6: 9 what are they a' so many?
43 them, Murmur not a' yourselves.
52 therefore strove a' themselves,
7:12 much murmuring a' the people
35 said the the Jews a' themselves,
35 unto the dispersed a' the Gentiles,
43 was a division a' the people
8: 7 He that is without sin a' you,
9:16 And there was a division a' them.
10:19 a' the Jews for these sayings.
11:54 no more openly a' the Jews;
56 they for Jesus, and spake a'
12:19 therefore said a' themselves,
20 Greeks a' them that came up to
42 a' the chief rulers also many
15:24 I had not done a' them the works
16:17 of his disciples a' themselves,
19 Do ye enquire a' yourselves of
19:24 said therefore a' themselves,
24 parted my raiment a' them, and
21:23 saying abroad a' the brethren,
Ac 1:21 Lord Jesus went in and out a' us,
2:22 of God a' you by miracles
3:23 destroyed from a' the people.
4:12 given a' men, whereby we must
15 they conferred a' themselves,
17 it spread no further a' the people,
34 there any a' them that lacked:
5:12 wonders wrought a' the people;
34 in reputation a' all the people,
6: 3 a' you seven men of honest report,
8 wonders and miracles a' the
10:22 of good report a' all the nation
12:18 was no small stir a' the soldiers,
13:26 whosoever a' you feareth God,
14:14 ran in a' the people, crying out,
15: 7 while ago God made choice a' us,
12 had wrought a' the Gentiles by
19 a' the Gentiles are turned to God.
22 Silas, chief men a' the brethren:
17:33 Paul departed from a' them.
34 a' the which was Dionysius the
18:11 teaching the word of God a' them.
20:25 a' whom I have gone preaching
29 grievous wolves enter in a' you,
32 an inheritance a' all them which
21:19 wrought a' the Gentiles by his
21 teachest all the Jews which are a'
34 some another, a' the multitude:
23:10 take him by force from a'
24: 5 a mover of sedition a' all the Jews
21 I cried standing a' them,
25: 5 which a' you are able, go down
6 And when he had tarried a' them
26: 3 customs which are a' the Jews:
4 a' mine own nation at Jerusalem,
18 inheritance a' them which are
27:22 no loss of any man's life a' you,
28: 4 said a' themselves, No doubt
25 when they agreed not a' themselves,
29 and had great reasoning a'
Ro 1: 5 obedience to the faith a' all nations,
6 A' whom are ye also the called
13 have some fruit a' you also,
13 even as a' other Gentiles.
2:24 the name of God is blasphemed a'
Ro 8:29 the firstborn a' many brethren.
11:17 wert graffed in a' them, and with
12: 3 to every man that is a' you,
15: 9 confess to thee a' the Gentiles,
16: 7 are of note a' the apostles, who
1Co 1:10 that there be no divisions a' you;
11 there are contentions a' you.
2: 2 not to know any thing a' you,
6 speak wisdom a' them that are
3: 3 there is a' you envying, and strife,
18 If any man a' you seemeth to be
5: 1 there is fornication a' you,
1 as named a' the Gentiles,
2 might be taken away from a' you.
13 put away from a' yourselves
6: 5 there is not a wise man a' you?
7 utterly a fault a' you, because
11:18 there be divisions a' you;
19 there must be also heresies a' you,
19 approved may be made manifest a'
30 many are weak and sickly a' you,
15:12 how say some a' you that there
2Co 1:19 Jesus Christ who was preached a'
6:17 come out from a' them,
10: 1 who in presence am base a' you,
12 comparing themselves a'
11: 6 manifest a' you in all things.
26 in perils a' false brethren;
12:12 a' you in all patience, in signs,
21 my God will humble me a' you,
Ga 1:16 I might preach him a' the heathen;
2: 2 which I preach a' the Gentiles,
3: 1 set forth, crucified a' you?
5 worketh miracles a' you, doeth he
Eph 2: 3 A' whom also we all had our
3: 8 I should preach a' the Gentiles
5: 3 not be once named a' you,
Ph'p 2:15 a' whom ye shine as lights in the
Col 1:27 mystery a' the Gentiles; which is
4:16 when this epistle is read a' you,
1Th 1: 5 men we are a' you for your sake.
2: 7 But we were gentle a' you,
10 we behaved ourselves a' you that
5:12 a' you, and are over you in the
13 And be at peace a' yourselves.
15 follow that which is good, both a'
2Th 1:10 testimony a' you was believed)
3: 7 not ourselves disorderly a' you;
11 which walk a' you disorderly,
2Ti 2: 2 heard of me a' many witnesses,
Heb 5: 1 priest taken from a' men is
Jas 1:26 If any man a' you seem to be
3: 6 so is the tongue a' our members,
13 endued with knowledge a' you?
4: 1 come wars and fightings a' you?
5:13 Is any a' you afflicted? let him pray.
14 Is any sick a' you?
1Pe 2:12 your conversation honest a' the
4: 8 have fervent charity a' yourselves:
5: 1 elders which are a' you I exhort,
2 flock of God which is a' you,
2Pe 2: 1 false prophets also a' the people,
1 shall be false teachers a' you,
8 righteous man dwelling a' them,
3Jo 9 loveth to have the preeminence a'
Jude 15 convince all that are ungodly a'
Re 2:13 who was slain a' you, where
7:15 shall dwell a' them.
14: 4 were redeemed from a' men,

amongst
Ge 3: 8 a' the trees of the garden.
23: 9 possession of a buryingplace a'

Amorite (*am'-o-rite*) See also AMORITES.
Ge 10:16 And the Jebusite, and the A',
14:13 dwelt in the plain of Mamre the A',
48:22 I took out of the hand of the A'
Ex 33: 2 will drive out the Canaanite, the A',
34:11 I drive out before thee the A',
Nu 32:39 dispossessed the A' which was in it.
De 2:24 given into thine hand Sihon the A',
Jos 9: 1 Hittite, and the A', the Canaanite,
11: 3 east and on the west, and to the A',
1Ch 1:14 The Jebusite also, and the A',
Eze 16: 3 thy father was an A', and thy
45 was a Hittite, and your father an A'.
Am 2: 9 destroyed I the A' before them,
10 to possess the land of the A'.

Amorites (*am'-o-rites*)
Ge 14: 7 and also the A', that dwelt in
15:16 iniquity of the A' is not yet full.
21 And the A' and the Canaanites,
Ex 3: 8 and the Hittites, and the A',
17 and the A', and the Perizzites,
13: 5 and the A', and the Hivites,
23:23 and bring thee in unto the A',
Nu 13:29 the A', dwell in the mountains:
21:13 cometh out of the coasts of the A':
13 between Moab and the A'.
21 unto Sihon king of the A',
25 dwelt in all the cities of the A',
26 city of Sihon the king of the A',
29 captivity unto Sihon king of the A'.
31 Israel dwelt in the land of the A'.
32 drove out the A' that were there.
34 didst unto Sihon king of the A',
22: 2 all that Israel had done to the A'.
32:33 the kingdom of Sihon king of the A',
De 1: 4 had slain Sihon the king of the A',
7 and go to the mount of the A',
19 the way of the mountain of the A',
20 come unto the mountain of the A',
27 deliver us into the hand of the A',
44 A', which dwell in that mountain,
3: 2 of the A', which dwelt at Heshbon.
8 the hand of the two kings of the A'
De 3: 9 and the A' call it Shenir;)
4:46 in the land of Sihon king of the A',
47 two kings of the A', which were on
7: 1 and the Girgashites, and the A',
20:17 namely, the Hittites, and the A',
31: 4 to Sihon and to Og, kings of the A',
Jos 2:10 ye did unto the two kings of the A',
3:10 and the A', and the Jebusites,
5: 1 when all the kings of the A',
7: 7 deliver us into the hand of the A',
9:10 the two kings of the A', that were
10: 5 Therefore the five kings of the A',
6 all the kings of the A' that dwell
12 when the Lord delivered up the A'
12: 2 Sihon king of the A', who dwelt in
8 the A', and the Canaanites,
13: 4 unto Aphek, to the borders of the A':
10 Sihon king of the A', which reigned
21 kingdom of Sihon king of the A',
24: 8 brought you into the land of the A',
11 fought against you, the A',
12 even the two kings of the A';
15 or the gods of the A', in whose land
18 even the A' which dwelt in the land:
J'g 1:34 the A' forced the children of Dan
35 A' would dwell in mount Heres
36 the coast of the A' was from the
3: 5 the Canaanites, Hittites, and A',
6:10 fear not the gods of the A',
10: 8 Jordan in the land of the A',
11 the Egyptians, and from the A',
11:19 Sihon king of the A', the king of
21 A', the inhabitants of that country.
22 possessed all the coasts of the A',
23 of Israel hath dispossessed the A'
1Sa 7:14 peace between Israel and the A'.
2Sa 21: 2 but of the remnant of the A';
1Ki 4:19 the country of Sihon king of the A',
9:20 the people that were left of the A',
21:26 according to all things as did the A',
2Ki 21:11 wickedly above all that the A' did,
2Ch 8: 7 of the Hittites, and the A',
Ezr 9: 1 Moabites, the Egyptians, and the A'.
Ne 9: 8 the A', and the Perizzites,
Ps 135:11 Sihon king of the A', and Og
136:19 Sihon king of the A': for his mercy

Amos (*a'-mos*)
Am 1: 1 The words of A', who was among
7: 8 And the Lord said unto me, A',
10 saying, A' hath conspired against
11 thus A' saith, Jeroboam shall die
12 Amaziah said unto A', O thou seer,
14 answered A', and said to Amaziah,
8: 2 And he said, A', what seest thou?
Lu 3:25 which was the son of A',

amounting
2Ch 3: 8 gold, a' to six hundred talents.

Amoz (*a'-moz*)
2Ki 19: 2 to Isaiah the prophet the son of A'.
20 the son of A' sent to Hezekiah,
20: 1 the son of A' came to him, and said
2Ch 26:22 did Isaiah the prophet, the son of A',
32:20 the son of A', prayed and cried to
32 Isaiah the prophet, the son of A',
Isa 1: 1 The vision of Isaiah the son of A',
2: 1 The word that Isaiah the son of A'
13: 1 which Isaiah the son of A' did see.
20: 2 the Lord by Isaiah the son of A',
37: 2 Isaiah the prophet the son of A'.
21 the son of A' sent unto Hezekiah,
38: 1 son of A' came unto him, and said

Amphipolis (*am-fip'-o-lis*)
Ac 17: 1 when they had passed through A'

Amplias (*am'-ple-as*)
Ro 16: 8 Greet A' my beloved in the Lord.

Amram (*am'-ram*) See also AMRAMITES; AMRAM'S; HEMDAN.
Ex 6:18 the sons of Kohath; A', and Izhar,
20 And A' took him Jochebed, his
20 and the years of the life of A' were
Nu 3:19 of Kohath by their families; A',
26:58 Korathites. And Kohath begat A'.
59 and she bare unto A' Aaron, and
1Ch 1:41 A', and Eshban, and Ithran, and
6: 2 A', Izhar, and Hebron, and Uzziel.
3 children of A'; Aaron and Moses,
18 sons of Kohath were, A', and Izhar,
23:12 sons of Kohath; A', Izhar, Hebron,
13 sons of A'; Aaron and Moses:
24:20 sons of A'; Shubael: of the sons
Ezr 10:34 sons of Bani; Maadai, A', and Uel,

Amramites (*am'-ram-ites*)
Nu 3:27 Kohath was the family of the A',
1Ch 26:23 Of the A', and the Izharites, the

Amram's (*am'-rams*)
Nu 26:59 name of A' wife was Jochebed,

Amraphel (*am'-raf-el*)
Ge 14: 1 it came to pass in the days of A'
9 and A' king of Shinar, and Arioch

Amzi (*am'-zi*)
1Ch 6:46 The son of A', the son of Bani,
Ne 11:12 the son of A', the son of Zechariah,

Anab (*a'-nab*)
Jos 11:21 from A', and from all the
15:50 And A', and Eshtemoh, and Anim,

Anah (*a'-nah*)
Ge 36: 2 Aholibamah, the daughter of A'
14, 18 Aholibamah, the daughter of A',
20 and Shobal, and Zibeon, and A',
24 of Zibeon; both Ajah and A';

Ge 36:24 was that A· that found the mules
25 And the children of A· were these;
25 Aholibamah the daughter of A·.
29 duke Shobal, duke Zibeon, duke A·,
1Ch 1:38 and Zibeon, and A·, and Dishon,
40 the sons of Zibeon; Aiah, and A·.
41 The sons of A·; Dishon. And the

Anaharath (*an-a-ha'-rath*)
Jos 19:19 Haphraim, and Shihon, and A·,

Anaiah (*an-a-i'-ah*)
Ne 8: 4 and Shema, and A·, and Urijah,
10:22 Pelatiah, Hanan, A·,

Anak (*a'-nak*) See also ANAKIMS.
Nu 13:22 and Talmai, the children of A·,
28 we saw the children of A· there.
33 we saw the giants, the sons of A·,
De 9: 2 stand before the children of A·!
Jos 15:13 the city of Arba the father of A·,
14 drove thence the three sons of A·,
14 and Talmai, the children of A·.
21:11 the city of Arba the father of A·,
J'g 1:20 expelled thence the three sons of A·.

Anakims (*an'-ak-ims*)
De 1:28 seen the sons of the A· there.
2:10 and many, and tall, as the A·;
11 were accounted giants, as the A·;
21 as the A·; but the Lord destroyed
9: 2 and tall, the children of the A·,
Jos 11:21 cut off the A· from the mountains,
22 There was none of the A· left
14:12 heardest in that day how the A·
15 was a great man among the A·.

Anamim (*an'-am-im*)
Ge 10:13 A·, and Lehabim, and Naphtuhim,
1Ch 1:11 Mizraim begat Ludim, and A·,

Anammelech (*a-nam'-mel-ek*)
2Ki 17:31 and A·, the gods of Sepharvaim.

Anan (*a'-nan*)
Ne 10:26 And Ahijah, Hanan, A·,

Anani (*an-a'-ni*)
1Ch 3:24 Johanan, and Dalaiah, and A·,

Ananiah (*an-an-i'-ah*) See also ANANIAS.
Ne 3:23 son of Maaseiah, the son of A·,
11:32 And at Anathoth, Nob, A·,

Ananias (*an-an-i'-as*) See also ANANIAH.
Ac 5: 1 a certain man named A·,
3 But Peter said, A·, why hath Satan
5 A· hearing these words fell down,
9:10 disciple at Damascus, named A·;
10 said the Lord in a vision, A·.
12 a vision a man named A· coming
13 Then A· answered, Lord,
17 A· went his way, and entered into
22:12 A·, a devout man according to the
23: 2 the high priest A· commanded
24: 1 after five days A· the high priest

Anath (*a'-nath*) See also BETH-ANATH.
J'g 3:31 was Shamgar the son of A·, which
5: 6 the days of Shamgar the son of A·,

Anathema (*a-nath'-em-ah*)
1Co 16:22 let him be A· Maran-atha.

Anathoth (*an'-a-thoth*) See also ANETOTHITE.
Jos 21:18 A· with her suburbs, and Almon
1Ki 2:26 Get thee to A·, unto thine own fields;
1Ch 6:60 and A· with her suburbs. All their
7: 8 and Abiah, and A·, and Alameth.
Ezr 2:23 A·, an hundred twenty and eight.
Ne 7:27 A·, an hundred twenty and eight.
10:19 Hariph, A·, Nebai,
11:32 And at A·, Nob, Ananiah,
Isa 10:30 be heard unto Laish, O poor A·.
Jer 1: 1 in A·, in the land of Benjamin:
11:21 saith the Lord of the men of A·,
23 will bring evil upon the men of A·,
29:27 thou not reproved Jeremiah of A·,
32: 7 Buy thee my field that is in A·:
8 field, I pray thee, that is in A·,
9 my uncle's son, that was in A·,

ancestors
Le 26:45 remember the covenant of their a·,

anchor See also ANCHORS.
Heb 6:19 hope we have as an a· of the soul,

anchors
Ac 27:29 they cast four a· out of the stern,
30 have cast a· out of the foreship
40 they had taken up the a·,

ancient See also ANCIENTS.
De 33:15 chief things of the a· mountains,
J'g 5:21 that a· river, the river Kishon.
2Ki 19:25 Hast thou not heard...of a· times
1Ch 4:22 And these are a· things.
Ezr 3:12 of the fathers, who were a· men,
Job 12:12 With the a· is wisdom;
Ps 77: 5 the years of a· times.
Pr 22:28 Remove not the a· landmark,
Isa 3: 2 and the prudent, and the a·,
5 himself proudly against the a·,
9:15 a· honourable, he is the head;
19:11 son of the wise, the son of a· kings?
23: 7 whose antiquity is of a· days?
37:26 Hast thou not heard...of a· times,
44: 7 since I appointed the a· people?
45:21 hath declared this from a· time?
46:10 a· times the things that are not
47: 6 upon the a· hast thou very
51: 9 a· days, in the generations of old.
Jer 5:15 mighty nation, it is an a· nation,
18:15 in their ways from the a· paths,
Eze 9: 6 Then they began at the a· men
36: 2 the a· high places are ours in
Da 7: 9 A· of days did sit, whose garment
13 and came to the A· of days,
22 A· of days came, and judgment

ancients
1Sa 24:13 As saith the proverb of the a·,
Ps 119:100 I understand more than the a·,
Isa 3:14 enter into judgment with the a·
24:23 and before his a· gloriously.
Jer 19: 1 and take of the a· of the people,
1 and of the a· of the priests;
Eze 7:26 priest, and counsel from the a·.
8:11 seventy men of the a· of the
12 the a· of the house of Israel do
27: 9 a· of Gebal and the wise men

ancle See also ANCLES.
Ac 3: 7 feet and a· bones received strength.

ancle-bones See ANCLE and BONES.

ancles
Eze 47: 3 the waters were to the a·.

Andrew (*an'-drew*)
M't 4:18 Simon called Peter, and A· his
10: 2 called Peter, and A· his brother;
M'k 1:16 Simon and A· his brother casting
29 into the house of Simon and A·,
3:18 A·, and Philip, and Bartholomew,
13: 3 John and A· asked him privately,
Lu 6:14 named Peter,) and A· his brother,
Joh 1:40 A·, Simon Peter's brother.
44 Bethsaida, the city of A· and Peter.
6: 8 One of his disciples, A·, Simon
12:22 Philip cometh and telleth A·:
22 and again A· and Philip tell Jesus.
Ac 1:13 A·, Philip, and Thomas,

Andronicus (*an-dro-ni'-cus*)
Ro 16: 7 Salute A· and Junia, my kinsmen,

Anem (*a'-nem*) See also EN-GANNIM.
1Ch 6:73 suburbs, and A· with her suburbs:

Aner (*a'-nur*)
Ge 14:13 of Eshcol, and brother of A·:
24 the men which went with me, A·,
1Ch 6:70 A· with her suburbs, and Bileam

Anethothite (*an'-e-thoth-ite*) See also ANETOTHITE.
2Sa 23:27 Abiezer the A·, Mebunnai the

Anetothite (*an'-e-toth-ite*) See also ANETHOTHITE; ANTOTHITE.
1Ch 27:12 Abiezer the A·, of the Benjamites:

angel See also ANGEL'S; ANGELS; ARCHANGEL.
Ge 16: 7 the a· of the Lord found her by a
9 the a· of the Lord said unto her,
10 a· of the Lord said unto her, I will
11 the a· of the Lord said unto her,
21:17 the a· of God called to Hagar out
22:11 the a· of the Lord called unto him
15 a· of the Lord called unto Abraham
24: 7 he shall send his a· before thee
40 will send his a· with thee,
31:11 the a· of God spake unto me in a
48:16 The A· which redeemed me from
Ex 3: 2 a· of the Lord appeared unto him,
14:19 the a· of God, which went before
23:20 Behold, I send an A· before thee,
23 mine A· shall go before thee,
32:34 mine A· shall go before thee:
33: 2 I will send an a· before thee;
Nu 20:16 he heard our voice, and sent an a·,
22:22 the a· of the Lord stood in the way
23 the ass saw the a· of the Lord
24 the a· of the Lord stood in a path
25 And when the ass saw the a· of the
26 the a· of the Lord went further,
27 the a· of the Lord, she fell down
31 he saw the a· of the Lord standing
32 the a· of the Lord said unto him,
34 Balaam said unto the a· of the
35 a· of the Lord said unto Balaam,
J'g 2: 1 an a· of the Lord came up from
4 when the a· of the Lord spake
5:23 Meroz, said the a· of the Lord,
6:11 there came an a· of the Lord,
12 a· of the Lord appeared unto him,
20 the a· of God said unto him, Take
21 a· of the Lord put forth the end
21 Then the a· of the Lord departed
22 perceived that he was an a·
22 I have seen an a· of the Lord
13: 3 the a· of the Lord appeared unto
6 like the countenance of an a·
9 the a· of God came again unto the
13, 16 the a· of the Lord said unto
15, 17 Manoah said unto the a· of the
16 Manoah knew not that he was an a·
18 And the a· of the Lord said
19 and the a· did wondrously;
20 the a· of the Lord ascended in the
21 a· of the Lord did no more appear
21 Manoah knew that he was an a·
1Sa 29: 9 good in my sight, as an a· of God:
2Sa 14:17 a· of God, so is my lord the king
20 to the wisdom of an a· of God,
19:27 the king is as an a· of God:
24:16 when the a· stretched out his hand
16 to the a· that destroyed the people,
16 a· of the Lord was by the threshing
17 the a· that smote the people,
1Ki 13:18 and an a· spake unto me by the
19: 5 an a· touched him, and said unto
7 the a· of the Lord came again
2Ki 1: 3 the a· of the Lord said to Elijah
15 the a· of the Lord said unto Elijah,
19:35 the a· of the Lord went out,
1Ch 21:12 and the a· of the Lord destroying
15 God sent an a· unto Jerusalem
15 a· that destroyed, It is enough,
15 And the a· of the Lord stood by
16 saw the a· of the Lord stand
18 the a· of the Lord commanded
20 Ornan turned back, and saw the a·;
27 And the Lord commanded the a·;
30 the sword of the a· of the Lord.
2Ch 32:21 the Lord sent an a·, which cut off
Ps 34: 7 The a· of the Lord encampeth
35: 5 let the a· of the Lord chase them.
6 let the a· of the Lord persecute
Ec 5: 6 neither say thou before the a·,
Isa 37:36 the a· of the Lord went forth,
63: 9 the a· of his presence saved them:
Da 3:28 who hath sent his a·, and delivered
6:22 My God hath sent his a·, and hath
Ho 12: 4 he had power over the a·,
Zec 1: 9 the a· that talked with me
11 they answered the a· of the Lord
12 a· of the Lord answered and said,
13 the Lord answered the a· that
14 the a· that communed with me
19 I said unto the a· that talked
2: 3 a· that talked with me went forth,
3 and another a· went out
3: 1 the a· of the Lord, and Satan
3 stood before the a·.
5 And the a· of the Lord stood by.
6 the a· of the Lord protested unto
4: 1 a· that talked with me came again,
4 spake to the a· that talked with
5 a· that talked with me answered
5: 5 a· that talked with me went forth,
10 said I to the a· that talked with me,
6: 4 I answered and said unto the a·
5 the a· answered and said unto me,
12: 8 as the a· of the Lord before them.
M't 1:20 a· of the Lord appeared unto him
24 did as the a· of the Lord had bidden
2:13 a· of the Lord appeareth to
19 behold, an a· of the Lord appeareth
28: 2 for the a· of the Lord descended
5 the a· answered and said unto the
Lu 1:11 appeared unto him an a· of the Lord
13 the a· said unto him, Fear not,
18 Zacharias said unto the a·,
19 the a· answering said unto him,
26 the a· Gabriel was sent from God
28 And the a· came in unto her,
30 a· said unto her, Fear not, Mary:
34 Then said Mary unto the a·,
35 the a· answered and said unto her,
38 And the a· departed from her.
2: 9 the a· of the Lord came upon them,
10 the a· said unto them, Fear not:
13 a· a multitude of the heavenly
21 which was so named of the a·
22:43 there appeared an a· unto him
Joh 5: 4 a· went down at a certain season
12:29 others said, An a· spake to him.
Ac 5:19 the a· of the Lord by night opened
6:15 as it had been the face of an a·.
7:30 an a· of the Lord in a flame
35 the hand of the a· which appeared
38 with the a· which spake to him
8:26 a· of the Lord spake unto Philip,
10: 3 an a· of God coming in to him,
7 the a· which spake unto Cornelius
22 warned from God by an holy a·
11:13 how he had seen an a· in his house,
12: 7 the a· of the Lord came upon him,
8 the a· said unto him, Gird thyself,
9 which was done by the a·;
10 forthwith the a· departed
11 the Lord hath sent his a·,
15 said they, It is his a·.
23 the a· of the Lord smote him,
23: 8 resurrection, neither a·, nor spirit:
9 if a spirit or an a· hath spoken
27:23 by me this night the a· of God,
2Co 11:14 transformed into an a· of light.
Ga 1: 8 we, or an a· from heaven, preach
4:14 received me as an a· of God,
Re 1: 1 he sent and signified it by his a·
2: 1 the a· of the church of Ephesus
8 the a· of the church in Smyrna
12 to the a· of the church in Pergamos
18 the a· of the church in Thyatira
3: 1 unto the a· of the church in Sardis
7 the a· of the church in Philadelphia
14 unto the a· of the church of the
5: 2 I saw a strong a· proclaiming
7: 2 another a· ascending from the east,
8: 3 a· came and stood at the altar,
5 the a· took the censer, and filled it
7 The first a· sounded, and there
8 the second a· sounded, and as it
10 the third a· sounded, and there fell
12 the fourth a· sounded, and the
13 an a· flying through the midst
9: 1 the fifth a· sounded, and I saw
11 which is the a· of the bottomless pit,
13 and the sixth a· sounded,
14 saying to the sixth a· which had the
10: 1 And I saw another mighty a· come
5 a· which I saw stand upon the sea
7 of the voice of the seventh a·,
8 open in the hand of the a·
9 I went unto the a·, and said unto
11: 1 and the a· stood, saying, Rise,
15 and the seventh a· sounded;
14: 6 I saw another a· fly in the midst
8 and there followed another a·,
9 the third a· followed them,

Re 14:15, 17 *a·* came out of the temple
18 another *a·* came out from the altar,
19 *a·* thrust in his sickle into the earth,
16: 3 the second *a·* poured out his vial
4 the third *a·* poured out his vial
5 I heard the *a·* of the waters say,
8 the fourth *a·* poured out his vial
10 the fifth *a·* poured out his vial
12 the sixth *a·* poured out his vial
17 the seventh *a·* poured out his vial
17: 7 and the *a·* said unto me,
18: 1 I saw another *a·* come down from
21 a mighty *a·* took up a stone
19:17 I saw an *a·* standing in the sun;
20: 1 and I saw an *a·* come down
21:17 measure of a man, that is, of the *a·*.
22: 6 his *a·* to shew unto his servants
8 before the feet of the *a·*
16 have sent mine *a·* to testify unto

angel's
Re 8: 4 before God out of the *a·* hand.
10:10 the little book out of the *a·* hand,

angels See also ANGELS'.
Ge 19: 1 there came two *a·* to Sodom
15 then the *a·* hastened Lot,
28:12 the *a·* of God ascending
32: 1 way, and the *a·* of God met him.
Job 4:18 and his *a·* he charged with folly:
Ps 8: 5 him a little lower than the *a·*,
68:17 thousand, even thousands of *a·*:
78:49 by sending evil *a·* among them.
91:11 shall give his *a·* charge over thee,
103:20 Bless the Lord, ye his *a·*,
104: 4 Who maketh his *a·* spirits;
148: 2 Praise ye him, all his *a·*:
M't 4: 6 He shall give his *a·* charge
11 *a·* came and ministered unto him.
13:39 and the reapers are the *a·*.
41 Son of man shall send forth his *a·*,
49 the *a·* shall come forth, and sever
16:27 the glory of his Father with his *a·*;
18:10 That in heaven their *a·* do always
22:30 are as the *a·* of God in heaven.
24:31 And he shall send his *a·* with a grea
36 no, not the *a·* of heaven,
25:31 all the holy *a·* with him,
41 prepared for the devil and his *a·*:
26:53 more than twelve legions of *a·*?
M'r 1:13 and the *a·* ministered unto him.
8:38 glory of his Father with the holy *a·*.
12:25 are as the *a·* which are in heaven.
13:27 then shall he send his *a·*,
32 not the *a·* which are in heaven,
Lu 2:15 as the *a·* were gone away from
4:10 He shall give his *a·* charge over thee
9:26 in his Father's, and of the holy *a·*.
12: 8 confess before the *a·* of God:
9 denied before the *a·* of God.
15:10 in the presence of the *a·* of God
16:22 carried by the *a·* into Abraham's
20:36 for they are equal unto the *a·*;
24:23 had also seen a vision of *a·*,
Joh 1:51 the *a·* of God ascending and
20:12 seeth two *a·* in white sitting, the
Ac 7:53 the law by the disposition of *a·*,
Ro 8:38 nor life, nor *a·*, nor principalities,
1Co 4: 9 world, and to *a·*, and to men.
6: 3 Know ye not that we shall judge *a·*?
11:10 on her head because of the *a·*.
13: 1 the tongues of men and of *a·*,
Ga 3:19 and it was ordained by *a·* in the
Col 2:18 humility and worshipping of *a·*,
2Th 1: 7 from heaven with his mighty *a·*,
1Ti 3:16 in the Spirit, seen of *a·*, preached
5:21 Jesus Christ, and the elect *a·*,
Heb 1: 4 made so much better than the *a·*,
5 unto which of the *a·* said he at
6 let all the *a·* of God worship him.
7 of the *a·* he saith,
7 Who maketh his *a·* spirits,
13 to which of the *a·* said he at any
2: 2 if the word spoken by *a·* was
5 unto the *a·* hath he not put in
7 a little lower than the *a·*;
9 made a little lower than the *a·*
16 not on him the nature of *a·*;
12:22 an innumerable company of *a·*,
13: 2 some have entertained *a·* unawares.
1Pe 1:12 things the *a·* desire to look into.
3:22 *a·* and authorities and powers being
2Pe 2: 4 spared not the *a·* that sinned,
11 Whereas *a·*, which are greater
Jude 6 *a·* which kept not their first estate,
Re 1:20 the *a·* of the seven churches:
3: 5 my Father, and before his *a·*.
5:11 I heard the voice of many *a·* round
7: 1 I saw four *a·* standing on the four
2 with a loud voice to the four *a·*,
11 all the *a·* stood round about the
8: 2 I saw the seven *a·* which stood
6 *a·* which had the seven trumpets
13 the trumpet of the three *a·*, which
9:14 Loose the four *a·* which are bound
15 and the four *a·* were loosed,
12: 7 Michael and his *a·* fought against
7 and the dragon fought and his *a·*,
9 his *a·* were cast out with him.
14:10 in the presence of the holy *a·*,
15: 1 seven *a·* having the seven last
6 seven *a·* came out of the temple,
7 gave unto the seven *a·* seven golden
8 of the seven *a·* were fulfilled.
16: 1 saying to the seven *a·*, Go your
17: 1 one of the seven *a·* which had the
21: 9 unto me one of the seven *a·* which

Re 21:12 at the gates twelve *a·*,

angels'
Ps 78:25 Man did eat *a·* food:

anger See also ANGERED.
Ge 27:45 Until thy brother's *a·* turn away
30: 2 Jacob's *a·* was kindled against
44:18 thine *a·* burn against thy servant:
49: 6 in their *a·* they slew a man,
7 Cursed be their *a·*, for it was fierce;
Ex 4:14 the *a·* of the Lord was kindled
11: 8 out from Pharaoh in a great *a·*.
32:19 Moses' *a·* waxed hot, and he cast
22 Let not the *a·* of my lord wax hot;
Nu 11: 1 heard it; and his *a·* was kindled;
10 the *a·* of the Lord was kindled
12: 9 *a·* of the Lord was kindled against
22:22 God's *a·* was kindled because he
27 Balaam's *a·* was kindled, and he
24:10 Balak's *a·* was kindled against
25: 3 the *a·* of the Lord was kindled
4 that the fierce *a·* of the Lord may
32:10, 13 the Lord's *a·* was kindled
14 to augment yet the fierce *a·* of the
De 4:25 Lord thy God, to provoke him to *a·*:
6:15 lest the *a·* of the Lord thy God be
7: 4 will the *a·* of the Lord be kindled
9:18 the Lord, to provoke him to *a·*.
19 I was afraid of the *a·* and hot
13:17 turn from the fierceness of his *a·*,
29:20 *a·* of the Lord and his jealousy
23 which the Lord overthrew in his *a·*,
24 meaneth the heat of this great *a·*?
27 the *a·* of the Lord was kindled
28 rooted them out of their land in *a·*,
31:17 Then my *a·* shall be kindled
29 to provoke him to *a·* through the
32:16 provoked they him to *a·*.
21 they have provoked me to *a·* with
21 I will provoke them to *a·* with a
22 For a fire is kindled in mine *a·*,
Jos 7: 1 the *a·* of the Lord was kindled
26 turned from the fierceness of his *a·*.
23:16 then shall the *a·* of the Lord be
J'g 2:12 and provoked the Lord to *a·*.
14 the *a·* of the Lord was hot against
20 And the *a·* of the Lord was hot
3: 8 *a·* of the Lord was hot against Israel,
6:39 Let not thine *a·* be hot against me,
8: 3 their *a·* was abated toward him,
9:30 son of Ebed, his *a·* was kindled.
10: 7 the *a·* of the Lord was hot against
14:19 his *a·* was kindled, and he went up
1Sa 11: 6 his *a·* was kindled greatly.
17:28 Eliab's *a·* was kindled against
20:30 Saul's *a·* was kindled against
34 arose from the table in fierce *a·*,
2Sa 6: 7 the *a·* of the Lord was kindled
12: 5 David's *a·* was greatly kindled
24: 1 again the *a·* of the Lord was
1Ki 14: 9 images, to provoke me to *a·*,
15 groves, provoking the Lord to *a·*.
15:30 the Lord God of Israel to *a·*.
16: 2 provoke me to *a·* with their sins;
7 provoking him to *a·* with the work
13 the Lord God of Israel to *a·*
26 provoke the Lord God of Israel to *a·*
33 Israel to *a·* than all the kings of
21:22 thou hast provoked me to *a·*,
22:53 and provoked to *a·* the Lord God
2Ki 13: 3 the *a·* of the Lord was kindled
17:11 things to provoke the Lord to *a·*:
17 the Lord, to provoke him to *a·*.
21: 6 to provoke him to *a·*.
15 provoked me to *a·*, since the day
22:17 that they might provoke me to *a·*
23:19 made to provoke the Lord to *a·*,
26 wherewith his *a·* was kindled
24:20 through the *a·* of the Lord it came
1Ch 13:10 the *a·* of the Lord was kindled
2Ch 25:10 wherefore their *a·* was greatly
10 they returned home in great *a·*.
15 the *a·* of the Lord was kindled
28:25 and provoked to *a·* the Lord God
33: 6 to provoke him to *a·*.
34:25 that they might provoke me to *a·*
Ne 4: 5 they have provoked thee to *a·*
9:17 merciful, slow to *a·*, and of great
Es 1:12 and his *a·* burned in him.
Job 9: 5 which overturneth them in his *a·*.
13 God will not withdraw his *a·*,
18: 4 He teareth himself in his *a·*:
21:17 God distributeth sorrows in his *a·*.
35:15 is not so, he hath visited in his *a·*;
Ps 6: 1 O Lord, rebuke me not in thine *a·*,
7: 6 Arise, O Lord, in thine *a·*, lift up
21: 9 fiery oven in the time of thine *a·*:
27: 9 put not thy servant away in *a·*:
30: 5 his *a·* endureth but a moment;
37: 8 Cease from *a·*, and forsake wrath:
38: 3 in my flesh because of thine *a·*;
56: 7 in thine *a·* cast down the people,
69:24 let thy wrathful *a·* take hold of
74: 1 doth thine *a·* smoke against the
77: 9 in *a·* shut up his tender mercies?
78:21 *a·* also came up against Israel;
38 many a time turned he his *a·* away,
49 upon them the fierceness of his *a·*,
50 He made a way to his *a·*;
58 For they provoked him to *a·* with
85: 3 from the fierceness of thine *a·*.
4 cause thine *a·* toward us to cease.
5 out thine *a·* to all generations?
90: 7 we are consumed by thine *a·*,
11 Who knoweth the power of thine *a·*?
103: 8 gracious, slow to *a·*, and plenteous

Ps 106:29 Thus they provoked him to *a·*
145: 8 slow to *a·*, and of great mercy.
Pr 15: 1 grievous words stir up *a·*.
18 that is slow to *a·* appeaseth strife.
16:32 slow to *a·* is better than the mighty
19:11 discretion of a man deferreth his *a·*:
20: 2 whoso provoketh him to *a·* sinneth
21:14 A gift in secret pacifieth *a·*:
22: 8 the rod of his *a·* shall fail.
27: 4 is cruel, and *a·* is outrageous;
Ec 7: 9 *a·* resteth in the bosom of fools.
Isa 1: 4 the Holy One of Israel unto *a·*,
5:25 the *a·* of the Lord kindled against
25 all this his *a·* is not turned away,
7: 4 the fierce *a·* of Rezin with Syria,
9:12 all this his *a·* is not turned away,
17 his *a·* is not turned away, but his
21 against Judah. For all this his *a·*
10: 4 under the slain. For all this his *a·*
5 O Assyrian, the rod of mine *a·*,
25 and mine *a·* in their destruction.
12: 1 thine *a·* is turned away, and thou
13: 3 called my mighty ones for mine *a·*,
9 both with wrath and fierce *a·*,
13 in the day of his fierce *a·*,
14: 6 he that ruled the nations in *a·*,
30:27 from far burning with his *a·*,
30 with the indignation of his *a·*,
42:25 poured upon him the fury of his *a·*,
48: 9 name's sake will I defer mine *a·*,
63: 3 for I will tread them in mine *a·*,
6 tread down the people in mine *a·*,
65: 3 A people that provoketh me to *a·*
66:15 to render his *a·* with fury, and his
Jer 2:35 surely his *a·* shall turn from me.
3: 5 Will he reserve his *a·* forever?
12 not cause mine *a·* to fall upon you:
12 and I will not keep *a·* forever.
4: 8 for the fierce *a·* of the Lord is not
26 presence of the Lord by his fierce *a·*.
7:18 that they may provoke me to *a·*.
19 Do they provoke me to *a·*?
20 mine *a·* and my fury shall be poured
8:19 Why have they provoked me to *a·*
10:24 not in thine *a·*, lest thou bring me
11:17 to provoke me to *a·* in offering
12:13 because of the fierce *a·* of the Lord.
15:14 for a fire is kindled in mine *a·*,
17: 4 have kindled a fire in mine *a·*,
18:23 with them in the time of thine *a·*.
21: 5 *a·*, and in fury, and in great wrath.
23:20 The *a·* of the Lord shall not return,
25: 6 provoke me not to *a·* with the
7 that ye might provoke me to *a·*
37 because of the fierce *a·* of the Lord.
38 because of his fierce *a·*.
30:24 *a·* of the Lord shall not return,
32:29 other gods, to provoke me to *a·*.
30 provoked me to *a·* with the work
31 to me as a provocation of mine *a·*
32 provoke me to *a·*, they, their kings.
37 I have driven them in mine *a·*,
33: 5 whom I have slain in mine *a·*
36: 7 for great is the *a·* and the fury
42:18 As mine *a·* and my fury hath been
44: 3 provoke me to *a·*, in that they
6 and mine *a·* was poured forth,
49:37 evil upon them, even my fierce *a·*,
51:45 from the fierce *a·* of the Lord.
52: 3 through the *a·* of the Lord it came
La 1:12 me in the day of his fierce *a·*.
2: 1 with a cloud in his *a·*,
1 his footstool in the day of his *a·*!
3 He hath cut off in his fierce *a·*
6 of his *a·* the king and the priest.
21 slain them in the day of thine *a·*;
22 day of the Lord's *a·* none escaped
3:43 covered with *a·*, and persecuted us:
66 Persecute and destroy them in *a·*
4:11 he hath poured out his fierce *a·*,
16 *a·* of the Lord hath divided them;
Eze 5:13 shall mine *a·* be accomplished,
15 in *a·* and in fury and in furious
7: 3 I will send mine *a·* upon thee,
8 accomplish mine *a·* upon thee:
8:17 returned to provoke me to *a·*:
13:13 overflowing shower in mine *a·*,
16:26 whoredoms, to provoke me to *a·*.
20: 8 to accomplish my *a·* against them
21 to accomplish my *a·* against them
22:20 so will I gather you in mine *a·*
25:14 in Edom according to mine *a·*
35:11 I will even do according to thine *a·*,
43: 8 I have consumed them in mine *a·*.
Da 9:16 let thine *a·* and thy fury be turned
11:20 neither in *a·*, nor in battle.
Ho 8: 5 mine *a·* is kindled against them:
11: 9 execute the fierceness of mine *a·*,
12:14 provoked him to *a·* most bitterly:
13:11 I gave thee a king in mine *a·*,
14: 4 for mine *a·* is turned away from him.
Joe 2:13 slow to *a·*, and of great kindness,
Am 1:11 his *a·* did tear perpetually,
Jon 3: 9 turn away from his fierce *a·*,
4: 2 slow to *a·*, and of great kindness,
Mic 5:15 I will execute vengeance in *a·*
7:18 he retaineth not his *a·* for ever,
Na 1: 3 The Lord is slow to *a·*, and great
6 abide in the fierceness of his *a·*?
Hab 3: 8 thine *a·* against the rivers?
12 thou didst thresh the heathen in *a·*.
Zep 2: 2 before the fierce *a·* of the Lord
2 before the day of the Lord's *a·* come
3 hid in the day of the Lord's *a·*.
3: 8 even all my fierce *a·*:
Zec 10: 3 Mine *a·* was kindled against the

M'r 3: 5 on them with a', being grieved
Ro 10:19 by a foolish nation I will a' you.
Eph 4:31 and wrath, and a', and clamour,
Col 3: 8 put off all these; a', wrath, malice.
21 provoke not your children to a'

angered
Ps 106:32 a' him also at the waters of strife,

angle
Isa 19: 8 they that cast a' into the brooks
Hab 1:15 take up all of them with the a',

angry
Ge 18:30, 32 Oh let not the Lord be a', and
45: 5 grieved, nor a' with yourselves,
Le 10:16 was a' with Eleazar and Ithamar,
De 1:37 was a' with me for your sakes,
4:21 was a' with me for your sakes,
9: 8 so that the Lord was a' with you
20 the Lord was very a' with Aaron
J'g 18:25 lest a' fellows run upon thee,
2Sa 19:42 then be ye a' for this matter?
1Ki 8:46 and thou be a' with them, and
11: 9 And the Lord was a' with Solomon,
2Ki 17:18 the Lord was very a' with Israel,
2Ch 6:36 be a' with them, and deliver them
Ezr 9:14 wouldest not thou be a' with us
Ne 5: 6 very a' when I heard their cry
Ps 2:12 Kiss the Son, lest he be a', and
7:11 God is a' with the wicked every
76: 7 in thy sight when once thou art a'?
79: 5 wilt thou be a' for ever? shall thy
80: 4 how long wilt thou be a' against
85: 5 Wilt thou be a' with us for ever?
Pr 14:17 that is soon a' dealeth foolishly:
21:19 a contentious and an a' woman.
22:24 no friendship with an a' man;
25:23 so doth an a' countenance a
29:22 An a' man stirreth up strife,
Ec 5: 6 should God be a' at thy voice,
7: 9 Be not hasty in thy spirit to be a':
Ca 1: 6 my mother's children were a'
Isa 12: 1 though thou wast a' with me,
Eze 16:42 be quiet and will be no more a'.
Da 2:12 the king was a' and very furious,
Jon 4: 1 and he was very a'.
4 Lord, Doest thou well to be a'?
9 thou well to be a' for the gourd?
9 I do well to be a', even unto death.
M't 5:22 whosoever is a' with his brother
Lu 14:21 the master of the house being a'
15:28 he was a', and would not go in:
Joh 7:23 are ye a' at me, because I have
Eph 4:26 Be ye a', and sin not: let not the
Tit 1: 7 not soon a', not given to wine,
Re 11:18 nations were a', and thy wrath

anguish
Ge 42:21 we saw the a' of his soul, when
Ex 6: 9 hearkened not...for a' of spirit,
De 2:25 and be in a' because of thee.
2Sa 1: 9 a' is come upon me, because my
Job 7:11 I will speak in the a' of my spirit;
15:24 and a' shall make him afraid;
Ps 119:143 Trouble and a' have taken hold
Pr 1:27 distress and a' cometh upon you.
Isa 8:22 and darkness, dimness of a';
30: 6 the land of trouble and a',
Jer 4:31 the a' as of her that bringeth
6:24 a' hath taken hold of us,
49:24 a' and sorrows have taken her,
50:43 a' took hold of him, and pangs as
Joh 16:21 she remembereth no more the a',
Ro 2: 9 and a', upon every soul of man
2Co 2: 4 of much affliction and a' of heart

an-hungered See HUNGRED.

Aniam (*a'-ne-am*)
1Ch 7:19 Shechem, and Likhi, and A'.

Anim (*a'-nim*)
Jos 15:50 And Anab, and Eshtemoh, and A',

anise
M't 23:23 tithe of mint, and a' and cummin,

ankle See ANCLE.

Anna (*an'-nah*)
Lu 2:36 there was one A', a prophetess,

Annas (*an'-nas*)
Lu 3: 2 A' and Caiaphas being the high
Joh 18:13 led him away to A' first;
24 A' had sent him bound unto
Ac 4: 6 A' the high priest, and Caiaphas,

annul See DISANNUL.

anoint See also ANOINTED; ANOINTEST; ANOINTING.
Ex 28:41 a' them, and consecrate them,
29: 7 pour it upon his head, and a' him.
36 and thou shalt a' it, to sanctify it.
30:26 And thou shalt a' the tabernacle
30 thou shalt a' Aaron and his sons,
40: 9 a' the tabernacle, and all that is
10 a' the altar of the burnt offering,
11 thou shalt a' the laver and his foot,
13 the holy garments, and a' him,
15 And thou shalt a' them,
15 as thou didst a' their father,
Le 16:32 And the priest, whom he shall a',
De 28:40 shalt not a' thyself with the oil;
J'g 9: 8 trees went forth on a time to a'
15 If in truth ye a' me king over you,
Ru 3: 3 Wash thyself therefore, and a'
1Sa 9:16 a' him to be captain over my
15: 1 The Lord sent me to a' thee
16: 3 shalt a' unto me him whom I name
12 the Lord said, Arise, a' him:
2Sa 14: 2 a' not thyself with oil,
1Ki 1:34 and Nathan the prophet a' him
19:15 a' Hazael to be king over Syria:
16 the son of Nimshi shalt thou a'
16 Elisha...shalt thou a' to be prophet
Isa 21: 5 arise, ye princes, and a' the shield.
Da 9:24 and to a' the most Holy.
10: 3 neither did I a' myself at all,
Am 6: 6 a' themselves with the chief
Mic 6:15 thou shalt not a' thee with oil;
M't 6:17 a' thine head, and wash thy face;
M'r 14: 8 to a' my body to the burying.
16: 1 they might come and a' him.
Lu 7:46 My head with oil thou didst not a':
Re 3:18 a' thine eyes with eyesalve, that

anointed See also ANOINTEDST.
Ex 29: 2 wafers unleavened a' with oil:
29 a' therein, and to be consecrated
Le 2: 4 unleavened wafers a' with oil.
4: 3 If the priest that is a' do sin
5 And the priest that is a' shall
16 is a' shall bring of the bullock's
6:20 the Lord in the day when he is a';
22 the priest of his sons that is a' in
7:12 a' with oil, and cakes mingled
36 in the day that he a' them,
8:10 a' the tabernacle and all that was
11 a' the altar and all his vessels,
12 and a' him, to sanctify him.
Nu 3: 3 of Aaron, the priests which were a',
6:15 wafers of unleavened bread a'
7: 1 set up the tabernacle, and had a' it,
1 vessels thereof, and had a' them,
10 the altar in the day that it was a',
84 it was a', by the princes of Israel;
88 of the altar after that it was a'.
35:25 which was a' with the holy oil.
1Sa 2:10 and exalt the horn of his a'.
35 shall walk before mine a' for ever.
10: 1 Lord hath a' thee to be captain
12: 3 before the Lord, and before his a':
5 his a' is witness this day,
15:17 the Lord a' thee king over Israel?
16: 6 Surely the Lord's a' is before him.
13 a' him in the midst of his brethren.
24: 6 unto my master, the Lord's a',
6 he is the a' of the Lord.
10 he is the Lord's a'.
26: 9 his hand against the Lord's a',
11 mine hand against the Lord's a':
16 kept your master, the Lord's a'.
23 against the Lord's a'.
2Sa 1:14 to destroy the Lord's a'?
16 I have slain the Lord's a'.
21 as though he had not been a' with
2: 4 and there they a' David king
7 house of Judah have a' me king
3:39 this day weak, though a' king;
5: 3 they a' David king over Israel.
17 heard that they had a' David king
12: 7 I a' thee king over Israel,
20 earth and washed, and a' himself,
19:10 Absalom, whom we a' over us,
21 because he cursed the Lord's a'?
22:51 sheweth mercy to his a',
23: 1 the a' of the God of Jacob,
1Ki 1:39 the tabernacle, and a' Solomon.
45 and Nathan...have a' him king
5: 1 a' him king in the room of his
2Ki 9: 3 I have a' thee king over Israel.
6 have a' thee king over the people
12 Thus saith the Lord, I have a' thee
11:12 they made him king, and a' him;
23:30 and a' him, and made him king
1Ch 11: 3 they a' David king over Israel,
14: 8 David was a' king over all Israel,
16:22 Touch not mine a', and do my
29:22 and a' him unto the Lord
2Ch 6:42 turn not away the face of thine a':
22: 7 a' to cut off the house of Ahab.
23:11 Jehoiada and his sons a' him,
28:15 to eat and to drink, and a' them,
Ps 2: 2 the Lord, and against his a',
18:50 sheweth mercy to his a',
20: 6 the Lord saveth his a';
28: 8 he is the saving strength of his a'.
45: 7 thy God, hath a' thee with the oil
84: 9 look upon the face of thine a'.
89:20 with my holy oil have I a' him:
38 hast been wroth with thine a'.
51 reproached the footsteps of thine a
92:10 I shall be a' with fresh oil.
105:15 Touch not mine a',
132:10 turn not away the face of thine a'.
17 I have ordained a lamp for mine a'.
Isa 45: 1 Thus saith the Lord to his a',
61: 1 the Lord hath a' me to preach
La 4:20 a' of the Lord, was taken in their
Eze 16: 9 and I a' thee with oil.
28:14 art the a' cherub that covereth;
Hab 3:13 for salvation with thine a';
Zec 4:14 the two a' ones, that stand †1121,
M'r 6:13 a' with oil many that were sick,
Lu 4:18 hath a' me to preach the gospel
7:38 a' them with the ointment.
46 hath a' my feet with ointment.
Joh 9: 6 a' the eyes of the blind man
11 made clay and a' mine eyes,
11: 2 was that Mary which a' the Lord
12: 3 a' the feet of Jesus, and wiped
Ac 4:27 child Jesus, whom thou hast a',
10:38 How God a' Jesus of Nazareth
2Co 1:21 and hath a' us is God.
Heb 1: 9 a' thee with the oil of gladness

anointedst
Ge 31:13 Bethel, where thou a' the pillar,

anointest
Ps 23: 5 thou a' my head with oil; my

anointing
Ex 25: 6 spices for a' oil, and for sweet
29: 7 Then shalt thou take the a' oil,
21 and of the a' oil, and sprinkle it
30:25 it shall be an holy a' oil.
31 This shall be an holy a' oil unto
31:11 And the a' oil, and sweet incense
35: 8 the light, and spices for the a' oil,
15 and his staves, and the a' oil,
28 and for the a' oil,
37:29 he made the holy a' oil,
39:38 the golden altar and the a' oil,
40: 9 thou shalt take the a' oil,
15 a' shall surely be an everlasting
Le 7:35 is the portion of the a' of Aaron,
35 and of the a' of his sons,
8: 2 and the a' oil, and a bullock for
10 Moses took the a' oil, and anointed
12 he poured of the a' oil upon
30 Moses took the a' oil,
10: 7 the a' oil of the Lord is upon you.
21:10 whose head the a' oil was poured,
12 the crown of the a' oil is of his
Nu 4:16 daily meat offering, and the a' oil,
18: 8 given them by reason of the a',
Isa 10:27 be destroyed because of the a'.
Jas 5:14 a' him with oil in the name of the
1Jo 2:27 But the a' which ye have received
27 same a' teacheth you of all things,

anon
M't 13:20 and a' with joy receiveth it;
M'r 1:30 a' they tell him of her.

Anoth See BETH-ANOTH.

another^ See also ANOTHER'S.
Ge 4:25 appointed me a' seed instead of
11: 3 said one to a', Go to, let us make
15:10 laid each piece one against a':
26:21 And they digged a' well, and
22 from thence, and digged a' well;
29:19 I should give her to a' man:
30:24 Lord shall add to me a' son.
31:49 when we are absent one from a'.
37: 9 he dreamed yet a' dream,
19 they said one to a', Behold, this
42: 1 Why do ye look one upon a'?
21 they said one to a', We are verily
28 they were afraid, saying one to a',
43: 7 yet alive? have ye a' brother? and
33 the men marvelled one at a'.
Ex 10:23 They saw not one a', neither rose
16:15 they said one to a', it is manna:
18:16 I judge between one and a',
21:10 If he take him a' wife, her food,
18 strive together, and one smite a'
22: 5 shall feed in a' man's field;
9 which a' challengeth to be his,
25:20 their faces shall look one to a';
26: 3 coupled together one to a';
3 curtains shall be coupled one to a';
4 uttermost edge of a' curtain;
5 loops may take hold one of a'.
17 set in order one against a':
19, 21, 25 and two sockets under a'
36:10 curtains one unto a': and the
10 curtains he coupled one unto a'.
11 the uttermost side of a' curtain,
12 the loops held one curtain to a'.
13 one unto a' with the taches:
22 equally distant one from a':
24, 26 and two sockets under a' board
37: 8 and a' cherub on the other end
9 with their faces one to a';
19 made like almonds in a' branch,
Le 7:10 Aaron have, one as much as a'.
19:11 deal falsely, neither lie one to a'.
20:10 adultery with a' man's wife,
25:14 ye shall not oppress one a':
17 not therefore oppress one a';
46 ye shall not rule one over a' with
26:37 they shall fall one upon a',
27:20 if he have sold the field to a' man,
Nu 5:19 with a' instead of thy husband,
20 to a' instead of thy husband,
29 when a wife goeth aside to a'
8: 8 a' young bullock shalt thou take
14: 4 they said one to a', Let us make
24 because he had a' spirit with him,
23:13 with me unto a' place,
27 I will bring thee unto a' place;
Nu 36: 9 remove from one tribe to a' tribe;
De 4:34 midst of a' nation, by temptations,
20: 5 the battle, and a' man dedicate it.
6 in the battle, and a' man eat of it.
7 in the battle, and a' man take her.
21:15 one beloved, and a' hated,
24: 2 she may go and be a' man's wife.
25:11 men strive together one with a',
28:30 a' man shall lie with her:
32 shall be given unto a' people,
29:28 cast them into a' land, as it is this
J'g 2:10 there arose a' generation after
6:29 said one to a', Who hath done this
9:37 a' company come along by the
10:18 princes of Gilead said one to a',
16: 7, 11 I be weak, and be as a' man.
Ru 2: 8 Go not to glean in a' field,
3:14 rose up before one could know a'.
1Sa 2:25 If one man sin against a',
10: 3 a' carrying three loaves of bread,
3 and a' carrying a bottle of wine:
6 shalt be turned into a' man.
9 God gave him a' heart:

1Sa 10:11 the people said one to a',
13:18 And a' company turned the way
18 and a' company turned to the way
14:16 went on beating down one a'.
17:30 he turned from him toward a',
18: 7 And the women answered one a'
20:41 and they kissed one a',
41 and wept one with a',
21:11 did they not sing one to a' of him
29: 5 sang one to a' in dances, saying,
2Sa 11:25 devoureth one as well as a':
18:20 thou shalt bear tidings a' day:
26 the watchman saw a' man running
26 Behold a' man running alone.
1Ki 6:27 and their wings touched one a'
7: 8 had a' court within the porch,
11:23 God stirred him up a' adversary,
13:10 So he went a' way, and returned
14: 5 shall feign herself to be a' woman.
6 why feignest thou thyself to be a'?
18: 6 Obadiah went a' way by himself.
20:37 Then he found a' man, and said,
21: 6 I will give thee a' vineyard for it:
22:20 one said on this manner, and a'
2Ki 1:11 he sent unto him a' captain of fifty
3:23 they have smitten one a':
7: 3 said one to a', why sit we here
6 they said one to a', Lo, the king
8 entered into a' tent, and carried
9 Then they said one to a', We do
10:21 Baal was full from one end to a'.
14: 8 let us look one a' in the face.
11 looked one a' in the face at
21:16 filled Jerusalem . . . one end to a';
1Ch 2:26 Jerahmeel had also a' wife,
16:20 from one kingdom to a' people;
17: 5 and from one tabernacle to a'.
24: 5 divided by lot, one sort with a';
26:12 having wards one against a',
2Ch 18:19 and a' saying after that manner.
20:23 every one helped to destroy a'.
25:17 Come, let us see one a' in the face.
21 and they saw one a' in the face,
32: 5 a' wall without, and repaired
Ezr 4:21 a' commandment shall be given
9:11 end to a' with their uncleanness.
Ne 3:19 a' piece over against the going
21 the son of Koz a' piece,
24 the son of Henadad a' piece,
27 the Tekoites repaired a' piece,
30 the sixth son of Zalaph, a' piece.
4:19 upon the wall, one far from a'.
9: 3 and a' fourth part they confessed,
Es 1: 7 vessels . . . diverse one from a',)
19 give her royal estate unto a'
4:14 arise to the Jews from a' place;
9:19 and of sending portions one to a'.
22 one to a', and gifts to the poor.
Job 1:16 came also a', and said, The fire
17 also a', and said, The Chaldeans
18 yet speaking, there came also a',
13: 9 as one man mocketh a', do ye
19:27 eyes shall behold, and not a';
21:25 And a' dieth in the bitterness of
31: 8 let me sow, and let a' eat;
10 let my wife grind unto a',
41:16 One is so near to a', that no air
17 They are joined one to a', they
Ps 16: 4 that hasten after a' god:
75: 7 down one, and setteth up a'.
105:13 they went from one nation to a',
13 from one kingdom to a' people;
109: 8 let a' take his office.
145: 4 shall praise thy works to a', and
Pr 25: 9 discover not a secret to a':
27: 2 Let a' man praise thee, and not
Ec 1: 4 away, and a' generation cometh:
4:10 for he hath not a' to help him up.
8: 9 wherein one man ruleth over a'
Ca 5: 9 beloved more than a' beloved, O
9 a' beloved, that thou dost so
Isa 3: 5 every one by a', and every one by
6: 3 And one cried unto a', and said,
13: 8 they shall be amazed one at a';
28:11 with stammering lips and a' tongue
42: 8 my glory will I not give to a',
44: 5 and a' shall call himself by
5 and a' shall subscribe with his
48:11 I will not give my glory unto a'.
57: 8 thou hast discovered thyself to a'
65:15 call his servants by a' name:
22 not build, and a' inhabit;
22 they shall not plant, and a' eat:
66:23 that from one new moon to a',
23 and from one sabbath to a', shall
Jer 3: 1 become a' man's, shall he return
13:14 I will dash them one against a',
18: 4 so he made it again a' vessel,
14 come from a' place be forsaken?
22:26 into a' country, where ye were not
25:26 far and near, one with a',
36:28 Take thee again a' roll, and write
32 Then took Jeremiah a' roll,
46:16 many to fall, yea, one fell upon a':
51:31 One post shall run to meet a',
31 and one messenger to meet a',
46 one year, and after that in a' year
Eze 1: 9 Their wings were joined one to a';
11 of every one were joined one to a',
3:13 creatures that touched one a',
4: 8 not turn thee from one side to a',
17 astonied one with a', and consume
10: 9 by one cherub, and a' wheel by
9 a' cherub: and the appearance
12: 3 remove from thy place to a' place
15: 7 and a' fire shall devour them;
Eze 17: 7 There was also a' great eagle
19: 5 she took a' of her whelps
22:11 a' hath lewdly defiled his daughter
11 a' in thee hath humbled his sister,
24:23 mourn one toward a'.
33:30 and speak one to a', every one to
37:16 then take a' stick, and write upon
17 join them one to a' into one stick:
40:13 little chamber to the roof of a':
26, 49 one on this side, and a' on that
41: 6 one over a', and thirty in order;
11 the north, and a' door toward the
47:14 shall inherit it, one as well as a':
Da 2:39 arise a' kingdom inferior to thee,
39 and a' third kingdom of brass,
43 they shall not cleave one to a',
5: 6 his knees smote one against a'.
17 to thyself, give thy rewards to a';
7: 3 diverse one from a'.
5 And behold a' beast, a second, like
6 I beheld, and lo a', like a leopard,
8 came up among them a' little horn,
24 and a' shall rise after them;
8:13 a' saint said unto that certain
Ho 3: 3 thou shalt not be for a' man:
4: 4 let no man strive, nor reprove a':
Joe 1: 3 their children a' generation.
2: 8 Neither shall one thrust a';
Am 4: 7 caused it not to rain upon a' city:
Na 2: 4 against a' in the broad ways:
Zec 2: 3 a' angel went out to meet him,
8:21 inhabitants of one city shall go to a',
11: 9 rest eat every one the flesh of a'.
Mal 3:16 they . . . . spake often one to a':
M't 2:12 into their own country a' way.
8: 9 and to a', Come, and he cometh;
21 And a' of his disciples said unto
10:23 you in this city, flee ye into a':
11: 3 should come, or do we look for a'?
13:24, 31 A' parable put he forth unto
33 A' parable spake he unto them;
19: 9 for fornication, and shall marry a',
21:33 Hear a' parable: There was a
35 and killed a', and stoned a'.
22: 5 his farm, a' to his merchandise:
24: 2 left here one stone upon a', that
10 shall betray one a',
10 and shall hate one a'.
25:15 to a' two, and to a' one; to every
32 he shall separate them one from a',
26:71 into the porch, a' maid saw him,
27:38 right hand, and a' on the left.
M'r 4:41 exceedingly, and said one to a',
9:10 questioning one with a' what the
50 and have peace one with a'.
10:11 put away his wife, and marry a',
12 her husband, and be married to a',
12: 4 he sent unto them a' servant;
5 he sent a'; and him they killed,
13: 2 not be left one stone upon a',
14:19 one, Is it I? and a' said, Is it I?
58 will build a' made without hands.
16:12 appeared in a' form unto two of
Lu 2:15 the shepherds said one to a',
6: 6 came to pass also on a' sabbath,
11 with a' what they might do to Jesus.
7: 8 and to a', Come, and he cometh;
19, 20 should come? or look we for a'?
32 marketplace, and calling one to a',
8:25 wondered, saying one to a', What
9:56 And they went to a' village.
59 And he said unto a', Follow me.
61 a' also said, Lord, I will follow
12: 1 that they trode one upon a',
14:19 a' said, I have bought five yoke of
20 a' said, I have married a wife,
31 to make war against a' king,
16: 7 said he to a', And how much owest
12 faithful in that which is a' man's,
18 marrieth a', committeth adultery:
19:20 a' came, saying, Lord, behold,
44 in thee one stone upon a';
20:11 he sent a' servant: and they beat
21: 6 not be left one stone upon a',
22:58 a' saw him, and said, Thou art also
59 a' confidently affirmed, saying,
24:17 these that ye have one to a', as ye
32 they said one to a', Did not our
Joh 4:33 said the disciples one to a',
37 true, One soweth, and a' reapeth.
5: 7 while I am coming, a' steppeth
32 There is a' that beareth witness
43 a' shall come in his own name,
44 which receive honor one of a',
13:22 disciples looked one on a', doubting
34 give unto you, That ye love one a';
34 loved you, that ye also love one a'.
35 if ye have love one to a'.
14:16 he shall give you a' Comforter,
15:12 love one a', as I have loved you.
17 command you, that love one a'.
18:15 Peter followed Jesus, and so did a'
19:37 a' scripture saith, They shall
21:18 and a' shall gird thee, and carry
Ac 1:20 His bishoprick let a' take.
2: 7 marvelled, saying one to a',
12 were in doubt, saying one to a',
7:18 a' king arose, which knew not
26 why do ye wrong one to a'?
10:28 or come unto one of a' nation;
12:17 departed and went into a' place.
13:35 Wherefore he saith also in a' psalm,
17: 7 that there is a' king, one Jesus.
19:32 cried one thing, and some a':
38 deputies: let them implead one a'.
21: 6 we had taken our leave one of a',
Ac 21:34 some cried one thing, some a',
Ro 1:27 burned in their lust one toward a';
2: 1 wherein thou judgest a', thou
15 accusing or else excusing one a';)
21 Thou therefore which teachest a',
7: 3 she be married to a' man,
3 though she be married to a' man.
4 that ye should be married to a',
23 But I see a' law in my members,
9:21 one vessel unto honour, and a'
12: 5 every one members one of a'.
10 one to a' with brotherly love;
10 in honour preferring one a';
16 Be of the same mind one toward a'.
13: 8 but to love one a': for he that
8 loveth a' hath fulfilled the law.
14: 2 a', who is weak, eateth herbs.
4 that judgest a' man's servant?
5 esteemeth one day above a':
5 a' esteemeth every day alike.
13 therefore judge one a' any more:
19 things wherewith one may edify a'.
15: 5 to be likeminded one toward a'
7 Wherefore receive ye one a',
14 able also to admonish one a'.
20 build upon a' man's foundation:
16:16 Salute one a' with an holy kiss.
1Co 3: 4 and a', I am of Apollos; are ye not
10 the foundation, and a' buildeth
4: 6 be puffed up for one against a'.
7 maketh thee to differ from a'?
6: 1 you, having a matter against a',
7 because ye go to law one with a'.
7: 7 one after this manner, and a'
10:29 judged of a' man's conscience?
11:21 one is hungry, and a' is drunken.
33 together to eat, tarry one for a'.
12: 8 to a' the word of knowledge by
9 To a' faith by the same Spirit;
9 to a' the gifts of healing by the
10 to a' the working of miracles;
10 to a' prophecy;
10 to a' discerning of spirits;
10 to a' divers kinds of tongues;
10 to a' the interpretation of tongues:
25 have the same care one for a'.
14:30 If anything be revealed to a' that
15:39 a' flesh of beasts,
39 a' of fishes, and a' of birds.
40 glory of the terrestrial is a'.
41 sun, and a' glory of the moon,
41 moon, and a' glory of the stars:
41 star differeth from a' star in glory.
16:20 Greet ye one a' with an holy kiss.
2Co 10:16 not to boast in a' man's line of
11: 4 a' Jesus, whom we have not
4 or if ye receive a' spirit,
4 or a' gospel, which ye have not
13:12 Greet one a' with a holy kiss.
Ga 1: 6 grace of Christ unto a' gospel:
7 Which is not a'; but there be
5:13 the flesh, but by love serve one a'.
15 if ye bite and devour one a', take
15 that ye be not consumed one of a'.
26 provoking one a', envying one a'.
6: 4 in himself alone, and not in a'.
Eph 4: 2 forbearing one a' in love;
25 for we are members one of a'.
32 be kind one to a', tenderhearted,
32 tenderhearted, forgiving one a',
5:21 Submitting yourselves one to a' in
Col 3: 9 Lie not one to a', seeing that ye
13 Forbearing one a',
13 and forgiving one a',
16 admonishing one a' in psalms
1Th 3:12 abound in love one toward a',
4: 9 are taught of God to love one a'.
18 comfort one a' with these words.
5:11 edify one a', even as also ye do.
1Ti 5:21 without preferring one before a',
Tit 3: 3 envy, hateful, and hating one a'.
Heb 3:13 exhort one a' daily, while it is
4: 8 afterward have spoken of a' day.
5: 6 As he saith also in a' place,
7:11 that a' priest should rise
13 pertaineth to a' tribe,
15 there ariseth a' priest,
10:24 let us consider one a' to provoke
25 but exhorting one a': and so
Jas 2:25 and had sent them out a' way?
4:11 Speak not evil one of a', brethren.
12 who art thou that judgest a'?
5: 9 Grudge not one against a',
16 Confess your faults one to a',
16 and pray one for a', that ye may be
1Pe 1:22 love one a' with a pure heart
3: 8 having compassion one of a',
4: 9 Use hospitality one to a' without
10 minister the same one to a',
5: 5 Yea, all of you be subject one to a',
14 Greet ye one a' with a kiss of
1Jo 1: 7 we have fellowship one with a',
3:11 that we should love one a'.
23 love one a', as he gave us
4: 7 Beloved, let us love one a':
11 us, we ought also to love one a'.
12 If we love one a', God dwelleth in
2Jo 5 beginning, that we love one a'.
Re 6: 4 there went out a' horse that was
4 they should kill one a':
7: 2 And I saw a' angel ascending
8: 3 And a' angel came and stood
10: 1 I saw a' mighty angel come
11:10 and shall send gifts one to a';
12: 3 And there appeared a' wonder in
13:11 And I beheld a' beast coming

Re 14: 6 And I saw a' angel fly in the
8 And there followed a' angel,
15, 17 a' angel came out of the temple
18 a' angel came out from the altar,
15: 1 And I saw a' sign in heaven, great
16: 7 And I heard a' out of the altar
18: 1 a' angel come down from heaven.
4 And I heard a' voice from heaven,
20:12 and a' book was opened, which

another's
Ge 11: 7 not understand one a' speech.
Ex 21:35 if one man's ox hurt a', that he die;
Joh 13:14 ye also ought to wash one a' feet.
1Co 10:24 but every man a' wealth.
Ga 6: 2 Bear ye one a' burdens, and so

answer See also ANSWERED; ANSWEREST; ANSWERETH; ANSWERING; ANSWERS.
Ge 30:33 shall my righteousness a' for me
41:16 God shall give Pharaoh an a' of
45: 3 his brethren could not a' him;
De 20:11 if it make thee a' of peace,
21: 7 And they shall a' and say,
25: 9 shall a' and say, So shall it be done
27:15 the people shall a' and say, Amen.
Jos 4: 7 Then ye shall a' them, That the
J'g 5:29 yea, she returned a' to herself,
1Sa 2:16 then he would a' him, Nay;
20:10 if thy father a' thee roughly?
2Sa 3:11 he could not a' Abner a word
24:13 see what a' I shall return to him
1Ki 9: 9 And they shall a', Because they
12: 6 do ye advise, that I may a'
7 and wilt serve them, and a' them,
9 that we may a' this people,
18:29 neither voice, nor any to a',
2Ki 4:29 if any salute thee, a' him not
18:36 commandment was, saying, A'
2Ch 10: 6 to return a' to this people?
9 we may return a' to this people,
10 Thus shalt thou a' the people
Ezr 4:17 sent the king an a' unto Rehum
5: 5 then they returned a' by letter
11 And thus they returned us a',
Ne 5: 8 peace, and found nothing to a'.
Es 4:13 commanded to a' Esther,
15 bade them return Mordecai this a'.
Job 5: 1 if there be any that will a' thee;
9: 3 cannot a' him one of a thousand.
14 How much less shall I a' him,
15 would I not a', but I would make
32 I should a' him, and we should
13:22 Then call thou, and I will a':
22 let me speak, and a' thou me.
14:15 Thou shalt call, and I will a' thee:
19:16 servant, and he gave me no a';
20: 2 do my thoughts cause me to a',
3 understanding causeth me to a'.
23: 5 the words which he would a' me,
31:14 when he visiteth, what shall I a'
35 that the Almighty would a' me,
32: 1 these three men ceased to a' Job,
3 they had found no a', and yet had
5 saw that there was no a'
14 will I a' him with your speeches.
17 I said, I will a' also my part,
20 I will open my lips and a'.
33: 5 If thou canst a' me, set thy
12 I will a' thee, that God is greater
32 If thou hast any thing to say, a'
35: 4 I will a' thee and thy
12 there they cry, but none giveth a',
38: 3 demand of thee, and a' thou me.
40: 2 he that reproveth God, let him a'
4 vile; what shall I a' thee?
5 have I spoken; but I will not a':
Ps 27: 7 mercy also upon me, and a' me.
65: 5 wilt thou a' us, O God
86: 7 call upon thee: for thou wilt a' me.
91:15 call upon me, and I will a' him:
102: 2 the day when I call a' me speedily.
108: 6 with thy right hand, and a' me.
119:42 to a' him that reproacheth me:
143: 1 in thy faithfulness a' me, and in
Pr 1:28 call upon me, but I will not a';
15: 1 A soft a' turneth away wrath:
23 hath joy by the a' of his mouth:
28 of the righteous studieth to a':
16: 1 a' of the tongue, is from the Lord
22:21 mightest a' the words of truth
24:26 his lips that giveth a right a'.
26: 4 A' not a fool according to his
5 A' a fool according to his folly,
27:11 a' him that reproacheth me.
29:19 he understand he will not a'.
Ca 5: 6 called him, but he gave me no a'
Isa 14:32 shall one then a' the messengers
30:19 he shall hear it, he will a' thee.
36:21 was, saying, A' him not.
41:28 I asked of them, could a'
46: 7 yet can he not a', nor save him
50: 2 I called, was there none to a'?
58: 9 thou call, and the Lord shall a';
65:12 when I called, ye did not answer;
24 before they call, I will a';
66: 4 when I called, none did a';
Jer 5:19 then shalt thou a' them, Like as
7:27 they will not a' thee.
22: 9 Then they shall a', Because they
33: 3 Call unto me, and I will a' thee,
42: 4 the Lord shall a' you,
44:20 which had given him that a',
Eze 14: 4 I the Lord will a' him that cometh
7 I the Lord will a' him by myself:
21: 7 thou shalt a', For the tidings;
Da 3:16 careful to a' thee in this matter,

Joe 2:19 Yea, the Lord will a' and say
Mic 3: 7 for there is no a' of God.
Hab 2: 1 what I shall a' when I am
11 beam out of the timber shall a'
Zec 13: 6 Then he shall a', Those with
M't 22:46 no man was able to a' him a word,
25:37 Then shall the righteous a' him,
40 King shall a' and say unto them,
44 Then shall they also a' him,
45 Then shall he a' them,
M'r 11:29 ask of you one question, and a' me,
30 from heaven, or of men? a' me.
14:40 wist they what to a' him.
Lu 11: 7 shall a' and say, Trouble me not:
12:11 how or what thing ye shall a',
13:25 he shall a' and say unto you,
14: 6 could not a' him again to these
20: 3 ask you one thing; and a' me:
26 they marvelled at his a', and held
21:14 meditate before what ye shall a':
22:68 ye will not a' me, nor let me go.
Joh 1:22 give an a' to them that sent us.
19: 9 Jesus gave him no a'.
Ac 24:10 more cheerfully a' for myself:
25:16 have licence to a' for himself
26: 2 a' for myself this day before thee
Ro 11: 4 what saith the a' of God unto him?
1Co 9: 3 a' to them that do examine me
2Co 5:12 somewhat to a' them which glory
Col 4: 6 how ye ought to a' every man.
2Ti 4:16 first a' no man stood with me,
1Pe 3:15 a' to every man that asketh you
21 a' of a good conscience toward

answerable
Ex 38:18 a' to the hangings of the court.

answered See also ANSWEREDST.
Ge 18:27 And Abraham a' and said,
23: 5 the children of Heth a' Abraham,
10 and Ephron the Hittite a' Abraham
14 and Ephron a' Abraham, saying
24:50 Laban and Bethuel a' and said,
27:37 And Isaac a' and said unto Esau,
39 And Isaac his father a' and said
31:14 And Rachel and Leah a' and said
31, 36 Jacob a' and said to Laban,
43 And Laban a' and said unto Jacob,
34:13 And the sons of Jacob a' Shechem
35: 3 unto God, who a' me in the day of
40:18 And Joseph a' and said, This is
41:16 And Joseph a' Pharaoh, saying,
42:22 And Reuben a' them, saying,
43:28 they a', Thy servant our father is
Ex 4: 1 Moses a' and said, But, behold,
15:21 And Miriam a' them,
19: 8 And all the people a' together,
19 and God a' him by a voice.
24: 3 and all the people a' with one voice,
Nu 11:28 And Joshua the son of Nun,...a'
22:18 And Balaam a' and said unto the
23:12 and he a' and said,
26 But Balaam a' and said unto Balak,
32:31 And the children of Gad...a',
De 1:14 And ye a' me, and said,
41 Then ye a' and said unto me,
Jos 1:16 And they a' Joshua, saying,
2:14 men a' her, Our life for yours,
7:20 And Achan a' Joshua,
9:24 And they a' Joshua,
15:19 Who a', Give me a blessing;
17:15 Joshua a' them, If thou be a great
22:21 the half tribe of Manasseh a',
24:16 the people a' and said, God forbid
J'g 5:29 Her wise ladies a' her,
7:14 And his fellow a' and said,
8: 8 and the men of Penuel a' him
8 as the men of Succoth had a' him.
18 they a', As thou art, so were they;
25 they a', We will willingly give them.
11:13 of Ammon a' unto the messengers
15: 6 they a', Samson, the son in law
10 And they a', To bind Samson
18:14 a' the five men that went to spy
19:28 and let us be going. But none a'.
20: 4 And the Levite...a' and said,
Ru 2: 4 they a' him, The Lord bless thee.
6 And the servant...a' and said,
11 And Boaz a' and said unto her,
3: 9 she a', I am Ruth thine handmaid;
1Sa 1:15 Hannah a' and said, No, my lord,
17 Then Eli a' and said, Go in peace·
3: 4 and he a', Here am I.
6 And he a', I called not, my son;
10 Then Samuel a', Speak; for thy
16 And he a', Here am I.
4:17 And the messenger a' and said,
20 she a' not, neither did she regard it.
5: 8 And they a', Let the ark of the God
6: 4 They a', Five golden emerods,
9: 8 the servant a' Saul again,
12 and they a' them, and said,
19 And Samuel a' Saul, and said,
21 And Saul a', and said,
10:12 And one of the same place a'
22 the Lord a', Behold, he hath hid
11: 2 Nahash the Ammonite a' them,
12: 5 And they a', He is witness.
14:12 men of the garrison a' Jonathan
28 Then a' one of the people,
37 he a' him not that day.
39 among all the people that a' him.
44 Saul a', God do so and more:
16:18 Then a' one of the servants,
17:27 people a' him after this manner.
30 the people a' him again after
58 David a', I am the son of thy servant

1Sa 18: 7 the women a' one another as
19:17 Michal a' Saul, He said unto me,
20:28 And Jonathan a' Saul, David
32 And Jonathan a' Saul his father,
21: 4 And the priest a' David,
5 And David a' the priest,
22: 9 Then a' Doeg the Edomite,
12 And he a', Here I am, my lord.
14 Then Ahimelech a' the king,
23: 4 the Lord a' him and said, Arise,
25:10 And Nabal a' David's servants,
26: 6 a' David and said to Ahimelech
14 Abner a' and said, Who art thou
22 David a' and said, Behold the king's
28: 6 the Lord a' him not, neither by
15 Saul a', I am sore distressed;
29: 9 And Achish a' and said to David,
30: 8 And he a' him, Pursue:
22 Then a' all the wicked men
2Sa 1: 4 And he a', That the people are fled
7 And I a', Here am I.
8 I a' him, I am an Amalekite.
13 he a', I am the son of a stranger,
2:20 Art thou Asahel? And he a', I am.
4: 9 David a' Rechab and Baanah his
9: 6 And he a', Behold thy servant!
13:12 she a' him, Nay, my brother,
32 And Jonadab,...David's brother, a'
14: 5 she a', I am indeed a widow woman,
18 king a' and said unto the woman,
19 And the woman a' and said,
32 Absalom a' Joab, Behold, I sent
15:21 And Ittai a' the king, and said,
18: 3 people a', Thou shalt not go
29 And Ahimaaz a', When Joab sent
32 Cushi a', The enemies of my lord
19:21 But Abishai the son of Zeruiah a'
26 he a', My lord, O king, my servant
38 the king a', Chimham shall go over
42 men of Judah a' the men of Israel,
43 men of Israel a' the men of Judah,
20:17 he a', I am he. Then she said
17 And he a', I do hear.
20 And Joab a' and said, Far be it,
21: 1 And the Lord a', It is for Saul,
5 And they a' the king, The man
22:42 the Lord, but he a' them not.
1Ki 1:28 Then king David a' and said,
36 And Benaiah...a' the king,
43 Jonathan a' and said to Adonijah,
2:22 And king Solomon a' and said
30 Thus said Joab, and thus he a' me.
3:27 Then the king a' and said,
11:22 he a', Nothing: howbeit let me go
12:13 the king a' the people roughly,
16 people a' the king, saying,
13: 6 king a' and said unto the man of
18: 8 And he a' him, I am:
18 he a', I have not troubled Israel;
21 the people a' him not a word.
24 people a' and said, It is well spoken.
26 was no voice, nor any that a'.
20: 4 And the king of Israel a' and
11 a' and said, Tell him, Let not him
14 And he a', Thou.
21: 6 a', I will not give thee my vineyard.
20 And he a', I have found thee:
22:15 he a' him, Go, and prosper:
2Ki 1: 8 they a' him, He was a hairy man,
10 Elijah a' and said to the captain
11 And he a' and said unto him,
12 And Elijah a' and said unto them,
2: 5 And he a', Yea, I know it; hold
3: 8 a', The way through the wilderness
11 of the king of Israel's servants a'
4:13 she a', I dwell among mine own
14 Gehazi a', Verily she hath no child,
26 the child? And she a', It is well.
6: 2 And he a', Go ye.
3 thy servants. And he a', I will go.
16 And he a', Fear not: for they that
22 he a', Thou shalt not smite them:
28 she a', This woman said unto me,
7: 2 king leaned a' the man of God,
13 one of his servants a' and said,
19 And that lord a' the man of God,
8:12 he a', Because I know the evil
13 Elisha a', The Lord hath shewed
14 And he a', He told me that thou
9:19 And Jehu a', What hast thou to do
22 And he a', What peace, so long as
10:13 And they a', We are the brethren
15 And Jehonadab a', It is. If it be,
18:36 and a' him not a word:
20:10 Hezekiah a', It is a light thing
15 And Hezekiah a', All the things
1Ch 12:17 David went out.... and a' and
21: 3 And Joab a', The Lord make his
26 he a' him from heaven by fire
28 the Lord had answered him in
2Ch 2:11 the king of Tyre a' in writing,
7:22 And it shall be a', Because they
10:13 And the king a' them roughly;
14 And a' them after the advice of
16 when.... the people a' the king,
18: 3 And he a' him, I am as thou art,
25: 9 the man of God a', The Lord is able
29:31 Then Hezekiah a' and said,
31:10 priest of the house of Zadok a'
34:15 Hilkiah a' and said to Shaphan
23 she a' them, Thus saith the Lord
Ezr 10: 2 sons of Elam, a' and said unto
12 all the congregation a' and said
Ne 2:20 Then a' I them, and said unto
6: 4 I a' them after the same manner.
8: 6 all the people a', Amen, Amen.

Es 1:16 And Memucan *a·* before the king
5: 4 Esther *a·*, If it seem good unto
7 Then *a·* Esther, and said, My
6: 7 And Haman *a·* the king, For the
7: 3 Esther the queen *a·* and said,
5 the king Ahasuerus *a·* and said
Job 1: 7, 9 Satan *a·* the Lord and said,
2: 2, 4 Satan *a·* the Lord, and said,
4: 1 Eliphaz the Temanite *a·* and said,
6: 1 But Job *a·* and said,
8: 1 Then *a·* Bildad the Shuhite,
9: 1 Then Job *a·* and said,
16 If I had called, and he had *a·* me;
11: 1 *a·* Zophar the Naamathite,
2 not the multitude of words be *a·*?
12: 1 And Job *a·* and said,
15: 1 Then *a·* Eliphaz the Temanite,
16: 1 Then Job *a·* and said,
18: 1 Then *a·* Bildad the Shuhite,
19: 1 Then Job *a·* and said,
20: 1 Then *a·* Zophar the Naamathite,
21: 1 But Job *a·* and said,
22: 1 Then Eliphaz the Temanite *a·*
23: 1 Then Job *a·* and said,
25: 1 Then *a·* Bildad the Shuhite,
26: 1 But Job *a·* and said,
32: 6 the son of Barachel the Buzite *a·*
12 convinced Job, or that *a·* his words:
15 were amazed they *a·* no more:
16 stood still, and *a·* no more,
34: 1 Furthermore Elihu *a·* and said,
38: 1 Lord *a·* Job out of the whirlwind,
40: 1 Moreover the Lord *a·* Job,
3 Then Job *a·* the Lord, and said,
6 Then *a·* the Lord unto Job
42: 1 Then Job *a·* the Lord,
Ps 18:41 the Lord, but he *a·* them not.
81: 7 I *a·* thee in the secret place of
99: 6 upon the Lord, and he *a·* them.
118: 5 Lord *a·* me, and set me in a large
Isa 6:11 And he *a·*, Until the cities
21: 9 he *a·* and said, Babylon is fallen,
36:21 peace, and *a·* him not a word:
39: 4 Hezekiah *a·*, All that is in mine
Jer 7:13 I called you, but ye *a·* not;
11: 5 Then *a·* I, and said, so be it, O Lord.
23:35 What hath the Lord *a·*?
37 What hath the Lord *a·* thee?
35:17 unto them, but they have not *a·*.
36:18 Then Baruch *a·* them,
44:15 all the men.... *a·* Jeremiah,
Eze 24:20 I *a·* them, The word of the Lord
37: 3 I *a·*, O Lord God, thou knowest.
Da 2: 5 king *a·* and said to the Chaldeans,
7 *a·* again and said, Let the king tell
8 *a·* and said, I know of certainty
10 Chaldeans *a·* before the king, and
14 *a·* with counsel and wisdom to
15 He *a·* and said to Arioch
20 Daniel *a·* and said, Blessed be the
26 The king *a·* and said to Daniel,
27 *a·* in the presence of the king,
47 The king *a·* unto Daniel,
3:16 *a·* and said to the king,
24 They *a·* and said unto the king,
25 He *a·* and said, Lo, I see four men
4:19 Belteshazzar *a·* and said, My lord,
5:17 Daniel *a·* and said before the king,
6:12 king *a·* and said, The thing is true,
13 *a·* they and said before the king,
Am 7:14 *a·* Amos, and said to Amaziah,
Mic 6: 5 Balaam the son of Beor *a·* him,
Hab 2: 2 And the Lord *a·* me, and said,
Hag 2:12 And the priests *a·* and said, No.
13 the priests *a·* and said, It shall be
14 Then *a·* Haggai, and said,
Zec 1:10 the man that stood.... *a·* and said,
11 And they *a·* the angel of the Lord
12 Then the angel of the Lord *a·*
13 And the Lord *a·* the angel
19 And he *a·* me, These are the horns
3: 4 And he *a·* and spake
4: 4 So I *a·* and spake to the angel
5 the angel that talked with me *a·*
6 Then he *a·* and spake unto me,
11 Then *a·* I, and said unto him,
12 And I *a·* again, and said unto him,
13 And he *a·* me and said,
5: 2 And I *a·*, I see a flying roll;
6: 4 Then I *a·* and said unto the angel
5 the angel *a·* and said unto me,
M't 4: 4 he *a·* and said, It is written,
8: 8 The centurion *a·* and said, Lord,
11: 4 Jesus *a·* and said unto them,
25 At that time Jesus *a·* and said,
12:38 scribes and of the Pharisees *a·*,
39 he *a·* and said unto them,
48 he *a·* and said unto him that told
13:11, 37 He *a·* and said unto them,
14:28 Peter *a·* him and said, Lord,
15: 3 he *a·* and said unto them,
13 he *a·* and said, Every plant,
15 Then *a·* Peter and said unto him,
23 he *a·* her not a word.
24 he *a·* and said, I am not sent
26 he *a·* and said, It is not meet
28 Then Jesus *a·* and said unto her,
16: 2 He *a·* and said unto them,
16 Simon Peter *a·* and said,
17 Jesus *a·* and said unto him,
17: 4 Then *a·* Peter, and said unto
11 Jesus *a·* and said unto them,
17 Then Jesus *a·* and said, O faithless
19: 4 he *a·* and said unto them,
27 Then *a·* Peter and said unto him,
20:13 he *a·* one of them, and said,

M't 20:22 Jesus *a·* and said, Ye know
21:21, 24 Jesus *a·* and said unto them,
27 they *a·* Jesus, and said, We cannot
29 He *a·* and said, I will not:
30 he *a·* and said, I go, sir:
22: 1 Jesus *a·* and spake unto them again
29 Jesus *a·* and said unto them,
24: 4 Jesus *a·* and said unto them,
25: 9 the wise *a·*, saying, Not so;
12 he *a·* and said, Verily I say unto
26 His lord *a·* and said unto him,
26:23 he *a·* and said, He that dippeth his
25 which betrayed him, *a·* and said,
33 Peter *a·* and said unto him,
63 the high priest *a·* and said unto
66 *a·* and said, He is guilty of death.
27:12 priests and elders, he *a·* nothing.
14 he *a·* him to never a word;
21 The governor *a·* and said unto them.
25 Then *a·* all the people, and said,
28: 5 the angel *a·* and said unto the
M'r 3:33 he *a·* them, saying, Who is my
5: 9 he *a·*, saying, My name is Legion:
6:37 He *a·* and said unto them,
7: 6 He *a·* and said unto them,
28 she *a·* and said unto him,
8: 4 his disciples *a·* him,
28 they *a·*, John the Baptist:
9: 5 Peter *a·* and said to Jesus,
12 he *a·* and told them, Elias verily
17 one of the multitude *a·* and said,
38 John *a·* him, saying, Master,
10: 3 he *a·* and said unto them,
5 Jesus *a·* and said unto them,
20 he *a·* and said unto him, Master,
29 Jesus *a·* and said, Verily I say
51 Jesus *a·* and said unto him,
11:14 Jesus *a·* and said unto it,
29 Jesus *a·* and said unto them,
33 they *a·* and said unto Jesus, We
12:28 perceiving that he had *a·* them well,
29 Jesus *a·* him, The first of all the
34 saw that he *a·* discreetly,
35 Jesus *a·* and said, while he taught
14:20 he *a·* and said unto them,
48 Jesus *a·* and said unto them,
61 held his peace and *a·* nothing.
15: 3 many things: but he *a·* nothing.
5 Jesus yet *a·* nothing; so that Pilate
9 Pilate *a·* them, saying,
12 Pilate *a·* and said again unto them
Lu 1:35 the angel *a·* and said unto her,
60 his mother *a·* and said,
3:16 John *a·*, saying unto them all,
4: 4 Jesus *a·* him, saying,
8 Jesus *a·* and said unto him,
7:43 Simon *a·* and said, I suppose that
8:21 he *a·* and said unto them,
50 he *a·* him, saying, Fear not:
9:49 John *a·* and said, Master, we saw
10:28 unto him, Thou hast *a·* right:
41 Jesus *a·* and said unto her,
11:45 Then *a·* one of the lawyers, and
13:14 the ruler of the synagogue *a·*
15 The Lord then *a·* him, and said,
14: 5 *a·* them, saying, Which of you
17:20 he *a·* them and said,
37 they *a·* and said unto him,
19:40 he *a·* and said unto them,
20: 3 he *a·* and said unto them,
7 they *a·*, that they could not tell
24 They *a·* and said, Cæsar's.
22:51 Jesus *a·* and said, Suffer ye thus
23: 3 he *a·* him and said, Thou sayest it.
9 he *a·* him nothing.
Joh 1:21 thou that prophet? And he *a·*, No.
26 John *a·* them, saying, I baptize
48 Jesus *a·* and said unto him,
49 Nathanael *a·* and saith
50 Jesus *a·* and said unto him,
2:18 Then *a·* the Jews and said
19 Jesus *a·* and said unto them,
3: 3 Jesus *a·* and said unto him,
5 Jesus *a·*, Verily, verily,
9 Nicodemus *a·* and said
10 Jesus *a·* and said unto him, Art
27 John *a·* and said, A man can
4:10, 13 Jesus *a·* and said unto her,
17 *a·* and said, I have no husband.
5: 7 The impotent man *a·*
11 He *a·* them, He that made me
17 Jesus *a·* them, My Father worketh
19 Then *a·* Jesus and said unto them,
6: 7 Philip *a·* him, Two hundred
26 Jesus *a·* them and said,
29 Jesus *a·* and said unto them,
43 Jesus therefore *a·* and said
68 Then Simon Peter *a·* him,
70 Jesus *a·* them, Have not I chosen
7:16 Jesus *a·* them, and said,
20 The people *a·* and said,
21 Jesus *a·* and said unto them,
46 The officers *a·*, Never man
47 Then *a·* them the Pharisees,
52 They *a·* and said unto him,
8:14 Jesus *a·* and said unto them,
19 Jesus *a·*, Ye neither know me,
33 *a·* him, We be Abraham's seed,
34 Jesus *a·* them, Verily,
39 They *a·* and said unto him,
48 Then *a·* the Jews, and said
49 Jesus *a·*, I have not a devil;
54 Jesus *a·*, If I honour myself, my
9: 3 Jesus *a·*, Neither hath this man
11 He *a·* and said, A man that is
20 His parents *a·* them

Joh 9:25 He *a·* and said, Whether he be a
27 He *a·* them, I have told
30 The man *a·* and said unto them,
34 They *a·* and said unto him,
36 He *a·* and said, Who is he,
10:25 Jesus *a·* them, I told you, and ye
32 Jesus *a·* them, Many good works
33 The Jews *a·* him, saying,
34 Jesus *a·* them, Is it not
11: 9 Jesus *a·*, Are there not twelve
12:23 Jesus *a·* them, saying,
30 Jesus *a·* and said, This voice
34 The people *a·* him, We have heard
13: 7 Jesus *a·* and said unto him,
8 Jesus *a·* him, If I wash thee not,
26 Jesus *a·*, He it is, to whom
36 Jesus *a·* him, Whither I go,
38 Jesus *a·* him, Wilt thou lay
14:23 Jesus *a·* and said unto him,
16:31 Jesus *a·* them, Do ye now believe?
18: 5 They *a·* him, Jesus of Nazareth.
8 Jesus *a·*, I have told you that I am
20 Jesus *a·* him, I spake openly to
23 Jesus *a·* him, If I have spoken evil,
30 They *a·* and said unto him,
34 Jesus *a·* him, Sayest thou this
35 Pilate *a·*, Am I a Jew?
36 Jesus *a·*, My kingdom is not of
37 Jesus *a·*, Thou sayest that I am
19: 7 The Jews *a·* him, We have a law,
11 Jesus *a·*, Thou couldest have no
15 chief priests *a·*, We have no king
22 Pilate *a·*, What I have written,
20:28 Thomas *a·* and said unto
21: 5 They *a·* him, No.
Ac 3:12 he *a·* unto the people, ye men of
4:19 Peter and John *a·* and said unto
5: 8 Peter *a·* unto her, Tell me
29 and the other apostles *a·* and said,
8:24 Then *a·* Simon, and said, Pray ye,
34 the eunuch *a·* Philip, and said,
37 he *a·* and said, I believe
9:13 Ananias *a·*, Lord, I have heard
10:46 magnify God. Then *a·* Peter,
11: 9 the voice *a·* me again from heaven,
15:13 James *a·*, saying, Men,
19:15 the evil spirit *a·* and said,
21:13 Then Paul *a·*, What mean ye to
22: 8 I *a·*, Who art thou, Lord?
28 chief captain *a·*, With a great sum
24:10 answered, Forasmuch as I know
25 trembled, and *a·*, Go thy way
25: 4 Festus *a·*, that Paul should be
8 While he *a·* for himself,
9 *a·* Paul, and said, Wilt thou go up
12 *a·*, Hast thou appealed unto
16 whom I *a·*, It is not the manner
26: 1 the hand, and *a·* for himself:
Re 7:13 one of the elders *a·*, saying unto

answeredst
Ps 99: 8 Thou *a·* them, O Lord our God:
138: 3 the day when I cried thou *a·* me,

answerest
1Sa 26:14 *A·* thou not, Abner?
Job 16: 3 emboldeneth thee that thou *a·*?
M't 26:62 unto him, *A·* thou nothing?
M'r 14:60 saying, *A·* thou nothing?
15: 4 him, saying, *a·* thou nothing?
Joh 18:22 *A·* thou the high priest so?

answereth^
1Sa 28:15 and *a·* me no more, neither by
1Ki 18:24 the God that *a·* by fire, let him
Job 12: 4 upon God, and he *a·* him:
Pr 18:13 He that *a·* a matter before
23 intreaties; but the rich *a·* roughly.
27:19 As in water face *a·* to face, so
Ec 5:20 God *a·* him in the joy of his
10:19 but money *a·* all things.
M'r 8:29 And Peter *a·* and saith unto
9:19 He *a·* him, and saith, O faithless
Lu 3:11 He *a·* and saith unto them,
Ga 4:25 and *a·* to Jerusalem which now is,

answering
M't 3:15 Jesus *a·* said unto him,
M'r 11:22 And Jesus *a·* saith unto them,
33 Jesus *a·* saith unto them,
12:17 Jesus *a·* said unto them,
24 Jesus *a·* said unto them,
13: 2 Jesus *a·* said unto him,
5 Jesus *a·* them, began to say,
15: 2 he *a·* said unto him, Thou sayest it.
Lu 1:19 the angel *a·* said unto him,
4:12 Jesus *a·* said unto him,
5: 5 Simon *a·* said unto him, Master,
22 *a·* said unto them, What reason
31 Jesus *a·* said unto them,
6: 3 Jesus *a·* them said, Have ye not
7:22 Then Jesus *a·* said unto
40 Jesus *a·* said unto him,
9:19 They *a·* said, John the Baptist;
20 Peter *a·* said, The Christ of God.
41 Jesus *a·* said, O faithless
10:27 he *a·* said, Thou shalt love the
30 And Jesus *a·* said, A certain man
13: 2 Jesus *a·* said unto them,
8 he *a·* said unto him, Lord,
14: 3 Jesus *a·* spake unto the lawyers
15:29 he *a·* said to his father,
17:17 Jesus *a·* said, Were there not ten
20:34 Jesus *a·* said unto them,
39 certain of the scribes *a·* said,
23:40 the other *a·* rebuked him,
24:18 Cleopas, *a·* said unto him,
Tit 2: 9 well in *a·* things; not *a·* again;

answers
Job 21:34 *a*' there remaineth falsehood?
34:36 of his *a*' for wicked men.
Lu 2:47 at his understanding and *a*'.

ant See also ANTS.
Pr 6: 6 Go to the *a*', thou sluggard;

antichrist See also ANTICHRISTS.
1Jo 2:18 ye have heard that *a*' shall come,
22 He is *a*', that denieth the Father
4: 3 this is that spirit of *a*', whereof
2Jo 7 This is a deceiver and an *a*'.

antichrists
1Jo 2:18 come, even now are there many *a*';

Antioch (*an'-te-ok*)
Ac 6: 5 and Nicolas a proselyte of *A*':
11:19 far as Phenice, and Cyprus, and *A*',
20 when they were come to *A*',
22 that he should go as far as *A*'.
26 brought him unto *A*'.
26 were called Christians first in *A*'.
27 from Jerusalem unto *A*'.
13: 1 in the church that was at *A*'
14 they came to *A*' in Pisidia,
14:19 certain Jews from *A*' and Iconium,
21 Iconium, and *A*',
26 and thence sailed to *A*',
15:22 men of their own company to *A*'
23 Gentiles in *A*' and Syria
30 were dismissed, they came to *A*':
35 Barnabas continued in *A*', teaching
18:22 the church, he went down to *A*'.
Ga 2:11 when Peter was come to *A*',
2Ti 3:11 which came unto me at *A*',

Antipas (*an'-tip-as*)
Re 2:13 *A*' was my faithful martyr,

Antipatris (*an-tip'-at-ris*)
Ac 23:31 and brought him by night to *A*'.

antiquity
Isa 23: 7 whose *a*' is of ancient days?

Antothijah (*an-to-thi'-jah*)
1Ch 8:24 And Hananiah, and Elam, and *A*',

Antothite (*an'-to-thite*) See also ANETOTHITE.
1Ch 11:28 the Tekoite, Abi-ezer the *A*',
12: 3 and Berachah, and Jehu the *A*',

ants
Pr 30:25 The *a*' are a people not strong,

Anub (*a'-nub*)
1Ch 4: 8 And Coz begat *A*', and Zobebah,

anvil
Isa 41: 7 hammer him that smote the *a*',

any^
Ge 3: 1 was more subtil than *a*' beast
4:15 a mark upon Cain, lest *a*' finding
8:12 not again unto him *a*' more.
21 not again curse the ground *a*' more
21 again smite *a*' more every thing
9:11 shall all flesh be cut off *a*' more
11 there *a*' more be a flood to destroy
14:23 not take *a*' thing that is thine,
17: 5 name *a*' more be called Abram,
12 bought with money of *a*' stranger,
18:14 Is *a*' thing too hard for the Lord?
19:12 Hast thou here *a*' besides?
22 I cannot do *a*' thing till thou be
22:12 neither do thou *a*' thing unto
24:16 neither had *a*' man known her:
30:31 Thou shalt not give me *a*' thing:
31:14 there yet *a*' portion or inheritance
35:10 shall not be called *a*' more Jacob,
36:31 reigned *a*' king over the children of
39: 9 neither hath he kept back *a*' thing
23 *a*' thing that was under his hand;
42:16 be proved, whether there be *a*'
47: 6 if thou knowest *a*' men of activity
Ex 8:29 Pharaoh deal deceitfully *a*' more
9:29 shall there be *a*' more hail;
10:23 neither rose *a*' from his place
11: 6 nor shall be like it *a*' more.
7 against *a*' of the children of Israel
16:24 neither was there *a*' worm
20: 4 unto thee *a*' graven image,
4 or *a*' likeness of
4 *a*' thing that is in heaven above
10 in it thou shalt not do *a*' work,
17 *a*' thing that is thy neighbour's.
21:23 And if *a*' mischief follow, then
22: 9 or for *a*' manner of lost thing,
10 or *a*' beast, to keep; and it die,
20 He that sacrificeth unto *a*' god,
22 Ye shall not afflict any widow,
23 If thou afflict them in *a*' wise,
31 neither shall ye eat *a*' flesh that
24:14 if *a*' man have *a*' matters to do,
30:32 neither shall ye make *a*' other
33 Whosoever compoundeth *a*' like it,
33 whosoever putteth *a*' of it upon
31:14 whosoever doeth *a*' work therein,
15 doeth *a*' work in the sabbath day,
32:24 Whosoever hath *a*' gold,
34: 3 neither let *a*' man be seen
10 done in all the earth, nor in *a*'
24 neither shall *a*' man desire thy
35:24 found shittim wood for *a*' work of
33 to make *a*' manner of cunning
35 even of them that do *a*' work,
36: 6 man nor woman make *a*' more
Le 1: 2 If *a*' man of you bring an offering
2: 1 when *a*' will offer a meat offering
11 burn no leaven, nor *a*' honey, in
11 *a*' offering of the Lord made by
4: 2 sin through ignorance against *a*'

Le 4: 2 be done, and shall do against *a*'
13 have done somewhat against *a*' of
22 through ignorance against *a*' of
27 if *a*' one of the common people sin
27 he doeth somewhat against *a*' of
5: 2 if a soul touch *a*' unclean thing,
11 he put *a*' frankincense thereon:
17 sin, and commit *a*' of these things
6: 3 *a*' of all these that a man doeth,
7 shall be forgiven him for *a*' thing
27 of the blood thereof upon *a*'
30 offering, whereof *a*' of the blood
7: 8 *a*' man's burnt offering, even the
15 not leave *a*' of it until the morning.
18 if *a*' of the flesh of the sacrifice of
19 that toucheth *a*' unclean thing
21 that shall touch *a*' unclean thing,
21 or *a*' unclean beast,
21 or *a*' abominable unclean
26 of beast, in *a*' of your dwellings.
27 he that eateth *a*' manner of blood,
11:10 of *a*' living thing which is in the
32 And upon whatsoever *a*' of them,
32 whether it be *a*' vessel of wood,
33 vessel, whereinto *a*' of them
35 whereupon *a*' part of their carcase
37 And if *a*' part of their carcase
37 fall upon *a*' sowing seed
38 if *a*' water be put upon the seed,
38 *a*' part of their carcase fall
39 if *a*' beast, of which he may eat,
43 abominable with *a*' creeping
44 defile yourselves with *a*' manner
13:24 Or if there be *a*' flesh, in the skin
48 or in *a*' thing made of skin;
49 the work, or in *a*' thing of skin;
51 in *a*' work that is made of skin;
52 or in linen, or *a*' thing of skin,
53 in the woof, or in *a*' thing of skin;
57 or in *a*' thing of skin; it is a
59 or *a*' thing of skins, to pronounce
15: 2 When *a*' man hath a running issue
6 he that sitteth on *a*' thing
10 whosoever toucheth *a*' thing that
10 he that beareth *a*' of those things
16 if *a*' man's seed of copulation go
22 whosoever toucheth *a*' thing that
23 or on *a*' thing whereon she sitteth,
24 And if *a*' man lie with her at all,
17:10 that eateth *a*' manner of blood;
12 shall eat blood, neither shall *a*'
13 catcheth *a*' beast or fowl that may
18: 6 shall approach to *a*' that is near
21 not let *a*' of thy seed pass through
23 lie with *a*' beast to defile thyself
23 neither shall *a*' woman stand before
24 yourselves in *a*' of these things:
26 commit *a*' of these abominations;
26 *a*' of your own nations, nor *a*'
29 commit *a*' of these abominations;
30 not *a*' one of these abominable
19:17 in *a*' wise rebuke thy neighbour,
18 nor bear *a*' grudge against the
26 not eat *a*' thing with the blood:
28 not make *a*' cuttings in your flesh
28 nor print *a*' marks upon you:
20: 2 giveth *a*' of his seed unto Molech;
4 people of the land do *a*' ways hide
16 a woman approach unto *a*' beast,
25 by *a*' manner of living thing that
21: 5 nor make *a*' cuttings in their flesh.
9 the daughter of *a*' priest, if she
11 shall he go into *a*' dead body,
17 that hath *a*' blemish, let him not
18 a flat nose, or *a*' thing superfluous.
22: 4 toucheth *a*' thing that is unclean
5 toucheth *a*' creeping thing,
6 soul which hath touched *a*' such
11 priest buy *a*' soul with his money,
23 that hath *a*' thing superfluous or
24 neither shall ye make *a*' offering
25 bread of your God of *a*' of these;
23:22 gather *a*' gleaning of thy harvest:
30 soul it be that doeth *a*' work
24:17 he that killeth *a*' man shall surely
25:25 if *a*' of his kin come to redeem it,
32 the Levites redeem at *a*' time.
49 *a*' that is nigh of kin unto him of
26: 1 neither shall ye set up *a*' image of
27: 9 all that *a*' man giveth of such
11 And if it be *a*' unclean beast,
19 sanctified the field will in *a*' wise
20 it shall not be redeemed *a*' more.
Nu 4:15 they shall not touch *a*' holy thing,
5: 6 man or woman shall commit *a*' sin
10 whatsoever *a*' man giveth the priest.
12 If *a*' man's wife go aside, and
6: 3 shall he drink *a*' liquor of grapes,
9 if *a*' man die very suddenly by him,
9:10 If *a*' man of you or of your posterity
12 morning, nor break any bone of
14:23 shall *a*' of them that provoked me
15:27 if *a*' soul sin through ignorance,
17:13 Whosoever cometh *a*' thing near
18: 5 wrath *a*' more upon the children
20 thou have *a*' part among them:
19:11, 13 toucheth the dead body of *a*'
20: 5 neither is there *a*' water to drink.
19 without doing *a*' thing else, go
21: 5 bread, neither is there *a*' water;
9 serpent had bitten *a*' man,
22:38 I now *a*' power...to say *a*' thing?
23:23 there *a*' divination against Israel:
29: 7 souls: ye shall not do *a*' work
30: 5 not *a*' of her vows, or of her
15 shall *a*' ways make them void

Nu 31:19 whosoever hath killed *a*' person,
19 whosoever hath touched *a*' slain,
35:11 killeth *a*' person at unawares.
15 Every one that killeth *a*' person
22 or have cast upon him *a*' thing
23 Or with *a*' stone, wherewith a man
26 if the slayer shall at *a*' time come
30 killeth *a*' person, the murderer
30 shall not testify against *a*' person
36: 3 be married to *a*' of the sons of the
8 possesseth an inheritance in *a*'
De 2:19 children of Ammon *a*' possession;
37 unto *a*' place of the river Jabbok,
4:16 graven image, the similitude of *a*'
17 The likeness of *a*' beast that is
17 the likeness of *a*' winged fowl
18 likeness of *a*' thing that creepeth
18 likeness of *a*' fish that is in the
23 likeness of *a*' thing, which the Lord
25 graven image, or the likeness of *a*'
32 there hath been *a*' such thing as
5: 8 *a*' graven image, or *a*' likeness
8 of *a*' thing that is in heaven above,
14 thou shalt not do *a*' work, thou,
14 nor *a*' of thy cattle, nor thy
21 or *a*' thing that is thy neighbour's.
25 voice of the Lord our God *a*' more
7: 7 more in number than *a*' people;
8: 9 thou shalt not lack *a*' thing in it;
12:17 nor *a*' of thy vows which thou
13:11 do no more *a*' such wickedness
14: 1 nor make *a*' baldness between
3 shalt not eat *a*' abominable thing.
21 shall not eat of *a*' thing that dieth
15: 7 brethren within *a*' of thy gates
21 if there be *a*' blemish therein, as
21 or have *a*' ill blemish, thou shalt
16: 4 shall there *a*' thing of the flesh,
5 passover within *a*' of thy gates,
21 thee a grove of *a*' trees near
22 shalt thou set thee up *a*' image;
17: 1 the Lord thy God *a*' bullock,
1 or *a*' evilfavouredness: for that
2 among you, within *a*' of thy gates
3 moon, or *a*' of the host of heaven,
15 in *a*' wise set him king over thee,
18: 6 a Levite come from *a*' of thy gates
10 not be found among you *a*' one
16 let me see this great fire *a*' more,
19:11 if *a*' man hate his neighbour, and
15 against a man for *a*' iniquity, or
15 for *a*' sin, in *a*' sin that he sinneth:
16 witness rise up against *a*' man to
20 commit no more *a*' such evil
21:23 in *a*' wise bury him that day
22: 1 shalt in *a*' case bring them again
6 before thee in the way in *a*' tree,
7 shalt in *a*' wise let the dam go,
8 house, if *a*' man fall from thence.
13 If *a*' man take a wife, and go in
23:10 among you *a*' man, that is not clean
18 of the Lord thy God for *a*' vow:
19 usury of *a*' thing that is lent
24 shalt not put *a*' in thy vessel.
24: 5 he be charged with *a*' business:
7 found stealing *a*' of his brethren
10 dost lend thy brother *a*' thing,
13 In *a*' case thou shalt deliver him
26:14 taken away ought thereof for *a*'
27: 5 not lift up *a*' iron tool upon them
15 Cursed be the man that maketh *a*'
21 with *a*' manner of beast. And all
28:14 go aside from any of the words
55 not give to *a*' of them of the flesh
29:23 nor *a*' grass groweth therein, like
30: 4 If *a*' of thine be driven out unto
31:13 have not known *a*' thing, may
32:28 there *a*' understanding in them.
39 neither is there *a*' that can deliver
Jos 1: 5 There shall not *a*' man be able
2:11 remain *a*' more courage in *a*' man,
19 our head, if *a*' hand be upon him.
5: 1 spirit in them *a*' more, because
12 children of Israel manna *a*' more:
6:10 shout, nor make *a*' noise with
10 neither shall *a*' word proceed out
18 And ye, in *a*' wise keep yourselves
7:12 neither will I be with you *a*' more,
8:31 no man hath lift up *a*' iron: and
10:21 against *a*' of the children of Israel.
11:11 there was not *a*' left to breathe:
14 them neither left they *a*'
13:33 Moses gave not *a*' inheritance:
20: 3 that killeth *a*' person unawares
9 killeth *a*' person at unawares
21:45 failed not ought of *a*' good thing
23:12 Else if ye do in *a*' wise go back,
13 God will no more drive out *a*' of
J'g 2:14 could not *a*' longer stand before
21 drive out *a*' from before them
4:20 when *a*' man doth come...and say,
20 Is there *a*' man here? that thou
11:25 art thou *a*' thing better than Balak
13: 4 and eat not *a*' unclean thing:
7 neither eat *a*' unclean thing: for
14 She may not eat of *a*' thing that
14 nor eat *a*' unclean thing: all
16:17 weak, and be like *a*' other man.
18: 7 put them to shame in *a*' thing;
7 and had no business with *a*' man.
10 there is no want of *a*' thing that
28 had no business with *a*' man; and
19:19 there is no want of *a*' thing:
20: 8 not *a*' of us go to his tent, neither
8 we *a*' of us turn into his house.
21: 1 shall not *a*' of us give his daughter

J'g 21:12 a' male: and they brought them
Ru 1:11 with me? are there yet a' more
2:22 meet thee not in a' other field.
1Sa 2: 2 is there a' rock like our God.
13 when a' man offered sacrifice,
16 if a' man said unto him, Let them
3:17 if thou hide a' thing from me of
5: 5 a' that come into Dagon's house,
6: 3 in a' wise return him a trespass
9: 2 was higher than a' of the people.
10:23 higher than a' of the people from
12: 3 of whose hand I received a' bribe
4 thou taken ought of a' man's hand.
13:22 nor spear found in the hand of a'
14:24 the man that eateth a' food until
24 none of the people tasted a' food.
28 Cursed be the man that eateth a'
52 Saul saw a' strong man, or a'
18:25 The king desireth not a' dowry,
20:12 my father about to morrow a'
26 Saul spake not a' thing that day:
39 the lad knew not a' thing:
21: 2 Let no man know a' thing of the
22:15 let not the king impute a' thing
25:15 neither missed we a' thing,
22 to him by the morning light a'
34 Nabal by the morning light a'
27: 1 to seek me a' more
1 in a' coast of Israel:
30: 2 slew not a', either great or small,
12 bread, nor drunk a' water,
19 nor a' thing that they had taken
2Sa 2: 1 up into a' of the cities of Judah?
28 more, neither fought they a' more.
7: 6 I have not dwelt in a' house
7 with a' of the tribes of Israel,
10 of wickedness afflict them a' more,
22 neither is there a' God beside thee,
9: 1 Is there yet a' that is left of the
3 not yet a' of the house of Saul,
10:19 help the children of Ammon a' more.
13: 2 hard for him to do a' thing to her.
14:10 he shall not touch thee a' more.
11 revengers of blood to destroy a',
14 doth God respect a' person:
32 and if there be a' iniquity in me,
15: 2 a' man that had a controversy
4 every man which hath a' suit or
5 when a' man came nigh to him
11 and they knew not a' thing.
19:22 there a' man be put to death
28 therefore have I yet to cry a' more
29 Why speakest thou a' more of thy
35 can I hear a' more the voice of
42 or hath he given us a' gift?
21: 4 shalt thou kill a' man in Israel.
5 in a' of the coasts of Israel,
1Ki 1: 6 had not displeased him at a' time
2:36 go not forth thence a' whither.
2:42 and walkest abroad a' whither,
3:12 neither after thee shall a' arise:
13 shall not be a' among the kings
5: 6 there is not among us a' that can
6: 7 nor ax nor a' tool of iron heard
8:31 If a' man trespass against his
38 supplication soever be made by a'
10: 3 all her questions: there was not a'
20 not the like made in a' kingdom.
11:22 howbeit let me go in a' wise.
15: 5 turned not aside from a' thing
17 he might not suffer a' to go out
29 not to Jeroboam a' that breathed,
18:26 was no voice, nor a' that answered.
29 neither voice, nor a' to answer,
29 nor a' that regarded.
20:33 diligently observe whether a'
39 if by a' means he be missing,
2Ki 2:21 there shall not be from thence a' more
4: 2 handmaid hath not a' thing
29 if thou meet a' man, salute him
29 if a' salute thee, answer him not
6:33 I wait for the Lord a' longer?
10: 5 we will not make a' king:
14 forty men; neither left he a' of
24 a' of the men whom I have brought
12: 4 that cometh into a' man's heart
5 a' breach shall be found.
14:26 for there was not a' shut up,
26 nor a' left,
26 nor a' helper for Israel.
18: 5 nor a' that were before him.
33 Hath a' of the gods of the nations
21: 8 the feet of Israel move a' more
23:25 after him arose there a' like him.
24: 7 of Egypt came not again a' more
1Ch 1:43 before a' king reigned over the
17: 6 word to a' of the judges of Israel,
9 of wickedness waste them a' more,
20 neither is there a' God beside thee,
19:19 help the children of Ammon a' more.
23:26 nor a' vessels of it for the service
26:28 whosoever had dedicated a' thing,
27: 1 that served the king in a' matter
28:21 skilful man, for a' manner of
29:25 as had not been on a' king
2Ch 1:12 there a' after thee have the like.
2:14 to grave a' manner of graving,
6: 5 neither chose I a' man to be a ruler
29 soever shall be made of a' man,
8:15 concerning a' matter, or
9: 9 neither was there a' such spice
19 not the like made in a' kingdom.
20 it was not a' thing accounted of
23:19 which was unclean in a' thing
32:13 a' ways able to deliver their lands
15 no god of a' nation or kingdom,

2Ch 33: 8 I a' more remove the foot of Israel
34:13 work in a' manner of service:
Ezr 1: 4 whosoever remaineth in a' place
7:24 a' of the priests and Levites,
Ne 2:12 neither told I a' man what my God
12 at Jerusalem: neither was there a'
5:16 wall, neither bought we a' land:
10:31 the land bring ware or a' victuals
Job 4:20 for ever without a' regarding it.
5: 1 there be a' that will answer thee;
4 neither is there a' to deliver them.
6: 6 a' taste in the white of an egg?
7:10 shall his place know him a' more.
8:12 it withered before a' other herb.
9:33 is there a' daysman betwixt us,
10:22 shadow of death, without a' order,
15:11 there a' secret thing with thee?
16:17 for a' injustice in mine hands:
18:19 people, nor a' remaining in his
20: 9 his place a' more behold him.
21:22 Shall a' teach God knowledge?
22: 3 Is it a' pleasure to the Almighty,
25: 3 Is there a' number of his armies?
31: 7 a' blot hath cleaved to mine hands;
19 a' perish for want of clothing,
19 or a' poor without covering;
32:21 pray you, accept a' man's person,
33:13 not account of a' of his matters.
27 upon men, and if a' say, I
32 [*In most editions*] hast a' thing to say,
34:27 would not consider a' of his ways:
31 I will not offend a' more:
36: 5 is mighty, and despiseth not a':
29 can a' understand the spreadings
37:24 respecteth not a' that are wise of
Ps 4: 6 say, Who will shew us a' good?
14: 2 there were a' that did understand,
33:17 deliver a' by his great strength.
34:10 shall not want a' good thing.
37: 8 fret not thyself in a' wise to do
38: 3 neither is there a' rest in my bones
49: 7 by a' means redeem his brother,
53: 2 there were a' that did understand,
59: 5 to a' wicked transgressors.
74: 9 signs: there is no more a' prophet:
9 is there a' among us that knoweth
81: 9 thou worship a' strange God.
86: 8 neither are there a' works like
91:10 neither shall a' plague come nigh
109:12 be a' to favour his fatherless
115:17 a' that go down into silence.
119:133 let not a' iniquity have dominion
135:17 neither is their a' breath in their
139:24 if there be a' wicked way in me,
141: 4 Incline not my heart to a' evil
146: 2 my God while I have a' being.
147:20 hath not dealt so with a' nation:
Pr 1:17 is spread in the sight of a' bird.
6:35 He will not regard a' ransom;
14:34 but sin is a reproach to a' people.
28:17 violence to the blood of a' person
30: 2 I am more brutish than a' man,
30 and turneth not away from a'.
31: 5 the judgment of a' of the afflicted.
Ec 1:10 Is there a' thing whereof it may
11 shall there be a' remembrance
2:10 withheld not my heart from a'
3:14 nothing can be put to it, nor a'
5: 2 heart be hasty to utter a' thing
6: 5 not seen the sun, nor known a'
9: 5 but the dead know not a' thing,
5 they a' more a reward; for the
6 have they a' more a portion ever
6 a' thing that is done under the
Isa 1: 5 should ye be stricken a' more?
2: 4 shall they learn war a' more.
7 there a' end of their treasures;
7 is their a' end of their chariots;
19:15 shall their be a' work for Egypt,
26:18 have not wrought a' deliverance
27: 3 lest a' hurt it, I will keep it night
30:20 removed into a corner a' more,
33:20 a' of the cords thereof be broken.
35: 9 nor a' ravenous beast shall
36:18 Hath a' of the gods of the
51:18 neither is there a' that taketh her
52:14 was so marred more than a' man,
53: 9 neither was a' deceit in his mouth.
54: 4 of thy widowhood a' more.
56: 2 his hand from doing a' evil.
59: 4 nor a' pleadeth for truth:
62: 4 land a' more be termed Desolate:
Jer 3:16 neither shall that be done a' more.
17 neither shall they walk a' more
5: 1 there be a' that executeth judgment,
9: 4 and trust ye not in a' brother:
10:20 to stretch forth my tent a' more,
14:22 Are there a' among the vanities
17:22 neither do ye a' work, but
18:18 not give heed to a' of his words.
20: 9 nor speak a' more in his name.
22:11 shall not return thither a' more:
30 and ruling a' more in Judah.
23:24 Can a' hide himself in secret
31:12 they shall not sorrow a' more at all.
40 nor thrown down a' more for ever.
32:27 is there a' thing too hard for me?
33:26 I will not take a' of his seed
34:10 serve themselves of them a' more
35: 7 nor plant vineyard, nor have a':
36:24 nor a' of his servants that heard
37:17 Is there a' word from the Lord?
38: 5 he that can do a' thing against you
42:21 voice of the Lord your God, nor a'
44:26 more be named in the mouth of a'
48: 9 without a' to dwell therein.

Jer 49:33 nor a' son of man dwell in it.
50:40 shall a' son of man dwell therein.
51:43 neither doth a' son of man pass
44 shall not flow together a' more
La 1:12 and see if there be a' sorrow like
3:49 down, and ceaseth not, without a'
Eze 5: 9 whereunto I will not do a' more
11 spare, neither will I have a' pity.
7:11 multitude, nor of a' of theirs:
13 neither shall a' strengthen himself
9: 6 a' man upon whom is the mark;
12:24 shall be no more a' vain vision
28 my words be prolonged a' more,
14:11 polluted a' more with all their
15: 3 be taken thereof to do a' work?
3 of it to hang a' vessel thereon?
4 burned. Is it meet for a' work?
5 shall it be meet yet for a' work,
16: 5 thee, to do a' of these unto thee,
41 also shalt give no hire a' more.
63 never open thy mouth a' more,
18: 3 ye shall not have occasion a' more
7 And hath not oppressed a', but
8 neither hath taken a' increase,
10 the like to a' one of these things,
11 that doeth not a' of those duties,
16 Neither hath oppressed a', hath
23 Have I a' pleasure at all that the
21: 5 it shall not return a' more.
23:27 nor remember Egypt a' more.
24:13 purged from thy filthiness a' more,
27:36 terror, and never shalt be a' more.
28:19 and never shalt thou be a' more.
24 nor a' grieving thorn of all that
29:15 itself a' more above the nations:
31: 8 nor a' tree in the garden of God
32:13 foot of man trouble them a' more,
33: 6 come, and take a' person from
34:10 shepherds feed themselves a' more;
29 the shame of the heathen a' more.
36:14 neither bereave thy nations a' more,
15 in thee the shame of the heathen a'
15 reproach of the people a' more,
37:22 into two kingdoms a' more
23 they defile themselves a' more
23 with a' of their transgressions:
39: 7 pollute my holy name a' more:
10 cut down a' out of the forests;
15 when a' seeth a man's bone, then
28 have left none of them a' more
29 hide my face a' more from them:
44: 9 sanctuary, of a' stranger that
13 come near to a' of my holy things,
18 with a' thing that causeth sweat.
21 Neither shall a' priest drink wine,
31 of a' thing that is dead of itself,
46:16 give a gift unto a' of his sons,
Da 2:10 asked such things at a' magician,
30 for a' wisdom that I have more
30 than a' living, but for their sakes
3:28 not serve nor worship a' god,
29 which speak a' thing amiss
6: 4 was there a' error or fault found
5 We shall not find a' occasion
7 ask a petition of a' God or man
12 that shall ask a petition of a' God
8: 4 before him, neither was there a'
11:15 neither shall there be a' strength
37 nor regard a' god: for he shall
Ho 13:10 where is a' other that may save
14: 3 neither will we say a' more to the
8 have I to do a' more with idols?
Joe 2: 2 neither shall be a' more after it,
3:17 pass through her a' more.
Am 6:10 Is there yet a' with thee? and he
7: 8 I will not pass by them a' more:
13 not again a' more at Beth-el:
8: 2 not again pass by them a' more.
7 never forget a' of their works.
Ob 18 a' remaining of the house of Esau;
Jon 3: 7 herd nor flock, taste a' thing:
Mic 4: 3 shall they learn war a' more.
Zep 3:15 thou shalt not see evil a' more.
Hag 2:12 or wine, or oil, or a' meat, shall
13 by a dead body touch a' of these,
Zec 8:10 nor a' hire for beast;
10 neither was there a' peace
9: 8 shall pass through them a' more:
13: 3 when a' shall yet prophesy, then
Mal 2:13 regardeth not the offering a' more,
M't 4: 6 lest at a' time thou dash thy foot
5:25 at a' time the adversary deliver
40 if a' man will sue thee at the law,
11:27 knoweth a' man the Father,
12:19 shall a' man hear his voice in
13:15 lest at a' time they should see
19 When a' one heareth the word
16:24 If a' man will come after me, let
18:19 agree on earth as touching a'
21: 3 if a' man say ought unto you,
22:16 neither carest thou for a' man:
46 a' man from that day forth
46 forth ask him a' more questions.
24:17 take a' thing out of his house:
23 if a' man shall say unto you,
M'r 1:44 See thou say nothing to a' man:
4:12 a' time they should be converted,
22 neither was a' thing kept secret,
23 If a' man have ears to hear, let
5: 4 neither could a' man tame him.
35 thou the Master a' further?
7:16 If a' man have ears to hear, let
8:26 nor tell it to a' in the town.
9: 8 they saw no man a' more, save
22 if thou canst do a' thing, have
30 that a' man should know it.

M'r 9:35 If *a'* man desire to be first, the
11: 3 And if *a'* man say unto you, Why
13 he might find *a'* thing thereon:
16 suffer that *a'* man should carry
16 carry *a'* vessel through the
25 if ye have ought against *a'*;
12:21 and died, neither left he *a'* seed:
34 that durst ask him *a'* question.
13: 5 heed lest *a'* man deceive you:
15 take *a'* thing out of his house:
21 if *a'* man shall say to you, Lo,
14:31 I will not deny thee in *a'* wise.
63 need we *a'* further witnesses?
15:44 whether he had been *a'* while dead.
16: 8 said they *a'* thing to
8 to *a'* man; for they were afraid.
18 and if they drink *a'* deadly thing,
Lu 3:14 man, neither accuse *a'* falsely;
4:11 lest at *a'* time thou dash thy foot
8:17 neither *a'* thing hid, that shall not
27 neither abode in *a'* house, but in
43 neither could be healed of *a'*,
9:23 If *a'* man will come after me, let
36 in those days *a'* of those things
10:19 shall by *a'* means hurt you.
11:11 son shall ask bread of *a'* of you
14: 8 art bidden of *a'* man to a wedding,
26 *a'* man come to me, and hate not
15:29 neither transgressed I at *a'* time
19: 8 taken *a'* thing from
8 *a'* man by false accusation, I
31 if *a'* man ask you, Why do ye
20:21 acceptest thou the person of *a'*,
27 deny that there is *a'* resurrection;
28 If *a'* man's brother die, having a
36 Neither can they die *a'* more:
40 not ask him *a'* question at all
21:34 lest at *a'* time your hearts
22:16 I will not *a'* more eat thereof,
35 lacked ye *a'* thing? And they
71 What need we *a'* further witness?
24:41 them, Have ye here *a'* meat?
Joh 1: 3 not *a'* thing made that was made.
18 No man hath seen God at *a'* time;
46 there *a'* good thing come out of
2:25 that *a'* should testify of man:
4:33 Hath *a'* man brought him ought
5:37 neither heard his voice at *a'* time,
6:46 Not that *a'* man hath seen the
51 if *a'* man eat of this bread, he shall
7: 4 no man that doeth *a'* thing in secret,
17 If *a'* man will do his will, he shall
37 If *a'* man thirst, let him come unto
48 Have *a'* of the rulers or of the
51 Doth our law judge *a'* man,
8:33 were never in bondage to *a'* man:
9:22 if *a'* man did confess that he was
31 if *a'* man be a worshipper of God,
32 that *a'* man opened the eyes of
10: 9 if *a'* man enter in, he shall be saved,
28 neither shall *a'* man pluck them
11: 9 If *a'* man walk in the day, he
57 if *a'* man knew where he were,
12:26 If *a'* man serve me, let him follow
26 if *a'* man serve me, him will my
47 And if *a'* man hear my words,
14:14 If ye shall ask *a'* thing in my name,
16:30 that *a'* man should ask thee:
18:31 for us to put *a'* man to death:
21: 5 Children, have ye *a'* meat?
Ac 4:12 is there salvation in *a'* other:
32 neither said *a'* of them that
34 there *a'* among them that lacked:
9: 2 that if he found *a'* of this way,
10:14 I have never eaten *a'* thing that
28 I should not call *a'* man common
47 Can *a'* man forbid water, that
11: 8 common or unclean hath at *a'* time
13:15 brethren, if ye have *a'* word of
17:25 as though he needed *a'* thing,
19: 2 whether there be *a'* Holy Ghost.
38 have a matter against *a'* man,
39 if ye enquire *a'* thing concerning
24:12 the temple disputing with *a'* man,
20 have found *a'* evil doing in me,
25: 5 if there be *a'* wickedness in him.
8 have I offended *a'* thing at all.
11 committed *a'* thing worthy of death,
16 to deliver *a'* man to die, before
17 without *a'* delay on the morrow
24 he ought not to live *a'* longer.
27:12 if by *a'* means they might attain
22 shall be no loss of *a'* man's life
34 hair fall from the head of *a'* of you.
42 lest *a'* of them should swim out,
28:21 neither *a'* of the brethren that
21 or spake *a'* harm of thee.
Ro 1:10 if by *a'* means now at length I
6: 2 to sin, live *a'* longer therein?
8: 9 if *a'* man have not the Spirit of
33 lay *a'* thing to the charge of God's
39 nor depth, nor *a'* other creature,
9:11 having done *a'* good or evil,
11:14 If by *a'* means I may provoke
13: 8 Owe no man *a'* thing, but to love
9 there be *a'* other commandment,
14:13 judge one another *a'* more:
14 esteemeth *a'* thing to be unclean,
21 nor *a'* thing whereby thy brother
15:18 dare to speak of *a'* of those things
1Co 1:15 Lest *a'* should say that I had
16 not whether I baptized *a'* other.
2: 2 not to know *a'* thing among you,
3: 7 neither is he that planteth *a'* thing,
12 *a'* man build upon this foundation
14 If *a'* man's work abide which he

1Co 3:15 If *a'* man's work shall be burned,
17 If *a'* man defile the temple of God,
18 If *a'* man among you seemeth to
5:11 if *a'* man that is called a brother
6: 1 Dare *a'* of you, having a matter
12 brought under the power of *a'*.
7:12 If *a'* brother hath a wife that
18 *a'* man called being circumcised?
18 Is *a'* called in uncircumcision?
36 But if *a'* man think that he
8: 2 if *a'* man think that he knoweth *a'*
3 But if *a'* man love God, the same
9 lest by *a'* means this liberty of
10 For if *a'* man see thee which hast
9: 7 a warfare *a'* time at his own
15 *a'* man should make my glorying
27 lest that by *a'* means, when I
10:19 that the idol is *a'* thing, or that
19 in sacrifice to idols is *a'* thing?
27 If *a'* of them that believe not bid
28 But if *a'* man say unto you,
11:16 if *a'* man seem to be contentious,
34 if *a'* man hunger, let him eat at
14:27 If *a'* man speak in an unknown
30 If *a'* thing be revealed to another
35 And if they will learn *a'* thing,
37 If *a'* man think himself to be a
38 But if *a'* man be ignorant, let him
16:22 If *a'*man love not the Lord Jesus
2Co 1: 4 them which are in *a'* trouble,
2: 5 But if *a'* have caused grief, he
10 To whom ye forgive *a'* thing,
10 if I forgave *a'* thing, to whom I
3: 5 to think *a'* thing as of ourselves;
5:17 Therefore if *a'* man be in Christ,
6: 3 Giving no offence in *a'* thing,
7:14 If I have boasted *a'* thing to him
8:23 Whether *a'* do enquire of Titus,
10: 7 If *a'* man trust to himself that he
11: 3 But I fear, lest by *a'* means, as
21 Howbeit whereinsoever *a'* is bold,
12: 6 lest *a'* man should think of me
17 *a'* of them whom I sent unto you?
Ga 1: 8 heaven, preach *a'* other gospel
9 If *a'* man preach *a'* other gospel
2: 2 lest by *a'* means I should run,
5: 6 neither circumcision availeth *a'*
6:15 neither circumcision availeth *a'*
Eph 2: 9 lest *a'* man should boast.
5: 5 an idolater, hath *a'* inheritance
27 or wrinkle, or *a'* such thing;
6: 8 whatsoever good thing *a'* man
Ph'p 2: 1 therefore *a'* consolation in Christ,
1 if *a'* comfort of love,
1 if *a'* fellowship of the Spirit,
1 if *a'* bowels and mercies,
3: 4 If *a'* other man thinketh that he
11 If by *a'* means I might attain unto
15 if in *a'* thing ye be otherwise
4: 8 *a'* virtue, and if there be *a'* praise,
Col 2: 4 lest *a'* man should beguile you
8 Beware lest *a'* man spoil you
23 not in *a'* honor to the satisfying
3:13 if *a'* man have a quarrel against *a'*:
1Th 1: 8 we need not to speak *a'* thing.
2: 5 at *a'* time used we flattering words,
9 not be chargeable unto *a'* of you,
4: 6 defraud his brother in *a'* matter:
5:15 render evil for evil unto *a'* man;
2Th 2: 3 man deceive you by *a'* means:
3: 8 we eat *a'* man's bread for nought;
8 not be chargeable to *a'* of you:
10 that if *a'* would not work, neither
14 And if *a'* man obey not our word
1Ti 1:10 if there be *a'* other thing that is
5: 4 But if *a'* widow have children
8 But if *a'* provide not for his own,
16 If *a'* man or woman that believeth
6: 3 If *a'* man teach otherwise, and
Tit 1: 6 If *a'* be blameless, the husband
Heb 1: 5 of the angels said he at *a'* time,
13 said he at *a'* time, Sit on my right
2: 1 lest at *a'* time we should let them
3:12 there be in *a'* of you an evil heart
13 lest *a'* of you be hardened through
4: 1 *a'* of you should seem to come
11 *a'* man fall after the same
12 sharper than *a'* twoedged sword,
13 Neither is there *a'* creature that
10:38 shall live by faith: but if *a'* man
12:15 lest *a'* man fail of the grace of God;
15 lest *a'* root of bitterness springing
16 Lest there be *a'* fornicator, or
19 not be spoken to them *a'* more:
Jas 1: 5 If *a'* of you lack wisdom, let him
7 shall receive *a'* thing of the Lord.
13 neither tempteth he *a'* man:
23 if *a'* man be a hearer of the word,
26 If *a'* man among you seem to be
3: 2 If *a'* man offend not in word,
5:12 neither by *a'* other oath: but let
13 Is *a'* among you afflicted? let him
13 Is *a'* merry? let him sing psalms.
14 Is *a'* sick among you? let him call
19 if *a'* of you do err from the truth,
1Pe 3: 1 if *a'* obey not the word, they also
6 not afraid with *a'* amazement.
4:11 If *a'* man speak, let him speak
11 if *a'* man minister, let him do it
16 if *a'* man suffer as a Christian,
2Pe 1:20 of the scripture is of *a'* private
3: 9 not willing that *a'* should perish,
1Jo 2: 1 if *a'* man sin, we have an advocate
15 If *a'* man love the world, the love
27 ye need not that *a'* man teach you:
4:12 No man hath seen God at *a'* time.

1Jo 5:14 if we ask *a'* thing according to his
16 If *a'* man see his brother sin a sin
2Jo 10 If there come *a'* unto you, and
Re 3:20 if *a'* man hear my voice, and open
7: 1 nor on the sea, nor on *a'* tree.
16 hunger no more, neither thirst *a'*
16 sun light on them, nor *a'* heat.
9: 4 neither *a'* green thing,
4 neither *a'* tree;
11: 5 And if *a'* man will hurt them, fire
5 if *a'* man will hurt them, he must
12: 8 place found *a'* more in heaven.
13: 9 If *a'* man have an ear, let him hear.
14: 9 If *a'* man worship the beast and
18:11 buyeth their merchandise *a'* more:
22 shall be found *a'* more in thee;
21: 4 shall there be *a'* more pain:
27 into it *a'* thing that defileth,
22:18 If *a'* man shall add unto these
19 if *a'* man shall take away from the

any-man See ANY and MAN.

any-one See ANY and ONE.

anything See also ANY and THING.
Job 33:32 [*In some editions*] If thou hast *a'* to say.

any-wise See ANY and WISE.

apace
2Sa 18:25 And he came *a'*, and drew near.
Ps 68:12 Kings of armies did flee *a'*:
Jer 46: 5 their mighty ones... are fled *a'*,

apart
Ex 13:12 thou shalt set *a'* unto the Lord
Le 15:19 she shall be put *a'* seven days:
18:19 as long as she is put *a'* for her
Ps 4: 3 the Lord hath set *a'* him that is
Eze 22:10 they humbled her that was set *a'*
Zec 12:12 land shall mourn, every family *a'*;
12 the family of the house of David *a'*,
12 and their wives *a'*;
12 family of the house of Nathan *a'*;
12 and their wives *a'*;
13 The family of.... Levi *a'*,
13 and their wives *a'*;
13 the family of Shimei *a'*,
13 and their wives *a'*;
14 every family *a'*,
14 and their wives *a'*.
M't 14:13 into a desert place *a'*;
23 into a mountain *a'* to pray:
17: 1 into an high mountain *a'*,
19 the disciples to Jesus *a'*,
20:17 took the twelve disciples *a'* in
M'r 6:31 ye yourselves *a'* into a desert
9: 2 mountain *a'* by themselves:
Jas 1:21 Wherefore lay *a'* all filthiness

ape See APES.

Apelles (*a-pel'-leze*)
Ro 16:10 Salute *A'* approved in Christ.

apes
1Ki 10:22 ivory, and *a'*, and peacocks.
2Ch 9:21 ivory, and *a'*, and peacocks.

Apharsachites (*a-far'-sak-ites*) See also APHARSATHCHITES.
Ezr 5: 6 and his companions the *A'*, which
6: 6 and your companions the *A'*, which

Apharsathchites (*a-far'-sath-kites*) See also APHARSACHITES; APHARSITES.
Ezr 4: 9 Dinaites, the *A'*, the Tarpelites,

Apharsites (*a-far'-sites*) See also APHARSATHCHITES.
Ezr 4: 9 Tarpelites, the *A'*, the Archevites,

Aphek (*a'-fek*) See also APHIK.
Jos 12:18 The king of *A'*, one; the king of
13: 4 unto *A'*, to the borders of the
19:30 Ummah also, and *A'*, and Rehob:
1Sa 4: 1 and the Philistines pitched in *A'*.
29: 1 together all their armies to *A'*:
1Ki 20:26 up to *A'*, to fight against Israel.
30 the rest fled to *A'*, into the city;
2Ki 13:17 thou shalt smite the Syrians in *A'*.

Aphekah (*af-e'-kah*)
Jos 15:53 Janum, and Beth-tappuah, and *A'*,

Aphiah (*af-i'-ah*)
1Sa 9: 1 son of *A'*, a Benjamite, a mighty

Aphik (*a'-fik*) See also APHEK.
J'g 1:31 nor of *A'*, nor of Rehob:

Aphrah (*af'-rah*) See also BETH-LEAPHRAH; OPHRAH.
Mic 1:10 house of *A'* roll thyself in the dust.

Aphses (*af'-seze*)
1Ch 24:15 Hezir, the eighteenth to *A'*,

apiece
Nu 3:47 take five shekels *a'* by the poll,
7:86 ten shekels *a'*, after the shekel
17: 6 their princes gave him a rod *a'*.
1Ki 7:15 eighteen cubits high *a'*:
Eze 10:21 Every one had four faces apiece,
41:24 and the doors had two leaves *a'*,
Lu 9: 3 money, neither have two coats *a'*.
Joh 2: 6 containing two or three firkins *a'*.

Apollonia (*ap-ol-lo'-ne-ah*)
Ac 17: 1 through Amphipolis and *A'*,

Apollos (*ap-ol'-los*)
Ac 18:24 a certain Jew named *A'*,
19: 1 while *A'* was at Corinth,

1Co 1:12 and I of A'; and I of Cephas;
3: 4 another, I am of A'; are ye not
5 Who then is Paul, and who is A',
6 A' watered; but God gave the
22 Whether Paul, or A', or Cephas.
4: 6 and to A' for your sakes;
16:12 touching our brother A',
Tit 3:13 Bring Zenas the lawyer and A'

Apollyon (*ap-ol'-le-on*)
Re 9:11 Greek tongue hath this name A'.

apostle^ See also APOSTLES.
Ro 1: 1 called to be an a', separated unto
11:13 as I am the a' of the Gentiles,
1Co 1: 1 called to be an a' of Jesus Christ
9: 1 Am I not an a'? am I not free?
2 If I be not an a' unto others,
15: 9 not meet to be called an a',
2Co 1: 1 Paul, an a' of Jesus Christ by the
12:12 the signs of an a' were wrought
Ga 1: 1 Paul, an a', (not of men, neither by
Eph 1: 1 Paul, an a' of Jesus Christ
Col 1: 1 Paul, an a' of Jesus Christ by the
1Ti 1: 1 Paul, an a' of Jesus Christ by the
2: 7 am ordained a preacher, and an a',
2Ti 1: 1 Paul, an a' of Jesus Christ
11 appointed a preacher, and an a',
Tit 1: 1 an a' of Jesus Christ, according to
Heb 3: 1 consider the A' and High Priest
1Pe 1: 1 Peter, an a' of Jesus Christ, to the
2Pe 1: 1 a servant and an a' of Jesus

apostles^ See also APOSTLES'.
M't 10: 2 names of the twelve a' are these;
M'r 6:30 the a' gathered themselves together
Lu 6:13 whom also he named a';
9:10 the a', when they were returned,
11:49 I will send them prophets and a',
17: 5 the a' said unto the Lord,
22:14 the twelve a' with him.
24:10 told these things unto the a'.
Ac 1: 2 commandments unto the a' whom
26 numbered with the eleven a'.
2:37 Peter, and to the rest of the a',
43 and signs were done by the a'.
4:33 the a' witness of the resurrection
36 by the a' was surnamed Barnabas,
5:12 hands of the a' were many signs
18 laid their hands on the a',
29 Peter and the other a' answered
34 to put the a' forth a little space;
40 called the a', and beaten them,
6: 6 Whom they set before the a':
8: 1 Judæa and Samaria, except the a'.
14 the a' which were at Jerusalem
9:27 him and brought him to the a',
11: 1 a' and brethren that were in Judæa,
14: 4 with the Jews, and part with the a'.
14 when the a', Barnabas and Paul,
15: 2 unto the a' and elders about this
4 of the a' and elders, and they
6 the a' and elders came together
22 Then pleased it the a' and elders,
23 The a' and elders and brethren
33 the brethren unto the a'.
16: 4 were ordained of the a' and elders
Ro 16: 7 who are of note among the a',
1Co 4: 9 God hath set forth us the a' last,
9: 5 as well as other a', and as the
12:28 first a', secondarily prophets,
29 Are all a'? are all prophets?
15: 7 of James; then of all the a'.
9 I am the least of the a', that am
2Co 11: 5 a whit behind the very chiefest a'
13 are false a', deceitful workers,
13 themselves into the a' of Christ.
12:11 the very chiefest a', though I be
Ga 1:17 to them which were a' before me;
19 other of the a' saw I none,
Eph 2:20 foundation of the a' and prophets,
3: 5 revealed unto his holy a'
4:11 gave some, a'; and some, prophets;
1Th 2: 6 burdensome, as the a' of Christ.
2Pe 3: 2 the a' of the Lord and Saviour:
Jude 17 before of the a' of our Lord Jesus
Re 2: 2 them which say they are a',
18:20 ye holy a' and prophets;
21:14 names of the twelve a' of the Lamb.

apostles'
Ac 2:42 in the a' doctrine and fellowship,
4:35 laid them down at the a' feet:
37 the money, and laid it at the a' feet.
5: 2 part, and laid it at the a' feet.
8:18 through laying on of the a' hands

apostleship
Ac 1:25 take part of this ministry and a',
Ro 1: 5 received grace and a', for obedience
1Co 9: 2 seal of mine a' are ye in the Lord.
Ga 2: 8 to the a' of the circumcision,

apothecaries See also APOTHECARIES'.
Ne 3: 8 Hananiah the son of one of the a',

apothecaries'
2Ch 16:14 spices prepared by the a' art:

apothecary See also APOTHECARIES.
Ex 30:25 compound after the art of the a':
35 confection after the art of the a',
37:29 according to the work of the a'.
Ec 10: 1 the ointment of the a'

Appaim (*ap'-pa-im*)
1Ch 2:30 the sons of Nadab; Seled, and A':
31 the sons of A'; Ishi. And the sons

apparel See also APPARELLED.
J'g 17:10 and a suit of a', and thy victuals.
1Sa 27: 9 the camels, and the a',
2Sa 1:24 ornaments of gold upon your a'.
12:20 himself, and changed his a',
14: 2 put on now mourning a',
1Ki 10: 5 his ministers, and their a',
2Ch 9: 4 his ministers, and their a'; his
4 cupbearers also, and their a';
Ezr 3:10 they set the priests in their a';
Es 5: 1 that Esther put on her royal a',
6: 8 Let the royal a' be brought
9 let this a' and horse be delivered
10 take the a' and the horse,
11 Then took Haman the a'
8:15 in royal a' of blue and white,
Isa 3:22 The changeable suits of a',
4: 1 own bread, and wear our own a':
63: 1 this that is glorious in his a',
2 Wherefore art thou red in thine a',
Eze 27:24 in chests of rich a', bound with
Zep 1: 8 as are clothed with strange a'.
Zec 14:14 gold, and silver, and a',
Ac 1:10 men stood by them in white a';
12:21 Herod, arrayed in royal a',
20:33 no man's silver, or gold, or a'.
1Ti 2: 9 adorn themselves in modest a',
Jas 2: 2 gold ring, in goodly a',
1Pe 3: 3 of gold or of putting on of a';

apparelled
2Sa 13:18 daughters that were virgins a'.
Lu 7:25 they which are gorgeously a',

apparently
Nu 12: 8 speak mouth to mouth, even a',

appeal See also APPEALED.
Ac 25:11 I a' unto Cæsar.
28:19 constrained to a' unto Cæsar;

appealed
Ac 25:12 Hast thou a' unto Cæsar?
21 when Paul had a' to be reserved
25 himself hath a' to Augustus,
26:32 if he had not a' unto Cæsar.

appear See also APPEARED; APPEARETH; APPEARING.
Ge 1: 9 let the dry land a': and it was so.
30:37 made the white a' which was in
Ex 23:15 none shall a' before me empty:)
17 all thy males shall a' before
34:20 none shall a' before me empty.
23 menchildren a' before the Lord
24 to a' before the Lord thy God
Le 9: 4 to day the Lord will a' unto you.
6 glory of the Lord shall a' unto you.
13:57 if it a' still in the garment,
16: 2 I will a' in the cloud upon the
De 16:16 males a' before the Lord thy God
16 they shall not a'...empty:
31:11 Israel is come to a' before the Lord
J'g 13:21 angel of the Lord did no more a'
1Sa 1:22 that he may a' before the Lord,
2:27 Did I plainly a' unto the house of
2Ch 1: 7 night did God a' unto Solomon,
Ps 42: 2 shall I come and a' before God?
90:16 thy work a' unto thy servants,
102:16 he shall a' in his glory.
Ca 2:12 The flowers a' on the earth;
4: 1 goats, that a' from mount Gilead.
6: 5 of goats that a' from Gilead.
7:12 whether the tender grape a',
Isa 1:12 When ye come to a' before me,
66: 5 but he shall a' to your joy, and
Jer 13:26 that thy shame may a'.
Eze 21:24 so that...your sins do a';
M't 6:16 they may a' unto men to fast.
18 thou a' not unto men to fast,
23:27 which indeed a' beautiful outward,
28 ye also outwardly a' righteous
24:30 shall a' the sign of the Son of man
Lu 11:44 are as graves which a' not,
19:11 of God should immediately a'.
Ac 22:30 and all their council to a',
26:16 in the which I will a' unto thee;
Ro 7:13 But sin, that it might a' sin,
2Co 5:10 all a' before the judgment seat
7:12 sight of God might a' unto you.
13: 7 not that we should a' approved,
Col 3: 4 Christ, who is our life, shall a',
4 then shall ye also a' with him in
1Ti 4:15 that thy profiting may a'
Heb 9:24 a' in the presence of God for us.
28 them that look for him shall he a'
11: 3 not made of things which do a'.
1Pe 4:18 the ungodly and the sinner a'?
5: 4 when the chief Shepherd shall a',
1Jo 2:28 when he shall a', we may have
3: 2 doth not yet a' what we shall be:
2 when he shall a', we shall be like
Re 3:18 of thy nakedness do not a';

appearance See also APPEARANCES.
Nu 9:15 as it were the a' of fire,
16 and the a' of fire by night.
1Sa 16: 7 man looketh on the outward a',
Eze 1: 5 this was their a'; they had the
13 their a' was like burning coals
13 and like the a' of lamps:
14 as the a' of a flash of lightning.
16 The a' of the wheels
16 and their a' and their work
26 as the a' of a sapphire
26 as the a' of a man above it.
27 as the a' of fire round about
Eze 1:27 the a' of his loins even upward,
27 the a' of his loins even downward,
27 as it were the a' of fire,
28 a' of the bow that is in the cloud
28 a' of the brightness round about.
28 This was the a' of the likeness
8: 2 a likeness as the a' of fire:
2 from the a' of his loins
2 as the a' of brightness, as the
10: 1 the a' of the likeness of a throne.
9 and the a' of the wheels
40: 3 whose a' was like the a' of brass,
41:21 a' of the one as the a' of the other.
42:11 like the a' of the chambers
43: 3 according to the a' of the vision,
Da 8:15 as the a' of a man.
10: 6 his face as the a' of lightning,
18 like the a' of a man, and he
Joe 2: 4 a' of them is as the a' of horses;
Joh 7:24 Judge not according to the a',
2Co 5:12 glory in a', and not in heart.
10: 7 on things after the outward a'?
1Th 5:22 Abstain from all a' of evil.

appearances
Eze 10:10 And as for their a', they four had
22 Chebar, their a' and themselves:

appeared
Ge 12: 7 And the Lord a' unto Abram,
7 unto the Lord, who a' unto him.
17: 1 And when...the Lord a' to Abram,
18: 1 And the Lord a' unto him in the
26: 2 And the Lord a' unto him,
24 a' unto him the same night,
35: 1 God, that a' unto thee when thou
7 because there God a' unto him,
9 And God a' unto Jacob again,
48: 3 God Almighty a' unto me at Luz
Ex 3: 2 And the angel of the Lord a'
16 The Lord God of your fathers,...a'
4: 1 The Lord hath not a' unto thee.
5 God of Jacob, hath a' unto thee.
6: 3 And I a' unto Abraham,
14:27 strength when the morning a';
16:10 glory of the Lord a' in the cloud.
Le 9:23 and the glory of the Lord a' unto
Nu 14:10 the glory of the Lord a' in the
16:19 Lord a' unto all the congregation.
42 and the glory of the Lord a'.
20: 6 the glory of the Lord a' unto them.
De 31:15 And the Lord a' in the tabernacle
J'g 6:12 the angel of the Lord a' unto him,
13: 3 a' unto the woman, and said unto
10 the man hath a' unto me,
1Sa 3:21 the Lord a' again in Shiloh:
2Sa 22:16 And the channels of the sea a',
1Ki 3: 5 In Gibeon the Lord a' to Solomon
9: 2 the Lord a' to Solomon the second
2 as he had a' unto him at Gibeon.
11: 9 Lord God of Israel, which had a'
2Ki 2:11 behold, there a' a chariot of fire,
2Ch 3: 1 where the Lord a' unto David
7:12 the Lord a' to Solomon by night,
Ne 4:21 of the morning till the stars a'.
Jer 31: 3 The Lord hath a' of old
Eze 10: 1 there a' over them as it were a
8 And there a' in the cherubims
19:11 and she a' in her height
Da 1:15 countenances a' fairer and fatter
8: 1 a' unto me,... after that which a'
M't 1:20 behold, the angel of the Lord a'
2: 7 what time the star a'.
13:26 then a' the tares also.
17: 3 a' unto them Moses and Elias
27:53 into the holy city, and a' unto
M'r 9: 4 a' unto them Elias with Moses:
16: 9 he a' first to Mary Magdalene,
12 a' in another form unto two of
14 Afterward he a' unto the eleven
Lu 1:11 there a' unto him an angel
9: 8 of some, that Elias had a';
31 Who a' in glory, and spake of his
22:43 And there a' an angel unto him
24:34 and hath a' to Simon.
Ac 2: 3 there a' unto them cloven tongues
7: 2 God of glory a' unto our father
30 there a' to him in the wilderness.
35 angel which a' to him in the bush.
9:17 Jesus, that a' unto thee in the way
16: 9 a vision a' to Paul in the night;
26:16 I a' unto thee for this purpose,
27:20 nor stars in many days a',
Tit 2:11 salvation hath a' to all men,
3: 4 of God our Saviour toward man a',
Heb 9:26 hath he a' to put away sin by
Re 12: 1 a' a great wonder in heaven,
3 a' another wonder in heaven;

appeareth
Le 13:14 when raw flesh a' in him,
43 a' in the skin of the flesh;
De 2:30 into thy hands, as a' this day.
Ps 84: 7 every one of them in Zion a'
Pr 27:25 The hay a', and the tender grass
Jer 6: 1 evil a' out of the north,
Mal 3: 2 who shall stand when he a'?
M't 2:13 angel of the Lord a' to Joseph in
19 a' in a dream to Joseph in Egypt,
Jas 4:14 a vapour, that a' for a little time,

appearing
1Ti 6:14 the a' of our Lord Jesus Christ:
2Ti 1:10 the a' of our Saviour Jesus Christ,
4: 1 at his a' and his kingdom;
8 them also that love his a'.

Tit 2:13 the glorious *a'* of the great God
1Pe 1: 7 glory at the *a'* of Jesus Christ:

appease See also APPEASED; APPEASETH.
Ge 32:20 will *a'* him with the present

appeased
Es 2: 1 wrath of king Ahasuerus was *a'*,
Ac 19:35 the townclerk had *a'* the people,

appeaseth
Pr 15:18 he that is slow to anger *a'* strife.

appertain See also APPERTAINED; APPERTAINETH; PURTENANCE.
Nu 16:30 with all that *a'* unto them,
Jer 10: 7 for to thee doth it *a'*:

appertained
Nu 16:32 all the men that *a'* unto Korah,
33 they, and all that *a'* to them,
Ne 2: 8 palace which *a'* to the house,

appertaineth
Le 6: 5 it unto him to whom it *a'*,
2Ch 26:18 It *a'* not unto thee, Uzziah

appetite
Job 38:39 or fill the *a'* of the young lions,
Pr 23: 2 if thou be a man given to *a'*.
Ec 6: 7 the *a'* is not filled.
Isa 29: 8 he is faint, and his soul hath *a'*:

Apphia (*af'-fee-ah*)
Ph'm 2 to our beloved *A'*, and Archippus

Appii (*ap'-pe-i*)
Ac 28:15 to meet us as far as *A'* forum,

Appii-forum See APPII and FORUM.

apple See also APPLES.
De 32:10 he kept him as the *a'* of his eye.
Ps 17: 8 Keep me as the *a'* of the eye,
Pr 7: 2 my law as the *a'* of thine eye.
Ca 2: 3 as the *a'* tree among the trees
8: 5 I raised thee up under the *a'* tree:
La 2:18 not the *a'* of thine eye cease.
Joe 1:12 palm tree also, and the *a'* tree,
Zec 2: 8 toucheth the *a'* of his eye.

apples
Pr 25:11 A word fitly spoken is like *a'* of
Ca 2: 5 flagons, comfort me with *a'*:
7: 8 the smell of thy nose like *a'*;

apple-tree See APPLE and TREE.

applied
Ec 7:25 I *a'* mine heart to know, and
8: 9 and *a'* my heart unto every work
16 I *a'* mine heart to know wisdom,

apply See also APPLIED.
Ps 90:12 may *a'* our hearts unto wisdom.
Pr 2: 2 *a'* thine heart to understanding;
22:17 *a'* thine heart unto my
23:12 *A'* thine heart unto instruction,

appoint See also APPOINTED; APPOINTETH; APPOINTING; DISAPPOINT.
Ge 30:28 *A'* me thy wages, and I will give
41:34 him *a'* officers over the land,
Ex 21:13 then I will *a'* thee a place,
30:16 and shalt *a'* it for the service of
Le 26:16 I will even *a'* over you terror,
Nu 1:50 thou shalt *a'* the Levites over
3:10 And thou shalt *a'* Aaron
4:19 and *a'* them every one to his
27 ye shall *a'* unto them in charge
35: 6 ye shall *a'* for the manslayer,
11 Then ye shall *a'* you cities to be
Jos 20: 2 *A'* out for you cities of refuge,
1Sa 8:11 and *a'* them for himself, for his
12 And he will *a'* him captains
2Sa 6:21 to *a'* me ruler over the people
7:10 I will *a'* a place for my people
15:15 my lord the king shall *a'*:
1Ki 5: 6 all that thou shalt *a'*:
9 the place that thou shalt *a'* me,
1Ch 15:16 the Levites to *a'* their brethren
Ne 7: 3 *a'* watches of the inhabitants
Es 2: 3 And let the king *a'* officers
Job 14:13 thou wouldst *a'* me a set time,
Isa 26: 1 salvation will God *a'* for walls
61: 3 To *a'* unto them that mourn in
Jer 15: 3 I will *a'* over them four kinds,
49:19 that I may *a'* over her?
19 who will *a'* me the time?
50:44 man, that I may *a'* over her?
44 and who will *a'* me the time?
51:27 *a'* a captain against her;
Eze 21:19 son of man, *a'* thee two ways,
20 *A'* a way, that the sword may
22 to *a'* captains, and to open the
22 to *a'* battering rams against the
45: 6 ye shall *a'* the possession of the
Ho 1:11 and *a'* themselves one head,
M't 24:51 and *a'* him his portion with
Lu 12:46 and will *a'* him his portion with
22:29 I *a'* unto you a kingdom, as my
Ac 6: 3 we may *a'* over this business.

appointed See also DISAPPOINTED.
Ge 4:25 said she, hath *a'* me another seed
18:14 At the time *a'* I will return
24:14 hast *a'* for thy servant Isaac;
44 woman whom the Lord hath *a'*
Ex 9: 5 And the Lord *a'* a set time,
23:15 the time *a'* of the month Abib;
Nu 9: 2 keep the passover at his *a'* season.
3 ye shall keep it in his *a'* season:
7 in his *a'* season among the children
13 of the Lord in his *a'* season,
Jos 8:14 at a time *a'*, before the plain;
20: 7 And they *a'* Kedesh in Galilee
9 These were the cities *a'* for all
J'g 18:11 men *a'* with weapons of war.
16 the six hundred men *a'*
17 men that were *a'* with weapons
20:38 there was an *a'* sign between
1Sa 13: 8 set time that Samuel had *a'*:
11 camest not within the days *a'*,
19:20 Samuel standing as *a'* over
20:35 field at the time *a'* with David,
21: 2 I have *a'* my servants to such
25:30 and shall have *a'* thee ruler over
29: 4 his place which thou hast *a'* him,
2Sa 17:14 Lord had *a'* to defeat the good
20: 5 the set time which he had *a'* him,
24:15 the morning even to the time *a'*:
1Ki 1:35 I have *a'* him to be ruler
11:18 *a'* him victuals, and gave him
12:12 as the king had *a'*, saying,
20:42 whom I *a'* to utter destruction,
2Ki 7:17 king *a'* the lord on whose hand
8: 6 king *a'* unto her a certain officer,
10:24 Jehu *a'* fourscore men without,
11:18 And the priest *a'* officers over the
18:14 the king of Assyria *a'* unto
1Ch 6:48 Levites were *a'* unto all manner
49 and were *a'* for all the work
9:29 were *a'* to oversee the vessels,
15:17 So the Levites *a'* Heman
19 And Ethan, were *a'* to sound
16: 4 And he *a'* certain of the Levites
2Ch 8:14 And he *a'*, according to the order
20:21 he *a'* singers unto the Lord,
23:18 Jehoiada *a'* the officers of the
31: 2 And Hezekiah *a'* the courses
3 He *a'* also the king's portion
33: 8 which I have *a'* for your fathers;
34:22 king had *a'*, went to Huldah
Ezr 3: 8 and *a'* the Levites, from twenty
8:20 David and the princes had *a'*
10:14 come at *a'* times, and with them
Ne 5:14 I was *a'* to be their governor
6: 7 thou hast also *a'* prophets to
7: 1 singers and the Levites were *a'*,
9:17 in their rebellion *a'* a captain
10:34 at times *a'* year by year
12:31 and *a'* two great companies
44 were some *a'* over the chambers
13:30 and *a'* the wards of the priests
31 for the wood offering, at times *a'*,
Es 1: 8 king had *a'* to all the officers
2:15 the keeper of the women, *a'*.
4: 5 whom he had *a'* to attend
9:27 and according to their *a'* time
31 days of Purim in their times *a'*,
Job 7: 1 *a'* time to man upon the earth?
3 wearisome nights are *a'* to me.
14: 5 thou hast *a'* his bounds that he
14 days of my *a'* time will I wait,
20:29 the heritage *a'* unto him by God.
23:14 the thing that is *a'* for me:
30:23 the house *a'* for all living.
Ps 44:11 given us like sheep *a'* for meat;
78: 5 *a'* a law in Israel, which he
79:11 preserve thou those that are *a'*
81: 3 in the new moon, in the time *a'*,
102:20 loose those that are *a'* to death;
104:19 He *a'* the moon for seasons:
Pr 7:20 will come home at the day *a'*.
8:29 when he *a'* the foundations of
31: 8 all such as are *a'* to destruction.
Isa 1:14 new moons and your *a'* feasts
14:31 shall be alone in his *a'* times.
28:25 wheat and the *a'* barley
44: 7 since I *a'* the ancient people?
Jer 5:24 reserveth unto us the *a'* weeks
8: 7 the stork...knoweth her *a'* times;
33:25 if I have not *a'* the ordinances
46:17 he hath passed the time *a'*.
47: 7 there hath he *a'* it.
Eze 4: 6 have *a'* thee each day for a year.
36: 5 have *a'* my land into their
43:21 he shall burn it in the *a'* place
Da 1: 5 And the king *a'* them a daily
10 who hath *a'* your meat, and
8:19 at the time *a'* the end shall be.
10: 1 but the time *a'* was long:
11:27 the end shall be at the time *a'*.
29 At the time *a'* he shall return,
35 it is yet for a time *a'*.
Mic 6: 9 the rod, and who hath *a'* it.
Hab 2: 3 the vision is yet for an *a'* time,
M't 26:19 disciples did as Jesus had *a'* them;
27:10 as the Lord *a'* me.
28:16 where Jesus had *a'* them.
Lu 3:13 than that which is *a'* you.
10: 1 the Lord *a'* other seventy also,
22:29 as my Father hath *a'* unto me;
Ac 1:23 *a'* two, Joseph called Barsabas,
7:44 as he had *a'*, speaking unto Moses,
17:26 determined the times before *a'*,
31 Because he hath *a'* a day,
20:13 for so he had *a'*, minding himself
22:10 which are *a'* for thee to do.
28:23 And when they had *a'* him a day,
1Co 4: 9 as it were *a'* to death;
Ga 4: 2 until the time *a'* of the father.
1Th 3: 3 know that we are *a'* thereunto.
5: 9 God hath not *a'* us to wrath,
2Ti 1:11 Whereunto I am *a'* a preacher,
Tit 1: 5 as I had *a'* thee:
Heb 1: 2 he hath *a'* heir of all things,
3: 2 faithful to him that *a'* him,
9:27 as it is *a'* unto men once to die,
1Pe 2: 8 whereunto also they were *a'*.

appointeth See also DISAPPOINTETH.
Da 5:21 he *a'* over it whomsoever he will.

appointment
Nu 4:27 At the *a'* of Aaron and his sons
2Sa 13:32 by the *a'* of Absalom this hath
Ezr 6: 9 according to the *a'* of the priests
Job 2:11 for they had made an *a'* together

apprehend See also APPREHENDED.
2Co 11:32 desirous to *a'* me:
Ph'p 3:12 if that I may *a'* that for which

apprehended
Ac 12: 4 when he had *a'* him,
Ph'p 3:12 for which also I am *a'* of Christ
13 I count not myself to have *a'*:

approach See also APPROACHED; APPROACHETH; APPROACHING.
Le 18: 6 None of you shall *a'* to any that
14 thou shalt not *a'* to his wife:
19 thou shalt not *a'* unto a woman
20:16 if a woman *a'* unto any beast,
21:17 let him not *a'* to offer the bread
18 hath a blemish, he shall not *a'*:
Nu 4:19 they *a'* unto the most holy things:
De 20: 2 that the priest shall *a'* and speak
3 Israel, ye *a'* this day unto battle
31:14 thy days *a'* that thou must die:
Jos 8: 5 people that are with me will *a'*
Job 40:19 make his sword to *a'* unto him.
Ps 65: 4 thou choosest and causest to *a'*
Jer 30:21 and he shall *a'* unto me:
21 engaged his heart to *a'* unto me?
Eze 42:13 the priests that *a'* unto the Lord
14 shall *a'* to those things which are
43:19 the Levites.... which *a'* unto me,
1Ti 6:16 in the light which no man can *a'*

approached
2Sa 11:20 Wherefore *a'* ye so nigh unto the
2Ki 16:12 and the king *a'* to the altar,

approacheth
Lu 12:33 where no thief *a'*, neither moth

approaching
Isa 58: 2 they take delight in *a'* to God.
Heb 10:25 the more, as ye see the day *a'*.

approve See also APPROVED; APPROVEST; APPROVETH; APPROVING.
Ps 49:13 their posterity *a'* their sayings.
1Co 16: 3 whomsoever ye shall *a'* by... letters
Ph'p 1:10 may *a'* things that are excellent;

approved
Ac 2:22 a man *a'* of God among you by
Ro 14:18 acceptable to God, and *a'* of men.
16:10 Salute Apelles *a'* in Christ.
1Co 11:19 which... *a'* may be made manifest
2Co 7:11 ye have *a'* yourselves to be clear
10:18 he that commendeth himself is *a'*,
13: 7 not that we should appear *a'*,
2Ti 2:15 Study to shew thyself *a'* unto God,

approvest
Ro 2:18 *a'* the things that are more

approveth
La 3:36 in his cause, the Lord *a'* not.

approving
2Co 6: 4 *a'* ourselves as the ministers of

appurtenance See PURTENANCE.

aprons
Ge 3: 7 together, and made themselves *a'*.
Ac 19:12 handkerchiefs or *a'*, and the

apt
2Ki 24:16 all that were strong and *a'* for war.
1Ch 7:40 that were *a'* to the war and to
1Ti 3: 2 given to hospitality, *a'* to teach;
2Ti 2:24 unto all men, *a'* to teach, patient,

Aquila (*ac'-quil-ah*)
Ac 18: 2 a certain Jew named *A'*, born in
18 with him Priscilla and *A'*;
26 when *A'* and Priscilla had heard,
Ro 16: 3 Greet Priscilla and *A'* my helpers
1Co 16:19 *A'* and Priscilla salute you much
2Ti 4:19 Salute Prisca and *A'*,

Ar (*ar*)
Nu 21:15 goeth down to the dwelling of *A'*,
28 it hath consumed *A'* of Moab,
De 2: 9 I have given *A'* unto the children
18 Thou art to pass over through *A'*,
29 the Moabites which dwell in *A'*,
Isa 15: 1 in the night *A'* of Moab is laid

Ara (*a'-rah*)
1Ch 7:38 Jephunneh, and Pispah, and *A'*.

Arab (*a'-rab*) See also ARBITE.
Jos 15:52 *A'*, and Dumah, and Eshean,

Arabah (*ar'-ab-ah*) See also BETH-ARABAH.
Jos 18:18 over against *A'* northward,
18 and went down unto *A'*:

Arabia (*a-ra'-be-ah*) See also ARABIAN.
1Ki 10:15 of all the kings of *A'*, and of the
2Ch 9:14 all the kings of *A'* and governors
Isa 21:13 The burden upon *A'*. In the forest
13 In the forest in *A'* shall ye lodge,
Jer 25:24 And all the kings of *A'*, and all
Eze 27:21 *A'*, and all the princes of Kedar,
Ga 1:17 I went into *A'*, and returned
4:25 this Agar is mount Sinai in *A'*,

Arabian (*a-ra'-be-un*) See also ARABIANS.
Ne 2:19 and Geshem the *A*, heard it, they
6: 1 Geshem the *A*, and the rest of
Isa 13:20 neither shall the *A* pitch tent
Jer 3: 2 thou sat for them, as the *A* in the

Arabians (*a-ra'-be-uns*)
2Ch 17:11 and the *A* brought him flocks,
21:16 of the Philistines, and of the *A*,
22: 1 band of men that came with the *A*,
26: 7 the *A* that dwelt in Gur-baal,
Ne 4: 7 and the *A*, and the Ammonites,
Ac 2:11 Cretes and *A*, we do hear them

Arad (*a'-rad*)
Nu 21: 1 And when king *A* the Canaanite,
33:40 *A* the Canaanite, which dwelt in
Jos 12:14 Hormah, one; the king of *A*, one;
J'g 1:16 which lieth in the south of *A*;
1Ch 8:15 And Zebadiah, and *A*, and Ader,

Arah (*a'-rah*)
1Ch 7:39 the sons of Ulla; *A*, and Haniel,
Ezr 2: 5 *A*, seven hundred seventy and five.
Ne 6:18 in law of Shechaniah the son of *A*;
7:10 the children of *A*, six hundred

Aram (*a'-ram*) See also ARAMITESS; ARAM-NAHARAIM; ARAM-ZOBAH; BETH-ARAM; PADAN-ARAM; SYRIA.
Ge 10:22 and Arphaxad, and Lud, and *A*.
23 the children of *A*: Uz, and Hul,
22:21 and Kemuel the father of *A*,
Nu 23: 7 of Moab that brought me from *A*,
1Ch 1:17 Arphaxad, and Lud, and *A*, and Uz,
2:23 he took Geshur, and *A*, with the
7:34 Rohgah, Jehubbah, and *A*.
M't 1: 3 Esrom begat *A*;
4 *A* begat Aminadab;
Lu 3:33 which was the son of *A*,

Aramitess (*a'-ram-i-tes*) See also SYRIAN.
1Ch 7:14 his concubine the *A* bare Machir

Aram-naharaim (*a''-ram-na-ha-ra'-im*) See also MESOPOTAMIA.
Ps 60:*title* when he strove with *A*

Aram-zobah (*a''-ram-zo'-bah*)
Ps 60:*title* and with *A*,

Aran (*a'-ran*) See also BETH-ARAN.
Ge 36:28 of Dishan are these; Uz and *A*.
1Ch 1:42 The sons of Dishan; Uz and *A*.

Ararat (*ar'-ar-at*) See also ARMENIA.
Ge 8: 4 upon the mountains of *A*.
Jer 51:27 against her the kingdoms of *A*,

Araunah (*a-raw'-nah*) See also ORNAN.
2Sa 24:16 threshingplace of *A* the Jebusite.
18 threshingfloor of *A* the Jebusite.
20 *A* looked, and saw the king and
20 *A* went out, and bowed himself
21 *A* said, Wherefore is my lord
22 *A* said unto David, Let my lord
23 All these things did *A*, as a king,
23 *A* said unto the king, The Lord
24 the king said unto *A*, Nay, but I

Arba (*ar'-bah*) See also ARBAH; ARBATHITE; ARBITE; KIRJATH-ARBA.
Jos 14:15 which *A* was a great man among
15:13 even the city of *A* the father of
21:11 they gave them the city of *A*

Arbah (*ar'-bah*) See also ARBA.
Ge 35:27 the city of *A*, which is Hebron,

Arbathite (*ar'-bath-ite*)
2Sa 23:31 Abi-albon the *A*, Azmaveth the
1Ch 11:32 brooks of Gaash, Abiel the *A*,

Arbel See BETH-ARBEL.

Arbite (*ar'-bite*)
2Sa 23:35 the Carmelite, Paarai the *A*,

arch See ARCHANGEL; ARCHES.

archangel
1Th 4:16 with the voice of the *a*,
Jude 9 Michael the *a*, when contending

Archelaus (*ar-ke-la'-us*)
M't 2:22 heard that *A* did reign in Judæa

archer See also ARCHERS.
Ge 21:20 he grew...and became an *a*.
Jer 51: 3 let the *a* bend his bow,

archers
Ge 49:23 *a* have sorely grieved him,
J'g 5:11 are delivered from the noise of *a*
1Sa 31: 3 the *a* hit him; and he
3 sore wounded of the *a*.
1Ch 8:40 mighty men of valour, *a*,
10: 3 the *a* hit him,
3 he was wounded of the *a*.
2Ch 35:23 the *a* shot at king Josiah;
Job 16:13 His *a* compass me round about,
Isa 21:17 the residue of the number of *a*,
22: 3 they are bound by the *a*:
Jer 50:29 Call together the *a* against

arches
Eze 40:16 about, and likewise to the *a*:
21 posts thereof and the *a* thereof
22 their windows, and their *a*,
24 and the *a* thereof according to
25 windows in it and in the *a* thereof
26 the *a* thereof were before them:
29 and the posts thereof, and the *a*
29 the *a* thereof round about: it was
30 *a* round about were five and twenty
31 *a* thereof were toward the outer
33 *a* thereof, were according to these
33 windows therein and in the *a*
34 the *a* thereof were toward the
36 and the *a* thereof, and the windows

Archevites (*ar'-ke-vites*)
Ezr 4: 9 the Apharsites, the *A*, the

Archi (*ar'-kee*) See also ARCHITE.
Jos 16: 2 along unto the borders of *A*

Archippus (*ar-kip'-pus*)
Col 4:17 say to *A*, Take heed to the
Ph'm 2 *A* our fellowsoldier,

Archite (*ar'-kite*) See also ARCHI.
2Sa 15:32 Hushai the *A* came to meet him
16:16 Hushai the *A*, David's friend,
17: 5 Call now Hushai the *A* also,
14 counsel of Hushai the *A* is better
1Ch 27:33 Hushai the *A* was the king's

Arcturus (*ark-tu'-rus*)
Job 9: 9 maketh *A*, Orion, and Pleiades,
38:32 thou guide *A* with his sons?

Ard (*ard*) See also ARDITES.
Ge 46:21 Muppim, and Huppim, and *A*.
Nu 26:40 sons of Bela were *A* and Naaman:
40 of *A*, the family of the Ardites:

Ardites (*ar'-dites*)
Nu 26:40 of Ard, the family of the *A*:

Ardon (*ar'-don*)
1Ch 2:18 Jesher, and Shobab, and *A*.

Areli (*a-re'-li*) See also ARELITES.
Ge 46:16 Ezbon, Eri, and Arodi, and *A*.
Nu 26:17 of *A*, the family of the Arelites.

Arelites (*a-re'-lites*) See also ARELI.
Nu 26:17 of Areli, the family of the *A*.

Areopagite (*a-re-op'-a-jite*)
Ac 17:34 which was Dionysius, the *A*,

Areopagus (*a-re-op'-a-gus*) See also AREOPAGITE; MARS'-HILL.
Ac 17:19 took him, and brought him unto *A*,

Aretas (*ar'-e-tas*)
2Co 11:32 under *A* the king kept the city

Argob (*ar'-gob*)
De 3: 4 all the region of *A*, the kingdom
13 the region of *A*, with all Bashan,
14 Manasseh took all the country of *A*
1Ki 4:13 him also pertained the region of *A*,
2Ki 15:25 with *A* and Arieh, and with him

arguing
Job 6:25 what doth your *a* reprove?

arguments
Job 23: 4 fill my mouth with *a*.

Aridai (*a-rid'-a-i*)
Es 9: 9 Parmashta, and Arisai, and *A*,

Aridatha (*a-rid'-a-thah*)
Es 9: 8 Poratha, and Adalia, and *A*,

Arieh (*a-ri'-eh*)
2Ki 15:25 with Argob and *A*, and with him

Ariel (*a'-re-el*) See also JERUSALEM.
Ezr 8:16 Then sent I for Eliezer, for *A*, for
Isa 29: 1 Woe to *A*, to *A*, the city where
2 Yet I will distress *A*, and there
2 it shall be unto me as *A*.
7 the nations that fight against *A*,

aright
Ps 50:23 that ordereth his conversation *a*
78: 8 that set not their heart *a*,
Pr 15: 2 of the wise useth knowledge *a*:
23:31 the cup, when it moveth itself *a*.
Jer 8: 6 heard, but they spake not *a*:

Arim See KIRJATH-ARIM.

Arimathæa (*ar-im-ath-e'-ah*)
M't 27:57 there came a rich man of *A*,
M'r 15:43 Joseph of *A*, an honourable
Lu 23:51 *A*, a city of the Jews:
Joh 19:38 Joseph of *A*, being a disciple of

Arioch (*a'-re-ok*)
Ge 14: 1 *A* king of Ellasar, Chedorlaomer
9 and *A* king of Ellasar; four kings
Da 2:14 *A* the captain of the king's guard,
15 He answered and said to *A*
15 *A* made the thing known to Daniel.
24 Therefore Daniel went in unto *A*,
25 Then *A* brought in Daniel before

Arisai (*a-ris'-a-i*)
Es 9: 9 Parmashta, and *A*, and Aridai,

arise See also ARISETH; ARISING; AROSE.
Ge 13:17 *A*, walk through the land
19:15 *A*, take thy wife, and thy two
21:18 *A*, lift up the lad, and hold him in
27:19 *a*, I pray thee, sit and eat of my
31 Let my father *a*, and eat of his
43 *a*, flee thou to Laban my brother
28: 2 *A*, go to Padan-aram, to the home
31:13 *a*, get thee out from this land,
35: 1 *A*, go up to Beth-el, and dwell
3 And let us *a*, and go up to Bethel;
41:30 And there shall *a* after them
43: 8 with me, and we will *a* and go;
13 Take also your brother, and *a*,
De 9:12 *A*, get thee down quickly from
10:11 *A*, take thy journey before the
13: 1 If there *a* among you a prophet,
17: 8 there *a* a matter too hard for thee
8 then shalt thou *a*, and get thee
Jos 1: 2 therefore *a*, go over this Jordan,
8: 1 and *a*, go up to Ai: see, I have
J'g 5:12 *a*, Barak, and lead thy captivity
7: 9 *A*, get thee down unto the host;
15 *A*; for the Lord hath delivered
18: 9 *A*, that we may go up against
20:40 when the flame began to *a* up
1Sa 9: 3 and *a*, go seek the asses.
16:12 *A*, anoint him: for this is he.
23: 4 *A*, go down to Keilah;
2Sa 2:14 Let the young men now *a*, and
14 And Joab said, Let them *a*.
3:21 Abner said unto David, I will *a*
11:20 if so be that the king's wrath *a*,
13:15 Ammon said unto her, *A*, be
15:14 *A*, and let us flee;
17: 1 I will *a* and pursue after David
21 *A*, and pass quickly over the
19: 7 Now therefore *a*, go forth,
22:39 them, that they could not *a*:
1Ki 3:12 after thee shall any *a* like thee.
14: 2 *A*, I pray thee, and disguise
12 *A* thou therefore, get thee to thine
17: 9 *A*, get thee to Zarephath,
19: 5 said unto him, *A* and eat.
7 *A* and eat; because the journey is
21: 7 *a*, and eat bread, and let thine
15 *A*, take possession of the
18 *A*, go down to meet Ahab king of
2Ki 1: 3 *A*, go up to meet the messengers
8: 1 *A*, and go thou and thine
9: 2 *a* up from among his brethren
1Ch 22:16 *A* therefore, and be doing,
19 *a* therefore, and build ye the
2Ch 6:41 Now therefore *a*, O Lord God,
Ezr 10: 4 *A*; for this matter belongeth unto
Ne 2:20 we his servants will *a* and build:
Es 1:18 *a* too much contempt and wrath.
4:14 and deliverance *a* to the Jews
Job 7: 4 When shall I *a*, and the night
25: 3 upon whom doth not his light *a*?
Ps 3: 7 *A*, O Lord; save me, O my God:
7: 6 *A*, O Lord, in thine anger,
9:19 *A*, O Lord; let not man prevail:
10:12 *A*, O Lord; O God, lift up thine
12: 5 now will I *a*, saith the Lord;
17:13 *A*, O Lord, disappoint him,
44:23 why sleepest thou, O Lord? *a*,
26 *A* for our help, and redeem us
68: 1 Let God *a*, let his enemies be
74:22 *A*, O God, plead thine own cause:
78: 6 who should *a* and declare them to
82: 8 *A*, O God, judge the earth:
88:10 shall the dead *a* and praise thee?
89: 9 when the waves thereof *a*, thou
102:13 Thou shalt *a*, and have mercy
109:28 they *a*, let them be ashamed;
132: 8 *A*, O Lord, into thy rest;
Pr 6: 9 when wilt thou *a* out of thy sleep?
31:28 children *a* up, and call her
Ca 2:13 *A*, my love, my fair one, and
Isa 21: 5 *a*, ye princes, and anoint the
23:12 *a*, pass over to Chittim;
26:19 with my dead body shall they *a*.
31: 2 but will *a* against the house of
49: 7 Kings shall see and *a*,
52: 2 *a*, and sit down, O Jerusalem:
60: 1 *A*, shine; for thy light is come,
2 but the Lord shall *a* upon thee,
Jer 1:17 gird up thy loins, and *a*,
2:27 they will say, *A*, and save us.
28 let them *a*, if they can save thee
6: 4 *a*, and let us go up at noon.
5 *A*, and let us go by night,
8: 4 Shall they fall, and not *a*?
13: 4 and *a*, go to Euphrates, and hide
6 *A*, go to Euphrates, and take the
18: 2 *A*, and go down to the potter's
31: 6 *A* ye, and let us go up to Zion
46:16 *A*, and let us go again to our own
49:28 *A* ye, go up to Kedar,
31 *A*, get you up unto the wealthy
La 2:19 *A*, cry out in the night:
Eze 3:22 *A*, go forth into the plain,
Da 2:39 And after thee shall *a* another
7: 5 *A*, devour much flesh.
17 which shall *a* out of the earth.
24 ten kings that shall arise:
Ho 10:14 a tumult *a* among thy people
Am 7: 2, 5 by whom shall Jacob *a*? for
Ob 1 *A* ye, and let us rise up against
Jon 1: 2 *A*, go to Nineveh, that great city,
6 *a*, call upon thy God,
3: 2 *A*, go unto Nineveh,
4: 8 when the sun did *a*,
Mic 2:10 *A* ye, and depart, for this is not
4:13 *A* and thresh, O daughter of
6: 1 *A*, contend thou before the
7: 8 enemy: when I fall, I shall *a*;
Hab 2:19 *A*, it shall teach! Behold, it is
Mal 4: 2 shall the Sun of righteousness *a*
M't 2:13 *A*, and take the young child
20 *A*, and take the young child
9: 5 or to say, *A*, and walk?
6 *A*, take up thy bed, and go unto
17: 7 said, *A*, and be not afraid.
24:24 For there shall *a* false Christs,
M'r 2: 9 or to say, *A*, and take up thy bed,
11 unto thee, *A*, and take up thy bed,
5:41 Damsel, I say unto thee, *a*.
Lu 5:24 I say unto thee, *A*, and take up thy
7:14 Young man, I say unto thee, *A*.
8:54 called, saying, Maid, *a*.
15:18 I will *a* and go to my father,
17:19 he said unto him, *A*, go thy way:
24:38 why do thoughts *a* in your hearts?
Joh 14:31 even so I do. *A*, let us go hence.
Ac 8:26 *A*, and go toward the south
9: 6 *A*, and go into the city, and it
11 *A*, and go into the street which
34 *a*, and make thy bed. And he
40 him to the body said, Tabitha, *a*.
10:20 *A* therefore, and get thee down,

Ac 11: 7 *A'*, Peter; slay and eat.
12: 7 raised him up, saying, *A'* up
20:30 of your own selves, shall men *a'*,
22:10 me, *A'*, and go unto Damascus;
16 *a'*, and be baptized, and wash away
Eph 5:14 *a'* from the dead, and Christ shall
2Pe 1:19 the day star *a'* in your hearts:

ariseth
1Ki 18:44 *a'* a little cloud out of the sea,
Ps 104:22 sun *a'*, they gather themselves
112: 4 Unto the upright there *a'* light
Ec 1: 5 The sun also *a'*, and the sun
Isa 2:19, 21 when he *a'* to shake terribly
Nah 3:17 when the sun *a'* they flee away
M't 13:21 tribulation or persecution *a'*
M'r 4:17 affliction or persecution *a'* for
Joh 7:52 for out of Galilee *a'* no prophet.
He 7:15 there *a'* another priest,

arising
Es 7: 7 the king *a'* from the banquet of

Aristarchus (*ar-is-tar'-cus*)
Ac 19:29 having caught Gaius and *A'*,
20: 4 Thessalonians, *A'* and Secundus;
27: 2 *A'*, a Macedonian of Thessalonica,
Col 4:10 *A'* my fellowprisoner saluteth you,
Ph'm 24 Marcus, *A'*, Demas,

Aristobulus' (*a-ris-to-bu'-lus*)
Ro 16:10 them which are of *A'* household.

ark
Ge 6:14 Make thee an *a'* of gopher wood;
14 rooms shalt thou make in the *a'*,
15 the length of the *a'* shall be three
16 window shalt thou make to the *a'*,
16 the door of the *a'* shalt thou set
18 thou shalt come into the *a'*,
19 shalt thou bring into the *a'*,
7: 1 thou and all thy house into the *a'*;
7 sons' wives with him, into the *a'*,
9 and two unto Noah into the *a'*,
13 of his sons with them, into the *a'*;
15 went in unto Noah into the *a'*,
17 increased, and bare up the *a'*,
18 the *a'* went upon the face of the
23 that were with him in the *a'*.
8: 1 cattle that was with him in the *a'*:
4 the *a'* rested in the seventh month,
6 Noah opened the window of the *a'*
9 she returned unto him into the *a'*,
9 pulled her in unto him into the *a'*.
10 sent forth the dove out of the *a'*;
13 removed the covering of the *a'*,
16 Go forth of the *a'*,
19 went forth out of the *a'*.
9:10 from all that go out of the *a'*,
18 that went forth of the *a'*,
Ex 2: 3 she took for him an *a'* of bulrushes,
5 she saw the *a'* among the flags,
25:10 shall make an *a'* of shittim wood:
14 into the rings by the sides of the *a'*,
14 the *a'* may be borne with them.
15 shall be in the rings of the *a'*:
16 shalt put into the *a'* the testimony
21 the mercy seat above upon the *a'*;
21 and in the *a'* thou shalt put
22 are upon the *a'* of the testimony
26:33 within the vail the *a'* of the
34 upon the *a'* of the testimony in the
30: 6 that is by the *a'* of the testimony,
26 therewith, and the *a'* of the
31: 7 the *a'* of the testimony, and the
35:12 The *a'*, and the staves thereof,
37: 1 Bezaleel made the *a'* of shittim
5 the sides of the *a'*, to bear the *a'*.
39:35 The *a'* of the testimony, and the
40: 3 therein the *a'* of the testimony,
3 and cover the *a'* with the vail.
5 before the *a'* of the testimony,
20 put the testimony into the *a'*,
20 and set the staves on the *a'*,
20 the mercy seat above upon the *a'*:
21 brought the *a'* into the tabernacle,
21 covered the *a'* of the testimony;
Le 16: 2 which is upon the *a'*;
Nu 3:31 the charge shall be the *a'*, and the
4: 5 cover the *a'* of testimony with it:
7:89 mercy seat that was upon the *a'*
10:33 and the *a'* of the covenant of the
35 when the *a'* set forward,
14:44 nevertheless the *a'* of the covenant
De 10:1 make thee an *a'* of wood.
2 thou shalt put them in the *a'*.
3 made an *a'* of shittim wood,
5 put the tables into the *a'* which
8 to bear the *a'* of the covenant
31: 9 the sons of Levi which bear the *a'*
25 which bare the *a'* of the covenant
26 the side of the *a'* of the covenant
Jos 3: 3 When ye see the *a'* of the covenant
6 Take up the *a'* of the covenant,
6 they took up the *a'* of the covenant,
8 that bear the *a'* of the covenant,
11 Behold the *a'* of the covenant
13 that bear the *a'* of the Lord,
14 the priests bearing the *a'*
15 as they that bare the *a'* were come
15 the priests that bare the *a'* were
17 the priests that bare the *a'* of the
4: 5 Pass over before the *a'* of the Lord
7 before the *a'* of the covenant
9 which bare the *a'* of the covenant
10 the priests which bare the *a'* stood
11 that the *a'* of the Lord passed over,
16 command the priests that bear the *a'*

Jos 4:18 when the priests that bare the *a'*
6: 4 priests shall bear before the *a'*
6 Take up the *a'* of the covenant,
6, 7 before the *a'* of the Lord.
8 and the *a'* of the covenant
9 the rereward came after the *a'*,
11 the *a'* of the Lord compassed the
12 the priests took up the *a'* of the
13 *a'* of the Lord went on continually,
13 but the rereward came after the *a'*
7: 6 before the *a'* of the Lord
8:33 judges, stood on this side the *a'*
33 which bare the *a'* of the covenant
Ju 20:27 the *a'* of the covenant of God was
1Sa 3: 3 where the *a'* of God was,
4: 3 Let us fetch the *a'* of the
4 bring from thence the *a'* of
4 there with the *a'* of the covenant
5 when the *a'* of the covenant
6 that the *a'* of the Lord was come
11 And the *a'* of God was taken;
13 his heart trembled for the *a'* of God.
17 and the *a'* of God is taken.
18 he made mention of the *a'* of God,
19 that the *a'* of God was taken,
21 because the *a'* of God was taken,
22 for the *a'* of God is taken.
5: 1 the Philistines took the *a'* of God,
2 When the Philistines took the *a'*
3, 4 before the *a'* of the Lord.
7 The *a'* of the God of Israel
8 What shall we do with the *a'* of
8 Let the *a'* of the God of Israel be
8 And they carried the *a'* of the God
10 Therefore they sent the *a'* of God
10 as the *a'* of God came to Ekron,
10 They have brought about the *a'* of
11 Send away the *a'* of the God of
6: 1 *a'* of the Lord was in the country
2 What shall we do to the *a'* of
3 If ye send away the *a'* of
8 take the *a'* of the Lord,
11 they laid the *a'* of the Lord upon
13 saw the *a'*, and rejoiced to see it.
15 the Levites took down the *a'* of
18 whereon they set down the *a'* of
19 because they had looked into the *a'*
21 Philistines have brought again the *a'*
7: 1 fetched up the *a'* of the Lord,
1 Eleazar his son to keep the *a'* of
2 the *a'* abode in Kirjath-jearim,
14:18 Bring hither the *a'* of God.
18 For the *a'* of God was at that time
2Sa 6: 2 bring up from thence the *a'* of God,
3 they set the *a'* of God upon a new
4 accompanying the *a'* of God:
4 and Ahio went before the *a'*.
6 put forth his hand to the *a'* of God,
7 there he died by the *a'* of God.
9 How shall the *a'* of the Lord
10 David would not remove the *a'* of
11 the *a'* of the Lord continued
12 because of the *a'* of God.
12 went and brought up the *a'* of
13 when they that bare the *a'* of
15 brought up the *a'* of the Lord
16 as the *a'* of the Lord came into the
17 they brought in the *a'* of the Lord,
7: 2 but the *a'* of God dwelleth within
11:11 The *a'*, and Israel, and Judah,
15:24 the *a'* of the covenant of God:
24 and they set down the *a'* of God;
25 Carry back the *a'* of God into the
29 carried the *a'* of God again to
1Ki 2:26 because thou barest the *a'* of
3:15 stood before the *a'* of the covenant
6:19 set there the *a'* of the covenant
8: 1 bring up the *a'* of the covenant
3 the priests took up the *a'*.
4 they brought up the *a'* of the Lord,
5 with him before the *a'*,
6 the priests brought in the *a'* of the
7 two wings over the place of the *a'*,
7 and the cherubims covered the *a'*
9 nothing in the *a'* save the two
21 I have set there a place for the *a'*,
1Ch 6:31 after that the *a'* had rest.
13: 3 let us bring again the *a'* of our God
5 bring the *a'* of God from
6 to bring up thence the *a'* of God
7 they carried the *a'* of God in a new
9 put forth his hand to hold the *a'*;
10 because he put his hand to the *a'*:
12 How shall I bring the *a'* of
13 David brought not the *a'*
14 the *a'* of God remained
15: 1 prepared a place for the *a'* of God,
2 None ought to carry the *a'* of God
2 the Lord chosen to carry the *a'* of
3, 14 to bring up the *a'* of the Lord
12 may bring up the *a'* of the Lord
15 the Levites bare the *a'* of God
23, 24 doorkeepers for the *a'*.
24 with the trumpets before the *a'* of
25 bring up the *a'* of the covenant
26 helped the Levites that bare the *a'*
27 the Levites that bare the *a'*,
28 Thus all Israel brought up the *a'*
29 the *a'* of the covenant of the Lord
16: 1 they brought the *a'* of God,
4 Levites to minister before the *a'*
6 before the *a'* of the covenant
37 he left there before the *a'* of the
37 minister before the *a'* continually,
17: 1 the *a'* of the covenant of the Lord
22:19 to bring the *a'* of the covenant

1Ch 28: 2 an house of rest for the *a'* of
18 covered the *a'* of the covenant
2Ch 1: 4 But the *a'* of God had David
5: 2 to bring up the *a'* of the covenant
4 the Levites took up the *a'*.
5 they brought up the *a'*,
6 assembled unto him before the *a'*,
7 the priests brought in the *a'*,
8 their wings over the place of the *a'*,
8 and the cherubims covered the *a'*
9 drew out the staves of the *a'*,
9 were seen from the *a'* before the
10 nothing in the *a'* save the two
6:11 in it have I put the *a'*,
41 and the *a'* of thy strength:
8:11 the *a'* of the Lord hath come.
35: 3 Put the holy *a'* in the house
Ps 132: 8 thou, and the *a'* of thy strength.
Jer 3:16 The *a'* of the covenant of the Lord:
M't 24:38 day that Noe entered into the *a'*,
Lu 17:27 Noe entered into the *a'*, and the
Heb 9: 4 censer, and the *a'* of the covenant
11: 7 prepared an *a'* to the saving of
1Pe 3:20 while the *a'* was a preparing
Re 11:19 was seen in his temple the *a'* of

Arkite (*ark'-kite*)
Ge 10:17 Hivite, and the *A'*, and the Sinite,
1Ch 1:15 and the *A'*, and the Sinite,

arm See also ARMED; ARMHOLES; ARMS.
Ex 6: 6 you with a stretched out *a'*,
15:16 by the greatness of thine *a'*
Nu 31: 3 *A'* some of yourselves unto the
De 4:34 and by a stretched out *a'*, and by
5:15 hand and by a stretched out *a'*:
7:19 and the stretched out *a'*,
9:29 and by thy stretched out *a'*.
11: 2 hand, and his stretched out *a'*,
26: 8 and with an outstretched *a'*,
33:20 teareth the *a'* with the crown of
1Sa 2:31 that I will cut off thine *a'*, and
31 the *a'* of thy father's house,
2Sa 1:10 the bracelet that was on his *a'*,
1Ki 8:42 and of thy stretched out *a'*;)
2Ki 17:36 great power and a stretched out *a'*,
2Ch 6:32 and thy stretched out *a'*;
32: 8 With him is an *a'* of flesh;
Job 26: 2 the *a'* that hath no strength?
31:22 *a'* fall from my shoulder blade,
22 mine *a'* be broken from the bone.
35: 9 by reason of the *a'* of the mighty.
38:15 and the high *a'* shall be broken.
40: 9 Hast thou an *a'* like God?
Ps 10:15 Break thou the *a'* of the wicked
44: 3 neither did their own *a'* save them:
3 but thy right hand, and thine *a'*,
77:15 with thine *a'* redeemed thy people,
89:10 thine enemies with thy strong *a'*.
13 Thou hast a mighty *a'*:
21 mine *a'* also shall strengthen him.
98: 1 *a'*, hath gotten him the victory.
136:12 and with a stretched out *a'*:)
Ca 8: 6 as a seal upon thine *a'*:
Isa 9:20 every man the flesh of his own *a'*:
17: 5 and reapeth the ears with his *a'*;
30:30 shew the lighting down of his *a'*,
33: 2 be thou their *a'* every morning,
40:10 and his *a'* shall rule for him:
11 shall gather the lambs with his *a'*,
48:14 his *a'* shall be on the Chaldeans.
51: 5 on mine *a'* shall they trust.
9 put on strength, O *a'* of the Lord;
52:10 Lord hath made bare his holy *a'*
53: 1 to whom is the *a'* of the Lord
59:16 his *a'* brought salvation unto him;
62: 8 and by the *a'* of his strength,
63: 5 own *a'* brought salvation unto me;
12 Moses with his glorious *a'*, dividing
Jer 17: 5 and maketh flesh his *a'*,
21: 5 and with a strong *a'*,
27: 5 and by my outstretched *a'*,
32:17 great power and stretched out *a'*,
21 and with a stretched out *a'*,
48:25 his *a'* is broken, saith the Lord.
Eze 4: 7 and thine *a'* shall be uncovered,
20:33 with a stretched out *a'*, and with
34 hand, and with a stretched out *a'*,
30:21 I have broken the *a'* of Pharaoh
31:17 and they that were his *a'*,
Da 11: 6 not retain the power of the *a'*;
6 neither shall he stand, nor his *a'*:
Zec 11:17 the sword shall be upon his *a'*,
17 his *a'* shall be clean dried up,
Lu 1:51 hath shewed strength with his *a'*;
Joh 12:38 to whom hath the *a'* of the Lord
Ac 13:17 with an high *a'* brought he them
1Pe 4: 1 *a'* yourselves likewise with the

Armageddon (*ar-mag-ed'-don*)
Re 16:16 in the Hebrew tongue *A'*.

armed
Ge 14:14 when...he *a'* his trained servants,
Nu 31: 5 twelve thousand *a'* for war.
32:17 we ourselves will go ready *a'*
20 if ye will go *a'* before the Lord
21 go all of you *a'* over Jordan
27 every man *a'* for war,
29 every man *a'* to battle,
30 they will not pass over with you *a'*,
32 will pass over *a'* before the Lord
De 3:18 pass over *a'* before your brethren
Jos 1:14 pass before your brethren *a'*,
4:12 Manasseh, passed over *a'* before
6: 7 that is *a'* pass on before the ark
9 the *a'* men went before the priests
13 the *a'* men went before them; but

J'g 7:11 the *a'* men that were in the host.
1Sa 17: 5 he was *a'* with a coat of mail;
38 Saul *a'* David with his armour,
38 also he *a'* him with a coat of mail.
1Ch 12: 2 They were *a'* with bows,
23 that were ready *a'* to the war,
24 ready *a'* to the war.
2Ch 17:17 *a'* men with bow and shield
28:14 the *a'* men left the captives and
Job 39:21 he goeth on to meet the *a'* men.
Ps 78: 9 The children of Ephraim, being *a'*,
Pr 6:11 and thy want as an *a'* man.
24:34 and thy want as an *a'* man.
Isa 15: 4 *a'* soldiers of Moab shall cry out
Lu 11:21 strong man *a'* keepeth his palace,

Armenia (*ar-me'-ne-ah*) See also ARARAT.
2Ki 19:37 they escaped into the land of *A'*:
Isa 37:38 they escaped into the land of *A'*:

armholes
Jer 38:12 rotten rags under thine *a'*
Eze 13:18 sew pillows to all *a'*,

armies
Ex 6:26 from...Egypt according to their *a'*.
7: 4 forth mine *a'*, and my people
12:17 your *a'* out of the land of Egypt:
51 of the land of Egypt by their *a'*.
Nu 1: 3 number them by their *a'*.
2: 3 pitch throughout their *a'*: and
9 throughout their *a'*. These shall
10 of Reuben according to their *a'*:
16 throughout their *a'*. And they
18 of Ephraim according to their *a'*:
24 throughout their *a'*. And they
25 on the north side by their *a'*:
10:14, 18 according to their *a'*: and
22 according to his *a'*; and over his
28 of Israel according to their *a'*,
33: 1 their *a'* under the hand of Moses
De 20: 9 make captains of the *a'* to lead
1Sa 17: 1 together their *a'* to battle,
8 and cried unto the *a'* of Israel,
10 I defy the *a'* of Israel this day;
23 out of the *a'* of the Philistines,
26 defy the *a'* of the living God?
36 defied the *a'* of the living God.
45 the God of the *a'* of Israel,
23: 3 against the *a'* of the Philistines?
28: 1 the Philistines gathered their *a'*
29: 1 together all their *a'* to Aphek:
2Ki 25:23 the captains of the *a'*, they and
26 captains of the *a'*, arose, and
1Ch 11:26 the valiant men of the *a'* were,
2Ch 16: 4 of his *a'* against the cities
Job 25: 3 Is there any number of his *a'*?
Ps 44: 9 goest not forth with our *a'*.
60:10 didst not go out with our *a'*?
68:12 Kings of *a'* did flee apace: and
Ca 6:13 As it were the company of two *a'*.
Isa 34: 2 his fury upon all their *a'*: he
M't 22: 7 he sent forth his *a'*, and destroyed
Lu 21:20 Jerusalem compassed with *a'*,
Heb 11:34 turned to flight the *a'* of the aliens.
Re 19:14 And the *a'* which were in heaven
19 and their *a'*, gathered together

Armoni (*ar-mo'-ni*)
2Sa 21: 8 unto Saul, *A'* and Mephibosheth;

armour See also ARMOURBEARER.
1Sa 14: 1 the young man that bare his *a'*,
6 that bare his *a'*, Come, and let us
17:38 Saul armed David with his *a'*,
39 girded his sword upon his *a'*,
54 he put his *a'* in his tent.
31: 9 his head, and stripped off his *a'*,
10 his *a'* in the house of Ashtaroth:
2Sa 2:21 take thee his *a'*. But Asahel would
18:15 young men that bare Joab's *a'*
1Ki 10:25 garments, and *a'*, and spices,
22:38 they washed his *a'*; according
2Ki 3:21 all that were able to put on *a'*,
10: 2 horses, a fenced city also, and *a'*;
20:13 of his *a'*, and all that was found
1Ch 10: 9 they took his head, and his *a'*,
10 his *a'* in the house of their gods,
Isa 22: 8 the *a'* of the house of the forest.
39: 2 the house of his *a'*, and all that
Eze 38: 4 clothed with all sorts of *a'*, even
Lu 11:22 him all his *a'* wherein he trusted,
Ro 13:12 let us put on the *a'* of light.
2Co 6: 7 by the *a'* of righteousness on the
Eph 6:11 Put on the whole *a'* of God, that
13 take unto you the whole *a'* of God,

armourbearer
J'g 9:54 the young man his *a'*,
1Sa 14: 7 his *a'* said unto him,
12 Jonathan and his *a'*, and said,
12 Jonathan said unto his *a'*,
13 and his *a'* after him:
13 and his *a'* slew after him.
14 Jonathan and his *a'* made,
17 Jonathan and his *a'* were not
16:21 he became his *a'*.
31: 4 Then said Saul unto his *a'*,
4 his *a'* would not; for he was
5 *a'* saw that Saul was dead,
6 Saul died,...and his *a'*, and
2Sa 23:37 *a'* to Joab the son of Zeruiah,
1Ch 10: 4 Then said Saul to his *a'*,
4 his *a'* would not;
5 his *a'* saw that Saul was dead,
11:39 *a'* of Joab the son of Zeruiah,

armoury
Ne 3:19 going up to the *a'* at the turning
Ca 4: 4 builded for an *a'*, whereon there
Jer 50:25 The Lord hath opened his *a'*,

arms
Ge 49:24 the *a'* of his hands were made
De 33:27 underneath are the everlasting *a'*:
J'g 15:14 the cords that were upon his *a'*
16:12 he brake them from off his *a'* like
2Sa 22:35 bow of steel is broken by mine *a'*.
2Ki 9:24 smote Jehoram between his *a'*,
Job 22: 9 the *a'* of the fatherless have been
Ps 18:34 bow of steel is broken by mine *a'*.
37:17 For the *a'* of the wicked shall be
Pr 31:17 strength, and strengtheneth her *a'*.
Isa 44:12 it with the strength of his *a'*:
49:22 bring thy sons in their *a'*, and thy
51: 5 mine *a'* shall judge the people;
Eze 13:20 I will tear them from your *a'*,
30:22 of Egypt, and will break his *a'*,
24 I will strengthen the *a'* of the king
24 but I will break Pharaoh's *a'*,
25 I will strengthen the *a'* of the king
25 the *a'* of Pharaoh shall fall down;
Da 2:32 his breast and his *a'* of silver,
10: 6 his *a'* and his feet like in colour
11:15 and the *a'* of the south shall not
22 with the *a'* of a flood shall they be
31 And *a'* shall stand on his part,
Ho 7:15 bound and strengthened their *a'*,
11: 3 taking them by their *a'*; but they
M'r 9:36 when he had taken him in his *a'*,
10:16 he took them up in his *a'*, put his
Lu 2:28 took he him up in his *a'*,

army See also ARMIES.
Ge 26:26 the chief captain of his *a'*.
Ex 14: 9 and his horsemen, and his *a'*,
De 11: 4 what he did unto the *a'* of Egypt,
J'g 4: 7 Sisera, the captain of Jabin's *a'*,
8: 6 should give bread unto thine *a'*?
9:29 Increase thine *a'*, and come out.
1Sa 4: 2 they slew of the *a'* in the field
12 a man of Benjamin out of the *a'*,
16 I am he that came out of the *a'*,
16 I fled to day out of the *a'*.
17:21 battle in array, *a'* against *a'*.
22 and ran into the *a'*, and came and
48 David hasted, and ran toward the *a'*
1Ki 20:19 and the *a'* which followed them.
25 number thee an *a'*,
25 like the *a'* that thou hast lost,
2Ki 25: 5 the *a'* of the Chaldees pursued
5 all his *a'* were scattered from him.
10 And all the *a'* of the Chaldees,
1Ch 20: 1 Joab led forth the power of the *a'*,
27:34 the general of the king's *a'*
2Ch 13: 3 in array with an *a'* of valiant
14: 8 Asa had an *a'* of men that bare
20:21 they went out before the *a'*,
24:24 *a'* of the Syrians came with a
25: 7 let not the *a'* of Israel go with
9 I have given to the *a'* of Israel?
10 the *a'* that was come to him out of
13 But the soldiers of the *a'* which
26:13 under their hand was an *a'*,
Ne 2: 9 had sent captains of the *a'*
4: 2 the *a'* of Samaria, and said, What
Job 29:25 dwelt as a king in the *a'*,
Ca 6: 4, 10 terrible as an *a'* with banners.
Isa 36: 2 king Hezekiah with a great *a'*.
43:17 horse, the *a'* and the power;
Jer 32: 2 Babylon's *a'* besieged Jerusalem:
34: 1 king of Babylon, and all his *a'*,
7 the king of Babylon's *a'* fought
21 hand of the king of Babylon's *a'*,
35:11 for fear of the *a'* of the Chaldeans,
11 for fear of the *a'* of the Syrians:
37: 5 Pharaoh's *a'* was come forth out
7 Pharaoh's *a'*, which is come
10 ye had smitten the whole *a'* of
11 when the *a'* of the Chaldeans was
11 for fear of Pharaoh's *a'*,
38: 3 the king of Babylon's *a'*,
39: 1 all his *a'* against Jerusalem,
5 Chaldeans' *a'* pursued after them,
46: 2 against the *a'* of Pharaoh-necho
22 they shall march with an *a'*,
52: 4 he and all his *a'*, against Jerusalem,
8 *a'* of the Chaldeans pursued after
8 all his *a'* was scattered from him.
14 all the *a'* of the Chaldeans,
Eze 17:17 Pharaoh with his mighty *a'*
27:10 Lud and Phut were in thine *a'*,
11 The men of Arvad with thine *a'*
29:18 caused his *a'* to serve a great service
18 yet had he no wages, nor his *a'*,
19 and it shall be the wages for his *a'*.
32:31 Pharaoh and all his *a'* slain by
37:10 an exceeding great *a'*.
38: 4 all thine *a'*, horses and horsemen,
15 a great company, and a mighty *a'*:
Da 3:20 mighty men that were in his *a'*
4:35 according to his will in the *a'* of
11: 7 which shall come with an *a'*,
13 after certain years with a great *a'*
25 of the south with a great *a'*;
25 with a very great and mighty *a'*;
26 and his *a'* shall overflow:
Joe 2:11 shall utter his voice before his *a'*:
20 far off from you the northern *a'*,
25 my great *a'* which I sent among
Zec 9: 8 mine house because of the *a'*,
Ac 23:27 then came I with an *a'*, and
Re 9:16 number of the *a'* of the horsemen
19:19 sat on the horse, and against his *a'*.

Arnan (*ar'-nan*)
1Ch 3:21 the sons of *A'*, the sons of Obadiah

Arnon (*ar'-non*)
Nu 21:13 and pitched on the other side of *A'*,
21:13 for *A'* is the border of Moab,
14 Red sea, and in the brooks of *A'*,
24 possessed his land from *A'* unto
26 land out of his hand, even unto *A'*.
28 the lords of the high places of *A'*.
22:36 Moab, which is in the border of *A'*,
De 2:24 and pass over the river *A'*:
36 is by the brink of the river of *A'*,
3: 8 river of *A'* unto mount Hermon;
12 Aroer, which is by the river *A'*,
16 from Gilead even unto the river *A'*
4:48 is by the bank of the river *A'*,
Jos 12: 1 rising of the sun, from the river *A'*
2 is upon the bank of the river *A'*,
13: 9 is upon the bank of the river *A'*,
16 the river *A'*, and the city that is
J'g 11:13 from *A'* even unto Jabbok, and
18 and pitched on the other side of *A'*,
18 for *A'* was the border of Moab.
22 from *A'* even unto Jabbok, and
26 that be along by the coasts of *A'*,
2Ki 10:33 by the river *A'*, even Gilead and
Isa 16: 2 of Moab shall be at the fords of *A'*.
Jer 48:20 tell ye it in *A'*, that Moab is spoiled,

Arod (*a'-rod*) See also ARODITES.
Nu 26:17 *A'*, the family of the Arodites:

Arodi (*ar'-o-di*) See also ARODITES.
Ge 46:16 Ezbon, Eri, and *A'*, and Areli.

Arodites (*a'-ro-dites*) See also ARODI.
Nu 26:17 Of Arod, the family of the *A'*:

Aroer (*ar'-o-ur*) See also AROERITE.
Nu 32:34 built Dibon, and Ataroth, and *A'*,
De 2:36 From *A'*, which is by the brink of
3:12 we possessed at that time, from *A'*,
4:48 From *A'*, which is by the bank of
Jos 12: 2 in Heshbon, and ruled from *A'*,
13: 9 From *A'*, that is upon the bank
16 And their coast was from *A'*, that
25 unto *A'* that is before Rabbah;
J'g 11:26 towns, and in *A'* and her towns,
33 And he smote them from *A'*, even
1Sa 30:28 And to them which were in *A'*,
2Sa 24: 5 over Jordan, and pitched in *A'*,
2Ki 10:33 from *A'*, which is by the river
1Ch 5: 8 the son of Joel, who dwelt in *A'*,
Isa 17: 2 The cities of *A'* are forsaken;
Jer 48:19 O inhabitant of *A'*, stand by the

Aroerite (*ar'-o-ur-ite*)
1Ch 11:44 Jehiel the sons of Hothan the *A'*,

arose
Ge 19:15 when the morning *a'*, then the
33 she lay down, nor when she *a'*.
35 and the younger *a'*, and lay with
35 she lay down, nor when she *a'*.
24:10 he *a'*, and went to Mesopotamia,
61 And Rebekah *a'*, and her damsels,
37: 7 my sheaf *a'*, and also stood upright;
38:19 And she *a'*, and went away,
Ex 1: 8 there *a'* up a new king over Egypt,
De 34:10 there *a'* not a prophet since in
Jos 8: 3 So Joshua *a'*, and all the people
19 the ambush *a'* quickly out of their
18: 8 And the men *a'*, and went away:
24: 9 *a'* and warred against Israel,
J'g 2:10 *a'* another generation after them,
3:20 And he *a'* out of his seat.
4: 9 Deborah *a'*, and went with Barak
5: 7 until that I Deborah *a'*,
7 that I *a'* a mother in Israel.
6:28 when the men of the city *a'* early
8:21 And Gideon *a'*, and slew Zebah
10: 1 after Abimelech there *a'* to defend
3 And after him *a'* Jair, a Gileadite,
13:11 And Manoah *a'*, and went after
16: 3 Samson lay till midnight, and *a'* at
19: 3 her husband *a'*, and went after her,
5 they *a'* early in the morning,
8 And he *a'* early in the morning on
20: 8 And all the people *a'* as one man,
18 And the children of Israel *a'*,
Ru 1: 6 she *a'* with her daughters in law,
1Sa 3: 6 And Samuel *a'* and went to Eli,
8 And he *a'* and went to Eli,
5: 3 And when they of Ashdod *a'* early
4 when they *a'* early on the morrow
9:26 And they *a'* early: and it came
26 Saul *a'*, and they went out both
13:15 Samuel *a'*, and gat him up from
17:35 he *a'* against me, I caught him
48 came to pass, when the Philistine *a'*,
52 the men of Israel and of Judah *a'*,
18:27 Wherefore David *a'* and went,
20:25 Jonathan *a'*, and Abner sat by
34 *a'* from the table in fierce anger,
41 soon as the lad was gone, David *a'*
42 And he *a'* and departed:
21:10 And David *a'*, and fled that day
23:13 David...*a'* and departed out of
16 And Jonathan Saul's son *a'*,
24 *a'*, and went to Ziph before Saul:
24: 4 Then David *a'*, and cut off the skirt
8 David also *a'* afterward, and went
25: 1 And David *a'*, and went down to
41 And she *a'*, and bowed herself
42 Abigail hasted, and *a'*,
26: 2 Then Saul *a'*, and went down
5 David *a'*, and came to the place
27: 2 David *a'*, and he passed over with
28:23 hearkened unto their voice. So he *a'*
31:12 All the valiant men *a'*,
2Sa 2:15 Then there *a'* and went over by
6: 2 And David *a'*, and went with all
11: 2 that David *a'* from off his bed,
12:17 And the elders of his house *a'*,

2Sa 12:20 Then David *a*· from the earth,
13:29 Then all the king's sons *a*·,
31 the king *a*·, and tare his garments,
14:23 So Joab *a*·, and went to Geshur,
31 Then Joab *a*·, and came to Absalom
15: 9 So he *a*·, and went to Hebron.
17:22 Then David *a*·, and all the people
23 he saddled his ass, and *a*·,
19: 8 the king *a*·, and sat in the gate,
23:10 He *a*·, and smote the Philistines
1Ki 1:50 and *a*·, and went, and caught hold
2:40 Shimei *a*·, and saddled his ass,
3:20 And she *a*· at midnight,
8:54 he *a*· from before the altar of the
11:18 And they *a*· out of Midian,
40 Jeroboam *a*·, and fled into Egypt,
14: 4 Jeroboam's wife did so, and *a*·,
17 Jeroboam's wife *a*·, and departed,
17:10 So he *a*· and went to Zarephath.
19: 3 And when he saw that, he *a*·,
8 And he *a*·, and did eat and drink,
21 Then he *a*·, and went after Elijah,
2Ki 1:15 he *a*·, and went down with him
4:30 And he *a*·, and followed her.
7: 7 they *a*· and fled in the twilight,
12 And the king *a*· in the night,
8: 2 woman *a*·, and did after the saying
9: 6 he *a*·, and went into the house;
10:12 And he *a*· and departed,
11: 1 she *a*· and destroyed all the seed
12:20 servants *a*·, and made a conspiracy,
19:35 they *a*· early in the morning,
23:25 after him *a*· there any like him.
25:26 the captains of the armies, *a*·,
1Ch 10:12 They *a*·, all the valiant men,
20: 4 *a*· war at Gezer with the
2Ch 22:10 she *a*· and destroyed all the seed
29:12 Then the Levites *a*·, Mahath the
30:14 they *a*· and took away the altars
27 Then the priests the Levites *a*·
36:16 the wrath of the Lord *a*· against
Ezr 9: 5 I *a*· up from my heaviness;
10: 5 *a*· Ezra, and made the chief priest,
Ne 2:12 And I *a*· in the night,
Es 8: 4 Esther *a*·, and stood before the
Job 1:20 Then Job *a*·, and rent his mantle,
19:18 I *a*·, and they spake against me.
29: 8 the aged *a*·, and stood up.
Ps 76: 9 When God *a*· to judgment,
Ec 1: 5 hasteth to his place where he *a*·.
Isa 37:36 when they *a*· early in the morning,
Jer 41: 2 *a*· Ishmael the son of Nethaniah,
Eze 3:23 Then I *a*·, and went forth into the
Da 6:19 king *a*· very early in the morning,
Jon 3: 3 Jonah *a*·, and went unto Nineveh,
6 and he *a*· from his throne,
M't 2:14 he *a*· he took the young child and
21 he *a*·, and took the young child
8:15 she *a*·, and ministered unto them.
24 there *a*· a great tempest in the sea,
26 he *a*·, and rebuked the winds
9: 7 he *a*·, and departed to his house.
9 And he *a*·, and followed him.
19 Jesus *a*·, and followed him,
25 her by the hand, and the maid *a*·.
25: 7 all those virgins *a*·, and trimmed
26:62 the high priest *a*·, and said
27:52 of the saints which slept *a*·,
M'r 2:12 immediately he *a*·, took up the bed,
14 And he *a*· and followed him.
4:37 there *a*· a great storm of wind,
39 he *a*·, and rebuked the wind,
5:42 the damsel *a*·, and walked;
7:24 he *a*·, and went into the borders
9:27 lifted him up; and he *a*·.
10: 1 he *a*· from thence, and cometh
14:57 *a*· certain, and bare false witness,
Lu 1:39 And Mary *a*· in those days, and
4:38 he *a*· out of the synagogue,
39 she *a*· and ministered unto them.
6: 8 he *a*· and stood forth.
48 *a*·, the stream beat vehemently
8:24 he *a*·, and rebuked the wind
55 again, and she *a*· straightway:
9:46 there *a*· a reasoning among them,
15:14 *a*· a mighty famine in that land;
20 he *a*·, and came to his father.
23: 1 the whole multitude of them *a*·,
24:12 *a*· Peter, and ran unto the sepulchre;
Joh 3:25 there *a*· a question between some
6:18 sea *a*· by reason of a great wind
11:29 she *a*· quickly, and came unto him.
Ac 5: 6 the young men *a*·, wound him
6: 1 *a*· a murmuring of the Grecians
9 there *a*· certain of the synagogue,
7:18 king *a*·, which knew not Joseph.
8:27 he *a*· and went: and, behold, a
9: 8 Saul *a*· from the earth; and when
18 *a*·, and was baptized.
34 thy bed. And he *a*· immediately.
39 Then Peter *a*· and went with them.
11:19 persecution that *a*· about Stephen
19:23 same time there *a*· no small stir.
23: 7 there *a*· a dissension between the
9 *a*· a great cry: and the scribes
9 of the Pharisees' part *a*·, and
10 when there *a*· a great dissension
27:14 *a*· against it a tempestuous wind
Re 9: 2 there *a*· a smoke out of the pit,

Arpad (*ar'-pad*) See also ARPHAD.
2Ki 18:34 the gods of Hamath, and of *A*·?
19:13 of Hamath, and the king of *A*·,
Isa 10: 9 not Hamath as *A*·? is not Samaria
Jer 49:23 Hamath is confounded, and *A*·:

Arphad (*ar'-fad*) See also ARPAD.
Isa 36:19 are the gods of Hamath and *A*·?
37:13 of Hamath, and the king of *A*·,

Arphaxad (*ar-fax'-ad*)
Ge 10:22 Elam, and Asshur, and *A*·, and
24 *A*· begat Salah; and Salah begat
11:10 begat *A*· two years after the flood:
11 Shem lived after he begat *A*· five
12 *A*· lived five and thirty years,
13 *A*· lived after he begat Salah four
1Ch 1:17 *A*·, and Lud, and Aram,
18 *A*· begat Shelah, and Shelah
24 Shem, *A*·, Shelah,
Lu 3:36 which was the son of *A*·,

array See also ARRAYED.
J'g 20:20 men of Israel put themselves in *a*·
22 battle again in *a*· in the place
22 where they put themselves in *a*·
30 themselves in *a*· against Gibeah,
33 themselves in *a*· at Baal-tamar:
1Sa 4: 2 Philistines put themselves in *a*·
17: 2 and set the battle in *a*·
8 come out to set your battle in *a*·?
21 Philistines had put the battle in *a*·,
2Sa 10: 8 put the battle in *a*· at the entering
9 and put them in *a*· against the
10 that he might put them in *a*·
17 the Syrians set themselves in *a*·
1Ki 20:12 his servants, Set yourselves in *a*·.
12 themselves in *a*· against the city.
1Ch 19: 9 and put the battle in array
10 and put them in *a*· against the
11 they set themselves in *a*· against
17 set the battle in *a*· against them.
17 when David had put the battle in *a*·
2Ch 13: 3 And Abijah set the battle in *a*·
3 Jeroboam also set the battle in *a*·
14:10 set the battle in *a*· in the valley
Es 6: 9 *a*· the man withal whom the king
Job 6: 4 set themselves in *a*· against me.
40:10 *a*· thyself with glory and beauty.
Isa 22: 7 set themselves in *a*· at the gate.
Jer 6:23 they ride upon horses, set in *a*·
43:12 and he shall *a*· himself with the
50: 9 and they shall set themselves in *a*·
14 yourselves in *a*· against Babylon
42 put in *a*·, like a man to the battle,
Joe 2: 5 a strong people set in battle *a*·.
1Ti 2: 9 or gold, or pearls, or costly *a*·;

arrayed
Ge 41:42 *a*· him in vestures of fine linen,
2Ch 5:12 *a*· in white linen, having cymbals
28:15 and *a*· them, and shod them,
Es 6:11 *a*· Mordecai, and brought him on
M't 6:29 was not *a*· like one of these.
Lu 12:27 was not *a*· like one of these.
23:11 *a*· him in a gorgeous robe, and
Ac 12:21 Herod, *a*· in royal apparel,
Re 7:13 these which are *a*· in white robes?
17: 4 And the woman was *a*· in purple
19: 8 she should be *a*· in fine linen,

arrived
Lu 8:26 *a*· at the country of the Gadarenes,
Ac 20:15 and the next day we *a*· at Samos,

arrogancy
1Sa 2: 3 not *a*· come out of your mouth:
Pr 8:13 pride, and *a*·, and the evil way,
Isa 13:11 the *a*· of the proud to cease,
Jer 48:29 his *a*·, and his pride,

arrow See also ARROWS.
1Sa 20:36 he shot an *a*· beyond him.
37 was come to the place of the *a*·
37 is not the *a*· beyond thee?
2Ki 9:24 the *a*· went out at his heart,
13:17 The *a*· of the Lord's deliverance,
17 and the *a*· of deliverance
19:32 nor shoot an *a*· there,
Job 41:28 *a*· cannot make him flee:
Ps 11: 2 they make ready their *a*·
64: 7 God shall shoot at them with an *a*·;
91: 5 for the *a*· that flieth by day;
Pr 25:18 a sword, and a sharp *a*·.
Isa 37:33 nor shoot an arrow there,
Jer 9: 8 Their tongue is as an *a*·
La 3:12 set me as a mark for the *a*·.
Zec 9:14 his *a*· shall go forth

arrows
Nu 24: 8 pierce them through with his *a*·.
De 32:23 I will spend mine *a*· upon them.
42 make mine *a*· drunk with blood,
1Sa 20:20 I will shoot three *a*· on the side
21 Go, find out the *a*·.
21 the *a*· are on this side of thee,
22 the *a*· are beyond thee;
36 find out now the *a*· which I shoot.
38 Jonathan's lad gathered up the *a*·,
2Sa 22:15 he sent out *a*·, and scattered them;
2Ki 13:15 Take bow and *a*·.
15 And he took unto him bow and *a*·.
18 he said, Take the *a*·.
1Ch 12: 2 in hurling stones and shooting *a*·
2Ch 26:15 to shoot *a*· and great stones
Job 6: 4 For the *a*· of the Almighty are
Ps 7:13 he ordaineth his *a*· against the
18:14 Yea, he sent out his arrows,
21:12 ready thine *a*· upon thy strings
38: 2 For thine *a*· stick fast in me,
45: 5 Thine *a*· are sharp in the heart
57: 4 whose teeth are spears and *a*·,
58: 7 bendeth his bow to shoot his *a*·,
64: 3 bend their bows to shoot their *a*·,
76: 3 brake he the *a*· of the bow,
77:17 thine *a*· also went abroad.

Ps 120: 4 Sharp *a*· of the mighty,
127: 4 As *a*· are in the hand of a mighty
144: 6 shoot out thine *a*·, and destroy
Pr 26:18 casteth firebrands, *a*·, and death,
Isa 5:28 Whose *a*· are sharp,
7:24 With *a*· and with bows shall men
Jer 50: 9 their *a*· shall be as of a mighty
14 shoot at her, spare no *a*·:
51:11 Make bright the *a*·;
La 3:13 hath caused the *a*· of his quiver
Eze 5:16 send upon them the evil *a*· of
21:21 he made his *a*· bright, he
39: 3 and will cause thine *a*· to fall
9 the bows and the *a*·, and the
Hab 3:11 at the light of thine *a*· they went,

art^ See also ARTS.
Ge 3: 9 and said unto him, Where *a*· thou?
14 thou *a*· cursed above all cattle,
19 for dust thou *a*·, and unto dust
4: 6 unto Cain, Why *a*· thou wroth?
11 now *a*· thou cursed from the earth,
12:11 *a*· a fair woman to look upon:
13 I pray thee, thou *a*· my sister:
13:14 look from the place where thou *a*·
16:11 Behold, thou *a*· with child, and
17: 8 land wherein thou *a*· a stranger,
20: 3 Behold, thou *a*· but a dead man,
23: 6 Thou *a*· a mighty prince among us:
24:23 And said, Whose daughter *a*· thou?
47 and said, Whose daughter *a*· thou?
60 Thou *a*· our sister; be thou the
26:16 thou *a*· much mightier than we.
29 *a*· now the blessed of the Lord.
27:18 Here am I; who *a*· thou, my son?
24 *A*· thou my very son Esau? And he
32 said unto him, Who *a*· thou?
28: 4 land wherein thou *a*· a stranger,
29:14 thou *a*· my bone and my flesh.
15 Because thou *a*· my brother,
32:17 thee, saying, Whose *a*· thou?
39: 9 thee, because thou *a*· his wife:
41:39 so discreet and wise as thou *a*·:
44:18 for thou *a*· even as Pharaoh.
45:19 Now thou *a*· commanded, this do
46:30 face, because thou *a*· yet alive.
47: 8 unto Jacob, How old *a*· thou?
49: 3 Reuben, thou *a*· my firstborn, my
8 thou *a*· he whom thy brethren
9 thou *a*· gone up: he stooped
Ex 4:25 a bloody husband *a*· thou to me!
26 said, A bloody husband thou *a*·,
18:18 thou *a*· not able to perform it
30:25, 35 the *a*· of the apothecary:
33: 3 for thou *a*· a stiffnecked people:
34:10 the people among which thou *a*·
Le 27:12 valuest it, who *a*· the priest
Nu 14:14 thou Lord *a*· among this people
14 that thou Lord *a*· seen face to face,
21:29 thou *a*· undone, O people of
De 2:18 Thou *a*· to pass over through Ar,
4:30 When thou *a*· in tribulation,
38 and mightier than thou *a*·,
7: 6 For thou *a*· an holy people unto
19 people of whom thou *a*· afraid.
8:10 thou hast eaten and *a*· full,
12 and *a*· full, and hast built goodly
9: 1 *a*· to pass over Jordan this day,
6 for thou *a*· a stiffnecked people.
14: 2 For thou *a*· an holy people unto the
21 *a*· an holy people unto the Lord
24 that thou *a*· not able to carry it;
17:14 When thou *a*· come unto the land
18: 9 *a*· come into the land which the
26: 1 when thou *a*· come in unto the
27: 3 law, when thou *a*· passed over,
9 *a*· become the people of the Lord
28:10 the earth shall see that thou *a*·
32:15 thou *a*· waxen fat,
15 thou *a*· grown thick,
15 thou *a*· covered with fatness;
18 that begat thee thou *a*· unmindful,
33:29 Happy *a*· thou, O Israel: who is
Jos 5:13 *A*· thou for us, or for our
13: 1 Thou *a*· old and stricken in years,
17:17 saying, Thou *a*· a great people,
J'g 8:18 As thou *a*·, so were they;
11: 2 *a*· the son of a strange woman.
12 thou *a*· come against me to fight
25 *a*· thou any thing better than Balak
35 *a*· one of them that trouble me:
12: 5 unto him, *A*· thou an Ephraimite?
13: 3 Behold now, thou *a*· barren, and
11 *A*· thou the man that spakest
Ru 2: 9 when thou *a*· athirst, go unto the
11 and *a*· come unto a people which
12 wings thou *a*· come to trust.
3: 9 And he said, Who *a*· thou?
9 for thou *a*· a near kinsman
11 that thou *a*· a virtuous woman.
16 said, Who *a*· thou, my daughter?
1Sa 8: 5 unto him, Behold, thou *a*· old,
10: 2 thou *a*· departed from me to day,
5 thou *a*· come thither to the city,
17:28 for thou *a*· come down that thou
33 Thou *a*· not able to go against
33 for thou *a*· but a youth, and he
58 Whose son *a*· thou, thou young
19: 3 father in the field where thou *a*·,
21: 1 Why *a*· thou alone, and no man
24:17 Thou *a*· more righteous than I:
26:14 Who *a*· thou that criest to the king?
15 Abner, *A*· not thou a valiant man?
28:12 deceived me? for thou *a*· Saul.
29: 9 that thou *a*· good in my sight,
30:13 thou? and whence *a*· thou?

2Sa 1: 8 he said unto me, Who a' thou?
13 that told him, Whence a' thou?
2:20 and said A' thou Asahel?
7:22 Wherefore thou a' great, O Lord
24 thou, Lord, a' become their God.
28 O Lord God, thou a' that God,
9: 2 king said unto him, A' thou Ziba?
12: 7 Nathan said to David, Thou a'
13: 4 he said unto him, Why a' thou,
15: 2 Of what city a' thou? and he said,
19 for thou art a stranger, and also
27 A' not thou a seer? return into
16: 8 thou a' taken in thy mischief,
8 because thou a' a bloody man.
21 shall hear that thou a' abhorred
18: 3 thou a' worth ten thousand of us:
19:13 A' thou not of my bone, and of my
20: 9 A' thou in health, my brother?
17 the woman said, A' thou Joab?
22:29 For thou a' my lamp, O Lord:
1Ki 1:42 for thou a' a valiant man, and
2: 9 for thou a' a wise man, and
6:12 concerning this house which thou a'
13:14 A' thou the man of God that
18 I am a prophet also as thou a':
17:18 a' thou come unto me to call my
24 I know that thou a' a man of God,
18: 7 A' thou that my lord Elijah?
17 A' thou he that troubleth Israel?
36 this day that thou a' God in Israel,
37 know that thou a' the Lord God,
20:36 as soon as thou a' departed from
22: 4 I am as thou a', my people as thy
2Ki 1: 4 bed on which thou a' gone up,
6 on which thou a' gone up, but
16 off that bed on which thou a' gone
3: 7 I am as thou a', my people as thy
4: 4 And when thou a' come in, thou
19:15 thou a' the God, even thou alone,
19 know that thou a' the Lord God,
1Ch 17:26 And now, Lord, thou a' God, and
29:11 and thou a' exalted as head above
2Ch 14:11 O Lord, thou a' our God; let not
16:14 prepared by the apothecaries' a':
18: 3 I am as thou a', and my people as
20: 6 of our fathers, a' not thou God in
7 A' not thou our God, who didst
25:16 A' thou made of the king's
Ezr 7:14 as thou a' sent to the king, and of
9:15 of Israel; thou a' righteous:
Ne 2: 2 sad, seeing thou a' not sick?
9: 6 Thou, even thou, a' Lord alone;
7 Thou a' the Lord the God, who
8 thy words; for thou a' righteous:
17 but thou a' a God ready to pardon,
31 a' a gracious and merciful God.
33 thou a' just in all that is brought
Es 4:14 knoweth whether thou a' come
Job 4: 5 thee, and thou a' troubled.
15: 7 A' thou the first man that was
17:14 Thou a' my father;
14 to the worm, Thou a' my
22: 3 Almighty, that thou a' righteous?
30:21 Thou a' become cruel to me: with
31:24 fine gold, thou a' my confidence;
33:12 Behold, in this thou a' not just;
34:18 say to a king, Thou a' wicked?
35: 8 may hurt a man as thou a'; and
Ps 2: 7 Thou a' my son; this day have I
3: 3 But thou, O Lord, art a shield
5: 4 For thou a' not a God that hath
8: 4 man, that thou a' mindful of him?
10:14 a' the helper of the fatherless.
16: 2 Thou a' my Lord: my goodness
22: 1 why a' thou so far from helping
3 But thou a' holy, O thou that
9 But thou a' he that took me out
10 thou a' my God from my mother's
23: 4 fear no evil; for thou a' with me;
25: 5 thou a' the God of my salvation;
31: 3 thou a' my rock and my fortress;
4 for me: for thou a' my strength.
14 O Lord: I said, Thou a' my God.
32: 7 Thou a' my hiding place; thou
40:17 thou a' my help and my deliverer;
42: 5 Why a' thou cast down, O my
5 why a' thou disquieted in me?
11 Why a' thou cast down, O my
11 why a' thou disquieted within me?
43: 2 For thou a' the God of my strength,
5 Why a' thou cast down, O my soul?
5 why a' thou disquieted within me?
44: 4 Thou a' my King, O God:
45: 2 Thou a' fairer than the children
63: 1 O God, thou a' my God; early will
65: 5 who a' the confidence of all the
66: 3 How terrible a' thou in thy works:
68:35 thou a' terrible out of thy holy
70: 5 thou a' my help and my deliverer;
71: 3 thou a' my rock and my fortress.
5 thou a' my hope, O Lord God:
5 thou a' my trust from my youth.
6 thou a' he that took me out of
7 but thou a' my strong refuge.
76: 4 Thou a' more glorious and excellent
7 Thou, even thou, a' to be feared:
7 sight when once thou a' angry?
77:14 Thou a' the God that doest
83:18 Jehovah, a' the most high over
86: 5 For thou, Lord, a' good, and
10 For thou a' great, and doest
10 thou a' God alone.
15 Lord, a' a God full of compassion,
89:17 thou a' the glory of their strength:
26 Thou a' my father, my God, and
90: 2 to everlasting, thou a' God.
Ps 92: 8 But thou, Lord, a' most high
93: 2 of old: thou a' from everlasting.
97: 9 Lord, a' high above all the earth:
9 thou a' exalted far above all gods.
102:27 But thou a' the same, and thy
104: 1 God, thou a' very great; thou a'
110: 4 Thou a' a priest for ever after the
118:21 and a' become my salvation.
28 Thou a' my God, I will praise thee;
28 thou a' my God, I will exalt thee.
119:12 Blessed a' thou, O Lord: teach
57 Thou a' my portion, O Lord:
68 Thou a' good, and doest good:
114 Thou a' my hiding place and my
137 Righteous a' thou, O Lord, and
151 Thou a' near, O Lord: and all thy
137: 8 Babylon who a' to be destroyed;
139: 3 a' acquainted with all my ways.
8 up into heaven, thou a' there:
8 bed in hell, behold, thou a' there:
140: 6 unto the Lord, Thou a' my God:
142: 5 Thou a' my refuge and my portion
143:10 for thou a' my God: thy spirit is
Pr 6: 2 Thou a' snared with the words of
2 thou a' taken with the words of
3 when thou a' come into the hand
7: 4 Thou a' my sister,
24:24 the wicked, Thou a' righteous;
Ec 10:17 Blessed a' thou, O land, when
Ca 1:15 Behold, thou a' fair, my love;
15 behold, thou a' fair;
16 Behold, thou a' fair, my beloved,
2:14 that a' in the clefts of the rock,
4: 1 Behold, thou a' fair, my love;
1 behold, thou a' fair;
7 Thou a' all fair, my love;
6: 4 Thou a' beautiful, O my love,
7: 6 How fair and how pleasant a' thou,
Isa 14: 8 saying, Since thou a' laid
10 A' thou also become weak as we?
10 a' thou become like unto us?
12 How a' thou fallen from heaven,
12 how a' thou cut down to the ground,
19 thou a' cast out of thy grave like
31 whole Palestina, a' dissolved:
22: 1 thou a' wholly gone up to the
2 Thou that a' full of stirs,
25: 1 O Lord, thou a' my God;
26:15 hast increased the nation: thou a'
37:16 thou a' the God, even thou alone,
20 may know that thou a' the Lord,
41: 8 But thou, Israel, a' my servant,
9 unto thee, Thou a' my servant;
43: 1 thee by thy name; thou a' mine.
44:17 Deliver me; for thou a' my God.
21 for thou a' my servant;
21 formed thee; thou a' my servant:
45:15 thou a' a God that hidest thyself,
47: 8 thou that a' given to pleasures,
13 Thou a' wearied in the multitude
48: 4 I knew that thou a' obstinate,
49: 3 Thou a' my servant, O Israel,
51: 9 A' thou not it that hath cut Rahab,
10 A' thou not it which hath dried
12 who a' thou that thou shouldest
16 and say unto Zion, Thou a' my
57: 8 thyself to another than me, and a'
10 Thou a' wearied in the greatness
63: 2 Wherefore a' thou red in thine
16 Doubtless thou a' our father,
16 thou, O Lord, a' our father
64: 5 behold, thou a' wroth; for we
8 But now, O Lord, thou a' our
Jer 2:21 wholly a right seed: how then a'
23 thou a' a swift dromedary
27 Thou a' my father;
3: 4 My father, thou a' the guide of
22 for thou a' the Lord our God.
4:30 And when thou a' spoiled, what
10: 6 thou a' great, and thy name is
12: 1 Righteous a' thou, O Lord, when I
2 thou a' near in their mouth, and
14: 9 O Lord, a' in the midst of us, and
22 A' not thou he, O Lord our God?
15: 6 saith the Lord, thou a' gone
17:14 and I shall be saved: for thou a'
17 Be not a terror unto me: thou a'
20: 7 thou a' stronger than I, and hast
22: 6 Thou a' Gilead unto me, and the
31:18 for thou a' the Lord my God.
39:17 the hand of men of whom thou a'
49:12 and a' thou he that shall
50:24 and thou a' also taken, O
24 was not aware: thou a' found,
51:20 Thou a' my battle ax and
La 5:22 hast utterly rejected us; thou a'
Eze 3: 5 For thou a' not sent to a people
16: 7 and thou a' come to excellent
34 therefore thou a' contrary.
45 Thou a' thy mother's daughter,
45 children; and thou a' the sister
54 in that thou a' a comfort unto
22: 4 Thou a' become guilty in thy
4 and a' come even unto thy years:
5 which a' infamous and much
24 Thou a' the land that is not
23:30 and because thou a' polluted
26:17 How a' thou destroyed, that wast
27: 3 Tyrus, O thou that a' situate
3 which a' a merchant of the
28: 2 yet thou a' a man, and not God,
3 Behold, thou a' wiser than
14 Thou a' the anointed cherub
31: 2 his multitude; whom a' thou
18 To whom a' thou thus like in
32: 2 Thou a' like a young lion of the
Eze 32: 2 and thou a' as a whale in the
33:32 And lo, thou a' unto them as a
38:13 A' thou come to take a spoil?
17 A' thou he of whom I have
40: 4 unto thee a' thou brought hither:
Dan 2:26 A' thou able to make known
37 Thou, O king, a' a king of kings:
38 Thou a' this head of gold.
4:18 but thou a' able; for the spirit
22 It is thou, O king, that a' grown
5:13 A' thou that Daniel,
13 which a' of the children of the
27 Tekel; Thou a' weighed in the
27 and a' found wanting.
9:23 for thou a' greatly beloved:
Ho 2:23 Thou a' my people; and they
23 Thou a' my God.
Ob 2 the heathen: thou a' greatly
5 by night, (how a' thou cut off!)
Jon 1: 8 and of what people a' thou?
4: 2 that thou a' a gracious God, and
Mic 2: 7 O thou that a' named the house
Na 1:14 make thy grave; for thou a' vile.
3: 8 A' thou better than populous No,
Hab 1:12 A' thou not from everlasting,
13 Thou a' of purer eyes than to
Zec 4: 7 Who a' thou, O great mountain?
M't 2: 6 in the land of Juda, a' not
5:25 whiles thou a' in the way with
6: 9 Our Father which a' in heaven,
8:29 a' thou come hither to torment
11: 3 A' thou he that should come, or
23 thou, Capernaum, which a'
14:33 Of a truth thou a' the Son of God.
16:14 Some say that thou a' John the
16 Thou a' the Christ, the Son of
17 Blessed a' thou, Simon Bar-jona;
18 That thou a' Peter,
23 thou a' an offence unto me:
22:16 we know that thou a' true, and
25:24 that thou a' an hard man,
26:50 him, Friend, wherefore a' thou
73 Surely thou also a' one of them;
27:11 A' thou the king of the Jews?
M'r 1:11 Thou a' my beloved Son, in
24 A' thou come to destroy us?
24 who thou a', the Holy One of God.
3:11 saying, Thou a' the Son of God.
8:29 saith unto him, Thou a' the
12:14 we know that thou a' true, and
34 Thou a' not far from the
14:61 A' thou the Christ, the Son of the
70 Surely thou a' one of them:
15: 2 Pilate asked him, A' thou the
Lu 1:28 Hail, thou that a' highly favoured,
28 blessed a' thou among women.
42 Blessed a' thou among women,
3:22 Thou a' my beloved Son;
4:34 a' thou come to destroy us?
34 I know thee who thou a':
41 Thou a' Christ the Son of God.
7:19, 20 A' thou he that should come?
10:15 Capernaum, which a' exalted to
41 Martha, Martha, thou a' careful
11: 2 Our Father which a' in heaven,
12:58 thou a' in the way, give diligence
13:12 thou a' loosed from thine infirmity.
14: 8 a' bidden of any man to a wedding,
10 when thou a' bidden, go and sit
15:31 Son, thou a' ever with me,
16:25 comforted, and thou a' tormented.
19:21 because thou a' an austere man;
22:32 and when thou a' converted,
58 Thou a' also of them. And Peter
67 A' thou the Christ? tell us.
70 A' thou then the Son of God?
23: 3 A' thou the king of the Jews?
40 a' in the same condemnation?
24:18 A' thou only a stranger in
Joh 1:19 to ask him, Who a' thou?
21 A' thou Elias? And he saith, I
21 A' thou that prophet? And he
22 Who a' thou? that we may give
42 Thou a' Simon the son of Jona:
49 thou a' the Son of God;
49 thou a' the king of Israel
3: 2 we know that thou a' a teacher
10 A' thou a master of Israel,
4:12 A' thou greater than our father
19 I perceive that thou a' a prophet.
5:14 Behold, thou a' made whole:
6:69 that thou a' that Christ, the Son
7:52 A' thou also of Galilee?
8:25 Who a' thou? And Jesus saith
48 that thou a' a Samaritan, and hast
53 A' thou greater than our father
57 Thou a' not yet fifty years old,
9:28 Thou a' his disciple; but we are
11:27 I believe that thou a' the Christ,
17:21 as thou, Father, a' in me, and I in
18:17 A' not thou also one of this man's
25 A' not thou also one of his
33 A' thou the king of the Jews?
37 A' thou a king then? Jesus
19: 9 Whence a' thou? But Jesus gave
12 thou a' not Cæsar's friend:
21:12 Who a' thou? knowing that it was
Ac 4:24 Lord, thou a' God, which hast
8:23 thou a' in the gall of bitterness,
9: 5 Who a' thou, Lord? And the Lord
10:33 hast well done that thou a' come.
12:15 Thou a' mad. But she constantly
13:33 Thou a' my Son, this day have I
17:29 graven by a' and man's device.
21:22 they will hear that thou a' come.
38 A' not thou that Egyptian, which

Ac 22: 8 Who a' thou, Lord? And he said
27 Tell me, a' thou a Roman?
26: 1 said unto Paul, Thou a' permitted
15 Who a' thou, Lord? And he said,
24 Paul, thou a' beside thyself;
Ro 2: 1 Therefore thou a' inexcusable,
1 whosoever thou a' that judgest:
17 Behold, thou a' called a Jew,
19 And a' confident
19 that thou thyself a' a guide
3: 4 overcome when thou a' judged.
9:20 who a' thou that repliest against
14: 4 Who a' thou that judgest another
1Co 7:21 A' thou called being a servant?
27 A' thou bound unto a wife?
27 A' thou loosed from a wife?
Ga 4: 7 thou a' no more a servant,
1Ti 6:12 whereunto thou a' also called,
Heb 1: 5 Thou a' my Son, this day have I
12 but thou a' the same, and thy
2: 6 man that thou a' mindful of him?
5: 5 Thou a' my Son, to day have I
6 Thou a' a priest for ever after the
7:17, 21 Thou a' a priest for ever after
Jas 2:11 a' become a transgressor of the
4:11 a' not a doer of the law, but a
12 Who a' thou that judgest another?
Re 2: 5 from whence thou a' fallen,
9 and poverty, (but thou a' rich)
3: 1 name that thou livest and a' dead.
15 that thou a' neither cold nor hot:
16 So then because thou a' lukewarm,
17 knowest not that thou a' wretched,
4:11 Thou a' worthy, O Lord, to receive
5: 9 Thou a' worthy to take the book,
11:17 O Lord God Almighty which a',
17 and wast, and a' to come;
15: 4 thou only a' holy: for all nations
16: 5 Thou a' righteous, O Lord,
5 which a', and wast, and

Artaxerxes (*ar-tax-erx'-ees*) See also ARTAXERXES'.
Ezr 4: 7 in the days of A', wrote Bishlam,
7 unto A' king of Persia; and the
8 to A' the king in this sort:
11 they sent unto him, even unto A'
6:14 and Darius, and A' king of Persia.
7: 1 in the reign of A' king of Persia,
7 in the seventh year of A' the king.
11 that the king A' gave unto Ezra
12 A', king of kings, unto Ezra the
21 And I, even I A' the king,
8: 1 in the reign of A', the king,
Ne 2: 1 in the twentieth year of A' the king,
5:14 the two and thirtieth year of A'
13: 6 in the two and thirtieth year of A'

Artaxerxes' (*ar-tax-erx'-eez*)
Ezr 4:23 the copy of king A' letter was read

Artemas (*ar'-te-mas*)
Tit 3:12 When I shall send A' unto thee,

artificer See also ARTIFICERS.
Ge 4:22 an instructer of every a'
Isa 3: 3 and the cunning a', and the

artificers
1Ch 29: 5 by the hands of a'.
2Ch 34:11 Even to the a' and builders

artillery
1Sa 20:40 Jonathan gave his a' unto his lad,

arts
Ac 19:19 them also which used curious a'

Aruboth (*ar'-u-both*)
1Ki 4:10 The son of Hesed, in A'; to him

Arumah (*a-ru'-mah*)
J'g 9:41 And Abimelech dwelt at A':

Arvad (*ar'-vad*) See also ARVADITE.
Eze 27: 8 The inhabitants of Zidon and A'
11 The men of A' with thine army

Arvadite (*ar'-vad-ite*)
Ge 10:18 And the A', and the Zemarite,
1Ch 1:16 And the A', and the Zemarite,

Arza (*ar'-zah*)
1Ki 16: 9 himself drunk in the house of A'

Asa (*a'-sah*) See also ASA'S.
1Ki 15: 8 and A' his son reigned in his stead.
9 of Israel reigned A' over Judah.
11 And A' did that which was right
13 A' destroyed her idol, and burnt it
16 was war between A' and Baasha
17 any to go out or come in to A'
18 A' took all the silver and the gold
18 king A' sent them to Ben-hadad,
20 Ben-hadad hearkened unto king A',
22 Then king A' made a proclamation
22 and king A' built with them Geba
23 The rest of all the acts of A',
24 And A' slept with his fathers,
25 over Israel in the second year of A'
28 Even in the third year of A' king of
32 was war between A' and Baasha
33 In the third year of A' king of
16: 8 In the twenty and sixth year of A'
10, 15 twenty and seventh year of A'
23 In the thirty and first year of A'
29 in the thirty and eighth year of A'
22:41 the son of A' began to reign
43 he walked in all the ways of A' his
46 in the days of his father A',
1Ch 3:10 Abia his son, A' his son,
9:16 and Berechiah, the son of A',
2Ch 14: 1 and A' his son reigned in his stead.
2Ch 14: 2 A' did that which was good and
8 A' had an army of men that bare
10 Then A' went out against him,
11 A' cried unto the Lord his God,
12 smote the Ethiopians before A',
13 And A' and the people that were
15: 2 And he went out to meet A', and
2 Hear ye me, A', and all Judah
8 when A' heard these words, and
10 fifteenth year of the reign of A'.
16 Maachah the mother of A' the king,
16 A' cut down her idol, and stamped
17 of A' was perfect all his days.
19 year of the reign of A'.
16: 1 year of the reign of A', Baasha
1 or come in to A' king of Judah.
2 Then A' brought out silver and gold
4 Ben-hadad hearkened unto king A',
6 Then A' the king took all Judah;
7 time Hanani the seer came to A'
10 Then A' was wroth with the seer,
10 A' oppressed some of the people
11 the acts of A', first and last, lo,
12 A' in the thirty and ninth year
13 A' slept with his fathers, and died
17: 2 which A' his father had taken.
20:32 walked in the way of A' his father,
21:12 the ways of A' king of Judah,
Jer 41: 9 which A' the king had made for
M't 1: 7 and Abia begat A';
8 and A' begat Josaphat;

Asahel (*as'-a-hel*)
2Sa 2:18 there, Joab, Abishai, and A':
18 A' was as light of foot as a wild
19 And A' pursued after Abner; and
20 him, and said, Art thou A'?
21 But A' would not turn aside from
22 And Abner said again to A', Turn
23 where A' fell down and died
30 servants nineteen men and A'.
32 And they took up A', and buried
3:27 for the blood of A' his brother.
30 slain their brother A' at Gibeon
23:24 A' the brother of Joab was one
1Ch 2:16 Abishai, and Joab, and A', three.
11:26 were, A' the brother of Joab,
27: 7 for the fourth month, was A' the
2Ch 17: 8 and Zebadiah, and A', and
31:13 and Nahath, and A', and Jerimoth,
Ezr 10:15 Only Jonathan the son of A', and

Asahiah (*as-a-hi'-ah*) See also ASAIAH.
2Ki 22:12 and A' a servant of the king's,
14 and A', went unto Huldah the

Asaiah (*as-a'-yah*) See also ASAHIAH.
1Ch 4:36 and A', and Adiel, and Jesimiel,
6:30 Haggiah his son, A' his son.
9: 5 A' the first born, and his sons.
15: 6 sons of Merari; A' the chief,
11 Uriel, A', and Joel, Shemaiah,
2Ch 34:20 the scribe, and A' a servant of

Asaph (*a'-saf*) See also ASAPH'S.
2Ki 18:18 Joah the son of A' the recorder.
37 the son of A' the recorder, to
1Ch 6:39 And his brother A', who stood on
39 right hand, even A' the son of
9:15 the son of Zichri, the son of A';
15:17 A' the son of Berechiah;
19 singers, Heman, A', and Ethan,
16: 5 A' the chief, and next to him
5 A' made a sound with cymbals;
7 the hand of A' and his brethren.
37 A' and his brethren, to minister
25: 1 to the service of the sons of A',
2 Of the sons of A'; Zaccur, and
2 the sons of A' under the
2 under the hands of A',
6 according to the king's order to A',
9 the first lot came forth for A'
26: 1 son of Kore, of the sons of A'.
2Ch 5:12 all of them of A', of Heman,
20:14 a Levite of the sons of A', came
29:13 of the sons of A'; Zechariah, and
30 words of David, and of A' the seer.
35:15 the sons of A' were in their place,
15 commandment of David, and A',
Ezr 2:41 the children of A', an hundred
3:10 the sons of A' with cymbals,
Ne 2: 8 A' the keeper of the king's forest,
7:44 The singers: the children of A'.
11:17 the son of A', was the principal
22 Of the sons of A', the singers were
12:35 the son of Zaccur, the son of A':
12:46 the days of David and A' of old
Ps 50:*title* A Psalm of A'. The mighty God,
73:*title* A Psalm of A'. Truly God is good
74:*title* Maschil of A'. O God, why hast
75:*title* A Psalm or Song of A'. Unto thee,
76:*title* A Psalm or Song of A'. In Judah
77:*title* A Psalm of A'. I cried unto God
78:*title* Maschil of A'. Give ear, O my
79:*title* A Psalm of A'. O God, the
80:*title* A Psalm of A'. Give ear, O
81:*title* A Psalm of A'. Sing aloud
82:*title* A Psalm of A'. God standeth in
83:*title* A Song or Psalm of A'. Keep not
Isa 36:22 Joah, the son of A', the recorder,

Asaph's (*a'-safs*)
Isa 36: 3 the scribe, and Joah, A' son,

Asareel (*a-sar'e-el*)
1Ch 4:16 Ziph, and Ziphah, Tiria, and A'.

Asarelah (*as-a-re'-lah*) See also JESHARELAH.
1Ch 25: 2 Joseph, and Nethaniah, and A',

Asa's (*a'-sahz*)
1Ki 15:14 nevertheless A' heart was perfect

ascend See also ASCENDED; ASCENDETH; ASCENDING.
Jos 6: 5 and the people shall a' up
Ps 24: 3 Who shall a' into the hill of the
135: 7 He causeth the vapours to a'
139: 8 If I a' up into heaven,
Isa 14:13 I will a' into heaven,
14 I will a' above the heights of the
Jer 10:13 and he causeth the vapours to a'
51:16 and he causeth the vapours to a'
Eze 38: 9 Thou shalt a' and come like a
Joh 6:62 ye shall see the Son of man a' up
20:17 I a' unto my Father, and your
Ro 10: 6 Who shall a' into heaven?
Re 17: 8 shall a' out of the bottomless pit,

ascended
Ex 19:18 and the smoke thereof a'
Nu 13:22 And they a' by the south,
Jos 8:20 the smoke of the city a' up
21 the smoke of the city a',
10: 7 So Joshua a' from Gilgal,
15: 3 and a' up on the south side
J'g 13:20 that the angel of the Lord a' in
20:40 flame of the city a' up to heaven,
Ps 68:18 Thou hast a' on high,
Pr 30: 4 Who hath a' up into heaven,
Joh 3:13 no man hath a' up to heaven,
20:17 for I am not yet a' to my Father:
Ac 2:34 David is not a' into the heavens:
25: 1 a' from Cæsarea to Jerusalem
Eph 4: 8 When he a' up on high,
9 (Now that he a', what is it
10 is the same also that a' up
Re 8: 4 a' up before God out of the angel's
11:12 they a' up to heaven in a cloud;

ascendeth
Re 11: 7 that a' out of the bottomless pit
14:11 their torment a' up for ever

ascending
Ge 28:12 angels of God a' and descending
1Sa 28:13 I saw gods a' out of the earth.
Lu 19:28 went before, a' up to Jerusalem.
Joh 1:51 angels of God a' and descending
Re 7: 2 another angel a' from the east,

ascent
Nu 34: 4 to the a' of Akrabbim,
2S 15:30 up by the a' of mount Olivet,
1Ki 10: 5 and his a' by which he went up
2Ch 9: 4 and his a' by which he went up

ascribe See also ASCRIBED.
De 32: 3 a' ye greatness unto our God.
Job 36: 3 a' righteousness to my Maker.
Ps 68:34 A' ye strength unto God:

ascribed
1Sa 18: 8 They have a' unto David
8 to me they have a' but thousands:

Asenath (*as'-e-nath*)
Ge 41:45 and he gave him to wife A' the
50 A' the daughter of Poti-pherah
46:20 Manasseh and Ephraim, which A'

Aser (*a'-sur*) See also ASHER.
Lu 2:36 of the tribe of A':
Re 7: 6 Of the tribe of A' were sealed

ash
Isa 44:14 he planteth an a', and the rain

ashamed
Ge 2:25 and were not a'.
Nu 12:14 should she not be a' seven days?
J'g 3:25 they tarried till they were a':
2Sa 10: 5 because the men were greatly a':
19: 3 as people being a' steal away
2Ki 2:17 they urged him till he was a',
8:11 until he was a': and the man of
1Ch 19: 5 the men were greatly a'.
2Ch 30:15 and the Levites were a',
Ezr 8:22 I was a' to require of the king
9: 6 I am a' and blush to lift up my face
Job 6:20 they came thither, and were a'.
11: 3 shall no man make thee a'?
19: 3 ye are not a' that ye make
Ps 6:10 Let all mine enemies be a'
10 them return and be a' suddenly.
25: 2 I trust in thee: let me not be a',
3 let none that wait on thee be a':
3 let them be a' which transgress
20 let me not be a'; for I put
31: 1 let me never be a':
17 Let me not be a', O Lord;
17 let the wicked be a',
34: 5 their faces were not a'.
35:26 be a' and brought to confusion
37:19 shall not be a' in the evil time:
40:14 Let them be a' and confounded
69: 6 them that wait on thee,...be a'
70: 2 Let them be a' and confounded
74:21 let not the oppressed return a':
86:17 may see it, and be a':
109:28 them be a'; but let thy servant
119: 6 Then shall I not be a',
46 and will not be a'.
78 Let the proud be a';
80 that I be not a'.
116 let me not be a' of my hope.
127: 5 they shall not be a',
Pr 12: 4 she that maketh a' is as rottenness
Isa 1:29 For they shall be a' of the oaks
20: 5 shall be afraid and a' of Ethiopia
23: 4 Be thou a', O Zidon:
24:23 and the sun a',
26:11 be a' for their envy at the people;

Isa 29:22 Jacob shall not now be *a*·,
30: 5 They were all *a*· of a people
33: 9 Lebanon is *a*· and hewn down:
41:11 shall be *a*· and confounded:
42:17 they shall be greatly *a*·,
44: 9 that they may be *a*·.
11 all his fellows shall be *a*·:
11 they shall be *a*· together.
45:16 shall be *a*·, and also confounded,
17 shall not be *a*· nor confounded
24 incensed against him shall be *a*·.
49:23 shall not be *a*· that wait for me.
50: 7 that I shall not be *a*·.
54: 4 for thou shalt not be *a*·:
65:13 but ye shall be *a*·:
66: 5 they shall be *a*·.
Jer 2:26 the thief is *a*· when he is found,
26 so is the house of Israel *a*·;
36 thou also shalt be *a*· of Egypt,
36 as thou wast *a*· of Assyria.
3: 3 thou refusedst to be *a*·.
6:15 Were they *a*· when they had
15 they were not at all *a*·,
8: 9 The wise men are *a*·,
12 Were they *a*· when they
12 at all *a*·, neither could they blush:
12:13 they shall be *a*· of your enemies
14: 3 they were *a*· and confounded,
4 the plowmen were *a*·,
15: 9 hath been *a*· and confounded,
17:13 all that forsake thee shall be *a*·,
20:11 they shall be greatly *a*·;
22:22 surely then shalt thou be *a*·
31:19 I was *a*·, yea, even confounded
48:13 And Moab shall be *a*· of Chemosh,
13 house of Israel was *a*· of Beth-el
50:12 she that bare you shall be *a*·:
Eze 16:27 of the Philistines, which are *a*·
61 remember thy ways, and be *a*·,
32:30 they are *a*· of their might;
36:32 be *a*· and confounded for your own
43:10 they may be *a*· of their iniquities:
11 if they be *a*· of all that
Ho 4:19 and they shall be *a*·
10: 6 Israel shall be *a*· of his own counsel.
Joe 1:11 Be ye *a*·, O ye husbandmen;
2:26, 27 My people shall never be *a*·.
Mic 3: 7 the seers be *a*·, and the diviners
Zep 3:11 In that day shalt thou not be *a*·
Zec 9: 5 her expectation shall be *a*·;
13: 4 the prophets shall be *a*· every one
M'r 8:38 therefore shall be *a*· of me
38 shall the Son of man be *a*·,
Lu 9:26 whosoever shall be *a*· of me
26 of him shall the Son of man be *a*·,
13:17 all his adversaries were *a*·:
16: 3 I cannot dig; to beg I am *a*·.
Ro 1:16 am not *a*· of the gospel of Christ:
5: 5 hope maketh not *a*·; because
6:21 whereof ye are now *a*·?
9:33 believeth on him shall not be *a*·.
10:11 on him shall not be *a*·.
2Co 7:14 I am not *a*·;
9: 4 we...should be *a*· in this same
10: 8 destruction, I should not be *a*·:
Ph'p 1:20 in nothing I shall be *a*·,
2Th 3:14 with him, that he may be *a*·.
2Ti 1: 8 thou therefore *a*· of the testimony
12 nevertheless I am not *a*·:
16 and was not *a*· of my chain:
2:15 workman that needeth not to be *a*·,
Tit 2: 8 the contrary part may be *a*·,
Heb 2:11 is not *a*· to call them brethren,
11:16 is not *a*· to be called their God:
1Pe 3:16 as of evildoers, they may be *a*·
4:16 a Christian, let him not be *a*·;
1Jo 2:28 not be *a*· before him.

Ashan (*a'-shan*) See also COR-ASHAN.
Jos 15:42 Libnah, and Ether, and *A*·,
19: 7 Ain, Remmon, and Ether, and *A*·;
1Ch 4:32 Rimmon, and Tochen, and *A*·, five
6:59 And *A*· with her suburbs, and

Ashbea (*ash'-be-ah*)
1Ch 4:21 of the house of *A*·,

Ashbel (*ash'-bel*) See also ASHBELITES.
Ge 46:21 Becher, and *A*·, Gera, and Naaman,
Nu 26:38 of *A*·, the family of the Ashbelites:
1Ch 8: 1 Bela his firstborn, *A*· the second,

Ashbelites (*ash'-bel-ites*)
Nu 26:38 of Ashbel, the family of the *A*·:

Ashchenaz (*ash'-ke-naz*) See also ASHKENAZ.
1Ch 1: 6 sons of Gomer; *A*·, and Riphath,
Jer 51:27 kingdoms of Ararat, Minni, and *A*·;

Ashdod (*ash'-dod*) See also ASHDODITES; AZOTUS.
Jos 11:22 only in Gaza, in Gath, and in *A*·,
15:46 lay near *A*·, with their villages:
47 *A*· with her towns and her villages;
1Sa 5: 1 brought it from Eben-ezer unto *A*·.
3 of *A*· rose early on the morrow,
5 the threshold of Dagon in *A*·
6 was heavy upon them of *A*·, and
6 even *A*· and the coasts thereof.
7 when the men of *A*· saw that it
6:17 for *A*· one, for Gaza one, for
2Ch 26: 6 of *A*·, and built cities about *A*·,
Ne 13:23 Jews that had married wives of *A*·,
24 spake half in the speech of *A*·,
Isa 20: 1 year that Tartan came unto *A*·,
1 and fought against *A*·, and took it;
Jer 25:20 and Ekron, and the remnant of *A*·,
Am 1: 8 cut off the inhabitant from *A*·,
3: 9 Publish in the palaces at *A*·,
Zep 2: 4 shall drive out *A*· at the noonday,
Zec 9: 6 And a bastard shall dwell in *A*·,

Ashdodites (*ash'-dod-ites*) See also ASHDOTHITES.
Ne 4: 7 and the *A*·, heard that the walls

Ashdoth See ASHDOTH-PISGAH.

Ashdothites (*ash'-doth-ites*) See also ASHDODITES.
Jos. 13: 3 *A*·, the Eshkalonites, the Gittites,

Ashdoth-pisgah (*ash''-doth-piz'-gah*)
De 3:17 salt sea, under *A*· eastward.
Jos 12: 3 from the south, under *A*·:
13:20 And Beth-peor, and *A*·, and

Asher (*ash'-ur*) See also ASER; ASHERITES.
Ge 30:13 and she called his name *A*·.
35:26 Leah's handmaid; Gad, and *A*·:
46:17 sons of *A*·; Jimnah, and Ishuah,
49:20 Out of *A*· his bread shall be fat,
Ex 1: 4 Dan, and Naphtali, Gad, and *A*·.
Nu 1:13 Of *A*·; Pagiel the son of Ocran.
40 children of *A*·, by their generations,
41 of the tribe of *A*·, were forty and
2:27 by him shall be the tribe of *A*·:
27 captain of the children of *A*· shall
7:72 prince of the children of *A*·, offered:
10:26 tribe of the children of *A*· was
13:13 of *A*·, Sethur the son of Michael.
26:44 children of *A*· after their families:
46 of the daughter of *A*· was Sarah.
47 are the families of the sons of *A*·
34:27 of *A*·, Ahihud the son of Shelomi.
De 27:13 Reuben, Gad, and *A*·, and Zebulun,
33:24 of *A*· he said, Let *A*· be blessed
Jos 17: 7 coast of Manasseh was from *A*· to
10 met together in *A*· on the north,
11 Manasseh had in Issachar and in *A*·
19:24 tribe of the children of *A*· according
31 of the tribe of the children of *A*·
34 reacheth to *A*· on the west side,
21: 6 out of the tribe of *A*·, and out of
30 of *A*·, Mishal with her suburbs,
J'g 1:31 did *A*· drive out the inhabitants of
5:17 *A*· continued on the sea shore,
6:35 and he sent messengers unto *A*·,
7:23 of *A*·, and out of all Manasseh,
1Ki 4:16 son of Hushai was in *A*· and in
1Ch 2: 2 Benjamin, Naphtali, Gad, and *A*·.
6:62 out of the tribe of *A*·, and out of
74 of *A*·; Mashal with her suburbs,
7:30 sons of *A*·; Imnah, and Isuah,
40 All these were the children of *A*·,
12:36 of *A*·, such as went forth to battle,
2Ch 30:11 divers of *A*· and Manasseh
Eze 48: 2 the west side, a portion for *A*·.
3 border of *A*·, from the east side,
34 gate of *A*·, one gate of Naphtali.

Asherites (*ash'-ur-ites*)
J'g 1:32 *A*· dwelt among the Canaanites,

ashes
Ge 18:27 which am but dust and *a*·:
Ex 9: 8 you handfuls of *a*· of the furnace,
10 And they took *a*· of the furnace,
27:3 pans to receive his *a*·,
Le 1:16 by the place of the *a*·:
4:12 where the *a*· are poured out, and
12 where the *a*· are poured out shall
6:10 take up the *a*·
11 carry forth the *a*·
Nu 4:13 And they shall take away the *a*·
19: 9 the *a*· of the heifer,
10 he that gathereth the *a*· of
17 they shall take of the *a*· of the
2Sa 13:19 Tamar put *a*· on her head,
1Ki 13: 3 the *a*· that are upon it
5 the *a*· poured out from the altar,
20:38 disguised himself with *a*· upon
41 took the *a*· away from his face;
2Ki 23: 4 the *a*· of them unto Beth-el.
Es 4: 1 put on sackcloth with *a*·,
3 many lay in sackcloth and *a*·.
Job 2: 8 he sat down among the *a*·.
13:12 remembrances are like unto *a*·,
30:19 I am become like dust and *a*·.
42: 6 repent in dust and *a*·.
Ps 102: 9 For I have eaten *a*· like bread.
147:16 he scattereth the hoarfrost like *a*·.
Isa 44:20 He feedeth on *a*·:
58: 5 spread sackcloth and *a*· under him?
61: 3 to give unto them beauty for *a*·,
Jer 6:26 wallow thyself in *a*·:
25:34 and wallow yourselves in the *a*·, ye
31:40 and of the *a*·, and all the fields
La 3:16 he hath covered me with *a*·.
Eze 27:30 wallow themselves in the *a*·:
28:18 I will bring thee to *a*·
Da 9: 3 with fasting, and sackcloth, and *a*·:
Jon 3: 6 and sat in *a*·.
Mal 4: 3 for they shall be *a*·
M't 11:21 long ago in sackcloth and *a*·.
Lu 10:13 sitting in sackcloth and *a*·.
Heb 9:13 the *a*· of an heifer sprinkling the
2Pe 2: 6 Sodom and Gomorrha into *a*·

Ashima (*ash'-im-ah*)
2Ki 17:30 and the men of Hamath made *A*·,

Ashkelon (*ash'-ke-lon*) See also ASKELON; ESHKALONITES.
J'g 14:19 and he went down to *A*·, and slew
Jer 25:20 *A*·, and Azzah, and Ekron,
47: 5 *A*· is cut off with the remnant
7 *A*·, and against the sea shore?
Am 1: 8 that holdeth the sceptre from *A*·,
Zep 2: 4 Gaza shall be forsaken, and *A*·
7 houses of *A*· shall they lie down
Zec 9: 5 *A*· shall see it, and fear;
5 and *A*· shall not be inhabited.

Ashkenaz (*ash'-ke-naz*) See also ASCHKENAZ.
Ge 10: 3 sons of Gomer; *A*·, and Riphath,

Ashnah (*ash'-nah*)
Jos 15:33 Eshtaol, and Zoreah, and *A*·,
43 Jiphtah, and *A*·, and Nezib,

Ashpenaz (*ash'-pe-naz*)
Da 1: 3 the king spake unto *A*· the master

Ashriel (*ash'-re-el*) See also ASRIEL
1Ch 7:14 of Manasseh; *A*·, whom she bare:

Ashtaroth (*ash'-ta-roth*). See also ASHTERATHITE; ASHTEROTH; ASTORETH; ASTAROTH; BEESHTERAH.
Jos 9:10 king of Bashan, which was at *A*·.
12: 4 that dwelt at *A*· and at Edrei,
13:12 Og in Bashan, which reigned in *A*·
31 half Gilead, and *A*·, and Edrei,
J'g 2:13 the Lord, and served Baal and *A*·.
10: 6 served Baalim, and *A*·, and the
1Sa 7: 3 put away the strange gods and *A*·
4 Israel did put away Baalim and *A*·,
12:10 and have served Baalim and *A*·:
31:10 put his armour in the house of *A*·;
1Ch 6:71 and *A*· with her suburbs:

Ashterathite (*ash'-ter-a-thite*)
1Ch 11:44 Uzzia the *A*·, Shama and Jehiel

Ashteroth (*ash'-te-roth*) See also ASHTAROTH.
Ge 14: 5 and smote the Rephaims in *A*·

Ashteroth-Karnaim See ASHTEROTH and KARNAIM.

Ashtoreth (*ash'-to-reth*) See also ASHTAROTH.
1Ki 11: 5 Solomon went after *A*· the
33 *A*· the goddess of the Sidonians,
2Ki 23:13 for *A*· the abomination of the

Ashur (*ash'-ur*) See also ASHURITES; ASSHUR; ASSUR; ASSYRIA.
1Ch 2:24 Hezron's wife bare him *A*· the
4: 5 *A*· the father of Tekoa had two

Ashurites (*ash'-ur-ites*) See also ASSHURIM.
2Sa 2: 9 over the *A*·, and over Jezreel,
Eze 27: 6 the *A*· have made thy benches

Ashvath (*ash'-vath*)
1Ch 7:33 and *A*·. These are the children

Asia (*a'-she-ah*)
Ac 2: 9 Pontus, and *A*·,
6: 9 them of Cilicia, and of *A*·,
16: 6 to preach the word in *A*·,
19:10 all they which dwelt in *A*·
22 stayed in *A*· for a season.
26 but almost throughout all *A*·,
27 all *A*· and the world worshippeth.
31 certain of the chief of *A*·,
20: 4 accompanied him into *A*·
4 of *A*·, Tychicus and Trophimus.
16 would not spend the time in *A*·:
18 that I came into *A*·,
21:27 the Jews which were of *A*·,
24:18 certain Jews from *A*·
27: 2 by the coasts of *A*·;
1Co 16:19 The churches of *A*· salute you.
2Co 1: 8 which came to us in *A*·,
2Ti 1:15 all they which are in *A*·
1Pe 1: 1 *A*· and Bithynia,
Re 1: 4 seven churches which are in *A*·:
11 seven churches which are in *A*·:

aside
Ex 3: 3 I will now turn *a*·, and see this
4 the Lord saw that he turned *a*·
32: 8 They have turned *a*· quickly out
Nu 5:12 If any man's wife go *a*·,
19 if thou hast not gone *a*·
20 if thou hast gone *a*·
29 when a wife goeth *a*·
22:23 and the ass turned *a*·
De 5:32 ye shall not turn *a*· to the right
9:12 they are quickly turned *a*· out of
16 ye had turned *a*· quickly out of
11:16 ye turn *a*·, and serve other gods,
28 but turn *a*· out of the way
17:20 that he turn not *a*· from the
28:14 thou shalt not go *a*· from any
31:29 corrupt yourselves, and turn *a*·
Jos 23: 6 that ye turn not *a*· therefrom
J'g 14: 8 he turned *a*· to see the carcase
19:12 We will not turn *a*· hither into
15 And they turned *a*· thither, to go
Ru 4: 1 Ho, such a one! turn *a*·, sit down
1 And he turned *a*·, and sat down,
1Sa 6:12 turned not *a*· to the right hand
8: 3 but turned *a*· after lucre,
12:20 turn not *a*· from following the
21 turn ye not *a*·: for then
2Sa 2:21 Turn thee *a*· to thy right hand, or
21 But Asahel would not turn *a*·
22 Turn thee *a*· from following me:
23 Howbeit he refused to turn *a*·:
3:27 And when...Joab took him *a*· in
6:10 but David carried it *a*·
18:30 Turn *a*·, and stand here.
30 And he turned *a*·, and stood still.
1Ki 15: 5 turned not *a*· from any thing
20:39 behold, a man turned *a*·,
22:32 And they turned *a*· to fight
43 he turned not *a*· from it,
2Ki 4: 4 thou shalt set *a*· that which is
22: 2 turned not *a*· to the right hand
1Ch 13:13 but carried it *a*· into the house of
Job 6:18 paths of their way are turned *a*·;
Ps 14: 3 They are all gone *a*·,
40: 4 nor such as turn *a*· to lies.
78:57 were turned *a*· like a deceitful
101: 3 the work of them that turn *a*·;

Ps 125: 5 As for such as turn *a*· unto their
Ca 1: 7 should I be as one that turneth *a*·
6: 1 whither is thy beloved turned *a*·?
Isa 10: 2 To turn *a*· the needy from
29:21 and turn *a*· the just for a thing of
30:11 turn *a*· out of the path,
44:20 heart hath turned him *a*·,
Jer 14: 8 a wayfaring man that turneth *a*·
15: 5 who shall go *a*· to ask how thou
La 3:11 He hath turned *a*· my ways,
35 To turn *a*· the right of a man
Am 2: 7 and turn *a*· the way of the meek:
5:12 they turn *a*· the poor
Mal 3: 5 and that turn *a*· the stranger
M't 2:22 he turned *a*· into the parts of
M'r 7: 8 laying *a*· the commandment of
33 *a*· from the multitude,
Lu 9:10 and went *a*· privately
Joh 13: 4 and laid *a*· his garments;
Ac 4:15 commanded them to go *a*· out of
23:19 went with him *a*· privately, and
26:31 when they were gone *a*·, they
1Ti 1: 6 turned *a*· unto vain jangling;
5:15 some are already turned *a*· after
Heb 12: 1 let us lay *a*· every weight, and
1Pe 2: 1 Wherefore laying *a*· all malice,

Asiel (*a'-se-el*).
1Ch 4:35 of Seraiah, the son of *A*·,

ask See also ASKED; ASKEST; ASKETH; ASKING.
Ge 32:29 thou dost *a*· after my name?
34:12 *A*· me never so much dowry and
Nu 27:21 who shall *a*· counsel for him
De 4:32 *a*· now of the days that are past,
32 *a*· from the one side of heaven
13:14 enquire, and make search, and *a*·
32: 7 *a*· thy father, and he will shew
Jos 4: 6 your children *a*· their fathers
21 When your children shall *a*·
15:18 she moved him to *a*· of her
J'g 1:14 she moved him to *a*· of her
18: 5 *A*· counsel, we pray thee, of God,
1Sa 12:19 our sins this evil, to *a*· us a king.
25: 8 *A*· thy young men, and they will
28:16 Wherefore then dost thou *a*· of me,
2Sa 14:18 thee, the thing that I shall *a*· thee.
20:18 shall surely *a*· counsel at Abel:
1Ki 2:16 I *a*· one petition of thee,
20 the king said unto her, *A*· on, my
22 why dost thou *a*· Abishag
22 *a*· for him the kingdom also;
3: 5 *A*· what I shall give thee.
14: 5 cometh to *a*· a thing of thee for
2Ki 2: 9 *A*· what I shall do for thee,
2Ch 1: 7 *A*· what I shall give thee.
20: 4 to *a*· help of the Lord:
Job 12: 7 *a*· now the beasts, and they shall
Ps 2: 8 *A*· of me, and I shall give thee
Isa 7:11 *A*· thee a sign of the Lord
11 *a*· it either in the depth, or in the
12 Ahaz said, I will not *a*·,
45:11 *A*· me of things to come
58: 2 *a*· of me the ordinances of justice;
Jer 6:16 and *a*· for the old paths,
15: 5 who shall go aside to *a*· how thou
18:13 *A*· ye now among the heathen,
23:33 prophet, or a priest, shall *a*· thee,
30: 6 *A*· ye now, and see
38:14 I will *a*· thee a thing;
48:19 *a*· him that fleeth,
50: 5 They shall *a*· the way to Zion
La 4: 4 the young children *a*· bread,
Da 6: 7 whosoever shall *a*· a petition of
12 every man that shall *a*· a petition
Ho 4:12 My people *a*· counsel at their
Hag 2:11 *A*· now the priests concerning
Zec 10: 1 *A*· ye of the Lord rain
M't 6: 8 have need of, before ye *a*· him.
7: 7 *A*·, and it shall be given you;
9 if his son *a*· bread, will he give
10 Or if he *a*· a fish, will he give him
11 good things to them that *a*· him?
14: 7 give her whatsoever she would *a*·.
18:19 any thing that they shall *a*·,
20:22 said, Ye know not what ye *a*·.
21:22 whatsoever ye shall *a*· in prayer
24 I also will *a*· you one thing,
22:46 *a*· him any more questions.
27:20 that they should *a*· Barabbas,
M'r 6:22 *A*· of me whatsoever thou wilt;
23 Whatsoever thou shalt *a*· of me,
24 unto her mother, What shall I *a*·?
9:32 saying, and were afraid to *a*· him.
10:38 Ye know not what ye *a*·:
11:29 I will also *a*· of you one question,
12:34 And no man after that durst *a*·
Lu 6: 9 I will *a*· you one thing; Is it
30 away thy goods *a*· them not
9:45 they feared to *a*· him of that
11: 9 *A*·, and it shall be given you;
11 If a son shall *a*· bread of any
11 if he *a*· a fish will he for a fish
12 Or if he shall *a*· an egg, will
13 Holy Spirit to them that *a*· him?
12:48 of him they will *a*· the more.
19:31 if any man *a*· you,
20: 3 I will also *a*· you one thing;
40 they durst not *a*· him any
22:68 And if I also *a*· you,
Joh 1:19 from Jerusalem to *a*· him, Who
9:21 he is of age; *a*· him: he shall
23 his parents, He is of age; *a*· him.
11:22 whatsoever thou wilt *a*· of God,
13:24 that he should *a*· who it should
14:13 whatsoever ye shall *a*· in my
14 If ye shall *a*· any thing in my
Joh 15: 7 abide in you, ye shall *a*· what
16 whatsoever ye shall *a*· of the
16:19 they were desirous to *a*· him,
23 ye shall *a*· me nothing.
23 Whatsoever ye shall *a*· the
24 *a*·, and ye shall receive, that your
26 At that day ye shall *a*· in my name:
30 that any man should *a*· thee:
18:21 Why askest thou me? *a*· them
21:12 none of the disciples durst *a*·
Ac 3: 2 to *a*· alms of them that entered
10:29 I *a*· therefore for what intent
1Co 14:35 let them *a*· their husbands at
Eph 3:20 above all that we *a*· or think,
Jas 1: 5 you lack wisdom, let him *a*· of
6 But let him *a*· in faith, nothing
4: 2 ye have not, because ye *a*· not.
3 Ye *a*·, and receive not, because
3 ye *a*· amiss, that ye may
1Jo 3:22 whatsoever we *a*·, we receive
5:14 if we *a*· any thing according to his
15 we *a*·, we know that we have the
16 not unto death, he shall *a*·, and

asked^
Ge 24:47 And I *a*· her, and said,
26: 7 the men of the place *a*· him of
32:29 And Jacob *a*· him,
37:15 and the man *a*· him,
38:21 Then he *a*· the men of that place,
40: 7 And he *a*· Pharaoh's officers
43: 7 The man *a*· us straitly
27 And he *a*· them of their welfare,
44:19 My lord *a*· his servants,
Ex 18: 7 they *a*· each other of their welfare;
Jos 9:14 *a*· not counsel at the mouth of the
19:50 gave him the city which he *a*·,
J'g 1: 1 that the children of Israel *a*·
5:25 *a*· water, and she gave him milk;
6:29 And when they enquired and *a*·,
13: 6 I *a*· him not whence he was,
20:18 and *a*· counsel of God,
23 and *a*· counsel of the Lord,
1Sa 1:17 thy petition that thou hast *a*·
20 I have *a*· him of the Lord.
27 my petition which I *a*· of him:
8:10 the people that *a*· of him a king.
14:37 And Saul *a*· counsel of God,
19:22 and he *a*· and said,
20: 6 David earnestly *a*· leave
28 *a*· leave of me to go to Beth-lehem:
1Ki 3:10 Solomon had *a*· this thing.
11 Because thou hast *a*· this thing,
11 hast not *a*· for thyself long life;
11 neither hast *a*· riches for thyself,
11 hast *a*· the life of thine enemies;
11 hast *a*· for thyself understanding
13 thee that which thou hast not *a*·,
10:13 whatsoever she *a*·,
2Ki 2:10 Thou hast *a*· a hard thing:
8: 6 when the king *a*· the woman,
2Ch 1:11 thou hast not *a*· riches,
11 neither yet hast *a*· long life;
11 hast *a*· wisdom and knowledge
9:12 all her desire, whatsoever she *a*·,
Ezr 5: 9 Then *a*· we those elders,
10 We *a*· their names also,
Ne 1: 2 and I *a*· them concerning the Jews
Job 21:29 Have ye not *a*· them that go by
Ps 21: 4 He *a*· life of thee,
105:40 The people *a*·, and he brought
Isa 30: 2 have not *a*· at my mouth;
41:28 when I *a*· of them, could answer
65: 1 I am sought of them that *a*· not
Jer 36:17 they *a*· Baruch,
37:17 the king *a*· him secretly in his
38:27 the princes unto Jeremiah, and *a*·
Da 2:10 *a*· such things at any magician,
7:16 and *a*· him the truth of all this.
M't 12:10 they *a*· him, saying,
16:13 he *a*· his disciples, saying, Whom
17:10 his disciples *a*· him, saying,
22:23 is no resurrection, and *a*· him,
35 them, which was a lawyer, *a*· him
41 gathered together, Jesus *a*· them,
27:11 and the governor *a*· him, saying,
M'r 4:10 about him with the twelve *a*· of
5: 9 And he *a*· him, What is thy name?
6:25 unto the king, and *a*·, saying,
7: 5 Pharisees and scribes *a*· him,
8: 5 he *a*· them, How many loaves
23 he *a*· him if he saw ought.
27 by the way he *a*· his disciples,
9:11 And they *a*· him saying, Why say
16 And he *a*· the scribes, What
21 And he *a*· his father, How long is it
28 his disciples *a*· him privately, Why
33 being in the house he *a*· them,
10: 2 Pharisees came to him, and *a*· him,
10 disciples *a*· him again of the same
17 and *a*· him, Good Master, what
12:18 no resurrection; and they *a*· him,
28 *a*· him, Which is the first
13: 3 John and Andrew *a*· him privately,
14:60 the midst, and *a*· Jesus, saying,
61 Again the high priest *a*· him, and
15: 2 And Pilate *a*· him, Art thou the
4 And Pilate *a*· him again, saying,
44 he *a*· him whether he had been
Lu 1:63 he *a*· for a writing table, and wrote,
3:10 And the people *a*· him, saying,
8: 9 And his disciples *a*· him, saying,
30 And Jesus *a*· him, saying, What is
9:18 and he *a*· them, saying, Whom say
15:26 and *a*· what these things meant.
18:18 a certain ruler *a*· him, saying,
36 pass by, he *a*· what it meant.
Lu 18:40 he was come near, he *a*· him,
20:21 they *a*· him, saying, Master, we
27 any resurrection; and they *a*· him,
21: 7 And they *a*· him, saying, Master,
22:64 and *a*· him, saying, Prophesy, who
23: 3 And Pilate *a*· him, saying, Art
6 he *a*· whether the man were a
Joh 1:21 And they *a*· him, What then?
25 they *a*· him, and said
4:10 thou wouldest have *a*· of him,
5:12 Then *a*· they him, What man is
9: 2 his disciples *a*· him,
15 the Pharisees also *a*· him
19 *a*· them, saying, Is this your son,
16:24 have ye *a*· nothing in my name:
18: 7 Then *a*· he them again, Whom
19 The high priest then *a*· Jesus of
Ac 1: 6 they *a*· of him, saying, Lord, wilt
3: 3 to go into the temple *a*· an alms.
4: 7 they *a*·, By what power, or by
5:27 and the high priest *a*· them,
10:18 and *a*· whether Simon,
23:19 aside privately, and *a*· him,
34 he *a*· of what province he was.
25:20 I *a*· him whether he would go
Ro 10:20 unto them that *a*· not after me.

Askelon (*as'-ke-lon*) See also ASHKELON.
J'g 1:18 and *A*· with the coast thereof,
1Sa 6:17 for Gaza one, for *A*· one, for Gath
2Sa 1:20 publish it not in the streets of *A*·;

askest
J'g 13:18 Why *a*· thou thus after my name,
Joh 4: 9 being a Jew, *a*· drink of me,
18:21 Why *a*· thou me? ask them which

asketh
Ge 32:17 my brother meeteth thee, and *a*·
Ex 13:14 when thy son *a*· thee
De 6:20 thy son *a*· thee in time to come,
Mic 7: 3 hands earnestly, the prince *a*·,
3 and the judge *a*· for a reward;
M't 5:42 Give to him that *a*· thee, and
7: 8 every one that *a*· receiveth;
Lu 6:30 Give to every man that *a*· of thee;
11:10 every one that *a*· receiveth;
Joh 16: 5 none of you *a*· me,
1Pe 3:15 every man that *a*· you a reason

asking
1Sa 12:17 in *a*· you a king.
1Ch 10:13 for *a*· counsel of one that had a
Ps 78:18 tempted God in their heart by *a*·
Lu 2:46 them, and *a*· them questions.
Joh 8: 7 So when they continued *a*· him,
1Co 10:25 *a*· no question for conscience sake:
27 eat, *a*· no question for conscience

asleep
J'g 4:21 he was fast *a*· and weary.
1Sa 26:12 for they were all *a*·;
Ca 7: 9 those that are *a*· to speak.
Jon 1: 5 and he lay, and was fast *a*·.
M't 8:24 but he was *a*·.
26:40 and findeth them *a*·,
43 came and found them *a*· again:
M'k 4:38 *a*· on a pillow: and they awake
14:40 he found them *a*· again,
Lu 8:23 as they sailed he fell *a*·:
Ac 7:60 when he had said this, he fell *a*·.
1Co 15: 6 but some are fallen *a*·.
18 also which are fallen *a*· in Christ
1Th 4:13 concerning them which are *a*·,
15 not prevent them which are *a*·.
2Pe 3: 4 since the fathers fell *a*·, all things

Asnah (*as'-nah*)
Ezr 2:50 The children of *A*·, the children

Asnapper (*as-nap'-pur*)
Ezr 4:10 great and noble *A*· brought over,

asp See also ASPS.
Isa 11: 8 shall play on the hole of the *a*·,

Aspatha (*as'-pa-thah*)
Es 9: 7 and Dalphon, and *A*·,

asps
De 32:33 and the cruel venom of *a*·.
Job 20:14 the gall of *a*· within him.
16 He shall suck the poison of *a*·:
Ro 3:13 poison of *a*· is under their lips:

Asriel (*as'-re-el*) See also ASHRIEL; ASRIELITES.
Nu 26:31 of *A*·, the family of the Asrielites:
Jos 17: 2 and for the children of *A*·,

Asrielites (*as'-re-el-ites*)
Nu 26:31 of Asriel, the family of the *A*·:

ass See also ASS'S; ASSES.
Ge 22: 3 saddled his *a*·, and took two of
5 Abide ye here with the *a*·;
42:27 give his *a*· provender in the inn,
44:13 laded every man his *a*·,
49:14 Issachar is a strong *a*· couching
Ex 4:20 set them upon an *a*·,
13:13 every firstling of an *a*· thou shalt
20:17 nor his ox, nor his *a*·, nor anything
21:33 an ox or an *a*· fall therein;
22: 4 whether it be ox, or *a*·, or sheep;
9 for ox, for *a*·, for sheep,
10 deliver unto his neighbour an *a*·,
23: 4 thine enemy's ox or his *a*· going
5 If thou see the *a*· of him that
12 thine ox and thine *a*· may rest,
34:20 firstling of an *a*· thou shalt redeem
Nu 16:15 I have not taken one *a*· from them,
22:21 and saddled his *a*·, and went with
22 Now he was riding upon his *a*·,
23 the *a*· saw the angel of the Lord
23 the *a*· turned aside out of the way,

Nu 22:23 Balaam smote the *a·*, to turn her
25, 27 the *a·* saw the angel of the Lord,
27 he smote the *a·* with a staff.
28 Lord opened the mouth of the *a·*,
29 Balaam said unto the *a·*,
30 the *a·* said unto Balaam,
30 Am not I thine *a·*,
32 hast thou smitten thine *a·*
33 And the *a·* saw me, and turned
De 5:14 nor thine ox, nor thine *a·*,
21 his ox, or his *a·*, or any thing
22: 3 shalt thou do with his *a·*;
4 see thy brother's *a·* or his ox fall
10 plow with an ox and an *a·* together
28:31 thine *a·* shall be violently taken
Jos 6:21 ox, and sheep, and *a·*, with the
15:18 she lighted off her *a·*;
J'g 1:14 she lighted from off her *a·*;
6: 4 neither sheep, nor ox, nor *a·*.
10: 4 sons that rode on thirty *a·* colts,
12:14 threescore and ten *a·* colts:
15:15 found a new jawbone of an *a·*,
16 With the jawbone of an *a·*,
16 upon heaps, with the jaw of an *a·*
19:28 the man took her up upon an *a·*,
1Sa 12: 3 or whose *a·* have I taken?
15: 3 ox and sheep, camel and *a·*.
16:20 Jesse took an *a·* laden with bread,
25:20 she rode on the *a·*,
23 hasted, and lighted off the *a·*,
42 arose, and rode upon an *a·*,
2Sa 17:23 he saddled his *a·*, and arose,
19:26 I will saddle me an *a·*,
1Ki 2:40 Shimei arose, and saddled his *a·*,
13:13 Saddle me the *a·*.
13 So they saddled him the *a·*:
23 that he saddled for him the *a·*,
24 cast in the way, and the *a·* stood by
27 Saddle me the *a·*.
28 and the *a·* and the lion standing
28 the carcase, nor torn the *a·*.
29 laid it upon the *a·*,
2Ki 4:24 Then she saddled an *a·*,
Job 6: 5 Doth the wild *a·* bray
24: 3 away the *a·* of the fatherless,
39: 5 hath sent out the wild *a·* free?
5 loosed the bands of the wild *a·*?
Pr 26: 3 a bridle for the *a·*,
Isa 1: 3 and the *a·* his master's crib:
32:20 the feet of the ox and the *a·*.
Jer 2:24 A wild *a·* used to the wilderness,
22:19 buried with the burial of an *a·*,
Hos 8: 9 a wild *a·* alone by himself:
Zec 9: 9 lowly, and riding upon an *a·*,
9 and upon a colt the foal of an *a·*.
14:15 mule, of the camel, and of the *a·*,
M't 21: 2 ye shall find an *a·* tied,
5 meek, and sitting upon an *a·*,
5 and a colt the foal of an *a·*.
7 And brought the *a·*, and the colt,
Lu 13:15 loose his ox or his *a·* from the stall,
14: 5 Which of you shall have an *a·* or
Joh 12:14 when he had found a young *a·*,
2Pe 2:16 *a·* speaking with man's voice

assault See also ASSAULTED.
Es 8:11 the people...that would *a·* them,
Ac 14: 5 when there was an *a·* made

assaulted
Ac 17: 5 *a·* the house of Jason, and sought

assay See also ASSAYED; ASSAYING.
Job 4: 2 If we *a·* to commune with thee,

assayed
De 4:34 hath God *a·* to go and take him
1Sa 17:39 and he *a·* to go; for he had not
Ac 9:26 *a·* to join himself to the disciples:
16: 7 they *a·* to go into Bithynia:

assaying
Heb 11:29 Egyptians *a·* to do were

ass-colts See ASS and COLTS.

assemble See also ASSEMBLED; ASSEMBLING.
Nu 10: 3 shall *a·* themselves to thee
2Sa 20: 4 *A·* me the men of Judah
5 went to *a·* the men of Judah:
Isa 11:12 shall *a·* the outcasts of Israel,
45:20 *A·* yourselves and come;
48:14 All ye, *a·* yourselves, and hear;
Jer 4: 5 and say, *A·* yourselves, and let us
8:14 do we sit still? *a·* yourselves,
12: 9 *a·* all the beasts of the field,
21: 4 and I will *a·* them into the midst
Eze 11:17 and *a·* you out of the countries
39:17 *A·* yourselves, and come;
Da 11:10 *a·* a multitude of great forces:
Ho 7:14 they *a·* themselves for corn
Joe 2:16 Gather the people,...*a·* the elders,
3:11 *A·* yourselves, and come, all ye
Am 3: 9 *A·* yourselves upon the mountains
Mic 2:12 surely *a·*, O Jacob, all of thee;
4: 6 will I *a·* her that halteth,
Zep 3: 8 that I may *a·* the kingdoms,

assembled
Ex 38: 8 *a·* at the door of the tabernacle
Nu 1:18 they *a·* all the congregation
Jos 18: 1 congregation...*a·* together at
J'g 10:17 of Israel *a·* themselves together,
1Sa 2:22 *a·* at the door of the tabernacle
14:20 all the people...*a·* themselves,
1Ki 8: 1 Solomon *a·* the elders of Israel,
2 *a·* themselves unto king Solomon
5 that were *a·* unto him,
12:21 he *a·* all the house of Judah,
1Ch 15: 4 David *a·* the children of Aaron,
28: 1 David *a·* all the princes of Israel,
2Ch 5: 2 Solomon *a·* the elders of Israel,
3 all the men of Israel *a·* themselves
6 were *a·* unto him before the ark,
20:26 they *a·* themselves in the valley
30:13 *a·* at Jerusalem much people,
Ezr 9: 4 Then were *a·* unto me every one
10: 1 there *a·* unto him...a very great
Ne 9: 1 the children of Israel were *a·*
Es 9:18 that were at Shushan *a·* together
Ps 48: 4 kings were *a·*, they passed by
Isa 43: 9 and let the people be *a·*:
Jer 5: 7 and *a·* themselves by troops
Eze 38: 7 company that are *a·* unto thee,
Da 6: 6 presidents and princes *a·* together
11 these men *a·*, and found Daniel
15 Then these men *a·* unto the king,
M't 26: 3 *a·* together the chief priests,
57 scribes and the elders were *a·*.
28:12 they were *a·* with the elders,
M'r 14:53 were *a·* all the chief priests,
Joh 20:19 where the disciples were *a·*
Ac 1: 4 And being *a·* together with them,
4:31 where they were *a·* together;
11:26 *a·* themselves with the church,
15:25 being *a·* with one accord,

assemblies
Ps 86:14 and the *a·* of violent men
Ec 12:11 fastened by the masters of *a·*,
Isa 1:13 calling of *a·*, I cannot away with;
4: 5 her *a·*, a cloud of smoke by day,
Eze 44:24 my statutes in all mine *a·*;
Am 5:21 not smell in your solemn *a·*.

assembling
Ex 38: 8 lookingglasses of the women *a·*,
Heb 10: 25 the *a·* of ourselves together,

assembly See also ASSEMBLIES.
Ge 49: 6 into their secret; unto their *a·*,
Ex 12: 6 *a·* of the congregation of Israel
16: 3 kill this whole *a·* with hunger.
Le 4:13 be hid from the eyes of the *a·*,
8: 4 the *a·* was gathered together
23:36 it is a solemn *a·*;
Nu 8: 9 thou shalt gather the whole *a·*
10: 2 the calling of the *a·*, and for the
3 *a·* shall assemble themselves to
14: 5 on their faces before all the *a·*
16: 2 princes of the *a·*, famous
20: 6 went from the presence of the *a·*
8 gather thou the *a·* together,
29:35 ye shall have a solemn *a·*:
De 5:22 the Lord spake unto all your *a·*
9:10 fire in the day of the *a·*.
10: 4 of the fire, in the day of the *a·*
16: 8 a solemn *a·* to the Lord thy God:
18:16 Horeb in the day of the *a·*,
J'g 20: 2 themselves in the *a·* of the people,
21: 8 from Jabesh-gilead to the *a·*.
1Sa 17:47 this *a·* shall know that the Lord
2Ki 10:20 Proclaim a solemn *a·* for Baal.
2Ch 7: 9 they made a solemn *a·*:
30:23 the whole *a·* took counsel
Ne 5: 7 And I set a great *a·* against them.
8:18 the eighth day was a solemn *a·*,
Ps 22:16 *a·* of the wicked have inclosed me:
89: 7 to be feared in the *a·* of the saints,
107:32 and praise him in the *a·* of the
111: 1 in the *a·* of the upright,
Pr 5:14 midst of the congregation and *a·*.
Jer 6:11 the *a·* of young men together:
9: 2 an *a·* of treacherous men.
15:17 I sat not in the *a·* of the mockers,
26:17 spake to all the *a·* of the people,
50: 9 Babylon an *a·* of great nations,
La 1:15 he hath called an *a·* against me,
2: 6 destroyed his places of the *a·*:
Eze 13: 9 not be in the *a·* of my people,
23:24 and with an *a·* of people,
Joe 1:14 call a solemn *a·*, gather the elders
2:15 sanctify a fast, call a solemn *a·*:
Zep 3:18 are sorrowful for the solemn *a·*,
Ac 19:32 for the *a·* was confused;
39 determined in a lawful *a·*.
41 thus spoken, he dismissed the *a·*.
Heb 12:23 *a·* and church of the firstborn,
Jas 2: 2 there come unto your *a·* a man

assent See also ASSENTED.
2Ch 18:12 good to the king with one *a·*;

assented
Ac 24: 9 And the Jews also *a·*, saying

ass's
Ge 49:11 his *a·* colt unto the choice vine;
2Ki 6:25 an *a·* head was sold for fourscore
Job 11:12 man be born like a wild *a·* colt.
Joh 12:15 King cometh, sitting on an *a·* colt.

asses
Ge 12:16 he *a·*, and menservants,
16 and maidservants, and she *a·*,
24:35 maidservants, and camels, and *a·*:
30:43 menservants, and camels, and *a·*.
32: 5 I have oxen, and *a·*, flocks,
15 twenty she *a·*, and ten foals.
34:28 their oxen, and their *a·*,
36:24 as he fed the *a·* of Zibeon
42:26 they laded their *a·* with the corn,
43:18 take us for bondmen, and our *a·*.
24 he gave their *a·* provender.
44: 3 sent away, they and their *a·*.
45:23 ten *a·* laden with the good things
23 she *a·* laden with corn and bread
47:17 herds, and for the *a·*:
Ex 9: 3 upon the horses, upon the *a·*,
Nu 31:28 of the beeves, and of the *a·*,
30 of the *a·*, and of the flocks,
Nu 31:34 threescore and one thousand *a·*,
39 And the *a·* were thirty thousand
45 thousand *a·* and five hundred,
Jos 7:24 his oxen, and his *a·*,
9: 4 took old sacks upon their *a·*,
J'g 5:10 speak, ye that ride on white *a·*,
19: 3 with him, and a couple of *a·*:
10 with him two *a·* saddled,
19 straw and provender for our *a·*;
21 gave provender unto the *a·*:
1Sa 8:16 goodliest young men, and your *a·*,
9: 3 *a·* of Kish, Saul's father were lost.
3 arise, go seek the *a·*.
5 leave caring for the *a·*,
20 And as for thine *a·* that were lost
10: 2 The *a·* which thou wentest to seek
2 hath left the care of the *a·*,
14 And he said, To seek the *a·*:
16 plainly that the *a·* were found.
22:19 oxen, and *a·*, and sheep,
25:18 laid them on *a·*.
27: 9 oxen, and the *a·*, and the camels,
2Sa 16: 1 with a couple of *a·* saddled,
2 The *a·* be for the king's household
2Ki 4:22 the young men, and one of the *a·*,
7: 7 their horses, and their *a·*,
10 horses tied, and *a·* tied,
1Ch 5:21 and of *a·* two thousand,
12:40 brought bread on *a·*,
27:30 and over the *a·* was Jehdeiah
2Ch 28:15 all the feeble of them upon *a·*,
Ezr 2:67 *a·*, six thousand seven hundred
Ne 7:69 seven hundred and twenty *a·*.
13:15 bringing in sheaves, and lading *a·*;
Job 1: 3 five hundred she *a·*,
14 and the *a·* feeding beside them
24: 5 as wild *a·* in the desert,
42:12 a thousand she *a·*.
Ps 104:11 the wild *a·* quench their thirst.
Isa 21: 7 a chariot of *a·*, and a chariot of
30: 6 upon the shoulders of young *a·*,
24 the young *a·* that ear the ground
32:14 joy of wild *a·*, a pasture of flocks;
Jer 14: 6 *a·* did stand in the high places,
Eze 23:20 whose flesh is as the flesh of *a·*,
Da 5:21 his dwelling was with the wild *a·*:

Asshur (*ash'-ur*) See also ASHUR; ASSUR; ASSYRIA.
Ge 10:11 Out of that land went forth *A·*,
22 Elam, and *A·*, and Arphaxad, and
Nu 24:22 *A·* shall carry thee away captive.
24 afflict *A·*, and shall afflict Eber,
1Ch 1:17 The sons of Shem; Elam, and *A·*,
Eze 27:23 the merchants of Sheba, *A·*, and
32:22 *A·* is there and all her company:
Hos 14: 3 *A·* shall not save us; we will not

Asshurim (*ash'-u-rim*) See also ASHURITES.
Ge 25: 3 the sons of Dedan were *A·*, and

assigned
Ge 47:22 priests had a portion *a·* them
Jos 20: 8 they *a·* Bezer in the wilderness
2Sa 11:16 that he *a·* Uriah unto a place

Assir (*as'-sur*)
Ex 6:24 *A·*, and Elkanah, and Abiasaph:
1Ch 3:17 Jeconiah; *A·*, Salathiel his son,
6:22 Korah his son, *A·* his son,
23 Ebiasaph his son, and *A·* his son,
37 The son of Tahath, the son of *A·*,

assist
Ro 16: 2 and that ye *a·* her in whatsoever

associate
Isa 8: 9 *A·* yourselves, O ye people,

Assos (*as'-sos*)
Ac 20:13 sailed unto *A·*, there intending to
14 he met with us at *A·*,

assuage See ASSWAGE.

Assur (*as'-sur*) See also ASSHUR.
Ezr 4: 2 days of Esar-haddon king of *A·*,
Ps 83: 8 *A·* also is joined with them: they

assurance
De 28:66 shalt have none *a·* of thy life:
Isa 32:17 quietness and *a·* for ever.
Ac 17:31 he hath given *a·* unto all men,
Col 2: 2 of the full *a·* of understanding,
1Th 1: 5 and in much *a·*; as ye know
He 6:11 the full *a·* of hope unto the end:
10:22 in full *a·* of faith, having our

assure See also ASSURED.
1Jo 3:19 and shall *a·* our hearts before him.

assured
Le 27:19 and it shall be *a·* to him.
Jer 14:13 *a·* peace in this place.
2Ti 3:14 and hast been *a·* of,

assuredly
1Sa 28: 1 know thou *a·*, that thou shalt go
1Ki 1:13 *A·* Solomon thy son shall reign
17, 30 saying, *A·* Solomon thy son
Jer 32:41 *a·* with my whole heart
38:17 wilt *a·* go forth unto the king
49:12 of the cup have *a·* drunken;
Ac 2:36 house of Israel know *a·*,
16:10 *a·* gathering that the Lord had

asswage See ASSWAGED.
Job 16: 5 my lips should *a·* your grief

asswaged
Ge 8: 1 and the waters *a·*;
Job 16: 6 my grief is not *a·*:

Assyria (*as-sir'-e-ah*) See also ASSHUR; ASSYRIAN.
Ge 2:14 which goeth toward the east of A·.
25:18 Egypt, as thou goest toward A·:
2Ki 15:19 Pul the king of A· came against
20 of silver, to give to the king of A·.
20 So the king of A· turned back,
29 came Tiglath-pileser king of A·,
29 and carried them captive to A·.
16: 7 to Tiglath-pileser king of A·,
8 for a present to the king of A·.
9 the king of A· hearkened unto him:
9 of A· went up against Damascus,
10 to meet Tiglath-pileser king of A·,
18 of the Lord for the king of A·.
17: 3 came up Shalmaneser king of A·;
4 the king of A· found conspiracy
4 brought no present to the king of A·,
4 therefore the king of A· shut him up,
5 Then the king of A· came up
6 the king of A· took Samaria,
6 and carried Israel away into A·,
23 away out of their own land to A·
24 the king of A· brought men from
26 they spake to the king of A·,
27 Then the king of A· commanded,
18: 7 he rebelled against the king of A·,
9 Shalmaneser king of A· came up
11 And the king of A· did carry away
11 did carry away Israel unto A·,
13 did Sennacherib king of A· come
14 sent to the king of A· to Lachish,
14 king of A· appointed unto Hezekiah
16 and gave it to the king of A·.
17 the king of A· sent Tartan and
19 the great king, the king of A·,
23 pledges to my lord the king of A·,
28 of the great king, the king of A·:
30 into the hand of the king of A·.
31 for thus saith the king of A·,
33 out of the hand of the king of A·?
19: 4 whom the king of A· his master
6 the servants of the king of A· have
8 and found the king of A· warring
10 into the hand of the king of A·.
11 what the kings of A· have done
17 the kings of A· have destroyed the
20 against Sennacherib king of A· I
32 Lord concerning the king of A·,
36 Sennacherib king of A· departed,
20: 6 out of the hand of the king of A·;
23:29 went up against the king of A·
1Ch 5: 6 whom Tilgath-pilneser king of A·
26 up the spirit of Pul king of A·,
26 spirit of Tilgath-pilneser king of A·,
2Ch 28:16 Ahaz send unto the kings of A· to
20 Tilgath-pilneser king of A· came
21 and gave it unto the king of A·:
30: 6 out of the hand of the kings of A·.
32: 1 Sennacherib king of A· came,
4 Why should the kings of A· come,
7 nor dismayed for the king of A·,
9 did Sennacherib king of A· send
10 Thus saith Sennacherib king of A·,
11 out of the hand of the king of A·?
21 in the camp of the king of A·.
22 hand of Sennacherib the king of A·,
33:11 of the host of the king of A·,
Ezr 6:22 turned the heart of the king of A·
Ne 9:32 since the time of the kings of A·
Isa 7:17 from Judah; even the king of A·.
18 the bee that is in the land of A·.
20 beyond the river, by the king of A·,
8: 4 taken away before the king of A·,
7 the king of A·, and all his glory:
10:12 of the stout heart of the king of A·,
11:11 which shall be left, from A·, and
16 which shall be left, from A·; like as
19:23 a highway out of Egypt to A·,
23 and the Egyptian into A·, and the
24 the third with Egypt and with A·,
25 and A· the work of my hands,
20: 1 Sargon the king of A· sent him,)
4 So shall the king of A· lead away
6 be delivered from the king of A·:
27:13 ready to perish in the land of A·,
36: 1 that Sennacherib king of A· came
2 the king of A· sent Rabshakeh
4 the king of A·, What confidence
8 thee, to my master the king of A·,
13 of the great king, the king of A·.
15 into the hand of the king of A·.
16 for thus saith the king of A·,
18 out of the hand of the king of A·?
37: 4 whom the king of A· his master hath
6 the servants of the king of A· have
8 and found the king of A· warring
10 into the hand of the king of A·.
11 what the kings of A· have done
18 the kings of A· have laid waste all
21 me against Sennacherib king of A·:
33 Lord concerning the king of A·,
37 Sennacherib king of A· departed,
38: 6 out of the hand of the king of A·:
Jer 2:18 hast thou to do in the way of A·,
36 Egypt, as thou wast ashamed of A·.
50:17 the king of A· hath devoured him;
18 as I have punished the king of A·.
Eze 23: 7 that were the chosen men of A·,
Ho 7:11 they call to Egypt, they go to A·.
8: 9 For they are gone up to A·, a wild
9: 3 they shall eat unclean things in A·.
10: 6 It shall be also carried unto A·
11:11 as a dove out of the land of A·:
Mic 5: 6 they shall waste the land of A·
7:12 shall come even to thee from A·,
Na 3:18 shepherds slumber, O king of A·:
Zep 2:13 against the north, and destroy A·;
Zec 10:10 Egypt, and gather them out of A·;
11 pride of A· shall be brought down,

Assyrian (*as-sir'-e'-un*) See also ASSYRIANS.
Isa 10: 5 O A·, the rod of mine anger,
24 in Zion, be not afraid of the A·:
14:25 I will break the A· in my land,
19:23 and the A· shall come into Egypt,
23:13 till the A· founded it for them that
30:31 shall the A· be beaten down,
31: 8 shall the A· fall with the sword,
52: 4 A· oppressed them without cause.
Eze 31: 3 the A· was a cedar in Lebanon with
Ho 5:13 then went Ephraim to the A·,
11: 5 but the A· shall be his king,
Mic 5: 5 the A· shall come into our land:
6 thus shall he deliver us from the A·

Assyrians (*as-sir'-e-uns*)
2Ki 19:35 and smote in the camp of the A·
Isa 19:23 shall serve with the A·.
37:36 and smote in the camp of the A·
La 5: 6 and to the A·, to be satisfied with
Eze 16:28 the whore also with the A·,
23: 5 her lovers, on the A· her neighbours,
9 into the hand of the A·, upon
12 upon the A· her neighbours,
23 and Koa, and all the A· with them:
Ho 12: 1 do make a covenant with the A·,

Astaroth (*as'-ta-roth*) See also ASHTAROTH.
De 1: 4 king of Bashan, which dwelt at A

astonied See also ASTONISHED.
Ezr 9: 3 of my beard, and sat down a·.
4 sat a· until the evening sacrifice.
Job 17: 8 upright men shall be a· at this,
18:20 that come after him shall be a·
Isa 52:14 As many were a· at thee;
Jer 14: 9 shouldest thou be as a man a·,
Eze 4:17 a· one with another, and
Da 3:24 Nebuchadnezzar the king was a·,
4:19 Daniel,....was a· for one hour,
5: 9 in him, and his lords were a·.

astonished See also ASTONIED.
Le 26:32 and your enemies...shall be a·
1Ki 9: 8 passeth by it shall be a·,
Job 21: 5 Mark me, and be a·, and lay your
26:11 and are a· at his reproof.
Jer 2:12 Be a·, O ye heavens, at this,
4: 9 and the priests shall be a·,
18:16 that passeth thereby shall be a·,
19: 8 that passeth thereby shall be a·
49:17 that goeth by it shall be a·,
50:13 that goeth by Babylon shall be a·,
Eze 3:15 remained there a· among them
26:16 every moment, and be a· at thee.
27:35 inhabitants of the isles shall be a·
28:19 the people shall be a· at thee:
Da 8:27 and I was a· at the vision,
M't 7:28 the people were a· at his doctrine:
13:54 insomuch that they were a·,
22:33 they were a· at his doctrine.
M'r 1:22 they were a· at his doctrine:
5:42 a· with a great astonishment.
6: 2 many hearing him were a·,
7:37 were beyond measure a·,
10:24 disciples were a· at his words.
26 they were a· out of measure,
11:18 the people was a· at his doctrine.
Lu 2:47 were a· at his understanding
4:32 they were a· at his doctrine:
5: 9 For he was a·, and all that
8:56 her parents were a·:
24:22 made us a·, which were early
Ac 9: 6 And he trembling and a· said,
10:45 were a·, as many as came with
12:16 saw him, they were a·.
13:12 a· at the doctrine of the Lord.

astonishment
De 28:28 and a· of heart:
37 thou shalt become an a·,
2Ch 7:21 shall be an a· to every one
29: 8 to trouble, to a·, and to hissing,
Ps 60: 3 made us to drink the wine of a·.
Jer 8:21 a· hath taken hold on me.
25: 9 make them an a·, and an hissing,
11 desolation, and an a·;
18 a desolation, an a·, an hissing,
29:18 a curse, and an a·,
42:18 execration, and an a·,
44:12 an a·, and a curse,
22 desolation, and an a·,
51:37 an a·, and an hissing,
41 Babylon become an a·,
Eze 4:16 water by measure, and with a·:
5:15 instruction and an a·
12:19 and drink their water with a·,
23:33 with the cup of a· and desolation,
Zec 12: 4 smite every horse with a·,
M'r 5:42 astonished with a great a·.

astray
Ex 23: 4 enemy's ox or his ass going a·,
De 22: 1 not see thy brother's ox...go a·,
Ps 58: 3 they go a· as soon as they be born,
119:67 Before I was afflicted I went a·:
176 I have gone a· like a lost sheep;
Pr 5:23 of his folly he shall go a·.
7:25 go not a· in her paths.
28:10 causeth the righteous to go a·
Isa 53: 6 All we like sheep have gone a·;
Jer 50: 6 have caused them to go a·,
Eze 14:11 Israel may go no more a· from me,
44:10 when Israel went a·,
10 which went a· away from me
Eze 44:15 the children of Israel went a·,
48:11 which went not a·
11 when the children of Israel went a·,
11 as the Levites went a·.
M't 18:12 and one of them be gone a·,
12 and seeketh that which is gone a·?
13 ninety and nine which went not a·.
1Pe 2:25 ye were as sheep going a·;
2Pe 2:15 and are gone a·, following the way

astrologer See also ASTROLOGERS.
Da 2:10 things at any magician, or a·.

astrologers.
Isa 47:13 now the a·, the stargazers,
Da 1:20 a· that were in all his realm,
2: 2 the magicians, and the a·,
27 cannot the wise men, the a·,
4: 7 came in the magicians, the a·,
5: 7 cried aloud to bring in the a·,
11 master of the magicians, a·,
15 the a·, have been brought in

asunder
Le 1:17 shall not divide it a·:
5: 8 his neck, but shall not divide it a·:
Nu 16:31 the ground clave a· that was
2Ki 2:11 and parted them both a·;
Job 16:12 but he hath broken me a·: he hath
13 about, he cleaveth my reins a·,
Ps 2: 3 Let us break their bands a·, and
129: 4 he hath cut a· the cords of the
Jer 50:23 hammer of the whole earth cut a·
Eze 30:16 No shall be rent a·,
Hab 3: 6 and drove a· the nations;
Zec 11:10 and cut it a·, that I might break
14 Then I cut a· mine other staff,
M't 19: 6 together, let not man put a·.
24:51 shall cut him a·, and appoint him
M'r 5: 4 had been plucked a· by him,
10: 9 let not man put a·.
Ac 1:18 he burst a· in the midst,
15:39 they departed a· one from the
Heb 4:12 even to the dividing a· of soul and
11:37 they were sawn a·, were tempted,

Asuppim
1Ch 26:15 to his sons, the house of A·.
17 and toward A· two and two.

Asyncritus (*a-sin'-cri-tus*).
Ro 16:14 Salute A·, Phlegon, Hermas,

at See also THEREAT.
Ge 3:24 and he placed a· the east of the
4: 7 doest not well, sin lieth a· the
6: 6 and it grieved him a· his heart.
8: 6 And it came to pass a· the end of
9: 5 a· the hand of every beast will I
5 require it, and a· the hand of man;
5 a· the hand of every man's brother
13: 3 where his tent had been a· the
4 he had made there a· the first:
14:17 a· the valley of Shaveh, which is
17:21 unto thee a· this set time in the
18:14 A· the time appointed I will
19: 1 angels to Sodom a· even; and Lot
6 And lot went out a· the door unto
11 that were a· the door of the house
20:13 a· every place whither we shall
21: 2 a· the set time of which God had
22 And it came to pass a· that time,
32 Thus they made a covenant a·
22:19 and Abraham dwelt a· Beer-sheba.
23:10 that went in a· the gate of his city,
18 that went in a· the gate of his city,
24:11 by a well of water a· the time of
21 And the man wondering a· her
30 stood by the camels a· the well.
55 with us a few days, a· the least ten;
57 damsel, and inquire a· her mouth.
63 in the field a· the eventide:
25:32 Behold, I am a· the point to die:
26: 8 looked out a· a window, and
27:41 for my father are a· hand;
28:19 city was called Luz a· the first.
31:10 And it came to pass a· the time
33:10 receive my present a· my hand:
19 tent, a· the hand of the children
38: 1 it came to pass a· that time, that
5 and he was at Chezib, when she
11 Remain a widow a· thy father's
41: 1 it came to pass a· the end of two
21 ill favored, as a· the beginning.
43:16 shall dine with me a· noon.
18 in our sacks a· the first time
19 communed with him a· the door
20 came indeed down a· the first time
25 against Joseph came a· noon:
33 men marvelled one a· another.
44:12 began a· the eldest, and left a· the
45: 3 they were troubled a· his presence.
48: 3 appeared unto me a· Luz in the
49:13 Zebulun shall dwell a· the haven
19 but he shall overcome a· the last.
23 and shot a· him, and hated him:
27 the prey, and a· night he shall
Ex 2: 5 wash herself a· the river; and her
4:25 of her son, and cast it a· his feet,
5:23 thou delivered the people a· all.
8:32 hardened his heart a· this time
9:14 For I will a· this time send all my
12: 9 raw, nor sodden a· all with water,
18 fourteenth day of the month, a· even.
18 twentieth day of the month a· even.
22 shall go out a· the door of his
29 a· midnight the Lord smote all
41 it came to pass a· the end of the
16: 6 A· even, then ye shall know that

Ex 16:12 A· even ye shall eat flesh, and in
13 it came to pass, that a· even the
18: 5 he encamped a· the mount of God:
22 judge the people a· all seasons:
26 judged the people a· all seasons:
19:15 third day: come not a· your wives.
17 and they stood a· the nether part
22:26 in any wise, and they cry a· all
26 If thou a· all take thy neighbour's
28: 7 joined a· the two edges thereof;
14 chains of pure gold a· the ends;
22 chains a· the ends of wreathen
29:39 lamb thou shalt offer a· even:
41 thou shalt offer a· even, and shalt
42 a· the door of the tabernacle of
30: 8 Aaron lighteth the lamps a· even,
32: 4 received them a· their hand, and
33: 8 stood every man a· his tent door,
9 stood a· the door of the tabernacle,
10 stand a· the tabernacle door:
34:22 of ingathering a· the year's end,
35:15 for the door a· the entering in of
36:29 together a· the head thereof,
38: 8 assembled a· the door of the
39:15 breastplate chains a· the ends,
40: 8 up the hanging a· the court gate.
28 set up the hanging a· the door of
Le 1: 3 voluntary will a· the door of the
15 shall be wrung out a· the side of
3: 2 of the offering, and kill it a· the
4: 7 of the bullock a· the bottom of the
7 which is a· the door of the
18 pour out all the blood a· the
18 a· the door of the tabernacle of the
25 a· the bottom of the altar of burnt
30 thereof a· the bottom of the altar.
34 the blood thereof a· the bottom
5: 9 wrung out a· the bottom of the
6:20 and half thereof a· night.
7:18 be eaten a· all on the third
8:15 blood a· the bottom of the altar,
31 Boil the flesh a· the door of the
33 your consecration be a· an end:
9: 9 the blood a· the bottom of the
13: 5 plague in his sight be a· a stay,
37 if the scall be in his sight a· a stay,
14:11 before the Lord, a· the door of the
15:24 man lie with her a· all, and her
16: 2 come not a· all times into the holy
7 before the Lord a· the door of the
29 do no work a· all, whether it be
17: 6 of the Lord a· the door of the
18: 9 be born a· home, or born abroad,
19: 5 ye shall offer it a· your will.
7 if it be eaten a· all on the third day,
20 not a· all redeemed, nor freedom
22:19 Ye shall offer a· your own will a
29 Lord, offer it a· your own will.
23: 5 the first month a· even is the
32 ninth day of the month a· even,
25:32 the Levites redeem a· any time.
26:32 therein shall be astonished a· it.
27:10 if he shall a· all change beast for
13 But if he will a· all redeem it,
16 shall be valued a· fifty shekels
31 And if a man will a· all redeem
33 if he change it a· all, then both it
Nu 3:39 numbered a· the commandment
4:27 A· the appointment of Aaron
6: 6 he shall come a· no dead body.
18 a· the door of the tabernacle of
9: 2 the passover a· his appointed
3 day of this month, a· even,
5 first month a· even in the
11 a· even they shall keep it, and eat
15 and a· even there was upon the
18 A· the commandment of the Lord
18 a· the commandment of the Lord
23 A· the commandment of the Lord
23 a· the commandment of the Lord
23 of the Lord, a· the commandment
10: 3 themselves to thee a· the door of
11: 6 there is nothing a· all besides this
20 until it come out a· your nostrils.
13:30 Let us go up a· once, and possess
16:34 round about them, fled a· the cry
19:19 and shall be clean a· even.
20:24 against my word a· the water
21:11 both, and pitched a· Ije-abarim,
15 And a· the stream of the brooks
30 We have shot a· them; Heshbon is
33 his people, to the battle a· Edrei.
34 Amorites, which dwelt a· Heshbon.
22: 4 king of the Moabites a· that time.
20 came unto Balaam a· night, and
38 I now any power a· all to say any
23:25 them a· all, nor bless them a· all.
24: 1 he went not, as a· other times, to
27:14 to sanctify me a· the water before
21 go out, and a· his word they shall
28: 4 lamb shalt thou offer a· even;
8 lamb shalt thou offer a· even;
30: 4 father shall hold his peace a· her;
6 And if she had a· all a husband,
7 it, and held his peace a· her
11 and held his peace a· her, and
30:14 altogether hold his peace a· her
14 because he held his peace a· her,
31:12 the camp a· the plains of Moab,
33:14 and encamped a· Rephidim,
16 pitched a· Kibroth-hattaavah.
17 and encamped a· Hazeroth.
19 and pitched a· Rimmon-parez.
21 Libnah, and pitched a· Rissah.
26 and encamped a· Tahath.
27 Tahath, and pitched a· Tarah.

Nu 33:30 and encamped a· Moseroth.
32 and encamped a· Hor-hagidgod,
34 and encamped a· Ebronah.
35 and encamped a· Ezion-gaber.
38 a· the commandment of the Lord,
34: 5 goings out of it shall be a· the sea.
9 out of it shall be a· Hazar-enan:
12 out of it shall be a· the salt sea:
35:11 killeth any person a· unawares.
20 or hurl a· him by laying of wait,
26 the slayer shall a· any time come
De 1: 4 dwelt a· Astaroth in Edrei:
9 And I spake unto you a· that time,
16 I charged your judges a· that time,
18 I commanded you a· that time
2:32 all his people, to fight a· Jahaz.
34 we took all his cities a· that time,
3: 2 Amorites, which dwelt a· Heshbon.
4 we took all his cities a· that time,
8 took a· that time out of the hand
12 which we possessed a· that time,
18 a· that time, saying, The Lord
21 I commanded Joshua a· that time,
23 I besought the Lord a· that time,
4:14 Lord commanded me a· that time
46 Amorites, who dwelt a· Heshbon,
5: 5 the Lord and you a· that time,
6:24 us alive, as it is a· this day.
7:21 shalt not be affrighted a· them:
22 not consume them a· once,
8:16 do thee good a· thy latter end;
19 if thou do a· all forget the Lord
9:11 it came to pass a· the end of
18 before the Lord, as a· the first,
19 hearkened unto me a· that time
22 And a· Taberah, and a· Massah,
22 and a· Kibroth-hattaavah,
25 as I fell down a· the first;
10: 1 A· that time the Lord said unto
8 A· that time the Lord separated
10 hearkened unto me a· that time
14:28 A· the end of three years thou
15: 1 A· the end of every seven years
9 the year of release is a· hand;
16: 4 sacrificedst the first day a· even,
6 But a· the place which the Lord
6 a· even, a· the going down of the
6 a· the season that thou camest
17: 6 A· the mouth of two witnesses,
6 but a· the mouth of one witness
19:15 a· the mouth of two witnesses,
15 a· the mouth of three witnesses,
21:14 shalt not sell her a· all for money,
23:24 thy fill a· thine own pleasure;
24: 5 shall be free a· home one year,
15 A· his day thou shalt give him
28:29 thou shalt grope a· noonday,
67 and a· even thou shalt say,
31:10 A· the end of every seven years,
32:35 day of their calamity is a· hand,
51 a· the waters of Meribah-kadesh,
33: 3 and they sat down a· thy feet;
8 whom thou didst prove a· Massah,
8 and with whom thou didst strive a·
Jos 5: 2 A· that time the Lord said unto
3 the children of Israel a· the hill
10 a· even in the plains of Jericho.
6:16 came to pass a· the seventh time,
26 Joshua adjured them a· that time,
7: 7 hast thou a· all brought this people
8: 5 out against us, as a· the first,
6 flee before us, as a· the first:
14 his people, a· a time appointed,
29 cast it a· the entering in of the
9: 6 Joshua unto the camp a· Gilgal,
10 Bashan, which was a· Ashtaroth,
14 counsel a· the mouth of the Lord.
16 to pass a· the end of three days
10:10 with a great slaughter a· Gibeon,
16 themselves in a cave a· Makkedah.
17 found hid in a cave a· Makkedah.
21 the camp to Joshua a· Makkedah.
27 it came to pass a· the time of the
42 land did Joshua take a· one time,
11: 5 pitched together a· the waters of
10 Joshua a· that time turned back,
21 And a· that time came Joshua,
12: 4 that dwelt a· Ashtaroth and a·
15: 4 out of that coast were a· the sea:
5 of the sea a· the uttermost part
7 out thereof were a· En-rogel:
8 westward, which is a· the end of
11 out of the border were a· the sea.
63 children of Judah a· Jerusalem
16: 3 goings out thereof are a· the sea.
7 to Jericho, and went out a· Jordan.
8 out thereof were a· the sea.
17: 9 the outgoings of it were a· the sea:
18: 1 Israel assembled together a· Shiloh,
9 to Joshua to the host a· Shiloh.
12 out thereof were a· the wilderness
14 out thereof were a· Kirjath-baal,
19 a· the north bay of the salt sea
19 a· the south end of Jordan:
19:22 of their border were a· Jordan:
29 are a· the sea from the coast to
33 outgoings thereof were a· Jordan:
51 a· the door of the tabernacle
20: 4 stand a· the entering of the gate
9 killeth any person a· unawares
21: 2 they spake unto them a· Shiloh
3 a· the commandment of the
22:11 a· the passage of the children of
12 themselves together a· Shiloh.
J'g 3: 2 a· the least such as before knew
29 slew of Moab a· that time about

J'g 4: 4 she judged Israel a· that time.
10 ten thousand men a· his feet:
5:27 A· her feet he bowed, he fell, he
27 a· her feet he bowed, he fell: where
28 Sisera looked out a· a window,
7:25 slew a· the winepress of Zeeb,
8:18 were they whom ye slew a· Tabor?
9: 5 unto his father's house a· Ophrah,
41 Abimelech dwelt a· Arumah:
11:39 it came to pass a· the end of two
12: 2 my people were a· great strife
6 him a· the passages of Jordan:
6 there fell a· that time of the
10 and was buried a· Beth-lehem.
13:23 a meat offering a· our hands,
23 as a· this time have told us such
25 began to move him a· times
14: 4 for a· that time the Philistines had
16: 3 midnight, and arose a· midnight,
20 I will go out as a· other times
28 I may be a· once avenged of the
30 dead which he slew a· his death
18:27 a people that were a· quiet and
29 of the city was Laish a· the first.
19:16 his work out of the field a· even,
22 beat a· the door, and spake to
26 fell down a· the door of the man's
27 was fallen down a· the door
20:15 were numbered a· that time
16 one could sling a stone a· an hair
30 against Gibeah, as a· other times.
31 and kill, as a· other times, in the
32 down before us, as a· the first.
21:14 Benjamin came again a· that time;
22 not give unto them a· this time,
24 of Israel departed thence a· that
Ru 2:14 A· mealtime come thou hither,
3: 7 he went to lie down a· the end of
8 And it came to pass a· midnight,
8 behold, a woman lay a· his feet.
10 latter end than a· the beginning,
14 And she lay a· his feet until the
1Sa 2:22 women that assembled a· the door
29 ye a· my sacrifice and a· mine
3: 2 pass a· that time, when Eli was
10 and called as a· other times,
11 in Israel, a· which both the ears
6:10 and shut up their calves a· home:
9: 8 I have here a· hand the fourth
10: 2 the border of Benjamin a· Zezah;
13:11 themselves together a· Michmash;
14:18 the ark of God was a· that time
16: 4 of the town trembled a· his
17: 1 were gathered together a· Shocoh,
15 his father's sheep a· Beth-lehem.
18:10 with his hand, as a· other times:
19 it came to pass a· the time when
19:19 David is a· Naioth in Ramah.
22 they be a· Naioth in Ramah.
20: 5 fail to sit with the king a· meat:
5 field unto the third day a· even.
6 If thy father a· all miss me,
16 a· the hand of David's enemies.
20 thereof, as though I shot a· a mark.
25 upon his seat, as a· other times,
33 Saul cast a javelin a· him to smite
35 went out into the field a· the time
21: 1 was afraid a· the meeting of
4 themselves a· least from women.
22: 8, 13 to lie in wait, as a· this day?
14 in law, and goeth a· thy bidding,
23:29 dwelt in strong holds a· En-gedi.
25: 1 buried him in his house a· Ramah.
24 And fell a· his feet, and said,
26: 7 stuck in the ground a· his bolster:
8 spear even to the earth a· once,
11 the spear that is a· his bolster,
16 of water that was a· his bolster.
27: 3 David dwelt with Achish a· Gath,
28: 7 hath a familiar spirit a· En-dor.
30: 8 David enquired a· the Lord,
21 also to abide a· the brook Besor:
31:13 them under a tree a· Jabesh,
2Sa 2:32 they came to Hebron a· break of
3:30 slain their brother Asahel a·
32 and wept a· the grave of Abner;
4: 5 who lay on a bed a· noon.
6: 4 which was a· Gibeah,
8: 3 to recover his border a· the river
9: 7 shalt eat bread a· my table
10 eat bread alway a· my table.
11 he shall eat a· my table, as one
13 did eat continually a· the king's
10: 5 the king said, Tarry a· Jericho
8 battle in array a· the entering in
11: 1 the year was expired, a· the time
1 But David tarried still a·
9 But Uriah slept a· the door of the
13 and a· even he went out to lie
13: 5 see it, and eat it a· her hand.
6 sight, that I may eat a· her hand.
14:26 for it was a· every year's end
26 the hair of his head a· two
15: 8 while I abode a· Geshur in Syria,
14 that were a· Jerusalem, Arise,
16: 3 he abideth a· Jerusalem: for he
6 And he cast stones a· David,
6 and a· all the servants of the
13 threw stones a· him, and cast
23 as if a man had inquired a· the
17: 7 given is not good a· this time.
9 of them be overthrown a· the
19: 9 And all the people were a· strife
28 them that did eat a· thine own
32 of sustenance while he lay a·
42 have we eaten a· all of the king's

2Sa 20: 3 David came to his house *a'*
8 When they were *a'* the great
18 surely ask counsel *a'* Abel: and
21:18 with the Philistines *a'* Gob:
22:16 *a'* the rebuking of the Lord,
16 *a'* the blast of the
23: 8 whom he slew *a'* one time.
24: 8 they came to Jerusalem *a'* the
24 I will surely buy it of thee *a'* a
1Ki 1: 6 had not displeased him *a'* any time
2: 7 of those that eat *a'* thy table: for
8 came down to meet me *a'* Jordan,
26 but I will not *a'* this time put thee
39 And it came to pass *a'* the end of
3:20 And she arose *a'* midnight, and
5:14 Lebanon, and two months *a'* home;
7:30 undersetters molten, *a'* the side of
8: 2 unto king Solomon *a'* the feast
9 which Moses put there *a'* Horeb,
59 cause of his people Israel *a'* all
61 keep his commandments as *a'* this
65 And *a'* that time Solomon held a
9: 2 had appeared unto him *a'* Gibeon.
6 But if ye shall *a'* all turn from
8 And *a'* this house, which is high,
10 And it came to pass *a'* the end of
10:22 For the king had *a'* sea a navy of
26 and with the king at Jerusalem.
28 received the linen yarn *a'* a price.
11:29 And it came to pass *a'* that time
12:27 house of the Lord *a'* Jerusalem,
13:20 it came to pass as they sat *a'* the
14: 1 *A'* that time Abijah the son of
6 as she came in *a'* the door, that he
15:18 king of Syria, that dwelt *a'*
27 Baasha smote him *a'* Gibbethon,
18:19 which eat *a'* Jezebel's table.
27 And it came to pass *a'* noon, that
36 it came to pass *a'* the time of the
36 I have done all these things *a'* thy
44 And it came to pass *a'* the seventh
19: 6 and a cruse of water *a'* his head.
20: 9 to thy servant *a'* the first I will do:
16 And they went out *a'* noon. But
22 *a'* the return of the year the king
26 And it came to pass *a'* the return
22: 5 I pray thee, *a'* the word of the Lord
20 go up and fall *a'* Ramoth-gilead?
28 if thou return *a'* all in peace, the
34 drew a bow *a'* a venture, and smote
35 died *a'* even: and the blood ran
48 ships were broken *a'* Ezion-geber.
2Ki 2: 3 prophets that were *a'* Beth-el came
5 prophets that were *a'* Jericho came
15 were to view *a'* Jericho, saw him,
18 he tarried *a'* Jericho,) he said unto,
4:17 and bare a son *a'* that season that
37 fell *a'* his feet, and bowed herself
5: 9 stood *a'* the door of the house of
20 not receiving *a'* his hands that
6:32 and hold him fast *a'* the door: is
7: 3 four leprous men *a'* the entering
8: 3 came to pass *a'* the seven years'
22 Then Libna revolted *a'* the same
29 the Syrians had given him *a'* Ramah,
9: 7 servants of the Lord, *a'* the hand
24 the arrow went out *a'* his heart,
27 they did so *a'* the going up to Gur,
30 and looked out *a'* a window.
31 And as Jehu entered in *a'* the gate,
10: 8 Lay ye them in two heaps *a'* the
12 as he was *a'* the shearing house
14 slew them *a'* the pit of the shearing
11: 6 shall be *a'* the gate of Sur; and a
6 *a'* the gate behind the guard:
12: 4 money that every man is set *a'*,
13:20 invaded the land *a'* the coming in
14:10 glory of this, and tarry *a'* home:
11 looked one another in the face *a'*
13 son of Ahaziah, *a'* Beth-shemesh.
20 and he was buried *a'* Jerusalem
16: 6 *A'* that time Rezin king of Syria
10 an altar that was *a'* Damascus:
17:25 And so it was *a'* the beginning of
18:10 And *a'* the end of three years they
16 *A'* that time did Hezekiah cut off
33 gods of the nations delivered *a'*
19:21 hath shaken her head *a'* thee.
36 returned, and dwelt *a'* Nineveh.
20:12 *A'* that time Berodach-baladan,
23: 6 burned it *a'* the brook Kidron,
8 left hand *a'* the gate of the city.
11 given to the sun, *a'* the entering in
15 altar that was *a'* Beth-el, and the
29 he slew him *a'* Megiddo, when he
33 put him in bands *a'* Riblah in the
24: 3 Surely *a'* the commandment of
10 *A'* that time the servants of
25:21 slew them *a'* Riblah in the land
25 the Chaldees that were with him *a'*
1Ch 2:55 the scribes which dwelt *a'* Jabez;
4:28 And they dwelt *a'* Beer-sheba,
29 *a'* Bilhah, and *a'* Ezem, and *a'* Tolad,
30 And *a'* Bethuel, and *a'* Hormah,
30 Hormah, and *a'* Ziklag,
31 And *a'* Beth-marcaboth, and
31 *a'* Beth-birei, and *a'* Shaaraim.
8:29 *a'* Gibeon dwelt the father of
9:34 their generations: these dwelt *a'*
38 with their brethren *a'* Jerusalem,
11:11 three hundred slain by him *a'* one
13 He was with David *a'* Pas-dammim,
16 Philistines' garrison was then *a'*
17 Bethlehem, that is *a'* the gate!
12:22 For *a'* that time day by day there
32 their brethren were *a'* their

1Ch 13: 3 inquired not *a'* it in the days of
14: 3 David took more wives *a'*
15:13 because ye did it not *a'* the first,
29 daughter of Saul looking out *a'* a
16:33 wood sing out *a'* the presence of
17: 9 them any more, as *a'* the beginning,
19: 5 Tarry *a'* Jericho until your beards
20: 1 year was expired, *a'* the time that
1 But David tarried *a'* Jerusalem.
4 that there arose war *a'* Gezer
4 *a'* which time Sibbechai the
6 was war *a'* Gath, where was a man
21:19 David went up *a'* the saying of Gad,
28 *A'* that time when David saw that
29 *a'* that season in the high place *a'*
23:30 praise the Lord, and likewise *a'*
26:18 *A'* Parbar westward,
18 four *a'* the causeway.
18 and two *a'* Parbar.
31 mighty men of valour *a'* Jazer of
28: 7 my judgments, as *a'* this day.
21 the people will be wholly *a'* thy
2Ch 1: 3 high place that was *a'* Gibeon;
4 pitched a tent for it *a'* Jerusalem.
6 which was *a'* the tabernacle of
13 the high place that was *a'* Gibeon
14 and with the king *a'* Jerusalem.
15 silver and gold *a'* Jerusalem
16 received the linen yarn *a'* a price.
3: 1 to build the house of the Lord *a'*
5:10 which Moses put therein *a'* Horeb,
12 stood *a'* the east end of the altar,
7: 8 Also *a'* the same time Solomon
8: 1 to pass *a'* the end of twenty years,
14 also by their courses *a'* every gate:
17 to Eloth, *a'* the sea side in the
9: 1 Solomon with hard questions *a'*
25 and with the king *a'* Jerusalem.
13:18 of Israel were brought under *a'*
14:10 in the valley of Zephathah *a'*
15:10 gathered themselves together *a'*
15 all Judah rejoiced *a'* the oath:
16 and burned it *a'* the brook Kidron.
16: 2 king of Syria, that dwelt *a'*
7 And *a'* that time Hanani the seer
18: 4 Enquire, I pray thee, *a'* the word
9 sat in a void place *a'* the entering
19 go up and fall *a'* Ramoth-gilead?
33 a certain man drew a bow *a'* a
19: 4 Jehoshaphat dwelt *a'* Jerusalem:
20:16 ye shall find them *a'* the end of
22: 5 against Hazael king of Syria *a'*
6 that were given him *a'* Ramah,
6 Ahab *a'* Jezreel, because he was
23: 5 part shall be *a'* the king's house;
5 part *a'* the gate of the foundation:
13 the king stood *a'* his pillar
13 *a'* the entering in, and the princes
19 porters *a'* the gates of the house
24: 8 And *a'* the king's commandment
8 and set it without *a'* the gate of
11 came to pass, that *a'* what time
21 and stoned him with stones *a'* the
23 came to pass *a'* the end of the year,
25:19 abide now *a'* home; why shouldest
21 king of Judah, *a'* Beth-shemesh,
23 son of Jehoahaz, *a'* Beth-shemesh,
26: 9 built towers in Jerusalem *a'* the
9 and *a'* the valley gate, and *a'*
28:16 *A'* that time did king Ahaz send
30: 1 house of the Lord *a'* Jerusalem,
3 could not keep it *a'* that time,
5 Lord God of Israel *a'* Jerusalem:
13 there assembled *a'* Jerusalem
21 that were present *a'* Jerusalem
31:13 brother, *a'* the commandment
32: 9 all Judah that were *a'* Jerusalem,
33 did honour him *a'* his death.
33:14 to the entering in *a'* the fish gate,
35:15 the porters waited *a'* every gate;
17 kept the passover *a'* that time,
23 the archers shot *a'* king Josiah;
36: 3 put him down *a'* Jerusalem,
7 put them in his temple *a'* Babylon.
Ezr 1: 2 him a house *a'* Jerusalem,
2:68 the Lord which is *a'* Jerusalem,
3: 8 unto the house of God *a'* Jerusalem,
4:10, 11 the river, and *a'* such a time.
17 Peace, and *a'* such a time.
24 of God which is *a'* Jerusalem.
5: 2 of God which is *a'* Jerusalem:
3 *A'* the same time came to them
17 which is there *a'* Babylon,
17 this house of God *a'* Jerusalem,
6: 2 there was found *a'* Achmetha,
3 the house of God *a'* Jerusalem,
5 the temple which is *a'* Jerusalem,
9 priests which are *a'* Jerusalem,
12 of God which is *a'* Jerusalem.
17 *a'* the dedication of this house of
18 of God, which is *a'* Jerusalem;
7:12 perfect peace, and *a'* such a time.
8:17 the chief *a'* the place Casiphia,
17 Nethinims, *a'* the place Casiphia,
21 a fast there, *a'* the river
29 *a'* Jerusalem, in the chambers
34 weight was written *a'* that time.
9: 4 trembled *a'* the words of the God
5 *a'* the evening sacrifice I arose up
10: 3 that tremble *a'* the commandment
14 in our cities come *a'* appointed
Ne 2:12 in my heart to do *a'* Jerusalem:
3:19 armoury *a'* the turning of the wall.
4:22 Likewise *a'* the same time said I
5:17 there were *a'* my table an
6: 1 *a'* that time I had not set up the

Ne 6: 7 to preach of thee *a'* Jerusalem,
7: 5 of them which came up *a'* the first,
9:37 over our cattle, *a'* their pleasure,
10:34 *a'* times appointed year by year,
11: 1 the people dwelt *a'* Jerusalem:
2 to dwell *a'* Jerusalem.
4 And *a'* Jerusalem dwelt certain
6 of Perez that dwelt *a'* Jerusalem
22 overseer of the Levites *a'* Jerusalem
24 of Judah, was *a'* the king's hand
25 dwelt *a'* Kirjath-arba, and in the
25 and *a'* Dibon, and in the villages
25 *a'* Jekabzeel, and in the villages
26 And *a'* Jeshua, and *a'* Moladah,
26 and *a'* Beth-phelet,
27 *a'* Hazar-shual, and *a'*
28 And *a'* Ziklag, and *a'* Mekonah,
29 *a'* En-rimmon, and *a'* Zareah,
29 and *a'* Jarmuth,
30 *a'* Lachish, and the fields
30 *a'* Azekah, and in the villages
31 dwelt *a'* Michmash, and Aija,
32 And *a'* Anathoth, Nob, Ananiah,
12:25 *a'* the thresholds of the gates.
27 And *a'* the dedication of the wall
37 *a'* the fountain gate, which was
37 David, *a'* the going up of the wall.
44 *a'* that time were some appointed
13: 6 this time was not I *a'* Jerusalem:
19 my servants set I *a'* the gates,
31 wood offering, *a'* times appointed,
Es 1:12 come *a'* the king's commandment,
4: 8 *a'* Shushan to destroy them,
14 thou holdest thy peace *a'* this time,
5: 6 said unto Esther *a'* the banquet
13 the Jew sitting *a'* the king's gate.
6:10 Jew, that sitteth *a'* the king's gate:
7: 2 second day *a'* the banquet of wine,
3 my life be given me *a'* my petition,
3 and my people *a'* my request:
8: 3 fell down *a'* his feet, and besought.
9 king's scribes called *a'* that time
14 the decree was given *a'* Shushan
9:14 decree was given *a'* Shushan;
15 three hundred men *a'* Shushan;
18 the Jews that were *a'* Shushan
Job 2:10 receive good *a'* the hand of God,
3:13 have slept: then had I been *a'* rest,
17 and there the weary be *a'* rest.
5:22 *A'* destruction and famine thou
23 beasts of the field shall be *a'* peace
9:23 laugh *a'* the trial of the innocent
12: 5 thought of him that is *a'* ease.
15:12 and what do thy eyes wink *a'*,
23 of darkness is ready *a'* his hand.
16: 4 and shake mine head *a'* you.
12 I was *a'* ease, but he hath broken
17: 8 men shall be astonied *a'* this,
18:12 destruction shall be ready *a'* his
20 shall be astonied *a'* his day,
19:25 he shall stand *a'* the latter day
21:12 rejoice *a'* the sound of the organ.
23 being wholly *a'* ease and quiet.
22:21 thyself with him, and be *a'* peace
23:15 am I troubled *a'* his presence:
26:11 and are astonished *a'* his reproof.
27:23 Men shall clap their hands *a'* him,
29:21 and kept silence *a'* my counsel.
31: 9 lain wait *a'* my neighbour's door;
29 rejoiced *a'* the destruction of him
34:20 shall be troubled *a'* midnight,
37: 1 *A'* this also my heart trembleth
39:22 He mocketh *a'* fear, and is not
27 eagle mount up *a'* thy command,
41: 9 down even *a'* the sight of him?
26 sword of him that layeth *a'* him
29 laugheth *a'* the shaking of a spear.
Ps 7: 4 him that was *a'* peace with me;
9: 3 fall and perish *a'* thy presence.
10: 5 his enemies, he puffeth *a'* them.
11: 2 may privily shoot *a'* the upright
12: 5 from him that puffeth *a'* him.
16: 8 because he is *a'* my right hand, I
11 *a'* thy right hand there are
18:12 *A'* the brightness that was before
15 *a'* thy rebuke, O Lord,
15 *a'* the blast of the breath
25:13 His soul shall dwell *a'* ease;
30:*title* Psalm and Song *a'* the dedication
4 give thanks *a'* the remembrance
34: 1 I will bless the Lord *a'* all times:
35: 8 come upon him *a'* unawares;
26 together that rejoice *a'* mine hurt:
37:13 The Lord shall laugh *a'* him:
39: 5 verily every man *a'* his best state
12 hold not thy peace *a'* my tears:
42: 7 Deep calleth unto deep *a'* the noise
52: 6 fear, and shall laugh *a'* him:
55: 6 would I fly away, and be *a'* rest.
17 and morning, and *a'* noon, will I
20 such as be *a'* peace with him.
59: 6 They return *a'* evening: they make
8 thou, O Lord, shalt laugh *a'* them;
14 And *a'* evening let them return;
62: 8 Trust in him *a'* all times;
64: 4 shoot in secret *a'* the perfect:
4 suddenly do they shoot *a'* him,
7 God shall shoot *a'* them with an
65: 8 parts are afraid *a'* thy tokens:
68: 2 perish *a'* the presence of God.
8 dropped *a'* the presence of God:
8 even Sinai itself was moved *a'* the
12 she that tarried *a'* home divided
29 of thy temple *a'* Jerusalem
73: 3 For I was envious *a'* the foolish,
74: 6 the carved work thereof *a'* once

Ps 76: 6 A' thy rebuke, O God of Jacob,
80:16 a' the rebuke of thy countenance.
81: 7 I proved thee a' the waters of
83: 9 Jabin, a' the brook of Kison:
10 which perished a' En-dor: they
91: 6 destruction that wasteth a' noonday.
7 A thousand shall fall a' thy side,
7 and ten thousand a' thy right hand;
97: 5 The hills melted like wax a' the
5 a' the presence of the Lord of the
12 give thanks a' the remembrance
99: 5 and worship a' his footstool;
9 and worship a' his holy hill;
104: 7 A' thy rebuke they fled;
7 a' the voice of thy
105:22 To bind his princes a' his pleasure;
106: 3 doeth righteousness a' all times.
7 but provoked him a' the sea,
7 even a' the Red sea.
32 angered him also a' the waters of
107:27 man, and are a' their wit's end.
109: 6 let Satan stand a' his right hand.
31 he shall stand a' the right hand
110: 1 Sit thou a' my right hand, until I
5 Lord a' thy right hand shall
114: 7 earth, a' the presence of the Lord,
7 a' the presence of the God of Jacob;
118:13 Thou hast thrust sore a' me that
119:20 unto thy judgments a' all times.
45 And I will walk a' liberty: for I
62 A' midnight I will rise to give
162 I rejoice a' thy word, as one that
123: 4 scorning of those that are a' ease,
132: 6 Lo, we heard of it a' Ephratah:
7 we will worship a' his footstool.
135:21 Zion, which dwelleth a' Jerusalem.
141: 7 are scattered a' the grave's mouth,
Pr 1:23 Turn you a' my reproof:
25 set a' nought all my counsel,
26 also will laugh a' your calamity;
4:19 know not a' what they stumble.
5:11 and thou mourn a' the last,
19 her breasts satisfy thee a' all times;
7: 6 For a' the window of my house I
12 and lieth in wait a' every corner.
19 For the goodman is not a' home,
20 come home a' the day appointed.
8: 3 She crieth a' the gates,
3 a' the entry of the city,
3 a' the coming in a' the doors:
34 watching daily a' my gates,
34 waiting a' the posts of my doors.
9:14 sitteth a' the door of her house,
14: 9 Fools make a mock a' sin:
19 a' the gates of the righteous.
16: 7 enemies to be a' peace with him.
17: 5 and he that is glad a' calamities
17 A friend loveth a' all times,
20:21 be gotten hastily a' the beginning;
21:13 his ears a' the cry of the poor,
23:30 They that tarry long a' the wine;
32 A' the last it biteth like a serpent,
24:19 be thou envious a' the wicked;
28:18 in his ways shall fall a' once.
29:21 become his son a' the length.
30:17 eye that mocketh a' his father,
Ec 5: 6 should God be angry a' thy voice,
8 marvel not a' the matter:
10: 2 man's heart is a' his right hand;
2 but a fool's heart a' his left.
12: 4 rise up a' the voice of the bird,
6 be broken a' the fountain,
6 wheel broken a' the cistern.
Ca 1: 7 makest thy flock to rest a' noon:
12 While the king sitteth a' his table,
2: 9 he looketh forth a' the windows,
7:13 and a' our gates are all manner
8:11 had a vineyard a' Baal-hamon;
Isa 1:12 hath required this a' your hand,
26 restore thy judges as a' the first,
26 counsellors as a' the beginning:
6: 4 door moved a' the voice of him
7: 3 a' the end of the conduit of the
23 vines a' a thousand silverlings,
9: 1 a' the first he lightly afflicted
10:26 of Midian a' the rock of Oreb:
28 a' Michmash he hath laid up his
29 taken up their lodging a' Geba;
32 shall remain a' Nob that day:
13: 6 for the day of the Lord is a' hand:
8 shall be amazed one a' another;
14: 7 The whole earth is a' rest,
8 Yea, the fir trees rejoice a' thee,
9 thee to meet thee a' thy coming:
16: 2 of Moab shall be a' the fords
4 for the extortioner is a' an end,
17: 7 A' that day shall a man look to
14 behold a' eveningtide trouble;
19: 1 idols of Egypt shall be moved a'
19 a' the border thereof to the Lord.
20: 2 A' the same time spake the Lord
21: 3 down a' the hearing of it;
3 I was dismayed a' the seeing of
22: 7 shall set themselves in array a'
23: 5 a' the report concerning Egypt,
5 pained a' the report of Tyre.
26:11 for their envy a' the people;
27:13 in the holy mount a' Jerusalem.
28:15 with hell are we a' agreement;
29: 5 it shall be a' an instant suddenly
30: 2 and have not asked a' my mouth;
4 For his princes were a' Zoan,
13 cometh suddenly a' an instant.
17 shall flee a' the rebuke of one;
17 a' the rebuke of five shall ye flee:
19 dwell in Zion a' Jerusalem:

Isa 30:19 gracious unto thee a' the voice
32: 9 Rise up, ye women that are a' ease;
11 Tremble, ye women that are a' ease;
33: 3 A' the noise of the tumult the
3 a' the lifting up of thyself the
37:22 hath shaken her head a' thee.
37 and dwelt a' Nineveh.
39: 1 A' that time Merodach-baladan,
42:14 destroy and devour a' once.
47:14 shall not be a coal to warm a',
50: 2 Is my hand shortened a' all,
2 a' my rebuke I dry up the sea,
51:17 drank a' the hand of the Lord
20 lie a' the head of all the streets,
52:14 As many were astonied a' thee;
15 shall shut their mouths a' him:
59:10 we stumble a' noon day as in the
60: 4 shall be nursed a' thy side.
14 down a' the soles of thy feet;
64: 1 might flow down a' thy
2 may tremble a' thy presence!
3 flowed down a' thy presence.
66: 2 and trembleth a' my word.
5 ye that tremble a' his word;
8 shall a nation be born a' once?
Jer 1:15 every one his throne a' the entering
17 be not dismayed a' their faces,
2:12 O ye heavens, a' this,
24 up the wind a' her pleasure;
3:17 A' that time they shall call
4: 9 shall come to pass a' that day,
11 A' that time shall it be said to this
19 I am pained a' my very heart;
26 down a' the presence of the Lord,
5:22 ye not tremble a' my presence,
6: 4 arise, and let us go up a' noon.
15 they were not a' all ashamed,
15 a' the time that I visit them they
7: 2 that enter in a' these gates to
12 where I set my name a' the first,
8: 1 A' that time, saith the Lord,
12 they were not a' all ashamed,
16 whole land trembled a' the sound
10: 2 dismayed a' the signs of heaven;
2 heathen are dismayed a' them.
10 a' his wrath the earth shall
18 of the land a' this once,
11:12 they shall not save them a' all
15: 8 young men a spoiler a' noonday;
17:11 and a' his end shall be a fool.
27 in a' the gates of Jerusalem
18: 7 A' what instant I shall speak
9 And a' what instant I shall speak
20:16 and the shouting a' noontide:
23:23 Am I a God a' hand, saith the
32 profit this people a' all, saith the
25:15 winecup of this fury a' my hand,
17 I took the cup a' the Lord's hand,
28 to take the cup a' thine hand
33 the Lord shall be a' that day from
26:19 Judah put him a' all to death?
27:18 a' Jerusalem, go not to Babylon.
29:10 years be accomplished a' Babylon
25 the people that are a' Jerusalem,
31: 1 A' the same time, saith the Lord,
12 shall not sorrow any more a' all.
32:20 thee a name, as a' this day;
33: 7 build them, as a' the first.
11 of the land, as a' the first, saith
15 In those days, and a' that time,
34: 8 people which were a' Jerusalem,
14 A' the end of seven years let ye go
16 whom he had set a' liberty
16 a' their pleasure, to return
35:11 so we dwell a' Jerusalem,
36:10 court, a' the entry of the new
17 write all these things a' his mouth?
27 wrote a' the mouth of Jeremiah
39:10 and fields a' the same time.
40:10 I will dwell a' Mizpah, to serve
41: 3 even with Gedaliah, a' Mizpah,
43: 9 a' the entry of Pharaoh's house in
44: 1 which dwell a' Migdol,
1 and a' Tahpanhes, and a' Noph,
6 and desolate, as a' this day.
22 an inhabitant as a' this day.
23 happened unto you, as a' this
45: 1 words in a book a' the mouth of
46:27 and be in rest and a' ease, and
47: 3 A' the noise of the stamping of
3 a' the rushing of his chariots,
3 and a' the rumbling of his wheels,
48:11 Moab hath been a' ease from his
41 hearts in Moab a' that day shall
49:17 hiss a' all the plagues thereof.
21 The earth is moved a' the noise
21 a' the cry the noise thereof was
22 a' that day shall the heart of the
50:11 ye are grown fat as the heifer a'
13 and hiss a' all her plagues.
14 shoot a' her, spare no arrows:
46 A' the noise of the taking of
51:31 that his city is taken a' one end,
49 so a' Babylon shall fall the slain
La 1: 7 and did mock a' her sabbaths.
20 sword bereaveth, a' home there
2:15 pass by clap their hands a' thee;
15 wag their head a' the daughter
3:56 ear a' my breathing, a' my cry.
Eze 2: 6 nor be dismayed a' their looks,
3: 9 neither be dismayed a' their looks,
15 of the captivity a' Tel-abib, that
16 came to pass a' the end of seven
17 hear the word a' my mouth,
18, 20 blood will I require a' thine hand.
8: 5 northward a' the gate of the

Eze 8:16 a' the door of the temple of the
9: 6 and begin a' my sanctuary.
6 Then they began a' the ancient
10:19 and every one stood a' the door
11: 1 behold a' the door of the gate
12: 4 go forth a' even in their sight
23 The days are a' hand, and the
14: 3 be enquired of a' all by them?
16: 4 thou wast not salted a' all,
4 nor swaddled a' all.
25 place a' every head of the way,
46 that dwell a' thy left hand:
46 that dwelleth a' thy right hand,
57 as a' the time of thy reproach of
18:23 a' all that the wicked should die?
20:32 into your mind shall not be a' all,
21:19 choose it a' the head of the way
21 of Babylon stood a' the parting
21 a' the head of the two ways, to
22 A' his right hand was the
22:13 mine hand a' thy dishonest gain
13 made, and a' thy blood which
23:42 voice of a multitude being a' ease
24:18 and a' even my wife died; and I
26:10 shake a' the noise of the horsemen,
15 not the isle shake a' the sound of
16 shall tremble a' every moment,
16 and be astonished a' thee.
18 shall be troubled a' thy departure.
27: 3 situate a' the entry of the sea
28 shake a' the sound of the cry of thy
35 isles shall be astonished a' thee,
36 the people shall hiss a' thee;
28:19 people shall be astonished a' thee:
29: 7 all their loins to be a' a stand.
13 God; A' the end of forty years
30:18 A' Tehaphnehes also the day
31:16 to shake a' the sound of his fall,
32:10 make many people amazed a' thee,
10 shall tremble a' every moment,
33: 6 require a' the watchman's hand.
7 shalt hear the word a' my mouth,
8 blood will I require a' thine hand.
34:10 require my flock a' their hand,
35:15 didst rejoice a' the inheritance
36: 8 for they are a' hand to come.
11 you than a' your beginnings:
37:22 into two kingdoms any more a' all:
38:10 a' the same time shall things
11 I will go to them that are a' rest.
18 it come to pass a' the same time
20 shall shake a' my presence, and
39:20 shall be filled a' my table with
40:40 And a' the side without, as one
40 which was a' the porch of the
44 which was a' the side of the north
44 one a' the side of the east gate
41:12 the separate place a' the end
44:11 having charge a' the gates of
17 they enter in a' the gates of the
25 they shall come a' no dead person
46: 2 he shall worship a' the threshold
3 shall worship a' the door of
19 which was a' the side of the gate,
47: 1 a' the south side of the altar
7 a' the bank of the river were
48:28 a' the south side southward,
32 a' the east side four thousand
33 a' the south side four thousand
34 A' the west side four thousand
Da 1: 5 that a' the end thereof they might
15 And a' the end of ten days their
18 Now a' the end of the days that
2:10 such things a' any magician,
3: 5 That a' what time ye hear the sound
7 Therefore a' that time, when all
8 Wherefore a' that time certain
15 that a' what time ye hear the
4: 4 was a' rest in mine house, and
8 But a' the last Daniel came in
29 A' the end of twelve months he
34 And a' the end of the days I
36 A' the same time my reason
5: 3 of God which was a' Jerusalem;
6:24 they came a' the bottom of the
8: 1 appeared unto me a' the first.
2 I was a' Shushan in the palace,
17 for a' the time of the end shall be
19 for a' the time appointed the end
27 I was astonished a' the vision,
9: 7 a' this day; to the men of Judah,
15 as a' this day; we have sinned,
21 in the vision a' the beginning,
23 A' the beginning of thy supplications
10: 3 did I anoint myself a' all, till
11:27 lies a' one table; but it shall not
27 yet the end shall be a' the time
29 A' the time appointed he shall
40 And a' the time of the end shall
40 king of the south push a' him:
43 Ethiopians shall be a' his steps.
12: 1 And a' that time Michael stand
1 and a' that time thy people shall
13 stand in thy lot a' the end of
Ho 1: 5 come to pass a' that day, that
2:16 And it shall be a' that day, saith
4:12 My people ask counsel a' their
5: 8 cry aloud a' Beth-aven, after thee,
9:10 in the fig tree a' her first time;
11: 7 none a' all would exalt him.
Joe 1:15 the Lord is a' hand, and as a
2: 1 cometh, for it is nigh a' hand;
9 shall enter in a' the windows like
Am 3: 5 and have taken nothing a' all?
9 Publish in the palaces a' Ashdod,
4: 3 ye shall go out a' the breaches,

Am 4: 3 every cow a' that which is before
4 transgress; a' Gilgal multiply
6: 1 to them that are a' ease in Zion,
7:13 not again any more a' Beth-el:
8: 9 the sun to go down a' noon, and
Ob 7 the men that were a' peace with
Mic 1:10 Declare ye it not a' Gath,
10 weep ye not a' all: in the house
3: 4 his face from them a' that time,
7:16 and be confounded a' all their
Na 1: 3 will not a' all acquit the wicked:
5 The mountains quake a' him, and
5 and the earth is burned a' his
3:10 dashed in pieces a' the top of
Hab 1:10 And they shall scoff a' the kings,
2: 3 but a' the end it shall speak,
5 neither keepeth a' home, who
19 there is no breath a' all in the
3: 5 coals went forth a' his feet.
11 a' the light of thine arrows they
11 a' the shining of thy glittering
16 my lips quivered a' the voice:
Zep 1: 7 Hold thy peace a' the presence
7 the day of the Lord is a' hand;
12 shall come to pass a' that time,
2: 4 out of Ashdod a' the noon day,
3:19 a' that time I will undo all
20 A' that time will I bring you
Zec 1:11 earth sitteth still, and is a' rest.
15 the heathen that are a' ease:
3: 1 Satan standing a' his right hand
8 for they are men wondered a':
7: 5 did ye a' all fast unto me, even
11:13 I was prised a' of them. And I
12: 8 feeble among them a' that day
14: 7 a' evening time it shall be light.
14 shall also fight a' Jerusalem;
Mal 1:10 accept an offering a' your hand.
13 ye have snuffed a' it, saith the
2: 7 should seek the law a' his mouth:
8 many to stumble a' the law;
13 it with good will a' your hand.
M't 3: 2 kingdom of heaven is a' hand.
4: 6 lest a' any time thou dash thy
17 kingdom of heaven is a' hand.
5:25 lest a' any time the adversary
34 Swear not a' all;
40 any man will sue thee a' the law
7:13 Enter ye in a' the strait gate
28 were astonished a' his doctrine:
8: 6 my servant lieth a' home
9: 9 sitting a' the receipt of custom;
10 as Jesus sat a' meat in the house,
10: 7 kingdom of heaven is a' hand.
35 am come to set a man a' variance
11:22 Tyre and Sidon a' the day of
25 A' that time Jesus answered and
12: 1 A' that time Jesus went on the
41 repented a' the preaching of
13:15 lest a' any time they should see
49 So shall it be a' the end of the
14: 1 A' that time Herod the tetrarch
9 them which sat a' meat with him
15:17 whatsoever entereth in a' the
30 and cast them a' Jesus' feet;
18: 1 A' the same time came the
29 fell down a' his feet
19: 4 a' the beginning made them male
22:33 were astonished a' his doctrine.
23: 6 the uppermost rooms a' feasts,
24 which strain a' a gnat, and
24:33 it is near, even a' the doors.
41 shall be grinding a' the mill;
25: 6 a' midnight there was a cry made,
27 and then a' my coming I should
26: 7 it on his head, as he sat a' meat.
18 My time is a' hand; I will keep
18 a' thy house with my disciples.
45 the hour is a' hand, and the Son
46 he is a' hand that doth betray me.
60 A' the last came two false
27:15 Now a' that feast the governor
M'r 1:15 the kingdom of God is a' hand:
22 were astonished a' his doctrine:
32 And a' even, when the sun did set,
33 gathered together a' the door.
2:14 Alphaeus sitting a' the
15 Jesus sat a' meat in his house,
4:12 lest a' any time they should be
5:22 he saw him, he fall a' his feet.
23 lieth a' the point of death:
6: 3 And they were offended a' him.
7:25 and came and fell a' his feet.
9:12 many things, and be set a' nought.
10:22 And he was sad a' that saying,
24 disciples were astonished a' his
11: 1 Bethany, a' the mount of Olives,
18 the people was astonished a' his
12: 2 And a' the season he sent to the
4 and a' him they cast stones, and
17 And they marvelled a' him.
39 the uppermost rooms a' feasts.
13:29 is nigh, even a' the doors.
35 of the house cometh, a' even,
35 a' midnight, or a' the cockcrowing,
14: 3 as he sat a' meat, there came a
42 that betrayeth me is a' hand.
54 and warmed himself a' the fire.
15: 6 Now a' that feast he released
34 a' the ninth hour Jesus cried
16: 2 sepulchre a' the rising of the sun.
14 the eleven as they sat a' meat,
Lu 1:10 praying without a' the time of
14 many shall rejoice a' his birth.
29 she was troubled a' this saying,
2:18 wondered a' those things which

Lu 2:33 marvelled a' those things which
41 Jerusalem every year a' the feast
47 astonished a' his understanding
4:11 up, lest a' any time thou dash
18 to set a' liberty them that are
22 wondered a' the gracious words
32 were astonished a' his doctrine;
5: 5 nevertheless a' thy word I will let
8 he fell down a' Jesus' knees,
9 were with him, a' the draught
27 Levi, sitting a' the receipt of
7: 9 he marvelled a' him, and turned
37 knew that Jesus sat a' meat in
38 stood a' his feet behind him
49 they that sat a' meat with him
8:19 could not come a' him for the
26 they arrived a' the country of
35 sitting a' the feet of Jesus,
41 and fell down a' Jesus' feet, and
9:31 should accomplish a' Jerusalem
9:43 amazed a' the mighty power of
43 wondered every one a' all things
61 farewell, which are a' home
61 home a' my house.
10:14 Tyre and Sidon a' the judgment,
32 when he was a' the place, came
39 which also sat a' Jesus' feet, and
11: 5 shall go unto him a' midnight,
32 they repented a' the preaching of
12:40 Son of man cometh a' an hour
46 not for him, and a' an hour when
13: 1 There were present a' that season
24 to enter in a' the strait gate:
25 and to knock a' the door, saying,
14:10 of them that sit a' meat with thee.
14 recompensed a' the resurrection
15 them that sat a' meat with him
17 sent his servant a' supper time
15:29 neither transgressed I a' any
16:20 which was laid a' his gate, full of
17:16 fell down on his face a' his feet,
19: 5 to day I must abide a' thy house.
23 bank, that a' my coming I might
29 Bethany, a' the mount called
30 in the which a' your entering ye
37 even now a' the descent of the
42 even thou, a' least in this thy day,
20:10 a' the season he sent a servant to
26 and they marvelled a' his answer,
37 Moses shewed a' the bush, when
40 not ask him any question a' all.
46 and the chief rooms a' feasts;
21:30 that summer is now nigh a' hand.
31 kingdom of God is nigh a' hand.
34 to yourselves, lest a' any time
37 a' night he went out, and abode
22:27 he that sitteth a' meat, or he that
27 is not he that sitteth a' meat?
30 eat and drink a' my table in my
40 And when he was a' the place, he
23: 7 to Herod, who himself also was a'
7 Jerusalem a' that time.
11 men of war set him a' nought, and
12 they were a' enmity between
17 release one unto them a' the
18 cried all a' once, saying, Away
24:12 wondering in himself a' that
22 which were early a' the sepulchre;
27 And beginning a' Moses and all
30 as he sat a' meat with them, he
47 nations, beginning a' Jerusalem.
Joh 1:18 No man hath seen God a' any
2:10 Every man a' the beginning doth
13 the Jews' passover was a' hand,
23 was in Jerusalem a' the passover,
4:21 nor yet a' Jerusalem, worship the
45 seen all the things that he did a'
45 Jerusalem a' the feast: for they
46 whose son was sick a' Capernaum.
47 for he was a' the point of death.
52 Yesterday a' the seventh hour the
53 knew that it was a' the same hour.
5: 2 Now there is a' Jerusalem by the
4 an angel went down a' a certain
28 Marvel not a' this: for the hour is
37 his voice a' any time, nor seen his
6:21 ship was a' the land whither they
39 raise it up again a' the last day.
40 I will raise him up a' the last day.
41 Jews then murmured a' him,
44 raise him up a' the last day.
54 I will raise him up a' the last day.
61 his disciples murmured a' it, he
7: 2 Jews' feast of tabernacles was a'
11 Jews sought him a' the feast, and
23 are ye angry a' me, because I have
8: 7 let him first cast a stone a' her.
9 beginning a' the eldest, even unto
59 took they up stones to cast a' him:
10:22 And it was a' Jerusalem the feast
40 place where John a' first baptized;
11:24 in the resurrection at the last day.
32 she fell down a' his feet, saying
49 Ye know nothing a' all,
55 Jews' passover was nigh a' hand:
12: 2 one of them that sat a' the table
16 understood not his disciples a' the
20 came up to worship a' the feast:
13:28 Now no man a' the table knew for
14:20 A' that day ye shall know that I
16: 4 not unto you a' the beginning,
26 A' that day ye shall ask in my
18:16 Peter stood a' the door without.
38 I find no fault in him a' all.
39 release unto you one a' the
19:11 couldest have no power a' all

Joh 19:39 Nicodemus, which a' the first
42 the sepulchre was nigh a' hand.
20:11 Mary stood without a' the
12 one a' the head, and the other a'
19 Then the same day a' evening,
21: 1 disciples a' the sea of Tiberias:
20 leaned on his breast a' supper,
Ac 1: 6 wilt thou a' this time restore
19 all the dwellers a' Jerusalem;
2: 5 were dwelling a' Jerusalem Jews,
14 all ye that dwell a' Jerusalem, be
3: 1 into the temple a' the hour of
2 whom they laid daily a' the gate
10 for alms a' the Beautiful gate of
10 amazement a' that which had
12 why marvel ye a' this? or why
4: 6 gathered together a' Jerusalem.
11 which was set a' nought of you
18 not to speak a' all nor teach in
35 laid them down a' the apostles'
37 and laid it a' the apostles' feet.
5: 2 and laid it a' the apostles' feet.
9 thy husband are a' the door, and
10 down straightway a' his feet, and
15 a' the least the shadow of Peter
7:13 a' the second time Joseph was
26 would have set them a' one again,
29 Then fled Moses a' this saying,
31 Moses saw it, he wondered a' the
58 laid down their clothes a' a young
8: 1 And a' that time there was a
1 church which was a' Jerusalem;
14 apostles which were a' Jerusalem
35 and began a' the same scripture,
40 But Philip was found a' Azotus:
9:10 a certain disciple a' Damascus,
13 done to thy saints a' Jerusalem:
19 disciples which were a' Damascus.
22 Jews which dwelt a' Damascus,
27 preached boldly a' Damascus in
28 in and going out a' Jerusalem,
32 the saints which dwelt a' Lydda.
35 all that dwelt a' Lydda and Saron,
36 Now there was a' Joppa a certain
10:11 sheet knit a' the four corners,
25 down a' his feet, and worshipped
30 a' the ninth hour I prayed in my
11: 8 unclean hath a' any time entered
15 them, as on us a' the beginning.
12:13 Peter knocked a' the door of the
13: 1 church that was a' Antioch
5 when they were a' Salamis, they
12 being astonished a' the doctrine
27 they that dwell a' Jerusalem, and
14: 8 sat a certain man a' Lystra,
15:14 declared how God a' the first did
16: 2 brethren that were a' Lystra and
4 elders which were a' Jerusalem.
25 And a' midnight Paul and Silas
17:13 God was preached of Paul a'
16 Paul waited for them a' Athens,
30 this ignorance God winked a':
18:22 when he had landed a' Cæsarea,
24 Apollos, born a' Alexandria, an
19: 1 Apollos was a' Corinth, Paul
17 Greeks also dwelling a' Ephesus;
26 not alone a' Ephesus, but almost
27 our craft is in danger to be set a'
20: 5 before tarried for us a' Troas.
14 when he met with us a' Assos,
15 we arrived a' Samos, and
15 tarried a' Trogyllium; and the
16 a' Jerusalem the day of Pentecost.
18 have been with you a' all seasons,
21: 3 into Syria, and landed a' Tyre:
11 So shall the Jews a' Jerusalem
13 but also to die a' Jerusalem for
24 and be a' charges with them, that
22: 3 brought up in this city a' the feet
23:11 thou bear witness also a' Rome.
23 two hundred, a' the third hour of
25: 4 should be kept a' Cæsarea, and
8 have I offended any thing a' all.
10 I stand a' Cæsar's judgment seat,
15 About whom, when I was a'
23 men of the city, a' Festus'
24 both a' Jerusalem, and also here,
26: 4 which was a' the first among
4 nation a' Jerusalem, know all the
13 A' midday, O king, I saw in the
20 and a' Jerusalem, and throughout
32 might have been set a' liberty, if
27: 3 the next day we touched a' Sidon.
28:12 And landing a' Syracuse, we
Ro 1:10 if by any means now a' length I
15 gospel to you that are a' Rome
3:26 To declare, I say, a' this time his
4:20 He staggered not a' the promise
8:34 who is even a' the right hand of
9: 9 A' this time will I come, and
32 stumbled a' that stumblingstone;
11: 5 Even so then a' this present time
13:12 spent, the day is a' hand: let us
14:10 set a' nought thy brother? for
15:26 saints which are a' Jerusalem.
16: 1 servant of the church a' Cenchrea:
1Co 1: 2 which is a' Corinth, to them that
7:39 she is a' liberty to be married to
8:10 sit a' meat in the idol's temple,
9: 7 time a' his own charges? who
13 and they which wait a' the altar
11:34 let him eat a' home; that ye come
14:16 say Amen a' thy giving of thanks,
27 or a' the most by three, and that
35 their husbands a' home: for it is
15: 6 five hundred brethren a' once;

1Co 15:23 that are Christ's *a'* his coming.
29 if the dead rise not *a'* all? why
32 fought with beasts *a'* Ephesus,
52 twinkling of an eye *a'* the last
16: 8 But I will tarry *a'* Ephesus until
12 but his will was not *a'* all
12 to come *a'* this time;
2Co 1: 1 which is *a'* Corinth, with all the
4:18 While we look not *a'* the things
18 but *a'* the things which are not
5: 6 whilst we are *a'* home in the
8:14 that now *a'* this time your
Ga 4:12 ye have not injured me *a'* all.
13 the gospel unto you *a'* the first.
Eph 1: 1 saints which are *a'* Ephesus,
20 and set him *a'* his own right
2:12 That *a'* that time ye were
3:13 faint not *a'* my tribulations
Ph'p 1: 1 Christ Jesus which are *a'* Philippi,
2:10 That *a'* the name of Jesus every
4: 5 to all men. The Lord is *a'* hand.
10 that now *a'* the last your care of
Col 1: 2 brethren in Christ which are *a'*
2: 1 for them *a'* Laodicea, and for
1Th 2: 2 know, *a'* Philippi we were bold
5 For neither *a'* any time used we
19 our Lord Jesus *a'* his coming?
3: 1 good to be left *a'* Athens alone;
13 even our Father, *a'* the coming of
5:13 And be *a'* peace among yourselves.
2Th 2: 2 the day of Christ is *a'* hand.
3:11 disorderly, working not *a'* all,
1Ti 1: 3 to abide still *a'* Ephesus, when
5: 4 to show piety *a'* home, and to
2Ti 1:18 ministered unto me *a'* Ephesus,
2:26 captive by him *a'* his will.
3:11 *a'* Antioch, *a'* Iconium, *a'* Lystra;
4: 1 and the dead *a'* his appearing
6 of my departure is *a'* hand.
8 shall give me *a'* that day:
13 left *a'* Troas with Carpus, when
16 *A'* my first answer no man stood
20 Erastus abode *a'* Corinth:
20 have I left *a'* Miletum sick.
Tit 2: 5 keepers *a'* home, good, obedient
Heb 1: 1 God, who *a'* sundry times and in
5, 13 the angels said he *a'* any time,
2: 1 lest *a'* any time we should let
3 which *a'* the first began to be
7:13 man gave attendance *a'* the altar.
9:17 no strength *a'* all while the
12: 2 and is set down *a'* the right hand
13:23 brother Timothy is set *a'* liberty;
Jas 3:11 send forth *a'* the same place
1Pe 1: 7 and glory *a'* the appearing
13 unto you *a'* the revelation of
2: 8 which stumble *a'* the word, being
4: 7 is *a'* hand: be ye therefore
17 begin *a'* the house of God; and if
17 it first begin *a'* us, what shall the
5:13 that is *a'* Babylon, elected
1Jo 1: 5 and in him is no darkness *a'* all.
2:28 before him *a'* his coming.
4:12 man hath seen God *a'* any time.
Re 1: 3 therein: for the time is *a'* hand.
17 saw him, I fell *a'* his feet as dead.
3:20 Behold I stand *a'* the door, and
8: 3 and stood *a'* the altar, having
18:14 shalt find them no more *a'* all.
21 shall be found no more *a'* all
22 shall be heard no more *a'* all in
22 shall be heard no more *a'* all in
23 shall shine no more *a'* all in thee:
23 shall be heard no more *a'* all in thee·
19: 2 blood of his servants *a'* her hand.
10 And I fell *a'* his feet to worship
21:12 twelve gates, and *a'* the gates
25 not be shut *a'* all by day; for
22:10 this book; for the time is *a'* hand.

Atad (*a'-tad*) See also ABEL-MIZRAIM.
Ge 50:10 came to the threshingfloor of *A'*,
11 saw the mourning in the floor of *A'*,

Atarah (*at'-a-rah*)
1Ch 2:26 another wife, whose name was *A'*;

Ataroth (*at'-a-roth*) See also ATAROTH-ADAR; ATROTH.
Nu 32: 3 *A'*, and Dibon, and Jazer,
34 of Gad built Dibon, and *A'*,
Jos 16: 2 unto the borders of Archi to *A'*,
7 went down from Janohah to *A'*,
1Ch 2:54 *A'*, the house of Joab, and half

Ataroth-adar (*at''-a-roth-a'-dar*) See also ATAROTH-ADDAR.
Jos 18:13 the border descended to *A'*,

Ataroth-addar (*at''-a-roth-ad'-dar*) See also ATAROTH-ADAR.
Jos 16: 5 on the east side was *A'*, unto

ate
Ps 106:28 and *a'* the sacrifices of the dead.
Da 10: 3 I *a'* no pleasant bread, neither
Re 10:10 of the angel's hand, and *a'* it up;

Ater (*a'-tur*)
Ezr 2:16 The children of *A'* of Hezekiah,
42 the children of *A'*, the children of
Ne 7:21 The children of *A'* of Hezekiah,
45 of Shallum, the children of *A'*,
10:17 *A'*, Hizkijah, Azzur,

Atha See MARAN-ATHA.

Athach (*a'-thak*)
1Sa 30:30 and to them which were in *A'*,

Athaiah (*ath-a-i'-ah*)
Ne 11: 4 of Judah; *A'* the son of Uzziah,

Athaliah (*ath-a-li'-ah*)
2Ki 8:26 and his mother's name was *A'*,
11: 1 And when *A'*, the mother of
2 from *A'*, so that he was not slain.
3 And *A'* did reign over the land.
13 when *A'* heard the noise of the
14 and *A'* rent her clothes, and cried
20 and they slew *A'* with the sword
1Ch 8:26 and Sheharian, and *A'*,
2Ch 22: 2 was *A'* the daughter of Omri.
10 when *A'* the mother of Ahaziah
11 hid him from *A'*, so that she slew
12 house of God in six years: and *A'*
23:12 Now when *A'* heard the noise
13 *A'* rent her clothes, and said,
21 they had slain *A'* with the sword.
24: 7 sons of *A'*, that wicked woman,
Ezr 8: 7 of Elam; Jeshaiah the son of *A'*,

Athenians (*a-the'-ne-uns*)
Ac 17:21 (For all the *A'* and strangers

Athens (*ath'-ens*) See also ATHENIANS.
Ac 17:15 brought him unto *A'*:
16 while Paul waited for them at *A'*,
22 Ye men of *A'*, I perceive
18: 1 Paul departed from *A'*,
1Th 3: 1 it good to be left at *A'* alone;
subscr. Thessalonians was written from *A'*
2Th *subscr.* Thessalonians was written from *A'*

athirst
J'g 15:18 he was sore *a'*, and called on the
Ru 2: 9 thou art *a'*, go unto the vessels,
M't 25:44 saw we thee an hungered, or *a'*,
Re 21: 6 I will give to him that is *a'*
22:17 let him that is *a'* come.

Athlai (*ath'-lahee*)
Ezr 10:28 Hananiah, Zabbai, and *A'*.

atonement See also ATONEMENTS:
Ex 29:33 wherewith the *a'* was made,
36 a bullock for a sin offering for *a'*:
36 when thou hast made an *a'* for it,
37 shalt make an *a'* for the altar,
30:10 shall make an *a'* upon the horns
10 once in the year shall he make *a'*
15 to make *a'* for your souls.
16 take the *a'* money of the children
16 to make an *a'* for your souls.
32:30 I shall make an *a'* for your sin.
Le 1: 4 to make *a'* for him.
4:20 priest shall make an *a'* for them,
26 and the priest shall make an *a'*
31 priest shall make an *a'* for him,
35 shall make an *a'* for his sin
5: 6, 10, 13 shall make an *a'* for him
16 the priest shall make an *a'*
18 an *a'* for him concerning his
6: 7 an *a'* for him before the Lord:
7: 7 the priest that maketh *a'*
8:34 to make an *a'* for you.
9: 7 and make an *a'* for thyself,
7 and make an *a'* for them;
10:17 make *a'* for them before the Lord?
12: 7 and make an *a'* for her;
8 priest shall make an *a'* for her,
14:18 and the priest shall make an *a'*
19 and make an *a'* for him
20 and the priest shall make an *a'*
21, 29 to make an *a'* for him,
31 and the priest shall make an *a'*
53 and make an *a'* for the house:
15:15, 30 the priest shall make an *a'* for
16: 6 and make an *a'* for himself,
10 to make an *a'* with him,
11 and shall make an *a'* for himself,
16 shall make an *a'* for the holy place,
17 to make an *a'* in the holy place,
17 and have made an *a'* for himself,
18 and make an *a'* for it;
24 and make an *a'* for himself,
27 blood was brought in to make *a'*
30 the priest make an *a'* for you,
32 And the priest,...shall make the *a'*,
33 make an *a'* for the holy sanctuary,
33 shall make an *a'* for the tabernacle
33 and he shall make an *a'* for the
34 an *a'* for the children of Israel.
17:11 to make an *a'* for your souls:
11 the blood that maketh an *a'* for
19:22 the priest shall make an *a'* for
23:27 there shall be a day of *a'*:
28 it is a day of *a'*,
28 to make an *a'* for you
25: 9 the day of *a'* shall ye make the
Nu 5: 8 the ram of the *a'*,
8 an *a'* shall be made for him.
6:11 and make an *a'* for him,
8:12 to make an *a'* for the Levites.
19 and to make an *a'* for the children
21 and Aaron made an *a'*
15:25 And the priest shall make an *a'*
28 shall make an *a'* for the soul
28 to make an *a'* for him;
16:46 and make an *a'* for them:
47 and made an *a'* for the people.
25:13 an *a'* for the children of Israel.
28:22 sin offering, to make an *a'* for you.
30 the goats; to make an *a'* for you.
29: 5 offering to make an *a'* for you:
11 the sin offering of *a'*,
31:50 to make an *a'* for our souls
2Sa 21: 3 wherewith shall I make the *a*,
1Ch 6:49 and to make an *a'* for Israel,
2Ch 29:24 to make an *a'* for all Israel:
Ne 10:33 to make an *a'* for Israel,
Ro 5:11 we have now received the *a'*.

atonements
Ex 30:10 the sin offering of *a'*:

Atroth (*a'-troth*) See also ATAROTH.
Nu 32:35 And *A'*, Shophan, and Jaazer,

Attai (*at'-tahee*)
1Ch 2:35 to wife, and she bare him *A'*.
36 And *A'* begat Nathan, and Nathan
12:11 *A'* the sixth, Eliel the seventh,
2Ch 11:20 which bare him Abijah, and *A'*,

attain See also ATTAINED.
Ps 139: 6 it is high, I cannot *a'* unto it.
Pr 1: 5 a man of understanding shall *a'*
Eze 46: 7 as his hand shall *a'* unto,
Ho 8: 5 will it be ere they *a'* to innocency?
Ac 27:12 means they might *a'* to Phenice,
Ph'p 3:11 I might *a'* unto the resurrection

attained
Ge 47: 9 not *a'* unto the days of the years
2Sa 23:19 he *a'* not unto the first three:
23 he *a'* not to the first
1Ch 11:21 howbeit he *a'* not to the first three.
25 but *a'* not to the first three.
Ro 9:30 have *a'* to righteousness,
31 not *a'* to the law of righteousness.
Ph'p 3:12 Not as though I had already *a'*,
16 whereto we have already *a'*,
1Ti 4: 6 whereunto thou hast *a'*.

Attalia (*at-ta-li'-ah*)
Ac 14:25 they went down into *A'*:

attend
Es 4: 5 he had appointed to *a'* upon her,
Ps 17: 1 *a'* unto my cry, give ear unto my
55: 2 *A'* unto me, and hear me:
61: 1 *a'* unto my prayer.
86: 6 *a'* to the voice of my supplications.
142: 6 *A'* unto my cry; for I am brought
Pr 4: 1 and *a'* to know understanding.
20 My son, *a'* to my words;
5: 1 My son, *a'* unto my wisdom,
7:24 and *a'* to the words of my mouth.
1Co 7:35 that ye may *a'* upon the Lord

attendance
1Ki 10: 5 and the *a'* of his ministers,
2Ch 9: 4 and the *a'* of his ministers,
1Ti 4:13 Till I come, give *a'* to reading,
Heb 7:13 no man gave *a'* at the altar.

attended
Job 32:12 Yea, I *a'* unto you, and, behold,
Ps 66:19 hath *a'* to the voice of my prayer.
Ac 16:14 she *a'* unto the things which were

attending
Ro 13: 6 *a'* continually upon this very thing.

attent
2Ch 6:40 thine ears be *a'* unto the prayer
7:15 mine ears *a'* unto the prayer

attentive
Ne 1: 6 let now thine ear be *a'*,
11 now thine ear be *a'* to the prayer
8: 3 were *a'* unto the book of the law.
Ps 130: 2 let thine ears be *a'* to the voice
Lu 19:48 were very attentive to hear him.

attentively
Job 37: 2 Hear *a'* the noise of his voice,

attire See also ATTIRED.
Pr 7:10 the *a'* of an harlot,
Jer 2:32 her ornaments, or a bride her *a'*?
Eze 23:15 in dyed *a'* upon their heads,

attired
Le 16: 4 the linen mitre shall he be *a'*:

audience
Ge 23:10 in the *a'* of the children of Heth,
13 in the *a'* of the people of the land,
16 named in the *a'* of the sons of Heth,
Ex 24: 7 read in the *a'* of the people:
1Sa 25:24 in thine *a'*, and hear the words
1Ch 28: 8 and in the *a'* of our God,
Ne 13: 1 in the *a'* of the people;
Lu 7: 1 sayings in the *a'* of the people,
20:45 in the *a'* of all the people he said
Ac 13:16 ye that fear God, give *a'*.
15:12 and gave *a'* to Barnabas and
22:22 they gave him *a'* unto this word,

aught See NAUGHT; OUGHT.

augment
Nu 32:14 to *a'* yet the fierce anger of the

Augustus (*aw-gus'-tus*) See also AUGUSTUS'; CÆSAR.
Lu 2: 1 a decree from Cæsar *A'*,
Ac 25:21 reserved unto the hearing of *A'*,
25 himself hath appealed to *A'*,

Augustus' (*aw-gus'-tus*)
Ac 27: 1 a centurion of *A'* band.

aul
Ex 21: 6 bore his ear through with an *a'*;
De 15:17 Then thou shalt take an *a'*,

aunt
Le 18:14 she is thine *a'*.

austere
Lu 19:21 because thou art an *a'* man:
22 that I was an *a'* man,

author
1Co 14:33 God is not the *a'* of confusion, but
Heb 5: 9 became the *a'* of eternal salvation
12: 2 the *a'* and finisher of our faith;

authorities
1Pe 3:22 *a'* and powers being made subject

authority See also AUTHORITIES.
Es 9:29 Mordecai the Jew,...with all a'.
Pr 29: 2 When the righteous are in a', the
M't 7:29 taught them as one having a'.
8: 9 For I am a man under a',
20:25 that are great exercise a' upon
21:23 what a' doest thou these things?
23 and who gave thee this a'
24, 27 by what a' I do these things.
M'r 1:22 as one that had a',
27 for with a' commandeth he even
10:42 their great ones exercise a' upon
11:28 what a' doest thou these things?
28 and who gave thee this a'
29, 33 by what a' I do these things.
13:34 gave a' to his servants,
Lu 4:36 with a' and power he commandeth
7: 8 am a man set under a',
9: 1 gave them power and a' over all
19:17 have thou a' over ten cities.
20: 2 what a' doest thou these things?
2 who is he that gave thee this a'?
8 by what a' I do these things.
20 power and a' of the governor.
22:25 that exercise a' upon them are
Joh 5:27 hath given him a' to execute
Ac 8:27 eunuch of great a' under Candace
9:14 he hath a' from the chief priests
26:10 having received a' from the chief
12 went to Damascus with a' and
1Co 15:24 all rule and all a' and power.
2Co 10: 8 somewhat more of our a',
1Ti 2: 2 and for all that are in a';
12 nor to usurp a' over the man, but
Tit 2:15 exhort, and rebuke with all a'.
Re 13: 2 power, and his seat, and great a'.

Ava *(a'-vah)* See also IVAH.
2Ki 17:24 and from Cuthah, and from A',

availeth
Es 5:13 all this a' me nothing,
Ga 5: 6 neither circumcision a' any thing,
6:15 neither circumcision a' any thing,
Jas 5:16 prayer of a righteous man a' much.

Aven See also BETH-AVEN.
Eze 30:17 young men of A' and of Pi-beseth
Ho 10: 8 high places also of A', the sin of
Am 1: 5 inhabitant from the plain of A',

avenge See also AVENGED; AVENGETH; AVENGING.
Le 19:18 Thou shalt not a', nor bear any
26:25 a sword...that shall a' the quarrel
Nu 31: 2 A' the children of Israel of
3 and a' the Lord of Midian.
De 32:43 will a' the blood of his servants,
1Sa 24:12 and the Lord a' me of thee:
2Ki 9: 7 I may a' the blood of my servants
Es 8:13 to a' themselves on their enemies.
Isa 1:24 and a' me of mine enemies:
Jer 46:10 he may a' him of his adversaries:
Ho 1: 4 and I will a' the blood of Jezreel
Lu 18: 3 saying, A' me of mine adversary.
5 I will a' her, lest by her continual
7 not God a' his own elect,
8 he will a' them speedily.
Ro 12:19 Dearly beloved, a' not yourselves,
Re 6:10 dost thou not judge and a' our

avenged
Ge 4:24 If Cain shall be a' sevenfold,
Jos 10:13 the people had a' themselves
J'd 15: 7 yet will I be a' of you,
16:28 that I may be at once a' of the
1Sa 14:24 that I may be a' on mine enemies.
18:25 to be a' of the king's enemies.
25:31 or that my Lord hath a' himself:
2Sa 4: 8 the Lord hath a' my lord
18:19 hath a' him of his enemies.
31 Lord hath a' thee this day of all
Jer 5: 9, 29 shall not my soul be a' on such
9: 9 shall not my soul be a' on such
Ac 7:24 a' him that was oppressed.
Re 18:20 God hath a' you on her.
19: 2 hath a' the blood of his servants

avenger
Nu 35:12 for refuge from the a'; that the
De 19: 6 Lest the a' of the blood pursue the
12 into the hand of the a' of blood,
Jos 20: 3 your refuge from the a' of blood.
5 if the a' of blood pursue after him,
9 by the hand of the a' of blood,
Ps 8: 2 still the enemy and the a'.
44:16 by reason of the enemy and a'.
1Th 4: 6 the Lord is the a' of all such,

avengeth
2Sa 22:48 It is God that a' me,
Ps 18:47 It is God that a' me,

avenging
J'g 5: 2 Praise ye the Lord for the a'
1Sa 25:26 from a' thyself with thine own
33 from a' myself with mine own

averse
Mic 2: 8 by securely as men a' from war.

Avim *(a'-vim)* See also AVIMS; AVITES.
Jos 18:23 And A', and Parah, and Ophrah,

Avims *(a'-vims)* See also AVIM.
De 2:23 And the A' which dwelt in

Avites *(a'-vites)* See also AVIM.
Jos 13: 3 and the Ekronites; also the A':
2Ki 17:31 the A' made Nibhaz and Tartak,

Avith *(a'-vith)*
Ge 36:35 and the name of his city was A'.
1Ch 1:46 and the name of his city was A'.

avoid See also AVOIDED; AVOIDING.
Pr 4:15 A' it, pass not by it, turn from it,
Ro 16:17 which ye have learned; and a'
1Co 7: 2 Nevertheless, to a' fornication,
2Ti 2:23 and unlearned questions a',
Tit 3: 9 But a' foolish questions, and

avoided See also AVOID.
1Sa 18:11 And David a' out of his presence

avoiding
2Co 8:20 A' this, that no man should
1Ti 6:20 a' profane and vain babblings,

avouched
De 26:17 Thou hast a' the Lord this day to
18 the Lord hath a' thee this day

await
Ac 9:24 laying a' was known of Saul.

awake See also AWAKED; AWAKEST; AWAKETH; AWAKING; AWOKE.
J'g 5:12 A', a', Deborah; a', a', utter a
Job 8: 6 surely now he would a' for thee,
14:12 they shall not a', nor be raised
Ps 7: 6 and a' for me to the judgment
17:15 I shall be satisfied, when I a', with
35:23 Stir up thyself, and a' to my
44:23 A', why sleepest thou, O Lord?
57: 8 A' up, my glory,
8 a', psaltery and harp:
8 I myself will a' early.
59: 4 a' to help me, and behold.
5 a' to visit all the heathen:
108: 2 A', psaltery and harp:
2 I myself will a' early.
139:18 when I a', I am still with thee.
Pr 23:35 when shall I a'? I will seek it yet
Ca 2: 7 nor a' my love, till he please.
3: 5 not up, nor a' my love, till he
4:16 A', O north wind; and come,
8: 4 ye stir not up, nor a' my love,
Isa 26:19 A' and sing, ye that dwell in dust:
51: 9 A', a', put on strength, O arm of
9 the Lord; a', as in the ancient
17 A', a'; stand up, O Jerusalem,
52: 1 A', a'; put on thy strength,
Da 12: 2 in the dust of the earth shall a',
Joe 1: 5 A', ye drunkards, and weep;
Hab 2: 7 and a' that shall vex thee,
19 him that saith to the wood, A';
Zec 13: 7 A', O sword, against my shepherd,
M'r 4:38 they a' him, and say unto him,
Lu 9:32 when they were a', they saw his
Joh 11:11 that I may a' him out of sleep.
Ro 13:11 is high time to a' out of sleep:
1Co 15:34 A' to righteousness, and sin not;
Eph 5:14 A' thou that sleepest, and arise

awaked See also AWOKE.
Ge 28:16 And Jacob a' out of his sleep,
J'g 16:14 And he a' out of his sleep,
1Sa 26:12 saw it, nor knew it, neither a':
1Ki 18:27 he sleepeth, and must be a'.
2Ki 4:31 The child is not a'.
Ps 3: 5 I a'; for the Lord sustained me.
78:65 the Lord a' as one out of sleep,
Jer 31:26 Upon this I a', and beheld;

awakest
Ps 73:20 when thou a', thou shalt despise
Pr 6:22 when thou a', it shall talk with

awaketh
Ps 73:20 As a dream when one a';
Isa 29: 8 but he a', and his soul is empty:
8 but he a', and, behold, he is faint,

awaking
Ac 16:27 a' out of his sleep, and

aware See also WARE.
Ca 6:12 Or ever I was a', my soul made
Jer 50:24 thou wast not a': thou art found,
M't 24:50 in an hour that he is not a' of,
Lu 11:44 over them are not a' of them.
12:46 and at an hour when he is not a',

away^ See also CASTAWAY.
Ge 12:20 and they sent him a', and his wife,
15:11 carcasses, Abram drove them a'.
18: 3 favour in thy sight, pass not a',
21:14 and the child, and sent her a':
25 servants had violently taken a'.
24:54 said, Send me a' unto my master.
56 send me a' that I may go to my
59 they sent a' Rebekah, their sister,
25: 6 gifts, and sent them a' from Isaac
26:27 me, and have sent me a' from you?
29 and have sent thee a' in peace:
31 Isaac sent them a', and they
27:35 and hath taken a' thy blessing.
36 times: he took a' my birthright;
36 now he hath taken a' my blessing.
44 until thy brother's fury turn a';
45 Until thy brother's anger turn a'
28: 5 And Isaac sent a' Jacob: and he
6 and sent him a' to Padan-aram,
30:15 take a' my son's mandrakes also?
23 Lord hath taken a' my reproach:
25 said unto Laban, Send me a',
31: 1 taken a' all that was our father's;
9 taken a' the cattle of your father,
18 And he carried a' all his cattle,
20 And Jacob stole a' unawares
26 stolen a' unawares to me,
26 and carried a' my daughters,
27 didst thou flee a' secretly,
27 and steal a' from me; and
27 that I might have sent thee a'
42 hadst sent me a' now empty.
35: 2 Put a' the strange gods that are
Ge 38:19 and she arose, and went a', and
40:15 I was stolen a' out of the land
42:36 and ye will take Benjamin a':
43:14 may send a' your other brother,
44: 3 the men were sent a', they and
45:24 So he sent his brethren a', and
Ex 2: 9 Take this child a', and nurse it
17 came and drove them a':
8: 8 may take a' the frogs from me,
28 not go very far a': intreat for me.
10:17 take a' from me this death only.
19 which took a' the locusts, and
12:15 first day ye shall put a' leaven
28 the children of Israel went a',
13:19 up my bones a' hence with you.
22 He took not a' the pillar of the
14:11 hast thou taken us a' to die in the
15:15 of Canaan shall melt a'.
18:18 Thou wilt surely wear a', both
19:24 the Lord said unto him, A', get
22:10 die, or be hurt, or driven a',
23:25 I will take sickness a' from the
33:23 And I will take a' mine hand,
Lev 1:16 he shall pluck a' his crop with his
3: 4, 10, 15 kidneys, it shall he take a'.
4: 9 the kidneys, it shall he take a'.
31 a' all the fat thereof,
31 as the fat is taken a'
35 shall take a' all the fat thereof,
35 the fat of the lamb is taken a'
6: 2 or in a thing taken a' by violence,
4 that which he took violently a',
7: 4 the kidneys, it shall he take a':
14:40 that they take a' the stones
43 that he hath taken a' the stones,
25:25 sold a' some of his possession,
26:39 that are left of you shall pine a'
39 of their fathers shall they pine a'
44 I will not cast them a', neither
Nu 4:13 take a' the ashes from the altar,
11: 6 But now our soul is dried a':
14:43 ye are turned a' from the Lord,
17:10 quite take a' their murmurings
20:21 wherefore Israel turned a' from
21: 7 he take a' the serpents from us.
24:22 Asshur shall carry thee a' captive.
25: 4 anger of the Lord may be turned a'
11 hath turned my wrath a' from
27: 4 name of our father be done a'
32:15 For if ye turn a' from after him,
36: 4 their inheritance be taken a' from
De 7: 4 turn a' thy son from following me,
15 take a' from thee all sickness,
13: 5 to turn you a' from the Lord
5 So shalt thou put the evil a'
10 he hath sought to thrust thee a'
15:13 shalt not let him go a' empty:
16 thee, I will not go a' from thee;
18 sendest him a' free from thee;
17: 7 put the evil a' from among you.
12 shalt put a' the evil from Israel.
17 that his heart turn not a';
19:13 put a' the guilt of innocent blood
19 put the evil a' from among you.
21: 9 put a' the guilt of innocent blood
21 thou put evil a' from among you;
22:19 may not put her a' all his days.
21 thou put evil a' from among you.
22 shalt thou put a' evil from Israel.
24 thou put a' evil from among you.
29 may not put her a' all his days.
23:14 in thee, and turn a' from thee.
24: 4 husband, which sent her a',
7 shalt put evil a' from among you.
26:13 brought a' the hallowed things
14 have I taken a' aught thereof
28:26 and no man shall fray them a'.
31 ass shall be violently taken a'
29:18 heart turneth a' this day from
30:17 But if thine heart turn a', so that
17 not hear, but shalt be drawn a',
Jos 2:21 And she sent them a', and they
5: 9 day have I rolled a' the reproach
7:13 ye take a' the accursed thing
8: 3 and sent them a' by night.
16 Joshua, and were drawn a' from
18: 8 the men arose, and went a':
22: 6 blessed them, and sent them a':
7 when Joshua sent them a' also
16 to turn a' this day from following
18 ye must turn a' this day from
24:14 a' the gods which your fathers
23 therefore put a', said he, the
J'g 3:18 sent a' the people that bare the
4:15 chariot, and fled a' on his feet.
17 Howbeit Sisera fled a' on his feet
5:21 river of Kishon swept them a',
8:21 and took a' the ornaments
9:21 And Jotham ran a', and fled,
10:16 And they put a' the strange gods
11:13 Because Israel took a' my land,
15 took not a' the land of Moab,
38 he sent her a' for two months:
15:17 cast a' the jawbone out of his hand,
16: 3 posts, and went a' with them,
14 went a' with the pin of the beam,
18:24 taken a' my gods which I made,
24 ye are gone a': and what have I
19: 2 went a' from him unto her
20:13 and put a' evil from Israel.
31 and were drawn a' from the city;
1Sa 1:14 put a' thy wine from thee.
5:11 Send a' the ark of the God of Israel,
6: 3 send a' the ark of the God of Israel,
8 by the side thereof; and send it a',
7: 3 then put a' the strange gods

1Sa 7: 4 the children of Israel did put a'
9:26 Up, that I may send thee a'.
10:25 And Samuel sent all the people a',
14:16 behold, the multitude melted a',
15:27 as Samuel turned about to go a',
17:26 taketh a' the reproach from Israel?
19:10 slipped a' out of Saul's presence,
17 me so, and sent a' mine enemy,
20:13 shew it thee, and send thee a',
22 for the Lord hath sent thee a'.
29 let me get a', I pray thee, and see
21: 6 in the day when it was taken a'.
23: 5 and brought a' their cattle,
26 haste to get a' for fear of Saul;
24:19 will he let him go well a'?
25:10 break a' every man from his
26:12 and gat them a', and no man
27: 9 alive, and took a' the sheep,
28: 3 had put a' those that had familiar
25 rose up, and went a' that night.
30: 2 but carried them a', and went on
18 the Amalekites had carried a':
22 that they may lead them a',
2Sa 1:21 of the mighty is vilely cast a',
3:21 And David sent Abner a'; and he
23 and he hath sent him a', and he is
24 thou hast sent him a', and he is
4: 7 gat them a' through the plain
11 and take you a' from the earth?
5: 6 Except thou take a' the blind and
7:15 But my mercy shall not depart a'
15 Saul, whom I put a' before thee.
10: 4 their buttocks, and sent them a'.
12:13 Lord also hath put a' thy sin;
13:16 this evil in sending me a' is
17:18 went both of them a' quickly,
18: 3 for if we flee a', they will not care
9 that was under him went a'.
19: 3 as people being ashamed steal a'
41 the men of Judah stolen thee a',
22:46 Strangers shall fade a', and they
23: 6 as thorns thrust a', because they
9 the men of Israel were gone a':
24:10 take a' the iniquity of thy
1Ki 2:31 thou mayest take a' the innocent
39 the servants of Shimei ran a'
8:46 that they carry them a' captives
48 which led them a' captive,
66 eighth day he sent the people a':
11: 2 surely they will turn a' your heart
3 and his wives turned a' his heart.
4 that his wives turned a' his heart
13 I will not rend a' all the kingdom;
14: 8 the kingdom a' from the house
10 take a' the remnant of the house
10 as a man taketh a' dung, till it
26 he took a' the treasures of the
26 he even took a' all:
26 and he took a' all the shields
15:12 he took a' the sodomites out of
22 took a' the stones of Ramah,
16: 3 I will take a' the posterity of
19: 4 now, O Lord, take a' my life;
10, 14 they seek my life, to take it a'.
20: 6 it in their hand, and take it a'.
24 Take the kings a', every man out
34 I will send thee a' with this
34 with him, and sent him a'.
41 took the ashes a' from his face;
21: 4 and turned a' his face, and would
21 and will take a' thy posterity,
22:43 the high places were not taken a';
2Ki 2: 3, 5 Lord will take a' thy master
9 before I be taken a' from thee.
3: 2 he put a' the image of Baal that
4:27 came near to thrust her a'.
5: 2 had brought a' captive out of
11 and went a', and said, Behold,
12 he turned and went a' in a rage.
6:23 he sent them a', and they went
32 hath sent to take a' mine head?
7:15 the Syrians had cast a' in their
12: 3 high places were not taken a':
18 and he went a' from Jerusalem.
14: 4 the high places were not taken a':
17: 6 and carried Israel a' into Assyria,
11 Lord carried a' before them;
23 So was Israel carried a' out of
28 had carried a' from Samaria
33 the nations whom they carried a'
18:11 king of Assyria did carry a' Israel
22 altars Hezekiah hath taken a',
24 How then wilt thou turn a' the
32 take you a' to a land like your own
20:18 thou shalt beget, shall they take a';
23:11 he took a' the horses that the
19 Josiah took a', and did to them
24 did Josiah put a', that he might
34 and took Jehoahaz a': and he
24:14 And he carried a' all Jerusalem,
15 And he carried a' Jehoiachin to
25:11 the fugitives that fell a' to the
11 the captain of the guard carry a'.
14 they ministered, took they a'.
15 the captain of the guard took a'.
21 So Judah was carried a' out of
1Ch 5: 6 king of Assyria carried a' captive:
21 And they took a' their cattle;
26 and he carried them a', even the
6:15 carried a' Judah and Jerusalem
7:21 came down to take a' their cattle
8: 8 after he had sent them a';
13 who drove a' the inhabitants of
9: 1 were carried a' to Babylon for
10:12 and took a' the body of Saul,
12:19 upon advisement sent him a',

1Ch 14:14 turn a' from them, and come upon
17:13 not take my mercy a' from him,
19: 4 their buttocks, and sent them a'.
21: 8 thee, do a' the iniquity of thy
2Ch 6:36 they carry them a' captives unto
42 O Lord God, turn not a' the face
7:10 sent the people a' into their tents,
19 But if ye turn a', and forsake my
9:12 and went a' to her own land,
12: 9 took a' the treasures of the house
9 he carried a' also the shields of
14: 3 took a' the altars of the strange
5 took a' out of all the cities of
13 they carried a' very much spoil.
15 and carried a' sheep and camels
15: 8 and put a' the abominable idols
17 the high places were not taken a'
16: 6 and they carried a' the stones of
17: 6 he took a' the high places and
19: 3 thou hast taken a' the groves out
20:25 came to take a' the spoil of them,
25 more than they could carry a':
33 high places were not taken a':
21:17 carried a' all the substance
25:12 children of Judah carry a' captive,
27 Amaziah did turn a' from following
28: 5 and carried a' a great multitude
8 children of Israel carried a' captive
8 and took also a' much spoil
17 and smitten Judah, and carried a'
21 Ahaz took a' a portion out of the
29: 6 have turned a' their faces from the
10 his fierce wrath may turn a' from
19 king Ahaz in his reign did cast a'
30: 8 his wrath may turn a' from you.
9 not turn a' his face from you,
14 they arose and took a' the altars
14 the altars for incense took they a',
32:12 Hezekiah taken a' his high places
33:15 And he took a' the strange gods,
34:33 took a' all the abominations
35:23 Have me a'; for I am sore
36:20 sword carried he a' to Babylon;
Ezr 2: 1 those which had been carried a',
1 the king of Babylon had carried a'
5:12 carried the people a' into Babylon.
8:35 of those that had been carried a',
9: 4 of those that had been carried a';
10: 3 our God to put a' all the wives,
6 of them that had been carried a'.
8 of those that had been carried a'.
19 that they would put a' their wives;
Ne 7: 6 had been carried a', whom
6 the king of Babylon had carried a',
Es 2: 6 been carried a' from Jerusalem
6 captivity which had been carried a'
6 the king of Babylon had carried a',
4: 4 take a' his sackcloth from him:
8: 3 with tears to put a' the mischief
Job 1:15 fell upon them, and took them a';
17 and have carried them a',
21 and the Lord hath taken a';
4:21 excellency which is in them go a'?
6:15 streams of brooks they pass a';
7: 9 is consumed and vanisheth a':
21 and take a' mine iniquity?
8: 4 he have cast them a' for their
20 God will not cast a' a perfect man,
9:12 Behold, he taketh a', who can
25 they flee a', they see no good.
26 are passed a' as the swift ships:
34 Let him take his rod a' from me,
11:14 put it far a', and let not wickedness
16 it as waters that pass a':
12:17 He leadeth counsellors a' spoiled,
19 He leadeth princes a' spoiled,
20 He removeth a' the speech of the
20 taketh a' the understanding of
24 He taketh a' the heart of the chief
14:10 But man dieth, and wasteth a':
19 thou washest a' the things which
20 countenance, and sendest him a',
15:12 doth thine heart carry thee a'?
30 breath of his mouth shall he go a'.
20: 8 He shall fly a' as a dream, and
8 he shall be chased a' as a vision
19 taken a' an house which he
28 his goods shall flow a' in the day
21:18 as chaff that the storm carrieth a'.
22: 9 Thou hast sent widows a' empty,
23 thou shalt put a' iniquity far from
24: 2 they violently take a' flocks, and
3 drive a' the ass of the fatherless,
10 take a' the sheaf from the hungry;
27: 2 who hath taken a' my judgment;
8 when God taketh a' his soul?
20 stealeth him a' in the night.
21 the east wind carrieth him a',
28: 4 up, they are gone a' from men.
30:12 they push a' my feet, and they
15 my welfare passeth a' as a cloud.
32:22 Maker would soon take me a'.
33:21 His flesh is consumed a', that
34: 5 God hath taken a' my judgment.
20 be troubled at midnight, and pass a':
20 and the mighty shall be taken a'
36:18 lest he take thee a' with his
Ps 1: 4 the chaff which the wind driveth a'.
2: 3 and cast a' their cords from us.
18:22 I did not put a' his statutes from
45 The strangers shall fade a',
27: 9 put not thy servant a' in anger:
28: 3 Draw me not a' with the wicked,
31:13 they devised to take a' my life.
34:*title* Abimelech; who drove him a',
37:20 into smoke shall they consume a'.

Ps 37:36 Yet he passed a', and, lo, he was
39:10 Remove thy stroke a' from me:
11 makest his beauty to consume a'
48: 5 were troubled, and hasted a'.
49:17 he dieth he shall carry nothing a':
51:11 Cast me not a' from thy presence;
52: 5 he shall take thee a', and pluck
55: 6 for then would I fly a', and be at
58: 7 Let them melt a' as waters which
8 let every one of them pass a':
9 he shall take them a' as with a
64: 8 all that see them shall flee a'.
65: 3 thou shalt purge them a'.
66:20 hath not turned a' my prayer,
68: 2 As smoke is driven a',
2 so drive them a':
69: 4 restored that which I took not a'.
78:38 turned his anger a', and did not
39 a wind that passeth a', and cometh
79: 9 and purge a' our sins, for thy
85: 3 Thou hast taken a' all thy wrath:
88: 8 hast put a' mine acquaintance
90: 5 carriest them a' as with a flood;
9 For all our days are passed a' in
10 it is soon cut off, and we fly a'.
102:24 O my God, take me not a' in the
104: 7 voice of thy thunder they hasted a'.
29 takest a' their breath, they die,
106:23 to turn a' his wrath, lest he should
112:10 gnash with his teeth, and melt a':
119:37 Turn a' mine eyes from beholding
39 Turn a' my reproach which I fear:
119 Thou puttest a' all the wicked of
132:10 David's sake turn not a' the face
137: 3 carried us a' captive required
144: 4 are as a shadow that passeth a'.
Pro 1:19 taketh a' the life of the owners
32 the turning a' of the simple shall
4:15 turn from it, and pass a'.
16 and their sleep is taken a', unless
24 Put a' from thee a froward mouth,
6:33 reproach shall not be wiped a'.
10: 3 casteth a' the substance of the
14:32 is driven a' in his wickedness:
15: 1 A soft answer turneth a' wrath:
19:26 and chaseth a' his mother,
20: 8 throne of judgment scattereth a'
30 blueness of a wound cleanseth a'
22:27 why should he take a' the bed
23: 5 they fly a' as an eagle toward
24:18 he turn a' his wrath from him.
25: 4 Take a' the dross from the silver,
5 Take a' the wicked from before
10 and thine infamy turn not a'.
20 taketh a' a garment in cold
23 The north wind driveth a' rain:
28: 9 turneth a' his ear from hearing the
29: 8 but wise men turn a' wrath.
30:30 and turneth not a' for any;
Ec 1: 4 One generation passeth a',
3: 5 A time to cast a' stones, and a
6 to keep, and a time to cast a';
5:15 he may carry a' in his hand.
11:10 and put a' evil from thy flesh:
Ca 2:10, 13 love, my fair one, and come a'.
17 day break, and the shadows flee a',
4: 6 day break, and the shadows flee a',
5: 7 keepers of the walls took a' my veil
6: 5 Turn a' thine eyes from me,
Isa 1: 4 they are gone a' backward.
13 of assemblies, I cannot a' with;
16 put a' the evil of your doings
25 and purely purge a' thy dross,
25 and take a' all thy tin:
3: 1 the Lord of hosts doth take a' from
18 the Lord will take a' the bravery
4: 1 to take a' our reproach.
4 Lord shall have washed a' the filth
5: 5 I will take a' the hedge thereof,
23 take a' the righteousness of the
24 because they have cast a' the law
25 all this his anger is not turned a',
29 shall carry it a' safe, and none shall
6: 7 and thine iniquity is taken a',
12 the Lord have removed men far a',
8: 4 spoil of Samaria shall be taken a'
9:12, 17, 21 his anger is not turned a',
10: 2 to take a' the right from the poor
4 all this his anger is not turned a',
27 his burden shall be taken a' from
12: 1 thine anger is turned a', and thou
15: 6 for the hay is withered a',
7 carry a' to the brook of the willows.
16:10 And gladness is taken a', and joy
17: 1 Damascus is taken a' from being
18: 5 a' and cut down the branches.
19: 6 they shall turn the rivers far a';
7 be driven a', and be no more.
20: 4 shall the king of Assyria lead a'
22: 4 Therefore said I, Look a' from me;
17 Behold, the Lord will carry thee a'
24: 4 The earth mourneth and fadeth a',
4 world languisheth and fadeth a',
25: 8 Lord God will wipe a' tears from
8 of his people shall he take a'
27: 9 is all the fruit to take a' his sin;
28:17 shall sweep a' the refuge of lies,
29: 5 shall be as chaff that passeth a':
30:22 them a' as a menstruous cloth;
31: 7 shall cast a' his idols of silver,
35:10 sorrow and sighing shall flee a'.
36: 7 altars Hezekiah hath taken a',
9 How then wilt thou turn a' the face
17 I come and take you a' to a land
39: 7 thou shalt beget, shall they take a';
40:24 shall take them a' as stubble.

Isa 41: 9 chosen thee, and not cast thee a'.
16 and the wind shall carry them a',
49:19 swallowed thee up shall be far a'.
25 of the mighty shall be taken a'.
50: 1 whom I have put a'?
1 transgressions is your mother put a'.
5 neither turned a' back.
51: 6 heavens shall vanish a' like smoke,
11 sorrow and mourning shall flee a'.
52: 5 my people is taken a' for nought?
57: 1 and merciful men are taken a',
1 that the righteousness is taken a'
13 the wind shall carry them all a';
58: 9 If thou take a' from the midst of
13 If thou turn a' thy foot from the
59:13 and departing a' from our God,
14 judgment is turned a' backward,
64: 6 like the wind, have taken us a'.
Jer 1: 3 carrying a' of Jerusalem captive
2:24 her occasion who can turn her a'?
3: 1 They say, If a man put a' his wife,
8 committed adultery I had put her a',
19 and shalt not turn a' from me
4: 1 put a' thine abominations
4 take a' the foreskins of your heart,
5:10 take a' her battlements;
25 Your iniquities have turned a' these
6: 4 unto us! for the day goeth a';
29 for the wicked are not plucked a'.
7:29 and cast it a', and take up a
33 and none shall fray them a'.
8: 4 shall he turn a', and not return?
13 I have given them shall pass a'
13:17 Lord's flock is carried a' captive.
19 Judah shall be carried a' captive
19 shall be wholly carried a' captive.
24 that passeth a' by the wind of the
15:15 me not a' in thy longsuffering:
16: 5 for I have taken a' my peace from
18:20 to turn a' thy wrath from them.
22:10 weep sore for him that goeth a':
23: 2 and driven them a', and have not
24: 1 Babylon had carried a' captive
5 are carried a' captive of Judah,
27:20 he carried a' captive Jeconiah
28: 3 king of Babylon took a' from this
6 and all that is carried a' captive,
29: 1 which were carried a' captives,
1 carried a' captive from Jerusalem
4 all that are carried a' captives,
4 to be carried a' from Jerusalem
7 you to be carried a' captives,
14 and I will turn a' your captivity,
14 I caused you to be carried a'
32:40 I will turn a' from them, to do
33:26 will I cast a' the seed of Jacob,
37:13 Thou fallest a' to the Chaldeans.
14 I fall not a' to the Chaldeans.
38:22 mire, and they are turned a' back.
39: 9 carried a' captive into Babylon
9 the city, and those that fell a',
40: 1 carried a' captive of Jerusalem
1 carried a' captive unto Babylon.
7 not carried a' captive to Babylon;
41:10 carried a' captive all the residue
10 carried them a' captive, and
14 people that Ishmael had carried a'
43: 3 carry us a' captives into Babylon.
12 carry them a' captives: and he
46: 5 turned a' back? and their mighty
6 Let not the swift flee a', nor the
15 Why are thy valiant men swept a'?
21 and are fled a' together: they did
48: 9 may flee and get a': for the cities
49:19 suddenly make him run a' from
29 their flocks shall they take a':
50: 6 they have turned them a' on the
17 the lions have driven him a':
44 suddenly run a' from her; and
51:50 go a', stand not still: remember
52:15 guard carried a' captive certain
15 and those that fell a', that
18 they ministered, took they a'.
19 took the captain of the guard a'.
27 Judah was carried a' captive
28 whom Nebuchadrezzar carried a'
29 carried a' captive from Jerusalem
30 the captain of the guard carried a'
La 2: 6 violently taken a' his tabernacle,
14 to turn a' thy captivity; but have
4: 9 for these pine a', stricken through
15 when they fled a' and wandered,
22 more carry thee a' into captivity:
Eze 3:14 spirit lifted me up, and took me a',
4:17 and consume a' for their iniquity.
11:18 take a' all the detestable things
14: 6 and turn a' your faces from all
16: 9 I thoroughly washed a' thy blood
50 I took them a' as I saw good.
18:24 But when the righteous turneth a'
26 a righteous man turneth a' from
27 when the wicked man turneth a'
28 he considereth, and turneth a'
31 Cast a' from you all your
20: 7 ye a' every man the abominations
8 they did not every man cast a' the
23:25 take a' thy nose and thine ears;
26 clothes, and take a' thy fair jewels.
29 and shall take a' all thy labour,
24:16 Son of man, behold, I take a' from
23 shall pine a' for your iniquities,
26:16 and lay a' their robes, and put off
30: 4 they shall take a' her multitude,
33: 4 and take him a', his blood shall
6 he is taken a' in his iniquity; but
10 we pine a' in them, how should
Eze 34: 4 again that which was driven a',
16 that which was driven a', and will
36:26 I will take a' the stony heart out
38:13 to carry a' silver and gold,
13 to take a' cattle and goods,
43: 9 let them put a' their whoredom,
44:10 are gone a' far from me, when
10 a' from me after their idols;
22 nor her that is put a': but they
45: 9 take a' your exactions from my
Da 1:16 Thus Melzar took a' the portion
2:35 carried them a', that no place was
4:14 the beasts get a' from under it,
7:12 had their dominion taken a':
14 which shall not pass a', and his
26 they shall take a' his dominion,
8:11 the daily sacrifice was taken a',
9:16 fury be turned a' from thy city
11:12 hath taken a' the multitude, his
31 shall take a' the daily sacrifice,
44 and utterly to make a' many.
12:11 be taken a', and the abomination
Ho 1: 6 I will utterly take them a'.
2: 2 therefore put a' her whoredoms
9 and take a' my corn in the time
17 I will take a' the names of Baalim
4: 3 the sea also shall be taken a'.
11 and new wine take a' the heart.
5:14 I, even I, will tear and go a';
14 I will take a', and none shall
6: 4 as the early dew it goeth a'.
9:11 their glory shall fly a' like a bird,
17 God will cast them a', because
13: 3 the early dew that passeth a', as
11 and took him a' in my wrath.
14: 2 Take a' all iniquity, and receive us
4 mine anger is turned a' from him.
Joe 1: 7 and cast it a'; the branches thereof
12 joy is withered a' from the sons of
Am 1: 3 I will not turn a' the punishment
6 not turn a' the punishment thereof;
6 because they carried a' captive
9, 11, 13 I will not turn a' the
2: 1, 4, 6 I will not turn a' the
16 the mighty shall flee a' naked in
4: 2 he will take you a' with hooks,
10 and have taken a' your horses;
5:23 Take thou a' from me the noise
6: 3 Ye that put far a' the evil day,
7:11 surely be led a' captive out of
12 flee thee a' into the land of Judah,
9: 1 shall not flee a', and he that
Ob 11 strangers carried a' captive his
Jon 3: 9 and turn a' from his fierce anger,
Mic 1:11 Pass ye a', thou inhabitant of
2: 2 and take them a'; so they oppress
4 turning a' he hath divided our
9 have ye taken a' my glory for ever.
Na 2: 2 hath turned a' the excellency
7 Huzzab shall be led a' captive, she
8 yet they shall flee a'. Stand, stand,
3:10 Yet was she carried a', she went
16 cankerworm spoileth, and fleeth a'.
17 the sun ariseth they flee a', and
Zep 2: 7 visit them, and turn a' their
3:11 then I will take a' out of the
15 The Lord hath taken a' thy
Zec 3: 4 Take a' the filthy garments from
7:11 and pulled a' the shoulder, and
9: 7 And I will take a' his blood out
10:11 sceptre of Egypt shall depart a'.
14:12 Their flesh shall consume a' while
12 their eyes shall consume a' in
12 and their tongue shall consume a'
Mal 2: 3 one shall take you a' with it.
6 and did turn many a' from iniquity.
16 saith that he hateth putting a':
3: 7 are gone a' from mine ordinances,
M't 1:11 they were carried a' to Babylon:
17 carrying a' into Babylon are
17 from the carrying a' into Babylon
19 was minded to put her a' privily.
5:31 Whosoever shall put a' his wife,
32 whosoever shall put a' his wife,
40 and take a' thy coat,
42 turn not thou a'.
8:31 suffer us to go a' into the herd of
13: 6 they had no root, they withered a'.
12 him shall be taken a' even that
19 and catcheth a' that which was
36 Then Jesus sent the multitude a',
48 but cast the bad a'.
14:15 send the multitude a',
22 while he sent the multitudes a'.
23 he had sent the multitudes a',
15:23 saying, Send her a'; for she crieth
32 I will not send them a' fasting,
39 And he sent a' the multitude,
19: 3 for a man to put a' his wife
7 and to put her a'?
8 suffered you to put a' your wives:
9 Whosoever shall put a' his wife,
9 whoso marrieth her which is put a'
22 he went a' sorrowful; for he had
21:19 presently the fig tree withered a'.
20 soon is the fig tree withered a'!
22:13 and take him a', and cast him into
24:35 Heaven and earth shall pass a',
35 but my word shall not pass a'.
39 flood came, and took them all a';
25:29 shall be taken a' even that which
46 these shall go a' into everlasting
26:42 He went a' again the second time,
42 cup may not pass a' from me,
44 and went a' again, and prayed
57 led him a' to Caiaphas the
M't 27: 2 they led him a', and delivered him
31 and led him a' to crucify him.
64 and steal him a', and say unto the
28:13 and stole him a' while we slept.
16 the eleven disciples went a' into
M'r 1:43 and forthwith sent him a';
2:20 bridegroom shall be taken a' from
21 taketh a' from the old, and the
4: 6 it had no root, it withered a'.
15 and taketh a' the word that was
36 when they had sent a' the
5:10 not send them a' out of the
6:36 Send them a', that they may go
45 while he sent a' the people.
46 he had sent them a', he departed
8: 3 if I send them a' fasting to their
9 thousand: and he sent them a'.
26 And he sent him a' to his house,
9:18 with his teeth, and pineth a': and I
10: 2 for a man to put a' his wife?
4 divorcement, and to put her a'.
11 Whosoever shall put a' his wife,
12 woman shall put a' her husband,
22 and went a' grieved: for he had
50 And he, casting a' his garment,
11:21 which thou cursedst is withered a'.
12: 3 and sent him a' empty.
4 and sent him a' shamefully
13:31 Heaven and earth shall pass a':
31 but my words shall not pass a'.
14:36 take a' this cup from me:
39 And again he went a', and prayed,
44 take him, and lead him a' safely.
53 And they led Jesus a' to the high
15: 1 and carried him a', and delivered
16 soldiers led him a' into the hall,
16: 3 Who shall roll a' the stone from
4 that the stone was rolled a': for it
Lu 1:25 to take a' my reproach among
53 the rich he hath sent empty a'.
2:15 the angels were gone a' from them
5:35 shall be taken a' from them, and
6:29 that taketh a' thy cloke forbid not
30 that taketh a' thy goods ask
8: 6 it withered a', because it lacked
12 and taketh a' the word out of
13 and in time of temptation fall a'.
38 but Jesus sent him a', saying,
9:12 when the day began to wear a',
12 Send the multitude a', that they
25 lose himself, or be cast a'?
10:42 which shall not be taken a' from
11:52 taken a' the key of knowledge:
13:15 and lead him a' to watering?
16: 3 for my lord taketh a' from me the
18 Whosoever putteth a' his wife, and
18 a' from her husband committeth
17:31 not come down to take it a': and
19:26 he hath shall be taken a' from him.
20:10 beat him, and sent him a' empty.
11 shamefully, and sent him a' empty.
21:24 and shall be led a' captive into
32 generation shall not pass a', till
33 earth shall pass a': but
33 my words shall not pass a'.
23:18 saying, A' with this man, and
26 And as they led him a', they laid
24: 2 stone rolled a' from the sepulchre.
Joh 1:29 taketh a' the sin of the world.
4: 8 his disciples were gone a' unto the
5:13 Jesus had conveyed himself a', a
6:22 his disciples were gone a' alone;
67 unto the twelve, Will ye also go a'?
10:40 And went a' again beyond Jordan
11:39 Take ye a' the stone. Martha, the
41 Then they took a' the stone from
48 come and take a' both our place
12:11 the Jews went a', and believed on
14:28 I go a' and come again unto you.
15: 2 he taketh a': and every branch
16: 7 is expedient for you that I go a':
7 if I go not a', the Comforter will
18:13 And led him a' to Annas first;
19:15 A' with him, a' with him, crucify
16 took Jesus, and led him a'.
31 and that they might be taken a'.
38 that he might take a' the body of
20: 1 stone taken a' from the sepulchre.
2 They have taken a' the Lord out of
10 disciples went a' again unto their
13 they have taken a' my Lord, and I
15 and I will take him a'.
Ac 3:26 in turning a' every one of you from
5:37 drew a' much people after him:
7:27 him a', saying, Who made thee
43 will carry you a' beyond Babylon.
8:33 his judgment was taken a': and
39 the Lord caught a' Philip, that the
10:23 morrow Peter went a' with them,
13: 3 hands on them, they sent them a'.
8 seeking to turn a' the deputy
17:10 immediately sent a' Paul and Silas
14 the brethren sent a' Paul to go as
19:26 turned a' much people, saying,
20: 6 And we sailed a' from Philippi
30 to draw a' disciples after them.
21:36 followed after, crying, A' with him.
22:16 wash a' thy sins, calling on the
22 A' with such a fellow from the
24: 7 great violence took him a' out of
27:20 should be saved was then taken a'.
Ro 11: 1 Hath God cast a' his people?
2 God hath not cast a' his people
15 For if the casting a' of them be
26 and shall turn a' ungodliness from
27 when I shall take a' their sins.

1Co 5: 2 might be taken *a'* from among you.
13 Therefore put *a'* from among
7:11 not the husband put *a'* his wife.
12 let him not put her *a'*.
31 fashion of this world passeth *a'*.
12: 2 carried *a'* unto these dumb idols,
13: 8 be knowledge, it shall vanish *a'*.
10 which is in part shall be done *a'*.
11 when I became a man, I put *a'*
2Co 3: 7 which glory was to be done *a'*:
11 For of that which is done *a'* was
14 vail untaken *a'* in the reading
14 which vail is done *a'* in Christ.
16 the vail shall be taken *a'*.
5:17 old things are passed *a'*; behold,
Ga 2:13 Barnabas also was carried *a'* with
Eph 4:25 Wherefore putting *a'* lying, speak
31 evil speaking, be put *a'* from you,
Col 1:23 be not moved *a'* from the hope of
2Th 2: 3 except there come a falling *a'* first,
1Ti 1:19 some having put *a'* concerning
2Ti 1:15 are in Asia be turned *a'* from me;
3: 5 power thereof: from such turn *a'*.
6 women laden with sins, led *a'*
4: 4 And they shall turn *a'* their ears
Heb 6: 6 they shall fall *a'*, to renew them
8:13 waxeth old, is ready to vanish *a'*.
9:26 *a'* sin by the sacrifice of himself.
10: 4 should take *a'* sins.
9 He taketh *a'* the first, that he may
11 which can never take *a'* sins:
35 Cast not *a'* therefore your
12:25 we turn *a'* from him that speaketh
Jas 1:10 of the grass he shall pass *a'*.
11 the rich man fade *a'* in his ways.
14 he is drawn *a'* of his own lust,
4:14 little time, and then vanisheth *a'*.
1Pe 1: 4 undefiled, and that fadeth not *a'*,
24 the flower thereof falleth *a'*:
3:21 (not the putting *a'* of the filth of the
5: 4 crown of glory that fadeth not *a'*.
2Pe 3:10 heavens shall pass *a'* with a great
17 *a'* with the error of the wicked,
1Jo 2:17 the world passeth *a'*, and the lust
3: 5 manifested to take *a'* our sins;
Re 7:17 God shall wipe *a'* all tears from
12:15 her to be carried *a'* of the flood.
16:20 And every island fled *a'*, and the
17: 3 So he carried me *a'* in the spirit
20:11 the earth and the heaven fled *a'*;
21: 1 first earth were passed *a'*; and
4 God shall wipe *a'* all tears from
4 the former things are passed *a'*.
10 he carried me *a'* in the spirit to a
22:19 if any man shall take *a'* from the
19 God shall take *a'* his part out of the

awe
Ps 4: 4 Stand in *a'*, and sin not:
33: 8 of the world stand in *a'*
119:161 heart standeth in *a'* of thy word.

awhile See WHILE.

awl See AUL.

awoke See also AWAKED.
Ge 9:24 And Noah *a'* from his wine,
41: 4 and fat kine. So Pharaoh *a'*.
7 and Pharaoh *a'*, and, behold, it
21 as at the beginning. So I *a'*.
J'g 16:20 And he *a'* out of his sleep,
1Ki 3:15 And Solomon *a'*; and, behold, it
M't 8:25 *a'* him, saying, Lord, save us:
Lu 8:24 they came to him, and *a'* him,

ax See also AXE.
M't 3:10 now also the *a'* is laid unto the

axe See also AXES. [*Most editions have* AX.]
De 19: 5 with the *a'* to cut down the tree,
20:19 by forcing an *a'* against them:
J'g 9:48 Abimelech took an *a'* in his hand,
1Sa 13:20 to sharpen every man...his *a'*,
1Ki 6: 7 neither hammer nor *a'* nor any
2Ki 6: 5 the *a'* head fell into the water:
Isa 10:15 Shall the *a'* boast itself
Jer 10: 3 of the workman, with the *a'*.
51:20 Thou art my battle *a'* and
Lu 3: 9 now also the *a'* is laid unto the

axes
1Sa 13:21 for the forks, and for the *a'*,
2Sa 12:31 and under *a'* of iron,
1Ch 20: 3 with harrows of iron, and with *a'*.
Ps 74: 5 he had lifted up *a'* upon the thick
6 with *a'* and hammers.
Jer 46:22 and come against her with *a'*,
Eze 26: 9 with his *a'* he shall break down

ax-head See AXE and HEAD.

axletrees
1Ki 7:32 and the *a'* of the wheels
33 their *a'*, and their naves,

ay See NAY.

Azal (*a'-zal*)
Zec 14: 5 mountains shall reach unto *A'*:

Azaliah (*az-a-li'-ah*)
2Ki 22: 3 king sent Shaphan the son of *A'*,
2Ch 34: 8 the son of *A'*, and Maaseiah

Azaniah (*az-a-ni'-ah*)
Ne 10: 9 both Jeshua the son of *A'*,

Azarael (*a-zar'-a-el*) See also AZAREEL.
Ne 12:36 his brethren, Shemaiah, and *A'*,

Azareel (*a-zar'-e-el*) See also AZARAEL.
1Ch 12: 6 and *A'*, and Joezer, and
25:18 The eleventh to *A'*, he, his sons,
27:22 Of Dan, *A'* the son of Jeroham.
Ezr 10:41 *A'*, and Shelemiah, Shemariah,
Ne 11:13 and Amashai the son of *A'*, the son

Azariah (*az-a-ri'-ah*) See also AHAZIAH.
1Ki 4: 2 *A'* the son of Zadok the priest,
5 And *A'* the son of Nathan was
2Ki 14:21 all the people of Judah took *A'*,
15: 1 began *A'* son of Amaziah king of
6 And the rest of the acts of *A'*, and
7 So *A'* slept with his fathers; and
8 In the thirty and eighth year of *A'*
17 In the nine and thirtieth year of *A'*
23 In the fiftieth year of *A'* king of
27 In the two and fiftieth year of *A'*
1Ch 2: 8 And the sons of Ethan; *A'*.
38 begat Jehu, and Jehu begat *A'*,
39 And *A'* begat Helez, and Helez
3:12 Amaziah his son, *A'* his son,
6: 9 And Ahimaaz begat *A'*,
9 And *A'* begat Johanan,
10 And Johanan begat *A'*, (he it is
11 And *A'* begat Amariah, and
13 and Hilkiah begat *A'*,
14 and *A'* begat Seraiah, and
36 the son of Joel, the son of *A'*,
9:11 And *A'* the son of Hilkiah, the son
2Ch 15: 1 the Spirit of God came upon *A'*
21: 2 the sons of Jehoshaphat, *A'*, and
2 Zechariah, and *A'*, and Michael,
22: 6 And *A'* the son of Jehoram king
23: 1 *A'* the son of Jeroham, and
1 *A'* the son of Obed, and Maaseiah
26:17 *A'* the priest went in after him,
20 And *A'* the chief priest, and all
28:12 *A'* the son of Johanan, Berechiah
29:12 Amasai, and Joel the son of *A'*,
12 and *A'* the son of Jehalelel:
31:10 And *A'* the chief priest of the
13 and *A'* the ruler of the house of
Ezr 7: 1 the son of Seraiah, the son of *A'*,
3 The son of Amariah, the son of *A'*,
Ne 3:23 After him repaired *A'* the son of
24 from the house of *A'* unto the
7: 7 Nehemiah, *A'*, Raamiah,
8: 7 Kelita, *A'*, Jozabad, Hanan,
10: 2 Seraiah, *A'*, Jeremiah,
12:33 And *A'*, Ezra, and Meshullam,
Jer 43: 2 spake *A'* the son of Hoshaiah,
Da 1: 6 Daniel, Hananiah, Mishael, and *A'*:
7 and to *A'*, of Abed-nego.
11 Daniel, Hananiah, Mishael, and *A'*.
19 and *A'*: therefore stood they
2:17 Mishael, and *A'*, his companions:

Azaz (*a'-zaz*)
1Ch 5: 8 And Bela the son of *A'*, the son of

Azaziah (*az-a-zi'-ah*)
1Ch 15:21 *A'*, with harps on the Sheminith
27:20 Ephraim, Hoshea the son of *A'*:
2Ch 31:13 And Jehiel, and *A'*, and Nahath,

Azbuk (*az'-buk*)
Ne 3:16 Nehemiah the son of *A'*, the ruler

Azekah (*a-ze'-kah*)
Jos 10:10 and smote them to *A'*, and unto
11 from heaven upon them unto *A'*,
15:35 and Adullam, Socoh, and *A'*,
1Sa 17: 1 pitched between Shochoh and *A'*,
2Ch 11: 9 Adoraim, and Lachish, and *A'*,
Ne 11:30 and the fields thereof, at *A'*,
Jer 34: 7 against Lachish, and against *A'*:

Azel (*a'-zel*) See also JAAZIEL.
1Ch 8:37 Eleasah his son, *A'* his son:
38 *A'* had six sons, whose names are
38 All these were the sons of *A'*.
9:43 Eleasah his son, *A'* his son.
44 *A'* had six sons, whose names are
44 these were the sons of *A'*.

Azem (*a'-zem*) See also EZEM.
Jos 15:29 Baalah, and Iim, and *A'*,
19: 3 Hazar-shual, and Balah, and *A'*,

Azgad (*az'-gad*)
Ezr 2:12 The children of *A'*, a thousand
8:12 And of the sons of *A'*; Johanan
Ne 7:17 The children of *A'*, two thousand
10:15 Bunni, *A'*, Bebai,

Aziel (*a'-ze-el*)
1Ch 15:20 And Zechariah, and *A'*, and

Aziza (*a-zi'-zah*)
Ezr 10:27 and Jeremoth, and Zabad, and *A'*.

Azmaveth (*az-ma'-veth*) See also BETH-AZMAVETH.
2Sa 23:31 Abi-albon the Arbathite, *A'* the
1Ch 8:36 Jehoadah begat Alemeth, and *A'*,
9:42 and Jarah begat Alemeth, and *A'*,
11:33 *A'* the Baharumite, Eliahba
12: 3 Jeziel, and Pelet, the sons of *A'*;
27:25 over the king's treasures was *A'*
Ezr 2:24 The children of *A'*, forty and two.
Ne 12:29 out of the fields of Geba and *A'*:

Azmon (*az'-mon*) See also HESHMON.
Nu 34: 4 Hazar-addar, and pass on to *A'*:
5 shall fetch a compass from *A'*
Jos 15: 4 From thence it passed toward *A'*,

Aznoth-tabor (*az''-noth-ta'-bor*)
Jos 19:34 the coast turneth westward to *A'*,

Azor (*a'-zor*)
M't 1:13 and Eliakim begat *A'*;
14 And *A'* begat Sadoc;

Azotus (*a-zo'-tus*) See also ASHDOD.
Ac 8:40 But Philip was found at *A'*:

Azriel (*az'-re-el*)
1Ch 5:24 and Ishi, and Eliel, and *A'*,
27:19 Naphtali, Jerimoth the son of *A'*:
Jer 36:26 and Seraiah the son of *A'*, and

Azrikam (*az'-ri-kam*)
1Ch 3:23 Elioenai, and Hezekiah, and *A'*,
8:38 whose names are these, *A'*,
9:14 son of *A'*, the son of Hashabiah,
44 sons, whose names are these, *A'*,
2Ch 28: 7 *A'*, the governor of the house,
Ne 11:15 the son of Hashub, the son of *A'*,

Azubah (*a-zu'-bah*)
1Ki 22:42 And his mother's name was *A'*,
1Ch 2:18 son of Hezron begat children of *A'*
19 And when *A'* was dead, Caleb
2Ch 20:31 And his mother's name was *A'*

Azur (*a'-zur*) See also AZZUR.
Jer 28: 1 that Hananiah the son of *A'* the
Eze 11: 1 I saw Jaazaniah the son of *A'*,

Azzah (*az'-zah*) See also GAZA.
De 2:23 dwelt in Hazerim, even unto *A'*,
1Ki 4:24 from Tiphsah even to *A'*, over all
Jer 25:20 and Ashkelon, and *A'*, and

Azzan (*az'-zan*)
Nu 34:26 Paltiel the son of *A'*.

Azzur (*az'-zur*) See also AZUR.
Ne 10:17 Ater, Hizkijah, *A'*,

B.

Baal (*ba'-al*) See also BAAL-BERITH; BAALE; BAAL-GAD; BAAL-HAMON; BAAL-HANAN; BAAL-HAZOR; BAAL-HERMON; BAALIM; BAAL-MEON; BAAL-PEOR; BAAL-PERAZIM; BAAL'S; BAAL-SHALISHA; BAAL-TAMAR; BAAL-ZEBUB; BAAL-ZEPHON; BAMOTH-BAAL; GUR-BAAL; BEL; KIRJATH-BAAL; MERIB-BAAL.
Nu 22:41 up into the high places of *B'*,
J'g 2:13 Lord, and served *B'* and Ashtaroth.
6:25 and throw down the altar of *B'*
28 the altar of *B'* was cast down,
30 hath cast down the altar of *B'*,
31 Will ye plead for *B'*? will ye save
32 Let *B'* plead against him, because
1Ki 16:31 and served *B'*, and worshipped
32 he reared up an altar for *B'*
32 in the house of *B'*,
18:19 the prophets of *B'* four hundred
21 but if *B'*, then follow him.
25 Elijah said unto the prophets of *B'*,
26 and called on the name of *B'*
26 saying, O *B'*, hear us.
40 them, Take the prophets of *B'*;
19:18 which have not bowed unto *B'*,
22:53 For he served *B'*, and worshipped
2Ki 3: 2 for he put away the image of *B'*
10:18 unto them, Ahab served *B'* a little;
19 unto me all the prophets of *B'*,
19 have a great sacrifice to do to *B'*;
19 destroy the worshippers of *B'*.
20 Proclaim a solemn assembly for *B'*.
21 all the worshippers of *B'* came,
21 they came into the house of *B'*;
21 and the house of *B'* was full
22 for all the worshippers of *B'*.
23 into the house of *B'*,
23 said unto the worshippers of *B'*,
23 but the worshippers of *B'* only.
25 went to the city of the house of *B'*.
26 the images out of the house of *B'*,
27 they brake down the image of *B'*,
27 and brake down the house of *B'*,
28 Jehu destroyed *B'* out of Israel.
11:18 the land went into the house of *B'*,
18 and slew Mattan the priest of *B'*
17:16 the host of heaven, and served *B'*.
21: 3 and he reared up altars for *B'*,
23: 4 the vessels that were made for *B'*,
5 also that burned incense unto *B'*,
1Ch 4:33 about the same cities, unto *B'*.
5: 5 Reaia his son, *B'* his son,
8:30 and Kish, and *B'*, and Nadab,
9:36 Kish, and *B'*, and Ner, and Nadab,
2Ch 23:17 the people went to the house of *B'*,
17 and slew Mattan the priest of *B'*
Jer 2: 8 the prophets prophesied by *B'*,
7: 9 falsely, and burn incense unto *B'*,
11:13 altars to burn incense unto *B'*.
17 anger in offering incense unto *B'*.
12:16 taught my people to swear by *B'*;
19: 5 built also the high places of *B'*,
5 fire for burnt offerings unto *B'*,
23:13 they prophesied in *B'*, and caused
27 have forgotten my name for *B'*.
32:29 they have offered incense unto *B'*,
35 they build the high places of *B'*,
Ho 2: 8 gold, which they prepared for *B'*.
13: 1 when he offended in *B'*, he died.
Zep 1: 4 I will cut off the remnant of *B'*
Ro 11: 4 bowed the knee to the image of *B'*.

Baalah (*ba'-al-ah*) See also BAALE; BALEH; BILHAH; KIRJATH-BAAL.
Jos 15: 9 and the border was drawn to *B'*,
10 the border compassed from *B'*

Jos 15:11 and passed along to mount *B*',
29 *B*', and Iim, and Azem,
1Ch 13: 6 went up, and all Israel, to *B*',

Baalath (*ba'-al-ath*) See also BAALATH-BEER.
Jos 19:44 Eltekeh, and Gibbethon, and *B*',
1Ki 9:18 *B*', and Tadmor in the wilderness,
2Ch 8: 6 *B*', and all the store cities

Baalath-beer (*ba''-al-ath-be'-ur*)
Jos 19: 8 round about these cities to *B*',

Baal-berith (*ba''-al-be'-rith*)
J'g 8:33 and made *B*' their god.
9: 4 of silver out of the house of *B*',

Baale (*ba'-al-eh*)
2Sa 6: 2 people that were with him from *B*'

Baal-gad (*ba''-al-gad'*)
Jos 11:17 even unto *B*' in the valley of
12: 7 the west, from *B*' in the valley
13: 5 from *B*' under mount Hermon

Baal-hamon (*ba''-al-ha'-mon*)
Ca 8:11 Solomon had a vineyard at *B*';

Baal-hanan (*ba''-al-ha'-nan*)
Ge 36:38 *B*' the son of Achbor reigned
39 And *B*' the son of Achbor died,
1Ch 1:49 when Shaul was dead, *B*' the son
50 when *B*' was dead, Hadad reigned
27:28 the low plains was *B*' the Gederite:

Baal-hazor (*ba''-al-ha'-zor*) See also HAZOR.
2Sa 13:23 Absalom had sheepshearers in *B*',

Baal-hermon (*ba''-al-her'-mon*)
J'g 3: 3 from mount *B*' unto the entering
1Ch 5:23 from Bashan unto *B*' and Senir,

Baali (*ba'-al-i*)
Hos 2:16 and shalt call me no more *B*'.

Baalim (*ba'-al-im*) See also BAAL.
J'g 2:11 sight of the Lord, and served *B*':
3: 7 and served *B*' and the groves.
8:33 went a whoring after *B*', and made
10: 6 and served *B*', and Ashtaroth,
10 our God, and also served *B*'.
1Sa 7: 4 children of Israel did put away *B*'
12:10 have served *B*' and Ashtaroth:
1Ki 18:18 and thou hast followed *B*'.
2Ch 17: 3 David, and sought not unto *B*';
24: 7 Lord did they bestow upon *B*'.
28: 2 made also molten images for *B*'.
33: 3 and he reared up altars for *B*',
34: 4 they brake down the altars of *B*'
Jer 2:23 polluted, I have not gone after *B*'?
9:14 after *B*', which their fathers
Ho 2:13 I will visit upon her the days of *B*',
17 I will take away the names of *B*'
11: 2 sacrificed unto *B*', and burned

Baalis (*ba'-al-is*)
Jer 40:14 *B*' the king of the Ammonites

Baal-meon (*ba''-al-me'-on*) See also BETH-BAAL-MEON.
Nu 32:38 Nebo, and *B*', (their names being
1Ch 5: 8 even unto Nebo and *B*':
Eze 25: 9 Beth-jeshimoth, *B*', and

Baal-peor (*ba''-al-pe'-or*) See also PEOR.
Nu 25: 3 Israel joined himself unto *B*':
5 his men that were joined unto *B*'.
De 4: 3 what the Lord did because of *B*':
3 for all the men that followed *B*',
Ps 106:28 joined themselves also unto *B*',
Ho 9:10 they went to *B*', and separated

Baal-perazim (*ba''-al-per'-a-zim*)
2Sa 5:20 David came to *B*', and David
20 called the name of that place *B*'.
1Ch 14:11 So they came up to *B*'; and David
11 called the name of that place *B*'.

Baal's (*ba'-als*)
1Ki 18:22 but *B*' prophets are four hundred

Baal-shalisha (*ba''-al-shal'-i-shah*)
2Ki 4:42 there came a man from *B*',

Baal-tamar (*ba''-al-ta'-mar*)
J'g 20:33 put themselves in array at *B*':

Baal-zebub (*ba''-al-ze'-bub*) See also BEELZEBUB.
2Ki 1: 2 Go, enquire of *B*' the god of Ekron
3 that ye go to enquire of *B*' the god
6 that thou sendest to enquire of *B*'
16 sent messengers to enquire of *B*'

Baal-zephon (*ba''-al-ze'-fon*)
Ex 14: 2 and the sea, over against *B*':
9 beside Pi-hahiroth, before *B*'.
Nu 33: 7 Pi-hahiroth, which is before *B*':

Baana (*ba'-an-ah*) See also BAANAH.
1Ki 4:12 *B*' the son of Ahilud; to him
Ne 3: 4 repaired Zadok the son of *B*'.

Baanah (*ba'-an-ah*) See also BAANA.
2Sa 4: 2 the name of the one was *B*',
5 Rechab and *B*', went, and came
6 Rechab and *B*' his brother
9 David answered Rechab and *B*'
23:29 Heleb the son of *B*, a Netophathite,
1Ki 4:16 *B*' the son of Hushai was in Asher
1Ch 11:30 Netophathite, Heled the son of *B*'
Ezr 2: 2 Mizpar, Bigvai, Rehum, *B*'.
Ne 7: 7 Mispereth, Bigvai, Nehum, *B*'.
10:27 Malluch, Harim, *B*'.

Baara (*ba'-ar-ah*)
1Ch 8: 8 Hushim and *B*' were his wives,

Baaseiah (*ba-as-i'-ah*)
1Ch 6:40 the son of *B*', the son of Malchiah,

Baasha (*ba'-ash-ah*)
1Ki 15:16 was war between Asa and *B*'
17 *B*' king of Israel went up against
1Ki 15:19 and break thy league with *B*'
21 to pass, when *B*' heard thereof,
22 wherewith *B*' had builded;
27 *B*' the son of Ahijah, of the house
27 and *B*' smote him at Gibbethon,
28 did *B*' slay him, and reigned
32 was war between Asa and *B*'
33 began *B*' the son of Ahijah to reign
16: 1 the son of Hanani against *B*',
3 will take away the posterity of *B*',
4 Him that dieth of *B*' in the city
5 Now the rest of the acts of *B*',
6 *B*' slept with his fathers, and was
7 the word of the Lord against *B*',
8 Elah the son of *B*' to reign
11 that he slew all the house of *B*':
12 Zimri destroy all the house of *B*',
12 which he spake against *B*' by Jehu
13 all the sins of *B*', and the sins of
21:22 like the house of *B*', the son of
2Ki 9: 9 like the house of *B*' the son of
2Ch 16: 1 *B*' king of Israel came up against
3 go, break thy league with *B*' king
5 it came to pass, when *B*' heard it,
6 wherewith *B*' was building;
Jer 41: 9 king had made for fear of *B*'

babbler
Ec 10:11 and a *b*' is no better.
Ac 17:18 said, What will this *b*' say?

babbling See also BABBLINGS.
Pr 23:29 who hath *b*'? who hath wounds

babblings
1Ti 6:20 avoiding profane and vain *b*',
2Ti 2:16 shun profane and vain *b*': for

babe See also BABES.
Ex 2: 6 behold, the *b*' wept.
Lu 1:41 the *b*' leaped in her womb;
44 the *b*' leaped in my womb for joy.
2:12 the *b*' wrapt in swaddling clothes,
16 Mary, and Joseph, and the *b*' lying
Heb 5:13 of righteousness: for he is a *b*'.

Babel (*ba'-bel*) See also BABYLON.
Ge 10:10 beginning of his kingdom was *B*',
11: 9 is the name of it called *B*';

babes
Ps 8: 2 of the mouth of *b*' and sucklings
17:14 rest of their substance to their *b*'.
Isa 3: 4 and *b*' shall rule over them.
M't 11:25 hast revealed them unto *b*'.
21:16 Out of the mouth of *b*'
Lu 10:21 hast revealed them unto *b*':
Ro 2:20 teacher of *b*', which hast the form
1Co 3: 1 as unto *b*' in Christ.
1Pe 2: 2 As newborn *b*', desire the sincere

Babylon (*bab'-il-un*) See also BABEL; BABYLONIANS; BABYLONISH; BABYLON'S; CHALDEA; SHESHACH.
2Ki 17:24 of Assyria brought men from *B*',
30 men of *B*' made Succoth-benoth,
20:12 son of Baladan, king of *B*', sent
14 from a far country, even from *B*'.
17 this day, shall be carried unto *B*':
18 in the palace of the king of *B*'.
24: 1 king of *B*' came up, and Jehoiakim
7 the king of *B*' had taken from
10 of *B*' came up against Jerusalem,
11 king of *B*' came against the city,
12 Judah went out to the king of *B*',
12 king of *B*' took him in the eighth
15 he carried away Jehoiachin to *B*',
15 into captivity from Jerusalem to *B*'.
16 king of *B*' brought captive to *B*'.
17 the king of *B*' made Mattaniah his
20 rebelled against the king of *B*'.
25: 1 of *B*' came, he, and all his host,
6 him up to the king of *B*' to Riblah;
7 of brass, and carried him to *B*',
8 of king Nebuchadnezzar king of *B*',
8 a servant of the king of *B*', unto
11 that fell away to the king of *B*',
13 carried the brass of them to *B*'.
20 them to the king of *B*' to Riblah:
21 king of *B*' smote them, and slew
22 Nebuchadnezzar king of *B*' had
23 of *B*' had made Gedaliah governor,
24 the land, and serve the king of *B*';
27 Evil-merodach king of *B*' in the
28 kings that were with him in *B*';
1Ch 9: 1 away to *B*' for their transgression.
2Ch 32:31 ambassadors of the princes of *B*',
33:11 with fetters, and carried him to *B*'.
36: 6 up Nebuchadnezzar king of *B*',
6 him in fetters, to carry him to *B*'.
7 of the house of the Lord to *B*',
7 put them in his temple at *B*'.
10 brought him to *B*', with the goodly
18 all these he brought to *B*'.
20 the sword carried he away to *B*';
Ezr 1:11 up from *B*' unto Jerusalem.
2: 1 of *B*' had carried away unto *B*',
5:12 the king of *B*', the Chaldean, who
12 carried the people away into *B*'.
13 first year of Cyrus the king of *B*'
14 brought them into the temple of *B*',
14 king take out of the temple of *B*',
17 treasure house, which is there at *B*',
6: 1 the treasures were laid up in *B*'.
5 and brought unto *B*', be restored,
7: 6 This Ezra went up from *B*'; and
9 began he to go up from *B*', and on
16 canst find in all the province of *B*',
8: 1 that went up with me from *B*'.
Ne 7: 6 the king of *B*' had carried away,
Ne 13: 6 of Artaxerxes king of *B*' came I
Es 2: 6 the king of *B*' had carried away.
Ps 87: 4 make mention of Rahab and *B*'
137: 1 the rivers of *B*', there we sat down,
8 O daughter of *B*', who art to be
Isa 13: 1 The burden of *B*', which Isaiah
19 And *B*', the glory of kingdoms,
14: 4 this proverb against the king of *B*',
22 and cut off from *B*' the name,
21: 9 and said, *B*' is fallen, is fallen;
39: 1 king of *B*', sent letters and a
3 far country unto me, even from *B*'.
6 this day, shall be carried to *B*':
7 in the palace of the king of *B*'.
43:14 For your sake I have sent to *B*',
47: 1 O virgin daughter of *B*', sit on the
48:14 he will do his pleasure on *B*',
20 Go ye forth of *B*', flee ye from the
Jer 20: 4 into the hand of the king of *B*',
4 he shall carry them captive into *B*',
5 take them, and carry them to *B*'.
6 and thou shalt come to *B*', and
21: 2 Nebuchadrezzar king of *B*'
4 ye fight against the king of *B*',
7 of Nebuchadrezzar king of *B*',
10 into the hand of the king of *B*',
22:25 king of *B*', and into the hand of the
24: 1 king of *B*' had carried away
1 and had brought them to *B*'.
25: 1 of Nebuchadrezzar king of *B*';
9 the king of *B*', my servant, and
11 serve the king of *B*' seventy years.
12 I will punish the king of *B*',
27: 6 the king of *B*', my servant; and
8 the king of *B*', and that will not
8 under the yoke of the king of *B*',
9 Ye shall not serve the king of *B*':
11, 12 under the yoke of the king of *B*',
13 that will not serve the king of *B*'?
14 Ye shall not serve the king of *B*':
16 shortly be brought again from *B*':
17 serve the king of *B*', and live:
18 and at Jerusalem, go not to *B*'.
20 Nebuchadnezzar king of *B*' took
20 from Jerusalem to *B*', and all the
22 They shall be carried to *B*',
28: 2 broken the yoke of the king of *B*'.
3 Nebuchadnezzar king of *B*' took
3 and carried them to *B*':
4 of Judah, that went into B',
4 break the yoke of the king of *B*'.
6 captive, from *B*' into this place.
11 king of *B*' from the neck of all
14 serve Nebuchadnezzar king of *B*';
29: 1 away captive from Jerusalem to *B*';
3 king of Judah sent unto *B*'
3 to Nebuchadnezzar king of *B*')
4 away from Jerusalem unto *B*';
10 years be accomplished at *B*'
15 hath raised us up prophets in *B*';
20 I have sent from Jerusalem to *B*':
21 king of *B*'; and he shall slay them
22 of Judah which are in *B*', saying,
22 the king of *B*' roasted in the fire;
28 therefore he sent unto us in *B*',
32: 3 the king of *B*', and he shall take it;
4 of the king of *B*', and shall speak
5 he shall lead Zedekiah to *B*',
28 Nebuchadrezzar king of *B*',
36 of the king of *B*' by the sword,
34: 1 king of *B*', and all his army,
2 the king of *B*', and he shall burn it
3 behold the eyes of the king of *B*',
3 to mouth, and thou shalt go to *B*'.
35:11 Nebuchadrezzar king of *B*' came up
36:29 king of *B*' shall certainly come.
37: 1 Nebuchadrezzar king of *B*' made
17 into the hand of the king of *B*'.
19 The king of *B*' shall not come
38:23 by the hand of the king of *B*':
39: 1 came Nebuchadrezzar king of *B*'
3 princes of the king of *B*' came in,
3 of the princes of the king of *B*'.
5 up to Nebuchadnezzar king of *B*'
6 Then the king of *B*' slew the sons
6 the king of *B*' slew all the nobles
7 with chains, to carry him to *B*'.
9 guard carried away captive into *B*'
11 king of *B*' gave charge concerning
40: 1 were carried away captive unto *B*'.
4 unto thee to come with me into *B*',
4 unto thee to come with me into *B*',
5 whom the king of *B*' hath made
7 the king of *B*' had made Gedaliah
7 not carried away captive to *B*';
9 and serve the king of *B*', and it
11 the king of *B*' had left a remnant
41: 2 and slew him, whom the king of *B*'
18 Ahikam, whom the king of *B*' made
42:11 Be not afraid of the king of *B*',
43: 3 and carry us away captives into *B*'.
10 Nebuchadrezzar the king of *B*',
44:30 king of *B*', his enemy, and that
46: 2 king of *B*' smote in the fourth year
13 Nebuchadrezzar king of *B*' should
26 hand of Nebuchadrezzar king of *B*',
49:28 which Nebuchadrezzar king of *B*'
30 king of *B*' hath taken counsel
50: 1 that the Lord spake against *B*'
2 *B*' is taken, Bel is confounded,
8 Remove out of the midst of *B*',
9 and cause to come up against *B*'
13 goeth by *B*' shall be astonished,
14 Put yourselves in array against *B*'
16 Cut off the sower from *B*',
17 king of *B*' hath broken his bones.

Jer 50:18 I will punish the king of B' and
23 how is B' become a desolation
24 and thou art also taken, O B',
28 and escape out of the land of B',
29 together the archers against B':
34 and disquiet the inhabitants of B'.
35 and upon the inhabitants of B',
42 against thee, O daughter of B'.
43 king of B' hath heard the report,
45 that he hath taken against B';
46 At the noise of the taking of B'
51: 1 Behold, I will raise up against B',
2 and will send unto B' fanners,
6 Flee out of the midst of B',
7 B' hath been a golden cup
8 B' is suddenly fallen and destroyed:
9 We would have healed B', but she
11 for his device is against B',
12 the standard upon the walls of B',
12 spake against the inhabitants of B'.
24 I will render unto B' and to all
29 shall be performed against B',
29 make the land of B' a desolation
30 mighty men of B' have forborn
31 shew the king of B' that his city
33 of B' is like a threshing floor,
34 the king of B' hath devoured me,
35 and to my flesh be upon B',
37 B' shall become heaps, a dwelling
41 how is B' become an astonishment
42 The sea is come up upon B':
44 I will punish Bel in B',
44 yea, the wall of B' shall fall.
47 upon the graven images of B':
48 that is therein, shall sing for B':
49 As B' hath caused the slain of
49 so at B' shall fall the slain of all
53 B' should mount up to heaven,
54 A sound of a cry cometh from B',
55 Because the Lord hath spoiled B',
56 is come upon her, even upon B',
58 walls of B' shall be utterly broken,
59 B' in the fourth year of his reign.
60 evil that should come upon B',
60 words that are written against B'.
61 When thou comest to B', and shalt
64 Thus shall B' sink, and shall not
52: 3 rebelled against the king of B'.
4 king of B' came, he and all his
9 carried him up unto the king of B'
10 king of B' slew the sons of Zedekiah
11 the king of B' bound him in chains,
11 and carried him to B',
12 year of Nebuchadrezzar king of B',
12 which served the king of B', into
15 that fell to the king of B',
17 carried all the brass of them to B'.
26 them to the king of B' to Riblah.
27 the king of B' smote them, and
31 Evil-merodach king of B', in the
32 of the kings that were with him in B',
34 diet given him of the king of B',
Eze 12:13 I will bring him to B' to the land
17:12 tell them, Behold, the king of B'
12 and led them with him to B';
16 in the midst of B' he shall die.
20 I will bring him to B', and will
19: 9 and brought him to the king of B':
21:19 the sword of the king of B' may
21 the king of B' stood at the parting
24: 2 the king of B' set himself against
26: 7 Nebuchadrezzar king of B', a king
29:18 of man, Nebuchadrezzar king of B'
19 unto Nebuchadrezzar king of B';
30:10 of Nebuchadrezzar king of B'.
24 the arms of the king of B',
25 the king of B', and the arms of
25 of the king of B', and he shall
32:11 The sword of the king of B'
Da 1: 1 Nebuchadnezzar king of B'
2:12 to destroy all the wise men of B'.
14 to slay the wise men of B':
18 with the rest of the wise men of B'.
24 to destroy the wise man of B':
24 Destroy not the wise men of B':
48 ruler over the whole province of B',
48 over all the wise men of B'.
49 the affairs of the province of B':
3: 1 of Dura, in the province of B'.
12 the affairs of the province of B',
30 Abed-nego, in the province of B'.
4: 6 to bring in all the wise men of B'
29 in the palace of the kingdom of B'.
30 Is not this great B', that I have
5: 7 and said to the wise men of B',
7: 1 first year of Belshazzar king of B'
Mic 4:10 and thou shalt go even to B';
Zec 2: 7 with the daughter of B'.
6:10 which are come from B',
M't 1:11 they were carried away to B':
12 after they were brought to B',
17 the carrying away into B'
17 carrying away from B' unto Christ
Ac 7:43 carry you away beyond B'.
1Pe 5:13 The church that is at B',
Re 14: 8 B' is fallen, is fallen,
16:19 great B' came in remembrance
17: 5 B' the great, the mother of
18: 2 B' the great is fallen,
10 that great city B', that mighty city!
21 great city B' be thrown down,

Babylonians (*bab-il-o'-ne-ans*) See also CHALDEANS.
Ezr 4: 9 the B', the Susanchites, the
Eze 23:15 manner of the B' of Chaldea,
23:17 the B' came to her into the
23 The B', and all the Chaldeans,

Babylonish (*bab-il-o'-nish*) See also BABYLONIANS.
Jos 7:21 spoils a goodly B' garment,

Babylon's (*bab'-il-ons*)
Jer 32: 2 the king of B' army besieged
34: 7 When the king of B' army fought
21 the hand of the king of B' army,
38: 3 of B' army, which shall take it.
17 go forth unto the king of B' princes,
18 to the king of B' princes, then shall
22 forth to the king of B' princes,
39:13 and all the king of B' princes;

Baca (*ba'-cah*)
Ps 84: 6 passing through the valley of B'

Bachrites (*bak'-rites*)
Nu 26:35 of Becher, the family of the B':

Bachuth See ALLON-BACHUTH.

back See also BACKBITERS; BACKBITETH; BACKBITING; BACKBONE; BACKS; BACKSIDE; BACKSLIDER; BACKSLIDING; BACKWARD; HORSEBACK.
Ge 14:16 And he brought b' all the goods,
19: 9 they said, Stand b'.
26 his wife looked b' from behind
38:29 as he drew b' his hand,
39: 9 neither hath he kept b' anything
Ex 14:21 Lord caused the sea to go b' by a
18: 2 after he had sent her b',
23: 4 surely bring it b' to him again.
33:23 thou shalt see my b' parts:
Nu 9: 7 wherefore are we kept b',
13:26 and brought b' word unto them,
22:34 thee, I will get me b' again.
24:11 hath kept thee b' from honour.
De 23:13 and shalt turn b' and cover that
Jos 8:20 wilderness turned b' upon the
26 Joshua drew not his hand b',
11:10 And Joshua at that time turned b',
23:12 if ye do in any wise go b',
J'g 11:35 the Lord, and I cannot go b'.
18:26 he turned and went b' unto his
Ru 1:15 is gone b' unto her people,
2: 6 Moabitish damsel that came b'
1Sa 10: 9 he had turned his b' to go from
15:11 he is turned b' from following me,
25:34 hath kept me b' from hurting
2Sa 1:22 the bow of Jonathan turned not b',
12:23 can I bring him b' again? I
15:20 and take b' thy brethren: mercy
25 Carry b' the ark of God into the
17: 3 I will bring b' all the people unto
18:16 Joab held b' the people.
19:10 a word of bringing the king b'?
11 to bring the king b' to his house?
12 ye the last to bring b' the king?
37 I pray thee, turn b' again,
43 first had in bringing b' our king?
1Ki 13:18 Bring him b' with thee into thine
19 So he went b' with him, and did eat
20 the prophet that brought him b':
22 But camest b', and hast eaten
23 prophet whom he had brought b'.
26 prophet that brought him b' from
29 upon the ass, and brought it b':
14: 9 hast cast me behind thy b':
28 and brought them b' into the
18:37 hast turned their heart b' again.
19:20 Go b' again: for what have I done
21 And he returned b' from him,
22:26 and carry him b' unto Amon the
33 they turned b' from pursuing him.
2Ki 1: 5 the messengers turned b' unto
5 Why are ye now turned b'?
2:13 and went b', and stood by the bank
24 And he turned b', and looked on
8:29 king Joram went b' to be healed
15:20 So the king of Assyria turned b',
19:28 and I will turn thee b' by the way
20: 9 ten degrees, or go b' ten degrees?
1Ch 21:20 And Ornan turned b', and saw the
2Ch 13:14 when Judah looked b', behold,
18:25 and carry him b' to Amon the
32 turned b' again from pursuing
19: 4 and brought them b' unto the Lord
25:13 the army which Amaziah sent b',
34:16 brought the king word b' again,
Ne 2:15 viewed the wall, and turned b', and
Job 23:12 I gone b' from the commandment
26: 9 He holdeth b' the face of his
33:18 He keepeth b' his soul from the
30 To bring b' his soul from the pit,
34:27 they turned b' from him, and
39:22 neither turneth he b' from the
Ps. 9: 3 enemies are turned b', they shall
14: 7 the Lord bringeth b' the captivity
19:13 Keep b' thy servant also from
21:12 make them turn their b', when
35: 4 let them be turned b' and brought
44:10 makest us to turn b' from the
18 Our heart is not turned b', neither
53: 3 Every one of them is gone b':
6 God bringeth b' the captivity of
56: 9 then shall mine enemies turn b':
70: 3 Let them be turned b' for a
78: 9 turned b' in the day of battle.
41 Yea, they turned b' and tempted
57 But turned b', and dealt
80:18 will not we go b' from thee:
85: 1 hast brought b' the captivity of
114: 3 and fled: Jordan was driven b'.
5 Jordan, that thou wast driven b'?
129: 3 plowed upon my b': they made
5 all be confounded and turned b'
Pr. 10:13 a rod is for the b' of him that is
19:29 and stripes for the b' of fools.
26: 3 a rod for the fool's b'.
Isa 14:27 out, and who shall turn it b'?
31: 2 will not call b' his words: but
37:29 and I will turn thee b' by the way
38:17 cast all my sins behind thy b'.
42:17 They shall be turned b', they shall
43: 6 and to the south, Keep not b':
50: 5 neither turned away b.
6 I gave my b' to the smiters, and
Jer 2:27 have turned their b' unto me,
4: 8 of the Lord is not turned b'
28 neither will I turn b' from it.
6: 9 turn b' thine hand as a grape
8: 5 of Jerusalem slidden b' by a
11:10 They are turned b' to the
18:17 shew them the b', and not the
21: 4 I will turn b' the weapons of war
32:33 they have turned unto me the b',
38:22 and they are turned away b'.
40: 5 he was not yet gone b', he said,
5 Go b' also to Gedaliah the son of
42: 4 I will keep nothing b' from you.
46: 5 dismayed and turned away b'?
5 are fled apace, and look not b':
21 also are turned b', and are fled
47: 3 fathers shall not look b' to their
48:10 he that keepeth b' his sword from
39 hath Moab turned the b' with
49: 8 Flee ye, turn b', dwell deep,
La 1:13 he hath turned me b': he hath
2: 3 he hath drawn b' his right hand
Eze 23:35 me behind thy b', therefore bear
24:14 I will not go b', neither will I
38: 4 And I will turn thee b',
8 the land that is brought b' from
39: 2 I will turn thee b', and leave but
44: 1 Then he brought me b' the way of
Da 7: 6 which had upon the b' of it four
Ho 4:16 Israel slideth b' as a backsliding
Na 2: 8 they cry; but none shall look b'.
Zep 1: 6 them that are turned b' from the
3:20 when I turn b' your captivity
M't 24:18 return b' to take his clothes.
28: 2 came and rolled b' the stone
M'r 13:16 that is in the field not turn b'
Lu 2:45 turned b' again to Jerusalem,
8:37 the ship, and returned b' again.
9:62 looking b', is fit for the kingdom
17:15 turned b', and with a loud voice
31 let him likewise not return b'.
Joh 6:66 many of his disciples went b',
20:14 turned herself b', and saw Jesus
Ac 5: 2 And kept b' part of the price,
3 to keep b' part of the price of the
7:39 hearts turned b' again into Egypt,
20:20 how I kept b' nothing that was
Ro 11:10 and bow down their b' alway.
Heb 10:38 but if any man draw b', my soul
39 we are not of them who draw b'
Jas 5: 4 is of you kept b' by fraud,

backbiters
Ro 1:30 B', haters of God, despiteful,

backbiteth
Ps 15: 3 He that b' not with his tongue,

backbiting See also BACKBITINGS.
Pr 25:23 angry countenance a b' tongue.

backbitings
2Co 12:20 strifes, b', whisperings,

backbone
Le 3: 9 it shall he take off hard by the b';

backed See BACKT.

backs
Ex 23:27 all thine enemies turn their b'
Jos 7: 8 when Israel turneth their b'
12 their b' before their enemies,
J'g 20:42 Therefore they turned their b'
2Ch 29: 6 of the Lord, and turned their b'.
Ne 9: 26 cast thy law behind their b',
Eze 8:16 with their b' toward the temple
10:12 and their b', and their hands,

backside
Ex 3: 1 flock to the b' of the desert, and
26:12 over the b' of the tabernacle.
Re 5: 1 book written within and on the b,

backslider
Pr 14:14 The b' in heart shall be filled

backsliding See also BACKSLIDINGS.
Jer 3: 6 that which b' Israel hath done?
8 b' Israel committed adultery
11 The b' Israel hath justified herself
12 Return, thou b' Israel, saith the
14 Turn, O b' children, saith the
22 Return, ye b' children, and I will
8: 5 slidden back by a perpetual b'?
31:22 O thou b' daughter?
49: 4 thy flowing valley, O b' daughter?
Ho 4:16 Israel slideth back as a b' heifer:
11: 7 my people are bent to b' from me:
14: 4 I will heal their b',

backslidings
Jer 2:19 and thy b' shall reprove thee:
3:22 and I will heal your b'.
5: 6 their b' are increased.
14: 7 our b' are many;

backward
Ge 9:23 both their shoulders, and went b',
23 and their faces were b', and they
49:17 so that his rider shall fall b'.
1Sa 4:18 he fell from off the seat b'
2Ki 20:10 shadow return b' ten degrees.

2Ki 20:11 brought the shadow ten degrees b'.
Job 23: 8 and b', but I cannot perceive
Ps 40:14 them be driven b' and put to shame
70: 2 be turned b', and put to confusion,
Isa 1: 4 unto anger, they are gone away b'.
28:13 that they might go, and fall b',
38: 8 sun dial of Ahaz, ten degrees b'.
44:25 that turneth wise men b',
59:14 judgment is turned away b',
Jer 7:24 went b', and not forward.
15: 6 saith the Lord, thou art gone b':
La 1: 8 she sigheth, and turneth b'.
Joh 18: 6 they went b', and fell to

bad See also WORSE; WORST.
Ge 24:50 cannot speak unto thee b' or good.
31:24, 29 not to Jacob either good or b'.
Le 27:10 nor change it, a good for a b',
10 or a b' for a good: and if he
12 value it, whether it be good or b':
14 estimate it, whether it be good or b',
33 not search whether it be good or b',
Nu 13:19 whether it be good or b'; and what
24:13 good or b' of mine own mind;
2Sa 13:22 brother Amnon neither good nor b':
14:17 the king to discern good and b':
1Ki 3: 9 discern between good and b':
Ezr 4:12 the rebellious and the b' city,
Jer 24: 2 not be eaten, they were so b'.
M't 13:48 into vessels, but cast the b' away.
22:10 as they found, both b' and good:
2Co 5:10 done, whether it be good or b'.

bade See also BADEST; FORBAD.
Ge 43:17 did as Joseph b'; and the man
Ex 16:24 up till the morning, as Moses b':
Nu 14:10 congregation b' stone them with
Jos 11: 9 unto them as the Lord b' him:
Ru 3: 6 all that her mother in law b' her.
1Sa 24:10 and some b' me kill thee: but
2Sa 1:18 b' them teach the children of Judah
14:19 thy servant Joab, he b' me, and
2Ch 10:12 the king b', saying, Come again
Es 4:15 Then Esther b' them return
M't 16:12 they how that he b' them not
Lu 14: 9 And he that b' thee and him come
10 when he that b' thee cometh, he
12 said he also to him that b' him,
16 made a great supper, and b' many:
Ac 11:12 the spirit b' me go with them,
18:21 b' them farewell, saying, I must
22:24 b' that he should be examined

badest
Ge 27:19 done according as thou b' me:

badgers'
Ex 25: 5 b' skins, and shittim wood,
26:14 a covering above of b' skins.
35: 7 dyed red, and b' skins, and
23 red skins of rams, and b' skins,
36:19 a covering of b' skins above that
39:34 the covering of b' skins,
Nu 4: 6 the covering of b' skins,
8 with a covering of b' skins,
10 within a covering of b' skins,
11 with a covering of b' skins,
12 a covering of b' skins, and shall
14 upon it a covering of b' skins,
25 the covering of the b' skins
Eze 16:10 shod thee with b' skin,

badger-skin See BADGERS' and SKIN.

badness
Ge 41:19 in all the land of Egypt for b':

bag See also BAGS.
De 25:13 not have in thy b' divers weights,
1Sa 17:40 in a shepherd's b' which he had,
49 David put his hand in his b',
Job 14:17 transgression is sealed up in a b',
Pr 7:20 taken a b' of money with him,
16:11 weights of the b' are his work.
Isa 46: 6 They lavish gold out of the b',
Mic 6:11 with the b' of deceitful weights?
Hag 1: 6 to put it into a b' with holes.
Joh 12: 6 he was a thief, and had the b',
13:29 thought, because Judas had the b',

bags
2Ki 5:23 two talents of silver in two b',
12:10 they put up in b', and told the
Lu 12:33 provide yourselves b' which wax

Bah See HEPHZI-BAH.

Baharumite (*ba-ha'-rum-ite*) See also BARHUMITE.
1Ch 11:33 Azmaveth the B', Eliahba the

Bahurim (*ba-hu'-rim*) See also BAHARUMITE.
2Sa 3:16 along weeping behind her to B'.
16: 5 And when king David came to B',
17:18 and came to a man's house in B',
19:16 a Benjamite, which was of B',
1Ki 2: 8 a Benjamite of B', which cursed

Bajith (*ba'-jith*)
Isa 15: 2 is gone up to B', and to Dibon,

Bakbakkar (*bak-bak'-kar*)
1Ch 9:15 B', Heresh, and Galal, and

Bakbuk (*bak'-buk*)
Ezr 2:51 The children of B', the children
Ne 7:53 The children of B', the children

Bakbukiah (*bak-buk-i'-ah*)
Ne 11:17 B' the second among his
12: 9 B' and Unni, their brethren,
25 Mattaniah, and B', Obadiah,

bake See also BAKED; BAKEMEATS; BAKEN; BAKETH.
Ge 19: 3 did b' unleavened bread, and they
Ex 16:23 b' that which ye will b'
Le 24: 5 and b' twelve cakes thereof:
26:26 ten women shall b' your bread in
1Sa 28:24 did b' unleavened bread thereof:
2Sa 13: 8 in his sight, and did b' the cakes.
Eze 4:12 thou shalt b' it with dung that
46:20 they shall b' the meat offering;

baked See also BAKEN.
Ex 12:39 And they b' unleavened cakes
Nu 11: 8 b' it in pans, and made cakes
1Ch 23:29 and for that which is b' in the pan,
Isa 44:19 I have b' bread upon the coals

bakemeats
Ge 40:17 of b' for Pharaoh;

baken See also BAKED.
Le 2: 4 a meat offering b' in the oven,
5 be a meat offering b' in a pan,
7 offering b' in the frying pan,
6:17 It shall not be b' with leaven.
21 when it is b', thou shalt
21 the b' pieces of the meat offering
7: 9 all the meat offering that is b'
23:17 they shall be b' with leaven;
1Ki 19: 6 there was a cake b' on the coals,

baketh
Isa 44:15 he kindleth it, and b' bread;

baker See also BAKERS.
Ge 40: 1 and his b' had offended their lord
5 and the b' of the king of Egypt,
16 When the chief b' saw that the
20 of the chief b' among his servants.
22 But he hanged the chief b':
41:10 both me and the chief b':
Ho 7: 4 as an oven heated by the b',
6 their b' sleepeth all the night;

bakers See also BAKERS'.
Ge 40: 2 against the chief of the b',
1Sa 8:13 and to be cooks, and to be b'.

bakers'
Jer 37:21 piece of bread out of the b' street,

Balaam (*ba'-la-am*) See also BALAAM'S.
Nu 22: 5 therefore unto B' the son of Beor
7 and they came unto B', and spake
8 princes of Moab abode with B'.
9 And God came unto B', and said,
10 And B' said unto God, Balak the
12 God said unto B', Thou shalt not
13 B' rose up in the morning, and said
14 said, B' refuseth to come with us.
16 they came to B', and said to him,
18 B' answered and said unto the
20 And God came unto B' at night,
21 And B' rose up in the morning,
23 and B' smote the ass, to turn her
27 fell down under B': and Balaam's
28 she said unto B', What have I done
29 And B' said unto the ass, Because
30 ass said unto B', Am not I thine
31 the Lord opened the eyes of B',
34 B' said unto the angel of the Lord,
35 angel of the Lord said unto B', Go
35 B' went with the princes of Balak.
36 Balak heard that B' was come,
37 And Balak said unto B', Did I not
38 B' said unto Balak, Lo, I am come
39 B' went with Balak, and they came
40 sent to B', and to the princes
41 Balak took B', and brought him
23: 1 And B' said unto Balak, Build me
2 Balak did as B' had spoken;
2 Balak and B' offered on every altar
3 B' said unto Balak, Stand by thy
4 And God met B': and he said unto
11 Balak said unto B', What hast thou
16 the Lord met B', and put a word
25 Balak said unto B', Neither curse
26 B' answered and said unto Balak,
27 Balak said unto B', Come, I pray
28 brought B' unto the top of Peor,
29 B' said unto Balak, Build me here
30 And Balak did as B' had said,
24: 1 B' saw that it pleased the Lord
2 And B' lifted up his eyes, and he
3 and said, B' the son of Beor
10 anger was kindled against B',
10 Balak said unto B', I called thee
12 B' said unto Balak, Spake I not
15 said, B' the son of Beor hath said,
25 B' rose up, and went and returned
31: 8 B' also the son of Beor they slew
16 through the counsel of B',
De 23: 4 they hired against thee B' the son
5 God would not hearken unto B';
Jos 13:22 B' also the son of Beor, the
24: 9 sent and called B' the son of Beor
10 But I would not hearken unto B';
Ne 13: 2 water, but hired B' against them,
Mic 6: 5 what B' the son of Beor answered
2Pe 2:15 following the way of B' the son of
Jude 11 the error of B' for reward)
Re 2:14 doctrine of B', who taught Balac

Balaam's (*ba'-la-ams*)
Nu 22:25 and crushed B' foot against
27 and B' anger was kindled,
23: 5 the Lord put a word in B' mouth,

Balac (*ba'-lak*) See also BALAK.
Re 2:14 taught B' to cast a stumblingblock

Baladan (*bal'-adan*) See also BERODACH-BALADAN; MERODACH-BALADAN.
2Ki 20:12 the son of B', king of Babylon,
Isa 39: 1 Merodach-baladan, the son of B',

Balah (*ba'-lah*) See also BAALAH.
Jos 19: 3 Hazar-shual, and B', and Azem,

Balak (*ba'-lak*) See also BALAC; BALAK'S.
Nu 22: 2 B' the son of Zippor saw all that
4 B' the son of Zippor was king of
7 spake unto him the words of B'.
10 B' the son of Zippor, king of
13 and said unto the princes of B',
14 went unto B', and said, Balaam
15 And B' sent yet again princes,
16 Thus saith B' the son of Zippor,
18 unto the servants of B',
18 If B' would give me
35 went with the princes of B'.
36 B' heard that Balaam was come,
37 B' said unto Balaam, Did I not
38 Balaam said unto B', Lo, I am
39 Balaam went with B', and they
40 And B' offered oxen and sheep,
41 B' took Balaam, and brought him
23: 1 Balaam said unto B', Build me
2 B' did as Balaam had spoken;
2 B' and Balaam offered on every
3 Balaam said unto B', Stand by thy
5 Return unto B', and thus thou
7 and said, B' the king of Moab
11 B' said unto Balaam, What hast
13 B' said unto him, Come, I pray
15 said unto B', Stand here by thy
16 Go again unto B', and say thus.
17 B' said unto him, What hath the
18 and said, Rise up, B', and hear;
25 And B' said unto Balaam,
26 and said unto B', Told not I thee,
27 B' said unto Balaam, Come, I pray
28 B' brought Balaam unto the top
29 Balaam said unto B', Build me
30 B' did as Balaam had said,
24:10 B' said unto Balaam, I called thee
12 Balaam said unto B', Spake I not
13 If B' would give me his house
25 to his place: and B' also went
Jos 24: 9 Then B' the son of Zippor, king of
J'g 11:25 art thou anything better than B'
Mic 6: 5 what B' king of Moab consulted,

Balak's (*ba'-laks*)
Nu 24:10 And B' anger was kindled against

balance See also BALANCES; BALANCINGS.
Job 31: 6 Let me be weighed in an even b',
Ps 62: 9 to be laid in the b', they are
Pr 11: 1 false b' is abomination to the
16:11 just weight and b' are the Lord's:
20:23 and a false b' is not good.
Isa 40:12 and the hills in a b'?
15 count as the small dust of the b':
46: 6 weigh silver in the b' and hire a

balances
Le 19:36 Just b', just weights, a just
Job 6: 2 my calamity laid in the b' together!
Jer 32:10 weighed him the money in the b'.
Eze 5: 1 then take thee b' to weigh, and
45:10 Ye shall have just b',
Da 5:27 Thou art weighed in the b',
Ho 12: 7 the b' of deceit are in his hand:
Am 8: 5 falsifying the b' by deceit?
Mic 6:11 pure with the wicked b',
Re 6: 5 had a pair of b' in his hand.

balancings
Job 37:16 thou know the b' of the clouds,

bald
Le 11:22 the b' locust after his kind, and
13:40 he is b'; yet is he clean.
41 he is forehead b': yet is he clean.
42 if there be in the b' head,
42 or b' forehead, a white
42 leprosy sprung up in his b' head,
42 head or his b' forehead.
43 be white reddish in his b' head,
43 or in her bald forehead,
2Ki 2:23 b' head; go up, thou b' head.
Jer 16: 6 make themselves b' for them:
48:37 every head shall be b', and every
Eze 27:31 themselves utterly b' for thee,
29:18 every head was made b', and every
Mic 1:16 Make thee b', and poll thee for thy

bald-head See BALD and HEAD.

bald-locust See BALD and LOCUST.

baldness
Le 21: 5 They shall not make b' upon their
De 14: 1 nor make any b' between your
Isa 3:24 instead of well set hair b';
15: 2 on all their heads shall be b',
22:12 to mourning, and to b',
Jer 47: 5 B' is come upon Gaza;
Eze 7:18 b' upon all their heads.
Am 8:10 b' upon every head; and I will
Mic 1:16 enlarge thy b' as the eagle;

ball
Isa 22:18 and toss thee like a b' into a

balm See also EMBALM.
Ge 37:25 spicery and b' and myrrh, going
43:11 a little b', and a little honey,
Jer 8:22 Is there no b' in Gilead;
46:11 Go up into Gilead, and take b',
51: 8 take b' for her pain, if so be she
Eze 27:17 and honey, and oil, and b'.

Bamah (*ba'-mah*) See also BAMOTH.
Eze 20:29 thereof is called B' unto this day.

Bamoth (*ba'-moth*) See also BAMOTH-BAAL.
Nu 21:19 from Nahaliel to B':
20 And from B' in the valley, that is

Bamoth-baal (*ba''-moth-ba'-al*)
Jos 13:17 Dibon, and B', and

band See also BANDED; BANDS; SWADDLING BAND.
Ex 39:23 a b' round about the hole, that it
1Sa 10:26 him a b' of men, whose hearts
1Ki 11:24 captain over a b', when David
2Ki 13:21 they spied a b' of men; and they
1Ch 12:18 made them captains of the b'.
21 David against the b' of the
2Ch 22: 1 the b' of men that came with the
Ezr 8:22 the king a b' of soldiers and
Job 39:10 unicorn with his b' in the furrow?
Da 4:15 even with a b' of iron and brass,
23 in the earth, even with a b' of iron
M't 27:27 gathered unto him the whole b'
M'r 15:16 they call together the whole b'.
Joh 18: 3 having received a b' of men and
12 Then the b' and the captain and
Ac 10: 1 of the b' called the Italian b',
21:31 chief captain of the b', that all
27: 1 Julius, a centurion of Augustus' b'.

banded
Ac 23:12 of the Jews b' together,

bands See also HEADBANDS.
Ge 32: 7 herds, and the camels, into two b';
10 and now I am become two b'.
Le 26:13 have broken the b' of your yoke,
J'g 15:14 his b' loosed from off his hands.
2Sa 4: 2 two men that were captains of b':
2Ki 6:23 So the b' of Syria came no more
13:20 And the b' of the Moabites invaded
23:33 Pharaoh-nechoh put him in b' at
24: 2 against him b' of the Chaldees,
2 and b' of the Syrians,
2 and b' of the Moabites,
2 and b' of the children of Ammon,
1Ch 7: 4 were b' of soldiers for war,
12:23 of the b. that were ready armed
2Ch 26:11 went out to war by b', according
Job 1:17 Chaldeans made out three b', and
38:31 Pleiades, or loose the b' of Orion?
39: 5 hath loosed the b' of the wild ass?
Ps 2: 3 break their b' asunder, and cast
73: 4 there are no b' in their death:
107:14 and break their b' in sunder.
119:61 The b' of the wicked have robbed
Pr 30:27 go they forth all of them by b';
Ec 7:26 and nets, and her hands as b':
Isa 28:22 lest your b' be made strong:
52: 2 loose thyself from the b' of thy
58: 6 loose the bands of wickedness, to
Jer 2:20 thy yoke, and burst thy b';
Eze 3:25 they shall put b' upon thee, and
4: 8 I will lay b. upon thee, and thou
12:14 to help him, and all his b';
17:21 with all his b' shall fall by the
34:27 have broken the b' of their yoke,
38: 6 Gomer, and all his b';
6 the north quarters, and all his b':
9 the land, thou, and all thy b',
22 upon him, upon his b',
39: 4 of Israel, thou, and all thy b',
Ho 11: 4 of a man, with b' of love:
Zec 11: 7 Beauty, the other I called B';
14 asunder mine other staff, even B',
Lu 8:29 he brake the b', and was driven
Ac 16:26 and every one's b' were loosed.
22:30 he loosed him from his b', and
27:40 loosed the rudder b', and hoised
Col 2:19 the body by joints and b' having

Bani *(ba'-ni)*
2Sa 23:36 Nathan of Zobah, B' the Gadite,
1Ch 6:46 The son of B', the son of Shamer,
9: 4 the son of B', of the children of
Ezr 2:10 The children of B', six hundred
10:29 sons of B'; Meshullam, and
34 Of the sons of B'; Maadai, Amram,
38 And B', and Binnui, and Shimei,
Ne 3:17 Rehum the son of B'. Next
8: 7 Jeshua, and B', and Sherebiah,
9: 4 Levites, Jeshua, and B', Kadmiel,
4 B', and Chenani, and cried
5 and Kadmiel, B', Hashabniah,
10:13 Hodijah, B', Beninu.
14 Pahath-moab, Elam, Zatthu, B',
11:22 Uzzi the son of B', the son of

banished
2Sa 14:13 doth not fetch home again his b'.
14 that his b' be not expelled

banishment
Ezr 7:26 it be unto death, or to b',
La 2:14 false burdens and causes of b'.

bank See also BANKS.
Ge 41:17 I stood upon the b' of the river:
De 4:48 is by the b' of the river Arnon,
Jos 12: 2 upon the b' of the river Arnon,
13: 9 is upon the b' of the river Arnon,
16 is on the b' of the river Arnon,
2Sa 20:15 cast up a b' against the city,
2Ki 2:13 and stood by the b' of Jordan;
19:32 shield, nor cast a b' against it.
Isa 37:33 shields, nor cast a b' against it.
Eze 47: 7 at the b' of the river were very
12 by the river upon the b' thereof,
Da 12: 5 this side of the b' of the river,
5 other on that side of the b' of
Lu 19:23 money into the b', that at my

banks
Jos 3:15 overfloweth all his b' all the time
4:18 flowed over all his b', as they did
1Ch 12:15 it had overflown all his b';
Isa 8: 7 channels, and go over all his b':
Da 8:16 man's voice between the b' of Ulai,

banner See also BANNERS.
Ps 60: 4 given a b' to them that fear
Ca 2: 4 and his b' over me was love.
Isa 13: 2 Lift ye up a b' upon the high

banners
Ps 20: 5 set up our b': the Lord fulfil all
Ca 6: 4 terrible as an army with b'.
10 and terrible as an army with b'?

banquet See also BANQUETING.
Es 5: 4 Haman come this day unto the b'
5 the king and Haman came to the b'
6 said unto Esther at the b' of wine,
8 the king and Haman come to the b'
12 come in with the king unto the b'
14 merrily with the king unto the b'.
6:14 hasted to bring Haman unto the b'
7: 1 the king and Haman came to b'
2 Esther on the second day at the b'
7 the king arising from the b' of
8 into the place of the b' of wine;
Job 41: 6 Shall the companions make a b'
Da 5:10 his lord, came into the b' house:
Am 6: 7 the b' of them that stretched

banqueting See also BANQUETINGS.
Ca 2: 4 He brought me to the b' house,

banquetings
1Pe 4: 3 b', and abominable idolatries:

baptism See also BAPTISMS.
M't 3: 7 and Sadducees come to his b',
20:22 the b' that I am baptized with?
23 be baptized with the b' that I am
21:25 The b' of John, whence was it?
M'r 1: 4 preach the b' of repentance for
10:38 the b' that I am baptized with?
39 with the b' that I am baptized
11:30 The b' of John, was it from heaven,
Lu 3: 3 preaching the b' of repentance
7:29 being baptized with the b' of John.
12:50 I have a b' to be baptized with,
20: 4 The b' of John, was it from heaven,
Ac 1:22 Beginning from the b' of John,
10:37 after the b' which John preached;
13:24 the b' of repentance to all the people
18:25 Lord, knowing only the b' of John.
19: 3 And they said, Unto John's b'.
4 with the b' of repentance, saying
Ro 6: 4 buried with him by b' into death:
Eph 4: 5 One Lord, one faith, one b',
Col 2:12 Buried with him in b', wherein
1Pe 3:21 even b' doth also now save us

baptisms
Heb 6: 2 Of the doctrine of b', and of laying

Baptist *(bap'-tist)* See also BAPTIST'S.
M't 3: 1 In those days came John the B',
11:11 risen a greater than John the B':
12 from the days of John the B' until
14: 2 This is John the B'; he is risen
16:14 Some say that thou art John the B':
17:13 he spake unto them of John the B'.
M'r 6:14 That John the B' was risen from
24 she said, The head of John the B'.
25 a charger the head of John the B'.
8:28 they answered, John the B':
Lu 7:20 John B' hath sent us unto thee,
28 greater prophet than John the B':
33 John the B' came neither eating
9:19 answering said, John the B';

Baptist's *(bap'-tists)*
M't 14: 8 Give me here John B' head in

baptize See also BAPTIZED; BAPTIZEST; BAPTIZETH; BAPTIZING.
M't 3:11 I indeed b' you with water
11 he shall b' you with the Holy Ghost,
M'r 1: 4 John did b' in the wilderness,
8 he shall b' you with the Holy Ghost
Lu 3:16 I indeed b' you with water;
16 he shall b' you with the Holy Ghost
Joh 1:26 saying, I b' with water: but
33 he that sent me to b' with water,
1Co 1:17 Christ sent me not to b', but to

baptized
M't 3: 6 And were b' of him in Jordan,
13 Jordan unto John, to be b' of him.
14 I have need to be b' of thee, and
16 Jesus, when he was b', went up
20:22 I shall drink of, and to be b',
22 the baptism that I am b' with?
23 and be b' with the baptism
23 that I am b' with:
M'r 1: 5 all b' of him in the river of Jordan,
8 I indeed have b' you with water:
9 and was b' of John in Jordan.
10:38 and be b' with the baptism
38 that I am b' with?
39 and with the baptism that I am b'
39 withal shall ye be b':
16:16 believeth and is b' shall be saved;
Lu 3: 7 came forth to be b' of him,
12 Then came also publicans to be b',
21 when all the people were b', it came
21 that Jesus also being b',
7:29 being b' with the baptism of John.
30 themselves, being not b' of him,
12:50 I have a baptism to be b' with;
Joh 3:22 there he tarried with them, and b'.
23 and they came, and were b'.
4: 1 Jesus made and b' more disciples
2 (Though Jesus himself b' not,
10:40 place where John at first b';
Ac 1: 5 John truly b' with water;

Ac 1: 5 ye shall be b' with the Holy Ghost
2:38 Repent, and be b' every one of you
41 gladly received his word were b':
8:12 were b', both men and women.
13 he was b', he continued with Philip,
16 only they were b' in the name
36 what doth hinder me to be b'?
38 and the eunuch; and he b' him.
9:18 forthwith, and arose, and was b'.
10:47 water, that these should not be b',
48 commanded them to be b' in the
11:16 John indeed b' with water;
16 ye shall be b' with the Holy Ghost.
16:15 when she was b', and her household,
33 was b', he and all his, straightway.
18: 8 hearing believed, and were b'.
19: 3 Unto what then were ye b'?
4 John verily b' with the baptism of
5 heard this, they were b' in the name
22:16 and be b', and wash away thy sins,
Ro 6: 3 of us as were b' into Jesus Christ
3 were b' into his death?
1Co 1:13 or were ye b' in the name of Paul?
14 I thank God that I b' none of you,
15 say that I had b' in mine own name.
16 I b' also the household of Stephanas:
16 I know not whether I b' any other.
10: 2 were all b' unto Moses in the cloud
12:13 For by one Spirit are we all b' into
15:29 they do which are b' for the dead,
29 why are they then b' for the dead?
Ga 3:27 as have been b' into Christ have put

baptizest
Joh 1:25 said unto him, Why b' thou then,

baptizeth
Joh 1:33 is he which b' with the Holy Ghost.
3:26 behold, the same b', and all men

baptizing
M't 28:19 b' them in the name of the Father,
Joh 1:28 Jordan, where John was b'.
31 therefore am I come b' with water.
3:23 John also was b' in Ænon

bar See also BARS.
Ex 26:28 And the middle b' in the midst of
36:33 he made the middle b' to shoot
Nu 4:10 skins, and shall put it upon a b'.
12 skins, and shall put them on a b':
J'g 16: 3 away with them, b' and all, and
Ne 7: 3 them shut the doors, and b' them:
Am 1: 5 break also the b' of Damascus,

Bar See BARABBAS; BAR-JESUS; BAR-JONAH; BARNABAS; BARSABAS; BARTHOLOMEW; BARTIMAEUS.

Barabbas *(ba-rab'-bas)*
M't 27:16 a notable prisoner, called B'.
17 B', or Jesus which is called Christ?
20 should ask B', and destroy Jesus.
21 release unto you? They said, B'.
26 Then released he B' unto them:
M'r 15: 7 And there was one named B',
11 that he should rather release B'
15 released B' unto them, and delivered
Lu 23:18 this man, and release unto us B':
Joh 18:40 Not this man, but B'.
40 Now B' was a robber.

Barachel *(bar'-ak-el)*
Job 32: 2 the wrath of Elihu the son of B'
6 Elihu the son of B' the Buzite

Barachias *(bar'-ak-i'-as)*
M't 23:35 Zacharias son of B', whom ye slew

Barah See BETH-BARAH.

Barak *(ba'-rak)*
J'g 4: 6 and called B' the son of Abinoam
8 B' said unto her, If thou wilt go
9 and went with B' to Kedesh.
10 B' called Zebulun and Naphtali to
12 they shewed Sisera that B' the son
14 Deborah said unto B', Up; for this
14 B' went down from mount Tabor,
15 the edge of the sword before B';
16 But B' pursued after the chariots,
22 behold, as B' pursued Sisera,
5: 1 Then sang Deborah and B' the son
12 arise, B', and lead thy captivity
15 even Issachar, and also B': he was
Heb 11:32 to tell of Gedeon, and of B',

barbarian See also BARBARIANS; BARBAROUS.
1Co 14:11 unto him that speaketh a b',
11 that speaketh shall be a b' unto me.
Col 3:11 B', Scythian, bond nor free:

barbarians
Ac 28: 4 when the b' saw the venomous
Ro 1:14 to the Greeks, and to the B';

barbarous
Ac 28: 2 the b' people shewed us no little

barbed
Job 41: 7 thou fill his skin with b' irons?

barber's
Eze 5: 1 sharp knife, take thee a b' rasor,

bare See also BAREFOOT; BAREST; FORBARE.
Ge 4: 1 she conceived, and b' Cain, and
2 she again b' his brother Abel.
17 she conceived, and b' Enoch:
20 Adah b' Jabal: he was the father
22 And Zillah, she also b' Tubal-cain,
25 b' a son, and called his name Seth:
6: 4 and they b' children to them,
7:17 increased, and b' up the ark,
16: 1 Abram's wife, b' him no children:

Ge 16:15 And Hagar b' Abram a son: and
15 his son's name, which Hagar b',
16 when Hagar b' Ishmael to Abram.
19:37 the firstborn b' a son, and called
38 And the younger, she also b' a son,
20:17 maidservants; and they b' children.
21: 2 Sarah conceived, and b' Abraham a
3 whom Sarah b' to him, Isaac.
22:24 she b' also Tebah, and Gaham,
24:24 Milcah, which she b' unto Nahor.
36 wife b' a son to my master
47 son, whom Milcah b' unto him:
25: 2 she b' him Zimran, and Jokshan,
12 handmaid, b' unto Abraham:
26 threescore years old when she b'
29:32 And Leah conceived, and b' a son,
33, 34, 35 conceived again, and b' a
30: 1 saw that she b' Jacob no children,
5 conceived, and b' Jacob a son.
7 maid conceived again, and b' Jacob
10 Zilpah Leah's maid b' Jacob a son.
12 Leah's maid b' Jacob a second
17 she conceived, and b' Jacob a fifth
19 again, and b' Jacob the sixth son.
21 And afterwards she b' a daughter,
23 And she conceived, and b' a son;
31: 8 then all the cattle b' speckled:
8 then b' all the cattle ringstraked.
39 I b' the loss of it; of my hand
34: 1 which she b' unto Jacob, went
36: 4 Adah b' to Esau Eliphaz;
4 and Bashemath b' Reuel;
5 Aholibamah b' Jeush, and Jaalam,
12 and she b' to Eliphaz Amalek:
14 she b' to Esau Jeush, and Jaalam,
38: 3 And she conceived, and b' a son;
4 she conceived again, and b' a son;
5 yet again conceived, and b' a son;
5 was at Chezib, when she b' him.
41:50 Poti-pherah priest of On b' unto
44:27 Ye know that my wife b' me two
46:15 she b' unto Jacob in Padan-aram,
18 and these she b' unto Jacob,
20 priest of On b' unto him.
25 and she b' these unto Jacob:
Ex 2: 2 the woman conceived, and b' a son:
22 And she b' him a son, and he called
6:20 and she b' him Aaron and Moses:
23 and she b' him Nadab, and Abihu,
25 and she b' him Phinehas: these are
19: 4 and how I b' you on eagles' wings,
Le 13:45 and his head b', and he shall put
55 whether it be b' within or
Nu 13:23 and they b' it between two
26:59 her mother b' to Levi in Egypt:
59 and she b' unto Amram Aaron
De 1:31 how that the Lord thy God b' thee,
31: 9 the sons of Levi, which b' the ark
25 the Levites, which b' the ark
Jos 3:15 they that b' the ark were come
15 and the feet of the priests that b'
17 the priests that b' the ark
4: 9 which b' the ark of the covenant
10 the priest which b' the ark stood
18 when the priests that b' the ark
8:33 the Levites, which b' the ark
J'g 3:18 the people that b' the present.
8:31 she also b' him a son, whose
11: 2 And Gilead's wife b' him sons;
13: 2 his wife was barren, and b' not.
24 And the woman b' a son,
Ru 4:12 Pharez whom Tamar b' unto
13 her conception and she b' a son.
1Sa 1:20 Hannah had conceived that she b'
2:21 she conceived, and b' three sons
14: 1 unto the young man that b' his
6 the young man that b' his armour,
17:41 man that b' the shield went before
2Sa 6:13 they that b' the ark of the Lord.
11:27 became his wife, and b' him a
12:15 the child that Uriah's wife b'
24 and she b' a son, and he called
18:15 ten young men that b' Joab's
21: 8 Aiah, whom she b' unto Saul,
1Ki 1: 6 his mother b' him after Absalom.
5:15 and ten thousand that b' burdens,
9:23 five hundred and fifty which b'
10: 2 camels that b' spices, and very
11:20 the sister of Tahpenes b' him
14:28 the guard b' them, and brought
2Ki 4:17 the woman conceived, and b' a son
5:23 and they b' them before him.
1Ch 1:32 she b' Zimran, and Jokshan,
2: 4 Tamar, his daughter in law, b' him
17 Abigail b' Amasa; and the father
19 Ephrath, which b' him Hur.
21 and she b' him Segub.
24 then Abiah Hezron's wife b' him
29 and she b' him Ahban, and Molid.
35 servant to wife; and she b' him
46 Ephah, Caleb's concubine, b'
48 Maachah, Caleb's concubine, b'
49 she b' also Shaaph the father
4: 6 And Naarah b' him Ahuzam, and
9 saying, Because I b' him with
17 and she b' Miriam, and Shammai,
18 And his wife Jehudijah b' Jered
7:14 Ashriel, whom she b'; but his
14 concubine the Aramitess b' Machir
16 Maachah the wife of Machir b' a
18 his sister Hammoleketh b' Ishod,
23 she conceived, and b' a son, and he
12:24 children of Judah that b' shield
15:15 children of the Levites b' the ark
26 the Levites that b' the ark of the
27 and all the Levites that b' the ark,
2Ch 8:10 two hundred and fifty, that b' rule
9: 1 camels that b' spices and gold in
11:19 Which b' him children; Jeush,
20 which b' him Abijah, and Attai,
14: 8 an army of men that b' targets
8 out of Benjamin, that b' shields
Ne 4:17 and they that b' burdens, with the
5:15 even their servants b' rule
Pr 17:25 and bitterness to her that b' him.
23:25 she that b' thee shall rejoice.
Ca 6: 9 is the choice one of her that b' her.
8: 5 brought thee forth that b' thee.
Isa 8: 3 she conceived, and b' a son.
22: 6 Elam b' the quiver with chariots
32:11 strip you, and make you b', and
47: 2 make b' the leg, uncover the
51: 2 father, unto Sarah that b' you:
52:10 Lord hath made b' his holy arm
53:12 and he b' the sin of many, and
63: 9 and he b' them, and carried them
Jer 13:22 discovered, and thy heels made b'.
16: 3 concerning their mothers that b'
20:14 day wherein my mother b' me be
22:26 out, and thy mother that b' thee,
49:10 I have made Esau b', I have
50:12 she that b' you shall be ashamed:
Eze 12: 7 I b' it upon my shoulder in their
16: 7 whereas thou wast naked and b'.
22 when thou wast naked and b',
39 jewels, and leave thee naked and b'.
19:11 the sceptres of them that b' rule,
23: 4 and they b' sons and daughters.
29 shall leave thee naked and b':
37 their sons, whom they b' unto me,
Ho 1: 3 which conceived, and b' him a son.
6 she conceived again, and b' him a
8 she conceived, and b' a son.
Joe 1: 7 he hath made clean b', and cast it
M't 8:17 our infirmities, and b' our
M'k 14:56 For many b' false witness against
57 and b' false witness against him,
Lu 4:22 all b' him witness, and wondered
7:14 they that b' him stood still.
8: 8 and sprang up, and b' fruit an
11:27 Blessed is the womb that b' thee,
23:29 and the wombs that never b',
Joh 1:15 John b' witness of him, and cried,
32 And John b' record, saying, I saw
34 I saw, and b' record that this
2: 8 of the feast. And they b' it.
5:33 and he b' witness unto the truth.
12: 6 had the bag, and b' what was put
17 from the dead, b' record.
19:35 he that saw it b' record, and his
Ac 15: 8 b' them witness, giving them the
1Co 15:37 body that shall be, but b' grain,
1Pe 2:24 who his own self b' our sins in his
Re 1: 2 Who b' record of the word of God,
22: 2 which b' twelve manner of fruits,

barefoot
2Sa 15:30 head covered, and he went b':
Isa 20: 2 he did so, walking naked and b'.
3 Isaiah hath walked naked and b'
4 young and old, naked and b',

barest
1Ki 2:26 because thou b' the ark of the
Isa 63:19 thou never b' rule over them:
Joh 3:26 to whom thou b' witness, behold,

Barhumite (*bar'-hu-mite*) See also BAHARUMITE.
2Sa 23:31 Azmaveth the B',

Bariah (*ba-ri'-ah*)
1Ch 3:22 Hattush, and Igeal, and B', and

Bar-jesus (*bar-je'-sus*) See also ELYMAS.
Ac 13: 6 a Jew, whose name was B':

Bar-jona (*bar-jo'-nah*) See also SIMON.
M't 16:17 Blessed art thou, Simon B':

bark See also BARKED.
Isa 56:10 all dumb dogs, they cannot b';

barked
Joe 1: 7 and b' my fig tree: he hath

Barkos (*bar'-cos*)
Ezr 2:53 The children of B', the children
Ne 7:55 The children of B',

barley
Ex 9:31 the flax and the b' was smitten:
31 for the b' was in the ear,
Le 27:16 an homer of b' seed shall be valued
Nu 5:15 tenth part of an ephah of b' meal;
De 8: 8 A land of wheat, and b', and vines,
J'g 7:13 and, lo, a cake of b' bread tumbled
Ru 1:22 in the beginning of b' harvest.
2:17 and it was about an ephah of b'.
23 to glean unto the end of b' harvest
3: 2 he winnoweth b' to-night in the
15 he measured six measures of b'.
17 six measures of b' gave he me;
2Sa 14:30 he hath b' there; go and set it on
17:28 wheat, and b', and flour
21: 9 beginning of b' harvest.
1Ki 4:28 B' also and straw for the horses
2Ki 4:42 twenty loaves of b', and full ears
7: 1 two measures of b' for a shekel,
16 two measures of b' for a shekel,
18 saying, Two measures of b' for a
1Ch 11:13 parcel of ground full of b';
2Ch 2:10 twenty thousand measures of b',
15 and the b', the oil, and the wine,
27: 5 of wheat, and ten thousand of b'.
Job 31:40 cockle instead of b'. The words
Isa 28:25 and the appointed b' and the rie
Jer 41: 8 of wheat, and of b', and of oil.
Eze 4: 9 unto thee wheat, and b', and beans,
12 thou shalt eat it as b' cakes,
Eze 13:19 for handfuls of b', and for pieces
45:13 part of an ephah of an homer of b':
Ho 3: 2 and for an homer of b',
2 and an half homer of b':
Joe 1:11 for the wheat and for the b';
Joh 6: 9 which hath five b' loaves and two
13 the fragments of the five b' loaves,
Re 6: 6 three measures of b' for a penny;

barn See also BARNFLOOR; BARNS.
Job 39:12 seed, and gather it into thy b'?
Hag 2:19 Is the seed yet in the b'?
M't 13:30 but gather the wheat into my b'.
Lu 12:24 neither have storehouse nor b';

Barnabas (*bar'-na-bas*) See also JOSES.
Ac 4:36 by the apostles was surnamed B',
9:27 But B' took him and brought him
11:22 and they sent forth B', that he
25 Then departed B' to Tarsus,
30 it to the elders by the hands of B'
12:25 And B' and Saul returned from
13: 1 as B', and Simeon that was called
2 Separate me B' and Saul for the
7 called for B' and Saul, and desired
43 proselytes followed Paul and B':
46 Then Paul and B' waxed bold,
50 persecution against Paul and B',
14:12 And they called B', Jupiter;
14 when the apostles, B' and Paul,
20 he departed with B' to Derbe.
15: 2 When therefore Paul and B' had
2 they determined that Paul and B',
12 and gave audience to B' and Paul,
22 to Antioch with Paul and B';
25 with our beloved B' and Paul,
35 also and B' continued in Antioch,
36 some days after, Paul said unto B',
37 B' determined to take with them
39 and so B' took Mark, and sailed
1Co 9: 6 Or I only and B', have not we
Ga 2: 1 up again to Jerusalem with B',
9 gave to me and B' the right hands
13 that B' also was carried away
Co 4:10 and Marcus, sister's son to B',

Barnea See KADESH-BARNEA.

barnfloor
2Ki 6:27 the b', or out of the winepress?

barns
Pr 3:10 shall thy b' be filled with plenty,
Joe 1:17 the b' are broken down;
M't 6:26 do they reap, nor gather into b';
Lu 12:18 I will pull down my b', and build

barrel See also BARRELS.
1Ki 17:12 a handful of meal in a b', and a
14 The b' of meal shall not waste,
16 the barrel of meal wasted not,

barrels
1Ki 18:33 Fill four b' with water, and pour

barren
Ge 11:30 Sarai was b'; she had no child.
25:21 for his wife, because she was b':
29:31 but Rachel was b'.
Ex 23:26 nothing cast their young, nor be b',
De 7:14 shall not be male or female b'
J'g 13: 2 his wife was b', and bare not.
3 Behold now, thou art b',
1Sa 2: 5 so that the b' hath born seven;
2Ki 2:19 is naught, and the ground b'.
21 any more death or b' land.
Job 24:21 He evil entreateth the b' that
39: 6 and the b' land his dwellings.
Ps 113: 9 maketh the b' woman to keep
Pr 30:16 The grave; and the b' womb;
Ca 4: 2 and none is b' among them.
6: 6 there is not one b' among them.
Isa 54: 1 Sing, O b', thou that didst not
Joe 2:20 him into a land b' and desolate,
Lu 1: 7 because that Elisabeth was b',
36 month with her, who was called b'.
23:29 Blessed are the b', and the wombs
Ga 4:27 Rejoice, thou b' that bearest not;
2Pe 1: 8 neither be b' nor unfruitful in the

barrenness
Ps 107:34 A fruitful land into b', for the

bars
Ex 26:26 shalt make b' of shittim wood;
27 b' for the boards of the other side
27 b' for the boards of the side of
29 rings of gold for places for the b':
29 thou shalt overlay the b' with gold.
35:11 his b', his pillars, and his sockets;
36:31 And he made b' of shittim wood;
32 five b' for the boards of the other
32 b' for the boards of the tabernacle
34 rings of gold to be places for the b',
34 and overlaid the b' with gold.
39:33 his b', and his pillars, and his
40:18 put in the b' thereof, and reared up
Nu 3:36 and the b' thereof, and the pillars
4:31 boards of the tabernacle, and the b'
De 3: 5 with high walls, gates, and b';
1Sa 23: 7 a town that hath gates and b'.
1Ki 4:13 cities with walls and brasen b':
2Ch 8: 5 cities, with walls, gates, and b';
14: 7 walls, and towers, gates, and b'.
Ne 3: 3 locks thereof, and the b' thereof.
6 and the b' thereof.
13 and the b' thereof, and a thousand
14 and the b' thereof.
15 and the b' thereof, and the wall of
Job 17:16 shall go down to the b' of the pit,
38:10 place, and set b' and doors,
40:18 his bones are like b' of iron.

Ps 107:16 and cut the b' of iron in sunder.
147:13 strengthened the b' of thy gates;
Pr 18:19 are like the b' of a castle.
Isa 45: 2 and cut in sunder the b' of iron:
Jer 49:31 which have neither gates nor b',
51:30 dwellingplaces; her b' are broken.
La 2: 9 hath destroyed and broken her b':
Eze 38:11 having neither b' nor gates,
Jon 2: 6 the earth with her b' was about me
Na 3:13 the fire shall devour thy b'.

Barsabas (*bar'-sab-as*) See also JOSEPH; JUDAS: JUSTUS.
Ac 1:23 B', who was surnamed Justus,
15:22 namely, Judas surnamed B',

Bartholomew (*bar-thol'-o-mew*) See also NATHANAEL.
M't 10: 3 Philip, and B'; Thomas,
M'k 3:18 Philip, and B', and Matthew,
Lu 6:14 Philip and B',
Ac 1:13 Philip, and Thomas, B',

Bartimæus (*bar-ti-me'-us*)
M'k 10:46 blind B', the son of Timæus, sat

Baruch (*ba'-rook*)
Ne 3:20 After him B' the son of Zabbai
10: 6 Daniel, Ginnethon, B',
11: 5 Maaseiah the son of B', the son of
Jer 32:12 evidence of the purchase unto B'
13 And I charged B' before them,
16 evidence of the purchase unto B'
36: 4 Then Jeremiah called B' the son of
4 and B' wrote from the mouth of
5 Jeremiah commanded B', saying,
8 B' the son of Neriah did according
10 Then read B' in the book the words
13 when B' read the book in the ears
14 unto B', saying, Take in thine
14 B' the son of Neriah took the roll
15 So B' read it in their ears.
16 and said unto B', We will surely
17 they asked B', saying, Tell us now,
18 B' answered them, He pronounced
19 Then said the princes unto B', Go,
26 to take B' the scribe and Jeremiah
27 and the words which B' wrote at
32 gave it to B' the scribe, the son
43: 3 B' the son of Neriah setteth thee
6 Jeremiah the prophet, and B' the
45: 1 the prophet spake unto B'
2 the God of Israel, unto thee, O B';

Barzillai (*bar-zil'-la-i*)
2Sa 17:27 and B' the Gileadite of Rogelim,
19:31 B' the Gileadite came down from
32 Now B' was a very aged man,
33 the king said unto B', Come thou
34 B' said unto the king, How long
39 king kissed B', and blessed him;
21: 8 brought up for Adriel the son of B'
1Ki 2: 7 shew kindness unto the sons of B'
Ezr 2:61 children of Koz, the children of B';
61 took a wife of the daughters of B'
Ne 7:63 the children of B', which took
63 one of the daughters of B'

base See also ABASE; BASER; BASES; BASEST: DEBASE.
2Sa 6:22 will be b' in mine own sight:
1Ki 7:27 cubits was the length of one b',
29 upon the ledges there was a b'
30 every b' had four brasen wheels,
31 work of the b', a cubit and a
32 axletrees...were joined to the b':
34 the four corners of one b':
34 undersetters were of the very b'
35 in the top of the b' was there a
35 and on the top of the b' the ledges
Job 30: 8 yea, children of b' men:
Isa 3: 5 the b' against the honourable.
Eze 17:14 That the kingdom might be b',
29:14 they shall be there a b' kingdom.
Zec 5:11 and set there upon her own b'.
Mal 2: 9 and b' before all the people,
1Co 1:28 And b' things of the world,
2Co 10: 1 who in presence am b' among

baser
Ac 17: 5 lewd fellows of the b' sort,

bases
1Ki 7:27 And he made ten b' of brass;
28 the work of the b' was on this
37 this manner he made the ten b':
38 upon every one of the ten b' one
39 he put five b' on the right side of
43 And the ten b',
43 and ten lavers on the b';
2Ki 16:17 Ahaz cut off the borders of the b',
25:13 and the b', and the brasen sea
16 the b' which Solomon had made
2Ch 4:14 He made also b',
14 and lavers made he upon the b';
Ezr 3: 3 they set the altar upon his b';
Jer 27:19 concerning the b', and concerning
52:17 and the b', and the brasen sea
20 bulls that were under the b',

basest
Eze 29:15 shall be the b' of the kingdoms;
Da 4:17 setteth up over it the b' of men.

Bashan (*ba'-shan*) See also BASHAN-HAVOTH-JAIR.
Nu 21:33 and went up by the way of B':
33 and Og the king of B' went out
32:33 the kingdom of Og king of B',
De 1: 4 and Og the king of B', which dwelt
3: 1 up the way to B':
1 and Og the king of B' came out
De 3: 3 our hands Og also, the king of B',
4 Argob, the kingdom of Og in B'.
10 all Gilead, and all B', unto Salchah
10 cities of the kingdom of Og in B'.
11 For only Og king of B' remained
13 And the rest of Gilead, and all B',
13 all the region of Argob, with all B',
4:43 Golan in B', of the Manassites.
47 and the land of Og king of B',
29: 7 Heshbon, and Og the king of B',
32:14 and rams of the breed of B',
33:22 lion's whelp: he shall leap from B'.
Jos 9:10 and to Og king of B', which was at
12: 4 And the coast of Og king of B',
5 and in Salcah, and in all B',
13:11 and all mount Hermon, and all B'
12 All the kingdom of Og in B',
30 coast was from Mahanaim, all B',
30 all the kingdom of Og king of B',
30 the towns of Jair, which are in B',
31 cities of the kingdom of Og in B',
17: 1 therefore he had Gilead and B'.
5 besides the land of Gilead and B',
20: 8 tribe of Gad, and Golan in B' out
21: 6 half tribe of Manasseh in B',
27 of Manasseh they gave Golan in B'
22: 7 Moses had given possession in B':
1Ki 4:13 the region of Argob, which is in B',
19 Amorites, and of Og king of B';
2Ki 10:33 river Arnon, even Gilead and B'.
1Ch 5:11 them, in the land of B' unto Salcah:
12 Jaanai, and Shaphat in B'.
16 dwelt in Gilead in B', and in her
23 they increased from B' unto
6:62 the tribe of Manasseh in B',
71 Golan in B' with her suburbs,
Ne 9:22 and the land of Og king of B'.
Ps 22:12 bulls of B' have beset me round.
68:15 The hill of God is as the hill of B';
15 a high hill as the hill of B'.
22 I will bring again from B', I will
135:11 Amorites, and Og king of B',
136:20 Og the king of B': for his mercy
Isa 2:13 up, and upon all the oaks of B',
33: 9 Sharon is like a wilderness; and B'
Jer 22:20 cry; and lift up thy voice in B',
50:19 feed on Carmel and B', and his
Eze 27: 6 of B' have they made thine oars;
39:18 bullocks, all of them fatlings of B'.
Am 4: 1 Hear this word, ye kine of B', that
Mic 7:14 let them feed in B' and Gilead,
Na 1: 4 B' languisheth, and Carmel,
Zec 11: 2 howl, O ye oaks of B'; for the

Bashan-havoth-jair (*ba'''-shan-ha''-voth-ja'-ur*)
De 3:14 own name, B', unto this day.

Bashemath (*bash'-e-math*) See also BASMATH.
Ge 26:34 and B' the daughter of Elon
36: 3 B' Ishmael's daughter, sister of
4 Esau Eliphaz; and B' bare Reuel;
10 the son of B' the wife of Esau.
13 were the sons of B' Esau's wife.
17 are the sons of B' Esau's wife.

basin See BASON.

basket See also BASKETS.
Ge 40:17 And in the uppermost b' there
17 birds did eat them out of the b'
Ex 29: 3 thou shalt put them into one b',
3 and bring them in the b',
23 wafer out of the b' of unleavened
32 and the bread that is in the b',
Le 8: 2 and a b' of unleavened bread;
26 out of the b' of unleavened bread,
31 that is in the b' of consecrations,
Nu 6:15 And a b' of unleavened bread,
17 with the b' of unleavened bread:
19 one unleavened cake out of the b',
De 26: 2 shalt put it in a b', and shalt go
4 the priest shall take the b' out of
28: 5 Blessed shall be thy b' and thy
17 Cursed shall be thy b' and thy
J'g 6:19 the flesh he put in a b', and he
Jer 24: 2 One b' had very good figs,
2 other b' had very naughty figs,
Am 8: 1 behold a b' of summer fruit.
2 And I said, A b' of summer fruit.
Ac 9:25 let him down by the wall in a b'.
2Co 11:33 in a b' was I let down by the wall,

baskets
Ge 40:16 I had three white b' on my head:
18 The three b' are three days:
2Ki 10: 7 put their heads in b', and sent
Jer 6: 9 as a grapegatherer into the b'.
24: 1 two b' of figs were set before the
M't 14:20 that remained twelve b' full.
15:37 meat that was left seven b' full.
16: 9 and how many b' ye took up?
10 and how many b' ye took up?
M'r 6:43 twelve b' full of the fragments,
8: 8 meat that was left seven b'.
19 how many b' full of fragments
20 how many b' full of fragments
Lu 9:17 remained to them twelve b'.
Joh 6:13 and filled twelve b' with the

Basmath (*bas'-math*) See also BASHEMATH.
1Ki 4:15 took B' the daughter of Solomon

bason See also BASONS.
Ex 12:22 in the blood that is in the b',
22 with the blood that is in the b';
1Ch 28:17 gave gold by weight for every b';
17 silver by weight for every b' of
Joh 13: 5 that he poureth water into a b',

basons
Ex 24: 6 half of the blood, and put it in b';
Ex 27: 3 ashes, and his shovels, and his b',
38: 3 the shovels, and the b', and the
Nu 4:14 the shovels, and the b', all the
2Sa 17:28 beds, and b', and earthen vessels,
1Ki 7:40 the shovels, and the b'. So Hiram
45 and the b': and all these vessels,
50 the snuffers, and the b', and the
2Ki 12:13 bowls of silver, snuffers, b',
1Ch 28:17 for the golden b' he gave gold by
2Ch 4: 8 he made an hundred b' of gold.
11 pots, and the shovels, and the b'.
22 the snuffers, and the b', and the
Ezr 1:10 Thirty b' of gold,
10 silver b' of a second sort
8:27 Also twenty b' of gold, of a
Ne 7:70 thousand drams of gold, fifty b',
Jer 52:19 the b', and the firepans, and the

bastard See also BASTARDS.
De 23: 2 A b' shall not enter into the
Zec 9: 6 and a b' shall dwell in Ashdod,

bastards
Heb 12: 8 then are ye b', and not sons.

bat See also BATS.
Le 11:19 kind, and the lapwing, and the b'.
De 14:18 the lapwing, and the b'.

bath See also BATHS.
Isa 5:10 of vineyard shall yield one b',
Eze 45:10 a just ephah, and a just b'.
11 the b' shall be of one measure,
11 that the b' may contain
14 the b' of oil, ye shall
14 offer the tenth part of a b'

Bath See BATH-RABBIM; BATH-SHEBA; BATH-SHUA.

bathe See also BATHED.
Le 15: 5 and b' himself in water, and be
6 wash his clothes, and b' himself
7 b' himself in water, and be unclean
8 wash his clothes, and b' himself
10 b' himself in water, and be unclean
11 wash his clothes, and b' himself
13 and b' his flesh in running water,
18 shall both b' themselves in water
21 wash his clothes, and b' himself
22 b' himself in water, and be unclean
27 wash his clothes, and b' himself
16:26 b' his flesh in water, and afterward
28 clothes, and b' his flesh in water,
17:15 b' himself in water, and be unclean
16 nor b' his flesh;
Nu 19: 7 he shall b' his flesh in water,
8 b' his flesh in water, and shall be
19 clothes, and b' himself in water,

bathed
Isa 34: 5 my sword shall be b' in heaven:

Bath-rabbim (*bath-rab'-bim*)
Ca 7: 4 Heshbon, by the gate of B': thy

baths
1Ki 7:26 it contained two thousand b'.
38 one laver contained forty b':
2Ch 2:10 twenty thousand b' of wine,
10 and twenty thousand b' of oil.
4: 5 received and held three thousand b'.
Ezr 7:22 and to an hundred b' of wine,
22 and to an hundred b' of oil,
Eze 45:14 an homer of ten b';
14 for ten b' are an homer.

Bath-sheba (*bath'-she-bah*) See also BATH-SHUA.
2Sa 11: 3 one said, Is not this B', the
12:24 David comforted B' his wife,
1Ki 1:11 Nathan spake unto B' the
15 And B' went in unto the king
16 And B' bowed, and did obeisance
28 answered and said, Call me B'.
31 Then B' bowed with her face to
2:13 came to B' the mother of Solomon.
18 And B' said, Well; I will speak
19 B' therefore went unto king
Ps 51:*title* him, after he had gone in to B'.

Bath-shua (*bath'-shu-ah*) See also BATH-SHEBA.
1Ch 3: 5 Solomon, four, of B' the daughter

bats
Isa 2:20 to the moles and to the b';

battered
2Sa 20:15 b' the wall, to throw it down.

battering
Eze 4: 2 set b' rams against it
21:22 appoint b' rams against the gates,

battering-ram See BATTERING and RAM.

battle See also BATTLES.
Ge 14: 8 they joined b' with them in the
Nu 21:33 all his people, to the b' at Edrei.
31:14 which came from the b'.
21 men of war which went to the b',
27 upon them, who went out to b',
28 men of war which went out to b':
32:27 before the Lord to b', as my lord
29 man armed to b', before the Lord,
De 2: 9 neither contend with them in b':
24 and contend with him in b'.
3: 1 and all his people, to b' at Edrei.
20: 1 When thou goest out to b' against
2 ye are come nigh unto the b',
3 ye approach this day unto b'
5, 6 his house, lest he die in the b',
7 lest he die in the b', and another
29: 7 came out against us unto b',
Jos 4:13 unto b', to the plains of Jericho.
8:14 went out against Israel to b',
11:19 of Gibeon: all other they took in b'.
20 should come against Israel in b',

Jos 22:33 to go up against them in *b'*, to
J'g 8:13 the son of Joash returned from *b'*
20:14 unto Gibeah, to go out to *b'*
18 of us shall go up first to the *b'*
20 the men of Israel went out to *b'*
22 and set their *b'* again in array
23 Shall I go up again to *b'*
28 Shall I yet again go out to *b'*
34 of all Israel, and the *b'* was sore:
39 the men of Israel retired in the *b'*,
39 as in the first *b'*.
42 but the *b'* overtook them; and
1Sa 4: 1 out against the Philistines to *b'*,
2 they joined *b'*, Israel was smitten
7:10 the Philistines drew near to *b'*
13:22 So it came to pass in the day of *b'*,
14:20 themselves, and they came to the *b'*:
22 followed hard after them in the *b'*.
23 the *b'* passed over unto Beth-aven.
17: 1 together their armies to *b'*,
2 and set the *b'* in array against
8 come out to set your *b'* in array?
13 went and followed Saul to the *b'*:
13 three sons that went to the *b'*
20 the fight, and shouted for the *b'*.
21 had put the *b'* in array,
28 that thou mightest see the *b'*.
47 for the *b'* is the Lord's, and he
26:10 he shall descend into *b'*, and perish.
28: 1 thou shalt go out with me to *b'*,
29: 4 not go down with us to *b'*,
4 lest in the *b'* he be an adversary
9 He shall not go up with us to the *b'*.
30:24 part is that goeth down to the *b'*,
31: 3 the *b'* went sore against Saul,
2Sa 1: 4 the people are fled from the *b'*,
25 fallen in the midst of the *b'*!
2:17 there was a very sore *b'* that day;
3:30 brother Asahel at Gibeon in the *b'*.
10: 8 put the *b'* in array at the entering
9 Joab saw that the front of the *b'*
13 unto the *b'* against the Syrians:
11: 1 the time when kings go forth to *b'*,
15 in the forefront of the hottest *b'*,
25 make thy *b'* more strong against
17:11 go to *b'* in thine own person.
18: 6 *b'* was in the wood of Ephraim;
8 the *b'* was there scattered
19: 3 steal away when they flee in *b'*.
10 anointed over us, is dead in *b'*.
21:17 go no more out with us to *b'*,
18 that there was again a *b'* with the
19 there was again a *b'* in Gob
20 And there was yet a *b'* in Gath,
22:40 girded me with strength to *b'*:
23: 9 gathered together to *b'*, and the
1Ki 8:44 go out to *b'* against their enemy,
20:14 Who shall order the *b'*? And he
29 the seventh day the *b'* was joined:
39 went out into the midst of the *b'*;
22: 4 Wilt thou go with me to *b'*
6 I go against Ramoth-gilead to *b'*,
15 go against Ramoth-gilead to *b'*,
30 enter into the *b'*; but put thou on
30 himself, and went into the *b'*.
35 the *b'* increased that day: and the
2Ki 3: 7 go with me against Moab to *b'*?
26 the king of Moab saw that the *b'*
1Ch 5:20 they cried to God in the *b'*, and he
7:11 fit to go out for war and *b'*.
40 were apt to the war and to *b'*
10: 3 the *b'* went sore against Saul,
11:13 were gathered together to *b'*,
12: 8 men of war fit for the *b'*, that
19 Philistines against Saul to *b'*:
33 Zebulun, such as went forth to *b'*,
36 of Asher, such as went forth to *b'*,
37 of instruments of war for the *b'*,
14:15 then thou shalt go out to *b'*:
19: 7 from their cities, and came to *b'*.
9 came out, and put the *b'* in array
10 Joab saw that the *b'* was set
14 before the Syrians unto the *b'*;
17 set the *b'* in array against them.
17 David had put the *b'* in array
20: 1 the time that kings go out to *b'*,
2Ch 13: 3 Abijah set the *b'* in array with an
3 Jeroboam also set the *b'* in array
14 the *b'* was before and behind:
14:10 set the *b'* in array in the valley
18: 5 we go to Ramoth-gilead to *b'*,
14 shall we go to Ramoth-gilead to *b'*,
29 myself, and will go to the *b'*;
29 himself, and they went to the *b'*.
34 And the *b'* increased that day:
20: 1 came against Jehoshaphat to *b'*.
15 for the *b'* is not yours, but God's.
17 shall not need to fight in this *b'*:
25: 8 will go, do it, be strong for the *b'*:
13 they should not go with him to *b'*,
Job 15:24 him, as a king ready to the *b'*.
38:23 against the day of *b'* and war?
39:25 he smelleth the *b'* afar off,
41: 8 remember the *b'*, do no more.
Ps 18:39 me with strength unto the *b'*:
24: 8 mighty, the Lord mighty in *b'*.
55:18 my soul in peace from the *b'*
76: 3 shield, and the sword, and the *b'*.
78: 9 turned back in the day of *b'*.
89:43 not made him to stand in the *b'*.
140: 7 covered my head in the day of *b'*.
Pr 21:31 is prepared against the day of *b'*:
Ec 9:11 nor the *b'* to the strong, neither
Isa 9: 5 For every *b'* of the warrior is
13: 4 mustereth the host of the *b'*.
22: 2 with the sword, nor dead in *b'*.
Isa 27: 4 and thorns against me in *b'*?
28: 6 strength to them that turn the *b'*
42:25 the strength of *b'*: and it hath set
Jer 8: 6 as the horse rusheth into the *b'*.
18:21 men be slain by the sword in *b'*.
46: 3 and shield, and draw near to *b'*.
49:14 against her, and rise up to the *b'*.
50:22 A sound of *b'* is in the land,
42 like a man to the *b'*, against thee,
51:20 Thou art my *b'* axe and weapons
Eze 7:14 none goeth to the *b'*: for my
13: 5 to stand in the *b'* in the day
Da 11:20 neither in anger, nor in *b'*.
25 stirred up to *b'* with a very great
Hos 1: 7 by bow, nor by sword, nor by *b'*,
2:18 the bow and the sword and the *b'*
10: 9 *b'* in Gibeah against the children
14 spoiled Beth-arbel in the day of *b'*:
Joe 2: 5 a strong people set in *b'* array.
Am 1:14 with shouting in the day of *b'*,
Ob 1 let us rise up against her in *b'*.
Zec 9:10 and the *b'* bow shall be cut off:
10: 3 them as his goodly horse in the *b'*.
4 out of him the *b'* bow, out of him
5 down their enemies...in the *b'*:
14: 2 nations against Jerusalem to *b'*;
3 when he fought in the day of *b'*.
1Co 14: 8 shall prepare himself to the *b'*?
Rev 9: 7 horses prepared unto *b'*; and on
9 of many horses running to *b'*.
16:14 to the *b'* of that great day of God
20: 8 to gather them together to *b'*:

battle-axe See BATTLE and AX.

battle-bow See BATTLE and BOW.

battlement See also BATTLEMENTS.
De 22: 8 thou shalt make a *b'* for thy roof,

battlements
Jer 5:10 take away her *b'*; for they are

battles
1Sa 8:20 go out before us, and fight our *b'*.
18:17 and fight the Lord's *b'*. For Saul
25:28 my lord fighteth the *b'* of the Lord,
1Ch 26:27 spoils won in *b'* did they dedicate
2Ch 32: 8 and to fight our *b'*. And the people
Isa 30:32 and in *b'* of shaking will he fight

Bavai (*bav'-a-i*)
Ne 3:18 *B'* the son of Henadad, the ruler

bay
Jos 15: 2 the *b'* that looketh southward:
5 the *b'* of the sea at the uttermost
18:19 the north *b'* of the salt sea
Ps 37:35 himself like a green *b'* tree.
Zec 6: 3 fourth chariot grisled and *b'* horses.
7 And the *b'* went forth, and sought

bay-tree See BAY and TREE.

Baz See MAHER-SHALAL-HASH-BAZ.

Bazlith (*baz'-lith*) See also BAZLUTH.
Ne 7:54 the children of *B'*, the children

Bazluth (*baz'-luth*) See also BAZLITH.
Ezr 2:52 the children of *B'*, the children

bdellium (*del'-le-um*)
Ge 2:12 there is *b'* and the onyx stone.
Nu 11: 7 colour thereof as the colour of *b'*.

beacon
Isa 30:17 left as a *b'* upon the top of a

Bealiah (*be-a-li'-ah*)
1Ch 12: 5 Eluzai, and Jerimoth, and *B'*,

Bealoth (*be'-a-loth*) See also ALOTH.
Jos 15:24 Ziph, and Telem, and *B'*,

beam See also BEAMS.
J'g 16:14 went away with the pin of the *b'*,
1Sa 17: 7 of his spear was like a weaver's *b'*;
2Sa 21:19 whose spear was like a weaver's *b'*.
1Ki 7: 6 the thick *b'* were before them
2Ki 6: 2 take thence every man a *b'*, and
5 as one was felling a *b'*, the axe head
1Ch 11:23 was a spear like a weaver's *b'*:
20: 5 spear staff was like a weaver's *b'*.
Hab 2:11 *b'* out of the timber shall answer
M't 7: 3 considerest not the *b'* that is in
4 behold, a *b'* is in thine own eye?
5 cast out the *b'* out of thine own eye;
Lu 6:41 perceivest not the *b'* that is in
42 beholdest not the *b'* that is in
42 cast out first the *b'* out of thine

beams
1Ki 6: 6 that the *b'* should not be fastened
9 covered the house with *b'* and
36 stone, and a row of cedar *b'*.
7: 2 with cedar *b'* upon the pillars.
3 with cedar above upon the *b'*,
12 a row of cedar *b'*, both for the
2Ch 3: 7 the *b'*, the posts, and the walls
Ne 2: 8 give me timber to make *b'* for the
3: 3 who also laid the *b'* thereof, and
6 they laid the *b'* thereof, and set up
Ps 104: 3 Who layeth the *b'* of his chambers
Ca 1:17 The *b'* of our house are cedar,

beans
2Sa 17:28 flour, and parched corn, and *b'*,
Eze 4: 9 barley, and *b'*, and lentiles,

bear^A See also BARE; BEAREST; BEARETH; BEARING; BEARS; FORBEAR.
Ge 4:13 is greater than I can *b'*.
13: 6 the land was not able to *b'* them,
16:11 art with child, and shalt *b'* a son,
Ge 17:17 Sarah, that is ninety years old, *b'*?
19 Sarah thy wife shall *b'* thee a son
21 Sarah shall *b'* unto thee at this set
18:13 Shall I of a surety *b'* a child,
22:23 these eight Milcah did *b'* to Nahor,
30: 3 and she shall *b'* upon my knees,
36: 7 were strangers could not *b'* them
43: 9 then let me *b'* the blame forever:
44:32 then I shall *b'* the blame to my
49:15 and bowed his shoulder to *b'*,
Ex 18:22 shall *b'* the burden with thee.
20:16 Thou shalt not *b'* false witness.
25:27 places of the staves to *b'* the table.
27: 7 the two sides of the altar, to *b'* it.
28:12 and Aaron shall *b'* their names
29 And Aaron shall *b'* the names
30 and Aaron shall *b'* the judgment
38 that Aaron may *b'* the iniquity
43 that they *b'* not iniquity, and die:
30: 4 for the staves to *b'* it withal.
37: 5 the sides of the ark, to *b'* the ark.
14 for the staves to *b'* the table.
15 them with gold, to *b'* the table.
27 for the staves to *b'* it withal.
38: 7 sides of the altar, to *b'* it withal;
Le 5: 1 it, then he shall *b'* his iniquity.
17 guilty, and shall *b'* his iniquity.
7:18 eateth of it shall *b'* his iniquity.
10:17 *b'* the iniquity of the congregation,
12: 5 But if she *b'* a maid child,
16:22 And the goat shall *b'* upon him
17:16 flesh; then he shall *b'* his iniquity.
19: 8 every one that eateth it shall *b'* his
18 nor *b'* any grudge against the
20:17 nakedness; he shall *b'* his
19 they shall *b'* their iniquity.
20 they shall *b'* their sin; they shall
22: 9 lest they *b'* sin for it, and die
16 Or suffer them to *b'* the iniquity
24:15 curseth his God shall *b'* his sin.
Nu 1:50 they shall *b'* the tabernacle, and
4:15 sons of Kohath shall come to *b'* it:
25 And they shall *b'* the curtains of
5:31 this woman shall *b'* her iniquity.
7: 9 should *b'* upon their shoulders.
9:13 season, that man shall *b'* his sin.
11:14 I am not able to *b'* all this people
17 shall *b'* the burden of the people
17 that thou *b'* it not thyself alone.
14:27 how long shall I *b'* with this evil
33 years, and *b'* your whoredoms,
34 shall ye *b'* your iniquities, even
18: 1 *b'* the iniquity of the sanctuary:
1 *b'* the iniquity of your priesthood.
22 congregation, lest they *b'* sin, and
23 and they shall *b'* their iniquity:
32 ye shall *b'* no sin by reason of it,
30:15 them; then he shall *b'* her iniquity.
De 1: 9 I am not able to *b'* you myself
12 I myself alone *b'* your cumbrance,
31 as a man doth *b'* his son, in all
5:20 Neither shalt thou *b'* false witness
10: 8 to *b'* the ark of the covenant of
28:57 her children which she shall *b'*:
Jos 3: 8 command the priests that *b'* the
13 feet of the priests that *b'* the ark
4:16 the priests that *b'* the ark of the
6: 4 seven priests shall *b'* before the
6 let seven priests *b'* seven trumpets
J'g 13: 3 thou shalt conceive, and *b'* a son.
5, 7 shalt conceive, and *b'* a son;
Ru 1:12 to-night, and should also *b'* sons;
1Sa 17:34 there came a lion, and a *b'*,
36 slew both the lion and the *b'*:
37 out of the paw of the *b'*, he will
2Sa 17: 8 as a *b'* robbed of her whelps
18:19 and *b'* the king tidings, how that
20 Thou shalt not *b'* tidings this
20 thou shalt *b'* tidings another day:
20 thou shalt *b'* no tidings, because
1Ki 3:21 it was not my son, which I did *b'*.
21:10 before him, to *b'* witness against
2Ki 18:14 thou puttest on me will I *b'*.
19:30 root downward, and *b'* fruit
1Ch 5:18 men able to *b'* buckler and sword,
2Ch 2: 2 ten thousand men to *b'* burdens,
Es 1:22 every man should *b'* rule in his
Ps 75: 3 dissolved: I *b'* up the pillars of
89:50 how I do *b'* in my bosom the
91:12 shall *b'* thee up in their hands,
Pr 9:12 scornest, thou alone shalt *b'* it.
12:24 The hand of the diligent shall *b'*
17:12 Let a *b'* robbed of her whelps
18:14 but a wounded spirit who can *b'*?
28:15 roaring lion, and a ranging *b'*;
30:21 and for four which it cannot *b'*:
Ca 4: 2 whereof every one *b'* twins, and
Isa 1:14 unto me; I am weary to *b'*
7:14 virgin shall conceive, and *b'* a son,
11: 7 the cow and the *b'* shall feed;
37:31 downward, and *b'* fruit upward:
46: 4 I have made, and I will *b'*;
7 They *b'* him upon the shoulder,
52:11 ye clean, that *b'* the vessels of the
53:11 for he shall *b'* their iniquities.
Jer 5:31 the priests *b'* rule
10:19 this is a grief, and I must *b'* it.
17:21 *b'* no burden on the sabbath day,
27 not to *b'* a burden, even entering
29: 6 they may *b'* sons and daughters;
31:19 I did *b'* the reproach of my youth.
44:22 that the Lord could no longer *b'*.
La 3:10 He was unto me as a *b'* lying in
27 good for a man that he *b'* the yoke
Eze 4: 4 upon it thou shalt *b'* their iniquity.
5 so shalt thou *b'* the iniquity of the

Eze 4: 6 thou shalt b' the iniquity of the
12: 6 In their sight shalt thou b' it upon
12 prince that is among them shall b'
14:10 And they shall b' the punishment
16:52 b' thine own shame for thy sins
52 confounded also, and b' thy shame,
54 thou mayest b' thine own shame,
17: 8 and that it might b' fruit,
23 bring forth boughs, and b' fruit,
18:19 doth not the son b' the iniquity
20 The son shall not b' the iniquity
20 neither shall the father b'
23:35 b' thou also thy lewdness and thy
49 ye shall b' the sins of your idols:
32:30 b' their shame with them that go
34:29 neither b' the shame of the
36: 7 they shall b' their shame.
15 neither shalt thou b' the reproach
44:10 they shall even b' their iniquity.
12 and they shall b' their iniquity.
13 and they shall b' their shame,
46:20 they b' them not out into the
Da 2:39 which shall b' rule over all the
7: 5 beast, a second, like to a b',
Ho 9:16 dried up, they shall b' no fruit:
13: 8 I will meet them as a b' that is
Am 5:19 from a lion, and a b' met him;
7:10 land is not able to b' all his words.
Mic 6:16 ye shall b' the reproach of my
7: 9 I will b' the indignation of the
Zep 1:11 they that b' silver are cut off.
Hag 2:12 If one b' holy flesh in the skirt
Zec 5:10 Whither do these b' the ephah?
6:13 he shall b' the glory, and sit and
M't 3:11 whose shoes I am not worthy to b':
4: 6 their hands they shall b' thee up,
19:18 Thou shalt not b' false witness,
27:32 him they compelled to b' his cross.
M'r 10:19 Do not b' false witness, Defraud
15:21 Alexander and Rufus, to b' his
Lu 1:13 wife Elisabeth shall b' thee a son,
4:11 their hands they shall b' thee up,
11:48 Truly ye b' witness that ye allow
13: 9 And if it b' fruit, well: and if not,
14:27 whosoever doth not b' his cross,
18: 7 though he b' long with them?
20 Do not b' false witness, Honour
23:26 that he might b' it after Jesus.
Joh 1: 7 to b' witness of the Light, that all
8 to b' witness of that Light.
2: 8 b' unto the governor of the feast.
3:28 yourselves b' me witness, that I
5:31 If I b' witness of myself, my witness
36 works that I do, b' witness of me,
8:14 Though I b' record of myself,
18 I am one that b' witness of myself,
10:25 Father's name, they b' witness of
15: 4 the branch cannot b' fruit of itself,
8 that ye b' much fruit; so shall ye
27 ye also shall b' witness, because
16:12 but ye cannot b' them now.
18:23 b' witness of the evil: but if well,
37 I should b' witness unto the truth.
Ac 9:15 to b' my name before the Gentiles,
15:10 our fathers nor we were able to b'?
18:14 would that I should b' with you:
22: 5 doth b' me witness, and all the
23:11 must thou b' witness also at Rome.
27:15 could not b' up in the wind,
Ro 10: 2 For I b' them record that they
13: 9 Thou shalt not b' false witness,
15: 1 to b' the infirmities of the weak,
1Co 3: 2 ye were not able to b' it,
10:13 that ye may be able to b' it.
15:49 also b' the image of the heavenly.
2Co 8: 3 I b' record, yea, and beyond their
11: 1 b' with me a little in my folly:
1 and indeed b' with me.
4 ye might well b' with him.
Ga 4:15 for I b' you record, that, if it had
5:10 shall b' his judgment, whosoever
6: 2 B' ye one another's burdens,
5 every man shall b' his own burden.
17 for I b' in my body the marks of
Col 4:13 For I b' him record, that he hath
1Ti 5:14 woman marry, b' children,
Heb 9:28 offered to b' the sins of many;
Jas 3:12 my brethren, b' olive berries?
1Jo 1: 2 and b' witness and shew unto you
5: 7 three that b' record in heaven,
8 three that b' witness in earth, the
3Jo 12 yea, and we also b' record;
Re 2: 2 canst not b' them which are evil:
13: 2 his feet were as the feet of a b',

beard See also BEARDS.
Le 13:29 plague upon the head or the b';
30 a leprosy upon the head or b'.
14: 9 head and his b' and his eyebrows,
19:27 thou mar the corners of thy b'.
21: 5 shave off the corner of their b',
1Sa 17:35 him by his b', and smote him
21:13 his spittle fall down upon his b'.
2Sa 19:24 his feet, nor trimmed his b',
20: 9 And Joab took Amasa by the b'
Ezr 9: 3 of my b', and sat down astonied
Ps 133: 2 that ran down upon the b',
2 even Aaron's b': that went down
Isa 7:20 and it shall also consume the b'.
15: 2 be baldness, and every b' cut off.
Jer 48:37 shall be bald and every b' clipped:
Eze 5: 1 upon thine head and upon thy b':
beards
2Sa 10: 4 shaved off the one half of their b',
5 at Jericho until your b' be grown,
1Ch 19: 5 Jericho until your b' be grown,

Jer 41: 5 b' shaven, and their clothes rent,
bearer See ARMOURBEARER; BEARERS; BEARER: STANDARDBEARER; TALEBEARER.
bearers
2Ch 2:18 of them to be b' of burdens,
34:13 they were over the b' of burdens,
Ne 4:10 of the b' of burdens is decayed,
bearest
J'g 13: 3 thou art barren and b' not:
Ps 106: 4 the favour that thou b' unto thy
Joh 8:13 Thou b' record of thyself; thy
Ro 11:18 thou b' not the root, but the root
Ga 4:27 Rejoice, thou barren that b' not;
beareth See also FORBEARETH.
Le 11:25 whosoever b' ought of the
28 he that b' the carcase of them
40 he also that b' the carcase of it
15:10 and he that b' any of those things
Nu 11:12 a nursing father b' the sucking
De 25: 6 the firstborn which she b' shall
29:18 a root that b' gall and wormwood;
23 is not sown, nor b,' nor any grass
32:11 b' them on her wings:
Job 16: 8 rising up in me b' witness
24:21 entreateth the barren that b' not:
Pr 25:18 A man that b' false witness
29: 2 but when the wicked b' rule,
Ca 6: 6 every one b' twins, and there is
Joe 2:22 tree that b' her fruit, the fig tree
M't 13:23 also b' fruit, and bringeth forth,
Joh 5:32 another that b' witness of me:
8:18 that sent me b' witness of me.
15: 2 branch in me that b' not fruit
2 branch that b' fruit, he purgeth it,
Ro 8:16 The Spirit itself b' witness with
13: 4 for he b' not the sword in vain:
1Co 13: 7 B' all things, believeth all things,
Heb 6: 8 that which b' thorns and briers
1Jo 5: 6 it is the Spirit that b' witness,
bearing See also CHILDBEARING; FORBEARING.
Ge 1:29 given you every herb b' seed,
16: 2 Lord hath restrained me from b':
29:35 his name Judah; and left b'.
30: 9 Leah saw that she had left b',
37:25 b' spicery and balm and myrrh,
Nu 10:17 set forward, b' the tabernacle.
21 set forward, b' the sanctuary:
Jos 3: 3 the priests the Levites b' it,
14 priests b' the ark of the covenant
6: 8 seven priests b' the seven trumpets
13 seven priests b' seven trumpets
1Sa 17: 7 one b' a shield went before him.
2Sa 15:24 b' the ark of the covenant of God:
Ps 126: 6 b' precious seed, shall doubtless
M'r 14:13 a man b' a pitcher of water:
Lu 22:10 meet you, b' a pitcher of water;
Joh 19:17 b' his cross went forth
Ro 2:15 conscience also b' witness, and
9: 1 conscience also b' me witness
2Co 4:10 Always b' about in the body the
Heb 2: 4 God also b' them witness both
13:13 without the camp, b' his reproach.
bears
2Ki 2:24 forth two she b' out of the wood,
Isa 59:11 We roar all like b', and mourn
beast See also BEAST'S; BEASTS.
Ge 1:24 and b' of the earth after his kind:
25 God made the b' of the earth
30 And to every b' of the earth,
2:19 God formed every b' of the field,
20 every b' of the field; but for Adam
3: 1 subtil than any b' of the field
14 above every b' of the field;
6: 7 man, and b', and the creeping
7: 2 Of every clean b' thou shalt take
14 every b' after his kind, and all the
21 of b', and of every creeping thing
8:19 Every b', every creeping thing, and
20 clean b', and of every clean fowl,
9: 2 be upon every b' of the earth,
5 hand of every b' will I require it,
10 every b' of the earth with you;
10 to every b' of the earth.
34:23 every b' of theirs be ours?
37:20 Some evil b' hath devoured him:
33 an evil b' hath devoured him;
Ex 8:17 became lice in man, and in b';
18 were lice upon man, and upon b'.
9: 9 blains upon man, and upon b',
10 blains upon man, and upon b'.
19 every man and b' which shall be
22 man, and upon b', and upon every
25 was in the field, both man and b';
11: 7 his tongue, against man or b':
12:12 land of Egypt, both man and b';
13: 2 of man and of b': it is mine.
12 cometh of a b' which thou hast;
15 of man, and the firstborn of b':
19:13 whether it be b' or man,
21:34 them; and the dead b' shall be his.
22: 5 shall put in his b', and shall feed
10 or an ox, or a sheep, or any b',
19 lieth with a b' shall surely
23:29 the b' of the field multiply against
Le 5: 2 the carcase of an unclean b',
7:21 unclean b', or any abominable
24 fat of the b' that dieth of itself
25 whosoever eateth the fat of the b',
26 or of b', in any of your dwellings.
11:26 every b' which divideth the hoof,
39 if any b', of which ye may eat, die:
47 between the b' that may be eaten
47 the b' that may not be eaten.

Le 17:13 hunteth and catcheth any b'
18:23 Neither shalt thou lie with any b'
23 shall any woman stand before a b'
20:15 And if a man lie with a b',
15 and ye shall slay the b'.
16 if a woman approach unto any b',
16 kill the woman and the b':
25 make your souls abominable by b',
24:18 that killeth a b' shall make it
18 good; b' for b'.
21 that killeth a b', he shall restore it.
25: 7 cattle, and for the b' that are
27: 9 And if it be a b', whereof men
10 if he shall at all change b' for b',
11 if it be any unclean b', of which
11 present the b' before the priest:
27 if it be an unclean b',
28 of man and b', and of the field
Nu 3:13 firstborn in Israel, both man and b':
8:17 Israel are mine, both man and b':
31:26 man and of b', thou, and Eleazar
47 of man and of b', and gave them
De 4:17 likeness of any b'...on the earth,
14: 6 And every b' that parteth the hoof,
27:21 that lieth with any manner of b'.
J'g 20:48 the men of every city, as the b',
2Ki 14: 9 passed by a wild b' that was in
2Ch 25:18 passed by a wild b' that was in
Ne 2:12 neither was there any b' with me,
12 save the b' that I rode upon.
14 for the b' that was under me to pass.
Job 39:15 that the wild b' may break them.
Ps 36: 6 thou preservest man and b'.
50:10 every b' of the forest is mine,
73:22 I was as a b' before thee.
80:13 wild b' of the field doth devour it.
104:11 give drink to every b' of the field:
135: 8 of Egypt, both of man and b'.
147: 9 He giveth to the b' his food,
Pr 12:10 regardeth the life of his b':
Ec 3:19 hath no preeminence above a b':
21 the spirit of the b' that goeth
Isa 35: 9 nor any ravenous b' shall go up
43:20 The b' of the field shall honour
46: 1 they are a burden to the weary b'.
63:14 As a b' goeth down into the valley,
Jer 7:20 upon man, and upon b', and upon
9:10 the fowl of the heavens and the b'
21: 6 of this city, both man and b':
27: 5 the b' that are upon the ground,
31:27 of man, and with the seed of b'.
32:43 desolate without man or b';
33:10 without man and without b',
10 without inhabitant, and without b',
12 without man and without b',
36:29 to cease from thence man and b'?
50: 3 shall depart, both man and b'.
51:62 neither man nor b', but that it shall
Eze 14:13 will cut off man and b' from it:
17 so that I cut off man and b'
19 to cut off from it man and b':
21 the famine, and the noisome b',
21 to cut off from it man and b'?
25:13 and will cut off man and b'
29: 8 cut off man and b' out of thee.
11 nor foot of b' shall pass through it.
34: 8 meat to every b' of the field,
28 neither shall the b' of the land
36:11 multiply upon you man and b';
39:17 to every b' of the field, Assemble
44:31 or torn, whether it be fowl or b'.
Da 7: 5 And behold another b', a second,
6 the b' had also four heads;
7 behold a fourth b', dreadful and
11 I beheld even till the b' was slain,
19 know the truth of the fourth b',
23 The fourth b' shall be the fourth
Ho 13: 8 the wild b' shall tear them.
Jon 3: 7 Let neither man nor b', herd nor
8 But let man and b' be covered
Mic 1:13 bind the chariot to the swift b':
Zep 1: 3 I will consume man and b';
Zec 8:10 no hire for man, nor any hire for b';
Lu 10:34 and set him on his own b', and
Ac 28: 4 the venomous b' hang on his hand,
5 shook off the beast into the fire.
Heb 12:20 And if so much as a b' touch the
Re 4: 7 the first b' was like a lion,
7 and the second b' like a calf,
7 third b' had a face as a man
7 and the fourth b' was like a
6: 3 I heard the second b' say,
5 I heard the third b' say, Come
7 the voice of the fourth b' say,
11: 7 the b' that ascendeth out of the
13: 1 saw a beast rise up out of the sea,
2 the b' which I saw was like
3 the world wondered after the b'.
4 power unto the b': and they
4 worshipped the b', saying,
4 Who is like unto the b'?
11 I beheld another b' coming up
12 all the power of the first b' before
12 therein to worship the first b',
14 to do in the sight of the b';
14 should make an image to the b',
15 unto the image of the b', that the
15 image of the b' should both speak,
15 worship the image of the b'
17 or the name of the b', or the
18 count the number of the b':
14: 9 If any man worship the b' and his
11 who worship the b' and his image
15: 2 the victory over the b', and over
16: 2 the mark of the b', and upon them
10 his vial upon the seat of the b':

Re 16:13 and out of the mouth of the b'.
17: 3 upon a scarlet coloured b',
7 of the b' that carrieth her, which
8 The b' that thou sawest was
8 the b' that was, and is not,
11 And the b' that was and is not,
12 as kings one hour with the b'.
13 power and strength unto the b'.
16 which thou sawest upon the b',
17 give their kingdom unto the b',
19:19 And I saw the b', and the kings
20 And the b' was taken,
20 had received the mark of the b',
20: 4 had not worshipped the b',
10 where the b' and the false prophet

beast's
Da 4:16 and let a b' heart be given unto

beasts
Ge 7: 2 of b' that are not clean by two,
8 Of clean b', and of b' that are not
31:39 That which was torn of b' I
36: 6 and all his b', and all his
45:17 lade your b', and go, get you
Ex 11: 5 and all the firstborn of b'.
22:31 flesh that is torn of b' in the field:
23:11 what they leave the b' of the field
Le 7:24 fat of that which is torn with b',
11: 2 These are the b' which ye shall
2 among all the b' that are on
3 cheweth the cud, among the b',
27 among all manner of b' that go
46 This is the law of the b', and of
17:15 or that which was torn with b',
20:25 between clean b' and unclean,
22: 8 or is torn with b', he shall not eat
26: 6 I will rid evil b' out of the land,
22 I will also send wild b' among
27:26 Only the firstling of the b',
Nu 18:15 whether it be of men or b',
15 the firstling of unclean b' shalt
20: 8 congregation and their b' drink.
11 drank, and their beasts also.
31:11 prey, both of men and of b'.
30 of all manner of b' and give
35: 3 their goods, and for all their b'.
De 7:22 lest the b' of the field increase
14: 4 These are the b' which ye shall
6 cheweth the cud among the b',
28:26 and unto the b' of the earth,
32:24 I will also send the teeth of b' upon
1Sa 17:44 of the air, and to the b' of the field.
46 and to the wild b' of the earth;
2Sa 21:10 nor the b' of the field by night.
1Ki 4:33 he spake also of b', and of fowl,
18: 5 that we lose not all the b'.
2Ki 3:17 and your cattle, and your b'.
2Ch 32:28 stalls for all manner of b',
Ezr 1: 4 with goods, and with b', beside
6 with goods, and with b', and with
Job 5:22 shalt thou be afraid of the b' of
23 and the b' of the field shall be at
12: 7 But ask now the b', and they shall
18: 3 Wherefore are we counted as b',
35:11 teacheth us more than the b' of
37: 8 Then the b' go into dens, and
40:20 where all the b' of the field play.
Ps 8: 7 oxen, yea, and the b' of the field;
49:12 he is like the b' that perish.
20 is like the b' that perish.
50:11 the wild b' of the field are mine.
79: 2 saints unto the b' of the earth.
104:20 all the b' of the forest do creep
25 both small and great b'.
148:10 B', and all cattle; creeping things,
Pr 9: 2 She hath killed her b'; she hath
30:30 lion which is strongest among b',
Ec 3:18 see that they themselves are b'.
19 the sons of men befalleth b';
Isa 1:11 the fat of fed b'; and I delight
13:21 wild b' of the desert shall lie
22 wild b' of the islands shall cry
18: 6 and to the b' of the earth:
6 the b' of the earth shall winter
30: 6 The burden of the beasts of the
34:14 The wild b' of the desert shall
14 with the wild b' of the island,
40:16 nor the b' thereof sufficient for a
46: 1 their idols were upon the b',
56: 9 ye b' of the field, come to devour,
9 all ye b' in the forest.
66:20 upon mules, and upon swift b',
Jer 7:33 and for the b' of the earth;
12: 4 the b' are consumed, and the birds;
9 assemble all the b' of the field,
15: 3 the b' of the earth, to devour
16: 4 and for the b' of the earth.
19: 7 for the b' of the earth.
27: 6 the b' of the field have I given him
28:14 given him the b' of the field also.
34:20 heaven, and to the b' of the earth.
50:39 Therefore the wild b' of the
39 with the wild b' of the islands
Eze 5:17 send upon you famine and evil b',
8:10 and abominable b', and all the
14:15 cause noisome b' to pass through
15 pass through because of the b':
29: 5 for meat to the b' of the field
31: 6 under his branches did all the b' of
13 all the b' of the field shall be upon
32: 4 I will fill the b' of the whole earth
13 destroy also all the b' thereof
13 nor the hoofs of b' trouble them.
33:27 will I give to the b' to be devoured,
34: 5 became meat to all the b' of the
25 the evil b' to cease out of the land:
Eze 38:20 and the b' of the field, and all
39: 4 and to the b' of the field, to be
Da 2:38 the b' of the field and the fowls
4:12 the b' of the field had shadow
14 let the b' get away from under it,
15 let his portion be with the b'
21 under which the b' of the field dwelt,
23 let his portion be with the b' of
25 dwelling shall be with the b' of the
32 shall be with the b' of the field:
5:21 his heart was made like the b',
7: 3 four great b' came up from the sea,
7 from all the b' that were before it;
12 concerning the rest of the b',
17 These great b', which are four,
8: 4 no b' might stand before him,
Ho 2:12 the b' of the field shall eat them.
18 a covenant for them with the b' of
4: 3 with the b' of the field, and with
Joe 1:18 How do the b' groan! the herds of
20 The b' of the field cry also
2:22 Be not afraid, ye b' of the field:
Am 5:22 the peace offerings of your fat b'.
Mic 5: 8 a lion among the b' of the forest,
Hab 2:17 the spoil of b', which made them
Zep 2:14 of her, all the b' of the nations:
15 a place for b' to lie down in!
Zec 14:15 all the b' that shall be in these
M'k 1:13 was with the wild b'; and the
Ac 7:42 have ye offered to me slain b'
10:12 all manner of fourfooted b'
12 of the earth, and wild b',
11: 6 and saw fourfooted b' of the earth,
6 and wild b', and creeping things,
23:24 And provide them b', that they
Ro 1:23 fourfooted b', and creeping things.
1Co 15:32 I have fought with b' at Ephesus,
39 another flesh of b', another of
Tit 1:12 alway liars, evil b', slow bellies.
Heb 13:11 of those b', whose blood is brought
Jas 3: 7 Every kind of b', and of birds,
2Pe 2:12 as natural brute b', made to be
Jude 10 they know naturally, as brute b',
Re 4: 6 were four b' full of eyes
8 And the four b' had each of them
9 those b' give glory and honour
5: 6 of the throne and of the four b',
8 the four b' and four and twenty
11 round about the throne and the b',
14 And the four b' said, Amen.
6: 1 one of the four b' saying, Come
6 voice in the midst of the four b'
8 death, and with the b' of the earth.
7:11 about the elders and the four b',
14: 3 before the four b', and the elders:
15: 7 one of the four b' gave unto the
18:13 and b', and sheep, and horses,
19: 4 elders and the four b' fell down

beat See also BEATEN; BEATEST; BEATETH; BEATING.
Ex 30:36 shalt b' some of it very small,
39: 3 did b' the gold into thin plates,
Nu 11: 8 it in mills, or b' it in a mortar,
De 25: 3 and b' him above these with
J'g 8:17 he b' down the tower of Penuel,
9:45 and b' down the city, and sowed
19:22 b' at the door, and spake to the
Ru 2:17 and b' out that she had gleaned:
2Sa 22:43 Then did I b' them as small as
2Ki 3:25 they b' down the cities, and on
13:25 Three times did Joash b' him,
23:12 did the king b' down, and brake
Ps 18:42 did I b' them small as the dust
89:23 b' down his foes before his face,
Pr 23:14 Thou shalt b' him with the rod,
Isa 2: 4 b' their swords into plowshares,
3:15 ye b' my people to pieces, and
27:12 Lord shall b' off from the channel
41:15 and b' them small, and shalt make
Joe 3:10 B' your plowshares into swords,
Jon 4: 8 the sun b' upon the head of Jonah,
Mic 4: 3 b' their swords into plowshares,
13 shalt b' in pieces many people:
M't 7:25 winds blew, and b' upon that
27 b' upon that house; and it fell:
21:35 took his servants, and b' one,
M'k 4:37 and the waves b' into the ship,
12: 3 they caught him, and b' him,
Lu 6:48 stream b' vehemently upon that
49 against which the stream did b'
12:45 shall begin to b' the menservants
20:10 the husbandmen b' him, and
11 servant: and they b' him also,
Ac 16:22 and commanded to b' them.
18:17 b' him before the judgment seat.
22:19 and b' in every synagogue

beaten
Ex 5:14 had set over them, were b',
16 and, behold, thy servants are b';
Ex 25:18 of b' work shalt thou make them,
31 of b' work shall the candlestick
36 one b' work of pure gold.
27:20 pure oil olive b' for the light,
29:40 fourth part of an hin of b' oil;
37: 7 of gold, b' out of one piece
17 b' work made he the candlestick;
22 it was one b' work of pure gold.
Le 2:14 even corn b' out of full ears.
16 of the b' corn thereof, and part
16:12 full of sweet incense b' small,
24: 2 pure oil olive b' for the light,
Nu 8: 4 the candlestick was of b' gold,
4 the flowers thereof, was b' work:
28: 5 fourth part of an hin of b' oil.
De 25: 2 the wicked man be worthy to be b',
De 25: 2 and to be b' before his face,
Jos 8:15 made as if they were b' before
2Sa 2:17 and Abner was b', and the men
1Ki 10:16 two hundred targets of b' gold:
17 three hundred shields of b' gold;
2Ch 2:10 measures of b' wheat,
9:15 two hundred targets of b' gold:
15 hundred shekels of b' gold
16 three hundred shields made he of b'
34: 7 b' the graven images into powder,
Pr 23:35 they have b' me, and I felt it not:
Isa 27: 9 chalkstones that are b' in sunder,
28:27 the fitches are b' out with a staff,
30:31 shall the Assyrian be b' down,
Jer 46: 5 and their mighty ones are b' down,
Mic 1: 7 images thereof shall be b' to pieces,
M'r 13: 9 in the synagogues ye shall be b':
Lu 12:47 shall be b' with many stripes.
48 shall be b' with few stripes.
Ac 5:40 called the apostles, and b' them,
16:37 have b' us openly uncondemned
2Co 11:25 Thrice was I b' with rods, once

beatest
De 24:20 When thou b' thine olive tree,
Pr 23:13 if thou b' him with the rod,

beateth
1Co 9:26 not as one that b' the air:

beating
1Sa 14:16 went on b' down one another.
M'r 12: 5 others; b' some, and killing some.
Ac 21:32 the soldiers, they left b' of Paul.

beauties
Ps 110: 3 in the b' of holiness from the

beautiful
Ge 29:17 Rachel was b' and well
De 21:11 among the captives a b' woman,
1Sa 16:12 withal of a b' countenance,
25: 3 and of a b' countenance:
2Sa 11: 2 was very b' to look upon.
Es 2: 7 the maid was fair and b';
Ps 48: 2 B' for situation, the joy of the
Ec 3:11 made every thing b' in his time:
Ca 6: 4 Thou art b', O my love,
7: 1 How b' are thy feet with shoes,
Isa 4: 2 shall the branch of the Lord be b'
52: 1 put on thy b' garments, O
7 How b' upon the mountains are
64:11 Our holy and our b' house,
Jer 13:20 was given thee, thy b' flock?
48:17 strong staff broken, and the b' rod!
Eze 16:12 a b' crown upon thine head.
13 thou wast exceeding b', and thou
23:42 b' crowns upon their heads.
M't 23:27 which indeed appear b' outward,
Ac 3: 2 the temple which is called B',
10 sat for alms at the B' gate
Ro 10:15 How b' are the feet of them that

beautify
Ezr 7:27 to b' the house of the Lord
Ps 149: 4 he will b' the meek with salvation.
Isa 60:13 to b' the place of my sanctuary;

beauty See also BEAUTIES.
Ex 28: 2 thy brother, for glory and for b'.
40 for them, for glory and for b'.
2Sa 1:19 The b' of Israel is slain upon thy
14:25 praised as Absalom for his b':
1Ch 16:29 the Lord in the b' of holiness.
2Ch 3: 6 house with precious stones for b':
20:21 should praise the b' of holiness,
Es 1:11 the people and the princes her b':
Job 40:10 array thyself with glory and b'.
Ps 27: 4 to behold the b' of the Lord,
29: 2 the Lord in the b' of holiness.
39:11 makest his b' to consume away
45:11 the king greatly desire thy b':
49:14 and their b' shall consume in the
50: 2 out of Zion, the perfection of b',
90:17 let the b' of the Lord our God
96: 6 and b' are in his sanctuary.
9 the Lord in the b' of holiness:
Pr 6:25 Lust not after her b' in thine
20:29 b' of old men is the gray head.
31:30 Favour is deceitful, and b' is vain:
Isa 3:24 burning instead of b'.
13:19 the b' of the Chaldees' excellency,
28: 1 glorious b' is a fading flower,
4 glorious b', which is on the head
5 of glory, and for a diadem of b',
33:17 eyes shall see the king in his b':
44:13 according to the b' of a man;
53: 2 no b' that we should desire him.
61: 3 to give unto them b' for ashes,
La 1: 6 her b' is departed: her princes
2: 1 the b' of Israel, and remembered
15 the perfection of b', The joy of
Eze 7:20 As for the b' of his ornament,
16:14 among the heathen for thy b':
15 thou didst trust in thine own b',
25 hast made thy b' to be abhorred,
27: 3 thou hast said, I am of perfect b'.
4 thy builders have perfected thy b'.
11 they have made thy b' perfect.
28: 7 against the b' of thy wisdom,
12 full of wisdom, and perfect in b'.
17 was lifted up because of thy b',
31: 8 God was like unto him in his b'.
32:19 Whom dost thou pass in b'?
Ho 14: 6 his b' shall be as the olive tree,
Zec 9:17 goodness, how great is his b'!
11: 7 the one I called B', and the other
10 I took my staff, even B', and cut

Bebai (*beb'-a-i*)
Ezr 2:11 The children of B', six hundred

Ezr 8:11 And of the sons of B';
11 Zechariah the son of B',
10:28 the sons also of B'; Jehohanan,
Ne 7:16 The children of B', six hundred
10:15 Bunni, Azgad, B',

became^ See also BECAMEST.
Ge 2: 7 of life; and man b' a living soul.
10 parted, and b' into four heads.
6: 4 the same b' mighty men which
19:26 and she b' a pillar of salt.
20:12 my mother; and she b' my wife.
24:67 Rebekah, and she b' his wife;
26:13 and grew until he b' very great:
44:32 thy servant b' surety for the lad
47:20 them: so the land b' Pharaoh's.
26 only, which b' not Pharaoh's.
49:15 and b' a servant unto tribute.
Ex 2:10 daughter, and he b' her son.
4: 3 it b' a serpent; and Moses fled
4 and it b' a rod in his hand:
7:10 his servants, and it b' a serpent.
12 his rod, and they b' serpents:
8:17 it b' lice in man, and in beast;
17 all the dust of the land b' lice
9:10 and it b' a boil breaking forth
24 land of Egypt since it b' a nation.
36:13 so it b' one tabernacle.
Nu 12:10 Miriam b' leprous, white as
26:10 and fifty men: and they b' a sign.
De 26: 5 b' there a nation, great, mighty,
Jos 7: 5 hearts of the people melted, and b'
14:14 therefore b' the inheritance
24:32 and it b' the inheritance of the
J'g 1:30 among them, and b' tributaries.
33 and of Beth-anath b' tributaries
35 so that they b' tributaries.
8:27 thing b' a snare unto Gideon,
15:14 b' as flax that was burnt with fire,
17: 5 one of his sons, who b' his priest.
12 and the young man b' his priest,
Ru 4:16 laid it in her bosom, and b' nurse
1Sa 10:12 b' a proverb, Is Saul also among
16:21 and he b' his armourbearer.
18:29 b' David's enemy continually.
22: 2 and he b' a captain over them:
25:37 and he b' as a stone.
42 messengers of David, and b'
2Sa 2:25 and b' one troop, and stood on
4: 4 he fell, and b' lame. And his
8: 2 the Moabites b' David's servants,
6 the Syrians b' servants to David,
14 they of Edom b' David's servants.
11:27 she b' his wife, and bare him a son.
1Ki 11:24 and b' captain over a band, when
12:30 And this thing b' a sin: for the
13: 6 again, and b' as it was before.
33 and he b' one of the priests of the
34 this thing b' sin unto the house
2Ki 17: 3 and Hoshea b' his servant,
15 and b' vain, and went after
24: 1 and Jehoiakim b' his servant
1Ch 18: 2 the Moabites b' David's servants,
6 the Syrians b' David's servants,
13 the Edomites b' David's servants.
19:19 with David, and b' his servants:
2Ch 27: 6 So Jotham b' mighty, because he
Ne 9:25 and were filled, and b' fat,
Es 8:17 people of the land b' Jews;
Ps 69:11 my garment; and I b' a proverb
83:10 perished at Endor: they b' as dung
109:25 I b' also a reproach unto them:
Jer 51:30 they b' as women: they have
Eze 17: 6 b' a spreading vine of low stature,
6 b' a vine, and brought forth
19: 3 whelps: it b' a young lion,
6 he b' a young lion, and learned
23:10 she b' famous among women;
31: 5 and his branches b' long because
34: 5 they b' meat to all the beasts
8 b' a prey, and my flock b'
36: 4 are forsaken, which b' a prey
Da 2:35 b' like the chaff of the summer
35 image b' a great mountain,
8: 4 according to his will, and b' great.
10:15 toward the ground, and I b' dumb.
Ob 12 in the day that he b' a stranger;
M't 28: 4 keepers did shake, and b' as dead
M'r 9: 3 his raiment b' shining, exceeding
Ac 10:10 he b' very hungry, and would have
Ro 1:21 but b' vain in their imaginations,
22 to be wise, they b' fools,
6:18 b' the servants of righteousness.
1Co 9:20 unto the Jews I b' as a Jew,
22 To the weak b' I as weak,
13:11 when I b' a man, I put away
2Co 8: 9 yet for your sakes he b' poor,
Ph'p 2: 8 and b' obedient unto death, even
1Th 1: 6 ye b' followers of us, and of the
2:14 ye, brethren, b' followers of the
Heb 2:10 For it b' him, for whom are all
5: 9 b' the author of eternal salvation
7:26 an high priest b' us, who is holy,
10:33 whilst ye b' companions of them
11: 7 b' heir of the righteousness which
Re 6:12 sun b' black as sackcloth of hair,
12 and the moon b' as blood;
8: 8 third part of the sea b' blood;
11 of the waters b' wormwood;
16: 3 it b' as the blood of a dead man:
4 of waters; and they b' blood.

becamest
1Ch 17:22 and thou, Lord, b' their God.
Eze 16: 8 and thou b' mine.

because^
Ge 2: 3 b' that in it he had rested
2:23 called Woman, b' she was taken
3:10 I was afraid, b' I was naked;
14 B' thou hast done this, thou art
17 he said, B' thou hast hearkened
20 B' she was the mother of all living.
5:29 b' of the ground which the Lord
7: 7 b' of the waters of the flood.
11: 9 it is called Babel; b' the Lord did
12:13 my soul shall live b' of thee.
17 plagues b' of Sarai Abram's
16:11 his name Ishmael; b' the Lord
18:20 the Lord said, B' the cry of Sodom
20 Gomorrah is great, and b' their
19:13 destroy this place, b' the cry of
20:11 Abraham said, B' I thought,
18 b' of Sarah Abraham's wife.
21:11 Abraham's sight b' of his
12 in thy sight b' of the lad,
12 and b' of thy bondwoman;
13 make a nation, b' he is thy seed
25 reproved Abimelech b' of a
22:16 b' thou hast done this thing,
18 b' thou hast obeyed my voice.
25:21 for his wife, b' she was barren:
28 loved Esau, b' he did eat of his
26: 5 B' that Abraham obeyed my
7 for Rebekah; b' she was fair
9 B' I said, Lest I die for her.
26:20 b' they strove with him.
27:20 he said, B' the Lord thy God
23 And he discerned him not, b'
41 Esau hated Jacob b' of the
46 weary of my life b' of the
28:11 tarried there all night, b' the sun
29:15 B' thou art my brother,
33 And said, B' the Lord hath heard
34 be joined unto me, b' I have born
30:18 my hire, b' I have given my hand
20 dwell with me, b' I have born him
31:30 be gone, b' thou sore longedst
31 said to Laban, B' I was afraid:
32:32 b' he touched the hollow of Jacob's
33:11 b' God hath dealt graciously
11 and b' I have enough.
34: 7 very wroth, b' he had wrought
13 said, B' he had defiled Dinah
19 to do the thing, b' he had delight
27 spoiled the city, b' they had
35: 7 El-beth-el: b' there God appeared
36: 7 could not bear them b' of their
37: 3 b' he was the son of his old age
38:15 an harlot; b' she had covered
26 more righteous than I; b' that I
39: 9 b' thou art his wife: how then can
23 b' the Lord was with him,
41:32 b' the thing is established by God,
57 to buy corn; b' that the famine
43:18 afraid, b' they were brought
18 B' of the money that was
32 b' the Egyptians might not eat
46:30 seen thy face, b' thou art yet
47:20 sold every man his field, b' the
49: 4 b' thou wentest up to thy
Ex 1:12 were grieved b' of the children of
19 B' the Hebrew women are not as
21 b' the midwives feared God
2:10 B' I drew him out of the water
4:26 bloody husband thou art, b' of the
5:21 and judge; b' ye have made our
8:12 b' of the frogs which he had
9:11 not stand before Moses b' of the
12:39 not leavened; b' they were
13: 8 b' of that which the Lord did
14:11 said unto Moses, B' there were no
17: 7 b' of the chiding of the children
7 and b' they tempted the Lord,
16 he said, B' the Lord hath
18:15 B' the people come unto me
19:18 b' the Lord descended upon
29:33 not eat thereof, b' they are holy.
34 shall not be eaten, b' it is holy.
32:35 plagued the people, b' they
40:35 b' the cloud abode thereon,
Le 6: 4 it shall be, b' he hath sinned,
9 burnt offering, b' of the burning
10:13 b' it is thy due, and thy son's
11: 4 as the camel, b' he cheweth the
5 and the coney, b' he cheweth the
6 and the hare, b' he cheweth the
14:18 the house clean, b' the plague
15: 2 b' of his issue he is unclean
16:16 b' of the uncleanness of the
16 and b' of their transgressions
19: 8 shall bear his iniquity, b' he
20 not be put to death, b' she was not
20: 3 b' he hath given of his seed
21:23 b' he hath a blemish;
22: 7 b' it is his food
25 b' their corruption is in them
26:10 bring forth the old b' of the new.
35 it shall rest; b' it did not rest
43 b', even b' they despised my
43 judgments, and b' their soul
Nu 3:13 B' all the firstborn are mine;
6: 7 b' the consecration of his God
12 shall be lost, b' his separation
7: 9 he gave none: b' the service
9:13 b' he brought not the offering
11: 3 Taberah: b' the fire of the Lord
14 this people alone, b' it is too
20 b' that ye have despised the Lord
34 Kibroth-hattaavah: b' there they
12: 1 against Moses b' of the
13:24 b' of the cluster of grapes
14:16 B' the Lord was not able to
22 B' all those men which have
Nu 14:24 b' he had another spirit with him,
43 b' ye are turned away
15:31 B' he hath despised the word
34 put him in ward, b' it was not
19:13 b' the water of separation
20 b' he hath defiled the sanctuary
20:12 unto Moses and Aaron, B' ye
13 b' the children of Israel strove
24 b' ye rebelled against my
21: 4 much discouraged b' of the way.
22: 3 of the people, b' they were many:
3 b' of the children of Israel.
22 God's anger was kindled b' he
29 unto the ass, B' thou hast
32 b' thy way is perverse before me:
25:13 b' he was zealous for his God,
26:62 b' there was no inheritance
27: 4 his family, b' he hath no son?
30: 5 forgive her, b' her father
14 b' he held his peace at her
32:11 b' they have not wholly followed
17 b' of the inhabitants of the land.
19 b' our inheritance is fallen
35:28 B' he should have remained
De 1:27 and said, B' the Lord hated
36 b' he hath wholly followed the
2: 5 b' I have given Mount Seir
9 for a possession; b' I have given
19 any possession; b' I have given it
25 and be in anguish b' of thee.
4: 3 the Lord did b' of Baal-peor:
37 And b' he loved thy fathers,
7: 7 nor choose you, b' ye were more
8 But b' the Lord loved you,
8 b' he would keep the oath which he
8:20 b' ye would not be obedient unto
12:20 I will eat flesh, b' thy soul
13: 5 put to death; b' he hath spoken
10 that he die; b' he hath sought to
14: 8 the swine, b' it divideth the hoof,
29 the Levite, (b' he hath no part
15: 2 b' it is called the Lord's release.
10 b' that for this thing the Lord
16 b' he loveth thee and thine house,
16 b' he is well with thee;
16:15 b' the Lord thy God shall bless
18:12 and b' of these abominations
19: 6 b' the way is long, and slay him;
20: 3 neither be ye terrified b' of them:
21:14 b' thou hast humbled her.
22:19 b' he hath brought up an evil
21 b' she hath wrought folly
24 damsel, b' she cried not,
24 man, b' he hath humbled
29 his wife; b' he hath humbled
23: 4 B' they met you not
5 blessing unto thee, b' the Lord
7 b' thou wast a stranger
24: 1 no favour in his eyes, b' he hath
27:20 b' he hath uncovered his
28:20 b' of the wickedness of thy doings,
45 destroyed; b' thou hearkenedst
47 B' thou servedst not the Lord
55 b' he hath nothing left him
62 b' thou wouldst not obey
29:25 say, B' they have forsaken
31:29 b' ye will do evil in the sight
32: 3 B' I will publish the name
19 abhorred them, b' of the provoking
47 vain thing for you; b' it is your
51 B' ye trespassed against me
33:21 part for himself, b' there, in a
Jos 2: 9 inhabitants of the land faint b' of
11 more courage in any man, b' of
24 the country do faint b' of us.
5: 1 them any more, b' of the children
6 were consumed, b' they obeyed
7 b' they had not circumcised
6: 1 up b' of the children of Israel:
17 b' she hid the messengers
25 unto this day; b' she hid the
7:12 before their enemies, b' they were
15 b' he hath transgressed the
15 b' he hath wrought folly in Israel.
9: 9 thy servants are come b' of the
18 smote them not, b' the princes
20 be upon us, b' of the oath which
24 B' it was certainly told thy
24 sore afraid of our lives b' of you,
10: 2 feared greatly, b' Gibeon was a
2 b' it was greater than Ai,
42 b' the Lord God...fought for Israel
11: 6 Be not afraid b' of them:
14: 9 for ever, b' thou hast wholly
14 unto this day, b' that he wholly
17: 1 b' he was a man of war,
6 B' the daughters of Manasseh
20: 5 b' he smote his neighbour
22:31 b' ye have not committed this
23: 3 done unto all these nations b' of
J'g 1:19 b' they had chariots
2:18 b' of their groanings by reason of
20 he said, B' that this people hath
3:12 against Israel, b' they had
5:23 b' they came not to the help of the
6: 2 against Israel: and b' of the
6 impoverished, b' of the Midianites;
7 cried unto the Lord b' of the
22 for b' I have seen an angel
27 so it was, b' he feared his father's
30 he may die: b' he hath cast down
30 and b' he hath cut down the grove
31 plead for himself, b' one hath cast
32 against him, b' he hath thrown
8:20 he feared, b' he was yet a youth.
24 b' they were Ishmaelites.)

J'g 9:18 b' he is your brother;)
10:10 sinned against thee, both b' we
11:13 B' Israel took away my land,
12: 4 smote Ephraim, b' they said,
13:22 surely die, b' we have seen God.
14:17 told her, b' she lay sore upon him
15: 6 b' he had taken his wife,
18:28 no deliverer, b' it was far
20:36 b' they trusted to the liers in wait
21:15 b' that the Lord had made a breach
22 b' we reserved not to each man
1Sa 1: 6 make her fret, b' the Lord had
20 B' I have asked him of the Lord.
2: 1 b' I rejoice in thy salvation.
25 b' the Lord would slay them.
3:13 b' his sons made themselves
4:21 b' the ark of God was taken,
21 and b' of her father in law
6:19 b' they had looked into the ark
19 people lamented, b' the Lord had
8:18 b' of your king which ye shall
9:13 until he come, b' he doth bless
16 my people, b' their cry is come
10: 1 it not b' the Lord hath anointed
12:10 sinned, b' we have forsaken
22 b' it hath pleased the Lord
13:11 B' I saw that the people
14 b' thou hast not kept
14:29 enlightened, b' I tasted a little
15:23 B' thou hast rejected the word
16: 7 b' I have refused him:
17:32 no man's heart fail b' of him;
18: 3 b' he loved him as his own
12 afraid of David, b' the Lord
16 loved David, b' he went out
19: 4 b' he hath not sinned against thee,
4 and b' his works have been
20:17 swear again, b' he loved him.
18 missed, b' thy seat will be empty.
34 b' his father had done him shame.
21: 8 with me, b' the king's business
22:17 b' their hand also is with David,
17 and b' they knew when he fled,
24: 5 smote him, b' he had cut off
25:28 b' my lord fighteth the battles
26:12 all asleep; b' a deep sleep from the
16 worthy to die, b' ye have not kept
21 b' my soul was precious
28:18 b' thou obeyedst not the voice of
20 b' of the words of Samuel:
30: 6 stoning him, b' the soul of all
13 left me, b' three days agone I fell
16 b' of all the great spoil
22 said, B' they went not with us,
2Sa 1: 9 b' my life is yet whole in me.
10 slew him, b' I was sure that he
12 b' they were fallen by the sword.
2: 6 b' ye have done this thing.
3:11 a word again, b' he feared him.
30 b' he had slain their brother
6: 8 displeased, b' the Lord had
12 b' of the ark of God.
8:10 bless him, b' he had fought
10: 5 b' the men were greatly
12: 6 b' he did this thing,
6 and b' he had no pity.
10 b' thou hast despised me,
14 b' by this deed thou hast given
25 name Jedidiah, b' of the Lord.
13:22 b' he had forced his
14:15 it is b' the people have made me
26 he polled it: b' the hair was heavy
16: 8 b' thou art a bloody man.
10 let him curse, b' the Lord hath said
18:20 bear no tidings, b' the king's
19:21 b' he cursed the Lord's anointed?
26 b' thy servant is lame.
42 B' the king is near of kin
21: 1 b' he slew the Gibeonites.
7 b' of the Lord's oath
22: 8 shook, b' he was wroth.
20 delivered me, b' he delighted in
23: 6 thrust away, b' they cannot be
1Ki 1:50 Adonijah feared b' of Solomon,
2: 7 I fled b' of Absalom thy brother.
26 b' thou bearest the ark of the Lord
26 and b' thou hast been afflicted
3: 2 b' there was no house built
11 B' thou hast asked this thing,
19 died in the night; b' she overlaid
7:47 b' they were exceeding many:
8:11 stand to minister b' of the cloud:
33 b' they have sinned against thee,
35 no rain, b' they have sinned
64 b' the brasen altar that was
9: 9 B' they forsook the Lord
10: 9 B' the Lord loved Israel for ever,
11: 9 b' his heart was turned
33 B' that they have forsaken
34 b' he kept my commandments
14:13 b' in him there is found some
15 b' they have made their groves,
16 b' of the sins of Jeroboam, who
15: 5 B' David did that which was right
13 from being queen, b' she had made
30 B' of the sins of Jeroboam
16: 7 and b' he killed him.
17: 7 up, b' there had been no rain
19: 7 Arise and eat; b' the journey is too
14 b' the children of Israel have
20:28 B' the Syrians have said,
36 B' thou hast not obeyed the
42 B' thou hast let go out of thy
21: 2 garden of herbs, b' it is near
4 displeased b' of the word which
6 B' I spake unto Naboth

1Ki 23:20 found thee: b' thou hast sold
29 b' he humbleth himself
2Ki 1: 3 Is it not b' there is not a God
6 Is it not b' there is not a God in
16 is it not b' there is no God in Israel,
17 king of Judah, b' he had no son.
5: 1 honourable, b' by him the Lord
8:12 answered, B' I know the evil that
29 b' he was sick.
9:14 b' of Hazael king of Syria.
10:30 unto Jehu, B' thou hast done
13: 4 b' the king of Syria oppressed
23 b' of his covenant with Abraham,
15:16 b' they opened not to him,
17:26 slay them, b' they know not
18:12 B' they obeyed not the voice
19:28 B' thy rage against me
21:11 B' Manasseh king of Judah
15 B' they have done that
22: 7 into their hand, b' they dealt
13 kindled against us, b' our
17 B' they have forsaken me,
19 B' thine heart was tender,
23:26 against Judah, b' of all the
1Ch 1:19 Peleg; b' in his days the earth
4: 9 saying, B' I bare him with sorrow.
41 b' there was pasture there
5: 9 b' their cattle were multiplied
20 intreated of them; b' they put
22 many slain, b' the war was of God.
7:21 b' they came down to take
23 Beriah, b' it went evil with his
9:27 b' the charge was upon them,
12: 1 close b' of Saul the son of Kish:
13:10 b' he put his hand to the ark:
11 displeased, b' the Lord had made
14: 2 b' of his people Israel.
15:13 For b' ye did it not at the first,
22 b' he was skilful.
16:33 b' he cometh to judge the earth.
41 thanks to the Lord, b' his mercy
18:10 congratulate him, b' he had
19: 2 b' his father showed kindness
21: 8 b' I have done this thing:
30 b' of the sword of the angel
22: 8 unto my name, b' thou hast shed
23:28 B' their office was to wait
27:23 b' the Lord had said
24 finished not, b' there fell wrath
28: 3 b' thou hast been a man of war,
29: 3 b' I have set my affection to the
9 b' with perfect heart
2Ch 1:11 to Solomon, B' this was in
2:11 B' the Lord hath loved his people,
6:24 b' they have sinned against
26 no rain, b' they have sinned
7: 2 b' the glory of the Lord
6 praise the Lord, b' his mercy
7 peace offerings, b' the brasen
22 B' they forsook the Lord God
8:11 b' the places are holy,
9: 8 b' thy God loved Israel,
12: 2 against Jerusalem, b' they had
5 to Jerusalem b' of Shishak,
14 did evil, b' he prepared not
13:18 b' they relied upon the Lord
14: 6 b' the Lord had given him
7 b' we have sought the Lord
15:16 b' she had made an idol
16: 7 B' thou hast relied on the king
8 yet, because thou didst rely on
10 rage with him b' of this thing.
17: 3 b' he walked in the first
20:37 B' thou hast joined thyself
21: 3 Jehoram; b' he was the firstborn
7 b' of the covenant
10 his hand; b' he had forsaken
12 B' thou hast not walked
22: 6 in Jezreel b' of the wounds
6 b' he was sick.
9 B', said they, he is the son
24:16 the kings, b' he had done good
20 b' ye have forsaken the Lord,
24 their hand, b' they had forsaken
25:16 thee, b' thou hast done this,
20 b' they sought after the gods
26:20 to go out, b' the Lord had smitten
27: 6 became mighty, b' he prepared
28: 6 b' they had forsaken the Lord
9 Behold, b' the Lord God
19 brought Judah low b' of Ahaz
23 he said, B' the gods of the kings
30: 3 at that time, b' the priests had
34:21 poured out upon us, b' our
25 B' they have forsaken me,
27 B' thine heart was tender,
35:14 for the priests: b' the priests
36:15 b' he had compassion on his
Ezr 3: 3 was upon them b' of the people
11 thanks unto the Lord; b' he is
11 the Lord, b' the foundation
4:14 Now b' we have
8:22 b' we had spoken unto the king
9: 4 b' of the transgression of those
15 cannot stand before thee b' of this.
10: 6 he mourned b' of the transgression
9 of God, trembling b' of this matter,
Ne 4: 9 against them day and night, b' of
5: 3 buy corn, b' of the dearth.
9 fear of our God, b' of the reproach
15 So did not I, b' of the fear of God.
18 b' the bondage was heavy upon
8:12 great mirth, b' they had
9:37 thou hast set over us b' of our
38 And b' of all this we make
13: 2 B' they met not the children

Ne 13:29 b' they have defiled the
Es 1:15 b' she hath not performed
8: 7 upon the gallows, b' he laid
9: 3 helped the Jews; b' the fear of
Job 3:10 B' it shut not up the doors
6:20 were confounded b' they had
11:16 B' thou shalt forget thy misery,
18 shalt be secure, b' there is hope;
15:27 B' he covereth his face
17:12 the light is short b' of darkness.
18:15 in his tabernacle, b' it is none
20:19 B' he hath oppressed
19 b' he hath violently taken away
23:17 B' I was not cut off
29:12 B' I delivered the poor that cried,
30:11 B' he hath loosed my cord,
31:25 I rejoiced b' my wealth was great,
25 and b' mine hand had gotten much;
32: 1 answer Job, b' he was righteous
2 his wrath kindled, b' he justified
3 b' they had found no answer,
4 Job had spoken, b' they were
34:27 B' they turned back
36 unto the end b' of his answers
35:12 b' of the pride of evil men.
15 But now, b' it is not so,
36:18 B' there is wrath,
38:21 thou it, b' thou wast then born?
21 b' the number of thy days is
39:11 trust him, b' his strength
17 B' God hath deprived her of
Ps 5: 8 in thy righteousness b' of mine
11 shout for joy, b' thou defendest
6: 7 Mine eye is consumed b' of grief;
7 it waxeth old b' of all mine
7: 6 lift up thyself b' of the rage
8: 2 strength b' of thine enemies,
13: 6 b' he hath dealt bountifully
14: 6 counsel of the poor, b' the Lord
16: 8 b' he is at my right hand,
18: 7 shaken, b' he was wroth.
19 he delivered me, b' he delighted
27:11 plain path, b' of mine enemies.
28: 5 B' they regard not the works
6 Blessed be the Lord, b' he hath
31:10 my strength faileth b' of mine
33:21 rejoice in him, b' we have
37: 1 Fret not thyself b' of evil doers,
7 fret not thyself b' of him who
7 his way, b' of the man
40 save them, b' they trust
38: 3 b' of thine anger; neither is
3 any rest in my bones b' of my sin.
5 corrupt b' of my foolishness.
20 b' I follow the thing that good is.
39: 9 not my mouth; b' thou didst it.
41:11 favourest me, b' mine enemy
42: 9 go I mourning b' of the oppression
43: 2 mourning b' of the oppression
44: 3 b' thou hadst a favour unto them.
45: 4 b' of truth and meekness
48:11 be glad, b' of thy judgments.
52: 9 forever, b' thou hast done it:
53: 5 put them to shame, b' God
55: 3 B' of the voice of the enemy,
3 b' of the oppression of the wicked:
19 B' they have no change,
59: 9 B' of his strength will I wait
60: 4 may be displayed b' of the truth.
8 triumph thou b' of me.
63: 3 B' thy loving kindness is better
7 B' thou hast been my help,
68:29 B' of thy temple at Jerusalem
69: 7 B' for thy sake I have borne
18 deliver me b' of mine enemies.
78:22 B' they believed not in God,
86:17 b' thou, Lord, hast holpen me,
91: 9 B' thou hast made the Lord,
14 B' he hath set his love upon me,
14 set him on high, b' he hath known
97: 8 Judah rejoiced b' of thy
102:10 B' of thine indignation and thy
106:33 B' they provoked his spirit,
107:11 B' they rebelled against the
17 b' of their transgression,
17 b' of their iniquities, are afflicted
26 their soul is melted b' of trouble.
30 glad b' they are quiet;
109:16 B' that he remembered not to
21 b' thy mercy is good,
116: 1 b' he hath heard my voice
2 B' he hath inclined his ear
118: 1 b' his mercy endureth for ever.
119:56 I had, b' I kept thy precepts.
62 give thanks unto thee b' of thy
74 b' I have hoped in thy word.
100 than the ancients, b' I keep
136 down mine eyes, b' they keep
139 consumed me, b' mine enemies
158 was grieved; b' they kept not
164 praise thee b' of thy righteous
122: 9 B' of the house of the Lord
Pr 1:24 B' I have called, and ye refused;
21: 7 destroy them; b' they refuse
22:22 Rob not the poor, b' he is poor:
24:13 eat honey, b' it is good;
19 Fret not thyself b' of evil men,
Ec 2:17 I hated life; b' the work
18 b' I should leave it
4: 9 Two are better than one; b' they
5:20 b' God answereth him in the joy
8: 6 B' to every purpose there is
11 B' sentence against an evil work
13 as a shadow; b' he feareth not
15 mirth, b' a man hath no better
17 b' though a man labor to seek it

Ec 10:15 b' he knoweth not how to go
12: 3 grinders cease b' they are few,
5 shall fail: b' man goeth to his
9 moreover, b' the preacher was wise,
Ca 1: 3 B' of the savour of thy good
6 not upon me, b' I am black,
6 b' the sun hath looked upon me:
3: 8 upon his thigh b' of fear
Isa 2: 6 b' they be replenished
3: 8 Judah is fallen: b' their tongue
16 B' the daughters of Zion
5:13 into captivity, b' they have no
24 b' they have cast away the law,
6: 5 I am undone; b' I am a man
7: 5 B' Syria, Ephraim, and the
24 men come thither; b' all the land
8:20 it is b' there is no light
10:27 destroyed b' of the anointing.
14:20 with them in burial, b' thou hast
29 Palestina, b' the rod of him
15: 1 B' in the night Ar of Moab
1 b' in the night Kir of Moab
17: 9 left b' of the children of Israel:
10 B' thou hast forgotten the God
19:16 b' of the shaking of the hand
17 b' of the counsel of the Lord of
20 b' of the oppressors, and he shall
22: 4 comfort me, b' of the spoiling
24: 5 b' they have transgressed
26: 3 b' he trusteth in thee.
28:15 B' ye have said,
28 is bruised; b' he will not ever
30:12 B' ye despise this word,
31: 1 b' they are many; and in
1 b' they are very strong;
32:14 B' the palaces shall be forsaken;
37:29 B' thy rage against me,
40: 7 fadeth: b' the spirit of the Lord
43:20 b' I give waters in the wilderness,
48: 4 B' I knew that thou art obstinate,
49: 7 shall worship, b' of the Lord
50: 2 fish stinketh, b' there is no water,
51:13 b' of the fury of the oppressor,
53: 9 b' he had done no violence,
53:12 b' he hath poured out his
55: 5 run unto thee b' of the Lord
60: 5 be enlarged; b' the abundance
9 Holy One of Israel, b' he hath
61: 1 b' the Lord hath anointed me
64: 7 us, b' of our iniquities.
65:12 down to the slaughter: b' when I
16 b' the former troubles are
16 forgotten, and b' they are hid
66: 4 fears upon them; b' when I
Jer 2:35 B' I am innocent,
35 plead with thee, b' thou sayest,
4: 4 b' of the evil of your doings.
17 b' she hath been rebellious.
18 b' it is bitter, b' it reacheth
19 hold my peace, b' thou hast
28 b' I have spoken it,
31 soul is wearied b' of murderers.
5: 6 in pieces: b' their transgressions
14 B' ye speak this word, behold,
6:19 b' they have not
30 them, b' the Lord hath rejected
7:13 now, b' ye have done all these
8:14 gall to drink, b' we have sinned
19 daughter of my people b' of them
9:10 lamentation, b' they are burned
13 saith, B' they have forsaken
19 confounded, b' we have forsaken
19 b' our dwellings have cast
10: 5 be borne, b' they cannot go,
12: 4 b' they said, He shall not see
11 made desolate, b' no man
13 b' of the fierce anger of the Lord.
13:17 b' the Lord's flock is carried
25 saith the Lord; b' thou hast
14: 4 B' the ground is chapt,
5 forsook it, b' there was no grass.
6 did fail, b' there was no grass.
16 b' of the famine and the sword;
15: 4 b' of Manasseh the son of
17 I sat alone b' of thy hand:
16:11 say unto them, B' your fathers
18 sin doubled; b' they have defiled
17:13 b' they have forsaken the Lord,
18:15 B' my people hath forgotten
19: 4 B' they have forsaken me,
8 hiss b' of all the plagues
13 Tophet, b' of all the houses
15 it, b' they have hardened
20: 8 violence and spoil; b' the word
17 B' he slew me not
21:12 b' of the evil of your doings.
22: 9 B' they have forsaken
15 reign, b' thou closest thyself
23: 9 is broken b' of the prophets;
9 b' of the Lord, and b' of the
10 b' of swearing the land mourneth;
38 B' ye say this word, The burden
25: 8 B' ye have not heard
16 b' of the sword that I will send
27 b' of the sword which I will send
37 b' of the fierce anger of the Lord.
38 b' of the fierceness of the oppressor,
38 and b' of his fierce anger.
26: 3 b' of the evil of their doings.
28:16 shalt die, b' thou hast taught
29:15 B' ye have said,
29:19 B' they have not hearkened
23 B' they have committed
25 saying, B' thou hast sent
31 B' that Shemaiah hath
32 b' he hath taught rebellion

Jer 30:14, 15 b' thy sins were increased.
17 b' they called thee an Outcast,
31:15 comforted for her children, b' they
19 even confounded, b' I did bear
32:24 against it, b' of the sword,
32 B' of all the evil of the children
35:16 B' the sons of Jonadab
17 against them: b' I have spoken
18 B' ye have obeyed
40: 3 b' ye have sinned against
41: 9 b' of Gedaliah, was it which Asa
18 B' of the Chaldeans: for they
18 b' Ishmael the son of Nethaniah
44: 3 B' of their wickedness which they
22 b' of the evil of your doings,
22 and b' of the abominations
23 B' ye have burned incense,
23 and b' ye have sinned against
46:15 stood not, b' the Lord did
21 did not stand, b' the day
23 be searched; b' they are more
47: 4 B' of the day that cometh
48: 7 For b' thou hast trusted
36 b' the riches that he hath
42 being a people, b' he hath
45 of Heshbon b' of the force:
50: 7 not, b' they have sinned
11 B' ye are glad, b' ye rejoiced,
11 b' ye are grown fat as the heifer
13 B' of the wrath of the Lord
24 caught, b' thou hast striven
51:11 destroy it; b' it is the vengeance
51 are confounded, b' we have heard
55 B' the Lord hath spoiled
56 B' the spoiler is come
La 1: 3 gone into captivity b' of affliction,
3 and b' of great servitude:
4 do mourn, b' none come
8 despise her, b' they have seen
16 down with water, b' the comforter
16 desolate, b' the enemy prevailed.
2:11 b' the children and the sucklings
3:22 not consumed, b' his compassions
28 keepeth silence, b' he hath borne
51 affecteth mine heart b' of all
5: 9 b' of the sword of the wilderness.
10 b' of the terrible famine.
18 B' of the mountain of Zion,
Eze 3:20 he shall die: b' thou hast not
21 surely live, b' he is warned;
5: 7 B' ye multiplied more
9 b' of all thine abominations.
11 Surely, b' thou hast defiled
6: 9 captives, b' I am broken
7:19 b' it is the stumbling block
12:19 b' of the violence of all them
13: 8 B' ye have spoken vanity, and
10 B', even b' they have seduced my
22 B' with lies ye have made the
14: 5 b' they are all estranged
15 pass through b' of the beasts:
15: 8 desolate, b' they have committed
16:15 the harlot b' of thy renown,
28 b' thou wast unsatiable; yea,
36 B' thy filthiness was poured
43 B' thou hast not remembered
63 b' of thy shame, when I am
18:18 b' he cruelly oppressed,
28 B' he considereth,
20:16 B' they despised my judgments
24 B' they had not executed
21: 7 For the tidings; b' it cometh:
13 B' it is a trial,
24 B' ye have made your iniquity
24 do appear; b', I say, ye are come
28 to consume b' of the glittering:
22:19 B' ye are all become dross,
23:30 unto thee, b' thou hast gone
30 and b' thou art polluted
35 B' thou hast forgotten me,
45 b' they are adulteresses,
24:13 lewdness: b' I have purged thee,
25: 3 B' thou saidst, Aha,
6 B' thou hast clapped thine hands
8 B' that Moab and Seir do say,
12 B' that Edom hath dealt
15 B' the Philistines have dealt
26: 2 Son of man, b' that Tyrus
28: 2 B' thine heart is lifted up,
5 heart is lifted up b' of thy riches:
6 B' thou hast set thine heart
17 was lifted up b' of thy beauty,
29: 6 am the Lord, b' they have been
9 am the Lord: b' he hath said,
20 served against it, b' they wrought
31: 5 became long b' of the multitude
10 B' thou hast lifted up thyself
33:29 most desolate b' of all their
34: 5 scattered, b' there is no shepherd:
8 surely b' my flock became
8 b' there was no shepherd,
21 B' ye have thrust with side
35:10 B' thou hast said,
15 of Israel, b' it was desolate,
36: 2 B' the enemy hath said
3 B' they have made you desolate,
6 and in my fury, b' ye have borne
13 B' they say unto you,
39:23 iniquity: b' they trespassed
44: 2 enter in by it; b' the Lord,
7 b' of all your abominations.
12 B' they ministered unto them
47: 9 of fish, b' these waters shall
12 b' their waters they issued
Da 2: 8 b' ye see the thing is
3:22 Therefore b' the king's

Da 3:29 b' there is no other God
4: 9 b' I know that the spirit
6: 3 b' an excellent spirit
23 upon him, b' he believed
7:11 b' of the voice of the great words
9: 7 driven them, b' of their trespass
8 to our fathers, b' we have sinned
11 b' we have sinned
16 b' for our sins,
11:35 b' it is yet for a time
Ho 4: 1 of the land, b' there is no truth,
6 knowledge, b' thou hast rejected
10 increase: b' they have left
13 and elms, b' the shadow
19 ashamed b' of their sacrifices.
5: 1 is toward you, b' ye have been
11 in judgment, b' he willingly
7:13 destruction unto them! b' they
8: 1 b' they have transgressed
11 B' Ephraim hath made
9: 6 they are gone b' of destruction:
17 cast them away, b' they did not
10: 3 king b' we feared not the Lord,
5 shall fear b' of the calves
5 thereof, b' it is departed from it.
13 b' thou didst trust in thy way,
15 b' of your great wickedness:
11: 5 be his king, b' they refused
6 them, b' of their own counsels.
Joe 1: 5 of wine, b' of the new wine;
11 b' the harvest of the field
12 withered: b' joy is withered away
18 perplexed, b' they have no pasture;
2:20 come up, b' he hath done great
3: 5 B' ye have taken my silver
19 b' they have shed innocent blood
Am 1: 3 b' they have threshed Gilead
6 b' they carried away captive the
9 b' they delivered up the whole
11 punishment thereof; b' he did
13 b' they have ripped up the women
2: 1 b' he burned the bones of the king
4 b' they have despised the law
6 b' they sold the righteous
4:12 b' I will do this unto thee,
Jon 1:10 presence of the Lord, b' he had told
Mic 2: 1 practise it, b' it is in the power
10 is not your rest: b' it is polluted,
6:13 thee desolate b' of thy sins.
7: 9 b' I have sinned against him,
13 be desolate b' of them that dwell
17 and shall fear b' of thee.
18 anger for ever, b' he delighteth
Na 3: 4 B' of the multitude of the
11 seek strength b' of the enemy.
Hab 1:16 b' by them their portion is fat,
2: 3 wait for it; b' it will surely come,
5 b' he transgresseth by wine,
17 them afraid, b' of men's blood,
Zep 1:17 blind men, b' they have sinned
2:10 pride, b' they have reproached
3:11 haughty b' of my holy mountain
Hag 1: 9 B' of mine house that is waste.
Zec 8:10 or came in b' of the affliction:
9: 8 about mine house b' of the army,
8 b' of him that passeth by,
8 and b' of him that returneth:
10: 2 troubled, b' there was no shepherd.
5 fight, b' the Lord is with them,
11: 2 fallen; b' the mighty are spoiled:
Mal 2: 2 b' ye do not lay it to heart.
14 B' the Lord hath been
M't 2:18 not be comforted, b' they are not.
5:36 b' thou canst not make one hair
7:14 B' strait is the gate, and narrow
9:36 b' they fainted, and were
11:20 were done, b' they repented not:
25 b' thou hast hid these things
12:41 b' they repented at the
13: 5 b' they had no deepness of earth:
6 b' they had no root, they withered
11 B' it is given unto you to know
13 b' they seeing see not;
21 ariseth b' of the word,
58 works there b' of their unbelief.
14: 5 b' they counted him as a prophet.
15:32 b' they continue with me now
16: 7 It is b' we have taken no bread.
8 b' ye have brought no bread?
17:20 unto them, B' of your unbelief:
18: 7 unto the world b' of offences!
32 that debt, b' thou desiredst me:
19: 8 b' of the hardness of your hearts
20: 7 B' no man hath hired us.
15 thine eye evil, b' I am good?
31 b' they should hold their peace:
21:46 b' they took him for a prophet.
23:29 b' ye build the tombs of the
24:12 b' iniquity shall abound, the
26:31 be offended b' of me this night:
33 shall be offended b' of thee, yet
27: 6 b' it is the price of blood.
19 this day in a dream b' of him.
M'r 1:34 devils to speak, b' they knew him.
3: 9 wait on him b' of the multitude,
30 B' they said, He hath an unclean
4: 5 b' it had no depth of earth:
6 b' it had no root, it withered away.
29 sickle, b' the harvest is come.
5: 4 B' that he had been often bound
6: 6 he marvelled b' of their unbelief.
34 b' they were as sheep not having
7:19 B' it entereth not into his heart,
8: 2 b' they have now been with me
16 It is b' we have no bread.
17 reason ye, b' ye have no bread?

M'r 9:38 forbad him, b' he followeth not us.
41 b' ye belong to Christ, verily I say
11:18 b' all the people was astonished
12:24 err, b' ye know not the scriptures,
14:27 be offended b' of me this night:
15:42 b' it was the preparation, that is,
16:14 b' they believed not them which
Lu 1: 7 b' that Elisabeth was barren,
20 b' thou believest not my
2: 4 (b' he was of the house and lineage
7 b' there was no room for them in
4:18 b' he hath anointed me to
5:19 bring him in b' of the multitude,
8: 6 away, b' it lacked moisture.
30 b' many devils were entered into
9: 7 b' that it was said of some, that
49 b' he followeth not with us.
53 b' his face was as though
10:20 b' your names are written in
11: 8 give him, b' he is his friend,
8 b' of his importunity he will rise
18 b' ye say that I cast out
12:17 b' I have no room where to
13: 2 b' they suffered such things?
14 b' that Jesus had healed on
15:27 b' he hath received him safe
16: 8 steward, b' he had done wisely:
17: 9 b' he did the things that were
18: 5 Yet b' this widow troubleth me,
19: 3 b' he was little of stature.
11 b' he was nigh to Jerusalem,
11 b' they thought that the kingdom
17 b' thou hast been faithful in a
21 b' thou art an austere man: thou
31 B' the Lord hath need of him.
44 b' thou knewest not the time
23: 8 b' he had heard many things of
Joh 1:50 B' I said unto thee, I saw thee
2:24 unto them, b' he knew all men,
3:18 b' he hath not believed in the
19 b' their deeds were evil.
23 b' there was much water there:
29 b' of the bridegroom's voice:
4:41 more believed b' of his own word;
42 we believe, not b' of thy saying:
5:16 b' he had done these things
18 b' he not only had broken the
27 b' he is the Son of man.
30 b' I seek not mine own will,
6: 2 b' they saw his miracles which he
26 not b' ye saw the miracles, but
26 b' ye did eat of the loaves,
41 b' he said, I am the bread which
7: 1 b' the Jews sought to kill him.
7 but me it hateth, b' I testify of
22 (not b' it is of Moses, but of the
23 are ye angry at me b' I have
30 b' his hour was not yet come.
39 b' that Jesus was not yet glorified.
43 a division among the people b' of
8:22 b' he saith, Whither I go, ye
37 b' my word hath no place in you.
43 b' ye cannot hear my word.
44 b' there is no truth in him.
45 And b' I tell you the truth,
47 them not, b' ye are not of God.
9:16 b' he keepeth not the sabbath
22 b' they feared the Jews: for the
10:13 fleeth, b' he is an hireling,
17 b' I lay down my life, that I might
26 b' ye are not of my sheep, as
33 and b' that thou, being a man,
36 b' I said, I am the son of God?
11: 9 b' he seeth the light of this world.
10 b' there is no light in him.
42 b' of the people which stand by
12: 6 but b' he was a thief, and had
11 B' that by reason of him many
30 This voice came not b' of me,
39 b' that Esaias said again,
42 b' of the Pharisees they did not
13:29 b' Judas had the bag, that Jesus
14:12 b' I go unto my Father.
17 b' it seeth him not, neither
19 b' I live, ye shall live also.
28 b' I said, I go unto the Father:
15:19 but b' ye are not of the world,
21 b' they know not him that sent me.
27 b' ye have been with me from
16: 3 b' they have not known the Father,
4 beginning, b' I was with you.
6 But b' I have said these things
9 b' they believe not on me;
10 b' I go to my Father, and ye see
11 b' the prince of this world is
16 see me, b' I go to the Father.
17 B' I go to the Father?
21 b' her hour is come: but as soon
27 b' ye have loved me, and have
32 b' the Father is with me.
17:14 b' they are not of the world, even
19: 7 b' he made himself the Son of God.
31 b' it was the preparation, that the
42 b' of the Jews' preparation day;
20:13 B' they have taken away my Lord,
29 Thomas, b' thou hast seen me,
21:17 Peter was grieved b' he said unto
Ac 2: 6 b' that every man heard them
24 b' it was not possible that he
27 B' thou wilt not leave my soul
4:21 punish them, b' of the people:
6: 1 b' their widows were neglected.
8:11 b' that of long time he had
20 b' thou hast thought that the
10:45 b' that on the Gentiles also
12: 3 And b' he saw it pleased the Jews,
Ac 12:20 b' their country was nourished
23 smote him, b' he gave not God
13:27 b' they knew him not.
14:12 Mercurius, b' he was the chief
16: 3 circumcised him b' of the Jews
17:18 b' he preached unto them Jesus,
31 B' he hath appointed a day, in
18: 2 b' that Claudius had commanded
3 b' he was of the same craft,
20:16 b' he would not spend the
22:29 Roman, and b' he had bound him.
30 the morrow, b' he would have
24:11 B' that thou mayest understand,
25:20 And b' I doubted of such
26: 2 Agrippa, b' I shall answer
3 Especially b' I know thee
27: 4 b' the winds were contrary.
9 b' the fast was now already past,
12 And b' the haven was not
28: 2 b' of the present rain,
2 and b' of the cold.
18 b' there was no cause of death in
20 b' that for the hope of Israel
Ro 1:19 B' that which may be known of
21 B' that, when they knew God,
3: 2 chiefly, b' that unto them were
4:15 B' the law worketh wrath: for
5: 5 b' the love of God is shed abroad
6:15 b' we are not under the law,
19 b' of the infirmity of your flesh:
8: 7 B' the carnal mind is enmity
10 body is dead b' of sin; but the
10 Spirit is life b' of righteousness.
21 b' the creature itself also shall be
27 b' he maketh intercession for the
9: 7 Neither, b' they are the seed
28 b' a short work will the Lord
32 B' they sought it not by faith,
11:20 Well; b' of unbelief they were
14:23 if he eat, b' he eateth not of faith:
15:15 b' of the grace that is given to me
1Co 1:25 B' the foolishness of God is wiser
2:14 b' they are spiritually discerned.
3:13 b' it shall be revealed by fire;
6: 7 b' ye go to law one with another.
11:10 power on her head b' of the angels.
12:15 B' I am not the hand, I am not of
16 B' I am not the eye, I am not of
15: 9 b' I persecuted the church of God.
15 b' we have testified of God that
2Co 2:13 my spirit, b' I found not Titus
5:14 b' we thus judge,
7:13 b' his spirit was refreshed by you
11: 7 b' I have preached to you the
11 Wherefore? b' I love you not?
Ga 2: 4 that b' of false brethren unawares
11 b' he was to be blamed.
3:19 It was added b' of transgressions,
4: 6 And b' ye are sons, God hath
16 your enemy, b' I tell you the truth?
Eph 4:18 b' of the blindness of their heart:
5: 6 for b' of these things cometh
16 the time, b' the days are evil.
Ph'p 1: 7 b' I have you in my heart;
2:26 b' that ye had heard that he
30 B' for the work of Christ he was
4:17 Not b' I desire a gift: but I desire
1Th 2: 8 b' ye were dear unto us.
9 night and day, b' we would not
13 b', when ye received the word
4: 6 b' that the Lord is the avenger
2Th 1: 3 b' that your faith groweth
10 (b' our testimony among you was
2:10 that perish; b' they received
13 b' God hath from the beginning
3: 9 Not b' we have not power,
1Ti 1:13 b' I did it ignorantly in unbelief.
4:10 b' we trust in the living God,
5:12 b' they have cast off their first
6: 2 despise them, b' they are brethren;
2 b' they are faithful and beloved,
Ph'm 7 b' the bowels of the saints are
Heb 3:19 could not enter in b' of unbelief.
4: 6 entered not in b' of unbelief:
6:13 b' he could swear by no greater,
7:23 many priests, b' they were not
24 this man, b' he continueth
8: 9 b' they continued not in my
10: 2 b' that the worshippers once
11: 5 not found, b' God had translated
11 b' she judged him faithful who
23 b' they saw he was a proper
Jas 1:10 b' as the flower of the grass
4: 2 ye have not, b' ye ask not.
3 and receive not, b' ye ask amiss.
1Pe 1:16 B' it is written, Be ye holy;
2:21 b' Christ also suffered us, leaving
5: 8 b' your adversary the devil, as a
1Jo 2: 8 b' the darkness is past, and the
11 b' that darkness hath blinded his
12 b' your sins are forgiven
13 b' ye have known him that is
13 b' ye have overcome the wicked
13 b' ye have known the Father.
14 b' ye have known him that is from
14 young men, b' ye are strong,
21 b' ye know not the truth,
21 but b' ye know it,
3: 1 us not, b' it knew him not.
9 cannot sin, b' he is born of God.
12 B' his own works were evil, and
14 b' we love the brethren. He that
16 b' he laid down his life for us:
22 b' we keep his commandments,
4: 1 b' many false prophets are gone
4 b' greater is he that is in you,
1Jo 4: 9 b' that God sent his only begotten
13 b' he hath given us of his Spirit.
17 b' as he is, so are we in this world.
18 b' fear hath torment. He that
19 We love him, b' he first loved us.
5: 6 beareth witness, b' the Spirit is
10 b' he believeth not the record
3Jo 7 B' that for his name's sake
Jude 16 in admiration b' of advantage.
Re 1: 7 shall wail b' of him. Even so,
2: 4 b' thou hast left thy first love.
14 b' thou hast there them that hold
20 b' thou sufferest that woman
3:10 B' thou hast kept the word of my
16 So then b' thou art lukewarm,
17 B' thou sayest, I am rich,
5: 4 b' no man was found worthy to
8:11 b' they were made bitter.
11:10 b' these two prophets tormented
17 b' thou hast taken to thee
12:12 great wrath, b' he knoweth
14: 8 b' she made all the nations drink
16: 5 b' thou hast judged thus.
11 b' of their pains and their sores,
21 b' of the plague of the hail;

Becher (*be'-ker*) See also BACHRITES.
Ge 46:21 Belah, and B', and Ashbel, Gera,
Nu 26:35 of B', the family of the Bachrites:
1Ch 7: 6 Bela, and B', and Jediael, three.
8 the sons of B'; Zemira, and Joash,
8 All these are the sons of B'.

Bechorath (*be-ko'-rath*)
1Sa 9: 1 Zeror, the son of B', the son of

beckoned
Lu 1:22 he b' unto them, and remained
5: 7 they b' unto their partners,
Joh 13:24 Peter therefore b' to him, that
Ac 19:33 Alexander b' with the hand, and
21:40 b' with the hand unto the people.
24:10 after that the governor had b'

beckoning
Ac 12:17 b' unto them with the hand
13:16 and b' with his hand, said

become^ See also BECAME; BECOMETH.
Ge 3:22 Behold, the man is b' as one of us,
9:15 the waters shall no more b' a
18:18 Abraham shall surely b' a great
24:35 and he is b' great: and he hath
32:10 and now I am b' two bands.
34:16 with you, and we will b' one
37:20 We shall see what will b' of his
48:19 he also shall b' a people, and he
19 shall b' a multitude of nations.
Ex 4: 9 of the river shall b' blood upon
7: 9 and it shall b' a serpent.
19 water, that they may b' blood;
8:16 that it may b' lice throughout all
9: 9 And it shall b' small dust in all
15: 2 and he is b' my salvation: he is
6 b' glorious in power: thy right
23:29 lest the land b' desolate, and the
32: 1, 23 we wot not what is b' of him.
Le 19:29 and the land b' full of wickedness.
Nu 5:24 shall enter into her, and b' bitter.
27 and b' bitter, and her belly shall
De 27: 9 thou art b' the people of the Lord
28:37 thou shalt b' an astonishment,
Jos 9:13 b' old by reason of the very long
J'g 16:17 and I shall b' weak, and be like
1Sa 28:16 from thee, and is b' thine enemy?
2Sa 7:24 and thou, Lord, art b' their God.
1Ki 2:15 about, and is b' my brother's;
14: 3 he shall tell thee what shall b' of
2Ki 21:14 they shall b' a prey and a spoil
22:19 that they should b' a desolation
Es 2:11 what should b' of her.
Job 7: 5 skin is broken, and b' loathsome.
15:28 which are ready to b' heaps.
21: 7 do the wicked live, b' old,
30:19 and I am b' like dust and ashes.
21 Thou art b' cruel to me: with
Ps 14: 3 they are all together b' filthy:
28: 1 I b' like them that go down into
53: 3 they are altogether b' filthy;
62:10 b' not vain in robbery: if riches
69: 8 I am b' a stranger unto my
22 Let their table b' a snare before
22 for their welfare, let it b' a trap.
79: 4 b' a reproach to our neighbours,
109: 7 and let his prayer b' sin.
118:14 and song, and is b' my salvation.
21 heard me, and art b' my salvation.
22 is b' the head stone of the corner.
119:83 For I am b' like a bottle in the
Isa 1:21 the faithful city b' an harlot!
22 Thy silver is b' dross, thy wine
7:24 land shall b' briers and thorns.
12: 2 he also is b' my salvation.
14:10 Art thou also b' weak as we?
10 art thou b' like unto us?
19:11 of Pharaoh is b' brutish:
13 The princes of Zoan are b' fools,
29:11 And the vision of all is b' unto
34: 9 thereof shall b' burning pitch.
35: 7 parched ground shall b' a pool,
59: 6 Their webs shall not b' garments,
60:22 A little one shall b' a thousand,
Jer 2: 5 after vanity, and are b' vain?
3: 1 from him, and b' another man's,
5:13 And the prophets shall b' wind,
27 they are b' great, and waxen rich.
7:11 b' a den of robbers in your eyes?
10:21 the pastors are b' brutish, and
22: 5 this house shall b' a desolation.

Jer 26:18 and Jerusalem shall b' heaps,
49:13 Bozrah shall b' a desolation,
50:23 how is Babylon b' a desolation
37 and they shall b' as women:
51:37 And Babylon shall b' heaps,
41 is Babylon b' an astonishment
La 1: 1 how is she b' as a widow! she
1 provinces, how is she b' tributary!
2 with her, they are b' her enemies.
6 her princes are b' like harts that
11 and consider; for I am b' vile.
4: 1 How is the gold b' dim! how is
3 daughter of my people is b' cruel,
8 is withered, it is b' like a stick.
Eze 22: 4 Thou art b' guilty in thy blood
18 Israel is to me b' dross: all they
19 Because ye are all b' dross,
26: 5 it shall b' a spoil to the nations.
36:35 land that was desolate is b' like
35 and ruined cities are b' fenced,
37:17 they shall b' one in thine hand.
Da 4:22 that art grown and b' strong:
9:16 people are b' a reproach to all
11:23 come up, and shall b' strong
Ho 12: 8 Ephraim said, Yet I am b' rich,
13:15 and his spring shall b' dry, and his
16 Samaria shall b' desolate;
Jon 4: 5 see what would b' of the city.
Mic 3:12 Jerusalem shall b' heaps, and
Zep 1:13 their goods shall b' a booty, and
2:15 is she b' a desolation, a place for
Zec 4: 7 Zerubbabel thou shalt b' a plain:
M't 18: 3 converted, and b' as little children,
21:42 is b' the head of the corner.
M'r 1:17 make you to b' fishers of men.
12:10 is b' the head of the corner:
Lu 20:17 is b' the head of the corner?
Joh 1:12 he power to b' the sons of God.
Ac 4:11 is b' the head of the corner:
7:40 we wot not what is b' of him.
12:18 the soldiers, what was b' of Peter.
Ro 3:12 they are together b' unprofitable;
19 world may b' guilty before God.
4:18 he might b' the father of many
6:22 and b' servants to God, ye have
7: 4 ye also are b' dead to the law
13 might b' exceeding sinful.
1Co 3:18 b' a fool, that he may be wise.
7:18 let him not b' uncircumcised.
8: 9 b' a stumblingblock to them that
13: 1 I am b' as sounding brass, or a
15:20 b' the firstfruits of them that slept.
2Co 5:17 behold, all things are b' new.
12:11 I am b' a fool in glorying;
Ga 4:16 Am I therefore b' your enemy,
5: 4 Christ is b' of no effect unto you,
Ti 2: 1 things which b' sound doctrine:
Ph'm 6 thy faith may b' effectual by
Heb 5:12 are b' such as have need of milk,
Jas 2: 4 are b' judges of evil thoughts?
11 art b' a transgressor of the law.
Re 11:15 The kingdoms of this world are b'
18: 2 is b' the habitation of devils, and

becometh
Ps 93: 5 holiness b' thine house, O Lord,
Pr 10: 4 He b' poor that dealeth with a
17: 7 Excellent speech b' not a fool:
18 b' surety in the presence of his
Ec 4:14 is born in his kingdom b' poor.
M't 3:15 for thus it b' us to fulfil all
13:22 the word, and he b' unfruitful.
32 among herbs, and b' a tree,
M'r 4:19 the word, and it b' unfruitful.
32 b' greater than all herbs,
Ro 16: 2 her in the Lord, as b' saints,
Eph 5: 3 named among you, as b' saints;
Ph'p 1:27 be as it b' the gospel of Christ:
1Ti 2:10 b' women professing godliness)
Tit 2: 3 be in behaviour as b' holiness,

bed See also BEDS; BEDCHAMBER; BEDSTEAD.
Ge 48: 2 himself, and sat upon the b'.
49: 4 thou wentest up to thy father's b';
33 gathered up his feet into the b',
Ex 8: 3 bedchamber, and upon thy b',
21:18 he die not, but keepeth his b':
Le 15: 4 Every b', whereon he lieth that
5 whosoever toucheth his b' shall
21 whosoever toucheth her b' shall
23 if it be on her b', or on any
24 all the b' whereon he lieth shall be
26 Every b' whereon she lieth all the
26 her as the b' of her separation:
1Sa 19:13 an image, and laid it in the b',
15 Bring him up to me in the b',
16 there was an image in the b',
28:23 the earth, and sat upon the b'.
2Sa 4: 5 who lay on a b' at noon.
7 lay on his b' in his bedchamber,
11 in his own house upon his b'?
11: 2 David arose from off his b',
13 he went out to lie on his b'
13: 5 Lay thee down on thy b', and
1Ki 1:47 king bowed himself upon the b'.
17:19 and laid him upon his own b',
21: 4 he laid him down upon his b',
2Ki 1: 4 that b' on which thou art gone up,
6 shalt not come down from that b'
16 shalt not come down off that b'
4:10 let us set for him there a b',
21 him on the b' of the man of God,
32 was dead, and laid upon his b'.
1Ch 5: 1 he defiled his father's b', his
2Ch 16:14 laid him in the b' which was
24:25 slew him on his b', and he died:
Es 7: 8 Haman was fallen upon the b'
Job 7:13 My b' shall comfort me, my couch
17:13 made my b' in the darkness.
33:15 men, in slumberings upon the b';
19 also with pain upon his b',
Ps 4: 4 with your own heart upon your b',
6: 6 the night make I my b' to swim;
36: 4 He deviseth mischief upon his b';
41: 3 strengthen him upon the b' of
3 make all his b' in his sickness,
63: 6 I remember thee upon my b',
132: 3 my house, nor go up into my b';
139: 8 if I make my b' in hell, behold,
Pr 7:16 decked my b' with coverings
17 perfumed my b' with myrrh,
22:27 why should he take away thy b'
26:14 So doth the slothful upon his b'.
Ca 1:16 pleasant: also our b' is green.
3: 1 By night on my b' I sought him
7 his b', which is Solomon's;
5:13 His cheeks are as a b' of spices,
Isa 28:20 the b' is shorter than that a man
57: 7 mountain hast thou set thy b':
8 thou hast enlarged thy b',
8 their b' where thou sawest it.
Eze 23:17 came to her into the b' of love,
41 And satest upon a stately b',
32:25 They have set her a b' in the
Da 2:28 visions of thy head upon thy b',
29 came into thy mind upon thy b',
4: 5 and the thoughts upon my b'
10 the visions of mine head in my b';
13 the visions of my head upon my b',
7: 1 visions of his head upon his b':
Am 3:12 in Samaria in the corner of a b',
M't 9: 2 sick of the palsy, lying on a b':
6 take up thy b', and go unto thine
M'r 2: 4 they let down the b' wherein
9 Arise, and take up thy b',
11 Arise, and take up thy b', and go
12 he arose, took up the b', and went
4:21 under a bushel, or under a b'?
7:30 and her daughter laid upon the b'.
Lu 5:18 men brought in a b' a man which
8:16 putteth it under a b'; but setteth
11: 7 my children are with me in b';
17:34 there shall be two men in one b';
Joh 5: 8 Rise, take up thy b', and walk.
9 and took up his b', and walked:
10 lawful for thee to carry thy b'.
11 unto me, Take up thy b', and walk.
12 Take up thy bed, and walk?
Ac 9:33 Æneas, which had kept his b'
34 arise, and make thy b'. And he
Heb 13: 4 b' undefiled: but whoremongers
Re 2:22 Behold, I will cast her into a b',

Bedad (*be'-dad*)
Ge 36:35 and Hadad the son of B', who
1Ch 1:46 Hadad the son of B', which smote

Bedan (*be'-dan*)
1Sa 12:11 the Lord sent Jerubbaal, and B',
1Ch 7:17 sons of Ulam; B'. These were

bedchamber
Ex 8: 3 into thy b', and upon thy bed,
2Sa 4: 7 he lay on his bed in his b',
2Ki 6:12 that thou speakest in thy b'.
11: 2 in the b' from Athalia,
2Ch 22:11 put him and his nurse in a b'.
Ec 10:20 curse not the rich in thy b':

Bedeiah (*be-de'-yah*)
Ezr 10:35 Benaiah, B', Chelluh,

bed's
Ge 47:31 bowed himself upon the b' head.

beds
2Sa 17:28 b', and basons, and earthen
Es 1: 6 the b' were of gold and silver,
Ps 149: 5 let them sing aloud upon their b'.
Ca 6: 2 to the b' of spices, to feed in
Isa 57: 2 they shall rest in their b', each
Ho 7:14 they howled upon their b':
Am 6: 4 That lie upon b' of ivory,
Mic 2: 1 and work evil upon their b'!
M'r 6:55 and began to carry about in b'
Ac 5:15 and laid them on b' and couches,

bedstead
De 3:11 his b' was a b' of iron;

bee See also BEES.
Isa 7:18 and for the b' that is in the land

Beeliada (*be-e-li'-ad-ah*)
1Ch 14: 7 Elishama, and B', and Eliphalet.

Beelzebub (*be-el'-ze-bub*) See also BAAL-ZEBUB.
M't 10:25 called the master of the house B',
12:24 but by B' the prince of the devils.
27 And if I by B' cast out devils,
M'r 3:22 said, He hath B', and by the prince
Lu 11:15 He casteth out devils through B'
18 I cast out devils through B'.
19 And if I by B' cast out devils,

been^
Ge 13: 3 place where his tent had b' at the
26: 8 when he had b' there a long time,
31: 5 God of my father hath b' with me.
38 twenty years have I b' with thee;
41 have I b' twenty years in thy house:
42 the fear of Isaac, had b' with me,
38:26 She hath b' more righteous than
45: 6 hath the famine b' in the land:
46:34 servants' trade hath b' about
47: 9 days of the years of my life b',
Ex 2:22 b' a stranger in a strange land.
9:18 such as hath not b' in Egypt
Ex 14:12 had b' better for us to serve the
18: 3 have b' an alien in a strange land:
21:29 it hath b' testified to his owner,
34:10 such as have not b' done in all
Le 10:19 should it have b' accepted
13: 7 he hath b' seen of the priest
De 2: 7 Lord thy God hath b' with thee;
4:32 there hath b' any such thing as
32 or hath b' heard like it?
9: 7 b' rebellious against the Lord.
24 b' rebellious against the Lord from
15:18 b' worth a double hired servant
21: 3 which hath not b' wrought with,
31:27 b' rebellious against the Lord;
Jos 7: 7 would to God we had b' content,
9: 4 as if they had b' ambassadors,
10:27 cave wherein they had b' hid,
23: 9 no man hath b' able to stand
J'g 16: 8 withs which had not b' dried,
17 for I have b' a Nazarite unto God
Ru 2:11 It hath fully been shewed me,
1Sa 1:13 Eli thought she had b' drunken.
4: 7 not b' such a thing heretofore.
9 Hebrews, as they have b' to you:
17 hath b' also a great slaughter
9:24 hath it b' kept for thee
14:29 how mine eyes have b' enlightened,
30 b' now a much greater slaughter
38 wherein this sin hath b' this
15:21 should have b' utterly destroyed,
18:19 daughter should have b' given
19: 4 have b' to thee-ward very good:
20:13 as he hath b' with my father.
21: 5 women have b' kept from us
25:28 evil hath not b' found in thee
34 there had not b' left unto Nabal
29: 3 which hath b' with me these days,
6 Lord liveth, thou hast b' upright,
8 so long as I have b' with thee
2Sa 1:21 he had not b' anointed
26 pleasant hast thou b' unto me:
12: 8 and if that had b' too little, I
13:20 Amnon thy brother b' with thee?
32 this hath b' determined
14:32 it had b' good for me
32 to have b' there still.
15:34 as I have b' thy father's servant
1Ki 1:37 As the Lord hath b' with my lord
2:26 because thou hast b' afflicted
14: 8 hast not b' as my servant David,
16:31 as if it had b' a light thing for him
17: 7 because there had b' no rain in
19:10, 14 have b' very jealous for the Lord
2Ki 4:13 Behold, thou hast b' careful for us
1Ch 17: 8 And I have b' with thee
28: 3 thou hast b' a man of war,
29:25 majesty as had not b' on any king
2Ch 1:12 kings have had that have b' before
15: 3 a long season Israel hath b' without
23: 9 shields, that had b' king David's,
Ezr 2: 1 those which had b' carried away,
4:18 hath b' plainly read before me.
19 and search hath b' made,
19 sedition have b' made therein.
20 There have b' mighty kings also
5:16 now hath it b' in building,
8:35 of those that had b' carried away,
9: 2 princes and rulers hath b' chief
4 those that had b' carried away;
7 our fathers have we b' in a great
7 and our priests, b' delivered
8 grace hath b' showed from the Lord
10: 6 of them that had b' carried away.
8 those that had b' carried away.
Ne 2: 1 I had not b' beforetime sad in
5:15 governors that had b' before me
7: 6 of those that had b' carried away,
13:10 portions of the Levites had not b'
Es 2: 6 Who had b' carried away
6 which had b' carried away
12 that she had b' twelve months,
4:11 I have not b' called to come
6: 3 honour and dignity hath b' done
7: 4 if we had b' sold for bondmen
Job 3:13 have lain still and b' quiet,
13 have slept: then had I b' at rest,
16 untimely birth I had not b;
10:19 I should have b' as though
19 as though I had not b';
19 I should have b' carried from
22: 9 arms of the fatherless have b' broken.
31: 9 If mine heart have b' deceived
27 my heart hath b' secretly enticed,
38:17 Have the gates of death b' opened
42:11 that had b' of his acquaintance
Ps 25: 6 for they have b' ever of old.
27: 9 thou hast b' my help: leave me
35:14 as though he had b' my friend
37:25 I have b' young, and now am old;
42: 3 My tears have b' my meat day and
50: 8 to have b' continually before,
18 hast b' partakers with adulterers.
59:16 hast b' my defence and refuge in
60: 1 thou hast b' displeased;
61: 3 thou hast b' a shelter for me,
63: 7 Because thou hast b' my help,
69:22 which should have b' for their
73:14 all the day long have I b' plagued,
85: 1 Lord, thou hast b' favourable unto
89:38 hast b' wroth with thine anointed.
90: 1 thou hast b' our dwelling place in
94:17 Unless the Lord had b' my help
115:12 The Lord hath b' mindful of us:
119:54 Thy statutes have b' my songs
71 good for me that I have b' afflicted;

Ps 119:92 Unless thy law had b' my delights,
124: 1, 2 If it had not b' the Lord who
143: 3 as those that have b' long dead.
Pr 7:26 many strong men have b' slain
Ec 1: 9 The thing that hath b', it is that
10 it hath b' already of old time,
16 than all they that have b' before
2:12 which hath b' already done.
3:15 that which hath b' is now;
15 that which is to be hath already b';
4: 3 which hath not yet b',
16 of all that have b' before them:
6:10 which hath b' is named already,
Isa 1: 6 they have not b' closed,
9 we should have b' as Sodom,
9 should have b' like unto Gomorrah.
5: 4 What could have b' done more
17:10 hast not b' mindful of the rock of
23:16 harlot that hast b' forgotten;
25: 4 hast b' a strength to the poor,
26:17 so have we b' in thy sight, O Lord.
18 We have b' with child,
18 we have b' in pain,
30:24 which hath b' winnowed
38: 9 king of Judah, when he had b' sick,
39: 1 he had heard that he had b' sick,
40:21 hath it not b' told you
43: 4 thou hast b' honourable, and I
22 thou hast b' weary of me, O Israel.
48:18 then had thy peace b' as a river,
19 Thy seed also had b' as the sand,
19 name should not have b' cut off
49:21 these, where had they b'?
52:15 which had not b' told them
57:11 And of whom hast thou b' afraid
60:15 thou hast b' forsaken and hated,
66: 2 and all those things have b',
Jer 2:31 Have I b' a wilderness unto Israel?
3: 2 where thou hast not b' lien with.
3 the showers have b' withholden,
3 and there hath b' no latter rain;
4:17 she hath b' rebellious against me,
20:17 mother might have b' my grave,
22:21 b' thy manner since thy youth,
28: 8 prophets that have b' before me
32:31 city hath b' to me as a provocation
42:18 and my fury hath b' poured
43: 5 whither they had b' driven,
44:18 and have b' consumed by the sword
48:11 Moab hath b' at ease from his youth,
50: 6 My people hath been lost sheep:
29 hath b' proud against the Lord,
51: 5 For Israel hath not b' forsaken,
7 Babylon hath b' a golden cup in
Eze 2: 5 hath b' a prophet among them.
4:14 my soul had not b' polluted:
10:10 as if a wheel had b' in the midst
11:17 where ye have b' scattered, and
20:41 wherein ye have b' scattered;
43 wherein ye have b' defiled;
22:13 blood which hath b' in the midst
28:13 Thou hast b' in Eden the garden
29: 6 because they have b' a staff of reed
33:33 that a prophet hath b' among them.
34:12 where they have b' scattered
38: 8 which have b' always waste:
Da 5:15 have b' brought in before me,
9:12 whole heaven hath not b' done
12 as hath b' done upon Jerusalem.
Hos 5: 1 because ye have b' a snare on
2 though I have b' a rebuker of
Joe 1: 2 Hath this b' in your days,
2: 2 there hath not b' ever the like,
Ob 1:16 be as though they had not b'.
Mic 5: 2 goings forth have b' from of old,
Zep 3:19 they have b' put to shame.
Zec 1: 2 The Lord hath b' sore displeased
Mal 1: 9 this hath b' by your means:
2: 9 but have b' partial in the law.
14 the Lord hath b' witness between
3:13 Your words have b' stout against
M't 1: 6 that had b' the wife of Urias;
5:31 It hath b' said,
33 heard that it hath b' said
38 that it hath b' said,
43 have heard that it hath b' said,
11:21 had b' done in Tyre
23 which have b' done in thee,
23 had b' done in Sodom,
13:35 which have b' kept secret
23:30 b' in the days of our fathers,
30 we would not have b' partakers
25:21, 23 thou hast b' faithful over a few
26: 9 might have b' sold for much,
24 it had b' good for that man
24 if he had not b' born.
M'r 5: 4 he had b' often bound
4 chains had b' plucked asunder
18 he that had b' possessed
6:49 they supposed he had b' a spirit,
8: 2 they have now b' with me three
14: 5 It might have b' sold
5 and have b' given to the poor.
21 if he had never b' born.
15:44 whether he had b' any while dead.
16:10 told them that had b' with him,
11 and had b' seen of her, believed
Lu 1: 4 wherein thou hast b' instructed.
70 which have b' since the world
2:44 supposing him to have b' in the
4:16 where he had b' brought up:
7:10 the servant whole that had b' sick.
8: 2 which had b' healed of evil spirits
10:13 mighty works had b' done
13 which have b' done in you,
16:11 ye have not b' faithful in the

Lu 16:12 And if ye have not b' faithful in
19:17 because thou hast b' faithful
24:21 trusted that it had b' he which
Joh 5: 6 that he had b' now a long time
9:18 that he had b' blind, and received
11:21, 32 if thou hadst b' here, my
39 for he hath b' dead four days.
12: 1 which had b' dead, whom he
38 arm of the Lord b' revealed?
14: 9 Have I b' so long time with you,
15:27 because ye have b' with me from
Ac 1:16 must needs have b' fulfilled,
4:13 that they had b' with Jesus.
16 miracle hath b' done by them
5:26 lest they should have b' stoned,
6:15 it had b' the face of an angel.
7:52 ye have b' now the betrayers
9:18 from his eyes as it had b' scales:
10:11 as it had b' a great sheet knit
11: 5 as it had b' a great sheet, let
13: 1 which had b' brought up
46 should first have b' spoken
14:19 city, supposing he had b' dead.
26 whence they had b' recommended
15: 7 there had b' much disputing,
16:27 that the prisoners had b' fled.
19:21 After I have b' there, I must also
20:18 what manner I have b' with you
23:10 Paul should have b' pulled
27 and should have b' killed
24:10 that thou hast b' of many years
19 ought to have b' here before thee,
26 that money should have b' given
25:14 they had b' there many days,
26:32 This man might have b' set
Ro 6: 5 For if we have b' planted
9:29 we have b' as Sodoma,
29 and b' made like unto Gomorrha.
11:34 or who hath b' his counsellor?
15:22 I have b' much hindered
27 Gentiles have b' made partakers
16: 2 hath b' a succourer of many,
1Co 1:11 it hath b' declared unto me of you,
12:13 and have b' all made to drink
2Co 11: 6 but we have b' throughly made
21 as though we had b' weak.
25 a night and a day I have been in
12:11 I ought to have b' commended
Gal 3: 1 Christ had b' evidently set forth,
21 if there had b' a law given
21 should have b' by the law.
27 as have b' baptized into Christ
4:15 if it had b' possible, ye would
5:13 ye have b' called unto liberty;
Eph 3: 9 of the world had b' hid in God,
4:21 heard him, and have b' taught
Col 1:26 which hath b' hid from ages
2: 7 as ye have b' taught,
4:11 which have b' a comfort unto me.
1Th 2: 6 when we might have b'
2Th 2:15 which ye have b' taught,
1Ti 5: 9 having b' the wife of one man,
2Ti 3:14 learned and hast b' assured of,
Tit 1: 9 word as he hath b' taught,
Heb 8: 7 first covenant had b' faultless,
7 no place have b' sought for the
11:15 if they had b' mindful,
13: 9 them that hath b' occupied
Ja 3: 7 and hath b' tamed of mankind:
5: 5 pleasures on the earth, and b'
2Pe 2:21 For it had b' better for them
1Jo 2:19 for if they had b' of us, they
Re 5: 6 stood a lamb as it had b' slain,
17: 2 of the earth have b' made drunk

Beer (*be'-ur*) See also BAALATH-BEER; BEER-ELIM; BEER-LAHAI-ROI; BEER-SHEBA.
Nu 21:16 from thence they went to B':
J'g 9:21 ran away, and fled, and went to B',

Beera (*be-e'-rah*)
1Ch 7:37 Shilshah, and Ithran, and B'.

Beerah (*be-e'-rah*)
1Ch 5: 6 B' his son, when Tilgath-pilneser

Beer-elim (*be''-ur-e'-lim*)
Isa 15: 8 and the howling thereof unto B'.

Beeri (*be-e'-ri*)
Ge 26:34 the daughter of B' the Hittite,
Ho 1: 1 Hosea, the son of B', in the days

Beer-lahai-roi (*be'''-ur-la''-hahe-ro'-e*)
Ge 16:14 Wherefore the well was called B';

Beeroth (*be-e'-roth*) See also BEEROTHITE.
De 10: 6 took their journey from B' of
Jos 9:17 and B', and Kirjath-jearim.
18:25 Gibeon, and Ramah, and B',
2Sa 4: 2 B' also was reckoned to Benjamin:
Ezr 2:25 Kirjath-arim, Chephirah, and B',
Neh 7:29 Kirjath-jearim, Chephirah, and B',

Beerothite (*be-er'-o-thite*) See also BEEROTHITES; BEROTHITE.
2Sa 4: 2 the sons of Rimmon a B', of the
5 Rimmon the B', Rechab and
9 brother, the sons of Rimmon the B',
23:37 Nahari the B', armourbearer

Beerothites (*be-er'-o-thites*)
2Sa 4: 3 the B' fled to Gittaim, and were

Beer-sheba (*be-ur'-she-bah*)
Ge 21:14 wandered in the wilderness of B'.
31 Wherefore he called that place B';
32 Thus they made a covenant at B':
33 Abraham planted a grove in B',
22:19 up and went together to B'; and
19 Abraham dwelt at B'.
26:23 he went up from thence to B'.
33 therefore the name of the city is B'

Ge 28:10 Jacob went out from B', and went
46: 1 came to B', and offered sacrifices.
5 rose up from B': and the sons
Jos 15:28 Hazar-shual, and B', and
19: 2 they had in their inheritance B',
J'g 20: 1 as one man, from Dan even to B',
1Sa 3:20 all Israel from Dan even to B'.
8: 2 they were judges in B'.
2Sa 3:10 over Judah, from Dan even to B'.
17:11 from Dan even to B', as the sand
24: 2 of Israel, from Dan even to B',
7 to the south of Judah even to B'.
15 from Dan even to B', seventy
1Ki 4:25 even to B', all the days of Solomon.
19: 3 went for his life, and came to B',
2Ki 12: 1 his mother's name was Zibiah of B'.
23: 8 from Geba to B', and brake down
1Ch 4:28 they dwelt at B', and Moladah,
21: 2 number Israel from B' even to Dan;
2Ch 19: 4 people from B' to mount Ephraim,
24: 1 name also was Zibiah of B'.
30: 5 all Israel, from B' even to Dan,
Ne 11:27 at B', and in the villages thereof,
30 from B' unto the valley of Hinnom.
Am 5: 5 into Gilgal, and pass not to B':
8:14 manner of B' liveth; even they shall

bees
De 1:44 you, as b' do, and destroyed you
J'g 14: 8 of b' and honey in the carcase
Ps 118:12 They compassed me about like b';

Beesh-terah (*be-esh'-te-rah*) See also ASHTAROTH.
Jos 21:27 and B' with her suburbs; two

beetle
Le 11:22 the b' after his kind, and the

beeves
Le 22:19 blemish, of the b', of the sheep,
21 a freewill offering in b' or sheep,
Nu 31:28 of persons, and of the b',
30 of the persons, of the b',
33 threescore and twelve thousand b',
38 And the b' were thirty and six
44 And thirty and six thousand b',

befall See also BEFALLEN; BEFALLETH; BEFELL.
Ge 42: 4 peradventure mischief b' him.
38 if mischief b' him by the way
44:29 mischief b' him, ye shall bring
49: 1 tell you that which shall b' you
De 31:17 evils and troubles shall b' them;
29 will b' you in the latter days;
Ps 91:10 There shall be no evil b' thee,
Da 10:14 what shall b' thy people
Ac 20:22 the things that shall b' me.

befallen
Le 10:19 and such things have b' me:
Nu 20:14 travel that hath b' us:
De 31:21 many evils and troubles are b'
J'g 6:13 why then is all this b' us?
1Sa 20:26 Something hath b' him, he is not
Es 6:13 every thing that had b' him.
M't 8:33 b' to the possessed of the devils.

befalleth
Ec 3:19 b' the sons of men b' beasts;
19 even one thing b' them:

befell
Ge 42:29 told him all that b' unto them;
Jos 2:23 told him all things that b' them:
2Sa 19: 7 evil that b' thee from thy youth
M'r 5:16 b' to him that was possessed
Ac 20:19 and temptations, which b' me by

before^ See also AFORE; BEFOREHAND; BEFORETIME.
Ge 2: 5 b' it was in the earth, and every
5 herb of the field b' it grew:
6:11 earth also was corrupt b' God;
13 flesh is come b' me; for the earth
7: 1 thee have I seen righteous b' me
10: 9 was a mighty hunter b' the Lord:
9 the mighty hunter b' the Lord.
11:28 died b' his father Terah
12:15 saw her, and commended her b'
13: 9 Is not the whole land b' thee?
10 b' the Lord destroyed Sodom
13 sinners b' the Lord exceedingly.
17: 1 walk b' me, and be thou perfect.
18 that Ishmael might live b' thee!
18: 8 and set it b' them; and he stood
22 Abraham stood yet b' the Lord.
19: 4 But b' they lay down, the men of
13 great b' the face of the Lord;
27 where he stood b' the Lord:
20:15 my land is b' thee: dwell where it
23: 3 stood up from b' his dead,
12 bowed down himself b' the
17 Machpelah, which was b' Mamre,
19 field of Machpelah b' Mamre:
24: 7 he shall send his angel b' thee,
33 there was set meat b' him to eat:
40 The Lord, b' whom I walk, will send
45 b' I had done speaking in mine
51 Behold, Rebekah is b' thee,
25: 9 Hittite, which is b' Mamre;
18 that is b' Egypt, as thou goest
27: 4 my soul may bless thee b' I die.
7 bless thee b' the Lord b' my
10 he may bless thee b' his death.
33 have eaten of all b' thou camest,
29:26 give the younger b' the firstborn.
30:30 which thou hadst b' I came.
33 for my hire b' thy face;
38 pilled b' the flocks in the gutters
39 the flocks conceived b' the rods,
41 the rods b' the eyes of the cattle
31: 2 was not toward him as b'.

Ge 31: 5 it is not toward me as b';
32 b' our brethren discern thou
35 I cannot rise up b' thee;
37 set it here b' my brethren
32: 3 sent messengers b' him to Esau
16 Pass over b' me, and put a space
17 and whose are these b' thee?
20 with the present that goeth b' me,
21 went the present over b' him:
33: 3 he passed over b' them, and bowed
12 and I will go b' thee.
14 thee, pass over b' his servant:
14 as the cattle that goeth b' me
18 and pitched his tent b' the city.
34:10 and the land shall be b' you;
36:31 b' there reigned any king over the
37:18 afar off, even b' he came near
40: 9 a vine was b' me;
41:43 cried b' him, Bow the knee:
46 stood b' Pharaoh king of Egypt.
50 born two sons b' the years
42: 6 bowed down themselves b' him
24 and bound him b' their eyes.
43: 9 and set him b' thee, then let me
14 give you mercy b' the man,
15 to Egypt, and stood b' Joseph.
33 And they sat b' him, the firstborn
34 messes unto them from b' him:
44:14 they fell b' him on the ground.
45: 1 Joseph could not refrain himself b'
5 did send me b' you to preserve
7 God sent me b' you to preserve
28 I will go and see him b' I die.
46:28 sent Judah b' him unto Joseph,
47: 6 The land of Egypt is b' thee;
7 set him b' Pharaoh, and Jacob
10 and went out b' Pharaoh.
19 shall we die b' thine eyes,
48: 5 b' I came unto thee into Egypt,
15 said, God, b' whom my fathers
20 and he set Ephraim b' Manasseh.
49: 8 shall bow down b' thee.
30 Machpelah, which is b' Mamre
50:13 of Ephron the Hittite, b' Mamre.
16 father did command b' he died,
18 went and fell down b' his face;
Ex 4: 3 and Moses fled from b' it.
21 do all those wonders b' Pharaoh,
6:12 Moses spake b' the Lord, saying,
30 Moses said b' the Lord, Behold,
7: 9 thy rod, and cast it b' Pharaoh,
10 cast down his rod b' Pharaoh,
10 and b' his servants,
8:20 morning, and stand b' Pharaoh;
26 of the Egyptians b' their eyes,
9:10 furnace and stood b' Pharaoh;
11 magicians could not stand b' Moses
13 morning, and stand b' Pharaoh,
10: 1 shew these my signs b' him:
3 refuse to humble thyself b' me?
10 look to it; for evil is b' you.
14 b' them there were no such
11:10 did all these wonders b' Pharaoh:
12:34 their dough b' it was leavened,
13:21 the Lord went b' them by day
22 fire by night, from b' the people.
14: 2 encamp b' Pi-hahiroth, between
2 b' it shall ye encamp by the sea.
9 Pi-hahiroth, b' Baal-zephon.
19 angel of God, which went b' the
19 pillar of cloud went from b' their
16: 9 Come near b' the Lord: for he
33 lay it up b' the Lord, to be kept
34 laid it up b' the Testimony, to be
17: 5 Go on b' the people, and take
6 I will stand b' thee there upon the
18:12 bread with Moses' father-in-law b'
19: 2 there Israel camped b' the mount.
7 and laid b' their faces
20: 3 shalt have no other gods b' me.
20 his fear may be b' your faces,
21: 1 judgments which thou shalt set b'
22: 9 parties shall come b' the judges;
23:15 none shall appear b' me empty:
17 males shall appear b' the Lord
20 I send an Angel b' thee to keep
23 mine Angel shall go b' thee,
27 I will send my fear b' thee, and
28 I will send hornets b' thee, which
28 and the Hittite, from b' thee,
29 not drive them out from b' thee
30 I will drive them out from b' thee,
31 thou shalt drive them out b' thee.
25:30 the table shewbread b' me alway
27:21 without the vail, which is b' the
21 evening to morning b' the Lord:
28:12 shall bear their names b' the Lord
25 of the ephod b' it.
29 for a memorial b' the Lord
30 when he goeth in b' the Lord:
30 his heart b' the Lord continually.
35 unto the holy place b' the Lord,
38 they may be accepted b' the Lord.
29:10 to be brought b' the tabernacle
11 kill the bullock b' the Lord,
23 unleavened bread that is b' the
24 a wave offering b' the Lord.
25 for a sweet savour b' the Lord:
26 a wave offering b' the Lord:
42 the congregation b' the Lord:
30: 6 b' the vail that is by the ark of
6 the testimony, b' the mercy seat
8 incense b' the Lord throughout
16 children of Israel b' the Lord,
36 b' the testimony in the tabernacle
Ex 32: 1 make us gods, which shall go b' us;
5 he built an altar b' it; and Aaron
23 shall go b' us: for as for this
34 behold, mine Angel shall go b' thee:
33: 2 I will send an angel b' thee;
19 my goodness pass b' thee, and
19 the name of the Lord b' thee;
34: 3 nor herds feed b' that mount.
6 the Lord passed by b' him,
10 a covenant: b' all thy people
11 I drive out b' thee the Amorite,
20 none shall appear b' me empty.
23 your menchildren appear b' the
24 I will cast out the nations b' thee,
24 go up to appear b' the Lord
34 when Moses went in b' the Lord
39:18 of the ephod, b' it.
40: 5 b' the ark of the testimony,
6 b' the door of the tabernacle
23 in order upon it b' the Lord;
25 he lighted the lamps b' the Lord;
26 b' the vail:
Le 1: 3 of the congregation b' the Lord.
5 shall kill the bullock b' the Lord:
11 the altar northward b' the Lord:
3: 1 it without blemish b' the Lord.
7 shall he offer it b' the Lord.
8 and kill it b' the tabernacle
12 then shall he offer it b' the Lord.
13 kill it b' the tabernacle
4: 4 the congregation b' the Lord;
4 kill the bullock b' the Lord.
6 blood seven times b' the Lord,
6 b' the vail of the sanctuary
7 incense b' the Lord, which is in
14 bring him b' the tabernacle of the
15 head of the bullock b' the Lord:
15 bullock shall be killed b' the Lord.
17 sprinkle it seven times b' the Lord,
17 even b' the vail.
18 the altar which is b' the Lord,
24 kill the burnt offering b' the Lord:
6: 7 an atonement for him b' the Lord:
14 offer it b' the Lord, b' the altar.
25 shall be killed b' the Lord:
7:30 for a wave offering b' the Lord.
8:26 bread that was b' the Lord,
27 them for a wave offering b' the
29 it for a wave offering b' the Lord:
9: 2 blemish, and offer them b' the Lord.
4 offerings, to sacrifice b' the Lord;
5 b' the tabernacle of the
5 near and stood b' the Lord.
21 for a wave offering b' the Lord;
24 there came a fire out from b'
10: 1 offered strange fire b' the Lord,
2 them, and they died b' the Lord.
3 b' all the people I will be
4 near, carry your brethren from b'
15 for a wave offering b' the Lord;
17 atonement for them b' the Lord?
19 their burnt offering b' the Lord;
12: 7 Who shall offer it b' the Lord,
14:11 clean, and those things, b' the Lord,
12 for a wave offering b' the Lord:
16 his finger seven times b' the Lord:
18 an atonement for him b' the Lord.
23 of the congregation, b' the Lord.
24 for a wave offering b' the Lord:
27 left hand seven times b' the Lord:
29 an atonement for him b' the Lord.
31 is to be cleansed b' the Lord.
36 they empty the house, b' the priest
15:14 come b' the Lord unto the door
15 him b' the Lord for his issue.
30 an atonement for her b' the Lord
16: 1 they offered b' the Lord, and died;
2 the vail b' the mercy seat,
7 present them b' the Lord at the
10 be presented alive b' the Lord,
12 from off the altar b' the Lord,
13 incense upon the fire b' the Lord,
14 eastward; and b' the mercy seat
15 seat, and b' the mercy seat:
18 that is b' the Lord, and make
30 from all your sins b' the Lord.
17: 4 b' the tabernacle of the
18:23 neither shall any woman stand b'
24 defiled which I cast out b' you:
27 which were b' you, and the land
28 the nations that were b' you.
30 which were committed b' you,
19:14 put a stumblingblock b' the blind,
22 trespass offering b' the Lord for
32 shalt rise up b' the hoary head,
20:23 nation, which I cast out b' you:
23:11 wave the sheaf b' the Lord,
20 for a wave offering b' the Lord,
28 for you b' the Lord your God.
40 rejoice b' the Lord your God
24: 3 morning b' the Lord continually:
4 pure candlestick b' the Lord
6 upon the pure table b' the Lord.
8 in order b' the Lord continually,
26: 7 they shall fall b' you by the sword.
8 your enemies shall fall b' you
17 ye shall be slain b' your enemies:
37 as it were b' a sword, when none
37 no power to stand b' your enemies.
27: 8 shall present himself b' the priest,
11 present the beast b' the priest:
Nu 3: 4 died b' the Lord, when they offered
4 strange fire b' the Lord,
6 present them b' Aaron the priest,
7 b' the tabernacle of the
Nu 3:38 b' the tabernacle toward the east,
38 even b' the tabernacle of the
5:16 near, and set her b' the Lord:
18 set the woman b' the Lord, and
25 wave the offering b' the Lord,
30 the woman b' the Lord,
6:12 days that were b' shall be lost,
16 priest shall bring them b' the Lord,
20 for a wave offering b' the Lord:
7: 3 brought their offering b' the Lord,
3 brought them b' the tabernacle.
10 offered their offering b' the altar.
8: 9 b' the tabernacle of the
10 bring the Levites b' the Lord:
11 shall offer the Levites b' the Lord
13 set the Levites b' Aaron, and b'
21 them as an offering b' the Lord;
22 congregation b' Aaron, and b' his
9: 6 they came b' Moses and b' Aaron
10: 9 b' the Lord your God, and ye shall
10 memorial b' your God: I am the
33 the Lord went b' them in the three
35 let them that hate thee flee b' thee.
11: 6 beside this manna, b' our eyes.
20 and have wept b' him, saying,
13:22 Hebron was built seven years b'
30 Caleb stilled the people b' Moses,
14: 5 Aaron fell on their faces b' all
10 of the congregation b' all the
14 thou goest b' them, by day time
37 died by the plague b' the Lord.
42 be not smitten b' your enemies.
43 the Canaanites are there b' you,
15:15 shall the stranger be b' the Lord.
25 their sin offering b' the Lord for
28 sinneth by ignorance b' the Lord,
16: 2 they rose up b' Moses, with certain
7 in them b' the Lord to morrow:
9 b' the congregation to minister
16 b' the Lord, thou, and they,
17 bring ye b' the Lord every man
38 for they offered them b' the Lord,
40 near to offer incense b' the Lord:
43 Moses and Aaron came b' the
17: 4 b' the testimony, where I will meet
7 laid up the rods b' the Lord
9 the rods from b' the Lord unto all
10 again b' the testimony, to be kept
18: 2 minister b' the tabernacle of
19 for ever b' the Lord unto thee
19: 3 one shall slay her b' his face:
4 blood directly b' the tabernacle
20: 3 our brethren died b' the Lord!
8 speak ye unto the rock b' their eyes;
9 Moses took the rod from b' the
10 congregation together b'...rock.
21:11 wilderness which is b' Moab,
22:32 thy way is perverse b' me:
25: 4 hang them up b' the Lord against
6 Who were weeping b' the door
26:61 offered strange fire b' the Lord.
27: 2 And they stood b' Moses,
2 and b' Eleazar the priest,
2 and b' the princes
5 brought their cause b' the Lord.
14 sanctify me at the water b' their
17 Which may go out b' them,
17 and which may go in b' them,
19 b' Eleazar the priest, and b' all
21 And he shall stand b' Eleazar the
21 of Urim b' the Lord:
22 b' Eleazar the priest, and b' all
31:50 atonement for our souls b' the Lord.
54 children of Israel b' the Lord.
32: 4 smote b' the congregation of Israel,
17 b' the children of Israel, until we
20 armed b' the Lord to war,
21 over Jordan b' the Lord, until he
21 driven out his enemies from b' him.
22 the land be subdued b' the Lord:
22 guiltless b' the Lord, and b' Israel;
22 be your possession b' the Lord.
27 b' the Lord to battle, as my lord
29 to battle, b' the Lord,
29 the land shall be subdued b' you;
32 pass over armed b' the Lord
33: 7 b' Baal-zephon:
7 and they pitched b' Migdol.
8 they departed from b' Pi-hahiroth,
47 the mountains of Abarim, b' Nebo.
52 inhabitants of the land from b' you,
55 the inhabitants of the land from b'
35:12 until he stand b' the congregation
36: 1 and spake b' Moses, and b' the
De 1: 8 I have set the land b' you:
21 thy God hath set the land b' thee:
22 We will send men b' us, and they
30 your God which goeth b' you,
30 did for you in Egypt b' your eyes;
33 Who went in the way b' you,
38 son of Nun, which standeth b' thee,
42 lest ye be smitten b' your enemies.
45 ye returned and wept b' the Lord;
2:12 had destroyed them from b' them,
21 the Lord destroyed them b' them;
22 destroyed the Horims from b' them;
31 to give Sihon and his land b' thee:
33 Lord our God delivered him b' us;
3:18 pass over armed b' your brethren
28 he shall go over b' this people,
4: 8 this law, which I set b' you
10 thou stoodest b' the Lord thy God
32 which were b' thee, since the day
34 did for you in Egypt b' your eyes?
38 To drive out nations from b' thee

De 4:44 Moses set b' the children of Israel:
5: 7 have none other gods b' me.
6:19 all thine enemies from b' thee,
22 all his household, b' our eyes:
25 b' the Lord our God, as he hath
7: 1 hath cast out many nations b' thee,
2 God shall deliver them b' thee;
22 put out those nations b' thee little
24 no man be able to stand b' thee,
8:20 the Lord destroyeth b' your face,
9: 2 Who can stand b' the children of
3 is he which goeth over b' thee;
3 shall bring them down b' thy face:
4 cast them out from b' thee,
4 drive them out from b' thee.
5 doth drive them out from b' thee,
17 and brake them b' your eyes.
18 And I fell down b' the Lord,
25 Thus I fell down b' the Lord
10: 8 of the Lord, to stand b' the Lord
11 take thy journey b' the people,
11:23 all these nations from b' you,
25 no man be able to stand b' you:
26 I set b' you this day a blessing
32 which I set b' you this day.
12: 7 there ye shall eat b' the Lord
12 And ye shall rejoice b' the Lord
18 thou must eat them b' the Lord
18 thou shalt rejoice b' the Lord
29 cut off the nations from b' thee,
30 that they be destroyed from b' thee;
14:23 thou shalt eat b' the Lord thy God,
26 thou shalt eat there b' the Lord
15:20 Thou shalt eat it b' the Lord
16:11 thou shalt rejoice b' the Lord
16 all thy males appear b' the Lord
16 they shall not appear b' the Lord
17:12 to minister there b' the Lord
18 that which is b' the priests
18: 7 which stand there b' the Lord.
12 drive them out from b' thee.
19:17 shall stand b' the Lord,
17 b' the priests and the judges,
21:16 firstborn b' the son of the hated,
22: 6 a bird's nest chance to be b' thee
17 cloth b' the elders of the city.
23:14 to give up thine enemies b' thee;
24: 4 that is abomination b' the Lord:
13 unto thee b' the Lord thy God.
25: 2 to be beaten b' his face,
26: 4 b' the altar of the Lord thy God.
5 shalt speak and say b' the Lord
10 set it b' the Lord thy God,
10 and worship b' the Lord thy God:
13 shalt say b' the Lord thy God,
27: 7 and rejoice b' the Lord thy God.
28: 7 thee to be smitten b' thy face:
7 and flee b' thee seven ways.
25 to be smitten b' thine enemies:
25 and flee seven ways b' them:
31 ox shall be slain b' thine eyes,
31 taken away from b' thy face,
66 life shall hang in doubt b' thee;
29: 2 all that the Lord did b' your eyes
10 all of you b' the Lord your God;
15 this day b' the Lord our God,
30: 1 curse, which I have set b' thee,
15 I have set b' thee this day
19 I have set b' you life and death,
31: 3 he will go over b' thee, and he will
3 destroy these nations from b' thee,
3 Joshua, he shall go over b' thee,
5 shall give them up b' your face,
8 he it is that doth go b' thee;
11 is come to appear b' the Lord
11 read this law b' all Israel
21 now, b' I have brought them
32:52 thou shalt see the land b' thee;
33: 1 the children of Israel b' his death.
10 shall put incense b' thee, and
27 thrust out the enemy from b' thee;
Jos 1: 5 any man be able to stand b' thee
14 ye shall pass b' your brethren
2: 8 And b' they were laid down,
3: 1 lodged there b' they passed over.
6 and pass over b' the people.
6 covenant, and went b' the people.
10 without fail drive out from b' you
11 the earth passeth over b' you
14 of the covenant b' the people;
4: 5 Pass over b' the ark of the Lord
7 b' the ark of the covenant
12 armed b' the children of Israel,
13 passed over b' the Lord unto
18 all his banks, as they did b'.
23 the waters of Jordan from b' you,
23 which he dried up from b' us,
5: 1 from b' the children of Israel,
6: 4 seven priests shall bear b' the ark
5 up every man straight b' him.
6 horns b' the ark of the Lord.
7 pass on b' the ark of the Lord.
8 horns passed on b' the Lord,
9 the armed men went b' the priests
13 rams' horns b' the ark of the Lord
13 the armed men went b' them;
20 every man straight b' him,
26 Cursed be the man b' the Lord,
7: 4 they fled b' the men of Ai.
5 b' the gate even unto Shebarim,
6 upon his face b' the ark
8 their backs b' their enemies!
12 could not stand b' their enemies,
12 but turned their backs b' their
13 canst not stand b' thine enemies,
23 and laid them out b' the Lord.

Jos 8: 5 first, that we will flee b' them,
6 They flee b' us, as at the first:
6 therefore we will flee b' them.
10 of Israel, b' the people to Ai.
11 drew nigh, and came b' the city,
14 a time appointed, b' the plain;
15 made as if they were beaten b'
33 and on that side b' the priests
33 had commanded b', that they
35 which Joshua read not b' all
9:24 of the land from b' you,
10: 5 and encamped b' Gibeon:
8 not a man of them stand b' thee.
10 Lord discomfited them b' Israel,
11 as they fled from b' Israel,
12 Amorites b' the children of Israel,
14 no day like that b' it or after it,
11: 6 deliver them up all slain b' Israel:
13: 3 Sihor, which is b' Egypt,
6 drive out from b' the children
25 Aroer that is b' Rabbah;
14:15 of Hebron b' was Kirjath-arba;
15: 7 b' the going up to Adummim,
8 that lieth b' the valley
15 of Debir b' was Kirjath-sepher.
17: 4 came near b' Eleazar the priest,
4 and b' Joshua the son of Nun,
4 and b' the princes,
7 that lieth b' Shechem;
18: 1 the land was subdued b' them.
6 cast lots for you here b' the Lord
8 for you b' the Lord in Shiloh.
10 for them in Shiloh b' the Lord:
14 hill that lieth b' Beth-horon
16 b' the valley of the son of
19:11 the river that is b' Jokneam;
46 the border b' Japho.
51 by lot in Shiloh b' the Lord,
20: 6 he stand b' the congregation
9 he stood b' the congregation.
21:44 of all their enemies b' them;
22:27 do the service of the Lord b' him
29 Lord our God that is b' his
23: 5 shall expel them from b' you,
9 Lord hath driven out from b' you
9 hath been able to stand b' you
13 any of these nations from b' you;
24: 1 they presented themselves b' God.
8 I destroyed them from b' you.
12 I sent the hornet b' you, which
12 drave them out from b' you,
18 the Lord drave out from b' us
J'g 1:10 now the name of Hebron b' was
11 and the name of Debir b'
23 the name of the city b' was Luz.)
2: 3 not drive them out from b' you;
14 any longer stand b' their enemies.
21 drive out any from b' them of the
3: 2 such as b' knew nothing thereof;
27 from the mount, and he b' them.
4:14 not the Lord gone out b' thee?
15 the edge of the sword b' Barak;
23 Canaan b' the children of Israel.
5: 5 mountains melted from b' the
5 even that Sinai from b' the Lord
6: 9 drave them out from b' you,
18 my present, and set it b' thee.
7:24 take b' them the waters
8:13 from battle b' the sun was up,
28 Midian subdued b' the children
9:39 Gaal went out b' the men of
40 chased him and he fled b' him,
11: 9 the Lord deliver them b' me,
11 Jephthah uttered all his words b'
23 from b' his people Israel,
24 God shall drive out from b' us,
33 subdued b' the children of Israel.
12: 5 of Jordan b' the Ephraimites:
14:16 Sampson's wife wept b' him,
17 she wept b' him the seven days,
18 seventh day b' the sun went down,
16: 3 of an hill that is b' Hebron.
20 as at other times b', and shake
18: 6 b' the Lord is your way wherein
21 cattle and the carriage b' them.
20:23 and wept b' the Lord until even,
26 and sat there b' the Lord,
26 and peace offerings b' the Lord.
28 Aaron, stood b' it in those days,)
32 They are smitten down b' us,
35 the Lord smote Benjamin b' Israel:
39 they are smitten down b' us,
42 turned their backs b' the men of
21: 2 abode there till even b' God,
Ru 3:14 she rose up b' one could know
4: 4 Buy it b' the inhabitants,
4 and b' the elders of my people.
1Sa 1:12 continued praying b' the Lord,
15 poured out my soul b' the Lord.
19 and worshipped b' the Lord,
22 that he may appear b' the Lord,
2:11 the Lord b' Eli the priest.
15 b' they burnt the fat, the priest's
17 was very great b' the Lord:
18 Samuel ministered b' the
21 child Samuel grew b' the Lord.
28 incense, to wear an ephod b' me?
30 of thy father, should walk b' me
35 he shall walk b' mine anointed
3: 1 ministered unto the Lord b'
4: 2 was smitten b' the Philistines:
3 us to day b' the Philistines?
17 Israel is fled b' the Philistines,
5: 3 to the earth b' the ark of the Lord.
4 ground b' the ark of the Lord;
6:20 is able to stand b' this holy Lord

1Sa 7: 6 drew water; and poured it out b'
10 and they were smitten b' Israel.
8:11 some shall run b' his chariots.
20 may judge us, and go out b' us,
9:12 He is; behold, he is b' you:
13 find him, b' he go up to the high
15 a day b' Saul came, saying,
19 go up b' me unto the high place;
24 and set it b' Saul. And Samuel
24 is left! set it b' thee, and eat:
27 Bid the servant pass on b' us,
10: 5 and a pipe, and a harp, b' them;
8 shalt go down b' me to Gilgal;
19 present yourselves b' the Lord
25 book, and laid it up b' the Lord.
11:15 they made Saul king b' the Lord
15 of peace offerings b' the Lord;
12: 2 the king walketh b' you: and I am
2 I have walked b' you from my
3 witness against me b' the Lord,
3 the Lord, and b' his anointed:
7 may reason with you b' the Lord
16 the Lord will do b' your eyes.
14:13 him; and they fell b' Jonathan;
21 the Philistines b' that time,
15:30 thee, b' the elders of my people,
30 and b' Israel, and turn again
33 hewed Agag in pieces b' the Lord,
16: 6 the Lord's anointed is b' him.
8 made him pass b' Samuel.
10 made seven of his sons to pass b'
16 thy servants, which are b' thee,
21 came to Saul, and stood b' him:
22 Let David, I pray thee, stand b' me;
17: 7 one bearing a shield went b' him.
31 they rehearsed them b' Saul:
41 that bare the shield went b' him.
57 brought him b' Saul with the head
18:13 out and came in b' the people.
16 he went out and came in b' them.
19:24 prophesied b' Samuel in like
20: 1 and came and said b' Jonathan,
1 what is my sin b' thy father,
21: 6 was taken from b' the Lord,
7 that day, detained b' the Lord;
13 he changed his behaviour b' them,
22: 4 he brought them b' the king
23:18 made a covenant b' the Lord:
24 arose and went to Ziph b' Saul:
25:19 Go on b' me; behold, I come after
23 fell b' David on her face,
26: 1 which is b' Jeshimon?
3 which is b' Jeshimon, by the
19 cursed be they b' the Lord;
20 fall to the earth b' the face of the
28:22 me set a morsel of bread b' thee;
25 And she brought it b' Saul,
25 and b' his servants;
30:20 they drave b' those other cattle,
31: 1 Israel fled from b' the Philistines,
2Sa 2:14 men now arise, and play b' us.
17 of Israel, b' the servants of David.
24 Ammah, that lieth b' Giah
3:28 are guiltless b' the Lord
31 sackcloth, and mourn b' Abner.
34 as a man falleth b' wicked men,
5: 3 with them in Hebron b' the Lord:
20 forth upon mine enemies b' me,
24 the Lord go out b' thee, to smite
6: 4 and Ahio went b' the ark.
5 played b' the Lord on all manner
14 David danced b' the Lord with all
16 leaping and dancing b' the Lord;
17 and peace offerings b' the Lord.
21 It was b' the Lord, which chose
21 which chose me b' thy father
21 and b' all his house,
21 therefore will I play b' the Lord.
7:15 Saul, whom I put away b' thee.
16 be established forever b' thee:
18 and sat b' the Lord, and he said,
23 for thy land, b' thy people,
26 David be established b' thee.
29 it may continue for ever b' thee:
10: 6 that they stank b' David,
9 was against him b' and behind,
13 the Syrians: and they fled b' him.
14 fled they also b' Abishai, and
15 were smitten b' Israel, they
16 host of Hadarezer went b' them.
18 And the Syrians fled b' Israel;
19 they were smitten b' Israel, they
11:13 he did eat and drink b' him;
12:11 I will take thy wives b' thine eyes,
12 I will do this thing b' all Israel,
12 and b' the sun.
20 they set bread b' him,
13: 9 pan and poured them out b' him;
14:33 face to the ground b' the king:
15: 1 and fifty men to run b' him.
18 from Gath, passed...b' the king.
18: 7 the people of Israel were slain b'
28 upon his face b' the king,
19: 8 all the people came b' the king:
13 captain of the host b' me
17 went over Jordan b' the king.
18 fell down b' the king, as he was
20: 8 in Gibeon, Amasa went b' them.
21: 9 them in the hill b' the Lord:
22:13 Through the brightness b' him
23 his judgments were b' me:
24 I was also upright b' him,
24:13 wilt thou flee three months b'
20 and bowed himself b' the king
1Ki 1: 2 let her stand b' the king, and let
5 and fifty men to run b' him.

1Ki 7:23 when he was come in b' the king,
25 behold, they eat and drink b' him,
28 king's presence, and stood b' the
32 And they came b' the king.
2: 4 heed to their way, to walk b' me
26 the ark of the Lord God b' David
45 shall be established b' the Lord
3: 6 according as he walked b' thee
12 there was none like thee b' thee,
15 stood b' the ark of the covenant
16 unto the king, and stood b' him.
22 Thus they spake b' the king.
24 they brought a sword b' the king.
6: 3 b' the temple of the house,
3 was the breadth thereof b'
7 ready b' it was brought thither:
17 the temple b' it, was forty cubits
21 b' the oracle; and he overlaid it
7: 6 the porch was b' them: and the
6 and the thick beam were b' them
49 left, b' the oracle, with the
8: 5 b' the ark, sacrificing sheep and
8 in the holy place b' the oracle,
22 stood b' the altar of the Lord
23 thy servants that walk b' thee
25 that they walk b' me as thou
25 hast walked b' me.
28 servant prayeth b' thee to day:
31 come b' thine altar in this house:
33 people Israel be smitten down b'
50 b' them who carried them captive,
54 from b' the altar of the Lord,
59 made supplication b' the Lord,
62 Israel with him offered sacrifice b'
64 that was b' the house of the Lord:
64 brasen altar that was b' the Lord
65 b' the Lord our God, seven days
9: 3 that thou hast made b' me:
4 if thou wilt walk b' me, as David
6 statutes which I have set b' you,
25 the altar that was b' the Lord.
10: 8 which stand continually b' thee,
11: 7 the hill that is b' Jerusalem,
36 a light alway b' me in Jerusalem,
12: 6 men, that stood b' Solomon
8 him, and which stood b' him:
30 people went to worship b' the one,
13: 6 again, and became as it was b'.
14: 9 evil above all that were b' thee:
24 cast out b' the children of Israel.
15: 3 father which he had done b' him:
16:25 worse than all that were b' him.
30 above all that were b' him.
33 kings of Israel that were b' him.
17: 1 of Israel liveth, b' whom I stand,
3 Cherith, that is b' Jordan.
5 Cherith, that is b' Jordan.
18:15 liveth, b' whom I stand, I will
46 ran b' Ahab to the entrance
19:11 stand upon the mount b' the Lord.
11 in pieces the rocks b' the Lord;
19 with twelve yoke of oxen b' him,
20:27 Israel pitched b' them like
21:10 sons of Belial, b' him, to bear
13 and sat b' him:
26 cast out b' the children of Israel.
29 how Ahab humbleth himself b' me?
29 he humbleth himself b' me,
22:10 the prophets prophesied b' them.
21 came forth a spirit, and stood b'
2Ki 1:13 and fell on his knees b' Elijah,
2: 9 do for thee, b' I be taken away
15 themselves to the ground b' him.
3:14 b' whom I stand, surely, were it
24 so that they fled b' them:
4:12 had called her, she stood b' him.
31 Gehazi passed on b' them, and laid
38 the prophets were sitting b' him:
43 I set this b' an hundred men?
44 So he set it b' them, and they
5:15 and came, and stood b' him:
16 the Lord liveth, b' whom I stand,
23 and they bare them b' him.
25 and stood b' his master.
6:22 set bread and water b' them,
32 the king sent a man from b' him:
8: 9 and came and stood b' him, and
10: 4 Behold, two kings stood not b' him:
11:18 the priest of Baal b' the altars.
14:12 was put to the worse b' Israel;
15:10 and smote him b' the people,
16: 3 cast out from b' the children
14 altar, which was b' the Lord,
17: 2 kings of Israel that were b' him.
8 out from b' the children of Israel,
11 the Lord carried away b' them;
18: 5 Judah, nor any that were b' him.
22 Ye shall worship b' this altar in
19:14 Lord, and spread it b' the Lord.
15 Hezekiah prayed b' the Lord,
26 corn blasted b' it be grown up.
32 nor come b' it with shield, nor
20: 3 I have walked b' thee in truth
21: 2 cast out b' the children of Israel.
9 destroyed b' the children of Israel.
11 Amorites did, which were b' him,
22:10 And Shaphan read it b' the king.
19 hast humbled thyself b' the Lord,
19 rent thy clothes, and wept b' me;
23: 3 made a covenant b' the Lord,
13 that were b' Jerusalem,
25 unto him was there no king b' him,
25: 7 sons of Zedekiah b' his eyes,
29 did eat bread continually b' him
1Ch 1:43 of Edom b' any king reigned over
5:25 land, whom God destroyed b' them.
1Ch 6:32 they ministered b' the dwelling
10: 1 Israel fled from b' the Philistines,
11: 3 with them in Hebron b' the Lord;
13 people fled from b' the Philistines.
13: 8 David and all Israel played b' God
10 the ark: and there he died b' God.
14:15 God is gone forth b' thee to smite
15:24 the trumpets b' the ark of God:
16: 1 and peace offerings b' God.
4 to minister b' the ark of the Lord,
6 b' the ark of the covenant of God.
29 an offering, and come b' him:
30 Fear b' him, all the earth: the
37 there b' the ark of the covenant
37 to minister b' the ark continually,
39 b' the tabernacle of the Lord
17: 8 off all thine enemies from b' thee,
13 it from him that was b' thee:
16 the king came and sat b' the Lord,
21 out nations from b' thy people,
24 thy servant be established b' thee.
25 found in his heart to pray b' thee.
27 that it may be b' thee for ever:
19: 7 who came and pitched b' Medeba.
9 the battle in array b' the gate
10 was set against him b' and behind,
14 b' the Syrians unto the battle;
14 and they fled b' him.
15 likewise fled b' Abishai his brother,
16 put to the worse b' Israel,
16 host of Hadarezer went b' them.
18 Syrians fled b' Israel; and David
19 put to the worse b' Israel, they
21:12 to be destroyed b' thy foes, while
30 not go b' it to enquire of God:
22: 5 prepared abundantly b' his death.
18 the land is subdued b' the Lord,
18 and b' his people.
23:13 to burn incense b' the Lord, to
31 unto them continually b' the Lord:
24: 2 and Abihu died b' their father,
6 wrote them b' the king,
6 and b' the chief of the fathers
28: 4 chose me b' all the house
29:10 the Lord b' all the congregation:
15 strangers b' thee, and sojourners
22 And did eat and drink b' the Lord
25 been on any king b' him in Israel.
2Ch 1: 5 b' the tabernacle of the Lord:
6 to the brasen altar b' the Lord,
10 go out and come in b' this people:
12 have had that have been b' thee,
13 from b' the tabernacle of the
2: 4 and to burn b' him sweet incense,
6 save only to burn sacrifice b' him?
3:15 he made b' the house two pillars
17 up the pillars b' the temple,
4:20 after the manner b' the oracle,
5: 6 assembled unto him b' the ark,
9 seen from the ark b' the oracle;
6:12 he stood b' the altar of the Lord
13 down upon his knees b' all
14 thy servants, that walk b' thee
16 my law as thou hast walked b' me.
19 which thy servant prayeth b' thee:
22 come b' thine altar in this house;
24 be put to the worse b' the enemy,
24 and make supplication b' thee
36 deliver them over b' their enemies,
7: 4 offered sacrifices b' the Lord.
6 priests sounded trumpets b' them,
7 was b' the house of the Lord:
17 if thou wilt walk b' me, as David
19 which I have set b' you,
8:12 which he had built b' the porch,
14 and minister b' the priests,
9: 7 which stand continually b' thee,
11 and there were none such seen b'
10: 6 men that had stood b' Solomon
8 up with him, that stood b' him.
13:13 they were b' Judah, and the
14 the battle was b' and behind:
15 Jeroboam and all Israel b' Abijah
16 children of Israel fled b' Judah:
14: 5 the kingdom was quiet b' him.
7 while the land is yet b' us;
12 the Lord smote the Ethiopians b'
12 Asa, and b' Judah;
13 they were destroyed b' the Lord,
13 and b' his host;
15: 8 that was b' the porch of the Lord.
18: 9 the prophets prophesied b' them.
20 and stood b' the Lord, and said,
19: 2 wrath upon thee from b' the Lord.
11 the Levites shall be officers b' you.
20: 5 b' the new court,
7 b' thy people Israel, and gavest
9 we stand b' this house, and in thy
13 and all Judah stood b' the Lord,
16 brook, b' the wilderness of Jeruel.
18 of Jerusalem fell b' the Lord,
21 as they went out b' the army,
23:17 slew Mattan the priest of Baal b'
24:14 the rest of the money b' the king
25: 8 shall make thee fall b' the enemy:
14 and bowed himself down b' them,
22 was put to the worse b' Israel,
26:19 forehead b' the priests in the
27: 6 he prepared his ways b' the Lord
28: 3 cast out b' the children of Israel.
9 he went out b' the host that came
14 b' the princes and all the
29:11 hath chosen you to stand b' him,
19 they are b' the altar of the Lord.
23 b' the king and the congregation,
30: 9 b' them that lead them captive,
2Ch 31:20 and truth b' the Lord his God.
32:12 Ye shall worship b' one altar, and
33: 2 cast out b' the children of Israel.
7 which I have chosen b' all the
9 destroyed b' the children of
12 himself greatly b' the God
19 graven images, b' he was humbled:
23 humbled not himself b' the Lord,
34:18 And Shaphan read it b' the king.
24 have read b' the king of Judah:
27 thou didst humble thyself b' God,
27 humbledst thyself b' me, and didst
27 rend thy clothes, and weep b' me;
31 and made a covenant b' the Lord,
36:12 humbled not himself b' Jeremiah
Ezr 3:12 this house was laid b' their eyes,
4:18 us hath been plainly read b' me.
23 letter was read b' Rehum,
7:19 vessels. . . deliver thou b' the God
28 extended mercy unto me b' the
28 b' all the king's mighty princes.
8:21 might afflict ourselves b' our God,
29 weigh them b' the chief of the
9:15 we are b' thee in our trespasses:
15 for we cannot stand b' thee
10: 1 himself down b' the house of God,
6 Ezra rose up from b' the house of
Ne 1: 4 and prayed b' the God of heaven,
6 I pray b' thee now, day and night,
2: 1 the king, that wine was b' him:
13 valley, even b' the dragon well,
4: 2 spake b' his brethren and the
5 sin be blotted out from b' thee:
5 to anger b' the builders.
5:15 governors that had been b' me
6:19 reported his good deeds b' me,
8: 1 street that was b' the water gate;
2 law b' the congregation both of
3 he read therein b' the street
3 that was b' the water gate
3 b' the men and the women, and
9: 8 foundest his heart faithful b' thee,
11 thou didst divide the sea b' them,
24 and thou subduedst b' them the
28 rest, they did evil again b' thee:
32 all the trouble seem little b' thee,
35 land which thou gavest b' them,
12:36 God, and Ezra the scribe b' them.
13: 4 And b' this, Eliashib the priest,
19 began to be dark b' the sabbath,
Es 1: 3 princes of the provinces, being b'
11 bring Vashti the queen b' the king
16 Memucan answered b' the king
17 the queen to be brought in b' him,
19 That Vashti come no more b' king
2:11 walked every day b' the court
23 book of the chronicles b' the king.
3: 7 the lot b' Haman from day to day,
4: 2 And came even b' the king's gate:
6 which was b' the king's gate.
8 to make request b' him for her
6: 1 And they were read b' the king.
9 and proclaim b' him, Thus shall
11 of the city, and proclaimed b' him,
13 b' whom thou hast begun to fall,
13 but shalt surely fall b' him.
7: 6 afraid b' the king and the queen.
8 queen also b' me in the house?
9 chamberlains, said b' the king,
8: 1 And Mordecai came b' the king;
3 Esther spake yet again b' the king,
4 Esther arose, and stood b' the
5 the thing seem right b' the king,
9:11 palace was brought b' the king.
25 when Esther came b' the king,
Job 1: 6 present themselves b' the Lord,
2: 1 present themselves b' the Lord,
3:24 my sighing cometh b' I eat, and
4:15 Then a spirit passed b' my face;
16 an image was b' mine eyes,
19 dust, which are crushed b' the
8:12 it withereth b' any other herb.
16 He is green b' the sun, and his
10:21 B' I go whence I shall not return,
13:15 maintain mine own ways b'
16 an hypocrite shall not come b' him.
15: 4 and restrainest prayer b' God.
7 or wast thou made b' the hills?
32 It shall be accomplished b' his
18:20 they that went b' were affrighted.
21: 8 and their offspring b' their eyes.
18 They are as stubble b' the wind,
33 as there are innumerable b' him.
23: 4 I would order my cause b' him,
17 I was not cut off b' the darkness,
30:11 have also let loose the bridle b' me.
33: 5 set thy words in order b' me,
35:14 judgment is b' him; therefore
41:10 who then is able to stand b' me?
22 sorrow is turned into joy b' him.
42:10 twice as much as he had b'
11 had been of his acquaintance b',
Ps 5: 8 make thy way straight b' my face.
16: 8 set the Lord always b' me:
18: 6 and my cry came b' him, even
12 brightness that was b' him
22 his judgments were b' me,
23 I was also upright b' him,
42 small as the dust b' the
22:27 the nations shall worship b' thee.
29 down to the dust shall bow b' him:
23: 5 Thou preparest a table b' me in
26: 3 thy loving kindness is b' mine
31:19 that trust in thee b' the sons of
22 I am cut off from b' thine eyes:
34:*title* his behaviour b' Abimelech;

Ps 35: 5 Let them be as chaff b' the wind:
36: 1 no fear of God b' his eyes,
38: 9 Lord, all my desire is b' thee;
17 my sorrow is continually b' me.
39: 1 while the wicked is b' me.
5 mine age is nothing b' thee:
13 I may recover strength b' I go
41:12 settest me b' thy face for ever.
42: 2 shall I come and appear b' God?
44:15 confusion is continually b' me,
50: 3 a fire shall devour b' him, and it
8 to have been continually b' me.
21 set them in order b' thine eyes.
51: 3 my sin is ever b' me.
52: 9 for it is good b' thy saints.
54: 3 they have not set God b' them.
56:13 that I may walk b' God in the
57: 6 they have digged a pit b' me,
58: 9 B' your pots can feel the thorns,
61: 7 He shall abide b' God for ever:
62: 8 people, pour out your heart b' him:
68: 1 also that hate him flee b' him.
2 as wax melteth b' the fire, so let
3 let them rejoice b' God: yea, let
4 his name Jah, and rejoice b' him.
7 thou wentest forth b' thy people,
25 The singers went b', the players
69:22 table become a snare b' them:
72: 9 the wilderness shall bow b' him;
11 all kings shall fall down b' him,
73:22 I was a beast b' thee.
78:55 cast out the heathen also b' them,
79:11 sighing of the prisoner come b' thee;
80: 2 B' Ephraim and Benjamin and
9 Thou preparedst room b' it,
83:13 as the stubble b' the wind.
84: 7 of them in Zion appeareth b' God.
85:13 Righteousness shall go b' him;
86: 9 and worship b' thee, O Lord;
14 have not set thee b' them.
88: 1 I have cried day and night b' thee:
2 Let my prayer come b' thee:
89:14 mercy and truth shall go b' thy
23 will beat down his foes b' his face,
90: 2 B' the mountains were brought
8 hast set our iniquities b' thee,
95: 2 Let us come b' his presence with
6 us kneel b' the Lord our maker.
96: 6 Honour and majesty are b' him:
9 fear b' him, all the earth.
13 B' the Lord: for he cometh, for he
97: 3 A fire goeth b' him, and burneth
98: 6 make a joyful noise b' the Lord,
9 B' the Lord; for he cometh
100: 2 come b' his presence with singing.
102:*title* poureth out his complaint b' the
28 seed shall be established b' thee.
105:17 He sent a man b' them, even
106:23 Moses his chosen stood b' him
109:15 them be b' the Lord continually,
116: 9 I will walk b' the Lord in the land
119:30 thy judgments have I laid b' me.
46 of thy testimonies also b' kings,
67 B' I was afflicted I went astray:
168 all my ways are b' thee.
169 Let my cry come near b' thee,
170 Let my supplication come b' thee:
138: 1 b' the gods will I sing praise
139: 5 Thou hast beset me behind and b',
141: 2 Let my prayer be set forth b' thee
3 a watch, O Lord, b' my mouth
142: 2 poured out my complaint b' him;
2 I shewed b' him my trouble.
147:17 who can stand b' his cold?
Pr 4:25 eyelids look straight b' thee.
5:21 ways of man are b' the eyes of
8:22 of his way, b' his works of old.
25 B' the mountains were settled,
25 b' the hills was I brought forth:
30 delight, rejoicing always b' him;
14:19 The evil bow b' the good; and the
15:33 wisdom; and b' honour is humility.
16:18 Pride goeth b' destruction,
18 and an haughty spirit b' a fall.
17:14 off contention, b' it be meddled
24 Wisdom is b' him that hath
18:12 B' destruction the heart of man is
12 and b' honour is humility.
13 that answereth a matter b' he
16 and bringeth him b' great men.
22:29 he shall stand b' kings;
29 he shall not stand b' mean men.
23: 1 consider diligently what is b' thee:
25: 5 Take away the wicked from b' the
26 man falling down b' the wicked
26:26 shewed b' the whole congregation.
27: 4 but who is able to stand b' envy?
30: 7 deny me them not b' I die:
Ec 1:10 of old time, which was b' us.
16 all they that have been b' me
2: 7 all that were in Jerusalem b' me:
9 more than all that were b' me
26 to him that is good b' God.
3:14 that men should fear b' him.
4:16 of all that have been b' them:
5: 2 hasty to utter any thing b' God:
6 neither say thou b' the angel, that
6: 8 knoweth to walk b' the living?
7:17 shouldest thou die b' thy time?
8:12 that fear God, which fear b' him:
13 he feareth not b' God.
9: 1 or hatred by all that is b' them.
Ca 8:12 vineyard, which is mine, is b' me:
Isa 1:12 When ye come to appear b' me,
16 of your doings from b' mine eyes;
7:16 For b' the child shall know

Isa 8: 4 b' the child shall have knowledge
4 taken away b' the king of Assyria.
9: 3 they joy b' thee according to the
12 Syrians b', and the Philistines
13:16 be dashed to pieces b' their eyes;
17:13 the chaff off the mountains b' the
13 and like a rolling thing b' the
14 b' the morning he is not.
23:18 them that dwell b' the Lord, to eat
24:23 b' his ancients gloriously.
28: 4 as the hasty fruit b' the summer;
30: 8 Now go, write it b' them
11 of Israel to cease from b' us.
36: 7 Ye shall worship b' this altar?
37:14 Lord, and spread it b' the Lord.
27 as corn blasted b' it be grown up.
33 come b' it with shields, nor cast
38: 3 I have walked b' thee in truth
40:10 with him, and his work b' him.
41: 1 Keep silence b' me,
2 gave the nations b' him,
42: 9 b' they spring forth I tell you
16 will make darkness light b' them,
43:10 b' me there was no God
13 b' the day was I am he;
45: 1 to subdue nations b' him; and I
1 open b' him the two leaved gates;
2 I will go b' thee, and make the
47:14 nor fire to sit b' it.
48: 5 b' it came to pass I shewed
7 even b' the day when thou
19 cut off nor destroyed from b' me.
49:16 thy walls are continually b' me.
52:12 will go b' you; and the God
53: 2 grow up b' him as a tender
7 sheep b' her shearers is dumb, so
55:12 the hills shall break forth b' you
57:16 should fail b' me, and the souls
58: 8 thy righteousness, shall go b' thee:
59:12 are multiplied b' thee,
61:11 to spring forth b' all the nations.
62:11 is with him, and his work b' him.
63:12 arm, dividing the water b' them,
65: 6 it is written b' me: I will not keep
12 but did evil b' mine eyes, and did
24 that b' they call, I will answer;
66: 4 did evil b' mine eyes, and chose
7 B' she travailed, she brought
7 b' her pain came,
22 remain b' me,...so shall your seed
23 all flesh come to worship b' me,
Jer 1: 5 B' I formed thee in the belly I
5 and b' thou camest forth
17 lest I confound thee b' them.
2:22 is marked b' me, saith the Lord
6: 7 b' me continually is grief
21 lay stumblingblocks b' this people,
7:10 and stand b' me in this house,
8: 2 spread them b' the sun,
9:13 my law which I set b' them,
13:16 b' he cause darkness, and
16 b' your feet stumble
15: 1 Moses and Samuel stood b' me,
9 to the sword b' their enemies,
19 shalt stand b' me: and if thou
17:16 of my lips was right b' thee.
18:17 with an east wind b' the enemy;
20 I stood b' thee to speak good for
23 let them be overthrown b' thee;
19: 7 fall by the sword b' their enemies,
21: 8 I set b' you the way of life,
24: 1 two baskets of figs were set b' the
26: 4 my law, which I have set b' you,
28: 8 prophets that have been b' me
8 and b' thee of old prophesied
29:21 he shall slay them b' your eyes;
30:20 shall be established b' me,
31:36 ordinances depart from b' me,
36 being a nation b' me for ever.
32:12 b' all the Jews that sat in the
13 charged Baruch b' them, saying,
30 Judah have only done evil b' me
31 should remove it from b' my face,
33: 9 an honour b' all the nations
18 the Levites want a man b' me
24 should be no more a nation b' them.
34: 5 former kings which were b' thee,
15 ye had made a covenant b' me
18 which they had made b' me,
35: 5 I set b' the sons of the house
19 not want a man to stand b' me
36: 7 their supplication b' the Lord,
9 proclaimed a fast b' the Lord to all
22 fire on the hearth burning b' him.
37:20 I pray thee, be accepted b' thee;
38:10 out of the dungeon, b' he die.
26 my supplication b' the king,
39: 6 Zedekiah in Riblah b' his eyes:
16 accomplished in that day b' thee.
40: 4 behold, all the land is b' thee:
42: 2 supplication be accepted b' thee,
9 present your supplication b' him;
44:10 statutes, that I set b' you and b'
49:19 shepherd that will stand b' me?
37 to be dismayed b' their enemies,
37 and b' them that seek their life:
50: 8 as the he goats b' the flocks.
44 shepherd that will stand b' me?
52:10 sons of Zedekiah b' his eyes:
33 did continually eat bread b' him
La 1: 5 gone into captivity b' the enemy.
6 without strength b' the pursuer.
22 all their wickedness come b' thee;
2: 3 right hand from b' the enemy,
19 water b' the face of the Lord:
3:35 man b' the face of the most High,

Eze 2:10 he spread it b' me; and it was
3:20 I lay a stumbling block b' him,
4: 1 thee a tile, and lay it b' thee,
6: 4 will cast down your slain men b'
5 children of Israel b' their idols;
8: 1 the elders of Judah sat b' me,
11 stood b' them seventy men of the
9: 6 men which were b' the house.
14: 1 of Israel unto me, and sat b' me.
3 their iniquity b' their face:
4 his iniquity b' his face, and cometh
7 his iniquity b' his face,
16:18 oil and mine incense b' them.
19 hast even set it b' them for a sweet
50 committed abomination b' me:
57 B' thy wickedness was discovered,
20: 1 inquire of the Lord, and sat b' me.
9 not be polluted b' the heathen,
14 that it should not be polluted b'
41 sanctified in you b' the heathen.
21: 6 with bitterness sigh b' their eyes.
22:30 stand in the gap b' me for the
23:24 and I will set judgment b' them,
41 bed, and a table prepared b' it,
28: 9 thou yet say b' him that slayeth
17 I will lay thee b' kings, that they
30:24 and he shall groan b' him with
32:10 brandish my sword b' them;
33:31 they sit b' thee as my people,
36:17 their way was b' me as the
23 sanctified in you b' their eyes.
37:20 be in thine hand b' their eyes.
38:16 in thee, O Gog, b' their eyes.
40:12 space also b' the little chambers
22 the arches thereof were b' them.
26 the arches thereof were b' them:
47 the altar that was b' the house.
41: 4 twenty cubits, b' the temple:
12 b' the separate place at the end
22 is the table that is b' the Lord.
42: 2 B' the length of an hundred
4 And b' the chambers was a walk
8 b' the temple was an hundred
11 And the way b' them was like
12 directly b' the wall toward the east,
13 which are b' the separate place,
43:24 thou shalt offer them b' the Lord,
44: 3 sit in it to eat bread b' the Lord;
4 of the north gate b' the house:
11 shall stand b' them to minister
12 they ministered unto them b' their
15 they shall stand b' me to offer
22 or a widow that had a priest b'.
45: 7 b' the oblation of the holy
7 b' the possession of the city,
46: 3 gate b' the Lord in the sabbaths
9 shall come b' the Lord in the
Da 1: 5 they might stand b' the king.
13 countenances be looked upon b'
18 them in b' Nebuchadnezzar.
19 therefore stood they b' the king.
2: 2 they came and stood b' the king.
9 corrupt words to speak b' me,
10 Chaldeans answered b' the king,
11 other that can shew it b' the king,
24 bring me in b' the king, and I will
25 brought in Daniel b' the king
31 brightness was excellent, stood b'
36 interpretation thereof b' the king.
3: 3 and they stood b' the image
13 brought these men b' the king.
4: 6 the wise men of Babylon b' me,
7 and I told the dream b' them;
8 at...last Daniel came in b' me,
8 and b' him I told the dream,
5: 1 and drank wine b' the thousand.
13 Daniel brought in b' the king,
15 have been brought in b' me,
17 answered and said b' the king,
19 trembled and feared b' him:
23 the vessels of his house b' thee,
6:10 and gave thanks b' his God,
11 making supplication b' his God.
12 and spake b' the king concerning
13 and said b' the king, That Daniel
18 of musick brought b' him;
22 b' him innocency was found in
22 and also b' thee,
26 and fear b' the God of Daniel:
7: 7 from all the beasts that were b' it;
8 b' whom there were three
10 and came forth from b' him:
10 times ten thousand stood b' him:
13 and they brought him near b' him.
20 up, and b' whom three fell;
8: 3 there stood b' the river a ram
4 no beasts might stand b' him,
6 had seen standing b' the river,
7 power in the ram to stand b' him,
15 stood b' me as the appearance
9:10 his laws, which he set b' us by
13 prayer b' the Lord our God,
18 present our supplications b' thee
20 supplication b' the Lord my God
10:12 and to chasten thyself b' thy God,
11:16 will, and none shall stand b' him:
22 they be overflown from b' him,
Ho 7: 2 them about; they are b' my face.
Joe 1:16 Is not the meat cut off b' our eyes,
2: 3 A fire devoureth b' them;
3 as the garden of Eden b' them,
6 B' their face the people shall be
10 The earth shall quake b' them;
11 Lord shall utter his voice b' his
31 b' the great and the terrible day
Am 1: 1 two years b' the earthquake.

Am 2: 9 destroyed I the Amorite *b'* them,
4: 3 at that which is *b'* her;
9: 4 go into captivity *b'* their enemies,
Jon 1: 2 their wickedness is come up *b'* me.
4: 2 Therefore I fled *b'* unto Tarshish
Mic 1: 4 as wax *b'* the fire, and as the
2:13 The breaker is come up *b'* them:
13 and their king shall pass *b'* them,
6: 1 contend thou *b'* the mountains,
4 I sent *b'* thee Moses, Aaron, and
6 Wherewith shall I come *b'* the
6 and bow myself *b'* the high God?
6 shall I come *b'* him with burnt
Na 1: 6 Who can stand *b'* his indignation?
2: 1 in pieces is come up *b'* thy face:
Hab 1: 3 spoiling and violence are *b'* me:
2:20 let all the earth keep silence *b'*
3: 5 *B'* him went the pestilence, and
Zep 3:20 turn back your captivity *b'* your
Hag 1:12 the people did fear *b'* the Lord.
2:14 so is this nation *b'* me, saith the
15 *b'* a stone was laid upon a stone
Zec 2:13 Be silent, O all flesh, *b'* the Lord:
3: 1 standing *b'* the angel of the Lord,
3 garments, and stood *b'* the angel.
4 those that stood *b'* him, saying,
8 and thy fellows that sit *b'* thee:
9 stone that I have laid *b'* Joshua;
4: 7 *b'* Zerubbabel thou shalt become
6: 5 from standing *b'* the Lord
7: 2 their men, to pray *b'* the Lord,
8:10 *b'* these days there was no hire
21, 22 speedily to pray *b'* the Lord,
12: 8 the angel of the Lord *b'* them.
14: 4 the mount of Olives, which is *b'*
5 as ye fled from *b'* the earthquake
20 shall be like the bowls *b'* the altar.
Mal 2: 5 me, and was afraid *b'* my name.
9 and base *b'* all the people,
3: 1 he shall prepare the way *b'* me:
11 vine cast her fruit *b'* the time
14 mournfully *b'* the Lord of hosts?
16 remembrance was written *b'* him
4: 5 *b'* the coming of the great and
M't 1:18 *b'* they came together,
2: 9 went *b'* them, till it came and
5:12 the prophets which were *b'* you.
16 Let your light so shine *b'* men,
24 Leave there thy gift *b'* the altar,
6: 1 do not your alms *b'* men,
2 do not sound a trumpet *b'* thee,
8 ye have need of, *b'* ye ask him.
7: 6 cast ye your pearls *b'* swine,
8:29 hither to torment us *b'* the time?
10:18 *b'* governors and kings for my
32 shall confess me *b'* men, him will
32 I confess also *b'* my Father
33 shall deny me *b'* men,
33 him will I also deny *b'* my
11:10 I send my messenger *b'* thy face,
10 shall prepare thy way *b'* thee.
14: 6 of Herodias danced *b'* them,
8 she, being *b'* instructed of her
22 to go *b'* him unto the other side,
17: 2 was transfigured *b'* them: and his
21: 9 the multitudes that went *b'*,
31 go into the kingdom of God *b'* you.
24:25 I have told you *b'*.
38 in the days that were *b'* the flood
25:32 *b'* him shall be gathered all
26:32 I will go *b'* you into Galilee.
34 That this night, *b'* the cock crow,
70 he denied *b'* them all, saying,
75 *B'* the cock crow, thou shalt deny
27:11 Jesus stood *b'* the governor:
24 washed his hands *b'* the multitude,
29 and they bowed the knee *b'* him,
28: 7 he goeth *b'* you into Galilee;
M'r 1: 2 I send my messenger *b'* thy face,
2 shall prepare thy way *b'* thee.
35 rising up a great while *b'* day,
2:12 bed, and went forth *b'* them all;
3:11 they saw him, fell down *b'* him,
5:33 came and fell down *b'* him,
6:41 to his disciples to set *b'* them;
45 to go to the other side *b'* unto
8: 6 to his disciples to set *b'* them;
6 they did set them *b'* the people.
7 commanded to set them also *b'*
9: 2 and he was transfigured *b'* them.
10:32 Jesus went *b'* them: and they
11: 9 And they that went *b'*, and they
13: 9 *b'* rulers and kings for my sake,
14:28 I will go *b'* you into Galilee.
30 night, *b'* the cock crow twice,
72 *B'* the cock crow twice, thou shalt
15:42 that is, the day *b'* the sabbath.
16: 7 that he goeth *b'* you into Galilee:
Lu 1: 6 they were both righteous *b'* God,
8 *b'* God in the order of his course,
17 shall go *b'* him in the spirit and
75 In holiness and righteousness *b'*
76 shalt go *b'* the face of the Lord
2:21 *b'* he was conceived in the womb.
26 *b'* he had seen the Lord's
31 *b'* the face of all people;
5:18 him in, and to lay him *b'* him.
19 his couch into the midst *b'* Jesus.
25 he rose up *b'* them, and took up
7:27 I send my messenger *b'* thy face,
27 shall prepare thy way *b'* thee.
8:28 and fell down *b'* him, and with a
47 and falling down *b'* him,
47 unto him *b'* all the people for
9:16 to set *b'* the multitude.
52 and sent messengers *b'* his face:

Lu 10: 1 two and two *b'* his face into every
8 such things as are set *b'* you:
11: 6 and I have nothing to set *b'* him?
38 he had not first washed *b'* dinner.
12: 6 one of them is forgotten *b'* God?
8 shall confess me *b'* men,
8 also confess *b'* the angels of God:
9 he that denieth me *b'* men shall
9 be denied *b'* the angels of God.
14: 2 there was a certain man *b'* him
15:18 against heaven, and *b'* thee,
16:15 which justify yourselves *b'* men;
18:39 they which went *b'* rebuked him,
19: 4 he ran *b'*, and climbed up
27 bring hither, and slay them *b'* me.
28 had thus spoken, he went *b'*,
20:26 his words *b'* the people: and they
21:12 But *b'* all these, they shall lay
12 brought *b'* kings and rulers for
14 meditate *b'* what ye shall answer:
36 to stand *b'* the Son of man.
22:15 this passover with you *b'* I suffer:
34 *b'* that thou shalt thrice
47 one of the twelve, went *b'* them,
61 *B'* the cock crow, thou shalt
23:12 for *b'* they were at enmity
14 having examined him *b'* you,
53 wherein never man *b'* was laid.
24:19 word *b'* God and all the people:
43 did eat *b'* them.
Joh 1:15 after me is preferred *b'* me:
15 for he was *b'* me.
27 after me is preferred *b'* me,
30 a man which is preferred *b'* me;
30 for he was *b'* me.
48 *B'* that Philip called thee, when
3:28 but that I am sent *b'* him.
5: 7 another steppeth down *b'* me.
6:62 ascend up where he was *b'*?
7:51 man, *b'* it hear him,
8:58 unto you, *B'* Abraham was, I am.
9: 8 they which *b'* had seen him
10: 4 he goeth *b'* them, and the sheep
8 that ever came *b'* me are thieves
11:55 up to Jerusalem *b'* the passover,
12: 1 Jesus six days *b'* the passover
37 done so many miracles *b'* them,
13: 1 Now *b'* the feast of the passover,
19 Now I tell you *b'* it come, that,
14:29 I have told you *b'* it come to pass,
15:18 hated me *b'* it hated you.
17: 5 I had with thee *b'* the world
24 *b'* the foundation of the world.
Ac 1:16 by the mouth of David spake *b'*
2:20 *b'* that great and notable
25 the Lord always *b'* my face,
31 He seeing this *b'* spake of the
3:18 which God *b'* had showed
20 which *b'* was preached unto you:
4:10 man stand here *b'* you whole.
28 counsel determined *b'* to be done.
5:23 standing without *b'* the doors:
27 set them *b'* the counsel: and the
36 *b'* these days rose up Theudas,
6: 6 Whom they set *b'* the apostles:
7: 2 *b'* he dwelt in Charran,
40 Make us gods to go *b'* us: for as
45 God drave out *b'* the face of our
46 Who found favour *b'* God,
52 which shewed *b'* the coming
8:32 like a lamb dumb *b'* his shearer,
9:15 to bear my name *b'* the Gentiles,
10: 4 come up for a memorial *b'* God.
17 stood *b'* the gate,
30 stood *b'* me in bright clothing,
33 are we all here present *b'* God
41 unto witnesses chosen *b'* of God,
12: 6 and the keepers *b'* the door kept
14 told how Peter stood *b'* the gate.
13:24 *b'* his coming the baptism
14:13 Jupiter, which was *b'* their city,
16:29 and fell down *b'* Paul and Silas,
34 he set meat *b'* them,
17:26 hath determined the times *b'*
18:17 beat him *b'* the judgment seat.
19: 9 that way *b'* the multitude,
19 burned them *b'* all men: and
20: 5 going *b'* tarried for us at Troas.
13 And we went *b'* to ship, and
21:29 (For they had seen *b'* with him
38 which *b'* these days madest
22:30 Paul down, and set him *b'* them.
23: 1 in all good conscience *b'* God
30 to say *b'* thee what they had
33 presented Paul also *b'* him.
24:19 to have been here *b'* thee, and
20 while I stood *b'* the council,
25: 9 judge of these things *b'* me?
16 *b'* that he which is accused have
26 brought him forth *b'* you,
26 and specially *b'* thee, O king
26: 2 for myself this day *b'* thee
26 *b'* whom also I speak freely:
27:24 thou must be brought *b'* Cæsar:
Ro 2:13 of the law are just *b'* God,
3: 9 *b'* proved both Jews and Gentiles,
18 no fear of God *b'* their eyes.
19 world may become guilty *b'* God.
4: 2 but not *b'* God.
17 *b'* him whom he believed, even
9:29 as Esaias said *b'*, Except the Lord
14:10 all stand *b'* the judgment seat
22 have it to thyself *b'* God. Happy
16: 7 who also were in Christ *b'* me.
1Co 2: 7 God ordained *b'* the world unto
4: 5 judge nothing *b'* the time,

1Co 6: 1 go to law *b'* the unjust,
1 and not *b'* the saints?
6 and that *b'* the unbelievers.
10:27 whatsoever is set *b'* you, eat,
11:21 taketh *b'* other his own supper:
2Co 1:15 was minded to come unto you *b'*,
5:10 *b'* the judgment seat of Christ;
7: 3 I have said *b'*, that ye are in our
14 which I made *b'* Titus, is found
8:10 who have begun *b'*, not only to
24 and *b'* the churches, the
9: 5 that they would go *b'* unto you,
5 whereof ye had notice *b'*, that
12:19 we speak *b'* God in Christ:
13: 2 I told you *b'*, and foretell you,
Gal 1: 9 As we said *b'*, so say I now again,
17 which were apostles *b'* me;
20 you, behold, *b'* God, I lie not.
2:12 *b'* that certain came from James,
14 I said unto Peter *b'* them all,
3: 1 *b'* whose eyes Jesus Christ hath
8 *b'* the gospel unto Abraham,
17 that was confirmed *b'* of God
23 But *b'* faith came,
5:21 of the which I tell you *b'*, as I
Eph 1: 4 us in him *b'* the foundation
4 and without blame *b'* him in love:
2:10 which God hath *b'* ordained that
Ph'p 3:13 unto those things which are *b'*,
Col 1: 5 heard *b'* in the word of the truth
17 he is *b'* all things, and by him
1Th 2: 2 after that we had suffered *b'*,
3: 4 you *b'* that we should suffer
9 joy for your sakes *b'* our God;
13 unblameable in holiness *b'* God,
1Ti 1:13 Who was *b'* a blasphemer, and a
18 to the prophecies which went *b'*
5: 4 that is good and acceptable *b'*
19 but *b'* two or three witnesses.
20 Them that sin rebuke *b'* all,
21 I charge thee *b'* God, and the
21 preferring one *b'* another,
24 going *b'* to judgment; and some
6:12 profession *b'* many witnesses.
13 and *b'* Christ Jesus,
13 *b'* Pontius Pilate witnessed
2Ti 1: 9 Christ Jesus *b'* the world began,
2:14 charging them *b'* the Lord
4: 1 therefore *b'* God, and the Lord
21 thy diligence to come *b'* winter.
Ti 1: 2 promised *b'* the world began;
Heb 6:18 lay hold upon the hope set *b'* us:
7:18 of the commandment going *b'*
10:15 after that he had said *b'*,
11: 5 *b'* his translation he had this
12: 1 the race that is set *b'* us,
2 for the joy that was set *b'* him
Jas 1:27 *b'* God and the Father is this,
2: 6 you *b'* the judgment seats?
5: 9 the judge standeth *b'* the door.
1Pe 1:20 *b'* the foundation of the world,
2Pe 2:11 against them *b'* the Lord.
3: 2 which were spoken *b'* by the holy
17 seeing ye know these things *b'*,
1Jo 2:28 be ashamed *b'* him at his coming.
3:19 shall assure our hearts *b'* him.
3Jo 6 of thy charity *b'* the church:
Jude 4 who were *b'* of old ordained to
17 were spoken *b'* of the apostles
24 faultless *b'* the presence of his
Re 1: 4 spirits which are *b'* his throne;
2:14 a stumblingblock *b'* the children
3: 2 found thy works perfect *b'* God.
5 *b'* my Father, and *b'* his angels.
8 I have set *b'* thee an open door,
9 to come and worship *b'* thy feet,
4: 5 of fire burning *b'* the throne,
6 *b'* the throne there was a sea
6 beasts full of eyes *b'* and behind.
10 elders fall down *b'* him that sat
10 and cast their crowns *b'* the throne,
5: 8 elders fell down *b'* the Lamb,
7: 9 *b'* the throne, and *b'* the Lamb,
11 fell *b'* the throne on their faces,
15 are they *b'* throne of God,
8: 2 seven angels which stood *b'* God;
3 altar which was *b'* the throne.
4 ascended up *b'* God out of the
9:13 golden altar which is *b'* God,
10:11 prophesy again *b'* many peoples,
11: 4 standing *b'* the God of the earth.
16 which sat *b'* God on their seats,
12: 4 the dragon stood *b'* the woman
10 accused them *b'* our God day and
13:12 power of the first beast *b'* him,
14: 3 *b'* the throne, and *b'* the four
5 without fault *b'* the throne of God.
15: 4 shall come and worship *b'* thee;
16:19 came in remembrance *b'* God,
19:20 that wrought miracles *b'* him,
20:12 small and great, stand *b'* God;
22: 8 *b'* the feet of the angel which

beforehand See also AFOREHAND.
M'r 13:11 take no thought *b'* what ye shall
2Co 9: 5 and make up *b'* your bounty,
1Ti 5:24 Some men's sins are open *b'*,
25 works of some are manifest *b'*;
1Pe 1:11 testified *b'* the sufferings of Christ.

beforetime See also AFORETIME.
De 2:12 The Horims also dwelt in Seir *b'*;
Jos 11:10 for Hazor *b'* was the head of all
20: 5 and hated him not *b'*.
1Sa 9: 9 (*B'* in Israel, when a man
9 a Prophet was *b'* called a Seer.)
10:11 when all that knew him *b'*

2Sa 7:10 afflict them any more, or b·
2Ki 13: 5 dwelt in their tents, as b·.
Ne 2: 1 Now I had not been b· sad
Isa 41:26 and b·, that we may say, He is
Ac 8: 9 called Simon, which b· in the same

beg See also BEGGED; BEGGING.
Ps 109:10 be continually vagabonds, and b·:
Pr 20: 4 therefore shall he b· in the harvest,
Lu 16: 3 cannot dig; to b· I am ashamed.

began
Ge 4:26 then b· men to call upon the name
6: 1 when men b· to multiply on the
9:20 And Noah b· to be an husbandman,
10: 8 b· to be a mighty one in the earth.
41:54 seven years of dearth b· to come,
44:12 he searched, and b· at the eldest,
Nu 25: 1 people b· to commit whoredom
De 1: 5 b· Moses to declare this law,
J'g 13:25 the Spirit of the Lord b· to move
16:19 and she b· to afflict him, and his
22 the hair of his head b· to grow
19:25 when the day b· to spring, they
20:31 they b· to smite of the people,
39 Benjamin b· to smite and kill
40 when the flame b· to arise up out
1Sa 3: 2 his eyes b· to wax dim, that he
2Sa 2:10 old when he b· to reign over Israel,
5: 4 years old when he b· to reign,
1Ki 6: 1 b· to build the house of the Lord.
14:21 when he b· to reign, and he
15:25 son of Jeroboam b· to reign over
33 b· Baasha the son of Ahijah to
16: 8 b· Elah the son of Baasha to reign
11 when he b· to reign, as soon as
23 b· Omri to reign over Israel,
29 b· Ahab the son of Omri to reign
22:41 son of Asa b· to reign over Judah
42 when he b· to reign; and he
51 the son of Ahab b· to reign over
2Ki 3: 1 the son of Ahab b· to reign over
8:16 king of Judah b· to reign.
17 when he b· to reign; and he
26 when he b· to reign; and he
9:29 b· Ahaziah to reign over Judah.
10:32 the Lord b· to cut Israel short:
11:21 Jehoash when he b· to reign.
12: 1 Jehoash b· to reign; and forty
13: 1 the son of Jehu b· to reign
10 b· Jehoash the son of Jehoahaz
14: 2 when he b· to reign, and reigned
23 Joash king of Israel b· to reign
15: 1 b· Azariah son of Amaziah king
2 old was he when he b· to reign,
13 the son of Jabesh b· to reign
17 b· Menahem the son of Gadi to reign
23 the son of Menahem b· to reign
27 the son of Remaliah b· to reign
32 b· Jotham the son of Uzziah king
33 old was he when he b· to reign,
37 In those days the Lord b· to send
16: 1 Jotham king of Judah b· to reign.
2 Ahaz when he b· to reign, and
17: 1 b· Hoshea the son of Elah to reign
18: 1 of Ahaz king of Judah b· to reign.
2 when he b· to reign; and he
21: 1 years old when he b· to reign,
19 twenty and two years old when he b·
22: 1 years old when he b· to reign,
23:31 years old when he b· to reign,
36 twenty and five years old when he b·
24: 8 years old when he b· to reign,
18 twenty and one years old when he b·
25:27 in the year that he b· to reign did
1Ch 1:10 b· to be mighty upon the earth.
27:24 the son of Zeruiah b· to number,
2Ch 3: 1 Solomon b· to build the house
2 And he b· to build in the second
12:13 years old when he b· to reign,
13: 1 b· Abijah to reign over Judah.
20:22 when they b· to sing and to praise,
31 years old when he b· to reign,
21: 5 years old when he b· to reign,
20 years old was he when he b· to
22: 2 was Ahaziah when he b· to reign,
24: 1 seven years old when he b· to reign,
25: 1 years old when he b· to reign,
26: 3 was Uzziah when he b· to reign,
27: 1 twenty and five years old when he b·
8 years old when he b· to reign,
28: 1 years old when he b· to reign,
29: 1 Hezekiah b· to reign when he was
17 Now they b· on the first day of
27 when the burnt offering b·,
27 the song of the Lord b·
31: 7 they b· to lay the foundation of
10 Since the people b· to bring the
21 And in every work that he b·
33: 1 twelve years old when he b· to
21 years old when he b· to reign,
34: 1 eight years old when he b· to reign.
3 b· to seek after the God of David
3 in the twelfth year he b· to purge
36: 2 twenty and three years old when he b·
5 twenty and five years old when he b·
9 eight years old when he b· to reign,
11 one and twenty years old when he b·
Ezr 3: 6 b· they to offer burnt offerings
8 b· Zerubbabel the son of Shealtiel
5: 2 and b· to build the house of God
7: 9 of the first month b· he to go up
Ne 4: 7 that the breaches b· to be stopped,
13:19 gates of Jerusalem b· to be dark
Jer 52: 1 years old when he b· to reign,
Eze 9: 6 Then they b· at the ancient men
Jon 3: 4 Jonah b· to enter into the city
M't 4:17 Jesus b· to preach, and to say,
11: 7 Jesus b· to say unto the multitudes
20 Then b· he to upbraid the cities
12: 1 b· to pluck the ears of corn, and to
16:21 b· Jesus to shew unto his disciples,
22 b· to rebuke him, saying, Be it far
26:22 b· every one of them to say unto
37 b· to be sorrowful and very heavy.
74 Then b· he to curse and to swear,
28: 1 as it b· to dawn toward the first
M'r 1:45 b· to publish it much, and to
2:23 his disciples b·, as they went,
4: 1 he b· again to teach by the sea side:
5:17 they b· to pray him to depart
20 b· to publish in Decapolis how great
6: 2 he b· to teach in the synagogue:
7 b· to send them forth by two and
34 he b· to teach them many things.
55 b· to carry about in beds those
8:11 b· to question with him, seeking
31 he b· to teach them, that the Son of
32 Peter took him, and b· to rebuke
10:28 Then Peter b· to say unto him,
32 b· to tell them what things should
41 they b· to be much displeased
47 he b· to cry out, and say, Jesus,
11:15 b· to cast out them that sold and
12: 1 b· to speak unto them by parables.
13: 5 Jesus answering them b· to say,
14:19 they b· to be sorrowful, and to
33 b· to be sore amazed, and to be
65 some b· to spit on him, and to cover
69 b· to say to them that stood by,
71 he b· to curse and to swear, saying,
15: 8 crying aloud, b· to desire him to do
18 b· to salute him, Hail, king of the
Lu 1:70 have been since the world b·:
3:23 Jesus himself b· to be about thirty
4:21 he b· to say unto them, This day
5: 7 the ships, so that they b· to sink.
21 scribes and the Pharisees b· to
7:15 he that was dead sat up, and b· to
24 he b· to speak unto the people
38 b· to wash his feet with tears, and
49 b· to say within themselves, Who is
9:12 when the day b· to wear away, then
11:29 gathered thick together, he b· to
53 scribes and the Pharisees b· to
12: 1 he b· to say unto his disciples first
14:18 with one consent b· to make excuse.
30 Saying, This man b· to build, and
15:14 famine in that land, and he b· to be
24 And they b· to be merry.
19:37 multitude of the disciples b· to
45 b· to cast out them that sold
20: 9 Then b· he to speak to the people
22:23 they b· to enquire among themselves
23: 2 they b· to accuse him, saying,
Joh 4:52 when he b· to amend. And they
9:32 Since the world b· was it not heard
13: 5 b· to wash the disciples' feet, and
Ac 1: 1 all that Jesus b· both to do and
2: 4 b· to speak with other tongues, as
3:21 holy prophets since the world b·.
8:35 b· at the same scripture, and
10:37 b· from Galilee, after the baptism
11:15 as I b· to speak, the Holy Ghost fell
18:26 he b· to speak boldly in the
24: 2 Tertullus b· to accuse him, saying,
27:35 when he had broken it, he b· to eat
Ro 16:25 kept secret since the world b·,
2Ti 1: 9 Christ Jesus before the world b·;
Tit 1: 2 promised before the world b·.
Heb 2: 3 which at the first b· to be

begat
Ge 4:18 Irad b· Mehujael:
18 and Mehujael b· Methusael:
18 and Methusael b· Lamech.
5: 3 and b· a son in his own likeness,
4 and he b· sons and daughters:
6 an hundred and five years, and b·
7 Seth lived after he b· Enos eight
7 and seven years, and b· sons and
9 Enos lived ninety years, and b·
10 Enos lived after he b· Cainan eight
10 fifteen years, and b· sons and
12 Cainan lived seventy years, and b·
13 And Cainan lived after he b·
13 forty years, and b· sons and
15 lived sixty and five years and b·
16 Mahalaleel lived after he b· Jared
16 and thirty years, and b· sons and
18 sixty and two years, and he b·
19 And Jared lived after he b· Enoch
19 hundred years, and b· sons and
21 lived sixty and five years, and b·
22 walked with God after he b·
22 three hundred years, and b· sons
25 eighty and seven years, and b·
26 And Methuselah lived after he b·
26 and two years, and b· sons and
28 eighty and two years, and b· a son:
30 And Lamech lived after he b· Noah
30 and five years, and b· sons and
32 Noah b· Shem, Ham, and Japheth.
6:10 Noah b· three sons, Shem, Ham,
10: 8 Cush b· Nimrod: he began to be
13 Mizraim b· Ludim, and Anamim,
15 Canaan b· Sidon his firstborn
24 Arphaxad b· Salah;
24 and Salah b· Eber
26 Joktan b· Almodad, and Sheleph,
11:10 and b· Arphaxad two years after
11 Shem lived after he b· Arphaxad
11 five hundred years, and b· sons and
Ge 11:12 and thirty years, and b· Salah:
13 Arphaxad lived after he b· Salah
13 and three years, and b· sons and
14 lived thirty years, and b· Eber;
15 Salah lived after he b· Eber four
15 hundred and three years, and b·
16 four and thirty years, and b· Peleg:
17 Eber lived after he b· Peleg four
17 hundred and thirty years, and b·
18 Peleg lived thirty years, and b·
19 Peleg lived after he b· Reu two
19 hundred and nine years and b·
20 two and thirty years, and b· Serug:
21 Reu lived after he b· Serug two
21 hundred and seven years, and b·
22 lived thirty years, and b· Nahor:
23 Serug lived after he b· Nahor two
23 Nahor two hundred years, and b·
24 nine and twenty years, and b·
25 Nahor lived after he b· Terah an
25 and nineteen years, and b· sons
26 Terah lived seventy years, and b·
27 Terah b· Abram, Nahor, and
27 Haran: and Haran b· Lot.
22:23 Bethuel b· Rebekah: these eight
25: 3 Jokshan b· Sheba, and Dedan.
19 Abraham b· Isaac:
Le 25:45 with you, which they b· in your
Nu 26:29 Machir b· Gilead: of Gilead come
58 Kohath b· Amram.
De 32:18 the Rock that b· thee thou art
J'g 11: 1 an harlot: and Gilead b· Jephthah.
Ru 4:18 Pharez b· Hezron,
19 Hezron b· Ram, and Ram b·
20 Amminadab b· Nahshon,
20 and Nahshon b· Salmon,
21 Salmon b· Boaz, and Boaz b· Obed,
22 Obed b· Jesse, and Jesse b· David.
1Ch 1:10 Cush b· Nimrod: he began to be
11 Mizraim b· Ludim, and Anamim,
13 Canaan b· Zidon his firstborn,
18 Arphaxad b· Shelah,
18 and Shelah b· Eber.
20 Joktan b· Almodad, and Sheleph,
34 Abraham b· Isaac. The sons of
2:10 Ram b· Amminadab;
10 and Amminadab b· Nahshon,
11 Nahshon b· Salma, and Salma b·
12 Boaz b· Obed, and Obed b· Jesse,
13 Jesse b· his firstborn Eliab,
18 Caleb, the son of Hezron b·
20 Hur b· Uri, and Uri b· Bezaleel,
22 Segub b· Jair, who had three
36 Attai b· Nathan, and Nathan b·
37 Zabad b· Ephlal, and Ephlal b·
38 Obed b· Jehu, and Jehu b· Azariah,
39 Azariah b· Helez, and Helez b·
40 Eleasah b· Sisamai, and Sisamai b·
41 Shallum b· Jekamiah,
41 and Jekamiah b· Elishama,
44 Shema b· Raham, the father of
44 Jorkoam: and Rekem b· Shammai.
46 Haran b· Gazez.
4: 2 Reaiah the son of Shobal b· Jahath;
2 and Jahath b· Ahumai,
8 Coz b· Anub, and Zobebah,
11 Chelub the brother of Shuah b·
12 Eshton b· Beth-rapha, and Paseah,
14 Meonothai b· Ophrah:
14 and Seraiah b· Joab,
6: 4 Eleazar b· Phinehas,
4 Phinehas b· Abishua,
5 And Abishua b· Bukki,
5 and Bukki b· Uzzi,
6 And Uzzi b· Zerahiah,
6 and Zerahiah b· Meraioth,
7 Meraioth b· Amariah,
7 and Amariah b· Ahitub,
8 And Ahitub b· Zadok,
8 and Zadok b· Ahimaaz,
9 And Ahimaaz b· Azariah,
9 and Azariah b· Johanan,
10 And Johanan b· Azariah (he it is
11 And Azariah b· Amariah,
11 and Amariah b· Ahitub,
12 And Ahitub b· Zadok,
12 and Zadok b· Shallum,
13 And Shallum b· Hilkiah,
13 and Hilkiah b· Azariah,
14 And Azariah b· Seraiah,
14 and Seraiah b· Jehozadak,
7:32 Heber b· Japhlet, and Shomer,
8: 1 Benjamin b· Belah his firstborn,
7 removed them, and b· Uzza, and
8 Shaharaim b· children in the
9 And he b· of Hodesh his wife,
11 of Hushim he b· Abitub, and
32 Mikloth b· Shimeah. And these
33 Ner b· Kish, and Kish b· Saul,
33 and Saul b· Jonathan,
34 Merib-baal b· Micah.
36 Ahaz b· Jehoadah; and
36 Jehoadah b· Alemeth, and
36 and Zimri b· Moza,
37 Moza b· Binea: Rapha was his son,
9:38 Mikloth b· Shimeam. And they also
39 Ner b· Kish; and Kish b· Saul;
39 and Saul b· Jonathan,
40 was Merib-baal: Merib-baal b·
42 Ahaz b· Jarah; and
42 Jarah b· Alemeth, and Azmaveth,
42 and Zimri b· Moza,
43 Moza b· Binea; and Rephaiah his
14: 3 and David b· more sons and
2Ch 11:21 and b· twenty and eight sons,
13:21 and b· twenty and two sons,

2Ch 24: 3 and he b' sons and daughters.
Ne 12:10 Jeshua b' Joiakim,
10 Joiakim also b' Eliashib,
10 and Eliashib b' Joiada,
11 Joiada b' Jonathan,
11 and Jonathan b' Jaddua.
Pr 23:22 unto thy father that b' thee,
Jer 16: 3 their fathers that b' them in this
Da 11: 6 brought her, and he that b' her,
Zec 13: 3 father and his mother that b' him
3 father and his mother that b' him
M't 1: 2 Abraham b' Isaac;
2 and Isaac b' Jacob;
2 and Jacob b' Judas
3 Judas b' Phares and Zara of
3 and Phares b' Esrom;
3 and Esrom b' Aram;
4 Aram b' Aminadab;
4 and Aminadab b' Naasson:
4 and Naasson b' Salmon;
5 Salmon b' Booz of Rachab;
5 and Booz b' Obed of Ruth;
5 and Obed b' Jesse;
6 Jesse b' David the king; and
6 David the king b' Solomon
7 Solomon b' Roboam;
7 and Roboam b' Abia;
7 and Abia b' Asa;
8 Asa b' Josaphat;
8 and Josaphat b' Joram;
8 and Joram b' Ozias;
9 Ozias b' Joatham;
9 and Joatham b' Achaz:
9 and Achaz b' Ezekias;
10 Ezekias b' Manasses;
10 and Manasses b' Amon;
10 and Amon b' Josias;
11 Josias b' Jechonias and his
12 Jechonias b' Salathiel;
12 and Salathiel b' Zorobabel;
13 Zorobabel b' Abiud;
13 and Abiud b' Eliakim;
13 and Eliakim b' Azor;
14 Azor b' Sadoc;
14 and Sadoc b' Achim;
14 and Achim b' Eliud;
15 Eliud b' Eleazar;
15 and Eleazar b' Matthan;
15 and Matthan b' Jacob;
16 Jacob b' Joseph the husband of
Ac 7: 8 Abraham b' Isaac, and circumcised
8 Isaac b' Jacob; and Jacob b' the
29 Madian, where he b' two sons.
Jas 1:18 own will b' he us with the word
1Jo 5: 1 every one that loveth him that b'

beget See also BEGAT; BEGETTEST; BEGETTETH; BEGOTTEN.
Ge 17:20 twelve princes shall he b',
De 4:25 When thou shalt b' children,
28:41 Thou shalt b' sons and daughters,
2Ki 20:18 which thou shalt b', shall they
Ec 6: 3 If a man b' a hundred children,
Isa 39: 7 from thee, which thou shalt b',
Jer 29: 6 Take ye wives, and b' sons and
Eze 18:10 If he b' a son that is a robber,
14 if he b' a son, that seeth all
47:22 which shall b' children among you:

begettest
Ge 48: 6 issue, which thou b' after them,
Isa 45:10 unto his father, What b' thou?

begetteth
Pr 17:21 He that b' a fool doeth it to his
23:24 and he that b' a wise child shall
Ec 5:14 he b' a son, and there is nothing

beggar
1Sa 2: 8 up the b' from the dunghill,
Lu 16:20 was a certain b' named Lazarus,
22 that the b' died, and was carried

beggarly
Ga 4: 9 to the weak and b' elements,

begged
M't 27:58 Pilate, and b' the body of Jesus.
Lu 23:52 Pilate, and b' the body of Jesus.
Joh 9: 8 Is not this he that sat and b'?

begging
Ps 37:25 forsaken, nor his seed b' bread.
M'r 10:46 sat by the highway side b'.
Lu 18:35 man sat by the wayside b':

begin See also BEGAN; BEGINNEST; BEGINNING; BEGUN.
Ge 11: 6 this they b' to do: and now
De 2:24 b' to possess it, and contend
25 will I b' to put the dread of thee
31 his land before thee: b' to possess,
16: 9 b' to number the seven weeks
Jos 3: 7 This day will I b' to magnify thee
J'g 10:18 What man is he that will b'
13: 5 he shall b' to deliver Israel
1Sa 3:12 I b', I will also make an end.
22:15 Did I then b' to enquire of God
2Ki 8:25 Jeroham king of Judah b' to reign.
Ne 11:17 to b' the thanksgiving in prayer:
Jer 25:29 I b' to bring evil on the city
Eze 9: 6 and b' at my sanctuary.
M't 24:49 b' to smite his fellowservants,
Lu 3: 8 b' not to say within yourselves,
12:45 shall b' to beat the menservants
13:25 ye b' to stand without, and to knock
26 Then shall ye b' to say, We have
14: 9 thou b' with shame to take the
29 behold it b' to mock him,
21:28 these things b' to come to pass,
23:30 they b' to say to the mountains,
2Co 3: 1 Do we b' again to commend
1Pe 4:17 must b' at the house of God:
17 and if it first b' at us, what shall
Re 10: 7 he shall b' to sound, the mystery

beginnest
De 16: 9 from such time as thou b' to put

beginning See also BEGINNINGS.
Ge 1: 1 In the b' God created the heaven
10:10 the b' of his kingdom was Babel,
13: 3 his tent had been at the b',
41:21 still ill favoured, as at the b'.
49: 3 might, and the b' of my strength,
Ex 12: 2 the b' of months: it shall be the
De 11:12 the b' of the year even unto the
21:17 for he is the b' of his strength;
32:42 b' of revenges upon the enemy.
J'g 7:19 in the b' of the middle watch;
Ru 1:22 Beth-lehem in the b' of barley
3:10 in the latter end than at the b'.
2Sa 21: 9 in the b' of barley harvest.
10 from the b' of harvest until water
2Ki 17:25 was at the b' of their dwelling
1Ch 17: 9 them any more, as at the b',
Ezr 4: 6 Ahasuerus, in the b' of his reign,
Job 8: 7 Though thy b' was small, yet thy
42:12 end of Job more than his b':
Ps 111:10 of the Lord is the b' of wisdom:
119:160 is true from the b': and every
Pr 1: 7 the b' of knowledge: but fools
8:22 possessed me in the b' of his
23 up from everlasting, from the b',
9:10 fear of the Lord is the b' of
17:14 The b' of strife is as when
20:21 hastily at the b'; but the end
Ec 3:11 that God maketh from the b'
7: 8 end of a thing than the b' thereof:
10:13 The b' of the words of his mouth
Isa 1:26 thy counsellors as at the b':
18: 2 terrible from their b' hitherto; a
7 a people terrible from their b'
40:21 you from the b'? have ye not
41: 4 the generations from the b'?
26 Who hath declared from the b',
46:10 Declaring the end from the b',
48: 3 the former things from the b':
5 I have even from the b' declared
7 now, and not from the b'; even
16 not spoken in secret from the b';
64: 4 For since the b' of the world men
Jer 17:12 glorious high throne from the b'
26: 1 the b' of the reign of
27: 1 the b' of the reign of Jehoiakim
28: 1 in the b' of the reign of Zedekiah
49:34 Elam in the b' of the reign
La 2:19 in the b' of the watches pour out
Eze 40: 1 in the b' of the year of our
Da 9:21 seen in the vision at the b',
23 At the b' of my supplications
Ho 1: 2 The b' of the word of the Lord
Am 7: 1 poured grasshoppers in the b' of
Mic 1:13 the b' of the sin to the daughter
M't 14:30 b' to sink, he cried, saying,
19: 4 which made them at the b'
8 from the b' it was not so.
20: 8 b' from the last unto the first.
24: 8 these are the b' of sorrows.
21 since the b' of the world to this
M'r 1: 1 The b' of the gospel of Jesus
10: 6 from the b' of the creation
13:19 such as was not from the b'
Lu 1: 2 from the b' were eyewitnesses,
23: 5 b' from Galilee to this place.
24:27 b' at Moses and all the prophets,
47 among all nations, b' at Jerusalem.
Joh 1: 1 In the b' was the Word, and the
2 The same was in the b' with God.
2:10 man at the b' doth set forth
11 This b' of miracles did Jesus
6:64 Jesus knew from the b' who
8: 9 b' at the eldest, even unto the last:
25 I said unto you from the b'.
44 was a murderer from the b',
15:27 ye have been with me from the b'.
16: 4 not unto you at the b', because I
Ac 1:22 B' from the baptism of John,
11: 4 rehearsed the matter from the b',
15 fell on them, as on us at the b'.
15:18 his works from the b' of the
26: 5 Which knew me from the b',
Eph 3: 9 which from the b' of the world
Ph'p 4:15 that in the b' of the gospel,
Col 1:18 who is the b', the firstborn
2Th 2:13 God hath from the b' chosen you
Heb 1:10 Thou, Lord, in the b' hast laid
3:14 if we hold the b' of our confidence
7: 3 having neither b' of days, nor end
2Pe 2:20 is worse with them than the b'.
3: 4 were from the b' of the creation.
1Jo 1: 1 That which was from the b',
2: 7 which ye had from the b'.
7 ye have heard from the b'.
13 him that is from the b'.
14 known him that is from the b'.
24 which ye have heard from the b'.
24 ye have heard from the b'
3: 8 the devil sinneth from the b'.
11 that ye heard from the b',
2Jo 5 which we had from the b',
6 as ye have heard from the b',
Re 1: 8 the b' and the ending,
3:14 the b' of the creation of God;
21: 6 the b' and the end. I will
22:13 Alpha and Omega, the b' and the

beginnings
Nu 10:10 and in the b' of your months,
28:11 And in the b' of your months
Eze 36:11 better unto you than at your b':
M'k 13: 8 these are the b' of sorrows.

begotten See also FIRSTBEGOTTEN.
Ge 5: 4 days of Adam after he had b' Seth
Le 18:11 b' of thy father, she is thy sister,
Nu 11:12 I b' them, that thou shouldest
De 23: 8 The children that are b' of them
J'g 8:30 and ten sons of his body b':
Job 38:28 who hath b' the drops of dew?
Ps 2: 7 my son; this day have I b' thee.
Isa 49:21 Who hath b' me these, seeing I
Hos 5: 7 for they have b' strange children:
Joh 1:14 as of the only b' of the Father,)
18 the only b' Son, which is
3:16 his only b' Son, that whosoever
18 name of the only b' Son of God.
Ac 13:33 my Son, this day have I b' thee.
1Co 4:15 I have b' you through the gospel.
Ph'm 10 whom I have b' in my bonds:
Heb 1: 5 my Son, this day have I b' thee?
5: 5 my Son, to day have I b' thee.
11:17 offered up his only b' son,
1Pe 1: 3 b' us again unto a lively hope
1Jo 4: 9 God sent his only b' Son
5: 1 loveth him also that is b' of him.
18 but he that is b' of God keepeth
Re 1: 5 first b' of the dead, and the prince

beguile See also BEGUILED; BEGUILING.
Col 2: 4 lest any man should b' you with
18 Let no man b' you of your reward

beguiled
Ge 3:13 The serpent b' me, and I did eat.
29:25 wherefore then hast thou b' me?
Nu 25:18 they have b' you in the matter of
Jos 9:22 Wherefore have ye b' us, saying,
2Co 11: 3 as the serpent b' Eve through his

beguiling
2Pe 2:14 b' unstable souls: an heart they

begun
Nu 16:46 from the Lord; the plague is b'.
47 plague was b' among the people:
De 2:31 I have b' to give Sihon and his
3:24 thou hast b' to shew thy servant
Es 6:13 before whom thou hast b' to fall,
9:23 undertook to do as they had b',
M't 18:24 when he had b' to reckon, one was
2Co 8: 6 that as he had b', so he would also
10 who have b' before, not only to do,
Ga 3: 3 having b' in the Spirit, are ye now
Ph'p 1: 6 that he which hath b' a good
1Ti 5:11 when they have b' to wax wanton

behalf
Ex 27:21 on the b' of the children of Israel.
2Sa 3:12 messengers to David on his b',
2Ch 16: 9 to shew himself strong in the b'
Job 36: 2 I have yet to speak on God's b'.
Da 11:18 but a prince for his own b' shall
Ro 16:19 I am glad therefore on your b':
1Co 1: 4 thank my God always on your b',
2Co 1:11 may be given by many on our b'.
5:12 you occasion to glory on our b',
8:24 and of our boasting on your b'.
9: 3 you should be in vain in this b';
Ph'p 1:29 it is given in the b' of Christ,
1Pe 4:16 let him glorify God on this b'.

behave See also BEHAVED; BEHAVETH.
De 32:27 lest their adversaries should b'
1Ch 19:13 and let us b' ourselves valiantly
Ps 101: 2 I will b' myself wisely in a perfect
Isa 3: 5 the child shall b' himself proudly
1Co 13: 5 Doth not b' itself unseemly,
1Ti 3:15 to b' thyself in the house of God,

behaved
1Sa 18: 5 sent him, and b' himself wisely:
14 David b' himself wisely in all his
15 saw that he b' himself very wisely,
30 David b' himself more wisely than
Ps 35:14 I b' myself as though he had been
131: 2 I have b' and quieted myself
Mic 3: 4 as they have b' themselves ill
1Th 2:10 unblameably we b' ourselves
2Th 3: 7 for we b' not ourselves disorderly

behaveth
1Co 7:36 think that he b' himself uncomely

behaviour
1Sa 21:13 he changed his b' before them.
Ps 34: *title* when he changed his b' before
1Ti 3: 2 vigilant, sober, of good b',
Tit 2: 3 that they be in b' as becometh

beheaded
De 21: 6 the heifer that is b' in the valley:
2Sa 4: 7 and slew him, and b' him,
M't 14:10 he sent, and b' John in the prison,
M'k 6:16 It is John, whom I b':
27 he went and b' him in the prison.
Lu 9: 9 Herod said, John have I b':
Re 20: 4 the souls of them that were b'

beheld
Ge 12:14 the Egyptians b' the woman that
13:10 and b' all the plain of Jordan,
19:28 and b', and, lo, the smoke of
31: 2 And Jacob b' the countenance
48: 8 And Israel b' Joseph's sons,
Nu 21: 9 when he b' the serpent of brass,
23:21 He hath not b' iniquity in Jacob,
J'g 16:27 men and women, that b'
1Sa 26: 5 and David b' the place where Saul
1Ch 21:15 the Lord b', and he repented him
Job 31:26 If I b' the sun when it shined,
Ps 119:158 I b' the transgressors, and was
142: 4 and b', but there was no man

Pr 7: 7 And b' among the simple ones,
Ec 8:17 Then I b' all the work of God,
Isa 41:28 For I b', and there was no man;
Jer 4:23 I b' the earth, and, lo, it was
24 I b' the mountains, and, lo, they
25 I b', and, lo, there was no man,
26 I b', and, lo, the fruitful place
31:26 I awaked, and b'; and my sleep
Eze 1:15 Now as I b' the living creatures,
8: 2 Then I b', and lo a likeness as the
37: 8 when I b', lo, the sinews and the
Da 7: 4 b' till the wings thereof were
6 b', and lo another, like a leopard,
9 b' till the thrones were cast down,
11 I b' then because of the voice
11 I b' even till the beast was slain,
21 I b', and the same horn made war
Hab 3: 6 he b', and drove asunder the
M't 19:26 b' them, and said unto them,
M'r 9:15 the people, when they b' him,
12:41 b' how the people cast money
15:47 mother of Joses b' where he was
Lu 10:18 I b' Satan as lightning fall from
19:41 b' the city, and wept over it,
20:17 b' them, and said, What is this
22:56 a certain maid b' him as he sat
23:55 b' the sepulchre, and how his
24:12 he b' the linen clothes laid by
Joh 1:14 we b' his glory, the glory as of
42 when Jesus b' him, he said,
Ac 1: 9 while they b', he was taken up;
17:23 passed by, and b' your devotions,
Re 5: 6 I b', and, lo, in the midst of the
11 I b', and I heard the voice of
6: 5 And I b', and lo a black horse;
12 b' when he had opened the sixth
7: 9 After this I b', and, lo, a great
8:13 I b', and heard an angel flying
11:12 and their enemies b' them.
13:11 I b' another beast coming up out

behemoth (*be'-he-moth*)
Job 40:15 Behold now b', which I made

behind
Ge 18:10 in the tent door, which was b' him.
19:17 look not b' thee, neither stay thou
26 his wife looked back from b' him,
22:13 b' him a ram, caught in a thicket
32:18 and, behold, also he is b' us.
20 Behold, thy servant Jacob is b' us.
Ex 10:26 there shall not an hoof be left b';
11: 5 the maidservant that is b' the mill;
14:19 removed and went b' them; and the
19 before their face, and stood b' them:
Le 25:51 If there be yet many years b',
Nu 3:23 pitch b' the tabernacle westward.
De 25:18 even all that were feeble b' thee,
Jos 8: 2 lay thee an ambush for the city b'
4 b' the city: go not very far from
14 in ambush against him b' the city.
20 when the men of Ai looked b' them,
J'g 18:12 behold, it is b' Kirjath-jearim.
20:40 the Benjamites looked b' them,
1Sa 21: 9 wrapped in a cloth b' the ephod:
24: 8 when Saul looked b' him, David
30: 9 those that were left b' stayed.
10 for two hundred abode b': which
2Sa 1: 7 when he looked b' him, he saw
2:20 Then Abner looked b' him,
23 the spear came out b' him; and he
3:16 weeping b' her to Bahurim.
5:23 fetch a compass b' them, and come
10: 9 was against him before and b',
13:34 by the way of the hill side b' him.
1Ki 10:19 top of the throne was round b':
14: 9 and hast cast me b' thy back:
2Ki 6:32 sound of his master's feet b' him?
9:18, 19 do with peace? turn thee b' me.
11: 6 third part at the gate b' the guard:
1Ch 19:10 was set against him before and b',
2Ch 13:13 an ambushment to come about b'
13 the ambushment was b' them.
14 the battle was before and b':
Ne 4:13 in the lower places b' the wall,
16 the rulers were b' all the house
9:26 cast thy law b' their backs, and slew
Ps 50:17 and castest my words b' thee.
139: 5 Thou hast beset me b' and before,
Ca 2: 9 he standeth b' our wall, he looketh
Isa 9:12 before, and the Philistines b';
30:21 Ears shall hear a word b',
38:17 hast cast all my sins b' thy back.
57: 8 B' the doors also and the posts
66:17 b' one tree in the midst, eating
Eze 3:12 I heard b' me a voice of a great
23:35 and cast me b' thy back, therefore
41:15 separate place which was b' it,
Joe 2: 3 and b' them a flame burneth:
3 and b' them a desolate wilderness;
14 leave a blessing b' him; even a
Zec 1: 8 and b' him were there red horses,
M't 9:20 came b' him, and touched the hem
16:23 Get thee b' me, Satan: thou art
M'k 5:27 came in the press b', and touched
8:33 Get thee b' me, Satan: for thou
12:19 brother die, and leave his wife b',
Lu 2:43 Jesus tarried b' in Jerusalem;
4: 8 Get thee b' me, Satan: for it is
7:38 And stood at his feet b' him
8:44 Came b' him, and touched the
1Co 1: 7 So that ye come b' in no gift;
2Co 11: 5 I suppose I was not a whit b' the
12:11 for in nothing am I b' the very
Ph'p 3:13 those things which are b',
Col 1:24 that which is b' of the afflictions
Re 1:10 and heard b' me a great voice,
4: 6 beasts full of eyes before and b'.

behold^ See also BEHELD; BEHOLDEST; BEHOLDETH; BEHOLDING.
Ge 1:29 God said, B', I have given you
31 had made, and, b', it was very good.
3:22 B', the man is become as one of
4:14 B', thou hast driven me out this
6:12 the earth, and, b', it was corrupt:
13 b', I will destroy them with the
17 And, b', I, even I, do bring a flood
8:13 b', the face of the ground was dry.
9: 9 And I, b', I establish my covenant
11: 6 the Lord said, B', the people is
12:11 B' now, I know that thou art
19 therefore b' thy wife, take her,
15: 3 B', to me thou hast given no seed:
4 And, b', the word of the Lord came
17 the sun went down, b' a smoking
16: 2 B' now, the Lord hath restrained
6 B', thy maid is in thy hand; do to
11 B', thou art with child, and shalt
14 b', it is between Kadesh and Bered.
17: 4 As for me, b', my covenant is
20 have heard thee: B', I have blessed
18: 9 And he said, B', in the tent.
27, 31 B' now, I have taken upon me
19: 2 B' now, my lords, turn in, I pray
8 B' now, I have two daughters
19 B' now, thy servant hath found
20 B' now, this city is near to flee
34 B', I lay yesternight with my
20: 3 B', thou art but a dead man,
15 said, B', my land is before thee:
16 unto Sarah he said, B', I have,
16 b', he is to thee a covering of the
22: 1 And he said, B', here I am.
24:51 B', Rebekah is before thee, take
63 and, b', the camels were coming.
25:24 were fulfilled, b', there were
32 B', I am at the point to die:
26: 8 b', Isaac was sporting with
9 B', of a surety she is thy wife:
27: 1 he said unto him, B', here I am.
2 And he said, B' now, I am
6 saying, B', I heard thy father
11 B', Esau my brother is a
36 and, b', now he hath taken away
37 B', I have made him thy lord,
39 B', thy dwelling shall be the
42 B', thy brother Esau, as touching
28:12 he dreamed, and b' a ladder set
12 b' the angels of God ascending
13 And, b', the Lord stood above it,
15 And, b', I am with thee, and will
29: 2 he looked, and b' a well in the field,
6 and, b', Rachel his daughter
25 in the morning, b', it was Leah:
30 3 she said, B' my maid Bilhah, go in
34 B', I would it might be according
31: 2 and, b', it was not toward him as
10 and, b', the rams which leaped
51 B' this heap, and b' this pillar,
32:18 unto my lord Esau: and, b', also
20 B', thy servant Jacob is behind us.
33: 1 and, b', Esau came, and with him
34:21 for the land, b', it is large enough
37: 7 For, b', we were binding sheaves
7 and, b', your sheaves stood round
9 B', I have dreamed a dream more;
9 and, b' the sun and the moon and
15 b', he was wandering in the field:
19 another, B', this dreamer cometh.
25 and, b', a company of Ishmeelites
38:13 B' thy father in law goeth up to
23 b', I sent this kid, and thou hast
24 and also, b', she is with child
27 that, b', twins were in her womb.
29 b', his brother came out: and she
39: 8 B', my master wotteth not what
40: 6 and looked upon them, and, b',
9 In my dream, b', a vine was before
16 and, b', I had three white baskets
41: 1 that Pharaoh dreamed: and, b',
2 And, b', there came up out of the
3 And, b', seven other kine came up
5 and, b', seven ears of corn came
6 b', seven thin ears and blasted
7 Pharaoh awoke, and, b', it was a
17 In my dream, b', I stood upon the
18 b', there came up out of the river
19 b', seven other kine came up after
22 b', seven ears came up in one stalk,
23 b', seven ears, withered, thin, and
29 B', there came seven years of great
42: 2 B', I have heard that there is corn
13 b', the youngest is this day with
22 b', also his blood is required.
27 for, b', it was in his sack's mouth.
35 b', every man's bundle of money
43:21 we opened our sacks, and, b',
44: 8 B', the money, which we found
16 b', we are my lord's servants,
45:12 And, b', your eyes see, and the
47: 1 b', they are in the land of Goshen.
48: 1 B', thy father is sick: and he took
2 B', thy son Joseph cometh unto
4 B', I will make thee fruitful, and
21 B', I die; but God shall be with
50:18 they said, B', we be thy servants.
Ex 2:13 b', two men of the Hebrews
3: 2 looked, and, b', the bush burned
9 b', the cry of the children of Israel
13 B', when I come unto the children
4: 1 But, b', they will not believe me,
6 b', his hand was leprous as snow.
7 b', it was turned again as his
Ex 4:14 b', he cometh forth to meet thee:
23 b', I will slay thy son, even thy
5: 5 B', the people of the land now are
16 and, b', thy servants are beaten;
6:12 B', the children of Israel have
30 Moses said before the Lord, B',
7:16 b', hitherto thou wouldest not
17 know that I am the Lord: b',
8: 2 if thou refuse to let them go, b', I
21 thou wilt not let my people go, b',
29 B', I go out from thee,
9: 7 b', there was not one of the cattle
18 B', to morrow about this time
10: 4 let my people go, b', to morrow
14:10 and, b', the Egyptians marched
17 And I, b', I will harden
16: 4 B', I will rain bread
10 b', the glory of the Lord
14 b', upon the face of the wilderness
17: 6 B', I will stand before thee
23:20 B', I send an Angel before thee,
24: 8 B' the blood of the covenant,
14 b', Aaron and Hur are with you:
31: 6 b', I have given with him Aholiab,
32: 9 and, b', it is a stiffnecked people:
34 b', mine Angel shall go before thee:
33:21 said, B', there is a place by me,
34:10 he said, B', I make a covenant:
11 b', I drive out before thee the
30 b', the skin of his face shone;
Le 10:16 and, b', it was burnt:
18 B', the blood of it was not brought
19 B', this day have they offered
13: 5 b', if the plague in his sight
6 b', if the plague be somewhat
8 b', the scab spreadeth in the skin,
10 b', if the rising be white
13 b', if the leprosy have covered
17 b', if the plague be turned
20 b', if it be in sight lower than
21 b', there be no white hairs
25 b', if the hair in the bright
26 b', there be no white hair
30 b', if it be in sight deeper
31 b', it be not in sight deeper
32 b', if the scall spread not,
34 b', if the scall be not spread
36 b', if the scall be spread
39 b', if the bright spots in the skin
53 b', the plague be not spread
55 b', if the plague have not changed
56 b', the plague be somewhat
14: 3 b', if the plague of leprosy
37 b', if the plague be in the walls
39, 44 b', if the plague be spread
48 b', the plague hath not spread
25:20 b', we shall not sow,
Nu 3:12 b', I have taken the Levites
12: 8 similitude of the Lord shall he b':
10 b', Miriam became leprous,
10 b', she was leprous.
16:42 b', the cloud covered it
47 b', the plague was begun
17: 8 b', the rod of Aaron for the house
12 B', we die, we perish,
18: 6 b', I have taken your brethren
21 b', I have given the children
20:16 b', we are in Kadesh,
22:11 B', there is a people come out
32 b', I went out to withstand
23: 9 him, and from the hills I b' him:
11 b', thou hast blessed them
17 b', he stood by his burnt
20 B', I have received commandment
24 B', the people shall rise up
24:14 b', I go unto my people:
17 I shall b' him, but not nigh:
25: 6 b', one of the children of Israel
12 B', I give unto him my covenant
31:16 B', these caused the children
32: 1 b', the place was a place
14 b', ye are risen up
23 b', ye have sinned
De 1: 8 B', I have set the land before you:
10 b', ye are this day as the stars
21 B', the Lord thy God hath set
2:24 b', I have given into thine hand
31 B', I have begun to give Sihon
3:11 b', his bedstead was a bedstead
27 and b' it with thine eyes:
4: 5 B', I have taught you statutes
5:24 B', the Lord our God hath shewed
9:16 I looked, and, b', ye had sinned
10:14 B', the heaven and the heaven
11:26 B', I set before you this day a
13:14 b', if it be truth,
17: 4 b', if it be true,
19:18 b', if the witness be a false
26:10 b', I have brought the firstfruits
31:14 B', thy days approach
16 B', thou shalt sleep with thy
27 b', while I am yet alive
32:49 and b' the land of Canaan, which
Jos 2: 2 B', there came men in hither
18 B', when we come into the land,
3:11 B', the ark of the covenant
5:13 b', there stood a man
7:21 b', they are hid in the earth
22 b', it was hid in his tent,
8: 4 B', ye shall lie in wait against the
20 b', the smoke of the city
9:12 b', it is dry,
13 b', they be rent:
25 And now, b', we are in thine hand:
14:10 b', the Lord hath kept me
22:11 B', the children of Reuben

Jos 22:28 *B'* the pattern of the altar
23: 4 *B'*, I have divided unto you by lot
14 And, *b'*, this day I am going
24:27 *B'*, this stone shall be a witness
J'g 1: 2 *b'*, I have delivered the land
3:24 *b'*, the doors of the parlour were
25 and, *b'*, he opened not
25 and, *b'*, their lord was fallen
4:22 And, *b'*, as Barak pursued
22 *b'*, Sisera lay dead,
6:15 *b'*, my family is poor
28 *b'*, the altar of Baal was cast
37 *B'*, I will put a fleece of wool
7:13 *b'*, there was a man
13 *B'*, I dreamed a dream,
17 and, *b'*, when I come
8:15 said, *B'*, Zebah and Zalmunna
9:31 saying, *B'*, Gaal the son of Obed
31 *b'*, they fortify the city
33 *b'*, when he and the people
36 *B'*, there come people
43 *b'*, the people were come
11:34 *b'*, his daughter came out
13: 3 *B'* now, thou art barren,
7 *B'*, thou shalt conceive,
10 *B'*, the man hath appeared
14: 5 and, *b'*, a young lion roared
8 *b'*, there was a swarm of bees
16 *B'*, I have not told it
16:10 *B'*, thou hast mocked me
17: 2 *b'*, the silver is with me;
18: 9 and, *b'*, it is very good:
12 *b'*, it is behind Kirjath-jearim.
19: 9 *B'*, now the day draweth
9 *b'*, the day groweth to an end,
16 And, *b'*, there came an old man
22 *b'*, the men of the city,
24 *B'*, here is my daughter
27 *b'*, the woman his concubine
20: 7 *B'*, ye are all children
40 *b'*, the flame of the city
21: 8 *b'*, there came none to the camp
9 *b'*, there were none of the
19 *B'*, there is a feast of the Lord
21 *b'*, if the daughters of Shiloh
Ru 1:15 *B'*, thy sister in law
2: 4 *b'*, Boaz came from Beth-lehem,
3: 2 *B'*, he winnoweth barley
8 *b'*, a woman lay at his feet.
4: 1 *b'*, the kinsman of whom Boaz
1Sa 2:31 *B'*, the days come, that I will cut
3:11 to Samuel, *B'*, I will do a thing in
5: 3, 4 *b'*, Dagon was fallen upon his
8: 5 *B'*, thou art old,
9: 6 *B'* now, there is in this city
7 *b'*, if we go, what shall we bring
8 *B'*, I have here at hand
12 He is; *b'*, he is before you:
14 *b'*, Samuel came out against
17 *B'* the man whom I spake
24 *B'* that which is left!
10: 8 *b'*, I will come down unto thee,
10 *b'*, a company of prophets
11 *b'*, he prophesied among
22 *B'*, he hath hid himself
11: 5 *b'*, Saul came after the herd
12: 1 *B'*, I have hearkened unto your
2 *b'*, the king walketh before you:
2 *b'*, my sons are with you:
13 Now therefore *b'* the king
13 And, *b'*, the Lord hath set
13:10 *b'*, Samuel came;
14: 7 *b'*, I am with thee according
8 *B'*, we will pass over unto these
11 *B'*, the Hebrews come forth
16 *b'*, the multitude melted
17 *b'*, Jonathan and his
20 *b'*, every man's sword
26 *b'*, the honey dropped;
33 *B'*, the people sin against
16:11 and, *b'*, he keepeth the sheep.
15 *B'* now, an evil spirit from God
18 *B'*, I have seen a son of Jesse, the
17:23 *b'*, there came up the champion,
18:17 *B'* my elder daughter
22 *B'*, the king hath delight
19:16 *b'*, there was an image
22 *B'*, they be at Naioth in Ramah.
20: 2 *b'*, my father will do nothing
5 *B'*, to morrow is the new moon,
12 *b'*, if there be good toward
21 And, *b'*, I will send a lad,
21 *B'*, the arrows are on this side
22 *B'*, the arrows are beyond
23 *b'*, the Lord be between
21: 9 *b'*, it is here wrapped in a cloth
23: 1 *B'*, the Philistines fight against
3 *B'*, we be afraid here
24: 1 *B'*, David is in the wilderness
4 *B'* the day of which the Lord said
4 *B'*, I will deliver thine enemy
9 *B'*, David seeketh thy hurt?
10 *B'*, this day thine eyes have seen
20 now, *b'*, I know well that
25:14 *B'*, David sent messengers
19 *b'*, I come after you.
20 and, *b'*, David and his men
36 *b'*, he held a feast in his
41 *B'*, let thine handmaid
26: 7 *b'*, Saul lay sleeping within
21 *b'*, I have played the fool,
22 *B'* the king's spear!
24 *b'*, as thy life was much
28: 7 *B'*, there is a woman
9 *B'*, thou knowest what Saul
21 *B'*, thine handmaid hath
1Sa 30: 3 *b'*, it was burned with fire;
16 *b'*, they were spread abroad
26 *B'* a present for you
2Sa 1: 2 *b'*, a man came out
6 *b'*, Saul leaned upon his spear
18 *b'*, it is written in the book
3:12 *b'*, my hand shall be with
22 *b'*, the servants of David
24 *b'*, Abner came unto thee;
4: 8 *B'* the head of Ish-bosheth
10 *B'*, Saul is dead,
5: 1 *B'*, we are thy bone and thy flesh.
9: 4 *B'*, he is in the house
6 answered, *B'* thy servant!
12:11 *B'*, I will raise up evil
18 *B'*, while the child was yet alive,
13:24 *B'* now, thy servant hath
34 *b'*, there came much people
35 *B'*, the king's sons come;
36 *B'*, the king's sons came,
14: 7 And, *b'*, the whole family
21 *B'* now, I have done this thing,
32 *B'*, I sent unto thee,
15:15 *B'*, thy servants are ready
26 *b'*, here am I, let him do
32 *b'*, Hushai, the Archite
36 *B'*, they have there with them
16: 1 *b'*, Ziba, the servant of
3 *B'*, he abideth at Jerusalem:
4 *B'*, thine are all that pertained
5 *b'*, thence came out a man
8 *b'*, thou art taken in thy
11 *B'*, my son, which came
17: 9 *B'*, he is hid now
18:11 *b'*, thou sawest him,
24 and *b'* a man running
26 *B'* another man running
31 And, *b'*, Cushi came;
19: 1 *B'*, the king weepeth
8 *B'*, the king doth sit
20 therefore, *b'*, I am come
37 But *b'* thy servant Chimham;
41 And, *b'*, all the men of Israel
20:21 *B'*, his head shall be thrown
24:22 *b'*, here be oxen for burnt
1Ki 1:14 *B'*, while thou yet talkest
18 *b'*, Adonijah reigneth;
23 *B'* Nathan the prophet.
25 *b'*, they eat and drink
42 *b'*, Jonathan the son of Abiathar
51 *B'*, Adonijah feareth king
2: 8 *b'*, thou hast with thee
29 *b'*, he is by the altar.
39 *B'*, thy servants be in Gath.
3:12 *B'*, I have done according
15 *b'*, it was a dream.
21 *b'*, it was dead:
21 *b'*, it was not my son,
5: 5 And, *b'*, I purpose to build
8:27 *b'* the heaven and heaven of
10: 7 *b'*, the half was not told me:
11:22 *b'*, thou seekest to go
31 *B'*, I will rend the kingdom
12:28 *b'* thy gods, O Israel,
13: 1 *b'*, there came a man of God
2 *B'*, a child shall be born
3 *B'*, the altar shall be rent,
25 *b'*, men passed by
14: 2 *b'*, there is Ahijah
5 *B'*, the wife of Jeroboam
10 *b'*, I will bring evil upon
19 *b'*, they are written in the book
15:19 *b'*, I have sent unto thee
16: 3 *B'*, I will take away the posterity
17: 9 *b'*, I have commanded
10 *b'*, the widow woman was
12 *b'*, I am gathering two sticks,
18: 7 *b'*, Elijah met him:
8, 11, 14 *B'*, Elijah is here:
44 *B'*, there ariseth a little cloud
19: 5 *b'*, then an angel touched
6 *b'*, there was a cake baken
9 *b'*, the word of the Lord came
11 And, *b'*, the Lord passed by,
13 *b'*, there came a voice
20:13 *b'*, there came a prophet
13 *b'*, I will deliver it
31 *B'* now, we have heard
36 *b'*, as soon as thou art
39 *b'*, a man turned aside,
21:18 *b'*, he is in the vineyard
21 *B'*, I will bring evil upon thee,
22:13 *B'* now, the words of the prophet
23 *b'*, the Lord hath put a lying
25 *B'*, thou shalt see in that
2Ki 1: 9 *b'*, he sat on the top of an hill.
14 *B'*, there came fire down from
2:11 *b'*, there appeared a chariot
16 *B'* now, there be with thy servants
19 *B'*, I pray thee, the situation
3:20 *b'*, there came water by the way
4: 9 *B'* now, I perceive that this
13 *B'*, thou hast been careful
25 *B'*, yonder is that Shunammite:
32 *b'*, the child was dead,
5: 6 *b'*, I have therewith sent
11 *B'*, I thought, He will surely
15 *B'*, now I know that there is
20 *B'*, my master hath spared
22 *B'*, even now there be come
6: 1 *B'* now, the place where
13 *B'*, he is in Dothan.
15 *b'*, an host compassed the city
17 *b'*, the mountain was full
20 *b'*, they were in the midst
25 *b'*, they besieged it,
2Ki 6:30 *b'*, he had sackcloth within
33 *b'*, the messenger came down
33 *B'*, this evil is of the Lord;
7: 2 *B'*, if the Lord would make
2 *B'*, thou shalt see it with thine
5 *b'*, there was no man there.
10 *b'*, there was no man there,
13 (*b'*, they are as all the multitude
13 *b'*, I say they are even as all
19 Now, *b'*, if the Lord should make
19 *B'*, thou shalt see it
8: 5 *b'*, the woman, whose son
9: 5 *b'*, the captains of the host
10: 4 *B'*, two kings stood not
9 *b'*, I conspired against my
11:14 when she looked, *b'*, the king stood
13:21 *b'*, they spied a band of men;
15:11, 15 *b'*, they are written in the book
26, 31 *b'*, they are written in the book
17:26 and, *b'*, they slay them,
18:21 *b'*, thou trustest upon the staff
19: 7 *B'*, I will send a blast upon him,
9 *B'*, he is come out to fight
11 *B'*, thou hast heard what
35 *b'*, they were all dead corpses.
20: 5 *b'*, I will heal thee:
17 *B'*, the days come, that all
21:12 *B'*, I am bringing such evil
22:16 *B'*, I will bring evil upon
20 *B'* therefore, I will gather thee
1Ch 9: 1 *b'*, they were written in the book
11: 1 *B'*, we are thy bone and thy flesh.
25 *B'*, he was honourable among
22: 9 *B'*, a son shall be born to thee,
14 *b'*, in my trouble I have
28:21 *b'*, the courses of the priests
29:29 *b'*, they are written in the book
2Ch 2: 4 *B'*, I build an house
8 *b'*, my servants shall be
10 *b'*, I will give to thy servants,
6:18 *b'*, heaven and the heaven of
9: 6 *b'*, the one half of the greatness
13:12 *b'*, God himself is with us
14 looked back, *b'*, the battle was
16: 3 *b'*, I have sent thee silver
11 *b'*, the acts of Asa,
18:12 *B'*, the words of the prophets
22 *b'*, the Lord hath put a lying
24 *B'*, thou shalt see on that day
19:11 *b'*, Amariah the chief priest
20: 2 *b'*, they be in Hazazon-tamar,
10 *b'*, the children of Ammon
11 *B'*, I say, how they reward us,
16 *b'*, they come up by the cliff
24 *b'*, they were dead bodies
34 *b'*, they are written in the book
21:14 *B'*, with a great plague will the
23: 3 *B'*, the king's son shall reign,
13 and, *b'*, the king stood at his pillar
24:27 *b'*, they are written in the story
25:26 *b'*, are they not written in the
26:20 *b'*, he was leprous in his forehead
28: 9 *B'*, because the Lord God of your
26 *b'*, they are written in the book
29:19 *b'*, they are before the altar
32:32 *b'*, they are written in the vision
33:18 *b'*, they are written in the book
19 *b'*, they are written among
34:24 *B'*, I will bring evil upon this
28 *B'*, I will gather thee to thy fathers
35:25 and, *b'*, they are written in the
27 *b'*, they are written in the book
36: 8 *b'*, they are written in the book
Ezr 9:15 *b'*, we are before thee in our
Ne 9:36 *B'*, we are servants this day,
36 *b'*, we are servants in it:
Es 6: 5 *B'*, Haman standeth
7: 9 *B'* also, the gallows fifty cubits
8: 7 *B'*, I have given Esther the house
Job 1:12 *B'*, all that he hath is in thy
19 *b'*, there came a great wind
2: 6 *B'*, he is in thine hand;
4: 3 *B'*, thou hast instructed many,
18 *B'*, he put no trust in his
5:17 *B'*, happy is the man whom
8:19 *B'*, this is the joy of his way,
20 *B'*, God will not cast away
9:12 *B'*, he taketh away, who can hinder
12:14 *B'*, he breaketh down,
15 *B'*, he withholdeth the waters,
13:18 *B'* now, I have ordered my
15:15 *B'*, he putteth no trust in his
16:19 *b'*, my witness is in heaven,
19: 7 *B'*, I cry out of wrong,
27 and mine eyes shall *b'*,
20: 9 shall his place any more *b'* him.
21:27 *B'*, I know your thoughts,
22:12 and *b'* the height of the stars,
23: 8 *B'*, I go forward,
9 but I cannot *b'* him: he hideth
24: 5 *B'*, as wild asses in the desert
25: 5 *B'* even to the moon,
27:12 *B'*, all ye yourselves have seen
28:28 *B'*, the fear of the Lord,
31:35 *b'*, my desire is,
32:11 *B'*, I waited for your words;
12 *b'*, there was none of you
19 *B'*, my belly is as wine
33: 2 *B'*, now I have opened my mouth,
6 *B'*, I am according to thy wish
7 *B'*, my terror shall not make
10 *B'*, he findeth occasions
12 *B'*, in this thou art not just:
34:29 who then can *b'* him? whether it
35: 5 and *b'* the clouds which are higher
36: 5 *B'*, God is mighty,

Job 36:22 B', God exalteth by his power:
24 his work, which men b'.
25 man may see it; man may b' it
26 B', God is great, and we know
30 B', he spreadeth his light
39:29 her eyes b' afar off.
40: 4 B', I am vile;
11 and b' every one that is proud,
15 B' now behemoth, which I made
23 B', he drinketh up a river,
41: 9 B', the hope of him is in vain:
Ps 7:14 B', he travaileth with iniquity,
11: 4 his eyes b', his eyelids try, the
7 his countenance doth b' the
17: 2 let thine eyes b' the things that
15 will b' thy face in righteousness:
27: 4 to b' the beauty of the Lord, and
33:18 B', the eye of the Lord is upon
37:37 and b' the upright: for the end of
39: 5 B', thou hast made my days
46: 8 come, b' the works of the Lord,
51: 5 B', I was shapen in iniquity;
6 B', thou desirest truth in the
54: 4 B', God is mine helper:
59: 4 awake to help me, and b',
7 B', they belch out with their
66: 7 power forever; his eyes b' the
73:12 B', these are the ungodly,
15 B', I should offend against
78:20 B', he smote the rock,
80:14 look down from heaven, and b',
84: 9 B', O God our shield, and look
87: 4 B' Philistia, and Tyre, with
91: 8 with thine eyes shalt thou b' and
102:19 from heaven did the Lord b' the
113: 6 to b' the things that are in
119:18 that I may b' wondrous things
40 B', I have longed after thy
121: 4 B', he that keepeth Israel shall
123: 2 B', as the eyes of servants look
128: 4 B', that thus shall the man be
133: 1 B', how good and how pleasant
134: 1 B', bless ye the Lord, all ye
139: 8 b', thou art there.
Pr 1:23 B', I will pour out my spirit unto
7:10 b', there met him a woman
11:31 B', the righteous shall be
23:33 Thine eyes shall b' strange
24:12 B', we knew it not;
Ec 1:14 b', all is vanity and vexation of
2: 1 b', this also is vanity.
11 b', all was vanity and vexation of
12 I turned myself to b' wisdom,
4: 1 B' the tears of such as were
5:18 B' that which I have seen: good
7:27 B', this have I found, saith the
11: 7 it is for the eyes to b' the sun:
Ca 1:15 B', thou art fair, my love;
15 b', thou art fair;
16 B', thou art fair, my beloved,
2: 8 b', he cometh leaping upon the
9 b', he standeth behind our wall,
3: 7 B' his bed,
11 and b' king Solomon with the
4: 1 B', thou art fair, my love;
1 b', thou art fair;
Isa 3: 1 B', the Lord, the Lord of hosts,
5: 7 but b' oppression;
7 but b' a cry.
26 b', they shall come with speed
30 b' darkness and sorrow,
7:14 B', a virgin shall conceive,
8: 7 b', the Lord bringeth up
18 B', I and the children whom
22 and b' trouble and darkness,
10:33 B', the Lord, the Lord of hosts,
12: 2 B', God is my salvation;
13: 9 B', the day of the Lord cometh,
17 B', I will stir up the Medes against
17: 1 B', Damascus is taken
14 and b' at eventide trouble;
19: 1 B', the Lord rideth upon a swift
20: 6 B', such is our expectation,
21: 9 b', here cometh a chariot of men
22:13 and b' joy and gladness,
17 B', the Lord will carry thee
23:13 B', the land of the Chaldeans;
24: 1 B', the Lord maketh the earth
26:10 will not b' the majesty of the
21 b', the Lord cometh out of his
28: 2 B', the Lord hath a mighty and
16 B', I lay in Zion for a foundation
29: 8 b', he eateth; but he awaketh,
8 b', he drinketh; but he awaketh,
8 b', he is faint, and his soul hath
14 b', I will proceed to do a marvelous
30:27 B', the name of the Lord cometh
32: 1 B', a king shall reign in
33: 7 B', their valiant ones shall cry
17 they shall b' the land that is very
34: 5 B', it shall come down upon
35: 4 b', your God will come with
37: 7 B', I will send a blast upon
11 B', thou hast heard what
36 b', they were all dead corpses.
38: 5 b', I will add unto thy days
8 B', I will bring again the shadow
11 I shall b' man no more with the
17 B', for peace I had great
39: 6 B', the days come,
40: 9 B' your God!
10 B', the Lord God will come with
10 b', his reward is with him,
15 B', the nations as a drop of a
15 b', he taketh up the isles as a
26 and b' who hath created these

Isa 41:11 B', all they that were incensed
15 B', I will make thee a new sharp
23 be dismayed, and b' it together.
24 B', ye are of nothing, and your
27 shall say to Zion, B', b' them:
29 B', they are all vanity;
42: 1 B' my servant, whom I uphold;
9 B', the former things are come
43:19 B', I will do a new thing;
44:11 B', all his fellows shall be
47:14 B', they shall be as stubble;
48: 7 B', I knew them.
10 B', I have refined thee,
49:12 B', these shall come from far:
16 B', I have graven thee upon
18 thine eyes round about, and b':
21 B', I was left alone;
22 B', I will lift up mine hand,
50: 1 B', for your iniquities have
2 b', at my rebuke I dry up the
9 B', the Lord God will help me;
11 B', all ye that kindle a fire,
51:22 B', I have taken out of
52: 6 b', it is I.
13 B', my servant shall deal
54:11 b', I will lay thy stones with
15 B', they shall surely gather
16 B', I have created the smith
55: 4 B', I have given him for
5 B', thou shalt call a nation
56: 3 B', I am a dry tree.
58: 3 B', in the day of your fast
4 B', ye fast for strife and debate,
59: 1 B', the Lord's hand is not
9 But b' obscurity;
60: 2 b', the darkness shall cover
62:11 B', the Lord hath proclaimed
11 B', thy salvation cometh:
11 b', his reward is with him,
63:15 Look down from heaven, and b'
64: 5 b', thou art wroth;
9 b', see, we beseech thee, we are all
65: 1 I said B' me, b' me, unto a
6 B', it is written before me:
13 B', my servants shall eat,
13 b', my servants shall drink,
13 b', my servants shall rejoice,
14 B', my servants shall sing for
17 B', I create new heavens and a new
18 b', I create Jerusalem a rejoicing,
66:12 B', I will extend peace to her
15 b', the Lord will come with fire,
Jer 1: 6 B', I cannot speak:
9 B', I have put my words in thy
18 b', I have made thee this day
2:35 B', I will plead with thee,
3: 5 B', thou hast spoken and done
22 B', we come unto thee;
4:13 B', he shall come up as clouds,
16 b', publish against Jerusalem,
5:14 b', I will make my words in
6:10 b', their ear is uncircumcised, and
10 b', the word of the Lord is unto
19 b', I will bring evil upon this
21 B', I will lay stumblingblocks
22 B', a people cometh from the
7: 8 B', ye trust in lying words,
11 B', even I have seen it,
20 B', mine anger and my fury
32 b', the days come,
8:15 and b' trouble!
17 b', I will send serpents,
19 B' the voice of the cry of the
9: 7 B', I will melt them, and try them;
15 B', I will feed them, even this
25 B', the days come, saith the Lord,
10:18 B', I will sling out the inhabitants
22 B', the noise of the bruit is come,
11:11 B', I will bring evil upon them,
22 B', I will punish them:
12:14 B', I will pluck them out of their
13: 7 b', the girdle was marred,
13 B', I will fill all the inhabitants of
20 Lift up your eyes, and b' them
14:13 b', the prophets say unto them,
18 B' the slain with the sword!
18 then b' them that are sick with
19 and b' trouble!
16: 9 B', I will cause to cease out of
12 for, b', ye walk every one after
14 b', the days come, saith the Lord,
16 B', I will send for many fishers,
21 b', I will this once cause them
17:15 B', they say unto me,
18: 3 and, b', he wrought a work
6 B', as the clay is in the potter's
11 B', I frame evil against you,
19: 3 B', I will bring evil upon this place,
6 b', the days come,
15 B', I will bring upon this city
20: 4 B', I will make thee a terror to
4 thine eyes shall b' it: and I will
21: 4 B', I will turn back the weapons
8 B', I set before you the way
13 B', I am against thee,
23: 2 b', I will visit upon you the evil
5, 7 B', the days come,
15 B', I will feed them...wormwood,
19 B', a whirlwind of the Lord
30, 31 B', I am against the prophets,
32 B', I am against them that
39 b', I, even I, will utterly forget
24: 1 b', two baskets of figs were
25: 9 B', I will send and take all
32 B', evil shall go forth from
26:14 b', I am in your hand:

Jer 27:16 B', the vessels of the Lord's house
28:16 B', I will cast thee from off
29:17 B', I will send upon them the
32 B', I will furnish Shemaiah the
32 neither shall he b' the good that
30:18 B', I will bring again the captivity
23 B', the whirlwind of the Lord
31: 8 B', I will bring them from the north
27, 31, 38 B', the days come,
32: 3 B', I will give this city into
4 and his eyes shall b' his eyes;
7 B', Hanameel the son of Shallum
17 b', thou hast made the heaven
24 B' the mounts, they are come
24 B', thou seest it.
27 B', I am the Lord,
28 B', I will give this city into
37 B', I will gather them out of
33: 6 B', I will bring it health and
14 B', the days come,
34: 2 B', I will give this city into the
3 thine eyes shall b' the eyes of
17 B', I proclaim a liberty for you,
22 B', I will command,
35:17 B', I will bring upon Judah
37: 7 B', Pharaoh's army,
38: 5 B', he is in your hand:
22 B', all the women that are left
39:16 b', I will bring my words upon
40: 4 b', I loose thee this day from the
4 b', all the land is before thee:
10 b', I will dwell at Mizpah,
42: 2 of many, as thine eyes do b' us)
4 b', I will pray unto the Lord
43:10 B', I will send and take
44: 2 b', this day they are a desolation,
11 B', I will set my face against
26 B', I have sworn by my great
27 B', I will watch over them
30 B', I will give Pharaoh-hophra
45: 4 B', that which I have built
5 b', I will bring evil upon all
46:25 B', I will punish the multitude
27 b', I will save thee from afar
47: 2 B', waters rise up out of the
48:12 b', the days come,
40 B', he shall fly as an eagle,
49: 2 b', the days come,
5 B', I will bring a fear upon thee,
12 B', they whose judgment was
22 B', he shall come up and fly
35 B', I will break the bow of Elam,
50:12 b', the hindermost of the nations
18 B', I will punish the king of
31 B', I am against thee,
44 B', he shall come up like a
51: 1 B', I will raise up against
25 B', I am against thee,
36 B', I will plead thy cause,
47 b', the days come, that I will do
52 b', the days come, saith the Lord,
La 1: 9 O Lord, b' my affliction: for the
12 b', and see if there be any sorrow
18 all people, and b' my sorrow:
20 B', O Lord; for I am in distress:
2:20 B', O Lord, and consider to whom
3:50 Till the Lord look down, and b'
63 B' their sitting down, and their
5: 1 consider, and b' our reproach.
Eze 1: 4 And I looked, and, b', a whirlwind
15 the living creatures, b', one wheel
2: 9 And when I looked, b', an hand
3: 8 B', I have made thy face strong
23 b', the glory of the Lord stood there,
25 b', they shall put bands upon
4: 8 b', I will lay bands upon
14 b', my soul hath not been
16 b', I will break the staff of bread
5: 8 B', I, even I, am against
6: 3 B', I, even I, will bring a sword
7: 5 an only evil, b', is come.
6 b', it is come.
10 B' the day, b', it is come:
8: 4 b', the glory of the God of Israel
5 and b' northward at the gate
7 b' a hole in the wall.
8 b' a door.
9 and b' the wicked abominations
10 and b' every form of creeping
14 b', there sat women weeping
16 b', at the door of the temple
9: 2 and, b', six men came from the
11 and, b', the man clothed with
10: 1 and, b', in the firmament
9 b' the four wheels by the
11: 1 and b' at the door of the gate
12:27 b', they of the house of Israel say,
13: 8 b', I am against you,
20 B', I am against your pillows,
14:22 b', therein shall be left a
22 b', they shall come forth unto you,
15: 4 B', it is cast into the fire for fuel;
5 B', when it was whole,
16: 8 b', thy time was the time of love;
27 B', therefore I have stretched out
37 B', therefore I will gather all thy
43 b', therefore I also will recompense
44 B', every one that useth proverbs
49 B', this was the iniquity of thy
17: 7 b', this vine did bend her
10 b', being planted,
12 B', the king of Babylon is come
18: 4 B', all souls are mine;
20:47 B', I will kindle fire in thee,
21: 3 B', I am against thee,
7 B', it cometh, and shall be brought

Eze 22: 6 B', the princes of Israel,
13 B', therefore I have smitten
19 b', therefore I will gather you
23:22 B', I will raise up thy lovers
28 B', I will deliver thee into the
24:16 b', I take away from thee the
21 B', I will profane my sanctuary,
25: 4 B', therefore I will deliver thee to
7 B', therefore I will stretch out
8 B', the house of Judah is like
9 b', I will open the side of Moab
16 B', I will stretch out mine
26: 3 B', I am against thee,
7 B', I will bring upon Tyrus
28: 3 B', thou art wiser than Daniel;
7 B', therefore I will bring strangers
17 kings, that they may b' thee.
18 the sight of all them that b' thee.
22 B', I am against thee,
29: 3 B', I am against thee,
8 B', I will bring a sword upon
10 B', therefore I am against thee,
19 B', I will give the land of
30:22 B', I am against Pharaoh
31: 3 B', the Assyrian was a cedar
34:10 B', I am against the shepherds;
11 B', I, even I, will both search my
17 B', I judge between cattle and
20 B', I, even I, will judge between
35: 3 B', O mount Seir, I am against
36: 6 B', I have spoken in my jealousy
9 b', I am for you, and I will
37: 2 b', there were very many in
5 B', I will cause breath to enter
11 b', they say, Our bones are
12 B', O my people, I will open
19 B', I will take the stick of Joseph,
21 B', I will take the children
38: 3 B', I am against thee,
39: 1 B', I am against thee,
8 B', it is come, and it is done,
40: 3 b', there was a man,
4 Son of man, b' with thine eyes,
5 and b' a wall on the outside
24 and b' a gate toward the south:
43: 2 b', the glory of the God of Israel
5 b', the glory of the Lord filled
12 B', this is the law of the house.
44: 4 and, b', the glory of the Lord filled
5 and b' with thine eyes, and hear
46:19 b', there was a place on the two
21 b', in every corner of the court
47: 1 b', waters issued out from
2 b', there ran out waters
7 b', at the bank of the river
Da 2:31 king, sawest, and b' a great image.
4:10 b' a tree in the midst of the earth,
13 and, b', a watcher and a holy
7: 2 b', the four winds of the heaven
5 And b' another beast, a second,
7 and b' a fourth beast, dreadful and
8 and, b', there came up among
8 and, b', in this horn were eyes like
13 and, b', one like the Son of man
8: 3 b', there stood before the river
5 b', an he goat came from
15 b', there stood before me
19 B', I will make thee know
9:18 thine eyes, and b' our desolations,
10: 5 b' a certain man clothed in linen,
10 b', an hand touched me,
16 b', one like the similitude of the
11: 2 b', there shall stand up yet three
12: 5 and b', there stood other two,
Ho 2: 6 b' I will hedge up thy way
14 b', I will allure her,
Joe 2:19 B', I will send you corn,
3: 7 B', I will raise them out of
Am 2:13 B', I am pressed under you,
3: 9 and b' the great tumults in
6:14 b', I will raise up against you,
7: 1 b', he formed grasshoppers
4 b', the Lord God called to contend
7 b', the Lord stood upon a wall
8 B', I will set a plumbline
8: 1 and b' a basket of summer fruit.
11 B', the days come,
9: 8 B', the eyes of the Lord God
13 B', the days come,
Ob 2 B', I have made thee small
Mic 1: 3 b', the Lord cometh forth out of
2: 3 B', against this family do I
7: 9 and I shall b' his righteousness.
10 mine eyes shall b' her: now shall
Na 1:15 B' upon the mountains the
2:13 B', I am against thee,
3: 5 B', I am against thee,
13 B', thy people in the midst of
Hab 1: 3 and cause me to b' grievance?
5 B' ye among the heathen, and
13 art of purer eyes than to b' evil,
2: 4 B', his soul which is lifted up
13 B', is it not of the Lord of hosts
19 B', it is laid over with gold and
Zep 3:19 B', at that time I will undo all
Zec 1: 8 and b' a man riding upon
11 b', all the earth sitteth still,
18 and b' four horns.
2: 1 and b' a man with a measuring
3 b', the angel that talked with me
9 b', I will shake mine hand upon
3: 4 B', I have caused thine iniquity
8 b', I will bring forth my servant
9 For b' the stone that I have laid
9 b', I will engrave the graving
4: 2 and b' a candlestick all of gold,
Zec 5: 1 and b' a flying roll.
7 b', there was lifted up a talent
9 b', there came out two women,
6: 1 b', there came four chariots out
8 B', these that go towards the
12 B', the man whose name is The
8: 7 B', I will save my people
9: 4 B', the Lord will cast her out,
9 b', thy king cometh unto thee:
12: 2 B', I will make Jerusalem a
14: 1 B', the day of the Lord cometh,
Mal 1:13 B', what a weariness is it!
2: 3 B', I will corrupt your seed,
3: 1 B', I will send my messenger,
1 b', he shall come,
4: 1 For, b', the day cometh,
5 B', I will send you Elijah the
M't 1:20 b', the angel of the Lord appeared
23 B', a virgin shall be with child,
2: 1 b' there came wise men from the
13 b', the angel of the Lord appeareth
19 was dead, b', an angel of the Lord
4:11 leaveth him, and, b', angels came
6:26 B' the fowls of the air: for they
7: 4 b', a beam is in thine own eye?
8: 2 And, b', there came a leper
24 b', there arose a great tempest
29 and, b', they cried out, saying,
32 b', the whole herd of swine ran
34 And, b', the whole city came out
9: 2 And, b', they brought to him
3 And, b', certain of the scribes
10 b', many publicans and sinners
18 b', there came a certain ruler,
20 b', a woman, which was diseased
32 b', they brought to him a dumb
10:16 B', I send you forth as sheep
11: 8 b', they that wear soft clothing
10 B', I send my messenger before
19 B' a man gluttonous, and a
12: 2 B', thy disciples do that which is
10 And, b', there was a man
18 B' my servant, whom I have
41 b', a greater than Jonas is here.
42 b', a greater than Solomon is here.
46 b', his mother and his brethren
47 B', thy mother and thy brethren
49 B', my mother and my brethren!
13: 3 B', a sower went forth to sow;
15:22 b', a woman of Canaan came out
17: 3 And, b', there appeared unto them
5 b', a bright cloud overshadowed
5 and b' a voice out of the cloud,
18:10 do always b' the face of my Father
19:16 b', one came and said unto him,
27 B', we have forsaken all, and
20:18 B', we go up to Jerusalem; and
30 And, b', two blind men sitting
21: 5 B', thy King cometh unto thee,
22: 4 B', I have prepared my dinner:
23:34 Wherefore, b', I send unto you
38 B', your house is left unto you
24:25 B', I have told you before.
26 B', he is in the desert; go not
26 b', he is in the secret chambers;
25: 6 B', the bridegroom cometh; go ye
20 b', I have gained beside them
22 b', I have gained two other
26:45 b', the hour is at hand, and the
46 b', he is at hand that doth betray
51 And, b', one of them which were
65 b', now ye have heard his
27:51 b', the veil of the temple was rent
28: 2 b', there was a great earthquake:
7 and, b', he goeth before you into
9 b', Jesus met them, saying, All hail.
11 were going, b', some of the watch
M'r 1: 2 B', I send my messenger before
2:24 B', why do they on the sabbath
3:32 B', thy mother and thy brethren
34 B' my mother and my brethren!
4: 3 B', there went out a sower to sow:
5:22 b', there cometh one of the rulers
10:33 saying, B', we go up to Jerusalem,
11:21 b', the fig tree which thou
13:23 b', I have foretold you all things.
14:41 b', the Son of man is betrayed
15: 4 b' how many things they witness
35 heard it, said, B', he calleth Elias.
16: 6 b' the place where they laid him.
Lu 1:20 And, b', thou shalt be dumb,
31 And, b', thou shalt conceive in thy
36 And, b', thy cousin Elisabeth, she
38 B' the handmaid of the Lord;
48 for, b', from henceforth all
2:10 for, b', I bring you good tidings of
25 b', there was a man in Jerusalem,
34 B', this child is set for the fall
48 b', thy father and I have sought
5:12 city, b' a man full of leprosy:
18 And, b', men brought in a bed
6:23 for, b', your reward is great
7:12 b', there was a dead man carried
25 B', they which are gorgeously
27 B', I send my messenger before
34 B' a gluttonous man, and a
37 And, b', a woman in the city,
8:41 And, b', there came a man named
9:30 And, b', there talked with him two
38 And, b', a man of the company
10: 3 b', I send you forth as lambs
19 B', I give unto you power to tread
25 And, b', a certain lawyer stood up,
11:31 and, b', a greater than Solomon
32 and, b', a greater than Jonas
41 and, b', all things are clean
Lu 13: 7 B', these three years I come
11 And, b', there was a woman which
30 And, b', there are last which shall
32 B', I cast out devils, and I do cures
35 B', your house is left unto you
14: 2 And, b', there was a certain man
29 all that b' it begin to mock him,
17:21 for, b', the kingdom of God
18:31 B', we go up to Jerusalem, and all
19: 2 And, b', there was a man named
8 B', Lord, the half of my goods
20 b', here is thy pound, which I have
21: 6 As for these things which ye b',
29 B' the fig tree, and all the trees;
22:10 B', when ye are entered into the
21 b', the hand of him that betrayeth
31 b', Satan hath desired to have you,
38 Lord, b', here are two swords.
47 b' a multitude, and he that was
23:14 and, b', I, having examined him
29 For, b', the days are coming, in
50 And, b', there was a man named
24: 4 b', two men stood by them in
13 b', two of them went that same
39 B' my hands and my feet, that it
49 And, b', I send the promise of
Joh 1:29 B' the Lamb of God, which taketh
36 B' the Lamb of God!
47 B' an Israelite indeed, in whom
3:26 b', the same baptizeth, and all
4:35 b', I say unto you, Lift up your
5:14 B', thou art made whole: sin no
11: 3 Lord, b', he whom thou lovest is
36 the Jews, B' how he loved him!
12:15 b', thy King cometh, sitting on an
19 b', the world is gone after him.
16:32 B', the hour cometh, yea, is now
17:24 that they may b' my glory, which
18:21 unto them: b' they know what I
19: 4 B', I bring him forth to you, that
5 Pilate saith unto them, B' the
14 unto the Jews, B' your king!
26 unto his mother, Woman, b' thy
27 B' thy mother! And from that
20:27 hither thy finger, and b' my
Ac 1:10 b', two men stood by them in
2: 7 B', are not all these which speak
4:29 now, Lord, b' their threatenings:
5: 9 b', the feet of them which have
25 B', the men whom ye put in prison
28 and, b', ye have filled Jerusalem
7:31 and as he drew near to b' it,
32 Moses trembled and durst not b'.
56 B', I see the heavens opened,
8:27 and, b', a man of Ethiopia, an
9:10 And he said, B', I am here, Lord.
11 Saul, of Tarsus: for, b', he
10:17 b', the men which were sent from
19 B', three men seek thee.
21 B', I am he whom ye seek: what
30 and, b', a man stood before me in
11:11 And, b', immediately there were
12: 7 And, b', the angel of the Lord
13:11 And now, b', the hand of the Lord
25 But, b', there cometh one after me,
41 B', ye despisers, and wonder,
16: 1 and, b', a certain disciple was
20:22 And now, b', I go bound in the
25 b', I know that ye all,
Ro 2:17 B', thou art called a Jew, and
9:33 B', I lay in Sion a stumblingstone
11:22 B' therefore the goodness and
1Co 10:18 B' Israel after the flesh: are not
15:51 B', I shew you a mystery; We
2Co 3: 7 Israel could not stedfastly b' the
5:17 b', all things are become new.
6: 2 b', now is the accepted time;
2 b', now is the day of salvation.)
9 and, b', we live; as chastened,
7:11 For b' this selfsame thing that ye
12:14 B', the third time I am ready to
Ga 1:20 unto you, b', before God, I lie not.
5: 2 B', I Paul say unto you, that if ye
Heb 2:13 B' I and the children which God
8: 8 B', the days come, saith the Lord,
Jas 3: 3 B', we put bits in the horses'
4 B' also the ships, which though
5 B', how great a matter a little fire
5: 4 B', the hire of the labourers who
7 B', the husbandman waiteth for
9 b', the judge standeth before the
11 B', we count them happy which
1Pe 2: 6 B', I lay in Sion a chief corner
12 good works, which they shall b',
3: 2 they b' your chaste conversation
1Jo 3: 1 B', what manner of love the
Jude 14 B', the Lord cometh with ten
Re 1: 7 B', he cometh with clouds; and
18 and, b', I am alive for evermore,
2:10 b', the devil shall cast some of you
22 B', I will cast her into a bed, and
3: 8 b', I have set before thee an open
9 B', I will make them of the
9 b', I will make them to come and
11 B', I come quickly: hold that
20 B', I stand at the door and knock:
4: 1 and, b', a door was opened in
2 and, b', a throne was set in heaven,
5: 5 b', the Lion of the tribe of Juda,
6: 2 And I saw, and b' a white horse:
8 And I looked, and b' a pale horse:
9:12 and, b', there come two woes more
11:14 and, b', the third woe cometh
12: 3 and b' a great red dragon, having
14:14 And I looked, and b' a white cloud,
15: 5 b', the temple of the tabernacle

Re 16:15 B', I come as a thief. Blessed
17: 8 when they b' the beast that was
19:11 opened, and b' a white horse;
21: 3 B', the tabernacle of God is with
5 said, B', I make all things new.
22: 7 B', I come quickly: blessed is he
12 And, b', I come quickly; and my

beholdest
Ps 10:14 thou b' mischief and spite, to
M't 7: 3 why b' thou the mote that is in thy
Lu 6:41 And why b' thou the mote that is
42 when thou thyself b' not the beam

beholdeth
Job 24:18 b' not the way of the vineyards.
41:34 He b' all high things: he is a
Ps 33:13 heaven; he b' all the sons of men.
Jas 1:24 For he b' himself, and goeth his

beholding
Ps 119:37 Turn away mine eyes from b'
Pr 15: 3 every place, b' the evil and the
Ec 5:11 the b' of them with their eyes?
M't 27:55 women were there b' afar off,
M'k 10:21 Jesus b' him loved him, and said
Lu 23:35 the people stood b'. And the
48 b' the things which were done,
49 stood afar off b' these things.
Ac 4:14 b' the man which was healed
8:13 b' the miracles and signs which
14: 9 who stedfastly b' him and
23: 1 Paul, earnestly b' the council,
2Co 3:18 b' as in a glass the glory of the
Col 2: 5 joying and b' your order, and the
Jas 1:23 like unto a man b' his natural

behoved
Lu 24:46 thus it b' Christ to suffer, and
Heb 2:17 in all things it b' him to be made

being^
Ge 18:12 I have pleasure, my lord b' old
19:16 the Lord b' merciful unto him:
21: 4 Isaac b' eight days old, as God
24:27 I b' in the way, the Lord led me
34:30 and I b' few in number, they shall
35:29 gathered unto his people, b' old
37: 2 Joseph, b' seventeen years old,
50:26 So Joseph died, b' an hundred and
Ex 12:34 their kneadingtroughs b' bound
13:15 all that openeth the matrix, b'
22:14 the owner thereof b' not with it,
28:16 it shall be b' doubled; a span
32:18 of them that cry for b' overcome:
39: 9 a span the breadth thereof, b'
Le 21: 4 b' a chief man among his people,
24: 8 b' taken from the children of
Nu 1:44 princes of Israel, b' twelve men:
22:24 of the vineyards, a wall b' on the
30: 3 bond, b' in her father's house in
16 b' yet in her youth in her father's
31:32 And the booty, b' the rest of the
32:38 Baal-meon, (their names b'
De 3:13 and all Bashan, b' the kingdom
17: 8 b' matters of controversy within
22:24 because she cried not, b' in the
32:31 even our enemies themselves b'
Jos 9:23 of you be freed from b' bondmen,
21:10 of Aaron, b' of the family of the
24:29 died, b' an hundred and ten years
J'g 2: 8 servant of the Lord died, b' an
9: 5 Jerubbaal, b' threescore and ten
1Sa 2:18 ministered before the Lord, b' a
15:23 also rejected thee from b' king.
26 hath rejected thee from b' king
26:13 a great space b' between them:
2Sa 8:13 salt, b' eighteen thousand men.
13: 4 Why art thou, b' the king's son,
14 but b' stronger than she, forced
19: 3 as people b' ashamed steal away
21:16 he b' girded with a new sword,
1Ki 1:41 noise of the city, b' in an uproar?
2:27 thrust out Abiathar from b' priest
11:17 Hadad b' yet a little child,
15:13 her he removed from b' queen,
16: 7 in b' like the house of Jeroboam;
20:15 of Israel, b' seven thousand.
2Ki 8:16 Jehoshaphat b' then king of Judah,
10: 6 king's sons, b' seventy persons,
12:11 gave the money, b' told, into the
1Ch 9:19 fathers, b' over the host of the
24: 6 household b' taken for Eleazar,
2Ch 5:12 b' arrayed in white linen,
13: 3 thousand chosen men, b' mighty
15:16 he removed her from b' queen,
21:20 and departed without b' desired.
26:21 in a several house, b' a leper;
Ezr 6:11 down from his house, and b'
10:19 and b' guilty, they offered a ram
Ne 6:11 and who is there, that, b' as I am,
Es 1: 3 of the provinces, b' before him:
3:15 out, b' hastened by the king's
8:14 b' hastened and pressed on by
Job 4: 7 who ever perished, b' innocent?
21:23 b' wholly at ease and quiet,
42:17 Job died, b' old and full of days,
Ps 49:12 man b' in honour abideth not:
65: 6 the mountains; b' girded with
69: 4 would destroy me, b' mine enemies
78: 9 children of Ephraim, b' armed,
38 But he, b' full of compassion,
83: 4 cut them off from b' a nation;
104:33 to my God while I have my b'.
107:10 b' bound in affliction and iron;
139:16 substance, yet b' unperfect;
146: 2 unto my God while I have any b'.
Pr 3:26 shall keep thy foot from b' taken.
29: 1 that b' often reproved hardeneth
Ca 3: 8 hold swords, b' expert in war:
10 midst thereof b' paved with love,
Isa 3:26 and she b' desolate shall set
17: 1 is taken away from b' a city,
40:13 b' his counseller hath taught him?
65:20 b' a hundred years old shall be
Jer 2:25 Withhold thy foot from b' unshod,
12:11 b' desolate it mourneth unto me;
17:16 not hastened from b' a pastor
31:36 shall cease from b' a nation
34: 9 his maidservant b' a Hebrew
40: 1 taken him b' bound in chains
48: 2 us cut it off from b' a nation.
42 Moab shall be destroyed from b' a
Eze 17:10 Yea, behold, b' planted, shall it
23:42 voice of the multitude b' at ease
48:22 b' in the midst of that which is
Da 3:27 king's counsellers, b' gathered
5:31 b' about threescore and two
6:10 and his windows b' open in his
8:22 Now that b' broken, whereas
9:21 b' caused to fly swiftly, touched
M't 1:19 Joseph her husband, b' a just
23 Emmanuel, which b' interpreted
24 Joseph b' raised from sleep did
2:12 b' warned of God in a dream
22 go thither: notwithstanding, b'
7:11 If ye then, b' evil, know
12:34 ye, b' evil, speak good things
14: 8 b' before instructed of her mother,
M'r 3: 5 with anger, b' grieved for the
5:41 which is, b' interpreted,
8: 1 the multitude b' very great,
9:33 b' in the house he asked them,
14: 3 b' in Bethany in the house of
15:22 Golgotha, which is, b' interpreted,
34 which is, b' interpreted, My God,
Lu 1:74 that we, b' delivered out of the
2: 5 wife, b' great with child.
3: 1 Pontius Pilate b' governor of
1 Herod b' tetrarch of Galilee,
2 and Caiaphas b' the high priest,
19 b' reproved by him for Herodias
21 that Jesus also b' baptized,
23 thirty years of age, b' (as was
4: 1 Jesus b' full of the Holy Ghost
2 B' forty days tempted of the devil.
15 taught in their synagogues, b'
7:29 justified God, b' baptized with
30 themselves, b' not baptized of
8:25 And they b' afraid wondered,
11:13 If ye then, b' evil, know how to
13:16 this woman, b' a daughter of
14:21 master of the house b' angry said
16:23 lift up his eyes, b' in torments,
20:36 children of God, b' the children
21:12 b' brought before kings and rulers
22: 3 Iscariot, b' of the number
44 And b' in an agony he prayed
Joh 1:38 is to say, b' interpreted, Master,)
41 which is, b' interpreted, the Christ.
4: 6 Jesus therefore, b' wearied with
9 How is it that thou, b' a Jew,
5:13 a multitude b' in that place,
6:71 betray him, b' one of the twelve,
7:50 Jesus by night, b' one of them,)
8: 9 b' convicted by their own
10:33 that thou, b' a man, makest
11:49 Caiaphas, b' the high priest that
51 but b' high priest that year,
13: 2 And supper b' ended, the devil
14:25 you, b' yet present with you.
18:26 high priest, b' his kinsman
19:38 Joseph of Arimathæa, b' a disciple
20:19 evening, b' the first day of the week,
26 came Jesus, the doors b' shut,
Ac 1: 3 b' seen of them forty days,
4 And, b' assembled together with
2:23 b' delivered by the determinate
30 Therefore b' a prophet, and
33 Therefore b' by the right hand
3: 1 of prayer, b' the ninth hour.
4: 2 B' grieved that they taught the
23 And b' let go, they went to their
36 (which is, b' interpreted, The son
5: 2 his wife also b' privy to it, and
7:55 b' full of the Holy Ghost,
13: 4 b' sent forth by the Holy Ghost,
12 b' astonished at the doctrine of
14: 8 in his feet, b' a cripple from
15: 3 And b' brought on their way
21 b' read in the synagogues every
25 good unto us, b' assembled with
32 b' prophets also themselves,
40 chose Silas, and departed, b'
16:20 These men, b' Jews, do
21 neither to observe, b' Romans.
37 openly uncondemned, b' Romans,
17:28 and move, and have our b';
18:25 and b' fervent in the spirit,
19:40 there b' no cause whereby we
20: 9 b' fallen into a deep sleep:
22:11 see for the glory of that light, b'
26:11 and b' exceedingly mad against
27: 2 Macedonian of Thessalonica, b'
18 And we b' exceedingly tossed
Ro 1:20 b' understood by the things
29 B' filled with all unrighteousness,
2:18 b' instructed out of the law;
3:21 b' witnessed by the law and the
24 B' justified freely by his grace
4:11 he had yet b' uncircumcised:
12 he had b' yet uncircumcised.
19 And b' not weak in faith, he
21 And b' fully persuaded that, what
5: 1 Therefore b' justified by faith,
Ro 5: 9 then, b' now justified by his
10 much more, b' reconciled,
6: 9 that Christ b' raised from the dead
18 B' then made free from sin, ye
22 But now b' made free from sin,
7: 6 b' dead wherein we were held;
9:11 (For the children b' not yet born,
10: 3 b' ignorant of God's righteousness
11:17 thou, b' a wild olive tree,
12: 5 So we, b' many, are one body
15:16 b' sanctified by the Holy Ghost.
1Co 4:12 b' reviled, we bless;
12 b' persecuted, we suffer it:
13 B' defamed, we intreat: we are
7:18 any man called b' circumcised?
21 Art thou called b' a servant?
22 b' a servant, is the Lord's
22 b' free is Christ's servant.
8: 7 conscience b' weak is defiled.
9:21 (b' not without law to God,
10:17 we b' many are one bread,
12:12 of that one body, b' many
2Co 5: 3 If so be that b' clothed we shall
4 tabernacle do groan, b' burdened:
8:17 b' more forward, of his own
9:11 B' enriched in every thing to all
10: 1 but b' absent am bold toward
11: 9 myself from b' burdensome
12:16 nevertheless, b' crafty, I caught
13: 2 and b' absent now I write to
10 these things b' absent,
10 lest b' present I should use
Ga 1:14 b' more exceedingly zealous of
2: 3 who was with me, b' a Greek,
14 if thou, b' a Jew, livest after
3:13 the curse of the law, b' made
Eph 1:11 inheritance, b' predestinated
18 understanding b' enlightened;
2:11 that ye b' in time past Gentiles
12 b' aliens from the commonwealth
20 Jesus Christ himself b' the chief
3:17 b' rooted and grounded in love,
4:18 b' alienated from the life of God
19 Who b' past feeling have given
Ph'p 1: 6 B' confident of this very thing,
11 B' filled with the fruits of
2: 2 the same love, b' of one accord,
6 Who, b' in the form of God,
8 And b' found in fashion as a man,
3:10 b' made conformable unto his
Col 1:10 b' fruitful in every good work,
2: 2 might be comforted, b' knit
13 And you, b' dead in your sins
1Th 2: 8 So b' desirous of you, we were
17 But we, brethren, b' taken from
1Ti 2:14 but the woman b' deceived
3: 6 novice, lest b' lifted up with
10 office of a deacon, b' found
2Ti 1: 4 b' mindful of thy tears, that I
3:13 worse, deceiving and b' deceived.
Tit 1:16 they deny him, b' abominable,
3: 7 That b' justified by his grace,
11 sinneth, b' condemned of himself.
Ph'm 9 b' such a one as Paul the aged,
Heb 1: 3 Who b' the brightness of his glory,
4 B' made so much better than
2:18 b' tempted, he is able to succour
4: 1 fear, lest, a promise b' left
2 not b' mixed with faith in them
5: 9 And b' made perfect, he became
7: 2 first b' by interpretation King
12 For the priesthood b' changed,
9:11 Christ b' come an high priest of
11: 4 and by it he b' dead yet speaketh.
7 Noah, b' warned of God of things
37 and goatskins; b' destitute,
13: 3 as b' yourselves also in the body.
Jas 1:25 he b' not a forgetful hearer, but
2:17 hath not works, is dead, b' alone.
1Pe 1: 7 your faith, b' much more precious
23 B' born again, not of corruptible
2: 8 stumble at the word, b' disobedient:
24 that we, b' dead to sins, should live
3: 5 b' in subjection unto their own
7 as b' heirs together of the grace of
18 bring us to God, b' put to death
22 b' made subject unto him.
5: 3 as b' lords over God's heritage,
3 but b' ensamples to the flock.
2Pe 3: 6 was, b' overflowed with water,
12 heavens b' on fire shall be dissolved,
17 b' led away with the error
Re 1:12 b' turned, I saw seven golden
12: 2 And she b' with child cried,
14: 4 b' the firstfruits unto God and

bekah (*be'-kah*)
Ex 38:26 A b' for every man, that is,

Bel (*bel*) See also BAAL.
Isa 46: 1 B' boweth down, Nebo stoopeth,
Jer 50: 2 Babylon is taken, B' is confounded,
51:44 I will punish B' in Babylon, and

Bela (*be'-lah*) See also BELAH; BELAITES.
Ge 14: 2 and the king of B', which is Zoar.
8 the king of B' (the same is Zoar;)
36:32 And B' the son of Beor reigned in
33 And B' died, and Jobab the son of
Nu 26:38 of B', the family of the Belaites:
40 sons of B' were Ard and Naaman:
1Ch 1:43 B' the son of Beor: and the name
44 And when B' was dead, Jobab the
5: 8 And B' the son of Azaz, the son of
7: 6 sons of Benjamin; B', and Becher,
7 the sons of B'; Ezbon, and Uzzi,
8: 1 Benjamin begat B' his firstborn,
3 sons of B' were, Addar, and Gera,

Belah (*be'-lah*) See also BELA.
Ge 46:21 sons of Benjamin were *B'*, and
Belaites (*be'-lah-ites*)
Nu 26:38 the family of the *B'*: of Ashbel,
belch
Ps 59: 7 they *b'* out with their mouth:
Belial (*be'-le-al*)
De 13:13 the children of *B'*, are gone out
J'g 19:22 certain sons of *B'*, beset the
20:13 the children of *B'*, which are in
1Sa 1:16 handmaid for a daughter of *B'*:
2:12 the sons of Eli were sons of *B'*;
10:27 But the children of *B'* said, How
25:17 for he is such a son of *B'*, that a
25 pray thee, regard this man of *B'*,
30:22 men of *B'*, of those that went
2Sa 16: 7 man, and thou man of *B'*:
20: 1 there a man of *B'*, whose name
23: 6 the sons of *B'* shall be all of
1Ki 21:10 set two men, sons of *B'*, before
13 came in two men, children of *B'*,
13 the men of *B'* witnessed against
2Ch 13: 7 him vain men, the children of *B'*,
2Co 6:15 what concord hath Christ with *B'*?
belied
Jer 5:12 They have *b'* the Lord, and said,
belief See also UNBELIEF.
2Th 2:13 of the Spirit and *b'* of the truth:
believe See also BELIEVED; BELIEVEST; BELIEVETH; BELIEVING.
Ex 4: 1 they will not *b'* me, nor hearken
5 That they may *b'* that the Lord
8 if they will not *b'* thee, neither
8 that they will *b'* the voice of the
9 if they will not *b'* also these two
19: 9 with thee, and *b'* thee for ever.
Nu 14:11 how long will it be ere they *b'* me,
De 1:32 ye did not *b'* the Lord your God,
2Ki 17:14 that did not *b'* in the Lord their
2Ch 20:20 *B'* in the Lord your God, so shall
20 *b'* his prophets, so shall ye prosper.
32:15 on this manner, neither yet *b'* him:
Job 9:16 I not *b'* that he had hearkened
39:12 Wilt thou *b'* him, that he will
Pr 26:25 When he speaketh fair, *b'* him not:
Isa 7: 9 If ye will not *b'*, surely ye shall not
43:10 that ye may know and *b'* me, and
Jer 12: 6 *b'* them not, though they speak
Hab 1: 5 ye will not *b'*, though it be told
M't 9:28 *B'* ye that I am able to do this?
18: 6 little ones which *b'* in me, it were
21:25 Why did ye not then *b'* him?
32 afterwards, that ye might *b'* him.
24:23 here is Christ, or there, *b'* it not.
26 in the secret chambers; *b'* it not.
27:42 and we will *b'* him.
M'r 1:15 repent ye, and *b'* the gospel.
5:36 Be not afraid, only *b'*.
9:23 If thou canst *b'*, all things are
24 Lord, I *b'*; help thou mine
42 little ones that *b'* in me,
11:23 but shall *b'* that those things which
24 *b'* that ye receive them, and ye
31 say, Why then did ye not *b'* him?
13:21 or, lo, he is there; *b'* him not:
15:32 that we may see and *b'*. And they
16:17 signs shall follow them that *b'*;
Lu 8:12 lest they should *b'* and be saved.
13 which for a while *b'*, and in time
50 *b'* only, and she shall be made
22:67 ye will not *b'*:
24:25 fools, and slow of heart to *b'*
Joh 1: 7 all men through him might *b'*.
12 even to them that *b'* on his name:
3:12 and ye *b'* not,
12 how shall ye *b'*, if I tell you of
4:21 Woman, *b'* me, the hour cometh,
42 Now we *b'*, not because of thy
48 signs and wonders, ye will not *b'*.
5:38 whom he hath sent, him ye *b'* not.
44 How can ye *b'*, which receive
47 But if ye *b'* not his writings,
47 how shall ye *b'* my words?
6:29 ye *b'* on him whom he hath sent.
30 that we may see, and *b'* thee?
36 ye also have seen me, and *b'* not.
64 there are some of you that *b'* not.
69 And we *b'* and are sure that thou
7: 5 neither did his brethren *b'* in him.
39 which they that *b'* on him should
8:24 if ye *b'* not that I am he, ye shall
45 I tell you the truth, ye *b'* me not.
46 the truth, why do ye not *b'* me?
9:18 the Jews did not *b'* concerning
35 Dost thou *b'* on the Son of God?
36 he, Lord, that I might *b'* on him?
38 Lord, I *b'*. And he worshipped
10:26 But ye *b'* not, because ye are not
37 the works of my Father, *b'* me not.
38 though ye *b'* not me,
38 *b'* the works: that ye may know,
38 and *b'*, that the Father
11:15 to the intent ye may *b'*; nevertheless
27 I *b'* that thou art the Christ, the
40 thou wouldest *b'*, thou shouldest
42 by I said it, that they may *b'* that
48 thus alone, all men will *b'* on him:
12:36 *b'* in the light, that ye may be
39 Therefore they could not *b'*,
47 man hear my words, and *b'* not,
13:19 come to pass, ye may *b'* that I am he.
14: 1 ye *b'* in God, *b'* also in me.
11 *B'* me that I am in the Father,
11 else *b'* me for the very works' sake.
Joh 14:29 it is come to pass, ye might *b'*.
16: 9 because they *b'* not on me;
30 by this we *b'* that thou camest
31 answered them, Do ye now *b'*?
17:20 for them also which shall *b'* on me
21 that the world may *b'* that thou
19:35 he saith true, that ye might *b'*.
20:25 my hand into his side, I will not *b'*.
31 might *b'* that Jesus is the Christ,
Ac 8:37 I *b'* that Jesus Christ is the Son of
13:39 by him all that *b'* are justified
41 which ye shall in no wise *b'*,
15: 7 hear the word of the gospel, and *b'*.
11 But we *b'* that through the grace
16:31 *B'* on the Lord Jesus Christ, and
19: 4 that they should *b'* on him which
21:20 of Jews there are which *b'*;
25 touching the Gentiles which *b'*,
27:25 for I *b'* God, that it shall be even
Ro 3: 3 For what if some did not *b'*?
22 unto all and upon all them that *b'*:
4:11 be the father of all them that *b'*,
24 if we *b'* on him that raised up
6: 8 we *b'* that we shall also live with
10: 9 shalt *b'* in thine heart that God
14 not believed? and how shall they *b'*
15:31 them that do not *b'* in Judæa;
1Co 1:21 preaching to save them that *b'*.
10:27 If any of them that *b'* not bid you
11:18 and I partly *b'* it.
14:22 not to them that *b'*,
22 but to them that *b'* not:
22 serveth not for them that *b'* not,
22 but for them which *b'*.
2Co 4: 4 minds of them which *b'* not,
13 spoken; we also *b'*, and therefore
Ga 3:22 might be given to them that *b'*.
Eph 1:19 to us-ward who *b'*, according to
Ph'p 1:29 not only to *b'* on him, but also to
1Th 1: 7 were ensamples to all that *b'*
2:10 ourselves among you that *b'*:
13 worketh also in you that *b'*.
4:14 if we *b'* that Jesus died and rose
2Th 1:10 be admired in all them that *b'*
2:11 delusion, that they should *b'* a lie:
1Ti 1:16 should hereafter *b'* on him to life
4: 3 them which *b'* and know the truth.
10 all men, specially of those that *b'*.
2Ti 2:13 If we *b'* not, yet he abideth
Heb 10:39 of them that *b'* to the saving
11: 6 must *b'* that he is, and that he is
Jas 2:19 the devils also *b'*, and tremble.
1Pe 1:21 Who by him do *b'* in God, that
2: 7 Unto you therefore which *b'* he is
1Jo 3:23 That we should *b'* on the name of
4: 1 Beloved, *b'* not every spirit, but
5:13 unto you that *b'* on the name of
13 ye may *b'* on the name of the Son
believed
Ge 15: 6 And he *b'* in the Lord; and he
45:26 Jacob's heart fainted, for he *b'*
Ex 4:31 And the people *b'*: and when they
14:31 and *b'* the Lord, and his servant
Nu 20:12 Because ye *b'* me not, to sanctify
De 9:23 and ye *b'* him not, nor hearkened
1Sa 27:12 And Achish *b'* David, saying, He
1Ki 10: 7 Howbeit I *b'* not the words, until
2Ch 9: 6 Howbeit I *b'* not their words, until
Job 29:24 I laughed on them, they *b'* it not;
Ps 27:13 unless I had *b'* to see the goodness
78:22 Because they *b'* not in God, and
32 *b'* not for his wondrous works.
106:12 Then *b'* they his words; they sang
24 pleasant land they *b'* not his word:
116:10 I *b'*, therefore have I spoken: I
119:66 for I have *b'* thy commandments.
Isa 53: 1 Who hath *b'* our report? and to
Jer 40:14 the son of Ahikam, *b'* them not.
La 4:12 of the world, would not have *b'* that
Da 6:23 upon him, because he *b'* in his
Jon 3: 5 So the people of Nineveh *b'* God,
M't 8:13 and as thou hast *b'*, so be it
21:32 and ye *b'* him not: but the
32 publicans and the harlots *b'* him:
M'r 16:11 and had been seen of her, *b'* not.
13 unto the residue: neither *b'* they
14 because they *b'* not them which
Lu 1: 1 things which are most surely *b'*
45 blessed is she that *b'*: for there
20: 5 say, Why then *b'* ye him not?
24:11 idle tales, and they *b'* them not.
41 while they yet *b'* not for joy, and
Joh 2:11 his disciples *b'* on him.
22 and they *b'* the scripture, and the
23 many *b'* in his name, when they
3:18 already, because he hath not *b'*
4:39 of the Samaritans of that city *b'* on
41 many more *b'* because of his own
50 the man *b'* the word that Jesus had
53 himself *b'*, and his whole house.
5:46 had ye *b'* Moses,
46 ye would have *b'* me.
6:64 who they were that *b'* not, and who
7:31 And many of the people *b'* on him,
48 or of the Pharisees *b'* on him?
8:30 spake these words, many *b'* on
31 to those Jews which *b'* on him,
10:25 ye *b'* not: the works that I do
42 And many *b'* on him there.
11:45 things which Jesus did, *b'* on him
12:11 of the Jews went away, and *b'* on
37 before them, yet they *b'* not on him:
38 Lord, who hath *b'* our report?
42 chief rulers also many *b'* on him;
16:27 have *b'* that I came out from God.
17: 8 and they have *b'* that thou didst
Joh 20: 8 the sepulchre, and he saw, and *b'*.
29 thou hast *b'*: blessed are they
29 have not seen, and yet have *b'*.
Ac 2:44 And all that *b'* were together,
4: 4 of them which heard the word *b'*;
32 of them that *b'* were of one heart
8:12 But when they *b'* Philip preaching
13 Then Simon himself *b'* also:
9:26 and *b'* not that he was a disciple.
42 Joppa; and many *b'* in the Lord.
10:45 they of the circumcision which *b'*
11:17 who *b'* on the Lord Jesus Christ;
21 a great number *b'*, and turned
13:12 when he saw what was done, *b'*,
48 as were ordained to eternal life *b'*.
14: 1 Jews and also of the Greeks *b'*.
23 them to the Lord, on whom they *b'*.
15: 5 of the Pharisees which *b'*, saying,
16: 1 which was a Jewess, and *b'*;
17: 4 And some of them *b'*, and
5 the Jews which *b'* not, moved
12 Therefore many of them *b'*; also
34 certain men clave unto him, and *b'*:
18: 8 *b'* on the Lord with all his house;
8 of the Corinthians hearing *b'*,
27 helped them much which had *b'*
19: 2 received the Holy Ghost since ye *b'*?
9 divers were hardened, and *b'* not,
18 And many that *b'* came, and
22:19 every synagogue them that *b'* on
27:11 the centurion *b'* the master and
28:24 And some *b'* the things which
24 were spoken, and some *b'* not.
Ro 4: 3 Abraham *b'* God, and it was
17 before him whom he *b'*, even God,
18 who against hope *b'* in hope,
10:14 on him in whom they have not *b'*?
16 saith, Lord, who hath *b'* our report?
11:30 ye in times past have not *b'* God,
31 so have these also now not *b'*,
13:11 salvation nearer than when we *b'*.
1Co 3: 5 ministers by whom ye *b'*, even as
15: 2 unless ye have *b'* in vain.
11 or they, so we preach, and so ye *b'*.
2Co 4:13 I *b'*, and therefore have I spoken;
Ga 2:16 even we have *b'* in Jesus Christ,
3: 6 as Abraham *b'* God, and it was
Eph. 1:13 in whom also after that ye *b'*,
2Th 1:10 our testimony among you was *b'*)
2:12 who *b'* not the truth, but had
1Ti 3:16 *b'* on in the world, received up into
2Ti 1:12 I know whom I have *b'*, and am
Tit 3: 8 that they which have *b'* in God
Heb 3:18 his rest, but to them that *b'* not?
4: 3 which have *b'* do enter into rest,
11:31 perished not with them that *b'*
Jas 2:23 Abraham *b'* God, and it was
1Jo 4:16 we have known and *b'* the love
Jude 5 destroyed them that *b'* not.
believers See also UNBELIEVERS.
Ac 5:14 And *b'* were the more added
1Ti 4:12 be thou an example of the *b'*, in
believest
Lu 1:20 because thou *b'* not my words,
Joh 1:50 thee under the fig tree, *b'* thou?
11:26 in me shall never die. *B'* thou
14:10 *B'* thou not that I am in the
Ac 8:37 If thou *b'* with all thine heart,
26:27 King Agrippa, *b'* thou the prophets?
27 I know that thou *b'*.
Jas 2:19 Thou *b'* that there is one God;
believeth
Job 15:22 He *b'* not that he shall return
39:24 neither *b'* he that it is the sound
Pr 14:15 The simple *b'* every word:
Isa 28:16 he that *b'* shall not make haste.
M'r 9:23 are possible to him that *b'*.
16:16 He that *b'* and is baptized shall
16 he that *b'* not shall be damned.
Joh 3:15, 16 whosoever *b'* in him should
18 He that *b'* on him is not
18 but he that *b'* not is condemned
36 He that *b'* on the Son hath
36 that *b'* not the Son shall not see
5:24 and *b'* on him that sent me,
6:35 he that *b'* on me shall never thirst.
40 and *b'* on him, may have
47 He that *b'* on me hath everlasting
7:38 He that *b'* on me, as the scripture
11:25 he that *b'* in me, though he were
26 and *b'* in me shall never die.
12:44 He that *b'* on me, *b'* not on me, but
46 that whosoever *b'* on me should not
14:12 He that *b'* on me, the works that I
Ac 10:43 whosoever *b'* in him shall receive
Ro 1:16 unto salvation to every one that *b'*;
3:26 justifier of him which *b'* in
4: 5 but *b'* on him that justifieth the
9:33 whosoever *b'* on him shall not be
10: 4 righteousness to every one that *b'*.
10 For with the heart man *b'* unto
11 Whosoever *b'* on him shall not be
14: 2 For one *b'* that he may eat all
1Co 7:12 hath a wife, that *b'* not, and she
13 hath an husband that *b'* not, and
13: 7 *b'* all things, hopeth all things,
14:24 there come in one that *b'* not, or
2Co 6:15 hath he that *b'* with an infidel?
1Ti 5:16 If any man or woman that *b'*
1Pe 2: 6 and he that *b'* on him shall not be
1Jo 5: 1 Whosoever *b'* that Jesus is the
5 he that *b'* that Jesus is the Son
10 He that *b'* on the Son of God
10 he that *b'* not God hath made
10 because he *b'* not the record

believing See also UNBELIEVING.
M't 21:22 ye shall ask in prayer, b', ye shall
Joh 20:27 and be not faithless, but b'.
31 and that b' ye might have life
Ac 16:34 rejoiced, b' in God with all his
24:14 b' all things which are written
Ro 15:13 you with all joy and peace in b',
1Ti 6: 2 And they that have b' masters,
1Pe 1: 8 yet b', ye rejoice with joy

bell See also BELLS.
Ex 28:34 b' and a pomegranate,
34 a golden b'
39:26 A b' and a pomegranate, a b'

bellies
Tit 1:12 always liars, evil beasts, slow b'.

bellow See also BELLOWS.
Jer 50:11 as the heifer at grass, and b' as

bellows
Jer 6:29 The b' are burned, the lead is

bells
Ex 28:33 and b' of gold between them
39:25 b' of pure gold, and put the b'
Zec 14:20 there be upon the b' of the horses,

belly See also BELLIES.
Ge 3:14 upon thy b' shalt thou go, and
Le 11:42 goeth upon the b', and whatsoever
Nu 5:21 thy thigh to rot, and thy b' to
22 to make thy b' to swell, and thy
27 her b' shall swell, and her thigh
25: 8 and the woman through her b'.
J'g 3:21 thrust it into his b':
22 not draw the dagger out of his b';
1Ki 7:20 over against the b' which was by
Job 3:11 ghost when I came out of the b'?
15: 2 and fill his b' with the east wind?
35 vanity, and their b' prepareth
20:15 God shall cast them out of his b'.
20 shall not feel quietness in his b',
23 he is about to fill his b', God
32:19 b' is as wine which hath no vent;
40:16 his force is in the navel of his b'.
Ps 17:14 whose b' thou fillest with thy hid
22:10 art my God from my mother's b'.
31: 9 grief, yea, my soul and my b'.
44:25 to the dust, our b' cleaveth unto
Pr 13:25 but the b' of the wicked shall want.
18: 8 the innermost parts of the b'.
20 A man's b' shall be satisfied with
20:27 all the inward parts of the b'.
30 stripes the inward parts of the b'.
26:22 into the innermost parts of the b'.
Ca 5:14 his b' is as bright ivory, overlaid
7: 2 thy b' is like an heap of wheat set
Isa 46: 3 borne by me from the b', which
Jer 1: 5 Before I formed thee in the b' I
51:34 he hath filled his b' with my
Eze 3: 3 cause thy b' to eat, and fill thy
Da 2:32 arms of silver, his b' and his
Jon 1:17 in the b' of the fish three days
2: 1 Lord his God out of the fish's b',
2 out of the b' of hell cried I, and
Hab 3:16 my b' trembled; my lips quivered
M't 12:40 three nights in the whale's b';
15:17 in at the mouth goeth into the b',
M'r 7:19 but into the b', and goeth out into
Lu 15:16 he would fain have filled his b'
Joh 7:38 out of his b' shall flow rivers of
Ro 16:18 Jesus Christ, but their own b';
1Co 6:13 Meats for the b',
13 and the b' for meats:
Ph'p 3:19 whose God is their b', and whose
Re 10: 9 it shall make thy b' bitter, but it
10 as I had eaten it, my b' was bitter.

belong See also BELONGED; BELONGETH; BELONGEST; BELONGING.
Ge 40: 8 Do not interpretations b' to God?
Le 27:24 the possession of the land did b'.
Nu 1:50 and over all things that b' to it:
De 29:29 The secret things b' unto the Lord
29 things which are revealed b' unto
Ps 47: 9 shields of the earth b' unto God
68:20 the Lord b' the issues from death.
Pr 24:23 These things also b' to the wise.
Da 9: 9 To the Lord our God b' mercies
M'r 9:41 because ye b' to Christ, verily I
Lu 19:42 things which b' unto thy peace!
1Co 7:32 careth for the things that b' to

belonged
Jos 17: 8 b' to the children of Ephraim;
1Sa 21: 7 the herdmen that b' to Saul.
1Ki 1: 8 mighty men which b' to David,
15:27 which b' to the Philistines;
16:15 which b' to the Philistines.
2Ki 14:28 and Hamath, which b' to Judah,
1Ch 2:23 these b' to the sons of Machir
13: 6 Kirjath-jearim, which b' to Judah,
2Ch 26:23 the burial which b' to the kings;
Es 1: 9 house which b' to king Ahasuerus
2: 9 things as b' to her, and seven
Lu 23: 7 he b' unto Herod's jurisdiction.

belongest
1Sa 30:13 unto him, To whom b' thou?

belongeth
Nu 8:24 This is it that b' unto the Levites:
De 32:35 To me b' vengeance, and
J'g 19:14 by Gibeah, which b' to Benjamin.
20: 4 into Gibeah that b' to Benjamin,
1Sa 17: 1 at Shochoh, which b' to Judah,
30:14 the coast which b' to Judah, and
1Ki 17: 9 Zarephath, which b' to Zidon,
19: 3 Beer-sheba, which b' to Judah,
2Ki 14:11 Beth-shemesh, which b' to Judah.
2Ch 25:21 Beth-shemesh, which b' to Judah.
Ezr 10: 4 for this matter b' unto thee:
Ps 3: 8 Salvation b' unto the Lord: thy
62:11 heard this; that power b' unto God.
12 unto thee, O Lord, b' mercy: for thou
94: 1 O Lord God, to whom vengeance b';
1 O God, to whom vengeance b', shew
Da 9: 7 O Lord, righteousness b' unto thee,
8 O Lord, to us b' confusion of face,
Heb 5:14 But strong meat b' to them that
10:30 Vengeance b' unto me, I will

belonging
Nu 7: 9 service of the sanctuary b' unto
Ru 2: 3 a part of the field b' unto Boaz
1Sa 6:18 of the Philistines b' to the five lords,
Pr 26:17 with strife b' not to him, is like
Lu 9:10 desert place b' to the city called

beloved See also BELOVED'S; WELL BELOVED.
De 21:15 wives, one b', and another hated,
15 both the b' and the hated;
16 not make the son of the b' firstborn
33:12 The b' of the Lord shall dwell in
Neh 13:26 was b' of his God, and God made
Ps 60: 5 That thy b' may be delivered;
108: 6 That thy b' may be delivered:
127: 2 for so he giveth his b' sleep.
Pr 4: 3 only b' in the sight of my mother.
Ca 1:14 My b' is unto me as a cluster
16 Behold, thou art fair, my b',
2: 3 so is my b' among the sons.
8 The voice of my b'! behold, he
9 My b' is like a roe or a young hart:
10 My b' spake, and said unto me,
16 My b' is mine, and I am his:
17 turn, my b', and be thou like a roe
4:16 b' come into his garden, and eat
5: 1 yea, drink abundantly, O b'.
2 the voice of my b' that knocketh,
4 My b' put in his hand by the hole
5 rose up to open to my b'; and my
6 to my b'; but my b' had withdrawn
8 if ye find my b', that ye tell him,
9 thy b' more than another b', O thou
9 b' more than another b', that thou
10 my b' is white and ruddy, the
16 This is my b', and this is my friend,
6: 1 Whither is thy b' gone, O thou
1 whither is thy b' turned aside?
2 My b' is gone down into his garden,
3 my beloved's, and my b' is mine:
7: 9 the best wine for my b' that goeth,
11 come my b', let us go forth
13 I have laid up for thee, O my b'.
8: 5 the wilderness, leaning upon her b'?
14 Make haste, my b', and be thou like
Isa 5: 1 to my wellbeloved a song of my b'
Jer 11:15 hath my b' to do in mine house,
12: 7 dearly b' of my soul into the hand
Da 9:23 greatly b': therefore understand
10:11 a man greatly b', understand the
19 said, O man greatly b', fear not:
Ho 3: 1 yet, love a woman b' of her friend,
9:16 even the b' fruit of their womb.
M't 3:17 saying, This is my b' Son, in whom
12:18 I have chosen; my b' in whom,
17: 5 which said, This is my b' Son,
M'r 1:11 Thou art my b' Son, in whom
9: 7 saying, This is my b' Son: hear him.
Lu 3:22 which said, Thou art my b' Son;
9:35 saying, This is my b' Son: hear
20:13 shall I do? I will send my b' son:
Ac 15:25 chosen men unto you with our b'
Ro 1: 7 To all that be in Rome, b' of God,
9:25 and her b', which was not b'.
11:28 touching the election, they are b'
12:19 Dearly b', avenge not yourselves,
16: 8 Greet Amplias my b' in the Lord.
9 helper in Christ, and Stachys my b'.
12 Salute the b' Persis, which laboured
1Co 4:14 but as my b' sons I warn you.
17 who is my b' son, and faithful in the
10:14 my dearly b', flee from idolatry.
15:58 Therefore, my b' brethren, be ye
2Co 7: 1 dearly b', let us cleanse ourselves
12:19 we do all things, dearly b', for your
Eph 1: 6 he hath made us accepted in the b'.
6:21 a b' brother and faithful minister
Ph'p 2:12 Wherefore, my b', as ye have
4: 1 brethren dearly b' and longed for,
1 stand fast in the Lord, my dearly b'.
Col 3:12 as the elect of God, holy and b',
4: 7 declare unto you, who is a b' brother
9 Onesimus, a faithful and b' brother,
14 Luke, the b' physician, and Demas,
1Th 1: 4 Knowing, brethren b', your election
2Th 2:13 for you, brethren b' of the Lord,
1Ti 6: 2 because they are faithful and b',
2Ti 1: 2 To Timothy, my dearly b' son:
Ph'm 1 unto Philemon our dearly b', and
2 to our b' Apphia, and Archippus
16 but above a servant, a brother b',
Heb 6: 9 b', we are persuaded better things
Jas 1:16 Do not err, my b' brethren.
19 Wherefore, my b' brethren, let every
2: 5 Hearken, my b' brethren, Hath not
1Pe 2:11 b', I beseech you as strangers
4:12 B', think it not strange concerning
2Pe 1:17 This is my b' Son, in whom I am
3: 1 This second epistle, b', I now write
8 But, b', be not ignorant of this
14 Wherefore, b', seeing that ye look
15 our b' brother Paul also according
17 Ye therefore, b', seeing ye know
1Jo 3: 2 B', now are we the sons of God,
21 B', if our heart condemn us not,
1Jo 4: 1 B', believe not every spirit, but try
7 B', let us love one another: for love
11 B', if God so loved us, we ought also
3Jo 2 B', I wish above all things that
5 B', thou doest faithfully whatsoever
11 B', follow not that which is evil,
Jude 3 B', when I gave all diligence to
17 b', remember ye the words which
20 But ye, b', building up yourselves
Re 20: 9 of the saints about, and the b' city:

beloved's
Ca 6: 3 my b', and my beloved is mine:
7:10 I am my b', and his desire is

Belshazzar (*bel-shaz'-ar*)
Da 5: 1 B' the king made a great feast to
2 B', whiles he tasted the wine,
9 was king B' greatly troubled, and
22 B', hast not humbled thine heart,
29 B', and they clothed Daniel
30 B' the king of the Chaldeans slain.
7: 1 B' king of Babylon Daniel had
8: 1 B' a vision appeared unto me,

Belteshazzar (*bel-te-shaz'-ar*) See also DANIEL.
Da 1: 7 gave unto Daniel the name of B';
2:26 to Daniel, whose name was B',
4: 8 in before me, whose name was B',
9 O B', master of the magicians,
18 B', declare the interpretation
19 whose name was B', was astonied
19 and said, B', let not the dream,
19 B' answered and said, My lord,
5:12 Daniel, whom the king named B':
10: 1 Daniel, whose name was called B':

bemoan See also BEMOANED; BEMOANING.
Jer 15: 5 who shall b' thee? or who shall go
16: 5 neither go to lament nor b' them:
22:10 ye not for the dead, neither b' him:
48:17 All ye that are about him, b' him;
Na 3: 7 is laid waste: who will b' her?

bemoaned
Job 42:11 and they b' him, and comforted

bemoaning
Jer 31:18 heard Ephraim b' himself thus;

Ben (*ben*) See also BEN-AMMI; BEN-HADAD; BEN-HAIL; BEN-HANAN; BEN-ONI; BEN-ZOHETH.
1Ch 15:18 second degree, Zechariah, B'

Benaiah (*ben-ay'-ah*)
2Sa 8:18 And B' the son of Jehoiada was
20:23 and B' the son of Jehoiada was
23:20 B' the son of Jehoiada, the son of
22 These things did B' the son of
30 B' the Pirathonite, Hiddai of the
1Ki 1: 8 priest, and B' the son of Jehoiada,
10 Nathan the prophet, and B',
26 and Zadok the priest, and B' the
32 and B' the son of Jehoiada.
36 B' the son of Jehoiada answered
38 and Nathan the prophet, and B'
44 B' the son of Jehoiada, and the
2:25 Solomon sent by the hand of B'
29 sent B' the son of Jehoiada,
30 And B' came to the tabernacle
30 B' brought the king word again,
34 B' the son of Jehoiada went up,
35 king put B' the son of Jehoiada
46 So the king commanded B' the son
4: 4 B' the son of Jehoiada was over
1Ch 4:36 and Adiel, and Jesimiel, and B',
11:22 B' the son of Jehoiada, the son of
24 These things did B' the son of
31 of Benjamin, B' the Pirathonite,
15:18 Eliab, and B', and Maaseiah,
20 and Eliab, and Maaseiah, and B',
24 Zechariah, and B', and Eliezer,
16: 5 and Eliab, and B', and Obed-edom:
6 B' also and Jahaziel the priests
18:17 And B' the son of Jehoiada was
27: 5 for the third month was B' the son
6 This is that B', who was mighty
14 month was B' the Pirathonite,
34 was Jehoiada the son of B',
2Ch 20:14 of Zechariah, the son of B', the
31:13 Mahath, and B', were overseers
Ezr 10:25 Eleazar, and Malchijah, and B',
30 Chelal, B', Maaseiah, Mattaniah,
35 B', Bedeiah, Chelluh,
43 Zebina, Jadau, and Joel, B'.
Eze 11: 1 and Pelatiah the son of B',
13 that Pelatiah the son of B' died.

Ben-ammi (*ben-am'-mi*)
Ge 19:38 bare a son, and called his name B':

benches
Eze 27: 6 made thy b' of ivory, brought out

bend See also BENDETH; BENDING; BENT.
Ps 11: 2 the wicked b' their bow, they
64: 3 b' their bows to shoot their
Jer 9: 3 they b' their tongues like their
46: 9 Lydians, that handle and b' the
50:14 all ye that b' the bow,
29 Babylon: all ye that b' the bow,
51: 3 bendeth let the archer b' his bow,
Eze 17: 7 vine did b' her roots toward him,

bendeth
Ps 58: 7 he b' his bow to shoot his arrows,
Jer 51: 3 Against him that b' let the archer

bending
Isa 60:14 thee shall come b' unto thee;

Bene See BENE-BERAK; BENE-JAAKAN.

beneath
Ge 35: 8 and she was buried b' Beth-el.
Ex 20: 4 or that is in the earth b', or that
26:24 they shall be coupled together b',
27: 5 under the compass of the altar b',
28:33 And b' upon the hem of it thou
32:19 and brake them b' the mount.
36:29 they were coupled b', and coupled
38: 4 thereof, b' unto the midst of it.
De 4:18 that is in the waters b' the earth:
39 upon the earth b': there is none
5: 8 or that is in the earth b',
8 or that is in the waters b'
28:13 above only, thou shalt not be b';
33:13 and for the deep that coucheth b',
Jos 2:11 in heaven above, and in earth b'.
J'g 7: 8 the host of Midian was b' him
1Ki 4:12 which is by Zartanah b' Jezreel,
7:29 and b' the lions and oxen were
8:23 in heaven above, or on earth b',
Job 18:16 His roots shall be dried up b', and
Pr 15:24 that he may depart from hell b'.
Isa 14: 9 Hell from b' is moved for thee to
51: 6 and look upon the earth b':
Jer 31:37 of the earth searched out b',
Am 2: 9 from above, and his roots from b'.
M'k 14:66 And as Peter was b' in the palace,
Joh 8:23 Ye are from b'; I am from above:
Ac 2:19 and signs in the earth b'; blood,

Bene-berak (*be''-ne-be'-rak*)
Jos 19:45 Jehud, and B', and Gath-rimmon,

benefactors
Lu 22:25 authority upon them are called b'.

benefit See also BENEFITS.
2Ch 32:25 according to the b' done unto
Jer 18:10 wherewith I said I would b' them.
2Co 1:15 that ye might have a second b';
1Ti 6: 2 and beloved, partakers of the b'.
Ph'm 14 that thy b' should not be as it

benefits
Ps 68:19 who daily loadeth us with b',
103: 2 and forget not all his b':
116:12 Lord for all his b' toward me?

Bene-jaakan (*be''-ne-ja'-a-kan*)
Nu 33:31 from Moseroth, and pitched in B'.
32 removed from B', and encamped

benevolence
1Co 7: 3 render unto the wife due b':

Ben-hadad (*ben'-ha-dad*)
1Ki 15:18 and king Asa sent them to B',
20 So B' hearkened unto king Asa,
20: 1 And B' the king of Syria gathered
2 said unto him, Thus saith B',
5 Thus speaketh B', saying,
9 unto the messengers of B', Tell
10 And B' sent unto him, and said,
12 when B' heard this message,
16 B' was drinking himself drunk
17 and B' sent out, and they told him,
20 and B' the king of Syria escaped
26 the year, that B' numbered the
30 And B' fled, and came into the city,
32 thy servant B' saith, I pray thee,
33 and they said, Thy brother B'.
33 Then B' came forth to him;
34 And B' said unto him,
2Ki 6:24 after this, that B' king of Syria
8: 7 and B' the king of Syria was sick;
9 and said, Thy son B' king of Syria
13: 3 the hand of B' the son of Hazael,
24 and B' his son reigned in his stead.
25 of the hand of B' the son of Hazael
2Ch 16: 2 and sent to B' king of Syria, that
4 And B' hearkened unto king Asa,
Jer 49:27 shall consume the palaces of B'.
Am 1: 4 shall devour the palaces of B'.

Ben-hail (*ben-ha'-il*)
2Ch 17: 7 sent to his princes, even to B',

Ben-hanan (*ben-ha'-nan*)
1Ch 4: 20 Amnon, and Rinnah, B', and

Beninu (*ben'-i-nu*)
Ne 10:13 Hodijah, Bani, B'.

Benjamin (*ben'-ja-min*) See also BENJAMIN'S; BENJAMITE.
Ge 35:18 but his father called him B'.
24 sons of Rachel; Joseph, and B':
42: 4 B', Joseph's brother, Jacob sent
36 and ye will take B' away:
43:14 away your other brother, and B'.
15 money in their hand, and B';
16 Joseph saw B' with them, he said
29 saw his brother B', his mother's
45:12 and the eyes of my brother B',
14 and wept; and B' wept upon
22 But to B' he gave three hundred
46:19 Jacob's wife; Joseph, and B'.
21 sons of B' were Belah, and Becher,
49:27 B' shall ravin as a wolf: in the
Ex 1: 3 Issachar, Zebulun, and B',
Nu 1:11 Of B'; Abidan the son of Gideoni.
36 Of the children of B', by their
37 even of the tribe of B', were thirty
2:22 Then the tribe of B':
22 the captain of the sons of B',
7:60 prince of the children of B', offered:
10:24 the children of B' was Abidan the
13: 9 Of the tribe of B', Palti the son of
26:38 The sons of B' after their families:
41 B' after their families: and they
34:21 Of the tribe of B', Elidad the son
De 27:12 and Issachar, and Joseph, and B':
33:12 And of B' he said, The beloved of
Jos 18:11 children of B' came up according
20 children of B', by the coasts
21 B' according to their families were
28 inheritance of the children of B'
21: 4 of the tribe of B', thirteen cities.
17 of B', Gibeon with her suburbs,
J'g 1:21 B' did not drive out the Jebusites
21 of B' in Jerusalem unto this day.
5:14 after thee, B', among thy people;
10: 9 against Judah, and against B',
19:14 by Gibeah, which belongeth to B'.
20: 3 children of B' heard that the
4 belongeth to B', I and my
10 come to Gibeah of B', according to
12 men through all the tribe of B',
13 B' would not hearken to the voice
14 children of B' gathered themselves
15 of B' were numbered at that time
17 Israel, beside B', were numbered
18 against the children of B'?
20 went out to battle against B';
21 of B' came forth out of Gibeah,
23 of B' my brother? And the Lord
24 near against the children of B'
25 B' went forth against them out of
28 against the children of B' my
30 against the children of B' on the
31 B' went out against the people,
32 B' said, They are smitten down
35 the Lord smote B' before Israel:
36 So the children of B' saw that they
39 in the battle, B' began to smite
41 the men of B' were amazed:
44 fell of B' eighteen thousand men;
46 fell that day of B' were twenty and
48 upon the children of B', and smote
21: 1 give his daughter unto B' to wife.
6 Israel repented them for B' their
13 speak to the children of B' that
14 And B' came again at that time;
15 repented them for B', because the
16 women are destroyed out of B'?
17 that be escaped of B', that a tribe
18 be he that giveth a wife to B'.
20 commanded the children of B',
21 Shiloh, and go to the land of B'.
23 children of B' did so, and took
1Sa 4:12 ran a man of B' out of the army,
9: 1 a man of B', whose name was Kish,
16 man out of the land of B', and thou
21 the families of the tribe of B'?
10: 2 in the border of B' at Zelzah;
20 near, the tribe of B' was taken.
21 tribe of B' to come near by their
13: 2 with Jonathan in Gibeah of B':
15 up from Gilgal unto Gibeah of B'.
16 with them, abode in Gibeah of B':
14:16 watchmen of Saul in Gibeah of B'
2Sa 2: 9 and over Ephraim, and over B',
15 went over by number twelve of B',
25 children of B' gathered themselves
31 of David had smitten of B', and
3:19 Abner also spake in the ears of B':
19 good to the whole house of B'.
4: 2 Beerothite, of the children of B':
2 Beeroth also was reckoned to B':
19:17 thousand men of B' with him,
21:14 in the country of B' in Zelah,
23:29 of Gibeah of the children of B',
1Ki 4:18 Shimei the son of Elah, in B':
12:21 Judah, with the tribe of B', an
23 unto all the house of Judah and B',
15:22 Asa built with them Geba of B',
1Ch 2: 2 Dan, Joseph, and B', Naphtali,
6:60 And out of the tribe of B'; Geba
65 children of B', these cities, which
7: 6 The sons of B'; Bela, and Becher,
10 Jeush, and B', and Ehud, and
8: 1 Now B' begat Bela his firstborn,
40 All these are of the sons of B'.
9: 3 children of B', and of the children
7 And of the sons of B'; Sallu the
11:31 to the children of B', Benaiah
12: 2 even of Saul's brethren of B'.
16 came of the children of B' and
29 children of B', the kindred of
21: 6 But Levi and B' counted he not
27:21 of B', Jaasiel the son of Abner:
2Ch 11: 1 house of Judah and B' an hundred
3 all Israel in Judah and B', saying,
10 which are in Judah and in B'
12 having Judah and B' on his side.
23 all the countries of Judah and B',
14: 8 and out of B', that bare shields
15: 2 ye me, Asa, and all Judah and B';
8 land of Judah and B', and out of
9 gathered all Judah and B', and
17:17 And of B'; Eliada a mighty man
25: 5 throughout all Judah and B':
31: 1 the altars out of all Judah and B',
34: 9 and all Judah and B'; and they
32 were present in Jerusalem and B'
Ezr 1: 5 fathers of Judah and B', and the
4: 1 adversaries of Judah and B' heard
10: 9 men of Judah and B' gathered
32 B', Malluch, and Shemariah.
Ne 3:23 After him repaired B' and Hashub
11: 4 of Judah, and of the children of B'.
7 All these are the sons of B'; Sallu
31 The children also of B' from Geba
36 were divisions in Judah, and in B'.
12:34 Judah, and B', and Shemaiah,
Ps 68:27 There is little B' with their ruler,
80: 2 Before Ephraim and B' and
Jer 1: 1 in Anathoth in the land of B':
6: 1 O ye children of B', gather
Jer 17:26 and from the land of B',
20: 2 that were in the high gate of B',
32: 8 which is in the country of B':
44 take witnesses in the land of B',
33:13 and in the land of B', and in the
37:12 to go into the land of B', to
13 was in the gate of B', a captain of
38: 7 king then sitting in the gate of B';
Eze 48:22 of Judah and the border of B',
23 west side, B' shall have a portion.
24 by the border of B', from the east
32 one gate of Joseph, one gate of B',
Hos 5: 8 at Beth-aven, after thee, O B'.
Ob 19 Samaria; and B' shall possess
Ac 13:21 a man of the tribe of B', by the
Ro 11: 1 of Abraham, of the tribe of B'.
Ph'p 3: 5 of the tribe of B', an Hebrew of
Re 7: 8 Of the tribe of B' were sealed

Benjamin's (*ben'-ja-mins*)
Ge 43:34 but B' mess was five times so
44:12 the cup was found in B' sack.
45:14 he fell upon his brother B' neck,
Zec 14:10 inhabited in her place, from B'

Benjamite (*ben'-ja-mite*) See also BENJAMITES.
J'g 3:15 Ehud the son of Gera, a B', a man
1Sa 9: 1 the son of Aphiah, a B', a mighty
21 Am not I a B', of the smallest of
2Sa 16:11 much more now may this B' do it?
19:16 Shimei the son of Gera, a B',
20: 1 Sheba, the son of Bichri, a B':
1Ki 2: 8 the son of Gera, a B' of Bahurim,
Es 2: 5 Shimei, the son of Kish, a B';
Ps 7:*title* the words of Cush the B'.

Benjamites (*ben'-ja-mites*)
J'g 19:16 but the men of the place were B'.
20:35 Israel destroyed of the B' that
36 Israel gave place to the B',
40 pillars of smoke, the B' looked
43 thus they inclosed the B' round
1Sa 9: 4 passed through the land of the B',
22: 7 Hear now, ye B'; will the son of
1Ch 27:12 Abiezer the Anetothite, of the B':

Beno (*be'-no*)
1Ch 24:26 Mushi: the sons of Jaaziah; B'.
27 B', and Shoham, and Zaccur, and

Benob See ISBI-BENOB.

Ben-oni (*ben-o'-ni*)
Ge 35:18 she called his name B': but his

Benoth See ISHBI-BENOTH.

bent
Ps 7:12 he hath b' his bow, and made it
37:14 and have b' their bow, to cast
Isa 5:28 all their bows b', their horses'
21:15 drawn sword, and from the b' bow,
La 2: 4 He hath b' his bow like an enemy:
3:12 He hath b' his bow, and set me as
Ho 11: 7 my people are b' to backsliding
Zec 9:13 When I have b' Judah for me,

Ben-zoheth (*ben-zo'-heth*)
1Ch 4:20 sons of Ishi were, Zoheth, and B'.

Beon (*be'-on*)
Nu 32: 3 and Shebam, and Nebo, and B',

Beor (*be'-or*)
Ge 36:32 And Bela the son of B' reigned in
Nu 22: 5 Balaam the son of B' to Pethor,
24: 3 Balaam the son of B' hath said,
15 the son of B' hath said, and the
31: 8 Balaam also the son of B' they
De 23: 4 against thee Balaam the son of B'
Jos 13:22 Balaam also the son of B', the
24: 9 called Balaam the son of B' to
1Ch 1:43 Bela the son of B': and the name
Mic 6: 5 Balaam the son of B' answered

Bera (*be'-rah*)
Ge 14: 2 these made war with B' king of

Berachah (*ber'-a-kah*)
1Ch 12: 3 Azmaveth; and B', and Jehu the
2Ch 20:26 themselves in the valley of B';
26 was called, The valley of B',

Berachiah (*ber-a-ki'-ah*) See also BERECHIAH.
1Ch 6:39 even Asaph the son of B', the son

Beraiah (*ber-a-i'-ah*)
1Ch 8:21 Adaiah, and B', and Shimrath,

Berea (*be-re'-a*)
Ac 17:10 Paul and Silas by night unto B':
13 was preached of Paul at B', they
20: 4 him into Asia Sopater of B';

bereave See also BEREAVED; BEREAVETH.
Ec 4: 8 I labour and b' my soul of good?
Jer 15: 7 I will b' them of children, I will
Eze 5:17 beasts, and they shall b' thee:
36:12 no more henceforth b' them of
14 neither b' thy nations any
Ho 9:12 yet will I b' them, that there shall

bereaved
Ge 42:36 Me have ye b' of my children:
43:14 I be b' of my children, I am b'.
Jer 18:21 wives be b' of their children,
Eze 36:13 up men, and hast b' thy nations;
Ho 13: 8 as a bear that is b' of her whelps,

bereaveth
La 1:20 abroad the sword b', at home

Berechiah (*ber-e-ki'-ah*) See also BERACHIAH.
1Ch 3:20 and Ohel, and B', and Hasadiah,
9:16 B' the son of Asa, the son of
15:17 his brethren, Asaph the son of B';
23 B' and Elkanah were doorkeepers
2Ch 28:12 B' the son of Meshillemoth, and

Ne 3: 4 Meshullam the son of B', the son
30 son of B' over against his chamber.
6:18 of Meshullam the son of B'.
Zec 1: 1, 7 the son of B', the son of Iddo

Bered (be'-red)
Ge 16:14 it is between Kadesh and B'.
1Ch 7:20 Shuthelah, and B' his son, and

Beri (be'-ri) See also BERITES.
1Ch 7:36 Shual, and B', and Imrah,

Beriah (be-ri'-ah) See also BERIITES.
Ge 46:17 and B', and Serah their sister:
17 sons of B'; Heber, and Malchiel.
Nu 26:44 Jesuites: of B', the family of the
45 Of the sons of B': of Heber, the
1Ch 7:23 he called his name B', because it
30 and B', and Serah their sister.
31 sons of B'; Heber, and Malchiel,
8:13 B' also, and Shema, who were
16 Ispah, and Joha, the sons of B';
23:10 Jahath, Zina, and Jeush, and B'.
11 Jeush and B' had not many sons;

Beriites (be-ri'-ites)
Nu 26:44 of Beriah, the family of the B'.

Berites (be'-rites)
2Sa 20:14 to Beth-maachah, and all the B':

Berith (be'-rith) See also BAAL-BERITH.
J'g 9:46 hold of the house of the god B'.

Bernice (bur-ni'-see)
Ac 25:13 and B' came unto Cæsarea to
23 come, and B', with great pomp,
26:30 B', and they that sat with them:

Berodach-baladan (ber-o''-dak-bal'-ad-an) See also MERODACH-BALADAN.
2Ki 20:12 At that time B', the son of

Berœa See BEREA.

Berothah (ber-o'-thah) See also BEROTHAI; BEROTHITE.
Eze 47:16 Hamath, B', Sibraim,

Berothai (ber'-o-thahee) See also BEROTHAH.
2Sa 8: 8 and from B', cities of Hadadezer,

Berothite (be'-ro-thite) See also BEEROTHITE.
1Ch 11:39 Naharai the B', the armourbearer

berries
Isa 17: 6 two or three b' in the top of the
Jas 3:12 tree, by brethren, bear olive b'?

beryl (ber'-il)
Ex 28:20 the fourth row a b', and an onyx,
39:13 a b', an onyx, and a jasper: they
Ca 5:14 are as gold rings set with the b':
Eze 1:16 was like unto the colour of a b':
10: 9 was as the colour of a b' stone.
28:13 topaz, and the diamond, the b',
Da 10: 6 His body also was like the b',
Re 21:20 seventh, chrysolyte; the eighth, b';

Besai (be'-sahee)
Ezr 2:49 of Paseah, the children of B',
Ne 7:52 of B', the children of Meunim,

beseech See also BESEECHING; BESOUGHT.
Ex 3:18 and now let us go, we b' thee,
33:18 I b' thee, shew me thy glory.
Nu 12:11 I b' thee, lay not the sin upon us,
13 Heal her now, O God, I b' thee.
14:17 And now, I b' thee, let the power
19 Pardon, I b' thee, the iniquity
1Sa 23:11 I b' thee, tell thy servant.
2Sa 13:24 let the king, I b' thee, and his
16: 4 I humbly b' thee that I may find
24:10 and now I b' thee, O Lord, take
2Ki 19:19 I b' thee, save thou us out of his
20: 3 I b' thee, O Lord, remember now
1Ch 21: 8 I b' thee, do away the iniquity
2Ch 6:40 Now, my God, let, I b' thee,
Ne 1: 5 And said, I b' thee, O Lord God
8 Remember, I b' thee, the word
11 O Lord, I b' thee, let now thine ear
Job 10: 9 Remember, I b' thee, that thou
42: 4 Hear, I b' thee, and I will speak:
Ps 80:14 Return, we b' thee, O God of hosts:
116: 4 O Lord, I b' thee, deliver my soul.
118:25 Save now, I b' thee, O Lord:
25 O Lord, I b' thee, send now
119:108 Accept, I b' thee, the freewill
Isa 38: 3 Remember now, O Lord, I b' thee,
64: 9 we b' thee, we are all thy people.
Jer 38: 4 We b' thee, let this man be put to
20 Obey, I beseech thee, the voice of
42: 2 we b' thee, our supplication be
Da 1:12 Prove thy servants, I b' thee, ten
9:16 I b' thee, let thine anger and thy
Am 7: 2 God, forgive, I b' thee: by whom
5 O Lord God, cease, I b' thee: by
Jon 1:14 We b' thee, O Lord, we b' thee,
4: 3 take, I b' thee, my life from me;
Mal 1: 9 b' God that he...be gracious
M'r 7:32 b' him to put his hand upon him.
Lu 8:28 high? I b' thee, torment me not.
9:38 I b' thee, look upon my son:
Ac 21:39 I b' thee, suffer me to speak unto
26: 3 I b' thee to hear me patiently.
Ro 12: 1 I b' you therefore, brethren, by
15:30 Now I b' you, brethren, for the
16:17 Now I b' you, brethren, mark
1Co 1:10 Now I b' you, brethren, by the
4:16 Wherefore I b' you, be ye followers
16:15 I b' you, brethren, (ye know the
2Co 2: 8 Wherefore I b' you that ye would
5:20 as though God did b' you by us:
6: 1 him, b' you also that ye receive
10: 1 I Paul myself b' you by the
2 I b' you, that I may not be bold
Ga 4:12 Brethren, I b' you, be as I am;
Eph 4: 1 b' you that ye walk worthy of the
Ph'p 4: 2 I b' Euodias, and b' Syntyche,
1Th 4: 1 we b' you, brethren, and exhort
10 but we b' you, brethren, that ye
5:12 And we b' you, brethren, to know
2Th 2: 1 Now we b' you, brethren, by the
Ph'm 9 for love's sake I rather b' thee,
10 I b' thee for my son Onesimus,
Heb 13:19 But I b' you the rather to do this,
22 I b' you, brethren, suffer the
1Pe 2:11 beloved, I b' you as strangers
2Jo 5 now I b' thee, lady, not as though

beseeching
M't 8: 5 unto him a centurion, b' him,
M'r 1:40 there came a leper to him, b' him,
Lu 7: 3 b' him that he would come and

beset
J'g 19:22 Belial, b' the house round about,
20: 5 and b' the house round about
Ps 22:12 of Bashan have b' me round.
139: 5 hast b' me behind and before,
Ho 7: 2 own doings have b' them about;
Heb 12: 1 the sin which doth so easily b' us,

Beseth See PI-BESETH.

beside See also BESIDES.
Ge 26: 1 b' the first famine that was in
31:50 take other wives b' my daughters,
Ex 12:37 that were men, b' children.
14: 9 the sea, b' Pi-hahiroth, before
29:12 blood b' the bottom of the altar.
Le 1:16 cast it b' the altar on the east part,
6:10 he shall put them b' the altar.
9:17 b' the burnt sacrifice of the
10:12 eat it without leaven b' the altar:
18:18 b' the other in her life time.
23:38 B' the sabbaths of the Lord,
38 and b' your gifts,
38 and b' all your vows,
38 and b' all your freewill offerings,
Nu 5: 8 b' the ram of the atonement,
20 lain with thee b' thine husband:
6:21 b' that that his hand shall get:
11: 6 at all, b' this manna, before our
16:49 b' them that died about the
24: 6 and as cedar trees b' the waters.
28:10 b' the continual burnt offering,
15 shall be offered, b' the continual
23 Ye shall offer these b' the burnt
24 it shall be offered b' the continual
31 shall offer them b' the continual
29: 6 B' the burnt offering of the month,
11 b' the sin offering of atonement,
16,19,22,25,28,31,34,38 b'...burntoffering,
39 b' your vows, and your freewill
31: 8 b' the rest of them that were
De 3: 5 b' unwalled towns a great many.
4:35 is God; there is none else b' him.
11:30 Gilgal, b' the plains of Moreh?
18: 8 to eat, b' that which cometh
139: 9 more for thee, b' these three;
29: 1 the land of Moab, b' the covenant
Jos 3:16 city Adam, that is b' Zaretan:
7: 2 to Ai, which is b' Beth-aven, on
12: 9 of Ai, which is b' Beth-el, one;
13: 4 Mearah that is b' the Sidonians,
17: 5 b' the land of Gilead
22:19 building you an altar b' the altar
29 or for sacrifices, b' the altar of
J'g 6:37 it be dry upon all the earth b'
7: 1 and pitched b' the well of Harod:
8:26 shekels of gold; b' ornaments,
26 b' the chains that were about
11:34 and she was his only child: b' her
20:15 drew sword, b' the inhabitants
17 the men of Israel, b' Benjamin,
36 wait which they had set b' Gibeah.
Ru 2:14 she sat b' the reapers: and he
4: 4 there is none to redeem it b' thee;
1Sa 2: 2 for there is none b' thee: neither
4: 1 battle, and pitched b' Ebenezer:
19: 3 go out and stand b' my father
2Sa 7:22 neither is there any God b' thee,
13:23 Baal-hazor, which is b' Ephraim:
15: 2 stood b' the way of the gate:
18 his servants passed on b' him;
1Ki 3:20 my son from b' me, while thine
4:23 sheep, b' harts, and roebucks,
5:16 B' the chief of Solomon's officers
9:26 Ezion-geber, which is b' Eloth,
10:13 asked, b' that which Solomon
15 B' that he had of the merchantmen
19 two lions stood b' the stays.
11:25 b' the mischief that Hadad did:
13:31 lay my bones b' his bones:
2Ki 11:20 the sword b' the king's house.
12: 9 set it b' the altar, on the right
21:16 b' his sin wherewith he made
1Ch 3: 9 sons of David, b' the sons
17:20 neither is there any God b'
2Ch 9:12 b' that which she had brought
14 B' that which chapmen and
17:19 waited on the king, b' those
20: 1 them other b' the Ammonites,
26:19 Lord, from b' the incense altar.
31:16 B' their genealogy of males,
Ezr 1: 4 beasts, b' the freewill offering
6 b' all that was willingly
2:65 B' their servants and their
Ne 5:15 wine, b' forty shekels of silver;
17 fifty of the Jews and rulers, b'
7:67 B' their manservants and their
8: 4 b' him stood Mattithiah, and
Job 1:14 the asses feeding b' them:
Ps 23: 2 leadeth me b' the still waters.
73:25 upon earth that I desire b' thee.
Ca 1: 8 thy kids b' the shepherds' tents.
Isa 26:13 our God, other lords b' thee
32:20 Blessed are ye that sow b' all
43:11 and b' me there is no saviour.
44: 6 and b' me there is no God.
8 Is there a God b' me? yea, there
45: 5 else, there is no God b' me:
6 west, that there is none b' me.
21 no God else b' me;
21 there is none b' me.
47: 8 I am, and none else b' me;
10 I am, and none else b' me.
56: 8 others to him, b' those that
64: 4 the eye seen, O God, b' thee,
Jer 36:21 princes which stood b' the king.
Eze 9: 2 and stood b' the brasen altar.
10: 6 went in, and stood b' the wheels.
16 turned not from b' them.
19 the wheels also were b' them,
11:22 wings, and the wheels b' them;
32:13 beasts thereof from b' the great
Da 11: 4 even for others b' those.
Ho 13: 4 for there is no saviour b' me.
Zep 2:15 there is none b' me: how is she
M't 14:21 men, b' women and children.
15:38 b' women and children.
25:20 I have gained b' them five
22 gained two other talents b' them.
M'r 3:21 for they said, He is b' himself.
Lu 16:26 b' all this, between us and you
24:21 and b' all this, to day
Ac 26:24 Paul, thou art b' thyself;
2Co 5:13 whether we be b' ourselves,
11:28 B' those things that are without.
2Pe 1: 5 And b' this, giving all

besides
Ge 19:12 Lot, Hast thou here any b'?
46:26 b' Jacob's sons' wives, all the
Le 7:13 B' the cakes, he shall offer for
1Ki 22: 7 not here a prophet of the Lord b',
2Ch 18: 6 here a prophet of the Lord b',
Jer 36:32 and there were added b' unto
1Co 1:16 b', I know not whether I
Ph'm 19 unto me even thine own self b'.

besiege See also BESIEGED.
De 20:12 thee, then thou shalt b' it:
19 When thou shalt b' a city a long
28:52 And he shall b' thee in all thy
52 b' thee in all thy gates
1Sa 23: 8 to b' David and his men.
1Ki 8:37 if their enemy b' them in the
2Ki 24:11 city, and his servants did b'
2Ch 6:28 if their enemies b' them in the
Isa 21: 2 Go up, O Elam: b', O Media;
Jer 21: 4 the Chaldeans, which b' you
9 to the Chaldeans that b' you,

besieged
2Sa 11: 1 of Ammon, and b' Rabbah.
20:15 And they came and b' him
1Ki 16:17 with him, and they b' Tirzah.
20: 1 and he went up and b' Samaria,
2Ki 6:24 and went up, and b' Samaria.
25 and, behold, they b' it, until
16: 5 they b' Ahaz, but could not
17: 5 Samaria, and b' it three years.
18: 9 came up against Samaria, and b' it.
19:24 up all the rivers of b' places.
24:10 and the city was b'.
25: 2 And the city was b' unto the
1Ch 20: 1 and came and b' Rabbah.
Ec 9:14 and b' it, and built great
Isa 1: 8 of cucumbers, as a b' city.
37:25 all the rivers of the b' places.
Jer 32: 2 the king of Babylon's army b'
37: 5 the Chaldeans that b' Jerusalem
39: 1 against Jerusalem, and they b' it.
52: 5 city was b' unto the eleventh
Eze 4: 3 it shall be b', and thou shalt
6:12 he that remaineth and is b' shall
Da 1: 1 unto Jerusalem, and b' it.

Besodeiah (bes-o-di'-ah)
Ne 3: 6 and Meshullam the son of B';

besom
Isa 14:23 it with the b' of destruction,

Besor (be'-sor)
1Sa 30: 9 and came to the brook B',
10 could not go over the brook B',
21 also to abide at the brook B':

besought
Ge 42:21 when he b' us, and we would not
Ex 32:11 And Moses b' the Lord his God,
De 3:23 And I b' the Lord at that time,
2Sa 12:16 David therefore b' God for the
1Ki 13: 6 And the man of God b' the Lord,
2Ki 1:13 knees before Elijah, and b' him,
13: 4 And Jehoahaz b' the Lord, and
2Ch 33:12 he b' the Lord his God,
Ezr 8:23 fasted and b' our God for this:
Es 8: 3 and b' him with tears to put
Jer 26:19 fear the Lord, and b' the Lord,
M't 8:31 the devils b' him, saying, If thou
34 they b' him that he would depart
14:36 And b' him that they might only
15:23 his disciples came and b' him,
18:29 b' him, saying, Have patience
M'r 5:10 And he b' him much that he
12 And all the devils b' him, saying,
23 And b' him greatly, saying,
6:56 streets, and b' him that they
7:26 and she b' him that he would
8:22 him, and b' him to touch him.
Lu 4:38 and they b' him for her.
5:12 Jesus fell on his face, and b'

Lu 7: 4 they b' him instantly, saying,
8:31 And they b' him that he would
32 and they b' him that he would
37 b' him to depart from them;
38 b' him that he might be with
41 b' him that he would come into
9:40 I b' thy disciples to cast him out;
11:37 certain Pharisee b' him to dine
Joh 4:40 they b' him that he would tarry
47 b' him that he would come down,
19:31 b' Pilate that their legs might
38 b' Pilate that he might take
Ac 13:42 the Gentiles b' that these words
16:15 she b' us, saying, If ye have
39 And they came and b' them,
21:12 b' him not to go up to Jerusalem.
25: 2 him against Paul, and b' him,
27:33 Paul b' them all to take meat,
2Co 12: 8 I b' the Lord thrice, that it might
1Ti 1: 3 As I b' thee to abide still at

best
Ge 43:11 take of the b' fruits in the land in
47: 6 in the b' of the land make thy
11 Egypt, in the b' of the land, in the
Ex 22: 5 of the b' of his own field, and of
5 the b' of his own vineyard,
Nu 18:12 All the b' of the oil,
12 and all the b' of the wine,
29 of all the b' thereof, even the
30 when ye have heaved the b'
32 ye have heaved from it the b' of it:
36: 6 to whom they think b';
De 23:16 where it liketh him b': thou
1Sa 8:14 your oliveyards, even the b' of
15: 9 the b' of the sheep, and of the
15 for the people spared the b' of the
2Sa 18: 4 What seemeth you b' I will do.
1Ki 10:18 and overlaid it with the b' gold.
2Ki 10: 3 Look even out the b' and meetest
Es 2: 9 her maids unto the b' place of the
Ps 39: 5 man at his b' state is altogether
Ca 7: 9 roof of thy mouth like the b' wine
Eze 31:16 the choice and b' of Lebanon,
Mic 7: 4 the b' of them is as a brier: the
Lu 15:22 Bring forth the b' robe, and put
1Co 12:31 but covet earnestly the b' gifts:

bestead
Isa 8:21 shall pass through it, hardly b'

bestir
2Sa 5:24 then thou shalt b' thyself: for

bestow See also BESTOWED.
Ex 32:29 he may b' upon you a blessing
De 14:26 And thou shalt b' that money for
2Ch 24: 7 of the Lord did they b' upon
Ezr 7:20 thou shalt have occasion to b',
20 b' it out of the king's treasure
Lu 12:17 I have no more room where to b'
18 there will I b' all my fruits and my
1Co 12:23 upon these we b' more abundant
13: 3 And though I b' all my goods to

bestowed
1Ki 10:26 horsemen, whom he b' in the
2Ki 5:24 their hand, and b' them in the
12:15 the money to be b' on workmen:
1Ch 29:25 b' upon him such royal majesty
2Ch 9:25 whom he b' in the chariot cities,
Isa 63: 7 to all that the Lord hath b' on us,
7 he hath b' on them according
Joh 4:38 whereon ye b' no labour: other
Ro 16: 6 Mary, who b' much labour on us.
1Co 15:10 his grace which was b' upon me
2Co 1:11 that for the gift b' upon us by the
8: 1 grace of God b' on the churches
Ga 4:11 lest I have b' upon you labour in
1Jo 3: 1 of love the Father hath b' on us.

Betah (*be'-tah*)
2Sa 8: 8 And from B', and from Berothai,

Beten (*be'-ten*)
Jos 19:25 and Hali, and B', and Achshaph,

Beth See BETH-ANATH; BETH-ANOTH; BETHANY; BETH-ARABAH; BETH-ARAM; BETH-ARBEL; BETH-AVEN; BETH-AZMAVETH; BETH-BAAL-MEON; BETH-BARAH; BERH-BIREI; BETH-CAR; BETH-DAGON; BETH-DIBLATHAIM; BETH-EL; BETH-EMEK; BETHESDA; BETH-EZEL; BETH-GADER; BETH-GAMUL; BETH-HACCEREM; BETH-HARAN; BETH-HOGLAH; BETH-HORON; BETH-JESHIMOTH; BETH-LEBAOTH; BETH-LEHEM; BETH-MAACHAH; BETH-MARCABOTH; BETH-MEON; BETH-NIMRAH; BETH-PALET; BETH-PAZZEZ; BETH-PEOR; BETHPHAGE; BETH-RAPHA; BETH-REHOB; BETHSAIDA; BETH-SHAN; BETH-SHEMESH; BETH-SHITTAH; BETH-TAPPUAH; BETH-ZUR.

Bethabara (*beth-ab'-ar-ah*) See also BETH-BARAH.
Joh 1:28 These things were done in B'

Beth-anath (*beth'-a-nath*)
Jos 19:38 Harem, and B', and
J'g 1:33 nor the inhabitants of B'; but he
33 Beth-shemesh, and of B' became

Beth-anoth (*beth'-a-noth*)
Jos 15:59 Maarath, and B', and Eltekon;

Bethany (*beth'-a-ny*)
M't 21:17 and went out of the city into B';
26: 6 Now when Jesus was in B', in the
M'k 11: 1 unto Bethphage and B', at the
11 he went out unto B' with the
12 when they were come from B', he
14: 3 And being in B' in the house of
Lu 19:29 come nigh to Bethphage and B',
24:50 he led them out as far as to B',
Joh 11: 1 named Lazarus, of B', the town
18 Now B' was nigh unto Jerusalem,
12: 1 before the passover came to B',

Beth-arabah (*beth-ar'-ab-ah*)
Jos 15: 6 passed along by the north of B';
61 In the wilderness, B', Middin, and
18:22 B', and Zemaraim, and Beth-el,

Beth-aram (*beth'-a-ram*)
Jos 13:27 And in the valley, B', and

Beth-arbel (*beth-ar'-bel*)
Ho 10:14 Shalman spoiled B' in the day of

Beth-aven (*beth-a'-ven*)
Jos 7: 2 to Ai, which is beside B', on the
18:12 were at the wilderness of B'.
1Sa 13: 5 in Michmash, eastward from B'.
14:23 and the battle passed over unto B'.
Ho 4:15 neither go ye up to B', nor swear,
5: 8 cry aloud at B', after thee, O
10: 5 because of the calves of B':

Beth-azmaveth (*beth-az'-maveth*) See also AZMAVETH.
Ne 7:28 The men of B', forty and two.

Beth-baal-meon (*beth-ba''-al-me'-on*) See also BAAL-MEON.
Jos 13:17 Dibon, and Bamoth-baal, and B',

Beth-barah (*beth-ba'-rah*) See also BETHABARA
J'g 7:24 before them the waters unto B'
24 and took the waters unto B' and

Beth-birei (*beth-bir-e-i*) See also BETH-LEBAOTH.
1Ch 4:31 Hazar-susim, and at B', and at

Beth-car (*beth'-car*)
1Sa 7:11 them, until they came under B'.

Beth-dagon (*beth-da'-gon*)
Jos 15:41 And Gederoth, B', and Naamah,
19:27 toward the sunrising to B',

Beth-diblathaim (*beth-dib-lath-a'-im*)
Jer 48:22 and upon Nebo, and upon B',

Beth-el (*beth'-el*) See also BETHELITE; EL-BETH-EL; LUZ.
Ge 12: 8 a mountain on the east of B',
8 pitched his tent, having B' on the
13: 3 from the south even to B',
3 beginning, between B' and Hai;
28:19 called the name of that place B':
31:13 I am the God of B', where thou
35: 1 unto Jacob, Arise, go up to B',
3 let us arise, and go up to B';
6 in the land of Canaan, that is, B',
8 she was buried beneath B' under
15 where God spake with him, B'.
16 they journeyed from B'; and
Jos 7: 2 Beth-aven, on the east side of B',
8: 9 and abode between B' and Ai,
12 lie in ambush between B' and Ai,
17 was not man left in Ai or B',
12: 9 king of Ai, which is beside B',
16 the king of B', one;
16: 1 from Jericho throughout mount B',
2 And goeth out from B' to Luz,
18:13 to the side of Luz, which is B',
22 Zemaraim, and B',
J'g 1:22 they also went up against B':
23 house of Joseph sent to descry B'.
4: 5 between Ramah and B' in mount
21:19 which is on the north side of B',
19 the highway that goeth up from B'
1Sa 7:16 from year to year in circuit to B',
10: 3 three men going up to God to B',
13: 2 in Michmash and in mount B',
30:27 To them which were in B', and
1Ki 12:29 he set the one in B', and the other
32 So did he in B', sacrificing unto
32 and he placed in B' the priests of
33 altar which he had made in B'
13: 1 by the word of the Lord unto B':
4 had cried against the altar in B',
10 by the way that he came to B'.
11 there dwelt an old prophet in B';
11 of God had done that day in B':
32 the Lord against the altar in B',
2Ki 2: 2 for the Lord hath sent me to B'.
2 So they went down to B'.
3 of the prophets that were at B'
23 he went up from thence unto B':
10:29 the golden calves that were in B',
17:28 came and dwelt in B', and taught
23: 4 carried the ashes of them unto B'.
15 Moreover the altar that was at B',
17 hast done against the altar of B'.
19 all the acts that he had done in B'.
1Ch 7:28 B' and the towns thereof, and
2Ch 13:19 B' with the towns thereof, and
Ezr 2:28 men of B' and Ai, two hundred
Ne 7:32 The men of B' and Ai, a hundred
11:31 and Aiji, and B', and in their
Jer 48:13 house of Israel was ashamed of B'
Ho 10:15 So shall B' do unto you because
12: 4 he found him in B', and there
Am 3:14 I will also visit the altars of B':
4: 4 Come to B', and transgress; at
5: 5 But seek not B', nor enter into
5 captivity, and B' shall come to
6 there be none to quench it in B'.
7:10 Then Amaziah the priest of B'
13 prophesy not again any more at B':

Beth-elite (*beth'-el-ite*)
1Ki 16:34 did Hiel the B' build Jericho:

Beth-emek (*beth-e'-mek*)
Jos 19:27 toward the north side of B',

Bether (*be'-thur*)
Ca 2:17 hart upon the mountains of B'.

Bethesda (*beth-ez'-dah*)
Joh 5: 2 is called in the Hebrew tongue B',

Beth-ezel (*beth-e'-zel*)
Mic 1:11 not forth in the mourning of B';

Beth-gader (*beth-ga'-der*) See also GEDER.
1Ch 2:51 Hareph the father of B'.

Beth-gamul (*beth-ga'-mul*)
Jer 48:23 upon B', and upon Beth-meon,

Beth-haccerem (*beth-hak'-se-rem*)
Ne 3:14 Rechab, the ruler of part of B';
Jer 6: 1 and set up a sign of fire in B':

Beth-hanan See ELON-BETH-HANAN.

Beth-haran (*beth-ha'-ran*) See also ELON-BETH-HARAN.
Nu 32:36 Beth-nimrah, and B', fenced

Beth-hogla (*beth-hog'-lah*) See also BETH-HOGLAH.
Jos 15: 6 went up to B', and passed

Beth-hoglah (*beth-hog'-lah*) See also BETH-HOGLA.
Jos 18:19 along to the side of B' northward
21 Jericho, and B', and the valley of

Beth-horon (*beth-ho'-ron*)
Jos 10:10 the way that goeth up to B',
11 and were in the going down to B',
16: 3 the coast of B' the nether, and
5 Ataroth-addar, unto B' the upper;
18:13 on the south side of the nether B'.
14 hill that lieth before B' southward;
21:22 B' with her suburbs; four cities.
1Sa 13:18 company turned the way to B':
1Ki 9:17 built Gezer, and B' the nether,
1Ch 6:68 B' with her suburbs,
7:24 Sherah, who built B' the nether,
2Ch 8: 5 Also he built B' the upper, and
5 B' the nether, fenced cities,
25:13 from Samaria even unto B', and

bethink
1Ki 8:47 b' themselves in the
2Ch 6:37 b' themselves in the

Beth-jesimoth (*beth-jes'-im-oth*) See also BETH-JESHIMOTH.
Nu 33:49 from B' even unto Abel-shittim

Beth-jeshimoth (*beth-jesh'-im-oth*) See also BETH-JESIMOTH.
Jos 12: 3 sea on the east, the way to B';
13:20 Ashdoth-pisgah, and B',
Eze 25: 9 of the country, B', Baal-meon,

Beth-lebaoth (*beth-leb'-a-oth*) See also BETH-BISEI.
Jos 19: 6 And B', and Sharuhen; thirteen

Beth-lehem (*beth'-le-hem*) See also BETH-LEHEMITE; BETH-LEHEM-JUDAH.
Ge 35:19 the way to Ephrath, which is B'.
48: 7 way of Ephrath; the same is B'.
Jos 19:15 Shimron, and Idalah, and B':
J'g 12: 8 after him Ibzan of B' judged Israel.
10 died Ibzan, and was buried at B'.
Ru 1:19 two went until they came to B'.
19 they were come to B', that all
22 came to B' in the beginning of
2: 4 Boaz came from B', and said
4:11 in Ephratah, and be famous in B':
1Sa 16: 4 and came to B'. And the elders
17:15 to feed his father's sheep at B'.
20: 6 that he might run to B' his city:
28 asked leave of me to go to B':
2Sa 2:32 of his father, which was in B'.
23:14 of the Philistines was then in B'.
15 the water of the well of B', which
16 drew water out of the well of B',
24 Elhanan the son of Dodo of B'.
1Ch 2:51 the father of B', Hareph the
54 Salma; B', and the Netophathites,
4: 4 of Ephratah, the father of B'.
11:16 Philistines' garrison was then at B'.
17 the well of B', that is at the gate!
18 drew water out of the well of B',
26 Elhanan the son of Dodo of B',
2Ch 11: 6 He built even B', and Etam, and
Ezr 2:21 children of B', an hundred twenty
Ne 7:26 The men of B' and Netophah,
Jer 41:17 of Chimham, which is by B', to go
Mic 5: 2 thou, B' Ephratah, though thou
M't 2: 1 Jesus was born in B' of Judæa
5 In B' of Judæa: for thus it is
6 And thou B', in the land of Juda,
8 And he sent them to B', and said,
16 all the children that were in B',
Lu 2: 4 city of David, which is called B';
15 Let us now go even unto B', and see
Joh 7:42 and out of the town of B', where

Beth-lehemite (*beth'-le-hem-ite*)
1Sa 16: 1 I will send thee to Jesse the B'.
18 I have seen a son of Jesse the B'.
17:58 the son of thy servant Jesse the B'.
2Sa 21:19 the son of Jaare-oregim, a B'.

Beth-lehem-judah (*beth''-le-hem-ju'-dah*)
J'g 17: 7 there was a young man out of B'
8 from B' to sojourn where he could
9 I am a Levite of B', and I
19: 1 to him a concubine out of B'.
2 unto her father's house to B',
18 We are passing from B' toward
18 and I went to B', but I
Ru 1: 1 a certain man of B' went to
2 and Chilion, Ephrathites of B'.
1Sa 17:12 son of that Ephrathite of B',

Beth-maachah *(beth-ma'-a-kah)* See also ABEL-BETH-MAACHAH.
2Sa 20:14 unto Abel, and to B', and all
15 and besieged him in Abel of B',
Beth-marcaboth *(beth-mar'-cab-oth)*
Jos 19: 5 Ziklag, and B', and Hazar-susah,
1Ch 4:31 at B', and Hazar-susim, and at
Beth-meon *(beth-me'-on)* See also BETH-BAAL-MEON.
Jer 48:23 upon Beth-gamul, and upon B',
Beth-nimrah *(beth-nim'-rah)* See also NIMRAH.
Nu 32:36 B', and Beth-haran, fenced cities:
Jos 13:27 in the valley, Beth-aram, and B',
Beth-palet *(beth-pa'-let)* See also BETH-PELET.
Jos 15:27 and Heshmon, and B',
Beth-pazzez *(beth-paz'-zez)*
Jos 19:21 and En-haddah, and B';
Beth-peor *(beth-pe'-or)*
De 3:29 in the valley over against B'.
4:46 against B', in the land of Sihon
34: 6 the land of Moab, over against B':
Jos 13:20 And B', and Ashdoth-pisgah, and
Bethphage *(beth'-fa-je)*
M't 21: 1 were come to B', unto the mount
M'r 11: 1 Jerusalem, unto B' and Bethany,
Lu 19:29 was come nigh to B' and Bethany,
Beth-phelet *(beth'-fe-let)* See also BETH-PALET.
Ne 11:26 and at Moladah, and at B',
Beth-rapha *(beth'-ra-fah)*
1Ch 4:12 And Eshton begat B', and
Beth-rehob *(beth'-re-hob)*
J'g 18:28 was in the valley that lieth by B'.
2Sa 10: 6 sent and hired the Syrians of B',
Bethsaida *(beth-sa'-dah)*
M't 11:21 woe unto thee, B'! for if the
M'r 6:45 go to the other side before unto B',
8:22 And he cometh to B'; and they
Lu 9:10 belonging to the city called B'.
10:13 woe unto thee, B'! for if the mighty
Joh 1:44 Now Philip was of B', the city of
12:21 therefore to Philip, which was of B'
Beth-shan *(beth'-shan)* See also BETH-SHEAN.
1Sa 31:10 his body to the wall of B'.
12 of his sons from the wall of B',
2Sa 21:12 stolen them from the street of B',
Beth-shean *(beth-she'-an)* See also BETH-SHAN.
Jos 17:11 B' and her towns, and Ibleam
16 both they who are of B' and her
J'g 1:27 drive out the inhabitants of B'
1Ki 4:12 and all B', which is by Zartanah
12 Jezreel, from B' to Abel-meholah,
1Ch 7:29 children of Manasseh, B' and her
Beth-shemesh *(beth'-she-mesh)* See also BETH-SHEMITE.
Jos 15:10 and went down to B', and passed
19:22 to Tabor, and Shahazimah, and B';
38 Horem, and Beth-anath, and B';
21:16 Juttah with her suburbs, and B'
J'g 1:33 drive out the inhabitants of B',
33 the inhabitants of B' and of
1Sa 6: 9 by the way of his own coast to B',
12 the straight way to the way of B',
12 after them unto the border of B'.
13 they of B' were reaping their
15 the men of B' offered burnt
19 smote the men of B', because they
20 And the men of B' said, Who is
1Ki 4: 9 Makaz, and in Shaalbim, and B',
2Ki 14:11 looked one another in the face at B'
13 the son of Ahaziah, at B', and
1Ch 6:59 Ashan with her suburbs, and B'
2Ch 25:21 Amaziah king of Judah, at B',
23 the son of Jehoahaz, at B', and
28:18 Judah, and had taken B', and
Jer 43:13 break also the images of B', that is
Beth-shemite *(beth'-shem-ite)*
1Sa 6:14 the field of Joshua, a B', and
18 day in the field of Joshua, the B'.
Beth-shittah *(beth-shit'-tah)*
J'g 7:22 and the host fled to B' in
Beth-tappuah *(beth-tap'-pu-ah)*
Jos 15:53 And Janum, and B', and Aphekah,
Bethuel *(beth-u'-el)* See also BETHUL.
Ge 22:22 and Pildash, and Jidlaph, and B'.
23 And B' begat Rebekah: these
24:15 who was born to B', son of Milcah,
24 I am the daughter of B' the son of
47 And she said, The daughter of B',
50 Then Laban and B' answered and
25:20 daughter of B' the Syrian of
28: 2 to the house of B' thy mother's
5 unto Laban, son of B' the Syrian,
1Ch 4:30 And at B', and at Hormah, and at
Bethul *(beth'-ul)* See also BETHUEL.
Jos 19: 4 And Eltolad, and B', and Hormah,
Beth-zur *(beth'-zur)*
Jos 15:58 Halhul, B', and Gedor,
1Ch 2:45 and Maon was the father of B'.
2Ch 11: 7 And B', and Shoco, and Adullam,
Ne 3:16 the ruler of the half part of B',
betimes
Ge 26:31 and they rose up b' in the
2Ch 36:15 rising up b', and sending;
Job 8: 5 thou wouldest seek unto God b',
24: 5 rising b' for a prey: the
Pr 13:24 loveth him chasteneth him b'.
Betonim *(bet'-o-nim)*
Jos 13:26 unto Ramath-mizpeh, and B';

betray See also BETRAYED; BETRAYEST; BETRAYETH; BEWRAY.
1Ch 12:17 but if ye be come to b' me to
M't 24:10 and shall b' one another, and
26:16 he sought opportunity to b' him.
21 one of you shall b' me.
23 in the dish, the same shall b' me.
46 he is at hand that doth b' me.
M'r 13:12 the brother shall b' the brother
14:10 the chief priests, to b' him unto
11 he might conveniently b' him.
18 eateth with me shall b' me.
Lu 22: 4 how he might b' him unto them.
6 sought opportunity to b' him
Joh 6:64 not, and who should b' him.
71 he it was that should b' him, being
12: 4 Simon's son, which should b' him,
13: 2 Iscariot, Simon's son, to b' him;
11 For he knew who should b' him;
21 you, that one of you shall b' me.
betrayed
M't 10: 4 Judas Iscariot, who also b' him.
17:22 The Son of man shall be b' into
20:18 The Son of man shall be b' unto
26: 2 Son of man is b' to be crucified.
24 by whom the Son of man is b'!
25 Then Judas, which b' him,
45 Son of man is b' into the hands of
48 Now he that b' him gave them a
27: 3 Then Judas, which had b' him,
4 I have sinned in that I have b'
M'r 3:19 Judas Iscariot, which also b' him:
14:21 by whom the Son of man is b'!
41 the Son of man is b' into the hands
44 And he that b' him had given them
Lu 21:16 And ye shall be b' both by
22:22 unto that man by whom he is b'!
Joh 18: 2 And Judas also, which b' him,
5 Judas also, which b' him, stood
1Co 11:23 night in which he was b' took
betrayers
Ac 7:52 ye have been now the b' and
betrayest
Lu 22:48 b' thou the Son of man with a
betrayeth See also BEWRAYETH.
M'r 14:42 lo, he that b' me is at hand.
Lu 22:21 the hand of him that b' me is with
Joh 21:20 Lord, which is he that b' thee?
betroth See also BETROTHED.
De 28:30 Thou shalt b' a wife, and another
Ho 2:19 And I will b' thee unto me for ever;
19 yea, I will b' thee unto me in
20 I will even b' thee unto me in
betrothed
Ex 21: 8 who hath b' her to himself,
9 And if he have b' her unto his
22:16 maid that is not b', and lie with
Le 19:20 that is a bondmaid, b' to an
De 20: 7 that hath b' a wife, and hath not
22:23 that is a virgin be b' unto an
25 But if a man find a b' damsel in the
27 the b' damsel cried, and there was
28 which is not b', and lay hold on her,
better See also BETTERED.
Ge 29:19 b' that I give her to thee, than
Ex 14:12 been b' for us to serve the
Nu 14: 3 not b' for us to return into Egypt?
J'g 8: 2 the grapes of Ephraim b' than the
9: 2 Whether is b' for you, either that
11:25 now art thou any thing b' than
18:19 is it b' for thee to be a priest unto
Ru 4:15 which is b' to thee than seven sons,
1Sa 1: 8 am not I b' to thee than ten sons?
15:22 Behold, to obey is b' than sacrifice,
28 neighbour of thine, that is b' than
27: 1 nothing b' for me than that I
2Sa 17:14 b' than the counsel of Ahithophel.
18: 3 b' that thou succour us out of the
1Ki 1:47 God make the name of Solomon b'
2:32 more righteous and b' than he,
19: 4 for I am not b' than my fathers.
21: 2 I will give thee for it a b' vineyard
2Ki 5:12 b' than all the waters of Israel?
2Ch 21:13 which were b' than thyself:
Es 1:19 estate unto another that is b' than
Ps 37:16 b' than the riches of many wicked.
63: 3 loving kindness is b' than life, my
69:31 This also shall please the Lord b'
84:10 a day in thy courts is b' than a
118: 8, 9 b' to trust in the Lord than to
119:72 the law of thy mouth is b' unto me
Pr 3:14 b' than the merchandise of silver,
8:11 For wisdom is b' than rubies;
19 My fruit is b' than gold, yea,
12: 9 is b' than he that honoureth
15:16 B' is little with the fear of the
17 B' is a dinner of herbs where love
16: 8 B' is a little with righteousness
16 how much b' is it to get wisdom
19 B' it is to be of an humble spirit
32 slow to anger is b' than the mighty
17: 1 B' is a dry morsel, and quietness
19: 1 B' is the poor that walketh in his
22 and a poor man is b' than a liar.
21: 9 b' to dwell in a corner of the
19 b' to dwell in the wilderness,
25: 7 b' it is that it be said unto thee,
24 It is b' to dwell in the corner
27: 5 Open rebuke is b' than secret love.
10 b' is a neighbour that is near than
28: 6 B' is the poor that walketh in his
Ec 2:24 nothing b' for a man, than that he
3:22 I perceive that there is nothing b',
4: 3 Yea, b' is he than both they, which
6 B' is an handful with quietness,
9 Two are b' than one; because they
13 B' is a poor and a wise child than
5: 5 B' is it that thou shouldest not
6: 3 an untimely birth is b' than he.
9 B' is the sight of the eyes than the
11 what is man the b'?
7: 1 A good name is b' than
2 b' to go to the house of mourning,
3 Sorrow is b' than laughter: for by
3 countenance the heart is made b'.
5 b' to hear the rebuke of the wise,
8 B' is the end of a thing than the
8 spirit is b' than the proud in spirit.
10 cause that the former days were b'
8:15 hath no b' thing under the sun,
9: 4 a living dog is b' than a dead lion.
16 said I, Wisdom is b' than strength:
18 Wisdom is b' than weapons of war:
10:11 and a babbler is no b'.
Ca 1: 2 for thy love is b' than wine.
4:10 how much b' is thy love than wine!
Isa 56: 5 b' than of sons and of daughters:
La 4: 9 b' than they that be slain with
Eze 36:11 will do b' unto you than at your
Da 1:20 ten times b' than all the magicians
Ho 2: 7 then it was b' with me than now.
Am 6: 2 be they b' than these kingdoms?
Jon 4: 3, 8 it is b' for me to die than to live.
Na 3: 8 Art thou b' than populous No,
M't 6:26 Are ye not much b' than they?
12:12 then is a man b' than a sheep?
18: 6 it were b' for him that a millstone
8, 9 it is b' for thee to enter into life
M'r 9:42 is b' for him that a millstone
43 it is b' for thee to enter into life
45 it is b' for thee to enter halt
47 it is b' for thee to enter into the
Lu 5:39 for he saith, The old is b'.
12:24 more are ye b' than the fowls?
17: 2 were b' for him that a millstone
Ro 3: 9 What then? are we b' than they?
1Co 7: 9 it is b' to marry than to burn.
38 her not in marriage doeth b'.
8: 8 neither, if we eat, are we the b';
9:15 it were b' for me to die,
11:17 not for the b', but for the worse.
Ph'p 1:23 to be with Christ; which is far b':
2: 3 esteem other b' than themselves.
Heb 1: 4 made so much b' than the angels,
6: 9 we are persuaded b' things of you,
7: 7 the less is blessed of the b'.
19 but the bringing in of a b' hope
22 made a surety of a b' testament.
8: 6 the mediator of a b' covenant,
6 was established upon b' promises.
9:23 with b' sacrifices than these.
10:34 in heaven a b' and an enduring
11:16 But now they desire a b' country,
35 they might obtain a b' resurrection:
40 provided some b' thing for us,
12:24 b' things than that of Abel.
1Pe 3:17 it is b', if the will of God be so,
2Pe 2:21 For it had been b' for them not to
bettered
M'r 5:26 nothing b', but rather grew worse,
between^ See also BETWIXT.
Ge 3:15 enmity b' thee and the woman,
15 and b' thy seed and her seed;
9:12 covenant which I make b' me and
13 a covenant b' me and the earth.
15 covenant, which is b' me and you
16 covenant b' God and every living
17 which I have established b' me and
10:12 And Resen b' Nineveh, and Calah
13: 3 the beginning, b' Beth-el and Hai;
7 there was a strife b' the herdmen
8 b' me and thee, and b' my
15:17 lamp that passed b' those pieces.
16: 5 the Lord judge b' me and thee.
14 behold, it is b' Kadesh and Bered.
17: 2 make my covenant b' me and thee,
7 establish my covenant b' me and
10 b' me and you and thy seed after
20: 1 and dwelled b' Kadesh and Shur,
31:44 be for a witness b' me and thee.
48 said, This heap is a witness b' me
49 The Lord watch b' me and thee,
48:12 them out from b' his knees,
49:10 nor a lawgiver from b' his feet,
14 is a strong ass couching down b' two
Ex 8:23 I will put a division b' my people
11: 7 a difference b' the Egyptians and
13: 9 and for a memorial b' thine eyes,
16 and for frontlets b' thine eyes:
14: 2 b' Migdol and the sea, over against
20 came b' the camp of the Egyptians
16: 1 the wilderness of Sin, which is b'
18:16 and I judge b' one and another,
22:11 an oath of the Lord be b' them both,
25:22 from b' the two cherubim which
26:33 vail shall divide unto you b' the holy
28:33 bells of gold b' them round about:
30:18 thou shalt put it b' the tabernacle
31:13 for it is a sign b' me and you
17 It is a sign b' me and the children of
39:25 put the bells b' the pomegranates
25 round about b' the pomegranates;
40: 7 thou shalt set the laver b' the tent
30 laver b' the tent of the congregation
Le 10:10 that ye may put difference b' holy
10 and b' unclean and clean;
11:47 make a difference b' the unclean

Le 11:47 and b' the beast that may be eaten
20:25 therefore put difference b' clean
25 and unclean, and b' unclean fowls
26:46 which the Lord made b' him and
Nu 7:89 from b' the two cherubim:
11:33 the flesh was yet b' their teeth,
13:23 and they bare it b' two upon a staff;
16:48 stood b' the dead and the living;
21:13 is the border of Moab, b' Moab
26:56 thereof be divided b' many and few.
30:16 b' a man and his wife,
16 b' the father and his daughter,
31:27 prey into two parts; b' them that
27 and b' all the congregation.
35:24 congregation shall judge b' the
De 1: 1 plain over against the Red sea, b'
16 Hear the causes b' your brethren,
16 and judge righteously b'
39 had no knowledge b' good and evil,
5: 5 (I stood b' the Lord and you at
6: 8 shall be as frontlets b' thine eyes.
11:18 may be as frontlets b' your eyes.
14: 1 baldness b' your eyes for the dead.
17: 8 b' blood and blood, b' plea and plea,
8 and b' stroke and stroke,
19:17 men, b' whom the controversy is,
25: 1 If there be a controversy b' men,
28:57 young one that cometh out from b'
33:12 he shall dwell b' his shoulders.
Jos 3: 4 there shall be a space b' you and it,
8: 9 to lie in ambush, and abode b'
11 there was a valley b' them and Ai.
12 to lie in ambush b' Beth-el and Ai,
18:11 coast of their lot came forth b' the
22:25 Lord hath made Jordan a border b'
27 But that it may be a witness b' us,
28 but it is a witness b' us and
34 witness b' us that the Lord is God.
24: 7 darkness b' you and the Egyptians,
J'g 4: 5 b' Ramah and Beth-el in mount
17 there was peace b' Jabin the king
9:23 God sent an evil spirit b' Abimelech
11:10 The Lord be witness b' us, if we do
27 the Judge be judge this day b' the
13:25 camp of Dan b' Zorah and Eshtaol.
15: 4 firebrand in the midst b' two tails.
16:25 and they set him b' the pillars.
20:38 there was an appointed sign b' the
1Sa 4: 4 which dwelleth b' the cherubim:
7:12 Samuel took a stone, and set it b'
14 was peace b' Israel and the Amorites.
14: 4 And b' the passages, by which
42 And Saul said, Cast lots b' me and
17: 1 pitched b' Shochoh and Azekah,
3 and there was a valley b' them.
6 a target of brass b' his shoulders.
20: 3 there is but a step b' me and death.
23 the Lord be b' thee and me for ever.
42 b' me and thee, and b' my seed
24:12 The Lord judge b' me and thee,
15 therefore be judge, and judge b'
26:13 a great space being b' them:
2Sa 3: 1 was long war b' the house of Saul
6 there was war b' the house of Saul
6: 2 that dwelleth b' the cherubim.
18: 9 up b' the heaven and the earth;
24 And David sat b' the two gates:
19:35 can I discern b' good and evil?
21: 7 the Lord's oath that was b' them, b'
1Ki 3: 9 I may discern b' good and bad:
5:12 peace b' Hiram and Solomon;
7:28 the borders were b' the ledges:
29 b' the ledges were lions, oxen,
46 in the clay ground b' Succoth
14:30 war b' Rehoboam and Jeroboam
15: 6 war b' Rehoboam and Jeroboam all
7 was war b' Abijam and Jeroboam.
16 was war b' Asa and Baasha king of
19 There is a league b' me and thee,
19 and b' my father and thy father:
32 was war b' Asa and Baasha king of
18: 6 divided the land b' them to pass
21 How long halt ye b' two opinions?
42 and put his face b' his knees,
22: 1 without war b' Syria and Israel.
34 smote the king of Israel b' the joints
2Ki 9:24 and smote Jehoram b' his arms,
11:17 made a covenant b' the Lord
17 b' the king also and the people.
16:14 from b' the altar and the house of
19:15 God of Israel, which dwellest b' the
25: 4 the way of the gate b' two walls,
1Ch 13: 6 that dwelleth b' the cherubim,
21:16 angel of the Lord stand b' the earth
2Ch 4:17 in the clay ground b' Succoth and
12:15 wars b' Rehoboam and Jeroboam
13: 2 And there was war b' Abijah and
16: 3 There is a league b' me and thee,
3 was b' my father and thy father:
18:33 and smote the king of Israel b'
19:10 b' blood and blood, b' law and
23:16 Jehoiada made a covenant b' him,
16 and b' all the people,
16 and b' the king, that they should
Ne 3:32 And b' the going up of the corner
Job 41:16 that no air can come b' them.
Ps 80: 1 that dwellest b' the cherubim,
99: 1 he sitteth b' the cherubim:
Pr 18:18 cease, and parteth b' the mighty.
Isa 22:11 Ye made also a ditch b' the
37:16 God of Israel, that dwellest b'
59: 2 b' you and your God, and your
Jer 7: 5 b' a man and his neighbour;
34:18 and passed b' the parts thereof,
19 passed b' the parts of the calf;
42: 5 faithful witness b' us, if we do
52: 7 way of the gate b' the two walls,
La 1: 3 persecutors overtook her b' the
Eze 4: 3 a wall of iron b' thee and the city:
8: 3 lifted me up b' the earth and the
16 b' the porch and the altar,
10: 2 Go in b' the wheels, even under
2 coals of fire from b' the cherubim
6 fire from b' the wheels, from b' the
7 his hand from b' the cherubim
7 that was b' the cherubim,
18: 8 executed true judgment b' man
20:12 to be a sign b' me and them, that
20 and they shall be a sign b'
22:26 difference b' the holy and profane,
26 they shewed difference b' the
34:17 I judge b' cattle and cattle,
17 b' the rams and the he goats.
20 will judge b' the fat cattle and
20 b' the lean cattle.
22 I will judge b' cattle and cattle.
40: 7 and b' the little chambers were
41:10 b' the chambers was the wideness
18 so that a palmtree was b' a cherub
42:20 a separation b' the sanctuary
43: 8 and the wall b' me and them, they
44:23 difference b' the holy and profane,
23 cause them to discern b' the
47:16 which is b' the border of Damascus
48:22 b' the border of Judah and the
Da 7: 5 three ribs in the mouth of it b' the
8: 5 goat had a notable horn b' his eyes.
16 a man's voice b' the banks of Ulai,
21 the great horn that is b' his eyes
11:45 the tabernacles of his palace b'
Ho 2: 2 her adulteries from b' her breasts;
Joe 2:17 weep b' the porch and the altar,
Jon 4:11 persons that cannot discern b'
Zec 5: 9 lifted up the ephah b' the earth
6: 1 out from b' two mountains;
13 counsel of peace shall be b' them
9: 7 his abominations from b' his teeth:
11:14 brotherhood b' Judah and Israel.
Mal 2:14 Lord hath been witness b' thee
3:18 shall ye return, and discern b' the
18 the wicked, b' him that serveth
M't 18:15 his fault b' thee and him alone:
23:35 b' the temple and the altar.
Lu 11:51 b' the altar and the temple:
16:26 b' us and you there is a great gulf
23:12 were at enmity b' themselves.
Joh 3:25 b' some of John's disciples
Ac 12: 6 was sleeping b' two soldiers,
15: 9 no difference b' us and them,
39 contention was so sharp b' them,
23: 7 dissension b' the Pharisees and
26:31 they talked b' themselves,
Ro 1:24 dishonour their own bodies b'
10:12 there is no difference b' the Jew
1Co 6: 5 able to judge b' his brethren?
7:34 There is difference also b' a wife
Eph 2:14 middle wall of partition b' us;
1Ti 2: 5 one God, and one mediator b' God

betwixt See also BETWEEN.
Ge 17:11 token of the covenant b' me and
23:15 what is that b' me and thee?
26:28 an oath b' us, even b' us and thee,
30:36 And he set three days' journey b'
31:37 that they may judge b' us both.
50 God is witness b' me and thee.
51 which I have cast b' me and thee;
53 God of their father, judge b' us.
32:16 put a space b' drove and drove.
Job 9:33 is there any daysman b' us, that
36:32 by the cloud that cometh b'.
Ca 1:13 he shall lie all night b' my breasts.
Isa 5: 3 pray you, b' me and my vineyard.
Jer 39: 4 the gate b' the two walls: and he
Ph'p 1:23 I am in a strait b' two, having

Beulah (*be-w'-lah*)
Isa 62: 4 and thy land B': for the Lord

bewail See also BEWAILED; BEWAILETH.
Le 10: 6 the whole house of Israel, b'
De 21:13 and b' her father and her mother
J'g 11:37 and b' my virginity, I and my
Isa 16: 9 I will b' with the weeping
2Co 12:21 and that I shall b' many which
Re 18: 9 shall b' her, and lament for her,

bewailed
J'g 11:38 companions, and b' her virginity
Lu 8:52 And all wept, and b' her: but he
23:27 which also b' and lamented

bewaileth
Jer 4:31 daughter of Zion, that b' herself,

beware
Ge 24: 6 B' thou that thou bring not my
Ex 23:21 B' of him, and obey his voice,
De 6:12 Then b' lest thou forget the Lord,
8:11 B' that thou forget not the Lord
15: 9 B' that there be not a thought in
J'g 13: 4 Now therefore b', I pray thee,
13 I said unto the woman let her b'.
2Sa 18:12 B' that none touch the young man
2Ki 6: 9 B' that thou pass not such a place;
Job 36:18 Because there is wrath, b' lest
Pr 19:25 a scorner, and the simple will b';
Isa 36:18 B' lest Hezekiah persuade you,
M't 7:15 B' of false prophets, which come
10:17 But b' of men: for they will
16: 6 Take heed and b' of the leaven
11 that ye should b' of the leaven
12 not b' of the leaven of bread, but
M'k 8:15 Take heed, b' of the leaven of the
12:38 B' of the scribes, which love to go
Lu 12: 1 B' ye of the leaven of the
15 heed, and b' of covetousness:
20:46 B' of the scribes, which desire
Ac 13:40 B' therefore, lest that come
Ph'p 3: 2 B' of dogs, b' of evil workers,
2 b' of the concision.
Col 2: 8 B' lest any man spoil you
2Pe 3:17 ye know these things before, b'

bewitched
Ac 8: 9 b' the people of Samaria, giving
11 he had b' them with sorceries.
Ga 3: 1 foolish Galatians, who hath b'

bewray See also BETRAY; BEWRAYETH.
Isa 16: 3 the outcasts; b' not him that

bewrayeth See also BETRAYETH.
Pr 27:16 of his right hand, which b' itself.
29:24 heareth cursing, and b' it not.
M't 26:73 for thy speech b' thee.

beyond
Ge 35:21 spread his tent b' the tower of
50:10 of Atad, which is b' Jordan,
11 called Abel-Mizraim, which is b'
Le 15:25 run b' the time of her separation;
Nu 22:18 I cannot go b' the word of the
24:13 go b' the commandment of the
De 3:20 God hath given them b' Jordan:
25 the good land that is b' Jordan,
30:13 Neither is it b' the sea, that thou
Jos 9:10 the Amorites, that were b' Jordan,
13: 8 Moses gave them, b' Jordan
18: 7 received their inheritance b'
J'g 3:26 and passed b' the quarries, and
5:17 Gilead abode b' Jordan: and why
1Sa 20:22 the arrows are b' thee; go thy
36 lad ran, he shot an arrow b' him.
37 and said, Is not the arrow b' thee?
2Sa 10:16 the Syrians that were b' the river:
1Ki 4:12 even unto the place that is b'
14:15 shall scatter them b' the river,
1Ch 19:16 the Syrians that were b' the river:
2Ch 20: 2 from b' the sea on this side Syria;
Ezr 4:17 and unto the rest b' the river,
20 have ruled over all countries b'
6: 6 therefore, Tatnai, governor b' the
6 which are b' the river, be ye far
8 even of the tribute b' the river,
7:21 treasurers which are b' the river,
25 the people that are b' the river, all
Ne 2: 7 to the governors b' the river, that
9 came to the governors b' the river,
12:38 b' the tower of the furnaces
Isa 7:20 by them b' the river, by the king
9: 1 b' Jordan, in Galilee of the nations.
18:1 which is b' the rivers of Ethiopia:
Jer 22:19 and cast forth b' the gates of
25:22 the isles which are b' the sea,
Am 5:27 you to go into captivity b'
Zep 3:10 From b' the rivers of Ethiopia
M't 4:15 the way of the sea, b' Jordan,
25 Judæa, and from b' Jordan.
19: 1 the coasts of Judæa b' Jordan;
M'r 3: 8 Idumæa, and from b' Jordan;
6:51 in themselves b' measure,
7:37 And were b' measure astonished,
Joh 1:28 in Bethabara b' Jordan, where
3:26 he that was with thee b' Jordan,
10:40 went away again b' Jordan into
Ac 7:43 I will carry you away b' Babylon.
2Co 8: 3 yea, and b' their power they
10:14 we stretch not ourselves b' our
16 the gospel in the regions b' you,
Gal 1:13 b' measure I persecuted
1Th 4: 6 no man go b' and defraud

Bezai (*be'-zahee*)
Ezr 2:17 The children of B', three
Ne 7:23 children of B', three hundred
10:18 Hodijah, Hashum, B',

Bezaleel (*be-zal'-e-el*)
Ex 31: 2 I have called by name B' the son
35:30 the Lord hath called by name B'
36: 1 Then wrought B' and Aholiab,
2 Moses called B' and Aholiab,
37: 1 B' made the ark of shittim wood:
38:22 B' the son of Uri, the son of Hur,
1Ch 2:20 Hur begat Uri, and Uri begat B'.
2Ch 1: 5 Moreover the brasen altar, that B'
Ezr 10:30 Mattaniah, B', and Binnui, and

Bezek (*be'-zek*) See also ADONI-BEZEK.
J'g 1: 4 they slew of them in B' ten
5 And they found Adoni-bezek in B':
1Sa 11: 8 And when he numbered them in B',

Bezer (*be'-zer*)
De 4:43 Namely, B' in the wilderness,
Jos 20: 8 assigned B' in the wilderness
21:36 Reuben, B' with her suburbs
1Ch 6:78 B' in the wilderness with her
7:37 B', and Hod, and Shamma, and

bibber See WINEBIBBER.

Bichri (*bik'-ri*)
2Sa 20: 1 the son of B', a Benjamite:
2 Sheba the son of B': but the men
6 Sheba the son of B' do us more
7 pursue after Sheba the son of B'.
10 pursued after Sheba the son of B'.
13 pursue after Sheba the son of B'.
21 Sheba the son of B' by name,
22 the head of Sheba the son of B',

bid See also BADE; BIDDEN; BIDDING; FORBID.
Nu 15:38 and b' them that they make them
Jos 6:10 until the day I b' you shout;
1Sa 9:27 B' the servant pass on before us,

2Sa 2:26 long shall it be then, ere thou *b'*
2Ki 4:24 riding for me, except I *b'* thee.
5:13 if the prophet had *b'* thee do
10: 5 will do all that thou shalt *b'* us;
Jo 3: 2 the preaching that I *b'* thee.
Zep 1: 7 prepared a sacrifice, he hath *b'*
M't 14:28 *b'* me come unto thee on the
22: 9 ye shall find, *b'* to the marriage.
23: 3 therefore whatsoever they *b'* you
Lu 9:61 let me first go *b'* them farewell,
10:40 *b'* her therefore that she help me.
14:12 lest they also *b'* thee again, and
1Co 10:27 any of them that believe not *b'*
2Jo 10 house, neither *b'* him God speed:

bidden See also FORBIDDEN.
1Sa 9:13 afterwards they eat that be *b'*.
22 among them that were *b'*, which
2Sa 16:11 for the Lord hath *b'* him.
M't 1:24 angel of the Lord had *b'* him,
22: 3 to call them that were *b'*
4 Tell them which are *b'*, Behold, I
8 which were *b'* were not worthy.
Lu 7:39 the Pharisee which had *b'* him
14: 7 a parable to those which were *b'*,
8 When thou art *b'* of any man
8 man than thou be *b'* of him;
10 when thou art *b'*, go and sit down
17 to say to them that were *b'*,
24 none of those men which were *b'*

biddeth See also FORBIDDETH.
2Jo 11 For he that *b'* him God speed

bidding See also FORBIDDING.
1Sa 22:14 and goeth at thy *b'*, and is

Bidkar (*bid'-kar*)
2Ki 9:25 said Jehu to *B'* his captain,

bier
2Sa 3:31 king David himself followed the *b'*.
Lu 7:14 And he came and touched the *b'*:

Bigtha (*big'-thah*)
Es 1:10 Harbona, *B'*, and Abagtha,

Bigthan (*big'-than*) See also BIGTHANA.
Es 2:21 king's chamberlains, *B'* and

Bigthana (*big'-than-ah*) See also BIGTHAN.
Es 6: 2 Mordecai had told of *B'* and

Bigvai (*big'-vahee*)
Ezr 2: 2 Mizpar, *B'*, Rehum, Baanah.
14 The children of *B'*, two thousand
8:14 Of the sons also of *B'*; Uthai, and
Ne 7: 7 Bilshan, Mispereth, *B'*, Nehum,
19 The children of *B'*, two thousand
10:16 Adonijah, *B'*, Adin,

Bildad (*bil'-dad*)
Job 2:11 *B'* the Shuhite, and Zophar
8: 1 Then answered *B'* the Shuhite,
18: 1 *B'* the Shuhite, and said,
25: 1 *B'* the Shuhite, and said,
42: 9 Temanite and *B'* the Shuhite

Bileam (*bil'-e-am*) See also IBLEAM.
1Ch 6:70 suburbs, and *B'* with her suburbs,

Bilgah (*bil'-gah*)
1Ch 24:14 The fifteenth to *B'*, the
Ne 12: 5 Miamin, Maadiah, *B'*,
18 Of *B'*, Shammua; of Shemaiah,

Bilgai (*bil'-gahee*)
Ne 10: 8 Maaziah, *B'*, Shemaiah: these

Bilhah (*bil'-hah*) See also BALAH.
Ge 29:29 *B'* his handmaid to be her
30: 3 Behold my maid *B'*, go in unto
4 gave him *B'* her handmaid to
5 And *B'* conceived, and bare
7 And *B'* Rachel's maid conceived
35:22 went and lay with *B'* his father's
25 And the sons of *B'*, Rachel's
37: 2 the lad was with the sons of *B'*,
46:25 These are the sons of *B'*, which
1Ch 4:29 And at *B'*, and at Ezem, and at
7:13 and Shallum, the sons of *B'*.

Bilhan (*bil'-han*)
Ge 36:27 *B'*, and Zaavan, and Akan.
1Ch 1:42 Ezer; *B'*, and Zavan, and Jakan.
7:10 The sons also of Jediael; *B'*:
10 and the sons of *B'*; Jeush,

bill
De 24: 1 write her a *b'* of divorcement,
3 and write her a *b'* of divorcement,
Isa 50: 1 Where is the *b'* of your mother's
Jer 3: 8 and given her a *b'* of divorce;
M'r 10: 4 to write a *b'* of divorcement,
Lu 16: 6, 7 he said unto him, Take thy *b'*,

billows
Ps 42: 7 all thy waves and thy *b'* are
Jon 2: 3 all thy *b'* and thy waves passed

Bilshan (*bil'-shan*)
Ezr 2: 2 Reelaiah, Mordecai, *B'*, Mizpar,
Ne 7: 7 Nahamani, Mordecai, *B'*,

Bimhal (*bim'-hal*)
1Ch 7:33 Pasach, and *B'*, and Ashvath.

bind See also BINDETH; BINDING; BOUND.
Ex 28:28 they shall *b'* the breastplate
39:21 And they did *b'* the breastplate
Nu 30: 2 swear an oath to *b'* his soul
3 Lord, and *b'* herself by a bond,
De 6: 8 thou shalt *b'* them for a sign
11:18 and *b'* them for a sign upon
14:25 *b'* up the money in thine hand,
Jos 2:18 thou shalt *b'* this line of scarlet
J'g 15:10 To *b'* Samson are we come up,
12 We are come down to *b'* thee,
J'g 15:13 but we will *b'* thee fast, and
16: 5 that we may *b'* him to afflict him:
7 they *b'* me with seven green withs
11 If they *b'* me fast with new ropes
Job 31:36 and *b'* it as a crown to me.
38:31 Canst thou *b'* the sweet
39:10 Canst thou *b'* the unicorn with
40:13 and *b'* their faces in secret.
41: 5 or wilt thou *b'* him for thy
Ps 105:22 To *b'* his princes at his pleasure;
118:27 *b'* the sacrifice with cords, even
149: 8 To *b'* their kings with chains,
Pro 3: 3 *b'* them about thy neck; write
6:21 *B'* them continually upon thine
7: 3 *B'* them upon thy fingers, write
Isa 8:16 *B'* up the testimony, seal the law
49:18 and *b'* them on thee, as a bride
61: 1 to *b'* up the brokenhearted,
Jer 51:63 thou shalt *b'* a stone to it, and
Eze 3:25 and shall *b'* thee with them, and
5: 3 and *b'* them in thy skirts.
24:17 *b'* the tire of thine head upon
30:21 to put a roller to *b'* it, to make
34:16 *b'* up that which was broken,
Da 3:20 were in his army to *b'* Shadrach,
Ho 6: 1 smitten, and he will *b'* us up.
10:10 when they shall *b'* themselves
Mic 1:13 *b'* the chariot to the swift beast:
M't 12:29 except he first *b'* the strong man?
13:30 *b'* them in bundles to burn them:
16:19 whatsoever thou shalt *b'* on earth
18:18 shall *b'* on earth shall be bound in
22:13 *B'* him hand and foot, and take
23: 4 For they *b'* heavy burdens and
M'r 3:27 he will first *b'* the strong man;
5: 3 no man could *b'* him, no, not with
Ac 9:14 to *b'* all that call on thy name.
12: 8 thyself, and *b'* on thy sandals.
21:11 the Jews at Jerusalem *b'* the man

bindeth
Job 5:18 for he maketh sore, and *b'* up:
26: 8 He *b'* up the waters in his thick
28:11 *b'* the floods from overflowing;
30:18 it *b'* me about as the collar of my
36:13 they cry not when he *b'* them.
Ps 129: 7 nor he that *b'* sheaves his bosom.
147: 3 in heart, and *b'* up their wounds.
Pr 26: 8 As he that *b'* a stone in a sling,
Isa 30:26 that the Lord *b'* up the breach

binding
Ge 37: 7 For, behold, we were *b'* sheaves
49:11 *B'* his foal unto the vine, and his
Ex 28:32 it shall have a *b'* of woven work
Nu 30:13 every *b'* oath to afflict the soul,
Ac 22: 4 *b'* and delivering into prisons

Binea (*bin'-e-ah*)
1Ch 8:37 Moza begat *B'*: Rapha was his
9:43 Moza begat *B'*; and Rephaiah

Binnui (*bin'-nu-ee*)
Ezr 8:33 Noadiah the son of *B'*, Levites;
10:30 Mattaniah, Bezaleel, and *B'*, and
38 And Bani, and *B'*, Shimei,
Ne 3:24 After him repaired *B'* the son of
7:15 The children of *B'*, six hundred
10: 9 the son of Azaniah, *B'* of the sons
12: 8 Moreover the Levites: Jeshua, *B'*,

bird See also BIRD'S; BIRDS.
Ge 7:14 his kind, every *b'* of every sort.
Le 14: 6 As for the living *b'*, he shall take
6 the living *b'* in the blood of the *b'*
7 and shall let the living *b'* loose
51 and the scarlet, and the living *b'*,
51 them in the blood of the slain *b'*,
52 the house with the blood of the *b'*,
52 living *b'*, and with the cedar wood,
53 But he shall let go the living *b'*
Job 41: 5 thou play with him as with a *b'*?
Ps 11: 1 Flee as a *b'* to your mountain?
124: 7 *b'* out of the snare of the fowlers:
Pr 1:17 spread in the sight of any *b'*.
6: 5 a *b'* from the hand of the fowler.
7:23 as a *b'* hasteth to the snare, and
26: 2 As the *b'* by wandering, as the
27: 8 As a *b'* that wandereth from
Ec 10:20 *b'* of the air shall carry the voice,
12: 4 the voice of the *b'*, and all the
Isa 16: 2 wandering *b'* cast out of the nest,
46:11 a ravenous *b'* from the east,
Jer 12: 9 heritage is unto me as a speckled *b'*,
La 3:52 enemies chased me sore, like a *b'*,
Ho 9:11 their glory shall fly away like a *b'*,
11:11 shall tremble as a *b'* out of Egypt,
Am 3: 5 Can a *b'* fall in a snare upon the
Re 18: 2 of every unclean and hateful *b'*.

bird's
De 22: 6 *b'* nest chance to be before thee

birds See also BIRDS'.
Ge 15:10 another: but the *b'* divided he not.
40:17 and the *b'* did eat them out of the
19 *b'* shall eat thy flesh from off thee.
Le 14: 4 cleansed two *b'* alive and clean,
5 that one of the *b'* be killed
49 take to cleanse the house two *b'*,
50 and he shall kill the one of the *b'*
De 14:11 Of all clean *b'* ye shall eat.
2Sa 21:10 neither the *b'* of the air to rest
Ps 104:17 Where the *b'* make their nests:
Ec 9:12 and as the *b'* that are caught in
Ca 2:12 time of the singing of *b'* is come,
Isa 31: 5 As *b'* flying, so will the Lord of
Jer 4:25 the *b'* of the heavens were fled.
5:27 As a cage is full of *b'*, so are their
12: 4 beasts are consumed, and the *b'*;
Jer 12: 9 as a speckled bird, the *b'* round
Eze 39: 4 give thee unto the ravenous *b'*
M't 8:20 and the *b'* of the air have nests;
13:32 so that the *b'* of the air come
Lu 9:58 holes, and *b'* of the air have nests;
Ro 1:23 like to corruptible man, and to *b'*,
1Co 15:39 of fishes, and another of *b'*.
Jas 3: 7 every kind of beasts, and of *b'*,

birds'
Da 4:33 and his nails like *b'* claws.

Birei See BETH-BIREI.

Birsha (*bur'-shah*)
Ge 14: 2 and with *B'* king of Gomorrah,

birth See also BIRTHDAY; BIRTHRIGHT.
Ex 28:10 other stone, according to their *b'*.
2Ki 19: 3 for the children are come to the *b'*,
Job 3:16 untimely *b'* I had not been;
Ps 58: 8 like the untimely *b'* of a woman,
Ec 6: 3 an untimely *b'* is better than he.
7: 1 of death than the day of one's *b'*.
Isa 37: 3 the children are come to the *b'*,
66: 9 I bring to the *b'*, and not cause
Eze 16: 3 Thy *b'* and thy nativity is of the
Ho 9:11 from the *b'*, and from the womb,
M't 1:18 the *b'* of Jesus Christ was on this
Lu 1:14 and many shall rejoice at his *b'*.
Joh 9: 1 man which was blind from his *b'*.
Ga 4:19 I travail in *b'* again until Christ
Re 12: 2 cried, travailing in *b'*, and pained

birthday
Ge 40:20 which was Pharaoh's *b'*,
M't 14: 6 when Herod's *b'* was kept, the
M'r 6:21 Herod on his *b'* made a supper

birthright
Ge 25:31 said, Sell me this day thy *b'*.
32 what profit shall this *b'* do to me?
33 and he sold his *b'* unto Jacob.
34 way: thus Esau despised his *b'*.
27:36 he took away my *b'*; and, behold,
43:33 the firstborn according to his *b'*,
1Ch 5: 1 his *b'* was given unto the sons
1 is not to be reckoned after the *b'*.
2 ruler; but the *b'* was Joseph's:)
Heb 12:16 for one morsel of meat sold his *b'*.

Birzavith (*bur'-za-vith*)
1Ch 7:31 Malchiel, who is the father of *B'*.

Bishlam (*bish'-lam*)
Ezr 4: 7 days of Artaxerxes, wrote *B'*,

bishop See also BISHOPRICK; BISHOPS.
1Ti 3: 1 If a man desire the office of a *b'*,
2 A *b'* then must be blameless, the
2Ti *subscr.* Timotheus, ordained the first *b'*
Tit 1: 7 For a *b'* must be blameless, as the
subscr. Titus, ordained the first *b'* of
1Pe 2:25 Shepherd and *B'* of your souls.

bishoprick
Ac 1:20 therein: and his *b'* let another

bishops
Ph'p 1: 1 Philippi, with the *b'* and deacons:

bit See also BITS
Nu 21: 6 people, and they *b'* the people;
Ps 32: 9 be held in with *b'* and bridle,
Am 5:19 on the wall, and a serpent *b'* him.

bite See also BACKBITE; BIT; BITETH; BITTEN.
Ec 10: 8 an hedge, a serpent shall *b'* him.
11 will *b'* without enchantment;
Jer 8:17 be charmed, and they shall *b'* you,
Am 9: 3 the serpent, and he shall *b'* them:
Mic 3: 5 that *b'* with their teeth, and cry,
Hab 2: 7 up suddenly that shall *b'* thee,
Ga 5:15 if ye *b'* and devour one another,

biteth See also BACKBITETH.
Ge 49:17 the path, that *b'* the horse heels,
Pr 23:32 it *b'* like a serpent, and stingeth

Bithiah (*bith-i'-ah*)
1Ch 4:18 the sons of *B'* the daughter of

Bithron (*bith'-ron*)
2Sa 2:29 went through all *B'*, and they

Bithynia (*bith-in'-e-ah*)
Ac 16: 7 Mysia, they assayed to go into *B'*:
1Pe 1: 1 Galatia, Cappadocia, Asia, and *B'*,

bits
Jas 3: 3 we put *b'* in the horses' mouths,

bitten See also HUNGERBITTEN.
Nu 21: 8 every one that is *b'*, when he
9 if a serpent had *b'* any man, when

bitter
Ge 27:34 with a great and exceeding *b'* cry,
Ex 1:14 made their lives *b'* with hard
12: 8 with *b'* herbs they shall eat it.
15:23 waters of Marah, for they were *b'*:
Nu 5:18 *b'* water that causeth the curse:
19 be thou free from this *b'* water
23 blot them out with the *b'* water:
24 drink the *b'* water that causeth
24 enter into her, and become *b'*.
27 into her, and become *b'*, and her
9:11 unleavened bread and *b'* herbs.
De 32:24 heat, and with *b'* destruction:
32 of gall, their clusters are *b'*:
2Ki 14:26 of Israel, that it was very *b'*
Es 4: 1 cried with a loud and a *b'* cry;
Job 3:20 and life unto the *b'* in soul;
13:26 thou writest *b'* things against me,
23: 2 Even to day is my complaint *b'*:
Ps 64: 3 to shoot their arrows, even *b'*
Pr 5: 4 her end is *b'* as wormwood, sharp
27: 7 to the hungry soul every *b'* thing

Ec 7:26 more b' than death the woman,
Isa 5:20 put b' for sweet, and sweet for b'!
24: 9 strong drink shall be b' to them
Jer 2:19 it is an evil thing and b', that thou
4:18 is thy wickedness, because it is b',
6:26 an only son, most b' lamentation:
31:15 in Ramah, lamentation, and b'
Eze 27:31 bitterness of heart and b' wailing.
Am 8:10 and the end thereof as a b' day.
Hab 1: 6 Chaldeans, that b' and hasty
Col 3:19 wives, and be not b' against them.
Jas 3:11 same place sweet water and b'?
14 if ye have b' envying and strife
Re 8:11 waters, because they were made b'.
10: 9 it shall make thy belly b', but it
10 I had eaten it, my belly was b'.

bitterly
J'g 5:23 curse ye b' the inhabitants thereof;
Ru 1:20 Almighty hath dealt very b' with
Isa 22: 4 I will weep b', labor not to comfort
33: 7 of peace shall weep b'.
Eze 27:30 and shall cry b', and shall cast up
Ho 12:14 provoked him to anger most b':
Zep 1:14 the mighty man shall cry there b'.
M't 26:75 And he went out, and wept b'.
Lu 22:62 Peter went out, and wept b'.

bittern
Isa 14:23 make it a possession for the b',
34:11 cormorant and the b' shall
Zep 2:14 cormorant and the b' shall lodge

bitterness
1Sa 1:10 she was in b' of soul, and prayed
15:32 said, Surely the b' of death is past.
2Sa 2:26 that it will be b' in the latter end?
Job 7:11 I will complain in the b' of my
9:18 breath, but filleth me with b'.
10: 1 I will speak in the b' of my soul.
21:25 another dieth in the b' of his soul,
Pr 14:10 The heart knoweth his own b';
17:25 father, and b' to her that bare
Isa 38:15 my years in the b' of my soul.
17 Behold, for peace I had great b':
La 1: 4 are afflicted, and she is in b'.
3:15 He hath filled me with b',
Eze 3:14 took me away, and I went in b',
21: 6 and with b' sigh before their eyes.
27:31 they shall weep for thee with b'
Zec 12:10 and shall be in b' for him,
10 as one that is in b'
Ac 8:23 thou art in the gall of b', and in
Ro 3:14 mouth is full of cursing and b':
Eph 4:31 Let all b', and wrath, and anger,
Heb 12:15 lest any root of b' springing up

Bizjothjah (*biz-joth'-jah*)
Jos 15:28 and Beer-sheba, and B',

Biztha (*biz'-thah*)
Es 1:10 he commanded Mehuman, B',

black See also BLACKER; BLACKISH.
Le 13:31 that there is no b' hair in it;
37 there is b' hair grown up therein;
1Ki 18:45 heaven was b' with clouds and
Es 1: 6 of red, and blue, and white, and b',
Job 30:30 My skin is b' upon me, and my
Pr 7: 9 in the evening, in the b' and
Ca 1: 5 I am b', but comely, O ye
6 not upon me, because I am b',
5:11 his locks are bushy, and b' as a
Jer 4:28 and the heavens above be b':
8:21 I am b'; astonishment hath taken
14: 2 they are b' unto the ground; and
La 5:10 Our skin was b' like an oven
Zec 6: 2 in the second chariot b' horses;
6 The b' horses which are therein
M't 5:36 not make one hair white or b'.
Re 6: 5 And I beheld, and lo a b' horse;
12 sun became b' as sackcloth of

blacker
La 4: 8 Their visage is b' than a coal;

blackish
Job 6:16 Which are b' by reason of the ice,

blackness
Job 3: 5 let the b' of the day terrify it.
Isa 50: 3 I clothe the heavens with b',
Joe 2: 6 pained: all faces shall gather b'.
Na 2:10 the faces of them all gather b'.
Heb 12:18 nor unto b', and darkness, and
Jude 13 to whom is reserved the b' of

blade
J'g 3:22 the haft also went in after the b';
22 and the fat closed upon the b',
Job 31:22 arm fall from my shoulder b',
M't 13:26 But when the b' was sprung up,
M'k 4:28 first the b', then the ear, after that

blains
Ex 9: 9 be a boil breaking forth with b'
10 a boil breaking forth with b'

blame See also BLAMED; BLAMELESS; UNBLAMEABLE.
Ge 43: 9 then let me bear the b' for ever:
44:32 then I shall bear the b' to my
2Co 8:20 that no man should b' us in this
Eph 1: 4 be holy and without b'

blamed
2Co 6: 3 that the ministry be not b':
Ga 2:11 the face, because he was to be b'.

blameless
Ge 44:10 my servant; and ye shall be b'.
Jos 2:17 We will be b' of this thine oath
J'g 15: 3 Now shall I be more b' than the
M't 12: 5 profane the sabbath, and are b'?
Lu 1: 6 and ordinances of the Lord b'.
1Co 1: 8 that ye may be b' in the day of
Ph'p 2:15 that ye may be b' and harmless,
3: 6 which is in the law, b'.
1Th 5:23 be preserved b' unto the coming
1Ti 3: 2 a bishop then must be b', the
10 office of a deacon, being found b'.
5: 7 in charge, that they may be b'.
Tit 1: 6 if any be b', the husband of one
7 For a bishop must be b', as the
2Pe 3:14 in peace, without spot, and b'.

blaspheme See also BLASPHEMED; BLASPHEMEST; BLASPHEMETH; BLASPHEMING.
2Sa 12:14 the enemies of the Lord to b',
1Ki 21:10 Thou didst b' God and the king.
13 Naboth did b' God and the king.
Ps 74:10 shall the enemy b' thy name for
M'r 3:28 wherewith soever they shall b':
29 he that shall b' against the Holy
Ac 26:11 and compelled them to b';
1Ti 1:20 that they may learn not to b'.
Jas 2: 7 Do not they b' that worthy name
Re 13: 6 to b' his name, and his tabernacle,

blasphemed
Le 24:11 Israelitish woman's son b' the
2Ki 19: 6 of the king of Assyria have b' me.
22 hast thou reproached and b'?
Ps 74:18 the foolish people have b' thy
Isa 37: 6 of the king of Assyria have b' me.
23 hast thou reproached and b'?
52: 5 name continually every day is b'.
65: 7 upon the mountains, and b' me
Eze 20:27 in this your fathers have b' me,
Ac 18: 6 they opposed themselves, and b',
Ro 2:24 the name of God is b' among the
1Ti 6: 1 God and his doctrine be not b'.
Tit 2: 5 that the word of God be not b'.
Re 16: 9 heat, and b' the name of God,
11 b' the God of heaven because of
21 men b' God because of the plague

blasphemer See also BLASPHEMERS.
1Ti 1:13 Who was before a b', and a

blasphemers
Ac 19:37 churches, nor yet b' of your
2Ti 3: 2 covetous, boasters, proud, b',

blasphemest
Joh 10:36 Thou b'; because I said, I am the

blasphemeth
Le 24:16 he that b' the name of the Lord,
16 when he b' the name of the Lord,
Ps 44:16 of him that reproacheth and b';
M't 9: 3 within themselves, This man b'.
Lu 12:10 unto him that b' against the Holy

blasphemies
Eze 35:12 I have heard all thy b' which thou
M't 15:19 thefts, false witness, b':
M'r 2: 7 Why doth this man thus speak b'?
3:28 b' wherewith soever they shall
Lu 5:21 Who is this which speaketh b'?
Re 13: 5 mouth speaking great things and b';

blaspheming
Ac 13:45 by Paul, contradicting and b'.

blasphemous
Ac 6:11 we have heard him speak b' words
13 ceaseth not to speak b' words

blasphemously
Lu 22:65 things b' spake they against him.

blasphemy See also BLASPHEMIES.
2Ki 19: 3 of trouble, and of rebuke, and b':
Isa 37: 3 trouble, and of rebuke, and of b':
M't 12:31 All manner of sin and b' shall be
31 the b' against the Holy Ghost
26:65 clothes, saying, He hath spoken b';
65 behold, now ye have heard his b'.
M'r 7:22 an evil eye, b', pride, foolishness:
14:64 Ye have heard the b': what think
Joh 10:33 for b'; and because that thou,
Col 3: 8 anger, wrath, malice, b', filthy
Re 2: 9 I know the b' of them which say
13: 1 and upon his heads the name of b'.
6 And he opened his mouth in b'
17: 3 full of names of b', having seven

blast See also BLASTED; BLASTING.
Ex 15: 8 And with the b' of thy nostrils
Jos 6: 5 when they make a long b' with the
2Sa 22:16 at the b' of the breath of his
2Ki 19: 7 I will send a b' upon him, and he
Job 4: 9 By the b' of God they perish, and
Ps 18:15 at the b' of the breath of thy
Isa 25: 4 when the b' of the terrible ones
37: 7 I will send a b' upon him, and he

blasted
Ge 41: 6 seven thin ears and b' with the
23 seven ears, withered, thin, and b'
27 seven empty ears b' with the east
2Ki 19:26 and as corn b' before it be grown
Isa 37:27 and as corn b' before it be grown

blasting
De 28:22 sword, and with b', and with
1Ki 8:37 famine, if there be pestilence, b',
2Ch 6:28 if there be b', or mildew, locusts,
Am 4: 9 I have smitten you with b' and
Hag 2:17 I smote you with b' and with

Blastus (*blas'tus*)
Ac 12:20 and having made B' the king's

blaze
M'r 1:45 and to b' abroad the matter,

bleating See also BLEATINGS.
1Sa 15:14 What meaneth then this b' of the

bleatings
J'g 5:16 to hear the b' of the flocks?

blemish See also BLEMISHES.
Ex 12: 5 Your lamb shall be without b', a
29: 1 and two rams without b',
Le 1: 3 let him offer a male without b':
10 he shall bring it a male without b'.
3: 1 he shall offer it without b' before
6 he shall offer it without b'.
4: 3 a young bullock without b' unto
23 of the goats, a male without b':
28 goats, a female without b', for his
32 shall bring it a female without b'.
5:15 a ram without b' out of the flocks,
18 he shall bring a ram without b'
6: 6 a ram without b' out of the flock,
9: 2 for a burnt offering without b', and
3 of the first year, without b', for a
14:10 shall take two he lambs without b',
10 lamb of the first year without b',
21:17 generations that hath any b',
18 man he be that hath a b',
20 or that hath a b' in his eye, or be
21 No man that hath a b' of the seed
21 he hath a b'; he shall not come
23 the altar, because he hath a b';
22:19 your own will a male without b',
20 whatsoever hath a b', that shall
21 there shall be no b' therein.
23:12 An he lamb without b' of the first
18 seven lambs without b' of the first
24:19 and if a man cause a b' in his
20 as he hath caused a b' in a
Nu 6:14 lamb of the first year without b'
14 lamb of the first year without b'
14 and one ram without b' for peace
19: 2 without spot, wherein is no b',
28:19 they shall be unto you without b':
31 (they shall be unto you without b')
29: 2 lambs of the first year without b':
8 they shall be unto you without b':
13 year: they shall be without b':
20 lambs of the first year without b';
23, 29, 32, 36 the first year without b':
De 15:21 be any b' therein, as if it be lame,
21 or blind, or have any ill b',
17: 1 bullock, or sheep, wherein is b',
2Sa 14:25 head there was no b' in him.
Eze 43:22 offer a kid of the goats without b'
23 a young bullock without b', and
23 a ram out of the flock without b'.
25 a ram out of the flock, without b'.
45:18 take a young bullock without b',
23 seven rams without b' daily the
46: 4 six lambs without b',
4 and a ram without b'.
6 a young bullock without b', and
6 a ram: they shall be without b'.
13 lamb of the first year without b':
Da 1: 4 Children in whom was no b', but
Eph 5:27 it should be holy and without b'.
1Pe 1:19 as of a lamb without b' and without

blemishes
Le 22:25 corruption in them, and b' be in
2Pe 2:13 Spots they are and b', sporting

bless See also BLESSED; BLESSEST; BLESSETH; BLESSING.
Ge 12: 2 and I will b' thee, and make thy
3 And I will b' them that b' thee,
17:16 And I will b' her, and give thee a
16 son also of her: yea, I will b' her,
22:17 in blessing I will b' thee, and in
26: 3 be with thee, and will b' thee: for
24 for I am with thee, and will b' thee,
27: 4 that my soul may b' thee before I
7 and b' thee before the Lord before
10 he may eat, and that he may b' thee
19 venison, that thy soul may b' me.
25 venison, that my soul may b' thee.
31 venison, that thy soul may b' me.
34 B' me, even me also, O my father.
38 b' me, even me also, O my father.
28: 3 God Almighty b' thee, and make
32:26 let thee go, except thou b' me.
48: 9 thee, unto me, and I will b' them.
16 me from all evil, b' the lads;
20 In thee shall Israel b', saying, God
49:25 the Almighty, who shall b' thee
Ex 12:32 said, and be gone; and b' me also.
20:24 come unto thee, and I will b' thee.
23:25 and he shall b' thy bread, and thy
Nu 6:23 on this wise ye shall b' the children
24 The Lord b' thee, and keep thee:
27 children of Israel; and I will b'
23:20 have received commandment to b':
25 Neither curse them at all, nor b'
24: 1 it pleased the Lord to b' Israel, he
De 1:11 and b' you, as he hath promised
7:13 will love thee, and b' thee, and
13 he will also b' the fruit of thy
8:10 then thou shalt b' the Lord thy
10: 8 unto him, and to b' in his name,
14:29 the Lord thy God may b' thee in all
15: 4 the Lord shall greatly b' thee in
10 thy God shall b' thee in all thy
18 thy God shall b' thee in all that
16:15 the Lord thy God shall b' thee in
21: 5 unto him, and to b' in the name of
23:20 the Lord thy God may b' thee in all
24:13 sleep in his own raiment, and b'
19 thy God may b' thee in all the work
26:15 from heaven, and b' thy people
27:12 upon mount Gerizim to b' the
28: 8 and he shall b' thee in the land
12 and to b' all the work of thine

De 29:19 that he b' himself in his heart,
30:16 and the Lord thy God shall b'
33:11 B', Lord, his substance, and accept
Jos 8:33 that they should b' the people of
J'g 5: 9 among the people. B' ye the Lord.
Ru 2: 4 answered him, the Lord b' thee.
1Sa 9:13 because he doth b' the sacrifice;
2Sa 6:20 Then David returned to b' his
7:29 let it please thee to b' the house of
8:10 to salute him, and to b' him,
21: 3 that ye may b' the inheritance of
1Ki 1:47 servants came to b' our lord king
1Ch 4:10 Oh that thou wouldest b' me
16:43 house: and David returned to b'
17:27 to b' the house of thy servant, that
23:13 minister unto him, and to b' in his
29:20 the congregation, Now b' the Lord
Ne 9: 5 b' the Lord your God for ever and
Ps 5:12 For thou, Lord, wilt b' the
16: 7 I will b' the Lord, who hath given
26:12 in the congregations will I b' the
28: 9 Save thy people, and b' thine
29:11 the Lord will b' his people with
34: 1 I will b' the Lord at all times: his
62: 4 they b' with their mouth, but they
63: 4 Thus will I b' thee while I live:
66: 8 O b' our God, ye people, and make
67: 1 God be merciful unto us and b' us;
6 God, even our own God, shall b' us.
7 God shall b' us; and all the ends of
68:26 B' ye God in the congregations,
96: 2 Sing unto the Lord, b' his name;
100: 4 be thankful unto him, and b' his
103: 1 B' the Lord, O my soul, and all
1 that is within me, b' his holy
2 B' the Lord, O my soul, and
20 B' the Lord, ye his angels, that
21 B' ye the Lord, all ye his hosts; ye
22 B' the Lord, all his works in all
22 places of his dominion; b' the Lord,
104: 1 B' the Lord, O my soul. O Lord,
35 B' thou the Lord, O my soul.
109:28 Let them curse, but b' thou: when
115:12 he will b' us; he will b' the house
12 of Israel; he will b' the house of
13 He will b' them that fear the Lord,
18 But we will b' the Lord from this
128: 5 The Lord shall b' thee out of Zion:
129: 8 upon you: we b' you in the name
132:15 I will abundantly b' her provision:
134: 1 b' ye the Lord, all ye servants of
2 in the sanctuary, and b' the Lord.
3 heaven and earth b' thee out of
135:19 B' the Lord, O house of Israel:
19 b' the Lord, O house of Aaron:
20 B' the Lord, O house of Levi:
20 ye that fear the Lord, b' the Lord.
145: 1 and I will b' thy name for ever
2 Every day will I b' thee; and I will
10 Lord; and thy saints shall b' thee.
21 and let all flesh b' his holy name
Pr 30:11 and doth not b' their mother.
Isa 19:25 Whom the Lord of hosts shall b',
65:16 shall b' himself in the God of truth;
Jer 4: 2 and the nations shall b' themselves
31:23 The Lord b' thee, O habitation of
Hag 2:19 forth: from this day will I b' you.
M't 5:44 b' them that curse you, do good
Lu 6:28 B' them that curse you, and pray
Ac 3:26 sent him to b' you, in turning
Ro 12:14 B' them which persecute you: b',
1Co 4:12 being reviled, we b'; being
10:16 The cup of blessing which we b',
14:16 Else, when thou shalt b' with the
Heb 6:14 Surely blessing I will b' thee, and
Jas 3: 9 Therewith b' we God, even the

blessed

Ge 1:22 And God b' them, saying,
28 God b' them, and God said unto
2: 3 And God b' the seventh day, and
5: 2 created he them; and b' them,
9: 1 And God b' Noah and his sons,
26 B' be the Lord God of Shem;
12: 3 shall all families of the earth be b'.
14:19 And he b' him, and said,
19 B' be Abram of the most high
20 And b' the most high God, which
17:20 Behold, I have b' him, and will
18:18 the nations of the earth shall be b'
22:18 all the nations of the earth be b';
24: 1 and the Lord had b' Abraham in
27 B' be the Lord God of my master
31 Come in, thou b' of the Lord;
35 Lord hath b' my master greatly;
48 and b' the Lord God of my master
60 And they b' Rebekah, and said unto
25:11 Abraham, that God b' his son Isaac;
26: 4 the nations of the earth be b';
12 hundredfold: and the Lord b' him.
29 thou art now the b' of the Lord.
27:23 brother Esau's hands: so he b' him.
27 and b' him, and said, See, the smell
27 of a field which the Lord hath b':
29 and b' be he that blesseth thee.
33 thou camest, and have b' him?
33 yea, and he shall be b'.
41 wherewith his father b' him:
28: 1 Isaac called Jacob, and b' him,
6 Esau saw that Isaac had b' Jacob,
6 and that as he b' him he gave him
14 all the families of the earth be b'.
30:13 for the daughters will call me b':
27 that the Lord hath b' me for thy
30 and the Lord hath b' thee since my
31:55 and b' them: and Laban departed,
32:29 my name? And he b' him there.
Ge 35: 9 out of Padan-aram, and b' him.
39: 5 the Lord b' the Egyptian's house
47: 7 Pharaoh: and Jacob b' Pharaoh.
10 Jacob b' Pharaoh, and went out
48: 3 in the land of Canaan, and b' me,
15 And he b' Joseph, and said, God,
20 And he b' them that day, saying,
49:28 spake unto them, and b' them;
28 according to his blessing he b' them.
Ex 18:10 Jethro said, B' be the Lord,
20:11 the Lord b' the sabbath day, and
39:43 they done it: and Moses b' them.
Le 9:22 toward the people, and b' them,
23 and came out, and b' the people:
Nu 22: 6 that he whom thou blessest is b',
12 curse the people: for they are b'.
23:11 thou hast b' them altogether.
20 he hath b'; and I cannot reverse it.
24: 9 B' is he that blesseth thee, and
10 thou hast altogether b' them these
De 2: 7 the Lord thy God hath b' thee in
7:14 Thou shalt be b' above all people:
12: 7 the Lord thy God hath b' thee.
14:24 the Lord thy God hath b' thee:
15:14 the Lord thy God hath b' thee
16:10 the Lord thy God hath b' thee:
28: 3 B' shalt thou be in the city,
3 and b' shalt thou be in the field.
4 B' shall be the fruit of thy body,
5 B' shall be thy basket and thy
6 B' shalt thou be when thou comest
6 and b' shalt thou be when thou
33: 1 Moses the man of God b' the
13 B' of the Lord be his land, for
20 B' be he that enlargeth Gad: he
24 Let Asher be b' with children;
Jos 14:13 And Joshua b' him, and gave unto
17:14 forasmuch as the Lord hath b' me
22: 6 So Joshua b' them, and sent them
7 unto their tents, then he b' them,
33 and the children of Israel b' God,
24:10 Balaam; therefore he b' you still:
J'g 5:24 B' above women shall Jael the wife
24 b' shall she be above women
13:24 child grew, and the Lord b' him.
17: 2 B' be thou of the Lord, my son.
Ru 2:19 b' be he that did take knowledge
20 B' be he of the Lord, who hath not
3:10 B' be thou of the Lord, my
4:14 B' be the Lord, which hath not
1Sa 2:20 And Eli b' Elkanah and his wife,
15:13 B' be thou of the Lord: I have
23:21 B' be ye of the Lord; for ye have
25:32 B' be the Lord God of Israel,
33 And b' be thy advice,
33 and b' be thou, which hast kept.
39 B' be the Lord, that hath pleaded
26:25 B' be thou, my son David: thou
2Sa 2: 5 B' be ye of the Lord, that ye have
6:11 and the Lord b' Obed-edom, and
12 The Lord hath b' the house of
18 he b' the people in the name of the
7:29 house of thy servant be b' forever.
13:25 he would not go, but b' him.
18:28 B' be the Lord thy God, which hath
19:39 king kissed Barzillai, and b' him;
22:47 the Lord liveth; and b' be my rock;
1Ki 1:48 B' be the Lord God of Israel,
2:45 and king Solomon shall be b',
5: 7 B' be the Lord this day, which
8:14 and b' all the congregation of
15 B' be the Lord God of Israel, which
55 stood, and b' all the congregation
56 B' be the Lord, that hath given
66 and they b' the king, and went
10: 9 B' be the Lord thy God, which
1Ch 13:14 And the Lord b' the house of
16: 2 he b' the people in the name of the
36 B' be the Lord God of Israel for
17:27 O Lord, and it shall be b' for ever.
26: 5 the eighth: for God b' him.
29:10 Wherefore David b' the Lord
10 B' be thou, Lord God of Israel our
20 all the congregation b' the Lord
2Ch 2:12 B' be the Lord God of Israel, that
6: 3 and b' the whole congregation of
4 B' be the Lord God of Israel, who
9: 8 B' be the Lord thy God, which
20:26 for there they b' the Lord:
30:27 Levites arose and b' the people:
31: 8 they b' the Lord, and his people
10 for the Lord hath b' his people;
Ezr 7:27 B' be the Lord God of our fathers,
Ne 8: 6 Ezra b' the Lord, the great God.
9: 5 and b' be thy glorious name, which
11: 2 And the people b' all the men,
Job 1:10 hast b' the work of his hands,
21 b' be the name of the Lord.
29:11 the ear heard me, then it b' me;
31:20 If his loins have not b' me, and if
42:12 So the Lord b' the latter end of
Ps 1: 1 B' is the man that walketh not
2:12 B' are all they that put their
18:46 Lord liveth; and b' be my rock;
21: 6 hast made him most b' for ever:
28: 6 B' be the Lord, because he hath
31:21 B' be the Lord: for he hath
32: 1 B' is he whose transgression is
2 B' is the man unto whom the Lord
33:12 B' is the nation whose God is the
34: 8 b' is the man that trusteth in him.
37:22 For such as be b' of him shall
26 and lendeth; and his seed is b'.
40: 4 B' is that man that maketh the
41: 1 B' is he that considereth the poor:
2 and he shall be b' upon the earth:
Ps 41:13 B' be the Lord God of Israel
45: 2 therefore God hath b' thee for ever.
49:18 while he lived he b' his soul: and
65: 4 B' is the man whom thou choosest,
66:20 B' be God, which hath not turned
68:19 B' be the Lord, who daily loadeth
35 power unto his people. B' be God.
72:17 sun: and men shall be b' in him:
17 him: all nations shall call him b'.
18 B' be the Lord God, the God of
19 b' be his glorious name for ever:
84: 4 B' are they that dwell in thy house:
5 B' is the man whose strength is in
12 b' is the man that trusteth in thee.
89:15 B' is the people that know the
52 B' be the Lord for evermore.
94:12 B' is the man whom thou
106: 3 B' are they that keep judgment,
48 B' be the Lord God of Israel from
112: 1 B' is the man that feareth the Lord,
2 of the upright shall be b'.
113: 2 B' be the name of the Lord from
115:15 Ye are b' of the Lord which made
118:26 B' be he that cometh in the name
26 we have b' you out of the house of
119: 1 B' are the undefiled in the way,
2 B' are they that keep his
12 B' art thou, O Lord: teach me
124: 6 B' be the Lord, who hath not
128: 1 B' is every one that feareth the
4 thus shall the man be b' that
135:21 B' be the Lord out of Zion, which
144: 1 B' be the Lord my strength,
147:13 he hath b' thy children within
Pr 5:18 Let thy fountain be b': and rejoice
8:32 for b' are they that keep my ways.
34 B' is the man that heareth me,
10: 7 The memory of the just is b': but
20: 7 his children are b' after him.
21 the end thereof shall not be b'.
22: 9 hath a bountiful eye shall be b';
31:28 children arise up, and call her b';
Ec 10:17 B' art thou, O land, when thy
Ca 6: 9 daughters saw her, and b' her;
Isa 19:25 B' be Egypt my people,
30:18 b' are all they that wait for him.
32:20 B' are ye that sow beside all
51: 2 I called him alone, and b' him,
56: 2 B' is the man that doeth this,
61: 9 the seed which the Lord hath b'.
65:23 the seed of the b' of the Lord,
66: 3 incense, as if he b' an idol.
Jer 17: 7 B' is the man that trusteth in the
20:14 wherein my mother bare me be b'.
Eze 3:12 B' be the glory of the Lord from
Da 2:19 Then Daniel b' the God of heaven.
20 B' be the name of God forever
3:28 B' be the God of Shadrach,
4:34 I b' the most High, and I praised
12:12 B' is he that waiteth, and cometh
Zec 11: 5 that sell them say, B' be the Lord;
Mal 3:12 And all nations shall call you b':
M't 5: 3 B' are the poor in spirit:
4 B' are they that mourn: for they
5 B' are the meek: for they shall
6 B' are they which do hunger and
7 B' are the merciful: for they shall
8 B' are the pure in heart: for they
9 B' are the peacemakers: for they
10 B' are they which are persecuted
11 B' are ye, when men shall revile
11: 6 And b' is he, whosoever shall not
13:16 But b' are your eyes, for they see:
14:19 he b', and brake, and gave
16:17 said unto him, B' art thou, Simon
21: 9 B' is he that cometh in the name
23:39 B' is he that cometh in the name
24:46 B' is that servant, whom his lord
25:34 ye b' of my Father, inherit the
26:26 b' it, and brake it, and gave it to
M'k 6:41 he looked up to heaven, and b',
8: 7 and he b', and commanded to set
10:16 hands upon them, and b' them.
11: 9 B' is he that cometh in the name
10 B' be the kingdom of our father
14:22 and b', and brake it, and gave to
61 thou the Christ, the Son of the B'?
Lu 1:28 thee: b' art thou among women,
42 B' art thou among women,
42 and b' is the fruit of thy womb.
45 b' is she that believed: for there
48 all generations shall call me b'.
68 B' be the Lord God of Israel;
2:28 him up in his arms, and b' God,
34 And Simeon b' them, and said
6:20 disciples, and said, B' be ye poor:
21 B' are ye that hunger now: for ye
21 B' are ye that weep now: for ye
22 B' are ye, when men shall hate
7:23 And b' is he, whosoever shall not
9:16 he b' them, and brake, and gave
10:23 B' are the eyes which see the
11:27 B' is the womb that bare thee,
28 Yea rather, b' are they that hear
12:37 B' are those servants, whom the
38 b' are those servants.
43 B' is that servant, whom his lord
13:35 B' is he that cometh in the name
14:14 thou shalt be b'; for they cannot
15 B' is he that shall eat bread in
19:38 B' be the king that cometh
23:29 they shall say, B' are the barren,
24:30 took bread, and b' it, and brake,
50 he lifted up his hands, and b' them.
51 while he b' them, he was parted
Joh 12:13 B' is the King of Israel that

Joh 20:29 *b*' are they that have not seen,
Ac 3:25 all the kindreds of the earth be *b*'.
20:35 more *b*' to give than to receive.
Ro 1:25 the Creator, who is *b*' for ever.
4: 7 *B*' are they whose iniquities are
8 *B*' is the man to whom the Lord
9: 5 who is over all, God *b*' for ever.
2Co 1: 3 *B*' be God, even the Father of our
11:31 Jesus Christ, which is *b*' for
Ga 3: 8 In thee shall all nations be *b*'.
9 are *b*' with faithful Abraham.
Eph 1: 3 *B*' be the God and Father of our
3 *b*' us with all spiritual blessings
1Ti 1:11 the glorious gospel of the *b*' God,
6:15 *b*' and only Potentate, the King
Tit 2:13 Looking for that *b*' hope, and the
Heb 7: 1 slaughter of the kings, and *b*' him;
6 *b*' him that had the promises.
7 contradiction the less is *b*' of
11:20 By faith Isaac *b*' Jacob and Esau
21 Jacob, when he was a dying, *b*'
Jas 1:12 *B*' is the man that endureth
25 this man shall be *b*' in his deed.
1Pe 1: 3 *B*' be the God and Father of our
Re 1: 3 *B*' is he that readeth, and they
14:13 *B*' are the dead which die in the
16:15 *B*' is he that watcheth, and
19: 9 *B*' are they which are called
20: 6 *B*' and holy is he that hath part
22: 7 *b*' is he that keepeth the sayings
14 *B*' are they that do his

blessedness
Ro 4: 6 also describeth the *b*' of the man,
9 Cometh this *b*' then upon the
Ga 4:15 Where is then the *b*' ye spake of?

blessest
Nu 22: 6 that he, whom thou *b*' is blessed,
1Ch 17:27 for thou *b*', O Lord, and it shall
Ps 65:10 it soft with showers: thou *b*' the

blesseth
Ge 27:29 and blessed be he that *b*' thee.
Nu 24: 9 Blessed is he that *b*' thee, and
De 15: 6 the Lord thy God *b*' thee, as he
Ps 10: 3 *b*' the covetous, whom the Lord
107:38 He *b*' them also, so that they are
Pr 3:33 but he *b*' the habitation of the just.
27:14 that *b*' his friend with a loud voice,
Isa 65:16 That he who *b*' himself in the earth

blessing See also BLESSINGS.
Ge 12: 2 great; and thou shalt be a *b*':
22:17 That in *b*' I will bless thee, and in
27:12 a curse upon me, and not a *b*'.
30 Isaac had made an end of *b*'
35 and hath taken away thy *b*'.
36 hath taken away my *b*'. And he
36 Hast thou not reserved a *b*'
38 Hast thou but one *b*', my father?
41 because of the *b*' wherewith his
28: 4 and give thee the *b*' of Abraham,
33:11 Take, I pray thee, my *b*' that is
39: 5 the *b*' of the Lord was upon all
49:28 every one according to his *b*' he
Ex 32:29 he may bestow upon you a *b*'
Le 25:21 I will command my *b*' upon you
De 11:26 you this day a *b*' and a curse;
27 A *b*', if ye obey the commandments
29 thou shalt put the *b*' upon mount
12:15 according to the *b*' of the Lord
16:17 according to the *b*' of the Lord
23: 5 thy God turned the curse into a *b*'
28: 8 The Lord shall command the *b*'
30: 1 the *b*' and the curse, which I have
19 life and death, *b*' and cursing:
33: 1 this is the *b*' wherewith Moses
7 And this is the *b*' of Judah:
16 *b*' come upon the head of Joseph,
23 and full with the *b*' of the Lord:
Jos 15:19 Who answereth, Give me a *b*';
J'g 1:15 Give me a *b*': for thou hast given
1Sa 25:27 now this *b*' with thine handmaid
2Sa 7:29 and with thy *b*' let the house of
2Ki 5:15 thee, take a *b*' of thy servant.
Ne 9: 5 is exalted above all *b*' and praise.
13: 2 God turned the curse into a *b*'.
Job 29:13 *b*' of him that was ready to perish
Ps 3: 8 thy *b*' is upon thy people.
24: 5 shall receive the *b*' from the Lord,
109:17 as he delighted not in *b*', so let it
129: 8 The *b*' of the Lord be upon you:
133: 3 there the Lord commanded the *b*',
Pr 10:22 The *b*' of the Lord, it maketh rich,
11:11 By the *b*' of the upright the city is
26 but *b*' shall be upon the head of
24:25 a good *b*' shall come upon them.
Isa 19:24 even a *b*' in the midst of the land:
44: 3 and my *b*' upon thine offspring:
65: 8 Destroy it not; for a *b*' is in it:
Eze 34:26 places round about my hill a *b*';
26 there shall be showers of *b*'.
44:30 that he may cause the *b*' to rest
Joe 2:14 repent, and leave a *b*' behind him;
Zec 8:13 I save you, and ye shall be a *b*':
Mal 3:10 pour you out a *b*', that there shall
Lu 24:53 in the temple, praising and *b*' God.
Ro 15:29 the fulness of the *b*' of the gospel
1Co 10:16 The cup of *b*' which we bless,
Ga 3:14 the *b*' of Abraham might come
Heb 6: 7 is dressed, receiveth *b*' from God:
14 Saying, Surely *b*' I will bless thee,
12:17 would have inherited the *b*',
Jas 3:10 mouth proceedeth *b*' and cursing.
1Pe 3: 9 but contrariwise *b*';
9 that ye should inherit a *b*'
Re 5:12 and honour, and glory, and *b*'.
5:13 *B*', and honour, and glory,
7:12 *B*', and glory, and wisdom,

blessings
Ge 49:25 bless thee with *b*' of heaven above,
25 *b*' of the deep that lieth under,
25 *b*' of the breasts, and of the womb:
26 The *b*' of thy father have prevailed
26 above the *b*' of my progenitors
De 28: 2 all these *b*' shall come on thee,
Jos 8:34 the *b*' and cursings, according to
Ps 21: 3 preventest with the *b*' of goodness:
Pr 10: 6 *B*' are upon the head of the just:
28:20 faithful man shall abound with *b*':
Mal 2: 2 I will curse your *b*': yea, I have
Eph 1: 3 with all spiritual *b*' in heavenly

blew
Jos 6: 8 Lord, and *b*' with the trumpets:
9 priests that *b*' with the trumpets,
13 went on continually, and *b*' with
16 the priests *b*' with the trumpets,
20 people shouted when the priests *b*'
J'g 3:27 he *b*' a trumpet in the mountain
6:34 upon Gideon, and he *b*' a trumpet;
7:19 they *b*' the trumpets, and brake
20 three companies *b*' the trumpets,
22 three hundred *b*' the trumpets,
1Sa 13: 3 *b*' the trumpet throughout all the
2Sa 2:28 So Joab *b*' a trumpet, and all
18:16 And Joab *b*' the trumpet, and the
20: 1 and he *b*' a trumpet, and said,
22 And he *b*' a trumpet, and they
1Ki 1:39 And they *b*' the trumpet; and all
2Ki 9:13 of the stairs, and *b*' with trumpets,
11:14 rejoiced, and *b*' with trumpets:
M't 7:25 winds *b*', and beat upon that
27 *b*', and beat upon that house;
Joh 6:18 by reason of a great wind that *b*'.
Ac 27:13 south wind *b*' softly, supposing
28:13 one day the south wind *b*', and

blind See also BLINDED; BLINDETH; BLINDFOLDED.
Ex 4:11 or deaf, or the seeing, or the *b*'?
Le 19:14 a stumblingblock before the *b*',
21:18 a *b*' man, or a lame, or he that
22:22 *B*', or broken, or maimed, or
De 15:21 it be lame, or *b*', or have any ill
16:19 a gift doth *b*' the eyes of the wise,
27:18 he that maketh the *b*' to wander
28:29 *b*' gropeth in darkness, and thou
1Sa 12: 3 bribe to *b*' mine eyes therewith?
2Sa 5: 6 take away the *b*' and the lame,
8 *b*', that are hated of David's soul,
8 The *b*' and the lame shall not come
Job 29:15 I was eyes to the *b*', and feet was I
Ps 146: 8 Lord openeth the eyes of the *b*':
Isa 29:18 the *b*' shall see out of obscurity,
35: 5 eyes of the *b*' shall be opened,
42: 7 open the *b*' eyes, to bring out the
16 bring the *b*' by a way that they
18 Hear, ye deaf; and look, ye *b*', that
19 Who is *b*', but my servant? or deaf
19 who is *b*' as he that is perfect, and
19 *b*' as the Lord's servant?
43: 8 forth the *b*' people that have eyes,
56:10 His watchmen are *b*': they are all
59:10 for the wall like the *b*', and we
Jer 31: 8 and with them the *b*' and the lame,
La 4:14 wandered as *b*' men in the streets,
Zep 1:17 walk like *b*' men, because they
Mal 1: 8 the *b*' for sacrifice, is it not evil?
M't 9:27 two *b*' men followed him, crying,
9:28 the house, the *b*' men came to him:
11: 5 The *b*' receive their sight, and the
12:22 one possessed with a devil, *b*',
22 that the *b*' and dumb both spake
15:14 Let them alone: they be *b*'
14 leaders of the *b*'. And
14 if the *b*' lead the *b*',
30 lame, *b*', dumb, maimed, and many
31 lame to walk, and the *b*' to see:
20:30 And, behold, two *b*' men sitting by
21:14 the *b*' and the lame came to him
23:16 Woe unto you, ye blind guides,
17, 19 Ye fools and *b*': for whether is
24 Ye *b*' guides, which strain at a
26 Thou *b*' Pharisee, cleanse first that
M'r 8:22 and they bring a *b*' man unto him,
23 he took the *b*' man by the hand,
10:46 *b*' Bartimæus, the son of Timæus,
49 they call the *b*' man, saying unto
51 The *b*' man said unto him, Lord,
Lu 4:18 and recovering of sight to the *b*',
6:39 Can the *b*' lead the *b*'?
7:21 many that were *b*' he gave sight.
22 how that the *b*' see, the lame walk,
14:13 the maimed, the lame, the *b*':
21 maimed, and the halt, and the *b*'.
18:35 a certain *b*' man sat by the way side
Joh 5: 3 *b*', halt, withered, waiting for the
9: 1 which was *b*' from his birth.
2 his parents, that he was born *b*'?
6 anointed the eyes of the *b*' man
8 had seen him that he was *b*',
13 him that aforetime was *b*'.
17 They say unto the *b*' man again,
18 he had been *b*', and received his
19 your son, who ye say was born *b*'?
20 and that he was born *b*':
24 called they the man that was *b*',
25 whereas I was *b*', now I see.
32 the eyes of one that was born *b*'.
39 they which see might be made *b*'.
40 and said unto him, Are we *b*' also?
41 If ye were *b*', ye should have no
10:21 a devil open the eyes of the *b*'?
11:37 opened the eyes of the *b*', have
Ac 13:11 shalt be *b*', not seeing the sun
Ro 2:19 thou thyself art a guide of the *b*',
2Pe 1: 9 he that lacketh these things is *b*',
Re 3:17 and poor, and *b*', and naked:

blinded
Joh 12:40 He hath *b*' their eyes, and
Ro 11: 7 obtained it, and the rest were *b*'
2Co 3:14 But their minds were *b*': for until
4: 4 of this world hath *b*' the minds
1Jo 2:11 that darkness hath *b*' his eyes.

blindeth
Ex 23: 8 *b*' the wise, and perverteth the

blindfolded
Lu 22:64 And when they had *b*' him, they

blindness
Ge 19:11 at the door of the house with *b*',
De 28:28 smite thee with madness, and *b*',
2Ki 6:18 this people, I pray thee, with *b*'.
18 And he smote them with *b*'
Zec 12: 4 every horse of the people with *b*'.
Ro 11:25 *b*' in part is happened to Israel,
Eph 4:18 because of the *b*' of their heart:

block See also STUMBLINGBLOCK.
Isa 57:14 take up the stumbling *b*' out of

blood See also BLOODGUILTINESS; BLOODTHIRSTY.
Ge 4:10 of thy brother's *b*' crieth unto me
11 thy brother's *b*' from thy hand;
9: 4 thereof, which is the *b*' thereof,
5 surely your *b*' of your lives will
6 sheddeth man's *b*',...his *b*' be shed:
37:22 Shed no *b*', but cast him into
26 our brother, and conceal his *b*'?
31 goats, and dipped the coat in the *b*';
42:22 behold, also his *b*' is required.
49:11 and his clothes in the *b*' of grapes:
Ex 4: 9 become *b*' upon the dry land.
7:17 and they shall be turned to *b*'.
19 that they may become *b*';
19 and that there may be *b*'
20 in the river were turned to *b*'.
21 *b*' throughout all the land of Egypt.
12: 7 shall take of the *b*', and strike it
13 the *b*' shall be to you for a token
13 when I see the *b*', I will pass over
22 dip it in the *b*' that is in the bason,
22 the *b*' that is in the bason;
23 he seeth the *b*' upon the lintel,
22: 2 shall no *b*' be shed for him.
3 there shall be *b*' shed for him;
23:18 not offer the *b*' of my sacrifice
24: 6 took half of the *b*' and put it
6 half of the *b*' he sprinkled on
8 Moses took the *b*', and sprinkled
8 Behold the *b*' of the covenant,
29:12 thou shalt take the *b*' of
12 pour all the *b*' beside the bottom
16 shalt take his *b*' and sprinkle it
20 kill the ram, and take of his *b*',
20 sprinkle the *b*' upon the altar
21 shalt take of the *b*' that is upon
30:10 with the *b*' of the sin offering
34:25 not offer the *b*' of my sacrifice
Le 1: 5 bring the *b*', and sprinkle the *b*'
11 sprinkle his *b*' round about upon
15 the *b*' thereof shall be wrung out
3: 2 sprinkle the *b*' upon the altar
8 sons shall sprinkle the *b*' thereof
13 Aaron shall sprinkle the *b*' thereof
17 that ye eat neither fat nor *b*'.
4: 5 shall take of the bullock's *b*', and
6 dip his finger in the *b*', and
6 sprinkle of the *b*' seven times
7 some of the *b*' upon the horns
7 pour all the *b*' of the bullock
16 shall bring of the bullock's *b*'
17 dip his finger in some of the *b*',
18 And he shall put some of the *b*'
18 pour out all the *b*' at the bottom
25 the priest shall take of the *b*' of
25 shall pour out his *b*' at the bottom
30 shall take of the *b*' thereof
30 shall pour out all the *b*' thereof
34 priest shall take of the *b*' of the
34 shall pour out all the *b*' thereof
5: 9 he shall sprinkle of the *b*' of the
9 the rest of the *b*' shall be wrung out
6:27 is sprinkled of the *b*' thereof
30 whereof any of the *b*' is brought
7: 2 the *b*' thereof shall he sprinkle
14 the priest's that sprinkleth the *b*' of
26 ye shall eat no manner of *b*',
27 that eateth any manner of *b*',
33 the *b*' of the peace offerings,
8:15 Moses took the *b*', and put it upon
15 poured the *b*' at the bottom of the
19 Moses sprinkled the *b*' upon the
23 and Moses took of the *b*' of it, and
24 Moses put of the *b*' upon the tip of
24 the *b*' upon the altar round about.
30 the *b*' which was upon the altar,
9: 9 brought the *b*' unto him: and he
9 dipped his finger in the *b*',
9 poured out the *b*' at the bottom of
12, 18 sons presented unto him the *b*',
10:18 Behold, the *b*' of it was not brought
12: 4 shall then continue in the *b*' of her
5 shall continue in the *b*' of her
7 cleansed from the issue of her *b*'.
14: 6 the living bird in the *b*' of the
14 the *b*' of the trespass offering,
17 upon the *b*' of the trespass offering:
25 some of the *b*' of the trespass
28 upon the place of the *b*' of the

Le 14:51 dip them in the b' of the slain
52 the house with the b' of the bird,
15:19 her issue in her flesh be b'.
25 if a woman have an issue of her b'
16:14 shall take of the b' of the bullock,
14 shall he sprinkle of the b'
15 bring his b' within the vail,
15 and do with that b' as he did
15 with the b' of the bullock,
18 take of the b' of the bullock,
18 and of the b' of the goat,
19 And he shall sprinkle of the b'
27 whose b' was brought in to make
17: 4 b' shall be imputed unto that man;
4 he hath shed b'; and that man
6 the priest shall sprinkle the b'
10 that eateth any manner of b';
10 against that soul that eateth b',
11 the life of the flesh is in the b':
11 the b' that maketh an atonement
12 No soul of you shall eat b',
12 that sojourneth among you eat b'.
13 shall even pour out the b' thereof,
14 the b' of it is for the life thereof:
14 Ye shall eat the b' of no manner
14 the life of all flesh is the b' thereof:
19:16 against the b' of thy neighbour:
26 shall not eat anything with the b':
20: 9 his b' shall be upon him.
11 their b' shall be upon them.
12 wrought confusion; their b' shall
13 their b' shall be upon them.
16 put to death; their b' shall be
18 uncovered the fountain of her b':
27 their b' shall be upon them.
Nu 18:17 thou shalt sprinkle their b' upon
19: 4 take of her b' with his finger,
4 and sprinkle of her b'
5 her skin, and her flesh, and her b',
23:24 prey, and drink the b' of the slain.
35:19 The revenger of b' himself shall
21 the revenger of b' shall slay
24 the slayer and the revenger of b'
25 of the hand of the revenger of b',
27 And the revenger of b' find him
27 the revenger of b' kill the slayer;
27 he shall not be guilty of b':
33 for b' it defileth the land: and the
33 cannot be cleansed of the b'
33 but by the b' of him that shed it.
De 12:16 Only ye shall not eat the b';
23 sure that thou eat not the b':
23 for the b' is the life;
27 the flesh, and the b', upon the
27 and the b' of thy sacrifices shall
15:23 thou shalt not eat the b' thereof;
17: 8 between b' and b', between plea
19: 6 Lest the avenger of the b' pursue
10 That innocent b' be not shed in
10 and so b' be upon thee.
12 into the hand of the avenger of b',
13 of innocent b' from Israel,
21: 7 Our hands have not shed this b',
8 lay not innocent b' unto thy people
8 And the b' shall be forgiven them.
9 put away the guilt of innocent b'
22: 8 that thou bring not b' upon
32:14 drink the pure b' of the grape.
42 make mine arrows drunk with b',
42 and that with the b' of the slain
43 will avenge the b' of his servants,
Jos 2:19 his b' shall be upon his head,
19 his b' shall be on our head, if any
20: 3 refuge from the avenger of b'.
5 if the avenger of b' pursue after
9 by the hand of the avenger of b',
J'g 9:24 their b' be laid upon Abimelech
1Sa 14:32 people did eat them with the b'.
33 Lord, in that they eat with the b'.
34 the Lord in eating with the b'.
19: 5 wilt thou sin against innocent b',
25:26 thee from coming to shed b',
31 either that thou hast shed b'
33 this day from coming to shed b',
26:20 let not my b' fall to the earth
2Sa 1:16 Thy b' be upon thy head;
22 From the b' of the slain,
3:27 that he died, for the b' of Asahel
28 from the b' of Abner the son
4:11 therefore now require his b'
14:11 the revengers of b' to destroy
16: 8 all the b' of the house of Saul,
20:12 Amasa wallowed in b' in the
23:17 the b' of the men that went in
1Ki 2: 5 shed the b' of war in peace,
5 put the b' of war upon his girdle
9 thou down to the grave with b'.
31 take away the innocent b', which
32 the Lord shall return his b'
33 Their b' shall therefore return
37 thy b' shall be upon thine own
18:28 lancets, till the b' gushed out
21:19 dogs licked the b' of Naboth
19 shall dogs lick thy b',
22:35 and the b' ran out of the wound
38 and the dogs licked up his b';
2Ki 3:22 on the other side as red as b':
23 they said, This is b': the kings
9: 7 avenge the b' of my servants
7 and the b' of all the servants
26 seen yesterday the b' of Naboth,
26 and the b' of his sons,
33 and some of her b' was sprinkled
16:13 sprinkled the b' of his peace
15 all the b' of the burnt offering,
15 and all the b' of the sacrifice:
2Ki 21:16 shed innocent b' very much,
24: 4 for the innocent b' that he shed:
4 filled Jerusalem with innocent b';
1Ch 11:19 shall I drink the b' of these men
22: 8 Thou hast shed b' abundantly,
8 thou hast shed much b' upon the
28: 3 man of war, and hast shed b'.
2Ch 19:10 between b' and b', between law
24:25 conspired against him for the b'
29:22 the priests received the b', and
22 sprinkled the b' upon the altar:
22 lambs, and they sprinkled the b'
24 reconciliation with their b' upon
30:16 the priests sprinkled the b', which
35:11 the priests sprinkled the b' from
Job 16:18 O earth, cover not thou my b',
39:30 Her young ones also suck up b':
Ps 9:12 he maketh inquisition for b',
16: 4 their drink offerings of b' will I
30: 9 What profit is their in my b', when
50:13 of bulls, or drink the b' of goats?
58:10 his feet in the b' of the wicked.
68:23 dipped in the b' of thine enemies,
72:14 precious shall their b' be in his
78:44 had turned their rivers into b';
79: 3 Their b' have they shed like water
10 revenging of the b' of thy servants
94:21 and condemn the innocent b'.
105:29 turned their waters into b', and
106:38 shed innocent b', even
38 even the b' of their sons
38 the land was polluted with b'.
Pr 1:11 let us lay wait for b', let us look
16 evil, and make haste to shed b'.
18 they lay wait for their own b';
6:17 and hands that shed innocent b',
12: 6 to lie in wait for b': but the mouth
28:17 violence to the b' of any person
30:33 of the nose bringeth forth b':
Isa 1:11 delight not in the b' of bullocks,
15 hear: your hands are full of b'.
4: 4 have purged the b' of Jerusalem
9: 5 noise, and garments rolled in b';
15: 9 of Dimon shall be full of b':
26:21 the earth also shall disclose her b',
33:15 his ears from hearing of b',
34: 3 shall be melted with their b'.
6 sword of the Lord is filled with b',
6 with the b' of lambs and goats,
7 their land shall be soaked with b',
49:26 be drunken with their own b',
59: 3 your hands are defiled with b',
7 make haste to shed innocent b':
63: 3 their b' shall be sprinkled upon
66: 3 as if he offered swine's b'; he that
Jer 2:34 skirts is found the b' of the souls
7: 6 shed not innocent b' in this place,
18:21 pour out their b' by the force
19: 4 this place with the b' of innocents;
22: 3 neither shed innocent b' in this
17 and for to shed innocent b', and
26:15 shall surely bring innocent b' upon
46:10 and made drunk with their b':
48:10 keepeth back his sword from b'.
51:35 and my b' upon the inhabitants of
Lam 4:13 that have shed the b' of the just
14 polluted themselves with b', so
Eze 3:18, 20 but his b' will I require at thine
5:17 pestilence and b' shall pass
9: 9 the land is full of b', and the city
14:19 and pour out my fury upon it in b',
16: 6 polluted in thine own b', I said
6 when thou wast in thy b', Live;
6 thee when thou wast in thy b',
9 washed away thy b' from thee, and
22 bare, and wast polluted in thy b'.
36 and by the b' of thy children,
38 that break wedlock and shed b'
38 will give thee b' in fury and
18:10 that is a robber, a shedder of b',
13 surely die; his b' shall be upon him.
19:10 Thy mother is like a vine in thy b',
21:32 thy b' shall be in the midst of the
22: 3 The city sheddeth b' in the midst of
4 Thou art become guilty in thy b'
6 in thee to their power to shed b'.
9 are men that carry tales to shed b':
12 have they taken gifts to shed b';
13 at thy b' which hath been in the
27 to shed b', and to destroy souls,
23:37 and b' is in their hands, and with
45 the manner of women that shed b';
45 are adulteresses, and b' is in their
24: 7 For her b' is in the midst of her;
8 I have set her b' upon the top of a
28:23 her pestilence, and b' into her
32: 6 I will also water with thy b' the
33: 4 his b' shall be upon his own head.
5 warning; his b' shall be upon him.
6 but his b' will I require at the
8 but his b' will I require at thine
25 Ye eat with the b', and lift up your
25 toward your idols, and shed b':
35: 5 shed the b' of the children of
6 I will prepare thee unto b',
6 and b' shall pursue thee: sith
6 thou hast not hated b', even b' shall
36:18 the b' that they had shed upon the
38:22 him with pestilence and with b';
39:17 that ye may eat flesh, and drink b'.
18 and drink the b' of the princes of
19 and drink b' till ye be drunken, of
43:18 thereon, and to sprinkle b' thereon.
20 thou shalt take of the b' thereof,
44: 7 my bread, the fat and the b', and
15 offer unto me the fat and the b',
Eze 45:19 the priest shall take of the b' of the
Ho 1: 4 I will avenge the b' of Jezreel upon
4: 2 they break out, and b' toucheth b'.
6: 8 iniquity, and is polluted with b'.
12:14 therefore shall he leave his b' upon
Joe 2:30 b', and fire, and pillars of smoke.
31 darkness, and the moon into b',
3:19 they have shed innocent b' in their
21 For I will cleanse their b' that I
Jon 1:14 and lay not upon us innocent b':
Mic 3:10 They build up Zion with b', and
7: 2 they all lie in wait for b'; they
Hab 2: 8 because of men's b', and for the
12 him that buildeth a town with b',
17 them afraid, because of men's b',
Zep 1:17 and their b' shall be poured out as
Zec 9: 7 I will take away his b' out of his
11 by the b' of thy covenant I have
M't 9:20 diseased with an issue of b' twelve
16:17 for flesh and b' hath not revealed
23:30 with them in the b' of the prophets.
35 the righteous b' shed upon the
35 from the b' of righteous Abel
35 unto the b' of Zacharias son of
26:28 for this is my b' of the new
27: 4 I have betrayed the innocent b'.
6 because it is the price of b'.
8 was called, The field of b', unto this
24 I am innocent of the b' of this just
25 His b' be on us, and on our children.
M'r 5:25 which had an issue of b' twelve
29 the fountain of her b' was dried up;
14:24 This is my b' of the new testament,
Lu 8:43 having an issue of b' twelve years,
44 and immediately her issue of b'
11:50 the b' of all the prophets, which
51 From the b' of Abel
51 unto the b' of Zacharias,
13: 1 whose b' Pilate had mingled with
22:20 new testament in my b', which is
44 great drops of b' falling down to
Joh 1:13 Which were born, not of b', nor of
6:53 Son of man, and drink his b', he
54 eateth my flesh, and drinketh my b',
55 is meat indeed, and my b' is drink
56 eateth my flesh, and drinketh my b',
19:34 forthwith came there out b' and
Ac 1:19 that is to say, The field of b'.
2:19 b', and fire, and vapour of smoke:
20 into darkness, and the moon into b',
5:28 intend to bring this man's b' upon
15:20 from things strangled, and from b'.
29 offered to idols, and from b', and
17:26 hath made of one b' all nations of
18: 6 Your b' be upon your own heads; I
20:26 that I am pure from the b' of all
28 hath purchased with his own b'.
21:25 from b', and from strangled, and
22:20 the b' of thy martyr Stephen was
Ro 3:15 Their feet are swift to shed b':
25 through faith in his b', to declare
5: 9 then, being now justified by his b',
1Co 10:16 the communion of the b' of Christ?
11:25 the new testament in my b':
27 of the body and b' of the Lord.
15:50 that flesh and b' cannot inherit the
Ga 1:16 I conferred not with flesh and b':
Eph 1: 7 have redemption through his b', the
2:13 are made nigh by the b' of Christ.
6:12 wrestle not against flesh and b,
Col 1:14 redemption through his b', even
20 made peace through the b' of his
Heb 2:14 partakers of flesh and b', he also
9: 7 once every year, not without b',
12 neither by the b' of goats and
12 calves, but by his own b' he
13 For if the b' of bulls and of goats,
14 How much more shall the b' of
18 testament was dedicated without b'.
19 he took the b' of calves and of
20 Saying, This is the b' of the
21 sprinkled with b' both the
22 are by the law purged with b'; and
22 without shedding of b' is no
25 the holy place every year with b' of
10: 4 that the b' of bulls and of goats
19 to enter into the holiest by the b' of
29 and hath counted the b' of the
11:28 passover, and the sprinkling of b',
12: 4 not yet resisted unto b', striving
24 to the b' of sprinkling, that
13:11 those beasts, whose b' is brought
12 sanctify the people with his own b',
20 through the b' of the everlasting
1Pe 1: 2 sprinkling of the b' of Jesus Christ:
19 with the precious b' of Christ, as of
1Jo 1: 7 the b' of Jesus Christ his Son
5: 6 water and b', even Jesus Christ;
6 by water only, but by water and b'.
8 spirit, and the water, and the b':
Re 1: 5 us from our sins in his own b',
5: 9 redeemed us to God by thy b' out of
6: 10 thou not judge and avenge our b'
12 of hair, and the moon became as b';
7:14 them white in the b' of the Lamb.
8: 7 hail and fire mingled with b', and
8 third part of the sea became b';
11: 6 over waters to turn them to b', and
12:11 by the b' of the Lamb, and by the
14:20 the city, and b' came out of the
16: 3 it became as the b' of a dead man:
4 of waters; and they became b'.
6 shed the b' of saints and prophets,
6 thou hast given them b' to drink;
17: 6 drunken with the b' of the saints,
6 and with the b' of the martyrs of

Re 18:24 And in her was found the *b*· of
19: 2 avenged the *b*· of his servants at
13 clothed with a vesture dipped in *b*·:

bloodguiltiness
Ps 51:14 Deliver me from *b*·, O God,

bloodthirsty
Pro 29:10 The *b*· hate the upright: but

bloody
Ex 4:25 Surely a *b*· husband art thou to
26 A *b*· husband thou art because of
2Sa 16: 7 come out, thou *b*· man, and thou
8 because thou art a *b*· man.
21: 1 for Saul, and for his *b*· house,
Ps 5: 6 Lord will abhor the *b*· and
26: 9 with sinners, nor my life with *b*·
55:23 *b*· and deceitful men shall not
59: 2 iniquity, and save me from *b*·
139:19 depart from me therefore, ye *b*·
Eze 7:23 the land is full of *b*· crimes, and
22: 2 wilt thou judge the *b*· city? yea,
24: 6 Woe to the *b*· city, to the pot
9 Woe to the *b*· city! I will even
Nah 3: 1 Woe to the *b*· city! it is all full
Ac 28: 8 lay sick of a fever and of a *b*· flux:

bloomed See also BLOSSOMED.
Nu 17: 8 and *b*· blossoms, and yielded

blossom See also BLOSSOMED; BLOSSOMS.
Nu 17: 5 whom I shall choose, shall *b*·:
Isa 5:24 and their *b*· shall go up as dust:
27: 6 Israel shall *b*· and bud, and fill
35: 1 shall rejoice, and *b*· as the rose.
2 It shall *b*· abundantly, and rejoice
Hab 3:17 Although the fig tree shall not *b*·,

blossomed See also BLOOMED.
Eze 7:10 rod hath *b*·, pride hath budded.

blossoms
Ge 40:10 it budded, and her *b*· shot forth;
Nu 17: 8 and bloomed *b*·, and yielded

blot See also BLOTTED; BLOTTETH; BLOTTING.
Ex 32:32 *b*· me, I pray thee, out of thy book
33 him will I *b*· out of my book.
Nu 5:23 and he shall *b*· them out with the
De 9:14 and *b*· out their name from under
25:19 *b*· out the remembrance of Amalek
29:20 the Lord shall *b*· out his name
2Ki 14:27 he would *b*· out the name of Israel
Job 31: 7 if any *b*· hath cleaved to mine
Ps 51: 1 mercies *b*· out my transgressions.
9 sins, and *b*· out all mine iniquities.
Pr 9: 7 wicked man getteth himself a *b*·.
Jer 18:23 neither *b*· out their sin from thy
Re 3: 5 I will not *b*· out his name out of

blotted
Ne 4: 5 let not their sin be *b*· out from
Ps 69:28 Let them be *b*· out of the book
109:13 following let their name be *b*· out.
14 the sin of his mother be *b*· out.
Isa 44:22 *b*· out, as a thick cloud, thy
Ac 3:19 your sins may be *b*· out, when

blotteth
Isa 43:25 he that *b*· out thy transgressions

blotting
Col 2:14 *B*· out the handwriting of

blow See also BLEW; BLOWETH; BLOWING; BLOWN.
Ex 15:10 Thou didst *b*· with thy wind, the
Nu 10: 3 when they shall *b*· with them,
4 they *b*· but with one trumpet,
5 When ye *b*· an alarm, then the
6 When ye *b*· an alarm the second
6 they shall *b*· an alarm for their
7 ye shall *b*·, but ye shall not sound
8 Aaron, the priests, shall *b*· with
9 then ye shall *b*· an alarm with
10 ye shall *b*· with the trumpets over
31: 6 the trumpets to *b*· in his hand.
Jos 6: 4 priests shall *b*· with the trumpets.
J'g 7:18 When I *b*· with the trumpet, I
18 with me, then *b*· ye the trumpets
20 trumpets in their right hands to *b*·
1Ki 1:34 and *b*· ye with the trumpet, and
1Ch 15:24 did *b*· with the trumpets before
Ps 39:10 I am consumed by the *b*· of thine
78:26 He caused an east wind to *b*· in
81: 3 *B*· up the trumpet in the new
147:18 he causeth his wind to *b*·, and
Ca 4:16 *b*· upon my garden, that the
Isa 40:24 he shall also *b*· upon them, and
Jer 4: 5 *B*· ye the trumpet in the land:
6: 1 *b*· the trumpet in Tekoa, and set
14:17 breach, with a very grievous *b*·.
51:27 *b*· the trumpet among the nations,
Eze 21:31 I will *b*· against thee in the fire
22:20 to *b*· the fire upon it, to melt it;
21 I will gather you, and *b*· upon
33: 3 upon the land, he *b*· the trumpet,
6 *b*· not the trumpet, and the
Ho 5: 8 *B*· ye the cornet in Gibeah, and
Joe 2: 1 *B*· ye the trumpet in Zion,
15 *B*· the trumpet in Zion, sanctify
Hag 1: 9 brought it home, I did *b*· upon it.
Zec 9:14 Lord God shall *b*· the trumpet,
Lu 12:55 when ye see the south wind *b*·,
Re 7: 1 wind should not *b*· on the earth,

bloweth
Isa 18: 3 when he *b*· a trumpet, hear ye.
40: 7 the spirit of the Lord *b*· upon it:
54:16 the smith that *b*· the coals in the
Joh 3: 8 the wind *b*· where it listeth,

blowing
Le 23:24 a memorial of *b*· of trumpets,
Nu 29: 1 a day of *b*· the trumpets unto you.
Jos 6: 9, 13 on and *b*· with the trumpets.

blown
Job 20:26 a fire not *b*· shall consume him;
Isa 27:13 the great trumpet shall be *b*·,
Eze 7:14 They have *b*· the trumpet, even
Am 3: 6 Shall a trumpet be *b*· in the city,

blue
Ex 25: 4 And *b*·, and purple, and scarlet,
26: 1 twined linen, and *b*·, and purple,
4 thou shalt make loops of *b*· upon
31 shalt make a vail of *b*·, and purple,
36 for the door of the tent, of *b*·,
27:16 an hanging of twenty cubits, of *b*·,
28: 5 shall take gold, and *b*·, and purple,
6 make the ephod of gold, of *b*·,
8 even of gold, of *b*·, and purple,
15 thou shalt make it; of gold, of *b*·,
28 the ephod with a lace of *b*·, that it
31 the robe of the ephod all of *b*·.
33 shalt make pomegranates of *b*·,
37 thou shalt put it on a *b*· lace, that
35: 6 And *b*·, and purple, and scarlet,
23 man with whom was found *b*·,
25 spun, both of *b*·, and of purple,
35 and of the embroiderer, in *b*·,
36: 8 twined linen, and *b*·, and purple,
11 he made loops of *b*· on the edge
35 he made a vail of *b*·, and purple,
37 for the tabernacle door of *b*·,
38:18 the court was needlework, of *b*·,
23 embroiderer in *b*·, and in purple,
39: 1 of the *b*·, and purple, and scarlet,
2 the ephod of gold, *b*·, and purple,
3 it into wires, to work it in the *b*·,
5 thereof; of gold, *b*·, and purple,
8 of gold, *b*·, and purple, and scarlet,
21 the ephod with a lace of *b*·, that it
22 ephod of woven work, all of *b*·.
24 of the robe pomegranates of *b*·,
29 twined linen, and *b*·, and purple,
31 they tied unto it a lace of *b*·, to
Nu 4: 6 spread over it a cloth wholly of *b*·,
7 they shall spread a cloth of *b*·,
9 they shall take a cloth of *b*·, and
11 spread a cloth of *b*·, and cover it
12 and put them in a cloth of *b*·,
15:38 of the borders a ribband of *b*·:
2Ch 2: 7 in purple, and crimson, and *b*·,
14 in *b*·, and in fine linen, and in
3:14 he made the vail of *b*·, and purple,
Es 1: 6 white, green, and *b*·, hangings,
6 *b*·, and white, and black, marble,
8:15 the king in royal apparel of *b*·
Jer 10: 9 *b*· and purple is their clothing:
Eze 23: 6 were clothed with *b*·, captains
27: 7 *b*· and purple from the isles
24 in *b*· clothes, and broidered work,

blueness
Pr 20:30 *b*· of a wound cleanseth away

blunt
Ec 10:10 If the iron be *b*·, and he do not

blush
Ezr 9: 6 I am ashamed and *b*· to lift
Jer 6:15 ashamed, neither could they *b*·:
8:12 neither could they *b*·: therefore

Boanerges (*bo-an-er'-jees*)
M'r 3:17 he surnamed them *B*·, which is,

boar
Ps 80:13 *b*· out of the wood doth waste it,

board See also ABOARD; BOARDS.
Ex 26:16 cubits shall be the length of a *b*·,
16 half shall be the breadth of one *b*·
17 tenons shall there be in one *b*·,
19 under one *b*· for his two tenons,
19 two sockets under another *b*· for
21, 25 two sockets under one *b*·, and
21, 25 two sockets under another *b*·.
36:21 *b*· was ten cubits,
21 and the breadth of a *b*· one cubit
22 One *b*· had two tenons, equally
24 two sockets under one *b*· for his
24 two sockets under another *b*· for
26 two sockets under one *b*·, and
26 two sockets under another *b*·.
30 of silver, under every *b*· two sockets.

boards
Ex 26:15 shalt make *b*· for the tabernacle
17 for all the *b*· of the tabernacle.
18 make the *b*· for the tabernacle,
18 twenty *b*· on the south side
19 of silver under the twenty *b*·;
20 north side there shall be twenty *b*·,
22 westward thou shalt make six *b*·.
23 two *b*· shalt thou make for the
25 And they shall be eight *b*·, and
26 for the *b*· of the one side of the
27 five bars for the *b*· of the other
27 five bars for the *b*· of the side of
28 in the midst of the *b*· shall reach
29 overlay the *b*· with gold, and make
27: 8 with *b*· shalt thou make it: as
35:11 his *b*·, his bars, his pillars, and
36:20 he made *b*· for the tabernacle of
22 for all the *b*· of the tabernacle.
23 he made *b*· for the tabernacle;
23 twenty *b*· for the south side
24 he made under the twenty *b*·;
25 north corner, he made twenty *b*·,
27 westward he made six *b*·.
28 two *b*· made he for the corners of
30 and there were eight *b*·; and their
31 for the *b*· of the one side of the
Ex 36:32 five bars for the *b*· of the other
32 bars for the *b*· of the tabernacle,
33 middle bar to shoot through the *b*·
34 And he overlaid the *b*· with gold,
38: 7 made the altar hollow with *b*·.
39:33 his furniture, his taches, his *b*·,
40:18 set up the *b*· thereof, and put in
Nu 3:36 the *b*· of the tabernacle, and the
4:31 the *b*· of the tabernacle, and the
1Ki 6: 9 the house with beams and *b*· of
15 walls of the house within with *b*·
16 and the walls with *b*· of cedar:
Ca 8: 9 we will inclose her with *b*· of
Eze 27: 5 thy ship *b*· of fir trees of Senir:
Ac 27:44 And the rest, some on *b*·, and

boast See also BOASTED; BOASTEST; BOASTETH; BOASTING.
1Ki 20:11 that girdeth on his harness *b*·
2Ch 25:19 thine heart lifteth thee up to *b*·:
Ps 34: 2 My soul shall make her *b*· in the
44: 8 In God we *b*· all the day long,
49: 6 trust in their wealth, and *b*·
94: 4 workers of iniquity *b*· themselves?
97: 7 images, that *b*· themselves of
Pr 27: 1 *B*· not thyself of to morrow; for
Isa 10:15 Shall the ax *b*· itself against him
61: 6 their glory shall ye *b*· yourselves.
Ro 2:17 law, and makest thy *b*· of God,
23 Thou that makest thy *b*· of the
11:18 *B*· not against the branches. But
18 if thou *b*·, thou bearest not
2Co 9: 2 for which I *b*· of you to them of
10: 8 though I should *b*· somewhat
13 we will not *b*· of things without
16 not to *b*· in another man's line
11:16 me, that I may *b*· myself a little.
Eph 2: 9 of works, lest any man should *b*·.

boasted
Eze 35:13 with your mouth ye have *b*·
2Co 7:14 I have *b*· any thing to him of

boasters
Ro 1:30 despiteful, proud, *b*·, inventors
2Ti 3: 2 covetous, *b*·, proud, blasphemers,

boastest
Ps 52: 1 Why *b*· thou thyself in mischief,

boasteth
Ps 10: 3 wicked *b*· of his heart's desire,
Pr 20:14 he is gone his way, then he *b*·.
25:14 Whoso *b*· himself of a false gift
Jas 3: 5 little member, and *b*· great

boasting See also BOASTINGS.
Ac 5:36 Theudas, *b*· himself to be
Ro 3:27 Where is *b*· then? It is excluded.
2Co 7:14 even so our *b*·, which I made
8:24 love, and of our *b*· on your behalf.
9: 3 lest our *b*· of you should be in
4 in this same confident *b*·.
10:15 Not *b*· of things without our
11:10 no man shall stop me of this *b*·
17 in this confidence of *b*·.

boastings
Jas 4:16 now ye rejoice in your *b*·: all

boat See also BOATS.
2Sa 19:18 And there went over a ferry *b*·
Joh 6:22 that there was none other *b*· there,
22 with his disciples into the *b*·,
Ac 27:16 much work to come by the *b*·:
30 when they had let down the *b*·
32 cut off the ropes of the *b*·, and

boats
Joh 6:23 (Howbeit there came other *b*·

Boaz (*bo'-az*) See also Booz.
Ru 2: 1 Elimelech; and his name was *B*·.
3 of the field belonging unto *B*·,
4 behold, *B*· came from Bethlehem,
5 Then said *B*· unto his servant
8 Then said *B*· unto Ruth, Hearest
11 *B*· answered and said unto her,
14 *B*· said unto her, At mealtime
15 *B*· commanded his young men,
19 with whom I wrought to day is *B*·.
23 she kept fast by the maidens of *B*·
3: 2 now is not *B*· of our kindred,
7 when *B*· had eaten and drunk,
4: 1 Then went *B*· up to the gate,
1 behold, the kinsman of whom *B*·
5 Then said *B*·, What day thou
8 the kinsman said unto *B*·, Buy it
9 And *B*· said unto the elders, and
13 So *B*· took Ruth, and she was his
21 Salmon begat *B*·, and *B*· begat
1Ki 7:21 and called the name thereof *B*·.
1Ch 2:11 begat Salma, and Salma begat *B*·,
12 *B*· begat Obed, and Obed begat
2Ch 3:17 the name of that on the left *B*·.

Bocheru (*bok'-er-u*)
1Ch 8:38 these, Azrikam, *B*·, and Ishmael,
9:44 *B*·, and Ishmael, and Sheariah,

Bochim (*bo'-kim*)
J'g 2: 1 came up from Gilgal to *B*·, and
5 called the name of that place *B*·:

bodies
Ge 47:18 lord, but our *b*·, and our lands:
1Sa 31:12 body of Saul and the *b*· of his
1Ch 10:12 away the body of Saul, and the *b*·
2Ch 20:24 they were dead *b*· fallen to the
25 riches with the dead *b*·, and
Ne 9:37 they have dominion over our *b*·,
Job 13:12 ashes, your *b*· to *b*· of clay.
Ps 79: 2 The dead *b*· of thy servants have
110: 6 fill the places with the dead *b*·,

Jer 31:40 the whole valley of the dead *b*',
33: 5 the dead *b*' of men, whom I have
34:20 and their dead *b*' shall be for
41: 9 the dead *b*' of the men, whom he
Eze 1:11 another, and two covered their *b*'.
23 covered on that side, their *b*'.
Da 3:27 upon whose *b*' the fire had no
28 and yielded their *b*', that they
Am 8: 3 there shall be many dead *b*' in
M't 27:52 and many *b*' of the saints which
Joh 19:31 the *b*' should not remain upon
Ro 1:24 to dishonour their own *b*' between
8:11 shall also quicken your mortal *b*'
12: 1 that ye present your *b*' a living
1Co 6:15 that your *b*' are the members of
15:40 also celestial *b*', and *b*' terrestrial:
Eph 5:28 to love their wives as their own *b*'.
Heb 10:22 and our *b*' washed with pure
13:11 For the *b*' of those beasts, whose
Re 11: 8 And their dead *b*' shall lie in the
9 shall see their dead *b*' three days
9 shall not suffer their dead *b*' to be

bodily
Lu 3:22 Holy Ghost descended in a *b*'
2Co 10:10 but his *b*' presence is weak, and
Col 2: 9 all the fulness of the Godhead *b*'.
1Ti 4: 8 For *b*' exercise profiteth little:

body See also BODIES; BODY'S; BUSYBODY; SOMEBODY.
Ex 24:10 and as it were the *b*' of heaven in
Le 21:11 any dead *b*', nor defile himself
Nu 6: 6 Lord he shall come at no dead *b*'.
9: 6 defiled by the dead *b*' of a man,
7 we are defiled by the dead *b*' of a
10 unclean by reason of a dead *b*',
19:11 He that toucheth the dead *b*' of
13 Whosoever toucheth the dead *b*' of
16 or a dead *b*', or a bone of a man,
De 21:23 His *b*' shall not remain all
28: 4 Blessed shall be the fruit of thy *b*',
11 in goods, in the fruit of thy *b*',
18 Cursed shall be the fruit of thy *b*',
53 shalt eat the fruit of thine own *b*',
30: 9 in the fruit of thy *b*', and in the
J'g 8:30 threescore and ten sons of his *b*'
1Sa 31:10 they fastened his *b*' to the wall of
12 took the *b*' of Saul and the bodies
2Ki 8: 5 he had restored a dead *b*' to life,
1Ch 10:12 took away the *b*' of Saul, and the
Job 19:17 children's sake of mine own *b*'.
26 worms destroy this *b*', yet in
20:25 drawn, and cometh out of the *b*'
Ps 132:11 fruit of thy *b*', will I set upon
Pr 5:11 when thy flesh and thy *b*' are
Isa 10:18 both soul and *b*': and they shall
26:19 with my dead *b*' shall they arise.
51:23 thou hast laid thy *b*' as the
Jer 26:23 and cast his dead *b*' into the
36:30 and his dead *b*' shall be cast out
La 4: 7 they were more ruddy in *b*' than
Eze 10:12 And their whole *b*', and their
Da 4:33 his *b*' was wet with the dew of
5:21 his *b*' was wet with the dew of
7:11 and his *b*' destroyed, and given to
15 in my spirit in the midst of my *b*',
10: 6 His *b*' also was like the beryl,
Mic 6: 7 the fruit of my *b*' for the sin of
Hag 2:13 unclean by a dead *b*' touch any
M't 5:29 not that thy whole *b*' should be
30 that thy whole *b*' should be cast
6:22 The light of the *b*' is the eye: if
22 thy whole *b*' shall be full of light.
23 thy whole *b*' shall be full of
25 nor yet for your *b*', what ye shall
25 more than meat, and the *b*' than
10:28 fear not them which kill the *b*',
28 able to destroy both soul and *b*' in
14:12 came, and took up the *b*', and
26:12 hath poured this ointment on my *b*',
26 and said, Take, eat; this is my *b*'.
27:58 begged the *b*' of Jesus. Then
58 Pilate commanded the *b*' to be
59 when Joseph had taken the *b*',
M'r 5:29 and she felt in her *b*' that she was
14: 8 aforehand to anoint my *b*' to the
22 and said, Take, eat: this is my *b*.
51 cloth cast about his naked *b*';
15:43 unto Pilate, and craved the *b*' of
45 of the centurion, he gave the *b*'
Lu 11:34 The light of the *b*' is the eye:
34 is single, thy whole *b*' also is full
34 evil, thy *b*' also is full of darkness.
36 If thy whole *b*' therefore be full of
12: 4 not afraid of them that kill the *b*',
22 neither for the *b*', what ye shall
23 than meat, and the *b*' is more
17:37 Wheresoever the *b*' is, thither will
22:19 This is my *b*' which is given for
23:52 unto Pilate, and begged the *b*' of
55 sepulchre, and how his *b*' was laid.
24: 3 and found not the *b*' of the Lord
23 when they found not his *b*', they
Joh 2:21 he spake of the temple of his *b*'.
19:38 that he might take away the *b*' of
38 came therefore, and took the *b*'
40 Then took they the *b*' of Jesus,
20:12 the feet, where the *b*' of Jesus had
Ac 9:40 and turning him to the *b*' said,
19:12 So that from his *b*' were brought
Ro 4:19 he considered not his own *b*' now
6: 6 the *b*' of sin might be destroyed,
12 reign in your mortal *b*', that ye
7: 4 dead to the law by the *b*' of Christ;
24 shall deliver me from the *b*' of this
8:10 the *b*' is dead because of sin; but
Ro 8:13 do mortify the deeds of the *b*', ye
23 to wit, the redemption of our *b*'.
12: 4 we have many members in one *b*',
5 being many, are one *b*' in Christ,
1Co 5: 3 For I verily, as absent in *b*', but
6:13 Now the *b*' is not for fornication,
13 and the Lord for the *b*'.
16 is joined to an harlot is one *b*'?
18 that a man doeth is without the *b*';
18 sinneth against his own *b*'.
19 your *b*' is the temple of the Holy
20 therefore glorify God in your *b*',
7: 4 wife hath not power of her own *b*',
4 hath not power of his own *b*',
34 she may be holy both in *b*' and in
9:27 But I keep under my *b*', and bring
10:16 is it not the communion of the *b*'
17 many are one bread, and one *b*':
11:24 Take, eat: this is my *b*', which is
27 shall be guilty of the *b*' and blood
29 not discerning the Lord's *b*'.
12:12 For as the *b*' is one, and hath many
12 the members of that one *b*', being
12 are one *b*': so also is Christ.
13 are we all baptized into one *b*',
14 For the *b*' is not one member, but
15 I am not of the *b*'; is it
15 therefore not of the *b*'?
16 I am not of the *b*'; is it
16 therefore not of the *b*'?
17 If the whole *b*' were an eye, where
18 every one of them in the *b*', as it
19 all one member, where were the *b*'?
20 many members, yet but one *b*'.
22 those members of the *b*' which
23 And those members of the *b*'
24 but God hath tempered the *b*'
25 should be no schism in the *b*';
27 Now ye are the *b*' of Christ, and
13: 3 though I give my *b*' to be burned,
15:35 and with what *b*' do they come?
37 thou sowest not that *b*' that shall
38 But God giveth it a *b*' as it hath
38 him, and to every seed his own *b*'.
44 It is sown a natural *b*';
44 it is raised a spiritual *b*'.
44 There is a natural *b*',
44 and there is a spiritual *b*'.
2Co 4:10 bearing about in the *b*' the dying
10 might be made manifest in our *b*'.
5: 6 whilst we are at home in the *b*', we
8 rather to be absent from the *b*',
10 receive the things done in his *b*',
12: 2 the *b*', I cannot tell;
2 or whether out of the *b*',
3 in the *b*', or out of the *b*', I cannot
Gal 6:17 I bear in my *b*' the marks of the
Eph 1:23 Which is his *b*', the fulness of him
2:16 unto God in one *b*' by the cross,
3: 6 fellow heirs, and of the same *b*',
4: 4 There is one *b*', and one Spirit,
12 ministry, for the edifying of the *b*'
16 From whom the whole *b*' fitly
16 maketh increase of the *b*' unto
5:23 and he is the saviour of the *b*'.
30 For we are members of his *b*', of
Php 1:20 Christ shall be magnified in my *b*',
3:21 Who shall change our vile *b*', that
21 like unto his glorious *b*', according
Col 1:18 And he is the head of the *b*', the
22 In the *b*' of his flesh through
2:11 putting off the *b*' of the sins of the
17 of things to come; but the *b*' is of
19 from which all the *b*' by joints and
23 humility, and neglecting of the *b*';
3:15 which also ye are called in one *b*';
1Th 5:23 and *b*' be preserved blameless
Heb 10: 5 but a *b*' hast thou prepared me:
10 through the offering of the *b*' of
13: 3 as being yourselves also in the *b*'.
Jas 2:16 things which are needful to the *b*';
26 as the *b*' without the spirit is dead,
3: 2 able also to bridle the whole *b*'.
3 and to turn about their whole *b*'.
6 that it defileth the whole *b*', and
1Pe 2:24 bare our sins in his own *b*' on the
Jude 9 he disputed about the *b*' of Moses,

body's
Col 1:24 in my flesh for his *b*' sake, which

Bohan (*Bo'-han*).
Jos 15: 6 border went up to the stone of *B*'
18:17 and descended to the stone of *B*'

boil See also BOILED; BOILING; BOILS.
Ex 9: 9 a *b*' breaking forth with blains
10 and it became a *b*' breaking forth
11 because of the boils; for the *b*'
Le 8:31 *B*' the flesh at the door of the
13:18 in the skin thereof, was a *b*', and
19 in the place of the *b*' there be a
20 of leprosy broken out of the *b*'.
23 it is a burning *b*'; and the priest
2Ki 20: 7 And they took and laid it on the *b*',
Job 41:31 He maketh the deep to *b*' like a
Isa 38:21 lay it for a plaister upon the *b*',
64: 2 the fire causeth the waters to *b*',
Eze 24: 5 make it *b*' well, and let them
46:20 the priests shall *b*' the trespass
24 the places of them that *b*', where
24 the ministers of the house shall *b*'

boiled
1Ki 19:21 *b*' their flesh with the instruments
2Ki 6:29 So we *b*' my son, and did eat him:
Job 30:27 My bowels *b*', and rested not:

boiling
Eze 46:23 and it was made with *b*' places

boiling-places See BOILING and PLACES.

boils
Ex 9:11 before Moses because of the *b*';
Job 2: 7 smote Job with sore *b*' from the

boisterous
M't 14:30 when he saw the wind *b*', he was

bold See also EMBOLDENED.
Pr 28: 1 but the righteous are *b*' as a lion.
Ac 13:46 Paul and Barnabas waxed *b*',
Ro 10:20 Esaias is very *b*', and saith, I was
2Co 10: 1 being absent am *b*' toward you:
2 that I may not be *b*' when I am
2 wherewith I think to be *b*' against
11:21 whereinsoever any is *b*', (I speak
21 foolishly,) I am *b*' also.
Ph'p 1:14 much more *b*' to speak the word
1Th 2: 2 we were *b*' in our God to speak
Ph'm 8 I might be much *b*' in Christ

boldly
Ge 34:25 came upon the city *b*', and slew
M'r 15:43 and went in *b*' unto Pilate, and
Joh 7:26 But, lo, he speaketh *b*', and they
Ac 9:27 he had preached *b*' at Damascus
29 spake *b*' in the name of the Lord
14: 3 speaking *b*' in the Lord, which
18:26 to speak *b*' in the synagogue:
19: 8 spake *b*' for the space of three
Ro 15:15 I have written the more *b*' unto
Eph 6:19 may open my mouth *b*', to make
20 may speak *b*', as I ought to speak.
Heb 4:16 Let us therefore come *b*' unto
13: 6 So that we may *b*' say, The Lord

boldness
Ec 8: 1 the *b*' of his face shall be changed.
Ac 4:13 they saw the *b*' of Peter and John,
29 all *b*' they may speak thy word,
31 they spake the word of God with *b*'.
2Co 7: 4 Great is my *b*' of speech toward
Eph 3:12 In whom we have *b*' and access
Ph'p 1:20 but that with all *b*', as always,
1Ti 3:13 great *b*' in the faith which is in
Heb 10:19 *b*' to enter into the holiest by the
1Jo 4:17 have *b*' in the day of judgment:

bolled
Ex 9:31 in the ear, and the flax was *b*'.

bolster
1Sa 19:13, 16 pillow of goats' hair for his *b*',
26: 7 stuck in the ground at his *b*':
11 the spear that is at his *b*', and
12 the cruse of water from Saul's *b*';
16 cruse of water that was at his *b*'.

bolt See also BOLTED; THUNDERBOLTS.
2Sa 13:17 woman out from me, and *b*' the

bolted
2Sa 13:18 out, and *b*' the door after her.

bond See also BONDMAID; BONDMAN; BONDSERVANT; BONDSERVICE; BONDWOMAN; BOUND.
Nu 30: 2 an oath to bind his soul with a *b*';
3 bind herself by a *b*', being in her
4 and her *b*' wherewith she hath
4 every *b*' wherewith she hath bound
10 bound her soul by a *b*' with an oath;
11 and every *b*' wherewith she bound
12 or concerning the *b*' of her soul,
Job 12:18 He looseth the *b*' of kings, and
Eze 20:37 I will bring you into the *b*' of the
Lu 13:16 be loosed from this *b*' on the
Ac 8:23 bitterness, and in the *b*' of
1Co 12:13 whether we be *b*' or free; and
Ga 3:28 there is neither *b*' nor free, there
Eph 4: 3 of the Spirit in the *b*' of peace.
6: 8 Lord, whether he be *b*' or free.
Col 3:11 Barbarian, Scythian, *b*' nor free:
14 which is the *b*' of perfectness.
Re 13:16 rich and poor, free and *b*', to
19:18 flesh of all men, both free and *b*',

bondage
Ex 1:14 their lives bitter with hard *b*',
2:23 sighed by reason of the *b*',
23 up unto God by reason of the *b*'.
6: 5 whom the Egyptians keep in *b*';
6 and I will rid you out of their *b*',
9 anguish of spirit, and for cruel *b*'.
13: 3 out of the house of *b*'; for by
14 from Egypt, from the house of *b*':
20: 2 of Egypt, out of the house of *b*'.
De 5: 6 of Egypt, from the house of *b*'.
6:12 of Egypt, from the house of *b*'.
8:14 of Egypt, from the house of *b*';
13: 5 you out of the house of *b*',
10 of Egypt, from the house of *b*'.
26: 6 us, and laid upon us hard *b*':
Jos 24:17 from the house of *b*', and which
J'g 6: 8 you forth out ot the house of *b*';
Ezr 9: 8 give us a little reviving in our *b*'.
9 hath not forsaken us in our *b*',
Ne 5: 5 we bring into *b*' our sons and our
5 our daughters are brought unto *b*'
18 because the *b*' was heavy upon
9:17 a captain to return to their *b*':
Isa 14: 3 the hard *b*' wherein thou wast
Joh 8:33 and were never in *b*' to any man:
Ac 7: 6 they should bring them into *b*',
7 to whom they shall be in *b*' will
Ro 8:15 received the spirit of *b*' again to
21 shall be delivered from the *b*' of
1Co 7:15 a sister is not under *b*' in such
2Co 11:20 if a man bring you into *b*',
Ga 2: 4 that they might bring us into *b*':
4: 3 were in *b*' under the elements of
9 ye desire again to be in *b*'?
24 which gendereth to *b*', which is

Ga 4:25 and is in b' with her children.
5: 1 again with the yoke of b'.
Heb 2:15 all their lifetime subject to b'.
2Pe 2:19 of the same is he brought in b'.

bondmaid See also BONDMAIDS.
Le 19:20 is a b', betrothed to an husband,
Ga 4:22 two sons, the one by a b', the

bondmaids
Le 25:44 Both thy bondmen, and thy b',
44 them shall ye buy bondmen and b'.

bondman See also BONDMEN.
Ge 44:33 instead of the lad a b' to my lord;
De 15:15 remember that thou wast a b' in
16:12 remember that thou wast a b' in
24:18 thou wast a b' in Egypt, and the
22 a b' in the land of Egypt:
Re 6:15 every b', and every free man, hid

bondmen
Ge 43:18 and take us for b', and our asses.
44: 9 and we also will be my lord's b'.
Le 25:42 Egypt: they shall not be sold as b'.
44 Both thy b', and thy bondmaids,
44 of them shall ye buy b' and
46 they shall be your b' for ever:
26:13 that ye should not be their b';
De 6:21 We were Pharaoh's b' in Egypt;
7: 8 you out of the house of b',
28:68 be sold unto your enemies for b'
Jos 9:23 none of you be freed from being b',
1Ki 9:22 Israel did Solomon make no b':
2Ki 4: 1 unto him my two sons to be b'.
2Ch 28:10 of Judah and Jerusalem for b'
Ezr 9: 9 For we were b'; yet our God hath
Es 7: 4 But if we had been sold for b'
Jer 34:13 of Egypt, out of the house of b',

bonds
Nu 30: 5 or of her b' wherewith she
7 and her b' wherewith she bound
14 or all her b', which are upon her:
Ps 116:16 handmaid:...hast loosed my b'.
Jer 5: 5 broken the yoke, and burst the b'.
27: 2 Make thee b' and yokes, and put
30: 8 burst thy b', and strangers shall
Na 1:13 and will burst thy b' in sunder.
Ac 20:23 saying that b' and afflictions
23:29 charge worthy of death or of b'.
25:14 a certain man left in b' by Felix:
26:29 such as I am, except these b'.
31 nothing worthy of death or of b'.
Eph 6:20 which I am an ambassador in b':
Ph'p 1: 7 as both in my b', and in the
13 So that my b' in Christ are
14 waxing confident by my b', are
16 to add affliction to my b':
Col 4: 3 for which I am also in b':
18 Remember my b'. Grace be with
2Ti 2: 9 as an evil doer, even unto b';
Ph'm 10 whom I have begotten in my b':
13 have ministered unto me in the b'
Heb 10:34 had compassion of me in my b',
11:36 moreover of b' and imprisonment:
13: 3 Remember them that are in b',

bondservant
Le 25:39 compel him to serve as a b': 5656.

bondservice
1Ki 9:21 Solomon levy a tribute of b'

bondwoman See also BONDWOMEN.
Ge 21:10 Cast out this b' and her son: for
10 the son of this b' shall not be heir
12 because of thy b'; in all that Sarah
13 the son of the b' will I make a
Gal 4:23 he who was of the b' was born
30 Cast out the b' and her son:
30 for the son of the b' shall not be
31 children of the b', but of the free.

bondwomen
De 28:68 for bondmen and b', and no man
2Ch 28:10 for bondmen and b' unto you:
Es 7: 4 bondmen and b', I had held my

bone See also BONES; JAWBONE.
Ge 2:23 This is now b' of my bones, and
29:14 thou art my b' and my flesh.
Ex 12:46 neither shall ye break a b' thereof.
Nu 9:12 nor break any b' of it:
19:16 a dead body, or a b' of a man,
18 him that touched a b', or one slain,
J'g 9: 2 that I am your b' and your flesh.
2Sa 5: 1 Behold, we are thy b' and thy flesh.
19:13 Art thou not of my b', and of my
1Ch 11: 1 Behold, we are thy b' and thy flesh.
Job 2: 5 touch his b' and his flesh, and he
19:20 My b' cleaveth to my skin and to
31:22 mine arm be broken from the b'.
Ps 3: 7 all mine enemies upon the cheek b';
Pr 25:15 a soft tongue breaketh the b'.
Eze 37: 7 bones came together, b' to his b'.
39:15 when any seeth a man's b', then
Joh 19:36 A b' of him shall not be broken.

bones
Ge 2:23 bone of my b', and flesh of my
50:25 shall carry up my b' from hence.
Ex 13:19 took the b' of Joseph with him:
19 ye shall carry up my b' away hence
Nu 24: 8 break their b', and pierce them
Jos 24:32 b' of Joseph, which the children
J'g 19:29 divided her, together with her b',
1Sa 31:13 took their b', and buried them
2Sa 19:12 ye are my b' and my flesh:
21:12 went and took the b' of Saul
12 and the b' of Jonathan
13 b' of Saul and the b' of Jonathan
13 the b' of them that were hanged.
2Sa 21:14 the b' of Saul and Jonathan
1Ki 13: 2 men's b' shall be burnt upon thee.
31 buried; lay my b' beside his b':
2Ki 13:21 and touched the b' of Elisha,
23:14 their places with the b' of men.
16 took the b' out of the sepulchres,
18 let no man move his b'. So they let
18 his b' alone, with the b' of the
20 men's b' upon them, and returned
1Ch 10:12 buried their b' under the oak in
2Ch 34: 5 b' of the priests upon their altars,
Job 4:14 which made all my b' to shake.
10:11 fenced me with b' and sinews.
20:11 His b' are full of the sin of his
21:24 his b' are moistened with marrow.
30:17 My b' are pierced in me in the
30 and my b' are burned with heat.
33:19 of his b' with strong pain:
21 b' that were not seen stick out.
40:18 b' are as strong as pieces of
18 his b' are like bars of iron.
Ps 6: 2 heal me; for my b' are vexed.
22:14 all my b' are out of joint:
17 all my b': they look and stare
31:10 and my b' are consumed.
32: 3 b' waxed old through my roaring
34:20 He keepeth all his b': not one of
35:10 All my b' shall say, Lord, who is
38: 3 neither is there any rest in my b'
42:10 with a sword in my b',
51: 8 the b' which thou hast broken
53: 5 God hath scattered the b' of him
102: 3 my b' are burned as an hearth.
5 my b' cleave to my skin.
109:18 water, and like oil into his b'.
141: 7 Our b' are scattered at the grave's
Pr 3: 8 thy navel, and marrow to thy b'.
12: 4 is as rottenness in his b'.
14:30 but envy the rottenness of the b'.
15:30 a good report maketh the b' fat.
16:24 to the soul and health to the b'.
17:22 a broken spirit drieth the b'.
Ec 11: 5 how the b' do grow in the womb
Isa 38:13 lion, so will he break all my b':
58:11 drought and make fat thy b':
66:14 and your b' shall flourish like an
Jer 8: 1 the b' of the kings of Judah,
1 and the b' of his princes,
1 and the b' of the priests,
1 and the b' of the prophets,
1 and the b' of the inhabitants
20: 9 as a burning fire shut up in my b',
23: 9 all my b' shake; I am like a
50:17 king of Babylon hath broken his b'.
La 1:13 he sent fire into my b', and it
3: 4 made old; he hath broken my b'.
4: 8 their skin cleaveth to their b';
Eze 6: 5 scatter your b' round about your
24: 4 fill it with the choice b'.
5 burn also the b' under it,
5 let them seethe the b' of it
10 it well, and let the b' be burned.
32:27 iniquities shall be upon their b',
37: 1 the valley which was full of b',
3 Son of man, can these b' live?
4 upon these b', and say unto them,
4 O ye dry b', hear the word
5 saith the Lord God unto these b':
7 b' came together bone to his bone.
11 these b' are the whole house of
11 Our b' are dried, and our hope is
Da 6:24 and brake all their b' in pieces or
Am 2: 1 burned the b' of the king of Edom
6:10 to bring out the b' out of the house,
Mic 3: 2 their flesh from off their b';
3 they break their b', and chop them
Hab 3:16 rottenness entered into my b', and
Zep 3: 3 gnaw not the b' till the morrow.
M't 23:27 full of dead men's b', and of all
Lu 24:39 hath not flesh and b', as ye see
Ac 3: 7 feet and ancle b' received
Eph 5:30 body, of his flesh, and of his b'.
Heb 11:22 commandment concerning his b'.

bonnets
Ex 28:40 and b' shalt thou make for them.
29: 9 put the b' on them: and the
39:28 goodly b' of fine linen, and linen
Le 8:13 put b' upon them; as the Lord
Isa 3:20 The b', and the ornaments of the
Eze 44:18 They shall have linen b' upon

book^ See also BOOKS.
Ge 5: 1 This is the b' of the generations of
Ex 17:14 Write this for a memorial in a b',
24: 7 he took the b' of the covenant, and
32:32 blot me, I pray thee, out of thy b'
33 me, him will I blot out of my b'.
Nu 5:23 shall write these curses in a b',
21:14 it is said in the b' of the wars of
De 17:18 him a copy of this law in a b' out
28:58 this law that are written in this b',
61 which is not written in the b' of
29:20 curses that are written in this b'
21 that are written in this b' of the
27 curses that are written in this b':
30:10 statutes which are written in this b'
31:24 the words of this law in a b',
26 Take this b' of the law and put it
Jos 1: 8 This b' of the law shall not depart
8:31 it is written in the b' of the law
34 all that is written in the b' of the
10:13 Is not this written in the b' of
18: 9 by cities into seven parts in a b',
23: 6 all that is written in the b' of the
24:26 wrote these words in the b' of the
1Sa 10:25 wrote it in a b', and laid it up
2Sa 1:18 behold, it is written in the b' of
1Ki 11:41 they not written in the b' of the
14:19 b' of the chronicles of...Israel?
29 b' of the chronicles of...Israel?
15: 7,23 b' of the chronicles of...Judah?
31 b' of the chronicles of...Israel?
16: 5, 14, 20, 27 b' of the...of Israel?
22:39 b' of the chronicles of...Israel?
45 b' of the chronicles of...Judah?
2Ki 1:18 b' of the chronicles of...Israel?
8:23 b' of the chronicles of...Judah?
10:34 b' of the chronicles of...Israel?
12:19 b' of the chronicles of...Judah?
13: 8 b' of the chronicles of...Israel?
12 are they not written in the b' of the
14: 6 which is written in the b' of the law
15 b' of the chronicles of...Israel?
18 b' of the chronicles of...Judah?
28 b' of the chronicles of...Israel?
15: 6, 11, 15, 21, 26, 31, 36 in the b' of the
chronicles of the kings of Judah?
16:19 b' of the chronicles of...Judah?
20:20 b' of the chronicles of...Judah?
21: 17, 25 b' of the chronicles of...Judah?
22: 8 I have found the b' of the law in
8 Hilkiah gave the b' to Shaphan
10 the priest hath delivered me a b'.
11 king had heard the words of the b'
13 concerning the words of this b'
13 hearkened unto the words of this b',
16 all the words of the b' which the
23: 2 all the words of the b' of the
3 that were written in this b'.
21 written in the b' of this covenant.
24 law which were written in the b'
28 written in the b' of the chronicles
24: 5 did, are they not written in the b'
1Ch 9: 1 were written in the b' of the kings
29:29 behold, they are written in the b'
29 in the b' of Nathan the prophet,
29 and in the b' of Gad the seer,
2Ch 9:29 in the b' of Nathan the prophet,
12:15 in the b' of Shemaiah the
16:11 are written in the b' of the kings
17: 9 had the b' of the law of the Lord
20:34 in the b' of Jehu the son of
34 who is mentioned in the b' of the
24:27 in the story of the b' of the kings.
25: 4 in the law in the b' of Moses,
26 in the b' of the kings of Judah and
27: 7 they are written in the b' of the
28:26 in the b' of the kings of Judah and
32:32 in the b' of the kings of Judah and
33:18 written in the b' of the kings of
34:14 Hilkiah the priest found a b' of
15 I have found the b' of the law in
15 And Hilkiah delivered the b' to
16 Shaphan carried the b' to the king,
18 the priest hath given me a b'.
21 concerning the words of the b'
21 after all that is written in this b'.
24 curses that are written in the b'
30 all the words of the b' of the
31 which are written in this b'.
35:12 as it is written in the b' of Moses.
27 in the b' of the kings of Israel
36: 8 they are written in the b' of the
Ezr 4:15 search may be made in the b' of
15 so shalt thou find it in the b' of the
6:18 as it is written in the b' of Moses.
Neh 8: 1 bring the b' of the law of Moses,
3 people were attentive unto the b'
5 And Ezra opened the b' in the
8 they read in the b' in the law of
18 last day, he read in the b' of the
9: 3 read in the b' of the law of the
12:23 written in the b' of the chronicles,
13: 1 they read in the b' of Moses in the
Es 2:23 written in the b' of the chronicles
6: 1 he commanded to bring the b' of
9:32 Purim; and it was written in the b'.
10: 2 in the b' of the chronicles of the
Job 19:23 oh that they were printed in a b'!
31:35 mine adversary had written a b'.
Ps 40: 7 in the volume of the b' it is
56: 8 thy bottle: are they not in thy b'?
69:28 Let them be blotted out of the b' of
139:16 in thy b' all my members were
Isa 29:11 the words of a b' that is sealed,
12 And the b' is delivered to him that
18 the deaf hear the words of the b',
30: 8 and note it in a b', that it may be
34:16 Seek ye out of the b' of the Lord
Jer 25:13 even all that is written in this b',
30: 2 I have spoken unto thee in a b'.
32:12 subscribed the b' of the purchase,
36: 2 Take thee a roll of a b', and write
4 unto him, upon a roll of a b'.
8 reading in the b' the words of the
10 Then read Baruch in the b' the
11 out of the b' all the words of the
13 Baruch read the b' in the ears of
18 I wrote them with ink in the b'.
32 all the words of the b' which
45: 1 he had written these words in a b'
51:60 Jeremiah wrote in a b' all the evil
63 made an end of reading this b',
Eze 2: 9 and, lo, a roll of a b' was therein;
Da 12: 1 shall be found written in the b'.
4 shut up the words, and seal the b',
Na 1: 1 The b' of the vision of Nahum the
Mal 3:16 and a b' of remembrance was
M't 1: 1 The b' of the generation of Jesus
M'r 12:26 have ye not read in the b' of Moses,
Lu 3: 4 As it is written in the b' of the
4:17 delivered unto him the b' of the

Lu 4:17 And when he had opened the b', he
20 he closed the b', and he gave it
20:42 David himself saith in the b' of
Joh 20:30 which are not written in this b':
Ac 1:20 For it is written in the b' of
7:42 as it is written in the b' of the
Ga 3:10 things which are written in the b'
Ph'p 4: 3 whose names are in the b' of life.
Heb 9:19 sprinkled both the b', and all the
10: 7 (in the volume of the b' it is
Re 1:11 What thou seest, write in a b', and
3: 5 blot out his name out of the b' of
5: 1 on the throne a b' written within
2 Who is worthy to open the b', and
3 was able to open the b', neither to
4 worthy to open and to read the b',
5 hath prevailed to open the b', and
7 he came and took the b' out of the
8 when he had taken the b', the four
9 Thou art worthy to take the b', and
10: 2 he had in his hand a little b' open:
8 Go and take the little b' which
9 said unto him, Give me the little b'.
10 I took the little b' out of the
13: 8 not written in the b' of life of the
17: 8 names were not written in the b'
20:12 and another b' was opened,
12 which is the b' of life:
15 was not found written in the b'
21:27 written in the Lamb's b' of life.
22: 7 sayings of the prophecy of this b'.
9 which keep the sayings of this b':
10 sayings of the prophecy of this b':
18 words of the prophecy of this b',
18 plagues that are written in this b':
19 take away from the words of the b'
19 take away his part out of the b' of
19 things which are written in this b'.

books
Ec 12:12 making many b' there is no end;
Da 7:10 judgment was set, and the b'
9: 2 I Daniel understood by b' the
Joh 21:25 could not contain the b' that
Ac 19:19 brought their b' together, and
2Ti 4:13 bring with thee, and the b', but
Re 20:12 the b' were opened: and another
12 which were written in the b',

booth See also BOOTHS.
Job 27:18 and as a b' that the keeper
Jon 4: 5 and there made him a b', and sat

booths
Ge 33:17 made b' for his cattle: therefore
Le 23:42 Ye shall dwell in b' seven days;
42 are Israelites born shall dwell in b':
43 children of Israel do dwell in b',
Ne 8:14 children of Israel should dwell in b'
15 branches of thick trees, to make b',
16 made themselves b', every one
17 again out of the captivity made b',
17 and sat under the b':

booties
Hab 2: 7 thou shalt be for b' unto them?

booty See also BOOTIES.
Nu 31:32 the b', being the rest of the prey
Jer 49:32 their camels shall be a b', and
Zep 1:13 their goods shall become a b',

Booz (*bo'-oz*) See also BOAZ.
M't 1: 5 And Salmon begat B' of Rachab;
5 and B' begat Obed of Ruth;
Lu 3:32 which was the son of B', which

border See also BORDERS.
Ge 10:19 the b' of the Canaanites was
49:13 and his b' shall be unto Zidon.
Ex 19:12 or touch the b' of it: whosoever
25:25 make unto it a b' of an hand
25 a golden crown to the b' thereof
27 Over against the b' shall the
28:26 breastplate in the b' thereof,
37:12 made thereunto a b' of an hand
12 a crown of gold for the b' thereof
14 Over against the b' were the rings,
39:19 b' of it, which was on the
Nu 20:16 a city in the uttermost of thy b':
21 passage through his b':
21:13 for Arnon is the b' of Moab,
15 and lieth upon the b' of Moab.
23 Israel to pass through his b':
24 the b' of the children of Ammon
22:36 which is in the b' of Arnon,
33:44 in Ije-abarim, in the b' of Moab.
34: 3 and your south b' shall be
4 And your b' shall turn from
5 the b' shall fetch a compass from
6 And as for the western b', ye
6 even have the great sea for a b':
6 this shall be your west b'.
7 And this shall be your north b':
8 shall point out your b' unto the
8 the goings forth of the b' shall be
9 the b' shall go on to Ziphron,
9 this shall be your north b'.
10 ye shall point out your east b'
11 the b' shall descend, and shall
12 the b' shall go down to Jordan,
35:26 the b' of the city of his refuge,
De 3:16 the b' even unto the river Jabbok
16 the b' of the children of Ammon;
12:20 God shall enlarge thy b', as he
Jos 4:19 in the east b' of Jericho.
12: 2 is the b' of the children of Ammon
5 unto the b' of the Geshurites
5 the b' of Sihon king of Heshbon.
13:10 the b' of the children of Ammon;
11 and the b' of the Geshurites and

Jos 13:23 the b' of the children of Reuben
23 Jordan, and the b' thereof.
26 Mahanaim unto the b' of Debir;
27 Jordan and his b', even unto the
15: 1 to the b' of Edom the wilderness
2 their south b' was from the shore
5 And the east b' was the salt sea,
5 And their b' in the north quarter
6 the b' went up to Beth-hogla,
6 b' went up to the stone of Bohan
7 And the b' went up toward Debir
7 the b' passed toward the waters of
8 the b' went up by the valley of
8 and the b' went up to the top of
9 the b' was drawn from the top
9 and the b' was drawn to Baalah,
10 the b' compassed from Baalah
11 b' went out unto the side of Ekron
11 and the b' was drawn to Shicron,
11 goings out of the b' were at the
12 the west b' was to the great sea,
47 the great sea, and the b' thereof.
16: 5 the b' of the children of Ephraim
5 even the b' of their inheritance
6 And the b' went out toward the
6 the b' went about eastward
8 The b' went out from Tappuah
17: 7 b' went along on the right hand
8 Tappuah on the b' of Manasseh
10 the sea is his b'; and they met
18:12 And their b' on the north side
12 b' went up to the side of Jericho
13 the b' went over from thence
13 the b' descended to Ataroth-adar,
14 the b' was drawn thence, and
15 b' went out on the west,
16 the b' came down to the end of
19 b' passed along to the side of
19 outgoings of the b' were at the
20 Jordan was the b' of it on the
19:10 the b' of their inheritance was
11 their b' went up toward the sea,
12 unto the b' of Chisloth-tabor,
14 the b' compasseth it on the north
18 their b' was toward Jezreel,
22 outgoings of their b' were at
25 their b' was Helkath, and Hali,
46 Rakkon, with the b' before Japho.
22:25 the Lord hath made Jordan a b'
24:30 in the b' of his inheritance in
J'g 2: 9 in the b' of his inheritance in
7:22 to the b' of Abel-meholah,
11:18 within the b' of Moab:
18 for Arnon was the b' of Moab.
1Sa 6:12 them unto the b' of Beth-shemesh.
10: 2 in the b' of Benjamin at Zelzah;
13:18 the way of the b' that looketh to
2Sa 8: 3 to recover his b' at the river
1Ki 4:21 and unto the b' of Egypt:
2Ki 3:21 and upward, and stood in the b'.
2Ch 9:26 Philistines, and to the b' of Egypt.
Ps 78:54 he brought them to the b' of his
Pr 15:25 will establish the b' of the widow.
Isa 19:19 at the b' thereof to the Lord.
37:24 into the height of his b', and the
Jer 31:17 shall come again to their own b'.
50:26 from the utmost b', open her
Eze 11:10 will judge you in the b' of Israel;
11 I will judge you in the b' of Israel:
29:10 even unto the b' of Ethiopia.
43:13 and the b' thereof by the edge
17 and the b' about it shall be half
20 and upon the b' round about:
45: 7 the west b' unto the east b'.
47:13 This shall be the b', whereby ye
15 this shall be the b' of the land
16 between the b' of Damascus
16 and the b' of Hamath;
17 the b' from the sea shall be
17 Hazar-enan, the b' of Damascus,
17 northward, and the b' of Hamath.
18 from the b' unto the east sea.
20 the great sea from the b', till a
48: 1 the b' of Damascus northward,
2 by the b' of Dan, from the east side
3 the b' of Asher, from the east side
4 b' of Naphtali, from the east side
5 b' of Manasseh, from the east side
6 b' of Ephraim, from the east side
7 b' of Reuben, from the east side
8 b' of Judah, from the east side
12 by the b' of the Levites.
13 against the b' of the priests
21 the oblation toward the east b',
21 thousand toward the west b',
22 between the b' of Judah
22 and the b' of Benjamin,
24 b' of Benjamin, from the east side
25 b' of Simeon, from the east side
26 b' of Issachar, from the east side
27 b' of Zebulun, from the east side
28 b' of Gad, at the south side
28 the b' shall be even from Tamar
Joe 3: 6 remove them far from their b'.
Am 1:13 that they might enlarge their b':
6: 2 or their b' greater than your b'?
Ob 7 have brought thee even to the b':
Zep 2: 8 themselves against their b'.
Zec 9: 2 Hamath also shall b' thereby;
Mal 1: 4 The b' of wickedness, and, The
5 magnified from the b' of Israel.
M'r 6:56 were but the b' of his garment:
Lu 8:44 touched the b' of his garment;

borders
Ge 23:17 in all the b' round about, were
47:21 from one end of the b' of Egypt
Ex 8: 2 I will smite all thy b' with frogs:
16:35 unto the b' of the land of Canaan.
34:24 before thee, and enlarge thy b':
Nu 15:38 in the b' of their garments
38 the fringe of the b' a ribband
20:17 until we have passed thy b'.
21:22 until we be passed thy b'.
35:27 him without the b' of the city of
Jos 11: 2 and in the b' of Dor on the west,
13: 2 all the b' of the Philistines,
3 unto the b' of Ekron northward,
4 Aphek, to the b' of the Amorites:
16: 2 unto the b' of Archi to Ataroth,
22:10 came unto the b' of Jordan, that
11 the b' of Jordan, at the passage
1Ki 7:28 they had b', and
28 the b' were between the ledges:
29 on the b' that were between the
31 with their b', foursquare
32 under the b' were four wheels;
35 the b' thereof were of the same.
36 b' thereof, he graved cherubim,
2Ki 16:17 Ahaz cut off the b' of the bases,
18: 8 the b' thereof, from the tower
19:23 into the lodgings of his b',
1Ch 5:16 suburbs of Sharon, upon their b'.
7:29 b' of the children of Manasseh,
Ps 74:17 hast set all the b' of the earth:
147:14 maketh peace in thy b', and filleth
Ca 1:11 b' of gold with studs of silver.
Isa 15: 8 gone round about the b' of Moab;
54:12 and all thy b' of pleasant stones.
60:18 nor destruction within thy b';
Jer 15:13 all thy sins, even in all thy b'.
17: 3 for sin, throughout all thy b'.
Eze 27: 4 Thy b' are in the midst of the seas,
45: 1 holy in all the b' thereof round
Mic 5: 6 when he treadeth within our b'.
M't 4:13 the b' of Zabulon and Nephthalim:
23: 5 enlarge the b' of their garments,
M'r 7:24 into the b' of Tyre and Sidon,

bore See also BARE; BORED.
Ex 21: 6 master shall b' his ear through
Job 41: 2 b' his jaw through with a thorn?

bored
2Ki 12: 9 and b' a hole in the lid of it,

born See also BORNE; FIRSTBORN; FORBORN; NEWBORN.
Ge 4:18 And unto Enoch was b' Irad:
26 to him also there was b' a son;
6: 1 and daughters were b' unto them,
10: 1 them were sons b' after the flood.
21 even to him were children b'.
25 unto Eber were b' two sons: the
14:14 b' in his own house, three
15: 3 one b' in my house is mine heir.
17:12 he that is b' in the house, or
13 He that is b' in thy house, and
17 Shall a child be b' unto him that
23 all that were b' in his house,
27 men of his house, b' in the house,
21: 3 his son that was b' unto him, whom
5 his son Isaac was b' unto him.
7 I have b' him a son in his old age.
9 which she had b' unto Abraham,
22:20 she hath also b' children unto
24:15 was b' to Bethuel, son of Milcah,
29:34 because I have b' him three sons:
30:20 I have b' him six sons: and she
25 Rachel had b' Joseph, that Jacob
31:43 children which they have b'?
35:26 were b' to him in Padan-aram.
36: 5 b' unto him in the land of Canaan.
41:50 And unto Joseph were b' two sons
46:20 land of Egypt were b' Manasseh
22 of Rachel, which were b' to Jacob:
27 which were b' him in Egypt, were
48: 5 Manasseh, which were b' unto thee
Ex 1:22 Every son that is b' ye shall cast
12:19 be a stranger, or b' in the land.
48 be as one that is b' in the land.
21: 4 have b' him sons or daughters;
Le 12: 2 and b' a man child, then she
7 law for her that hath b' a male
18: 9 whether she be b' at home,
9 or b' abroad,
19:34 unto you as one b' among you,
22:11 and he that is b' in his house:
23:42 all that are Israelites b' shall
24:16 as he that is b' in the land, when
Nu 9:14 him that was b' in the land.
15:13 All that are b' of the country
29 him that is b' among the children
30 be b' in the land, or a stranger,
26:60 unto Aaron was b' Nadab and
De 21:15 and they have b' him children,
Jos 5: 5 the people that were b' in the
8:33 as he that was b' among them;
J'g 13: 8 do unto the child that shall be b'.
18:29 father, who was b' unto Israel:
Ru 4:15 than seven sons, hath b' him.
17 There is a son b' to Naomi;
1Sa 2: 5 so that the barren hath b' seven;
4:20 Fear not, for thou hast b' a son.
2Sa 3: 2 unto David were sons b' in Hebron:
5 These were b' to David in Hebron.
5:13 sons and daughters b' to David.
14 names of those that were b' unto
12:14 the child also that is b' unto thee
14:27 Absalom there were b' three sons,
21:20 and he also was b' to the giant.
22 four were b' to the giant in Gath,
1Ki 13: 2 be b' unto the house of David,
1Ch 1:19 And unto Eber were b' two sons:
2: 3 which three were b' unto him of

1Ch 2: 9 of Hezron, that were b' unto him;
3: 1 which were b' unto him in Hebron;
4 six were b' unto him in Hebron;
5 were b' unto him in Jerusalem;
7:21 of Gath that were b' in that land
20: 8 were b' unto the giant in Gath;
22: 9 a son shall be b' to thee, who shall
26: 6 Shemaiah his son were sons b',
Ezr 10: 3 such as are b' of them, according
Job 1: 2 there were b' unto him seven sons
3: 3 the day perish wherein I was b',
5: 7 man is b' unto trouble, as the
11:12 man be b' like a wild ass's colt.
14: 1 Man that is b' of a woman is of
15: 7 Art thou the first man that was b'?
14 he which is b' of a woman, that he
25: 4 he be clean that is b' of a woman?
38:21 thou it, because thou wast then b'?
Ps 22:31 a people that shall be b', that he
58: 3 go astray as soon as they be b',
78: 6 the children which should be b';
87: 4 Ethiopia; this man was b' there.
5 that man was b' in her: and the
6 people, that this man was b' there.
Pr 17:17 and a brother is b' for adversity.
Ec 2: 7 and had servants b' in my house;
3: 2 A time to be b', and a time to die;
4:14 is b' in his kingdom becometh
Isa 9: 6 unto us a child is b', unto us a son
66: 8 shall a nation be b' at once? for as
Jer 16: 3 daughters that are b' in this place,
20:14 be the day wherein I was b':
15 A man child is b' unto thee;
22:26 country, where ye were not b';
Eze 16: 4 in the day thou wast b' thy
5 in the day that thou wast b'.
47:22 shall be unto you as b' in the
Ho 2: 3 her as in the day that she was b',
M't 1:16 of whom was b' Jesus, who is
2: 1 when Jesus was b' in Bethlehem
2 is he that is b' King of the Jews?
4 of them where Christ should be b'.
11:11 Among them that are b' of women
19:12 so b' from their mother's womb:
26:24 that man if he had not been b'.
M'r 14:21 that man if he had never been b'.
Lu 1:35 that holy thing which shall be b'
2:11 For unto you is b' this day in the
7:28 Among those that are b' of women
Joh 1:13 Which were b', not of blood, nor
3: 3 Except a man be b' again, he
4 can a man be b' when he is old?
4 into his mother's womb, and be b'?
5 Except a man be b' of water and
6 which is b' of the flesh is flesh;
6 which is b' of the Spirit is spirit.
7 unto thee, Ye must be b' again.
8 every one that is b' of the Spirit.
8:41 We be not b' of fornication; we
9: 2 or his parents, that he was b' blind?
19 your son, who ye say was b' blind?
20 our son, and that he was b' blind:
32 the eyes of one that was b' blind.
34 Thou wast altogether b' in sins,
16:21 joy that a man is b' into the world.
18:37 To this end was I b', and for this
Ac 2: 8 own tongue, wherein we were b'?
7:20 In which time Moses was b', and
18: 2 Aquila, b' in Pontus, lately come
24 named Apollos, b' at Alexandria,
22: 3 which am a Jew, b' in Tarsus,
28 Paul said, But I was free b'.
Ro 9:11 (For the children being not yet b',
1Co 15: 8 also, as of one b' out of due time.
Ga 4:23 bondwoman was b' after the flesh;
29 he that was b' after the flesh
29 him that was b' after the Spirit,
Heb 11:23 By faith Moses, when he was b',
1Pe 1:23 b' again not of corruptible seed,
1Jo 2:29 doeth righteousness is b' of him.
3: 9 Whosoever is b' of God doth not
9 sin, because he is b' of God.
4: 7 every one that loveth is b' of God,
5: 1 Jesus is the Christ is b' of God:
4 For whatsoever is b' of God
18 whosoever is b' of God sinneth not;
Re 12: 4 her child as soon as it was b'.

borne See also BORN.
Ex 25:14 the ark may be b' with them.
28 the table may be b' with them.
J'g 16:29 and on which it was b' up,
Job 34:31 I have b' chastisement, I will not
Ps 55:12 then I could have b' it: neither
69: 7 I have b' reproach; shame hath
Isa 46: 3 are b' by me from the belly,
53: 4 Surely he hath b' our griefs,
66:12 ye shall be b' upon her sides,
Jer 10: 5 they must needs be b', because
15: 9 that hath b' seven languisheth:
10 thou hast b' me a man of strife
La 3:28 because he hath b' it upon him.
5: 7 and we have b' their iniquities.
Eze 16:20 daughters, whom thou hast b'
58 Thou hast b' thy lewdness
32:24, 25 yet have they b' their shame
36: 6 ye have b' the shame of the
39:26 that they have b' their shame,
Am 5:26 b' the tabernacle of your Moloch
M't 20:12 which have b' the burden and heat
23: 4 burdens and grievous to be b',
M'k 2: 3 the palsy, which was b' of four.
Lu 11:46 with burdens grievous to be b',
Joh 5:37 hath sent me, hath b' witness of me.
20:15 Sir, if thou have b' him hence,
Ac 21:35 that he was b' of the soldiers
1Co 15:49 have b' the image of the earthy,
3Jo 6 have b' witness of thy charity
Re 2: 3 And hast b', and hast patience,

borrow See also BORROWED; BORROWETH.
Ex 3:22 woman shall b' of her neighbour,
11: 2 every man b' of his neighbour,
22:14 borrow ought of his neighbour,
De 15: 6 nations, but thou shalt not b';
28:12 nations, and thou shalt not b'.
2Ki 4: 3 b' thee vessels abroad of all thy
3 even empty vessels; b' not a few.
M't 5:42 from him that would b' of thee

borrowed
Ex 12:35 they b' of the Egyptians jewels
2Ki 6: 5 Alas, master! for it was b'.
Ne 5: 4 We have b' money for the king's

borrower
Pr 22: 7 the b' is servant to the lender.
Isa 24: 2 so with the b'; as with the taker

borroweth
Ps 37:21 The wicked b', and payeth not

Boscath (*bos'-cath*) See also BOSKETH.
2Ki 22: 1 the daughter of Adaiah of B'.

Bosketh See ISH-BOSKETH.

bosom
Ge 16: 5 I have given my maid into thy b';
Ex 4: 6 Put now thine hand into thy b'.
6 And he put his hand into his b':
7 Put thine hand into thy b' again.
7 he put his hand into his b' again;
7 and plucked it out of his b',
Nu 11:12 Carry them in thy b', as a nursing
De 13: 6 or the wife of thy b', or thy friend,
28:54 toward the wife of his b',
56 evil toward the husband of her b',
Ru 4:16 laid it in her b', and became nurse
2Sa 12: 3 lay in his b', and was unto him
8 thy master's wives into thy b',
1Ki 1: 2 let her lie in thy b', that my lord
3:20 and laid it in her b', and laid her
20 and laid her dead child in my b'.
17:19 he took him out of her b',
Job 31:33 by hiding mine iniquity in my b':
Ps 35:13 prayer returned into mine own b'.
74:11 hand? pluck it out of thy b'.
79:12 sevenfold into their b' their
89:50 I do bear in my b' the reproach of
129: 7 he that bindeth sheaves his b'.
Pr 5:20 and embrace the b' of a stranger?
6:27 Can a man take fire in his b', and
17:23 man taketh a gift out of the b' to
19:24 man hideth his hand in his b',
21:14 a reward in the b' strong wrath.
26:15 slothful hideth his hand in his b';
Ec 7: 9 anger resteth in the b' of fools.
Isa 40:11 and carry them in his b', and shall
65: 6 even recompense into their b',
7 their former work into their b'.
Jer 32:18 into the b' of their children after
La 2:12 poured out into their mother's b'.
Mic 7: 5 from her that lieth in thy b'.
Lu 6:38 shall men give into your b'.
16:22 by the angels into Abraham's b':
23 afar off, and Lazarus in his b'.
Joh 1:18 which is in the b' of the Father,
13:23 leaning on Jesus' b' one of his

Bosor (*bo'-sor*)
2Pe 2:15 Balaam the son of B', who loved

bosses
Job 15:26 upon the thick b' of his bucklers:

botch
De 28:27 smite thee with the b' of Egypt,
35 with a sore b' that cannot be

both^
Ge 2:25 they were b' naked, the man and
3: 7 the eyes of them b' were opened,
6: 7 b' man, and beast, and the
7:21 upon the earth, b' of fowl, and of
23 upon the face of the ground, b'
8:17 all flesh, b' of fowl, and of cattle,
9:23 laid it upon b' their shoulders,
19: 4 b' old and young, all the people
11 with blindness, b' small and great:
36 b' the daughters of Lot with child
21:27 b' of them made a covenant.
31 and there they sware b' of them.
22: 6 they went b' of them together.
8 so they went b' of them together.
24:25 We have b' straw and provender
27:45 deprived also of you b' in one day?
31:37 they may judge betwixt us b'.
36:24 children of Zibeon; b' Ajah, and
40: 5 dreamed a dream b' of them,
41:10 b' me and the chief baker:
42:35 when b' they and their father
43: 8 live, and not die, b' we, and thou,
44: 9 it be found, b' let him die,
16 my lord's servants, b' we, and he
46:34 now, b' we, and also our fathers:
47: 3 b' we, and also our fathers.
19 we die before thine eyes, b' we
48:13 Joseph took them b', Ephraim in
50: 9 went up with him b' chariots
Ex 5:14 making brick b' yesterday and to
8: 4 the frogs shall come up b' on thee,
12:31 forth from among my people, b'
13: 2 b' of man and of beast: it is mine.
15 of Egypt, b' the firstborn of man,
18:18 surely wear away, b' thou, and
22: 9 the cause of b' parties shall come
11 the Lord be between them b',
26:24 thus shall it be for them b';
29:44 sanctify also b' Aaron and his
32:15 tables were written on b' their
35:22 b' men and women, as many as
25 that which they had spun, b' of
34 may teach, b' he, and Aholiab,
36:29 thus he did to b' of them in
29 of them in b' the corners.
37:26 overlaid it with pure gold, b' the
Le 6:28 brasen pot, it shall be b' scoured,
8:11 b' the laver and his foot,
9: 3 and a lamb, b' of the first year,
15:18 shall b' bathe themselves in water,
16:21 And Aaron shall lay b' his hands
17:15 he shall b' wash his clothes,
20:11 b' of them shall surely be put to
12 daughter in law, b' of them shall
13 b' of them have committed an
14 burnt with fire, b' he and they;
18 and b' of them shall be cut off
21:22 eat the bread of his God, b' of the
22:28 kill it and her young b' in one
25:41 shall he depart from thee, b' he
44 B' thy bondmen, and thy
54 go out in the year of jubile, b'
27:28 b' of man and beast, and of the
33 then b' it and the change thereof
Nu 3:13 b' man and beast: mine shall they
5: 3 B' male and female shall ye put
7: 1 b' the altar and all the vessels
13 b' of them were full of fine flour
19, 25, 31, 37, 43, 49, 55, 61, 67, 73, 79
b' of them full of fine flour
8:17 of Israel are mine, b' man and
9:14 ordinance, b' for the stranger,
12: 5 Aaron and Miriam, and they b'
15:15 One ordinance shall be b' for you
29 b' for him that is born among
16:11 For which cause b' thou and all
25: 8 thrust b' of them through,
27:21 his word they shall come in, b' he,
31:11 and all the prey, b' of men and of
19 any slain, purify b' yourselves
26 prey that was taken, b' of man
28 of five hundred, b' of the persons,
47 portion of fifty, b' of man and
35:15 be a refuge, b' for the children
De 19:17 Then b' the men, between whom
21:15 b' the beloved, and the hated;
22:22 then they shall b' of them die,
22 b' the man that lay with the
24 bring them b' out unto the gate
23:18 for even b' these are abomination
30:19 life, that b' thou and thy seed
32:25 shall destroy b' the young man
Jos 6:21 all that was in the city, b' man
8:25 fell that day, b' of men and women,
14:11 war, b' to go out, and to come in.
17:16 b' they who are of Beth-shean
J'g 5:30 colours of needlework on b' sides,
6: 5 for b' they and their camels were
8:22 Rule thou over us, b' thou, and
10:10 against thee, b' because we have
15: 5 and burnt up b' the shocks,
19: 6 did eat and drink b' of them
8 afternoon, and they did eat b' of
19 there is b' straw and provender
Ru 1: 5 Mahlon and Chilion died also b'
1Sa 2:26 was in favour b' with the Lord,
34 one day they shall die b' of them.
3:11 b' the ears of every one that
5: 4 b' the palms of his hands were cut
9 smote the men of the city, b' small
9:26 they went out b' of them, he and
12:14 then shall b' ye and also the king
25 be consumed, b' ye and your king.
14:11 b' of them discovered themselves
15: 3 spare them not; but slay b' man
17:36 Thy servant slew b' the lion and
20:11 they went out b' of them into the
42 we have sworn b' of us in the name
22:19 b' men and women, children and
25: 6 Peace be b' to thee, and peace be
16 wall unto us b' by night and day,
43 were also b' of them his wives.
26:25 thou shalt b' do great things,
2Sa 8:18 the son of Jehoiada was over b'
9:13 and was lame on b' his feet.
15:25 shew me b' it, and his habitation:
16:23 of Ahithophel b' with David
17:18 went b' of them away quickly,
1Ki 3:13 thou hast not asked, b' riches,
6: 5 b' of the temple and of the oracle:
15 b' the floor of the house, and the
16 b' the floor and the walls with
25 b' the cherubims were of one
7:12 b' for the inner court of the
50 hinges of gold, b' for the doors
2Ki 2:11 parted them b' asunder; and
3:17 that ye may drink, b' ye, and your
6:15 host compassed the city b' with
17:41 served their graven images, b'
21:12 of it, b' his ears shall tingle.
23: 2 all the people, b' small and great:
15 b' that altar and the high place
25:26 people, b' small and great, and the
1Ch 12: 2 and could use b' the right hand
15 b' toward the east, and toward
15:12 sanctify yourselves, b' ye and
16: 3 one of Israel, b' man and woman,
23:29 B' for the shewbread, and for
28:15 by weight, b' for the candlestick,
29:12 B' riches and honour come of thee,
2Ch 20:25 abundance b' riches with the dead
24:16 done good in Israel, b' toward
25:21 face, b' he and Amaziah king
26:10 cattle, b' in the low country,
27: 5 of Ammon pay unto him, b' the

2Ch 31:17 B' to the genealogy of the priests
32:26 pride of his heart, b' he and the
Ezr 3: 5 burnt offering, b' of the new
6: 9 have need of, b' young bullocks,
Ne 1: 6 b' I and my father's house have
4:16 half of them held b' the spears,
8: 2 congregation b' of men and
10: 9 And the Levites: b' Jeshua the
12:27 gladness, b' with thanksgivings,
28 b' out of the plain country round
45 b' the singers and the porters
Es 1: 5 the palace, b' unto great and small,
20 husbands honour, b' to great and
2:23 therefore they were b' hanged on
3:13 to perish, all Jews, b' young and
8:11 them, b' little ones and women,
9:20 the king Ahasuerus, b' nigh, and
Job 9:33 might lay his hand upon us b'.
15:10 With us are b' the greyheaded
Ps 4: 8 I will b' lay me down in peace,
49: 2 B' low and high, rich and poor,
58: 9 whirlwind, b' living, and in his
64: 6 b' the inward thought of every
76: 6 O God of Jacob, b' the chariot
104:25 innumerable, b' small and great
115:13 that fear the Lord, b' small and
135: 8 the firstborn of Egypt, b' of man
139:12 darkness and the light are b' alike
148:12 B' young men and maidens; old
Pr 17:15 they b' are abomination
20:10 b' of them are alike abomination
12 the Lord hath made even b' of them.
24:22 who knoweth the ruin of them b'?
26:10 formed all things b' rewardeth
27: 3 wrath is heavier than them b'
29:13 the Lord lighteneth b' their eyes.
Ec 4: 3 better is he than b' they, which
6 than b' the hands full with
8: 5 a wise man's heart discerneth b'
11: 6 whether they b' shall be alike
Isa 1:31 they shall b' burn together, and
7:16 shall be forsaken of b' her
8:14 to b' the houses of Israel, for a gin
10:18 fruitful field, b' soul and body:
13: 9 Lord cometh, cruel b' with
18: 5 he shall b' cut off the sprigs
38:15 What shall I say? he hath b'
44:12 with the tongs b' worketh it in
Jer 5:24 that giveth rain, b' the former and
9:10 b' the fowl of the heavens and the
14:18 yea, b' the prophet and the priest
16: 6 B' the great and the small shall
21: 6 of this city, b' man and beast:
23:11 For b' prophet and priest are
26: 5 sent unto you, b' rising up early
28: 8 prophesied b' against many
31:13 b' young men and old together
32:11 purchase, b' that which was
14 of the purchase, b' which is
36:16 were afraid b' one and other, and
44:25 wives have b' spoken with your
46:12 the mighty, and they are fallen b'
50: 3 they shall depart, b' man and
51:12 for the Lord hath b' devised and
46 a rumor shall b' come one year,
La 3:26 good that a man should b' hope
Eze 9: 6 young, b' maids, and little
14:22 that shall be brought forth, b' sons
15: 4 the fire devoureth b' the ends of
21:19 b' twain shall come forth out of
23:13 defiled, that they took b' one way,
29 b' thy lewdness and thy whoredoms.
34:11 I, will b' search my sheep, and
39: 9 b' the shields and the bucklers,
42:11 their goings out were b' according
Da 8:13 to give b' the sanctuary and the
11:27 And b' these kings' hearts shall
Mic 5: 8 he go through, b' treadeth down
7: 3 they may do evil with b' hands
Na 3: 3 horseman lifteth up b' the bright
Zep 2:14 b' the cormorant and the bittern
Zec 6:13 of peace shall be between them b'.
12: 2 siege b' against Judah and
M't 9:17 new bottles, and b' are preserved.
10:28 to destroy b' soul and body in
12:22 blind and dumb b' spake and
13:30 Let b' grow together until the
15:14 blind, b' shall fall into the ditch.
22:10 many as they found, b' bad
M'r 6:30 him all things, b' what they had
7:37 he maketh b' the deaf to hear,
Lu 1: 6 they were b' righteous before God,
7 they b' were now well stricken in
2:46 doctors, b' hearing them and
5: 7 they came, and filled b' the ships,
36 then b' the new maketh a rent,
38 into new bottles; and b' are
6:39 shall they not b' fall into the ditch?
7:42 to pay, he frankly forgave them b'
21:16 shall be betrayed b' by parents
22:33 thee, b' into prison, and to death.
Joh 2: 2 And b' Jesus was called, and his
4:36 that b' he that soweth and he
7:28 Ye b' know me, and ye know
9:37 Thou hast b' seen him, and it is
11:48 take away b' our place and nation.
57 Now b' the chief priests and the
12:28 saying, I have b' glorified it, and
15:24 they b' seen and hated b' me and
20: 4 So they ran b' together: and the
Ac 1: 1 Jesus began b' to do and teach,
8 b' in Jerusalem, and in all Judæa,
13 b' Peter, and James, and John,
2:29 patriarch David, that he is b'
36 have crucified, b' Lord and Christ.
4:27 b' Herod, and Pontius Pilate,
Ac 5:14 to the Lord, multitudes b' of men
8:12 they were baptized, b' men and
38 and they went down b' into the
38 b' Philip and the eunuch; and he
10:39 b' in the land of the Jews, and in
14: 1 that they went b' together into
1 b' of the Jews and also of the
5 b' of the Gentiles, and also of the
19:10 Lord Jesus, b' Jews and Greeks.
20:21 b' to the Jews, and also to the
21:12 b' we, and they of that place,
22: 4 delivering into prisons b' men and
23: 8 but the Pharisees confess b'.
24:15 of the dead, b' of the just and
25:24 b' at Jerusalem, and also here,
26:16 a witness b' of these things which
22 witnessing b' to small and great,
29 hear me this day, were b'
28:23 b' out of the law of Moses, and out
Ro 1:12 by the mutual faith b' of you and
14 b' to the Greeks, and to the
14 b' to the wise, and to the unwise.
3: 9 b' Jews and Gentiles, that they
11:33 the riches b' of the wisdom and
14: 9 For to this end Christ b' died,
9 be Lord b' of the dead and living.
1Co 1: 2 Jesus Christ our Lord, b' theirs
24 b' Jews and Greeks, Christ the
4: 5 Lord come, who b' will bring to
11 we b' hunger, and thirst, and are
6:13 God shall destroy b' it and them.
14 And God hath b' raised up the
7:29 it remaineth, that b' they that
34 that she may be holy b' in body
2Co 9:10 to the sower b' minister bread
Eph 1:10 b' which are in heaven, and
2:14 our peace, who hath made b' one,
16 he might reconcile b' unto God
18 through him we b' have access
Ph'p 1: 7 inasmuch as b' in my bonds, and
2:13 God which worketh in you b' to
4: 9 things which ye have b' learned,
12 I know b' how to be abased, and
12 b' to be full and to be hungry, b'
1Th 2:15 Who b' killed the Lord Jesus, and
5:15 is good, b' among yourselves,
1Ti 4:10 For therefore we b' labour and
16 shalt b' save thyself, and them
Tit 1: 9 able by sound doctrine b' to exhort
Ph'm 16 thee, b' in the flesh, and in the
Heb 2: 4 b' with signs and wonders, and
11 For b' he that sanctifieth and they
5: 1 that he may offer b' gifts and
14 exercised to discern b' good and
6:19 an anchor of the soul, b' sure and
9: 9 offered b' gifts and sacrifices,
19 sprinkled b' the book, and all the
21 he sprinkled with blood b' the
10:33 b' by reproaches and afflictions;
11:21 blessed b' the sons of Joseph;
Jas 3:12 so can no fountain b' yield salt
2Pe 3: 1 in b' which I stir up your pure
18 To him be glory b' now and for
2Jo 9 he hath b' the Father and the Son.
Jude 25 dominion and power, b' now and
Re 13:15 image of the beast should b' speak,
16 And he causeth all, b' small and
19: 5 ye that fear him, b' small and
18 all men, b' free and bond,
18 b' small and great.
20 These b' were cast alive into a

bottle See also BOTTLES.
Ge 21:14 took bread, and a b' of water,
15 the water was spent in the b', and
19 filled the b' with water, and gave
J'g 4:19 she opened a b' of milk, and gave
1Sa 1:24 one ephah of flour, and a b' of
10: 3 another carrying a b' of wine:
16:20 and a b' of wine, and a kid, and
2Sa 16: 1 summer fruits, and a b' of wine,
Ps 56: 8 put thou my tears into thy b':
119:83 am become like a b' in the smoke;
Jer 13:12 Every b' shall be filled with wine:
12 not certainly know that every b'
19: 1 get a potter's earthen b', and take
10 Then shalt thou break the b' in
Hab 2:15 that puttest thy b' to him, and

bottles
Jos 9: 4 and wine b', old, and rent, and
13 these b' of wine, which we filled,
1Sa 25:18 two b' of wine, and five sheep
Job 32:19 it is ready to burst like new b'.
38:37 or who can stay the b' of heaven,
Jer 48:12 his vessels, and break their b'.
Ho 7: 5 have made him sick with b' of
M't 9:17 put new wine into old b':
17 else the b' break, and the wine
17 runneth out, and the b' perish:
17 put new wine into new b',
M'r 2:22 putteth new wine into old b':
22 new wine doth burst the b',
22 spilled, and the b' will be
22 wine must be put into new b'.
Lu 5:37 putteth new wine into old b';
37 new wine will burst the b', and
37 spilled, and the b' shall perish.
38 wine must be put into new b';

bottom See also BOTTOMLESS; BOTTOMS.
Ex 15: 5 they sank into the b' as a stone.
29:12 blood beside the b' of the altar.
Le 4: 7 blood of the bullock at the b' of
18 blood at the b' of the altar of the
25 pour out his blood at the b' of the
30 thereof at the b' of the altar.
34 thereof at the b' of the altar:
Le 5: 9 blood shall be wrung out at the b'
8:15 the blood at the b' of the altar.
9: 9 poured out the blood at the b' of
Job 36:30 and covereth the b' of the sea.
Ca 3:10 b' thereof of gold, the covering
Eze 43:13 even the b' shall be a cubit, and
14 And from the b' upon the ground
17 and the b' thereof shall be a cubit
Dan 6:24 or ever they came at the b' of the
Am 9: 3 in the b' of the sea, thence will I
Zec 1: 8 myrtle trees that were in the b';
M't 27:51 from the top to the b'; and the
M'k 15:38 in twain from the top to the b'.

bottoms
Jon 2: 6 I went down to the b' of the

bottomless
Rev 9: 1 was given the key of the b' pit.
2 And he opened the b' pit;
11 the angel of the b' pit, whose
11: 7 that ascendeth out of the b' pit
17: 8 and shall ascend out of the b' pit,
20: 1 having the key of the b' pit and a
3 cast him into the b' pit, and shut

bough See also BOUGHS.
Ge 49:22 Joseph is a fruitful b',
22 even a fruitful b' by a well;
J'g 9:48 and cut down a b' from the trees,
49 cut down every man his b', and
Isa 10:33 the Lord of hosts, shall lop the b'
17: 6 the top of the uppermost b', four
9 strong cities be as a forsaken b',

boughs
Le 23:40 the b' of goodly trees, branches
40 and the b' of thick trees, and
De 24:20 thou shalt not go over the b'
2Sa 18: 9 the thick b' of a great oak, and
Job 14: 9 will bud, and bring forth b' like
Ps 80:10 and the b' thereof were like the
11 She sent out her b' unto the sea,
Ca 7: 8 I will take hold of the b' thereof:
Isa 27:11 When the b' thereof are
Eze 17:23 it shall bring forth b', and bear
31: 3 his top was among the thick b'.
5 his b' were multiplied, and his
6 heaven made their nests in his b',
8 the fir trees were not like his b',
10 up this top among the thick b',
12 his b' are broken by all the rivers
14 up their top among the thick b',
Da 4:12 of the heaven dwelt in the b'

bought
Ge 17:12 or b' with money of any stranger,
13 and he that is b' with thy money,
23 all that were b' with his money,
27 b' with money of the stranger,
33:19 And he b' a parcel of a field,
39: 1 b' him of the hands of the
47:14 for the corn which they b':
20 And Joseph b' all the land of
22 Only the land of the priests b' he
23 Behold, I have b' you this day and
49:30 which Abraham b' with the field
50:13 which Abraham b' with the field
Ex 12:44 man's servant that is b' for
Le 25:28 hand of him that hath b' it until
30 to him that b' it throughout his
50 him that b' him from the year
51 of the money that he was b' for.
27:22 field which he hath b', which is
24 unto him of whom it was b', even
De 32: 6 he thy father that hath b' thee?
Jos 24:32 which Jacob b' of the sons of
Ru 4: 9 that I have b' all that was
2Sa 12: 3 which he had b' and nourished up:
24:24 So David b' the threshingfloor and
1Ki 16:24 And he b' the hill Samaria of
Ne 5:16 of this wall, neither b' we any
Isa 43:24 Thou hast b' me no sweet cane
Jer 32: 9 And I b' the field of Hanameel my
43 And fields shall be b' in this land,
Ho 3: 2 So I b' her to me for fifteen pieces
M't 13:46 and sold all that he had, and b' it.
21:12 sold and b' in the temple, and
27: 7 b' with them the potter's field, to
M'r 11:15 cast out them that sold and b' in
15:46 he b' fine linen, and took him
16: 1 had b' sweet spices, that they
Lu 14:18 I have b' a piece of ground, and I
19 I have b' five yoke of oxen, and I go
17:28 they did eat, they drank, they b',
19:45 that sold therein, and them that b';
Ac 7:16 Abraham b' for a sum of money of
1Co 6:20 For ye are b' with a price:
7:23 Ye are b' with a price; be not ye
2Pe 2: 1 denying the Lord that b' them, and

bound^ See also BOUNDS.
Ge 22: 9 and b' Isaac his son, and laid
38:28 and b' upon his hand a scarlet
39:20 where the king's prisoners were b':
40: 3 the place where Joseph was b'.
5 Egypt, which were b' in the prison.
42:19 let one of your brethren be b' in
24 Simeon, and b' him before their
44:30 seeing that his life is b' up in the
49:26 the utmost b' of the everlasting
Ex 12:34 their kneadingtroughs being b'
Le 8: 7 and b' it unto him therewith.
Nu 19:15 vessel, which hath no covering b'
30: 4 her bond wherein she hath b' her
4 wherewith she hath b' her soul,
5 bonds wherewith she hath b' her
6 out of her lips, wherewith she b'
7 wherewith she b' her soul shall
8 wherewith she b' her soul, of none

Nu 30: 9 have b' their souls, shall stand
10 house, or b' her soul by a bond
11 every bond wherewith she b' her
Jos 2:21 and she b' the scarlet line in the
9: 4 wine bottles, old, and rent, and b'
J'g 15:13 they b' him with two new cords,
16: 6 wherewith thou mightest be b' to
8 not been dried, and she b' him
10 thee, wherewith thou mightest be b'.
13 me wherewith thou mightest be b'.
21 and b' him with fetters of brass;
1Sa 25:29 the soul of my lord shall be b' in
2Sa 3:34 Thy hands were not b', nor thy
2Ki 5:23 and b' two talents of silver in two
17: 4 of Assyria shut him up, and b' him
25: 7 and b' him with fetters of brass,
2Ch 33:11 and b' him with fetters, and
36: 6 and b' him in fetters, to carry him
Job 36: 8 if they be b' in fetters, and be
38:20 to the b' thereof, and that thou
Ps 68: 6 bringeth out those which are b'
104: 9 Thou hast set a b' that they may
107:10 shadow of death, being b' in
Pr 22:15 Foolishness is b' in the heart of a
30: 4 who hath b' the waters in a
Isa 1: 6 have not been closed, neither b'
22: 3 they are b' by the archers:
3 all that are found in thee are b'
61: 1 of the prison to them that are b';
Jer 5:22 the b' of the sea by a perpetual
30:13 thy cause, that thou mayest be b'
39: 7 and b' him with chains to carry
40: 1 being b' in chains among all that
52:11 and the king of Babylon b' him
La 1:14 yoke of my transgressions is b' by
Eze 27:24 apparel, b' with cords, and made
30:21 it shall not be b' up to be healed,
34: 4 neither have ye b' up that which
Da 3:21 Then these men were b' in their
23 fell down b' into the midst of the
24 Did not we cast three men b' into
Ho 4:19 The wind hath b' her up in her
5:10 them that remove the b':
7:15 I have b' and strengthened their
13:12 The iniquity of Ephraim is b' up;
Na 3:10 and all her great men were b' in
M't 14: 3 laid hold on John, and b' him,
16:19 on earth shall be b' in heaven;
18:18 on earth shall be b' in heaven;
27: 2 when they had b' him, they led him
M'r 5: 4 had been often b' with fetters and
6:17 laid hold upon John, and b' him in
15: 1 and b' Jesus, and carried him
7 Barabbas, which lay b' with them
Lu 8:29 he was kept b' with chains and in
10:34 And went to him, and b' up his
13:16 whom Satan hath b', lo, these
Joh 11:44 b' hand and foot with
44 his face was b' about with a
18:12 the Jews took Jesus and b' him,
24 Now Annas had sent him b' unto
Ac 9: 2, 21 he might bring them b' unto
12: 6 b' with two chains: and the
20:22 I go b' in the spirit unto
21:11 b' his own hands and feet, and
13 I am ready not to be b' only, but
33 commanded him to be b' with
22: 5 b' unto Jerusalem, for to be
25 as they b' him with thongs, Paul
29 a Roman, and because he had b'
23:12 and b' themselves under a curse,
14 b' ourselves under a great curse,
21 have b' themselves with an oath,
24:27 the Jews a pleasure, left Paul b'.
28:20 hope of Israel I am b' with this
Ro 7: 2 which hath an husband is b' by
1Co 7:27 Art thou b' unto a wife? seek not
39 The wife is b' by the law as long as
2Th 1: 3 We are b' to thank God always
2:13 we are b' to give thanks alway
2Ti 2: 9 but the word of God is not b'.
Heb 13: 3 them that are in bonds, as b'
Re 9:14 Loose the four angels which are b'
20: 2 Satan, and b' him a thousand

bounds
Ex 19:12 thou shalt set b' unto the people
23 Set b' about the mount, and
23:31 set thy b' from the Red sea even
De 32: 8 he set the b' of the people
Job 14: 5 hast appointed his b' that he
26:10 waters with b', until the day
Isa 10:13 removed the b' of the people,
Ac 17:26 and the b' of their habitation;

bountiful
Pr 22: 9 hath a b' eye shall be blessed;
Isa 32: 5 nor the churl said to be b'.

bountifully
Ps 13: 6 he hath dealt b' with me.
116: 7 the Lord hath dealt b' with thee.
119:17 Deal b' with thy servant, that I
142: 7 thou shalt deal b' with me.
2Co 9: 6 which soweth b' shall reap also b'.

bountifulness
2Co 9:11 thing to all b', which causeth

bounty
1Ki 10:13 Solomon gave her of his royal b'.
2Co 9: 5 your b', whereof ye had notice
5 might be ready, as a matter of b',

bow see also BOWED; BOWETH; BOWING; BOWMEN; BOWS; BOWSHOT.
Ge 9:13 I do set my b' in the cloud, and it
14 the b' shall be seen in the cloud:
16 And the b' shall be in the cloud;
27: 3 thy weapons, thy quiver and thy b',
Ge 27:29 and nations b' down to thee:
29 thy mother's sons b' down to thee:
37:10 come to b' down ourselves to thee
41:43 cried before him, B' the knee:
48:22 with my sword and with my b'.
49: 8 children shall b' down before thee.
24 his b' abode in strength, and the
Ex 11: 8 and b' down themselves unto me,
20: 5 Thou shalt not b' down thyself
23:24 Thou shalt not b' down to their
Le 26: 1 in your land, to b' down unto it:
De 5: 9 Thou shalt not b' down thyself
Jos 23: 7 nor b' yourselves unto them:
24:12 with thy sword, nor with thy b'.
J'g 2:19 them, and to b' down unto them;
1Sa 18: 4 and to his b', and to his girdle.
2Sa 1:18 of Judah the use of the b':
22 the b' of Jonathan turned not back,
22:35 a b' of steel is broken by mine
1Ki 22:34 certain man drew a b' at a venture,
2Ki 5:18 b' myself in the house of Rimmon:
18 when I b' down myself in the
6:22 with thy sword and with thy b'?
9:24 drew a b' with his full strength,
13:15 said unto him, Take b' and arrows.
15 he took unto him b' and arrows.
16 Put thine hand upon the b'. And
17:35 other gods, nor b' yourselves to
19:16 Lord, b' down thine ear and
1Ch 5:18 to shoot with b', and skilful in
12: 2 arrows out of a b', even of Saul's
2Ch 17:17 armed men with b' and shield
18:33 certain man drew a b' at a venture,
Job 20:24 the b' of steel shall strike him
29:20 my b' was renewed in my hand.
31:10 and let others b' down upon her.
39: 3 They b' themselves, they bring
Ps 7:12 bent his b', and made it ready.
11: 2 bend their b', they make ready
18:34 a b' of steel is broken by mine
22:29 go down to the dust shall b'
31: 2 B' down thine ear to me; deliver
37:14 have bent their b', to cast down
44: 6 I will not trust in my b', neither
46: 9 he breaketh the b', and cutteth
58: 7 bendeth his b' to shoot his arrows,
72: 9 wilderness shall b' before him;
76: 3 the arrows of the b', the shield,
78:57 turned aside like a deceitful b'.
86: 1 B' down thine ear, O Lord, hear
95: 6 let us worship and b' down:
144: 5 B' thy heavens, O Lord, and
Pr 5: 1 b' thine ear to my understanding:
14:19 The evil b' before the good; and
22:17 B' down thine ear, and hear the
Ec 12: 3 strong men shall b' themselves,
Isa 10: 4 Without me they shall b' down
21:15 sword, and from the bent b',
41: 2 and as driven stubble to his b'.
45:23 unto me every knee shall b', every
46: 2 stoop, they b' down together;
49:23 b' down to thee with their face
51:23 B' down, that we may go over:
58: 5 b' down his head as a bulrush,
60:14 shall b' themselves down at the
65:12 all b' down to the slaughter:
66:19 Pul, and Lud, that draw the b',
Jer 6:23 shall lay hold on b' and spear;
9: 3 bend their tongues like their b'
46: 9 that handle and bend the b'.
49:35 I will break the b' of Elam, the
50:14 all ye that bend the b', shoot at
29 all ye that bend the b', camp
42 shall hold the b' and the lance:
51: 3 bend his b', and against him
La 2: 4 hath bent his b' like an enemy:
3:12 He hath bent his b', and set me as
Eze 1:28 As the appearance of the b' that is
39: 3 smite thy b' out of thy left hand,
Ho 1: 5 I will break the b' of Israel
7 not save them by b', nor by sword,
2:18 and I will break the b' and the
7:16 they are like a deceitful b':
Am 2:15 he stand that handleth the b';
Mic 6: 6 b' myself before the high God?
Hab 3: 6 the perpetual hills did b':
9 Thy b' was made quite naked,
Zec 9:10 and the battle b' shall be cut off:
13 filled the b' with Ephraim, and
10: 4 out of him the battle b', out of
Ro 11:10 and b' down their back alway.
14:11 every knee shall b' to me, and
Eph 3:14 I b' my knees unto the Father
Ph'p 2:10 of Jesus every knee should b',
Re 6: 2 he that sat on him had a b';

bowed
Ge 18: 2 and b' himself toward the ground,
19: 1 b' himself with his face toward
23: 7 and b' himself to the people
12 b' down himself before the people
24:26 the man b' down his head, and
48 b' down my head, and worshipped
33: 3 and b' himself to the ground
6 children, and they b' themselves.
7 came near, and b' themselves:
7 and Rachel, and they b' themselves.
42: 6 and b' down themselves before
43:26 and b' themselves to him to the
28 And they b' down their heads,
47:31 Israel b' himself upon the bed's
48:12 b' himself with his face to the
49:15 and b' his shoulder to bear, and
Ex 4:31 b' their heads and worshipped.
12:27 b' the head and worshipped.
34: 8 Moses made haste, and b' his head
Nu 22:31 he b' down his head, and fell flat
Nu 25: 2 eat, and b' down to their gods.
Jos 23:16 gods, and b' yourselves to them;
J'g 2:12 and b' themselves unto them, and
17 and b' themselves unto them:
5:27 he b', he fell, he lay down:
27 at her feet he b', he fell:
27 where he b', there he fell
7: 6 people b' down upon their knees
16:30 he b' himself with all his might;
Ru 2:10 and b' herself to the ground, and
1Sa 4:19 she b' herself and travailed: for
20:41 and b' himself three times:
24: 8 face to the earth, and b' himself.
25:23 and b' herself to the ground,
41 b' herself on her face to the earth
28:14 to the ground, and b' himself.
2Sa 9: 8 And he b' himself, and said,
14:22 b' himself, and thanked the king:
33 the king, and b' himself on his face
18:21 And Cushi b' himself unto Joab,
19:14 And he b' the heart of all the men
22:10 He b' the heavens also, and
24:20 b' himself before the king on his
1Ki 1:16 Bath-sheba b', and did obeisance
23 he b' himself before the king
31 Bath-sheba b' with her face to the
47 the king b' himself upon the bed.
53 and b' himself to king Solomon:
2:19 to meet her, and b' himself unto
19:18 which have not b' unto Baal,
2Ki 2:15 and b' themselves to the ground
4:37 and b' herself to the ground,
1Ch 21:21 b' himself to David with his face
29:20 and b' down their heads, and
2Ch 7: 3 the house, they b' themselves
20:18 Jehoshaphat b' his head with his
25:14 b' down himself before them, and
29:29 present with him b' themselves
30 b' their heads and worshipped.
Ne 8: 6 b' their heads, and worshipped
Es 3: 2 b', and reverenced Haman:
2 Mordecai b' not, nor did him
5 Haman saw that Mordecai b' not,
Ps 18: 9 He b' the heavens also, and
35:14 I b' down heavily, as one that
38: 6 b' down greatly; I go mourning
44:25 our soul is b' down to the dust:
57: 6 my soul is b' down: they have
145:14 all those that be b' down.
146: 8 raiseth them that are b' down:
Isa 2:11 of men shall be b' down,
17 loftiness of man shall be b' down,
21: 3 I was b' down at hearing of it;
M't 27:29 and they b' the knee before him,
Lu 13:11 was b' together, and could in no
24: 5 afraid, and b' down their faces
Joh 19:30 b' his head, and gave up the ghost.
Ro 11: 4 have not b' the knee to the image

bowels
Ge 15: 4 of thine own b' shall be thine
25:23 shall be separated from thy b';
43:30 his b' did yearn upon his brother:
Nu 5:22 the curse shall go into thy b',
2Sa 7:12 which shall proceed out of thy b',
16:11 which came forth of my b',
20:10 and shed out his b' to the ground,
1Ki 3:26 her b' yearned upon her son,
2Ch 21:15 of thy b', until thy b' fall out by
18 the Lord smote him in his b' with
19 his b' fell out by reason of his
32:21 they that came forth of his own b'
Job 20:14 his meat in his b' is turned, it is
30:27 My b' boiled, and rested not:
Ps 22:14 it is melted in the midst of my b'.
71: 6 took me out of my mother's b':
109:18 into his b' like water, and like
Ca 5: 4 and my b' were moved for him.
Isa 16:11 my b' shall sound like an harp for
48:19 the offspring of thy b' like the
49: 1 from the b' of my mother hath
63:15 the sounding of my b' and of thy
Jer 4:19 My b', my b'! I am pained at my
31:20 my b' are troubled for him;
La 1:20 my b' are troubled; mine heart
2:11 my b' are troubled, my liver is
Eze 3: 3 and fill thy b' with this roll that
7:19 their souls, neither fill their b':
Ac 1:18 and all his b' gushed out.
2Co 6:12 are straightened in your own b'.
Ph'p 1: 8 you all in the b' of Jesus Christ.
2: 1 Spirit, if any b' and mercies,
Col 3:12 b' of mercies, kindness.
Ph'm 7 the b' of the saints are refreshed
12 receive him, that is, mine own b':
20 refresh my b' in the Lord.
1Jo 3:17 shutteth up his b' of compassion

boweth
J'g 7: 5 every one that b' down upon
Isa 2: 9 And the mean man b' down,
46: 1 Bel b' down, Nebo stoopeth,

bowing
Ge 24:52 worshipped the Lord, b'
Ps 17:11 have set their eyes b' down
62: 3 as a b' wall shall ye be, and as a
M'r 15:19 b' their knees worshipped him.

bowl See also BOWLS.
Nu 7:13, 19, 25, 31, 37, 43, 49, 55, 61, 67, 73,
79 one silver b' of seventy shekels,
85 and thirty shekels, each b' seventy:
J'g 6:38 of the fleece, a b' full of water.
Ec 12: 6 or the golden b' be broken,
Zec 4: 2 with a b' upon the top of it, and his
3 upon the right side of the b',

bowls
Ex 25:29 covers thereof, and *b*' thereof,
31 his branches, his *b*', his knops,
33 Three *b*' made like unto almonds,
33 three *b*' made like almonds in
34 four *b*' made like unto almonds,
37:16 his spoons, and his *b*', and his
17 his branch, his *b*', his knops,
19 Three *b*' made after the fashion
19 and three *b*' made like almonds
20 in the candlestick were four *b*'
Nu 4: 7 the spoons, and the *b*', and
7:84 twelve silver *b*', twelve spoons
1Ki 7:41 the two *b*' of the chapiters that
41 the two *b*' of the chapiters which
42 cover the two *b*' of the chapiters
50 And the *b*', and the snuffers,
2Ki 12:13 house of the Lord *b*' of silver,
25:15 firepans, and the *b*', and such
1Ch 28:17 for the fleshhooks, and the *b*',
Jer 52:18 the snuffers, and the *b*', and the
19 the firepans, and the *b*', and the
Am 6: 6 That drink wine in *b*', and anoint
Zec 9:15 they shall be filled like *b*', and as
14:20 shall be like *b*' before the altar.

bowmen
Jer 4:29 of the horsemen and *b*';

bows^
1Sa 2: 4 *b*' of the mighty men are broken,
1Ch 12: 2 They were armed with *b*',
2Ch 14: 8 bare shields and drew *b*',
26:14 helmets, and habergeons, and *b*',
Ne 4:13 swords, their spears, and their *b*'.
16 spears, the shields, and the *b*',
Ps 37:15 and their *b*' shall be broken.
64: 3 and bend their *b*' to shoot their
78: 9 being armed, and carrying *b*',
Isa 5:28 all their *b*' bent, their horses
7:24 With arrows and with *b*' shall
13:18 Their *b*' also shall dash the young
Jer 51:56 every one of their *b*' is broken:

bowshot
Ge 21:16 way off, as it were a *b*':

box
2Ki 9: 1 take this *b*' of oil in thine hand,
3 Then take the *b*' of oil, and pour
Isa 41:19 pine, and the *b*' tree together:
60:13 and the *b*' together, to beautify
M't 26: 7 having an alabaster *b*' of very
M'r 14: 3 having an alabaster *b*' of
3 she brake the *b*', and poured it
Lu 7:37 brought an alabaster *b*' of

box-tree See BOX and TREE.

boy See also BOYS.
Joe 3: 3 given a *b*' for an harlot, and

boys
Ge 25:27 And the *b*' grew: and Esau was
Zec 8: 5 *b*' and girls playing in the streets

Bozez (*bo'-zez*)
1Sa 14: 4 and the name of the one was *B*',

Bozkath (*boz'-kath*) See also BOSCATH.
Jos 15:39 Lachish, and *B*', and Eglon,

Boznai See SHETHAR-BOZNAI.

Bozrah (*boz'-rah*)
Ge 36:33 the son of Zerah of *B*' reigned
1Ch 1:44 Jobab the son of Zerah of *B*',
Isa 34: 6 the Lord hath a sacrifice in *B*',
63: 1 with dyed garments from *B*'?
Jer 48:24 And upon Kerioth, and upon *B*',
49:13 that *B*' shall become a desolation,
22 and spread his wings over *B*':
Am 1:12 shall devour the palaces of *B*'.
Mic 2:12 them together as the sheep of *B*',

bracelet See also BRACELETS.
2Sa 1:10 and the *b*' that was on his arm,

bracelets
Ge 24:22 two *b*' for her hands of ten
30 *b*' upon his sister's hands,
47 and the *b*' upon her hands.
38:18 Thy signet, and thy *b*', and thy
25 the signet, and *b*', and staff.
Ex 35:22 brought *b*', and earrings, and
Nu 31:50 jewels of gold, chains, and *b*',
Isa 3:19 The chains, and the *b*', and the
Eze 16:11 I put *b*' upon thy hands,
23:42 *b*' upon their hands, and

braided See BROIDED.

brake See also BRAKEST.
Ex 9:25 *b*' every tree of the field.
32: 3 people *b*' off the golden earrings
19 and *b*' them beneath the mount.
De 9:17 and *b*' them before your eyes.
J'g 7:19 the trumpets, and *b*' the pitchers
20 the trumpets, and *b*' the pitchers,
9:53 head, and all to *b*' his skull.
16: 9 And he *b*' the withs, as a thread
12 he *b*' them from off his arms
1Sa 4:18 and his neck *b*', and he died:
2Sa 23:16 three mighty men *b*' through
1Ki 19:11 and *b*' in pieces the rocks before
2Ki 10:27 they *b*' down the image of Baal,
27 and *b*' down the house of Baal,
11:18 house of Baal, and *b*' it down;
18 his images *b*' they in pieces
14:13 *b*' down the wall of Jerusalem
18: 4 and *b*' the images, and cut down
4 *b*' in pieces the brasen serpent
23: 7 And he *b*' down the houses of
8 and *b*' down the high places
12 and *b*' them down from thence,
14 And he *b*' in pieces the images,
2Ki 23:15 the high place he *b*' down, and
25:10 *b*' down the walls of Jerusalem
1Ch 11:18 And the three *b*' through the host
2Ch 14: 3 and *b*' down the images, and cut
21:17 and *b*' into it, and carried away
23:17 the house of Baal, and *b*' it down,
17 and *b*' his altars and his images
25:23 *b*' down the wall of Jerusalem
26: 6 and *b*' down the wall of Gath,
31: 1 and *b*' the images in pieces,
34: 4 they *b*' down the altars of Baalim
4 images, he *b*' in pieces,
36:19 *b*' down the wall of Jerusalem,
Job 29:17 I *b*' the jaws of the wicked,
38: 8 when it *b*' forth, as if it had
10 *b*' up for it my decreed place,
Ps 76: 3 *b*' he the arrows of the bow,
105:16 he *b*' the whole staff of bread.
33 and *b*' the trees of their coasts.
106:29 inventions: and the plague *b*' in
107:14 and *b*' their bands in sunder.
Jer 28:10 off...Jeremiah's neck, and *b*' it.
31:32 my covenant they *b*', although
39: 8 *b*' down the walls of Jerusalem.
52:14 *b*' down all the walls of Jerusalem
17 the Chaldeans *b*', and carried
Eze 17:16 whose covenant he *b*', even with
Da 2: 1 and his sleep *b*' from him.
34 and clay, and *b*' them to pieces.
45 that it *b*' in pieces the iron,
6:24 and *b*' all their bones in pieces
7: 7 it devoured and *b*' in pieces,
19 which devoured, *b*' in pieces,
8: 7 the ram, and *b*' his two horns:
M't 14:19 he blessed, and *b*', and gave
15:36 and gave thanks, and *b*' them,
26:26 bread, and blessed it, and *b*'
M'r 6:41 and *b*' the loaves, and gave them
8: 6 and gave thanks, and *b*', and
19 When I *b*' the five loaves among
14: 3 and she *b*' the box, and poured
22 took bread, and blessed, and *b*'
Lu 5: 6 of fishes: and their net *b*'.
8:29 he *b*' the bands, and was
9:16 he blessed them, and *b*', and
22:19 and gave thanks, and *b*' it,
24:30 and blessed it, and *b*', and gave
Joh 19:32 and *b*' the legs of the first, and of
33 already, they *b*' not his legs:
1Co 11:24 he *b*' it, and said, Take, eat:

brakest
Ex 34: 1 the first tables, which thou *b*'.
De 10: 2 the first tables which thou *b*',
Ps 74:13 thou *b*' the heads of the dragons
14 Thou *b*' the heads of leviathan
Eze 29: 7 they leaned upon thee, thou *b*',

bramble See also BRAMBLES.
J'g 9:14 said all the trees unto the *b*',
15 the *b*' said unto the trees, If in
15 let fire come out of the *b*', and
Lu 6:44 of a *b*' bush gather they grapes.

brambles
Isa 34:13 nettles and *b*' in the fortresses

branch See also BRANCHES.
Ex 25:33 in one *b*'; and three bowls made
33 like almonds in the other *b*',
37:17 his shaft, and his *b*', his bowls,
19 fashion of the almonds in one *b*',
19 made like almonds in another *b*',
Nu 13:23 cut down from thence a *b*' with
Job 8:16 *b*' shooteth forth in his garden.
14: 7 tender *b*' thereof will not cease.
15:32 and his *b*' shall not be green.
18:16 above shall his *b*' be cut off.
29:19 dew lay all night upon my *b*'.
Ps 80:15 the *b*' that thou madest strong
Pr 11:28 righteous shall flourish as a *b*'.
Isa 4: 2 day shall the *b*' of the Lord
9:14 head and tail, *b*' and rush,
11: 1 *B*' shall grow out of his roots:
14:19 like an abominable *b*', and as the
17: 9 bough, and an uppermost *b*',
19:15 the head or tail, *b*' or rush, may
25: 5 the *b*' of the terrible ones shall
60:21 the *b*' of my planting, the work of
Jer 23: 5 raise unto David a righteous *B*',
33:15 at that time, will I cause the *B*' of
Eze 8:17 and, lo, they put the *b*' to their
15: 2 a *b*' which is among the trees of
17: 3 and took the highest *b*' of the
22 the highest *b*' of the high cedar,
Da 11: 7 out of a *b*' of her roots shall
Zec 3: 8 bring forth my servant the *B*'.
6:12 the man whose name is The *B*';
Mal 4: 1 leave them neither root nor *b*'.
M't 24:32 When his *b*' is yet tender, and
M'k 13:28 When her *b*' is yet tender, and
Joh 15: 2 Every *b*' in me that beareth not
2 and every *b*' that beareth fruit,
4 As the *b*' cannot bear fruit of
6 he is cast forth as a *b*', and is

branches
Ge 40:10 And in the vine were three *b*':
12 The three *b*' are three days:
49:22 a well; whose *b*' run over the
Ex 25:31 his shaft, and his *b*', his bowls,
32 six *b*' shall come out of the sides
32 three *b*' of the candlestick out of
32 and three *b*' of the candlestick
33 so in the six *b*' that come out of
35 a knop under two *b*' of the same,
35 and a knop under two *b*' of the
35 a knop under two *b*' of the same,
35 according to the six *b*'
Ex 25:36 and their *b*' shall be of the same:
37:18 six *b*' going out of the sides
18 three *b*' of the candlestick out of
18 three *b*' of the candlestick out of
19 so throughout the six *b*' going out
21 a knop under two *b*' of the same,
21 a knop under two *b*' of the same,
21 a knop under two *b*' of the same,
21 according to the six *b*' going out of
22 Their knops and their *b*' were of
Le 23:40 *b*' of palm trees, and the boughs
Ne 8:15 and fetch olive *b*', and pine *b*',
15 and myrtle *b*', and palm *b*',
15 and *b*' of thick trees,
Job 15:30 the flame shall dry up his *b*', and
Ps 80:11 unto the sea, and her *b*' unto the
104:12 which sing among the *b*'.
Isa 16: 8 her *b*' are stretched out, they
17: 6 in the outmost fruitful *b*' thereof,
18: 5 take away and cut down the *b*'.
27:10 lie down, and consume the *b*'
Jer 11:16 it, and the *b*' of it are broken.
Eze 17: 6 whose *b*' turned toward him, and
6 brought forth *b*', and shot forth
7 and shot forth her *b*' toward him,
8 that it might bring forth *b*', and
23 the shadow of the *b*' thereof shall
19:10 fruitful and full of *b*' by reason
11 was exalted among the thick *b*',
11 with the multitude of her *b*'.
14 fire is gone out of a rod of her *b*',
31: 3 a cedar in Lebanon with fair *b*',
5 his *b*' became long because of the
6 under his *b*' did all the beasts
7 greatness, in the length of his *b*':
8 chestnut trees were not like his *b*';
9 fair by the multitude of his *b*':
12 in all the valleys his *b*' are fallen,
13 of the field shall be upon his *b*':
36: 8 ye shall shoot forth your *b*', and
Da 4:14 cut off his *b*', shake off his leaves,
14 under it, and the fowls from his *b*':
21 and upon whose *b*' the fowls of
Ho 11: 6 consume his *b*', and devour them,
14: 6 His *b*' shall spread, and his
Joe 1: 7 the *b*' thereof are made white.
Na 2: 2 out, and marred their vine *b*'.
Zec 4:12 these two olive *b*' which through
M't 13:32 come and lodge in the *b*' thereof.
21: 8 others cut down *b*' from the trees,
M'r 4:32 shooteth out great *b*'; so that
11: 8 others cut down *b*' off the trees,
Lu 13:19 fowls of the air lodged in the *b*'
Joh 12:13 Took *b*' of palm trees, and went
15: 5 I am the vine, ye are the *b*'.
Ro 11:16 if the root be holy so are the *b*'.
17 if some of the *b*' be broken off,
18 Boast not against the *b*'. But if
19 The *b*' were broken off, that I
21 if God spared not the natural *b*',
24 these, which be the natural *b*', be

brand See also BRANDS; FIREBRAND.
Zec 3: 2 is not this a *b*' plucked out of the

brandish
Eze 32:10 I shall *b*' my sword before them;

brands See also FIREBRANDS.
J'g 15: 5 when he had set the *b*' on fire, he

brasen
Ex 27: 4 make four *b*' rings in the four
35:16 burnt offering with his *b*' grate,
38: 4 he made for the altar a *b*' grate
10 their *b*' sockets twenty; the
30 and the *b*' altar, and the *b*' grate
39:39 *b*' altar, and his grate of brass,
Le 6:28 sodden in a *b*' pot, it shall be both
Nu 16:39 the priest took the *b*' censers,
1Ki 4:13 great cities walls and *b*' bars:
7:30 every base had four *b*' wheels,
8:64 *b*' altar that was before the Lord
14:27 made in their stead *b*' shields,
2Ki 16:14 he brought also the *b*' altar,
15 the *b*' altar shall be for me to
17 down the sea from off the *b*' oxen
18: 4 brake in pieces the *b*' serpent that
25:13 the *b*' sea that was in the house of
1Ch 18: 8 wherewith Solomon made the *b*'
2Ch 1: 5 Moreover the *b*' altar, that Bezaleel
6 the *b*' altar before the Lord, which
6:13 Solomon had made a *b*' scaffold,
7: 7 *b*' altar which Solomon had made
Jer 1:18 an iron pillar, and *b*' walls
15:20 unto this people a fenced *b*' wall:
52:17 the *b*' sea that was in the house of
20 twelve *b*' bulls that were under the
Eze 9: 2 and stood beside the *b*' altar.
M'r 7: 4 of cups, and pots, *b*' vessels,

brass
Ge 4:22 of every artificer in *b*' and iron:
Ex 25: 3 of them; gold, and silver, and *b*',
26:11 thou shalt make fifty taches of *b*',
37 cast five sockets of *b*' for them.
27: 2 and thou shalt overlay it with *b*'.
3 thereof thou shalt make of *b*'.
4 for it a grate of network of *b*';
6 wood, and overlay them with *b*'.
10 their twenty sockets shall be of *b*';
11 and their twenty sockets of *b*';
17 of silver, and their sockets of *b*'.
18 twined linen, and their sockets of *b*'.
19 the pins of the court, shall be of *b*'.
30:18 Thou shalt also make a laver of *b*',
18 and his foot also of *b*',
31: 4 in gold, and in silver, and in *b*',
35: 5 the Lord; gold, and silver, and *b*',

Ex 35:24 an offering of silver and b'
32 in gold, and in silver, and in b',
36:18 he made fifty taches of b' to couple
38 but their five sockets were of b'.
38: 2 same: and he overlaid it with b'.
3 the vessels thereof made he of b'.
5 the four ends of the grate of b',
6 wood, and overlaid them with b'.
8 he made the laver of b',
8 and the foot of it of b',
11 and their sockets of b' twenty;
17 sockets for the pillars were of b';
19 four, and their sockets of b' four;
20 court round about, were of b'.
29 And the b' of the offering was
39:39 brasen altar, and his grate of b'.
Le 26:19 as iron, and your earth as b':
Nu 21: 9 Moses made a serpent of b', and
9 when he beheld the serpent of b',
31:22 the gold, and the silver, the b',
De 8: 9 of whose hills thou mayest dig b'.
28:23 that is over thy head shall be b',
33:25 Thy shoes shall be iron and b';
Jos 6:19 vessels of b' and iron, are
24 the vessels of b' and of iron, they
22: 8 with gold, and with b', and with
J'g 16:21 bound him with fetters of b'; and
1Sa 17: 5 had an helmet of b' upon his head,
5 was five thousand shekels of b'.
6 had greaves of b' upon his legs,
6 and a target of b' between his
38 an helmet of b' upon his head;
2Sa 8: 8 David took exceeding much b'.
10 vessels of gold, and vessels of b':
21:16 three hundred shekels of b' in
1Ki 7:14 a man of Tyre, a worker in b':
14 cunning to work all works in b'.
15 he cast two pillars of b', of
16 two chapiters of molten b', to set
27 he made ten bases of b'; four
30 brasen wheels, and plates of b':
38 Then made he ten lavers of b':
45 of the Lord, were of bright b'.
47 the weight of the b' found out.
2Ki 25: 7 bound him with fetters of b', and
13 pillars of b' that were in the house
13 carried the b' of them to Babylon.
14 all the vessels of b' wherewith
16 b' of all these vessels was without
17 and the chapiter upon it was b':
17 the chapiter round about, all of b':
1Ch 15:19 to sound with cymbals of b';
18: 8 brought David very much b',
8 the pillars, and the vessels of b'.
10 vessels of gold and silver and b'.
22: 3 b' in abundance without weight;
14 and of b' and iron without weight;
16 the gold, the silver, and the b',
29: 2 the b' for things of b', the iron for
7 of b' eighteen thousand talents,
2Ch 2: 7 in silver, and in b', and in iron,
14 in gold, and in silver, and in b',
4: 1 made an altar of b', twenty cubits
9 overlaid the doors of them with b'.
16 house of the Lord, of bright b'.
18 the weight of the b' could not be
12:10 king Rehoboam made shields of b'
24:12 also such as wrought iron and b'
Job 6:12 of stones? or is my flesh of b'?
28: 2 b' is molten out of the stone.
40:18 bones are as strong pieces of b';
41:27 as straw, and b' as rotten wood.
Ps 107:16 he hath broken the gates of b',
Isa 45: 2 break in pieces the gates of b',
48: 4 is an iron sinew, and thy brow b';
60:17 For b' I will bring gold, and for
17 bring silver, and for wood b',
Jer 6:28 they are b' and iron; they are all
52:17 Also the pillars of b' that were in
17 and carried all the b' of them to
18 of b' wherewith they ministered,
20 the b' of all these vessels was
22 a chapiter of b' was upon it; and
22 the chapiters round about, all of b'.
Eze 1: 7 like the colour of burnished b'.
22:18 all they are b', and tin, and iron,
20 they gather silver, and b', and iron,
24:11 that the b' of it may be hot, and
27:13 persons of men and vessels of b'
40: 3 was like the appearance of b',
Da 2:32 his belly and his thighs of b',
35 the clay, the b', the silver, and
39 another third kingdom of b',
45 the iron, the b', the clay, the
4:15, 23 with a band of iron and b',
5: 4 gods of gold, and of silver, of b',
23 the gods of silver, and gold, of b',
7:19 were of iron, and his nails of b';
10: 6 feet like in colour to polished b',
Mic 4:13 I will make thy hoofs b': and
Zec 6: 1 mountains were mountains of b'.
M't 10: 9 nor silver, nor b' in your purses,
1Co 13: 1 I am become as sounding b',
Re 1:15 and his feet like unto fine b', as
2:18 and his feet are like fine brass;
9:20 idols of gold, and silver, and b',
18:12 and of b', and iron, and marble,

bravery
Isa 3:18 b' of their tinkling ornaments

brawler See also BRAWLERS.
1Ti 3: 3 patient, not a b', not covetous;

brawlers
Tit 3: 2 evil of no man, to be no b', but

brawling
Pr 21: 9 with a b' woman in a wide house.
Pr 25:24 with a b' woman in a wide house.

bray See also BRAYED.
Job 6: 5 Doth the wild ass b' when he
Pr 27:22 shouldest b' a fool in a mortar

brayed
Job 30: 7 Among the bushes they b';

brazen See BRASEN.

breach See also BREACHES; BREAKING.
Ge 38:29 this b' be upon thee: therefore
Le 24:20 B' for b', eye for eye, tooth for
Nu 14:34 ye shall know my b' of promise.
J'g 21:15 made a b' in the tribes of Israel.
2Sa 5:20 before me, as the b' of waters.
6: 8 Lord had made a b' upon Uzzah:
2Ki 12: 5 wheresoever any b' shall be found.
1Ch 13:11 Lord had made a b' upon Uzzah:
15:13 our God made a b' upon us,
Ne 6: 1 there was no b' left therein;
Job 16:14 He breaketh me with b' upon b',
Ps 106:23 chosen stood before him in the b',
Pr 15: 4 therein is a b' in the spirit.
Isa 7: 6 let us make a b' therein for us,
30:13 as a b' ready to fall, swelling out
26 bindeth up the b' of his people,
58:12 repairer of the b', the restorer
Jer 14:17 people is broken with a great b',
La 2:13 thy b' is great like the sea:
Eze 26:10 into a city wherein is made a b'.

breaches
J'g 5:17 seashore, and abode in his b'.
1Ki 11:27 repaired the b' of the city of
2Ki 12: 5 them repair the b' of the house,
6 not repaired the b' of the house.
7 repair ye not the b' of the house?
7 deliver it for the b' of the house.
8 to repair the b' of the house.
12 stone to repair the b' of the house
22: 5 Lord, to repair the b' of the house,
Ne 4: 7 the b' began to be stopped, then
Ps 60: 2 heal the b' thereof; for it shaketh.
Isa 22: 9 b' of the city of David, that they
Am 4: 3 And ye shall go out at the b',
6:11 smite the great house with b',
9:11 and close up the b' thereof;

bread See also SHEWBREAD.
Ge 3:19 sweat of thy face shalt thou eat b',
14:18 Salem brought forth b' and wine:
18: 5 I will fetch a morsel of b',
19: 3 and did bake unleavened b',
21:14 and took b', and a bottle of water,
25:34 Jacob gave Esau b' and pottage
27:17 gave the savoury meat and the b',
28:20 and will give me b' to eat,
31:54 called his brethren to eat b':
54 and they did eat b',
37:25 they sat down to eat b': and they
39: 6 save the b' which he did eat.
41:54 all the land of Egypt there was b'.
55 the people cried to Pharaoh for b':
43:25 they heard that they should eat b'
31 himself, and said, Set on b'.
32 the Egyptians might not eat b'
45:23 laden with corn and b' and meat
47:12 with b', according to their
13 And there was no b' in all the land;
15 unto Joseph, and said, Give us b':
17 Joseph gave them b' in exchange
17 fed them with b' for all their cattle
19 buy us and our land for b', and we
49:20 Out of Asher his b' shall be fat,
Ex 2:20 call him, that he may eat b'.
12: 8 roast with fire, and unleavened b';
15 shall ye eat unleavened b';
15 whosoever eateth leavened b'
17 observe the feast of unleavened b';
18 ye shall eat unleavened b', until
20 shall ye eat unleavened b'.
13: 3 shall no leavened b' be eaten.
6 thou shalt eat unleavened b',
7 Unleavened b' shall be eaten
7 there shall no leavened b' be seen
16: 3 when we did eat b' to the full;
4 I will rain b' from heaven for you;
8 and in the morning b' to the full;
12 morning ye shall be filled with b';
15 the b' which the Lord hath given
22 they gathered twice as much b',
29 on the sixth day the b' of two days;
32 the b' wherewith I have fed you
18:12 to eat b' with Moses' father in law
23:15 the feast of unleavened b':
15 (thou shalt eat unleavened b'
18 of my sacrifice with leavened b';
25 shall bless thy b', and thy water;
29: 2 And unleavened b', and cakes
23 loaf of b', and one cake of oiled b',
23 basket of the unleavened b' that is
32 the b' that is in the basket, by the
34 of the b', remain until the morning,
34:18 The feast of unleavened b' shalt
18 (thou shalt eat unleavened b',
28 he did neither eat b', nor drink
40:23 he set the b' in order upon it
Le 6:16 with unleavened b' shall it be
7:13 leavened b' with the sacrifice of
8: 2 and a basket of unleavened b';
26 the basket of unleavened b', that
26 a cake of oiled b', and one wafer,
31 the b' that is in the basket of
32 of the b' shall ye burn with fire.
21: 6 by fire, and the b' of their God,
8 for he offereth the b' of thy God:
17 approach to offer the b' of his God.
21 nigh to offer the b' of his God.
22 He shall eat the b' of his God,
22:25 the b' of your God of any of these;
23: 6 the feast of unleavened b' unto
6 ye must eat unleavened b'.
14 ye shall eat neither b', nor
18 offer with the b' seven lambs
20 the b' of the firstfruits for a wave
24: 7 may be on the b' for a memorial,
26: 5 ye shall eat your b' to the full,
26 the staff of your b',
26 ten women shall bake your b'
26 and they shall deliver you your b'
Nu 4: 7 the continual b' shall be thereon:
6:15 a basket of unleavened b', cakes
15 wafers of unleavened b' anointed
17 the basket of unleavened b':
9:11 eat it with unleavened b' and bitter
14: 9 they are b' for us: their defence
15:19 when ye eat of the b' of the land,
21: 5 for there is no b', neither is there
5 our soul loatheth this light b'.
28: 2 my b' for my sacrifices made by
17 shall unleavened b' be eaten.
De 8: 3 man doth not live by b' only,
9 A land wherein thou shalt eat b'
9: 9 I neither did eat b' nor drink
18 I did neither eat b', nor drink
16: 3 shalt eat no leavened b' with it;
3 shalt thou eat unleavened b'
3 even the b' of affliction; for thou
4 there shall be no leavened b'
8 thou shalt eat unleavened b':
16 the feast of unleavened b', and in
23: 4 they met you not with b' and with
29: 6 Ye have not eaten b', neither have
Jos 9: 5 all the b' of their provision was
12 This our b' we took hot for our
J'g 7:13 and, lo, a cake of barley b'
8: 5 Give, I pray you, loaves of b'
6 should give b' unto thine army?
15 we should give b' unto thy men
13:16 detain me, I will not eat of thy b':
19: 5 thine heart with a morsel of b',
19 there is b' and wine also for me,
Ru 1: 6 visited his people in giving them b'.
2:14 eat of the b', and dip thy
1Sa 2: 5 hired out themselves for b';
36 and a morsel of b', and shall say,
36 that I may eat a piece of b'.
9: 7 the b' is spent in our vessels,
10: 3 another carrying three loaves of b',
4 and give thee two loaves of b';
16:20 an ass laden with b', and a bottle
21: 3 give me five loaves of b' in mine
4 no common b' under mine hand,
4 but there is hallowed b':
5 the b' is in a manner common,
6 the priest gave him hallowed b':
6 b' there but the shewbread,
6 to put hot b' in the day when it
22:13 in that thou hast given him b',
25:11 Shall I then take my b', and my
28:20 he had eaten no b' all the day,
22 let me set a morsel of b' before
24 did bake unleavened b' thereof:
30:11 to David, and gave him b', and he
12 for he had eaten no b', nor drunk
2Sa 3:29 on the sword, or that lacketh b'.
35 if I taste b', or ought else, till the
6:19 to every one a cake of b', and a
9: 7 thou shalt eat b' at my table
10 thy master's son shall eat b' always
12:17 neither did he eat b' with them.
20 they set b' before him, and he did
21 dead, thou didst rise and eat b'.
16: 1 two hundred loaves of b', and an
2 b' and summer fruit for the young
1Ki 13: 8 neither will I eat b' nor drink
9 Eat no b', nor drink water, nor
15 Come home with me, and eat b'.
16 neither will I eat b' nor drink
17 Thou shalt eat no b', nor drink
18 he may eat b' and drink water.
19 went back with him, and did eat b'
22 hast eaten b' and drunk water in
22 Eat no b', and drink no water;
23 after he had eaten b', and after he
17: 6 ravens brought him b' and flesh
6 and b' and flesh in the evening;
11 me, I pray thee, a morsel of b'
18: 4 and fed them with b' and water.)
13 and fed them with b' and water?
21: 4 away his face, and would eat no b'.
5 so sad that thou eatest no b'?
7 arise, and eat b', and let thine
22:27 feed him with b' of affliction and
2Ki 4: 8 and she constrained him to eat b'.
8 he turned in thither to eat b'.
42 b' of the firstfruits, twenty loaves
6:22 set b' and water before them, that
18:32 a land of b' and vineyards, a land
23: 9 they did eat of the unleavened b'
25: 3 there was no b' for the people of
29 he did eat b' continually before
1Ch 12:40 b' on asses, and on camels, and
16: 3 to every one a loaf of b', and a
2Ch 8:13 in the feast of unleavened b', and
18:26 feed him with b' of affliction and
30:13 the feast of unleavened b' in the
21 feast of unleavened b' seven days
35:17 feast of unleavened b' seven days.
Ezr 6:22 feast of unleavened b' seven days
10: 6 he did eat no b', nor drink water:
Ne 5:14 brethren have not eaten the b' of
15 had taken of them b' and wine,
18 the b' of the governor, because

Ne 9:15 And gavest them b' from heaven
13: 2 not the children of Israel with b'
Job 15:23 wandereth abroad for b', saying,
22: 7 thou hast withholden b' from the
27:14 shall not be satisfied with b'.
28: 5 for the earth, out of it cometh b':
33:20 his life abhorreth b', and his soul
42:11 and did eat b' with him in his
Ps 14: 4 up my people as they eat b', and
37:25 forsaken, nor his seed begging b'.
41: 9 which did eat of my b', hath lifted
53: 4 eat up my people as they eat b':
78:20 he give b' also? can he provide
80: 5 feedest them with the b' of tears;
102: 4 grass; so that I forget to eat my b'.
9 I have eaten ashes like b', and
104:15 and b' which strengtheneth man's
105:16 he brake the whole staff of b'.
40 and satisfied them with the b' of
109:10 and beg: let them seek their b' also
127: 2 to eat the b' of sorrows: for so
132:15 I will satisfy her poor with b'.
Pr 4:17 they eat the b' of wickedness, and
6:26 a man is brought to a piece of b':
9: 5 Come, eat of my b', and drink of
17 are sweet, and b' eaten in secret is
12: 9 honoureth himself, and lacketh b'.
11 his land shall be satisfied with b':
20:13 and thou shalt be satisfied with b'.
17 B' of deceit is sweet to a man;
22: 9 for he giveth of his b' to the poor.
23: 6 the b' of him that hath an evil eye,
25:21 enemy be hungry, give him b' to
28:19 his land shall have plenty of b':
21 For a piece of b' that man will
31:27 and eateth not the b' of idleness.
Ec 9: 7 eat thy b' with joy, and drink
11 neither yet b' to the wise, nor
11: 1 Cast thy b' upon the waters: for
Isa 3: 1 the whole stay of b', and the whole
7 house is neither b' nor clothing:
4: 1 We will eat our own b', and wear
21:14 they prevented with their b' him
28:28 B' corn is bruised; because he
30:20 the b' of adversity, and the water
23 and b' of the increase of the earth,
33:16 of rocks: b' shall be given him;
36:17 wine, a land of b' and vineyards.
44:15 he kindleth it and baketh b'; yea,
19 I have baked b' upon the coals
51:14 pit, nor that his b' should fail.
55: 2 money for that which is not b'?
10 seed to the sower, and b' to the
58: 7 to deal thy b' to the hungry, and
Jer 5:17 eat up thine harvest, and thy b',
37:21 give him daily a piece of b' out of
21 the bakers' street, until all the b'
38: 9 for there is no more b' in the city.
41: 1 they did eat b' together in Mizpah.
42:14 nor have hunger of b'; and there
52: 6 there was no b' for the people of
33 did continually eat b' before him
La 1:11 All her people sigh, they seek b';
4: 4 the young children ask b', and no
5: 6 Assyrians, to be satisfied with b'.
9 We gat our b' with the peril of
Eze 4: 9 make thee b' thereof, according
13 their defiled b' among the Gentiles,
15 thou shalt prepare thy b'
16 I will break the staff of b' in
16 and they shall eat b' by weight,
17 That they may want b' and water,
5:16 and will break your staff of b':
12:18 of man, eat thy b' with quaking,
19 shall eat their b' with carefulness,
13:19 of barley and for pieces of b',
14:13 will break the staff of the b'
16:49 fulness of b', and abundance of
18: 7 given his b' to the hungry, and
16 hath given his b' to the hungry,
24:17 thy lips, and eat not the b' of men.
22 your lips, nor eat the b' of men.
44: 3 sit in it to eat b' before the Lord;
7 when ye offer my b', the fat and
45:21 days; unleavened b' shall be eaten.
Da 10: 3 I ate no pleasant b', neither
Ho 2: 5 give me my b' and my water,
9: 4 unto them as the b' of mourners;
4 their b' for their soul shall not
Am 4: 6 and want of b' in all your places:
7:12 and there eat b', and prophesy
8:11 not a famine of b', nor a thirst for
Ob 7 they that eat thy b' have laid a
Hag 2:12 and with his skirt do touch b',
Mal 1: 7 Ye offer polluted b' upon mine
M't 4: 3 that these stones be made b'.
4 Man shall not live by b' alone,
6:11 Give us this day our daily b'.
7: 9 whom if his son ask b', will he
15: 2 not their hands, when they eat b'.
26 not meet to take the children's b',
33 should we have so much b' in
16: 5 they had forgotten to take b'.
7 It is because we have taken no b'.
8 because ye have brought no b'?
11 not to you concerning b', that
12 not beware of the leaven of b', but
26:17 the feast of unleavened b' the
26 Jesus took b', and blessed it, and
M'r 3:20 could not so much as eat b'.
6: 8 no scrip, no b', no money in their
36 villages, and buy themselves b':
37 two hundred pennyworth of b',
7: 2 saw some of his disciples eat b'
5 but eat b' with unwashen hands?
27 not meet to take the children's b',
M'r 8: 4 satisfy these men with b' here in
14 disciples had forgotten to take b',
16 saying, It is because we have no b'.
17 reason ye, because ye have no b'?
14: 1 the passover, and of unleavened b':
12 the first day of unleavened b',
22 Jesus took b', and blessed, and
Lu 4: 3 this stone that it be made b'.
4 man shall not live by b' alone, but
7:33 neither eating b' nor drinking
9: 3 scrip, neither b', neither money;
11: 3 Give us day by day our daily b'.
11 If a son shall ask b' of any of you
14: 1 to eat b' on the sabbath day, that
15 he that shall eat b' in the kingdom
15:17 servants of my father's have b'
22: 1 Now the feast of unleavened b' drew
7 came the day of unleavened b',
19 he took b', and gave thanks, and
24:30 he took b', and blessed it, and
35 known of them in breaking of b'.
Joh 6: 5 Whence shall we buy b', that these
7 Two hundred pennyworth of b'
23 place where they did eat b', after
31 He gave them b' from heaven to
32 Moses gave you not that b' from
32 my Father giveth you the true b'
33 For the b' of God is he which
34 Lord, evermore give us this b'.
35 I am the b' of life: he that cometh
41 I am the b' which came down from
48 I am that b' of life.
50 This is the b' which cometh down
51 I am the living b' which came
51 if any man eat of this b', he shall
51 the b' that I will give is my flesh,
58 This is that b' which came down
58 he that eateth of this b' shall live
13:18 He that eateth b' with me hath
21: 9 there, and fish laid thereon, and b'.
13 Jesus then cometh, and taketh b'
Ac 2:42 in breaking of b', and in prayers.
46 breaking b' from house to house,
12: 3 were the days of unleavened b'.)
20: 6 after the days of unleavened b',
7 came together to break b', Paul
11 had broken b', and eaten, and
27:35 he took b', and gave thanks to God
1Co 5: 8 unleavened b' of sincerity and
10:16 The b' which we break, is it not
17 we being many are one b', and
17 are all partakers of that one b'.
11:23 which he was betrayed took b':
26 as often as ye eat this b', and drink
27 whosoever shall eat this b', and
28 so let him eat of that b', and drink
2Co 9:10 minister b' for your food, and
2Th 3: 8 Neither did we eat any man's b'
12 they work, and eat their own b'.

breadth See also HANDBREADTH.
Ge 6:15 the b' of it fifty cubits, and the
13:17 the length of it and in the b' of it;
Ex 25:10 a cubit and a half the b' thereof,
17 and a cubit and a half the b'
23 a cubit the b' thereof, and a cubit
25 border of an hand b' round
26: 2 and the b' of one curtain four
8 shall be thirty cubits, and the b'
16 cubit and a half shall be the b' of
27:12 And for the b' of the court on the
13 And the b' of the court on the
18 and the b' fifty every where, and
28:16 and a span shall be the b' thereof.
30: 2 a cubit the b' thereof; four
36: 9 and the b' of one curtain four
15 four cubits was the b' of one
21 the b' of a board one cubit and a
37: 1 a cubit and a half the b' of it, and
6 and one cubit and a half the b'
10 a cubit the b' thereof, and a cubit
25 the b' of it a cubit; it was four
38: 1 five cubits the b' thereof; it was
18 length, and the height in the b'
39: 9 thereof, and span the b' thereof,
De 2: 5 so much as a foot b';
3:11 four cubits the b' of it, after the
J'g 20:16 could sling stones at an hair b',
1Ki 6: 2 the b' thereof twenty cubits, and
3 according to the b' of the house;
3 the b' thereof before the house.
20 in length, and twenty cubits in b',
7: 2 the b' thereof fifty cubits, and the
6 fifty cubits, and the b' thereof
26 And it was an hand b' thick,
27 four cubits the b' thereof, and
2Ch 3: 3 threescore cubits, and the b'
4 the b' of the house, twenty cubits,
8 was according to the b' of the
8 twenty cubits, and the b' thereof
4: 1 twenty cubits the b' thereof, and
Ezr 6: 3 and the b' thereof threescore
Job 37:10 and the b' of the waters is
38:18 Hast thou perceived the b' of the
Isa 8: 8 shall fill the b' of thy land, O
Eze 40: 5 by the cubit and an hand b':
5 he measured the b' of the
11 the b' of the entry of the gate, ten
13 the b' was five and twenty cubits,
19 the b' from the forefront of
20 the length thereof and the b'
21, 25, 36 and the b' five and twenty
48 and the b' of the gate was three
49 twenty cubits, and the b' eleven
41: 1 other side, which was the b' of the
2 And the b' of the door was ten
2 forty cubits; and the b', twenty
Eze 41: 3 and the b' of the door, seven
4 and the b', twenty cubits, before
5 and the b' of every side chamber,
7 therefore the b' of the house was
11 and the b' of the place that was
14 Also the b' of the face of the house
42: 2 north door, and the b' was fifty
4 a walk of ten cubits b' inward,
43:13 cubit is a cubit and an hand b';
13 and the b' a cubit, and the border
14 shall be two cubits, and the b'
14 shall be four cubits, and the b'
45: 1 and the b' shall be ten thousand.
2 five hundred in b', square round
3 and the b' of ten thousand: and
5 the ten thousand of b', shall also
48: 8 and twenty thousand reeds in b',
9 length, and of ten thousand in b'.
10 the west ten thousand in b'
10 the east ten thousand in b',
13 and ten thousand in b': all the
13 twenty thousand, and the b' ten
15 in the b' over against the five
Da 3: 1 threescore cubits, and the b'
Hab 1: 6 through the b' of the land, to
Zec 2: 2 to see what is the b' thereof, and
5: 2 twenty cubits, and the b' thereof
Eph 3:18 what is the b', and length, and
Re 20: 9 they went up on the b' of the
21:16 the length is as large as the b':
16 and the b' and the height of it are

break See also BRAKE; BREAKEST; BREAKETH; BREAKING; BROKEN.
Ge 19: 9 even Lot, came near to b' the
27:40 that thou shalt b' his yoke from
Ex 12:46 neither shall ye b' a bone
13:13 then thou shalt b' his neck: and
19:21 lest they b' through unto the
22 lest the Lord b' forth upon them.
24 the people b' through to come up
24 lest he b' forth upon them.
22: 6 If fire b' out, and catch in thorns,
23:24 overthrow them, and quite b'
32: 2 B' off the golden earrings, which
24 hath any gold, let them b' it off.
34:13 b' their images, and cut down
20 him not, then shalt thou b' his
Le 11:33 shall be unclean: and ye shall b'
13:12 if a leprosy b' out abroad in the
14:43 and b' out in the house, after that
45 And he shall b' down the house,
26:15 but that ye b' my covenant:
19 I will b' the pride of your power;
44 to b' my covenant with them: for
Nu 9:12 of it unto the morning, nor b'
24: 8 shall b' their bones, and pierce
30: 2 he shall not b' his word, he shall
De 7: 5 b' down their images, and cut
12 a border of an hand b' round
12: 3 and b' their pillars, and burn
31:16 and b' my covenant which I have
20 provoke me, and b' my covenant.
J'g 2: 1 I will never b' my covenant with
8: 9 again in peace, I will b' down this
1Sa 25:10 servants now a days that b' away
2Sa 2:32 they came to Hebron at b' of day.
1Ki 15:19 and b' thy league with Baasha
2Ki 3:26 that drew swords, to b' through
25:13 did the Chaldees b' in pieces, and
2Ch 16: 3 go, b' thy league with Baasha
Ezr 9:14 Should we again b' thy
Ne 4: 3 he shall even b' down their
Job 13:25 Wilt thou b' a leaf driven to and
19: 2 vex my soul, and b' me in pieces
34:24 He shall b' in pieces mighty
39:15 that the wild beast may b' them.
Ps 2: 3 Let us b' their bands asunder,
9 Thou shalt b' them with a rod of
10:15 B' thou the arm of the wicked
58: 6 B' their teeth, O God, in their
6 b' out the great teeth of the
72: 4 shall b' in pieces the oppressor.
74: 6 But now they b' down the carved
89:31 If they b' my statutes, and keep
34 My covenant will I not b', nor
94: 5 They b' in pieces thy people,
141: 5 shall not b' my head: forget my
Ec 3: 3 a time to b' down, and a time to
Ca 2:17 Until the day b', and the
4: 6 day b', and the shadows flee
Isa 5: 5 and b' down the wall thereof,
14: 7 and is quiet: they b' forth into
25 That I will b' the Assyrian in my
28:24 doth he open and b' the clods of
28 nor b' it with the wheel of his
30:14 And he shall b' it as the breaking
35: 6 in the wilderness shall waters b'
38:13 as a lion, so will he b' all my
42: 3 A bruised reed shall he not b',
44:23 b' forth into singing, ye
45: 2 I will b' in pieces the gates of
49:13 and b' forth into singing, O
52: 9 B' forth into joy, sing together,
54: 1 b' forth into singing, and cry
3 thou shalt b' forth on the right
55:12 mountains and the hills shall b'
58: 6 go free, and that ye b' every yoke?
8 Then shall thy light b' forth as
Jer 1:14 an evil shall b' forth upon all the
4: 3 B' up your fallow ground, and
14:21 remember, b' not thy covenant
15:12 Shall iron b' the northern iron
19:10 Then shalt thou b' the bottle in
11 Even so will I b' this people and
28: 4 I will b' the yoke of the king of
11 Even so will I b' the yoke of

Jer 30: 8 I will b' his yoke from off thy
31:28 to pluck up, and to b' down,
33:20 If ye can b' my covenant of the
43:13 He shall b' also the images of
45: 4 which I have built will I b' down,
48:12 empty his vessels, and b' their
49:35 I will b' the bow of Elam, the
51:20 for with thee will I b' in pieces
21 And with thee will I b' in pieces
21 rider; and with thee will I b' in
22 With thee also will I b' in pieces
22 and with thee will I b' in pieces old
22 and with thee will I b' in pieces
23 I will also b' in pieces with thee
23 and with thee will I b' in pieces
23 And with thee will I b' in pieces
Eze 4:16 I will b' the staff of bread in
5:16 and will b' your staff of bread:
13:14 So will I b' down the wall that ye
14:13 and will b' the staff of the bread
16:38 women that b' wedlock and shed
39 shall b' down thy high places:
17:15 or shall he b' the covenant, and
23:34 thou shalt b' the sherds thereof,
26: 4 Tyrus, and b' down her towers:
9 he shall b' down thy towers.
12 and they shall b' down thy walls,
29: 7 thou didst b', and rend all their
30:18 when I shall b' there the yokes of
22 and will b' his arms, the strong
24 but I will b' Pharaoh's arms, and
Da 2:40 all these shall it b' in pieces
44 it shall b' in pieces and consume
4:27 b' off thy sins by righteousness,
7:23 shall tread it down, and b' it in
Ho 1: 5 that I will b' the bow of Israel in
2:18 I will b' the bow and the sword
4: 2 they b' out, and blood toucheth
10: 2 he shall b' down their altars, he
11 shall plow, and Jacob shall b' his
12 mercy; b' up your fallow ground:
Joe 2: 7 and they shall not b' their ranks:
Am 1: 5 I will b' also the bar of Damascus,
5: 6 lest he b' out like fire in the
Mic 3: 3 they b' their bones, and chop
Na 1:13 now will I b' his yoke from off
Zec 11:10 that I might b' my covenant
14 that I might b' the brotherhood
M't 5:19 shall b' one of these least
6:19 where thieves b' through and
20 where thieves do not b' through
9:17 else the bottles b', and the wine
12:20 A bruised reed shall he not b',
Ac 20: 7 came together to b' bread, Paul
11 a long while, even to b' of day,
21:13 What mean ye to weep and to b'
1Co 10:16 The bread which we b', is it not
Ga 4:27 b' forth and cry, thou that

breaker See also COVENANTBREAKERS; TRUCE-BREAKERS.
Mic 2:13 The b' is come up before them:
Ro 2:25 but if thou be a b' of the law,

breakest
Ps 48: 7 Thou b' the ships of Tarshish

breaketh
Ge 32:26 he said, Let me go, for the day b'.
Job 9:17 he b' me with a tempest, and
12:14 Behold, he breaketh down, and it
16:14 He b' me with breach upon
28: 4 The flood b' out from the
Ps 29: 5 The voice of the Lord b' the
5 yea, the Lord b' the cedars
46: 9 he b' the bow, and cutteth the
119:20 My soul b' for the longing that it
Pr 25:15 and a soft tongue b' the bone.
Ec 10: 8 whoso b' an hedge, a serpent
Isa 59: 5 is crushed b' out into a viper.
Jer 19:11 as one b' a potter's vessel, that
23:29 like a hammer that b' the rock in
La 4: 4 ask bread, and no man b' it unto
Da 2:40 forasmuch as iron b' in pieces
40 as iron that b' all these, shall it

breaking See also BREACH; BREAKINGS.
Ge 32:24 a man with him until the b' of
Ex 9: 9 a boil b' forth with blains upon
10 it became a boil b' forth with
22: 2 If a thief be found b' up, and be
1Ch 14:11 like the b' forth of waters:
Job 30:14 me as a wide b' in of waters:
Ps 144:14 that there be no b' in, nor going
Isa 22: 5 b' down the walls, and of crying
30:13 whose b' cometh suddenly at an
14 as the b' of the potters' vessel
Eze 16:59 despised the oath in b' the
17:18 by b' the covenant, when, lo, he
21: 6 with the b' of thy loins; and
Ho 13:13 in the place of the b' forth of
Lu 24:35 known of them in b' of bread.
Ac 2:42 in b' of bread, and in prayers.
46 and b' bread from house to house,
Ro 2:23 b' the law dishonourest thou

breakings
Job 41:25 by reason of b' they purify

breast See also BREASTPLATE; BREASTS.
Ex 29:26 thou shalt take the b' of the
27 sanctify the b' of the wave
Le 7:30 the fat with the b', it shall he
30 that the b' may be waved
31 but the b' shall be Aaron's and his
34 the wave b' and the heave
8:29 Moses took the b', and waved it
10:14 the wave b' and heave shoulder
15 heave shoulder and the wave b'
Nu 6:20 priest, with the wave b' and heave
Nu 18:18 as the wave b' and as the right
Job 24: 9 pluck the fatherless from the b',
Isa 60:16 shalt suck the b' of kings; and
La 4: 3 the sea monsters draw out the b',
Da 2:32 his b' and his arms of silver, his
Lu 18:13 but smote upon his b', saying,
Joh 13:25 He then lying on Jesus' b' saith
21:20 which also leaned on his b' at

breastplate See also BREASTPLATES.
Ex 25: 7 be set in the ephod, and in the b'.
28: 4 they shall make; a b', and an
15 shalt make the b' of judgment
22 make upon the b' chains at the
23 make upon the b' two rings of
23 two rings on the two ends of the b'.
24 which are on the ends of the b'.
26 two ends of the b' in the border
28 they shall bind the b' by the rings
28 that the b' be not loosed from the
29 the children of Israel in the b' of
30 put in the b' of judgment the
29: 5 the ephod, and the b', and gird
35: 9 set for the ephod, and for the b'.
27 set, for the ephod, and for the b';
39: 8 he made the b' of cunning work,
9 they made the b' double:
15 upon the b' chains at the ends,
16 rings in the two ends of the b'.
17 two rings on the ends of the b'.
19 put them on the two ends of the b',
21 bind the b' by his rings unto the
21 that the b' might not be loosed
Le 8: 8 he put the b' upon him:
8 also he put in the b' the Urim
Isa 59:17 put on righteousness as a b',
Eph 6:14 having on the b' of righteousness;
1Th 5: 8 putting on the b' of faith and love;

breastplates
Re 9: 9 b', as it were b' of iron;
17 b' of fire, and of jacinth, and

breasts
Ge 49:25 blessings of the b', and of the
Le 9:20 they put the fat upon the b', and
21 the b' and the right shoulder
Job 3:12 or why the b' that I should suck?
21:24 His b' are full of milk, and his
Ps 22: 9 when I was upon my mother's b'.
Pr 5:19 let her b' satisfy thee at all times;
Ca 1:13 shall lie all night betwixt my b'.
4: 5 Thy two b' are like two young roes
7: 3 thy two b' are like two young roes
7 and thy b' to clusters of grapes.
8 thy b' shall be as clusters of the
8: 1 that sucked the b' of my mother!
8 little sister, and she hath no b':
10 and my b' like towers: then was
Isa 28: 9 the milk, and drawn from the b'.
66:11 satisfied with the b' of her
Eze 16: 7 thy b' are fashioned, and thine
23: 3 there were their b' pressed, and
8 bruised the b' of her virginity,
34 and pluck off thine own b':
Ho 2: 2 adulteries from between her b';
9:14 miscarrying womb and dry b'.
Joe 2:16 and those that suck the b':
Na 2: 7 of doves, tabering upon their b'.
Lu 23:48 smote their b', and returned.
Re 15: 6 their b' girded with golden girdles.

breath
Ge 2: 7 into his nostrils the b' of life;
6:17 wherein is the b' of life, from
7:15 flesh, wherein is the b' of life.
22 in whose nostrils was the b' of life.
2Sa 22:16 at the blast of the b' of his nostrils.
1Ki 17:17 that there was no b' left in him.
Job 4: 9 and by the b' of his nostrils are
9:18 will not suffer me to take my b',
12:10 and the b' of all mankind.
15:30 by the b' of his mouth shall he go
17: 1 My b' is corrupt, my days are
19:17 My b' is strange to my wife,
27: 3 while my b' is in me, and the
33: 4 and the b' of the Almighty hath
34:14 unto himself his spirit and his b';
37:10 By the b' of God frost is given:
41:21 His b' kindleth coals, and a flame
Ps 18:15 the blast of the b' of thy nostrils.
33: 6 the host of them by the b' of his
104:29 thou takest away their b', they
135:17 neither is their any b' in their
146: 4 His b' goeth forth, he returneth
150: 6 every thing that hath b' praise
Ec 3:19 yea, they have all one b'; so that
Isa 2:22 from man, whose b' is in his
11: 4 and with the b' of his lips shall
30:28 And his b', as an overflowing
33 the b' of the Lord, like a stream
33:11 your b', as fire, shall devour you.
42: 5 he that giveth b' unto the people
Jer 10:14 falsehood, and there is no b' in
51:17 falsehood, and there is no b' in
La 4:20 b' of our nostrils, the anointed
Eze 37: 5 I will cause b' to enter into you,
6 and put b' in you, and ye shall
8 but there was no b' in them.
9 the four winds, O b', and breathe
10 the b' came into them, and they
Da 5:23 God in whose hand thy b' is, and
10:17 me, neither is there b' left in me.
Hab 2:19 there is no b' at all in the midst
Ac 17:25 he giveth to all life, and b', and

breathe See also BREATHED; BREATHEST; BREATHING.
Jos 11:11 there was not any left to b': and
Jos 11:14 them, neither left they any to b'.
Ps 27:12 me, and such as b' out cruelty.
Eze 37: 9 and b' upon these slain, that

breathed
Ge 2: 7 and b' into his nostrils the breath
Jos 10:40 utterly destroyed all that b', as
1Ki 15:29 left not to Jeroboam any that b',
Joh 20:22 said this, he b' on them, and said

breatheth
De 20:16 shalt save alive nothing that b':

breathing
La 3:56 hide not thine ear at my b', at
Ac 9: 1 Saul, yet b' out threatenings and

bred
Ex 16:20 morning, and it b' worms, and

breeches
Ex 28:42 thou shalt make them linen b' to
39:28 and linen b' of fine twined linen,
Le 6:10 and his linen b' shall he put upon
16: 4 and he shall have the linen b' upon
Eze 44:18 and shall have linen b' upon their

breed See also BRED; BREEDING.
Ge 8:17 that they may b' abundantly in
De 32:14 rams of the b' of Bashan, and

breeding
Zep 2: 9 the b' of nettles, and salt pits,

brethren See also BRETHREN'S; BROTHERS'.
Ge 9:22 his father, and told his two b'
25 of servants shall he be unto his b'.
13: 8 and thy herdmen; for we be b'.
16:12 dwell in the presence of his b'.
19: 7 pray you, b', do not so wickedly.
24:27 to the house of my master's b'.
25:18 died in the presence of all his b'.
27:29 be lord over thy b', and let thy
37 all his b' have I given to him for
29: 4 unto them, My b', whence be ye?
31:23 he took his b' with him, and
25 Laban with his b' pitched in the
32 before our b' discern thou what
37 it here before my b' and thy b',
46 Jacob said unto his b', Gather
54 called his b' to eat bread: and they
34:11 unto her father and unto her b',
25 Simeon and Levi, Dinah's b', took
37: 2 feeding the flock with his b'; and
4 his b' saw that their father loved
4 him more than all his b',
5 a dream, and he told it his b':
8 his b' said to him, Shalt thou
9 another dream, and told it his b',
10 told it to his father, and to his b':
10 Shall I and thy mother and thy b'
11 his b' envied him; but his father
12 his b' went to feed their father's
13 Do not thy b' feed the flock in
14 whether it be well with thy b',
16 he said, I seek my b': tell me, I pray
17 Joseph went after his b', and found
23 when Joseph was come unto his b',
26 Judah said unto his b', What profit
27 our flesh: and his b' were content.
30 he returned unto his b', and said,
38: 1 Judah went down from his b', and
11 peradventure he die also, as his b'
42: 3 Joseph's ten b' went down to buy
4 not with his b'; for he said, Lest
6 Joseph's b' came, and bowed
7 Joseph saw his b', and he knew
8 Joseph knew his b', but they knew
13 Thy servants are twelve b', the
19 let one of your b' be bound in the
28 he said unto his b', My money is
32 We be twelve b', sons of our father;
33 leave one of your b' here with me,
44:14 Judah and his b' came to Joseph's
33 and let the lad go up with his b'.
45: 1 made himself known unto his b'.
3 Joseph said unto his b', I am
3 And his b' could not answer him;
4 Joseph said unto his b', Come
15 Moreover he kissed all his b', and
15 after that his b' talked with him.
16 Joseph's b' are come: and it
17 Say unto thy b', This do ye; lade
24 So he sent his b' away, and they
46:31 Joseph said unto his b', and unto
31 My b', and my father's house,
47: 1 My father and my b', and their
2 he took some of his b', even five
3 Pharaoh said unto his b', What is
5 saying, Thy father and thy b' are
6 make thy father and b' to dwell;
11 placed his father and his b', and
12 nourished his father, and his b',
48: 6 the name of their b' in their
22 to thee one portion above thy b',
49: 5 Simeon and Levi are b';
8 art he whom thy b' shall praise:
26 him that was separate from his b'.
50: 8 the house of Joseph, and his b',
14 returned into Egypt, he, and his b',
15 when Joseph's b' saw that their
17 trespass of thy b', and their sin
18 his b' also went and fell down
24 And Joseph said unto his b',
Ex 1: 6 And Joseph died, and all his b',
2:11 that he went out unto his b',
11 smiting an Hebrew, one of his b'.
4:18 unto my b' which are in Egypt,
Le 10: 4 carry your b' from before the
6 but let your b', the whole house of
21:10 the high priest among his b',

Le 25:46 over your b' the children of Israel,
48 one of his b' may redeem him:
Nu 8:26 with their b' in the tabernacle
16:10 thy b' the sons of Levi with thee:
18: 2 thy b' also of the tribe of Levi,
6 I have taken your b' the Levites
20: 3 when our b' died before the Lord!
25: 6 brought unto his b' a Midianitish
27: 4 possession among the b' of our
7 among their father's b', and thou
9 give his inheritance unto his b'.
10 if he have no b', then ye shall give
10 his inheritance unto his father's b'.
11 if his father have no b', then ye
32: 6 Shall your b' go to war, and shall
De 1:16 Hear the causes between your b',
28 our b' have discouraged our heart,
2: 4 pass through the coast of your b'
8 when we passed by from our b'
3:18 pass over armed before your b'
20 Lord have given rest unto your b',
10: 9 no part nor inheritance with his b';
15: 7 a poor man of one of thy b' within
17:15 from among thy b' shalt thou set
20 heart be not lifted up above his b',
18: 2 no inheritance among their b':
7 as all his b' the Levites do, which
15 from the midst of thee, of thy b',
18 a Prophet from among their b',
24: 7 any of his b' of the children of
14 whether he be of thy b', or of
25: 5 If b' dwell together, and one of
33: 9 neither did he acknowledge his b',
16 him that was separated from his b'.
24 let him be acceptable to his b',
Jos 1:14 ye shall pass before your b' armed,
15 Until the Lord have given your b'
2:13 father, and my mother, and my b',
18 and thy b', and all thy father's
6:23 father, and her mother, and her b',
14: 8 Nevertheless my b' that went up
17: 4 us an inheritance among our b'.
4 among the b' of their father.
22: 3 Ye have not left your b' these many
4 God hath given rest unto your b',
7 gave Joshua among their b' on
8 spoil of your enemies with your b',
J'g 8:19 They were my b', even the sons of
9: 1 to Shechem unto his mother's b',
3 his mother's b' spake of him in
5 slew his b' the sons of Jerubbaal,
24 aided him in the killing of his b'.
26 son of Ebed came with his b',
31 and his b' be come to Shechem;
41 Zebul thrust out Gaal and his b',
56 his father, in slaying his seventy b':
11: 3 Jepthah fled from his b', and dwelt
14: 3 among the daughters of thy b',
16:31 Then his b' and all the house
18: 8 they came unto their b' to Zorah
8 and their b' said unto them,
14 said unto their b', Do ye know
19:23 said unto them, Nay, my b', nay,
20:13 hearken to the voice of their b'
21:22 their b' come unto us to complain,
Ru 4:10 not cut off from among his b',
1Sa 16:13 anointed him in the midst of his b':
17:17 Take now for thy b' an ephah of
17 and run to the camp to thy b';
18 look how thy b' fare, and take their
22 and came and saluted his b'.
20:29 I pray thee, and see my b'.
22: 1 his b' and all his father's house
30:23 Ye shall not do so, my b', with that
2Sa 2:26 return from following their b'?
3: 8 to his b', and to his friends,
15:20 take back thy b': mercy and truth
19:12 Ye are my b', ye are my bones
41 Why have our b' the men of Judah
1Ki 1: 9 called all his b' the king's sons,
12:24 nor fight against your b' the
2Ki 9: 2 him arise up from among his b',
10:13 Jehu met with the b' of Ahaziah
13 We are the b' of Ahaziah; and we
23: 9 unleavened bread among their b'.
1Ch 4: 9 was more honourable than his b':
27 but his b' had not many children,
5: 2 Judah prevailed above his b',
7 And his b' by their families,
13 And their b' of the house of their
6:44 And their b' the sons of Merari
48 Their b' also the Levites were
7: 5 And their b' among all the families
22 and his b' came to comfort him.
8:32 dwelt with their b' in Jerusalem,
9: 6 sons of Zerah; Jeuel, and their b',
9 And their b', according to their
13 And their b', heads of the house of
17 Talmon, and Ahiman, and their b':
19 the son of Korah, and his b',
25 And their b', which were in their
32 other of their b', of the sons of the
38 And they also dwelt with their b' at
38 Jerusalem, over against their b'.
12: 2 even of Saul's b' of Benjamin.
32 b' were at their commandment.
39 for their b' had prepared for them.
13: 2 let us send abroad unto our b'
15: 5 and his b' an hundred and twenty:
6 and his b' two hundred and twenty:
7 and his b' an hundred and thirty:
8 the chief, and his b' two hundred:
9 the chief, and his b' fourscore:
10 and his b' an hundred and twelve.
12 both ye and your b', that ye may
16 appoint their b' to be the singers

1Ch 15:17 the son of Joel, and of his b',
17 of the sons of Merari their b',
18 with them their b' of the second
16: 7 into the hand of Asaph and his b'.
37 Asaph and his b', to minister before
38 Obed-edom with their b',
39 Zadok the priest, and his b'
23:22 and their b' the sons of Kish
32 charge of the sons of Aaron their b',
24:31 cast lots over against their b' the
31 over against their younger b'.
25: 7 their b' that were instructed in
9 with his b' and sons were twelve:
10, 11, 12, 13, 14, 15, 16, 17, 18, 19, 20,
21, 22, 23, 24, 25, 26, 27, 28, 29, 30, 31,
his sons, and his b', were twelve:
26: 7 whose b' were strong men, Elihu,
8 they and their sons, and their b',
9 Meshelemiah had sons and b',
11 all the sons and b' of Hosah were
25 And his b' by Eliezer; Rehabiah
26 Shelomith and his b' were over
28 the hand of Shelomith, and of his b'.
30 Hashabiah and his b', men of
32 And his b', men of valour, were
27:18 Elihu, one of the b' of David:
28: 2 Hear me, my b', and my people:
2Ch 5:12 with their sons and their b', being
11: 4 go up, nor fight against your b':
22 chief, to be ruler among his b':
19:10 shall come to you of your b' that
10 come upon you, and upon your b':
21: 2 he had b' the sons of Jehoshaphat,
4 slew all his b' with the sword,
13 hast slain thy b' of thy father's
22: 8 the sons of the b' of Ahaziah,
28: 8 carried away captive of their b'
11 ye have taken captive of your b':
15 the city of palm trees, to their b':
29:15 they gathered their b', and
34 their b' the Levites did help
30: 7 and like your b', which trespassed
9 your b' and your children shall
31:15 to give to their b' by courses,
35: 5 families of the fathers of your b'
6 prepare your b', that they may
9 Shemaiah and Nethaneel, his b',
15 for their b' the Levites prepared
Ezr 3: 2 his b' the priests, and Zerubbabel
2 the son of Shealtiel, and his b',
8 their b' the priests and the Levites,
9 Jeshua with his sons and his b',
9 their sons and their b' the Levites.
6:20 for their b' the priests, and for
7:18 seem good to thee, and to thy b',
8:17 to his b' the Nethinims at the place
18 with his sons and his b',
19 sons of Merari, his b' and their
24 and ten of their b' with them,
10:18 the son of Jozadak, and his b';
Ne 1: 2 That Hanani, one of my b', came,
3: 1 with his b' the priests, and they
18 After him repaired their b',
4: 2 he spake before his b' and the
14 fight for your b', your sons, and
23 So neither I, nor my b', nor my
5: 1 wives against their b' the Jews.
5 our flesh is as the flesh of our b',
8 have redeemed our b' the Jews,
8 and will ye even sell your b'?
10 I likewise, and my b', and my
14 and my b' have not eaten the bread
10:10 And their b', Shebaniah, Hodijah,
29 They clave to their b', their nobles,
11:12 And their b' that did the work of
13 And his b', chief of the fathers,
14 And their b', mighty men of valour,
17 Bakbukiah the second among his b',
19 and their b' that kept the gates,
12: 7 of their b' in the days of Jeshua.
8 the thanksgiving, he and his b'.
9 Bakbukiah and Unni, their b',
24 with their b' over against them,
36 his b', Shemaiah, and Azarael,
13:13 was to distribute unto their b'.
Es 10: 3 accepted of the multitude of his b',
Job 6:15 My b' have dealt deceitfully as a
19:13 He hath put my b' far from me,
42:11 came there unto him all his b',
15 them inheritance among their b'.
Ps 22:22 will declare thy name unto my b':
69: 8 become a stranger unto my b',
122: 8 For my b' and companions' sakes,
133: 1 is for b' to dwell together in unity!
Pr 6:19 he that soweth discord among b'.
17: 2 of the inheritance among the b'.
19: 7 All the b' of the poor do hate him:
Isa 66: 5 Your b' that hated you, that cast
20 they shall bring all your b' for an
Jer 7:15 I have cast out all your b',
12: 6 For even thy b', and the house of
29:16 of your b' that are not gone forth
35: 3 son of Habaziniah, and his b',
41: 8 and slew them not among their b'.
49:10 and his b', and his neighbours,
Eze 11:15 Son of man, thy b', even thy
15 even thy b', the men of thy kindred,
Hos 2: 1 Say ye unto your b', Ammi; and to
13:15 he be fruitful among his b',
Mic 5: 3 the remnant of his b' shall return
M't 1: 2 and Jacob begat Judas and his b';
11 Josias begat Jechonias and his b',
4:18 by the sea of Galilee, saw two b',
21 he saw other two b', James the son
5:47 if ye salute your b' only, what do ye
12:46 his mother and his b' stood without,

M't 12:47 thy mother and thy b' that stand
48 my mother? and who are my b'?
49 said, Behold my mother and my b'!
13:55 b', James, and Joses, and Simon,
19:29 b', or sisters, or father, or mother,
20:24 with indignation against the two b'.
22:25 there were with us seven b': and
23: 8 even Christ; and all ye are b'.
25:40 the least of these my b', ye have
28:10 tell my b' that they go into Galilee,
M'r 3:31 came then his b' and his mother,
32 and thy b' without seek for thee.
33 Who is my mother, or my b'?
34 Behold my mother and my b'!
10:29 left house, or b', or sisters,
30 and b', and sisters, and mothers,
12:20 Now there were seven b': and the
Lu 8:19 his mother, and his b', and could
20 Thy mother and thy b' stand
21 My mother and my b' are these
14:12 not thy friends, nor thy b', neither
26 children, and b', and sisters, yea,
16:28 I have five b'; that he may testify
18:29 parents, or b', or wife, or children,
20:29 There were therefore seven b':
21:16 by parents, and b', and kinsfolks,
22:32 art converted, strengthen thy b'.
Joh 2:12 his mother, and his b', and his
7: 3 His b' therefore said unto him,
5 neither did his b' believe in him.
10 But when his b' were gone up,
20:17 go to my b', and say unto them,
21:23 saying abroad among the b',
Ac 1:14 mother of Jesus, and with his b'.
16 Men and b', this scripture must
2:29 Men and b', let me freely speak
37 Men and b', what shall we do?
3:17 b', I wot that through ignorance
22 unto you of your b', like unto me;
6: 3 Wherefore, b', look ye out among
7: 2 said, Men, b', and fathers, hearken;
13 Joseph was made known to his b';
23 visit his b' the children of Israel.
25 his b' would have understood
26 saying, Sirs, ye are b'; why do ye
37 unto you of your b', like unto me;
9:30 Which when the b' knew, they
10:23 b' from Joppa accompanied him.
11: 1 apostles and b' that were in Judæa
12 these six b' accompanied me,
29 send relief unto the b' which dwelt
12:17 things unto James, and to the b'.
13:15 saying, Ye men and b', if ye have
26 Men and b', children of the stock of
38 unto you therefore, men and b',
14: 2 minds evil affected against the b'.
15: 1 from Judæa taught the b',
3 caused great joy unto all the b'.
7 and said unto them, Men and b',
13 Men and b', hearken unto me:
22 and Silas, chief men among the b':
23 The apostles and elders and b'
23 send greeting unto the b'
32 exhorted the b' with many words
33 peace from the b' unto the apostles.
36 and visit our b' in every city where
40 being recommended by the b' unto
16: 2 b' that were at Lystra and Iconium.
40 and when they had seen the b',
17: 6 they drew Jason and certain b'
10 the b' immediately sent away Paul
14 the b' sent away Paul to go as it
18:18 took his leave of the b', and sailed
27 b' wrote, exhorting the disciples
20:32 now, b', I commend you to God,
21: 7 saluted the b', and abode with them
17 the b' received us gladly.
22: 1 Men, b', and fathers, hear ye my
5 I received letters unto the b',
23: 1 Men and b', I have lived in all good
5 I wist not, b', that he was the high
6 Men and b', I am a Pharisee,
28:14 we found b', and were desired to
15 when the b' heard of us, they came
17 Men and b', though I have committed
21 any of the b' that came shewed or
Ro 1:13 you ignorant, b', that oftentimes I
7: 1 Know ye not, b', (for I speak to them
4 my b', ye also are become dead to
8:12 Therefore, b', we are debtors,
29 be the firstborn among many b'.
9: 3 accursed from Christ for my b',
10: 1 B', my heart's desire and prayer to
11:25 not, b', that ye should be ignorant
12: 1 I beseech you therefore, b', by the
15:14 persuaded of you, my b', that ye
15 b', I have written the more
30 Now I beseech you, b', for the Lord
16:14 and the b' which are with them.
17 I beseech you, b', mark them which
1Co 1:10 I beseech you, b', by the name of
11 declared unto me of you, my b',
26 ye see your calling, b', how that not
2: 1 I, b', when I came to you, came not
3: 1 I, b', could not speak unto you as
4: 6 these things, b', I have in a figure
6: 5 be able to judge between his b'?
8 and defraud, and that your b'.
7:24 B', let every man, wherein he is
29 But this I say, b', the time is short:
8:12 ye sin so against the b', and wound
9: 5 the b' of the Lord, and Cephas?
10: 1 b', I would not that ye should be
11: 2 praise you, b', that ye remember
33 Wherefore, my b', when ye come
12: 1 Now concerning spiritual gifts, b',

1Co 14: 6 b', if I come unto you speaking
20 B', be not children in
26 How is it then, b'? when ye come
39 Wherefore, b', covet to prophesy,
15: 1 Moreover, b', I declare unto you
6 of above five hundred b' at once;
50 this I say, b', that flesh and blood
58 Therefore, my beloved b', be ye
16:11 me: for I look for him with the b'.
12 him to come unto you with the b':
15 beseech you, b', (ye know the house
20 All the b' greet you. Greet ye one
2Co 1: 8 b', have you ignorant of our trouble
8: 1 Moreover, b', we do you to wit of
23 or our b' be enquired of, they are
9: 3 Yet have I sent the b', lest our
5 necessary to exhort the b', that
11: 9 the b' which came from Macedonia
26 the sea, in perils among false b';
13:11 Finally, b', farewell. Be perfect,
Ga 1: 2 And all the b' which are with me,
11 I certify you, b', that the gospel
2: 4 that because of false b' unawares
3:15 B', I speak after the manner of men;
4:12 B', I beseech you, be as I am; for I
28 Now we, b', as Isaac was, are the
31 So then, b', we are not children of
5:11 I, b', if I yet preach circumcision,
13 b', ye have been called unto liberty;
6: 1 B', if a man be overtaken in a fault,
18 B', the grace of our Lord Jesus
Eph 6:10 Finally, my b', be strong in the
23 Peace be to the b', and love with
Ph'p 1:12 ye should understand, b', that the
14 many of the b' in the Lord, waxing
3: 1 Finally, my b', rejoice in the Lord.
13 B', I count not myself to have
17 B', be followers together of me,
4: 1 my b' dearly beloved and longed
8 Finally, b', whatsoever things are
21 The b' which are with me greet you.
Col 1: 2 saints and faithful b' in Christ
4:15 Salute the b' which are in Laodicea,
1Th 1: 4 Knowing, b' beloved, your election
2: 1 yourselves, b', know our entrance
9 ye remember, b', our labour and
14 For ye, b', became followers of the
17 we, b', being taken from you for a
3: 7 Therefore, b', we were comforted
4: 1 we beseech you, b', and exhort you
10 toward all the b' which are in all
10 we beseech you, b', that ye increase
13 not have you to be ignorant, b',
5: 1 the times and the seasons, b', ye
4 ye, b', are not in darkness, that
12 we beseech you, b', to know them
14 we exhort you, b', warn them that
25 B', pray for us.
26 Greet all the b' with an holy kiss.
27 epistle be read unto all the holy b'.
2Th 1: 3 thank God always for you, b', as it
2: 1 we beseech you, b', by the coming
13 for you, b' beloved of the Lord,
15 Therefore, b', stand fast, and hold
3: 1 Finally, b', pray for us, that the
6 we command you, b', in the name
13 ye, b' be not weary in well doing.
1Ti 4: 6 put the b' in remembrance of these
5: 1 father; and the younger men as b';
6: 2 despise them, because they are b';
2Ti 4:21 Linus, and Claudia, and all the b'.
Heb 2:11 he is not ashamed to call them b',
12 I will declare thy name unto my b',
17 made like unto his b', that he
3: 1 Wherefore, holy b', partakers of
12 Take heed, b', lest there be in any
7: 5 that is, of their b', though they
10:19 Having therefore, b', boldness to
13:22 I beseech you, b', suffer the word
Jas 1: 2 My b', count it all joy when ye fall
16 Do not err, my beloved b'.
19 Wherefore, my beloved b', let every
2: 1 My b', have not the faith of our
5 Hearken, my beloved b', Hath not
14 What doth it profit, my b', though
3: 1 My b', be not many masters,
10 My b', these things ought not so to
12 Can the fig tree, my b', bear olive
4:11 Speak not evil one of another, b'.
5: 7 Be patient therefore, b', unto the
9 Grudge not one against another, b',
10 Take, my b', the prophets, who
12 above all things, my b', swear not
19 B', if any of you do err from the
1Pe 1:22 unto unfeigned love of the b', see
3: 8 love as b', be pitiful, be courteous:
5: 9 accomplished in your b' that are
2Pe 1:10 the rather, b', give diligence to
1Jo 2: 7 B', I write no new commandment
3:13 Marvel not, my b', if the world
14 because we love the b'. He that
16 to lay down our lives for the b'.
3Jo 3 when the b' came and testified of
5 thou doest to the b', and to
10 he himself receive the b', and
Re 6:11 fellowservants also and their b',
12:10 the accuser of our b' is cast down,
19:10 of thy b' that have the testimony
22: 9 of thy b' the prophets, and of them

brethren's See also BROTHERS'.
De 20: 8 lest his b' heart faint as well as

bribe See also BRIBES.
1Sa 12: 3 hand have I received any b'
Am 5:12 they take a b', and they turn aside

bribery
Job 15:34 consume the tabernacles of b'.

bribes
1Sa 8: 3 aside after lucre, and took b',
Ps 26:10 and their right hand is full of b'.
Isa 33:15 his hands from holding of b',

brick See also BRICKKILN; BRICKS.
Ge 11: 3 Go to, let us make b', and burn
3 they had b' for stone, and slime
Ex 1:14 in morter, and in b', and in all
5: 7 give the people straw to make b',
14 fulfilled your task in making b'
16 and they say to us, Make b': and
Isa 65: 3 burneth incense upon altars of b';

brickkiln
2Sa 12:31 made them pass through the b':
Jer 43: 9 the clay in the b', which is at the
Na 3:14 morter, make strong the b'.

bricks
Ex 5: 8 the tale of the b', which they did
18 yet shall ye deliver the tale of b'.
19 from your b' of your daily task.
Isa 9:10 The b' are fallen down, but we will

bride See also BRIDECHAMBER; BRIDEGROOM.
Isa 49:18 bind them on thee, as a b' doeth.
61:10 a b' adorneth herself with jewels.
62: 5 bridegroom rejoiceth over the b',
Jer 2:32 maid forget her ornaments, or a b'
7:34 bridegroom, and the voice of the b':
16: 9 and the voice of the b'.
25:10 the voice of the b', the sound of
33:11 the voice of the b', the voice of
Joe 2:16 and the b' out of her closet.
Joh 3:29 that hath the b' is the bridegroom:
Re 18:23 of the b' shall be heard no more
21: 2 prepared as a b' adorned for her
9 shew thee the b', the Lamb's wife.
22:17 the Spirit and the b' say, Come.

bridechamber
M't 9:15 Can the children of the b' mourn,
M'r 2:19 Can the children of the b' fast,
Lu 5:34 make the children of the b' fast,

bridegroom See also BRIDEGROOM'S.
Ps 19: 5 a b' coming out of his chamber,
Isa 61:10 as a b' decketh himself with
62: 5 the b' rejoiceth over the bride, so
Jer 7:34 the voice of the b', and the voice
16: 9 of gladness, the voice of the b',
25:10 the voice of the b', and the voice
33:11 the voice of the b', and the voice
Joe 2:16 let the b' go forth of his chamber,
M't 9:15 as long as the b' is with them?
15 when the b' shall be taken from
25: 1 and went forth to meet the b'.
5 While the b' tarried, they all
6 Behold, the b' cometh; go ye out
10 they went to buy, the b' came;
M'r 2:19 while the b' is with them?
19 as long as they have the b'
20 when the b' shall be taken away
Lu 5:34 fast, while the b' is with them?
35 come, when the b' shall be taken
Joh 2: 9 governor of the feast called the b',
3:29 that hath the bride is the b':
29 but the friend of the b',
Re 18:23 and the voice of the b' and of the

bridegroom's
Joh 3:29 greatly because of the b' voice:

bridle See also BRIDLES; BRIDLETH.
2Ki 19:28 my b' in thy lips, and I will turn
Job 30:11 they have also let loose the b'
41:13 come to him with his double b'?
Ps 32: 9 must be held in with bit and b',
39: 1 I will keep my mouth with a b',
Pr 26: 3 a b' for the ass, and a rod for the
Isa 30:28 be a b' in the jaws of the people,
37:29 in thy nose, and my b' in thy lips,
Jas 3: 2 able also to b' the whole body.

bridles
Re 14:20 even unto the horse b', by the

bridleth
Jas 1:26 b' not his tongue, but deceiveth

briefly
Ro 13: 9 b' comprehended in this saying,
1Pe 5:12 I have written b', exhorting

brier See also BRIERS.
Isa 55:13 instead of the b' shall come up
Eze 28:24 shall be no more a pricking b'
Mic 7: 4 The best of them is as a b': the

briers
J'g 8: 7 of the wilderness and with b'.
16 thorns of the wilderness, and b',
Isa 5: 6 but there shall come up b' and
7:23 it shall even be for b' and thorns.
24 all the land shall become b' and
25 come thither the fear of b' and
9:18 it shall devour the b' and thorns,
10:17 and devour his thorns and his b'
27: 4 who would set the b' and thorns
32:13 shall come up thorns and b';
Eze 2: 6 b' and thorns be with thee, and
Heb 6: 8 which beareth thorns and b'

brigandine See also BRIGANDINES.
Jer 51: 3 that lifteth himself up in his b':

brigandines
Jer 46: 4 the spears, and put on the b'.

bright
Le 13: 2 a rising, a scab, or b' spot, and it
4 If the b' spot be white in the skin
19 or a b' spot, white, and somewhat
23 if the b' spot stay in his place, and
24 have a white b' spot, somewhat
25 the hair in the b' spot be turned
26 no white hair in the b' spot, and it
28 if the b' spot stay in his place, and
38 in the skin of their flesh b' spots,
38 even white b' spots;
39 the b' spots in the skin of their
14:56 and for a scab, and for a b' spot:
1Ki 7:45 of the Lord, were of b' brass.
2Ch 4:16 for the house of the Lord of b'
Job 37:11 he scattereth his b' cloud:
21 now men see not the b' light
Ca 5:14 his belly is as b' ivory overlaid
Jer 51:11 Make b' the arrows; gather the
Eze 1:13 and the fire was b', and out of
21:15 ah! it is made b', it is wrapped
21 he made his arrows b', he
27:19 b' iron, cassia, and calamus,
32: 8 All the b' lights of heaven will I
Na 3: 3 both the b' sword and the
Zec 10: 1 so the Lord shall make b' clouds,
M't 17: 5 behold, a b' cloud overshadowed
Lu 11:36 as when the b' shining of a candle
Ac 10:30 stood before me in b' clothing,
Re 22:16 and the b' and morning star.

brightness
2Sa 22:13 Through the b' before him were
Job 31:26 shined, or the moon walking in b';
Ps 18:12 At the b' that was before him his
Isa 59: 9 for b', but we walk in darkness.
60: 3 and kings to the b' of thy rising.
19 neither for b' shall the moon give
62: 1 righteousness thereof go forth as b'
Eze 1: 4 and a b' was about it, and out of
27 of fire, and it had b' round about.
28 the appearance of the b' round
8: 2 as the appearance of b', as the
10: 4 the court was full of the b' of the
28: 7 wisdom, they shall defile thy b'.
17 thy wisdom by reason of thy b':
Da 2:31 This great image, whose b' was
4:36 mine honour and b' returned
12: 3 shall shine as the b' of the
Am 5:20 even very dark, and no b' in it?
Hab 3: 4 And his b' was as the light;
Ac 26:13 light from heaven above, the b' of
2Th 2: 8 with the b' of his coming;
Heb 1: 3 Who being the b' of his glory

brim See also BRIMSTONE.
Jos 3:15 were dipped in the b' of the
1Ki 7:23 ten cubits from the one b' to the
24 under the b' of it round about
26 and the b' thereof was wrought
26 like the b' of a cup,
2Ch 4: 2 from b' to b', round in compass,
5 and the b' of it like the work
5 like the work of the b' of a cup,
Joh 2: 7 And they filled them up to the b'.

brimstone
Ge 19:24 Sodom and upon Gomorrah b'
De 29:23 the whole land thereof is b', and
Job 18:15 b' shall be scattered upon his
Ps 11: 6 he shall rain snares, fire and b',
Isa 30:33 like a stream of b', doth kindle it.
34: 9 the dust thereof into b', and the
Eze 38:22 and great hail stones, fire and b'.
Lu 17:29 fire and b' from heaven, and
Rev 9:17 of fire, and of jacinth, and b',
17 issued fire and smoke and b'.
18 the smoke, and by the b', which
14:10 with fire and b' in the presence of
19:20 a lake of fire burning with b'.
20:10 the lake of fire and b', where the
21: 8 lake which burneth with fire and b':

bring See also BRINGEST; BRINGETH; BRINGING; BROUGHT.
Ge 1:11 Let the earth b' forth grass, the
20 the waters b' forth abundantly
24 Let the earth b' forth the living
3:16 in sorrow thou shalt b' forth
18 also and thistles shall it b' forth
6:17 do b' a flood of waters upon the
19 two of every sort shalt thou b' into
8:17 B' forth with thee every living
9: 7 b' forth abundantly in the earth
14 when I b' a cloud over the earth,
18:16 went with them to b' them on the
19 the Lord may b' upon Abraham
19: 5 b' them out unto us, that we may
8 let me, I pray thee, b' them out
12 hast in the city, b' them out of
24: 5 must I needs b' thy son again
6 Beware thou that thou b' not my
8 my oath: only b' not my son
27: 4 and b' it to me, that I may eat;
5 to hunt for venison, and to b' it.
7 B' me venison, and make me
10 And thou shalt b' it to thy father,
12 and I shall b' a curse upon me, and
25 B' it near to me, and I will eat of
28:15 and will b' thee again into this
37:14 well with the flocks; and b' me
38:24 B' her forth, and let her be burnt.
40:14 and b' me out of this house:
41:32 and God will shortly b' it to pass.
42:20 b' your youngest brother unto
34 And b' your youngest brother
37 Slay my two sons, if I b' him not
37 and I will b' him to thee again.
38 then shall ye b' down my gray
43: 7 know that he would say, B' your
9 if I b' him not unto thee, and set
16 B' these men home, and slay, and

Ge 44:21 *B'* him down unto me, that I may
29 ye shall *b'* down my gray hairs
31 and thy servants shall *b'* down
32 If I *b'* him not unto thee, then I
45:13 ye shall haste and *b'* down my
19 and for your wives, and *b'* your
46: 4 and I will also surely *b'* thee up
48: 9 *B'* them, I pray thee, unto me,
21 and *b'* you again unto the land of
50:20 to *b'* to pass, as it is this day, to
24 and *b'* you out of this land into
Ex 3: 8 and to *b'* them up out of that
10 that thou mayest *b'* forth my
11 I should *b'* forth the children of
17 I will *b'* you up out of the
6: 6 and I will *b'* you out from under
8 And I will *b'* you in unto the land,
13 to *b'* the children of Israel out of
26 *B'* out the children of Israel from
27 to *b'* out the children of Israel
7: 4 and *b'* forth mine armies, and my
5 and *b'* out the children of Israel
8: 3 And the river shall *b'* forth
18 enchantments to *b'* forth lice,
10: 4 to morrow will I *b'* the locusts
11: 1 Yet will I *b'* one plague more upon
12:51 the Lord did *b'* the children of
13: 5 the Lord shall *b'* thee into the
11 shall be when the Lord shall *b'*
15:17 Thou shalt *b'* them in, and plant
16: 5 prepare that which they *b'* in;
18:19 that thou mayest *b'* the causes
22 they shall *b'* unto thee, but
21: 6 Then his master shall *b'* him
6 the judges; he shall also *b'* him
22:13 let him *b'* it for witness, and he
23: 4 thou shalt surely *b'* it back to
19 thou shalt *b'* into the house of the
20 and to *b'* thee into the place which
23 and *b'* thee in unto the Amorites,
25: 2 that they *b'* me an offering:
26:33 that thou mayest *b'* in thither
27:20 that they *b'* thee pure oil olive
29: 3 and *b'* them in the basket, with
4 Aaron and his sons thou shalt *b'*
8 thou shalt *b'* his sons, and put
32: 2 your daughters, and *b'* them unto
12 For mischief did he *b'* them out,
33:12 *B'* up this people: and thou hast
34:26 firstfruits of thy land thou shalt *b'*
35: 5 let him *b'* it, an offering
29 made them willing to *b'* for all
36: 5 The people *b'* much more than
40: 4 And thou shalt *b'* in the table,
4 thou shalt *b'* in the candlestick,
12 And thou shalt *b'* Aaron and his
14 thou shalt *b'* his sons, and
Le 1: 2 If any man of you *b'* an offering
2 unto the Lord, ye shall *b'* your
5 the priests, Aaron's sons, shall *b'*
10 he shall *b'* it a male without
13 and the priest shall *b'* it all, and
14 he shall *b'* his offering of turtle
15 And the priest shall *b'* it unto
2: 2 And he shall *b'* it to Aaron's sons
4 if thou *b'* an oblation of a meat
8 thou shalt *b'* the meat offering
8 priest, he shall *b'* it unto the
11 meat offering, which ye shall *b'*
4: 3 then let him *b'* for his sin,
4 And he shall *b'* the bullock unto
5 and *b'* it to the tabernacle of the
14 and *b'* him before the tabernacle
16 priest that is anointed shall *b'* of
23 he shall *b'* his offering, a kid of
28 then he shall *b'* his offering, a
32 if he *b'* a lamb for a sin offering,
32 shall *b'* it a female without blemish
5: 6 And he shall *b'* his trespass
7 And if he be not able to *b'* a lamb,
7 then he shall *b'* for his trespass,
5: 8 he shall *b'* them unto the priest,
11 not able to *b'* two turtledoves,
11 sinned shall *b'* for his offering
12 Then shall he *b'* it to the priest,
15 *b'* for his trespass unto the Lord
18 And he shall *b'* a ram without
6: 6 he shall *b'* his trespass offering
21 it is baken, thou shalt *b'* it in:
7:29 shall *b'* his oblation unto the
30 His own hands shall *b'* the
30 he *b'*, that the breast may be
10:15 the wave breast shall they *b'*
12: 6 she shall *b'* a lamb of the first
8 if she not be able to *b'* a lamb,
8 then she shall *b'* two turtles,
14:23 And he shall *b'* them on the
15:29 and *b'* them unto the priest,
16: 9 And Aaron shall *b'* the goat
11 And Aaron shall *b'* the bullock
12 small, and *b'* it within the vail:
15 and *b'* his blood within the vail,
20 altar, he shall *b'* the live goat:
17: 5 may *b'* their sacrifices, which
5 even that they may *b'* them unto
18: 3 whither I *b'* you, shall ye not do:
19:21 he shall *b'* his trespass offering
20:22 whither I *b'* you to dwell therein,
23:10 then ye shall *b'* a sheaf of the
17 Ye shall *b'* out of your habitations
24: 2 that they *b'* unto thee pure oil
14 *B'* forth him that hath cursed
23 they should *b'* forth him that
25:21 and it shall *b'* forth fruit for three
26:10 and *b'* forth the old because of
21 I will *b'* seven times more

Le 26:25 And I will *b'* a sword upon you,
31 and *b'* your sanctuaries unto
32 *b'* the land into desolation:
27: 9 *b'* an offering unto the Lord,
Nu 3: 6 *B'* the tribe of Levi near, and
5: 9 *b'* unto the priest, shall be his.
15 *b'* his wife unto the priest,
15 and he shall *b'* her offering
16 And the priest shall *b'* her near,
6:10 he shall *b'* two turtles, or two
12 and shall *b'* a lamb of the first
16 *b'* them before the Lord,
8: 9, 10 And thou shalt *b'* the Levites
11:16 and *b'* them unto the tabernacle
13:20 and *b'* of the fruit of the land.
14: 8 then he will *b'* us into the land,
16 was not able to *b'* this people
24 him will I *b'* into the land
31 them will I *b'* in, and they shall
37 that did *b'* up the evil report
15: 4 his offering unto the Lord *b'*
9 shall he *b'* with a bullock
10 thou shalt *b'* for a drink offering
18 into the land whither I *b'* you,
25 they shall *b'* their offering, a
27 then he shall *b'* a she goat of
16: 9 to *b'* you near to himself to do
17 and *b'* ye before the Lord every
17:10 *B'* Aaron's rod again before the
18: 2 *b'* thou with thee, that they may
13 they shall *b'* unto the Lord,
15 which they *b'* unto the Lord,
19: 2 that they *b'* thee a red heifer
3 *b'* her forth without the camp,
20: 5 to *b'* us in unto this evil place?
8 and thou shalt *b'* forth to them
12 therefore ye shall not *b'* this
25 and *b'* them up unto mount Hor:
22: 8 I will *b'* you word again, as the
23:27 I will *b'* thee unto another place;
27:17 which may *b'* them in; that the
28:26 when ye *b'* a new meat offering
32: 5 and *b'* us not over Jordan.
De 1:17 *b'* it unto me, and I will hear it.
22 and *b'* us word again by what
4:38 to *b'* thee in, to give thee their
6:23 that he might *b'* us in, to give us
7: 1 shall *b'* thee into the land
26 Neither shalt thou *b'* an
9: 3 *b'* them down before thy face:
28 to *b'* them into the land which
12: 6 And thither ye shall *b'* your
11 thither ye shall *b'* all that I
14:28 thou shalt *b'* forth all the tithe
17: 5 Then shalt thou *b'* forth that man
21: 4 elders of that city shall *b'* down
12 Then thou shalt *b'* her home
19 and *b'* him out unto the elders
22: 1 any case *b'* them again unto
2 shalt *b'* it unto thine own house,
8 that thou *b'* not blood upon
14 and *b'* up an evil name upon her,
15 and *b'* forth the tokens of the
21 Then they shall *b'* out the damsel
24 Then ye shall *b'* them both out
23:18 Thou shalt not *b'* the hire of a
24:11 shall *b'* out the pledge abroad
26: 2 which thou shalt *b'* of thy land
28:36 The Lord shall *b'* thee, and thy
49 shall *b'* a nation against thee
60 *b'* upon thee all the diseases
61 them will the Lord *b'* upon thee,
63 and to *b'* you to nought; and ye
68 shall *b'* thee into Egypt again
29:27 to *b'* upon it all the curses that
30: 5 And the Lord thy God will *b'* thee
12 us to heaven, and *b'* it unto us,
13 the sea for us, and *b'* it unto us,
31:23 for thou shalt *b'* the children
33: 7 and *b'* him unto his people:
Jos 2: 3 *B'* forth the men that are come
18 *b'* thy father, and thy mother,
6:22 and *b'* out thence the woman,
10:22 and *b'* out those five kings
18: 6 and *b'* the description hither
23:15 so shall the Lord *b'* upon you
J'g 6:13 Did not the Lord *b'* us up
18 and *b'* forth my present, and
30 *B'* out thy son, that he may die:
7: 4 *b'* them down unto the water,
11: 9 If ye *b'* me home again to fight
19: 3 unto her, and to *b'* her again,
22 *B'* forth the man that came into
24 I will *b'* out now, and humble ye
Ru 3:15 *B'* the vail that thou hast upon
1Sa 1:22 and then I will *b'* him, that he
4: 4 might *b'* from thence the ark
6: 7 *b'* their calves home from them:
9: 7 what shall we *b'* the man?
7 not a present to *b'* to the man
23 *B'* the portion which I gave thee,
11:12 *b'* the men, that we may put them
13: 9 *B'* hither a burnt offering to me,
14:18 *B'* hither the ark of God. For the
34 *B'* me hither every man his ox,
15:32 *B'* ye hither to me Agag the king
16:17 well, and *b'* him to me.
19:15 *B'* him up to me in the bed,
20: 8 why shouldest thou *b'* me to thy
23: 9 priest, *B'* hither the ephod.
27:11 to *b'* tidings to Gath, saying,
28: 8 and *b'* me him up, whom I shall
11 Whom shall I *b'* up unto thee?
11 And he said, *B'* me up Samuel.
15 disquieted me, to *b'* me up?
30: 7 *b'* me hither the ephod,

1Sa 30:15 Canst thou *b'* me down to this
15 and I will *b'* thee down to this
2Sa 2: 3 were with him did David *b'* up,
3:12 to *b'* about all Israel unto thee.
13 except thou first *b'* Michal
6: 2 to *b'* up from thence the ark
9:10 and thou shalt *b'* in the fruits,
12:23 can I *b'* him back again? I shall
13:10 *B'* the meat into the chamber,
14:10 *b'* him to me, and he shall not
21 *b'* the young man Absalom
15: 8 shall *b'* me again indeed to
14 and *b'* evil upon us, and smite
25 he will *b'* me again, and shew
17: 3 I will *b'* back all the people unto
13 then shall all Israel *b'* ropes
14 that the Lord might *b'* evil
19:11 the last to *b'* the king back
12 the last to *b'* back the king?
22:28 that thou mayest *b'* them down.
1Ki 1:33 and *b'* him down to Gihon:
2: 9 head *b'* thou down to the grave
3:24 king said, *B'* me a sword.
5: 9 My servants shall *b'* them down
8: 1 that they might *b'* up the ark
4 priests and the Levites *b'* up.
32 to *b'* his way upon his head;
34 and *b'* them again unto the land
10:29 did they *b'* them out by their
12:21 to *b'* the kingdom again to
13:18 *B'* him back with thee unto thine
14:10 I will *b'* evil upon the house of
17:11 *B'* me, I pray thee, a morsel of
13 and *b'* it unto me, and after
20:33 Go ye, *b'* him. Then Ben-hadad
21:21 I will *b'* evil upon thee, and will
29 I will not *b'* evil in his days:
29 son's days will I *b'* evil upon his
2Ki 2:20 *B'* me a new cruse, and put salt
3:15 *b'* me a minstrel. And it came to
4: 6 unto her son, *B'* me yet a vessel.
41 Then *b'* meal. And he cast it
6:19 and I will *b'* you to the man
10:22 *B'* forth vestments for all the
12: 4 *b'* into the house of the Lord,
19: 3 there is not strength to *b'* forth.
22:16 I will *b'* evil upon this place,
20 which I will *b'* upon this place.
23: 4 to *b'* forth out of the temple
1Ch 9:28 that they should *b'* them in
13: 3 And let us *b'* again the ark of our
5 to *b'* the ark of God from
6 to *b'* up thence the ark of God
12 How shall I *b'* the ark of God
15: 3 to *b'* up the ark of the Lord unto
12 that ye may *b'* up the ark of the
14 sanctified themselves to *b'* up the
25 to *b'* up the ark of the covenant of
16:29 *b'* an offering, and come before
21: 2 and *b'* the number of them to me,
12 what word I shall *b'* again
22:19 to *b'* the ark of the covenant of the
2Ch 2:16 and we will *b'* it to thee in floats
5: 2 to *b'* up the ark of the covenant
5 did the priests and the Levites *b'*
6:25 and *b'* them again unto the land
11: 1 that he might *b'* the kingdom
24: 6 required of the Levites to *b'* in
9 to *b'* in to the Lord the collection
19 to *b'* them again unto the Lord;
28:13 Ye shall not *b'* in the captives
29:31 *b'* sacrifices and thank offerings
31:10 Since the people began to *b'* the
34:24 I will *b'* evil upon this place, and
28 all the evil that I will *b'* upon this
Ezr 1: 8 did Cyrus king of Persia *b'* forth
11 All these did Sheshbazzar *b'* up
3: 7 to *b'* cedar trees from Lebanon to
8:17 they should *b'* unto us ministers
30 to *b'* them to Jerusalem unto the
Ne 1: 9 and will *b'* them unto the place
5: 5 we *b'* into bondage our sons and
8: 1 to *b'* the book of the law of Moses,
9:29 that thou mightest *b'* them again
10:31 the people of the land *b'* ware
34 to *b'* it into the house of our God,
35 And to *b'* the firstfruits of our
36 to *b'* to the house of our God,
37 we should *b'* the firstfruits of our
38 the Levites shall *b'* up the tithe
39 *b'* the offering of the corn, of the
11: 1 *b'* one of ten to dwell in Jerusalem
12:27 to *b'* them to Jerusalem, to keep
13:18 and did not our God *b'* all this
18 *b'* more wrath upon Israel by
Es 1:11 To *b'* Vashti the queen before the
3: 9 business to *b'* it into the king's
6: 1 to *b'* the book of records of the
9 *b'* him on horseback through
14 hasted to *b'* Haman unto the
Job 6:22 Did I say, *B'* unto me? or, Give
10: 9 and wilt thou *b'* me into dust
14: 4 Who can *b'* a clean thing out of
9 will bud, and *b'* forth boughs
15:35 They conceive mischief, and *b'*
18:14 and it shall *b'* him to the king of
30:23 thou wilt *b'* me to death, and the
33:30 To *b'* back his soul from the pit,
38:32 Canst thou *b'* forth Mazzaroth
39: 1 when the wild goats of the rock *b'*
2 thou the time when they *b'*
3 They bow themselves, they *b'*
12 he will *b'* home thy seed, and
40:12 and *b'* him low; and tread down
20 the mountains *b'* him forth food,
Ps 18:27 afflicted; but wilt *b'* down high

Ps 25:17 O *b'* thou me out of my distresses.
37: 5 him; and he shall *b'* it to pass.
6 shall *b'* forth thy righteousness
38:*title* A Psalm of David, to *b'* to
43: 3 let them *b'* me unto thy holy hill,
55:23 thou, O God, shalt *b'* them down
59:11 and *b'* them down, O Lord our
60: 9 Who will *b'* me into the strong
68:22 I will *b'* again from Bashan,
22 I will *b'* my people again
29 Jerusalem shall kings *b'* presents
70:*title* A Psalm of David, to *b'* to
71:20 *b'* me up again from the depths
72: 3 The mountains shall *b'* peace to
10 Tarshish and of the isles shall *b'*
76:11 all that be round about him *b'*
81: 2 and *b'* hither the timbrel, the
92:14 They shall still *b'* forth fruit in
94:23 And he shall *b'* upon them their
96: 8 *b'* an offering, and come into his
104:14 that he may *b'* forth food out of
108:10 Who will *b'* me into the strong
142: 7 *B'* my soul out of prison, that I
143:11 sake *b'* my soul out of trouble.
144:13 our sheep may *b'* forth thousands
Pr 4: 8 she shall *b'* thee to honour, when
19:24 will not so much as *b'* it to his
26:15 him to *b'* it again to his mouth.
27: 1 knowest not what a day may *b'*
29: 8 Scornful men *b'* a city into a
23 A man's pride shall *b'* him low:
Ec 3:22 for who shall *b'* him to see what
11: 9 God will *b'* thee into judgment.
12:14 God shall *b'* every work into
Ca 8: 2 I would lead thee, and *b'* thee
11 was to *b'* a thousand pieces of
Isa 1:13 *B'* no more vain oblations; incense
5: 2 he looked that it should *b'* forth
4 when I looked that it should *b'*
7:17 The Lord shall *b'* upon thee, and
14: 2 and *b'* them to their place: and
15: 9 I will *b'* more upon Dimon, lions
23: 4 I travail not, nor *b'* forth
4 up young men, nor *b'* up virgins.
9 to *b'* into contempt all the
25: 5 Thou shalt *b'* down the noise
11 and he shall *b'* down their pride
12 of thy walls shall he *b'* down,
12 lay low, and *b'* to the ground,
28:21 and *b'* to pass his act, his strange
31: 2 and will *b'* evil, and will not call
33:11 ye shall *b'* forth stubble: your
37: 3 and there is not strength to *b'*
38: 8 I will *b'* again the shadow of the
41:21 *b'* forth your strong reasons,
22 Let them *b'* them forth, and shew
42: 1 he shall *b'* forth judgment to the
3 he shall *b'* forth judgment unto
7 to *b'* out the prisoners from the
16 And I will *b'* the blind by a way
43: 5 I will *b'* thy seed from the east,
6 *b'* my sons from far, and my
8 *B'* forth the blind people that
9 let them *b'* forth their witnesses,
45: 8 and let them *b'* forth salvation,
21 Tell ye, and *b'* them near; yea,
46: 8 *b'* it again to mind, O ye
11 I will also *b'* it to pass; I have
13 I *b'* near my righteousness; it
49: 5 to *b'* Jacob again to him, Though
22 and they shall *b'* thy sons in their
52: 8 the Lord shall *b'* again Zion.
55:10 and maketh it *b'* forth and bud
56: 7 Even them will I *b'* to my holy
58: 7 that thou *b'* the poor that are cast
59: 4 they conceive mischief, and *b'*
60: 6 they shall *b'* gold and incense;
9 to *b'* thy sons from far, their
11 that men may *b'* unto thee the
17 For brass I will *b'* gold,
17 and for iron I will *b'* silver,
63: 6 and I will *b'* down their strength
65: 9 And I will *b'* forth a seed out of
23 in vain, nor *b'* forth for trouble;
66: 4 will *b'* their fears upon them;
8 Shall the earth be made to *b'*
9 Shall I *b'* to the birth,
9 and not cause to *b'* forth?
9 shall I cause to *b'* forth, and
20 And they shall *b'* all your brethren
20 as the children of Israel *b'* an
Jer 3:14 family, and I will *b'* you to Zion:
4: 6 for I will *b'* evil from the north,
5:15 I will *b'* a nation upon you from
6:19 I will *b'* evil upon this people,
8: 1 they shall *b'* out the bones of the
10:24 anger, lest thou *b'* me to nothing.
11: 8 therefore I will *b'* upon them all
11 I will *b'* evil upon them, which
23 for I will *b'* evil upon the men of
12: 2 they grow, yea, they *b'* forth
15 and will *b'* them again, every
15:19 then will I *b'* thee again, and thou
16:15 and I will *b'* them again into their
17:18 *b'* upon them the day of evil, and
21 sabbath day, nor *b'* it in by the
24 to *b'* in no burden through the
18:22 when thou shalt *b'* a troop suddenly
19: 3 I will *b'* evil upon this place, the
15 I will *b'* upon this city and upon all
23: 3 and will *b'* them again to their
12 for I will *b'* evil upon them, even
40 I will *b'* an everlasting reproach
24: 6 And I will *b'* them again to this
25: 9 and will *b'* them against this
13 And I will *b'* upon that land all

Jer 25:29 I begin to *b'* evil on the city
26:15 ye shall surely *b'* innocent blood
27:11 But the nations that *b'* their neck
12 *B'* your necks under the yoke of
22 will I *b'* them up, and restore
28: 3 will I *b'* again into this place all
4 will *b'* again to this place Jeconiah
6 to *b'* again the vessels of the
29:14 and I will *b'* you again into the
30: 3 that I will *b'* again the captivity
18 I will *b'* again the captivity of
31: 8 I will *b'* them from the north
23 I shall *b'* again their captivity
32 *b'* them out of the land of Egypt;
32:37 and I will *b'* them again unto
42 so will I *b'* upon them all the
33: 6 I will *b'* it health and cure, and
11 of them that shall *b'* the sacrifice
35: 2 and *b'* them into the house of the
17 I will *b'* upon Judah and upon all
36:31 and I will *b'* upon them, and upon
38:23 they shall *b'* out all thy wives
39:16 I will *b'* my words upon this city
41: 5 *b'* them to the house of the Lord.
42:17 the evil that I will *b'* upon them.
45: 5 I will *b'* evil upon all flesh, saith
48:44 for I will *b'* upon it, even upon
47 Yet will I *b'* again the captivity
49: 5 I will *b'* a fear upon thee, saith
6 I will *b'* again the captivity of
8 I will *b'* the calamity of Esau
16 I will *b'* thee down from thence,
32 I will *b'* their calamity from all
36 And upon Elam will I *b'* the four
37 and I will *b'* evil upon them, even
39 I will *b'* again the captivity of
50:19 And I will *b'* Israel again to his
51:40 I will *b'* them down like lambs to
44 I will *b'* forth out of his mouth
64 the evil that I will *b'* upon her:
La 1:21 thou wilt *b'* the day that thou hast
Eze 5:17 I will *b'* the sword upon thee.
6: 3 will *b'* a sword upon you, and I
7:24 Wherefore I will *b'* the worst of
11: 7 I will *b'* you forth out of the
8 I will *b'* a sword upon you, saith
9 And I will *b'* you out of the midst
12: 4 Then shalt thou *b'* forth thy stuff
13 and I will *b'* him to Babylon to the
13:14 and *b'* it down to the ground, so
14:17 Or if I *b'* a sword upon that land,
16:40 They shall also *b'* up a company
53 When I shall *b'* again their
53 then will I *b'* again the captivity
17: 8 that it might *b'* forth branches,
20 and I will *b'* him to Babylon, and
23 and it shall *b'* forth boughs, and
20: 6 to *b'* them forth of the land of
15 I would not *b'* them into the land
34 I will *b'* you out from the people,
35 I will *b'* you into the wilderness
37 and I will *b'* you into the bond of
38 I will *b'* them forth out of the
41 when I *b'* you out from the people,
42 when I shall *b'* you into the land
21:29 to *b'* thee upon the necks of them
23:22 and I will *b'* them against thee on
46 I will *b'* up a company upon
24: 6 *b'* it out piece by piece; let no lot
26: 7 *b'* upon Tyrus Nebuchadrezzar
19 when I shall *b'* up the deep upon
20 When I shall *b'* thee down with
28: 7 I will *b'* strangers upon thee, the
8 They shall *b'* thee down to the
18 therefore will I *b'* forth a fire
18 and I will *b'* thee to ashes upon
29: 4 I will *b'* thee up out of the midst
8 I will *b'* a sword upon thee, and
14 And I will *b'* again the captivity
31: 6 did all the beasts of the field *b'*
32: 3 and they shall *b'* thee up in my
9 when I shall *b'* thy destruction
33: 2 When I *b'* the sword upon a land,
34:13 will *b'* them out from the people,
13 and will *b'* them to their own land,
16 and *b'* again that which was
36:11 they shall increase and *b'* fruit:
24 and will *b'* you into your own land.
37: 6 and will *b'* up flesh upon you,
12 your graves, and *b'* you into the
21 every side, and *b'* them into their
38: 4 and I will *b'* thee forth, and all
16 and I will *b'* thee against my land,
17 I would *b'* thee against them?
39: 2 *b'* thee upon the mountains of
25 Now will I *b'* again the captivity
47:12 it shall *b'* forth...fruit according
Da 1: 3 that he should *b'* certain of the
18 he should *b'* them in, then the
2:24 *b'* me in before the king, and I
3:13 his rage and fury commanded to *b'*
4: 6 made I a decree to *b'* in all the
5: 2 commanded to *b'* the golden and
7 The king cried aloud to *b'* in the
9:24 *b'* in everlasting righteousness,
Ho 2:14 and *b'* her into the wilderness,
7:12 I will *b'* them down as the fowls
9:12 Though they *b'* up their children,
13 Ephraim shall *b'* forth his
16 though they *b'* forth, yet will I
Joe 3: 1 I shall *b'* again the captivity of
2 and will *b'* them down into the
Am 3:11 and he shall *b'* down thy strength
4: 1 masters, *B'*, and let us drink.
4 and *b'* your sacrifices every
6:10 to *b'* out the bones out of the

Am 8:10 and I will *b'* up sackcloth upon
9: 2 heaven, thence will I *b'* them
14 And I will *b'* again the captivity
Ob 3 Who shall *b'* me down to the
4 thence will I *b'* thee down, saith
Jon 1:13 the men rowed hard to *b'* it to
Mic 1:15 Yet will I *b'* an heir unto thee,
4:10 and labour to *b'* forth, O daughter
7: 9 he will *b'* me forth to the light,
Zep 1:17 And I will *b'* distress upon men,
2: 2 Before the decree *b'* forth,
3: 5 doth he *b'* his judgment to
10 dispersed, shall *b'* mine offering.
20 At that time will I *b'* you again,
Hag 1: 6 and *b'* in little; yet eat, but ye
8 Go up to the mountain, and *b'* wood,
Zec 3: 8 I will *b'* forth my servant the
4: 7 he shall *b'* forth the headstone
5: 4 I will *b'* it forth, saith the Lord of
8: 8 And I will *b'* them, and they shall
10: 6 and I will *b'* them again to place
10 I will *b'* them again also out of
10 I will *b'* them into the land of
13: 9 And I will *b'* the third part
Mal 3:10 *B'* ye all the tithes into the
M't 1:21 And she shall *b'* forth a son, and
23 and shall *b'* forth a son, and they
2: 8 *b'* me word again, that I may
13 until I *b'* thee word: for Herod
3: 8 *B'* forth therefore fruits meet for
5:23 if thou *b'* thy gift to the altar,
7:18 A good tree cannot *b'* forth evil
18 a corrupt tree *b'* forth good fruit.
14:18 He said, *B'* them hither to me,
17:17 suffer you? *b'* him hither to me.
21: 2 loose them, and *b'* them unto me.
28: 8 did run to *b'* his disciples word.
M'r 4:20 *b'* forth fruit, some thirtyfold,
7:32 And they *b'* unto him one that
8:22 and they *b'* a blind man unto him,
9:19 shall I suffer you? *b'* him unto me.
11: 2 never man sat; loose him, and *b'*
12:15 tempt ye me? *b'* me a penny,
15:22 And they *b'* him unto the place
Lu 1:31 and *b'* forth a son, and shall call
2:10 I *b'* you good tidings of great joy,
3: 8 *B'* forth therefore fruits worthy
5:18 sought means to *b'* him in, and to
19 they might *b'* him in because of
6:43 neither doth a corrupt tree *b'*
8:14 pleasures of this life, and *b'* no
15 keep it, and *b'* forth fruit with
9:41 suffer you? *B'* thy son hither.
12:11 when they *b'* you unto the
14:21 *b'* in hither the poor, and the
15:22 *B'* forth the best robe, and put it
23 *b'* hither the fatted calf, and kill
19:27 reign over them, *b'* hither, and
30 sat: loose him, and *b'* him hither.
Joh 10:16 this fold: them also I must *b'*,
14:26 shall teach you all things, and *b'*
15: 2 that it may *b'* forth more fruit.
16 that ye should go and *b'* forth
18:29 What accusation *b'* ye against
19: 4 Behold, I *b'* him forth to you,
21:10 *B'* of the fish which ye have now
Ac 5:28 and intend to *b'* this man's blood
7: 6 they should *b'* them into bondage,
9: 2 he might *b'* them bound unto
21 he might *b'* them bound unto the
12: 4 after Easter to *b'* him forth to the
17: 5 and sought to *b'* them out to the
22: 5 to *b'* them which were there bound
23:10 them, and to *b'* him into the castle.
15 *b'* him down unto you to morrow
17 *B'* this young man unto the chief
18 to *b'* this young man unto thee,
20 that thou wouldest *b'* down Paul
24 and *b'* him safe unto Felix the
24:17 I came to *b'* alms to my nation,
Ro 7: 4 we should *b'* forth fruit unto God.
5 to *b'* forth fruit unto death.
10: 6 (that is, to *b'* Christ down from
7 to *b'* up Christ again from the
15 and *b'* glad tidings of good things!
1Co 1:19 *b'* to nothing the understanding
28 to *b'* to nought things that are:
4: 5 who both will *b'* to light the
17 *b'* you into remembrance of my
9:27 under my body, and *b'* it into
16: 3 them will I send to *b'* your
6 ye may *b'* me on my journey
2Co 11:20 if any man *b'* you into bondage,
Ga 2: 4 they might *b'* us into bondage:
3:24 schoolmaster to *b'* us unto Christ,
Eph 6: 4 *b'* them up in the nurture and
1Th 4:14 in Jesus will God *b'* with him.
2Ti 4:11 Take Mark, and *b'* him with thee:
13 *b'* with thee, and the books, but
Tit 3:13 *B'* Zenas the lawyer and Apollos
1Pe 3:18 that he might *b'* us to God, being
2Pe 2: 1 who privily shall *b'* in damnable
1 and *b'* upon themselves swift
11 *b'* not railing accusation against
2Jo 10 and *b'* not this doctrine, receive
3Jo 6 thou *b'* forward on their journey
Jude 9 durst not *b'* against him a railing
Re 21:24 do *b'* their glory and honour into
26 shall *b'* the glory and honour of

bringers
2Ki 10: 5 and the *b'* up of the children,

bringest
1Ki 1:42 art a valiant man, and *b'* good
Job 14: 3 *b'* me into judgment with thee?
Isa 40: 9 O Zion, that *b'* good tidings, get

Isa 40: 9 O Jerusalem, that b' good
Ac 17:20 thou b' certain strange things to

bringeth
Ex 6: 7 b' you out from under the
Le 11:45 I am the Lord that b' you up
17: 4 b' it not unto the door of the
9 b' it not unto the door of the
De 8: 7 the Lord thy God b' thee into a
14:22 the field b' forth year by year.
1Sa 2: 6 he b' down to the grave,
6 to the grave, and b' up.
7 rich: he b' low, and lifteth up.
2Sa 18:26 He also b' tidings.
22:48 and that b' down the people
49 And that b' me forth from mine
Job 12: 6 into whose hand God b'
22 and b' out to light the shadow of
19:29 for wrath b' the punishments
28:11 that is hid b' he forth to light.
Ps 1: 3 b' forth his fruit in his season;
14: 7 when the Lord b' back the
33:10 The Lord b' the counsel of the
37: 7 of the man who b' wicked
53: 6 When God b' back the captivity
68: 6 he b' out those which are bound
107:28 he b' them out of their distresses.
30 b' them unto their desired haven.
135: 7 b' the wind out of his treasuries.
Pr 10:31 The mouth of the just b' forth
16:30 moving his lips he b' evil to pass.
18:16 and b' him before great men.
19:26 causeth shame, and b' reproach.
20:26 and b' the wheel over them.
21:27 he b' it with a wicked mind?
29:15 himself b' his mother to shame.
21 He that delicately b' up his
25 The fear of man b' a snare: but
30:33 churning of milk b' forth butter,
33 wringing of the nose b' forth
33 forcing of wrath b' forth strife.
31:14 ships; she b' her food from afar.
Ec 2: 6 the wood that b' forth trees:
Isa 8: 7 the Lord b' up upon them the
26: 5 he b' down them that dwell on
5 ground; he b' it even to the dust.
40:23 That b' the princes to nothing;
26 that b' out their host by number:
41:27 to Jerusalem one that b' good
43:17 Which b' forth the chariot and
52: 7 the feet of him that b' good
7 peace; that b' good tidings
54:16 b' forth an instrument for his
61:11 as the earth b' forth her bud,
Jer 4:31 her that b' forth her first child,
10:13 and b' forth the wind out of his
51:16 and b' forth the wind out of his
Eze 29:16 which b' their iniquity to
Ho 10: 1 he b' forth fruit unto himself:
Na 1:15 feet of him that b' good tidings,
Hag 1:11 that which the ground b' forth,
M't 3:10 tree which b' not forth good fruit
7:17 good tree b' forth good fruit;
17 but a corrupt tree b' forth evil
19 tree that b' not forth good fruit is
12:35 of the heart b' forth good things:
35 evil treasure b' forth evil things.
13:23 and b' forth some an hundredfold,
52 b' forth out of his treasure things
17: 1 b' them up into an high mountain
M'r 4:28 earth b' forth fruit of herself;
Lu 3: 9 which b' not forth good fruit is
6:43 b' not forth corrupt fruit; neither
45 b' forth that which is good;
45 an evil b' forth that which is evil:
Joh 12:24 if it die, it b' forth much fruit.
15: 5 the same b' forth much fruit:
Col 1: 6 and b' forth fruit, as it doth also
Tit 2:11 grace of God that b' salvation
Heb 1: 6 when he b' in the firstbegotten
6: 7 b' forth herbs meet for them by
Jas 1:15 when lust hath conceived, it b'
15 when it is finished, b' forth death.

bringing
Ex 12:42 for b' them out from the land of
36: 6 people were restrained from b'.
Nu 5:15 b' iniquity to remembrance.
14:36 by b' up a slander upon the land,
2Sa 19:10 speak ye not a word of b' the king
43 be first had in b' back our king?
1Ki 10:22 b' gold, and silver, ivory, and
2Ki 21:12 am b' such evil upon Jerusalem
2Ch 9:21 the ships of Tarshish b' gold, and
Ne 13:15 b' in sheaves, and lading asses;
Ps 126: 6 rejoicing, b' his sheaves with him.
Jer 17:26 b' burnt offerings, and sacrifices,
26 and b' sacrifices of praise unto the
Eze 20: 9 b' them forth out of the land of
Da 9:12 by b' upon us a great evil:
M't 21:43 a nation b' forth the fruits thereof.
M'r 2: 3 b' one sick of the palsy, which was
Lu 24: 1 b' the spices which they had
Ac 5:16 unto Jerusalem, b' sick folks, and
Ro 7:23 b' me into captivity to the law of
2Co 10: 5 b' into captivity every thought to
Heb 2:10 b' many sons unto glory, to make
7:19 the b' in of a better hope did;
2Pe 2: 5 b' in the flood upon the world

brink
Ge 41: 3 kine upon the b' of the river.
Ex 2: 3 in the flags by the river's b'.
7:15 stand by the river's b' against he
De 2:36 is by the b' of the river Arnon,
Jos 3: 8 When ye are come to the b' of
Eze 47: 6 to return to the b' of the river.

broad See also ABROAD; BROADER.
Ex 27: 1 five cubits long, and five cubits b';
Nu 16:38 let them make them b' plates for
39 and they were made b' plates for
1Ki 6: 6 chamber was five cubits b',
6 and the middle was six cubits b',
6 and the third was seven cubits b':
2Ch 6:13 five cubits long, and five cubits b',
Ne 3: 8 Jerusalem unto the b' wall.
12:38 furnaces even unto the b' wall;
Job 36:16 out of the strait into a b' place,
Ps 119:96 commandment is exceeding b'.
Ca 3: 2 in the streets, and in the b' ways
Isa 33:21 of b' rivers and streams; 7338,
Jer 5: 1 seek in the b' places thereof, if ye
51:58 The b' walls of Babylon shall be
Eze 40: 6 the gate, which was one reed b';
6 the other threshold...one reed b'.
7 one reed long, and one reed b';
29 and five and twenty cubits b'.
30 cubits long, and five cubits b'.
33 and five and twenty cubits b'.
42 and a cubit and a half b'. and one
43 hooks, an hand b', fastened
47 and an hundred cubits b', four
41: 1 six cubits b' on the one side,
1 six cubits b' on the other side,
12 the west was seventy cubits b';
42:11 long as they, and as b' as they:
20 and five hundred b', to make a
43:16 twelve cubits long, twelve b',
17 cubits long and fourteen b' in the
45: 6 of the city five thousand b',
46:22 forty cubits long and thirty b':
Na 2: 4 against another in the b' ways:
M't 7:13 b' is the way, that leadeth to
23: 5 they make b' their phylacteries,

broader
Job 11: 9 the earth, and b' than the sea.

broided See also BROIDERED.
1Ti 2: 9 not with b' hair, or gold, or

broidered
Ex 28: 4 a b' coat, a mitre, and a girdle:
Eze 16:10 I clothed thee also with b' work,
13 fine linen, and silk, and b' work;
18 tookest thy b' garments, and
26:16 and put off their b' garments:
27: 7 linen with b' work from Egypt
16 b' work, and fine linen, and coral,
24 blue clothes, and b' work, and in

broiled
Lu 24:42 they gave him a piece of a b' fish,

broke See BRAKE.

broken See also BROKENFOOTED; BROKENHANDED; BROKENHEARTED.
Ge 7:11 fountains of the great deep b' up,
17:14 he hath b' my covenant.
38:29 How hast thou b' forth? this
Le 6:28 wherein it is sodden shall be b':
11:35 they shall be b' down: for they
13:20 a plague of leprosy b' out of the
25 a leprosy b' out of the burning:
15:12 which hath the issue, shall be b':
21:20 scabbed, or hath his stones b';
22:22 Blind, or b', or maimed, or having
24 bruised, or crushed, or b', or cut;
26:13 I have b' the bands of your yoke,
26 I have b' the staff of your bread,
Nu 15:31 and hath b' his commandment,
J'g 5:22 Then were the horsehoofs b' by
16: 9 as a thread of tow is b' when it
1Sa 2: 4 bows of the mighty men are b',
10 shall be b' to pieces; out of
2Sa 5:20 hath b' forth upon mine enemies
22:35 a bow of steel is b' by mine arms.
1Ki 18:30 altar of the Lord that was b'
22:48 the ships were b' at Ezion-geber.
2Ki 11: 6 the house, that it be not b' down.
25: 4 And the city was b' up, and all
1Ch 14:11 God hath b' in upon mine enemies
2Ch 20:37 the Lord hath b' thy works.
37 And the ships were b', that they
24: 7 that wicked woman, had b' up
25:12 that they all were b' in pieces.
32: 5 the wall that was b', and raised
33: 3 his father had b' down, and he
34: 7 when he had b' down the altars
Ne 1: 3 wall of Jerusalem also is b' down,
2:13 of Jerusalem, which were b' down,
Job 4:10 teeth of the young lions, are b'.
7: 5 my skin is b', and become
16:12 but he hath b' me asunder:
17:11 my purposes are b' off, even the
22: 9 of the fatherless have been b'.
24:20 wickedness shall be b' as a tree.
31:22 mine arm be b' from the bone.
38:15 and the high arm shall be b'.
Ps 3: 7 hast b' the teeth of the ungodly.
18:34 a bow of steel is b' by mine arms.
31:12 of mind: I am like a b' vessel.
34:18 unto them that are of a b' heart:
20 his bones: not one of them is b'.
37:15 and their bows shall be b'.
17 the arms of the wicked shall be b':
38: 8 I am feeble and sore b': I have
44:19 Though thou hast sore b' us in
51: 8 the bones which thou hast b' may
17 sacrifices of God are a b' spirit:
17 a b' and a contrite heart,
55:20 him: he hath b' his covenant.
60: 2 earth to tremble; thou hast b' it:
69:20 Reproach hath b' my heart;
80:12 thou then b' down her hedges,
89:10 Thou hast b' Rahab in pieces,
Ps 89:40 thou hast b' down all his hedges;
107:16 he hath b' the gates of brass,
109:16 might even slay the b' in heart.
124: 7 snare is b', and we are escaped.
147: 3 He healeth the b' in heart,
Pr 3:20 knowledge the depths are b' up,
6:15 suddenly shall he be b' without
15:13 sorrow of the heart the spirit is b'.
17:22 but a b' spirit drieth the bones.
24:31 stone wall thereof was b' down.
25:19 is like a b' tooth, and a foot out
28 is like a city that is b' down,
Ec 4:12 a threefold cord is not quickly b'.
12: 6 or the golden bowl be b',
6 the pitcher be b' at the fountain,
6 or the wheel b' at the cistern.
Isa 5:27 the latchet of their shoes be b':
7: 8 five years shall Ephraim be b',
8: 9 people, and ye shall be b' in pieces;
9 be b' in pieces; gird yourselves,
9 and ye shall be b' in pieces.
15 shall stumble, and fall, and be b',
9: 4 hast b' the yoke of his burden,
14: 5 hath b' the staff of the wicked,
29 rod of him that smote thee is b':
16: 8 the heathen have b' down the
19:10 they shall be b' in the purposes
21: 9 images of her gods he hath b'
22:10 and the houses have ye b' down
24: 5 b' the everlasting covenant.
10 The city of confusion is b' down:
19 The earth is utterly b' down,
27:11 withered, they shall be b' off:
28:13 and fall backward, and be b',
30:14 potter's vessel that is b' in pieces
33: 8 he hath b' the covenant, he hath
20 any of the cords thereof be b'.
36: 6 staff of this b' reed, on Egypt;
Jer 2:13 b' cisterns, that can hold no
16 have b' the crown of thy head.
20 I have b' thy yoke, and burst thy
4:26 all the cities thereof were b' down
5: 5 have altogether b' the yoke,
10:20 all my cords are b': my children
11:10 of Judah have b' my covenant
16 it, and the branches of it are b'.
14:17 virgin daughter of my people is b'
22:28 man Coniah a despised b' idol?
23: 9 Mine heart within me is b'
28: 2 b' the yoke of the king of Babylon.
12 had b' the yoke from off the neck
13 Thou hast b' the yokes of wood;
33:21 Then may also my covenant be b'
37:11 the army of the Chaldeans was b'
39: 2 the month, the city was b' up.
48:17 How is the strong staff b', and
20 for it is b' down: howl and cry;
25 his arm is b', saith the Lord.
38 I have b' Moab like a vessel
39 howl, saying, How is it b' down!
50: 2 Merodach is b' in pieces; her
2 her images are b' in pieces.
17 king of Babylon hath b' his bones
23 whole earth cut asunder and b'!
51:30 dwelling places; her bars are b'.
56 every one of their bows is b':
58 of Babylon shall be utterly b',
52: 7 Then the city was b' up, and all
La 2: 9 destroyed and b' her bars:
3: 4 made old; he hath b' my bones.
16 b' my teeth with gravel stones,
Eze 6: 4 and your images shall be b':
6 and your idols may be b' and
9 I am b' with their whorish heart,
17:19 and my covenant that he hath b',
19:12 her strong rods were b' and
26: 2 b' that was the gates of the people:
27:26 the east wind hath b' thee in the
34 thou shalt be b' by the seas in
30: 4 her foundations shall be b'
21 I have b' the arm of Pharaoh
22 strong, and that which was b';
31:12 and his boughs are b' by all the
32:28 thou shalt be b' in the midst of
34: 4 ye bound up that which was b',
16 will bind up that which was b',
27 have b' the bands of their yoke,
44: 7 and they have b' my covenant
Da 2:35 silver, and the gold, b' to pieces
42 be partly strong, and partly b'.
8: 8 strong, the great horn was b';
22 Now that being b', whereas
25 but he shall be b' without hand.
11: 4 his kingdom shall be b', and shall
22 and shall be b'; yea, also the prince
Ho 5:11 Ephraim is oppressed and b'
8: 6 Samaria shall be b' in pieces.
Joe 1:17 the barns are b' down; for the
Jon 1: 4 that the ship was like to be b'.
Mic 2:13 they have b' up, and have passed
Zec 11:11 And it was b' in that day; and so
16 nor heal that that is b', nor feed
M't 15:37 they took up of the b' meat that
21:44 fall on this stone shall be b':
24:43 suffered his house to be b' up.
M'r 2: 4 when they had b' it up, they let
5: 4 and the fetters b' in pieces:
8: 8 they took up the b' meat that
Lu 12:39 suffered his house to be b'
20:18 fall upon that stone shall be b';
Joh 5:18 he not only had b' the sabbath,
7:23 law of Moses should not be b';
10:35 and the scripture cannot be b';
19:31 that their legs might be b',
36 A bone of him shall not be b'.
21:11 many, yet was not the net b'.

Ac 13:43 when the congregation was b'
20:11 and had b' bread, and eaten,
27:35 when he had b' it, he began to
41 the hinder part was b' with the
44 some on b' pieces of the ship.
Ro 11:17 some of the branches be b' off,
19 The branches were b' off, that I
20 because of unbelief they were b' off,
1Co 11:24 is my body, which is b' for you:
Eph 2:14 hath b' down the middle wall
Re 2:27 of the potter shall they be b'

brokenfooted
Le 21:19 Or a man that is b',

brokenhanded
Le 21:19 that is brokenfooted, or b',

brokenhearted
Isa 61: 1 bind up the b', to proclaim
Lu 4:18 hath sent me to heal the b',

brood
Lu 13:34 as a hen doth gather her b'

brook See also BROOKS.
Ge 32:23 and sent them over the b',
Le 23:40 willows of the b'; and ye shall
Nu 13:23 they came unto the b' of Eschol,
24 The place was called the b'
De 2:13 you over the b' Zered.
13 And we went over the b' Zered.
14 until we were come over the b'
9:21 I cast the dust thereof into the b'
1Sa 17:40 five smooth stones out of the b',
30: 9 and came to the b' Besor, where
10 could not go over the b' Besor.
21 to abide at the b' Besor: and they
2Sa 15:23 himself passed over the b' Kidron,
17:20 They be gone over the b' of water.
1Ki 2:37 out and passest over the b' Kidron,
15:13 and burnt it by the b' Kidron.
17: 3 hide thyself by the b' Cherith,
4 thou shalt drink of the b';
5 and dwelt by the b' Cherith, that
6 evening; and he drank of the b'.
7 the b' dried up, because there
18:40 brought them down to the b'
2Ki 23: 6 unto the b' Kidron, and
6 burned it at the b' Kidron,
12 dust of them into the b' Kidron.
2Ch 15:16 and burnt it at the b' Kidron.
20:16 at the end of the b', before
29:16 abroad into the b' Kidron.
30:14 cast them into the b' Kidron.
32: 4 the b' that ran through the midst
Ne 2:15 went I up in the night by the b',
Job 6:15 have dealt deceitfully as a b',
40:22 willows of the b' compass him
Ps 83: 9 as to Jabin, at the b' of Kison:
110: 7 He shall drink of the b' in the way:
Pr 18: 4 of wisdom as a flowing b'.
Isa 15: 7 away to the b' of the willows.
Jer 31:40 the fields unto the b' of Kidron,
Joh 18: 1 over the b' Cedron, where was

brooks
Nu 21:14 in the b' of Arnon,
15 the stream of the b' that goeth
De 8: 7 good land, a land of b' of water,
2Sa 23:30 Hiddai of the b' of Gaash,
1Ki 18: 5 and unto all b': peradventure
1Ch 11:32 Hurai of the b' of Gaash,
Job 6:15 and as a stream of b' they pass
20:17 the b' of honey and butter.
22:24 of Ophir as the stones of the b'.
Ps 42: 1 hart panteth after the water b',
Isa 19: 6 and the b' of defence shall be
7 the paper reeds by the b',
7 by the mouth of the b',
7 and everything sown by the b',
8 they that cast angle into the b'

broth
J'g 6:19 and he put the b' in a pot, and
20 this rock, and pour out the b'.
Isa 65: 4 and b' of abominable things

brother See also BRETHREN; BROTHERHOOD; BROTHER'S; BROTHERS'.
Ge 4: 2 And she again bare his b' Abel.
8 And Cain talked with Abel his b':
8 Cain rose up against Abel his b',
9 Where is Abel thy b'?
9: 5 at the hand of every man's b'
10:21 the b' of Japheth the elder, even
14:13 b' of Eschol, and b' of Aner:
14 Abram heard that his b' was taken
16 also brought his b' Lot, and his
20: 5 she herself said, He is my b':
13 come, say of me, He is my b'.
16 Behold, I have given thy b'
22:20 born children unto thy b' Nahor;
21 Huz his firstborn, and Buz his b',
23 did bear to Nahor, Abraham's b'.
24:15 the wife of Nahor, Abraham's b',
29 Rebekah had a b', and his name
53 he gave also to her b' and to her
55 her b' and her mother said, Let the
25:26 after that came his b' out, and his
27: 6 thy father speak unto Esau thy b',
11 Esau my b' is a hairy man, and
23 as his b' Esau's hands: so he
30 Esau his b' came in from his
35 Thy b' came with subtilty,
40 thou live, and shalt serve thy b';
41 then will I slay my b' Jacob.
42 Behold, thy b' Esau, as touching
43 flee thou to Laban my b' to Haran;
28: 2 daughters of Laban thy mother's b'.
5 the Syrian, the b' of Rebekah,
Ge 29:10 daughter of Laban his mother's b',
10 sheep of Laban his mother's b',
10 the flock of Laban his mother's b'.
12 Rachel that he was her father's b',
15 Because thou art my b',
32: 3 before him to Esau his b'
6 We came to thy b' Esau, and also
11 from the hand of my b', from the
13 hand a present for Esau his b';
17 When Esau my b' meeteth thee,
33: 3 until he came near to his b'.
9 Esau said, I have enough, my b';
35: 1 from the face of Esau thy b'.
7 he fled from the face of his b'.
36: 6 from the face of his b' Jacob.
37:26 is it if we slay our b', and conceal
27 for he is our b' and our flesh:
38: 8 her, and raise up seed to thy b'.
9 that he should give seed to his b'.
29 behold, his b' came out: and she
30 afterward came out his b', that
42: 4 But Benjamin, Joseph's b',
15 except your youngest b' come
16 let him fetch your b', and ye shall
20 bring your youngest b' unto me;
21 guilty concerning our b', in that
42:34 bring your youngest b' unto me:
34 I deliver you your b', and ye shall
38 his b' is dead, and he is left alone:
43: 3 face, except your b' be with you.
4 If thou wilt send our b' with us, we
5 face, except your b' be with you.
6 the man whether ye had yet a b'?
7 have ye another b'? and we told
7 he would say, Bring your b' down?
13 Take also your b', and arise, and
14 he may send away your other b',
29 saw his b' Benjamin, his mother's
29 Is this your younger b', of whom
30 his bowels did yearn upon his b':
44:19 saying, Have ye a father, or a b'?
20 and his b' is dead, and he alone is
23 Except your youngest b' come
26 if our youngest b' be with us, then
26 except our youngest b' be with us.
45: 4 he said, I am Joseph your b', whom
12 the eyes of my b' Benjamin, that
14 fell upon his b' Benjamin's neck,
48:19 younger b' shall be greater than he,
Ex 4:14 Is not Aaron the Levite thy b'?
7: 1 Aaron thy b' shall be thy prophet.
2 thy b' shall speak unto Pharoah,
28: 1 take thou unto thee Aaron thy b',
2, 4 holy garments for Aaron thy b',
41 put them upon Aaron thy b', and
32:27 slay every man his b', and every
29 man upon his son, and upon his b';
Le 16: 2 Speak unto Aaron thy b', that he
18:14 the nakedness of thy father's b',
19:17 Thou shalt not hate thy b' in thine
21: 2 for his daughter, and for his b',
25:25 If thy b' be waxen poor, and hath
25 he redeem that which his b' sold.
35 if thy b' be waxen poor, and fallen
36 God; that thy b' may live with thee.
39 if thy b' that dwelleth by thee be
47 b' that dwelleth by him wax poor,
Nu 6: 7 for his b', or for his sister, when
20: 8 thou, and Aaron thy b', and speak
14 Thus saith thy b' Israel, Thou
27:13 as Aaron thy b' was gathered,
36: 2 our b' unto his daughters.
De 1:16 between every man and his b', and
13: 6 If thy b', the son of thy mother, or
15: 2 of his neighbour, or of his b';
3 that which is thine with thy b'
7 shut thine hand from thy poor b':
9 eye be evil against thy poor b', and
11 open thine hand wide unto thy b',
12 if thy b', an Hebrew man, or an
17:15 over thee, which is not thy b'.
19:18 hath testified falsely against his b';
19 thought to have done unto his b':
22: 1 case bring them again unto thy b'.
2 if thy b' be not nigh unto thee, or if
2 until thy b' seek after it, and thou
23: 7 an Edomite; for he is thy b':
19 not lend upon usury to thy b';
20 unto thy b' thou shalt not lend upon
24:10 When thou dost lend thy b'
25: 3 thy b' should seem vile unto thee.
5 husband's b' shall go in unto her,
5 the duty of an husband's b'
6 shall succeed in the name of his b'
7 My husband's b' refuseth to raise
7 his b' a name in Israel, he will not
7 the duty of my husband's b'.
28:54 his eye shall be evil toward his b',
32:50 Aaron thy b' died in mount Hor,
Jos 15:17 son of Kenaz, the b' of Caleb, took
J'g 1: 3 And Judah said unto Simeon his b',
13 son of Kenaz, Caleb's younger b',
17 Judah went with Simeon his b',
3: 9 son of Kenaz, Caleb's younger b'.
9: 3 for they said, He is our b'.
18 Shechem, because he is your b';
21 there, for fear of Abimelech his b'.
24 upon Abimelech their b', which
20:23 the children of Benjamin my b'?
28 of Benjamin my b', or shall I cease?
21: 6 repented them for Benjamin their b',
Ru 4: 3 which was our b' Elimelech's:
1Sa 14: 3 the son of Ahitub, I-chabod's b',
17:28 Eliab his eldest b' heard when he
20:29 my b', he hath commanded me to
26: 6 the son of Zeruiah, b' to Joab,
2Sa 1:26 distressed for thee, my b' Jonathan:
2:22 I hold up my face to Joab thy b'?
27 every one from following his b'.
3:27 died, for the blood of Asahel his b'.
30 Joab and Abishai his b' slew Abner,
30 because he had slain their b'
4: 6 Rechab and Baanah his b' escaped.
9 answered Rechab and Baanah his b',
10:10 into the hand of Abishai his b',
13: 3 the son of Shimeah David's b':
4 Tamar, my b' Absalom's sister.
7 Go now to thy b' Amnon's house,
8 Tamar went to her b' Amnon's
10 into the chamber to Amnon her b'.
12 she answered him, Nay, my b', do
20 Absalom her b' said unto her, Hath
20 Amnon thy b' been with thee?
20 peace, my sister: he is thy b';
20 desolate in her b' Absalom's house.
22 Absalom spake unto his b' Amnon
26 thee, let my b' Amnon go with us.
32 the son of Shimeah David's b',
14: 7 Deliver him that smote his b', that
7 life of his b' whom he slew;
18: 2 the son of Zeruiah, Joab's b', and
20: 9 said, Art thou in health, my b'?
10 Abishai his b' pursued after Sheba
21:19 slew the b' of Goliath the Gittite,
21 Shimeah the b' of David slew him.
23:18 Abishai, the b' of Joab, the son of
24 Asahel the b' of Joab was one of
1Ki 1:10 and Solomon his b', he called not.
2: 7 I fled because of Absalom thy b'.
21 be given to Adonijah thy b' to wife.
22 for he is mine elder b'; even for
9:13 which thou hast given me, my b'?
13:30 over him, saying, Alas, my b'!
20:32 said, Is he yet alive? he is my b'.
33 Thy b' Ben-hadad. Then he said,
2Ki 24:17 made Mattaniah his father's b' king
1Ch 2:32 sons of Jada the b' of Shammai;
42 sons of Caleb the b' of Jerahmeel
4:11 Chelub the b' of Shuah begat Mehir,
6:39 And his b' Asaph, who stood on
7:16 the name of his b' was Sheresh;
35 the sons of his b' Helem; Zophah,
8:39 the sons of Eshek his b' were, Ulam
11:20 Abishai the b' of Joab, he was chief
26 Asahel the b' of Joab, Elhanan
38 Joel the b' of Nathan, Mibhar the
45 Shimei, and Joha his b', the Tizite,
19:11 unto the hand of Abishai his b',
15 fled before Abishai his b', and
20: 5 Jair slew Lahmi the b' of Goliath
7 son of Shimea David's b' slew him.
24:25 The b' of Michah was Isshiah: of
26:22 Zetham, and Joel his b', which
27: 7 Asahel the b' of Joab, and Zebadiah
2Ch 31:12 and Shimei his b' was the next.
13 Cononiah and Shimei his b', at the
36: 4 Eliakim his b' king over Judah
4 Necho took Jehoahaz his b', and
10 Zedekiah his b' king over Judah
Ne 5: 7 Ye exact usury, every one of his b'.
7: 2 That I gave my b' Hanani, and
Job 22: 6 hast taken a pledge from thy b'
30:29 I am a b' to dragons, and a
Ps 35:14 though he had been my friend or b':
49: 7 can by any means redeem his b',
50:20 sittest and speakest against thy b';
Pr 17:17 times, and a b' is born for adversity.
18: 9 is b' to him that is a great waster.
19 A b' offended is harder to be won
24 friend that sticketh closer than a b'.
27:10 that is near than a b' far off.
Ec 4: 8 yea, he hath neither child nor b':
Ca 8: 1 O that thou wert as my b', that
Isa 3: 6 a man shall take hold of his b' of
9:19 the fire: no man shall spare his b'.
19: 2 fight every one against his b', and
41: 6 every one said to his b', Be of good
Jer 9: 4 trust ye not in any b': for
4 every b' will utterly supplant,
22:18 saying, Ah my b'! or, Ah sister!
23:35 every one to his b', What hath the
31:34 every man his b', saying, Know the
34: 9 of them, to wit, of a Jew his b'.
14 ye go every man his b' an Hebrew,
17 liberty, every one to his b',
Eze 18:18 spoiled his b' by violence, and did
33:30 every one to his b', saying, Come,
38:21 man's sword shall be against his b'.
44:25 for son, or for daughter, for b', or
Ho 12: 3 He took his b' by the heel in the
Am 1:11 because he did pursue his b' with
Ob 10 thy violence against thy b' Jacob,
12 have looked on the day of thy b'
Mic 7: 2 hunt every man his b' with a net.
Hag 2:22 every one by the sword of his b'.
Zec 7: 9 compassions every man to his b':
10 evil against his b' in your heart.
Mal 1: 2 Was not Esau Jacob's b'? saith
2:10 every man against his b',
M't 4:18 called Peter, and Andrew his b',
21 of Zebedee, and John his b',
5:22 whosoever is angry with his b'
22 whosoever shall say to his b', Raca,
23 thy b' hath ought against thee;
24 first be reconciled to thy b', and
7: 4 wilt thou say to thy b', Let me
10: 2 called Peter, and Andrew his b';
2 son of Zebedee, and John his b';
21 b' shall deliver up the b' to death,
12:50 the same is my b', and sister, and
14: 3 Herodias' sake, his b' Philip's wife.
17: 1 James, and John his b', and

M't 18:15 thy b' shall trespass against thee,
15 hear thee, thou hast gained thy b'.
21 how oft shall my b' sin against me,
35 every one his b' their trespasses.
22:24 his b' shall marry his wife,
24 and raise up seed unto his b'.
25 no issue, left his wife unto his b':
M'r 1:16 saw Simon and Andrew his b'
19 the son of Zebedee and John his b',
3:17 and John the b' of James; and he
35 will of God, the same is my b', and
5:37 James, and John the b' of James.
6: 3 son of Mary, the b' of James, and
17 Herodias' sake, his b' Philip's wife:
12:19 If a man's b' die, and leave his wife
19 that his b' should take his wife,
19 and raise up seed unto his b'.
13:12 the b' shall betray the b' to death,
Lu 3: 1 and his b' Philip tetrarch of Ituræa
19 for Herodias his b' Philip's wife,
6:14 named Peter,) and Andrew his b',
16 And Judas the b' of James, and
42 say to thy b', B', let me pull out the
12:13 Master, speak to my b', that he
15:27 said unto him, Thy b' is come;
32 for this thy b' was dead, and is alive
17: 3 If thy b' trespass against thee,
20:28 If any man's b' die, having a wife,
28 that his b' should take his wife,
28 and raise up seed unto his b'.
Joh 1:40 was Andrew, Simon Peter's b'.
41 findeth his own b' Simon, and saith
6: 8 Andrew, Simon Peter's b', saith
11: 2 hair, whose b' Lazarus was sick.)
19 to comfort them concerning their b'.
21 hadst been here, my b' had not died.
23 unto her, Thy b' shall rise again.
32 hadst been here, my b' had not died.
Ac 1:13 Zelotes, and Judas the b' of James.
9:17 said, B' Saul, the Lord, even Jesus,
12: 2 he killed James the b' of John with
21:20 Thou seest, b', how many thousands
22:13 unto me, B' Saul, receive thy sight.
Ro 14:10 why dost thou judge thy b'? or why
10 dost thou set at nought thy b'?
15 if thy b' be grieved with thy meat,
21 thing whereby thy b' stumbleth,
16:23 city saluteth you, and Quartus a b'.
1Co 1: 1 will of God, and Sosthenes our b',
5:11 that is called a b' be a fornicator,
6: 6 b' goeth to law with b', and that
7:12 If any b' hath a wife that
15 A b' or a sister is not under
8:11 shall the weak b' perish, for
13 meat make my b' to offend,
13 lest I make my b' to offend.
16:12 As touching our b' Apollos,
2Co 1: 1 will of God, and Timothy our b',
2:13 I found not Titus my b': but
8:18 have sent with him the b', whose
22 have sent with them our b',
12:18 Titus, and with him I sent a b'.
Ga 1:19 none, save James the Lord's b'.
Eph 6:21 a beloved b' and faithful minister
Ph'p 2:25 send to you Epaphroditus, my b',
Col 1: 1 will of God, and Timotheus our b',
4: 7 you, who is a beloved b', and a
9 a faithful and beloved b', who is
1Th 3: 2 sent Timotheus, our b', and
4: 6 and defraud his b' in any matter:
2Th 3: 6 from every b' that walketh
15 but admonish him as a b'.
Ph'm 1 Timothy our b'; unto Philemon
7 the saints are refreshed by thee, b'.
16 above a servant, a b' beloved,
20 Yea, b', let me have
Heb 8:11 neighbour, and every man his b',
13:23 Know ye that our b' Timothy
Jas 1: 9 Let the b' of low degree rejoice
2:15 If a b' or sister be naked, and
4:11 evil of his b', and judgeth his b',
1Pe 5:12 a faithful b' unto you, as I suppose,
2Pe 3:15 as our beloved b' Paul also
1Jo 2: 9 in the light, and hateth his b',
10 He that loveth his b' abideth in the
11 he that hateth his b' is in darkness,
3:10 neither he that loveth not his b'.
12 wicked one, and slew his b'.
14 loveth not his b' abideth in death.
15 Whosoever hateth his b' is a
17 seeth his b' have need, and
4:20 hateth his b', he is a liar: for he
20 that loveth not his b' whom he
21 who loveth God, love his b' also.
5:16 any man see his b' sin a sin which
Jude 1 of Jesus Christ, and b' of James,
Re 1: 9 I John who also am your b', and

brotherhood
Zec 11:14 the b' between Judah and Israel.
1Pe 2:17 Love the b'. Fear God. Honour

brotherly
Am 1: 9 remembered not the b' covenant:
Ro 12:10 one to another with b' love;
1Th 4: 9 But as touching b' love ye need
Heb 13: 1 Let b' love continue.
2Pe 1: 7 godliness b' kindness; and to b'

brother's
Ge 4: 9 I know not: Am I my b' keeper?
10 the voice of thy b' blood crieth
11 her mouth to receive thy b' blood
21 And his b' name was Jubal:
10:25 and his b' name was Joktan.
12: 5 Sarah his wife, and Lot his b' son,
14:12 And they took Lot, Abram's b' son,
24:48 to take my master's b' daughter
Ge 27:44 until thy b' fury turn away;
45 Until thy b' anger turn away
38: 8 in unto thy b' wife, and marry her,
9 he went in unto his b' wife, that he
Le 18:16 the nakedness of thy b' wife:
16 it is thy b' nakedness.
20:21 if a man shall take his b' wife,
21 hath uncovered his b' nakedness;
De 22: 1 Thou shalt not see thy b' ox
3 with all lost thing of thy b',
4 Thou shalt not see thy b' ass or
25: 7 like not to take his b' wife,
7 then let his b' wife go up to the
9 Then shall his b' wife come unto
9 will not build up his b' house
1Ki 2:15 turned about, and is become my b':
1Ch 1:19 and his b' name was Joktan.
Job 1:13 drinking wine in their eldest b'
18 wine in their eldest b' house:
Pr 27:10 neither go into thy b' house in
M't 7: 3 the mote that is in thy b' eye,
5 out the mote out of thy b' eye.
M'r 6:18 lawful for thee to have thy b' wife,
Lu 6:41 mote that is in thy b' eye,
42 out the mote that is in thy b' eye.
Ro 14:13 an occasion to fall in his b' way.
1Jo 3:12 were evil, and his b' righteous.

brothers' See also BRETHREN'S.
Nu 36:11 unto their father's b' sons:

brought^ See also BROUGHTEST.
Ge 1:12 And the earth b' forth grass,
21 the waters b' forth abundantly,
2:19 and b' them unto Adam to see
22 and b' her unto the man.
4: 3 that Cain b' of the fruit of the
4 he also b' of the firstlings of his
14:16 b' back all the goods, and also
16 b' again his brother Lot,
18 king of Salem b' forth bread and
15: 5 And he b' him forth abroad, and
7 I am the Lord that b' thee out of
19:16 and they b' him forth, and set him
17 when they had b' them forth
20: 9 thou hast b' on me and on my
24:53 And the servant b' forth jewels
67 And Isaac b' her into his mother
26:10 and thou shouldest have b'
27:14 and b' them to his mother:
20 the Lord thy God b' it to me.
25 And he b' it near to him, and
25 he b' him wine, and he drank.
31 and b' it unto his father, and
33 hath taken venison, and b' it me,
29:13 and b' him to his house.
23 and b' her to him; and he went
30:14 and b' them unto his mother Leah.
39 and b' forth cattle ringstraked,
31:39 I b' not unto thee; I bear the loss
33:11 I pray thee, my blessing that is b'
37: 2 and Joseph b' unto his father
28 and they b' Joseph into Egypt.
32 and they b' it to their father;
38:25 When she was b' forth, she sent
39: 1 Joseph was b' down to Egypt;
1 which had b' him down thither.
14 he hath b' in an Hebrew unto us
17 which thou hast b' unto us,
40:10 thereof b' forth ripe grapes:
41:14 b' him hastily out of the dungeon:
47 the earth b' forth by handfuls.
43: 2 which they had b' out of Egypt,
12 the money that was b' again
17 and the man b' the men into
18 they were b' into Joseph's house;
18 at the first time are we b' in;
21 have b' it again in our hand.
22 other money have we b' down
23 And he b' Simeon out unto them.
24 b' the men into Joseph's house,
26 they b' him the present
44: 8 we b' again unto thee out of the
46: 7 seed b' he with him into Egypt.
32 they have b' their flocks, and
47: 7 And Joseph b' in Jacob his father,
14 and Joseph b' the money into
17 they b' their cattle unto Joseph:
48:10 And he b' them near unto him;
12 And Joseph b' them out from
13 hand, and b' them near unto him.
50:23 were b' up upon Joseph's knees.
Ex 2:10 b' him unto Pharaoh's daughter,
3:12 When thou hast b' forth the
8: 7 and b' up frogs upon the land
12 the frogs which he had b' against
9:19 be b' home, the hail shall come
10: 8 And Moses and Aaron were b'
13 the Lord b' an east wind upon
13 the east wind b' the locusts.
12:17 day have I b' your armies out
39 the dough which they b' forth
13: 3 Lord b' you out from this place:
9 hand hath the Lord b' thee out
14 the Lord b' us out from Egypt,
16 the Lord b' us forth out of Egypt.
15:19 b' again the waters of the sea
22 So Moses b' Israel from the Red
26 I have b' upon the Egyptians:
16: 3 ye have b' us forth into this
6 the Lord hath b' you out from
32 when I brought you forth from
17: 3 thou hast b' us up out of Egypt,
18: 1 had b' Israel out of Egypt;
26 the hard causes they b' unto
19: 4 and b' you unto myself.
17 And Moses b' forth the people
Ex 20: 2 have b' thee out of the land of
22: 8 master of the house shall be b'
29:10 shalt cause a bullock to be b'
46 that b' them forth out of the land
32: 1 the man that b' us up out of the
3 ears, and b' them unto Aaron.
4 gods, O Israel, which b' thee up
6 and b' peace offerings; and the
8 Israel, which have b' thee up
11 b' forth out of the land of Egypt
21 hast b' so great a sin upon them?
23 the man that b' us up out of the
33: 1 thou hast b' up out of the land
35:21 they b' the Lord's offering to the
22 b' bracelets, and earrings, and rings,
23 rams, and badgers' skins, b' them.
24 b' the Lord's offering: and every
24 for any work of the service, b' it.
25 and b' that which they had spun,
27 the rulers b' onyx stones, and
29 Israel b' a willing offering
36: 3 Israel had b' for the work of the
3 they b' yet unto him free offerings
39:33 And they b' the tabernacle unto
40:21 he b' the ark into the tabernacle,
Le 6:30 whereof any of the blood is b' into
8: 6 And Moses b' Aaron and his
13 And Moses b' Aaron's sons, and
14 And he b' the bullock for the sin
18 And he b' the ram for the
22 And he b' the other ram, the
24 And he b' Aaron's sons, and
9: 5 And they b' that which Moses
9 And the sons of Aaron b' the
15 And he b' the people's offering,
16 And he b' the burnt offering,
17 And he b' the meat offering,
10:18 the blood of it was not b' in
13: 2 then he shall be b' unto Aaron
9 in a man, then he shall be b' unto
14: 2 He shall be b' unto the priest:
16:27 whose blood was b' in to make
19:36 which b' you out of the land of
22:27 or a sheep, or a goat, is b' forth,
33 That b' you out of the land of
23:14 that ye have b' an offering unto
15 the day that ye b' the sheaf of
43 when I b' them out of the land of
24:11 And they b' him unto Moses: (and
25:38 which b' you forth out of the land
42 which I b' forth out of the land of
55 whom I b' forth out of the land of
26:13 which b' you forth out of the land
41 and have b' them into the land of
45 whom I b' forth out of the land
Nu 6:13 he shall be b' unto the door of
7: 3 And they b' their offering before
3 and they b' them before the
9:13 he b' not the offering of the Lord
11:31 and b' quails from the sea, and
12:15 not till Miriam was b' in again.
13:23 and they b' of the pomegranates,
26 and b' back word unto them, and
32 And they b' up an evil report of
14: 3 wherefore hath the Lord b' us
15:33 him gathering sticks b' him
36 And all the congregation b' him
41 which b' you out of the land of
16:10 And he hath b' thee near to him,
13 thou hast b' us up out of a land
14 thou hast not b' us into a land
17: 8 and b' forth buds, and bloomed
9 And Moses b' out all the rods
20: 4 And why have ye b' up the
16 hath b' us forth out of Egypt:
21: 5 Wherefore have ye b' us up out
22:41 and b' him up into the high
23: 7 Balak the king of Moab hath b'
14 And he b' him into the field of
22 God b' them out of Egypt; he
28 And Balak b' Balaam unto the
24: 8 God b' him forth out of Egypt;
25: 6 and b' unto his brethren a
27: 5 And Moses b' their cause before
31:12 And they b' the captives, and the
50 We have therefore b' an oblation
54 and b' it into the tabernacle of
32:17 until we have b' them unto their
De 1:25 in their hands, and b' it down
25 unto us, and b' us word again,
27 he has b' us forth out of the land
4:20 hath taken you, and b' you forth
37 and b' thee out in his sight with
5: 6 which b' thee out of the land of
15 the Lord thy God b' thee out
6:10 Lord thy God shall have b' thee
12 which b' thee forth out of the
21 and the Lord b' us out of Egypt
23 he b' us out from thence, that he
7: 8 b' you out with a mighty hand,
19 the Lord thy God b' thee out:
8:14 which b' thee forth out of the land
15 who b' thee forth water out of the
9: 4 hath b' me in to possess this land:
12 people which thou hast b' forth
26 which thou hast b' forth out of
28 he hath b' them out to slay them
11:29 hath b' thee in unto the land
13: 5 which b' you out of the land of
10 which b' thee out of the land of
16: 1 the Lord thy God b' thee forth out
20: 1 God is with thee, which b' thee
22:19 he hath b' up an evil name upon
26: 8 And the Lord b' us forth out of
9 And he hath b' us into this place,
10 I have b' the firstfruits of the land,

De 26:13 I have b' away the hallowed
29:25 when he b' them forth out of the
31:20 For when I shall have b' them
21 before I have b' them into the land
33:14 precious fruits b' forth by the sun.
Jos 2: 6 she had b' them up to the roof
6:23 and b' out Rahab, and her father,
23 they b' out all her kindred, and
7: 7 hast thou at all b' this people
14 ye shall be b' according to your
16 and b' Israel by their tribes; and
17 And he b' the family of Judah;
17 he b' the family of the Zarhites
18 And he b' his household man by
23 and b' them unto Joshua, and
24 and they b' them unto the valley
8:23 took alive, and b' him to Joshua.
10:23 and b' forth those five kings unto
24 when they b' out those kings unto
14: 7 and I b' him word again as it was
22:32 of Israel, and b' them word again.
24: 5 them: and afterward I b' you out.
6 And I b' your fathers out of Egypt:
7 and b' the sea upon them, and
8 And I b' you into the land of the
17 he it is that b' us up and our
32 which the children of Israel b' up
J'g 1: 7 And they b' him to Jerusalem,
2: 1 and have b' you unto the land
12 b' them out of the land of Egypt,
3:17 he b' the present unto Eglon
5:25 she b' forth butter in a lordly dish.
6: 8 I b' you up from Egypt, and
8 b' you forth out of the house of
19 b' it out unto him under the oak,
7: 5 So he b' down the people unto the
25 and b' the heads of Oreb and Zeeb
11:35 thou hast b' me very low, and
14:11 that they b' thirty companions to
15:13 and b' him up from the rock.
16: 8 the lords of the Philistines b' up
18 her, and b' money in their hand.
21 b' him down to Gaza, and bound
31 and b' him up, and buried him
18: 3 unto him, Who b' thee hither?
19: 3 b' him into her father's house:
21 So he b' him into his house, and
25 took his concubine, and b' her
21:12 and they b' them unto the camp
Ru 1:21 the Lord hath b' me home again
2:18 and she b' forth, and gave to her
1Sa 1:24 and b' him unto the house of the
25 a bullock, and b' the child to Eli.
2:14 all that the fleshhook b' up the
19 and b' it to him from year to year,
5: 1 and b' it from Eben-ezer unto
2 they b' it into the house of Dagon,
10 They have b' about the ark of the
6:21 Philistines have b' again the ark
7: 1 b' it into the house of Abinadab
8: 8 that I b' them up out of Egypt
9:22 and b' them into the parlour, and
10:18 I b' up Israel out of Egypt, and
27 him, and b' him no presents.
12: 6 that b' your fathers up out of the
8 b' forth your fathers out of Egypt,
14:34 the people b' every man his ox
15:15 Saul said, They have b' them from
20 have b' Agag the king of Amalek,
16:12 he sent, and b' him in. Now he
17:54 and b' it to Jerusalem; but he put
57 b' him before Saul with the head
18:27 David b' their foreskins, and they
19: 7 And Jonathan b' David to Saul,
20: 8 b' thy servant into a covenant of
21: 8 I have neither b' my sword nor
14 then have ye b' him to me?
15 b' this fellow to play the mad man
22: 4 he b' them before the king of
23: 5 b' away their cattle, and smote
25:27 which thine handmaid hath b'
35 which she had b' him, and said
28:25 she b' it before Saul, and before
30: 7 Abiathar b' thither the ephod to
11 b' him to David, and gave him
16 And when he had b' him down,
2Sa 1:10 have b' them hither unto my Lord.
2: 8 and b' him over to Mahanaim;
3:22 b' in a great spoil with them:
26 messengers after Abner, which b'
4: 8 b' the head of Ish-bosheth unto
10 thinking to have b' good tidings,
6: 3, 4 b' it out of the house of Abinadab
12 David went and b' up the ark
15 b' up the ark of the Lord with
17 they b' in the ark of the Lord,
7: 6 I b' up the children of Israel out
18 that thou hast b' me hitherto?
8: 2 became David's servants, and b'
6 servants to David, and b' gifts.
7 of Hadadezer, and b' them to
10 Joram b' with him vessels of
10:16 and b' out the Syrians that were
12:30 he b' forth the spoil of the city in
31 And he b' forth the people that
13:10 and b' them into the chamber to
11 when she had b' them unto him to
18 Then his servant b' her out, and
14:23 went to Geshur, and b' Absalom to
17:28 B' beds, and basons, and earthen
19:41 and have b' the king, and his
21: 8 whom she b' up for Adriel the son
13 And he b' up from thence the
22:20 He b' me forth also into a large
23:16 and b' it to David: nevertheless
1Ki 1: 3 Shunammite, and b' her to the

1Ki 1:38 king David's mule, and b' him
53 and they b' him down from the
2:30 And Benaiah b' the king word
40 and b' his servants from Gath.
3: 1 and b' her into the city of David,
24 And they b' a sword before the
4:21 they b' presents, and served
28 dromedaries b' they unto the
5:17 and they b' great stones, costly
6: 7 made ready before it was b'
7:51 And Solomon b' in the things
8: 4 And they b' up the ark of the
6 And the priests b' in the ark of
16 the day that I b' forth my people
21 when he b' them out of the land
9: 9 who b' forth their fathers out of
9 therefore hath the Lord b' upon
28 twenty talents, and b' it to king
10:11 that b' gold from Ophir,
11 b' in from Ophir great plenty
25 they b' every man his present,
28 And Solomon had horses b' out
12:28 gods, O Israel, which b' thee up
13:20 unto the prophet that b' him
23 the prophet whom he had b' back.
26 And when the prophet that b' him
29 it upon the ass, and b' it back:
14:28 and b' them back into the guard
15:15 And he b' in the things which
17: 6 the ravens b' him bread and flesh
20 hast thou also b' evil upon the
23 b' him down out of the chamber
18:40 and Elijah b' them down to the
20: 9 the messengers departed, and b'
39 and b' a man unto me, and said,
22:37 and was b' to Samaria; and they
2Ki 2:20 salt therein. And they b' it to
4: 5 who b' the vessels to her; and
20 and b' him to his mother, he sat
42 and b' the man of God bread of
5: 2 and had b' away captive out of
6 And he b' the letter to the king
20 at his hands that which he b':
10: 1 them that b' up Ahab's children,
6 of the city, which b' them up.
8 They have b' the heads of the
22 And he b' them forth vestments.
24 any of the men whom I have b'
26 And they b' forth the images out
11: 4 b' them to him into the house of
12 And he b' forth the king's son,
19 and they b' down the king from
12: 4 that is b' into the house of the
9 money that was b' into the house
13 that was b' into the house of the
16 money was not b' into the house
14:20 And they b' him on horses: and
16:14 And he b' also the brasen altar,
17: 4 and b' no present to the king of
7 Lord their God, which had b'
24 And the king of Assyria b' men
27 whom ye b' from thence; and let
36 But the Lord, who b' you up out
19:25 now have I b' it to pass, that
20:11 and he b' the shadow ten degrees
20 and b' water into the city, are
22: 4 the silver which is b' into the house
9 and b' the king word again, and
20 And they b' the king word again.
23: 6 And he b' out the grove from the
8 And he b' all the priests out of the
30 and b' him to Jerusalem, and
24:16 the king of Babylon b' captive to
25: 6 So they took the king, and b'
20 b' them to the king of Babylon
1Ch 5:26 and b' them unto Halah, and
10:12 and b' them to Jabesh, and buried
11:18 and b' it to David: but David
19 jeopardy of their lives they b' it.
12:40 b' bread on asses, and on camels,
13:13 David b' not the ark home to
14:17 and the Lord b' the fear of him
15:28 Thus all Israel b' up the ark of
16: 1 So they b' the ark of God, and set
17: 5 since the day that I b' up Israel
16 that thou hast b' me hitherto?
18: 2, 6 David's servants, and b' gifts.
7 servants of Hadarezer, and b' them
8 b' David very much brass,
11 silver and the gold that he b'
20: 2 he b' also exceeding much spoil
3 he b' out the people that were in
22: 4 they of Tyre b' much cedar wood
2Ch 1: 4 the ark of God had David b' up
16 And Solomon had horses b' out of
17 b' forth out of Egypt a chariot
17 and so b' they out horses for all
5: 1 and Solomon b' in all the things
5 And they b' up the ark, and the
7 And the priests b' in the ark of the
6: 5 Since the day that I b' forth my
7:22 of their fathers, which b' them
22 hath he b' all this evil upon them.
8:11 Solomon b' up the daughter of
18 gold, and b' them to king Solomon.
9:10 which b' gold from Ophir, b' algum
12 which she had b' unto the king.
14 which chapmen and merchants b'.
14 b' gold and silver to Solomon.
24 they b' every man his present,
28 And they b' unto Solomon horses
10: 8 that were b' up with him, that
10 the young men that were b' up
12:11 and b' them again into the guard
13:18 the children of Israel were b'
15:11 of the spoil which they had b',

2Ch 15:18 And he b' into the house of God
16: 2 Then Asa b' out silver and gold
17: 5 and all Judah b' to Jehoshaphat
11 the Philistines b' Jehoshaphat
11 the Arabians b' him flocks, seven
19: 4 and b' them back unto the Lord
22: 9 and b' him to Jehu: and when
23:11 Then they b' out the king's son,
14 Then Jehoiada the priest b' out
20 and b' down the king from the
24:10 and b' in, and cast into the chest,
11 at what time the chest was b' unto
14 they b' the rest of the money
25:12 and b' them unto the top of the
14 that he b' the gods of the children
23 and b' him to Jerusalem, and
28 And they b' him upon horses, and
28: 5 captives, and b' them to Damascus.
8 and b' the spoil to Samaria.
15 and b' them to Jericho, the
19 the Lord b' Judah low because
27 they b' him not into the sepulchres
29: 4 And he b' in the priests and the
16 and b' out all the uncleanness
21 And they b' seven bullocks, and
23 And they b' forth the he goats
31 the congregation b' in sacrifices
32 which the congregation b', was
30:15 and b' in the burnt offerings into
31: 5 children of Israel b' in abundance
5 all things b' they in abundantly.
6 they also b' in the tithe of oxen
12 And b' in the offerings and the
32:23 many b' gifts unto the Lord to
30 b' it straight down to the west
33:11 Wherefore the Lord b' upon them
13 and b' him again to Jerusalem
34: 9 the money that was b' into the
14 they b' out the money
14 that was b' into the
16 b' the king word back again.
28 So they b' the king word again.
35:24 and they b' him to Jerusalem,
36:10 and b' him to Babylon, with the
17 Therefore he b' upon them the
18 all these he b' to Babylon.
Ezr 1: 7 the king b' forth the vessels of the
7 which Nebuchadnezzar had b'
11 were b' up from Babylon unto
4: 2 of Assur, which b' us up hither.
10 and noble Asnapper b' over, and
5:14 and b' them into the temple of
6: 5 and b' unto Babylon, be restored,
5 and b' again unto the temple
8:18 they b' us a man of understanding,
Ne 4:15 and God had b' their counsel
5: 5 daughters are b' unto bondage
8: 2 And Ezra the priest b' the law
16 went forth, and b' them, and made
9:18 This is thy God that b' thee up
33 in all that is b' upon us; for
12:31 Then I b' up the princes of
13: 9 and thither b' I again the vessels
12 Then b' all Judah the tithe of the
15 which they b' into Jerusalem
16 which b' fish, and all manner of
19 there should no burden be b' in
Es 1:17 Vashti the queen to be b' in before
2: 7 And he b' up Hadassah, that is,
8 that Esther was b' also unto the
20 like as when she was b' up with
6: 8 Let the royal apparel be b' which
11 b' him on horseback through
9:11 palace was b' before the king.
Job 4:12 a thing was secretly b' to me,
10:18 Wherefore then hast thou b' me
14:21 and they are b' low, but he
21:30 they shall be b' forth to the day
32 Yet shall he be b' to the grave,
24:24 are gone and b' low; they are
31:18 he was b' up with me, as with a
42:11 evil the Lord had b' upon him:
Ps 7:14 mischief, and b' forth falsehood.
18:19 He b' me forth also into a large
20: 8 They are b' down and fallen:
22:15 thou hast b' me into the dust
30: 3 thou hast b' up my soul from
35: 4 turned back and b' to confusion
26 be ashamed and b' to confusion
40: 2 He b' me up also out of an
45:14 She shall be b' unto the king
14 that follow her shall be b' unto
15 and rejoicing shall they be b':
71:24 for they are b' unto shame.
73:19 How are they b' into desolation,
78:16 b' streams also out of the rock.
26 his power he b' in the south wind.
54 And he b' them to the border of
71 he b' him to feed Jacob his people,
79: 8 us: for we are b' very low.
80: 8 Thou hast b' a vine out of Egypt:
81:10 Lord thy God, which b' thee out
85: 1 b' back the captivity of Jacob.
89:40 hast b' his strong holds to ruin.
90: 2 Before the mountains were b'
105:30 b' forth frogs in abundance,
37 He b' them forth also with silver
40 and he b' quails, and satisfied
43 And he b' forth his people with
106:42 and they were b' into subjection
43 and were b' low for their iniquity.
107:12 Therefore he b' down their heart
14 He b' them out of darkness and
39 they are minished and b' low
116: 6 I was b' low, and he helped me.
136:11 b' out Israel from among them:

Ps 142: 6 for I am b' very low: deliver me
Pr 6:26 a man is b' to a piece of bread:
8:24 no depths, I was b' forth; when
25 before the hills was I b' forth:
30 as one b' up with him: and I
Ec 12: 4 of music shall be b' low;
Ca 1: 4 the king hath b' me into his
2: 4 He b' me to the banqueting house,
3: 4 b' him into my mother's house,
8: 5 there thy mother b' thee forth:
5 she b' thee forth that bare thee.
Isa 1: 2 nourished and b' up children,
2:12 lifted up; and he shall be b' low:
5: 2 grapes, and it b' forth wild grapes.
4 grapes, b' it forth wild grapes?
15 the mean man shall be b' down,
14:11 Thy pomp is b' down to the
15 thou shalt be b' down to hell,
15: 1 is laid waste, and b' to silence;
1 is laid waste, and b' to silence;
18: 7 shall the present be b' unto
21:14 land of Tema b' water to him
23:13 thereof; and he b' it to ruin.
25: 5 the terrible ones shall be b' low.
26:18 have as it were b' forth wind;
29: 4 And thou shalt be b' down,
20 the terrible one is b' to nought,
37:26 now have I b' it to pass, that thou
43:14 have b' down all their nobles,
23 Thou hast not b' me the small
45:10 What hast thou b' forth?
48:15 I have b' him, and he shall make
49:21 who hath b' up these? Behold,
51:18 the sons whom she hath b' forth;
18 the sons that she hath b' up.
53: 7 is b' as a lamb to the slaughter,
59:16 therefore his arm b' salvation
60:11 and that their kings may be b'.
62: 9 they that have b' it together
63: 5 mine own arm b' salvation unto
11 Where is he that b' them up out
66: 7 Before she travailed, she b' forth;
8 she b' forth her children.
Jer 2: 6 where is the Lord that b' us up
7 b' you into a plentiful country,
27 Thou hast b' me forth: for they
7:22 the day that I b' them out of the
10: 9 Silver spread into plates is b'
11: 4 the day that I b' them forth out
7 in the day that I b' them up
19 ox that is b' to the slaughter;
15: 8 I have b' upon them against
16:14, 15 liveth, that b' up the children
20: 3 that Pashur b' forth Jeremiah
15 man who b' tidings to my father,
23: 7, 8 The Lord liveth, which b' up
24: 1 and had b' them to Babylon.
26:23 and b' him unto Jehoiakim the
27:16 shortly be b' again from Babylon:
32:21 And hast b' forth thy people
42 Like as I have b' all this great
34:11 and b' them into subjection for
13 the day that I b' them forth out
16 and b' them into subjection,
35: 4 And I b' them into the house
37:14 and b' him to the princes.
38:22 b' forth to the king of Babylon's
39: 5 they b' him up to Nebuchadnezzar
40: 3 Now the Lord hath b' it, and done
41:16 whom he had b' again from
44: 2 all the evil that I have b' upon
50:25 and hath b' forth the weapons
51:10 The Lord hath b' forth our
52:26 b' them to the king of Babylon
31 and b' him forth out of prison,
La 2: 2 hath b' them down to the ground:
22 that I have swaddled and b' up
3: 2 led me, and b' me into darkness,
4: 5 they that were b' up in scarlet
Eze 8: 3 and b' me in the visions of God
7 he b' me to the door of the court;
14 Then he b' me to the door of the
16 And he b' me into the inner court
11: 1 and b' me unto the east gate
24 and b' me in a vision by the Spirit
12: 7 I b' forth my stuff by day,
7 I b' it forth in the twilight,
14:22 remnant that shall be b' forth,
22 the evil that I have b' upon
22 all that I have b' upon it.
17: 6 a vine, and b' forth branches,
24 I the Lord have b' down the high
19: 3 she b' up one of her whelps:
4 and they b' him with chains
9 b' him to the king of Babylon:
9 they b' him into holds,
20:10 and b' them into the wilderness.
14 in whose sight I b' them out.
22 in whose sight I b' them forth.
28 I had b' them into the land,
21: 7 cometh, and shall be b' to pass,
23: 8 her whoredoms b' from Egypt:
27 whoredom b' from the land of
42 the common sort were b'
27: 6 b' out of the isles of Chittim.
15 they b' thee for a present
26 Thy rowers have b' thee into
29: 5 thou shalt not be b' together,
30:11 shall be b' to destroy the land:
31:18 thou be b' down with the trees
34: 4 have ye b' again that which
37:13 b' you up out of your graves,
38: 8 the land that is b' back from the
8 it is b' forth out of the nations,
39:27 b' them again from the people,
40: 1 was upon me, and b' me thither
Eze 40: 2 In the visions of God b' he me
3 And he b' me thither, and,
4 art thou b' hither: declare all
17 Then b' he me into the outward
24 that he b' me toward the south,
28 And he b' me to the inner court
32 And he b' me into the inner court
35 And he b' me to the north gate,
48 And he b' me to the porch of the
49 cubits; and he b' me by the steps
41: 1 Afterward he b' me to the temple,
42: 1 Then he b' me forth into the
1 and he b' me into the chamber
15 he b' me forth toward the gate
43: 1 Afterward he b' me to the gate
5 and b' me into the inner court;
44: 1 Then he b' me back the way of
4 Then b' he me the way of the
7 that ye have b' into my sanctuary
46:19 After he b' me through the entry,
21 Then he b' me forth into the
47: 1 Afterward he b' me again unto
2 Then b' he me out of the way of
3 he b' me through the waters;
4 and b' me through the waters;
4 b' me through; the waters were
6 b' me, and caused me to return
8 b' forth into the sea, the waters
Da 1: 2 b' the vessels into the treasure
9 God had b' Daniel into favour
18 then the prince of the eunuchs b'
2:25 Then Arioch b' in Daniel
3:13 b' these men before the king.
5: 3 Then they b' the golden vessels
13 was Daniel b' in before the king.
13 king my father b' out of Jewry?
15 been b' in before me, that they
23 and they have b' the vessels of
6:16 and they b' Daniel, and cast him
17 And a stone was b', and laid
18 b' before him: and his sleep
24 and they b' those men which
7:13 and they b' him near before him.
9:14 upon the evil, and b' it upon us:
15 that hast b' thy people forth out
11: 6 and they that b' her, and he that
Ho 12:13 the Lord b' Israel out of Egypt,
Am 2:10 I b' you up from the land of
3: 1 I b' up from the land of Egypt,
9: 7 Have not I b' up Israel out of the
Ob 7 of thy confederacy have b' thee
Jon 2: 6 yet hast thou b' up my life
Mic 5: 3 which travaileth hath b' forth:
6: 4 I b' thee up out of the land of
Na 2: 7 she shall be b' up, and her maids
Hag 1: 9 and when ye b' it home, I did
2:19 the olive tree, hath not b' forth:
Zec 10:11 of Assyria shall be b' down,
Mal 1:13 and ye b' that which was torn,
13 thus ye b' an offering: should I
M't 1:12 after they were b' to Babylon,
25 b' forth her firstborn son:
4:24 they b' unto him all sick people
8:16 they b' unto him many that were
9: 2 b' to him a man sick of the palsy,
32 they b' to him a dumb man
10:18 ye shall be b' before governors
11:23 heaven, shalt be b' down to hell:
12:22 Then was b' unto him one
25 is b' to desolation; and every city
13: 8 unto good ground, and b' forth
26 and b' forth fruit, then appeared
14:11 his head was b' in a charger,
11 and she b' it to her mother.
35 and b' unto him all that were
16: 8 because ye have b' no bread?
17:16 And I b' him to thy disciples,
18:24 one was b' unto him, which owed
19:13 these b' unto him little children
21: 7 And b' the ass, and the colt,
22:19 And they b' unto him a penny.
25:20 came and b' other five talents,
27: 3 b' again the thirty pieces of
M'r 1:32 they b' unto him all that were
4: 8 and b' forth, some thirty, and
21 b' to be put under a bushel,
29 when the fruit is b' forth,
6:27 commanded his head to be b':
28 And b' his head in a charger,
9:17 I have b' unto thee my son,
20 And they b' him unto him: and
10:13 they b' young children to him,
13 disciples rebuked those that b'
11: 7 And they b' the colt to Jesus,
12:16 And they b' it. And he saith
13: 9 ye shall be b' before rulers and
Lu 1:57 delivered; and she b' forth a son.
2: 7 she b' forth her firstborn son,
22 they b' him to Jerusalem to
27 when the parents b' in the child
3: 5 mountain and hill shall be b' low:
4: 9 And he b' him to Jerusalem, and
16 Nazareth, where he had been b' up:
40 divers diseases b' them unto him;
5:11 they had b' their ships to land,
18 And, behold, men b' in a bed
7:37 b' an alabaster box of ointment,
10:34 b' him to an inn, and took care
11:17 against itself is b' to desolation;
12:16 of a certain rich man b' forth
18:15 they b' unto him also infants,
40 commanded him to be b' unto him:
19:35 And they b' him to Jesus: and
21:12 being b' before kings and rulers
22:54 b' him into the high priest's
23:14 Ye have b' this man unto me,
Joh 1:42 And he b' him to Jesus. And
4:33 any man b' him ought to eat?
7:45 Why have ye not b' him?
8: 3 the scribes and Pharisees b'
9:13 They b' to the Pharisees him
18:16 kept the door, and b' in Peter.
19:13 he b' Jesus forth, and sat down
39 b' a mixture of myrrh and aloes,
Ac 4:34 and b' the prices of the things
37 and b' the money, and laid it at
5: 2 and b' a certain part, and laid it
15 b' forth the sick into the streets,
19 b' them forth, and said,
21 to the prison to have them b'.
26 officers and b' them without
27 And when they had b' them,
36 scattered, and b' to nought.
6:12 and caught him, and b' him
7:36 He b' them out, after that
40 Moses, which b' us out of the
45 b' in with Jesus into the
9: 8 hand, and b' him to Damascus.
27 took him, and b' him to the
30 they b' him down to Cæsarea,
39 b' him into the upper chamber:
11:26 when he had found him, he b' him
12: 6 Herod would have b' him forth,
17 Lord had b' him out of the prison.
13: 1 which had been b' up with
17 b' he them out of it.
14:13 b' oxen and garlands unto the
15: 3 And being b' on their way by
16:16 which b' her masters much gain
20 And b' them to the magistrates,
30 And b' them out, and said, Sirs,
34 he had b' them into his house,
39 b' them out, and desired them
17:15 conducted Paul b' him unto Athens:
19 him, and b' him unto Areopagus,
18:12 against Paul, and b' him to the
19:12 his body were b' unto the sick
19 b' their books together, and
24 b' no small gain unto the
37 b' hither these men, which are
20:12 they b' the young man alive, and
21: 5 and they all b' us on our way,
16 b' with them one Mnason of
28 b' Greeks also into the temple,
29 that Paul had b' into the temple.)
22: 3 yet b' up in this city at the feet
24 him to be b' into the castle,
30 b' Paul down, and set him before
23:18 and b' him to the chief captain,
28 I b' him forth into their council:
31 and b' him by night to Antipatris.
25: 6 seat commanded Paul to be b'.
17 commanded the man to be b' forth.
18 they b' none accusation of such
23 commandment Paul was b' forth.
26 Wherefore I have b' him forth
27:24 thou must be b' before Cæsar
Ro 15:24 to be b' on my way thitherward
1Co 6:12 not be b' under the power of any.
15:54 then shall be b' to pass the
2Co 1:16 b' on my way toward Judæa.
Ga 2: 4 false brethren unawares b' in,
1Th 3: 6 b' us good tidings of your faith
1Ti 5:10 if she have b' up children, if she
6: 7 we b' nothing into this world,
2Ti 1:10 and hath b' life and immortality
subscr. when Paul was b' before Nero
Heb 13:11 b' into the sanctuary by the high
20 that b' again from the dead our
Jas 5:18 and the earth b' forth her fruit.
1Pe 1:13 be b' unto you at the revelation
2Pe 2:19 of the same is he b' in bondage.
Re 12: 5 And she b' forth a man child.
13 which b' forth the man child.

broughtest
Ex 32: 7 thy people, which thou b' out of
Nu 14:13 thou b' up this people in thy
De 9:28 land whence thou b' us out say,
29 which thou b' out by thy mighty
2Sa 5: 2 that leddest out and b' in Israel:
1Ki 8:51 thou b' forth out of Egypt, from
53 thou b' our fathers out of Egypt,
1Ch 11: 2 and b' in Israel: and the Lord
Ne 9: 7 and b' him forth out of Ur of the
15 b' forth water for them out of
23 and b' them into the land,
Ps 66:11 Thou b' us into the net; thou
12 thou b' us out into a wealthy place.

brow See also EYEBROW.
Isa 48: 4 an iron sinew, and thy b' brass;
Lu 4:29 and led him unto the b' of the hill

brown
Ge 30:32 the b' cattle among the sheep,
33 b' among the sheep, that shall
35 all the b' among the sheep, and
40 all the b' in the flock of Laban;

bruise See also BRUISED; BRUISES; BRUISING.
Ge 3:15 it shall b' thy head,
15 and thou shalt b' his heel.
Isa 28:28 cart, nor b' it with his horsemen.
53:10 Yet it pleased the Lord to b' him;
Jer 30:12 Thy b' is incurable, and thy
Da 2:40 shall it break in pieces and b'.
Na 3:19 no healing of thy b'; thy wound
Ro 16:20 b' Satan under your feet shortly.

bruised
Le 22:24 unto the Lord that which is b',
2Ki 18:21 the staff of this b' reed, even
Isa 28:28 Bread corn is b'; because he
42: 3 A b' reed shall he not break, and

Isa 53: 5 he was *b*' for our iniquities: the
Eze 23: 3 they *b*' the teats of their virginity.
8 *b*' the breasts of her virginity,
M't 12:20 A *b*' reed shall he not break, and
Lu 4:18 to set at liberty them that are *b*',

bruises
Isa 1: 6 and *b*', and putrifying sores:

bruising
Eze 23:21 in *b*' thy teats by the Egyptians
Lu 9:39 *b*' him, hardly departeth from

bruit
Jer 10:22 the noise of the *b*' is come, and
Na 3:19 that hear the *b*' of thee shall

brute
2Pe 2:12 these, as natural *b*' beasts, made
Jude 10 know naturally, as *b*' beasts, in

brutish
Ps 49:10 the fool and the *b*' person perish,
92: 6 A *b*' man knoweth not; neither
94: 8 ye *b*' among the people: and ye
Pr 12: 1 but he that hateth reproof is *b*'.
30: 2 Surely I am more *b*' than any
Isa 19:11 of Pharaoh is become *b*':
Jer 10: 8 they are altogether *b*' and foolish:
14 Every man is *b*' in his knowledge:
21 the pastors are become *b*', and
51:17 Every man is *b*' by his knowledge:
Eze 21:31 into the hand of *b*' men, and skilful

buck See ROEBUCK.

bucket See also BUCKETS.
Isa 40:15 the nations are as a drop of a *b*',

buckets
Nu 24: 7 pour the water out of his *b*', and

buckler See also BUCKLERS.
2Sa 22:31 a *b*' to all them that trust in him.
1Ch 5:18 men able to bear *b*' and sword,
12: 8 that could handle shield and *b*',
Ps 18: 2 my *b*', and the horn of my
30 he is a *b*' to all those that trust
35: 2 Take hold of shield and *b*', and
91: 4 truth shall be thy shield and *b*'.
Pr 2: 7 a *b*' to them that walk uprightly
Jer 46: 3 Order ye the *b*' and shield, and
Eze 23:24 set against thee *b*' and shield
26: 8 and lift up the *b*' against thee.

bucklers
2Ch 23: 9 spears, and *b*', and shields, that
Job 15:26 upon the thick bosses of his *b*':
Ca 4: 4 there hang a thousand *b*', all
Eze 38: 4 company with *b*' and shields,
39: 9 the shields and the *b*', the bows

bud See also BUDDED; BUDS.
Job 14: 9 the scent of water it will *b*', and
38:27 to cause the *b*' of the tender herb
Ps 132:17 I make the horn of David to *b*':
Ca 7:12 the pomegranates *b*' forth: there
Isa 18: 5 when the *b*' is perfect, and the
27: 6 Israel shall blossom and *b*', and
55:10 maketh it bring forth and *b*', that
61:11 the earth bringeth forth her *b*',
Eze 16: 7 to multiply as the *b*' of the field,
29:21 of the house of Israel to *b*' forth,
Ho 8: 7 the *b*' shall yield no meal: if so

budded
Ge 40:10 it was as though it *b*', and her
Nu 17: 8 Aaron for the house of Levi was *b*',
Ca 6:11 and the pomegranates *b*'.
Eze 7:10 hath blossomed, pride hath *b*'.
Heb 9: 4 Aaron's rod that *b*', and the tables

buds
Nu 17: 8 was budded, and brought forth *b*',

buffet See also BUFFETED.
M'r 14:65 to cover his face, and to *b*' him,
2Co 12: 7 messenger of Satan to *b*' me, lest

buffeted
M't 26:67 they spit in his face and *b*' him;
1Co 4:11 and are *b*', and have no certain
1Pe 2:20 when ye be *b*' for your faults, ye

build^ See also BUILDED; BUILDEST; BUILDETH; BUILDING; BUILT.
Ge 11: 4 Go to, let us *b*' us a city and
8 and they left off to *b*' the city.
Ex 20:25 thou shalt not *b*' it of hewn stone:
Nu 23: 1, 29 *B*' me here seven altars, and
32:16 We will *b*' sheepfolds here for our
24 *B*' you cities for your little ones,
De 20:20 and thou shalt *b*' bulwarks against
25: 9 will not *b*' up his brother's house.
27: 5 there shalt thou *b*' an altar unto
6 Thou shalt *b*' the altar of the Lord
28:30 thou shalt *b*' an house, and thou
Jos 22:26 Let us now prepare to *b*' us an
29 to *b*' an altar for burnt offerings,
J'g 6:26 And *b*' an altar unto the Lord
Ru 4:11 two did *b*' the house of Israel:
1Sa 2:35 and I will *b*' him a sure house;
2Sa 7: 5 Shalt thou *b*' me an house for me
7 Why *b*' ye not me an house of
13 shall *b*' an house for my name,
27 saying, I will *b*' thee an house:
24:21 to *b*' an altar unto the Lord, that
1Ki 2:36 *B*' thee an house in Jerusalem
5: 3 my father could not *b*' an house
5 behold, I purpose to *b*' an house
5 shall *b*' an house unto my name.
18 timber and stones to *b*' the house.
6: 1 that he began to *b*' the house of
8:16 tribes of Israel to *b*' an house,
17 David my father to *b*' an house
18 to *b*' an house unto my name, thou
1Ki 8:19 thou shalt not *b*' the house; but
19 shall *b*' the house unto my name.
9:15 to *b*' the house of the Lord, and
19 which Solomon desired to *b*' in
24 built for her: then did he *b*' Millo.
11: 7 Then did Solomon *b*' an high place
38 and *b*' thee a sure house,
16:34 did Hiel the Beth-elite *b*' Jericho:
1Ch 14: 1 carpenters, to *b*' him an house.
17: 4 Thou shalt not *b*' me an house
10 the Lord will *b*' thee an house.
12 He shall *b*' me an house, and I will
25 that thou wilt *b*' him an house:
21:22 that I may *b*' an altar therein unto
22: 2 stones to *b*' the house of God.
6 him to *b*' an house for the Lord
7 it was in my mind to *b*' an house
8 thou shalt not *b*' an house unto
10 shall *b*' an house for my name;
11 *b*' the house of the Lord thy God,
19 and *b*' the sanctuary of the Lord
28: 2 in mine heart to *b*' an house of
3 Thou shalt not *b*' an house for my
6 shall *b*' my house and my courts,
10 to *b*' an house for the sanctuary:
29:16 to *b*' thee an house for thine holy
19 and to *b*' the palace, for the which
2Ch 2: 1 Solomon determined to *b*' an house
3 send him cedars to *b*' him an
4 Behold, I *b*' an house to the name
5 the house which I *b*' is great: for
6 who is able to *b*' him an house,
6 that I should *b*' him an house,
9 the house which I am about to *b*'
12 that might *b*' an house for the Lord,
3: 1 Solomon began to *b*' the house
2 And he began to *b*' in the second
6: 5 to *b*' an house in, that my name
7 David my father to *b*' an house
8 heart to *b*' an house for my name,
9 thou shalt not *b*' the house; but
9 he shall *b*' the house for my name.
8: 6 desired to *b*' in Jerusalem,
14: 7 Let us *b*' these cities, and make
35: 3 son of David king of Israel did *b*';
36:23 to *b*' him an house in Jerusalem.
Ezr 1: 2 to *b*' him an house at Jerusalem,
3 and *b*' the house of the Lord God
5 to *b*' the house of the Lord which
4: 2 Let us *b*' with you: for we seek
3 to *b*' an house unto our God;
3 but we ourselves together will *b*'
5: 2 and began to *b*' the house of God
3 Who hath commanded you to *b*'
9 commanded you to *b*' this house,
13 made a decree to *b*' this house of
17 was made of Cyrus the king to *b*'
6: 7 the elders of the Jews *b*' this house
Ne 2: 5 sepulchres, that I may *b*' it.
17 let us *b*' up the wall of Jerusalem,
18 Let us rise up and *b*'. So they
20 we his servants will arise and *b*':
3: 3 did the sons of Hassenaah *b*', who
4: 3 Even that which they *b*', if a fox
10 that we are not able to *b*' the wall.
Ps 28: 5 destroy them, and not *b*' them up.
51:18 *b*' thou the walls of Jerusalem.
69:35 and will *b*' the cities of Judah:
89: 4 *b*' up thy throne to all generations.
102:16 the Lord shall *b*' up Zion, he shall
127: 1 Except the Lord *b*' the house, they
147: 2 The Lord doth *b*' up Jerusalem:
Pr 24:27 and afterwards *b*' thine house.
Ec 3: 3 break down, and a time to *b*' up;
Ca 8: 9 will *b*' upon her a palace of silver:
Isa 9:10 but we will *b*' with hewn stones:
45:13 he shall *b*' my city, and he shall
58:12 they that shall be of thee shall *b*'
60:10 the sons of strangers shall *b*' up
61: 4 And they shall *b*' the old wastes,
65:21 shall *b*' houses, and inhabit them;
22 shall not *b*', and another inhabit;
66: 1 where is the house that ye *b*' unto
Jer 1:10 to throw down, to *b*', and to plant.
18: 9 concerning a kingdom, to *b*' and
22:14 I will *b*' me a wide house and large
24: 6 I will *b*' them, and not pull them
29: 5, 28 *B*' ye houses, and dwell in them;
31: 4 Again I will *b*' thee, and thou shalt
28 so will I watch over them, to *b*',
33: 7 and will *b*' them, as at the first.
35: 7 Neither shall ye *b*' house, nor sow
9 Nor to *b*' houses for us to dwell in:
42:10 then will I *b*' you, and not pull you
Eze 4: 2 and *b*' a fort against it, and cast a
11: 3 let us *b*' houses: this city is the
21:22 to cast a mount, and to *b*' a fort.
28:26 and shall *b*' houses, and plant
36:36 that I the Lord *b*' the ruined
Da 9:25 to restore and to *b*' Jerusalem
Am 9:11 I will *b*' it as in the days of old:
14 and they shall *b*' the waste cities,
Mic 3:10 They *b*' up Zion with blood, and
Zep 1:13 they shall also *b*' houses, but not
Hag 1: 8 and *b*' the house; and I will take
Zec 5:11 To *b*' it an house in the land of
6:12 and he shall *b*' the temple of the
13 Even he shall *b*' the temple of
15 and *b*' in the temple of the Lord,
9: 3 Tyrus did *b*' herself a strong hold,
Mal 1: 4 return and *b*' the desolate places;
4 shall *b*', but I will throw down;
M't 16:18 upon this rock I will *b*' my
23:29 because ye *b*' the tombs of the
26:61 God, and to *b*' it in three days.
M'r 14:58 within three days I will *b*' another
Lu 11:47 *b*' the sepulchres of the prophets,
48 them, and ye *b*' their sepulchres.
12:18 I will pull down my barns, and *b*'
14:28 intending to *b*' a tower, sitteth
30 This man began to *b*', and was not
Ac 7:49 what house will ye *b*' me? saith
15:16 *b*' again the tabernacle of David,
16 I will *b*' again the ruins thereof,
20:32 to *b*' you up, and to give you an
Ro 15:20 lest I should *b*' upon another
1Co 3:12 Now if any man *b*' upon this
Gal 2:18 if I *b*' again the things which I

builded See also BUILDEDST; BUILT.
Ge 4:17 and he *b*' a city, and called the
8:20 Noah *b*' an altar unto the Lord;
10:11 and *b*' Nineveh, and the city
11: 5 which the children of men *b*'.
12: 7 there *b*' he an altar unto the Lord,
8 and there he *b*' an altar unto the
26:25 And he *b*' an altar there, and
Ex 24: 4 and *b*' an altar under the hill,
Nu 32:38 unto the cities which they *b*'.
Jos 22:16 in that ye have *b*' you an altar,
1Ki 8:27 less this house that I have *b*?
43 this house, which I have *b*', is
15:22 thereof, wherewith Baasha had *b*';
2Ki 23:13 Solomon the king of Israel had *b*'
1Ch 22: 5 to be *b*' for the Lord must be
Ezr 3: 2 and *b*' the altar of the God of Israel,
4: 1 children of the captivity *b*' the
13 if this city be *b*', and the walls set
16 if this city be *b*' again, and the
21 and that this city be not *b*', until
5: 8 which is *b*' with great stones,
11 *b*' these many years ago, which
11 which a great king of Israel *b*' and
15 let the house of God be *b*' in this
6: 3 Let the house be *b*', the place
14 And the elders of the Jews *b*',
14 And they *b*', and finished it,
Ne 3: 1 and they *b*' the sheep gate;
2 And next unto him *b*' the men
2 And next to him *b*' Zaccur
4: 1 heard that we *b*' the wall, he was
17 They which *b*' on the wall, and
18 girded by his side, and so *b*'.
6: 1 heard that I had *b*' the wall, and
7: 4 and the houses were not *b*'.
12:29 the singers had *b*' them villages
Job 20:19 away an house which he *b*' not;
Ps 122: 3 Jerusalem is *b*' as a city that is
Pr 9: 1 Wisdom hath *b*' her house, she
24: 3 Through wisdom is an house *b*';
Ec 2: 4 I *b*' me houses; I planted me
Ca 4: 4 tower of David *b*' for an armoury,
Jer 30:18 and the city shall be *b*' upon
La 3: 5 He hath *b*' against me, and
Eze 36:10 and the wastes shall be *b*':
33 cities, and the wastes shall be *b*'.
Lu 17:28 they sold, they planted, they *b*';
Eph 2:22 In whom ye also are *b*' together
Heb 3: 3 as he who hath *b*' the house hath
4 every house is *b*' by some man;

buildedst
De 6:10 goodly cities, which thou *b*' not,

builder See also BUILDERS; MASTERBUILDER.
Heb 11:10 whose *b*' and maker is God.

builders
1Ki 5:18 Solomon's *b*' and Hiram's *b*'
2Ki 12:11 to the carpenters and *b*', that
22: 6 Unto carpenters, and *b*', and
2Ch 34:11 to the artificers and *b*' gave they it,
Ezr 3:10 when the *b*' laid the foundation
Ne 4: 5 thee to anger before the *b*'.
18 For the *b*', every one had his
Ps 118:22 the stone which the *b*' refused
Eze 27: 4 thy *b*' have perfected thy beauty.
M't 21:42 The stone which the *b*' rejected,
M'r 12:10 The stone which the *b*' rejected
Lu 20:17 The stone which the *b*' rejected,
Ac 4:11 which was set at nought of you *b*',
1Pe 2: 7 the stone which the *b*' disallowed,

buildest
De 22: 8 When thou *b*' a new house,
Neh 6: 6 which cause thou *b*' the wall,
Eze 16:31 In that thou *b*' thine eminent
M't 27:40 temple and *b*' it in three days,
M'r 15:29 temple, and *b*' it in three days,

buildeth
Jos 6:26 and *b*' this city Jericho: he shall
Job 27:18 he *b*' his house as a moth, and
Pr 14: 1 Every wise woman *b*' her house:
Jer 22:13 Woe unto him that *b*' his house
Ho 8:14 and *b*' temples; and Judah
Am 9: 6 that *b*' his stories in the heaven,
Hab 2:12 Woe to him that *b*' a town with
1Co 3:10 foundation, and another *b*'
10 take heed how he *b*' thereupon.

building See also BUILDINGS.
Jos 22:19 in *b*' you an altar beside the
1Ki 3: 1 made an end of *b*' his own house,
6: 7 when it was in *b*', was built of
7 in the house, while it was in *b*'.
12 which thou art in *b*', if thou wilt
38 So was he seven years in *b*' it.
7: 1 Solomon was *b*' his own house
9: 1 Solomon had finished the *b*' of
15:21 that he left off *b*' of Ramah,
1Ch 28: 2 and had made ready for the *b*':
2Ch 3: 3 for the *b*' of the house of God.
16: 5 that he left off *b*' of Ramah,
6 wherewith Baasha was *b*'; and
Ezr 4: 4 Judah, and troubled them in *b*',

Ezr 4:12 b' the rebellious and the bad
5: 4 of the men that make this b'?
16 even until now hath it been in b',
6: 8 for the b' of this house of God:
Ec 10:18 By much slothfulness the b'
Eze 17:17 and b' forts, to cut off many
40: 5 the breadth of the b', one reed;
41:12 Now the b' that was before the
12 broad; and the wall of the b'
13 and the b', with the walls thereof,
15 the length of the b' over against
42: 1 before the b' toward the north.
5 and than the middlemost of the b'.
42: 6 therefore the b' was straitened
10 place, and over against the b'.
46:23 there was a row of b' round about
Joh 2:20 was this temple in b', and wilt
1Co 3: 9 husbandry, ye are God's b'.
2Co 5: 1 we have a b' of God, an house
Eph 2:21 In whom all the b' fitly framed
Heb 9:11 that is to say, not of this b';
Jude 20 b' up yourselves on your most
Re 21:18 the b' of the wall of it was of

buildings
M't 24: 1 to shew him the b' of the temple.
M'r 13: 1 stones and what b' are here!
2 him, Seest thou these great b'?

built^ See also BUILDED.
Ge 13:18 b' there an altar unto the Lord.
22: 9 and Abraham b' an altar there,
33:17 and b' him an house, and made
35: 7 And he b' there an altar,
Ex 1:11 b' for Pharaoh treasure cities,
17:15 And Moses b' an altar, and called
32: 5 he b' an altar before it; and Aaron
Nu 13:22 Hebron was b' seven years before
21:27 let the city of Sihon be b' and
23:14 and b' seven altars, and offered
32:34 And the children of Gad b' Dibon,
37 the children of Reuben b' Heshbon,
De 8:12 and hast b' goodly houses, and
13:16 for ever; it shall not be b' again.
20: 5 that hath b' a new house, and
Jos 8:30 Joshua b' an altar unto the Lord
19:50 Ephraim: and he b' the city,
22:10 tribe of Manasseh b' there an altar
11 b' an altar over against the land
23 That we have b' us an altar to
24:13 cities which ye b' not, and ye
J'g 1:26 and b' a city, and called the name
6:24 Then Gideon b' an altar there
28 offered upon the altar that was b'.
18:28 And they b' a city, and dwelt
21: 4 and b' there an altar, and offered
1Sa 7:17 there he b' an altar unto the Lord.
14:35 And Saul b' an altar unto the Lord:
35 same was the first altar that he b'
2Sa 5: 9 And David b' round about from
11 and they b' David an house.
24:25 And David b' there an altar unto
1Ki 3: 2 b' unto the name of the Lord,
6: 2 the house which king Solomon b'
5 against the wall of the house he b'
7 was b' of stone made ready before
9 So he b' the house, and finished it;
10 And then he b' chambers against
14 So Solomon b' the house, and
15 And he b' the walls of the house
16 And he b' twenty cubits on the
16 with boards of cedar: he even b'
36 And he b' the inner court with
7: 2 He b' also the house of the forest
8:13 I have surely b' thee an house to
20 promised, and have b' an house
44 house that I have b' for thy name:
48 and the house which I have b'
9: 3 thou hast b', to put my name
10 Solomon had b' the two houses,
17 And Solomon b' Gezer, and
24 house which Solomon had b' for
25 altar which he b' unto the Lord,
10: 4 and the house that he had b',
11:27 Solomon b' Millo, and repaired the
38 a sure house, as I b' for David,
12:25 Then Jeroboam b' Shechem in
25 out from thence, and b' Penuel.
14:23 they also b' them high places,
15:17 up against Judah, and b' Ramah,
22 and king Asa b' with them Geba
23 the cities which he b', are they
16:24 and b' on the hill, and called
24 the name of the city which he b',
32 Baal, which he had b' in Samaria.
18:32 And with the stones he b' an altar
22:39 made, and all the cities that he b',
2Ki 14:22 He b' Elath, and restored it to
15:35 He b' the higher gate of the house
16:11 And Urijah the priest b' an altar
18 that they had b' in the house, and
17: 9 and they b' them high places in all
21: 3 he b' up again the high places
4 And he b' altars in the house of
5 And he b' altars for all the host of
25: 1 they b' forts against it round about.
1Ch 6:10 that Solomon b' in Jerusalem:)
32 until Solomon had b' the house of
7:24 who b' Beth-horon the nether, and
8:12 who b' Ono,and Lod, with the towns
11: 8 And he b' the city round about,
17: 6 Why have ye not b' me an house
21:26 And David b' there an altar unto
29:19 the house that is to be b' to the
2Ch 6: 2 I have b' an house of habitation
10 and have b' the house for the name
18 less this house which I have b'!
2Ch 6:33 this house which I have b' is called
34 which I have b' for thy name;
38 toward the house which I have b'
8: 1 Solomon had b' the house of the
2 Solomon b' them, and caused the
4 he b' Tadmor in the wilderness,
4 store cities, which he b' in Hamath.
5 Also he b' Beth-horon the upper,
11 house that he had b' for her:
12 which he had b' before the porch,
9: 3 and the house that he had b',
11: 5 b' cities for defence in Judah.
6 He b' even Beth-lehem, and Etam,
14: 6 And he b' fenced cities in Judah:
7 So they b' and prospered.
16: 1 and b' Ramah, to the intent that
6 he b' therewith Geba and Mizpah.
17:12 he b' in Judah castles, and cities
20: 8 b' thee a sanctuary therein for thy
26: 2 He b' Eloth, and restored it to
6 and b' cities about Ashdod, and
9 Uzziah b' towers in Jerusalem at
10 Also he b' towers in the desert,
27: 3 He b' the high gate of the house of
3 and on the wall of Ophel he b'
4 he b' cities in the mountains of
4 and in the forests he b' castles
32: 5 and b' up all the wall that was
33: 3 For he b' again the high places
4 Also he b' altars in the house of
5 And he b' altars for all the host of
14 after this he b' a wall without the
15 all the altars that he had b' in the
19 places wherein he b' high places,
Ne 3:13 they b' it, and set up the doors
14 he b' it, and set up the doors
15 he b' it, and covered it, and set up
4: 6 So b' we the wall; and all the wall
7: 1 when the wall was b', and I had set
Job 3:14 b' desolate places for themselves;
12:14 down, and it cannot be b' again:
22:23 thou shalt be b' up, thou shalt put
Ps 78:69 b' his sanctuary like high palaces,
89: 2 Mercy shall be b' up for ever: thy
Ec 9:14 and b' great bulwarks against it:
Isa 5: 2 and b' a tower in the midst of it,
25: 2 to be no city; it shall never be b'.
44:26 Ye shall be b', and I will raise up
28 Thou shalt be b'; and to the
Jer 7:31 And they have b' the high places
12:16 then shall they be b' in the midst
19: 5 They have b' also the high places
31: 4 thou shalt be b', O virgin of Israel:
38 the city shall be b' to the Lord
32:35 And they b' the high places of Baal,
45: 4 which I have b' will I break down,
52: 4 and b' forts against it round about.
Eze 13:10 one b' up a wall, and, lo, others
16:24 also b' unto thee an eminent place,
25 Thou hast b' thy high place at
26:14 Thou shalt be b' no more: for I the
Da 4:30 I have b' for the house of the
9:25 the street shall be b' again,
Am 5:11 ye have b' houses of hewn stone,
Mic 7:11 the day that thy walls are to be b',
Hag 1: 2 that the Lord's house should be b'.
Zec 1:16 my house shall be b' in it, saith
8: 9 laid, that the temple might be b'.
M't 7:24 which b' his house upon a rock:
26 which b' his house upon the sand:
21:33 winepress in it, and b' a tower,
M'r 12: 1 and b' a tower, and let it out to
Lu 4:29 whereon their city was b', that
6:48 a man which b' an house, and
49 a man that . . . b' an house upon
7: 5 and he hath b' us a synagogue.
Ac 7:47 But Solomon b' him an house.
1Co 3:14 abide which he hath b' thereupon,
Eph 2:20 And are b' upon the foundation
Col 2: 7 Rooted and b' up in him, and
Heb 3: 4 but he that b' all things is God.
1Pe 2: 5 are b' up a spiritual house,

Bukki (*buk'-ki*)
Nu 34:22 of Dan, B' the son of Jogli.
1Ch 6: 5 Abishua begat B', and B' begat
51 B' his son, Uzzi his son, Zerahiah
Ezr 7: 4 the son of Uzzi, the son of B',

Bukkiah (*buk-ki'-ah*)
1Ch 25: 4 B', Mattaniah, Uzziel, Shebuel,
13 The sixth to B', he, his sons, and

Bul (*bul*)
1Ki 6:38 in the month B', which is the

bull See also BULLS; BULRUSH.
Job 21:10 Their b' gendereth, and faileth
Isa 51:20 as a wild b' in a net: they are

bullock See also BULLOCK'S; BULLOCKS.
Ex 29: 1 Take one young b', and two rams
3 with the b' and the two rams.
10 thou shalt cause a b' to be brought
10 hands upon the head of the b'.
11 shalt kill the b' before the Lord,
12 take of the blood of the b', and
14 the flesh of the b', and his skin,
36 And thou shalt offer every day a b'
Le 1: 5 kill the b' before the Lord:
4: 3 a young b' without blemish unto
4 he shall bring the b' unto the door
4 the bullock's head, and kill the b'
7 the blood of the b' at the bottom
8 fat of the b' for the sin offering;
10 from the b' of the sacrifice of
11 skin of the b', and all his flesh,
12 Even the whole b' shall he carry
14 congregation shall offer a young b'
Le 4:15 upon the head of the b' before the
15 Lord: and the b' shall be killed
20 And he shall do with the b'
20 as he did with the b' for
21 he shall carry forth the b' without
21 burn him as he burned the first b':
8: 2 a b' for the sin offering, and two
14 the b' for the sin offering: and
14 hands upon the head of the b' for
17 the b', and his hide, his flesh, and
9: 4 Also a b' and a ram for peace
18 He slew also the b' and the ram
19 the fat of the b' and of the ram,
16: 3 a young b' for a sin offering, and
6 shall offer his b' of the sin offering,
11 Aaron shall bring the b' of the
11 shall kill the b' of the sin offering
14 take of the blood of the b', and
15 as he did with the blood of the b',
18 and shall take of the blood of the b',
27 the b' for the sin offering, and
22:23 Either a b' or a lamb, that hath
27 When a b', or a sheep, or a goat,
23:18 and one young b', and two rams:
Nu 7:15, 21, 27, 33, 39, 45, 51, 57, 63, 69, 75, 81
One young b', one ram, one lamb
8: 8 Then let them take a young b' with
8 another young b' shalt thou take
15: 8 when thou preparest a b' for
9 with a b' a meat offering of
11 Thus shall it be done for one b',
24 offer one young b' for a burnt
23: 2 offered on every altar a b' and a
4 offered upon every altar a b' and
14, 30 offered a b' and a ram on every
28:12 mingled with oil, for one b';
14 half an hin of wine unto a b', and
20 tenth deals shall ye offer for a b',
28 three tenth deals unto one b', two
29: 2 one young b', one ram, and seven
3 three tenth deals for a b', and two
8 for a sweet savour; one young b',
9 three tenth deals to a b', and two
14 deals unto every b' of the thirteen
36 one b', one ram, seven lambs of
37 for the b', for the ram, and for the
De 15:19 the firstling of thy b', nor shear
17: 1 any b', or sheep, wherein is
33:17 like the firstling of his b', and his
J'g 6:25 Take thy father's young b',
25 even the second b' of seven years
26 and take the second b', and offer
28 the second b' was offered upon the
1Sa 1:25 And they slew a b', and brought
1Ki 18:23 and let them choose one b' for
23 and I will dress the other b',
25 Choose you one b' for yourselves,
26 they took the b' which was given
33 and cut the b' in pieces; and laid
2Ch 13: 9 consecrate himself with a young b'
Ps 50: 9 I will take no b' out of thy house,
69:31 or b' that hath horns and hoofs.
Isa 65:25 lion shall eat straw like the b':
Jer 31:18 a b' unaccustomed to the yoke:
Eze 43:19 a young b' for a sin offering.
21 take the b' also of the sin offering,
22 as they did cleanse it with the b'.
23 offer a young b' without blemish,
25 they shall also prepare a young b',
45:18 take a young b' without blemish,
22 for all the people of the land a b'
24 an ephah for a b', and an ephah
46: 6 a young b' without blemish,
7 an ephah for a b', and an ephah
11 shall be an ephah to a b', and an

bullock's
Le 4: 4 his hand upon the b' head,
5 shall take of the b' blood,
16 anointed, shall bring of the b'

bullocks
Nu 7:87 were twelve b', the rams twelve,
88 were twenty and four b', the rams
8:12 upon the heads of the b':
23:29 prepare me here seven b' and
28:11 unto the Lord; two young b',
19 two young b', and one ram,
27 unto the Lord; two young b',
29:13 thirteen young b', two rams,
14 every bullock of the thirteen b',
17 ye shall offer twelve young b',
18 their drink offerings for the b',
20 the third day eleven b', two rams,
21 for the b', for the rams, and for
23 on the fourth day ten b', two rams,
24 drink offerings for the b', for the
26 And on the fifth day nine b', two
27 offerings for the b', for the rams,
29 on the sixth day eight b', two
30 b', for the rams, and for the lambs,
32 And on the seventh day seven b',
33 and their drink offerings for the b',
1Sa 1:24 him up with her, with three b',
1Ki 18:23 them therefore give us two b';
1Ch 15:26 they offered seven b', and seven
29:21 a thousand b', a thousand rams,
2Ch 29:21 they brought seven b', and seven
22 they killed the b', and the priests
32 threescore and ten b', an hundred
30:24 thousand b' and seven thousand
24 to the congregation a thousand b'
35: 7 three thousand b': these were
Ezr 6: 9 both young b', and rams, and
17 an hundred b', two hundred rams,
7:17 buy speedily with this money b',
8:35 twelve b' for all Israel, ninety

Job 42: 8 take unto you now seven b' and
Ps 51:19 then shall they offer b' upon thine
66:15 I will offer b' with goats.
Isa 1:11 I delight not in the blood of b',
34: 7 and the b' with the bulls; and
Jer 46:21 in the midst of her like fatted b';
50:27 Slay all her b'; let them go down
Eze 39:18 of lambs, and of goats, of b', all of
45:23 seven b' and seven rams without
Hos 12:11 they sacrifice b' in Gilgal; yea,

bulls
Ge 32:15 forty kine, and ten b', twenty
Ps 22:12 Many b' have compassed me:
12 strong b' of Bashan have beset me
50:13 Will I eat the flesh of b', or drink
68:30 the multitude of the b', with the
Isa 34: 7 the bullocks with the b'; and their
Jer 50:11 heifer at grass, and bellow as b';
52:20 and twelve brasen b' that were
Heb 9:13 if the blood of b' and of goats,
10: 4 not possible that the blood of b'

bulrush See also BULRUSHES.
Isa 58: 5 bow down his head as a b',

bulrushes
Ex 2: 3 took for him an ark of b',
Isa 18: 2 in vessels of b' upon the waters,

bulwarks
De 20:20 shalt build b' against the city
2Ch 26:15 be on the towers and upon the b',
Ps 48:13 Mark ye well her b', consider her
Ec 9:14 and built great b' against it:
Isa 26: 1 will God appoint for walls and b'.

Bunah *(boo'-nah)*
1Ch 2:25 Ram the firstborn, and B', and

bunch See also BUNCHES.
Ex 12:22 ye shall take a b' of hyssop, and

bunches
2Sa 16: 1 an hundred b' of raisins, and an
1Ch 12:40 cakes of figs, and b' of raisins,
Isa 30: 6 upon the b' of camels, to a

bundle See also BUNDLES.
Ge 42:35 every man's b' of money was in
1Sa 25:29 bound in the b' of life with the
Ca 1:13 A b' of myrrh is my wellbeloved
Ac 28: 3 gathered a b' of sticks, and laid

bundles
Ge 42:35 their father saw the b' of money,
M't 13:30 bind them in b' to burn them:

Bunni *(bun'-ni)*
Ne 9: 4 Shebaniah, B', Sherebiah, Bani,
10:15 B', Azgad, Bebai,
11:15 son of Hashabiah, the son of B';

burden See also BURDENED; BURDENS; BURDENSOME.
Ex 18:22 they shall bear the b' with thee.
23: 5 lying under his b', and wouldest
Nu 4:15 the b' of the sons of Kohath in the
19 one to his service and to his b':
31 And this is the charge of their b',
32 of the charge of their b'.
47 service of the b' in the tabernacle
49 according to his b': thus were they
11:11 the b' of all this people upon me?
17 they shall bear the b' of the people
De 1:12 and your b', and your strife?
2Sa 15:33 then thou shalt be a b' unto me:
19:35 should thy servant be yet a b'
2Ki 5:17 servant two mules' b' of earth?
8: 9 forty camels' b', and came and
9:25 the Lord laid this b' upon him;
2Ch 35: 3 not be a b' upon your shoulders:
Ne 13:19 there should no b' be brought in
Job 7:20 so that I am a b' to myself?
Ps 38: 4 as an heavy b' they are too heavy
55:22 Cast thy b' upon the Lord, and he
81: 6 removed his shoulder from the b':
Ec 12: 5 and the grasshopper shall be a b',
Isa 9: 4 broken the yoke of his b', and the
10:27 his b' shall be taken away from off
13: 1 The b' of Babylon, which Isaiah
14:25 and his b' depart from off their
28 that king Ahaz died was this b'.
15: 1 The b' of Moab. Because in the
17: 1 The b' of Damascus. Behold,
19: 1 The b' of Egypt. Behold, the Lord
21: 1 The b' of the desert of the sea.
11 The b' of Dumah. He calleth to
13 The b' upon Arabia. In the forest
22: 1 The b' of the valley of vision.
25 fall; and the b' that was upon it
23: 1 The b' of Tyre. Howl, ye ships
30: 6 The b' of the beasts of the south:
27 the b' thereof is heavy: his lips
46: 1 they are a b' to the weary beast.
2 they could not deliver the b', but
Jer 17:21 bear no b' on the sabbath day,
22 Neither carry forth a b' out of
24 to bring in no b' through the gates
27 not to bear a b', even entering in at
23:33 saying, What is the b' of the Lord?
33 then say unto them, What b'?
34 that shall say, The b' of the Lord,
36 And the b' of the Lord shall ye
36 every man's word shall be his b';
38 ye say, The b' of the Lord;
38 this word, The b' of the Lord,
38 shall not say, The b' of the Lord;
Eze 12:10 This b' concerneth the prince
Ho 8:10 for the b' of the king of princes.
Na 1: 1 The b' of Nineveh. The book of
Hab 1: 1 b' which Habakkuk the prophet
Zep 3:18 whom the reproach of it was a b'.
Zec 9: 1 The b' of the word of the Lord in
12: 1 The b' of the word of the Lord
3 all that b' themselves with it
Mal 1: 1 The b' of the word of the Lord to
M't 11:30 yoke is easy, and my b' is light.
20:12 which have borne the b' and heat
Ac 15:28 upon you no greater b' than these
21: 3 the ship was to unlade her b'.
2Co 12:16 I did not b' you: nevertheless,
Ga 6: 5 every man shall bear his own b'.
Re 2:24 will put upon you none other b'.

burdened
2Co 5: 4 do groan, being b': not for that
8:13 other men be eased, and ye b':

burdens
Ge 49:14 crouching down between two b':
Ex 1:11 to afflict them with their b'.
2:11 looked on their b': and he spied
5: 4 their works? get you unto your b'.
5 ye make them rest from their b'.
6: 6 from under the b' of the Egyptians,
7 bringeth you out from under the b'
Nu 4:24 Gershonites, to serve, and for b':
27 the Gershonites, in all their b',
27 unto them in charge all their b'.
1Ki 5:15 and ten thousand that bare b',
2Ch 2: 2 ten thousand men to bear b',
18 to be bearers of b', and fourscore
24:27 the greatness of the b' laid upon
34:13 over the bearers of b', and were
Ne 4:10 The strength of the bearers of b'
17 and they that bare b', with those
13:15 all manner of b', which they
Isa 58: 6 to undo the heavy b', and to
La 2:14 false b' and causes of banishment.
Am 5:11 ye take from him b' of wheat:
M't 23: 4 For they bind heavy b' and
Lu 11:46 with b' grievous to be borne, and
46 ye yourselves touch not the b'
Ga 6: 2 Bear ye one another's b', and

burdensome
Zec 12: 3 will I make Jerusalem a b' stone
2Co 11: 9 kept myself from being b' unto
12:13 I myself was not b' to you?
14 I will not be b' to you: for I seek
1Th 2: 6 we might have been b', as the

burial
2Ch 26:23 in the field of the b' which
Ec 6: 3 good, and also that ye have no b';
Isa 14:20 not be joined with them in b',
Jer 22:19 with the b' of an ass, drawn and
M't 26:12 my body, she did it for my b'.
Ac 8: 2 men carried Stephen to his b',

buried
Ge 15:15 thou shalt be b' in a good old age.
23:19 Abraham b' Sarah his wife in the
25: 9 his sons Isaac and Ishmael b' him
10 there was Abraham b', and Sarah
35: 8 nurse died, and she was b'
19 Rachel died, and was b' in the
29 his sons Esau and Jacob b' him.
48: 7 and I b' her there in the way of
49:31 There they b' Abraham and Sarah
31 there they b' Isaac and Rebekah
31 and there I b' Leah.
50:13 and b' him in the cave of the field
14 after he had b' his father.
Nu 11:34 because there they b' the people
20: 1 Miriam died there, and was b'
33: 4 For the Egyptians b' all their
De 10: 6 Aaron died, and there he was b';
34: 6 And he b' him in a valley in the
Jos 24:30 And they b' him in the border of
32 b' they in Shechem, in a parcel
33 and they b' him in a hill that
J'g 2: 9 And they b' him in the border of
8:32 died in a good old age, and was b'
10: 2 and died, and was b' in Shamir.
5 Jair died, and was b' in Camon.
12: 7 the Gileadite, and was b' in one of
10 Ibzan, and was b' at Beth-lehem.
12 died, and was b' in Aijalon
15 died, and was b' in Pirathon in
16:31 b' him between Zorah and Eshtaol
Ru 1:17 and there will I be b': the Lord
1Sa 25: 1 and b' him in his house at Ramah.
28: 3 and b' him in Ramah, even in
31:13 b' them under a tree at Jabesh,
2Sa 2: 4 Jabesh-gilead were they that b'
5 even unto Saul, and have b' him.
32 and b' him in the sepulchre of his
3:32 And they b' Abner in Hebron:
4:12 head of Ish-bosheth, and b' it
17:23 and was b' in the sepulchre of his
19:37 be b' by the grave of my father
21:14 and Jonathan his son b' they
1Ki 2:10 slept with his fathers, and was b'
34 and he was b' in his own house
11:43 slept with his fathers, and was b'
13:31 after he had b' him, that he spake
31 wherein the man of God is b';
14:18 And they b' him; and all Israel
31 slept with his fathers, and was b'
15: 8 they b' him in the city of David:
24 slept with his fathers, and was b'
16: 6, 28 with his fathers, and was b'
22:37 and they b' the king in Samaria.
50 slept with his fathers, and was b'
2Ki 8:24 slept with his fathers, and was b'
9:28 and b' him in his sepulchre with
10:35 fathers: and they b' him in
12:21 and they b' him with his fathers
13: 9 and they b' him in Samaria: and
13 and Joash was b' in Samaria with
2Ki 13:20 And Elisha died, and they b' him.
14:16 slept with his fathers, and was b'
20 and he was b' at Jerusalem with
15: 7 and they b' him with his fathers
38 slept with his fathers, and was b'
16:20 slept with his fathers, and was b'
21:18 slept with his fathers, and was b'
26 And he was b' in his sepulchre
23:30 and b' him in his own sepulchre.
1Ch 10:12 and b' their bones under the oak
2Ch 9:31 and he was b' in the city of David
12:16 slept with his fathers, and was b'
14: 1 they b' him in the city of David:
16:14 b' him in his own sepulchres,
21: 1 slept with his fathers, and was b'
20 Howbeit they b' him in the city of
22: 9 they had slain him, they b' him:
24:16 they b' him in the city of David
25 and they b' him in the city of David,
25 they b' him not in the sepulchres
25:28 and b' him with his fathers in the
26:23 b' him with his fathers in the field
27: 9 they b' him in the city of David:
28:27 and they b' him in the city, even
32:33 and they b' him in the chiefest of
33:20 and they b' him in his own house:
35:24 and was b' in one of the sepulchres
Job 27:15 remain of him shall be b' in death:
Ec 8:10 And so I saw the wicked b', who
Jer 8: 2 shall not be gathered, nor be b';
16: 4 lamented; neither shall they be b';
6 they shall not be b', neither shall
20: 6 thou shalt die, and shalt be b'
22:19 He shall be b' with the burial of an
25:33 lamented, neither gathered, nor b';
Eze 39:15 till the buriers have b' it in the
M't 14:12 and b' it, and went and told Jesus.
Lu 16:22 rich man also died, and was b';
Ac 2:29 he is both dead and b', and his
5: 6 and carried him out, and b' him.
9 the feet of them which have b' thy
10 carrying her forth, b' her by her
Ro 6: 4 we are b' with him by baptism
1Co 15: 4 And that he was b', and that he
Col 2:12 B' with him in baptism, wherein

buriers
Eze 39:15 till the b' have buried it in the

burn See also BURNED; BURNETH; BURNING; BURNT.
Ge 11: 3 let us make brick, and b' them
44:18 let not thine anger b' against thy
Ex 12:10 until the morning ye shall b' with
27:20 light, to cause the lamp to b'
29:13 them, and b' them upon the altar.
14 his dung, shalt thou b' with fire
18 And thou shalt b' the whole ram
25 and b' them upon the altar for a
34 then thou shalt b' the remainder
30: 1 make an altar to b' incense upon:
7 And Aaron shall b' thereon sweet
7 lamps, he shall b' incense upon it.
8 at even, he shall b' incense upon
20 to b' offering made by fire unto
Le 1: 9 the priest shall b' all on the altar,
13 and b' it upon the altar: it is a
15 b' it on the altar; and the blood
17 the priest shall b' it upon the altar,
2: 2 the priest shall b' the memorial
9 and shall b' it upon the altar:
11 ye shall b' no leaven, nor any
16 the priest shall b' the memorial of
3: 5 And Aaron's sons shall b' it on the
11 And the priest shall b' it upon the
16 And the priest shall b' them upon
4:10 and the priest shall b' them upon
12 are poured out, and b' him on the
19 from him, and b' it upon the altar.
21 bullock without the camp, and b'
26 he shall b' all his fat upon the
31 and the priest shall b' it upon the
35 and the priest shall b' them upon
5:12 and b' it on the altar, according
6:12 and the priest shall b' wood on it
12 and he shall b' thereon the fat
15 and shall b' it upon the altar
7: 5 the priest shall b' them upon the
31 And the priest shall b' the fat
8:32 of the bread shall ye b' with fire.
13:52 He shall therefore b' that garment,
55 thou shalt b' it in the fire;
57 thou shalt b' that wherein the
16:25 offering shall he b' upon the altar.
27 and they shall b' in the fire their
17: 6 and b' the fat for a sweet savour
24: 2 cause the lamps to b' continually.
Nu 5:26 and b' it upon the altar, and
18:17 shalt b' their fat for an offering
19: 5 And one shall b' the heifer in his
5 blood, with her dung, shall he b':
De 5:23 the mountain did b' with fire,)
7: 5 b' their graven images with fire.
25 images of their gods shall ye b'
12: 3 b' their groves with fire; and ye
13:16 and shalt b' with fire the city,
32:22 and shall b' unto the lowest hell,
Jos 11: 6 and b' their chariots with fire.
13 Hazor only; that did Joshua b'.
J'g 9:52 the door of the tower to b' it
12: 1 we will b' thine house upon thee
14:15 lest we b' thee and thy father's
1Sa 2:16 Let them not fail to b' the fat
28 to b' incense, to wear an ephod
1Ki 13: 1 stood by the altar to b' incense.
2 the high places that b' incense
2Ki 16:15 Upon the great altar b' the morning

2Ki 18: 4 children of Israel did b' incense
23: 5 ordained to b' incense in the
1Ch 23:13 to b' incense before the Lord,
2Ch 2: 4 to b' before him sweet incense,
6 save only to b' sacrifice before
4:20 that they should b' after the
13:11 And they b' unto the Lord
11 to b' every evening: for we keep
26:16 the temple of the Lord to b'
18 to b' incense unto the Lord,
18 that are consecrated to b' incense:
19 a censer in his hand to b' incense:
28:25 places to b' incense unto other
29:11 unto him, and b' incense.
32:12 altar, and b' incense upon it?
Ne 10:34 to b' upon the altar of the Lord
Ps 79: 5 shall thy jealousy b' like fire?
89:46 shall thy wrath b' like fire?
Isa 1:31 and they shall both b' together,
10:17 and it shall b' and devour his
27: 4 I would b' them together.
40:16 Lebanon is not sufficient to b',
44:15 shall it be for a man to b': for he
47:14 the fire shall b' them; they shall
Jer 4: 4 and b' that none can quench it,
7: 9 and b' incense unto Baal, and
20 and it shall b',and shall not be
31 b' their sons and their daughters
11:13 altars to b' incense unto Baal.
15:14 anger, which shall b' upon you.
17: 4 anger, which shall b' for ever.
19: 5 to b' their sons with fire for
21:10 and he shall b' it with fire.
12 and b' that none can quench it,
32:29 and b' it with the houses, upon
34: 2 and he shall b' it with fire:
5 so shall they b' odours for thee;
22 and b' it with fire: and I will
36:25 that he would not b' the roll:
37: 8 and take it, and b' it with fire.
10 and b' this city with fire.
38:18 and they shall b' it with fire,
43:12 and he shall b' them, and carry
13 the Egyptians shall he b' with fire.
44: 3 in that they went to b' incense,
5 to b' no incense unto other gods.
17 to b' incense unto the queen of
18 since we left off to b' incense
25 b' incense to the queen of heaven,
Eze 5: 2 Thou shalt b' with fire a third
4 and b' them in the fire; for
16:41 And they shall b' thine houses
23:47 and b' up their houses with fire.
24: 5 b' also the bones under it, and
11 may be hot, and may b', and
39: 9 set on fire and b' the weapons,
9 and they shall b' them with fire
10 shall b' the weapons with fire:
43:21 and he shall b' it in the appointed
Ho 4:13 b' incense upon the hills,
Na 2:13 and I will b' her chariots in the
Hab 1:16 and b' incense unto their drag;
Mal 4: 1 that shall b' as an oven; and all
1 and the day that cometh shall b'
M't 3:12 but he will b' up the chaff with
13:30 bind them in bundles to b'
Lu 1: 9 his lot was to b' incense when
3:17 but the chaff he will b' with fire
24:32 Did not our heart b' within us,
1Co 7: 9 it is better to marry than to b'.
2Co 11:29 who is offended, and I b' not?
Re 17:16 and b' her with fire.

burned^ See also BURNT.
Ex 3: 2 the bush b' with fire, and the
Le 4:21 him as he b' the first bullock:
8:16 and Moses b' it upon the altar.
De 4:11 the mountain b' with fire unto
9:15 and the mount b' with fire:
Jos 7:25 and b' them with fire, after
11:13 Israel b' none of them, save Hazor
1Sa 30: 1 Ziklag, and b' it with fire;
3 behold, it was b' with fire; and
14 Caleb; and we b' Ziklag with fire.
2Sa 5:21 and David and his men b' them.
23: 7 they shall be utterly b' with fire
2Ki 10:26 the house of Baal, and b' them.
15:35 b' incense still in the high places.
22:17 have b' incense unto other gods,
23: 4 he b' them without Jerusalem
5 also that b' incense unto Baal,
6 and b' it at the brook Kidron,
8 where the priest had b' incense,
11 and b' the chariots of the sun
15 to powder, and b' the grove.
16 and b' them upon the altar,
20 and b' men's bones upon them,
1Ch 14:12 and they were b' with fire.
2Ch 25:14 them, b' incense unto them.
29: 7 have not b' incense nor offered
34:25 have b' incense unto other gods,
Neh 1: 3 gates thereof are b' with fire.
2:17 and the gates thereof are b' with
4: 2 heaps of rubbish which are b'?
Es 1:12 wroth, and his anger b' in him.
Job 1:16 and hath b' up the sheep,
30:30 and my bones are b' with heat.
Ps 39: 3 while I was musing the fire b':
74: 8 have b' up all the synagogues
80:16 It is b' with fire, it is cut down:
102: 3 and my bones are b' as an hearth.
106:18 the flame b' up the wicked.
Pr 6:27 and his clothes not be b'?
28 hot coals, and his feet not be b'?
Isa 1: 7 your cities are b' with fire: your
24: 6 inhabitants of the earth are b',
Isa 33:12 as thorns cut up shall they be b'
42:25 and it b' him, yet he laid it not
43: 2 thou shalt not be b'; neither
44:19 I have b' part of it in the fire;
64:11 is b' up with fire: and all our
65: 7 b' incense upon the mountains,
Jer 1:16 have b' incense unto other gods,
2:15 cities are b' without inhabitant.
6:29 The bellows are b', the lead is
9:10 they are b' up, so that none can
12 the land perisheth and is b' up
18:15 they have b' incense to vanity,
19: 4 b' incense in it unto other gods,
13 they have b' incense unto all the
36:27 after that the king had b' the roll,
28 the king of Judah hath b'.
29 Thou hast b' this roll, saying,
32 Jehoiakim king of Judah had b'
38:17 this city shall not be b' with fire;
23 cause this city to be b' with fire.
39: 8 the Chaldeans b' the king's house,
44:15 wives had b' incense unto other
19 b' incense to the queen of heaven,
21 that ye b' in the cities of Judah,
23 Because ye have b' incense, and
49: 2 her daughters shall be b' with fire:
51:30 they have b' her dwellingplaces;
32 the reeds they have b' with fire,
58 high gates shall be b' with fire;
52:13 And b' the house of the Lord,
13 of the great men, b' he with fire:
La 2: 3 he b' against Jacob like a flaming
Eze 15: 4 of it, and the midst of it is b'.
5 fire hath devoured it, and it is b'?
20:47 the south to the north shall be b'
24:10 it well, and let the bones be b'.
Ho 2:13 wherein she b' incense to them,
11: 2 and b' incense to graven images.
Joe 1:19 the flame hath b' all the trees of
Am 2: 1 b' the bones of the king of Edom
Mic 1: 7 the hires thereof shall be b' with
Na 1: 5 the earth is b' at his presence,
M't 13:40 the tares are gathered and b' in
22: 7 murderers, and b' up their city.
Joh 15: 6 into the fire, and they are b'.
Ac 19:19 and b' them before all men: and
Ro 1:27 b' in their lust one toward
1Co 3:15 If any man's work shall be b', he
13: 3 I give my body to be b', and have
Heb 6: 8 cursing, whose end is to be b'.
12:18 and that b' with fire, nor unto
13:11 high priest for sin, are b' without
2Pe 3:10 works that are therein shall be b'
Re 1:15 as if they b' in a furnace; and his
18: 8 she shall be utterly b' with fire:

burneth
Le 13:24 that b' have a white bright spot,
16:28 And he that b' them shall wash
Nu 19: 8 And he that b' her shall wash his
Ps 46: 9 he b' the chariot in the fire.
83:14 As the fire b' a wood, and as the
97: 3 A fire goeth before him, and b' up
Isa 9:18 For wickedness b' as a fire: it shall
44:16 He b' part thereof in the fire;
62: 1 thereof as a lamp that b'.
64: 2 As when the melting fire b', the
65: 3 b' incense upon altars of brick;
5 nose, a fire that b' all the day.
66: 3 he that b' incense, as if he
Jer 48:35 and him that b' incense to his gods.
Ho 7: 6 in the morning it b' as a flaming
Joe 2: 3 behind them a flame b': the land
Am 6:10 that b' him, to bring out the bones
Re 21: 8 in the lake which b' with fire and

burning See also BURNINGS.
Ge 15:17 a b' lamp that passed between
Ex 21:25 B' for b', wound for wound,
Le 6: 9 because of the b' upon the altar
9 the fire of the altar shall be b' in
12 the fire upon the altar shall be b'
13 The fire shall ever be b' upon
10: 6 b' which the Lord hath kindled.
13:23 it is a b' boil; and the priest
24 skin thereof there is a hot b',
25 a leprosy broken out of the b':
25 a rising of the b', and the priest
28 it is an inflammation of the b'.
16:12 shall take a censer full of b' coals
26:16 consumption, and the b' ague,
Nu 16:37 take up the censers out of the b',
19: 6 cast it into the midst of the b' of
De 28:22 and with an extreme b', and with
29:23 brimstone, and salt, and b', that
32:24 devoured with b' heat, and with
2Ch 16:14 they made a very great b' for him.
21:19 his people made no b' for him,
19 like the b' of his fathers.
Job 41:19 Out of his mouth go b' lamps,
Ps 140:10 Let b' coals fall upon them: let
Pr 16:27 in his lips there is as a b' fire.
26:21 As coals are to b' coals, and
23 B' lips and a wicked heart are
Isa 3:24 and b' instead of beauty.
4: 4 and by the spirit of b'.
9: 5 but this shall be with b' and fuel
10:16 kindle a b' like the b' of a fire.
30:27 b' with his anger, and the burden
34: 9 land thereof shall become b' pitch.
Jer 20: 9 was in mine heart as a b' fire
36:22 fire on the hearth b' before him.
44: 8 b' incense unto other gods in
Eze 1:13 like b' coals of fire, and like the
Da 3: 6 into the midst of a b' fiery furnace.
11 should be cast into the midst of a b
15 same hour into the midst of a b'
Da 3:17 able to deliver us from the b' fiery
20 cast them into the b' fiery furnace.
21, 23 the midst of the b' fiery furnace.
26 to the mouth of the b' fiery furnace,
7: 9 flame, and his wheels as b' fire.
11 and given to the b' flame.
Am 4:11 firebrand plucked out of the b':
Hab 3: 5 b' coals went forth at his feet.
Lu 12:35 girded about, and your lights b';
Joh 5:35 He was a b' and a shining light:
Jas 1:11 no sooner risen with a b' heat,
Re 4: 5 lamps of fire b' before the throne,
8: 8 a great mountain b' with fire was
10 b' as it were a lamp, and it fell
18: 9 they shall see the smoke of her b',
18 saw the smoke of her b', saying,
19:20 a lake of fire b' with brimstone.

burnings
Isa 33:12 people shall be as the b' of lime:
14 us shall dwell with everlasting b'?
Jer 34: 5 and with the b' of thy fathers,

burnished
Eze 1: 7 like the colour of b' brass.

burnt See also BURNED.
Ge 8:20 offered b' offerings on the altar.
22: 2 offer him there for a b' offering
3 clave the wood for the b' offering,
6 took the wood of the b' offering,
7 where is the lamb for a b' offering?
8 himself a lamb for a b' offering:
13 offered him up for a b' offering in
38:24 Bring her forth, and let her be b'.
Ex 3: 3 sight, why the bush is not b'.
10:25 b' offerings, that we may sacrifice
18:12 father in law, took a b' offering
20:24 sacrifice thereon thy b' offerings,
24: 5 of Israel, which offered b' offerings,
29:18 it is a b' offering unto the Lord:
25 upon the altar for a b' offering,
42 continual b' offering throughout
30: 9 nor b' sacrifice, nor meat offering;
28 of b' offering with all his vessels,
31: 9 of b' offering with all his furniture,
32: 6 offered b' offerings, and brought
20 and b' it in the fire, and ground
35:16 of b' offering, with his brasen
38: 1 he made the altar of b' offering
40: 6 shalt set the altar of the b' offering
10 anoint the altar of the b' offering,
27 And he b' sweet incense thereon;
29 he put the altar of b' offering by
29 and offered upon it the b' offering
Le 1: 3 If his offering be a b' sacrifice of
4 upon the head of the b' offering;
6 shall flay the b' offering, and cut
9 on the altar, to be a b' sacrifice,
10 or of the goats, for a b' sacrifice;
13 a b' sacrifice, an offering made by
14 the b' sacrifice for his offering to
17 it is a b' sacrifice, an offering
2:12 they shall not be b' on the altar
3: 5 upon the b' sacrifice, which is
4: 7 of the altar of the b' offering,
10 upon the altar of the b' offering.
12 are poured out shall he be b'.
18 the altar of the b' offering, which
24 kill the b' offering before the Lord:
25 horns of the altar of b' offering,
25 bottom of the altar of b' offering.
29 in the place of the b' offering.
30 horns of the altar of b' offering,
33 where they kill the b' offering.
34 altar of b' offering, and shall pour
5: 7 and the other for a b' offering.
10 offer the second for a b' offering,
6: 9 the law of the b' offering:
9 It is the b' offering, because of
10 with the b' offering on the altar,
12 lay the b' offering in order upon it;
22 the Lord; it shall be wholly b'.
23 shall be wholly b': it shall not
25 place where the b' offering is killed
30 eaten: it shall be b' in the fire.
7: 2 where they kill the b' offering
8 offereth any man's b' offering,
8 himself the skin of the b' offering
17 the third day shall be b' with fire.
19 it shall be b' with fire: and as for
37 This is the law of the b' offering,
8:17 he b' with fire without the camp;
18 the ram for the b' offering:
20 b' the head, and the pieces, and
21 Moses b' the whole ram upon the
21 a b' sacrifice for a sweet savour,
28 from off their hands, and b' them
28 on the altar upon the b' offering:
9: 2 a ram for a b' offering, without
3 without blemish, for a b' offering;
7 sin offering, and thy b' offering,
10 sin offering, he b' upon the altar;
11 he b' with fire without the camp.
12 he slew the b' offering; and
13 presented the b' offering unto him,
13 and he b' them upon the altar.
14 inwards and the legs, and b' them
14 upon the b' offering on the
16 the b' offering, and offered it
17 and b' it upon the altar,
17 the b' sacrifice of the morning.
20 and he b' the fat upon the altar:
22 sin offering, and the b' offering,
24 upon the altar the b' offering
10:16 it was b': and he was angry with
19 sin offering and their b' offering
12: 6 of the first year for a b' offering,

Le 12: 8 the one for the b' offering, and the
13:52 leprosy; it shall be b' in the fire.
14:13 sin offering and the b' offering, in
19 he shall kill the b' offering:
20 the priest shall offer the b' offering
22 and the other a b' offering.
31 and the other for a b' offering,
15:15 and the other for a b' offering;
30 and the other for a b' offering.
16: 3 a ram for a b' offering.
5 and one ram for a b' offering.
24 and offer his b' offering, and the
24 b' offering of the people,
17: 8 offereth a b' offering or sacrifice,
19: 6 it shall be b' in the fire.
20:14 they shall be b' with fire, both he
21: 9 she shall be b' with fire.
22:18 unto the Lord for a b' offering;
23:12 for a b' offering unto the Lord.
18 a b' offering unto the Lord,
37 a b' offering, and a meat offering,
Nu 6:11 the other for a b' offering,
14 without blemish for a b' offering,
16 sin offering, and his b' offering:
7:15, 21, 27, 33, 39, 45, 51, 57, 63, 69, 75,
81 the first year, for a b' offering:
87 the oxen for the b' offering
8:12 for a b' offering, unto the Lord,
10:10 over your b' offerings, and over
11: 1 fire of the Lord b' among them,
3 the fire of the Lord b' among them
15: 3 a b' offering, or a sacrifice
5 with the b' offering or sacrifice,
8 a bullock for a b' offering,
24 one young bullock for a b' offering,
16:39 they that were b' had offered;
19:17 take of the ashes of the b' heifer
23: 3 Stand by thy b' offering, and I
6 he stood by his b' sacrifice,
15 Stand here by thy b' offering,
17 he stood by his b' offering, and
28: 3 by day, for a continual b' offering.
6 a continual b' offering, which was
10 the b' offering of every Sabbath,
10 beside the continual b' offering,
11 ye shall offer a b' offering unto
13 a b' offering of a sweet savour,
14 the b' offering of every month
15 the continual b' offering, and his
19 for a b' offering unto the Lord;
23 the b' offering in the morning,
23 is for a continual b' offering.
24 the continual b' offering, and his
27 ye shall offer the b' offering for a
31 beside the continual b' offering,
29: 2 ye shall offer a b' offering for a
6 Beside the b' offering of the month,
6 and the daily b' offering,
8 a b' offering unto the Lord
11 and the continual b' offering,
13 And ye shall offer a b' offering,
16, 19, 22, 28, 31, 34 beside the continual b' offering,
36 ye shall offer a b' offering,
38 b' offering, and his meat offering,
39 for your b' offerings, and for your
31:10 they b' all their cities wherein
De 9:21 and b' it with fire, and stamped it,
12: 6 ye shall bring your b' offerings,
11 b' offerings, and your sacrifices,
13 thou offer not thy b' offerings
14, 27 thou shalt offer thy b' offerings,
31 daughters they have b' in the fire
27: 6 shalt offer b' offerings thereon
32:24 They shall be b' with hunger,
33:10 whole b' sacrifice upon thine altar.
Jos 6:24 they b' the city with fire, and
7:15 the accursed thing shall be b'
8:28 And Joshua b' Ai, and made it
31 they offered thereon b' offerings
11: 9 and b' their chariots with fire.
11 and he b' Hazor with fire.
22:23 to offer thereon b' offering
26 not for b' offering, nor for sacrifice:
27 before him with our b' offerings,
28 b' offerings, nor for sacrifices;
29 to build an altar for b' offerings,
J'g 6:26 and offer a b' sacrifice with the
11:31 will offer it up for a b' offering.
13:16 if thou wilt offer a b' offering,
23 not have received a b' offering
15: 5 and b' up both the shocks, and
6 b' her and her father with fire.
14 as flax that was b' with fire,
18:27 sword, and b' the city with fire.
20:26 and offered b' offerings and
21: 4 and offered b' offerings and
1Sa 2:15 before they b' the fat, the priest's
6:14 a b' offering unto the Lord.
15 Beth-shemesh offered b' offerings
7: 9 a b' offering wholly unto the Lord:
10 b' offering, the Philistines drew
10: 8 unto thee, to offer b' offerings,
13: 9 Bring hither a b' offering to me,
9 And he offered the b' offering.
10 an end of offering the b' offering,
12 therefore, and offered a b' offering.
15:22 as great delight in b' offerings
31:12 Jabesh, and b' them there.
2Sa 6:17 and David offered b' offerings
18 an end of offering b' offerings
24:22 here be oxen for b' sacrifice,
24 neither will I offer b' offerings
25 the Lord, and offered b' offerings
1Ki 3: 3 and b' incense in high places.
4 a thousand b' offerings did
1Ki 3:15 and offered up b' offerings,
8:64 there he offered b' offerings,
64 too little to receive the b' offerings.
9:16 and b' it with fire, and slain
25 did Solomon offer b' offerings
25 and he b' incense upon the altar
11: 8 which b' incense and sacrificed
12:33 upon the altar, and b' incense.
13: 2 bones shall be b' upon thee.
15:13 her idol, and b' it by the brook
16:18 and b' the king's house over him
18:33 pour it on the b' sacrifice, and
38 fell, and consumed the b' sacrifice,
22:43 the people offered and b' incense
2Ki 1:14 and b' up the two captains of
3:27 and offered him for a b' offering
5:17 neither b' offering nor sacrifice
10:24 to offer sacrifices and b' offerings,
25 an end of offering the b' offering,
12: 3 sacrificed and b' incense in the
14: 4 b' incense on the high places.
15: 4 people sacrificed and b' incense
16: 4 And he sacrificed and b' incense
13 And he b' [6999] his b' offering and
15 the morning b' offering, and the
15 the king's b' sacrifice, and his
15 the b' offering of all the people
15 the blood of the b' offering,
17:11 And there they b' incense in all
31 Sepharvites b' their children
25: 9 And he b' the house of the Lord,
9 every great man's house b' he
1Ch 6:49 the altar of the b' offering, and
16: 1 they offered b' sacrifices and
2 end of offering the b' offerings
40 To offer b' offerings unto the Lord
40 the altar of the b' offering
21:23 the oxen also for b' offerings,
24 nor offer b' offerings without cost.
26 offered b' offerings and peace
26 by fire upon the altar of b' offering.
29 the altar of the b' offering,
22: 1 is the altar of the b' offering
23:31 offer all b' sacrifices unto the Lord
29:21 offered b' offerings unto the Lord,
2Ch 1: 6 offered a thousand b' offerings
2: 4 and for the b' offerings morning
4: 6 as they offered for the b' offering
7: 1 and consumed the b' offering
7 there he offered b' offerings,
7 to receive the b' offerings,
8:12 Solomon offered b' offerings
13:11 b' sacrifices and sweet incense:
15:16 and b' it at the brook Kidron.
23:18 the b' offerings of the Lord, as it
24:14 they offered b' offerings in the
28: 3 he b' incense in the valley of the
3 and b' his children in the fire,
4 and b' incense in the high place,
29: 7 nor offered b' offerings in the
18 the altar of b' offering, with all
24 the b' offering and the sin
27 offer the b' offering upon the altar.
27 And when the b' offering began,
28 until the b' offering was finished.
31 as were of a free heart b' offerings.
32 the number of the b' offerings,
32 for a b' offering to the Lord.
34 could not flay all the b' offerings:
35 the b' offerings were in abundance,
35 drink offerings for every b' offering.
30:15 brought in the b' offerings unto
31: 2 priests and Levites for b' offerings
3 his substance for the b' offerings,
3 morning and evening b' offerings,
3 the b' offerings for the sabbaths,
34: 5 he b' the bones of the priests,
35:12 they removed the b' offerings,
14 in offering of b' offerings
16 to offer b' offerings upon the altar
36:19 And they b' the house of God,
19 and b' all the palaces thereof
Ezr 3: 2 to offer b' offerings thereon,
3 they offered b' offerings thereon
3 b' offerings morning and evening.
4 and offered the daily b' offerings
5 offered the continual b' offering,
6 to offer b' offerings unto the Lord.
6: 9 for the b' offerings of the God of
8:35 b' offerings unto the God of Israel,
35 a b' offering unto the Lord.
Ne 10:33 and for the continual b' offering,
Job 1: 5 and offered b' offerings according
42: 8 up for yourselves a b' offering;
Ps 20: 3 and accept thy b' sacrifice;
40: 6 b' offering and sin offering hast
50: 8 thy sacrifices or thy b' offerings,
51:16 thou delightest not in b' offering.
19 b' offering and whole b' offering:
66:13 go into thy house with b' offerings:
15 I will offer unto thee b' sacrifices
Isa 1:11 I am full of the b' offerings of
40:16 thereof sufficient for a b' offering.
43:23 the small cattle of thy b' offerings;
56: 7 b' offerings and their sacrifices
61: 8 I hate robbery for b' offering;
Jer 6:20 your b' offerings are not acceptable,
7:21 Put your b' offerings unto your
22 concerning b' offerings or
14:12 when they offer b' offering and
17:26 bringing b' offerings, and sacrifices,
19: 5 burn their sons with fire for b'
33:18 before me to offer b' offerings,
51:25 will make thee a b' mountain.
Eze 40:38 they washed the b' offering.
39 to slay thereon the b' offering
Eze 40:42 of hewn stone for the b' offering,
42 they slew the b' offering, and
43:18 to offer b' offerings thereon,
24 for a b' offering unto the Lord.
27 priests shall make your b' offerings
44:11 they shall slay the b' offering
45:15 and for a b' offering, and for
17 prince's part to give b' offerings,
17 meat offering, and the b' offering,
23 a b' offering to the Lord, seven
25 according to the b' offering,
46: 2 priests shall prepare his b' offering
4 And the b' offering that the prince
12 prepare a voluntary b' offering
12 he shall prepare his b' offering
13 a b' offering unto the Lord of
15 for a continual b' offering.
Ho 6: 6 of God more than b' offerings.
Am 5:22 ye offer me b' offerings and your
Mic 6: 6 come before him with b' offerings,
M'r 12:33 more than all whole b' offerings
Heb 10: 6 In b' offerings and sacrifices for
8 and b' offerings and offering for
Re 8: 7 the third part of trees was b' up,
7 and all green grass was b' up.

burnt-offering See BURNT and OFFERING.

burnt-sacrifice See BURNT and SACRIFICE.

burst See also BURSTING.
Job 32:19 it is ready to b' like new bottles.
Pr 3:10 and thy presses shall b' out
Jer 2:20 thy yoke, and b' thy bands;
5: 5 broken the yoke, and b' the bonds.
30: 8 and will b' thy bonds, and
Na 1:13 and will b' thy bonds in sunder.
M'r 2:22 doth b' the bottles, and the wine
Lu 5:37 new wine will b' the bottles,
Ac 1:18 he b' asunder in the midst,

bursting
Isa 30:14 shall not be found in the b' of it

bury See also BURIED; BURYING.
Ge 23: 4 I may b' my dead out of my sight.
6 of our sepulchres b' thy dead;
6 but that thou mayest b' thy dead.
8 mind that I should b' my dead
11 people give I it thee; b' thy dead.
13 me, and I will b' my dead there.
15 and thee: b' therefore thy dead.
47:29 b' me not, I pray thee, in Egypt:
30 and b' me in their buryingplace.
49:29 b' me with my fathers in the
50: 5 Canaan, there shalt thou b' me.
5 and b' my father, and I will come
6 Go up, and b' thy father, according
7 Joseph went up to b' his father:
14 went up with him to b' his father,
De 21:23 shalt in any wise b' him that day;
1Ki 2:31 and fall upon him, and b' him;
11:15 host was gone up to b' the slain,
13:29 the city, to mourn and to b' him.
31 When I am dead, then b' me in
14:13 shall mourn for him, and b' him:
2Ki 9:10 and there shall be none to b' her.
34 and b' her: for she is the king's
35 they went to b' her: but they
Ps 79: 3 and there was none to b' them.
Jer 7:32 for they shall b' in Tophet,
14:16 they shall have none to b' them,
19:11 they shall b' them in Tophet,
11 till there be no place to b'.
Eze 39:11 and there shall they b' Gog and
13 all the people of the land shall b'
14 to b' with the passengers those
Ho 9: 6 them up, Memphis shall b' them:
M't 8:21 me first to go and b' my father.
22 and let the dead b' their dead.
27: 7 potter's field, to b' strangers in.
Lu 9:59 me first to go and b' my father.
60 Let the dead b' their dead:
Joh 19:40 the manner of the Jews is to b'.

burying See also BURYINGPLACE.
2Ki 13:21 as they were b' a man, that,
Eze 39:12 house of Israel be b' of them,
M'r 14: 8 to anoint my body to the b'.
Joh 12: 7 against the day of my b' hath she

buryingplace
Ge 23: 4 give me a possession of a b'
9 possession of a b' amongst you.
20 possession of a b' by the sons
47:30 bury me in their b'. And he said,
49:30 Hittite for a possession of a b'.
50:13 for a possession of a b' of Ephron
J'g 16:31 in the b' of Manoah his father.

bush See also BUSHES.
Ex 3: 2 fire out of the midst of a b':
2 behold, the b' burned with fire,
2 and the b' was not consumed.
3 sight, why the b' is not burnt.
4 him out of the midst of the b'.
De 33:16 will of him that dwelt in the b':
M'r 12:26 how in the b' God spake unto him,
Lu 6:44 of a bramble b' gather they grapes.
20:37 even Moses shewed at the b',
Ac 7:30 Lord in a flame of fire in a b'.
35 which appeared to him in the b'.

bushel
M't 5:15 a candle, and put it under a b',
M'r 4:21 brought to be put under a b',
Lu 11:33 neither under a b', but on a

bushes
Job 30: 4 Who cut up mallows by the b',
7 Among the b' they brayed; under
Isa 7:19 all thorns, and upon all b'.

bushy
Ca 5:11 his locks are b', and black as a

busied
2Ch 35:14 priests the sons of Aaron were b'

business
Ge 39:11 went into the house to do his b';
De 24: 5 shall he be charged with any b':
Jos 2:14 yours, if ye utter not this our b'.
20 if thou utter this our b', then we
J'g 18: 7 and had no b' with any man.
28 they had no b' with any man;
1Sa 20:19 when the b' was in hand,
21: 2 hath commanded me a b', and
2 man know any thing of the b'
8 the king's b' required haste.
1Ch 26:29 his sons were for the outward b'
30 westward in all the b' of the Lord,
2Ch 13:10 the Levites wait upon their b':
17:13 much b' in the cities of Judah:
32:31 in the b' of the ambassadors of
Ne 11:16 outward b' of the house of God.
22 over the b' of the house of God.
13:30 Levites, every one in his b';
Es 3 : 9 that have the charge of the b',
Ps 107:23 ships, that do b' in great waters;
Pr 22:29 thou a man diligent in his b'?
Ec 5: 3 through the multitude of b';
8:16 the b' that is done upon the earth:
Da 8:27 rose up, and did the king's b';
Lu 2:49 must be about my father's b'?
Ac 6: 3 we may appoint over this b'.
Ro 12:11 Not slothful in b'; fervent in
16: 2 in whatsoever b' she hath need of
1Th 4:11 to do your own b', and to work

busy See also BUSIED; BUSYBODY.
1Ki 20:40 servant was b' here and there,

busybodies
2Th 3:11 working not at all, but are b'.
1Ti 5:13 but tattlers also and b', speaking

busybody See also BUSYBODIES.
1Pe 4:15 or as a b' in other men's matters.

butler See also BUTLERS; BUTLERSHIP.
Ge 40: 1 the b' of the king of Egypt and
5 the b' and the baker of the king of
9 chief b' told his dream to Joseph,
13 manner when thou wast his b'.
20 lifted up the head of the chief b'
21 he restored the chief b' unto his
23 Yet did not the chief b' remember
41: 9 spake the chief b' unto Pharaoh,

butlers
Ge 40: 2 against the chief of the b', and

butlership
Ge 40:21 the chief butler unto his b'

butter
Ge 18: 8 he took b', and milk, and the calf
De 32:14 B' of kine, and milk of sheep,
J'g 5:25 brought forth b' in a lordly dish.
2Sa 17:29 honey, and b', and sheep, and
Job 20:17 floods, the brooks of honey and b'.
29: 6 When I washed my steps with b',
Ps 55:21 his mouth were smoother than b',
Pr 30:33 of milk bringeth forth b', and the
Isa 7:15 B' and honey shall he eat, that he
22 they shall give, he shall eat b':
22 for b' and honey shall every one

buttocks
2Sa 10: 4 in the middle, even to their b',
1Ch 19: 4 in the midst hard by their b',
Isa 20: 4 with their b' uncovered, to the

buy See also BUYEST; BUYETH; BOUGHT.
Ge 41:57 Egypt to Joseph for to b' corn;
42: 2 b' for us from thence; that we
3 went down to b' corn in Egypt.
5 the sons of Israel came to b' corn
7 From the land of Canaan to b' food.
10 to b' food are thy servants come.
43: 2 Go again, b' us a little food.
4 we will go down and b' thee food:
20 down at the first time to b' food:
22 money have we brought...to b'
44:25 Go again, and b' us a little food.
47:19 b' us and our land for bread,
Ex 21: 2 If thou b' an Hebrew servant,
Le 22:11 But if the priest b' any soul with
25:15 thou shalt b' of thy neighbour,
44 of them shall ye b' bondmen
45 of them shall ye b', and of their
De 2: 6 shall b' meat of them for money,
6 ye shall also b' water of them for
28:68 bondwomen, and no man shall b'
Ru 4: 4 B' it before the inhabitants,
5 b' it also of Ruth the Moabitess,
8 said unto Boaz, B' it for thee.
2Sa 24:21 To b' the threshingfloor of thee to
24 will surely b' it of thee at a price:
2Ki 12:12 to b' timber and hewed stone
22: 6 and to b' timber and hewn stone
1Ch 21:24 I will verily b' it for the full price:
2Ch 34:11 to b' hewn stone, and timber for
Ezr 7:17 b' speedily with this money
Ne 5: 3 that we might b' corn, because
10:31 not b' it of them on the sabbath,
Pr 23:23 B' the truth, and sell it not;
Isa 55: 1 come ye, b', and eat:
1 yea, come, b' wine and milk
Jer 32: 7 B' thee my field that is in
7 of redemption is thine to b' it.
Jer 32: 8 B' my field, I pray thee, that is in
8 is thine; b' it for thyself.
25 B' thee the field for money, and
44 Men shall b' fields for money,
Am 8: 6 That we may b' the poor for silver,
M't 14:15 villages, and b' themselves victuals.
25: 9 that sell, and b' for yourselves.
10 while they went to b', the
M'r 6:36 villages, and b' themselves bread:
37 b' two hundred pennyworth of bread,
Lu 9:13 go and b' meat for all this people.
22:36 let him sell his garment, and b' one.
Joh 4: 8 away unto the city to b' meat.)
6: 5 Whence shall we b' bread, that
13:29 B' those things that we have need
1Co 7:30 they that b', as though they
Jas 4:13 and b' and sell, and get gain:
Re 3:18 I counsel thee to b' of me gold
13:17 that no man might b' or sell,

buyer
Pr 20:14 it is naught, saith the b': but
Isa 24: 2 as with the b', so with the seller;
Eze 7:12 let not the b' rejoice, nor the seller

buyest
Le 25:14 b' ought of thy neighbour's hand,
Ru 4: 5 What day thou b' the field of the

buyeth
Pr 31:16 She considereth a field, and b' it:
M't 13:44 all that he hath, and b' that field.
Re 18:11 for no man b' their merchandise

Buz (*buz*)
Ge 22:21 his firstborn, and B' his brother,
1Ch 5:14 the son of Jahdo, the son of B';
Jer 25:23 Dedan, and Tema, and B',

Buzi (*boo'-zi*) See also BUZITE.
Eze 1: 3 Ezekiel the priest, the son of B',

Buzite (*boo'-zite*)
Job 32: 2 of Barachel the B', of the kindred
6 Elihu the son of Barachel the B'

by-and-by See BY and AND.

byways
J'g 5: 6 travellers walked through b'.

byword
De 28:37 a b', among all nations whither
1Ki 9: 7 and a b' among all people:
2Ch 7:20 and a b' among all nations.
Job 17: 6 made me also a b' of the people;
30: 9 their song, yea, I am their b'.
Ps 44:14 us a b' among the heathen,

C.

cab
2Ki 6:25 fourth part of a c' of dove's dung

Cabbon (*cab'-bon*)
Jos 15:40 C', and Lahmam, and Kithlish,

cabins
Jer 37:16 into the c', and Jeremiah

Cabul (*ca'-bul*)
Jos 19:27 goeth out to C' on the left hand,
1Ki 9:13 he called them the land of C'

Cæsar (*se'-zur*) See also CÆSAR'S.
M't 22:17 to give tribute unto C', or not?
21 unto C' the things which are
M'r 12:14 to give tribute to C', or not?
17 C' the things that are Cæsar's,
Lu 2: 1 a decree from C' Augustus,
3: 1 the reign of Tiberius C', Pontius
20:22 to give tribute unto C', or no?
25 C' the things which be Cæsar's,
23: 2 forbidding to give tribute to C',
Joh 19:12 himself a king speaketh against C'.
15 answered, We have no king but C'.
Ac 11:28 pass in the days of Claudius C'.
17: 7 contrary to the decrees of C',
25: 8 nor yet against C', have I offended
11 unto them. I appeal unto C'.
12 Hast thou appealed unto C'?
12 unto C' shalt thou go.
21 be kept till I might send him to C'.
26:32 if he had not appealed unto C'.
27:24 thou must be brought before C':
28:19 constrained to appeal unto C';

Cæsar-Augustus See CÆSAR and AUGUSTUS.

Cæsarea (*ses-a-re'-ah*)
M't 16:13 into the coasts of C' Philippi,
M'k 8:27 into the towns of C' Philippi:
Ac 8:40 all the cities, till he came to C'.
9:30 they brought him down to C',
10: 1 certain man in C' called Cornelius,
24 morrow after they entered into C'.
11:11 I was, sent from C' unto me.
12:19 went down from Judæa to C',
18:22 he had landed at C', and gone up,
21: 8 came unto C': and we entered
16 of the disciples of C', and brought
23:23 soldiers to go to C',
33 they came to C', and delivered
25: 1 ascended from C' to Jerusalem.
4 that Paul should be kept at C',
6 ten days, he went down unto C';
13 Bernice came unto C' to salute

Cæsarea-Philippi See CÆSAREA and PHILIPPI.

Cæsar's (*se'-zurs*)
M't 22:21 They say unto him, C'. Then
21 Cæsar the things which are C';
M'k 12:16 And they said unto him, C'.
17 to Cæsar the things that are C',
Lu 20:24 They answered and said, C'.
25 unto Cæsar the things which be C',
Jo 19:12 thou art not C' friend: whosoever
Ac 25:10 I stand at C' judgment seat,
Ph'p 4:22 they that are of C' household.

cage
Jer 5:27 As a c' is full of birds, so are their
Re 18: 2 a c' of every unclean and hateful

Caiaphas (*cah'-ya-fus*)
M't 26: 3 high priest, who was called C',
57 led him away to C' the high priest,
Lu 3: 2 Annas and C' being the high
Joh 11:49 And one of them, named C',
18:13 he was father in law to C',
14 C' was he, which gave counsel to
24 Annas had sent him bound unto C'
28 Then led they Jesus from C' unto
Ac 4: 6 Annas the high priest, and C',

Cain See also TUBAL-CAIN.
Ge 4: 1 and she conceived, and bare C',
2 but C' was a tiller of the ground.
3 pass, that C' brought of the fruit
5 unto C' and to his offering he had
5 And C' was very wroth, and his
6 And the Lord said unto C', Why
8 C' talked with Abel his brother:
8 C' rose up against Abel his
9 And the Lord said unto C', Where
13 And C' said unto the Lord,
15 Therefore whosoever slayeth C',
15 And the Lord set a mark upon C',
16 C' went out from the presence of
17 And C' knew his wife; and she
24 If C' shall be avenged seven fold,
25 instead of Abel, whom C' slew.
Jos 15:57 C', Gibeah, and Timnah; ten cities
Heb 11: 4 a more excellent sacrifice than C',
1Jo 3:12 Not as C', who was of that wicked
Jude 11 gone in the way of C', and ran

Cainan (*ca'-nun*) See also KENAN.
Ge 5: 9 lived ninety years, and begat C':
10 Enos lived after he begat C'
12 C' lived seventy years, and
13 C' lived after he begat
Ge 5:14 the days of C' were nine hundred
Lu 3:36, 37 Which was the son of C',

cake See also CAKES.
Ex 29:23 and one c' of oiled bread, and one
Le 8:26 he took one unleavened c',
26 and a c' of oiled bread,
24: 5 two tenth deals shall be in one c'.
Nu 6:19 unleavened c' out of the basket,
15:20 Ye shall offer up a c' of the first
J'g 7:13 a c' of barley bread tumbled into
1Sa 30:12 gave him a piece of a c' of figs,
2Sa 6:19 to every one a c' of bread, and a
1Ki 17:12 I have not a c', but an handful of
13 make me thereof a little c' first,
19: 6 there was a c' baken on the coals,
Hos 7: 8 Ephraim is a c' not turned.

cakes
Ge 18: 6 it, and make c' upon the hearth.
Ex 12:39 baked unleavened c' of the dough
29: 2 bread, and c' unleavened
Le 2: 4 unleavened c' of fine flour
7:12 unleavened c' mingled with oil,
12 with oil, and c' mingled with oil,
13 Besides the c', he shall offer for
24: 5 bake twelve c' thereof: two tenth
Nu 6:15 c' of fine flour mingled with oil,
11: 8 baked it in pans, and make c' of it:
Jos 5:11 unleavened c', and parched corn
J'g 6:19 unleavened c' of an ephah of flour:
20, 21 flesh and the unleavened c',
1Sa 25:18 two hundred c' of figs, and laid
2Sa 13: 6 make me a couple of c' in my sight,
8 made c' in his sight,
8 and did bake the c'.
10 Tamar took the c' which she had
1Ch 12:40 meal, c' of figs, and bunches of
23:29 for the unleavened c', and
Jer 7:18 make c' to the queen of heaven,
44:19 we make her c' to worship her,
Eze 4:12 And thou shalt eat it as barley c',

Calah (*ca'-lah*)
Ge 10:11 and the city Rehoboth, and C',
12 Resen between Nineveh and C':

calamities
Ps 57: 1 refuge, until these c' be overpast.
141: 5 prayer also shall be in their c'.
Pr 17: 5 he that is glad at c' shall not be

calamity See also CALAMITIES.
De 32:35 the day of their c' is at hand, and
2Sa 22:19 prevented me in the day of my c':

Job 6: 2 and my c' laid in the balances
30:13 they set forward my c', they have
Ps 18:18 prevented me in the day of my c':
Pr 1:26 I also will laugh at your c'; I will
6:15 shall his c' come suddenly;
19:13 foolish son is the c' of his father:
24:22 For their c' shall rise suddenly;
27:10 brother's house in the day of thy c':
Jer 18:17 the face, in the day of their c'.
46:21 the day of their c' was come upon
48:16 The c' of Moab is near to come,
49: 8 will bring the c' of Esau upon him,
32 bring their c' from all sides thereof,
Eze 35: 5 the sword in the time of their c',
Ob 13 in the day of their c'; yea, thou
13 their affliction in the day of their c',
13 substance in the day of their c';

calamus *(cal'-a-mus)*
Ex 30:23 of sweet c' two hundred and fifty
Ca 4:14 and saffron; c' and cinnamon,
Eze 27:19 cassia, and c', were in thy market.

Calcol *(cal'-col)* See also CHALCOL.
1Ch 2: 6 and Heman, and C' and Dara:

caldron See also CALDRONS.
1Sa 2:14 the pan, or kettle, or c', or pot;
Job 41:20 as out of a seething pot or c'.
Eze 11: 3 city is the c', and we be the flesh.
7 this city is the c': but I will bring
11 This city shall not be your c',
Mic 3: 3 the pot, and as flesh within the c'.

caldrons
2Ch 35:13 sod they in pots, and in c', and in
Jer 52:18 The c' also, and the shovels,
19 the c', and the candlesticks,

Caleb *(ca'-leb)* See also CALEB'S; CALEB-EPHRATAH; CHELLUBAI.
Nu 13: 6 Judah, C' the son of Jephunneh.
30 C' stilled the people before Moses,
14: 6 Joshua the son of Nun, and C' the
24 But my servant C', because he had
30 to make you dwell therein, save C'
38 Joshua, the son of Nun, and C' the
26:65 was not left a man of them, save C'
32:12 Save C' the son of Jephunneh
34:19 Judah, C' the son of Jephunneh.
De 1:36 Save C' the son of Jephunneh;
Jos 14: 6 C' the son of Jephunneh the
13 blessed him, and gave unto C'
14 became the inheritance of C'
15:13 unto C' the son of Jephunneh he
14 C' drove thence the three sons of
16 And C' said, He that smiteth
17 Kenaz, the brother of C', took:
18 C' said unto her, What wouldest
21:12 villages thereof, gave they to C'
J'g 1:12 And C' said, He that smiteth
14 C' said unto her, What wilt thou?
15 And C' gave her the upper springs
20 they gave Hebron unto C', as
1Sa 25: 3 and he was of the house of C'.
30:14 Judah, and upon the south of C';
1Ch 2:18 And C' the son of Hezron begat
19 Azubah was dead, C' took unto
42 Now the sons of C' the brother of
49 and the daughter of C' was Achsa.
50 These were the sons of C' the son
4:15 sons of C' the son of Jephunneh;
6:56 villages thereof, they gave to C'

Caleb-ephratah *(ca''-leb-ef'-ra-tah)*
1Ch 2:24 after that Hezron was dead in C',

Caleb's *(ca'-lebs)*
J'g 1:13 son of Kenaz, C' younger brother,
3: 9 son of Kenaz, C' younger brother.
1Ch 2:46 Ephah, C' concubine, bare Haran,
48 Maachah, C' concubine, bare

calf See also CALF'S; CALVES.
Ge 18: 7 fetcht a c' tender and good,
8 the c' which he had dressed,
Ex 32: 4 after he had made it a molten c':
8 they have made them a molten c',
19 he saw the c', and the dancing:
20 took the c' which they had made,
24 fire, and there came out this c'.
35 made the c', which Aaron made
Le 9: 2 a young c' for a sin offering,
3 a c' and a lamb, both of the first
8 slew the c' of the sin offering,
De 9:16 and had made you a molten c':
21 the c' which ye had made, and
1Sa 28:24 woman had a fat c' in the house;
Ne 9:18 They had made them a molten c',
Job 21:10 cow calveth, and casteth not her c'.
Ps 29: 6 maketh them also to skip like a c';
106:19 They made a c' in Horeb, and
Isa 11: 6 and the c' and the young lion and
27:10 wilderness: there shall the c' feed,
Jer 34:18 when they cut the c' in twain, and
19 passed between the parts of the c';
Ho 8: 5 Thy c', O Samaria, hath cast thee
6 the c' of Samaria shall be broken
Lu 15:23 bring hither the fatted c', and kill
27 thy father hath killed the fatted c',
30 hast killed for him the fatted c'.
Ac 7:41 they made a c' in those days, and
Re 4: 7 the second beast like a c', and the

calf's
Eze 1: 7 feet was like the sole of a c' foot:

calkers
Eze 27: 9 thereof were in thee thy c':
27 mariners, and thy pilots, thy c',

call^ See also CALLED; CALLEST; CALLETH; CALLING; RECALL.
Ge 2:19 to see what he would c' them:
4:26 began men to c' upon the name
16:11 shalt c' his name Ishmael;
17:15 thou shalt not c' her name Sarai,
19 and thou shalt c' his name Isaac:
24:57 We will c' the damsel, and enquire
30:13 the daughters will c' me blessed:
46:33 when Pharaoh shall c' you, and
Ex 2: 7 Shall I go and c' to thee a nurse
20 c' him, that he may eat bread.
34:15 c' thee, and thou eat of his sacrifice;
Nu 16:12 Moses sent to c' Dathan and
22: 5 of his people, to c' him, saying,
20 If the men come to c' thee, rise
37 earnestly send unto thee to c' thee?
De 2:11 but the Moabites c' them Emims.
20 Ammonites c' them Zamzummims;
3: 9 Hermon the Sidonians c' Sirion;
9 and the Amorites c' it Shenir;)
4: 7 things that we c' upon him for?
26 I c' heaven and earth to witness
25: 8 the elders of his city shall c' him,
30: 1 thou shalt c' them to mind among
19 I c' heaven and earth to record
31:14 c' Joshua, and present yourselves
28 and c' heaven and earth to record
33:19 c' the people unto the mountain;
J'g 12: 1 didst not c' us to go with thee?
16:25 C' for Samson, that he may make
21:13 and to c' peaceably unto them.
Ru 1:20 C' me not Naomi, c' me Mara: for
21 why then c' ye me Naomi, seeing
1Sa 3: 6 Here am I; for thou didst c' me.
8 for thou didst c' me. And Eli
9 if he c' thee, that thou shalt say,
12:17 I will c' unto the Lord, and he
16: 3 And c' Jesse to the sacrifice, and I
22:11 Then the king sent to c' Ahimelech
2Sa 17: 5 C' now Hushai the Archite also,
22: 4 I will c' on the Lord, who is worthy
1Ki 1:28 C' me Bath-sheba. And she came
32 C' me Zadok the priest, and Nathan
8:52 in all that they c' for unto thee.
17:18 to c' my sin to remembrance, and
18:24 c' ye on the name of your gods,
24 I will c' on the name of the Lord:
25 and c' on the name of your gods,
22:13 messenger that was gone to c'
2Ki 4:12 C' this Shunammite. And when he
15 And he said, C' her. And when he
36 and said, C' this Shunammite.
5:11 c' on the name of the Lord his
10:19 c' unto me all the prophets of Baal,
1Ch 16: 8 c' upon his name, make known his
2Ch 18:12 messenger that went to c' Micaiah
Job 5: 1 C' now, if there be any that will
13:22 Then c' thou, and I will answer:
14:15 Thou shalt c', and I will answer
27:10 will he always c' upon God?
Ps 4: 1 Hear me when I c', O God of my
3 the Lord will hear when I c' unto
14: 4 bread, and c' not upon the Lord.
18: 3 I will c' upon the Lord, who is
20: 9 let the king hear us when we c'.
49:11 c' their lands after their own names.
50: 4 shall c' to the heavens from above,
15 c' upon me in the day of trouble:
55:16 I will c' upon God; and the Lord
72:17 all nations shall c' him blessed.
77: 6 I c' to remembrance my song in
80:18 and we will c' upon thy name.
86: 5 unto all them that c' upon thee.
7 In the day of my trouble I will c'
91:15 He shall c' upon me, and I will
99: 6 among them that c' upon his name;
102: 2 day when I c' answer me speedily.
105: 1 c' upon his name: make known his
116:13 and c' upon the name of the Lord.
17 will c' upon the name of the Lord.
145:18 unto all them that c' upon him,
18 to all that c' upon him
Pr 1:28 Then shall they c' upon me, but I
7: 4 c' understanding thy kinswoman:
8: 4 Unto thee, O men, I c'; and my
9:15 To c' passengers who go right on
31:28 arise up, and c' her blessed;
Isa 5:20 that c' evil good, and good evil;
7:14 and shall c' his name Immanuel.
8: 3 C' his name Maher-shalal-hash-baz
12: 4 Praise the Lord, c' upon his name,
22:12 Lord God of hosts c' to weeping,
20 that I will c' my servant Eliakim
31: 2 will not c' back his words: but
34:12 They shall c' the nobles thereof
41:25 shall he c' upon my name: and
44: 5 c' himself by the name of Jacob;
7 who, as I, shall c', and shall
45: 3 the Lord, which c' thee by thy name,
48: 2 they c' themselves of the holy city,
13 when I c' unto them, they stand
55: 5 c' a nation that thou knowest not,
6 c' ye upon him while he is near:
58: 5 wilt thou c' this a fast, and an
9 thou c', and the Lord shall answer;
13 and c' the sabbath a delight, the
60:14 shall c' thee, The city of the Lord,
18 thou shalt c' thy walls Salvation,
61: 6 c' you the Ministers of our God:
62:12 they shall c' them, The holy people
65:15 c' his servants by another name:
24 and before they c', I will answer;
Jer 1:15 I will c' all the families of the
3:17 c' Jerusalem the throne of the Lord;
19 Thou shalt c' me, My father; and
Jer 6:30 Reprobate silver shall men c'
7:27 thou shalt also c' unto them; but
9:17 and c' for the mourning women,
10:25 families that c' not on thy name:
25:29 I will call for a sword upon all the
29:12 Then shall ye c' upon me, and ye
33: 3 C' unto me, and I will answer
50:29 C' together the archers against
51:27 c' together against her the
La 2:15 city that men c' The perfection of
Eze 21:23 c' to remembrance the iniquity,
36:29 and I will c' for the corn, and will
38:21 And I will c' for a sword against
39:11 shall c' it The valley of Hamon-gog.
Da 2: 2 commanded to c' the magicians,
Ho 1: 4 C' his name Jezreel: for yet a
6 C' her name Lo-ruhamah: for I
9 C' his name Lo-ammi: for ye are
2:16 thou shalt c' me Ishi;
16 and shalt c' me no more Baali.
7:11 they c' to Egypt, they go to Assyria.
Joe 1:14 c' a solemn assembly, gather the
2:15 a fast, c' a solemn assembly:
32 whosoever shall c' on the name of
32 remnant whom the Lord shall c'.
Am 5:16 and they shall c' the husbandman
Jon 1: 6 arise, c' upon thy God, if so be
Zep 3: 9 all c' upon the name of the Lord,
Zec 3:10 ye c' every man his neighbour
13: 9 they shall c' on my name, and I
Mal 1: 4 c' them, The border of wickedness,
3:12 all nations shall c' you blessed:
15 now we c' the proud happy; yea,
M't 1:21 thou shalt c' his name Jesus:
23 shall call his name Emmanuel,
9:13 I am not come to c' the righteous,
20: 8 C' the labourers, and give them
22: 3 to c' them that were bidden
43 doth David in spirit c' him Lord,
45 If David then c' him Lord, how is
23: 9 And c' no man your father upon
M'r 2:17 came not to c' the righteous, but
10:49 they c' the blind man, saying unto
15:12 whom ye c' the King of the Jews?
16 and they c' together the whole
Lu 1:13 thou shalt c' his name John.
31 son, and shalt c' his name Jesus.
48 generations shall c' me blessed.
5:32 I came not to c' the righteous,
6:46 And why c' ye me, Lord, Lord,
14:12 c' not thy friends, nor thy brethren
13 when thou makest a feast, c' the
Joh 4:16 Go, c' thy husband, and come
13:13 Ye c' me Master and Lord: and ye
15:15 Henceforth I c' you not servants;
Ac 2:21 whosoever shall c' on the name of
39 many as the Lord our God shall c'.
9:14 to bind all that c' on thy name.
10: 5 to Joppa, and c' for one Simon
15 that c' not thou common.
28 I should not c' any man common
32 c' hither Simon, whose surname
11: 9 that c' not thou common.
13 and c' for Simon, whose surname
19:13 c' over them which had evil
24:14 c' heresy, so worship I the God
25 season, I will c' for thee.
Ro 9:25 I will c' them my people which
10:12 rich unto all that c' upon him.
13 whosoever shall c' upon the name
14 How then shall they c' on him in
1Co 1: 2 in every place c' upon the name
2Co 1:23 I c' God for a record upon my
2Ti 1: 5 When I c' to remembrance the
2:22 with them that c' on the Lord
He 2:11 not ashamed to c' them brethren,
10:32 c' to remembrance the former days,
Jas 5:14 c' for the elders of the church;
1Pe 1:17 And if ye c' on the Father, who

called^ See also CALLEDST.
Ge 1: 5 And God c' the light Day,
5 and the darkness he c' Night.
8 God c' the firmament Heaven.
10 and God c' the dry land Earth;
10 together of the waters c' he Seas:
2:19 Adam c' every living creature,
23 she shall be c' Woman, because
3: 9 And the Lord God c' unto Adam,
20 And Adam c' his wife's name Eve;
4:17 c' the name of the city, after the
25 and c' his name Seth:
26 and he c' his name Enos:
5: 2 and c' their name Adam,
3 his image; and c' his name Seth:
29 And he c' his name Noah,
11: 9 therefore is the name of it c' Babel;
12: 8 and c' upon the name of the Lord.
18 And Pharoah c' Abram, and said,
13: 4 Abram c' on the name of the Lord.
16:13 And she c' the name of the Lord
14 the well was c' Beer-lahai-roi;
15 Abram c' his son's name, which
17: 5 thy name any more be c' Abram,
19: 5 And they c' unto Lot, and said
22 the name of the city was c' Zoar.
37 and c' his name Moab:
38 and c' his name Ben-ammi:
20: 8 and c' all his servants, and told all
9 Then Abimelech c' Abraham, and
21: 3 And Abraham c' the name of his
12 in Isaac shall thy seed be c'.
17 the angel of God c' to Hagar
31 he c' that place Beer-sheba;
33 c' there on the name of the Lord,
22:11 angel of the Lord c' unto him out
14 Abraham c' the name of that place

Ge 22:15 angel of the Lord c' unto Abraham
24:58 And they c' Rebekah, and said
25:25 and they c' his name Esau.
26 and his name was c' Jacob:
30 therefore was his name c' Edom.
26: 9 And Abimelech c' Isaac, and said,
18 he c' their names after the names
18 by which his father had c' them.
20 he c' the name of the well Esek;
21 and he c' the name of it Sitnah.
22 and he c' the name of it Rehoboth;
25 and c' upon the name of the Lord,
33 and he c' it Shebah:
27: 1 he called Esau his eldest son, and
42 she sent and c' Jacob
28: 1 Isaac c' Jacob, and blessed him,
19 c' the name of that place Beth-el:
19 the name of that city was c' Luz
29:32 and she c' his name Reuben:
33 and she c' his name Simeon.
34 therefore was his name c' Levi.
35 she c' his name Judah;
30: 6 therefore c' she his name Dan.
8 and she c' his name Naphtali.
11 and she c' his name Gad.
13 and she c' his name Asher.
18 and she c' his name Issachar.
20 and she c' his name Zebulun.
21 and c' her name Dinah.
24 And she c' his name Joseph;
31: 4 Jacob sent and c' Rachel and Leah
47 And Laban c' it Jegar-sahadutha:
47 Jacob c' it Galeed.
31:48 was the name of it c' Galeed;
54 and c' his brethren to eat bread:
32: 2 and he c' the name of that place
28 name shall be c' no more Jacob,
30 c' the name of the place Peniel:
33:17 name of the place is c' Succoth.
20 and c' it El-elohe-Israel.
35: 7 and c' the place El-Beth-el:
8 name of it was c' Allon-bachuth.
10 shall not be c' any more Jacob,
10 and he c' his name Israel.
15 And Jacob c' the name of the place
18 that she c' his name Ben-oni:
18 his father c' him Benjamin.
38: 3 and he c' his name Er.
4 and she c' his name Onan.
5 and c' his name Shelah:
29 therefore his name was c' Pharez.
30 and his name was c' Zarah.
39:14 she c' unto the men of her house,
41: 8 and c' for all the magicians
14 Pharaoh sent and c' Joseph,
45 And Pharaoh c' Joseph's name
51 c' the name of the firstborn
52 of the second c' he Ephraim:
47:29 and he c' his son Joseph,
48: 6 c' after the name of their brethren
49: 1 And Jacob c' unto his sons,
50:11 name of it was c' Abel-mizraim,
Ex 1:18 king of Egypt c' for the midwives,
2: 8 went and c' the child's mother.
10 And she c' his name Moses:
22 and he c' his name Gershom:
3: 4 God c' unto him out of the midst
7:11 Pharaoh also c' the wise men
8: 8 Pharaoh c' for Moses and Aaron,
25 c' for Moses and for Aaron,
9:27 Pharaoh sent, and c' for Moses
10:16 Pharaoh c' for Moses and Aaron
24 And Pharaoh c' unto Moses,
12:21 Then Moses c' for all the elders
31 And he c' for Moses and Aaron
15:23 the name of it was c' Marah.
16:31 c' the name thereof Manna:
17: 7 c' the name of the place Massah,
15 c' the name of it Jehovah-nissi:
19: 3 c' unto him out of the mountain,
7 Moses came and c' for the elders
20 and the Lord c' Moses up
24:16 the seventh day he c' unto Moses
31: 2 I have c' by name Bezaleel
33: 7 and c' it the Tabernacle of the
34:31 Moses c' unto them; and Aaron
35:30 the Lord hath c' by name Bezaleel
36: 2 c' Bezaleel and Aholiab,
Le 1: 1 And the Lord c' unto Moses,
9: 1 Moses c' Aaron and his sons,
10: 4 Moses c' Mishael and Elzaphan,
Nu 11: 3 c' the name of the place Taberah:
34 And he c' the name of that place
12: 5 and c' Aaron and Miriam:
13:16 And Moses c' Oshea the son of Nun
24 The place was c' the brook Eshcol,
21: 3 c' the name of the place Hormah.
24:10 I c' thee to curse mine enemies,
25: 2 c' the people unto the sacrifices
32:41 and c' them Havoth-jair.
42 c' it Nobah, after his own name.
De 3:13 which was c' the land of giants.
14 and c' them after his own name,
5: 1 c' all Israel, and said unto them,
15: 2 because it is c' the Lord's release.
25:10 And his name shall be c' in Israel,
28:10 art c' by the name of the Lord;
29: 2 And Moses c' unto all Israel,
31: 7 And Moses c' unto Joshua,
Jos 4: 4 Then Joshua c' the twelve men,
5: 9 the name of the place is c' Gilgal
6: 6 the son of Nun c' the priests,
7:26 place was c', The valley of Achor,
8:16 c' together to pursue after them:
9:22 And Joshua c' for them,
10:24 Joshua c' for all the men of Israel,

Jos 19:47 c' Leshem, Dan, after the name
22: 1 Then Joshua c' the Reubenites,
34 and the children of Gad c' the altar
23: 2 And Joshua c' for all Israel,
24: 1 and c' for the elders of Israel,
9 sent and c' Balaam the son of Beor
J'g 1:17 name of the city was c' Hormah.
26 and c' the name thereof Luz:
2: 5 c' the name of that place Bochim:
4: 6 c' Barak the son of Abinoam
10 Barak c' Zebulun and Naphtali
6:24 and c' it Jehovah-shalom:
32 on that day he c' him Jerubbaal,
8:31 son, whose name he c' Abimelech.
9:54 he c' hastily unto the young man
10: 4 cities, which are c' Havoth-jair
12: 2 I c' you, ye delivered me not
13:24 and c' his name Samson:
14:15 have ye c' us to take that we have?
15:17 and c' that place Ramath-lehi.
18 and c' on the Lord, and said,
19 c' the name thereof En-hakkore,
16:18 c' for the lords of the Philistines,
19 and she c' for a man, and she
25 c' for Samson out of the prison
28 And Samson c' unto the Lord,
18:12 they c' that place Mahaneh-dan
29 they c' the name of the city Dan,
Ru 4:17 and they c' his name Obed:
1Sa 1:20 a son, and c' his name Samuel,
3: 4 That the Lord c' Samuel:
5 he said, I c' not; lie down again.
6 the Lord c' yet again, Samuel.
6 I c' not, my son; lie down again.
8 Lord c' Samuel again the third
8 that the Lord had c' the child.
10 the Lord came, and stood, and c'
16 Then Eli c' Samuel, and said,
6: 2 the Philistines c' for the priests
7:12 and c' the name of it Eben-ezer,
9: 9 he that is now c' a Prophet was
9 beforetime c' a Seer.)
26 c' Saul to the top of the house,
10:17 And Samuel c' the people together
12:18 So Samuel c' unto the Lord;
13: 4 were c' together after Saul,
16: 5 and c' them to the sacrifice.
8 Then Jesse c' Abinadab, and
19: 7 And Jonathan c' David, and
23: 8 Saul c' all the people together
28 c' that place Sela-hammahlekoth.
28:15 I have c' thee, that thou mayest
29: 6 Then Achish c' David, and said
2Sa 1: 7 he saw me, and c' unto me.
15 David c' one of the young men,
2:16 place was c' Helkath-hazzurim,
26 Then Abner c' to Joab, and said,
5: 9 and c' it the city of David.
20 he c' the name of that place
6: 2 whose name is c' by the name of
8 and he c' the name of the place
9: 2 when they had c' him unto David,
9 king c' to Ziba, Saul's servant,
11:13 David had c' him, he did eat
12:24 and he c' his name Solomon:
25 and he c' his name Jedidiah,
28 and it be c' after my name.
13:17 Then he c' his servant that
14:33 he had c' for Absalom, he came
15: 2 Absalom c' unto him, and said,
11 out of Jerusalem, that were c';
18:18 c' the pillar after his own name:
18 and it is c' unto this day,
26 the watchman c' unto the porter,
28 Ahimaaz c', and said unto the king,
21: 2 And the king c' the Gibeonites,
22: 7 In my distress I c' upon the Lord,
1Ki 1: 9 c' all his brethren the king's sons,
10 Solomon his brother, he c' not.
19 and hath c' all the sons of the king,
19 Solomon thy servant hath he not c'.
25 and hath c' all the king's sons,
26 servant Solomon, hath he not c'.
2:36 the king sent and c' for Shimei,
42 sent and c' for Shimei, and said
7:21 and c' the name thereof Jachin:
21 and c' the name thereof Boaz.
8:43 have builded, is c' by thy name.
9:13 And he c' them the land of Cabul
12: 3 and c' him. And Jeroboam
20 and c' him unto the congregation,
16:24 and c' the name of the city
17:10 he c' to her, and said, Fetch me,
11 he c' to her, and said, Bring me,
18: 3 And Ahab c' Obadiah, which was
26 and c' on the name of Baal
20: 7 the king of Israel c' all the elders
22: 9 the king of Israel c' an officer,
2Ki 3:10 that the Lord hath c' these three
13 for the Lord hath c' these three
4:12 had c' her, she stood before him.
15 had c' her, she stood in the door.
22 And she c' unto her husband,
36 And he c' Gehazi, and said, Call
36 this Shunammite. So he c' her.
6:11 and he c' his servants, and said
7:10 they came and c' unto the porter
11 c' the porters; and they told
8: 1 for the Lord hath c' for a famine;
9: 1 the prophet c' one of the children
12: 7 Jehoash c' for Jehoiada the priest,
14: 7 and c' the name of it Joktheel
18: 4 and he c' it Nehushtan.
18 when they had c' to the king,
1Ch 4: 9 c' his name Jabez, saying,
10 And Jabez c' on the God of Israel,

1Ch 6:65 which are c' by their names.
7:16 and she c' his name Peresh;
23 he c' his name Beriah, because
11: 7 they c' it the city of David.
13: 6 cherubims, whose name is c' on it.
11 that place is c' Perez-uzza
14:11 they c' the name of that place
15:11 David c' for Zadok and Abiathar
21:26 and c' upon the Lord;
22: 6 Then he c' for Solomon his son,
2Ch 3:17 and c' the name of that on the
6:33 I have built is c' by thy name.
7:14 people, which are c' by my name,
10: 3 And they sent and c' him.
18: 8 Israel c' for one of his officers,
20:26 the name of the same place was c',
24: 6 And the king c' for Jehoiada
Ezr 2:61 and was c' after their name:
Ne 5:12 Then I c' the priests, and took
7:63 and was c' after their name.
Es 2:14 that she were c' by name.
3:12 scribes c' on the thirteenth day
4: 5 Then c' Esther for Hatach,
11 who is not c', there is one law
11 I have not been c' to come in
5:10 and c' for his friends, and
8: 9 king's scribes c' at that time
9:26 they c' these days Purim after
Job 1: 4 and c' for their three sisters to eat
9:16 I had c', and he had answered me;
19:16 I c' my servant, and he gave me
42:14 c' the name of the first, Jemima;
Ps 17: 6 I have c' upon thee, for thou
18: 6 In my distress I c' upon the Lord,
31:17 O Lord; for I have c' upon thee:
50: 1 Lord hath spoken and c' the earth
53: 4 they have not c' upon God.
79: 6 kingdoms that have not c' upon
88: 9 Lord, I have c' daily upon thee,
99: 6 they c' upon the Lord, and he
105:16 c' for a famine upon the land,
116: 4 c' I upon the name of the Lord;
118: 5 I c' upon the Lord in distress: the
Pr 1:24 I have c', and ye refused; I have
16:21 wise in heart shall be c' prudent:
24: 8 be c' a mischievous person.
Ca 5: 6 c' him, but he gave me no answer.
Isa 1:26 c', The city of righteousness,
4: 1 only let us be c' by thy name,
3 c' holy, even every one that is
9: 6 his name shall be c' Wonderful,
13: 3 I have also c' my mighty ones
19:18 be c', The city of destruction.
31: 4 multitude of shepherds is c' forth
32: 5 person shall be no more c' liberal,
35: 8 it shall be c' The way of holiness;
41: 2 man from the east, c' him
9 c' thee from the chief men thereof,
42: 6 I the Lord have c' thee
43: 1 I have c' thee by thy name;
7 every one that is c' by my name:
22 thou hast not c' upon me, O Jacob,
45: 4 I have even c' thee by thy name:
47: 1 thou shalt no more be c' tender
5 be c', The lady of kingdoms.
48: 1 which are c' by the name of Israel,
8 and wast c' a transgressor
12 O Jacob and Israel, my c'; I am he;
15 yea, I have c' him: I have
49: 1 The Lord hath c' me from the
50: 2 I c', was there none to answer?
51: 2 I c' him alone, and blessed him,
54: 5 of the whole earth shall he be c'.
6 the Lord hath c' thee as a woman
56: 7 mine house shall be c' an house of
58:12 and thou shalt be c', The repairer
61: 3 might be c' trees of righteousness,
62: 2 thou shalt be c' by a new name,
4 thou shalt be c' Hephzi-bah, and
12 thou shalt be c', Sought out,
63:19 they were not c' by thy name.
65: 1 a nation that was not c' by my
12 when I c', ye did not answer;
66: 4 when I c', none did answer;
Jer 7:10 in this house, which is c' by my
11 Is this house, which is c' by my
13 I c' you, but ye answered not;
14 this house, which is c' by my name,
30 the house which is c' by my name,
32 it shall no more be c' Tophet,
11:16 The Lord c' thy name, A green
12: 6 they have c' a multitude after
14: 9 we are c' by thy name; leave us
15:16 I am c' by thy name, O Lord God
19: 6 place shall no more be c' Tophet,
20: 3 Lord hath not c' thy name Pashur,
23: 6 he shall be c', The Lord our
25:29 the city which is c' by my name,
30:17 they c' thee an Outcast, saying,
32:34 house, which is c' by my name,
33:16 name wherewith she shall be c',
34:15 house which is c' by my name:
35:17 and I have c' unto them, but they
36: 4 Then Jeremiah c' Baruch the
42: 8 Then c' he Johanan the son of
La 1:15 he hath c' an assembly against me
19 I c' for my lovers, but they
21 bring the day that thou hast c',
2:22 Thou hast c' as in a solemn day
3:55 I c' upon thy name, O Lord,
57 in the day that I c' upon thee:
Eze 9: 3 he c' to the man clothed with linen,
20:29 And the name thereof is c' Bamah
Da 5:12 now let Daniel be c', and he will
8:16 which c', and said, Gabriel, make
9:18 the city which is c' by thy name:

Da 9:19 thy people are c· by thy name.
10: 1 whose name was c· Belteshazzar;
Ho 11: 1 c· my son out of Egypt.
2 As they c· them, so they went
7 though they c· them to the most
Am 7: 4 Lord God c· to contend by fire,
9:12 heathen, which are c· by my name,
Hag 1:11 And I c· for a drought upon the
Zec 8: 3 Jerusalem shall be c· a city of
11: 7 the one I c· Beauty,
7 and the other I c· Bands;
M't 1:16 born Jesus, who is c· Christ.
25 and he c· his name Jesus.
2: 7 privily c· the wise men, enquired
15 Out of Egypt have I c· my son.
23 and dwelt in a city c· Nazareth:
23 He shall be c· a Nazarene.
4:18 Simon c· Peter, and Andrew his
21 mending their nets; and he c·
5: 9 they shall be c· the children of God.
19 he shall be c· the least in the
19 the same shall be c· great in the
10: 1 And when he had c· unto him his
2 The first, Simon, who is c· Peter,
25 If they have c· the master of the
13:55 is not his mother c· Mary? and
15:10 And he c· the multitude, and said
32 Then Jesus c· his disciples unto
18: 2 Jesus c· a little child unto him,
32 after that he had c· him, said
20:16 for many be c·, but few chosen.
25 But Jesus c· them unto him, and
32 Jesus stood still, and c· them,
21:13 My house shall be c· the house of
22:14 many are c·, but few are chosen.
23: 7 and to be c· of men, Rabbi, Rabbi.
8 be not ye c· Rabbi: for one is your
10 Neither be ye c· masters: for one
25:14 c· his own servants, and delivered
26: 3 high priest, who was c· Caiaphas,
14 Then one of the twelve, c· Judas
36 unto a place c· Gethsemane, and
27: 8 that field was c·, The field of
16 a notable prisoner, c· Barabbas.
17 or Jesus which is c· Christ?
22 do then with Jesus which is c·
33 unto a place c· Golgotha, that is
M'r 1:20 straightway he c· them: and they
3:23 And he c· them unto him, and said
6: 7 And he c· unto him the twelve,
7:14 when he had c· all the people unto
8: 1 Jesus c· his disciples unto him,
34 when he had c· the people unto
9:35 and c· the twelve, and saith unto
10:42 But Jesus c· them to him, and
49 and commanded him to be c·.
11:17 My house shall be c· of all nations
12:43 he c· unto him his disciples, and
14:72 Peter c· to mind the word that
15:16 into the hall, c· Prætorium;
Lu 1:32 shall be c· the Son of the Highest:
35 shall be c· the Son of God.
36 with her, who was c· barren.
59 and they c· him Zacharias, after
60 Not so, but he shall be c· John.
61 kindred that is c· by this name.
62 father, how he would have him c·.
76 shalt be c· the prophet of the
2: 4 David, which is c· Bethlehem;
21 his name was c· Jesus, which was
23 shall be c· holy to the Lord;)
6:13 he c· unto him his disciples:
15 and Simon c· Zelotes,
7:11 he went into a city c· Nain;
8: 2 Mary c· Magdalene, out of whom
54 and c·, saying, Maid, arise.
9: 1 c· his twelve disciples together,
10 belonging to the city c· Bethsaida.
10:39 she had a sister c· Mary, which
13:12 he c· her to him,
15:19 no more worthy to be c· thy son:
21 no more worthy to be c· thy son.
26 he c· one of the servants, and
16: 2 And he c· him, and said unto
5 So he c· every one of his lord's
18:16 But Jesus c· them unto him,
19:13 And he c· his ten servants, and
15 these servants to be c· unto him,
29 the mount c· the mount of Olives,
21:37 that is c· the mount of Olives.
22: 1 which is c· the Passover.
25 upon them are c· benefactors.
47 he that was c· Judas, one of the
23:13 when he had c· together the
33 to the place which is c· Calvary,
24:13 to a village c· Emmaus, which
Joh 1:42 thou shalt be c· Cephas, which
48 Before that Philip c· thee, when
2: 2 Jesus was c·, and his disciples,
9 governor of the feast c· the
4: 5 of Samaria, which is c· Sychar,
25 Messias cometh, which is c· Christ:
5: 2 which is c· in the Hebrew tongue
9:11 A man that is c· Jesus made clay,
18 until they c· the parents of him
24 Then again c· they the man that
10:35 If he c· them gods, unto whom
11:16 Thomas, which is c· Didymus,
28 and c· Mary her sister secretly,
54 into a city c· Ephraim, and there
12:17 when he c· Lazarus out of his
15:15 but I have c· you friends;
18:33 c· Jesus, and said unto him, Art
19:13 in a place that is c· the Pavement,
17 a place c· the place of a skull,
17 is c· in the Hebrew Golgotha:

Joh 20:24 one of the twelve, c· Didymus,
21: 2 and Thomas c· Didymus, and
Ac 1:12 from the mount c· Olivet, which
19 insomuch as that field is c· in
23 Joseph c· Barsabas, who was
3: 2 gate of the temple which is c·
11 the porch that is c· Solomon's,
4:18 they c· them, and commanded
5:21 and c· the council together, and
40 when they had c· the apostles,
6: 2 Then the twelve c· the multitude
9 of the synagogue, which is c·
7:14 and c· his father Jacob to him,
8: 9 a certain man, c· Simon, which
9:11 the street which is c· Straight,
11 for one c· Saul, of Tarsus: for
21 them which c· on his name in
36 by interpretation is c· Dorcas:
41 when he had c· the saints and
10: 1 man in Cæsarea c· Cornelius,
1 of the band c· the Italian band,
7 c· two of his household servants,
18 And c·, and asked whether Simon,
23 Then c· he them in, and lodged
24 and had c· together his kinsmen
11:26 the disciples were c· Christians
13: 1 and Simeon that was c· Niger,
2 work whereunto I have c· them.
7 who c· for Barnabas and Saul,
9 Then Saul, (who also is c· Paul,)
14:12 they c· Barnabas, Jupiter; and
15:17 upon whom my name is c·,
16:10 that the Lord had c· us for to
29 Then he c· for a light, and
19:25 Whom he c· together with the
40 we are in danger to be c· in
20: 1 Paul c· unto him the disciples,
17 and c· the elders of the church.
23: 6 I am c· in question.
17 c· one of the centurions unto him,
18 Paul the prisoner c· me unto him,
23 he c· unto him two centurions,
24: 2 when he was c· forth, Tertullus
21 I am c· in question by you this
27: 8 which is c· The fair havens;
14 tempestuous wind, c· Euroclydon.
16 a certain island which is c· Clauda,
28: 1 knew that the island was c· Melita.
17 Paul c· the chief of the Jews
20 have I c· for you, to see you,
Ro 1: 1 c· to be an apostle, separated
6 are ye also the c· of Jesus Christ:
7 c· to be saints: grace to you
2:17 Behold, thou art c· a Jew, and
7: 3 she shall be c· an adulteress:
8:28 to them who are the c· according
30 them he also c·: and whom he c·,
9: 7 In Isaac shall thy seed be c·.
24 Even us, whom he hath c·, not of
26 there shall they be c· the children
1Co 1: 1 c· to be an apostle of Jesus Christ
2 in Christ Jesus, c· to be saints,
9 by whom ye were c· unto the
24 But unto them which are c·, both
26 mighty, not many noble, are c·:
5:11 if any man that is c· a brother
7:15 but God hath c· us to peace.
17 as the Lord hath c· every one, so
18 Is any man c· being circumcised?
18 Is any c· in uncircumcision? let
20 same calling wherein he was c·.
21 Art thou c· being a servant? care
22 For he that is c· in the Lord, being
22 he that is c·, being free, is
24 wherein he is c·, therein abide
8: 5 though there be that are c· gods,
15: 9 am not meet to be c· an apostle,
Ga 1: 6 from him that c· you into the
15 and c· me by his grace,
5:13 ye have been c· unto liberty;
Eph 2:11 c· Uncircumcision by
11 that which is c· the Circumcision
4: 1 wherewith ye are c·,
4 even as ye are c· in one hope
Col 3:15 to the which also ye are c·
4:11 Jesus, which is c· Justus, who are
1Th 2:12 worthy of God, who hath c· you
4: 7 hath not c· us unto uncleanness,
2Th 2: 4 himself above all that is c· God,
14 he c· you by our gospel, to the
1Ti 6:12 life, whereunto thou art also c·,
20 of science falsely so c·:
2Ti 1: 9 and c· us with an holy calling,
Heb 3:13 while it is c· To day; lest any
5: 4 but he that is c· of God, as was
10 C· of God an high priest after
7:11 not be c· after the order of Aaron?
9: 2 which is c· the sanctuary.
3 tabernacle which is c· the Holiest
15 are c· might receive the promise
11: 8 Abraham, when he was c· to go
16 not ashamed to be c· their God:
18 in Isaac shall thy seed be c·:
24 refused to be c· the son of
Jas 2: 7 name by the which ye are c·?
23 he was c· the Friend of God.
1Pe 1:15 as he which hath c· you is holy,
2: 9 who hath c· you out of darkness
21 hereunto were ye c·: because
3: 9 that ye are thereunto c·, that ye
5:10 the God of all grace, who hath c·
2Pe 1: 3 of him that hath c· us to glory
1Jo 3: 1 we should be c· the sons of God:
Jude 1 preserved in Jesus Christ, and c·:
Re 1: 9 was in the isle that is c· Patmos,
8:11 name of the star is c· Wormwood:

Re 11: 8 spiritually is c· Sodom and Egypt,
12: 9 serpent, c· the Devil, and Satan,
16:16 c· in the Hebrew tongue
17:14 they that are with him are c·,
19: 9 which are c· unto the marriage
11 him was c· Faithful and True,
13 his name is c· The Word of God.

calledst
J'g 8: 1 that thou c· us not, when thou
1Sa 3: 5 for thou c· me. And he said, I
Ps 81: 7 c· in trouble, and I delivered thee;
Eze 23:21 Thus thou c· to remembrance the

callest
M't 19:17 Why c· thou me good? there is
M'k 10:18 unto him, Why c· thou me good?
Lu 18:19 Why c· thou me good? none is

calleth
1Ki 8:43 that the stranger c· to thee for:
2Ch 6:33 that the stranger c· to thee for;
Job 12: 4 c· upon God, and he answereth
Ps 42: 7 Deep c· unto deep at the noise
147: 4 he c· them all by their names.
Pro 18: 6 and his mouth c· for strokes.
Isa 21:11 He c· to me out of Seir, Watchman,
40:26 he c· them all by names by the
59: 4 None c· for justice, nor any
64: 7 there is none that c· upon thy
Hos 7: 7 there is none among them that c·
Am 5: 8 that c· for the waters of the sea,
9: 6 he that c· for the waters of the sea,
M't 27:47 that, said, This man c· for Elias.
M'r 3:13 and c· unto him whom he would:
10:49 of good comfort, rise; he c· thee.
12:37 therefore himself c· him Lord;
15:35 heard it, said, Behold, he c· Elias.
Lu 15: 6 home, he c· together his friends
9 c· her friends and her neighbours
20:37 c· the Lord the God of Abraham,
44 David therefore c· him Lord, how
Joh 10: 3 and he c· his own sheep by name,
11:28 The Master is come, and c· for thee.
Ro 4:17 c· those things which be not as
9:11 not of works, but of him that c·;)
1Co 12: 3 c· Jesus accursed: and that no
Gal 5: 8 cometh not of him that c· you.
1Th 5:24 Faithful is he that c· you, who
Re 2:20 which c· herself a prophetess, to

calling
Nu 10: 2 for the c· of the assembly, and for
Isa 1:13 the c· of assemblies, I cannot
41: 4 c· the generations from the
46:11 C· a ravenous bird from the east,
Eze 23:19 in c· to remembrance the days of
M't 11:16 and c· unto their fellows,
M'r 3:31 without, sent unto him, c· him.
11:21 Peter c· to remembrance saith
15:44 and c· unto him the centurion, he
Lu 7:19 And John c· unto him two of his
32 c· one to another, and saying,
Ac 7:59 stoned Stephen, c· upon God, and
22:16 sins, c· on the name of the Lord.
Ro 11:29 gifts and c· of God are without
1Co 1:26 For ye see your c·, brethren, how
7:20 abide in the same c· wherein he
Eph 1:18 what is the hope of his c·, and
4: 4 are called in one hope of your c·;
Ph'p 3:14 for the prize of the high c· of
2Th 1:11 would count you worthy of this c·,
2Ti 1: 9 us, and called us with an holy c·,
Heb 3: 1 partakers of the heavenly c·,
1Pe 3: 6 Even as Sara obeyed Abraham, c·
2Pe 1:10 give diligence to make your c·

calm
Ps 107:29 He maketh the storm a c·, so that
Jon 1:11 unto thee, that the sea may be c·
12 so shall the sea be c· unto you:
M't 8:26 the sea; and there was a great c·.
M'k 4:39 ceased, and there was a great c·.
Lu 8:24 they ceased, and there was a c·.

Calneh *(cal'-neh)* See also CALNO; CANNEH.
Ge 10:10 and Erech, and Accad, and C·,
Am 6: 2 Pass ye unto C·, and see; and

Calno *(cal'-no)* See also CALNEH.
Isa 10: 9 Is not C· as Carchemish? is not

Calvary *(cal'-va-ry)*
Lu 23:33 which is called C·, there they

calve See also CALVED; CALVETH.
Job 39: 1 thou mark when the hinds do c·?
Ps 29: 9 the Lord maketh the hinds to c·,

calved
Jer 14: 5 the hind also c· in the field, and

calves
1Sa 6: 7 bring their c· home from them:
10 and shut up their c· at home:
14:32 took sheep, and oxen, and c·,
1Ki 12:28 made two c· of gold, and said
32 unto the c· that he had made:
2Ki 10:29 golden c· that were in Beth-el,
17:16 them molten images, even two c·,
2Ch 11:15 and for the c· which he had made.
13: 8 there are with you golden c·, which
Ps 68:30 with the c· of the people, till
Hos 10: 5 shall fear because of the c· of
13: 2 the men that sacrifice kiss the c·,
14: 2 will we render the c· of our lips.
Am 6: 4 the c· out of the midst of the stall;
Mic 6: 6 offerings, with c· of a year old?
Mal 4: 2 and grow up as c· of the stall.
Heb 9:12 by the blood of goats and c·, but
19 took the blood of c· and of goats,

calveth
Job 21:10 their cow c·, and casteth not her

came^ See also BECAME; CAMEST; OVERCAME.
Ge 4: 3 c' to pass, that Cain brought of
8 c' to pass, when they were in the
6: 1 c' to pass, when men began to
4 sons of God c' in unto the daughters
7:10 c' to pass after seven days, that
8: 6 it c' to pass at the end of forty
11 And the dove c' in to him in the
13 it c' to pass in the six hundredth
10:14 (out of whom c' Philistim,) and
11: 2 it c' to pass, as they journeyed
5 the Lord c' down to see the city
31 and they c' unto Haran, and
12: 5 and into the land of Canaan they c'.
11 it c' to pass, when he was come
14 it c' to pass, that, when Abram was
13:18 c' and dwelt in the plain of Mamre,
14: 1 c' to pass in the days of Amraphel
5 fourteenth year c' Chedorlaomer,
7 and c' to En-mishpat, which is
13 there c' one that had escaped,
15: 1 word of the Lord c' unto Abram
4 the word of the Lord c' unto him,
11 when the fowls c' down upon the
17 And it c' to pass, that, when the
19: 1 And there c' two angels to Sodom
5 Where are the men which c' in to
8 c' they under the shadow
9 This one fellow c' in to sojourn
9 Lot, and c' near to break the door.
17 c' to pass, when they had brought
29 it c' to pass, when God destroyed
34 c' to pass on the morrow, that the
20: 3 God c' to Abimelech in a dream
13 c' to pass when God caused me
21:22 And it c' to pass at that time, that
22: 1 c' to pass after these things, that
9 they c' to the place which God had
20 it c' to pass after these things,
23: 2 Abraham c' to mourn for Sarah,
24:15 it c' to pass, before he had done
15 behold, Rebekah c' out, who was
16 and filled her pitcher, and c' up.
22 it c' to pass, as the camels had
30 it c' to pass, when he saw the
30 that he c' unto the man; and,
32 And the man c' into the house:
42 And I c' this day unto the well,
45 Rebekah c' forth with her pitcher
52 c' to pass, that when Abraham's
62 Isaac c' from the way of the well
25:11 it c' to pass after the death of
25 And the first c' out red, all over
26 after that c' his brother out,
29 and Esau c' from the field,
26: 8 And it c' to pass, when he had
32 And it c' to pass the same day,
32 that Isaac's servants c', and told
27: 1 And it c' to pass, that when Isaac
18 And he c' unto his father, and
27 And he c' near, and kissed him:
30 And it c' to pass, as soon as
30 that Esau his brother c' in from
35 Thy brother c' with subtilty,
29: 1 on his journey, and c' into the
9 Rachel c' with her father's sheep:
10 And it c' to pass, when Jacob
13 And it c' to pass, when Laban
23 And it c' to pass in the evening,
25 it c' to pass, that in the morning,
30:16 And Jacob c' out of the field in
25 And it c' to pass, when Rachel
30 little which thou hadst before I c',
38 when the flocks c' to drink,
38 when they c' to drink.
41 And it c' to pass, whensoever
31:10 And it c' to pass at the time that
24 And God c' to Laban...in a dream
32: 6 We c' to thy brother Esau,
13 took of that which c' to his hand
33: 1 Esau c', and with him four hundred
3 until he c' near to his brother.
6 Then the handmaidens c' near,
7 Leah also with her children c' near,
7 after c' Joseph near and Rachel,
18 And Jacob c' to Shalem, a city of
18 when he c' from Padan-aram;
34: 7 c' out of the field when they heard
20 And Hamor and Shechem his son c'
25 And it c' to pass on the third day,
25 and c' upon the city boldly,
27 The sons of Jacob c' upon the slain,
35: 6 So Jacob c' to Luz, which is in the
9 when he c' out of Padan-aram, and
22 And it c' to pass when Israel dwelt
27 Jacob c' unto Isaac his father
36:16 dukes that c' of Eliphaz in the
17 these are the dukes that c' of Reuel
18 the dukes that c' of Aholibamah
29 the dukes that c' of the Horites;
40 names of the dukes that c' of Esau,
37:14 Hebron, and he c' to Shechem.
18 before he c' near unto them,
23 And it c' to pass, when Joseph
25 a company of Ishmeelites c'
38: 1 it c' to pass at that time,
9 and it c' to pass, when he
18 and c' in unto her, and she
24 it c' to pass about three months
27 And it c' to pass in the time of
28 it c' to pass, when she travailed,
28 thread, saying, This c' out first.
29 And it c' to pass, as he drew back
29 behold, his brother c' out: and
30 afterward c' out his brother,
Ge 39: 5 And it c' to pass from the time
7 And it c' to pass after these things,
10 And it c' to pass, as she spake
11 And it c' to pass about this time,
13 And it c' to pass, when she saw
14 he c' in unto me to lie with me,
15 And it c' to pass, when he heard
16 by her, until his lord c' home.
17 us, c' in unto me to mock me:
18 And it c' to pass, as I lifted
19 And it c' to pass, when his master
40: 1 it c' to pass after these things,
6 And Joseph c' in unto them
20 And it c' to pass the third day,
41: 1 And it c' to pass at the end of
2 there c' up out of the river seven
3 seven other kine c' up after them
5 seven ears of corn c' up upon
8 And it c' to pass in the morning
13 And it c' to pass, as he interpreted
14 raiment, and c' in unto Pharaoh.
18 there c' up out of the river seven
19 seven other kine c' up after them,
22 seven ears c' up in one stalk,
27 ill favoured kine that c' up
50 sons before the years of famine c',
57 all countries c' into Egypt to
42: 5 And the sons of Israel c' to buy
6 and Joseph's brethren c', and
29 they c' unto Jacob their father,
35 And it c' to pass as they emptied
43: 2 And it c' to pass, when they had
19 And they c' near to the steward
20 we c' indeed down at the first
21 And it c' to pass, when we
21 when we c' to the inn, that we
25 against Joseph c' at noon: for they
26 And when Joseph c' home, they
44:14 And Judah and his brethren c'
18 Then Judah c' near unto him,
24 And it c' to pass when we
24 when we c' up unto thy servant
45: 4 And they c' near. And he said,
25 and c' into the land of Canaan
46: 1 and c' to Beer-sheba, and offered
6 and c' into Egypt, Jacob, and all
8 of the children of Israel, which c'
26 All the souls that c' with Jacob
26 which c' out of his loins,
27 which c' into Egypt, were
28 they c' into the land of Goshen.
47: 1 Then Joseph c' and told Pharaoh,
15 the Egyptians c' unto Joseph,
18 they c' unto him the second year,
48: 1 And it c' to pass after these
5 before I c' unto thee into Egypt,
7 for me, when I c' from Padan,
50:10 And they c' to the threshingfloor
Ex 1: 1 of Israel, which c' into Egypt;
1 and his household c' with Jacob.
5 all the souls that c' out of the
21 And it c' to pass, because the
2: 5 And the daughter of Pharaoh c'
11 And it c' to pass in those days,
16 and they c' and drew water,
17 And the shepherds c' and drove
18 And when they c' to Reuel their
23 And it c' to pass in process of
23 and their cry c' up unto God
3: 1 and c' to the mountain of God,
4:24 And it c' to pass by the way in
5:15 officers of the children of Israel c'
20 as they c' forth from Pharaoh:
23 For since I c' to Pharaoh to speak
6:28 And it c' to pass on the day when
8: 6 and the frogs c' up, and covered
24 and there c' a grievous swarm
10: 3 And Moses and Aaron c' in unto
12:29 it c' to pass, that at midnight
41 And it c' to pass at the end of the
41 the selfsame day it c' to pass,
51 And it c' to pass the selfsame day,
13: 3 ye c' out from Egypt, out of the
4 c' ye out in the month Abib.
8 when I c' forth out of Egypt.
15, 17 it c' to pass, when Pharaoh
14:20 And it c' between the camp of
20 the one c' not near the other
24 it c' to pass, that in the morning
28 that c' into the sea after them;
15:23 And when they c' to Marah,
27 And they c' to Elim, where were
16: 1 Israel c' unto the wilderness of
10 And it c' to pass, as Aaron spake
13 And it c' to pass, that at even
13 that at even the quails c' up,
22 c' to pass, that on the sixth day
22 the rulers of the congregation c'
27 And it c' to pass, that there
35 until they c' to a land inhabited;
35 until they c' unto the borders
17: 8 Then c' Amalek, and fought with
11 And it c' to pass, when Moses
18: 5 Jethro, Moses' father in law, c'
7 welfare; and they c' into the tent.
12 and Aaron c', and all the elders
13 it c' to pass on the morrow,
19: 1 day c' they into the wilderness
7 Moses c' and called for the elders
16 And it c' to pass on the third day
20 Lord c' down upon mount Sinai,
21: 3 If he c' in by himself, he shall
22:15 hired thing, it c' for his hire.
24: 3 And Moses c' and told the people
32:19 c' [1961] to pass, as soon as he c' nigh
Ex 32:24 fire, and there c' out this calf.
30 And it c' to pass on the morrow,
33: 7 c' to pass, that every one which
8 And it c' to pass, when Moses
9 And it c' to pass, as Moses entered
34:29 And it c' to pass, when Moses
29 Moses c' down from mount Sinai
29 when he c' down from the mount,
32 all the children of Israel c' nigh:
34 took the vail off, until he c' out.
34 And he c' out, and spake unto
35:21 And they c', every one whose
22 And they c', both men and women,
36: 4 sanctuary, c' every man from his
40:17 it c' to pass in the first month
32 when they c' near unto the altar,
Le 9:22 and c' down from offering of the
23 c' out, and blessed the people:
24 And there c' a fire out from before
Nu 4:47 every one that c' to do the service
7: 1 And it c' to pass on the day that
9: 6 c' before Moses and before Aaron
10:11 it c' to pass on the twentieth day
21 the tabernacle against they c'.
35 And it c' to pass when the ark
11:20 Why c' we forth out of Egypt?
25 And the Lord c' down in a cloud,
25 and it c' to pass, that, when the
12: 4 And they three c' out.
5 And the Lord c' down in the pillar
5 Miriam: and they both c' forth.
13:22 the south, and c' unto Hebron;
23 they c' unto the brook of Eshcol,
26 they went and c' to Moses, and to
27 We c' unto the land whither thou
14:45 Amalekites c' down, and the
16:27 Dathan and Abiram c' out, and
31 And it c' to pass, as he had made
35 there c' out a fire from the Lord,
42 c' to pass, when the congregation
43 And Moses and Aaron c' before
17: 8 it c' to pass, that on the morrow
19: 2 and upon which never c' yoke.
20: 1 Then c' the children of Israel, even
11 and the water c' out abundantly,
20 And Edom c' out against him with
22 Kadesh, and c' unto Mount Hor.
28 Eleazar c' down from the mount.
21: 1 heard tell that Israel c' by the way
7 Therefore the people c' to Moses,
9 and it c' to pass, that if a serpent
23 and he c' to Jahaz, and fought
22: 7 they c' unto Balaam, and spake
9 And God c' unto Balaam, and said,
16 And they c' to Balaam, and said to
20 And God c' unto Balaam at night,
39 and they c' unto Kirjath-huzoth,
41 And it c' to pass on the morrow,
23:17 And when he c' to him, behold, he
24: 2 the spirit of God c' upon him.
25: 6 one of the children of Israel c'
26: 1 And it c' to pass after the plague,
27: 1 c' the daughters of Zelophehad,
31:14 hundreds, which c' from the battle.
48 of hundreds, c' near unto Moses:
32: 2 Reuben c' and spake unto Moses,
11 none of the men that c' up out of
16 they c' near unto him, and said,
33: 9 from Marah, and c' unto Elim:
36: 1 of the sons of Joseph, c' near, and
De 1: 3 it c' to pass in the fortieth year,
19 and we c' to Kadesh-barnea.
22 And ye c' near unto me every one
24 and c' unto the valley of Eshcol,
31 ye went, until ye c' into this place.
44 c' out against you, and chased
2:14 which we c' from Kadesh-barnea,
16 it c' to pass, when all the men
23 which c' forth out of Caphtor,
32 Then Sihon c' out against us, he
3: 1 king of Bashan c' out against us,
4:11 And ye c' near and stood under
45 after they c' forth out of Egypt,
5:23 c' to pass, when ye heard the voice
23 that ye c' near unto me, even all
9: 7 until ye c' unto this place, ye have
11 c' to pass at the end of forty days
15 So I turned and c' down from the
10: 5 I turned myself and c' down from
11: 5 until ye c' into this place;
10 from whence ye c' out, where
22:14 took this woman, and when I c'
23: 4 when ye c' forth out of Egypt;
29: 7 And when ye c' unto this place,
7 Og the king of Bashan, c' out
16 how we c' through the nations
31:24 And it c' to pass, when Moses
32:17 to new gods that c' newly up,
44 And Moses c' and spake all the
33: 2 The Lord c' from Sinai, and
2 and he c' with ten thousands of
21 c' with the heads of the people, he
Jos 1: 1 it c' to pass, that the Lord spake
2: 1 and c' into an harlot's house,
2 there c' men in hither to night of
4 There c' men unto me, but I
5 it c' to pass about the time of
8 c' up unto them upon the roof;
10 when ye c' out of Egypt; and
22 c' unto the mountain, and abode
23 and c' to Joshua the son of Nun,
3: 1 c' to Jordan, he and all the
2 And it c' to pass after three
14 And it c' to pass, when the people
16 waters which c' down from

Jos 3:16 those that c' down toward the sea
4: 1, 11 it c' to pass, when all the people
18 it c' to pass, when the priests
19 the people c' up out of Jordan on
22 Israel c' over this Jordan on dry
5: 1 it c' to pass, when all the kings
4 the people that c' out of Egypt,
4 the way, after they c' out of Egypt.
5 all the people that c' out were
5 as they c' forth out of Egypt,
6 c' out of Egypt, were consumed,
8 it c' to pass, when they had done
13 And it c' to pass, when Joshua was
6: 1 none went out, and none c' in.
8 c' to pass, when Joshua had
9 the rereward c' after the ark,
11 and they c' into the camp, and
13 the rereward c' after the ark of
15 it c' to pass on the seventh day,
16 it c' to pass at the seventh time,
20 c' to pass, when the people heard
8:11 c' before the city, and pitched
14 it c' to pass, when the king of Ai
24 And it c' to pass, when Israel
9: 1 it c' to pass, when all the kings
12 we c' forth to go unto you; but
16 it c' to pass, at the end of three
17 c' unto their cities on the third
10: 1 it c' to pass, when Adoni-zedec
9 Joshua therefore c' unto them
11 And it c' to pass, as they fled
20 And it c' to pass, when Joshua
24 it c' to pass, when they brought
24 they c' near, and put their feet
27 And it c' to pass at the time of
33 king of Gezer c' up to help
11: 1 c' to pass, when Jabin king of
5 they c' and pitched together at
7 So Joshua c', and all the people of
21 And at that time c' Joshua, and
14: 6 Then the children of Judah c'
15:18 And it c' to pass, as she
18 as she c' unto him, that she
16: 7 and c' to Jericho, and went out
17: 4 they c' near before Eleazar the
13 it c' to pass, when the children of
18: 9 and c' again to Joshua to the host
11 the children of Benjamin c' up
11 the coast of their lot c' forth
16 And the border c' down to the
19: 1 the second lot c' forth to Simeon,
10 And the third lot c' up for the
17 And the fourth lot c' out to
24 the fifth lot c' out for the tribe
32 The sixth lot c' out to the children
40 And the seventh lot c' out for the
21: 1 c' near the heads of the fathers
4 the lot c' out for the families of
45 the house of Israel; all c' to pass.
22:10 And when they c' unto the borders
15 they c' unto the children of Reuben.
23: 1 it c' to pass a long time after that
24: 6 and ye c' unto the sea; and the
11 and c' unto Jericho: and the men
29 it c' to pass after these things,
J'g 1: 1 after the death of Joshua it c' to
14 And it c' to pass, when she
14 when she c' to him, that she
28 c' to pass, when Israel was strong,
2: 1 an angel of the Lord c' up from
4 it c' to pass, when the angel of the
19 c' to pass, when the judge was
3:10 the Spirit of the Lord c' upon him,
20 Ehud c' unto him; and he was
22 of his belly; and the dirt c' out.
24 his servants c'; and when they
27 it c' to pass, when he was come,
4: 5 and the children of Israel c' up to
22 Jael c' out to meet him, and said
22 and when he c' into her tent,
5:14 out of Machir c' down governors,
19 The kings c' and fought, then
23 because they c' not to the help of
6: 3 that the Midianites c' up, and
3 east, even they c' up against them;
5 they c' up with their cattle and
5 and they c' as grasshoppers
7 it c' to pass, when the children of
11 And there c' an angel of the Lord,
25 And it c' to pass the same night,
34 Spirit of the Lord c' upon Gideon,
35 and they c' up to meet them.
7: 9 And it c' to pass the same night,
13 and c' unto a tent, and smote it
19 were with him, c' unto the outside
8: 4 Gideon c' to Jordan, and passed
15 And he c' unto the men of Succoth,
33 it c' to pass, as soon as Gideon
9:25 they robbed all that c' along that
26 And Gaal the son of Ebed c' with
42 And it c' to pass on the morrow,
52 And Abimelech c' unto the tower,
57 and upon them c' the curse of
11: 4 c' to pass in process of time, that
13 when they c' up out of Egypt,
16 when Israel c' up from Egypt,
16 the Red sea, and c' to Kadesh;
18 c' by the east side of the land of
18 c' not within the border of Moab:
29 Spirit of the Lord c' upon
34 Jephthah c' to Mizpeh unto his
34 his daughter c' out to meet him
35 it c' to pass, when he saw her,
39 c' to pass at the end of two months,
13: 6 woman c' and told her husband,
6 A man of God c' unto me,
J'g 13: 9 the angel of God c' again unto the
10 that c' unto me the other day.
11 c' to the man, and said unto him,
20 it c' to pass, when the flame went
14: 2 And he c' up, and told his father
5 c' to the vineyards of Timnath:
6 Spirit of the Lord c' mightily
9 and c' to his father and mother,
11 it c' to pass, when they saw him,
14 Out of the eater c' forth meat,
14 out of the strong c' forth sweetness.
15, 17 c' to pass on the seventh day,
19 Spirit of the Lord c' upon him,
15: 1 it c' to pass, within a while after,
6 the Philistines c' up, and burnt
14 he c' unto Lehi, the Philistines
14 Spirit of the Lord c' mightily
17 c' to pass, when he had made an
19 there c' water thereout; and when
19 spirit c' again, and he revived:
16: 4 it c' to pass afterward, that he
5 lords of the Philistines c' up unto
16 c' to pass, when she pressed him
18 lords of the Philistines c' up unto
25 it c' to pass, when their hearts
31 the house of his father c' down,
17: 8 he c' to mount Ephraim to the
18: 2 when they c' to mount Ephraim,
7 c' to Laish, and saw the people
8 they c' unto their brethren to Zorah
13 and c' unto the house of Micah.
15 c' to the house of the young man
17 c' in thither, and took the graven
27 and c' unto Laish, unto a people
19: 1 And it c' to pass in those days,
5 it c' to pass on the fourth day,
10 and c' over against Jebus, which
16 there c' an old man from his work
22 the man that c' into thine house,
26 Then c' the woman in the dawning
30 day that the children of Israel c'
20: 4 I c' into Gibeah that belongeth to
21 the children of Benjamin c' forth
24 And the children of Israel c' near
26 c' unto the house of God, and wept,
33 c' forth out of their places, even
34 there c' against Gibeah ten
42 them which c' out of the cities
48 all that c' to hand: also they set
48 all the cities that they c' to.
21: 2 the people c' to the house of God,
4 And it c' to pass on the morrow,
5 c' not up with the congregation
5 him that c' not up to the Lord
8 c' not up to Mizpeh to the Lord?
8 there c' none to the camp from
14 Benjamin c' again at that time;
Ru 1: 1 it c' to pass in the days when
2 they c' into the country of Moab,
19 until they c' to Beth-lehem. And it
19 And it c' to pass, when they were
22 until they c' to Beth-lehem in the
2: 3 she went, and c', and gleaned in
4 Boaz c' from Beth-lehem, and said
6 the Moabitish damsel that c' back
7 among the sheaves: so she c',
3: 7 she c' softly, and uncovered his
8 it c' to pass at midnight, that the
14 that a woman c' into the floor.
16 when she c' to her mother in law,
4: 1 of whom Boaz spake c' by; unto
1Sa 1:12 c' to pass, as she continued
19 and c' to their house to Ramah:
20 it c' to pass, when the time was
2:13 sacrifice, the priest's servant c',
14 all the Israelites that c' thither.
15 the priest's servant c', and said
19 when she c' up with her husband
27 there c' a man of God unto Eli,
3: 2 And it c' to pass at that time,
10 the Lord c', and stood, and called
4: 1 the word of Samuel c' to all Israel.
5 ark of the covenant of the Lord c'
12 and c' to Shiloh the same day with
13 when he c', lo, Eli sat upon a seat
13 when the man c' into the city,
14 the man c' in hastily, and told Eli.
16 I am he that c' out of the army,
18 c' to pass, when he made mention
19 for her pains c' upon her.
5:10 it c' to pass, as the ark of God
10 as the ark of God c' to Ekron,
6:14 the cart c' into the field of Joshua,
7: 1 And the men of Kirjath-jearim c',
2 it c' to pass, while the ark abode
11 them, until they c' under Beth-car.
13 c' no more into the coast of Israel:
8: 1 c' to pass, when Samuel was old,
4 and c' to Samuel unto Ramah,
9:12 for he c' to day to the city; for
14 Samuel c' out against them, for
15 a day before Saul c', saying,
26 c' to pass about the spring of the
10: 9 all those signs c' to pass that day.
10 when they c' thither to the hill,
10 the Spirit of God c' upon him,
11 c' to pass, when all that knew
13 made an end of prophesying, he c'
14 were no where, we c' to Samuel.
11: 1 Then Nahash the Ammonite c' up,
4 Then c' the messengers to Gibeah
5 Saul c' after the herd out of the
6 the Spirit of God c' upon Saul
7 and they c' out with one consent.
9 the messengers that c', Thus shall
9 the messengers c' and shewed it
1Sa 11:11 they c' into the midst of the
11 and it c' to pass that they which
12:12 Ammon c' against you, ye said
13: 5 c' up and pitched in Michmash,
8 Samuel c' not to Gilgal; and the
10 it c' to pass, that as soon as he
10 behold, Samuel c'; and Saul went
17 the spoilers c' out of the camp
22 it c' to pass in the day of battle,
14: 1 Now it c' to pass upon a day,
19 it c' to pass, while Saul talked
20 they c' to the battle: and, behold,
25 all they of the land c' to a wood;
15: 2 way, when he c' up from Egypt.
5 And Saul c' to a city of Amalek,
6 when they c' up out of Egypt.
10 c' the word of the Lord unto
12 Saul c' to Carmel, and, behold,
13 Samuel c' to Saul: and Saul said
32 And Agag c' unto him delicately.
35 Samuel c' no more to see Saul
16: 4 spake, and c' to Beth-lehem.
6 c' to pass, when they were come,
13 Spirit of the Lord c' upon David
21 David c' to Saul, and stood before
23 it c' to pass, when the evil spirit
17:20 he c' to the trench, as the host
22 and c' and saluted his brethren.
23 there c' up the champion, the
34 and there c' a lion, and a bear,
41 the Philistine c' on and drew
48 it c' to pass, when the Philistine
48 and c' and drew nigh to meet
18: 1 c' to pass, when he had made
6 And it c' to pass as they
6 as they c', when David was
6 the women c' out of all cities
10 And it c' to pass on the morrow,
10 spirit from God c' upon Saul,
13 out and c' in before the people.
16 he went out and c' in before them.
19 c' to pass at the time when Merab
30 it c' to pass, after they went forth,
19:18 c' to Samuel to Ramah, and told
22 c' to a great well that is in Sechu:
23 until he c' to Naioth in Ramah.
20: 1 and c' and said before Jonathan,
27 it c' to pass on the morrow,
35 And it c' to pass in the morning,
38 the arrows, and c' to his master.
21: 1 c' David to Nob to Ahimelech
5 these three days, since I c' out,
22: 5 and c' into the forest of Hareth.
11 they c' all of them to the king.
23: 6 it c' to pass, when Abiathar
6 c' down with an ephod in his
19 Then c' up the Ziphites to Saul
25 wherefore he c' down into a rock,
27 there c' a messenger unto Saul,
24: 1 c' to pass, when Saul was
3 he c' to the sheepcotes by the way,
5 c' to pass afterward, that David
16 And it c' to pass, when David
25: 9 when David's young men c', they
12 went again, and c' and told him all
20 c' down by the covert of the hill,
20 and his men c' down against her;
36 Abigail c' to Nabal; and, behold,
37 But it c' to pass in the morning,
38 it c' to pass about ten days after,
26: 1 And the Ziphites c' unto Saul to
3 he saw that Saul c' after him into
5 and c' to the place where Saul had
7 David and Abishai c' to the people
15 for there c' one of the people in to
27: 9 and returned, and c' to Achish.
28: 1 And it c' to pass in those days,
4 and c' and pitched in Shunem:
8 they c' to the woman by night:
21 And the woman c' unto Saul,
30: 1 And it c' to pass, when David
3 David and his men c' to the city,
9 and c' to the brook Besor, where
12 when he had eaten, his spirit c'
21 David c' to the two hundred men,
21 when David c' near to the people,
23 the company that c' against us
26 when David c' to Ziklag, he sent
31: 7 Philistines c' and dwelt in them.
8 And it c' to pass on the morrow,
8 Philistines c' to strip the slain,
12 c' to Jabesh, and burnt them
2Sa 1: 1 c' to pass after the death of Saul,
2 It c' even to pass on the third day,
2 a man c' out of the camp from Saul
2 when he c' to David, that he fell to
2: 1 And it c' to pass after this, that
4 the men of Judah c', and there
23 that the spear c' out behind
23 that as many as c' to the place
29 and they c' to Mahanaim.
32 they c' to Hebron at break of day
3: 6 it c' to pass, while there was war
20 So Abner c' to David to Hebron,
22 Joab c' from pursuing a troop,
23 Abner the son of Ner c' to the king,
24 Then Joab c' to the king, and said,
24 behold, Abner c' unto thee; why is
25 he c' to deceive thee, and to know
35 all the people c' to cause David to
4: 4 when the tidings c' of Saul and
4 c' to pass, as she made haste to
5 c' about the heat of the day to the
6 And they c' thither into the midst
7 For when they c' into the house,
5: 1 c' all the tribes of Israel to David

2Sa 5: 3 the elders of Israel c' to the king
17 Philistines c' up to seek David;
18 Philistines also c' and spread
20 And David c' to Baal-perazim,
22 Philistines c' up yet again, and
6: 6 they c' to Nachon's threshingfloor,
16 the ark of the Lord c' into the city
20 daughter of Saul c' out to meet
7: 1 it c' to pass, when the king sat in
4 c' to pass that night, that the
4 word of the Lord c' unto Nathan,
8: 1 c' to pass, that David smote the
5 Syrians of Damascus c' to succour
10: 1 And it c' to pass after this, that
2 David's servants c' into the land
8 the children of Ammon c' out,
14 of Ammon, and c' to Jerusalem.
16 and they c' to Helam; and Shobach
17 over Jordan, and c' to Helam.
11: 1 And it c' to pass, after the year
2 it c' to pass in an evening tide,
4 and she c' in unto him, and he lay
14 And it c' to pass in the morning
16 it c' to pass, when Joab observed
22 and c' and shewed David all that
23 and c' out unto us into the field,
12: 1 he c' unto him, and said unto him,
4 And there c' a traveller unto the
18 it c' to pass on the seventh day,
20 and c' into the house of the Lord,
20 then he c' to his own house;
13: 1 c' to pass after this, that Absalom
23 it c' to pass after two full years,
24 Absalom c' to the king,
30 And it c' to pass, while they were
30 that tidings c' to David, saying,
34 there c' much people by the way
36 it c' to pass, as soon as he had
36 behold, the king's sons c',
14:31 and c' to Absalom unto his house,
33 Joab c' to the king, and told him:
33 called for Absalom, he c' to the
15: 1 c' to pass after this, that
2 c' to the king for judgment,
5 when any man c' nigh to him to
6 all Israel that c' to the king for
7 And it c' to pass after forty years,
13 there c' a messenger to David,
18 six hundred men which c' after
32 it c' to pass, that when David
32 Hushai the Archite c' to meet him
37 Hushai David's friend c' into the
37 Absalom c' into Jerusalem.
16: 5 when king David c' to Bahurim,
5 behold, thence c' out a man
5 he c' forth, and cursed still as he
5 and cursed still as he c'.
11 my son, which c' forth of my
14 the people that were with him, c'
15 the men of Israel, c' to Jerusalem,
16 it c' to pass, when Hushai the
17:18 c' to a man's house in Bahurim,
20 And when Absalom's servants c'
21 c' to pass, after they were
21 that they c' up out of the well,
24 Then David c' to Mahanaim.
27 And it c' to pass, when David
18: 4 all the people c' out by hundreds
25 And he c' apace, and drew near.
31 And, behold, Cushi c'; and Cushi
19: 5 Joab c' into the house to the king,
8 all the people c' before the king:
15 king returned, and c' to Jordan.
15 And Judah c' to Gilgal,
16 c' down with the men of Judah
24 the son of Saul c' down to meet
24 until the day he c' again in peace.
25 And it c' to pass, when he was
31 Gileadite c' down from Rogelim,
41 all the men of Israel c' to the king,
20: 3 David c' to his house at Jerusalem;
12 every one that c' by him stood still.
15 they c' and besieged him in Abel
21:18 c' to pass after this, that there
22:10 bowed the heavens also, and c'
23:13 c' to David in the harvest time
24: 6 Then they c' to Gilead, and to the
6 and they c' to Dan-jaan,
7 And c' to the stronghold of Tyre,
8 all the land, they c' to Jerusalem
11 the word of the Lord c' unto the
13 So Gad c' to David, and told him,
18 And Gad c' that day to David,
1Ki 1:22 Nathan the prophet also c' in.
28 And she c' into the king's presence,
32 And they c' before the king.
40 all the people c' up after him,
42 Abiathar the priest c': and
47 the king's servants c' to bless our
53 he c' and bowed himself to king
2: 7 they c' to me when I fled because
8 he c' down to meet me at Jordan,
13 son of Haggith c' to Bathsheba
28 Then tidings c' to Joab: for Joab
30 And Benaiah c' to the tabernacle
39 c' to pass at the end of three
3:15 And he c' to Jerusalem, and stood
16 Then c' there two women, that
18 And it c' to pass the third day
4:27 that c' unto king Solomon's table,
34 And there c' of all people to hear
5: 7 it c' to pass, when Hiram heard
6: 1 it c' to pass in the four hundred
11 word of the Lord c' to Solomon,
7:14 And he c' to king Solomon,
8: 3 And all the elders of Israel c',

1Ki 8: 9 they c' out of the land of Egypt.
10 c' to pass, when the priests were
9: 1 And it c' to pass, when Solomon
10 c' to pass at the end of twenty
12 And Hiram c' out from Tyre
24 Pharaoh's daughter c' up out of
28 And they c' to Ophir, and fetched
10: 1 c' to prove him with hard questions.
2 And she c' to Jerusalem with a
7 believed not the words, until I c',
10 c' no more such abundance of spices
12 there c' no such almug trees,
14 gold that c' to Solomon in one year
22 once in three years c' the navy of
29 And a chariot c' up and went out
11: 4 c' to pass, when Solomon was old,
15 c' to pass, when David was in
18 and c' to Paran: and they took
18 out of Paran, and they c' to Egypt,
29 it c' to pass at that time when
12: 2 And it c' to pass, when Jeroboam
3 all the congregation of Israel c',
12 Jeroboam and all the people c' to
20 And it c' to pass, when all Israel
22 word of God c' unto Shemaiah
13: 1 there c' a man of God out of Judah
4 it c' to pass, when king Jeroboam
10 returned not by the way that he c'
11 and his sons c' and told him all
12 God went, which c' from Judah.
20 c' to pass, as they sat at the table,
20 the word of the Lord c' unto the
21 that c' from Judah, saying,
23 c' to pass, after he had eaten
25 and they c' and told it in the city
29 and the old prophet c' to the city,
31 c' to pass, after he had buried
14: 4 and c' to the house of Ahijah.
6 as she c' in at the door, that he
17 and departed, and c' to Tirzah:
17 c' to the threshold of the door,
25 And it c' to pass in the fifth year
25 of Egypt c' up against Jerusalem:
15:21 it c' to pass, when Baasha heard
29 it c' to pass, when he reigned,
16: 1 the word of the Lord c' to Jehu
7 Jehu the son of Hanani c' the
11 c' to pass, when he began to reign,
18 c' to pass, when Zimri saw that
31 c' to pass, as if it had been a light
17: 2 the word of the Lord c' unto him,
7 And it c' to pass after a while, that
8 word of the Lord c' unto him,
10 when he c' to the gate of the city,
17 it c' to pass after these things,
22 soul of the child c' into him again,
18: 1 it c' to pass after many days,
1 the word of the Lord c' to Elijah
17 c' to pass, when Ahab saw Elijah,
21 And Elijah c' unto all the people,
27 it c' to pass at noon, that Elijah
29 c' to pass, when midday was past,
30 all the people c' near unto him.
31 word of the Lord c', saying, Israel
36 And it c' to pass at the time of the
36 that Elijah the prophet c' near,
44 c' to pass at the seventh time,
45 it c' to pass in the mean while,
19: 3 and c' to Beer-sheba, which
4 c' and sat down under a juniper
7 the angel of the Lord c' again
9 And he c' thither unto a cave,
9 behold, the word of the Lord c' to
20: 5 the messengers c' again, and said,
12 c' to pass, when Benhadad heard
13 there c' a prophet unto Ahab king
19 the princes of the provinces c'
22 the prophet c' to the king of Israel,
26 c' to pass at the return of the year,
28 there c' a man of God, and spake
30 Ben-hadad fled, and c' into the
32 c' to the king of Israel, and said,
33 Then Ben-hadad c' forth to him;
43 and displeased, and c' to Samaria.
21: 1 it c' to pass after these things,
4 Ahab c' into his house heavy and
5 But Jezebel his wife c' to him, and
13 there c' in two men, children of
15 c' to pass, when Jezebel heard
16 And it c' to pass, when Ahab heard
17 word of the Lord c' to Elijah
27 And it c' to pass, when Ahab heard
28 the word of the Lord c' to Elijah
22: 2 it c' to pass in the third year,
2 the king of Judah c' down
15 So he c' to the king. And the
21 there c' forth a spirit, and stood
32, 33 it c' to pass, when the captains
2Ki 1: 6 There c' a man up to meet us,
7 manner of man was he which c'
10 there c' down fire from heaven,
12 fire of God c' down from heaven,
13 c' and fell on his knees before
14 there c' fire down from heaven,
2: 1 c' to pass, when the Lord would
3 that were at Beth-el c' forth
4 leave thee. So they c' to Jericho.
5 that were at Jericho c' to Elisha,
9 it c' to pass, when they were
11 c' to pass, as they still went on,
15 they c' to meet him, and bowed
18 when they c' again to him, (for he
23 there c' forth little children out
24 there c' forth two she bears out
3: 5 it c' to pass, when Ahab was dead,
15 it c' to pass, when the minstrel

2Ki 3:15 the hand of the Lord c' upon him.
20 c' to pass in the morning, when
20 there c' water by the way of Edom,
24 when they c' to the camp of Israel,
4: 6 it c' to pass, when the vessels
7 Then she c' and told the man of
11 that he c' thither, and he turned
25 went, and c' unto the man of God
25 it c' to pass, when the man of God
27 when she c' to the man of God to
27 Gehazi c' near to thrust her away.
38 Elisha c' again to Gilgal: and
39 c' and shred them into the pot of
40 it c' to pass, as they were eating
42 there c' a man from Baal-shalisha,
5: 7 it c' to pass, when the king of
9 So Naaman c' with his horses
13 his servants c' near, and spake
14 his flesh c' again like unto the
15 and c', and stood before him:
24 And when he c' to the tower, he
6: 4 when they c' to Jordan, they cut
14 they c' by night, and compassed
18 when they c' down to him, Elisha
20 it c' to pass, when they were come
23 the bands of Syria c' no more into
24 c' to pass after this, that
30 it c' to pass, when the king heard
32 ere the messenger c' to him, he
33 behold, the messenger c' down
7: 8 when these lepers c' to the
8 c' again, and entered into
10 they c', and called unto the porter
10 We c' to the camp of the Syrians,
17 when the king c' down to him.
18 it c' to pass as the man of God
8: 3 c' to pass at the seven years' end,
5 it c' to pass, as he was telling the
7 And Elisha c' to Damascus; and
9 c' and stood before him, and said,
14 and c' to his master; who said to
15 it c' to pass on the morrow, that
9: 5 when he c', behold, the captains of
11 Jehu c' forth to the servants of
11 wherefore c' this mad fellow to
17 spied the company of Jehu as he c',
18 The messenger c' to them, but he
19 on horseback, which c' to them,
20 He c' even unto them, and cometh
22 c' to pass, when Joram saw Jehu,
36 Wherefore they c' again, and told
10: 7 And it c' to pass, when the letter
7 when the letter c' to them,
8 And there c' a messenger, and told
9 it c' to pass in the morning, that
12 and departed, and c' to Samaria.
17 And when he c' to Samaria, he slew
21 and all the worshippers of Baal c',
21 not a man left that c' not.
21 And they c' into the house of Baal;
25 it c' to pass, as soon as he had
11: 9 and c' to Jehoiada the priest,
13 she c' to the people into the temple
16 way by the which the horses c'
19 and c' by the way of the gate of
12:10 scribe and the high priest c' up,
13:14 Joash the king of Israel c' down
21 it c' to pass, as they were burying
14: 5 c' to pass, as soon as the kingdom
13 and c' to Jerusalem, and brake
15:12 And so it c' to pass.
14 and c' to Samaria, and smote
19 of Assyria c' against the land:
29 c' Tiglath-pileser king of Assyria,
16: 5 son of Remaliah king of Israel c'
6 the Syrians c' to Elath, and dwelt
11 against king Ahaz c' from Damascus.
17: 3 Against him c' up Shalmaneser
5 Then the king of Assyria c' up
28 had carried away from Samaria c'.
18: 1 it c' to pass in the third year of
9 it c' to pass in the fourth year of
9 Shalmaneser king of Assyria c' up
17 and c' to Jerusalem. And when
17 they were come up, they c' and
18 there c' out to them Eliakim the
37 Then c' Eliakim the son of Hilkiah,
19: 1 it c' to pass, when king Hezekiah
5 So the servants of king Hezekiah c'
33 By the way that he c', by the same
35 c' to pass that night, that the
37 And it c' to pass, as he was
20: 1 prophet Isaiah the son of Amoz c'
4 c' to pass, afore Isaiah was gone
4 word of the Lord c' to him, saying,
14 Then c' Isaiah the prophet unto
14 from whence c' they unto thee?
21:15 the day their fathers c' forth out
22: 3 it c' to pass in the eighteenth year
9 Shaphan the scribe c' to the king,
11 c' to pass, when the king had
23: 9 the priests of the high places c'
17 which c' from Judah, and
18 prophet that c' out of Samaria.
34 he c' to Egypt, and died there.
24: 1 king of Babylon c' up, and
3 c' this upon Judah, to remove
7 And the king of Egypt c' not
10 king of Babylon c' up against
11 Nebuchadnezzar king of Babylon c'
20 c' to pass in Jerusalem and
25: 1 it c' to pass in the ninth year of
1 king of Bayblon c', he, and all
8 king of Babylon, c' Nebuzar-adan,
23 there c' to Gedaliah, to Mizpah,
25 c' to pass in the seventh month.

2Ki 25:25 c' and ten men with him, and
26 and c' to Egypt: for they were
27 it c' to pass in the seven and
1Ch 1:12 (of whom c' the Philistines,) and
2:53 of them c' the Zareathites, and
55 the Kenites that c' of Hemath, the
4:41 And these written by name c' in
5: 2 and of him c' the chief ruler; but
7:21 because they c' down to take away
22 and his brethren c' to comfort him.
10: 7 the Philistines c' and dwelt in
8 it c' to pass on the morrow,
8 when the Philistines c' to strip the
11: 3 Therefore c' all the elders of Israel
12: 1 these are they that c' to David
16 And there c' of the children of
18 the spirit c' upon Amasai, who
19 when he c' with the Philistines
22 there c' to David to help him,
23 c' to David to Hebron, to turn the
38 c' with a perfect heart to Hebron,
13: 9 they c' unto the threshingfloor
14: 9 the Philistines c' and spread
11 So they c' up to Baal-perazim;
15:26 c' to pass, when God helped the
29 And it c' to pass, as the ark of the
29 ark of the covenant of the Lord c'
17: 1 it c' to pass, as David sat in his
3 And it c' to pass the same night,
16 And David the king c' and sat
18: 1 it c' to pass, that David smote the
5 Syrians of Damascus c' to help
19: 1 c' to pass after this, that Nahash
2 So the servants of David c' into
7 who c' and pitched before Medeba.
7 from their cities, and c' to battle.
9 the children of Ammon c' out,
15 city. Then Joab c' to Jerusalem.
17 and c' upon them, and set the
20: 1 it c' to pass, that after the year
1 and c' and besieged Rabbah.
4 And it c' to pass after this, that
21: 4 all Israel, and c' to Jerusalem.
11 So Gad c' to David, and said unto
21 And as David c' to Ornan, Ornan
22: 8 But the word of the Lord c' to me,
24: 7 the first lot c' forth to Jehoiarib,
28 Mahli c' Eleazar, who had no son
25: 9 the first lot c' forth for Asaph
26:14 lots; and his lot c' out northward.
16 Hosah the lot c' forth westward,
27: 1 which c' in and went out month
2Ch 1:13 Solomon c' from his journey to
5: 4 And all the elders of Israel c';
10 children of Israel, when they c' out
11 And it c' to pass, when the priests
13 It c' even to pass, as the trumpeters
7: 1 the fire c' down from heaven, and
3 Israel saw how the fire c' down,
11 all that c' into Solomon's heart to
8: 1 it c' to pass at the end of twenty
9: 1 she c' to prove Solomon with hard
6 believed not their words, until I c',
13 Now the weight of gold that c' to
21 c' the ships of Tarshish bringing
10: 2 And it c' to pass, when Jeroboam
3 So Jeroboam and all Israel c' and
12 So Jeroboam and all the people c'
11: 2 word of the Lord c' to Shemaiah
14 and c' to Judah and Jerusalem:
16 c' to Jerusalem, to sacrifice unto
12: 1 it c' to pass, when Rehoboam had
2 it c' to pass, that in the fifth year
2 Shishak king of Egypt c' up
3 that c' with him out of Egypt;
4 to Judah, and c' to Jerusalem.
5 Then c' Shemaiah, the prophet to
7 word of the Lord c' to Shemaiah,
9 So Shishak king of Egypt c' up
11 the guard c' and fetched them,
13:15 of Judah shouted, it c' to pass,
14: 9 there c' out against them Zerah
9 chariots; and c' unto Mareshah.
14 the fear of the Lord c' upon them:
15: 1 the Spirit of God c' upon Azariah
5 nor to him that c' in, but great
16: 1 Baasha king of Israel c' up
5 it c' to pass, when Baasha heard
7 Hanani the seer c' to Asa king of
18:20 Then there c' out a spirit, and
23 the son of Chenaanah c' near,
31 it c' to pass, when the captains of
32 For it c' to pass, that, when the
20: 1 c' to pass after this also, that the
1 Ammonites c' against Jehoshaphat
2 c' some that told Jehoshaphat,
4 of Judah they c' to seek the Lord.
10 invade, when they c' out of the land,
14 Asaph, c' the Spirit of the Lord
24 Judah c' toward the watch tower
25 when Jehoshaphat and his people c
28 And they c' to Jerusalem with
21:12 And there c' a writing to him from
17 And they c' up into Judah, and
19 c' to pass, that in process of time,
22: 1 the band of men that c' with the
8 c' to pass, that, when Jehu was
23: 2 Israel, and they c' to Jerusalem.
12 and praising the king, she c' to
20 they c' through the high gate into
24: 4 it c' to pass after this, that Joash
11 it c' to pass, that at what time
11 high priest's officer c' and emptied
17 c' the princes of Judah, and made
18 c' upon Judah and Jerusalem
20 the Spirit of God c' upon Zechariah
2Ch 24:23 it c' to pass at the end of the year,
23 host of Syria c' up against him:
23 and they c' to Judah
24 c' with a small company of men,
25: 3 it c' to pass, when the kingdom
7 But there c' a man of God to him,
14 it c' to pass, after that Amaziah
16 it c' to pass, as he talked with
20 would not hear; for it c' of
28: 9 went out before the host that c' to
12 against them that c' from the war,
20 Tilgath-pilneser king of Assyria c'
29:15 sanctified themselves, and c',
17 c' they to the porch of the Lord:
30:11 themselves, and c' to Jerusalem.
25 all the congregation that c' out of
25 and the strangers that c'
27 their prayer c' up to his holy
31: 5 as the commandment c' abroad,
8 Hezekiah and the princes c' and
32: 1 Sennacherib king of Assyria c', and
21 they that c' forth of his own bowels
26 the wrath of the Lord c' not upon
34: 9 And when they c' to Hilkiah the
19 And it c' to pass, when the king
35:20 Necho king of Egypt c' up to fight
22 c' to fight in the valley of Megiddo.
36: 6 c' up Nebuchadnezzar king of
Ezr 2: 1 and c' again unto Jerusalem and
2 Which c' with Zerubbabel: Jeshua,
68 they c' to the house of the Lord
4: 2 Then they c' to Zerubbabel, and
12 the Jews which c' up from thee
5: 3 At the same time c' to them Tatnai,
5 till the matter c' to Darius: and
16 Then c' the same Sheshbazzar, and
7: 8 c' to Jerusalem in the fifth month,
9 c' he to Jerusalem, according to
8:32 And we c' to Jerusalem, and abode
9: 1 the princes c' to me, saying,
10: 6 he c' thither, he did eat no bread,
Ne 1: 1 it c' to pass in the month Chisleu,
2 Hanani, one of my brethren, c', he
4 it c' to pass, when I heard these
2: 1 it c' to pass in the month Nisan
9 Then I c' to the governors beyond
11 So I c' to Jerusalem, and was there
4: 1, 7 c' to pass, that when Sanballat,
12 it c' to pass, that when the Jews
12 the Jews which dwelt by them c'
15 it c' to pass, when our enemies
16 And it c' to pass from that time
5:17 beside those that c' unto us from
6: 1 Now it c' to pass, when Sanballat,
10 I c' unto the house of Shemaiah
16 it c' to pass, that when all our
17 the letters of Tobiah c' unto them.
7: 1 it c' to pass, when the wall was
5 the genealogy of them which c' up
6 and c' again to Jerusalem and
7 Who c' with Zerubbabel, Jeshua,
73 when the seventh month c', the
13: 3 c' to pass, when they had heard
6 c' I unto the king, and after
7 I c' to Jerusalem, and understood
19 it c' to pass, that when the gates
21 c' they no more on the sabbath.
Es 1: 1 Now it c' to pass in the days of
17 in before him, but she c' not.
2: 8 So it c' to pass, when the king's
13 Then thus c' every maiden unto
14 she c' in unto the king no more,
3: 4 Now it c' to pass, when they
4: 2 c' even before the king's gate:
3 commandment and his decree c',
4 maids and her chamberlains c'
9 And Hatach c' and told Esther
5: 1 it c' to pass on the third day
5 So the king and Haman c' to the
10 and when he c' home, he sent
6: 6 So Haman c' in. And the king
12 Mordecai c' again to the king's
14 c' the king's chamberlains,
7: 1 king and Haman c' to banquet
8: 1 Mordecai c' before the king;
17 commandment and his decree c',
9:25 when Esther c' before the king,
Job 1: 6 a day when the sons of God c'
6 and Satan c' also among them.
14 there c' a messenger unto Job,
16, 17, 18 c' also another, and said,
19 there c' a great wind from the
21 c' I out of my mother's womb,
2: 1 a day when the sons of God c'
1 and Satan c' also among them
11 c' every one from his own place;
3:11 when I c' out of the belly?
26 was I quiet; yet trouble c'.
4:14 Fear c' upon me, and trembling,
6:20 they c' thither, and were ashamed.
26: 4 and whose spirit c' from thee?
29:13 was ready to perish c' upon me:
30:14 They c' upon me as a wide
26 then evil c' unto me: and when I
26 waited for light, there c' darkness.
38:29 Out of whose womb c' the ice?
42:11 Then c' there unto him all his
Ps 18: 6 and my cry c' before him, even
9 the heavens also, and c' down:
27: 2 c' upon me to eat up my flesh,
51:*title* when Nathan the prophet c'
52:*title* when Doeg the Edomite c' and
54:*title* when the Ziphims c' and said
78:21 anger also c' up against Israel;
31 The wrath of God c' upon them,
88:17 They c' round about me daily
Ps 105:19 Until the time that his word c':
23 Israel also c' into Egypt; and
31 and there c' divers sorts of flies,
34 He spake, and the locusts c',
Pr 7:15 Therefore c' I forth to meet thee,
Ec 5:15 he c' forth of his mother's
15 shall he return to go as he c',
16 in all points as he c', so shall he go:
9:14 there c' a great king against it,
Ca 4: 2 which c' up from the washing;
Isa 7: 1 And it c' to pass in the day of
11:16 in the days that he c' up out of
20: 1 that Tartan c' unto Ashdod,
30: 4 his ambassadors c' to Hanes.
36: 1 Now it c' to pass in the fourteenth
1 Sennacherib king of Assyria c' up
3 Then c' forth unto him Eliakim,
22 Then c' Eliakim, the son of
37: 1 c' to pass, when king Hezekiah
5 servants of king Hezekiah c' to
34 By the way that he c', by the same
38 c' to pass, as he was worshipping
38: 1 the son of Amoz c' unto him,
4 Then c' the word of the Lord to
39: 3 Then c' Isaiah the prophet unto
3 from whence c' they unto thee?
41: 5 were afraid, drew near, and c'.
48: 3 suddenly, and they c' to pass.
5 before it c' to pass I shewed it
50: 2 when I c', was there no man?
66: 7 before her pain c', she was
Jer 1: 2 word of the Lord c' in the days
3 c' also in the day of Jehoiakim
4 word of the Lord c' unto me,
11 the word of the Lord c' unto me
13 word of the Lord c' unto me the
2: 1 word of the Lord c' to me,
3: 9 it c' to pass through the lightness
7: 1 The word that c' to Jeremiah from
25 day that your fathers c' forth
31 neither c' it into my heart.
8:15 looked for peace, but no good c';
11: 1 The word that c' to Jeremiah
13: 3 And the word of the Lord c' unto
6 it c' to pass after many days,
8 the word of the Lord c' unto me,
14: 1 c' to Jeremiah concerning the
3 they c' to the pits, and found no
16: 1 The word of the Lord c' also unto
17:16 that which c' out of my lips was
18: 1 The word which c' to Jeremiah
5 Then the word of the Lord c' to
19: 5 neither c' it into my mind:
14 Then c' Jeremiah from Tophet,
20: 3 And it c' to pass on the morrow,
18 Wherefore c' I forth out of the
21: 1 the word which c' unto Jeremiah
24: 4 the word of the Lord c' unto me,
25: 1 The word that c' to Jeremiah
26: 1 Judah c' this word from the Lord,
8 Now it c' to pass, when Jeremiah
10 they c' up from the king's house
27: 1 came this word unto Jeremiah
28: 1 And it c' to pass the same year,
12 word of the Lord c' unto Jeremiah
29:30 Then c' the word of the Lord unto
30: 1 The word that c' to Jeremiah from
32: 1 The word that c' to Jeremiah from
6 The word of the Lord c' unto me,
8 Hanameel mine uncle's son c' to
23 And they c' in, and possessed it;
26 Then c' the word of the Lord unto
35 neither c' it into my mind, that
33: 1 word of the Lord c' unto Jeremiah
19 word of the Lord c' unto Jeremiah,
23 word of the Lord c' to Jeremiah,
34: 1 The word which c' unto Jeremiah
8 This is the word that c' unto
12 word of the Lord c' to Jeremiah
35: 1 The word which c' unto Jeremiah
11 But it c' to pass, when
11 king of Babylon c' up into the land,
12 Then c' the word of the Lord
36: 1 And it c' to pass in the fourth
1 c' unto Jeremiah from the Lord,
9 And it c' to pass in the fifth year
9 to all the people that c' from the
14 in his hand, and c' unto them.
16 Now it c' to pass when they had
23 it c' to pass, that when Jehudi
27 word of the Lord c' to Jeremiah,
37: 4 Jeremiah c' in and went out
6 Then c' the word of the Lord
11 it c' to pass, that when the army
38:27 c' all the princes unto Jeremiah,
39: 1 c' Nebuchadrezzar king of Babylon
3 of the king of Babylon c' in,
4 it c' to pass, that when Zedekiah
15 c' unto Jeremiah, while he was
40: 1 The word that c' to Jeremiah
8 Then they c' to Gedaliah to
12 and c' to the land of Judah, to
13 fields, c' to Gedaliah to Mizpah,
41: 1 it c' to pass in the seventh month,
1 c' unto Gedaliah the son of Ahikam
4 it c' to pass the second day after
5 there c' certain from Shechem,
6 and it c' to pass, as he met them,
7 when they c' into the midst of
13 Now it c' to pass, that when all
42: 1 even unto the greatest, c' near,
7 And it c' to pass after ten days,
7 that the word of the Lord c' unto
43: 1 it c' to pass, that when Jeremiah
7 they c' into the land of Egypt:
7 the Lord: thus c' they even to

Jer 43: 8 Then c' the word of the Lord
44: 1 The word that c' to Jeremiah
21 and c' it not into his mind?
46: 1 The word of the Lord which c' to
47: 1 word of the Lord that c' to
49:34 of the Lord that c' to Jeremiah
52: 3 anger of the Lord it c' to pass
4 it c' to pass in the ninth year of
4 Nebuchadrezzar king of Babylon c',
12 c' Nebuzar-adan, captain of the
31 And it c' to pass in the seven
La 1: 9 end; therefore she c' down
Eze 1: 1 it c' to pass in the thirtieth year
3 word of the Lord c' expressly
4 whirlwind c' out of the north,
5 the midst thereof c' the likeness
3:15 Then I c' to them of the captivity
16 it c' to pass at the end of seven
16 of the Lord c' unto me, saying,
4:14 neither c' there abominable
6: 1 the word of the Lord c' unto me,
7: 1 the word of the Lord c' unto me,
8: 1 And it c' to pass in the sixth
9: 2 six men c' from the way of the
8 it c' to pass, while they were
10: 6 it c' to pass, that when he had
11:13 it c' to pass, when I prophesied,
14 the word of the Lord c' unto me,
12: 1 The word of the Lord also c' unto
8 in the morning c' the word of the
17 word of the Lord c' to me, saying,
21 word of the Lord c' unto me,
26 word of the Lord c' to me, saying,
13: 1 word of the Lord c' unto me,
14: 1 Then c' certain of the elders of
2 word of the Lord c' unto me,
12 word of the Lord c' again to me,
15: 1 word of the Lord c' unto me,
16: 1 the word of the Lord c' unto me,
23 c' to pass after all thy
17: 1 word of the Lord c' unto me,
3 c' unto Lebanon, and took the
11 word of the Lord c' unto me,
18: 1 word of the Lord c' unto me again,
20: 1 it c' to pass in the seventh year,
1 certain of the elders of Israel c'
2 Then c' the word of the Lord
45 of the Lord c' unto me, saying,
21: 1 word of the Lord c' unto me,
8 the word of the Lord c' unto me,
18 word of the Lord c' unto me again,
22: 1, 17, 23 word of the Lord c' unto me,
23: 1 word of the Lord c' again unto me,
17 And the Babylonians c' to her into
39 then they c' the same day into
40 lo, they c': for whom thou didst
24: 1, 15, 20 word of the Lord c' unto
25: 1 word of the Lord c' again unto me,
26: 1 it c' to pass in the eleventh year,
1 of the Lord c' unto me, saying,
27: 1 word of the Lord c' again unto me,
28: 1 The word of the Lord c' again
11 Moreover the word of the Lord c'
20 word of the Lord c' unto me,
29: 1 of the Lord c' unto me, saying,
17 And it c' to pass in the seven and
17 the word of the Lord c' unto me,
30: 1 word of the Lord c' again unto
20 it c' to pass in the eleventh year,
20 the word of the Lord c' unto me,
31: 1 it c' to pass in the eleventh year,
1 the word of the Lord c' unto me,
32: 1 it c' to pass in the twelfth year,
1 the word of the Lord c' unto me,
17 c' to pass also in the twelfth year,
17 of the Lord c' unto me, saying,
33: 1 word of the Lord c' unto me,
21 it c' to pass in the twelfth year of
21 c' unto me, saying, The city is
22 afore he that was escaped c'; and
22 until he c' to me in the morning;
23 the word of the Lord c' unto me,
34: 1 the word of the Lord c' unto me,
35: 1 the word of the Lord c' unto me,
36:16 the word of the Lord c' unto me,
37: 7 the bones c' together, bone to his
8 the sinews and the flesh c' up
10 the breath c' into them, and they
15 The word of the Lord c' again
38: 1 the word of the Lord c' unto me,
40: 6 Then c' he unto the gate which
43: 2 the glory of the God of Israel c'
3 when I c' to destroy the city: and
4 the glory of the Lord c' into the
46: 9 whereby he c' in, but shall go forth
47: 1 the waters c' down from under
Da 1: 1 c' Nebuchadnezzar king of
2: 2 they c' and stood before the king.
29 O king, thy thoughts c' into thy
3: 8 at that time certain Chaldeans c'
26 Nebuchadnezzar c' near to the
26 c' forth of the midst of the fire.
4: 7 Then c' in the magicians, the
8 But at the last Daniel c' in before
13 an holy one c' down from heaven;
28 All this c' upon the king
5: 5 In the same hour c' forth fingers
8 Then c' in all the king's wise men:
10 c' into the banquet house: and
6:12 Then they c' near, and spake
20 when he c' to the den, he cried
24 they c' at the bottom of the den.
7: 3 great beasts c' up from the sea,
8 there c' up among them another
10 A fiery stream issued and c' forth
13 one like the Son of man c'

Da 7:13 and c' to the Ancient of days,
16 I c' near unto one of them that
20 and of the other which c' up,
22 Until the Ancient of days c', and
22 time c' that the saints possessed
8: 2 c' to pass, when I saw, that I
3 other, and the higher c' up last.
5 an he goat c' from the west on
6 c' to the ram that had two horns,
8 for it c' up four notable ones
9 one of them c' forth a little horn,
15 c' to pass, when I, even I Daniel,
17 So he c' near where I stood:
17 and when he c', I was afraid,
9: 2 word of the Lord c' to Jeremiah
23 the commandment came forth,
10: 3 neither c' flesh nor wine in my
13 c' to help me; and I remained
18 there c' again and touched
Ho 1: 1 word of the Lord that c' unto
2:15 c' up out of the land of Egypt.
Joe 1: 1 word of the Lord that c' to Joel
Am 6: 1 to whom the house of Israel c'!
7: 2 it c' to pass, that when they had
Ob 5 If thieves c' to thee, if robbers
5 if the grapegatherers c' to thee,
Jon 1: 1 word of the Lord c' unto Jonah
6 So the shipmaster c' to him, and
2: 7 and my prayer c' in unto thee,
3: 1 word of the Lord c' unto Jonah
6 word c' unto the king of Nineveh,
4: 8 it c' to pass, when the sun did
10 c' up in a night, and perished
Mic 1: 1 word of the Lord that c' to Micah
11 inhabitant of Zaanan c' not forth
12 evil c' down from the Lord unto
Hab 3: 3 God c' from Teman, and the
14 they c' out as a whirlwind to
Zep 1: 1 which c' unto Zephaniah the son
Hag 1: 1, 3 c' the word of the Lord by
9 for much, and, lo, it c' to little;
14 they c' and did work in the house
2: 1 c' the word of the Lord by the
5 when ye c' out of Egypt, so my
10 in the second year of Darius, c'
16 when one c' to an heap of twenty
16 when one c' to the pressfat for to
20 word of the Lord c' unto Haggai
Zec 1: 1 year of Darius, c' the word of
7 Darius, c' the word of the Lord
4: 1 angel that talked with me c' again,
8 the word of the Lord c' unto me,
5: 9 there c' out two women, and the
6: 1 there c' four chariots out from
9 And the word of the Lord c' unto
7: 1 And it c' to pass in the fourth year
1 word of the Lord c' unto Zechariah
4 Then c' the word of the Lord of
8 word of the Lord c' unto Zechariah,
12 therefore c' a great wrath from
8: 1 word of the Lord of hosts c' to me,
10 to him that went out or c' in
18 word of the Lord of hosts c' unto
10: 4 Out of him c' forth the corner,
14:16 which c' against Jerusalem shall
M't 1:18 before they c' together, she was
2: 1 behold, there came wise men
9 till it c' and stood over where the
21 and c' into the land of Israel.
23 he c' and dwelt in a city called
3: 1 those days c' John the Baptist.
4: 3 when the tempter c' to him,
11 angels c' and ministered unto him.
13 he c' and dwelt in Capernaum,
5: 1 was set, his disciples c' unto him:
7:25, 27 the floods c', and the winds
28 it c' to pass, when Jesus had
8: 2 there c' a leper and worshipped
5 there c' unto him a centurion,
19 a certain scribe c', and said unto
25 his disciples c' to him, and awoke
34 whole city c' out to meet Jesus:
9: 1 over, and c' into his own city.
10 it c' to pass, as Jesus sat at meat
10 sinners c' and sat down with him
14 c' to him the disciples of John,
18 there c' a certain ruler, and
20 c' behind him, and touched the
23 when Jesus c' unto the ruler's
28 the blind men c' to him: and Jesus
10:34 I c' not to send peace, but a sword.
11: 1 it c' to pass, when Jesus had made
18 For John c' neither eating nor
19 The Son of man c' eating and
12:42 she c' from the uttermost parts
44 from whence I c' out; and when
13: 4 fowls c' and devoured them up:
10 disciples c', and said unto him,
25 his enemy c' and sowed tares
27 c' and said unto him, Sir, didst
36 his disciples c' unto him, saying,
53 it c' to pass, that when Jesus had
14:12 disciples c', and took up the body,
15 his disciples c' to him, saying,
33 c' and worshipped him, saying,
34 when they were gone over, they c'
15: 1 Then c' to Jesus scribes and
12 Then c' his disciples, and said
22 a woman of Canaan c' out of the
23 his disciples c' and besought him,
25 Then c' she and worshipped him,
29 c' nigh unto the sea of Galilee;
30 great multitudes c' unto him,
39 and c' into the coasts of Magdala.
16: 1 the Sadducees c', and tempting
13 When Jesus c' into the coasts

M't 17: 7 Jesus c' and touched them, and
9 they c' down from the mountain,
14 there c' to him a certain man,
19 c' the disciples to Jesus apart,
24 c' to Peter, and said, Doth not
18: 1 time c' the disciples unto Jesus,
21 Then c' Peter to him, and said,
31 and c' and told unto their lord
19: 1 it c' to pass, that when Jesus had
1 and c' into the coasts of Judæa
3 The Pharisees also c' unto him,
16 And, behold, one c' and said unto
20: 9 when they c' that were hired
10 when the first c', they supposed
20 Then c' to him the mother of
28 c' not to be ministered unto,
21:14 the blind and the lame c' to him
19 he c' to it, and found nothing
23 the elders of the people c' unto
28 and he c' to the first, and said,
30 And he c' to the second, and said
32 For John c' unto you in the way
22:11 when the king c' in to see the
23 same day c' to him the Sadducees,
24: 1 and his disciples c' to him for to
3 Olives, the disciples c' unto him
39 until the flood c', and took them
25:10 went to buy, the bridegroom c';
11 Afterward c' also the other
20 c' and brought other five talents,
22 c' and said, Lord, thou deliveredst
24 c' and said, Lord, I knew thee
36 in prison, and ye c' unto me.
39 or in prison, and c' unto thee?
26: 1 it c' to pass, when Jesus had
7 There c' unto him a woman
17 the disciples c' to Jesus, saying,
43 he c' and found them asleep
47 one of the twelve, c', and with
49 he c' to Jesus, and said, Hail,
50 Then c' they, and laid hands on
60 though many false witnesses c',
60 At the last c' two false witnesses,
69 a damsel c' unto him, saying,
73 c' unto him they that stood by,
27:32 as they c' out, they found a man
53 c' out of the graves after his
57 there c' a rich man of Arimathæa,
62 priests and Pharisees c' together
28: 1 c' Mary Magdalene and the other
2 and c' and rolled back the stone
9 they c' and held him by the feet,
11 c' into the city, and shewed unto
13 c' by night, and stole him away
18 Jesus c' and spake unto them,
M'r 1: 9 it c' to pass in those days, that
9 Jesus c' from Nazareth
11 And there c' a voice from heaven,
14 Jesus c' into Galilee, preaching
26 with a loud voice, he c' out of him.
31 he c' and took her by the hand,
38 also: for therefore c' I forth.
40 c' a leper to him, beseeching
45 they c' to him from every quarter.
2:15 it c' to pass, that, as Jesus sat at
17 I c' not to call the righteous, but
23 it c' to pass, that he went through
3: 8 what great things he did, c' unto
13 whom he would: and they c'
22 And the scribes which c' down
31 There c' then his brethren and
4: 4 it c' to pass, as he sowed, some
4 and the fowls of the air c'
5: 1 they c' over unto the other side of
27 c' in the press behind, and touched
33 c' and fell down before him, and
35 c' from the ruler of the
6: 1 and c' into his own country; and
22 daughter of the said Herodias c'
25 c' in straightway with haste unto
29 his disciples heard of it, they c'
33 outwent them, and c' together
34 Jesus, when he c' out, saw much
35 his disciples c' unto him, and said,
53 when they had passed over, they c'
7: 1 c' together unto him the Pharisees,
1 certain of the scribes, which c'
25 him, and c' and fell at his feet:
31 he c' unto the sea of Galilee,
8: 3 for divers of them c' from far.
10 c' into the parts of Dalmanutha.
11 the Pharisees c' forth, and began
9: 7 a voice c' out of the cloud, saying,
9 they c' down from the mountain,
14 when he c' to his disciples, he
21 is it ago since this c' unto him?
25 the people c' running together,
26 rent him sore, and c' out of him:
33 And he c' to Capernaum: and
10: 2 the Pharisees c' to him, and asked
17 there c' one running, and kneeled
45 c' not to be ministered unto, but
46 they c' to Jericho: and as he
50 garment, rose, and c' to Jesus.
11: 1 when they c' nigh to Jerusalem,
13 he c', if haply he might find
13 thereon: and when he c' to it,
12:28 And one of the scribes c', and
42 There c' a certain poor widow, and
14: 3 c' a woman having an alabaster
16 and c' into the city, and found as
32 And they c' to a place which was
15:41 many other women which c' up
43 for the kingdom of God, c',
16: 2 they c' unto the sepulchre at the
Lu 1: 8 c' to pass, that while he executed

Lu 1:22 when he c' out, he could not
23 it c' to pass, that, as soon as the
28 the angel c' in unto her, and said,
41 c' to pass, that, when Elisabeth
57 Now Elisabeth's full time c' that
59 c' to pass, that on the eighth day
59 they c' to circumcise the child;
65 fear c' on all that dwelt round
2: 1 it c' to pass in those days, that
9 the angel of the Lord c' upon
15 it c' to pass, as the angels were
16 they c' with haste, and found
27 he c' by the Spirit into the temple:
46 it c' to pass, that after three days
51 c' to Nazareth, and was subject
3: 2 the word of God c' unto John the
3 he c' into all the country about
7 to the multitude that c' forth to
12 c' also publicans to be baptized,
21 it c' to pass, that Jesus also being
22 a voice c' from heaven, which said,
4:16 he c' to Nazareth, where he had
31 c' down to Capernaum, a city of
35 c' out of him, and hurt him not.
41 devils also c' out of many, crying
42 c' unto him, and stayed him, that
5: 1 c' to pass, that, as the people
7 they c', and filled both the ships,
12 it c' to pass, when he was in a
15 great multitudes c' together to
17 it c' to pass on a certain day, as
32 I c' not to call the righteous, but
6: 1 c' to pass on the second sabbath
6 it c' to pass also on another
12 And it c' to pass in those days,
17 he c' down with them, and stood
17 which c' to hear him, and to be
7: 4 when they c' to Jesus, they
11 it c' to pass the day after, that he
12 when he c' nigh to the gate of the
14 And he c' and touched the bier:
16 And there c' a fear on all: and
33 For John the Baptist c' neither
45 since the time I c' in hath not
8: 1 it c' to pass afterward, that he
19 c' to him his mother and his
22 it c' to pass on a certain day, that
23 there c' down a storm of wind on
24 And they c' to him, and awoke him,
35 c' to Jesus, and found the man,
40 c' to pass, that, when Jesus was
41 there c' a man named Jairus, and
44 C' behind him, and touched the
47 was not hid, she c' trembling,
51 when he c' into the house, he
55 her spirit c' again, and she arose
9:12 then c' the twelve, and said unto
18 c' to pass, as he was alone
28 it c' to pass about an eight days
33 it c' to pass, as they departed
34 c' a cloud, and overshadowed
35 there c' a voice out of the cloud,
37 it c' to pass, that on the next day,
51 c' to pass, when the time was come
57 c' to pass, that, as they went in
10:31 by chance there c' down a certain
32 c' and looked on him, and passed
33 as he journeyed, c' where he was:
38 Now it c' to pass, as they went,
40 and c' to him, and said, Lord,
11: 1 c' to pass, that, as he was praying
14 it c' to pass, when the devil was
24 unto my house whence I c' out.
27 c' to pass, as he spake these
31 c' from the utmost parts of the
13: 6 he c' and sought fruit thereon,
31 The same day there c' certain of
14: 1 c' to pass, as he went into the
21 So that servant c', and shewed
15:17 And when he c' to himself, he
20 he arose, and c' to his father.
25 c' and drew nigh to the house, he
28 therefore c' his father out, and
16:21 the dogs c' and licked his sores.
22 it c' to pass that the beggar died,
17:11 it c' to pass, as he went to
14 it c' to pass, that, as they went,
27 and the flood c', and destroyed
18: 3 she c' unto him, saying, Avenge
35 c' to pass, that as he was come
19: 5 when Jesus c' to the place, he
6 And he made haste, and c' down,
15 it c' to pass, that when he was
16 Then c' the first, saying, Lord,
18 And the second c', saying, Lord,
20 another c' saying, Lord, behold,
29 c' to pass, when he was come nigh
20: 1 c' to pass, that on one of those
1 chief priests and the scribes c'
27 c' to him certain of the Sadducees,
21:38 And all the people c' early in the
22: 7 c' the day of unleavened bread,
39 c' out, and went, as he was wont,
66 priests and the scribes c' together,
23:48 all the people that c' together to
55 which c' with him from Galilee,
24: 1 very early in the morning, they c'
4 it c' to pass, as they were much
15 it c' to pass, that, while they
23 found not his body, they c', saying,
30 c' to pass, as he sat at meat with
51 it c' to pass, while he blessed
Joh 1: 7 The same c' for a witness, to bear
11 He c' unto his own, and his own
17 grace and truth c' by Jesus Christ.
39 They c' and saw where he dwelt,

Joh 3: 2 The same c' to Jesus by night, and
13 but he that c' down from heaven,
22 After these things c' Jesus and
23 and they c', and were baptized.
26 c' unto John, and said unto him,
4:27 upon this c' his disciples, and
30 out of the city, and c' unto him.
46 So Jesus c' again into Cana of
6:23 (Howbeit there c' other boats from
24 shipping, and c' to Capernaum,
38 For I c' down from heaven, not to
41 I am the bread which c' down from
42 I c' down from heaven?
51 bread which c' down from heaven:
58 This is that bread which c' down
7:45 Then c' the officers to the chief
50 (he that c' to Jesus by night,
8: 2 early in the morning he c' again
2 the people c' unto him;
14 for I know whence I c', and
42 I proceeded forth and c' from
42 neither c' I of myself,
9: 7 therefore, and washed, and c'
10: 8 All that ever c' before me are
24 c' the Jews round about him,
35 unto whom the word of God c',
11:17 Then when Jesus c', he found that
19 many of the Jews c' to Martha
29 arose quickly, and c' unto him.
33 Jews also weeping which c' with
44 he that was dead c' forth, bound
45 of the Jews which c' to Mary,
12: 1 before the passover c' to Bethany,
9 they c' not for Jesus' sake only,
20 Greeks among them that c' up to
21 The same c' therefore to Philip,
27 for this cause c' I unto this hour.
28 Then c' there a voice from heaven,
30 This voice c' not because of me,
47 for I c' not to judge the world,
16:27 believed that I c' out from God.
28 I c' forth from the Father, and am
17: 8 that I c' out from thee, and they
18:37 for this cause c' I into the world,
19: 5 then c' Jesus forth, wearing the
32 Then c' the soldiers, and
33 But when they c' to Jesus,
34 forthwith c' there out blood and
38 He c' therefore, and took the body
39 And there c' also Nicodemus,
39 at the first c' to Jesus by night,
20: 3 disciple, and c' to the sepulchre.
4 Peter, and c' first to the sepulchre.
8 which c' first to the sepulchre,
18 Mary Magdalene c' and told the
19 c' Jesus and stood in the midst,
24 was not with them when Jesus c'.
26 c' Jesus, the doors being shut,
21: 8 other disciples c' in a little ship;
Ac 2: 2 suddenly there c' a sound from
6 multitude c' together, and were
43 And fear c' upon every soul:
4: 1 and the Sadducees, c' upon them,
5 it c' to pass on the morrow, that
5: 5 great fear c' on all them that
7 knowing what was done, c' in.
10 young men c' in, and found
11 great fear c' upon all the church,
16 There c' also a multitude out of
21 But the high priest c', and they
22 But when the officers c', and found
25 Then c' one and told them, saying,
6:12 c' upon him, and caught him,
7: 4 Then c' he out of the land of the
11 c' a dearth over all the land of
23 it c' into his heart to visit his
31 the voice of the Lord c' unto him,
45 also our fathers that c' after
8: 7 c' out of many that were possessed
36 they c' unto a certain water:
40 the cities, till he c' to Cæsarea.
9: 3 journeyed, he c' near Damascus:
21 and c' hither for that intent, that
32 it c' to pass, as Peter passed
32 he c' down also to the saints
37 it c' to pass in those days, that
43 it c' to pass, that he tarried many
10:13 there c' a voice to him, Rise,
29 Therefore c' I unto you without
45 as many as c' with Peter, because
11: 5 four corners; and it c' even to me:
22 tidings of these things c' unto the
23 Who, when he c', and had seen
26 it c' to pass, that a whole year
27 c' prophets from Jerusalem unto
28 which c' to pass in the days of
12: 7 angel of the Lord c' upon him,
10 they c' unto the iron gate that
12 c' to the house of Mary the mother
13 a damsel c' to hearken, named
20 they c' with one accord to him,
13:13 they c' to Perga in Pamphylia:
14 they c' to Antioch in Pisidia,
31 of them which c' up with him
44 c' almost the whole city together
51 them, and c' unto Iconium.
14: 1 it c' to pass in Iconium, that they
19 there c' thither certain Jews
20 he rose up, and c' into the city:
24 Pisidia, they c' to Pamphylia.
15: 1 men which c' down from Judæa
6 apostles and elders c' together
30 dismissed, they c' to Antioch:
16: 1 Then c' he to Derbe and Lystra:
8 passing by Mysia c' down to Troas.
11 we c' with a straight course to

Ac 16:16 it c' to pass, as he went to prayer,
18 And he c' out the same hour.
29 and c' trembling, and fell down
39 they c' and besought them,
17: 1 they c' to Thessalonica, where
13 they c' thither also, and stirred up
18: 1 from Athens, and c' to Corinth;
2 from Rome:) and c' unto them.
19 he c' to Ephesus, and left them
24 mighty in the scriptures, c' to
19: 1 it c' to pass, that, while Apollos
1 the upper coasts c' to Ephesus:
6 the Holy Ghost c' on them;
18 that believed c', and confessed,
20: 2 exhortation, he c' into Greece,
6 c' unto them to Troas in five days:
7 when the disciples c' together to
14 took him in, and c' to Mitylene.
15 c' the next day over against Chios;
15 and the next day we c' to Miletus.
18 first day that I c' into Asia,
21: 1 it c' to pass, that after we were
1 we c' with a straight course unto
7 we c' to Ptolemais, and saluted
8 departed, and c' unto Cæsarea:
10 there c' down from Judæa a
31 tidings c' unto the chief captain of
33 Then the chief captain c' near,
35 when he c' upon the stairs, so it
22: 6 it c' to pass, that, as I made my
11 with me, I c' into Damascus.
13 C' unto me, and stood, and said
17 And it c' to pass, that, when I
27 Then the chief captain c', and
23:14 And they c' to the chief priests
27 c' I with an army, and rescued
33 Who, when they c' to Cæsarea,
24: 7 chief captain Lysias c' upon us,
17 I c' to bring alms to my nation,
24 Felix c' with his wife Drusilla,
27 Porcius Festus c' into Felix'
25: 7 the Jews which c' down from
13 Agrippa and Bernice c' unto
27: 5 we c' to Myra, a city of Lycia.
8 hardly passing it, c' unto a place
44 so it c' to pass, that they escaped
28: 3 c' a viper out of the heat,
8 it c' to pass, that the father of
9 in the island, c', and were healed:
13 c' to Rhegium: and after one day
13 and we c' the next day to Puteoli:
15 they c' to meet us as far as Appii
16 when we c' to Rome, the
17 it c' to pass, that after three days
21 any of the brethren that c'
23 c' many to him into his lodging;
30 received all that c' in unto him,
Ro 5:18 one judgment c' upon all men to
18 the free gift c' upon all men unto
7: 9 but when the commandment c',
9: 5 concerning the flesh Christ c',
1Co 2: 1 I, brethren, when I c' to you,
1 c' not with excellency of speech
14:36 c' the word of God out from you?
36 or c' it unto you only?
15:21 since by man c' death, by man c' also
2Co 1: 8 trouble which c' to us in Asia,
23 I c' not as yet unto Corinth.
2: 3 lest, when I c', I should have
12 when I c' to Troas to preach
11: 9 brethren which c' from Macedonia
Ga 1:21 I c' into the regions of Syria and
2: 4 who c' in privily to spy out our
12 before that certain c' from James,
3:23 But before faith c', we were kept
Eph 2:17 And c' and preached peace to you
1Th 1: 5 our gospel c' not unto you in
3: 4 even as it c' to pass, and ye know.
6 now when Timotheus c' from you
1Ti 1:15 Christ Jesus c' into the world to
2Ti 3:11 afflictions, which c' unto me at
Heb 3:16 not all that c' out of Egypt
11:15 from whence they c' out, they
2Pe 1:17 when there c' such a voice to him
18 this voice which c' from heaven
21 the prophecy c' not in old time
1Jo 5: 6 he that c' by water and blood,
3Jo 3 the brethren c' and testified of the
Re 5: 7 And he c' and took the book out
7:13 in white robes? and whence c'
14 These are they which c' out of
8: 3 angel c' and stood at the altar,
4 smoke of the incense, which c'
9: 3 there c' out of the smoke locusts
14:15 another angel c' out of the temple,
17 And another angel c' out of the
18 angel c' out from the altar,
20 blood c' out of the winepress,
15: 6 seven angels c' out of the temple,
16:17 c' a great voice out of the temple
19 Babylon c' in remembrance
17: 1 there c' one of the seven angels
19: 5 And a voice c' out of the throne,
20: 9 and fire c' down from God out of
21: 9 c' unto me one of the seven angels

came to pass See CAME and PASS.

camel See also CAMEL'S; CAMELS.
Ge 24:64 saw Isaac, she lighted off the c'.
Le 11: 4 c', because he cheweth the cud,
De 14: 7 the c', and the hare, and the
1Sa 15: 3 suckling, ox and sheep, c' and ass.
Zec 14:15 of the mule, of the c',
M't 19:24 easier for a c' to go through the
23:24 at a gnat, and swallow a c'.
M'k 10:25 easier for a c' to go through the

Lu 18:25 easier for a c' to go through a
camel's
Ge 31:34 put them in the c' furniture, and
M't 3: 4 his raiment of c' hair, and a
M'k 1: 6 clothed with c' hair, and with a
camels See also CAMELS'.
Ge 12:16 and she asses, and c'.
24:10 took ten c' of the c' of his master,
11 he made his c' to kneel down
14 I will give thy c' drink also: let
19 draw water for thy c' also, until
20 water, and drew for all his c'.
22 as the c' had done drinking, that
30 he stood by the c' at the well.
31 the house, and room for the c'.
32 and he ungirded his c', and gave
32 and provender for the c',
35 maidservants, and c', and asses.
44 I will also draw for thy c': let the
46 I will give thy c' drink also: so I
46 and she made the c' drink
61 they rode upon the c', and
63 and, behold, the c' were coming.
30:43 menservants, and c', and asses.
31:17 set his sons and his wives upon c';
32: 7 herds, and the c', into two bands;
15 Thirty milch c' with their colts,
37:25 came from Gilead with their c'
Ex 9: 3 upon the asses, upon the c', upon
J'g 6: 5 both they and their c' were
7:12 and their c' were without number,
1Sa 27: 9 the asses, and the c', and the
30:17 young men, which rode upon c',
1Ki 10: 2 with c' that bare spices, and very
1Ch 5:21 cattle; of their c' fifty thousand,
12:40 bread on asses, and on c', and on
27:30 Over the c' also was Obil the
2Ch 9: 1 company, and c' that bare spices,
14:15 carried away sheep and c' in
Ezr 2:67 Their c', four hundred thirty and
Ne 7:69 c', four hundred thirty and five:
Es 8:10 c', and young dromedaries:
14 rode upon mules and c' went out,
Job 1: 3 three thousand c', and five
17 fell upon the c', and have carried
42:12 six thousand c', and a thousand
Isa 21: 7 of asses, and a chariot of c';
30: 6 treasures upon the bunches of c',
60: 6 The multitude of c' shall cover
Jer 49:29 and all their vessels, and their c';
32 And their c' shall be a booty, and
Eze 25: 5 make Rabbah a stable for c', and
camels'
J'g 8:21 that were on their c' necks.
26 chains that were about their c'
2Ki 8: 9 of Damascus, forty c' burden,
camest See also BECAMEST.
Ge 16: 8 whence c' thou? and whither wilt
24: 5 the land from whence thou c'?
27:33 eaten of all before thou c', and
Ex 23:15 in it thou c' out from Egypt:
34:18 Abib thou c' out from Egypt.
Nu 22:37 wherefore c' thou not unto me?
De 2:37 children of Ammon thou c' not,
16: 3 for thou c' forth out of the land of
3 when thou c' forth out of the land
6 season that thou c' forth out of
1Sa 13:11 thou c' not within the days
17:28 Why c' thou down hither? and
2Sa 11:10 C' thou not from thy journey?
15:20 Whereas thou c' but yesterday,
1Ki 13: 9 by the same way that thou c'.
14 man of God that c' from Judah?
17 to go by the way that thou c'.
22 But c' back, and hast eaten bread
2Ki 19:28 back by the way by which thou c'.
Ne 9:13 Thou c' down also upon mount
Isa 37:29 back by the way by which thou c'.
64: 3 thou c' down, the mountains
Jer 1: 5 before thou c' forth out of the
Eze 32: 2 thou c' forth with thy rivers, and
M't 22:12 Friend, how c' thou in hither
Joh 6:25 him, Rabbi, when c' thou hither?
16:30 that thou c' forth from God.
Ac 9:17 in the way as thou c', hath sent
Camon *(ca'-mon)*
J'g 10: 5 Jair died, and was buried in C'.
camp See also CAMPED; CAMPS; ENCAMP.
Ex 14:19 which went before the c' of Israel,
20 between the c' of the Egyptians
20 and the c' of Israel;
16:13 quails came up, and covered the c':
19:16 people that was in the c' trembled.
17 all the people out of the c' to meet
29:14 burn with fire without the c':
32:17 There is a noise of war in the c'.
19 as he came nigh unto the c', that
26 stood in the gate of the c', and
27 gate to gate throughout the c',
33: 7 without the c', afar off from the c',
7 which was without the c'.
11 he turned again into the c': but
36: 6 proclaimed throughout the c'.
Le 4:12 he carry forth without the c' unto
21 forth the bullock without the c',
6:11 the ashes without the c' unto a
8:17 he burnt with fire without the c';
9:11 he burnt with fire without the c'.
10: 4 before the sanctuary out of the c'.
5 their coats out of the c'; as Moses
13:46 without the c' shall his habitation
14: 3 shall go forth out of the c'; and
8 come into the c', and shall tarry
16:26 and afterward come into the c'.
Le 16:27 carry forth without the c'; and
28 afterward he shall come into the c'.
17: 3 lamb, or goat, in the c', or that
3 killeth it out of the c',
24:10 strove together in the c':
14 that hath cursed without the c';
23 had cursed out of the c', and
Nu 1:52 every man by his own c', and
2: 3 standard of the c' of Judah pitch
9 All that were numbered in the c'
10 the standard of the c' of Reuben
16 All that were numbered in the c'
17 with the c' of the Levites
17 in the midst of the c':
18 standard of the c' of Ephraim
24 that were numbered of the c' of
25 The standard of the c' of Dan
31 that were numbered in the c' of
4: 5 when the c' setteth forward,
15 as the c' is to set forward;
5: 2 put out of the c' every leper,
3 without the c' shall ye put them;
4 and put them out without the c':
10:14 standard of the c' of the children
18 standard of the c' of Reuben set
22 c' of the children of Ephraim set
25 the c' of the children of Dan set
34 when they went out of the c'.
11: 1 in the uttermost parts of the c'.
9 dew fell upon the c' in the night,
26 remained two of the men in the c',
26 and they prophesied in the c'.
27 and Medad do prophesy in the c'.
30 Moses gat him into the c',
31 let them fall by the c', as it were
31 the other side, round about the c',
32 themselves round about the c'.
12:14 let her be shut out from the c'
15 Miriam was shut out from the c'
14:44 Moses departed not out of the c'.
15:35 him with stones without the c'.
36 brought him without the c', and
19: 3 bring her forth without the c', and
7 afterward he shall come into the c',
9 without the c' in a clean place,
31:12 unto the c' at the plains of Moab,
13 forth to meet them without the c'.
19 do ye abide without the c' seven
24 afterward ye shall come into the c'.
De 23:10 shall he go abroad out of the c',
10 he shall not come within the c':
11 he shall come into the c' again.
12 have a place also without the c',
14 God walketh in the midst of thy c',
14 therefore shall thy c' be holy:
29:11 thy stranger that is in thy c',
Jos 5: 8 abode in their places in the c', till
6:11 into the c', and lodged in the c'.
14 returned into the c': so they did
18 make the c' of Israel a curse, and
23 left them without the c' of Israel.
9: 6 to Joshua unto the c' at Gilgal,
10: 6 sent unto Joshua to the c' to Gilgal,
15 and all Israel with him, unto the c'
21 all the people returned to the c' to
43 with him, unto the c' to Gilgal.
J'g 7:17 I come to the outside of the c',
18 also on every side of all the c',
19 came unto the outside of the c'
21 in his place round about the c':
13:25 him at times in the c' of Dan
21: 8 there came none to the c' from
12 brought them unto the c' to Shiloh,
1Sa 4: 3 the people were come into the c',
5 of the Lord came into the c',
6 noise of this great shout in the c'
6 of the Lord was come into the c'.
7 they said, God is come into the c'.
13:17 out of the c' of the Philistines
14:21 went up with them into the c'
17: 4 out of the c' of the Philistines,
17 run to the c' to thy brethren;
26: 6 down with me to Saul to the c'?
2Sa 1: 2 a man came out of the c' from
3 Out of the c' of Israel am I
1Ki 16:16 king over Israel that day in the c'.
2Ki 3:24 when they came to the c' of Israel,
6: 8 and such a place shall be my c'.
7: 5 to go unto the c' of the Syrians:
5 to the uttermost part of the c'
7 even the c' as it was, and fled
8 to the uttermost part of the c',
10 We came to the c' of the Syrians,
12 are they gone out of the c' to hide
19:35 smote in the c' of the Assyrians
2Ch 22: 1 came with the Arabians to the c'
32:21 the leaders and captains in the c'
Ps 78:28 let it fall in the midst of their c',
106:16 They envied Moses also in the c',
Isa 29: 3 And I will c' against thee round
37:36 smote in the c' of the Assyrians
Jer 50:29 c' against it round about; and
Eze 4: 2 set the c' also against it, and set
Joe 2:11 for his c' is very great: for he is
Na 3:17 c' in the hedges in the cold day,
Heb 13:11 sin, are burned without the c'.
13 unto him without the c', bearing
Re 20: 9 compassed the c' of the saints
camped
Ex 19: 2 and there Israel c' before the
camphire
Ca 1:14 a cluster of c' in the vineyards
4:13 c', with spikenard,
camps
Nu 2:32 that were numbered of the c'
Nu 5: 3 that they defile not their c', in
10: 2 for the journeying of the c'.
5 then the c' that lie on the east
6 then the c' that lie on the south
25 the rereward of all the c'
Am 4:10 the stink of your c' to come up
can^ See also CANNOT; CANST.
Ge 4:13 punishment is greater than I c' bear.
13:16 c' number the dust of the
31:43 and what c' I do this day unto
39: 9 then c' I do this great wickedness,
41:15 is none that c' interpret it:
38 C' we find such a one as this is)
44: 1 as much as they c' carry,
15 a man as I c' certainly divine?
Ex 4:14 I know that he c' speak well.
5:11 you straw where ye c' find it:
Le 14:30 pigeons such as he c' get;
Nu 23:10 Who c' count the dust of Jacob,
De 3:24 c' do according to thy works,
7:17 how c' I dispossess them?
9: 2 Who c' stand before the children
31: 2 I c' no more go out and
32:39 that c' deliver out of my hand.
J'g 14:12 if ye c' certainly declare it me
1Sa 9: 6 peradventure he c' shew us our
16: 2 Samuel said, How c' I go?
17 me now a man that c' play well,
18: 8 and what c' he have more but
26: 9 c' stretch forth his hand against
28: 2 know what thy servant c' do.
2Sa 7:20 And what c' David say more unto
12:22 Who c' tell whether God will
23 c' I bring him back again?
14:19 none c' turn to the right hand
15:36 me every thing that ye c' hear.
19:35 c' I discern between good and evil?
35 c' thy servant taste what I eat
35 c' I hear any more the voice of
1Ch 17:18 What c' David speak more to thee
2Ch 1:10 who c' judge this thy people,
2: 7 and that c' skill to grave with the
8 I know that thy servants c'
Es 8: 6 c' I endure to see the evil
6 people? or how c' I endure to
Job 3:22 when they c' find the grave?
4: 2 but who c' withhold himself
6: 6 C' that which is unsavoury be
8:11 C' the rush grow up without mire?
11 c' the flag grow without water?
9:12 taketh away, who c' hinder him?
10: 7 there is none that c' deliver out
11:10 together, then who c' hinder him?
12:14 man, and there c' be no opening.
14: 4 Who c' bring a clean thing out of
15: 3 wherewith he c' do no good?
22: 2 C' a man be profitable unto God,
13 doth God know? c' he judge
17 and what c' the Almighty do for
23:13 one mind and who c' turn him?
25: 4 How then c' man be justified with
4 how c' he be clean that is born of
26:14 of his power who c' understand?
34:29 who then c' make trouble?
29 his face, who then c' behold him?
36:23 or who c' say, Thou hast wrought
26 neither c' the number of his
29 c' any understand the spreadings
38:37 c' number the clouds in wisdom?
37 who c' stay the bottles of heaven,
40:14 thine own right hand c' save thee.
19 he that made him c' make his
23 he trusteth that he c' draw
41:13 Who c' discover the face of his
13 who c' come to him with his double
14 c' open the doors of his face?
16 that no air c' come between
42: 2 that no thought c' be withholden
Ps 11: 3 destroyed, what c' the righteous
19:12 Who c' understand his errors?
22:29 none c' keep alive his own soul.
40: 5 they are more than c' be numbered.
49: 7 None of them c' by any means
56: 4 fear what flesh c' do unto me.
11 not be afraid what man c' do unto
58: 9 Before your pots c' feel the thorns,
78:19 C' God furnish a table in
20 c' he give bread also?
20 c' he provide flesh
89: 6 who in the heaven c' be compared
6 sons of the mighty c' be likened
106: 2 Who c' utter the mighty acts
2 who c' shew forth all his praise?
118: 6 fear: what c' man do unto me?
147:17 who c' stand before his cold?
Pr 6:27 C' a man take fire in his bosom,
28 C' one go upon hot coals, and his
18:14 but a wounded spirit who c' bear?
20: 6 but a faithful man who c' find?
9 Who c' say, I have made my heart
24 how c' a man then understand
26:16 seven men that c' render a reason.
31:10 Who c' find a virtuous woman?
Ec 2:12 for what c' the man do that
25 For who c' eat,
25 or who else c' hasten hereunto,
3:11 no man c' find out the work
14 nothing c' be put to it, nor
4:11 but how c' one be warm alone?
6:12 for who c' tell a man what shall
7:13 who c' make that straight,
24 who c' find it out?
8: 7 for who c' tell him when it shall
10:14 be after him, who c' tell him?
Ca 8: 7 neither c' the floods drown it:
Isa 28:20 shorter than a man c' stretch

Isa 28:20 narrower than that he c' wrap
43: 9 among them c' declare this.
13 that c' deliver out of my hand:
46: 7 unto him, yet c' he not answer,
49:15 C' a woman forget her sucking
56:11 greedy dogs which c' never have
Jer 2:13 cisterns, that c' hold no water.
24 occasion who c' turn her away?
28 if they c' save thee in the time of
32 C' a maid forget her ornaments,
4: 4 and burn that none c' quench it,
5: 1 if ye c' find a man, if there be any
22 yet c' they not prevail;
22 yet c' they not pass over it?
13:23 C' the Ethiopian change his skin,
14:22 the Gentiles that c' cause rain?
22 or c' the heavens give showers?
17: 9 desperately wicked: who c' know
21:12 and burn that none c' quench it,
23:24 C' any hide himself in secret
31:37 If heaven above c' be measured,
33:20 If ye c' break my covenant of the
38: 5 king is not he that c' do
47: 7 How c' it be quiet, seeing the
La 2:13 like the sea: who c' heal thee?
Eze 22:14 C' thine heart endure, or c' thine
28: 3 no secret that they c' hide from
33:32 c' play well on an instrument:
37: 3 c' these bones live? And I
Da 2: 9 know that ye c' shew me the
10 upon the earth that c' shew the
11 none other that c' shew it before
3:29 God that c' deliver after this
4:35 none c' stay his hand,
10:17 c' the servant of this my lord
Joel 2:11 terrible; and who c' abide it?
Am 3: 3 C' two walk together, except
5 C' a bird fall in a snare upon the
8 hath spoken, who c' but prophesy?
Jon 3: 9 Who c' tell if God will turn and
Mic 3:11 none evil c' come upon us.
5: 8 in pieces, and none c' deliver.
Na 1: 6 Who c' stand before his indignation?
6 and who c' abide in the fierceness
M't 6:24 No man c' serve two masters:
27 Which of you by taking thought c'
7:18 neither c' a corrupt tree bring
9:15 C' the children of the
12:29 Or else how c' one enter into a
34 how c' ye, being evil, speak good
16: 3 ye c' discern the face of the sky;
3 but c' ye not discern the signs of
19:25 saying, Who then c' be saved?
23:33 how c' ye escape the damnation
27:65 way, make it as sure as ye c'.
M'r 2: 7 who c' forgive sins but God only?
19 C' the children of the
3:23 How c' Satan cast out Satan?
27 No man c' enter into a strong
7:15 entering into him c' defile him:
8: 4 From whence c' a man satisfy
9: 3 no fuller on earth c' white them.
29 This kind c' come forth by nothing,
39 name, that c' lightly speak evil
10:26 themselves, Who then c' be saved?
38 know not what ye ask: c' ye
39 And they said unto him, We c'.
Lu 5:21 Who c' forgive sins, but God alone?
34 C' ye make the children of the
6:39 C' the blind lead the blind?
12: 4 have no more that they c' do.
25 thought c' add to his stature
56 ye c' discern the face of the sky
16:13 No servant c' serve two masters:
26 neither c' they pass to us, that
18:26 it said, Who then c' be saved?
20:36 Neither c' they die any more:
Joh 1:46 C' there any good thing come out
3: 2 for no man c' do these miracles
4 How c' a man be born when he is
4 c' he enter the second time into
9 unto him, How c' these things be?
27 A man c' receive nothing except it
5:19 The Son c' do nothing of himself,
30 I c' of mine own self do nothing:
44 How c' ye believe, which received
6:44 No man c' come to me, except the
52 How c' this man give us his flesh
60 an hard saying; who c' hear it?
65 that no man c' come unto me,
9: 4 cometh, when no man c' work.
16 How c' a man that is a sinner do
10:21 C' a devil open the eyes of the
14: 5 and how c' we know the way?
15: 4 no more c' ye, except ye abide in me.
5 for without me ye c' do nothing.
Ac 8:31 How c' I, except some man should
10:47 C' any man forbid water, that
24:13 Neither c' they prove the things
Ro 8: 7 law of God, neither indeed c' be.
31 If God be for us, who c' be against
1Co 2:14 neither c' he know them, for
3:11 other foundation c' no man lay
12: 3 no man c' say that Jesus is the
2Co 13: 8 we c' do nothing against the truth,
Ph'p 4:13 I c' do all things through Christ
1Th 3: 9 what thanks c' we render to God
1Ti 6: 7 is certain we c' carry nothing out.
16 light which no man c' approach
16 no man hath seen, nor c' see:
Heb 5: 2 Who c' have compassion on the
10: 1 very image of the things, c' never
11 the same sacrifices, which c' never
Jas 2:14 not works? C' faith save him?
3: 8 But the tongue c' no man tame;
12 C' the fig tree, my brethren, bear
Jas 3:12 so c' no fountain both yield salt
1Jo 4:20 how c' he love God whom he
Re 3: 8 open door, and no man c' shut it:
9:20 neither c' see, nor hear, nor walk:

Cana (*ca'-nah*)
Joh 2: 1 in C' of Galilee; and the mother
11 did Jesus in C' of Galilee,
4:46 Jesus came again into C' of
21: 2 Nathanael of C' in Galilee,

Canaan (*ca'-na-an*) See also CANAANITE; CHANAAN.
Ge 9:18 and Ham is the father of C'.
22 Ham, the father of C', saw the
25 And he said, Cursed be C';
26 God of Shem; and C' shall be his
27 tents of Shem; and C' shall be his
10: 6 and Mizraim, and Phut, and C'.
15 And C' begat Sidon his firstborn,
11:31 Chaldees, to go into the land of C';
12: 5 forth to go into the land of C';
5 into the land of C' they came.
13:12 Abram dwelt in the land of C',
16: 3 dwelt ten years in the land of C',
17: 8 the land of C', for an everlasting
23: 2 same is Hebron in the land of C':
19 same is Hebron in the land of C'.
28: 1 take a wife of the daughters of C'.
6 take a wife of the daughters of C';
8 daughters of C' pleased not Isaac
31:18 Isaac his father in the land of C'.
33:18 which is in the land of C',
35: 6 to Luz, which is in the land of C',
36: 2 his wives of the daughters of C';
5 born unto him in the land of C'.
6 which he had got in the land of C';
37: 1 was a stranger, in the land of C'.
42: 5 the famine was in the land of C'.
7 From the land of C' to buy food.
13 sons of one man in the land of C';
29 their father unto the land of C',
32 with our father in the land of C'.
44: 8 unto thee out of the land of C':
45:17 go, get you unto the land of C';
25 came into the land of C' unto
46: 6 they had gotten in the land of C',
12 Er and Onan died in the land of C'.
31 which were in the land of C',
47: 1 are come out of the land of C';
4 famine is sore in the land of C':
13 the land of C' fainted by reason
14 of Egypt, and in the land of C',
15 in the land of C', all the Egyptians
48: 3 at Luz in the land of C',
7 Rachel died by me in the land of C'
49:30 is before Mamre, in the land of C',
50: 5 digged for me in the land of C',
13 carried him into the land of C',
Ex 6: 4 them, to give them the land of C',
15:15 inhabitants of C' shall melt away.
16:35 unto the borders of the land of C'.
Le 14:34 come into the land of C', which
18: 3 the doings of the land of C',
25:38 to give you the land of C', and
Nu 13: 2 they may search the land of C',
17 them to spy out the land of C',
26:19 Onan died in the land of C'.
32:30 among you in the land of C'.
32 before the Lord into the land of C',
33:40 in the south in the land of C',
51 over Jordan into the land of C';
34: 2 When ye come into the land of C';
2 land of C' with the coasts thereof:)
29 children of Israel in the land of C'.
35:10 over Jordan into the land of C';
14 shall ye give in the land of C',
De 32:49 the land of C', which I give
Jos 5:12 the fruit of the land of C' that
14: 1 of Israel inherited the land of C',
21: 2 at Shiloh in the land of C', saying,
22: 9 Shiloh, which is in the land of C',
10 Jordan, that are in the land of C',
11 an altar over against the land of C',
32 unto the land of C', to the children
24: 3 throughout all the land of C',
J'g 3: 1 had not known all the wars of C';
4: 2 the hand of Jabin the king of C',
23 on that day Jabin the king of C',
24 against Jabin the king of C',
24 had destroyed Jabin king of C'.
5:19 fought the kings of C' in Taanach
21:12 to Shiloh, which is in the land of C'.
1Ch 1: 8 Cush, and Mizraim, Put, and C'.
13 And C' begat Zidon his firstborn,
16:18 Unto thee will I give the land of C',
Ps 105:11 Unto thee will I give the land of C',
106:38 they sacrificed unto the idols of C':
135:11 and all the kingdoms of C':
Isa 19:18 speak the language of C', and
Eze 16: 3 thy nativity is of the land of C';
29 thy fornication in the land of C'
Zep 2: 5 O C', the land of the Philistines,
M't 15:22 behold, a woman of C' came out

Canaanite (*ca'-na-an-ite*) See also CANAANITES; CANAANITESS; CANAANITISH; ZELOTES.
Ge 12: 6 And the C' was then in the land.
13: 7 the C' and the Perizzite dwelled
38: 2 certain C', whose name was Shuah;
Ex 23:28 shall drive out the Hivite, the C'
33: 2 and I will drive out the C',
34:11 before thee the Amorite, and the C',
Nu 21: 1 king Arad the C', which dwelt in
33:40 king Arad the C', which dwelt in
Jos 9: 1 Hittite, and the Amorite, the C',
11: 3 the C' on the east and on the west,
13: 3 which is counted to the C':
Zec 14:21 the C' in the house of the Lord
M't 10: 4 Simon the C', and Judas Iscariot,
M'r 3:18 Thaddæus, and Simon the C',

Canaanites (*ca'-na-an-ites*)
Ge 10:18 families of the C' spread abroad
19 border of the C' was from Sidon,
15:21 And the Amorites, and the C',
24: 3 my son of the daughters of the C',
37 my son of the daughters of the C',
34:30 among the C', and the Perizzites:
50:11 the C', saw the mourning in the
Ex 3: 8 place of the C', and the Hittites,
17 land of the C', and the Hittites,
13: 5, 11 thee into the land of the C',
23:23 C', the Hivites, and the Jebusites;
Nu 13:29 and the C' dwell by the sea,
14:25 and the C' dwelt in the valley.
43 the C' are there before you,
45 the C' which dwelt in that hill,
21: 3 and delivered up the C'; and they
De 1: 7 sea side, to the land of the C',
7: 1 and the Amorites, and the C',
11:30 goeth down in the land of the C',
20:17 and the Amorites, the C',
Jos 3:10 drive out from before you the C',
5: 1 the kings of the C', which were
7: 9 the C' and all the inhabitants
12: 8 the Amorites, and the C',
13: 4 the south, all the land of the C',
16:10 And they drove not out the C'
10 the C' dwell among the Ephraimites
17:12 the C' would dwell in that land.
13 that they put the C' to tribute;
16 all the C' that dwell in the land
18 for thou shalt drive out the C',
24:11 and the Perizzites, and the C',
J'g 1: 1 shall go up for us against the C'
3 that we may fight against the C';
4 and the Lord delivered the C'
5 slew the C' and the Perizzites.
9 went down to fight against the C',
10 went against the C' that dwelt
17 they slew the C' that inhabited
27 the C' would dwell in that land.
28 that they put the C' to tribute,
29 did Ephraim drive out the C'
29 the C' dwelt in Gezer among them.
30 but the C' dwelt among them,
32 the Asherites dwelt among the C',
33 but he dwelt among the C',
3: 3 the Philistines, and all the C',
5 of Israel dwelt among the C',
2Sa 24: 7 of the Hivites, and of the C':
1Ki 9:16 slain the C' that dwelt in the city,
Ezr 9: 1 their abominations, even of the C',
Ne 9: 8 him to give the land of the C'
24 inhabitants of the land, the C',
Ob 20 Israel shall possess that of the C',

Canaanitess (*ca'-na-an-ite-ess*)
1Ch 2: 3 of the daughter of Shua the C'.

Canaanitish (*ca'-na-an-i-tish*)
Ge 46:10 Shaul the son of a C' woman.
Ex 6:15 Shaul the son of a C' woman.

Candace (*can'-da-see*)
Ac 8:27 under C' queen of the Ethiopians,

candle See also CANDLES; CANDLESTICK.
Job 18: 6 and his c' shall be put out
21:17 is the c' of the wicked put out!
29: 3 When his c' shined upon my
Ps 18:28 For thou wilt light my c':
Pr 20:27 the c' of the Lord, searching
24:20 c' of the wicked shall be put out.
31:18 her c' goeth not out by night.
Jer 25:10 and the light of the c'.
M't 5:15 men light a c', and put it under
M'r 4:21 Is a c' brought to be put under
Lu 8:16 when he hath lighted a c',
11:33 when he hath lighted a c',
36 the bright shining of a c' doth
15: 8 doth not light a c', and sweep
Re 18:23 And the light of a c' shall shine
22: 5 they need no c', neither light of

candles
Zep 1:12 I will search Jerusalem with c',

candlestick See also CANDLESTICKS.
Ex 25:31 thou shalt make a c' of pure gold:
31 beaten work shall the c' be made:
32 branches of the c' out of the one
32 branches of the c' out of the other
33 branches that come out of the c'.
34 And in the c' shall be four bowls
35 branches that proceed out of the c'.
26:35 the c' over against the table
30:27 the c' and his vessels, and the
31: 8 the pure c' with all his furniture,
35:14 The c' also for the light,
37:17 he made the c' of pure gold:
17 of beaten work made he the c';
18 c' out of the one side thereof,
18 and three branches of the c'
19 six branches going out of the c'.
20 And in the c' were four bowls
39:37 The pure c', with the lamps
40: 4 thou shalt bring in the c',
24 he put the c' in the tent of the
Le 24: 4 the lamps upon the pure c'
Nu 3:31 c', and the altars, and the vessels
4: 9 and cover the c' of the light,
8: 2 give light over against the c'.
3 over against the c', as the Lord
4 work of the c' was of beaten gold,
4 Moses, so he made the c'.
2Ki 4:10 a table, a stool, and a c':
1Ch 28:15 by weight for every c', and for the

1Ch 28:15 the *c'*, and also for the lamps
15 according to the use of every *c'*.
2Ch 13:11 and the *c'* of gold with the lamps
Da 5: 5 and wrote over against the *c'*
Zec 4: 2 a *c'* all of gold, with a bowl
11 upon the right side of the *c'*
M't 5:15 but on a *c'*; and it giveth light
M'r 4:21 abed? and not to be set on a *c'*?
Lu 8:16 but setteth it on a *c'*, that they
11:33 but on a *c'*, that they which
Heb 9: 2 wherein was the *c'*, and the table,
Re 2: 5 remove thy *c'* out of his place,

candlesticks
1Ki 7:49 the *c'* of pure gold, five on the
1Ch 28:15 the weight for the *c'* of gold, and
15 and for the *c'* of silver by weight,
2Ch 4: 7 he made ten *c'* of gold according
20 the *c'* with their lamps, that they
Jer 52:19 the *c'*, and the spoons, and the
Re 1:12 turned, I saw seven golden *c'*;
13 in the midst of the seven *c'* one
20 hand, and the seven golden *c'*.
20 and the seven *c'* which thou sawest
2: 1 the midst of the seven golden *c'*;
11: 4 and the two *c'* standing before the

cane
Isa 43:24 Thou hast bought me no sweet *c'*
Jer 6:20 Sheba, and the sweet *c'* from a far

canker See also CANKERED; CANKERWORM.
2Ti 2:17 their word will eat as doth a *c'*:

cankered
Jas 5: 3 Your gold and silver is *c'*; and

cankerworm
Joe 1: 4 hath the *c'* eaten;
4 and that which the *c'* hath left
2:25 the *c'*, and the caterpillar, and the
Na 3:15 it shall eat thee up like the *c'*:
15 make thyself many as the *c'*,
16 the *c'* spoileth, and fleeth away.

Canneh (*can'-neh*) See also CALNEH.
Eze 27:23 *C'*, and Eden, the merchants of

cannot^ See also CAN and NOT.
Ge 19:19 I *c'* escape to the mountain,
22 I *c'* do any thing till thou be
24:50 we *c'* speak unto thee bad or
29: 8 We *c'*, until all the flocks be
31:35 I *c'* rise up before thee: for
32:12 the sand of the sea, which *c'* be
34:14 We *c'* do this thing, to give
38:22 and said, I *c'* find her; and also
43:22 *c'* tell who put our money
44:22 The lad *c'* leave his father:
26 *c'* go down: if our youngest
Ex 10: 5 one *c'* be able to see the earth:
19:23 people *c'* come up to mount
Nu 22:18 I *c'* go beyond the word of
23:20 he hath blessed; and I *c'* reverse
24:13 I *c'* go beyond the
35:33 and the land *c'* be cleansed of
De 28:35 a sore botch that *c'* be
Jos 24:19 Ye *c'* serve the Lord: for he is
J'g 11:35 mouth unto the Lord, and I *c'*
14:13 if ye *c'* declare it me, then
Ru 4: 6 I *c'* redeem it for myself, lest
6 my right to thyself; for I *c'*
1Sa 12:21 things, which *c'* profit nor deliver:
17:39 I *c'* go with these; for I
55 As thy soul liveth, O king, I *c'* tell.
25:17 that a man *c'* speak to him.
2Sa 5: 6 thinking, David *c'* come in hither.
14:14 which *c'* be gathered up again;
23: 6 they *c'* be taken with hands:
1Ki 3: 8 that *c'* be numbered nor counted
8:27 heaven of heavens *c'* contain
18:12 tell Ahab, and he *c'* find thee,
2Ch 2: 6 heaven of heavens *c'* contain him?
6:18 heaven of heavens *c'* contain
24:20 of the Lord, that ye *c'* prosper?
Ezr 9:15 we *c'* stand before thee because
Ne 6: 3 so that I *c'* come down:
Job 5:12 their hands *c'* perform their
6:30 *c'* my taste discern perverse things?
9: 3 *c'* answer him one of a thousand.
12:14 *c'* be built again: he shutteth
14: 5 appointed his bounds that he *c'*
17:10 *c'* find one wise man among you
23: 8 backward, but I *c'* perceive him:
9 doth work, but I *c'* behold him:
9 the right hand, that I *c'* see him:
28:15 It *c'* be gotten for gold, neither
16 It *c'* be valued with the gold of
17 gold and the crystal *c'* equal it:
31:31 of his flesh! we *c'* be satisfied.
33:21 that it *c'* be seen; and his bones
36:18 then a great ransom *c'* deliver
37: 5 which we *c'* comprehend.
19 we *c'* order our speech by reason
23 Almighty, we *c'* find him out:
41:17 stick together, that they *c'* be
23 in themselves; they *c'* be moved.
26 him *c'* hold: the spear, the dart,
28 The arrow *c'* make him flee:
Ps 40: 5 they *c'* be reckoned up in order
77: 4 I am so troubled that I *c'* speak.
93: 1 is stablished, that it *c'* be moved.
125: 1 mount Zion, which *c'* be removed,
139: 6 for me; it is high, I *c'* attain
Pr 30:21 and for four which it *c'* bear:
Ec 1: 8 man *c'* utter it: the eye is not
15 crooked *c'* be made straight:
15 that which is wanting *c'* be
8:17 man *c'* find out the work that
10:14 a man *c'* tell what shall be;
Ca 8: 7 Many waters *c'* quench love,
Isa 1:13 the calling of assemblies, I *c'*
29:11 and he saith, I *c'*; for it is
38:18 For the grave *c'* praise thee,
18 go down into the pit *c'* hope for
44:18 shut their eyes, that they *c'* see;
18 and their hearts, that they *c'*
20 that he *c'* deliver his soul, nor
45:20 and pray unto a god that *c'* save.
50: 2 hand shortened at all, that it *c'*
56:10 all dumb dogs, they *c'* bark;
11 shepherds that *c'* understand:
57:20 troubled sea, when it *c'* rest,
59: 1 is not shortened, that it *c'* save;
1 his ear heavy, that it *c'* hear:
14 and equity *c'* enter.
Jer 1: 6 Ah, Lord God! behold, I *c'* speak:
4:19 noise in me; I *c'* hold my peace,
6:10 they *c'* hearken: behold,
7: 8 trust in lying words, that *c'* profit.
10: 5 needs be borne, because they *c'* go.
5 for they *c'* do evil, neither also
14: 9 as a mighty man that *c'*
18: 6 of Israel, *c'* I do with you as
19:11 vessel, that *c'* be made whole
24: 3 that *c'* be eaten, they are so evil.
8 evils figs, which *c'* be eaten, they
29:17 them like vile figs, that *c'* be
33:22 host of heaven *c'* be numbered.
36: 5 am shut up; I *c'* go into
46:23 Lord, though it *c'* be searched;
49:23 on the sea; it *c'* be quiet.
La 3: 7 I *c'* get out: he hath made my
4:18 that we *c'* go in our streets:
Da 2:27 *c'* the wise men, the
Ho 1:10 sea, which *c'* be measured nor
Jon 4:11 that *c'* discern between their
Hab 2: 5 and *c'* be satisfied, but gathereth
M't 5:14 city that is set on an hill *c'* be
6:24 Ye *c'* serve God and mammon.
7:18 A good tree *c'* bring forth evil
19:11 All men *c'* receive this saying,
21:27 We *c'* tell. And he said unto
26:53 Thinkest thou that I *c'* now
27:42 saved others; himself he *c'*
M'r 2:19 bridegroom with them, they *c'*
3:24 itself, that kingdom *c'* stand.
25 itself, that house *c'* stand.
26 he *c'* stand, but hath an end.
7:18 it *c'* defile him;
11:33 *c'* tell. And Jesus answering
15:31 others; himself he *c'* save.
Lu 11: 7 in bed; I *c'* rise and give thee.
13:33 it *c'* be that a prophet perish
14:14 for they *c'* recompense thee:
20 wife, and therefore I *c'* come.
26 life also, he *c'* be my disciple.
27 after me, *c'* be my disciple.
33 he hath, he *c'* be my disciple.
16: 3 I *c'* dig; to beg I am ashamed.
13 Ye *c'* serve God and mammon.
26 pass from hence to you *c'*;
Joh 3: 3 *c'* see the kingdom of God.
5 *c'* enter into the kingdom of
7: 7 world *c'* hate you; but me it
34, 36 I am, thither ye *c'* come.
8:14 ye *c'* tell whence I come,
21 whither I go, ye *c'* come.
22 Whither I go, ye *c'* come.
43 because ye *c'* hear my word.
10:35 the scripture *c'* be broken;
13:33 Whither I go, ye *c'* come; so
37 why *c'* I follow thee now? I
14:17 whom the world *c'* receive,
15: 4 As the branch *c'* bear fruit of
16:12 but ye *c'* bear them now.
18 we *c'* tell what he saith.
Ac 4:16 Jerusalem; and we *c'* deny
20 we *c'* but speak the things
5:39 ye *c'* overthrow it lest; haply
15: 1 of Moses, ye *c'* be saved.
19:36 these things *c'* be spoken against,
27:31 in the ship, ye *c'* be saved.
Ro 8: 8 are in the flesh *c'* please God.
26 groanings which *c'* be uttered.
1Co 7: 9 But if they *c'* contain, let them
10:21 *c'* drink the cup of the Lord,
21 ye *c'* be partakers of the
12:21 the eye *c'* say unto the hand, I
15:50 flesh and blood *c'* inherit the
2Co 12: 2 I *c'* tell; or whether out
2 of the body, I *c'* tell:
3 the body, I *c'* tell: God
Ga 3:17 *c'* disannul, that it should make
5:17 ye *c'* do the things that ye would.
1Ti 5:25 that are otherwise *c'* be hid.
2Ti 2:13 abideth faithful: he *c'* deny
Tit 1: 2 which God, that *c'* lie, promised
2: 8 speech, that *c'* be condemned;
Heb 4:15 priest which *c'* be touched
9: 5 of which we *c'* now speak
12:27 things which *c'* be shaken may
28 a kingdom which *c'* be moved,
Jas 1:13 for God *c'* be tempted with evil,
4: 2 desire to have, and *c'* obtain:
2Pe 1: 9 is blind, and *c'* see afar off, and
2:14 that *c'* cease from sin; beguiling
1Jo 3: 9 he *c'* sin, because he is born

canst^
Ge 41:15 that thou *c'* understand a dream to
Ex 33:20 And he said, Thou *c'* not see
De 28:27 the itch, whereof thou *c'* not
Jos 7:13 thou *c'* not stand before
J'g 16:15 unto him, How *c'* thou say, I love
1Sa 30:15 David said to him, *C'* thou bring
2Ki 8: 1 sojourn wheresoever thou *c'* sojourn:
Ezr 7:16 silver and gold that thou *c'* find
Job 11: 7 *C'* thou by searching find out God?
7 *c'* thou find out the Almighty unto
8 is as high as heaven; what *c'* thou do?
8 deeper than hell; what *c'* thou know?
22:11 Or darkness, that thou *c'* not see;
33: 5 If thou *c'* answer me, set thy
38:31 *C'* thou bind the sweet influences of
32 *C'* thou bring forth Mazzaroth in his
32 or *c'* thou guide Arcturus with his
33 *c'* thou set the dominion thereof in
34 *C'* thou lift up thy voice to the clouds,
35 *C'* thou send lightnings, that they
39: 1 or *c'* thou mark when the hinds do
2 *C'* thou number the months that they
10 *C'* thou bind the unicorn with his
20 *C'* thou make him afraid as a
40: 9 or *c'* thou thunder with a voice
41: 1 *C'* thou draw out leviathan with an
2 *C'* thou put an hook into his nose?
7 *C'* thou fill his skin with barbed
42: 2 I know that thou *c'* do every
Pr 3:15 and all the things thou *c'* desire are
5: 6 ways are moveable, that thou *c'*
30: 4 is his son's name, if thou *c'* tell?
Isa 33:19 deeper speech than thou *c'* perceive;
19 tongue, that thou *c'* not understand
Jer 12: 5 how *c'* thou contend with horses?
Eze 3: 6 words thou *c'* not understand.
Da 5:16 that thou *c'* make interpretations,
16 doubts: now if thou *c'* read
Hab 1:13 and *c'* not look on iniquity:
M't 5:36 because thou *c'* not make
8: 2 thou *c'* make me clean.
M'r 1:40 If thou wilt, thou *c'* make me
9:22 but if thou *c'* do any thing, have
23 If thou *c'* believe, all things are
Lu 5:12 if thou wilt, thou *c'* make me clean.
6:42 how *c'* thou say to thy brother,
Joh 3: 8 but *c'* not tell whence it cometh,
13:36 Whither I go, thou *c'* not follow
Ac 21:37 Who said, *C'* thou speak Greek?
Re 2: 2 and how thou *c'* not bear them

Capernaum (*ca-pur'-na-um*)
M't 4:13 he came and dwelt in *C'*, which is
8: 5 when Jesus was entered into *C'*,
11:23 And thou, *C'*, which art exalted
17:24 were come to *C'*, they that
M'r 1:21 they went into *C'*; and straightway
2: 1 he entered into *C'* after some days;
9:33 he came to *C'*: and being in the
Lu 4:23 have heard done in *C'*, do also here
31 And came down to *C'*, a city of
7: 1 of the people, he entered into *C'*.
10:15 And thou, *C'*, which art exalted to
Joh 2:12 After this he went down to *C'*,
4:46 whose son was sick at *C'*.
6:17 and went over the sea toward *C'*.
24 came to *C'*, seeking for Jesus.
59 synagogue, as he taught in *C'*.

Caphthorim (*caf'-tho-rim*) See also CAPHTORIM.
1Ch 1:12 came the Philistines,) and *C'*.

Caphtor (*caf'-tor*) See also CAPHTORIM.
De 2:23 which came forth out of *C'*,
Jer 47: 4 the remnant of the country of *C'*.
Am 9: 7 the Philistines from *C'*, and the

Caphtorim (*caf'-to-rim*) See also CAPHTHORIM; CAPHTORIMS.
Ge 10:14 came Philistim,) and *C'*.

Caphtorims (*caf'-to-rims*) See also CAPHTORIM.
De 2:23 the *C'*, which came forth out of

capital See CHAPITER.

Cappadocia (*cap-pa-do'-she-ah*)
Ac 2: 9 and *C'*, in Pontus, and Asia,
1Pe 1: 1 Galatia, *C'*, Asia, and Bithynia,

captain See also CAPTAINS.
Ge 21:22 *c'* of his host spake unto
32 Phichol, the chief *c'* of his host,
26:26 Phichol, the chief *c'* of his army.
37:36 Pharaoh's, and *c'* of the guard.
39: 1 *c'* of the guard, an Egyptian,
40: 3 the house of the *c'* of the guard,
4 *c'* of the guard charged Joseph
41:10 *c'* of the guard's house, both me
12 Hebrew, servant to the *c'* of the
Nu 2: 3 be *c'* of the children of Judah.
5 be *c'* of the children of Issachar.
7 be *c'* of the children of Zebulun.
10 the *c'* of the children of Reuben
12 the *c'* of the children of Simeon
14 the *c'* of the sons of Gad shall be
18 the *c'* of the sons of Ephraim
20 *c'* of the children of Manasseh
22 the *c'* of the sons of Benjamin
25 the *c'* of the children of Dan
27 the *c'* of the children of Asher
29 the *c'* of the children of Naphtali
14: 4 Let us make a *c'*, and let us
Jos 5:14 but as *c'* of the host of the Lord
15 *c'* of the Lord's host said unto
J'g 4: 2 the *c'* of whose host was Sisera,
7 the *c'* of Jabin's army, with his
11: 6 and be our *c'*, that we may fight
11 made him head and *c'* over them:
1Sa 9:16 to be *c'* over my people Israel,
10: 1 thee to be *c'* over his inheritance?
12: 9 *c'* of the host of Hazor, and into
13:14 to be *c'* over his people, because
14:50 the name of the *c'* of his host was
17:18 unto the *c'* of their thousand,
55 the *c'* of the host, Abner, whose
18:13 made him his *c'* over a thousand;
22: 2 he became a *c'* over them: and

1Sa 26: 5 Abner the son of Ner, the c' of his
2Sa 2: 8 Abner the son of Ner, c' of Saul's
5: 2 and thou shalt be a c' over Israel.
8 soul, he shall be chief and c'.
10:16 Shobach, the c' of the host of
18 Shobach, the c' of their host, who
17:25 And Absalom made Amasa c'
19:13 c' of the host before me
23:19 therefore he was their c': howbeit
24: 2 Joab the c' of the host, which was
1Ki 1:19 Joab the c' of the host: but
2:32 c' of the host of Israel, and Amasa
32 Jether, c' of the host of Judah.
11:15 Joab the c' of the host was gone up
21 Joab the c' of the host was dead,
24 became c' over a band, when
16: 9 c' of half his chariots, conspired
16 Omri, the c' of the host, king over
2Ki 1: 9 unto him a c' of fifty with his fifty.
10 said to the c' of fifty, If I be a man
11 unto him another c' of fifty
13 a c' of the third fifty with his
13 And the third c' of fifty went up,
4:13 the c' of the host? And she
5: 1 c' of the host of the king of Syria,
9: 5 I have an errand to thee, O c'.
5 all us? And he said, To thee, O c'.
25 Then said Jehu to Bidkah his c',
15:25 Pekah, the son of Remaliah, a c'
18:24 one c' of the least of my master's
20: 5 Hezekiah the c' of my people,
25: 8 Nebuzar-adan, c' of the guard,
10 were with the c' of the guard,
11 Nebuzar-adan the c' of the guard
12 But the c' of the guard left of the
15 in silver, the c' of the guard took
18 the c' of the guard took Seraiah
20 c' of the guard took these, and
1Ch 11: 6 first shall be the chief and c'.
21 than the two; for he was their c':
42 a c' of the Reubenites, and
19:16 the c' of the host of Hadarezer
18 killed Shophach the c' of the host.
27: 5 The third c' of the host for the
7 The fourth c' for the fourth month
8 fifth c' for the fifth month was
9 The sixth c' for the sixth month
10 The seventh c' for the seventh
11 The eighth c' for the eighth month
12 The ninth c' for the ninth month
13 The tenth c' for the tenth month
14 The eleventh c' for the eleventh
15 The twelfth c' for the twelfth
2Ch 13:12 himself is with us for our c',
17:15 Jehohanan the c', and with him
Ne 9:17 in their rebellion appointed a c'
Isa 3: 3 c' of fifty, and the honourable
36: 9 one c' of the least of my master's
Jer 37:13 a c' of the ward was there,
39: 9 the c' of the guard carried away
10 the c' of the guard left of the poor
11 Nebuzar-adan, the c' of the guard,
13 the c' of the guard sent,
40: 1 after that Nebuzar-adan the c' of
2 c' of the guard took Jeremiah,
5 the c' of the guard gave him
41:10 Nebuzar-adan the c' of the guard
43: 6 person that Nebuzar-adan the c'
51:27 appoint a c' against her; cause
52:12 Nebuzar-adan, c' of the guard,
14 that were with the c' of the guard,
15 the c' of the guard carried away
16 the c' of the guard left certain
19 took the c' of the guard away.
24 the c' of the guard took Seraiah
26 Nebuzar-adan the c' of the guard
30 the c' of the guard carried away
Da 2:14 the c' of the king's guard, which
15 said to Arioch the king's c', Why
Joh 18:12 band and the c' and officers
Ac 4: 1 and the c' of the temple, and the
5:24 and the c' of the temple and the
26 went the c' with the officers,
21:31 tidings came unto the chief c'
32 the chief c' and the soldiers,
33 Then the chief c' came near,
37 he said unto the chief c', May I
22:24 The chief c' commanded him to
26 he went and told the chief c',
27 Then the chief c' came, and said
28 And the chief c' answered, With a
29 the chief c' also was afraid, after
23:10 the chief c', fearing lest Paul
15 signify to the chief c' that he
17 this young man unto the chief c':
18 and brought him to the chief c',
19 chief c' took him by the hand,
22 chief c' then let the young man
24: 7 But the chief c' Lysias came
22 When Lysias the chief c' shall
28:16 delivered the prisoners to the c'
Heb 2:10 make the c' of their salvation

captains
Ex 14: 7 and c' over every one of them.
15: 4 his chosen c' also are drowned
Nu 31:14 the c' over thousands,
14 and c' over hundreds,
48 the c' of thousands,
48 and c' of hundreds,
52 of the c' of thousands,
52 and of the c' of hundreds,
54 c' of thousands and of hundreds,
De 1:15 c' over thousands,
15 and c' over hundreds,
15 and c' over fifties,
15 and c' over tens,
De 20: 9 c' of the armies to lead the
29:10 your c' of your tribes, your
Jos 10:24 unto the c' of the men of war
1Sa 8:12 c' over thousands,
12 and c' over fifties;
22: 7 make you all c' of thousands,
7 and c' of hundreds;
2Sa 4: 2 two men that were c' of bands:
18: 1 c' of thousands
1 and c' of hundreds
5 the king gave all the c' charge
23: 8 chief among the c'; the same
24: 4 against the c' of the host.
4 and the c' of the host went out
1Ki 1:25 and the c' of the host, and
2: 5 two c' of the hosts of Israel, unto
9:22 his princes, and his c', and rulers
15:20 the c. of the hosts which he had
20:24 and put c' in their rooms:
22:31 thirty and two c' that had rule
32 the c' of the chariots saw
33 the c' of the chariots perceived
2Ki 1:14 the two c' of the former fifties
8:21 the c' of the chariots: and the
9: 5 the c' of the host were sitting;
10:25 said to the guard and to the c',
25 guard and the c' cast them out,
11: 4 with the c' and the guard,
9 the c' over the hundreds did
10 to the c' over hundreds did the
15 the c' of the hundreds, and
19 the c', and the guard, and all
25:23 all the c' of the armies,
26 and the c' of the armies,
1Ch 4:42 having for their c' Pelatiah,
11:11 chief of the c': he lifted up
15 three of the thirty c' went down
12:14 the sons of Gad, c' of the host:
18 chief of the c', and he said,
18 and made them c' of the band.
20 c' of the thousands that were
21 and were c' of the host.
28 father's house twenty and two c'.
34 of Naphtali a thousand c', and
13: 1 c' of thousands and hundreds,
15:25 and the c' over thousands, went
25: 1 and the c' of the host separated
26:26 the c' over thousands and
26 hundreds, and the c' of the host,
27: 1 c' of thousands and hundreds,
3 the chief of all the c' of the host
28: 1 and the c' of the companies that
1 and the c' over the thousands,
1 and c' over the hundreds,
29: 6 c' of thousands and of hundreds,
2Ch 1: 2 c' of thousands and of hundreds,
8: 9 and chief of his c',
9 and c' of his chariots
11:11 strong holds, and put c' in them,
16: 4 the c' of his armies against the
17:14 the c' of thousands; Adnah the
18:30 Syria had commanded the c' of
31 when the c' of the chariots saw
32 the c' of the chariots perceived
21: 9 and the c' of the chariots.
23: 1 took the c' of hundreds, Azariah
9 to the c' of hundreds spears,
14 the priest brought out the c' of
20 he took the c' of hundreds, and
25: 5 c' over thousands,
5 and c' over hundreds,
26:11 Hananiah, one of the king's c'.
32: 6 set c' of war over the people,
21 the leaders and c' in the camp
33:11 the c' of the host of the king
14 c' of war in all the fenced cities
Ne 2: 9 king had sent c' of the army
Job 39:25 the thunder of the c', and the
Jer 13:21 hast taught them to be c',
40: 7 Now when all the c' of the
13 and all the c' of the forces that
41:11, 13, 16 all the c' of the forces that
42: 1 Then all the c' of the forces, and
8 all the c' of the forces which were
43: 4 all the c' of the forces, and all
5 and all the c' of the forces, took
51:23 will I break in pieces c' and
28 the Medes, the c' thereof, and
57 her c', and her rulers, and her
Eze 21:22 to appoint c', to open the mouth
23: 6 c' and rulers, all of them
12 c' and rulers clothed most
23 desirable young men, c' and
Da 3: 2 and the c', the judges, the
3 the governors, and c', the judges,
27 c', and the king's counsellers,
6: 7 counsellers, and the c', have
Na 3:17 locusts, and thy c' as the great
M'r 6:21 a supper to his lords, high c',
Lu 22: 4 with the chief priest and c',
52 and c' of the temple, and the
Ac 25:23 with the chief c', and principal
Rev 6:15 the rich men, and the chief c',
19:18 of kings, and the flesh of c',

captive See also CAPTIVES.
Ge 14:14 that his brother was taken c',
34:29 their wives took they c', and
Ex 12:29 the firstborn of the c' that was
Nu 24:22 Asshur shall carry thee away c'.
De 21:10 and thou hast taken them c',
J'g 5:12 and lead thy captivity c', thou son
1Ki 8:48 enemies, which led them away c',
50 who carried them c', that they
2Ki 5: 2 and had brought away c' out of
6:22 those whom thou hast taken c'
15:29 and carried them c' to Assyria.
2Ki 16: 9 and carried the people of it c' to
24:16 king of Babylon brought c' to
1Ch 5: 6 king of Assyria carried away c':
2Ch 6:37 whither they are carried c', and
25:12 children of Judah carry away c',
28: 8 carried away c' of their brethren
11 again, which ye have taken c'
30: 9 them that lead them c', so that
Ps 68:18 thou hast led captivity c': thou
137: 3 that carried us away c' required
Isa 49:21 am desolate, a c', and removing
24 the mighty, or the lawful c'
51:14 The c' exile hasteneth that he
52: 2 thy neck, O c' daughter of Zion.
Jer 1: 3 carrying away of Jerusalem c'
13:17 Lord's flock is carried away c'.
19 shall be carried away c' all of it,
19 it shall be wholly carried away c'.
20: 4 and he shall carry them c' into
22:12 they have led him c', and shall
24: 1 had carried away c' Jeconiah the
5 are carried away c' of Judah,
27:20 he carried away c' Jeconiah the
28: 6 all that is carried away c', from
29: 1 carried away c' from Jerusalem
14 caused you to be carried away c'.
39: 9 carried away c' into Babylon the
40: 1 all that were carried away c' of
1 which were carried away c' unto
7 not carried away c' to Babylon;
41:10 Then Ishmael carried away c'
10 carried them away c', and
14 Ishmael had carried away c' from
52:15 carried away c' certain of the
27 Thus Judah was carried away c'
28 Nebuchadrezzar carried away c':
29 he carried away c' from Jerusalem
30 carried away c' of the Jews seven
Am 1: 6 they carried away c' the whole
6: 7 therefore now shall they go c'
7 with the first that go c',
7:11 Israel shall surely be led away c'
Ob 11 the strangers carried away c'
Na 2: 7 Huzzab shall be led away c',
Lu 21:24 shall be led away c' into all
Eph 4: 8 upon high, he led captivity c', and
2Ti 2:26 who are taken c' by him at his
3: 6 lead c' silly women laden with

captives
Ge 31:26 away my daughters, as c' taken
Nu 31: 9 took all the women of Midian c',
12 they brought the c', and the prey,
19 purify both yourselves and your c'
De 21:11 And seest among the c' a
32:42 blood of the slain and of the c',
1Sa 30: 2 And had taken the women c',
3 their daughters, were taken c'.
5 David's two wives were taken c',
1Ki 8:46 they carry them away c' unto
47 whither they were carried c',
47 of them that carried them c',
2Ki 24:14 ten thousand c', and all the
2Ch 6:36 they carry them away c' unto a
38 they have carried them c', and
28: 5 a great multitude of them c',
11 deliver the c' again, which ye
13 Ye shall not bring in the c' hither:
14 the armed men left the c' and the
15 by name rose up, and took the c',
17 Judah, and carried away c'.
Ps 106:46 of all those that carried them c'.
Isa 14: 2 and they shall take them c',
2 whose c' they were; and they shall
20: 4 the Ethiopians c', young and old,
45:13 and he shall let go my c', not
49:25 the c' of the mighty shall be
61: 1 to proclaim liberty to the c', and
Jer 28: 4 with all the c' of Judah, that went
29: 1 which were carried away c',
4 all that are carried away c',
7 caused you to be carried away c',
43: 3 death, and carry us away c': and he
12 and carry them away c': and he
48:46 thy sons are taken c', and
46 and thy daughters c'.
50:33 and all that took them c' held
Eze 1: 1 as I was among the c' by the
6: 9 they shall be carried c', because
16:53 captivity of thy c' in the midst of
Da 2:25 found a man of the c' of
11: 8 shall also carry c' into Egypt
Lu 4:18 to preach deliverance to the c',

captivity
Nu 21:29 and his daughters, into c'
De 21:13 the raiment of her c' from off
28:41 them; for they shall go into c'.
30: 3 the Lord thy God will turn thy c',
J'g 5:12 and lead thy c' captive, thou son
18:30 Dan until the day of the c' of the
2Ki 24:15 carried he into c' from Jerusalem
25:27 thirtieth year of the c' of
1Ch 5:22 dwelt in their steads until the c'.
6:15 And Jehozadak went into c',
2Ch 6:37 the land of their c', saying, We
38 in the land of their c', whither
29: 9 daughters and our wives are in c'
Ezr 1:11 bring up with them of the c' that
2: 1 that went up out of the c',
3: 8 that were come out of the c' unto
4: 1 that the children of the c'
6:16 the rest of the children of the c',
19 And the children of the c' kept
20 all the children of the c', and for
21 were come again out of c', and all
8:35 which were come out of the c',

Ezr 9: 7 to the sword, to *c*, and to a spoil,
10: 7 all the children of the *c*, that
16 the children of the *c* did so. And
Ne 1: 2 escaped, which were left of the *c*,
3 remnant that are left of the *c*
4: 4 them for a prey in the land of *c*:
7: 6 went up out of the *c*, of those
8:17 come again out of the *c* made
Es 2: 6 from Jerusalem with the *c*,
Job 42:10 Lord turned the *c* of Job when
Ps 14: 7 Lord bringeth back the *c* of his
53: 6 God bringeth back the *c* of his
68:18 high, thou hast led *c* captive:
78:61 delivered his strength into *c*, and
85: 1 brought back the *c* of Jacob.
126: 1 the Lord turned again the *c* of
4 Turn again our *c*, O Lord, as the
Isa 5:13 my people are gone into *c*,
22:17 thee away with a mighty *c*,
46: 2 but themselves are gone into *c*.
Jer 15: 2 such as are for the *c*, to the *c*.
20: 6 in thine house, shall go into *c*:
22:22 and thy lovers shall go into *c*:
29:14 and I will turn away your *c*,
16 not gone forth with you into *c*;
20 word of the Lord, all ye of the *c*,
22 a curse by all the *c* of Judah
28 This *c* is long: build ye houses,
31 Send to all them of the *c*, saying,
30: 3 I will bring again the *c* of my
10 seed from the land of their *c*;
16 every one of them, shall go into *c*;
18 will bring again the *c* of Jacob's
31:23 when I shall bring again their *c*;
32:44 I will cause their *c* to return,
33: 7 I will cause the *c* of Judah and the
7 and the *c* of Israel to return,
11 I will cause to return the *c* of the
26 I will cause their *c* to return, and
43:11 and such as are for *c* to *c*;
46:19 furnish thyself to go into *c*:
27 seed from the land of their *c*;
48: 7 Chemosh shall go forth into *c*
11 neither hath he gone into *c*:
47 Yet will I bring again the *c* of
49: 3 their king shall go into *c*, and
6 I will bring again the *c* of the
39 I will bring again the *c* of Elam,
52:31 and thirtieth year of the *c* of
La 1: 3 Judah is gone into *c* because
5 her children are gone into *c*
18 my young men are gone into *c*.
2:14 to turn away thy *c*; but have
4:22 more carry thee away into *c*:
Eze 1: 2 fifth year of king Jehoiachin's *c*,
3:11 get thee to them of the *c*, unto
15 I came to them of the *c* at
11:24 God into Chaldea, to them of the *c*.
25 Then I spake unto them of the *c*
12: 4 as they that go forth into *c*.
7 as stuff for *c*, and in the even
11 they shall remove and go into *c*.
16:53 I shall bring again their *c*,
53 the *c* of Sodom and her daughters,
53 and the *c* of Samaria and her
53 the *c* of thy captives in the midst
25: 3 Judah, when they went into *c*;
29:14 And I will bring again the *c* of
30:17 and these cities shall go into *c*.
18 her daughters shall go into *c*.
33:21 the twelfth year of our *c*, in the
39:23 Israel went into *c* for their
25 will I bring again the *c* of Jacob,
28 them to be led into *c* among the
40: 1 year of our *c*, in the beginning
Da 5:13 art of the children of the *c* of
6:13 which is of the children of the *c*
11:33 the sword, and by flame, by *c*,
Ho 6:11 when I returned the *c* of my
Joe 3: 1 shall bring again the *c* of Judah,
Am 1: 5 people of Syria shall go into *c*
6 carried away captive the whole *c*,
9 they delivered up the whole *c* to
15 their king shall go into *c*, he
5: 5 Gilgal shall surely go into *c*, and
27 will I cause you to go into *c*
7:17 Israel shall surely go into *c*
9: 4 though they go into *c* before
14 I will bring again the *c* of my
Ob 20 And the *c* of this host of the
20 and the *c* of Jerusalem, which
Mic 1:16 for they are gone into *c* from
Na 3:10 she went into *c*: her young
Hab 1: 9 they shall gather the *c* as the
Zep 2: 7 them, and turn away their *c*.
3:20 when I turn back your *c* before
Zec 6:10 Take of them of the *c*, even of
14: 2 of the city shall go forth into *c*,
Ro 7:23 bringing me into *c* to the law of
2Co 10: 5 bringing into *c* every thought to
Eph 4: 8 he led *c* captive, and gave gifts
Re 13:10 that leadeth into *c* shall go into *c*:

Car See BETH-CAR.

carbuncle See also CARBUNCLES.
Ex 28:17 topaz, and a *c*: this shall be the
39:10 was a sardius, a topaz, and a *c*:
Eze 28:13 emerald, and the *c*, and gold:

carbuncles
Isa 54:12 and thy gates of *c*, and all thy

Carcas (*car'-cas*)
Es 1:10 Abagtha, Zethar, and *C*,

carcase See also CARCASES.
Le 5: 2 a *c* of an unclean beast,
5: 2 or a *c* of unclean cattle,
2 the *c* of unclean creeping things,
11: 8 and their *c* shall ye not touch;
24 whosoever toucheth the *c* of them
25 beareth ought of the *c* of them
27 whoso toucheth their *c* shall be
28 he that beareth the *c* of them
35 any part of their *c* falleth
36 that which toucheth their *c* shall
37 if any part of their *c* fall upon any
38 any part of their *c* fall thereon,
39 he that toucheth the *c* thereof
40 he that eateth of the *c* of it shall
40 he also that beareth the *c* of it
De 14: 8 flesh, nor touch their dead *c*.
28:26 thy *c* shall be meat unto all fowls
Jos 8:29 they should take his *c* down from
J'g 14: 8 aside to see the *c* of the lion:
8 and honey in the *c* of the lion.
9 honey out of the *c* of the lion.
1Ki 13:22 thy *c* shall not come unto the
24 his *c* was cast in the way,
24 the lion also stood by the *c*.
25 and saw the *c* cast in the way,
25 and the lion standing by the *c*:
28 and found his *c* cast in the way,
28 ass and the lion standing by the *c*:
28 the lion had not eaten the *c*,
29 prophet took up the *c* of the man
30 he laid his *c* in his own grave;
2Ki 9:37 the *c* of Jezebel shall be as dung
Isa 14:19 as a *c* trodden under feet.
M't 24:28 For wheresoever the *c* is, there

carcases
Ge 15:11 the fowls came down upon the *c*,
Le 11:11 shall have their *c* in abomination.
26:30 cast your *c* upon the *c* of your
Nu 14:29 Your *c* shall fall in this wilderness;
32 for you, your *c*, they shall fall
33 your *c* be wasted in the wilderness.
1Sa 17:46 the *c* of the host of the Philistines
Isa 5:25 their *c* were torn in the midst of
34: 3 stink shall come up out of their *c*,
66:24 upon the *c* of the men that have
Jer 7:33 the *c* of this people shall be meat
9:22 the *c* of men shall fall as dung
16: 4 their *c* shall be meat for the fowls
18 with the *c* of their detestable
19: 7 their *c* will I give to be meat for
Eze 6: 5 dead *c* of the children of Israel
43: 7 nor by the *c* of their kings in
9 the *c* of their kings, far from me,
Na 3: 3 slain, and a great number of *c*;
Heb 3:17 whose *c* fell in the wilderness?

carcass See CARCASE.

Carchemish (*car'-ke-mish*) See also CHARCHEMISH.
Isa 10: 9 Is not Calno as *C*? is not Hamath
Jer 46: 2 was by the river Euphrates in *C*,

care See also CARED; CAREFUL; CARELESS; CARES; CAREST; CARETH; CARING.
1Sa 10: 2 hath left the *c* of the asses,
2Sa 18: 3 they will not *c* for us;
3 of us die, will they *c* for us:
2Ki 4:13 been careful for us with all this *c*;
Jer 49:31 nation, that dwelleth without *c*,
Eze 4:16 eat bread by weight, and with *c*;
M't 13:22 the *c* of this world, and the
Lu 10:34 to an inn, and took *c* of him.
35 Take *c* of him; and whatsoever
40 Lord, dost thou not *c* that my
1Co 7:21 being a servant? *c* not for it;
9: 9 Doth God take *c* for oxen?
12:25 the same *c* one for another.
2Co 7:12 or *c* for you in the sight of God
8:16 earnest *c* into the heart of Titus
11:28 daily, the *c* of all the churches.
Ph'p 2:20 will naturally *c* for your state.
4:10 your *c* of me hath flourished
1Ti 3: 5 shall he take *c* of the church of
1Pe 5: 7 Casting all your *c* upon him;

Careah (*ca-re'-ah*) See also KAREAH.
2Ki 25:23 and Johanan the son of *C*,

cared
Ps 142: 4 failed me; no man *c* for my soul.
Joh 12: 6 not that he *c* for the poor;
Ac 18:17 Gallio *c* for none of those things.

careful
2Ki 4:13 thou hast been *c* for us with all
Jer 17: 8 not be *c* in the year of drought,
Da 3:16 we are not *c* to answer thee in
Lu 10:41 Martha, thou art *c* and troubled
Ph'p 4: 6 Be *c* for nothing; but in
10 wherein ye were also *c*, but ye
Tit 3: 8 be *c* to maintain good works.

carefully
De 15: 5 Only if thou *c* hearken unto the
Mic 1:12 inhabitant of Maroth waited *c*
Ph'p 2:28 sent him therefore the more *c*,
Heb 12:17 though he sought it *c* with tears.

carefulness
Eze 12:18 water with trembling and with *c*;
19 eat their bread with *c*, and drink
1Co 7:32 But I would have you without *c*.
2Co 7:11 sort, what *c* it wrought in you,

careless
J'g 18: 7 how they dwelt *c*, after the
Isa 32: 9 ye *c* daughters; give ear unto my
10 ye be troubled, ye *c* women: for
Isa 32:11 at ease; be troubled, ye *c* ones:
Eze 30: 9 to make the *c* Ethiopians afraid,

carelessly
Isa 47: 8 that dwellest *c*, that sayest in
Eze 39: 6 and among them that dwell *c* in
Zep 2:15 is the rejoicing city that dwelt *c*,

cares
M'r 4:19 the *c* of this world, and the
Lu 8:14 are choked with *c* and riches and
21:34 and *c* of this life, and so that day

carest
M't 22:16 neither *c* thou for any man: for
M'r 4:38 Master, *c* thou not that we perish?
12:14 thou art true, and *c* for no man:

careth
De 11:12 which the Lord thy God *c* for:
Joh 10:13 hireling, and *c* not for the sheep.
1Co 7:32 He that is unmarried *c* for the
33 he that is married *c* for the
34 unmarried woman *c* for the
34 married *c* for the things of the
1Pe 5: 7 upon him, for he *c* for you.

caring
1Sa 9: 5 lest my father leave *c* for the asses,

Carmel (*car'-mel*) See also CARMELITE.
Jos 12:22 the king of Jokneam of *C*, one;
15:55 Maon, *C*, and Ziph, and Juttah,
19:26 Misheal; and reacheth to *C*
1Sa 15:12 Samuel, saying, Saul came to *C*,
25: 2 whose possessions were in *C*;
2 he was shearing his sheep in *C*.
5 Get you up to *C*, and go to Nabal,
7 them, all the while they were in *C*.
40 of David were come to Abigail to *C*,
1Ki 18:19 to me all Israel unto mount *C*,
20 prophets together unto mount *C*.
42 Elijah went up to the top of *C*;
2Ki 2:25 he went from thence to mount *C*,
4:25 unto the man of God to mount *C*.
19:23 and into the forest of his *C*.
2Ch 26:10 in the mountains, and in *C*:
Ca 7: 5 Thine head upon thee is like *C*,
Isa 33: 9 and *C* shake off their fruits.
35: 2 the excellency of *C* and Sharon,
37:24 border, and the forests of his *C*.
Jer 46:18 and as *C* by the sea, so shall he
50:19 he shall feed on *C* and Bashan,
Am 1: 2 shall mourn, and the top of *C*
9: 3 hide themselves in the top of *C*,
Mic 7:14 in the wood, in the midst of *C*:
Na 1: 4 Bashan languisheth, and *C*, and

Carmelite (*car'-mel-ite*) See also CARMELITESS.
1Sa 30: 5 Abigail the wife of Nabal the *C*.
2Sa 2: 2 and Abigail Nabal's wife the *C*.
3: 3 Abigail the wife of Nabal the *C*;
23:35 Hezrai the *C*, Paarai the Arbite,
1Ch 11:37 Hezro the *C*, Naarai the son of

Carmelitess (*car'-mel-i-tess*)
1Sa 27: 3 and Abigail the *C*, Nabal's wife.
1Ch 3: 1 second Daniel, of Abigail the *C*:

Carmi (*car'-mi*) See also CARMITES.
Ge 46: 9 and Phallu, and Hezron, and *C*.
Ex 6:14 Hanoch, and Pallu, Hezron, and *C*:
Nu 26: 6 Hezronites: of *C*, the family of
Jos 7: 1 for Achan, the son of *C*, the son
18 by man; and Achan, the son of *C*,
1Ch 2: 7 And the sons of *C*; Achar, the
4: 1 of Judah; Pharez, Hezron, and *C*,
5: 3 Hanoch, and Pallu, Hezron, and *C*.

Carmites (*car'-mites*)
Nu 26: 6 of Carmi, the family of the *C*.

carnal
Ro 7:14 but I am *c*, sold under sin.
8: 7 Because the *c* mind is enmity
15:27 to minister unto them in *c* things.
1Co 3: 1 but as unto *c*, even as unto
3 For ye are yet *c*: for whereas
3 are ye not *c*, and walk as men?
4 I am of Apollos; are ye not *c*?
9:11 if we shall reap your *c* things?
2Co 10: 4 weapons of our warfare are not *c*,
He 7:16 the law of a *c* commandment,
9:10 and *c* ordinances, imposed on

carnally
Le 18:20 thou shalt not lie *c* with thy
19:20 whosoever lieth *c* with a
Nu 5:13 And a man lie with her *c*, and
Ro 8: 6 to be *c* minded is death; but to

carpenter See also CARPENTER'S; CARPENTERS.
Isa 41: 7 the *c* encouraged the goldsmith,
44:13 The *c* stretched out his rule;
M'r 6: 3 Is not this the *c*, the son of

carpenter's
M't 13:55 Is not this the *c* son? is not his

carpenters
2Sa 5:11 *c*, and masons: and they
2Ki 12:11 they laid it out to the *c* and
22: 6 Unto *c*, and builders, and
1Ch 14: 1 with masons and *c*, to build
2Ch 24:12 and hired masons and *c* to repair
Ezr 3: 7 unto the masons, and to the *c*;
Jer 24: 1 with the *c* and smiths, from
29: 2 and the *c*, and the smiths,
Zec 1:20 And the Lord shewed me four *c*.

Carpus (*car'-pus*)
2Ti 4:13 cloak that I left at Troas with *C*,

carriage See also CARRIAGES.
J'g 18:21 the cattle and the c' before them.
1Sa 17:22 David left his c' in the hand
22 the hand of the keeper of the c',

carriages
Isa 10:28 Michmash he hath laid up his c':
46: 1 your c' were heavy loaden;
Ac 21:15 we took up our c', and went up

carried
Ge 31:18 And he c' away all his cattle,
26 and c' away my daughters,
46: 5 of Israel c' Jacob their father,
50:13 For his sons c' him into the land
Le 10: 5 and c' them in their coats out of
Jos 4: 8 and c' them over with them
J'g 16: 3 c' them up to the top of an hill
1Sa 5: 8 ark of the God of Israel be c'
8 c' the ark of the God of Israel
9 so, that, after they had c' it about,
30: 2 or small, but c' them away,
18 the Amalekites had c' away:
2Sa 6:10 David c' it aside into the house
15:29 and Abiathar c' the ark of God
1Ki 8:47 whither they were c' captives,
47 of them that c' them captives,
50 before them who c' them captive,
17:19 and c' him up into a loft,
21:13 c' him forth out of the city,
2Ki 7: 8 and c' thence silver, and gold,
8 and c' thence also, and went
9:28 c' him in a chariot to Jerusalem,
15:29 and c' them captive to Assyria.
16: 9 and c' the people of it captive
17: 6 and c' Israel away into Assyria,
11 the Lord c' away before them;
23 So was Israel c' away out of their
28 had c' away from Samaria
33 whom they c' away from thence,
20:17 shall be c' unto Babylon:
23: 4 c' the ashes of them unto Beth-el.
30 his servants c' him in a chariot
24:13 he c' out thence all the treasures
14 And he c' away all Jerusalem,
15 And he c' away Jehoiachin
15 those c' he into captivity from
25: 7 of brass, and c' him to Babylon.
13 c' the brass of them to Babylon.
21 So Judah was c' away
1Ch 5: 6 king of Assyria c' away captive:
26 of Assyria, and he c' them away,
6:15 when the Lord c' away Judah
9: 1 were c' away to Babylon
13: 7 And they c' the ark of God
13 but c' it aside into the house of
2Ch 6:37 whither they are c' captive,
38 they have c' them captives,
12: 9 he c' away also the shields
14:13 they c' away very much spoil.
15 and c' away sheep and camels
16: 6 they c' away the stones of Ramah,
21:17 and c' away all the substance
24:11 it, and c' it to his place again.
28: 5 and they smote him, and c' away
8 c' away captive of their brethren
15 and c' all the feeble of them
17 Judah, and c' away captives.
33:11 fetters, and c' him to Babylon.
34:16 Shaphan c' the book to the king,
36: 4 brother, and c' him to Egypt.
7 Nebuchadnezzar also c' of the
20 sword c' he away to Babylon;
Ezr 2: 1 of those which had been c' away,
1 king of Babylon had c' away
5:12 c' the people away into Bablyon.
8:35 those that had been c' away,
9: 4 those that had been c' away;
10: 6 them that had been c' away.
8 those that had been c' away.
Ne 7: 6 of those that had been c' away,
6 king of Babylon had c' away,
Es 2: 6 been c' away from Jerusalem
6 captivity which had been c' away
6 king of Babylon had c' away.
Job 1:17 and have c' them away, yea,
5:13 of the froward is c' headlong.
10:19 I should have been c' from the
Ps 46: 2 though the mountains be c' into
106:46 those that c' them captives.
137: 3 they that c' us away captive
Isa 39: 6 shall be c' to Babylon: nothing
46: 3 are c' from the womb:
49:22 thy daughters shall be c' upon
53: 4 our grief, and c' our sorrows:
63: 9 and c' them all the days of old.
Jer 13:17 Lord's flock is c' away captive.
19 shall be c' away captive all of
19 shall be wholly c' away captive,
24: 1 had c' away captive Jeconiah
5 them that are c' away captive,
27:20 he c' away captive Jeconiah the
22 They shall be c' to Babylon,
28: 3 this place, and c' them to Babylon:
6 all that is c' away captive,
29: 1 which were c' away captives,
1 Nebuchadnezzar had c' away
4 all that are c' away captives,
4 whom I have caused to be c' away
7 caused you to be c' away captives,
14 caused you to be c' away captive.
39: 9 the guard c' away captive into
40: 1 c' away captive of Jerusalem
1 which were c' away captive unto
7 that were not c' away captive
41:10 Then Ishmael c' away captive
10 c' them away captive, and
Jer 41:14 Ishmael had c' away captive
52: 9 they took the king and c' him up
11 and c' him to Babylon, and put
15, 30 captain of the guard c' away
17 and c' all the brass of them to
27 Thus Judah was c' away captive
28 Nebuchadnezzar c' away captive
29 Nebuchadrezzar he c' away
Eze 6: 9 they shall be c' captives,
17: 4 and c' it into a land of traffick;
37: 1 and c' me out in the spirit
Da 1: 2 he c' into the land of Shinar
2:35 and the wind c' them away,
Ho 10: 6 It shall be also c' unto Assyria
12: 1 and oil is c' into Egypt.
Joe 3: 5 have c' into your temples
Am 1: 6 because they c' away captive
Ob 11 the strangers c' away captive
Na 3:10 Yet was she c' away, she went
M't 1:11 the time they were c' away
M'r 15: 1 bound Jesus, and c' him away,
Lu 7:12 there was a dead man c' out,
16:22 was c' by the angels into
24:51 them, and c' up into heaven.
Ac 3: 2 from his mother's womb was c',
5: 6 up, and c' him out, and buried
7:16 And were c' over into Sychem,
8: 2 c' Stephen to his burial,
21:34 him to be c' into the castle.
1Co 12: 2 c' away unto these dumb idols,
Ga 2:13 Barnabas also was c' away with
Eph 4:14 and c' about with every wind
Heb 13: 9 Be not c' about with divers
2Pe 2:17 that are c' with a tempest;
Jude 12 without water, c' about of winds;
Re 12:15 her to be c' away of the flood.
17: 3 So he c' me away in the spirit
21:10 c' me away in the spirit to a great

carriest
Ps 90: 5 c' them away as with a flood;

carrieth
Job 21:18 chaff that the storm c' away.
27:21 The east wind c' him away,
Re 17: 7 and of the beast that c' her,

carry See also CARRIED; CARRIEST; CARRIETH; CARRYING.
Ge 37:25 going to c' it down to Egypt.
42:19 go ye, c' corn for the famine of
43:11 and c' down the man a present,
12 sacks, c' it again in your hand;
44: 1 as much as they can c', and put
45:27 which Joseph had sent to c' him,
46: 5 which Pharaoh had sent to c' him.
47:30 and thou shalt c' me out of Egypt,
50:25 shall c' up my bones from hence.
Ex 12:46 thou shalt not c' forth ought of
13:19 ye shall c' up my bones away
14:11 us, to c' us forth out of Egypt?
33:15 with me, c' us not up hence.
Le 4:12 whole bullock shall he c' forth
21 And he shall c' forth the bullock
6:11 c' forth the ashes without the
10: 4 c' your brethren from before the
14:45 and he shall c' them forth out of
16:27 shall one c' forth without the
Nu 11:12 C' them in thy bosom, as a
24:22 Asshur shall c' thee away captive.
De 14:24 so that thou art not able to c' it;
28:38 Thou shalt c' much seed out
Jos 4: 3 ye shall c' them over with you,
1Sa 17:18 And c' these ten cheeses unto
20:40 him, Go, c' them to the city.
2Sa 15:25 C' back the ark of God into the
19:18 to c' over the king's household,
1Ki 8:46 c' them away captives unto the
18:12 the Spirit of the Lord shall c' thee
21:10 And then c' him out and stone
22:26 and c' him back unto Amon
34 Turn thine hand, and c' me out
2Ki 4:19 C' him to his mother.
9: 2 and c' him to an inner chamber;
17:27 C' thither one of the priests
18:11 the king of Assyria did c' away
25:11 the captain of the guard c' away.
1Ch 10: 9 to c' tidings unto their idols, and
15: 2 None ought to c' the ark of God
2 the Lord chosen to c' the ark
23:26 shall no more c' the tabernacle,
2Ch 2:16 shalt c' it up to Jerusalem.
6:36 enemies, and they c' them away captives
18:25 Micaiah, and c' him back to Amon
33 mayest c' me out of the host;
20:25 more than they could c' away;
25:12 the children of Judah c' away captives
29: 5 and c' forth the filthiness out of
16 And the Levites took it, to c' it
36: 6 in fetters, to c' him to Babylon.
Ezr 5:15 go, c' them into the temple that
7:15 And to c' the silver and gold,
Job 15:12 Why doth thine heart c' thee
Ps 49:17 he shall c' nothing away: his glory
Ec 5:15 he may c' away in his hand.
10:20 a bird of the air shall c' the voice
Isa 5:29 the prey, and shall c' it away
15: 7 laid up, shall they c' away to the
22:17 the Lord will c' thee away with a
23: 7 her own feet shall c' her afar off
30: 6 they will c' their riches upon the
40:11 and c' them in his bosom, and
41:16 and the wind shall c' them away,
46: 4 to hoar hairs will I c' you: I have
4 even I will c', and will deliver you.
7 c' him, and set him in his place,
57:13 the wind shall c' them all away;
Jer 17:22 Neither c' forth a burden out of
20: 4 shall c' them captive into Babylon,
5 them, and c' them to Babylon.
39: 7 with chains, to c' him to Babylon.
14 Shaphan, that he should c' him
43: 3 c' us away captives into Babylon.
12 and c' them away captives: and
La 4:22 no more c' thee...into captivity:
Eze 12: 5 their sight, and c' out thereby.
6 and c' it forth in the twilight:
12 the wall to c' out thereby:
22: 9 In thee are men that c' tales to
38:13 to c' away silver and gold, to
Da 11: 8 And shall also c' captives into
M'r 6:55 to c' about in beds those that
11:16 any man should c' any vessel
Lu 10: 4 C' neither purse, nor scrip, nor
Joh 5:10 it is not lawful for thee to c' thy
21:18 shall gird thee, and c' thee whither
Ac 5: 9 at the door, and shall c' thee out.
7:43 c' you away beyond Babylon.
1Ti 6: 7 is certain we can c' nothing out.

carrying See also MISCARRYING.
1Sa 10: 3 one c' three kids, and another
3 another c' three loaves of bread,
3 and another c' a bottle of wine:
Ps 78: 9 c' bows, turned back in the day
Jer 1: 3 c' away of Jerusalem captive
M't 1:17 from David until the c' away
17 from the c' away into Babylon
Ac 5:10 c' her forth, buried her by her

Carshena *(car-she'-nah)*
Es 1:14 And the next unto him was C',

cart
1Sa 6: 7 Now therefore make a new c',
7 tie the kine to the c', and bring
8 the Lord, and lay it upon the c';
10 milch kine, and tied them to the c',
11 the ark of the Lord upon the c',
14 And the c' came into the field of
14 they clave the wood of the c', and
2Sa 6: 3 set the ark of God upon a new c',
3 of Abinadab, drave the new c'.
1Ch 13: 7 carried the ark of God in a new c'
7 And Uzza and Ahio drave the c'.
Isa 5:18 and sin as it were with a c' rope:
28:27 neither is a c' wheel turned about
28 break it with the wheel of his c',
Am 2:13 as a c' is pressed that is full of

carved
J'g 18:18 fetched the c' image, the ephod,
1Ki 6:18 the house within was c' with
29 he c' all the walls of the house
29 c' figures of cherubims and palm
32 and he c' upon them carvings of
35 And he c' thereon cherubims
35 with gold fitted upon the c' work.
2Ch 33: 7 he set a c' image, the idol which
22 sacrificed unto all the c' images
34: 3 the c' images, and the molten
4 the groves, and the c' images,
Ps 74: 6 now they break down the c' work
Pr 7:16 with c' works, with fine linen of

carving See also CARVINGS.
Ex 31: 5 and in c' of timber, to work in all
35:33 and in c' of wood, to make any

carvings
1Ki 6:32 c' of cherubims and palm trees

case See also CASES.
Ex 5:19 did see that they were in evil c',
De 19: 4 this is the c' of the slayer, which
22: 1 thou shalt in any c' bring them
24:13 In any c' thou shalt deliver him
Ps 144:15 that people, that is in such a c':
M't 5:20 ye shall in no c' enter into the
19:10 If the c' of the man be so with his
Joh 5: 6 a long time in that c', he saith unto

casement
Pro 7: 6 I looked through my c',

cases
1Co 7:15 is not under bondage in such c':

Casiphia *(cas-if'-e-ah)*
Ezr 8:17 Iddo the chief at the place C',
17 the Nethinims, at the place C',

Casluhim *(cas'-loo-him)*
Ge 10:14 and C', (out of whom came
1Ch 1:12 and C', (of whom came the

cassia
Ex 30:24 And of c' five hundred shekels,
Ps 45: 8 smell of myrrh, and aloes, and c',
Eze 27:19 bright iron, c', and calamus,

cast See also CASTAWAY; CASTEDST; CASTEST; CASTETH; CASTING; FORECAST; OUTCAST.
Ge 21:10 C' out this bondwoman and her
15 and she c' the child under one of
31:38 she goats have not c' their young,
51 behold this pillar, which I have c'
37:20 him, and c' him into some pit,
22 c' him into this pit that is in the
24 took him, and c' him into a pit:
39: 7 master's wife c' her eyes upon
Ex 1:22 is born ye shall c' into the river,
4: 3 And he said, C' it on the ground.
3 And he c' it on the ground,
25 and c' it at his feet, and said,
7: 9 Take thy rod, and c' it before

Ex 7:10 and Aaron c' down his rod before
12 For they c' down every man his
10:19 locusts, and c' them into the Red
15: 4 his host hath he c' into the sea:
25 when he had c' into the waters,
22:31 ye shall c' it to the dogs.
23:26 shall nothing c' their young.
25:12 thou shalt c' four rings of gold
26:37 thou shalt c' five sockets of brass
32:19 he c' the tables out of his hands,
24 then I c' it into the fire, and
34:24 I will c' out the nations before
36:36 and he c' for them four sockets of
37: 3, 13 he c' for it four rings of gold,
38: 5 he c' four rings for the four ends
27 hundred talents of silver were c'
Le 1:16 and c' it beside the altar on the
14:40 and they shall c' them into an
16: 8 Aaron shall c' lots upon the two
18:24 nations are defiled which I c' out
20:23 nation, which I c' out before you:
26:30 and c' your carcases upon the
44 I will not c' them away, neither
Nu 19: 6 and c' it into the midst of the
35:22 or have c' upon him any thing
23 and c' it upon him, that he die,
De 6:19 To c' out all thine enemies from
7: 1 hath c' out many nations before
9: 4 Lord thy God hath c' them out
17 and c' them out of my two hands,
21 and I c' the dust thereof into the
28:40 for thine olive shall c' his fruit.
29:28 and c' them into another land, as
Jos 8:29 and c' it at the entering of the
10:11 the Lord c' down great stones
27 and c' them into the cave
13:12 Moses smite, and c' them out.
18: 6 that I may c' lots for you here
8 that I may here c' lots for you
10 And Joshua c' lots for them
J'g 6:28 the altar of Baal was c' down,
30 he hath c' down the altar of Baal,
31 because one hath c' down his
8:25 and did c' therein every man the
9:53 a certain woman c' a piece of
15:17 that he c' away the jawbone out
1Sa 14:42 C' lots between me and Jonathan
18:11 And Saul c' the javelin; for he
20:33 And Saul c' a javelin at him to
2Sa 1:21 of the mighty is vilely c' away,
11:21 did not a woman c' a piece of a
16: 6 And he c' stones at David, and at
13 threw stones at him, and c' dust.
18:17 and c' him into a great pit in
20:12 and c' a cloth upon him,
15 c' up a bank against the city,
22 Bichri, and c' it out to Joab.
1Ki 7:15 For he c' two pillars of brass,
24 knops were c' in two rows,
in two rows, when it was c'.
46 plain of Jordan did the king c'
9: 7 name, will I c' out of my sight;
13:24 his carcase was c' in the way,
25 passed by, and saw the carcase c'
28 he went and found his carcase c'
14: 9 and hast c' me behind thy back:
24 the nations which the Lord c'
18:42 c' himself down upon the earth,
19:19 and c' his mantle upon him.
21:26 whom the Lord c' out before the
2Ki 2:16 and c' him upon some mountain
21 and c' the salt in there, and said,
3:25 c' every man his stone, and
4:41 And he c' it into the pot;
6: 6 and c' it in thither; and the iron
7:15 Syrians had c' away in their haste.
9:25 c' him in the portion of the field
26 c' him into the plat of ground,
10:25 and the captain c' them out,
13:21 c' the man into the sepulchre
23 neither c' he them from his
16: 3 whom the Lord c' out from
17: 8 c' out from before the children
20 had c' them out of his sight.
19:18 have c' their gods into the fire:
32 shield, nor c' a bank against it.
21: 2 heathen, whom the Lord c' out
23: 6 and c' the powder thereof upon
12 and c' the dust of them into the
27 will c' off this city Jerusalem
24:20 until he had c' them out from
1Ch 24:31 These likewise c' lots over
25: 8 And they c' lots, hard against
26:13 And they c' lots, as well the small
14 they c' lots; and his lot came out
28: 9 thou forsake him, he will c' thee
2Ch 4: 3 rows of oxen were c',
3 when it was c'.
17 plain of Jordan did the king c'
7:20 will I c' out of my sight, and
11:14 and his sons had c' them off
13: 9 Have ye not c' out the priests
20:11 to come to c' us out of thy
24:10 in, and c' into the chest,
25: 8 power to help, and to c' down.
12 and c' them down from the top of
26:14 and bows, and slings to c' stones.
28: 3 whom the Lord had c' out
29:19 king Ahaz in his reign did c'
30:14 and c' them into the brook
33: 2 whom the Lord had c' out before
15 and c' them out of the city.
Neh 1: 9 there were of you c' out unto
6:16 they were much c' down in their
9:26 and c' thy law behind their backs,
10:34 we c' the lots among the priests,

Ne 11: 1 the rest of the people also c' lots,
13: 8 therefore I c' forth all the
Es 3: 7 they c' Pur, that is, the lot,
9:24 and had c' Pur, that is, the lot,
Job 8: 4 and he have c' them away for their
20 God will not c' away a perfect
15:33 and shall c' off his flower as the
18: 7 his own counsel shall c' him down.
8 he is c' into a net by his own
20:15 God shall c' them out of his belly.
23 God shall c' the fury of his wrath
22:29 When men are c' down, then thou
27:22 For God shall c' upon him, and
29:24 my countenance they c' not down.
30:19 He hath c' me into the mire,
39: 3 ones, they c' out their sorrows.
40:11 C' abroad the rage of thy wrath:
41: 9 shall not one be c' down even
Ps 2: 3 and c' away their cords from us.
5:10 c' them out in the multitude
17:13 disappoint him, c' him down:
18:42 I did c' them out as the dirt
22:10 I was c' upon thee from the womb:
18 and c' lots upon my vesture.
36:12 they are c' down, and shall not
37:14 to c' down the poor and needy,
24 he shall not be utterly c' down:
42: 5 Why art thou c' down, O my soul?
6 my soul is c' down within me:
11 Why art thou c' down, O my soul?
43: 2 why dost thou c' me off?
5 Why art thou c' down, O my soul?
44: 2 the people, and c' them out.
9 But thou hast c' off, and put us
23 arise, c' us not off for ever.
51:11 C' me not away from thy presence;
55: 3 they c' iniquity upon me, and in
22 C' thy burden upon the Lord,
56: 7 in thine anger c' down the people,
60: 1 O God, thou hast c' us off, thou
8 over Edom will I c' out my shoe:
10 O God, which hadst c' us off?
62: 4 They only consult to c' him down
71: 9 C' me not off in the time of old
74: 1 hast thou c' us off for ever?
7 have c' fire into thy sanctuary,
76: 6 the chariot and horse are c' into
77: 7 Will the Lord c' off for ever?
78:49 He c' upon them the fierceness
55 He c' out the heathen also
80: 8 thou hast c' out the heathen,
89:38 thou hast c' off and abhorred,
44 c' his throne down to the ground.
94:14 Lord will not c' off his people,
102:10 lifted me up, and c' me down.
108: 9 over Edom will I c' out my shoe;
11 O God, who hast c' us off?
140:10 let them be c' into the fire;
144: 6 C' forth lightning, and scatter
Pr 1:14 C' in thy lot among us; let us all
7:26 she hath c' down many wounded:
16:33 The lot is c' into the lap; but
22:10 C' out the scorner, and contention
Ec 3: 5 A time to c' away stones, and a
6 and a time to c' away;
11: 1 C' thy bread upon the waters:
Isa 2:20 a man shall c' his idols of silver,
5:24 because they have c' away the
6:13 when they c' their leaves:
14:19 thou art c' out of thy grave
16: 2 wandering bird c' out of the nest,
19: 8 all they that c' angle into the
25: 7 the covering c' over all people,
26:19 the earth shall c' out the dead.
28: 2 shall c' down to the earth with
25 doth he not c' abroad the fitches,
25 and c' in the principal wheat
30:22 gold: thou shalt c' them away
31: 7 every man shall c' away his idols
34: 3 Their slain also shall be c' out,
17 he hath c' the lot for them,
37:19 have c' their gods into the fire:
33 nor c' a bank against it.
38:17 c' all my sins behind thy back.
41: 9 chosen thee, and not c' thee away.
57:14 C' ye up, c' ye up, prepare the
20 whose waters c' up mire and
58: 7 poor that are c' out to thy house?
62:10 c' up, c' up the highway;
66: 5 c' you out for my name's sake,
Jer 6: 6 c' a mount against Jerusalem:
15 I visit them they shall be c' down,
7:15 I will c' you out of my sight,
15 I have c' out all your brethren,
29 O Jerusalem, and c' it away,
8:12 visitation, they shall be c' down,
9:19 our dwellings have c' us out.
14:16 shall be c' out in the streets of
15: 1 people: c' them out of my sight,
16:13 Therefore will I c' you out of
18:15 in paths, in a way not c' up;
22: 7 cedars, and c' them into the fire.
19 burial of an ass, drawn and c' forth
26 And I will c' thee out, and thy
28 wherefore are they c' out, he and
28 and are c' into a land which
23:39 your fathers, and c' you out of
26:23 and c' his dead body into the
28:16 will c' thee from off the face of
31:37 also c' off all the seed of Israel
33:24 he hath even c' them off?
26 I will c' away the seed of Jacob,
36:23 and c' it into the fire that was
30 his dead body shall be c' out in
38: 6 and c' him into the dungeon
9 whom they have c' into the

Jer 38:11 took thence old c' clouts and old
12 Put now these old c' clouts and
41: 7 and c' them into the midst of the
9 Ishmael had c' all the dead
14 from Mizpah c' about and
50:26 c' her up as heaps, and destroy
51:34 my delicates, he hath c' me out.
63 and c' it into the midst of
52: 3 till he had c' them out from his
La 2: 1 c' down from heaven unto the
7 The Lord hath c' off his altar, he
10 they have c' up dust upon their
3:31 the Lord will not c' off for ever:
53 and c' a stone upon me.
Eze 4: 2 against it, and c' a mount against
5: 4 and c' them into the midst of the
6: 4 and I will c' down your slain
7:19 They shall c' their silver in the
11:16 I have c' them far off among the
15: 4 Behold, it is c' into the fire for
16: 5 but thou wast c' out in the open
18:31 C' away from you all your
19:12 in fury, she was c' down to the
20: 7 C' ye away every man the
8 they did not every man c' away
21:22 to c' a mount, and to build a fort.
23:35 forgotten me, and c' me behind
26: 8 and c' a mount against thee,
27:30 shall c' up dust upon their heads,
28:16 therefore I will c' thee as profane
17 I will c' thee to the ground, I will
31:16 when I c' him down to hell with
32: 4 I will c' thee forth upon the open
18 of Egypt, and c' them down, even
36: 5 to c' it out for a prey.
43:24 and the priests shall c' salt upon
Da 3: 6 shall the same hour be c' into
11 he should be c' into the midst of
15 ye shall be c' the same hour into
20 and to c' them into the burning
21 and were c' into the midst of the
24 Did not we c' three men bound
6: 7 he shall be c' into the den of lions.
12 shall be c' into the den of lions?
16 they brought Daniel, and c' him
24 they c' them into the den of lions,
7: 9 till the thrones were c' down,
8: 7 but he c' him down to the
10 and it c' down some of the host
11 the place of his sanctuary was c'
12 and it c' down the truth to the
11:12 and he shall c' down many ten
15 and c' up a mount, and take the
Ho 8: 3 Israel hath c' off the thing that
5 Thy calf, O Samaria, hath c' thee
9:17 My God will c' them away,
14: 5 and c' forth his roots as Lebanon.
Joe 1: 7 made it clean bare, and c' it away;
3: 3 they have c' lots for my people;
Am 1:11 and did c' off all pity, and his
4: 3 and ye shall c' them into the
8: 3 they shall c' them forth with
8 and it shall be c' out and
Ob 11 and c' lots upon Jerusalem,
Jon 1: 5 and c' forth the wares that were
7 Come, and let us c' lots, that we
7 So they c' lots, and the lot fell
12 and c' me forth into the sea;
15 and c' him forth into the sea:
2: 3 For thou hadst c' me into the
4 I said, I am c' out of thy sight;
Mic 2: 5 none that shall c' a cord by lot
9 women of my people have ye c'
4: 7 and her that was c' far off a
7:19 and thou wilt c' all their sins
Na 3: 6 And I will c' abominable filth
10 they c' lots for her honourable
Zep 3:15 thy judgments, he hath c' out,
Zec 1:21 c' out the horns of the Gentiles,
5: 8 And he c' it into the midst of the
8 and he c' the weight of lead upon
9: 4 the Lord will c' her out, and he
10: 6 though I had not c' them off:
11:13 C' it unto the potter: a goodly
13 and c' them to the potter in the
Mal 3:11 shall your vine c' her fruit before
M't 3:10 hewn down, and c' into the fire.
4: 6 the Son of God, c' thyself down:
12 had heard that John was c' into
5:13 good for nothing, but to be c' out,
25 to the officer, and thou be c' into
29 pluck it out, and c' it from thee:
29 thy whole body should be c' into
30 cut it off, and c' it from thee:
30 that thy whole body should be c'
6:30 and to morrow is c' into the oven.
7: 5 first c' out the beam out of thine
5 see clearly to c' out the mote out
6 neither c' ye your pearls before
19 hewn down, and c' into the fire.
22 in thy name have c' out devils?
8:12 shall be c' out into outer darkness;
16 he c' out the spirits with his word,
31 saying, If thou c' us out, suffer us
9:33 when the devil was c' out, the
10: 1 unclean spirits, to c' them out,
8 lepers, raise the dead, c' out devils:
12:24 doth not c' out devils, but by
26 if Satan c' out Satan, he is divided
27 And if I by Beelzebub c' out devils,
27 do your children c' them out?
28 if I c' out devils by the Spirit
13:42 shall c' them into a furnace of fire:
47 like unto a net, that was c' into the
48 good into vessels, but c' the bad
50 shall c' them into the furnace of

M't 15:17 and is c' out into the draught?
26 children's bread, and to c' it to
30 and c' them down at Jesus' feet;
17:19 Why could not we c' him out?
27 go thou to the sea, and c' an hook,
18: 8 cut them off, and c' them from thee:
8 feet to be c' into everlasting fire.
9 pluck it out, and c' it from thee:
9 having two eyes to be c' into hell
30 went and c' him into prison, till he
21:12 c' out all that sold and bought
21 and be thou c' into the sea;
39 they caught him, and c' him out
22:13 and c' him into outer darkness;
25:30 And c' ye the unprofitable servant
27: 5 And he c' down the pieces of
35 upon my vesture did they c' lots.
44 him, c' the same in his teeth.
M'r 1:34 and c' out many devils; and
39 throughout all Galilee, and c' out
3:15 sicknesses, and to c' out devils:
23 How can Satan c' out Satan?
4:26 a man should c' seed into the
6:13 they c' out many devils, and
7:26 he would c' forth the devil out of
27 children's bread, and to c' it unto
9:18 that they should c' him out;
22 it hath c' him into the fire,
28 Why could not we c' him out?
42 his neck, and he were c' into the
45 two feet to be c' into hell, into the
47 two eyes to be c' into hell fire:
11: 7 and c' their garments on him;
15 and began to c' out them that
23 removed, and be thou c' into the
12: 4 at him they c' stones, and
8 killed him, and c' him out of the
41 people c' money into the treasury:
41 and many that were rich c' in
43 this poor widow hath c' more in,
43 than all they which have c' into
44 they did c' in of their abundance,
44 but she of her want did c' in all
14:51 having a linen cloth c' about his
16: 9 out of whom he had c' seven
17 In my name shall they c' out
Lu 1:29 c' in her mind what manner of
3: 9 is hewn down, and c' into the fire.
4: 9 Son of God, c' thyself down from
29 that they might c' him down
6:22 shall reproach you, and c' out
42 c' out first the beam out of thine
9:25 and lose himself, or be c' away?
40 I besought thy disciples to c' him
11:18 ye say that I c' out devils through
19 if I by Beelzebub c' out devils,
19 by whom do your sons c' them out?
20 if I with the finger of God c' out
12: 5 hath power to c' into hell; yea, I
28 and to morrow is c' into the oven;
58 and the officer c' thee into prison.
13:19 a man took, and c' into his garden;
32 Behold, I c' out devils, and I do
14:35 for the dunghill; but men c' it out.
17: 2 about his neck, and he c' into
19:35 they c' their garments upon the
43 thine enemies shall c' a trench
45 began to c' out them that sold
20:12 wounded him also, and c' him out.
15 c' him out of the vineyard, and
21: 3 this poor widow hath c' in more
4 of their abundance c' in unto the
4 but she of her penury hath c' in
22:41 from them about a stone's c',
23:19 for murder, was c' into prison.
25 and murder was c' into prison,
34 parted his raiment, and c' lots.
Joh 3:24 John was not yet c' into prison.
6:37 to me I will in no wise c' out.
8: 7 let him first c' a stone at her.
59 took they up stones to c' at him:
9:34 teach us? And they c' him out.
35 heard that they had c' him out;
12:31 the prince of this world be c' out.
15: 6 he is c' forth as a branch, and is
6 c' them into the fire, and they are
19:24 Let us not rend it, but c' lots for it,
24 and for my vesture they did c' lots.
21: 6 C' the net on the right side of the
6 They c' therefore, and now they
7 and did c' himself into the sea.
Ac 7:19 they c' out their young
21 when he was c' out, Pharaoh's
58 c' him out of the city, and stoned
12: 8 C' thy garment about thee, and
16:23 they c' them into prison, charging
37 have c' us into prison; and now do
22:23 they cried out, and c' off their
27:19 we c' out with our own hands the
26 we must be c' upon a certain
29 they c' four anchors out of the
30 as though they would have c'
38 and c' out the wheat into the sea.
43 should c' themselves first into the
Ro 11: 1 Hath God c' away his people?
2 God hath not c' away his people
13:12 let us therefore c' off the works of
1Co 7:35 not that I may c' a snare upon you,
2Co 4: 9 but not forsaken; c' down, but
7: 6 comforteth those that are c' down,
Ga 4:30 C' out the bondwoman and her
1Ti 5:12 they have c' off their first faith.
Heb 10:35 C' not away therefore your
2Pe 2: 4 but c' them down to hell, and
Re 2:10 the devil shall c' some of you into
14 Balac to c' a stumblingblock

Re 2:22 Behold, I will c' her into a bed,
4:10 and c' their crowns before the
8: 5 c' it into the earth: and there were
7 they were c' upon the earth: and
8 burning with fire was c' into the
12: 4 stars of heaven, and did c' them to
9 the great dragon was c' out, that
9 he was c' out into the earth,
9 and his angels were c' out with
10 accuser of our brethren is c' down,
13 dragon saw that he was c' unto
15 the serpent c' out of his mouth
16 the dragon c' out of his mouth.
14:19 c' it into the great winepress of
18:19 they c' dust on their heads, and
21 millstone, and c' it into the sea,
19:20 These both were c' alive into a
20: 3 c' him into the bottomless pit, and
10 was c' into the lake of fire and
14 death and hell were c' into the
15 was c' into the lake of fire.

castaway
1Co 9:27 to others, I myself should be a c'.

castedst
Ps 73:18 c' them down into destruction.

castest
Job 15: 4 thou c' off fear, and restrainest
Ps 50:17 instruction, and c' my words
88:14 Lord, why c' thou off my soul?

casteth
Job 21:10 their cow calveth, and c' not her
Ps 147: 6 he c' the wicked down to the
17 He c' forth his ice like morsels:
Pr 10: 3 but he c' away the substance of
19:15 Slothfulness c' into a deep sleep;
21:22 and c' down the strength of the
26:18 who c' firebrands, arrows, and
Isa 40:19 with gold, and c' silver chains.
Jer 6: 7 As a fountain c' out her waters,
7 so she c' out her wickedness:
M't 9:34 He c' out devils through the prince
M'r 3:22 prince of the devils c' he out devils.
Lu 11:15 He c' out devils through Beelzebub
1Jo 4:18 perfect love c' out fear: because
3Jo 10 and c' them out of the church.
Re 6:13 as a fig tree c' her untimely figs,

casting
2Sa 8: 2 c' them down to the ground;
1Ki 7:37 all of them had one c', one
Ezr 10: 1 c' himself down before the house
Job 6:21 ye see my c' down, and are afraid.
Ps 74: 7 sanctuary, have they defiled by c'
89:39 his crown by c' it to the ground.
Eze 17:17 by c' up mounts, and building
Mic 6:14 and thy c' down shall be in the
M't 4:18 c' a net into the sea: for they were
27:35 parted his garments, c' lots: that
M'r 1:16 Andrew his brother c' a net into
9:38 we saw one c' out devils in thy
10:50 he, c' away his garment, rose, and
15:24 parted his garments, c' lots upon
Lu 9:49 we saw one c' out devils in thy
11:14 he was c' out a devil, and it was
21: 1 the rich men c' their gifts into the
2 a certain poor widow c' in thither
Ro 11:15 For if the c' away of them be the
2Co 10: 5 C' down imaginations, and every
1Pe 5: 7 C' all your care upon him; for he

castle See also CASTLES.
1Ch 11: 5 David took the c' of Zion, which
7 David dwelt in the c'; therefore
Pr 18:19 contentions are like the bars of a c'.
Ac 21:34 him to be carried into the c'.
37 Paul was to be led into the c', he
22:24 to be brought into the c', and bade
23:10 and to bring him into the c'.
16 he went and entered into the c',
32 and returned to the c':

castles
Ge 25:16 by their towns, and by their c';
Nu 31:10 they dwelt, and all their goodly c',
1Ch 6:54 places throughout their c'
27:25 in the villages, and in the c',
2Ch 17:12 he built in Judah c', and cities
27: 4 and in the forests he built c' and

Castor (*cas'-tor*)
Ac 28:11 whose sign was C' and Pollux.

catch See also CATCHETH; CAUGHT.
Ex 22: 6 If fire break out, and c' in
J'g 21:21 and c' you every man his wife of
1Ki 20:33 from him, and did hastily c' it:
2Ki 7:12 we shall c' them alive, and get
Ps 10: 9 in wait to c' the poor: he doth c'
35: 8 let his net that he hath hid c'
109:11 Let the extortioner c' all that he
Jer 5:26 snares; they set a trap, they c'
Eze 19: 3 it learned to c' the prey; it
6 and learned to c' the prey, and
Hab 1:15 they c' them in their net, and
M'r 12:13 of the Herodians, to c' him in his
Lu 5:10 henceforth thou shalt c' men.
11:54 seeking to c' something out of his

catcheth
Le 17:13 which hunteth and c' any beast
M't 13:19 cometh the wicked one, and c'
Joh 10:12 the wolf c' them, and scattereth

caterpiller [*some editions* CATERPILLAR] See also CATERPILLERS.
1Ki 8:37 if there be c'; if their enemy
Ps 78:46 their increase unto the c', and
Isa 33: 4 the gathering of the c': as the

Joe 1: 4 cankerworm hath left hath the c'
2:25 cankerworm, and the c', and the

caterpillers
2Ch 6:28 mildew, locusts, or c'; if their
Ps 105:34 the locusts came, and c', and
Jer 51:14 fill thee with men, as with c':
27 horses to come up as the rough c'.

cattle
Ge 1:24 c', and creeping thing, and beast
25 c' after their kind, and every thing
26 and over the c', and over all the
2:20 Adam gave names to all c', and to
3:14 thou art cursed above all c', and
4:20 in tents, and of such as have c'.
6:20 c' after their kind, of every
7:14 all the c' after their kind, and every
21 of fowl, and of c', and of beast, and
23 both man, and c', and the creeping
8: 1 all the c' that was with him in the
17 of fowl, and of c', and of every
9:10 of the fowl, of the c', and of every
13: 2 Abram was very rich in c', in
7 between the herdmen of Abram's c'
7 and the herdmen of Lot's c':
29: 7 neither is it time that the c' should
30:29 I have served thee, and how thy c'
32 all the speckled and spotted c',
32 and all the brown c' among the
39 and brought forth c' ringstraked,
40 and put them not unto Laban's c'.
41 the stronger c' did conceive, that
41 the rods before the eyes of the c'
42 when the c' were feeble, he put
43 had much c', and maidservants,
31: 8 all the c' bare speckled: and if
8 then bare all the c' ringstraked.
9 the c' of your father, and given
10 the time that the c' conceived,
10 the rams which leaped upon the c
12 the rams which leap upon the c'
18 carried away all his c', and all
18 the c' of his getting, which he had
41 and six years for thy c': and
43 and these c' are my c', and all
33:14 according as the c' that goeth
17 house, and made booths for his c':
34: 5 his sons were with his c' in the
23 Shall not their c' and their
36: 6 his c', and all his beasts, and all
7 bear them because of their c'.
46: 6 And they took their c', and their
32 their trade hath been to feed c';
34 trade hath been about c' from our
47: 6 then make them rulers over my c'.
16 Joseph said, Give your c'; and I
16 will give you for your c',
17 they brought their c' unto Joseph:
17 and for the c' of the herds, and for
17 bread for all their c' for that year.
18 hath our herds of c'; there is not
Ex 9: 3 hand of the Lord is upon thy c'
4 sever between the c' of Israel
4 and the c' of Egypt: and there shall
6 all the c' of Egypt died:
6 but of the c' of the children of
7 not one of the c' of the Israelites
19 now, and gather thy c', and all
20 his servants and his c' flee into the
21 his servants and his c' in the field.
10:26 Our c' also shall go with us; there
12:29 and all the firstborn of c'.
38 and herds, even very much c'.
17: 3 kill us and our children and our c'
20:10 thy maidservant nor thy c', nor
34:19 firstling among thy c', whether
Le 1: 2 bring your offering of the c', even
5: 2 or a carcase of unclean c', or the
19:19 Thou shalt not let thy c' gender
25: 7 And for thy c', and for the beast
26:22 and destroy your c', and make you
Nu 3:41 the c' of the Levites, instead of all
41 all the firstlings among the c' of the
45 c' of the Levites instead of their c':
20: 4 that we and our c' should die
19 I and my c' drink of thy water,
31: 9 the spoil of all their c', and all
32: 1 had a very great multitude of c':
1 the place was a place for c';
4 Israel, is a land for c',
4 and thy servants have c';
16 sheepfolds here for our c', and
26 and all our c', shall be there in the
35: 3 shall be for their c', and for their
De 2:35 Only the c' we took for a prey
3: 7 But all the c', and the spoil of the
19 your little ones, and your c',
19 (for I know that ye have much c',)
5:14 nor any of thy c', nor thy stranger
7:14 among you, or among your c'.
11:15 send grass in thy fields for thy c',
13:15 and the c' thereof, with the edge of
20:14 the little ones, and the c', and all
28: 4 the fruit of thy c', the increase of
11 thy body, and in the fruit of thy c',
51 he shall eat the fruit of thy c', and
30: 9 in the fruit of thy c', and in the
Jos 1:14 your little ones, and your c', shall
8: 2 and the c' thereof, shall ye take
27 Only the c' and the spoil of that
11:14 these cities, and the c', the children
14: 4 with their suburbs for their c' and
21: 2 the suburbs thereof for our c'.
22: 8 with very much c', with silver,
J'g 6: 5 came up with their c', and their
18:21 the little ones and the c' and the

1Sa 23: 5 and brought away their *c*, and
30:20 before those other *c*, and said,
1Ki 1: 9 slew sheep and oxen and fat *c*
19 hath slain oxen and fat *c* and
25 fat *c* in abundance, and hath
2Ki 3: 9 for the *c* that followed them.
17 ye, and your *c*, and your beasts.
1Ch 5: 9 because their *c* were multiplied in
21 they took away their *c*; of their
7:21 came down to take away their *c*.
2Ch 14:15 also the tents of *c*, and carried
26:10 for he had much *c*, both in the
35: 8 small *c*, and three hundred oxen.
9 offerings five thousand small *c*, and
Ne 9:37 over our bodies, and over our *c*,
10:36 of our *c*, as it is written in the
Job 36:33 the *c* also concerning the vapour.
Ps 50:10 the *c* upon a thousand hills.
78:48 He gave up their *c* also to the
104:14 the grass to grow for the *c*, and
107:38 and suffereth not their *c* to decrease.
148:10 Beasts, and all *c*; creeping
Ec 2: 7 possessions of great and small *c*
Isa 7:25 for the treading of lesser *c*.
30:23 thy *c* feed in large pastures.
43:23 small *c* of thy burnt offerings;
46: 1 upon the beasts, and upon the *c*:
Jer 9:10 can men hear the voice of the *c*;
49:32 multitude of their *c* a spoil: and
Eze 34:17 between *c* and *c*, between the
20 I, will judge between the fat *c*
20 and between the lean *c*.
22 I will judge between *c* and *c*.
38:12 nations, which have gotten *c* and
13 to take away *c* and goods,
Joe 1:18 the herds of *c* are perplexed,
Jon 4:11 left hand; and also much *c*?
Hag 1:11 upon men, and upon *c*, and upon
Zec 2: 4 for the multitude of men and *c*
13: 5 to keep *c* from my youth.
Lu 17: 7 a servant plowing or feeding *c*,
Joh 4:12 and his children, and his *c*?

caught
Ge 22:13 ram *c* in a thicket by his horns:
39:12 And she *c* him by his garment,
Ex 4: 4 put forth his hand, and *c* it,
Nu 31:32 which the men of war had *c*,
J'g 1: 6 pursued after him, and *c* him,
8:14 And *c* a young man of the men
15: 4 went and *c* three hundred foxes,
21:23 whom they *c*: and they went
1Sa 17:35 he arose against me, I *c* him
2Sa 2:16 And they *c* every one his fellow
18: 9 and his head *c* hold of the oak,
1Ki 1:50 and *c* hold on the horns of the
51 he hath *c* hold on the horns of
2:28 and *c* hold on the horns of the
11:30 And Ahijah *c* the new garment
2Ki 4:27 she *c* him by the feet: but
2Ch 22: 9 sought Ahaziah: and they *c* him,
Pr 7:13 So she *c* him, and kissed him,
Ec 9:12 birds that are *c* in the snare;
Jer 50:24 thou art found, and also *c*,
M't 14:31 *c* him, and said unto him,
21:39 they *c* him, and cast him out
M'r 12: 3 And they *c* him and beat him,
Lu 8:29 For oftentimes it had *c* him:
Joh 21: 3 and that night they *c* nothing.
10 the fish which we have now *c*.
Ac 6:12 *c* him, and brought him to the
8:39 Spirit of the Lord *c* away Philip,
16:19 they *c* Paul and Silas, and drew
19:29 *c* Gaius and Aristarchus, men
26:21 the Jews *c* me in the temple,
27:15 And when the ship was *c*,
2Co 12: 2 one *c* up to the third heaven.
4 he was *c* up into paradise,
16 being crafty, I *c* you with guile.
1Th 4:17 shall be *c* up together with
Re 12: 5 her child was *c* up unto God,

caul See also CAULS.
Ex 29:13 the *c* that is above the liver,
22 and the *c* above the liver,
Le 3: 4 *c* above the liver, with the kidneys,
10 and the *c* above the liver,
15 *c* above the liver, with the kidneys,
4: 9 *c* above the liver, with the kidneys,
7: 4 and the *c* that is above the liver,
8:16 and the *c* above the liver, and
25 the *c* above the liver, and the two
9:10 and the *c* above the liver of the
19 and the *c* above the liver:
Ho 13: 8 and will rend the *c* of their heart,

cauls
Isa 3:18 about their feet, and their *c*,

cause See also BECAUSE; CAUSED; CAUSES; CAUSEST; CAUSETH; CAUSING; CAUSELESS; CAUSEWAY.
Ge 7: 4 I will *c* it to rain upon the earth
45: 1 *C* every man to go out from me.
Ex 8: 5 and *c* frogs to come up upon
9:16 And in very deed for this *c* have I
18 I will *c* it to rain a very grievous
21:19 shall *c* him to be thoroughly healed.
22: 5 *c* a field or vineyard to be eaten,
9 the *c* of both parties shall come
23: 2 speak in a *c* to decline after
3 countenance a poor man in his *c*.
6 the judgment of thy poor in his *c*.
27:20 to *c* the lamp to burn always.
29:10 shalt *c* a bullock to be brought
Le 14:41 he shall *c* the house to be scraped
19:29 to *c* her to be a whore; lest the
24: 2 the light, to *c* the lamps to burn
Le 24:19 *c* a blemish in his neighbor;
25: 9 Then shalt thou *c* the trumpet
26:16 the eyes, and *c* sorrow of heart:
Nu 5:24 he shall *c* the woman to drink
26 shall *c* the woman to drink the
16: 5 and will *c* him to come near
5 will he *c* to come near unto him.
11 which *c* both thou and all thy
27: 5 brought their *c* before the Lord.
7 and thou shalt *c* the inheritance
8 then ye shall *c* his inheritance
28: 7 shalt thou *c* the strong wine
35:30 any person to *c* him to die.
De 1:17 the *c* that is too hard for you,
38 he shall *c* Israel to inherit it.
3:28 he shall *c* them to inherit the land
12:11 choose to *c* his name to dwell
17:16 nor *c* the people to return to Egypt,
24: 4 thou shalt not *c* the land to sin,
25: 2 the judge shall *c* him to lie down,
28: 7 shall *c* thine enemies that rise
25 shall *c* thee to be smitten before
31: 7 thou shalt *c* them to inherit it.
Jos 5: 4 the *c* why Joshua did circumcise:
20: 4 his *c* in the ears of the elders
23: 7 nor *c* to swear by them,
1Sa 17:29 now done? Is there not a *c*?
19: 5 blood, to slay David without a *c*?
24:15 plead my *c*, and deliver me out
25:39 pleaded the *c* of my reproach
28: 9 for my life to *c* me to die?
2Sa 3:35 to *c* David to eat meat while it
13:13 whither shall I *c* my shame
16 said unto him, There is no *c*:
15: 4 suit or *c* might come unto me,
1Ki 1:33 and *c* Solomon my son to ride
5: 9 *c* them to be discharged there,
8:31 laid upon him to *c* him to swear,
45 supplication, and maintain their *c*.
49 place, and maintain their *c*,
59 maintain the *c* of his servant,
59 and the *c* of his people Israel
11:27 the *c* that he lifted up his hand
12:15 the *c* was from the Lord,
2Ki 19: 7 *c* him to fall by the sword
1Ch 21: 3 he be a *c* of trespass to Israel?
2Ch 6:35 supplication, and maintain their *c*.
39 maintain their *c*, and forgive
10:15 for the *c* was of God, that the
19:10 And what *c* soever shall come
32:20 And for this *c* Hezekiah the
Ezr 4:15 which *c* was this city destroyed.
21 to *c* these men to cease,
5: 5 they could not *c* them to cease,
Ne 4:11 slay them, and *c* the work to cease.
6: 6 for which *c* thou buildest the wall,
13:26 did outlandish women *c* to sin.
Es 3:13 and to *c* to perish, all Jews,
5: 5 *C* Haman to make haste,
8:11 to slay, and to *c* to perish, all the
Job 2: 3 him, to destroy him without *c*.
5: 8 unto God would I commit my *c*:
6:24 and *c* me to understand wherein
9:17 multiplieth my wounds without *c*.
13:18 I have ordered my *c*; I know
20: 2 do my thoughts *c* me to answer,
23: 4 I would order my *c* before him,
24: 7 They *c* the naked to lodge
10 They *c* him to go naked
29:16 and the *c* which I knew not I
31:13 If I did despise the *c* of my
34:11 *c* every man to find according to
28 So that they *c* the cry of the
38:26 To *c* it to rain on the earth,
27 and to *c* the bud of the tender
Ps 7: 4 delivered him that without *c* is
9: 4 maintained my right and my *c*;
10:17 their heart, thou wilt *c* thine ear
25: 3 which transgress without *c*.
35: 1 Plead my *c*, O Lord, with them
7 For without *c* have they hid for
7 in a pit, which without *c* they
19 the eye that hate me without a *c*.
23 my judgment, even unto my *c*,
27 glad, that favour my righteous *c*:
43: 1 plead my *c* against an ungodly
67: 1 bless us; and *c* his face to shine
69: 4 that hate me without a *c* are
71: 2 and *c* me to escape: incline
74:22 Arise, O God, plead thine own *c*:
76: 8 Thou didst *c* judgment to be
80: 3 and *c* thy face to shine; and we
7 of hosts, and *c* thy face to shine;
9 and didst *c* it to take deep root,
19 God of hosts, *c* thy face to shine;
85: 4 and *c* thine anger toward us to
109: 3 fought against me without a *c*.
119:78 perversely with me without a *c*:
154 Plead my *c*, and deliver me:
161 persecuted me without a *c*:
140:12 Lord will maintain the *c* of the
143: 8 *C* me to hear thy lovingkindness
8 *c* me to know the way wherein
Pr 1:11 for the innocent without *c*:
3:30 Strive not with a man without *c*,
4:16 away, unless they *c* some to fall.
8:21 That I may *c* those that love me
18:17 He that is first in his own *c*;
22:23 the Lord will plead their *c*, and
23:11 mighty; he shall plead their *c*
29 who hath wounds without *c*?
24:28 against thy neighbour without *c*;
25: 9 Debate thy *c* with thy neighbour
29: 7 The righteous considereth the *c*
31: 8 dumb in the *c* of all such as are
9 and plead the *c* of the poor and
Ec 2:20 to *c* my heart to despair of all
5: 6 Suffer not thy mouth to *c* thy
7:10 What is the *c* that the former
10: 1 *c* the ointment of the apothecary
Ca 8: 2 I would *c* thee to drink of spiced
13 hearken to thy voice: *c* me to
Isa 1:23 neither doth the *c* of the widow
3:12 they which lead thee *c* thee to
9:16 leaders of this people *c* them to
10:30 *c* it to be heard unto Laish, O
13:10 moon shall not *c* her light to
11 and I will *c* the arrogancy of the
27: 6 He shall *c* them that come of
28:12 ye may *c* the weary to rest;
30:11 *c* the Holy One of Israel to cease
30 And the Lord shall *c* his glorious
32: 6 he will *c* the drink of the thirsty
37: 7 and I will *c* him to fall by the
41:21 Produce your *c*, saith the Lord;
42: 2 nor *c* his voice to be heard in the
49: 8 the earth, to *c* to inherit the
51:22 thy God that pleadeth the *c* of
52: 4 oppressed them without *c*.
58:14 and I will *c* thee to ride upon
61:11 the Lord God will *c* righteousness
66: 9 to the birth, and not *c* to bring
9 shall I *c* to bring forth, and shut
Jer 3:12 and I will not *c* mine anger to
5:28 judge not the *c*, the *c* of the
7: 3 and I will *c* you to dwell in this
7 Then will I *c* you to dwell in this
34 Then will I *c* to cease from the
11:20 unto thee have I revealed my *c*.
13:16 before he *c* darkness, and before
14:22 of the Gentiles that can *c* rain?
15: 4 And I will *c* them to be removed
11 *c* the enemy to entreat thee well
16: 9 Behold, I will *c* to cease out of
21 I will this once *c* them to know,
21 I will *c* them to know mine hand
17: 4 and I will *c* thee to serve thine
18: 2 and there I will *c* thee to hear
19: 7 and I will *c* them to fall by the
9 And I will *c* them to eat the flesh
20:12 unto thee have I opened my *c*.
22:16 He judged the *c* of the poor and
23:27 which think to *c* my people to
32 and *c* my people to err by their
25:15 and *c* all the nations, to whom I
29: 8 to your dreams which ye *c* to be
30: 3 and I will *c* them to return to
13 none to plead thy *c*, that thou
21 and I will *c* him to draw near,
31: 2 when I went to *c* him to rest.
9 I will *c* them to walk by the
32:35 *c* their sons and their daughters
35 abomination, to *c* Judah to sin.
37 this place, and I will *c* them to
44 I will *c* their captivity to return,
33: 7 And I will *c* the captivity of
11 I will *c* to return the captivity of
15 *c* the Branch of righteousness
26 I will *c* their captivity to return,
34:22 the Lord, and *c* them to return
36:29 and shall *c* to cease from thence
37:20 that thou *c* me not to return to
38:23 thou shalt *c* this city to be
26 that he would not *c* me to return
42:12 and *c* you to return to your own
48:12 that shall *c* him to wander, and
35 Moreover I will *c* to cease in
49: 2 that I will *c* an alarm of war to
37 For I will *c* Elam to be dismayed
50: 9 I will raise and *c* to come up
34 he shall throughly plead their *c*,
51:27 *c* the horses to come up as the
36 I will plead thy *c*, and take
La 3:32 though he *c* grief, yet will he
36 To subvert a man in his *c*, the
52 me sore, like a bird, without *c*.
59 seen my wrong: judge thou my *c*.
Eze 3: 3 *c* thy belly to eat, and fill thy bowels
5: 1 and *c* it to pass upon thine head
13 I will *c* my fury to rest upon
9: 1 *C* them that have charge over the
14:15 If I *c* noisome beasts to pass through
23 that I have not done without *c* all
16: 2 *c* Jerusalem to know her
21 *c* them to pass through the fire
41 and I will *c* thee to cease from
20: 4 *c* them to know the abominations
37 I will *c* you to pass under the rod,
21:17 and I will *c* my fury to rest:
30 Shall I *c* it to return into his sheath?
23:48 Thus will I *c* lewdness to cease out of
24: 8 That it might *c* fury to come up to
26 to *c* thee to hear it with thine ears?
25: 7 and I will *c* thee to perish out of the
26: 3 and will *c* many nations to come up
13 And I will *c* the noise of thy songs to
17 inhabitants, which *c* their terror
27:30 shall *c* their voice to be heard
29: 4 I will *c* the fish of thy rivers to stick
14 will *c* them to return into the land
21 I *c* the horn of the house of Israel
30:13 I will *c* their images to cease out of
22 and I will *c* the sword to fall out of
32: 4 will *c* all the fowls of the heaven to
12 will I *c* thy multitude to fall, the
14 *c* their rivers to run like oil, saith the
34:10 *c* them to cease from feeding the
15 I will *c* them to lie down, saith the
25 and will *c* the evil beasts to cease out
26 I will *c* the shower to come down in
36:12 Yea, I will *c* men to walk upon
15 Neither will I *c* men to hear in

Eze 36:15 neither shalt thou c· thy nations to fall
27 and c· you to walk in my statutes,
33 I will also c· you to dwell in the cities.
37: 5 Behold, I will c· breath to enter into
12 open your graves, and c· you to come
39: 2 will c· thee to come up from the
3 and will c· thine arrows to fall out of
44:23 and c· them to discern between the
30 he may c· the blessing to rest in
Da 2:12 For this c· the king
8:25 also he shall c· craft to prosper in
9:17 and c· thy face to shine upon thy
27 shall c· the sacrifice and the oblation
11:18 shall c· the reproach offered by him
18 his own reproach he shall c· it to cease;
39 he shall c· them to rule over many,
Ho 1: 4 will c· to cease the kingdom of the
2:11 I will also c· all her mirth to cease,
Joe 2:23 he will c· to come down for you the
3:11 c· thy mighty ones to come down,
Am 5:27 Therefore will I c· you to go into
6: 3 and c· the seat of violence to come
8: 9 I will c· the sun to go down at noon,
Jon 1: 7 may know for whose c· this evil is
8 for whose c· this evil is upon us?
Mic 7: 9 until he plead my c·, and execute
Hab 1: 3 and c· me to behold grievance?
Zec 8:12 and I will c· the remnant of this
13: 2 I will c· the prophets and the unclean
M't 5:22 with his brother without a c·
32 saving for the c· of fornication
10:21 and c· them to be put to death.
19: 3 put away his wife for every c·?
5 For this c· shall a man leave father
M'r 10: 7 For this c· shall a man leave his
13:12 shall c· them to be put to death.
Lu 8:47 for what c· she had touched him,
21:16 some of you shall they c· to be put
23:22 I have found no c· of death in him:
Joh 12:18 For this c· the people also met him,
27 for this c· came I unto this hour.
15:25 law. They hated me without a c·.
18:37 this c· came I into the world,
Ac 10:21 what is the c· wherefore ye are
13:28 though they found no c· of death
19:40 there being no c· whereby we may
23:28 when I would have known the c·
25:14 Festus declared Paul's c·
28:18 there was no c· of death in me.
20 For this c· therefore have I called
Ro 1:26 For this c· God gave them
13: 6 For for this c· pay ye tribute
15: 9 For this c· I will confess to
22 For which c· also I have been
16:17 mark them which c· divisions
1Co 4:17 For this c· have I sent unto
11:10 For this c· ought the woman
30 For this c· many are weak
2Co 4:16 For which c· we faint not; but
5:13 we be sober, it is for your c·.
7:12 not for his c· that had done the
12 nor for his c· that suffered wrong,
Eph 3: 1 For this c· I Paul, the prisoner of
14 For this c· I bow my knees unto
5:31 For this c· shall a man leave his
Ph'p 2:18 For the same c· also do ye joy,
Col 1: 9 For this c· we also, since
4:16 c· that it be read also in the
1Th 2:13 For this c· also thank we God
3: 5 For this c·, when I could no longer
2Th 2:11 for this c· God shall send them
1Ti 1:16 Howbeit for this c· I obtained
2Ti 1:12 For the which c· I also suffer
Tit 1: 5 For this c· left I thee in Crete,
Heb 2:11 for which c· he is not ashamed to
9:15 for this c· he is the mediator
1Pe 4: 6 for this c· was the gospel
Re 12:15 he might c· her to be carried
13:15 and c· that as many as would not

caused^
Ge 2: 5 the Lord God had not c· it to rain
21 And the Lord God c· a deep sleep to
20:13 when God c· me to wander from my
41:52 God hath c· me to be fruitful
Ex 14:21 and the Lord c· the sea to go
36: 6 and they c· it to be proclaimed
Le 24:20 as he hath c· a blemish in a man,
Nu 31:16 Behold, these c· the children of
De 34: 4 I have c· thee to see it with
J'g 16:19 she c· him to shave off the seven
1Sa 10:20 when Samuel had c· all the tribes
21 When he had c· the tribe of Benjamin
20:17 Jonathan c· David to swear again,
2Sa 7:11 and have c· thee to rest from all
1Ki 1:38 and c· Solomon to ride upon king
44 and they have c· him to ride upon
2:19 and c· a seat to be set for the king's
20:33 he c· him to come up into the chariot.
2Ki 17:17 And they c· their sons and their
2Ch 8: 2 and c· the children of Israel to dwell
13:13 Jeroboam c· an ambushment to come
21:11 c· the inhabitants of Jerusalem
33: 6 he c· his children to pass through the
Ezr 6:12 God that hath c· his name to dwell
Ne 8: 7 c· the people to understand the law:
8 and c· them to understand the
Es 5:14 and he c· the gallows to be made.
Job 29:13 I c· the widow's heart to sing for joy.
31:16 have c· the eyes of the widow to fail;
39 have c· the owners thereof to lose
37:15 and c· the light of his cloud to
38:12 c· the dayspring to know his place;
Ps 66:12 Thou hast c· men to ride over our
78:13 the sea, and c· them to pass through;
16 and c· waters to run down like rivers.
26 He c· an east wind to blow

Ps 119:49 upon which thou hast c· me to
Pr 7:21 With her much fair speech she c·
Isa 19:14 and they have c· Egypt to err
43:23 I have not c· thee to serve with
48:21 he c· the waters to flow out of the rock
63:14 the Spirit of the Lord c· him to rest:
Jer 12:14 I have c· my people Israel to inherit;
13:11 so have I c· to cleave unto me
15: 8 I have c· him to fall upon it
18:15 they have c· them to stumble in
23:13 and c· my people Israel to err.
22 had c· my people to hear my words,
29: 4 whom I have c· to be carried away
7 I have c· you to be carried away
14 I c· you to be carried away captive.
32:23 therefore thou hast c· all this evil to
34:11 c· the servants and the handmaids,
16 c· every man his servant, and every
48: 4 little ones have c· a cry to be heard.
33 I have c· wine to fail from the
50: 6 shepherds have c· them to go astray,
51:49 As Babylon hath c· the slain
La 2: 6 c· the solemn feasts and sabbaths to
17 he hath c· thine enemy to rejoice
3:13 He hath c· the arrows of his quiver
Eze 3: 2 mouth, and he c· me to eat that roll.
16: 7 I have c· thee to multiply as the
20:10 Wherefore I c· them to go forth out of
26 in that they c· to pass through the fire
22: 4 and thou hast c· thy days to draw near,
23:37 c· their sons, whom they bare unto me,
24:13 have c· my fury to rest upon thee,
29:18 king of Babylon c· his army to serve
31:15 down to the grave I c· a mourning:
15 and I c· Lebanon to mourn for him,
32:23 c· terror in the land of the living.
24 which c· their terror in the land
25 their terror was c· in the land
26 they c· their terror in the land of
32 I have c· my terror in the land
37: 2 And c· me to pass by them round
39:28 which c· them to be led into captivity
44:12 c· the house of Israel to fall into
46:21 and c· me to pass by the four corners
47: 6 and c· me to return to the brink
Da 9:21 being c· to fly swiftly, touched me
Ho 4:12 hath c· them to err, and they have
Am 2: 4 and their lies c· them to err, after the
4: 7 and I c· it to rain upon one city,
7 c· it not to rain upon another city:
Jon 3: 7 And he c· it to be proclaimed and
Zec 3: 4 c· thine iniquity to pass from thee,
Mal 2: 8 ye have c· many to stumble at the law;
Joh 11:37 eyes of the blind, have c· that
Ac 15: 3 they c· great joy unto all the
2Co 2: 5 if any have c· grief, he hath not

causeless
1Sa 25:31 that thou hast shed blood c·,
Pr 26: 2 by flying, so the curse c· shall

causes
Ex 18:19 that thou mayest bring the c·
26 hard c· they brought unto Moses.
De 1:16 Hear the c· between your brethren,
Jer 3: 8 I saw, when for all the c· whereby
La 2:14 for thee false burdens and c· of
3:58 O Lord, thou hast pleaded the c·
Ac 26:21 For these c· the Jews caught me

causest
Job 30:22 thou c· me to ride upon it, and
Ps 65: 4 man whom thou choosest, and c· to

causeth
Nu 5:18 the bitter water that c· the curse:
19 free from this bitter water that c·
22 this water that c· the curse shall go
24 the bitter water that c· the curse:
24 and the water that c· the curse
27 that the water that c· the curse shall
Job 12:24 c· them to wander in a wilderness
20: 3 my understanding c· me to answer.
37:13 He c· it to come, whether for
Ps 104:14 He c· the grass to grow for the cattle,
107:40 c· them to wander in the wilderness,
135: 7 He c· the vapours to ascend from the
147:18 he c· his wind to blow, and the
Pr 10: 5 in harvest is a son that c· shame.
10 winketh with the eye c· sorrow:
14:35 wrath is against him that c· shame.
17: 2 have rule over a son that c· shame,
18:18 The lot c· contentions to cease,
19:26 a son that c· shame, and bringeth
27 hear the instruction that c· to err
28:10 c· the righteous to go astray in an
Isa 61:11 the garden c· the things that are
64: 2 fire burneth, the fire c· the waters to
Jer 10:13 and he c· the vapours to ascend from
51:16 in the heavens; and he c· the vapours
Eze 26: 3 as the sea c· his waves to come up.
44:18 gird themselves with anything that c·
M't 5:32 c· her to commit adultery: and
2Co 2:14 c· us to triumph in Christ, and
9:11 c· through us thanksgiving to
Re 13:12 beast before him, and c· the
16 he c· all, both small and great,

causeway
1Ch 26:16 by the c· of the going up, ward
18 four at the c·, and two at Parbar.

causing
Ca 7: 9 c· the lips of those that are asleep
Isa 30:28 in the jaws of the people, c· them to
Jer 29:10 in c· you to return to this place.
33:12 of shepherds, c· their flocks to lie

cave^ See also CAVE'S; CAVES.
Ge 19:30 and he dwelt in a c·, he and his two
23: 9 That he may give me the c· of
11 the field give I thee, and the c·
17 field, and the c· which was therein,
19 in the c· of the field of Machpelah
20 field, and the c· that is therein,
25: 9 buried him in the c· of Machpelah,
49:29 in the c· that is in the field of
30 In the c· that is in the field of
32 purchase of the field and of the c·
50:13 buried him in the c· of the field
Jos 10:16 hid themselves in a c· at
17 five kings are found hid in a c·
18 stones upon the mouth of the c·,
22 Open the mouth of the c·, and
22 five kings unto me out of the c·.
23 five kings unto him out of the c·,
27 cast them into the c· wherein they
1Sa 22: 1 and escaped to the c· Adullam:
24: 3 where was a c·; and Saul went in
3 remained in the sides of the c·.
7 Saul rose up out of the c·, and
8 went out of the c·, and cried after
10 to day into mine hand in the c·:
2Sa 23:13 in the harvest time unto the c·
1Ki 18: 4 hid them by fifty in a c·, and fed
13 Lord's prophets by fifty in a c·,
19: 9 he came thither unto a c·, and
1Ch 11:15 into the c· of Adullam; and the
Ps 57 title he fled from Saul in the c·.
142 title A Prayer when he was in the c·.
Joh 11:38 It was a c·, and a stone lay upon

cave's
Jos 10:27 laid great stones in the c·

caves
J'g 6: 2 in the mountains, and c·, and
1Sa 13: 6 people did hide themselves in c·,
Job 30: 6 cliffs of the valleys, in c· of the
Isa 2:19 into the c· of the earth, for fear
Eze 33:27 in the forts and in the c· shall die
Heb 11:38 mountains, and in dens and c·

cease See also CEASED; CEASETH; CEASING.
Ge 8:22 and day and night shall not c·.
Ex 9:29 the thunder shall c·, neither shall
Nu 8:25 years they shall c· waiting upon
11:25 they prophesied, and did not c·.
17: 5 and I will make to c· from me the
De 15:11 For the poor shall never c· out of
32:26 the remembrance of them to c·
Jos 22:25 children make our children c·
J'g 15: 7 of you, and after that I will c·.
20:28 or shall I c·? And the Lord said,
1Sa 7: 8 C· not to cry unto the Lord our
2Ch 16: 5 of Ramah, and let his work c·.
Ezr 4:21 to cause these men to c·,
23 and made them to c· by force and
5: 5 they could not cause them to c·,
Ne 4:11 them, and cause the work to c·.
6: 3 why should the work c·, whilst I
Job 3:17 the wicked c· from troubling;
10:20 c· then, and let me alone, that I
14: 7 tender branch thereof will not c·.
Ps 37: 8 C· from anger, and forsake
46: 9 He maketh wars to c· unto the
85: 4 cause thine anger toward us to c·.
89:44 Thou hast made his glory to c·,
Pr 18:18 The lot causeth contentions to c·,
19:27 C·, my son, to hear the instruction
20: 3 It is an honour for a man to c·
22:10 yea, strife and reproach shall c·.
23: 4 c· from thine own wisdom.
Ec 12: 3 and the grinders c· because they
Isa 1:16 before mine eyes; c· to do evil;
2:22 C· ye from man, whose breath is
10:25 and the indignation shall c·,
13:11 the arrogancy of the proud to c·,
16:10 their vintage shouting to c·.
17: 3 The fortress also shall c· from
21: 2 sighing thereof have I made to c·.
30:11 cause the Holy One of Israel to c·
33: 1 when thou shalt c· to spoil, thou
Jer 7:34 Then will I cause to c· from the
14:17 and day, and let them not c·:
16: 9 I will cause to c· out of this place
17: 8 drought, neither shall c· from
31:36 the seed of Israel also shall c·
36:29 and shall cause to c· from thence
48:35 I will cause to c· in Moab, saith
La 2:18 let not the apple of thine eye c·.
Eze 6: 6 your idols may be broken and c·,
7:24 the pomp of the strong to c·;
12:23 I will make this proverb to c·,
16:41 and I will cause thee to c· from
23:27 will I make thy lewdness to c·
48 Thus will I cause lewdness to c·
26:13 cause the noise of thy songs to c·;
30:10 make the multitude of Egypt to c·
13 I will cause their images to c·,
18 the pomp of her strength shall c·
33:28 the pomp of her strength shall c·;
34:10 and cause them to c· from feeding
25 and will cause the evil beasts to c·
Da 9:27 sacrifice and the oblation to c·,
11:18 reproach offered by him to c·;
Ho 1: 4 and will cause to c· the kingdom
2:11 will also cause all her mirth to c·,
Am 7: 5 O Lord God, c·, I beseech thee:
Ac 13:10 wilt thou not c· to pervert the
1Co 13: 8 there be tongues, they shall c·;
Eph 1:16 C· not to give thanks for you,
Col 1: 9 do not c· to pray for you, and to
2Pe 2:14 that cannot c· from sin; beguiling

ceased
Ge 18:11 it c· to be with Sarah after the
Ex 9:33 and the thunders and hail c·,
34 hail and the thunders were c·,

Jos 5:12 and the manna *c'* on the morrow
J'g 2:19 *c'* not from their own doings,
5: 7 the villages *c'*, they *c'* in Israel,
1Sa 2: 5 they that were hungry *c'*: so that
25: 9 in the name of David, and *c'*.
Ezr 4:24 Then *c'* the work of the house of
24 So it *c'* unto the second year
Job 32: 1 these three men *c'* to answer Job,
Ps 35:15 they did tear me, and *c'* not:
77: 2 my sore ran in the night, and *c'*
Isa 14: 4 How hath the oppressor *c'*!
4 the golden city *c'*!
La 5:14 The elders have *c'* from the gate,
15 The joy of our heart is *c'*; our
Jon 1:15 and the sea *c'* from her raging.
M't 14:32 come into the ship, the wind *c'*.
M'r 4:39 the wind *c'*, and there was a great
6:51 the wind *c'*: and they were sore
Lu 7:45 came in hath not *c'* to kiss my feet,
8:24 they *c'*, and there was a calm.
11: 1 when he *c'*, one of his disciples
Ac 5:42 they *c'* not to teach and preach
20: 1 And after the uproar was *c'*, Paul
31 I *c'* not to warn every one night
21:14 not be persuaded, we *c'*, saying,
Ga 5:11 then is the offence of the cross *c'*.
Heb 4:10 he also hath *c'* from his own
10: 2 would they not have *c'* to be
1Pe 4: 1 suffered in the flesh hath *c'* from

ceaseth
Ps 12: 1 Help, Lord; for the godly man *c'*:
49: 8 is precious, and it *c'* for ever:)
Pr 26:20 there is no talebearer, the strife *c'*.
Isa 16: 4 the spoiler *c'*, the oppressors are
24: 8 The mirth of tabrets *c'*, the noise
8 endeth, the joy of the harp *c'*.
33: 8 lie waste, the wayfaring man *c'*:
La 3:49 eye trickleth down, and *c'* not,
Ho 7: 4 who *c'* from raising after he hath
Ac 6:13 This man *c'* not to speak

ceasing
1Sa 12:23 the Lord in *c'* to pray for you:
Ac 12: 5 prayer was made without *c'* of
Ro 1: 9 that without *c'* I make mention of
1Th 1: 3 Remembering without *c'* your
2:13 also thank we God without *c'*,
5:17 Pray without *c'*.
2Ti 1: 3 without *c'* I have remembrance

cedar See also CEDARS.
Le 14: 4 *c'* wood, and scarlet, and hyssop:
6 the *c'* wood, and the scarlet, and
49 two birds, and *c'* wood, and scarlet,
51 he shall take the *c'* wood, and the
52 the *c'* wood, and with the hyssop,
Nu 19: 6 the priest shall take *c'* wood,
24: 6 and as *c'* trees beside the waters.
2Sa 5:11 *c'* trees, and carpenters, and
7: 2 I dwell in an house of *c'*, but the
7 build ye not me an house of *c'*?
1Ki 4:33 from the *c'* tree that is in Lebanon
5: 6 hew me *c'* trees out of Lebanon;
8 concerning timber of *c'*, and
10 Hiram gave Solomon *c'* trees and fir
6: 9 house with beams and boards of *c'*.
10 on the house with timber of *c'*.
15 the house within with boards of *c'*,
16 and the walls with boards of *c'*:
18 *c'* of the house within was carved
18 was *c'*; there was no stone seen.
20 covered the altar which was of *c'*.
36 hewed stone, and a row of *c'* beams.
7: 2 upon four rows of *c'* pillars,
2 with *c'* beams upon the pillars.
3 And it was covered with *c'* above
7 covered with *c'* from one side of
12 a row of *c'* beams, both for the inner
9:11 furnished Solomon with *c'* trees
2Ki 14: 9 sent to the *c'* that was in Lebanon,
19:23 and will cut down the tall *c'* trees
1Ch 22: 4 Also *c'* trees in abundance: for the
4 they of Tyre brought much *c'* wood
2Ch 1:15 *c'* trees made he as the sycomore
2: 8 Send me also *c'* trees, fir trees, and
9:27 in Jerusalem as stones, and *c'*
25:18 was in Lebanon sent to the *c'* that
Ezr 3: 7 to bring *c'* trees from Lebanon
Job 40:17 He moveth his tail like a *c'*: the
Ps 92:12 he shall grow like a *c'* in Lebanon.
Ca 1:17 The beams of our house are *c'*,
8: 9 we will inclose her with boards of *c'*.
Isa 41:19 plant in the wilderness the *c'*, the
Jer 22:14 cieled with *c'*, and painted with
15 thou closest thyself in *c'*? did not
Eze 17: 3 took the highest branch of the *c'*:
22 the highest branch of the high *c'*,
23 be a goodly *c'*: and under it shall
27:24 bound with cords, and made of *c'*,
31: 3 the Assyrian was a *c'* in Lebanon
Zep 2:14 for he shall uncover the *c'* work.
Zec 11: 2 for the *c'* is fallen; because the

cedars
J'g 9:15 and devour the *c'* of Lebanon.
1Ki 7:11 measures of hewed stones, and *c'*.
10:27 *c'* made he to be as the sycomore
1Ch 14: 1 timber of *c'*, with masons and
17: 1 I dwell in an house of *c'*, but the
6 ye not built me an house of *c'*?
2Ch 2: 3 send him *c'* to build him an house
Ps 29: 5 the Lord breaketh the *c'*; yea,
5 the Lord breaketh the *c'* of
80:10 thereof were like the goodly *c'*.
104:16 *c'* of Lebanon, which he hath
148: 9 all hills; fruitful trees, and all *c'*:
Ca 5:15 as Lebanon, excellent as the *c'*.
Isa 2:13 upon all the *c'* of Lebanon, that
9:10 but we will change them into *c'*.
14: 8 the *c'* of Lebanon, saying, Since
37:24 cut down the tall *c'* thereof, and
44:14 He heweth him down *c'*, and taketh
Jer 22: 7 shall cut down thy choice *c'*, and
23 that makest thy nest in the *c'*, how
Eze 27: 5 they have taken *c'* from Lebanon to
31: 8 The *c'* in the garden of God could
Am 2: 9 like the height of the *c'*, and he
Zec 11: 1 that the fire may devour thy *c'*.

cedar-tree See CEDAR and TREE.

cedar-wood See CEDAR and WOOD.

Cedron (*se'-drun*) See also KIDRON.
Joh 18: 1 over the brook *C'*, where was a

ceiled See CIELED.

ceiling See CIELING.

celebrate
Le 23:32 even, shall ye *c'* your sabbath.
41 shall *c'* it in the seventh month.
Isa 38:18 praise thee, death can not *c'* thee:

celestial
1Co 15:40 There are also *c'* bodies, and
40 but the glory of the *c'* is one,

cellars
1Ch 27:27 for the wine *c'* was Zabdi the
28 and over the *c'* of oil was Joash:

Cenchrea (*sen'-kre-ah*)
Ac 18:18 having shorn his head in *C'*:
Ro 16: 1 of the church which is at *C'*:
subscr. servant of the church at *C'*.

censer See also CENSERS.
Le 10: 1 took either of them his *c'*, and put
16:12 shall take a *c'* full of burning coals
Nu 16:17 take every man his *c'*, and put
17 before the Lord every man his *c'*,
17 and Aaron, each of you his *c'*.
18 took every man his *c'*, and put fire
46 Take a *c'*, and put fire therein
2Ch 26:19 a *c'* in his hand to burn incense:
Eze 8:11 with every man his *c'* in his hand;
Heb 9: 4 Which had the golden *c'*, and the
Re 8: 3 at the altar, having a golden *c'*;
5 took the *c'*, and filled it with fire

censers
Nu 4:14 the *c'*, the fleshhooks, and the
16: 6 This do; Take you *c'*, Korah, and
17 two hundred and fifty *c'*; thou
37 take up the *c'* out of the burning,
38 The *c'* of these sinners against their
39 the priest took the brasen *c'*,
1Ki 7:50 spoons, and the *c'* of pure gold;
2Ch 4:22 spoons, and the *c'*, of pure gold:

centurion (*sen-too'-ree-un*) See also CENTURION'S; CENTURIONS.
M't 8: 5 unto him a *c'*, beseeching him,
8 The *c'* answered and said, Lord,
13 Jesus said unto the *c'*, Go thy way;
27:54 *c'*, and they that were with him,
M'r 15:39 *c'*, which stood over against him,
44 calling unto him the *c'*, he asked
45 when he knew it of the *c'*, he gave
Lu 7: 6 the *c'* sent friends to him, saying
23:47 when the *c'* saw what was done,
Ac 10: 1 *c'* of the band called the Italian
22 they said, Cornelius the *c'*, a just
22:25 Paul said unto the *c'* that stood by,
26 When the *c'* heard that, he went
24:23 commanded a *c'* to keep Paul,
27: 1 Julius, a *c'* of Augustus' band.
6 there the *c'* found a ship of
11 the *c'* believed the master and the
31 Paul said to the *c'* and to the
43 the *c'*, willing to save Paul, kept
28:16 the *c'* delivered the prisoners to

centurion's (*sen-too'-ree-uns*)
Lu 7: 2 a certain *c'* servant, who was dear

centurions (*sen-too'-ree-uns*).
Ac 21:32 immediately took soldiers and *c'*,
23:17 Paul called one of the *c'* unto him,
23 he called unto him two *c'*, saying,

Cephas (*se'-fas*) See also PETER.
Joh 1:42 thou shalt be called *C'*, which is
1Co 1:12 and I of Apollos; and I of *C'*;
3:22 Whether Paul, or Apollos, or *C'*,
9: 5 as the brethren of the Lord, and *C'*?
15: 5 he was seen of *C'*, then of the
Ga 2: 9 And when James, *C'*, and John,

ceremonies
Nu 9: 3 all the *c'* thereof, shall ye keep it.

certain See also UNCERTAIN.
Ge 28:11 And he lighted upon a *c'* place,
37:15 And a *c'* man found him, and
38: 1 turned in to a *c'* Adullamite,
2 there a daughter of a *c'* Canaanite.
Ex 16: 4 gather a *c'* rate every day, that I
Nu 9: 6 there were *c'* men, who were
16: 2 with *c'* of the children of Israel,
De 13:13 *C'* men, the children of Belial,
14 thing *c'*, that such abomination
17: 4 behold, it be true, and the thing *c'*.
25: 2 to his fault, by a *c'* number.
J'g 9:53 a *c'* woman cast a piece of a
13: 2 a *c'* man of Zorah, of the family of
19: 1 there was a *c'* Levite sojourning
22 men of the city, *c'* sons of Belial,
Ru 1: 1 And a *c'* man of Beth-lehem-judah
1Sa 1: 1 a *c'* man of Ramathaim-zophim,
21: 7 a *c'* man of the servants of Saul
2Sa 18:10 a *c'* man saw it, and told Joab,
1Ki 2:37 thou shalt know for *c'* that thou
42 Know for a *c'*, on the day thou
7:29 *c'* additions made of thin work.
11:17 Hadad fled, he and *c'* Edomites
20:35 *c'* man of the sons of the prophets
22:34 And a *c'* man drew a bow at a
2Ki 4: 1 Now there cried a *c'* woman of the
8: 6 unto her a *c'* officer, saying,
1Ch 9:28 And *c'* of them had the charge
16: 4 he appointed *c'* of the Levites to
19: 5 Then there went *c'*, and told David
2Ch 8:13 Even after a *c'* rate every day,
18: 2 And after *c'* years he went down
33 And a *c'* man drew a bow at a
28:12 *c'* of the heads of the children of
Ezr 10:16 *c'* chief of the fathers, after the
Ne 1: 2 came, he and *c'* men of Judah;
4 and wept, and mourned *c'* days,
11: 4 And at Jerusalem dwelt *c'* of the
23 that a *c'* portion should be for
12:35 and *c'* of the priests' sons with
13: 6 after *c'* days obtained I leave of
25 smote *c'* of them, and plucked off
Es 2: 5 *c'* Jew whose name was Mordecai,
3: 8 There is a *c'* people scattered
Jer 26:15 for *c'*, that if ye put me to death,
17 rose up *c'* of the elders of the land,
22 and *c'* men with him into Egypt,
41: 5 there came *c'* from Shechem
52:15 away captive *c'* of the poor of the
16 of the guard left *c'* of the poor
Eze 14: 1 came *c'* of the elders of Israel
20: 1 *c'* of the elders of Israel came to
Da 1: 3 bring *c'* of the children of Israel,
2:45 and the dream is *c'*, and the
3: 8 that time *c'* Chaldeans came near,
12 There are *c'* Jews whom thou hast
8:13 another saint said unto that *c'*
27 Daniel fainted, and was sick *c'* days;
10: 5 behold a *c'* man clothed in linen,
11:13 come after *c'* years with a great
M't 8:19 a *c'* scribe came, and said unto
9: 3 And, behold, *c'* of the scribes said
18 behold, there came a *c'* ruler,
12:38 Then *c'* of the scribes and of the
17:14 came to him a *c'* man, kneeling
18:23 heaven likened unto a *c'* king,
20:20 and desiring a *c'* thing of him.
21:28 A *c'* man had two sons; and he
33 There was a *c'* householder,
22: 2 of heaven is like unto a *c'* king,
M'r 2: 6 But there were *c'* of the scribes
5:25 a *c'* woman, which had an issue
35 *c'* which said, Thy daughter is
7: 1 and *c'* of the scribes, which came
25 *c'* woman, whose young daughter
11: 5 And *c'* of them that stood there
12: 1 A *c'* man planted a vineyard,
13 send unto him *c'* of the Pharisees
42 there came a *c'* poor widow, and
14:51 followed him a *c'* young man,
57 And there arose *c'*, and bear false
Lu 1: 5 a *c'* priest named Zacharias, of the
5:12 when he was in a *c'* city, behold
17 it came to pass on a *c'* day, as he
6: 2 And *c'* of the Pharisees said unto
7: 2 And a *c'* centurion's servant, who
41 There was a *c'* creditor which had
8: 2 *c'* women, which had been healed
20 And it was told him by *c'* which
22 it came to pass on a *c'* day, that
27 *c'* man, which had devils long time,
9:57 a *c'* man said unto him, Lord, I
10:25 a *c'* lawyer stood up, and tempted
30 A *c'* man went down from
31 came down a *c'* priest that way:
33 a *c'* Samaritan, as he journeyed,
38 he entered into a *c'* village:
38 and a *c'* woman named Martha
11: 1 as he was praying in a *c'* place,
27 a *c'* woman of the company lifted
37 a *c'* Pharisee besought him to
12:16 ground of a *c'* rich man brought
13: 6 A *c'* man had a fig tree planted
31 there came *c'* of the Pharisees,
14: 2 there was a *c'* man before him
16 A *c'* man made a great supper,
15:11 A *c'* man had two sons:
16: 1 There was a *c'* rich man, which
19 a *c'* rich man, which was clothed
20 was a *c'* beggar named Lazarus,
17:12 as he entered into a *c'* village,
18: 9 *c'* which trusted in themselves
18 And a *c'* ruler asked him, saying,
35 a *c'* blind man sat by the wayside
19:12 A *c'* nobleman went into a far
20: 9 A *c'* man planted a vineyard,
27 came to him *c'* of the Sadducees
39 *c'* of the scribes answering said,
21: 2 saw also a *c'* poor widow casting
22:56 a *c'* maid beheld him as he sat
23:19 for a *c'* sedition made in the city,
24: 1 prepared, and *c'* others with them.
22 Yea, and *c'* women also of our
24 *c'* of them which were with us
Joh 4:46 there was a *c'* nobleman, whose
5: 4 angel went down at a *c'* season
5 And a *c'* man was there, which
11: 1 Now a *c'* man was sick, named
12:20 there were *c'* Greeks among them
Ac 3: 2 And a *c'* man lame from his
5: 1 But a *c'* man named Ananias,
2 brought a *c'* part, and laid it at
6: 9 there arose *c'* of the synagogue,
8: 9 there was a *c'* man, called Simon,
36 way, they came unto a *c'* water:

Ac 9:10 was a c' disciple at Damascus,
19 Then was Saul c' days with the
33 And there he found a c' man
36 at Joppa a c' disciple named
10: 1 a c' man in Cæsarea called
11 a c' vessel descending unto him,
23 and c' brethren from Joppa
48 prayed they him to tarry c' days.
11: 5 A c' vessel descend, as it had been
12: 1 his hands to vex c' of the church.
13: 1 c' prophets and teachers;
6 a c' sorcerer, a false prophet,
14: 8 And there sat a c' man at Lystra,
19 And there came thither c' Jews
15: 1 And c' men which came down
2 Barnabas, and c' other of them,
5 up c' of the sect of the Pharisees
24 that c' which went out from us
16: 1 a c' disciple was there, named
1 Timotheus, the son of a c' woman,
12 were in that city abiding c' days.
14 a c' woman named Lydia, a seller
16 a c' damsel possessed with a spirit
17: 5 took unto them c' lewd fellows of
6 they drew Jason and c' brethren
18 c' philosophers of the Epicureans,
20 thou bringest c' strange things
28 c' also of your own poets have said
34 c' men clave unto him, and
18: 2 a c' Jew named Aquila, born in
7 entered into a c' man's house,
24 And a c' Jew named Apollos, born
19: 1 Ephesus: and finding c' disciples,
13 Then c' of the vagabond Jews,
24 a c' man named Demetrius, a
31 And c' of the chief of Asia, which
20: 9 a window a c' young man named
21:10 a c' prophet, named Agabus.
16 also c' of the disciples of Cæsarea,
23:12 c' of the Jews banded together,
17 for he hath a c' thing to tell him.
24: 1 with a c' orator named Tertullus,
18 Whereupon c' Jews from Asia
24 And after c' days, when Felix
25:13 c' days king Agrippa and Bernice
14 is a c' man left in bonds by Felix:
19 had c' questions against him of
26 Of whom I have no c' thing to
27: 1 Paul and c' other prisoners
16 running under a c' island which
26 we must be cast upon a c' island.
39 they discovered a c' creek
Ro 15:26 a c' contribution for the poor
1Co 4:11 and have no c' dwellingplace;
Ga 2:12 before that c' came from James,
1Ti 6: 7 it is c' we can carry nothing out.
Heb 2: 6 But one in a c' place testified,
4: 4 spake in a c' place of the seventh
7 Again, he limiteth a c' day, saying
10:27 c' fearful looking for of judgment
Jude 4 For there are c' men crept in

certainly^ See also UNCERTAINLY.
Ge 26:28 We saw c' that the Lord was with
43: 7 could we c' know that he would
44:15 such a man as I can c' divine?
50:15 will c' requite us all the evil
Ex 3:12 he said, C' I will be with thee;
22: 4 If the theft be c' found in his
Le 5:19 hath c' trespassed against the
24:16 the congregation shall c' stone
Jos 9:24 Because it was c' told thy
J'g 14:12 if ye can c' declare it me within
1Sa 20: 3 Thy father c' knoweth that I
9 if I knew c' that evil were
23:10 thy servant hath c' heard
25:28 the Lord will c' make my lord a
1Ki 1:30 even so will I c' do this day.
2Ki 8:10 him, Thou mayest c' recover:
2Ch 18:27 If thou c' return in peace,
Pr 23: 5 riches c' make themselves wings
Jer 8: 8 Lo, c' in vain made he it;
13:12 Do we not c' know that every
25:28 Lord of hosts; Ye shall c' drink.
36:29 king of Babylon shall c' come
40:14 Dost thou c' know that Baalis
42:19 know c' that I have admonished
22 Now therefore know c' that ye shall
44:17 we will c' do whatsoever thing
La 2:16 c' this is the day that we looked
Da 11:10 one shall c' come, and overflow,
13 c' come after certain years
Lu 23:47 C' this was a righteous man.

certainty
Jos 23:13 Know for a c' that the Lord your God
1Sa 23:23 come ye again to me with the c',
Pr 22:21 the c' of the words of truth; that
Da 2: 8 I know of c' that ye would gain
Lu 1: 4 know the c' of those things,
Ac 21:34 not know the c' for the tumult,
22:30 he would have known the c'

certified
Ezr 4:14 have we sent and c' the king;
Es 2:22 and Esther c' the king thereof in

certify See also CERTIFIED.
2Sa 15:28 come word from you to c' me.
Ezr 4:16 We c' the king that, if this city
5:10 asked their names also, to c' thee,
7:24 Also we c' you that touching any
Ga 1:11 But I c' you, brethren, that the

Cesar See CÆSAR.
Cesarea See CÆSAREA.
Chabod See I-CHABOD.

chafed
2Sa 17: 8 be c' in their minds, as a bear

chaff
Job 21:18 c' that the storm carrieth away.
Ps 1: 4 c' which the wind driveth away.
35: 5 Let them be as c' before the wind:
Isa 5:24 and the flame consumeth the c',
17:13 chased as the c' of the mountains
29: 5 the terrible ones shall be as c'
33:11 Ye shall conceive c', ye shall
41:15 and shalt make the hills as c'.
Jer 23:28 What is the c' to the wheat?
Da 2:35 like the c' of the summer
Ho 13: 3 as the c' that is driven with the
Zep 2: 2 before the day pass as the c',
M't 3:12 burn up the c' with unquenchable
Lu 3:17 the c' he will burn with fire

chain See also CHAINS.
Ge 41:42 put a gold c' about his neck;
1Ki 7:17 wreaths of c' work, for the
Ps 73: 6 compasseth them about as a c';
Ca 4: 9 eyes, with one c' of thy neck.
La 3: 7 he hath made my c' heavy.
Eze 7:23 Make a c': for the land is full of
16:11 thy hands, and a c' on thy neck.
Da 5: 7 have a c' of gold about his neck,
16 have a c' of gold about thy neck,
29 put a c' of gold about his neck,
Ac 28:20 of Israel I am bound with this c'.
2Ti 1:16 and was not ashamed of my c':
Re 20: 1 pit and a great c' in his hand.

chains^
Ex 28:14 two c' of pure gold at the ends;
14 the wreathen c' to the ouches.
22 upon the breastplate c' at the ends
24 thou shalt put the two wreathen c'
39:15 upon the breastplate c' at the ends,
17 c' of gold in the two rings
18 the two wreathen c' they fastened
Nu 31:50 of gold, c', and bracelets, rings,
J'g 8:26 c' that were about their camels'
1Ki 6:21 made a partition by the c' of gold
2Ch 3: 5 and set thereon palm trees and c'.
16 And he made c', as in the oracle,
16 and put them on the c'.
Ps 68: 6 those which are bound with c':
149: 8 To bind their kings with c',
Pr 1: 9 thy head, and c' about thy neck.
Ca 1:10 jewels, thy neck with c' of gold.
Isa 3:19 The c', and the bracelets, and the
40:19 with gold, and casteth silver c'.
45:14 in c' they shall come over,
Jer 39: 7 and bound him with c', to carry
40: 1 being bound in c' among all that
4 I loose thee this day from the c'
52:11 king of Babylon bound him in c',
Eze 19: 4 brought him with c' unto the land
9 put him in ward in c', and
Na 3:10 her great men were bound in c'.
M'r 5: 3 could bind him, no, not with c':
4 often bound with fetters and c',
4 the c' had been plucked asunder
Lu 8:29 he was kept bound with c' and in
Ac 12: 6 two soldiers, bound with two c':
7 And his c' fell off from his hands.
21:33 him to be bound with two c';
2Pe 2: 4 delivered them into c' of darkness,
Jude 6 hath reserved in everlasting c'

chain-work See CHAIN and WORK.

chalcedony (*kal-sed'-o-nee*)
Re 21:19 the third, a c'; the fourth,

Chalcol (*kal'-kol*) See also CALCOL.
1Ki 4:31 the Ezrahite, and Heman, and C',

Chaldæans (*kal-de'-uns*) See also CHALDEANS.
Ac 7: 4 out of the land of the C',

Chaldea (*kal-de'-ah*) See also BABYLON; CHALDEAN.
Jer 50:10 And C' shall be a spoil: all that
51:24 the inhabitants of C' all their evil
35 blood upon the inhabitants of C',
Eze 11:24 vision by the Spirit of God into C',
16:29 in the land of Canaan unto C';
23:15 manner of the Babylonians of C',
16 messengers unto them into C'.

Chaldean (*kal-de'-un*) See also BABYLONIAN; CHALDEANS; CHALDEANS'.
Ezr 5:12 the C', who destroyed this house,
Da 2:10 any magician, or astrologer, or C'.

Chaldeans (*kal-de'-uns*) See also BABYLONIANS; CHALDÆANS; CHALDEANS'; CHALDEES.
Job 1:17 The C' made out three bands,
Isa 23:13 Behold the land of the C'; this
43:14 nobles, and the C', whose cry is in
47: 1 no throne, O daughter of the C':
5 darkness, O daughter of the C':
48:14 and his arm shall be on the C'.
20 flee ye from the C', with a voice of
Jer 21: 4 and against the C', which besiege
9 out, and falleth to the C' that
22:25 and into the hand of the C'.
24: 5 the land of the C' for their good.
25:12 iniquity, and the land of the C',
32: 4 escape out of the hand of the C',
5 though ye fight with the C',
24, 25 is given into the hand of the C',
28 this city into the hand of the C',
29 the C', that fight against the city,
43 is given into the hand of the C'.
33: 5 They come to fight with the C',
35:11 for fear of the army of the C',
37: 5 the C' that besieged Jerusalem
8 the C' shall come again, and fight
Jer 37: 9 The C' shall surely depart from us:
10 smitten the whole army of the C'
11 the army of the C' was broken up
13 saying, Thou fallest away to the C'.
14 is false: I fall not away to the C'.
38: 2 goeth forth to the C' shall live,
18 be given into the hand of the C',
19 the Jews that are fallen to the C',
23 wives and thy children to the C':
39: 8 And the C' burned the king's house,
40: 9 saying, Fear not to serve the C':
10 dwell at Mizpah, to serve the C',
41: 3 and the C' that were found there,
18 Because of the C': for they were
43: 3 deliver us into the hand of the C',
50: 1 and against the land of the C'
8 go forth out of the land of the C',
25 God of hosts in the land of the C'.
35 A sword is upon the C', saith the
45 purposed against the land of the C':
51: 4 shall fall in the land of the C',
54 destruction from the land of the C':
52: 7 C' were by the city round about:)
8 of the C' pursued after the king,
14 the C', that were with the captain
17 C' brake, and carried all the brass
Eze 1: 3 land of the C' by the river Chebar;
12:13 to Babylon to the land of the C';
23:14 images of the C' pourtrayed with
23 The Babylonians, and all the C',
Da 1: 4 learning and the tongue of the C'.
2: 2 C', for to shew the king his dreams.
4 Then spake the C' to the king
5 king answered and said to the C',
10 C' answered before the king,
3: 8 at that time certain C' came near,
4: 7 magicians, the astrologers, the C',
5: 7 to bring in the astrologers, the C',
11 astrologers, C', and soothsayers;
30 Belshazzar the king of the C' slain.
9: 1 king over the realm of the C';
Hab 1: 6 For, lo, I raise up the C', that

Chaldeans' (*kal-de'uns*) See also CHALDEES.
Jer 39: 5 the C' army pursued after them,

Chaldees (*kal'-dees*) See also CHALDEES'.
Ge 11:28 of his nativity, in Ur of the C'.
31 forth with them from Ur of the C',
15: 7 brought thee out of Ur of the C',
2Ki 24: 2 sent against him bands of the C',
25: 4 the C' were against the city round
5 of the C' pursued after the king,
10 And all the army of the C', that
13 C' break in pieces, and carried
24 to be the servants of the C':
25 Jews and the C' that were with
26 for they were afraid of the C'.
2Ch 36:17 upon them the king of the C',
Ne 9: 7 him forth out of Ur of the C',

Chaldeans' (*kal-de'-uns*) See also CHALDEES.
Jer 39: 5 the C' army pursued after them,

chalkstones
Isa 27: 9 of the altar as c' that are beaten

challengeth
Ex 22: 9 which another c' to be his,

chamber See also BEDCHAMBER; CHAMBERING; CHAMBERLAIN; CHAMBERS; GUESTCHAMBER.
Ge 43:30 he entered into his c',
J'g 3:24 covereth his feet in his summer c'.
15: 1 I will go in to my wife into the c'.
16: 9 wait, abiding with her in the c'.
12 were liers in wait abiding in the c'.
2Sa 13:10 Bring the meat into the c', that I
10 brought them into the c' to
18:33 the c' over the gate, and wept:
1Ki 1:15 in unto the king into the c':
6: 6 The nethermost c' was five cubits
8 The door for the middle c' was
8 into the middle c', and out of the
14:28 them back into the guard c'.
17:23 brought him down out of the c'
20:30 into the city, into an inner c'.
22:25 when thou shalt go into an inner c
2Ki 1: 2 through a lattice in his upper c'
4:10 Let us make a little c', I pray thee,
11 he turned into the c', and lay
9: 2 and carry him to an inner c';
23:11 the c' of Nathan-melech the
12 the upper c' of Ahaz, which the
2Ch 12:11 them again into the guard c'.
18:24 thou shalt go into an inner c'
Ezr 10: 6 c' of Johanan the son of Eliashib:
Ne 3:30 Berechiah over against his c'.
13: 4 of the c' of the house of our God,
5 had prepared for him a great c',
7 a c' in the courts of the house
8 stuff of Tobiah out of the c'.
Ps 19: 5 bridegroom coming out of his c',
Ca 3: 4 the c' of her that conceived me.
Jer 35: 4 the c' of the sons of Hanan,
4 by the c' of the princes, which
4 was above the c' of Maaseiah
36:10 in the c' of Gemariah the son of
12 king's house, into the scribe's c':
20 in the c' of Elishama the scribe,
21 it out of Elishama the scribe's c'.
Eze 40: 7 every little c' was one reed long,
13 from the roof of one little c' to
45 This c', whose prospect is toward
46 c' whose prospect is toward the
41: 5 and the breadth of every side c',
7 from the lowest c' to the highest
9 which was for the side c' without,
42: 1 into the c' that was over against
Da 6:10 windows being open in his c'

Joe 2:16 the bridegroom go forth of his *c*.
Ac 9:37 they laid her in an upper *c*.
39 they brought him into the upper *c*
20: 8 were many lights in the upper *c*.

chambering
Ro 13:13 not in *c* and wantonness, nor in

chamberlain See also CHAMBERLAINS.
2Ki 23:11 chamber of Nathan-melech the *c*,
Es 2: 3 custody of Hege the king's *c*,
14 of Shaashgaz, the king's *c*, which
15 Hegai the king's *c*, the keeper of
Ac 12:20 Blastus the king's *c* *1909, 3588.*
Ro 16:23 Erastus the *c* of the city saluteth

chamberlains
Es 1:10 the seven *c* that served in the
12 king's commandment by his *c*:
15 of the king Ahasuerus by the *c*?
2:21 two of the king's *c*, Bigthan and
4: 4 maids and her *c* came and told it
5 for Hatach, one of the king's *c*,
6: 2 two of the king's *c*, the keepers of
14 came the king's *c*, and hasted
7: 9 Harbonah, one of the *c*, said

chambers
1Ki 6: 5 built *c* round about, against the
5 of the oracle: and he made *c*
10 he built *c* against all the house
1Ch 9:26 were over the *c* and treasuries
33 Levites, who remaining in the *c*
23:28 in the courts, and in the *c*, and in
28:11 and of the upper *c* thereof, and
12 all the *c* round about, of the
2Ch 3: 9 he overlaid the upper *c* with gold.
31:11 to prepare *c* in the house of the
Ezr 8:29 the *c* of the house of the Lord.
Ne 10:37 to the *c* of the house of our God;
38 the *c*, into the treasure house.
39 the *c*, where are the vessels of the
12:44 the *c* for the treasures, for the
13: 9 and they cleansed the *c*:
Job 9: 9 Pleiades, and the *c* of the south.
Ps 104: 3 Who layeth the beams of his *c*
13 He watereth the hills from his *c*:
105:30 abundance, in the *c* of their
Pr 7:27 going down to the *c* of death.
24: 4 by knowledge shall the *c* be filled
Ca 1: 4 king hath brought me into his *c*:
Isa 26:20 people, enter thou into my *c*, and
Jer 22:13 and his *c* by wrong;
14 a wide house and large *c*, and
35: 2 into one of the *c*, and give them
Eze 8:12 man in the *c* of his imagery?
21:14 which entereth into their privy *c*.
40: 7 between the little *c* were five
10 the little *c* of the gate eastward
12 The space also before the little *c*
12 the little *c* were six cubits on
16 narrow windows to the little *c*,
17 there were *c*, and a pavement
17 thirty *c* were upon the pavement.
21 And the little *c* thereof were
29 And the little *c* thereof, and the
33 the little *c* thereof, and the posts
36 The little *c* thereof, the posts
38 the *c* and the entries thereof
44 the *c* of the singers in the inner
41: 6 the side *c* were three, one over
6 house for the side *c* round about,
7 upward to the side *c*: for the
8 the foundations of the side *c* were
9 the place of the side *c* that were
10 And between the *c* was the
11 the doors of the side *c* were
26 and upon the side *c* of the house,
42: 4 before the *c* was a walk of ten
5 Now the upper *c* were shorter:
7 over against the *c*, toward the
7 court on the forepart of the *c*,
8 For the length of the *c* that were
9 from under these *c* was the entry
10 The *c* were in the thickness of
11 the appearance of the *c* which
12 according to the doors of the *c*
13 The north *c* and the south *c*,
13 separate place, they be holy *c*,
44:19 in the holy *c*, and they shall put
45: 5 for a possession for twenty *c*.
46:19 into the holy *c* of the priests,
M't 24:26 behold, he is in the secret *c*;

chameleon *(ca-me'-le-un)*
Le 11:30 ferret, and the *c*, and the lizard,

chamois *(sham'-my)*
De 14: 5 and the wild ox, and the *c*.

champaign *(sham-pane')*
De 11:30 in the *c* over against Gilgal,

champion
1Sa 17: 4 went out a *c* out of the camp
23 the *c*, the Philistine of Gath,
51 when the Philistines saw their *c*

Chanaan *(ka'-na-un)* See also CANAAN.
Ac 7:11 over all the land of Egypt and *C*,
13:19 seven nations in the land of *C*,

chance See also CHANCETH.
De 22: 6 If a bird's nest *c* to be before thee
1Sa 6: 9 it was a *c* that happened to us.
2Sa 1: 6 I happened by *c* upon mount
Ec 9:11 time and *c* happeneth to them
Lu 10:31 by *c* there came down a certain
1Co 15:37 grain, it may *c* of wheat,

chancellor
Ezr 4: 8 Rehum the *c*, and Shimshai
Ezr 4: 9 Then wrote Rehum the *c*,
17 an answer unto Rehum the *c*,

chanceth
De 23:10 by reason of uncleanness that *c*

change See also CHANGEABLE; CHANGED; CHANGES; CHANGEST; CHANGETH; CHANGING; EXCHANGE.
Ge 35: 2 be clean, and *c* your garments:
Le 27:10 nor *c* it, a good for a bad, or a
10 and if he shall at all *c*
33 neither shall he *c* it:
33 and if he *c* it at all,
33 and the *c* thereof shall be holy;
J'g 14:12, 13 and thirty *c* of garments:
19 gave *c* of garments unto them
Job 14:14 time will I wait, till my *c* come.
17:12 They *c* the night into day: and
Ps 102:26 as a vesture shalt thou *c* them,
Pr 24:21 with them that are given to *c*:
Isa 9:10 but we will *c* them into cedars.
Jer 2:36 about so much to *c* thy way?
13:23 Can the Ethiopian *c* his skin, or
Da 7:25 and think to *c* times and laws:
Ho 4: 7 will I *c* their glory into shame.
Hab 1:11 Then shall his mind *c*, and he
Zec 3: 4 clothe thee with *c* of raiment.
Mal 3: 6 I am the Lord, I *c* not; therefore
Ac 6:14 shall *c* the customs which Moses
Ro 1:26 their women did *c* the natural
Ga 4:20 with you now, and to *c* my voice;
Ph'p 3:21 Who shall *c* our vile body, that it
Heb 7:12 of necessity a *c* also of the law.

changeable See also UNCHANGEABLE.
Isa 3:22 The *c* suits of apparel, and the

changed
Ge 31: 7 and *c* my wages ten times; but
41 thou hast *c* my wages ten times.
41:14 *c* his raiment, and came in unto
Le 13:16 turn again, and be *c* unto white,
55 the plague have not *c* his colour,
Nu 32:38 (their names being *c*,) and
1Sa 21:13 he *c* his behaviour before them,
2Sa 12:20 *c* his apparel, and came into the
2Ki 24:17 and *c* his name to Zedekiah.
25:29 *c* his prison garments: and he
Job 30:18 of my disease is my raiment *c*:
Ps 34 *title* when he *c* his behaviour
102:26 and they shall be *c*:
106:20 Thus they *c* their glory into the
Ec 8: 1 boldness of his face shall be *c*.
Isa 24: 5 have transgressed the laws, *c* the
Jer 2:11 Hath a nation *c* their gods,
11 my people have *c* their glory for
48:11 in him, and his scent is not *c*.
52:33 And *c* his prison garments: and
La 4: 1 how is the most fine gold *c*!
Eze 5: 6 And she had *c* my judgments
Da 2: 9 before me, till the time be *c*:
3:19 the form of his visage was *c*
27 neither were their coats *c*, nor
28 and have *c* the king's word, and
4:16 Let his heart be *c* from man's, and
5: 6 the king's countenance was *c*, and
9 his countenance was *c* in him,
10 nor let thy countenance be *c*:
6: 8 that it be not *c*, according to the
15 the king establisheth may be *c*.
17 might not be *c* concerning Daniel.
7:28 my countenance *c* in me: but I
Mic 2: 4 hath *c* the portion of my people:
Ac 28: 6 they *c* their minds, and said that
Ro 1:23 *c* the glory of the uncorruptible
25 Who *c* the truth of God into a
1Co 15:51 all sleep, but we shall all be *c*,
52 incorruptible, and we shall be *c*.
2Co 3:18 are *c* into the same image from
Heb 1:12 them up, and they shall be *c*:
7:12 priesthood being *c*, there is made

changers See also CHANGERS'; MONEYCHANGERS.
Joh 2:14 doves, and the *c* of money sitting:

changers'
Joh 2:15 poured out the *c* money, and

changes
Ge 45:22 he gave each man *c* of raiment;
22 of silver, and five *c* of raiment.
2Ki 5: 5 of gold, and ten *c* of raiment.
22 of silver, and two *c* of garments.
23 two bags, with two *c* of garments,
Job 10:17 me; *c* and war are against me.
Ps 55:19 Because they have no *c*, therefore

changest
Job 14:20 thou *c* his countenance, and

changeth
Ps 15: 4 to his own hurt, and *c* not.
Da 2:21 he *c* the times and the seasons:

changing
Ru 4: 7 redeeming and concerning *c*,

channel See also CHANNELS.
Isa 27:12 from the *c* of the river unto the

channels
2Sa 22:16 the *c* of the sea appeared, the
Ps 18:15 Then the *c* of waters were seen,
Isa 8: 7 he shall come up over all his *c*,

chant
Am 6: 5 That *c* to the sound of the viol,

chapel
Am 7:13 it is the king's *c*, and it is the

chapiter See also CHAPITERS.
1Ki 7:16 the height of the one *c* was five
16 and the height of the other *c*
17 seven for the one *c*,
1Ki 7:17 and seven for the other *c*.
18 and so he did for the other *c*.
20 round about upon the other *c*.
31 the mouth of it within the *c* and
2Ki 25:17 and the *c* upon it was brass:
17 the height of the *c* three cubits;
17 the pomegranates upon the *c*
2Ch 3:15 the *c* that was on the top of each
Jer 52:22 And a *c* of brass was upon it;
22 and the height of one *c* was five

chapiters
Ex 36:38 he overlaid their *c* and their
38:17 overlaying of their *c* of silver;
19 their *c* and their fillets of silver.
28 overlaid their *c*, and filleted
1Ki 7:16 he made two *c* of molten brass,
17 the *c* which were upon the top
18 the *c* that were upon the top,
19 the *c* that were upon the top of
20 And the *c* upon the two pillars
41 the two bowls of the *c* that were
41 to cover the two bowls of the *c*
42 the two bowls of the *c* that were
2Ch 4:12 the *c* which were on the top
12 cover the two pommels of the *c*
13 *c* which were upon the pillars.
Jer 52:22 and pomegranates upon the *c*

chapmen
2Ch 9:14 *c* and merchants brought.

chapped See CHAPT.

chapt
Jer 14: 4 Because the ground is *c*, for

Charashim *(car'-a-shim)*
1Ch 4:14 of *C*; for they were craftsmen.

Charchemish *(car'-ke-mish)* See also CARCHEMISH.
2Ch 35:20 to fight against *C* by Euphrates:

charge See also CHARGEABLE; CHARGED; CHARGES; CHARGEST; CHARGING; OVERCHARGE.
Ge 26: 5 obeyed my voice, and kept my *c*,
28: 6 he blessed him he gave him a *c*,
Ex 6:13 gave them a *c* unto the children
19:21 *c* the people, lest they break
Le 8:35 keep the *c* of the Lord, that ye
Nu 1:53 Levites shall keep the *c* of the
3: 7 they shall keep his *c*, and the
7 *c* of the whole congregation
8 the *c* of the children of Israel,
25 And the *c* of the sons of Gershon
28 keeping the *c* of the sanctuary.
31 And their *c* shall be the ark,
32 that keep the *c* of the sanctuary.
36 the custody and *c* of the sons
38 keeping the *c* of the sanctuary for
38 the *c* of the children of Israel;
4:27 unto them in *c* all their burdens.
28 their *c* shall be under the hand of
31 this is the *c* of their burden,
32 instruments of the *c* of their burden.
5:19 the priest shall *c* her by an oath,
21 the priest shall *c* the woman
8:26 congregation, to keep the *c*, and
26 the Levites touching their *c*.
9:19 the children of Israel kept the *c*
23 they kept the *c* of the Lord,
18: 3 shall keep thy *c*, and the *c* of
4 keep the *c* of the tabernacle of
5 keep the *c* of the sanctuary,
5 and the *c* of the altar:
8 I also have given thee the *c* of
27:19 and give him a *c* in their sight.
23 and gave him a *c*, as the Lord
31:30 keep the *c* of the tabernacle of
47 kept the *c* of the tabernacle of
49 which are under our *c*, and
De 3:28 *c* Joshua, and encourage him,
11: 1 keep his *c*, and his statutes,
21: 8 unto thy people of Israel's *c*.
31:14 that I may give him a *c*.
23 gave Joshua the son of Nun a *c*,
Jos 22: 3 kept the *c* of the commandment
2Sa 14: 8 I will give *c* concerning thee.
18: 5 the king gave all the captains *c*
1Ki 2: 3 keep the *c* of the Lord thy God,
4:28 every man according to his *c*.
11:28 the *c* of the house of Joseph.
2Ki 7:17 hand he leaned to have the *c*
1Ch 9:27 because the *c* was upon them,
28 And certain of them had the *c*
22:12 give thee *c* concerning Israel,
23:32 the *c* of the tabernacle of the
32 and the *c* of the holy place,
32 and the *c* of the sons of Aaron.
2Ch 13:11 for we keep the *c* of the Lord
30:17 Levites had the *c* of the killing
Ne 7: 2 the palace, *c* over Jerusalem:
10:32 to *c* ourselves yearly with the
Es 3: 9 that have the *c* of the business,
4: 8 to *c* her that she should go in
Job 34:13 Who hath given him a *c* over
Ps 35:11 to my *c* things that I knew not.
91:11 shall give his angels *c* over thee,
Ca 2: 7 I *c* you, O ye daughters of
3: 5 I *c* you, O ye daughters of
5: 8 I *c* you, O daughters of
9 beloved, that thou dost so *c* us?
8: 4 I *c* you, O daughters of
Isa 10: 6 of my wrath will I give him a *c*,
Jer 39:11 King of Babylon gave *c* concerning
47: 7 the Lord hath given it a *c* against
52:25 which had the *c* of the men
Eze 9: 1 them that have *c* over the city
40:45 keepers of the *c* of the house.

Eze 40:46 the keepers of the c' of the altar:
44: 8 kept the c' of mine holy things:
8 but ye have set keepers of my c'
11 c' at the gates of the house,
14 keepers of the c' of the house,
15 kept a c' of my sanctuary when
16 me, and they shall keep my c'.
48:11 which have kept my c', which
Zec 3: 7 keep my c', then thou shalt also
M't 4: 6 give his angels c' concerning
M'r 9:25 I c' thee, come out of him, and
Lu 4:10 shall give his angels c' over thee,
Ac 7:60 Lord, lay not this sin to their c'.
8:27 who had the c' of all her treasure,
16:24 Who, having received such a c',
23:29 to have nothing laid to his c'
Ro 8:33 shall lay anything to the c' of
1Co 9:18 the gospel of Christ without c',
1Th 5:27 I c' you by the Lord that this.
1Ti 1: 3 that thou mightest c' some that
18 This c' I commit unto thee, son
5: 7 And these things give in c', that
21 I c' thee before God, and the Lord
6:13 I give thee c' in the sight of God,
17 C' them that are rich in this world,
2Ti 4: 1 I c' thee therefore before God,
16 it may not be laid to their c'.

chargeable
2Sa 13:25 now go, lest we be c' unto thee.
Ne 5:15 before me were c' unto the people,
2Co 11: 9 I was c' to no man: for that
1Th 2: 9 not be c' unto any of you,
2Th 3: 8 that we might not be c' to any

charged See also CHARGEDST; OVERCHARGED.
Ge 26:11 And Abimelech c' all his people,
28: 1 and c' him, and said unto him,
40: 4 the captain of the guard c' Joseph
49:29 he c' them, and said unto them,
Ex 1:22 Pharaoh c' all his people, saying,
De 1:16 I c' your judges at that time,
24: 5 be c' with any business: 5674,
27:11 Moses c' the people the same day,
Jos 18: 8 and Joshua c' them that went
22: 5 Moses the servant of the Lord c'
Ru 2: 9 have I not c' the young men
1Sa 14:27 father c' the people with the oath:
28 straitly c' the people with an oath,
2Sa 11:19 And c' the messenger, saying,
18:12 c' thee and Abishai and Ittai,
1Ki 2: 1 he c' Solomon his son, saying,
43 that I have c' thee with?
13: 9 For so was it c' me by the word
2Ki 17:15 the Lord had c' them, that they
35 had made a covenant, and c' them,
1Ch 22: 6 and c' him to build an house
13 c' Moses with concerning Israel:
2Ch 19: 9 c' them, saying, Thus shall ye do
36:23 hath c' me to build him an house
Ezr 1: 2 and he hath c' me to build him
Ne 13:19 c' that they should not be opened
Es 2:10 Mordecai had c' her that she
20 Mordecai had c' her: for Esther
Job 1:22 sinned not, nor c' God foolishly.
4:18 and his angels he c' with folly:
Jer 32:13 And I c' Baruch before them,
35: 8 he hath c' us, to drink no wine
M't 9:30 Jesus straitly c' them, saying,
12:16 And c' them that they should not
16:20 Then c' he his disciples that they
17: 9 Jesus c' them, saying, Tell the
M'r 1:43 he straitly c' him, and forthwith
3:12 straitly c' them that they should
5:43 he c' them straitly that no man
7:36 c' them that they should tell no
36 but the more he c' them,
8:15 he c' them, saying, Take heed,
30 he c' them that they should tell
9: 9 c' them they should tell no man
10:48 And many c' him that he should
Lu 5:14 And he c' him to tell no man:
8:56 but he c' them that they should
9:21 straitly c' them, and commanded
Ac 23:22 c' him, See thou tell no man
1Th 2:11 c' every one of you, as a father
1Ti 5:16 and let not the church be c';

chargedst
Ex 19:23 thou c' us, saying, Set bounds

charger See also CHARGERS.
Nu 7:13 And his offering was one silver c',
19 for his offering one silver c',
25, 31, 37, 43, 49, 55, 61, 67, 73 79,
His offering was one silver c',
85 c' of silver weighing an hundred
M't 14: 8 here John Baptist's head in a c'.
11 was brought in a c', and given to
M'r 6:25 by and by in a c' the head of John
28 brought his head in a c', and gave

chargers
Nu 7:84 c' of silver, twelve silver bowls,
Ezr 1: 9 thirty c' of gold, and a thousand
9 c' of silver, nine and twenty.

charges
2Ch 8:14 the Levites to their c', to praise
31:16 service in their c' according to
17 in their c' by their courses;
35: 2 And he set the priests in their c',
Ac 21:24 c' with them, that they may shave
1Co 9: 7 warfare any time at his own c'?

chargest
2Sa 3: 8 thou c' me to day with a fault

charging
Ac 16:23 c' the jailor to keep them safely:
2Ti 2:14 c' them before the Lord that they

chariot See also CHARIOTS.
Ge 41:43 made him to ride in the second c'
46:29 Joseph made ready his c', and
Ex 14: 6 ready his c', and took his people
25 their c' wheels, that they drave
J'g 4:15 Sisera lighted down off his c', and
5:28 Why is his c' so long in coming?
2Sa 8: 4 David houghed all the c' horses,
1Ki 7:33 like the work of a c' wheel:
10:29 c' came up and went out of Egypt
12:18 speed to get him up to his c',
18:44 say unto Ahab, Prepare thy c',
20:25 horse for horse, and c' for c':
33 caused him to come up into the c'.
22:34 he said unto the driver of his c',
35 the king was stayed up in his c'
35 wound into the midst of the c'.
38 the c' in the pool of Samaria;
2Ki 2:11 appeared a c' of fire, and horses
12 c' of Israel, and the horsemen
5: 9 with his horses and with his c',
21 down from the c' to meet him,
26 again from his c' to meet thee?
7:14 took therefore two c' horses;
9:16 Jehu rode in a c', and went to Jezreel
21 And his c' was made ready.
21 of Judah went out, each in his c',
24 heart, and he sunk down in his c'.
27 and said, Smite him also in the c'.
28 carried him in a c' to Jerusalem,
10:15 took him up to him into the c'.
16 So they made him ride in his c'.
13:14 c' of Israel, and the horsemen
23:30 servants carried him in a c' dead
1Ch 18:4 also houghed all the c' horses,
28:18 c' of the cherubims, that spread
2Ch 1:14 which he placed in the c' cities,
17 brought forth out of Egypt a c'
8: 6 all the c' cities, and the cities
9:25 in the c' cities, and with the king
10:18 speed to get him up to his c',
18:33 to his c' man, Turn thine hand,
34 Israel stayed himself up in his c'
35:24 therefore took him out of that c',
24 him in the second c' that he had;
Ps 46: 9 he burneth the c' in the fire.
76: 6 the c' and horse are cast into
104: 3 who maketh the clouds his c':
Ca 3: 9 King Solomon made himself a c'
Isa 21: 7 a c' with a couple of horsemen,
7 a c' of asses, and a c' of camels;
9 behold, here cometh a c' of men,
43:17 bringeth forth the c' and horse,
Jer 51:21 thee will I break in pieces the c'
Mic 1:13 bind the c' to the swift beast:
Zec 6: 2 In the first c' were red horses;
2 and in the second c' black horses;
3 in the third c' white horses;
3 in the fourth c' grisled and bay
9:10 will cut off the c' from Ephraim,
Ac 8:28 and sitting in his c' read Esaias
29 Go near, and join thyself to this c'.
38 he commanded the c' to stand still:

chariot-cities See CHARIOT and CITIES.

chariot-horses See CHARIOT and HORSES.

chariot-man See CHARIOT and MAN.

chariots
Ge 50: 9 there went up with him both c'
Ex 14: 7 he took six hundred chosen c',
7 and all the c' of Egypt,
9 c' of Pharaoh, and his horsemen,
17 upon all his host, upon his c',
18 his c', and upon his horsemen.
23 even all Pharaoh's horses, his c',
26 the Egyptians, upon their c',
28 returned, and covered the c',
15: 4 Pharaoh's c' and his host hath he
19 of Pharaoh went in with his c'
De 11: 4 unto their horses, and to their c';
20: 1 seest horses, and c', and a people
Jos 11: 4 with horses and c' very many.
6 and burn their c' with fire.
9 and burnt their c' with fire.
17:16 have c' of iron, both they who are
18 have iron c', and though they
24: 6 c' and horsemen unto the Red sea.
J'g 1:19 because they had c' of iron.
4: 3 he had nine hundred c' of iron;
7 Jabin's army, with his c' and his
13 Sisera gathered together all his c',
13 even nine hundred c' of iron,
15 discomfited Sisera, and all his c',
16 Barak pursued after the c', and
5:28 why tarry the wheels of his c'?
1Sa 8:11 them for himself, for his c',
11 and some shall run before his c'.
12 war, and instruments of his c'.
13: 5 with Israel, thirty thousand c',
2Sa 1: 6 c' and horsemen followed hard
8: 4 took from him a thousand c',
4 of them for an hundred c'.
10:18 of seven hundred c of the Syrians,
15: 1 prepared him c' and horses,
1Ki 1: 5 prepared him c' and horsemen,
4:26 stalls of horses for his c',
9:19 cities for his c', and cities for his
22 his captains, and rulers of his c',
10:26 Solomon gathered together c'
26 a thousand and four hundred c',
26 he bestowed in the cities for c',
16: 9 Zimri, captain of half his c',
20: 1 with him, and horses, and c':
21 and c', and slew the Syrians
22:31 captains that had rule over his c',
1Ki 22:32 captains of the c' saw Jehoshaphat,
33 the captains of the c' perceived
2Ki 6:14 sent he thither horses, and c',
15 the city both with horses and c'.
17 mountain was full of horses and c'
7: 6 noise of c', and a noise of horses,
8:21 went over to Zair, and all the c'
21 of the c': and the people fled
10: 2 there are with you c' and horses,
13: 7 but fifty horsemen, and ten c',
18:24 put thy trust on Egypt for c'
19:23 the multitude of my c' I am come
23:11 burned the c' of the sun with fire.
1Ch 18: 4 c', and seven thousand horsemen,
4 reserved of them an hundred c'.
19: 6 hire them c' and horsemen out of
7 hired thirty and two thousand c',
18 thousand men which fought in c',
2Ch 1:14 gathered c' and horsemen:
14 a thousand and four hundred c',
8: 9 captains of his c' and horsemen.
9:25 thousand stalls for horses and c',
12: 3 twelve hundred c', and threescore
14: 9 and three hundred c'; and came
16: 8 with very many c' and horsemen?
18:30 of the c' that were with him,
31 when the captains of the c' saw
32 the captains of the c' perceived
21: 9 princes, and all his c' with him:
9 him in, and the captains of the c'.
Ps 20: 7 trust in c', and some in horses:
68:17 c' of God are twenty thousand,
Ca 1: 9 company of horses in Pharaoh's c'.
6:12 my soul made me like the c' of
Isa 2: 7 neither is there any end of their c':
22: 6 Elam bare the quiver with c' of
7 choicest valleys shall be full of c',
18 c' of thy glory shall be the shame
31: 1 trust in c', because they are
36: 9 and put thy trust on Egypt for c'
37:24 By the multitude of my c' am I
66:15 with his c' like a whirlwind, to
20 upon horses, and in c', and in
Jer 4:13 his c' shall be as a whirlwind:
17:25 riding in c' and on horses, they,
22: 4 David, riding in c' and on horses,
46: 9 rage, ye c'; and let the mighty
47: 3 the rushing of his c', and at the
50:37 upon their c', and upon all the
Eze 23:24 come against thee with c',
26: 7 with horses, and with c', and
10 of the wheels, and of the c', when
27:20 in precious clothes for c'.
39:20 with horses and c', with mighty
Da 11:40 with c', and with horsemen, and
Joe 2: 5 Like the noise of c' on the tops of
Mic 5:10 I will destroy thy c':
Na 2: 3 c' shall be with flaming torches
4 The c' shall rage in the streets,
13 I will burn her c' in the smoke,
3: 2 horses, and of the jumping c'.
Hab 3: 8 thine horses and thy c' of
Hag 2:22 I will overthrow the c', and those
Zec 6: 1 came four c' out from between
Re 9: 9 as the sound of c' of many horses
18:13 and horses, and c', and slaves,

charitably
Ro 14:15 meat, now walkest thou not c'.

charity
1 Co 8: 1 Knowledge puffeth up, but c'
13: 1 of angels, and have not c', I am
2 mountains, and have not c',
3 to be burned, and have not c'.
4 C' suffereth long, and is kind;
4 c' envieth not; c' vaunteth not
8 C' never faileth: but whether
13 now abideth faith, hope, c', these
13 the greatest of these is c'.
14: 1 Follow after c', and desire
16:14 all your things be done with c'.
Col 3:14 above all these things put on c',
1 Th 3: 6 good tidings of your faith and c',
2 Th 1: 3 the c' of every one of you all
1 Ti 1: 5 commandment is c' out of a
2:15 in faith and c' and holiness with
4:12 in conversation, in c', in spirit, in
2 Ti 2:22 follow righteousness, faith, c',
3:10 faith, longsuffering, c', patience,
Tit 2: 2 temperate, sound in faith, in c',
1 Pe 4: 8 fervent c' among yourselves:
8 for c' shall cover the multitude
5:14 ye one another with a kiss of c'.
2 Pe 1: 7 and to brotherly kindness c'.
3 Jo 6 have borne witness of thy c'
Jude 12 spots in your feasts of c', when
Re 2:19 I know thy works, and c', and

charmed
Jer 8:17 which will not be c', and they

charmer See also CHARMERS.
De 18:11 Or a c', or a consulter with

charmers
Ps 58: 5 hearken to the voice of c',
Isa 19: 3 seek to the idols, and to the c',

charming
Ps 58: 5 to the voice of charmers, c'

Charran (*car'-ran*) See also HARAN.
Ac 7: 2 before he dwelt in C',
4 and dwelt in C': and from thence,

chase See also CHASED; CHASETH; CHASING.
Le 26: 7 And ye shall c' your enemies, and
8 And five of you shall c' an hundred,
36 the sound of a shaken leaf shall c'
De 32:30 How should one c' a thousand,

Jos 23:10 man of you shall c' a thousand:
Ps 35: 5 and let the angel of the Lord c'

chased
De 1:44 came out against you, and c' you,
Jos 7: 5 for they c' them from before the
8:24 the wilderness wherein they c'
10:10 and c' them along the way that
11: 8 and c' them unto great Zidon,
J'g 9:40 And Abimelech c' him, and he
20:43 c' them, and trode them down
Ne 13:28 Horonite: therefore I c' him from
Job 18:18 into darkness, and c' out of the
20: 8 he shall be c' away as a vision of
Isa 13:14 it shall be as the c' roe, and as a
17:13 and shall be c' as the chaff of the
La 3:52 Mine enemies c' me sore, like a

chaseth
Pr 19:26 c' away his mother, is a son that

chasing
1 Sa 17:53 of Israel returned from c' after

chaste
2 Co 11: 2 present you as a c' virgin to
Tit 2: 5 discreet, c', keepers at home,
1 Pe 3: 2 they behold your c' conversation

chasten See also CHASTENED; CHASTENEST; CHASTENETH; CHASTENING; CHASTISE.
2 Sa 7:14 I will c' him with the rod of men,
Ps 6: 1 neither c' me in thy hot
38: 1 c' me in thy hot displeasure.
Pr 19:18 C' thy son while there is hope,
Da 10:12 and to c' thyself before thy God,
Re 3:19 many as I love, I rebuke and c':

chastened
De 21:18 when they have c' him, will not
Job 33:19 He is c' also with pain upon his
Ps 69:10 When I wept, and c' my soul
73:14 have I been plagued, and c' every
118:18 The Lord hath c' me sore: but he
1 Co 11:32 we are c' of the Lord, that we
2 Co 6: 9 as c', and not killed;
Heb 12:10 for a few days c' us after their own

chastenest
Ps 94:12 Blessed is the man whom thou c',

chasteneth
De 8: 5 as a man c' his son, so
5 the Lord thy God c' thee.
Pr 13:24 he that loveth him c' him
Heb 12: 6 For whom the Lord loveth he c',
7 son is he whom the father c' not?

chastening
Job 5:17 therefore despise not thou the c'
Pr 3:11 despise not the c' of the Lord;
Isa 26:16 a prayer when thy c' was upon
Heb 12: 5 despise not thou the c' of the
7 If ye endure c', God dealeth with
11 Now no c' for the present

chastise See also CHASTEN; CHASTISED; CHASTISETH.
Le 26:28 and I, even I, will c' you seven
De 22:18 city shall take that man and c'
1 Ki 12:11 but I will c' you with scorpions.
14 with whips, but I will c' you with
2Ch 10:11, 14 I will c' you with scorpions.
Hos 7:12 I will c' them, as their
10:10 in my desire that I should c'
Lu 23:16 I will therefore c' him, and release
22 I will therefore c' him, and let him

chastised
1K 12:11 my father hath c' you with whips,
14 my father also c' you with whips,
2Ch 10:11 my father c' you with whips, but
14 will add thereto: my father c' you
Jer 31:18 Thou hast c' me, and I was c',

chastisement
De 11: 2 not seen the c' of the Lord your
Job 34:31 I have borne c', I will not offend
Isa 53: 5 the c' of our peace was upon
Jer 30:14 the c' of a cruel one, for the
Heb 12: 8 But if ye be without c', whereof

chastiseth
Ps 94:10 He that c' the heathen, shall not

chatter
Isa 38:14 so did I c': I did mourn as a

Chebar (*ke'-bar*)
Eze 1: 1 the captives by the river of C',
3 the Chaldeans by the river C';
3:15 that dwelt by the river of C',
23 which I saw by the river of C':
10:15 that I saw by the river of C'.
20 God of Israel by the river of C';
22 which I saw by the river of C',
43: 3 vision that I saw by the river C';

check
Job 20: 3 heard the c' of my reproach,

checker
1Ki 7:17 nets of c' work, and wreaths of

checker-work See CHECKER and WORK.

Chedorlaomer (*ked''-or-la'-o-mer*)
Ge 14: 1 C' king of Elam, and Tidal king
4 Twelve years they served C', and
5 in the fourteenth year came C',
9 With C' the king of Elam, and
17 his return from the slaughter of C',

cheek See also CHEEKS.
1Ki 22:24 and smote Micaiah on the c', and
2Ch 18:23 and smote Micaiah upon the c',
Job 16:10 they have smitten me upon the c'
Ps 3: 7 all mine enemies upon the c' bone;
La 3:30 He giveth his c' to him that
Joe 1: 6 hath the c' teeth of a great lion.
Mic 5: 1 Israel with a rod upon the c'.
M't 5:39 smite thee upon thy right c',
Lu 6:29 smiteth thee on the one c'

cheek-bone See CHEEK and BONE.

cheeks
De 18: 3 the shoulder, and the two c',
Ca 1:10 Thy c' are comely with rows of
5:13 His c' are as a bed of spices, as
Isa 50: 6 and my c' to them that plucked
La 1: 2 and her tears are on her c':

cheek-teeth See CHEEK and TEETH.

cheer See also CHEERETH; CHEERFUL.
De 24: 5 and shall c' up his wife which he
Ec 11: 9 and let thy heart c' thee in the
M't 9: 2 be of good c'; thy sins be forgiven
14:27 Be of good c'; it is I; be not afraid.
M'r 6:50 saith unto them, Be of good c': it
Joh 16:33 but be of good c'; I have overcome
Ac 23:11 Be of good c', Paul: for as thou
27:22 I exhort you to be of good c': for
25 Wherefore, sirs, be of good c':
36 Then were they all of good c',

cheereth
J'g 9:13 which c' God and man, and go to

cheerful
Pr 15:13 A merry heart maketh a c'
Zec 8:19 gladness, and c' feasts; therefore
9:17 shall make the young men c',
2Co 9: 7 for God loveth a c' giver.

cheerfully
Ac 24:10 the more c' answer for myself:

cheerfulness
Ro 12: 8 he that sheweth mercy, with c'.

cheese See also CHEESES.
2Sa 17:29 sheep, and c' of kine, for David,
Job 10:10 as milk, and curdled me like c'?

cheeses
1Sa 17:18 carry these ten c' unto the

Chelal (*ke'-lal*)
Ezr 10:30 Adna, and C', Benaiah, Maaseiah,

Chelluh (*kel'-loo*)
Ezr 10:35 Benaiah, Bedeiah, C',

Chelub (*ke'-lub*)
1Ch 4:11 And C' the brother of Shuah
27:26 the ground was Ezri the son of C'.

Chelubai (*ke-loo'-bahee*) See also CALEB.
1Ch 2: 9 Jerahmeel, and Ram, and C'.

Chemarims (*kem'-a-rims*)
Zep 1: 4 name of the C' with the priests;

Chemosh (*ke'-mosh*)
Nu 21:29 thou art undone, O people of C':
J'g 11:24 that which C' thy god giveth
1Ki 11: 7 Solomon build an high place for C',
33 C' the god of the Moabites, and
2Ki 23:13 C' the abomination of the Moabites,
Jer 48: 7 and C' shall go forth into captivity
13 Moab shall be ashamed of C', as
46 O Moab! the people of C' perisheth:

Chenaanah (*ke-na'-a-nah*)
1Ki 22:11 C' made him horns of iron:
24 C' went near, and smote Micaiah
1Ch 7:10 Benjamin, and Ehud, and C',
2Ch 18:10 C' had made him horns of iron,
23 Zedekiah the son of C' came near,

Chenani (*ken'-a-ni*)
Ne 9: 4 Bani, and C', and cried with

Chenaniah (*ken-a-ni'-ah*) See also CONONIAH.
1Ch 15:22 And C', chief of the Levites, was
27 and C' the master of the song
26:29 C' and his sons were for the

Chephar-haammonai (*ke''-far-ha-am'-mo-nahee*)
Jos 18:24 And C', and Ophni, and Gaba;

Chephirah (*ke-fi'-rah*)
Jos 9:17 their cities were Gibeon, and C',
18:26 Mizpeh, and C', and Mozah,
Ezr 2:25 Kirjath-arim, C', and Beeroth,
Ne 7:29 of Kirjath-jearim, C', and Beeroth,

Cheran (*ke'-ran*)
Ge 36:26 and Eshban, and Ithran, and C'.
1Ch 1:41 and Eshban, and Ithran, and C'.

Cherethims (*ker'-e-thims*) See also CHERETHITES.
Eze 25:16 I will cut off the C', and destroy

Cherethites (*ker'-e-thites*) See also CHERETHIMS.
1Sa 30:14 invasion upon the south of the C'.
2Sa 8:18 both the C' and the Pelethites;
15:18 all the C', and all the Pelethites,
20: 7 and the C', and the Pelethites,
23 was over the C' and over
1Ki 1:38 and the C', and the Pelethites,
44 and the C', and the Pelethites,
1Ch 18:17 was over the C' and the Pelethites;
Zep 2: 5 the nation of the C'! the word of

cherish See also CHERISHED.
1Ki 1: 2 let her c' him, and let her lie in

cherished
1Ki 1: 4 was very fair, and c' the king,

cherisheth
Eph 5:29 but nourisheth and c' it, even
1Th 2: 7 even as a nurse c' her children:

Cherith (*ke'-rith*)
1Ki 17: 3 and hide thyself by the brook C',
5 went and dwelt by the brook C',

Cherub (*ke'-rub*)
Ezr 2:59 up from Tel-melah, Tel-harsa, C',
Ne 7:61 from Tel-melah, Tel-haresha, C',

cherub (*cher'-ub*) See also CHERUBIMS.
Ex 25:19 one c' on the one end,
19 and the other c' on the other end:
37: 8 One c' on the end on this side,
8 and another c' on the other
2Sa 22:11 he rode upon a c', and did fly:
1Ki 6:24 the one wing of the c', and five
24 cubits the other wing of the c':
25 the other c' was ten cubits: both
26 height of the one c' was ten cubits,
26 and so was it of the other c'.
27 of the other c' touched the wall;
2Ch 3:11 one wing of the one c' was five
11 to the wing of the other c'.
12 one wing of the other c' was five
12 joining to the wing of the other c'.
Ps 18:10 he rode upon a c', and did fly:
Eze 9: 3 was gone up from the c',
10: 2 under the c', and fill thine hand
4 went up from the c', and stood
7 one c' stretched forth his hand
9 one wheel by one c', and another
9 another wheel by another c':
14 the first face was the face of a c',
28:14 Thou art the anointed c' that
16 I will destroy thee, O covering c',
41:18 between a c' and a c'; and
18 every c' had two faces;

cherubims (*cher'-u-bims*) See also CHERUBIMS'.
Ge 3:24 of the garden of Eden C', and
Ex 25:18 thou shalt make two c' of gold,
19 mercy seat shall ye make the c'
20 c' shall stretch forth their wings
20 seat shall the faces of the c'
22 between the two c' which are
26: 1 c' of cunning work shalt thou
31 work: with c' shall it be made:
36: 8 c' of cunning work made he
35 c' made he it of cunning work.
37: 7 he made two c' of gold, beaten
8 the mercy seat made he the c'
9 the c' spread out their wings on
9 seatward were the faces of the c'.
Nu 7:89 from between the two c':
1Sa 4: 4 which dwelleth between the c':
2Sa 6: 2 that dwelleth between the c'.
1Ki 6:23 oracle he made two c' of olive
25 the c' were of one measure and
27 set the c' within the inner house:
27 stretched forth the wings of the c',
28 And he overlaid the c' with gold.
29 about with carved figures of c'
32 carvings of c' and palm trees
32 spread gold upon the c', and upon
35 carved thereon c' and palm trees
7:29 ledges were lions, oxen, and c':
36 graved c', lions, and palm trees,
8: 6 even under the wings of the c'.
7 c' spread forth their two wings
7 ark, and the c' covered the ark
2Ki 19:15 which dwellest between the c',
1Ch 13: 6 that dwelleth between the c',
28:18 the chariot of the c', that spread
2Ch 3: 7 gold; and graved c' on the walls.
10 he made two c' of image work,
11 wings of the c' were twenty
13 The wings of these c' spread
14 linen, and wrought c' thereon.
5: 7 even under the wings of the c':
8 the c' spread forth their wings
8 c' covered the ark and the staves
Ps 80: 1 that dwellest between the c',
99: 1 he sitteth between the c'; let
Isa 37:16 that dwellest between the c',
Eze 10: 1 head of the c' there appeared
2 coals of fire from between the c',
3 c' stood on the right side of the
6 the wheels, from between the c';
7 from between the c' unto the fire
7 the fire that was between the c',
8 there appeared in the c' the form
9 behold the four wheels by the c',
15 the c' were lifted up. This is the
16 when the c' went, the wheels
16 them: and when the c' lifted
18 house, and stood over the c'.
19 the c' lifted up their wings, and
20 and I knew that they were the c'.
11:22 the c' lift up their wings, and the
41:18 was made with c' and palm trees
20 door were c' and palm trees
25 c' and palm trees, like as were
Heb 9: 5 c' of glory shadowing the

cherubims'
Eze 10: 5 sound of the c' wings was heard

Chesalon (*kes'-a-lon*)
Jos 15:10 of mount Jearim, which is C',

Chesed (*ke'-sed*)
Ge 22:22 And C', and Hazo, and Pildash,

Chesil (*ke'-sil*)
Jos 15:30 And Eltolad, and C', and Hormah,

chesnut
Ge 30:37 and of the hazel and c' tree
Eze 31: 8 and the c' trees were not like

chesnut-tree See CHESNUT and TREE.

chest See also CHESTS.
2Ki 12: 9 Jehoiada the priest took a c', and
10 much money in the c', that the
2Ch 24: 8 made a c', and set it without at the
10 cast into the c', until they had
11 c' was brought unto the king's
11 came and emptied the c', and took

chestnut See CHESNUT.

chests
Eze 27:24 in c' of rich apparel, bound with
Chesulloth (*ke-sul'-loth*) See also CHISLOTH-TABOR.
Jos 19:18 was toward Jezreel, and C'
chew See also CHEWED; CHEWETH.
Le 11: 4 shall ye not eat of them that c'
De 14: 7 of them that c' the cud, or of them
7 c' the cud, but divide not the hoof;
chewed
Nu 11:33 between their teeth, ere it was c'.
cheweth
Le 11: 3 and c' the cud, among the beasts,
4 he c' the cud, but divideth not the
5 the coney, because he c' the cud,
6 because he c' the cud, but divideth
7 he c' not the cud; he is unclean
26 not clovenfooted, nor c' the cud,
De 14: 6 and c' the cud among the beasts,
8 yet c' not the cud, it is unclean
Chezib (*ke'-zib*) See also ACHZIB; CHOZEBA.
Ge 38: 5 he was at C', when she bare him.
chickens
M't 23:37 as a hen gathereth her c' under
chid See CHODE.
chide See also CHIDING; CHODE.
Ex 17: 2 Wherefore the people did c' with
2 Why c' ye with me? wherefore
J'g 8: 1 they did c' with him sharply.
Ps 103: 9 He will not always c': neither will
chided See CHODE.
chiding
Ex 17: 7 of the c' of the children of Israel,
Chidon (*ki'-don*) See also NACHON.
1Ch 13: 9 unto the threshingfloor of C',
chief See also CHIEFEST.
Ge 21:22 Phichol the c' captain of his host
32 Phichol the c' captain of his host,
26:26 Phichol the c' captain of his army.
40: 2 against the c' of the butlers,
2 and against the c' of the bakers.
9 c' butler told his dream to Joseph,
16 When the c' baker saw that the
20 of the c' butler and of the c' baker
21 he restored the c' butler unto his
22 he hanged the c' baker: as Joseph
23 Yet did not the c' butler remember
41: 9 spake the c' butler unto Pharaoh,
10 house, both me and the c' baker:
Le 21: 4 a c' man among his people, to
Nu 3:24 the c' of the house of the father
30 the c' of the house of the father
32 be c' over the c' of the Levites,
35 And the c' of the house of the
4:34 and the c' of the congregation
46 and the c' of Israel numbered,
25:14 prince of a c' house among the
15 and of a c' house in Midian.
31:26 c' fathers of the congregation:
32:28 the c' fathers of the tribes of the
36: 1 the c' fathers of the families of
1 c' fathers of the children of
De 1:15 I took the c' of your tribes, wise
33:15 for the c' things of the ancient
Jos 22:14 c' house a prince throughout all
J'g 20: 2 c' of all the people, even of all
1Sa 14:38 Draw ye near thither, all the c' of
15:21 c' of the things which should
2Sa 5: 8 of David's soul, he shall be c'
8:18 and David's sons were c' rulers.
20:26 was a c' ruler about David.
23: 8 c' among the captains; the same
13 three of the thirty c' went down,
18 of Zeruiah, was c' among three.
1Ki 5:16 Beside the c' of Solomon's officers
8: 1 c' of the fathers of the children
9:23 the c' of the officers that were
14:27 c' of the guard, which kept the
2Ki 25:18 guard took Seraiah the c' priest,
1Ch 5: 2 and of him came the c' ruler;
7 the c', Jeiel, and Zechariah,
12 Joel the c', and Shapham the
15 c' of the house of their fathers.
7: 3 Isheah, five: all of them c' men.
40 men of valour, c' of the princes.
8:28 by their generations, c' men.
9: 9 these men were c' of the fathers
17 brethren: Shallum was the c';
26 four c' porters, were in their set
33 c' of the fathers of the Levites,
34 c' fathers of the Levites were
34 c' throughout their generations;
11: 6 the Jebusites first shall be c'
6 Zeruiah went first up, and was c',
10 c' of the mighty men whom David
11 Hachmonite, the c' of the captains:
20 of Joab, he was c' of the three:
12: 3 The c' was Ahiezer, then Joash,
18 Amasai, who was c' of the captains,
15: 5 the sons of Kohath; Uriel the c',
6 the sons of Merari; Asaiah the c',
7 the sons of Gershom; Joel the c',
8 of Elizaphan; Shemaiah the c',
9 the sons of Hebron; Eliel the c',
10 sons of Uzziel; Amminadab the c',
12 c' of the fathers of the Levites:
16 spake to the c' of the Levites
22 Chenaniah, c' of the Levites, was
16: 5 Asaph the c', and next to him
18:17 sons of David were c' about the
23: 8 the c' was Jehiel, and Zetham,
9 the c' of the fathers of Laadan.
1Ch 23:11 Jahath was the c', and Zizah the
16 of Gershom, Shebuel was the c'.
17 of Eliezer were, Rehabiah the c'.
18 sons of Izhar; Shelomith the c'.
24 c' of the fathers, as they were
24: 4 more c' men found of the sons of
4 were sixteen c' men of the house
6 and before the c' of the fathers
31 c' of the fathers of the priests
26:10 Simri the c', (for though he was
10 yet his father made him the c';)
12 even among the c' men, having
21 c' fathers, even of Laadan the
26 the c' fathers, the captains over
31 Jerijah the c', even among the
32 two thousand and seven hundred c'
27: 1 the c' fathers and captains of
3 Of the children of Perez was the c
5 Benaiah the son of Jehoiada, a c'
29: 6 the c' of the fathers and princes
22 to be the c' governor, and Zadok
2Ch 1: 2 all Israel, the c' of the fathers.
5: 2 c' of the fathers of the children
8: 9 c' of his captains, and captains of
10 c' of king Solomon's officers,
11:22 c', to be ruler among his brethren:
12:10 the c' of the guard, that kept the
17:14 Adnah the c', and with him
19: 8 of the c' of the fathers of Israel,
11 Amariah the c' priest is over you
23: 2 the c' of the fathers of Israel,
24: 6 king called for Jehoiada the c',
26:12 c' of the fathers of the mighty
20 the c' priest, and all the priests,
31:10 Azariah the c' priest of the house
35: 9 and Jozabad, c' of the Levites,
36:14 c' of the priests, and the people
Ezr 1: 5 the c' of the fathers of Judah
2:68 some of the c' of the fathers,
3:12 and c' of the fathers, who were
4: 2 the c' of the fathers, and said
3 of the c' of the fathers of Israel,
5:10 men that were the c' of them.
7: 5 the son of Aaron the c' priest:
28 Israel c' men to go up with me.
8: 1 are now the c' of their fathers,
16 and for Meshullam, c' men;
17 Iddo the c' at the place Casiphia,
24 twelve of the c' of the priests,
29 c' of the priests and the Levites,
29 and c' of the fathers of Israel,
9: 2 hath been c' in this trespass.
10: 5 Ezra, and made the c' priests,
16 c' of the fathers, after the house
Ne 7:70 some of the c' of the fathers
71 the c' of the fathers gave to the
8:13 c' of the fathers of all the people,
10:14 The c' of the people; Parosh,
11: 3 the c' of the province that dwelt
13 his brethren, c' of the fathers,
16 of the c' of the Levites, had the
12: 7 These were the c' of the priests
12 the c' of the fathers: of Seraiah,
22 were recorded c' of the fathers:
23 sons of Levi, the c' of the fathers,
24 the c' of the Levites: Hashabiah,
46 old there were c' of the singers,
Job 12:24 the c' of the people of the earth,
29:25 I chose out their way, and sat c',
40:19 the c' of the ways of God:
Ps 4:*title* To the c' Musician on Neginoth,
5:*title* the c' Musician upon Nehiloth,
6:*title* To the c' Musician on Neginoth
8:*title* To the c' Musician upon Gittith,
9:*title* c' Musician upon Muth-labben,
11:*title* c' Musician, A Psalm of David.
12:*title* the c' Musician upon Sheminith,
13:*title* c' Musician, A Psalm of David.
14:*title* c' Musician, A Psalm of David.
18:*title* c' Musician, A Psalm of David.
19:*title* c' Musician, A Psalm of David.
20:*title* c' Musician, A Psalm of David.
21:*title* c' Musician, A Psalm of David.
22:*title* c' Musician upon Aijeleth
31:*title* c' Musician, A Psalm of David.
36:*title* c' Musician, A Psalm of David
39:*title* c' Musician, even to Jeduthun,
40:*title* c' Musician, A Psalm of David.
41:*title* c' Musician, A Psalm of David.
42:*title* the c' Musician, Maschil, for the
44:*title* To the c' Musician for the sons
45:*title* c' Musician upon Shoshannim,
46:*title* To the c' Musician for the sons
47:*title* To the c' Musician, A Psalm for
49:*title* To the c' Musician, A Psalm for
51:*title* c' Musician, A Psalm of David,
52:*title* c' Musician, Maschil, A Psalm of
53:*title* the c' Musician upon Mahalath,
54:*title* To the c' Musician on Neginoth,
55:*title* To the c' Musician on Neginoth,
56:*title* To the c' Musician upon
57:*title* To the c' Musician, Al-taschith,
58:*title* To the c' Musician, Al-taschith,
59:*title* To the c' Musician, Al-taschith,
60:*title* c' Musician upon Shushan-eduth,
61:*title* the c' Musician upon Neginah,
62:*title* To the c' Musician, to Jeduthun,
64:*title* c' Musician, A Psalm of David.
65:*title* c' Musician, A Psalm and Song
66:*title* c' Musician, A Song or Psalm.
67:*title* To the c' Musician on Neginoth,
68:*title* c' Musician, A Psalm or Song of
69:*title* c' Musician upon Shoshannim,
70:*title* c' Musician, A Psalm of David,
75:*title* To the c' Musician, Al-taschith,
76:*title* To the c' Musician on Neginoth,
Ps 77:*title* To the c' Musician, to Jeduthun,
78:51 the c' of their strength in the
80:*title* To the c' Musician upon
81:*title* To the c' Musician upon Gittith,
84:*title* To the c' Musician upon Gittith,
85:*title* To the c' Musician, A Psalm for
88:*title* the c' Musician upon Mahalath
105:36 land, the c' of all their strength.
109:*title* c' Musician, A Psalm of David.
137: 6 not Jerusalem above my c' joy.
139:*title* c' Musician, A Psalm of David.
140:*title* c' musician, A Psalm of David.
Pr 1:21 in the c' place of concourse,
16:28 a whisperer separateth c' friends.
Ca 4:14 and aloes, with all the c' spices:
Isa 14: 9 even all the c' ones of the earth;
41: 9 thee from the c' men thereof,
Jer 13:21 them to be captains, and as c'
20: 1 c' governor in the house of the
31: 7 among the c' of the nations:
49:35 of Elam, the c' of their might.
52:24 guard took Seraiah the c' priest,
La 1: 5 Her adversaries are the c', her
Eze 27:22 in thy fairs with c' of all spices,
38: 2 c' prince of Meshech and Tubal,
3 I am against thee, O Gog, the c'
39: 1 c' prince of Meshech and Tubal:
Da 2:48 and c' of the governors over all
10:13 lo, Michael, one of the c' princes,
11:41 the c' of the children of Ammon.
Am 6: 1 which are named c' of the nations,
6 themselves with the c' ointments:
Hab 3:19 to the c' singer on my stringed
M't 2: 4 all the c' priests and scribes
16:21 elders and c' priests and scribes,
20:18 be betrayed unto the c' priests
27 whosoever will be c' among you,
21:15 when the c' priests and scribes
23 the c' priests and the elders of the
45 the c' priests and Pharisees had
23: 6 the c' seats in the synagogues,
26: 3 assembled together the c' priests,
14 Iscariot, went unto the c' priests,
47 from the c' priests and elders
59 Now the c' priests, and elders,
27: 1 c' priests and elders of the people
3 silver to the c' priests and elders,
6 the c' priests took the silver pieces,
12 he was accused of the c' priests
20 the c' priests and elders persuaded
41 also the c' priests mocking him,
62 the c' priests and Pharisees came
28:11 shewed unto the c' priests all the
M'r 6:21 captains, and c' estates of Galilee;
8:31 of the c' priests, and scribes,
10:33 be delivered unto the c' priests,
11:18 the scribes and c' priests heard it,
27 there come to him the c' priests,
12:39 the c' seats in the synagogues,
14: 1 the c' priests and the scribes
10 went unto the c' priests, to betray
43 from the c' priests and the scribes
53 all the c' priests and the elders
55 the c' priests and all the council
15: 1 the c' priests held a consultation
3 c' priests accused him of many
10 the c' priests had delivered him for
11 the c' priests moved the people,
31 also the c' priests mocking said
Lu 9:22 c' priests and scribes, and be slain,
11:15 devils through Beelzebub the c'
14: 1 house of one of the c' Pharisees
7 how they chose out the c' rooms;
19: 2 was the c' among the publicans,
47 the c' priests and the scribes
47 and the c' of the people sought
20: 1 the c' priests and the scribes came
19 the c' priests and the scribes the
46 and the c' rooms at feasts;
22: 2 the c' priests and scribes sought
4 communed with the c' priests
26 that is c', as he that doth serve.
52 Jesus said unto the c' priests,
66 the c' priests and the scribes came
23: 4 said Pilate to the c' priests and to
10 the c' priests and scribes stood
13 together the c' priests and the
23 of them and of the c' priests
24:20 how the c' priests and our rulers
Joh 7:32 the Pharisees and the c' priests
45 came the officers to the c' priests
11:47 the c' priests and the Pharisees
57 both the c' priests and the Pharisees
12:10 c' priests consulted that they might
42 Nevertheless among the c' rulers
18: 3 from the c' priests and Pharisees,
35 Thine own nation and the c' priests
19: 6 c' priests therefore and officers
15 The c' priests answered, We have
21 Then said the c' priests of the Jews
Ac 4:23 the c' priests and elders had said
5:24 the c' priests heard these things
9:14 authority from the c' priests to
21 them bound unto the c' priests?
13:50 and the c' men of the city,
14:12 because he was the c' speaker.
15:22 c' men among the brethren:
16:12 c' city of that part of Macedonia,
17: 4 and of the c' women not a few.
18: 8 the c' ruler of the synagogue,
17 the c' ruler of the synagogue,
19:14 a Jew, and c' of the priests,
31 and certain of the c' of Asia,
21:31 unto the c' captain of the band,
32 when they saw the c' captain and
33 Then the c' captain came near,

Ac 21:37 he said unto the *c'* captain, May
22:24 The *c'* captain commanded him
26 he went and told the *c'* captain,
27 Then the *c'* captain came, and said
28 And the *c'* captain answered, With
29 and the *c'* captain also was afraid,
30 commanded the *c'* priests and all
23:10 the *c'* captain, fearing lest Paul
14 came to the *c'* priests and elders,
15 signify to the *c'* captain that he
17 this young man to the *c'* captain:
18 brought him to the *c'* captain,
19 Then the *c'* captain took him by
22 the *c'* captain then let the young
24: 7 But the *c'* captain Lysias came
22 When Lysias the *c'* captain shall
25: 2 the *c'* of the Jews informed him
15 the *c'* priests and the elders of
23 with the *c'* captains, and principal
26:10 authority from the *c'* priests;
12 commission from the *c'* priests,
28: 7 of the *c'* man of the island,
17 Paul called the *c'* of the Jews
Eph 2:20 himself being the *c'* corner stone;
1Ti 1:15 to save sinners; of whom I am *c'*.
1Pe 2: 6 I lay in Sion a *c'* corner stone,
5: 4 when the *c'* Shepherd shall appear,
Re 6:15 *c'* captains, and the mighty men,

chiefest
1Sa 2:29 with the *c'* of all the offerings
9:22 in the *c'* place among them that
21: 7 Edomite,the *c'* of the herdmen
2Ch 32:33 they buried him in the *c'* of the
Ca 5:10 ruddy, the *c'* among ten thousand.
M'r 10:44 the *c'*, shall be servant of all.
2Co 11: 5 behind the very *c'* apostles.
12:11 behind the very *c'* apostles,
1Ti *subscr.* which is the *c'* city

chiefly
Ro 3: 2 *c'*, because that unto them were
Ph'p 4:22 *c'* they that are of Cæsar's
2Pe 2:10 *c'* them that walk after the flesh

chief-priest See CHIEF and PRIEST.

child See also CHILDBEARING; CHILDHOOD; CHILDLESS; CHILDREN; CHILD'S.
Ge 11:30 Sarai was barren; she had no *c'*.
16:11 her, Behold, thou art with *c'*,
17:10 Every man *c'* among you shall
12 every man *c'* in your generations,
14 the uncircumcised man *c'* whose
19:36 both the daughters of Lot with *c'*
21: 8 the *c'* grew, and was weaned:
14 and the *c'*, and sent her away:
15 cast the *c'* under one of the shrubs.
16 Let me not see the death of the *c'*.
37:30 The *c'* is not; and I, whither shall
38:24 she is with *c'* by whoredom.
25 am I with *c'*: and she said,
42:22 Do not sin against the *c'*;
44:20 and a *c'* of his old age, a little one;
Ex 2: 2 saw him that he was a goodly *c'*,
3 and put the *c'* therein; and she
6 had opened it, she saw the *c'*:
7 women, that she may nurse the *c'*
9 Take this *c'* away, and nurse it
9 the woman took the *c'*, and nursed
10 And the *c'* grew, and she brought
21:22 hurt a woman with *c'*, so that her
22:22 afflict any widow, or fatherless *c'*.
Le 12: 2 and born a man *c'*: then she shall
5 if she bear a maid *c'*, then she
22:13 and have no *c'*, and is returned
Nu 11:12 father beareth the sucking *c'*,
De 25: 5 and have no *c'*, the wife of the
Jud 11:34 she was his only *c'*; beside her he
13: 5 for the *c'* shall be a Nazarite unto
7 the *c'* shall be Nazarite to God
8 what we shall do unto the *c'* that
12 How shall we order the *c'*, and
24 and the *c'* grew, and the Lord
Ru 4:16 Naomi took the *c'*, and laid it in
1Sa 1:11 unto thine handmaid a man *c'*,
22 I will not go up until the *c'* be
24 in Shiloh: and the *c'* was young,
25 and brought the *c'* to Eli.
27 For this *c'* I prayed; and the
2:11 the *c'* did minister unto the Lord
18 before the Lord, being a *c'*,
21 *c'* Samuel grew before the Lord.
26 And the *c'* Samuel grew on, and
3: 1 And the *c'* Samuel ministered
8 that the Lord had called the *c'*.
4:19 Phinehas' wife, was with *c'*, near
21 she named the *c'* I-chabod,
2Sa 6:23 the daughter of Saul had no *c'*
11: 5 told David, and said, I am with *c'*.
12:14 the *c'* also that is born unto thee
15 And the Lord struck the *c'* that
16 therefore besought God for the *c'*;
18 the seventh day, that the *c'* died.
18 to tell him that the *c'* was dead:
18 while the *c'* was yet alive, we
18 if we tell him that the *c'* is dead?
19 David perceived that the *c'* was
19 unto his servants, Is the *c'* dead?
21 thou didst fast and weep for the *c'*,
21 when the *c'* was dead, thou didst
22 While the *c'* was yet alive, I fasted
22 gracious to me, that the *c'* may live?
1Ki 3: 7 I am but a little *c'*: I know not
17 and I was delivered of a *c'* with her
19 this woman's *c'* died in the night;
20 and laid her dead *c'* in my bosom.
21 in the morning to give my *c'* suck,
1Ki 3:25 Divide the living *c'* in two, and
26 the woman whose the living *c'* was
26 O my Lord, give her the living *c'*,
27 Give her the living *c'*, and in no
11:17 Egypt; Hadad being yet a little *c'*.
13: 2 a *c'* shall be born unto the house
14: 3 what shall become of the *c'*.
12 enter into the city, the *c'* shall die.
17 threshold of the door, the *c'* died;
17:21 he stretched himself upon the *c'*
22 the soul of the *c'* came into him
23 Elijah took the *c'*, and brought
2Ki 4:14 Verily she hath no *c'*, and her
18 when the *c'* was grown, it fell on
26 is it well with the *c'*? And she
29 my staff upon the face of the *c'*.
30 the mother of the *c'* said, As the
31 laid the staff on the face of the *c'*;
31 him, saying, The *c'* is not awaked.
32 the *c'* was dead and laid upon his
34 he went up, and lay upon the *c'*,
34 stretched himself upon the *c'*;
34 the flesh of the *c'* waxed warm.
35 the *c'* sneezed seven times,
35 and the *c'* opened his eyes.
5:14 like unto the flesh of a little *c'*,
8:12 and rip up their women with *c'*.
15:16 women therein that were with *c'*
Job 3: 3 said, There is a man *c'* conceived.
Ps 131: 2 *c'* that is weaned of his mother:
2 my soul is even as a weaned *c'*.
Pr 20:11 a *c'* is known by his doings,
22: 6 Train up a *c'* in the way he
15 is bound in the heart of a *c'*;
23:13 Withhold not correction from the *c'*:
24 he that begetteth a wise *c'* shall
29:15 but a *c'* left to himself bringeth
21 his servant from a *c'* shall have
Ec 4: 8 he hath neither *c'* nor brother:
13 Better is a poor and a wise *c'*
15 the second *c'* that shall stand up
10:16 O land, when thy king is a *c'*,
11: 5 in the womb of her that is with *c'*:
Isa 3: 5 the *c'* shall behave himself
7:16 before the *c'* shall know to refuse
8: 4 the *c'* shall have knowledge to cry,
9: 6 unto us a *c'* is born, unto us a
10:19 shall be few, that a *c'* may write
11: 6 and a little *c'* shall lead them.
8 the sucking *c'* shall play on the
8 and the weaned *c'* shall put his
26:17 Like as a woman with *c'*, that
18 We have been with *c'*, we have
49:15 a woman forget her sucking *c'*,
54: 1 that didst not travail with *c'*:
65:20 the *c'* shall die an hundred years
66: 7 she was delivered of a man *c'*.
Jer 1: 6 I cannot speak: for I am a *c'*.
7 Say not, I am a *c'*: for thou shalt
4:31 that bringeth forth her first *c'*,
20:15 A man *c'* is born unto thee;
30: 6 a man doth travail with *c'*?
31: 8 the lame, the woman with *c'*
8 and her that travaileth with *c'*
20 dear son? Is he a pleasant *c'*?
44: 7 off from you man and woman, *c'*
La 4: 4 The tongue of the sucking *c'*
Hos 11: 1 When Israel was a *c'*, then I
13:16 women with *c'* shall be ripped up.
Am 1:13 have ripped up the women with *c'*
M't 1:18 with *c'* of the Holy Ghost.
23 a virgin shall be with *c'*,
2: 8 search diligently for the young *c'*;
9 stood over where the young *c'* was.
11 they saw the young *c'* with Mary
13 Arise, and take the young *c'* and
13 Herod will seek the young *c'* to
14 took the young *c'* and his mother
20 Arise, and take the young *c'* and
21 took the young *c'* and his mother,
10:21 and the father the *c'*: and the
17:18 *c'* was cured from that very hour.
18: 2 And Jesus called a little *c'* unto
4 humble himself as this little *c'*,
5 whoso shall receive one such little *c'*
23:15 twofold more the *c'* of hell than
24:19 them that are with *c'*,
M'r 9:21 unto him? And he said, Of a *c'*.
24 straightway the father of the *c'*
36 And he took a *c'*, and set him in
10:15 the kingdom of God as a little *c'*,
13:17 them that are with *c'*,
Lu 1: 7 And they had no *c'*, because that
59 they came to circumcise the *c'*;
66 What manner of *c'* shall this be!
76 And thou, *c'*, shalt be called the
80 the *c'* grew, and waxed strong
2: 5 wife, being great with *c'*.
17 was told them concerning this *c'*.
21 for the circumcising of the *c'*,
27 parents brought in the *c'* Jesus,
34 Behold, this *c'* is set for the fall
40 And the *c'* grew, and waxed strong
43 the *c'* Jesus tarried behind
9:38 my son: for he is mine only *c'*.
42 and healed the *c'*, and delivered
47 their heart, took a *c'*, and set him
48 Whosoever shall receive this *c'*
18:17 the kingdom of God as a little *c'*
21:23 them that are with *c'*,
Joh 4:49 Sir, come down ere my *c'* die.
16:21 soon as she is delivered of the *c'*,
Ac 4:27 against thy holy *c'* Jesus, whom
30 by the name of thy holy *c'* Jesus.
7: 5 him, when as yet he had no *c'*.
13:10 thou *c'* of the devil, thou enemy
1Co 13:11 When I was a *c'*, I spake as a *c'*,
11 I understood as a *c'*,
11 I thought as a *c'*:
Gal 4: 1 the heir, as long as he is a *c'*.
1Th 5: 3 upon a woman with *c'*;
2Ti 3:15 from a *c'* thou hast known the
Heb 11:11 and was delivered of a *c'* when
23 they saw he was a proper *c'*;
Re 12: 2 And she being with *c'*
4 to devour her *c'* as soon as it
5 she brought forth a man *c'*, who
5 her *c'* was caught up unto God,
13 which brought forth the man *c'*.

childbearing
1Ti 2:15 she shall be saved in *c'*, if they

childhood
1Sa 12: 2 walked before you from my *c'*
Ec 11:10 evil from thy flesh: for *c'* and

childish
1Co 13:11 a man, I put away *c'* things.

childless
Ge 15: 2 wilt thou give me, seeing I go *c'*,
Le 20:20 bear their sins; they shall die *c'*.
21 nakedness; they shall be *c'*.
1Sa 15:33 thy sword hath made women *c'*,
33 so shall thy mother be *c'*
Jer 22:30 Write ye this man *c'*, a man that
Lu 20:30 took her to wife, and he died *c'*.

children See also CHILDREN'S; MENCHILDREN.
Ge 3:16 sorrow thou shalt bring forth *c'*;
6: 4 and they bare *c'* to them, the same
10:21 *c'* of Eber, the brother of Japheth
21 the elder, even to him were *c'* born.
22 *c'* of Shem; Elam, and Asshur,
23 And the *c'* of Aram; Uz, and Hul,
11: 5 which the *c'* of men builded.
16: 1 Sarai Abram's wife bare him no *c'*:
2 that I may obtain *c'* by her.
18:19 he will command his *c'* and his
19:38 the father of the *c'* of Ammon
20:17 maidservants; and they bare *c'*.
21: 7 Sarah should have given *c'* suck?
22:20 also born *c'* unto thy brother
23: 5 *c'* of Heth answered Abraham,
7 the land, even to the *c'* of Heth.
10 dwelt among the *c'* of Heth:
10 in the audience of the *c'* of Heth,
18 in the presence of the *c'* of Heth,
25: 4 these were the *c'* of Keturah.
22 *c'* struggled together within her;
30: 1 she bare Jacob no *c'*, Rachel
1 Give me *c'*, or else I die.
3 that I may also have *c'* by her.
26 Give me my wives and my *c'*,
31:43 and these *c'* are my *c'*, and these
43 their *c'* which they have born?
32:11 me, and the mother with the *c'*.
32 Therefore the *c'* of Israel eat not
33: 1 the *c'* unto Leah, and unto Rachel,
2 handmaids and their *c'* foremost,
2 and Leah and her *c'* after,
5 and saw the women and the *c'*;
5 The *c'* which God hath graciously
6 came near, they and their *c'*,
7 Leah also with her *c'* came near,
13 knoweth that the *c'* are tender,
14 and the *c'* be able to endure,
19 at the hand of the *c'* of Hamor,
36:21 the *c'* of Seir in the land of Edom.
22 *c'* of Lotan were Hori and Hemam;
23 the *c'* of Shobal were these; Alvan,
24 *c'* of Zibeon; both Ajah, and Anah:
25 the *c'* of Anah were these; Dishon,
26 *c'* of Dishon; Hemdan, and Eshban,
27 *c'* of Ezer are these; Bilhan and
28 *c'* of Dishan are these; Uz, and
31 any king over the *c'* of Israel.
37: 3 loved Joseph more than all his *c'*,
42:36 bereaved of my *c'*: Joseph is not,
43:14 If I be bereaved of my *c'*, I am
45:10 and thy *c'*, and thy children's *c'*,
21 the *c'* of Israel did so: and Joseph
46: 8 the names of the *c'* of Israel,
49: 8 thy father's *c'* shall bow down
32 therein was from the *c'* of Heth.
50:23 saw Ephraim's *c'* of the third
23 *c'* also of Machir the son of Manasseh
25 took an oath of the *c'* of Israel,
Ex 1: 1 are the names of the *c'* of Israel,
7 And the *c'* of Israel were fruitful,
9 people of the *c'* of Israel are more
12 grieved because of the *c'* of Israel.
13 the *c'* of Israel to serve with rigour:
17 but saved the men *c'* alive.
18 have saved the men *c'* alive?
2: 6 This is one of the Hebrews' *c'*.
23 the *c'* of Israel sighed by reason
25 God looked upon the *c'* of Israel,
3: 9 the cry of the *c'* of Israel is come
10 the *c'* of Israel out of Egypt.
11 I should bring forth the *c'* of Israel
13 come unto the *c'* of Israel,
14 thou say unto the *c'* of Israel, I AM
15 thou say unto the *c'* of Israel, The
4:29 all the elders of the *c'* of Israel:
31 Lord had visited the *c'* of Israel,
5:14 the officers of the *c'* of Israel,
15 the *c'* of Israel came and cried
19 And the officers of the *c'* of Israel
6: 5 the groaning of the *c'* of Israel,
6 say unto the *c'* of Israel, I am the
9 Moses spake so unto the *c'* of
11 let the *c'* of Israel go out of his land.
12 *c'* of Israel have not hearkened

Ex 6:13 a charge unto the c' of Israel,
13 to bring the c' of Israel out of the
26 the c' of Israel from the land of
27 out the c' of Israel from Egypt:
7: 2 send the c' of Israel out of his land.
4 and my people the c' of Israel, out
5 bring out the c' of Israel from
9: 6 cattle of the c' of Israel died not
26 Goshen, where the c' of Israel were,
35 would he let the c' of Israel go;
10:20 would not let the c' of Israel go.
23 all the c' of Israel had light in their
11: 7 against any of the c' of Israel shall
10 would not let the c' of Israel go
12:26 when your c' shall say unto you,
27 over the houses of the c' of Israel
28 the c' of Israel went away,
31 both ye and the c' of Israel;
35 And the c' of Israel did according
37 the c' of Israel journeyed from
37 on foot that were men, beside c'.
40 the sojourning of the c' of Israel,
42 of all the c' of Israel in their
50 Thus did all the c' of Israel;
51 the Lord did bring the c' of Israel
13: 2 among the c' of Israel, both of
13 the firstborn of man among thy c'
15 the firstborn of my c' I redeem.
18 the c' of Israel went up harnessed
19 had straitly sworn the c' of Israel,
14: 2 Speak unto the c' of Israel, that
3 Pharaoh will say of the c' of Israel,
8 pursued after the c' of Israel: and
8 the c' of Israel went out with an
10 the c' of Israel lifted up their eyes,
10 c' of Israel cried out unto the Lord
15 c' of Israel, that they go forward:
16 c' of Israel shall go on dry ground
22 the c' of Israel went into the midst
29 But the c' of Israel walked upon
15: 1 sang Moses and the c' of Israel this
19 but the c' of Israel went on dry
16: 1 congregation of the c' of Israel
2 the c' of Israel murmured against
3 the c' of Israel said unto them,
6 Aaron said unto all the c' of Israel,
9 the c' of Israel, Come near before
10 the c' of Israel, that they looked
12 the murmurings of the c' of Israel:
15 when the c' of Israel saw it,
17 the c' of Israel did so, and gathered,
35 And the c' of Israel did eat manna
17: 1 congregation of the c' of Israel
3 kill us and our c' and our cattle
7 the chiding of the c' of Israel,
19: 1 when the c' of Israel were gone
3 and tell the c' of Israel;
6 shalt speak unto the c' of Israel.
20: 5 the fathers upon the c' unto
22 shalt say unto the c' of Israel,
21: 4 the wife and her c' shall be her
5 my master, my wife, and my c';
22:24 widows, and your c' fatherless.
24: 5 sent young men of the c' of Israel,
11 upon the nobles of the c' of Israel
17 mount in the eyes of the c' of Israel.
25: 2 Speak unto the c' of Israel, that
22 commandment unto the c' of Israel.
27:20 shalt command the c' of Israel,
21 on the behalf of the c' of Israel,
28: 1 among the c' of Israel, that he
9 them the names of the c' of Israel:
11 with the names of the c' of Israel:
12 stones of memorial unto the c' of
21 the c' of Israel, twelve, according
29 the c' of Israel in the breastplate
30 the judgment of the c' of Israel
38 which the c' of Israel shall hallow
29:28 for ever from the c' of Israel:
28 offering from the c' of Israel
43 I will meet with the c' of Israel,
45 I will dwell among the c' of Israel,
30:12 takest the sum of the c' of Israel
16 atonement money of the c' of Israel,
16 memorial unto the c' of Israel
31 speak unto the c' of Israel, saying,
31:13 thou also unto the c' of Israel,
16 c' of Israel shall keep the sabbath,
17 between me and the c' of Israel
32:20 made the c' of Israel drink of it.
28 the c' of Levi did according to
33: 5 Moses, Say unto the c' of Israel,
6 c' of Israel stripped themselves
34: 7 the fathers upon the c', and upon
7 the children's c', unto the third
23 [shall all your men c' appear]
30 all the c' of Israel saw Moses,
32 all the c' of Israel came nigh:
34 spake unto the c' of Israel that
35 c' of Israel saw the face of Moses,
35: 1 of the c' of Israel together, and said
4 congregation of the c' of Israel,
20 the c' of Israel departed from the
29 The c' of Israel brought a willing
30 Moses said unto the c' Israel,
36: 3 the c' of Israel had brought for
39: 6 graven, with the names of the c' of
7 for a memorial to the c' of Israel;
14 names of the c' of Israel, twelve,
32 the c' of Israel did according to
42 the c' of Israel made all the work.
40:36 the c' of Israel went onward in all
Le 1: 2 Speak unto the c' of Israel, and say
4: 2 Speak unto the c' of Israel, saying,
6:18 among the c' of Aaron shall eat
7:23, 29 Speak unto the c' of Israel,

Le 7:34 have I taken of the c' of Israel
34 ever from among the c' of Israel.
36 be given them of the c' of Israel,
38 he commanded the c' of Israel
9: 3 the c' of Israel thou shalt speak,
10:11 ye may teach the c' of Israel all
14 peace offerings of the c' of Israel.
11: 2 unto the c' of Israel, saying, These
12: 2 unto the c' of Israel, saying, If a
15: 2 Speak unto the c' of Israel, and say
31 shall ye separate the c' of Israel
16: 5 congregation of the c' of Israel two
16 of the uncleanness of the c' of Israel,
19 from the uncleanness of the c' of
21 the iniquities of the c' of Israel,
34 an atonement for the c' of Israel
17: 2 sons, and unto all the c' of Israel,
5 the c' of Israel may bring their
12 I said unto the c' of Israel,
13 whatsoever man there be of the c'
14 therefore I said unto the c' of
18: 2 c' of Israel, and say unto them, I
19: 2 c' of Israel, and say unto them, Ye
18 against the c' of thy people,
20: 2 say to the c' of Israel, Whosoever
2 he be of the c' of Israel, or of the
21:24 sons, and unto all the c' of Israel.
22: 2 the holy things of the c' of Israel,
3 c' of Israel hallow unto the Lord,
15 the holy things of the c' of Israel,
18 and unto all the the c' of Israel,
32 hallowed among the c' of Israel:
23: 2, 10 unto the c' of Israel, and say
24, 34 Speak unto the c' of Israel,
43 the c' of Israel to dwell in booths,
44 Moses declared unto the c' of
24: 2 the c' of Israel, that they bring
8 being taken from the c' of Israel
10 Egyptian, went out among the c' of
15 speak unto the c' of Israel, saying,
23 Moses spake to the c' of Israel,
23 the c' of Israel did as the Lord
25: 2 Speak unto the c' of Israel, and say
33 their possession among the c' of
41 both he and his c' with him, and
45 c' of the strangers that do sojourn
46 inheritance for your c' after you,
46 over your brethren the c' of Israel,
54 both he, and his c' with him.
55 me the c' of Israel are servants;
26:22 which shall rob you of your c',
46 him and the c' of Israel in mount
27: 2 c' of Israel, and say unto them,
34 for the c' of Israel in mount Sinai.
Nu 1: 2 congregation of the c' of Israel,
10 Of the c' of Joseph; of Ephraim;
20 c' of Reuben, Israel's eldest son,
22 c' of Simeon, by their generations,
24 c' of Gad, by their generations,
26 Of the c' of Judah, by their
28 Of the c' of Issachar, by their
30 Of the c' of Zebulun, by their
32 Of the c' of Joseph, namely,
32 Of the c' of Ephraim, by their
34 Of the c' of Manasseh, by their
36 Of the c' of Benjamin, by their
38 Of the c' of Dan,
40 Of the c' of Asher, by their
42 Of the c' of Naphtali, throughout
45 were numbered of the c' of Israel,
49 of them among the c' of Israel:
52 c' of Israel shall pitch their tents,
53 upon the congregation of the c' of
54 the c' of Israel did according to all
2: 2 man of the c' of Israel shall pitch
3 shall be captain of the c' of Judah.
5 be captain of the c' of Issachar.
7 be captain of the c' of Zebulun.
10 and the captain of the c' of Reuben
12 captain of the c' of Simeon shall be
20 the captain of the c' of Manasseh
25 captain of the c' of Dan shall be
27 captain of the c' of Asher shall be
29 the captain of the c' of Naphtali
32 were numbered of the c' of Israel
33 numbered among the c' of Israel;
34 the c' of Israel did according to all
3: 4 and they had no c': and Eleazar
8 the charge of the c' of Israel, to do
9 unto him out of the c' of Israel.
12 from among the c' of Israel instead
12 the matrix among the c' of Israel:
15 the c' of Levi after the house of
38 for the charge of the c' of Israel;
40 of the males of the c' of Israel
41 firstborn among the c' of Israel;
41 among the cattle of the c' of Israel
42 firstborn among the c' of Israel.
45 firstborn among the c' of Israel,
46 the firstborn of the c' of Israel,
50 the c' of Israel took he the money;
5: 2 Command the c' of Israel, that they
4 the c' of Israel did so, and put
4 unto Moses, so did the c' of Israel.
6 Speak unto the c' of Israel, When
9 the holy things of the c' of Israel,
12 unto the c' of Israel, and say
6: 2 unto the c' of Israel, and say
23 wise ye shall bless the c' of Israel,
27 put my name upon the c' of Israel;
7:24 prince of the c' of Zebulun, did
30 prince of the c' of Reuben, did offer:
36 prince of the c' of Simeon, did offer:
42 prince of the c' of Gad, offered:
48 prince of the c' of Ephraim, offered:
54 prince of the c' of Manasseh:

Nu 7:60 prince of the c' of Benjamin,
66 prince of the c' of Dan, offered:
72 prince of the c' of Asher, offered:
78 prince of the c' of Naphtali, offered:
8: 6 the Levites from among the c' of
9 whole assembly of the c' of Israel
10 c' of Israel shall put their hands
11 for an offering of the c' of Israel,
14 the Levites from among the c' of
16 me from among the c' of Israel;
16 of the firstborn of all the c' of
17 For all the firstborn of the c' of
18 for all the firstborn of the c' of
19 sons from among the c' of Israel,
19 do the service of the c' of Israel in
19 an atonement for the c' of Israel:
19 no plague among the c' of Israel,
19 when the c' of Israel come nigh
20 congregation of the c' of Israel,
20 so did the c' of Israel unto them.
9: 2 c' of Israel also keep the passover
4 Moses spake unto the c' of Israel,
5 Moses, so did the c' of Israel.
7 season among the c' of Israel?
10 unto the c' of Israel, saying, If any
17 after that the c' of Israel journeyed:
17 the c' of Israel pitched their tents.
18 the Lord the c' of Israel journeyed,
19 then the c' of Israel kept the charge
22 c' of Israel abode in their tents,
10:12 c' of Israel took their journeys
14 of the camp of the c' of Judah
15 the tribe of the c' of Issachar was
16 the tribe of the c' of Zebulun was
19 the c' of Simeon was Shelumiel
20 of the c' of Gad was Eliasaph the
22 of the camp of the c' of Ephraim
23 of the tribe of the c' of Manasseh
24 of the tribe of the c' of Benjamin
25 the camp of the c' of Dan set
26 the tribe of the c' of Asher was
27 tribe of the c' of Naphtali was
28 these were the journeyings of the c'
11: 4 and the c' of Israel also wept
13: 2 which I give unto the c' of Israel:
3 men were heads of the c' of Israel.
22 and Talmai, the c' of Anak, were.
24 which the c' of Israel cut down
26 c' of Israel, unto the wilderness of
28 moreover we saw the c' of Anak
32 had searched unto the c' of Israel
14: 2 c' of Israel murmured against
3 our wives and our c' should be a
5 congregation of the c' of Israel.
7 all the company of the c' of Israel,
10 before all the c' of Israel.
18 iniquity of the fathers upon the c'
27 heard the murmurings of the c' of
33 c' shall wander in the wilderness
39 sayings unto all the c' of Israel:
15: 2, 18 Speak unto the c' of Israel, and
25, 26 congregation of the c' of Israel,
29 that is born among the c' of Israel,
32 c' of Israel were in the wilderness,
38 Speak unto the c' of Israel, and say
16: 2 with certain of the c' of Israel,
27 and their sons, and their little c'.
38 be a sign unto the c' of Israel.
40 To be a memorial unto the c' of
41 all the congregation of the c' of
17: 2 Speak unto the c' of Israel, and take
5 me the murmurings of the c' of
6 spake unto the c' of Israel, and
9 before the Lord unto all the c' of
12 the c' of Israel spake unto Moses,
18: 5 any more upon the c' of Israel.
6 the Levites from among the c' of
8 hallowed things of the c' of Israel;
11 wave offering of the c' of Israel:
19 the c' of Israel offer unto the Lord,
20 inheritance among the c' of Israel.
21 behold, I have given the c' of Levi
22 Neither must the c' of Israel
23 among the c' of Israel they have no
24 But the tithes of the c' of Israel,
24 Among the c' of Israel they shall
26 When ye take of the c' of Israel
28 which ye receive of the c' of Israel;
32 the holy things of the c' of Israel,
19: 2 Speak unto the c' of Israel, that they
9 of the c' of Israel for a water of
10 it shall be unto the c' of Israel,
20: 1 Then came the c' of Israel, even
12 in the eyes of the c' of Israel,
13 because the c' of Israel strove with
19 the c' of Israel said unto him,
22 And the c' of Israel, even the
24 I have given unto the c' of Israel,
21:10 the c' of Israel set forward, and
24 even unto the c' of Ammon: for
24 the border of the c' of Ammon
22: 1 And the c' of Israel set forward,
3 was distressed because of the c' of
5 the land of the c' of his people,
24:17 and destroy all the c' of Sheth.
25: 6 one of the c' of Israel came and
6 the c' of Israel, who were weeping
8 plague was stayed from the c' of
11 wrath away from the c' of Israel,
11 I consumed not the c' of Israel
13 an atonement for the c' of Israel.
26: 2 the congregation of the c' of Israel,
4 Moses and the c' of Israel, which
5 c' of Reuben; Hanoch, of whom
11 Notwithstanding the c' of Korah
15 The c' of Gad after their families:

Nu 26:18 are the families of the c' of Gad
44 c' of Asher after their families:
51 the numbered of the c' of Israel,
62 numbered among the c' of Israel,
62 given them among the c' of Israel.
63 the c' of Israel in the plains of Moab
64 they numbered the c' of Israel in
27: 8 shalt speak unto the c' of Israel,
11 c' of Israel a statute of judgment,
12 I have given unto the c' of Israel.
20 the c' of Israel may be obedient.
21 and all the c' of Israel with him,
28: 2 Command the c' of Israel, and say
29:40 And Moses told the c' of Israel
30: 1 concerning the c' of Israel, saying,
31: 2 Avenge the c' of Israel of the
9 the c' of Israel took all the women
12 unto the c' of Israel, unto the camp
16 Behold, these caused the c' of
18 But all the women c', that have
30, 42 And of the c' of Israel's half,
47 even of the c' of Israel's half, Moses
54 for a memorial for the c' of Israel
32: 1 Now the c' of Reuben and the
1 and the c' of Gad had a very
2 c' of Gad and the c' of Reuben came
6 Moses said unto the c' of Gad and
6 of Gad and to the c' of Reuben,
7 the heart of the c' of Israel from
9 the heart of the c' of Israel, that
17 ready armed before the c' of Israel,
18 until the c' of Israel have inherited
25 the c' of Gad and the c' of Reuben
28 of the tribes of the c' of Israel:
29 If the c' of Gad and the c' of Reuben
31 the c' of Gad and the c' of Reuben
33 even to the c' of Gad, and to the
33 and to the c' of Reuben,
34 And the c' of Gad built Dibon,
37 the c' of Reuben built Heshbon,
39 c' of Machir the son of Manasseh
33: 1 are the journeys of the c' of Israel,
3 the c' of Israel went out with an
5 c' of Israel removed from Rameses,
38 after the c' of Israel were come
40 of the coming of the c' of Israel.
51 Speak unto the c' of Israel, and
34: 2 Command the c' of Israel, and
13 Moses commanded the c' of Israel,
14 for the tribe of the c' of Reuben
14 and the tribe of the c' of Gad
20 And of the tribe of the c' of Simeon,
22 prince of the tribe of the c' of Dan,
23 The prince of the c' of Joseph,
23 of the tribe of the c' of Manasseh,
24 of the tribe of the c' of Ephraim,
25 of the tribe of the c' of Zebulun,
26 of the tribe of the c' of Issachar,
27 of the tribe of the c' of Asher,
28 of the tribe of the c' of Naphtali,
29 inheritance unto the c' of Israel
35: 2 Command the c' of Israel, that they
8 the possession of the c' of Israel:
10 Speak unto the c' of Israel, and
15 a refuge, both for the c' of Israel,
34 Lord dwell among the c' of Israel.
36: 1 families of the c' of Gilead, the son
1 chief fathers of the c' of Israel:
2 for an inheritance by lot to the c' of
3 the other tribes of the c' of Israel,
4 the jubile of the c' of Israel shall
5 Moses commanded the c' of Israel
7 the inheritance of the c' of Israel
7 every one of the c' of Israel shall
8 any tribe of the c' of Israel, shall
8 that the c' of Israel may enjoy
9 the tribes of the c' of Israel shall
13 hand of Moses unto the c' of Israel
De 1: 3 Moses spake unto the c' of Israel,
36 and to his c', because he hath
39 and your c', which in that day had
2: 4 your brethren the c' of Esau,
8 from our brethren the c' of Esau,
9 unto the c' of Lot for a possession.
12 the c' of Esau succeeded them,
19 nigh over against the c' of Ammon,
19 the land of the c' of Ammon any
19 unto the c' of Lot for a possession.
22 As he did to the c' of Esau, which
29 the c' of Esau which dwell in Seir,
37 the c' of Ammon thou camest not,
3: 6 men, women, and c', of every city.
11 in Rabbath of the c' of Ammon?
16 is the border of the c' of Ammon;
18 your brethren the c' of Israel, all
4:10 and that they may teach their c'.
25 shalt beget c', and children's c',
40 with thee, and with thy c' after
44 Moses set before the c' of Israel:
45 Moses spake unto the c' of Israel,
46 whom Moses and the c' of Israel
5: 9 iniquity of the fathers upon the c'
29 them, and with their c' for ever!
6: 7 teach them diligently unto thy c',
9: 2 and tall, the c' of the Anakims,
2 can stand before the c' of Anak!
10: 6 the c' of Israel took their journey
6 from Beeroth of the c' of Jaakan
11: 2 for I speak not with your c' which
19 ye shall teach them your c',
21 the days of your c', in the land
12:25 thy c' after thee, when thou shalt
28 well with thee, and with thy c'
13:13 Certain men, the c' of Belial, are
14: 1 are the c' of the Lord your God:
17:20 and his c', in the midst of Israel.

De 21:15 hated, and they have born him c',
23: 8 The c' that are begotten of them
24: 7 of his brethren of the c' of Israel,
16 shall not be put to death for the c',
16 neither shall the c' be put to death
54 remnant of his c' which he shall
55 flesh of his c' whom he shall eat:
57 toward her c' which she shall bear:
29: 1 with the c' of Israel in the land
22 the generation to come of your c'
29 unto us and to our c' for ever,
30: 2 thee this day, thou and thy c',
31:12 men, and women, and c',
13 And that their c', which have not
19 and teach it the c' of Israel:
19 for me against the c' of Israel.
22 and taught it the c' of Israel.
23 thou shalt bring the c' of Israel
32: 5 their spot is not the spot of his c':
8 according to the number of the c'
20 generation, c' in whom is no faith.
46 command your c' to observe to do,
49 which I give unto the c' of Israel
51 among the c' of Israel at the waters,
51 in the midst of the c' of Israel.
52 land which I give the c' of Israel.
33: 1 blessed the c' of Israel before his
9 his brethren, nor knew his own c':
24 Let Asher be blessed with c';
34: 8 the c' of Israel wept for Moses
9 c' of Israel hearkened unto him,
Jos 1: 2 to them, even to the c' of Israel.
2: 2 men in hither to night of the c' of
3: 1 he and all the c' of Israel, and
9 Joshua said unto the c' of Israel,
4: 4 he had prepared of the c' of Israel,
5 of the tribes of the c' of Israel:
6 your c' ask their fathers in time
7 a memorial unto the c' of Israel
8 the c' of Israel did so as Joshua
8 of the tribes of the c' of Israel,
12 And the c' of Reuben, and the
12 of Reuben, and the c' of Gad,
12 over armed before the c' of Israel,
21 he spake unto the c' of Israel,
21 saying, When your c' shall ask
22 ye shall let your c' know, saying,
5: 1 Jordan from before the c' of Israel,
1 more, because of the c' of Israel.
2 circumcise again the c' of Israel
3 circumcised the c' of Israel at the
6 the c' of Israel walked forty years
7 And their c', whom he raised up
10 c' of Israel encamped in Gilgal,
12 neither had the c' of Israel manna
6: 1 shut up because of the c' of Israel:
7: 1 c' of Israel committed a trespass
1 kindled against the c' of Israel.
12 the c' of Israel could not stand
23 unto all the c' of Israel, and laid
8:31 Lord commanded the c' of Israel,
32 in the presence of the c' of Israel.
9:17 the c' of Israel journeyed, and
18 the c' of Israel smote them not,
26 out of the hand of the c' of Israel,
10: 4 peace with Joshua and with the c'
11 the c' of Israel slew with the sword.
12 Amorites before the c' of Israel,
20 the c' of Israel had made an end
21 against any of the c' of Israel.
11:14 the c' of Israel took for a prey
19 made peace with the c' of Israel,
22 Anakims left in the land of the c'
12: 1 which the c' of Israel smote,
2 the border of the c' of Ammon;
6 Lord and the c' of Israel smite:
7 Joshua and the c' of Israel smote
13: 6 will I drive out from before the c'
10 the border of the c' of Ammon;
13 the c' of Israel expelled not the
15 the tribe of the c' of Reuben
22 soothsayer, did the c' of Israel slay
23 the border of the c' of Reuben
23 inheritance of the c' of Reuben
24 unto the c' of Gad according to
25 the land of the c' of Ammon,
28 the inheritance of the c' of Gad
29 half tribe of the c' of Manasseh
31 unto the c' of Machir the son of
31 the one half of the c' of Machir
14: 1 which the c' of Israel inherited
1 of the tribes of the c' of Israel,
4 the c' of Joseph were two tribes,
5 Moses, so the c' of Israel did,
6 Then the c' of Judah came unto
10 while the c' of Israel wandered
15: 1 the tribe of the c' of Judah
12 the coast of the c' of Judah
13 gave a part among the c' of Judah,
14 and Talmai, the c' of Anak.
20 inheritance of the . . . c' of Judah
21 cities of the tribe of the c' of Judah
63 the c' of Judah could not drive
63 Jebusites dwell with the c' of Judah
16: 1 the lot of the c' of Joseph fell
4 So the c' of Joseph, Manasseh
5 the border of the c' of Ephraim
8 of the tribe of the c' of Ephraim
9 separate cities for the c' of Ephraim
9 inheritance of the c' of Manasseh,
17: 2 c' of Manasseh by their families;
2 for the c' of Abiezer,
2 and for the c' of Helek,
2 and for the c' of Asriel,
2 and for the c' of Shechem,
2 and for the c' of Hepher,

Jos 17: 2 and for the c' of Shemida:
2 these were the male c' of Manasseh
8 belonged to the c' of Ephraim;
12 the c' of Manasseh could not drive
13 when the c' of Israel were waxen
14 c' of Joseph spake unto Joshua,
16 the c' of Joseph said, The hill
18: 1 c' of Israel assembled together
2 remained among the c' of Israel
3 Joshua said unto the c' of Israel,
10 the land unto the c' of Israel
11 the tribe of the c' of Benjamin
11 between the c' of Judah and the
11 of Judah and the c' of Joseph.
14 a city of the c' of Judah:
20 the c' of Benjamin, by the coasts
21 of the tribe of the c' of Benjamin
28 inheritance of the c' of Benjamin
19: 1 c' of Simeon according to their
1 the inheritance of the c' of Judah.
8 of the tribe of the c' of Simeon
9 the portion of the c' of Judah was
9 the inheritance of the c' of Simeon:
9 for the part of the c' of Judah was
9 therefore the c' of Simeon had
10 came up for the c' of Zebulun
16 inheritance of the c' of Zebulun
17 Issachar, for the c' of Issachar
23 the tribe of the c' of Issachar
24 the c' of Asher according to their
31 the tribe of the c' of Asher
32 came out to the c' of Naphtali,
32 even for the c' of Naphtali
39 the tribe of the c' of Naphtali
40 out for the tribe of the c' of Dan
47 the coast of the c' of Dan went out
47 c' of Dan went up to fight against
48 the c' of Dan according to their
49 c' of Israel gave an inheritance
51 of the tribes of the c' of Israel,
20: 2 Speak to the c' of Israel, saying,
9 appointed for all the c' of Israel,
21: 1 of the tribes of the c' of Israel;
3 c' of Israel gave unto the Levites
4 the c' of Aaron the priest, which
5 And the rest of the c' of Kohath
6 And the c' of Gershon had by lot
7 The c' of Merari by their families
8 the c' of Israel gave by lot unto
9 out of the tribe of the c' of Judah,
9 out of the tribe of the c' of Simeon,
10 Which the c' of Aaron, being of
10 of the c' of Levi, had: for theirs
13 Thus they gave to the c' of Aaron
19 the cities of the c' of Aaron,
20 families of the c' of Kohath, the
20 which remained of the c' of Kohath,
26 the c' of Kohath that remained.
27 And unto the c' of Gershon, of the
34 families of the c' of Merari, the
40 the c' of Merari by their families,
41 the possession of the c' of Israel
22: 9 And the c' of Reuben
9 and the c' of Gad and the half
9 and departed from the c' of Israel
10 the c' of Reuben and the c' of Gad
11 And the c' of Israel heard say,
11 Behold the c' of Reuben
11 and the c' of Gad and the half
11 at the passage of the c' of Israel.
12 when the c' of Israel heard of it,
12 congregation of the c' of Israel
13 And the c' of Israel sent unto
13 sent unto the c' of Reuben,
13 of Reuben, and to the c' of Gad,
15 they came unto the c' of Reuben,
15 of Reuben, and to the c' of Gad,
21 Then the c' of Reuben and the
21 and the c' of Gad and the half
24 your c' might speak unto our c',
25 ye c' of Reuben and c' of Gad; ye
25 so shall your c' make our c' cease
27 your c' may not say to our c' in time
30 that the c' of Reuben and the
30 of Reuben and the c' of Gad
30 and the c' of Manasseh spake,
31 priest said unto the c' of Reuben,
31 and to the c' of Gad,
31 and to the c' of Manasseh, This
31 ye have delivered the c' of Israel
32 returned from the c' of Reuben,
32 and from the c' of Gad,
32 to the c' of Israel, and brought
33 the thing pleased the c' of Israel;
33 and the c' of Israel blessed God,
33 the c' of Reuben and Gad dwelt.
34 And the c' of Reuben and
34 the c' of Gad called the altar Ed:
24: 4 Jacob and his c' went down into
32 which the c' of Israel brought up
32 the inheritance of the c' of Joseph.
J'g 1: 1 the c' of Israel asked the Lord,
8 Now the c' of Judah had fought
9 afterward the c' of Judah went
16 And the c' of the Kenite, Moses'
16 the c' of Judah into the wilderness
21 And the c' of Benjamin did not
21 dwell with the c' of Benjamin
34 the Amorites forced the c' of Dan
2: 4 words unto all the c' of Israel,
6 the c' of Israel went every man
11 the c' of Israel did evil in the sight
3: 2 the generations of the c' of Israel
5 the c' of Israel dwelt among the
7 And the c' of Israel did evil
8 and the c' of Israel served

J'g 3: 9 And when the c' of Israel cried
9 up a deliverer to the c' of Israel,
12 the c' of Israel did evil again
13 gathered unto him the c' of Ammon
14 c' of Israel served Eglon the king
15 c' of Israel cried unto the Lord,
15 the c' of Israel sent a present unto
27 c' of Israel went down with him
4: 1 the c' of Israel again did evil
3 c' of Israel cried unto the Lord:
3 oppressed the c' of Israel.
5 the c' of Israel came up to her
6 men of the c' of Naphtali and of
6 and of the c' of Zebulun?
11 the c' of Hobab the father in law
23 of Canaan before the c' of Israel.
24 hand of the c' of Israel prospered.
6: 1 c' of Israel did evil in the sight of
2 c' of Israel made them the dens
3 and the c' of the east, even they
6 c' of Israel cried unto the Lord.
7 when the c' of Israel cried unto
8 sent a prophet unto the c' of Israel,
33 and the c' of the east were gathered
7:12 the c' of the east lay along
8:10 the hosts of the c' of the east:
18 one resembled the c' of a king.
28 subdued before the c' of Israel,
33 the c' of Israel turned again, and
34 c' of Israel remembered not the
10: 6 the c' of Israel did evil again
6 the gods of the c' of Ammon,
7 the hands of the c' of Ammon.
8 and oppressed the c' of Israel:
8 the c' of Israel that were on the
9 c' of Ammon passed over Jordan
10 the c' of Israel cried unto the Lord,
11 Lord said unto the c' of Israel,
11 Amorites, from the c' of Ammon,
15 the c' of Israel said unto the Lord,
17 the c' of Ammon were gathered
17 c' of Israel assembled themselves
18 to fight against the c' of Ammon?
11: 4 that the c' of Ammon made war
5 the c' of Ammon made war against
6 may fight with the c' of Ammon.
8 and fight against the c' of Ammon,
9 to fight against the c' of Ammon,
12 king of the c' of Ammon, saying,
13 king of the c' of Ammon answered
14 unto the king of the c' of Ammon:
15 nor the land of the c' of Ammon:
27 c' of Israel and the c' of Ammon.
28 of the c' of Ammon hearkened not
29 passed over unto the c' of Ammon.
30 the c' of Ammon into mine hands,
31 in peace from the c' of Ammon,
32 passed over unto the c' of Ammon
33 Thus the c' of Ammon were subdued
33 before the c' of Israel.
36 enemies, even of the c' of Ammon.
12: 1 to fight against the c' of Ammon,
2 great strife with the c' of Ammon;
3 the c' of Ammon, and the Lord
13: 1 the c' of Israel did evil again
14:16 a riddle unto the c' of my people,
17 the riddle to the c' of her people.
18: 2 the c' of Dan sent of their family
16 were of the c' of Dan, stood by
22 and overtook the c' of Dan.
23 they cried unto the c' of Dan.
25 c' of Dan said unto him, Let not
26 the c' of Dan went their way:
30 the c' of Dan set up the graven
19:12 that is not of the c' of Israel;
30 the day that the c' of Israel came
20: 1 Then all the c' of Israel went out,
3 the c' of Benjamin heard that the
3 c' of Israel were gone up to Mizpeh.)
3 Then said the c' of Israel,
7 Behold, ye are all c' of Israel;
13 c' of Belial, which are in Gibeah,
13 c' of Benjamin would not hearken
13 of their brethren the c' of Israel:
14 But the c' of Benjamin gathered
14 to battle against the c' of Israel.
15 the c' of Benjamin were numbered
18 the c' of Israel arose, and went up
18 battle against the c' of Benjamin?
19 the c' of Israel rose up in the
21 the c' of Benjamin came forth
23 the c' of Israel went up and wept
23 against the c' of Benjamin my
24 the c' of Israel came near against
24 the c' of Benjamin the second day,
25 to the ground of the c' of Israel
26 the c' of Israel, and all the people,
27 c' of Israel enquired of the Lord,
28 the c' of Benjamin my brother,
30 c' of Israel went up against the
30 c' of Benjamin on the third day,
31 c' of Benjamin went out against
32 the c' of Benjamin said, They are
32 the c' of Israel said, Let us flee,
35 the c' of Israel destroyed of the
36 So the c' of Benjamin saw that
48 again upon the c' of Benjamin,
21: 5 the c' of Israel said, Who is there
6 the c' of Israel repented them for
10 sword with the women and the c'.
13 to speak to the c' of Benjamin
18 c' of Israel have sworn, saying,
20 commanded the c' of Benjamin,
23 the c' of Benjamin did so, and
24 the c' of Israel departed thence
1Sa 1: 2 and Peninnah had c',
1Sa 1: 3 but Hannah had no c'.
2: 5 hath many c' is waxed feeble.
28 made by fire of the c' of Israel?
7: 4 c' of Israel did put away Baalim
6 judged the c' of Israel in Mizpeh.
7 Philistines heard that the c' of
7 And when the c' of Israel heard it,
8 the c' of Israel said to Samuel,
9: 2 was not among the c' of Israel
10:18 And said unto the c' of Israel,
27 the c' of Belial said, How shall
11: 8 the c' of Israel were three hundred
12:12 the king of the c' of Ammon
14:18 at that time with the c' of Israel.
47 and against the c' of Ammon,
15: 6 kindness to all the c' of Israel,
16:11 unto Jesse, Are here all thy c'?
17:53 c' of Israel returned from chasing
22:19 and women, c' and sucklings,
26:19 the c' of men, cursed be they
30:22 to every man his wife and his c',
2Sa 1:18 bade them teach the c' of Judah
2:25 the c' of Benjamin gathered
4: 2 Beerothite, of the c' of Benjamin:
7: 6 up the c' of Israel out of Egypt,
7 walked with all the c' of Israel
10 the c' of wickedness afflict them
7:14 with the stripes of the c' of men:
8:12 c' of Ammon, and of the Philistines,
10: 1 the king of the c' of Ammon died,
2 into the land of the c' of Ammon.
3 the c' of Ammon said unto Hanun
6 when the c' of Ammon saw that
6 the c' of Ammon sent and hired
8 the c' of Ammon came out, and
10 in array against the c' of Ammon.
11 if the c' of Ammon be too strong
14 c' of Ammon saw that the Syrians
14 returned from the c' of Ammon,
19 feared to help the c' of Ammon
11: 1 they destroyed the c' of Ammon,
12: 3 together with him, and with his c';
9 the sword of the c' of Ammon.
26 Rabbah of the c' of Ammon,
31 all the cities of the c' of Ammon.
17:27 of Rabbah of the c' of Ammon,
21: 2 were not of the c' of Israel,
2 c' of Israel had sworn unto them:
2 zeal to the c' of Israel and Judah.)
23:29 of Gibeah of the c' of Benjamin,
1Ki 2: 4 If thy c' take heed to their way,
4:30 the wisdom of all the c' of the east
6: 1 the c' of Israel were come out of
13 I will dwell among the c' of Israel,
8: 1 of the fathers of the c' of Israel,
9 a covenant with the c' of Israel,
25 that thy c' take heed to their way,
39 the hearts of all the c' of men;
63 and all the c' of Israel dedicated
9: 6 from following me, ye or your c',
20 which were not of the c' of Israel,
21 Their c' that were left after them in
21 in the land, whom the c' of Israel
22 the c' of Israel did Solomon make
11: 2 Lord said unto the c' of Israel,
7 abomination of the c' of Ammon.
33 the god of the c' of Ammon,
12:17 But as for the c' of Israel which
24 your brethren the c' of Israel:
33 a feast unto the c' of Israel:
14:24 cast out before the c' of Israel.
18:20 Ahab sent unto all the c' of Israel,
19:10 the c' of Israel have forsaken thy
14 because the c' of Israel have
20: 3 thy wives also and thy c', even the
5 thy gold, and thy wives, and thy c';
7 me for my wives, and for my c',
15 c' of Israel, being seven thousand,
27 the c' of Israel were numbered,
27 c' of Israel pitched before them
29 the c' of Israel slew of the Syrians
21:13 came in two men, c' of Belial,
26 cast out before the c' of Israel.
2Ki 2:23 came forth little c' out of the city,
24 and tare forty and two c' of them.
4: 7 live thou and thy c' of the rest.
8:12 wilt do unto the c' of Israel:
12 and wilt dash their c', and rip
19 him alway a light, and to his c',
9: 1 one of the c' of the prophets,
10: 1 them that brought up Ahab's c',
5 and the bringers up of the c'
13 down to salute the c' of the king
13 and the c' of the queen.
30 thy c' of the fourth generation
13: 5 the c' of Israel dwelt in their tents,
14: 6 But the c' of the murderers he
6 shall not be put to death for the c',
6 nor the c' be put to death for the
16: 3 Lord cast out from before the c'
17: 7 that the c' of Israel had sinned
8 the Lord cast out from before the c'
9 the c' of Israel did secretly those
22 c' of Israel walked in all the sins
24 Samaria instead of the c' of Israel:
31 Sepharvites burnt their c' in fire
34 Lord commanded the c' of Jacob,
41 their c', and their children's c':
18: 4 the c' of Israel did burn incense
19: 3 for the c' are come to the birth,
12 and the c' of Eden which were in
21: 2 cast out before the c' of Israel.
9 destroyed before the c' of Israel.
23: 6 the graves of the c' of the people.
10 in the valley of the c' of Hinnom,
13 abomination of the c' of Ammon,
2Ki 24: 2 bands of the c' of Ammon, and
1Ch 1:43 king reigned over the c' of Israel;
2:10 Nahshon, prince of the c' of Judah
18 Caleb the son of Hezron begat c'
30 Appaim: but Seled died without c'
31 And the c' of Sheshan; Ahlai.
32 and Jether died without c'.
4:27 his brethren had not many c',
27 multiply, like to the c' of Judah.
5:11 And the c' of Gad dwelt over
14 These are the c' of Abihail the
23 c' of the half tribe of Manasseh
6: 3 c' of Amram; Aaron, and Moses,
33 are they that waited with their c'.
64 the c' of Israel gave to the Levites
65 the tribe of the c' of Judah, and
65 of the tribe of the c' of Simeon,
65 of the tribe of the c' of Benjamin,
77 Unto the rest of the c' of Merari
7:12 and Huppim, the c' of Ir, and
29 the borders of the c' of Manasseh,
29 dwelt the c' of Joseph the son of
33 These are the c' of Japhlet.
40 All these were the c' of Asher,
8: 8 And Shaharaim begat c' in the
9: 3 dwelt of the c' of Judah,
3 and of the c' of Benjamin,
3 and of the c' of Ephraim,
4 the c' of Pharez the son of Judah.
18 in the companies of the c' of Levi.
23 and their c' had the oversight
11:31 Gibeah, that pertained to the c' of
12:16 there came of the c' of Benjamin
24 The c' of Judah that bare shield
25 Of the c' of Simeon, mighty men
26 Of the c' of Levi four thousand
29 And of the c' of Benjamin, the
30 the c' of Ephraim twenty thousand
32 of the c' of Issachar, which were
14: 4 these are the names of his c'
15: 4 David assembled the c' of Aaron,
15 the c' of the Levites bare the ark
16:13 ye c' of Jacob, his chosen ones.
17: 9 neither shall the c' of wickedness
18:11 Moab, and from the c' of Ammon,
19: 1 king of the c' of Ammon died,
2 into the land of the c' of Ammon
3 the princes of the c' of Ammon
6 when the c' of Ammon saw that
6 the c' of Ammon sent a thousand
7 And the c' of Ammon gathered
9 the c' of Ammon came out, and put
11 in array against the c' of Ammon.
12 if the c' of Ammon be too strong
15 c' of Ammon saw that the Syrians
19 the Syrians help the c' of Ammon
20: 1 the country of the c' of Ammon,
3 all the cities of the c' of Ammon.
4 that was of the c' of the giant:
24: 2 before their father, and had no c':
26:10 Hosah, of the c' of Merari, had
27: 1 the c' of Israel after their number,
3 Of the c' of Perez was the chief
10 the Pelonite, of the c' of Ephraim:
14 Pirathonite, of the c' of Ephraim:
20 Of the c' of Ephraim, Hoshea the
28: 8 inheritance for your c' after you
2Ch 5: 2 of the fathers of the c' of Israel,
10 a covenant with the c' of Israel,
6:11 that he made with the c' of Israel.
16 yet so that thy c' take heed to
30 knowest the hearts of the c' of men:)
7: 3 all the c' of Israel saw how the fire
8: 2 caused the c' of Israel to dwell
8 of their c', who were left after
8 whom the c' of Israel consumed
9 of the c' of Israel did Solomon
10:17 as for the c' of Israel that dwelt
18 and the c' of Israel stoned him
11:19 Which bare him c'; Jeush, and
23 wisely, and dispersed of all his c'
13: 7 unto him vain men, the c' of Belial,
12 O c' of Israel, fight ye not against
16 the c' of Israel fled before Judah:
18 the c' of Israel were brought
18 the c' of Judah prevailed, because
20: 1 c' of Moab, and the c' of Ammon,
10 the c' of Ammon and Moab and
13 little ones, their wives, and their c'.
19 of the c' of the Kohathites,
19 and of the c' of the Korhites,
22 against the c' of Ammon, Moab,
23 the c' of Ammon and Moab stood
21:14 people, and thy c', and thy wives,
25: 4 But he slew not their c', but did
4 The fathers shall not die for the c',
4 neither shall the c' die for the
7 to wit, with all the c' of Ephraim.
11 of the c' of Seir ten thousand.
12 the c' of Judah carry away captive,
14 brought the gods of the c' of Seir,
27: 5 the c' of Ammon gave him the
5 So much did the c' of Ammon pay
28: 3 burnt his c' in the fire, after the
3 had cast out before the c' of Israel.
8 c' of Israel carried away captive
10 to keep under the c' of Judah
12 the heads of the c' of Ephraim,
30: 6 Ye c' of Israel, turn again unto
9 your brethren and your c' shall
21 the c' of Israel that were present
31: 1 Then all the c' of Israel returned,
5 c' of Israel brought in abundance
6 And concerning the c' of Israel
33: 2 had cast out before the c' of Israel.
6 caused his c' to pass through the

2Ch 33: 9 Lord had destroyed before the c' of
34:33 that pertained to the c' of Israel,
35:17 the c' of Israel that were present
Ezr 2: 1 Now these are the c' of the province
3 c' of Parosh, two thousand an
4 c' of Shephatiah, three hundred
5 c' of Arah, seven hundred seventy
6 The c' of Pahath-moab, of the
6 of the c' of Jeshua and Joab, two
7 The c' of Elam, a thousand two
8 The c' of Zattu, nine hundred forty
9 The c' of Zaccai, seven hundred and
10 The c' of Bani, six hundred forty
11 The c' of Bebai, six hundred twenty
12 The c' of Azgad, a thousand two
13 The c' of Adonikam, six hundred
14 The c' of Bigvai, two thousand fifty
15 The c' of Adin, four hundred fifty
16 The c' of Ater of Hezekiah, ninety
17 The c' of Bezai, three hundred
18 The c' of Jorah, an hundred and
19 The c' of Hashum, two hundred
20 The c' of Gibbar, ninety and five.
21 The c' of Beth-lehem, an hundred
24 The c' of Azmaveth, forty and two.
25 The c' of Kirjath-arim, Chephirah,
26 The c' of Ramah and Gaba, six
29 The c' of Nebo, fifty and two.
30 The c' of Magbish, an hundred fifty
31 The c' of the other Elam, a thousand
32 The c' of Harim, three hundred and
33 The c' of Lod, Hadid, and Ono, seven
34 The c' of Jericho, three hundred
35 The c' of Senaah, three thousand
36 The priests: the c' of Jedaiah, of
37 The c' of Immer, a thousand fifty
38 The c' of Pashur, a thousand two
39 The c' of Harim, a thousand and
40 the c' of Jeshua and Kadmiel,
40 of the c' of Hodaviah, seventy
41 The singers: the c' of Asaph, an
42 The c' of the porters: the
42 the c' of Shallum, the c' of Ater,
42 the c' of Talmon, the c' of Akkub,
42 the c' of Hatita, the c' of Shobai,
43 the c' of Ziha, the c' of Hasupha,
43 the c' of Tabbaoth, in all an
44 The c' of Keros, the c' of Siaha,
44 the c' of Padon,
45 The c' of Lebanah,
45 the c' of Hagabah,
45 the c' of Akkub,
46 The c' of Hagab, the c' of Shalmai,
46 the c' of Hanan,
47 The c' of Giddel, the c' of Gahar,
47 the c' of Reaiah,
48 The c' of Rezin, the c' of Nekoda,
48 the c' of Gazzam,
49 The c' of Uzza, the c' of Paseah,
49 the c' of Besai,
50 The c' of Asnah, the c' of Mehunim,
50 the c' of Nephusim,
51 The c' of Bakbuk, the c' of Hakupha,
51 the c' of Harhur,
52 The c' of Bazluth, the c' of Mehida,
52 the c' of Harsha,
53 The c' of Barkos, the c' of Sisera,
53 the c' of Thamah,
54 The c' of Neziah, the c' of Hatipha.
55 The c' of Solomon's servants:
55 the c' of Sotai, the c' of Sophereth,
55 the c' of Peruda,
56 The c' of Jaalah, the c' of Darkon,
56 the c' of Giddel,
57 The c' of Shephatiah,
57 the c' of Hattil,
57 the c' of Pochereth of Zebaim,
57 the c' of Ami.
58 and the c' of Solomon's servants,
60 The c' of Delaiah, the c' of Tobiah,
60 the c' of Nekoda,
61 And of the c' of the priests:
61 the c' of Habaiah, the c' of Koz,
61 the c' of Barzillai;
3: 1 and the c' of Israel were in the
4: 1 heard that the c' of the captivity
6:16 And the c' of Israel, the priests,
16 the rest of the c' of the captivity,
19 the c' of the captivity kept the
20 for all the c' of the captivity, and
21 And the c' of Israel, which were
7: 7 went up some of the c' of Israel,
8:35 c' of those that had been carried
9:12 an inheritance to your c' forever.
10: 1 of men and women and c':
7 unto all the c' of the captivity,
16 the c' of the captivity did so.
44 and wives by whom they had c'.
Ne 1: 6 for the c' of Israel thy servants,
6 confess the sins of the c' of Israel,
2:10 seek the welfare of the c' of Israel.
5: 5 our c' as their c': and, lo, we bring
7: 6 These are the c' of the province,
8 The c' of Parosh, two thousand
9 The c' of Shephatiah, three
10 The c' of Arah, six hundred fifty
11 The c' of Pahath-moab, of the
11 c' of Jeshua and Joab,
12 The c' of Elam, a thousand two
13 The c' of Zattu, eight hundred
14 The c' of Zaccai, seven hundred
15 The c' of Binnui, six hundred
16 The c' of Bebai, six hundred
17 The c' of Azgad, two thousand
18 The c' of Adonikam, six hundred
19 The c' of Bigvai, two thousand

Ne 7:20 The c' of Adin, six hundred fifty
21 The c' of Ater of Hezekiah, ninety
22 The c' of Hashum, three hundred
23 The c' of Bezai, three hundred
24 The c' of Hariph, an hundred
25 The c' of Gibeon, ninety and five.
34 The c' of the other Elam,
35 The c' of Harim, three hundred
36 The c' of Jericho, three hundred
37 The c' of Lod, Hadid, and Ono,
38 The c' of Senaah, three thousand
39 the c' of Jedaiah, of the house of
40 The c' of Immer, a thousand
41 The c' of Pashur, a thousand
42 The c' of Harim, a thousand
43 the c' of Jeshua of Kadmiel, and
43 of the c' of Hodevah, seventy and
44 the c' of Asaph, an hundred forty
45 the c' of Shallum, the c' of Ater,
45 the c' of Talmon, the c' of Akkub,
45 the c' of Hatita, the c' of Shobai,
46 the c' of Ziha, the c' of Hashupha,
46 the c' of Tabbaoth,
47 The c' of Keros, the c' of Sia,
47 the c' of Padon,
48 The c' of Lebana, the c' of Hagaba,
48 the c' of Shalmai,
49 The c' of Hanan, the c' of Giddel,
49 the c' of Gahar,
50 The c' of Reaiah, the c' of Rezin,
50 the c' of Nekoda,
51 The c' of Gazzam, the c' of Uzza,
51 the c' of Phaseah,
52 The c' of Besai, the c' of Meunim,
52 the c' of Nephishesim,
53 The c' of Bakbuk, the c' of Hakupha,
53 the c' of Harhur,
54 The c' of Bazlith, the c' of Mehida,
54 the c' of Harsha,
55 The c' of Barkos, the c' of Sisera,
55 the c' of Tamah,
56 The c' of Neziah, the c' of Hatipha,
57 The c' of Solomon's servants:
57 the c' of Sotai, the c' of Sophereth,
57 the c' of Perida,
58 The c' of Jaala, the c' of Darkon,
58 the c' of Giddel,
59 The c' of Shephatiah,
59 the c' of Hattil,
59 the c' of Pochereth of Zebaim,
59 the c' of Amon.
60 and the c' of Solomon's servants,
62 The c' of Delaiah, the c' of Tobiah,
62 the c' of Nekoda,
63 the c' of Habaiah, the c' of Koz,
63 the c' of Barzillai,
73 the c' of Israel were in their cities,
8:14 the c' of Israel should dwell in
17 had not the c' of Israel done so.
9: 1 the c' of Israel were assembled
23 Their c' also multipliedst thou
24 c' went in and possessed the land,
10:39 the c' of Israel and the c' of Levi
11: 3 and the c' of Solomon's servants.
4 certain of the c' of Judah, and of the
4 c' of Benjamin. Of the c' of Judah;
4 of Mahalaleel, of the c' of Perez;
24 the c' of Zerah the son of Judah,
25 c' of Judah dwelt at Kirjath-arba,
31 c' also of Benjamin from Geba
12:43 the wives also and the c' rejoiced:
47 them unto the c' of Aaron.
13: 2 they met not the c' of Israel
16 sabbath unto the c' of Judah,
24 their c' spake half in the speech
Es 3:13 and old, little c' and women,
5:11 and the multitude of his c',
Job 5: 4 His c' are far from safety, and
8: 4 If thy c' have sinned against him,
17: 5 even the eyes of his c' shall fail.
19:18 young c' despised me; I arose,
20:10 His c' shall seek to please the poor,
21:11 like a flock, and their c' dance.
19 layeth up his iniquity for his c':
24: 5 food for them and for their c'.
27:14 If his c' be multiplied, it is for
29: 5 my c' were about me;
30: 8 c' of fools, yea, c' of base men:
41:34 a king over all the c' of pride.
Ps 11: 4 his eyelids try, the c' of men.
12: 1 fail from among the c' of men.
14: 2 from heaven upon the c' of men, to
17:14 are full of c', and leave the rest
21:10 seed from among the c' of men.
34:11 Come, ye c', hearken unto me:
36: 7 the c' of men put their trust
45: 2 art fairer than the c' of men:
16 of thy fathers shall be thy c',
53: 2 from heaven upon the c' of men, to
66: 5 in his doing toward the c' of men.
69: 8 and an alien unto my mother's c'.
72: 4 he shall save the c' of the needy,
73:15 against the generation of thy c'.
78: 4 will not hide them from their c',
5 make them known to their c':
6 the c' which should be born;
6 and declare them to their c':
9 The c' of Ephraim, being armed,
82: 6 of you are c' of the most High.
83: 8 they have holpen the c' of Lot.
89:30 If his c' forsake my law, and walk
90: 3 and sayest, Return, ye c' of men.
16 and thy glory unto their c'.
102:28 c' of thy servants shall continue,
103: 7 his acts unto the c' of Israel.
13 Like as a father pitieth his c', so

Ps 103:17 righteousness unto children's c';
105: 6 ye c' of Jacob his chosen.
107: 8, 15, 21, 31 works to the c' of men!
109: 9 Let his c' be fatherless, and his wife
10 Let his c' be continually vagabonds,
12 be any to favour his fatherless c'.
113: 9 and to be a joyful mother of c'.
115:14 more and more, you and your c'.
16 earth hath he given to the c' of men.
127: 3 Lo, c' are an heritage of the Lord:
4 so are the c' of the youth.
128: 3 thy c' like olive plants round about
6 thou shalt see thy children's c',
132:12 If thy c' will keep my covenant
12 c' shall also sit upon the throne
137: 7 c' of Edom in the day of Jerusalem;
144: 7 from the hand of strange c';
11 me from the hand of strange c',
147:13 he hath blessed thy c' within thee.
148:12 and maidens; old men, and c':
14 even of the c' of Israel, a people
149: 2 c' of Zion be joyful in their king.
Pr 4: 1 Hear, ye c', the instruction of a
5: 7 Hear me now therefore, O ye c',
7:24 unto me now therefore, O ye c',
8:32 hearken unto me, O ye c':
13:22 an inheritance to his children's c':
14:26 his c' shall have a place of refuge.
15:11 the hearts of the c' of men?
17: 6 Children's c' are the crown of old
6 and the glory of c' are their fathers.
20: 7 his c' are blessed after him.
31:28 her c' arise up and call her blessed;
Ec 6: 3 If a man beget an hundred c',
Ca 1: 6 mother's c' were angry with me;
Isa 1: 2 I have nourished and brought up c',
4 c' that are corrupters: they have
2: 6 themselves in the c' of strangers,
3: 4 I will give c' to be their princes,
12 people, c' are their oppressors,
8:18 c' whom the Lord hath given me
11:14 the c' of Ammon shall obey them.
13:16 c' also shall be dashed to pieces
18 their eye shall not spare c'.
14:21 Prepare slaughter for his c' for
17: 3 be as the glory of the c' of Israel,
9 left because of the c' of Israel:
21:17 the mighty men of the c' of Kedar,
23: 4 nor bring forth c', neither do I
27:12 one by one, O ye c' of Israel.
29:23 he seeth his c', the work of mine
30: 1 the rebellious c', saith the Lord,
9 lying c', that will not hear the
31: 6 c' of Israel have deeply revolted.
37: 3 for the c' are come to the birth,
12 and the c' of Eden which were in
38:19 the c' shall make known thy truth.
47: 8 neither shall I know the loss of c':
9 day, the loss of c', and widowhood:
49:17 Thy c' shall make haste; thy
20 The c' which thou shalt have,
21 I have lost my c', and am desolate,
25 and I will save thy c'.
54: 1 for more are the c' of the desolate
1 than the c' of the married wife,
13 thy c' shall be taught of the Lord;
13 great shall be the peace of thy c'.
57: 4 are ye not c' of transgression,
5 slaying c' in the valleys under the
63: 8 my people, c' that will not lie:
66: 8 travailed, she brought forth her c'.
20 the c' of Israel bring an offering
Jer 2: 9 your children's c' will I plead.
16 the c' of Noph and Tahapanes
30 In vain have I smitten your c';
3:14 O backsliding c', saith the Lord;
19 shall I put thee among the c',
21 supplications of the c' of Israel:
22 Return, ye backsliding c', and I
4:22 are sottish c', and they have none
5: 7 thy c' have forsaken me, and sworn
6: 1 O ye c' of Benjamin, gather
11 pour it out upon the c' abroad,
7:18 c' gather wood, and the fathers
30 c' of Judah have done evil in my
9:21 to cut off the c' from without, and
26 and Edom, and the c' of Ammon,
10:20 my c' are gone forth of me, and
15: 7 will bereave them of c', I will destroy
16:14 the c' of Israel out of the land of
15 that brought up the c' of Israel
17: 2 their c' remember their altars
19 in the gate of the c' of the people,
18:21 deliver up their c' to the famine,
21 wives be bereaved of their c',
23: 7 brought up the c' of Israel out of
25:21 Moab, and the c' of Ammon,
30:20 Their c' also shall be as aforetime,
31:15 Rahel weeping for her c' refused
15 to be comforted for her c',
17 Lord, that thy c' shall come again
32:18 the bosom of their c' after them:
30 For the c' of Israel and the
30 c' of Judah have done evil before
30 c' of Israel have only provoked me
32 c' of Israel and of the c' of Judah,
39 them, and of their c' after them:
38:23 wives and thy c' to the Chaldeans:
40: 7 men, and women, and c', and of
41:16 women, and the c', and the eunuchs,
43: 6 and c', and the king's daughters,
47: 3 shall not look back to their c'
49: 6 the captivity of the c' of Ammon,
11 Leave thy fatherless c', I will preserve
50: 4 the c' of Israel shall come,
4 they and the c' of Judah together

Jer 50:33 The c' of Israel and the c' of Judah
La 1: 5 her c' are gone into captivity
16 my c' are desolate, because the
2:11 the c' and the sucklings swoon
19 the life of thy young c', that faint
20 their fruit, and c' of a span long?
3:33 nor grieve the c' of men.
4: 4 young c' ask bread, and no man
10 women have sodden their own c':
5:13 and the c' fell under the wood.
Eze 2: 3 I send thee to the c' of Israel,
4 are impudent c' and stiffhearted.
3:11 captivity, unto the c' of thy people,
4:13 c' of Israel eat their defiled bread
6: 5 dead carcases of the c' of Israel
9: 6 maids, and little c', and women:
16:21 hast slain my c', and delivered
36 blood of thy c', which thou didst
45 lotheth her husband and her c';
45 lothed their husbands and their c':
20:18 unto their c' in the wilderness,
21 the c' rebelled against me: they
23:39 had slain their c' to their idols,
31:14 in the midst of the c' of men,
33: 2 man, speak to the c' of thy people,
12 man, say unto the c' of thy people,
17 Yet the c' of thy people say, The
30 c' of thy people still are talking
35: 5 shed the blood of the c' of Israel
37:16 the c' of Israel his companions:
18 the c' of thy people shall speak
21 take the c' of Israel from among
25 their c', and their children's c'
43: 7 in the midst of the c' of Israel
44: 9 any stranger that is among the c'
15 c' of Israel went astray from me,
47:22 shall beget the c' among you:
22 country among the c' of Israel;
48:11 when the c' of Israel went astray,
Da 1: 3 bring certain of the c' of Israel,
4 C' in whom was no blemish, but
6 c' of Judah, Daniel, Hananiah,
10 the c' which are of your sort?
13 countenance of the c' that eat
15 the c' which did eat the portion
17 for these four c', God gave them
2:38 wheresoever the c' of men dwell,
5:13 which art of the c' of the captivity
6:13 Daniel, which is of the c' of the
24 the den of lions, them, their c',
11:41 and the chief of the c' of Ammon.
12: 1 standeth for the c' of thy people:
Ho 1: 2 and c' of whoredoms:
10 number of the c' of Israel shall be
11 the c' of Judah and the c' of Israel
2: 4 will not have mercy upon her c';
4 for they be the c' of whoredoms.
3: 1 toward the c' of Israel, who look to
4 c' of Israel shall abide many days
5 shall the c' of Israel return,
4: 1 word of the Lord, ye c' of Israel:
6 I will also forget thy c'.
5: 7 for they have begotten strange c':
9:12 Though they bring up their c',
13 Ephraim shall bring forth his c'
10: 9 Gibeah against the c' of iniquity
14 was dashed in pieces upon her c'.
11:10 the c' shall tremble from the west.
13:13 place of the breaking forth of c'.
Joe 1: 3 Tell ye your c' of it, and
3 let your c' tell their c',
3 and their c' another generation.
2:16 gather the c', and those that suck
23 Be glad then, ye c' of Zion, and
3: 6 The c' also of Judah and the
6 c' of Jerusalem have ye sold unto
8 into the hand of the c' of Judah,
16 the strength of the c' of Israel.
19 violence against the c' of Judah,
Am 1:13 transgressions of the c' of Ammon,
2:11 not even thus, O ye c' of Israel?
3: 1 spoken against you, O c' of Israel,
12 so shall the c' of Israel be taken
4: 5 ye c' of Israel, saith the Lord God.
9: 7 Are ye not as c' of the Ethiopians
7 unto me, O c' of Israel?
Ob 12 have rejoiced over the c' of Judah
20 host of the c' of Israel shall possess
Mic 1:16 and poll thee for thy delicate c';
2: 9 c' have ye taken away my glory
5: 3 shall return unto the c' of Israel.
Na 3:10 young c' also were dashed in pieces
Zep 1: 8 the princes, and the king's c',
2: 8 the revilings of the c' of Ammon,
9 the c' of Ammon as Gomorrah,
Zec 10: 7 their c' shall see it, and be glad;
9 they shall live with their c', and
Mal 4: 6 the heart of the fathers to the c',
6 the heart of the c' to their fathers,
M't 2:16 and slew all the c' that were in
18 Rachel weeping for her c', and
3: 9 to raise up c' unto Abraham.
5: 9 they shall be called the c' of God.
45 That ye may be the c' of your
7:11 to give good gifts unto your c',
8:12 But the c' of the kingdom shall be
9:15 Can the c' of the bridechamber
10:21 and the c' shall rise up against
11:16 It is like unto c' sitting in the
19 But wisdom is justified of her c'.
12:27 by whom do your c' cast them
13:38 seed are the c' of the kingdom;
38 tares are the c' of the wicked
14:21 men, beside women and c'.
15:38 men, beside women and c'.
M't 17:25 of their own c', or of strangers?
26 saith unto him, Then are the c'
18: 3 and become as little c', ye shall
25 him to be sold, and his wife, and c',
19:13 brought unto him little c', that
14 Jesus said, Suffer little c', and forbid
29 or c', or lands, for my name's
20:20 him the mother of Zebedee's c'
21:15 and the c' crying in the temple,
22:24 If a man die, having no c', his
23:31 that ye are the c' of them which
37 would I have gathered thy c'
27: 9 they of the c' of Israel did value;
25 His blood be on us, and on our c'.
56 and the mother of Zebedee's c'.
M'r 2:19 Can the c' of the bridechamber
7:27 said unto her, Let the c' first be
9:37 receive one of such c' in my
10:13 And they brought young c' to
14 Suffer the little c' to come unto
24 C', how hard is it for them that
29 or wife, or c', or lands, for my
30 mothers, and c', and lands, with
12:19 and leave no c', that his brother
13:12 and c' shall rise up against their
Lu 1:16 many of the c' of Israel shall he
17 the hearts of the fathers to the c',
3: 8 to raise up c' unto Abraham.
5:34 Can ye make the c' of the
6:35 ye shall be the c' of the Highest:
7:32 like unto c' sitting in the
35 wisdom is justified of all her c'.
11: 7 my c' are with me in bed; I cannot
13 to give good gifts unto your c':
13:34 have gathered thy c' together, as
14:26 c', and brethren, and sisters, yea,
16: 8 for the c' of this world are
8 wiser than the c' of light.
18:16 Suffer little c' to come unto me,
29 or wife, or c', for the kingdom of
19:44 and thy c' within thee; and they
20:28 he died without c', that his
29 took a wife, and died without c'.
31 and they left no c', and died.
34 The c' of this world marry, and
36 and are the c' of God, being
36 the c' of the resurrection.
23:28 for yourselves, and for your c'.
Joh 4:12 drank thereof himself, and his c',
8:39 If ye were Abraham's c', ye would
11:52 c' of God that were scattered
12:36 that ye may be the c' of light.
13:33 Little c', yet a little while I am
21: 5 Jesus saith unto them, C', have ye
Ac 2:39 is unto you, and to your c',
3:25 Ye are the c' of the prophets,
5:21 all the senate of the c' of Israel,
7:19 they cast out their young c', to
23 visit his brethren the c' of Israel.
37 which said unto the c' of Israel,
9:15 Gentiles, and kings, and the c' of
10:36 God sent unto the c' of Israel,
13:26 c' of the stock of Abraham,
33 fulfilled the same unto us their c',
21: 5 on our way, with wives and c',
21 ought not to circumcise their c',
Ro 8:16 spirit, that we are the c' of God:
17 And if c', then heirs; heirs of God,
21 the glorious liberty of the c' of God.
9: 7 seed of Abraham, are they all c':
8 They which are the c' of the flesh,
8 these are not the c' of God:
8 the c' of the promise are counted
11 (For the c' being not yet born,
26 be called the c' of the living God.
27 the number of the c' of Israel be
1Co 7:14 else were your c' unclean; but
14:20 be not c' in understanding,
20 howbeit in malice be ye c', but
2Co 3: 7 so that the c' of Israel could not
13 that the c' of Israel could not
6:13 (I speak as unto my c',) be ye also
12:14 the c' ought not to lay up for the
14 but the parents for the c'.
Ga 3: 7 the same are the c' of Abraham.
26 ye are all the c' of God by faith
4: 3 when we were c', were in
19 My little c', of whom I travail
25 and is in bondage with her c'.
27 the desolate hath many more c'
28 as Isaac was, are the c' of promise.
31 we are not c' of the bondwoman,
Eph 1: 5 us unto the adoption of c' by
2: 2 worketh in the c' of disobedience:
3 were by nature the c' of wrath,
4:14 be no more c', tossed to and fro,
5: 1 followers of God, as dear c';
6 God upon the c' of disobedience.
8 in the Lord: walk as c' of light:
6: 1 C', obey your parents in the Lord:
4 provoke not your c' to wrath,
Col 3: 6 cometh on the c' of disobedience:
20 C', obey your parents in all
21 provoke not your c' to anger,
1Th 2: 7 even as a nurse cherisheth her c':
11 as a father doth his c',
5: 5 Ye are all the c' of light,
5 and the c' of the day:
1Ti 3: 4 having his c' in subjection with
12 ruling their c' and their own
5: 4 But if any widow have c' or
10 if she have brought up c', if she
14 younger women marry, bear c',
Tit 1: 6 having faithful c', not accused of
2: 4 their husbands, to love their c',
Heb 2:13 Behold I and the c' which God
14 then as the c' are partakers
11:22 of the departing of the c' of Israel;
12: 5 speaketh unto you as unto c',
1Pet 1:14 As obedient c', not fashioning
2Pet 2:14 with covetous practices; cursed c':
1Jo 2: 1 My little c', these things write I
12 I write unto you, little c', because
13 I write unto you, little c', because
18 Little c', it is the last time: and
28 And now, little c', abide in him;
3: 7 Little c', let no man deceive you:
10 In this the c' of God are manifest,
10 and the c' of the devil:
18 My little c', let us not love in
4: 4 Ye are of God, little c', and have
5: 2 know that we love the c' of God,
21 Little c', keep yourselves from
2Jo 1 unto the elect lady and her c',
4 that I found of thy c' walking in
13 The c' of thy elect sister greet
3Jo 4 joy I have to hear that my c' walk
Re 2:14 before the c' of Israel, to eat
23 And I will kill her c' with death;
7: 4 of all the tribes of the c' of Israel.
21:12 the twelve tribes of the c' of Israel:

children of Israel See CHILDREN and ISRAEL.

children of men See CHILDREN and MEN.

children's
Ge 31:16 father, that is ours, and our c':
45:10 thy c' children, and thy flocks, and
Ex 9: 4 die of all that is the c' of Israel.
34: 7 the c' children, unto the third
Jos 14: 9 inheritance, and thy c' for ever,
2Ki 17:41 children, and their c' children:
Job 19:17 I entreated for the c' sake of
Ps 103:17 righteousness unto c' children;
128: 6 see thy c' children, and peace
Pro 13:22 leaveth an inheritance to his c'
17: 6 C' children are the crown of old men;
Jer 2: 9 and with your c' children will
31:29 and the c' teeth are set on edge.
Eze 18: 2 the c' teeth are set on edge?
37:25 their c' children for ever: and my
M't 15:26 It is not meet to take the c' bread,
M'r 7:27 it is not meet to take the c' bread,
28 the table eat of the c' crumbs.

child's
Ex 2: 8 went and called the c' mother.
1Ki 17:21 let this c' soul come into him again.
Job 33:25 flesh shall be fresher than a c':
M't 2:20 which sought the young c' life.

Chileab (*kil'-e-ab*) See also DANIEL.
2Sa 3: 3 And his second, C', of Abigail the

Chilion (*kil'-e-on*) See also CHILION'S.
Ru 1: 2 of his two sons Mahlon and C',
5 And Mahlon and C' died also

Chilion's (*kil'-e-ons*)
Ru 4: 9 Elimelech's, and all that was C'

Chilmad (*kil'-mad*)
Eze 27:23 of Sheba, Asshur, and C',

Chimham (*kim'-ham*)
2Sa 19:37 But behold thy servant C'; let
38 the king answered, C' shall go
40 and C' went on with him: and all
Jer 41:17 and dwelt in the habitation of C',

chimney
Hos 13: 3 and as the smoke out of the c'.

Chinnereth (*kin'-ne-reth*) See also CHINNEROTH; CINNEROTH; GENNESARET.
Nu 34:11 the side of the sea of C' eastward:
Deu 3:17 C' even unto the sea of the plain,
Jos 13:27 even unto the edge of the sea of C'.
19:35 and Hammath, Rakkath, and C',

Chinneroth (*kin'-ne-roth*) See also CHINNERETH.
Jos 11: 2 and the plains south of C',
12: 3 from the plain to the sea of C'

Chios (*ki'-os*)
Ac 20:15 the next day over against C';

Chisleu (*kis'-lew*)
Ne 1: 1 month C', in the twentieth year,
Zec 7: 1 of the ninth month, even in C';

Chislon (*kis'-lon*)
Nu 34:21 Benjamin, Elidad the son of C'

Chisloth-tabor (*kis''-loth-ta'-bor*) See also CHESULLOTH.
Jos 19:12 sunrising unto the border of C'.

Chittim (*kit'-tim*) See also KITTIM.
Nu 24:24 shall come from the coast of C',
Isa 23: 1 from the land of C' it is revealed
12 pass over to C'; there also shalt
Jer 2:10 For pass over the isles of C',
Eze 27: 6 brought out of the isles of C'.
Da 11:30 ships of C' shall come against him:

Chiun (*ki'-un*) See also REMPHAN.
Am 5:26 tabernacle of your Moloch and C'

Chloe (*clo'-e*)
1Co 1:11 which are of the house of C',

chode
Ge 31:36 was wroth, and c' with Laban:
Nu 20: 3 And the people c' with Moses,

choice See also CHOICEST.
Ge 23: 6 c' of our sepulchres bury thy dead:
49:11 his ass's colt unto the c' vine;

De 12:11 your c' vows which ye vow unto
1Sa 9: 2 a c' young man, and a goodly:
2Sa 10: 9 chose of all the c' men of Israel,
2Ki 3:19 fenced city, and every c' city,
19:23 and the c' fir trees thereof:
1Ch 7:40 c' and mighty men of valour,
19:10 all the c' of Israel, and put them
2Ch 25: 5 three hundred thousand c' men,
Ne 5:18 one ox and six c' sheep; also
Pr 8:10 knowledge rather than c' gold.
19 and my revenue than c' silver.
10:20 tongue of the just is as c' silver:
Ca 6: 9 is the c' one of her that bare her.
Isa 37:24 the c' fir trees thereof: and I will
Jer 22: 7 shall cut down thy c' cedars,
Eze 24: 4 shoulder, fill it with the c' bones.
5 Take the c' of the flock, and burn
31:16 Eden, the c' and best of Lebanon,
Ac 15: 7 God made c' among us, that the

choicest
Isa 5: 2 planted it with the c' vine,
22: 7 c' valleys shall be full of chariots,

choke See also CHOKED.
M't 13:22 deceitfulness of riches, c' the
M'r 4:19 entering in, c' the word, and it

choked
M't 13: 7 thorns sprung up, and c' them:
M'r 4: 7 c' it, and it yielded no fruit.
5:13 and were c' in the sea.
Lu 8: 7 sprang up with it, and c' it.
14 and are c' with cares and riches
33 place into the lake, and were c'.

choler (*col'-ur*)
Dan 8: 7 was moved with c' against him,
11:11 the south shall be moved with c',

choose See also CHOOSEST; CHOOSETH; CHOOSING; CHOSE; CHOSEN.
Ex 17: 9 C' us out men, and go out,
Nu 16: 7 the man whom the Lord doth c',
17: 5 the man's rod, whom I shall c',
De 7: 7 nor c' you, because ye were more
12: 5 the Lord your God shall c' out
11 God shall c' to cause his name
14 the place which the Lord shall c'
18 which the Lord thy God shall c',
26 the place which the Lord shall c':
14:23 the place which he shall c' to
24 which the Lord thy God shall c'
25 which the Lord thy God shall c':
15:20 the place which the Lord shall c',
16: 2 the place which the Lord shall c'
6 which the Lord thy God shall c'
7 which the Lord thy God shall c':
15 the place which the Lord shall c':
16 in the place which he shall c';
17: 8 which the Lord thy God shall c';
10 which the Lord shall c' shall shew
15 whom the Lord thy God shall c':
18: 6 the place which the Lord shall c';
23:16 that place which he shall c' in one
26: 2 God shall c' to place his name
30:19 therefore c' life, that both
31:11 in the place which he shall c',
Jos 9:27 in the place which he should c'.
24:15 c' you this day whom ye will serve;
1Sa 2:28 did I c' him out of all the tribes
17: 8 c' you a man for you, and let
2Sa 16:18 and all the men of Israel, c',
17: 1 Let me now c' out twelve thousand
21: 6 of Saul, whom the Lord did c'.
24:12 c' thee one of them, that I may do
1Ki 14:21 which the Lord did c' out of all
18:23 and let them c' one bullock for
25 C' you one bullock for yourselves,
1Ch 21:10 c' thee one of them, that I may
11 Thus saith the Lord, C' thee
Ne 9: 7 the God, who didst c' Abram,
Job 9:14 and c' out my words to reason
34: 4 Let us c' to us judgment: let us
33 thou refuse, or whether thou c';
Ps 25:12 teach in the way that he shall c'.
47: 4 He shall c' our inheritance for us,
Pr 1:29 did not c' the fear of the Lord:
3:31 oppressor, and c' none of his ways.
Isa 7:15, 16 refuse the evil, and c' the good,
14: 1 and will yet c' Israel, and set them
49: 7 of Israel, and he shall c' thee.
56: 4 and c' the things that please me,
65:12 c' that wherein I delighted not.
66: 4 I also will c' their delusions,
Eze 21:19 c' thou a place, c' it at the head
Zec 1:17 Zion, and shall yet c' Jerusalem.
2:12 and shall c' Jerusalem again.
Phil 1:22 yet what I shall c' I wot not.

choosest
Job 15: 5 thou c' the tongue of the crafty.
Ps 65: 4 Blessed is the man whom thou c',

chooseth
Job 7:15 So that my soul c' strangling,
Isa 40:20 he hath no oblation c' a tree that
41:24 an abomination is he that c' you.

choosing
Heb 11:25 C' rather to suffer affliction with

chop
Mic 3: 3 their bones, and c' them in pieces,

Chor-ashan (*cor-a'-shan*)
1Sa 30:30 and to them which were in C',

Chorazin (*co-ra'-zin*)
M't 11:21 Woe unto thee, C'! woe unto
Lu 10:13 Woe unto thee, C'! woe unto

chose
Ge 6: 2 them wives of all which they c'.
13:11 Lot c' him all the plain of Jordan;
Ex 18:25 Moses c' able men out of all Israel,
De 4:37 therefore he c' their seed after them,
10:15 and he c' their seed after them,
Jos 8: 3 Joshua c' out thirty thousand
J'g 5: 8 They c' new gods; then was war in
1Sa 13: 2 Saul c' him three thousand men
17:40 and c' him five smooth stones out
2Sa 6:21 which c' me before thy father,
10: 9 behind, he c' of all the choice men
1Ki 8:16 I c' no city out of all the tribes of
16 but I c' David to be over my people
11:34 David my servant's sake whom I c',
1Ch 19:10 c' out of all the choice of Israel,
28: 4 the Lord God of Israel c' me before
2Ch 6: 5 I c' no city among all the tribes
5 neither c' I any man to be a ruler
Job 29:25 I c' out their way, and sat chief,
Ps 78:67 and c' not the tribe of Ephraim:
68 But c' the tribe of Judah, the
70 He c' David also his servant,
Isa 66: 4 and c' that in which I delighted not.
Eze 20: 5 In the day when I c' Israel,
Lu 6:13 of them he c' twelve, whom also
14: 7 they c' out the chief rooms; saying
Ac 6: 5 they c' Stephen, a man full of faith
13:17 c' our fathers, and exalted the
15:40 And Paul c' Silas, and departed,

chosen
Ex 14: 7 he took six hundred c' chariots,
15: 4 his c' captains also are drowned
Nu 16: 5 even him whom he hath c' will
De 7: 6 the Lord thy God hath c' thee to be
12:21 which the Lord thy God hath c'
14: 2 the Lord hath c' thee to be a
16:11 the Lord thy God hath c' to place
18: 5 For the Lord thy God hath c' him
21: 5 Lord thy God hath c' to minister
Jos 24:22 that ye have c' you the Lord to
J'g 10:14 cry unto the gods which ye have c';
20:15 numbered seven hundred c' men.
16 there were seven hundred c' men
34 ten thousand c' men out of all
1Sa 8:18 your king which ye shall have c'
10:24 See ye him whom the Lord hath c',
12:13 the king whom ye have c', and
16: 8, 9 Neither hath the Lord c' this.
10 Jesse, The Lord hath not c' these.
20:30 that thou hast c' the son of Jesse
24: 2 Saul took three thousand c' men
26: 2 having three thousand c' men of
2Sa 6: 1 together all the c' men of Israel,
1Ki 3: 8 thy people which thou hast c',
8:44 toward the city which thou hast c',
48 the city which thou hast c', and the
11:13 Jerusalem's sake which I have c'.
32 sake, the city which I have c' out of
36 Jerusalem, the city which I have c'
12:21 hundred and fourscore thousand c'
2Ki 21: 7 which I have c' out of all tribes
23:27 Jerusalem, which I have c', and the
1Ch 9:22 c' to be porters in the gates
15: 2 them hath the Lord c' to carry the
16:13 ye children of Jacob, his c' ones.
41 the rest that were c', who were
28: 4 he hath c' Judah to be the ruler;
5 he hath c' Solomon my son to sit
6 I have c' him to be my son, and I
10 heed now; for the Lord hath c' thee
29: 1 whom alone God hath c', is yet
2Ch 6: 6 But I have c' Jerusalem, that my
6 and have c' David to be over my
34 toward this city which thou hast c',
38 toward the city which thou hast c',
7:12 and have c' this place to myself for
16 For now have I c' and sanctified
11: 1 fourscore thousand c' men which
12:13 which the Lord had c' out of all
13: 3 four hundred thousand c' men:
3 eight hundred thousand c' men,
17 five hundred thousand c' men.
29:11 Lord hath c' you to stand before
33: 7 which I have c' before all the tribes
Ne 1: 9 the place that I have c' to set
Job 36:21 for this hast thou c' rather than
Ps 33:12 the people whom he hath c' for his
78:31 smote down the c' men of Israel.
89: 3 I have made a covenant with my c',
19 exalted one c' out of the people.
105: 6 servant, ye children of Jacob his c'.
26 and Aaron whom he had c'.
43 with joy, and his c' with gladness:
106: 5 That I may see the good of thy c',
23 had not Moses his c' stood before
119:30 I have c' the way of truth: thy
173 help me; for I have c' thy precepts.
132:13 the Lord hath c' Zion; he hath
135: 4 the Lord hath c' Jacob unto himself,
Pr 16:16 rather to be c' than silver!
22: 1 A good name is rather to be c'
Isa 1:29 for the gardens that ye have c'.
41: 8 servant, Jacob whom I have c',
9 I have c' thee, and not cast thee
43:10 and my servant whom I have c':
20 to give drink to my people, my c'.
44: 1 Israel, whom I have c':
2 and thou, Jesurun, whom I have c'.
48:10 c' thee in the furnace of affliction.
58: 5 Is it such a fast that I have c'?
6 Is not this the fast that I have c'?
65:15 your name for a curse unto my c':
66: 3 they have c' their own ways, and
Jer 8: 3 death shall be c' rather than life
Jer 33:24 families which the Lord hath c',
48:15 and his c' young men are gone
49:19 and who is a c' man, that I may
50:44 from her: and who is a c' man,
Eze 23: 7 with all them that were the c'
Da 11:15 neither his c' people, neither
Hag 2:23 for I have c' thee, saith the Lord
Zec 3: 2 the Lord that hath c' Jerusalem
M't 12:18 my servant, whom I have c';
20:16 for many be called, but few c'.
22:14 many are called, but few are c'.
M'r 13:20 the elect's sake, whom he hath c',
Lu 10:42 Mary hath c' that good part, which
23:35 if he be Christ, the c' of God.
Joh 6:70 Have not I c' you twelve, and one
13:18 I know whom I have c':
15:16 Ye have not c' me,
16 but I have c' you, and
19 I have c' you out of the world,
Ac 1: 2 the apostles whom he had c':
24 whether of these two thou hast c',
9:15 he is a c' vessel unto me, to bear
10:41 unto witnesses c' before of God,
15:22 to send c' men of their own
25 to send c' men unto you with our
22:14 hath c' thee, that thou shouldest
Ro 16:13 Salute Rufus c' in the Lord, and
1Co 1:27 God hath c' the foolish things of
27 God hath c' the weak things of
28 which are despised, hath God c',
2Co 8:19 who was also c' of the churches
Eph 1: 4 as he hath c' us in him before the
2Th 2:13 God hath from the beginning c'
2Ti 2: 4 he may please him who hath c'
Jas 2: 5 Hath not God c' the poor of this
1Pe 2: 4 but c' of God, and precious,
9 ye are a c' generation, a royal
Re 17:14 him are called, and c', and faithful.

Chozeba (*ko-ze'-bah*) See also CHEZIB.
1Ch 4:22 and the men of C', and Joash,

Christ (*krist*) See also ANTICHRIST; CHRISTIAN; CHRIST'S; CHRISTS; JESUS; MESSIAH.
M't 1: 1 book of the generation of Jesus C',
16 was born Jesus, who is called C'.
17 unto C' are fourteen generations.
18 the birth of Jesus C' was on this
2: 4 of them where C' should be born.
11: 2 heard in the prison the works of C',
16:16 Thou art the C', the Son of the
20 no man that he was Jesus the C'.
22:42 What think ye of C'? whose son
23: 8 one is your Master, even C'; and
10 for one is your Master, even C'.
24: 5 my name, saying, I am C'; and
23 Lo, here is C', or there; believe it
26:63 whether thou be the C', the Son
68 Prophesy unto us, thou C', Who is
27:17 or Jesus which is called C'?
22 with Jesus which is called C'?
M'r 1: 1 of the gospel of Jesus C',
8:29 saith unto him, Thou art the C'.
9:41 because ye belong to C', verily I
12:35 How say the scribes that C' is the
13: 6 saying, I am C'; and shall
21 Lo, here is C'; or, lo, he is there;
14:61 Art thou the C', the Son of the
15:32 Let C' the King of Israel descend
Lu 2:11 a Saviour, which is C' the Lord.
26 before he had seen the Lord's C'.
3:15 whether he were the C', or not;
4:41 Thou art C' the Son of God.
41 for they knew that he was C'.
9:20 answering said, The C' of God.
20:41 say they that C' is David's son?
21: 8 in my name, saying, I am C'; and
22:67 Art thou the C'? tell us. And he
23: 2 saying that he himself is C' a king.
35 if he be C', the chosen of God.
39 saying, If thou be C', save thyself
24:26 Ought not C' to have suffered
46 thus it behoved C' to suffer, and to
Joh 1:17 grace and truth came by Jesus C'.
20 but confessed, I am not the C'.
25 if thou be not that C', nor Elias,
41 which is, being interpreted, the C'.
3:28 said, I am not the C', but that I am
4:25 Messias cometh, which is called C':
29 that even I did: is not this the C'?
42 this is indeed the C', the Saviour of
6:69 are sure that thou art that C',
7:26 indeed that this is the very C'?
27 when C' cometh, no man knoweth
31 When C' cometh, will he do more
41 Others said, This is the C'. But
41 Shall C' come out of Galilee?
42 C' cometh of the seed of David, and
9:22 man did confess that he was C',
10:24 If thou be the C', tell us plainly.
11:27 I believe that thou art the C',
12:34 the law that C' abideth for ever:
17: 3 Jesus C', whom thou hast sent.
20:31 might believe that Jesus is the C'.
Ac 2:30 raise up C' to sit on his throne;
31 spake of the resurrection of C',
36 ye have crucified, both Lord and C'.
38 in the name of Jesus C' for the
3: 6 In the name of Jesus C' of
18 prophets, that C' should suffer, he
20 And he shall send Jesus C', which
4:10 that by the name of Jesus C' of
26 the Lord, and against his C'.
5:42 to teach and preach Jesus C'.
8: 5 Samaria, and preached C' unto
12 and the name of Jesus C', they were

Ac 8:37 that Jesus C' is the Son of God.
9:20 preached C' in the synagogues,
22 proving that this is very C'.
34 Jesus C' maketh thee whole:
10:36 peace by Jesus C': (he is Lord of
11:17 believed on the Lord Jesus C';
15:11 the grace of the Lord Jesus C'
26 for the name of our Lord Jesus C'.
16:18 thee in the name of Jesus C' to
31 Believe on the Lord Jesus C', and
17: 3 C' must needs have suffered, and
3 whom I preach unto you, is C'.
18: 5 to the Jews that Jesus was C'.
28 the scriptures that Jesus was C'.
19: 4 after him, that is, on C' Jesus.
20:21 faith toward our Lord Jesus C'.
24:24 him concerning the faith in C'.
26:23 That C' should suffer, and that
28:31 which concern the Lord Jesus C',
Ro 1: 1 Paul, a servant of Jesus C', called
3 Concerning his Son Jesus C' our
6 ye also the called of Jesus C':
7 our Father, and the Lord Jesus C'.
8 I thank my God through Jesus C'
16 not ashamed of the gospel of C':
2:16 judge the secrets of men by Jesus C'
3:22 is by faith of Jesus C' unto all
24 redemption that is in C' Jesus:
5: 1 God through our Lord Jesus C':
6 in due time C' died for the ungodly.
8 were yet sinners, C' died for us.
11 through our Lord Jesus C', by
15 which is by one man, Jesus C',
17 shall reign in life by one, Jesus C'.)
21 eternal life by Jesus C' our Lord.
6: 3 were baptized into Jesus C' were
4 as C' was raised up from the dead
8 if we be dead with C', we believe
9 Knowing that C' being raised from
11 God, through Jesus C' our Lord.
23 eternal life through Jesus C' our
7: 4 dead to the law by the body of C';
25 God through Jesus C' our Lord.
8: 1 to them which are in C' Jesus,
2 Spirit of life in C' Jesus hath
9 any man have not the Spirit of C',
10 if C' be in you, the body is dead
11 that raised up C' from the dead
17 of God, and joint-heirs with C';
34 It is C' that died, yea rather, that
35 separate us from the love of C'?
39 love of God, which is in C' Jesus
9: 1 say the truth in C', I lie not, my
3 accursed from C' for my brethren,
5 C' came, who is over all, God
10: 4 C' is the end of the law for
6 (that is, to bring C' down from
7 (that is, to bring up C' again from
12: 5 being many, are one body in C',
13:14 But put ye on the Lord Jesus C',
14: 9 C' both died, and rose, and revived,
10 before the judgment seat of C'.
15 with thy meat, for whom C' died.
18 that in these things serveth C' is
15: 3 For even C' pleased not himself;
5 another according to C' Jesus:
6 the Father of our Lord Jesus C'.
7 as C' also received us to the glory
8 Jesus C' was a minister of the
16 minister of Jesus C' to the Gentiles,
17 I may glory through Jesus C' in
18 things which C' hath not wrought
19 fully preached the gospel of C'.
20 not where C' was named, lest I
29 the blessing of the gospel of C'.
16: 3 Aquila my helpers in C' Jesus:
5 the firstfruits of Achaia unto C'.
7 who also were in C' before me.
9 Urbane, our helper in C', and
10 Salute Apelles approved in C'.
16 The churches of C' salute you.
18 such serve not our Lord Jesus C',
20 of our Lord Jesus C' be with you.
24 our Lord Jesus C' be with you all.
25 and the preaching of Jesus C',
27 wise, be glory through Jesus C'
1Co 1: 1 apostle of Jesus C' through the will
2 them that are sanctified in C' Jesus,
2 call upon the name of Jesus C'
3 and from the Lord Jesus C'.
4 which is given you by Jesus C';
6 of C' was confirmed in you:
7 the coming of our Lord Jesus C':
8 in the day of our Lord Jesus C'.
9 of his Son Jesus C' our Lord.
10 by the name of our Lord Jesus C',
12 and I of Cephas; and I of C'.
13 Is C' divided? was Paul crucified
17 C' sent me not to baptize, but to
17 C' should be made of none effect.
23 But we preach C' crucified,
24 C' the power of God, and the
30 But of him are ye in C' Jesus,
2: 2 save Jesus C', and him crucified.
16 But we have the mind of C'.
3: 1 even as unto babes in C'.
11 that is laid, which is Jesus C'.
23 ye are Christ's; and C' is God's.
4: 1 ministers of C', and stewards of
10 sake, but ye are wise in C';
15 ten thousand instructors in C', yet
15 for in C' Jesus I have begotten
17 of my ways which be in C',
5: 4 the name of our Lord Jesus C',
4 the power of our Lord Jesus C',
1Co 5: 7 C' our passover is sacrificed for
6:15 bodies are the members of C'?
15 I then take the members of C',
8: 6 Jesus C', by whom are all things,
11 brother perish, for whom C' died?
12 conscience, ye sin against C'.
9: 1 have I not seen Jesus C' our Lord?
12 we should hinder the gospel of C'.
18 the gospel of C' without charge,
21 under the law to C',) that I might
10: 4 and that rock was C'.
9 neither let us tempt C', as some
16 communion of the blood of C'?
16 communion of the body of C'?
11: 1 of me, even as I also am of C'.
3 that the head of every man is C';
3 man; and the head of C' is God.
12:12 are one body: so also is C'.
27 are the body of C', and members
15: 3 C' died for our sins according to
12 if C' be preached that he rose
13 of the dead, then is C' not risen:
14 if C' be not risen, then is our
15 of God that he raised up C':
16 rise not, then is not C' raised:
17 C' be not raised, your faith is vain;
18 also which are fallen asleep in C'
19 this life only we have hope in C',
20 now is C' risen from the dead,
22 in C' shall all be made alive.
23 C' the firstfruits; afterward they
31 which I have in C' Jesus our Lord,
57 victory through our Lord Jesus C'.
16:22 man love not the Lord Jesus C',
23 of our Lord Jesus C' be with you.
24 love be with you all in C' Jesus.
2Co 1: 1 of Jesus C' by the will of God,
2 and from the Lord Jesus C'.
3 the Father of our Lord Jesus C',
5 sufferings of C' abound in us,
5 consolation also aboundeth by C'.
19 C', who was preached among you
21 stablisheth us with you in C',
2:10 forgave I it in the person of C';
14 always causeth us to triumph in C',
15 unto God a sweet savour of C',
17 in the sight of God speak we in C'.
3: 3 the epistle of C' ministered by us,
4 have we through C' to God-ward:
14 which vail is done away in C'.
4: 4 light of the glorious gospel of C',
5 ourselves, but C' Jesus the Lord;
6 glory of God in the face of Jesus C'.
5:10 judgment seat of C'; that every
14 For the love of C' constraineth us;
16 we have known C' after the flesh,
17 if any man be in C', he is a new
18 us to himself by Jesus C', and hath
19 God was in C', reconciling the
20 we are ambassadors for C', as
6:15 what concord hath C' with Belial?
8: 9 the grace of our Lord Jesus C',
23 the churches, and the glory of C'.
9:13 subjection unto the gospel of C',
10: 1 meekness and gentleness of C',
5 thought to the obedience of C';
14 in preaching the gospel of C':
11: 2 you as a chaste virgin to C'.
3 from the simplicity that is in C'.
10 truth of C' is in me, no man shall
13 themselves into the apostles of C'.
23 Are they ministers of C'? (I speak
31 the Father of our Lord Jesus C',
12: 2 a man in C' above fourteen years
9 power of C' may rest upon me.
19 we speak before God in C': but
13: 3 seek a proof of C' speaking in me,
5 Jesus C' is in you, except ye be
14 grace of the Lord Jesus C', and
Ga 1: 1 neither by man, but by Jesus C',
3 and from our Lord Jesus C',
6 grace of C' unto another gospel:
7 would pervert the gospel of C'.
10 should not be the servant of C'.
12 but by the revelation of Jesus C'.
22 of Judæa which were in C':
2: 4 in C' Jesus, that they might bring
16 law, but by the faith of Jesus C',
16 we have believed in Jesus C',
16 be justified by the faith of C',
17 we seek to be justified by C',
17 is therefore C' the minister of sin?
20 I am crucified with C':
20 yet not I, but C' liveth in me:
21 by the law, then C' is dead in vain.
3: 1 C' hath been evidently set forth,
13 C' hath redeemed us from the
14 on the Gentiles through Jesus C';
16 one, And to thy seed, which is C'.
17 confirmed before of God in C',
22 promise by faith of Jesus C'
24 schoolmaster to bring us unto C',
26 of God by faith in C' Jesus.
27 baptized into C' have put on C'.
28 for ye are all one in C' Jesus.
4: 7 then an heir of God through C'.
14 angel of God, even as C' Jesus.
19 in birth again until C' be formed
5: 1 wherewith C' hath made us free,
2 C' shall profit you nothing.
4 C' is become of no effect unto you,
6 in Jesus C' neither circumcision
6: 2 burdens, and so fulfil the law of C'.
12 persecution for the cross of C'.
14 cross of our Lord Jesus C', by
Ga 6:15 in C' Jesus neither circumcision
18 Lord Jesus C' be with your spirit.
Eph 1: 1 Paul, an apostle of Jesus C' by the
1 and to the faithful in C' Jesus:
2 and from the Lord Jesus C'.
3 Father of our Lord Jesus C', who
3 in heavenly places in C':
5 children by Jesus C' to himself,
10 all things in C', both which are in
12 his glory, who first trusted in C'.
17 God of our Lord Jesus C', the
20 Which he wrought in C', when he
2: 5 quickened us together with C',
6 in heavenly places in C' Jesus:
7 toward us through C' Jesus.
10 in C' Jesus unto good works,
12 without C', being aliens from the
13 now in C' Jesus, ye who sometimes
13 are made nigh by the blood of C'.
20 C' himself being the chief corner
3: 1 prisoner of Jesus C' for you
4 knowledge in the mystery of C')
6 his promise in C' by the gospel:
8 the unsearchable riches of C';
9 created all things by Jesus C':
11 which he purposed in C' Jesus
14 Father of our Lord Jesus C',
17 C' may dwell in your hearts by
19 the love of C', which passeth
21 by C' Jesus throughout all ages,
4: 7 to the measure of the gift of C'.
12 for the edifying of the body of C':
13 of the stature of the fulness of C':
15 which is the head, even C':
20 ye have not so learned C';
5: 2 as C' also hath loved us, and hath
5 in the kingdom of C' and of God.
14 dead, and C' shall give thee light.
20 in the name of our Lord Jesus C';
23 C' is the head of the church:
24 as the church is subject unto C',
25 even as C' also loved the church,
32 concerning C' and the church.
6: 5 of your heart, as unto C';
6 the servants of C', doing the will
23 Father and the Lord Jesus C'.
24 our Lord Jesus C' in sincerity.
Ph'p 1: 1 the servants of Jesus C', to all
1 to all the saints in C' Jesus
2 Father, and from the Lord Jesus C'.
6 perform it until the day of Jesus C':
8 you all in the bowels of Jesus C'.
10 without offence till the day of C';
11 are by Jesus C', unto the glory
13 my bonds in C' are manifest in all
15 indeed preach C' even of envy and
16 The one preach C' of contention,
18 or in truth, C' is preached;
19 supply of the Spirit of Jesus C',
20 C' shall be magnified in my body,
21 For me to live is C', and to die is
23 to depart, and to be with C';
26 may be more abundant in Jesus C'
27 as it becometh the gospel of C':
29 it is given in the behalf of C', not
2: 1 be therefore any consolation in C',
5 you, which was also in C' Jesus:
11 Jesus C' is Lord, to the glory of God
16 I may rejoice in the day of C',
30 for the work of C' he was nigh
3: 3 rejoice in C' Jesus, and have no
7 those I counted loss for C'.
8 knowledge of C' Jesus my Lord:
8 but dung, that I may win C',
9 which is through the faith of C',
12 I am apprehended of C' Jesus.
14 the high calling of God in C' Jesus.
18 are the enemies of the cross of C':
20 for the Saviour, the Lord Jesus C':
4: 7 hearts and minds through C' Jesus.
13 C' which strengtheneth me.
19 to his riches in glory by C' Jesus.
21 Salute every saint in C' Jesus.
23 The grace of our Lord Jesus C' be
Col 1: 1 an apostle of Jesus C' by the will
2 saints and faithful brethren in C'
2 Father and the Lord Jesus C'.
3 the Father of our Lord Jesus C',
4 we heard of your faith in C' Jesus,
7 for you a faithful minister of C';
24 the afflictions of C' in my flesh for
27 is C' in you, the hope of glory:
28 every man perfect in C' Jesus:
2: 2 and of the Father, and of C';
5 stedfastness of your faith in C'.
6 therefore received C' Jesus the
8 of the world, and not after C'.
11 flesh by the circumcision of C':
17 but the body is of C'.
20 dead with C' from the rudiments
3: 1 If ye then be risen with C',
1 where C' sitteth on the right hand
3 your life is hid with C' in God.
4 C', who is our life, shall appear,
11 but C' is all, and in all.
13 as C' forgave you, so also do ye.
16 the word of C' dwell in you richly
24 for ye serve the Lord C'.
4: 3 speak the mystery of C', for which
12 a servant of C', saluteth you.
1Th 1: 1 Father and in the Lord Jesus C':
1 Father, and the Lord Jesus C'.
3 hope in our Lord Jesus C', in
2: 6 burdensome, as the apostles of C'.
14 which in Judæa are in C' Jesus:

1Th 2:19 our Lord Jesus C' at his coming?
3: 2 fellowlabourer in the gospel of C',
11 Lord Jesus C', direct our way
13 the coming of our Lord Jesus C'
4:16 the dead in C' shall rise first:
5: 9 salvation by our Lord Jesus C',
18 this is the will of God in C' Jesus
23 the coming of our Lord Jesus C'.
28 The grace of our Lord Jesus C' be
2Th 1: 1 our Father and the Lord Jesus C':
2 our Father and the Lord Jesus C'.
8 the gospel of our Lord Jesus C':
12 the name of our Lord Jesus C'
12 of our God and the Lord Jesus C'.
2: 1 the coming of our Lord Jesus C'.
2 as that the day of C' is at hand.
14 the glory of our Lord Jesus C'.
16 Now our Lord Jesus C' himself,
3: 5 into the patient waiting for C'.
6 in the name of our Lord Jesus C',
12 and exhort by our Lord Jesus C',
18 The grace of our Lord Jesus C' be
1Ti 1: 1 Paul, an apostle of Jesus C' by the
1 our Saviour, and Lord Jesus C',
2 our Father and Jesus C' our Lord.
12 thank C' Jesus our Lord, who hath
14 and love which is in C' Jesus.
15 that C' Jesus came into the world
16 first Jesus C' might shew forth
2: 5 and men, the man C' Jesus;
7 speak the truth in C', and lie not;)
3:13 in the faith which is in C' Jesus.
4: 6 be a good minister of Jesus C',
5:11 begun to wax wanton against C',
21 before God, and the Lord Jesus C',
6: 3 the words of our Lord Jesus C',
13 C' Jesus, who before Pontius Pilate
14 appearing of our Lord Jesus C':
2Ti 1: 1 an apostle of Jesus C' by the will
1 promise of life which is in C' Jesus,
2 the Father and C' Jesus our Lord.
9 in C' Jesus before the world began,
10 appearing of our Saviour Jesus C',
13 and love which is in C' Jesus.
2: 1 in the grace that is in C' Jesus.
3 as a good soldier of Jesus C'.
8 Remember that Jesus C' of the
10 is in C' Jesus with eternal glory.
19 that nameth the name of C'
3:12 live godly in C' Jesus shall suffer
15 through faith which is in C' Jesus.
4: 1 Lord Jesus C', who shall judge
22 Lord Jesus C' be with thy spirit.
Tit 1: 1 an apostle of Jesus C', according to
4 and the Lord Jesus C' our Saviour.
2:13 great God and our Saviour Jesus C';
3: 6 through Jesus C' our Saviour;
Ph'm 1 Paul, a prisoner of Jesus C',
3 our Father and the Lord Jesus C'.
6 thing which is in you in C' Jesus.
8 be much bold in C' to enjoin thee
9 now also a prisoner of Jesus C'.
23 my fellowprisoner in C' Jesus;
25 grace of our Lord Jesus C' be with
Heb 3: 1 Priest of our profession, C' Jesus:
6 C' as a son over his own house;
14 For we are made partakers of C',
5: 5 also C' glorified not himself to be
6: 1 the principles of the doctrine of C',
9:11 But C' being come an high priest
14 much more shall the blood of C',
24 C' is not entered in to the holy places
28 C' was once offered to bear the sins
10:10 of the body of Jesus C' once for all.
11:26 the reproach of C' greater riches
13: 8 Jesus C' the same yesterday, and
21 in his sight, through Jesus C';
Jas 1: 1 Lord Jesus C', to the twelve tribes
2: 1 faith of our Lord Jesus C', the Lord
1Pe 1: 1 Peter, an apostle of Jesus C', to
2 sprinkling of the blood of Jesus C':
3 and Father of our Lord Jesus C',
3 resurrection of Jesus C' from the
7 glory at the appearing of Jesus C':
11 the spirit of C' which was in them
11 beforehand the sufferings of C',
13 you at the revelation of Jesus C';
19 precious blood of C', as of a lamb
2: 5 acceptable to God by Jesus C'.
21 because C' also suffered for us,
3:16 your good conversation in C'.
18 C' also hath once suffered for sins,
21 by the resurrection of Jesus C':
4: 1 Forasmuch then as C' hath suffered
11 may be glorified through Jesus C',
14 be reproached for the name of C',
5: 1 a witness of the sufferings of C',
10 his eternal glory by C' Jesus,
14 with you all that are in C' Jesus.
2Pe 1: 1 Peter, an apostle of Jesus C', to
1 of God and our Saviour Jesus C':
8 knowledge of our Lord Jesus C'.
11 of our Lord and Saviour Jesus C'.
14 as our Lord Jesus C' hath shewed
16 and coming of our Lord Jesus C',
2:20 of the Lord and Saviour Jesus C',
3:18 of our Lord and Saviour Jesus C'.
1Jo 1: 3 Father, and with his Son Jesus C'.
7 and the blood of Jesus C' his Son
2: 1 the Father, Jesus C' the righteous:
22 that denieth that Jesus is the C'?
3:23 on the name of his son Jesus C',
4: 2 that Jesus C' is come in the flesh
3 confesseth not that Jesus C' is
5: 1 believeth that Jesus is the C' is
1Jo 5: 6 water and blood, even Jesus C';
20 is true, even in his Son Jesus C'.
2Jo 3 Lord Jesus C', the son of the Father,
7 that Jesus C' is come in the flesh.
9 abideth not in the doctrine of C',
9 that abideth in the doctrine of C',
Jude 1 the servant of Jesus C', and brother
1 preserved in Jesus C', and called:
4 Lord God, and our Lord Jesus C'.
17 the apostles of our Lord Jesus C';
21 the mercy of our Lord Jesus C'
Re 1: 1 Revelation of Jesus C' which God
2 testimony of Jesus C', and of all
5 from Jesus C', who is the faithful
9 kingdom and patience of Jesus C',
9 and for the testimony of Jesus C'.
11:15 of our Lord, and of his C';
12:10 our God, and the power of his C':
17 have the testimony of Jesus C'.
20: 4 reigned with C' a thousand years.
6 shall be priests of God and of C',
22:21 Lord Jesus C' be with you all.

Christ Jesus See CHRIST and JESUS.

Christ's (*krīsts*)
Ro 15:30 for the Lord Jesus C' sake, and
1Co 3:23 ye are C'; and Christ is God's.
4:10 for C' sake, but ye are wise in
7:22 is called, being free, is C' servant.
15:23 fruits; afterward they that are C'
2Co 2:12 C' gospel, and a door was opened
5:20 in C' stead, be ye reconciled to
10: 7 man trust to himself that he is C',
7 think this again, that, as he is C',
7 even so are we C'.
12:10 in distresses for C' sake:
Ga 3:29 if ye be C', then are ye Abraham's
5:24 are C' have crucified the flesh
Eph 4:32 God for C' sake hath forgiven
Ph'p 2:21 not the things which are Jesus C'.
1Pe 4:13 as ye are partakers of C'

Christs (*krīsts*)
M't 24:24 For there shall arise false C', and
M'r 13:22 For false C' and false prophets

Christian (*kris'-tyan*) See also CHRISTIANS.
Ac 26:28 thou persuadest me to be a C'.
1Pe 4:16 if any man suffer as a C', let him

Christians (*kris'-tyans*)
Ac 11:26 disciples were called C' first in

chronicles^A
1Ki 14:19 c' of the kings of Israel?
29 c' of the kings of Judah?
15: 7, 23 c' of the kings of Judah?
31 c' of the kings of Israel?
16: 5, 14, 20, 27 c' of . . . Israel?
22:39 c' of the kings of Israel?
45 c' of the kings of Judah?
2Ki 1:18 c' of the kings of Israel?
8:23 c' of the kings of Judah?
10:34 c' of the kings of Israel?
12:19 c' of the kings of Judah?
13: 8, 12 c' of the kings of Israel?
14:15 c' of the kings of Israel?
18 c' of the kings of Judah?
28 c' of the kings of Israel?
15: 6 c' of the kings of Judah?
11, 15, 21, 26, 31 c' of . . . Israel?
36 c' of the kings of Judah?
20:20 c' of the kings of Judah?
21:17, 25 c' of the kings of Judah?
23:28 c' of the kings of Judah?
24: 5 c' of the kings of Judah?
1Ch 27:24 c' of King David.
Neh 12:23 book of the c' even until
Es 2:23 book of the c' before the king
6: 1 records of the c'; and they
10: 2 c' of the kings of Media and

chrysolite (*cris'-o-lite*)
Re 21:20 the seventh, c'; the eighth, beryl:

chrysoprasus (*cris'-o-pra-sus*)
Re 21:20 the tenth, a c'; the eleventh, a

Chub (*cub*)
Eze 30: 5 all the mingled people, and C',

Chun (*kun*)
1Ch 18: 8 from Tibhath, and from C', cities

church See also CHURCHES.
M't 16:18 upon this rock I will build my c';
18:17 tell it unto the c':
17 but if he neglect to hear the c',
Ac 2:47 the Lord added to the c' daily
5:11 fear came upon all the c', and
7:38 he, that was in the c' in the
8: 1 against the c' which was at
3 he made havock of the c',
11:22 the c' which was in Jerusalem:
26 assembled themselves with the c',
12: 1 his hands to vex certain of the c'.
5 without ceasing of the c' unto God
13: 1 Now there were in the c' that was
14:23 ordained them elders in every c',
27 and had gathered the c' together,
15: 3 brought on their way by the c',
4 they were received of the c', and of
22 and elders, with the whole c',
18:22 gone up, and saluted the c', he
20:17 and called the elders of the c'.
28 overseers, to feed the c' of God,
Ro 16: 1 is a servant of the c' which is at
Ro 16: 5 greet the c' that is in their house.
23 mine host, and of the whole c',
subscr. by Phebe servant of the c'
1Co 1: 2 Unto the c' of God which is at
4:17 I teach everywhere in every c'.
6: 4 who are least esteemed in the c'.
10:32 Gentiles; nor to the c' of God:
11:18 when ye come together in the c',
22 or despise ye the c' of God, and
12:28 God hath set some in the c',
14: 4 that prophesieth edifieth the c'.
5 interpret, that the c' may receive
12 excel to the edifying of the c'.
19 in the c' I had rather speak five
23 therefore the whole c' be come
28 let him keep silence in the c';
35 for women to speak in the c'.
15: 9 I persecuted the c' of God.
16:19 with the c' that is in their house.
2Co 1: 1 unto the c' of God which is
Ga 1:13 I persecuted the c' of God, and
Eph 1:22 the head over all things to the c',
3:10 might be known by the c' the
21 glory in the c' by Christ Jesus
5:23 Christ is the head of the c':
24 Therefore as the c' is subject unto
25 as Christ also loved the c', and
27 present it to himself a glorious c',
29 even as the Lord the c':
32 concerning Christ and the c'.
Ph'p 3: 6 Concerning zeal, persecuting the c';
4:15 no c' communicated with me
Col 1:18 the head of the body, the c':
24 for his body's sake, which is the c':
4:15 and the c' which is in his house.
16 it be read also in the c' of the
1Th 1: 1 unto the c' of the Thessalonians
2Th 1: 1 unto the c' of the Thessalonians
1Ti 3: 5 take care of the c' of God?)
15 the c' of the living God, the pillar
5:16 let not the c' be charged;
2Ti *subscr.* first bishop of the c' of the
Tit *subscr.* first bishop of the c' of the
Ph'm 2 to the c' in thy house:
Heb 2:12 in the midst of the c' will I sing
12:23 general assembly and c' of the
Jas 5:14 call for the elders of the c';
1Pe 5:13 The c' that is at Babylon, elected
3Jo 6 of thy charity before the c':
9 I wrote unto the c': but
10 and casteth them out of the c'.
Rev 2: 1 the angel of the c' of Ephesus
8 the angel of the c' in Smyrna
12 to the angel of the c' in Pergamos
18 the angel of the c' in Thyatira.
3: 1 the angel of the c' in Sardis write;
7 the angel of the c' in Philadelphia
14 the angel of the c' of the Laodiceans

churches
Ac 9:31 Then had the c' rest throughout
15:41 and Cilicia, confirming the c'.
16: 5 so were the c' established in the
19:37 which are neither robbers of c',
Ro 16:4 but also all the c' of the Gentiles.
16 The c' of Christ salute you.
1Co 7:17 And so ordain I in all c'.
11:16 custom, neither the c' of God.
14:33 of peace, as in all c' of the saints.
34 your women keep silence in the c':
16: 1 I have given order to the c' of
19 The c' of Asia salute you.
2Co 8: 1 bestowed on the c' of Macedonia;
18 gospel throughout all the c';
19 was also chosen of the c' to travel
23 they are the messengers of the c',
24 ye to them, and before the c',
11: 8 I robbed other c', taking wages of
28 me daily, the care of all the c'.
12:13 ye were inferior to other c',
Ga 1: 2 unto the c' of Galatia:
22 unto the c' of Judæa which were
1Th 2:14 became followers of the c' of God
2Th 1: 4 glory in you in the c' of God
Re 1: 4 John to the seven c' which are in
11 and send it unto the seven c'
20 are the angels of the seven c':
20 which thou sawest are the seven c'.
2: 7 what the Spirit saith unto the c';
11 the Spirit saith unto the c'; He
17 the Spirit saith unto the c'; To
23 all the c' shall know that I am he
29 what the Spirit saith unto the c'.
3: 6, 13, 22 the Spirit saith unto the c'.
22:16 unto you these things in the c'.

churl
Isa 32: 5 nor the c' said to be bountiful.
7 The instruments also of the c'

churlish
1Sa 25: 3 the man was c' and evil in his

churning
Pr 30:33 c' of milk bringeth forth butter,

Chushan-rishathaim (*cu''-shan-rish-a-tha'-im*)
J'g 3: 8 he sold them into the hand of C'
8 of Israel served C' eight years.
10 Lord delivered C' into his hand;
10 and his hand prevailed against C'.

Chuza (*cu'-zah*)
Lu 8: 3 the wife of C' Herod's steward,

cieled
2Ch 3: 5 greater house he c' with fir tree,
Jer 22:14 it is c' with cedar, and painted

Eze 41:16 door, c' with wood round about,
Hag 1: 4 to dwell in your c' houses,

cieling
1Ki 6:15 the house, and the walls of the c':

Cilicia (*sil-ish'-yah*)
Ac 6: 9 and of them of C' and of Asia,
15:23 in Antioch and Syria and C':
41 And he went through Syria and C',
21:39 am a Jew of Tarsus, a city in C',
22: 3 born in Tarsus, a city in C',
23:34 he understood that he was of C';
27: 5 we had sailed over the sea of C'
Gal 1:21 into the regions of Syria and C';

cinnamon
Ex 30:23 and of sweet c' half so much,
Pr 7:17 my bed with myrrh, aloes, and c'.
Ca 4:14 calamus and c', with all trees of
Re 18:13 c', and odours, and ointments,

Cinneroth (*sin'-ne-roth*) See also CHINNEROTH.
1Ki 15:20 and all C', with all the land of

circle
Isa 40:22 sitteth upon the c' of the earth,

circuit See also CIRCUITS.
1Sa 7:16 he went from year to year in c'
Job 22:14 he walketh in the c' of heaven.
Ps 19: 6 and his c' unto the ends of it:

circuits
Ec 1: 6 again according to his c'.

circumcise See also CIRCUMCISED; CIRCUMCISING.
Ge 17:11 shall c' the flesh of your foreskin;
De 10:16 C' therefore the foreskin of your
30: 6 And the Lord thy God will c' thine
Jos 5: 2 c' again the children of Israel the
4 is the cause why Joshua did c':
Jer 4: 4 C' yourselves to the Lord, and take
Lu 1:59 day they came to c' the child;
Joh 7:22 ye on the sabbath day c' a man.
Ac 15: 5 That it was needful to c' them,
21:21 saying that they ought not to c'

circumcised See also UNCIRCUMCISED.
Ge 17:10 man child among you shall be c'.
12 that is eight days old shall be c'
13 must needs be circumcised:
14 whose flesh of his foreskin is not c',
23 and c' the flesh of their foreskin
24 was c' in the flesh of his foreskin.
25 when he was c' in the flesh of his
26 the selfsame day was Abraham c',
27 the stranger, were c' with him.
21: 4 And Abraham c' his son Isaac
34:15 that every male of you be c';
17 will not hearken unto us, to be c';
22 if every male among us be c',
22 as they are c'.
24 and every male was c', all that
Ex 12:44 when thou hast c' him, then shall
48 let all his males be c', and then let
Le 12: 3 flesh of his foreskin shall be c'.
Jos 5: 3 c' the children of Israel at the hill
5 the people that came out were c',
5 of Egypt, them they had not c'.
7 them Joshua c': for they were
7 they had not c' them by the way.
Jer 9:25 all them which are c' with the
Ac 7: 8 Isaac, and c' him the eighth day;
15: 1 be c' after the manner of Moses,
24 Ye must be c', and keep the law:
16: 3 and took and c' him because of
Ro 4:11 believe, though they be not c';
1Co 7:18 Is any man called being c'?
18 let him not be c'.
Ga 2: 3 a Greek, was compelled to be c':
5: 2 if ye be c', Christ shall profit you
3 again to every man that is c',
6:12 they constrain you to be c'; only
13 they themselves who are c' keep
13 desire to have you c', that they may
Ph'p 3: 5 C' the eighth day, of the stock of
Col 2:11 In whom also ye are c' with the

circumcising
Jos 5: 8 they had done c' all the people,
Lu 2:21 accomplished for the c' of the

circumcision See also UNCIRCUMCISION.
Ex 4:26 husband thou art, because of the c'.
Joh 7:22 Moses therefore gave unto you c';
23 man on the sabbath day receive c',
Ac 7: 8 he gave him the covenant of c':
10:45 they of the c' which believed
11: 2 they that were of the c' contended
Ro 2:25 For c' verily profiteth, if thou keep
25 thy c' is made uncircumcision.
26 uncircumcision be counted for c'?
27 the letter and c' dost transgress
28 is that c', which is outward in the
29 c' is that of the heart, in the spirit,
3: 1 what profit is there of c'?
30 shall justify the c' by faith, and
4: 9 blessedness then upon the c' only,
10 when he was in c', or in
10 Not in c', but in uncircumcision.
11 And he received the sign of c',
12 the father of c' to them who are not
12 them who are not of the c' only,
15: 8 a minister of the c' for the truth
1Co 7:19 C' is nothing, and uncircumcision
Ga 2: 7 gospel of the c' was unto Peter;
8 Peter to the apostleship of the c',
9 heathen, and they unto the c'.
12 fearing them which were of the c'.
5: 6 neither c' availeth any thing,
11 if I yet preach c', why do I yet
Ga 6:15 neither c' availeth any thing,
Eph 2:11 C' in the flesh made by hands;
Ph'p 3: 3 For we are the c', which worship
Col 2:11 with the c' made without hands,
11 sins of the flesh by the c' of Christ:
3:11 c' nor uncircumcision, Barbarian,
4:11 called Justus, who are of the c'.
Tit 1:10 deceivers, specially they of the c':

circumspect
Ex 23:13 that I have said unto you be c':

circumspectly
Eph 5:15 that ye walk c', not as fools,

Cis (*sis*) See also KISH.
Ac 13:21 Saul the son of C', a man of the

cistern See also CISTERNS.
2Ki 18:31 every one the waters of his c':
Pr 5:15 Drink waters out of thine own c',
Ec 12: 6 or the wheel broken at the c'.
Isa 36:16 every one the waters of his own c';

cisterns
Jer 2:13 hewed them out c', broken c',

cities
Ge 13:12 Lot dwelled in the c' of the plain,
19:25 overthrew those c', and all the plain,
25 and all the inhabitants of the c',
29 God destroyed the c' of the plain,
29 overthrew the c' in which Lot dwelt.
35: 5 the terror of God was upon the c'
41:35 let them keep food in the c'.
48 and laid up the food in the c':
47:21 removed them to c' from one end
Ex 1:11 built for Pharaoh treasure c',
Lev 25:32 Notwithstanding the c' of the
32 and the houses of the c' of their
33 houses of the c' of the Levites
34 the field of the suburbs of their c'
26:25 gathered together within your c',
31 I will make your c' waste, and
33 shall be desolate, and your c' waste.
Nu 13:19 what c' they be that they dwell in,
28 and the c' are walled, and very
21: 2 then I will utterly destroy their c'.
3 utterly destroyed them and their c':
25 Israel took all these c': and Israel
25 dwelt in all the c' of the Amorites,
31:10 burnt all their c' wherein they
32:16 cattle, and c' for our little ones:
17 ones shall dwell in the fenced c'
24 Build you c' for your little ones,
26 shall be there in the c' of Gilead:
33 with the c' thereof in the coasts,
33 the c' of the country round about.
36 and Beth-haran, fenced c':
38 unto the c' which they builded.
35: 2 of their possession c' to dwell in;
2 unto the Levites suburbs for the c'
3 the c' shall they have to dwell in;
4 And the suburbs of the c', which
5 be to them the suburbs of the c'.
6 among the c' which ye shall give
6 there shall be six c' for refuge,
6 them ye shall add forty and two c'.
7 all the c' which ye shall give to
7 Levites shall be forty and eight c':
8 And the c' which ye shall give
8 give of his c' unto the Levites
11 ye shall appoint you c' to be
11 to be c' of refuge for you;
12 they shall be unto you c' for refuge
13 And of these c' which ye shall give
13 six c' shall ye have for refuge.
14 give three c' on this side Jordan,
14 three c' shall ye give in the land
14 which shall be c' of refuge.
15 These six c' shall be a refuge,
De 1:22 and into what c' we shall come.
28 the c' are great and walled up
2:34 took all his c' at that time,
35 the spoil of the c' which we took.
37 nor unto the c' in the mountains,
3: 4 we took all his c' at that time,
4 took not from them, threescore c',
5 All these c' were fenced with high
7 spoil of the c', we took for a prey
10 the c' of the plain, and all Gilead,
10 c' of the kingdom of Og in Bashan.
12 half mount Gilead, and the c'
19 abide in your c' which I have given
4:41 Then Moses severed three c' on
42 that fleeing unto one of these c' he
6:10 to give thee great and goodly c',
9: 1 c' great and fenced up to heaven,
13:12 thou shalt hear say in one of thy c',
19: 1 and dwellest in their c', and in
2 three c' for thee in the midst of
5 he shall flee unto one of those c',
7 Thou shalt separate three c' for
9 then shalt thou add three c' more
11 and fleeth into one of these c':
20:15 Thus shalt thou do unto all the c'
15 are not of the c' of these nations.
16 But of the c' of these people, which
21: 2 they shall measure unto the c'
Jos 9:17 and came unto their c' on the third
17 c' were Gibeon, and Chephirah,
10: 2 a great city, as one of the royal c',
19 them not to enter into their c':
20 of them entered into fenced c'.
37 all the c' thereof, and all the souls
39 king thereof, and all the c' thereof;
11:12 all the c' of those kings, and all the
13 c' that stood still in their strength,
14 all the spoil of these c', and the
Jos 11:21 them utterly with their c'.
13:10 c' of Sihon king of the Amorites,
17 Heshbon, and all her c' that are in
21 all the c' of the plain, and all the
23 families, the c' and the villages
25 all the c' of Gilead, and half the
28 families, the c', and their villages.
30 which are in Bashan, threescore c':
31 c' of the kingdom of Og in Bashan,
14: 4 c' to dwell in, with their suburbs
12 that the c' were great and fenced:
15: 9 out to the c' of mount Ephron;
21 uttermost c' of the tribe of the
32 all the c' are twenty and nine,
36 fourteen c' with their villages.
41 sixteen c' with their villages.
44 nine c' with their villages.
51 eleven c' with their villages.
54 nine c' with their villages;
57 ten c' with their villages.
59 six c' with their villages.
60 two c' with their villages.
62 six c' with their villages.
16: 9 separate c' for the children
9 all the c' with their villages.
17: 9 these c' of Ephraim are among
9 are among the c' of Manasseh;
12 out the inhabitants of those c';
18: 9 the land, and described it by c'
21 c' of the tribe of the children of
24 twelve c' with their villages:
28 fourteen c' with their villages.
19: 6 thirteen c' with their villages:
7 four c' and their villages:
8 that were round about these c'
15 twelve c' with their villages.
16 these c' with their villages.
22 sixteen c' with their villages.
23 the c' and their villages.
30 twenty and two c' with their
31 these c' with their villages.
35 And the fenced c' are Ziddim, Zer,
38 nineteen c' with their villages.
39 the c' and their villages.
48 these c' with their villages.
20: 2 Appoint out for you c' of refuge,
4 flee unto one of those c' shall stand
9 c' appointed for all the children of
21: 2 to give us c' to dwell in, with the
3 Lord, these c' and their suburbs.
4 the tribe of Benjamin, thirteen c'.
5 the half tribe of Manasseh, ten c'.
6 of Manasseh in Bashan, thirteen c'.
7 of the tribe of Zebulun, twelve c'.
8 by lot unto the Levites these c'
9 these c' which are here mentioned
16 nine c' out of those two tribes.
18 Almon with her suburbs; four c'.
19 All the c' of the children of Aaron,
19 were thirteen c' with their suburbs.
20 they had the c' of their lot out of
22, 24 with her suburbs; four c'.
25 with her suburbs; two c'.
26 All the c' were ten with their
27 with her suburbs; two c'.
29 with her suburbs; four c'.
31 Rehob with her suburbs; four c'.
32 Kartan with her suburbs; three c'.
33 All the c' of the Gershonites were
33 were thirteen c' with their suburbs.
35 Nahalal with her suburbs; four c'.
37 Mephaath with her suburbs; four c'.
39 Jazer with her suburbs; four c'
40 the c' for the children of Merari by
40 Levites, were by their lot twelve c.
41 All the c' of the Levites within the
41 forty and eight c' with their
42 These c' were every one with their
42 about them: thus were all these c'.
24:13 c' which ye built not, and ye dwell
J'g 10: 4 they had thirty c', which are called
11:26 the c' that be along by the coasts
33 come to Minnith, even twenty c',
12: 7 buried in one of the c' of Gilead.
20:14 themselves together out of the c'
15 numbered at that time out of the c'
42 them which came out of the c'
48 they set on fire all the c' that they
21:23 repaired the c', and dwelt in them.
1Sa 6:18 the number of all the c' of the
18 of fenced c', and of country villages,
7:14 the c' which the Philistines had
18: 6 women came out of all c' of Israel,
30:29 in the c' of the Jerahmeelites, and
29 which were in the c' of the Kenites,
31: 7 dead, they forsook the c', and fled;
2Sa 2: 1 go up into any of the c' of Judah?
3 and they dwelt in the c' of Hebron.
8: 8 and from Berothai, c' of Hadadezer,
10:12 people, and for the c' of our God:
12:31 the c' of the children of Ammon.
20: 6 he get him fenced c', and escape
24: 7 all the c' of the Hivites, and of the
1Ki 4:13 threescore great c' with walls and
8:37 besiege them in the land of their c';
9:11 Solomon gave Hiram twenty c' in
12 came out from Tyre to see the c'
13 What c' are these which thou hast
19 the c' of store that Solomon had,
19 and c' for his chariots,
19 and c' for his horsemen,
10:26 he bestowed in the c' for chariots,
12:17 Israel which dwelt in the c' of
13:32 high places which are in the c' of
15:20 he had against the c' of Israel,
23 he did, and the c' which he built,

1Ki 20:34 The c', which my father took from
22:39 all the c' that he built, are they
2Ki 3:25 And they beat down the c', and on
13:25 son of Hazael the c', which he had
25 and recovered the c' of Israel.
17: 6 Gozan, and in the c' of the Medes.
9 them high places in all their c',
24 placed them in the c' of Samaria
24 Samaria, and dwelt in the c'
26 and placed in the c' of Samaria,
29 every nation in their c' wherein
18:11 and in the c' of the Medes:
13 come up against all the fenced c'
19:25 shouldest be to lay waste fenced c'
23: 5 the high places in the c' of Judah,
8 all the priests out of the c' of Judah,
19 the high places that were in the c'
1Ch 2:22 Jair, who had three and twenty c'
23 towns thereof, even threescore c'.
4:31 These were their c' unto the reign
32 and Tochen, and Ashan, five c':
33 that were round about the same c',
6:57 the sons of Aaron they gave the c'
60 All their c' throughout their
60 their families were thirteen c'.
61 of the family of that tribe, were c'
61 tribe of Manasseh, by lot, ten c'.
62 Manasseh in Bashan, thirteen c'.
63 of the tribe of Zebulun, twelve c'.
64 Israel gave to the Levites these c'
65 these c', which are called by their
66 the sons of Kohath had c' of their
67 unto them, of the c' of refuge,
9: 2 dwelt in their possessions in their c'
10: 7 they forsook their c', and fled:
13: 2 Levites which are in their c' and
18: 8 and from Chun, c' of Hadarezer,
19: 7 themselves together from their c',
13 people, and for the c' of our God:
20: 3 so dealt David with all the c' of
27:25 the fields, in the c', and in the
2Ch 1:14 which he placed in the chariot c',
6:28 besiege them in the c' of their
8: 2 c' which Huram had restored
4 wilderness, and all the store c',
5 fenced c', with walls, gates, and
6 all the store c' that Solomon had,
6 and all the chariot c',
6 and the c' of the horsemen,
9:25 he bestowed in the chariot c', and
10:17 Israel that dwelt in the c' of Judah,
11: 5 in Jerusalem, and built c' for
10 Judah and in Benjamin fenced c'.
12: 4 he took the fenced c' which
13:19 and took c' from him, Bethel with
14: 5 out of all the c' of Judah the high
6 he built fenced c' in Judah: for
7 unto Judah, Let us build these c',
14 they smote all the c' round about
14 them: and they spoiled all the c';
15: 8 c' which he had taken from mount
16: 4 captains of his armies against the c'
4 and all the store c' of Naphtali.
17: 2 placed forces in all the fenced c' of
2 and in the c' of Ephraim, which
7 to teach in the c' of Judah.
9 throughout all the c' of Judah,
12 in Judah castles, and c' of store.
13 much business in the c' of Judah:
19 fenced c' throughout all Judah.
19: 5 fenced c' of Judah, city by city,
10 brethren that dwell in their c',
20: 4 out of all the c' of Judah they
21: 3 things, with fenced c' in Judah:
23: 2 the Levites out of all the c' of
24: 5 Go out unto the c' of Judah and
25:13 fell upon the c' of Judah, from
26: 6 and built c' about Ashdod,
27: 4 he built c' in the mountains
28:18 invaded the c' of the low country,
31: 1 went out to the c' of Judah,
1 his possession, into their own c'.
6 Judah, that dwelt in the c' of
15 in the c' of the priests, in their
19 fields of the suburbs of their c',
32: 1 encamped against the fenced c',
29 Moreover he provided him c', and
33:14 war in all the fenced c' of Judah.
34: 6 so did he in the c' of Manasseh,
Ezr 2:70 the Nethinims, dwelt in their c',
70 and all Israel in their c'.
3: 1 children of Israel were in the c',
4:10 and set in the c' of Samaria,
10:14 taken strange wives in our c'
Ne 7:73 and all Israel, dwelt in their c';
73 children of Israel were in their c'.
8:15 and proclaim in all their c',
9:25 took strong c', and a fat land,
10:37 tithes in all the c' of our tillage.
11: 1 nine parts to dwell in other c'.
3 in the c' of Judah dwelt every one
3 in his possesion in their c',
20 the c' of Judah, every one in his
12:44 of the fields of the c' the portions
Es 9: 2 themselves together in their c'
Job 15:28 he dwelleth in desolate c', and in
Ps 9: 6 and thou hast destroyed c'; their
69:35 and will build the c' of Judah:
Isa 1: 7 c' are burned with fire: your land,
6:11 c' be wasted without inhabitant,
14:17 and destroyed the c' thereof;
21 fill the face of the world with c'.
17: 2 The c' of Aroer are forsaken:
9 strong c' be as a forsaken bough,
19:18 five c' in the land of Egypt speak
33: 8 hath despised the c', he regardeth

Isa 36: 1 all the defenced c' of Judah,
37:26 be to lay waste defenced c'
40: 9 say unto the c' of Judah, Behold
42:11 the wilderness and the c' thereof
44:26 and to the c' of Judah, Ye shall be
54: 3 the desolate c' to be inhabited.
61: 4 they shall repair the waste c', the
64:10 Thy holy c' are a wilderness,
Jer 1:15 and against all the c' of Judah.
2:15 c' are burned without inhabitant.
28 the number of thy c' are thy gods,
4: 5 and let us go into the defenced c'.
7 thy c' shall be laid waste, without
16 their voice against the c' of Judah.
26 the c' thereof were broken down
5: 6 leopard shall watch over their c':
17 shall impoverish thy fenced c',
7:17 what they do in the c' of Judah
34 to cease from the c' of Judah,
8:14 let us enter into the defenced c',
9:11 will make the c' of Judah desolate,
10:22 to make the c' of Judah desolate,
11: 6 all these words in the c' of Judah,
12 Then shall the c' of Judah and
13 number of thy c' were thy gods,
13:19 c' of the south shall be shut up,
17:26 shall come from the c' of Judah,
20:16 the c' which the Lord overthrew,
22: 6 and c' which are not inhabited.
25:18 Jerusalem, and the c' of Judah,
26: 2 speak unto all the c' of Judah,
31:21 turn again to these thy c'.
23 of Judah and in the c' thereof,
24 in Judah itself, and in all the c'
32:44 Jerusalem, and in the c' of Judah,
44 and in the c' of the mountains,
44 and in the c' of the valley,
44 and in the c' of the south:
33:10 c' of Judah, and in the streets of
12 c' thereof, shall be an habitation
13 In the c' of the mountains, in the
13 c' of the vale, and in the c' of the
13 Jerusalem, and in the c' of Judah,
34: 1 and against all the c' thereof,
7 and against all the c' of Judah
7 Azekah: for these defenced c'
7 remained of the c' of Judah.
22 make the c' of Judah a desolation
36: 6 all Judah that come out of their c'.
9 the c' of Judah unto Jerusalem.
40: 5 governor over the c' of Judah,
10 in your c' that ye have taken.
44: 2 upon all the c' of Judah; and,
6 and was kindled in the c' of Judah
17 and our princes, in the c' of Judah,
21 that ye burned in the c' of Judah,
48: 9 for the c' thereof shall be desolate,
15 spoiled, and gone up out of her c',
24 all the c' of the land of Moab, far
28 ye that dwell in Moab, leave the c',
49: 1 and his people dwell in his c'?
13 the c' thereof shall be perpetual
18 and the neighbour c' thereof,
50:32 I will kindle a fire in his c', and it
40 Gomorrah and the neighbour c'
51:43 c' are a desolation, a dry land,
La 5:11 and the maids in the c' of Judah.
Eze 6: 6 the c' shall be laid waste,
12:20 And the c' that are inhabited shall
19: 7 palaces, and he laid waste their c';
25: 9 open the side of Moab from the c',
9 his c' which are on his frontiers,
26:19 like the c' that are not inhabited;
29:12 that are desolate, and her c'
12 among the c' that are laid waste
30: 7 and her c' shall be in the midst
7 of the c' that are wasted.
17 and these c' shall go into captivity.
35: 4 I will lay thy c' waste, and thou
9 and thy c' shall not return: and
36: 4 and to the c' that are forsaken,
10 the c' shall be inhabited, and the
33 also cause you to dwell in the c',
35 ruined c' are become fenced,
38 waste c' be filled with flocks of
39: 9 in the c' of Israel shall go forth,
Da 11:15 and take the most fenced c':
Ho 8:14 Judah hath multiplied fenced c':
14 but I will send a fire upon his c',
11: 6 the sword shall abide on his c',
13:10 that may save thee in all thy c'?
Am 4: 6 cleanness of teeth in all your c',
8 three c' wandered unto one city,
9:14 they shall build the waste c', and
Ob 20 shall possess the c' of the south.
Mic 5:11 I will cut off the c' of thy land,
14 so will I destroy thy c'.
7:12 Assyria, and from the fortified c',
Zep 1:16 and alarm against the fenced c',
3: 6 their c' are destroyed, so that
Zec 1:12 Jerusalem and on the c' of Judah,
17 My c' through prosperity shall yet
7: 7 in prosperity, and the c' thereof
8:20 and the inhabitants of many c':
M't 9:35 Jesus went about all the c' and
10:23 over the c' of Israel, till the Son
11: 1 to teach and to preach in their c'.
20 Then began he to upbraid the c'
14:13 followed him on foot out of the c'.
M'r 6:33 and ran afoot thither out of all c',
56 into villages, or c', or country,
Lu 4:43 kingdom of God to other c' also:
13:22 went through the c' and villages,
19:17 have thou authority over ten c'.
19 to him, Be thou also over five c'.
Ac 5:16 out of the c' round about

Ac 8:40 he preached in all the c', till he
14: 6 Lystra and Derbe, c' of Lycaonia,
16: 4 through the c', they delivered
26:11 them even unto strange c'.
2Pe 2: 6 c' of Sodom and Gomorrha into
Jude 7 Gomorrha, and the c' about them
Re 16:19 parts, and the c' of the nations

citizen See also CITIZENS.
Lu 15:15 himself to a c' of that country;
Ac 21:39 in Cilicia, a c' of no mean city:

citizens see also FELLOWCITIZENS.
Lu 19:14 But his c' hated him, and sent a

city See also CITIES.
Ge 4:17 and he builded a c', and called
17 called the name of the c', after
10:11 and the c' Rehoboth, and Calah,
12 and Calah: the same is a great c'.
11: 4 let us build us a c' and a tower,
5 the Lord came down to see the c'
8 and they left off to build the c'.
18:24 be fifty righteous within the c':
26 Sodom fifty righteous within the c',
28 destroy all the c' for lack of five?
19: 4 of the c', even the men of Sodom,
12 whatsoever thou hast in the c',
14 for the Lord will destroy this c'.
15 consumed in the iniquity of the c'.
16 forth, and set him without the c'.
20 this c' is near to flee unto, and it
21 I will not overthrow this c', for the
22 the name of the c' was called Zoar.
23:10 in at the gate of his c', saying,
18 that went in at the gate of his c'.
24:10 Mesopotamia, unto the c' of Nahor.
11 to kneel down without the c'
13 of the men of the c' come out
26:33 the name the c' is Beer-sheba
28:19 name of that c' was called Luz
33:18 Jacob came to Shalem, a c' of
18 and pitched his tent before the c'.
34:20 came unto the gate of their c',
20 with the men of their c', saying,
24 that went out of the gate of his c';
24 that went out of the gate of his c'.
25 c' boldly, and slew all the males.
27 upon the slain, and spoiled the c',
28 and that which was in the c',
35:27 c' of Arbah, which is Hebron,
36:32 name of his c' was Dinhabah.
35 the name of his c' was Avith.
39 the name of his c' was Pau; and
41:48 which was round about every c',
44: 4 when they were gone out of the c',
13 his ass, and returned to the c'.
Ex 9:29 As soon as I am gone out of the c',
33 Moses went out of the c' from
Le 14:40 an unclean place without the c':
41 that they scrape off without the c'
45 carry them forth out of the c'
53 let go the living bird out of the c'
25:29 a dwelling house in a walled c',
30 the house that is in the walled c'
33 sold, and the c' of his possession,
Nu 20:16 Kadesh, a c' in the uttermost of
21:26 Heshbon was the c' of Sihon the
27 c' of Sihon be built and prepared:
28 a flame from the c' of Sihon:
22:36 meet him unto a c' of Moab,
24:19 him that remaineth of the c'.
35: 4 the wall of the c' and outward a
5 shall measure from without the c'
5 the c' shall be in the midst:
25 shall restore him to the c'
26 the border of the c' of his refuge,
27 him without the borders of the c'
28 remained in the c' of his refuge
32 that is fled to the c' of his refuge,
De 2:34 and the little ones, of every c',
36 and from the c' that is by the
36 there was not one c' too strong
3: 4 not a c' which we took not from
6 women, and children, of every c'.
13:13 the inhabitants of their c', saying,
15 smite the inhabitants of that c'
16 and shalt burn with fire the c',
19:12 elders of his c' shall send and fetch
20:10 When thou comest nigh unto a c'
14 and all that is in the c', even all the
19 When thou shalt besiege a c' a long
20 shalt build bulwarks against the c'
21: 3 the c' which is next unto the slain
3 even the elders of that c' shall take
4 elders of that c' shall bring down
6 all the elders of that c', that are
19 him out unto the elders of his c',
20 shall say unto the elders of his c',
21 all the men of his c' shall stone
22:15 the elders of the c' in the gate:
17 the cloth before the elders of the c'.
18 elders of that c' shall take that
21 the men of her c' shall stone her
23 and a man find her in the c',
24 both out unto the gate of that c',
24 she cried not, being in the c';
25: 8 the elders of his c' shall call him,
28: 3 Blessed shalt thou be in the c',
16 Cursed shalt thou be in the c', and
34: 3 of Jericho, the c' of palm
Jos 3:16 far from the c' Adam, that is
6: 3 And ye shall compass the c', all ye
3 go round about the c' once. Thus
4 seventh day ye shall compass the c'
5 wall of the c' shall fall down flat,
7 Pass on, and compass the c', and
11 ark of the Lord compassed the c',

Jos 6:14 second day they compassed the c'
15 compassed the c' after the same
15 day they compassed the c' seven
16 for the Lord hath given you the c'.
17 the c' shall be accursed, even it,
20 people went up into the c', every
20 before him, and they took the c'.
21 destroyed all that was in the c',
24 And they burnt the c' with fire,
26 that riseth up and buildeth this c'
8: 1 king of Ai, and his people, and his c',
2 lay thee an ambush for the c' behind
4 lie in wait against the c',
4 even behind the c':
4 go not very far from the c',
5 with me, will approach unto the c':
6 we have drawn them from the c';
7 the ambush, and seize upon the c':
8 when ye have taken the c',
8 that ye shall set the c' on fire:
11 drew nigh, and came before the c',
12 and Ai, on the west side of the c'.
13 host that was on the north of the c',
13 liers in wait on the west of the c',
14 the men of the c' went out against
14 ambush against him behind the c'.
16 and were drawn away from the c'.
17 and they left the c' open, and
18 he had in his hand toward the c'.
19 they entered into the c', and took it,
19 and hasted and set the c' on fire.
20 the smoke of the c' ascended up to
21 the ambush had taken the c', and
21 that the smoke of the c' ascended
22 And the other issued out of the c'
27 the spoil of that c' Israel took for
29 the entering of the gate of the c',
10: 2 Gibeon was a great c', as one of
11:19 not a c' that made peace with the
13: 9, 16 c'... in the midst of the river,
15:13 the c' of Arba the father of Anak,
13 which c' is Hebron.
62 Nibshan, and the c' of Salt,
18:14 Kirjath-jearim, a c' of the
19:29 the strong c' Tyre; and the coast
50 gave him the c' which he asked,
50 he built the c', and dwelt therein.
20: 4 at the entering of the gate of the c',
4 in the ears of the elders of that c',
4 shall take him into the c' unto them,
6 shall dwell in that c', until he stand
6 return, and come unto his own c',
6 unto the c' from whence he fled.
21:11 they gave them the c' of Arba
11 which c' is Hebron, in the hill
12 fields of the c', and the villages
13, 21, 27, 32, 38 c' of refuge ... slayer;
J'g 1: 8 the sword, and set the c' on fire.
16 out of the c' of palm trees with
17 name of the c' was called Hormah.
23 the name of the c' before was Luz.)
24 saw a man come forth out of the c',
24 the entrance into the c', and we will
25 them the entrance into the c',
25 they smote the c' with the edge of
26 land of the Hittites and built a c',
3:13 and possessed the c' of palm trees.
6:27 household, and the men of the c',
28 when the men of the c' arose early
30 the men of the c' said unto Joash,
8:16 And he took the elders of the c',
17 and slew the men of the c'.
27 ephod thereof, and put it in his c',
9:30 Zebul the ruler of the c' heard
31 they fortify the c' against thee.
33 rise early, and set upon the c':
35 the entering of the gate of the c':
43 were come forth out of the c';
44 in the entering of the gate of the c':
45 Abimelech fought against the c' all
45 that day; and he took the c',
45 and beat down the c' and sowed it
51 was a strong tower within the c',
51 and women, and all they of the c',
14:18 the men of the c' said unto him on
16: 2 him all night in the gate of the c',
3 took the doors of the gate of the c',
17: 8 the man departed out of the c'
18:27 and burnt the c' with fire.
28 they built a c' and dwelt therein.
29 they called the name of the c' Dan,
29 name of the c' was Laish at the first.
19:11 turn in into this c' of the Jebusites,
12 hither into the c' of a stranger,
15 sat him down in a street of the c':
17 man in the street of the c':
22 men of the c', certain sons of Belial,
20:11 Israel were gathered against the c',
31 were drawn away from the c'; and
32 them from the c' unto the highways.
37 smote all the c' with the edge of
38 with smoke rise up out of the c'.
40 began to arise up out of the c'
40 the flame of the c' ascended up to
48 as well the men of every c', as the
Ru 1:19 all the c' was moved about them,
2:18 took it up, and went into the c':
3:11 the c' of my people doth know
15 on her: and she went into the c'.
4: 2 took ten men of the elders of the c',
1Sa 1: 3 this man went up out of his c'
4:13 when the man came into the c',
13 told it, all the c' cried out.
5: 9 hand of the Lord was against the c'
9 he smote the men of the c',

1Sa 5:11 destruction throughout all the c';
12 cry of the c' went up to heaven,
8:22 Go ye every man unto his c'.
9: 6 there is in this c' a man of God,
10 the c' where the man of God was.
11 as they went up the hill to the c',
12 for he came to day to the c'; for
13 As soon as ye be come into the c',
14 they went up into the c': and
14 when they were come into the c',
25 from the high place into the c',
27 going down to the end of the c',
10: 5 thou art come thither to the c',
15: 5 Saul came to a c' of Amalek, and
20: 6 he might run to Beth-lehem his c':
29 family hath a sacrifice in the c';
40 him, Go, carry them to the c'.
42 and Jonathan went into the c'.
22:19 Nob, the c' of the priests, smote he
23:10 to destroy the c' for my sake.
27: 5 thy servant dwell in the royal c'
28: 3 him in Ramah, even in his own c'.
30: 3 David and his men came to the c',
2Sa 5: 7 Zion: the same is the c' of David.
9 fort, and called it the c' of David.
6:10 unto him into the c' of David: but
12 the house of Obed-edom into the c'
16 ark of the Lord came into the c'
10: 3 to search the c', and to spy it out,
14 and entered into the c'. So Joab
11:16 to pass, when Joab observed the c',
17 the men of the c' went out, and
20 approached ye so nigh unto the c'
25 battle more strong against the c',
12: 1 There were two men in one c';
26 of Ammon, and took the royal c'.
27 and have taken the c' of waters.
28 encamp against the c', and take it:
28 lest I take the c', and it be called
30 he brought forth the spoil of the c'
15: 2 Of what c' art thou? And he said,
12 David's counseller, from his c',
14 smite the c' with the edge of the
24 had done passing out of the c'.
25 back the ark of God into the c':
27 return into the c' in peace, and
34 But if thou return to the c', and say
37 David's friend came into the c',
17:13 if he be gotten into a c', then shall
13 all Israel bring ropes to that c',
17 not be seen to come into the c':
23 him home to his house, to his c',
18: 3 that thou succour us out of the c'.
19: 3 by stealth that day into the c',
37 die in mine own c', and be buried
20:15 they cast up a bank against the c',
16 cried a wise woman out of the c',
19 to destroy a c' and a mother in
21 and I will depart from the c'.
22 they retired from the c', every man
24: 5 on the right side of the c' that lieth
1Ki 1:41 of the c' being in an uproar?
45 c' rang again. This is the noise
2:10 and was buried in the c' of David.
3: 1 brought her into the c' of David,
8: 1 of the Lord out of the c' of David,
16 I chose no c' out of all the tribes
44 pray unto the Lord toward the c'
48 the c' which thou hast chosen,
9:16 the Canaanites that dwelt in the c',
24 came up out of the c' of David
11:27 the breaches of the c' of David
32 sake, the c' which I have chosen
36 Jerusalem, the c' which I have
43 was buried in the c' of David his
13:25 they came and told it in the c'
29 the old prophet came to the c', to
14:11 that dieth of Jeroboam in the c'
12 when thy feet enter into the c', the
21 the c' which the Lord did choose
31 buried with his fathers in the c' of
15: 8 they buried him in the c' of David:
24 buried with his fathers in the c' of
16: 4 Him that dieth of Baasha in the c'
18 when Zimri saw that the c' was
24 called the name of the c' which he
17:10 when he came to the gate of the c',
20: 2 to Ahab king of Israel into the c',
12 themselves in array against the c'.
19 the provinces came out of the c',
30 the rest fled to Aphek, into the c';
30 Ben-hadad fled and came into the c',
21: 8 to the nobles that were in his c',
11 the men of his c', even the elders
11 who were the inhabitants in his c',
13 they carried him forth out of the c',
24 Him that dieth of Ahab in the c'
22:26 Amon the governor of the c', and
36 saying, Every man to his c', and
50 buried with his fathers in the c' of
2Ki 2:19 the men of the c' said unto Elisha,
19 the situation of this c' is pleasant,
23 forth little children out of the c',
3:19 ye shall smite every fenced c',
19 and every choice c',
6:14 by night, and compassed the c'
15 an host compassed the c' both
19 not the way, neither is this the c':
7: 4 If we say, We will enter into the c',
4 then the famine is in the c',
10 and called unto the porter of the c':
12 When they come out of the c', we
7:12 them alive, and get into the c'.
13 remain, which are left in the c',
8:24 with his fathers in the c' of David:

2Ki 9:15 go forth nor escape out of the c'
28 with his fathers in the c' of David.
10: 2 chariots and horses, a fenced c'
5 he that was over the c', the elders
6 the great men of the c', which
25 went to the c' of the house of Baal.
11:20 the land rejoiced, and the c' was in
12:21 with his fathers in the c' of David:
14:20 with his fathers in the c' of David,
15: 7 with his fathers in the c' of David:
38 in the c' of David his father: and
16:20 with his fathers in the c' of David:
17: 9 of the watchman to the fenced c'.
18: 8 of the watchman to the fenced c'.
30 this c' shall not be delivered into
19:13 the king of the c' of Sepharvaim,
32 He shall not come into this c',
33 and shall not come into this c',
34 I will defend this c', to save it,
20: 6 I will deliver thee and this c' out
6 I will defend this c' for mine own
20 and brought water into the c', are
23: 8 of Joshua the governor of the c',
8 left hand at the gate of the c'.
17 And the men of the c' told him,
27 and will cast off this c' Jerusalem
24:10 and the c' was besieged.
11 of Babylon came against the c',
25: 2 the c' was besieged unto the
3 the famine prevailed in the c',
4 And the c' was broken up, and all
4 the Chaldees were against the c'
11 the people that were left in the c',
19 out of the c' he took an officer that
19 which were found in the c', and
19 the land that were found in the c':
1Ch 1:43 the name of his c' was Dinhabah.
46 the name of his c' was Avith.
50 name of his c' was Pai; and his
6:56 the fields of the c', and the villages
57 namely, Hebron, the c' of refuge,
11: 5 castle of Zion, which is the c' of
7 they called it the c' of David.
8 he built the c' round about, even
8 and Joab repaired the rest of the c'.
13:13 home to himself to the c' of David,
15: 1 David made him houses in the c' of
29 came to the c' of David, that
19: 9 in array before the gate of the c':
15 his brother, and entered into the c'.
20: 2 exceeding much spoil out of the c'.
2Ch 5: 2 of the Lord out of the c' of David,
6: 5 I chose no c' among all the tribes
34 they pray unto thee toward this c'
38 and toward the c' which thou hast
8:11 of Pharaoh out of the c' of David
9:31 he was buried in the c' of David
11:12 in every several c' he put shields
23 Benjamin, unto every fenced c':
12:13 the c' which the Lord had chosen
16 and was buried in the c' of David:
14: 1 they buried him in the c' of David:
15: 6 was destroyed of nation, and c' of c':
16:14 made for himself in the c' of David,
18:25 to Amon the governor of the c',
19: 5 the fenced cities of Judah, c' by c',
21: 1 with his fathers in the c' of David,
20 they buried him in the c' of David,
23:21 and the c' was quiet, after that
24:16 in the c' of David among the kings,
25 they buried him in the c' of David,
25:28 with his fathers in the c' of Judah.
27: 9 they buried him in the c' of David:
28:15 Jericho, the c' of palm trees,
25 in every several c' of Judah he
27 they buried him in the c', even in
29:20 and gathered the rulers of the c',
30:10 the posts passed from c' to c'
31:19 in every several c', the men that
32: 3 which were without the c':
5 repaired Millo in the c' of David,
6 in the street of the gate of the c',
18 them; that they might take the c'.
30 to the west side of the c' of David.
33:14 built a wall without the c' of David,
15 and cast them out of the c'.
34: 8 Maaseiah the governor of the c',
Ezr 2: 1 Judah, every one unto his c';
4:12 the rebellious and the bad c',
13 if this c' be builded, and the walls
15 know that this c' is a rebellious c',
15 which cause was this c' destroyed.
16 if this c' be builded again, and the
19 and it is found that this c' of old
21 and that this c' be not builded,
10:14 the elders of every c', and the
Neh 2: 3 when the c', the place of my father's
5 the c' of my father's sepulchres,
8 house, and for the wall of the c',
3:15 the stairs that go down from the c'
7: 4 the c' was large and great: but the
6 to Judah, every one unto his c';
11: 1 to dwell in Jerusalem the holy c',
9 of Senuah was second over the c'.
18 the Levites in the holy c' were
12:37 by the stairs of the c' of David,
13:18 this evil upon us, and upon this c'?
Es 3:15 but the c' Shushan was perplexed.
4: 1 went out into the midst of the c',
6 unto the street of the c', which
6: 9, 11 through the street of the c',
8:11 the Jews which were in every c'
15 and the c' of Shushan rejoiced
17 in every province, and in every c',
9:28 every province, and every c';

Job 24:12 Men groan from out of the c',
29: 7 out to the gate through the c',
39: 7 scorneth the multitude of the c',
Ps 31:21 kindness in a strong c'.
46: 4 shall make glad the c' of God,
48: 1 the c' of our God, in the mountain
2 north, the c' of the great King.
8 in the c' of the Lord of hosts,
8 in the c' of our God:
55: 9 seen violence and strife in the c'.
59: 6, 14 dog, and go round about the c'.
60: 9 will bring me into the strong c'?
72:16 they of the c' shall flourish like
87: 3 are spoken of thee, O c' of God.
101: 8 doers from the c' of the Lord.
107: 4 they found no c' to dwell in.
7 they might go to a c' of habitation.
36 may prepare a c' for habitation;
108:10 will bring me into the strong c'?
122: 3 is builded as a c' that is compact
127: 1 except the Lord keep the c',
Pr 1:21 in the c' she uttereth her words,
8: 3 the gates, at the entry of the c',
9: 3 upon the highest places of the c',
14 in the high places of the c',
10:15 rich man's wealth is his strong c':
11:10 the righteous, the c' rejoiceth:
11 of the upright the c' is exalted:
16:32 spirit than he that taketh a c'.
18:11 rich man's wealth is his strong c',
19 harder to be won than a strong c':
21:22 man scaleth the c' of the mighty,
25:28 like a c' that is broken down,
29: 8 men bring a c' into a snare:
Ec 7:19 mighty men which are in the c'.
8:10 they were forgotten in the c'
9:14 There was a little c', and few men
15 he by his wisdom delivered the c';
10:15 knoweth not how to go to the c'.
Ca 3: 2 will rise now, and go about the c'
3 that go about the c' found me:
5: 7 that went about the c' found me,
Isa 1: 8 of cucumbers, as a besieged c'.
21 is the faithful c' become an harlot!
26 be called, The c' of righteousness,
26 of righteousness, the faithful c'
14: 4 the golden c' ceased!
31 Howl, O gate; cry, O c';
17: 1 is taken away from being a c',
19: 2 against his neighbour; c' against c',
18 The c' of destruction.
22: 2 of stirs, a tumultuous c',
2 a joyous c': thy slain men
9 the breaches of the c' of David,
23: 7 this your joyous c', whose
8 against Tyre, the crowning c',
11 against the merchant c',
16 Take an harp, go about the c',
24:10 c' of confusion is broken down:
12 In the c' is left desolation,
25: 2 thou hast made of a c' an heap;
2 of a defenced c' a ruin:
2 a palace of strangers to be no c';
3 the c' of the terrible nations shall
26: 1 We have a strong c'; salvation
5 the lofty c', he layeth it low;
27:10 the defenced c' shall be desolate,
29: 1 Ariel, the c' where David dwelt!
32:13 houses of joy in the joyous c':
14 multitude of the c' shall be left;
19 the c' shall be low in a low place.
33:20 Zion, the c' of our solemnities:
36:15 this c' shall not be delivered into
37:13 the king of the c' of Sepharvaim,
33 He shall not come into this c', nor
34 and shall not come into this c', saith
35 I will defend this c' to save it
38: 6 I will deliver thee and this c' out
6 and I will defend this c'.
45:13 he shall build my city, and he
48: 2 they call themselves of the holy c',
52: 1 O Jerusalem, the holy c':
60:14 call thee, The c' of the Lord,
62:12 Sought out, A c' not forsaken.
66: 6 A voice of noise from the c',
Jer 1:18 made thee this day a defenced c',
3:14 I will take you one of a c',
4:29 whole c' shall flee for the noise
29 every c' shall be forsaken, and not
6: 6 this is the c' to be visited;
8 16 the c', and those that dwell therein.
14:18 if I enter into the c', then behold
15: 8 suddenly, and terrors upon the c'.
17:24 burden through the gates of this c'
25 there enter into the gates of this c'
25 and this c' shall remain for ever.
19: 8 I will make this c' desolate, and an
11 will I break this people and this c',
12 and even make this c' as Tophet:
15 upon this c' and upon all her towns
20: 5 deliver all the strength of this c',
21: 4 them into the midst of this c'.
6 will smite the inhabitants of this c',
7 left in this c' from the pestilence,
9 He that abideth in this c' shall
10 have set my face against this c'
22: 8 many nations shall pass by this c',
8 Lord done thus unto this great c'?
23:39 you, and the c' that I gave you
25:29 I begin to bring evil on the c'
26: 6 and will make this c' a curse to all
9 this c' shall be desolate without
11 he hath prophesied against this c',
12 this house and against this c'
15 upon yourselves, and upon this c',
26:20 who prophesied against this c'

Jer 27:17 should this c' be laid waste?
19 the vessels that remain in this c',
29: 7 And seek the peace of the c'
16 the people that dwelleth in this c',
30:18 c' shall be builded upon her own
31:38 the c' shall be built to the Lord
32: 3 this c' into the hand of the king
24 mounts, they are come unto the c'
24 and the c' is given into the hand of
25 for the c' is given into the hand of
28 I will give this c' into the hand of
29 that fight against this c',
29 shall come and set fire on this c',
31 For this c' hath been to me as a
36 concerning this c', whereof ye say
33: 4 concerning the houses of this c',
5 I have hid my face from this c'.
34: 2 I will give this c' into the hand of
22 cause them to return to this c';
37: 8 and fight against this c', and take
10 tent; and burn this c' with fire.
21 all the bread in the c' were spent.
38: 2 that remaineth in this c' shall die
3 This c' shall surely be given into
4 men of war that remain in this c',
9 there is no more bread in the c'.
17 and this c' shall not be burned
18 shall this c' be given into the hand
23 shalt cause this c' to be burned
39: 2 of the month, the c' was broken up.
4 went forth out of the c' by night,
9 the people that remained in the c',
16 will bring my words upon this c'
41: 7 they came into the midst of the c',
46: 8 the c' and the inhabitants thereof.
47: 2 c', and them that dwell therein:
48: 8 spoiler shall come upon every c',
8 and no c' shall escape:
49:25 is the c' of praise not left,
25 the c' of my joy!
51:31 king of Babylon that his c' is taken
52: 5 the c' was besieged unto the
6 the famine was sore in the c', so
7 the c' was broken up, and all the
7 went forth out of the c' by night
7 were by the c' round about:)
15 the people that remained in the c',
25 took also out of the c' an eunuch,
25 which were found in the c';
25 were found in the midst of the c'.
La 1: 1 How doth the c' sit solitary,
19 elders gave up the ghost in the c',
2:11 swoon in the streets of the c'.
12 wounded in the streets of the c',
15 c' that men call The perfection
3:51 of all the daughters of my c'.
Eze 4: 1 thee, and pourtray upon it the c',
3 of iron between thee and the c':
5: 2 a third part in the midst of the c',
7:15 and he that is in the c', famine and
23 and the c' is full of violence.
9: 1 that have charge over the c'
4 Go through the midst of the c',
5 Go ye after him through the c',
7 went forth, and slew in the c'.
9 and the c' full of perverseness:
10: 2 and scatter them over the c'.
11: 2 and give wicked counsel in this c':
3 this c' is the caldron, and we be the
6 multiplied your slain in this c',
7 and this c' is the caldron: but I will
11 This c' shall not be your caldron,
23 up from the midst of the c',
23 which is on the east side of the c'.
17: 4 he set it in a c' of merchants.
21:19 at the head of the way to the c'.
22: 2 wilt thou judge the bloody c'?
3 The c' sheddeth blood in the midst
24: 6 Woe to the bloody c', to the pot
9 Woe to the bloody c'! I will even
26:10 enter into a c' wherein is made
17 the renowned c', which wast
19 I shall make thee a desolate c',
27:32 saying, What c' is like Tyrus,
33:21 me, saying, The c' is smitten.
39:16 name of the c' shall be Hamonah.
40: 1 year after that the c' was smitten,
2 the frame of a c' on the south.
43: 3 when I came to destroy the c':
45: 6 possession of the c' five thousand
7 possession of the c', before the
7 before the possession of the c',
48:15 place for the c', for dwelling,
15 c' shall be in the midst thereof.
17 suburbs of the c' shall be toward
18 food unto them that serve the c'.
19 that serve the c' shall serve it
20 with the possession of the c'.
21 and of the possession of the c',
22 from the possession of the c',
30 out of the c' on the north side,
31 the gates of the c' shall be after
35 name of the c' from that day shall
Da 9:16 away from thy c' Jerusalem,
18 c' which is called by thy name:
19 thy c' and thy people are called by
24 thy people and upon thy holy c',
26 destroy the c' and the sanctuary;
Ho 6: 8 is a c' of them that work iniquity,
11: 9 and I will not enter into the c'.
Joe 2: 9 shall run to and fro in the c';
Am 3: 6 a trumpet be blown in the c',
6 there be evil in a c', and the Lord
4: 7 I caused it to rain upon one c',
7 it not to rain upon another c':
8 cities wandered unto one c',

Am 5: 3 c' that went out by a thousand
6: 8 deliver up the c' with all that is
7:17 wife shall be an harlot in the c',
Jon 1: 2 go to Nineveh, that great c', and
3: 2 go unto Nineveh, that great c',
3 Nineveh was an exceeding great c'
4 Jonah began to enter into the c'
4: 5 Jonah went out of the c', and sat
5 on the east side of the c',
5 see what would become of the c'.
11 not I spare Nineveh, that great c',
Mic 4:10 shalt thou go forth out of the c',
6: 9 Lord's voice crieth unto the c',
Na 3: 1 Woe to the bloody c'! it is all full
Hab 2: 8 the violence of the land, of the c',
12 and stablisheth a c' by iniquity!
17 of the c', and of all that dwell
Zep 2:15 rejoicing c' that dwelt carelessly,
3: 1 and polluted, to the oppressing c'!
Zec 8: 3 shall be called a c' of truth;
5 c' shall be full of boys and girls
21 the inhabitants of one c' shall go to
14: 2 c' shall be taken, and the houses
2 the c' shall go forth into captivity,
2 shall not be cut off from the c'.
M't 2:23 and dwelt in a c' called Nazareth:
4: 5 taketh him up into the holy c',
5:14 A c' that is set on an hill cannot be
35 for it is the c' of the great King.
8:33 and went their ways into the c',
34 whole c' came out to meet Jesus:
9: 1 over, and came into his own c'.
10: 5 c' of the Samaritans enter ye not:
11 c' or town ye shall enter,
14 ye depart out of that house or c',
15 day of judgment, than for that c'.
23 when they persecute you in this c',
12:25 c' or house divided against itself
21:10 all the c' was moved, saying, Who
17 went out of the c' into Bethany;
18 returned into the c', he hungered.
22: 7 and burned up their c'.
23:34 and persecute them from c' to c':
26:18 Go into the c' to such a man, and
27:53 went into the holy c', and appeared
28:11 of the watch came into the c',
M'r 1:33 all the c' was gathered together
45 no more openly enter into the c',
5:14 told it in the c', and in the country.
6:11 day of judgment, than for that c'.
11:19 was come, he went out of the c'.
14:13 Go ye into the c', and there shall
16 went forth, and came into the c',
Lu 1:26 a c' of Galilee, named Nazareth,
39 with haste, into a c' of Juda;
2: 3 taxed, every one into his own c'.
4 out of the c' of Nazareth, into
4 Judæa, unto the c' of David,
11 day in the c' of David a Saviour,
39 Galilee, to their own c' Nazareth.
4:26 save unto Sarepta, a c' of Sidon,
29 up, and thrust him out of the c',
29 hill whereon their c' was built,
31 to Capernaum, a c' of Galilee,
5:12 was in a certain c', behold a man
7:11 he went into a c' called Nain;
12 he came nigh to the gate of the c',
12 much people of the c' was with her.
37 And, behold, a woman in the c',
8: 1 throughout every c' and village,
4 were come to him out of every c',
27 him out of the c' a certain man,
34 and went and told it in the c'
39 published throughout the whole c'
9: 5 when ye go out of that c', shake
10 to the c' called Bethsaida.
10: 1 into every c' and place, whither
8, 10 whatsoever c' ye enter, and
11 Even the very dust of your c',
12 day for Sodom, than for that c'.
14:21 into the streets and lanes of the c',
18: 2 There was in a c' a judge, which
3 And there was a widow in that c';
19:41 beheld the c', and wept over it,
22:10 when ye are entered into the c',
23:19 a certain sedition made in the c',
51 of Arimathæa, a c' of the Jews:
24:49 tarry ye in the c' of Jerusalem,
Joh 1:44 the c' of Andrew and Peter.
4: 5 Then cometh he to a c' of Samaria,
8 gone away unto the c' to buy meat.
28 went her way into the c', and saith
30 Then they went out of the c', and
39 the Samaritans of that c' believed
11:54 into a c' called Ephraim, and
19:20 was crucified was nigh to the c':
Ac 7:58 And cast him out of the c', and
8: 5 went down to the c' of Samaria,
8 And there was great joy in that c'.
9 in the same c' used sorcery, and
9: 6 Arise, and go into the c', and it
10: 9 and drew nigh unto the c',
11: 5 I was in the c' of Joppa praying:
12:10 iron gate that leadeth unto the c';
13:44 came almost the whole c' together
50 and the chief men of the c',
14: 4 multitude of the c' was divided:
13 Jupiter, which was before their c',
19 drew him out of the c', supposing
20 he rose up, and came into the c':
21 preached the gospel to that c',
15:21 in every c' them that preach him,
36 and visit our brethren in every c'
16:12 chief c' of that part of Macedonia,
12 in that c' abiding certain days.
13 went out of the c' by a river side,

Ac 16:14 of purple, of the *c'* of Thyatira,
20 do exceedingly trouble our *c'*,
39 them to depart out of the *c'*.
17: 5 set all the *c'* on an uproar,
6 unto the rulers of the *c'*, crying,
8 rulers of the *c'*, when they heard
16 the *c'* wholly given to idolatry.
18:10 for I have much people in this *c'*.
19:29 whole *c'* was filled with confusion:
19:35 how that the *c'* of the Ephesians
20:23 Holy Ghost witnesseth in every *c'*,
21: 5 till we were out of the *c'*: and we
29 in the *c'* Trophimus an Ephesian,
30 the *c'* was moved, and the people
39 which am a Jew of Tarsus, a *c'*
39 in Cilicia, a citizen of no mean *c'*:
22: 3 am a Jew, born in Tarsus, a *c'*
3 Cilicia, yet brought up in this *c'*
24:12 in the synagogues, nor in the *c'*:
25:23 principal men of the *c'*, at Festus'
27: 5 we came to Myra, a *c'* of Lycia.
8 whereunto was the *c'* of Lasea.
Ro 16:23 Erastus the chamberlain of the *c'*
2Co 11:26 in perils in the *c'*, in perils in
32 king kept the *c'* of the Damascenes
subscr. written from Philippi, a *c'*
1Ti *subscr.* is the chiefest *c'* of Phrygia
Tit 1: 5 ordain elders in every *c'*, as I had
Heb 11:10 For he looked for a *c'* which hath
16 he hath prepared for them a *c'*.
12:22 *c'* of the living God, the heavenly
13:14 have we no continuing *c'*, but we
Jas 4:13 go into such a *c'*, and continue
Re 3:12 the name of the *c'* of my God,
11: 2 holy *c'* shall they tread under foot
8 lie in the street of the great *c'*,
13 and the tenth part of the *c'* fell,
14: 8 is fallen, is fallen, that great *c'*,
20 was trodden without the *c'*,
16:19 the great *c'* was divided into three
17:18 is that great *c'*, which reigneth
18:10 great *c'* Babylon, that mighty *c'*!
16 that great *c'*, that was clothed
18 What *c'* is like unto this great *c'*!
19 alas that great *c'*, wherein were
21 great *c'* Babylon be thrown down,
20: 9 saints about, and the beloved *c'*:
21: 2 saw the holy *c'*, new Jerusalem,
10 and shewed me that great *c'*, the
14 of the *c'* had twelve foundations,
15 a golden reed to measure the *c'*,
16 And the *c'* lieth foursquare, and
16 he measured the *c'* with the reed,
18 the *c'* was pure gold, like unto
19 the foundations of the wall of the *c'*
21 the street of the *c'* was pure gold,
23 the *c'* had no need of the sun,
22:14 in through the gates into the *c'*.
19 out of the holy *c'*, and from the

clad See also CLOTHED.
1Ki 11:29 *c'* himself with a new garment;
Isa 59:17 and was *c'* with zeal as a cloke.

clamorous
Pr 9:13 foolish woman is *c'*: she is simple,

clamour
Eph 4:31 anger, and *c'*, and evil speaking,

clap See also CLAPPED; CLAPPETH.
Job 27:23 Men shall *c'* their hands at him,
Ps 47: 1 O *c'* your hands, all ye people;
98: 8 Let the floods *c'* their hands: let
Isa 55:12 of the field shall *c'* their hands.
La 2:15 pass by *c'* their hands at thee;
Na 3:19 shall *c'* the hands over thee:

clapped
2Ki 11:12 and they *c'* their hands, and said,
Eze 25: 6 thou hast *c'* thine hands, and

clappeth
Job 34:37 he *c'* his hands among us, and

Clauda (*claw'-dah*)
Ac 27:16 certain island which is called *C'*,

Claudia (*claw'-de-ah*)
2Ti 4:21 and *C'*, and all the brethren.

Claudius (*claw'-de-us*)
Ac 11:28 to pass in the days of *C'* Cæsar.
18: 2 *C'* had commanded all Jews to
23:26 *C'* Lysias unto the most excellent

clave
Ge 22: 3 and *c'* the wood for the burnt
34: 3 And his soul *c'* unto Dinah the
Nu 16:31 ground *c'* asunder that was under
J'g 15:19 But God *c'* an hollow place that
Ru 1:14 but Ruth *c'* unto her.
1Sa 6:14 and they *c'* the wood of the cart,
2Sa 20: 2 men of Judah *c'* unto their king,
23:10 and his hand *c'* unto the sword:
1Ki 11: 2 Solomon *c'* unto these in love.
2Ki 18: 6 he *c'* to the Lord, and departed not
Ne 10:29 They *c'* to their brethren, their
Ps 78:15 He *c'* the rocks in the wilderness,
Isa 48:21 he *c'* the rock also, and the
Ac 17:34 men *c'* unto him, and believed:

claws
De 14: 6 cleaveth the cleft into two *c'*, and
Da 4:33 feathers, and his nails like birds' *c'*.
Zec 11:16 fat, and tear their *c'* in pieces.

clay
1Ki 7:46 king cast them, in the *c'* ground
2Ch 4:17 in the *c'* ground between Succoth
Job 4:19 them that dwell in houses of *c'*,
10: 9 thou hast made me as the *c'*; and
13:12 ashes, your bodies to bodies of *c'*.
Job 27:16 and prepare raiment as the *c'*;
33: 6 I also am formed out of the *c'*.
38:14 It is turned as *c'* to the seal; and
Ps 40: 2 out of the miry *c'*, and set my feet
Isa 29:16 be esteemed as the potter's *c'*:
41:25 and as the potter treadeth *c'*.
45: 9 *c'* say to him that fashioneth it,
64: 8 thou art our father; we are the *c'*,
Jer 18: 4 that he made of *c'* was marred
6 as the *c'* is in the potter's hand, so
43: 9 them in the *c'* in the brickkiln,
Da 2:33 feet part of iron and part of *c'*.
34 were of iron and *c'*, and brake them
35 iron, the *c'*, the brass, the silver,
41 part of potter's *c'*, and part of iron,
41 sawest the iron mixed with miry *c'*.
42 were part of iron, and part of *c'*,
43 sawest iron mixed with miry *c'*,
43 even as iron is not mixed with *c'*.
45 in pieces the iron, the brass, the *c'*,
Na 3:14 go into *c'*, and tread the morter,
Hab 2: 6 that ladeth himself with thick *c*!
Joh 9: 6 and made *c'* of the spittle, and he
6 eyes of the blind man with the *c'*,
11 man that is called Jesus made *c'*,
14 when Jesus made the *c'*, and
15 He put *c'* upon mine eyes, and
Ro 9:21 not the potter power over the *c'*,

clean See also UNCLEAN.
Ge 7: 2 Of every *c'* beast thou shalt take
2 of beasts that are not *c'* by two,
8 Of *c'* beasts, and of
8 beasts that are not *c'*,
8:20 every *c'* beast, and of every *c'* fowl,
35: 2 be *c'*, and change your garments:
Le 4:12 a *c'* place where the ashes are
6:11 without the camp unto a *c'* place.
7:19 all that be *c'* shall eat thereof.
10:10 and between unclean and *c'*;
14 shoulder shall ye eat in a *c'* place;
11:36 is plenty of water, shall be *c'*:
37 which is to be sown, it shall be *c'*.
47 between the unclean and the *c'*,
12: 8 for her, and she shall be *c'*.
13: 6 the priest shall pronounce him *c'*:
6 he shall wash his clothes, and be *c'*.
13 he shall pronounce him *c'* that
13 it is all turned white: he is *c'*.
17 the priest shall pronounce him *c'*
17 that hath the plague: he is *c'*.
23 the priest shall pronounce him *c'*.
28 the priest shall pronounce him *c'*:
34 pronounce him *c'*: and he shall
34 wash his clothes, and be *c'*.
37 the scall is healed, he is *c'*:
37 the priest shall pronounce him *c'*.
39 groweth in the skin; he is *c'*.
40 he is bald; yet is he *c'*.
41 he is forehead bald: yet is he *c'*.
58 the second time, and shall be *c'*.
59 to pronounce it *c'*, or to pronounce
14: 4 be cleansed two birds alive and *c'*,
7 and shall pronounce him *c'*, and
8 himself in water, that he may be *c'*:
9 flesh in water, and he shall be *c'*.
11 the priest that maketh him *c'*
11 the man that is to be made *c'*, and
20 for him, and he shall be *c'*.
48 priest shall pronounce the house *c'*,
53 for the house: and it shall be *c'*.
57 unclean, and when it is *c'*: this is
15: 8 spit upon him that is *c'*; then he
13 in running water, and shall be *c'*.
28 days, and after that she shall be *c'*.
16:30 ye may be *c'* from all your sins
17:15 until the even: then shall he be *c'*.
20:25 between *c'* beasts and unclean,
25 and between unclean fowls and *c'*:
22: 4 of the holy things, until he be *c'*.
7 the sun is down, he shall be *c'*,
23:22 thou shalt not make *c'* riddance
Nu 5:28 woman be not defiled, but be *c'*;
8: 7 and so make themselves *c'*.
9:13 But the man that is *c'*, and is not
18:11 every one that is *c'* in thy house
13 every one that is *c'* in thine house
19: 9 a man that is *c'* shall gather up
9 up without the camp in a *c'* place,
12 on the seventh day he shall be *c'*:
12 the seventh day he shall not be *c'*.
18 a *c'* person shall take hyssop, and
19 and the *c'* person shall sprinkle
19 himself in water, and shall be *c'*
31:23 through the fire, and it shall be *c'*:
24 and ye shall be *c'*, and afterward
De 12:15 the unclean and the *c'* may eat
22 the unclean and the *c'* shall eat of
14:11 Of all *c'* birds ye shall eat.
20 But of all *c'* fowls ye may eat.
15:22 unclean and the *c'* person shall
23:10 not *c'* by reason of uncleanness
Jos 3:17 all the people were passed *c'* over
4: 1 people were *c'* passed over Jordan,
11 people were *c'* passed over, that
1Sa 20:26 he is not *c'*; surely he is not *c'*.
2Ki 5:10 again to thee, and thou shalt be *c'*.
12 may I not wash in them, and be *c'*?
13 he saith to thee, Wash, and be *c'*?
14 of a little child, and he was *c'*.
2Ch 30:17 for every one that was not *c'*, to
Job 9:30 and make my hands never so *c'*;
11: 4 doctrine is pure, and I am *c'* in
14: 4 Who can bring a *c'* thing out of an
15:14 What is man, that he should be *c'*?
15 the heavens are not *c'* in his sight.
Job 17: 9 and he that hath *c'* hands shall
25: 4 or how can he be *c'* that is born
33: 9 I am *c'* without transgression, I
Ps 19: 9 The fear of the Lord is *c'*,
24: 4 He that hath *c'* hands, and a pure
51: 7 me with hyssop, and I shall be *c'*:
10 Create in me a *c'* heart, O God;
73: 1 even to such as are of a *c'* heart.
77: 8 Is his mercy *c'* gone for ever?
Pr 14: 4 Where no oxen are, the crib is *c'*:
16: 2 ways of a man are *c'* in his own
20: 9 can say, I have made my heart *c'*,
Ec 9: 2 to the good and to the *c'*, and to
Isa 1:16 Wash you, make you *c'*; put away
24:19 broken down, the earth is *c'*
28: 8 so that there is no place *c'*.
30:24 that ear the ground shall eat *c'*
52:11 be ye *c'*, that bear the vessels of
66:20 bring an offering in a *c'* vessel
Jer 13:27 wilt thou not be made *c'*?
Eze 22:26 between the unclean and the *c'*,
36:25 Then will I sprinkle *c'* water
25 and ye shall be *c'*: from all your
44:23 between the unclean and the *c'*.
Joe 1: 7 he hath made it *c'* bare, and cast
Zec 11:17 his arm shall be *c'* dried up, and
M't 8: 2 thou wilt, thou canst make me *c'*.
3 him, saying, I will; be thou *c'*.
23:25 for ye make *c'* the outside of the
26 the outside of them may be *c'*.
27:59 the body, he wrapped it in a *c'*
M'k 1:40 wilt, thou canst make me *c'*.
41 saith unto him, I will; be thou *c'*.
Lu 5:12 thou wilt, thou canst make me *c'*.
13 him, saying, I will: be thou *c'*.
11:39 Now do ye Pharisees make *c'*
41 behold, all things are *c'* unto you.
Joh 13:10 but is *c'* every whit:
10 and ye are *c'*, but not all.
11 therefore said he, Ye are not all *c'*.
15: 3 Now ye are *c'* through the word
Ac 18: 6 upon your own heads; I am *c'*:
2Pe 2:18 those that were *c'* escaped from
Re 19: 8 arrayed in fine linen, *c'* and white:
14 clothed in fine linen, white and *c'*.

cleanness See also UNCLEANNESS.
2Sa 22:21 to the *c'* of my hands hath he
25 according to my *c'* in his eye sight.
Ps 18:20 to the *c'* of my hands hath he
24 the *c'* of my hands in his eyesight.
Am 4: 6 I also have given you *c'* of teeth

cleanse See also CLEANSED; CLEANSETH; CLEANSING.
Ex 29:36 and thou shalt *c'* the altar, when
Lev 14:49 he shall take to *c'* the house two
52 And he shall *c'* the house with the
16:19 seven times, and *c'* it, and hallow
30 an atonement for you, to *c'* you,
Nu 8: 6 children of Israel, and *c'* them.
7 shalt thou do unto them, to *c'*
15 and thou shalt *c'* them, and offer
21 an atonement for them to *c'* them.
2Ch 29:15 of the Lord, to *c'* the house of the
16 house of the Lord, to *c'* it.
Neh 13:22 the Levites that they should *c'*
Ps 19:12 *c'* thou me from secret faults.
51: 2 mine iniquity, and *c'* me from my
119: 9 Wherewithal shall a young man *c'*
Jer 4:11 people, not to fan, nor to *c'*,
33: 8 And I will *c'* them from all their
Eze 36:25 from all your idols, will I *c'* you.
37:23 they have sinned, and will *c'* them:
39:12 of them, that they may *c'* the land.
14 upon the face of the earth, to *c'* it:
16 Thus shall they *c'* the land.
43:20 thus shalt thou *c'* and purge it.
22 and they shall *c'* the altar,
22 as they did *c'* it with the bullock.
45:18 blemish, and *c'* the sanctuary:
Joe 3:21 For I will *c'* their blood that I
M't 10: 8 *c'* the lepers, raise the dead, cast
23:26 *c'* first that which is within the
2Co 7: 1 let us *c'* ourselves from all
Eph 5:26 That he might sanctify and *c'* it
Jas 4: 8 *C'* your hands, ye sinners; and
1Jo 1: 9 to *c'* us from all unrighteousness.

cleansed
Lev 11:32 until the even; so it shall be *c'*
12: 7 and she shall be *c'* from
14: 4 take for him that is to be *c'* two
7 upon him that is to be *c'* from the
8 he that is to be *c'* shall wash his
14, 17 right ear of him that is to be *c'*,
18 the head of him that is to be *c'*:
19 for him that is to be *c'* from his
25, 28 right ear of him that is to be *c'*,
29 the head of him that is to be *c'*, to
31 atonement for him that is to be *c'*
15:13 when he that hath an issue is *c'*
28 if she be *c'* of her issue, then she
Nu 35:33 the land cannot be *c'* of the blood
Jos 22:17 which we are not *c'* until this day,
2Ch 29:18 have *c'* all the house of the Lord,
30:18 not *c'* themselves, yet did they eat
19 though he be not *c'* according to
34: 5 their altars, and *c'* Judah and
Ne 13: 9 and they *c'* the chambers:
30 Thus *c'* I them from all strangers,
Job 35: 3 I have, if I be *c'* from my sin?
Ps 73:13 Verily I have *c'* my heart in vain,
Eze 22:24 Thou art the land that is not *c'*,
36:33 In the day that I shall have *c'* you
44:26 after he is *c'*, they shall reckon
Da 8:14 then shall the sanctuary be *c'*.
Joe 3:21 their blood that I have not *c'*:

M't 8: 3 immediately his leprosy was c'.
11: 5 lepers are c', and the deaf hear,
M'r 1:42 departed from him and he was c'.
Lu 4:27 and none of them was c', saving
7:22 the lepers are c', the deaf hear,
17:14 to pass, as they went, they were c'.
17 Were there not ten c'? but where
Ac 10:15 What God hath c', that call not thou
11: 9 What God hath c', that call not thou

cleanseth
Job 37:21 the wind passeth, and c' them.
Pr 20:30 blueness of a wound c' away evil:
1Jo 1: 7 blood of Jesus Christ his Son c' us

cleansing
Le 13: 7 been seen of the priest for his c',
35 much in the skin after his c';
14: 2 law of the leper in the day of his c':
23 them on the eighth day for his c'
32 get that which pertaineth to his c'.
15:13 to himself seven days for his c',
Nu 6: 9 shave his head in the day of his c',
Eze 43:23 When thou hast made an end of c'
M'r 1:44 and offer for thy c' those things
Lu 5:14 and offer for thy c', according as

clear See also CLEARER; CLEARING.
Ge 24: 8 shalt be c' from this my oath:
41 shalt thou be c' from this my oath,
41 thou shalt be c' from my oath.
44:16 or how shall we c' ourselves?
Ex 34: 7 will by no means c' the guilty;
2Sa 23: 4 the earth by c' shining after rain.
Ps 51: 4 speakest, and be c' when thou
Ca 6:10 fair as the moon, c' as the sun,
Isa 18: 4 like a c' heat upon herbs, and like
Am 8: 9 will darken the earth in the c' day:
Zec 14: 6 the light shall not be c', nor dark:
2Co 7:11 approved yourselves to be c' in
Re 21:11 like a jasper stone, c' as crystal;
18 was pure gold, like unto c' glass.
22: 1 river of water of life, c' as crystal,

clearer
Job 11:17 age shall be c' than the noonday;

clearing
Nu 14:18 no means c' the guilty, visiting
2Co 7:11 in you, yea, what c' of yourselves,

clearly
Job 33: 3 my lips shall utter knowledge c'.
M't 7: 5 then shalt thou see c' to cast out
M'r 8:25 restored, and saw every man c'.
Lu 6:42 then shalt thou see c' to pull out
Ro 1:20 are c' seen, being understood by

clearness
Ex 24:10 were the body of heaven in his c'.

cleave See also CLAVE; CLEAVED; CLEAVETH; CLEFT; CLOVEN.
Ge 2:24 shall c' unto his wife: and they
Le 1:17 shall c' it with the wings thereof,
De 4: 4 But ye that did c' unto the Lord
10:20 to him shalt thou c', and swear by
11:22 in all his ways, and to c' unto him;
13: 4 shall serve him, and c' unto him.
17 shall c' nought of the cursed thing
28:21 make the pestilence c' unto thee,
60 they shall c' unto thee.
30:20 and that thou mayest c' unto him:
Jos 22: 5 to c' unto him and to serve him,
23: 8 But c' unto the Lord your God, as
12 and c' unto the remnant of these
2Ki 5:27 of Naaman shall c' unto thee,
Job 38:38 and the clods c' fast together?
Ps 74:15 c' the fountain and the flood:
101: 3 it shall not c' to me.
102: 5 groaning my bones c' to my skin.
137: 6 tongue c' to the roof of my mouth;
Isa 14: 1 they shall c' to the house of Jacob.
Jer 13:11 so have I caused to c' unto me the
Eze 3:26 tongue c' to the roof of thy mouth,
Da 2:43 they shall not c' one to another,
11:34 shall c' to them with flatteries.
Hab 3: 9 didst c' the earth with rivers.
Zec 14: 4 of Olives shall c' in the midst
M't 19: 5 c' to his wife: and they twain
M'r 10: 7 and mother, and c' to his wife;
Ac 11:23 they would c' unto the Lord.
Ro 12: 9 c' to that which is good.

cleaved
2Ki 3: 3 Nevertheless he c' unto the sins
Job 29:10 tongue c' to the roof of their
31: 7 if any blot hath c' to mine hands;

cleaveth
De 14: 6 and c' the cleft into two claws,
Job 16:13 he c' my reins asunder, and doth
19:20 My bone c' to my skin and to my
Ps 22:15 and my tongue c' to my jaws;
41: 8 disease, say they, c' fast unto him:
44:25 our belly c' unto the earth.
119:25 My soul c' unto the dust: quicken
141: 7 when one cutteth and c' wood
Ec 10: 9 that c' wood shall be endangered
Jer 13:11 the girdle c' to the loins of a man,
La 4: 4 The tongue of the sucking child c'
8 their skin c' to their bones; it is
Lu 10:11 dust of your city, which c' on us,

cleft See also CLEFTS; CLIFT.
De 14: 6 cleaveth the c' into two claws,
Mic 1: 4 the valleys shall be c', as wax

clefts See also CLIFTS.
Ca 2:14 in the c' of the rock, in the secret
Isa 2:21 To go into the c' of the rocks,
Jer 49:16 thou that dwellest in the c' of the
Am 6:11 and the little house with c'.
Ob 3 that dwellest in the c' of the rock,

clemency
Ac 24: 4 hear us of thy c' a few words.

Clement (*clem'-ent*)
Ph'p 4: 3 in the gospel, with *C'* also, and

Cleopas (*cle'-o-pas*) See also ALPHÆUS; CLEOPHAS.
Lu 24:18 one of them, whose name was *C'*,

Cleophas (*cle'-o-fas*) See also CLEOPAS.
Joh 19:25 Mary the wife of *C'*, and Mary

clerk See TOWNCLERK.

cliff See also CLIFFS.
2Ch 20:16 they come up by the c' of Ziz;

cliffs
Job 30: 6 in the c' of the valleys, in caves

clift See also CLEFT.
Ex 33:22 put thee in a c' of the rock,

clifts See also CLEFTS.
Isa 57: 5 under the c' of the rocks?

climb See also CLIMBED; CLIMBETH.
Jer 4:29 and c' up upon the rocks:
Joe 2: 7 shall c' the wall like men of war;
9 they shall c' up upon the houses;
Am 9: 2 though they c' up to heaven,

climbed
1Sa 14:13 Jonathan c' up upon his hands
Lu 19: 4 c' up into a sycomore tree to see

climbeth
Joh 10: 1 c' up some other way, the same

clipped
Jer 48:37 shall be bald, and every beard c':

cloak See CLOKE.

clods
Job 7: 5 with worms and c' of dust;
21:33 The c' of the valley shall be sweet
38:38 and the c' cleave fast together?
Isa 28:24 and break the c' of his ground?
Ho 10:11 and Jacob shall break his c'.
Joe 1:17 seed is rotten under their c',

cloke
Isa 59:17 was clad with zeal as a c'.
M't 5:40 thy coat, let him have thy c' also.
Lu 6:29 him that taketh away thy c'
Joh 15:22 they have no c' for their sin
1Th 2: 5 nor a c' of covetousness; God is
2Ti 4:13 The c' that I left at Troas with
1Pe 2:16 liberty for a c' of maliciousness,

close See also CLOSED; CLOSER; CLOSEST; DISCLOSE; INCLOSE.
Nu 5:13 of her husband, and be kept c',
2Sa 22:46 be afraid out of their c' places.
1Ch 12: 1 he yet kept himself c' because of
Job 28:21 kept c' from the fowls of the air.
41:15 shut up together as with a c' seal.
Ps 18:45 be afraid out of their c' places.
Jer 42:16 c' after you there in Egypt;
Da 8: 7 saw him come c' unto the ram,
Am 9:11 and c' up the breaches thereof;
Lu 9:36 And they kept it c', and told no
Ac 27:13 thence, they sailed c' by Crete.

closed See also INCLOSED.
Ge 2:21 c' up the flesh instead thereof;
20:18 the Lord had fast c' up all the
Nu 16:33 and the earth c' upon them:
J'g 3:22 and the fat c' upon the blade,
Isa 1: 6 they have not been c', neither
29:10 sleep, and hath c' your eyes:
Da 12: 9 the words are c' up and sealed
Jon 2: 5 the depth c' me round about,
M't 13:15 their eyes they have c'; lest at
Lu 4:20 c' the book, and he gave it again
Ac 28:27 their eyes have they c'; lest they

closer
Pr 18:24 that sticketh c' than a brother.

closest
Jer 22:15 because thou c' thyself in cedar?

closet See also CLOSETS.
Joe 2:16 and the bride out of her c'.
M't 6: 6 thou prayest, enter into thy c',

closets
Lu 12: 3 ye have spoken in the ear in c'

cloth See CLOTHS; SACKCLOTH.
Nu 4: 6 spread over it a c' wholly of blue,
7 they shall spread a c' of blue,
8 spread upon them a c' of scarlet,
9 they shall take a c' of blue,
11 they shall spread a c' of blue,
12 put them in a c' of blue, and cover
13 and spread a purple c' thereon:
De 22:17 spread the c' before the elders
1Sa 19:13 bolster, and covered it with a c'.
21: 9 wrapped in a c' behind the ephod:
2Sa 20:12 cast a c' upon him, when he saw
2Ki 8:15 he took a thick c', and dipped it
Isa 30:22 them away as a menstruous c';
M't 9:16 of new c' unto an old garment,
27:59 wrapped it in a clean linen c',
M'r 2:21 of new c' on an old garment:
14:51 linen c' cast about his naked body;
52 And he left the linen c', and fled

clothe See also CLOTHED; CLOTHES; CLOTHEST; CLOTHING.
Ex 40:14 his sons, and c' them with coats:
Est 4: 4 she sent raiment to c' Mordecai,
Ps 132:16 also c' her priests with salvation:
18 His enemies will I c' with shame:
Pr 23:21 shall c' a man with rags.
Isa 22:21 And I will c' him with thy robe,
49:18 shalt surely c' thee with them all,
50: 3 I c' the heavens with blackness,
Eze 26:16 c' themselves with trembling;
34: 3 ye c' you with the wool, ye kill them
Hag 1: 6 ye c' you, but there is none warm;
Zec 3: 4 c' thee with change of raiment.
M't 6:30 if God so c' the grass of the field,
30 shall he not much more c' you,
Lu 12:28 If then God so c' the grass, which
28 how much more will he c' you,

clothed See also CLAD; UNCLOTHED.
Ge 3:21 make coats of skins, and c' them.
Le 8: 7 and c' him with the robe, and put
2Sa 1:24 over Saul, who c' you in scarlet,
1Ch 15:27 was c' with a robe of fine linen,
21:16 the elders of Israel, who were c'
2Ch 6:41 thy priests... be c' with salvation,
18: 9 c' in their robes, and they sat
28:15 c' all that were naked among them.
Es 4: 2 the king's gate c' with sackcloth.
Job 7: 5 My flesh is c' with worms and
8:22 hate thee shall be c' with shame;
10:11 hast c' me with skin and flesh,
29:14 on righteousness, and it c' me:
39:19 thou c' his neck with thunder?
Ps 35:26 let them be c' with shame and
65:13 The pastures are c' with flocks;
93: 1 he is c' with majesty;
1 the Lord is c' with strength,
104: 1 art c' with honour and majesty.
109:18 As he c' himself with cursing
29 mine adversaries be c' with shame,
132: 9 priests be c' with righteousness;
Pr 31:21 her household are c' with scarlet.
Isa 61:10 he hath c' me with the garments of
Eze 7:27 prince shall be c' with desolation,
9: 2 among them was c' with linen,
3 called to the man c' with linen,
11 And, behold, the man c' with linen,
10: 2 spake unto the man c' with linen,
6 commanded the man c' with linen,
7 of him that was c' with linen:
16:10 c' thee also with broidered work,
23: 6 c' with blue, captains and rulers,
12 and rulers c' most gorgeously,
38: 4 c' with all sorts of armour,
44:17 shall be c' with linen garments;
Da 5: 7 shall be c' with scarlet, and have
16 thou shalt be c' with scarlet,
29 and they c' Daniel with scarlet,
10: 5 behold a certain man c' in linen,
12: 6 one said to the man c' in linen,
7 I heard the man c' in linen,
Zep 1: 8 as are c' with strange apparel.
Zec 3: 3 Joshua was c' with filthy garments,
5 head, and c' him with garments.
M't 6:31 or, Wherewithal shall we be c'?
11: 8 A man c' in soft raiment?
25:36 Naked, and ye c' me: I was sick,
38 thee in? or naked, and c' thee?
43 naked and ye c' me not: sick,
M'r 1: 6 And John was c' with camel's hair,
5:15 and c', and in his right mind:
15:17 c' him with purple, and platted
16: 5 c' in a long white garment;
Lu 7:25 see? A man c' in soft raiment?
8:35 at the feet of Jesus, c', and in his
16:19 was c' in purple and fine linen,
2Co 5: 2 earnestly desiring to be c' upon
3 being c' we shall not be found
4 would be unclothed, but c' upon,
1Pe 5: 5 be c' with humility: for God
Re 1:13 c' with a garment down to the
3: 5 shall be c' in white raiment;
18 raiment, that thou mayest be c',
4: 4 sitting, c' in white raiment;
7: 9 c' with white robes, and palms in
10: 1 from heaven, c' with a cloud:
11: 3 threescore days, c' in sackcloth.
12: 1 a woman c' with the sun, and the
15: 6 c' in pure and white linen, and
18:16 city, that was c' in fine linen,
19:13 c' with a vesture dipped in blood:
14 c' in fine linen, white and clean.

clothes See also SACKCLOTHES.
Ge 37:29 in the pit; and he rent his c'.
34 And Jacob rent his c', and put
44:13 Then they rent their c', and
49:11 in wine, and his c' in the blood
Ex 12:34 being bound up in their c' upon
19:10 let them wash their c',
14 people, and they washed their c'.
Le 10: 6 your heads, neither rend your c';
11:25 shall wash his c', and be unclean
28 carcase of them shall wash his c',
40 carcase of it shall wash his c',
40 shall wash his c', and be unclean
13: 6, 34 shall wash his c', and be clean.
45 c' shall be rent, and his head bare,
14: 8 wash his c', and shave off all his hair,
9 he shall wash his c', also he shall
47 lieth in the house shall wash his c';
47 eateth in the house shall wash his c'.
15: 5, 6, 7, 8, 10, 11, 13, 21, 22, 27 wash his c',
16:26, 28 shall wash his c', and bathe
32 shall put on the linen c', even
17:15 he shall both wash his c', and
21:10 uncover his head, nor rend his c';
Nu 8: 7 let them wash their c', and so make
21 purified, and they washed their c';
14: 6 that searched the land, rent their c':
19: 7 Then the priest shall wash his c',
8 that burneth her shall wash his c'

Nu 19:10 of the heifer shall wash his c',
19 purify himself, and wash his c',
21 of separation shall wash his c';
31:24 wash your c' on the seventh day,
De 29: 5 c' are not waxen old upon you,
Jos 7: 6 Joshua rent his c', and fell to the
J'g 11:35 that he rent his c', and said, Alas,
1Sa 4:12 with his c' rent, and with earth
19:24 he stripped off his c' also, and
2Sa 1: 2 camp from Saul with his c' rent,
11 David took hold on his c', and rent
3:31 Rend your c', and gird you with
13:31 servants stood by with their c' rent.
19:24 nor washed his c', from the day the
1Ki 1: 1 they covered him with c', but he gat
21:27 that he rent his c', and put
2Ki 2:12 he took hold of his own c', and
5: 7 that he rent his c', and said, Am I
8 the king of Israel had rent his c',
8 hast thou rent thy c'? let him come
6:30 the woman, that he rent his c';
11:14 Athaliah rent her c', and cried,
18:37 to Hezekiah with their c' rent,
19: 1 rent his c', and covered himself
22:11 book of the law, that he rent his c'.
19 hast rent thy c', and wept before
2Ch 23:13 Then Athaliah rent her c', and said,
34:19 words of the law, that he rent his c'.
27 before me, and didst rend thy c',
Ne 4:23 none of us put off our c', saving
9:21 their c' waxed not old, and their
Es 4: 1 Mordecai rent his c', and put on
Job 9:31 and mine own c' shall abhor me.
Pr 6:27 bosom, and his c' not be burned?
Isa 36:22 to Hezekiah with their c' rent,
37: 1 heard it, that he rent his c',
Jer 41: 5 and their c' rent, and having cut
Eze 16:39 shall strip thee also of thy c',
23:26 strip thee out of thy c', and take
27:20 in precious c' for chariots.
24 in blue c', and broidered work,
Am 2: 8 lay themselves down upon c' laid
M't 21: 7 put on them their c', and they
24:18 field return back to take his c'.
26:65 Then the high priest rent his c',
M'r 5:28 If I may but touch his c', I shall
30 and said, Who touched my c'?
14:63 Then the high priest rent his c',
15:20 and put his own c' on him,
Lu 2: 7 and wrapped him in swaddling c',
12 the babe wrapped in swaddling c',
8:27 and ware no c', neither abode in
19:36 they spread their c' in the way.
24:12 the linen c' laid by themselves,
Joh 19:40 and wound it in linen c' with the
20: 5 looking in, saw the linen c' lying;
6 and seeth the linen c' lie,
7 not lying with the linen c', but
Ac 7:58 the witnesses laid down their c'
14:14 rent their c', and ran in among
16:22 the magistrates rent off their c',
22:23 cast off their c', and threw dust

clothest
Jer 4:30 thou c' thyself with crimson,

clothing
Job 22: 6 and stripped the naked of their c'.
24: 7 the naked to lodge without c',
10 cause him to go naked without c',
31:19 seen any perish for want of c',
Ps 35:13 were sick, my c' was sackcloth:
45:13 within: her c' is of wrought gold.
Pr 27:26 lambs are for thy c', and the goats
31:22 her c' is silk and purple.
25 Strength and honour are her c';
Isa 3: 6 Thou hast c', be thou our ruler,
7 my house is neither bread nor c':
23:18 sufficiently, and for durable c'.
59:17 the garments of vengeance for c',
Jer 10: 9 blue and purple is their c': they
M't 7:15 come to you in sheep's c', but
11: 8 wear soft c' are in kings' houses.
M'r 12:38 which love to go in long c', and
Ac 10:30 stood before me in bright c',
Jas 2: 3 to him that weareth the gay c',

cloths
Ex 31:10 the c' of service, and the holy
35:19 The c' of service, to do service in
39: 1 they made c' of service, to do
41 The c' of service to do service in

cloud See also CLOUDS.
Ge 9:13 I do set my bow in the c', and it
14 when I bring a c' over the earth,
14 the bow shall be seen in the c':
16 And the bow shall be in the c';
Ex 13:21 them by day in a pillar of a c',
22 took not away the pillar of the c'
14:19 the c' went from before their face,
20 it was a c' and darkness to them,
24 the pillar of fire and of the c',
16:10 of the Lord appeared in the c'.
19: 9 I come unto thee in a thick c',
16 and a thick c' upon the mount,
24:15 a c' covered the mount.
16 the c' covered it six days: and
16 Moses out of the midst of the c'.
18 went into the midst of the c',
34: 5 And the Lord descended in the c',
40:34 a c' covered the tent of the
35 c' abode thereon, and the glory
36 when the c' was taken up from
37 But if the c' were not taken up,
38 the c' of the Lord was upon the
Le 16: 2 in the c' upon the mercy seat.
13 that the c' of the incense may
Nu 9:15 the c' covered the tabernacle,
Nu 9:16 the c' covered it by day, and the
17 And when the c' was taken up
17 in the place where the c' abode,
18 as long as the c' abode upon the
19 c' tarried long upon the tabernacle
20 when the c' was a few days upon
21 when the c' abode from even unto
21 c' was taken up in the morning,
21 by night that the c' was taken up,
22 the c' tarried upon the tabernacle,
10:11 that the c' was taken up
12 the c' rested in the wilderness of
34 the c' of the Lord was upon them
11:25 And the Lord came down in a c',
12: 5 came down in the pillar of the c',
10 And the c' departed from off the
14:14 that thy c' standeth over them,
14 by day time in a pillar of a c',
16:42 behold, the c' covered it, and the
De 1:33 ye should go, and in a c' by day.
5:22 the c', and of the thick darkness,
31:15 the tabernacle in a pillar of a c':
15 and the pillar of the c' stood over
1Ki 8:10 the c' filled the house of the Lord,
11 stand to minister because of the c':
18:44 ariseth a little c' out of the sea,
2Ch 5:13 the house was filled with a c',
14 to minister by reason of the c':
Ne 9:19 the pillar of the c' departed not
Job 3: 5 let a c' dwell upon it; let the
7: 9 c' is consumed and vanisheth away:
22:13 he judge through the dark c'?
26: 8 the c' is not rent under them.
9 and spreadeth his c' upon it.
30:15 my welfare passeth away as a c'.
36:32 by the c' that cometh betwixt.
37:11 he wearieth the thick c':
11 he scattereth his bright c':
15 caused the light of his c' to shine?
38: 9 made the c' the garment thereof,
Ps 78:14 daytime also he led them with a c',
105:39 He spread a c' for a covering; and
Pr 16:15 favour is as a c' of the latter rain.
Isa 4: 5 a c' and smoke by day, and the
18: 4 a c' of dew in the heat of harvest.
19: 1 the Lord rideth upon a swift c',
25: 5 the heat with the shadow of a c':
44:22 I have blotted out, as a thick c',
22 as a c', thy sins: return unto me;
60: 8 Who are these that fly as a c',
La 2: 1 the daughter of Zion with a c'
3:44 hast covered thyself with a c',
Eze 1: 4 a great c', and a fire infolding itself,
28 that is in the c' in the day of rain,
8:11 and a thick c' of incense went up.
10: 3 and the c' filled the inner court.
4 the house was filled with the c',
30:18 as for her, a c' shall cover her,
32: 7 I will cover the sun with a c', and
38: 9 shalt be like a c' to cover the land,
16 as a c' to cover the land; it shall
Ho 6: 4 your goodness is as a morning c',
13: 3 they shall be as the morning c',
M't 17: 5 a bright c' overshadowed them:
5 and behold a voice out of the c',
M'r 9: 7 a c' that overshadowed them:
7 and a voice came out of the c',
Lu 9:34 a c', and overshadowed them:
34 as they entered into the c'.
35 there came a voice out of the c',
12:54 ye see a c' rise out of the west,
21:27 in a c' with power and great glory.
Ac 1: 9 a c' received him out of their sight.
1Co 10: 1 all our fathers were under the c',
2 Moses in the c' and in the sea;
Heb 12: 1 with so great a c' of witnesses,
Re 10: 1 from heaven, clothed with a c':
11:12 ascended up to heaven in a c';
14:14 and behold a white c', and upon the
14 upon the c' one sat like unto the Son
15 to him that sat on the c', Thrust
16 sat on the c' thrust in his sickle

clouds
De 4:11 darkness, c', and thick darkness.
J'g 5: 4 the c' also dropped water.
2Sa 22:12 waters, and thick c' of the skies,
23: 4 even a morning without c';
1Ki 18:45 was black with c' and wind,
Job 20: 6 and his head reach unto the c';
22:14 Thick c' are a covering to him,
26: 8 up the waters in his thick c';
35: 5 c' which are higher than thou.
36:28 c' do drop and distil upon man
29 the spreadings of the c',
32 With c' he covereth the light;
37:16 know the balancings of the c',
21 bright light which is in the c':
38:34 thou lift up thy voice to the c',
37 can number the c' in wisdom?
Ps 18:11 waters and thick c' of the skies.
12 before him his thick c' passed,
36: 5 faithfulness reacheth unto the c'.
57:10 and thy truth unto the c'.
68:34 and his strength is in the c'.
77:17 The c' poured out water: the
78:23 commanded the c' from above,
97: 2 C' and darkness are round about
104: 3 who maketh the c' his chariot:
108: 4 thy truth reacheth unto the c'.
147: 8 Who covereth the heaven with c',
Pr 3:20 and the c' drop down the dew.
8:28 When he established the c' above:
25:14 is like c' and wind without rain.
Ec 11: 3 If the c' be full of rain, they empty
4 regardeth the c' shall not reap.
12: 2 nor the c' return after the rain:
Isa 5: 6 I will also command the c' that
14:14 ascend above the heights of the c';
Jer 4:13 he shall come up as c', and his
Da 7:13 of man came with the c' of heaven,
Joe 2: 2 a day of c' and of thick darkness,
Na 1: 3 and the c' are the dust of his feet.
Zep 1:15 a day of c' and thick darkness,
Zec 10: 1 the Lord shall make bright c',
M't 24:30 in the c' of heaven with power
26:64 and coming in the c' of heaven.
M'r 13:26 the Son of man coming in the c'
14:62 and coming in the c' of heaven.
1Th 4:17 up together with them in the c',
2Pe 2:17 c' that are carried with a
Jude 12 c' they are without water, carried
Re 1: 7 Behold he cometh with c'; and

cloudy
Ex 33: 9 c' pillar descended, and stood
10 the people saw the c' pillar stand
Ne 9:12 them in the day by a c' pillar;
Ps 99: 7 spake unto them in the c' pillar:
Eze 30: 3 day of the Lord is near, a c' day;
34:12 scattered in the c' and dark day.

clouted
Jos 9: 5 old shoes and c' upon their feet,

clouts
Jer 38:11 old cast c' and old rotten rags,
12 Put now these old cast c' and

clove See CLAVE.

cloven See also CLOVENFOOTED.
De 14: 7 or of them that divide the c' hoof;
Ac 2: 3 appeared unto them c' tongues

clovenfooted
Le 11: 3 the hoof, and is c',
7 the hoof, and be c',
26 the hoof, and is not c',

cluster See also CLUSTERS.
Nu 13:23 a branch with one c' of grapes,
24 the c' of grapes which the children
Ca 1:14 My beloved is unto me as a c' of
Isa 65: 8 As the new wine is found in the c',
Mic 7: 1 there is no c' to eat: my soul

clusters
Ge 40:10 the c' thereof brought forth ripe
De 32:32 grapes of gall, their c' are bitter:
1Sa 25:18 and an hundred c' of raisins,
30:12 cake of figs, and two c' of raisins:
Ca 7: 7 and thy breasts to c' of grapes.
8 breasts shall be as c' of the vine,
Re 14:18 the c' of the vine of the earth;

Cnidus (*ni'-dus*)
Ac 27: 7 scarce were come over against C'

coal See also COALS.
2Sa 14: 7 so they shall quench my c' which
Isa 6: 6 having a live c' in his hand,
47:14 there shall not be a c' to warm at,
La 4: 8 Their visage is blacker than a c';

coals
Le 16:12 take a censer full of burning c'
2Sa 22: 9 devoured: c' were kindled by it.
13 before him were c' of fire
1Ki 19: 6 there was a cake baken on the c',
Job 41:21 His breath kindleth c', and a
Ps 18: 8 devoured: c' were kindled by it.
12 passed, hail stones and c' of fire.
13 his voice; hail stones and c' of fire.
120: 4 of the mighty, with c' of juniper.
140:10 let burning c' fall upon them: let
Pr 6:28 Can one go upon hot c', and his
25:22 thou shalt heap c' of fire upon his
26:21 As c' are to burning
21 are to burning c', and wood to
Ca 8: 6 the c' thereof are c' of fire, which
Isa 44:12 the tongs both worketh in the c',
19 baked bread upon the c' thereof;
54:16 the smith that bloweth the c'
Eze 1:13 was like burning c' of fire,
10: 2 and fill thine hand with c' of fire
24:11 Then set it empty upon the c'
Hab 3: 5 and burning c' went forth at his
Joh 18:18 who had made a fire of c'; for it
21: 9 they saw a fire of c' there, and fish
Ro 12:20 thou shalt heap c' of fire on his

coast See also COASTS.
Ex 10: 4 I bring the locusts into thy c':
Nu 13:29 the sea, and by the c' of Jordan.
20:23 by the c' of the land of Edom,
22:36 Arnon, which is in the utmost c'.
24:24 shall come from the c' of Chittim,
34: 3 of Zin along by the c' of Edom,
3 the outmost c' of the salt sea
11 c' shall go down from Shepham
De 2: 4 through the c' of your brethren
18 over through Ar, the c' of Moab,
3:17 Jordan, and the c' thereof,
11:24 uttermost sea shall your c' be.
16: 4 seen with thee in all thy c' seven
19: 8 the Lord thy God enlarge thy c',
Jos 1: 4 down of the sun, shall be your c'.
12: 4 And the c' of Og king of Bashan,
23 The king of Dor in the c' of Dor,
13:16 their c' was from Aroer, that is
25 their c' was Jazer, and all the
30 And their c' was from Mahanaim,
15: 1 uttermost part of the south c'.
4 out of that c' were at the sea:
4 this shall be your south c'.
12 the great sea, and the c' thereof.
12 is the c' of the children of Judah,
21 toward the c' of Edom southward
16: 3 to the c' of Japhleti, unto the c'

Jos 17: 7 the c' of Manasseh was from
9 And the c' descended unto the
9 the c' of Manasseh also was on
18: 5 Judah shall abide in their c' on
11 and the c' of their lot came forth
19 of Jordan: this was the south c'.
19:22 the c' reacheth to Tabor, and
29 the c' turneth to Ramah, and to
29 and the c' turneth to Hosah;
29 at the sea from the c' to Achzib:
33 their c' was from Heleph, from
34 then the c' turneth westward to
41 the c' of the inheritance was
47 the c' of the children of Dan went
J'g 1:18 Gaza with the c' thereof,
18 and Askelon with the c' thereof,
18 and Ekron with the c' thereof.
36 And the c' of the Amorites was
11:20 not Israel to pass through his c':
1Sa 6: 9 by the way of his own c' to
7:13 no more into the c' of Israel:
27: 1 any more in any c' of Israel:
30:14 the c' which belongeth to Judah,
2Ki 14:25 He restored the c' of Israel from
1Ch 4:10 me indeed, and enlarge my c',
Eze 25:16 destroy the remnant of the sea c'.
47:16 which is by the c' of Hauran.
48: 1 the c' of the way of Hethlon, as
1 northward, to the c' of Hamath;
Zep 2: 5 unto the inhabitants of the sea c',
6 the sea c' shall be dwellings and
7 the c' shall be for the remnant of
M't 4:13 which is upon the sea c',
Lu 6:17 from the sea c' of Tyre and Sidon,

coasts
Ex 10:14 and rested in all the c' of Egypt:
19 one locust in all the c' of Egypt.
Nu 21:13 out of the c' of the Amorites:
32:33 with the cities thereof in the c',
34: 2 the land of Canaan with the c'
12 your land with the c' thereof
De 3:14 of Argob unto the c' of Geshuri
19: 3 divide the c' of thy land, which
28:40 olive trees throughout all thy c',
Jos 9: 1 in all the c' of the great sea over
18: 5 Joseph shall abide in their c' on
20 Benjamin by the c' thereof
19:49 land for inheritance by their c',
J'g 11:22 all the c' of the Amorites,
26 that be along by the c' of Arnon,
18: 2 five men from their c', men of
19:29 sent her into all the c' of Israel.
1Sa 5: 6 even Ashdod and the c' thereof.
7:14 and the c' thereof did Israel
11: 3 unto all the c' of Israel:
7 throughout all the c' of Israel
2Sa 21: 5 in any of the c' of Israel,
1Ki 1: 3 throughout all the c' of Israel,
2Ki 10:32 smote them in all the c' of Israel;
15:16 therein, and the c' thereof from
1Ch 6:54 their castles in their c',
66 had cities of their c' out of the
21:12 throughout all the c' of Israel.
2Ch 11:13 resorted to him out of all their c'.
Ps 105:31 flies, and lice in all their c'.
33 brake the trees of their c'.
Jer 25:32 up from the c' of the earth.
31: 8 them from the c' of the earth,
50:41 up from the c' of the earth.
Eze 33: 2 take a man of their c', and set
Joe 3: 4 Zidon, and all the c' of Palestine?
M't 2:16 and in all the c' thereof, from
8:34 he would depart out of their c'.
15:21 departed into the c' of Tyre and
22 out of the same c', and cried
39 came into the c' of Magdala.
16:13 Jesus came into the c' of Caesarea
19: 1 and came into the c' of Judæa
M'r 5:17 pray him to depart out of their c'.
7:31 departing from the c' of Tyre
31 the midst of the c' of Decapolis.
10: 1 and cometh into the c' of Judæa
Ac 13:50 and expelled them out of their c'.
19: 1 passed through the upper c'
26:20 throughout all the c' of Judæa,
27: 2 meaning to sail by the c' of Asia;

coat See also COATS.
Ge 37: 3 made him a c' of many colours.
23 out of his c', his c' of many colours
31 they took Joseph's c', and killed
31 and dipped the c' in the blood;
32 they sent the c' of many colours,
32 whether it be thy son's c' or no.
33 it, and said, It is my son's c';
Ex 28: 4 and a broidered c', a mitre, and
39 embroider the c' of fine linen,
29: 5 put upon Aaron the c', and the
Le 8: 7 he put upon him the c', and
16: 4 He shall put on the holy linen c',
1Sa 2:19 his mother made him a little c',
17: 5 he was armed with a c' of mail;
5 and the weight of the c' was
38 he armed him with a c' of mail.
2 Sa 15:32 came to meet him with his c' rent,
Job 30:18 me about as the collar of my c'.
Ca 5: 3 I have put off my c'; how shall I
M't 5:40 at the law, and take away thy c',
Lu 6:29 forbid not to take thy c' also.
Joh 19:23 and also his c': now the c' was
21: 7 he girt his fisher's c' unto him,

coat of mail See COAT and MAIL.

coats
Gen 3:21 did the Lord God make c' of skins,
Ex 28:40 Aaron's sons thou shalt make c',
29: 8 his sons, and put c' upon them.
39:27 they made c' of fine linen of
40:14 sons, and clothe them with c':
Le 8:13 put c' upon them, and girded them
10: 5 carried them in their c' out of the
Da 3:21 bound in their c', their hosen
27 neither were their c' changed,
M't 10:10 neither two c', neither shoes,
M'r 6: 9 sandals; and not put on two c'.
Lu 3:11 He that hath two c', let him
9: 3 money; neither have two c' apiece.
Ac 9:39 shewing the c' and garments which

cock See also COCKCROWING; PEACOCKS.
M't 26:34 this night, before the c' crow, thou
74 And immediately the c' crew.
75 Before the c' crow, thou shalt deny
M'r 14:30 before the c' crow twice, thou shalt
68 into the porch; and the c' crew.
72 the second time the c' crew.
72 said unto him, Before the c' crow
Lu 22:34 the c' shall not crow this day,
60 while he yet spake, the c' crew.
61 Before the c' crow, thou shalt deny
Joh 13:38 The c' shall not crow, till thou hast
18:27 and immediately the c' crew.

cockatrice See also COCKATRICE'; COCKATRICES.
Isa 14:29 shall come forth a c', and his

cockatrice'
Isa 11: 8 shall put his hand on the c' den.
59: 5 They hatch c' eggs, and weave the

cockatrices
Jer 8:17 I will send serpents, c', among,

cockcrowing
M'r 13:35 at midnight, or at the c', or in the

cockle
Job 31:40 instead of wheat, and c' instead of

coffer
1Sa 6: 8 a trespass offering, in a c' by the
11 the c' with the mice of gold and
15 and the c' that was with it, wherein

coffin
Ge 50:26 and he was put in a c' in Egypt.

cogitations
Da 7:28 my c' much troubled me, and

Col See COL-HOZEH.

cold
Ge 8:22 and c' and heat, and summer
Job 24: 7 they have no covering in the c'.
37: 9 whirlwind: and c' out of the north.
Ps 147:17 who can stand before his c'?
Pr 20: 4 will not plow by reason of the c';
25:13 As the c' of snow in the time of
20 away a garment in c' weather,
25 c' waters to a thirsty soul, so is
Jer 18:14 shall the c' flowing waters that
Na 3:17 camp in the hedges in the c' day,
M't 10:42 these little ones a cup of c' water
24:12 the love of many shall wax c'.
Joh 18:18 made a fire of coals; for it was c':
Ac 28: 2 present rain, and because of the c'.
2Co 11:27 in fastings often, in c' and
Re 3:15 that thou art neither c' nor hot:
15 I would thou wert c' or hot.
16 and neither c' nor hot, I will spue

Col-hozeh (*col-ho'-zeh*)
Ne 3:15 repaired Shallum the son of C',
11: 5 the son of Baruch, the son of C',

collar See also COLLARS.
Job 30:18 me about as the c' of my coat.

collars
J'g 8:26 and c', and purple raiment

collection
2Ch 24: 6 out of Jerusalem the c', according
9 to the Lord the c' that Moses
1Co 16: 1 concerning the c' for the saints,

college
2Ki 22:14 she dwelt in Jerusalem in the c';)
2Ch 34:22 she dwelt in Jerusalem in the c':)

collops
Job 15:27 maketh c' of fat on his flanks.

colony
Ac 16:12 part of Macedonia, and a c':

color See COLOUR.

Colossæ See COLOSSE.

Colosse (*co-los'-see*) See also COLOSSIANS.
Col 1: 2 in Christ which are at C':

Colossians^ (*co-los'-yuns*)
Col *subscr.* Written from Rome to the C'

colour See also COLOURED; COLOURS.
Le 13:55 plague have not changed his c',
Nu 11: 7 c' thereof as the c' of bdellium.
Pr 23:31 when it giveth his c' in the cup,
Eze 1: 4 midst thereof as the c' of amber,
7 like the c' of burnished brass.
16 was like unto the c' of a beryl:
22 as the c' of the terrible crystal,
27 And I saw as c' of amber, as
8: 2 of brightness, as the c' of amber.
10: 9 wheels was as the c' of a beryl
Da 10: 6 feet like in c' to polished brass,
Ac 27:30 under c' as though they would
Re 17: 4 arrayed in purple and scarlet c',

coloured
Re 17: 3 sit upon a scarlet c' beast,

colours
Ge 37: 3 he made him a coat of many c'.
23 coat of many c' that was on him;
32 And they sent the coat of many c',
J'g 5:30 to Sisera a prey of divers c',
30 a prey of divers c' of needlework,
30 of divers c' of needlework on both
2Sa 13:18 a garment of divers c' upon her:
19 rent her garment of divers c'
1Ch 29: 2 glistering stones, and of divers c',
Isa 54:11 I will lay thy stones with fair c',
Eze 16:16 thy high places with divers c',
17: 3 of feathers, which had divers c',

colt See also COLTS
Ge 49:11 ass's c' unto the choice vine;
Job 11:12 man be born like a wild ass's c'.
Zec 9: 9 and upon a c' the foal of an ass.
M't 21: 2 find an ass tied, and a c' with her:
5 an ass, and a c' the foal of an ass.
7 brought the ass, and the c', and put
M'r 11: 2 ye shall find a c' tied, whereon
4 and found the c' tied by the door
5 them, What do ye, loosing the c'?
7 brought the ass c' to Jesus, and cast
Lu 19:30 entering ye shall find a c' tied,
33 as they were loosing the c', the
33 unto them, Why loose ye the c'?
35 cast their garments upon the c',
Joh 12:15 king cometh, sitting on an ass's c'.

colts
Ge 32:15 milch camels with their c', forty
J'g 10: 4 sons that rode on thirty ass c',
12:14 rode on threescore and ten ass c':

combs See HONEYCOMBS.

come^ See also CAME; COMEST; COMETH; COMING; BECOME; OVERCOME.
Ge 4:14 it shall c' to pass, that every one
6:13 end of all flesh is c' before me;
18 and thou shalt c' into the ark, thou,
20 two of every sort shall c' unto thee,
7: 1 C' thou and all thy house into the
12:11 was c' near to enter into Egypt,
14 when Abram was c' into Egypt,
15: 4 shall c' forth out of thine own
14 they c' out with great substance.
16 they shall c' hither again: for the
17: 6 thee, and kings shall c' out of thee.
18: 5 therefore are ye c' to your servant.
21 the cry of it, which is c' unto me;
19:22 cannot do any thing till thou be c'
31 to c' in unto us after the manner
32 C', let us make our father drink
20: 4 Abimelech had not c' near her:
13 whither we shall c', say of me,
22: 5 and worship, and c' again to you.
24:13 of the city c' out to draw water:
31 C' in, thou blessed of the Lord;
43 c' to pass, that when the virgin
26:27 Wherefore c' ye to me, seeing ye
27:21 C' near, I pray thee, that I may
26 C' near now, and kiss me, my son.
40 it shall c' to pass when thou shalt
28:21 I c' again to my father's house
30:16 Thou must c' in unto me; for
33 answer for me in time to c',
33 c' for my hire before thy face:
31:44 c' thou, let us make a covenant,
32: 8 If Esau c' to the one company,
11 him, lest he will c' and smite me,
33:14 until I c' unto my Lord unto Seir.
34: 5 his peace until they were c'.
35:11 kings shall c' out of thy loins;
16 but a little way to c' to Ephrath:
37:10 mother and thy brethren indeed c'
13 c', and I will send thee unto them.
20 C' now therefore, and let us slay
23 Joseph was c' unto his brethren,
27 C', and let us sell him to the
38:16 pray thee, let me c' in unto thee;
16 that thou mayest c' in unto me?
41:29 there c' seven years of great plenty
35 the food of those good years that c',
54 seven years of dearth began to c',
42: 7 Whence c' ye? And they said,
9 the nakedness of the land ye are c'.
10 but to buy food are thy servants c'.
12 the nakedness of the land ye are c'.
15 your youngest brother c' hither.
21 therefore is this distress c' upon us.
44:23 Except your youngest brother c'
30 when I c' to thy servant my father,
31 It shall c' to pass, when he seeth
34 the evil that shall c' on my father.
45: 4 C' near to me, I pray you. And
9 c' down unto me, tarry not:
11 all that thou hast, c' to poverty.
16 Joseph's brethren are c': and it
18 and c' unto me: and I will give you
19 wives, and bring your father, and c'.
46:31 My brethren, ... are c' unto me;
33 it shall c' to pass, when Pharaoh
47: 1 they have, are c' out of the land
4 to sojourn in the land are we c';
5 and thy brethren are c' unto thee:
24 it shall c' to pass in the increase
48: 7 a little way to c' unto Ephrath:
49: 6 soul, c' not thou into their secret;
10 until Shiloh c'; and unto him shall
50: 5 my father, and I will c' again.
Ex 1:10 C' on, let us deal wisely with
10 and it c' to pass, that, when there
19 ere the midwives c' in unto them.
2:18 is it that ye are c' so soon to day?

Ex 3: 8 And I am c' down to deliver them
9 children of Israel is c' unto me:
10 C' now therefore, and I will send
13 I c' unto the children of Israel,
18 c', thou and the elders of Israel,
21 and it shall c' to pass, that, when
4: 8, 9 c' to pass, if they will not believe
7:15 by the river's brink against he c',
8: 3 c' into thine house, and into thy
4 the frogs shall c' up both on thee,
5 cause frogs to c' up upon the land
9:19 the hail shall c' down upon them,
10:12 they may c' up upon the land
26 serve the Lord, until we c' thither.
11: 8 these thy servants shall c' down
12:23 not suffer the destroyer to c' in
25 And it shall c' to pass, when ye
25 be c' to the land which the Lord
26 it shall c' to pass, when your
48 then let him c' near and keep it;
13:14 thy son asketh thee in time to c',
14:26 may c' again upon the Egyptians,
16: 5 And it shall c' to pass, that on
9 C' near before the Lord: for he
17: 6 and there shall c' water out of it,
18: 6 father in law Jethro am c' unto
8 the travail that had c' upon them
15 the people c' unto me to enquire
16 have a matter, they c' unto me;
19: 2 and were c' to the desert of Sinai,
9 c' unto thee in a thick cloud,
11 third day the Lord will c' down
13 they shall c' up to the mount.
15 third day: c' not at your wives.
22 also, which c' near to the Lord,
23 cannot c' up to mount Sinai:
24 thou shalt c' up, thou, and Aaron
24 through to c' up unto the Lord,
20:20 for God is c' to prove you, and
24 I will c' unto thee, and I will bless
21:14 if a man c' presumptuously upon
22: 9 parties shall c' before the judges;
27 and it shall c' to pass, when
23:27 to whom thou shalt c', and I will
24: 1 C' up unto the Lord, thou, and
2 Moses alone shall c' near the Lord:
2 they shall not c' nigh; neither
12 Lord said unto Moses, C' up to me
14 until we c' again unto you: and,
14 to do, let him c' unto them.
25:32 shall c' out of the sides of it;
33 the six branches that c' out of
28:43 when they c' in unto the tabernacle
43 when they c' near unto the altar
30:20 c' near to the altar to minister,
32: 1 to c' down out of the mount,
26 Lord's side? let him c' unto me.
33: 5 I will c' up into the midst of thee
22 it shall c' to pass, while my glory
34: 2 and c' up in the morning unto
3 And no man shall c' up with thee,
30 they were afraid to c' nigh him.
35:10 wise hearted among you shall c',
36: 2 him up to c' unto the work
Le 4:23 hath sinned, c' to his knowledge;
28 hath sinned, c' to his knowledge:
10: 3 sanctified in them that c' nigh
4 C' near, carry your brethren
6 wrath c' upon all the people:
12: 4 nor c' into the sanctuary, until
13:16 he shall c' unto the priest;
14: 8 that he shall c' into the camp,
34 ye be c' into the land of Canaan,
35 he that owneth the house shall c'
39 shall c' again the seventh day,
43 if the plague c' again, and break
44 Then the priest shall c' and look,
48 priest shall c' in, and look upon it,
15:14 and c' before the Lord unto the door
16: 2 that he c' not at all times into the
3 shall Aaron c' into the holy place:
17 until he c' out, and have made an
23 Aaron shall c' into the tabernacle
24 put on his garments, and c' forth,
26 and afterward c' into the camp.
28 afterward he shall c' into the camp.
19:19 of linen and woollen c' upon thee.
23 when ye shall c' into the land,
21:21 shall c' nigh to offer the offering
21 shall not c' nigh to offer the bread
23 nor c' nigh unto the altar, because
23:10 When ye be c' into the land which
25: 2 c' into the land which I give you,
22 c' in ye shall eat of the old store.
25 if any of his kin c' to redeem it,
Nu 1: 1 were c' out of the land of Egypt,
4: 5 setteth forward, Aaron shall c',
15 sons of Kohath shall c' to bear it:
5:14 spirit of jealousy c' upon him,
14 the spirit of jealousy c' upon him,
27 it shall c' to pass, that if she
6: 5 shall no rasor c' upon his head:
6 he shall c' at no dead body.
8:19 when the children of Israel c' nigh
9: 1 after they were c' out of the land
10:29 c' thou with us, and we will do
11:17 I will c' down and talk with thee
20 until it c' out at your nostrils,
23 shall c' to pass unto thee or not.
12: 4 C' out ye three unto the
13:21 Rehob, as men c' to Hamath.
33 sons of Anak, which c' of the giants:
14:30 ye shall not c' into the land,
15: 2 When ye be c' into the land of
18 When ye c' into the land whither I

Nu 16: 5 cause him to c' near unto him:
5 will he cause to c' near unto him.
12 which said, We will not c' up:
14 of these men? we will not c' up.
40 c' near to offer incense before
17: 5 c' to pass, that the man's rod,
18: 3 they shall not c' nigh the vessels
4 stranger shall not c' nigh unto you.
22 c' nigh the tabernacle of the
19: 7 he shall c' into the camp,
14 all that c' into the tent, and all
20: 5 have ye made us to c' up
18 lest I c' out against thee with the
21: 8 it shall c' to pass, that every one
27 C' into Heshbon, let the city of
22: 5 is a people c' out from Egypt:
6 C' now therefore, I pray thee,
11 there is a people c' out of Egypt,
11 c' now, curse me them;
14 Balaam refuseth to c' with us.
17 c' therefore, I pray thee, curse
20 If the men c' to call thee, rise up,
36 Balak heard that Balaam was c',
38 Lo, I am c' unto thee: have I now
23: 3 the Lord will c' to meet me: and
7 C', curse me Jacob, and c', defy
13 C', I pray thee, with me unto
27 C', I pray thee, I will bring thee
24:14 c' therefore, and I will advertise
17 there shall c' a Star out of Jacob,
19 Out of Jacob shall c' he that
24 shall c' from the coast of Chittim,
26:29 c' the family of the Gileadites.
27:21 at his word they shall c' in, both
31:24 ye shall c' into the camp.
33:38 the children of Israel were c'
55 then it shall c' to pass, that those
56 Moreover it shall c' to pass,
34: 2 ye c' into the land of Canaan;
35:10 When ye be c' over Jordan into
26 if the slayer shall at any time c'
32 c' again to dwell in the land,
De 1:20 Ye are c' unto the mountain of the
22 into what cities we shall c'.
2:14 we were c' over the brook Zered,
4:30 all these things are c' upon thee,
46 they were c' forth out of Egypt:
6:20 thy son asketh thee in time to c',
7:12 Wherefore it shall c' to pass, if ye
10: 1 c' up unto me into the mount,
11:13 And it shall c' to pass, if ye shall
29 it shall c' to pass, when the Lord
12: 5 seek, and thither thou shalt c':
9 For ye are not as yet c' to the rest
13: 2 the sign or the wonder c' to pass,
14:29 shall c', and shall eat and be
15:19 firstling males that c' of thy herd
17: 9 And thou shalt c' unto the priests
14 thou art c' unto the land which
18: 6 if a Levite c' from any of thy gates
6 c' with all the desire of his mind
9 When thou art c' into the land
19 it shall c' to pass, that whosoever
22 thing follow not, nor c' to pass,
20: 2 ye are c' nigh unto the battle,
21: 2 and thy judges shall c' forth,
5 the sons of Levi shall c' near;
23:10 he shall not c' within the camp:
11 he shall c' into the camp again.
24: 1 and it c' to pass that she find no
9 ye were c' forth out of Egypt.
25: 1 and they c' unto judgment,
9 Then shall his brother's wife c'
17 ye were c' forth out of Egypt;
26: 1 when thou art c' in unto the land
3 c' unto the country which the Lord
27:12 when ye are c' over Jordan;
28: 1 c' to pass, if thou shalt hearken
2 these blessings shall c' on thee,
7 shall c' out against thee one way,
15 it shall c' to pass, if thou wilt not
15 all these curses shall c' upon thee,
24 shall it c' down upon thee,
43 and thou shalt c' down very low.
45 all these curses shall c' upon thee,
52 high and fenced walls c' down,
63 shall c' to pass, that as the Lord
29:19 And it c' to pass, when he heareth
22 So that the generation to c' of
22 that shall c' from a far land,
30: 1 And it shall c' to pass, when
1 all these things are c' upon thee,
31: 2 can no more go out and c' in:
11 When all Israel is c' to appear
17 Are not these evils c' upon us,
21 shall c' to pass, when many evil
32:35 shall c' upon them make haste.
33:16 c' upon the head of Joseph,
Jos 2: 3 forth the men that are c' to thee,
3 c' to search out all the country.
18 Behold, when we c' into the land,
3: 4 c' not near unto it, that ye may
8 ye are c' to the brink of the water
9 C' hither, and hear the words of
13 And it shall c' to pass, as soon as
13 waters that c' down from above;
15 as they that bare the ark were c'
4: 6 ask their fathers in time to c',
16 that they c' up out of Jordan.
17 saying, C' ye up out of Jordan.
18 c' up out of the midst of Jordan,
21 in time to c', saying, What men
5:14 the host of the Lord am I now c'.
6: 5 c' to pass, that when they make
19 c' into the treasury of the Lord.

Jos 7:14 which the Lord taketh shall c'
14 which the Lord shall take shall c'
8: 5 and it shall c' to pass, when they
5 c' out against us, as at the first,
6 (For they will c' out after us) till
9: 6 We be c' from a far country: now
8 are ye? and from whence c' ye?
9 thy servants are c' because of the
10: 4 C' up unto me, and help me, that
6 c' up to us quickly, and save us,
24 C' near, put your feet upon the
11:20 should c' against Israel in battle,
14:11 war, both to go out, and to c' in.
18: 4 and they shall c' again to me,
8 and describe it, and c' again to me,
20: 6 and c' unto his own city, and unto
22:24 In time to c' your children might
27 say to our children in time to c',
28 to our generations in time to c',
23: 7 ye c' not among these nations,
14 all are c' to pass unto you, and not
15 Therefore it shall c' to pass, that
15 as all good things are c' upon you,
J'g 1: 3 C' up with me into my lot, that
24 the spies saw a man c' forth out
34 would not suffer them to c' down
3:27 when he was c', that he blew a
4:20 man doth c' and enquire of thee,
22 C', and I will shew thee the
6: 4 till thou c' unto Gaza, and left no
18 pray thee, until I c' unto thee,
18 I will tarry until thou c' again.
7:13 And when Gideon was c', behold,
17 I c' to the outside of the camp,
24 C' down against the Midianites,
8: 9 When I c' again in peace, I will
9:10 tree, C' thou, and reign over us.
12 vine, C' thou, and reign over us.
14 bramble, C' thou, and reign over us.
15 c' and put your trust in my
15 let fire c' out of the bramble, and
20 let fire c' out from Abimelech,
20 fire c' out from the men of Shechem,
24 and ten sons of Jerubbaal might c',
29 Increase thine army, and c' out.
31 his brethren be c' to Shechem;
33 is with him c' out against thee,
36 there c' people down from the top
37 c' people down by the middle
37 another company c' along by the
43 were c' forth out of the city;
11: 6 C', and be our captain, that we
7 why are ye c' unto me now when
12 thou art c' against me to fight in
33 Aroer, even till thou c' to Minnith,
12: 3 are ye c' up unto me this day,
13: 5 and no rasor shall c' on his head:
8 which thou didst send c' again
12 said, Now let thy words c' to pass.
17 that when thy sayings c' to pass we
15:10 Why are ye c' up against us? And
10 To bind Samson are we c'
12 We are c' down to bind thee, that
16: 2 saying, Samson is c' hither.
17 There hath not c' a rasor upon
18 C' up this once, for he hath
18:10 ye shall c' unto a people secure,
19:11 C', I pray thee, and let us turn in
13 C', and let us draw near to one of
23 that this man is c' into mine house,
29 And when he was c' into his house,
20:10 they c' to Gibeah of Benjamin,
41 saw that evil was c' upon them.
21: 3 why is this c' to pass in Israel,
21 daughters of Shiloh c' out to dance
21 then c' ye out of the vineyards, and
22 brethren c' unto us to complain,
Ru 1:19 when they were c' to Beth-lehem,
2:11 art c' unto a people which thou
12 whose wings thou art c' to trust.
14 At mealtime c' thou hither, and
4: 3 Naomi, that is c' again out of the
11 woman that is c' into thine house
1Sa 1:11 shall no rasor c' upon his head.
20 when the time was c' about after
2: 3 arrogancy c' out of your mouth:
31 Behold, the days c', that I will cut
34 that shall c' upon thy two sons, on
36 shall c' to pass, that every one
36 c' and crouch to him for a piece
4: 3 the people were c' into the camp,
6 of the Lord was c' into the camp.
7 they said, God is c' into the camp.
5: 5 nor any that c' into Dagon's house,
6: 7 on which there hath c' no yoke,
21 c' ye down, and fetch it up to you.
9: 5 when they were c' to the land of
5 C', and let us return; lest my
9 spake C', and let us go to the seer:
10 Well said; c', let us go. So they
13 As soon as ye be c' into the city,
13 the people will not eat until he c',
14 and when they were c' into the city,
16 because their cry is c' unto me.
25 they were c' down from the high
10: 3 thou shalt c' to the plain of Tabor,
5 that thou shalt c' to the hill of God,
5 it shall c' to pass, when thou art
5 thou art c' thither to the city,
6 of the Lord will c' upon thee,
7 when these signs are c' unto thee,
8 c' down unto thee, to offer burnt
8 till I c' to thee, and shew thee what
11 that is c' unto the son of Kish?
20 to c' near, the tribe of Benjamin

1Sa 10:21 to c' near by their families, the
22 if the man should yet c' thither.
11: 3 to save us, we will c' out to thee.
10 To morrow we will c' out unto you,
14 C', and let us go to Gilgal, and
12: 8 When Jacob was c' into Egypt,
13:12 The Philistines will c' down now
14: 1 C', and let us go over to the
6 C', and let us go over unto the
9 Tarry until we c' to you; then we
10 if they say thus, C' up unto us;
11 Hebrews c' forth out of the holes
12 C' up to us, and we will shew you
12 C' up after me: for the Lord hath
26 when the people were c' into the
16: 2 say, I am c' to sacrifice to the Lord.
5 I am c' to sacrifice unto the Lord:
5 and c' with me to the sacrifice.
6 when they were c', that he looked
11 will not sit down till he c' hither.
16 c' to pass, when the evil spirit
17: 8 Why are ye c' out to set your
8 you, and let him c' down to me.
25 ye seen this man that is c' up?
25 surely to defy Israel is he c' up:
28 art c' down that thou mightest
44 C' to me, and I will give thy flesh
45 but I c' to thee in the name of the
52 until thou c' to the valley, and to
19:16 And when the messengers were c'
20: 9 were determined by my father to c'
11 C', and let us go out into the
19 c' to the place where thou didst
21 then c' thou: for there is peace to
24 when the new moon was c', the
37 when the lad was c' to the place
21:15 shall this fellow c' into my house?
22: 3 my mother, I pray thee, c' forth,
23: 3 much more then if we c' to Keilah
7 told Saul that David was c' to
10 that Saul seeketh to c' to Keilah,
11 will Saul c' down, as thy servant
11 And the Lord said, He will c' down.
15 David saw that Saul was c' out to
20 Now therefore, O king, c' down
20 the desire of thy soul to c' down;
23 and c' ye again to me with the
23 c' to pass, if he be in the land,
27 Haste thee, and c'; for the
24:14 After whom is the king of Israel c'
25: 8 we c' in a good day: give, I pray
19 before me; behold, I c' after you.
30 c' to pass, when the Lord shall
34 hadst hasted and c' to meet me,
40 when the servants of David were c'
26: 4 and understood that Saul was c' in
10 him; or his day shall c' to die;
20 king of Israel is c' out to seek a
22 let one of the young men c' over
29:10 servants that are c' with thee:
30: 1 when David and his men were c' to
31: 4 lest these uncircumcised c' and
2Sa 1: 9 me: for anguish is c' upon me,
2:24 went down when they were c' to
3:23 the host that was with him were c',
26 when Joab was c' out from David,
5: 6 thou shalt not c' in hither:
6 David cannot c' in hither.
8 the lame shall not c' into the house.
13 of Jerusalem, after he was c' from
23 and c' upon them over against the
25 from Geba until thou c' to Gazer.
6: 9 How shall the ark of the Lord c' to
7:19 house for a great while to c'.
9: 6 the son of Saul, was c' unto David,
10:11 thee, then I will c' and help thee.
11: 7 And when Uriah was c' unto him,
12: 4 the wayfaring man that was c' unto
4 it for the man that was c' to him.
13: 5 let my sister Tamar c', and give me
6 when the king was c' to see him,
6 I pray thee, let Tamar my sister c',
11 unto her, C' lie with me, my sister.
35 Behold, the king's sons c': as thy
14: 3 And c' to the king, and speak on
15 Now therefore that I am c' to speak
29 but he would not c' to him: and
29 the second time, he would not c'.
32 C' hither, that I may send thee to
32 Wherefore am I c' from Geshur? it
15: 4 any suit or cause might c' unto me,
28 until there c' word from you to
32 that when David was c' to the top of
16: 7 C' out, c' out, thou bloody man,
16 David's friend, was c' unto
17: 2 And I will c' upon him while he is
6 when Hushai was c' to Absalom,
9 and it will c' to pass, when some
12 So shall we c' upon him in some
17 they might not be seen to c' into
27 it came to pass, when David was c'
19:11 all Israel is c' to the king, even to
18 before the king, as he was c' over
20 I am c' the first this day of all the
25 when he was c' to Jerusalem to
30 as my lord the king is c' again in
33 C' thou over with me, and I will
39 when the king was c' over, the
20:16 C' near hither, that I may speak
17 when he was c' near unto her,
24:13 Shall seven years of famine c' unto
21 my lord the king c' to his servant?
1Ki 1:12 therefore c', let me, I pray thee,
14 I also will c' in after thee, and
21 c' to pass, when my lord the king
23 And when he was c' in before the

1Ki 1: 35 Then ye shall c' up after him,
35 that he may c' and sit upon my
42 C' in; for thou art a valiant man,
45 are c' up from thence rejoicing,
2:30 Thus saith the king, C' forth.
41 Jerusalem to Gath, and was c'
3: 7 I know not how to go out or c' in.
6: 1 the children of Israel were c' out
8:10 when the priests were c' out of the
19 thy son that shall c' forth out of
31 and the oath c' before thine altar
42 when he shall c' and pray toward
10: 2 and when she was c' to Solomon,
11: 2 neither shall they c' in unto you:
12: 1 all Israel were c' to Shechem to
5 yet for three days, then c' again
12 saying, C' to me again the third
20 heard that Jeroboam was c' again,
21 And when Rehoboam was c' to
13: 7 C' home with me, and refresh
15 said unto him, C' home with me,
22 thy carcase shall not c' unto the
32 Samaria, shall surely c' to pass.
14: 6 C' in, thou wife of Jeroboam;
13 of Jeroboam shall c' to the grave,
15:17 to go out or c' in to Asa king of
19 c' and break thy league with
17:18 art thou c' unto me to call my sin
21 let this child's soul c' into him
18:12 c' to pass, as soon as I am gone
12 and so when I c' and tell Ahab,
30 said unto all the people, C' near
19:17 c' to pass, that him that escapeth
20:17 There are men c' out of Samaria.
18 Whether they be c' out for peace,
18 alive; or whether they be c' out
22 king of Syria will c' up against
33 whether anything would c' from
33 he caused him to c' up into the
22:27 of affliction, until I c' in peace.
2Ki 1: 4 c' down from that bed on which
6 thou shalt not c' down from that
9 God, the king hath said, C' down.
10 then let fire c' down from heaven,
11 the king said, C' down quickly.
12 let fire c' down from heaven, and
16 shalt not c' down off that bed
3:21 heard that the kings were c' up
4: 1 c' to take unto him my two sons
4 And when thou art c' in, thou
22 to the man of God, and c' again.
32 when Elisha was c' into the house,
36 And when she was c' in unto him,
5: 6 when this letter is c' unto thee,
8 let him c' now to me, and
10 and thy flesh shall c' again to thee,
11 He will surely c' out to me,
22 be c' to me from mount Ephraim
6: 9 thither the Syrians are c' down.
20 when they were c' into Samaria,
7: 4 Now therefore c', and let us fall
5 they were c' to the uttermost part
6 of the Egyptians, to c' upon us.
9 some mischief will c' upon us:
9 c', that we may go and tell the
12 When they c' out of the city, we
8: 1 c' upon the land seven years.
7 saying, The man of God is c' hither.
9:16 Ahaziah king of Judah was c'
30 when Jehu was c' to Jezreel,
34 And when he was c' in, he did eat
10: 6 c' to me to Jezreel by to morrow
16 C' with me, and see my zeal
25 and slay them; let none c' forth.
11: 9 that were to c' in on the sabbath,
14: 8 C', let us look one another in the
16: 7 c' up, and save me out of the hand
12 the king was c' from Damascus,
18:13 did Sennacherib king of Assyria c'
17 And when they were c' up, they
25 Am I now c' up without the Lord
31 and c' out to me, and then eat ye
32 Until I c' and take you away to a
19: 3 the children are c' to the birth,
9 he is c' out to fight against thee:
23 multitude of my chariots I am c'
28 thy tumult is c' up into mine ears,
32 He shall not c' into this city,
32 nor c' before it with shield,
33 not c' into this city, saith the Lord.
20:14 They are c' from a far country,
17 Behold, the days c', that all that
1Ch 9:25 to c' after seven days from time
10: 4 lest these uncircumcised c'
11: 5 David, Thou shalt not c' hither.
12:17 c' peaceably unto me to help me,
17 c' to betray me to mine enemies,
31 name, to c' and make David king.
14:14 and c' upon them over against
16:29 c' before him: worship the Lord
17:11 And it shall c' to pass, when thy
17 house for a great while to c',
19: 3 are not his servants c' unto thee
9 the kings that were c' were by
24:19 to c' into the house of the Lord,
29:12 Both riches and honour c' of thee,
14 for all things c' of thee, and of
2Ch 1:10 out and c' in before this people:
5:11 were c' out of the holy place:
6: 9 but thy son which shall c' forth
22 and the oath c' before thine altar
32 but is c' from a far country for
32 if they c' and pray in this house;
8:11 the ark of the Lord hath c'.
9: 1 and when she was c' to Solomon,
10: 1 to Shechem were all Israel c'

2Ch 10: 5 C' again unto me after three days.
12 C' again to me on the third day.
11: 1 Rehoboam was c' to Jerusalem,
13:13 caused an ambushment to c'
16: 1 let none go out or c' in to Asa
18:14 And when he was c' to the king,
19:10 what cause soever shall c' to you
10 Lord, and so wrath c' upon you.
20:11 c' to cast us out of thy possession,
16 they c' up by the cliff of Ziz;
22 which were c' against Judah;
22: 7 for when he was c', he went out
23: 6 But let none c' into the house of
8 his men that were to c' in on the
15 when she was c' to the entering
25:10 the army that was c' to him out
14 Amaziah was c' from the slaughter
17 C', let us see one another in the
28:17 Edomites had c' and smitten Judah,
29:31 c' near and bring sacrifices and
30: 1 that they should c' to the house
5 should c' to keep the passover
9 they shall c' again into this land:
32: 2 saw that Sennacherib was c',
4 should the kings of Assyria c',
21 when he was c' into the house
35:21 I c' not against thee this day,
Ezr 3: 1 when the seventh month was c',
8 that were c' out of the captivity
4:12 are c' unto Jerusalem, building
6:21 of Israel, which were c' again out
8:35 which were c' out of the captivity
9:13 after all that is c' upon us for
10: 8 would not c' within three days,
14 c' at appointed times, and with
Ne 2: 7 convey me over till I c' to Judah;
10 that there was c' a man to seek
17 c', and let us build up the wall
4: 8 together to c' and to fight against
11 we c' in the midst among them,
6: 2 C', let us meet together in some
3 work, so that I cannot c' down:
3 whilst I leave it, and c' down to
7 C' now therefore, and let us take
10 for they will c' to slay thee;
10 yea, in the night will they c'
8:17 were c' again out of the captivity
9:32 hath c' upon us, on our kings,
13: 1 not c' into the congregation
22 and that they should c' and keep
Es 1:12 Vashti refused to c' at the kings
17 shall c' abroad unto all women,
19 Vashti c' no more before king
2:12 when every maid's turn was c'
15 was c' to go in unto the king,
4:11 shall c' unto the king into the
11 to c' in unto the king these thirty
14 thou art c' to the kingdom
5: 4 c' this day unto the banquet
8 let the king and Haman c' to the
12 the queen did let no man c' in
6: 4 Haman was c' into the outward
5 And the king said, Let him c' in.
8: 6 evil that shall c' unto my people?
9:26 and which had c' unto them,
Job 2:11 heard of all this evil that was c'
11 to c' to mourn with him and
3: 6 let it not c' into the number
7 let no joyful voice c' therein.
25 which I greatly feared is c' upon
25 which I was afraid of is c' unto me.
4: 5 But now it is c' upon thee, and
5:26 Thou shalt c' to thy grave in a
7: 9 down to the grave shall c' up no
8:22 of the wicked shall c' to nought.
9:32 should c' together in judgment.
13:13 speak, and let c' on me what will.
16 hypocrite shall not c' before him.
14:14 time will I wait, till my change c'.
21 His sons c' to honour, and he
15:21 the destroyer shall c' upon him.
16:22 When a few years are c',
17:10 you all, do ye return, and c' now:
18:20 They that c' after him shall be
19:12 His troops c' together, and raise
20:22 hand of the wicked shall c' upon
22:21 thereby good shall c' unto thee.
23: 3 that I might c' even to his seat!
10 tried me, I shall c' forth as gold.
26:10 the day and night c' to an end.
34:28 cry of the poor to c' unto him,
37:13 He causeth it to c', whether for
38:11 Hitherto shalt thou c', but no
41:13 who can c' to him with his double
16 that no air can c' between them.
Ps 5: 7 c' into thy house in the multitude
7: 9 of the wicked c' to an end;
16 his violent dealing shall c' down
9: 6 destructions are c' to a perpetual
14: 7 salvation of Israel were c' out
17: 2 c' forth from thy presence;
22:31 They shall c', and shall declare
24: 7, 9 and the King of glory shall c' in.
32: 6 they shall not c' nigh unto him.
9 bridle, lest they c' near unto thee.
34:11 C', ye children, hearken unto me:
35: 8 Let destruction c' upon him
36:11 not the foot of pride c' against me,
40: 7 Then said I, Lo, I c': in the
41: 6 if he c' to see me, he speaketh
42: 2 shall I c' and appear before God?
44:17 All this is c' upon us; yet have we
46: 8 C', behold the works of the Lord,
50: 3 Our God shall c', and shall not
52:title David is c' to the house of
53: 6 salvation of Israel were c' out of Zion

Ps 55: 5 and trembling are c' upon me,
65: 2 prayer, unto thee shall all flesh c'.
66: 5 C' and see the works of God:
16 C' and hear, all ye that fear God,
68:31 Princes shall c' out of Egypt;
69: 1 waters are c' in unto my soul.
2 I am c' into deep waters, where
27 them not c' into thy righteousness.
71:18 power to every one that is to c'.
72: 6 He shall c' down like rain upon
78: 4 shewing to the generation to c'
6 That the generation to c' might
79: 1 O God, the heathen are c' into
11 Let the sighing of the prisoner c'
80: 2 strength, and c' and save us.
83: 4 C', and let us cut them off from
86: 9 whom thou hast made shall c'
88: 2 Let my prayer c' before thee:
8 shut up, and I cannot c' forth.
91: 7 but it shall not c' nigh thee.
10 neither shall any plague c' nigh
95: 1 O c', let us sing unto the Lord:
2 Let us c' before his presence
6 O c', let us worship and bow down:
96: 8 offering, and c' into his courts.
100: 2 c' before his presence with singing.
101: 2 O when wilt thou c' unto me?
102: 1 O Lord, and let my cry c' unto thee.
13 favour her, yea, the set time, is c'.
18 be written for the generation to c':
109:17 cursing, so let it c' unto him:
18 it c' into his bowels like water,
119:41 Let thy mercies c' also unto me,
77 Let thy tender mercies c' unto me,
169 Let my cry c' near before thee,
170 my supplication c' before thee:
126: 6 doubtless c' again with rejoicing,
132: 3 I will not c' into the tabernacle
144: 5 thy heavens, O Lord, and c' down:
Pr 1:11 C' with us, let us lay wait for
3:28 thy neighbour, Go, and c' again,
5: 8 c' not nigh the door of her house:
6: 3 c' into the hand of thy friend;
11 So shall thy poverty c' as one that
15 Therefore shall his calamity c'
7:18 C', let us take our fill of love until
20 will c' home at the day appointed.
9: 5 C', eat of my bread, and drink
10:24 the wicked, it shall c' upon him:
11:27 mischief, it shall c' unto him.
12:13 the just shall c' out of trouble.
20:13 not sleep, lest thou c' to poverty;
22:16 the rich, shall surely c' to want.
23:21 the glutton shall c' to poverty:
24:25 good blessing shall c' upon them.
34 So shall thy poverty c' as one that
25: 4 shall c' forth a vessel for the finer.
7 said unto thee, C' up hither; than
26: 2 the curse causeless shall not c'.
28:22 that poverty shall c' upon him.
31:25 she shall rejoice in time to c'.
Ec 1: 7 place from whence the rivers c'
11 remembrance of things that are to c'
11 with those that shall c' after.
16 Lo, I am c' to great estate,
2:16 the days to c' shall all be forgotten.
4:16 also that c' after shall not rejoice
7:18 he that feareth God shall c' forth
8:10 had c' and gone from the place
9: 2 All things c' alike to all: there is
12: 1 while the evil days c' not, nor
Ca 2:10 love, my fair one, and c' away.
12 of the singing of birds is c',
13 love, my fair one, and c' away.
4: 8 C' with me from Lebanon,
16 O north wind; and c', thou south;
16 Let my beloved c' into his garden,
5: 1 I am c' into my garden, my sister,
7:11 C', my beloved, let us go forth
Isa 1:12 When ye c' to appear before me,
18 C' now, and let us reason
23 doth the cause of the widow c'
2: 2 And it shall c' to pass in the last
3 C' ye, and let us go up to the
5 O house of Jacob, c' ye, and let us
3:24 it shall c' to pass, that instead of
4: 3 c' to pass, that he that is left in
5: 6 shall c' up briers and thorns:
19 One of Israel draw nigh and c',
26 behold, they shall c' with speed
7: 7 stand, neither shall it c' to pass.
17 house, days that have not c',
18 shall c' to pass in that day, that
19 And they shall c', and shall rest
21 c' to pass in that day, that a man
22 c' to pass, for the abundance of
23 c' to pass in that day, that every
24 and with bows shall men c'
25 not c' thither the fear of briers
8: 7 shall c' up over all his channels,
10 and it shall c' to nought;
21 shall c' to pass, that when they
10: 3 desolation which shall c' from far?
12 c' to pass, that when the Lord
20 c' to pass in that day, that the
27 c' to pass in that day, that his
28 c' to Aiath, he is passed to Migron;
11: 1 And there shall c' forth a rod out
11 c' to pass in that day, that the
13: 5 They c' from a far country, from
6 it shall c' as a destruction from
22 her time is near to c', and her days
14: 3 c' to pass in the day that the Lord
8 no feller is c' up against us.
24 thought, so shall it c' to pass;
29 of the serpent's root shall c' forth

Isa 14:31 shall c' from the north a smoke,
16: 8 they are c' even unto Jazer,
12 c' to pass, when it is seen that
12 shall c' to his sanctuary to pray;
17: 4 And in that day it shall c' to pass,
19: 1 cloud, and shall c' into Egypt:
23 the Assyrian shall c' into Egypt,
21:12 enquire, enquire ye: return, c'.
22: 7 shall c' to pass, that thy choicest
20 And it shall c' to pass in that day,
23:15 c' to pass in that day, that Tyre
17 c' to pass after the end of seventy
24:10 is shut up, that no man may c' in.
18 shall c' to pass that he who fleeth
21 And it shall c' to pass in that day,
26:20 C', my people, enter thou into thy
27: 6 shall cause them that c' of Jacob
11 women c', and set them on fire:
12 c' to pass in that day, that the
13 And it shall c' to pass in that day,
13 shall c' which were ready to perish
28:15 it shall not c' unto us: for we have
29:24 shall c' to understanding,
30: 6 whence c' the young and old lion,
8 the time to c' for ever and ever:
29 c' into the mountain of the Lord,
31: 4 so shall the Lord of hosts c' down
32:10 fail, the gathering shall not c'.
13 of my people shall c' up thorns
34: 1 C' near, ye nations, to hear; and
1 and all things that c' forth of it.
3 shall c' up out of their carcases,
5 it shall c' down upon Idumea,
7 unicorns shall c' down with them,
13 thorns shall c' up in her palaces,
35: 4 God will c' with vengeance,
4 he will c' and save you.
10 and c' to Zion with songs and
36:10 am I now c' up without the Lord
16 c' out to me: and eat ye every one
17 Until I c' and take you away to a
37: 3 the children are c' to the birth,
9 is c' forth to make war with thee.
24 multitude of my chariots am I c'
29 tumult, is c' up into mine ears,
33 He shall not c' into this city, nor
33 nor c' before it with shields,
34 not c' into this city, saith the Lord.
39: 3 are c' from a far country unto me,
6 Behold, the days c', that all that is
40:10 Lord God will c' with strong hand,
41: 1 c' near; then let them speak:
1 us c' near together to judgment.
22 declare us things for to c'.
23 things that are to c' hereafter,
25 the north, and he shall c':
25 c' upon princes as upon morter,
42: 9 the former things are c' to pass,
23 hearken and hear for the time to c'?
44: 7 are coming, and shall c',
45:11 things to c' concerning my sons,
14 stature, shall c' over unto thee,
14 be thine: they shall c' after thee;
14 in chains they shall c' over, and
20 Assemble yourselves and c';
24 even to him shall men c';
47: 1 C' down, and sit in the dust, O
9 these two things shall c' to thee
9 they shall c' upon thee in their
11 Therefore shall evil c' upon thee;
11 shall c' upon thee suddenly,
13 things that shall c' upon thee.
48: 1 are c' forth out of the waters of
16 C' ye near unto me, hear ye this;
49:12 these shall c' from far: and, lo,
18 themselves together, and c' to thee.
50: 8 let him c' near to me.
51:11 and c' with singing unto Zion;
19 two things are c' unto thee;
52: 1 there shall no more c' into thee
54:14 for it shall not c' near thee.
55: 1 c' ye to the waters, and he that
1 hath no money; c' ye, buy, and eat;
1 yea, c', buy wine and milk
3 Incline your ear, and c' unto me:
13 the thorn shall c' up the fir tree,
13 and instead of the brier shall c' up
56: 1 for my salvation is near to c',
9 ye beasts of the field, c' to devour,
12 C' ye, say they, I will fetch wine,
57: 1 is taken away from the evil to c'.
59:19 the enemy shall c' in like a flood,
20 And the Redeemer shall c' to Zion,
60: 1 Arise, shine; for thy light is c',
3 the Gentiles shall c' to thy light,
4 together, they c' to thee:
4 thy sons shall c' from far, and thy
5 forces of the Gentiles shall c' unto
6 all they from Sheba shall c': they
7 they shall c' up with acceptance
13 of Lebanon shall c' unto thee,
14 of them that afflicted thee shall c'
63: 4 and the year of my redeemed is c'.
64: 1 that thou wouldest c' down, that
65: 5 c' not near to me; for I am holier
17 shall not be remembered, nor c'
24 c' to pass, that before they call,
66:15 behold, the Lord will c' with fire,
18 and their thoughts: it shall c',
18 they shall c', and see my glory.
23 And it shall c' to pass, that from
23 all flesh c' to worship before me,
Jer 1:15 and they shall c', and they shall
2: 3 shall c' upon them, saith the Lord.
31 we will c' no more unto thee?
3:16 c' to pass, when ye be multiplied

Jer 3:16 neither shall it c' to mind:
18 shall c' together out of the land
22 we c' unto thee; for thou art the
4: 4 lest my fury c' forth like fire,
7 lion is c' up from his thicket,
9 it shall c' to pass at that day,
12 from those places shall c' unto me:
13 he shall c' up as clouds,
16 watchers c' from a far country,
5:12 neither shall evil c' upon us;
19 it shall c' to pass, when ye shall
6: 3 their flocks shall come unto her;
26 spoiler shall suddenly c' upon us.
7:10 And c' and stand before me in this
32 behold, the days c', saith the Lord,
8:16 for they are c', and have devoured
9:17 mourning women, that they may c';
17 cunning women, that they may c':
21 death is c' up into our windows,
25 Behold, the days c', saith the Lord,
10:22 Behold, the noise of the bruit is c',
12: 9 c' ye, assemble all the beasts
9 beasts of the field, c' to devour,
12 The spoilers are c' upon all high
13:18 your principalities shall c' down,
20 them that c' from the north:
22 Wherefore c' these things upon
15: 2 c' to pass, if they say unto thee,
16:10 And it shall c' to pass, when thou
14 behold, the days c', saith the Lord,
19 the Gentiles shall c' unto thee
17:15 word of the Lord? let it c' now.
19 whereby the kings of Judah c' in,
24 it shall c' to pass, if ye diligently
26 And they shall c' from the cities
18:14 waters that c' from another place
18 C', and let us devise devices
18 C', and let us smite him with the
19: 6 the days c', saith the Lord, that
20: 6 thou shalt c' to Babylon, and
21:13 Who shall c' down against us?
22:23 thou be when pangs c' upon thee,
23: 5 days c', saith the Lord, that I will
7 days c', saith the Lord, that they
17 No evil shall c' upon you.
25: 3 word of the Lord hath c' unto me,
12 c' to pass, when seventy years
31 c' even to the ends of the earth;
26: 2 c' to worship in the Lord's house,
27: 3 c' to Jerusalem unto Zedekiah king
7 until the very time of his land c':
8 c' to pass, that the nation and
28: 9 of the prophet shall c' to pass,
30: 3 For, lo, the days c', saith the Lord,
8 For it shall c' to pass in that day,
31: 9 They shall c' with weeping,
12 Therefore they shall c' and sing
16 and they shall c' again from the
17 shall c' again to their own border;
27, 31, 38 Behold, the days c', saith
28 And it shall c' to pass, that like
32: 7 thine uncle shall c' unto thee,
23 hast caused all this evil to c'
24 they are c' unto the city to take
24 thou hast spoken is c' to pass;
29 shall c' and set fire on this city,
33: 5 They c' to fight with the Chaldeans,
14 days c', saith the Lord, that I will
35:11 C', and let us go to Jerusalem for
36: 6 all Judah that c' out of their cities.
14 in the ears of the people, and c'.
29 king of Babylon shall certainly c'
37: 5 Pharaoh's army was c' forth out
7 Pharaoh's army, which is c' forth
8 And the Chaldeans shall c' again,
19 The king of Babylon shall not c'
38:25 and they c' unto thee, and say
40: 3 therefore this thing is c' upon
4 to c' with me into Babylon,
4 c'; and I will look well unto thee:
4 but if it seem ill unto thee to c'
10 the Chaldeans, which will c' unto us:
41: 6 unto them, C' to Gedaliah the son
42: 4 c' to pass, that whatsoever thing
16 it shall c' to pass, that the sword,
46: 9 C' up, ye horses; and rage, ye
9 let the mighty men c' forth;
13 king of Babylon should c' and
18 as Carmel by the sea, so shall he c'.
21 the day of their calamity was c'
22 c' against her with axes, as hewers
47: 5 Baldness is c' upon Gaza;
48: 2 c', and let us cut it off from being
8 And the spoiler shall c' upon
12 days c', saith the Lord, that I will
16 The calamity of Moab is near to c'.
18 Dibon, c' down from thy glory,
18 the spoiler of Moab shall c' upon
21 judgment is c' upon the plain
45 fire shall c' forth out of Heshbon,
49: 2 behold, the days c', saith the Lord,
4 her treasures, saying, Who shall c'
9 If grapegatherers c' to thee,
14 and c' against her, and rise up to
19 he shall c' up like a lion from the
22 he shall c' up and fly as the eagle,
36 the outcasts of Elam shall not c'.
39 it shall c' to pass in the latter days,
50: 4 the children of Israel shall c', they
5 C', and let us join ourselves to the
9 I will raise and cause to c' up
26 C' against her from the utmost
27 for their day is c', the time of their
31 for thy day is c', the time that I will
41 Behold, a people shall c' from the
44 he shall c' up like a lion from the

Jer 51:10 c', and let us declare in Zion the
13 thine end is c', and the measure
27 cause the horses to c' up as the
33 and the time of her harvest shall c'.
42 The sea is c' up upon Babylon:
46 a rumour shall both c' one year,
46 in another year shall c' a rumour,
47 behold, the days c', that I will do
48 for the spoilers shall c' unto her
50 and let Jerusalem c' into your
51 for strangers are c' into the
52 behold, the days c', saith the Lord,
53 from me shall spoilers c' unto her,
56 Because the spoiler is c' upon her,
60 all the evil that should c' upon
La 1: 4 none c' to the solemn feasts:
14 they are wreathed, and c' up upon
22 Let all their wickedness c' before
3:47 Fear and a snare is c' upon us,
4:18 days are fulfilled; for our end is c'.
5: 1 what is c' upon us: consider, and
Eze 5: 4 thereof shall a fire c' forth into
7: 2 the end is c' upon the four corners
3 Now is the end c' upon thee, and
5 evil, an only evil, behold, is c'.
6 An end is c', the end is c': it
6 for thee; behold, it is c'.
7 c' unto thee, O thou that dwellest
7 the time is c', the day of trouble is
10 Behold the day, behold, it is c':
12 The time is c', the day draweth
26 Mischief shall c' upon mischief,
9: 6 c' not near any man upon whom
11: 5 for I know the things that c' into
16 the countries where they shall c'.
18 And they shall c' thither, and they
12:16 among the heathen whither they c';
25 that I shall speak shall c' to pass
27 he seeth is for many days to c',
13:18 the souls alive that c' unto you?
14:22 they shall c' forth unto you, and
16: 7 art c' to excellent ornaments;
16 the like things shall not c',
33 that they may c' unto thee on
17:12 the king of Babylon is c' to
18: 6 neither hath c' near to a
20: 3 Are ye c' to enquire of me? As I
21:19 of the king of Babylon may c':
19 both twain shall c' forth out of
20 that the sword may c' to Rabbath
24 I say, that ye are c' to remembrance.
25 whose day is c', when iniquity
27 until he c' whose right it is; and I
29 wicked, whose day is c', when
22: 3 that her time may c', and maketh
4 to draw near, and art c' even unto
23:24 And they shall c' against thee
40 ye have sent for men to c' from far,
24: 8 That it might cause fury to c' up
14 it shall c' to pass, and I will do it;
26 escapeth in that day shall c' unto
26: 3 will cause many nations to c' up
3 the sea causeth his waves to c' up.
16 princes of the sea shall c' down
27:29 pilots of the sea, shall c' down from
30: 4 And the sword shall c' upon Egypt,
6 pride of her power shall c' down:
9 great pain shall c' upon them,
32:11 of the king of Babylon shall c'
33: 3 If when he seeth the sword c' upon
4 if the sword c', and take him away,
6 if the watchman see the sword c',
6 if the sword c', and take any
30 C', I pray you, and hear what is
31 And they c' unto thee as the people
33 this cometh to pass, (lo, it will c',)
34:26 I will cause the shower to c' down
36: 8 Israel; for they are at hand to c'.
37: 9 C' from the four winds, O breath,
12 graves, and cause you to c' up
38: 8 thou shalt c' into the land that is
9 Thou shalt ascend and c' like
10 It shall also c' to pass, that at the
10 same time shall things c' into thy
13 Art thou c' to take a spoil? hast
15 And thou shalt c' from thy place
16 And thou shalt c' up against my
18 And it shall c' to pass at the same
18 time when Gog shall c' against the
18 that my fury shall c' up in my
39: 2 will cause thee to c' up from the
8 Behold, it is c', and it is done,
11 And it shall c' to pass in that
17 Assemble yourselves, and c';
40:46 the sons of Levi, which c' near to
44:13 they shall not c' near unto me,
13 nor to c' near to any of my holy
15 they shall c' near to me to
16 they shall c' near to my table, to
17 it shall c' to pass, that when they
17 no wool shall c' upon them,
25 they shall c' at no dead person
45: 4 which shall c' near to minister
46: 9 the people of the land shall c'
47: 9 And it shall c' to pass, that every
9 whithersoever the rivers shall c',
9 because these waters shall c'
10 And it shall c' to pass, that the
20 the border, till a man c' over
22 And it shall c' to pass, that ye
23 shall c' to pass, that in what tribe
Da 2:29 what should c' to pass hereafter:
29 to thee what shall c' to pass.
45 to the king what shall c' to pass
3: 2 to c' to the dedication of the
Da 3:26 of the most high God, c' forth,
26 forth, and c' hither. Then
4:24 which is c' upon my lord the
8: 7 I saw him c' close unto the ram,
23 when the transgressors are c' to the full,
9:13 all this evil is c' upon us: yet
22 I am now c' forth to give thee
23 I am c' to shew thee; for thou art
26 people of the prince that shall c'
10:12 words were heard, and I am c' for
14 Now I am c' to make thee
20 knowest thou wherefore I c' unto
20 lo, the prince of Grecia shall c'.
11: 6 shall c' to the king of the north to
7 which shall c' with an army,
9 So the king of the south shall c'
10 and one shall certainly c', and
11 and shall c' forth and fight with
13 and shall certainly c' after certain
15 So the king of the north shall c',
21 but he shall c' in peaceably, and
23 for he shall c' up, and shall
29 he shall return, and c' toward the
30 For the ships of Chittim shall c'
11:40 king of the north shall c' against
45 yet he shall c' to his end, and
Ho 1: 5 it shall c' to pass at that day,
10 c' to pass, that in the place where
11 they shall c' up out of the land:
2:21 c' to pass in that day, I will hear,
4:15 c' not ye unto Gilgal, neither go
6: 1 C', and let us return unto the
3 and he shall c' unto us as the rain,
8: 1 He shall c' as an eagle against the
9: 4 not c' into the house of the Lord.
7 The days of visitation are c',
7 the days of recompence are c';
10: 8 thistle shall c' up on their altars;
12 till he c' and rain righteousness
13:13 c' upon him: he is an unwise son;
15 an east wind shall c', the wind of
15 the wind of the Lord shall c' up
Joe 1: 6 a nation is c' up upon my land,
13 c', lie all night in sackcloth, ye
15 from the Almighty shall it c'.
2:20 and his stink shall c' up,
20 and his ill savour shall c' up,
23 cause to c' down for you the rain,
28 And it shall c' to pass afterward,
31 and the terrible day of the Lord c'.
32 c' to pass, that whosoever shall
3: 9 of war draw near; let them c' up:
11 Assemble yourselves, and c', all ye
11 cause thy mighty ones to c' down,
12 c' up to the valley of Jehoshaphat:
13 c', get you down; for the press is
18 And it shall c' to pass in that day,
18 a fountain shall c' forth out of the
Am 4: 2 the days shall c' upon you, that he
4 C' to Beth-el, and transgress; at
10 the stink of your camps to c' up
5: 5 and Beth-el shall c' to nought.
9 shall c' against the fortress.
6: 3 the seat of violence to c' near;
9 shall c' to pass, if there remain ten
8: 2 is c' upon my people of Israel;
9 And it shall c' to pass in that day,
11 days c', saith the Lord God, that
9:13 the days c', saith the Lord, that the
Ob 21 saviours shall c' up on mount
Jon 1: 2 wickedness is c' up before me.
7 C', and let us cast lots, that we
4: 6 and made it to c' up over Jonah,
Mic 1: 3 will c' down, and tread upon the
9 for it is c' unto Judah; he is
9 is c' unto the gate of my people
15 c' unto Adullam, the glory of
2:13 The breaker is c' up before them:
3:11 none evil can c' upon us.
4: 1 c' to pass, that the mountain of
2 many nations shall c', and say,
2 C', and let us go up to the
8 unto thee shall it c', even the first
8 kingdom shall c' to the daughter
5: 2 out of thee shall he c' forth unto
5 Assyrian shall c' into our land:
10 shall c' to pass in that day, saith
6: 6 Wherewith shall I c' before the
6 c' before him with burnt offerings,
7:12 c' even to thee from Assyria,
Na 1:11 There is one c' out of thee,
2: 1 that dasheth in pieces is c' up
3: 7 c' to pass, that all they that look
Hab 1: 8 their horsemen shall c' from far;
9 They shall c' all for violence:
2: 3 it will surely c', it will not tarry.
Zep 1: 8 c' to pass in the day of the Lord's
10 it shall c' to pass in that day,
12 And it shall c' to pass at that time
2: 2 of the Lord c' upon you, before
2 the day of the Lord's anger c'
Hag 1: 2 The time is not c', the time that
2: 7 the desire of all nations shall c':
22 and their riders shall c' down,
Zec 1:21 Then said I, What c' these to do?
21 but these are c' to fray them, to
2: 6 Ho, ho, c' forth, and flee from the
10 I c', and I will dwell in the midst
6:10 c' from Babylon, and c' thou the
15 that are far off shall c' and build
15 And this shall c' to pass, if ye will
7:13 it is c' to pass, that as he cried,
8:13 c' to pass, that as ye were a curse
20 shall yet c' to pass, that there shall
20 c' people, and the inhabitants
Zec 8:22 people and strong nations shall c'
23 In those days it shall c' to pass,
11: 2 forest of the vintage is c' down.
12: 9 it shall c' to pass in that day, that
9 nations that c' against Jerusalem.
13: 2 And it shall c' to pass in that day,
3 And it shall c' to pass, that when
4 And it shall c' to pass in that day,
8 And it shall c' to pass, that in all
14: 5 my God shall c', and all the saints
6, 13 it shall c' to pass in that day,
16 And it shall c' to pass, that every
17 will not c' up of all the families,
18 of Egypt go not up, and c' not,
18, 19 that c' not up to keep the feast
21 they that sacrifice shall c' and take
Mal 3: 1 shall suddenly c' to his temple,
1 behold, he shall c', saith the Lord
5 I will c' near to you to judgment;
4: 6 lest I c' and smite the earth
M't 2: 2 east, and are c' to worship him.
6 out of thee shall c' a Governor,
8 I may c' and worship him also.
11 when they were c' into the house,
3: 7 and Sadducees c' to his baptism,
7 to flee from the wrath to c'?
5:17 that I am c' to destroy the law,
17 I am not c' to destroy, but to fulfil.
24 and then c' and offer thy gift.
26 shalt by no means c' out thence,
6:10 Thy kingdom c'. Thy will be done
7:15 which c' to you in sheep's clothing,
8: 1 was c' down from the mountain,
7 unto him, I will c' and heal him.
8 thou shouldest c' under my roof:
9 to another, C', and he cometh;
11 shall c' from the east and west,
14 Jesus was c' into Peter's house,
16 When the even was c', they
28 when he was c' to the other side
29 art thou c' hither to torment us
32 when they were c' out, they went
9:13 I am not c' to call the righteous,
15 days will c', when the bridegroom
18 c' and lay thy hand upon her, and
28 And when he was c' into the house,
10:12 ye c' into an house, salute it.
13 worthy, let your peace c' upon it;
23 of Israel, till the Son of man be c'.
34 I am c' to send peace on earth:
35 I am c' to set a man at variance
11: 3 Art thou he that should c', or do
14 is Elias, which was for to c'.
28 C' unto me, all ye that labour
12:28 kingdom of God is c' unto you.
32 neither in the world to c'.
44 when he is c', he findeth it empty,
13:32 so that the birds of the air c'
49 the angels shall c' forth, and
54 he was c' into his own country,
14:23 when the evening was c', he was
28 bid me c' unto thee on the water.
29 And he said, C'. And when
29 Peter was c' down out of the ship,
32 when they were c' into the ship,
15:18 c' forth from the heart; and they
16: 5 when his disciples were c' to the
24 If any man will c' after me,
27 Son of man shall c' in the glory
17:10 scribes that Elias must first c'?
11 Elias truly shall first c', and
12 unto you, That Elias is c' already,
14 when they were c' to the multitude,
24 when they were c' to Capernaum,
25 when he was c' into the house,
18: 7 must needs be that offences c';
11 For the Son of man is c' to save
19:14 forbid them not, to c' unto me:
21 in heaven: and c' and follow me.
20: 8 So when even was c', the lord of
21: 1 and were c' to Bethphage, unto
10 when he was c' into Jerusalem,
23 when he was c' into the temple,
38 c', let us kill him, and let us seize
22: 3 wedding: and they would not c'.
4 ready: c' unto the marriage.
23:35 That upon you may c' all the
36 shall c' upon this generation.
24: 5 For many shall c' in my name,
6 all these things must c' to pass,
14 and then shall the end c'.
17 is on the housetop not c' down
42 not what hour your Lord doth c'.
43 what watch the thief would c',
50 The lord of that servant shall c'
25:31 When the Son of man shall c' in
34 C', ye blessed of my Father,
26:20 Now when the even was c', he sat
50 Friend, wherefore art thou c'?
55 Are ye c' out as against a thief
27: 1 When the morning was c', all the
33 when they were c' unto a place
40 of God, c' down from the cross.
42 let him now c' down from the cross,
49 whether Elias will c' to save him.
57 When the even was c', there
64 lest his disciples c' by night,
28: 6 C', see the place where the Lord
14 if this c' to the governor's ears,
M'r 1:17 C' ye after me, and I will make
24 art thou c' to destroy us? I know
25 thy peace, and c' out of him.
29 when they were c' out of the
2: 3 And they c' unto him, bringing
4 And when they could not c' nigh

M'r 2:18 they c' and say unto him, Why do
20 But the days will c', when the
4:22 but that it should c' abroad.
29 sickle, because the harvest is c'.
35 same day, when the even was c',
5: 2 when he was c' out of the ship,
8 C' out of the man, thou unclean
15 And they c' to Jesus, and see him
18 when he was c' into the ship,
23 c' and lay thy hands on her,
39 when he was c' in, he saith unto
6: 2 when the sabbath day was c',
21 when a convenient day was c',
31 C' ye yourselves apart into a
47 when even was c', the ship was in
54 when they were c' out of the ship,
7: 4 And when they c' from the market,
15 the things which c' out of him,
23 these evil things c' from within,
30 when she was c' to her house,
8:34 Whosoever will c' after me, let
9: 1 kingdom of God c' with power.
11 scribes that Elias must first c'?
13 That Elias is indeed c', and they
25 I charge thee, c' out of him,
28 when he was c' into the house,
29 This kind can c' forth by nothing,
10:14 Suffer the little children to c'
21 c', take up the cross, and follow
30 in the world to c' eternal life.
35 c' unto him, saying, Master, we
11:11 and now the eventide was c',
12 when they were c' from Bethany
15 And they c' to Jerusalem: and
19 when even was c', he went out
23 which he saith shall c' to pass;
27 And they c' again to Jerusalem:
27 there c' to him the chief priests,
12: 7 is the heir; c', let us kill him,
9 c' and destroy the husbandmen,
14 And when they were c', they say
18 Then c' unto him the Sadducees,
13: 6 For many shall c' in my name,
29 shall see these things c' to pass,
14: 8 she is c' aforehand to anoint
41 it is enough, the hour is c';
45 And as soon as he was c', he goeth
48 Are ye c' out, as against a thief,
15:30 Save thyself, and c' down from
33 when the sixth hour was c', there
36 Elias will c' to take him down.
42 now when the even was c',
16: 1 they might c' and anoint him.
Lu 1:35 Holy Ghost shall c' upon thee,
43 the mother of my Lord should c'
2:15 this thing which is c' to pass,
3: 7 to flee from the wrath to c'?
4:34 art thou c' to destroy us? I know
35 Hold thy peace, and c' out of him.
36 unclean spirits, and they c' out.
5: 7 that they should c' and help them.
17 which were c' out of every town
35 But the days will c', when the
7: 3 he would c' and heal his servant.
7 I myself worthy to c' unto thee:
8 and to another, C', and he cometh;
19 Art thou he that should c'?
20 When the men were c' unto him,
20 Art thou he that should c'?
34 The Son of man is c' eating and
8: 4 were c' to him out of every city,
17 not be known and c' abroad.
19 could not c' at him for the press.
29 spirit to c' out of the man.
41 that he would c' into his house:
9:23 If any man will c' after me,
26 when he shall c' in his own glory,
37 they were c' down from the hill,
51 when the time was c' that he
54 that we command fire to c' down
56 is not c' to destroy men's lives,
10: 1 whither he himself would c'.
9 The kingdom of God is c' nigh
11 that the kingdom of God is c' nigh
35 when I c' again, I will repay thee.
11: 2 Thy kingdom c'. Thy will be
6 mine in his journey is c' to me,
20 kingdom of God is c' upon you.
22 he shall c' upon him, and
33 which c' in may see the light.
12:37 and will c' forth and serve them.
38 if he shall c' in the second watch,
38 or c' in the third watch,
39 what hour the thief would c',
46 The lord of that servant will c'
49 I am c' to send fire on the earth;
51 Suppose ye that I am c' to give
13: 7 I c' seeking fruit on this fig tree,
14 them therefore c' and be healed,
29 they shall c' from the east, and
35 the time c' when we shall say,
14: 9 that bade thee and him c' and
17 C'; for all things are now ready.
20 a wife, and therefore I cannot c'.
23 compel them to c' in, that my
26 If any man c' to me, and hate not
27 bear his cross, and c' after me,
15:27 Thy brother is c'; and thy father
30 as soon as this thy son was c',
16:26 that would c' from thence.
28 lest they also c' into this place
17: 1 but that offences will c': but woe
1 unto him, through whom they c'!
7 when he is c' from the field,
20 the kingdom of God should c',
22 The days will c', when ye shall

Lu 17:31 let him not c' down to take it
18:16 little children to c' unto me,
22 in heaven: and c', follow me.
30 in the world to c' life everlasting.
35 as he was c' nigh unto Jericho,
40 when he was c' near, he asked
19: 5 make haste, and c' down; for
9 day is salvation c' to this house,
10 For the Son of man is c' to seek
13 said unto them, Occupy till I c'.
29 he was c' nigh to Bethphage and
37 when he was c' nigh, even now
41 when he was c' near, he beheld
43 the days shall c' upon thee, that
20:14 is the heir: c', let us kill him,
16 c' and destroy these husbandmen,
21: 6 the days will c', in the which
7 these things shall c' to pass?
8 for many shall c' in my name,
9 these things must first c' to pass;
28 these things begin to c' to pass,
31 ye see these things c' to pass,
34 that day c' upon you unawares.
35 as a snare shall it c' on all them
36 these things that shall c' to pass,
22:14 when the hour was c', he sat down,
18 the kingdom of God shall c'.
45 and was c' to his disciples, he
52 the elders, which were c' to him,
52 Be ye c' out, as against a thief,
23:33 when they were c' to the place,
24:12 at that which was c' to pass.
18 things which are c' to pass there
Joh 1:31 am I c' baptizing with water.
39 He saith unto them, C' and see.
46 good thing c' out of Nazareth?
46 Philip saith unto him, C' and see.
2: 4 with thee? mine hour is not yet c'.
3: 2 thou art a teacher c' from God:
19 light is c' into the world, and men
26 baptizeth, and all men c' to him.
4:15 not, neither c' hither to draw.
16 call thy husband, and c' hither.
25 is called Christ: when he is c',
29 C', see a man, which told me all
40 the Samaritans were c' unto him,
45 Then when he was c' into Galilee,
47 that Jesus was c' out of Judæa
47 would c' down, and heal his son:
49 Sir, c' down ere my child die.
54 was c' out of Judæa into Galilee.
5:14 lest a worse thing c' unto thee.
24 shall not c' into condemnation;
29 And shall c' forth; they that have
40 ye will not c' to me, that ye might
43 I am c' in my Father's name, and
43 another shall c' in his own name,
6: 5 saw a great company c' unto him,
14 a truth that prophet that should c'
15 would c' and take him by force,
16 And when even was now c', his
17 and Jesus was not c' to them.
37 Father giveth me shall c' to me;
44 No man can c' to me, except the
65 c' unto me, except it were given
7: 6 My time is not yet c': but your
8 for my time is not yet full c'.
28 I am not c' of myself, but he that
30 because his hour was not yet c'.
34 where I am, thither ye cannot c'.
36 where I am, thither ye cannot c'?
37 let him c' unto me, and drink.
41 Shall Christ c' out of Galilee?
8:14 ye cannot tell whence I c', and
20 him; for his hour was not yet c'.
21 sins: whither I go, ye cannot c'.
22 saith, Whither I go, ye cannot c'.
9:39 I am c' into this world, that they
10:10 I am c' that they might have life,
11:27 Son of God, which should c' into
28 Master is c', and calleth for thee.
30 Jesus was not yet c' into the town,
32 Mary was c' where Jesus was,
34 said unto him, Lord, c' and see.
43 a loud voice, Lazarus, c' forth.
48 the Romans shall c' and take
56 that he will not c' to the feast?
12:12 people that were c' to the feast,
23 the hour is c', that the Son of man
35 lest darkness c' upon you:
46 I am c' a light into the world,
13: 1 Jesus knew that his hour was c'
3 was c' from God, and went to God;
19 Now I tell you before it c', that,
19 when it is c' to pass, ye may
33 Whither I go, ye cannot c'; so
14: 3 I will c' again, and receive you
18 you comfortless: I will c' to you.
23 we will c' unto him, and make our
28 I go away, and c' again unto you.
29 c' to pass, that, when it is c' to
15:22 not c' and spoken unto them,
26 But when the Comforter is c',
16: 4 that when the time shall c', ye
7 Comforter will not c' unto you;
8 And when he is c', he will reprove
13 when he, the Spirit of truth, is c',
13 he will shew you things to c'.
21 because her hour is c': but as
28 Father, and am c' into the world:
32 cometh, yea, is now c', that ye shall
17: 1 Father, the hour is c'; glorify thy
11 are in the world, and I c' to thee.
13 And now c' I to thee; and these
18: 4 all things that should c' upon him,
21: 4 when the morning was now c',

Joh 21: 9 then as they were c' to land,
12 Jesus saith unto them, C' and dine.
22, 23 he tarry till I c', what is that to
Ac 1: 6 they therefore were c' together,
8 the Holy Ghost is c' upon you:
11 shall so c' in like manner as ye
13 when they were c' in, they went
2: 1 the day of Pentecost was fully c',
17 And it shall c' to pass in the last
20 and notable day of the Lord c':
21 it shall c' to pass, that whosoever
3:19 the times of refreshing shall c'
23 shall c' to pass, that every soul,
5:38 be of men, it will c' to nought:
7: 3 c' into the land which I shall
7 after that shall they c' forth, and
34 and am c' down to deliver them.
34 c', I will send thee into Egypt.
8:15 were c' down, prayed for them,
24 which ye have spoken c' upon me.
27 c' to Jerusalem for to worship,
31 he would c' up and sit with him.
39 they were c' up out of the water,
9:26 when Saul was c' to Jerusalem,
38 he would not delay to c' to them.
39 When he was c', they brought
10: 4 c' up for a memorial before God.
21 is the cause wherefore ye are c'?
27 many that were c' together.
28 or c' unto one of another nation;
33 hast well done that thou art c'.
11: 2 Peter was c' up to Jerusalem,
11 were three men already c' unto the
20 when they were c' to Antioch,
12:11 Peter was c' to himself, he said,
13:40 lest that c' upon you, which is
14:11 The gods are c' down to us in the
27 And when they were c', and had
15: 4 when they were c' to Jerusalem,
16: 7 After they were c' to Mysia, they
9 saying, C' over into Macedonia,
15 c' into my house, and abide there.
18 of Jesus Christ to c' out of her.
37 c' themselves and fetch us out.
17: 6 upside down are c' hither also;
15 for to c' to him with all speed,
18: 2 lately c' from Italy, with his wife
5 Silas and Timotheus were c' from
27 who, when he was c', helped them
19: 4 him which should c' after him,
32 wherefore they were c' together.
20:11 therefore was c' up again, and
18 And when they were c' to him, he
21:11 when he was c' unto us, he took
17 when we were c' to Jerusalem,
22 multitude must needs c' together:
22 for they will hear that thou art c'.
22: 6 my journey, and was c' nigh
17 I was c' again to Jerusalem, even
23:15 he c' near, are ready to kill him.
35 when thine accusers are also c'.
24: 8 his accusers to c' unto thee:
22 the chief captain shall c' down,
23 to minister or c' unto him.
25 judgment to c', Felix.
25: 1 Festus was c' into the province,
7 And when he was c', the Jews
17 when they were c' hither, without
23 when Agrippa was c', and Bernice,
26: 7 God day and night, hope to c'.
22 and Moses did say should c':
27: 7 were c' over against Cnidus,
16 much work to c' by the boat:
27 when the fourteenth night was c',
28: 6 no harm c' to him, they changed
17 they were c' together, he said
Ro 1:10 by the will of God to c' unto you.
13 oftentimes I purposed to c' unto
3: 8 Let us do evil, that good may c'?
23 For all have sinned, and c' short
5:14 the figure of him that was to c'.
8:38 things present, nor things to c',
9: 9 At this time will I c', and Sarah
26 shall c' to pass, that in the place
11:11 salvation is c' unto the Gentiles,
25 fulness of the Gentiles be c' in.
26 shall c' out of Sion the Deliverer,
15:23 these many years to c' unto you;
24 journey into Spain, I will c' to
28 I will c' by you into Spain.
29 when I c' unto you, I shall c' in
32 That I may c' unto you with joy
16:19 obedience is c' abroad unto all men.
1Co 1: 7 So that ye c' behind in no gift;
2: 6 of this world, that c' to nought:
3:22 or things to c'; all are yours;
4: 5 the Lord c', who both will bring
18 as though I would not c' to you
19 c' to you shortly, if the Lord will,
21 shall I c' unto you with a rod, or
7: 5 c' together again, that Satan
10:11 whom the ends of the world are c'.
11:17 ye c' together not for the better,
18 when ye c' together in the church,
20 When ye c' together therefore
26 shew the Lord's death till he c'.
33 when ye c' together to eat, tarry
34 c' not together unto condemnation.
34 rest will I set in order when I c'.
13:10 when that which is perfect is c',
14: 6 if I c' unto you speaking with
23 the whole church be c' together
23 c' in those that are unlearned,
24 there c' in one that believeth not,
26 when ye c' together, every one of
15:35 and with what body do they c'?

1Co 16: 2 there be no gatherings when I *c*'.
3 And when I *c*', whomsoever ye
5 Now I will *c*' unto you, when I
10 Now if Timotheus *c*', see that he
11 in peace, that he may *c*' unto me:
12 I greatly desired him to *c*' unto
12 but his will was not at all to *c*' at
12 this time: but he will *c*' when he
2Co 1:15 I was minded to *c*' unto you before,
16 to *c*' again out of Macedonia unto
2: 1 that I would not *c*' again to you in
6:17 *c*' out from among them, and be
7: 5 For when we were *c*' into
9: 4 haply if they of Macedonia *c*' with
10:14 for we are *c*' as far as to you also
12: 1 I will *c*' to visions and revelations
14 third time I am ready to *c*' to you;
20 lest, when I *c*', I shall not find you
21 lest, when I *c*' again, my God will
13: 2 other, that, if I *c*' again, I will not
Ga 2:11 But when Peter was *c*' to Antioch,
12 but when they were *c*', he
21 for if righteousness *c*' by the law,
3:14 blessing of Abraham might *c*' on
19 till the seed should *c*' to whom
25 But after that faith is *c*', we are
4: 4 the fulness of the time was *c*',
Eph 1:21 but also in that which is to *c*':
2: 7 that in the ages to *c*' he might
4:13 Till we all *c*' in the unity of the
Ph'p 1:27 that whether I *c*' and see you, or
2:24 Lord that I also myself shall *c*'
Col 1: 6 Which is *c*' unto you, as it is in all
2:17 are a shadow of things to *c*';
4:10 if he *c*' unto you, receive him;)
1Th 1:10 delivered us from the wrath to *c*'.
2:16 for the wrath is *c*' upon them to
18 we would have *c*' unto you, even
2Th 1:10 When he shall *c*' to be glorified in
2: 3 for that day shall not *c*', except
3 except there *c*' a falling away
1Ti 2: 4 *c*' unto the knowledge of the truth.
3:14 hoping to *c*' unto thee shortly:
4: 8 now is, and of that which is to *c*'.
13 Till I *c*', give attendance to
6:19 foundation against the time to *c*',
2Ti 3: 1 last days perilous times shall *c*'.
7 never able to *c*' to the knowledge
4: 3 the time will *c*' when they will not
9 Do thy diligence to *c*' shortly
21 Do thy diligence to *c*' before winter.
Tit 3:12 be diligent to *c*' unto me to
Heb 2: 5 put in subjection the world to *c*',
4: 1 any of you should seem to *c*' short
16 Let us therefore *c*' boldly unto
6: 5 and the powers of the world to *c*',
7: 5 *c*' out of the loins of Abraham:
25 that *c*' unto God by him, seeing
8: 8 Behold, the days *c*', saith the
9:11 But Christ being *c*' an high priest
11 high priest of good things to *c*',
10: 1 a shadow of good things to *c*',
7 Then said I, Lo, I *c*' (in the
9 Then said he, Lo, I *c*' to do thy
37 and he that shall *c*' will
37 will *c*', and will not tarry.
11:20 Esau concerning things to *c*'.
24 Moses, when he was *c*' to years,
12:18 For ye are not *c*' unto the mount
22 But ye are *c*' unto mount Sion,
13:14 city, but we seek one to *c*'.
23 with whom, if he *c*' shortly, I will
Jas 2: 2 if there *c*' unto your assembly a
2 there *c*' in also a poor man in vile
4: 1 From whence *c*' wars and fightings
1 *c*' they not hence, even of your lusts
5: 1 miseries that shall *c*' upon you.
1Pe 1:10 the grace that should *c*' unto you:
4:17 For the time is *c*' that judgment
2Pe 3: 3 there shall *c*' in the last days
9 that all should *c*' to repentance.
10 But the day of the Lord will *c*' as
1Jo 2:18 heard that antichrist shall *c*',
4: 2 that Jesus Christ is *c*' in the flesh
3 Christ is *c*' in the flesh is not of
3 ye have heard that it should *c*';
5:20 know that the Son of God is *c*',
2Jo 7 confess not that Jesus Christ is *c*'
10 If there *c*' any unto you,and bring
12 I trust to *c*' unto you, and speak
3Jo 10 Wherefore, if I *c*', I will remember
Re 1: 1 which must shortly *c*' to pass;
4 and which was, and which is to *c*';
8 and which was, and which is to *c*',
2: 5 or else I will *c*' unto thee quickly,
16 I will *c*' unto thee quickly, and will
25 ye have already, hold fast till I *c*'.
3: 3 I will *c*' on thee as a thief, and thou
3 shalt not know what hour I will *c*'
9 behold, I will make them to *c*' and
10 of temptation, which shall *c*' upon
11 Behold, I *c*' quickly: hold that fast
20 open the door, I will *c*' in to him,
4: 1 which said, *C*' up hither, and I
8 which was, and is, and is to *c*'.
6: 1 one of the four beasts saying, *C*'
3 I heard the second beast say, *C*'
5 the third beast say, *C*' and see.
7 the fourth beast say, *C*' and see.
17 the great day of his wrath is *c*';
9:12 and, behold, there *c*' two woes
10: 1 I saw another mighty angel *c*'
11:12 saying unto them, *C*' up hither.
17 which art, and wast, and art to *c*';
18 thy wrath is *c*', and the time of *
12:10 Now is *c*' salvation, and strength,
Re 12:12 the devil is *c*' down unto you,
13:13 so that he maketh fire *c*' down
14: 7 for the hour of his judgment is *c*':
15 the time is *c*' for thee to reap; for
15: 4 all nations shall *c*' and worship
16:13 unclean spirits like frogs *c*' out
15 I *c*' as a thief. Blessed is he that
17: 1 *C*' hither; I will shew unto thee
10 the other is not yet *c*'; and when
18: 1 I saw another angel *c*' down from
4 *C*' out of her, my people, that ye
8 Therefore shall her plagues *c*' in
10 in one hour is thy judgment *c*'.
17 so great riches is *c*' to nought.
19: 7 the marriage of the Lamb is *c*',
17 *C*' and gather yourselves together
20: 1 I saw an angel *c*' down from
21: 9 *C*' hither, I will shew thee the
22: 7 Behold, I *c*' quickly: blessed is he
12 behold, I *c*' quickly; and my
17 the Spirit and the bride say, *C*'.
17 And let him that heareth say, *C*'.
17 And let him that is athirst *c*'.
20 Surely I *c*' quickly. Amen.
20 Even so, *c*', Lord Jesus.

comeliness
Isa 53: 2 he hath no form nor *c*'; and when
Eze 16:14 for it was perfect through my *c*',
27:10 they set forth thy *c*'.
Da 10: 8 for my *c*' was turned in me into
1Co 12:23 parts have more abundant *c*'.

comely See also UNCOMELY.
1Sa 16:18 in matters, and a *c*' person,
Job 41:12 his power, nor his *c*' proportion.
Ps 33: 1 for praise is *c*' for the upright.
147: 1 for it is pleasant; and praise is *c*'.
Pr 30:29 go well, yea, four are *c*' in going:
Ec 5:18 it is good and *c*' for one to eat and
Ca 1: 5 I am black, but *c*', O ye daughters
10 Thy cheeks are *c*' with rows of
2:14 voice, and thy countenance is *c*'.
4: 3 thy speech is *c*': thy temples are
6: 4 love, as Tirzah, *c*' as Jerusalem,
Isa 4: 2 earth shall be excellent and *c*' for
Jer 6: 2 daughter of Zion to a *c*' and
1Co 7:35 you, but for that which is *c*',
11:13 is it *c*' that a woman pray unto
12:24 For our *c*' parts have no need: but

comers
Heb 10: 1 continually make the *c*' thereunto

comest
Ge 10:19 Sidon, as thou *c*' to Gerar, unto
13:10 of Egypt, as thou *c*' unto Zoar.
24:41 this my oath, when thou *c*' to my
De 2:19 And when thou *c*' nigh over
20:10 When thou *c*' nigh unto a city to
23:24 When thou *c*' into thy neighbour's
25 When thou *c*' into the standing corn
28: 6 when thou *c*' in, and blessed shalt
19 when thou *c*' in, and cursed shalt
J'g 17: 9 said unto him, Whence *c*' thou?
18:23 that thou *c*' with such a company?
19:17 goest thou? and whence *c*' thou?
1Sa 15: 7 thou *c*' to Shur, that is over against
16: 4 *C*' thou peaceably?
17:43 Am I a dog, that thou *c*' to me
45 Thou *c*' to me with a sword, and
2Sa 1: 3 unto him, From whence *c*' thou?
3:13 when thou *c*' to see my face.
1Ki 2:13 she said, *C*' thou peaceably? And
19:15 and when thou *c*', anoint Hazael to
2Ki 5:25 Elisha said unto him, Whence *c*'
9: 2 And when thou *c*' thither, look out
Job 1: 7 said unto Satan, Whence *c*' thou?
2: 2 From whence *c*' thou? And Satan
Jer 51:61 When thou *c*' to Babylon, and shalt
Jon 1: 8 and whence *c*' thou? What is thy
M't 3:14 and *c*' thou to me?
Lu 23:42 remember me when thou *c*' into
2Ti 4:13 when thou *c*', bring with thee, and

cometh See also BECOMETH; OVERCOMETH.
Ge 24:43 when the virgin *c*' forth to draw
29: 6 his daughter *c*' with the sheep.
30:11 And Leah said, A troop *c*': and
32: 6 he *c*' to meet thee, and four
37:19 Behold, this dreamer *c*'.
48: 2 thy son Joseph *c*' unto thee:
Ex 4:14 he *c*' forth to meet thee: and when
8:20 he *c*' forth to the water; and say
13:12 every firstling that *c*' of a beast
28:35 when he *c*' out, that he die not.
29:30 when he *c*' into the tabernacle of
Le 11:34 on which such water *c*' shall be
Nu 1:51 the stranger that *c*' nigh shall be
3:10, 38 stranger that *c*' nigh shall be
5:30 the spirit of jealousy *c*' upon him,
12:12 he *c*' out of his mother's womb.
17:13 Whosoever *c*' any thing near unto
18: 7 the stranger that *c*' nigh shall be
21:13 that *c*' out of the coasts of the
26: 5 Hanoch, of whom *c*' the family of
De 18: 8 that which *c*' of the sale of his
23:11 when evening *c*' on, he shall wash
13 and cover that which *c*' from thee:
28:57 that *c*' out from between her feet,
J'g 11:31 whatsoever *c*' forth of the doors
13:14 eat of any thing that *c*' of the vine,
1Sa 4: 3 when it *c*' among us, it may save
9: 6 all that he saith *c*' surely to pass:
11: 7 Whosoever *c*' not forth after Saul
20:27 Wherefore *c*' not the son of Jesse
29 he *c*' not unto the king's table.
25: 8 whatsoever *c*' to thine hand unto
28:14 An old man *c*' up; and he is
2Sa 13: 5 and when thy father *c*' to see thee,
18:27 good man, and *c*' with good tidings.
1Ki 8:41 but *c*' out of a far country for thy
14: 5 wife of Jeroboam *c*' to ask a thing
5 when she *c*' in, that she shall feign
2Ki 4:10 when he *c*' to us, that he shall turn
6:32 when the messenger *c*', shut the
9:18 came to them, but he *c*' not again.
20 even unto them, and *c*' not again:
10: 2 Now as soon as this letter *c*' to you,
11: 8 and he that *c*' within the ranges, let
8 king as he goeth out and as he *c*' in.
12: 4 all the money that *c*' into any
9 on the right side as one *c*' into the
1Ch 16:33 because he *c*' to judge the earth.
29:16 thine holy name *c*' of thine hand,
2Ch 13: 9 so that whosoever *c*' to consecrate
20: 2 There *c*' a great multitude against
9 If, when evil *c*' upon us, as the
12 this great company that *c*' against
23: 7 whosoever else *c*' into the house,
7 be ye with the king when he *c*' in.
Job 3:21 long for death, but it *c*' not; and
24 For my sighing *c*' before I eat, and
5: 6 affliction *c*' not forth of the dust,
21 be afraid of destruction when it *c*'.
26 a shock of corn *c*' in in his season.
14: 2 He *c*' forth like a flower, and is
18 the mountain falling *c*' to nought,
20:25 is drawn, and *c*' out of the body;
25 glittering sword *c*' out of his gall:
21:17 oft *c*' their destruction upon them!
27: 9 his cry when trouble *c*' upon him?
28: 5 for the earth, out of it *c*' bread:
20 Whence then *c*' wisdom? and
36:32 by the cloud that *c*' betwixt.
37: 9 Out of the south *c*' the whirlwind:
22 Fair weather *c*' out of the north:
Ps 30: 5 a night, but joy *c*' in the morning.
62: 1 God: from him *c*' my salvation.
75: 6 For promotion *c*' neither from the
78:39 passeth away, and *c*' not again.
96:13 Lord: for he *c*', for he *c*' to judge
98: 9 Lord; for he *c*' to judge the earth:
118:26 Blessed be he that *c*' in the name
121: 1 the hills, from whence *c*' my help.
2 My help *c*' from the Lord, which
Pr 1:26 I will mock when your fear *c*';
27 When your fear *c*' as desolation,
27 and your destruction *c*' as a
27 distress and anguish *c*' upon
2: 6 out of his mouth *c*' knowledge and
3:25 desolation of the wicked, when it *c*'.
11: 2 When pride *c*', then *c*' shame:
8 and the wicked *c*' in his stead.
13: 5 man is loathsome, and *c*' to shame.
10 by pride *c*' contention: but with
12 but when the desire *c*', it is a tree
18: 3 When the wicked *c*', then *c*' also
17 but his neighbour *c*' and searcheth
29:26 every man's judgment *c*' from the Lord.
Ec 1: 4 another generation *c*': but the
2:12 the man do that *c*' after the king?
4:14 For out of prison he *c*' to reign;
5: 3 a dream *c*' through the multitude
6: 4 For he *c*' in with vanity, and
11: 8 All that *c*' is vanity.
Ca 2: 8 he *c*' leaping upon the mountains,
3: 6 Who is this that *c*' out of the
8: 5 Who is this that *c*' up from the
Isa 13: 9 Behold, the day of the Lord *c*',
21: 1 it *c*' from the desert, from a terrible
9 here *c*' a chariot of men, a couple
12 The morning *c*', and also the night:
24:18 and he that *c*' up out of the midst
26:21 Lord *c*' out of his place to punish
28:29 This also *c*' forth from the Lord
30:13 whose breaking *c*' suddenly at an
27 the name of the Lord *c*' from far,
42: 5 earth, and that which *c*' out of it;
55:10 as the rain *c*' down, and the snow
62:11 salvation *c*'; behold, his reward is
63: 1 Who is this that *c*' from Edom,
Jer 6:20 To what purpose *c*' there to me
22 a people *c*' from the north country,
17: 6 shall not see when good *c*'; but
8 shall not see when heat *c*', but her
18:14 Lebanon which *c*' from the rock
43:11 when he *c*', he shall smite the
46: 7 Who is this that *c*' up as a flood,
20 *c*'; it *c*' out of the north.
47: 4 Because of the day that *c*' to spoil
50: 3 there *c*' up a nation against her,
La 3:37 he that saith, and it *c*' to pass,
Eze 4:12 with dung that *c*' out of man,
7:25 destruction *c*'; and they shall seek
14: 4 and *c*' to the prophet; I the Lord
4 will answer him that *c*' according
7 and *c*' to a prophet to enquire of
20:32 And that which *c*' into your mind
21: 7 For the tidings; because it *c*': and
7 be weak as water: behold, it *c*',
24:24 and when this *c*', ye shall know
30: 9 in the day of Egypt: for, lo, it *c*'.
33:30 the word that *c*' forth from the
31 as the people *c*', and they sit
33 And when this *c*' to pass, (lo, it will
47: 9 shall live whither the river *c*'.
Da 11:16 But he that *c*', against him shall do
12:12 waiteth, and *c*' to the thousand
Ho 7: 1 and the thief *c*' in, and the troop
Joe 2: 1 for the day of the Lord *c*', for it is
Mic 1: 3 the Lord *c*' forth out of his place,
5: 6 when he *c*' into our land, and when
7: 4 watchmen and thy visitation *c*';
Hab 3:16 when he *c*' up unto the people, he

Zec 9: 9 thy King c' unto thee: he is just,
14: 1 day of the Lord c', and thy spoil
Mal 4: 1 the day c', that shall burn as an
1 the day that c' shall burn them up,
M't 3:11 but he that c' after me is mightier
13 Then c' Jesus from Galilee to
5:37 is more than these c' of evil.
8: 9 and to another, Come, and he c';
13:19 then c' the wicked one, and
15:11 that which c' out of the mouth,
17:27 and take up the fish that first c' up;
18: 7 that man by whom the offence c'!
21: 5 c' unto thee, meek, and sitting
9 Blessed is he that c' in the name of
40 lord therefore of the vineyard c',
23:39 Blessed is he that c' in the name of
24:27 as the lightning c' out of the east,
44 as ye think not the Son of man c'.
46 whom his lord when he c' shall
25: 6 made, Behold, the bridegroom c';
13 hour wherein the Son of man c'.
19 the lord of those servants c', and
26:36 Then c' Jesus with them unto a
40 And he c' unto the disciples, and
45 Then c' he to his disciples, and
M'r 1: 7 There c' one mightier than I
3:20 the multitude c' together again,
4:15 Satan c' immediately, and taketh
5:22 there c' one of the rulers of the
38 he c' to the house of the ruler
6:48 he c' unto them, walking upon the
7:20 That which c' out of the man,
8:22 c' to Bethsaida; and they bring
38 he c' in the glory of his Father
9:12 Elias verily c' first, and restoreth
10: 1 thence, and c' into the coasts
11: 9 he that c' in the name of the Lord:
10 of our father David, that c' in the
13:35 master of the house c', at even,
14:17 the evening he c' with the twelve.
37 he c', and findeth them sleeping,
41 And he c' the third time, and saith
43 while he yet spake, c' Judas, one
66 there c' one of the maids of the
Lu 3:16 but one mightier than I c',
6:47 c' to me, and heareth my sayings,
7: 8 and to another, Come, and he c';
8:12 then c' the devil, and taketh away
49 spake, there c' one from the ruler
11:25 And when he c', he findeth it swept
12:36 When he c' and knocketh, they
37 the lord when he c' shall find
40 the Son of man c' at an hour when
43 when he c' shall find so doing.
54 There c' a shower; and so it is.
55 will be heat; and it c' to pass.
13:35 Blessed is he that c' in the name
14:10 he that bade thee c', he may say
31 meet him that c' against him with
15: 6 he c' home, he calleth together
17:20 of God c' not with observation:
18: 8 Son of man c', shall he find faith
19:38 that c' in the name of the Lord:
Joh 1: 9 every man that c' into the world.
15 c' after me is preferred before me:
30 me c' a man which is preferred
3: 8 canst not tell whence it c', and
20 c' to the light, lest his deeds
21 he that doeth truth c' to the light,
31 He that c' from above is above all:
31 that c' from heaven is above all.
4: 5 Then c' he to a city of Samaria,
7 There c' a woman of Samaria to
21 the hour c', when ye shall neither
23 But the hour c', and now is, when
25 Messias c', which is called Christ:
35 four months, and then c' harvest?
5:44 not the honour that c' from God
6:33 bread of God is he which c' down
35 that c' to me shall never hunger;
37 c' to me I will in no wise cast out.
45 learned of the Father, c' unto me.
50 bread which c' down from heaven,
7:27 when Christ c', no man knoweth
31 Christ c', will he do more miracles
42 Christ c' of the seed of David,
9: 4 night c', when no man can work.
10:10 The thief c' not, but for to steal,
11:38 in himself c' to the grave.
12:13 that c' in the name of the Lord.
15 King c', sitting on an ass's colt.
22 Philip c' and telleth Andrew: and
13: 6 c' he to Simon Peter: and Peter
14: 6 man c' unto the Father, but by me.
30 the prince of this world c', and hath
15:25 But this c' to pass, that the word
16: 2 the time c', that whosoever killeth
25 time c', when I shall no more speak
32 the hour c', yea, is now come,
18: 3 c' thither with lanterns and
20: 1 c' Mary Magdalene early, when it
2 she runneth, and c' to Simon Peter,
6 Then c' Simon Peter following
21:13 Jesus then c', and taketh bread,
Ac 10:32 when he c', shall speak unto thee.
13:25 there c' one after me, whose shoes
18:21 this feast that c' in Jerusalem:
Ro 4: 9 C' this blessedness then upon
10:17 So then faith c' by hearing, and
1Co 15:24 Then c' the end, when he shall
2Co 11: 4 For if he that c' preacheth another
28 that which c' upon me daily,
Ga 5: 8 This persuasion c' not of him
Eph 5: 6 of these things c' the wrath of God
Col 3: 6 the wrath of God c' on the children
1Th 5: 2 the day of the Lord so c' as a thief
1Th 5: 3 sudden destruction c' upon them,
1Ti 6: 4 strifes of words, whereof c' envy,
Heb 6: 7 in the rain that c' oft upon it,
10: 5 when he c' into the world, he
11: 6 for he that c' to God must believe
Jas 1:17 c' down from the Father of lights
Jude 14 the Lord c' with ten thousands of
Re 1: 7 Behold, he c' with clouds; and
3:12 new Jerusalem, which c' down
11:14 behold, the third woe c' quickly.
17:10 when he c', he must continue a

come to pass See COME and PASS.

comfort See also COMFORTABLE; COMFORTED; COMFORTETH; COMFORTLESS; COMFORTS.
Ge 5:29 shall c' us concerning our work
18: 5 and c' ye your hearts; after that
27:42 c' himself, purposing to kill thee.
37:35 all his daughters rose up to c' him;
J'g 19: 5 C' thine heart with a morsel of
8 said, C' thine heart, I pray thee.
2Sa 10: 2 David sent to c' him by the hand
1Ch 7:22 and his brethren came to c' him.
19: 2 David sent messengers to c' him
2 of Ammon to Hanun, to c' him.
Job 2:11 to mourn with him and to c' him.
6:10 should I yet have c'; yea, I would
7:13 My bed shall c' me, my couch
9:27 my heaviness, and c' myself:
10:20 alone, that I may take c' a little,
21:34 How then c' ye me in vain, seeing
Ps 23: 4 thy rod and thy staff they c' me.
71:21 and c' me on every side.
119:50 This is my c' in my affliction: for
76 merciful kindness be for my c',
82 saying, When wilt thou c' me?
Ca 2: 5 with flagons, c' me with apples:
Isa 22: 4 to c' me, because of the spoiling
40: 1 C' ye, c' ye my people, saith your
51: 3 the Lord shall c' Zion:
3 he will c' all her waste places;
19 by whom shall I c' thee?
57: 6 Should I receive c' in these?
61: 2 to c' all that mourn;
66:13 comforteth, so will I c' you;
Jer 8:18 I would c' myself against sorrow,
16: 7 to c' them for the dead; neither
31:13 into joy, and will c' them,
La 1: 2 none to c' her: all her friends
17 is none to c' her: the Lord hath
21 I sigh: there is none to c' me:
2:13 I may c' thee, O virgin daughter
Eze 14:23 And they shall c' you, when ye see
16:54 in that thou art a c' unto them.
Zec 1:17 and the Lord shall yet c' Zion,
10: 2 they c' in vain: therefore they
M't 9:22 Daughter, be of good c'; thy faith
M'r 10:49 of good c', rise; he calleth thee.
Lu 8:48 Daughter, be of good c': thy faith
Joh 11:19 to Martha and Mary, to c' them
Ac 9:31 and in the c' of the Holy Ghost,
Ro 15: 4 patience and c' of the scriptures
1Co 14: 3 and exhortation, and c'.
2Co 1: 3 of mercies, and the God of all c';
4 that we may be able to c' them
4 by the c' wherewith we ourselves
2: 7 to forgive him, and c' him, lest
7: 4 I am filled with c', I am exceeding
13 we were comforted in your c':
13:11 Be perfect, be of good c', be of
Eph 6:22 and that he might c' your hearts.
Ph'p 2: 1 if any c' of love, if any fellowship
19 that I also may be of good c',
Col 4: 8 your estate, and c' your hearts;
11 which have been a c' unto me.
1Th 3: 2 to c' you concerning your faith:
4:18 c' one another with these words.
5:11 c' yourselves together, and edify
14 c' the feebleminded, support the
2Th 2:17 C' your hearts, and stablish you

comfortable
2Sa 14:17 my lord the king shall now be c':
Zec 1:13 with good words and c' words.

comfortably
2Sa 19: 7 speak c' unto thy servants:
2Ch 30:22 spake c' unto all the Levites
32: 6 spake c' to them, saying,
Isa 40: 2 Speak ye c' to Jerusalem,
Ho 2:14 speak c' unto her.

comforted See also COMFORTEDST.
Ge 24:67 Isaac was c' after his mother's
37:35 he refused to be c'; and he said,
38:12 wife died; and Judah was c',
50:21 And he c' them, and spake kindly
Ru 2:13 for that thou hast c' me, and for
2Sa 12:24 And David c' Bath-sheba his wife,
13:39 he was c' concerning Amnon,
Job 42:11 they bemoaned him, and c' him
Ps 77: 2 not: my soul refused to be c'.
86:17 Lord, hast holpen me, and c' me.
119:52 of old, O Lord; and have c' myself.
Isa 49:13 the Lord hath c' his people, and
52: 9 the Lord hath c' his people, he
54:11 tossed with tempest, and not c',
66:13 ye shall be c' in Jerusalem.
Jer 31:15 children refused to be c' for her
Eze 5:13 rest upon them, and I will be c':
14:22 and ye shall be c' concerning
31:16 shall be c' in the nether parts
32:31 shall be c' over all his multitude,
M't 2:18 would not be c', because they
5: 4 that mourn: for they shall be c'.
Lu 16:25 but now he is c', and thou art
Joh 11:31 in the house, and c' her, when
Ac 16:40 the brethren, they c' them, and
20:12 alive, and were not a little c'.
Ro 1:12 that I may be c' together with you.
1Co 14:31 may learn, and all may be c'.
2Co 1: 4 wherewith we ourselves are c'
6 or whether we be c', it is for your
7: 6 down, c' us by the coming of Titus;
7 wherewith he was c' in you,
13 we were c' in your comfort: yea,
Col 2: 2 That their hearts might be c',
1Th 2:11 ye know how we exhorted and c'
3: 7 we were c' over you in all our

comfortedst
Isa 12: 1 is turned away, and thou c' me.

comforter See also COMFORTERS.
Ec 4: 1 oppressed, and they had no c';
1 was power; but they had no c'.
La 1: 9 down wonderfully: she had no c'.
16 the c' that should relieve my soul
Joh 14:16 and he shall give you another C',
26 the C', which is the Holy Ghost,
15:26 But when the C' is come, whom I
16: 7 the C' will not come unto you; but

comforters
2Sa 10: 3 that he hath sent c' unto thee?
1Ch 19: 3 he hath sent c' unto thee? are not
Job 16: 2 miserable c' are ye all.
Ps 69:20 none; and for c', but I found none.
Na 3: 7 whence shall I seek c' for thee?

comforteth
Job 29:25 as one that c' the mourners.
Isa 51:12 I, even I, am he that c' you:
66:13 As one whom his mother c', so will
2Co 1: 4 Who c' us in all our tribulation,
7: 6 that c' those that are cast down,

comfortless
Joh 14:18 I will not leave you c': I will

comforts
Ps 94:19 within me thy c' delight my soul.
Isa 57:18 and restore c' unto him and to

coming See also COMINGS.
Ge 24:63 and, behold, the camels were c'.
30:30 hath blessed thee since my c':
Nu 22:16 hinder them from c' unto me:
33:40 of the c' of the children of Israel.
J'g 5:28 Why is his chariot so long in c'?
1Sa 10: 5 a company of prophets c' down
16: 4 of the town trembled at his c',
22: 9 saw the son of Jesse c' to Nob,
25:26 withholden thee from c' to shed
33 me this day from c' to shed blood,
29: 6 thy going out and thy c' in with me
6 of thy c' unto me unto this day:
2Sa 3:25 know thy going out and thy c' in,
24:20 saw the king and his servants c'
2Ki 10:15 son of Rechab c' to meet him:
13:20 invaded the land at the c' in of the
19:27 and thy going out, and thy c' in,
2Ch 22: 7 was of God by c' to Joram: for
Ezr 3: 8 in the second year of their c' unto
Ps 19: 5 bridegroom c' out of his chamber,
37:13 for he seeth that his day is c'.
121: 8 and thy c' in from this time forth,
Pr 8: 3 city, at the c' in at the doors.
Isa 14: 9 to meet thee at thy c': it stirreth
32:19 When it shall hail, c' down on
37:28 and thy c' in, and thy rage against
44: 7 and the things that are c', and
Jer 8: 7 swallow observe the time of their c';
Da 4:23 watcher and an holy one c' down
Mic 7:15 According to the days of thy c'
Hab 3: 4 he had horns c' out of his hand:
Mal 3: 2 who may abide the day of his c'?
4: 5 before the c' of the great and
M't 8:28 devils, c' out of the tombs,
16:28 the Son of man c' in his kingdom.
24: 3 what shall be the sign of thy c',
27 also the c' of the Son of man be.
30 they shall see the Son of man c'
37, 39 also the c' of the Son of man
48 heart, My lord delayeth his c';
25:27 at my c' I should have received
26:64 and c' in the clouds of heaven.
M'r 1:10 straightway c' up out of the water,
6:31 for there were many c' and going,
13:26 see the Son of man c' in the clouds
36 c' suddenly he find you sleeping.
14:62 and c' in the clouds of heaven.
15:21 passed by, c' out of the country,
Lu 2:38 she c' in that instant gave thanks
9:42 And as he was yet a c', the devil
12:45 My lord delayeth his c'; and
18: 5 by her continual c' she weary me.
19:23 at my c' I might have required
21:26 things which are c' on the earth:
27 shall they see the Son of man c'
23:26 a Cyrenian, c' out of the country,
29 behold, the days are c', in the which
36 c' to him, and offering him
Joh 1:27 c' after me is preferred before me,
29 John seeth Jesus c' unto him,
47 Jesus saw Nathanael c' to him,
5: 7 but while I am c', another steppeth
25 The hour is c', and now is, when
28 for the hour is c', in the which all
10:12 seeth the wolf c', and leaveth the
11:20 as she heard that Jesus was c',
12:12 that Jesus was c' to Jerusalem,
Ac 7:52 before of the c' of the Just One;
9:12 a man named Ananias c' in,
28 with them c' in and going out
10: 3 an angel of God c' in to him,
25 as Peter was c' in, Cornelius met

Ac 13:24 had first preached before his c'
17:10 Berea: who c' thither went into
27:33 while the day was c' on,
Ro 15:22 much hindered from c' to you.
1Co 1: 7 waiting for the c' of our Lord
15:23 they that are Christ's at his c'.
16:17 glad of the c' of Stephanus and
2Co 7: 6 comforted us by the c' of Titus;
7 And not by his c' only, but by the
13: 1 This is the third time I am c'
Ph'p 1:26 for me by my c' to you again.
1Th 2:19 our Lord Jesus Christ at his c'?
3:13 at the c' of our Lord Jesus Christ
4:15 remain unto the c' of the Lord
5:23 the c' of our Lord Jesus Christ.
2Th 2: 1 by the c' of our Lord Jesus
8 with the brightness of his c':
9 him, whose c' is after the working
Jas 5: 7 brethren, unto the c' of the Lord.
8 the c' of the Lord draweth nigh.
1Pe 2: 4 To whom c', as unto a living stone,
2Pe 1:16 power and c' of our Lord Jesus
3: 4 Where is the promise of his c'?
12 unto the c' of the day of God,
1Jo 2:28 be ashamed before him at his c'.
Re 13:11 beast c' up out of the earth;
21: 2 new Jerusalem, c' down from God

comings
Eze 43:11 and the c' in thereof, and all

command See also COMMANDED; COMMANDEST; COMMANDETH; COMMANDING; COMMANDMENT.
Ge 18:19 c' his children and his household
27: 8 according to that which I c' thee.
50:16 Thy father did c' before he died,
Ex 7: 2 shalt speak all that I c' thee:
8:27 Lord our God, as he shall c' us.
18:23 do this thing, and God c' thee
27:20 And thou shalt c' the children of
34:11 thou that which I c' thee this day:
Le 6: 9 C' Aaron and his sons, saying,
13:54 the priest shall c' that they wash
14: 4 Then shall the priest c' to take
5 priest shall c' that one of the birds
36 the priest shall c' that they empty
40 priest shall c' that they take away
24: 2 C' the children of Israel that they
25:21 I will c' my blessing upon you
Nu 5: 2 C' the children of Israel, that they
9: 8 the Lord will c' concerning you.
28: 2 C' the children of Israel, and say
34: 2 C' the children of Israel, and say
35: 2 C'...children of Israel, that they give
36: 6 which the Lord doth c' concerning
De 2: 4 c' thou the people, saying, Ye are
4: 2 add unto the word which I c' you,
2 of the Lord your God which I c'
40 I c' thee this day, that it may go
6: 2 commandments, which I c' thee,
6 words, which I c' thee this day,
7:11 judgments, which I c' thee this
8: 1 the commandments which I c' thee
11 statutes, which I c' thee this day:
10:13 and his statutes, which I c' thee
11: 8 the commandments which I c' you
13 my commandments which I c'
22 these commandments which I c'
27 your God, which I c' you this day:
28 the way which I c' you this day,
12:11 shall ye bring all that I c' you;
14 thou shalt do all that I c' thee.
28 all these words which I c' thee,
32 What thing soever I c' you,
13:18 his commandments which I c' thee
15: 5 these commandments which I c'
11 therefore I c' thee, saying, Thou
15 therefore I c' thee this thing to day.
18:18 unto them all that I shall c' him.
19: 7 Wherefore I c' thee, saying, Thou
9 which I c' thee this day, to love the
24:18, 22 I c' thee to do this thing.
27: 1 which I c' you this day.
4 set up these stones, which I c' you
10 statutes, which I c' thee this day.
28: 1 I c' thee this day, that the Lord
8 Lord shall c' the blessing upon thee
13 which I c' thee this day, to observe
14 the words which I c' thee this day,
15 statutes which I c' thee this day;
30: 2 all that I c' thee this day, thou and
8 his commandments which I c' thee
11 which I c' thee this day, it is not
16 In that I c' thee this day to love
32:46 shall c' your children to observe to
Jos 1:11 c' the people, saying, Prepare you
3: 8 c' the priests that bear the ark
4: 3 c' ye them, saying, Take you hence
16 C' the priests that bear the ark
11:15 so did Moses c' Joshua, and so did
1Sa 16:16 Let our lord now c' thy servants,
1Ki 5: 6 c' thou that they hew me cedar
11:38 hearken unto all that I c' thee,
2Ch 7:13 I c' the locusts to devour the land,
Job 39:27 the eagle mount up at thy c',
Ps 42: 8 Lord will c' his lovingkindness
44: 4 God: c' deliverances for Jacob.
Isa 5: 6 also c' the clouds that they rain
45:11 the work of my hands c' ye me.
Jer 1: 7 I c' thee thou shalt speak.
17 speak unto them all that I c' thee:
11: 4 according to all which I c' you:
26: 2 the words that I c' thee to speak
27: 4 And c' them to say unto their
34:22 I will c', saith the Lord, and cause
La 1:10 whom thou didst c' that they
Am 9: 3 thence will I c' the serpent, and
4 thence will I c' the sword, and it
9 For, lo, I will c', and I will sift
M't 4: 3 c' that these stones be made bread.
19: 7 Why did Moses then c' to give a
27:64 C' therefore that the sepulchre be
M'r 10: 3 unto them, What did Moses c' you?
Lu 4: 3 c' this stone that it be made bread.
8:31 he would not c' them to go out
9:54 wilt thou that we c' fire to come
Joh 15:14 if ye do whatsoever I c' you.
17 These things I c' you, that ye love
Ac 5:28 Did not we straitly c' you that ye
15: 5 c' them to keep the law of Moses.
16:18 I c' thee in the name of Jesus
1Co 7:10 unto the married I c', yet not I,
2Th 3: 4 and will do the things which we c'
6 we c' you, brethren, in the name
12 that are such we c' and exhort
1Ti 4:11 These things c' and teach.

commanded See also COMMANDEDST.
Ge 2:16 And the Lord God c' the man,
3:11 the tree, whereof I c' thee that
17 the tree, of which I c' thee, saying,
6:22 all that God c' him, so did he.
7: 5 unto all that the Lord c' him.
9 the female, as God had c' Noah.
16 of all flesh, as God had c' him:
12:20 Pharaoh c' his men concerning
21: 4 eight days old, as God had c' him.
32: 4 And he c' them, saying, Thus shall
17 And he c' the foremost, saying,
19 so c' he the second, and the third,
42:25 Then Joseph c' to fill their sacks,
44: 1 And he c' the steward of his house,
45:19 Now thou art c', this do ye;
47:11 of Rameses, as Pharaoh had c'.
50: 2 And Joseph c' his servants the
12 unto him according as he c' them:
Ex 1:17 not as the king of Egypt c' them,
4:28 all the signs which he had c' him.
5: 6 And Pharaoh c' the same day the
7: 6 as the Lord c' them, so did they.
10 Aaron did so as the Lord had c':
20 and Aaron did so, as the Lord c';
12:28 and did as the Lord had c' Moses
50 as the Lord c' Moses and Aaron,
16:16 the Lord hath c', Gather of it every
34 As the Lord c' Moses, so Aaron laid
19: 7 these words which the Lord c' him.
23:15 as I c' thee, in the time appointed
29:35 which I have c' thee: seven days
31: 6 all that I have c' thee;
11 that I have c' thee shall they do.
32: 8 out of the way which I c' them:
34: 4 as the Lord had c' him, and took
18 as I c' thee, in the time of the month
34 that which he was c'.
35: 1 words which the Lord hath c',
4 the thing which the Lord c',
10 make all that the Lord hath c';
29 which the Lord had c' to be made
36: 1 all that the Lord had c'.
5 work, which the Lord c' to make.
38:22 made all that the Lord c' Moses.
39: 1 for Aaron; as the Lord c' Moses.
5 twined linen; as the Lord c' Moses.
7 of Israel; as the Lord c' Moses.
21 ephod; as the Lord c' Moses.
26 to minister in; as the Lord c' Moses.
29 needlework; as the Lord c' Moses.
31 the mitre; as the Lord c' Moses.
32 that the Lord c' Moses, so did they.
42 all that the Lord c' Moses, so
43 the Lord had c', even so had they
40:16 that the Lord c' him, so did he.
19 upon it; as the Lord c' Moses.
21 testimony; as the Lord c' Moses.
23 Lord; as the Lord had c' Moses.
25 the Lord; as the Lord c' Moses.
27 thereon; as the Lord c' Moses.
29 meat offering; as the Lord c'
32 they washed; as the Lord c' Moses.
Le 7:36 Which the Lord c' to be given them
38 the Lord c' Moses in mount Sinai,
38 in the day that he c' the children of
8: 4 And Moses did as the Lord c' him;
5 thing which the Lord c' to be done.
9 holy crown; as the Lord c' Moses.
13 bonnets upon them; as the Lord c'
17 without the camp; as the Lord c'
21 unto the Lord; as the Lord c'
29 it was Moses' part; as the Lord c'
31 as I c', saying, Aaron and his sons
34 the Lord hath c' to do, to make an
35 that ye die not: for so I am c'.
36 which the Lord c' by the hand
9: 5 Moses c' before the tabernacle
6 the Lord c' that ye should do:
7 for them; as the Lord c'.
10 upon the altar; as the Lord c' Moses.
21 before the Lord; as Moses c'.
10: 1 the Lord, which he c' them not.
13 made by fire: for so I am c'.
15 for ever; as the Lord hath c'.
18 eaten it in the holy place, as I c'.
16:34 And he did as the Lord c' Moses.
17: 2 the Lord hath c', saying,
24:23 Israel did as the Lord c' Moses.
27:34 the Lord c' Moses for the children
Nu 1:19 the Lord c' Moses, so he numbered
54 according to all that the Lord c'
2:33 of Israel; as the Lord c' Moses.
34 all that the Lord c' Moses: so they
3:16 of the Lord, as he was c'.
Nu 3:42 the Lord c' him, all the firstborn
51 of the Lord, as the Lord c' Moses.
4:49 of him, as the Lord c' Moses.
8: 3 candlestick, as the Lord c' Moses.
20 that the Lord c' Moses concerning
22 the Lord had c' Moses concerning
9: 5 Lord c' Moses, so did the children
15:23 the Lord hath c' you by the hand
23 the day that the Lord c' Moses,
36 and he died; as the Lord c' Moses.
16:47 Aaron took as Moses c', and ran
17:11 did so: as the Lord c' him, so did
19: 2 the Lord hath c', saying, Speak
20: 9 before the Lord, as he c' him.
27 Moses did as the Lord c': and they
26: 4 the Lord c' Moses and the children
27:11 of judgment, as the Lord c' Moses.
22 And Moses did as the Lord c' him:
23 gave him a charge, as the Lord c'
29:40 according to all that the Lord c'
30: 1 the thing which the Lord hath c'.
16 the Lord c' Moses, between a man
31: 7 the Lord c' Moses; and they slew
21 the law which the Lord c' Moses;
31 the priest did as the Lord c' Moses.
41 the priest, as the Lord c' Moses.
47 of the Lord; as the Lord c' Moses.
32:28 So concerning them Moses c'
34:13 c' the children of Israel, saying,
13 Lord c' to give unto the nine tribes,
29 Lord c' to divide the inheritance
36: 2 Lord c' my lord to give the land
2 my lord was c' by the Lord to give
5 And Moses c' the children of
10 as the Lord c' Moses, so did the
13 the Lord c' by the hand of Moses
De 1:18 I c' you at that time all the things
19 as the Lord our God c' us; and we
41 all that the Lord our God c' us.
3:18 And I c' you at that time,
21 And I c' Joshua at that time,
4: 5 even as the Lord my God c' me,
13 which he c' you to perform,
14 the Lord c' me at that time to
5:12 it, as the Lord thy God hath c'
15 the Lord thy God c' thee to keep
16 the Lord thy God hath c' thee;
32 the Lord your God hath c' you:
33 which the Lord your God hath c'
6: 1 the Lord your God c' to teach
17 statutes, which he hath c' thee.
20 the Lord our God hath c' you?
24 And the Lord c' us to do all these
25 the Lord our God, as he hath c' us.
9:12 out of the way which I c' them;
16 the way which the Lord had c' you.
10: 5 they be, as the Lord c' me.
12:21 as I have c' thee, and thou shalt
13: 5 the Lord thy God c' thee to walk
17: 3 of heaven, which I have not c';
18:20 I have not c' him to speak, or that
20:17 as the Lord thy God hath c' thee:
24: 8 as I c' them, so ye shall observe
26:13 which thou hast c' me: I have not
14 to all that thou hast c' me.
16 the Lord thy God hath c' thee to
27: 1 c' the people, saying, Keep all the
28:45 and his statutes which he c' thee:
29: 1 the Lord c' Moses to make with
31: 5 commandments which I have c' you.
10 And Moses c' them, saying, At the
25 That Moses c' the Levites,
29 the way which I have c' you; and
33: 4 Moses c' us a law, even the
34: 9 and did as the Lord c' Moses.
Jos 1: 7 which Moses my servant c' thee:
9 Have not I c' thee? Be strong
10 Then Joshua c' the officers of the
13 the servant of the Lord c' you,
3: 3 And they c' the people, saying,
4: 8 as Joshua c', and took up twelve
10 the Lord c' Joshua to speak unto
10 according to all that Moses c'
17 Joshua therefore c' the priests.
6:10 Joshua had c' the people, saying,
7:11 my covenant which I c' them: for
8: 4 And he c' them, saying, Behold, ye
8 See, I have c' you.
27 word of the Lord, which he c'
29 Joshua c' that they should take
31 the servant of the Lord c' the
33 the servant of the Lord had c'
35 all that Moses c', which Joshua
9:24 the Lord thy God c' his servant
10:27 Joshua c', and they took them
40 as the Lord God of Israel c'.
11:12 Moses the servant of the Lord c'.
15 As the Lord c' Moses his servant,
15 undone of all that the Lord c'
20 destroy them, as the Lord c' Moses.
13: 6 for an inheritance, as I have c'
14: 2 as the Lord c' by the hand of Moses,
5 As the Lord c' Moses, so the
17: 4 The Lord c' Moses to give us an
21: 2 The Lord c' by the hand of Moses
8 with their suburbs, as the Lord c'
22: 2 the servant of the Lord c' you,
2 obeyed my voice in all that I c' you:
23:16 which he c' you, and have gone
J'g 2:20 my covenant which I c' their
3: 4 which he c' their fathers by the
4: 6 the Lord God of Israel c', saying,
13:14 all that I c' her let her observe.
21:10 and c' them, saying, Go and smite
20 Therefore they c' the children of

Ru 2:15 Boaz c· his young men, saying,
1Sa 2:29 I have c· in my habitation; and
13:13 which he c· thee: for now would
14 and the Lord hath c· him to be
14 not kept that which the Lord c·
17:20 and went, as Jesse had c· him;
18:22 And Saul c· his servants, saying,
20:29 he hath c· me to be there: and
21: 2 The king hath c· me a business,
2 I send thee, and what I have c·
2Sa 4:12 And David c· his young men, and
5:25 David did so, as the Lord had c·
7: 7 whom I c· to feed my people
11 the time that I c· judges to be over
9:11 my lord the king hath c· his
13:28 Now Absalom had c· his servants,
28 have not I c· you? be courageous,
29 unto Amnon as Absalom had c·.
18: 5 And the king c· Joab and Abishai
21:14 they performed all that the king c·.
24:19 of Gad, went up as the Lord c·.
1Ki 2:46 So the king c· Benaiah the son of
5:17 And the king c·, and they brought
8:58 his judgments, which he c· our
9: 4 all that I have c· thee, and wilt
11:10 And had c· him concerning this
10 kept not that which the Lord c·.
11 which I have c· thee, I will surely
13:21 which the Lord thy God c· thee,
15: 5 any thing that he c· him all the
17: 4 I have c· the ravens to feed thee
9 I have c· a widow woman there to
22:31 the king of Syria c· his thirty and
2Ki 11: 5 And he c· them, saying, This is the
9 Jehoiada the priest c·: and they
15 But Jehoiada the priest c· the
14: 6 wherein the Lord c·, saying, The
16:15 And king Ahaz c· Urijah the priest,
16 according to all that king Ahaz c·.
17:13 the law which I c· your fathers,
27 Then the king of Assyria c·, saying,
34 which the Lord c· the children of
18: 6 which the Lord c· Moses.
12 Moses the servant of the Lord c·,
21: 8 all that I have c· them, and
8 the law that my servant Moses c·
22:12 And the king c· Hilkiah the priest,
23: 4 And the king c· Hilkiah the high
21 And the king c· all the people,
1Ch 6:49 Moses the servant of God had c·.
14:16 David therefore did as God c· him:
15:15 thereon, as Moses c· according to
16:15 which he c· to a thousand
40 of the Lord, which he c· Israel;
17: 6 whom I c· to feed my people,
10 I c· judges to be over my people
21:17 Is it not I that c· the people to be
18 Then the angel of the Lord c· Gad
27 And the Lord c· the angel; and he
22: 2 And David c· to gather together
17 David also c· all the princes of
23:31 according to the order c· unto
24:19 as the Lord God of Israel had c·
2Ch 7:17 I have c· thee, and shalt observe
8:14 so had David the man of God c·.
14: 4 And c· Judah to seek the Lord God
18:30 king of Syria had c· the captains
23: 8 that Jehoiada the priest had c·,
25: 4 Lord c·, saying, The fathers shall
29:21 And he c· the priests the sons of
24 the king c· that the burnt offering
27 And Hezekiah c· to offer the burnt
30 king and the princes c· the Levites
31: 4 Moreover he c· the people that
11 Hezekiah c· to prepare chambers
32:12 c· Judah and Jerusalem, saying,
33: 8 to do all that I have c· them,
16 c· Judah to serve the Lord God of
34:20 the king c· Hilkiah, and Ahikam
35:21 God c· me to make haste: forbear
Ezr 4: 3 the king of Persia hath c· us.
19 And I c·, and search hath
5: 3 Who hath c· you to build
9 Who c· you to build this
7:23 Whatsoever is c· by the God
9:11 Which thou hast c· by thy servants
Ne 8: 1 which the Lord had c· to Israel.
14 the Lord had c· by Moses, that the
13: 5 which was c· to be given to the
9 Then I c·, and they cleansed the
19 I c· that the gates should be shut,
22 And I c· the Levites that they should
Es 1:10 he c· Mehuman, Biztha, Harbona,
17 king Ahasuerus c· Vashti the queen
3: 2 king had so c· concerning him.
12 Haman had c· unto the king's
4:13 Mordecai c· to answer Esther,
17 according to all that Esther had c·
6: 1 he c· to bring the book of records
8: 9 that Mordecai c· unto the Jews,
9:14 And the king c· it so to be done:
25 he c· by letters that his wicked
Job 38:12 Hast thou c· the morning since
42: 9 and did according as the Lord c·
Ps 7: 6 to the judgment that thou hast c·.
33: 9 was done; he c·, and it stood fast.
68:28 Thy God hath c· thy strength:
78: 5 he c· our fathers, that they should
23 Though he had c· the clouds from
105: 8 forever, the word which he c· to a
106:34 concerning whom the Lord c·
111: 9 he hath c· his covenant for ever:
119: 4 hast c· us to keep thy precepts
138 testimonies that thou hast c· are
133: 3 the Lord c· the blessing, even life

Ps 148: 5 for he c·, and they were created.
Isa 13: 3 I have c· my sanctified ones, I have
34:16 my mouth it hath c·, and his spirit
45:12 and all their host have I c·.
48: 5 my molten image, hath c· them.
Jer 7:22 c· them in the day that I brought
23 But this thing c· I them, saying,
23 the ways that I have c· you, that it
31 I c· them not, neither came it into
11: 4 I c· your fathers in the day that I
8 I c· them to do: but they did them
13: 5 it by Euphrates, as the Lord c· me.
6 from thence, which I c· thee to hide
14:14 neither have I c· them, neither
17:22 sabbath day, as I c· your fathers.
19: 5 offerings unto Baal, which I c· not,
23:32 nor c· them: therefore they shall
26: 8 Lord had c· him to speak unto all
29:23 I have not c· them; even I know,
32:35 I c· them not, neither came it into
35: 6 of Rechab our father c· us, saying,
10 all that Jonadab our father c· us.
14 he c· his sons not to drink wine,
16 of their father, which he c· them.
18 all that he hath c· you:
36: 5 And Jeremiah c· Baruch, saying,
8 Jeremiah the prophet c· him,
26 the king c· Jerahmeel the son of
37:21 Then Zedekiah the king c· that
38:10 Then the king c· Ebed-melech the
27 all these words that the king had c·.
50:21 to all that I have c· thee.
51:59 Jeremiah the prophet c· Seraiah
La 1:17 the Lord hath c· concerning Jacob,
2:17 his word that he had c· in the days
Eze 9:11 saying, I have done as thou hast c·
10: 6 when he had c· the man clothed
12: 7 And I did so as I was c·: I brought
24:18 I did in the morning as I was c·.
37: 7 I prophesied as I was c·: and as I
10 I prophesied as he c· me, and the
Da 2: 2 the king c· to call the magicians,
12 and c· to destroy all the wise men
46 c· that they should offer an oblation
3: 4 To you it is c·, O people, nations,
13 in his rage and fury c·
19 he spake, and c· that they should
20 And he c· the most mighty men
4:26 whereas they c· to leave the stump
5: 2 c· to bring the golden and silver
29 c· Belshazzar, and they clothed
6:16 Then the king c·, and they brought
23 and c· that they should take Daniel
24 And the king c·, and they brought
Am 2:12 c· the prophets, saying, Prophesy
Zec 1: 6 I c· my servants the prophets,
Mal 4: 4 which I c· unto him in Horeb for
M't 8: 4 offer the gift that Moses c·, for a
10: 5 and c· them, saying, Go not into
14: 9 he c· it to be given her.
19 he c· the multitude to sit down on
15: 4 For God c·, saying, Honour thy
35 he c· the multitude to sit down
18:25 his lord c· him to be sold, and his
21: 6 went, and did as Jesus c· them,
27:58 Pilate c· the body to be delivered.
28:20 whatsoever I have c· you: and, lo,
M'r 1:44 those things which Moses c·, for
5:43 c· that something should be given
6: 8 And c· them that they should
27 and c· his head to be brought
39 he c· them to make all sit down
8: 6 And he c· the people to sit down
7 c· to set them also before them.
10:49 stood still, and c· him to be called.
11: 6 even as Jesus had c·: and they let
13:34 and c· the porter to watch.
Lu 5:14 according as Moses c·, for a
8:29 (For he had c· the unclean spirit
55 and he c· to give her meat.
9:21 and c· them to tell no man
14:22 it is done as thou hast c·, and yet
17: 9 he did the things that were c· him?
10 those things which are c· you, say,
18:40 c· him to be brought unto him:
19:15 c· these servants to be called unto
Joh 8: 5 Now Moses in the law c· us,
Ac 1: 4 c· them that they should not
4:15 when they had c· them to go aside
18 and c· them not to speak at all nor
5:34 c· to put the apostles forth a little
40 they c· that they should not speak
8:38 he c· the chariot to stand still:
10:33 all things that are c· thee of God.
42 he c· us to preach unto the people,
48 he c· them to be baptized in the
12:19 c· that they should be put to
13:47 the Lord c· us, saying, I have set
16:22 their clothes, and c· to beat them.
18: 2 Claudius had c· all Jews to depart
21:33 and c· him to be bound with two
34 he c· him to be carried into the
22:24 chief captain c· him to be brought
30 c· the chief priests and all their
23: 2 Ananias c· them that stood by him
10 c· the soldiers to go down, and to
31 the soldiers, as it was c· them,
35 he c· him to be kept in Herod's
24:23 he c· a centurion to keep Paul,
25: 6 seat c· Paul to be brought.
17 and c· the man to be brought forth.
21 c· him to be kept till I might send
27:43 c· that they which could swim
1Co 14:34 c· to be under obedience, as
2Co 4: 6 For God, who c· the light to shine

1Th 4:11 with your own hands, as we c·
2Th 3:10 this we c· you, that if any would
Heb 12:20 not endure that which was c·,
Re 9: 4 was c· them that they should not

commandedst
Ne 1: 7 thou c· thy servant Moses.
8 the word that thou c· thy servant
9:14 c· them precepts, statutes, and laws,
Jer 32:23 of all that thou c· them to do:

commander
Isa 55: 4 a leader and c· to the people.

commandest
Jos 1:16 All that thou c· us we will do,
18 thy word in all that thou c· him,
Ac 23: 3 and c· me to be smitten contrary

commandeth
Ex 16:32 is the thing which the Lord c·,
Nu 32:25 Thy servants will do as my lord c·.
Job 9: 7 Which c· the sun, and it riseth not;
36:10 c· that they return from iniquity.
32 and c· it not to shine by the cloud
37:12 they may do whatsoever he c·
Ps 107:25 For he c·, and raiseth the stormy
La 3:37 to pass, when the Lord c· it not?
Am 6:11 the Lord c·, and he will smite
M'r 1:27 c· he even the unclean spirits,
Lu 4:36 power he c· the unclean spirits
8:25 he c· even the winds and water,
Ac 17:30 but now c· all men every where to

commanding
Ge 49:33 Jacob had made an end of c· his
M't 11: 1 an end of c· his twelve disciples,
Ac 24: 8 C· his accusers to come unto
1Ti 4: 3 c· to abstain from meats, which

commandment See also COMMANDMENTS.
Ge 45:21 according to the c· of Pharaoh,
Ex 17: 1 journeys, according to the c· of
25:22 give thee in c· unto the children
34:32 gave them in c· all that the Lord
36: 6 Moses gave c·, and they caused
38:21 was counted according to the c·
Nu 3:39 numbered at the c· of the Lord,
4:37 did number according to the c· of
41 according to the c· of the Lord.
49 According to the c· of the Lord they
9:18 At the c· of the Lord the children
18 Israel journeyed, and at the c· of
20 the tabernacle; according to the c·
20 the c· of the Lord they journeyed.
23 At the c· of the Lord they rested
23 the c· of the Lord they journeyed:
23 c· of the Lord by the hand of Moses.
10:13 their journey according to the c· of
13: 3 by the c· of the Lord sent them
14:41 do ye transgress the c· of the Lord?
15:31 hath broken his c·, that soul shall
23:20 Behold, I have received c· to bless:
24:13 c· of the Lord to do either good
27:14 ye rebelled against my c· in the
33: 2 their journeys by the c· of the Lord:
38 the c· of the Lord, and died there,
De 1: 3 the Lord had given him in c· unto
26 rebelled against the c· of the Lord
43 against the c· of the Lord, and
9:23 against the c· of the Lord your God
17:20 that he turn not aside from the c·,
30:11 For this c· which I command thee
Jos 1:18 be that doth rebel against thy c·,
8: 8 city on fire: according to the c·
15:13 the c· of the Lord to Joshua, even
17: 4 according to the c· of the Lord, he
21: 3 at the c· of the Lord, these cities
22: 3 of the c· of the Lord your God.
5 But take diligent heed to do the c·
1Sa 12:14 and not rebel against the c· of the
15 but rebel against the c· of the Lord.
13:13 hast not kept the c· of the Lord
15:13 have performed the c· of the Lord.
24 transgressed the c· of the Lord,
2Sa 12: 9 despised the c· of the Lord, to do
1Ki 2:43 c· that I have charged thee with?
13:21 not kept the c· which the Lord
2Ki 17:34 after the law and c· which the Lord
37 the law, and the c·, which he wrote
18:36 king's c· was, saying, Answer him
23:35 according to the c· of Pharaoh:
24: 3 c· of the Lord came this upon Judah,
1Ch 12:32 all their brethren were at their c·.
14:12 David gave a c·, and they were
28:21 people will be wholly at thy c·.
2Ch 8:13 according to the c· of Moses,
15 not from the c· of the king
14: 4 and to do the law and the c·.
19:10 between law and c·, statutes and
24: 6 according to the c· of Moses the
8 at the king's c· they made a chest,
21 at the c· of the king in the court
29:15 according to the c· of the king, by
25 to the c· of David, and of Gad the
25 the c· of the Lord by his prophets.
30: 6 and Judah, and according to the c·
12 c· of the king and of the princes,
31: 5 as soon as the c· came abroad,
13 at the c· of Hezekiah the king,
35:10 courses according to the king's c·.
15 to the c· of David, and Asaph,
16 according to the c· of king Josiah.
Ezr 4:21 Give ye now c· to cause these men
21 until another c· shall be given
6:14 according to the c· of the God of
14 and according to the c· of Cyrus,
8:17 And I sent them with c· unto Iddo
10: 3 that tremble at the c· of our God;

Ne 11:23 the king's c· concerning them,
12:24 the c· of David the man of God,
45 the c· of David, and of Solomon
Es 1:12 refused to come at the king's c·
15 she hath not performed the c· of
19 let there go a royal c· from him,
2: 8 when the king's c· and his decree
20 for Esther did the c· of Mordecai,
3: 3 transgressest thou the king's c·?
14 a c· to be given in every province
15 being hastened by the king's c·,
4: 3 the king's c· and his decree came,
5 and gave him a c· to Mordecai,
10 and gave him c· unto Mordecai;
8:13 the writing for a c· to be given
14 and pressed on by the king's c·.
17 the king's c· and his decree came,
9: 1 when the king's c· and his decree
Job 23:12 gone back from the c· of his lips;
Ps 19: 8 c· of the Lord is pure, enlightening
71: 3 thou hast given c· to save me;
119:96 but thy c· is exceeding broad.
147:15 sendeth forth his c· upon earth:
Pr 6:20 keep thy father's c·, and forsake
23 c· is a lamp; and the law is light;
8:29 the waters should not pass his c·:
13:13 feareth the c· shall be rewarded.
19:16 keepeth the c· keepeth his own
Ec 8: 2 counsel thee to keep the king's c·,
5 keepeth the c· shall feel no evil
Isa 23:11 the Lord hath given a c· against
36:21 not a word: for the king's c· was,
Jer 35:14 none, but obey their father's c·:
16 performed the c· of their father,
18 the c· of Jonadab your father,
La 1:18 for I have rebelled against his c·:
Da 3:22 because the king's c· was urgent,
9:23 the c· came forth, and I am come
25 the going forth of the c· to restore
Ho 5:11 he willingly walked after the c·.
Na 1:14 Lord hath given a c· concerning
Mal 2: 1 O ye priests, this c· is for you.
4 that I have sent this c· unto you,
M't 8:18 he gave c· to depart unto the
15: 3 Why do ye also transgress the c·
6 made the c· of God of none effect
22:36 which is the great c· in the law?
38 This is the first and great c·.
M'r 7: 8 laying aside the c· of God, ye hold
9 Full well ye reject the c· of God,
12:28 Which is the first c· of all?
30 strength: this is the first c·.
31 there is none other c· greater than
Lu 15:29 transgressed I at any time thy c·:
23:56 the sabbath day according to the c·.
Joh 10:18 This c· have I received of my
11:57 the Pharisees had given a c·,
12:49 he gave me a c·, what I should
50 And I know that his c· is life
13:34 A new c· I give unto you, that ye
14:31 as the Father gave me c·, even so
15:12 This is my c·, That ye love
Ac 15:24 to whom we gave no such c·:
17:15 and receiving a c· unto Silas and
23:30 gave c· to his accusers also to say
25:23 at Festus' c· Paul was brought
Ro 7: 8 taking occasion by the c·, wrought
9 but when the c· came, sin revived
10 And the c·, which was ordained
11 taking occasion by the c·, deceived
12 the c· holy, and just, and good.
13 that sin by the c· might appear
13: 9 and if there be any other c·,
16:26 the c· of the everlasting God,
1Co 7: 6 this by permission, and not of c·.
25 I have no c· of the Lord: yet I give
2Co 8: 8 I speak not by c·, but by occasion
Eph 6: 2 which is the first c· with promise;
1Ti 1: 1 by the c· of God our Saviour,
5 Now the end of the c· is charity
6:14 That thou keep this c· without
Tit 1: 3 according to the c· of God our
Heb 7: 5 priesthood, have a c· to take tithes
16 not after the law of a carnal c·,
18 disannulling of the c· going before
11:22 and gave c· concerning his bones.
23 were not afraid of the king's c·.
2Pe 2:21 to turn from the holy c· delivered
3: 2 and of the c· of us the apostles of
1Jo 2: 7 I write no new c· unto you,
7 but an old c· which ye had from the
7 The old c· is the word which ye
8 Again, a new c· I write unto you,
3:23 And this is his c·, That we should
23 love one another, as he gave us c·.
4:21 And this c· have we from him, That
2Jo 4 have received a c· from the Father.
5 though I wrote a new c· unto thee,
6 This is the c·, That, as ye have

commandments
Ge 26: 5 my c·, my statutes, and my laws.
Ex 15:26 and wilt give ear to his c·, and keep
16:28 refuse ye to keep my c· and my
20: 6 them that love me, and keep my c·.
24:12 a law, and c· which I have written;
34:28 words of the covenant, the ten c·.
Le 4: 2 against any of the c· of the Lord
13 any the c· of the Lord concerning
22 ignorance against any of the c·
27 against any of the c· of the Lord
5:17 to be done by the c· of the Lord;
22:31 Therefore shall ye keep my c·,
26: 3 and keep my c·, and do them;
14 and will not do all these c·;
15 that ye will not do all my c·, but
27:34 These are the c·, which the Lord
Nu 15:22 all these c·, which the Lord hath
39 remember all the c· of the Lord,
40 do all my c·, and be holy unto your
36:13 These are the c· and the judgments
De 4: 2 ye may keep the c· of the Lord
13 to perform, even ten c·; and he
40 his statutes, and his c·, which I
5:10 them that love me and keep my c·.
29 keep all my c· always, that it might
31 all the c·, and the statutes, and
6: 1 Now these are the c·, the statutes,
2 his statutes and his c·, which I
17 keep the c· of the Lord your God,
25 to do all these c· before the Lord
7: 9 and keep his c· to a thousand
11 keep the c·, and the statutes, and
8: 1 All the c· which I command thee
2 whether thou wouldest keep his c·,
6 the c· of the Lord thy God, to walk
11 keeping his c·, and his judgments,
10: 4 the ten c·, which the Lord spake
13 To keep the c· of the Lord, and
11: 1 his judgments, and his c·, alway.
8 keep all the c· which I command
13 my c· which I command you this
22 shall diligently keep all these c·
27 A blessing, if ye obey the c· of the
28 if ye will not obey the c· of the Lord
13: 4 keep his c·, and obey his voice, and
18 Lord thy God, to keep all his c·
15: 5 observe to do all these c· which I
19: 9 shalt keep all these c· to do them,
26:13 to all thy c· which thou hast
13 I have not transgressed thy c·,
17 and his c·, and his judgments, and
18 thou shouldest keep all his c·;
27: 1 Keep all the c· which I command
10 and do his c·, and his statutes,
28: 1 to do all his c· which I command
9 keep the c· of the Lord thy God,
13 if that thou hearken unto the c· of
15 to observe to do all his c· and his
45 thy God, to keep his c· and his
30: 8 do all his c· which I command thee
10 thy God, to keep his c· and his
16 walk in his ways, and to keep his c
31: 5 unto all the c· which I have
Jos 22: 5 and to keep his c·, and to cleave
J'g 2:17 walked in, obeying the c· of the
3: 4 they would hearken unto the c· of
1Sa 15:11 and hath not performed my c·.
1Ki 2: 3 his statutes, and his c·, and his
3:14 to keep my statutes and my c·, as
6:12 and keep all my c· to walk in them;
8:58 to keep his c·, and his statutes,
61 and to keep his c·, as at this day.
9: 6 keep my c· and my statutes which
11:34 he kept my c· and my statutes:
38 my statutes and my c·, as David my
14: 8 David, who kept my c·, and who
18:18 ye have forsaken the c· of the Lord,
2Ki 17:13 your evil ways, and keep my c· and
16 they left all the c· of the Lord
19 Judah kept not the c· of the Lord
18: 6 but kept his c·, which the Lord
23: 3 to keep his c· and his testimonies
1Ch 28: 7 if he be constant to do my c·
8 seek for all the c· of the Lord
29:19 son a perfect heart, to keep thy c·,
2Ch 7:19 my statutes and my c·, which I
17: 4 and walked in his c·, and not after
24:20 Why transgress ye the c· of the
31:21 and in the c·, to seek his God, he
34:31 after the Lord, and to keep his c·,
Ezr 7:11 of the words of the c· of the Lord,
9:10 for we have forsaken thy c·,
14 break thy c·, and join in affinity
Ne 1: 5 that love him, and observe his c·:
7 and have not kept the c·, nor the
9 and keep my c·, and do them;
9:13 and true laws, good statutes and c·:
16 necks, and hearkened not to thy c·,
29 and hearkened not unto thy c·, but
34 nor hearkened unto thy c· and
10:29 do all the c· of the Lord our God,
Ps 78: 7 works of God, but keep his c·:
89:31 my statutes, and keep not my c·;
103:18 those that remember his c· to do
20 do his c·, hearkening unto the
111: 7 judgment; all his c· are sure.
10 have all they that do his c·:
112: 1 that delighteth greatly in his c·.
119: 6 when I have respect unto all thy c·.
10 O let me not wander from thy c·.
19 hide not thy c· from me.
21 cursed, which do err from thy c·.
32 I will run the way of thy c·, when
35 Make me to go in the path of thy c·:
47 I will delight myself in thy c·,
48 hands also will I lift up unto thy c·,
60 and delayed not to keep thy c·.
66 for I have believed thy c·.
73 that I may learn thy c·.
86 All thy c· are faithful: they
98 Thou through thy c· hast made me
115 For I will keep the c· of my God.
127 I love thy c· above gold; yea,
131 and panted: for I longed for thy c·.
143 yet thy c· are my delights.
151 O Lord; and all thy c· are truth.
166 for thy salvation, and done thy c·.
172 for all thy c· are righteousness.
176 servant; for I do not forget thy c·.
Pr 2: 1 words, and hide my c· with thee;
3: 1 but let thine heart keep my c·:
4: 4 my words: keep my c·, and live.
Pr 7: 1 and lay up my c· with thee.
2 Keep my c·, and live; and my law
10: 8 The wise in heart will receive c·:
Ec 12:13 Fear God, and keep his c·: for this
Isa 48:18 thou hadst hearkened to my c·!
Da 9: 4 and to them that keep his c·;
Am 2: 4 and have not kept his c·, and
M't 5:19 shall break one of these least c·,
15: 9 teaching for doctrines the c· of
19:17 wilt enter into life, keep the c·.
22:40 On these two c· hang all the law
M'r 7: 7 teaching for doctrines the c· of
10:19 Thou knowest the c·, Do not kill,
12:29 of all the c· is, Hear, O Israel;
Lu 1: 6 in all the c· and ordinances of the
18:20 Thou knowest the c·, Do not commit
Joh 14:15 If ye love me, keep my c·.
21 He that hath my c·, and keepeth
15:10 If ye keep my c·, ye shall abide in
10 kept my Father's c·, and abide in
Ac 1: 2 had given c· unto the apostles
1Co 7:19 but the keeping of the c· of God.
14:37 I write unto you are the c· of the
Eph 2:15 law of c· contained in ordinances;
Col 2:22 after the c· and doctrines of men?
4:10 touching whom ye received c·:
1Th 4: 2 ye know what c· we gave you
Tit 1:14 Jewish fables, and c· of men,
1Jo 2: 3 that we know him, if we keep his c·.
4 and keepeth not his c·, is a liar,
3:22 because we keep his c·, and do those
24 he that keepeth his c· dwelleth in
5: 2 when we love God, and keep his c·.
3 love of God, that we keep his c·:
3 and his c· are not grievous.
2Jo 6 this is love, that we walk after his c·.
Re 12:17 her seed, which keep the c· of God,
14:12 here are they that keep the c· of God,
22:14 Blessed are they that do his c·,

commend See also COMMENDED; COMMENDETH; COMMENDING.
Lu 23:46 into thy hands I c· my spirit:
Ac 20:32 brethren, I c· you to God, and to
Ro 3: 5 But if our unrighteousness c· the
16: 1 I c· unto you Phebe our sister,
2Co 3: 1 Do we begin again to c· ourselves?
5:12 c· not ourselves again unto you,
10:12 with some that c· themselves:

commendation
2Co 3: 1 some others, epistles of c· to you,
1 or letters of c· from you?

commended
Ge 12:15 her, and c· her before Pharaoh:
Pr 12: 8 be c· according to his wisdom:
Ec 8:15 Then I c· mirth, because a man
Lu 16: 8 the lord c· the unjust steward,
Ac 14:23 they c· them to the Lord, on whom
2Co 12:11 I ought to have been c· of you:

commendeth
Ro 5: 8 But God c· his love toward us,
1Co 8: 8 But meat c· us not to God:
2Co 10:18 not he that c· himself is approved,
18 but whom the Lord c·.

commending
2Co 4: 2 truth c· ourselves to every man's

commission See also COMMISSIONS.
Ac 26:12 with authority and c· from the

commissions
Ezr 8:36 And they delivered the king's c·

commit See also COMMITTED; COMMITTEST; COMMITTETH; COMMITTING.
Ex 20:14 Thou shalt not c· adultery.
Le 5:15 If a soul c· a trespass, and sin
17 and c· any of these things which
6: 2 If a soul sin, and c· a trespass
18:26 and shall not c· any of these
29 whosoever shall c· any of these
29 the souls that c· them shall be
30 that ye c· not any one of these
20: 5 to c· whoredom with Molech,
Nu 5: 6 When a man or woman shall c·
6 any sin that men c·, to do a
12 and c· a trespass against him,
25: 1 the people began to c· whoredom
31:16 to c· trespass against the Lord
De 5:18 Neither shalt thou c· adultery.
19:20 c· no more any such evil among
Jos 22:20 the son of Zerah c· a trespass
2Sa 7:14 If he c· iniquity, I will chasten
2Ch 21:11 of Jerusalem to c· fornication,
Job 5: 8 unto God would I c· my cause:
34:10 from the Almighty, that he should c·
Ps 31: 5 Into thine hand I c· my spirit:
37: 5 C· thy way unto the Lord; trust
Pr 16: 3 C· thy works unto the Lord,
12 to kings to c· wickedness: for the
Isa 22:21 c· thy government into his hand:
23:17 and shall c· fornication with
Jer 7: 9 ye steal, murder, and c· adultery,
9: 5 weary themselves to c· iniquity.
23:14 they c· adultery, and walk in lies·
37:21 should c· Jeremiah into the court
44: 7 Wherefore c· ye this great evil
Eze 3:20 his righteousness, and c· iniquity,
8:17 that they c· the abominations
17 which they c· here?
16:17 didst c· whoredom with them,
34 followeth thee to c· whoredoms:
43 thou shalt not c· this lewdness
20:30 and c· ye whoredom after their
22: 9 midst of thee they c· lewdness.
23:43 Will they now c· whoredoms with
33:13 and c· iniquity, all his

Ho 4:10 they shall c' whoredom, and
13 daughters shall c' whoredom,
13 your spouses shall c' adultery.
14 when they c' whoredom, nor your
14 spouses when they c' adultery:
6: 9 consent: for they c' lewdness.
7: 1 they c' falsehood; and the thief
M't 5:27 Thou shalt not c' adultery:
32 causeth her to c' adultery:
19: 9 which is put away doth c' adultery.
18 Thou shalt not c' adultery,
M'r 10:19 Do not c' adultery,
Lu 12:48 did c' things worthy of stripes,
16:11 c' to your trust the true riches?
18:20 Do not c' adultery,
Joh 2:24 Jesus did not c' himself unto
Ro 1:32 which c' such things are worthy
2: 2 them which c' such things.
22 a man should not c' adultery,
22 dost thou c' adultery?
22 idols, dost thou c' sacrilege?
13: 9 Thou shalt not c' adultery,
1Co 10: 8 Neither let us c' fornication,
1Ti 1:18 This charge I c' unto thee,
2Ti 2: 2 the same c' thou to faithful men,
Jas 2: 9 ye c' sin, and are convinced of the
11 that said, Do not c' adultery,
11 Now if thou c' no adultery,
1Pe 4:19 c' the keeping of their souls to
1Jo 3: 9 is born of God doth not c' sin;
Re 2:14 unto idols, and to c' fornication.
20 to c' fornication, and to eat things
22 them that c' adultery with her

committed^
Ge 39: 8 he hath c' all that he hath to my
22 of the prison c' to Joseph's hand
Le 4:35 for his sin that he hath c', it
5: 7 his trespass, which he hath c',
18:30 which were c' before you,
20:13 of them have c' an abomination:
23 for they c' all these things, and
Nu 15:24 be c' by ignorance without the
De 17: 5 or that woman, which have c'
21:22 man have c' a sin worthy of death,
Jos 7: 1 children of Israel c' a trespass
22:16 that ye have c' against the God
31 c' this trespass against the Lord:
J'g 20: 6 c' lewdness and folly in Israel.
1Ki 8:47 we have c' wickedness;
14:22 with their sins which they had c',
27 and c' them unto the hands of the
1Ch 10:13 for his transgression which he c'
2Ch 12:10 shields of brass, and c' them
34:16 All that was c' to thy servants,
Ps 106: 6 we have c' iniquity, we have done
Jer 2:13 For my people have c' two evils;
3: 8 backsliding Israel c' adultery
9 and c' adultery with stones and
5: 7 then c' adultery, and assembled
30 horrible thing is c' in the land;
6:15 when they had c' abomination?
8:12 they had c' abomination? nay,
16:10 that we have c' against the Lord
29:23 they have c' villany in Israel, and
39:14 and c' him unto Gedaliah the son
40: 7 c' unto him men, and women,
41:10 of the guard had c' to Gedaliah
44: 3 wickedness which they have c' to
9 which they have c' in the land
22 abominations which ye have c';
Eze 6: 9 the evils which they have c' in all
15: 8 have c' a trespass, saith the Lord
16:26 c' fornication with the Egyptians
50 and c' abomination before me:
51 hath Samaria c' half of thy sins;
52 c' more abominable than they:
18:12 to the idols, hath c' abomination,
21 from all his sins that he hath c',
22 his trangressions that he hath c',
27 his wickedness that he hath c',
28 his transgressions that he hath c',
20:27 have c' a trespass against me.
43 for all your evils that ye have c'.
22:11 And one hath c' abomination with
23: 3 they c' whoredoms in Egypt;
3 c' whoredoms in their youth:
7 she c' her whoredoms with them,
37 they have c' adultery, and blood
37 their idols have they c' adultery,
33:13 for his iniquity that he hath c',
16 None of his sins that he hath c'
29 abominations which they have c'.
43: 8 abominations that they have c':
44:13 abominations which they have c'.
Da 9: 5 sinned, and have c' iniquity,
Ho 1: 2 land hath c' great whoredom,
4:18 have c' whoredom continually:
Mal 2:11 an abomination is c' in Israel
M't 5:28 hath c' adultery with her already
M'r 15: 7 c' murder in the insurrection.
Lu 12:48 to whom men have c' much, of
Joh 5:22 c' all judgment unto the Son:
Ac 8: 3 men and women c' them to prison.
25:11 or have c' any thing worthy of
25 he had c' nothing worthy of death.
27:40 they c' themselves unto the sea,
28:17 c' nothing against the people,
Ro 3: 2 them were c' the oracles of God.
1Co 9:17 a dispensation of the gospel is c'
10: 8 fornication, as some of them c',
2Co 5:19 and hath c' unto us the word of
11: 7 I c' an offence in abasing myself
12:21 lasciviousness which they have c'.
Ga 2: 7 uncircumcision was c' unto me,
1Ti 1:11 which was c' to my trust.
6:20 keep that which is c' to thy trust,
2Ti 1:12 able to keep that which I have c'
14 That good thing which was c' unto
Tit 1: 3 preaching, which is c' unto me
Jas 5:15 if he have c' sins, they shall be
1Pe 2:23 but c' himself to him that judgeth
Jude 15 deeds which they have ungodly c',
Re 17: 2 of the earth have c' fornication,
18: 3 have c' fornication with her, and
9 who have c' fornication and lived

committest
Ho 5: 3 O Ephraim, thou c' whoredom,

committeth
Le 20:10 man that c' adultery with another
10 c' adultery with his neighbour's
Ps 10:14 the poor c' himself unto thee;
Pr 6:32 whoso c' adultery with a woman
Eze 8: 6 that the house of Israel c' here,
16:32 But as a wife that c' adultery,
18:24 c' iniquity, and doeth according
26 and c' iniquity, and dieth in them;
33:18 and c' iniquity, he shall even die
M't 5:32 her that is divorced c' adultery,
19: 9 marry another, c' adultery: and
M'r 10:11 another, c' adultery against her.
12 married to another, she c' adultery.
Lu 16:18 marrieth another c' adultery:
18 away from her husband c' adultery.
Joh 8:34 c' sin is the servant of sin.
1Co 6:18 but he that c' fornication sinneth
1Jo 3: 4 Whosoever c' sin transgresseth
8 He that c' sin is of the devil; for

committing
Eze 33:15 without c' iniquity; he shall
Ho 4: 2 stealing, and c' adultery, they

commodious
Ac 27:12 the haven was not c' to winter in,

common See also COMMONWEALTH.
Le 4:27 c' people sin through ignorance,
Nu 16:29 If these men die the c' death of
1Sa 21: 4 is no c' bread under mine hand,
5 and the bread is in a manner c',
Ec 6: 1 and it is c' among men:
Jer 26:23 into the graves of the c' people.
31: 5 and shall eat them as c' things.
Eze 23:42 men of the c' sort were brought
M't 27:27 took Jesus into the c' hall, and
M'r 12:37 the c' people heard him gladly.
Ac 2:44 and had all things c';
4:32 but they had all things c'.
5:18 put them in the c' prison.
10:14 any thing that is c' or unclean.
15 cleansed, that call not thou c'.
28 not call any man c' or unclean.
11: 8 for nothing c' or unclean hath at
9 cleansed, that call not thou c'.
1Co 10:13 you but such as is c' to man:
Tit 1: 4 mine own son after the c' faith:
Jude 3 write unto you of the c' salvation,

common hall See COMMON and HALL.

commonly^
M't 28:15 is c' reported among the Jews
1Co 5: 1 It is reported c' that there is

common people See COMMON, and PEOPLE.

commonwealth
Eph 2:12 being aliens from the c' of Israel,

commotion See also COMMOTIONS.
Jer 10:22 great c' out of the north country,

commotions
Lu 21: 9 ye shall hear of wars and c',

commune See also COMMUNED; COMMUNING.
Ge 34: 6 out unto Jacob to c' with him.
Ex 25:22 and I will c' with thee from above
1Sa 18:22 C' with David secretly, and say,
19: 3 I will c' with my father of thee;
Job 4: 2 we assay to c' with thee, wilt thou
Ps 4: 4 c' with your own heart upon your
64: 5 they c' of laying snares privily;
77: 6 I c' with mine own heart: and my

communed
Ge 23: 8 And he c' with them, saying, If it
34: 8 And Hamor c' with them, saying,
20 and c' with the men of their city,
42:24 and c' with them, and took from
43:19 and they c' with him at the door
J'g 9: 1 and c' with them, and with all
1Sa 9:25 Samuel c' with Saul upon the top
25:39 David sent and c' with Abigail,
1Ki 10: 2 she was come to Solomon, she c'
2Ki 22:14 and they c' with her.
2Ch 9: 1 she was come to Solomon, she c'
Ec 1:16 I c' with mine own heart, saying,
Da 1:19 And the king c' with them; and
Zec 1:14 that c' with me said unto me,
Lu 6:11 c' one with another what they
22: 4 and c' with the chief priests and
24:15 they c' together and reasoned,
Ac 24:26 him the oftener, and c' with him.

communicate See also COMMUNICATED.
Ga 6: 6 c' unto him that teacheth in all
Ph'p 4:14 that ye did c' with my affliction.
1Ti 6:18 ready to distribute, willing to c';
Heb 13:16 to do good and to c' forget not:

communicated
Ga 2: 2 c' unto them that gospel which I
Ph'p 4:15 church c' with me as concerning

communication See also COMMUNICATIONS.
2Sa 3:17 And Abner had c' with the elders
2Ki 9:11 Ye know the man, and his c'.
M't 5:37 your c' be, Yea, yea; Nay, nay:
Eph 4:29 Let no corrupt c' proceed out of
Col 3: 8 filthy c' out of your mouth.
Ph'm 6 The c' of thy faith may become

communications
Lu 24:17 What manner of c' are these that
1Co 15:33 evil c' corrupt good manners.

communion
1Co 10:16 not the c' of the blood of Christ?
16 it not the c' of the body of Christ?
2Co 6:14 what c' hath light with darkness?
13:14 the c' of the Holy Ghost, be with

communing
Ge 18:33 as he had left c' with Abraham:
Ex 31:18 he had made an end of c' with him

compact See also COMPACTED.
Ps 122: 3 as a city that is c' together:

compacted
Eph 4:16 and c' by that which every joint

companied See also ACCOMPANIED.
Ac 1:21 these men which have c' with us

companies
J'g 7:16 three hundred men into three c',
20 the three c' blew the trumpets,
9:34 wait against Shechem in four c'.
43 divided them into three c', and
44 other c' ran upon all the people
1Sa 11:11 Saul put the people in three c';
13:17 camp of the Philistines in three c':
2Ki 5: 2 the Syrians had gone out by c',
1Ch 9:18 they were porters in the c' of the
28: 1 c' that ministered to the king by
Ne 12:31 two great c' of them that gave thanks,
40 So stood the two c' of them that gave
Job 6:19 the c' of Sheba waited for them.
Isa 21:13 O ye travelling c' of Dedanim.
57:13 criest, let thy c' deliver thee;
Eze 26: 7 with horsemen, and c', and much
M'r 6:39 sat down by c' upon the green

companion See COMPANIONS.
Ex 32:27 brother, and every man his c',
J'g 14:20 Samson's wife was given to his c',
15: 2 I gave her to thy c': is not her
6 his wife, and given her to his c'.
1Ch 27:33 the Archite was the king's c':
Job 30:29 brother to dragons, and a c' to owls.
Ps 119:63 am a c' of all them that fear thee,
Pr 13:20 but a c' of fools shall be destroyed.
28: 7 but he that is a c' of riotous men
24 the same is the c' of a destroyer.
Mal 2:14 yet is she thy c', and the wife of
Ph'p 2:25 my brother, and c' in labour,
Re 1: 9 and c' in tribulation, and in the

companions See also COMPANIONS'.
J'g 11:38 she went with her c', and bewailed
14:11 they brought thirty c' to be with
Ezr 4: 7 Tabeel, and the rest of their c',
9 the rest of their c'; the Dinaites,
17 the rest of their c' that dwell in
23 Shimshai the scribe, and their c',
5: 3 Shethar-boznai, and their c', and
6 Shethar-boznai, and his c' the
6: 6 Shethar-boznai, and your c' the
13 Shethar-boznai, and their c',
Job 35: 4 will answer thee, and thy c' with
41: 6 Shall the c' make a banquet of
Ps 45:14 the virgins her c' that follow her
Ca 1: 7 aside by the flocks of thy c'?
8:13 the c' hearken to thy voice:
Isa 1:23 are rebellious, and c' of thieves:
Eze 37:16 and for the children of Israel his c':
16 for all the house of Israel his c':
Da 2:17 Mishael, and Azariah, his c':
Ac 19:29 of Macedonia, Paul's c' in travel,
Heb 10:33 ye became c' of them that were so

companions'
Ps 122: 8 For my brethren and c' sakes,

company See also ACCOMPANY; COMPANIED; COMPANIES.
Ge 32: 8 If Esau come to the one c',
8 then the other c' which is left
21 himself lodged that night in the c'.
35:11 a c' of nations shall be of thee,
37:25 a c' of Ishmeelites came from
50: 9 and it was a very great c'.
Nu 14: 7 they spake unto all the c' of the
16: 5 unto all his c', saying, Even
6 you censers, Korah, and all his c';
11 thou and all thy c' are gathered
16 and all thy c' before the Lord,
40 he be not as Korah, and as his c':
22: 4 Now shall this c' lick up all that
26: 9 in the c' of Korah, when they
10 when that c' died, what time the
27: 3 in the c' of them that gathered
3 against the Lord in the c' of Korah:
J'g 9:37 and another c' come along by the
44 Abimelech, and the c' that was
18:23 that thou comest with such a c'?
1Sa 10: 5 thou shalt meet a c' of prophets
10 behold, a c' of prophets met him;
13:17 one c' turned unto the way that
18 And another c' turned the way to
18 Beth-horon: and another c' turned
19:20 they saw the c' of the prophets
30:15 thou bring me down to this c'?
15 I will bring thee down to this c'.
23 the c' that came against us into
2Ki 5:15 he and all his c', and came,
9:17 he spied the c' of Jehu as he came,
17 and said, I see a c'. And Joram
2Ch 9: 1 with a very great c', and camels
20:12 have no might against this great c'
24:24 Syrians came with a small c' of

Ne 12:38 And the other c' of them that
Job 16: 7 thou hast made desolate all my c'.
34: 8 Which goeth in c' with the
Ps 55:14 unto the house of God in c'.
68:11 great was the c' of those that
30 Rebuke the c' of spearmen, the
106:17 and covered the c' of Abiram.
18 And a fire was kindled in their c';
Pr 29: 3 he that keepeth c' with harlots
Ca 1: 9 c' of horses in Pharaoh's chariots.
6:13 As it were the c' of two armies.
Jer 31: 8 a great c' shall return thither.
Eze 16:40 They shall also bring up a c'
17:17 with his mighty army and great c'
23:46 I will bring up a c' upon them,
47 And the c' shall stone them with
27: 6 the c' of the Ashurites have made
27 in all thy c' which is in the midst
34 all thy c' in the midst of thee shall
32: 3 my net over thee with a c' of many
22 Asshur is there and all her c': his
23 and her c' is round about her
38: 4 great c' with bucklers and shields,
7 all thy c' that are assembled unto
13 hast thou gathered thy c' to take a
15 horses, a great c', and a mighty
Ho 6: 9 c' of priests murder in the way
Lu 2:44 him to have been in the c', went
5:29 c' of publicans and of others that
6:17 and the c' of his disciples, and a
22 shall separate you from their c',
9:14 them sit down by fifties in a c'.
38 a man of the c' cried out, saying,
11:27 certain woman of the c' lifted up
12:13 And one of the c' said unto him,
23:27 great c' of people, and of women,
24:22 certain women also of our c' made us
Joh 6: 5 saw a great c' come unto him,
Ac 4:23 go, they went to their own c',
6: 7 and a great c' of the priests were
10:28 is a Jew to keep c', or come unto
13:13 when Paul and his c' loosed
15:22 chosen men of their own c'
17: 5 gathered a c', and set all the city
21: 8 day we that were of Paul's c'
Ro 15:24 somewhat filled with your c'.
1Co 5: 9 epistle not to c' with fornicators:
11 written unto you not to keep c',
2Th 3:14 that man, and have no c' with him,
Heb 12:22 to an innumerable c' of angels,
Re 18:17 all the c' in ships, and sailors,

comparable
La 4: 2 The precious sons of Zion, c' to

compare See also COMPARABLE; COMPARED; COMPARING.
Isa 40:18 what likeness will ye c' unto him?
46: 5 and c' me, that we may be like?
M'r 4:30 what comparison shall we c' it?
2Co 10:12 or c' ourselves with some that

compared
Ps 89: 6 who in the heaven can be c' unto
Pr 3:15 thou canst desire are not to be c'
8:11 may be desired are not to be c' to
Ca 1: 9 I have c' thee, O my love, to a
Ro 8:18 not worthy to be c' with the glory

comparing
1Co 2:13 c' spiritual things with spiritual.
2Co 10:12 c' themselves among themselves,

comparison
J'g 8: 2 have I done now in c' of you?
3 what was I able to do in c' of you?
Hag 2: 3 is it not in your eyes in c' of it as
M'r 4:30 or with what c' shall we compare

compass See also COMPASSED; COMPASSEST; COMPASSETH; COMPASSING.
Ex 27: 5 put it under the c' of the altar
38: 4 under the c' thereof beneath unto
Nu 21: 4 way of the Red sea, to c' the land
34: 5 And the border shall fetch a c'
Jos 6: 3 And ye shall c' the city, all ye men
4 ye shall c' the city seven times,
7 Pass on, and c' the city, and let him
15: 3 and fetched a c' to Karkaa:
2Sa 5:23 fetch a c' behind them, and come
1Ki 7:15 line of twelve cubits did c' either
23 of thirty cubits did c' it round
35 was there a round c' of half a cubit
2Ki 3: 9 they fetched a c' of seven days'
11: 8 And ye shall c' the king round
2Ch 4: 2 from brim to brim, round in c',
2 a line of thirty cubits did c' it
3 oxen, which did c' it round about:
23: 7 And the Levites shall c' the king
Job 16:13 His archers c' me round about,
40:22 willows of the brook c' him about.
Ps 5:12 with favour wilt thou c' him as
7: 7 congregation of the people c' thee
17: 9 from my deadly enemies, who c'
26: 6 so will I c' thine altar, O Lord:
32: 7 thou shalt c' me about with songs
10 Lord, mercy shall c' him about.
49: 5 the iniquity of my heels shall c' me
140: 9 for the head of those that c' me
142: 7 the righteous shall c' me about;
Pr 8:27 he set a c' upon the face of the
Isa 44:13 and he marketh it out with the c',
50:11 c' yourselves about with sparks:
Jer 31:22 earth, A woman shall c' a man.
39 hill Gareb, and shall c' about to
52:21 a fillet of twelve cubits did c' it;
Hab 1: 4 for the wicked doth c' about the
M't 23:15 for ye c' sea and land to make one
Lu 19:43 a trench about thee, and c' thee
Ac 28:13 thence we fetched a c', and came

compassed
Ge 19: 4 c' the house round, both old and
De 2: 1 and we c' mount Seir many days.
3 Ye have c' this mountain long
Jos 6:11 So the ark of the Lord c' the city,
14 the second day they c' the city once,
15 c' the city after the same manner
15 on that day they c' the city seven
15:10 And the border c' from Baalah
18:14 and c' the corner of the sea
J'g 11:18 and c' the land of Edom, and the
16: 2 And they c' him in, and laid wait
1Sa 23:26 Saul and his men c' David and his
2Sa 18:15 c' about and smote Absalom,
22: 5 waves of death c' me, the floods
6 The sorrows of hell c' me about;
2Ki 6:14 they came by night, and c' the city
15 host c' the city both with horses
8:21 smote the Edomites which c' him
2Ch 18:31 Therefore they c' about him to
21: 9 smote the Edomites which c' him
33:14 and c' about Ophel, and raised it
Job 19: 6 and hath c' me with his net.
26:10 hath c' the waters with bounds,
Ps 17:11 They have now c' us in our steps:
18: 4 The sorrows of death c' me, and
5 The sorrows of hell c' me about:
22:12 Many bulls have c' me: strong
16 For dogs have c' me: the assembly
40:12 innumerable evils have c' me
88:17 water; they c' me about together.
109: 3 They c' me about also with words
116: 3 The sorrows of death c' me, and
118:10 All nations c' me about: but in
11 c' me about; yea, they c' me about:
12 They c' me about like bees: they
La 3: 5 me, and c' me with gall and travel.
Jon 2: 3 the floods c' me about: all thy
5 The waters c' me about, even to
Lu 21:20 shall see Jerusalem c' with armies,
Heb 5: 2 himself also is c' with infirmity.
11:30 they were c' about seven days.
12: 1 are c' about with so great a cloud
Re 20: 9 and c' the camp of the saints about,

compassest
Ps 139: 3 Thou c' my path and my lying

compasseth
Ge 2:11 c' the whole land of Havilah,
13 that c' the whole land of Ethiopia.
Jos 19:14 the border c' it on the north side
Ps 73: 6 pride c' them about as a chain;
Ho 11:12 Ephraim c' me about with lies,

compassing
1Ki 7:24 were knops c' it, ten in a cubit,
24 c' the sea round about: the knops
2Ch 4: 3 c' the sea round about. Two rows

compassion See also COMPASSIONS.
Ex 2: 6 And she had c' on him, and said,
De 13:17 thee mercy, and have c' upon thee,
30: 3 captivity, and have c' upon thee,
1Sa 23:21 of the Lord: for ye have c' on me.
1Ki 8:50 c' before them who carried them
50 that they may have c' on them:
2Ki 13:23 had c' on them, and had respect
2Ch 30: 9 children shall find c' before them
36:15 because he had c' on his people,
17 had no c' on young man or maiden,
Ps 78:38 he, being full of c', forgave their
86:15 a God full of c', and gracious,
111: 4 Lord is gracious and full of c'.
112: 4 and full of c', and righteous.
145: 8 Lord is gracious, and full of c';
Isa 49:15 she should not have c' on the son
Jer 12:15 I will return, and have c' on them,
La 3:32 will he have c' according to the
Eze 16: 5 to have c' upon thee; but thou
Mic 7:19 he will have c' upon us; he will
M't 9:36 he was moved with c' on them,
14:14 was moved with c' toward them,
15:32 I have c' on the multitude, because
18:27 was moved with c', and loosed him,
33 have had c' on thy fellow servant,
20:34 Jesus had c' on them, and touched
M'r 1:41 Jesus, moved with c', put forth
5:19 for thee, and hath had c' on thee.
6:34 was moved with c' toward them,
8: 2 I have c' on the multitude, because
9:22 have c' on us, and help us.
Lu 7:13 he had c' on her, and said unto her,
10:33 when he saw him, he had c' on him,
15:20 his father saw him, and had c',
Ro 9:15 will have c' on whom I will have c'
Heb 5: 2 Who can have c' on the ignorant,
10:34 For ye had c' of me in my bonds,
1Pe 3: 8 having c' one of another, love
1Jo 3:17 shutteth up his bowels of c' from him,
Jude 22 have c', making a difference:

compassions
La 3:22 consumed, because his c' fail not.
Zec 7: 9 shew mercy and c' every man to

compel See also COMPELLED.
Le 25:39 thou shalt not c' him to serve as
Es 1: 8 none did c': for so the king had
M't 5:41 shall c' thee to go a mile, go with
M'r 15:21 they c' one Simon a Cyrenian, who
Lu 14:23 c' them to come in, that my house

compelled
1Sa 28:23 together with the woman, c' him;
2Ch 21:11 fornication, and c' Judah thereto.
M't 27:32 him they c' to bear his cross.
Ac 26:11 and c' them to blaspheme; and
2Co 12:11 a fool in glorying; ye have c' me:
Ga 2: 3 a Greek, was c' to be circumcised:

compellest
Ga 2:14 why c' thou the Gentiles to live

complain See also COMPLAINED; COMPLAINING.
J'g 21:22 come unto us to c', that we will say
Job 7:11 c' in the bitterness of my soul.
31:38 the furrows likewise thereof c';
La 3:39 Wherefore doth a living man c',

complained
Nu 11: 1 when the people c', it displeased
Ps 77: 3 I c', and my spirit was

complainers
Jude 16 are murmurers, c', walking after

complaining
Ps 144:14 that there be no c' in our streets.

complaint See also COMPLAINTS.
1Sa 1:16 abundance of my c' and grief have
Job 7:13 my couch shall ease my c';
9:27 I will forget my c', I will leave off
10: 1 I will leave my c' upon myself;
21: 4 is my c' to man? And if it were so,
23: 2 to day is my c' bitter: my stroke is
Ps 55: 2 I mourn in my c', and make a
102 *title* poureth out his c' before the Lord.
142: 2 I poured out my c' before him;

complaints
Ac 25: 7 and grievous c' against Paul,

complete
Le 23:15 seven sabbaths shall be c':
Col 2:10 are c' in him, which is the head
4:12 perfect and c' in all the will of God.

composition
Ex 30:32 any other like it, after the c' of it:
37 according to the c' thereof: it shall

compound See also COMPOUNDETH.
Ex 30:25 an ointment c' after the art of the

compoundeth
Ex 30:33 Whosoever c' any like it, or

comprehend See also COMPREHENDED.
Job 37: 5 doeth he, which we cannot c'.
Eph 3:18 able to c' with all saints what is

comprehended
Isa 40:12 and c' the dust of the earth in a
Joh 1: 5 and the darkness c' it not.
Ro 13: 9 it is briefly c' in this saying,

Conaniah (*co-na-ni'-ah*) See also CONONIAH.
2Ch 35: 9 C' also, and Shemaiah, and

conceal See also CONCEALED; CONCEALETH.
Ge 37:26 slay our brother, and c' his blood?
De 13: 8 neither shalt thou c' him:
Job 27:11 is with the Almighty will I not c'.
41:12 I will not c' his parts, nor his
Pr 25: 2 It is the glory of God to c' a thing:
Jer 50: 2 publish and c' not: say,

concealed
Job 6:10 not c' the words of the Holy One.
Ps 40:10 I have not c' thy lovingkindness

concealeth
Pr 11:13 is of a faithful spirit c' the matter.
12:23 A prudent man c' knowledge: but

conceit See also CONCEITS.
Pr 18:11 and as an high wall in his own c'.
26: 5 lest he be wise in his own c'.
12 thou a man wise in his own c'?
16 The sluggard is wiser in his own c'
28:11 The rich man is wise in his own c';

conceits
Ro 11:25 be wise in your own c';
12:16 Be not wise in your own c'.

conceive See also CONCEIVED; CONCEIVING.
Ge 30:38 should c' when they came to drink.
41 cattle did c', that Jacob laid
41 that they might c' among the rods.
Nu 5:28 shall be free, and shall c' seed.
J'g 13: 3 but thou shalt c', and bear a son.
5 lo, thou shalt c', and bear a son;
7 thou shalt c', and bear a son;
Job 15:35 They c' mischief, and bring forth
Ps 51: 5 and in sin did my mother c' me.
Isa 7:14 a virgin shall c', and bear a son,
33:11 shall c' chaff, ye shall bring forth
59: 4 c' mischief, and bring forth iniquity.
Lu 1:31 thou shalt c' in thy womb, and
Heb 11:11 received strength to c' seed,

conceived
Ge 4: 1 and she c', and bare Cain, and
17 and she c', and bare Enoch: and
16: 4 went in unto Hagar, and she c':
4 when she saw that she had c', her
5 when she saw that she had c', I
21: 2 Sarah c', and bare Abraham a son
25:21 and Rebekah his wife c'.
29:32 And Leah c', and bare a son,
33, 34 she c' again, and bare a son;
35 And she c' again, and bare a son:
30: 5 Bilhah c', and bare Jacob a son.
7 And Bilhah Rachel's maid c' again,
17 she c', and bare Jacob the fifth son.
19 And Leah c' again, and bare Jacob
23 And she c', and bare a son;
39 And the flocks c' before the rods,
31:10 pass at the time that the cattle c',
38: 3 And she c', and bare a son;
4 and she c' again, and bare a son;
5 And she yet again c', and bare
18 in unto her, and she c' by him.
Ex 2: 2 the woman c', and bare a son:
Le 12: 2 If a woman have c' seed, and
Nu 11:12 Have I c' all this people? have I
1Sa 1:20 after Hannah had c', that she bare

1Sa 2:21 that she c', and bare three sons
2Sa 11: 5 And the woman c', and sent and
2Ki 4:17 And the woman c', and bare a son
1Ch 7:23 she c', and bare a son, and he
Job 3: 3 was said, There is a man child c'.
Ps 7:14 and hath c' mischief, and brought
Ca 3: 4 into the chamber of her that c' me.
Isa 8: 3 and she c', and bare a son.
Jer 49:30 hath c' a purpose against you.
Ho 1: 3 which c', and bare him a son.
6 she c' again, and bare a daughter.
8 Loruhamah, she c', and bare a son.
2: 5 harlot: she that c' them hath done
M't 1:20 that which is c' in her is of the
Lu 1:24 his wife Elisabeth c', and hid
36 hath also c' a son in her old age:
2:21 before he was c' in the womb.
Ac 5: 4 why hast thou c' this thing in
Ro 9:10 when Rebecca also had c'
Jas 1:15 Then when lust hath c', it bringeth

conceiving
Isa 59:13 c' and uttering from the heart

conception
Ge 3:16 multiply thy sorrow and thy c';
Ru 4:13 the Lord gave her c', and she bare
Ho 9:11 from the womb, and from the c'.

concern See also CONCERNETH; CONCERNING.
Ac 28:31 things which c' the Lord Jesus
2Co 11:30 glory of the things which c' mine

concerneth
Ps 138: 8 that which c' me: thy mercy,
Eze 12:10 This burden c' the prince in

concerning^
Ge 5:29 comfort us c' our work and toil
19:21 accepted thee c' this thing also,
24: 9 and sware to him c' that matter.
26:32 c' the well which they had
42:21 are verily guilty c' our brother,
Ex 6: 8 the land, c' the which I did swear
24: 8 made with you c' all these words.
Le 4: 2 the Lord c' things which ought
13, 22 c' things which should not be
26 atonement for him as c' his sin,
27 c' things which ought not to be
5: 6 atonement for him c' his sin.
18 for him c' his ignorance
6: 3 which was lost, and lieth c' it,
18 c' the offerings of the Lord
23: 2 C' the feasts of the Lord,
27:32 And c' the tithe of the herd,
Nu 8:20 Lord commanded Moses c' the
22 commanded Moses c' the Levites,
9: 8 the Lord will command c' you.
10:29 Lord hath spoken good c' Israel.
14:30 the land, c' which I sware to
30: 1 tribes c' the children of Israel,
12 out of her lips c' her vows,
12 or c' the bond of her soul,
32:28 So c' them Moses commanded
36: 6 c' the daughters of Zelophehad
Jos 14: 6 man of God c' me and thee in 5921.
23:14 Lord your God spake c' you;
J'g 15: 3 Samson said c' them, Now shall
21: 5 a great oath c' him that came not
Ru 4: 7 c' redeeming and c' changing,
1Sa 3:12 which I have spoken c' his house:
25:30 good that he hath spoken c' thee,
2Sa 3: 8 to day with a fault c' this woman?
7:25 c' thy servant, and c' his house,
11:18 David all the things c' the war;
13:39 for he was comforted c' Amnon,
14: 8 and I will give charge c' thee.
18: 5 captains charge c' Absalom. 5921.
1Ki 2: 4 his word which he spake c' me,
27 which he spake c' the house of Eli
5: 8 will do all thy desire c' timber
8 of cedar, and c' timber of fir.
6:12 C' this house which thou art
8:41 Moreover c' a stranger, that is
10: 1 c' the name of the Lord, she
11: 2 nations c' which the Lord said
10 had commanded him c' this thing,
22: 8 doth not prophesy good c' me,
18 would prophesy no good c' me,
23 Lord hath spoken evil c' thee.
2Ki 10:10 Lord spake c' the house of Ahab:
17:15 c' whom the Lord hath charged
19:21 that the Lord hath spoken c' him;
32 the Lord c' the king of Assyria,
22:13 c' the words of this book that is
13 unto all that which is written c' us.
1Ch 11:10 to the word of the Lord c' Israel.
17:23 that thou hast spoken c' thy servant
23 and c' his house be established for
19: 2 to comfort him c' his father.
22:12 and give thee charge c' Israel.
23:14 Now c' Moses the man of God,
24:21 C' Rehabiah: of the sons of
29 C' Kish: the son of Kish was
26: 1 C' the divisions of the porters:
21 As c' the sons of Laadan; the
2Ch 6:32 Moreover c' the stranger, which
8:15 c' any matter, or c' the treasures.
12:15 of Iddo the seer c' genealogies?
15:16 c' Maachah the mother of Asa
24:27 Now c' his sons, and the greatness
31: 6 And c' the children of Israel
9 and the Levites c' the heaps.
34:21 c' the words of the book that
26 God of Israel c' the words which
Ezr 5: 5 answer by letter c' this matter.
17 pleasure to us c' this matter.
6: 3 a decree c' the house of God
7:14 enquire c' Judah and Jerusalem,
Ezr 10: 2 hope in Israel c' this thing.
Ne 1: 2 and I asked them c' the Jews
2 of the captivity, and c' Jerusalem.
9:23 them into the land, c' which thou
11:23 king's commandment c' them,
24 in all matters c' the people.
13:14 Remember me, O my God, c' this,
22 Remember me, O my God, c' this also,
Es 3: 2 king had so commanded c' him.
9:26 of that which they had seen c' this
Job 36:33 noise thereof sheweth c' it,
33 the cattle also c' the vapour.
Ps 7 *title* the Lord, c' the words of Cush
17: 4 C' the works of men, by the
73: 8 speak wickedly c' oppression:
90:13 let it repent thee c' thy servants.
106:34 not destroy the nations, c' whom
119:128 I esteem all thy precepts c' all things
152 C' thy testimonies, I have
135:14 repent himself c' his servants.
Ec 1:13 search out by wisdom c' all things
3:18 I said in mine heart c' the estate
7:10 dost not enquire wisely c' this.
Isa 1: 1 of Amoz, which he saw c' Judah
2: 1 Amoz saw c' Judah and Jerusalem.
3: 1 write in it with a man's pen c'
16:13 Lord hath spoken c' Moab since
23: 5 As at the report c' Egypt, so
29:22 Abraham, c' the house of Jacob,
30: 7 therefore have I cried c' this,
37: 9 he heard say c' Tirhakah king
22 Lord hath spoken c' him; The
33 Lord c' the king of Assyria, He
45:11 c' my sons, and c' the work of my
Jer 7:22 c' burnt offerings or
14: 1 to Jeremiah c' the dearth.
15 saith the Lord c' the prophets
16: 3 c' the sons, and c' the daughters
3 and c' their mothers that bare
3 and c' their fathers that begat
18: 7, 9 c' a nation, and c' a kingdom,
22:18 thus saith the Lord c' Jehoiakim
23:15 the Lord of hosts c' the prophets;
25: 1 came to Jeremiah c' all the people
27:19 c' [413] the pillars, and c' the sea,
19 c' the bases, and c' the residue
21 c' the vessels that remain in the
29:31 Thus saith the Lord c' Shemaiah
30: 4 Lord spake c' Israel and c' Judah.
32:36 c' the city, whereof ye say,
33: 4 of Israel, c' the houses of this city,
4 and c' the houses of the kings
39:11 gave charge c' Jeremiah to
42:19 The Lord hath said c' you,
44: 1 c' all the Jews which dwell in
49: 1 C' the Ammonites, thus saith
7 C' Edom, thus saith the Lord
23 C' Damascus. Hamath is
28 C' Kedar, and c' the kingdoms
52:21 And c' the pillars, the height
La 1:17 Lord hath commanded c' Jacob
Eze 13:16 which prophesy c' Jerusalem,
14: 7 to enquire of him c' me;
22 c' the evil that I have brought
22 c' all that I have brought upon
18: 2 proverb c' the land of Israel,
21:28 the Lord God c' the Ammonites,
28 and c' their reproach;
36: 6 Prophesy therefore c' the land
44: 5 I say unto thee c' all the ordinances
45:14 C' the ordinance of oil,
47:14 c' the which I lifted up mine hand
Da 2:18 God of heaven c' this secret;
5:29 made a proclamation c' him,
6: 4 against Daniel c' the kingdom;
5 against him c' the law of his God.
12 the king c' the king's decree;
17 might not be changed c' Daniel.
7:12 As c' the rest of the beasts,
8:13 the vision c' the daily sacrifice,
Am 1: 1 which he saw c' Israel in the
Ob 1 saith the Lord God c' Edom;
Mic 1: 1 c' Samaria and Jerusalem.
3: 5 saith the Lord c' the prophets
Na 1:14 given a commandment c' thee,
Hag 2:11 Ask now the priests c' the law,
M't 4: 6 give his angels charge c' thee:
11: 7 to say unto the multitudes c' John,
16:11 I spake it not to you c' bread,
M'r 5:16 and also c' the swine.
7:17 disciples asked him c' the parable
Lu 2:17 which was told them c' this child.
7:24 to speak unto the people c' John,
18:31 by the prophets c' the Son of man
22:37 for the things c' me have an end.
24:19 C' Jesus of Nazareth, which was
27 scriptures the things c' himself.
44 and in the psalms, c' me.
Joh 7:12 among the people c' him:
32 murmured such things c' him;
9:18 believe c' him, that he had been
11:19 to comfort them c' their brother.
Ac 1:16 c' Judas, which was guide to them
2:25 David speaketh c' him, I foresaw
8:12 the things c' the kingdom of God,
13:34 And as c' that he raised him up
19: 8 the things c' the kingdom of God.
39 any thing c' other matters,
21:24 whereof they were informed c' thee.
22:18 will not receive thy testimony c' me.
23:15 something more perfectly c' him:
24:24 and heard him c' the faith in Christ.
25:16 for himself c' the crime laid against
28:21 received letters out of Judæa c' thee,
22 as c' this sect, we know that every
23 persuading them c' Jesus, both
Ro 1: 3 C' his son Jesus Christ our Lord,
9: 5 as c' the flesh Christ came, who
27 Esaias also crieth c' Israel,
11:28 As c' the gospel, they are enemies
16:19 which is good, and simple c' evil.
1Co 5: 3 present, c' him that hath so done
7: 1 Now c' the things whereof ye
25 Now c' virgins I have no
8: 4 As c' therefore the eating of those
12: 1 Now c' spiritual gifts, brethren, I
16: 1 c' the collection for the saints, as I
2Co 8:23 and fellowhelper c' you:
11:21 I speak as c' reproach, as though
Eph 4:22 c' the former conversation the old
5:32 I speak c' Christ and the church.
Ph'p 3: 6 C' zeal, persecuting the church:
4:15 with me as c' giving and
1Th 3: 2 and to comfort you c' your faith:
4:13 c' them which are asleep, that ye
5:18 will of God in Christ Jesus c' you.
1Ti 1:19 c' faith have made shipwreck:
6:21 professing have erred c' the faith.
2Ti 2:18 Who c' the truth have erred,
3: 8 minds, reprobate c' the faith.
Heb 7:14 Moses spake nothing c' priesthood.
11:20 blessed Jacob and Esau c' things
22 gave commandment c' his bones
1Pe 4:12 c' the fiery trial which is to try you,
2Pe 3: 9 Lord is not slack c' his promise,
1Jo 2:26 have I written unto you c' them

concision
Ph'p 3: 2 of evil workers, beware of the c'.

conclude See also CONCLUDED.
Ro 3:28 Therefore we c' that a man is

concluded
Ac 21:25 we have written and c' that they
Ro 11:32 For God hath c' them all in
Ga 3:22 the scripture hath c' all under

conclusion
Ec 12:13 Let us hear the c' of the whole

concord
2Co 6:15 And what c' hath Christ with

concourse
Pr 1:21 She crieth in the chief place of c',
Ac 19:40 we may give an account of this c'.

concubine See also CONCUBINES.
Ge 22:24 And his c', whose name was
35:22 Bilhah his father's c': and Israel
36:12 Timna was c' to Eliphaz Esau's son;
J'g 8:31 And his c' that was in Shechem,
19: 1 who took to him a c' out of
2 his c' played the whore against
9 and his c', and his servant, his
10 his c' also was with him.
24 my daughter a maiden, and his c';
25 so the man took his c', and brought
27 the woman his c' was fallen down
29 laid hold on his c', and divided her
20: 4 I and my c', to lodge.
5 my c' have they forced, that she is
6 And I took my c', and cut her in
2Sa 3: 7 And Saul had a c', whose name was
7 thou gone in unto my father's c'?
21:11 the daughter of Aiah, the c' of Saul,
1Ch 1:32 the sons of Keturah, Abraham's c':
2:46 And Ephah, Caleb's c', bare Haran,
48 Maachah, Caleb's c', bare Sheber.
7:14 his c' the Aramitess bare Machir

concubines
Ge 25: 6 the sons of the c', which Abraham
2Sa 5:13 David took him more c' and wives
15:16 ten women, which were c', to keep
16:21 Go in unto thy father's c', which
22 Absalom went in unto his father's c'
19: 5 of thy wives, and the lives of thy c';
20: 3 the ten women his c', whom he had
1Ki 11: 3 and three hundred c': and his
1Ch 3: 9 beside the sons of the c', and
2Ch 11:21 above all his wives and his c':
21 and threescore c'; and begat
Es 2:14 chamberlain, which kept the c':
Ca 6: 8 and fourscore c', and virgins
9 the queens and the c', and they
Da 5: 2 his wives, and his c', might drink
3 his wives, and his c', drank in them.
23 and thy c', have drunk wine in

concupiscence
Ro 7: 8 wrought in me all manner of c'.
Col 3: 5 evil c', and covetousness, which
1Th 4: 5 Not in the lust of c', even as the

condemn See also CONDEMNED; CONDEMNEST; CONDEMNETH; CONDEMNING.
Ex 22: 9 whom the judges shall c', he shall
De 25: 1 the righteous, and c' the wicked.
Job 9:20 mine own mouth shall c' me:
10: 2 Do not c' me; shew me wherefore
34:17 wilt thou c' him that is most just?
40: 8 wilt thou c' me, that thou mayest
Ps 37:33 in his hand, nor c' him when he is
94:21 the righteous, and c' the innocent
109:31 him from those that c' his soul.
Pr 12: 2 a man of wicked devices will he c'.
Isa 50: 9 who is he that shall c' me? lo, they
54:17 in judgment thou shalt c'. This is
M't 12:41 and shall c' it: because they
42 and shall c' it: for she came from
20:18 they shall c' him to death,
M'r 10:33 they shall c' him to death, and shall
Lu 6:37 c' not, and ye shall not be
11:31 of this generation, and c' them:
32 with this generation, and shall c' it
Joh 3:17 Son into the world to c' the world:

Joh 8:11 Neither do I c· thee: go, and sin
2Co 7: 3 I speak not this to c· you: for I
1Jo 3:20 For if our heart c· us, God is
21 if our heart c· us not, then have

condemnation
Lu 23:40 seeing thou art in the same c·?
Joh 3:19 And this is the c·, that light is
5:24 shall not come into c·; but is
Ro 5:16 for the judgment was by one to c·,
18 judgment came upon all men to c·;
8: 1 now no c· to them which are in
1Co 11:34 ye come not together unto c·.
2Co 3: 9 For if the administration of c· be
1Ti 3: 6 he fall into the c· of the devil.
Jas 3: 1 we shall receive the greater c·.
5:12 your way, nay; lest ye fall into c·.
Jude 4 before of old ordained to this c·,

condemned
2Ch 36:3 and c· the land in an hundred
Job 32: 3 no answer, and yet had c· Job.
Ps 109: 7 be judged, let him be c·:
Am 2: 8 drink the wine of the c· in the
M't 12: 7 ye would not have c· the guiltless.
37 and by thy words thou shalt be c·.
27: 3 when he saw that he was c·,
M'r 14:64 they all c· him to be guilty of death.
Lu 6:37 and ye shall not be c·: forgive,
24:20 delivered him to be c· to
Joh 3:18 believeth on him is not c·: but he
18 that believeth not is c· already,
8:10 hath no man c· thee?
Ro 8: 3 c· sin in the flesh:
1Co 11:32 that we should not be c· with
Tit 2: 8 Sound speech, that cannot be c·
3;11 and sinneth, being c· of himself.
Heb 11: 7 by the which he c· the world, and
Jas 5: 6 Ye have c· and killed the just;
9 lest ye be c·: behold, the judge
2Pe 2: 6 c· them with an overthrow,

condemnest
Ro 2: 1 judgest another, thou c· thyself;

condemneth
Job 15: 6 Thine own mouth c· thee, and
Pr 17:15 and he that c· the just, even they
Ro 8:34 Who is he that c·? It is Christ
14:22 Happy is he that c· not himself

condemning
1Ki 8:32 c· the wicked, to bring his way
Ac 13:27 they have fulfilled them in c· him.

condescend
Ro 12:16 but c· to men of low estate.

condition See also CONDITIONS.
1Sa 11: 2 On this c· will I make a covenant

conditions
Lu 14:32 and desireth c· of peace.

conduct See also CONDUCTED.
2Sa 19:15 king, to c· the king over Jordan.
31 the king, to c· him over Jordan.
1Co 16:11 but c· him forth in peace, that he

conducted
2Sa 19:40 the people of Judah c· the king,
Ac 17:15 c· Paul brought him unto Athens:

conduit *(con'-dit)*
2Ki 18:17 stood by the c· of the upper pool,
20:20 he made a pool, and a c·, and
Isa 7: 3 the end of the c· of the upper pool
36: 2 he stood by the c· of the upper pool

coney See also CONIES.
Le 11: 5 c·, because he cheweth the cud,
De 14: 7 camel, and the hare, and the c·:

confection
Ex 30:35 c· after the art of the apothecary,

confectionaries
1Sa 8:13 take your daughters to be c·,

confederacy
Isa 8:12 Say ye not, A c·, to all them to
12 this people shall say, A c·; neither
Ob 7 All the men of thy c· have brought

confederate
Ge 14:13 these were c· with Abram.
Ps 83: 5 they are c· against thee:
Isa 7: 2 Syria is c· with Ephraim. And

conference
Ga 2: 6 in c· added nothing to me:

conferred
1Ki 1: 7 And he c· with Joab the son
Ac 4:15 they c· among themselves,
25:12 Then Festus, when he had c· with
Ga 1:16 I c· not with flesh and blood:

confess See also CONFESSED; CONFESSETH; CONFESSING.
Le 5: 5 he shall c· that he hath sinned
16:21 and c· over him all the iniquities
26:40 If they shall c· their iniquity, and
Nu 5: 7 c· their sin which they have done:
1Ki 8:33 and c· thy name, and pray, and
35 and c· thy name, and turn from
2Ch 6:24 c· thy name, and pray and make
26 toward this place, and c· thy name,
Ne 1: 6 c· the sins of the children of Israel,
Job 40:14 Then will I also c· unto thee that
Ps 32: 5 I will c· my transgressions unto
M't 10:32 shall c· me before men, him will I
32 will I c· also before my Father
Lu 12: 8 shall c· me before men, him
8 shall the Son of man also c· before
Joh 9:22 any man did c· that he was Christ,
12:42 the Pharisees they did not c· him,
Ac 23: 8 but the Pharisees c· both.
Ac 24:14 But this I c· unto thee, that after
Ro 10: 9 c· with thy mouth the Lord Jesus,
14:11 and every tongue shall c· to God.
15: 9 c· to thee among the Gentiles,
Ph'p 2:11 should c· that Jesus Christ is Lord,
Jas 5:16 C· your faults one to another, and
1Jo 1: 9 If we c· our sins, he is faithful and
4:15 c· that Jesus is the Son of God,
2Jo 7 who c· not that Jesus Christ is
Re 3: 5 will c· his name before my Father,

confessed
Ezr 10: 1 when he had c·, weeping and
Ne 9: 2 stood and c· their sins, and the
3 another fourth part they c·, and
Joh 1:20 he c·, and denied not; but
20 c·, I am not the Christ.
Ac 19:18 and c·, and showed their deeds.
Heb 11:13 and c· that they were strangers

confesseth
Pr 28:13 c· and forsaketh them shall have
1Jo 4: 2 Every spirit that c· that Jesus
3 every spirit that c· not that Jesus

confessing
Da 9:20 praying, and c· my sin and the
M't 3: 6 of him in Jordan, c· their sins.
M'r 1: 5 in the river of Jordan, c· their sins.

confession
Jos 7:19 make c· unto him; and tell me
2Ch 30:22 and making c· to the Lord God of
Ezr 10:11 make c· unto the Lord God of
Da 9: 4 Lord my God, and made my c·,
Ro 10:10 mouth c· is made unto salvation;
1Ti 6:13 Pontius Pilate witnessed a good c·:

confidence See also CONFIDENCES.
J'g 9:26 men of Shechem put their c· in
2Ki 18:19 c· is this wherein thou trustest?
Job 4: 6 not this thy fear, thy c·, thy hope,
18:14 His c· shall be rooted out of his
31:24 to the fine gold, Thou art my c·;
Ps 65: 5 the c· of all the ends of the earth,
118: 8 in the Lord than to put c· in man.
9 the Lord than to put c· in princes.
Pr 3:26 the Lord shall be thy c·, and
14:26 the fear of the Lord is strong c·:
21:22 the strength of the c· thereof.
25:19 C· in an unfaithful man in time of
Isa 30:15 and in c· shall be your strength:
36: 4 c· is this wherein thou trustest?
Jer 48:13 was ashamed of Beth-el their c·.
Eze 28:26 they shall dwell with c·, when I
29:16 be no more the c· of the house
Mic 7: 5 a friend, put ye not c· in a guide:
Ac 28:31 with all c·, no man forbidding
2Co 1:15 in this c· I was minded to come
2: 3 having c· in you all, that my joy
7:16 I have c· in you in all things.
8:22 the great c· which I have in you.
10: 2 c·, wherewith I think to be bold
11:17 foolishly, in this c· of boasting.
Ga 5:10 have c· in you through the Lord,
Eph 3:12 and access with c· by the faith
Ph'p 1:25 And having this c·, I know that I
3: 3 and have no c· in the flesh.
3: 4 might also have c· in the flesh.
2Th 3: 4 have c· in the Lord touching you,
Ph'm 21 Having c· in thy obedience I wrote
Heb 3: 6 if we hold fast the c· and the
14 if we hold the beginning of our c·
10:35 therefore your c·, which hath
1Jo 2:28 we may have c·, and not be
3:21 then have we c· toward God.
5:14 is the c· that we have in him,

confidences
Jer 2:37 the Lord hath rejected thy c·, and

confident
Ps 27: 3 against me, in this will I be c·.
Pr 14:16 but the fool rageth, and is c·.
Ro 2:19 c· that thou thyself art a guide
2Co 5: 6 Therefore we are always c·,
8 are c·, I say, and willing rather
9: 4 in this same c· boasting.
Ph'p 1: 6 Being c· of this very thing, that
14 waxing c· by my bonds, are much

confidently
Lu 22:59 another c· affirmed, saying, Of a

confirm See also CONFIRMED; CONFIRMETH; CONFIRMING.
Ru 4: 7 changing, for to c· all things;
1Ki 1:14 in after thee, and c· thy words.
2Ki 15:19 be with him to c· the kingdom
Es 9:29 to c· this second letter of Purim.
31 To c· these days of Purim in their
Ps 68: 9 thou didst c· thine inheritance,
Isa 35: 3 and c· the feeble knees.
Eze 13: 6 hope that they would c· the word.
Da 9:27 And he shall c· the covenant
11: 1 stood to c· and to strengthen him.
Ro 15: 8 to c· the promises made unto the
1Co 1: 8 Who shall also c· you unto the end,
2Co 2: 8 would c· your love toward him.

confirmation
Ph'p 1: 7 in the defence and c· of the gospel,
Heb 6:16 an oath for c· is to them an end of

confirmed
2Sa 7:24 thou hast c· to thyself thy people
2Ki 14: 5 the kingdom was c· in his hand,
1Ch 14: 2 Lord had c· him king over Israel,
16:17 And hath c· the same to Jacob
Es 9:32 Esther c· these matters of Purim;
Ps 105:10 c· the same unto Jacob for a law,
Da 9:12 And he hath c· his words, which
Ac 15:32 with many words, and c· them.
1Co 1: 6 testimony of Christ was c· in you:
Ga 3:15 a man's covenant, yet if it be c·,
17 that was c· before of God in Christ,
Heb 2: 3 c· unto us by them that heard him
6:17 of his counsel, c· it by an oath:

confirmeth
Nu 30:14 he c· them, because he held his
De 27:26 Cursed be he that c· not all the
Isa 44:26 That c· the word of his servant,

confirming
M'r 16:20 c· the word with signs following.
Ac 14:22 C· the souls of the disciples, and
15:41 Syria and Cilicia, c· the churches.

confiscation
Ezr 7:26 c· of goods, or to imprisonment.

conflict
Ph'p 1:30 the same c· which ye saw in me,
Col 2: 1 knew what great c· I have for you,

conformable
Ph'p 3:10 being made c· unto his death;

conformed
Ro 8:29 to be c· to the image of his Son,
12: 2 And be not c· to this world: but

confound See also CONFOUNDED.
Ge 11: 7 and there c· their language,
9 the Lord did there c· the language
Jer 1:17 faces, lest I c· thee before them.
1Co 1:27 things of the world to c· the wise;
27 c· the things which are mighty;

confounded
2Ki 19:26 they were dismayed and c·;
Job 6:20 were c· because they had hoped;
Ps 22: 5 trusted in thee, and were not c·.
35: 4 Let them be c· and put to shame
40:14 Let them be ashamed and c·
69: 6 let not those that seek thee be c·
70: 2 Let them be ashamed and c·
71:13 Let them be c· and consumed
24 for they are c·, for they are brought
83:17 Let them be c· and troubled for
97: 7 C· be all they that serve graven
129: 5 Let them all be c· and turned
Isa 1:29 ye shall be c· for the gardens
19: 9 that weave net works, shall be c·.
24:23 Then the moon shall be c·,
37:27 they were dismayed and c·;
41:11 shall be ashamed and c·: they
45:16 They shall be ashamed, and also c·,
17 ye shall not be ashamed nor c·
50: 7 me; therefore shall I not be c·:
54: 4 neither be thou c·; for thou shalt
Jer 9:19 we are greatly c·, because we have
10:14 founder is c· by the graven image:
14: 3 they were ashamed and c·,
15: 9 she hath been ashamed and c·:
17:18 them be c· that persecute me,
18 let not me be c·: let them be
22:22 then shalt thou be ashamed and c·
31:19 I was ashamed, yea, even c·,
46:24 daughter of Egypt shall be c·;
48: 1 Kiriathaim is c· and taken:
1 Misgab is c· and dismayed.
20 Moab is c·; for it is broken down:
49:23 Hamath is c·, and Arpad: for
50: 2 Bel is c·, Merodach is broken
2 her idols are c·, her images are
12 Your mother shall be sore c·;
51:17 founder is c· by the graven image:
47 her whole land shall be c·,
51 We are c·, because we have
Eze 16:52 be thou c· also, and bear thy shame,
54 and mayest be c· in all that thou
63 thou mayest remember, and be c·,
36:32 be ashamed and c· for your own
Mic 3: 7 ashamed, and the diviners c·:
7:16 The nations shall see and be c·
Zec 10: 5 the riders on horses shall be c·.
Ac 2: 6 came together, and were c·,
9:22 and c· the Jews which dwelt at
1Pe 2: 6 believeth on him shall not be c·.

confused
Isa 9: 5 of the warrior is with c· noise,
Ac 19:32 for the assembly was c·;

confusion
Le 18:23 to lie down thereto: it is c·.
20:12 they have wrought c·; their blood
1Sa 20:30 to thine own c·, and unto the c· of
Ezr 9: 7 and to c· of face, as it is this day.
Job 10:15 I am full of c·; therefore see
Ps 35: 4 be turned back and brought to c·
26 be ashamed and brought to c·
44:15 My c· is continually before me,
70: 2 and put to c·, that desire my hurt.
71: 1 let me never be put to c·.
109:29 themselves with their own c·,
Isa 24:10 The city of c· is broken down:
30: 3 in the shadow of Egypt your c·.
34:11 stretch out upon it the line of c·,
41:29 molten images are wind and c·.
45:16 they shall go to c· together that
61: 7 and for c· they shall rejoice
Jer 3:25 our c· covereth us: for we have
7:19 to the c· of their own faces?
20:11 their everlasting c· shall never
Da 9: 7 but unto us c· of faces, as at this
8 Lord, to us belongeth c· of face,
Ac 19:29 the whole city was filled with c·:
1Co 14:33 For God is not the author of c·,
Jas 3:16 there is c· and every evil work.

congealed
Ex 15: 8 the depths were c· in the heart of

congratulate
1Ch 18:10 and to c' him, because he had

congregation See also CONGREGATIONS.
Ex 12: 3 Speak ye unto all the c' of Israel,
6 whole assembly of the c' of Israel
19 be cut off from the c' of Israel,
47 All the c' of Israel shall keep it.
16: 1 the c' of the children of Israel came
2 And the whole c' of the children of
9 Say unto all the c' of the children
10 Aaron spake unto the whole c' of
22 all the rulers of the c' came and
17: 1 all the c' of the children of Israel
27:21 the tabernacle of the c' without
28:43 in unto the tabernacle of the c',
29: 4 door of the tabernacle of the c',
10 before the tabernacle of the c':
11 door of the tabernacle of the c'.
30 into the tabernacle of the c' of
32 door of the tabernacle of the c'.
42 door of the tabernacle of the c' of
44 sanctify the tabernacle of the c'.
30:16 service of the tabernacle of the c';
18 between the tabernacle of the c'
20 go into the tabernacle of the c',
26 anoint the tabernacle of the c'
36 in the tabernacle of the c', where
31: 7 tabernacle of the c', and the ark
33: 7 called it the Tabernacle of the c'.
7 out unto the tabernacle of the c',
34:31 all the rulers of the c' returned
35: 1 And Moses gathered all the c' of the
4 spake unto all the c' of the children
20 c' of the children of Israel departed
21 work of the tabernacle of the c',
38: 8 door of the tabernacle of the c'.
25 that were numbered of the c'
30 door of the tabernacle of the c',
39:32 tabernacle of the tent of the c'
40 for the tent of the c',
40: 2, 6 tabernacle of the tent of the c'.
7 the tent of the c' and the altar,
12 door of the tabernacle of the c',
22 the table in the tent of the c',
24 candlestick in the tent of the c',
26 the tent of the c' before the vail:
29 tabernacle of the tent of the c',
30 the tent of the c' and the altar,
32 they went into the tent of the c',
34 cloud covered the tent of the c',
35 to enter into the tent of the c',
Le 1: 1 out of the tabernacle of the c',
3 the tabernacle of the c' before
5 door of the tabernacle of the c'.
3: 2 door of the tabernacle of the c':
8, 13 before the tabernacle of the c':
4: 4 tabernacle of the c' before the
5 it to the tabernacle of the c':
7 is in the tabernacle of the c';
7 door of the tabernacle of the c'.
13 And if the whole c' of Israel sin
14 the c' shall offer a young bullock,
14 before the tabernacle of the c'.
15 And the elders of the c' shall lay
16 blood to the tabernacle of the c':
18 that is in the tabernacle of the c',
18 door of the tabernacle of the c'.
21 it is a sin offering for the c'.
6:16 tabernacle of the c' they shall eat
26 court of the tabernacle of the c'.
30 into the tabernacle of the c' to
8: 3 gather thou all the c' together
3, 4 door of the tabernacle of the c'.
5 And Moses said unto the c',
31 door of the tabernacle of the c':
33 tabernacle of the c' in seven days,
35 door of the tabernacle of the c'
9: 5 before the tabernacle of the c';
5 the c' drew near and stood before
23 went into the tabernacle of the c',
10: 7 door of the tabernacle of the c',
9 go into the tabernacle of the c',
17 the iniquity of the c', to make
12: 6 door of the tabernacle of the c',
14:11 door of the tabernacle of the c':
23 door of the tabernacle of the c',
15:14 door of the tabernacle of the c',
29 door of the tabernacle of the c'.
16: 5 shall take of the c' of the children
7 door of the tabernacle of the c'.
16 he do for the tabernacle of the c',
17 man in the tabernacle of the c'
17 and for all the c' of Israel.
20 and the tabernacle of the c',
23 come into the tabernacle of the c',
33 for the tabernacle of the c',
33 and for all the people of the c'.
17: 4, 5, 6, 9 of the tabernacle of the c',
19: 2 Speak unto all the c' of the
21 door of the tabernacle of the c',
24: 3 in the tabernacle of the c', shall
14 and let all the c' stone him.
16 the c' shall certainly stone him:
Nu 1: 1 Sinai, in the tabernacle of the c',
2 Take ye the sum of all the c'
16 were the renowned of the c',
18 they assembled all the c' together
53 there be no wrath upon the c'
2: 2 about the tabernacle of the c'
17 the tabernacle of the c' shall set
3: 7 and the charge of the whole c'
7 before the tabernacle of the c',
8 of the tabernacle of the c',
25 in the tabernacle of the c'
25 door of the tabernacle of the c',
38 before the tabernacle of the c',

Nu 4: 3 work in the tabernacle of the c'.
4 Kohath in the tabernacle of the c',
15 Kohath in the tabernacle of the c'.
23 work in the tabernacle of the c'.
25 and the tabernacle of the c',
25 door of the tabernacle of the c',
28 in the tabernacle of the c':
30 work of the tabernacle of the c'.
31 service in the tabernacle of the c':
33 service in the tabernacle of the c',
34 the chief of the c' numbered the
35 work in the tabernacle of the c':
37 service in the tabernacle of the c',
39 work in the tabernacle of the c',
41 service in the tabernacle of the c',
43 work in the tabernacle of the c',
47 burden in the tabernacle of the c',
6:10, 13 door of the tabernacle of the c':
18 door of the tabernacle of the c',
7: 5 service of the tabernacle of the c';
89 gone into the tabernacle of the c'
8: 9 before the tabernacle of the c':
15 service of the tabernacle of the c':
19 Israel in the tabernacle of the c',
20 all the c' of the children of Israel,
22 service in the tabernacle of the c'
24 service of the tabernacle of the c':
26 brethren in .. tabernacle of the c',
10: 3 door of the tabernacle of the c'.
7 But when the c' is to be gathered
11:16 them unto the tabernacle of the c',
12: 4 three unto the tabernacle of the c'.
13:26 all the c' of the children of Israel,
26 and unto all the c', and shewed
14: 1 And all the c' lifted up their voice,
2 And the whole c' said unto them,
5 assembly of the c' of the children
10 all the c' bade stone them with
10 the tabernacle of the c' before all
27 shall I bear with this evil c',
35 surely do it unto all this evil c',
36 made all the c' to murmur against
15:15 shall be both for you of the c',
24 without the knowledge of the c',
24 that all the c' shall offer one young
25 for the c' of the children of Israel,
26 forgiven all the c' of the children
33 and Aaron, and unto all the c'.
35 the c' shall stone him with stones
36 c' brought him without the camp,
16: 2 the assembly, famous in the c',
3 seeing all the c' are holy, every
3 lift ye up yourselves above the c'
9 separated you from the c' of Israel,
9 to stand before the c' to minister
18 door of the tabernacle of the c'
19 Korah gathered all the c' against
19 door of the tabernacle of the c':
19 the Lord appeared unto all the c'.
21 yourselves from among this c',
22 thou be wroth with all the c'?
24 Speak unto the c', saying, Get you
26 he spake unto the c', saying,
33 they perished from among the c'.
41 morrow all the c' of the children
42 where the c' was gathered against
42 toward the tabernacle of the c':
43 before the tabernacle of the c'.
45 Get you up from among this c',
46 go quickly unto the c', and make
47 and ran into the midst of the c';
50 door of the tabernacle of the c':
17: 4 them up in the tabernacle of the c'
18: 4 charge of the tabernacle of the c',
6 service of the tabernacle of the c'.
21 service of the tabernacle of the c'.
22 come nigh the tabernacle of the c',
23 service of the tabernacle of the c',
31 service in the tabernacle of the c'.
19: 4 tabernacle of the c' seven times:
9 for the c' of the children of Israel
20 shall be cut off from among the c',
20: 1 even the whole c', into the desert
2 And there was no water for the c':
4 have ye brought up the c' of the
6 door of the tabernacle of the c',
8 thou shalt give the c' and their
10 Moses and Aaron gathered the c'
11 the c' drank, and their beasts
12 ye shall not bring this c' into the
22 even the whole c', journeyed from
27 mount Hor in the sight of all the c'.
29 when all the c' saw that Aaron
25: 6 in the sight of all the c' of the
6 door of the tabernacle of the c'.
7 he rose up from among the c',
26: 2 Take the sum of all the c' of the
9 which were famous in the c', who
27: 2 the princes and all the c',
2 door of the tabernacle of the c',
14 in the strife of the c', to sanctify
16 set a man over the c',
17 the c' of the Lord be not as sheep
19 and before all the c'; and give him
20 the c' of the children of Israel may
21 Israel with him, even all the c'.
22 and before all the c':
31:12 unto the c' of the children of Israel,
13 all the princes of the c', went forth
16 was a plague among the c' of the
26 and the chief fathers of the c':
27 to battle, and between all the c':
43 half that pertained unto the c'
54 unto the tabernacle of the c', for a
32: 2 and unto the princes of the c',
4 before the c' of Israel, is a land for

Nu 35:12 until he stand before the c' in
24 c' shall judge between the slayer
25 c' shall deliver the slayer out of
25 the c' shall restore him to the city
De 23: 1, 2 shall not enter into the c' of the
2 shall he not enter into the c' of the
3 Moabite shall not enter into the c'
3 shall they not enter into the c' of
8 of them shall enter into the c'
31:14 in the tabernacle of the c',
14 in the tabernacle of the c'.
30 spake in the ears of all the c' of
33: 4 even the inheritance of the c' of
Jos 8:35 Joshua read not before all the c'
9:15 the princes of the c' sware unto
18 because the princes of the c' had
18 all the c' murmured against the
19 all the princes said unto all the c',
21 drawers of water unto all the c';
27 drawers of water for the c', and for
18: 1 whole c' of the children of Israel
1 set up the tabernacle of the c'
19:51 door of the tabernacle of the c'.
20: 6 until he stand before the c' for
9 until he stood before the c'.
22:12 c' of the children of Israel gathered
16 Thus saith the whole c' of the Lord,
17 was a plague in the c' of the Lord,
18 will be wroth with the whole c' of
20 wrath fell on all the c' of Israel?
30 the princes of the c' and heads of
J'g 20: 1 c' was gathered together as one
21: 5 came not up with the c' unto the
10 c' sent thither twelve thousand
13 the whole c' sent some to speak
16 elders of the c' said, How shall we
1Sa 2:22 door of the tabernacle of the c'.
1Ki 8: 4 the tabernacle of the c', and all
5 c' of Israel, that were assembled
14 blessed all the c' of Israel:
14 (and all the c' of Israel stood;)
22 in the presence of all the c' of
55 blessed all the c' of Israel with a
65 all Israel with him, a great c',
12: 3 Jeroboam and all the c' of Israel
20 sent and called him unto the c',
1Ch 6:32 place of the tabernacle of the c'
9:21 door of the tabernacle of the c'.
13: 2 David said unto all the c' of
4 the c' said that they would do so:
23:32 charge of the tabernacle of the c',
28: 8 of all Israel the c' of the Lord,
29: 1 the king said unto all the c',
10 blessed the Lord before all the c':
20 David said to all the c', Now bless
20 all the c' blessed the Lord God
2Ch 1: 3 Solomon, and all the c' with him,
3 there was the tabernacle of the c'
5 Solomon and the c' sought unto it.
6 was at the tabernacle at the c',
13 before the tabernacle of the c',
5: 5 ark, and the tabernacle of the c',
6 c' of Israel that were assembled
6: 3 blessed the whole c' of Israel:
3 and all the c' of Israel stood.
12 the presence of all the c' of Israel,
13 upon his knees before all the c' of
7: 8 Israel with him, a very great c',
20: 5 stood in the c' of Judah and
14 of the Lord in the midst of the c';
23: 3 all the c' made a covenant with
24: 6 and of the c' of Israel, for the
28:14 before the princes and all the c'.
29:23 offering before the king and the c';
28 all the c' worshipped, and the
31 the c' brought in sacrifices and
32 burnt offerings, which the c' brought,
30: 2 all the c' in Jerusalem, to keep
4 pleased the king and all the c'.
13 the second month, a very great c'.
17 there were many in the c' that
24 give to the c' a thousand bullocks
24 princes gave to the c' a thousand
25 all the c' of Judah, with the priests
25 all the c' that came out of Israel,
31:18 their daughters, through all the c':
Ezr 2:64 whole c' together was forty and two
10: 1 a very great c' of men and women
8 himself separated from the c' of
12 Then all the c' answered and said
14 now our rulers of all the c' stand,
Ne 5:13 all the c' said, Amen, and praised
7:66 whole c' together was forty and two
8: 2 brought the law before the c' both
17 all the c' of them that were come
13: 1 not come into the c' of God
Job 15:34 c' of hypocrites shall be desolate,
30:28 I stood up, and I cried in the c'.
Ps 1: 5 sinners in the c' of the righteous.
7: 7 shall the c' of the people compass
22:22 midst of the c' will I praise thee.
25 shall be of thee in the great c':
26: 5 have hated the c' of evil doers;
35:18 give thee thanks in the great c':
40: 9 righteousness in the great c':
10 and thy truth from the great c'.
58: 1 speak righteousness, O c'?
68:10 Thy c' hath dwelt therein: thou,
74: 2 Remember thy c', which thou hast
19 forget not the c' of thy poor
75: 2 When I shall receive the c' I will
82: 1 God standeth in the c' of the
89: 5 faithfulness also in the c' of the
107:32 him also in the c' of the people,
111: 1 of the upright, and in the c'.
149: 1 and his praise in the c' of saints.

Pr 5:14 in all evil in the midst of the c·
21:16 shall remain in the c· of the dead.
26:26 be shewed before the whole c·.
Isa 14:13 sit also upon the mount of the c·,
Jer 6:18 know, O c·, what is among them.
30:20 and their c· shall be established
La 1:10 they should not enter into thy c·.
Ho 7:12 chastise them, as their c· hath
Joe 2:16 Gather the people, sanctify the c·,
Mic 2: 5 a cord by lot in the c· of the Lord.
Ac 13:43 Now when the c· was broken up,

congregations
Ps 26:12 in the c· will I bless the Lord.
68:26 Bless ye God in the c·, even the
74: 4 roar in the midst of thy c·;

Coniah *(co-ni'-ah)* See also JEHOIACHIN.
Jer 22:24 though C· the son of Jehoiakim
28 this man C· a despised broken idol?
37: 1 son of Josiah reigned instead of C·

conies
Ps 104:18 goats; and the rocks for the c·.
Pr 30:26 The c· are but a feeble folk, yet

Cononiah *(co-no-ni'-ah)* See also CONANIAH.
2Ch 31:12 over which C· the Levite was ruler,
13 overseers under the hand of C·

conquer See also CONQUERING.
Re 6: 2 went forth conquering, and to c·.

conquering
Re 6: 2 he went forth c·, and to conquer.

conquerors
Ro 8:37 we are more than c· through him

conscience See also CONSCIENCES.
Joh 8: 9 being convicted by their own c·,
Ac 23: 1 have lived in all good c· before God
24:16 to have always a c· void of offence
Ro 2:15 their c· also bearing witness, and
9: 1 my c· also bearing me witness.
13: 5 for wrath, but also for c· sake.
1Co 8: 7 for some with c· of the idol unto
7 and their c· being weak is defiled.
10 shall not the c· of him which is weak
12 and wound their weak c·, ye sin
10:25 eat, asking no question for c· sake:
27 eat, asking no question for c· sake.
28 sake that showed it, and for c· sake:
29 C·, I say, not thine own, but of the
29 liberty judged of another man's c·?
2Co 1:12 is this, the testimony of our c·,
4: 2 ourselves to every man's c· in the
1Ti 1: 5 a good c·, and of faith unfeigned:
19 Holding faith, and a good c;
3: 9 mystery of the faith in a pure c·.
4: 2 their c· seared with a hot iron;
2Ti 1: 3 from my forefathers with pure c·,
Tit 1:15 even their mind and c· is defiled.
Heb 9: 9 perfect, as pertaining to the c·;
14 purge your c· from dead works
10: 2 should have had no more c· of sins.
22 hearts sprinkled from an evil c·,
13:18 we trust we have a good c·,
1Pe 2:19 if a man for c· toward God endure
3:16 Having a good c·; that whereas
21 answer of a good c· toward God,)

consciences
2Co 5:11 also are made manifest in your c·.

consecrate See also CONSECRATED.
Ex 28: 3 make Aaron's garments to c· him,
41 anoint them, and c· them,
29: 9 shalt c· Aaron and his sons.
33 to c· and to sanctify them:
35 seven days shalt thou c· them.
30:30 Aaron and his sons, and c· them,
32:29 C· yourselves to day to the
Le 8:33 for seven days shall he c· you.
16:32 he shall c· to minister in
Nu 6:12 And he shall c· unto the Lord the
1Ch 29: 5 c· his service this day unto
2Ch 13: 9 to c· himself with a young
Eze 43:26 and they shall c· themselves.
Mic 4:13 and I will c· their gain unto the

consecrated
Ex 29:29 anointed therein, and to be c·
Le 21:10 and that is c· to put on the
Nu 3: 3 whom he c· to minister in the
Jos 6:19 of brass and iron, are c· unto the
J'g 17: 5 and c· one of his sons,
12 And Micah c· the Levite;
1Ki 13:33 he c· him, and he became one
2Ch 26:18 Aaron, that are c· to burn incense:
29:31 have c· yourselves unto the
33 the c· things were six hundred
31: 6 which were c· unto the Lord their
Ezr 3: 5 set feasts of the Lord that were c·
Heb 7:28 the Son, who is c· for evermore.
10:20 way, which he hath c· for us,

consecration See also CONSECRATIONS.
Ex 29:22 for it is a ram of c·:
26 breast of the ram of Aaron's c·,
27 of the ram of the c·, even of that
31 thou shalt take the ram of the c·,
Le 8:22 the other ram, the ram of c·:
29 of the ram of c· it was Moses' part;
33 until the days of your c· be at an
Nu 6: 7 because the c· of his God is upon
9 he hath defiled the head of his c·;

consecrations
Ex 29:34 And if ought of the flesh of the c·,
Le 7:37 and of the c·, and of the sacrifice
8:28 they were c· for a sweet savour:
31 bread that is in the basket of c·,

consent See also CONSENTED; CONSENTING.
Ge 34:15 But in this will we c· unto you:
22 Only herein will the men c· unto us
23 only let us c· unto them, and they
De 13: 8 Thou shalt not c· unto him,
J'g 11:17 but he would not c·:
1Sa 11: 7 and they came out with one c·.
1Ki 20: 8 him, Hearken not unto him, nor c·.
Ps 83: 5 consulted together with one c·:
Pr 1:10 if sinners entice thee, c· thou not.
Ho 6: 9 priests murder in the way by c·:
Zep 3: 9 the Lord, to serve him with one c·.
Lu 14:18 with one c· began to make excuse.
Ro 7:16 I c· unto the law that it is good.
1Co 7: 5 except it be with c· for a time,
1Ti 6: 3 and c· not to wholesome words,

consented See also CONSENTEDST.
2Ki 12: 8 the priests c· to receive no more
Da 1:14 So he c· to them in this matter,
Lu 23:51 same had not c· to the counsel and
Ac 18:20 longer time with them, he c· not;

consentedst
Ps 50:18 then thou c· with him, and hast

consenting
Ac 8: 1 And Saul was c· unto his death.
22:20 standing by, and c· unto his death,

consider See also CONSIDERED; CONSIDEREST; CONSIDERETH; CONSIDERING.
Ex 33:13 and c· that this nation is thy
Le 13:13 Then the priest shall c·: and,
De 4:39 Know therefore this day, and c·
8: 5 Thou shalt also c· in thine heart,
32: 7 c· the years of many generations:
29 that they would c· their latter end!
J'g 18:14 now therefore c· what ye have to
19:30 c· of it, take advice, and speak
1Sa 12:24 for c· how great things he hath
25:17 therefore know and c· what thou
2Ki 5: 7 wherefore c·, I pray you, and see
Job 11:11 wickedness also; will he not then c·
23:15 when I c·, I am afraid of him.
34:27 and would not c· any of his ways:
37:14 and c· the wondrous works of God.
Ps 5: 1 O Lord, c· my meditation.
8: 3 When I c· thy heavens, the work
9:13 c· my trouble which I suffer of
13: 3 C· and hear me, O Lord my God:
25:19 C· mine enemies; for they are
37:10 thou shalt diligently c· his place,
45:10 Hearken, O daughter, and c·,
48:13 well her bulwarks, c· her palaces;
50:22 Now c· this, ye that forget God,
64: 9 they shall wisely c· of his doing.
119:95 I will c· thy testimonies.
153 C· mine affliction, and deliver me:
159 C· how I love thy precepts:
Pr 6: 6 the ant, thou sluggard; c· her ways,
23: 1 c· diligently what is before thee:
24:12 he that pondereth the heart c· it?
Ec 5: 1 for they c· not that they do evil.
7:13 C· the work of God: for who
14 in the day of adversity c·: God also
Isa 1: 3 not know, my people doth not c·.
5:12 neither c· the operation of his
14:16 narrowly look upon thee, and c· thee
18: 4 I will c· in my dwelling place
41:20 they may see, and know, and c·,
22 that we may c· them, and
43:18 neither c· the things of old.
52:15 they had not heard shall they c·.
Jer 2:10 and c· diligently, and see if there
9:17 C· ye, and call for the mourning
23:20 in the latter days ye shall c· it
30:24 in the latter days ye shall c· it.
La 1:11 see, O Lord, and c·; for I am
2:20 Behold, O Lord, and c· to whom
5: 1 c·, and behold our reproach.
Eze 12: 3 may be they will c·, though they
Da 9:23 the matter, and c· the vision.
Ho 7: 2 they c· not in their hearts that I
Hag 1: 5, 7 hosts; C· your ways.
2:15 c· from this day and upward,
18 C· now from this day and
18 Lord's temple was laid, c· it.
M't 6:28 C· the lilies of the field, how they
Lu 12:24 C· the ravens: for they neither
27 C· the lilies how they grow: they
Joh 11:50 Nor c· that it is expedient for us,
Ac 15: 6 came together for to c· of this
2Ti 2: 7 C· what I say; and the Lord give
Heb 3: 1 c· the Apostle and High Priest
7: 4 Now c· how great this man was,
10:24 let us c· one another to provoke
12: 3 For c· him that endured such

considered
1Ki 3:21 but when I had c· it in the morning,
5: 8 I have c· the things which thou
Job 1: 8 Hast thou c· my servant Job,
2: 3 Hast thou c· my servant Job,
Ps 31: 7 thou hast c· my trouble; thou
77: 5 have c· the days of old, the years
Pr 24:32 I saw, and c· it well: I looked 7896,
Ec 4: 1 and c· all the oppressions that
4 Again, I c· all travail, and every
15 I c· all the living which walk
9: 1 I c· in my heart even to declare
Da 7: 8 I c· the horns, and, behold, there
M'r 6:52 For they c· not the miracle of the
Ac 11: 6 I c·, and saw fourfooted beasts
12:12 And when he had c· the thing,
Ro 4:19 he c· not his own body now dead,

considerest
Jer 33:24 C· thou not what this people have
M't 7: 3 but c· not the beam that is in

considereth
Ps 33:15 hearts alike; he c· all their works.
41: 1 Blessed is he that c· the poor:
Pr 21:12 wisely c· the house of the wicked:
28:22 c· not that poverty shall come
29: 7 The righteous c· the cause of the
31:16 She c· a field, and buyeth it:
Isa 44:19 none c· in his heart, neither is
Eze 18:14 and c·, and doeth not such like,
28 Because he c·, and turneth away

considering
Isa 57: 1 none c· that the righteous is taken
Da 8: 5 I was c·, behold, an he goat came
Ga 6: 1 c· thyself, lest thou also be
Heb 13: 7 c· the end of their conversation.

consist See also CONSISTETH.
Col 1:17 things, and by him all things c·.

consisteth
Lu 12:15 man's life c· not in the abundance

consolation See also CONSOLATIONS.
Jer 16: 7 give them the cup of c· to drink
Lu 2:25 waiting for the c· of Israel:
6:24 for ye have received your c·.
Ac 4:36 being interpreted, The son of c·,)
15:31 had read, they rejoiced for the c·.
Ro 15: 5 the God of patience and c· grant
2Co 1: 5 in us, so our c· also aboundeth
6 it is for your c· and salvation,
6 we be comforted, it is for your c·
7 so shall ye be also of the c·.
7: 7 but by the c· wherewith he was
Ph'p 2: 1 any c· in Christ, if any comfort
2Th 2:16 given us everlasting c· and good
Ph'm 7 we have great joy and c· in thy
Heb 6:18 we might have a strong c·, who

consolations
Job 15:11 Are the c· of God small with thee?
21: 2 my speech, and let this be your c·.
Isa 66:11 satisfied with the breasts of her c·;

consorted
Ac 17: 4 believed, and c· with Paul and

conspiracy
2Sa 15:12 the c· was strong; for the people
2Ki 12:20 servants arose, and made a c·, and
14:19 Now they made a c· against
15:15 acts of Shallum, and his c·
30 the son of Elah made a c·
17: 4 the king of Assyria found c· in
2Ch 25:27 they made a c· against him
Jer 11: 9 the Lord said unto me, A c· is
Eze 22:25 There is a c· of her prophets in the
Ac 23:13 than forty which had made this c·.

conspirators
2Sa 15:31 Ahithophel is among the c· with

conspired
Ge 37:18 they c· against him to slay him.
1Sa 22: 8 all of you have c· against me, and
13 Why have ye c· against me, thou
1Ki 15:27 c· against him; and Baasha smote
16: 9 c· against him, as he was in Tirzah
16 Zimri hath c·, and hath also slain
2Ki 9:14 Jehoshaphat the son of Nimshi c·
10: 9 I c· against my master, and slew
15:10 And Shallum the son of Jabesh c·
25 c· against him, and smote him in
21:23 And the servants of Amon c·
24 that had c· against king Amon;
2Ch 24:21 And they c· against him, and
25 his own servants c· against him for
26 And these are they that c· against
33:24 And his servants c· against him,
25 slew all them that had c· against
Ne 4: 8 c· all of them together to come
Am 7:10 Amos hath c· against thee in the

constant
1Ch 28: 7 he be c· to do my commandments

constantly
Pr 21:28 man that heareth speaketh c·.
Ac 12:15 she c· affirmed that it was even
Tit 3: 8 things I will that thou affirm c·,

constellations
Isa 13:10 stars of heaven and the c· thereof

constrain See also CONSTRAINED; CONSTRAINETH.
Ga 6:12 they c· you to be circumcised;

constrained
2Ki 4: 8 she c· him to eat bread. And so
M't 14:22 Jesus c· his disciples to get into a
M'r 6:45 straightway he c· his disciples to
Lu 24:29 But they c· him, saying, Abide
Ac 16:15 And she c· us.
28:19 I was c· to appeal unto Cæsar;

constraineth
Job 32:18 the spirit within me c· me.
2Co 5:14 the love of Christ c· us; because

constraint
1Pe 5: 2 thereof, not by c·, but willingly;

consult See also CONSULTED; CONSULTETH.
Ps 62: 4 They only c· to cast him down

consultation
M'r 15: 1 priests held a c· with the elders

consulted
1Ki 12: 6 Rehoboam c· with the old men,
8 and c· with the young men that
1Ch 13: 1 And David c· with the captains of
2Ch 20:21 when he had c· with the people,
Ne 5: 7 Then I c· with myself, and I
Ps 83: 3 and c· against thy hidden ones.
5 have c· together with one consent:
Eze 21:21 he c· with images, he looked in

Da 6: 7 have c' together to establish a
Mic 6: 5 now what Balak, king of Moab c',
Hab 2:10 Thou hast c' shame to thy house
M't 26: 4 c' that they might take Jesus by
Joh 12:10 the chief priests c' that they

consulter
De 18:11 or a c' with familiar spirits, or a

consulteth
Lu 14:31 c' whether he be able with ten

consume See also CONSUMED; CONSUMETH; CONSUMING.
Ge 41:30 and the famine shall c' the land;
Ex 32:10 that I may c' them: and I will
12 c' them from the face of the earth?
33: 3 people: lest I c' thee in the way.
5 in a moment, and c' thee: therefore
Le 26:16 that shall c' the eyes, and cause
Nu 16:21 that I may c' them in a moment.
45 that I may c' them as in a moment.
De 5:25 this great fire will c' us: if we
7:16 And thou shalt c' all the people
22 thou mayest not c' them at once,
28:38 for the locust shall c' it.
42 of thy land shall the locust c'.
32:22 and shall c' the earth with her
Jos 24:20 turn and do you hurt, and c' you,
1Sa 2:33 to c' thine eyes, and to grieve thine
2Ki 1:10, 12 heaven, and c' thee and thy fifty.
Ne 9:31 thou didst not utterly c' them,
Es 9:24 to c' them, and to destroy them;
Job 15:34 shall c' the tabernacles of bribery.
20:26 a fire not blown shall c' him; it
24:19 and heat c' the snow waters:
Ps 37:20 c'; into smoke shall they c' away.
39:11 thou makest his beauty to c' away
49:14 their beauty shall c' in the grave
59:13 C' them in wrath, c' them, that
78:33 their days did he c' in vanity,
Isa 7:20 and it shall also c' the beard.
10:18 shall c' the glory of his forest,
27:10 down, and c' the branches thereof.
Jer 8:13 surely c' them, saith the Lord:
14:12 I will c' them by the sword, and
49:27 shall c' the palaces of Ben-hadad.
Eze 4:17 and c' away for their iniquity.
13:13 hailstones in my fury to c' it.
20:13 them in the wilderness, to c' them.
21:28 to c' because of the glittering:
22:15 will c' thy filthiness out of thee.
24:10 kindle the fire, c' the flesh, and
35:12 desolate, they are given us to c'.
Da 2:44 and c' all these kingdoms, and it
7:26 c' and to destroy it unto the end.
Ho 11: 6 and shall c' his branches, and
Zep 1: 2 c' all things from off the land,
3 I will c' man and beast;
3 I will c' the fowls of heaven,
Zec 5: 4 and shall c' it with the timber
14:12 Their flesh shall c' away
12 eyes shall c' away in their holes,
12 and their tongue shall c' away in
Lu 9:54 down from heaven, and c' them,
2Th 2: 8 the Lord shall c' with the spirit
Jas 4: 3 that ye may c' it upon your lusts.

consumed
Ge 19:15 lest thou be c' in the iniquity of
17 to the mountain, lest thou be c'.
31:40 in the day the drought c' me, and
Ex 3: 2 with fire, and the bush was not c'.
15: 7 wrath, which c' them as stubble.
22: 6 standing corn, or the field, be c'
Le 6:10 which the fire hath c' with the
9:24 and c' upon the altar the burnt
Nu 11: 1 and c' them that were in the
12:12 the flesh is half c' when he cometh
14:35 in this wilderness they shall be c',
16:26 lest ye be c' in all their sins.
35 c' the two hundred and fifty men
17:13 shall we be c' with dying?
21:28 hath c' Ar of Moab, and the lords
25:11 I c' not the children of Israel in
32:13 in the sight of the Lord, was c'.
De 2:15 among the host, until they were c'.
16 when all the men of war were c'
28:21 he have c' thee from off the land,
Jos 5: 6 which came out of Egypt, were c',
8:24 of the sword, until they were c',
10:20 great slaughter, till they were c',
J'g 6:21 and c' the flesh and the unleavened
1Sa 12:25 ye shall be c', both ye and your
15:18 fight against them until they be c'.
2Sa 21: 5 The man that c' us, and that
22:38 not again until I had c' them.
39 I have c' them, and wounded them,
1Ki 18:38 and c' the burnt sacrifice, and the
22:11 Syrians, until thou have c' them.
2Ki 1:10 heaven, and c' him and his fifty.
12 God came down from heaven, and c'
7:13 of the Israelites that are c':)
13:17 Syrians in Aphek, till thou have c'
19 smitten Syria till thou hadst c' it:
2Ch 7: 1 and c' the burnt offering and the
8: 8 whom the children of Israel c' not,
18:10 shalt push Syria until they be c'.
Ezr 9:14 till thou hadst c' us, so that
Ne 2: 3 the gates thereof are c' with fire?
13 the gates thereof were c' with fire.
Job 1:16 sheep, and the servants, and c' them;
4: 9 breath of his nostrils are they c'.
6:17 hot, they are c' out of their place.
7: 9 cloud is c' and vanisheth away:
19:27 though my reins be c' within me.
33:21 His flesh is c' away, that it cannot
Ps 6: 7 Mine eye is c' because of grief;
18:37 did I turn again till they were c'.
31: 9 mine eye is c' with grief, yea,
10 iniquity, and my bones are c'.
39:10 I am c' by the blow of thine hand.
71:13 Let them be confounded and c'
73:19 they are utterly c' with terrors.
78:63 The fire c' their young men; and
90: 7 we are c' by thine anger, and
102: 3 For my days are c' like smoke,
104:35 Let the sinners be c' out of the
119:87 They had almost c' me upon
139 My zeal hath c' me, because mine
Pr 5:11 thy flesh and thy body are c',
Isa 1:28 that forsake the Lord shall be c'.
16: 4 the oppressors are c' out of the
29:20 scorner is c', and all that watch
64: 7 c' us, because of our iniquities.
66:17 shall be c' together, saith the
Jer 5: 3 thou hast c' them, but they have
6:29 the lead is c' of the fire; the
9:16 after them, till I have c' them.
10:25 devoured him, and c' him, and
12: 4 the beasts are c', and the birds;
14:15 famine shall those prophets be c'.
16: 4 they shall be c' by the sword, and
20:18 my days should be c' with shame?
24:10 till they be c' from off the land
27: 8 until I have c' them by his hand.
36:23 until all the roll was c' in the fire
44:12 and they shall all be c', and fall
12 they shall even be c' by the sword
18 have been c' by the sword and by
27 are in the land of Egypt shall be c'
49:37 after them, till I have c' them:
La 2:22 brought up hath mine enemy c'.
3:22 Lord's mercies that we are not c',
Eze 5:12 with famine shall they be c' in the
13:14 ye shall be c' in the midst thereof:
19:12 and withered; the fire c' them.
22:31 I have c' them with the fire of my
24:11 that the scum of it may be c'.
34:29 be no more c' with hunger in the
43: 8 wherefore I have c' them in mine
47:12 shall the fruit thereof be c':
Da 11:16 which by his hand shall be c'.
Mal 3: 6 ye sons of Jacob are not c'.
Ga 5:15 take heed that ye be not c' one of

consumeth
Job 13:28 he, as a rotten thing, c', as a
22:20 the remnant of them the fire c'.
31:12 it is a fire that c' to destruction,
Isa 5:24 flame c' the chaff, so their root

consuming
De 4:24 the Lord thy God is a c' fire,
9: 3 as a c' fire he shall destroy them,
Heb 12:29 For our God is a c' fire.

consummation
Da 9:27 until the c', and that determined

consumption
Le 26:16 terror, c', and the burning ague,
De 28:22 The Lord shall smite thee with a c',
Isa 10:22 the c' decreed shall overflow with
23 God of hosts shall make a c',
28:22 a c', even determined upon the

contain See also CONTAINED; CONTAINETH; CONTAINING.
1Ki 8:27 heaven of heavens cannot c' thee;
18:32 great as would c' two measures of
2Ch 2: 6 heaven of heavens cannot c' him?
6:18 heaven of heavens cannot c' thee;
Eze 45:11 that the bath may c' the tenth
Joh 21:25 even the world itself could not c'
1Co 7: 9 if they cannot c', let them marry:

contained
1Ki 7:26 of lilies: it c' two thousand baths.
38 of brass: one laver c' forty baths:
Ro 2:14 by nature the things c' in the law,
Eph 2:15 of commandments c' in ordinances;
1Pe 2: 6 also it is c' in the scripture,

containeth
Eze 23:32 and had in derision; it c' much.

containing
Joh 2: 6 of the Jews, c' two or three firkins

contemn See also CONTEMNED; CONTEMNETH.
Ps 10:13 Wherefore doth the wicked c' God?
Eze 21:13 what if the sword c' even the rod?

contemned
Ps 15: 4 In whose eyes a vile person is c';
107:11 c' the council of the most High:
Ca 8: 7 for love, it would utterly be c'.
Isa 16:14 and the glory of Moab shall be c',

contemneth
Eze 21:10 it c' the rod of my son, as every

contempt See also CONTEMPTIBLE.
Es 1:18 shall there arise too much c' and
Job 12:21 He poureth c' upon princes, and
31:34 or did the c' of families terrify me,
Ps 107:40 He poureth c' upon princes, and
119:22 Remove from me reproach and c';
123: 3 for we are exceedingly filled with c'.
4 at ease, and with the c' of the proud.
Pr 18: 3 wicked cometh, then cometh also c',
Isa 23: 9 to bring into c' all the honourable
Da 12: 2 some to shame and everlasting c'.

contemptible
Mal 1: 7 ye say, The table of the Lord is c'.
12 the fruit thereof, even his meat, is c'.
2: 9 have I also made you c' and base
2Co 10:10 is weak, and his speech c'.

contemptuously
Ps 31:18 and c' against the righteous.

contend See also CONTENDED; CONTENDEST; CONTENDETH; CONTENDING.
De 2: 9 neither c' with them in battle:
24 possess it, and c' with him in battle.
Job 9: 3 If he will c' with him, he cannot
13: 8 his person? will ye c' for God?
Pr 28: 4 such as keep the law c' with them.
Ec 6:10 neither may he c' with him that
Isa 49:25 I will c' with him that contendeth
50: 8 who will c' with me? let us stand
57:16 I will not c' for ever, neither will I
Jer 12: 5 how canst thou c' with horses?
18:19 the voice of them that c' with me.
Am 7: 4 the Lord God called to c' by fire,
Mic 6: 1 c' thou before the mountains, and
Jude 3 ye should earnestly c' for the faith

contended
Ne 13:11 Then c' I with the rulers, and
17 Then I c' with the nobles of Judah,
25 I c' with them, and cursed them,
Job 31:13 when they c' with me;
Isa 41:12 them, even them that c' with thee:
Ac 11: 2 of the circumcision c' with him,

contendest
Job 10: 2 me wherefore thou c' with me.

contendeth
Job 40: 2 Shall he that c' with the Almighty
Pr 29: 9 If a wise man c' with a foolish
Isa 49:25 with him that c' with thee, and

contending
Jude 9 when c' with the devil he disputed

content
Ge 37:27 flesh. And his brethren were c'.
Ex 2:21 And Moses was c' to dwell with
Le 10:20 Moses heard that, he was c'.*3190.
Jos 7: 7 would to God we had been c', and
J'g 17:11 And the Levite was c' to dwell
19: 6 Be c', I pray thee, and tarry all
2Ki 5:23 Naaman said, Be c', take two
6: 3 one said, Be c', I pray thee, and go
Job 6:28 Now therefore be c', look upon
Pr 6:35 neither will he rest c', though thou
M'r 15:15 Pilate, willing to c' the
Lu 3:14 and be c' with your wages.
Ph'p 4:11 state I am, therewith to be c'.
1Ti 6: 8 raiment let us be therewith c'.
Heb 13: 5 be c' with such things as ye have:
3Jo 10 with malicious words: and not c'

contention See CONTENTIONS.
Pr 13:10 by pride cometh c': but with the
17:14 leave off c', before it be meddled
18: 6 A fool's lips enter into c', and his
22:10 out the scorner, and c' shall go out;
Jer 15:10 a man of c' to the whole earth!
Hab 1: 3 there are that raise up strife and c'.
Ac 15:39 And the c' was so sharp between
Ph'p 1:16 The one preach Christ of c', not
1Th 2: 2 the gospel of God with much c'.

contentions
Pr 18:18 The lot causeth c' to cease, and
19 and their c' are like the bars of a
19:13 the c' of a wife are a continual
23:29 who hath c'? who hath babbling?
1Co 1:11 that there are c' among you.
Tit 3: 9 genealogies, and c', and strivings

contentious
Pr 21:19 with a c' and an angry woman.
26:21 so is a c' man to kindle strife.
27:15 rainy day and a c' woman are alike.
Ro 2: 8 But unto them that are c',
1Co 11:16 But if any man seem to be c',

contentment
1Ti 6: 6 godliness with c' is great gain.

continence See INCONTINENCY.

continual
Ex 29:42 a c' burnt offering throughout
Nu 4: 7 the c' bread shall be thereon:
28: 3 day by day, for a c' burnt offering.
6 It is a c' burnt offering, which was
10 the c' burnt offering, and his drink
15 offered, beside the c' burnt offering,
23 which is for a c' burnt offering.
24 offered beside the c' burnt offering,
31 them beside the c' burnt offering,
29:11 and the c' burnt offering, and the
16 beside the c' burnt offering, his
19, 22 beside the c' burnt offering, and
25 beside the c' burnt offering, his
28 beside the c' burnt offering, and
31, 34 beside the c' burnt offering, his
38 beside the c' burnt offering, and
2Ki 25:30 his allowance was a c' allowance
2Ch 2: 4 for the c' shewbread, and for the
Ezr 3: 5 the c' burnt offering, both of the
Ne 10:33 for the c' meat offering,
33 and for the c' burnt offering,
Pr 15:15 of a merry heart hath a c' feast.
19:13 of a wife are a c' dropping.
27:15 A c' dropping in a very rainy day
Isa 14: 6 wrath with a c' stroke,
Jer 48: 5 c' weeping shall go up; for in
52:34 a c' diet given him of the king
Eze 39:14 sever out men of c' employment,
46:15 morning for a c' burnt offering.
Lu 18: 5 lest by her c' coming
Ro 9: 2 great heaviness and c' sorrow

continually
Ge 6: 5 of his heart was only evil c'.
8: 3 returned from off the earth c':
5 decreased c' until the tenth month:
Ex 28:29 a memorial before the Lord c'.
30 upon his heart before the Lord c'.

Ex 29:38 of the first year day by day c'.
Le 24: 2 to cause the lamps to burn c'.
3 the morning before the Lord c':
4 pure candlestick before the Lord c'.
8 set it in order before the Lord c',
Jos 6:13 went on c', and blew with the
1Sa 18:29 became David's enemy c'.
2Sa 9: 7 shalt eat bread at my table c'.
13 he did eat c' at the king's table;
15:12 people increased c' with Absalom.
19:13 of the host before me c'
1Ki 10: 8 which stand c' before thee,
2Ki 4: 9 of God, which passeth by us c'.
25:29 he did eat bread c' before him
1Ch 16: 6 with trumpets c' before the ark
11 his strength, seek his face c'.
37 to minister before the ark c',
40 the altar of the burnt offering c'
23:31 unto them, c' before the Lord:
2Ch 9: 7 which stand c' before thee,
12:15 Rehoboam and Jeroboam c'.
24:14 house of the Lord c' all the days
Job 1: 5 Thus did Job c'.
Ps 34: 1 praise shall c' be in my mouth.
35:27 let them say c', Let the Lord be
38:17 and my sorrow is c' before me.
40:11 and thy truth c' preserve me.
16 salvation say c', The Lord be
42: 3 and night, while they c' say
44:15 My confusion is c' before
50: 8 to have been c' before me.
52: 1 goodness of God endureth c'.
58: 7 away as waters which run c':
69:23 and make their loins c' to shake.
70: 4 say c', Let God be magnified.
71: 3 whereunto I may c' resort:
6 my praise shall be c' of thee.
14 I will hope c', and will yet praise
72:15 also shall be made for him c';
73:23 Nevertheless I am c' with thee:
74:23 rise up against thee increaseth c'.
109:10 his children be c' vagabonds,
15 Let them be before the Lord c',
19 girdle wherewith he is girded c'.
119:44 So shall I keep thy law c' for ever
109 My soul is c' in my hand:
117 have respect unto thy statutes c'.
140: 2 c' are they gathered together
Pr 6:14 he deviseth mischief c';
21 Bind them c' upon thine heart,
Ec 1: 6 it whirleth about c', and the wind
Isa 21: 8 I stand c' upon the watchtower
49:16 thy walls are c' before me.
51:13 hast feared c' every day because
52: 5 name c' every day is blasphemed.
58:11 And the Lord shall guide thee c',
60:11 thy gates shall be open c';
65: 3 that provoketh me to anger c'
Jer 6: 7 before me c' is grief and wounds.
33:18 and to do sacrifice c'.
52:33 he did c' eat bread before him
Eze 46:14 offering c' by a perpetual ordinance
Da 6:16 Thy God whom thou servest c',
20 is thy God, whom thou servest c',
Ho 4:18 they have committed whoredom c':
12: 6 and wait on thy God c'.
Ob 16 so shall all the heathen drink c',
Na 3:19 hath not thy wickedness passed c'?
Hab 1:17 not spare c' to slay the nations?
Lu 24:53 And were c' in the temple,
Ac 6: 4 will give ourselves c' to prayer,
10: 7 of them that waited on him c';
Ro 13: 6 attending c' upon this very thing.
Heb 7: 3 of God; abideth a priest c'.
10: 1 offered year by year c' make
13:15 the sacrifice of praise to God c',

continuance
De 28:59 great plagues, and of long c',
59 and sore sicknesses, and of long c'.
Ps 139:16 which in c' were fashioned,
Isa 64: 5 in those is c', and we shall be
Ro 2: 7 by patient c' in well doing seek

continue See also CONTINUED; CONTINUETH; CONTINUING.
Ex 21:21 if he c' a day or two, he shall not
Le 12: 4 she shall then c' in the blood of
5 she shall c' in the blood of her
1Sa 12:14 c' following the Lord your God:
13:14 now thy kingdom shall not c':
2Sa 7:29 it may c' for ever before thee:
1Ki 2: 4 That the Lord may c' his word
Job 15:29 neither shall his substance c',
17: 2 doth not mine eye c' in their
Ps 36:10 c' thy lovingkindness unto them
49:11 is, that their houses shall c' for ever,
102:28 children of thy servants shall c',
119:91 They c' this day according to
Isa 5:11 that c' until night, till wine
Jer 32:14 that they may c' many days.
Da 11: 8 shall c' more years than the king
M't 15:32 they c' with me now three days,
Joh 8:31 If ye c' in my word, then are ye
15: 9 I loved you: c' ye in my love.
Ac 13:43 them to c' in the grace of God.
14:22 exhorting them to c' in the faith,
26:22 I c' unto this day, witnessing
Ro 6: 1 Shall we c' in sin, that grace
11:22 if thou c' in his goodness:
Gal 2: 5 of the gospel might c' with you.
Ph'p 1:25 I shall abide and c' with you all
Col 1:23 If ye c' in the faith grounded
4: 2 C' in prayer, and watch in the
1Ti 2:15 if they c' in faith and charity
4:16 c' in them: for in doing this thou
2Ti 3:14 c' thou in the things which thou
Heb 7:23 suffered to c' by reason of death:
13: 1 Let brotherly love c'.
Jas 4:13 and c' there a year, and buy,
2Pe 3: 4 all things c' as they were from
1Jo 2:24 remain in you, ye also shall c'
Re 13: 5 him to c' forty and two months.
17:10 cometh, he must c' a short space.

continued
Ge 40: 4 and they c' a season in ward.
J'g 5:17 Asher c' on the seashore,
Ru 1: 2 country of Moab, and c' there.
2: 7 hath c' even from the morning
1Sa 1:12 she c' praying before the Lord,
2Sa 6:11 ark of the Lord c' in the house
1Ki 22: 1 they c' three years without war
2Ch 29:28 this c' until the burnt offering
Ne 5:16 also I c' in the work of this wall,
Job 27: 1 Moreover Job c' his parable, and
29: 1 Moreover Job c' his parable, and
Ps 72:17 shall be c' as long as the sun:
Da 1:21 And Daniel c' even unto the
Lu 6:12 and c' all night in prayer to God.
22:28 c' with me in my temptations
Joh 2:12 they c' there not many days.
8: 7 So when they c' asking him,
11:54 and there c' with his disciples.
Ac 1:14 all c' with one accord in prayer
2:42 they c' steadfastly in the apostles'
8:13 he c' with Philip, and wondered,
12:16 But Peter c' knocking, and when
15:35 Paul also and Barnabas c' in
18:11 c' there a year and six months,
19:10 c' by the space of two years;
20: 7 and c' his speech until midnight.
27:33 c' fasting, having taken nothing.
Heb 8: 9 they c' not in my covenant,
1Jo 2:19 would no doubt have c' with us:

continueth
Job 14: 2 fleeth also as a shadow, and c' not.
Gal 3:10 every one that c' not in all things
1Ti 5: 5 c' in supplications and prayers
Heb 7:24 this man, because he c' ever,
Jas 1:25 law of liberty, and c' therein,

continuing
Jer 30:23 a c' whirlwind: it shall fall with
Ac 2:46 And they, c' daily with one accord
Ro 12:12 tribulations; c' instant in prayer;
Heb 13:14 here have we no c' city, but we

contradicting
Ac 13:45 were spoken by Paul, c' and

contradiction
Heb 7: 7 without all c' the less is blessed
12: 3 c' of sinners against himself,

contrariwise
2Co 2: 7 that c' ye ought rather to forgive
Ga 2: 7 But c', when they saw that the
1Pe 3: 9 railing for railing: but c' blessing;

contrary See also CONTRARIWISE.
Le 26:21 if ye walk c' unto me, and will
23 but will walk c' unto me;
24 Then will I also walk c' unto you,
27 but walk c' unto me;
28 I will walk c' unto you also in fury;
40 and that also they have walked c'
41 I also have walked c' unto them,
Es 9: 1 (though it was turned to the c',
Eze 16:34 the c' is in thee from other women
34 unto thee, therefore thou art c'.
M't 14:24 for the wind was c'.
M'r 6:48 for the wind was c' unto them:
Ac 17: 7 these all do c' to the decrees of
18:13 men to worship God c' to the law.
23: 3 commandest me to be smitten c' to
26: 9 many things c' to the name of
27: 4 Cyprus, because the winds were c'.
Ro 11:24 graffed c' to nature into a good
16:17 c' to the doctrine which ye have
Ga 5:17 these are c' the one to the other:
Col 2:14 which was c' to us, and took it out
1Th 2:15 not God, and are c' to all men:
1Ti 1:10 thing that is c' to sound doctrine;
Tit 2: 8 is of the c' part may be ashamed,

contribution
Ro 15:26 to make a certain c' for the poor

contrite
Ps 34:18 saveth such as be of a c' spirit.
51:17 a broken and a c' heart, O God,
Isa 57:15 also that is of a c' and humble
15 to revive the heart of the c' ones.
66: 2 him that is poor and of a c' spirit,

controversies
2Ch 19: 8 judgment of the Lord, and for c',

controversy See also CONTROVERSIES.
De 17: 8 being matters of c' within thy
19:17 the men, between whom the c' is,
21: 5 by their word shall every c' and
25: 1 If there be a c' between men,
2Sa 15: 2 any man that had a c' came to
Isa 34: 8 year of recompences for the c' of
Jer 25:31 Lord hath a c' with the nations,
Eze 44:24 in c' they shall stand in judgment;
Ho 4: 1 the Lord hath a c' with the
12: 2 Lord hath also a c' with Judah,
Mic 6: 2 Hear ye, O mountains, the Lord's c',
2 the Lord hath a c' with his people,
1Ti 3:16 without c' great is the mystery

convenient
Pr 30: 8 feed me with food c' for me:
Jer 40: 4 whither it seemeth good and c'
5 go wheresoever it seemeth c' unto
M'r 6:21 And when a c' day was come,
Ac 24:25 when I have a c' season, I will call
Ro 1:28 do those things which are not c';
1Co 16:12 come when he shall have c' time.
Eph 5: 4 nor jesting, which are not c':
Ph'm 8 to enjoin thee that which is c',

conveniently
M'r 14:11 he sought how he might c' betray

conversant
Jos 8:35 the strangers that were c' among
1Sa 25:15 as long as we were c' with them,

conversation
Ps 37:14 to slay such as be of upright c'.
50:23 him that ordereth his c' aright
2Co 1:12 we have had our c' in the world,
Ga 1:13 ye have heard of my c' in time
Eph 2: 3 we all had our c' in times past
4:22 put off concerning the former c'
Ph'p 1:27 let your c' be as it becometh the
3:20 our c' is in heaven; from whence
1Ti 4:12 in word, in c', in charity, in spirit,
Heb 13: 5 your c' be without covetousness;
7 considering the end of their c'.
Jas 3:13 shew out of a good c' his works
1Pe 1:15 so be ye holy in all manner of c';
18 from your vain c' received by
2:12 Having your c' honest among
3: 1 be won by the c' of the wives;
2 While they behold your chaste c'
16 falsely accuse your good c' in
2Pe 2: 7 with the filthy c' of the wicked:
3:11 be in all holy c' and godliness,

conversion
Ac 15: 3 declaring the c' of the Gentiles:

convert See also CONVERTED; CONVERTETH; CONVERTING; CONVERTS.
Isa 6:10 with their heart, and c', and be
Jas 5:19 from the truth, and one c' him;

converted
Ps 51:13 and sinners shall be c' unto thee.
Isa 60: 5 of the sea shall be c' unto thee,
M't 13:15 and should be c', and I should
18: 3 Except ye be c', and become as
M'r 4:12 they should be c', and their sins
Lu 22:32 and when thou art c', strengthen
Joh 12:40 and be c', and I should heal them.
Ac 3:19 Repent ye therefore, and be c',
28:27 should be c', and I should heal

converteth
Jas 5:20 he which c' the sinner from the

converting
Ps 19: 7 of the Lord is perfect, c' the soul:

converts
Isa 1:27 with judgment, and her c' with

convey See also CONVEYED.
1Ki 5: 9 will c' them by sea in floats unto
Ne 2: 7 river, that they may c' me over

conveyed
Joh 5:13 for Jesus had c' himself away,

convicted
Joh 8: 9 being c' by their own conscience,

convince See also CONVINCED; CONVINCETH.
Tit 1: 9 exhort and to c' the gainsayers.
Jude 15 to c' all that are ungodly among

convinced
Job 32:12 there was none of you that c' Job,
Ac 18:28 For he mightily c' the Jews,
1Co 14:24 unlearned, he is c' of all, he is
Jas 2: 9 c' of the law as transgressors.

convinceth
Joh 8:46 Which of you c' me of sin?

convocation See also CONVOCATIONS.
Ex 12:16 first day there shall be an holy c',
16 seventh day there shall be an holy c'
Le 23: 3 is the sabbath of rest, an holy c';
7 first day ye shall have an holy c':
8 in the seventh day is an holy c':
21 that it may be an holy c' unto you:
24 of blowing of trumpets, an holy c'.
27 of atonement: it shall be an holy c'
35 On the first day shall be an holy c':
36 the eighth day shall be an holy c'
Nu 28:18 In the first day shall be an holy c';
25 seventh day ye shall have an holy c';
26 be out, ye shall have an holy c';
29: 1 the month, ye shall have an holy c';
7 of this seventh month an holy c';
12 month ye shall have an holy c';

convocations
Le 23: 2 ye shall proclaim to be holy c',
4 the feasts of the Lord, even holy c',
37 ye shall proclaim to be holy c', to

cook See also COOKS.
1Sa 9:23 Samuel said unto the c', Bring the
24 And the c' took up the shoulder,

cooks
1Sa 8:13 to be confectionaries, and to be c',

cool
Ge 3: 8 in the garden in the c' of the day;
Lu 16:24 finger in water, and c' my tongue;

Coos (co'-os)
Ac 21: 1 with a straight course unto C',

copied
Pr 25: 1 Hezekiah king of Judah c' out.

coping
1Ki 7: 9 from the foundation unto the c',

copper See also COPPERSMITH.
Ezr 8:27 two vessels of fine c', precious as

coppersmith
2Ti 4:14 Alexander the c' did me much
copulation
Le 15:16 if any man's seed of c' go out
17 whereon is the seed of c', shall be
18 whom man shall lie with seed of c',
copy See also COPIED.
De 17:18 he shall write him a c' of this law
Jos 8:32 a c' of the law of Moses, which he
Ezr 4:11 This is the c' of the letter that
23 when the c' of king Artaxerxes'
5: 6 The c' of the letter that Tatnai,
7:11 Now this is the c' of the letter that
Es 3:14 The c' of the writing for a
4: 8 the c' of the writing of the decree
8:13 The c' of the writing for a
cor
Eze 45:14 tenth part of a bath out of the c',
coral
Job 28:18 No mention shall be made of c',
Eze 27:16 and fine linen, and c', and agate.
Corban (*cor'-ban*)
M'r 7:11 It is C', that is to say, a gift,
cord See also ACCORD; CORDS; DISCORD; RECORD.
Jos 2:15 down by a c' through the window:
Job 30:11 hath loosed my c', and afflicted
41: 1 or his tongue with a c' which
Ec 4:12 threefold c' is not quickly broken.
12: 6 Or ever the silver c' be loosed, or
Mic 2: 5 cast a c' by lot in the congregation
cords
Ex 35:18 the pins of the court, and their c',
39:40 his c', and his pins, and all the
Nu 3:26 c' of it for all the service thereof.
37 sockets, their pins, and their c'.
4:26 their c', and all the instruments of
32 their pins, and their c', with all
J'g 15:13 they bound him with two new c',
14 the c' that were upon his arms
Es 1: 6 fastened with c' of fine linen and
Job 36: 8 and be holden in c' of affliction;
Ps 2: 3 and cast away their c' from us.
118:27 with c', even unto the horns
129: 4 cut asunder the c' of the wicked.
140: 5 have hid a snare for me, and c';
Pr 5:22 be holden with the c' of his sins.
Isa 5:18 that draw iniquity with c' of vanity,
33:20 any of the c' thereof be broken.
54: 2 lengthen thy c', and strengthen
Jer 10:20 is spoiled, all my c' are broken:
38: 6 they let down Jeremiah with c'.
11 them down by c' into the dungeon
12 under thine armholes under the c'.
13 they drew up Jeremiah with c',
Eze 27:24 of rich apparel, bound with c',
Ho 11: 4 I drew them with c' of a man, with
Joh 2:15 he had made a scourge of small c',
Core (*co'-ree*) See also KORAH.
Jude 11 perished in the gainsaying of C'.
coriander
Ex 16:31 and it was like c' seed, white;
Nu 11: 7 And the manna was as c' seed, and
Corinth (*cor'-inth*) See also CORINTHIANS; CORINTHUS.
Ac 18: 1 from Athens, and came to C';
19: 1 while Apollos was at C', Paul
1Co 1: 2 the church of God which is at C', to
2Co 1: 1 church of God which is at C', with
23 spare you I came not as yet unto C'.
2Ti 4:20 Erastus abode at C': but
Corinthians^ (*co-rin'-the-uns*)
Ac 18: 8 many of the C' hearing believed,
1Co *subscr.* The first epistle to the C' was
2Co 6:11 O ye C', our mouth is open unto
subscr. The second epistle to the C' was
Corinthus (*co-rin'-thus*) See also CORINTH.
Ro *subscr.* Written to the Romans from C',
cormorant
Le 11:17 the little owl, and the c', and the
De 14:17 and the gier eagle, and the c',
Isa 34:11 c' and the bittern shall possess
Zep 2:14 the c' and the bittern shall lodge
corn^ See also CORNFLOOR.
Ge 27:28 earth, and plenty of c' and wine:
37 c' and wine have I sustained him:
41: 5 seven ears of c' came up upon
35 and lay up c' under the hand of
49 Joseph gathered c' as the sand
57 into Egypt to Joseph for to buy c';
42: 1 saw that there was c' in Egypt,
2 heard that there is c' in Egypt:
3 went down to buy c' in Egypt.
5 the sons of Israel came to buy c'
19 c' for the famine of your houses:
25 to fill their sacks with c', and to
26 laded their asses with the c',
43: 2 the c' which they had brought
44: 2 and his c' money. And he did
45:23 ten she asses laden with c' and
47:14 the c' which they had bought:
Ex 22: 6 so that the stacks of c',
6 or the standing c, or the field,
Le 2:14 of the firstfruits green ears of c'
14 even c' beaten out of full ears.
16 part of the beaten c' thereof, and
23:14 eat neither bread, nor parched c',
Nu 18:27 the c' of the threshingfloor,
De 7:13 of thy land, thy c', and thy wine,
11:14 gather in thy c', and thy wine,
12:17 the tithe of thy c', or of thy wine,
14:23 the tithe of thy c', of thy wine.
De 16: 9 to put the sickle to the c'.
13 that thou hast gathered in thy c',
18: 4 also of thy c', of thy wine
23:25 the standing c' of thy neighbour,
25 unto thy neighbour's standing c'.
25: 4 ox when he treadeth out the c'.
28:51 leave thee either c', wine, or oil,
33:28 be upon a land of c' and wine;
Jos 5:11 did eat of the old c' of the land
11 parched c' in the selfsame day.
12 eaten of the old c' of the land;
J'g 15: 5 the standing c' of the Philistines,
5 shocks, and also the standing c',
Ru 2: 2 glean ears of c' after him in
14 he reached her parched c', and
3: 7 down at the end of the heap of c':
1Sa 17:17 an ephah of this parched c', and
25:18 five measures of parched c', and
2Sa 17:19 and spread ground c' thereon;
28 and parched c', and beans, and
2Ki 4:42 and full ears of c' in the husk
18:32 a land of c' and wine, a land of
2Ch 31: 5 in abundance the firstfruits of c',
32:28 for the increase of c', and wine,
Ne 5: 2 therefore we take up c' for them,
3 buy c', because of the dearth.
10 exact of them money and c':
11 of the c', the wine, and the oil,
10:39 offering of the c', of the new wine,
13: 5 vessels, and the tithes of the c',
12 all Judah the tithe of the c' and
Job 5:26 age, like as a shock of c' cometh
24: 6 reap every one his c' in the field:
24 off as the tops of the ears of c'.
39: 4 grow up with c'; they go forth,
Ps 4: 7 than in the time that their c' and
65: 9 thou preparest them c', when
13 also are covered over with c';
72:16 be an handful of c' in the earth
78:24 given them of the c' of heaven.
Pr 11:26 He that withholdeth c', the
Isa 17: 5 the harvestman gathereth the c',
21:10 threshing, and the c' of my floor:
28:28 Bread c' is bruised; because he
36:17 own land, a land of c' and wine,
37:27 as c' blasted before it be grown up.
62: 8 no more give thy c' to be meat
La 2:12 mothers, Where is c' and wine?
Eze 36:29 call for the c', and will increase it,
Ho 2: 8 I gave her c', and wine, and oil,
9 and take away my c' in the time
22 the earth shall hear the c', and
7:14 assemble themselves for c' and
10:11 and loveth to tread out the c';
14: 7 they shall revive as the c', and
Joe 1:10 the c' is wasted: the new wine is
17 down; for the c' is withered.
2:19 I will send you c', and wine, and
Am 8: 5 be gone, that we may sell c'?
9: 9 like as c' is sifted in a sieve,
Hag 1:11 the mountains, and upon the c',
Zec 9:17 c' shall make the young men
M't 12: 1 the sabbath day through the c';
1 and began to pluck the ears of c',
M'r 2:23 that he went through the c' fields
23 they went to pluck the ears of c'.
4:28 ear, after that the full c' in the ear.
Lu 6: 1 that he went through the c' fields;
1 disciples plucked the ears of c',
Joh 12:24 Except a c' of wheat fall into the
Ac 7:12 heard that there was c' in Egypt,
1Co 9: 9 of the ox that treadeth out the c'.
1Ti 5:18 muzzle the ox that treadeth out the c'.
Cornelius (*cor-ne'-le-us*)
Ac 10: 1 C', a centurion of the band
3 to him, and saying unto him, C'.
7 which spake unto C' was departed,
17 the men which were sent from C'
21 which were sent unto him from C';
22 said, C' the centurion, a just man,
24 C' waited for them, and had called
25 C' met him, and fell down at his
30 C' said, Four days ago I was fasting
31 C', thy prayer is heard, and thine
corner See also CORNERS.
Ex 36:25 north c', he made twenty boards,
Le 21: 5 shave off the c' of their beard,
Jos 18:14 the c' of the sea southward, from
2Ki 11:11 from the right c' of the temple
11 to the left c' of the temple,
14:13 gate of Ephraim unto the c' gate,
2Ch 25:23 gate of Ephraim to the c' gate,
26: 9 towers in Jerusalem at the c' gate,
28:24 altars in every c' of Jerusalem.
Ne 3:24 of the wall, even unto the c'.
31 and to the going up of the c'.
32 between the going up of the c'
Job 38: 6 or who laid the c' stone thereof;
Ps 118:22 become the head stone of the c'.
144:12 daughters may be as c' stones,
Pr 7: 8 through the street near her c';
12 and lieth in wait at every c'.)
21: 9 to dwell in a c' of the housetop,
25:24 to dwell in the c' of the housetop,
Isa 28:16 precious c' stone, a sure foundation:
30:20 thy teachers be removed into a c'
Jer 31:38 Hananeel unto the gate of the c'.
40 unto the c' of the horse gate
48:45 shall devour the c' of Moab, and
51:26 not take of thee a stone for a c',
Eze 46:21 behold, in every c' of the court
Am 3:12 in Samaria in the c' of a bed,
Zec 10: 4 Out of him came forth the c',
14:10 the c' gate, and from the tower
M't 21:42 same is become the head of the c':
M'r 12:10 is become the head of the c':
Lu 20:17 same is become the head of the c'?
Ac 4:11 which is become the head of the c'.
26:26 for this thing was not done in a c'.
Eph 2:20 Christ himself being the chief c'
1Pe 2: 6 I lay in Sion a chief c' stone, elect,
7 same is made the head of the c',
corner-gate See CORNER and GATE.
corners
Ex 25:12 put them in the four c' thereof;
26 the rings in the four c' that are
26:23 make for the c' of the tabernacle
24 both; they shall be for the two c'.
27: 2 horns of it upon the four c' thereof:
4 brasen rings in the four c' thereof.
30: 4 by the two c' thereof, upon the
36:28 made he for the c' of the tabernacle
29 did to both of them in both the c'.
37: 3 gold, to be set by the four c' of it;
13 put the rings upon the four c' that
27 by the two c' of it, upon the two
38: 2 horns thereof on the four c' of it;
Le 19: 9 not wholly reap the c' of thy field,
27 shall not round the c' of your heads,
27 shalt thou mar the c' of thy beard.
23:22 riddance of the c' of thy field
Nu 24:17 and shall smite the c' of Moab,
De 32:26 said, I would scatter them into c',
1Ki 7:30 four c' thereof had undersetters:
34 to the four c' of one base: and the
Ne 9:22 and didst divide them into c':
Job 1:19 smote the four c' of the house,
Isa 11:12 from the four c' of the earth.
Jer 9:26 are in the utmost c', that dwell
25:23 all that are in the utmost c',
49:32 them that are in the utmost c';
Eze 7: 2 come upon the four c' of the land.
41:22 and the c' thereof, and the length
43:20 and on the four c' of the settle,
45:19 upon the four c' of the settle of the
46:21 to pass by the four c' of the court;
22 In the four c' of the court there
22 these four c' were of one measure.
Zec 9:15 bowls, and as the c' of the altar.
M't 6: 5 in the c' of the streets, that they
Ac 10:11 knit at the four c', and let down
11: 5 let down from heaven by four c';
Re 7: 1 standing on the four c' of the earth,
corner-stone See CORNER and STONE.
cornet See also CORNETS.
1Ch 15:28 with sound of the c', and with
Ps 98: 6 With trumpets and sound of c'
Da 3: 5 ye hear the sound of the c', flute,
7 people heard the sound of the c',
10 that shall hear the sound of the c',
15 ye hear the sound of the c', flute,
Ho 5: 8 Blow ye the c' in Gibeah, and the
cornets
2Sa 6: 5 on timbrels, and on c', and on
2Ch 15:14 and with trumpets, and with c'.
cornfloor
Ho 9: 1 loved a reward upon every c'.
corpse See also CORPSES.
M'r 6:29 they came and took up his c',
corpses
2Ki 19:35 behold, they were all dead c'.
Isa 37:36 behold, they were all dead c'.
Na 3: 3 c'; they stumble upon their c':
correct See also CORRECTED; CORRECTETH.
Ps 39:11 thou with rebukes dost c' man
94:10 the heathen, shall not he c'?
Pr 29:17 C' thy son, and he shall give thee
Jer 2:19 thine own wickedness shall c' thee,
10:24 O Lord, c' me, but with judgment;
30:11 I will c' thee in measure, and will
46:28 but c' thee in measure; yet will I
corrected
Pr 29:19 A servant will not be c' by words:
Heb 12: 9 fathers of our flesh which c' us,
correcteth
Job 5:17 happy is the man whom God c':
Pr 3:12 For whom the Lord loveth he c';
correction
Job 37:13 whether for c', or for his land,
Pr 3:11 neither be weary of his c':
7:22 as a fool to the c' of the stocks;
15:10 C' is grievous unto him that
22:15 rod of c' shall drive it far from him.
23:13 Withhold not c' from the child:
Jer 2:30 they received no c': your own
5: 3 they have refused to receive c':
7:28 nor receiveth c': truth is perished,
Hab 1:12 thou hast established them for c'.
Zep 3: 2 she received not c'; she trusted
2Ti 3:16 for reproof, for c', for instruction
corrupt See also CORRUPTED; CORRUPTETH; CORRUPTIBLE; CORRUPTING.
Ge 6:11 The earth also was c' before God,
12 it was c'; for all flesh had corrupted
De 4:16 Lest ye c' yourselves, and make you
25 and shall c' yourselves, and make a
31:29 ye will utterly c' yourselves,
Job 17: 1 breath is c', my days are extinct,
Ps 14: 1 They are c', they have done
38: 5 My wounds stink and are c'
53: 1 C' are they, and have done
73: 8 They are c', and speak wickedly
Pr 25:26 troubled fountain, and a c' spring.
Eze 20:44 according to your c' doings, O ye
23:11 was more c' in her inordinate love
Da 2: 9 have prepared lying and c' words

Da 11:32 shall he c' by flatteries: but the
Mal 1:14 sacrificeth unto the Lord a c'
2: 3 I will c' your seed, and spread
M't 6:19 where moth and rust doth c', and
20 neither moth nor dust doth c',
7:17 a c' tree bringeth forth evil fruit.
18 neither can a c' tree bring forth
12:33 make the tree c', and his fruit c':
Lu 6:43 tree bringeth not forth c' fruit;
43 neither doth a c' tree bring forth
1Co 15:33 evil communications c' good
2Co 2:17 many, which c' the word of God:
Eph 4:22 old man, which is c' according to
29 Let no c' communication proceed
1Ti 6: 5 disputings of men of c' minds,
2Ti 3: 8 men of c' minds, reprobate
Jude 10 those things they c' themselves.
Re 19: 2 which did c' the earth with her

corrupted
Ge 6:12 flesh had c' his way upon the earth.
Ex 8:24 land was c' by reason of the swarm
32: 7 out of Egypt, have c' themselves:
De 9:12 out of Egypt have c' themselves;
32: 5 They have c' themselves, their
J'g 2:19 c' themselves more than their
Eze 16:47 wast c' more than they in all thy
28:17 thou hast c' thy wisdom by reason
Ho 9: 9 They have deeply c' themselves,
Zep 3: 7 rose early, and c' all their doings.
Mal 2: 8 ye have c' the covenant of Levi,
2Co 7: 2 we have c' no man, we have
11: 3 your minds should be c' from the
Jas 5: 2 Your riches are c', and your

corrupters
Isa 1: 4 children that are c': they have
Jer 6:28 brass and iron; they are all c'.

corrupteth
Lu 12:33 approacheth, neither moth c'.

corruptible See also INCORRUPTIBLE.
Ro 1:23 into an image made like to c' man,
1Co 9:25 they do it to obtain a c' crown;
15:53 this c' must put on incorruption,
54 So when this c' shall have put on
1Pe 1:18 were not redeemed with c' things,
23 not of c' seed, but of incorruptible,
3: 4 in that which is not c', even the

corrupting
Da 11:17 the daughter of women, c' her:

corruption See also INCORRUPTION.
Le 22:25 their c' is in them, and blemishes
2Ki 23:13 the right hand of the mount of c',
Job 17:14 said to c', Thou art my father:
Ps 16:10 suffer thine Holy One to see c'.
49: 9 still live for ever, and not see c'.
Isa 38:17 delivered it from the pit of c':
Da 10: 8 was turned in me into c', and I
Jon 2: 6 thou brought up my life from c',
Ac 2:27 suffer thine Holy One to see c'.
31 in hell, neither his flesh did see c'.
13:34 to return to c', he said on this wise,
35 not suffer thine Holy One to see c'.
36 laid unto his fathers, and saw c':
37 whom God raised again, saw no c'.
Ro 8:21 delivered from the bondage of c'
1Co 15:42 It is sown in c'; it is raised in
50 neither doth c' inherit incorruption.
Ga 6: 8 shall of the flesh reap c'; but he
2Pe 1: 4 escaped the c' that is in the world
2:12 utterly perish in their own c';
19 themselves are the servants of c':

corruptly
2Ch 27: 2 And the people did yet c'.
Ne 1: 7 We have dealt very c' against thee,

Cosam *(co'-sam)*
Lu 3:28 Addi, which was the son of C',

cost See COSTLY.
2Sa 19:42 have we eaten at all of the king's c'?
24:24 of that which doth c' me nothing.
1Ch 21:24 nor offer burnt offerings without c'.
Lu 14:28 not down first, and counteth the c',

costliness
Re 18:19 ships in the sea by reason of her c'!

costly
1Ki 5:17 c' stones, and hewed stones,
7: 9 All these were of c' stones,
10 the foundation was of c' stones,
11 And above were c' stones, after the
Joh 12: 3 of ointment of spikenard, very c',
1Ti 2: 9 or gold, or pearls, or c' array;

cotes See also SHEEPCOTES.
2Ch 32:28 of beasts, and c' for flocks.

cottage See also COTTAGES.
Isa 1: 8 daughter of Zion is left as a c' in
24:20 and shall be removed like a c';

cottages
Zep 2: 6 c' for shepherds, and folds for

couch See also COUCHED; COUCHES; COUCHETH; COUCHING.
Ge 49: 4 thou it: he went up to my c'.
Job 7:13 my c' shall ease my complaint;
38:40 When they c' in their dens, and
Ps 6: 6 I water my c' with my tears.
Am 3:12 of a bed, and in Damascus in a c'.
Lu 5:19 through the tiling with his c' into
24 take up thy c', and go unto thine

couched
Ge 49: 9 he c' as a lion, and as an old lion;
Nu 24: 9 He c', he lay down as a lion, and

couches
Am 6: 4 stretch themselves upon their c',
Ac 5:15 and laid them on beds and c',

coucheth
De 33:13 and for the deep that c' beneath,

couching See also COUCHINGPLACE.
Ge 49:14 Issachar is a strong ass c' down

couchingplace
Eze 25: 5 and the Ammonites a c' for flocks:

could See also COULDEST.
Ge 13: 6 so that they c' not dwell together.
27: 1 his eyes were dim, so that he c' not see,
36: 7 were strangers c' not bear them
37: 4 they hated him, and c' not speak
41: 8 there was none that c' interpret them
21 it c' not be known that they had
24 there was none that c' declare it to me.
43: 7 c' we certainly know that he
45: 1 Then Joseph c' not refrain himself
3 his brethren c' not answer him;
48:10 dim for age, so that he c' not see.
Ex 2: 3 when she c' not longer hide him,
7:21 and the Egyptians c' not drink of
24 for they c' not drink of the water of
8:18 bring forth lice, but they c' not.
9:11 magicians c' not stand before Moses
12:39 out of Egypt, and c' not tarry,
15:23 c' not drink of the waters of Marah,
Nu 9: 6 c' not keep the passover on that
Jos 7:12 the children of Israel c' not stand
15:63 of Judah c' not drive them out:
17:12 children of Manasseh c' not drive
J'g 1:19 c' not drive out the inhabitants of the
2:14 that they c' not any longer stand
3:22 that he c' not draw the dagger out
6:27 of the city, that he c' not do it by day,
12: 6 he c' not frame to pronounce it right.
14:14 they c' not in three days expound
17: 8 to sojourn where he c' find a place:
20:16 one c' sling stones at an hair breadth,
Ru 3:14 rose up before one c' know another.
1Sa 3: 2 to wax dim, that he c' not see;
4:15 eyes were dim, that he c' not see.
10:21 they sought him, he c' not be found.
23:13 and went whithersoever they c' go.
30:10 they c' not go over the brook Besor.
21 so faint that they c' not follow David,
2Sa 1:10 I was sure that he c' not live after that
3:11 he c' not answer Abner a word
17:20 had sought and c' not find them,
22:39 wounded them, that they c' not
1Ki 5: 3 David my father c' not build an
8: 5 oxen, that c' not be told nor numbered
11 priests c' not stand to minister
13: 4 he c' not pull it in again to him.
14: 4 But Ahijah c' not see; for his eyes
2Ki 3:26 the king of Edom; but they c' not.
4:40 And they c' not eat thereof.
16: 5 besieged Ahaz, but c' not overcome
1Ch 12: 2 and c' use both the right hand and the
8 for the battle, that c' handle shield and
33 which c' keep rank; they were not of
38 All these men of war, that c' keep rank,
21:30 But David c' not go before it to
2Ch 4:18 weight of the brass c' not be found out.
5: 6 which c' not be told nor numbered for
14 priests c' not stand to minister by
7: 2 priests c' not enter into the house
13: 7 tenderhearted, and c' not withstand
14:13 that they c' not recover themselves;
20:25 more than they c' carry away: and
25: 5 war, that c' handle spear and shield.
15 c' not deliver their own people
29:34 c' not flay all the burnt offerings:
30: 3 For they c' not keep it at that time,
32:14 c' deliver his people out of mine
34:12 all that c' skill of instruments
Ezr 2:59 c' not show their father's house,
3:13 the people c' not discern the noise of
5: 5 they c' not cause them to cease,
Ne 7:61 c' not show their father's house,
8: 2 all that c' hear with understanding,
3 and those that c' understand; and
13:24 c' not speak in the Jews' language,
Es 6: 1 that night c' not the king sleep,
7: 4 the enemy c' not countervail the king's
9: 2 no man c' withstand them; for the fear
Job 4:16 It stood still, but I c' not discern the
16: 4 I also c' speak as ye do: if your souls
4 c' heap up words against you,
31:23 his highness I c' not endure.
Ps 37:36 I sought him, but he c' not be found.
55:12 then I c' have borne it: neither was
73: 7 they have more than heart c' wish.
78:44 their floods, that they c' not drink.
Ca 5: 6 I sought him, but I c' not find him;
Isa 5: 4 c' have been done more to my vineyard,
7: 1 but c' not prevail against it.
30: 5 of a people that c' not profit
33:23 c' not well strengthen their mast,
23 they c' not spread the sail:
41:28 asked of them, c' answer a word.
46: 2 they c' not deliver the burden,
Jer 6:15 ashamed, neither c' they blush:
8:12 ashamed, neither c' they blush:
15: 1 my mind c' not be toward this people:
20: 9 with forbearing, and I c' not stay.
24: 2 c' not be eaten, they were so bad.
44:22 So that the Lord c' no longer bear,
La 4:14 men c' not touch their garments.
17 for a nation that c' not save us.
Eze 31: 8 in the garden of God c' not hide him:
47: 5 a river that I c' not pass over:
5 a river that c' not be passed over.
Da 5: 8 but they c' not read the writing,
15 they c' not shew the interpretation
6: 4 but they c' find none occasion, nor
8: 4 any that c' deliver out of his hand;
7 none that c' deliver the ram out of his
Ho 5:13 c' he not heal you, nor cure you
Jon 1:13 they c' not: for the sea wrought,
M't 17:16 and they c' not cure him.
19 Why c' not we cast him out?
26:40 What, c' ye not watch with me
27:24 When Pilate saw that he c' prevail
M'r 1:45 insomuch that Jesus c' no more
2: 4 And when they c' not come nigh
3:20 that c' not so much as eat bread.
5: 3 and no man c' bind him, no, not
4 neither c' any man tame him.
6: 5 he c' there do no mighty work,
19 have killed him; but she c' not:
7:24 man know it: but he c' not be hid.
9:18 cast him out; and they c' not.
28 privately, Why c' not we cast him
14: 8 She hath done what she c': she is
Lu 1:22 he came out, he c' not speak unto
5:19 And when they c' not find by what
6:48 that house, and c' not shake it:
8:19 and c' not come to him for the
43 physicians, neither c' be healed
9:40 cast him out; and they c' not.
13:11 and c' in no wise lift up herself.
14: 6 And they c' not answer him again
19: 3 who he was; and c' not for the
48 And c' not find what they might do:
20: 7 that they c' not tell whence it
26 And they c' not take hold of his
Joh 9:33 were not of God, he c' do nothing.
11:37 C' not this man, which opened the
12:39 Therefore they c' not believe,
21:25 even the world itself c' not contain
Ac 4:14 they c' say nothing against it.
11:17 what was I, that I c' withstand
13:39 from which ye c' not be justified
21:34 and when he c' not know the
22:11 And when I c' not see for the
25: 7 Paul, which they c' not prove.
27:15 and c' not bear up into the wind,
43 that they which c' swim should
Ro 8: 3 For what the law c' not do,
9: 3 For I c' wish that myself were
1Co 3: 1 And I, brethren, c' not speak unto
13: 2 all faith, so that I c' remove
2Co 3: 7 Israel c' not stedfastly behold
13 Israel c' not stedfastly look to
11: 1 Would to God ye c' bear with me
Ga 3:21 a law given which c' have given
1Th 3: 1 when we c' no longer forbear,
5 cause, when I c' no longer forbear,
Heb 3:19 So we see that they c' not enter
6:13 because he c' swear by no greater,
9: 9 and sacrifices, that c' not make
12:20 (For they c' not endure that which
Re 7: 9 great multitude, which no man c'
14: 3 and no man c' learn that song but

couldest
Jer 3: 5 and done evil things as thou c'.
Eze 16:28 and yet c' not be satisfied.
Da 2:47 seeing thou c' reveal this secret.
M'r 14:37 c' not thou watch one hour?
Joh 19:11 Thou c' have no power at all

coulter See also COULTERS.
1Sa 13:20 every man his share, and his c',

coulters
1Sa 13:21 and for the c', and for the forks,

council See also COUNCILS.
Ps 68:27 princes of Judah and their c',
M't 5:22 Raca, shall be in danger of the c':
12:14 Pharisees went out, and held a c'
26:59 and elders, and all the c', sought
M'r 14:55 chief priests and all the c' sought
15: 1 and scribes and the whole c', and
Lu 22:66 and led him into their c', saying,
Joh 11:47 chief priests and the Pharisees a c',
Ac 4:15 to go aside out of the c', they
5:21 and called the c' together, and all
27 they set them before the c':
34 Then stood there up one in the c',
41 from the presence of the c',
6:12 him, and brought him to the c',
15 And all that sat in the c', looking
22:30 and all their c' to appear, and
23: 1 Paul, earnestly beholding the c',
6 he cried out in the c', Men and
15 Now therefore ye with the c' signify
20 down Paul to morrow into the c',
28 I brought him forth into their c':
24:20 while I stood before the c',
25:12 he had conferred with the c',

councils
M't 10:17 they will deliver you up to the c',
M'r 13: 9 they shall deliver you up to c':

counsel See also COUNSELLED; COUNSELS.
Ex 18:19 I will give thee c', and God shall
Nu 27:21 the priest, who shall ask c', for
31:16 through the c' of Balaam, to
De 32:28 For they are a nation void of c',
Jos 9:14 and asked not c' at the mouth of
J'g 18: 5 Ask c', we pray thee, of God,
20: 7 give here your advice and c'.
18 and asked c' of God, and said,
23 and asked c' of the Lord, saying,
1Sa 14:37 And Saul asked c' of God, Shall I
2Sa 15:31 turn the c' of Ahithophel into
34 for me defeat the c' of Ahithophel.
16:20 Give c' among you what we shall
23 And the c' of Ahithophel, which he

2Sa 16:23 so was all the c' of Ahithophel both
17: 7 The c' that Ahithophel hath given
11 I c' that all Israel be generally
14 The c' of Hushai the Archite
14 is better than the c' of Ahithophel.
14 to defeat the good c' of Ahithophel,
15 Thus and thus did Ahithophel c'
23 saw that his c' was not followed,
20:18 They shall surely ask c' at Abel:
1Ki 1:12 let me, I pray thee, give thee c',
12: 8 he forsook the c' of the old men,
9 What c' give ye that we may
13 forsook the old men's c' that they
14 to them after the c' of the young
28 Whereupon the king took c', and
2Ki 6: 8 and took c' with his servants,
18:20 I have c' and strength for the war.
1Ch 10:13 asking c' of one that had a familiar
2Ch 10: 6 Rehoboam took c' with the old
6 What c' give ye me to return
8 forsook the c' which the old men
8 and took c' with the young men
13 forsook the c' of the old men,
22: 5 He walked also after their c', and
25:16 Art thou made of the king's c'?
16 hast not hearkened unto my c'.
30: 2 For the king had taken c', and
23 whole assembly took c' to keep
32: 3 He took c' with his princes and
Ezr 10: 3 according to the c' of my lord,
8 according to the c' of the princes
Ne 4:15 God had brought their c' to nought,
6: 7 and let us take c' together.
Job 5:13 the c' of the froward is carried
10: 3 shine upon the c' of the wicked?
12:13 strength, he hath c' and
18: 7 and his own c' shall cast him down.
21:16 the c' of the wicked is far from me.
22:18 but the c' of the wicked is far from
29:21 waited, and kept silence at my c'.
38: 2 Who is this that darkeneth c' by
42: 3 Who is he that hideth c' without
Ps 1: 1 walketh not in the c' of the ungodly,
2: 2 the rulers take c' together,
13: 2 How long shall I take c' in my
14: 6 Ye have shamed the c' of the poor,
16: 7 the Lord, who hath given me c':
20: 4 own heart, and fulfil all thy c'.
31:13 while they took c' together
33:10 The Lord bringeth the c' of the
11 The c' of the Lord standeth for
55:14 We took sweet c' together, and
64: 2 Hide me from the secret c' of the
71:10 that lay wait for my soul take c'
73:24 Thou shalt guide me with thy c',
83: 3 They have taken crafty c' against
106:13 works; they waited not for his c':
43 they provoked him with their c',
107:11 contemned the c' of the most High,
Pr 1:25 ye have set at nought all my c',
30 They would none of my c':
8:14 C' is mine, and sound wisdom:
11:14 Where no c' is, the people fall:
12:15 that hearkeneth unto c' is wise.
15:22 Without c' purposes are
19:20 Hear c', and receive instruction,
21 nevertheless the c' of the Lord,
20: 5 C' in the heart of man is like deep
18 Every purpose is established by c':
21:30 nor c' against the Lord.
24: 6 wise c' thou shalt make thy war:
27: 9 of a man's friend by hearty c'.
Ec 8: 2 I c' thee to keep the king's
Isa 5:19 the c' of the Holy One of Israel
7: 5 have taken evil c' against thee,
8:10 Take c' together, and it shall
11: 2 the spirit of c' and might,
16: 3 Take c', execute judgment; make
19: 3 and I will destroy the c' thereof:
11 the c' of the wise counsellers
17 because of the c' of the Lord of
23: 8 hath taken this c' against Tyre,
28:29 which is wonderful in c',
29:15 hide their c' from the Lord,
30: 1 Lord, that take c', but not of me;
36: 5 I have c' and strength for war:
40:14 With whom took he c', and who
44:26 the c' of his messengers;
45:21 let them take c' together:
46:10 My c' shall stand, and I will do
11 the man that executeth my c'
Jer 18:18 nor c' from the wise, nor the word
23 thou knowest all their c' against
19: 7 I will make void the c' of Judah
23:18 hath stood in the c' of the Lord,
22 if they had stood in my c',
32:19 Great in c', and mighty in work:
38:15 if I give thee c', wilt thou not
49: 7 is c' perished from the prudent?
20 hear the c' of the Lord, that he
30 hath taken c' against you,
50:45 hear ye the c' of the Lord,
Eze 7:26 priest, and c' from the ancients.
11: 2 and give wicked c' in this city:
Da 2:14 answered with c' and wisdom
4:27 let my c' be acceptable unto thee,
Ho 4:12 My people ask c' at their stocks,
10: 6 shall be ashamed of his own c'.
Mic 4:12 neither understand they his c':
Zec 6:13 c' of peace shall be between them
M't 22:15 took c' how they might entangle
27: 1 and elders of the people took c'
7 And they took c', and bought
28:12 and had taken c', they gave large
M'r 3: 6 took c' with the Herodians
Lu 7:30 lawyers rejected the c' of God
Lu 23:51 consented to the c' and deed of
Joh 11:53 they took c' together for to put
18:14 was he which gave c' to the Jews,
Ac 2:23 determinate c' and foreknowledge
4:28 thy hand and thy c' determined
5:33 heart, and took c' to slay them.
38 this c' or this work be of men,
9:23 the Jews took c' to kill him:
20:27 declare unto you all the c' of God.
27:42 soldiers' c' was to kill the prisoners,
Eph 1:11 after the c' of his own will:
Heb 6:17 the immutability of his c',
Re 3:18 I c' thee to buy of me gold

counselled

2Sa 16:23 which he c' in those days, was as if
17:15 and thus and thus have I c'.
21 hath Ahithophel c' against you.
Job 26: 3 How hast thou c' him that hath

counseller See also COUNSELLERS; COUNSELLOR. [*Most editions have uniformly* COUNSELLOR *and* COUNSELLORS.]

2Sa 15:12 David's c', from his city, even
1Ch 26:14 for Zechariah his son, a wise c',
27:32 Jonathan David's uncle was a c',
33 Ahithophel was the king's c':
2Ch 22: 3 mother was his c' to do wickedly.
Isa 3: 3 the c', and the cunning artificer,
9: 6 shall be called Wonderful, C',
40:13 Who being his c' hath taught him?
41:28 there was no c', that, when I asked
Mic 4: 9 is thy c' perished? for pangs have
Na 1:11 against the Lord, a wicked c'.

counsellers

2Ch 22: 4 they were his c' after the death
Ezr 4: 5 hired c' against them, to frustrate
7:14 of the king, and of his seven c',
15 king and his c' have freely offered
28 me before the king, and his c',
8:25 which the king, and his c',
Job 3:14 With kings and c' of the earth,
12:17 He leadeth c' away spoiled,
Ps 119:24 also are my delight and my c'.
Pr 11:14 multitude of c' there is safety.
12:20 but to the c' of peace is joy.
15:22 in the multitude of c' they are
24: 6 multitude of c' there is safety.
Isa 1:26 and thy c' as at the beginning:
19:11 counsel of the wise c' of Pharaoh
Da 3: 2, 3 treasurers, the c', the sheriffs,
24 said unto his c', Did not we cast
27 king's c', being gathered together,
4:36 c' and my lords sought unto me;
6: 7 c', and the captains, have consulted

counsellor See also COUNSELLER.

M'r 15:43 of Arimathæa, an honourable c',
Lu 23:50 was a man named Joseph, a c';
Ro 11:34 or who hath been his c'?

counsels

Job 37:12 turned round about by his c':
Ps 5:10 let them fall by their own c';
81:12 and they walked in their own c'.
Pr 1: 5 shall attain unto wise c':
12: 5 the c' of the wicked are deceit.
22:20 things in c' and knowledge,
Isa 25: 1 thy c' of old are faithfulness
47:13 in the multitude of thy c'.
Jer 7:24 in the c' and in the imagination
Ho 11: 6 them, because of their own c'.
Mic 6:16 ye walk in their c'; that I should
1Co 4: 5 manifest the c' of the hearts:

count See also ACCOUNT; COUNTED; COUNTETH; COUNTING; RECOUNT.

Ex 12: 4 shall make your c' for the lamb.
Le 19:23 c' the fruit thereof as uncircumcised:
23:15 c' unto you from the morrow
25:27 c' the years of the sale thereof,
52 then he shall c' with him,
Nu 23:10 Who can c' the dust of Jacob,
1Sa 1:16 C' not thine handmaid for a
Job 19:15 my maids, c' me for a stranger:
31: 4 see my ways, and c' all my steps?
Ps 87: 6 The Lord shall c', when he writeth
139:18 If I should c' them, they are
22 I c' them mine enemies.
Mic 6:11 Shall I c' them pure with the
Ac 20:24 neither c' I my life dear unto
Ph'p 3: 8 I c' all things but loss for the
8 do c' them but dung, that I may
13 Brethren, I c' not myself to have
2Th 1:11 God would c' you worthy of this
3:15 c' him not as an enemy, but
1Ti 6: 1 c' their own masters worthy of
Ph'm 17 If thou c' me therefore a partner,
Jas 1: 2 c' it all joy when ye fall into
5:11 we c' them happy which endure.
2Pe 2:13 as they that c' it pleasure to riot
3: 9 as some men c' slackness; but is
Re 13:18 hath understanding c' the number

counted

Ge 15: 6 he c' it to him for righteousness.
30:33 that shall be c' stolen with me.
31:15 Are we not c' of him strangers?
Ex 38:21 as it was c', according to the
Le 25:31 shall be c' as the fields of the
Nu 18:30 it shall be c' unto the Levites
Jos 13: 3 is c' to the Canaanite: five lords
1Ki 1:21 son Solomon shall be c' offenders.
3: 8 be numbered nor c' for multitude.
1Ch 21: 6 But Levi and Benjamin c' he not
23:24 they were c' by number of names
Ne 13:13 they were c' faithful, and their
Job 18: 3 Wherefore are we c' as beasts,
41:29 Darts are c' as stubble: he
Ps 44:22 we are c' as sheep for the slaughter.
Ps 88: 4 I am c' with them that go down
106:31 was c' unto him for righteousness
Pr 17:28 he holdeth his peace, is c' wise:
27:14 it shall be c' a curse to him.
Isa 5:28 horses' hoofs shall be c' like flint,
32:15 the fruitful field be c' for a forest.
33:18 where is he that c' the towers?
40:15 are c' as the small dust of the
17 are c' to him less than nothing,
Ho 8:12 they were c' as a strange thing.
M't 14: 5 because they c' him as a prophet
M'r 11:32 men c' John, that he was a prophet.
Ac 5:41 that they were c' worthy to suffer
19:19 they c' the price of them, and found
Ro 2:26 shall not his uncircumcision be c'
4: 3 c' unto him for righteousness.
5 his faith is c' for righteousness
9: 8 of the promise are c' for the seed.
Ph'p 3: 7 gain to me, those I c' loss for
2Th 1: 5 may be c' worthy of the kingdom
1Ti 1:12 that he c' me faithful, putting me
5:17 well be c' worthy of double honour,
Heb 3: 3 was c' worthy of more glory than
7: 6 whose descent is not c' from them
10:29 hath c' the blood of the covenant,

countenance See also COUNTENANCES.

Ge 4: 5 Cain was very wroth, and his c' fell.
6 why is thy c' fallen?
31: 2 Jacob beheld the c' of Laban,
5 I see your father's c', that it is
Ex 23: 3 Neither shalt thou c' a poor man
Nu 6:26 The Lord lift up his c' upon thee,
De 28:50 nation of fierce c', which shall not
J'g 13: 6 his c' was like the c' of an angel
1Sa 1:18 eat, and her c' was no more sad.
16: 7 Look not on his c', or on the
12 of a beautiful c', and goodly
17:42 youth, and ruddy, and of a fair c'.
25: 3 and of a beautiful c':
2Sa 14:27 she was a woman of a fair c'.
2Ki 8:11 And he settled his c' stedfastly,
Ne 2: 2 Why is thy c' sad, seeing thou art
3 why should not my c' be sad,
Job 14:20 thou changest his c', and sendest
29:24 light of my c' they cast not down.
Ps 4: 6 lift thou up the light of thy c'
10: 4 through the pride of his c',
11: 7 his c' doth behold the upright.
21: 6 him exceeding glad with thy c'.
42: 5 praise him for the help of his c'.
11 health of my c', and my God.
43: 5 health of my c', and my God.
44: 3 light of thy c', because thou hadst
80:16 they perish at the rebuke of thy c'.
89:15 walk, O Lord, in the light of c':
90: 8 secret sins in the light of thy c'.
Pr 15:13 merry heart maketh a cheerful c':
16:15 the light of the king's c' is life;
25:23 an angry c' a backbiting tongue.
27:17 sharpeneth the c' of his friend.
Ec 7: 3 by the sadness of the c' the heart
Ca 2:14 let me see thy c', let me hear
14 is thy voice, and thy c' is comely.
5:15 his c' is as Lebanon, excellent as
Isa 3: 9 The shew of their c' doth witness
Eze 27:35 they shall be troubled in their c'.
Da 1:13 and the c' of the children that
5: 6 the king's c' was changed, and
9 his c' was changed in him, and
10 nor let thy c' be changed:
7:28 and my c' changed in me: but I
8:23 a king of fierce c', and
M't 6:16 the hypocrites, of a sad c':
28: 3 His c' was like lightning, and his
Lu 9:29 fashion of his c. was altered, and
Ac 2:28 make me full of joy with thy c.
2Co 3: 7 of Moses for the glory of his c';
Re 1:16 and his c' was as the sun shineth

countenances

Da 1:13 Then let our c' be looked upon
15 their c' appeared fairer and

countervail

Es 7: 4 the enemy could not c' the king's

counteth

Job 19:11 he c' me unto him as one of his
33:10 he c' me for his enemy,
Lu 14:28 and c' the cost, whether he hath

counting

Ec 7:27 saith the preacher, c' one by one,

countries

Ge 10:20 after their tongues, in their c',
26: 3 give all these c', and I will
4 give unto thy seed all these c';
41:57 all c' came into Egypt to Joseph
Jos 13:32 These are the c' which Moses did
14: 1 And these are the c' which the
17:11 and her towns, even three c'.
2Ki 18:35 gods of the c', that have delivered
1Ch 22: 5 and of glory throughout all c':
29:30 over all the kingdoms of the c'.
2Ch 11:23 all the c' of Judah and Benjamin,
12: 8 service of the kingdoms of the c'.
15: 5 upon all the inhabitants of the c'.
20:29 on all the kingdoms of those c',
34:33 out of all the c' that pertained
Ezr 3: 3 because of the people of those c':
4:20 over all c' beyond the river;
Ps 110: 6 wound the heads over many c'.
Isa 8: 9 and give ear, all ye of far c':
37:18 waste all the nations, and their c',
Jer 23: 3 my flock out of all c' whither I have
8 from all c' whither I had driven
28: 8 prophesied both against many c'
32:37 will gather them out of all c',

Jer 40:11 that were in all the c', heard that
Eze 5: 5 the nations and c' that are round
6 more than the c' that are round
6: 8 be scattered throughout the c'.
11:16 have scattered them among the c',
16 them as a little sanctuary in the c'
17 assemble you out of the c' where
12:15 and disperse them in the c'.
20:23 and disperse them through the c';
32 heathen, as the families of the c',
34 gather you out of the c' wherein
41 c' wherein ye have been scattered;
22: 4 and a mocking to all c'.
15 disperse thee in the c', and will
25: 7 cause thee to perish out of the c':
29:12 midst of the c' that are desolate,
12 will disperse them through the c'.
30: 7 midst of the c' that are desolate,
23 disperse them through the c'.
26 and disperse them among the c';
32: 9 the c' which thou hast not known.
34:13 and gather them from the c',
35:10 and these two c' shall be mine,
36:19 were dispersed through the c':
24 gather you out of all c', and will
Da 9: 7 all the c' whither thou hast driven
11:40 he shall enter in the c', and shall
41 many c' shall be overthrown:
42 forth his hand also upon the c':
Zec 10: 9 they shall remember me in far c';
Lu 21:21 that are in the c' enter thereinto.

country See also COUNTRIES; COUNTRYMEN.
Ge 12: 1 Get thee out of thy c', and from thy
14: 7 smote all the c' of the Amalekites,
19:28 the smoke of the c' went up as
20: 1 toward the south c', and dwelled
24: 4 thou shalt go unto my c', and to
62 for he dwelt in the south c'.
25: 6 lived, eastward, unto the east c'.
29:26 It must not be so done in our c',
30:25 mine own place, and to my c'.
32: 3 the land of Seir, the c' of Edom.
9 Return unto thy c', and to thy
34: 2 Hivite, prince of the c', saw her,
36: 6 went into the c' from the face of
42:30 and took us for spies of the c'.
33 man, the lord of the c', said unto
47:27 of Egypt, in the c' of Goshen;
Le 16:29 whether it be one of your own c',
17:15 whether it be one of your own c',
24:22 stranger, as for one of your own c':
25:31 be counted as the fields of the c':
Nu 15:13 All that are born of the c' shall do
20:17 pass, I pray thee, through thy c':
21:20 c' of Moab, to the top of Pisgah,
32: 4 the c' which the Lord smote
33 the cities of the c' round about.
De 3:14 Manasseh took all the c' of Argob
4:43 in the plain c', of the Reubenites;
26: 3 come unto the c' which the Lord
Jos 2: 2 of Israel to search out the c'.
3 be come to search out all the c'.
24 the inhabitants of the c' do faint
6:22 men that had spied out the c',
27 was noised throughout all the c'.
7: 2 Go up and view the c'. And the
9: 6 We be come from a far c': now
9 From a very far c' thy servants are
11 inhabitants of our c' spake to us,
10:40 Joshua smote all the c' of the hills,
41 and all the c' of Goshen, even unto
11:16 all the south c', and all the land
12: 7 the kings of the c' which Joshua
8 and in the south c'; the Hittites,
13: 6 of the hill c' from Lebanon
21 of Sihon, dwelling in the c'.
17:15 then get thee up to the wood c',
19:51 made an end of dividing the c'.
21:11 Hebron, in the hill c' of Judah,
22: 9 to go unto the c' of Gilead, to the
J'g 8:28 c' was in quietness forty years
11:21 Amorites, the inhabitants of that c'.
12:12 in Aijalon in the c' of Zebulun.
16:24 the destroyer of our c', which slew
18:14 that went to spy out the c' of Laish,
20: 6 the c' of the inheritance of Israel:
Ru 1: 1 to sojourn in the c' of Moab, he,
2 And they came into the c' of Moab,
6 might return from the c' of Moab:
6 for she had heard in the c' of Moab
22 returned out of the c' of Moab:
2: 6 with Naomi out of the c' of Moab:
4: 3 come again out of the c' of Moab,
1Sa 6: 1 c' of the Philistines seven months.
18 of fenced cities, and of c' villages,
14:21 the camp from the c' round about,
27: 5 me a place in some town in the c',
7 the time that David dwelt in the c'
11 dwelleth in the c' of the Philistines.
2Sa 15:23 all the c' wept with a loud voice,
18: 8 scattered over the face of all the c':
21:14 in the c' of Benjamin in Zelah,
1Ki 4:19 the son of Uri was in the c' of
19 Gilead, in the c' of Sihon king
30 the children of the east c', and all
8:41 out of a far c' for thy name's sake;
10:13 turned and went to her own c',
15 and of the governors of the c'.
11:21 that I may go to mine own c'.
22 thou seekest to go to thine own c'?
20:27 but the Syrians filled the c'.
22:36 and every man to his own c'.
2Ki 3:20 and the c' was filled with water.
24 the Moabites, even in their c'.
18:35 delivered their c' out of mine hand,
20:14 They are come from a far c', even
1Ch 8: 8 begat children in the c' of Moab,
20: 1 the c' of the children of Ammon,
2Ch 6:32 a far c' for thy great name's sake,
9:14 governors of the c' brought gold
26:10 in the low c', and in the plains:
28:18 invaded the cities of the low c',
30:10 the c' of Ephraim and Manasseh
Ne 12:28 plain c' round about Jerusalem,
Pr 25:25 soul, so is good news from a far c'.
Isa 1: 7 Your c' is desolate, your cities are
13: 5 They come from a far c', from the
22:18 toss thee like a ball into a large c':
39: 3 are come from a far c' unto me,
46:11 executeth my counsel from a far c':
Jer 2: 7 I brought you into a plentiful c',
4:16 watchers come from a far c', and
6:20 and the sweet cane from a far c'?
22 a people cometh from the north c',
8:19 them that dwell in a far c':
10:22 great commotion out of the north c',
22:10 no more, nor see his native c'.
26 another c', where ye were not born;
23: 8 out of the north c', and from all
31: 8 I will bring them from the north c',
32: 8 which is in the c' of Benjamin:
44: 1 Noph, and in the c' of Pathros,
46:10 hath a sacrifice in the north c' by
47: 4 the remnant of the c' of Caphtor.
48:21 upon the plain c'; upon Holon,
50: 9 great nations from the north c':
51: 9 let us go every one into his own c':
Eze 20:38 out of the c' where they sojourn,
42 into the c' for the which I lifted up
25: 9 the glory of the c', Beth-jeshimoth,
32:15 and the c' shall be destitute of
34:13 in all the inhabited places of the c'.
47: 8 issue out toward the east c'.
22 be unto you as born in the c'
Ho 12:12 Jacob fled into the c' of Syria,
Jon 1: 8 what is thy c'? and of what people
4: 2 saying, when I was yet in my c'?
Zec 6: 6 go forth into the north c'; and the
6 go forth toward the south c'.
8 that go toward the north c' have
8 quieted my spirit in the north c'.
8: 7 save my people from the east c',
7 and from the west c';
M't 2:12 into their own c' another way.
8:28 side into the c' of the Gergesenes,
9:31 abroad his fame in all that c'.
13:54 he was come into his own c', he
57 without honour, save in his own c',
14:35 all that c' round about, and
21:33 and went into a far c':
25:14 a man travelling into a far c', who
M'r 5: 1 into the c' of the Gadarenes.
10 not send them away out of the c'.
14 told it in the city, and in the c'.
6: 1 and came into his own c'; and
4 without honour, but in his own c',
36 go into the c' round about, and into
56 into villages, or cities, or c',
12: 1 husbandmen, and went into a far c'.
15:21 coming out of the c', the father of
16:12 they walked, and went into the c'.
Lu 1:39 and went into the hill c' with haste,
65 throughout all the hill c' of Judæa.
2: 8 were in the same c' shepherds
3: 3 into all the c' about Jordan,
4:23 Capernaum, do also here in thy c'.
24 prophet is accepted in his own c'.
37 every place of the c' round about.
8:26 at the c' of the Gadarenes, which
34 and told it in the city and in the c'.
37 c' of the Gadarenes round about
9:12 may go into the towns and c' round
15:13 took his journey into a far c', and
15 joined himself to a citizen of that c';
19:12 went into a far c' to receive for
20: 9 went into a far c' for a long time.
23:26 a Cyrenian, coming out of the c',
Joh 4:44 hath no honour in his own c'.
11:54 unto a c' near to the wilderness,
55 went out of the c' up to Jerusalem
Ac 4:36 a Levite, and of the c' of Cyprus,
7: 3 Get thee out of thy c', and from
12:20 c' was nourished by the king's c'.
13: 7 deputy of the c', Sergius Paulus,
18:23 all the c' of Galatia and Phrygia
27:27 that they drew near to some c';
Heb 11: 9 of promise, as in a strange c',
14 declare plainly that they seek a c'.
15 mindful of that c' from whence
16 But now they desire a better c',

countrymen
2Co 11:26 in perils by mine own c', in perils
1Th 2:14 suffered like things of your own c',

couple See also COUPLED; COUPLETH; COUPLING.
Ex 26: 6 and c' the curtains together with
9 c' five curtains by themselves,
11 and c' the tent together, that it
36:18 of brass to c' the tent together,
39: 4 shoulderpieces for it, to c' it
J'g 19: 3 servant with him, and a c' of asses:
2Sa 13: 6 make me a c' of cakes in my sight,
16: 1 him, with a c' of asses saddled,
Isa 21: 7 a chariot with a c' of horsemen,
9 of men, with a c' of horsemen.

coupled
Ex 26: 3 five curtains shall be c' together
3 c' one to another.
24 they shall be c' together beneath,
24 they shall be c' together above
36:10 And he c' the five curtains one
10 five curtains he c' one unto another.
Ex 36:13 and c' the curtains one unto
16 And he c' five curtains by
29 And they were c' beneath,
29 c' together at the head thereof,
39: 4 by the two edges was it c'
1Pe 3: 2 chaste conversation c' with fear.

coupleth
Ex 26:10 the edge of the curtain which c'
36:17 of the curtain which c' the second.

coupling See also COUPLINGS.
Ex 26: 4 from the selvedge in the c';
4 curtain, in the c' of the second.
5 that is in the c' of the second;
10 curtain that is outmost in the c',
28:27 over against the other c' thereof,
36:11 from the selvedge in the c':
11 side of another curtain, in the c'
12 which was in the c' of the second:
17 edge of the curtain in the c',
39:20 over against the other c' thereof,

couplings
2Ch 34:11 buy hewn stone, and timber for c',

courage See also DISCOURAGE; ENCOURAGE.
Nu 13:20 And be ye of good c', and bring
De 31: 6 Be strong and of a good c', fear not
7, 23 Be strong and of a good c': for
Jos 1: 6 Be strong and of a good c': for unto
9 Be strong and of a good c'; be not
18 only be strong and of a good c'.
2:11 did there remain any more c'
10:25 be strong and of good c': for thus
2Sa 10:12 Be of good c', and let us play the
1Ch 19:13 Be of good c', and let us behave
22:13 be strong, and of good c'; dread not,
28:20 Be strong and of good c', and do it:
2Ch 15: 8 Oded the prophet, he took c', and
Ezr 10: 4 with thee: be of good c', and do it.
Ps 27:14 Wait on the Lord: be of good c',
31:24 Be of good c', and he shall
Isa 41: 6 said to his brother, Be of good c'.
Da 11:25 shall stir up his power and his c'
Ac 28:15 saw, he thanked God, and took c'.

courageous
Jos 1: 7 Only be thou strong and very c',
23: 6 Be ye therefore very c' to keep
2Sa 13:28 I commanded you? be c', and be
2Ch 32: 7 Be strong and c', be not afraid
Am 2:16 And he that is c' among the

courageously
2Ch 19:11 Deal c', and the Lord shall be

course See also CONCOURSE; COURSES; WATERCOURSE.
1Ch 27: 1 of every c' were twenty and four
2 Over the first c' for the first month
2 in his c' were twenty and four
4 over the c' of the second month
4 and of his c' was Mikloth also the
4 in his c' likewise were twenty and
5 and in his c' were twenty and four
6 and in his c' was Ammizabad his
7, 8, 9, 10, 11, 12, 13, 14, 15 and in his
c' were twenty and four thousand.
28: 1 that ministered to the king by c',
2Ch 5:11 and did not then wait by c':
Ezr 3:11 And they sang together by c' in
Ps 82: 5 of the earth are out of c'.
Jer 8: 6 every one turned to his c', as the
23:10 their c' is evil, and their force is
Lu 1: 5 Zacharias, of the c' of Abia:
8 before God in the order of his c',
Ac 13:25 as John fulfilled his c', he said,
16:11 we came with a straight c' to
20:24 that I might finish my c' with joy,
21: 1 we came with a straight c' unto
7 when we had finished our c' from
1Co 14:27 three, and that by c'; and let one
Eph 2: 2 according to the c' of this world,
2Th 3: 1 word of the Lord may have free c',
2Ti 4: 7 I have finished my c', I have kept
Jas 3: 6 setteth on fire the c' of nature;

courses
J'g 5:20 stars in their c' fought against
1Ki 5:14 ten thousand a month by c': a
1Ch 23: 6 divided them into c' among the
27: 1 the king in any matter of the c',
28:13 Also for the c' of the priests and
21 behold, the c' of the priests and the
2Ch 8:14 the c' of the priests to their service,
14 the porters also by their c' at every
23: 8 the priest dismissed not the c'.
31: 2 appointed the c' of the priests and
2 and the Levites after their c',
15 to give to their brethren by c', as
16 their charges according to their c';
17 in their charges by their c';
35: 4 fathers, after your c', according to
10 the Levites in their c', according to
Ezr 6:18 and the Levites in their c', for the
Isa 44: 4 as willows by the water c'.

court See also COURTS.
Ex 27: 9 thou shalt make the c' of the
9 hangings for the c' of fine twined
12 the breadth of the c' on the west
13 the breadth of the c' on the east
16 for the gate of the c' shall be an
17 the pillars round about the c' shall
18 The length of the c' shall be an
19 all the pins of the c', shall be of
35:17 The hangings of the c', his pillars,
17 the hanging for the door of the c',
18 the pins of the c', and their cords,
38: 9 he made the c': on the south side
9 the hangings of the c' were of fine

Ex 38:15 And for the other side of the c'
16 All the hangings of the c' round
17 and all the pillars of the c' were
18 the hanging for the gate of the c'
18 answerable to the hangings of the c'.
20 and of the c' round about, were of
31 the sockets of the c' round about,
31 and the sockets of the c' gate,
31 all the pins of the c' round about.
39:40 The hangings of the c', his pillars,
40 the hanging for the c' gate, his
40: 8 thou shalt set up the c' round
8 hang up the hanging at the c' gate.
33 he reared up the c' round about
33 set up the hanging of the c' gate.
Le 6:16 place; in the c' of the tabernacle
26 be eaten, in the c' of the tabernacle
Nu 3:26 the hangings of the c', and the
26 curtain for the door of the c',
37 And the pillars of the c' round
4:26 And the hangings of the c', and the
26 the door of the gate of the c',
32 the pillars of the c' round about,
2Sa 17:18 which had a well in his c'; whither
1Ki 6:36 he built the inner c' with three
7: 8 another c' within the porch, which
9 on the outside toward the great c'.
12 And the great c' round about was
12 both for the inner c' of the house
8:64 hallow the middle of the c' that
2Ki 20: 4 was gone out into the middle c',
2Ch 4: 9 he made the c' of the priests,
9 and the great c',
9 and doors for the c',
6:13 and had set it in the midst of the c':
7: 7 hallowed the middle of the c' that
20: 5 house of the Lord, before the new c',
24:21 in the c' of the house of the Lord.
29:16 into the c' of the house of the Lord.
Ne 3:25 that was by the c' of the prison.
Es 1: 5 in the c' of the garden of the king's
2:11 before the c' of the women's house,
4:11 unto the king into the inner c',
5: 1 stood in the inner c' of the king's
2 Esther the queen standing in the c',
6: 4 the king said, Who is in the c'?
4 into the outward c' of the king's
5 Behold, Haman standeth in the c'.
Isa 34:13 of dragons, and a c' for owls.
Jer 19:14 he stood in the c' of the Lord's
26: 2 Stand in the c' of the Lord's house,
32: 2 was shut up in the c' of the prison,
8 came to me in the c' of the prison
12 Jews that sat in the c' of the prison.
33: 1 yet shut up in the c' of the prison,
36:10 in the higher c', at the entry of the
20 they went in to the king into the c',
37:21 Jeremiah into the c' of the prison,
21 remained in the c' of the prison.
38: 6 that was in the c' of the prison:
13 remained in the c' of the prison.
28 abode in the c' of the prison until
39:14 Jeremiah out of the c' of the prison,
15 shut up in the c' of the prison,
Eze 8: 7 brought me to the door of the c';
16 brought me into the inner c' of the
10: 3 and the cloud filled the inner c'.
4 the c' was full of the brightness
5 was heard even to the outer c',
40:14 unto the post of the c' round about
17 brought he me into the outer c',
17 a pavement made for the c' round
19 forefront of the inner c' without,
20 gate of the outward c' that looked
23 the gate of the inner c' was over
27 a gate in the inner c' toward
28 he brought me to the inner c'
31 thereof were toward the utter c';
32 he brought me into the inner c'
34 were toward the outward c';
37 thereof were toward the utter c';
44 the singers in the inner c', which
47 measured the c', an hundred cubits
41:15 temple, and the porches of the c';
42: 1 brought me forth into the utter c',
3 cubits which were for the inner c',
3 which was for the utter c',
7 toward the utter c' on the forepart
8 chambers that were in the utter c'
9 goeth into them from the utter c'.
10 the thickness of the wall of the c'
14 the holy place into the utter c',
43: 5 and brought me into the inner c';
44:17 enter in at the gates of the inner c',
17 minister in the gates of the inner c',
19 they go forth into the utter c',
19 even into the utter c' to the people,
21 when they enter into the inner c'.
27 unto the inner c', to minister
45:19 posts of the gate of the inner c'.
46: 1 gate of the inner c' that looketh
20 bear them not out into the utter c',
21 brought me forth into the utter c',
21 me to pass by the corners of the c';
21 corner of the c' there was a c'.
22 corners of the c' there were courts
Am 7:13 chapel, and it is the king's c'.
Re 11: 2 the c' which is without the temple

courteous
1Pe 3: 8 as brethren, be pitiful, be c':

courteously
Ac 27: 3 Julius c' entreated Paul,
28: 7 us, and lodged us three days c'.

courts
2Ki 21: 5 two c' of the house of the Lord.
23:12 Manasseh had made in the two c'
1Ch 23:28 in the c', and in the chambers,
28: 6 he shall build my house and my c':
12 of the c' of the house of the Lord,
2Ch 23: 5 all the people shall be in the c' of
33: 5 two c' of the house of the Lord.
Ne 8:16 roof of his house, and in their c',
16 and in the c' of the house of God,
13: 7 preparing him a chamber in the c'
Ps 65: 4 thee, that he may dwell in thy c':
84: 2 even fainteth for the c' of the Lord:
10 For a day in thy c' is better than
92:13 shall flourish in the c' of our God.
96: 8 an offering, and come into his c'.
100: 4 into his c' with praise: be thankful
116:19 In the c' of the Lord's house,
135: 2 in the c' of the house of our God,
Isa 1:12 this at your hand, to tread my c'?
62: 9 drink it in the c' of my holiness.
Eze 9: 7 and fill the c' with the slain:
42: 6 not pillars as the pillars of the c':
46:22 were c' joined of forty cubits long
Zec 3: 7 and shalt also keep my c', and I will
Lu 7:25 live delicately, are in kings' c'.

cousin See also COUSINS.
Lu 1:36 And, behold, thy c' Elizabeth,

cousins
Lu 1:58 her neighbours and her c' heard

covenant See also COVENANTBREAKERS; COVENANTED; COVENANTS.
Ge 6:18 with thee will I establish my c';
9: 9 behold, I establish my c' with you,
11 I will establish my c' with you;
12 This is the token of the c' which
13 shall be for a token of a c' between
15 I will remember my c', which is
16 the everlasting c' between God
17 This is the token of the c', which
15:18 the Lord made a c' with Abram,
17: 2 I will make my c' between me and
4 for me, behold, my c' is with thee,
7 I will establish my c' between me
7 for an everlasting c', to be a God
9 Thou shalt keep my c' therefore,
10 This is my c', which ye shall keep,
11 a token of the c' betwixt me and
13 and my c' shall be in your flesh
13 in your flesh for an everlasting c'.
14 his people; he hath broken my c'.
19 I will establish my c' with him
19 with him for an everlasting c',
21 my c' will I establish with Isaac,
21:27 and both of them made a c'.
32 Thus they made a c' at Beer-sheba:
26:28 and let us make a c' with thee;
31:44 let us make a c', I and thou;
Ex 2:24 God remembered his c' with
6: 4 I have also established my c' with
5 and I have remembered my c'.
19: 5 and keep my c', then ye shall be
23:32 Thou shalt make no c' with them,
24: 7 And he took the book of the c',
8 Behold, the blood of the c', which
31:16 generations, for a perpetual c'.
34:10 Behold, I make a c': before all
12 lest thou make a c' with the
15 Lest thou make a c' with the
27 of these words I have made a c'
28 upon the tables the words of the c',
Le 2:13 the salt of the c' of thy God to be
24: 8 of Israel by an everlasting c'.
26: 9 and establish my c' with you.
15 but that ye break my c':
25 shall avenge the quarrel of my c':
42 will I remember my c' with Jacob,
42 and also my c' with Isaac,
42 and also my c' with Abraham
44 and to break my c' with them: for
45 remember the c' of their ancestors,
Nu 10:33 the ark of the c' of the Lord went
14:44 the ark of the c' of the Lord, and
18:19 it is a c' of salt for ever before the
25:12 I give unto him my c' of peace:
13 the c' of an everlasting priesthood;
De 4:13 And he declared unto you his c',
23 lest ye forget the c' of the Lord
31 nor forget the c' of thy fathers
5: 2 Lord our God made a c' with us in
3 The Lord made not this c' with our
7: 2 thou shalt make no c' with them,
9 keepeth c' and mercy with them
12 God shall keep unto thee the c' and
8:18 that he may establish his c' which
9: 9 the tables of the c' which the Lord
11 stone, even the tables of the c'.
15 the two tables of the c' were in my
10: 8 to bear the ark of the c' of the Lord,
17: 2 in transgressing his c',
29: 1 These are the words of the c',
1 the c' which he made with them
9 Keep therefore the words of this c',
12 That thou shouldest enter into c'
14 with you only do I make this c'
21 curses of the c' that are written
25 have forsaken the c' of the Lord
31: 9 which bare the ark of the c' of the
16 break my c' which I have made
20 and provoke me, and break my c'.
25 which bare the ark of the c' of the
26 in the side of the ark of the c' of
33: 9 thy word, and kept thy c'.
Jos 3: 3 When ye see the ark of the c' of
6 Take up the ark of the c', and pass
6 they took up the ark of the c',
8 that bear the ark of the c', saying,
Jos 3:11 the ark of the c' of the Lord of the
14 bearing the ark of the c' before the
17 priests that bare the ark of the c'
4: 7 cut off before the ark of the c' of
9 which bare the ark of the c' stood:
18 bare the ark of the c' of the Lord
6: 6 Take up the ark of the c',
8 and the ark of the c' of the Lord
7:11 also transgressed my c' which I
15 he hath transgressed the c' of the
8:33 which bare the ark of the c' of
23:16 When ye have transgressed the c'
24:25 Joshua made a c' with the people
J'g 2: 1 I will never break my c' with you.
20 people hath transgressed my c'
20:27 the ark of the c' of God was there
1Sa 4: 3 Let us fetch the ark of the c' of the
4 from thence the ark of the c' of the
4 there with the ark of the c' of God.
5 the ark of the c' of the Lord came
11: 1 Make a c' with us, and we will
2 condition will I make a c' with you,
18: 3 Jonathan and David made a c',
20: 8 brought thy servant into a c' of the
16 Jonathan made a c' with the house
23:18 two made a c' before the Lord:
2Sa 15:24 bearing the ark of the c' of God:
23: 5 made with me an everlasting c',
1Ki 3:15 and stood before the ark of the c'
6:19 there the ark of the c' of the Lord.
8: 1 might bring up the ark of the c' of
6 brought in the ark of the c' of the
9 when the Lord made a c' with the
21 wherein is the c' of the Lord,
23 who keepest c' and mercy with
11:11 thou hast not kept my c' and my
19:10, 14 of Israel have forsaken thy c',
20:34 send thee away with this c'.
34 So he made a c' with him,
2Ki 11: 4 and made a c' with them, and took
17 Jehoiada made a c' between the
13:23 because of his c' with Abraham,
17:15 c' that he made with their fathers,
35 With whom the Lord had made a c',
38 the c' that I have made with you
18:12 but transgressed his c', and all
23: 2 words of the book of the c' which
3 made a c' before the Lord, to walk
3 words of this c' that were written
3 And all the people stood to the c'.
21 it is written in the book of this c'.
1Ch 11: 3 David made a c' with them in
15:25 went to bring up the ark of the c'
26 Levites that bare the ark of the c'
28 Israel brought up the ark of the c'
29 the ark of the c' of the Lord came
16: 6 before the ark of the c' of God.
15 Be ye mindful always of his c';
16 Even of the c' which he made
17 to Israel for an everlasting c',
37 before the ark of the c' of the Lord
17: 1 but the ark of the c' of the Lord
22:19 bring the ark of the c' of the Lord,
28: 2 house of rest for the ark of the c'
18 and covered the ark of the c' of
2Ch 5: 2 the ark of the c' of the Lord out
7 brought in the ark of the c' of
10 when the Lord made a c' with
6:11 wherein is the c' of the Lord,
14 which keepest c', and shewest
13: 5 and to his sons by a c' of salt?
15:12 into a c' to seek the Lord
21: 7 because of the c' that he had made
23: 1 son of Zichri, into c' with him.
3 congregation made a c' with the
16 Jehoiada made a c' between him,
29:10 a c' with the Lord God of Israel,
34:30 the book of the c' that was found
31 made a c' before the Lord,
31 to perform the words of the c'
32 did according to the c' of God,
Ezr 10: 3 let us make a c' with our God
Ne 1: 5 that keepeth c' and mercy for them
9: 8 madest a c' with him to give the land
32 God, who keepest c' and mercy,
38 we make a sure c', and write
13:29 and the c' of the priesthood, and
Job 31: 1 I made a c' with mine eyes; why
41: 4 Will he make a c' with thee?
Ps 25:10 as keep his c' and his testimonies.
14 and he will shew them his c'.
44:17 have we dealt falsely in thy c'.
50: 5 made a c' with me by sacrifice.
16 shouldest take my c' in thy mouth?
55:20 with him: he hath broken his c'.
74:20 have respect unto the c': for
78:10 They kept not the c' of God, and
37 neither were they stedfast in his c'.
89: 3 I have made a c' with my chosen,
28 my c' shall stand fast with him.
34 My c' will I not break, nor alter
39 made void the c' of thy servant:
103:18 To such as keep his c', and to those
105: 8 hath remembered his c' for ever,
9 Which c' he made with Abraham,
10 and to Israel for an everlasting c':
106:45 he remembered for them his c',
111: 5 he will ever be mindful of his c'.
9 he hath commanded his c' for ever:
132:12 If thy children will keep my c' and
Pr 2:17 and forgetteth the c' of her God.
Isa 24: 5 ordinance, broken the everlasting c'.
28:15 We have made a c' with death, and
18 c' with death shall be disannulled,
33: 8 he hath broken the c', he hath
42: 6 give thee for a c' of the people, for

Isa 49: 8 give thee for a *c* of the people, to
54:10 neither shall the *c* of my peace be
55: 3 make an everlasting *c* with you,
56: 4 please me, and take hold of my *c*;
6 and taketh hold of my *c*;
57: 8 and made thee a *c* with them;
59:21 As for me, this is my *c* with them,
61: 8 make an everlasting *c* with them.
Jer 3:16 The ark of the *c* of the Lord:
11: 2 Hear ye the words of this *c*, and
3 obeyeth not the words of this *c*,
6 Hear ye the words of this *c*, and do
8 upon them all the words of this *c*,
10 of Judah having broken my *c*
14:21 remember, break not thy *c* with us.
22: 9 Because they have forsaken the *c*
31:31 will make a new *c* with the house
32 Not according to the *c* that I made
32 which my *c* they brake, although I
33 shall be the *c* that I will make
32:40 I will make an everlasting *c* with
33:20 If ye can break my *c* of the day,
20 and my *c* of the night,
21 also my *c* be broken with David
25 If my *c* be not with day and night,
34: 8 had made a *c* with all the people
10 which had entered into the *c*,
13 a *c* with your fathers in the day
15 made a *c* before me in the house
18 men that have transgressed my *c*,
18 not performed the words of the *c*
50: 5 to the Lord in a perpetual *c* that
Eze 16: 8 and entered into a *c* with thee, saith
59 despised the oath in breaking the *c*.
60 I will remember my *c* with thee in
60 establish unto thee an everlasting *c*.
61 for daughters, but not by thy *c*.
62 I will establish my *c* with thee;
17:13 and made a *c* with him, and hath
14 by keeping of his *c* it might stand.
15 he break the *c*, and be delivered?
16 whose *c* he brake, even with him
18 despised the oath by breaking the *c*,
19 and my *c* that he hath broken,
20:37 bring you into the bond of the *c*:
34:25 will make with them a *c* of peace,
37:26 will make a *c* of peace with them;
26 shall be an everlasting *c* with them:
44: 7 they have broken my *c* because
Da 9: 4 keeping the *c* and mercy to them
27 he shall confirm the *c* with many
11:22 yea, also the prince of the *c*.
28 heart shall be against the holy *c*;
30 indignation against the holy *c*:
30 with them that forsake the holy *c*.
32 such as do wickedly against the *c*
Ho 2:18 in that day will I make a *c* for them
6: 7 like men have transgressed the *c*:
8: 1 they have transgressed my *c*,
10: 4 swearing falsely in making a *c*:
12: 1 do make a *c* with the Assyrians,
Am 1: 9 remembered not the brotherly *c*:
Zec 9:11 by the blood of thy *c* I have sent
11:10 that I might break my *c* which I
Mal 2: 4 that my *c* might be with Levi,
5 My *c* was with him of life and
8 ye have corrupted the *c* of Levi,
10 by profaning the *c* of our fathers?
14 companion, and the wife of thy *c*.
3: 1 the messenger of the *c*, whom ye
Lu 1:72 to remember his holy *c*;
Ac 3:25 *c* which God made with our fathers,
7: 8 And he gave him the *c* of
Ro 11:27 this is my *c* unto them, when I shall
Ga 3:15 Though it be but a man's *c*,
17 the *c*, that was confirmed before
Heb 8: 6 he is the mediator of a better *c*,
7 if that first *c* had been faultless,
8 will make a new *c* with the house
9 Not according to the *c* that I made
9 they continued not in my *c*, and
10 this is the *c* that I will make with
13 In that he saith, A new *c*, he
9: 1 Then verily the first *c* had also
4 the ark of the *c* overlaid round
4 and the tables of the *c*;
10:16 This is the *c* that I will make with
29 the blood of the *c*, wherewith he
12:24 Jesus the mediator of the new *c*,
13:20 the blood of the everlasting *c*,

covenantbreakers
Ro 1:31 *c*, without natural affection.

covenanted
2Ch 7:18 as I have *c* with David thy father
Hag 2: 5 I *c* with you when ye came out of
M't 26:15 they *c* with him for thirty pieces
Lu 22: 5 glad, and *c* to give him money.

covenants
Ro 9: 4 glory, and the *c*, and the giving
Ga 4:24 for these are the two *c*; the one
Eph 2:12 strangers from the *c* of promise,

cover See also COVERED; COVERETH; COVERING; DISCOVER; RECOVER; UNCOVER.
Ex 10: 5 they shall *c* the face of the earth,
21:33 a man shall dig a pit, and not *c* it.
25:29 and bowls thereof, to *c* withal: of
26:13 side and on that side, to *c* it.
28:42 breeches to *c* their nakedness;
33:22 and will *c* thee with my hand while
37:16 bowls, and his covers to *c* withal,
40: 3 and *c* the ark with the vail.
Le 13:12 the leprosy *c* all the skin of him
16:13 the incense may *c* the mercy seat
17:13 blood thereof, and *c* it with dust.
Nu 4: 5 *c* the ark of testimony with it:
7 the bowls, and covers to *c* withal:
8 and *c* the same with a covering
9 and *c* the candlestick of the light,
11 and *c* it with a covering of badgers'
12 *c* them with a covering of badgers'
22: 5 they *c* the face of the earth, and
De 23:13 and *c* that which cometh from thee:
33:12 Lord shall *c* him all the day
1Sa 24: 3 Saul went in to *c* his feet: and
1Ki 7:18 to *c* the chapiters that were upon
41 two networks, to *c* the two bowls of
42 to *c* the two bowls of the chapiters
2Ch 4:12 two wreaths to *c* the two pommels
13 each wreath, to *c* the two pommels
Ne 4: 5 And *c* not their iniquity, and let
Job 16:18 *c* not thou my blood, and let my
21:26 and the worms shall *c* them.
22:11 and abundance of waters *c* thee.
38:34 abundance of waters may *c* thee?
40:22 trees *c* him with their shadow;
Ps 91: 4 He shall *c* thee with his feathers,
104: 9 they turn not again to *c* the earth
109:29 them *c* themselves with their own
139:11 Surely the darkness shall *c* me;
140: 9 mischief of their own lips *c* them.
Isa 11: 9 the Lord, as the waters *c* the sea.
14:11 under thee, and the worms *c* thee.
22:17 captivity, and will surely *c* thee.
26:21 and shall no more *c* her slain.
30: 1 that *c* with a covering, but not
58: 7 seest the naked, that thou *c* him;
59: 6 neither shall they *c* themselves
60: 2 darkness shall *c* the earth, and
6 multitude of camels shall *c* thee.
Jer 46: 8 I will go up, and will *c* the earth;
Eze 7:18 and horror shall *c* them;
12: 6 thou shalt *c* thy face, that thou
12 he shall *c* his face, that he see not
24: 7 the ground, to *c* it with dust;
17 and *c* not thy lips, and eat not the
22 ye shall not *c* your lips, nor eat
26:10 his horses their dust shall *c* thee:
19 and great waters shall *c* thee;
30:18 a cloud shall *c* her, and her
32: 7 I will *c* the heaven, and make the
7 I will *c* the sun with a cloud,
37: 6 and *c* you with skin, and put
38: 9 like a cloud to *c* the land, thou,
16 as a cloud to *c* the land; it shall
Ho 2: 9 flax given to *c* her nakedness.
10: 8 shall say to the mountains, *C* us;
Ob 10 shame shall *c* thee, and thou shalt
Mic 3: 7 yea, they shall all *c* their lips;
7:10 and shame shall *c* her which said
Hab 2:14 glory of the Lord, as the waters *c*
17 violence of Lebanon shall *c* thee,
M'r 14:65 to spit on him, and to *c* his face,
Lu 23:30 Fall on us; and to the hills, *C* us.
1Co 11: 7 For a man indeed ought not to *c*
1Pe 4: 8 charity shall *c* the multitude of

covered See also COVEREDST; DISCOVERED; RECOVERED; UNCOVERED.
Ge 7:19 under the whole heaven, were *c*.
20 and the mountains were *c*.
9:23 *c* the nakedness of their father;
24:65 she took a vail, and *c* herself.
38:14 and *c* her with a vail, and wrapped
15 because she had *c* her face.
Ex 8: 6 the frogs came up, and *c* the land
10:15 For they *c* the face of the whole
14:28 waters returned, and *c* the chariots
15: 5 depths have *c* them: they sank
10 the sea *c* them: they sank as lead
16:13 quails came up, and *c* the camp:
24:15 and a cloud *c* the mount.
16 and the cloud *c* it six days:
37: 9 and *c* with their wings over the
40:21 and *c* the ark of the testimony;
34 Then a cloud *c* the tent of the
Le 13:13 if the leprosy have *c* all his flesh,
Nu 4:20 when the holy things are *c*,
7: 3 six *c* wagons, and twelve oxen;
9:15 cloud *c* the tabernacle, namely,
16 the cloud *c* it by day, and the
16:42 the cloud *c* it, and the glory of
De 32:15 thick, thou art *c* with fatness;
Jos 24: 7 the sea upon them, and *c* them;
J'g 4:18 she *c* him with a mantle.
19 and gave him drink, and *c* him.
1Sa 19:13 for his bolster, and *c* it with a
28:14 and he is *c* with a mantle.
2Sa 15:30 had his head *c*, and he went
30 *c* every man his head, and they
19: 4 the king *c* his face, and the king
1Ki 1: 1 and they *c* him with clothes,
6: 9 and *c* the house with beams and
15 he *c* them on the inside with
15 and *c* the floor of the house with
20 and so *c* the altar which was of
35 and *c* them with gold fitted upon
7: 3 And it was *c* with cedar above
7 and it was *c* with cedar from one
8: 7 and the cherubims *c* the ark and
2Ki 19: 1 and *c* himself with sackcloth,
2 of the priests, *c* with sackcloth,
1Ch 28:18 and *c* the ark of the covenant
2Ch 5: 8 and the cherubims *c* the ark and
Ne 3:15 he built it, and *c* it, and set up
Es 6:12 mourning, and having his head *c*.
7: 8 mouth, they *c* Haman's face.
Job 23:17 neither hath he *c* the darkness
31:33 If I *c* my transgressions as Adam,
Ps 32: 1 is forgiven, whose sin is *c*.
44:15 the shame of my face hath *c* me,
19 and *c* us with the shadow of death.
Ps 65:13 valleys also are *c* over with corn;
68:13 the wings of a dove *c* with silver,
69: 7 reproach; shame hath *c* my face.
71:13 let them be *c* with reproach and
80:10 The hills were *c* with the shadow
85: 2 people, thou hast *c* all their sin.
89:45 thou hast *c* him with shame.
106:11 And the waters *c* their enemies:
17 and *c* the company of Abiram.
139:13 thou hast *c* me in my mother's
140: 7 thou hast *c* my head in the day
Pr 24:31 nettles had *c* the face thereof,
26:23 a potsherd *c* with silver dross.
26 Whose hatred is *c* by deceit,
Ec 6: 4 his name shall be *c* with darkness.
Isa 6: 2 with twain he *c* his face,
2 and with twain he *c* his feet,
29:10 your rulers, the seers hath he *c*.
37: 1 and *c* himself with sackcloth,
2 of the priests *c* with sackcloth,
51:16 I have *c* thee in the shadow of mine
61:10 he hath *c* me with the robe of
Jer 14: 3 confounded, and *c* their heads.
4 ashamed, they *c* their heads.
51:42 she is *c* with the multitude of the
51 shame hath *c* our faces: for
La 2: 1 Lord *c* the daughter of Zion with
3:16 stones, he hath *c* me with ashes.
43 Thou hast *c* with anger, and
44 Thou hast *c* thyself with a cloud,
Eze 1:11 and two *c* their bodies.
23 had two, which *c* on this side, and
23 had two, which *c* on that side, their
16: 8 over thee, and *c* thy nakedness:
10 fine linen, and I *c* thee with silk.
18: 7 hath *c* the naked with a garment;
16 hath *c* the naked with a garment,
24: 8 of a rock, that it should not be *c*.
27: 7 Elishah was that which *c* thee.
31:15 I *c* the deep for him, and I
37: 8 them, and the skin *c* them above:
41:16 and the windows were *c*;
Jon 3: 6 and *c* him with sackcloth, and sat
8 man and beast be *c* with sackcloth,
Hab 3: 3 His glory *c* the heavens, and the
M't 8:24 the ship was *c* with the waves:
10:26 there is nothing *c*, that shall not
Lu 12: 2 there is nothing *c*, that shall not
Ro 4: 7 forgiven, and whose sins are *c*.
1Co 11: 4 having his head *c*, dishonoureth
6 the woman be not *c*, let her also
6 shorn or shaven, let her be *c*.

coveredst
Ps 104: 6 Thou *c* it with the deep as with a
Eze 16:18 broidered garments, and *c* them:

coverest
De 22:12 vesture, wherewith thou *c* thyself.
Ps 104: 2 Who *c* thyself with light as with

covereth See also UNCOVERETH.
Ex 29:13 all the fat that *c* the inwards,
22 and the fat that *c* the inwards,
Le 3: 3, 9, 14 the fat that *c* the inwards,
4: 8 the fat that *c* the inwards,
7: 3 and the fat that *c* the inwards,
9:19 and that which *c* the inwards,
Nu 22:11 which *c* the face of the earth:
J'g 3:24 he *c* his feet in his summer
Job 9:24 he *c* the faces of the judges
15:27 Because he *c* his face with his
36:30 it, and *c* the bottom of the sea.
32 With clouds he *c* the light;
Ps 73: 6 violence *c* them as a garment.
109:19 him as the garment which *c* him,
147: 8 Who *c* the heaven with clouds,
Pr 10: 6, 11 but violence *c* the mouth of the
12 up strifes: but love *c* all sins.
12:16 but a prudent man *c* shame.
17: 9 He that *c* a transgression seeketh
28:13 that *c* his sins shall not prosper:
Jer 3:25 and our confusion *c* us: for we
Eze 28:14 art the anointed cherub that *c*;
Mal 2:16 one *c* violence with his garment,
Lu 8:16 a candle, *c* it with a vessel,

covering See also COVERINGS; DISCOVERING; RECOVERING.
Ge 8:13 Noah removed the *c* of the ark,
20:16 he is to thee a *c* of the eyes, unto
Ex 22:27 For that is his *c* only, it is his
25:20 *c* the mercy seat with their wings,
26: 7 to be a *c* upon the tabernacle:
14 a *c* for the tent of rams' skins,
14 and a *c* above of badgers' skins.
35:11 tabernacle, his tent, and his *c*,
12 mercy seat, and the vail of the *c*,
36:19 a *c* for the tent of rams' skins
19 a *c* of badgers' skins above that.
39:34 the *c* of rams' skins dyed red,
34 and the *c* of badgers' skins,
34 and the vail of the *c*,
40:19 the *c* of the tent above upon it;
21 set up the vail of the *c*, and
Le 13:45 shall put a *c* upon his upper lip,
Nu 3:25 the tent, the *c* thereof, and the
4: 5 they shall take down the *c* vail,
6 the *c* of badgers' skins, and
8 same with a *c* of badgers' skins,
10 within a *c* of badgers' skins,
11 cover it with a *c* of badgers' skins,
12 them with a *c* of badgers' skins,
14 upon it a *c* of badgers' skins, and
15 made an end of *c* the sanctuary,
25 his *c*, and the *c* of the badgers'
16:38, 39 plates for a *c* of the altar:
19:15 no *c* bound upon it, is unclean.

2Sa 17:19 spread a c' over the well's mouth,
Job 22:14 Thick clouds are a c' to him, that
24: 7 that they have no c' in the cold.
26: 6 him, and destruction hath no c'.
31:19 clothing, or any poor without c';
Ps 105:39 He spread a cloud for a c'; and
Ca 3:10 the c' of it of purple, the midst
Isa 22: 8 he discovered the c' of Judah,
25: 7 face of the c' cast over all people,
28:20 and the c' narrower than that he
30: 1 that cover with a c', but not of
22 c' of thy graven images of silver,
50: 3 and I make sackcloth their c'.
Eze 28:13 every precious stone was thy c',
16 I will destroy thee, O c' cherub,
Mal 2:13 c' the altar of the Lord with tears,
1Co 11:15 for her hair is given her for a c'.

coverings
Pr 7:16 decked my bed with c' of tapestry,
31:22 She maketh herself c' of tapestry;

covers
Ex 25:29 and c' thereof, and bowls thereof,
37:16 and his c' to cover withal, of pure
Nu 4: 7 the bowls, and c' to cover withal:

covert
1Sa 25:20 came down by the c' of the hill,
2Ki 16:18 c' for the sabbath that they had
Job 38:40 and abide in the c' to lie in wait?
40:21 in the c' of the reed, and fens.
Ps 61: 4 I will trust in the c' of thy wings.
Isa 4: 6 a c' from storm and from rain.
16: 4 be thou a c' to them from the face
32: 2 wind, and a c' from the tempest;
Jer 25:38 hath forsaken his c', as the lion:

covet See also COVETED; COVETETH.
Ex 20:17 shalt not c' thy neighbour's house,
17 shalt not c' thy neighbour's wife,
De 5:21 shalt thou c' thy neighbour's house,
Mic 2: 2 And they c' fields, and take them
Ro 7: 7 law had said, Thou shalt not c'.
13: 9 Thou shalt not c'; and if there be
1Co 12:31 But c' earnestly the best gifts:
14:39 c' to prophesy, and forbid not to

coveted
Jos 7:21 then I c' them, and took them;
Ac 20:33 I have c' no man's silver, or gold,
1Ti 6:10 while some c' after, they have

coveteth
Pr 21:26 He c' greedily all the day long:
Hab 2: 9 him that c' an evil covetousness

covetous See COVETOUSNESS.
Ps 10: 3 blesseth the c', whom the Lord
Lu 16:14 the Pharisees also, who were c',
1Co 5:10 or with the c', or extortioners, or
11 or c', or an idolator, or a railer, or
6:10 nor c', nor drunkards, nor revilers,
Eph 5: 5 nor c' man, who is an idolater,
1Ti 3: 3 patient, not a brawler, not c';
2Ti 3: 2 lovers of their own selves, c',
2Pe 2:14 have exercised with c' practices;

covetousness
Ex 18:21 fear God, men of truth, hating c';
Ps 119:36 thy testimonies, and not to c'.
Pr 28:16 hateth c' shall prolong his days.
Isa 57:17 the iniquity of his c' was I wroth,
Jer 6:13 them every one is given to c'; and
8:10 the greatest is given to c', from
22:17 are not but for c', and for to shed
51:13 is come, and the measure of thy c'
Eze 33:31 their heart goeth after their c'.
Hab 2: 9 coveteth an evil c' to his house,
M'r 7:22 Thefts, c', wickedness, deceit,
Lu 12:15 Take heed, and beware of c':
Ro 1:29 wickedness, c', maliciousness;
2Co 9: 5 of bounty, and not as of c'.
Eph 5: 3 all uncleanness, or c', let it not be
Col 3: 5 and c', which is idolatry:
1Th 2: 5 as ye know, nor a cloke of c';
Heb 13: 5 your conversation be without c';
2Pe 2: 3 through c' shall they with feigned

cow See also COW'S; KINE.
Le 22:28 And whether it be c' or ewe, ye
Nu 18:17 But the firstling of a c', or the
Job 21:10 their c' calveth, and casteth not
Isa 7:21 man shall nourish a young c',
11: 7 And the c' and the bear shall feed;
Am 4: 3 every c' at that which is before her,

cow's
Eze 4:15 me, Lo, I have given thee c' dung

Coz (*coz*)
1Ch 4: 8 And C' begat Anub, and Zobebah,

Cozbi (*coz'-bi*)
Nu 25:15 woman that was slain was C',
18 of Peor, and in the matter of C',

crackling
Ec 7: 6 as the c' of thorns under a pot,

cracknels
1Ki 14: 3 take with thee ten loaves and c',

craft See also CRAFTSMAN; WITCHCRAFT.
Da 8:25 cause c' to prosper in his hand;
M'r 14: 1 how they might take him by c',
Ac 18: 3 because he was of the same c',
19:25 by this c' we have our wealth.
27 not only this our c' is in danger
Re 18:22 craftsman, of whatsoever c' he be,

craftiness
Job 5:13 taketh the wise in their own c':
Lu 20:23 But he perceived their c', and
1Co 3:19 He taketh the wise in their own c'.
2Co 4: 2 not walking in c', nor handling the
Eph 4:14 the sleight of men, and cunning c',

craftsman See also CRAFTSMEN.
De 27:15 the work of the hands of the c',
Re 18:22 no c', of whatsoever craft he be,

craftsmen
2Ki 24:14 and all the c' and smiths: none
16 and c' and smiths a thousand, all
1Ch 4:14 of Charashim; for they were c'.
Ne 11:35 Lod, and Ono, the valley of c'.
Ho 13: 2 all of it the work of the c':
Ac 19:24 brought no small gain unto the c';
38 and the c' which are with him,

crafty
Job 5:12 disappointeth the devices of the c',
15: 5 thou choosest the tongue of the c'.
Ps 83: 3 They have taken c' counsel against
2Co 12:16 being c', I caught you with guile.

crag
Job 39:28 upon the c' of the rock, and the

crane
Isa 38:14 a c' or a swallow, so did I chatter:
Jer 8: 7 the c' and the swallow observe

crashing
Zep 1:10 and a great c' from the hills.

craved
M'r 15:43 Pilate, and c' the body of Jesus.

craveth
Pr 16:26 for his mouth c' it of him,

create See also CREATED; CREATETH.
Ps 51:10 C' in me a clean heart, O God;
Isa 4: 5 Lord will c' upon every dwelling
45: 7 I form the light, and c' darkness:
7 I make peace, and c' evil:
57:19 I c' the fruit of the lips; Peace,
65:17 I c' new heavens and a new earth:
18 rejoice for ever in that which I c':
18 behold, I c' Jerusalem a rejoicing,

created
Ge 1: 1 God c' the heaven and the earth.
21 And God c' great whales, and every
27 So God c' man in his own image,
27 in the image of God c' he him;
27 male and female c' he them.
2: 3 his work which God c' and made.
4 and of the earth, when they were c',
5: 1 In the day that God c' man, in the
2 Male and female c' he them; and
2 in the day when they were c'.
6: 7 I will destroy man whom I have c'
De 4:32 that God c' man upon the earth,
Ps 89:12 and the south thou hast c' them:
102:18 the people which shall be c' shall
104:30 sendest forth thy spirit, they are c':
148: 5 he commanded, and they were c'.
Isa 40:26 behold who hath c' these things,
41:20 the Holy One of Israel hath c' it.
42: 5 he that c' the heavens, and
43: 1 thus saith the Lord that c' thee,
7 I have c' him for my glory, I have
45: 8 I the Lord have c' it.
12 made the earth, and c' man upon it:
18 the Lord that c' the heavens; God
18 he c' it not in vain, he formed it to
48: 7 They are c' now, and not from the
54:16 c' the smith that bloweth the coals
16 I have c' the waster to destroy.
Jer 31:22 hath c' a new thing in the earth,
Eze 21:30 in the place where thou wast c',
28:13 thee in the day that thou wast c'.
15 from the day that thou wast c', till
Mal 2:10 hath not one God c' us? why do we
M'r 13:19 which God c' unto this time, neither
1Co 11: 9 was the man c' for the woman; but
Eph 2:10 c' in Christ Jesus unto good works,
3: 9 in God, who c' all things by Jesus
4:24 after God is c' in righteousness
Col 1:16 by him were things c', that are in
16 all things were c' by him, and for
3:10 after the image of him that c' him:
1Ti 4: 3 which God hath c' to be received
Re 4:11 for thou hast c' all things, and for
11 thy pleasure they are and were c'.
10: 6 who c' heaven, and the things that

createth
Am 4:13 and c' the wind, and declareth

creation
M'r 10: 6 But from the beginning of the c'
13:19 not from the beginning of the c'
Ro 1:20 from the c' of the world are clearly
8:22 that the whole c' groaneth and
2Pe 3: 4 were from the beginning of the c'
Re 3:14 the beginning of the c' of God;

Creator
Ec 12: 1 Remember now thy C' in the days
Isa 40:28 the C' of the ends of the earth,
43:15 your Holy One, the c' of Israel,
Ro 1:25 more than the C', who is blessed
1Pe 4:19 well doing, as unto a faithful C'.

creature See also CREATURES.
Ge 1:20 the moving c' that hath life, and
21 every living c' that moveth, which
24 the earth bring forth the living c'
2:19 called every living c', that was the
9:10 every living c' that is with you, of
12 me and you and every living c'
15 and every living c' of all flesh;
16 between God and every living c'
Le 11:46 every living c' that moveth in the
46 every c' that creepeth upon the
Eze 1:20, 21 spirit of the living c' was in the
22 upon the heads of the living c'
10:15 This is the living c' that I saw by
Eze 10:17 spirit of the living c' was in them.
20 This is the living c' that I saw by
M'r 16:15 and preach the gospel to every c'.
Ro 1:25 and served the c' more than the
8:19 the earnest expectation of the c'
20 For the c' was made subject to
21 Because the c' itself also shall be
39 nor any other c', shall be able to
2Co 5:17 he is a new c': old things are
Ga 6:15 uncircumcision, but a new c'.
Col 1:15 God, the firstborn of every c':
23 which was preached to every c'
1Ti 4: 4 For every c' of God is good and
Heb 4:13 Neither is there any c' that is not
Re 5:13 And every c' which is in heaven,

creatures
Isa 13:21 houses shall be full of doleful c';
Eze 1: 5 came the likeness of four living c'.
13 the likeness of the living c', their
13 up and down among the living c';
14 And the living c' ran and returned
15 Now as I beheld the living c',
15 upon the earth by the living c',
19 when the living c' went, the wheels
19 and when the living c' were lifted
3:13 noise of the wings of the living c'
Jas 1:18 be a kind of firstfruits of his c'.
Re 8: 9 third part of the c' which were in

credible See INCREDIBLE.

creditor See CREDITORS.
De 15: 2 Every c' that lendeth
2Ki 4: 1 and the c' is come to take unto
Lu 7:41 There was a certain c' which had

creditors
Isa 50: 1 which of my c' is it to whom I

creek
Ac 27:39 they discovered a certain c' with

creep See also CREEPETH; CREEPING; CREPT.
Le 11:20 All fowls that c', going upon all
29 the creeping things that c' upon
31 unclean to you among all that c':
42 all creeping things that c' upon
Ps 104:20 the beasts of the forest do c' forth
Eze 38:20 and all creeping things that c'
2Ti 3: 6 are they which c' into houses,

creepeth
Ge 1:25 and every thing that c' upon the
26 every creeping thing that c' upon
30 to every thing that c' upon the
7: 8 and of every thing that c' upon the
14 and every creeping thing that c'
21 and of every creeping thing that c'
8:17 and of every creeping thing that c'
19 fowl, and whatsoever c' upon the
Le 11:41 every creeping thing that c' upon
43 with any creeping thing that c',
44 manner of creeping thing that c'
46 of every creature that c' upon the
20:25 manner of living thing that c' on
De 4:18 The likeness of any thing that c'

creeping
Ge 1:24 cattle, and c' thing, and beast of
26 over every c' thing that creepeth
6: 7 the c' thing, and the fowls of the
20 every c' thing of the earth after
7:14 and every c' thing that creepeth
21 and of beast, and of every c' thing
23 the c' things, and the fowl of the
8:17 of every c' thing that creepeth
19 Every beast, every c' thing, and
Le 5: 2 carcase of unclean c' things, and
11:21 every flying c' thing that goeth
23 all other flying c' things, which
29 among the c' things that creep
41 every c' thing that creepeth upon
42 hath more feet among all c' things
43 abominable with any c' thing that
44 with any manner of c' thing that
22: 5 whosoever toucheth any c' thing,
De 14:19 every c' thing that flieth is unclean
1Ki 4:33 of fowl, and of c' things, and of
Ps 104:25 things c' innumerable, both small
148:10 c' things, and flying fowl:
Eze 8:10 and behold every form of c' things,
38:20 field, and all c' things that creep
Hos 2:18 with the c' things of the ground:
Hab 1:14 as the c' things, that have no ruler
Ac 10:12 and wild beasts, and c' things, and
11: 6 and wild beasts, and c' things, and
Ro 1:23 fourfooted beasts, and c' things.

crept
Jude 4 For there are certain men c' in

Crescens (*cres'-sens*)
2Ti 4:10 C' to Galatia, Titus unto

Cretans See CRETES; CRETIANS.

Crete (*creet*) See also CRETES.
Ac 27: 7 suffering us, we sailed under C',
12 which is an haven of C', and lieth
13 thence, they sailed close by C'.
21 me, and not have loosed from C',
Tit 1: 5 For this cause left I thee in C',

Cretes (*creets*) See also CRETIANS.
Ac 2:11 C' and Arabians, we do hear

Cretians ((*cre'-shuns*) See also CRETES.
Tit 1:12 The C' are always liars, evil
subscr bishop of the church of the C'

crew
M't 26:74 And immediately the cock c'.
M'r 14:68 out into the porch; and the cock c'.
72 And the second time the cock c'.

Lu 22:60 while he yet spake, the cock c·.
Joh 18:27 again: and immediately the cock c·.

crib
Job 39: 9 to serve thee, or abide by thy c·?
Pr 14: 4 Where no oxen are, the c· is clean:
Isa 1: 3 owner, and the ass his master's c·:

cried
Ge 27:34 he c· with a great and exceeding
39:14 me, and I c· with a loud voice:
15 that I lifted up my voice and c·,
18 as I lifted up my voice and c·, that
41:43 they c· before him, Bow the knee:
55 people c· to Pharaoh for bread:
45: 1 and he c·, Cause every man to go
Ex 2:23 and they c·, and their cry came up
5:15 the children of Israel came and c·
8:12 Moses c· unto the Lord because of
14:10 and the children of Israel c· out
15:25 And he c· unto the Lord; and the
17: 4 And Moses c· unto the Lord, saying,
Nu 11: 2 And the people c· unto Moses;
12:13 And Moses c· unto the Lord, saying,
14: 1 lifted up their voice, and c·;
20:16 And when we c· unto the Lord,
De 22:24 the damsel, because she c· not,
27 the betrothed damsel c·, and there
26: 7 And when we c· unto the Lord God
Jos 24: 7 And when they c· unto the Lord,
J'g 3: 9 And when the children of Israel c·
15 But when the children of Israel c·
4: 3 And the children of Israel c· unto
5:28 and c· through the lattice,
6: 6 and the children of Israel c· unto
7 when the children of Israel c· unto
7:20 they c·, The sword of the Lord,
21 all the host ran, and c·, and fled.
9: 7 and lifted up his voice, and c·,
10:10 and the children of Israel c· unto
12 and ye c· to me, and I delivered
18:23 they c· unto the children of Dan.
1Sa 4:13 and told it, all the city c· out.
5:10 that the Ekronites c· out, saying,
7: 9 and Samuel c· unto the Lord for
12: 8 and your fathers c· unto the Lord,
10 they c· unto the Lord, and said,
15:11 and he c· unto the Lord all night.
17: 8 and c· unto the armies of Israel,
20:37 Jonathan c· after the lad, and said,
38 Jonathan c· after the lad, make
24: 8 out of the cave, and c· after Saul,
26:14 And David c· to the people, and to
28:12 woman saw Samuel, she c· with a
2Sa 18:25 watchman c·, and told the king.
19: 4 and the king c· with a loud voice,
20:16 Then c· a wise woman out of the
22: 7 and c· to my God: and he did hear
1Ki 13: 2 he c· against the altar in the word
4 had c· against the altar in Beth-el,
21 And he c· unto the man of God
32 which he c· by the word of the Lord
17:20 he c· unto the Lord, and said,
21 the child three times, and c· unto
18:28 they c· aloud, and cut themselves
20:39 he c· unto the king: and he said,
22:32 against him: and Jehoshaphat c·
2Ki 2:12 and he c·, My father, my father,
4: 1 Now there c· a certain woman of
40 they c· out, and said, O thou man
6: 5 and he c·, and said, Alas, master!
26 there c· a woman unto him, saying,
8: 5 c· to the king for her house and
11:14 Athaliah rent her clothes, and c·,
18:28 Then Rab-shakeh stood and c· with
20:11 And Isaiah the prophet c· unto the
1Ch 5:20 they c· to God in the battle, and he
2Ch 13:14 and they c· unto the Lord, and the
14:11 And Asa c· unto the Lord his God,
18:31 Jehoshaphat c· out, and the Lord
32:18 Then they c· with a loud voice in
20 the son of Amoz, prayed and c· to
Ne 9: 4 and c· with a loud voice unto the
27 they c· unto thee, thou heardest
28 when they returned, and c· unto
Es 4: 1 and c· with a loud and a bitter cry;
Job 29:12 I delivered the poor that c·,
30: 5 c· after them as after a thief;)
28 up, and I c· in the congregation.
Ps 3: 4 I c· unto the Lord with my voice,
18: 6 and c· unto my God: he heard
41 They c·, but there was none to
22: 5 They c· unto thee, and were
24 when he c· unto him, he heard.
30: 2 O Lord my God, I c· unto thee,
8 I c· to thee, O Lord; and unto the
31:22 supplications when I c· unto thee.
34: 6 This poor man c·, and the Lord
66:17 I c· unto him with my mouth,
77: 1 I c· unto God with my voice,
88: 1 I have c· day and night before thee:
13 unto thee have I c·, O Lord; and
107: 6 Then they c· unto the Lord in
13 Then they c· unto the Lord in
119:145 I c· with my whole heart;
146 I c· unto thee; save me, and I
147 dawning of the morning, and c·:
120: 1 In my distress I c· unto the Lord,
130: 1 Out of the depths have I c· unto
138: 3 day when I c· thou answeredst
142: 1 I c· unto the Lord with my voice;
5 I c· unto thee, O Lord: I said,
Isa 6: 3 And one c· unto another, and said,
4 moved at the voice of him that c·,
21: 8 And he c·, A lion: My lord,
30: 7 therefore have I c· concerning
36:13 Then Rabshakeh stood, and c· with
Jer 4:20 Destruction upon destruction is c·;
20: 8 For since I spake, I c· out,
8 I c· violence and spoil;
La 2:18 Their heart c· unto the Lord,
4:15 they c· unto them, Depart ye;
Eze 9: 1 He c· also in mine ears with a loud
8 I fell upon my face, and c·,
10:13 As for the wheels, it was c· unto
11:13 fell I down upon my face, and c·
Da 3: 4 Then an herald c· aloud, To you
4:14 He c· aloud, and said thus,
5: 7 The king c· aloud to bring in the
6:20 he c· with a lamentable voice unto
Ho 7:14 And they have not c· unto me
Jon 1: 5 and c· every man unto his god,
14 they c· unto the Lord, and said,
2: 2 And said, I c· by reason of mine
2 out of the belly of hell c· I, and
3: 4 he c·, and said, Yet forty days, and
Zec 1: 4 former prophets have c·, saying,
6: 8 Then c· he unto me, and spake
7: 7 the Lord hath c· by the former
13 as he c·, and they would not hear;
13 so they c·, and I would not hear,
M't 8:29 behold, they c· out, saying,
14:26 is a spirit; and they c· out for fear.
30 beginning to sink, he c·, saying,
15:22 c· unto him, saying, Have mercy
20:30 c· out, saying, Have mercy on us,
31 but they c· the more, saying,
21: 9 c·, saying, Hosanna to the son of
27:23 But they c· out the more, saying,
46 Jesus c· with a loud voice, saying,
50 Jesus, when he had c· again with
M'r 1:23 with an unclean spirit; and he c·
26 torn him, and c· with a loud voice,
3:11 c·, saying, Thou art the Son of God.
5: 7 c· with a loud voice, and said,
6:49 it had been a spirit, and c· out:
9:24 c· out, and said with tears, Lord,
26 the spirit c·, and rent him sore,
10:48 but he c· the more a great deal,
11: 9 and they that followed, c·, saying,
15:13 they c· out again, Crucify him.
14 they c· out the more exceedingly,
34 hour Jesus c· with a loud voice,
37 And Jesus c· with a loud voice,
39 saw that he so c· out, and gave
Lu 4:33 unclean devil, and c· out with a
8: 8 he had said these things, he c·,
28 When he saw Jesus, he c· out, and
9:38 a man of the company c· out,
16:24 he c· and said, Father Abraham,
18:38 he c·, saying, Jesus, thou son of
39 he c· so much the more, Thou son
23:18 they c· out all at once, saying,
21 But they c·, saying, Crucify him,
46 when Jesus had c· with a loud
Joh 1:15 and c·, saying, This was he of
7:28 Then c· Jesus in the temple as he
37 Jesus stood and c·, saying, If any
11:43 he c· with a loud voice, Lazarus,
12:13 to meet him, and c·, Hosanna:
44 Jesus c· and said, He that
18:40 Then c· they all again, saying,
19: 6 saw him, they c· out, saying,
12 the Jews c· out, saying, If thou
15 they c· out, Away with him,
Ac 7:57 they c· out with a loud voice,
60 and c· with a loud voice, Lord,
16:17 and c·, saying, These men are the
28 Paul c· with a lond voice, saying,
19:28 and c· out, saying, Great is Diana
32 Some therefore c· one thing, and
34 c· out, Great is Diana of the
21:34 some c· one thing, some another,
22:23 And as they c· out, and cast off
24 he might know wherefore they c·
23: 6 he c· out in the council, Men and
24:21 I c· standing among them,
Re 6:10 they c· with a loud voice, saying,
7: 2 and he c· with a loud voice to the
10 And c· with a loud voice, saying,
10: 3 And c· with a loud voice, as when
3 when he had c·, seven thunders
12: 2 And she being with child c,
14:18 c· with a loud cry to him that had
18: 2 And he c· mightily with a strong
18 And c· when they saw the smoke
19 and c·, weeping and wailing,
19:17 and he c· with a loud voice,

cries
Jas 5: 4 the c· of them which have reaped

criest
Ex 14:15 Wherefore c· thou unto me?
1Sa 26:14 Who art thou that c· to the king?
Pr 2: 3 Yea, if thou c· after knowledge,
Isa 57:13 When thou c·, let thy companies
Jer 30:15 Why c· thou for thine affliction?

crieth
Ge 4:10 the voice of thy brother's blood c·
Ex 22:27 he c· unto me, that I will hear;
Job 24:12 the soul of the wounded c· out:
Ps 72:12 shall deliver the needy when he c·;
84: 2 my heart and my flesh c· out for
Pr 1:20 Wisdom c· without; she uttereth
21 c· in the chief place of concourse,
8: 3 She c· at the gates, at the entry
9: 3 she c· upon the highest places of
Isa 26:17 in pain, and c· out in her pangs;
40: 3 of him that c· in the wilderness,
Jer 12: 8 it c· out against me:
Mic 6: 9 The Lord's voice c· unto the city,
M't 15:23 for she c· after us.
Lu 9:39 him, and he suddenly c· out;
Ro 9:27 Esaias also c· concerning Israel,
Jas 5: 4 is of you kept back by fraud, c·:

crime See also CRIMES.
Job 31:11 For this is an heinous c·; yea,
Ac 25:16 concerning the c· laid against him.

crimes
Eze 7:23 for the land is full of bloody c·,
Ac 25:27 signify the c· laid against him.

crimson
2Ch 2: 7 in purple, and c·, and blue,
14 blue, and in fine linen, and in c·;
3:14 purple, and c·, and fine linen,
Isa 1:18 though they be red like c·,
Jer 4:30 thou clothest thyself with c·,

cripple
Ac 14: 8 a c· from his mother's womb,

crisping
Isa 3:22 the wimples, and the c· pins,

crisping-pins See CRISPING and PINS.

Crispus (*cris'-pus*)
Ac 18: 8 And C·, the chief ruler of the
1Co 1:14 I baptized none of you, but C· and

crookbackt
Le 21:20 Or c·, or a dwarf, or that hath a

crooked
De 32: 5 are a perverse and c· generation.
Job 26:13 hand hath formed the c· serpent.
Ps 125: 5 turn aside unto their c· ways,
Pr 2:15 Whose ways are c·, and they
Ec 1:15 is c· cannot be made straight:
7:13 straight, which he hath made c·?
Isa 27: 1 even leviathan that c· serpent;
40: 4 and the c· shall be made straight,
42:16 them, and c· things straight.
45: 2 and make the c· places straight:
59: 8 they have made them c· paths:
La 3: 9 he hath made my paths c·.
Lu 3: 5 the c· shall be made straight,
Ph'p 2:15 midst of a c· and perverse nation,

crop See also CROPPED.
Le 1:16 pluck away his c· with his feathers,
Eze 17:22 I will c· off from the top of his

cropped
Eze 17: 4 c· off the top of his young twigs,

cross See also CROSSWAY.
M't 10:38 And he that taketh not his c·,
16:24 deny himself, and take up his c·,
27:32 him they compelled to bear his c·.
40 Son of God, come down from the c·.
42 let him now come down from the c·,
M'r 8:34 deny himself, and take up his c·,
10:21 take up the c·, and follow me.
15:21 and Rufus, to bear his c·.
30 and come down from the c·.
32 descend now from the c·, that we
Lu 9:23 himself, and take up his c· daily,
14:27 whosoever doth not bear his c·,
23:26 and on him they laid the c·, that
Joh 19:17 And he bearing his c· went forth
19 wrote a title, and put it on the c·.
25 stood by the c· of Jesus his mother,
31 should not remain upon the c· on
1Co 1:17 lest the c· of Christ should be made
18 the preaching of the c· is to them
Ga 5:11 then is the offence of the c· ceased.
6:12 should suffer persecution for the c·
14 save in the c· of our Lord Jesus
Eph 2:16 unto God in one body by the c·,
Ph'p 2: 8 death, even the death of the c·.
3:18 are the enemies of the c· of Christ:
Col 1:20 peace through the blood of his c·,
2:14 out of the way, nailing it to his c·;
Heb 12: 2 endured the c·, despising the shame,

crossway
Ob 14 shouldest thou have stood in the c·,

crouch See also CROUCHETH.
1Sa 2:36 c· to him for a piece of silver

croucheth
Ps 10:10 He c·, and humbleth himself,

crow See also COCKCROWING; CREW.
M't 26:34 this night, before the cock c·, thou
75 Before the cock c·, thou shalt deny
M'r 14:30 before the cock c· twice, thou shalt
72 him, Before the c· crow twice, thou
Lu 22:34 the cock shall not c· this day, before
61 him, Before the cock c·, thou shalt
Joh 13:38 The cock shall not c·, till thou hast

crown See also CROWNED; CROWNEST; CROWNETH; CROWNING; CROWNS.
Ge 49:26 and on the c· of the head of him
Ex 25:11 make upon it a c· of gold round
24 and make thereto a c· of gold
25 make a golden c· to the border.
29: 6 put the holy c· upon the mitre.
30: 3 shalt make unto it a c· of gold
4 thou make to it under the c· of it,
37: 2 and made a c· of gold to it round
11 and made thereunto a c· of gold
12 made a c· of gold for the border
26 also he made unto it a c· of gold
27 of gold for it under the c· thereof,
39:30 they made the plate of the holy c·
Le 8: 9 put the golden plate, the holy c·;
21:12 c· of the anointing oil of his God
De 33:20 the arm with the c· of the head.
2Sa 1:10 took the c· that was upon his head,
12:30 And he took their king's c· from
14:25 his foot even to the c· of his head
2Ki 11:12 and put the c· upon him,
1Ch 20: 2 David took the c· of their king

2Ch 23:11 son, and put upon him the c',
Es 1:11 queen before the king with the c'
2:17 he set the royal c' upon her head,
6: 8 c' royal which is set upon his head.
8:15 and with a great c' of gold,
Job 2: 7 the sole of his foot unto his c'.
19: 9 and taken the c' from my head.
31:36 and bind it as a c' to me.
Ps 21: 3 a c' of pure gold on his head.
89:39 hast profaned his c' by casting it
132:18 upon himself shall his c' flourish.
Pr 4: 9 a c' of glory shall she deliver to
12: 4 woman is a c' to her husband:
14:24 The c' of the wise is their riches:
16:31 The hoary head is a c' of glory,
17: 6 Children's children are the c' of
27:24 the c' endure to every generation?
Ca 3:11 behold king Solomon with the c'
Isa 3:17 Lord will smite with a scab the c'
28: 1 the c' of pride, to the drunkards
3 The c' of pride, the drunkards of
5 Lord of hosts be for a c' of glory,
62: 3 Thou shalt also be a c' of glory
Jer 2:16 have broken the c' of thy head.
13:18 down, even the c' of your glory.
48:45 c' of the head of the tumultuous
La 5:16 The c' is fallen from our head:
Eze 16:12 and a beautiful c' upon thine head.
21:26 the diadem, and take off the c':
Zec 9:16 shall be as the stones of a c',
M't 27:29 they had platted a c' of thorns,
M'r 15:17 and platted a c' of thorns,
Joh 19: 2 the soldiers platted a c' of thorns,
5 wearing the c' of thorns, and the
1Co 9:25 to obtain a corruptible c'; but we
Ph'p 4: 1 and longed for, my joy and c',
1Th 2:19 hope, or joy, or c' of rejoicing?
2Ti 4: 8 up for me a c' of righteousness,
Jas 1:12 he shall receive the c' of life,
1Pe 5: 4 a c' of glory that fadeth not away.
Re 2:10 and I will give thee a c' of life.
3:11 thou hast, that no man take thy c'.
6: 2 and a c' was given unto him:
12: 1 upon her head a c' of twelve stars:
14:14 having on his head a golden c',

crowned See also CROWNEDST.
Ps 8: 5 c' him with glory and honour.
Pr 14:18 prudent are c' with knowledge.
Ca 3:11 wherewith his mother c' him in
Na 3:17 Thy c' are as the locusts, and thy
2Ti 2: 5 yet is he not c', except he strive
Heb 2: 9 death, c' with glory and honour;

crownedst
Heb 2: 7 thou c' him with glory and honour,

crownest
Ps 65:11 c' the year with thy goodness;

crowneth
Ps 103: 4 who c' thee with lovingkindness

crowning
Isa 23: 8 counsel against Tyre, the c' city,

crowns
Eze 23:42 and beautiful c' upon their heads.
Zec 6:11 take silver and gold, and make c',
14 And the c' shall be to Helem,
Re 4: 4 they had on their heads c' of gold.
10 and cast their c' before the throne,
9: 7 heads were as it were c' like gold,
12: 3 and seven c' upon his heads.
13: 1 and upon his horns ten c', and
19:12 and on his head were many c';

crucified
M't 26: 2 Son of man is betrayed to be c'.
27:22 all say unto him, Let him be c'.
23 out the more, saying, Let him be c'.
26 he delivered him to be c'.
35 And the c' him, and parted his
38 were there two thieves c' with him,
44 also, which were c' with him,
28: 5 that ye seek Jesus, which was c'.
M'r 15:15 when he had scourged him, to be c'.
24 when they had c' him, they parted
25 was the third hour, and they c' him.
32 that were c' with him reviled him.
16: 6 Jesus of Nazareth, which was c':
Lu 23:23 requiring that he might be c'.
33 called Calvary, there they c' him,
24: 7 and be c', and the third day rise
20 to death, and have c' him.
Joh 19:16 him therefore unto them to be c'.
18 Where they c' him, and two others
20 place where Jesus was c' was nigh
23 soldiers, when they had c' Jesus,
32 the other which was c' with him.
41 Now in the place where he was c'
Ac 2:23 wicked hands have c' and slain:
36 same Jesus, whom ye have c',
4:10 Christ of Nazareth, whom ye c',
Ro 6: 6 that our old man is c' with him,
1Co 1:13 was Paul c' for you? or were ye
23 we preach Christ c', unto the Jews
2: 2 you, save Jesus Christ, and him c'.
8 would not have c' the Lord of glory.
2Co 13: 4 he was c' through weakness,
Ga 2:20 I am c' with Christ: nevertheless
3: 1 evidently set forth, c' among you?
5:24 have c' the flesh with the affections
6:14 by whom the world is c' unto me,
Re 11: 8 Egypt, where also our Lord was c'.

crucify See also CRUCIFIED.
M't 20:19 and to scourge, and to c' him:
23:34 some of them ye shall kill and c';
27:31 and led him away to c' him.
M'r 15:13 they c' out again, C' him.
15:14 out the more exceedingly, C' him.
20 and led him out to c' him.
27 And with him they c' two thieves;
Lu 23:21 they cried, saying, C' him, c' him.
Joh 19: 6 cried out, saying, C' him, c' him.
6 Take ye him, and c' him: for I find
10 not that I have power to c' thee,
15 away with him, c' him. Pilate saith
15 Shall I c' your King? The chief
Heb 6: 6 they c' to themselves the Son of God

cruel
Ge 49: 7 and their wrath, for it was c':
Ex 6: 9 of spirit, and for c' bondage.
De 32:33 dragons, and the c' venom of asps.
Job 30:21 Thou art become c' to me: with thy
Ps 25:19 and they hate me with c' hatred.
71: 4 of the unrighteous and c' man.
Pr 5: 9 others, and thy years unto the c':
11:17 he that is c' troubleth his own flesh.
12:10 tender mercies of the wicked are c'.
17:11 a c' messenger shall be sent against
27: 4 is c', and anger is outrageous;
Ca 8: 6 jealousy is c' as the grave: the coals
Isa 13: 9 Lord cometh, c' both with wrath
19: 4 over into the hand of a c' lord;
Jer 6:23 they are c', and have no mercy;
30:14 the chastisement of a c' one, for
50:42 they are c', and will not shew mercy
La 4: 3 daughter of my people is become c',
Heb 11:36 others had trial of c' mockings

cruelly
Eze 18:18 father, because he c' oppressed,

cruelty
Ge 49: 5 instruments of c' are in their
J'g 9:24 the c' done to the threescore and
Ps 27:12 against me, and breathe out c'.
74:20 are full of the habitations of c'.
Eze 34: 4 and with c' have ye ruled them.

crumbs
M't 15:27 dogs eat of the c' which fall from
M'r 7:28 the table eat of the children's c'.
Lu 16:21 to be fed with the c' which fell

cruse
1Sa 26:11 and the c' of water, and let us go.
12 the c' of water from Saul's bolster;
16 and the c' of water that was at his
1Ki 14: 3 and a c' of honey, and go to him:
17:12 in a barrel, and a little oil in a c':
14 waste, neither shall the c' of oil fail,
16 not, neither did the c' of oil fail,
19: 6 and a c' of water at his head.
2Ki 2:20 Bring me a new c', and put salt

crush See also CRUSHED.
Job 39:15 that the foot may c' them, or that
La 1:15 against me to c' my young men:
3:34 c' under his feet all the prisoners
Am 4: 1 which c' the needy, which say to

crushed
Le 22:24 bruised, or c', or broken, or cut;
Nu 22:25 c' Balaam's foot against the wall:
De 28:33 be only oppressed and c' alway:
Job 4:19 which are c' before the moth?
5: 4 they are c' in the gate, neither is
Isa 59: 5 is c' breaketh out into a viper.
Jer 51:34 he hath c' me, he hath made me

cry See also CRIED; CRIES; CRIEST; CRIETH; CRYING.
Ge 18:20 c' of Sodom and Gomorrah is
21 altogether according to the c' of it,
19:13 the c' of them is waxen great
27:34 a great and exceeding bitter c',
Ex 2:23 their c' came up unto God by
3: 7 and have heard their c' by reason
9 c' of the children of Israel is come
5: 8 they c', saying, Let us go and
11: 6 shall be great c' throughout all
12:30 there was a great c' in Egypt;
22:23 and they c' at all unto me,
23 I will surely hear their c';
32:18 is it the voice of them that c'
Le 13:45 and shall c', Unclean, unclean.
Nu 16:34 about them fled at the c' of them:
De 15: 9 he c' unto the Lord against thee,
24:15 he c' against thee unto the Lord,
J'g 10:14 Go and c' unto the gods which ye
1Sa 5:12 c' of the city went up to heaven.
7: 8 Cease not to c' unto the Lord our
8:18 And ye shall c' out in that day
9:16 because their c' is come unto me.
2Sa 19:28 have I yet to c' any more unto the
22: 7 and my c' did enter into his ears.
1Ki 8:28 unto the c' and to the prayer,
18:27 C' aloud: for he is a god; either
2Ki 8: 3 she went forth to c' unto the king
2Ch 6:19 to hearken unto the c' and the
13:12 sounding trumpets to c' alarm
20: 9 and c' unto thee in our affliction,
Ne 5: 1 there was a great c' of the people
6 I heard their c' and these words.
9: 9 heardest their c' by the Red sea;
Es 4: 1 cried with a loud and a bitter c';
9:31 matters of the fastings and their c'.
Job 16:18 and let my c' have no place.
19: 7 I c' out of wrong, but I am not
7 I c' aloud, but there is no
27: 9 Will God hear his c' when trouble
30:20 I c' unto thee, and thou dost not
24 though they c' in his destruction.
31:38 If my land c' against me, or
34:28 c' of the poor to come unto him,
28 and he heareth the c' of the
35: 9 they make the oppressed to c':
9 they c' out by reason of the arm
Job 35:12 they c', but none giveth answer,
36:13 they c' not when he bindeth them.
38:41 when his young ones c' unto God,
Ps 5: 2 unto the voice of my c', my King,
9:12 forgetteth not the c' of the humble.
17: 1 attend unto my c', give ear unto
18: 6 and my c' came before him, even
22: 2 O my God, I c' in the daytime,
27: 7 Hear, O Lord, when I c' with my
28: 1 Unto thee will I c', O Lord my
2 when I c' unto thee, when I lift
34:15 his ears are open unto their c'.
17 The righteous c', and the Lord
39:12 and give ear unto my c'; hold not
40: 1 inclined unto me, and heard my c'.
55:17 at noon; will I pray, and c' aloud:
56: 9 I c' unto thee, then shall mine
57: 2 I will c' unto God most high; unto
61: 1 Hear my c', O God; attend unto
2 of the earth will I c' unto thee,
86: 3 O Lord: for I c' unto thee daily.
88: 2 incline thine ear unto my c';
89:26 He shall c' unto me, Thou art my
102: 1 and let my c' come unto thee.
106:44 affliction, when he heard their c':
107:19 c' unto the Lord in their trouble,
28 c' unto the Lord in their trouble,
119:169 Let my c' come near before thee,
141: 1 Lord, I c' unto thee: make haste
1 my voice, when I c' unto thee.
142: 6 Attend unto my c'; for I am
145:19 hear their c', and will save them.
147: 9 and to the young ravens which c'.
Pr 8: 1 Doth not wisdom c'? and
21:13 his ears at the c' of the poor,
13 he also shall c' himself,
Ec 9:17 c' of him that ruleth among fools.
Isa 5: 7 for righteousness, but behold a c'.
8: 4 child shall have knowledge to c',
12: 6 C' out and shout, thou inhabitant
13:22 wild beasts of the islands shall c'
14:31 Howl, O gate; c', O city; thou,
15: 4 Heshbon shall c', and Elealeh:
4 soldiers of Moab shall c' out;
5 My heart shall c' out for Moab;
5 shall raise up a c' of destruction.
8 For the c' is gone round about the
19:20 shall c' unto the Lord because of
24:14 they shall c' aloud from the sea.
29: 9 and wonder; c' ye out, and c':
30:19 unto thee at the voice of thy c';
33: 7 their valiant ones shall c' without:
34:14 the satyr shall c' to his fellow;
40: 2 and c' unto her, that her warfare is
6 The voice said, C'.
6 And he said, what shall I c'?
42: 2 He shall not c', nor lift up, nor
13 he shall c', yea, roar; he shall
14 will I c' like a travailing woman;
43:14 the Chaldeans, whose c' is in the
46: 7 yea, one shall c' unto him, yet
54: 1 forth into singing, and c' aloud,
58: 1 C' aloud, spare not, lift up thy
9 thou shalt c', and he shall say,
65:14 ye shall c' for sorrow of heart,
Jer 2: 2 and c' in the ears of Jerusalem,
3: 4 thou not from this time c' unto me,
4: 5 in the land: c', gather together,
7:16 lift up c' nor prayer for them,
8:19 c' of the daughter of my people
11:11 though they shall c' unto me,
12 go, and c' unto the gods unto
14 lift up a c' or prayer for them:
14 the time that they c' unto me for
14: 2 the c' of Jerusalem is gone up.
12 they fast, I will not hear their c';
18:22 a c' be heard from their houses,
20:16 let him hear the c' in the morning,
22:20 Go up to Lebanon, and c'; and lift
20 up thy voice in Bashan, and c' from
25:34 Howl, ye shepherds, and c'; and
36 A voice of the c' of the shepherds,
31: 6 shall c', Arise ye, and let us go
46:12 and thy c' hath filled the land:
17 They did c' there, Pharaoh king
47: 2 then the men shall c', and all the
48: 4 her little ones have caused a c'
5 have heard a c' of destruction.
20 it is broken down: howl and c';
31 I will c' out for all Moab; mine
34 c' of Heshbon even unto Elealeh,
49: 3 c', ye daughters of Rabbah, gird
21 at the c' the noise thereof was
29 they shall c' unto them, Fear is
50:46 c' is heard among the nations.
51:54 sound of a c' cometh from Babylon,
La 2:19 Arise, c' out in the night: in the
3: 8 Also when I c' and shout, he
56 ear at my breathing, at my c'.
Eze 8:18 though they c' in mine ears with
9: 4 that c' for all the abominations
21:12 C' and howl, son of man: for it
24:17 Forbear to c', make no mourning
26:15 wounded c', when the slaughter
27:28 the sound of the c' of thy pilots
30 and shall c' bitterly, and shall cast
Ho 5: 8 Ramah: c' aloud at Beth-aven,
8: 2 Israel shall c' unto me, My God,
Joe 1:14 and c' unto the Lord,
19 O Lord, to thee will I c': for the
20 beasts of the field c' also unto
Am 3: 4 young lion c' out of his den,
Jon 1: 2 that great city, and c' against it;
3: 8 and c' mightily unto God:
Mic 3: 4 Then shall they c' unto the Lord,
5 with their teeth, and c', Peace;

Mic 4: 9 why dost thou c' out aloud. is
Na 2: 8 Stand, stand, shall they c'; but none
Hab 1: 2 O Lord, how long shall I c', and
2 c' out unto thee of violence, and
2:11 the stone shall c' out of the wall,
Zep 1:10 noise of a c' from the fish gate,
14 mighty man shall c' there bitterly.
Zec 1:14 C' thou, saying, Thus saith the
17 C' yet, saying, Thus saith the Lord
M't 12:19 He shall not strive, nor c';
25: 6 at midnight there was a c' made,
M'r 10:47 he began to c' out, and say, Jesus,
Lu 18: 7 own elect, which c' day and night
19:40 stones would immediately c' out.
Ac 23: 9 And there arose a great c': and
Ro 8:15 whereby we c', Abba, Father.
Ga 4:27 and c' thou that travailest not:
Re 14:18 and cried with a loud c' to him

crying
1Sa 4:14 Eli heard the noise of the c',
2Sa 13:19 hand on her head, and went on c'.
Job 39: 7 regardeth he the c' of the driver.
Ps 69: 3 I am weary of my c': my throat
Pr 19:18 let not thy soul spare for his c'.
30:15 hath two daughters, c', Give, give.
Isa 22: 5 walls, and of c' to the mountains.
24:11 is a c' for wine in the streets;
65:19 heard in her, nor the voice of c'.
Jer 48: 3 of c' shall be from Horonaim,
Zec 4: 7 thereof with shoutings, c', Grace,
Mal 2:13 with weeping, and with c' out,
M't 3: 3 voice of one c' in the wilderness,
9:27 c', and saying, Thou son of David,
21:15 and the children c' in the temple,
M'r 1: 3 voice of one c' in the wilderness,
5: 5 and in the tombs, c', and cutting
15: 8 the multitude c' aloud began to
Lu 3: 4 voice of one c' in the wilderness,
4:41 out of many, c' out, and saying,
Joh 1:23 the voice of one c' in the wilderness,
Ac 8: 7 unclean spirits, c' with loud voice,
14:14 ran in among the people, c' out,
17: 6 unto the rulers of the city, c',
21:28 C' out, Men of Israel, help: This
36 followed after, c', Away with him.
25:24 c' that he ought not to live any
Ga 4: 6 into your hearts, c', Abba, Father.
Heb 5: 7 with strong c' and tears unto him
Re 14:15 c' with a loud voice to him that
21: 4 neither sorrow, nor c', neither

crystal
Job 28:17 The gold and the c' cannot equal
Eze 1:22 as the colour of the terrible c',
Re 4: 6 was a sea of glass like unto c':
21:11 like a jasper stone, clear as c';
22: 1 river of water of life, clear as c',

cubit See also CUBITS.
Ge 6:16 a c' shalt thou finish it above;
Ex 25:10 a c' and a half the breadth thereof,
10 a c' and a half the height thereof.
17 a c' and a half the breadth thereof.
23 and a c' the breadth thereof, and
23 a c' and a half the height thereof.
26:13 And a c' on the one side,
13 and a c' on the other side of that
16 a c' and a half shall be the breadth
30: 2 A c' shall be the length thereof, and
2 a c' the breadth thereof; foursquare
36:21 and the breadth of a board one c'
37: 1 and a c' and a half the breadth of it,
1 and a c' and a half the height of it:
6 one c' and a half the breadth thereof,
10 and a c' the breadth thereof,
10 a c' and a half the height thereof.
25 the length of it was a c',
25 and the breadth of it a c';
De 3:11 breadth of it, after the c' of a man.
J'g 3:16 had two edges, of a c' length;
1Ki 7:24 knops compassing it, ten in a c',
31 the chapiter and above was a c':
31 work of the base, a c' and an half:
32 a wheel was a c' and half a c'.
35 a round compass of half a c' high:
2Ch 4: 3 ten in a c', compassing the sea
Eze 40: 5 six cubits long by the c' and an hand
12 one c' on this side,
12 the space was one c' on that side:
42 of a c' and an half long,
42 and a c' and an half broad,
42 and one c' high:
42: 4 breadth inward, a way of one c';
43:13 The c' is a c' and an hand breadth;
13 even the bottom shall be a c',
13 and the breadth a c',
14 two cubits, and the breadth one c';
14 four cubits, and the breadth one c'.
17 border about it shall be half a c';
17 bottom thereof shall be a c' about;
M't 6:27 can add one c' unto his stature?
Lu 12:25 can add to his stature one c'?

cubits
Ge 6:15 the ark shall be three hundred c',
15 the breadth of it fifty c',
15 and the height of it thirty c'.
7:20 Fifteen c' upward did the waters
Ex 25:10, 17 two c' and a half shall be the
23 two c' shall be the length thereof,
26: 2 curtain shall be eight and twenty c',
2 the breadth of one curtain four c':
8 of one curtain shall be thirty c', and
8 the breadth of one curtain four c':
16 Ten c' shall be the length of a
27: 1 wood, five c' long, and five c' broad;
1 the height thereof shall be three c'.
9 fine twined linen of an hundred c'
Ex 27:11 be hangings of an hundred c' long,
12 side shall be hangings of fifty c':
13 east side eastward shall be fifty c'.
14 side of the gate shall be fifteen c':
15 side shall be hangings fifteen c':
16 shall be an hanging of twenty c',
18 of the court shall be an hundred c',
18 and the height five c' of fine twined
30: 2 two c' shall be the height thereof;
36: 9 one curtain was twenty and eight c',
9 the breadth of one curtain four c':
15 length of one curtain was thirty c',
15 and four c' was the breadth of one
21 The length of a board was ten c',
37: 1 two c' and a half was the length of
6 c' and a half was the length thereof,
10 two c' was the length thereof, and
25 and two c' was the height of it; the
38: 1 five c' was the length thereof,
1 and five c' the breadth thereof;
1 and three c' the height thereof.
9 of fine twined linen, an hundred c':
11 the hangings were an hundred c',
12 side were hangings of fifty c',
13 for the east side eastward fifty c'.
14 one side of the gate were fifteen c';
15 hand, were hangings of fifteen c';
18 twenty c' was the length, and the
18 the breadth was five c', answerable
Nu 11:31 and as it were two c' high upon the
35: 4 and outward a thousand c' round
5 east side two thousand c',
5 the south side two thousand c',
5 the west side two thousand c',
5 on the north side two thousand c';
De 3:11 nine c' was the length thereof,
11 and four c' the breadth of it,
Jos 3: 4 about two thousand c' by measure:
1Sa 17: 4 whose height was six c' and a span.
1Ki 6: 2 the length thereof was threescore c',
2 the breadth thereof twenty c',
2 and the height thereof thirty c'.
3 twenty c' was the length thereof,
3 and ten c' was the breadth thereof
6 nethermost chamber was five c'
6 and the middle was six c' broad,
6 and the third was seven c' broad:
10 against all the house, five c' high:
16 he built twenty c' on the sides of
17 temple before it, was forty c' long.
20 forepart was twenty c' in length,
20 and twenty c' in breadth,
20 and twenty c' in the height thereof.
23 cherubims of olive tree, each ten c'
24 c' was the one wing of the cherub,
24 five c' the other wing of the cherub:
24 part of the other were ten c'.
25 And the other cherub was ten c':
26 height of the one cherub was ten c',
7: 2 the length thereof was an hundred c',
2 and the breadth thereof fifty c',
2 and the height thereof thirty c',
6 the length thereof was fifty c',
6 and the breadth thereof thirty c':
10 stones of ten c', and stones of eight c'.
15 of brass, of eighteen c' high apiece:
15 line of twelve c' did compass either
16 one chapiter was five c', and the
16 of the other chapiter was five c':
19 of lily work in the porch, four c'.
23 a molten sea, ten c' from the one
23 and his height was five c': and
23 a line of thirty c' did compass it
27 four c' was the length of one base,
27 and four c' the breadth thereof,
27 and three c' the height of it.
38 every laver was four c': and upon
2Ki 14:13 the corner gate, four hundred c'.
25:17 one pillar was eighteen c', and the
17 the height of the chapiter three c';
1Ch 11:23 a man of great stature, five c' high;
2Ch 3: 3 The length, by c' after the first
3 measure was threescore c',
3 and the breadth twenty c'.
4 the breadth of the house, twenty c',
8 length whereof was twenty c',
8 and the breadth thereof twenty c':
11 the cherubims were twenty c' long:
11 wing of the one cherub was five c',
11 the other wing was likewise five c',
12 wing of the other cherub was five c',
12 the other wing was five c' also,
13 spread themselves forth twenty c':
15 house two pillars of thirty and five c'
15 the top of each of them was five c'.
4: 1 twenty c' the length thereof,
1 and twenty c' the breadth thereof,
1 and ten c' the height thereof.
2 a molten sea of ten c' from brim to
2 brim, round in compass, and five c'
2 a line of thirty c' did compass
6:13 a brasen scaffold, of five c' long,
13 and five c' broad, and three c' high,
25:23 to the corner gate, four hundred c'.
Ezr 6: 3 the height thereof threescore c',
3 the breadth thereof threescore c';
Neh 3:13 and a thousand c' on the wall unto
Es 5:14 Let a gallows be made of fifty c'
7: 9 Behold also, the gallows fifty c' high,
Jer 52:21 height of one pillar was eighteen c';
21 and a fillet of twelve c' did compass
22 height of one chapiter was five c',
Eze 40: 5 a measuring reed of six c' long by
7 the little chambers were five c';
9 the porch of the gate, eight c';
9 and the posts thereof, two c';
Eze 40:11 the entry of the gate, ten c'; and
11 the length of the gate, thirteen c'.
12 chambers were six c' on this side,
12 and six c' on that side.
13 breadth was five and twenty c', door
14 He made also posts of threescore c',
15 porch of the inner gate were fifty c'.
19 without, an hundred c' eastward and
21 the length thereof was fifty c',
21 and the breadth five and twenty c'.
23 from gate to gate an hundred c'.
25 the length was fifty c', and the
25 breadth five and twenty c'.
27 gate toward the south an hundred c'.
29 it was fifty c' long, and
29 and five and twenty c' broad.
30 about were five and twenty c' long,
30 and five c' broad.
33 it was fifty c' long,
33 and five and twenty c' broad.
36 the length was fifty c', and the
36 breadth five and twenty c'.
47 an hundred c' long, and
47 an hundred c' broad, four square;
48 post of the porch, five c' on this side,
48 and five c' on that side:
48 of the gate was three c' on this side,
48 and three c' on that side.
49 length of the porch was twenty c',
49 and the breadth eleven c';
41: 1 posts, six c' broad on the one side,
1 and six c' broad on the other side,
2 breadth of the door was ten c';
2 sides of the door were five c' on the
2 side, and five c' on the other side:
2 the length thereof, forty c':
2 and the breadth, twenty c'.
3 door two c'; and the door, six c';
3 the breadth of the door, seven c'.
4 the length thereof, twenty c';
4 and the breadth, twenty c'.
5 the wall of the house, six c';
5 of every side chamber, four c',
8 were a full reed of six great c'.
9 side chamber without, was five c':
10 was the wideness of twenty c' round
11 place that was left was five c' round
12 the west was seventy c' broad;
12 was five c' thick round about,
12 and the length thereof ninety c'.
13 the house an hundred c' long; and
13 walls thereof, an hundred c' long;
14 place toward the east, an hundred c'.
15 the other side, an hundred c', with
22 altar of wood was three c' high,
22 and the length thereof two c';
42: 2 Before the length of an hundred c'
2 door, and the breadth was fifty c'.
3 Over against the twenty c' which
4 a walk of ten c' breadth inward,
7 the length thereof was fifty c'.
8 were in the utter court was fifty c':
8 the temple were an hundred c'.
43:13 measures of the altar after the c':
14 to the lower settle shall be two c',
14 the greater settle shall be four c',
15 the altar shall be four c'; and from
16 the altar shall be twelve c' long,
17 the settle shall be fourteen c' long
45: 2 fifty c' round about for the suburbs
46:22 were courts joined of forty c' long
47: 3 he measured a thousand c', and
Da 3: 1 whose height was threescore c',
1 and the breadth thereof six c':
Zec 5: 2 the length thereof is twenty c',
2 and the breadth thereof ten c'.
Joh 21: 8 but as it were two hundred c',)
Re 21:17 an hundred and forty and four c',

cuckow
Le 11:16 the night hawk, and the c', and
De 14:15 the night hawk, and the c', and

cucumbers
Nu 11: 5 freely; the c', and the melons,
Isa 1: 8 as a lodge in a garden of c',

cud
Le 11: 3 cheweth the c', among the beasts,
4 of them that chew the c', or of
4, 5, 6 because he cheweth the c', but
7 yet he cheweth not the c'; he is
26 nor cheweth the c', are unclean
De 14: 6 cheweth the c' among the beasts,
7 of them that chew the c', or of
7 for they chew the c', but divide
8 yet cheweth not the c', it is

cumbered
Lu 10:40 But Martha was c' about much

cumbereth
Lu 13: 7 cut it down; why c' it the ground?

cumbrance
De 1:12 can I myself alone bear your c',

cumi *(coo'-mi)*
M'r 5:41 unto her, Talitha c'; which is,

cummin
Isa 28:25 and scatter the c', and cast in the
27 wheel turned about upon the c';
27 with a staff, and the c' with a rod.
M't 23:23 pay tithe of mint and anise and c',

cunning
Ge 25:27 Esau was a c' hunter, a man of
Ex 26: 1 cherubims of c' work shalt thou
31 and fine twined linen of c' work:
28: 6 fine twined linen, with c' work,
15 breastplate of judgment with c'

Ex 31: 4 devise c' works, to work in gold,
35:33 to make any manner of c' work.
35 and of the c' workman, and of the
35 and of those that devise c' work.
36: 8 cherubims of c' work made he
35 cherubims made he it of c' work.
38:23 an engraver and a c' workman,
39: 3 in the fine linen, with c' work.
8 the breastplate of c' work, like
1Sa 16:16 seek out a man, who is a c' player
18 that is c' in playing, and a mighty
1Ki 7:14 c' to work all works in brass.
1Ch 22:15 c' men for every manner of work.
25: 7 all that were c', was two hundred
2Ch 2: 7 c' to work in gold, and in silver,
7 skill to grave with c' the men that
13 now I have sent a c' man, endued
14 be put to him, with thy c' men,
14 and with the c' men of my lord
26:15 engines, invented by c' men, to be
Ps 137: 5 let my right hand forget her c'
Ca 7: 1 of the hands of a c' workman.
Isa 3: 3 counseller, and the c' artificer,
40:20 seeketh unto a him c' workman
Jer 9:17 may come; and send for c' women,
10: 9 they are all the work of c' men.
Da 1: 4 and c' in knowledge, and
Eph 4:14 sleight of men, and c' craftiness.

cunningly
2Pe 1:16 have not followed c' devised fables,

cup See also CUPBEARER; CUPS.
Ge 40:11 and Pharaoh's c' was in my hand:
11 pressed them into Pharaoh's c',
11 I gave the c' into Pharaoh's hand.
13 deliver Pharaoh's c' into his hand,
21 he gave the c' into Pharaoh's hand:
44: 2 And put my c', the silver c', in the
12 c' was found in Benjamin's sack.
16 he also with whom the c' is found.
17 man in whose hand the c' is found,
2Sa 12: 3 and drank of his own c', and lay
1Ki 7:26 was wrought like the brim of a c',
2Ch 4: 5 like the work of the brim of a c',
Ps 11: 6 this shall be the portion of their c'.
16: 5 of mine inheritance and of my c':
23: 5 head with oil; my c' runneth over.
73:10 and waters of a full c' are wrung out
75: 8 hand of the Lord there is a c',
116:13 I will take the c' of salvation, and
Pr 23:31 when it giveth his colour in the c',
Isa 51:17 of the Lord the c' of his fury;
17 the dregs of the c' of trembling,
22 of thine hand the c' of trembling,
22 even the dregs of the c' of my fury;
Jer 16: 7 the c' of consolation to drink for
25:15 the wine c' of this fury at my hand,
17 took I the c' at the Lord's hand,
28 take the c' at thine hand to drink,
49:12 judgment was not to drink of the c'
51: 7 Babylon hath been a golden c' in
La 4:21 the c' also shall pass through unto
Eze 23:31 will I give her c' into thine hand.
32 of thy sister's c' deep and large:
33 c' of astonishment and desolation,
33 with the c' of thy sister Samaria.
Hab 2:16 c' of the Lord's right hand shall be
Zec 12: 2 make Jerusalem a c' of trembling
M't 10:42 c' of cold water only in the name
20:22 drink of the c' that I shall drink of,
23 Ye shall drink indeed of my c', and
23:25 outside of the c' and of the platter,
26 first that which is within the c'
26:27 he took the c', and gave thanks,
39 possible, let this c' pass from me:
42 this c' may not pass away from me,
M'r 9:41 give you a c' of water to drink
10:38 ye drink of the c' that I drink of?
39 indeed drink of the c' that I drink
14:23 And he took the c', and when he
36 take away this c' from me:
Lu 11:39 make clean the outside of the c'
22:17 he took the c', and gave thanks,
20 Likewise also the c' after supper,
20 This c' is the new testament in my
42 if thou be willing, remove this c'
Joh 18:11 c' which my Father hath given me,
1Co 10:16 The c' of blessing which we bless,
21 Ye cannot drink the c' of the Lord,
21 and the c' of devils:
11:25 same manner also he took the c',
25 This c' is the new testament in my
26 and drink this c', ye do show
27 drink this c' of the Lord, unworthily,
28 of that bread, and drink of that c'.
Re 14:10 into the c' of his indignation;
16:19 the c' of the wine of the fierceness
17: 4 having a golden c' in her hand full
18: 6 in the c' which she hath filled, fill

cupbearer See also CUPBEARERS.
Ne 1:11 For I was the king's c'.

cupbearers
1Ki 10: 5 their apparel, and his c', and his
2Ch 9: 4 their apparel; his c' also, and their

cups
1Ch 28:17 and the bowls, and the c':
Isa 22:24 from the vessels of c', even to all
Jer 35: 5 pots full of wine, and c', and I
52:19 and the spoons, and the c'; that
M'r 7: 4 as the washing of c', and pots,
8 as the washing of pots and c':

curdled
Job 10:10 as milk, and c' me like cheese?

cure See also CURED; CURES; INCURABLE; PROCURE.
Jer 33: 6 I will bring it health and c',
6 and I will c' them, and will reveal
Ho 5:13 you, nor c' you of your wound.
M't 17:16 and they could not c' him.
Lu 9: 1 over all devils, and to c' diseases.

cured
Jer 46:11 for thou shalt not be c'.
M't 17:18 child was c' from that very hour.
Lu 7:21 he c' many of their infirmities and
Joh 5:10 said unto him that was c', It is the

cures
Lu 13:32 and I do c' to day and to morrow,

curious
Ex 28: 8 And the c' girdle of the ephod,
27, 28 above the c' girdle of the
29: 5 with the c' girdle of the ephod:
35:32 devise c' works, to work in gold,
39: 5 And the c' girdle of his ephod,
20, 21 above the c' girdle of the
Le 8: 7 with the c' girdle of the ephod,
Ac 19:19 used c' arts brought their books

curiously
Ps 139:15 c' wrought in the lowest parts

current
Ge 23:16 c' money with the merchant.

curse See also CURSED; CURSES; CURSEST; CURSETH; CURSING.
Ge 8:21 I will not again c' the ground any
12: 3 and c' him that curseth thee: and in
27:12 I shall bring a c' upon me, and not
13 Upon me be thy c', my son:
Ex 22:28 gods, nor c' the ruler of thy people.
Le 19:14 Thou shalt not c' the deaf, nor
Nu 5:18, 19 bitter water that causeth the c':
21 Lord make thee a c' and an oath
22 water that causeth the c' shall go
24 bitter water that causeth the c':
24, 27 water that causeth the c' shall
27 woman shall be a c' among her
22: 6 I pray thee, c' me this people:
11 come now, c' me them;
12 shalt not c' the people: for they
17 I pray thee, c' me this people.
23: 7 Come, c' me Jacob, and come,
8 How shall I c', whom God hath not
11 I took thee to c' mine enemies,
13 all: and c' me them from thence.
25 c' them at all, nor bless them at all.
27 mayest c' me them from thence.
24:10 I called thee to c' mine enemies,
De 11:26 you this day a blessing and a c';
28 a c', if ye will not obey the
29 and the c' upon mount Ebal.
23: 4 Pethor of Mesopotamia, to c' thee.
5 God turned the c' into a blessing
27:13 shall stand upon mount Ebal to c'
29:19 he heareth the words of this c',
30: 1 the blessing and the c', which I
Jos 6:18 and make the camp of Israel a c',
24: 9 Balaam the son of Beor to c' you:
J'g 5:23 C' ye Meroz, said the angel
23 c' ye bitterly the inhabitants
9:57 upon them came the c' of Jotham
2Sa 16: 9 should this dead dog c' my lord
10 let him c', because the Lord hath
10 Lord hath said unto him, C' David.
11 let him alone, and let him c': for
1Ki 2: 8 a grievous c' in the day when I
2Ki 22:19 should become a desolation and a c',
Ne 10:29 entered into a c', and into an oath,
13: 2 against them, that he should c'
2 God turned the c' into a blessing.
Job 1:11 and he will c' thee to thy face.
2: 5 and he will c' thee to thy face.
9 c' God, and die.
3: 8 Let them c' it that
8 that c' the day, who are
31:30 to sin by wishing a c' to his soul.
Ps 62: 4 their mouth, but they c' inwardly.
109:28 Let them c', but bless thou:
Pr 3:33 The c' of the Lord is in the house
11:26 corn, the people shall c' him: but
24:24 him shall the people c', nations
26: 2 the c' causeless shall not come.
27:14 morning, it shall be counted a c'
28:27 his eyes shall have many a c'.
30:10 lest he c' thee, and thou be found
Ec 7:21 lest thou hear thy servant c' thee:
10:20 C' not the king, no not in thy
20 c' not the rich in thy bedchamber:
Isa 8:21 and c' their king and their God,
24: 6 hath the c' devoured the earth,
34: 5 and upon the people of my c', to
43:28 given Jacob to the c', and Israel
65:15 ye shall leave your name for a c'
Jer 15:10 every one of them doth c' me.
24: 9 and a proverb, a taunt and a c',
25:18 astonishment, an hissing, and a c'
26: 6 will make this city a c' to all the
29:18 to be a c', and an astonishment,
22 them shall be taken up a c' by all
42:18 an astonishment, and a c', and a
44: 8 ye might be a c' and a reproach
12 an astonishment, and a c', and a
22 astonishment, and a c', without an
49:13 a reproach, a waste, and a c'; and
La 3:65 sorrow of heart, thy c' unto them.
Da 9:11 the c' is poured upon us, and the
Zec 5: 3 is the c' that goeth forth over the
8:13 ye were a c' among the heathen,
Mal 2: 2 I will even send a c' upon you,
2 and I will c' your blessings:
Mal 3: 9 are cursed with a c': for ye have
4: 6 come and smite the earth with a c'
M't 5:44 bless them that c' you, do good to
26:74 Then began he to c' and to swear,
M'r 14:71 But he began to c' and to swear,
Lu 6:28 Bless them that c' you, and pray
Ac 23:12 and bound themselves under a c',
14 bound ourselves under a great c',
Ro 12:14 persecute you: bless, and c' not.
Ga 3:10 works of the law are under the c':
13 redeemed us from the c' of the
13 law, being made a c' for us:
Jas 3: 9 therewith c' we men, which are
Re 22: 3 there shall be no more c': but the

cursed See also ACCURSED; CURSEDST.
Ge 3:14 thou art c' above all cattle, and
17 c' is the ground for thy sake; in
4:11 now art thou c' from the earth,
5:29 ground which the Lord hath c'.
9:25 he said, C' be Canaan; a servant of
27:29 c' be every one that curseth thee,
49: 7 C' be their anger, for it was fierce:
Le 20: 9 hath c' his father or his mother;
24:11 the name of the Lord, and c'.
14 forth him that hath c' without the
23 forth him that had c' out of the
Nu 22: 6 and he whom thou cursest is c'.
23: 8 I curse, whom God hath not c'?
24: 9 and c' is he that curseth thee.
De 7:26 lest thou be a c' thing like it:
26 abhor it; for it is a c' thing.
13:17 cleave nought of the c' thing to
27:15 C' be the man that maketh any
16 C' be he that setteth light by his
17 C' be he that removeth his
18 C' be he that maketh the blind to
19 C' be he that perverteth the
20 C' be he that lieth with his father's
21 C' be he that lieth with any manner
22 C' be he that lieth with his sister,
23 C' be he that lieth with his mother
24 C' be he that smiteth his neighbour
25 C' be he that taketh reward to slay
26 C' be he that confirmeth not all the
28:16 C' shalt thou be in the city,
16 and c' shalt thou be in the field.
17 C' shall be thy basket and thy store.
18 C' shall be the fruit of thy body,
19 C' shalt thou be when thou comest
19 c' shalt thou be when thou goest
Jos 6:26 C' be the man before the Lord, that
9:23 therefore ye are c', and there shall
J'g 9:27 eat and drink, and c' Abimelech.
21:18 C' be he that giveth a wife to
1Sa 14:24, 28 C' be the man that eateth any
17:43 Philistine c' David by his gods:
26:19 of men, c' be they before the Lord;
2Sa 16: 5 came forth, and c' still as he came.
7 said Shimei when he c', Come out,
13 and c' as he went, and threw stones
19:21 because he c' the Lord's anointed?
1Ki 2: 8 which c' me with a grievous curse
2Ki 2:24 c' them in the name of the Lord.
9:34 now this c' woman, and bury her:
Ne 13:25 contended with them, and c' them,
Job 1: 5 sinned, and c' God in their hearts.
3: 1 Job his mouth, and c' his day.
5: 3 but suddenly I c' his habitation.
24:18 their portion is c' in the earth: he
Ps 37:22 they that be c' of him shall be cut
119:21 hast rebuked the proud that are c'.
Ec 7:22 thyself likewise hast c' others.
Jer 11: 3 C' be the man that obeyeth not the
17: 5 C' be the man that trusteth in man,
20:14 C' be the day wherein I was born:
15 C' be the man who brought tidings
48:10 C' be he that doeth the work
10 c' be he that keepeth back his
Mal 1:14 c' be the deceiver, which hath in
2: 2 yea, I have c' them already, because
3: 9 Ye are c' with a curse: for ye have
M't 25:41 Depart from me, ye c', into
Joh 7:49 who knoweth not the law are c'.
Ga 3:10 C' is every one that continueth
13 C' is every one that hangeth on a
2Pe 2:14 covetous practices; c' children:

cursedst
J'g 17: 2 about which thou c', and spakest
M'r 11:21 behold, the fig tree which thou c'

curses
Nu 5:23 the priest shall write these c' in
De 28:15, 45 these c' shall come upon thee,
29:20 all the c' that are written in this
21 according to all the c' of the
27 to bring upon it all the c' that are
30: 7 put all these c' upon thine enemies,
2Ch 34:24 all the c' that are written in the

cursest
Nu 22: 6 and he whom thou c' is cursed.

curseth
Ge 12: 3 and curse him that c' thee: and in
27:29 cursed be every one that c' thee,
Ex 21:17 And he that c' his father, or his
Le 20: 9 every one that c' his father or his
24:15 Whosoever c' his God shall bear
Nu 24: 9 thee, and cursed is he that c' thee.
Pr 20:20 Whoso c' his father or his mother,
30:11 There is a generation that c' their
M't 15: 4 He that c' father or mother, let
M'r 7:10 Whoso c' father or mother, let him

cursing See also CURSINGS.
Nu 5:21 the woman with an oath of c',
De 28:20 The Lord shall send upon thee c',
30:19 life and death, blessing and c':

2Sa 16:12 will requite me good for his c'
Ps 10: 7 His mouth is full of c' and deceit
59:12 for c' and lying which they speak.
109:17 As he loved c', so let it come unto
18 he clothed himself with c' like as
Pr 29:24 he heareth c', and bewrayeth it
Ro 3:14 Whose mouth is full of c' and
Heb 6: 8 nigh unto c'; whose end is to be
Jas 3:10 mouth proceedeth blessing and c'.

cursings
Jos 8:34 of the law, the blessings and c',

curtain See also CURTAINS.
Ex 26:2 The length of one c' shall be eight
2 the breadth of one c' four cubits:
4 upon the edge of the one c' from
4 in the uttermost edge of another c',
5 loops shalt thou make in the one c',
5 the edge of the c' that is in the
8 length of one c' shall be thirty
8 breadth of one c' four cubits; and
9 double the sixth c' in the forefront
10 edge of the one c' that is outmost
10 fifty loops in the edge of the c'
12 the half c' that remaineth, shall
36: 9 The length of one c' was twenty
9 the breadth of one c' four cubits:
11 loops of blue on the edge of one c'
11 the uttermost side of another c',
12 Fifty loops made he in one c', and
12 the edge of the c' which was
12 the loops held one c' to another.
15 length of one c' was thirty cubits,
15 cubits was the breadth of one c':
17 upon the uttermost edge of the c'
17 made he upon the edge of the c',
Nu 3:26 the c' for the door of the court,
Ps 104: 2 out the heavens like a c':
Isa 40:22 stretcheth out the heavens as a c',

curtains
Ex 26: 1 ten c' of fine twined linen, and
2 every one of the c' shall have one
3 five c' shall be coupled together
3 other five c' shall be coupled one to
6 couple the c' together with the
7 thou shalt make c' of goats' hair
7 eleven c' shalt thou make.
8 the eleven c' shall be all of one
9 thou shalt couple five c' by
9 and six c' by themselves, and shalt
12 remaineth of the c' of the tent,
13 in the length of the c' of the tent,
36: 8 ten c' of fine twined linen, and blue
9 the c' were all of one size.
10 he coupled the five c' one unto
10 the other five c' he coupled one
13 coupled the c' one unto another
14 made c' of goats' hair for the tent
14 eleven c' he made them.
15 the eleven c' were of one size.
16 five c' by themselves, and six c' by
Nu 4:25 shall bear the c' of the tabernacle,
2Sa 7: 2 the ark of God dwelleth within c'.
1Ch 17: 1 of the Lord remaineth under c'.
Ca 1: 5 of Kedar, as the c' of Solomon.
Isa 54: 2 and let them stretch forth the c' of
Jer 4:20 spoiled, and my c' in a moment.
10:20 and to set up my c'.
49:29 shall take to themselves their c',
Hab 3: 7 the c' of the land of Midian did

Cush (*cush*) See also ETHIOPIA.
Ge 10: 6 the sons of Ham; C', and Mizraim,
7 the sons of C'; Seba, and Havilah,
8 C' begat Nimrod: he began to be
1Ch 1: 8 sons of Ham; C', and Mizraim,
9 the sons of C'; Seba, and Havilah,
10 C' begat Nimrod: he began to be
Ps 7 *title* the words of C' the Benjamite.
Isa 11:11 from Pathros, and from C', and

Cushan (*cu'-shan*) See also CHUSHAN-RISHATHAIM.
Hab 3: 7 I saw the tents of C' in affliction:

Cushi (*cu'-shi*)
2Sa 18:21 said Joab to C', Go tell the king
21 And C' bowed himself unto Joab,
22 I pray thee, also run after C'.
23 way of the plain, and overran C'.
31 And, behold, C' came; and C' said,
32 said unto C', Is the young man
32 C' answered, The enemies of my
Jer 36:14 the son of C', unto Baruch, saying,
Zep 1: 1 unto Zephaniah the son of C',

custody
Nu 3:36 under the c' and charge of the
Es 2: 3 the women, unto the c' of Hege the
8 the palace, to the c' of Hegai, that
8 the king's house, to the c' of Hegai,
14 the women, to the c' of Shaashgaz,

custom See also ACCUSTOM; CUSTOMS.
Ge 31:35 for the c' of women is upon me.
J'g 11:39 And it was a c' in Israel,
1Sa 2:13 priest's c' with the people was,
Ezr 3: 4 according to the c', as the duty
4:13 they not pay toll, tribute, and c',
20 and toll, tribute, and c', was paid
7:24 toll, tribute, or c', upon them.
Jer 32:11 sealed according to the law and c',
M't 9: 9 sitting at the receipt of c':
17:25 of the earth take c' or tribute?
M'r 2:14 sitting at the receipt of c',
Lu 1: 9 to the c' of the priest's office, his
2:27 do for him after the c' of the law,
42 Jerusalem after the c' of the feast.
4:16 as his c' was, he went into
5:27 Levi, sitting at the receipt of c':
Joh 18:39 ye have a c', that I should release
Ro 13: 7 is due; c' to whom c'; fear to whom
1Co 11:16 we have no such c', neither the

customs
Le 18:30 any one of these abominable c',
Jer 10: 3 the c' of the people are vain:
Ac 6:14 the c' which Moses delivered us.
16:21 teach c' which are not lawful for us
21:21 neither to walk after the c'.
26: 3 to be expert in all c' and questions
28:17 the people, or c' of our fathers,

cut See also CUTTEST; CUTTETH; CUTTING.
Ge 9:11 neither shall all flesh be c' off any
17:14 shall be c' off from his people;
Ex 4:25 and c' off the foreskin of her son,
9:15 shalt be c' off from the earth.
12:15 soul shall be c' off from Israel.
19 be c' off from the congregation
23:23 Jebusites; and I will c' them off.
29:17 thou shalt c' the ram in pieces,
30:33, 38 even be c' off from his people.
31:14 that soul shall be c' off from among
34:13 images, and c' down their groves:
39: 3 and c' it into wires, to work it in
Le 1: 6 offering, and c' it into his pieces.
12 And he shall c' it into his pieces,
7:20, 21 even that soul shall be c' off
25 the soul that eateth it shall be c' off
27 even that soul shall be c' off from
8:20 And he c' the ram into pieces;
17: 4 and that man shall be c' off from
9 even that man shall be c' off from
10 c' him off from among his people.
14 whosoever eateth it shall be c' off.
18:29 that commit them shall be c' off
19: 8 and that soul shall be c' off from
20: 3 c' him off from among his people;
5 and will c' him off, and all that go
6 and will c' him off from among
17 c' off in the sight of their people:
18 and both of them shall be c' off
22: 3 shall be c' off from my presence:
24 or crushed, or broken, or c';
23:29 day, he shall be c' off from among
26:30 places, and c' down your images,
Nu 4:18 C' ye not off the tribe of the families
9:13 even the same soul shall be c' off
13:23 and c' down from thence a branch
24 the children of Israel c' down from
15:30 that soul shall be c' off from among
31 that soul shall utterly be c' off;
19:13 that soul shall be c' off from Israel:
20 that soul shall be c' off from among
De 7: 5 c' down their groves, and burn
12:29 thy God shall c' off the nations
14: 1 ye shall not c' yourselves, nor
19: 1 thy God hath c' off the nations,
5 with the axe to c' down the tree,
20:19 and thou shalt not c' them down
20 shalt destroy and c' them down;
23: 1 or hath his privy member c' off,
25:12 Then thou shalt c' off her hand,
Jos 3:13 the waters of Jordan shall be c' off
16 salt sea, failed, and were c' off:
4: 7 of Jordan were c' off before the ark
7 the waters of Jordan were c' off:
7: 9 and c' off our name from the earth:
11:21 and c' off the Anakims from the
17:15 and c' down for thyself there in
18 a wood, and thou shalt c' it down:
23: 4 all the nations that I have c' off.
J'g 1: 6 c' off his thumbs and his great toes,
7 thumbs and their great toes c' off,
6:25 c' down the grove that is by it:
26 the grove which thou shalt c' down.
28 grove was c' down that was by it,
30 because he hath c' down the grove
9:48 c' down a bough from the trees,
49 c' down every man his bough,
20: 6 and c' her in pieces, and sent her
21: 6 There is one tribe c' off from Israel
Ru 4:10 the name of the dead be not c' off
1Sa 2:31 that I will c' off thine arm, and
33 I shall not c' off from mine altar,
5: 4 the palms of his hands were c' off
17:51 him, and c' off his head therewith.
20:15 thou shalt not c' off thy kindness
15 the Lord hath c' off the enemies
24: 4 and c' off the skirt of Saul's robe
5 because he had c' off Saul's skirt.
11 that I c' off the skirt of thy robe,
21 thou wilt not c' off my seed after
28: 9 he hath c' off those that have
31: 9 they c' off his head, and stripped
2Sa 4:12 c' off their hands and their feet,
7: 9 and have c' off all thine enemies
10: 4 and c' off their garments in the
20:22 And they c' off the head of Sheba
1Ki 9: 7 will I c' off Israel out of the land
11:16 until he had c' off every male
13:34 even to c' it off, and to destroy it
14:10 will c' off from Jeroboam him
14 shall c' off the house of Jeroboam
18: 4 when Jezebel c' off the prophets of
23 c' it in pieces, and lay it on wood,
28 cried aloud, and c' themselves
33 c' the bullock in pieces, and laid
21:21 and will c' off from Ahab him that
2Ki 6: 4 they came to Jordan, they c' down
6 he c' down a stick, and cast it in
9: 8 and I will c' off from Ahab him
10:32 the Lord began to c' Israel short:
16:17 And king Ahaz c' off the borders
18: 4 c' down the groves, and brake
16 Hezekiah c' off the gold from the
2Ki 19:23 will c' down the tall cedar trees
23:14 and c' down the groves, and filled
24:13 c' in pieces all the vessels of gold
1Ch 17: 8 and have c' off all thine enemies
19: 4 and c' off their garments in the
20: 3 and c' them with saws, and with
2Ch 2: 8 skill to c' timber in Lebanon;
10 servants, the hewers that c' timber,
16 we will c' wood out of Lebanon,
14: 3 images, and c' down the groves:
15:16 Asa c' down her idol, and stamped
22: 7 anointed to c' off the house of Ahab.
26:21 c' off from the house of the Lord:
28:24 and c' in pieces the vessels of
31: 1 and c' down the groves, and
32:21 Lord sent an angel, which c' off all
34: 4 on high above them, he c' down;
7 c' down all the idols throughout
Job 4: 7 where were the righteous c' off?
6: 9 loose his hand, and c' me off!
8:12 in his greenness, and not c' down,
14 Whose hope shall be c' off, and
11:10 If he c' off, and shut up, or
14: 2 flower, and is c' down: he fleeth
7 is hope of a tree, if it be c' down,
18:16 above shall his branch be c' off.
21:21 his months is c' off in the midst?
22:16 Which were c' down out of time,
20 our substance is not c' down, but
23:17 was not c' off before the darkness,
24:24 and c' off as the tops of the ears
30: 4 Who c' up mallows by the bushes,
36:20 people are c' off in their place.
Ps 12: 3 Lord shall c' off all flattering lips,
31:22 I am c' off from before thine eyes:
34:16 to c' off the remembrance of them
37: 2 they shall soon be c' down like
9 evildoers shall be c' off: but those
22 be cursed of him shall be c' off.
28 seed of the wicked shall be c' off.
34 when the wicked are c' off, thou
38 the end of the wicked shall be c' off.
54: 5 enemies: c' them off in thy truth.
58: 7 let them be as c' in pieces.
75:10 of the wicked also will I c' off;
76:12 He shall c' off the spirit of princes:
80:16 It is burned with fire, it is c' down:
83: 4 Come, and let us c' them off from
88: 5 and they are c' off from thy hand.
16 thy terrors have c' me off.
90: 6 it is c' down, and withereth.
10 it is soon c' off, and we fly away.
94:23 c' them off in their own wickedness;
23 the Lord our God shall c' them off.
101: 5 his neighbour, him will I c' off:
8 that I may c' off all wicked doers
107:16 and c' the bars of iron in sunder.
109:13 Let his posterity be c' off; and in
15 he may c' off the memory of them
129: 4 c' asunder the cords of the wicked.
143:12 of thy mercy c' off mine enemies,
Pr 2:22 shall be c' off from the earth,
10:31 the froward tongue shall be c' out.
23:18 thine expectation shall not be c' off.
24:14 thy expectation shall not be c' off.
Isa 9:10 the sycomores are c' down, but we
14 Lord will c' off from Israel head
10: 7 destroy and c' off nations not a few.
34 And he shall c' down the thickets
11:13 adversaries of Judah shall be c' off:
14:12 art thou c' down to the ground,
22 and c' off from Babylon the name,
15: 2 be baldness, and every beard c' off.
18: 5 both c' off the sprigs with pruning
5 away and c' down the branches.
22:25 removed, and be c' down, and fall;
25 that was upon it shall be c' off:
29:20 that watch for iniquity are c' off:
33:12 thorns c' up shall they be burned
37:24 c' down the tall cedars thereof,
38:12 have c' off like a weaver my life:
12 c' me off with pining sickness:
45: 2 and c' in sunder the bars of iron:
48: 9 for thee, that I c' thee not off.
19 name should not have been c' off
51: 9 Art thou not it that hath c' Rahab,
53: 8 c' off out of the land of the living:
55:13 sign that shall not be c' off.
56: 5 name, that shall not be c' off.
66: 3 lamb, as if he c' off a dog's neck;
Jer 7:28 and is c' off from their mouth.
29 C' off thine hair, O Jerusalem,
9:21 to c' off the children from without,
11:19 and let us c' him off from the land
16: 6 nor c' themselves, nor make
22: 7 shall c' down thy choice cedars,
25:37 peaceable habitations are c' down
34:18 c' the calf in twain, and passed
36:23 he c' it with the penknife, and
41: 5 and having c' themselves, with
44: 7 c' off from you man and woman,
8 that ye might c' yourselves off,
11 you for evil, and to c' off all Judah.
46:23 They shall c' down her forest,
47: 4 c' off from Tyrus and Zidon every
5 Ashkelon is c' off with the
5 how long wilt thou c' thyself?
48: 2 let us c' it off from being a nation.
2 thou shalt be c' down, O Madmen;
25 The horn of Moab is c' off, and
49:26 men of war shall be c' off in that
50:16 C' off the sower from Babylon.
23 the hammer of the whole earth c'
30 of war shall be c' off in that day,
51: 6 soul: be not c' off in her iniquity;
62 against this place, to c' it off,

La 2: 3 He hath *c'* off in his fierce anger
3:53 have *c'* off my life in the dungeon,
54 then I said, I am *c'* off.
Eze 6: 6 and your images may be *c'* down,
14: 8 *c'* him off from the midst of my
13 will *c'* off man and beast from it:
17 that I *c'* off man and beast from it:
19 to *c'* off from it man and beast:
21 to *c'* off from it man and beast?
16: 4 thy navel was not *c'*, neither wast
17: 9 and *c'* off the fruit thereof, that it
17 forts, to *c'* off many persons:
21: 3 will *c'* off from thee the righteous
4 I will *c'* off from thee the righteous
25: 7 I will *c'* thee off from the people,
13 will *c'* off man and beast from it;
16 and I will *c'* off the Cherethims,
29: 8 and *c'* off man and beast out of thee.
30:15 I will *c'* off the multitude of No.
31:12 of the nations, have *c'* him off,
35: 7 *c'* off from it him that passeth out
37:11 is lost: we are *c'* off for our parts.
39:10 out of the field, neither *c'* down
Da 2: 5 ye shall be *c'* in pieces, and your
34 a stone was *c'* out without hands,
45 stone was *c'* out of the mountain
3:29 shall be *c'* in pieces, and their
4:14 and *c'* off his branches, shake off
9:26 shall Messiah be *c'* off, but not for
Ho 8: 4 them idols, that they may be *c'* off.
10: 7 her king is *c'* off as the foam upon
15 the king of Israel utterly be *c'* off.
Joe 1: 5 for it is *c'* off from your mouth.
9 the drink offering is *c'* off from the
16 not the meat *c'* off before our eyes,
Am 1: 5 and *c'* off the inhabitants from the
8 *c'* off the inhabitant from Ashdod,
2: 3 *c'* off the judge from the midst
3: 14 horns of the altar shall be *c'* off,
9: 1 *c'* them in the head, all of them;
Ob 5 (how art thou *c'* off!) would
9 Esau may be *c'* off by slaughter.
10 and thou shalt be *c'* off for ever.
14 *c'* off those of his that did escape;
Mic 5: 9 all thine enemies shall be *c'* off.
10 I will *c'* off thy horses out of the
11 I will *c'* off the cities of thy land,
12 *c'* off witchcrafts out of thine hand;
13 Thy graven images also will I *c'* off,
Na 1:12 shall they be *c'* down, when he
14 will I *c'* off the graven image and
15 through thee; he is utterly *c'* off.
2:13 I will *c'* off thy prey from the earth,
3:15 the sword shall *c'* thee off, it shall
Hab 3:17 flock shall be *c'* off from the fold,
Zep 1: 3 I will *c'* off man from off the land,
4 *c'* off the remnant of Baal from
11 the merchant people are *c'* down;
11 all they that bear silver are *c'* off.
3: 6 I have *c'* off the nations: their
7 their dwelling should not be *c'* off,
Zec 5: 3 every one that stealeth shall be *c'*
3 every one that sweareth shall be *c'*
9: 6 *c'* off the pride of the Philistines.
10 *c'* off the chariot from Ephraim,
Zec 9:10 and the battle bow shall be *c'* off:
11: 8 Three shepherds also I *c'* off in
9 and that that is to be *c'* off,
9 let it be *c'* off;
10 even Beauty, and *c'* it asunder,
14 Then I *c'* asunder mine other staff,
16 those that be *c'* off, neither shall
12: 3 with it shall be *c'* in pieces,
13: 2 will *c'* off the names of the idols
8 therein shall be *c'* off and die;
14: 2 of the people shall not be *c'* off
Mal 2:12 The Lord will *c'* off the man that
M't 5:30 *c'* it off, and cast it from thee:
18: 8 *c'* them off, and cast them from
21: 8 *c'* down branches from the trees,
24:51 shall *c'* him asunder, and appoint
M'r 9:43 if thy hand offend thee, *c'* it off:
45 if thy foot offend thee, *c'* it off:
11: 8 *c'* down branches off the trees,
14:47 the high priest, and *c'* off his ear.
Lu 12:46 will *c'* him in sunder, and will
13: 7 *c'* it down; why cumbereth it the
9 after that thou shalt *c'* it down.
22:50 priest, and *c'* off his right ear.
Joh 18:10 servant, and *c'* off his right ear.
26 kinsman whose ear Peter *c'* off,
Ac 5:33 that, they were *c'* to the heart,
7:54 they were *c'* to the heart, and they
27:32 soldiers *c'* off the ropes of the boat,
Ro 9:28 and *c'* it short in righteousness:
11:22 otherwise thou also shalt be *c.* off.
24 thou wert *c'* out of the olive tree
2Co 11:12 I may *c'* off occasion from them
Ga 5:12 were even *c'* off which trouble you.

Cuth (*cuth*) See also CUTHAH.
2Ki 17:30 and the men of *C'* made Nergal,

Cuthah (*cu'-thah*) See also CUTH.
2Ki 17:24 men from Babylon, and from *C'*

cuttest
De 24:19 thou *c'* down thine harvest in

cutteth
Job 28:10 *c'* out rivers among the rocks;
Ps 46: 9 bow, and *c'* the spear in sunder;
141: 7 when one *c'* and cleaveth wood
Pr 26: 6 hand of the fool *c'* off the feet,
Jer 10: 3 for one *c'* a tree out of the forest,
22:14 and *c'* him out windows;

cutting See also CUTTINGS.
Ex 31: 5 And in *c'* of stones, to set them,
35:33 And in the *c'* of stones, to set them,
Isa 38:10 I said in the *c'* off of my days,
Hab 2:10 thy house by *c'* off many people,
M'r 5: 5 crying, and *c'* himself with stones.

cuttings
Le 19:28 not make any *c'* in your flesh for
21: 5 nor make any *c'* in their flesh.
Jer 48:37 upon all the hands shall be *c'*,

cymbal See also CYMBALS.
1Co 13: 1 sounding brass, or a tinkling *c'*.

cymbals
2Sa 6: 5 and on cornets, and on *c'*.
1Ch 13: 8 with timbrels, and with *c'*.
15:16 psalteries and harps and *c'*,
19 to sound with *c'* of brass;
28 with trumpets, and with *c'*,
16: 5 but Asaph made a sound with *c'*;
42 with trumpets and *c'* for those
25: 1 harps, with psalteries, and with *c'*:
6 with *c'*, psalteries, and harps,
2Ch 5:12 having *c'* and psalteries and harps,
13 trumpets and *c'* and instruments
29:25 the Lord with *c'*, with psalteries,
Ezr 3:10 the sons of Asaph with *c'*, to praise
Ne 12:27 with singing, with *c'*, psalteries,
Ps 150: 5 Praise him upon the loud *c'*:
5 him upon the high sounding *c'*.

cypress
Isa 44:14 and taketh the *c'* and the oak,

Cyprus (*si'-prus*)
Ac 4:36 Levite, and of the country of *C'*.
11:19 and *C'*, and Antioch, preaching
20 them were men of *C'* and Cyrene,
13: 4 and from thence they sailed to *C'*.
15:39 took Mark, and sailed unto *C'*;
21: 3 when we had discovered *C'*, we left
16 with them one Mnason of *C'*,
27: 4 we sailed under *C'*, because the

Cyrene (*si-re'-ne*) See also CYRENIAN.
M't 27:32 a man of *C'*, Simon by name:
Ac 2:10 of Libya about *C'*, and strangers
11:20 were men of Cyprus and *C'*, which
13: 1 and Lucius of *C'*, and Manaen,

Cyrenian (*si-re'-ne-an*) See also CYRENIANS.
M'r 15:21 compel one Simon a *C'*, who
Lu 23:26 laid hold upon one Simon, a *C'*,

Cyrenians (*si-re'-ne-ans*)
Ac 6: 9 of the Libertines, and *C'*, and

Cyrenius (*si-re'-ne-us*)
Lu 2: 2 when *C'* was governor of Syria.)

Cyrus (*si'-rus*)
2Ch 36:22 the first year of *C'* king of Persia,
22 the Lord stirred up the spirit of *C'*
23 Thus saith *C'* king of Persia,
Ezr 1: 1 the first year of *C'* king of Persia,
1 the Lord stirred up the spirit of *C'*
2 Thus saith *C'* king of Persia,
7 *C'* the king brought forth the
8 those did *C'* king of Persia bring
3: 7 to the grant that they had of *C'*
4: 3 as king *C'* the king of Persia hath
5 all the days of *C'* king of Persia,
5:13 first year of *C'* the king of Babylon
13 the same king *C'* made a decree
14 those did *C'* the king take out of
17 was made of *C'* the king to build
6: 3 year of *C'* the king the same *C'*
14 to the commandment of *C'*,
Isa 44:28 saith of *C'*, He is my shepherd,
45: 1 the Lord to his anointed, to *C'*,
Da 1:21 even unto the first year of king *C'*.
6:28 and in the reign of *C'* the Persian.
10: 1 the third year of *C'* king of Persia

D.

Dabareh (*dab'-a-reh*) See also DABARETH.
Jos 21:28 *D'* with her suburbs,

Dabbasheth (*dab'-ba-sheth*)
Jos 19:11 and reached to *D'*, and reached

Daberath (*dab'-e-rath*) See also DABASEH.
Jos 19:12 and then goeth out to *D'*,
1Ch 6:72 *D'* with her suburbs,

dagger
J'g 3:16 Ehud made him a *d'* which had two
21 took the *d'* from his right thigh,
22 he could not draw the *d'* out

Dagon See also BETH-DAGON; DAGON'S.
J'g 16:23 great sacrifice unto *D'* their god,
1Sa 5: 2 brought it into the house of *D'*,
2 and set it by *D'*.
3 behold, *D'* was fallen upon his face
3 took *D'*, and set him in his place
4 behold, *D'* was fallen upon his face
4 the head of *D'* and both the palms
4 the stump of *D'* was left to him.
5 neither the priests of *D'*, nor any
5 house, tread on the threshold of *D'*
7 is sore upon us, and upon *D'*
1Ch 10:10 his head in the temple of *D'*.

Dagon's
1Sa 5: 5 any that come into *D'* house,

daily
Ex 5:13 Fulfill your works, your *d'* tasks,
19 your bricks of your *d'* tasks.
16: 5 twice as much as they gather *d'*.
Nu 4:16 the *d'* meat offering, and the
28:24 this manner ye shall offer *d'*,
29: 6 *d'* burnt offering, and his meat
J'g 16:16 pressed him *d'* with her words,
2Ki 25:30 a *d'* rate for every day,
2Ch 31:16 his *d'* portion for their service
Ezr 3: 4 the *d'* burnt offerings by number.
Ne 5:18 prepared for me *d'* was one
Es 3: 4 when they spake *d'* unto him,
Ps 13: 2 having sorrow in my heart *d'*?
42:10 while they say *d'* unto me,
56: 1 he fighting *d'* oppresseth me.
Ps 56: 2 enemies would *d'* swallow me
61: 8 I may *d'* perform my vows.
68:19 who *d'* loadeth us with benefits,
72:15 and *d'* shall he be praised.
74:22 foolish...reproacheth thee *d'*.
86: 3 O Lord for I cry unto thee *d'*
88: 9 Lord, I...called *d'* upon thee,
17 They came round about me *d'*
Pr 8:30 and I was *d'* his delight,
34 watching *d'* at my gates,
Isa 58: 2 Yet they seek me *d'*, and delight
Jer 7:25 *d'* rising up early and sending
20: 7 I am in derision *d'*, every one
8 unto me and a derision, *d'*.
37:21 *d'* a piece of bread out of the
Eze 30:16 Noph shall have distresses *d'*.
45:23 without blemish *d'* the seven days;
23 and a kid of the goats *d'*
46:13 shalt *d'* prepare a burnt offering
Da 1: 5 appointed them a *d'* provision
8:11 the *d'* sacrifice was taken away,
12 given him against the *d'* sacrifice
13 vision concerning the *d'* sacrifice,
11:31 shall take away the *d'* sacrifice,
12:11 *d'* sacrifice shall be taken away,
Ho 12: 1 *d'* increaseth lies and
M't 6:11 Give us this day our *d'* bread.
26:55 I sat *d'* with you teaching
M'r 14:49 was *d'* with you in the temple
Lu 9:23 and take up his cross *d'*,
11: 3 us day by day our *d'* bread.
19:47 he taught *d'* in the temple.
22:53 *d'* with you in the temple,
Ac 2:46 continuing *d'* with one accord
47 Lord added to the church *d'*
3: 2 whom they laid *d'* at the gate
5:42 And *d'* in the temple, and in
6: 1 neglected in the *d'* ministration.
16: 5 increased in number *d'*.
17:11 searched the scriptures *d'*,
17 the market *d'* with them
19: 9 disputing *d'* in the school
1Co 15:31 Jesus our Lord, I die *d'*.
2Co 11:28 which cometh upon me *d'*,
Heb 3:13 exhort one another *d'*,
7:27 Who needeth not *d'*, as
10:11 priest standeth *d'* ministering
Jas 2:15 naked, and destitute of *d'* food,

dainties
Ge 49:20 fat, and he shall yield royal *d'*.
Ps 141: 4 and let me not eat of their *d'*.
Pr 23: 3 not desirous of his *d'*: for they

dainty See also DAINTIES.
Job 33:20 abhorreth bread, and his soul *d'*
Pr 23: 6 neither desire thou his *d'* meats:
Re 18:14 things which were *d'* and goodly

Dalaiah (*dal-a-i'-ah*) See also DELAIAH.
1Ch 3:24 Johanan, and *D'*, and Anani,

dale
Ge 14:17 of Shaveh, which is the king's *d'*.
2Sa 18:18 a pillar, which is in the king's *d'*:

Dalmanutha (*dal-ma-nu'-thah*)
M'r 8:10 and came into the parts of *D'*.

Dalmatia (*dal-ma'-she-ah*)
2Ti 4:10 Crescens to Galatia, Titus unto *D'*.

Dalphon (*dal'-fon*)
Es 9: 7 Parshandatha, and *D'*, and

dam
Ex 22:30 seven days it shall be with his *d'*;
Le 22:27 shall be seven days under the *d'*;
De 22: 6 and the *d'* sitting upon the young,
6 shalt not take the *d'* with the
7 thou shalt in any wise let the *d'* go,

damage See also ENDAMAGE.
Ezr 4:22 why should *d'* grow to the hurt
Es 7: 4 not countervail the king's *d'*.
Pr 26: 6 off the feet, and drinketh *d'*.
Da 6: 2 and the king should have no *d'*.
Ac 27:10 will be with hurt and much *d'*,
2Co 7: 9 that ye might receive *d'* by us in

Damaris (*dam'-a-ris*)
Ac 17:34 and a woman named *D'*, and

Damascenes (*dam-as-senes'*)
2Co 11:32 the king kept the city of the *D'*

Damascus (*da-mas'-cus*) See also DAMASCENES; SYRIA-DAMASCUS.
Ge 14:15 which is on the left hand of *D*.
15: 2 of my house is this Eliezer of *D*?
2Sa 8: 5 when the Syrians of *D* came to
6 David put garrisons in Syria of *D*:
1Ki 11:24 they went to *D*, and dwelt therein,
24 and reigned in *D*.
15:18 king of Syria, that dwelt at *D*,
19:15 on thy way to the wilderness of *D*:
20:34 shalt make streets for thee in *D*,
2Ki 5:12 Abana and Pharpar, rivers of *D*,
8: 7 Elisha came to *D*; and Ben-hadad
9 even of every good thing of *D*,
14:28 how he recovered *D*, and Hamath,
16: 9 king of Assyria went up against *D*,
10 king Ahaz went to *D* to meet
10 and saw an altar that was at *D*:
11 that king Ahaz had sent from *D*:
11 against king Ahaz came from *D*.
12 when the king was come from *D*,
1Ch 18: 5 when the Syrians of *D* came to
2Ch 16: 2 king of Syria, that dwelt at *D*,
24:23 spoil of them unto the king of *D*.
28: 5 captives, and brought them to *D*.
23 he sacrificed unto the gods of *D*,
Ca 7: 4 Lebanon which looketh toward *D*.
Isa 7: 8 the head of Syria is *D*,
8 and the head of *D* is Rezin;
8: 4 the riches of *D* and the spoil of
10: 9 is not Samaria as *D*?
17: 1 The burden of *D*. Behold,
1 *D* is taken away from being a city,
3 and the kingdom from *D*, and the
Jer 49:23 Concerning *D*. Hamath is
24 *D* is waxed feeble, and turneth
27 I will kindle a fire in the wall of *D*,
Eze 27:18 *D* was thy merchant in the
47:16 which is between the border of *D*
17 the border of *D*, and the north
18 and from *D*, and from Gilead,
48: 1 the border of *D* northward, to the
Am 1: 3 For three transgressions of *D*,
5 I will break also the bar of *D*,
3:12 and in *D* in a couch.
5:27 to go into captivity beyond *D*,
Zec 9: 1 and *D* shall be the rest thereof:
Ac 9: 2 And desired of him letters to *D*
3 as he journeyed, he came near *D*:
8 the hand, and brought him into *D*.
10 there was a certain disciple at *D*,
19 with the disciples which were at *D*.
22 the Jews which dwelt at *D*,
27 how he had preached boldly at *D*
22: 5 and went to *D*, to bring them
6 and was come nigh unto *D*
10 Arise, and go into *D*; and there it
11 that were with me, I came into *D*.
26:12 Whereupon as I went to *D* with
20 But shewed first unto them of *D*,
2Co 11:32 In *D* the governor under Aretas
Ga 1:17 Arabia, and returned again unto *D*.

Dammim (*dam'-mim*) See EPHES-DAMMIM; PAS-DAMMIM.

damnable
2Pe 2: 1 privily shall bring in *d* heresies,

damnation
M't 23:14 ye shall receive the greater *d*.
33 how can ye escape the *d* of hell?
M'r 3:29 but is in danger of eternal *d*:
12:40 these shall receive greater *d*.
Lu 20:47 the same shall receive greater *d*.
Joh 5:29 unto the resurrection of *d*.
Ro 3: 8 good may come? whose *d* is just.
13: 2 shall receive to themselves *d*.
1Co 11:29 eateth and drinketh *d* to himself,
1Ti 5:12 Having *d*, because they have cast
2Pe 2: 3 not, and their *d* slumbereth not.

damned
M'r 16:16 he that believeth not shall be *d*.
Ro 14:23 he that doubteth is *d* if he eat,
2Th 2:12 That they all might be *d* who

damsel See also DAMSEL'S; DAMSELS.
Ge 24:14 the *d* to whom I shall say,
16 And the *d* was very fair to look
28 And the *d* ran, and told them of
55 Let the *d* abide with us a few
57 We will call the *d*, and enquire
34: 3 and he loved the *d*, and
3 spake kindly unto the *d*.
4 saying, Get me this *d* to wife.
12 unto me: but give me the *d* to
De 22:15 father of the *d*, and her mother,
19 unto the father of the *d*, because
20 of virginity be not found for the *d*:
21 they shall bring out the *d* to the
23 a *d* that is a virgin be betrothed
24 the *d*, because she cried not,
25 if a man find a betrothed *d* in the
26 unto the *d* thou shalt do nothing;
26 there is in the *d* no sin
27 the betrothed *d* cried, and there
28 If a man find a *d* that is a virgin,
J'g 5:30 to every man a *d* or two;
19: 3 the father of the *d* saw him,
Ru 2: 5 over the reapers, Whose *d* is this?
6 It is the Moabitish *d* that came
1Ki 1: 3 So they sought for a fair *d*
4 And the *d* was very fair,
M't 14:11 in a charger, and given to the *d*:
26:69 and a *d* came unto him, saying,
M'r 5:39 the *d* is not dead, but sleepeth.
40 father and the mother of the *d*,
40 and entereth in where the *d* was
M'r 5:41 he took the *d* by the hand,
41 interpreted, *D*, I say unto thee,
42 the *d* arose, and walked; for she
6:22 the king said unto the *d*, Ask of
28 and gave it to the *d*: and
28 the *d* gave it to her mother.
Joh 18:17 Then saith the *d* that kept the
Ac 12:13 a *d* came to hearken, named
16:16 a certain *d* possessed with a

damsel's
De 22:15 bring forth the tokens of the *d*
16 And the *d* father shall say unto
29 shall give unto the *d* father fifty
J'g 19: 4 the *d* father, retained him; and
5 *d* father said unto his son in law,
6 the *d* father had said unto the
8 and the *d* father said, Comfort
9 his father in law, the *d* father,

damsels
Ge 24:61 Rebekah arose, and her *d*, and
1Sa 25:42 with five *d* of hers that went
Ps 68:25 were the *d* playing with timbrels.

Dan (*dan*) See also DANITES; DAN-JAAN; LAISH; MAHANEH-DAN.
Ge 14:14 and pursued them unto *D*.
30: 6 therefore called she his name *D*.
35:25 of Bilhah, Rachel's handmaid; *D*,
46:23 And the sons of *D*; Hushim.
49:16 *D* shall judge his people, as one of
17 *D* shall be a serpent by the way,
Ex 1: 4 *D*, and Naphtali, Gad, and Asher.
31: 6 of Ahisamach, of the tribe of *D*:
35:34 Ahisamach, of the tribe of *D*.
38:23 of the tribe of *D*, an engraver,
Le 24:11 of Dibri, of the tribe of *D*:)
Nu 1:12 Of *D*; Ahiezer the son of
38 children of *D*, by their generations,
39 of them, even of the tribe of *D*,
2:25 The standard of the camp of *D*
25 the captain of the children of *D*
31 were numbered in the camp of *D*
7:66 prince of the children of *D*,
10:25 of the camp of the children of *D*
13:12 the tribe of *D*, Ammiel the son of
26:42 the sons of *D* after their families:
42 families of *D* after their families
34:22 of the tribe of the children of *D*,
De 27:13 Gad, and Asher, and Zebulun, *D*,
33:22 of *D* he said, *D* is a lion's whelp:
34: 1 all the land of Gilead, unto *D*,
Jos 19:40 for the tribe of the children of *D*
47 of the children of *D* went out
47 the children of *D* went up to fight
47 and called Leshem, *D*, after
47 the name of *D* their father.
48 of the tribe of the children of *D*
21: 5 and out of the tribe of *D*, and out
23 of the tribe of *D*, Eltekeh with her
J'g 1:34 Amorites forced the children of *D*
5:17 and why did *D* remain in ships?
13:25 him at times in the camp of *D*
18: 2 children of *D* sent of their family
16 which were of the children of *D*,
22 and overtook the children of *D*.
23 they cried unto the children of *D*.
25 the children of *D* said unto him,
26 the children of *D* went their way:
29 they called the name of the city *D*,
29 after the name of *D* their father,
30 children of *D* set up the graven
30 sons were priests to the tribe of *D*
20: 1 man, from *D* even to Beer-sheba,
1Sa 3:20 Israel from *D* even to Beer-sheba
2Sa 3:10 Judah, from *D* even to Beer-sheba
17:11 thee, from *D* even to Beer-sheba,
24: 2 Israel, from *D* even to Beer-sheba,
15 people from *D* even to Beer-sheba
1Ki 4:25 fig tree, from *D* even to Beer-sheba,
12:29 Bethel, and the other put he in *D*.
30 before the one, even unto *D*.
15:20 and *D*, and Abel-beth-maachah,
2Ki 10:29 in Beth-el, and that were in *D*.
1Ch 2: 2 *D*, Joseph, and Benjamin,
21: 2 Israel from Beer-sheba even to *D*;
27:22 Of *D*, Azareel the son of Jeroham.
2Ch 2:14 a woman of the daughters, of *D*,
16: 4 smote Ijon, and *D*, and Abel-maim,
30: 5 Israel, from Beer-sheba even to *D*,
Jer 4:15 For a voice declareth from *D*, and
8:16 of his horses was heard from *D*:
Eze 27:19 *D* also and Javan going to and
48: 1 east and west; a portion for *D*.
2 the border of *D*, from the east side
32 gate of Benjamin, one gate of *D*.
Am 8:14 and say, Thy god, O *D*, liveth;

dance See also DANCED; DANCES; DANCING.
J'g 21:21 of Shiloh come out to *d* in dances,
Job 21:11 like a flock, and their children *d*.
Ps 149: 3 praise his name in the *d*: let
150: 4 Praise him with the timbrel and *d*:
Ec 3: 4 a time to mourn, and a time to *d*;
Isa 13:21 there, and satyrs shall *d* there.
Jer 31:13 shall the virgin rejoice in the *d*,
La 5:15 our *d* is turned into mourning.

danced
J'g 21:23 to their number, of them that *d*,
2Sa 6:14 David *d* before the Lord with all
M't 11:17 unto you, and ye have not *d*;
14: 6 the daughter of Herodias *d* before
M'r 6:22 the said Herodias came in, and *d*,
Lu 7:32 unto you, and ye have not *d*;

dances
Ex 15:20 her with timbrels and with *d*.
J'g 11:34 him with timbrels and with *d*:
J'g 21:21 of Shiloh come out to dance in *d*,
1Sa 21:11 sing one to another of him in *d*,
29: 5 they sang one to another in *d*,
Jer 31: 4 shalt go forth in the *d* of them

dancing
Ex 32:19 that he saw the calf, and the *d*:
1Sa 18: 6 singing and *d*, to meet king Saul.
30:16 eating and drinking, and *d*,
2Sa 6:16 saw king David leaping and *d*
1Ch 15:29 saw king David *d* and playing:
Ps 30:11 for me my mourning into *d*:
Lu 15:25 the house, he heard musick and *d*.

dandled
Isa 66:12 and be *d* upon her knees.

danger See also ENDANGER.
M't 5:21, 22 shall be in *d* of the judgment:
22 shall be in *d* of the council: but
22 thou fool, shall be in *d* of hell fire.
M'r 3:29 is in *d* of eternal damnation:
Ac 19:27 not only this our craft is in *d*
40 we are in *d* to be called in question

dangerous
Ac 27: 9 when sailing was now *d*,

Daniel (*dan'-yel*) See also BELTESHAZZAR.
1Ch 3: 1 *D*, of Abigail the Carmelitess:
Ezr 8: 2 of the sons of Ithamar; *D*: of the
Ne 10: 6 *D*, Ginnethon, Baruch,
Eze 14:14 three men, Noah, *D*, and Job,
20 Noah, *D*, and Job, were in it,
28: 3 Behold, thou art wiser than *D*;
Da 1: 6 children of Judah, *D*, Hananiah,
7 for he gave unto *D* the name of
8 But *D* purposed in his heart that
9 God had brought *D* into favour
10 prince of the eunuchs said unto *D*,
11 said *D* to Melzar, whom the prince
11 of the eunuchs had set over *D*,
17 *D* had understanding in all visions
19 them all was found none like *D*,
21 *D* continued even unto the first
2:13 they sought *D* and his fellows
14 Then *D* answered with counsel
15 made the thing known to *D*.
16 Then *D* went in, and desired of the
17 Then *D* went to his house, and
18 that *D* and his fellows should not
19 was the secret revealed unto *D*.
19 Then *D* blessed the God of heaven.
20 *D* answered and said, Blessed be
24 Therefore *D* went in unto Arioch,
25 Then Arioch brought in *D* before
26 The king answered and said to *D*,
27 *D* answered in the presence of the
46 upon his face, and worshipped *D*,
47 king answered unto *D*, and said,
48 the king made *D* a great man,
49 Then *D* requested of the king, and
49 but *D* sat in the gate of the king.
4: 8 at the last *D* came in before me,
19 *D*, whose name was Belteshazzar,
5:12 in the same *D*, whom the king
12 now let *D* be called, and he will
13 was *D* brought in before the king.
13 the king spake and said unto *D*,
13 Art thou that *D*, which art of
17 Then *D* answered and said before
29 and they clothed *D* with scarlet,
6: 2 presidents; of whom *D* was first:
3 Then this *D* was preferred above
4 sought to find occasion against *D*
5 find any occasion against this *D*,
10 when *D* knew that the writing was
11 and found *D* praying and making
13 *D*, which is of the children of the
14 set his heart on *D* to deliver him:
16 and they brought *D*, and cast him
16 the king spake and said unto *D*,
17 not be changed concerning *D*.
20 with a lamentable voice unto *D*:
20 and the king spake and said to *D*,
20 O *D*, servant of the living God,
21 Then said *D* unto the king, O king
23 that they should take *D* up out of
23 the den. So *D* was taken up
24 those men which had accused *D*,
26 and fear before the God of *D*:
27 hath delivered *D* from the power
28 *D* prospered in the reign of Darius.
7: 1 *D* had a dream and visions of
2 *D* spake and said, I saw in my
15 I *D* was grieved in my spirit
28 As for me *D*, my cogitations much
8: 1 unto me, even unto me *D*,
15 it came to pass, when I, even I *D*,
27 And I *D* fainted, and was sick
9: 2 In the first year of his reign I *D*
22 and said, O *D*, I am now come forth
10: 1 a thing was revealed unto *D*,
2 In those days I *D* was mourning
7 And I *D* alone saw the vision:
11 he said unto me, O *D*, a man
12 Then said he unto me, Fear not, *D*:
12: 4 But thou, O *D*, shut up the words,
5 *D* looked, and behold, there stood
9 And he said, Go thy way, *D*:
M't 24:15 spoken of by *D* the prophet,
M'r 13:14 spoken of by *D* the prophet,

Danites (*dan'-ites*)
J'g 13: 2 of Zorah, of the family of the *D*,
18: 1 the tribe of the *D* sought them
11 from thence of the family of the *D*,
1Ch 12:35 And of the *D* expert in war

Dan-jaan (*dan-ja'-an*)
2Sa 24: 6 they came to *D*, and about to

Dannah (dan'-nah)
Jos 15:49 D', and Kirjath-sannah, which is
Dara (da'-rah) See also DARDA.
1Ch 2: 6 and Heman, and Calcol, and D':
Darda (dar'-dah) See also DARA.
1Ki 4:31 Chalcol, and D', the son of Mahol:
dare See also DURST.
Job 41:10 None is so fierce that d' stir him
Ro 5: 7 man some would even d' to die.
15:18 For I will not d' to speak of
1Co 6: 1 D' any of you, having a matter
2Co 10:12 For we d' not make ourselves
Darius (da-ri'-us)
Ezr 4: 5 until the reign of D' king of
24 the second year of the reign of D'
5: 5 till the matter came to D': and then
6 this side of the river, sent unto D'
7 thus; Unto D' the king, all peace.
6: 1 Then D' the king made a decree,
12 I D' have made a decree; let it be
13 to that which D' the king had sent,
14 the commandment of Cyrus, and D',
15 the sixth year of the reign of D'
Ne 12:22 also the priests, to the reign of D'
Da 5:31 D' the Median took the kingdom,
6: 1 It pleased D' to set over the
6 thus unto him, King D', live forever.
9 Wherefore king D' signed the
25 Then king D' wrote unto all people,
28 Daniel prospered in the reign of D'.
9: 1 year of D' the son of Ahasuerus,
11: 1 I in the first year of D' the Mede,
Hag 1: 1 In the second year of D' the king,
15 in the second year of D' the king.
2:10 month, in the second year of D',
Zec 1: 1 month, in the second year of D',
7 Sebat, in the second year of D',
7: 1 in the fourth year of king D',
dark See also DARKISH.
Ge 15:17 the sun went down, and it was d',
Le 13: 6 if the plague be somewhat d',
21 the skin, but be somewhat d';
26 other skin, but be somewhat d';
28 the skin, but it be somewhat d';
56 the plague be somewhat d' after
Nu 12: 8 apparently, and not in d' speeches;
Jos 2: 5 when it was d', that the men went
2Sa 22:12 round about him, d' waters,
Ne 13:19 gates of Jerusalem began to be d'
Job 3: 9 stars of the twilight thereof be d';
12:25 grope in the d' without light,
18: 6 light shall be d' in his tabernacle,
22:13 he judge through the d' cloud?
24:16 In the d' they dig through houses,
Ps 18:11 round about him were d' waters
35: 6 Let their way be d' and slippery:
49: 4 open my d' saying upon the harp.
74:20 the d' places of the earth are full
78: 2 I will utter d' sayings of old:
88:12 thy wonders be known in the d'?
105:28 He sent darkness, and made it d';
Pr 1: 6 of the wise, and their d' sayings.
7: 9 evening, in the black and d' night:
Isa 29:15 their works are in the d', and they
45:19 secret, in a d' place of the earth:
Jer 13:16 stumble upon the d' mountains,
La 3: 6 He hath sent me in d' places,
Eze 8:12 the house of Israel do in the d',
32: 7 and make the stars thereof d';
8 of heaven will I make d' over thee,
34:12 scattered in the cloudy and d' day.
Da 8:23 and understanding d' sentences,
Joe 2:10 the sun and the moon shall be d',
Am 5: 8 maketh the day d' with night:
20 very d', and no brightness in it?
Mic 3: 6 and it shall be d' unto you, that
6 and the day shall be d' over them.
Zec 14: 6 light shall not be clear, nor d':
Lu 11:36 full of light, having no part d',
Joh 6:17 And it was now d', and Jesus was
20: 1 Magdalene early, when it was yet d',
2Pe 1:19 light that shineth in a d' place,
darken See also DARKENED; DARKENETH.
Am 8: 9 will d' the earth in the clear day:
darkened
Ex 10:15 earth, so that the land was d';
Ps 69:23 Let their eyes be d', that they see
Ec 12: 2 stars, be not d', nor the clouds
3 that look out of the windows be d',
Isa 5:30 light is d' in the heavens thereof.
9:19 the Lord of hosts is the land d',
13:10 sun shall be d' in his going forth,
24:11 all joy is d', the mirth of the
Eze 30:18 shall be d', when I shall break
Joe 3:15 sun and the moon shall be d',
Zec 11:17 his right eye shall be utterly d'.
M't 24:29 of those days shall the sun be d',
M'r 13:24 the sun shall be d', and the moon
Lu 23:45 And the sun was d', and the veil
Ro 1:21 and their foolish heart was d'.
11:10 Let their eyes be d', that they may
Eph 4:18 Having the understanding d',
Re 8:12 so as the third part of them was d',
9: 2 and the sun and the air were d'
darkeneth
Job 38: 2 Who is this that d' counsel by
darkish
Le 13:39 skin of their flesh be d' white;
darkly
1Co 13:12 we see through a glass, d';
darkness
Ge 1: 2 d' was upon the face of the deep.
Ge 1: 4 God divided the light from the d'.
5 Day, and the d' he called Night.
18 and to divide the light from the d':
15:12 horror of great d' fell upon him.
Ex 10:21 may be d' over the land of Egypt,
21 even d' which may be felt.
22 there was a thick d' in all the land
14:20 it was a cloud and d' to them,
20:21 drew near unto the thick d'
De 4:11 unto the midst of heaven, with d',
11 clouds, and thick d'.
5:22 the cloud, and of the thick d', with
23 voice out of the midst of the d',
28:29 as the blind gropeth in d',
Jos 24: 7 d' between you and the Egyptians,
1Sa 2: 9 the wicked shall be silent in d';
2Sa 22:10 and d' was under his feet.
12 he made d' pavilions round about
29 and the Lord will lighten my d'.
1Ki 8:12 he would dwell in the thick d'.
2Ch 6: 1 he would dwell in the thick d'.
Job 3: 4 Let that day be d'; let not God
5 Let d' and the shadow of death
6 for that night, let d' seize upon it;
5:14 meet with d' in the day time,
10:21 Even to the land of d', and the
22 A land of d', as
22 as d' itself; and of the shadow
22 and where the light is as d'.
12:22 discovereth deep things out of d',
15:22 that he shall return out of d',
23 knoweth that the day of d' is ready
30 He shall not depart out of d';
17:12 the light is short because of d'.
13 I have made my bed in the d'.
18:18 be driven from light into d', and
19: 8 he hath set d' in my paths.
20:26 d' shall be hid in his secret places:
22:11 Or d', that thou canst not see;
23:17 I was not cut off before the d',
17 neither hath he covered the d'
28: 3 He setteth an end to d', and
3 the stones of d', and the
29: 3 by his light I walked through d';
30:26 I waited for light, there came d'.
34:22 There is no d', nor shadow of
37:19 order our speech by reason of d'
38: 9 thick d' a swaddlingband for it,
19 and as for d', where is the place
Ps 18: 9 and d' was under his feet.
11 He made d' his secret place;
28 my God will enlighten my d'.
82: 5 understand; they walk on in d':
88: 6 lowest pit, in d', in the deeps.
18 me, and mine acquaintance into d'.
91: 6 the pestilence that walketh in d';
97: 2 and d' are round about him:
104:20 Thou makest d', and it is night:
105:28 He sent d', and made it dark;
107:10 Such as sit in d' and in the shadow
14 He brought them out of d' and the
112: 4 upright there ariseth light in the d':
139:11 I say, Surely the d' shall cover me;
12 Yea, the d' hideth not from thee;
12 d' and the light are both alike to
143: 3 he hath made me to dwell in d',
Pr 2:13 to walk in the ways of d';
4:19 The way of the wicked is as d':
20:20 shall be put out in obscure d'.
Ec 2:13 folly, as far as light excelleth d'.
14 head; but the fool walketh in d':
5:17 All his days also he eateth in d',
6: 4 vanity, and departeth in d', and
4 his name shall be covered with d'.
11: 8 let him remember the days of d';
Isa 5:20 put d' for light, and light for d';
30 behold d' and sorrow, and the light
8:22 behold trouble and d', dimness of
22 and they shall be driven to d'.
9: 2 The people that walked in d' have
29:18 out of obscurity, and out of d'.
42: 7 them that sit in d' out of the prison
16 I will make d' light before them,
45: 3 I will give thee the treasures of d',
7 I form the light, and create d':
47: 5 Sit thou silent, and get thee into d',
49: 9 to them that are in d', Shew
50:10 walketh in d', and hath no light?
58:10 and thy d' be as the noon day:
59: 9 for brightness, but we walk in d'.
60: 2 the d' shall cover the earth,
2 and gross d' the people:
Jer 2:31 unto Israel? a land of d'?
13:16 before he cause d', and before
16 of death, and make it gross d'.
Jer 23:12 as slippery ways in the d':
La 3: 2 led me, and brought me into d',
Eze 32: 8 over thee, and set d' upon thy land
Da 2:22 he knoweth what is in the d',
Joe 2: 2 A day of d' and of gloominess,
2 a day of clouds and of thick d',
31 The sun shall be turned into d',
Am 4:13 that maketh the morning d', and
5:18 the day of the Lord is d', and not
20 shall not the day of the Lord be d',
Mic 7: 8 I sit in d', the Lord shall be a light
Na 1: 8 and d' shall pursue his enemies.
Zep 1:15 a day of d' and gloominess,
15 a day of clouds and thick d',
M't 4:16 The people which sat in d' saw
6:23 thy whole body shall be full of d'.
23 in thee be d', how great is that d'!
8:12 shall be cast out into outer d':
10:27 What I tell you in d', that speak
22:13 away, and cast him into outer d';
25:30 unprofitable servant into outer d':
M't 27:45 there was d' over all the land
M'r 15:33 there was d' over the whole land
Lu 1:79 To give light to them that sit in d'
11:34 is evil, thy body also is full of d'.
35 light which is in thee be not d'.
12: 3 whatsoever ye have spoken in d'
22:53 is your hour, and the power of d'.
23:44 there was a d' over all the earth
Joh 1: 5 And the light shineth in d'; and
5 and the d' comprehended it not.
3:19 men loved d' rather than light,
8:12 followeth me shall not walk in d',
12:35 the light, lest d' come upon you:
35 for he that walketh in d' knoweth
46 on me should not abide in d'.
Ac 2:20 The sun shall be turned into d',
13:11 there fell on him a mist and a d';
26:18 to turn them from d' to light,
Ro 2:19 a light of them which are in d',
13:12 cast off the works of d', and let us
1Co 4: 5 to light the hidden things of d',
2Co 4: 6 the light to shine out of d', hath
6:14 communion hath light with d'?
Eph 5: 8 ye were sometimes d', but now are
11 with the unfruitful works of d',
6:12 the rulers of the d' of this world,
Col 1:13 delivered us from the power of d',
1Th 5: 4 But ye, brethren, are nor in d',
5 we are not of the night, not of d'.
Heb 12:18 nor unto blackness, and d', and
1Pe 2: 9 hath called you out of d' into his
2Pe 2: 4 delivered them into chains of d',
17 the mist of d' is reserved for ever.
1Jo 1: 5 light, and in him is no d' at all.
6 and walk in d', we lie, and do not
2: 8 because the d' is past, and the
9 brother, is in d' even until now.
11 is in d', and walketh in d', and
11 goeth, because that d' hath blinded
Jude 6 in everlasting chains under d'
13 the blackness of d' for ever.
Re 16:10 and his kingdom was full of d';
Darkon (dar'-kon)
Ezr 2:56 of Jaalah, the children of D', the
Ne 7:58 of Jaala, the children of D', the
darling
Ps 22:20 my d' from the power of the dog.
35:17 my d' from the lions.
dart See also DARTS.
Job 41:26 spear, the d', nor the habergeon.
Pr 7:23 Till a d' strike through his liver;
Heb 12:20 or thrust through with a d':
darts
2Sa 18:14 he took three d' in his hand,
2Ch 32: 5 d' and shields in abundance.
Job 41:29 D' are counted as stubble: he
Eph 6:16 all the fiery d' of the wicked.
dash See also DASHED; DASHETH.
2Ki 8:12 wilt d' their children, and rip up
Ps 2: 9 thou shalt d' them in pieces like
91:12 thou d' thy foot against a stone.
Isa 13:18 shall d' the young men to pieces;
Jer 13:14 d' them one against another,
M't 4: 6 thou d' thy foot against a stone.
Lu 4:11 thou d' thy foot against a stone.
dashed
Ex 15: 6 hand, O Lord, hath d' in pieces
Isa 13:16 children also shall be d' to pieces
Ho 10:14 the mother was d' in pieces upon
13:16 their infants shall be d' in pieces,
Na 3:10 children also were d' in pieces
dasheth
Ps 137: 9 that taketh and d' thy little ones
Na 2: 1 He that d' in pieces is come
Dathan (da'-than)
Nu 16: 1 D' and Abiram, the sons of Eliab,
12 Moses sent to call D' and Abiram,
24 of Korah, D', and Abiram.
25 Moses rose up and went unto D'
27 from the tabernacle of Korah, D',
27 side: and D' and Abiram came out,
26: 9 Nemuel, and D', and Abiram.
9 This is that D' and Abiram, which
De 11: 6 what he did unto D' and Abiram,
Ps 106:17 earth opened and swallowed up D',
daub See also DAUBED; DAUBING.
Eze 13:11 d' it with untempered morter,
daubed
Ex 2: 3 d' it with slime and with pitch,
Eze 13:10 d' it with untempered morter:
12 daubing wherewith ye have d' it?
14 down the wall that ye have d'
15 have d' it with untempered morter,
15 no more, neither they that d' it;
22:28 And her prophets have d' them
daubing
Eze 13:12 Where is the d' wherewith ye
daughter See also DAUGHTER'S; DAUGHTERS.
Ge 11:29 Milcah, the d' of Haran, the
31 and Sarai his d' in law, his son
20:12 she is the d' of my father,
12 but not the d' of my mother;
24:23 Whose d' art thou: tell me, I pray
24 d' of Bethuel the son of Milcah,
47 Whose d' art thou? And she said,
47 The d' of Bethuel, Nahor's son,
48 master's brother's d' unto his son.
25:20 the d' of Bethuel the Syrian of
26:34 Judith the d' of Beeri the Hittite,
34 and Bashemath the d' of Elon the
28: 9 Mahalath the d' of Ishmael
29: 6 his d' cometh with the sheep.

Ge 29:10 Jacob saw Rachel the d' of Laban
18 years for Rachel thy younger d'.
23 took Leah his d', and brought her
24 gave unto his d' Leah Zilpah his
28 gave him Rachel his d' to wife also.
29 Laban gave to Rachel his d'
30:21 afterwards she bare a d', and
34: 1 And Dinah the d' of Leah,
3 clave unto Dinah the d' of Jacob,
5 that he had defiled Dinah his d':
7 Israel in lying with Jacob's d';
8 son Shechem longeth for your d':
17 then will we take our d', and we
19 he had delight in Jacob's d':
36: 2 the d' of Elon the Hittite,
2 d' of Anah the d' of Zibeon the
3 Bashemath Ishmael's d', sister of
14 Aholibamah the d' of Anah
14 the d' of Zibeon, Esau's wife
18 the d' of Anah, Esau's wife.
25 and Aholibamah the d' of Anah.
39 the d' of Matred, the d' of Mezahab.
38: 2 there a d' of a certain Canaanite,
11 said Judah to Tamar his d' in law,
12 the d' of Shuah Judah's wife died;
16 not that she was his d' in law.)
24 Tamar thy d' in law hath played
41:45 gave him to wife Asenath the d' of
50 Asenath the d' of Poti-pherah
46:15 with his d' Dinah: all the souls of
18 whom Laban gave to Leah his d',
20 Asenath the d' of Poti-pherah
25 Laban gave unto Rachel his d',
Ex 1:16 but if it be a d', then she shall live.
22 every d' ye shall save alive.
2: 1 took to wife a d' of Levi.
5 And the d' of Pharaoh came down
7 said his sister to Pharaoh's d',
8 And Pharaoh's d' said to her, Go.
9 Pharaoh's d' said unto her, Take
10 she brought him unto Pharaoh's d',
21 he gave Moses Zipporah his d'.
6:23 Elisheba, d' of Amminadab, sister
20:10 thou, nor thy son, nor thy d',
21: 7 man sell his d' to be a maidservant,
31 a son, or have gored a d',
Le 12: 6 or for a d', she shall bring
18: 9 d' of thy father, or d' of thy mother,
10 The nakedness of thy son's d',
10 or of thy daughter's d',
11 nakedness of thy father's wife's d'.
15 the nakedness of thy d' in law:
17 nakedness of a woman and her d',
17 shalt thou take her son's d',
17 or her daughter's d',
19:29 Do not prostitute thy d', to cause
20:12 if a man lie with his d' in law,
17 take his sister, his father's d',
17 or his mother's d',
21: 2 for his son, and for his d', and for
9 d' of any priest, if she profane
22:12 if the priest's d' also be married
13 But if the priest's d' be a widow,
24:11 was Shelomith, the d' of Dibri,
Nu 25:15 slain was Cozbi, the d' of Zur;
18 Cozbi, the d' of a prince of Midian,
26:46 of the d' of Asher was Sarah.
59 wife was Jochebed, the d' of Levi,
27: 8 his inheritance to pass unto his d'.
9 if he have no d', then he shall give
30:16 between the father and his d',
36: 8 every d', that possesseth an
De 5:14 work, thou, nor thy son, nor thy d',
7: 3 d' thou shalt not give unto his son,
3 d' shalt thou take unto thy son.
12:18 thou, and thy son, and thy d',
13: 6 thy mother, or thy son, or thy d',
16:11 thy d', and thy manservant, and
14 thou, and thy son, and thy d',
18:10 his son or his d' to pass through
22:16 I gave my d' unto this man to wife,
17 I found not thy d' a maid; and yet
27:22 the d' of his father, or the d' of his
28:56 toward her son, and toward her d',
Jos 15:16 will I give Achsah my d' to wife.
17 he gave him Achsah his d' to wife.
J'g 1:12 will I give Achsah my d' to wife.
13 he gave him Achsah his d' to wife.
11:34 his d' came out to meet him
34 her he had neither son nor d'.
35 Alas, my d'! thou hast brought me
40 yearly to lament the d' of Jephthah
19:24 Behold, here is my d' a maiden,
21: 1 any of us give his d' unto Benjamin
Ru 1:22 the Moabitess, her d' in law, with
2: 2 she said unto her, Go, my d'.
8 unto Ruth, Hearest thou not, my d'?
20 Naomi said unto her d' in law,
22 Naomi said unto Ruth her d' in law,
22 It is good, my d', that thou go
3: 1 My d', shall I not seek rest for thee,
10 Blessed be thou of the Lord, my d':
11 And now, my d', fear not; I will do
16 Who art thou, my d'? And she told
18 Then said she, Sit still, my d',
4:15 thy d' in law, which loveth thee,
1Sa 1:16 thine handmaid for a d' of Belial:
4:19 And his d' in law, Phinehas' wife,
14:50 was Ahinoam, the d' of Ahimaaz:
17:25 riches, and will give him his d',
18:17 Behold my elder d' Merab, her will
19 Saul's d' should have been given
20 And Michal Saul's d' loved David:
27 gave him Michal his d' to wife.
28 that Michal Saul's d' loved him.
25:44 But Saul had given Michal his d',

2Sa 3: 3 Maacah the d' of Talmai king of
7 name was Rizpah, the d' of Aiah:
13 thou first bring Michal Saul's d',
6:16 Michal Saul's d' looked through a
20 And Michal the d' of Saul come out
23 Michal the d' of Saul had no child
11: 3 this Bath-sheba, the d' of Eliam,
12: 3 bosom, and was unto him as a d'.
14:27 three sons, and one d', whose name
17:25 went in to Abigail the d' of Nahash,
21: 8 the d' of Aiah, whom she bare unto
8 five sons of Michal the d' of Saul,
10 the d' of Aiah took sackcloth, and
11 David what Rizpah the d' of Aiah,
1Ki 3: 1 took Pharaoh's d', and brought her
4:11 Taphath the d' of Solomon to wife:
15 took Basmath the d' of Solomon to
7: 8 also an house for Pharaoh's d',
9:16 given it for a present unto his d',
24 Pharaoh's d' came up out of the
11: 1 together with the d' of Pharaoh,
15: 2, 10 Maachah, the d' of Abishalom.
16:31 to wife Jezebel the d' of Ethbaal
22:42 name was Azubah the d' of Shilhi.
2Ki 8:18 for the d' of Ahab was his wife:
26 the d' of Omri king of Israel.
9:34 bury her for she is a king's d'.
11: 2 Jehosheba the d' of king Joram,
14: 9 Give thy d' to my son to wife:
15:33 name was Jerusha the, d' of Zadok.
18: 2 also was Abi, the d' of Zachariah.
19:21 virgin the d' of Zion hath despised
21 the d' of Jerusalem hath shaken
21:19 Meshullemeth, the d' of Haruz of
22: 1 Jedidah, the d' of Adaiah of
23:10 or his d' to pass through the fire
31 Hamutal, the d' of Jeremiah of
36 Zebudah, the d' of Pedaiah of
24: 8 Nehushta, the d' of Elnathan of
18 Hamutal, the d' of Jeremiah of
1Ch 1:50 the d' of Matred, the d' of Mezahab.
2: 3 of the d' of Shua the Canaanitess.
4 Tamar his d' in law bare him
21 Hezron went in to the d' of Machir
35 Sheshan gave his d' to Jarha his
49 and the d' of Caleb was Achsa.
3: 2 son of Maachah the d' of Talmai
5 of Bath-shua the d' of Ammiel:
4:18 the d' of Pharaoh, which Mered
7:24 (And his d' was Sherah, who built
15:29 Michal the d' of Saul looking out at
2Ch 8:11 Solomon brought up the d' of
11:18 Mahalath the d' of Jerimoth the
18 Abihail the d' of Eliab
20 took Maachah the d' of Absalom;
21 the d' of Absalom above all his
13: 2 Michaiah the d' of Uriel of Gibeah.
20:31 was Azubah the d' of Shilhi.
21: 6 he had the d' of Ahab to wife:
22: 2 also was Athaliah the d' of Omri.
11 Jehoshabeath, the d' of the king,
11 So Jehoshabeath, the d' of king
25:18 Give thy d' to my son to wife:
27: 1 also was Jerushah, the d' of Zadok.
29: 1 was Abijah, the d' of Zechariah.
Ne 6:18 had taken the d' of Meshullam
Es 2: 7 that is, Esther, his uncle's d':
7 were dead, took for his own d'.
15 Esther, the d' of Abihail the uncle
15 who had taken her for his d',
9:29 Esther the queen, the d' of Abihail,
Ps 9:14 in the gates of the d' of Zion:
45:10 Hearken, O d', and consider, and
12 And the d' of Tyre shall be there
13 The king's d' is all glorious within:
137: 8 O d' of Babylon, who art to be
Ca 7: 1 O prince's d'! the joints of thy
Isa 1: 8 the d' of Zion is left as a cottage
10:30 Lift up thy voice, O d' of Gallim:
32 against the mount of the d' of Zion.
16: 1 unto the mount of the d' of Zion.
22: 4 the spoiling of the d' of my people.
23:10 d' of Tarshish: there is no more
12 thou oppressed virgin, d' of Zidon:
37:22 virgin, the d' of Zion, hath despised
22 the d' of Jerusalem hath shaken
47: 1 O virgin d' of Babylon, sit on the
1 no throne, O d' of the Chaldeans:
5 darkness, O d' of the Chaldeans:
52: 2 of thy neck, O captive d' of Zion.
62:11 Say ye to the d' of Zion,
Jer 4:11 wilderness toward the d' of my
31 the voice of the d' of Zion,
6: 2 I have likened the d' of Zion
14 the hurt of the d' of my people
23 war against thee, O d' of Zion.
26 O d' of my people, gird thee
8:11 hurt of the d' of my people slightly,
19 the cry of the d' of my people
21 the hurt of the d' of my people
22 the health of the d' of my people
9: 1 the slain of the d' of my people!
7 I do for the d' of my people?
14:17 for the virgin d' of my people is
31:22 go about, O thou backsliding d'?
46:11 balm, O virgin, the d' of Egypt:
19 O thou d' dwelling in Egypt,
24 d' of Egypt shall be confounded;
48:18 Thou d' that dost inhabit Dibon,
49: 4 O backsliding d'? that trusted
50:42 against thee, O d' of Babylon.
51:33 The d' of Babylon is like a
52: 1 the d' of Jeremiah of Libnah.
La 1: 6 from the d' of Zion all her beauty
15 the virgin, the d' of Judah,
2: 1 the Lord covered the d' of Zion

La 2: 2 strongholds of the d' of Judah;
4 the tabernacle of the d' of Zion:
5 hath increased in the d' of Judah
8 destroy the wall of the d' of Zion:
10 The elders of the d' of Zion sit
11 destruction of the d' of my people;
13 liken to thee, O d' of Jerusalem?
13 comfort thee, O virgin d' of Zion?
15 their head at the d' of Jerusalem,
18 O wall of the d' of Zion, let tears
3:48 destruction of the d' of my people.
4: 3 the d' of my people is become cruel,
6 the iniquity of the d' of my people
10 destruction of the d' of my people.
21 and be glad, O d' of Edom,
22 is accomplished, O d' of Zion;
22 O d' of Edom; he will discover thy
Eze 14:20 shall deliver neither son nor d';
16:44 As is the mother, so is her d'.
45 Thou art thy mother's d', that
22:11 hath lewdly defiled his d' in law;
11 humbled his sister, his father's d'.
44:25 for son, or for d', for brother,
Da 11: 6 for the king's d' of the south
17 shall give him the d' of women,
Ho 1: 3 took Gomer the d' of Diblaim;
6 conceived again, and bare a d'.
Mic 1:13 of the sin to the d' of Zion:
4: 8 the strong hold of the d' of Zion,
8 shall come to the d' of Jerusalem.
10 O d' of Zion, like a woman in travail:
13 Arise and thresh, O d' of Zion:
5: 1 thyself in troops, O d' of troops:
7: 6 d' riseth up against her mother,
6 d' in law against her mother in
Zep 3:10 even the d' of my dispersed, shall
14 Sing, O d' of Zion; shout, O Israel;
14 all the heart, O d' of Jerusalem.
Zec 2: 7 dwellest with the d' of Babylon.
10 Sing and rejoice, O d' of Zion:
9: 9 Rejoice greatly, O d' of Zion;
9 shout, O d' of Jerusalem:
Mal 2:11 hath married the d' of a strange god.
M't 9:18 My d' is even now dead: but
22 D', be of good comfort; thy faith
10:35 and the d' against her mother,
35 and the d' in law against her
37 loveth son or d' more than me
14: 6 the d' of Herodias danced before
15:22 my d' is grievously vexed with a
28 And her d' was made whole from
21: 5 Tell ye the d' of Sion, Behold,
M'r 5:23 little d' lieth at the point of death:
34 D', thy faith hath made thee whole;
35 Thy d' is dead: why troublest thou
6:22 the d' of the said Herodias came
7:25 young d' had an unclean spirit,
26 cast forth the devil out of her d'.
29 the devil is gone out of thy d'.
30 and her d' laid upon the bed.
Lu 2:36 the d' of Phanuel, of the tribe of
8:42 he had one only d', about twelve
48 D', be of good comfort: thy faith
49 Thy d' is dead: trouble not the
12:53 against the d', and the d' against
53 d' in law, and the d' in law against
13:16 a d' of Abraham, whom Satan
Joh 12:15 Fear not, d' of Sion: behold, thy
Ac 7:21 Pharaoh's d' took him up and
Heb 11:24 be called the son of Pharaoh's d';

daughter-in-law See DAUGHTER and LAW.

daughter's
Le 18:10 daughter, or thy d' daughter,
17 or her d' daughter, to uncover her
De 22:17 are the tokens of my d' virginity.

daughters
Ge 5: 4 years: and he begat sons and d':
7, 10, 13, 16, 19, 22, 26, 30 and begat
sons and d':
6: 1 earth, and d' were born unto them.
2 the sons of God saw the d' of men
4 came in unto the d' of men, and they
11:11, 13, 15, 17, 19, 21, 23, 25, and begat
sons and d'.
19: 8 have two d' which have not known
12 in law, and thy sons, and thy d',
14 sons in law, which married his d',
15 and thy two d', which are here;
16 and upon the hand of his two d';
30 in the mountain, and his two d'
30 dwelt in a cave, he and his two d'.
36 Thus were both the d' of Lot with
24: 3 my son of the d' of the Canaanites,
13 and the d' of the men of the city
37 of the Canaanites, in whose land
27:46 my life because of the d' of Heth:
46 Jacob take a wife of the d' of Heth,
46 these which are of the d' of the land,
28: 1 not take a wife of the d' of Canaan.
2 d' of Laban thy mother's brother.
6 not take a wife of the d' of Canaan;
8 Esau seeing that the d' of Canaan
29:16 Laban had two d': the name of the
30:13 for the d' will call me blessed:
31:26 carried away my d', as captives
28 me to kiss my sons and my d'?
31 take by force thy d' from me.
41 thee fourteen years for thy two d',
43 These d' are my d', and these
43 can I do this day unto these my d',
50 If thou shalt afflict my d', or if thou
50 shalt take other wives beside my d',
55 and kissed his sons and his d',
34: 1 went out to see the d' of the land.
9 and give your d' unto us, and take

Ge 34: 9 and take our d' unto you.
16 Then we will give our d' unto you,
16 and we will take your d' unto us,
21 let us take their d' to us for wives,
21 and let us give them our d'.
36: 2 wives of the d' of Canaan; Adah
6 his wives, and his sons, and his d',
37:35 and his d' rose up to comfort
46: 7 his d', and his sons' d', and all
15 and his d' were thirty and three.
Ex 2:16 the priest of Midian had seven d':
20 And he said unto his d', And where
3:22 upon your sons, and upon your d';
6:25 took him one of the d' of Putiel to
10: 9 with our sons and with our d',
21: 4 she have born him sons or d';
9 with her after the manner of d'.
32: 2 wives, of your sons, and of your d',
34:16 take of their d' unto thy sons,
16 and their d' go a whoring after
Le 10:14 and thy sons, and thy d' with thee:
26:29 the flesh of your d' shall ye eat.
Nu 18:11 to thy sons and to thy d' with thee,
19 and thy sons and thy d' with thee,
21:29 and his d', into captivity unto Sihon
25: 1 whoredom with the d' of Moab.
26:33 Hepner had no sons, but d': and
33 names of the d' of Zelophehad were
27: 1 Then came the d' of Zelophehad,
1 these are the names of his d';
7 The d' of Zelophehad speak right:
36: 2 Zelophehad our brother unto his d'.
6 concerning the d' of Zelophehad,
10 so did the d' of Zelophehad:
11 the d' of Zelophehad, were married
De 12:12 ye, and your sons, and your d',
31 sons and their d' they have burnt
23:17 be no whore of the d' of Israel,
28:32 Thy sons and thy d' shall be given
41 Thou shalt beget sons and d', but
53 the flesh of thy sons and of thy d',
32:19 provoking of his sons, and of his d'.
Jos 7:24 of gold, and his sons, and his d',
17: 3 had no sons, but d': and these
3 and these are the names of his d',
6 Because the d' of Manasseh had an
J'g 3: 6 they took their d' to be their wives,
6 and gave their d' to their sons,
11:40 d' of Israel went yearly to lament
12: 9 he had thirty sons, and thirty d',
9 thirty d' from abroad for his sons.
14: 1, 2 of the d' of the Philistines:
3 among the d' of thy brethren, or
21: 7 give them of our d' to wives?
18 may not give them wives of our d':
21 the d' of Shiloh come out to dance
21 man his wife of the d' of Shiloh,
Ru 1: 6 she arose with her d' in law,
7 her two d' in law with her;
8 Naomi said unto her two d' in law,
11 my d': why will ye go with me?
12 Turn again, my d', go your way;
13 nay, my d'; for it grieveth me
1Sa 1: 4 to all her sons and her d', portions:
2:21 and bare three sons and two d'.
8:13 And he will take your d' to be
14:49 names of his two d' were these;
30: 3 their sons, and their d', were taken
6 man for his sons and for his d':
19 neither sons nor d', neither spoil,
2Sa 1:20 lest the d' of the Philistines rejoice,
20 d' of the uncircumcised triumph.
24 Ye d' of Israel, weep over Saul,
5:13 were yet sons and d' born to David.
13:18 with such robes were the king's d'
19: 5 the lives of thy sons and of thy d',
2Ki 17:17 their d' to pass through the fire,
1Ch 2:34 Sheshon had no sons, but d'.
4:27 Shimei had sixteen sons and six d';
7:15 and Zelophehad had d'.
14: 3 and David begat more sons and d'.
23:22 died, and had no sons, but d':
25: 5 Heman fourteen sons and three d'.
2Ch 2:14 son of a woman of the d' of Dan,
11:21 and eight sons, and threescore d'.)
13:21 twenty and two sons, and sixteen d'.
24: 3 wives; and he begat sons and d'.
28: 8 women, sons, and d', and took also
29: 9 our sons and our d' and our wives
31:18 their sons, and their d', through all
Ezr 2:61 of the d' of Barzillai the Gileadite,
9: 2 taken of their d' for themselves,
12 give not your d' unto their sons,
12 neither take their d' unto your sons,
Ne 3:12 part of Jerusalem, he and his d'.
4:14 your sons, and your d', your wives,
5: 2 our sons, and our d', are many:
5 our sons and our d' to be servants,
5 our d' are brought unto bondage
7:63 which took one of the d' of Barzillai,
10:28 their sons, and their d', every one
30 our d' unto the people of the land,
30 nor take their d' for our sons:
13:25 not give your d' unto their sons,
25 nor take their d' unto your sons,
Job 1: 2 unto him seven sons and three d'.
13 his sons and his d' were eating and
18 Thy sons and thy d' were eating
42:13 had also seven sons and three d'.
15 found so fair as the d' of Job:
Ps 45: 9 Kings' d' were among thy
48:11 let the d' of Judah be glad,
97: 8 the d' of Judah rejoiced because of
106:37 sacrificed their sons and their d'
38 blood of their sons and of their d',
144:12 that our d' may be as corner stones,

Pr 30:15 horseleach hath two d', crying,
31:29 Many d' have done virtuously, but
Ec 12: 4 d' of musick shall be brought low;
Ca 1: 5 O ye d' of Jerusalem, as the tents
2: 2 so is my love among the d'.
7 I charge you, O ye d' of Jerusalem,
3: 5 I charge you, O ye d' of Jerusalem,
10 with love, for the d' of Jerusalem.
11 Go forth, O ye d' of Zion, and
5: 8 I charge you, O d' of Jerusalem,
16 is my friend, O d' of Jerusalem.
6: 9 The d' saw her, and blessed her;
8: 4 I charge you, O d' of Jerusalem,
Isa 3:16 Because the d' of Zion are haughty,
17 crown of the head of the d' of Zion,
4: 4 away the filth of the d' of Zion,
16: 2 the d' of Moab shall be at the fords
32: 9 hear my voice, ye careless d';
43: 6 and my d' from the ends of the earth;
49:22 thy d' shall be carried upon their
56: 5 name better than of sons and of d':
60: 4 thy d' shall be nursed at thy side.
Jer 3:24 their herds, their sons and their d'.
5:17 which thy sons and thy d' should eat:
7:31 their sons and their d' in the fire;
9:20 teach your d' wailing, and every
11:22 and their d' shall die by famine:
14:16 wives, nor their sons, nor their d':
16: 2 neither shalt thou have sons or d'
3 concerning the d' that are born in
19: 9 flesh of their d', and they shall eat
29: 6 beget sons and d'; and take wives
6 and give your d' to husbands,
6 that they may bear sons and d';
32:35 their d' to pass through the fire
35: 8 our wives, our sons, nor our d';
41:10 the king's d', and all the people
43: 6 and the king's d', and every person
48:46 taken captives, and thy d' captives.
49: 2 her d' shall be burned with fire:
3 cry, ye d' of Rabbah, gird you with
La 3:51 because of all the d' of my city.
Eze 13:17 against the d' of thy people, which
14:16 deliver neither sons nor d'; they
18 deliver neither sons nor d', but they
22 both sons and d': behold, they shall
16:20 thou hast taken thy sons and thy d',
27 the d' of the Philistines, which are
46 Samaria, she and her d' that dwell
46 thy right hand, is Sodom and her d'.
48 hast not done, she nor her d', as
48 thou hast done, thou and thy d'.
49 idleness was in her and in her d',
53 the captivity of Sodom and her d',
53 the captivity of Samaria and her d',
55 When thy sisters, Sodom and her d',
55 Samaria and her d', shall return
55 then thou and thy d' shall return
57 of thy reproach of the d' of Syria,
57 about her, the d' of the Philistines,
61 I will give them unto thee for d',
23: 2 two women, the d' of one mother:
4 mine, and they bare sons and d'.
10 they took her sons and her d', and
25 they shall take thy sons and thy d';
47 shall slay their sons and their d',
24:21 your sons and your d' whom ye
25 their minds, their sons and their d',
26: 6 And her d' which are in the field
8 He shall slay with the sword thy d'
30:18 and her d' shall go into captivity.
32:16 the d' of the nations shall lament
18 and the d' of the famous nations,
Hos 4:13 your d' shall commit whoredom,
14 I will not punish your d' when they
Joe 2:28 sons and your d' shall prophesy,
3: 8 I will sell your sons and d' into the
Am 7:17 and thy d' shall fall by the sword,
Lu 1: 5 his wife was of the d' of Aaron,
23:28 D' of Jerusalem, weep not for me,
Ac 2:17 sons and your d' shall prophesy,
21: 9 four d', virgins, which did prophesy
2Co 6:18 ye shall be my sons and d', saith
1Pe 3: 6 whose d' ye are, as long as ye do

David^ (*da'-vid*) See also DAVID'S.
Ru 4:17 father of Jesse, the father of D'.
22 begat Jesse, and Jesse begat D'.
1Sa 16:13 the Spirit of the Lord came upon D'
19 Send me D' thy son, which is with
20 sent them by D' his son unto Saul.
21 D' came to Saul, and stood before
22 Let D', I pray thee, stand before
23 D' took a harp, and played with his
17:12 Now D' was the son of that
14 D' was the youngest: and the three
15 D' went and returned from Saul
17 Jesse said unto D' his son, Take
20 D' rose up early in the morning,
22 D' left his carriage in the hand of
23 same words: and D' heard them.
26 D' spake to the men that stood by
28 anger was kindled against D',
29 D' said, What have I now done?
31 words were heard which D' spake,
32 D' said to Saul, Let no man's heart
33 Saul said to D', Thou art not able
34 D' said unto Saul, Thy servant
37 D' said moreover, The Lord that
37 Saul said unto D', Go, and the
38 Saul armed D' with his armour,
39 D' girded his sword upon his
39 D' said unto Saul, I cannot go
39 And D' put them off him.
41 came on and drew near unto D';
42 looked about, and saw D',
43 the Philistine said unto D', Am I a

1Sa 17:43 Philistine cursed D' by his gods.
44 the Philistine said to D', Come to
45 Then said D' to the Philistine,
48 and came and drew nigh to meet D',
48 that D' hasted and ran toward the
49 D' put his hand in his bag, and
50 So D' prevailed over the Philistine
50 was no sword in the hand of D'.
51 Therefore D' ran, and stood upon
54 D' took the head of the Philistine,
55 when Saul saw D' go forth against
57 as D' returned from the slaughter
58 D' answered, I am the son of thy
18: 1 was knit with the soul of D', and
3 Jonathan and D' made a covenant,
4 and gave it to D', and his garments,
5 D' went out whithersoever Saul
6 when D' was returned from the
7 slain his thousands, and D' his ten
8 They have ascribed unto D' ten
9 Saul eyed D' from that day and
10 and D' played with his hand, as at
11 I will smite D' even to the wall
11 And D' avoided out of his presence
12 Saul was afraid of D', because the
14 D' behaved himself wisely in all
16 But all Israel and Judah loved D',
17 Saul said to D', Behold my elder
18 D' said unto Saul, Who am I? and
19 should have been given to D', that
20 Michal Saul's daughter loved D':
21 Wherefore Saul said to D', Thou
22 Commune with D' secretly, and say,
23 spake these words in the ears of D'.
23 And D' said, Seemeth it to you a
24 On this manner spake D'.
25 Thus shall ye say to D', The king
25 Saul thought to make D' fall by the
26 when his servants told D' these
26 it pleased D' well to be the king's
27 Wherefore D' arose and went, he
27 D' brought their foreskins, and
28 knew that the Lord was with D',
29 Saul was yet the more afraid of D';
30 D' behaved himself more wisely
19: 1 servants, that they should kill D'.
2 Saul's son delighted much in D':
2 Jonathan told D', saying, Saul my
4 Jonathan spake good of D' unto
4 sin against his servant, against D';
5 against innocent blood, to slay D'
7 Jonathan called D', and Jonathan
7 Jonathan brought D' to Saul, and
8 and D' went out, and fought with
9 hand: and D' played with his hand.
10 Saul sought to smite D' even to the
10 and D' fled, and escaped that night.
12 So Michal let D' down through a
14 Saul sent messengers to take D',
15 the messengers again to see D',
18 So D' fled, and escaped, and came
19 Behold, D' is at Naioth in Ramah.
20 Saul sent messengers to take D':
22 said, Where are Samuel and D'?
20: 1 D' fled from Naioth in Ramah, and
3 D' sware moreover, and said, Thy
4 Then said Jonathan unto D',
5 D' said unto Jonathan, Behold,
6 D' earnestly asked leave of me that
10 Then said D' to Jonathan, Who
11 Jonathan said unto D', Come, and
12 Jonathan said unto D', O Lord God
12 if there be good toward D', and I
15 Lord hath cut off the enemies of D'
16 a covenant with the house of D',
17 Jonathan caused D' to swear again,
18 Jonathan said to D', To morrow
24 So D' hid himself in the field: and
28 And Jonathan answered Saul, D'
33 determined of his father to slay D'.
34 for he was grieved for D', because
35 at the time appointed with D', and
39 only Jonathan and D' knew the
41 D' arose out of a place toward the
41 with another, until D' exceeded.
42 Jonathan said to D', Go in peace,
21: 1 Then came D' to Nob to Ahimelech
1 was afraid at the meeting of D',
2 D' said unto Ahimelech the priest,
4 the priest answered D', and said,
5 D' answered the priest, and said
8 D' said unto Ahimelech, And is
9 D' said, There is none like that;
10 D' arose, and fled that day for fear
11 Is not this D' the king of the land?
11 slain his thousands, and D' his ten
12 D' laid up these words in his heart,
22: 1 D' therefore departed thence, and
3 D' went thence to Mizpeh of Moab:
4 the while that D' was in the hold.
5 the prophet Gad said unto D',
5 Then D' departed, and came into
6 Saul heard that D' was discovered,
14 among all thy servants as D',
17 because their hand also is with D',
20 Abiathar, escaped, and fled after D'.
21 Abiathar shewed D' that Saul had
22 D' said unto Abiathar, I knew it
23: 1 Then they told D', saying, Behold,
2 Therefore D' enquired of the Lord,
2 the Lord said unto D', Go, and
4 D' enquired of the Lord yet again.
5 So D' and his men went to Keilah,
5 D' saved the inhabitants of Keilah.
6 the son of Ahimelech fled to D'
7 it was told Saul that D' was come

1Sa 23: 8 to Keilah, to besiege D· and his
9 D· knew that Saul secretly practised
10 Then said D·, O Lord God of Israel,
12 Then said D·, Will the men of
13 Then D· and his men, which were
13 was told Saul that D· was escaped
14 D· abode in the wilderness in
15 D· saw that Saul was come out to
15 D· was in the wilderness of Ziph
16 arose, and went to D· into the wood,
18 and D· abode in the wood, and
19 Doth not D· hide himself with us
24 but D· and his men were in the
25 they told D·: wherefore he came
25 pursued after D· in the wilderness
26 and D· and his men on that side of
26 and D· made haste to get away
26 Saul and his men compassed D·
28 returned from pursuing after D·,
29 D· went up from thence, and dwelt
24: 1 D· is in the wilderness of En-gedi.
2 and went to seek D· and his men
3 D· and his men remained in the
4 the men of D· said unto him,
4 D· arose, and cut off the skirt of
7 So D· stayed his servants with
8 D· also arose afterward, and went
8 D· stooped with his face to the
9 D· said to Saul, Wherefore hearest
9 saying, Behold, D· seeketh thy
16 when D· had made an end of
16 said, Is this thy voice, my son D·?
17 he said to D·, Thou art more
22 And D· sware unto Saul. And Saul
22 but D· and his men gat them up
25: 1 D· arose, and went down to the
4 D· heard in the wilderness that
5 And D· sent out ten young men,
5 and D· said unto the ten young
8 unto thy servants, and to thy son D·.
9 words in the name of D·, and ceased.
10 Who is D·? and who is the son of
13 D· said unto his men, Gird ye on
13 and D· also girded on his sword:
13 went up after D· about four hundred
14 D· sent messengers out of the
20 D· and his men came down against
21 D· had said, Surely in vain have I
22 also do God unto the enemies of D·,
23 when Abigail saw D·, she hasted,
23 lighted off the ass, and fell before D·
32 D· said to Abigail, Blessed be the
35 So D· received of her hand that
39 when D· heard that Nabal was dead,
39 And D· sent and communed with
40 when the servants of D· were come
40 D· sent us unto thee, to take thee
42 went after the messengers of D·,
43 D· also took Ahinoam of Jezreel;
26: 1 Doth not D· hide himself in the
2 to seek D· in the wilderness of Ziph.
3 But D· abode in the wilderness, and
4 D· therefore sent out spies, and
5 D· arose, and came to the place
5 D· beheld the place where Saul lay,
6 Then answered D· and said to
7 D· and Abishai came to the people
8 Then said Abishai to D·, God hath
9 D· said to Abishai, Destroy him not:
10 D· said furthermore, As the Lord
12 So D· took the spear and the cruse
13 Then D· went over to the other side,
14 D· cried to the people, and to Abner
15 D· said to Abner, Art not thou a
17 Is this thy voice, my son D·?
17 And D· said, It is my voice, my lord,
21 I have sinned: return, my son D·;
22 D· answered and said, Behold the
25 Then Saul said to D·,
25 Blessed be thou, my son D·:
25 So D· went on his way, and Saul
27: 1 D· said in his heart, I shall now
2 D· arose, and he passed over with
3 D· dwelt with Achish at Gath,
3 even D· with his two wives,
4 it was told Saul that D· was fled to
5 D· said unto Achish, If I have now
7 And the time that D· dwelt in the
8 D· and his men went up, and
9 D· smote the land, and left neither
10 D· said, Against the south of Judah,
11 D· saved neither man nor woman
11 So did D·, and so will be his
12 Achish believed D·, saying, He hath
28: 1 Achish said unto D·, Know thou
2 D· said to Achish, Surely thou
2 Achish said to D·, Therefore will I
17 given it to thy neighbor, even to D·:
29: 2 D· and his men passed on in the
3 Is not this D·, the servant of Saul
5 Is not this D·, of whom they sang
5 slew his thousands, and D· his ten
6 Then Achish called D·, and said
8 D· said unto Achish, But what
9 Achish answered and said to D·, I
11 So D· and his men rose up early
30: 1 when D· and his men were come to
3 So D· and his men came to the
4 Then D· and the people that were
6 D· was greatly distressed; for the
6 D· encouraged himself in the Lord
7 D· said to Abiathar the priest,
7 brought thither the ephod to D·.
8 D· enquired at the Lord, saying,
9 So D· went, he and the six hundred
10 D· pursued, he and four hundred

1Sa 30:11 and brought him to D·, and gave
13 And D· said unto him, To whom
15 D· said to him, Canst thou bring
17 D· smote them from the twilight
18 D· recovered all that the
18 and D· rescued his two wives.
19 taken to them: D· recovered all.
20 D· took all the flocks and the herds
21 D· came to the two hundred men,
21 faint that they could not follow D·,
21 and they went forth to meet D·,
21 when D· came near to the people,
22 Belial, of those that went with D·,
23 Then said D·, Ye shall not do so,
26 when D· came to Ziklag, he sent of
31 where D· himself and his men were
2Sa 1: 1 D· was returned from the slaughter
1 D· had abode two days in Ziklag;
2 And so it was, when he came to D·,
3 D· said unto him, From whence
4 D· said unto him, How went the
5 D· said unto the young man that
11 Then D· took hold on his clothes,
13 D· said unto the young man that
14 D· said unto him, How wast thou
15 D· called one of the young men,
16 D· said unto him, Thy blood be
17 D· lamented with this lamentation
2: 1 D· enquired of the Lord, saying,
1 D· said, Whither shall I go up?
2 D· went up thither, and his two
3 were with him did D· bring up,
4 And there they anointed D· king
4 they told D·, saying, That the men
5 D· sent messengers unto the men
10 the house of Judah followed D·.
11 time that D· was king in Hebron
13 of Zeruiah, and the servants of D·,
15 and twelve of the servants of D·,
17 Israel, before the servants of D·.
31 the servants of D· had smitten of
3: 1 house of Saul and the house of D·:
1 D· waxed stronger and stronger,
2 unto D· were sons born in Hebron:
5 These were born to D· in Hebron.
6 house of Saul and the house of D·,
8 delivered thee into the hand of D·,
9 as the Lord hath sworn to D·, even
10 set up the throne of D· over Israel
12 sent messengers to D· on his behalf.
14 D· sent messengers to Ish-bosheth
17 Ye sought for D· in times past to
18 for the Lord hath spoken of D·,
18 By the hand of my servant D· I will
19 went also to speak in the ears of D·
20 So Abner came to D· to Hebron,
20 D· made Abner and the men that
21 Abner said unto D·, I will arise and
21 D· sent Abner away; and he went
22 the servants of D· and Joab came
22 Abner was not with D· in Hebron;
26 when Joab was come out from D·,
26 well of Sirah: but D· knew it not.
28 afterward when D· heard it, he said,
31 And D· said to Joab, and to all the
31 king D· himself followed the bier.
35 people came to cause D· to eat
35 while it was yet day, D· sware,
4: 8 the head of Ish-bosheth unto D·
9 And D· answered Rechab and
12 D· commanded his young men, and
5: 1 came all the tribes of Israel to D·
3 king D· made a league with them
3 they anointed D· king over Israel.
4 D· was thirty years old when he
6 spake unto D·, saying, Except thou
6 thinking, D· cannot come in hither.
7 D· took the strong hold of Zion:
7 the same is the city of D·.
8 D· said on that day, Whosoever
9 So D· dwelt in the fort,
9 and called it the city of D·.
9 D· built round about from Millo
10 D· went on, and grew great,
11 king of Tyre sent messengers to D·,
11 and they built D· an house.
12 D· perceived that the Lord had
13 D· took him more concubines and
13 yet sons and daughters born to D·.
17 had anointed D· king over Israel,
17 Philistines came up to seek D·;
17 and D· heard of it, and went
19 D· enquired of the Lord, saying,
19 the Lord said unto D·, Go up:
20 And D· came to Baal-perazim,
20 and D· smote them there,
21 and D· and his men burned them.
23 when D· enquired of the Lord, he
25 And D· did so, as the Lord had
6: 1 D· gathered together all the chosen
2 D· arose, and went with all the
5 And D· and all the house of Israel
8 D· was displeased, because the
9 D· was afraid of the Lord that day,
10 D· would not remove the ark of the
10 Lord unto him in the city of D·:
10 but D· carried it aside into the
12 was told king D·, saying, The Lord
12 So D· went and brought up the ark
12 into the city of D· with gladness.
14 D· danced before the Lord with all
14 and D· was girded with a linen
15 So D· and all the house of Israel
16 the Lord came into the city of D·,
16 saw king D· leaping and dancing
17 tabernacle that D· had pitched for

2Sa 6:17 and D· offered burnt offerings
18 as D· had made an end of offering
20 D· returned to bless his household.
20 daughter of Saul came to meet D·,
21 D· said unto Michal, It was before
7: 5 Go and tell my servant D·, Thus
8 shalt thou say unto my servant D·,
17 so did Nathan speak unto D·.
18 Then went king D· in, and sat
20 what can D· say more unto thee?
26 of thy servant D· be established
8: 1 D· smote the Philistines, and
1 D· took Metheg-ammah out of the
3 D· smote also Hadadezer, the son
4 D· took from him a thousand
4 D· houghed all the chariot horses,
5 D· slew of the Syrians two and
6 D· put garrisons in Syria of
6 the Syrians became servants to D·,
6 preserved D· whithersoever he
7 D· took the shields of gold that
8 king D· took exceeding much brass.
9 Toi king of Hamath heard that D·
10 sent Joram his son unto king D·,
11 Which also king D· did dedicate
13 D· gat him a name when he
14 And the Lord preserved D·
15 And D· reigned over all Israel;
15 D· executed judgment and justice
9: 1 D· said, Is there yet any that is left
2 when they had called him unto D·,
5 Then king D· sent, and fetched
6 come unto D·, he fell on his face,
6 And D· said, Mephibosheth.
7 D· said unto him, Fear not: for I
10: 2 Then said D·, I will shew kindness
2 D· sent to comfort him by the hand
3 that D· doth honour thy father,
3 hath not D· rather sent his servants
5 When they told it unto D·, he sent
6 saw that they stank before D·,
7 when D· heard of it, he sent Joab,
17 was told D·, he gathered all Israel
17 set themselves in array against D·,
18 D· slew the men of seven hundred
11: 1 D· sent Joab, and all his servants
1 But D· tarried still at Jerusalem.
2 that D· arose from off his bed, and
3 D· sent and enquired after the
4 D· sent messengers, and took her;
5 conceived, and sent and told D·,
6 D· sent to Joab, saying, Send me
6 And Joab sent Uriah to D·.
7 D· demanded of him how Joab did,
8 D· said to Uriah, Go down to thy
10 had told D·, saying, Uriah went
10 D· said unto Uriah, camest thou
11 Uriah said unto D·, The ark, and
12 And D· said to Uriah, Tarry here
13 when D· had called him, he did eat
14 D· wrote a letter to Joab, and sent
17 of the people of the servants of D·;
18 Joab sent and told D· all the things
22 come and shewed D· all that Joab
23 messenger said unto D·, Surely the
25 Then D· said unto the messenger,
27 the mourning was passed, D· sent
27 thing that D· had done displeased
12: 1 the Lord sent Nathan unto D·.
7 Nathan said to D·, Thou art the
13 D· said unto Nathan, I have sinned
13 Nathan said unto D·, The Lord
15 that Uriah's wife bare unto D·,
16 D· therefore besought God for the
16 and D· fasted, and went in,
18 servants of D· feared to tell him
19 D· saw that his servants whispered,
19 D· perceived that the child was
19 D· said unto his servants, Is the
20 Then D· arose from the earth, and
24 D· comforted Bath-sheba his wife,
27 Joab sent messengers to D·, and
29 D· gathered all the people together,
31 So D· and all the people returned
13: 1 Absalom the son of D· had a fair
1 Amnon the son of D· loved her.
7 Then D· sent home to Tamar,
21 king D· heard of all these things,
30 came to D·, saying, Absalom hath
37 D· mourned for his son every day.
39 the soul of king D· longed to go
15:13 came a messenger to D·, saying,
14 D· said unto all his servants that
22 D· said to Ittai, Go and pass over.
30 D· went up by the ascent of mount
31 told D·, saying, Ahithophel is among
31 D· said, O Lord, I pray thee, turn
32 when D· was come up to the top of
33 Unto whom D· said, If thou passest
16: 1 when D· was a little past the top of
5 when king D· came to Bahurim,
6 And he cast stones at D·, and
6 at all the servants of king D·:
10 Lord hath said unto him, Curse D·.
11 D· said to Abishai, and to all his
13 as D· and his men went by the way,
23 of Ahithophel both with D· and
17: 1 I will arise and pursue after D·
16 and tell D·, saying, Lodge not this
17 and they went and told king D·.
21 and told king D·, and said unto
21 said unto D·, Arise, and pass quickly
22 Then D· arose, and all the people
24 D· came to Mahanaim. And Absalom
27 when D· was come to Mahanaim,
29 sheep, and cheese of kine, for D·,

2Sa 18: 1 D· numbered the people that were
2 D· sent forth a third part of the
7 slain before the servants of D·,
9 Absalom met the servants of D·.
24 D· sat between the two gates: and
19:11 D· sent to Zadok and to Abiathar
16 the men of Judah to meet king D·.
22 D· said, What have I to do with
43 have also more right in D· than ye:
20: 1 We have no part in D·, neither
2 man of Israel went up from after D·,
3 D· came to his house at Jerusalem;
6 D· said to Abishai, Now shall Sheba
11 favoureth Joab, and he that is for D·,
21 against the king, even against D·:
26 Jairite was a chief ruler about D·.
21: 1 was a famine in the days of D·,
1 and D· enquired of the Lord. And
3 D· said unto the Gibeonites, What
7 D· and Jonathan the son of Saul.
11 it was told D· what Rizpah the
12 D· went and took the bones of Saul
15 D· went down, and his servants
15 Philistines: and D· waxed faint,
16 new sword, thought to have slain D·.
17 the men of D· sware unto him,
21 the brother of D· slew him.
22 and fell by the hand of D·, and by
22: 1 D· spake unto the Lord the words
51 mercy to his anointed, unto D·,
23: 1 these be the last words of D·.
1 D· the son of Jesse said, and the
8 of the mighty men whom D· had:
9 of the three mighty men with D·,
13 came to D· in the harvest time
14 D· was then in an hold, and the
15 D· longed, and said, Oh that one
16 and took it, and brought it to D·:
23 And D· set him over his guard.
24: 1 he moved D· against them to say,
10 D· said unto the Lord, I have
11 when D· was up in the morning,
12 Go and say unto D·, Thus saith the
13 So Gad came to D·, and told him,
14 D· said unto Gad, I am in a great
17 D· spake unto the Lord when he
18 Gad came that day to D·, and said
19 D·, according to the saying of Gad,
21 D· said, To buy the threshingfloor
22 Araunah said unto D·, Let my lord
24 So D· bought the threshingfloor
25 D· built there an altar unto the
1Ki 1: 1 Now king D· was old and stricken
8 mighty men which belonged to D·,
11 and D· our lord knoweth it not?
13 Go and get thee in unto king D·,
28 Then king D· answered and said,
31 Let my lord king D· live for ever.
32 D· said, Call me Zadok the priest,
37 than the throne of my lord king D·.
43 king D· hath made Solomon king.
47 came to bless our lord king D·,
2: 1 of D· drew nigh that he should die;
10 So D· slept with his fathers,
10 and was buried in the city of D·.
11 the days that D· reigned over Israel
12 sat Solomon upon the throne of D·
24 and set me on the throne of D·
26 the ark of the Lord God before D·
32 my father D· not knowing thereof,
33 but upon D·, and upon his seed,
44 that thou didst to D· my father:
45 throne of D· shall be established
3: 1 and brought her into the city of D·,
3 in the statutes of D· his father:
6 hast shewed unto thy servant D·
7 made thy servant king instead of D·
14 as thy father D· did walk, then I
5: 1 for Hiram was ever a lover of D·.
3 Thou knowest how that D· my
5 the Lord spake unto D· my father,
7 hath given unto D· a wise son
6:12 which I spake unto D· thy father:
7:51 which D· his father had dedicated;
8: 1 out of the city of D·, which is Zion.
15 which spake with his mouth unto D·
16 but I chose D· to be over my people
17 it was in the heart of D· my father
18 the Lord said unto D· my father,
20 I am risen up in the room of D·
24 Who hast kept with thy servant D·
25 keep with thy servant D· my father
26 thou spakest unto thy servant D·
66 that the Lord had done for D· his
9: 4 D· thy father walked, in integrity
5 I promised to D· thy father, saying,
24 came up out of the city of D· unto
11: 4 as was the heart of D· his father.
6 not fully after the Lord, as did D·
12 not do it for D· thy father's sake:
13 to thy son for D· my servant's sake,
15 to pass, when D· was in Edom,
21 Hadad heard in Egypt that D· slept
24 when D· slew them of Zobah:
27 the breaches of the city of D·
33 my judgments, as did D· his father
34 D· my servant's sake, whom I chose.
36 D· my servant may have a light
38 commandments, as D· my servant
38 thee a sure house, as I built for D·,
39 I will for this afflict the seed of D·,
43 buried in the city of D· his father:
12:16 What portion have we in D·?
16 now see to thine own house, D·.
19 rebelled against the house of D·
20 none that followed the house of D·,

1Ki 12:26 kingdom return to the house of D·:
13: 2 shall be born unto the house of D·,
14: 8 kingdom away from the house of D·,
8 hast not been as my servant D·,
31 with his fathers in the city of D·.
15: 3 Lord his God, as the heart of D·
5 D· did that which was right in the
8 they buried him in the city of D·
11 in the eyes of the Lord, as did D·
24 of D· his father: and Jehoshaphat
22:50 fathers in the city of D· his father:
2Ki 8:19 Judah for D· his servant's sake,
24 with his fathers in the city of D·:
9:28 with his fathers in the city of D·.
12:21 with his fathers in the city of D·:
14: 3 yet not like D· his father: he did
20 with his fathers in the city of D·.
15: 7 with his fathers in the city of D·:
38 fathers in the city of D· his father
16: 2 Lord his God, like D· his father.
20 with his fathers in the city of D·:
17:21 rent Israel from the house of D·;
18: 3 according to all that D· his father
20: 5 Thus saith the Lord, the God of D·
21: 7 house, of which the Lord said to D·,
22: 2 and walked in all the way of D·
1Ch 2:15 Ozem the sixth, D· the seventh
3: 1 these were the sons of D·, which
9 These were all the sons of D·,
4:31 their cities unto the reign of D·.
6:31 D· set over the service of song
7: 2 whose number was in the days of D·
9:22 D· and Samuel the seer did ordain
10:14 and turned the kingdom unto D·
11: 1 Israel gathered themselves to D·
3 and D· made a covenant with them
3 they anointed D· king over Israel,
4 D· and all Israel went to Jerusalem,
5 the inhabitants of Jebus said to D·,
5 Nevertheless D· took the castle
5 of Zion, which is the city of D·.
6 D· said, Whosoever smiteth the
7 D· dwelt in the castle; therefore
7 they called it the city of D·.
9 So D· waxed greater and greater:
10 chief of the mighty men whom D·
11 number of the mighty men whom D·
13 He was with D· at Pas-dammim,
15 went down to the rock to D·,
16 D· was then in the hold, and the
17 D· longed, and said, Oh that one
18 and took it, and brought it to D·:
18 but D· would not drink of it,
25 and D· set him over his guard.
12: 1 they that came to D· to Ziklag,
8 there separated themselves unto D·
16 and Judah to the hold unto D·.
17 D· went out to meet them, and
18 Thine are we, D·, and on thy side,
18 D· received them, and made them
19 there fell some of Manasseh to D·,
21 D· against the band of the rovers:
22 day there came to D· to help him,
23 came to D· to Hebron, to turn the
31 name, to come and make D· king.
38 to make D· king over all Israel:
38 were of one heart to make D· king.
39 there they were with D· three days,
13: 1 D· consulted with the captains of
2 D· said unto all the congregation
5 So D· gathered all Israel together,
6 D· went up, and all Israel, to
8 D· and all Israel played before God
11 D· was displeased, because the
12 D· was afraid of God that day,
13 So D· brought not the ark home
13 to himself to the city of D·,
14: 1 king of Tyre sent messengers to D·,
2 D· perceived that the Lord had
3 D· took more wives at Jerusalem:
3 D· begat more sons and daughters.
8 when the Philistines heard that D·
8 the Philistines went up to seek D·.
8 And D· heard of it, and went out
10 D· enquired of God, saying, Shall I
11 and D· smote them there. Then
11 D· said, God hath broken in upon
12 D· gave a commandment, and they
14 Therefore D· enquired again of God;
16 D· therefore did as God commanded
17 fame of D· went out into all lands;
15: 1 D· made him houses in the city
1 houses in the city of D·,
2 Then D· said, None ought to carry
3 D· gathered all Israel together to
4 D· assembled the children of Aaron,
11 D· called for Zadok and Abiathar
16 D· spake to the chief of the Levites
25 So D·, and the elders of Israel, and
27 D· was clothed with a robe of fine
27 D· also had upon him an ephod of
29 came to the city of D·, that Michal
29 at a window saw king D· dancing
16: 1 the tent that D· had pitched for it:
2 D· had made an end of offering
7 day D· delivered first this psalm
43 D· returned to bless his house.
17: 1 to pass, as D· sat in his house,
1 that D· said to Nathan the prophet,
2 Nathan said unto D·, Do all that is
4 Go and tell D· my servant, Thus
7 shalt thou say unto my servant D·,
15 so did Nathan speak unto D·.
16 D· the king came and sat before
18 What can D· speak more to thee
24 let the house of D· thy servant be

1Ch 18: 1 pass, that D· smote the Philistines,
3 D· smote Hadarezer king of Zobah
4 D· took from him a thousand
4 D· also houghed all the chariot
5 D· slew of the Syrians two and
6 D· put garrisons in
6 Thus the Lord preserved D·
7 D· took the shields of gold that
8 brought D· very much brass,
9 Tou king of Hamath heard how D·
10 sent Hadoram his son to king D·,
11 king D· dedicated unto the Lord,
13 Thus the Lord preserved D·
14 So D· reigned over all Israel, and
17 of D· were chief about the king.
19: 2 D· said, I will shew kindness unto
2 D· sent messengers to comfort
2 servants of D· came into the land
3 Thinkest thou that D· doth honour
5 told D· how the men were served.
6 had made themselves odious to D·,
8 when D· heard of it, he sent Joab,
17 And it was told D·; and he gathered
17 D· had put the battle in array
18 D· slew of the Syrians seven
19 they made peace with D·, and
20: 1 But D· tarried at Jerusalem. And
2 D· took the crown of their king
3 Even so dealt D· with all the cities
3 D· and all the people returned to
8 and they fell by the hand of D·, and
21: 1 and provoked D· to number Israel.
2 D· said to Joab, and to the rulers of
5 of the number of people unto D·.
8 D· said unto God, I have sinned
10 Go and tell D·, saying, Thus saith
11 Gad came to D·, and said unto him,
13 D· said unto Gad, I am in a great
16 D· lifted up his eyes, and saw the
16 Then D· and the elders of Israel,
17 D· said unto God, Is it not I that
18 Lord commanded Gad to say to D·,
18 that D· should go up, and set up
19 D· went up at the saying of Gad,
21 as D· came to Ornan, Ornan looked
21 and saw D·, and went out of the
21 bowed himself to D· with his face
22 Then D· said to Ornan, Grant me
23 Ornan said unto D·, Take it to thee,
24 king D· said to Ornan, Nay; but I
25 So D· gave to Ornan for the place
26 D· built there an altar unto the
28 time when D· saw that the Lord
30 D· could not go before it to enquire
22: 1 Then D· said, This is the house of
2 D· commanded to gather together
3 D· prepared iron in abundance for
4 brought much cedar wood to D·
5 D· said, Solomon my son is young
5 So D· prepared abundantly before
7 D· said to Solomon, My son, as for
17 D· also commanded all the princes
23: 1 when D· was old and full of days,
6 D· divided them into courses
25 For D· said, The Lord God of Israel
27 last words of D· the Levites were
24: 3 D· distributed them, both Zadok of
31 sons of Aaron in the presence of D·
25: 1 Moreover D· and the captains of
26:26 D· the king, and the chief fathers,
31 the fortieth year of the reign of D·
32 D· made rulers over the Reubenites,
27:18 Elihu, one of the brethren of D·:
23 D· took not the number of them
24 of the chronicles of king D·.
28: 1 D· assembled all the princes of
2 D· the king stood up upon his feet,
11 Then D· gave to Solomon his son
19 All this, said D·, the Lord made me
20 D· said to Solomon his son, Be
29: 1 Furthermore D· the king said unto
9 D· the king also rejoiced with great
10 D· blessed the Lord before all the
10 D· said, Blessed be thou, Lord God
20 D· said to all the congregation,
22 the son of D· king the second time,
23 as king instead of D· his father, and
24 all the sons likewise of king D·,
26 Thus D· the son of Jesse reigned
29 acts of D· the king, first and last,
2Ch 1: 1 And Solomon the son of D· was
4 ark of God had D· brought up from
4 the place which D· had prepared
8 hast shewed great mercy unto D·
9 let thy promise unto D· my father
2: 3 thou didst deal with D· my father,
7 whom D· my father did provide.
12 hath given to D· the king a wise son,
14 with the cunning men of my lord D·
17 D· his father had numbered them;
3: 1 Lord appeared unto D· his father,
1 the place that D· had prepared
5: 1 brought in all the things that D· his
2 out of the city of D·, which is Zion.
6: 4 with his mouth to my father D·,
6 and have chosen D· to be over my
7 it was in the heart of D· my father
8 But the Lord said to D· my father,
10 I am risen up in the room of D·
15 which hast kept with thy servant D·
16 keep with thy servant D· my father
17 hast spoken unto thy servant D·.
42 remember the mercies of D· thy
7: 6 which D· the king had made to
6 when D· praised by their ministry;
10 that the Lord had shewed unto D·,

2Ch 7:17 as D' thy father walked, and do
18 as I have covenanted with D' thy
8:11 out of the city of D' unto the house
11 shall not dwell in the house of D'
14 according to the order of D' his
14 had D' the man of God commanded
9:31 he was buried in the city of D' his
10:16 What portion have we in D'? and
16 now, D', see to thine own house.
19 rebelled against the house of D'
11:17 years they walked in the way of D'
18 daughter of Jerimoth the son of D'
12:16 and was buried in the city of D':
13: 5 kingdom over Israel to D' forever,
6 servant of Solomon the son of D',
8 in the hand of the sons of D';
14: 1 they buried him in the city of D':
16:14 made for himself in the city of D',
17: 3 in the first ways of his father D',
21: 1 with his fathers in the city of D'.
7 would not destroy the house of D',
7 covenant that he had made with D',
12 saith the Lord God of D' thy father,
20 they buried him in the city of D',
23: 3 Lord hath said of the sons of D'.
18 whom D' had distributed in the
18 singing, as it was ordained by D'.
24:16 in the city of D' among the kings,
25 in the city of D', but they buried
27: 9 they buried him in the city of D':
28: 1 of the Lord, like D' his father:
29: 2 according to all that D' his father
25 to the commandment of D', and of
26 stood with the instruments of D',
27 the instruments ordained by D'
30 with the words of D', and of Asaph
30:26 the time of Solomon the son of D'
32: 5 repaired Millo in the city of D',
30 to the west side of the city of D'.
33 of the sepulchres of the sons of D':
33: 7 God had said to D' and to Solomon
14 built a wall without the city of D',
34: 2 walked in the ways of D' his father,
3 began to seek after the God of D'
35: 3 house which Solomon the son of D'
4 according to the writing of D'
15 to the commandment of D', and of
Ezr 3:10 after the ordinance of D' king of
8: 2 of the sons of D'; Hattush.
20 of the Nethinims, whom D' and
Ne 3:15 that go down from the city of D'.
16 over against the sepulchres of D',
12:24 to the commandment of D' the man
36 with the musical instruments of D'
37 up by the stairs of the city of D',
37 above the house of D', even unto
45 to the commandment of D', and of
46 For in the days of D' and Asaph of
Ps 3:*title* A Psalm of D', when he fled from
4:*title* on Neginoth, A Psalm of D'.
5:*title* upon Nehiloth, A Psalm of D'.
6:*title* upon Sheminith, A Psalm of D'.
7:*title* Shiggaion of D', which he sang
8:*title* upon Gittith, A Psalm of D'.
9:*title* upon Muth-labben, A Psalm of D'.
11:*title* chief Musician, A Psalm of D'.
12:*title* upon Sheminith, A Psalm of D'.
13:*title* chief Musician, A Psalm of D'.
14:*title* chief Musician, A Psalm of D'.
15:*title* A Psalm of D'.
16:*title* Michtam of D'.
17:*title* A Prayer of D'.
18:*title* A Psalm of D', the servant of the
50 to D', and to his seed for evermore.
19:*title* chief Musician, A Psalm of D'.
20:*title* chief Musician, A Psalm of D'.
21:*title* chief Musician, A Psalm of D'.
22:*title* Aijeleth Shahar, A Psalm of D'.
23:*title* A Psalm of D'.
24:*title* A Psalm of D'.
25:*title* A Psalm of D'.
26:*title* A Psalm of D'.
27:*title* A Psalm of D'.
28:*title* A Psalm of D'.
29:*title* A Psalm of D'.
30:*title* the dedication of the house of D'.
31:*title* chief Musician, A Psalm of D'.
32:*title* A Psalm of D', Maschil.
34:*title* A Psalm of D', when he changed
35:*title* A Psalm of D.'
36:*title* A Psalm of D' the servant of the
37:*title* A Psalm of D'.
38:*title* A Psalm of D', to bring to
39:*title* even to Jeduthun, A Psalm of D'.
40:*title* chief Musician, A Psalm of D'.
41:*title* chief Musician, A Psalm of D'.
51:*title* A Psalm of D', when Nathan, the
52:*title* A Psalm of D', when Doeg the
title D' is come to the house of
53:*title* Mahalath, Maschil, A Psalm of D'.
54:*title* A Psalm of D', when the Ziphims
title said to Saul, Doth not D' hide
55:*title* Neginoth, Maschil, A Psalm of D'.
56:*title* Michtam of D', when the
57:*title* Michtam of D', when he fled from
58:*title* Al-taschith, Michtam of D'.
59:*title* Michtam of D'; when Saul sent,
60:*title* Michtam of D', to teach; when he
61:*title* upon Neginah, A Psalm of D'.
62:*title* to Jeduthun, A Psalm of D'.
63:*title* A Psalm of D', when he was in the
64:*title* chief Musician, A Psalm of D'.
65:*title* Musician, A Psalm and Song of D'.
68:*title* Musician, A Psalm or Song of D'.
69:*title* upon Shoshannim, A Psalm of D'.
70:*title* A Psalm of D', to bring to
Ps 72:20 The prayers of D' the son of Jesse
78:70 He chose D' also his servant, and
86:*title* A Prayer of D'.
89: 3 I have sworn unto D' my servant,
20 I have found D' my servant; with
35 that I will not lie unto D'.
49 which thou swearest unto D' in
101:*title* A Psalm of D'.
103:*title* A Psalm of D'.
108:*title* A Song or Psalm of D'.
109:*title* chief Musician, A Psalm of D'.
110:*title* A Psalm of D'.
122:*title* A Song of degrees of D'.
5 the thrones of the house of D'.
124:*title* A Song of degrees of D'.
131:*title* A Song of degrees of D'.
132: 1 Lord, remember D', and all his
11 Lord hath sworn in truth unto D';
17 There will I make the horn of D'
133:*title* A Song of degrees of D'.
138:*title* A Psalm of D'.
139:*title* chief Musician, A Psalm of D'.
140:*title* chief Musician, A Psalm of D'.
141:*title* A Psalm of D'.
142:*title* Maschil of D'; A Prayer when he
143:*title* A Psalm of D'.
144:*title* A Psalm of D'.
10 who delivereth D' his servant from
Pr 1: 1 Proverbs of Solomon, the son of D',
Ec 1: 1 words of the Preacher, the son of D',
Ca 4: 4 Thy neck is like the tower of D'
Isa 7: 2 it was told the house of D', saying,
13 said, Hear ye now, O house of D';
9: 7 upon the throne of D', and upon
16: 5 in truth in the tabernacle of D',
22: 9 the breaches of the city of D',
22 key of the house of D' will I lay
29: 1 to Ariel, the city where D' dwelt!
38: 5 the Lord, the God of D' thy father,
55: 3 even the sure mercies of D'.
Jer 17:25 sitting upon the throne of D',
21:12 O house of D', thus saith the Lord;
22: 2 that sittest upon the throne of D',
4 kings sitting upon the throne of D',
30 sitting upon the throne of D', and
23: 5 raise unto D' a righteous Branch,
29:16 that sitteth upon the throne of D',
30: 9 D' their king, whom I will raise up
33:15 righteousness to grow up unto D';
17 D' shall never want a man to sit
21 my covenant be broken with D'
22 so will I multiply the seed of D'
26 seed of Jacob, and D' my servant,
36:30 none to sit upon the throne of D':
Eze 34:23 feed them, even my servant D';
24 servant D' a prince among them;
37:24 D' my servant shall be king over
25 my servant D' shall be their prince
Ho 3: 5 Lord their God, and D' their king;
Am 6: 5 instruments of musick, like D';
9:11 will I raise up the tabernacle of D'
Zec 12: 7 that the glory of the house of D'
8 them at that day shall be as D';
8 the house of D' shall be as God,
10 I will pour upon the house of D',
12 the family of the house of D' apart,
13: 1 fountain opened to the house of D'
M't 1: 1 son of D', the son of Abraham.
6 Jesse begat D' the king; and D'
17 generations from Abraham to D'
17 D' until the carrying away into
20 Joseph, thou son of D', fear not to
9:27 Thou son of D', have mercy on us.
12: 3 have ye not read what D' did,
23 said, Is not this the son of D'?
15:22 Lord, thou son of D'; my daughter
20:30, 31 on us, O Lord, thou son of D'.
21: 9 Hosanna to the son of D': Blessed
15 Hosanna to the son of D'; they
22:42 They say unto him, The son of D'.
43 How then doth D' in spirit call him
45 If D' then call him Lord, how is
M'r 2:25 Have ye never read what D' did,
10:47 Jesus, thou son of D', have mercy
48 Thou son of D', have mercy on me.
11:10 of our father D', that cometh in
12:35 that Christ is the son of D'?
36 D' himself said by the Holy Ghost,
37 D' therefore himself calleth him
Lu 1:27 was Joseph, of the house of D';
32 him the throne of his father D':
69 in the house of his servant D';
2: 4 unto the city of D', which is called
4 was of the house and lineage of D':)
11 is born this day in the city of D'
3:31 Nathan, which was the son of D',
6: 3 what D' did, when himself was an
18:38 Jesus, thou son of D', have mercy
39 Thou son of D', have mercy on me.
20:42 And D' himself saith in the book
44 D' therefore calleth him Lord, how
Joh 7:42 Christ cometh of the seed of D',
42 town of Bethlehem, where D' was?
Ac 1:16 the Holy Ghost by the mouth of D'
2:25 For D' speaketh concerning him,
29 speak unto you of the patriarch D',
34 D' is not ascended into the heavens:
4:25 Who by the mouth of thy servant D'
7:45 of our fathers, unto the days of D';
13:22 up unto them D' to be their king;
22 I have found D' the son of Jesse,
34 give you the sure mercies of D'.
36 For D', after he had served his own
15:16 build again the tabernacle of D',
Ro 1: 3 which was made of the seed of D'
4: 6 D' also describeth the blessedness
Ro 11: 9 D' saith, Let their table be made
2Ti 2: 8 Jesus Christ of the seed of D'
Heb 4: 7 limiteth a certain day, saying in D',
11:32 D' also, and Samuel, and of the
Re 3: 7 he that hath the key of D', he that
5: 5 Root of D', hath prevailed to open
22:16 am the root and the offspring of D'.

David's (*da'-vids*)
1Sa 18:29 became D' enemy continually.
19:11 sent messengers unto D' house,
11 Michal D' wife told him, saying,
20:16 require it at the hand of D' enemies,
25 side, and D' place was empty:
27 month, that D' place was empty:
23: 3 And D' men said unto him, Behold,
24: 5 afterward, that D' heart smote him,
25: 9 when D' young men came, they
12 So D' young men turned their way,
44 D' wife, to Phalti the son of Laish,
26:17 Saul knew D' voice, and said, Is
30: 5 D' two wives were taken captives,
20 cattle, and said, this is D' spoil.
2Sa 2:30 lacked of D' servants, nineteen
3: 5 sixth, Ithream, by Eglah D' wife.
5: 8 the blind that are hated of D' soul,
8: 2 the Moabites became D' servants,
14 they of Edom became D' servants.
18 and D' sons were chief rulers.
10: 2 D' servants came into the land of
4 D' servants, and shaved off the one
12: 5 D' anger was greatly kindled
30 stones: and it was set on D' head.
13: 3 son of Shimeah D' brother: and
32 of Shimeah D' brother, answered
15:12 the Gilonite, D' counseller, from
37 So Hushai D' friend came into the
16:16 Hushai the Archite, D' friend,
19:41 all D' men with him, over Jordan?
24:10 D' heart smote him after that he
11 unto the prophet Gad, D' seer,
1Ki 1:38 Solomon to ride upon king D' mule,
11:32 one tribe for my servant D' sake,
15: 4 for D' sake did the Lord his God
2Ki 11:10 give king D' spears and shields,
19:34 sake, and for my servant D' sake.
20: 6 sake, and for my servant D' sake.
1Ch 18: 2 the Moabites became D' servants,
6 the Syrians became D' servants,
13 the Edomites became D' servants.
19: 4 Wherefore Hanun took D' servants,
20: 2 in it: and it was set upon D' head:
7 of Shimea D' brother slew him.
21: 9 the Lord spake unto Gad, D' seer,
27:31 the substance which was king D'.
32 D' uncle was a counseller,
2Ch 23: 9 and shields, that had been king D'.
Ps 132:10 For thy servant D' sake turn not
145:*title* D' Psalm of praise.
Isa 37:35 sake, and for my servant D' sake.
Jer 13:13 kings that sit upon D' throne,
Lu 20:41 say they that Christ is D' son?

dawn See also DAWNING.
M't 28: 1 began to d' toward the first day
2Pe 1:19 until the day d', and the day star

dawning
Jos 6:15 rose early about the d' of the day,
J'g 19:26 the woman in the d' of the day,
Job 3: 9 neither let it see the d' of the day:
7: 4 to and fro unto the d' of the day.
Ps 119:147 prevented the d' of the morning,

day^ See also DAY'S; DAYS; DAYSMAN; DAY-SPRING; DAYTIME; HOLYDAY; MIDDAY; NOON-DAY; YESTERDAY.
Ge 1: 5 God called the light D', and the
5 and the morning were the first d'.
8 and the morning were the second d'.
13 and the morning were the third d'.
14 to divide the d' from the night;
16 the greater light to rule the d',
18 rule over the d' and over the night,
19 and the morning were the fourth d'.
23 and the morning were the fifth d'.
31 and the morning were the sixth d'.
2: 2 the seventh d' God ended his work
2 and he rested on the seventh d'
3 God blessed the seventh d', and
4 in the d' that the Lord God made
17 in the d' that thou eatest thereof
3: 5 in the d' ye eat thereof, then your
8 the garden in the cool of the d':
4:14 thou hast driven me out this d'
5: 1 In the d' that God created man,
2 in the d' when they were created.
7:11 the seventeenth d' of the month,
11 the same d' were all the fountains
13 In the selfsame d' entered Noah,
8: 4 on the seventeenth d' of the month,
14 seven and twentieth d' of the month,
22 and d' and night shall not cease.
15:18 same d' the Lord made a covenant
17:23 the selfsame d', as God had said
26 d' was Abraham circumcised,
18: 1 the tent door in the heat of the d';
19:37 father of the Moabites unto this d'.
38 children of Ammon unto this d'.
21: 8 made a great feast the same d'
26 neither yet heard I of it, but to d'.
22: 4 third d' Abraham lifted up his eyes,
14 as it is said to this d', In the mount
24:12 send me good speed this d', and
42 I came this d' unto the well, and
25:31 said, Sell me this d' thy birthright.
33 Swear to me this d'; and he sware
26:32 it came to pass the same d', that

Ge 26:33 the city is Beer-sheba unto this d'.
27: 2 I know not the d' of my death:
45 deprived also of you both in one d'?
29: 7 it is yet high d', neither is it time
30:32 will pass through all thy flock to d',
35 he removed that d' the he goats
31:22 it was told Laban on the third d'
39 whether stolen by d', or stolen by
40 the d' the drought consumed me,
43 this d' unto these my daughters,
48 between me and thee this d'.
32:24 him until the breaking of the d'.
26 Let me go, for the d' breaketh.
32 hollow of the thigh, unto this d':
33:13 men should overdrive them one d',
16 Esau returned that d' on his way
34:25 it came to pass on the third d',
35: 3 answered me in the d' of my distress,
20 pillar of Rachel's grave unto this d'.
39:10 as she spake to Joseph d' by d',
40: 7 Wherefore look ye so sadly to d'?
20 it came to pass the third d', which
41: 9 I do remember my faults this d':
42:13 youngest is this d' with our father,
18 Joseph said unto them the third d',
32 youngest is this d' with our father
47:23 bought you this d' and your land
26 over the land of Egypt unto this d'.
48:15 fed me all my life long unto this d',
20 he blessed them that d', saying,
50:20 as it is this d', to save much people
Ex 2:13 he went out the second d', behold,
18 it that ye are come so soon to d'?
5: 6 Pharaoh commanded the same d'
14 yesterday and to d', as heretofore?
6:28 the d' when the Lord spake unto
8:22 I will sever in that d' the land of
10: 6 have seen, since the d' that they
6 were upon the earth unto this d'.
13 east wind upon the land all that d',
28 in that d' thou seest my face thou
12: 3 In the tenth d' of this month
6 fourteenth d' of the same month:
14 d' shall be unto you for a memorial;
15 first d' ye shall put away leaven
15 the first d' until the seventh d',
16 in the first d' there shall be an holy
16 the seventh d' there shall be an
17 in this selfsame d' have I brought
17 observe this d' in your generations
18 fourteenth d' of the month at even,
18 one and twentieth d' of the month
41 the selfsame d' it came to pass,
51 it came to pass the selfsame d',
13: 3 Remember this d', in which ye
4 This d' came ye out in the month
6 and in the seventh d' shall be a
8 thou shalt shew thy son in that d',
21 the Lord went before them by d'
21 them light; to go by d' and night:
22 the pillar of the cloud by d', nor
14:13 which he will shew to you to d':
13 Egyptians whom ye have seen to d',
30 the Lord saved Israel that d' out of
16: 1 the fifteenth d' of the second month
4 gather a certain rate every d', that
5 on the sixth d' they shall prepare
22 on the sixth d' they gathered twice
23 bake that which ye will bake to d',
25 that to d'; for to d' is a sabbath
25 to d' ye shall not find it in the
26 but on the seventh d', which is the
27 on the seventh d' for to gather,
29 he giveth you on the sixth d' the
29 out of his place on the seventh d'.
30 the people rested on the seventh d'.
19: 1 the same d' came they into the
10 sanctify them to d' and to morrow,
11 be ready against the third d': for
11 the third d' the Lord will come
15 Be ready against the third d': come
16 it came to pass on the third d' in
20: 8 Remember the sabbath d', to keep
10 But the seventh d' is the sabbath
11 rested the seventh d': wherefore
11 the Lord blessed the sabbath d',
21:21 if he continue a d' or two he shall
22:30 on the eighth d' thou shalt give it
23:12 the seventh d' thou shalt rest: that
24:16 and the seventh d' he called unto
29:36 thou shalt offer every d' a bullock
38 two lambs of the first year d' by d'
31:15 doeth any work in the sabbath d',
17 and on the seventh d' he rested,
32:28 there fell of the people that d'
29 Consecrate yourselves to d' to the
29 bestow upon you a blessing this d'.
34 nevertheless in the d' when I visit
34:11 that which I command thee this d':
21 but on the seventh d' thou shalt
35: 2 but on the seventh d' there shall be
2 to you an holy d', a sabbath of
3 habitations upon the sabbath d'.
40: 2 On the first d' of the first month
17 second year, on the first d' of the
37 they journeyed not till the d' that
38 was upon the tabernacle by d',
Le 6: 5 in the d' of his trespass offering.
20 Lord in the d' when he is anointed;
7:15 eaten the same d' that it is offered;
16 the same d' that he offereth his
17 the sacrifice on the third d' shall be
18 be eaten at all on the third d',
35 in the d' when he presented them
36 in the d' that he anointed them,
38 in the d' that he commanded the

Le 8:34 As he hath done this d', so the
35 d' and night seven days, and keep
9: 1 it came to pass on the eighth d',
4 to d' the Lord will appear unto you.
10:19 this d' have they offered their sin
19 I had eaten the sin offering to d',
12: 3 And in the eighth d' the flesh of
13: 5 shall look on him the seventh d':
6 look on him again the seventh d':
27 shall look upon him the seventh d':
32, 34 in the seventh d' the priest shall
51 on the plague on the seventh d':
14: 2 the leper in the d' of his cleansing:
9 it shall be on the seventh d', that
10 And on the eighth d' he shall take
23 shall bring them on the eighth d'
39 shall come again the seventh d',
15:14 And on the eighth d' he shall take
29 And on the eighth d' she shall take
16:29 on the tenth d' of the month, ye
30 in that d' shall the priest make an
19: 6 it shall be eaten the same d' ye
6 if ought remain until the third d',
7 if it be eaten at all on the third d',
22:27 from the eighth d' and thenceforth
28 it and her young both in one d'.
30 On the same d' it shall be eaten up;
23: 3 but the seventh d' is the sabbath of
5 In the fourteenth d' of the first
6 the fifteenth d' of the same month
7 In the first d' ye shall have an holy
8 seventh d' is an holy convocation
12 ye shall offer that d' when ye wave
14 until the selfsame d' that ye have
15 from the d' that ye brought the
21 shall proclaim on the selfsame d',
24 seventh month in the first d' of the
27 Also on the tenth d' of this seventh
27 there shall be a d' of atonement:
28 ye shall do no work in that same d':
28 for it is a d' of atonement,
29 not be afflicted in that same d',
30 doeth any work in that same d',
32 in the ninth d' of the month at even,
34 The fifteenth d' of this seventh
35 On the first d' shall be an holy
36 on the eighth d' shall be an holy
37 every thing upon his d':
39 in the fifteenth d' of the seventh
39 on the first d' shall be a sabbath,
39 on the eighth d' shall be a sabbath.
40 ye shall take you on the first d'
25: 9 the jubile to sound on the tenth d'
9 in the d' of atonement shall ye
27:23 give thine estimation in that d',
Nu 1: 1, 18 on the first d' of the second month,
3: 1 in the d' that the Lord spake with
13 the d' that I smote all the firstborn
6: 9 his head in the d' of his cleansing,
9 on the seventh d' shall he shave it.
10 And on the eighth d' he shall bring
11 shall hallow his head that same d'.
7: 1 to pass on the d' that Moses
10 in the d' that it was anointed, even
11 each prince on his d', for the
12 offered his offering the first d'
18 On the second d' Nethaneel the son
24 On the third d' Eliab the son of
30 On the fourth d' Elizur the son of
36 On the fifth d' Shelumiel the son of
42 On the sixth d' Eliasaph the son of
48 On the seventh d' Elishama the son
54 On the eighth d' offered Gamaliel
60 On the ninth d' Abidan the son of
66 On the tenth d' Ahiezer the son of
72 On the eleventh d' Pagiel the son of
78 On the twelfth d' Ahira the son of
84 in the d' when it was anointed,
8:17 on the d' that I smote every
9: 3 In the fourteenth d' of this month,
5 the fourteenth d' of the first month
6 not keep the passover on that d':
6 Moses and before Aaron on that d':
11 The fourteenth d' of the second
15 And on the d' that the tabernacle
16 alway: the cloud covered it by d',
21 whether it was by d' or by night
10:10 Also in the d' of your gladness,
11 the twentieth d' of the second
34 of the Lord was upon them by d',
11:19 Ye shall not eat one d', nor two
32 the people stood up all that d', and
32 all that night, and all the next d',
14:14 by d' time in a pillar of a cloud,
34 each d' for a year, shall ye bear
15:23 the d' that the Lord commanded
32 gathered sticks upon the sabbath d'.
19:12 himself with it on the third d',
12 and on the seventh d' he shall be
12 he purify not himself the third d',
12 then the seventh d' he shall not be
19 upon the unclean on the third d',
19 and on the seventh d': and on the
19 seventh d' he shall purify himself,
22:30 since I was thine unto this d'?
25:18 the d' of the plague for Peor's sake.
28: 3 without spot d' by d', for a
9 And on the sabbath d' two lambs of
16 in the fourteenth d' of the first
17 in the fifteenth d' of this month
18 In the first d' shall be an holy
25 And on the seventh d' ye shall
26 Also in the d' of the first fruits,
29: 1 On the first d' of the month,
1 it is a d' of blowing the trumpets
7 on the tenth d' of this seventh

Nu 29:12 the fifteenth d' of the seventh
17 And on the second d' ye shall offer
20 And on the third d' eleven bullocks,
23 And on the fourth d' ten bullocks,
26 And on the fifth d' nine bullocks,
29 And on the sixth d' eight bullocks,
32 And on the seventh d' seven
35 On the eighth d' ye shall have a
30: 5 her in the d' that he heareth;
7 at her in the d' that he heard it:
8 her on the d' that he heard it;
12 void on the d' he heard them;
14 hold his peace at her from d' to d';
14 at her in the d' that he heard them.
31:19 and your captives on the third d',
19 and on the seventh d'.
24 wash your clothes on the seventh d'
33: 3 the fifteenth d' of the first month;
38 Egypt, in the first d' of the fifth
De 1: 3 on the first d' of the month, that
10 are this d' as the stars of heaven
33 should go, and in a cloud by d'.
39 which in that d' had no knowledge
2:18 Ar, the coast of Moab, this d':
22 in their stead even unto this d':
25 This d' will I begin to put the dread
30 thy hand, as appeareth this d'.
3:14 Bashan-havoth-jair, unto this d'.
4: 4 are alive every one of you this d'.
8 which I set before you this d'?
10 the d' that thou stoodest before
15 on the d' that the Lord spake unto
20 of inheritance, as ye are this d'.
26 earth to witness against you this d',
32 since the d' that God created man
38 for an inheritance, as it is this d'.
39 Know therefore this d', and
40 which I command thee this d', that
5: 1 which I speak in your ears this d',
3 who are all of us here alive this d'.
12 Keep the sabbath d' to sanctify it,
14 But the seventh d' is the sabbath
15 thee to keep the sabbath d'.
24 we have seen this d' that God doth
6: 6 which I command thee this d',
24 preserve us alive, as it is at this d'.
7:11 command thee this d', to do them.
8: 1 this d' shall ye observe to do, that
11 which I command thee this d':
18 unto thy fathers, as, it is this d'.
19 testify against you this d' that ye
9: 1 art to pass over Jordan this d',
3 Understand therefore this d', that
7 the d' that thou didst depart out
10 the fire in the d' of the assembly.
24 Lord from the d' that I knew you.
10: 4 of the fire in the d' of the assembly:
8 to bless in his name, unto this d'.
13 command thee this d' for thy good?
15 above all people, as it is this d'.
11: 2 And know ye this d': for I speak not
4 hath destroyed them unto this d';
8 command you this d', that ye may
13 command you this d', to love the
26 I set before you this d' a blessing
27 God, which I command you this d':
28 I command you this d', to go after
32 which I set before you this d'.
12: 8 the things that we do here this d',
13:18 command thee this d', to do that
15: 5 which I command thee this d'.
15 I command thee this thing to d'.
16: 3 mayest remember the d' when
4 sacrificedst the first d' at even,
8 the seventh d' shall be a solemn
18:16 in the d' of the assembly, saying,
19: 9 command thee this d', to love the
20: 3 ye approach this d' unto battle
21:23 shalt in any wise bury him that d';
24:15 his d' thou shalt give him his hire,
26: 3 I profess this d' unto the Lord
16 This d' the Lord thy God hath
17 the Lord this d' to be thy God,
18 Lord hath avouched thee this d' to
27: 1 which I command you this d'.
2 on the d' when ye shall pass over
4 which I command you this d', in
9 d' thou art become the people of
10 which I command thee this d'.
11 charged his people the same d',
28: 1 thee this d', that the Lord thy God,
13 I command thee this d', to observe
14 I command thee this d', to the
15 which I command thee this d;
32 longing for them all the d' long:
66 thou shalt fear d' and night, and
29: 4 and ears to hear, unto this d'.
10 Ye stand this d' all of you before
12 thy God maketh with thee this d':
13 That he may establish thee to d'
15 that standeth here with us this d'
15 that is not here with us this d':
18 whose heart turneth away this d'
28 into another land, as it is this d'.
30: 2 I command thee this d', thou and
8 which I command thee this d'.
11 I command thee this d', it is not
15 I have set before thee this d' life
16 this d' to love the Lord thy God,
18 I denounce unto you this d', that ye
19 heaven and earth to record this d'
31: 2 and twenty years old this d':
17 kindled against them in that d',
17 so that they will say in that d',
18 I will surely hide my face in that d'
22 wrote this song the same d'.

De 31:27 I am yet alive with you this d'.
32:35 the d' of their calamity is at hand,
46 I testify among you this d', which
48 spake unto Moses that selfsame d',
33:12 shall cover him all the d' long,
34: 6 of his sepulchre unto this d'.
Jos 1: 8 meditate therein d' and night,
3: 7 d' will I begin to magnify thee
4: 9 and they are there unto this d'.
14 that d' the Lord magnified Joshua
19 on the tenth d' of the first month,
5: 9 This d' have I rolled away the
9 place is called Gilgal unto this d'.
10 on the fourteenth d' of the month
11 parched corn in the selfsame d'.
6: 4 and the seventh d' ye shall compass
10 mouth, until the d' I bid you shout;
14 the second d' they compassed the
15 it came to pass on the seventh d',
15 about the dawning of the d',
15 that d' they compassed the city
25 even unto this d'; because she hid
7:25 the Lord shall trouble thee this d'.
26 a great heap of stones unto this d'.
26 The valley of Achor, unto this d'.
8:25 all that fell that d', both of men
28 ever, even a desolation unto this d'.
29 stones, that remaineth unto this d'.
9:12 on the d' we came forth to go unto
17 unto their cities on the third d'.
27 Joshua made them that d' hewers
27 of the Lord, even unto this d',
10:12 in the d' when the Lord delivered
13 not to go down about a whole d'.
14 no d' like that before it or after it,
27 which remain until this very d'.
28 that d' Joshua took Makkedah,
32 it on the second d', and smote it
35 they took it on that d', and smote it
35 therein he utterly destroyed that d',
13:13 among the Israelites until this d'.
14: 9 Moses sware on that d', saying,
10 this d' fourscore and five years old.
11 d' as I was in the d' that Moses sent
12 the Lord spake in that d';
12 for thou heardest in that d'
14 unto this d', because that he wholly
15:63 of Judah at Jerusalem unto this d'.
16:10 this d', and serve under tribute.
22: 3 these many days unto this d',
16 to turn away this d' from following
16 rebel this d' against the Lord.
17 we are not cleansed until this d',
18 ye must turn away this d' from
18 and it will be, seeing ye rebel to d'
22 the Lord, (save us not this d',)
29 this d' from following the Lord,
31 This d' we perceive that the Lord
23: 8 as ye have done unto this d'.
9 stand before you unto this d'.
14 this d' I am going the way of all
24:15 choose you this d' whom ye will
25 a covenant with the people that d',
J'g 1:21 in Jerusalem unto this d'.
26 is the name thereof unto this d'.
3:30 So Moab was subdued that d'
4:14 this is the d' in which the Lord
23 God subdued on that d' Jabin the
5: 1 son of Abinoam on that d', saying,
6:24 unto this d' it is yet in Ophrah
27 could not do it by d', that he did
32 that d' he called him Jerubbaal,
9:18 against my father's house this d',
19 his house this d', then rejoice ye
45 fought against the city all that d';
10: 4 are called Havoth-jair unto this d',
15 us only, we pray thee, this d'.
11:27 the Judge be judge this d' between
12: 3 are ye come up unto me this d',
13: 7 the womb to the d' of his death.
10 that came unto me the other d'.
14:15 the seventh d', that they said unto
17 it came to pass on the seventh d',
18 said unto him on the seventh d'
15:19 which is in Lehi unto this d'.
16: 2 when it is d', we shall kill him.
18: 1 that d' all their inheritance had
12 Mahaneh-dan unto this d': behold,
30 the d' of the captivity of the land.
19: 5 it came to pass on the fourth d',
8 morning on the fifth d' to depart:
9 the d' draweth toward evening, I
9 behold, the d' groweth to an end,
11 d' was far spent; and the servant
25 when the d' began to spring, they
26 dawning of the d', and fell down
30 the d' that the children of Israel
30 of the land of Egypt unto this d':
20:21 d' twenty and two thousand men.
22 put themselves in array the first d'
24 children of Benjamin the second d'
25 them out of Gibeah the second d',
26 fasted that d' until even, and
30 of Benjamin on the third d',
35 that d' twenty and five thousand
46 all which fell that d' of Benjamin
21: 3 should be to d' one tribe lacking
6 one tribe cut off from Israel this d'
Ru 2:19 Where hast thou gleaned to d'?
19 name with whom I wrought to d' is
3:18 he hath finished the thing this d'.
4: 5 What d' thou buyest the field of
9 witnesses this d', that I have
10 this place: ye are witnesses this d'.
14 which hath not left thee this d'
1Sa 2:34 one d' they shall die both of them.
1Sa 3:12 In that d' I will perform against Eli
4: 3 the Lord smitten us to d' before the
12 came to Shiloh the same d' with his
16 I fled to d' out of the army.
5: 5 of Dagon in Ashdod unto this d'.
6:15 sacrifices the same d' unto the Lord.
16 they returned to Ekron the same d'.
18 unto this d' in the field of Joshua,
7: 6 and fasted on that d',
10 a great thunder on that d'
8: 8 since the d' that I brought them up
8 out of Egypt even unto this d',
18 ye shall cry out in that d' because
18 Lord will not hear you in that d'.
9:12 he came to d' to the city; for there
12 a sacrifice of the people to d'
15 in his ear a d' before Saul came,
19 ye shall eat with me to d',
24 Saul did eat with Samuel that d'.
26 about the spring of the d', that
10: 2 art departed from me to d', then
9 those signs came to pass that d'.
19 ye have this d' rejected your God,
11:11 Ammonites until the heat of the d':
13 not a man be put to death this d':
13 for to d' the Lord hath wrought
12: 2 you from my childhood unto this d'.
5 his anointed is witness this d', that
17 Is it not wheat harvest to d'?
18 Lord sent thunder and rain that d':
13:22 it came to pass in the d' of battle,
14: 1 it came to pass upon a d',
23 the Lord saved Israel that d':
24 of Israel were distressed that d':
28 man that eateth any food this d'.
30 the people had eaten freely to d'
31 they smote the Philistines that d'
33 roll a great stone unto me this d'.
37 he answered him not that d'.
38 wherein this sin hath been this d'.
45 he hath wrought with God this d'.
15:28 kingdom of Israel from thee this d',
35 to see Saul until the d' of his death:
16:13 upon David from that d' forward.
17:10 I defy the armies of Israel this d';
46 This d' will the Lord deliver thee
46 this d' unto the fowls of the air,
18: 2 Saul took him that d', and would
9 Saul eyed David from that d' and
21 Thou shalt this d' be my son in law
19:24 lay down naked all that d' and all
20: 5 in the field unto the third d' at even.
12 to morrow any time, or the third d',
26 Saul spake not any thing that d':
27 was the second d' of the month,
27 neither yesterday, nor to d'?
34 meat the second d' of the month:
21: 5 though it were sanctified this d'
6 in the d' when it was taken away.
7 servants of Saul was there that d',
10 fled that d' for fear of Saul,
22: 8, 13 me, to lie in wait, as at this d'?
18 slew on that d' fourscore and five
22 I knew it that d', when Doeg the
23:14 Saul sought him every d', but God
24: 4 Behold the d' of which the Lord
10 this d' thine eyes have seen how
10 the Lord had delivered thee to d'
18 thou hast shewed this d' how that
19 that thou hast done unto me this d'.
25: 8 we come in a good d': give, I pray
16 both by night and d', all the while
32 sent thee this d' to meet me:
33 which hast kept me this d' from
26: 8 enemy into thine hand this d':
10 his d' shall come to die;
19 they have driven me out this d'
21 was precious in thine eyes this d':
23 delivered thee into my hand to d',
24 thy life was much set by this d'
27: 1 I shall now perish one d' by the
6 Achish gave him Ziklag that d':
6 the kings of Judah unto this d'.
10 Whither have ye made a road to d'?
28:18 done this thing unto thee this d'.
20 he had eaten no bread all the d',
29: 3 since he fell unto me unto this d'?
6 d' of thy coming... unto this d':
8 I have been with thee unto this d',
30: 1 were come to Ziklag on the third d',
17 unto the evening of the next d':
25 it was so from that d' forward,
25 an ordinance for Israel unto this d'.
31: 6 all his men, that same d' together.
2Sa 1: 2 came even to pass on the third d',
2:17 was a very sore battle that d';
32 they came to Hebron at break of d'.
3: 8 shew kindness this d' unto the
8 thou chargest me to d' with a fault
35 eat meat while it was yet d',
37 all Israel understood that d' that it
38 great man fallen this d' in Israel?
39 I am this d' weak, though anointed
4: 3 were sojourners there until this d'.)
5 about the heat of the d' to the
8 avenged my lord the king this d'
5: 8 David said on that d', Whosoever
6: 8 of the place Perez-uzzah to this d'.
9 was afraid of the Lord that d',
20 glorious was the king of Israel to d',
20 who uncovered himself to d'
23 no child unto the d' of her death.
7: 6 even to this d', but have walked in
11:12 Tarry here to d' also, and to
12 Uriah abode in Jerusalem that d',
12:18 it came to pass on the seventh d',
2Sa 13: 4 the king's son, lean from d' to d'?
32 from the d' that he forced his sister
37 David mourned for his son every d'.
14:22 d' thy servant knoweth that I have
15:20 should I this d' make thee go up
16: 3 To d' shall the house of Israel
12 me good for his cursing this d'.
18: 7 was there a great slaughter that d'
8 wood devoured more people that d'
18 unto this d', Absalom's place.
20 Thou shalt not bear tidings this d',
20 thou shalt bear tidings another d':
20 this d' thou shalt bear no tidings,
31 the Lord hath avenged thee this d'
19: 2 the victory that d' was turned into
2 for the people heard say that d'
3 people gat them by stealth that d'
5 shamed this d' the faces of all thy
5 which this d' have saved thy life,
6 thou hast declared this d', that
6 this d' I perceive, that if Absalom
6 lived, and all we had died this d',
19 the d' that my lord the king went
20 I am come the first this d'
22 ye should this d' be adversaries
22 put to death this d' in Israel? for do
22 not I know that I am this d' king
24 from the d' the king departed until
24 the d' he came again in peace.
35 I am this d' fourscore years old:
20: 3 shut up unto the d' of their death,
21:10 of the air to rest on them by d',
22: 1 the d' that the Lord had delivered
19 me in the d' of my calamity:
23:10 wrought a great victory that d';
24:18 Gad came that d' to David, and
1Ki 1:25 gone down this d', and hath slain
30 so will I certainly do this d'.
48 one to sit on my throne this d',
51 king Solomon swear unto me to d'
2: 8 the d' when I went to Mahanaim:
24 shall be put to death this d'.
37 the d' thou goest out, and passest
42 the d' thou goest out, and walkest
3: 6 to sit on his throne, as it is this d'.
18 came to pass the third d' after that
4:22 Solomon's provision for one d' was
5: 7 Blessed be the Lord this d', which
8: 8 and there they are unto this d'.
16 Since the d' that I brought forth
24 with thine hand, as it is this d'.
28 servant prayeth before thee to d':
29 toward this house night and d',
59 the Lord our God d' and night,
61 his commandments, as at this d'.
64 The same d' did the king hallow
66 eighth d' he sent the people away:
9:13 the land of Cabul unto this d'.
21 tribute of bondservice unto this d'.
10:12 trees, nor were seen unto this d'.
12: 7 servant unto this people this d',
12 came to Rehoboam the third d',
12 Come to me again the third d'.
19 the house of David unto this d'.
32 the fifteenth d' of the month, like
33 fifteenth d' of the eighth month,
13: 3 he gave a sign the same d',
11 the man of God had done that d'
14:14 off the house of Jeroboam that d':
16:16 over Israel that d' in the camp.
17:14 d' that the Lord sendeth rain
18:15 surely shew thyself unto him to d'.
36 known this d' that thou art God
20:13 deliver it into thine hand this d';
29 seventh d' the battle was joined:
29 thousand footmen in one d'.
22: 5 at the word of the Lord to d'.
25 thou shalt see in that d', when thou
35 the battle increased that d': and
2Ki 2: 3, 5 thy master from thy head to d'?
22 the waters were healed unto this d',
4: 8 it fell on a d', that Elisha passed to
11 it fell on a d', that he came thither,
18 it fell on a d', that he went out
23 Wherefore wilt thou go to him to d'?
6:28 thy son, that we may eat him to d',
29 I said unto her on the next d',
31 Shaphat shall stand on him this d'.
7: 9 this d' is a d' of good tidings,
8: 6 since the d' that she left the land,
22 the hand of Judah unto this d'.
10:27 it a draught house unto this d'.
14: 7 name of it Joktheel unto this d'.
15: 5 was a leper unto the d' of his death,
16: 6 Elath, and dwelt there unto this d'.
17:23 own land to Assyria unto this d'.
34 this d' they do after the former
41 fathers, so do they unto this d'.
19: 3 This d' is a d' of trouble,
20: 5 on the third d' thou shalt go up
8 the house of the Lord the third d'?
17 laid up in store unto this d',
21:15 the d' their fathers came forth out
15 of Egypt, even unto this d'.
25: 3 d' of the fourth month of the famine
8 on the seventh d' of the month
27 seven and twentieth d' of the month,
30 daily rate for every d', all the days
1Ch 4:41 destroyed them utterly unto this d',
43 and dwelt there unto this d'.
5:26 to the river Gozan, unto this d'.
9:33 in that work d' and night.
11:22 slew a lion in a pit in a snowy d'.
12:22 d' by d' there came to David to
13:11 place is called Perez-uzza to this d'.
12 David was afraid of God that d',

1Ch 16: 7 d' David delivered first this psalm
23 forth from d' to d' his salvation.
17: 5 dwelt in an house since the d' that
5 I brought up Israel unto this d';
26:17 Levites northward four a d',
17 southward four a d', and toward
28: 7 and my judgments, as at this d'.
29: 5 his service this d' unto the Lord?
21 on the morrow after that d', even a
22 drink before the Lord on that d'
2Ch 3: 2 began to build in the second d' of
5: 9 And there it is unto this d'.
6: 5 since the d' that I brought forth
15 with thine hand, as it is this d'.
20 open upon this house d' and night,
7: 9 d' they made a solemn assembly:
10 And on the three and twentieth d'
8: 8 make to pay tribute until this d'.
13 Even after a certain rate every d',
14 as the duty of every d' required:
16 d' of the foundation of the house of
10:12 came to Rehoboam on the third d',
12 Come again to me on the third d'.
19 the house of David unto this d'.
18: 4 at the word of the Lord to d'.
24 thou shalt see on that d' when
34 battle increased that d': howbeit
20:26 on the fourth d' they assembled
26 valley of Berachah, unto this d'.
21:10 the hand of Judah unto this d'.
15 by reason of the sickness d' by d'.
24:11 they did d' by d', and gathered
26:21 the d' of his death, and dwelt in a
28: 6 twenty thousand in one d', which
29:17 on the first d' of the first month
17 and on the eighth d' of the month
17 in the sixteenth d' of the first month
30:15 fourteenth d' of the second month:
21 priests praised the Lord d' by d',
35: 1 the fourteenth d' of the first month.
16 Lord was prepared the same d',
21 I come not against thee this d',
25 their lamentations to this d', and
Ezr 3: 4 as the duty of every d' required;
6 the first d' of the seventh month
6: 9 let it be given them d' by d'
15 finished on the third d' of the month
19 the fourteenth d' of the first month.
7: 9 upon the first d' of the first month
9 on the first d' of the fifth month
8:31 river of Ahava on the twelfth d' of
33 fourth d' was the silver and the
9: 7 a great trespass unto this d'; and
7 to confusion of face, as it is this d'.
15 remain yet escaped, as it is this d':
10: 9 on the twentieth d' of the month;
13 work of one d' or two: for we are
16 in the first d' of the tenth month
17 by the first d' of the first month.
Ne 1: 6 pray before thee now, d' and night,
11 I pray thee, thy servant this d',
4: 2 will they make an end in a d'?
9 watch against them d' and night,
22 guard to us, and labour on the d'.
5:11 I pray you, to them, even this d',
6:15 twenty and fifth d' of the month
8: 2 the first d' of the seventh month.
9 d' is holy unto the Lord your God;
10 this d' is holy unto our Lord:
11 Hold your peace, for the d' is holy;
13 And on the second d' were gathered
17 d' had not the children of Israel
18 Also d' by d', from the first
18 d' unto the last d',
18 and on the eighth d' was a solemn
9: 1 Now in the twenty and fourth d'
3 one fourth part of the d';
10 get thee a name, as it is this d'.
12 them in the d' by a cloudy pillar;
19 departed not from them by d',
32 the kings of Assyria unto this d'.
36 Behold, we are servants this d',
10:31 victuals on the sabbath d' to sell,
31 on the sabbath, or on the holy d':
11:23 for the singers, due for every d'.
12:43 that d' they offered great sacrifices,
47 the porters, every d' his portion:
13: 1 On that d' they read in the book
15 into Jerusalem on the sabbath d':
15 in the d' wherein they sold victuals.
17 ye do, and profane the sabbath d'?
19 be brought in on the sabbath d'.
22 gates, to sanctify the sabbath d'.
Es 1:10 d', when the heart of the king
18 of Persia and Media say this d'
2:11 Mordecai walked every d' before
3: 7 d' to d', and from month to month,
12 thirteenth d' of the first month,
13 one d', even upon the thirteenth d'
14 should be ready against that d'.
4:16 nor drink three days, night or d':
5: 1 it came to pass on the third d',
4 the king and Haman come this d'
9 Then went Haman forth that d'
7: 2 again unto Esther on the second d'
8: 1 On that d' did the king Ahasuerus
9 the three and twentieth d' thereof;
12 Upon one d' in all the provinces
12 upon the thirteenth d' of the twelfth
13 should be ready against that d'
17 gladness, a feast and a good d'.
9: 1 on the thirteenth d' of the same,
1 the d' that the enemies of the Jews
11 On that d' the number of those that
15 together on the fourteenth d'
17 On the thirteenth d' of the month

Es 9:17 on the fourteenth d' of the same
17 and made it a d' of feasting and
18 on the thirteenth d' thereof,
18 the fifteenth d' of the same they
18 made it a d' of feasting and
19 the fourteenth d' of the month Adar
19 month Adar a d' of gladness and
19 and feasting, and a good d',
21 the fourteenth d' of the month Adar,
21 and the fifteenth d' of the same,
22 from mourning into a good d': that
Job 1: 4 in their houses, every one his d';
6 Now there was a d' when the sons of
13 there was a d' when his sons and
2: 1 Again there was a d' when the sons
3: 1 Job his mouth, and cursed his d'.
3 Let the d' perish wherein I was
4 Let that d' be darkness; let not
5 let the blackness of the d' terrify it.
8 Let them curse it that curse the d'.
9 let it see the dawning of the d':
7: 4 and fro unto the dawning of the d'.
14: 6 accomplish, as an hireling, his d'.
15:23 the d' of darkness is ready at his
17:12 They change the night into d': the
18:20 shall be astonied at his d', as they
19:25 stand at the latter d' upon the
20:28 flow away in the d' of his wrath.
21:30 to the d' of destruction? they shall
30 brought forth to the d' of wrath.
23: 2 Even to d' is my complaint bitter:
26:10 until the d' and night come to an
38:23 against the d' of battle and war?
Ps 1: 2 in his law doth he meditate d' and
2: 7 Son; this d' have I begotten thee.
7:11 angry with the wicked every d'.
18:*title* in the d' that the Lord delivered
18 in the d' of my calamity: but the
19: 2 D' unto d' uttereth speech, and
20: 1 Lord hear thee in the d' of trouble;
25: 5 on thee do I wait all the d'.
32: 3 through my roaring all the d' long.
4 d' and night thy hand was heavy
35:28 of thy praise all the d' long.
37:13 for he seeth that his d' is coming.
38: 6 I go mourning all the d' long.
12 and imagine deceits all the d' long.
42: 3 My tears have been my meat d'
44: 8 In God we boast all the d' long,
22 For thy sake are we killed all the d'
50:15 call upon me in the d' of trouble:
55:10 D' and night they go about it upon
56: 5 Every d' they wrest my words:
59:16 and refuge in the d' of my trouble.
71: 8 and with thy honour all the d'.
15 and thy salvation all the d';
24 thy righteousness all the d' long:
73:14 all the d' long have I been plagued,
74:16 The d' is thine, the night also is
77: 2 in the d' of my trouble I sought the
78: 9 turned back in the d' of battle.
42 the d' when he delivered them from
81: 3 appointed, on our solemn feast d'.
84:10 a d' in thy courts is better than a
86: 7 the d' of my trouble I will call upon
88: 1 have cried d' and night before thee:
89:16 name shall they rejoice all the d':
91: 5 for the arrow that flieth by d';
92:*title* Psalm or Song for the sabbath d'.
95: 7 To d' if ye will hear his voice,
8 in the d' of temptation in the
96: 2 forth his salvation from d' to d'.
102: 2 in the d' when I am in trouble;
2 in the d' when I call answer me
8 enemies reproach me all the d';
110: 3 be willing in the d' of thy power,
5 through kings in the d' of his wrath.
118:24 This is the d' which the Lord hath
119:91 They continue this d' according to
97 it is my meditation all the d'.
164 Seven times a d' do I praise thee
121: 6 The sun shall not smite thee by d',
136: 8 The sun to rule by d': for his
137: 7 of Edom in the d' of Jerusalem;
138: 3 In the d' when I cried thou
139:12 the night shineth as the d': the
140: 7 hast covered my head in the d' of
145: 2 Every d' will I bless thee;
146: 4 in that very d' his thoughts perish.
Pr 4:18 more and more unto the perfect d'.
6:34 not spare in the d' of vengeance.
7:14 this d' have I payed my vows.
20 come home at the d' appointed.
11: 4 Riches profit not in the d' of wrath:
16: 4 the wicked for the d' of evil.
21:26 He coveteth greedily all the d' long:
31 horse is prepared against the d'
22:19 I have made known to thee this d',
23:17 the fear of the Lord all the d' long.
24:10 If thou faint in the d' of adversity,
27: 1 for thou knowest not what a d' may
10 house in the d' of thy calamity:
15 dropping in a very rainy d' and a
Ec 7: 1 the d' of death than the d' of one's
14 In the d' of prosperity be joyful,
14 but in the d' of adversity consider:
8: 8 hath he power in the d' of death:
16 there is that neither d' nor night
12: 3 In the d' when the keepers of the
Ca 2:17 Until the d' break, and the shadows
3:11 in the d' of his espousals, and in
11 the d' of the gladness of his heart.
4: 6 Until the d' break, and the shadows
8: 8 in the d' when she shall be spoken
Isa 2:11 alone shall be exalted in that d'.
12 the d' of the Lord of hosts shall be

Isa 2:17 alone shall be exalted in that d'.
20 In that d' a man shall cast his idols
3: 7 In that d' shall he swear, saying, I
18 In that d' the Lord will take away
4: 1 In that d' seven women shall take
2 In that d' shall the branch of the
5 a cloud and smoke by d', and the
5:30 in that d' they shall roar against
7:17 from the d' that Ephraim departed
18 to pass in that d', that the Lord
20 In the same d' shall the Lord shave
21 to pass in that d', that a man shall
23 to pass in that d', that every place
9: 4 oppressor, as in the d' of Midian.
14 tail, branch and rush, in one d'.
10: 3 will ye do in the d' of visitation,
17 his thorns and his briers in one d';
20 to pass in that d', that the remnant
27 to pass in that d', that his burden
32 yet shall he remain at Nob that d':
11:10 in that d' there shall be a root of
11 to pass in that d', that the Lord
16 in the d' that he came up out of the
12: 1 in that d' thou shalt say, O Lord, I
4 And in that d' shall ye say, Praise
13: 6 the d' of the Lord is at hand;
9 the d' of the Lord cometh, cruel
13 and in the d' of his fierce anger.
14: 3 to pass in the d' that the Lord
17: 4 in that d' it shall come to pass, that
7 At that d' shall a man look to his
9 In that d' shall his strong cities be
11 In the d' shalt thou make thy plant
11 in the d' of grief and of desperate
19:16 In that d' shall Egypt be like unto
18 In that d' shall five cities in the
19 In that d' shall there be an altar to
21 shall know the Lord in that d',
23 In that d' shall there be a highway
24 In that d' shall Israel be the third
20: 6 isle shall say in that d', Behold,
22: 5 it is a d' of trouble, and of treading
8 thou didst look in that d' to the
12 in that d' did the Lord God of
20 to pass in that d', that I will call
25 In that d', saith the Lord of hosts,
23:15 to pass in that d', that Tyre shall
24:21 to pass in that d', that the Lord
25: 9 it shall be said in that d', Lo, this
26: 1 In that d' shall this song be sung
27: 1 In that d' the Lord with his sore
2 In that d' sing ye unto her, A
3 it, I will keep it night and d'.
8 wind in the d' of the east wind.
12 to pass in that d', that the Lord
13 to pass in that d', that the great
28: 5 In that d' shall the Lord of hosts
19 shall it pass over, by d' and by
24 Doth the plowman plow all d' to
29:18 in that d' shall the deaf hear the
30:23 in that d' shall thy cattle feed in
25 in the d' of the great slaughter,
26 in the d' that the Lord bindeth up
31: 7 in that d' every man shall cast
34: 8 is the d' of the Lord's vengeance,
10 not be quenched night nor d';
37: 3 This d' is a d' of trouble,
38:12, 13 from d' even to night wilt thou
19 he shall praise thee, as I do this d':
39: 6 have laid up in store until this d',
43:13 before the d' was I am he;
47: 9 come to thee in a moment in one d',
48: 7 before the d' when thou heardest
49: 8 and in a d' of salvation have I
51:13 hast feared continually every d'
52: 5 continually every d' is blasphemed.
6 they shall know in that d' that I
56:12 to morrow shall be as this d',
58: 3 in the d' of your fast ye find
4 ye shall not fast as ye do this d',
5 a d' for a man to afflict his soul?
5 and an acceptable d' to the Lord?
10 thy darkness be as the noon d':
13 doing thy pleasure on my holy d';
59:10 We stumble at noon d' as in the
60:11 they shall not be shut d' nor night;
19 shall be no more thy light by d';
61: 2 the d' of vengeance of our God;
62: 6 never hold their peace d' nor night;
63: 4 the d' of vengeance is in mine
65: 2 have spread out my hands all the d'
5 a fire that burneth all the d'.
66: 8 be made to bring forth in one d'?
Jer 1:10 I have this d' set thee over the
18 I have made thee this d' a defenced
3:25 from our youth even unto this d',
4: 9 it shall come to pass at that d',
6: 4 the d' goeth away, for the shadows
7:22 in the d' that I brought them out
25 Since the d' that your fathers came
25 of the land of Egypt unto this d'
9: 1 that I might weep d' and night for
11: 4 in the d' that I brought them
5 milk and honey, as it is this d'.
7 in the d' that I brought them up
7 the land of Egypt even unto this d',
12: 3 prepare them for the d' of slaughter
14:17 run down with tears night and d',
15: 9 is gone down while it was yet d':
16:13 there shall ye serve other gods d'
19 my refuge in the d' of affliction,
17:16 have I desired the woeful d';
17 thou art my hope in the d' of evil.
18 bring upon them the d' of evil,
21 bear no burden on the sabbath d',
22 of your houses on the sabbath d',

Jer 17:22 work, but hallow ye the sabbath *d'*,
24 gates of this city on the sabbath *d'*,
24 hallow the sabbath *d'*, to do no
27 hallow the sabbath *d'*, and not to
27 of Jerusalem on the sabbath *d'*;
18:17 the face, in the *d'* of their calamity.
20:14 Cursed be the *d'* wherein I was
14 let not the *d'* wherein my mother
25: 3 even unto this *d'*, that is the three
18 and a curse; as it is this *d'*;
33 slain of the Lord shall be at that *d'*
27:22 until the *d'* that I visit them,
30: 7 Alas! for that *d'* is great, so that
8 come to pass in that *d'*, saith the
31: 6 For there shall be a *d'*, that the
32 in the *d'* that I took them by the
35 giveth the sun for a light by *d'*,
32:20 even unto this *d'*, and in Israel,
20 made thee a name, as at this *d'*;
31 *d'* that they built it even unto this *d'*;
33:20 break my covenant of the *d'*,
20 there should not be *d'* and night
25 covenant be not with *d'* and night,
34:13 the *d'* that I brought them forth
35:14 unto this *d'* they drink none, but
36: 2 from the *d'* I spake unto thee,
2 days of Josiah, even unto this *d'*.
6 Lord's house upon the fasting *d'*:
30 body shall be cast out in the *d'*
38:28 the *d'* that Jerusalem was taken:
39:16 accomplished in that *d'* before thee.
17 I will deliver thee in that *d'*,
40: 4 I loose thee this *d'* from the chains
41: 4 *d'* after he had slain Gedaliah,
42:19 that I have admonished you this *d'*.
21 I have this *d'* declared it to you;
44: 2 this *d'* they are a desolation,
6 wasted and desolate, as at this *d'*.
10 not humbled even unto this *d'*,
22 without an inhabitant, as at this *d'*.
23 happened unto you, as at this *d'*.
46:10 For this is the *d'* of the Lord God
10 of hosts, a *d'* of vengeance,
21 *d'* of their calamity was come upon
47: 4 the *d'* that cometh to spoil all the
48:41 men's hearts in Moab at that *d'*
49:22 at that *d'* shall the heart of the
26 shall be cut off in that *d'*,
50:27 their *d'* is come, the time of their
30 of war shall be cut off in that *d'*,
31 thy *d'* is come, the time that I will
51: 2 in the *d'* of trouble they shall be
52: 4 month, in the tenth *d'* of the month,
6 ninth day of the month, the famine
11 in prison till the *d'* of his death.
12 in the tenth *d'* of the month, which
31 in the five and twentieth *d'* of the
34 every *d'* a portion until the *d'* of
La 1:12 me in the *d'* of his fierce anger.
13 me desolate and faint all the *d'*.
21 bring the *d'* that thou hast called,
2: 1 his footstool in the *d'* of his anger!
7 as in the *d'* of a solemn feast.
16 this is the *d'* that we looked for;
18 down like a river *d'* and night:
21 thou hast slain them in the *d'* of
22 solemn *d'* my terrors round about,
22 so that in the *d'* of the Lord's anger
3: 3 his hand against me all the *d'*.
14 people; and their song all the *d'*.
57 Thou drewest near in the *d'* that I
62 their device against me all the *d'*.
Eze 1: 1 in the fifth *d'* of the month, as I was
2 In the fifth *d'* of the month, which
28 is in the cloud in the *d'* of rain,
2: 3 against me, even unto this very *d'*.
4: 6 appointed thee each *d'* for a year.
10 be by weight, twenty shekels a *d'*:
7: 7 the *d'* of trouble is near, and not
10 Behold the *d'*, behold, it is come:
12 is come, the *d'* draweth near:
19 in the *d'* of the wrath of the Lord:
8: 1 in the fifth *d'* of the month, as I
12: 3 and remove by *d'* in their sight;
4 forth thy stuff by *d'* in their sight,
7 I brought forth my stuff by *d'*,
13: 5 the battle in the *d'* of the Lord.
16: 4 in the *d'* thou wast born thy navel
5 in the *d'* that thou wast born.
56 by thy mouth in the *d'* of thy pride,
20: 1 the tenth *d'* of the month, that
5 In the *d'* when I chose Israel,
6 In the *d'* that I lifted up mine hand
29 is called Bamah unto this *d'*.
31 all your idols, even unto this *d'*:
21:25 prince of Israel, whose *d'* is come,
29 of the wicked, whose *d'* is come,
22:24 rained upon in the *d'* of indignation.
23:38 defiled my sanctuary in the same *d'*,
39 came the same *d'* into my sanctuary
24: 1 month, in the tenth *d'* of the month,
2 write thee the name of the *d'*,
2 even of this same *d'*:
2 against Jerusalem this same *d'*.
25 in the *d'* when I take from them
26 in that *d'* shall come unto thee,
27 that *d'* shall thy mouth be opened
26: 1 year, in the first *d'* of the month,
18 isles tremble in the *d'* of thy fall;
27:27 of the seas in the *d'* of thy ruin.
28:13 in the *d'* that thou wast created.
15 from the *d'* that thou wast created,
29: 1 in the twelfth *d'* of the month, the
17 the first *d'* of the month, the word
21 In that *d'* will I cause the horn of
30: 2 Howl ye, Woe worth the *d'*!
Eze 30: 3 For the *d'* is near, even the *d'* of
3 the Lord is near, a cloudy *d'*;
9 In that *d'* shall messengers go forth
9 upon them, as in the *d'* of Egypt:
18 the *d'* shall be darkened, when I
20 in the seventh *d'* of the month, that
31: 1 the first *d'* of the month, that the
15 In the *d'* when he went down to
32: 1 first *d'* of the month, that the word
10 his own life, in the *d'* of thy fall.
17 in the fifteenth day of the month,
33:12 in the *d'* of his transgression:
12 in the *d'* that he turneth from his
12 in the *d'* that he sinneth.
21 in the fifth *d'* of the month, that one
34:12 the *d'* that he is among his sheep
12 scattered in the cloudy and dark *d'*.
36:33 In the *d'* that I shall have cleansed
38:14 In that *d'* when my people of Israel
19 in that *d'* there shall be a great
39: 8 this is the *d'* whereof I have spoken.
11 to pass in that *d'*, that I will
13 the *d'* that I shall be glorified,
22 their God from that *d'* and forward.
40: 1 in the tenth *d'* of the month,
1 in the selfsame *d'* the hand of the
43:18 in the *d'* when they shall make it,
22 the second *d'* thou shalt offer a kid
25 every *d'* a goat for a sin offering:
27 upon the eighth *d'*, and so forward,
44:27 *d'* that he goeth into the sanctuary,
45:18 the first month, in the first *d'* of the
20 And so shalt thou do the seventh *d'*
21 the fourteenth *d'* of the month,
22 upon that *d'* shall the prince
25 the fifteenth *d'* of the month,
46: 1 in the *d'* of the new moon it shall
4 in the sabbath *d'* shall be six lambs
6 the day of the new moon it shall be
12 as he did on the sabbath *d'*: then
48:35 of the city from that *d'* shall be,
Da 6:10 upon his knees three times a *d'*,
13 maketh his petition three times a *d'*.
9: 7 confusion of faces, as at this *d'*;
15 gotten thee renown, as at this *d'*;
10: 4 And in the four and twentieth *d'*
12 from the first *d'* that thou didst set
Ho 1: 5 it shall come to pass at that *d'*,
11 great shall be the *d'* of Jezreel.
2: 3 as in the *d'* that she was born,
15 as in the *d'* when she came up out
16 shall be at that *d'*, saith the Lord,
18 in that *d'* will I make a covenant
21 it shall come to pass in that *d'*,
4: 5 Therefore shalt thou fall in the *d'*,
5: 9 Ephraim shall be desolate in the *d'*
6: 2 in the third *d'* he will raise us up,
7: 5 in the *d'* of our king the princes
9: 5 Whtat will ye do in the solemn *d'*,
5 in the *d'* of the feast of the Lord?
10:14 Beth-arbel in the *d'* of battle:
Joe 1:15 for the *d'*! for the *d'* of the Lord
2: 1 the *d'* of the Lord cometh, for it is
2 A *d'* of darkness and of gloominess
2 *d'* of clouds and of thick darkness,
11 the *d'* of the Lord is great and very
31 and the terrible *d'* of the Lord come.
3:14 *d'* of the Lord is near in the valley
18 it shall come to pass in that *d'*,
Am 1:14 in the *d'* of battle, with a tempest
14 in the *d'* of the whirlwind:
2:16 shall flee away naked in that *d'*,
3:14 in the *d'* that I shall visit the
5: 8 and maketh the *d'* dark with night:
18 you that desire the *d'* of the Lord!
18 the *d'* of the Lord is darkness,
20 not the *d'* of the Lord be darkness,
6: 3 Ye that put far away the evil *d'*,
8: 3 temple shall be howlings in that *d'*,
9 it shall come to pass in that *d'*,
9 darken the earth in the clear *d'*:
10 the end thereof as a bitter *d'*.
13 In that *d'* shall the fair virgins
9:11 In that *d'* will I raise up the
Ob 8 shall I not in that *d'*, saith the Lord,
11 in the *d'* that thou stoodest on the
11 in the *d'* that the strangers
12 *d'* of thy brother in the *d'* that he
12 in the *d'* of their destruction;
12 spoken proudly in the *d'* of distress.
13 people in the *d'* of their calamity;
13 affliction in the *d'* of their calamity,
13 in the *d'* of their calamity;
14 did remain in the *d'* of distress.
15 the *d'* of the Lord is near upon all
Jon 4: 7 the morning rose the next *d'*,
Mic 2: 4 In that *d'* shall one take up
3: 6 the *d'* shall be dark over them.
4: 6 In that *d'*, saith the Lord, will I
5:10 it shall come to pass in that *d'*,
7: 4 the *d'* of thy watchmen and thy
11 *d'* that thy walls are to be built,
11 *d'* shall the decree be far removed.
12 In that *d'* also he shall come
Na 1: 7 a strong hold in the *d'* of trouble;
2: 3 in the *d'* of his preparation, and
3:17 camp in the hedges in the cold *d'*,
Hab 3:16 I might rest in the *d'* of trouble:
Zep 1: 7 the *d'* of the Lord is at hand:
8 come to pass in the *d'* of the Lord's
9 In the same *d'* also will I punish
10 it shall come to pass in that *d'*,
14 The great *d'* of the Lord is near,
14 the voice of the *d'* of the Lord:
15 That *d'* is a *d'* of wrath,
15 a *d'* of trouble and distress,
Zep 1:15 a *d'* of wasteness and desolation,
15 a *d'* of darkness and gloominess,
15 a *d'* of clouds and thick darkness,
16 A *d'* of the trumpet and alarm
18 in the *d'* of the Lord's wrath;
2: 2 before the *d'* pass as the chaff,
2 before the *d'* of the Lord's anger
3 hid in the *d'* of the Lord's anger.
4 drive out Ashdod at the noon *d'*,
3: 8 the *d'* that I rise up to the prey:
11 that *d'* shalt thou not be ashamed
16 that *d'* it shall be said to Jerusalem,
Hag 1: 1 in the first *d'* of the month, came
15 In the four and twentieth *d'* of the
2: 1 one and twentieth *d'* of the month,
10 In the four and twentieth *d'* of the
15 consider from this *d'* and upward,
18 now from this *d'* and upward,
18 four and twentieth *d'* of the ninth
18 from the *d'* that the foundation of
19 from this *d'* will I bless you.
20 four and twentieth *d'* of the month,
23 In that *d'*, saith the Lord of hosts,
Zec 1: 7 the four and twentieth *d'* of the
2:11 be joined to the Lord in that *d'*,
3: 9 the iniquity of that land in one *d'*.
10 In that *d'*, saith the Lord of hosts,
4:10 despised the *d'* of small things?
6:10 come thou the same *d'*, and go
7: 1 the fourth *d'* of the ninth month,
8: 9 in the *d'* that the foundation of
9:12 even to *d'* do I declare that I will
16 their God shall save them in that *d'*
11:11 And it was broken in that *d'*: and
12: 3 in that *d'* will I make Jerusalem
4 that *d'*, saith the Lord, I will smite
6 that *d'* will I make the governors
8 that *d'* shall the Lord defend the
8 he that is feeble . . . at that *d'*
9 it shall come to pass in that *d'*,
11 in that *d'* shall there be a great
13: 1 In that *d'* there shall be a fountain
2 it shall come to pass in that *d'*,
4 in that *d'*, that the prophets shall
14: 1 *d'* of the Lord cometh, and thy
3 when he fought in the *d'* of battle.
4 his feet shall stand in that *d'*
6 it shall come to pass in that *d'*,
7 be one *d'* which shall be known
7 to the Lord, not *d'*, nor night:
8 be in that *d'*, that living waters
9 in that *d'* shall there be one Lord,
13 it shall come to pass in that *d'*,
20 In that *d'* shall there be upon the
21 in that *d'* there shall be no more
Mal 3: 2 who may abide the *d'* of his coming?
17 that *d'* when I make up my jewels;
4: 1 the *d'* cometh, that shall burn as an
1 and the *d'* that cometh shall burn
3 in the *d'* that I shall do this,
5 great and dreadful *d'* of the Lord:
M't 6:11 Give us this *d'* our daily bread.
30 the grass of the field, which to *d'* is,
34 Sufficient unto the *d'* is the evil
7:22 Many will say to me in that *d'*,
10:15 in the *d'* of judgment, than for that
11:22 for Tyre and Sidon at the *d'* of
23 would have remained until this *d'*.
24 of Sodom in the *d'* of judgment,
12: 1 Jesus went on the sabbath *d'*
2 lawful to do upon the sabbath *d'*.
8 is Lord even of the sabbath *d'*.
11 fall into a pit on the sabbath *d'*,
36 thereof in the *d'* of judgment.
13: 1 The same *d'* went Jesus out of
16: 3 It will be foul weather to *d'*: for
21 and be raised again the third *d'*.
17:23 third *d'* he shall be raised again.
20: 2 with the laborers for a penny a *d'*,
6 Why stand ye here all the *d'* idle?
12 the burden and heat of the *d'*.
19 the third *d'* he shall rise again.
21:28 Son, go work to *d'* in my vineyard.
22:23 *d'* came to him the Sadducees,
46 any man from that *d'* forth ask
24:20 winter, neither on the sabbath *d'*:
36 *d'* and hour knoweth no man,
38 until the *d'* that Noe entered into
50 a *d'* when he looketh not for him,
25:13 know neither the *d'* nor the hour
26: 5 But they said, not on the feast *d'*,
17 the first *d'* of the feast of unleavened
29 *d'* when I drink it new with you
27: 8 The field of blood, unto this *d'*.
19 suffered many things this *d'* in a
62 Now the next *d'*, that followed
62 the *d'* of the preparation,
64 be made sure until the third *d'*,
28: 1 began to dawn toward the first *d'*
15 among the Jews until this *d'*.
M'r 1:21 on the sabbath *d'* he entered into
35 rising up a great while before *d'*,
2:23 the corn fields on the sabbath *d'*;
24 why do they on the sabbath *d'*
3: 2 would heal him on the sabbath *d'*;
4:27 sleep, and rise night and *d'*, and
35 same *d'*, when the even was come,
5: 5 And always, night and *d'*, he was
6: 2 when the sabbath *d'* was come,
11 Gomorrha in the *d'* of judgment,
21 when a convenient *d'* was come,
35 And when the *d'* was now far spent,
9:31 killed, he shall rise the third *d'*.
10:34 the third *d'* he shall rise again.
13:32 of that *d'* and that hour knoweth
14: 2 But they said, Not on the feast *d'*,

M'r 14:12 the first d' of unleavened bread,
25 until that d' that I drink it new
30 That this d', even in this night,
15:42 that is, the d' before the sabbath,
16: 2 first d' of the week, they came unto
9 risen early the first d' of the week,
Lu 1:20 not able to speak, until the d' that
59 eighth d' they came to circumcise
80 deserts till the d' of his shewing
2:11 unto you is born this d' in the city
37 fastings and prayers night and d'.
4:16 the synagogue on the sabbath d',
21 This d' is this scripture fulfilled
42 And when it was d', he departed
5:17 a certain d', as he was teaching,
26 We have seen strange things to d'.
6: 7 he would heal on the sabbath d';
13 when it was d', he called
23 Rejoice ye in that d', and leap for
7:11 the d' after, that he went into a
8:22 it came to pass on a certain d',
9:12 when the d' began to wear away,
22 slain, and be raised the third d'.
37 that on the next d', when they
10:12 more tolerable in that d' for Sodom,
11: 3 d' by d' our daily bread.
12:28 grass, which is to d' in the field
46 d' when he looketh not for him,
13:14 healed on the sabbath d', and
14 healed, and not on the sabbath d'.
16 from this bond on the sabbath d'?
31 The same d' there came certain
32 I do cures to d' and to morrow,
32 the third d' I shall be perfected
33 Nevertheless I must walk to d',
33 and the d' following: for it cannot
14: 1 to eat bread on the sabbath d',
3 lawful to heal on the sabbath d'?
5 pull him out on the sabbath d'?
16:19 fared sumptuously every d':
17: 4 seven times in a d', and seven
4 times in a d' turn again to thee,
24 also the Son of man be in his d'.
27 d' that Noe entered into the ark,
29 same d' that Lot went out of Sodom
30 d' when the Son of man is revealed.
31 In that d', he which shall be upon
18: 7 which cry d' and night unto him,
33 the third d' he shall rise again.
19: 5 to d' I must abide at thy house.
9 d' is salvation come to this house,
42 at least in this thy d', the things
21:34 that d' come upon you unawares.
37 And in the d' time he was teaching
22: 7 came the d' of unleavened bread,
34 the cock shall not crow this d',
66 as soon as it was d', the elders
23:12 the same d' Pilate and Herod were
43 I say unto thee, To d' shalt thou
54 that d' was the preparation, and
56 rested the sabbath d' according to
24: 1 Now upon the first d' of the week,
7 and the third d' rise again.
13 them went that same d' to a village
21 and beside all this, to d' is
21 is the third d' since these things
29 evening, and the d' is far spent.
46 rise from the dead the third d':
Joh 1:29 next d' John seeth Jesus coming
35 the next d' after John stood, and
39 abode with him that d': for it
43 d' following Jesus would go forth
2: 1 the third d' there was a marriage
23 at the passover, in the feast d',
5: 9 on the same d' was the sabbath.
10 is the sabbath d': it is not lawful
16 these things on the sabbath d'.
6:22 The d' following, when the people
39 raise it up again at the last d'.
40, 44, 54 raise him up at the last d'.
7:22 ye on the sabbath d' circumcise a
23 If a man on the sabbath d' receive
23 whit whole on the sabbath d'?
37 In the last d', that great
37 that great d' of the feast, Jesus
8:56 Abraham rejoiced to see my d':
9: 4 him that sent me, while it is d':
14 And it was the sabbath d' when
16 he keepeth not the sabbath d'.
11: 9 there not twelve hours in the d'?
9 If any man walk in the d',
24 in the resurrection at the last d'.
53 Then from that d' forth they took
12: 7 against the d' of my burying hath
12 On the next d' much people that
48 same shall judge him in the last d'.
14:20 At that d' ye shall know that I
16:23 in that d' ye shall ask me nothing.
26 At that d' ye shall ask in my name:
19:31 upon the cross on the sabbath d',
31 (for that sabbath d' was an high
31 was an high d') besought
42 of the Jews' preparation d';
20: 1 The first d' of the week cometh
19 the same d' at evening, being the
19 first d' of the week, when the doors
Ac 1: 2 Until the d' in which he was taken
22 John, unto that same d' that he was
2: 1 the d' of Pentecost was fully come,
15 it is but the third hour of the d'.
20 before that great and notable d' of
29 sepulchre is with us unto this d'.
41 the same d' there were added unto
4: 3 put them in hold unto the next d':
9 If we this d' be examined of the
7: 8 and circumcised him the eighth d';

Ac 7:26 And the next d' he shewed himself
9:24 watched the gates d' and night to
10: 3 the ninth hour of the d' an angel of
40 Him God raised up the third d',
12:18 Now as soon as it was d', there was
21 And upon a set d' Herod, arrayed in
13:14 the synagogue on the sabbath d',
27 which are read every sabbath d',
33 Son, this d' have I begotten thee.
44 And the next sabbath d' came
14:20 the next d' he departed with
15:21 the synagogues every sabbath d'.
16:11 Samothracia, and the next d' to
35 when it was d', the magistrates
17:31 Because he hath appointed a d', in
20: 7 And upon the first d' of the week,
11 a long while, even till break of d',
15 next d' over against Chios; and
15 the next d' we arrived at Samos,
15 and the next d' we came to Miletus.
16 at Jerusalem the d' of Pentecost.
18 from the first d' that I came into
26 I take you to record this d',
31 warn every one night and d' with
21: 1 and the d' following unto Rhodes,
7 and abode with them one d'.
8 the next d' we that were of Paul's
18 And the d' following Paul went
26 and the next d' purifying himself
22: 3 toward God, as ye all are this d'.
23: 1 conscience before God until this d'.
12 And when it was d', certain of the
24:21 called in question by you this d'.
25: 6 and the next d' sitting on the
26: 2 I shall answer for myself this d'
7 serving God d' and night, hope to
22 I continue unto this d', witnessing
29 but also all that hear me this d',
27: 3 And the next d' we touched at Sidon.
18 the next d' they lightened the ship;
19 And the third d' we cast out with
29 stern, and wished for the d'.
33 while the d' was coming on,
33 to take meat, saying, This d' is
33 is the fourteenth d' that ye have
39 And when it was d', they knew not
28:13 after one d' the south wind blew,
16 we came the next d' to Puteoli:
23 when they had appointed him a d',
Ro 2: 5 the d' of wrath and revelation
16 In the d' when God shall judge
8:36 we are killed all the d' long;
10:21 All d' long I have stretched forth
11: 8 not hear;) unto this d'.
13:12 the d' is at hand: let us therefore
13 Let us walk honestly, as in the d';
14: 5 esteemeth one d' above another:
5 another esteemeth every d' alike.
6 that regardeth the d', regardeth
6 and he that regardeth not the d',
1Co 1: 8 in the d' of our Lord Jesus Christ.
3:13 for the d' shall declare it, because
4:13 of all things unto this d'.
5: 5 saved in the d' of the Lord Jesus.
10: 8 one d' three and twenty thousand.
15: 4 he rose again the third d' according
16: 2 Upon the first d' of the week let
2Co 1:14 ours in the d' of the Lord Jesus.
3:14 for until this d' remaineth
15 unto this d', when Moses is read,
4:16 inward man is renewed d' by d'.
6: 2 d' of salvation have I succoured
2 behold, now is the d' of salvation.)
11:25 a night and a d' I have been in the
Eph 4:30 sealed unto the d' of redemption.
6:13 to withstand in the evil d', and
Ph'p 1: 5 gospel from the first d' until now;
6 it until the d' of Jesus Christ:
10 without offence till the d' of Christ;
2:16 I may rejoice in the d' of Christ,
3: 5 Circumcised the eighth d', of the
Col 1: 6 since the d' ye heard of it, and
9 we also, since the d' we heard it,
1Th 2: 9 for labouring night and d', because
3:10 Night and d' praying exceedingly
5: 2 d' of the Lord so cometh as a thief
4 that that d' should overtake you
5 of light, and the children of the d':
8 But let us, who are of the d',
2Th 1:10 among you was believed) in that d'.
2: 2 as that the d' of Christ is at hand.
3 for that d' shall not come, except
3: 8 labour and travail night and d',
1Ti 5: 5 and prayers night and d'.
2Ti 1: 3 thee in my prayers night and d';
12 committed unto him against that d'.
18 find mercy of the Lord in that d':
4: 8 judge, shall give me at that d':
Heb 1: 5 this d' have I begotten thee?
3: 7 saith, To d' if ye will hear his voice,
8 d' of temptation in the wilderness:
13 while it is called To d'; lest any of
15 While it is said, To d' if ye will hear
4: 4 in a certain place of the seventh d'
4 And God did rest the seventh d'
7 Again, he limiteth a certain d',
7 To d', after so long a time,
7 To d' if ye will hear his voice,
8 have spoken of another d'.
5: 5 my Son, to d' have I begotten thee.
8: 9 d' when I took them by the hand
10:25 as ye see the d' approaching.
13: 8 yesterday, and to d', and for ever.
Jas 4:13 ye that say, To d' or to morrow we
5: 5 hearts, as in a d' of slaughter.
1Pe 2:12 glorify God in the d' of visitation.

2Pe 1:19 in a dark place, until the d' dawn,
19 the d' star arise in your hearts:
2: 8 his righteous soul from d' to d'
9 the d' of judgment to be punished:
13 in pleasure to riot in the d' time.
3: 7 against the d' of judgment and
8 d' is with the Lord as a thousand
8 and a thousand years as one d'.
10 But the d' of the Lord will come
12 unto the coming of the d' of God,
1Jo 4:17 boldness in the d' of judgment:
Jude 6 unto the judgment of the great d'.
Re 1:10 I was in the Spirit on the Lord's d',
4: 8 and they rest not d' and night,
6:17 the great d' of his wrath is come;
7:15 him d' and night in his temple:
8:12 d' shone not for a third part of it,
9:15 for an hour, and a d', and a month,
12:10 them before our God d' and night.
14:11 and they have no rest d' nor night,
16:14 of that great d' of God Almighty.
18: 8 shall her plagues come in one d',
20:10 d' and night for ever and ever.
21:25 shall not be shut at all by d':

day's
Nu 11:31 it were a d' journey on this side,
31 were a d' journey on the other side,
1Ki 19: 4 he himself went a d' journey
1Ch 16:37 continually, as every d' work
Es 9:13 according unto this d' decree, and
Jon 3: 4 a d' journey, and he cried, and said,
Lu 2:44 a d' journey; and they sought
Ac 1:12 Jerusalem a sabbath d' journey.
19:40 in question for this d' uproar,

days
Ge 1:14 for seasons, and for d', and years:
3:14 shalt thou eat all the d' of thy life:
17 eat of it all the d' of thy life;
5: 4 d' of Adam after he had begotten
5 the d' that Adam lived were nine
8 the d' of Seth were nine hundred
11 the d' of Enos were nine hundred
14 d' of Cainan were nine hundred
17 d' of Mahalaleel were eight hundred
20 the d' of Jared were nine hundred
23 the d' of Enoch were three hundred
27 d' of Methuselah were nine hundred
31 d' of Lamech were seven hundred
6: 3 d' shall be an hundred and twenty
4 giants in the earth in those d';
7: 4 For yet seven d', and I will cause it
4 to rain upon the earth forty d'
10 it came to pass after seven d',
12 the rain was upon the earth forty d'
17 flood was forty d' upon the earth;
24 the earth an hundred and fifty d'.
8: 3 the end of the hundred and fifty d'
6 at the end of forty d', that Noah
10, 12 he stayed yet other seven d';
9:29 the d' of Noah were nine hundred
10:25 in his d' was the earth divided;
11:32 d' of Terah were two hundred and
14: 1 to pass in the d' of Amraphel
17:12 he that is eight d' old shall be
21: 4 being eight d' old, as God had
34 in the Philistines' land many d'.
24:55 the damsel abide with us a few d',
25: 7 the d' of the years of Abraham's
24 her d' to be delivered were fulfilled,
26: 1 that was in the d' of Abraham.
15 servants had digged in the d'
18 in the d' of Abraham his father;
27:41 The d' of mourning for my father
44 him a few d', until thy brother's
29:20 they seemed unto him but a few d',
21 my d' are fulfilled, that I may go
30:14 in the d' of wheat harvest, and
35:28 the d' of Isaac were an hundred
29 his people, being old and full of d':
37:34 and mourned for his son many d'.
40:12 The three branches are three d':
13 Yet within three d' shall Pharaoh
18 The three baskets are three d':
19 within three d' shall Pharaoh lift
42:17 all together into ward three d'.
47: 9 d' of the years of my pilgrimage
9 and evil have the d' of the years of
9 and have not attained unto the d'
9 in the d' of their pilgrimage.
49: 1 which shall befall you in the last d'.
50: 3 forty d' were fulfilled for him; for
3 d' of those which are embalmed:
3 for him threescore and ten d'.
4 the d' of his mourning were past,
10 a mourning for his father seven d'.
Ex 2:11 And it came to pass in those d',
7:25 seven d' were fulfilled, after that
10:22 in all the land of Egypt three d':
23 any from his place for three d':
12:15 d' shall ye eat unleavened bread;
19 Seven d' shall there be no leaven
13: 6 d' thou shalt eat unleavened bread,
7 bread shall be eaten seven d';
15:22 went three d' in the wilderness,
16:26 Six d' ye shall gather it;
29 the sixth day the bread of two d';
20: 9 Six d' shalt thou labour, and do all
11 d' the Lord made heaven and earth,
12 thy d' may be long upon the land
22:30 seven d' it shall be with his dam;
23:12 Six d' thou shalt do thy work,
15 eat unleavened bread seven d',
26 the number of thy d' I will fulfil.
24:16 the cloud covered it six d': and the
18 Moses was in the mount forty d'

Ex 29:30 shall put them on seven d', when
35 d' shalt thou consecrate them.
37 Seven d' thou shalt make an
31:15 Six d' may work be done; but in
17 in six d' the Lord made heaven and
34:18 Seven d' thou shalt eat unleavened
21 Six d' thou shalt work, but on the
28 he was there with the Lord forty d'
35: 2 Six d' shall work be done, but on
Le 8:33 in seven d', until the d' of your
33 seven d' shall he consecrate you.
35 congregation day and night seven d',
12: 2 she shall be unclean seven d';
2 according to the d' of the separation
4 her purifying three and thirty d';
4 the d' of her purifying be fulfilled.
5 her purifying threescore and six d'.
6 the d' of her purifying are fulfilled,
13: 4 him that hath the plague seven d':
5 shall shut him up seven d' more:
21, 26 shall shut him up seven d':
31 the plague of the scall seven d':
33 up him that hath the scall seven d'
46 All the d' wherein the plague shall
50 up it that hath the plague seven d':
54 he shall shut it up seven d' more:
14: 8 abroad out of his tent seven d'.
38 and shut up the house seven d':
15:13 he shall number to himself seven d'
19 she shall be put apart seven d':
24 he shall be unclean seven d'; and
25 many d' out of the time of her
25 d' of the issue of her uncleanness
25 shall be as the d' of her separation:
26 she lieth all the d' of her issue
28 shall number to herself seven d',
22:27 it shall be seven d' under the dam;
23: 3 Six d' shall work be done: but the
6 seven d' ye must eat unleavened
8 made by fire unto the Lord seven d':
16 sabbath shall ye number fifty d';
34 tabernacles for seven d' unto the
36 Seven d' ye shall offer an offering
39 a feast unto the Lord seven d':
40 before the Lord your God seven d'.
41 unto the Lord seven d' in the year.
42 Ye shall dwell in booths seven d';
Nu 6: 4 All the d' of his separation shall he
5 the d' of the vow of his separation
5 his head: until the d' be fulfilled,
6 the d' that he separateth himself
8 All the d' of his separation he is
12 the d' of his separation, and shall
12 the d' that were before shall be lost,
13 d' of his separation are fulfilled:
9:19 upon the tabernacle many d', then
20 when the cloud was a few d'
22 whether it were two d', or a month,
10:10 and in your solemn d', and in the
11:19 shall not eat one day nor two d',
19 five d', neither ten d', nor twenty d';
12:14 she not be ashamed seven d'?
14 shut out from the camp seven d',
15 shut out from the camp seven d':
13:25 searching of the land after forty d'.
14:34 After the number of the d' in
34 even forty d', each day for a year,
19:11 any man shall be unclean seven d'.
14 the tent, shall be unclean seven d'.
16 a grave, shall be unclean seven d'.
20:29 they mourned for Aaron thirty d',
24:14 do to thy people in the latter d'.
28:17 seven d' shall unleavened bread be
24 daily, throughout the seven d',
29:12 a feast unto the Lord seven d':
31:19 abide without the camp seven d':
De 1:46 ye abode in Kadesh many d',
46 according unto the d' that ye abode
2: 1 we compassed mount Seir many d'.
4: 9 from thy heart all the d' of thy life:
10 fear me all the d' that they shall live
26 shall not prolong your d' upon it,
30 even in the latter d', if thou turn
32 ask now of the d' that are past,
40 prolong thy d' upon the earth,
5:13 Six d' thou shalt labour, and do all
16 that thy d' may be prolonged, and
33 that ye may prolong your d' in the
6: 2 all the d' of thy life; and that thy d'
9: 9 I abode in the mount forty d'
11 at the end of forty d' and forty
18 the Lord, as at the first, forty d'
25 I fell down before the Lord forty d'
10:10 according to the first time, forty d'
11: 9 that ye may prolong your d' in the
21 That your d' may be multiplied,
21 and the d' of your children,
21 give them, as the d' of heaven
12: 1 all the d' that ye live upon the
16: 3 seven d' shalt thou eat unleavened
3 of Egypt all the d' of thy life.
4 with thee in all thy coast seven d';
8 Six d' thou shalt eat unleavened
13 the feast of tabernacles seven d',
15 Seven d' shalt thou keep a solemn
17: 9 the judge that shall be in those d',
19 read therein all the d' of his life:
20 that he may prolong his d' in his
19:17 judges, which shall be in those d';
22: 7 that thou mayest prolong thy d'.
19, 29 may not put her away all his d'.
23: 6 their prosperity all thy d' for ever.
25:15 that thy d' may be lengthened in
26: 3 the priest that shall be in those d',
30:18 ye shall not prolong your d' upon
20 is thy life, and the length of thy d':

De 31:14 thy d' approach that thou must die:
29 evil will befall you in the latter d';
32: 7 Remember the d' of old, consider
47 ye shall prolong your d' in the land,
33:25 and as thy d', so shall thy strength
34: 8 in the plains of Moab thirty d':
8 so the d' of weeping and mourning
Jos 1: 5 before thee all the d' of thy life:
11 within three d' ye shall pass over
2:16 hide yourselves there three d'.
22 mountain and abode there three d',
3: 2 it came to pass after three d',
4:14 feared Moses, all the d' of his life.
6: 3 once. Thus shalt thou do six d'.
14 the camp: so they did six d'.
9:16 the end of three d' after they had
20: 6 priest that shall be in those d':
22: 3 left your brethren these many d'
24:31 Israel served the Lord all the d' of
31 Joshua, and all the d' of the elders
J'g 2: 7 people served the Lord all the d' of
7 Joshua, and all the d' of the elders
18 their enemies all the d' of the judge:
5: 6 In the d' of Shamgar the son of
6 Anath, in the d' of Jael,
8:28 forty years in the d' of Gideon.
11:40 of Jephthah the Gileadite four d'
14:12 the seven d' of the feast, and find it
14 they could not in three d' expound
17 she wept before him the seven d',
15:20 d' of the Philistines twenty years.
17: 6 In those d' there was no king in
18: 1 those d' there was no king in Israel:
1 in those d' the tribe of the Danites
19: 1 it came to pass in those d', when
4 he abode with him three d': so
20:27 of God was there in those d',
28 stood before it in those d'), saying,
21:25 those d' there was no king in Israel:
Ru 1: 1 in the d' when the judges ruled,
1Sa 1:11 unto the Lord all the d' of his life,
2:31 d' come, that I will cut off thine
3: 1 the Lord was precious in those d';
7:13 against the Philistines all the d' of
15 Samuel judged Israel all the d' of
9:20 thine asses that were lost three d'
10: 8 d' shalt thou tarry, till I come
13: 8 he tarried seven d', according to
11 thou camest not within the d'
14:52 against the Philistines all the d' of
17:12 an old man in the d' of Saul.
16 and presented himself forty d'.
18:26 law: and the d' were not expired.
20:19 when thou hast staid three d',
21: 5 kept from us about these three d',
25:10 there be many servants now a d'
28 not been found in thee all thy d'.
38 it came to pass about ten d' after,
28: 1 it came to pass in those d', that the
29: 3 which hath been with me these d',
30:12 nor drunk any water, three d' and
13 because three d' agone I fell sick.
31:13 at Jabesh, and fasted seven d'.
2Sa 1: 1 David had abode two d' in Ziklag;
7:12 when thy d' be fulfilled, and thou
16:23 which he counselled in those d',
20: 4 the men of Judah within three d',
21: 1 was a famine in the d' of David
9 the d' [3117] of harvest, in the first d',
24: 8 end of nine months and twenty d'.
1Ki 2: 1 the d' of David drew nigh that he
11 And the d' that David reigned over
38 Shimei dwelt in Jerusalem many d'.
3: 2 the name of the Lord, until those d'.
13 the kings like unto thee all thy d'.
14 walk, then I will lengthen thy d'.
4:21 served Solomon all the d' of his life.
25 Beer-sheba, all the d' of Solomon.
8:40 fear thee all the d' that they live
65 d' and seven d', even fourteen d'.
10:21 nothing accounted of in the d' of
11:12 in thy d' I will not do it for David
25 to Israel all the d' of Solomon,
34 him prince all the d' of his life.
12: 5 Depart yet for three d', then come
14:20 the d' which Jeroboam reigned
30 and Jeroboam all their d'.
15: 5 commanded him all the d' of his
6 and Jeroboam all the d' of his life.
14 perfect with the Lord all his d'.
16, 32 Baasha king of Israel all their d'.
16:15 did Zimri reign seven d' in Tirzah.
34 In his d' did Hiel the Beth-elite
17:15 and her house, did eat many d'.
18: 1 it came to pass after many d',
19: 8 the strength of that meat forty d'
20:29 one over against the other seven d'.
21:29 evil in his d': but in his son's d'
22:46 which remained in the d' of his
2Ki 2:17 sought three d', but found him not.
8:20 In his d' Edom revolted from
10:32 In those d' the Lord began to cut
12: 2 d' wherein Jehoiada the priest
13: 3 the son of Hazael, all their d'.
22 oppressed Israel all the d' of
15:18 he departed not all his d' from the
29 In the d' of Pekah king of Israel
37 In those d' the Lord began to send
18: 4 unto those d' the children of Israel
20: 1 In those d' was Hezekiah sick
6 I will add unto thy d' fifteen years;
17 Behold, the d' come, that all that is
19 if peace and truth be in my d'?
23:22 from the d' of the judges that
22 Israel, nor in all the d' of the kings
29 In his d' Pharaoh-nechoh king of

2Ki 24: 1 In his d' Nebuchadnezzar king of
25:29 continually before him all the d' of
30 for every day, all the d' of his life.
1Ch 1:19 because in his d' the earth was
4:41 the d' of Hezekiah king of Judah,
5:10 in the d' of Saul they made war
17 In the d' of Jotham king of Judah,
17 in the d' of Jeroboam king of Israel.
7: 2 number was in the d' of David
22 their father mourned many d', and
9:25 and were to come after seven d'
10:12 oak in Jabesh, and fasted seven d'.
12:39 they were with David three d',
13: 3 enquired not at it in the d' of Saul.
17:11 when thy d' be expired that thou
21:12 else three d' the sword of the Lord,
22: 9 and quietness unto Israel in his d'.
23: 1 when David was old and full of d',
29:15 our d' on the earth are as a shadow,
28 age, full of d', riches, and honour:
2Ch 7: 8 Solomon kept the feast seven d',
9 seven d', and the feast seven d'.
9:20 accounted of in the d' of Solomon.
10: 5 Come again unto me after three d'.
13:20 recover strength again in the d' of
14: 1 In his d' the land was quiet
15:17 heart of Asa was perfect all his d'.
20:25 three d' in gathering of the spoil,
21: 8 In his d' the Edomites revolted
24: 2 in the sight of the Lord all the d'
14 continually all the d' of Jehoiada.
15 was full of d' when he died;
26: 5 sought God in the d' of Zechariah,
29:17 the house of the Lord in eight d';
30:21 feast of unleavened bread seven d'
22 eat throughout the feast seven d',
23 took counsel to keep other seven d':
23 and they kept other seven d'
32:24 In those d' Hezekiah was sick to
26 upon them in the d' of Hezekiah.
34:33 all his d' they departed not from
35:17 feast of unleavened bread seven d'.
18 from the d' of Samuel the prophet;
36: 9 reigned three months and ten d'
Ezr 4: 2 him since the d' of Esar-haddon
5 their purpose, all the d' of Cyrus
7 d' of Artaxerxes wrote Bishlam,
6:22 feast of unleavened bread seven d'
8:15 there abode we in tents three d':
32 and abode there three d'.
9: 7 d' of our fathers have we been
10: 8 would not come within three d',
9 unto Jerusalem within three d'.
Ne 1: 4 wept, and mourned certain d',
2:11 Jerusalem, and was there three d'.
5:18 in ten d' store of all sorts of wine:
6:15 month Elul, in fifty and two d'.
17 in those d' the nobles of Judah
8:17 since the d' of Jeshua the son of
18 they kept the feast seven days;
12: 7 their brethren in the d' of Jeshua.
12 in the d' of Joiakim were priests,
22 The Levites in the d' of Eliashib,
23 until the d' of Johanan the son of
26 These were in the d' of Joiakim
26 the d' of Nehemiah the governor,
46 in the d' of David and Asaph of old
47 in the d' of Zerubbabel,
47 and in the d' of Nehemiah,
13: 6 after certain d' obtained I leave of
15 In those d' saw I in Judah some
23 In those d' also saw I Jews that
Es 1: 1 to pass in the d' of Ahasuerus,
2 That in those d', when the king
4 excellent majesty many d', even
4 an hundred and fourscore d'.
5 when these d' were expired, the
5 both unto great and small, seven d',
2:12 so were the d' of their purifications
21 In those d', while Mordecai sat in
4:11 in unto the king these thirty d'.
16 neither eat nor drink three d',
9:22 As the d' wherein the Jews rested
22 should make them d' of feasting
26 they called these d' Purim after
27 that they would keep these two d'
28 these d' should be remembered
28 these d' of Purim should not fail
31 confirm these d' of Purim in their
Job 1: 5 the d' of their feasting were gone
2:13 with him upon the ground seven d'
3: 6 be joined unto the d' of the year,
7: 1 d' also like the d' of an hireling?
6 My d' are swifter than a weaver's
16 me alone; for my d' are vanity.
8: 9 our d' upon earth are a shadow:)
9:25 Now my d' are swifter than a post:
10: 5 Are thy d' as the d' of man?
5 are thy years as man's d',
20 Are not my d' few? cease then,
12:12 in length of d' understanding.
14: 1 born of a woman is of few d',
5 Seeing his d' are determined, the
14 all the d' of my appointed time
15:20 man travaileth with pain all his d',
17: 1 my d' are extinct, the graves are
11 My d' are past, my purposes are
21:13 They spend their d' in wealth, and
24: 1 they that know him not see his d'?
29: 2 in the d' when God preserved me;
4 As I was in the d' of my youth,
18 I shall multiply my d' as the sand.
30:16 the d' of affliction have taken hold
27 the d' of affliction prevented me.
32: 7 D' should speak, and multitude
33:25 shall return to the d' of his youth:

Job 36:11 shall spend their d· in prosperity,
38:12 the morning since thy d·;
21 the number of thy d· is great?
42:17 Job died, being old and full of d·.
Ps 21: 4 length of d· for ever and ever.
23: 6 shall follow me all the d· of my life:
27: 4 of the Lord all the d· of my life,
34:12 loveth many d·, that he may see
37:18 The Lord knoweth the d· of the
19 d· of famine they shall be satisfied.
39: 4 the measure of my d·, what it is;
5 made my d· as an hand breadth;
44: 1 what work thou didst in their d·,
49: 5 should I fear in the d· of evil,
55:23 shall not live out half their d·;
72: 7 his d· shall the righteous flourish;
77: 5 I have considered the d· of old,
78:33 their d· did he consume in vanity,
89:29 his throne as the d· of heaven.
45 d· of his youth hast thou shortened:
90: 9 d· are passed away in thy wrath:
10 The d· of our years are threescore
12 So teach us to number our d·,
14 may rejoice and be glad all our d·.
15 d· wherein thou hast afflicted us,
94:13 him rest from the d· of adversity,
102: 3 my d· are consumed like smoke,
11 d· are like a shadow that declineth;
23 in the way, he shortened my d·.
24 me not away in the midst of my d·:
103:15 As for man, his d· are as grass:
109: 8 Let his d· be few; and let another
119:84 many are the d· of thy servant?
128: 5 of Jerusalem all the d· of thy life.
143: 5 I remember the d· of old;
144: 4 his d· are as a shadow that passeth
Pr 3: 2 For length of d·, and long life,
16 Length of d· is in her right hand;
9:11 by me thy d· shall be multiplied,
10:27 The fear of the Lord prolongeth d·:
15:15 All the d· of the afflicted are evil:
28:16 covetousness shall prolong his d·.
31:12 and not evil all the d· of her life.
Ec 2: 3 heaven all the d· of their life.
16 d· to come shall all be forgotten.
23 all his d· are sorrows, and his
5:17 his d· also he eateth in darkness,
18 all the d· of his life, which God
20 much remember the d· of his life;
6: 3 the d· of his years be many,
12 all the d· of his vain life which he
7:10 former d· were better than these?
15 In the d· of my vanity: there is a
8:12 times, and his d· be prolonged, yet
13 neither shall he prolong his d·,
15 d· of his life, which God giveth
9: 9 the d· of the life of thy vanity,
9 sun, all the d· of thy vanity:
11: 1 thou shalt find it after many d·.
8 him remember the d· of darkness;
9 cheer thee in the d· of thy youth,
12: 1 now thy Creator in the d· of thy
1 youth, while the evil d· come not,
Isa 1: 1 in the d· of Uzziah, Jotham, Ahaz,
2: 2 it shall come to pass in the last d·,
7: 1 it came to pass in the d· of Ahaz
17 d· that have not come, from the day
13:22 and her d· shall not be prolonged.
23: 7 whose antiquity is of ancient d·?
15 according to the d· of one king:
24:22 after many d· shall they be visited.
30:26 sevenfold, as the light of seven d·,
32:10 Many d· and years shall ye be
38: 1 In those d· was Hezekiah sick unto
5 I will add unto thy d· fifteen years.
10 I said in the cutting off of my d·,
20 all the d· of our life in the house of
39: 6 Behold, the d· come, that all that
8 shall be peace and truth in my d·.
51: 9 awake, as in the ancient d·, in the
53:10 he shall also prolong his d·, and
60:20 d· of thy mourning shall be ended.
63: 9 and carried them all the d· of old.
11 he remembered the d· of old,
65:20 thence an infant of d·, nor an old
20 man that hath not filled his d·:
22 as the d· of a tree are the d· of my
Jer 1: 2 in the d· of Josiah the son of
3 in the d· of Jehoiakim the son of
2:32 forgotten me d· without number.
3: 6 me in the d· of Josiah the king,
16 in those d·, saith the Lord, they
18 In those d· the house of Judah
5:18 in those d·, saith the Lord, I will
6:11 the aged with him that is full of d·.
7:32 behold, the d· come, saith the Lord,
9:25 d· come, saith the Lord, that I will
13: 6 it came to pass after many d·,
16: 9 and in your d·, the voice of mirth,
14 the d· come, saith the Lord, that it
17:11 leave them in the midst of his d·,
19: 6 the d· come, saith the Lord, that
20:18 d· should be consumed with shame?
22:30 that shall not prosper in his d·:
23: 5 Behold, the d· come, saith the Lord,
6 In his d· Judah shall be saved,
7 the d· come, saith the Lord, that
20 in the latter d· ye shall consider it
25:34 the d· of your slaughter and of your
26:18 the d· of Hezekiah king of Judah,
30: 3 the d· come, saith the Lord, that I
24 in the latter d· ye shall consider it.
31:27 Behold, the d· come, saith the Lord,
29 In those d· they shall say no more,
31 the d· come, saith the Lord, that I
33 After those d·, saith the Lord, I will

Jer 31:38 the d· come, saith the Lord, that
32:14 that they may continue many d·.
33:14 the d· come, saith the Lord, that I
15 In those d·, and at that time,
16 In those d· shall Judah be saved,
35: 1 d· of Jehoiakim the son of Josiah
7 all your d· ye shall dwell in tents;
7 that ye may live many d· in the
8 us, to drink no wine all our d·,
36: 2 from the d· of Josiah, even unto
37:16 had remained there many d·;
42: 7 it came to pass after ten d·,
46:26 as in the d· of old, saith the Lord.
48:12 the d· come, saith the Lord, that I
47 in the latter d·, saith the Lord.
49: 2 the d· come, saith the Lord, that I
39 shall come to pass in the latter d·,
50: 4, 20 In those d·, and in that time,
51:47 Therefore, behold, the d· come, that
52 Wherefore, behold, the d· come,
52:33 before him all the d· of his life.
34 his death, all the d· of his life.
La 1: 7 in the d· of her affliction and of her
7 that she had in the d· of old,
2:17 he had commanded in the d· of old:
4:18 end is near, our d· are fulfilled;
5:21 be turned; renew our d· as of old.
Eze 3:15 astonished among them seven d·.
16 came to pass at the end of seven d·,
4: 4 according to the number of the d·
5 according to the number of the d·,
5 three hundred and ninety d·: so
6 of the house of Judah forty d·:
8 thou hast ended the d· of thy siege.
9 the d· that thou shalt lie upon thy
9 side, three hundred and ninety d·
5: 2 when the d· of the siege are fulfilled:
12:22 The d· are prolonged, and every
23 The d· are at hand, and the effect
25 in your d·, O rebellious house, will
27 d· to come, and he prophesieth
16:22 the d· of thy youth, when thou wast
43 the d· of thy youth, but hast fretted
60 with thee in the d· of thy youth,
22: 4 hast caused thy d· to draw near,
14 in the d· that I shall deal with thee?
23:19 to remembrance the d· of her youth,
38: 8 After many d· thou shalt be visited:
16 it shall be in the latter d·, and I
17 which prophesied in those d·
43:25 Seven d· shalt thou prepare every
26 Seven d· shall they purge the altar
27 when these d· are expired, it shall
44:26 shall reckon unto him seven d·.
45:21 a feast of seven d·; unleavened
23 seven d· of the feast he shall
23 without blemish daily the seven d·;
25 the feast of the seven d·, according
46: 1 six working d·; but on the sabbath
Da 1:12 thy servants, I beseech thee, ten d·;
14 matter, and proved them ten d·.
15 end of ten d· their countenances
18 at the end of the d· that the king
2:28 what shall be in the latter d·.
44 And in the d· of these kings
4:34 the end of the d· I Nebuchadnezzar
5:11 and in the d· of thy father
6: 7 of any God or man for thirty d·,
12 of any God or man within thirty d·,
7: 9 and the Ancient of d· did sit,
13 and came to the Ancient of d·,
22 Until the Ancient of d· came, and
8:14 and three hundred d·;
26 for it shall be for many d·.
27 fainted, and was sick certain d·;
10: 2 In those d· I Daniel was mourning
13 withstood me one and twenty d·:
14 befall thy people in the latter d·:
14 for yet the vision is for many d·.
11:20 within few d· he shall be destroyed,
33 by captivity, and by spoil, many d·.
12:11 thousand two hundred and ninety d·.
12 hundred and five and thirty d·.
13 stand in thy lot at the end of the d·.
Ho 1: 1 in the d· of Uzziah, Jotham, Ahaz,
1 Judah, and in the d· of Jeroboam
2:11 her feast d·, her new moons,
13 I will visit upon her the d· of
15 as in the d· of her youth, and as in
3: 3 Thou shalt abide for me many d·;
4 of Israel shall abide many d·
5 and his goodness in the latter d·.
6: 2 After two d· will he revive us:
9: 7 The d· of visitation are come,
7 the d· of recompence are come;
9 as in the d· of Gibeah: therefore he
10: 9 hast sinned from the d· of Gibeah:
12: 9 as in the d· of the solemn feast.
Joe 1: 2 in your d·, or even in the d· of your
2: 29 those d· will I pour out my spirit.
3: 1 behold, in those d·, and in that
Am 1: 1 in the d· of Uzziah king of Judah,
1 in the d· of Jeroboam the son of
4: 2 the d· shall come upon you, that he
5:21 I hate, I despise your feast d·,
8:11 the d· come, saith the Lord God,
9:11 I will build it as in the d· of old:
13 the d· come, saith the Lord, that
Jon 1:17 was in the belly of the fish three d·
3: 4 Yet forty d·, and Nineveh shall be
Mic 1: 1 in the d· of Jotham, Ahaz, and
4: 1 in the last d· it shall come to pass,
7:14 and Gilead, as in the d· of old.
15 According to the d· of thy coming
20 unto our fathers from the d· of old.
Hab 1: 5 I will work a work in your d·,

Zep 1: 1 in the d· of Josiah the son of
Hag 2:16 Since those d· were, when one
Zec 8: 6 remnant of this people in these d·,
9 ye that hear in these d· these words
10 before these d· there was no hire
11 this people as in the former d·,
15 have I thought in these d· to do
23 In those d· it shall come to pass,
14: 5 in the d· of Uzziah king of Judah:
Mal 3: 4 unto the Lord, as in the d· of old,
7 from the d· of your fathers ye are
M't 2: 1 in the d· of Herod the king,
3: 1 In those d· came John the Baptist,
4: 2 when he had fasted forty d·
9:15 but the d· will come, when the
11:12 from the d· of John the Baptist
12: 5 on the sabbath d· the priests in
10 it lawful to heal on the sabbath d·?
12 lawful to do well on the sabbath d·.
40 Jonas was three d· and three
40 three d· and three nights in the
15:32 continue with me now three d·,
17: 1 And after six d· Jesus taketh Peter,
23:30 If we had been in the d· of our
24:19 to them that give suck in those d·!
22 except those d· should be shortened,
22 sake those d· shall be shortened.
29 After the tribulation of those d·
37 But as the d· of Noe were,
38 For as in the d· that were before
26: 2 after two d· is the feast of the
61 and to build it in three d·.
27:40 and buildest it in three d·, save
63 After three d· I will rise again.
M'r 1: 9 in those d·, that Jesus came from
13 there in the wilderness forty d·,
2: 1 into Capernaum after some d·;
20 But the d· will come, when the
20 then shall they fast in those d·.
26 of God in the d· of Abiathar
3: 4 to do good on the sabbath d·, or
8: 1 In those d· the multitude being
2 have now been with me three d·,
31 killed, and after three d· rise again.
9: 2 after six d· Jesus taketh with him
13:17 to them that give suck in those d·!
19 For in those d· shall be affliction,
20 had shortened those d·, no flesh
20 chosen, he hath shortened the d·.
24 in those d·, after that tribulation,
14: 1 After two d· was the feast of the
58 within three d· I will build another
15:29 temple, and buildest it in three d·,
Lu 1: 5 There was in the d· of Herod,
23 soon as the d· of his ministration
24 after those d· his wife Elisabeth
25 in the d· wherein he looked on me,
39 Mary arose in those d·, and went
75 before him, all the d· of our life.
2: 1 in those d·, that there went out a
6 the d· were accomplished that she
21 eight d· were accomplished for the
22 when the d· of her purification
43 when they had fulfilled the d·,
46 that after three d· they found him
4: 2 forty d· tempted of the devil. And
2 in those d· he did eat nothing:
25 were in Israel in the d· of Elias,
31 taught them on the sabbath d·.
5:35 But the d· will come, when the
35 then shall they fast in those d·.
6: 2 not lawful to do on the sabbath d·?
9 lawful on the sabbath d· to do good,
12 it came to pass in those d·, that he
9:28 about an eight d· after these
36 told no man in those d· any of those
13:14 There are six d· in which men
15:13 not many d· after the younger son
17:22 The d· will come, when ye shall
22 to see one of the d· of the Son of
26 as it was in the d· of Noe, so shall
26 be also in the d· of the Son of man.
28 as it was in the d· of Lot;
19:43 For the d· shall come upon thee,
20: 1 on one of those d·, as he taught
21: 6 the d· will come, in the which there
22 For these be the d· of vengeance,
23 that give suck, in these d·!
23:29 behold, the d· are coming, in the
24:18 come to pass there in these d·?
Joh 2:12 they continued there not many d·.
19 in three d· I will raise it up.
20 wilt thou rear it up in three d·?
4:40 and he abode there two d·.
43 after two d· he departed thence,
11: 6 abode two d· still in the same place
17 he had lain in the grave four d·
39 for he hath been dead four d·.
12: 1 Jesus six d· before the passover
20:26 after eight d· again his disciples
Ac 1: 3 being seen of them forty d·, and
5 the Holy Ghost not many d· hence.
15 And in those d· Peter stood up
2:17 it shall come to pass in the last d·,
18 pour out in those d· of my Spirit;
3:24 have likewise foretold of these d·.
5:36 before these d· rose up Theudas,
37 in the d· of the taxing, and drew
6: 1 And in those d·, when the number
7:41 they made a calf in those d·,
45 our fathers, unto the d· of David;
9: 9 And he was three d· without sight,
19 Saul certain d· with the disciples
23 d· were fulfilled, the Jews took
37 came to pass in those d·, that she
43 tarried many d· in Joppa with one

Ac 10:30 Four *d'* ago I was fasting until this
48 prayed they him to tarry certain *d'*
11:27 And in these *d'* came prophets
28 pass in the *d'* of Claudius Cæsar.
12: 3 were the *d'* of unleavened bread.
13:31 he was seen many *d'* of them
41 for I work a work in your *d'*,
15:36 some *d'* after Paul said unto
16:12 in that city abiding certain *d'*.
18 this did she many *d'*. But Paul,
17: 2 three sabbath *d'* reasoned with them
20: 6 Philippi after the *d'* of unleavened
6 five *d'*; where we abode seven *d'*.
21: 4 we tarried there seven *d'*: who said
5 we had accomplished those *d'*,
10 And as we tarried there many *d'*,
15 And after those *d'* we took up our
26 the accomplishment of the *d'* of
27 the seven *d'* were almost ended,
38 Egyptian, which before these *d'*
24: 1 And after five *d'* Ananias the high
11 there are yet but twelve *d'* since I
24 after certain *d'*, when Felix came
25: 1 three *d'* he ascended from Cæsarea
6 among them more than ten *d'*,
13 And after certain *d'* king Agrippa
14 when they had been there many *d'*,
27: 7 when we had sailed slowly many *d'*,
20 sun nor stars in many *d'* appeared,
28: 7 and lodged us three *d'* courteously.
12 Syracuse, we tarried there three *d'*.
14 desired to tarry with them seven *d'*:
17 after three *d'* Paul called the chief
Ga 1:18 and abode with him fifteen *d'*.
4:10 Ye observe *d'*, and months,
Eph 5:16 the time, because the *d'* are evil.
Col 2:16 the new moon, or of the sabbath *d'*.
2Ti 3: 1 last *d'* perilous times shall come.
Heb 1: 2 in these last *d'* spoken unto us
5: 7 Who in the *d'* of his flesh, when
7: 3 beginning of *d'*, nor end of life;
8: 8 Behold, the *d'* come, saith the Lord,
10 the house of Israel after those *d'*,
10:16 will make with them after those *d'*,
32 call to remembrance the former *d'*,
11:30 were compassed about seven *d'*.
12:10 they verily for a few *d'* chastened
Jas 5: 3 treasure together for the last *d'*.
1Pe 3:10 that will love life, and see good *d'*,
20 of God waited in the *d'* of Noah,
2Pe 3: 3 shall come in the last *d'* scoffers,
Re 2:10 ye shall have tribulation ten *d'*:
13 in those *d'* wherein Antipas was
9: 6 in those *d'* shall men seek death,
10: 7 But in the *d'* of the voice of the
11: 3 two hundred and threescore *d'*,
6 rain not in the *d'* of their prophecy:
9 dead bodies three *d'* and a half,
11 three *d'* and a half the Spirit of life
12: 6 two hundred and threescore *d'*.

days'
Ge 30:36 three *d'* journey betwixt himself
31:23 pursued after him seven *d'* journey;
Ex 3:18 we beseech thee, three *d'* journey
5: 3 we pray thee, three *d'* journey into
8:27 *d'* journey into the wilderness,
Nu 10:33 of the Lord three *d'* journey:
33 them in the three *d'* journey:
33: 8 three *d'* journey in the wilderness
De 1: 2 are eleven *d'* journey from Horeb
1Sa 11: 3 Give us seven *d'* respite, that we
2Sa 24:13 three *d'* pestilence in thy land?
2Ki 3: 9 a compass of seven *d'* journey:
Jon 3: 3 great city of three *d'* journey.

daysman
Job 9:33 Neither is there any *d'* betwixt us,

dayspring
Job 38:12 caused the *d'* to know his place;
Lu 1:78 *d'* from on high hath visited us,

daystar See DAY and STAR.

daytime See also DAY and TIME.
Job 5:14 They meet with darkness in the *d'*,
24:16 marked for themselves in the *d'*:
Ps 22: 2 O my God, I cry in the *d'*, but thou
42: 8 his lovingkindness in the *d'*, and in
78:14 *d'* also he led them with a cloud,
Isa 4: 6 a shadow in the *d'* from the heat,
21: 8 upon the watchtower in the *d'*,

deacon See also DEACONS.
1Ti 3:10 let them use the office of a *d'*,
13 that have used the office of a *d'*,

deacons
Ph'p 1: 1 Philippi, with the bishops and *d'*:
1Ti 3: 8 Likewise must the *d'* be grave,
12 the *d'* be the husbands of one wife,

dead
Ge 20: 3 art but a *d'* man, for the woman
23: 3 stood up from before his *d'*,
4 that I may bury my *d'* out of my
6 of our sepulchres bury thy *d'*;
6 but that thou mayest bury thy *d'*.
8 that I should bury my *d'* out of my
11 people give I it thee: bury thy *d'*.
13 and I will bury my *d'* there.
15 me and thee? bury therefore thy *d'*.
42:38 for his brother is *d'*, and he is
44:20 and his brother is *d'*, and he alone
50:15 that their father was *d'*, they said,
Ex 4:19 men are *d'* which sought thy life.
9: 7 one of the cattle of the Israelites *d'*.
12:30 a house where there was not one *d'*.
33 for they said, We be all *d'* men.
14:30 Israel saw the Egyptians *d'* upon
21:34 and the *d'* beast shall be his.
35 the *d'* ox also they shall divide.
36 and the *d'* shall be his own.
Le 11:31 when they be *d'*, shall be unclean
32 when they are *d'*, doth fall, it shall
19:28 cuttings in your flesh for the *d'*,
21: 1 shall none be defiled for the *d'*
11 shall he go in to any *d'* body,
22: 4 thing that is unclean by the *d'*,
Nu 5: 2 whosoever is defiled by the *d'*:
6: 6 he shall come at no *d'* body.
11 him, for that he sinned by the *d'*,
9: 6, 7 defiled by the *d'* body of a man,
10 unclean by the reason of a *d'* body,
12:12 Let her not be as one *d'*,
16:48 stood between the *d'* and the living;
19:11 He that toucheth the *d'* body of any
13 Whosoever toucheth the *d'* body
13 of any man that is *d'*, and
16 or a *d'* body, or a bone of a man,
18 or one slain, or one *d'*, or a grave:
20:29 that Aaron was *d'*, they mourned
De 2:16 men of war were consumed and *d'*
14: 1 between your eyes for the *d'*.
8 flesh, nor touch their *d'* carcass.
25: 5 the wife of the *d'* shall not marry
6 the name of his brother which is *d'*,
26:14 nor given ought thereof for the *d'*:
Jos 1: 2 Moses my servant is *d'*; now
J'g 2:19 the judge was *d'*, that they returned
3:25 their lord was fallen down *d'*
4: 1 of the Lord, when Ehud was *d'*.
22 into her tent, behold, Sisera lay *d'*,
5:27 he bowed, there he fell down *d'*.
8:33 as soon as Gideon was *d'*, that the
9:55 Israel saw that Abimelech was *d'*,
16:30 the *d'* which he slew at his death
20: 5 have they forced, that she is *d'*.
Ru 1: 8 as ye have dealt with the *d'*,
2:20 to the living and to the *d'*.
4: 5 the *d'*, to raise up the name of the *d'*
10 name of the *d'* upon his inheritance,
10 the name of the *d'* be not cut off
1Sa 4:17 Hophni and Phinehas, are *d'*, and
19 in law and her husband were *d'*,
17:51 saw their champion was *d'*, they
24:14 after a *d'* dog, after a flea.
25:39 David heard that Nabal was *d'*,
28: 3 Now Samuel was *d'*, and all Israel
31: 5 armourbearer saw that Saul was *d'*,
7 Saul and his sons were *d'*, they
2Sa 1: 4 the people also are fallen and *d'*;
4 Saul and Jonathan his son are *d'*
5 Saul and Jonathan his son be *d'*?
2: 7 your master Saul is *d'*, and also the
4: 1 Abner was *d'* in Hebron, his hands
10 Saul is *d'*, thinking to have brought
9: 8 such a *d'* dog as I am?
11:21 Thy servant Uriah the Hittite is *d'*
24 some of the king's servants be *d'*,
24 Uriah the Hittite is *d'* also,
26 Uriah her husband was *d'*, she
12:18 to tell him that the child was *d'*:
18 if we tell him that the child is *d'*?
19 perceived that the child was *d'*:
19 unto his servants, Is the child *d'*?
19 And they said, He is *d'*.
21 the child was *d'*, thou didst rise
23 he is *d'*, wherefore should I fast?
13:32 Amnon only is *d'*: for by the
33 that all the king's sons are *d'*:
33 for Amnon only is *d'*.
39 Amnon, seeing he was *d'*.
14: 2 a long time mourned for the *d'*:
5 woman, and mine husband is *d'*.
16: 9 this *d'* dog curse my lord the king?
18:20 because the king's son is *d'*.
19:10 we anointed over us, is *d'* in battle.
28 my father's house were but *d'* men
1Ki 3:20 laid her *d'* child in my bosom.
21 my child suck, behold, it was *d'*:
22 the *d'* is thy son. And this said,
22 No; but the *d'* is thy son, and
23 and thy son is the *d'*: and the other
23 saith, Nay; but thy son is the *d'*,
11:21 Joab the captain of the host was *d'*,
13:31 When I am *d'*, then bury me in the
21:14 saying, Naboth is stoned, and is *d'*.
15 that Naboth was stoned, and was *d'*,
15 for Naboth is not alive, but *d'*.
16 Ahab heard that Naboth was *d'*,
2Ki 3: 5 when Ahab was *d'*, that the king
4: 1 Thy servant my husband is *d'*; and
32 child was *d'*, and laid upon his bed.
8: 5 he had restored a *d'* body to life,
11: 1 of Ahaziah saw that her son was *d'*,
19:35 morning, behold, they were all *d'*
23:30 servants carried him in a chariot *d'*
1Ch 1:44 when Bela was *d'*, Jobab the son
45 And when Jobab was *d'*, Husham
46 when Husham was *d'*, Hadad
47 And when Hadad was *d'*, Samlah
48 And when Samlah was *d'*, Shaul
49 when Shaul was *d'*, Baal-hanan
50 And when Baal-hanan was *d'*,
2:19 And when Azubah was *d'*, Caleb
24 after that Hezron was *d'* in
10: 5 saw that Saul was *d'*, he fell
7 Saul and his sons were *d'*, then
2Ch 20:24 they were *d'* bodies fallen to the
25 riches with the *d'* bodies, and
22:10 Ahaziah saw that her son was *d'*,
Es 2: 7 her father and mother were *d'*,
Job 1:19 the young men, and they are *d'*;
26: 5 *D'* things are formed from under
Ps 31:12 I am forgotten as a *d'* man
76: 6 and horse are cast into a *d'* sleep.
79: 2 The *d'* bodies of thy servants
88: 5 Free among the *d'*, like the slain
10 Wilt thou shew wonders to the *d'*?
10 shall the *d'* arise and praise thee?
106:28 and ate the sacrifices of the *d'*.
110: 6 fill the places with the *d'* bodies;
115:17 The *d'* praise not the Lord,
143: 3 as those that have been long *d'*.
Pr 2:18 death, and her paths unto the *d'*.
9:18 knoweth not that the *d'* are there;
21:16 in the congregation of the *d'*.
Ec 4: 2 praised the *d'* which are already *d'*
9: 3 and after that they go to the *d'*,
4 a living dog is better than a *d'* lion.
5 but the *d'* know not any thing,
10: 1 *D'* flies cause the ointment of the
Isa 8:19 their God? for the living to the *d'*?
14: 9 it stirreth up the *d'* for thee,
22: 2 slain with the sword, nor *d'* in
26:14 They are *d'*, they shall not live;
19 Thy *d'* men shall live, together
19 with my *d'* body shall they arise.
19 the earth shall cast out the *d'*.
37:36 behold, they were all *d'* corpses.
59:10 are in desolate places as *d'* men
Jer 16: 7 to comfort them for the *d'*,
22:10 Weep ye not for the *d'*, neither
26:23 cast his *d'* body into the graves
31:40 the whole valley of the *d'* bodies,
33: 5 fill them with the *d'* bodies of men,
34:20 their *d'* bodies shall be for meat
36:30 and his *d'* body shall be cast out
41: 9 cast all the *d'* bodies of the men,
La 3: 6 as they that be *d'* of old.
Eze 6: 5 And I will lay the *d'* carcasses
24:17 make no mourning for the *d'*,
44:25 they shall come at no *d'* person
31 any thing that is *d'* of itself, or
Am 8: 3 there shall be many *d'* bodies
Hag 2:13 unclean by a *d'* body touch any of
M't 2:19 But when Herod was *d'*, behold,
20 for they are *d'* which sought the
8:22 me; and let the *d'* bury their *d'*.
9:18 My daughter is even now *d'*: but
24 for the maid is not *d'*, but sleepeth.
10: 8 lepers, raise the *d'*, cast out
11: 5 the *d'* are raised up, and the poor
14: 2 Baptist; he is risen from the *d'*;
17: 9 of man be risen again from the *d'*.
22:31 touching the resurrection of the *d'*,
32 God is not the God of the *d'*, but
23:27 within full of *d'* men's bones, and
27:64 He is risen from the *d'*: so the last
28: 4 did shake, and became as *d'* men.
7 that he is risen from the *d'*;
M'r 5:35 which said, Thy daughter is *d'*:
39 the damsel is not *d'*, but sleepeth.
6:14 the Baptist was risen from the *d'*,
16 beheaded: he is risen from the *d'*.
9: 9 Son of man were risen from the *d'*.
10 what the rising from the *d'* should
26 out of him: and he was as one *d'*;
26 insomuch that many said, He is *d'*.
12:25 when they shall rise from the *d'*,
26 as touching the *d'*, that they rise:
27 He is not the God of the *d'*,
15:44 marvelled if he were already *d'*:
44 whether he had been any while *d'*.
Lu 7:12 there was a *d'* man carried out,
15 And he that was *d'* sat up,
22 the deaf hear, the *d'* are raised,
8:49 Thy daughter is *d'*; trouble not
52 not; she is not *d'*, but sleepeth.
53 to scorn, knowing that she was *d'*.
9: 7 that John was risen from the *d'*;
60 unto him, Let the *d'* bury the *d'*:
10:30 and departed, leaving him half *d'*.
15:24 For this my son was *d'*, and is
32 for this thy brother was *d'*, and is
16:30 if one went unto them from the *d'*,
31 though one rose from the *d'*.
20:35 and the resurrection from the *d'*,
37 Now that the *d'* are raised, even
38 For he is not a God of the *d'*,
24: 5 seek ye the living among the *d'*?
46 to rise from the *d'* the third day:
Joh 2:22 therefore he was risen from the *d'*,
5:21 as the Father raiseth up the *d'*,
25 when the *d'* shall hear the voice
6:49 in the wilderness, and are *d'*.
58 fathers did eat manna, and are *d'*:
8:52 Abraham is *d'*, and the prophets;
53 Abraham, which is *d'*?
53 and the prophets are *d'*:
11:14 unto them plainly, Lazarus is *d'*.
25 though he were *d'*, yet shall he live:
39 the sister of him that was *d'*,
39 for he hath been *d'* four days.
41 the place where the *d'* was laid.
44 And he that was *d'* came forth,
12: 1 Lazarus was which had been *d'*,
1 *d'* whom he raised from the *d'*,
9 whom he had raised from the *d'*.
17 him from the *d'*, bare record.
19:33 that he was *d'* already, they brake
20: 9 he must rise again from the *d'*.
21:14 after that he was risen from the *d'*.
Ac 2:29 that he is both *d'* and buried,
3:15 God hath raised from the *d'*;
4: 2 Jesus the resurrection from the *d'*.
10 whom God raised from the *d'*, even
5:10 men came in and found her *d'*,
7: 4 thence, when his father was *d'*, he
10:41 with him after he rose from the *d'*.
42 to be the Judge of quick and *d'*.

Ac 13:30 But God raised him from the d':
34 that he raised him up from the d',
14:19 city, supposing he had been d'.
17: 3 and risen again from the d';
31 he hath raised him from the d'.
32 heard of the resurrection of the d',
20: 9 the third loft, and was taken up d'.
23: 6 the hope and resurrection of the d'
24:15 shall be a resurrection of the d',
21 Touching the resurrection of the d'
25:19 of one Jesus, which was d', whom
26: 8 you, that God should raise the d'?
23 first that should rise from the d',
28: 6 or fallen down d' suddenly: but
Ro 1: 4 by the resurrection from the d':
4:17 God, who quickeneth the d',
19 not his own body now d',
24 Jesus our Lord from the d'; Who
5:15 the offence of one many be d',
6: 2 How shall we, that are d' to sin,
4 Christ was raised up from the d'
7 For he that is d' is freed from sin.
8 if we be d' with Christ, we believe
9 raised from the d' dieth no more:
11 to be d' indeed unto sin, but alive
13 as those that are alive from the d',
7: 2 if the husband be d', she is loosed
3 if her husband be d', she is free
4 ye also are become d' to the law
4 to him who is raised from the d',
6 being d' wherein we were held;
8 For without the law sin was d'.
8:10 the body is d' because of sin;
11 up Jesus from the d' dwell in you,
11 that raised up Christ from the d'
10: 7 bring up Christ again from the d'.
9 hath raised him from the d', thou
11:15 of them be, but life from the d'?
14: 9 be Lord both of the d' and living.
1Co 7:39 but if her husband be d', she is at
15:12 preached that he rose from the d',
12 there is no resurrection of the d'?
13 if there be no resurrection of the d',
15 if so be that the d' rise not.
16 For if the d' rise not, then is not
20 now is Christ risen from the d',
21 came also the resurrection of the d'.
29 which are baptized for the d',
29 if the d' rise not at all? why are
29 they then baptized for the d'?
32 it me, if the d' rise not?
35 How are the d' raised up? and with
42 also is the resurrection of the d'.
52 the d' shall be raised incorruptible,
2Co 1: 9 but in God which raiseth the d':
5:14 one died for all, then were all d':
Ga 1: 1 who raised him from the d';
2:19 I through the law am d' to the
21 the law, then Christ is d' in vain.
Eph 1:20 when he raised him from the d',
2: 1 were d' in trespasses and sins;
5 when we were d' in sins, hath
5:14 and arise from the d', and Christ
Ph'p 3:11 unto the resurrection of the d'.
Col 1:18 the firstborn from the d';
2:12 who hath raised him from the d'.
13 And you, being d' in your sins
20 if ye be d' with Christ from the
3: 3 For ye are d', and your life is hid
1Th 1:10 whom he raised from the d', even
4:16 the d' in Christ shall rise first:
1Ti 5: 6 in pleasure is d' while she liveth.
2Ti 2: 8 of David was raised from the d'
11 For if we be d' with him, we shall
4: 1 shall judge the quick and the d'
Heb 6: 1 repentance from d' works, and of
2 and of resurrection of the d', and
9:14 your conscience from d' works to
17 of force after men are d':
11: 4 by it he being d' yet speaketh.
12 even of one, and him as good as d',
19 to raise him up, even from the d';
35 received their d' raised to life
13:20 brought again from the d' our Lord
Jas 2:17 hath not works, is d', being alone.
20 that faith without works is d'?
26 the body without the spirit is d',
26 so faith without works is d' also.
1Pe 1: 3 of Jesus Christ from the d',
21 that raised him up from the d', and
2:24 that we, being d' to sins, should
4: 5 to judge the quick and the d'.
6 preached also to them that are d',
Jude 12 without fruit, twice d', plucked
Re 1: 5 the first begotten of the d', and
17 saw him, I fell at his feet as d'.
18 I am he that liveth, and was d';
2: 8 last, which was d', and is alive;
3: 1 a name that thou livest, and art d'.
11: 8 d' bodies shall lie in the streets
9 shall see their d' bodies three days
9 shall not suffer their d' bodies to
18 time of the d', that they should
14:13 Blessed are the d' which die in the
16: 3 became as the blood of a d' man:
20: 5 the rest of the d' lived not again
12 And I saw the d', small and great,
12 and the d' were judged out of
13 gave up the d' which were in it,
13 death and hell delivered up the d'

deadly
1Sa 5:11 was a d' destruction throughout
Ps 17: 9 my d' enemies, who compass me
Eze 30:24 groanings of a d' wounded man.
M'r 16:18 and if they drink any d' thing,
Jas 3: 8 an unruly evil, full of d' poison.

Re 13: 3 d' wound was healed: and all
12 whose d' wound was healed.

deadness
Ro 4:19 yet the d' of Sarah's womb:

deaf
Ex 4:11 who maketh the dumb, or d', or
Le 19:14 Thou shalt not curse the d', nor
Ps 38:13 But I, as a d' man, heard not;
58: 4 the d' adder that stoppeth her ear;
Isa 29:18 in that day shall the d' hear
35: 5 ears of the d' shall be unstopped.
42:18 Hear, ye d'; and look, ye blind,
19 d', as my messenger that I sent?
43: 8 eyes, and the d' that have ears.
Mic 7:16 their mouth, their ears shall be d'.
M't 11: 5 and the d' hear, the dead are
M'r 7:32 was d', and had an impediment
37 he maketh both the d' to hear, and
9:25 Thou dumb and d' spirit, I charge
Lu 7:22 the d' hear, the dead are raised,

deal See also DEALEST; DEALETH; DEALING; DEALS; DEALT.
Ge 19: 9 now will we d' worse with thee,
21:23 thou wilt not d' falsely with me,
24:49 if ye will d' kindly and truly with
32: 9 and I will d' well with thee:
34:31 Should he d' with our sister as
47:29 and d' kindly and truly with me;
Ex 1:10 let us d' wisely with them; lest
8:29 let not Pharaoh d' deceitfully any
21: 9 d' with her after the manner
23:11 thou shalt d' with thy vineyard,
Ex 29:40 the one lamb a tenth d' of flour
Le 14:21 and one tenth d' of fine flour
19:11 shall not steal, neither d' falsely,
Nu 11:15 if thou d' thus with me, kill me,
15: 4 a tenth d' of flour mingled with
28:13 And a several tenth d' of flour
21 several tenth d' shalt thou offer
29 several tenth d' unto one lamb
29: 4 And one tenth d' for one lamb,
10 A several tenth d' for one lamb,
15 a several tenth d' to each lamb
De 7: 5 shall ye d' with them; ye shall
Jos 2:14 will d' kindly and truly with thee.
Ru 1: 8 the Lord d' kindly with you, as ye
1Sa 20: 8 shalt d' kindly with thy servant;
2Sa 18: 5 D' gently for my sake with the
2Ch 2: 3 didst d' with David my father,
3 dwell therein, even so d' with me
19:11 D' courageously, and the Lord
Job 42: 8 lest I d' with you after your folly,
Ps 75: 4 D' not foolishly: and to the
105:25 to d' subtilly with his servants.
119:17 D' bountifully with thy servant,
124 D' with thy servant according
142: 7 thou shalt d' bountifully with me.
Pr 12:22 they that d' truly are his delight.
Isa 26:10 of uprightness will he d' unjustly,
33: 1 an end to d' treacherously,
1 shall d' treacherously with thee.
48: 8 wouldest d' very treacherously,
52:13 my servant shall d' prudently,
58: 7 to d' thy bread to the hungry,
Jer 12: 1 happy that d' very treacherously?
18:23 d' thus with them in the time of
21: 2 Lord will d' with us according to
Eze 8:18 Therefore will I also d' in fury:
16:59 d' with thee as thou hast done
18: 9 kept my judgments, to d' truly;
22:14 the days that I shall d' with thee?
23:25 they shall d' furiously with thee:
29 they shall d' with thee hatefully,
31:11 he shall surely d' with him:
Da 1:13 thou seest, d' with thy servants.
11: 7 and shall d' against them, and
Hab 1:13 upon them that d' treacherously,
Mal 2:10 why do we d' treacherously every
15 let none d' treacherously against
16 spirit, that ye d' not treacherously.
M'r 7:36 so much the more a great d'
10:48 he cried the more a great d'.

dealer See also DEALERS.
Isa 21: 2 the treacherous d' dealeth

dealers
Isa 24:16 the treacherous d' have dealt
16 yea, the treacherous d' have dealt very

dealest
Ex 5:15 d' thou thus with thy servants?
Isa 33: 1 d' treacherously, and they dealt

dealeth
J'g 18: 4 d' Micah with me, and hath
1Sa 23:22 told me that he d' very subtilly.
Pr 10: 4 He becometh poor that d' with
13:16 prudent man d' with knowledge:
14:17 He that is soon angry d' foolishly:
21:24 his name, who d' in proud wrath.
Isa 21: 2 treacherous dealer d' treacherously;
Jer 6:13 the priest every one d' falsely.
8:10 unto the priest every one d' falsely.
Heb 12: 7 God d' with you as with sons;

dealing See also DEALINGS.
Ps 7:16 his violent d' shall come down

dealings
1Sa 2:23 of your evil d' by all this people
Joh 4: 9 had no d' with the Samaritans.

deals
Le 14:10 three tenth d' of fine flour for
23:13 two tenth d' of fine flour mingled
17 two wave loaves of two tenth d':
24: 5 two tenth d' shall be in one cake.
Nu 15: 6 two tenth d' of flour mingled

Nu 15: 9 three tenth d' of flour mingled
28: 9 and two tenth d' of flour for a
12 three tenth d' of flour for a meat
12 two tenth d' of flour for a meat
20 three tenth d' shall ye offer for a
20 and two tenth d' for a ram;
28 three tenth d' unto one bullock,
28 two tenth d' unto one ram,
29: 3 three tenth d' for a bullock,
3 and two tenth d' for a ram,
9 three tenth d' to a bullock,
9 and two tenth d' to one ram,
14 three tenth d' unto every bullock
14 two tenth d' to each ram

dealt
Ge 16: 6 when Sarai d' hardly with her
33:11 God hath d' graciously with me,
43: 6 Wherefore d' ye so ill with me,
Ex 1:20 God d' well with the midwives:
14:11 wherefore hast thou d' thus with
18:11 the thing wherein they d' proudly
21: 8 seeing he hath d' deceitfully with
J'g 9:16 if ye have d' well with Jerubbaal
19 ye then have d' truly and sincerely
23 men of Shechem d' treacherously
Ru 1: 8 as ye have d' with the dead,
20 the Almighty hath d' very bitterly
1Sa 24:18 thou hast d' well with me: for as
25:31 when the Lord shall have d' well
2Sa 6:19 And he d' among all the people,
2Ki 12:15 workmen: for they d' faithfully.
21: 6 and d' with familiar spirits and
22: 7 hand, because they d' faithfully.
1Ch 16: 3 And he d' to every one of Israel,
20: 3 so d' David with all the cities
2Ch 6:37 done amiss, and have d' wickedly;
11:23 And he d' wisely, and dispersed of
33: 6 d' with a familiar spirit, and with
Ne 1: 7 d' very corruptly against thee,
9:10 that they d' proudly against them.
16 they and our fathers d' proudly
29 yet they d' proudly and hearkened
Job 6:15 My brethren have d' deceitfully as
Ps 13: 6 he hath d' bountifully with me.
44:17 have we d' falsely in thy covenant.
78:57 d' unfaithfully like their fathers:
103:10 hath not d' with us after our sins;
116: 7 hath d' bountifully with thee.
119:65 hast d' well with thy servant,
78 for they d' perversely with me
147:20 He hath not d' so with any nation:
Isa 24:16 dealers have d' treacherously; yea,
16 have d' very treacherously.
33: 1 d' not treacherously with thee!
Jer 3:20 have ye d' treacherously with me,
5:11 d' very treacherously against me,
12: 6 have d' treacherously with thee;
La 1: 2 have d' treacherously with her,
Eze 22: 7 of thee have they d' by oppression
25:12 d' against the house of Judah
15 the Philistines have d' by revenge,
Ho 5: 7 d' treacherously against the Lord:
6: 7 have d' treacherously against me.
Joe 2:26 your God that hath d' wondrously
Zec 1: 6 our doings, so hath he d' with us.
Mal 2:11 Judah hath d' treacherously, and
14 hast d' treacherously: yet is she
Lu 1:25 Thus hath the Lord d' with me
2: 48 why hast thou thus d' with us?
Ac 7:19 The same d' subtilly with our
25:24 the Jews have d' with me, both
Ro 12: 3 as God hath d' to every man

dear
Jer 31:20 Is Ephraim my d' son? is he a
Lu 7: 2 who was d' unto him, was sick,
Ac 20:24 count I my life d' unto myself,
Eph 5: 1 followers of God, as d' children;
Col 1: 7 our d' fellowservant, who is
13 into the kingdom of his d' Son:
1Th 2: 8 souls, because ye were d' unto us.

dearly
Jer 12: 7 the d' beloved of my soul
Ro 12:19 D' beloved, avenge not
1Co 10:14 Wherefore, my d' beloved, flee
2Co 7: 1 these promises d' beloved, let us
12:19 do all things d' beloved for
Ph'p 4: 1 my brethren d' beloved and longed
1 fast in the Lord, my d' beloved
2Ti 1: 2 To Timothy my d' beloved son:
Ph'm 1: 1 unto Philemon our d' beloved
1Pe 2:11 D' beloved, I beseech you as

dearth
Ge 41:54 seven years of d' began to come,
54 said, and the d' was in all lands;
2Ki 4:38 and there was a d' in the land;
2Ch 6:28 If there be d' in the land,
Ne 5: 3 might buy corn, because of the d'.
Jer 14: 1 to Jeremiah concerning the d'.
Ac 7:11 there came a d' over all the land
11:28 be great d' throughout all the

death See also DEATHS.
Ge 21:16 Let me not see the d' of the child.
24:67 was comforted after his mother's d'
25:11 after the d' of Abraham, that God
26:11 his wife shall surely be put to d'.
18 after the d' of Abraham: and he
27: 2 I know not the day of my d':
7 before the Lord before my d'.
10 he may bless thee before his d'.
Ex 10:17 take away from me this d' only.
19:12 mount shall be surely put to d':
21:12 he die shall be surely put to d'.
15 his mother, shall be surely put to d'
16 hand, he shall surely be put to d'.

Ex 21:17 his mother shall surely be put to *d'*.
29 his owner also shall be put to *d'*.
22:19 a beast shall surely be put to *d'*.
31:14 defileth it shall surely be put to *d'*:
15 day, he shall surely be put to *d'*.
35: 2 work therein shall be put to *d'*.
Le 16: 1 after the *d'* of the two sons of
19:20 they shall not be put to *d'*, because
20: 2 he shall surely be put to *d'*: the
9 shall be surely put to *d'*: he hath
10 adulteress shall surely be put to *d'*.
11, 12 them shall surely be put to *d'*;
13 they shall surely be put to *d'*; their
15 he shall surely be put to *d'*: and ye
16 they shall surely be put to *d'*; their
27 a wizard, shall surely be put to *d'*:
24:16 he shall surely be put to *d'*, and all
16 of the Lord, shall be put to *d'*.
17 any man shall surely be put to *d'*.
21 a man, he shall be put to *d'*.
27:29 but shall surely be put to *d'*.
Nu 1:51 that cometh nigh shall be put to *d'*.
3:10, 38 cometh nigh shall be put to *d'*.
15:35 The man shall be surely put to *d'*:
16:29 these men die the common *d'* of all
18: 7 that cometh nigh shall be put to *d'*.
23:10 Let me die the *d'* of the righteous,
35:16, 17, 18 murderer . . . be put to *d'*.
21 smote him shall surely be put to *d'*:
25 unto the *d'* of the high priest,
28 until the *d'* of the high priest:
28 but after the *d'* of the high priest
35:30 the murderer shall be put to *d'* by
31 a murderer, which is guilty of *d'*.
31 but he shall surely be put to *d'*.
32 land, until the *d'* of the priest.
De 13: 5 of dreams, shall be put to *d'*;
9 be first upon him to put him to *d'*,
17: 6 shall he that is worthy of *d'* be
6 be put to *d'*; but at the mouth of
6 witness he shall not be put to *d'*.
7 upon him to put him to *d'*, and
19: 6 whereas he was not worthy of *d'*,
21:22 committed a sin worthy of *d'*,
22 and he be to be put to *d'*,
22:26 in the damsel no sin worthy of *d'*.
24:16 The fathers shall not be put to *d'*
16 the children be put to *d'* for the
16 shall be put to *d'* for his own sin.
30:15 life and good, and *d'* and evil;
19 I have set before you life and *d'*,
31:27 how much more after my *d'*?
29 I know that after my *d'* ye will
33: 1 the children of Israel before his *d'*.
Jos 1: 1 after the *d'* of Moses the servant of
18 he shall be put to *d'*: only be
2:13 have, and deliver our lives from *d'*.
20: 6 until the *d'* of the high priest
J'g 1: 1 after the *d'* of Joshua it came to
5:18 jeoparded their lives unto the *d'*
6:31 let him be put to *d'* whilst it is yet
13: 7 the womb to the day of his *d'*.
16:16 his soul was vexed unto *d'*;
30 the dead which he slew at his *d'*
20:13 that we may put them to *d'*, and
21: 5 saying, He shall surely be put to *d'*.
Ru 1:17 if ought but *d'* part thee and me.
2:11 since the *d'* of thine husband:
1Sa 4:20 about the time of her *d'* the women
11:12 men, that we may put them to *d'*.
13 There shall not a man be put to *d'*
15:32 Surely the bitterness of *d'* is past.
35 to see Saul until the day of his *d'*:
20: 3 but a step between me and *d'*.
22:22 I have occasioned the *d'* of all the
2Sa 1: 1 came to pass after the *d'* of Saul,
23 in their *d'* they were not divided:
6:23 had no child unto the day of her *d'*.
8: 2 two lines measured he to put to *d'*,
15:21 whether in *d'* or life, even there
19:21 shall not Shimei be put to *d'* for
22 shall there any man be put to *d'*
20: 3 shut up unto the day of their *d'*,
21: 9 and were put to *d'* in the days of
22: 5 When the waves of *d'* compassed
6 the snares of *d'* prevented me;
1Ki 2: 8 I will not put thee to *d'* with the
24 Adonijah shall be put to *d'* this day.
26 thou art worthy of *d'*: but
26 not at this time put thee to *d'*.
11:40 in Egypt until the *d'* of Solomon.
2Ki 1: 1 against Israel after the *d'* of Ahab.
2:21 thence any more *d'* or barren land.
4:40 man of God, there is *d'* in the pot.
14: 6 fathers shall not be put to *d'* for
6 nor the children be put to *d'*
6 but every man shall be put to *d'*
17 after the *d'* of Jehoash son of
15: 5 a leper unto the day of his *d'*,
20: 1 days was Hezekiah sick unto *d'*.
1Ch 22: 5 prepared abundantly before his *d'*.
2Ch 15:13 God of Israel should be put to *d'*,
22: 4 after the *d'* of his father to his
23: 7 the house, he shall be put to *d'*:
24:17 after the *d'* of Jehoiada came the
25:25 after the *d'* of Joash son of
26:21 a leper unto the day of his *d'*,
32:24 Hezekiah was sick to the *d'*, and
33 did him honour at his *d'*.
Ezr 7:26 whether it be unto *d'*, or to
Es 4:11 one law of his to put him to *d'*,
Job 3: 5 Let darkness and the shadow of *d*
21 long for *d'*, but it cometh not;
5:20 he shall redeem thee from *d'*:
7:15 and *d'* rather than my life.
10:21 of darkness and the shadow of *d'*;
Job 10:22 itself; and of the shadow of *d'*,
12:22 out to light the shadow of *d'*.
16:16 on my eyelids is the shadow of *d'*:
18:13 firstborn of *d'* shall devour his
24:17 to them even as the shadow of *d'*:
17 the terrors of the shadow of *d'*.
27:15 of him shall be buried in *d'*:
28: 3 of darkness, and the shadow of *d'*.
22 Destruction and *d'* say, We have
30:23 thou wilt bring me to *d'*, and to the
34:22 is no darkness, nor shadow of *d'*,
38:17 Have the gates of *d'* been opened
17 the doors of the shadow of *d'*?
Ps 6: 5 in *d'* there is no remembrance of
7:13 for him the instruments of *d'*; he
9:13 liftest me up from the gates of *d'*:
13: 3 lest I sleep the sleep of *d'*;
18: 4 The sorrows of *d'* compassed me,
5 the snares of *d'* prevented me.
22:15 brought me into the dust of *d'*.
23: 4 the valley of the shadow of *d'*,
33:19 To deliver their soul from *d'*, and
44:19 covered us with the shadow of *d'*.
48:14 he will be our guide even unto *d'*.
49:14 *d'* shall feed on them; and the
55: 4 the terrors of *d'* are fallen upon me.
15 Let *d'* seize upon them, and
56:13 hast delivered my soul from *d'*:
68:20 the Lord belong the issues from *d'*.
73: 4 there are no bands in their *d'*:
78:50 spared not their soul from *d'*,
89:48 he that liveth, and shall not see *d'*?
102:20 those that are appointed to *d'*;
107:10 darkness and in the shadow of *d'*,
14 of darkness and the shadow of *d'*,
18 they draw near unto the gates of *d'*.
116: 3 The sorrows of *d'* compassed me,
8 delivered my soul from *d'*, mine
15 of the Lord is the *d'* of his saints.
118:18 he hath not given me over unto *d'*.
Pr 2:18 her house inclineth unto *d'*, and
5: 5 Her feet go down to *d'*; her steps
7:27 going down to the chambers of *d'*.
8:36 all they that hate me love *d'*.
10: 2 righteousness delivereth from *d'*.
11: 4 righteousness delivereth from *d'*.
19 evil pursueth it to his own *d'*.
12:28 the pathway thereof there is no *d'*.
13:14 to depart from the snares of *d'*.
14:12 the end thereof are the ways of *d'*.
27 to depart from the snares of *d'*.
32 the righteous hath hope in his *d'*.
16:14 of a king is as messengers of *d'*:
25 the end thereof are the ways of *d'*.
18:21 *D'* and life are in the power of the
21: 6 to and fro of them that seek *d'*.
24:11 them that are drawn unto *d'*, and
26:18 casteth firebrands, arrows, and *d'*,
Ec 7: 1 day of *d'* than the day of one's birth.
26 more bitter than *d'* the woman,
8: 8 power in the day of *d'*: and there is
Ca 8: 6 love is strong as *d'*; jealousy is
Isa 9: 2 the land of the shadow of *d'*, upon
25: 8 He will swallow up *d'* in victory;
28:15 We have made a covenant with *d'*,
18 your covenant with *d'* shall be
38: 1 days was Hezekiah sick unto *d'*.
18 *d'* can not celebrate thee: they
53: 9 wicked, and with the rich in his *d'*;
12 hath poured out his soul unto *d'*:
Jer 2: 6 drought, and of the shadow of *d'*,
8: 3 *d'* shall be chosen rather than
9:21 *d'* is come up into our windows,
13:16 he turn it into the shadow of *d'*,
15: 2 Such as are for *d'*, to *d'*; and such
18:21 let their men be put to *d'*; let
21: 8 the way of life, and the way of *d'*.
26:15 if ye put me to *d'*, ye shall surely
19 and all Judah put him at all to *d'*?
21 the king sought to put him to *d'*:
24 hand of the people to put him to *d'*.
38: 4 let this man be put to *d'*: for thus
15 wilt thou not surely put me to *d'*?
16 I will not put thee to *d'*, neither
25 we will not put thee to *d'*; also
43: 3 that they might put us to *d'*, and
11 such as are for *d'* to *d'*; and such
52:11 in prison till the day of his *d'*.
27 smote them, and put them to *d'*
34 a portion until the day of his *d'*,
La 1:20 bereaveth, at home there is as *d'*.
Eze 18:32 pleasure in the *d'* of him that dieth,
31:14 they are all delivered unto *d'*, to the
33:11 no pleasure in the *d'* of the wicked;
Ho 13:14 I will redeem them from *d'*: O *d'*,
Am 5: 8 turneth the shadow of *d'* into the
Jon 4: 9 well to be angry, even unto *d'*.
Hab 2: 5 his desire as hell, and is as *d'*,
M't 2:15 was there until the *d'* of Herod:
4:16 in the region and shadow of *d'*
10:21 deliver up the brother to *d'*,
21 and cause them to be put to *d'*.
14: 5 he would have put him to *d'*,
15: 4 or mother, let him die the *d'*.
16:28 shall not taste of *d'*, till they see
20:18 and they shall condemn him to *d'*,
26:38 exceeding sorrowful, even unto *d'*:
59 against Jesus, to put him to *d'*;
66 and said, He is guilty of *d'*.
27: 1 against Jesus, to put him to *d'*:
M'r 5:23 daughter lieth at the point of *d'*:
7:10 let him die the *d'*: But ye say,
9: 1 shall not taste of *d'*, till they have
10:33 shall condemn him to *d'*, and shall
13:12 shall betray the brother to *d'*,
12 shall cause them to be put to *d'*.
M'r 14: 1 him by craft, and put him to *d'*.
34 is exceeding sorrowful unto *d'*:
55 against Jesus to put him to *d'*; and
64 condemned him to be guilty of *d'*.
Lu 1:79 and in the shadow of *d'*, to guide
2:26 that he should not see *d'*, before
9:27 which shall not taste of *d'*, till they
18:33 scourge him, and put him to *d'*:
21:16 shall they cause to be put to *d'*.
22:33 thee; both into prison, and to *d'*.
23:15 nothing worthy of *d'* is done unto
22 found no cause of *d'* in him: I will
32 led with him to be put to *d'*.
24:20 to be condemned to *d'*, and have
Joh 4:47 for he was at the point of *d'*.
5:24 but is passed from *d'* unto life.
8:51 my saying, he shall never see *d'*.
52 saying, he shall never taste of *d'*.
11: 4 This sickness is not unto *d'*, but
13 Jesus spake of his *d'*: but they
53 together for to put him to *d'*.
12:10 they might put Lazarus also to *d'*;
33 signifying what *d'* he should die.
18:31 lawful for us to put any man to *d'*
32 signifying what *d'* he should die.
21:19 by what *d'* he should glorify God.
Ac 2:24 up, having loosed the pains of *d'*:
8: 1 Saul was consenting unto his *d'*.
12:19 that they should be put to *d'*.
13:28 they found no cause of *d'* in him,
22: 4 I persecuted this way unto the *d'*,
20 by, and consenting unto his *d'*,
23:29 charge worthy of *d'* or of bonds.
25:11 committed any thing worthy of *d'*,
25 committed nothing worthy of *d'*,
26:10 when they were put to *d'*, I gave
31 nothing worthy of *d'* or of bonds.
28:18 there was no cause of *d'* in me.
Ro 1:32 such things are worthy of *d'*,
5:10 by the *d'* of his Son, much more,
12 and *d'* by sin; and so *d'* passed
14 *d'* reigned from Adam to Moses,
17 man's offence *d'* reigned by one;
21 That as sin hath reigned unto *d'*,
6: 3 Christ were baptized into his *d'*?
4 with him by baptism into *d'*:
5 in the likeness of his *d'*, we shall be
9 *d'* hath no more dominion over him.
16 of sin unto *d'*, or of obedience
21 the end of those things is *d'*.
23 For the wages of sin is *d'*; but the
7: 5 to bring forth fruit unto *d'*.
10 life, I found to be unto *d'*.
13 which is good made *d'* unto me?
13 might appear sin, working *d'* in me
24 me from the body of this *d'*?
8: 2 free from the law of sin and *d'*.
6 to be carnally minded is *d'*;
38 neither *d'*, nor life, nor angels, nor
1Co 3:22 or life, or *d'*, or things present,
4: 9 last, as it were appointed to *d'*:
11:26 ye do shew the Lord's *d'* till he
15:21 by man came *d'*, by man came
26 that shall be destroyed is *d'*.
54 *D'* is swallowed up in victory.
55 O *d'*, where is thy sting? O grave
56 sting of *d'* is sin; and the strength
2Co 1: 9 had the sentence of *d'* in ourselves,
10 delivered us from so great a *d'*,
2:16 one we are the savour of *d'* unto *d'*;
3: 7 the ministration of *d'*, written and
4:11 delivered unto *d'* for Jesus' sake,
12 then *d'* worketh in us, but life in
7:10 the sorrow of the world worketh *d'*.
Ph'p 1:20 whether it be by life, or by *d'*.
2: 8 and became obedient unto *d'*,
8 even the *d'* of the cross.
27 he was sick nigh unto *d'*: but God
30 he was nigh unto *d'*, not regarding
3:10 made comformable unto his *d'*;
Col 1:22 In the body of his flesh through *d'*,
2Ti 1:10 who hath abolished *d'*, and
Heb 2: 9 for the suffering of *d'*, crowned
9 God should taste *d'* for every man.
14 through *d'* he might destroy him
14 that had the power of *d'*,
15 fear of *d'* were all their lifetime
5: 7 to save him from *d'*, and was heard
7:23 to continue by reason of *d'*:
9:15 by means of *d'*, for the redemption
16 must also of necessity be the *d'*
11: 5 that he should not see *d'*;
Jas 1:15 it is finished, bringeth forth *d'*.
5:20 save a soul from *d'*, and shall hide
1Pe 3:18 being put to *d'* in the flesh,
1Jo 3:14 we have passed from *d'* unto life,
14 not his brother abideth in *d'*.
5:16 a sin which is not unto *d'*, he shall
16 life for them that sin not unto *d'*.
16 There is a sin unto *d'*: I do not
17 and there is a sin not unto *d'*.
Re 1:18 the keys of hell and of *d'*.
2:10 be thou faithful unto *d'*, and I will
11 shall not be hurt of the second *d'*.
23 I will kill her children with *d'*;
6: 8 his name that sat on him was *D'*,
8 and with hunger, and with *d'*,
9: 6 men seek *d'*, and shall not find it;
6 and *d'* shall flee from them.
12:11 loved not their lives unto the *d'*.
13: 3 as it were wounded to *d'*; and his
18: 8 day, *d'*, and mourning, and famine;
20: 6 the second *d'* hath no power, but
13 *d'* and hell delivered up the dead
14 *d'* and hell were cast into the
14 lake of fire. This is the second *d'*.

Re 21: 4 be no more *d*, neither sorrow,
8 brimstone: which is the second *d*.

deaths
Jer 16: 4 They shall die of grievous *d*;
Eze 28: 8 the *d* of them that are slain
10 die the *d* of the uncircumcised
2Co 11:23 prisons more frequent in *d* oft.

Debar See LO-DEBAR.

debase
Isa 57: 9 didst *d* thyself even unto hell.

debate See also DEBATES.
Pr 25: 9 *D* thy cause with thy neighbour
Isa 27: 8 forth, thou wilt *d* with it:
58: 4 fast for strife and *d*, and to smite
Ro 1:29 murder, *d*, deceit, malignity;

debates
2Co 12:20 there be *d*, envyings, wraths,

Debir (*de'-bur*) See also KIRJATH-SANNAH; KIRJATH-SEPHER.
Jos 10: 3 unto *D* king of Eglon, saying,
38 and all Israel with him, to *D*;
39 did to *D*, and to the king thereof;
11:21 from Hebron, from *D*, from Anab,
12:13 king of *D*, one; the king of Geder,
13:26 Mahanaim unto the border of *D*;
15: 7 the border went up toward *D*
15 up thence to the inhabitants of *D*:
15 of *D* before was Kirjath-sepher.
49 and Kirjath-sannah, which is *D*,
21:15 Holon with her suburbs, and *D*
J'g 1:11 up against the inhabitants of *D*:
11 of *D* before was Kirjath-sepher.
1Ch 6:58 Hilen with her suburbs, *D* with

Deborah (*deb'-o-rah*)
Ge 35: 8 But *D* Rebekah's nurse died,
J'g 4: 4 *D*, a prophetess, the wife of
5 dwelt under the palm tree of *D*,
9 *D* arose, and went with Barak
10 and *D* went up with him.
14 *D* said unto Barak, Up; for this
5: 1 Then sang *D* and Barak the son of
7 until that I *D* arose, that I arose
12 Awake, awake, *D*: awake, awake,
15 princes of Issachar were with *D*;

debt See also DEBTS; INDEBTED.
1Sa 22: 2 every one that was in *d*, and
2Ki 4: 7 sell the oil, and pay thy *d*,
Ne 10:31 and the exaction of every *d*.
M't 18:27 him, and forgave him the *d*.
30 prison, till he should pay the *d*.
32 I forgave thee all that *d*, because
Ro 4: 4 not reckoned of grace, but of *d*.

debtor See also DEBTORS.
Eze 18: 7 hath restored to the *d* his pledge,
M't 23:16 the gold of the temple, he is a *d*!
Ro 1:14 I am *d* both to the Greeks, and
Ga 5: 3 he is a *d* to do the whole law.

debtors
M't 6:12 our debts, as we forgive our *d*.
Lu 7:41 certain creditor which had two *d*:
16: 5 called every one of his lord's *d*
Ro 8:12 we are *d*, not to the flesh,
15:27 them verily; and their *d* they are.

debts
Pr 22:26 of them that are sureties for *d*.
M't 6:12 forgive us our *d*, as we forgive

Decapolis (*de-cap'-o-lis*)
M't 4:25 and from *D*, and from Jerusalem,
M'r 5:20 and began to publish in *D* how
7:31 the midst of the coasts of *D*.

decay See also DECAYED; DECAYETH.
Le 25:35 and fallen in *d* with thee;

decayed
Ne 4:10 of the bearers of burdens is *d*,
Isa 44:26 and I will raise up the *d* places

decayeth
Job 14:11 the flood *d* and drieth up:
Ec 10:18 slothfulness the building *d*;
Heb 8:13 that which *d* and waxeth old

decease See also DECEASED.
Lu 9:31 spake of his *d* which he should
2Pe 1:15 may be able after my *d* to have

deceased
Isa 26:14 they are *d*, they shall not rise:
M't 22:25 when he had married a wife, *d*,

deceit See also DECEITFUL; DECEITS.
Job 15:35 and their belly prepareth *d*.
27: 4 nor my tongue utter *d*.
31: 5 if my foot hath hasted to *d*;
Ps 10: 7 His mouth is full of cursing and *d*
36: 3 of his mouth are iniquity and *d*:
50:19 to evil, and thy tongue frameth *d*.
55:11 *d* and guile depart not from her
72:14 shall redeem their soul from *d*
101: 7 *d* shall not dwell within my
119:118 statutes: for their *d* is falsehood.
Pr 12: 5 the counsels of the wicked are *d*.
17 but a false witness *d*.
20 *D* is in the heart of them that
14: 8 but the folly of fools is *d*.
20:17 Bread of *d* is sweet to a man;
26:24 and layeth up *d* within him;
26 Whose hatred is covered by *d*,
Isa 53: 9 neither was any *d* in his mouth.
Jer 5:27 their houses full of *d*: therefore
8: 5 hold fast *d*, they refuse to return.
9: 6 habitation is in the midst of *d*;
6 through *d* they refuse to know me,
8 it speaketh *d*: one speaketh
14:14 nought, and the *d* of their heart.
23:26 of the *d* of their own heart;
Ho 11:12 and the house of Israel with *d*:
12: 7 the balances of *d* are in his hand:
Am 8: 5 and falsifying the balances by *d*?
Zep 1: 9 houses with violence and *d*.
M'r 7:22 wickedness, *d*, lasciviousness, an
Ro 1:29 full of envy, murder, debate, *d*,
3:13 their tongues they have used *d*;
Col 2: 8 through philosophy and vain *d*,
1Th 2: 3 our exhortation was not of *d*,

deceitful
Ps 5: 6 will abhor the bloody and *d* man.
35:20 devise *d* matters against them
43: 1 me from the *d* and unjust man.
52: 4 words, O thou *d* tongue.
55:23 bloody and *d* men shall not live
78:57 were turned aside like a *d* bow.
109: 2 of the *d* are opened against me:
120: 2 from lying lips, and from a *d*
Pr 11:18 The wicked worketh a *d* work:
14:25 but a *d* witness speaketh lies.
23: 3 his dainties: for they are *d* meat.
27: 6 but the kisses of an enemy are *d*.
29:13 and the *d* man meet together:
31:30 Favour is *d*, and beauty is vain:
Jer 17: 9 The heart is *d* above all things,
Ho 7:16 High: they are like a *d* bow:
Mic 6:11 and with the bag of *d* weights?
12 their tongue is *d* in their mouth.
Zep 3:13 *d* tongue be found in their mouth:
2Co 11:13 false apostles, *d* workers,
Eph 4:22 corrupt according to the *d* lusts;

deceitfully
Ge 34:13 Shechem and Hamor his father *d*,
Ex 8:29 let not Pharaoh deal *d* any more
21: 8 seeing he hath dealt *d* with her.
Le 6: 4 thing which he hath *d* gotten.
Job 6:15 brethren have dealt *d* as a brook,
13: 7 for God? and talk *d* for him?
Ps 24: 4 his soul unto vanity, nor sworn *d*.
52: 2 like a sharp razor, working *d*.
Jer 48:10 doeth the work of the Lord *d*,
Da 11:23 he shall work *d*: for he shall
2Co 4: 2 nor handling the word of God *d*,

deceitfulness
M't 13:22 the *d* of riches, choke the word,
M'r 4:19 the *d* of riches, and the lusts of
Heb 3:13 be hardened through the *d* of sin.

deceits
Ps 38:12 and imagine *d* all the day long.
Isa 30:10 us smooth things, prophesy *d*:

deceivableness
2Th 2:10 with all *d* of unrighteousness in

deceive See also DECEIVED; DECEIVETH; DECEIVING.
2Sa 3:25 that he came to *d* thee, and to
2Ki 4:28 did I not say, Do not *d* me?
18:29 Let not Hezekiah *d* you: for he
19:10 God in whom thou trustest *d* thee,
2Ch 32:15 let not Hezekiah *d* you, nor
Pr 24:28 cause; and *d* not with thy lips.
Isa 36:14 Let not Hezekiah *d* you: for he
37:10 God, in whom thou trustest, *d* thee,
Jer 9: 5 will *d* every one his neighbour,
29: 8 that be in the midst of you *d* you,
37: 9 *D* not yourselves, saying, The
Zec 13: 4 they wear a rough garment to *d*:
M't 24: 4 Take heed that no man *d* you.
5 I am Christ; and shall *d* many.
11 shall rise and shall *d* many.
24 they shall *d* the very elect.
M'r 13: 5 Take heed lest any man *d* you:
6 I am Christ; and shall *d* many.
Ro 16:18 speeches *d* the hearts of the
1Co 3:18 Let no man *d* himself. If any
Eph 4:14 whereby they lie in wait to *d*;
5: 6 Let no man *d* you with vain words:
2Th 2: 3 Let no man *d* you by any means:
1Jo 1: 8 we *d* ourselves, and the truth
3: 7 let no man *d* you: he that doeth
Re 20: 3 that he should *d* the nations no
8 go out to *d* the nations which are

deceived
Ge 31: 7 your father hath *d* me, and
Le 6: 2 violence, or hath *d* his neighbour;
De 11:16 that your heart be not *d*,
1Sa 19:17 Why hast thou *d* me so, and sent
28:12 Why hast thou *d* me? for thou art
2Sa 19:26 my servant *d* me: for thy servant
Job 12:16 the *d* and the deceiver are his.
15:31 not him that is *d* trust in vanity:
31: 9 If mine heart have been *d* by a
Pr 20: 1 whosoever is *d* thereby is not
Isa 19:13 the princes of Noph are *d*:
44:20 a *d* heart hath turned him aside,
Jer 4:10 thou hast greatly *d* this people
20: 7 thou hast *d* me, and I was *d*:
49:16 Thy terribleness hath *d* thee,
La 1:19 I called for my lovers, but they *d*
Eze 14: 9 if the prophet be *d* when he hath
9 I the Lord have *d* that prophet,
Ob 3 pride of thine heart hath *d* thee,
7 at peace with thee hath *d* thee,
Lu 21: 8 Take heed that ye be not *d*:
Joh 7:47 the Pharisees, Are ye also *d*?
Ro 7:11 *d* me, and by it slew me.
1Co 6: 9 Be not *d*: neither fornicators, nor
15:33 Be not *d*: evil communications
Ga 6: 7 Be not *d*; God is not mocked:
1Ti 2:14 Adam was not *d*, but the woman
14 being *d* was in the transgression.
2Ti 3:13 worse, deceiving, and being *d*.
Tit 3: 3 *d*, serving divers lusts and
Re 18:23 thy sorceries were all nations *d*.
19:20 with which he *d* them that had
20:10 the devil that *d* them was cast

deceiver See also DECEIVERS.
Ge 27:12 I shall seem to him as a *d*;
Job 12:16 the deceived and the *d* are his.
Mal 1:14 cursed be the *d*, which hath in
M't 27:63 we remember that that *d* said,
2Jo 7 This is a *d* and an antichrist.

deceivers
2Co 6: 8 good report: as *d*, and yet true;
Tit 1:10 unruly and vain talkers and *d*,
2Joh 7 For many *d* are entered into the

deceiveth
Pr 26:19 the man that *d* his neighbour,
Joh 7:12 said, Nay; but he *d* the people.
Ga 6: 3 when he is nothing, he *d* himself.
Jas 1:26 his tongue, but *d* his own heart,
Re 12: 9 Satan, which *d* the whole world:
13:14 *d* them that dwell on the earth

deceiving See also DECEIVINGS.
2Ti 3:13 worse and worse, *d*, and being
Jas 1:22 hearers only, *d* your own selves.

deceivings
2Pe 2:13 their own *d* while they feast,

decently
1Co 14:40 all things be done *d* and in order.

decided
1Ki 20:40 judgment be; thyself hast *d* it.

decision
Joe 3:14 multitudes in the valley of *d*: for
14 the Lord is near in the valley of *d*

deck See also DECKED; DECKEST; DECKETH.
Job 40:10 *D* thyself now with majesty
Jer 10: 4 *d* it with silver and with gold;

decked See also DECKEDST.
Pr 7:16 I have *d* my bed with coverings
Eze 16:11 I *d* thee also with ornaments,
13 wast thou *d* with gold and silver;
Ho 2:13 she *d* herself with her earrings
Re 17: 4 *d* with gold and precious stones
18:16 *d* with gold, and precious stones,

deckedst
Eze 16:16 and *d* thy high places with divers
23:40 and *d* thyself with ornaments,

deckest
Jer 4:30 thou *d* thee with ornaments of

decketh
Isa 61:10 as a bridegroom *d* himself with

declaration
Es 10: 2 *d* of the greatness of Mordecai
Job 13:17 and my *d* with your ears.
Lu 1: 1 to set forth in order a *d* of those
2Co 8:19 and *d* of your ready mind:

declare See also DECLARED; DECLARETH; DECLARING.
Ge 41:24 was none that could *d* it to me.
De 1: 5 began Moses to *d* this law, saying,
Jo 20: 4 and shall *d* his cause in the ears
J'g 14:12 *d* it me within the seven days of
13 if ye cannot *d* it me, then shall ye
15 that he may *d* unto us the riddle,
1Ki 22:13 prophets *d* good unto the king
1Ch 16:24 *D* his glory among the heathen;
2Ch 18:12 the words of the prophets *d* good
Es 4: 8 and to *d* unto her, and to charge
Job 12: 8 the fishes of the sea shall *d* unto
15:17 that which I have seen I will *d*;
21:31 Who shall *d* his way to his face?
28:27 Then did he see it, and *d* it;
31:37 I would *d* unto him the number
38: 4 *d*, if thou hast understanding.
18 earth? *d* if thou knowest it all.
40: 7 of thee, and *d* thou unto me.
42: 4 of thee, and *d* thou unto me.
Ps 2: 7 I will *d* the decree: the Lord
9:11 *d* among the people his doings.
19: 1 The heavens *d* the glory of God;
22:22 *d* thy name unto my brethren:
31 *d* his righteousness unto a people
30: 9 praise thee? shall it *d* thy truth?
38:18 For I will *d* mine iniquity;
40: 5 if I would *d* and speak of them,
50: 6 heavens shall *d* his righteousness:
16 hast thou to do to *d* my statutes,
64: 9 and shall *d* the work of God;
66:16 and I will *d* what he hath done
73:28 that I may *d* all thy works.
75: 1 is near thy wondrous works *d*.
9 But I will *d* for ever; I will
78: 6 and *d* them to their children:
96: 3 *D* his glory among the heathen,
97: 6 The heavens *d* his righteousness,
102:21 To *d* the name of the Lord in
107:22 and *d* his works with rejoicing.
118:17 but live, and *d* the works of the
145: 4 and shall *d* thy mighty acts.
6 acts: and I will *d* thy greatness.
Ec 9: 1 to *d* all this, that the righteous,
Isa 3: 9 they *d* their sin as Sodom, they
12: 4 *d* his doings among the people,
21: 6 let him *d* what he seeth.
41:22 or *d* us things for to come.
42: 9 new things do I *d*: before they
12 unto the Lord, and *d* his praise
43: 9 who among them can *d* this,
26 *d* thou, that thou mayest be
44: 7 as I, shall call, and shall *d* it,
45:19 I *d* things that are right.
48: 6 all this; and will not ye *d* it?
20 with a voice of singing *d* ye,

Isa 53: 8 and who shall *d'* his generation?
57:12 I will *d'* thy righteousness, and
66:19 and they shall *d'* my glory among
Jer 4: 5 *D'* ye in Judah, and publish in
5:20 *D'* this in the house of Jacob,
9:12 *d'* it, for what the land perisheth
31:10 and *d'* it in the isles afar off,
38:15 If I *d'* it unto thee, wilt thou not
25 *D'* unto us now what thou hast
42: 4 I will *d'* it unto you; I will keep
20 *d'* unto us, and we will do it.
46:14 *D'* ye in Egypt, and publish in
50: 2 *D'* ye among the nations, and
28 to *d'* in Zion the vengeance of the
51:10 and let us *d'* in Zion the work of
Eze 12:16 they may *d'* all their abomination.
23:36 *d'* unto them their abominations;
40: 4 *d'* all that thou seest to the house
Da 4:18 *d'* the interpretation thereof,
Mic 1:10 *D'* ye it not at Gath, weep ye not
3: 8 to *d'* unto Jacob his transgression,
Zec 9:12 even to day do I *d'* that I will
M't 13:36 *D'* unto us the parable of the
15:15 unto him, *D'* unto us this parable.
Joh 17:26 them thy name, and will *d'* it:
Ac 8:33 and who shall *d'* his generation?
13:32 we *d'* unto you glad tidings, how
41 though a man *d'* it unto you.
17:23 worship, him *d'* I unto you.
20:27 to *d'* unto you the counsel of God.
Ro 3:25 to *d'* his righteousness for the
26 To *d'*, I say, at this time his
1Co 3:13 for the day shall *d'* it, because
11:17 Now in this that I *d'* unto you
15: 1 brethren I *d'* unto you the gospel
Col 4: 7 state shall Tychicus *d'* unto you,
Heb 2:12 will *d'* thy name unto my brethren
11:14 *d'* plainly that they seek a
1Jo 1: 3 seen and heard *d'* we unto you,
5 *d'* unto you, that God is light,

declared
Ex 9:16 my name may be *d'* throughout
Le 23:44 And Moses *d'* unto the children
Nu 1:18 and they *d'* their pedigrees after
15:34 was not *d'* what should be done
De 4:13 And he *d'* unto you his covenant
2Sa 19: 6 thou hast *d'* this day, that thou
Ne 8:12 the words that were *d'* unto them.
Job 26: 3 hast thou plentifully *d'* the thing
Ps 40:10 I have *d'* thy faithfulness and thy
71:17 have I *d'* thy wondrous works.
77:14 *d'* thy strength among the people.
88:11 Shall thy lovingkindness be *d'*
119:13 With my lips have I *d'* all the
26 I have *d'* my ways, and thou
Isa 21: 2 A grievous vision is *d'* unto me;
10 of Israel, have I *d'* unto you.
41:26 Who hath *d'* from the beginning,
43:12 I have *d'*, and have saved, and I
44: 8 from that time, and have *d'* it?
45:21 who hath *d'* this from ancient
48: 3 I have *d'* the former things from
5 from the beginning *d'* it to thee;
14 among them hath *d'* these things?
Jer 36:13 Then Michaiah *d'* unto them all
42:21 And now I have this day *d'* it
Lu 8:47 *d'* unto him before all the people
Joh 1:18 the Father, he hath *d'* him:
17:26 I have *d'* unto them thy name,
Ac 9:27 *d'* unto them how he had seen the
10: 8 when he had *d'* all these things
12:17 *d'* unto them how the Lord had
15: 4 *d'* all things that God had done
14 Simeon hath *d'* how God at the
21:19 *d'* particularly what things God
25:14 *d'* Paul's cause unto the king,
Ro 1: 4 *d'* to be the Son of God with power,
9:17 my name might be *d'* throughout
1Co 1:11 it hath been *d'* unto me of you,
2Co 3: 3 manifestly *d'* to be the epistle of
Col 1: 8 Who also *d'* unto us your love
Re 10: 7 *d'* to his servants the prophets.

declareth
Isa 41:26 there is none that *d'*, yea, there is
Jer 4:15 For a voice *d'* from Dan, and
Ho 4:12 and their staff *d'* unto them: for
Am 4:13 *d'* unto man what is his thought,

declaring
Isa 46:10 *D'* the end from the beginning,
Ac 15: 3 *d'* the conversion of the Gentiles:
12 *d'* what miracles and wonders
1Co 2: 1 *d'* unto you the testimony of God.

decline See also DECLINED; DECLINETH.
Ex 23: 2 *d'* after many to wrest judgment:
De 17:11 shalt not *d'* from the sentence
Ps 119:157 do I not *d'* from thy testimonies.
Pr 4: 5 neither *d'* from the words of my
7:25 Let not thine heart *d'* to her ways,

declined
2Ch 34: 2 *d'* neither to the right hand, nor
Job 23:11 his way have I kept, and not *d'*.
Ps 44:18 have our steps *d'* from thy way;
119:51 yet have I not *d'* from thy law.

declineth
Ps 102:11 days are like a shadow that *d'*;
109:23 gone like the shadow when it *d'*:

decrease See also DECREASED.
Ps 107:38 and suffereth not their cattle to *d'*.
Joh 3:30 He must increase, but I must *d'*.

decreased
Ge 8: 5 the waters *d'* continually until

decree See also DECREED; DECREES.
2Ch 30: 5 So they established a *d'* to make
Ezr 5:13 Cyrus made a *d'* to build this
17 that a *d'* was made of Cyrus the
6: 1 Darius the king made a *d'*, and
3 same Cyrus the king made a *d'*
8 I make a *d'* what ye shall do to
11 I have made a *d'*, that whosoever
12 I Darius have made a *d'*: let it
7:13 I make a *d'*, that all they of the
21 I Artaxerxes the king, do make a *d'*
Es 1:20 the king's *d'* which he shall make
2: 8 and his *d'* was heard, and when
3:15 and the *d'* was given in Shushan
4: 3 commandment and his *d'* came,
8 the copy of the writing of the *d'*
8:14 And the *d'* was given at Shushan
17 commandment and his *d'* came,
9: 1 and his *d'* drew near to be put in
13 according unto this day's *d'*, and let
14 the *d'* was given at Shushan; and
32 And the *d'* of Esther confirmed
Job 22:28 Thou shalt also *d'* a thing, and it
28:26 When he made a *d'* for the rain,
Ps 2: 7 I will declare the *d'*: the Lord hath
148: 6 made a *d'* which shall not pass.
Pr 8:15 reign, and princes *d'* justice.
29 When he gave to the sea his *d'*,
Isa 10: 1 unto them that *d'* unrighteous
Jer 5:22 of the sea by a perpetual *d'*,
Da 2: 9 there is but one *d'* for you:
13 And the *d'* went forth that wise men
15 is the *d'* so hasty from the king?
3:10 Thou, O king, hast made a *d'*,
29 I make a *d'*, That every people,
4: 6 Therefore made I a *d'* to bring in
17 by the *d'* of the watchers, and the
24 and this is the *d'* of the most High.
6: 7 to make a firm *d'*, that whosoever
8 O king, establish the *d'*, and sign
9 signed the writing and the *d'*.
12 king concerning the king's *d'*;
12 Hast thou not signed a *d'*, that
13 nor the *d'* that thou hast signed,
15 no *d'* nor statute which the king
26 I make a *d'*, That in every
Jon 3: 7 the *d'* of the king and his nobles,
Mic 7:11 day shall the *d'* be far removed.
Zep 2: 2 Before the *d'* bring forth, before
Lu 2: 1 there went out a *d'* from Cæsar

decreed
Es 2: 1 and what was *d'* against her.
9:31 and as they had *d'* for themselves
Job 38:10 brake up for it my *d'* place
Isa 10:22 the consumption *d'* shall overflow
1Co 7:37 hath so *d'* in his heart that he

decrees
Isa 10: 1 that decree unrighteous *d'*, and
Ac 16: 4 delivered them the *d'* for to keep,
17: 7 all do contrary to the *d'* of Cæsar

Dedan (*de'-dan*) See also DEDANIM.
Ge 10: 7 sons of Raamah; Sheba, and *D'*.
25: 3 Jokshan begat Sheba and *D'*.
3 the sons of *D'* were Asshurim, and
1Ch 1: 9 sons of Raamah; Sheba, and *D'*.
32 sons of Jokshan; Sheba, and *D'*.
Jer 25:23 *D'*, and Tema, and Buz, and all
49: 8 dwell deep, O inhabitants of *D'*;
Eze 25:13 they of *D'* shall fall by the sword.
27:15 The men of *D'* were thy merchants;
20 *D'* was thy merchant in precious
38:13 Sheba, and *D'*, and the merchants

Dedanim (*ded'-a-nim*) See also DODANIM.
Isa 21:13 O ye travelling companies of *D'*.

dedicate See also DEDICATED; DEDICATING.
De 20: 5 battle, and another man *d'* it.
2Sa 8:11 Which also king David did *d'*
1Ch 26:27 did they *d'* to maintain the house
2Ch 2: 4 to *d'* it to him, and to burn

dedicated
De 20: 5 new house, and hath not *d'* it?
J'g 17: 3 wholly *d'* the silver unto the Lord
2Sa 8:11 the silver and gold that he had *d'*
1Ki 7:51 which David his father had *d'*;
8:63 and all the children of Israel *d'*
15:15 things which his father had *d'*,
15 the things which himself had *d'*,
2Ki 12: 4 money of the *d'* things that is
18 kings of Judah, had *d'*, and his
1Ch 18:11 king David *d'* unto the Lord,
26:20 over the treasures of the *d'* things
26 all the treasures of the *d'* things,
26 the captains of the host, had *d'*.
28 Joab the son of Zeruiah, had *d'*;
28 and whosoever had *d'* any thing,
28:12 of the treasuries of the *d'* things:
2Ch 5: 1 things that David his father had *d'*;
7: 5 and all the people *d'* the house
15:18 the things that his father had *d'*,
18 and that he himself had *d'*,
24: 7 *d'* things of the house of the Lord
31:12 and the *d'* things faithfully: over
Eze 44:29 every *d'* thing in Israel shall be
Heb 9:18 testament was *d'* without blood.

dedicating
Nu 7:10 princes offered for *d'* of the altar
11 on his day, for the *d'* of the altar.

dedication
Nu 7:84 the *d'* of the altar, in the day
88 This was the *d'* of the altar,
2Ch 7: 9 they kept the *d'* of the altar
Ezr 6:16 kept the *d'* of this house of God
17 And offered at the *d'* of this house
Ne 12:27 at the *d'* of the wall of Jerusalem
27 to keep the *d'* with gladness,
Ps 30:*title* at the *d'* of the house of David.
Da 3: 2 come to the *d'* of the image
3 together unto the *d'* of the image
Joh 10:22 at Jerusalem the feast of the *d'*,

deed See also DEEDS; INDEED.
Ge 44:15 What *d'* is this that ye have done?
Ex 9:16 And in very *d'* for this cause
J'g 19:30 There was no such *d'* done nor
1Sa 25:34 For in very *d'*, as the Lord God of
26: 4 that Saul was come in very *d'*.
2Sa 12:14 by this *d'* thou hast given great
2Ch 6:18 But will God in very *d'* dwell with men
Es 1:17 For this *d'* of the queen shall
18 have heard of the *d'* of the queen.
Lu 23:51 to the counsel and *d'* of them;
24:19 mighty in *d'* and word before God
Ac 4: 9 good *d'* done to the impotent man,
Ro 15:18 Gentiles obedient, by word and *d'*,
1Co 5: 2 hath done this *d'* might be taken
3 him that hath so done this *d'*,
2Co 10:11 also in *d'* when we are present.
Col 3:17 ye do in word or *d'*, do all in the
Jas 1:25 man shall be blessed in his *d'*.
1Jo 3:18 tongue; but in *d'* and in truth.

deeds See also ALMSDEEDS.
Ge 20: 9 thou hast done *d'* unto me that
1Ch 16: 8 make known his *d'* among the
2Ch 35:27 And his *d'*, first and last, behold,
Ezr 9:13 for our evil *d'*, and for our
Ne 6:19 reported his good *d'* before him,
13:14 wipe not out my good *d'* that I
Ps 28: 4 Give them according to their *d'*,
105: 1 make known his *d'* among the
Isa 59:18 According to their *d'*,
Jer 5:28 overpass the *d'* of the wicked:
25:14 them according to their *d'*, and
Lu 11:48 ye allow the *d'* of your fathers:
23:41 the due reward of our *d'*:
Joh 3:19 because their *d'* were evil.
20 lest his *d'* should be reproved.
21 his *d'* may be made manifest,
8:41 Ye do the *d'* of your father.
Ac 7:22 was mighty in words and in *d'*.
19:18 confessed, and shewed their *d'*.
24: 2 and that very worthy *d'* are done
Ro 2: 6 to every man according to his *d'*:
3:20 by the *d'* of the law there shall no
28 faith without the *d'* of the law.
8:13 do mortify the *d'* of the body,
2Co 12:12 and wonders, and mighty *d'*.
Col 3: 9 put off the old man with his *d'*;
2Pe 2: 8 to day with their unlawful *d'*;
2Jo 11 speed is partaker of his evil *d'*.
3Jo 10 his *d'* which he doeth, prating
Jude 15 of all their ungodly *d'* which
Re 2: 6 hatest the *d'* of the Nicolaitanes
22 except they repent of their *d'*.
16:11 and repented not of their *d'*.

deemed
Ac 27:27 shipmen *d'* that they drew near

deep See also DEEPER; DEEPS.
Ge 1: 2 was upon the face of the *d'*.
2:21 God caused a *d'* sleep to fall upon
7:11 fountains of the great *d'* broken
8: 2 The fountains also of the *d'* and
15:12 down, a *d'* sleep fell upon Abram;
49:25 blessings of the *d'* that lieth under,
De 33:13 for the *d'* that coucheth beneath,
1Sa 26:12 *d'* sleep from the Lord was fallen
Job 4:13 when *d'* sleep falleth on men,
12:22 He discovereth *d'* things out of
33:15 when *d'* sleep falleth upon men,
38:30 and the face of the *d'* is frozen.
41:31 maketh the *d'* to boil like a pot:
32 would think the *d'* to be hoary.
Ps 36: 6 thy judgments are a great *d'*:
42: 7 *D'* calleth unto *d'* at the noise of
64: 6 one of them, and the heart, is *d'*.
69: 2 I sink in *d'* mire, when there is no
2 I am come into *d'* waters, where
14 hate me, and out of the *d'* waters.
15 neither let the *d'* swallow me up,
80: 9 and didst cause it to take *d'* root,
92: 5 and thy thoughts are very *d'*.
95: 4 In his hand are the *d'* places of the
104: 6 Thou coveredst it with the *d'* as
107:24 Lord, and his wonders in the *d'*.
135: 6 in the seas, and all *d'* places.
140:10 into the fire; into *d'* pits, that
Pr 8:28 the fountains of the *d'*:
18: 4 of a man's mouth are as *d'* waters,
19:15 casteth into a *d'* sleep: and an
20: 5 in the heart of man is like *d'* water;
22:14 mouth of strange women is a *d'* pit;
23:27 whore is a *d'* ditch; and a strange
Ec 7:24 far off, and exceeding *d'*, who can
Isa 29:10 the spirit of *d'* sleep, and hath
15 Woe unto them that seek *d'* to
30:33 he hath made it *d'* and large:
44:27 That saith to the *d'*, Be dry,
51:10 sea, the waters of the great *d'*;
63:13 That led them through the *d'*, as
Jer 49: 8 dwell *d'*, O inhabitants of Dedan;
30 dwell *d'* O ye inhabitants of Hazor,
Eze 23:32 shalt drink of thy sister's cup *d'*
26:19 when I shall bring up the *d'* upon
31: 4 the *d'* set him up on high with her
15 I covered the *d'* for him, and I
32:14 Then will I make their waters *d'*,
34:18 to have drunk of the *d'* waters,
Da 2:22 revealeth the *d'* and secret things:
8:18 I was in a *d'* sleep on my face
10: 9 then was I in a *d'* sleep on my face,
Am 7: 4 it devoured the great *d'*, and did

Jon 2: 3 thou hadst cast me into the *d'*,
Hab 3:10 the *d'* uttered his voice, and lifted
Lu 5: 4 Launch out into the *d'*, and let
6:48 built an house, and digged *d'*,
8:31 them to go out into the *d'*.
Joh 4:11 to draw with, and the well is *d'*:
Ac 20: 9 being fallen into a *d'* sleep:
Ro 10: 7 Who shall descend into the *d'*?
1Co 2:10 things, yea, the *d'* things of God.
2Co 8: 2 their *d'* poverty abounded unto the
11:25 and a day I have been in the *d'*;

deeper
Le 13: 3 plague in sight be *d'* than the skin,
4 and in sight be not *d'* than the skin,
25 and it be in sight *d'* than the skin;
30 if it be in sight *d'* than the skin;
31 it be not in sight *d'* than the skin
32 in sight *d'* than the skin;
34 nor be in sight *d'* than the skin;
Job 11: 8 *d'* than hell; what canst thou know?
Isa 33:19 a people of *d'* speech than thou

deeply
Isa 31: 6 children of Israel have *d'* revolted
Ho 9: 9 They have *d'* corrupted themselves,
M'r 8:12 he sighed *d'* in his spirit, and saith,

deepness
M't 13: 5 because they had no *d'* of earth:

deeps
Ne 9:11 thou threwest into the *d'*, as a
Ps 88: 6 lowest pit, in darkness, in the *d'*.
148: 7 the earth, ye dragons, and all *d'*:
Zec 10:11 the *d'* of the river shall dry up:

deer See also FALLOWDEER.
De 14: 5 the roebuck, and the fallow *d'*,

defamed
1Co 4:13 Being *d'*, we intreat: we are made

defaming
Jer 20:10 For I heard the *d'* of many, fear

defeat
2Sa 15:34 me *d'* the counsel of Ahithophel.
17:14 *d'* the good counsel of Ahithophel,

defence See also DEFENCED.
Nu 14: 9 their *d'* is departed from them,
2Ch 11: 5 Jerusalem, and built cities for *d'*
Job 22:25 the Almighty shall be thy *d'*, and
Ps 7:10 My *d'* is of God, which saveth
31: 2 for an house of *d'* to save me.
59: 9 wait upon thee: for God is my *d'*.
16 thou hast been my *d'* and refuge
17 God is my *d'*, and the God of my
62: 2 and my salvation; he is my *d'*;
6 he is my *d'*; I shall not be moved.
89:18 For the Lord is our *d'*; and the
94:22 the Lord is my *d'*; and my God
Ec 7:12 wisdom is a *d'*, and money is a *d'*:
Isa 4: 5 upon all the glory shall be a *d'*.
19: 6 the brooks of *d'* shall be emptied
33:16 place of *d'* shall be the munition
Na 2: 5 and the *d'* shall be prepared.
Ac 19:33 have made his *d'* unto the people.
22: 1 hear ye my *d'*, which I make
Ph'p 1: 7 *d'* and confirmation of the gospel.
17 I am set for the *d'* of the gospel.

defenced
Isa 25: 2 of a *d'* city a ruin: a palace of
27:10 Yet the *d'* city shall be desolate
36: 1 against all the *d'* cities of Judah,
37:26 to lay waste *d'* cities into ruinous
Jer 1:18 have made thee this day a *d'* city,
4: 5 and let us go into the *d'* cities.
8:14 and let us enter into the *d'* cities,
34: 7 for these *d'* cities remained of
Eze 21:20 and to Judah in Jerusalem the *d'*.

defend See also DEFENDED; DEFENDEST; DEFENDING.
J'g 10: 1 arose to *d'* Israel Tola the son of
2Ki 19:34 For I will *d'* this city, to save it,
20: 6 will *d'* this city for mine own sake.
Ps 20: 1 name of the God of Jacob *d'* thee;
59: 1 *d'* me from them that rise up
82: 3 *D'* the poor and fatherless: do
Isa 31: 5 the Lord of hosts *d'* Jerusalem;
37:35 For I will *d'* this city to save it
38: 6 of Assyria: and I will *d'* this city.
Zec 9:15 The Lord of hosts shall *d'* them;
12: 8 In that day shall the Lord *d'* the

defended
2Sa 23:12 and *d'* it, and slew the Philistines:
Ac 7:24 suffer wrong, he *d'* him; and smote

defendest
Ps 5:11 because thou *d'* them: let them

defending
Isa 31: 5 *d'* also he will deliver it; and

defer See also DEFERRED; DEFERRETH.
Ec 5: 4 *d'* not to pay it; for he hath no
Isa 48: 9 will I *d'* mine anger, and for my
Da 9:19 *d'* not, for thine own sake, O my

deferred
Ge 34:19 young man *d'* not to do the thing,
Pr 13:12 Hope *d'* maketh the heart sick:
Ac 24:22 of that way, he *d'* them, and said,

deferreth
Pr 19:11 discretion of a man *d'* his anger;

defied
Nu 23: 8 defy, whom the Lord hath not *d'*?
1Sa 17:36 seeing he hath *d'* the armies of
45 armies of Israel, whom thou hast *d'*.
2Sa 21:21 And when he *d'* Israel, Jonathan
23: 9 when they *d'* the Philistines that
1Ch 20: 7 But when he *d'* Israel, Jonathan

defile See also DEFILED; DEFILETH.
Le 11:44 neither shall ye *d'* yourselves
15:31 when they *d'* my tabernacle that is
18:20 neighbour's wife, to *d'* thyself with
23 thou lie with any beast to *d'* thyself
24 *D'* not ye yourselves in any of these
28 spue not you out also, when ye *d'* it,
30 that ye *d'* not yourselves therein:
20: 3 to *d'* my sanctuary, and to profane
21: 4 shall not *d'* himself, being a chief
11 nor *d'* himself for his father, or for
22: 8 not eat to *d'* himself therewith:
Nu 5: 3 that they *d'* not their camps, in the
35:34 *D'* not therefore the land which ye
2Ki 23:13 children of Ammon, did the king *d'*.
Ca 5: 3 my feet; how shall I *d'* them?
Isa 30:22 Ye shall *d'* also the covering of thy
Jer 32:34 called by my name, to *d'* it.
Eze 7:22 robbers shall enter into it, and *d'*
9: 7 he said unto them, *D'* the house,
20: 7 *d'* not yourselves with the idols of
18 nor *d'* yourselves with their idols:
22: 3 maketh idols against herself to *d'*
28: 7 and they shall *d'* thy brightness.
33:26 ye *d'* every one his neighbour's
37:23 Neither shall they *d'* themselves
43: 7 shall the house of Israel no more *d'*,
44:25 no dead person to *d'* themselves:
25 husband, they may *d'* themselves.
Da 1: 8 he would not *d'* himself with the
8 that he might not *d'* himself.
M't 15:18 the heart; and they *d'* the man.
20 are the things which *d'* a man:
M'k 7:15 entering into him can *d'* him: but
15 him, those are they that *d'* the man.
18 into the man, it cannot *d'* him;
23 come from within, and *d'* the man.
1Co 3:17 If any man *d'* the temple of God,
1Ti 1:10 that *d'* themselves with mankind,
Jude 8 these filthy dreamers *d'* the flesh,

defiled See also DEFILEDST.
Ge 34: 2 and lay with her, and *d'* her.
5 Jacob heard that he had *d'* Dinah
13 he had *d'* Dinah their sister:
27 because they had *d'* their sister.
Le 5: 3 that a man shall be *d'* withal, and
11:43 them, that ye should be *d'* thereby.
13:46 shall be in him he shall be *d'*;
15:32 from him, and is *d'* therewith;
18:24 all these the nations are *d'* which
25 the land is *d'*: therefore I do visit
27 before you, and the land is *d'*;
19:31 wizards, to be *d'* by them: I am the
21: 1 There shall none be *d'* for the
3 no husband; for her may he be *d'*.
Nu 5: 2 and whosoever is *d'* by the dead:
13 kept close, and she be *d'*, and
14 jealous of his wife, and she be *d'*:
14 of his wife, and she be not *d'*:
20 if thou be *d'*, and some man have
27 if she be *d'*, and have done trespass
28 if the woman be not *d'*, but be
29 instead of her husband, and is *d'*;
6: 9 and he hath *d'* the head of his
12 lost, because his separation was *d'*.
9: 6 men, who were *d'* by the dead
7 We are *d'* by the dead body of a
19:20 hath *d'* the sanctuary of the Lord:
De 21:23 that thy land be not *d'*, which the
22: 9 the fruit of thy vineyard, be *d'*.
24: 4 after that she is *d'*; for that is
2Ki 23: 8 and *d'* the high places where the
10 And he *d'* Topheth, which is in
1Ch 5: 1 forasmuch as he *d'* his father's
Neh 13:29 they have *d'* the priesthood,
Job 16:15 and *d'* my horn in the dust.
Ps 74: 7 they have *d'* by casting down the
79: 1 thy holy temple have they *d'*;
106:39 Thus were they *d'* with their own
Isa 24: 5 The earth also is *d'* under the
59: 3 your hands are *d'* with blood, and
Jer 2: 7 when ye entered, ye *d'* my land,
3: 9 she *d'* the land, and committed
16:18 because they have *d'* my land,
19:13 be *d'* as the place of Tophet,
Eze 4:13 Israel eat their *d'* bread among
5:11 thou hast *d'* my sanctuary with
7:24 and their holy places shall be *d'*.
18: 6 hath *d'* his neighbour's wife,
11 and *d'* his neighbour's wife,
15 hath not *d'* his neighbour's wife,
20:43 wherein ye have been *d'*: and ye
22: 4 and hast *d'* thyself in thine idols
11 hath lewdly *d'* his daughter in law;
23: 7 with all their idols she *d'* herself.
13 Then I saw that she was *d'*, that
17 they *d'* her with their whoredom,
38 they have *d'* my sanctuary in the
28:18 Thou hast *d'* thy sanctuaries by
36:17 dwelt in their own land, they *d'* it
43: 8 they have even *d'* my holy name
Hos 5: 3 whoredom, and Israel is *d'*.
6:10 whoredom of Ephraim, Israel is *d'*.
Mic 4:11 that say, Let her be *d'*, and let our
M'k 7: 2 eat bread with *d'*, that is to say,
Joh 18:28 lest they should be *d'*; but that
1Co 8: 7 their conscience being weak is *d'*.
Tit 1:15 but unto them that are *d'* and
15 their mind and conscience is *d'*.
Heb 12:15 you, and thereby many be *d'*;
Rev 3: 4 which have not *d'* their garments;
14: 4 which were not *d'* with women;

defiledst
Ge 49: 4 then *d'* thou it: he went up to

defileth
Ex 31:14 every one that *d'* it shall surely
Nu 19:13 *d'* the tabernacle of the Lord;
35:33 for blood it *d'* the land: and the
M't 15:11 into the mouth *d'* a man; but that
11 out of the mouth, this *d'* a man.
20 with unwashen hands *d'* not a man.
M'k 7:20 of the man, that *d'* the man.
Jas 3: 6 members, that it *d'* the whole body,
Re 21:27 enter into it any thing that *d'*,

defraud See also DEFRAUDED.
Le 19:13 Thou shalt not *d'* thy neighbour,
M'r 10:19 *D'* not, Honour thy father and
1Co 6: 8 Nay, ye do wrong, and *d'*, and that
7: 5 *D'* ye not one the other, except it
1Th 4: 6 and *d'* his brother in any matter:

defrauded
1Sa 12: 3 I taken? or whom have I *d'*?
4 Thou hast not *d'* us, nor oppressed
1Co 6: 7 rather suffer yourselves to be *d'*?
2Co 7: 2 no man, we have *d'* no man.

defy See also DEFIED.
Nu 23: 7 me Jacob, and come, *d'* Israel.
8 hath not cursed? or how shall I *d'*,
1Sa 17:10 I *d'* the armies of Israel this day;
25 surely to *d'* Israel is he come up:
26 that he should *d'* the armies of the

degenerate
Jer 2:21 art thou turned into the *d'* plant

degree See also DEGREES.
1Ch 15:18 of the second *d'*, Zechariah, Ben,
17:17 to the estate of a man of high *d'*,
Ps 62: 9 *d'* are vanity, and men of high *d'*
Lu 1:52 seats, and exalted them of low *d'*.
1Ti 3:13 purchase to themselves a good *d'*,
Jas 1: 9 Let the brother of low *d'* rejoice

degrees
2Ki 20: 9 the shadow go forward ten *d'*,
9 or go back ten *d'*?
10 for the shadow to go down ten *d'*:
10 shadow return backward ten *d'*.
11 the shadow ten *d'* backward, by
Ps 120 *title* A Song of *d'*.
121 *title* A Song of *d'*.
122 *title* A Song of *d'* of David.
123 *title* A Song of *d'*.
124 *title* A Song of *d'* of David.
125 *title* A Song of *d'*.
126 *title* A Song of *d'*.
127 *title* A Song of *d'* for Solomon.
128 *title* A Song of *d'*.
129 *title* A Song of *d'*.
130 *title* A Song of *d'*.
131 *title* A Song of *d'* of David.
132 *title* A Song of *d'*.
133 *title* A Song of *d'* of David.
134 *title* A Song of *d'*.
Isa 38: 8 bring again the shadow of the *d'*,
8 Ahaz, ten *d'* backward. So the sun
8 ten *d'*, by which *d'* it was gone

Dehavites (*de-ha'-vites*)
Ezr 4: 9 the *D'*, and the Elamites,

Dekar (*de'-kar*)
1Ki 4: 9 The son of *D'*, in Makaz, and in

Delaiah (*del-a-i'-ah*) See also DALAIAH.
1Ch 24:18 The three and twentieth to *D'*,
Ezr 2:60 The children of *D'*, the children of
Ne 6:10 house of Shemaiah the son of *D'*
7:62 The children of *D'*, the children of
Jer 36:12 and *D'* the son of Shemaiah,
25 Nevertheless Elnathan and *D'* and

delay See also DELAYED; DELAYETH.
Ex 22:29 Thou shalt not *d'* to offer the
Ac 9:38 that he would not *d'* to come
25:17 without any *d'* on the morrow

delayed
Ex 32: 1 Moses *d'* to come down out of the
Ps 119:60 I made haste, and *d'* not to keep

delayeth
M't 24:48 My lord *d'* his coming; and shall
Lu 12:45 My lord *d'* his coming; and shall

delectable
Isa 44: 9 their *d'* things shall not profit;

delicacies
Rev 18: 3 through the abundance of her *d'*.

delicate See also DELICATES.
De 28:54 is tender among you, and very *d'*,
56 The tender and *d'* woman among
Isa 47: 1 no more be called tender and *d'*.
Jer 6: 2 to a comely and *d'* woman.
Mic 1:16 and poll thee for thy *d'* children;

delicately
1Sa 15:32 And Agag came unto him *d'*.
Pr 29:21 He that *d'* bringeth up his servant
La 4: 5 They that did feed *d'* are desolate
Lu 7:25 and live *d'*, are in kings' courts.

delicateness
De 28:56 of her foot upon the ground for *d'*

delicates
Jer 51:34 he hath filled his belly with my *d'*,

deliciously
Re 18: 7 glorified herself, and lived *d'*,
9 and lived *d'* with her, shall

delight See also DELIGHTED; DELIGHTEST; DELIGHTETH; DELIGHTS; DELIGHTSOME.
Ge 34:19 he had *d'* in Jacob's daughter:
Nu 14: 8 If the Lord *d'* in us, then he will
De 10:15 the Lord had a *d'* in thy fathers
21:14 if thou have no *d'* in her, then

1Sa 15:22 Hath the Lord as great d' in burnt
18:22 the king hath d' in thee, and all
2Sa 15:26 I have no d' in thee; behold, here
24: 3 doth my lord the king d' in this
Es 6: 6 To whom would the king d' to do
Job 22:26 then shalt thou have thy d' in the
27:10 Will he d' himself in the Almighty?
34: 9 that he should d' himself with God.
Ps 1: 2 But his d' is in the law of the Lord;
16: 3 excellent, in whom is all my d'.
37: 4 D' thyself also in the Lord; and
11 d' themselves in the abundance
40: 8 I d' to do thy will, O my God:
62: 4 they d' in lies: they bless with
68:30 thou the people that d' in war.
94:19 me thy comforts d' my soul.
119:16 I will d' myself in thy statutes:
24 Thy testimonies also are my d'
35 for therein do I d'.
47 d' myself in thy commandments,
70 fat as grease; but I d' in thy law.
77 I may live: for thy law is my d'.
174 O Lord; and thy law is my d'.
Pr 1:22 the scorners d' in their scorning,
2:14 and d', in the frowardness of the
8:30 I was daily his d', rejoicing always
11: 1 but a just weight is his d'.
20 but such as are upright are his d'.
12:22 but they that deal truly are his d'.
15: 8 the prayer of the upright is his d'.
16:13 Righteous lips are the d' of kings;
18: 2 fool hath no d' in understanding,
19:10 D' is not seemly for a fool;
24:25 them that rebuke him shall be d',
29:17 he shall give d' unto thy soul.
Ca 2: 3 under his shadow with great d',
Isa 1:11 I d' not in the blood of bullocks,
13:17 as for gold, they shall not d' in it.
55: 2 let your soul d' itself in fatness.
58: 2 me daily, and d' to know my ways,
Isa 58: 2 take d' in approaching to God.
13 call the sabbath a d', the holy of
14 shalt thou d' thyself in the Lord;
Jer 6:10 reproach; they have no d' in it.
9:24 these things I d', saith the Lord.
Mal 3: 1 of the covenant, whom ye d' in:
Ro 7:22 For I d' in the law of God after

delighted
1Sa 19: 2 Saul's son d' much in David:
2Sa 22:20 delivered me, because he d' in me.
1Ki 10: 9 which d' in thee, to set thee on the
2Ch 9: 8 which d' in thee to set thee on his
Ne 9:25 and d' themselves in thy great
Es 2:14 no more, except the king d' in her,
Ps 18:19 delivered me, because he d' in me.
22: 8 deliver him, seeing he d' in him.
109:17 as he d' not in blessing, so let it be
Isa 65:12 did choose that wherein I d' not.
66: 4 and chose that in which I d' not.
11 and be d' with the abundance

delightest
Ps 51:16 thou d' not in burnt offering.

delighteth
Es 6: 6 man whom the king d' to honour?
7 man whom the king d' to honour,
9 withal whom the king d' to honour
9, 11 whom the king d' to honour.
Ps 37:23 Lord: and he d' in his way.
112: 1 d' greatly in his commandments.
147:10 d' not in the strength of the horse:
Pr 3:12 a father the son in whom he d'.
Isa 42: 1 mine elect, in whom my soul d';
62: 4 the Lord d' in thee, and thy land
66: 3 their soul d' in their abominations.
Mic 7:18 for ever, because he d' in mercy.
Mal 2:17 and he d' in them; or, Where is the

delights
2Sa 1:24 you in scarlet, with other d',
Ps 119:92 Unless thy law had been my d',
143 thy commandments are my d'.
Pr 8:31 my d' were with the sons of men.
Ec 2: 8 and the d' of the sons of men,
Ca 7: 6 pleasant art thou, O love, for d'!

delightsome
Mal 3:12 for ye shall be a d' land,

Delilah (*de-li'-lah*)
J'g 16: 4 of Sorek, whose name was D'.
6 D' said to Samson, Tell me, I pray
10 D' said unto Samson, Behold, thou
12 D' therefore took new ropes, and
13 D' said unto Samson, Hitherto thou
18 D' saw that he had told her all

deliver See also DELIVERED; DELIVEREST; DELIVERETH; DELIVERING.
Ge 32:11 D' me, I pray thee, from the hand
37:22 to d' him to his father again.
40:13 d' Pharaoh's cup into his hand,
42:34 will I d' you your brother, and ye
37 d' him into my hand, and I will
Ex 3: 8 I am come down to d' them
5:18 yet shall ye d' the tale of bricks.
21:13 but God d' him into his hand;
22: 7 a man shall d' unto his neigbour
10 If a man d' unto his neighbour
26 thou shalt d' it unto him by that
23:31 d' the inhabitants of the land into
Le 26:26 shall d' you your bread again
Nu 21: 2 If thou wilt indeed d' this people
35:25 congregation shall d' the slayer
De 1:27 to d' us into the hand of the
2:30 that he might d' him into thy hand.
3: 2 d' him, and all his people, into
De 7: 2 Lord thy God shall d' them before
16 the Lord thy God shall d' thee;
23 the Lord thy God shall d' them unto
24 shall d' their kings into thine hand,
19:12 d' him into the hand of the avenger
23:14 the midst of thy camp, to d' thee,
15 not d' unto his master the servant
24:13 shalt d' him the pledge again
25:11 to d' her husband out of the hand
32:39 any that can d' out of my hand.
Jos 2:13 have, and d' our lives from death.
7: 7 to d' us into the hand of the
8: 7 the Lord your God will d' it into
11: 6 about this time will I d' them up
20: 5 d' the slayer up into his hand;
J'g 4: 7 and I will d' him into thine hand.
7: 7 I save you, and d' the Midianites
10:11 not I d' you from the Egyptians
13 wherefore I will d' you no more.
14 let them d' you in the time of
15 d' us only, we pray thee, this day.
11: 9 and the Lord d' them before me,
30 d' the children of Ammon into mine
13: 5 he shall begin to d' Israel out of
15:12 that we may d' thee into the hand
13 fast, and d' thee into their hand:
20:13 Now therefore d' us the men, the
28 I will d' them into thine hand.
1Sa 4: 8 who shall d' us out of the hand of
7: 3 he will d' you out of the hand of the
14 the coasts thereof did Israel d' out
12:10 but now d' us out of the hand of our
21 things, which cannot profit nor d';
14:37 d' them into the hand of Israel?
17:37 he will d' me out of the hand of
46 the Lord d' thee into mine hand;
23: 4 d' the Philistines into thine hand.
11 Will the men of Keilah d' me up
12 Will the men of Keilah d' me and
12 Lord said, They will d' thee up.
20 to d' him into the king's hand.
24: 4 I will d' thine enemy into thine
15 and d' me out of thine hand.
26:24 him d' me out of all tribulation.
28:19 Lord will also d' Israel with thee
19 the Lord also shall d' the host into
30:15 nor d' me into the hands of my
2Sa 3:14 D' me my wife Michal, which I
5:19 wilt thou d' them into mine hand?
19 will doubtless d' the Philistines into
14: 7 D' him that smote his brother that
16 d' his handmaid out of the hand
20:21 d' him only, and I will depart
1Ki 8:46 d' them to the enemy, so that they
18: 9 thou wouldst d' thy servant into
20: 5 Thou shalt d' me thy silver, and
13 I will d' it into thine hand
28 I d' all this great multitude into
22: 6 shall d' it into the hand of the king.
12 Lord shall d' it into the king's hand
15 shall d' into the hand of the king.
2Ki 3:10, 13 d' them into the hand of Moab!
18 he will d' the Moabites also into
12: 7 d' it for the breaches of the house.
17:39 he shall d' you out of the hand of
18:23 will d' thee two thousand horses,
29 he shall not be able to d' you
30 The Lord will surely d' us, and this
32 you, saying, The Lord will d' us.
35 the Lord should d' Jerusalem out
20: 6 I will d' thee and this city out of the
21:14 and d' them into the hand of their
22: 5 And let them d' it into the hand of
1Ch 14:10 thou d' them into mine hand?
10 for I will d' them into thine hand.
16:35 and d' us from the heathen, that
2Ch 6:36 angry with them, and d' them over
18: 5 God will d' it into the king's hand.
11 shall d' it into the hand of the king.
25:15 could not d' their own people
20 that he might d' them into the
28:11 and d' the captives again, which
32:11 The Lord our God shall d' us out
13 d' their lands out of mine hand?
14 d' his people out of mine hand,
14 God should be able to d' you out
15 able to d' his people out of mine
15 your God d' you out of mine hand?
17 God of Hezekiah d' his people out
Ezr 7:19 those d' thou before the God of
Ne 9:28 many times didst thou d' them
Job 5: 4 neither is there any to d' them.
19 He shall d' thee in six troubles:
6:23 D' me from the enemy's hand?
10: 7 there is none that can d' out of
22:30 d' the island of the innocent:
33:24 D' him from going down to the
28 He will d' his soul from going
36:18 a great ransom cannot d' thee.
Ps 6: 4 Return, O Lord, d' my soul: oh
7: 1 that persecute me, and d' me:
2 in pieces, while there is none to d'.
17:13 d' my soul from the wicked,
22: 4 trusted, and thou didst d' them.
8 on the Lord that he would d' him:
8 d' him, seeing he delighted in
20 D' my soul from the sword; my
25:20 O keep my soul, and d' me:
27:12 D' me not over unto the will of
31: 1 d' me in thy righteousness.
2 d' me speedily: be thou my strong
15 d' me from the hand of mine
33:17 he d' any by his great strength.
19 To d' their soul from death, and
37:40 d' them: he shall d' them from
Ps 39: 8 D' me from all my transgressions:
40:13 Be pleased, O Lord, to d' me:
41: 1 Lord will d' him in time of trouble.
2 thou wilt not d' him unto the will
43: 1 O d' me from the deceitful and
50:15 the day of trouble: I will d' thee,
22 in pieces, and there be none to d'.
51:14 D' me from bloodguiltiness, O God,
56:13 not thou d' my foot from falling,
59: 1 D' me from mine enemies, O my
2 D' me from the workers of iniquity,
69:14 D' me out of the mire, and let me
18 d' me because of mine enemies.
70: 1 Make haste, O God, to d' me:
71: 2 D' me in thy righteousness, and
4 D' me, O my God, out of the
11 for there is none to d' him.
72:12 shall d' the needy when he crieth;
74:19 O d' not the soul of thy turtledove
79: 9 d' us, and purge away our sins,
82: 4 D' the poor and needy: rid them
89:48 shall he d' his soul from the hand
91: 3 he shall d' thee from the snare
14 will I d' him: I will set him on
15 I will d' him, and honour him
106:43 Many times did he d' them; but
109:21 thy mercy is good, d' thou me.
116: 4 Lord, I beseech thee, d' my soul.
119:134 D' me from the oppression of
153 mine affliction and d' me: for I
154 Plead my cause, and d' me:
170 d' me according to thy word.
120: 2 D' my soul, O Lord, from lying
140: 1 D' me, O Lord, from the evil man:
142: 6 d' me from my persecutors; for
143: 9 D' me, O Lord, from mine enemies:
144: 7 and d' me out of great waters,
11 and d' me from the hand of strange
Pr 2:12 To d' thee from the way of the evil
16 To d' thee from the strange woman,
4: 9 a crown of glory shall she d' to
6: 3 this now, my son, and d' thyself,
5 D' thyself as a roe from the hand
11: 6 of the upright shall d' them:
12: 6 mouth of the upright shall d' them.
19:19 if thou d' him, yet thou must
23:14 and shall d' his soul from hell.
24:11 If thou forbear to d' them that are
Ec 8: 8 neither shall wickedness d' those
Isa 5:29 away safe, and none shall d' it.
19:20 a great one, and he shall d' them.
29:11 men d' to one that is learned,
31: 5 defending also he will d' it.
36:14 he shall not be able to d' you.
15 The Lord will surely d' us: this city
18 you, saying, The Lord will d' us.
20 that the Lord should d' Jerusalem
38: 6 And I will d' thee and this city
43:13 there is none that can d' out of my
44:17 D' me; for thou art my god.
20 he cannot d' his soul, nor say,
46: 2 they could not d' the burden, but
4 I will carry, and will d' you.
47:14 they shall not d' themselves from
50: 2 or have I no power to d'?
57:13 let thy companies d' thee; but the
Jer 1: 8 I am with thee to d' thee, saith
19 with thee, saith the Lord, to d' thee.
15: 9 the residue of them will I d' to the
20 to save thee and to d' thee,
21 And I will d' thee out of the hand
18:21 d' up their children to the famine
20: 5 will d' all the strength of the city,
21: 7 I will d' Zedekiah king of Judah,
12 and d' him that is spoiled out of
22: 3 and d' the spoiled out of the hand
24: 9 And I will d' them to be removed
29:18 and will d' them to be removed
21 I will d' them into the hand of
38:19 lest they d' me into their hand,
20 They shall not d' thee. Obey, I
39:17 But I will d' thee in that day,
18 I will surely d' thee, and thou
42:11 and to d' you from his hand.
43: 3 to d' us into the hand of the
11 and d' such as are for death to
46:26 and I will d' them into the hand
51: 6 and d' every man his soul: be
45 and d' ye every man his soul
La 5: 8 there is none that doth d' us out
Eze 7:19 gold shall not be able to d' them
11: 9 and d' you into the hands of
13:21 and d' my people out of your
23 for I will d' my people out of your
14:14 they should d' but their own souls
16 d' neither sons nor daughters; they
18 d' neither sons nor daughters, but
20 shall d' neither son nor daughter;
20 they shall but d' their own souls
21:31 and d' thee into the hand of
23:28 I will d' thee into the hand of them
25: 4 I will d' thee to the men of the
7 and will d' thee for a spoil to the
33: 5 taketh warning shall d' his soul.
12 of the righteous shall not d' him
34:10 I will d' my flock from their mouth,
12 and will d' them out of all places
Da 3:15 who is that God that shall d' you
17 is able to d' us from the burning
17 he will d' us out of thine hand,
29 God that can d' after this sort.
6:14 set his heart on Daniel to d' him:
14 going down of the sun to d' him.
16 servest continually, he will d' thee.
20 able to d' thee from the lions?

Da 8: 4 was there any that could *d'* out of
7 was none that could *d'* the ram
Hos 2:10 shall *d'* her out of mine hand.
11: 8 how shall I *d'* thee, Israel?
Am 1: 6 captivity, to *d'* them up to Edom:
2:14 shall the mighty *d'* himself:
15 swift of foot shall not *d'* himself:
15 he that rideth the horse *d'* himself.
6: 8 therefore will I *d'* up the city
Jon 4: 6 head, to *d'* him from his grief.
Mic 5: 6 shall he *d'* us from the Assyrian,
8 teareth in pieces, and none can *d'*.
6:14 shalt take hold, but shalt not *d'*;
Zep 1:18 shall be able to *d'* them in the day
Zec 2: 7 *D'* thyself, O Zion, that dwellest
11: 6 I will *d'* the men every one
6 out of their hand I will not *d'* them.
M't 5:25 adversary *d'* thee to the judge,
25 and the judge *d'* thee to the officer,
6:13 temptation, but *d'* us from evil:
10:17 will *d'* you up to the councils,
19 But when they *d'* you up, take
21 the brother shall *d'* up the brother
20:19 And shall *d'* him to the Gentiles
24: 9 Then shall they *d'* you up to the
26:15 and I will *d'* him unto you?
27:43 let him *d'* him now, if he will have
M'r 10:33 and shall *d'* him to the Gentiles:
13: 9 they shall *d'* you up to councils;
11 and *d'* you up, take no thought
Lu 11: 4 temptation; but *d'* us from evil.
12:58 the judge *d'* thee to the officer,
20:20 that so they might *d'* him unto the
Ac 7:25 God by his hand would *d'* them:
34 and am come down to *d'* them.
21:11 and shall *d'* him into the hands of
25:11 no man may *d'* me unto them.
16 to *d'* any man to die, before that
Ro 7:24 who shall *d'* me from the body of
1Co 5: 5 To *d'* such an one unto Satan
2Co 1:10 a death, and doth *d'*: in whom
10 we trust that he will yet *d'* us;
Ga 1: 4 that he might *d'* us from this
2Ti 4:18 the Lord shall *d'* me from every
Heb 2:15 and *d'* them who through fear of
2Pe 2: 9 The Lord knoweth how to *d'* the

deliverance See also DELIVERANCES.
Ge 45: 7 save your lives by a great *d'*.
J'g 15:18 Thou hast given this great *d'*
2Ki 5: 1 Lord had given *d'* unto Syria:
13:17 The arrow of the Lord's *d'*,
17 the arrow of *d'* from Syria
1Ch 11:14 Lord saved them by a great *d'*.
2Ch 12: 7 but I will grant them some *d'*;
Ezr 9:13 hast given us such *d'* as this;
Es 4:14 enlargement and *d'* arise to the
Ps 18:50 Great *d'* giveth he to his king;
32: 7 me about with the songs of *d'*.
Isa 26:18 we have not wrought any *d'* in
Joe 2:32 and in Jerusalem shall be *d'*
Ob 17 upon Mount Zion shall be *d'*
Lu 4:18 to preach *d'* to the captives, and
Heb 11:35 were tortured, not accepting *d'*;

deliverances
Ps 44: 4 O God: command *d'* for Jacob.

delivered See also DELIVEREDST.
Ge 9: 2 sea; into your hand are they *d'*.
14:20 hath *d'* thine enemies into thy
25:24 her days to be *d'* were fulfilled,
32:16 And he *d'* them into the hand of
37:21 and he *d'* him out of their hands;
Ex 1:19 and are *d'* ere the midwives come
2:19 An Egyptian *d'* us out of the hand
5:23 neither hast thou *d'* thy people at
12:27 the Egyptians, and *d'* our houses.
18: 4 *d'* me from the sword of Pharaoh:
8 way, and how the Lord *d'* them.
9 whom he had *d'* out of the hand
10 who hath *d'* you out of the hand of
10 of Pharaoh, who hath *d'* the people
Le 6: 2 which was *d'* him to keep, or in
4 which was *d'* him to keep, or the
26:25 and ye shall be *d'* into the
Nu 21: 3 and *d'* up the Canaanites; and they
34 I have *d'* him into thy hand,
31: 5 they were *d'* out of the thousands
De 2:33 And the Lord our God *d'* him
36 the Lord our God *d'* all unto us:
3: 3 So the Lord our God *d'* into our
5:22 of stone, and *d'* them unto me.
9:10 And the Lord *d'* unto me two tables
20:13 God hath *d'* it into thine hands,
21:10 the Lord thy God hath *d'* them
31: 9 and *d'* it unto the priests the sons
Jos 2:24 the Lord hath *d'* into our hands
9:26 and *d'* them out of the hand of the
10: 8 I have *d'* them into thine hand;
12 the Lord *d'* up the Amorites before
19 the Lord your God hath *d'* them
30 And the Lord *d'* it also, and the
32 And the Lord *d'* Lachish into the
11: 8 *d'* them into the hand of Israel,
21:44 the Lord *d'* all their enemies into
22:31 ye have *d'* the children of Israel
24:10 so I *d'* you out of his hand.
11 and I *d'* them into your hand.
J'g 1: 2 I have *d'* the land into his hand.
4 and the Lord *d'* the Canaanites
2:14 and he *d'* them into the hands of
16 which *d'* them out of the hand of
18 and *d'* them out of the hand of
23 neither *d'* he them into the hand
3: 9 children of Israel who *d'* them,
10 the Lord *d'* Chushan-rishathaim
28 hath *d'* your enemies the Moabites
J'g 3:31 ox-goad: and he also *d'* Israel.
4:14 hath *d'* Sisera into thine hand:
5:11 are *d'* from the noise of archers
6: 1 *d'* them into the hand of Midian
9 And I *d'* you out of the hand of
13 and *d'* us into the hands of the
7: 9 I have *d'* it into thine hand.
14 into his hand hath God *d'* Midian,
15 the Lord hath *d'* into your hand
8: 3 God hath *d'* into your hands the
7 when the Lord hath *d'* Zebah and
22 *d'* us from the hand of Midian.
34 Lord their God, who had *d'* them
9:17 *d'* you out of the hand of Midian:
10:12 and I *d'* you out of their hand.
11:21 the Lord God of Israel *d'* Sihon
32 the Lord *d'* them into his hands.
12: 2 ye *d'* me not out of their hands.
3 And when I saw that ye *d'* me not,
3 the Lord *d'* them into my hand:
13: 1 and the Lord *d'* them into the hand
16:23 hath *d'* Samson our enemy into our
24 hath *d'* into our hands our enemy,
1Sa 4:19 was with child, near to be *d'*:
10:18 and *d'* you out of the hand of the
12:11 and *d'* you out of the hand of your
14:10 hath *d'* them into our hand:
12 *d'* them into the hand of Israel.
48 *d'* Israel out of the hands of them
17:35 and *d'* it out of his mouth:
37 *d'* me out of the paw of the lion,
23: 7 God hath *d'* him into mine hand;
14 God *d'* him not into his hand.
24:10 the Lord had *d'* thee to day
18 Lord had *d'* me into thine hand,
26: 8 *d'* thine enemy into thine hand
23 the Lord *d'* thee into my hand
30:23 and *d'* the company that came
2Sa 3: 8 not *d'* thee into the hand of David,
10:10 the rest of the people he *d'*
12: 7 I *d'* thee out of the hand of Saul;
16: 8 and the Lord hath *d'* the kingdom
18:28 hath *d'* up the men that lifted
19: 9 and he *d'* us out of the hand of
21: 6 Let seven men of his sons be *d'*
9 And he *d'* them into the hands of
22: 1 the Lord had *d'* him out of the
18 He *d'* me from my strong enemy,
20 he *d'* me, because he delighted in
44 *d'* me from the strivings of my
49 hast *d'* me from the violent man.
1Ki 3:17 *d'* of a child with her in the house
18 the third day after that I was *d'*,
18 that this woman was *d'* also:
13:26 Lord hath *d'* him unto the lion,
15:18 and *d'* them into the hand of his
17:23 and *d'* him unto his mother: and
2Ki 12:15 they *d'* the money to be bestowed
13: 3 *d'* them into the hand of Hazael
17:20 *d'* them into the hand of spoilers,
18:30 shall not be *d'* into the hand
33 any of the gods of the nations, *d'*
34 *d'* Samaria out of mine hand?
35 *d'* their country out of mine hand.
19:10 Jerusalem shall not be *d'* into
11 utterly: and shalt thou be *d'*?
12 the gods of the nation *d'* them
22: 7 the money that was *d'* into their
9 and have *d'* it into the hand of
10 Hilkiah the priest hath *d'* me a
1Ch 5:20 Hagarites were *d'* into their hand,
11:14 *d'* it, and slew the Philistines;
16: 7 David *d'* first this psalm to thank
19:11 the rest of the people he *d'* unto
2Ch 13:16 and God *d'* them into their hand.
16: 8 Lord, he *d'* them into thine hand.
18:14 and they shall be *d'* into your hand
23: 9 Moreover Jehoiada the priest *d'* to
24:24 *d'* a very great host into their hand,
28: 5 Lord his God *d'* him into the hand
5 he was also *d'* into the hand of
9 he hath *d'* them into your hand,
29: 8 and he hath *d'* them to trouble,
32:17 not *d'* their people out of mine
34: 9 the high priest, they *d'* the money
15 Hilkiah *d'* the book to Shaphan
17 *d'* it into the hand of the overseers,
Ezr 5:14 and they were *d'* unto one,
8:31 *d'* us from the hand of the enemy,
36 they *d'* the king's commissions
9: 7 our priests, been *d'* into the hand
Es 6: 9 let this apparel and horse be *d'*
Job 16:11 God hath *d'* me to the ungodly,
22:30 *d'* by the pureness of thine hands.
23: 7 I be *d'* for ever from my judge
29:12 I *d'* the poor that cried, and the
Ps 7: 4 have *d'* him that without cause
18:*title* the Lord *d'* him from the hand
17 He *d'* me from my strong enemy,
19 he *d'* me, because he delighted in
43 hast *d'* me from the strivings
48 *d'* me from the violent man.
22: 5 They cried unto thee and were *d'*:
33:16 a mighty man is not *d'* by much
34: 4 and *d'* me from all my fears.
54: 7 he hath *d'* me out of all trouble:
55:18 He hath *d'* my soul in peace
56:13 thou hast *d'* my soul from death:
60: 5 That thy beloved may be *d'*; save
69:14 me be *d'* from them that hate me,
78:42 he *d'* them from the enemy.
61 And *d'* his strength into captivity,
81: 6 his hands were *d'* from the pots.
7 calledst in trouble, and I *d'* thee;
86:13 and thou hast *d'* my soul from the
107: 6 he *d'* them out of their distresses.
Ps 107:20 *d'* them from their destructions.
108: 6 That thy beloved may be *d'*: save
116: 8 thou hast *d'* my soul from death,
Pr 11: 8 The righteous is *d'* out of trouble,
9 knowledge shall the just be *d'*.
21 seed of the righteous shall be *d'*.
28:26 walketh wisely, he shall be *d'*.
Ec 9:15 and he by his wisdom *d'* the city;
Isa 20: 6 to be *d'* from the king of Assyria:
29:12 And the book is *d'* to him that is
34: 2 he hath *d'* them to the slaughter.
36:15 this city shall not be *d'* into the
18 the gods of the nations *d'* his land
19 have they *d'* Samaria out of my
20 that have *d'* their land out of my
37:11 them utterly; and shalt thou be *d'*?
12 Have the gods of the nations *d'* them
38:17 hast in love to my soul *d'* it from the
49:24 mighty, or the lawful captive *d'*?
25 the prey of the terrible shall be *d'*:
66: 7 came, she was *d'* of a man child.
Jer 7:10 are *d'* to do all these abominations?
20:13 he hath *d'* the soul of the poor
32: 4 surely be *d'* into the hand of the
16 when I had *d'* the evidence of the
36 It shall be *d'* into the hand of the
34: 3 shalt surely be taken, and *d'* into
37:17 thou shalt be *d'* into the hand of the
46:24 she shall be *d'* into the hand of the
La 1:14 Lord hath *d'* me into their hands,
Eze 3:19 iniquity; but thou hast *d'* thy soul.
21 warned; also thou hast *d'* thy soul.
14:16 they only shall be *d'*, but the land
18 they only shall be *d'* themselves.
16:21 and *d'* them to cause them to pass
27 and *d'* thee unto the will of them
17:15 he break the covenant, and be *d'*?
23: 9 I have *d'* her into the hand of her
31:11 I have therefore *d'* him into the
14 they are all *d'* unto death, to the
32:20 she is *d'* to the sword: draw her
33: 9 iniquity; but thou hast *d'* thy soul.
34:27 and *d'* them out of the hand of those
Da 3:28 hath sent his angel, and *d'* his
6:27 who hath *d'* Daniel from the power
12: 1 thy people shall be *d'*, every one
Joel 2:32 the name of the Lord shall be *d'*:
Am 1: 9 they *d'* up the whole captivity to
9: 1 escapeth of them I shall not be *d'*
Ob 14 neither shouldest thou have *d'* up
Mic 4:10 there shalt thou be *d'*; there the
Hab 2: 9 that he may be *d'* from the power
Mal 3:15 they that tempt God are even *d'*.
M't 11:27 All things are *d'* unto me of my
18:34 and *d'* him to the tormentors, till
25:14 and *d'* unto them his goods.
27: 2 and *d'* him to Pontius Pilate the
18 that for envy they had *d'* him.
26 Jesus, he *d'* him to be crucified.
58 commanded the body to be *d'*.
M'r 7:13 your tradition, which ye have *d'*:
9:31 is *d'* into the hands of men, and
10:33 the Son of man shall be *d'* unto the
15: 1 him away, and *d'* him to Pilate.
10 chief priests had *d'* him for envy.
15 and *d'* Jesus, when he had scourged
Lu 1: 2 Even as they *d'* them unto us,
57 time came that she should be *d'*;
74 that we being *d'* out of the hand
2: 6 accomplished that she should be *d'*.
4: 6 of them; for that is *d'* unto me;
17 was *d'* unto him the book of the
7:15 And he *d'* him to his mother.
9:42 and *d'* him again to his father.
44 Son of man shall be *d'* into the
10:22 things are *d'* to me of my Father.
12:58 that thou mayest be *d'* from him;
18:32 For he shall be *d'* unto the Gentiles.
19:13 *d'* them ten pounds, and said unto
23:25 but he *d'* Jesus to their will.
24: 7 must be *d'* into the hands of sinful
20 and our rulers *d'* him to be
Joh 16:21 as soon as she is *d'* of the child,
18:30 we would not have *d'* him up unto
35 chief priests have *d'* thee unto me:
36 that I should not be *d'* to the Jews:
19:11 therefore he that *d'* me unto thee
16 Then *d'* he him therefore unto
Ac 2:23 Him being *d'* by the determinate
3:13 whom ye *d'* up, and denied him
6:14 the customs which Moses *d'* us.
7:10 And *d'* him out of all his afflictions,
12: 4 and *d'* him to four quaternions of
11 and hath *d'* me out of the hand of
15:30 together, they *d'* the epistle:
16: 4 *d'* them the decrees for to keep
23:33 *d'* the epistle to the governor,
27: 1 they *d'* Paul and certain other
28:16 the centurion *d'* the prisoners to
17 yet was I *d'* prisoner from
Ro 4:25 Who was *d'* for our offences, and
6:17 form of doctrine which was *d'* you.
7: 6 now we are *d'* from the law,
8:21 shall be *d'* from the bondage of
32 own Son, but *d'* him up for us all,
15:31 That I may be *d'* from them that
1Co 11: 2 ordinances, as I *d'* them to you.
23 which also I *d'* unto you, that the
15: 3 For I *d'* unto you first of all that
24 when he shall have *d'* up the
2Co 1:10 Who *d'* us from so great a death,
4:11 are alway *d'* unto death for Jesus'
Col 1:13 *d'* us from the power of darkness,
1Th 1:10 Jesus which *d'* us from the wrath
2Th 3: 2 we may be *d'* from unreasonable
1Ti 1:20 whom I have *d'* unto Satan, that

2Ti 3:11 out of them all the Lord *d'* me.
4:17 was *d'* out of the mouth of the lion.
Heb 11:11 and was *d'* of a child when she
2Pe 2: 4 *d'* them into chains of darkness,
7 And *d'* just Lot, vexed with the
21 holy commandment *d'* unto them.
Jude 3 faith which was once *d'* unto the
Re 12: 2 in birth, and pained to be *d'*.
4 woman which was ready to be *d'*,
20:13 death and hell *d'* up the dead

deliveredst
Ne 9:27 Therefore thou *d'* them into the
M't 25:20 Lord, thou *d'* unto me five talents:
22 Lord, thou *d'* unto me two talents:

deliverer
J'g 3: 9 the Lord raised up a *d'* to the
15 the Lord raised them up a *d'*,
18:28 there was no *d'*, because it was
2Sa 22: 2 rock, and my fortress, and my *d'*;
Ps 18: 2 my fortress, and my *d'*; my God,
40:17 thou art my help and my *d'*; make
70: 5 thou art my help and my *d'*; O Lord,
144: 2 my high tower, and my *d'*; my
Ac 7:35 God send to be a ruler and a *d'* by
Ro 11:26 shall come out of Sion the *D'*,

deliverest
Ps 35:10 which *d'* the poor from him that
Mic 6:14 which thou *d'* will I give up to

delivereth
Job 36:15 He *d'* the poor in his affliction,
Ps 18:48 He *d'* me from mine enemies:
34: 7 them that fear him, and *d'* them.
17 *d'* them out of all their troubles.
19 the Lord *d'* him out of them all.
97:10 he *d'* them out of the hand of the
144:10 who *d'* David his servant from
Pr 10: 2 but righteousness *d'* from death.
11: 4 but righteousness *d'* from death.
14:25 A true witness *d'* souls: but a
31:24 and *d'* girdles unto the merchant.
Isa 42:22 for a prey, and none *d'*; for a spoil,
Da 6:27 He *d'* and rescueth, and he

delivering
Lu 21:12 *d'* you up to the synagogues, and
Ac 22: 4 and *d'* into prisons both men and
26:17 *D'* thee from the people, and from

delivery
Isa 26:17 draweth near the time of her *d'*,

delusion See also DELUSIONS.
2Th 2:11 God shall send them strong *d'*.

delusions
Isa 66: 4 I also will choose their *d'*,

demand See also DEMANDED.
Job 38: 3 for I will *d'* of thee, and answer
40: 7 like a man: I will *d'* of thee, and
42: 4 will speak: I will *d'* of thee, and
Da 4:17 the *d'* by the word of the holy ones:

demanded
Ex 5:14 were beaten, and *d'*, Wherefore
2Sa 11: 7 David *d'* of him how Joab did,
Da 2:27 The secret which the king hath *d'*
M't 2: 4 he *d'* of them where Christ should
Lu 3:14 soldiers likewise *d'* of him, saying,
17:20 when he was *d'* of the Pharisees,
Ac 21:33 and *d'* who he was, and what

Demas (*de'-mas*)
Col 4:14 the beloved physician, and *D'*,
2Ti 4:10 For *D'* hath forsaken me, having
Ph'm 24 Marcus, Aristarchus, *D'*, Lucas,

Demetrius (*de-me'-tre-us*)
Ac 19:24 For a certain man named *D'*, a
38 Wherefore if *D'*, and the craftsmen
3Jo 12 *D'* hath good report of all men,

demonstration
1Co 2: 4 in *d'* of the Spirit and of power:

den See also DENS.
Ps 10: 9 in wait secretly as a lion in his *d'*:
Isa 11: 8 his hand on the cockatrice' *d'*.
Jer 7:11 a *d'* of robbers in your eyes?
9:11 heaps, and a *d'* of dragons; and I
10:22 desolate, and a *d'* of dragons.
Da 6: 7 shall be cast into the *d'* of lions.
12 *d'* of lions? The king answered
16 and cast him into the *d'* of lions.
17 and laid upon the mouth of the *d'*;
19 went in haste unto the *d'* of lions.
20 when he came to the *d'* he cried
23 should take Daniel up out of the *d'*.
23 Daniel was taken up out of the *d'*,
24 they cast them into the *d'* of lions,
24 they came at the bottom of the *d'*.
Am 3: 4 will a young lion cry out of his *d'*,
M't 21:13 but ye have made it a *d'* of thieves.
M'r 11:17 but ye have made it a *d'* of thieves.
Lu 19:46 but ye have made it a *d'* of thieves.

denied
Ge 18:15 Sarah *d'*, saying, I laughed not;
1Ki 20: 7 my gold; and I *d'* him not.
Job 31:28 have *d'* the God that is above.
M't 26:70 he *d'* before them all, saying,
72 again he *d'* with an oath, I do not
M'r 14:68 But he *d'*, saying, I know not,
70 And he *d'* it again. And a little after,
Lu 8:45 When all *d'*, Peter and they that
12: 9 be *d'* before the angels of God.
22:57 he *d'* him, saying, Woman, I know
Joh 1:20 he confessed, and *d'* not; but
13:38 crow, till thou hast *d'* me thrice.
18:25 He *d'* it, and said, I am not.
27 Peter then *d'* again: and
Ac 3:13 *d'* him in the presence of Pilate,
14 ye *d'* the Holy One and the Just,
1Ti 5: 8 he hath *d'* the faith, and is worse
Re 2:13 hast not *d'* my faith, even in those
3: 8 word, and hast not *d'* my name.

denieth
Lu 12: 9 he that *d'* me before men shall be
1Jo 2:22 he that *d'* that Jesus is the Christ?
22 that *d'* the Father and the Son.
23 Whosoever *d'* the Son, the same

denounce
De 30:18 I *d'* unto you this day, that ye

dens
J'g 6: 2 of Israel made them the *d'* which
Job 37: 8 Then the beasts go into *d'*, and
38:40 When they couch in their *d'*, and
Ps 104:22 and lay them down in their *d'*.
Ca 4: 8 from the lions' *d'*, from the
Isa 32:14 forts and towers shall be for *d'*
Na 2:12 with prey, and his *d'* with ravin.
Heb 11:38 and in *d'* and caves of the earth
Re 6:15 hid themselves in the *d'* and in

deny See also DENIED; DENIETH; DENYING.
Jos 24:27 unto you, lest ye *d'* your God.
1Ki 2:16 one petition of thee, *d'* me not.
Job 8:18 then it shall *d'* him, saying, I have
Pr 30: 7 *d'* me them not before I die:
9 be full, and *d'* thee, and say, Who
M't 10:33 whosoever shall *d'* me before men,
33 him will I also *d'* before my Father
16:24 come after me, let him *d'* himself,
26:34 cock crow, thou shalt *d'* me thrice.
35 die with thee, yet will I not *d'* thee.
75 cock crow, thou shalt *d'* me thrice.
M'r 8:34 let him *d'* himself, and take up
14:30 crow twice, thou shalt *d'* me thrice.
31 I will not *d'* thee in any wise.
72 twice, thou shalt *d'* me thrice.
Lu 9:23 come after me, let him *d'* himself,
20:27 *d'* that there is any resurrection;
22:34 thrice *d'* that thou knowest me.
61 cock crow, thou shalt *d'* me thrice.
Ac 4:16 Jerusalem; and we cannot *d'* it.
2Ti 2:12 if we *d'* him, he also will *d'* us:
13 faithful: he cannot *d'* himself.
Tit 1:16 but in works they *d'* him, being

denying
2Ti 3: 5 of godliness, but *d'* the power
Tit 2:12 *d'* ungodliness and worldly lusts,
2Pe 2: 1 *d'* the Lord that bought them,
Jude 4 *d'* the only Lord God, and our Lord

depart See also DEPARTED; DEPARTETH; DEPARTING.
Ge 13: 9 or if thou *d'* to the right hand,
49:10 sceptre shall not *d'* from Judah,
Ex 8:11 And the frogs shall *d'* from thee,
29 that the swarms of flies may *d'*
18:27 And Moses let his father in law *d'*;
21:22 so that her fruit *d'* from her,
33: 1 *D'*, and go up hence, thou and
Le 25:41 And then shall he *d'* from thee,
Nu 10:30 but I will *d'* to mine own land,
16:26 *D'*, I pray you, from the tents of
De 4: 9 lest they *d'* from thy heart all the
9: 7 from the day that thou didst *d'*
Jos 1: 8 This book of the law shall not *d'*
24:28 So Joshua let the people *d'*,
J'g 6:18 *D'* not hence, I pray thee,
7: 3 let him return and *d'* early from
19: 5 he rose up to *d'*: and the damsel's
7 the man rose up to *d'*, his father
8 the morning on the fifth day to *d'*:
9 the man rose up to *d'*, he, and his
1Sa 15: 6 *d'*, get you down from among
22: 5 *d'*, and get thee into the land of
29:10 in the morning, and have light, *d'*.
11 and his men rose up early to *d'*
30:22 they may lead them away, and *d'*.
2Sa 7:15 mercy shall not *d'* away from him,
11:12 and to morrow I will let thee *d'*.
12:10 shall never *d'* from thine house;
15:14 make speed to *d'*, lest he overtake
20:21 and I will *d'* from the city.
22:23 statutes, I did not *d'* from them.
1Ki 11:21 Let me *d'*, that I may go to mine
12: 5 unto them, *D'* yet for three days,
24 returned to *d'*, according to the
15:19 king of Israel, that he may *d'* from
2Ch 16: 3 king of Israel, that he may *d'* from
18:31 God moved them to *d'* from him.
35:15 might not *d'* from their service;
Job 7:19 long wilt thou not *d'* from me,
15:30 He shall not *d'* out of darkness;
20:28 The increase of his house shall *d'*,
21:14 they say unto God, *D'* from us;
22:17 Which said unto God, *D'* from us:
28:28 to *d'* from evil is understanding.
Ps 6: 8 *D'* from me, all ye workers of
34:14 *D'* from evil, and do good; seek
37:27 *D'* from evil, and do good; and
55:11 and guile *d'* not from her streets.
101: 4 froward heart shall *d'* from me:
119:115 *D'* from me, ye evildoers: for I
139:19 *d'* from me therefore, ye bloody
Pr 3: 7 fear the Lord, and *d'* from evil.
21 let not them *d'* from thine eyes:
4:21 Let them not *d'* from thine eyes;
5: 7 *d'* not from the words of my
13:14 to *d'* from the snares of death.
19 abomination to fools to *d'* from
14:27 to *d'* from the snares of death.
15:24 that he may *d'* from hell beneath.
16: 6 fear of the Lord men *d'* from evil.
Pr 16:17 of the upright is to *d'* from evil:
17:13 evil shall not *d'* from his house.
22: 6 he is old, he will not *d'* from it.
27:22 not his foolishness *d'* from him.
Isa 11:13 The envy also of Ephraim shall *d'*,
14:25 shall his yoke *d'* from off them,
25 burden *d'* from off their shoulders.
52:11 *D'* ye, *d'* ye, go ye out from thence,
54:10 the mountains shall *d'*, and the
10 but my kindness shall not *d'* from
59:21 have put in thy mouth, shall not *d'*
Jer 6: 8 lest my soul *d'* from thee; lest
17:13 and they that *d'* from me shall be
31:36 ordinances *d'* from before me,
32:40 that they shall not *d'* from me.
37: 9 The Chaldeans shall surely *d'*
9 from us: for they shall not *d'*.
50: 3 they shall *d'*, both man and beast.
La 4:15 They cried unto them, *D'* ye; it
15 it is unclean; *d'*, *d'*, touch not:
Eze 16:42 my jealously shall *d'* from thee,
Hos 9:12 woe also to them when I *d'* from
Mic 2:10 Arise ye, and *d'*; for this is not
Zec 10:11 sceptre of Egypt shall *d'* away.
M't 7:23 *d'* from me, ye that work iniquity.
8:18 gave the commandment to *d'* unto
34 he would *d'* out of their coasts.
10:14 ye *d'* out of that house or city,
14:16 unto them, They need not *d'*;
25:41 *D'* from me, ye cursed, into
M'r 5:17 pray him to *d'* out of their coasts.
6:10 abide till ye *d'* from that place.
11 ye *d'* thence, shake off the dust
Lu 2:29 lettest thou thy servant *d'* in peace,
4:42 that he should not *d'* from them.
5: 8 saying, *D'* from me; for I am a
8:37 besought him to *d'* from them;
9: 4 into, there abide, and thence *d'*.
12:59 thou shalt not *d'* thence, till thou
13:27 *d'* from me, all ye workers of
31 Get thee out, and *d'* hence: for
21:21 which are in the midst of it *d'* out;
Joh 7: 3 *D'* hence, and go into Judæa,
13: 1 that he should *d'* out of this world
16: 7 but if I *d'*, I will send him unto
Ac 1: 4 they should not *d'* from Jerusalem
16:36 therefore *d'*, and go in peace.
39 desired them to *d'* out of the city.
18: 2 all Jews to *d'* from Rome:
20: 7 them, ready to *d'* on the morrow;
22:21 *D'*: for I will send thee far hence
23:22 then let the young man *d'*, and
25: 4 himself would *d'* shortly thither.
27:12 part advised to *d'* thence also,
1Co 7:10 not the wife *d'* from her husband
11 she *d'*, let her remain unmarried,
15 if the unbelieving *d'*, let him *d'*.
2Co 12: 8 thrice, that it might *d'* from me.
Ph'p 1:23 having a desire to *d'*, and to be
1Ti 4: 1 some shall *d'* from the faith,
2Ti 2:19 name of Christ *d'* from iniquity.
Jas 2:16 say unto them, *D'* in peace, be ye

departed
Ge 12: 4 Abram *d'*, as the Lord had spoken
4 old when he *d'* out of Haran.
14:12 and his goods, and *d'*.
21:14 and she *d'*, and wandered in the
24:10 the camels of his master, and *d'*;
26:17 And Isaac *d'* thence, and pitched
31 and they *d'* from him in peace.
31:40 and my sleep *d'* from mine eyes.
55 and Laban *d'*, and returned unto
37:17 They are *d'* hence; for I heard
42:26 asses with the corn, and *d'* thence.
45:24 his brethren away, and they *d'*:
Ex 19: 2 For they were *d'* from Rephidim,
33:11 *d'* not out of the tabernacle.
35:20 of the children of Israel *d'*
Le 13:58 if the plague be *d'* from them,
Nu 10:33 *d'* from the mount of the Lord
12: 9 kindled against them; and he *d'*.
10 cloud *d'* from off the tabernacle;
14: 9 their defence is *d'* from them,
44 Moses, *d'* not out of the camp.
22: 7 the elders of Midian *d'* with the
33: 3 they *d'* from Rameses in the first
6 And they *d'* from Succoth, and
8 they *d'* from before Pi-hahiroth,
13 And they *d'* from Dophkah, and
15 And they *d'* from Rephidim, and
17 they *d'* from Kibroth-hattaavah,
18 And they *d'* from Hazeroth, and
19 And they *d'* from Rithmah, and
20 And they *d'* from Rimmon-parez,
27 And they *d'* from Tahath, and
30 And they *d'* from Hashmonah,
31 And they *d'* from Moseroth, and
35 And they *d'* from Ebronah, and
41 And they *d'* from mount Hor, and
42 And they *d'* from Zalmonah, and
43 And they *d'* from Punon, and
44 And they *d'* from Oboth, and
45 And they *d'* from Iim, and pitched
48 *d'* from the mountains of Abarim,
De 1:19 when we *d'* from Horeb, we went
24: 2 when she is *d'* out of his house,
Jos 2:21 she sent them away, and they *d'*:
22: 9 and *d'* from the children of Israel
J'g 6:21 angel of the Lord *d'* out of his
9:55 that Abimelech was dead they *d'*
16:20 he wist not that the Lord was *d'*
17: 8 And the man *d'* out of the city
18: 7 Then the five men *d'*, and came to
21 So they turned and *d'*, and put
19:10 he rose up and *d'*, and came over

J'g 21:24 And the children of Israel *d'*
1Sa 4:21 saying, The glory is *d'* from Israel:
22 is *d'* from Israel: for the ark of God
6: 6 let the people go, and they *d'*?
10: 2 When thou art *d'* from me to day,
15: 6 So the Kenites *d'* from among the
16:14 the Spirit of the Lord *d'* from Saul,
23 and the evil spirit *d'* from him.
18:12 with him, and was *d'* from Saul.
20:42 he arose and *d'*: and Jonathan
22: 1 David therefore *d'* thence, and
5 David *d'*, and came into the forest
23:13 six hundred, *d'* out of Keilah,
28:15 God is *d'* from me, and answereth
16 seeing the Lord is *d'* from thee,
2Sa 6:19 So all the people *d'* every one
11: 8 Uriah *d'* out of the king's house,
12:15 And Nathan *d'* unto his house.
17:21 after they were *d'*, that they came
19:24 the day the king *d'* until the day
22:22 have not wickedly *d'* from my God.
1Ki 12: 5 again to me. And the people *d'*.
16 So Israel *d'* unto their tents.
14:17 Jeroboam's wife arose, and *d'*, and
19:19 So he *d'* thence, and found Elisha
20: 9 the messengers *d'*, and brought
36 as thou art *d'* from me a lion shall
36 as soon as he was *d'* from him,
38 So the prophet *d'*, and waited
2Ki 1: 4 shalt surely die. And Elijah *d'*.
3: 3 to sin; he *d'* not therefrom.
27 they *d'* from him, and returned
5: 5 *d'*, and took with him ten talents
19 So he *d'* from him a little way.
24 he let the men go, and they *d'*.
8:14 So he *d'* from Elisha, and came to
10:12 he arose and *d'*, and came to
15 when he was *d'* thence, he lighted
29 Jehu *d'* not from after them,
31 *d'* not from the sins of Jeroboam,
13: 2 Israel to sin; he *d'* not therefrom.
6 They *d'* not from the sins of the
11 *d'* not from all the sins of Jeroboam
14:24 *d'* not from all the sins of Jeroboam
15: 9 he *d'* not from the sins of Jeroboam
18 he *d'* not all his days from the sins
24, 28 *d'* not from the sins of Jeroboam
17:22 he did; they *d'* not from them;
18: 6 and *d'* not from following him,
19: 8 that he was *d'* from Lachish.
36 So Sennacherib king of Assyria *d'*,
1Ch 16:43 And all the people *d'* every man
21: 4 Joab *d'*, and went throughout all
2Ch 8:15 *d'* not from the commandment
10: 5 three days. And the people *d'*.
20:32 *d'* not from it, doing that which
21:20 and *d'* without being desired.
24:25 And when they were *d'* from him,
34:33 *d'* not from following the Lord,
Ezr 8:31 we *d'* from the river of Ahava
Ne 9:19 cloud *d'* not from them by day,
Ps 18:21 have not wickedly *d'* from my God.
34:*title* who drove him away, and he *d'*.
105:38 Egypt was glad when they *d'*:
119:102 have not *d'* from thy judgments:
Isa 7:17 from the day that Ephraim *d'*
37: 8 that he was *d'* from Lachish.
37 So Sennacherib king of Assyria *d'*,
38:12 Mine age is *d'*, and is removed
Jer 29: 2 smiths were *d'* from Jerusalem:
37: 5 of them, they *d'* from Jerusalem.
41:10 *d'* to go over to the Ammonites.
17 they *d'*, and dwelt in the habitation
La 1: 6 of Zion all her beauty is *d'*:
Eze 6: 9 their whorish heart, which hath *d'*
10:18 the glory of the Lord *d'* from off
Da 4:31 The kingdom is *d'* from thee.
Ho 10: 5 thereof, because it is *d'* from it.
Mal 2: 8 ye are *d'* out of the way;
M't 2: 9 they *d'*; and, lo, the star, which
12 *d'* into their own country another
13 when they were *d'*, behold, the angel
14 mother by night, and *d'* into Egypt:
4:12 into prison, he *d'* into Galilee;
9: 7 And he arose and *d'* to his house
27 And when Jesus *d'* thence, two
31 when they were *d'*, spread abroad
11: 1 he *d'* thence to teach and to preach
7 as they *d'*, Jesus began to say
12: 9 And when he was *d'* thence, he
13:53 these parables, he *d'* thence.
14:13 he *d'* thence by ship into a desert
15:21 and *d'* into the coasts of Tyre and
29 Jesus *d'* from thence, and came
16: 4 Jonas. And he left them, and *d'*.
17:18 he *d'* out of him: and the child
19: 1 he *d'* from Galilee, and came unto
15 his hands on them, and *d'* thence.
20:29 *d'* from Jericho, a great multitude
24: 1 and *d'* from the temple: and his
27: 5 in the temple, and *d'*, and went
60 the door of the sepulchre, and *d'*.
28: 8 they *d'* quickly from the sepulchre
M'r 1:35 he went out, and *d'* into a solitary
42 the leprosy *d'* from him, and he was
5:20 he *d'*, and began to publish in
6:32 they *d'* into a desert place by ship
46 he *d'* into a mountain to pray.
8:13 the ship again *d'* to the other side.
9:30 And they *d'* thence, and passed
Lu 1:23 he *d'* to his own house.
38 word. And the angel *d'* from her.
2:37 which *d'* not from the temple,
4:13 he *d'* from him for a season.
42 was day, he *d'* and went into
Lu 5:13 the leprosy *d'* from him.
25 *d'* to his own house, glorifying God.
7:24 the messengers of John were *d'*,
8:35, 38 out of whom the devils were *d'*
9: 6 *d'*, and went through the towns,
33 as they *d'* from him, Peter said
10:30 him, *d'*, leaving him half dead.
35 morrow when he *d'*, he took out
24:12 clothes laid by themselves, and *d'*,
Joh 4: 3 Judæa, and *d'* again into Galilee.
43 after two days he *d'* thence, and
5:15 The man *d'*, and told the Jews
6:15 *d'* again into a mountain himself
12:36 These things spake Jesus, and *d'*,
Ac 5:41 And they *d'* from the presence of
10: 7 spake unto Cornelius was *d'*, he
11:25 Then *d'* Barnabas to Tarsus, for
12:10 forthwith the angel *d'* from him.
17 And he *d'*, and went into another
13: 4 *d'* unto Seleucia; and from thence
14 when they *d'* from Perga, they
14:20 he *d'* with Barnabas to Derbe.
15:38 *d'* from them from Pamphylia,
39 they *d'* asunder one from the
40 Paul chose Silas, and *d'*, being
16:40 they comforted them, and *d'*.
17:15 come to him with all speed, they *d*.
33 So Paul *d'* from among them.
18: 1 Paul *d'* from Athens, and came to
7 he *d'* thence, and entered into a
23 he *d'*, and went over all the country
19: 9 he *d'* from them, and separated
12 and the diseases *d'* from them,
20: 1 and *d'* for to go into Macedonia.
11 even till break of day, so he *d'*.
21: 5 we *d'* and went our way; and they
8 that were of Paul's company *d'*, and
22:29 Then straightway they *d'* from him
28:10 when we *d'*, they laded us with
11 we *d'* in a ship of Alexandria,
25 not among themselves, they *d'*,
29 Jews *d'*, and had great reasoning
Ph'p 4:15 when I *d'* from Macedonia, no
Ph'm 15 For perhaps he therefore *d'* for a
2Ti 4:10 and is *d'* unto Thessalonica;
Re 6:14 the heaven *d'* as a scroll when it is
18:14 lusted after are *d'* from thee, and
14 and goodly are *d'* from thee, and

departeth
Job 27:21 carrieth him away, and he *d'*:
Pr 14:16 A wise man feareth, and *d'* from
Ec 6: 4 and *d'* in darkness, and his name
Isa 59:15 and he that *d'* from evil maketh
Jer 3:20 a wife treacherously *d'* from her
17: 5 and whose heart *d'* from the Lord.
Na 3: 1 lies and robbery; the prey *d'* not;
Lu 9:39 bruising him hardly *d'* from him,

departing
Ge 35:18 her soul was in *d'* (for she died),
Ex 16: 1 after their *d'* out of the land of
Isa 59:13 *d'* away from our God, speaking
Da 9: 5 even by *d'* from thy precepts and
11 transgressed thy law, even by *d'*,
Ho 1: 2 great whoredom, *d'* from the Lord.
M'r 6:33 And the people saw them *d'*, and
7:31 again, *d'* from the coast of Tyre
Ac 13:13 John *d'* from them returned to
20:29 I know this, that after my *d'*
Heb 3:12 unbelief, in *d'* from the living God.
11:22 the *d'* of the children of Israel

departure
Eze 26:18 the sea shall be troubled at thy *d'*.
2Ti 4: 6 and the time of my *d'* is at hand.

deposed
Da 5:20 he was *d'* from his kingly throne,

deprived
Ge 27:45 why should I be *d'* also of you
Job 39:17 God hath *d'* her of wisdom,
Isa 38:10 I am *d'* of the residue of my years.

depth See also DEPTHS.
Job 28:14 The *d'* saith, It is not in me:
38:16 walked in the search of the *d'*?
Ps 33: 7 layeth up the *d'* in storehouses.
Pr 8:27 compass upon the face of the *d'*:
25: 3 for height, and the earth for *d'*,
Isa 7:11 ask it either in the *d'* or in the
Jon 2: 5 the *d'* closed me round about, the
M't 18: 6 were drowned in the *d'* of the sea.
M'r 4: 5 because it had no *d'* of earth:
Ro 8:39 Nor height, nor *d'*, nor any other
11:33 O the *d'* of the riches both of the
Eph 3:18 the breadth, and length, and *d'*, and

depths
Ex 15: 5 The *d'* have covered them; they
8 *d'* were congealed in the heart
De 8: 7 of fountains and *d'* that spring out
Ps 68:22 again from the *d'* of the sea:
71:20 up again from the *d'* of the earth.
77:16 afraid: the *d'* also were troubled.
78:15 them drink as out of the great *d'*.
106: 9 so he led them through the *d'*,
107:26 they go down again to the *d'*:
130: 1 Out of the *d'* have I cried unto thee,
Pr 3:20 By his knowledge the *d'* are
8:24 When there were no *d'*, I was
9:18 her guests are in the *d'* of hell.
Isa 51:10 that hath made the *d'* of the sea
Eze 27:34 by the seas in the *d'* of the waters
Mic 7:19 their sin into the *d'* of the sea.
Re 2:24 have not known the *d'* of Satan,

deputed
2Sa 15: 3 there is no man *d'* of the king to hear

deputies
Es 8: 9 the *d'* and rulers of the provinces
9: 3 the *d'* and officers of the king,
Ac 19:38 the law is open, and there are *d'*:

deputy See also DEPUTIES.
1Ki 22:47 no king in Edom: a *d'* was king.
Ac 13: 7 was with the *d'* of the country,
8 turn away the *d'* from the faith.
12 Then the *d'*, when he saw what
18:12 when Gallio was *d'* of Achaia,

Derbe (*der'-by*)
Ac 14: 6 and fled unto Lystra and *D'*,
20 he departed with Barnabas to *D'*.
16: 1 Then came he to *D'* and Lystra:
20: 4 and Secundus; and Gaius of *D'*, and

deride See also DERIDED.
Hab 1:10 they shall *d'* every strong hold;

derided
Lu 16:14 all these things: and they *d'* him.
23:35 the rulers also with them *d'* him,

derision
Job 30: 1 are younger than I have me in *d'*,
Ps 2: 4 the Lord shall have them in *d'*.
44:13 a scorn and a *d'* to them that are
59: 8 shalt have all the heathen in *d'*.
79: 4 a scorn and *d'* to them that are
119:51 proud have had me greatly in *d'*:
Jer 20: 7 am in *d'* daily, every one mocketh
8 a reproach unto me, and a *d'*,
48:26 and he also shall be in *d'*.
27 was not Israel a *d'* unto thee?
39 so shall Moab be a *d'* and a
La 3:14 I was a *d'* to all my people;
Eze 23:32 laughed to scorn and had in *d'*;
36: 4 which became a prey and *d'* to the
Ho 7:16 shall be their *d'* in the land of Egypt.

descend See also DESCENDED; DESCENDETH; DESCENDING.
Nu 34:11 and the border shall *d'*, and shall
1Sa 26:10 he shall *d'* into battle, and perish.
Ps 49:17 his glory shall not *d'* after him.
Isa 5:14 he that rejoiceth, shall *d'* into it.
Eze 26:20 them that *d'* into the pit, with the
31:16 them that *d'* into the pit: and all
M'r 15:32 Let Christ the king of Israel *d'*
Ac 11: 5 A certain vessel *d'*, as it had been
Ro 10: 7 Or, Who shall *d'* into the deep?
1Th 4:16 Lord himself shall *d'* from heaven

descended
Ex 19:18 the Lord *d'* upon it in fire: and
33: 9 the cloudy pillar *d'*, and stood at
34: 5 And the Lord *d'* in the cloud,
De 9:21 the brook that *d'* out of the mount.
Jos 2:23 returned, and *d'* from the mountain,
17: 9 And the coast *d'* unto the river
18:13 the border *d'* to Ataroth-adar,
16 and *d'* to the valley of Hinnom,
16 south, and *d'* to En-rogel,
17 and *d'* to the stone of Bohan the
Ps 133: 3 *d'* upon the mountains of Zion:
Pr 30: 4 ascended up into heaven, or *d'*?
M't 7:25, 27 And the rain *d'*, and the floods
28: 2 for the angel of the Lord *d'* from
Lu 3:22 the Holy Ghost *d'* in a bodily shape
Ac 24: 1 the high priest *d'* with the elders,
Eph 4: 9 but that he also *d'* first into the
10 He that *d'* is the same also that

descendeth
Jas 3:15 This wisdom *d'* not from above,

descending
Ge 28:12 angels of God ascending and *d'*
M't 3:16 Spirit of God *d'* like a dove,
M'r 1:10 the Spirit like a dove *d'* upon him
Joh 1:32 I saw the Spirit *d'* from heaven
33 whom thou shalt see the Spirit *d'*,
51 angels of God ascending and *d'*
Ac 10:11 a certain vessel *d'* unto him,
Re 21:10 Jerusalem, *d'* out of heaven from

descent
Lu 19:37 at the *d'* of the mount of Olives,
Heb 7: 3 without mother, without *d'*,
6 whose *d'* is not counted from

describe See also DESCRIBED; DESCRIBETH.
Jos 18: 4 and go through the land, and *d'* it
6 Ye shall therefore *d'* the land into
8 them that went to *d'* the land,
8 walk through the land, and *d'* it,

described
Jos 18: 9 and *d'* it by cities into seven parts
J'g 8:14 and he *d'* unto him the princes of

describeth
Ro 4: 6 as David also *d'* the blessedness
10: 5 Moses *d'* the righteousness which

description
Jos 18: 6 and bring the *d'* hither to me

descry
J'g 1:23 the house of Joseph sent to *d'*

desert See also DESERTS.
Ex 3: 1 to the backside of the *d'*, and
5: 3 three days' journey into the *d'*,
19: 2 were come to the *d'* of Sinai, and
23:31 and from the *d'* unto the river:
Nu 20: 1 into the *d'* of Zin in the first
27:14 in the *d'* of Zin, in the strife of
33:16 removed from the *d'* of Sinai, and
De 32:10 He found him in a *d'* land, and
2Ch 26:10 he built towers in the *d'*, and
Job 24: 5 wild asses in the *d'*, go they forth

Ps 28: 4 hands: render to them their *d*.
78:40 and grieve him in the *d*!
102: 6 I am like an owl of the *d*.
106:14 and tempted God in the *d*.
Isa 13:21 beasts of the *d* shall lie there;
21: 1 burden of the *d* of the sea.
1 through; so it cometh from the *d*.
34:14 The wild beasts of the *d* shall
35: 1 the *d* shall rejoice, and blossom
6 break out,and streams in the *d*.
40: 3 make straight in the *d* a highway
41:19 I will set in the *d* the fir tree,
43:19 wilderness, and rivers in the *d*.
20 rivers in the *d*, to give drink to my
51: 3 her *d* like the garden of the Lord;
Jer 17: 6 like the heath in the *d*, and shall
25:24 people that dwell in the *d*,
50:12 wilderness, a dry land, and a *d*.
39 Therefore the wild beasts of the *d*
Eze 47: 8 go down into the *d*, and go into
M't 14:13 by ship into a *d* place apart:
15 This is a *d* place, and the time is
24:26 Behold, he is in the *d*; go not
M'r 1:45 was without in *d* places: and they
6:31 yourselves apart into a *d* place,
32 they departed into a *d* place by
35 This is a *d* place, and now the
Lu 4:42 departed and went into a *d* place:
9:10 into a *d* place belonging to the
12 for we are here in a *d* place.
Joh 6:31 fathers did eat manna in the *d*;
Ac 8:26 Jerusalem unto Gaza, which is *d*.

deserts
Isa 48:21 he led them through the *d*: he
Jer 2: 6 a land of *d* and of pits,
Eze 7:27 and according to their *d* will I
13: 4 are like the foxes in the *d*.
Lu 1:80 and was in the *d* till the day of
Heb 11:38 wandered in *d*, and in mountains,

deserve See also DESERVETH; DESERVING.
Ezr 9:13 us less than our iniquities *d*, and

deserveth
Job 11: 6 of thee less than thine iniquity *d*.

deserving
J'd 9:16 according to the *d* of his hands;

desirable
Eze 23: 6 rulers, all of them *d* young men,
12 riding upon horses, all of them *d*
23 *d* young men, captains and rulers,

desire See also DESIRABLE; DESIRED; DESIRES; DESIREST; DESIRETH; DESIRING.
Ge 3:16 thy *d* shall be to thy husband,
4: 7 unto thee shall be his *d*, and thou
Ex 10:11 serve the Lord; for that ye did *d*.
34:24 neither shall any man *d* thy land
De 5:21 shalt thou *d* thy neighbour's wife
7:25 shalt not *d* the silver or gold
18: 6 come with all the *d* of his mind
21:11 and hast a *d* unto her, that thou
J'g 8:24 I would *d* a request of you,
1Sa 9:20 on whom is all the *d* of Israel?
23:20 according to all the *d* of thy soul
2Sa 23: 5 all my salvation, and all my *d*,
1Ki 2:20 I *d* one small petition of thee;
5: 8 I will do all thy *d* concerning
9 thou shalt accomplish my *d*, in
10 fir trees according to all his *d*.
9: 1 all Solomon's *d* which he was
11 according to all his *d*,) that then
10:13 unto the queen of Sheba all her *d*,
2Ki 4:28 Did I *d* a son of my lord?
2Ch 9:12 to the queen of Sheba all her *d*,
15:15 sought him with their whole *d*;
Ne 1:11 who *d* to fear thy name: and
Job 13: 3 and I *d* to reason with God.
14:15 thou wilt have a *d* to the work of
21:14 we *d* not the knowledge of thy
31:16 withheld the poor from their *d*,
35 my *d* is, that the Almighty would
33:32 speak, for I *d* to justify thee.
34:36 My *d* is that Job may be tried
36:20 *D* not the night, when people are
Ps 10: 3 wicked boasteth of his heart's *d*,
17 hast heard the *d* of the humble:
21: 2 Thou hast given him his heart's *d*,
38: 9 Lord, all my *d* is before thee;
40: 6 and offering thou didst not *d*;
45:11 shall the king greatly *d* thy beauty:
54: 7 mine eye hath seen his *d* upon mine
59:10 let me see my *d* upon mine enemies.
70: 2 put to confusion, that *d* my hurt.
73:25 upon earth that I *d* beside thee.
78:29 for he gave them their own *d*;
92:11 shall see my *d* upon mine enemies,
11 ears shall hear my *d* of the wicked
112: 8 he see his *d* upon his enemies.
10 the *d* of the wicked shall perish.
118: 7 therefore shall I see my *d* upon them
145:16 satisfiest the *d* of every living
19 He will fulfil the *d* of them that
Pr 3:15 all the things thou canst *d* are
10:24 but the *d* of the righteous shall
11:23 The *d* of the righteous is only good
13:12 when the *d* cometh, it is a tree of
19 The *d* accomplished is sweet to
18: 1 Through *d* a man, having separated
19:22 The *d* of a man is his kindness:
21:25 The *d* of the slothful killeth him;
23: 6 neither *d* thou his dainty meats:
24: 1 men, neither *d* to be with them.
Ec 6: 9 than the wandering of the *d*:
12: 5 be a burden, and *d* shall fail:
Ca 7:10 beloved's, and his *d* is toward me.
Isa 26: 8 the *d* of our soul is to thy name,
53: 2 no beauty that we should *d* him.
Jer 22:27 whereunto they *d* to return,
42:22 the place whither ye *d* to go
44:14 which they have a *d* to return
Eze 24:16 away from thee the *d* of thine
21 strength, the *d* of your eyes,
25 of their glory, the *d* of their eyes,
Da 2:18 That they would *d* mercies of the
11:37 nor the *d* of women, nor regard
Ho 10:10 It is in my *d* that I should chastise
Am 5:18 Woe unto you that *d* the day of
Mic 7: 3 he uttereth his mischievous *d*:
Hab 2: 5 who enlargeth his *d* as hell, and
Hag 2: 7 the *d* of all nations shall come:
M'r 9:35 If any man *d* to be first,
10:35 do for us whatsoever we shall *d*.
11:24 What things soever ye *d*, when
15: 8 began to *d* him to do as he had
Lu 17:22 ye shall *d* to see one of the days
20:46 the scribes, which *d* to walk in
22:15 With *d* I have desired to eat this
Ac 23:20 The Jews have agreed to *d* thee
28:22 we *d* to hear of thee what thou
Ro 10: 1 Brethren, my heart's *d* and prayer
15:23 having a great *d* these many
1Co 14: 1 and *d* spiritual gifts, but rather
2Co 7: 7 he told us your earnest *d*, your
11 yea, what vehement *d*, yea, what
11:12 from them which *d* occasion;
12: 6 For though I would *d* to glory,
Ga 4: 9 ye *d* again to be in bondage?
20 I *d* to be present with you now,
21 Tell me, ye that *d* to be under the
6:12 As many as *d* to make a fair shew
13 but *d* to have you circumcised,
Eph 3:13 I *d* that ye faint not at my
Ph'p 1:23 having a *d* to depart, and to be
4:17 Not because I *d* a gift:
17 but I *d* fruit that may abound
Col 1: 9 and to *d* that ye might be filled
1Th 2:17 to see your face with great *d*.
1Ti 3: 1 If a man *d* the office of a bishop,
Heb 6:11 And we *d* that every one of you
11:16 But now they *d* a better country,
Jas 4: 2 kill, and *d* to have, and cannot
1Pe 1:12 which things the angels *d* to look
2: 2 *d* the sincere milk of the word,
Re 9: 6 and shall *d* to die, and death shall

desired See also DESIREDST.
Ge 3: 6 and a tree to be *d* to make one
1Sa 12:13 chosen, and whom ye have *d*!
1Ki 9:19 that which Solomon *d* to build in
2Ch 8: 6 all that Solomon *d* to build in
11:23 And he *d* many wives.
21:20 and departed without being *d*.
Es 2:13 whatsoever she *d* was given her
Job 20:20 shall not save of that which he *d*.
Ps 19:10 More to be *d* are they than gold,
27: 4 One thing have I *d* of the Lord,
107:30 bringeth them unto their *d* haven.
132:13 he hath *d* it for his habitation.
14 here will I dwell; for I have *d* it.
Pr 8:11 all the things that may be *d* are
21:20 There is treasure to be *d* and oil
Ec 2:10 whatsoever mine eyes *d* I kept
Isa 1:29 the oaks which ye have *d*, and ye
26: 9 With my soul have I *d* thee
Jer 17:16 neither have I *d* the woeful day;
Da 2:16 Daniel went in, and *d* of the king
23 known unto me now what we *d*
Ho 6: 6 For I *d* mercy, and not sacrifice
Mic 7: 1 my soul *d* the first ripe fruit
Zep 2: 1 gather together, O nation not *d*;
M't 13:17 righteous men have *d* to see those
16: 1 *d* him that he would shew them
M'r 15: 6 one prisoner, whomsoever they *d*.
Lu 7:36 And one of the Pharisees *d* him
9: 9 things? And he *d* to see him.
10:24 prophets and kings have *d* to see
22:15 With desire I have *d* to eat this
31 Satan hath *d* to have you, that
23:25 into prison, whom they had *d*;
Jo 12:21 *d* him, saying, Sir, we would see
Ac 3:14 the Just, and *d* a murderer to
7:46 *d* to find a tabernacle for the God
8:31 And he *d* Philip that he would
9: 2 *d* of him letters to Damascus to
12:20 their friend, *d* peace; because
13: 7 and *d* to hear the word of God.
21 afterward they *d* a king: and
28 yet *d* they Pilate that he should
16:39 them out, and *d* them to depart
18:20 When they *d* him to tarry longer
25: 3 *d* favour against him, that he
28:14 and were *d* to tarry with them
1Co 16:12 Apollos, I greatly *d* him to come
2Co 8: 6 Insomuch that we *d* Titus, that
12:18 I *d* Titus, and with him I sent
1Jo 5:15 the petitions that we *d* of him.

desiredst
De 18:16 According to all that thou *d* of the
M't 18:32 all that debt, because thou *d* me:

desires
Ps 37: 4 give thee the *d* of thine heart.
140: 8 Grant not, O Lord, the *d* of the
Eph 2: 3 fulfilling the *d* of the flesh and of

desirest
Ps 51: 6 thou *d* truth in the inward parts:
16 For thou *d* not sacrifice; else

desireth
De 14:26 or for whatsoever thy soul *d*:
1Sa 2:16 take as much as thy soul *d*;
18:25 The king *d* not any dowry,
1Sa 20: 4 Whatsoever thy soul *d*,
2Sa 3:21 reign over all that thine heart *d*.
1Ki 11:37 according to all that thy soul *d*,
Job 7: 2 As a servant earnestly *d* the
23:13 what his soul *d*, even that he
Ps 34:12 What man is he that *d* life,
68:16 the hill which God *d* to dwell in;
Pr 12:12 The wicked *d* the net of evil men:
13: 4 The soul of the sluggard *d*, and
21:10 The soul of the wicked *d* evil:
Ec 6: 2 for his soul of all that he *d*,
Lu 5:39 drunk old wine straightway *d* new:
14:32 and *d* conditions of peace.
1Ti 3: 1 of a bishop, he *d* a good work.

desiring
M't 12:46 without, *d* to speak with him.
47 without, *d* to speak with thee.
20:20 and *d* a certain thing of him.
Lu 8:20 stand without, *d* to see thee.
16:21 *d* to be fed with the crumbs
Ac 9:38 *d* him that he would not delay
19:31 *d* him that he would not
25:15 *d* to have judgment against him.
2Co 5: 2 earnestly *d* to be clothed upon
1Th 3: 6 *d* greatly to see us, as we also
1Ti 1: 7 *D* to be teachers of the law;
2Ti 1: 4 Greatly *d* to see thee, being

desirous
Pr 23: 3 Be not *d* of his dainties: for they
Lu 23: 8 for he was *d* to see him a long
Joh 16:19 they were *d* to ask him, and said
2Co 11:32 garrison, *d* to apprehend me:
Gal 5:26 Let us not be *d* of vain glory,
1Th 2: 8 So being affectionately *d* of you,

desolate
Ge 47:19 not die, that the land be not *d*.
Ex 23:29 lest the land become *d*, and the
Le 26:22 and your high ways shall be *d*.
33 your land shall be *d*, and your
34 as long as it lieth *d*, and ye be in
35 As long as it lieth *d*, it shall rest;
43 while she lieth *d* without them:
2Sa 13:20 Tamar remained *d* in her brother
2Ch 36:21 as long as she lay *d*, she kept
Job 3:14 built *d* places for themselves;
15:28 he dwelleth in *d* cities, and in
34 of hypocrites shall be *d*, and fire
16: 7 hast made *d* all my company.
30: 3 in former time *d* and waste.
38:27 satisfy the *d* and waste ground,
Ps 25:16 upon me; for I am *d* and afflicted.
34:21 hate the righteous shall be *d*.
22 them that trust in him shall be *d*.
40:15 Let them be *d* for a reward of
69:25 Let their habitation be *d*; and
109:10 bread also out of their *d* places.
143: 4 me; my heart within me is *d*.
Isa 1: 7 Your country is *d*, your cities are
7 in your presence, and it is *d*,
3:26 being *d* shall sit upon the ground.
5: 9 many houses shall be *d*, even
6:11 and the land be utterly *d*,
7:19 all of them in the *d* valleys,
13: 9 fierce anger, to lay the land *d*:
22 shall cry in their *d* houses,
15: 6 the waters of Nimrim shall be *d*:
24: 6 they that dwell therein are *d*:
27:10 the defenced city shall be *d*,
49: 8 cause to inherit the *d* heritages;
19 thy waste and thy *d* places, and
21 children, and am *d*, a captive,
54: 1 the children of the *d* than the
3 make the *d* cities to be inhabited.
59:10 we are in *d* places as dead men.
62: 4 thy land any more be termed *D*:
Jer 2:12 be ye very *d*, saith the Lord.
4: 7 his place to make thy land *d*;
27 The whole land shall be *d*; yet
6: 8 lest I make thee *d*, a land not
7:34 bride: for the land shall be *d*.
9:11 will make the cities of Judah *d*,
10:22 to make the cities of Judah *d*,
25 and have made his habitation *d*.
12:10 pleasant portion a *d* wilderness.
11 They have made it *d*, and
11 being *d* it mourneth unto me;
11 the whole land is made *d*, because
18:16 To make their land *d*, and a
19: 8 I will make this city *d*, and an
25:38 for their land is *d* because of
26: 9 this city shall be *d* without an
32:43 It is *d* without man or beast;
33:10 which ye say shall be *d* without
10 streets of Jerusalem, that are *d*,
12 Again in this place, which is *d*
44: 6 they are wasted and *d*, as at
46:19 for Noph shall be waste and *d*
48: 9 for the cities thereof shall be *d*,
34 waters also of Nimrim shall be *d*.
49: 2 it shall be a *d* heap, and her
20 shall make their habitations *d*
50: 3 shall make her land *d*, and none
13 but it shall be wholly *d*:
45 he shall make their habitation *d*
51:26 but thou shalt be *d* for ever,
62 but that it shall be *d* for ever.
La 1: 4 feasts: all her gates are *d*: and
13 made me *d* and faint all the day.
16 my children are *d*, because the
3:11 in pieces: he hath made me *d*.
4: 5 They that did feed delicately are *d*
5:18 the mountain of Zion, which is *d*,
Eze 6: 4 And your altars shall be *d*, and
6 the high places shall be *d*: that
6 may be laid waste and made *d*,

Eze 6:14 and make the land d'. yea,
14 more d' than the wilderness
12:19 that her land may be d' from all
20 waste, and the land shall be d';
14:15 spoil it, so that it be d',
16 delivered, but the land shall be d'.
15: 8 I will make the land d', because
19: 7 he knew their d' places, and he
7 their cities; and the land was d',
20:26 that I might make them d', to the
25: 3 land of Israel, when it was d';
13 I will make it d' from Teman;
26:19 I shall make thee a d' city,
20 of the earth, in places d' of old,
29: 9 the land of Egypt shall be d'
10 of Egypt utterly waste and d',
12 I will make the land of Egypt d'
12 midst of the countries that are d',
12 laid waste shall be d' forty years:
30: 7 they shall be d' in the midst of
7 midst of the countries that are d',
14 And I will make Pathros d', and
32:15 I shall make the land of Egypt d',
33:28 For I will lay the land most d',
28 mountains of Israel shall be d',
29 when I have laid the land most d'
35: 3 I will make thee most d'.
4 cities waste, and thou shalt be d',
7 will I make mount Seir most d',
12 They are laid d', they are given
14 rejoiceth, I will make thee d'.
15 house of Israel, because it was d',
15 I do unto thee: thou shalt be d',
36: 3 Because they have made you d',
4 to the valleys, to the d' wastes,
34 And the d' land shall be tilled,
34 whereas it lay d' in the sight
35 This land that was d' is become
35 waste and d and ruined cities
36 places, and plant that that was d':
38:12 thine hand upon the d' places
Da 9:17 upon thy sanctuary that is d',
27 he shall make it d', even until the
27 shall be poured upon the d'.
11:31 the abomination that maketh d'.
12:11 abomination that maketh d' set up,
Ho 5: 9 Ephraim shall be d' in the day
13:16 Samaria shall become d'; for she
Joe 1:17 the garners are laid d', the barns
18 the flocks of sheep are made d'.
2: 3 behind them a d' wilderness;
20 him into a land barren and d',
3:19 and Edom shall be a d' wilderness,
Am 7: 9 high places of Isaac shall be d',
Mic 1: 7 the idols thereof will I lay d':
6:13 making thee d' because of thy sins.
7:13 land shall be d' because of them
Zep 3: 6 their towers are d'; I made their
Zec 7:14 the land was d' after them, that
14 for they laid the pleasant land d'.
Mal 1: 4 return and build the d' places;
M't 23:38 your house is left unto you d'.
Lu 13:35 your house is left unto you d':
Ac 1:20 Let his habitation be d', and let
Ga 4:27 the d' hath many more children
1Ti 5: 5 that is a widow indeed, and d',
Re 17:16 shall make her d' and naked,
18:19 for in one hour is she made d'.

desolation See also DESOLATIONS.
Le 26:31 bring your sanctuaries unto d',
32 And I will bring the land into d':
Jos 8:28 for ever, even a d' unto this day.
2Ki 22:19 should become a d' and a curse,
2Ch 30: 7 gave them up to d', as ye see.
Job 30:14 in the d' they rolled themselves
Ps 73:19 How are they brought into d',
Pr 1:27 When your fear cometh as d',
3:25 neither of the d' of the wicked,
Isa 10: 3 and in the d' which shall come
17: 9 of Israel: and there shall be d'.
24:12 In the city is left d', and the gate
47:11 d' shall come upon thee suddenly,
51:19 d', and destruction, and the
64:10 is a wilderness, Jerusalem a d'.
Jer 22: 5 that this house shall become a d'.
25:11 this whole land shall be a d',
18 make them a d', an astonishment,
34:22 Judah a d' without an inhabitant.
44: 2 this day they are a d', and no man
22 therefore is your land a d', and an
49:13 Bozrah shall become a d',
17 Edom shall be a d': every one
33 for dragons, and a d' for ever:
50:23 Babylon become a d' among the
51:29 Babylon a d' without an inhabitant.
43 Her cities are a d', a dry land,
La 3:47 come upon us, d' and destruction.
Eze 7:27 prince shall be clothed with d',
23:33 the cup of astonishment and d',
Da 8:13 transgression of d', to give both
Ho 12: 1 he daily increaseth lies and d';
Joe 3:19 Egypt shall be a d', and Edom
Mic 6:16 that I should make thee a d',
Zep 1:13 a booty, and their houses a d':
15 a day of wasteness, and d', a day
2: 4 be forsaken, and Ashkelon a d':
9 and salt pits, and a perpetual d':
13 will make Nineveh a d', and dry
14 d' shall be in the thresholds:
15 how is she become a d', a place
M't 12:25 against itself is brought to d';
24:15 the abomination of d', spoken of
M'r 13:14 ye shall see the abomination of d',
Lu 11:17 against itself is brought to d';
21:20 know that the d' thereof is nigh.

desolations
Ezr 9: 9 to repair the d' thereof, and to
Ps 46: 8 what d' he hath made in the
74: 3 thy feet unto the perpetual d';
Isa 61: 4 they shall raise up the former d',
4 cities, the d' of many generations.
Jer 25: 9 and an hissing, and perpetual d'.
12 and will make it perpetual d'.
Eze 35: 9 I will make thee perpetual d', and
Da 9: 2 years in the d' of Jerusalem.
18 thine eyes, and behold our d',
26 end of the war d' are determined.

despair See also DESPAIRED.
1Sa 27: 1 and Saul shall d' of me, to seek
Ec 2:20 my heart to d' of all the labour
2Co 4: 8 we are perplexed, but not in d';

despaired
2Co 1: 8 insomuch that we d' even of life:

desperate
Job 6:26 and speeches of one that is d',
Isa 17:11 the day of grief and of d' sorrow.

desperately
Jer 17: 9 above all things, and d' wicked:

despise See also DESPISED; DESPISEST; DESPISETH; DESPISING.
Le 26:15 if ye shall d' my statutes, or if
1Sa 2:30 and they that d' me shall be lightly
2Sa 19:43 why then did ye d' us, that our
Es 1:17 that they shall d' their husbands
Job 5:17 d' not thou the chastening of the
9:21 my soul: I would d' my life.
10: 3 shouldst d' the work of thine hands,
31:13 did d' the cause of my manservant
Ps 51:17 heart, O God, thou wilt not d'.
73:20 awakest, thou shalt d' their image.
102:17 destitute, and not d' their prayer.
Pr 1: 7 fools d' wisdom and instruction.
3:11 d' not the chastening of the Lord;
6:30 Men do not d' a thief, if he steal
23: 9 he will d' the wisdom of thy words.
22 d' not thy mother when she is old.
Isa 30:12 Because ye d' this word, and trust
Jer 4:30 thy lovers will d' thee, they
23:17 They say still unto them that d'
La 1: 8 all that honoured her d' her,
Eze 16:57 of the Philistines, which d' thee
28:26 upon all those that d' them
Am 5:21 I hate, I d' your feast days, and I
Mal 1: 6 you, O priests, that d' my name.
M't 6:24 hold to the one, and d' the other.
18:10 ye d' not one of these little ones;
Lu 16:13 hold to the one, and d' the other.
Ro 14: 3 Let not him that eateth d' him
1Co 11:22 or d' ye the church of God,
16:11 Let no man therefore d' him:
1Th 5:20 D' not prophesyings. Prove all
1Ti 4:12 Let no man d' thy youth; but be
6: 2 masters, let them not d' them,
Tit 2:15 authority. Let no man d' thee.
Heb 12: 5 d' not thou the chastening of
2Pe 2:10 uncleanness, and d' government.
Jude 8 d' dominion, and speak evil of

despised^
Ge 16: 4 her mistress was d' in her eyes.
5 conceived, I was d' in her eyes:
25:34 way: thus Esau d' his birthright.
Le 26:43 because they d' my judgments,
Nu 11:20 ye have d' the Lord which is
14:31 know the land which ye have d'.
15:31 he hath d' the word of the Lord,
J'g 9:38 this the people that thou hast d'?
1Sa 10:27 And they d' him, and brought him
2Sa 6:16 and she d' him in her heart.
12: 9 d' the commandment of the Lord,
10 because thou hast d' me, and hast
2Ki 19:21 the daughter of Zion hath d' thee,
1Ch 15:29 and she d' him in her heart.
2Ch 36:16 and d' his words, and misused his
Ne 2:19 and d' us, and said, What is this
4: 4 Hear, O our God; for we are d':
Job 12: 5 a lamp d' in the thought of him
19:18 young children d' me; I arose,
Ps 22: 6 of men, and d' of the people.
24 not d' nor abhorred the affliction
53: 5 because God hath d' them.
106:24 Yea, they d' the pleasant land,
119:141 I am small and d': yet do not I
Pr 1:30 counsel: they d' all my reproof.
5:12 and my heart d' reproof;
12: 8 is of a perverse heart shall be d'.
9 He that is d', and hath a servant,
Ec 9:16 the poor man's wisdom is d',
Ca 8: 1 kiss thee; yea, I should not be d'.
Isa 5:24 d' the word of the Holy One of
33: 8 he hath d' the cities, he regardeth
37:22 d' thee, and laughed thee to scorn;
53: 3 He is d' and rejected of men; a
3 he was d', and we esteemed him not.
60:14 all they that d' thee shall bow
Jer 33:24 they have d' my people, that they
49:15 the heathen, and d' among men.
La 2: 6 d' in the indignation of his anger
Eze 16:59 hast d' the oath in breaking the
17:16 oath he d', and whose covenant
18 Seeing he d' the oath by breaking
19 surely mine oath that he hath d',
20:13 they d' my judgments, which if
16 they d' my judgments, and walked
24 d' my statutes, and had polluted
22: 8 Thou hast d' mine holy things,
28:24 round about them, that d' them;
Am 2: 4 they have d' the law of the Lord,
Ob 2 the heathen: thou art greatly d'.

Zec 4:10 hath d' the day of small things?
Mal 1: 6 Wherein have we d' thy name?
Lu 18: 9 were righteous, and d' others:
Ac 19:27 Diana should be d',
1Co 1:28 things which are d', hath God
4:10 ye are honourable, but we are d'.
Ga 4:14 in my flesh ye d' not, nor rejected;
Heb 10:28 He that d' Moses' law died without
Jas 2: 6 But ye have d' the poor. Do not

despisers
Ac 13:41 Behold, ye d', and wonder, and
2Ti 3: 3 fierce, d' of those that are good,

despisest
Ro 2: 4 d' thou the riches of his goodness

despiseth
Job 36: 5 God is mighty, and d' not any:
Ps 69:33 the poor, and d' not his prisoners.
Pr 11:12 void of wisdom d' his neighbour:
13:13 Whoso d' the word shall be
14: 2 that is perverse in his ways d' him.
21 He that d' his neighbour sinneth:
15: 5 A fool d' his father's instruction:
20 but a foolish man d' his mother.
32 refuseth instruction d' his own
19:16 but he that d' his ways shall die.
30:17 father, and d' to obey his mother,
Isa 33:15 he that d' the gain of oppressions,
49: 7 to him whom man d', to him whom
Lu 10:16 he that d' you d' me;
16 and he that d' me d' him that sent
1Th 4: 8 He therefore that d', d' not man,

despising
Heb 12: 2 the cross, d' the shame, and is

despite See also DESPITEFUL.
Eze 25: 6 rejoiced in heart with all thy d'
Heb 10:29 and hath done d' unto the Spirit

despiteful
Eze 25:15 taken vengeance with a d' heart,
36: 5 with d' minds, to cast it out for
Ro 1:30 Backbiters, haters of God, d',

despitefully
M't 5:44 pray for them which d' use you,
Lu 6:28 pray for them which d' use you.
Ac 14: 5 to use them d', and to stone them,

destitute
Ge 24:27 not left d' my master of his mercy
Ps 102:17 will regard the prayer of the d',
141: 8 is my trust; leave not my soul d'.
Pr 15:21 joy to him that is d' of wisdom:
Eze 32:15 and the country shall be d' of that
1Ti 6: 5 corrupt minds and d' of the truth,
Heb 11:37 being d', afflicted, tormented;
Jas 2:15 be naked, and d' of daily food,

destroy See also DESTROYED; DESTROYEST; DESTROYETH; DESTROYING.
Ge 6: 7 And the Lord said, I will d' man
13 I will d' them with the earth.
17 to d' all flesh, wherein is the breath
7: 4 that I have made will I d' from off
9:11 more be a flood to d' the earth.
15 more become a flood to d' all flesh.
18:23 d' the righteous with the wicked?
24 wilt thou also d' and not spare
28 thou d' all the city for lack of five?
28 there forty and five, I will not d' it.
31 I will not d' it for twenty's sake.
32 I will not d' it for ten's sake.
19:13 we will d' this place, because the
13 the Lord hath sent us to d' it.
14 place; for the Lord will d' this city.
Ex 8: 9 to d' the frogs from thee and thy
12:13 be upon you to d' you, when I
15: 9 my sword, my hand shall d' them.
23:27 d' all the people to whom thou
34:13 But ye shall d' their altars,
Le 23:30 same soul will I d' from among his
26:22 d' your cattle, and make you few
30 And I will d' your high places,
44 to d' them utterly, and to break
Nu 21: 2 then I will utterly d' their cities.
24:17 and d' all the children of Sheth.
19 and shall d' him that remaineth
32:15 and ye shall d' all this people.
33:52 before you, and d' all their pictures,
52 and d' all their molten images,
De 1:27 hand of the Amorites, to d' us.
2:15 to d' them from among the host,
4:31 d' thee, nor forget the covenant of
6:15 and d' thee from off the face of
7: 2 smite them, and utterly d' them;
4 against you, and d' thee suddenly.
5 ye shall d' their altars, and break
10 hate him to their face, to d' them:
23 and shall d' them with a mighty
24 thou shalt d' their name from
9: 3 a consuming fire he shall d' them,
3 thou drive them out, and d' them
14 Let me alone, that I may d' them,
19 was wroth against you to d' you.
25 the Lord had said he would d' you.
26 God, d' not thy people and thine
10:10 and the Lord would not d' thee.
12: 2 Ye shall utterly d' all the places,
3 and d' the names of them out of
20:17 But thou shalt utterly d' them;
19 shalt not d' the trees thereof by
20 thou shalt d' and cut them down;
28:63 Lord will rejoice over you to d' you
31: 3 d' these nations from before thee,
32:25 shall d' both the young man and
33:27 thee; and shall say, D' them.

Jos 7: 7 hand of the Amorites, to d' us?
12 d' the accursed from among you.
9:24 to d' all the inhabitants of the land
11:20 that he might d' them utterly,
20 favour, but that he might d' them,
22:33 d' the land wherein the children
J'g 6: 5 they entered into the land to d' it.
21:11 Ye shall utterly d' every male,
1Sa 15: 3 smite Amalek, and utterly d' all
6 the Amalekites, lest I d' you with
9 and would not utterly d' them:
18 d' the sinners the Amalekites,
23:10 to d' the city for my sake.
24:21 that thou wilt not d' my name
26: 9 D' him not: for who can stretch
15 came one of the people in to d' the
2Sa 1:14 hand to d' the Lord's anointed?
14: 7 and we will d' the heir also:
11 revengers of blood to d' any more,
11 lest they d' my son. And he said,
16 the man that would d' me and my
20:19 seekest to d' a city and a mother
20 that I should swallow up or d'.
22:41 I might d' them that hate me.
24:16 his hand upon Jerusalem to d' it,
1Ki 9:21 also were not able utterly to d',
13:34 and to d' it from off the face of the
16:12 did Zimri d' all the house Baasha,
2Ki 8:19 Yet the Lord would not d' Judah
10:19 he might d' the worshippers of Baal
13:23 would not d' them, neither cast
18:25 Lord against this place to d' it?
25 Go up against this land, and d' it.
24: 2 sent them against Judah to d' it,
1Ch 21:15 an angel unto Jerusalem to d' it:
2Ch 12: 7 I will not d' them, but I will grant
12 he would not d' him altogether:
20:23 Seir, utterly to slay and d' them:
23 every one helped to d' another,
21: 7 would not d' the house of David,
25:16 God hath determined to d' thee,
35:21 who is with me, that he d' thee not.
Ezr 6:12 d' all kings and people, that shall
12 to alter and to d' this house of God
Es 3: 6 Haman sought to d' all the Jews
13 to d', to kill, and to cause to perish,
4: 7 treasuries for the Jews, to d' them.
8 was given at Shushan to d' them,
8: 5 which he wrote to d' the Jews which
11 d', to slay, and to cause to perish,
9:24 devised against the Jews to d' them,
24 to consume them, and to d' them;
Job 2: 3 him, to d' him without cause.
6: 9 it would please God to d' me;
8:18 If he d' him from his place,
10: 8 round about; yet thou dost d' me.
19:26 my skin worms d' this body,
Ps 5: 6 shalt d' them that speak leasing:
10 D' thou them, O God; let them
18:40 I might d' them that hate me.
21:10 fruit shalt thou d' from the earth,
28: 5 d' them, and not build them up.
40:14 that seek after my soul to d' it;
52: 5 God shall likewise d' thee for ever,
55: 9 D', O Lord, and divide their
63: 9 those that seek my soul, to d' it,
69: 4 they that would d' me, being
74: 8 Let us d' them together: they
101: 8 early d' all the wicked of the land;
106:23 he would d' them, had not Moses
23 his wrath, lest he should d' them.
34 They did not d' the nations,
118:10, 11, 12 of the Lord will I d' them.
119:95 wicked have waited for me to d' me:
143:12 and d' all them that afflict my soul:
144: 6 out thine arrows, and d' them.
145:20 but all the wicked will he d'.
Pr 1:32 the prosperity of fools shall d' them.
11: 3 of transgressors shall d' them.
15:25 will d' the house of the proud:
21: 7 of the wicked shall d' them;
Ec 5: 6 and d' the work of thine hands?
7:16 why shouldest thou d' thyself?
Isa 3:12 and d' the way of thy paths.
10: 7 d' and cut off nations not a few.
11: 9 shall not hurt nor d' in all my
15 Lord shall utterly d' the tongue of
13: 5 indignation, to d' the whole land.
9 d' the sinners thereof out of it.
19: 3 and I will d' the counsel thereof:
23:11 city, to d' the strong holds thereof.
25: 7 And he will d' in this mountain
32: 7 wicked devices to d' the poor with
36:10 Lord against this land to d' it?
10 Go up against this land, and d' it.
42:14 I will d' and devour at once.
51:13 as if he were ready to d'?
54:16 I have created the waster to d'.
65: 8 D' it not; for a blessing is in it:
8 sakes, that I may not d' them all.
25 They shall not hurt nor d' in all my
Jer 1:10 to pull down, and to d', and to
5:10 Go ye up upon her walls, and d';
6: 5 by night, and let us d' her palaces.
11:19 Let us d' the tree with the fruit
12:17 pluck up and d' that nation,
13:14 nor have mercy, but d' them.
15: 3 of the earth, to devour and d'.
6 my hand against thee, and d' thee;
7 I will d' my people, since they return
17:18 d' them with double destruction.
18: 7 to pull down, and to d' it;
23: 1 Woe be unto the pastors that d' and
25: 9 utterly d' them, and make them
31:28 break down, and to d', and to afflict:
36:29 certainly come and d' this land,

Jer 46: 8 I will d' the city and the inhabitants
48:18 and he shall d' thy strong holds.
49: 9 they will d' till they have enough.
38 and will d' from thence the king
50:21 waste and utterly d' after them,
26 her up as heaps, and d' her utterly:
51: 3 men, d' ye utterly all her host.
11 device is against Babylon, to d' it;
20 and with thee will I d' kingdoms;
La 2: 8 Lord hath purposed to d' the wall
3:66 Persecute and d' them in anger
Eze 5:16 and which I will send to d' you:
6: 3 and I will d' your high places.
9: 8 wilt thou d' all the residue of Israel
14: 9 and will d' him from the midst
21:31 of brutish men, and skilful to d'.
22:27 to shed blood, and to d' souls,
30 the land, that I should not d' it;
25: 7 I will d' thee; and thou shalt know
15 heart, to d' it for the old hatred;
16 and d' the remnant of the sea coast.
26: 4 they shall d' the walls of Tyrus,
12 walls, and d' thy pleasant houses:
28:16 I will d' thee; O covering cherub,
30:11 shall be brought to d' the land:
13 I will also d' the idols, and I will
32:13 I will d' also all the beasts thereof
34:16 I will d' the fat and the strong;
43: 3 saw when I came to d' the city:
Da 2:12 to d' all the wise men of Babylon.
24 to d' the wise men of Babylon.
24 D' not the wise men of Babylon:
4:23 Hew the tree down, and d' it;
7:26 consume and to d' it unto the end.
8:24 d' wonderfully, and shall prosper,
24 d' the mighty and the holy people.
25 heart, and by peace shall d' many:
9:26 shall d' the city and the sanctuary;
11:26 portion of his meat shall d' him,
44 shall go forth with great fury to d',
Ho 2:12 will d' her vines and her fig trees,
4: 5 the night, and I will d' thy mother
11: 9 I will not return to d' Ephraim:
Am 9: 8 and I will d' it from off the face of
8 I will not utterly d' the house of
Ob 8 even d' the wise men out of Edom.
Mic 2:10 it is polluted, it shall d' you,
5:10 of thee, and I will d' thy chariots:
14 of thee: so will I d' thy cities.
Zep 2: 5 the Philistines, I will even d' thee,
13 against the north, and d' Assyria;
Hag 2:22 d' the strength of the kingdoms
Zec 12: 9 seek to d' all the nations that come
Mal 3:11 he shall not d' the fruits of your
M't 2:13 seek the young child to d' him.
5:17 not that I am come to d' the law,
17 I am not come to d', but to fulfil.
10:28 able to d' both soul and body in
12:14 against him, how they might d' him.
21:41 He will miserably d' those wicked
26:61 said, I am able to d' the temple
27:20 should ask Barabbas, and d' Jesus.
M'r 1:24 art thou come to d' us? I know thee
3: 6 against him, how they might d' him.
9:22 and into the waters, to d' him:
11:18 sought how they might d' him:
12: 9 will come and d' the husbandmen,
14:58 I will d' this temple that is made
Lu 4:34 Nazareth? art thou come to d' us?
6: 9 or to do evil? to save life, or to d' it?
9:56 is not come to d' men's lives, but
19:47 chief of the people sought to d' him,
20:16 come and d' these husbandmen,
Joh 2:19 D' this temple, and in three days
10:10 for to steal, and to kill, and to d':
Ac 6:14 Jesus of Nazareth shall d' this
Ro 14:15 D' not him with thy meat, for whom
14:20 For meat d' not the work of God.
1Co 1:19 I will d' the wisdom of the wise,
3:17 temple of God, him shall God d';
6:13 God shall d' both it and them.
2Th 2: 8 and shall d' with the brightness
Heb 2:14 through death he might d' him
Jas 4:12 who is able to save and to d':
1Jo 3: 8 that he might d' the works of the
Re 11:18 d' them which d' the earth.

destroyed

Ge 7:23 And every living substance was d'
23 and they were d' from the earth:
13:10 before the Lord d' Sodom and
19:29 when God d' the cities of the plain,
34:30 and I shall be d', I and my house.
Ex 10: 7 knowest thou not yet that Egypt is d'?
22:20 Lord only, he shall be utterly d'.
Nu 21: 3 and they utterly d' them and their
De 1:44 and d' you in Seir, even unto
2:12 them, when they had d' them from
21 but the Lord d' them before them;
22 in Seir, when he d' the Horims
23 out of Caphtor, d' them, and dwelt
34 and utterly d' the men, and the
3: 6 And we utterly d' them, as we did
4: 3 thy God hath d' them from among
26 days upon it, but shall utterly be d'.
7:20 hide themselves from thee, be d'.
23 destruction, until they be d'.
24 before thee, until they have d' them.
9: 8 was angry with you to have d' you.
20 angry with Aaron to have d' him:
11: 4 how the Lord hath d' them unto this
12:30 after that they be d' from before
28:20 until thou be d', and until thou
24 down upon thee, until thou be d'.
45 and overtake thee, till thou be d';
48 thy neck, until he have d' thee.

De 28:51 fruit of thy land, until thou be d'.
51 thy sheep, until he have d' thee.
61 bring upon thee, until thou be d'.
31: 4 the land of them, whom he d'.
Jos 2:10 Sihon and Og, whom ye utterly d'.
6:21 And they utterly d' all that was in
8:26 until he had utterly d' all the
10: 1 taken Ai, and had utterly d' it,
28 and the king thereof he utterly d',
35 were therein he utterly d' that day,
37 but d' it utterly, and all the souls
39 and utterly d' all the souls that
40 but utterly d' all that breathed,
11:12 he utterly d' them, as Moses the
14 until they had d' them, neither left
21 Joshua d' them utterly with their
23:15 until he have d' you from off this
24: 8 and d' them from before you.
J'g 1:17 Zephath, and utterly d' it.
4:24 until they had d' Jabin king of
6: 4 and d' the increase of the earth,
20:21 Gibeah, and d' down to the ground
25 second day, and d' down to the
35 and the children of Israel d' of the
42 the cities they d' in the midst of
21:16 remain, seeing the women are d'
17 Benjamin, that a tribe be not d'
1Sa 5: 6 Ashdod, and he d' them, and smote
15: 8 and utterly d' all the people with
9 and refuse, that they d' utterly.
15 and the rest we have utterly d'.
20 and have utterly d' the Amalekites.
21 which should have been utterly d'.
2Sa 11: 1 they d' the children of Ammon,
21: 5 we should be d' from remaining
22:38 pursued mine enemies, and d' them;
24:16 the angel that d' the people,
1Ki 15:13 and Asa d' her idol, and burnt it
29 that breathed, until he had d' him.
2Ki 10:17 in Samaria, till he had d' him,
28 Thus Jehu d' Baal out of Israel.
11: 1 she arose and d' all the seed royal.
13: 7 the king of Syria had d' them,
19:12 them which my fathers have d';
17 of Assyria have d' the nations
18 stone, therefore they have d' them.
21: 3 which Hezekiah his father had d';
9 nations whom the Lord d' before
1Ch 4:41 and d' them utterly unto this day,
5:25 land, whom God d' before them.
20: 1 Joab smote Rabbah, and d' it,
21:12 three months to be d' before thy
15 and said to the angel that d',
2Ch 14:13 for they were d' before the Lord,
15: 6 And nation was d' of nation,
20:10 turned from them, and d' them not;
22:10 she arose and d' all the seed royal
24:23 and d' all the princes of the people
31: 1 until they had utterly d' them all.
32:14 nations that my fathers utterly d',
33: 9 whom the Lord had d' before the
34:11 which the kings of Judah had d'.
36:19 d' all the goodly vessels thereof.
Ezr 4:15 for which cause was this city d'.
5:12 who d' this house, and carried the
Es 3: 9 it be written that they may be d':
4:14 and thy father's house shall be d'
7: 4 to be d', to be slain, and to perish.
9: 6 Jews slew and d' five hundred men.
12 Jews have slain and d' five hundred
Job 4:20 They are d' from morning to
19:10 He hath d' me on every side,
34:25 in the night, so that they are d'.
Ps 9: 5 thou hast d' the wicked, thou hast
6 hast d' cities; their memorial
11: 3 If the foundations be d', what can
37:38 transgressors shall be d' together:
73:27 thou hast d' all them that go a
78:38 their iniquity, and d' them not:
45 them; and frogs, which d' them.
47 he d' their vines with hail, and
92: 7 it is that they shall be d' for ever:
137: 8 of Babylon, who art to be d';
Pr 13:13 despiseth the word shall be d':
13:20 a companion of fools shall be d'.
23 there is that is d' for want of
29: 1 shall suddenly be d', and that
Isa 9:16 they that are led of them are d'.
10:27 and the yoke shall be d' because
14:17 and d' the cities thereof;
20 because thou hast d' thy land,
26:14 therefore hast thou visited and d'
34: 2 he hath utterly d' them, he hath
37:12 them which my fathers have d',
19 stone: therefore they have d' them.
48:19 not have been cut off nor d' from
Jer 12:10 Many pastors have d' my vineyard,
22:20 passages: for all thy lovers are d'.
48: 4 Moab is d'; her little ones have
8 and the plain shall be d', as the
42 And Moab shall be d' from being a
51: 8 Babylon is suddenly fallen and d':
51:55 Babylon, and d' out of her the great
La 2: 5 he hath d' his strong holds, and
6 hath d' his places of the assembly:
9 he hath d' and broken her bars:
Eze 26:17 How art thou d', that wast inhabited
27:32 the d' in the midst of the sea?
30: 8 when all her helpers shall be d'.
32:12 the multitude thereof shall be d'.
Da 2:44 kingdom, which shall never be d':
6:26 kingdom that which shall not be d',
7:11 the beast was slain, and his body d',
14 kingdom that which shall not be d'
11:20 but within few days he shall be d',
Ho 4: 6 My people are d' for lack of

Ho 10: 8 Aven, the sin of Israel, shall be *d*:
13: 9 O Israel, thou hast *d* thyself, but
Am 2: 9 Yet *d* I the Amorite before them,
9 yet I *d* his fruit from above,
Zep 3: 6 passeth by: their cities are *d*,
M't 22: 7 and *d* those murderers, and burned
Lu 17:27 the flood came, and *d* them all.
29 from heaven, and *d* them all.
Ac 3:23 shall be *d* from among the people.
9:21 Is not this he that *d* them which
13:19 And when he had *d* seven nations
19:27 her magnificence should be *d*,
Ro 6: 6 that the body of sin might be *d*,
1Co 10: 9 tempted and were *d* of serpents.
10 and were *d* of the destroyer.
15:26 The last enemy that shall be *d*
2Co 4: 9 forsaken; cast down, but not *d*;
Ga 1:23 the faith which once he *d*.
2:18 build again the things which I *d*,
Heb 11:28 lest he that *d* the first born
2Pe 2:12 beasts, made to be taken and *d*,
Jude 5 afterward *d* them that believed not.
Re 8: 9 the third part of the ships were *d*.

destroyer See also DESTROYERS.
Ex 12:23 will not suffer the *d* to come in
J'g 16:24 the *d* of our country, which slew
Job 15:21 the *d* shall come upon him.
Ps 17: 4 kept me from the paths of the *d*.
Pr 28:24 the same is the companion of a *d*.
Jer 4: 7 and the *d* of the Gentiles is on his
1Co 10:10 and were destroyed of the *d*.

destroyers
Job 33:22 the grave, and his life to the *d*.
Isa 49:17 thy *d* and they that made thee
Jer 22: 7 And I will prepare *d* against thee,
50:11 O ye *d* of mine heritage, because

destroyest
Job 14:19 earth; and thou *d* the hope of man.
Jer 51:25 the Lord, which *d* all the earth:
M't 27:40 Thou that *d* the temple, and
M'r 15:29 Ah, thou that *d* the temple, and

destroyeth
De 8:20 As the nations which the Lord *d*
Job 9:22 He *d* the perfect and the wicked.
12:23 increaseth the nations, and *d* them:
Pr 6:32 he that doeth it *d* his own soul.
11: 9 with his mouth *d* his neighbour:
31: 3 thy ways to that which *d* kings.
Ec 7: 7 man mad; and a gift *d* the heart.
9:18 war: but one sinner *d* much good.

destroying
De 3: 6 of Heshbon, utterly *d* the men,
13:15 *d* it utterly, and all that is therein,
Jos 11:11 edge of the sword, utterly *d* them:
2Ki 19:11 to all lands, by *d* them utterly:
1Ch 21:12 angel of the Lord *d* throughout
15 and as he was *d*, the Lord beheld
Isa 28: 2 a tempest of hail and a *d* storm,
37:11 by *d* them utterly; and shalt thou
Jer 2:30 your prophets, like a *d* lion.
51: 1 that rise up against me, a *d* wind;
25 I am against thee, O *d* mountain,
La 2: 8 not withdrawn his hand from *d*:
Eze 9: 1 every man with his *d* weapon in
20:17 eye spared them from *d* them,

destruction See also DESTRUCTIONS.
De 7:23 destroy them with a mighty *d*,
32:24 burning heat, and with bitter *d*:
1Sa 5: 9 the city with a very great *d*:
11 there was a deadly *d* throughout
1Ki 20:42 whom I appointed to utter *d*,
2Ch 22: 4 the death of his father to his *d*.
7 the *d* of Ahaziah was of God by
26:16 his heart was lifted up to his *d*:
Es 8: 6 how can I endure to see the *d* of my
9: 5 slaughter, and *d*, and did what
Job 5:21 neither shalt thou be afraid of *d*
22 At *d* and famine thou shalt laugh:
18:12 and *d* shall be ready at his side.
21:17 oft cometh their *d* upon them!
20 His eyes shall see his *d*, and he
30 is reserved to the day of *d*?
26: 6 him, and *d* hath no covering.
28:22 *D* and death say, We have heard
30:12 against me the ways of their *d*.
24 grave, though they cry in his *d*.
31: 3 Is not *d* to the wicked?
12 it is a fire that consumeth to *d*,
23 *d* from God was a terror to me,
29 If I rejoiced at the *d* of him that
Ps 35: 8 *d* come upon him at unawares;
8 into that very *d* let him fall.
55:23 bring them down into the pit of *d*:
73:18 thou castedst them down into *d*.
88:11 grave? or thy faithfulness in *d*?
90: 3 turnest man to *d*; and sayest,
91: 6 the *d* that wasteth at noonday.
103: 4 Who redeemeth thy life from *d*;
Pr 1:27 your *d* cometh as a whirlwind;
10:14 the mouth of the foolish is near *d*.
15 the *d* of the poor is their poverty.
29 but *d* shall be to the workers of
13: 3 openeth wide his lips shall have *d*.
14:28 want of people is the *d* of the prince.
15:11 Hell and *d* are before the Lord:
16:18 Pride goeth before *d*, and an
17:19 that exalteth his gate seeketh *d*.
18: 7 A fool's mouth is his *d*, and his
12 Before *d* the heart of man is
21:15 but *d* shall be to the workers of
24: 2 their heart studieth *d*, and their
27:20 Hell and *d* are never full;
31: 8 all such as are appointed to *d*.
Isa 1:28 And the *d* of the transgressors
10:25 cease, and mine anger in their *d*.
13: 6 come as a *d* from the Almighty.
14:23 will sweep it with the besom of *d*,
15: 5 they shall raise up a cry of *d*.
19:18 one shall be called, The city of *d*.
24:12 and the gate is smitten with *d*.
49:19 the land of thy *d*, shall even now
51:19 desolation, and *d*, and the famine,
59: 7 wasting and *d* are in their paths.
60:18 wasting nor *d* within thy borders;
Jer 4: 6 evil from the north and a great *d*.
20 *D* upon *d* is cried; for the whole
6: 1 out of the north, and great *d*.
17:18 and destroy them with double *d*.
46:20 but *d* cometh; it cometh out of
48: 3 Horonaim, spoiling and great *d*.
5 the enemies have heard a cry of *d*.
50:22 battle is in the land and of great *d*.
51:54 and great *d* from the land of the
La 2:11 *d* of the daughter of my people;
3:47 come upon us, desolation and *d*.
48 *d* of the daughter of my people.
4:10 *d* of the daughter of my people.
Eze 5:16 which shall be for their *d*,
7:25 *D* cometh; and they shall seek
32: 9 bring thy *d* among the nations,
Ho 7:13 *d* unto them! because they have
9: 6 lo, they are gone because of *d*:
13:14 O grave, I will be thy *d*:
Joe 1:15 and as a *d* from the Almighty
Ob 12 of Judah in the day of their *d*;
Mic 2:10 destroy you, even with a sore *d*.
Zec 14:11 there shall be no more utter *d*;
M't 7:13 broad is the way that leadeth to *d*
Ro 3:16 *D* and misery are in their ways:
9:22 vessels of wrath fitted to *d*:
1Co 5: 5 unto Satan for the *d* of the flesh,
2Co 10: 8 edification, and not for your *d*,
13:10 me to edification, and not to *d*.
Ph'p 3:19 Whose end is *d*, whose God is
1Th 5: 3 sudden *d* cometh upon them,
2Th 1: 9 be punished with everlasting *d*
1Ti 6: 9 drown men in *d* and perdition.
2Pe 2: 1 bring upon themselves swift *d*.
3:16 other scriptures, unto their own *d*.

destructions
Ps 9: 6 *d* are come to a perpetual end:
35:17 rescue my soul from their *d*,
107:20 and delivered them from their *d*.

detain See also DETAINED.
J'g 13:15 I pray thee, let us *d* thee,
16 Though thou *d* me, I will not eat

detained
1Sa 21: 7 there that day, *d* before the Lord;

determinate
Ac 2:23 delivered by the *d* counsel and

determination
Zep 3: 8 for my *d* is to gather the nations,

determine See DETERMINED.
Ex 21:22 and he shall pay as the judges *d*

determined
1Sa 20: 7 be sure that evil is *d* by him.
9 evil were *d* by my father to come
1Sa 20:33 Jonathan knew that it was *d* of his
25:17 evil is *d* against our master.
2Sa 13:32 this hath been *d* from the day
2Ch 2: 1 Solomon *d* to build an house for
25:16 know that God hath *d* to destroy
Es 7: 7 there was evil *d* against him by
Job 14: 5 Seeing his days are *d*, the number
Isa 10:23 consumption, even *d*, in the midst
19:17 hosts, which he hath *d* against it.
28:22 a consumption, even *d* upon
Da 9:24 Seventy weeks are *d* upon thy
26 end of the war desolations are *d*.
27 that *d* shall be poured upon the
11:36 for that that is *d* shall be done.
Lu 22:22 Son of man goeth, as it was *d*:
Ac 3:13 Pilate, when he was *d* to let him
4:28 counsel *d* before to be done.
11:29 *d* to send relief unto the brethren
15: 2 they *d* that Paul and Barnabas,
37 Barnabas *d* to take with them
17:26 hath *d* the times before appointed,
19:39 shall be *d* in a lawful assembly.
20:16 Paul had *d* to sail by Ephesus,
25:25 Augustus, I have *d* to send him.
27: 1 when it was *d* that we should sail
1Co 2: 2 For I *d* not to know any thing
2Co 2: 1 But I *d* this with myself, that I
Tit 3:12 for I have *d* there to winter.

detest See also DETESTABLE.
De 7:26 thou shalt utterly *d* it, and thou

detestable
Jer 16:18 their *d* and abominable things.
Eze 5:11 sanctuary with all thy *d* things,
7:20 and of their *d* things therein:
11:18 all the *d* things thereof from
21 *d* things and their abominations,
37:23 idols, nor with their *d* things,

Deuel (*de-oo'-el*) See also REUEL.
Nu 1:14 of Gad; Eliasaph the son of *D*.
7:42 sixth day Eliasaph the son of *D*,
47 offering of Eliasaph the son of *D*.
10:20 Gad was Eliasaph the son of *D*.

device See also DEVICES.
2Ch 2:14 to find out every *d* which shall
Es 8: 3 his *d* that he had devised against
9:25 by letters that his wicked *d*, which
Ps 21:11 they imagined a mischievous *d*,
140: 8 further not his wicked *d*; lest
Ec 9:10 for there is no work, nor *d*, nor
Jer 18:11 and devise a *d* against you:
51:11 for his *d* is against Babylon,
La 3:62 their *d* against me all the day.
Ac 17:29 stone, graven by art and man's *d*.

devices
Job 5:12 He disappointeth the *d* of the
21:27 *d* which ye wrongfully imagine
Ps 10: 2 let them be taken in the *d* that
33:10 he maketh the *d* of the people
37: 7 who bringeth wicked *d* to pass.
Pr 1:31 and be filled with their own *d*.
12: 2 man of wicked *d* will he condemn.
14:17 a man of wicked *d* is hated.
19:21 are many *d* in a man's heart;
Isa 32: 7 he deviseth wicked *d* to destroy
Jer 11:19 they had devised *d* against me,
18:12 we will walk after our own *d*,
18 let us devise *d* against Jeremiah;
Da 11:24 forecast his *d* against the strong
25 they shall forecast *d* against him.
2Co 2:11 we are not ignorant of his *d*.

devil See also DEVILS.
M't 4: 1 wilderness to be tempted of the *d*.
5 *d* taketh him up into the holy city,
8 Again the *d* taketh him up into
11 Then the *d* leaveth him, and,
9:32 a dumb man possessed with a *d*.
33 when the *d* was cast out, the
11:18 and they say, He hath a *d*.
12:22 one possessed with a *d*, blind,
13:39 enemy that sowed them is the *d*;
15:22 is grievously vexed with a *d*.
17:18 Jesus rebuked the *d*; and he
25:41 prepared for the *d* and his angels:
M'r 5:15, 16 was possessed with the *d*,
18 that had been possessed with a *d*,
7:26 that he would cast forth the *d*
29 *d* is gone out of thy daughter.
30 she found the *d* gone out, and her
Lu 4: 2 Being forty days tempted of the *d*
3 the *d* said unto him, If thou be
5 *d*, taking him up into an high
6 the *d* said unto him, All this will
13 *d* had ended all the temptation,
33 had a spirit of an unclean *d*,
35 when the *d* had thrown him in
7:33 wine; and ye say, He hath a *d*.
8:12 cometh the *d*, and taketh away
29 of the *d* into the wilderness
9:42 *d* threw him down, and tare him.
11:14 casting out a *d*, and it was dumb.
14 to pass when the *d* was gone out,
Joh 6:70 twelve, and one of you is a *d*?
7:20 and said, Thou hast a *d*:
8:44 Ye are of your father the *d*,
48 art a Samaritan, and hast a *d*?
49 Jesus answered, I have not a *d*;
52 Now we know that thou hast a *d*.
10:20 many of them said, He hath a *d*,
21 the words of him that hath a *d*.
21 a *d* open the eyes of the blind?
13: 2 *d* having now put into the heart
Ac 10:38 all that were oppressed of the *d*;
13:10 thou child of the *d*, thou enemy
Eph 4:27 Neither give place to the *d*.
6:11 stand against the wiles of the *d*.
1Ti 3: 6 into the condemnation of the *d*.
7 reproach and the snare of the *d*.
2Ti 2:26 out of the snare of the *d*, who
Heb 2:14 power of death, that is, the *d*;
Jas 4: 7 Resist the *d*, and he will flee from
1Pe 5: 8 because your adversary the *d*,
1Jo 3: 8 that committeth sin is of the *d*;
8 *d* sinneth from the beginning.
8 might destroy the works of the *d*.
10 manifest, and the children of the *d*:
Jude 9 when contending with the *d* he
Re 2:10 the *d* shall cast some of you into
12: 9 that old serpent, called the *D*, and
12 the *d* is come down unto you,
20: 2 that old serpent, which is the *D*,
10 the *d* that deceived them was cast

devilish
Jas 3:15 above, but is earthly, sensual, *d*.

devils
Le 17: 7 offer their sacrifices unto *d*, after
De 32:17 sacrificed unto *d*, not to God;
2Ch 11:15 and for the *d*, and for the calves
Ps 106:37 sons and their daughters unto *d*,
M't 4:24 which were possessed with *d*,
7:22 in thy name have cast out *d*?
8:16 that were possessed with *d*:
28 met him two possessed with *d*,
31 So the *d* besought him, saying, If
33 befallen to the possessed of the *d*.
9:34 Pharisees said, He casteth out *d*
34 through the prince of the *d*.
10: 8 lepers, raise the dead, cast out *d*:
12:24 This fellow doth not cast out *d*,
24 by Beelzebub the prince of the *d*.
27 if I by Beelzebub cast out *d*,
28 if I cast out *d* by the Spirit of
M'r 1:32 them that were possessed with *d*.
34 diseases, and cast out many *d*;
34 and suffered not the *d* to speak,
39 all Galilee, and cast out *d*.
3:15 sicknesses, and to cast out *d*:
22 and by the prince of the *d*
22 casteth he out *d*.

M'r 5:12 all the *d'* besought him, saying,
6:13 they cast out many *d'*, and
9:38 one casting out *d'* in thy name,
16: 9 out of whom he had cast seven *d'*.
17 my name shall they cast out *d'*;
Lu 4:41 *d'* also came out of many, crying
8: 2 out of whom went seven *d'*,
27 a certain man, which had *d'* long
30 because many *d'* were entered
33 Then went the *d'* out of the man,
35 of whom the *d'* were departed,
36 possessed of the *d'* was healed.
38 the man out of whom the *d'* were
9: 1 power and authority over all *d'*,
49 Master, we saw one casting out *d'*
10:17 even the *d'* are subject unto us
11:15 casteth out *d'* through Beelzebub
15 the chief of the *d'*.
18 I cast out *d'* through Beelzebub.
19 if I by Beelzebub cast out *d'*,
20 with the finger of God cast out *d'*,
13:32 I cast out *d'*, and I do cures
1Co 10:20 sacrifice to *d'*, and not to God:
20 ye should have fellowship with *d'*.
21 cup of the Lord, and the cup of *d'*:
21 Lord's table, and of the table of *d'*.
1Ti 4: 1 spirits, and doctrines of *d'*;
Jas 2:19 the *d'* also believe, and tremble.
Re 9:20 that they should not worship *d'*,
16:14 For they are the spirits of *d'*,
18: 2 is become the habitation of *d'*,

devise See also DEVISED; DEVISETH.
Ex 31: 4 To *d'* cunning works, to work in
35:32 And to *d'* curious works, to work in
35 and of those that *d'* cunning work.
2Sa 14:14 yet doth he *d'* means, that his
Ps 35: 4 to confusion that *d'* my hurt.
20 *d'* deceitful matters against them
41: 7 against me do they *d'* my hurt.
Pr 3:29 *D'* not evil against thy neighbour,
14:22 Do they not err that *d'* evil? but
22 shall be to them that *d'* good.
16:30 shutteth his eyes to *d'* froward
Jer 18:11 and *d'* a device against you: return
18 let us *d'* devices against Jeremiah;
Eze 11: 2 the men that *d'* mischief, and give
Mic 2: 1 Woe to them that *d'* iniquity, and
3 against this family do I *d'* an evil,

devised
2Sa 21: 5 that *d'* against us that we should
1Ki 12:33 in the month which he had *d'*
Es 8: 3 that he had *d'* against the Jews.
5 reverse the letters *d'* by Haman
9:24 had *d'* against the Jews to destroy
25 which he *d'* against the Jews,
Ps 31:13 they *d'* to take away my life.
Jer 11:19 they had *d'* devices against me,
48: 2 in Heshbon they had *d'* evil
51:12 the Lord hath both *d'* and done
La 2:17 hath done that which he had *d'*;
2Pe 1:16 not followed cunningly *d'* fables,

deviseth
Ps 36: 4 He *d'* mischief upon his bed; he
52: 2 tongue *d'* mischiefs; like a sharp
Pr 6:14 heart, he *d'* mischief continually;
18 heart that *d'* wicked imaginations,
16: 9 A man's heart *d'* his ways; but the
24: 8 He that *d'* to do evil shall be
Isa 32: 7 he *d'* wicked devices to destroy
8 But the liberal *d'* liberal things;

devote See also DEVOTED.
Le 27:28 that a man shall *d'* unto the Lord

devoted
Le 27:21 unto the Lord, as a field *d'*;
28 no *d'* thing, that a man shall devote
28 every *d'* thing is most holy unto
29 None *d'*, which shall be
29 which shall be *d'* of men,
Nu 18:14 Every thing *d'* in Israel shall be
Ps 119:38 servant, who is *d'* to thy fear.

devotions
Ac 17:23 I passed by, and beheld your *d'*,

devour See also DEVOURED; DEVOUREST; DEVOURETH; DEVOURING.
Ge 49:27 the morning he shall *d'* the prey,
De 32:42 blood, and my sword shall *d'* flesh;
J'g 9:15 and *d'* the cedars of Lebanon.
20 and *d'* the men of Shechem, and the
20 house of Millo, and *d'* Abimelech.
2Sa 2:26 Shall the sword *d'* for ever?
2Ch 7:13 command the locusts to *d'* the land,
Job 18:13 It shall *d'* the strength of his skin:
13 born of death shall *d'* his strength.
Ps 21: 9 wrath, and the fire shall *d'* them.
50: 3 silence: a fire shall *d'* before him,
80:13 wild beasts of the field doth *d'* it.
Pr 30:14 to *d'* the poor from off the earth,
Isa 1: 7 strangers *d'* it in your presence,
9:12 shall *d'* Israel with open mouth.
18 it shall *d'* the briers and thorns,
10:17 and it shall burn and *d'* his thorns
26:11 of thine enemies shall *d'* them.
31: 8 not of a mean man, shall *d'* him:
33:11 your breath, as fire, shall *d'* you.
42:14 I will destroy and *d'* at once.
56: 9 beasts of the field, come to *d'*,
Jer 2: 3 all that *d'* him shall offend:
5:14 people wood, and it shall *d'* them.
12: 9 the beasts of the field, come to *d'*.
12 the sword of the Lord shall *d'*
15: 3 of the earth, to *d'* and destroy.
17:27 shall *d'* the palaces of Jerusalem,
21:14 and it shall *d'* all things round
30:16 Therefore all they that *d'* shall be
Jer 46:10 and the sword shall *d'*, and it shall
14 sword shall *d'* round about thee.
48:45 and shall *d'* the corner of Moab,
50:32 and it shall *d'* all round about him.
Eze 7:15 famine and pestilence shall *d'* him.
15: 7 fire, and another fire shall *d'* them;
20:47 it shall *d'* every green tree in thee,
23:37 them through the fire to *d'* them.
28:18 it shall *d'* thee, and I will bring
34:28 the beast of the land *d'* them;
36:14 thou shalt *d'* men no more, neither
Da 7: 5 thus unto it, Arise, *d'* much flesh.
23 and shall *d'* the whole earth,
Ho 5: 7 now shall a month *d'* them with
8:14 and it shall *d'* the palaces thereof.
11: 6 and *d'* them, because of their own
13: 8 and there will I *d'* them like a lion:
Am 1: 4 shall *d'* the palaces of Ben-hadad.
7 which shall *d'* the palaces thereof:
10 of Tyrus, which shall *d'* the palaces
12 shall *d'* the palaces of Bozrah.
14 and it shall *d'* the palaces thereof,
2: 2 Moab, and it shall *d'* the palaces
5 shall *d'* the palaces of Jerusalem.
5: 6 in the house of Joseph, and *d'* it,
Ob 18 shall kindle in them, and *d'* them;
Na 2:13 the sword shall *d'* thy young lions:
3:13 enemies: the fire shall *d'* thy bars.
15 There shall the fire *d'* thee: the
Hab 3:14 was as to *d'* the poor secretly.
Zec 9:15 and they shall *d'*, and subdue with
11: 1 that the fire may *d'* thy cedars.
12: 6 and they shall *d'* all the people
M't 23:14 ye *d'* widows' houses, and for
M'r 12:40 which *d'* widows' houses, and for
Lu 20:47 Which *d'* widows' houses, and for
2Co 11:20 if a man *d'* you, if a man take
Ga 5:15 if ye bite and *d'* one another,
Heb 10:27 which shall *d'* the adversaries.
1Pe 5: 8 about, seeking whom he may *d'*:
Re 12: 4 for to *d'* her child as soon as

devoured
Ge 31:15 and hath quite *d'* also our money.
37:20 Some evil beast hath *d'* him: and
33 an evil beast hath *d'* him: Joseph
41: 7 And the seven thin ears *d'* the
24 And the thin ears *d'* the seven
Le 10: 2 and *d'* them, and they died before
Nu 26:10 the fire *d'* two hundred and fifty
De 31:17 and they shall be *d'*, and many evils
32:24 and *d'* with burning heat, and
2Sa 18: 8 the wood *d'* more people
8 that day than the sword *d'*.
22: 9 and fire out of his mouth *d'*:
Ps 18: 8 and fire out of his mouth *d'*:
78:45 flies among them, which *d'* them;
79: 7 For they have *d'* Jacob, and laid
105:35 and *d'* the fruit of their ground.
Isa 1:20 ye shall be *d'* with the sword:
24: 6 hath the curse *d'* the earth,
Jer 2:30 own sword hath *d'* your prophets,
3:24 shame hath *d'* the labour of our
8:16 they are come, and have *d'* the land,
10:25 have eaten up Jacob, and *d'* him,
30:16 they that devour thee shall be *d'*;
50: 7 All that found them have *d'* them:
17 the king of Assyria hath *d'* him;
51:34 the king of Babylon hath *d'* me,
La 4:11 it hath *d'* the foundations thereof.
Eze 15: 5 when the fire hath *d'* it, and it is
16:20 thou sacrificed unto them to be *d'*.
19: 3 learned to catch the prey; it *d'* men.
6 to catch the prey, and *d'* men.
14 branches, which hath *d'* her fruit,
22:25 they have *d'* souls; they have taken
23:25 thy residue shall be *d'* by the fire.
33:27 will I give to the beasts to be *d'*,
39: 4 to the beasts of the field to be *d'*.
Da 7: 7 teeth: it *d'* and brake in pieces,
19 which *d'*, brake in pieces, and
Ho 7: 7 an oven, and have *d'* their judges;
9 Strangers have *d'* his strength, and
Joe 1:19 to thee will I cry for the fire hath *d'*
20 the fire hath *d'* the pastures of the
Am 4: 9 increased, the palmerworm *d'* them:
7: 4 and it *d'* the great deep, and did eat
Na 1:10 they shall be *d'* as stubble fully
Zep 1:18 shall be *d'* by the fire of his jealousy:
3: 8 be *d'* with the fire of my jealousy.
Zec 9: 4 and she shall be *d'* with fire.
M't 13: 4 the fowls came and *d'* them up:
M'r 4: 4 fowls of the air came and *d'* it up.
Lu 8: 5 and the fowls of the air *d'* it.
15:30 hath *d'* thy living with harlots,
Re 20: 9 out of heaven, and *d'* them.

devourer
Mal 3:11 I will rebuke the *d'* for your sakes,

devourest
Eze 36:13 Thou land *d'* up men, and hast

devoureth
2Sa 11:25 sword *d'* one as well as another:
Pr 19:28 mouth of the wicked *d'* iniquity.
20:25 man who *d'* that which is holy,
Isa 5:24 Therefore as the fire *d'* the stubble,
La 2: 3 a flaming fire, which *d'* round about.
Eze 15: 4 the fire *d'* both the ends of it,
Joe 2: 3 A fire *d'* before them; and behind
5 a flame of fire that *d'* the stubble
Hab 1:13 when the wicked *d'* the man that
Re 11: 5 their mouth, and *d'* their enemies:

devouring
Ex 24:17 like *d'* fire on the top of the mount
Ps 52: 4 Thou lovest all *d'* words, O thou
Isa 29: 6 tempest, and the flame of *d'* fire.
30:27 and his tongue as a *d'* fire:
30 and with the flame of a *d'* fire,
33:14 us shall dwell with the *d'* fire?

devout
Lu 2:25 the same man was just and *d'*,
Ac 2: 5 Jews, *d'* men, out of every nation
8: 2 And *d'* men carried Stephen to his
10: 2 A *d'* man, and one that feared God
7 a *d'* soldier of them that waited on
13:50 stirred up the *d'* and honourable
17: 4 of the *d'* Greeks a great multitude,
17 the Jews, and with the *d'* persons,
22:12 a *d'* man according to the law,

dew
Ge 27:28 God give thee of the *d'* of heaven,
39 and of the *d'* of heaven from above;
Ex 16:13 the *d'* lay round about the host.
14 when the *d'* that lay was gone
Nu 11: 9 when the *d'* fell upon the camp
De 32: 2 my speech shall distil as the *d'*,
33:13 for the *d'*, and for the deep
28 also his heavens shall drop down *d'*.
J'g 6:37 if the *d'* be on the fleece only,
38 wringed the *d'* out of the fleece,
39 upon all the ground let there be *d'*.
40 there was *d'* on all the ground.
2Sa 1:21 Gilboa, let there be no *d'*, neither
17:12 light upon him as the *d'* falleth
1Ki 17: 1 there shall not be *d'* nor rain
Job 29:19 the *d'* lay all night upon my branch.
38:28 who hath begotten the drops of *d'*?
Ps 110: 3 thou hast the *d'* of thy youth.
133: 3 the *d'* [2919] of Hermon, and as the *d'*
Pr 3:20 and the clouds drop down the *d'*.
19:12 his favour is as *d'* upon the grass.
Ca 5: 2 for my head is filled with *d'*,
Isa 18: 4 like a cloud of *d'* in the heat of
26:19 for thy *d'* is as the *d'* of herbs,
Da 4:15 let it wet with the *d'* of heaven,
23 *d'* of heaven, and let his portion be
25 they shall wet thee with the *d'* of
33 and his body was wet with the *d'* of
5:21 body was wet with the *d'* of heaven;
Ho 6: 4 and as the early *d'* it goeth away.
13: 3 and as the early *d'* that passeth
14: 5 I will be as the *d'* unto Israel;
Mic 5: 7 many people as a *d'* from the Lord,
Hag 1:10 heaven over you is stayed from *d'*,
Zec 8:12 the heavens shall give their *d'*;

diadem
Job 29:14 judgment was as a robe and a *d'*.
Isa 28: 5 and for a *d'* of beauty, unto the
62: 3 a royal *d'* in the hand of thy God.
Eze 21:26 Remove the *d'*, and take off the

dial
2Ki 20:11 which it had gone down in the *d'*
Isa 38: 8 which is gone down in the sun *d'*

diamond
Ex 28:18 an emerald, a sapphire, and a *d'*.
39:11 an emerald, a sapphire, and a *d'*.
Jer 17: 1 and with the point of a *d'*:
Eze 28:13 the sardius, topaz, and the *d'*,

Diana (*di-an'-ah*)
Ac 19:24 which made silver shrines for *D'*
27 the temple of the great goddess *D'*
28 Great is *D'* of the Ephesians.
34 out, Great is *D'* of the Ephesians.
35 worshipper of the great goddess *D'*,

Diblaim (*dib'-la-im*)
Ho 1: 3 took Gomer the daughter of *D'*;

Diblath (*dib'-lath*)
Eze 6:14 than the wilderness toward *D'*,

Diblathaim See ALMON-DIBLATHAIM; BETH-DIBLATHAIM.

Dibon (*di'-bon*) See also DIBON-GAD; DIMON.
Nu 21:30 Heshbon is perished even unto *D'*,
32: 3 Ataroth, and *D'*, and Jazer, and
34 And the children of Gad built *D'*,
Jos 13: 9 all the plain of Medeba unto *D'*;
17 *D'*, and Bamoth-baal, and
Ne 11:25 at *D'*, and in the villages thereof,
Isa 15: 2 He is gone up to Bajith, and to *D'*,
Jer 48:18 daughter that dost inhabit *D'*,
22 And upon *D'*, and upon Nebo, and

Dibon-gad (*di''-bon-gad'*)
Nu 33:45 from Iim, and pitched in *D'*.
46 removed from *D'*, and encamped

Dibri (*dib'-ri*)
Le 24:11 Shelomith, the daughter of *D'*,

did^ See also DIDDEST; DIDST.
Ge 3: 6 and *d'* eat, and gave also unto her
6 husband with her; and he *d'* eat.
12 she gave me of the tree, and I *d'* eat.
13 serpent beguiled me, and I *d'* eat.
21 unto his wife *d'* the Lord God make
6:22 Thus *d'* Noah; according to all
22 God commanded him, so *d'* he.
7: 5 Noah *d'* according unto all that the
20 cubits upward *d'* the waters prevail;
11: 9 because the Lord *d'* there confound
9 thence *d'* the Lord scatter them
18: 8 under the tree, and they *d'* eat.
13 Wherefore *d'* Sarah laugh,
19: 3 and *d'* bake unleavened bread,
21: 1 *d'* unto Sarah as he had spoken.
22: 1 that God *d'* tempt Abraham and
23 these eight Milcah *d'* bear to Nahor,
24:54 and they *d'* eat and drink,
25:28 because he *d'* eat of his venison:
34 and he *d'* eat and drink, and rose up,

Ge 26:20 the herdmen of Gerar *d'* strive
30 and they *d'* eat and drink,
27:25 brought it near to him, and he *d'* eat:
29:25 *d'* not I serve with thee for
28 Jacob *d'* so, and fulfilled her week:
30:40 And Jacob *d'* separate the lambs,
41 the stronger cattle *d'* conceive,
31:46 and they *d'* eat thereupon the heap.
54 and they *d'* eat bread,
35: 5 and they *d'* not pursue after the
38:10 which he *d'* displeased the Lord:
11 he die also, as his brethren *d'*.
39: 3 Lord made all that he *d'* to prosper
6 save the bread which he *d'* eat.
19 this manner *d'* thy servant to me;
22 they *d'* there, he was the doer of it.
23 that which he *d'*, the Lord made
40:17 birds *d'* eat them out of the basket
23 Yet *d'* not the chief butler remember
41: 4 and the lean fleshed kine *d'* eat up
12 to his dream he *d'* interpret.
20 illfavored kine *d'* eat up the first
42:20 ye shall not die. And they *d'* so.
25 way: and thus *d'* he unto them.
43: 3 man *d'* solemnly protest unto us,
17 And the man *d'* as Joseph bade;
30 bowels *d'* yearn upon his brother:
32 which *d'* eat with him,
44: 2 And he *d'* according to the word
45: 5 for God *d'* send me before you to
21 And the children of Israel *d'* so:
47:22 *d'* eat their portion which Pharaoh
48:15 fathers Abraham and Isaac *d'* walk,
50:12 his sons *d'* unto him according as
15 all the evil which we *d'* unto him.
16 father *d'* command before he died,
17 they *d'* unto thee evil: and now,
Ex 1:11 *d'* set over them taskmasters
17 and *d'* not as the king of Egypt
2:13 he said to him that *d'* the wrong,
4:30 and *d'* the signs in the sight of the
5: 8 which they *d'* make heretofore,
19 the children of Israel *d'* see that
6: 8 the which I *d'* swear to give it to
7: 6 Aaron *d'* as the Lord commanded
6 Lord commanded them, so *d'* they.
10 *d'* so as the Lord had commanded:
11 magicians of Egypt, they also *d'* in
20 And Moses and Aaron *d'* so, as the
22 magicians of Egypt *d'* so with their
23 *d'* he set his heart to this also.
8: 7 *d'* so with their enchantments,
13 *d'* according to the word of Moses;
17 they *d'* so; for Aaron stretched
18 *d'* so with their enchantments
24 the Lord *d'* so; and there came
31 the Lord *d'* according to the word
9: 6 Lord *d'* that thing on the morrow,
7 and he *d'* not let the people go.
10:11 for that ye *d'* desire.
15 they *d'* eat every herb of the land,
11:10 And Moses and Aaron *d'* all these
12:28 children of Israel went away, and *d'*
28 Moses and Aaron, so *d'* they.
35 the children of Israel *d'* according
50 Thus *d'* all the children of Israel;
50 Moses and Aaron, so *d'* they.
51 Lord *d'* bring the children of Israel
13: 8 that which the Lord *d'* unto me
14: 4 I am the Lord. And they *d'* so.
12 the word that we *d'* tell thee in
31 the Lord *d'* upon the Egyptians:
16: 3 and when we *d'* eat bread to the full;
17 And the children of Israel *d'* so,
18 and when they *d'* mete it with an
24 and it *d'* not stink, neither was
35 the children of Israel *d'* eat manna
35 they *d'* eat manna, until they
17: 2 the people *d'* chide with Moses
6 And Moses *d'* so in the sight of
10 Joshua *d'* as Moses had said to him,
18: 7 his father in law, and *d'* obeisance,
14 father in law saw all that he *d'* to
24 in law, and *d'* all that he had said.
19: 4 seen what I *d'* unto the Egyptians,
24:11 nobles of the children of....and *d'* eat
32:12 For mischief *d'* he bring them out,
21 What *d'* this people unto thee,
28 the children of Levi *d'* according
33: 4 and no man *d'* put on him his
34:28 *d'* neither eat bread, nor drink water.
35:24 that *d'* offer an offering of silver
25 that were wise hearted *d'* spin
36:22 thus *d'* he make for all the boards
29 *d'* both of them in both the corners.
39: 3 And they *d'* beat the gold into
21 *d'* bind the breastplate by his rings
32 children of Israel *d'* according to
32 Lord commanded Moses, so *d'* they.
43 And Moses *d'* look upon all the
40:16 Thus *d'* Moses: according to all
16 command him, so *d'* he. And it
Le 4:20 bullock as he *d'* with the bullock
8: 4 Moses *d'* as the Lord commanded
9 *d'* he put the golden plate
36 Aaron and his sons *d'* all the
9:14 *d'* wash the inwards and the legs,
10: 7 *d'* according to the word of Moses.
16:15 he *d'* with the blood of the bullock,
34 *d'* as the Lord commanded Moses.
24:23 Israel *d'* as the Lord commanded
26:35 it *d'* not rest in your sabbaths,
27:24 possession of the land *d'* belong.
Nu 1:54 commanded Moses, so *d'* they.
54 the children of Israel *d'* according

Nu 2:34 the children of Israel *d'* according
4:37 Moses and Aaron *d'* number
41 Moses and Aaron *d'* number
5: 4 so *d'* the children of Israel.
4 And the children of Israel *d'* so,
7:18 prince of Issachar, *d'* offer:
24 children of Zebulun, *d'* offer:
30 the children of Reuben, *d'* offer:
36 the children of Simeon, *d'* offer:
8: 3 Aaron *d'* so; he lighted the lamps
20 *d'* the children of Israel unto them.
20 *d'* to the Levites according unto all
22 the Levites, so *d'* they unto them.
9: 5 Moses, so *d'* the children of Israel.
10:21 the other *d'* set up the tabernacle
11: 5 which we *d'* eat in Egypt freely;
25 they prophesied, and *d'* not cease.
14:22 my miracles, which I *d'* in Egypt,
37 those men that *d'* bring up the evil
17:11 *d'* so: as the Lord commanded
11 commanded him, so *d'* he.
20:27 Moses *d'* as the Lord commanded:
21:14 What he *d'* in the Red sea, and
23: 2 Balak *d'* as Balaam had spoken;
30 And Balak *d'* as Balaam had said,
25: 2 and the people *d'* eat,
27:22 Moses *d'* as the Lord commanded
31:31 *d'* as the Lord commanded Moses.
32: 8 *d'* your fathers, when I sent them
36:10 so *d'* the daughters of Zelophehad:
De 1:30 to all that he *d'* for you in Egypt
32 ye *d'* not believe the Lord your God,
2:12 as Israel *d'* unto the land of his
22 As he *d'* to the children of Esau,
29 Moabites which dwell in Ar, *d'* unto
3: 6 we *d'* unto Sihon king of Heshbon,
4: 3 eyes have seen what the Lord *d'*
4 *d'* cleave unto the Lord your God
33 *D'* ever people hear the voice of God
34 to all that the Lord your God *d'*
5:23 for the mountain *d'* burn with fire,
7:18 Lord thy God *d'* unto Pharaoh,
8: 3 neither *d'* thy fathers know;
4 neither *d'* thy foot swell,
9: 9 I neither *d'* eat nor drink water:
18 I *d'* neither eat bread nor drink
11: 3 which he *d'* in the midst of Egypt
4 what he *d'* unto the army of Egypt,
5 he *d'* unto you in the wilderness,
6 he *d'* unto Dathan and Abiram,
7 great acts of the Lord which he *d'*
12:30 How *d'* these nations serve their
24: 9 what the Lord thy God *d'* unto
25:17 Remember what Amalek *d'* unto
29: 2 Ye have seen all that the Lord *d'*
31: 4 do unto them as he *d'* to Sihon and
32:12 the Lord alone *d'* lead him,
38 which *d'* eat the fat of their sacrifices
33: 9 neither *d'* he acknowledge his
34: 9 and *d'* as the Lord commanded
Jos 2:10 what ye *d'* unto the two kings of
11 hearts *d'* melt, neither *d'* there remain
4: 8 children of Israel *d'* so as Joshua
18 over all his banks, as they *d'* before.
20 *d'* Joshua pitch in Gilgal.
23 as the Lord your God *d'* to the Red
5: 4 cause why Joshua *d'* circumcise
11 and they *d'* eat of the old corn
12 but they *d'* eat of the fruit of the
14 and *d'* worship, and said unto him,
15 is holy. And Joshua *d'* so.
6:14 into the camp: so they *d'* six days.
9: 4 They *d'* work wilily, and went
9 fame of him, and all that he *d'* in
10 *d'* to the two kings of the Amorites,
26 And so *d'* he unto them, and
10:23 And they *d'* so, and brought forth
28 *d'* to the king of Makkedah as he *d'*
30 *d'* unto the king thereof as he *d'*
39 he had done to Hebron, so he *d'* to
42 kings and their land *d'* Joshua take
11: 9 Joshua *d'* unto them as the Lord
12 all the kings of them, *d'* Joshua take
13 Hazor only; that *d'* Joshua burn.
15 Moses command Joshua, and so *d'*
12: 6 Them *d'* Moses the...smite:
13:12 for these *d'* Moses smite,
22 *d'* the children of Israel slay with the
32 which Moses *d'* distribute for
14: 5 Moses, so the children of Israel *d'*,
17:13 but *d'* not utterly drive them out.
22:20 *D'* not Achan the son of Zerah commit
33 and *d'* not intend to go up against
24: 5 according to that which I *d'* among
13 a land for which ye *d'* not labour,
17 and which *d'* those great signs in
J'g 1:21 children of Benjamin *d'* not drive out
27 Neither *d'* Manasseh drive out the
28 and *d'* not utterly drive them out.
29 Neither *d'* Ephraim drive out the
30 Neither *d'* Zebulun drive out the
31 Neither *d'* Asher drive out the
32 for they *d'* not drive them out.
33 Neither *d'* Naphtali drive out the
2: 7 works of the Lord, that he *d'* for
11 And the children of Israel *d'* evil in
17 of the Lord; but they *d'* not so.
22 As their fathers *d'* keep it, or not.
3: 7 And the children of Israel *d'* evil
12 the children of Israel *d'* evil again.
16 he *d'* gird it under his raiment
4: 1 the children of Israel again *d'* evil
5:17 and why *d'* Dan remain in ships?
6: 1 the children of Israel *d'* evil in the
20 pour out the broth. And he *d'* so.

J'g 6:27 and *d'* as the Lord had said unto
27 do it by day, that he *d'* it by night.
40 And God *d'* so that night: for it was
8: 1 And they *d'* chide with him sharply.
15 with whom ye *d'* upbraid me,
25 and *d'* cast therein every man the
9:27 and *d'* eat and drink,
56 of Abimelech, which he *d'* unto
57 the men of Shechem *d'* God render
10: 6 And the children of Israel *d'* evil
11 *D'* not I deliver you from the
12 and the Maonites, *d'* oppress you;
11: 7 *D'* not ye hate me, and expel me,
25 *d'* he ever strive against Israel,
26 Why therefore *d'* ye not recover them
39 father, who *d'* with her, according
13: 1 Israel *d'* evil again in the sight of
19 and the angel *d'* wondrously;
21 angel of the Lord *d'* no more appear
14: 9 and they *d'* eat: but he told not
15:11 As they *d'* unto me, so have I done
16:21 and he *d'* grind in the prison house
17: 6 every man *d'* that which was right
19: 4 so they *d'* eat and drink,
6 and *d'* eat and drink both of them
8 and they *d'* eat both of them.
21 and *d'* eat and drink.
21:22 for ye *d'* not give unto them at this
23 the children of Benjamin *d'* so,
25 every man *d'* that which was right
Ru 2:14 and she *d'* eat, and was sufficed,
19 blessed be he that *d'* take knowledge
3: 6 unto the floor, and *d'* according
4:11 which two *d'* build the house of Israel:
1Sa 1: 7 And as he *d'* so year by year, when
18 went her way, and *d'* eat,
2:11 And the child *d'* minister unto the
14 So they *d'* in Shiloh unto all the
22 heard all that his sons *d'* unto all
27 *D'* I plainly appear unto the house
28 and *d'* I choose him out of all the
28 and *d'* I give unto the house of thy
3: 7 Now Samuel *d'* not yet know the Lord,
19 and *d'* let none of his words fall to the
4:20 neither *d'* she regard it.
6: 6 *d'* they not let the people go,
10 And the men *d'* so; and took two
7: 4 children of Israel *d'* put away Baalim
14 and the coasts thereof *d'* Israel deliver
9:24 So Saul *d'* eat with Samuel that day.
12: 7 Lord, which he *d'* to you and to
13: 6 then the people *d'* hide themselves in
14:32 and the people *d'* eat them with the
43 I *d'* but taste a little honey with the
15: 2 remember that which Amalek *d'* to
16: 4 Samuel *d'* that which the Lord
19: 5 for he *d'* put his life in his hand,
20:34 and *d'* eat no meat the second day
21:11 *d'* they not sing one to another of
22:15 *D'* I then begin to enquire of God
17 and *d'* not shew it to me.
18 and five persons that *d'* wear
25: 4 David heard...that Nabal *d'* shear
27:11 saying, So *d'* David, and so will be
28:24 and *d'* bake unleavened bread thereof;
25 and they *d'* eat. Then they rose up,
30:11 and he *d'* eat; and they made
2Sa 1: 2 he fell to the earth, and *d'* obeisance.
2: 3 were with him *d'* David bring up,
3:36 whatsoever the king *d'* pleased
5:25 And David *d'* so, as the Lord had
7:17 so *d'* Nathan speak unto David.
8:11 king David *d'* dedicate unto the
9: 6 fell on his face, and *d'* reverence.
13 he *d'* eat continually at the king's
11: 7 Joab *d'*, and how the people *d'*,
13 he *d'* eat and drink before him;
20 ye so nigh...when ye *d'* fight?
21 *d'* not a woman cast a piece of
12: 3 it *d'* eat of his own meat,
6 because he *d'* this thing, and
17 neither *d'* he eat bread with them.
20 bread before him, and he *d'* eat.
31 and thus *d'* he unto all the cities
13: 8 and *d'* bake the cakes.
29 the servants of Absalom *d'* unto
14: 4 face to the ground, and *d'* obeisance,
15: 6 this manner *d'* Absalom to all
17:15 Thus and thus *d'* Ahithophel counsel
19:19 that which thy servant *d'* perversely
28 among them that *d'* eat at thine own
43 why then *d'* ye despise us,
20: 6 more harm than *d'* Absalom: take
21: 6 whom the Lord *d'* choose.
22: 7 and he *d'* hear my voice out of his
7 my cry *d'* enter into his ears.
11 he rode upon a cherub, and *d'* fly:
23 I *d'* not depart from them.
37 so that my feet *d'* not slip.
43 then *d'* I beat them as small as the
43 I *d'* stamp them as the mire of the
43 and *d'* spread them abroad.
23:17 These things *d'* these three
22 These things *d'* Benaiah the son of
24:23 things *d'* Araunah, as a king,
1Ki 1:16 Bath-sheba bowed, and *d'* obeisance
31 and *d'* reverence to the king,
2: 5 the son of Zeruiah *d'* to me, and
5 what he *d'* to the two captains
35 and Zadok the priest *d'* the king put
42 *D'* I not make thee to swear by the
3: 4 burnt offerings *d'* Solomon offer upon
14 as thy father David *d'* walk,
21 it was not my son, which I *d'* bear.
5:18 builders and Hiram's *d'* hew them,

1Ki 7:15 a line of twelve cubits *d'* compass
18 and so *d'* he for the other chapiter
23 a line of thirty cubits *d'* compass it
46 the plain of Jordan *d'* the king cast
51 the gold, and the vessels, *d'* he put
8: 4 even those *d'* the priests...bring up.
64 the same day *d'* the king hallow
9:21 upon those *d'* Solomon levy a tribute
22 the children of Israel *d'* Solomon
24 then *d'* he build Millo.
25 And three times in a year *d'* Solomon
10:29 kings of Syria, *d'* they bring them out
11: 6 And Solomon *d'* evil in the sight
6 after the Lord, as *d'* David his
7 Then *d'* Solomon build an high place
8 likewise *d'* he for all his strange
16 For six months *d'* Joab remain
25 beside the mischief that Hadad *d'*:
33 and my judgments as *d'* David his
38 as David my servant *d'*;
41 and all that he *d'*, and his wisdom,
12: 9 which thy father *d'* put upon us
11 now whereas my father *d'* lade
32 So *d'* he in Beth-el, sacrificing
13:19 and *d'* eat bread in his house,
22 which the Lord *d'* say to thee,
14: 4 And Jeroboam's wife *d'* so, and
16 who *d'* sin, and who made Israel
21 the city which the Lord *d'* choose
22 And Judah *d'* evil in the sight of
24 and they *d'* according to all the
29 and all that he *d'*, are they not
15: 4 for David's sake *d'* the Lord...give him
5 Because David *d'* that which was
7 and all that he *d'*, are they not
11 And Asa *d'* that which was right in
11 of the Lord, as *d'* David his father.
23 and all that he *d'*, and the cities
26 he *d'* evil in the sight of the Lord,
28 king of Judah *d'* Baasha slay him
31 and all that he *d'*, are they not
34 he *d'* evil in the sight of the Lord,
16: 5 and what he *d'*, and his might, are
7 the evil that he *d'* in the sight of
12 Thus *d'* Zimri destroy all the house
14 Elah, and all that he *d'*, are they
15 of Asa king of Judah *d'* Zimri reign
19 in his sin which he *d'*, to make
25 and *d'* worse than all that were
27 the acts of Omri which he *d'*, and
30 And Ahab the son of Omri *d'* evil
33 Ahab *d'* more to provoke the Lord
34 In his days *d'* Hiel the Bethelite build
17: 5 So he went and *d'* according unto
15 And she went and *d'* according to
16 neither *d'* the cruse of oil fail,
18:13 told my lord what I *d'* when
34 And they *d'* it the second time.
34 And they *d'* it the third time.
19: 6 And he *d'* eat and drink,
8 And he arose, and *d'* eat and drink,
21 gave unto the people, and they *d'* eat.
20:25 unto their voice, and *d'* so.
33 Now the men *d'* diligently observe
33 and *d'* hastily catch it:
21:11 in his city, *d'* as Jezebel had
13 Naboth *d'* blaspheme God and the
25 which *d'* sell himself to work wicked
26 he *d'* very abominably in following
26 to all things as *d'* the Amorites,
22:18 *D'* I not tell thee that he would
39 acts of Ahab, and all that he *d'*,
52 he *d'* evil in the sight of the Lord,
2Ki 1:18 the acts of Ahaziah which he *d'*,
2:18 *D'* I not say unto you, Go not?
4: 1 thy servant *d'* fear the Lord:
28 *D'* I desire a son of my Lord?
28 *D'* I not say, do not deceive me?
44 he set it before them, and they *d'* eat,
6: 6 and the iron *d'* swim.
29 we boiled my son, and *d'* eat him:
7: 8 into one tent, and *d'* eat and drink,
8: 2 *d'* after the saying of the man
18 as *d'* the house of Ahab: for the
18 was his wife: and he *d'* evil in the
23 of Joram, and all that he *d'*, are
25 Ahab king of Israel *d'* Ahaziah...begin
27 *d'* evil in the sight of the Lord,
27 as *d'* the house of Ahab: for he
9:27 they *d'* so at the going up to Gur,
34 was come in, he *d'* eat and drink,
10:19 But Jehu *d'* it in subtilty, to the
34 and all that he *d'*, and all his might,
11: 3 Athaliah *d'* reign over the land.
9 captains over the hundreds *d'*
10 over hundreds *d'* the priest give
12: 2 And Jehoash *d'* that which was
11 the hands of them that *d'* the work,
19 and all that he *d'*, are they not
13: 2 And he *d'* that which was evil in the
7 neither *d'* he leave of the people
8 and all that he *d'*, and his might,
11 And he *d'* that which was evil in
12 acts of Joash, and all that he *d'*,
25 three times *d'* Joash beat him,
14: 3 And he *d'* that which was right
3 he *d'* according to all things
3 as Joash his father *d'*.
4 as yet the people *d'* sacrifice and
15 acts of Jehoash which he *d'*, and
24 and he *d'* that which was evil in
28 of Jeroboam, and all that he *d'*,
15: 3 And he *d'* that which was right
6 and all that he *d'*, are they not
8 king of Judah *d'* Zachariah...reign

2Ki 15: 9 And he *d'* that which was evil in
18 *d'* that which was evil in the sight
21 and all that he *d'*, are they not
24 And he *d'* that which was evil in
26 and all that he *d'*, behold, they are
28 And he *d'* that which was evil in
31 the acts of Pekah, and all that he *d'*,
34 And he *d'* that which was right in
34 he *d'* according to all that his
36 acts of Jotham, and all that he *d'*,
16: 2 and *d'* not that which was right
16 *d'* Urijah the priest, according to all
19 the acts of Ahaz which he *d'*, are
17: 2 And he *d'* that which was evil in
9 children of Israel *d'* secretly those
11 the high places, as *d'* the heathen
14 that *d'* not believe in the Lord
22 the sins of Jeroboam which he *d'*;
40 Howbeit they *d'* not hearken,
40 *d'* after their former manner.
41 as *d'* their fathers, so do they unto
18: 3 And he *d'* that which was right in
3 to all that David his father *d'*.
4 children of Israel *d'* burn incense
11 of Assyria *d'* carry away Israel
13 king Hezekiah *d'* Sennacherib...come
16 time *d'* Hezekiah cut off the gold
21: 2 And he *d'* that which was evil in
3 grove, as *d'* Ahab king of Israel
9 do more evil than *d'* the nations
11 above all that the Amorites *d'*,
17 and all that he *d'*, and his sin that
20 And he *d'* that which was evil in
20 Lord, as his father Manasseh *d'*.
25 the acts of Amon which he *d'*,
22: 2 And he *d'* that which was right in
23: 9 *d'* eat of the unleavened bread
13 of Ammon, *d'* the king defile.
19 and *d'* to them according to all
24 *d'* Josiah put away, that he might
28 and all that he *d'*, are they not
32 And he *d'* that which was evil in
37 he *d'* that which was evil in the
24: 3 according to all that he *d'*;
5 all that he *d'*, are they not written
9 And he *d'* that which was evil in
11 and his servants *d'* besiege it.
19 And he *d'* that which was evil in
25:11 *d'* Nebuzar-adan...carry away.
13 *d'* the Chaldees break in pieces,
27 *d'* lift up the head of Jehoiachin
29 and he *d'* eat bread continually
1Ch 4:27 *d'* all their family multiply,
9:22 David and Samuel the Seer *d'* ordain
11:19 things *d'* these three mightiest.
24 *d'* Benaiah the son of Jehoiada
14:16 therefore *d'* as God commanded
15:13 because ye *d'* it not at the first,
24 *d'* blow with the trumpets before
17:15 so *d'* Nathan speak unto David
23:24 that *d'* the work for the service
26:27 *d'* they dedicate to maintain
27:26 And over them that *d'* the work
29:22 And *d'* eat and drink before the Lord
2Ch 1: 7 In that night *d'* God appear unto
2: 7 whom David my father *d'* provide
4: 2 line of thirty cubits *d'* compass
3 which *d'* compass it round about:
16 *d'* Huram his father make to
17 of the Jordan *d'* the king cost them
5: 5 *d'* the priests and the Levites bring
11 and *d'* not then wait by course:
8: 8 *d'* Solomon make to pay tribute
9 of Israel *d'* Solomon make no
10: 9 that thy father *d'* put upon us?
12:14 *d'* evil, because he prepared not
13:20 Neither *d'* Jeroboam recover
14: 2 And Asa *d'* that which was good
15: 4 when they in their trouble *d'* turn
6 *d'* vex them with all adversity.
18:16 I *d'* see all Israel scattered upon
17 *D'* I not tell thee that he would
19: 8 in Jerusalem *d'* Jehoshaphat set
20:35 after this *d'* Jehoshaphat join
35 of Israel, who *d'* very wickedly:
21: 6 like as *d'* the house of Ahab: for
10 same time also *d'* Libnah revolt
22: 4 Wherefore he *d'* evil in the sight
23: 8 Levites and all Judah *d'* according
24: 2 Joash *d'* that which was right
7 *d'* they bestow on Baalim.
11 Thus they *d'* day by day, and
12 gave it to such as *d'* the work of
25: 2 And he *d'* that which was right in
4 but *d'* as it is written in the law
12 alive *d'* the children of Judah carry
27 the time that Amaziah *d'* turn
26: 4 And he *d'* that which was right in
4 to all that his father Amaziah *d'*
22 *d'* Isaiah the prophet,...write.
27: 2 And he *d'* that which was right
2 to all that his father Uzziah *d'*:
2 And the people *d'* yet corruptly.
5 So much *d'* the children of Ammon pay
28: 1 he *d'* not that which was right
16 *d'* king Ahaz send unto the kings
22 of his distress *d'* he trespass yet
29: 2 And he *d'* that which was right
19 Ahaz in his reign *d'* cast away
34 the Levites *d'* help them,
30:18 yet *d'* they eat the passover
22 they *d'* eat throughout the feast
24 Hezekiah king of Judah *d'* give
31:20 *d'* Hezekiah throughout all Judah
21 he *d'* it with all his heart, and

2Ch 32: 3 and they *d'* help him.
9 After this *d'* Sennacherib...send
33 Jerusalem *d'* him honour at his
33: 2 *d'* that which was evil in the sight
17 *d'* sacrifice still in the high places,
22 But he *d'* that which was evil
22 Lord, as *d'* Manasseh his father:
34: 2 And he *d'* that which was right in
6 *d'* he in the cities of Manasseh,
12 the men *d'* the work faithfully:
32 the inhabitants of Jerusalem *d'*
35: 3 David king of Israel *d'* build
12 And so *d'* they with the oxen.
36: 5 and he *d'* that which was evil in
8 and his abominations which he *d'*,
9 and he *d'* that which was evil in
12 he *d'* that which was evil in the
Ezr 1: 8 *d'* Cyrus king of Persia bring forth
11 All these *d'* Sheshbazzar bring up with
5:14 those *d'* Cyrus the king take out
6:13 the king had sent, so they *d'* speedily.
21 had separated themselves.... *d'* eat,
10: 6 he *d'* eat no bread, nor drink
16 the children of the captivity *d'* so.
Ne 2:16 not whither I went, or what I *d'*;
16 nor to the rest that *d'* the work.
3: 3 gate *d'* the sons of Hassenaah build,
5:13 *d'* according to this promise.
15 but so *d'* not I, because of the fear
9:25 so they *d'* eat, and were filled,
28 they *d'* evil again before thee:
11:12 their brethren that *d'* the work
13: 7 evil that Eliashib *d'* for Tobiah,
10 and the singers, that *d'* the work
18 *D'* [6213] not your fathers thus, and *d'*
26 *D'* not Solomon king of Israel sin
26 *d'* outlandish women cause to sin.
Es 1: 8 none *d'* compel: for so the king
21 king *d'* according to the word of
2: 4 pleased the king; and he *d'* so.
11 to know how Esther *d'*, and what
20 for Esther *d'* the commandment
3: 1 things *d'* king Ahasuerus promote
2, 5 bowed not, nor *d'* him reverence.
4:17 *d'* according to all that Esther
5:12 Esther the Queen *d'* let no man
8: 1 that day *d'* the king Ahasuerus give
9: 5 and *d'* what they would unto those
Job 1: 5 Thus *d'* Job continually.
2:10 In all this *d'* not Job sin with his lips.
3:11 why *d'* I not give up the ghost
12 Why *d'* the knees prevent me?
6:22 *D'* I say, Bring unto me?
28:27 Then *d'* he see it, and declare it;
30:25 *D'* not I weep for him that was in
31:13 If I *d'* despise the cause of my
15 *D'* not he that made me in the
15 *d'* not one fashion us in the womb?
32 The stranger *d'* not lodge in the
34 *D'* I fear a great multitude,
34 or *d'* the contempt of families
42: 9 and *d'* according as the Lord
11 and *d'* eat bread with him in his
Ps 14: 2 if there any that *d'* understand,
18:10 upon a cherub, and *d'* fly: yea,
10 he *d'* fly upon the wings of the
22 I *d'* not put away his statutes
36 that my feet *d'* not slip.
37 neither *d'* I turn again till they
42 Then *d'* I beat them small as the dust
42 I *d'* cast them out as the dirt in the
31:11 they that *d'* see me without fled
35:11 False witnesses *d'* rise up;
15 they *d'* tear me, and ceased not:
41: 9 which *d'* eat of my bread,
44: 3 neither *d'* their own arm save them:
45: 9 upon the right hand *d'* stand the
51: 5 and in sin *d'* my mother conceive me.
53: 2 there were any that *d'* understand,
2 that *d'* seek God.
55:12 that *d'* magnify himself against me;
66: 6 there *d'* we rejoice in him.
68:12 Kings of armies *d'* flee apace:
78:12 Marvellous things *d'* he in the
25 Man *d'* eat angel's food:
29 so they *d'* eat, and were well filled:
33 their days *d'* he consume in vanity.
36 Nevertheless they *d'* flatter him
38 and *d'* not stir up all his wrath.
40 How oft *d'* they provoke him
102:19 from heaven *d'* the Lord behold the
105:35 And *d'* eat up all the herbs in
106:34 They *d'* not destroy the nations,
43 Many times *d'* he deliver them;
119:23 also *d'* sit and speak against
23 but thy servant *d'* meditate in thy
135: 6 pleased, that *d'* he in heaven,
139:16 Thine eyes *d'* see my substance, yet
142: 1 unto the Lord *d'* I make my
Pr 1:29 and *d'* not choose the fear of the
Isa 5:25 and the hills *d'* tremble,
6: 2 and with twain he *d'* fly.
9: 1 afterward *d'* more grievously
10:10 and whose graven images *d'* excel
13: 1 which Isaiah the son of Amoz *d'* see.
14:16 that *d'* shake kingdoms;
20: 2 And he *d'* so, walking naked and
22:12 that day *d'* the Lord God of hosts call
38:14 or a swallow, so *d'* I chatter:
14 I *d'* mourn as a dove:
42:24 *d'* not the Lord, he against whom
48: 3 I *d'* them suddenly, and they came
53: 4 yet we *d'* esteem him stricken
58: 2 as a nation that *d'* righteousness,
65:12 when I called, ye *d'* not answer;

Isa 65:12 when I spake, ye d' not hear:
12 d' evil before mine eyes, and d'
66: 4 when I called, none d' answer;
4 when I spake, they d' not hear:
4 but they d' evil before mine eyes,
Jer 7:12 and see what I d' to it for the
26 they d' worse than their fathers.
11: 8 but they d' them not.
14: 6 the wild asses d' stand in the high
6 their eyes d' fail,
15: 4 for that which he d' in Jerusalem.
16 and I d' eat them;
22:15 d' not thy father eat and drink,
26:19 D' Hezekiah king of Judah...put him
19 d' he not fear the Lord,
31:19 I d' bear the reproach of my youth.
36: 8 the son of Neriah d' according to
37: 2 d' hearken unto the words of the
38:12 the cords. And Jeremiah d' so,
44:19 d' we make her cakes to worship
21 d' not the Lord remember them,
46:15 because the Lord d' drive them.
17 They d' cry there, Pharaoh king
21 they d' not stand, because the day
52: 2 And he d' that which was evil in
21 fillet of twelve cubits d' compass it;
33 and he d' continually eat bread
La 1: 7 and none d' help her:
7 and d' mock at her sabbaths.
4: 5 They that d' feed delicately are
Eze 3: 3 Then d' I eat it; and it was in
6:13 the place where they d' offer sweet
11:22 Then d' the cherubims lift up their
12: 7 And I d' so as I was commanded:
16:49 neither d' she strengthen the hand
17: 7 this vine d' bend her roots toward
18:18 and d' that which is not good
20: 8 they d' not every man cast away
8 neither d' they forsake the idols of
17 neither d' I make an end of them
24:18 I d' in the morning as I was
27:25 ships of Tarshish d' sing of thee,
31: 6 branches d' all the beasts...bring
34: 6 and none d' search or seek after
8 neither d' my shepherds search for
43:22 as they d' cleanse it with the
46:12 as he d' on the sabbath day:
Da 1:15 children which d' eat the portion of
3:24 D' not we cast three men bound
4: 7 but they d' not make known unto
33 and d' eat grass as oxen,
6:10 as he d' aforetime.
7: 9 and the Ancient of days d' sit,
8: 4 but he d' according to his will,
27 I rose up, and d' the king's
10: 3 neither d' I anoint myself at all,
Ho 2: 8 For she d' not know that I gave her
9:17 because they d' not hearken unto
10: 9 of iniquity d' not overtake them.
13: 5 I d' know thee in the wilderness,
Am 1:11 because he d' pursue his brother
11 and d' cast off all pity,
11 and his anger d' tear perpetually,
5:19 As if a man d' flee from a lion.
7: 4 and d' eat up a part.
Ob 14 to cut off those of his that d' escape;
14 those of his that d' remain in the
Jon 3:10 do unto them: and he d' it not.
4: 8 when the sun d' arise,
Na 2:12 The lion d' tear in pieces enough
Hab 1: 1 which Habakkuk the prophet d' see.
3: 6 the perpetual hills d' bow:
7 of the land of Midian d' tremble.
Hag 1: 9 I d' blow upon it.
12 the people d' fear before the Lord.
14 they came and d' work in the
Zec 1: 4 but they d' not hear,
6 d' they not take hold of your
21 so that no man d' lift up his head:
7: 5 seventy years d' ye at all fast
6 when ye d' eat, and when ye d' drink
6 d' not ye eat for yourselves,
9: 3 Tyrus d' build herself a stronghold,
Mal 2: 6 and d' turn many away from
15 And d' not he make one?
M't 1:24 being raised from sleep d' as
2:22 that Archelaus d' reign in Judæa
9:19 and so d' his disciples.
12: 3 Have ye not read what David d'
4 and d' eat the shewbread,
13:58 And he d' not many mighty works
14:20 And they d' all eat, and were filled:
15: 7 well d' Esaias prophesy of you,
37 And they d' all eat, and were filled:
38 they that d' eat were four thousand
17: 2 and his face d' shine as the sun,
19: 7 Why d' Moses then command to give
20: 5 and ninth hour, and d' likewise.
21: 6 went and d' as Jesus commanded
15 the wonderful things that he d',
25 Why d' ye not them believe him?
31 twain d' the will of his father?
36 and they d' unto them likewise.
42 D' ye never read in the scriptures,
25:44 and d' not minister unto thee?
45 as ye d' it not to one of the least
45 of these, ye d' it not to me.
26:12 on my body, she d' it for my burial.
19 disciples d' as Jesus had appointed
21 And as they d' eat, he said,
67 Then d' they spit in his face,
27: 9 of the children of Israel d' value;
35 upon my vesture d' they cast lots,
51 and the earth d' quake,
28: 4 for fear of him the keepers d' shake,
8 d' run to bring his disciples word.
M't 28:15 money and d' as they were taught.
M'r 1: 4 John d' baptize in the wilderness,
6 he d' eat locusts and wild honey;
32 And at even, when the sun d' set,
2:25 read what David d', when he had
26 and d' eat the shewbread,
3: 8 great things he d', came unto him.
4: 8 and d' yield fruit that sprang up
5:20 and all men d' marvel.
6:20 he d' many things, and heard
42 And they d' all eat, and were filled.
44 they that d' eat of the loaves were
8: 6 d' set them before the people.
8 So they d' eat, and were filled:
10: 3 What d' Moses command you?
11:31 Why then d' ye not believe him?
12:44 they d' cast in of their abundance;
44 of her want d' cast in all that she had,
14:18 and as they sat and d' eat;
22 as they d' eat, Jesus took bread,
59 neither so d' their witness agree
65 the servants d' strike him with
15:19 and d' spit upon him,
Lu 4: 2 and in those days he d' eat nothing:
6: 1 and d' eat, rubbing them in their
3 what David d', when himself was
4 and d' take and eat the shewbread,
10 and he d' so: and his hand was
23 the like manner d' their fathers
26 for so d' their fathers to the false
49 the stream d' beat vehemently,
7:38 and d' wipe them with the hairs of
9:15 And they d' so, and made them all
17 And they d' eat, and were all filled:
43 at all things which Jesus d', he
53 And they d' not receive him,
54 consume them, even as Elias did?
11:40 d' not he that made that which is
12:47 neither d' according to his will,
48 d' commit things worthy of stripes,
15:16 with the husks that the swine d' eat:
17: 9 because he d' things that were
27, 28 They d' eat, they drank,
19:22 and reaping that I d' not sow:
24:32 D' not our heart burn within us,
43 and d' eat before them.
Joh 1:45 the law, and the prophets, d' write,
2:11 of miracles d' Jesus in Cana of
23 they saw the miracles which he d'.
24 But Jesus d' not commit himself
4:29 all things that ever I d': is not
39 He told me all that ever I d'.
45 the things that he d' at Jerusalem
54 miracle that Jesus d', when he was
5:16 therefore d' the Jews persecute Jesus,
6: 2 which he d' on them that were
14 miracle that Jesus d', said, This
23 where they d' eat bread,
26 but because ye d' eat of the loaves,
31 fathers d' eat manna in the desert;
49 your fathers d' eat manna in the
58 not as your fathers d' eat manna,
7: 5 For neither d' his brethren believe
19 D' not Moses give you the law,
8:40 of God: this d' not Abraham,
9: 2 Master, who d' sin, this man, or his
18 But the Jews d' not believe
22 man d' confess that he was Christ,
26 What d' he to thee? how opened
27 and ye d' not hear:
10: 8 but the sheep d' not hear them.
41 John d' no miracle: but all things
11:45 seen the things which Jesus d',
12:36 and d' hide himself from them.
42 the Pharisees they d' not confess him,
15:24 which none other man d', they
18:15 followed Jesus, and so d' another
26 D' not I see thee in the garden with
34 or d' others tell it thee of me?
19:24 for my vesture they d' cast lots.
24 things therefore the soldiers d',
20: 4 other disciples d' outrun Peter
30 other signs truly d' Jesus in
21: 7 and d' cast himself into the sea.
25 many other things which Jesus d',
Ac 2:22 which God d' by him in the midst
26 Therefore d' my heart rejoice,
31 neither his flesh d' see corruption.
40 many other words d' he testify
46 d' eat their meat with gladness and
3:17 through ignorance ye d' it,
17 as d' also your rulers.
4:25 Why d' the heathen rage, and the
5:28 D' not we straitly command you
6: 8 faith and power, d' great wonders
7:27 that d' his neighbour wrong thrust
35 the same d' God send to be a ruler
51 as your fathers d', so do ye.
8: 6 seeing the miracles which he d'.
9: 9 and neither d' eat nor drink.
36 works and almsdeeds which she d'.
10:39 of all things which he d' both in
41 who d' eat and drink with him after
11:17 God gave them the like gift as he d'
30 Which also they d', and sent it to
12: 8 bind on thy sandels, so he d'.
14:17 in that he d' good, and gave us rain
15: 8 Holy Ghost, even as he d' unto us;
14 God at the first d' visit the Gentiles
16:18 And this d' she many days. But
19:14 and chief of the priests which d' so.
21: 9 virgins, which d' prophesy.
26:10 thing I also d' in Jerusalem:
22 and Moses d' say should come:
Ro 1:26 even their women d' change the
28 even as they d' not like to retain
Ro 3: 3 For what if some d' not believe?
5:20 grace d' much more abound:
7: 5 d' work in our members to bring
8:29 For whom he d' foreknow,
29 d' predestinate to be conformed
30 whom he d' predestinate,
10:19 D' not Israel know?
1Co 4: 8 and I would to God ye d' reign,
10: 3 d' all eat the same spiritual meat;
4 d' all drink the same spiritual drink:
15:27 which d' put all things under him.
2Co 1:17 d' I use lightness?
2: 9 For to this end also d' I write,
5:20 as though God d' beseech you
7: 8 though I d' repent:
12 I d' it not for his cause that had
8: 5 this they d', not as we hoped,
12:16 But be it so, I d' not burden you:
17 D' I make a gain of you by any of
18 D' Titus make a gain of you?
Ga 2:12 he d' eat with the Gentiles:
4: 8 ye d' service unto them which
5: 7 Ye d' run well: who
7 who d' hinder you that ye should not
Ph'p 4:14 d' communicate with my affliction.
2Th 3: 8 Neither d' we eat any man's bread
1Ti 1:13 because I d' it ignorantly in
2Ti 4:14 Alexander the coppersmith d' me
Heb 3:16 when they had heard, d' provoke:
4: 2 word preached d' not profit them:
4 God d' rest the seventh day from
10 his own works, as God d' from his.
7:19 bringing in of a better hope d'.
27 for this he d' once, when he offered
9: 9 him that d' the service perfect,
1Pe 1:11 Christ which was in them d' signify,
12 unto us they d' minister the things,
2:22 Who d' no sin, neither was guile
Re 12: 4 and d' cast them to the earth:
13:14 the wound by a sword, and d' live.
19: 2 which d' corrupt the earth with her
21:23 for the glory of God d' lighten it,

diddest See also DIDST.
Ac 7:28 thou d' the Egyptian yesterday?

didst^ See also DIDDEST.
Ge 12:18 Why d' thou not tell me that
18:15 Nay; but thou d' laugh.
20: 6 I know that thou d' this in the
21:26 neither d' thou tell me,
31:27 Wherefore d' thou flee away
27 and d' not tell me,
39 of my hand d' thou require it,
Ex 15:10 Thou d' blow with thy wind,
40:15 as thou d' anoint their father,
De 3: 2 as thou d' unto Sihon king of
9: 7 from the day that thou d' depart
32:14 and thou d' drink the pure
33: 8 whom thou d' prove at Massah,
8 and with whom thou d' strive
Jos 2:18 window which thou d' let us down by:
8: 2 thou d' unto Jericho and her king:
1Sa 3: 6, 8 Here am I; for thou d' call me.
15:19 Wherefore d' thou not obey the
19 but d' fly upon the spoil,
19 and d' evil in the sight of the
19: 5 thou sawest it, and d' rejoice:
20:19 the place where thou d' hide thyself
25:25 of my lord, whom thou d' send.
2Sa 11:10 Why then d' thou not go down
12:12 For thou d' it secretly: but I will
21 thou d' fast and weep for the child,
21 thou d' rise and eat bread.
13:16 the other that thou d' unto me.
18:11 and why d' thou not smite him
19:28 yet d' thou set thy servant among
1Ki 1:13 D' not thou, my lord, O king, swear
2:44 that thou d' to David my father:
8:18 thou d' well that it was in thine
20: 9 All that thou d' send for to thy
21:10 Thou d' blaspheme God and the king.
1Ch 17:22 For thy people Israel d' thou make
2Ch 2: 3 As thou d' deal with David my father,
3 and d' send him cedars to build him
6: 8 d' well in that it was in thine heart:
16: 8 because thou d' rely on the Lord,
20: 7 who d' drive out the inhabitants
34:27 thou d' humble thyself before God,
27 and d' rend thy clothes, and weep
Ne 9: 7 the God, who d' choose Abram,
9 and d' see the affliction of our
10 So d' thou get thee a name, as it is
11 And thou d' divide the sea before them,
17 wonders that thou d' among them;
21 forty years d' thou sustain them in the
22 and d' divide them into corners:
28 and many times d' thou deliver them
30 Yet many years d' thou forbear them,
31 thou d' not utterly consume them,
34 wherewith thou d' testify against
Ps 22: 4 they trusted, and thou d' deliver them.
9 thou d' make me hope when I was upon
30: 7 thou d' hide thy face, and I was
39: 9 not my mouth; because thou d' it.
40: 6 and offering thou d' not desire;
44: 1 what work thou d' in their days,
2 how thou d' drive out the heathen
2 how thou d' afflict the people,
60:10 d' not go out with our armies?
68: 7 thou d' march through the wilderness;
9 Thou, O God, d' send a plentiful rain,
9 thou d' confirm thine inheritance,
73:18 d' set them in slippery places:
74:13 Thou d' divide the sea by thy strength:
15 Thou d' cleave the fountain and the
76: 8 Thou d' cause judgment to be heard

Ps 80: 9 and d' cause it to take deep root,
Isa 14:12 which d' weaken the nations!
22: 8 and thou d' look in that day to the
47: 6 thou d' shew them no mercy;
7 so that thou d' not lay these things to
7 d' remember the latter end of it.
48: 6 and thou d' not know them.
54: 1 barren, thou that d' not bear;
1 thou that d' not travail with child:
57: 9 and d' increase thy perfumes,
9 and d' send thy messengers far off,
9 and d' debase thyself even unto hell.
63:14 so d' thou lead thy people,
64: 3 When thou d' terrible things
Jer 32:22 which thou d' swear to their fathers
36:17 How d' thou write all these words
45: 3 Thou d' say, Woe is me now!
La 1:10 thou d' command that they should
Eze 16:13 thou d' eat fine flour, and honey,
13 and thou d' prosper into a kingdom,
15 But thou d' trust in thine own beauty,
16 And of thy garments thou d' take, and
17 and d' commit whoredom with them,
36 which thou d' give unto them;
23:40 for whom thou d' wash thyself,
27:33 d' enrich the kings of the earth with
29: 7 thou d' break, and rend all their
35:15 As thou d' rejoice at the inheritance
Da 10:12 d' set thine heart to understand,
Ho 10:13 because thou d' trust in thy way,
Hab 3: 8 that thou d' ride upon thine horses
9 Thou d' cleave the earth with rivers.
12 Thou d' march through the land in
12 thou d' thresh the heathen in anger
14 Thou d' strike through with his slaves
15 Thou d' walk through the sea with
M't 14:31 wherefore d' thou doubt?
20:13 d' not thou agree with me for a penny?
Lu 7:46 My head with oil thou d' not anoint.
19:21 and reapest that thou d' not sow.
Joh 17: 8 believed that thou d' send me.
Ac 11: 3 uncircumcised, and d' eat with them.
1Co 4: 7 hast thou that thou d' not receive?
7 now if thou d' receive it, why dost thou
Heb 2: 7 and d' set him over the works of thy
Re 17: 7 Wherefore d' thou marvel?

Didymus (*did'-i-mus*) See also THOMAS.
Joh 11:16 said Thomas, which is called D',
20:24 one of the twelve, called D',
21: 2 Simon Peter, and Thomas called D',

die See also DEAD; DIED; DIETH; DYING.
Ge 2:17 eatest thereof thou shalt surely d'.
3: 3 neither shall ye touch it, lest ye d'.
4 the woman, Ye shall not surely d':
6:17 thing that is in the earth shall d'.
19:19 lest some evil take me, and I d':
20: 7 thou shalt surely d', thou, and all
25:32 Behold, I am at the point to d':
26: 9 Because I said, Lest I d' for her.
27: 4 my soul may bless thee before I d'.
30: 1 Give me children, or else I d'.
33:13 them one day, all the flock will d'.
38:11 Lest peradventure he d' also, as
42: 2 thence; that we may live, and not d'.
20 be verified, and ye shall not d'.
43: 8 go; that we may live, and not d',
44: 9 it be found, both let him d', and we
22 leave his father, his father would d'.
31 lad is not with us, that he will d':
45:28 I will go and see him before I d'.
46:30 Now let me d', since I have seen
47:15 why should we d' in thy presence?
19 Wherefore shall we d' before thine
19 seed, that we may live, and not d',
29 time drew nigh that Israel must d':
48:21 said unto Joseph, Behold, I d':
50: 5 made me swear, saying, Lo, I d':
24 Joseph said unto his brethren, I d':
Ex 7:18 the fish that is in the river shall d',
9: 4 there shall nothing d' of all that is
19 down upon them, and they shall d'.
10:28 thou seest my face thou shalt d'.
11: 5 in the land of Egypt shall d',
14:11 us away to d' in the wilderness?
12 that we should d' in the wilderness.
20:19 not God speak with us, lest we d'.
21:12 that smiteth a man, so that he d',
14 from mine altar, that he may d'.
18 or with his fist, and he d' not,
20 a rod, and he d' under his hand;
28 a man or a woman, that they d':
35 man's ox hurt another's, that he d';
22: 2 up, and be smitten that he d',
10 it d', or be hurt, or driven away,
14 and it be hurt, or d', the owner
28:35 he cometh out, that he d' not.
43 that they bear not iniquity, and d':
30:20 wash with water that they d' not;
21 and their feet, that they d' not:
Le 8:35 charge of the Lord, that ye d' not;
10: 6 rend your clothes, lest ye d',
7 of the congregation, lest ye d':
9 of the congregation, lest ye d':
11:39 any beast of which ye may eat, d';
15:31 they d' not in their uncleanness,
16: 2 is upon the ark; that he d' not:
13 the testimony, that he d' not:
20:20 their sin: they shall d' childless.
22: 9 lest they bear sin for it, and d'
Nu 4:15 touch any holy thing, lest they d'.
19 that they may live, and not d',
20 holy things are covered, lest they d'.
6: 7 or for his sister, when they d':
9 any man d' very suddenly by him,

Nu 14:35 consumed, and there they shall d'.
16:29 If these men d' the common death
17:10 from me, that they d' not.
12 saying, Behold we d', we perish,
13 tabernacle of the Lord shall d':
18: 3 that neither they, nor ye also, d'.
22 lest they bear sin, and d'.
32 the children of Israel, lest ye d'.
20: 4 that we and our cattle should d'
26 unto his people, and shall d' there.
21: 5 of Egypt to d' in the wilderness?
23:10 me d' the death of the righteous,
26:65 They shall surely d' in the
27: 8 If a man d', and have no son,
35:12 that the manslayer d' not, until he
16 instrument of iron, so that he d',
17, 18 wherewith he may d', and he d',
20 him by laying of wait, that he d';
21 him with his hand, that he d':
23 wherewith a man may d', seeing
23 cast it upon him, that he d',
30 any person to cause him to d'.
De 4:22 I must d' in this land, I must not
5:25 Now therefore why should we d'?
25 our God any more, then we shall d'.
13:10 stone him with stones, that he d';
17: 5 stone them with stones, till they d'.
12 the judge, even that man shall d':
18:16 great fire any more that I d' not.
20 gods, even that prophet shall d'.
19: 5 upon his neighbour, that he d';
11 smite him mortally that he d',
12 avenger of blood, that he may d'.
20: 5, 6, 7 lest he d' in the battle, and
21:21 stone him with stones, that he d':
22:21 stone her with stones that she d':
22 then they shall both of them d',
24 stone them with stones that they d';
25 man only that lay with her shall d':
24: 3 if the latter husband d', which took
7 that thief shall d'; and thou shalt
25: 5 dwell together, and one of them d',
31:14 days approach that thou must d':
32:50 And d' in the mount whither thou
33: 6 Let Reuben live, and not d'; and let
Jos 20: 9 not d' by the hand of the avenger
J'g 6:23 thee; fear not: thou shalt not d'.
30 Bring out thy son, that he may d':
13:22 We shall surely d', because we have
15:18 and now shall I d' for thirst, and
16:30 Let me d' with the Philistines.
Ru 1:17 Where thou diest, will I d', and
1Sa 2:33 the increase of thine house shall d'
34 in one day they shall d' both of
12:19 the Lord thy God, that we d' not:
14:39 my son, he shall surely d'.
43 in mine hand, and, lo, I must d'.
44 for thou shalt surely d', Jonathan.
45 Shall Jonathan d', who hath
20: 2 God forbid; thou shalt not d':
14 kindness of the Lord, that I d' not:
31 unto me, for he shall surely d'.
22:16 Thou shalt surely d', Ahimelech,
26:10 his day shall come to d'; or he
16 ye are worthy to d', because ye
28: 9 for my life, to cause me to d'?
2Sa 11:15 that he may be smitten, and d'.
12: 5 done this thing shall surely d':
13 away thy sin; thou shalt not d'.
14 is born unto thee shall surely d'.
14:14 For we must needs d', and are as
18: 3 neither if half of us d', will they
19:23 said unto Shimei, Thou shalt not d'.
37 that I may d' in mine own city,
1Ki 1:52 shall be found in him, he shall d'.
2: 1 David drew nigh that he should d';
30 he said, Nay; but I will d' here.
37 certain that thou shalt surely d':
42 whither, that thou shalt surely d'?
14:12 into the city, the child shall d'.
17:12 that we may eat it, and d'.
19: 4 for himself that he might d';
21:10 out, and stone him, that he may d'.
2Ki 1: 4, 6, 16 gone up, but shalt surely d'.
7: 3 Why sit we here until we d'?
4 is in the city and we shall d' there:
4 and if we sit still here, we d' also.
4 and if they kill us, we shall but d'.
8:10 showed me that he shall surely d'.
18:32 that ye may live, and not d':
20: 1 for thou shalt d', and not live.
2Ch 25: 4 The fathers shall not d' for the
4 neither shall the children d' for the
4 but every man shall d' for his own
32:11 to d' by famine and by thirst,
Job 2: 9 thine integrity? curse God, and d'.
4:21 they d', even without wisdom.
12: 2 and wisdom shall d' with you.
14: 8 the stock thereof d' in the ground;
14 If a man d', shall he live again?
27: 5 that I should justify you: till I d'
29:18 Then I said, I shall d' in my nest,
34:20 In a moment shall they d', and the
36:12 they shall d' without knowledge.
14 They d' in youth, and their life is
Ps 41: 5 When shall he d', and his name
49:10 For he seeth that wise men d',
79:11 those that are appointed to d';
82: 7 But ye shall d' like men, and fall
88:15 I am afflicted and ready to d' from
104:29 they d', and return to their dust.
118:17 I shall not d', but live, and declare
Pr 5:23 He shall d' without instruction;
10:21 but fools d' for want of wisdom.
15:10 he that hateth reproof shall d'.

Pr 19:16 he that despiseth his ways shall d'.
23:13 him with the rod, he shall not d'.
30: 7 deny me them not before I d':
Ec 3: 2 A time to be born, and a time to d';
7:17 why shouldest thou d' before thy
9: 5 the living know that they shall d':
Isa 22:13 drink; for to-morrow we shall d'.
14 not be purged from you till ye d',
18 there shalt thou d', and there the
38: 1 for thou shalt d', and not live.
51: 6 they that dwell therein shall d' in
12 be afraid of a man that shall d',
14 that he should not d' in the pit,
65:20 the child shall d' an hundred years
66:24 their worm shall not d', neither
Jer 11:21 Lord, that thou d' not by our hand:
22 young men shall d' by the sword;
22 sons and their daughters shall d'
16: 4 They shall d' of grievous deaths;
6 the great and the small shall d' in
20: 6 Babylon, and there thou shalt d',
21: 6 they shall d' of a great pestilence.
9 He that abideth in this city shall d'
22:12 he shall d' in the place whither they
26 not born; and there shall ye d'.
26: 8 him, saying, Thou shalt surely d'.
11 This man is worthy to d'; for he
16 This man is not worthy to d';
27:13 will ye d', thou and thy people,
28:16 this year thou shalt d', because
31:30 But every one shall d' for his own
34: 4 Thou shalt not d' by the sword:
5 Thou shalt d' in peace: and with
37:20 Jonathan the scribe, lest I d' there.
38: 2 that remaineth in this city shall d'
9 and he is like to d' for hunger
10 out of the dungeon, before he d'.
24 these words, and thou shalt not d'.
26 to Jonathan's house, to d' there.
42:16 in Egypt; and there ye shall d'.
17 they shall d' by the sword, by the
22 know certainly that ye shall d' by
44:12 they shall d', from the least even
Eze 3:18 Thou shalt surely d'; and thou
18 the same wicked man shall d' in
19 way, he shall d' in his iniquity;
20 he shall d': because thou hast not
20 him warning, he shall d' in his sin,
5:12 of thee shall d' with the pestilence,
6:12 He that is far off shall d' of the
12 remaineth and is besieged shall d'
7:15 he that is in the field shall d' with
12:13 not see it, though he shall d' there.
13:19 to slay the souls that should not d',
17:16 in the midst of Babylon he shall d'.
18: 4 the soul that sinneth, it shall d'.
13 he shall surely d'; his blood shall
17 he shall not d' for the iniquity of
18 even he shall d' in his iniquity.
20 The soul that sinneth, it shall d'.
21 he shall surely live, he shall not d'.
23 at all that the wicked should d'?
24 hath sinned, in them shall he d'.
26 that he hath done shall he d'.
28 he shall surely live, he shall not d'.
31 why will ye d', O house of Israel?
28: 8 and thou shalt d' the deaths of them
10 Thou shalt d' the deaths of the
33: 8 thou shalt surely d'; if thou dost
8 his way, that wicked man shall d'
9 his way he shall d' in his iniquity;
11 why will ye d', O house of Israel?
13 hath committed, he shall d' for it.
14 Thou shalt surely d'; if he turn
15 he shall surely live, he shall not d'.
18 iniquity, he shall even d' thereby.
27 the caves shall d' of the pestilence.
Am 2: 2 and Moab shall d' with tumult,
6: 9 in one house, that they shall d'.
7:11 Jeroboam shall d' by the sword,
17 thou shalt d' in a polluted land:
9:10 the sinners of my people shall d'
Jon 4: 3 is better for me to d' than to live.
8 wished in himself to d', and said,
8 It is better for me to d' than to live.
Hab 1:12 mine Holy One? we shall not d'.
Zec 11: 9 feed you: that that dieth, let it d';
13: 8 therein shall be cut off and d';
M't 15: 4 or mother, let him d' the death.
22:24 Master, Moses said, If a man d',
26:35 Though I should d' with thee, yet
M'r 7:10 let him d' the death: But ye say,
12:19 If a man's brother d', and leave
14:31 If I should d' with thee, I will not
Lu 7: 2 him, was sick, and ready to d'.
20:28 If any man's brother d', having a
28 wife, and he d' without children,
36 Neither can they d' any more: for
Joh 4:49 Sir, come down ere my child d'.
6:50 a man may eat thereof, and not d'.
8:21 seek me, and shall d' in your sins:
24 that ye shall d' in your sins: for if
24 unto you ye shall d' in your sins.
11:16 also go, that we may d' with him.
26 and believeth in me shall never d'.
50 one man should d' for the people,
51 that Jesus should d' for that nation;
12:24 wheat fall into the ground and d',
24 it abideth alone: but if it d', it
33 signifying what death he should d'.
18:14 one man should d' for the people.
32 signifying what death he should d'.
19: 7 and by our law he ought to d',
21:23 that disciple should not d': yet
23 said not unto him, He shall not d':

Ac 21:13 also to d' at Jerusalem for the
25:11 worthy of death, I refuse not to d':
16 Romans to deliver any man to d',
Ro 5: 7 for a righteous man will one d':
7 man some would even dare to d'.
8:13 ye live after the flesh, ye shall d':
14: 8 whether we d', we d' unto the Lord:
8 therefore, or d', we are the Lord's.
1Co 9:15 better for me to d', than that any
15:22 For as in Adam all d', even so
31 in Christ Jesus our Lord, I d' daily.
32 eat and drink; for to morrow we d'.
36 is not quickened, except it d':
2Co 7: 3 our hearts to d' and live with you.
Ph'p 1:21 to live is Christ, and to d' is gain.
Heb 7: 8 here men that d' receive tithes;
9:27 it is appointed unto men once to d',
Re 3: 2 which remain, that are ready to d':
9: 6 not find it; and shall desire to d',
14:13 are the dead which d' in the Lord

died
Ge 5: 5 and thirty years: and he d'.
8 and twelve years: and he d'.
11 hundred and five years: and he d'.
14 hundred and ten years: and he d'.
17 ninety and five years: and he d'.
20 sixty and two years: and he d'.
27 sixty and nine years: and he d'.
31 seventy and seven years: and he d'.
7:21 And all flesh d' that moved upon
22 all that was in the dry land, d'.
9:29 hundred and fifty years: and he d'.
11:28 Haran d' before his father Terah
32 five years: and Terah d' in Haran.
23: 2 And Sarah d' in Kirjath-arba; the
25: 8 d' in a good old age, an old man,
17 and he gave up the ghost and d';
18 he d' in the presence of all his
35: 8 But Deborah Rebekah's nurse d',
18 soul was in departing, (for she d')
19 And Rachel d', and was buried in
29 Isaac gave up the ghost, and d',
36:33 And Bela d', and Jobab the son of
34 And Jobab d', and Husham of the
35 And Husham d', and Hadad the son
36 And Hadad d', and Samlah of
37 Samlah d', and Saul of Rehoboth
38 Saul d', and Baal-hanan the son of
39 Baal-hanan the son of Achbor d',
38:12 daughter of Shuah Judah's wife d';
46:12 and Onan d' in the land of Canaan.
48: 7 Rachel d' by me in the land of
50:16 father did command before he d',
26 Joseph d', being an hundred and
Ex 1: 6 Joseph d', and all his brethren,
2:23 of time that the king of Egypt d':
7:21 the fish that was in the river d';
8:13 and the frogs d' out of the houses,
9: 6 and all the cattle of Egypt d':
6 of the children of Israel d' not one.
16: 3 Would to God we had d' by the
Lev 10: 2 them, and they d' before the Lord.
16: 1 offered before the Lord, and d';
17:15 soul that eateth that which d' of
Nu 3: 4 and Abihu d' before the Lord,
14: 2 we had d' in the land of Egypt!
2 God we had d' in this wilderness!
37 up the evil report upon the land, d'
15:36 stoned him with stones, and he d';
16:49 they that d' in the plague were
49 that d' about the matter of Korah.
20: 1 Miriam d' there, and was buried
3 Would God that we had d' when
3 our brethren d' before the Lord!
28 Aaron d' there in the top of the
21: 6 and much people of Israel d'.
25: 9 those that d' in the plague were
26:10 when that company d', what time
11 the children of Korah d' not.
19 and Onan d' in the land of Canaan.
61 And Nadab and Abihu d', when
27: 3 Our father d' in the wilderness, and
3 d' in his own sin, and had no sons.
33:38 of the Lord, and d' there,
39 old when he d' in mount Hor.
De 10: 6 Aaron d', and there he was buried;
32:50 Aaron thy brother d' in mount Hor,
34: 5 Moses the servant of the Lord d'
7 and twenty years old when he d':
Jos 5: 4 d' in the wilderness by the way,
10:11 them unto Azekah, and they d':
11 more which d' with hailstones than
24:29 of Nun, the servant of the Lord, d',
33 Eleazar the son of Aaron d'; and
J'g 1: 7 him to Jerusalem, and there he d'.
2: 8 of Nun, the servant of the Lord, d',
21 which Joshua left when he d':
3:11 And Othniel the son of Kenaz d'.
4:21 fast asleep and weary. So he d'.
8:32 And Gideon the son of Joash d'
9:49 the men of the tower of Shechem d'
54 man thrust him through, and he d'.
10: 2 twenty and three years, and d',
5 And Jair d', and was buried in
12: 7 Then d' Jephthah the Gileadite, and
10 Then d' Ibzan, and was buried at
12 And Elon the Zebulonite d', and was
15 son of Hillel the Pirathonite d',
Ru 1: 3 Elimelech Naomi's husband d';
5 and Chilion d' also both of them;
1Sa 4:18 and his neck brake, and he d':
5:12 the men that d' not were smitten
14:45 rescued Jonathan, that he d' not.
25: 1 Samuel d'; and all the Israelites
37 that his heart d' within him, and he

1Sa 25:38 the Lord smote Nabal, that he d'.
31: 5 upon his sword, and d' with him.
6 So Saul d', and his three sons,
2Sa 1:15 And he smote him that he d'.
2:23 and d' in the same place: and it
23 Asahel fell down and d' stood still.
31 hundred and threescore men d'.
3:27 under the fifth rib, that he d',
33 said, D' Abner as a fool dieth?
6: 7 and there he d' by the ark of God.
10: 1 king of the children of Ammon d',
18 captain of their host, who d' there.
11:17 and Uriah the Hittite d' also.
21 the wall, that he d' in Thebez?
12:18 the seventh day, that the child d'.
17:23 and hanged himself, and d', and
18:33 would God I had d' for thee,
19: 6 all we had d' this day, then it had
20:10 struck him not again; and he d'.
24:15 there d' of the people from Dan
1Ki 2:25 and he fell upon him that he d'.
46 and fell upon him, that he d'.
3:19 woman's child d' in the night;
12:18 stoned him with stones, that he d'.
14:17 threshold of the door, the child d';
16:18 house over him with fire, and d',
22 so Tibni d', and Omri reigned.
21:13 stoned him with stones, that he d'.
22:35 against the Syrians, and d' at even:
37 So the king d', and was brought to
2Ki 1:17 So he d' according to the word of
4:20 on her knees till noon, and then d'.
7:17 upon him in the gate, and he d', as
20 upon him in the gate, and he d'.
8:15 spread it on his face, so that he d':
9:27 he fled to Megiddo, and d' there.
12:21 his servants, smote him, and he d';
13:14 sick of his sickness whereof he d'.
20 And Elisha d', and they buried him.
24 So Hazael king of Syria d'; and
23:34 he came to Egypt, and d' there.
25:25 and smote Gedaliah, that he d',
1Ch 1:51 Hadad d' also. And the dukes of
2:30 but Seled d' without children.
32 and Jether d' without children.
10: 5 fell likewise on the sword, and d'.
6 So Saul d', and his three sons,
6 and all his house d' together.
13 So Saul d' for his transgression
13:10 and there he d' before God.
19: 1 king of the children of Ammon d',
23:22 And Eleazar d', and had no sons,
24: 2 Nadab and Abihu d' before their
29:28 And he d' in a good old age,
2Ch 10:18 stoned him with stones, that he d'.
13:20 the Lord struck him, and he d'.
16:13 and d' in the one and fortieth year
18:34 time of the sun going down he d'.
21:19 sickness: so he d' of sore diseases.
24:15 and was full of days when he d';
15 years old was he when he d'.
22 And when he d', he said, The Lord
25 slew him on his bed, and he d';
35:24 him to Jerusalem, and he d',
Job 3:11 Why d' I not from the womb?
42:17 Job d', being old and full of days.
Isa 6: 1 In the year that king Uzziah d'
14:28 In the year that king Ahaz d'
Jer 28:17 So Hananiah the prophet d' the
Eze 11:13 Pelatiah the son of Benaiah d'.
24:18 and at even my wife d'; and I did
Ho 13: 1 when he offended in Baal, he d'.
M't 22:27 And last of all the woman d' also.
M'r 12:21 the second took her, and d', neither
22 seed: last of all the woman d' also.
Lu 16:22 it came to pass, that the beggar d',
22 rich man also d', and was buried;
20:29 a wife, and d' without children.
30 her to wife, and he d' childless.
31 and they left no children, and d'.
32 Last of all the woman d' also.
Joh 11:21, 32 here, my brother had not d'.
37 even this man should not have d'?
Ac 7:15 Egypt, and d', he, and our fathers,
9:37 days, that she was sick, and d':
Ro 5: 6 time Christ d' for the ungodly.
8 were yet sinners, Christ d' for us.
6:10 in that he d', he d' unto sin once:
7: 9 came, sin revived, and I d'.
8:34 It is Christ that d', yea rather,
14: 9 To this end Christ both d', and rose,
15 with thy meat, for whom Christ d'.
1Co 8:11 brother perish, for whom Christ d'?
15: 3 how that Christ d' for our sins
2Co 5:14 one d' for all, then were all dead:
15 that he d' for all, that they which
15 but unto him which d' for them,
1Th 4:14 that Jesus d' and rose again, even
5:10 Who d' for us, that, whether we
Heb 10:28 Moses' law d' without mercy under
11:13 These all d' in faith, not having
22 By faith Joseph when he d', made
Re 8: 9 were in the sea, and had life, d';
11 many men d' of the waters,
16: 3 every living soul d' in the sea.

diest
Ru 1:17 Where thou d', will I die, and

diet
Jer 52:34 And for his d', there was a
34 there was a continual d' given

dieth
Le 7:24 fat of the beast that d' of itself,
22: 8 That which d' of itself, or is torn
Nu 19:14 when a man d' in a tent:
De 14:21 eat of any thing that d' of itself:
2Sa 3:33 said, Died Abner as a fool d'?
1Ki 14:11 Him that d' of Jeroboam in the
11 eat; and him that d' in the field
16: 4 Him that d' of Baasha in the city
4 and him that d' of his in the fields
21:24 Him that d' of Ahab in the city
24 eat; and him that d' in the field
Job 14:10 But man d', and wasteth away:
21:23 One d' in his full strength, being
25 d' in the bitterness of his soul,
Ps 49:17 when he d' he shall carry nothing
Pr 11: 7 a wicked man d', his expectation
Ec 2:16 And how d' the wise man? as the
3:19 as the one d', so d' the other;
Isa 50: 2 is no water, and d' for thirst.
59: 5 he that eateth of their eggs d',
Eze 4:14 eaten of that which d' of itself,
18:26 iniquity, and d' in them;
32 pleasure in the death of him that d',
Zec 11: 9 feed you: that that d', let it die;
M'r 9:44, 46 Where their worm d' not, and
48 Where their worm d' not, and
Ro 6: 9 raised from the dead, d' no more;
14: 7 himself, and no man d' to himself.

differ See also DIFFERETH; DIFFERING.
1Co 4: 7 maketh thee to d' from another?

difference See also DIFFERENCES.
Ex 11: 7 the Lord doth put a d' between
Le 10:10 And that ye may put d' between holy
11:47 d' between the unclean and the
20:25 shall therefore put d' between
Eze 22:26 they have put no d' between the
26 have they showed d' between
44:23 the d' between the holy and
Ac 15: 9 no d' between us and them,
Ro 3:22 that believe: for there is no d':
10:12 no d' between the Jew and the
1Co 7:34 There is d' also between a wife
Jude 22 have compassion, making a d':

differences
1Co 12: 5 there are d' of administrations,

differeth
1Co 15:41 for one star d' from another star
Ga 4: 1 a child, d' nothing from a servant,

differing
Ro 12: 6 gifts d' according to the grace

dig See also DIGGED; DIGGETH.
Ex 21:33 if a man shall d' a pit, and not
De 8: 9 whose hills thou mayest d' brass.
23:13 thou shalt d' therewith, and shalt
Job 3:21 d' for it more than for hid treasures:
6:27 and ye d' a pit for your friend.
11:18 yea, thou shalt d' about thee,
24:16 the dark they d' through houses,
Eze 8: 8 Son of man, d' now in the wall:
12: 5 D' thou through the wall in their
12 d' through the wall to carry out,
Am 9: 2 Though they d' into hell, thence
Lu 13: 8 till I shall d' about it, and dung it:
16: 3 I cannot d'; to beg I am ashamed.

digged See also DIGGEDST.
Ge 21:30 unto me, that I have d' this well.
26:15 had d' in the days of Abraham
18 Isaac d' again the wells of water;
18 which they had d' in the days of
19 Isaac's servants d' in the valley,
21 And they d' another well, and
22 from thence, and d' another well;
25 there Isaac's servants d' a well.
32 the well which they had d', and
49: 6 their selfwill they d' down a wall.
50: 5 in my grave which I have d' for
Ex 7:24 the Egyptians d' round about the
Nu 21:18 The princes d' the well,
18 the nobles of the people d' it,
De 6:11 wells d', which thou diggedst not,
2Ki 19:24 d' and drunk strange waters,
2Ch 26:10 in the desert, and d' many wells:
Ne 9:25 houses full of all goods, wells d',
Ps 7:15 He made a pit, and d' it, and is
35: 7 cause they have d' for my soul.
57: 6 they have d' a pit before me, into
94:13 until the pit be d' for the wicked.
119:85 The proud have d' pits for me,
Isa 5: 6 it shall not be pruned, nor d';
7:25 on all hills that shall be d' with
37:25 I have d', and drunk water; and
51: 1 hole of the pit whence ye are d'.
Jer 13: 7 Then I went to Euphrates, and d',
18:20 they have d' a pit for my soul,
22 they have d' a pit to take me,
Eze 8: 8 and when I had d' in the wall,
12: 7 in the even I d' through the wall
M't 21:33 and d' a winepress in it, and built
25:18 and d' in the earth, and hid his
M'r 12: 1 and d' a place for the winefat,
Lu 6:48 d' deep, and laid the foundation
Ro 11: 3 and d' down thine altars;

diggedst
De 6:11 wells digged, which thou d' not,

diggeth
Pr 16:27 An ungodly man d' up evil: and
26:27 Whoso d' a pit shall fall therein:
Ec 10: 8 He that d' a pit shall fall into it;

dignities
2Pe 2:10 are not afraid to speak evil of d'.
Jude 8 dominion, and speak evil of d'.

dignity See also DIGNITIES.
Ge 49: 3 the excellency of d', and the
Es 6: 3 What honour and d' has been done

Ec 10: 6 Folly is set in great *d*, and the
Hab 1: 7 *d* shall proceed of themselves.

Diklah (*dik'-lah*)
Ge 10:27 And Hadoram, and Uzal, and *D*,
1Ch 1:21 Hadoram also, and Uzal, and *D*,

Dilean (*dil'-e-an*)
Jos 15:38 and *D*, and Mizpeh, and Joktheel,

diligence
Pr 4:23 Keep thy heart with all *d*; for out
Lu 12:58 way, give *d* that thou mayest be
Ro 12: 8 he that ruleth, with *d*; he that
2Co 8: 7 and knowledge, and in all *d*, and
2Ti 4: 9 thy *d* to come shortly unto me:
21 Do thy *d* to come before winter.
Heb 6:11 the same *d* to the full assurance
2Pe 1: 5 giving all *d*, add to your faith
10 give *d* to make your calling and
Jude 3 when I gave all *d* to write unto

diligent
De 19:18 judges shall make *d* inquisition:
Jos 22: 5 *d* heed to do the commandment
Ps 64: 6 they accomplish a *d* search:
77: 6 heart: and my spirit made *d* search.
Pr 10: 4 the hand of the *d* maketh rich.
12:24 The hand of the *d* shall bear rule:
27 substance of a *d* man is precious.
13: 4 the soul of the *d* shall be made fat
21: 5 The thoughts of the *d* tend only to
22:29 thou a man *d* in his business?
27:23 Be thou *d* to know the state of
2Co 8:22 often proved *d* in many things,
22 but now much more *d*, upon
Tit 3:12 *d* to come unto me to Nicopolis:
2Pe 3:14 *d* that ye may be found of him in

diligently
Ex 15:26 If thou wilt *d* hearken to the voice
Le 10:16 And Moses *d* sought the goat of
De 4: 9 keep thy soul *d*, lest thou forget
6: 7 teach them *d* unto thy children,
17 Ye shall *d* keep the commandments
11:13 hearken *d* unto my commandments
22 For if ye shall *d* keep all these
13:14 make search, and ask *d*; and,
17: 4 hast heard of it, and enquired *d*,
24: 8 of leprosy, that thou observe *d*,
28: 1 if thou shalt hearken *d* unto the
1Ki 20:33 did *d* observe whether any thing
Ezr 7:23 let it be *d* done for the house of
Job 13:17 Hear *d* my speech, and my
21: 2 Hear *d* my speech, and let this be
Ps 37:10 thou shalt *d* consider his place,
119: 4 us to keep thy precepts *d*.
Pr 7:15 *d* to seek thy face, and I have
11:27 He that *d* seeketh good procureth
23: 1 ruler, consider *d* what is before thee:
Isa 21: 7 he hearkened *d* with much heed
55: 2 hearken *d* unto me, and eat ye that
Jer 2:10 and consider *d*, and see if there
12:16 if they will *d* learn the ways
17:24 if ye *d* hearken unto me, saith the
Zec 6:15 will *d* obey the voice of the Lord
M't 2: 7 of them *d* what time the star
8 search *d* for the young child;
16 had *d* enquired of the wise men,
Lu 15: 8 house, and seek *d* till she find it?
Ac 18:25 he spake and taught *d* the things
1Ti 5:10 *d* followed every good work.
2Ti 1:17 Rome, he sought me out very *d*,
Tit 3:13 and Apollos on their journey *d*,
Heb 11: 6 reward of them that *d* seek him.
12:15 Looking *d* lest any man fail of
1Pe 1:10 have enquired and searched *d*,

dim
Ge 27: 1 was old, and his eyes were *d*,
48:10 the eyes of Israel were *d* for age,
De 34: 7 his eye was not dim, nor his
1Sa 3: 2 his eyes began to wax *d*, that he
4:15 his eyes were *d*, that he could
Job 17: 7 eye also is *d* by reason of sorrow,
Isa 32: 3 of them that see shall not be *d*,
La 4: 1 How is the gold become *d*! how
5:17 for these things our eyes are *d*.

diminish See also DIMINISHED; DIMINISHING; MINISH.
Ex 5: 8 ye shall not *d* ought thereof: for
21:10 duty of marriage, shall he not *d*.
Le 25:16 thou shalt *d* the price of it:
De 4: 2 neither shall ye *d* ought from it,
12:32 not add thereto, nor *d* from it.
Jer 26: 2 speak unto them; *d* not a word:
Eze 5:11 therefore will I also *d* thee;
29:15 for I will *d* them, that they shall

diminished See also MINISHED.
Ex 5:11 ought of your work shall be *d*.
Pr 13:11 gotten by vanity shall be *d*:
Isa 21:17 children of Kedar, shall be *d*:
Jer 29: 6 may be increased there, and not *d*.
Eze 16:27 and have *d* thine ordinary food,

diminishing
Ro 11:12 and the *d* of them the riches of

Dimnah (*dim'-nah*)
Jos 21:35 *D* with her suburbs, Nahalal

dimness
Isa 8:22 and darkness, *d* of anguish;
9: 1 the *d* shall not be such as was

Dimon (*di'-mon*) See also DIBON; DIMONAH.
Isa 15: 9 waters of *D* shall be full of blood:
9 I will bring more upon *D*,

Dimonah (*di-mo'-nah*) See also DIMON.
Jos 15:22 Kinah, and *D*, and Adadah,

Dinah See also DINAH'S.
Ge 30:21 daughter, and called her name *D*.
34: 1 *D* the daughter of Leah, which
3 soul clave unto *D* the daughter of
5 Jacob heard that he had defiled *D*
13 he had defiled *D* their sister:
26 took *D* out of Shechem's house,
46:15 Padan-aram, with his daughter *D*:

Dinah's
Ge 34:25 Simeon, and Levi, *D* brethren,

Dinaites (*di'-na-ites*)
Ezr 4: 9 the *D*, the Apharsathchites,

dine See also DINED.
Ge 43:16 these men shall *d* with me at noon.
Lu 11:37 besought him to *d* with him:
Joh 21:12 saith unto them, Come and *d*.

dined
Joh 21:15 So when they had *d*, Jesus saith

Dinhabah (*din'-ha-bah*)
Ge 36:32 and the name of his city was *D*.
1Ch 1:43 and the name of his city was *D*.

dinner
Pr 15:17 is a *d* of herbs where love is,
M't 22: 4 Behold, I have prepared my *d*:
Lu 11:38 had not first washed before *d*.
14:12 When thou makest a *d* or a supper,

Dionysius (*di-on-ish'-yus*)
Ac 17:34 the which was *D* the Areopagite,

Diotrephes (*di-ot'-re-feez*)
3Jo 9 I wrote unto the church: but *D*,

dip See also DIPPED; DIPPETH.
Ex 12:22 *d* it in the blood that is in the
Le 4: 6 shall *d* his finger in the blood,
17 *d* his finger in some of the blood,
14: 6 shall *d* them and the living bird
16 the priest shall *d* his right finger
51 *d* them in the blood of the slain
Nu 19:18 and *d* it in the water, and sprinkle
De 33:24 and let him *d* his foot in oil.
Ru 2:14 and *d* thy morsel in the vinegar.
Lu 16:24 that he may *d* the tip of his finger

dipped
Ge 37:31 and *d* the coat in the blood;
Le 9: 9 and he *d* his finger in the blood,
Jos 3:15 were *d* in the brim of the water,
1Sa 14:27 and *d* it in an honeycomb, and put
2Ki 5:14 *d* himself seven times in Jordan,
8:15 and *d* it in water, and spread it on
Ps 68:23 thy foot may be *d* in the blood
Joh 13:26 give a sop when I have *d* it.
26 had *d* the sop, he gave it to Judas
Re 19:13 with a vesture *d* in blood:

dippeth
M't 26:23 He that *d* his hand with me in
M'r 14:20 that *d* with me in the dish.

direct See also DIRECTED; DIRECTETH.
Ge 46:28 to *d* his face unto Goshen;
Ps 5: 3 will I *d* my prayer unto thee,
Pr 3: 6 him, and he shall *d* thy paths.
11: 5 of the perfect shall *d* his way:
Ec 10:10 but wisdom is profitable to *d*.
Isa 45:13 and I will *d* all his ways:
61: 8 and I will *d* their work in truth,
Jer 10:23 man that walketh to *d* his steps.
1Th 3:11 Christ, *d* our way unto you.
2Th 3: 5 *d* your hearts into the love of God,

directed
Job 32:14 hath not *d* his words against me:
Ps 119: 5 ways were *d* to keep thy statutes!
Isa 40:13 Who hath *d* the spirit of the Lord,

directeth
Job 37: 3 He *d* it under the whole heaven,
Pr 16: 9 way: but the Lord *d* his steps.
21:29 as for the upright, he *d* his way.

direction
Nu 21:18 it, by the *d* of the lawgiver,

directly
Nu 19: 4 blood *d* before the tabernacle
Eze 42:12 even the way *d* before the wall

dirt
J'g 3:22 his belly; and the *d* came out.
Ps 18:42 them out as the *d* in the streets.
Isa 57:20 whose waters cast up mire and *d*.

disallow See also DISALLOWED.
Nu 30: 5 if her father *d* her in the day that

disallowed
Nu 30: 5 her, because her father *d* her.
8 her husband *d* her on the day that
11 his peace at her, and *d* her not:
1Pe 2: 4 *d* indeed of men, but chosen of
7 the stone which the builders *d*,

disannul See also DISANNULLED; DISANNULLETH; DISANNULLING.
Job 40: 8 Wilt thou also *d* my judgment?
Isa 14:27 purposed, and who shall *d* it?
Ga 3:17 years after, cannot *d*, that it

disannulled
Isa 28:18 covenant with death shall be *d*,

disannulleth
Ga 3:15 no man *d*, or addeth thereto.

disannulling
Heb 7:18 verily a *d* of the commandment

disappoint See also DISAPPOINTED; DISAPPOINTETH.
Ps 17:13 Arise, O Lord, *d* him, cast him

disappointed
Pr 15:22 Without counsel purposes are *d*:

disappointeth
Job 5:12 He *d* the devices of the crafty,

discern See also DISCERNED; DISCERNETH; DISCERNING.
Ge 31:32 *d* thou what is thine with me,
38:25 *D*, I pray thee, whose are these,
2Sa 14:17 lord the king to *d* good and bad:
19:35 can I *d* between good and evil?
1Ki 3: 9 I may *d* between good and bad:
11 understanding to *d* judgment;
Ezr 3:13 the people could not *d* the noise
Job 4:16 I could not *d* the form thereof:
6:30 cannot my taste *d* perverse things?
Eze 44:23 them to *d* between the unclean
Jon 4:11 that cannot *d* between their right
Mal 3:18 and *d* between the righteous and
M't 16: 3 ye can *d* the face of the sky;
3 but can ye not *d* the signs of the
Lu 12:56 ye can *d* the face of the sky and
56 is it that ye do not *d* this time?
Heb 5:14 exercised to *d* both good and evil.

discerned
Ge 27:23 he *d* him not, because his hands
1Ki 20:41 and the king of Israel *d* him that
Pr 7: 7 I *d* among the youths, a young
1Co 2:14 because they are spiritually *d*.

discerner
Heb 4:12 and is a *d* of the thoughts and

discerneth
Ec 8: 5 and a wise man's heart *d* both

discerning
1Co 11:29 himself, not *d* the Lord's body.
12:10 to another *d* of spirits; to another

discharge See also DISCHARGED.
Ec 8: 8 and there is no *d* in that war;

discharged
1Ki 5: 9 and will cause them to be *d* there,

disciple See also DISCIPLES.
M't 10:24 The *d* is not above his master,
25 It is enough for the *d* that he be as
42 water only in the name of a *d*,
27:57 who also himself was Jesus' *d*:
Lu 6:40 The *d* is not above his master:
14:26 own life also, he cannot be my *d*.
27 come after me, cannot be my *d*.
33 that he hath, he cannot be my *d*.
Joh 9:28 Thou art his *d*; but we are Moses'
18:15 another *d*: that *d* was known
16 Then went out that other *d*, which
19:26 and the *d* standing by, whom he
27 Then saith he to the *d*, Behold thy
27 from that hour that *d* took her
38 of Arimathea, being a *d* of Jesus,
20: 2 to the other *d*, whom Jesus loved,
3 went forth, and that other *d*,
4 and the other *d* did outrun Peter,
8 Then went in also that other *d*,
21: 7 Therefore that *d* whom Jesus loved
20 seeth the *d* whom Jesus loved
23 that that *d* should not die;
24 This is the *d* which testifieth of
Ac 9:10 *d* at Damascus, named Ananias;
26 believed not that he was a *d*.
36 Joppa a certain *d* named Tabitha,
16: 1 *d* was there, named Timotheus,
21:16 *d*, with whom we should lodge.

disciples See also DISCIPLES'; FELLOWDISCIPLES.
Isa 8:16 seal the law among my *d*.
M't 5: 1 he was set, his *d* came unto him:
8:21 another of his *d* said unto him,
23 into a ship, his *d* followed him.
25 his *d* came to him, and awoke
9:10 and sat down with him and his *d*.
11 they said unto his *d*, Why eateth
14 came to him the *d* of John, saying,
14 fast oft, but thy *d* fast not?
19 and followed him, and so did his *d*.
37 saith he unto his *d*, The harvest
10: 1 had called unto him his twelve *d*,
11: 1 end of commanding his twelve *d*,
2 of Christ, he sent two of his *d*,
12: 1 *d* were an hungred, and began to
2 thy *d* do that which is not lawful
49 forth his hand toward his *d*,
13:10 And the *d* came, and said unto him,
36 into the house: and his *d* came
14:12 his *d* came, and took up the body,
15 his *d* came to him, saying, This is
19 loaves to his *d*, and the *d* to the
22 constrained his *d* to get into a ship,
26 the *d* saw him walking on the sea,
15: 2 Why do thy *d* transgress the
12 Then came his *d*, and said unto him,
23 And his *d* came and besought him,
32 Jesus called his *d* unto him, and
33 his *d* say unto him, Whence
36 and brake them, and gave to his *d*,
36 and the *d* to the multitude.
16: 5 his *d* were come to the other side,
13 he asked his *d*, saying, Whom do
20 Then charged he his *d* that they
21 to shew unto his *d*, how that he
24 said Jesus unto his *d*, If any man
17: 6 when the *d* heard it, they fell
10 his *d* asked him, saying, Why then
13 Then the *d* understood that he
16 I brought him to thy *d*, and they
19 Then came the *d* to Jesus apart,
18: 1 came the *d* unto Jesus, saying,
19:10 His *d* say unto him, If the case
13 and pray: and the *d* rebuked them.
23 Then said Jesus unto his *d*, Verily
25 When his *d* heard it, they were

M't 20:17 took the twelve d' apart in the way,
21: 1 of Olives, then sent Jesus two d',
6 And the d' went, and did as Jesus
20 when the d' saw it, they marvelled,
22:16 sent out unto him their d' with the
23: 1 to the multitude, and to his d',
24: 1 his d' came to him for to shew him
3 the d' came unto him privately,
26: 1 he said unto his d', Ye know that
8 his d' saw it, they had indignation,
17 the d' came to Jesus, saying unto
18 passover at thy house with my d'.
19 the d' did as Jesus had appointed
26 gave it to the d', and said, Take,
35 thee. Likewise also said all the d'.
36 and saith unto the d', Sit ye here
40 he cometh unto the d', and findeth
45 Then cometh he to his d', and saith
56 Then all the d' forsook him, and
27:64 lest his d' come by night, and steal
28: 7 d' that he is risen from the dead;
8 and did run to bring his d' word.
9 And as they went to tell his d',
13 Say ye, His d' came by night,
16 eleven d' went away into Galilee,
M'r 2:15 together with Jesus and his d':
16 they said unto his d', How is it
18 And the d' of John and of the
18 Why do the d' of John and of the
18 Pharisees fast, but thy d' fast not?
23 his d' began, as they went, to pluck
3: 7 himself with his d' to the sea:
9 spake to his d', that a small ship
4:34 he expounded all things to his d'.
5:31 his d' said unto him, Thou seest
6: 1 own country; and his d' follow him.
29 when his d' heard of it, they came
35 his d' came unto him, and said,
41 them to his d' to set before them:
45 constrained his d' to get into the
7: 2 they saw some of his d' eat bread
5 Why walk not thy d' according to
17 his d' asked him concerning the
8: 1 Jesus called his d' unto him, and
4 his d' answered him, From whence
6 gave to his d' to set before them;
10 entered into a ship with his d',
14 Now the d' had forgotten to take
27 went out, and his d', into the towns
27 and by the way he asked his d',
33 looked on his d', he rebuked Peter,
34 people unto him with his d' also,
9:14 when he came to his d', he saw a
18 I spake to thy d' that they should
28 his d' asked him privately, Why
31 taught his d', and said unto them,
10:10 in the house his d' asked him
13 his d' rebuked those that brought
23 and saith unto his d', How hardly
24 the d' were astonished at his words.
46 went out of Jericho with his d'
11: 1 he sendeth forth two of his d',
14 for ever. And his d' heard it.
12:43 he called unto him his d', and saith
13: 1 one of his d' saith unto him,
14:12 d' said unto him, Where wilt thou
13 he sendeth forth two of his d',
14 shall eat the passover with my d'?
16 his d' went forth, and came into
32 and he saith to his d', Sit ye here,
16: 7 tell his d' and Peter that he goeth
Lu 5:30 murmured against his d', saying,
33 Why do the d' of John fast often,
33 likewise the d' of the Pharisees
6: 1 his d' plucked the ears of corn,
13 was day, he called unto him his d':
17 company of his d', and a great
20 And he lifted up his eyes on his d',
7:11 and many of his d' went with him,
18 the d' of John shewed him of all
19 John calling unto him two of his d'
8: 9 his d' asked him, saying, What
22 he went into a ship with his d':
9: 1 he called his twelve d' together,
14 he said to his d', Make them sit
16 and gave to the d' to set before
18 praying, his d' were with him:
40 I besought thy d' to cast him out;
43 said unto his d', Let these sayings
54 And when his d' James and John
10:23 he turned him unto his d', and said
11: 1 one of his d' said unto him, Lord,
1 as John also taught his d'.
12: 1 he began to say unto his d' first of
22 he said unto his d', Therefore I say
16: 1 he said also unto his d', There was
17: 1 Then said he unto the d', It is
22 said unto the d', The days will come,
18:15 his d' saw it, they rebuked them.
19:29 of Olives, he sent two of his d',
37 d' began to rejoice and praise God
39 unto him, Master, rebuke thy d'.
20:45 unto his d', Beware of the scribes,
22:11 eat the passover with my d'?
39 Olives; and his d' also followed him.
45 was come to his d', he found them
Joh 1:35 John stood, and two of his d';
37 And the two d' heard him speak,
2: 2 called, and his d', to the marriage.
11 glory; and his d' believed on him.
12 and his brethren, and his d':
17 his d' remembered that it was
22 his d' remembered that he had said
3:22 came Jesus and his d' into the land
25 between some of John's d' and the
4: 1 and baptized more d' than John,
Joh 4: 2 himself baptized not, but his d',)
8 (For his d' were gone away unto
27 upon this came his d', and marvelled
31 the meanwhile his d' prayed him,
33 Therefore said the d' one to
6: 3 and there he sat with his d'.
8 One of his d', Andrew, Simon
11 distributed to the d', and the d' to
12 he said unto his d', Gather up the
16 his d' went down unto the sea,
22 whereinto his d' were entered,
22 Jesus went not with his d' into the
22 that his d' were gone away alone;
24 was not there, neither his d', they
60 Many therefore of his d', when they
61 himself that his d' murmured at it,
66 many of his d' went back, and
7: 3 that thy d' also may see the works
8:31 word, then are ye my d' indeed;
9: 2 his d' asked him, saying, Master,
27 it again? will ye also be his d'?
28 his disciple; but we are Moses' d'.
11: 7 saith he to his d', Let us go into
8 His d' say unto him, Master, the
12 Then said his d', Lord, if he sleep,
54 and there continued with his d'.
12: 4 Then saith one of his d', Judas
16 understood not his d' at the first:
13:22 Then the d' looked one on another,
23 one of his d', whom Jesus loved.
35 know that ye are my d', if ye have
15: 8 much fruit; so shall ye be my d'.
16:17 Then said some of his d' among
29 His d' said unto him, Lo, now
18: 1 he went forth with his d' over the
1 the which he entered, and his d'.
2 resorted thither with his d'.
17 not thou also one of this man's d'?
19 priest then asked Jesus of his d',
25 Art not thou also one of his d'?
20:10 Then the d' went away unto their
18 Magdalene came and told the d'
19 shut where the d' were assembled
20 Then were the d' glad, when they
25 The other d' therefore said unto
26 his d' were within, and Thomas
30 did Jesus in the presence of his d',
21: 1 himself again to the d' at the sea
2 of Zebedee, and two other of his d'.
4 the d' knew not that it was Jesus.
8 And the other d' came in a little
12 And none of the d' durst ask him,
14 Jesus shewed himself to his d',
Ac 1:15 stood up in the midst of the d',
6: 1 number of the d' was multiplied,
2 called the multitude of the d' unto
7 the number of the d' multiplied in
9: 1 against the d' of the Lord, went
19 certain days with the d' which
25 Then the d' took him by night,
26 assayed to join himself to the d':
38 and the d' had heard that Peter
11:26 And the d' were called Christians
29 Then the d', every man according
13:52 And the d' were filled with joy,
14:20 Howbeit, as the d' stood round
22 Confirming the souls of the d', and
28 they abode long time with the d'.
15:10 a yoke upon the neck of the d',
18:23 in order, strengthening all the d'.
27 exhorting the d' to receive him:
19: 1 Ephesus; and finding certain d',
9 and separated the d', disputing
30 people, the d' suffered him not.
20: 1 Paul called unto him the d', and
7 the d' came together to break
30 things, to draw away d' after them.
21: 4 And finding d', we tarried there
16 also certain of the d' of Cæsarea,

disciples'
Joh 13: 5 to wash the d' feet, and to wipe

discipline
Job 36:10 He openeth also their ear to d',

disclose
Isa 26:21 the earth also shall d' her blood,

discomfited
Ex 17:13 And Joshua d' Amalek and his
Nu 14:45 smote them, and d' them, even
Jos 10:10 And the Lord d' them before
J'g 4:15 And the Lord d' Sisera, and all his
8:12 and Zalmunna, and d' all the host.
1Sa 7:10 the Philistines, and d' them; and
2Sa 22:15 them; lightning, and d' them.
Ps 18:14 shot out lightnings, and d' them.
Isa 31: 8 and his young men shall be d'.

discomfiture
1Sa 14:20 and there was a very great d'.

discontented
1Sa 22: 2 every one that was d',

discontinue
Jer 17: 4 And thou, even thyself, shalt d'

discord
Pr 6:14 continually; he soweth d'.
19 that soweth d' among brethren.

discourage See also DISCOURAGED.
Nu 32: 7 d' ye the heart of the children of

discouraged
Nu 21: 4 the soul of the people was much d'
32: 9 they d' the heart of the children
De 1:21 thee: fear not, neither be d'.
28 our brethren have d' our heart,
Isa 42: 4 He shall not fail nor be d', till
Col 3:21 children to anger, lest they be d'.

discover See also DISCOVERED; DISCOVERETH; DISCOVERING.
De 22:30 wife, nor d' his father's skirt.
1Sa 14: 8 and we will d' ourselves unto them.
Job 41:13 can d' the face of his garment?
Pr 18: 2 but that his heart may d' itself.
25: 9 and d' not a secret to another:
Isa 3:17 Lord will d' their secret parts.
Jer 13:26 Therefore will I d' thy skirts
La 4:22 of Edom; he will d' thy sins.
Eze 16:37 will d' thy nakedness unto them,
Ho 2:10 now will I d' her lewdness in the
Mic 1: 6 I will d' the foundations thereof.
Na 3: 5 will d' thy skirts upon thy face,

discovered
Ex 20:26 that thy nakedness be not d'
Le 20:18 he hath d' her fountain, and she
1Sa 14:11 And both of them d' themselves
22: 6 Saul heard that David was d',
2Sa 22:16 foundations of the world were d',
Ps 18:15 foundations of the world were d'
Isa 22: 8 And he d' the covering of Judah,
57: 8 thou hast d' thyself to another
Jer 13:22 thine iniquity are thy skirts d',
La 2:14 they have not d' thine iniquity,
Eze 13:14 foundation thereof shall be d',
16:36 thy nakedness d' through thy
57 thy wickedness was d', as at the
21:24 that your transgressions are d',
22:10 In thee have they d' their fathers'
23:10 These d' her nakedness: they
18 she d' her whoredoms, and d' her
29 thy whoredoms shall be d', both
Ho 7: 1 the iniquity of Ephraim was d',
Ac 21: 3 when we had d' Cyprus, we left
27:39 they d' a certain creek with a

discovereth
Job 12:22 He d' deep things out of darkness,
Ps 29: 9 and d' the forests: and in his

discovering
Hab 3:13 d' the foundation unto the neck.

discreet
Ge 41:33 look out a man d' and wise,
39 none so d' and wise as thou art:
Tit 2: 5 To be d', chaste, keepers at home,

discreetly
M'r 12:34 saw that he answered d', he said

discretion
Ps 112: 5 he will guide his affairs with d'.
Pr 1: 4 the young man knowledge and d'.
2:11 D' shall preserve thee,
3:21 eyes: keep sound wisdom and d':
5: 2 That thou mayest regard d', and
11:22 a fair woman which is without d'.
19:11 d' of a man deferreth his anger;
Isa 28:26 his God doth instruct him to d',
Jer 10:12 out the heavens by his d'.

disdained
1Sa 17:42 and saw David, he d' him: for he
Job 30: 1 whose fathers I would have d' to

disease See also DISEASED; DISEASES.
2Ki 1: 2 whether I shall recover of this d'.
8: 8, 9 Shall I recover of this d'?
2Ch 16:12 until his d' was exceeding great:
12 yet in his d' he sought not to the
21:15 sickness by d' of thy bowels, until
18 his bowels with an incurable d'.
Job 30:18 By the great force of my d' is my
Ps 38: 7 are filled with a loathsome d':
41: 8 An evil d', say they, cleaveth fast
Ec 6: 2 this is vanity, and it is an evil d'.
M't 4:23 all manner of d' among the people.
9:35 and every d' among the people.
10: 1 of sickness and all manner of d'.
Joh 5: 4 whole of whatsoever d' he had.

diseased
1Ki 15:23 his old age he was d' in his feet.
2Ch 16:12 year of his reign was d' in his feet,
Eze 34: 4 The d' have ye not strengthened,
21 pushed all the d' with your horns.
M't 9:20 was d' with an issue of blood
14:35 unto him all that were d';
M'r 1:32 unto him all that were d',
Joh 6: 2 which he did on them that were d'.

diseases
Ex 15:26 put none of these d' upon thee,
De 7:15 put none of the evil d' of Egypt,
28:60 bring upon thee all the d' of Egypt,
2Ch 21:19 his sickness: so he died of sore d'
24:25 (for they left him in great d',) his
Ps 103: 3 iniquities; who healeth all thy d'
M't 4:24 that were taken with divers d'
M'r 1:34 many that were sick of divers d',
Lu 4:40 any sick with divers d' brought
6:17 him; and to be healed of their d':
9: 1 over all devils, and to cure d'.
Ac 19:12 and the d' departed from them,
28: 9 which had d' in the island, came,

disfigure
M't 6:16 for they d' their faces, that they

disgrace
Jer 14:21 do not d' the throne of thy glory:

disguise See also DISGUISED; DISGUISETH.
1Ki 14: 2 Arise, I pray thee, and d' thyself,
22:30 I will d' myself and enter into the
2Ch 18:29 I will d' myself and will go to the

disguised
1Sa 28: 8 And Saul d' himself, and put on

1Ki 20:38 and *d'* himself with ashes upon
22:30 And the king of Israel *d'* himself,
2Ch 18:29 So the king of Israel *d'* himself;
35:22 but *d'* himself, that he might fight

disguiseth
Job 24:15 shall see me: and *d'* his face.

dish See DISHES; SNUFFDISH.
J'y 5:25 brought forth butter in a lordly *d'*.
2Ki 21:13 as a man wipeth a *d'*, wiping it,
M't 26:23 dippeth his hand with me in the *d'*,
M'r 14:20 that dippeth with me in the *d'*,

Dishan (*di'-shan*) See also DISHON.
Ge 36:21 And Dishon, and Ezer, and *D'*:
28 The children of *D'* are these; Uz
30 Duke Dishon, duke Ezer, duke *D'*:
1Ch 1:38 and Dishon, and Ezar, and *D'*.
42 The sons of *D'*; Uz, and Aran.

dishes
Ex 25:29 thou shalt make the *d'* thereof,
37:16 the table, his *d'*, and his spoons,
Nu 4: 7 put thereon the *d'*, and the spoons,

Dishon (*di'-shon*) See also DISHAN.
Ge 36:21 And *D'*, and Ezer, and Dishan:
25 *D'*, and Aholibamah the daughter
26 are the children of *D'*; Hemdan,
30 Duke *D'*, duke Ezer, duke Dishan:
1Ch 1:38 and *D'*, and Ezar, and Dishan.
41 The sons of Anah; *D'*. And the
41 sons of *D'*; Amram, and Eshban,

dishonest
Eze 22:13 smitten mine hand at thy *d'* gain
27 to destroy souls, to get *d'* gain.

dishonesty
2Co 4: 2 renounced the hidden things of *d'*,

dishonour See also DISHONOUREST; DISHONOURETH.
Ezr 4:14 meet for us to see the king's *d'*,
Ps 35:26 be clothed with shame and *d'* that
69:19 and my shame, and my *d'*: mine
71:13 be covered with reproach and *d'*
Pr 6:33 A wound and *d'* shall he get;
Joh 8:49 honour my Father, and ye do *d'* me.
Ro 1:24 to *d'* their own bodies between
9:21 unto honour, and another unto *d'*?
1Co 15:43 It is sown in *d'*; it is raised in
2Co 6: 8 By honour and *d'*, by evil report
2Ti 2:20 some to honour, and some to *d'*.

dishonourest
Ro 2:23 breaking the law *d'* thou God?

dishonoureth
Mic 7: 6 son *d'* the father, the daughter
1Co 11: 4 his head covered, *d'* his head.
5 her head uncovered *d'* her head:

disinherit
Nu 14:12 with the pestilence, and *d'* them,

dismayed
De 31: 8 thee: fear not, neither be *d'*.
Jos 1: 9 neither be thou *d'*: for the Lord
8: 1 neither be thou *d'*: take all the
10:25 Fear not, nor be *d'*, be strong and
1Sa 17:11 Philistine, they were *d'*, and greatly
2Ki 19:26 they were *d'* and confounded;
1Ch 22:13 courage; dread not, nor be *d'*.
28:20 fear not, nor be *d'*: for the Lord
2Ch 20:15 Be not afraid nor *d'* by reason of
17 fear not, nor be *d'*; to morrow go
32: 7 be not afraid nor *d'* for the king of
Isa 21: 3 of it; I was *d'* at the seeing of it.
37:27 they were *d'* and confounded:
41:10 be not *d'*; for I am thy God:
23 that we may be *d'*, and behold it
Jer 1:17 be not *d'* at their faces, lest I
8: 9 ashamed, they are *d'* and taken:
10: 2 be not *d'* at the signs of heaven;
2 for the heathen are *d'* at them.
17:18 be confounded: let them be *d'*,
18 but let not me be *d'*: bring upon
23: 4 they shall fear no more, nor be *d'*,
30:10 neither be *d'*, O Israel: for, lo,
46: 5 Wherefore have I seen them *d'*
27 be not *d'*, O Israel: for, behold,
48: 1 Misgab is confounded and *d'*.
49:37 For I will cause Elam to be *d'*
50:36 mighty men; and they shall be *d'*.
Eze 2: 6 of their words, nor be *d'* at their
3: 9 neither be *d'* at their looks, though
Ob 9 mighty men, O Teman, shall be *d'*,

dismaying
Jer 48:39 a derision and a *d'* to all them

dismissed
2Ch 23: 8 Jehoiada the priest *d'* not the
Ac 15:30 So when they were *d'*, they came
19:41 thus spoken, he *d'* the assembly.

disobedience
Ro 5:19 by one man's *d'* many were made
2Co 10: 6 to revenge all *d'*, when your
Eph 2: 2 now worketh in the children of *d'*:
5: 6 of God upon the children of *d'*.
Col 3: 6 of God cometh on the children of *d'*:
Heb 2: 2 transgression and *d'* received a

disobedient
1Ki 13:26 the man of God, who was *d'* unto
Ne 9:26 Nevertheless they were *d'*, and
Lu 1:17 the *d'* to the wisdom of the just;
Ac 26:19 was not *d'* unto the heavenly vision:
Ro 1:30 of evil things, *d'* to parents,
10:21 unto a *d'* and gainsaying people.
1Ti 1: 9 but for the lawless and *d'*, for the
2Ti 3: 2 blasphemers, *d'* to parents,
Tit 1:16 being abominable, and *d'*, and unto
3: 3 sometimes foolish, *d'*, deceived,

1Pe 2: 7 but unto them which be *d'*,
8 stumble at the word, being *d'*:
3:20 Which sometime were *d'*, when

disobeyed
1Ki 13:21 hast *d'* the mouth of the Lord,

disorderly
2Th 3: 6 every brother that walketh *d'*,
7 behaved not ourselves *d'* among
11 some which walk among you *d'*,

dispatch
Eze 23:47 and *d'* them with their swords;

dispensation
1Co 9:17 a *d'* of the gospel is committed
Eph 1:10 That in the *d'* of the fulness of
3: 2 heard of the *d'* of the grace of God
Col 1:25 according to the *d'* of God which

disperse See also DISPERSED.
1Sa 14:34 *D'* yourselves among the people,
Pr 15: 7 The lips of the wise *d'* knowledge:
Eze 12:15 and *d'* them in the countries.
20:23 and *d'* them through the countries;
22:15 and *d'* thee in the countries, and
29:12 and *d'* them through the countries.
30:23 will *d'* them through the countries.
26 and *d'* them among the countries;

dispersed
2Ch 11:23 *d'* of all his children throughout
Es 3: 8 and *d'* among the people in all
Ps 112: 9 He hath *d'*, he hath given to the
Pr 5:16 Let thy fountains be *d'* abroad,
Isa 11:12 gather together the *d'* of Judah
Eze 36:19 were *d'* through the countries:
Zep 3:10 the daughter of my *d'*, shall bring
Joh 7:35 unto the *d'* among the Gentiles?
Ac 5:37 as many as obeyed him, were *d'*.
2Co 9: 9 He hath *d'* abroad; he hath given

dispersions
Jer 25:34 of your slaughter and of your *d'*

displayed
Ps 60: 4 may be *d'* because of the truth.

displease See also DISPLEASED.
Ge 31:35 Let it not *d'* my lord that I cannot
Nu 22:34 *d'* thee, I will get me back
1Sa 29: 7 thou *d'* not the lords of the
2Sa 11:25 Let not this thing *d'* thee, for
Pr 24:18 the Lord see it, and it *d'* him,

displeased^
Ge 38:10 which he did *d'* the Lord:
48:17 And when Joseph...it *d'* him:
Nu 11: 1 complained, it *d'* the Lord:
1Sa 8: 6 But the thing *d'* Samuel,
18: 8 and the saying *d'* him; and he
2Sa 6: 8 And David was *d'*, because the
11:27 thing that David had done *d'*
1Ki 1: 6 his father had not *d'* him at any
20:43 went to his house heavy and *d'*,
21: 4 came into his house heavy and *d'*
1Ch 13:11 And David was *d'*, because the
21: 7 God was *d'* with this thing;
Ps 60: 1 thou hast been *d'*; O turn thyself
Isa 59:15 it *d'* him that there was no
Da 6:14 was sore *d'* with himself, and set
Jon 4: 1 But it *d'* Jonah exceedingly,
Hab 3: 8 the Lord *d'* against the rivers?
Zec 1: 2 The Lord hath been sore *d'* with
15 I am very sore *d'* with the heathen
15 at ease: for I was but a little *d'*,
M't 21:15 son of David; they were sore *d'*,
M'r 10:14 Jesus saw it, he was much *d'*,
41 began to be much *d'* with James
Ac 12:20 Herod was highly *d'* with them of

displeasure
De 9:19 was afraid of the anger and hot *d'*,
J'g 15: 3 though I do them a *d'*.
Ps 2: 5 and vex them in his sore *d'*.
6: 1 neither chasten me in thy hot *d'*.
38: 1 neither chasten me in thy hot *d'*.

disposed
Job 34:13 who hath *d'* the whole world?
37:15 thou know when God *d'* them,
Ac 18:27 he was *d'* to pass into Achaia,
1Co 10:27 you to a feast, and ye be *d'* to go;

disposing
Pr 16:33 the whole *d'* thereof is of the Lord.

disposition
Ac 7:53 the law by the *d'* of angels,

dispossess See also DISPOSSESSED.
Nu 33:53 And ye shall *d'* the inhabitants
De 7:17 more than I; how can I *d'* them?

dispossessed
Nu 32:39 and *d'* the Amorite which was
J'g 11:23 God of Israel hath *d'* the Amorites

disputation See also DISPUTATIONS.
Ac 15: 2 no small dissension and *d'* with

disputations
Ro 14: 1 receive ye, but not to doubtful *d'*.

dispute See also DISPUTED; DISPUTING.
Job 23: 7 the righteous might *d'* with him;

disputed
M'r 9:33 that ye *d'* among yourselves by
34 they had *d'* among themselves,
Ac 9:29 and *d'* against the Grecians:
17:17 *d'* he in the synagogue with the
Jude 9 he *d'* about the body of Moses,

disputer
1Co 1:20 where is the *d'* of this world?

disputing See also DISPUTINGS.
Ac 6: 9 and of Asia, *d'* with Stephen.

Ac 15: 7 when there had been much *d'*,
19: 8 three months, *d'* and persuading
9 *d'* daily in the school of one
24:12 me in the temple *d'* with any man,

disputings
Ph'p 2:14 without murmurings and *d'*:
1Ti 6: 5 Perverse *d'* of men of corrupt

disquiet See also DISQUIETED.
Jer 50:34 and *d'* the inhabitants of Babylon.

disquieted
1Sa 28:15 Why hast thou *d'* me, to bring me
Ps 39: 6 shew: surely they are *d'* in vain:
42: 5 and why art thou *d'* in me? hope
11 why art thou *d'* within me? hope
43: 5 why art thou *d'* within me? hope
Pr 30:21 For three things the earth is *d'*,

disquietness
Ps 38: 8 I have roared by reason of the *d'*

dissembled See also DISSEMBLETH.
Jos 7:11 and have also stolen, and *d'* also,
Jer 42:20 For ye *d'* in your hearts, when ye
Ga 2:13 other Jews *d'* likewise with him;

dissemblers
Ps 26: 4 neither will I go in with *d'*.

dissembleth
Pr 26:24 he that hateth *d'* with his lips,

dissension
Ac 15: 2 had no small *d'* and disputation
23: 7 a *d'* between the Pharisees and the
10 And when there arose a great *d'*,

dissimulation
Ro 12: 9 Let love be without *d'*. Abhor
Ga 2:13 was carried away with their *d'*.

dissolve See also DISSOLVED; DISSOLVEST; DISSOLVING.
Da 5:16 interpretations, and *d'* doubts:

dissolved
Ps 75: 3 the inhabitants therefore are *d'*:
Isa 14:31 thou, whole Palestina, art *d'*:
24:19 the earth is clean *d'*, the earth
34: 4 all the host of heaven shall be *d'*,
Na 2: 6 and the palace shall be *d'*.
2Co 5: 1 house of this tabernacle were *d'*,
2Pe 3:11 that all these things shall be *d'*,
12 heavens being on fire shall be *d'*,

dissolvest
Job 30:22 upon it, and *d'* my substance.

dissolving
Da 5:12 hard sentences, and *d'* of doubts,

distaff
Pr 31:19 and her hands hold the *d'*.

distant
Ex 36:22 equally *d'* one from another:

distil
De 32: 2 my speech shall *d'* as the dew,
Job 36:28 clouds do drop and *d'* upon man

distinction
1Co 14: 7 they give a *d'* in the sounds,

distinctly
Ne 8: 8 in the book in the law of God *d'*,

distracted
Ps 88:15 while I suffer thy terrors I am *d'*.

distraction
1Co 7:35 attend upon the Lord without *d'*.

distress See also DISTRESSED; DISTRESSES.
Ge 35: 3 answered me in the day of my *d'*,
42:21 therefore is this *d'* come upon us.
De 2: 9 *D'* not the Moabites, neither
19 Ammon, *d'* them not, nor meddle
28:53 thine enemies shall *d'* thee:
55 thine enemies shall *d'* thee in all
57 enemy shall *d'* thee in thy gates.
J'g 11: 7 unto me now when ye are in *d'*?
1Sa 22: 2 And every one that was in *d'*,
2Sa 22: 7 In my *d'* I called upon the Lord,
1Ki 1:29 redeemed my soul out of all *d'*,
2Ch 28:22 And in the time of his *d'* did he
Ne 2:17 Ye see the *d'* that we are in,
9:37 pleasure, and we are in great *d'*.
Ps 4: 1 enlarged me when I was in *d'*;
18: 6 In my *d'* I called upon the Lord,
118: 5 I called upon the Lord in *d'*:
120: 1 In my *d'* I cried unto the Lord,
Pr 1:27 *d'* and anguish cometh upon you.
Isa 25: 4 a strength to the needy in his *d'*,
29: 2 Yet I will *d'* Ariel, and there shall
7 and her munition, and that *d'* her.
Jer 10:18 and will *d'* them, that they may
La 1:20 O Lord; for I am in *d'*: my bowels
Ob 12 spoken proudly in the day of *d'*.
14 that did remain in the day of *d'*.
Zep 1:15 a day of trouble and *d'*, a day of
17 And I will bring *d'* upon men,
Lu 21:23 there shall be great *d'* in the land,
25 and upon the earth *d'* of nations,
Ro 8:35 tribulation, or *d'*, or persecution,
1Co 7:26 this is good for the present *d'*,
1Th 3: 7 our affliction and *d'* by your faith:

distressed
Ge 32: 7 Jacob was greatly afraid and *d'*:
Nu 22: 3 and Moab was *d'* because of the
J'g 2:15 them: and they were greatly *d'*.
10: 9 so that Israel was sore *d'*.
1Sa 13: 6 (for the people were *d'*,) then the
14:24 the men of Israel were *d'* that day:
28:15 And Saul answered, I am sore *d'*;
30: 6 And David was greatly *d'*; for the
2Sa 1:26 I am *d'* for thee, my brother

2Ch 28:20 d' him, but strengthened him not.
2Co 4: 8 troubled on every side, yet not d';

distresses
Ps 25:17 O bring thou me out of my d'.
107: 6 he delivered them out of their d'.
13 he saved them out of their d'.
19 he saveth them out of their d'.
28 he bringeth them out of their d'.
Eze 30:16 and Noph shall have d' daily.
2Co 6: 4 in afflictions, in necessities, in d',
12:10 persecutions, in d' for Christ's sake:

distribute See also DISTRIBUTED; DISTRIBUTETH; DISTRIBUTING.
Jos 13:32 Moses did d' for inheritance in
2Ch 31:14 to d' the oblations of the Lord,
Ne 13:13 was to d' unto their brethren.
Lu 18:22 d' unto the poor, and thou shalt
1Ti 6:18 works, ready to d', willing to

distributed
Jos 14: 1 Israel, d' for inheritance to them.
1Ch 24: 3 David d' them, both Zadok of
2Ch 23:18 whom David had d' in the house of
Joh 6:11 he d' to the disciples, and the
1Co 7:17 as God hath d' to every man,
2Co 10:13 rule which God hath d' to us,

distributeth
Job 21:17 God d' sorrows in his anger.

distributing
Ro 12:13 D' to the necessity of saints;

distribution
Ac 4:35 feet: and d' was made unto every
2Co 9:13 and for your liberal d' unto them,

ditch See also DITCHES.
Job 9:31 Yet shalt thou plunge me in the d',
Ps 7:15 is fallen into the d' which he
Pr 23:27 For a whore is a deep d'; and a
Isa 22:11 Ye made also a d' between the
M't 15:14 blind, both shall fall into the d'
Lu 6:39 they not both fall into the d'?

ditches
2Ki 3:16 Make this valley full of d':

divers See also DIVERSE.
De 22: 9 sow thy vineyard with d' seeds:
11 a garment of d' sorts, as of
25:13 shalt not have in thy bag d' weights,
14 not have in thine house d' measures,
J'g 5:30 to Sisera a prey of d' colours,
30 a prey of d' colours of needlework,
30 of d' colours of needlework
2Sa 13:18 she had a garment of d' colours
19 rent her garment of d' colours
1Ch 29: 2 glistering stones, and of d' colours,
2Ch 16:14 filled with sweet odours and d' kinds
21: 4 and d' also of the princes of Israel.
30:11 d' of Asher and Manasseh and
Ps 78:45 sent d' sorts of flies among them,
105:31 came d' sorts of flies, and lice
Pr 20:10 D' weights, and d' measures,
23 D' weights are an abomination
Ec 5: 7 words there are also d' vanities:
Eze 16:16 thy high places with d' colours,
17: 3 of feathers, which had d' colours,
M't 4:24 with d' diseases and torments,
24: 7 and earthquakes, in d' places.
M'r 1:34 many that were sick of d' diseases,
8: 3 for d' of them came from far.
13: 8 shall be earthquakes in d' places,
Lu 4:40 sick with d' diseases brought
21:11 great earthquakes shall be in d'
Ac 19: 9 But when d' were hardened, and
1Co 12:10 to another d' kind of tongues;
2Ti 3: 6 with sins, led away with d' lusts,
Tit 3: 3 serving d' lusts and pleasures,
Heb 1: 1 times and in d' manners spake in
2: 4 and with d' miracles, and gifts of
9:10 meats and drinks, and d' washings,
13: 9 with d' and strange doctrines.
Jas 1: 2 when ye fall into d' temptations;

diverse See also DIVERS.
Le 19:19 cattle gender with a d' kind:
Es 1: 7 vessels being d' one from another,)
3: 8 their laws are d' from all people;
Da 7: 3 the sea, d' one from another.
7 and it was d' from all the beasts
19 which was d' from all the others,
23 which shall be d' from all kingdoms,
24 and he shall be d' from the first.

diversities
1Co 12: 4 Now there are d' of gifts, but the
6 there are d' of operations, but it
28 helps, governments, d' of tongues.

divide See also DIVIDED; DIVIDETH; DIVIDING.
Ge 1: 6 let it d' the waters from the waters.
14 to d' the day from the night;
18 to d' the light from the darkness:
49: 7 will d' them in Jacob, and scatter
27 at night he shall d' the spoil.
Ex 14:16 thine hand over the sea, and d' it:
15: 9 I will overtake, I will d' the spoil;
21:35 the live ox, and d' the money of it;
35 the dead ox also they shall d'.
26:33 the vail shall d' unto you between
Le 1:17 thereof, but shall not d' it asunder:
5: 8 neck, but shall not d' it asunder:
11: 4 cud, or of them that d' the hoof:
7 the swine, though he d' the hoof,
Nu 31:27 And d' the prey into two parts;
33:54 And ye shall d' the land by lot for
34:17 which shall d' the land unto you:
18 tribe, to d' the land by inheritance.
29 Lord commanded to d' the inheritance
De 14: 7 or of them that d' the cloven hoof;
7 chew the cud, but d' not the hoof;
19: 3 d' the coasts... into three parts,
Jos 1: 6 shalt thou d' for an inheritance
13: 6 d' thou it by lot unto the Israelites
7 d' this land for an inheritance
18: 5 And they shall d' it into seven
22: 8 d' the spoil of your enemies with
2Sa 19:29 said, Thou and Ziba d' the land.
1Ki 3:25 D' the living child in two, and
26 be neither mine nor thine, but d' it.
Ne 9:11 thou didst d' the sea before them,
22 and didst d' them into corners:
Job 27:17 and the innocent shall d' the silver.
Ps 55: 9 Destroy, O Lord, and d' their
60: 6 I will d' Shechem, and mete out
74:13 Thou didst d' the sea by thy
108: 7 will rejoice, I will d' Shechem, and
Pr 16:19 than to d' the spoil with the proud.
Isa 9: 3 rejoice when they d' the spoil.
53:12 Therefore will I d' him a portion
12 he shall d' the spoil with the strong;
Eze 5: 1 balances to weigh, and d' the hair.
45: 1 Moreover, when ye shall d' by lot
47:21 So shall ye d' this land unto you
22 shall d' it by lot for an inheritance
48:29 ye shall d' by lot unto the tribes
Da 11:39 and shall d' the land for gain.
Lu 12:13 that he d' the inheritance with me.
22:17 Take this, and d' it among

divided
Ge 1: 4 God d' the light from the darkness.
7 and d' the waters which were under
10: 5 were the isles of the Gentiles d'
25 in his days was the earth d';
32 by these were the nations d' in the
14:15 And he d' himself against them,
15:10 and d' them in the midst, and laid
10 another: but the birds d' he not.
32: 7 and he d' the people that was with
33: 1 And he d' the children unto Leah,
Ex 14:21 dry land, and the waters were d'.
Nu 26:53 Unto these the land shall be d'
55 the land shall be d' by lot:
56 shall the possession thereof be d'
31:42 which Moses d' from the men that
De 4:19 which the Lord thy God hath d'
32: 8 d' to the nations their inheritance,
Jos 14: 5 Israel did, and they d' the land.
18:10 there Joshua d' the land unto the
19:51 d' for an inheritance by lot in
23: 4 I have d' unto you by lot
J'g 5:30 have they not d' the prey; to
7:16 And he d' the three hundred men
9:43 and d' them into three companies,
19:29 and d' her, together with her
2Sa 1:23 in their death they were not d':
1Ki 16:21 Then were the people of Israel d'
18: 6 So they d' the land between them
2Ki 2: 8 they were d' hither and thither,
1Ch 1:19 in his days the earth was d':
23: 6 And David d' them into courses
24: 4 of Ithamar; and thus were they d'.
5 Thus were they d' by lot, one sort
2Ch 35:13 and d' them speedily among all
Job 38:25 Who hath d' a watercourse for the
Ps 68:12 that tarried at home d' the spoil.
78:13 He d' the sea, and caused them
55 and d' them an inheritance by
136:13 To him which d' the Red sea into
Isa 33:23 is the prey of a great spoil d';
34:17 his hand hath d' it unto them by
51:15 the Lord thy God, that d' the sea,
La 4:16 anger of the Lord hath d' them;
Eze 37:22 neither shall they be d' into two
Da 2:41 of iron, the kingdom shall be d';
5:28 Thy kingdom is d', and given
11: 4 and shall be d' toward the four
Ho 10: 2 Their heart is d'; now shall they
Am 7:17 and thy land shall be d' by line;
Mic 2: 4 away he hath d' our fields.
Zec 14: 1 and thy spoil shall be d' in the
M't 12:25 Every kingdom d' against itself is
25 city or house d' against itself
26 Satan, he is d' against himself;
M'r 3:24 if a kingdom be d' against itself,
25 if a house be d' against itself,
26 and be d', he cannot stand, but hath
6:41 the two fishes d' he among them all.
Lu 11:17 Every kingdom d' against itself is
17 house d' against a house falleth
18 If Satan also be d' against himself,
12:52 there shall be five in one house d',
53 father shall be d' against the son,
15:12 And he d' unto them his living.
Ac 13:19 he d' their land to them by lot.
14: 4 the multitude of the city was d':
23: 7 and the multitude was d'.
1Co 1:13 Is Christ d'? was Paul crucified
Re 16:19 the great city was d' into three

divider
Lu 12:14 made me a judge or a d' over you?

divideth
Le 11: 4, 5 the cud; but d' not the hoof;
6 the cud, but d' not the hoof;
26 every beast which d' the hoof,
De 14: 8 the swine, because it d' the hoof,
Job 26:12 He d' the sea with his power,
Ps 29: 7 the Lord d' the flames of fire.
Jer 31:35 which d' the sea when the waves
M't 25:32 as a shepherd d' his sheep from
Lu 11:22 he trusted, and d' his spoils.

dividing
Jos 19:49 end of d' the land for inheritance
51 made an end of d' the country.
Isa 63:12 d' the water before them, to
Da 7:25 a time and times and the d' of
1Co 12:11 d' to every man severally as he
2Ti 2:15 rightly d' the word of truth.
Heb 4:12 even to the d' asunder of soul and

divination See also DIVINATIONS.
Nu 22: 7 with the rewards of d' in their
23:23 is there any d' against Israel:
De 18:10 or that useth d', or an observer
2Ki 17:17 used d' and enchantments, and
Jer 14:14 a false vision and d', and a thing
Eze 12:24 vain vision nor flattering d' within
13: 6 vanity and lying d', saying, The
7 have ye not spoken a lying d',
21:21 head of the two ways, to use d':
22 hand was the d' for Jerusalem,
23 be unto them as a false d' in their
Ac 16:16 possessed with a spirit of d' met us,

divinations
Eze 13:23 see no more vanity, nor divine d':

divine See also DIVINETH; DIVINING.
Ge 44:15 such a man as I can certainly d'?
1Sa 28: 8 d' unto me by the familiar spirit,
Pr 16:10 A d' sentence is in the lips of the
Eze 13: 9 that see vanity, and that d' lies:
23 no more vanity, nor d' divinations
21:29 whiles they d' a lie unto thee,
Mic 3: 6 unto you, that ye shall not d';
11 the prophets thereof d' for money:
Heb 9: 1 had also ordinances of d' service,
2Pe 1: 3 According as his d' power hath
4 might be partakers of the d' nature,

diviners
De 18:14 observers of times, and unto d':
1Sa 6: 2 called for the priests and the d',
Isa 44:25 of the liars, and maketh d' mad;
Jer 27: 9 to your d', nor to your dreamers,
29: 8 Let not your prophets and your d',
Mic 3: 7 ashamed, and the d' confounded:
Zec 10: 2 and the d' have seen a lie,

divineth
Ge 44: 5 and whereby indeed he d'?

divining
Eze 22:28 seeing vanity, and d' lies unto

division See also DIVISIONS.
Ex 8:23 I will put a d' between my people
2Ch 35: 5 and after the d' of the families
Lu 12:51 I tell you, Nay; but rather d':
Joh 7:43 there was a d' among the people
9:16 there was a d' among them.
10:19 There was a d' therefore again

divisions
Jos 11:23 to their d' by their tribes.
12: 7 a possession according to their d';
18:10 of Israel according to their d'.
J'g 5:15 For the d' of Reuben... thoughts
16 the d' of Reuben... searchings
1Ch 24: 1 are the d' of the sons of Aaron.
26: 1 Concerning the d' of the porters:
12 these were the d' of the porters,
19 These are the d' of the porters
2Ch 35: 5 according to the d' of the families
12 according to the d' of the families
Ezr 6:18 they set the priests in their d',
Ne 11:36 of the Levites were d' in Judah.
Ro 16:17 them which cause d' and offences
1Co 1:10 that there be no d' among you;
3: 3 you envying, and strife, and d',
11:18 hear that there be d' among you;

divorce See also DIVORCED; DIVORCEMENT.
Jer 3: 8 away, and given her a bill of d';

divorced
Le 21:14 widow, or a d' woman, or profane,
22:13 priest's daughter be a widow, or d',
Nu 30: 9 of a widow, and of her that is d',
M't 5:32 her that is d' committeth adultery.

divorcement
De 24: 1 then let him write her a bill of d',
3 hate her, and write her a bill of d',
Isa 50: 1 Where is the bill of your mother's d',
M't 5:31 let him give her a writing of d':
19: 7 command to give a writing of d',
M'r 10: 4 Moses suffered to write a bill of d',

Dizahab (*diz'-a-hab*)
De 1: 1 and Laban, and Hazeroth, and D'.

do See also ADO; DID; DOEST; DOETH; DOING; DONE; UNDO.
Ge 6:17 I, even I, d' bring a flood of waters
9:13 I d' set my bow in the cloud, and it
11: 6 and this they begin to d': and now
6 which they have imagined to d'.
16: 6 hand; d' to her as it pleaseth thee.
18: 5 they said, So d', as thou hast said.
17 Abraham that thing which I d';
19 Lord, to d' justice and judgment;
25 from thee to d' after this manner,
25 the Judge of all the earth d' right?
29 said, I will not d' it for forty's sake.
30 I will not d' it, if I find thirty there.
19: 7 you, brethren, d' not so wickedly.
8 you, and d' ye to them as is good
8 only unto these men d' nothing;
22 for I cannot d' any thing till thou
21:23 thou shalt d' unto me, and to the
22:12 the lad, neither d' thou any thing
24:42 thou d' prosper my way which I go:
25:32 profit shall this birthright d' to me?
26:29 That thou wilt d' us no hurt, as
27:37 and what shall I d' now unto thee,
46 what good shall my life d' me?
30:31 if thou wilt d' this thing for me, I

Ge 31:16 God hath said unto thee, d'.
29 power of my hand to d' you hurt:
43 and what can I d' this day unto
32:12 saidst, I will surely d' thee good,
34:14 We cannot d' this thing, to give
19 man deferred not to d' the thing,
37:13 D' not thy brethren feed the flock in
39: 9 can I d' this great wickedness,
11 into the house to d' his business;
40: 8 D' not interpretations belong to God?
41: 9 I d' remember my faults this day:
25 Pharaoh what he is about to d'.
28 to d' he sheweth unto Pharaoh.
34 Let Pharaoh d' this, and let him
55 Joseph; what he saith to you, d'.
42: 1 Why d' ye look one upon another?
18 This d', and live; for I fear God:
22 D' not sin against the child;
43:11 so now, d' this; take of the best
44: 7 thy servants should d' according
17 said, God forbid that I should d' so:
45:17 Say unto your brethren, This d' ye;
19 thou art commanded, this d' ye;
47:30 he said, I will d' as thou hast said.
Ex 1:16 When ye d' the office of a midwife to
3:20 I will d' in the midst thereof:
4:15 will teach you what ye shall d'.
17 wherewith thou shalt d' signs.
21 d' all those wonders before Pharaoh,
5: 4 Wherefore d' ye, Moses and Aaron,
17 Let us go and d' sacrifice to the
6: 1 see what I will d' to Pharaoh:
8: 8 may d' sacrifice unto the Lord.
26 Moses said, It is not meet so to d';
9: 5 To morrow the Lord shall d' this
15:26 d' that which is right in his sight,
17: 2 wherefore d' ye tempt the Lord?
4 What shall I d' unto this people?
18:16 d' make them know the statutes
20 and the work that they must d'.
23 If thou shalt d' this thing, and God
19: 8 the Lord hath spoken we will d'.
20: 9 thou labour, and d' all thy work:
10 in it thou shalt not d' any work,
21: 7 not go out as the menservants d'.
11 if he d' not these three unto her,
22:30 shalt thou d' with thine oxen, and
23: 2 shalt not follow a multitude to d' evil;
12 Six days thou shalt d' thy work,
22 his voice, and d' all that I speak;
24 them, nor d' after their works:
24: 3 which the Lord hath said will we d'.
7 that the Lord hath said will we d',
14 any man have any matters to d',
29: 1 is the thing that thou shalt d' unto
35 And thus shalt thou d' unto Aaron,
41 shalt d' according to the meat
31:11 commanded thee shall they d'.
32:14 he thought to d' unto his people.
18 the noise of them that sing d' I hear.
33: 5 may know what to d' unto thee.
17 I will d' this thing also that thou
34:10 all thy people I will d' marvels,
10 thing that I will d' with thee.
15 gods, and d' sacrifice unto their gods,
35: 1 commanded, that ye should d'
19 to d' service in the holy place,
35 weaver, even of them that d' any
36: 2 up to come unto the work to d' it:
39: 1, 41 to d' service in the holy place,
Le 4: 2 and shall d' against any of them:
3 that is anointed d' sin according
20 And he shall d' with the bullock
20 offering, so shall he d' with this:
5: 1 if he d' not utter it, then he shall
4 his lips to d' evil, or to d' good,
8:34 the Lord hath commanded to d',
9: 6 commanded that ye should d':
10: 9 D' not drink wine nor strong
16:15 and d' with that blood as he did
16 so shall he d' for the tabernacle
29 souls, and d' no work at all,
18: 3 wherein ye dwelt, shall ye not d':
3 whither I bring you, shall ye not d':
4 Ye shall d' my judgments, and
5 if a man d', he shall live in them:
25 therefore I d' visit the iniquity
19:15 Ye shall d' no unrighteousness in
29 D' not prostitute thy daughter,
35 Ye shall d' no unrighteousness in
37 judgments, and d' them: I am the
20: 4 d' any ways hide their eyes from
8 keep my statutes, and d' them:
22 all my judgments, and d' them:
21: 6 the bread of their God, they d' offer:
15 for I the Lord d' sanctify him.
23 for I the Lord d' sanctify them.
22: 9 it: I the Lord d' sanctify them.
16 for I the Lord d' sanctify them.
31 my commandments, and d' them:
28: 3 ye shall d' no work therein:
7 ye shall d' no servile work therein.
8 ye shall d' no servile work
21 ye shall d' no servile work therein:
25 Ye shall d' no servile work therein:
28 shall d' no work in that same day:
31 Ye shall d' no manner of work: it
35 ye shall d' no servile work therein.
36 and ye shall d' no servile work
25:18 Wherefore ye shall d' my statutes,
18 keep my judgments, and d' them;
45 strangers that d' sojourn among you,
26: 3 my commandments, and d' them;
14 not d' all these commandments;
15 will not d' all my commandments,
16 I also will d' this unto you; I will

Le 27:11 of which they d' not offer a sacrifice
Nu 2: 5 those that d' pitch next unto him
3: 7 congregation, to d' the service of
8 of Israel, to d' the service of the
4: 3 to d' the work in the tabernacle of
19 d' unto them, that they may live,
23 the service, to d' the work in the
30 the service, to d' the work of the
37, 41 d' service in the tabernacle
47 to d' the service of the ministry,
5: 6 to d' a trespass against the Lord,
6:21 d' after the law of his separation.
7: 5 to d' the service of the tabernacle
8: 7 And thus shalt thou d' unto them,
15 the Levites go in to d' the service
19 to d' the service of the children of
22 Levites in to d' their service
26 the charge, and shall d' no service.
26 Thus shalt thou d' unto the
9:14 the manner thereof, so shall ye d':
10:29 with us, and we will d' thee good:
32 goodness the Lord shall d' unto us,
32 the same will we d' unto thee.
11:27 and Medad d' prophesy in the camp.
14:28 in mine ears, so will I d' to you:
35 will surely d' it unto all this evil
41 Wherefore d' ye now transgress
15:12 shall ye d' to every one according
13 of the country shall d' these things
14 as ye d', so he shall d'.
20 ye d' the heave offering of the
39 of the Lord, and d' them;
40 and d' all my commandments,
16: 6 This d'; Take you censers, Korah,
9 near to himself to d' the service
28 sent me to d' all these works;
18: 6 gift for the Lord, to d' the service
23 But the Levites shall d' the service
21:34 d' to him as thou didst unto Sihon
22:17 d' whatsoever thou sayest unto me:
18 Lord my God, to d' less or more.
20 say unto thee, that shalt thou d'.
30 was I ever wont to d' so unto thee?
23:19 he said, and shall he not d' it?
26 the Lord speaketh, that I must d'?
24:13 d' either good or bad of mine own
14 thee what this people shall d'
18 and Israel shall d' valiantly.
28:18 shall d' no manner of servile work
25 ye shall d' no servile work.
26 ye shall d' no servile work:
29: 1 ye shall d' no servile work: it is a
7 ye shall not d' any work therein:
12 ye shall d' no servile work, and ye
35 ye shall d' no servile work therein:
39 things ye shall d' unto the Lord
30: 2 he shall d' according to all that
32:20 If ye will d' this thing, if ye will
23 But if ye will not d' so, behold, ye
24 and d' that which hath proceeded
25 Thy servants will d' as my lord
31 unto thy servants, so will we d'.
33:56 shall d' unto you, as I thought to d'
De 1:14 hast spoken is good for us to d'.
18 all the things which ye should d'.
44 you, and chased you, as bees d',
3: 2 thou shalt d' unto him as thou
21 so shall the Lord d' unto all the
24 or in earth, that can d' according
4: 1 which I teach you, for to d' them,
5 that ye should d' so in the land
6 Keep therefore and d' them; for
14 that ye might d' them in the land
25 shall d' evil in the sight of the Lord
5: 1 learn them, and keep, and d' them.
13 Six days thou shall labour, and d'
14 in it thou shalt not d' any work,
27 and we will hear it, and d' it.
31 teach them, that they may d' them
32 Ye shall observe to d' therefore as
6: 1 to teach you, that ye might d' them
3 O Israel, and observe to d' it;
18 And thou shalt d' that which is
24 Lord commanded us to d' all these
25 if we observe to d' all these
7:11 I command thee this day, to d' them.
12 and keep, and d' them, that the
19 shall the Lord thy God d' unto all
8: 1 shall ye observe to d', that ye may
16 prove thee, to d' thee good at thy
19 if thou d' at all forget the Lord
11:22 to d' them, to love the Lord your
32 And ye shall observe to d' all the
12: 1 which ye shall observe to d' in the
4 Ye shall not d' so unto the Lord
8 not d' after all the things that we d'
14 and there thou shalt d' all that I
25 d' that which is right in the sight
30 serve their gods? even so will I d'
31 Thou shalt not d' so unto the Lord
32 I command you, observe to d' it:
13:11 and shall d' no more any such
18 d' that which is right in the sight
15: 5 to observe to d' all these
17 maidservant thou shalt d' likewise.
19 shalt d' no work with the firstling
16: 8 Lord thy God: thou shalt d' no
12 and thou shalt observe and d'
17:10 And thou shalt d' according to the
10 to d' according to all that they
11 they shall tell thee, thou shalt d':
12 man that will d' presumptuously,
13 and d' no more presumptuously.
18: 7 as all his brethren the Levites d',
9 shalt not learn to d' after the
12 all that d' these things are an

De 18:14 God hath not suffered thee so to d'.
19: 9 to d' them, which I command
19 Then shall ye d' unto him, as he
20: 3 fear not, and d' not tremble,
15 Thus shalt thou d' unto all the
18 That they teach you not to d' after
21: 9 when thou shalt d' that which is
22: 3 d' with his ass; and so shalt thou d'
3 hast found, shalt thou d' likewise:
5 all that d' so are an abomination
24: 8 and d' according to all that the
8 them, so ye shall observe to d'.
18, 22 therefore I command thee to d'
25:16 For all that d' such things, and all
16 all that d' unrighteously, are an
26:16 hath commanded thee to d' these
16 thou shalt therefore keep and d'
27:10 and d' his commandments and his
26 not all the words of this law to d'
28: 1 thy God, to observe and to d' all his
13 thee this day, to observe and to d'
15 thy God, to observe to d' all his
20 settest thine hand unto for to d',
58 If thou wilt not observe to d' all the
63 rejoiced over you to d' you good,
29: 9 this covenant, and d' them, that
9 ye may prosper in all that ye d'.
14 Neither with you only d' I make this
29 that we may d' all the words of
30: 5 and he will d' thee good, and
8 and d' all his commandments
12, 13 that we may hear it, and d' it?
14 thy heart, that thou mayest d' it.
31: 4 And the Lord shall d' unto them as
5 that ye may d' unto them according
12 and observe to d' all the words of
29 ye will d' evil in the sight of the
32: 6 D' ye thus requite the Lord,
46 your children to observe to d',
34:11 the Lord sent him to d' in the land
Jos 1: 2 the land which I d' give to them,
7 to d' according to all the law,
8 to d' according to all that is written
16 thou commandest us we will d',
2:24 the country d' faint because of us.
3: 5 morrow the Lord will d' wonders
6: 3 Thus shalt thou d' six days.
7: 9 what wilt thou d' unto thy great
8: 2 And thou shalt d' to Ai and her king
8 of the Lord shall ye d'.
9:20 This we will d' to them: we will
25 right unto thee to d' unto us, d'.
10:25 thus shall the Lord d' to all your
22: 5 take diligent heed to d' the
24 What have ye to d' with the Lord
27 that we might d' the service of the
23: 6 courageous to keep and to d' all
12 Else if ye d' in any wise go back,
24:13 which ye planted not d' ye eat.
20 will turn and d' you hurt, and consume
J'g 6:27 of the city, that he could not d'
7:17 unto them, Look on me, and d'
17 it shall be that, as I d', so shall ye d'.
8: 3 was I able to d' in comparison of
9:33 thou d' to them as thou shalt find
48 What ye have seen me d', make
48 make haste, and d' as I have done.
10:15 d' thou unto us whatsoever seemeth
11:10 if we d' not so according to thy
12 What hast thou to d' with me, that
36 unto the Lord, d' to me according
13: 8 teach us what we shall d' unto the
12 child, and how shall we d' unto
17 come to pass we may d' thee honour?
14:10 for so used the young men to d'.
15: 3 Philistines, though I d' them a
10 come up, to d' to him as he hath
17:13 know I that the Lord will d' me good.
18:14 D' ye know that there is in these
14 consider what ye have to d'
18 the priest unto them, What d' ye?
19:23 nay, I pray you, d' not so wickedly:
23 into mine house, d' not this folly.
24 d' with them what seemeth good
24 but unto this man d' not so vile a
20: 9 the thing which we will d' to
10 that they may d', when they come
21: 7 How shall we d' for wives for them
11 this is the thing that ye shall d',
16 How shall we d' for wives for them
Ru 1:17 the Lord d' so to me, and more also,
2: 9 eyes be on the field that they d' reap,
3: 4 he will tell thee what thou shalt d'.
5 All thou sayest unto me I will d'.
11 I will d' for thee all that thou
13 well; let him d' the kinsman's part:
13 but if he will not d' the part of a
13 will I d' the part of a kinsman to
4:11 and d' thou worthily in Ephratah,
1Sa 1:23 said unto her, D' what seemeth
2:23 he said unto them, Why d' ye such
35 priest, that shall d' according to
3:11 Behold, I will d' a thing in Israel,
17 God d' so to thee, and more also, if
18 let him d' what seemeth him good.
5: 8 What shall we d' with the ark of the
6: 2 What shall we d' to the ark of the
6 Wherefore then d' ye harden your
7: 3 If ye d' return unto the Lord with
8: 8 served other gods, so d' they also
10: 2 you, saying, What shall I d' for my
7 that thou d' as occasion serve thee;
8 and shew thee what thou shalt d'.
11:10 ye shall d' with us all that seemeth
12:16 which the Lord will d' before your
25 But if ye shall still d' wickedly, ye

1Sa 14: 7 said unto him, D' all that is in
36 D' whatsoever seemeth good unto
40 unto Saul, D' what seemeth good
44 And Saul answered, God d' so and
16: 3 will shew thee what thou shalt d':
20: 2 my father will d' nothing either
4 thy soul desireth, I will even d' it
13 The Lord d' so and much more to
13 if it please my father to d' thee evil,
30 d' not I know that thou hast
22: 3 till I know what God will d' for me.
24: 4 that thou mayest d' to him as it
6 Lord forbid that I should d' this
25:17 and consider what thou wilt d';
22 So and more also d' God unto the
26:21 I will no more d' thee harm, because
25 David: thou shalt both d' great
28: 2 shalt know what thy servant can d'.
15 known unto me what I shall d'.
29: 3 the Philistines, What d' these Hebrews
30:23 Ye shall not d' so, my brethren,
2Sa 3: 8 which against Judah d' shew
9 So d' God to Abner, and more
9 sworn to David, even so I d' to him;
18 Now then d' it: for the Lord hath
35 So d' God to me, and more also, if
7: 3 Nathan said to the king, Go, d' all
23 to make him a name, and to d' for
25 establish it for ever, and d' as thou
9:11 his servant, so shall thy servant d'.
10:12 Lord d' that which seemeth him
11:11 soul liveth, I will not d' this thing.
12: 9 commandment of the Lord, to d'
12 but I will d' this thing before all
13: 2 thought it hard for him to d' any
12 in Israel: d' not thou this folly.
15: 4 unto me, and I would d' him justice!
5 nigh to him to d' him obeisance,
15 thy servants are ready to d'
26 let him d' to me as seemeth good
16:10 What have I to d' with you, ye sons of
11 more now may this Benjamite d' it?
20 among you what we shall d'.
17: 6 shall we d' after his saying? if not,
18: 4 What seemeth you best I will d'.
32 rise against thee to d' thee hurt, be as
19:13 God d' so to me, and more also, if
18 and to d' what he thought good.
19 neither d' thou remember that which
22 What have I to d' with you, ye sons of
22 for d' not I know that I am this day
27 d' therefore what is good in thine
37 and d' to him what shall seem
38 will d' to him that which shall seem
38 shalt require of me, that will I d'
20: 6 the son of Bichri d' us more harm
17 And he answered, I d' hear.
21: 3 What shall I d' for you? and
4 ye shall say, that will I d' for you.
23:17 that I should d' this: is not this the
24:12 of them, that I may d' it unto thee.
1Ki 1:30 even so will I certainly d' this day.
2: 6 D' therefore according to thy
9 knowest what thou oughtest to d'
23 God d' so to me, and more also, if
31 the king said unto him, D' as he
38 hath said, so will thy servant d'.
3:28 wisdom of God was in him, to d'
5: 8 and I will d' all thy desire
8:32 Then hear thou in heaven, and d',
39 and forgive, and d', and give to
43 and d' according to all that the
43 fear thee, as d' thy people Israel;
9: 1 which he was pleased to d', That
4 to d' according to all that I have
10: 9 made he thee king, to d' judgment
11:12 I will not d' it for David thy
33 have not walked in my ways, to d'
38 and d' that is right in my sight, to
12: 6 d' ye advise that I may answer
27 If this people go up to d' sacrifice
14: 8 to d' that only which was right in
17:13 go and d' as thou hast said: but
18 What have I to d' with thee, O thou
18:34 And he said, D' it the second time.
34 And he said, D' it the third time.
19: 2 So let the gods d' to me, and more
20: 9 I will d': but this thing I may not d'.
10 The gods d' so unto me, and more
24 And d' this thing, Take the kings
22:22 prevail also: go forth, and d' so.
2Ki 2: 9 Ask what I shall d' for thee, before
3:13 What have I to d' with thee? get
4: 2 What shall I d' for thee? tell me,
16 thou man of God, d' not lie unto thine
28 did I not say, D' not deceive me?
5:13 the prophet had bid thee d' some
6:15 Alas, my master! how shall we d'?
27 And he said, If the Lord d' not help
31 God d' so and more also to me, if
7: 9 We d' not well: this day is a day of
8:12 the evil that thou wilt d' unto the
13 servant a dog, that he should d'
9:18, 19 What hast thou to d' with peace?
10: 5 and will d' all that thou shalt bid
5 d' thou that which is good in thine
19 I have a great sacrifice to d' to Baal:
11: 5 This is the thing that ye shall d';
17:12 said unto them, Ye shall not d' this
15 that they should not d' like them.
17 sold themselves to d' evil in the
34 Unto this day they d' after the
34 they fear not the Lord, neither d'
36 and to him shall ye d' sacrifice,
37 shall observe to d' for evermore;
41 so d' they unto this day.

2Ki 18:12 would not hear them, nor d' them.
19:31 of the Lord of hosts shall d' this.
20: 9 that the Lord will d' the thing that
21: 8 observe to d' according to all that
9 seduced them to d' more evil than
22: 9 hand of them that d' the work,
13 this book, to d' according unto all
1Ch 11:19 that I should d' this thing: shall I
12:32 to know what Israel ought to d';
13: 4 said that they would d' so: for
16:21 He suffered no man to d' them wrong:
22 anointed, and d' my prophets no harm.
40 d' according to all that is written
17: 2 D' all that is in thine heart; for
23 for ever, and d' as thou hast said.
19:13 the Lord d' that which is good in
21: 8 thee, d' away the iniquity of thy
10 them, that I may d' it unto thee.
23 let my lord the king d' that which
28: 7 constant to d' my commandments
10 sanctuary: be strong, and d' it.
20 and of good courage, and d' it:
29:19 and to d' all these things, and to
2Ch 6:23 hear thou from heaven, and d',
33 and d' according to all that the
7:17 d' according to all that I have
9: 8 king over them, to d' judgment
14: 4 d' the law and the commandment.
18:21 also prevail: go out, and d' even so.
19: 6 Take heed what ye d': for ye judge
7 be upon you; take heed and d' it:
9 shall ye d' in the fear of the Lord,
10 this d', and ye shall not trespass.
20:12 neither know we what to d':
22: 3 was his counseller to d' wickedly.
23: 4 This is the thing that ye shall d';
25: 8 But if thou wilt go, d' it, be strong
9 shall we d' for the hundred talents
30:12 one heart to d' the commandment
32:10 Whereon d' ye trust, that ye abide
33: 8 will take heed to d' all that I have
9 and to d' worse than the heathen,
34:16 to thy servants, they d' it.
21 d' after all that is written in this
35: 6 they may d' according to the word
21 What have I to d' with thee, thou king
Ezr 4: 2 for we seek your God, as ye d';
2 we d' sacrifice unto him since the
3 Ye have nothing to d' with us
22 now that ye fail not to d' this:
6: 8 what ye shall d' to the elders of
7:10 and to d' it, and to teach in Israel
18 to d' with the rest of the silver
18 that d' after the will of your God.
21 I Artaxerxes the king, d' make
26 whosoever will not d' the law of
10: 4 be of good courage, and d' it.
5 should d' according to this word.
11 your fathers, and d' his pleasure:
12 As thou hast said, so must we d'.
Ne 1: 9 my commandments, and d' them;
2:12 in my heart to d' at Jerusalem:
19 What is this thing that ye d'?
4: 2 What d' these feeble Jews?
5: 9 I said, It is not good that ye d':
12 them; so will we d' as thou sayest.
12 should d' according to this promise.
6: 2 they thought to d' me mischief.
13 should be afraid, and d' so, and sin,
9:24 might d' with them as they would.
29 which if a man d', he shall live in
10:29 and d' all the commandments of
13:17 What evil thing is this that ye d',
21 d' so again, I will lay hands on you.
27 hearken unto you to d' all this
Es 1: 8 should d' according to every man's
15 shall we d' unto the queen Vashti
3:11 to d' with them as it seemeth good
4:11 of the king's provinces, d' know, that
5: 5 he may d' as Esther hath said.
8 d' to morrow as the king hath said.
6: 6 the king delight to d' honour more
10 said, and d' even so to Mordecai
7: 5 presume in his heart to d' so?
9:13 in Shushan to d' to morrow also
23 undertook to d' as they had begun,
Job 6: 4 terrors of God d' set themselves in
26 D' ye imagine to reprove words,
7:20 what shall I d' unto thee, O thou
9:13 proud helpers d' stoop under him.
10: 2 D' not condemn me; shew me
11: 8 as heaven; what canst thou d'?
13: 2 ye know, the same d' I know also:
9 another, d' ye so mock him?
10 if ye d' secretly accept persons.
14 Wherefore d' I take my flesh in
20 Only d' not two things unto me:
15: 3 wherewith he can d' no good?
12 and what d' thy eyes wink at,
16: 4 I also could speak as ye d':
17:10 all, d' ye return, and come now:
19:22 Why d' ye persecute me as God,
20: 2 Therefore d' my thoughts cause me
21: 7 Wherefore d' the wicked live, become
29 and d' ye not know their tokens,
22:17 can the Almighty d' for them?
24: 1 d' they that know him not see
31:14 shall I d' when God riseth up?
32: 9 d' the aged understand judgment.
34:10 God, that he should d' wickedness;
12 God will not d' wickedly, neither
32 done iniquity, I will d' no more.
36:28 Which the clouds d' drop and
37:12 d' whatsoever he commandeth
39: 1 thou mark when the hinds d' calve?
41: 8 him, remember the battle, d' no more.

Job 42: 2 know that thou canst d' every thing,
Ps 2: 1 Why d' the heathen rage, and the
7: 1 my God, in thee d' I put my trust:
11: 3 what can the righteous d'?
12: 2 with a double heart d' they speak.
16: 1 for in thee d' I put my trust.
25: 1 thee, O Lord, d' I lift up my soul.
5 on thee d' I wait all the day.
34:14 Depart from evil, and d' good;
16 Lord is against them that d' evil,
36: 3 off to be wise, and to d' good.
37: 3 Trust in the Lord and d' good;
8 not thyself in any wise to d' evil
27 Depart from evil, and d' good;
38:15 For in thee, O Lord, d' I hope:
40: 8 I delight to d' thy will, O my God:
41: 7 against me d' they devise my hurt.
50:16 hast thou to d' to declare my statutes,
51:18 D' good in thy good pleasure
56: 4 fear what flesh can d' unto me.
11 afraid what man can d' unto me.
58: 1 D' ye indeed speak righteousness,
1 d' ye judge uprightly, O ye sons of
60:12 God we shall d' valiantly: for he
64: 4 suddenly d' they shoot at him, and fear
71: 1 In thee, O Lord, d' I put my trust:
82: 3 d' justice to the afflicted and needy.
83: 9 D' unto them as unto the
86: 4 unto thee, O Lord, d' I lift up my soul.
89:50 how d' I bear in my bosom the
92: 7 all the workers of iniquity d' flourish;
95:10 a people that d' err in their heart,
103:18 his commandments to d' them.
20 that d' his commandments,
21 of his, that d' his pleasure.
104:20 beasts of the forest d' creep forth.
105:14 suffered no man to d' them wrong:
15 anointed, and d' my prophets no harm.
107:23 that d' business in great waters;
108:13 Through God we shall d' valiantly:
109:21 But d' thou for me, O God the
111:10 they that d' his commandments:
118: 6 fear: what can man d' unto me?
119: 3 They also d' no iniquity: they
21 which d' err from thy commandments.
35 commandments; for therein d' I
83 yet d' I not forget thy statutes.
109 yet d' I not forget thy law.
113 vain thoughts: but thy law d' I love.
132 as thou usest to d' unto those that
141 yet d' not I forget thy precepts.
153 for I d' not forget thy law.
157 yet d' I not decline from thy
163 lying: but thy law d' I love.
164 seven times a day d' I praise thee
176 I d' not forget thy commandments.
125: 4 D' good, O Lord, unto those that
129: 8 Neither d' they which go by say,
130: 5 and in his word d' I hope.
131: 1 neither d' I exercise myself in
137: 6 If I d' not remember thee, let my
139:21 D' not I hate them, O Lord, that hate
143: 8 morning: for in thee d' I trust:
10 Teach me to d' thy will; for thou
Pr 2:14 Who rejoice to d' evil, and delight
3:27 in the power of thine hand to d' it.
6: 3 D' this now, my son, and deliver
30 Men d' not despise a thief, if he
8:13 and the froward mouth, d' I hate.
10:23 as sport to a fool to d' mischief:
14:22 D' they not err that devise evil?
17: 7 much less d' lying lips a prince.
19: 7 brethren of the poor d' hate him:
7 how much more d' his friends go
19 deliver him, yet thou must d' it again.
20:30 so d' stripes the inward parts of
21: 3 To d' justice and judgment is
7 because they refuse to d' judgment.
15 It is joy to the just to d' judgment:
24: 8 He that deviseth to d' evil shall be
29 I will d' so to him as he hath done
25: 8 lest thou know not what to d' in
28:12 When righteous men d' rejoice,
31:12 She will d' him good and not evil
Ec 2: 3 which they should d' under the
11 labour that I had laboured to d':
12 what can the man d' that cometh
3:12 rejoice, and to d' good in his life.
4: 8 For whom d' I labour, and bereave
5: 1 they consider not that they d' evil.
6: 6 no good: d' not all go to one place?
8:11 men is fully set in them to d' evil.
12 Though a sinner d' evil an hundred
9:10 hand findeth to d', d' it with thy
10:10 iron be blunt, and he d' not whet the
11: 5 how the bones d' grow in the womb
Ca 1: 3 therefore d' the virgins love thee.
8: 8 what shall we d' for our sister in
Isa 1:16 before mine eyes; cease to d' evil;
17 Learn to d' well; seek judgment,
5: 5 you what I will d' to my vineyard.
9:13 neither d' they seek the Lord of
10: 3 will ye d' in the day of visitation,
11 so d' to Jerusalem and her idols?
14:21 that they d' not rise, nor possess
19:15 or tail, branch or rush, may d'.
21 shall d' sacrifice and oblation;
23: 4 neither d' I nourish up young men,
24: 4 people of the earth d' languish.
7 all the merryhearted d' sigh.
18 the foundations of the earth d' shake.
27: 3 I the Lord d' keep it; I will water
28:21 that he may d' his work, his
29:13 and with their lips d' honour me,
14 I will proceed to d' a marvellous work
37:32 of the Lord of hosts shall d' this

Isa 38: 7 that the Lord will d· this thing that
19 he shall praise thee, as I d· this day:
41:23 yea, d· good, or d· evil, that we
42: 9 and new things d· I declare:
16 These things will I d· unto them,
43:19 Behold, I will d· a new thing;
45: 7 I the Lord d· all these things.
46:10 and I will d· all my pleasure:
11 I have purposed it, I will also d· it.
48:11 even for mine own sake, will I d· it:
14 will d· his pleasure on Babylon,
55: 2 Wherefore d· ye spend money for that
56: 1 Keep ye judgment, and d· justice:
57: 4 Against whom d· ye sport yourselves?
58: 4 ye shall not fast as ye d· this day,
64: 6 and we all d· fade as a leaf;
65: 8 so will I d· for my servants' sakes,
Jer 2: 8 walked after things that d· not profit.
18 hast thou to d· in the way of Egypt,
18 hast thou to d· in the way of Assyria,
4:22 they are wise to d· evil, but to
22 to d· good they have no knowledge.
30 thou art spoiled, what wilt thou d·?
5:28 right of the needy d· they not judge.
31 what will ye d· in the end thereof?
7:10 We are delivered to d· all these
14 Therefore will I d· unto this house,
17 Seest thou not what they d· in the
19 D· they provoke me to anger?
19 d· they not provoke themselves to
8: 8 How d· ye say, We are wise,
14 Why d· we sit still? assemble
9: 7 for how shall I d· for the daughter
10: 5 for they cannot d· evil, neither
5 also is it in them to d· good.
11: 4 Obey my voice, and d· them,
6 words of this covenant, and d· them.
8 which I commanded them to d·;
15 hath my beloved to d· in mine house,
12: 5 then how wilt thou d· in the
13:12 D· we not certainly know that every
23 then may ye also d· good, that are
23 that are accustomed to d· evil.
14: 7 d· thou it for thy name's sake:
21 D· not abhor us, for thy name's sake,
21 d· not disgrace the throne of thy glory:
17:22 neither d· ye any work, but hallow
24 sabbath day, to d· no work therein;
18: 6 cannot I d· with you as this potter?
8 evil that I thought to d· unto them
10 If it d· evil in my sight, that it obey
12 we will every one d· the imagination
19:12 Thus will I d· unto this place, saith
22: 3 and d· no wrong, d· no violence to
4 For if ye d· this thing indeed,
15 and d· judgment and justice, and
17 oppression, and for violence, to d· it.
23:24 D· not I fill heaven and earth?
25: 6 hands; and I will d· you no hurt.
26: 3 which I purpose to d· unto them
14 d· with me as seemeth good and
28: 6 the Lord d· so: the Lord perform
29:32 good that I will d· for my people,
30: 6 wherefore d· I see every man with
31:20 I d· earnestly remember him still:
32:23 that thou commandest them to d·:
35 they should d· this abomination,
40 away from them, to d· them good;
41 rejoice over them to d· them good,
33: 9 shall hear all the good that I d·
18 meat offerings, and to d· sacrifice
36: 3 which I purpose to d· unto them;
38: 5 is not he that can d· any thing
39:12 d· him no harm; but d· unto him
40:16 Thou shalt not d· this thing: for
42: 2 as thine eyes d· behold us:)
3 and the thing that we may d·.
5 if we d· not even according to all
20 declare unto us, and we will d· it.
44: 4 Oh, d· not this abominable thing
17 we will certainly d· whatsoever
50:15 as she hath done, d· unto her.
21 saith the Lord, and d· according to
29 that she hath done, d· unto her:
51:47 that I will d· judgment upon the
52 that I will d· judgment upon her
55 when her waves d· roar like great
La 1: 4 The ways of Zion d· mourn,
22 and d· unto them, as thou hast
2:11 Mine eyes d· fail with tears,
Eze 2: 4 I d· send thee unto them;
5: 9 And I will d· in thee that which I
9 and whereunto I will not d· any
6:10 I would d· this evil unto them.
7:27 I will d· unto them after their way,
8: 6 seest thou what they d·? even the
9 abominations that they d· here.
12 of the house of Israel d· in the dark,
13 greater abominations that they d·.
11:20 and d· them: and they shall be my
15: 3 be taken thereof to d· any work?
16: 5 pitied thee, to d· any of these unto
18: 5 but if a man be just and d· that
21 d· that which is lawful and right,
20:11 man d·, he shall even live in them.
13 man d·, he shall even live in them;
19 keep my judgments, and d· them;
21 to d· them, which if a man d·, he
21:24 all your doings your sins d· appear:
22:14 Lord have spoken it, and will d· it.
23:48 taught not to d· after your lewdness.
24:14 and I will d· it; I will not go back,
22 And ye shall d· as I have done: ye
24 to all that he hath done shall ye d·:
25: 8 Because that Moab and Seir d· say,
14 they shall d· in Edom according

Eze 33: 9 if he d· not turn from his way,
14, 19 and d· that which is lawful and
31 but they will not d· them: for with
32 thy words, but they d· them not.
34: 2 to the shepherds of Israel that d· feed
35:11 even d· according to thine anger,
15 so will I d· unto thee: thou shalt
36:11 and will d· better unto you than at
22 I d· not this for your sakes, O
27 keep my judgments and d· them.
32 Not for your sakes d· I this, saith
36 Lord have spoken it, and I will d· it.
37 house of Israel, to d· it for them;
37:24 observe my statues, and d· them.
28 I the Lord d· sanctify Israel,
39:17 my sacrifice that I d· sacrifice for
43:11 ordinances thereof, and d· them.
44:13 near unto me, to d· the office of a
45:20 And so shalt thou d· the seventh
25 shall he d· the like in the feast of
Da 3:14 d· not ye serve my gods, nor
4:26 have known that the heavens d· rule.
9:18 for we d· not present our supplications
19 O Lord, hearken and d·; defer not
11: 3 dominion, and d· according to his
16 shall d· according to his own will,
17 thus shall he d·: and he shall give
24 he shall d· that which his fathers
27 shall be to d· mischief, and they
28 he shall d· exploits, and return to
30 so shall he d·; he shall even return
32 and such as d· wickedly against
32 the people that d· know their God
32 shall be strong, and d· exploits,
36 king shall d· according to his will;
39 he d· in the most strong holds
12:10 but the wicked shall d· wickedly:
Ho 4:18 her rulers with shame d· love,
6: 4 Ephraim, what shall I d· unto thee?
4 Judah, what shall I d· unto thee?
7:10 d· not return to the Lord their God,
15 yet d· they imagine mischief against
9: 5 What will ye d· in the solemn day
10: 3 what then should a king d· to us?
15 So shall Beth-el d· unto you
12: 1 and they d· make a covenant with
14: 8 What have I to d· any more with idols?
Joe 1:18 How d· the beasts groan?
2:21 for the Lord will d· great things,
22 pastures of the wilderness d· spring
3: 4 what have ye to d· with me, O Tyre,
Am 3: 7 the Lord God will d· nothing, but
10 know not to d· right, saith the Lord,
4:12 thus will I d· unto thee, O Israel:
12 because I will d· this unto thee,
Jon 1:11 What shall we d· unto thee, that
3:10 that he would d· unto them: and
4: 9 he said, I d· well to be angry,
Mic 2: 3 against this family d· I devise an evil,
7 d· not my words d· good to him
11 in the spirit and falsehood d· lie,
6: 8 to d· justly, and to love mercy,
7: 3 that they may d· evil with both hands
Na 1: 9 What d· ye imagine against the Lord?
Zep 1:12 will not d· good,
12 neither will he d· evil.
3: 5 not d· iniquity: every morning
13 Israel shall not d· iniquity, nor
Hag 2: 3 and how d· ye see it now?
12 and with his skirt d· touch bread,
Zec 1: 5 and the prophets, d· they live for ever?
6 Lord of hosts thought to d· unto us,
21 What come these to d·? And he
5:10 Whither d· these bear the ephah?
8:15 days to d· well unto Jerusalem
16 things that ye shall d·; Speak ye
9:12 even to day d· I declare that I will
12: 7 of Jerusalem d· not magnify
Mal 1:10 d· ye kindle fire on mine altar
2: 2 because ye d· not lay it to heart.
10 why d· we deal treacherously every
4: 1 and all that d· wickedly shall be
3 day that I d· this, saith the Lord
M't 5: 6 Blessed are they which d· hunger
15 neither d· men light a candle, and
19 whosoever shall d· and teach them,
44 d· good to them that hate you,
46 d· not even the publicans the same?
47 what d· ye more than others?
47 d· not even the publicans so?
6: 1 Take heed that ye d· not your alms
2 d· not sound a trumpet before thee,
2 as the hypocrites d· in the
7 repetitions, as the heathen d·:
20 where thieves d· not break through
26 they sow not, neither d· they reap,
28 they toil not, neither d· they spin:
32 all these things d· the Gentiles seek:
7:12 ye would that men should d· to you,
12 d· ye even so to them: for this is
16 D· men gather grapes of thorns,
8: 9 D· this, and he doeth it.
9:14 Why d· we and the Pharisees fast oft,
17 Neither d· men put new wine into old
28 ye that I am able to d· this?
11: 3 or d· we look for another?
4 again these things which ye d· hear
12: 2 thy disciples d· that which is not
2 not lawful to d· upon the sabbath
12 Wherefore it is lawful to d· well
27 whom d· your children cast them out?
50 For whosoever shall d· the will
13:13 neither d· they understand.
41 and them which d· iniquity;
14: 2 mighty works d· shew forth
15: 2 Why d· thy disciples transgress the

M't 15: 3 Why d· ye also transgress the
16: 9 D· ye not yet understand,
11 How is it that ye d· not understand
13 Whom d· men say that I the Son of
17:25 of whom d· the kings of the earth take
18:10 in heaven their angels d· always behold
35 heavenly Father d· also unto you,
19:16 what good thing shall I d·, that I
18 Thou shalt d· no murder. Thou
20:13 I d· thee no wrong: didst not thou
15 for me to d· what I will with mine
32 will ye that I shall d· unto you?
21:21 ye shall not only d· this which is
24, 27 by what authority I d· these
40 will he d· unto those husbandmen?
22:29 Ye d· err, not knowing the Scriptures,
23: 3 you observe, that observe and d·;
3 but d· not ye after their works:
3 for they say and d· not.
5 But all their works they d· for to
26:72 I d· not know the man.
27:19 thou nothing to d· with that just man:
22 What shall I d· then with Jesus
M'r 1:24 have we to d· with thee, thou Jesus
27 spirits, and they d· obey him.
2:18 Why d· the disciples of John and of
24 why d· they on the sabbath day
3: 4 to d· good on the sabbath days,
4 to d· evil? to save life, or to kill?
35 whosoever shall d· the will of God,
5: 7 What have I to d· with thee, Jesus
6: 5 he could there d· no mighty work,
14 d· shew forth themselves in him.
7: 7 Howbeit in vain d· they worship me,
8 many other such like things ye d·.
12 ye suffer him no more to d· ought
13 and many such like things d· ye.
18 D· ye not perceive, that whatsoever
8:18 and d· ye not remember?
21 How is it that ye d· not understand?
27 Whom d· men say that I am?
9:22 canst d· any thing, have compassion
39 no man which shall d· a miracle
10:17 what shall I d· that I may inherit
19 D· not commit adultery, D· not kill,
19 D· not steal, D· not bear false witness,
35 that thou shouldest d· for us
36 What would ye that I should d·
51 What wilt thou that I should d·
11: 3 Why d· ye this? say ye that the
5 them, What d· ye, loosing the colt?
26 But if ye d· not forgive, neither
28 this authority to d· these things?
29, 33 by what authority I d· these
12: 9 the lord of the vineyard d·? he
24 D· ye not therefore err, because
27 living: ye therefore d· greatly err.
13:11 neither d· ye premeditate:
14: 7 ye will ye may d· them good: but
15: 8 desire him to d· as he had ever done
12 I shall d· unto him whom ye call
Lu 2:27 to d· for him after the custom of
3:10 saying, What shall we d· then?
11 that hath meat, let him d· likewise.
12 him, Master, what shall we d·?
14 And what shall we d·? And he
14 D· violence to no man, neither
4:23 d· also here in thy country.
34 have we to d· with thee, thou Jesus
5:30 Why d· ye eat and drink with publicans
33 Why d· the disciples of John fast
6: 2 Why d· ye that which is not lawful
2 to d· on the sabbath days?
9 on the sabbath days to d· good,
9 or to d· evil?
11 what they might d· to Jesus.
27 Love your enemies, d· good to them
31 would that men should d· to you,
31 d· ye also to them likewise.
33 And if ye d· good to them which
33 d· good to you, what thank have ye?
33 for sinners also d· even the same.
35 love your enemies, and d· good,
44 For of thorns men d· not gather figs,
46 and d· not the things which I say?
7: 4 worthy for whom he should d· this:
8 servant, D· this, and he doeth it.
8:21 hear the word of God, and d· it.
28 What have I to d· with thee, Jesus,
10:11 dust. . .we d· wipe off against you:
25 shall I d· to inherit eternal life?
28 answered right: this d·, and thou
37 unto him, Go, and d· thou likewise.
11:19 by whom d· your sons cast them out?
39 Now d· ye Pharisees make clean the
12: 4 have no more that they can d·.
17 What shall I d·, because I have no
18 will I d·: I will pull down my barns,
26 not able to d· that thing which is least,
30 all these things d· the nations of the
56 that ye d· not discern this time?
13:32 I d· cures to day and to morrow,
15:29 these many years d· I serve thee,
16: 3 What shall I d·? for my lord
4 I am resolved what to d·, that,
17:10 that which was our duty to d·.
18:18 shall I d· to inherit eternal life?
20 D· not commit adultery, D· not kill,
20 D· not steal, D· not bear false witness,
41 thou that I shall d· unto thee?
19:31 Why d· ye loose him?
48 could not find what they might d·:
20: 8 by what authority I d· these things.
13 What shall I d·? I will send my
15 lord of the vineyard d· unto them?
22:19 you: this d· in remembrance of me.

Lu 22:23 it was that should *d·* this thing.
23:31 *d·* these things in a green tree
34 for they know not what they *d·*.
24:38 why *d·* thoughts arise in your hearts?
Joh 2: 4 what have I to *d·* with thee? mine
5 Whatsoever he saith unto you, *d·*
3: 2 for no man can *d·* these miracles
11 We speak that we *d·* know,
4:34 My meat is to *d·* the will of him
5:19 The Son can *d·* nothing of himself,
19 what he seeth the Father *d·*: for
30 I can of mine own self *d·* nothing;
36 same works that I *d·*, bear witness
45 *D·* not think that I will accuse you to
6: 6 himself knew what he would *d·*.
28 What shall we *d·*, that we might
38 not to *d·* mine own will, but the
7: 4 thou *d·* these things, shew thyself
17 If any man will *d·* his will, he shall
26 *D·* the rulers know indeed that
31 will he *d·* more miracles than
8:11 neither *d·* I condemn thee: go and
28 and that I *d·* nothing of myself;
29 for I *d·* always those things that
38 and ye *d·* that which ye have seen
39 ye would *d·* the works of Abraham.
41 Ye *d·* the deeds of your father.
43 *d·* ye not understand my speech?
44 the lusts of your father ye will *d·*.
46 the truth, why *d·* ye not believe me?
49 and ye *d·* dishonour me.
9:15 and I washed, and *d·* see.
16 that is a sinner *d·* such miracles?
33 not of God, he could *d·* nothing.
10:25 that I *d·* in my Father's name,
32 for which of these works *d·* ye stone me?
37 If I *d·* not the work of my Father,
38 if I *d·*, though ye believe not me,
11:12 Lord, if he sleep, he shall *d·* well.
47 What *d·* we? for this man doeth
13: 7 What I *d·* thou knowest not now;
15 ye should *d·* as I have done to you.
17 things, happy are ye if ye *d·* them.
27 That thou doest, *d·* quickly.
14:12 the works that I *d·* shall he *d·* also;
12 works than these shall he *d·*;
13 that will I *d·*, that the Father may
14 any thing in my name, I will *d·* it.
31 commandment, even so I *d·*. Arise,
15: 5 for without me ye can *d·* nothing.
14 ye *d·* whatsoever I command you.
21 But all these things will they *d·*
16: 3 these things will they *d·* unto you,
19 *D·* ye enquire among yourselves of
31 *D·* ye now believe?
17: 4 work which thou gavest me to *d·*.
21:21 Lord, and what shall this man *d·*?
Ac 1: 1 Jesus began both to *d·* and teach,
2:11 we *d·* hear them speak in our tongues
37 and brethren, what shall we *d·*?
4:16 What shall we *d·* to these men?
28 For to *d·* whatsoever thy hand and
5:35 to *d·* as touching these men.
7:26 why *d·* ye wrong one to another?
51 as your fathers did, so *d·* ye.
9: 6 have me to *d·*? And the Lord
6 be told thee what thou must *d·*.
10: 6 thee what thou oughtest to *d·*
14:15 Sirs, why *d·* ye these things?
15:29 ye shall *d·* well. Fare ye well.
36 of the Lord, and see how they *d·*.
16:20 Jews, *d·* exceedingly trouble our city.
28 *D·* thyself no harm: for we are
30 Sirs, what must I *d·* to be saved?
37 now *d·* they thrust us out privily?
17: 7 all *d·* contrary to the decrees
19:36 be quiet, and to *d·* nothing rashly,
21:23 *D·* therefore this that we say to
22:10 I said, What shall I *d·*, Lord?
10 which are appointed for thee to *d·*.
23:21 But *d·* not thou yield unto them:
24:10 I *d·* the more cheerfully answer for
16 and herein *d·* I exercise myself,
25: 9 willing to *d·* the Jews a pleasure,
26: 9 ought to *d·* many things contrary
20 *d·* works meet for repentance,
Ro 1:28 to *d·* those things which are not
32 not only *d·* the same, but have
32 pleasure in them that *d·* them.
2: 3 them which *d·* such things, and
8 and *d·* not obey the truth,
14 have not the law, *d·* by nature
3: 8 Let us *d·* evil, that good may come?
31 *D·* we then make void the law
7:15 For that which I *d·* I allow not:
15 for what I would, that *d·* I not;
15 but what I hate, that *d·* I.
16 If then I *d·* that which I would not
17 it is no more I that *d·* it, but sin
19 the good that I would I *d·* not: but
19 evil which I would not, that I *d·*.
20 Now if I *d·* that I would not,
20 no more I that *d·* it, but sin that
21 I would *d·* good, evil is present
8: 3 law could not *d·*, in that it was weak
5 flesh *d·* mind the things of the flesh;
13 *d·* mortify the deeds of the body,
25 then *d·* we with patience wait for it.
12: 8 giveth, let him *d·* it with simplicity;
15 Rejoice with them that *d·* rejoice,
13: 3 *d·* that which is good, and thou
4 But if thou *d·* that which is evil,
15:31 that *d·* not believe in Judæa;
1Co 5:12 I to *d·* to judge them also that are
12 *d·* not ye judge them that are
6: 2 *D·* ye not know that the saints shall

1Co 6: 7 Why *d·* ye not rather take wrong?
7 *d·* ye not rather suffer yourselves
8 Nay, ye *d·* wrong, and defraud,
7:36 let him *d·* what he will,
9: 3 answer to them that *d·* examine me
13 *D·* ye not know that they which
17 For if I *d·* this thing willingly, I
23 And this I *d·* for the gospel's sake,
25 *d·* it to obtain a corruptible crown;
10:22 *D·* we provoke the Lord to jealousy?
31 ye *d·*, *d·* all to the glory of God.
11:24 this *d·* in remembrance of me.
25 this *d·* ye, as oft as ye drink it in
26 ye *d·* show the Lord's death till
12:30 *d·* all speak with tongues?
30 *d·* all interpret?
15:29 Else what shall they *d·* which are
35 and with what body *d·* they come?
16: 1 even so *d·* ye. Upon the first day
5 for I *d·* pass through Macedonia.
10 the work of the Lord, as I also *d·*.
2Co 1:17 *d·* I purpose according to the flesh,
3: 1 *D·* we begin again to commend
5: 4 that are in this tabernacle *d·* groan,
7: 8 I *d·* not repent, though I did repent:
8: 1 *d·* you to wit of the grace of God
10 only to *d·*, but also to be forward
23 Whether any *d·* enquire of Titus,
10: 3 we *d·* not war after the flesh:
7 *D·* ye look on things after the
11: 8 wages of them to *d·* you service.
12 But what I *d·*, that I will *d·*, that
12:19 but we *d·* all things, dearly
13: 7 *d·* no evil; *d·* that which is honest,
8 we can *d·* nothing against the truth,
Ga 1:10 *d·* I now persuade men, or God?
10 or *d·* I seek to please men?
2:10 which I also was forward to *d·*.
14 and not as *d·* the Jews,
14 to live as *d·* the Jews? We who
21 *d·* not frustrate the grace of God:
3:10 in the book of the law to *d·* them.
4:21 *d·* ye not hear the law?
5: 3 he is a debtor to *d·* the whole law.
11 why *d·* I yet suffer persecution?
17 *d·* the things that ye would.
21 that they which *d·* such things
6:10 let us *d·* good unto all men,
Eph 3:20 is able to *d·* exceeding abundantly
6: 9 *d·* the same things unto them,
21 know my affairs, and how I *d·*,
Ph'p 1:18 and I therefore *d·* rejoice,
2:13 and to *d·* of his good pleasure.
14 *D·* all things without murmurings
18 For the same cause also *d·* ye joy,
3: 8 loss of all things, and *d·* count them
13 but this one thing I *d·*, forgetting
4: 9 heard, and seen in me, *d·*: and
13 can *d·* all things through Christ
Col 1: 9 *d·* not cease to pray for you,
3:13 as Christ forgave you, so also *d·* ye.
17 ye *d·* in word or deed, *d·* all in
23 And whatsoever ye *d·*,
23 *d·* it heartily, as to the Lord,
1Th 3:12 even as we *d·* toward you:
4:10 And indeed ye *d·* it toward all the
11 be quiet, and to *d·* your business
5: 6 let us not sleep, as *d·* others; but
11 one another, even as also ye *d·*.
24 calleth you, who also will *d·* it.
2Th 3: 4 that ye both *d·*, and will *d·* the
1Ti 1: 4 edifying which is in faith: so *d·*.
6: 2 rather *d·* them service, because
18 That they *d·* good, that they be rich
2Ti 2:23 knowing that they *d·* gender strifes.
3: 8 so *d·* these also resist the truth: men
4: 5 *d·* the work of an evangelist, make
9 *D·* thy diligence to come shortly
21 *D·* thy diligence to come before
Ph'm 14 thy mind would I *d·* nothing;
21 thou wilt also *d·* more than I say.
Heb 3:10 They *d·* always err in their heart;
4: 3 For we which have believed *d·* enter
13 him with whom we have to *d·*. *3588*.
6: 3 And this will we *d·* if God permit.
10 have ministered to the saints and *d·*
11 every one of you *d·* shew the same
10: 7 written of me,) to *d·* thy will, O God
9 Lo, I come to *d·* thy will, O God.
11: 3 not made of things which *d·* appear.
29 assaying to *d·* were drowned.
13: 6 not fear what man shall *d·* unto me.
16 to *d·* good and to communicate
17 that they may *d·* it with joy,
19 beseech you the rather to *d·* this,
21 in every good work to *d·* his will,
Jas 1:16 *D·* not err, my beloved brethren.
2: 6 *D·* not rich men oppress you,
7 *D·* they not blaspheme that worthy
8 neighbour as thyself, ye *d·* well:
11 that said, *D·* not commit adultery,
11 said also, *D·* not kill.
12 So speak ye, and so *d·*, as they
4: 5 *D·* ye think that the scripture saith
15 we shall live, and *d·* this, or that.
17 to him that knoweth to *d·* good,
5:19 any of you *d·* err from the truth,
1Pe 1:21 Who by him *d·* believe in God,
2:14 for the praise of them that *d·* well.
20 if, when ye *d·* well, and suffer for it,
3: 6 daughters ye are, as long as ye *d·*
11 him eschew evil, and *d·* good;
12 Lord is against them that *d·* evil.
4:11 let him *d·* it as of the ability
2Pe 1:10 for if ye *d·* these things, ye shall
19 ye *d·* well that ye take heed, as

2Pe 3:16 they *d·* also the other Scriptures,
1Jo 1: 6 we lie, and *d·* not the truth:
2: 3 hereby we *d·* know that we know
3:22 *d·* those things that are pleasing
4:14 and *d·* testify that the Father
5:16 I *d·* not say that he shall pray for it.
3Jo 1: 6 a godly sort, thou shalt *d·* well:
Re 2: 5 and repent, and *d·* the first works;
3: 9 they are Jews, and are not, but *d·* lie;
18 thy nakedness *d·* not appear;
9:19 and with them they *d·* hurt.
13:14 which he had the power to *d·* in
14:13 and their works *d·* follow them.
19:10 See thou *d·* it not: I am thy fellow
21:24 the kings of the earth *d·* bring their
22: 9 saith he unto me, See thou *d·* it not;
14 they that *d·* his commandments,

doctor See also DOCTORS.
Ac 5:34 named Gamaliel, a *d·* of the law,

doctors
Lu 2:46 sitting in the midst of the *d·*,
5:17 and *d·* of the law sitting by,

doctrine See also DOCTRINES.
De 32: 2 My *d·* shall drop as the rain,
Job 11: 4 My *d·* is pure, and I am clean in
Pr 4: 2 I give you good *d·*, forsake ye not
Isa 28: 9 shall he make to understand *d·*?
29:24 that murmured shall learn *d·*.
Jer 10: 8 the stock is a *d·* of vanities.
M't 7:28 people were astonished at his *d·*:
16:12 of the *d·* of the Pharisees and of
22:33 they were astonished at his *d·*.
M'r 1:22 they were astonished at his *d·*:
27 what new *d·* is this? for with
4: 2 and said unto them in his *d·*,
11:18 people was astonished at his *d·*.
12:38 he said unto them in his *d·*,
Lu 4:32 they were astonished at his *d·*:
Joh 7:16 My *d·* is not mine, but his that
17 he shall know of the *d·*, whether
18:19 of his disciples, and of his *d·*.
Ac 2:42 in the apostles' *d·* and fellowship,
5:28 filled Jerusalem with your *d·*,
13:12 astonished at the *d·* of the Lord.
17:19 what this new *d·*, whereof thou
Ro 6:17 form of *d·* which was delivered
16:17 offences contrary to the *d·* which
1Co 14: 6 or by prophesying, or by *d·*?
26 of you hath a psalm, hath a *d·*,
Eph 4:14 about with every wind of *d·*,
1Ti 1: 3 some that they teach no other *d·*,
10 that is contrary to sound *d·*;
4: 6 up in words of faith and of good *d·*,
13 to reading, to exhortation, to *d·*.
16 unto thyself, and unto the *d·*;
5:17 who labour in the word and *d·*.
6: 1 God and his *d·* be not blasphemed.
3 to the *d·* which is according to
2Ti 3:10 thou hast fully known my *d·*,
16 is profitable for *d·*, for reproof,
4: 2 with all longsuffering and *d·*.
3 they will not endure sound *d·*;
Tit 1: 9 able by sound *d·* both to exhort
2: 1 things which become sound *d·*:
7 in *d·* shewing uncorruptness,
10 to adorn the *d·* of God our Saviour
Heb 6: 1 leaving the principles of the *d·*
2 Of the *d·* of baptisms, and of
2Jo 9 abideth not in the *d·* of Christ,
9 that abideth in the *d·* of Christ,
10 bring not this *d·*, receive him not
Re 2:14 that hold the *d·* of Balaam, who
15 hold the *d·* of the Nicolaitanes,
24 as many as have not this *d·*,

doctrines
M't 15: 9 for *d·* the commandments of men.
M'r 7: 7 for *d·* the commandments of men.
Col 2:22 the commandments and *d·* of men?
1Ti 4: 1 seducing spirits, and *d·* of devils;
Heb 13: 9 about with divers and strange *d·*.

Dodai (*do'-dahee*) See also DODO.
1Ch 27: 4 second month was *D·* an Ahohite,

Dodanim (*do'-da-nim*) See also RODANIM.
Ge 10: 4 and Tarshish, Kittim, and *D·*.
1Ch 1: 7 and Tarshish, Kittim, and *D·*.

Dodavah (*do'-da-vah*)
2Ch 20:37 Then Eliezer the son of *D·* of

Dodo (*do'-do*) See also DODAI.
J'g 10: 1 the son of *D·*, a man of Issachar;
2Sa 23: 9 Eleazar the son of *D·* the Ahohite,
24 Elhanan the son of *D·* of Beth-lehem,
1Ch 11:12 him was Eleazar the son of *D·*,
26 Elhanan the son of *D·* of Beth-lehem,

Doeg (*do'-eg*)
1Sa 21: 7 his name was *D·*, an Edomite,
22: 9 Then answered *D·* the Edomite,
18 the king said to *D·*, Turn thou,
18 *D·* the Edomite turned, and he fell
22 when *D·* the Edomite was there,
Ps 52 *title* when *D·* the Edomite came and

doer See also DOERS.
Ge 39:22 did there, he was the *d·* of it.
2Sa 3:39 Lord shall reward the *d·* of evil
Ps 31:23 plentifully rewardeth the proud *d·*.
Pr 17: 4 wicked *d·* giveth heed to false lips;
2Ti 2: 9 as an evil *d·*, even unto bonds;
Jas 1:23 hearer of the word, and not a *d·*,
25 hearer, but a *d·* of the work,
4:11 not a *d·* of the law, but a judge.

doers
2Ki 22: 5 the hand of the *d·* of the work.
5 them give it to the *d·* of the work.

Job 8:20 neither will he help the evil *d'*:
Ps 26: 5 hated the congregation of evil *d'*;
101: 8 that I may cut off all wicked *d'*
Ro 2:13 *d'* of the law shall be justified.
Jas 1:22 be ye *d'* of the word, and not

doest^ See also DOST.
Ge 4: 7 If thou *d'* well, shalt thou not be
7 and if thou *d'* not well, sin lieth at
21:22 is with thee in all that thou *d'*:
Ex 18:14 What is this thing that thou *d'* to
17 unto him, The thing that thou *d'* is
De 12:28 when thou *d'* that which is good
14:29 work of thine hand which thou *d'*.
15:18 shall bless thee in all that thou *d'*.
J'g 11:27 thou *d'* me wrong to war against
1Ki 2: 3 mayest prosper in all that thou *d'*,
19: 9 he said unto him, What *d'* thou here,
13 and said, What *d'* thou here, Elijah?
20:22 mark, and see what thou *d'*: for
Job 9:12 will say unto him, What *d'* thou?
35: 6 what *d'* thou against him? or if
6 be multiplied, what *d'* thou unto
Ps 49:18 men will praise thee, when thou *d'* well
77:14 Thou art the God that *d'* wonders:
86:10 thou art great, and *d'* wondrous
119:68 Thou art good, and *d'* good; teach me
Ec 8: 4 may say unto him, What *d'* thou?
Jer 11:15 when thou *d'* evil, then thou rejoicest.
15: 5 go aside to ask how thou *d'*?
Eze 12: 9 said unto thee, What *d'* thou?
16:30 seeing thou *d'* all these things, the
24:19 these things are to us, that thou *d'*
Da 4:35 or say unto him, What *d'* thou?
Jon 4: 4 the Lord, *D'* thou well to be angry?
9 *D'* thou well to be angry for the gourd?
M't 6: 2 when thou *d'* thine alms, do not
3 But when thou *d'* alms, let not
21:23 By what authority *d'* thou these
M'r 11:28 By what authority *d'* thou these
Lu 20: 2 by what authority *d'* thou these
Joh 2:18 seeing that thou *d'* these things?
3: 2 that thou *d'*, except God be with
7: 3 may see the works that thou *d'*.
13:27 That thou *d'*, do quickly.
Ac 22:26 Take heed what thou *d'*: for this
Ro 2: 1 thou that judgest *d'* the same
3 and *d'* the same, that thou shalt
Jas 2:19 that there is one God; thou *d'* well:
3Jo 5 *d'* faithfully whatsoever thou *d'* to

doeth See also DOTH.
Ge 31:12 seen all that Laban *d'* unto thee.
Ex 31:14 whosoever *d'* any work therein,
15 whosoever *d'* any work in the
35: 2 whosoever *d'* work therein shall be
Le 4:27 while he *d'* somewhat against
6: 3 of all these that a man *d'*, sinning
23:30 whatsoever soul it be that *d'* any
Nu 15:30 soul that *d'* ought presumptuously,
24:23 who shall live when God *d'* this!
Job 5: 9 *d'* great things and unsearchable;
9:10 Which *d'* great things past finding
23:13 his soul desireth, even that he *d'*.
24:21 and *d'* not good to the widow.
37: 5 great things *d'* he, which we
Ps 1: 3 and whatsoever he *d'* shall prosper.
14: 1 works, there is none that *d'* good.
3 there is none that *d'* good, no, not
15: 3 nor *d'* evil to his neighbour, nor
5 He that *d'* these things shall never
53: 1 iniquity: there is none that *d'* good.
3 there is none that *d'* good, no, not
72:18 of Israel, who only *d'* wondrous
106: 3 and he that *d'* righteousness at all
118:15, 16 hand of the Lord *d'* valiantly.
136: 4 him who alone *d'* great wonders:
Pr 6:32 he that *d'* it destroyeth his own soul.
11:17 The merciful man *d'* good to his
15: 7 but the heart of the foolish *d'* not so.
17:21 He that begetteth a fool *d'* it to his
22 A merry heart *d'* good like a
28:17 A man that *d'* violence to the
Ec 2: 2 is mad: and of mirth, What *d'* it?
3:14 I know that, whatsoever God *d'*, it
14 and God *d'* it, that men should fear
7:20 just man upon earth, that *d'* good,
8: 3 for he *d'* whatsoever pleaseth him.
Isa 49:18 bind them on thee, as a bride *d'*.
56: 2 Blessed is the man that *d'* this,
Jer 5:19 Wherefore *d'* the Lord our God all
48:10 Cursed be he that *d'* the work of the
Eze 17:15 shall he escape that *d'* such things?
18:10 and that *d'* the like to any one of
11 And that *d'* not any of those duties,
14 and considereth, and *d'* not such
24 iniquity, and *d'* according to all the
24 that the wicked man *d'*, shall he
27 and *d'* that which is lawful and
Da 4:35 and he *d'* according to his will
9:14 in all his work which he *d'*:
Am 9:12 saith the Lord that *d'* this.
Mal 2:12 the man that *d'* this, the master
17 Every one that *d'* evil is good in
M't 6: 3 what thy right hand *d'*:
7:21 but he that *d'* the will of my Father
24 and *d'* them, I will liken him unto
26 and *d'* them not, shall be likened
8: 9 my servant, Do this, and he *d'* it.
Lu 6:47 my sayings, and *d'* them, I will
49 heareth, and *d'* not, is like a man
7: 8 my servant, Do this, and he *d'* it.
Joh 3:20 For every one that *d'* evil hateth
21 But he that *d'* truth cometh to the
5:19 for what things soever he *d'*,
19 these also *d'* the Son likewise.
20 him all things that himself *d'*: and

Joh 7: 4 there is no man that *d'* any thing
51 hear him, and know what he *d'*?
9:31 and *d'* his will, him he heareth.
11:47 What do we? for this man *d'* many
14:10 dwelleth in me, he *d'* the works.
15:15 knoweth not what his lord *d'*: but
16: 2 will think that he *d'* God service.
Ac 15:17 the Lord who *d'* all these things.
26:31 This man *d'* nothing worthy of
Ro 2: 9 soul of man that *d'* evil, of the
3:12 there is none that *d'* good, no, not
10: 5 the man which *d'* those things
13: 4 wrath upon him that *d'* evil.
1Co 6:18 that a man *d'* is without the body;
7:37 he will keep his virgin, *d'* well.
38 giveth her in marriage, *d'* well;
38 her not in marriage *d'* better.
Ga 3: 5 *d'* he it by the works of the law, or
12 The man that *d'* them shall live
Eph 6: 8 whatsoever good thing any man *d'*,
Col 3:25 But he that *d'* wrong shall receive
Jas 4:17 knoweth to do good, and *d'* it not,
1Jo 2:17 but he that *d'* the will of God
29 that *d'* righteousness is born of him.
3: 7 that *d'* righteousness is righteous,
10 Whosoever *d'* not righteousness is
3Jo 10 remember his deeds which he *d'*,
11 He that *d'* good is of God: but he
11 he that *d'* evil hath not seen God.
Re 13:13 And he *d'* great wonders, so that

dog See also DOG'S; DOGS.
Ex 11: 7 shall not a *d'* move his tongue,
De 23:18 the price of a *d'*, into the house
J'g 7: 5 with his tongue, as a *d'* lappeth,
1Sa 17:43 Am I a *d'*, that thou comest to me
24:14 after a dead *d'*, after a flea.
2Sa 9: 8 look upon such a dead *d'* as I am?
16: 9 Why should this dead *d'* curse my
2Ki 8:13 is thy servant a *d'*, that he should
Ps 22:20 darling from the power of the *d'*.
59: 6 they make a noise like a *d'*, and go
14 let them make a noise like a *d'*,
Pr 26:11 As a *d'* returneth to his vomit,
17 one that taketh a *d'* by the ears.
Ec 9: 4 living *d'* is better than a dead lion.
2Pe 2:22 The *d'* is turned to his own vomit

dog's
2Sa 3: 8 Am I a *d'* head, which against
Isa 66: 3 a lamb, as if he cut off a *d'* neck;

dogs
Ex 22:31 the field; ye shall cast it to the *d'*.
1Ki 14:11 in the city shall the *d'* eat; and him
16: 4 Baasha in the city shall the *d'* eat;
21:19 place where *d'* licked the blood of
19 Naboth shall *d'* lick thy blood,
23 The *d'* shall eat Jezebel by the wall
24 Ahab in the city, the *d'* shall eat;
22:38 and the *d'* licked up his blood;
2Ki 9:10 the *d'* shall eat Jezebel in the
36 shall *d'* eat the flesh of Jezebel:
Job 30: 1 to have set with the *d'* of my flock.
Ps 22:16 For *d'* have compassed me: the
68:23 and the tongue of thy *d'* in the
Isa 56:10 all ignorant, they are all dumb *d'*,
11 Yea, they are greedy *d'* which can
Jer 15: 3 and the *d'* to tear, and the fowls
M't 7: 6 not that which is holy unto the *d'*,
15:26 bread, and to cast it to *d'*.
27 yet the *d'* eat of the crumbs which
M'r 7:27 bread, and to cast it unto the *d'*.
28 yet the *d'* under the table eat of the
Lu 16:21 the *d'* came and licked his sores.
Ph'p 3: 2 Beware of *d'*, beware of evil
Re 22:15 For without are *d'*, and sorcerers,

doing See also DOINGS.
Ge 31:28 hast now done foolishly in so *d'*
44: 5 ye have done evil in so *d'*.
Ex 15:11 fearful in praises, *d'* wonders?
Nu 20:19 I will only, without *d'* any thing
De 9:18 in *d'* wickedly in the sight of the
1Ki 7:40 Hiram made an end of *d'* all the
16:19 he sinned in *d'* evil in the sight of
22:43 *d'* that which was right in the eyes
2Ki 21:16 in *d'* that which was evil in the
1Ch 22:16 Arise therefore and be *d'*, and the
2Ch 20:32 and departed not from it, *d'* that
Ezr 9: 1 *d'* according to their abominations.
Ne 6: 3 I am doing a great work, so that
Job 32:22 in so *d'* my Maker would soon
Ps 64: 9 shall wisely consider of his *d'*.
66: 5 is terrible in his *d'* toward the
118:23 This is the Lord's *d'*; it is
Isa 56: 2 keepeth his hand from *d'* any evil.
58:13 *d'* thy pleasure on my holy day;
13 honour him, not *d'* thine own ways,
M't 21:42 this is the Lord's *d'*, and it is
24:46 when he cometh shall find so *d'*.
M'r 12:11 This was the Lord's *d'*, and it is
Lu 12:43 when he cometh shall find so *d'*.
Ac 10:38 who went about *d'* good, and
24:20 found any evil *d'* in me, while I
Ro 2: 7 by patient continuance in well *d'*
12:20 for in so *d'* thou shalt heap coals
2Co 8:11 Now therefore perform the *d'* of it;
Ga 6: 9 be weary in well *d'*: for in due
Eph 6: 6 servants of Christ, *d'* the will of
7 With good will *d'* service, as to
2Th 3:13 brethren, be not weary in well *d'*.
1Ti 4:16 for in *d'* this thou shalt both save
5:21 one before another, *d'* nothing by
1Pe 2:15 that with well *d'* ye may put to
3:17 be so, that ye suffer for well *d'*
17 than for evil *d'*.
4:19 of their souls to him in well *d'*, as

doings^
Le 18: 3 after the *d'* of the land of Egypt,
3 and after the *d'* of the land of
De 28:20 of the wickedness of thy *d'*,
J'g 2:19 they ceased not from their own *d'*,
1Sa 25: 3 was churlish and evil in his *d'*;
2Ch 17: 4 and not after the *d'* of Israel.
Ps 9:11 declare among the people his *d'*.
77:12 all thy work, and talk of thy *d'*.
Pr 20:11 Even a child is known by his *d'*,
Isa 1:16 put away the evil of your *d'* from
3: 8 and their *d'* are against the Lord,
10 they shall eat the fruit of their *d'*.
12: 4 declare his *d'* among the people,
Jer 4: 4 it, because of the evil of your *d'*.
18 Thy way and thy *d'* have procured
7: 3 Amend your ways and your *d'*,
5 amend your ways and your *d'*;
11:18 then thou shewedst me their *d'*.
17:10 and according to the fruit of his *d'*.
18:11 make your ways and your *d'* good.
21:12 because of the evil of your *d'*.
14 according to the fruit of your *d'*,
23: 2 visit upon you the evil of your *d'*,
22 way, and from the evil of their *d'*.
25: 5 and from the evil of your *d'*, and
26: 3 because of the evil of their *d'*.
13 amend your ways and your *d'*,
32:19 according to the fruit of his *d'*:
35:15 his evil way, and amend your *d'*,
44:22 because of the evil of your *d'*, and
Eze 14:22 shall see their way and their *d'*:
23 ye see their ways and their *d'*:
20:44 nor according to your corrupt *d'*,
21:24 in all your *d'*, your sins do appear;
24:14 and according to thy *d'*, shall they
36:17 by their own way and by their *d'*:
19 according to their *d'* I judged them
31 own evil ways, and your *d'* that
Hos 4: 9 ways, and reward them their *d'*.
5: 4 They will not frame their *d'* to turn
7: 2 now their own *d'* have beset them
9:15 for the wickedness of their *d'* I
12: 2 to his *d'* will he recompense him.
Mic 2: 7 are these his *d'*? do not my words
3: 4 behaved themselves ill in their *d'*.
7:13 therein, for the fruit of their *d'*.
Zep 3: 7 early, and corrupted all their *d'*.
11 thou not be ashamed for all thy *d'*.
Zec 1: 4 and from your evil *d'*: but they did
6 according to our *d'*, so hath he

doleful
Isa 13:21 houses shall be full of *d'* creatures;
Mic 2: 4 and lament with a *d'* lamentation,

dominion See also DOMINIONS.
Ge 1:26 and let them have *d'* over the fish
28 and have *d'* over the fish of the sea,
27:40 pass when thou shalt have the *d'*,
37: 8 shalt thou indeed have *d'* over us?
Nu 24:19 shall come he that shall have *d'*,
J'g 5:13 made him that remaineth have *d'*
13 made me have *d'* over the mighty.
14: 4 the Philistines had *d'* over Israel.
1Ki 4:24 he had *d'* over all the region on
9:19 and in all the land of his *d'*.
2Ki 20:13 in his house, nor in all his *d'*,
1Ch 4:22 Saraph, who had the *d'* in Moab,
18: 3 his *d'* by the river Euphrates.
2Ch 8: 6 throughout all the land of his *d'*,
21: 8 from under the *d'* of Judah, and
Ne 9:28 so that they had the *d'* over them:
37 also they have *d'* over our bodies,
Job 25: 2 *D'* and fear are with him, he
38:33 canst thou set the *d'* thereof in
Ps 8: 6 Thou madest him to have *d'* over
19:13 let them not have *d'* over me:
49:14 and the upright shall have *d'* over
72: 8 He shall have *d'* also from sea to
103:22 his works in all places of his *d'*:
114: 2 was his sanctuary, and Israel his *d'*.
119:133 let not iniquity have *d'* over me.
145:13 and thy *d'* endureth throughout
Isa 26:13 beside thee have had *d'* over us:
39: 2 nor in all his *d'*, that Hezekiah
Jer 34: 1 the kingdoms of the earth of his *d'*,
51:28 thereof, and all the land of his *d'*.
Da 4: 3 and his *d'* is from generation to
22 and thy *d'* to the end of the earth.
34 whose *d'* is an everlasting *d'*,
6:26 That in every *d'* of my kingdom
26 his *d'* shall be even unto the end.
7: 6 four heads; and *d'* was given to it.
12 they had their *d'* taken away:
14 there was given him *d'*, and glory,
14 his *d'* is an everlasting *d'*,
26 and they shall take away his *d'*,
27 And the kingdom and *d'*, and the
11: 3 up, that shall rule with great *d'*,
4 according to his *d'* which he ruled:
5 be strong above him, and have *d'*;
5 his *d'* shall be a great
5 shall be a great *d'*.
Mic 4: 8 shall it come, even the first *d'*;
Zec 9:10 and his *d'* shall be from sea to
M't 20:25 princes of the Gentiles exercise *d'*
Ro 6: 9 death hath no more *d'* over him.
14 sin shall not have *d'* over you:
7: 1 the law hath *d'* over a man as long
2Co 1:24 that we have *d'* over your faith,
Eph 1:21 might, and *d'*, and every name that
1Pe 4:11 be praise and *d'* for ever and ever.
5:11 To him be glory and *d'* for ever
Jude 8 despise *d'*, and speak evil of
25 *d'* and power, both now and ever.
Re 1: 6 to him be glory and *d'* for ever

dominions
Da 7:27 all d' shall serve and obey him.
Col 1:16 or d', or principalities, or powers:
done See also UNDONE.
Ge 3:13 What is this that thou hast d'?
14 Because thou hast d' this, thou art
4:10 What hast thou d'? the voice of
8:21 every living thing, as I have d'.
9:24 knew what his younger son had d'
12:18 is this that thou hast d' unto me?
18:21 whether they have d' altogether
20: 5 of my hands have I d' this.
9 What hast thou d' unto us?
9 thou hast d' deeds unto me that
9 unto me that ought not to be d'.
10 thou, that thou hast d' this thing?
21:23 kindness that I have d' unto thee,
26 I wot not who hath d' this thing:
22:16 because thou hast d' this thing,
24:15 pass, before he had d' speaking,
19 when she had d' giving him drink,
19 also, until they have d' drinking.
22 pass,as the camels had d' drinking,
45 I had d' speaking in mine heart,
66 Isaac all things that he had d'.
26:10 What is this thou hast d' unto us?
29 have d' unto thee nothing but good,
27:19 d' according as thou badest me:
45 that which thou hast d' to him:
28:15 I have d' that which I have spoken
29:25 What is this thou hast d' unto me?
26 It must not be so d' in our country,
30:26 my service which I have d' thee.
31:26 What hast thou d', that thou hast
28 hast now d' foolishly in so doing.
34: 7 which thing ought not to be d'.
40:15 and here also have I d' nothing
42:28 is this that God hath d' unto us?
44: 5 divineth? ye have d' evil in so doing.
15 What deed is this that ye have d'?
Ex 1:18 Why have ye d' this thing, and
2: 4 to wit what would be d' to him.
3:16 that which is d' to you in Egypt:
5:23 he hath d' evil to this people;
10: 2 which I have d' among them;
12:16 no manner of work shall be d' in
16 eat, that only may be d' of you.
13: 8 This is d' because of that which
14: 5 Why have we d' this, that we have
18: 1 of all that God had d' for Moses,
8 that the Lord had d' unto Pharaoh
9 which the Lord had d' to Israel,
21:31 judgment shall it be d' unto him.
31:15 Six days may work be d'; but in
34:10 have not been d' in all the earth,
33 Moses had d' speaking with them,
35: 2 Six days shall work be d', but on
39:43 d' it as the Lord had commanded,
43 even so had they d' it: and Moses
Le 4: 2 things which ought not to be d',
13 and they have d' somewhat against
13 should not be d', and are guilty;
22 When a ruler hath sinned, and d'
22 things which should not be d',
27 things which ought not to be d',
5:16 for the harm that he hath d' in
17 to be d' by the commandments
6: 7 he hath d' in trespassing therein.
8: 5 the Lord commanded to be d'.
34 As he hath d' this day, so the Lord
11:32 vessel it be, wherein any work is d',
18:27 have the men of the land d', which
19:22 for his sin which he hath d':
22 he hath d' shall be forgiven him.
23: 3 six days shall work be d': but
24:19 he hath d', so shall it be d' to him;
20 so shall it be d' to him again.
Nu 5: 7 their sin which they have d':
27 d' trespass against her husband,
12:11 wherein we have d' foolishly, and
15:11 Thus shall it be d' for one bullock,
34 declared what should be d' to him.
16:28 have not d' them of mine own mind.
22: 2 that Israel had d' to the Amorites.
28 What have I d' unto thee, that
23:11 What hast thou d' unto me?
27: 4 name of our father be d' away
32:13 d' evil in the sight of the Lord,
De 3:21 God hath d' unto these two kings:
10:21 d' for thee these great and terrible
12:31 Lord, which he hateth, have they d'
19:19 to have d' unto his brother:
25: 9 So shall it be d' unto that man
26:14 d' according to all that thou hast
29:24 Wherefore hath the Lord d' thus
32:27 and the Lord hath not d' all this.
Jos 5: 8 d' circumcising all the people,
7:19 tell me now what thou hast d';
20 and thus and thus have I d':
9: 3 what Joshua had d' unto Jericho
24 of you, and have d' this thing.
10: 1 d' to Jericho and her king,
1 so he had d' to Ai and her
32 to all that he had d' to Libnah.
35 to all that he had d' to Lachish.
37 to all that he had d' to Eglon;
39 as he had d' to Hebron, so he did
39 as he had d' also to Libnah, and to
22:24 rather d' it for fear of this thing,
23: 3 all that the Lord your God hath d'
8 God, as ye have d' unto this day.
24: 7 seen what I have d' in Egypt:
20 you, after that he hath d' you good.
31 Lord, that he had d' for Israel.
J'g 1: 7 have d', so God hath requited me.
2: 2 my voice: why have ye d' this?

J'g 2:10 yet the works which he had d'
3:12 Israel, because they had d' evil
6:29 another, Who hath d' this thing?
29 the son of Joash hath d' this thing.
8: 2 What have I d' now, in comparison
9:16 Now therefore, if ye have d' truly
16 d' unto him according to the
24 That the cruelty d' to the three
48 do, make haste, and do as I have d'.
11:37 Let this thing be d' for me:
14: 6 or his mother what he had d'.
15: 6 Philistines said, Who hath d' this?
7 Though ye have d' this, yet will
10 up, to do to him as he hath d' to us.
11 is this that thou hast d' unto us?
11 unto me, so have I d' unto them.
19:30 There was no such deed d' nor
20:12 wickedness is this that is d'
Ru 2:11 hast d' unto thy mother in law
3: 3 shall have d' eating and drinking.
16 told her all that the man had d'
1Sa 4:16 What is there d', my son?
6: 9 to Beth-shemesh, then he hath d'
8: 8 works which they have d' since the
11: 7 Samuel, so shall it be d' unto his
12:17 ye have d' in the sight of the Lord,
20 not: ye have d' all this wickedness:
24 consider how great things he hath d'
13:11 Samuel said, What hast thou d'?
13 said to Saul, Thou hast d' foolishly:
14:43 Tell me what thou hast d'.
17:26 shall be d' to the man that killeth
27 it be d' to the man that killeth him.
29 David said, What have I now d'?
19:18 told him all that Saul had d' to him.
20: 1 before Jonathan, What have I d'?
32 shall he be slain? what hath he d'?
34 because his father had d' him shame.
24:19 that thou hast d' unto me this day.
25:30 the Lord shall have d' to my lord
26:16 thing is not good that thou hast d'.
18 for what have I d'? or what evil is
28: 9 thou knowest what Saul hath d',
17 the Lord hath d' to him, as he
18 therefore hath the Lord d' this
29: 8 unto Achish, But what have I d'?
31:11 the Philistines had d' to Saul;
2Sa 2: 6 because ye have d' this thing.
3:24 and said, What hast thou d'?
7:21 thou d' all these great things,
11:27 But the thing that David had d'
12: 5 the man that hath d' this thing
21 thing is this that thou hast d'?
13:12 such thing ought to be d' in Israel:
14:20 hath thy servant Joab d' this thing:
21 Behold now, I have d' this thing:
15:24 all the people had d' passing out
16:10 Wherefore hast thou d' so?
21:11 Aiah, the concubine of Saul, had d'.
23:20 who had d' many acts, he slew
24:10 sinned greatly in that I have d':
10 for I have d' very foolishly. For
17 sinned, and I have d' wickedly:
17 but these sheep what have they d'?
1Ki 1: 6 Why hast thou d' so?
27 thing d' by my lord the king,
3:12 Behold, I have d' according to thy
8:47 have sinned, and have d' perversely,
66 that the Lord had d' for David
9: 8 Why hath the Lord d' thus unto
11:11 Forasmuch as this is d' of thee,
13:11 the man of God had d' that day
14: 9 But hast d' evil above all that were
22 above all that their fathers had d'.
15: 3 which he had d' before him: and
18:36 d' all these things at thy word.
19: 1 all that Elijah had d', and withal
20 for what have I d' to thee?
22:53 to all that his father had d'.
2Ki 4:13 what is to be d' for thee? wouldest
14 what is then to be d' for her?
5:13 wouldest thou not have d' it?
7:12 what the Syrians have d' to us.
8: 4 great things that Elisha hath d'.
10:10 Lord hath d' that which he spake
30 thou hast d' well in executing that
30 hast d' unto the house of Ahab
15: 3 all that his father Amaziah had d';
9 as his fathers had d': he departed
34 to all that his father Uzziah had d'.
17: 4 he had d' year by year: therefore
19:11 what the kings of Assyria have d'
25 long ago how I have d' it, and of
20: 3 have d' that which is good in thy
21:11 Judah hath d' these abominations,
11 and hath d' wickedly above all
15 they have d' that which was evil
23:17 that thou hast d' against the altar
19 the acts that he hath d' in Beth-el.
32, 37 to all that his fathers had d'.
24: 9 to all that his father had d'.
19 to all that Jehoiakim had d'.
1Ch 10:11 that the Philistines had d' to Saul,
11:22 who had d' many acts; he slew two
16:12 marvellous works that he hath d'.
17:19 hast thou d' all this greatness,
21: 8 because I have d' this thing;
8 for I have d' very foolishly.
17 have sinned and d' evil indeed;
17 for these sheep, what have they d'?
2Ch 6:37 We have sinned, we have d' amiss,
7:21 Why hath the Lord d' thus unto
11: 4 for this thing is d' of me.
16: 9 Herein thou hast d' foolishly:
24:16 because he had d' good in Israel,
22 Jehoiada his father had d' to

2Ch 25:16 because thou hast d' this, and hast
29: 2 to all that David his father had d'.
6 d' that which was evil in the sight
36 for the thing was d' suddenly.
30: 5 they had not d' it of a long time
32:13 what I and my fathers have d'
25 according to the benefit d' unto him;
31 wonder that was d' in the land,
Ezr 6:12 made a decree; let it be d' with
7:21 require of you, it be d' speedily,
23 let it be diligently d' for the house
9: 1 Now when these things were d',
10: 3 let it be d' according to the law.
Ne 5:19 all that I have d' for this people.
6: 8 There are no such things d' as
9 from the work, that it be not d'.
8:17 not the children of Israel d' so.
9:33 for thou hast d' right,
33 but we have d' wickedly:
13:14 deeds that I have d' for the house
Es 1:16 hath not d' wrong unto the king
2: 1 and what she had d', and what
4: 1 Mordecai perceived all that was d',
6: 3 hath been d' to Mordecai for this?
3 him, There is nothing d' for him.
6 What shall be d' unto the man
9 Thus shall it be d' to the man
11 Thus shall it be d' unto the man
9:12 they d' in the rest of the king's
12 request further? and it shall be d'.
14 the king commanded it so to be d':
Job 21:31 shall repay him what he hath d'?
34:29 whether it be d' against a nation,
32 if I have d' iniquity, I will do no
Ps 7: 3 O Lord my God, if I have d' this;
14: 1 they have d' abominable works,
22:31 be born, that he hath d' this.
33: 4 and all his works are d' in truth.
9 For he spake, and it was d'; he
40: 5 works which thou hast d', and thy
50:21 These things hast thou d', and I
51: 4 sinned, and d' this evil in thy sight:
52: 9 because thou hast d' it: and I will
53: 1 and have d' abominable iniquity:
66:16 what he hath d' for my soul.
71:19 who hast d' great things: O God,
74: 3 hath d' wickedly in the sanctuary.
78: 4 wonderful works that he hath d'.
98: 1 for he hath d' marvellous things:
105: 5 marvellous works that he hath d';
106: 6 iniquity, we have d' wickedly.
21 saviour, which had d' great things
109:27 hand; that thou, Lord, hast d' it.
111: 8 are d' in truth and uprightness.
115: 3 d' whatsoever he hath pleased.
119:121 I have d' judgment and justice:
166 and d' thy commandments.
120: 3 what shall be d' unto thee, thou
126: 2 hath d' great things for them.
3 Lord hath d' great things for us;
Pr 3:30 if he have d' thee no harm.
4:16 sleep not, except they have d' mischief;
24:29 do so to him as he hath d' to me:
30:20 saith, I have d' no wickedness.
32 hast d' foolishly in lifting up thyself,
31:29 daughters have d' virtuously,
Ec 1: 9 which is d' is that which shall be d':
13 things that are d' under heaven:
14 works that are d' under the sun;
2:12 that which hath been already d'.
4: 1 that are d' under the sun:
3 the evil work that is d' under the
8: 9 my heart unto every work that is d'
10 in the city where they had so d':
14 a vanity which is d' upon the earth;
16 business that is d' upon the earth:
17 cannot find out the work that is d'
9: 3 things that are d' under the sun,
6 any thing that is d' under the sun.
Isa 5: 4 have been d' more to my vineyard,
4 that I have not d' in it?
10:11 d' unto Samaria and her idols, so
13 strength of my hand I have d' it,
12: 5 for he hath d' excellent things:
24:13 grapes when the vintage is d'.
25: 1 thou hast d' wonderful things;
33:13 that are far off, what I have d';
37:11 the kings of Assyria have d' to all
26 heard long ago, how I have d' it;
38: 3 and have d' that which is good in
15 unto me, and himself hath d' it:
41: 4 Who hath wrought and d' it,
20 the hand of the Lord hath d' this,
44:23 ye heavens; for the Lord hath d' it:
46:10 the things that are not yet d',
48: 5 say, Mine idol hath d' them,
53: 9 because he had d' no violence,
Jer 2:23 the valley, know what thou hast d':
3: 5 thou hast spoken and d' evil things
6 which backsliding Israel hath d'?
7 after she had d' all these things,
16 neither shall that be d' any more.
5:13 thus shall it be d' unto them.
7:13 because ye have d' all these works,
14 your fathers, as I have d' to Shiloh.
30 children of Judah have d' evil in
8: 6 saying, What have I d'?
11:17 d' against themselves to provoke
16:12 have d' worse than your fathers;
18:13 the virgin of Israel hath d' a very
22: 8 hath the Lord d' thus unto this
30:15 I have d' these things unto thee.
24 until he have d' it, and until he
31:37 that they have d', saith the Lord,
32:23 they have d' nothing of all that
30 children of Judah have only d' evil

Jer 32:32 have *d'* to provoke me to anger,
34:15 *d'* right in my sight, in proclaiming
35:10 obeyed, and *d'* according to all
18 *d'* according unto all that he hath
38: 9 these men have *d'* evil in all that
9 have *d'* to Jeremiah the prophet,
40: 3 brought it, and *d'* according as he
41:11 the son of Nethaniah had *d'*,
42:10 the evil that I have *d'* unto you.
44:17 as we have *d'*, we, and our fathers,
48:19 that escapeth, and say, What is *d'*?
50:15 as she hath *d'*, do unto her.
29 according to all that she hath *d'*,
51:12 both devised and *d'* that which
24 they have *d'* in Zion in your sight
35 The violence *d'* to me and to my flesh
52: 2 all that Jehoiakim had *d'*.
La 1:12 which is *d'* unto me, wherewith
21 they are glad that thou hast *d'* it:
22 unto them, as thou hast *d'* unto
2:17 The Lord hath *d'* that which he
20 to whom thou hast *d'* this.
Eze 3:20 his righteousness which he hath *d'*
5: 7 *d'* according to the judgments
9 which I have not *d'*, and whereunto
9: 4 that be *d'* in the midst thereof.
11 *d'* as thou hast commanded me.
11:12 *d'* after the manners of the heathen
12:11 have *d'*, so shall it be *d'* unto them
28 shall be *d'*, saith the Lord God.
14:23 I have not *d'* without cause all that
23 I have *d'* in it, saith the Lord God.
16:47 nor *d'* after their abominations:
48 hath not *d'*, she nor her daughters,
48 hast *d'*, thou and thy daughters.
51 abominations which thou hast *d'*.
54 confounded in all that thou hast *d'*,
59 deal with thee as thou hast *d'*,
63 toward thee for all that thou hast *d'*
17:18 and hath *d'* all these things, he
24 Lord have spoken and have *d'* it.
18:13 he hath *d'* all these abominations;
14 his father's sins which he hath *d'*,
19 *d'* that which is lawful and right,
19 hath *d'* them, he shall surely live.
22 that he hath *d'* he shall live.
24 he hath *d'* shall not be mentioned:
26 that he hath *d'* shall he die.
23:38 Moreover this they have *d'* unto me:
39 they *d'* in the midst of mine house.
24:22 And ye shall do as I have *d'*: ye
24 according to all that he hath *d'*
33:16 *d'* that which is lawful and right;
39: 8 Behold, it is come, and it is *d'*,
24 have I *d'* unto them, and hid my
43:11 of all that they have *d'*, shew them
44:14 and for all that shall be *d'* therein.
Da 6:22 thee, O King, have I *d'* no hurt.
9: 5 have *d'* wickedly, and have rebelled,
12 hath not been *d'* as hath been *d'*
15 we have sinned, we have *d'* wickedly.
11:24 which his fathers have not *d'*, nor
36 that that is determined shall be *d'*.
Hos 2: 5 conceived them hath *d'* shamefully:
Joel 2:20 because he hath *d'* great things.
Am 3: 6 and the Lord hath not *d'* it?
Ob 1:15 as thou hast *d'*, it shall be *d'* unto
Jo 1:10 Why hast thou *d'* this? For the
14 O Lord, hast *d'* as it pleased thee.
Mic 6: 3 what have I *d'* unto thee? and
Zep 3: 4 they have *d'* violence to the law.
Zec 7: 3 as I have *d'* these so many years?
Mal 2:13 And this have ye *d'* again,
M't 1:22 Now all this was *d'*, that it might
6:10 Thy will be *d'* in earth
7:22 in thy name *d'* many wonderful
8:13 so be it *d'* unto thee.
11:20 most of his mighty works were *d'*,
21 which were *d'* in you,
21 had been *d'* in Tyre and Sidon,
23 which have been *d'* in thee,
23 had been *d'* in Sodom, it would
13:28 An enemy hath *d'* this.
17:12 but have *d'* unto him whatsoever
18:19 it shall be *d'* for them of my Father
31 saw what was *d'*, they were very
31 told unto their lord all that was *d'*.
21: 4 All this was *d'*, that it might be
21 this which is *d'* to the fig tree, but
21 cast into the sea; and it shall be *d'*.
23:23 these ought ye to have *d'*, and not
25:21 Well *d'*, thou good and faithful
23 Well *d'*, good and faithful servant;
40 as ye have *d'* it unto one of the
40 brethren, ye have *d'* it unto me.
26:13 that this woman hath *d'*, be told for
42 except I drink it, thy will be *d'*.
56 But all this was *d'* that the
27:23 Why, what evil hath he *d'*? But
54 and those things that were *d'*,
28:11 priests all the things that were *d'*.
M'r 4:11 all these things are *d'* in parables:
5:14 to see what it was that was *d'*.
19 the Lord hath *d'* for thee, and
20 great things Jesus had *d'* for him:
32 to see her that had *d'* this thing.
33 knowing what was *d'* in her, came
6:30 both what they had *d'*, and what
7:37 He hath *d'* all things well;
9:13 they have *d'* unto him whatsoever
13:30 pass, till all these things be *d'*.
14: 8 She hath *d'* what she could: she
9 this also that she hath *d'* shall be
15: 8 do as he had ever *d'* unto them.
14 what evil hath he *d'*? And thy
Lu 1:49 he that is mighty hath *d'* to me

Lu 3:19 all the evils which Herod had *d'*.
4:23 whatsoever we have heard *d'* in
5: 6 when they had this *d'*, they inclosed
8:34 that fed them saw what was *d'*,
35 they went out to see what was *d'*;
39 great things God hath *d'* unto
39 how great things Jesus had *d'* unto
56 should tell no man what was *d'*.
9: 7 heard all that was *d'* by him: and
10 told him all that they had *d'*.
10:13 works had been *d'* in Tyre and
13 which have been *d'* in you, they
11: 2 Thy will be *d'*, as in heaven, so in
42 these ought ye to have *d'*, and not
13:17 glorious things that were *d'* by
14:22 it is *d'* as thou hast commanded
16: 8 because he had *d'* wisely; for the
17:10 when ye shall have *d'* all those
10 unprofitable servants: we have *d'*
22:42 not my will, but thine, be *d'*.
23: 8 have seen some miracle *d'* by him.
15 worthy of death is *d'* unto him
22 time, Why, what evil hath he *d'*?
31 what shall be *d'* in the dry?
41 this man hath *d'* nothing amiss.
47 saw what was *d'*, he glorified God,
48 the things which were *d'*, smote
24:21 day since these things were *d'*.
35 what things were *d'* in the way,
Joh 1:28 These things were *d'* in Bethabara
5:16 because he had *d'* these things on
29 they that have *d'* good, unto the
29 of life; and they that have *d'* evil
7:21 I have *d'* one work, and ye all
31 than these which this man hath *d'*?
11:46 them what things Jesus had *d'*.
12:16 and that they had *d'* these things
18 they heard that he had *d'* this
37 But though he had *d'* so many
13:12 Know ye what I have *d'* to you?
15 ye should do as I have *d'* to you.
15: 7 what ye will, and it shall be *d'*
24 If I had not *d'* among them the
18:35 thee unto me: what hast thou *d'*?
19:36 For these things were *d'*, that the
Ac 2:43 wonders and were *d'* by the
4: 7 by what name, have ye *d'* this?
9 the good deed *d'* to the impotent
16 notable miracle hath been *d'* by
21 glorified God for that which was *d'*.
28 determined before to be *d'*.
30 may be *d'* by the name of thy holy
5: 7 not knowing what was *d'*, came in.
8:13 miracles and signs which were *d'*,
9:13 much evil he hath *d'* to thy saints
10:16 This was *d'* thrice: and the vessel
33 and thou hast *d'* well that thou
11:10 And this was *d'* three times: and
12: 9 true which was *d'* by the angel;
13:12 when he saw what was *d'*,
14: 3 signs and wonders to be *d'* by their
11 saw what Paul had *d'*, they lifted
13 and would have *d'* sacrifice with the
18 that they had not *d'* sacrifice unto
27 all that God had *d'* with them, and
15: 4 all things that God had *d'* with
21:14 The will of the Lord be *d'*.
33 who he was, and what he had *d'*.
24: 2 worthy deeds are *d'* unto this
25:10 have I *d'* no wrong, as thou very
26:26 this thing was not *d'* in a corner.
28: 9 So when this was *d'*, others also,
Ro 9:11 neither having *d'* any good or evil,
1Co 5: 2 that he that hath *d'* this deed
3 him that hath so *d'* this deed,
9:15 that it should be so *d'* unto me:
13:10 which is in part shall be *d'* away.
14:26 Let all things be *d'* unto edifying.
40 Let all things be *d'* decently and in
16:14 all your things be *d'* with charity.
2Co 3: 7 which glory was to be *d'* away:
11 For if that which is *d'* away was
14 which vail is *d'* away in Christ.
5:10 may receive the things *d'* in his body,
10 according to that he hath *d'*,
7:12 that had *d'* the wrong, nor for his
Eph 5:12 those things which are *d'* of them
6:13 in the evil day, and having *d'* all,
Ph'p 2: 3 Let nothing be *d'* through strife or
4:14 Notwithstanding ye have well *d'*,
Col 3:25 for the wrong which he hath *d'*:
4: 9 unto you all things which are *d'* here.
Tit 3: 5 righteousness which we have *d'*,
Heb 10:29 hath *d'* despite unto the Spirit of
36 after ye have *d'* the will of God,
Re 16:17 from the throne, saying, It is *d'*.
21: 6 And he said unto me, It is *d'*.
22: 6 things which must shortly be *d'*.

door See also DOORKEEPER; DOORS.
Ge 4: 7 doest not well, sin lieth at the *d'*.
6:16 and the *d'* of the ark shalt thou set
18: 1 he sat in the tent *d'* in the heat of
2 ran to meet them from the tent *d'*,
10 Sarah heard it in the tent *d'*,
19: 6 Lot went out at the *d'* unto them,
6 and shut the *d'* after him,
9 and came near to break the *d'*.
10 house to them, and shut to the *d'*.
11 the men that were at the *d'*
11 wearied themselves to find the *d'*.
43:19 with him at the *d'* of the house
Ex 12: 7 on the *d'* post of the houses,
22 go out at the *d'* of his house
23 the Lord will pass over the *d'*,
21: 6 he shall also bring him to the *d'*,
6 unto the *d'* post; and his master

Ex 26:36 shalt make an hanging for the *d'*
29: 4 bring unto the *d'* of the tabernacle
11 Lord, by the *d'* of the tabernacle
32 in the basket, by the *d'* of the
42 at the *d'* of the tabernacle of
33: 8 and stood every man at his tent *d'*,
9 stood at the *d'* of the tabernacle,
10 pillar stand at the tabernacle *d'*:
10 worshipped, every man in his tent *d'*.
35:15 and the hanging for the *d'* at the
17 hanging for the *d'* of the court,
36:37 for the tabernacle *d'* of blue,
38: 8 which assembled at the *d'* of the
30 the sockets to the *d'* of the
39:38 the hanging for the tabernacle *d'*,
40: 5 and put the hanging of the *d'* to the
6 before the *d'* of the tabernacle of
12 and his sons unto the *d'* of the
28 he set up the hanging at the *d'*
29 by the *d'* of the tabernacle of the
Le 1: 3 voluntary will at the *d'* of the
5 the altar that is by the *d'* of the
3: 2 kill it at the *d'* of the tabernacle
4: 4 unto the *d'* of the tabernacle
7 which is at the *d'* of the tabernacle
18 burnt offering, which is at the *d'* of
8: 3 congregation together unto the *d'*
4 was gathered together unto the *d'*
31 the flesh at the *d'* of the tabernacle
33 And ye shall not go out of the *d'*
35 Therefore shall ye abide at the *d'*
10: 7 And ye shall not go out from the *d'*
12: 6 sin offering, unto the *d'* of the
14:11 Lord, at the *d'* of the tabernacle
23 the priest, unto the *d'* of the
38 the house to the *d'* of the house,
15:14 Lord unto the *d'* of the tabernacle
29 the priest, to the *d'* of the
16: 7 at the *d'* of the tabernacle of the
17: 4 And bringeth it not unto the *d'* of
5 unto the Lord, unto the *d'* of the
6 altar of the Lord at the *d'* of
9 bringeth it not unto the *d'* of the
19:21 offering unto the Lord, unto the *d'*
Nu 3:25 for the *d'* of the tabernacle
26 the curtain for the *d'* of the court,
4:25 for the *d'* of the tabernacle
26 the hanging for the *d'* of the gate
6:10 priest, to the *d'* of the tabernacle
13 unto the *d'* of the tabernacle
18 his separation at the *d'* of the
10: 3 at the *d'* of the tabernacle
11:10 every man in the *d'* of his tent:
12: 5 stood in the *d'* of the tabernacle,
16:18 stood in the *d'* of the tabernacle
19 them unto the *d'* of the tabernacle
27 and stood in the *d'* of their tents,
50 returned unto Moses unto the *d'* of
20: 6 unto the *d'* of the tabernacle of the
25: 6 before the *d'* of the tabernacle
27: 2 the congregation, by the *d'* of the
De 11:20 upon the *d'* posts of thine house,
15:17 it through his ear unto the *d'*,
22:21 to the *d'* of her father's house,
31:15 stood over the *d'* of the tabernacle.
Jos 19:51 Lord, at the *d'* of the tabernacle
J'g 4:20 Stand in the *d'* of the tent, and it
9:52 went hard unto the *d'* of the tower
19:22 beat at the *d'*, and spake to the
26 down at the *d'* of the man's house
27 fallen down at the *d'* of the house,
1Sa 2:22 that assembled at the *d'* of the
2Sa 11: 9 Uriah slept at the *d'* of the king's
13:17 from me, and bolt the *d'* after her.
18 her out, and bolted the *d'* after her.
1Ki 6: 8 The *d'* for the middle chamber
33 made he for the *d'* of the temple
34 leaves of the one *d'* were folding,
34 and the two leaves of the other *d'*
14: 6 her feet, as she came in at the *d'*,
17 threshold of the *d'*, the child died;
27 kept the *d'* of the king's house.
2Ki 4: 4 thou shalt shut the *d'* upon thee
5 shut the *d'* upon her and upon her
15 had called her, she stood in the *d'*.
21 shut the *d'* upon him, and went out.
33 and shut the *d'* upon them twain,
5: 9 at the *d'* of the house of Elisha.
6:32 the *d'*, and hold him fast at the *d'*:
9: 3 Then open the *d'*, and flee, and
10 And he opened the *d'*, and fled.
12: 9 that kept the *d'* put therein
22: 4 keepers of the *d'* have gathered
23: 4 keepers of the *d'*, to bring forth
25:18 and the three keepers of the *d'*:
1Ch 9:21 porter of the *d'* of the tabernacle
Ne 3:20 unto the *d'* of the house of Eliashib
21 from the *d'* of the house of Eliashib
Es 2:21 which kept the *d'*, were wroth,
6: 2 the keepers of the *d'*, who sought
Job 31: 9 laid wait at my neighbour's *d'*;
34 silence, and went not out of the *d'*?
Ps 141: 3 my mouth; keep the *d'* of my lips.
Pr 5: 8 come not nigh the *d'* of her house:
9:14 she sitteth at the *d'* of her house,
26:14 As the *d'* turneth upon his hinges,
Ca 5: 4 the hole of the *d'*, and my bowels
8: 9 if she be a *d'*, we will enclose
Isa 6: 4 posts of the *d'* moved at the voice
Jer 35: 4 of Shallum, the keeper of the *d'*:
52:24 and the three keepers of the *d'*:
Eze 8: 3 to the *d'* of the inner gate that
7 brought me to the *d'* of the court;
8 had digged in the wall, behold a *d'*.
14 he brought me to the *d'* of the gate
16 at the *d'* of the temple of the Lord,

Eze 10:19 one stood at the *d'* of the east gate
11: 1 and behold at the *d'* of the gate five
40:13 and twenty cubits, *d'* against *d'*.
41: 2 breadth of the *d'* was ten cubits;
2 the sides of the *d'* were five cubits
3 and measured the post of the *d'*,
3 two cubits; and the *d'*, six cubits.
3 the breadth of the *d'*, seven cubits
11 one *d'* toward the north, and
11 another *d'* toward the south:
16 The *d'* posts, and the narrow
16 against the *d'*, cieled with wood
17 To that above the *d'*, even unto
20 From the ground unto above the *d'*
24 leaves for the one *d'*, and...other *d'*.
42: 2 hundred cubits was the north *d'*,
12 was a *d'* in the head of the way,
46: 3 shall worship at the *d'* of this gate
47: 1 me again unto the *d'* of the house;
Hos 2:15 the valley of Achor for a *d'* of hope:
Am 9: 1 he said, Smite the lintel of the *d'*,
M't 6: 6 when thou hast shut thy *d'*,
25:10 marriage; and the *d'* was shut.
27:60 stone to the *d'* of the sepulchre,
28: 2 rolled back the stone from the *d'*,
M'r 1:33 was gathered together at the *d'*.
2: 2 no, not so much as about the *d'*:
11: 4 colt tied by the *d'* without in a place
15:46 stone unto the *d'* of the sepulchre.
16: 3 stone from the *d'* of the sepulchre?
Lu 11: 7 the *d'* is now shut, and my children
13:25 is risen up, and hath shut to the *d'*,
25 to knock at the *d'*, saying, Lord,
Joh 10: 1 by the *d'* into the sheepfold, but
2 the *d'* is the shepherd of the sheep.
7 unto you, I am the *d'* of the sheep.
9 I am the *d'*: by me if any man
18:16 Peter stood at the *d'* without.
16 spake unto her that kept the *d'*,
17 the damsel that kept the *d'*
Ac 5: 9 at the *d'*, and shall carry thee out.
12: 6 before the *d'* kept the prison.
13 Peter knocked at the *d'* of the gate,
16 and when they had opened the *d'*,
14:27 opened the *d'* of faith unto the
1Co 16: 9 a great *d'* and effectual is opened
2Co 2:12 and a *d'* was opened unto me
Col 4: 3 open unto us a *d'* of utterance,
Jas 5: 9 the judge standeth before the *d'*.
Re 3: 8 set before thee an open *d'*,
20 I stand at the *d'*, and knock: if any
20 man hear my voice, and open the *d'*,
4: 1 a *d'* was opened in heaven:

doorkeeper See also DOORKEEPERS.
Ps 84:10 I had rather be a *d'* in the house

doorkeepers
1Ch 15:23 and Elkanah were *d'* for the ark.
24 and Jehiah were *d'* for the ark.

door-post See DOOR and POST.

doors
Jos 2:19 shall go out of the *d'* of thy house
J'g 3:23 the *d'* of the parlour upon him,
24 the *d'* of the parlour were locked,
25 he opened not the *d'* of the parlour;
11:31 cometh forth of the *d'* of my house
16: 3 took the *d'* of the gate of the city,
19:27 and opened the *d'* of the house, and
1Sa 3:15 the *d'* of the house of the Lord.
21:13 scrabbled on the *d'* of the gate, and
1Ki 6:31 the oracle he made *d'* of olive tree:
32 The two *d'* also were of olive tree;
34 the two *d'* were of fir tree: the two
7: 5 all the *d'* and posts were square,
50 of the *d'* of the inner house, the
50 place, and for the *d'* of the house,
2Ki 18:16 the *d'* of the temple of the Lord,
1Ch 22: 3 the nails of the *d'* of the gates,
2Ch 3: 7 and the *d'* thereof, with gold;
4: 9 great court and *d'* for the court,
9 and overlaid the *d'* of them with
22 the inner *d'* thereof for the most
22 and the *d'* of the house of the
23: 4 Levites, shall be porters of the *d'*;
28:24 up the *d'* of the house of the Lord,
29: 3 the *d'* of the house of the Lord,
7 have shut up the *d'* of the porch,
34: 9 the Levites that kept the *d'* had
Ne 3: 1 set up the *d'* of it; even unto the
3,6,13,14,15 and set up the *d'* thereof,
6: 1 that time I had not set up the *d'*
10 let us shut the *d'* of the temple:
7: 1 I had set up the *d'*, and the porters,
3 let them shut the *d'* and bar them:
Job 3:10 up the *d'* of my mother's womb,
31:32 but I opened my *d'* to the traveller.
38: 8 Or who shut up the sea with *d'*,
10 decreed place, and set bars and *d'*,
17 thou seen the *d'* of the shadow
41:14 Who can open the *d'* of his face?
Ps 24: 7 be ye lift up, ye everlasting *d'*;
9 lift them up, ye everlasting *d'*;
78:23 and opened the *d'* of heaven,
Pr 8: 3 city, at the coming in at the *d'*.
34 waiting at the posts of my *d'*.
Ec 12: 4 the *d'* shall be shut in the streets,
Isa 26:20 shut thy *d'* about thee: hide
57: 8 Behind the *d'* also and the posts
Eze 33:30 and in the *d'* of the houses,
41:11 And the *d'* of the side chambers
23 and the sanctuary had two *d'*.
24 the *d'* had two leaves apiece,
25 on the *d'* of the temple, cherubims
42: 4 and their *d'* toward the north.
11 fashions, and according to their *d'*.
Eze 42:12 according to the *d'* of the chambers
Mic 7: 5 keep the *d'* of my mouth from her
Zec 11: 1 Open thy *d'*, O Lebanon, that the
Mal 1:10 that would shut the *d'* for nought?
M't 24:33 it is near, even at the *d'*.
M'r 13:29 it is nigh, even at the *d'*.
Joh 20:19 when the *d'* were shut where the
26 the *d'* being shut, and stood in the
Ac 5:19 opened the prison *d'*, and brought
23 standing without before the *d'*:
16:26 immediately all the *d'* were opened
27 seeing the prison *d'* open, he drew
21:30 and forthwith the *d'* were shut.

Dophkah (*dof'-kah*)
Nu 33:12 of Sin, and encamped in *D'*.
13 And they departed from *D'*, and

Dor (*dor*) See also EN-DOR.
Jos 11: 2 the borders of *D'* on the west,
12:23 The king of *D'* in the coast of *D'*,
17:11 the inhabitants of *D'* and her towns,
J'g 1:27 the inhabitants of *D'* and her towns,
1Ki 4:11 of Abinadab, in all the region of *D'*;
1Ch 7:29 and her towns, *D'* and her towns.

Dorcas (*dor'-cas*) See also TABITHA.
Ac 9:36 by interpretation is called *D'*:
39 *D'* made, while she was with them.

dost See also DOEST.
Ge 32:29 is it that thou *d'* ask after my name?
44: 4 thou *d'* overtake them, say unto them,
De 9: 5 *d'* thou go to possess their land:
24:10 thou *d'* lend thy brother any thing,
11 the man to whom thou *d'* lend shall
J'g 14:16 Thou *d'* but hate me, and lovest me
1Sa 24:14 after whom *d'* thou pursue? after
28:16 Wherefore then *d'* thou ask of me,
1Ki 2:22 *d'* thou ask Abishag the Shunammite
21: 7 *D'* thou now govern the kingdom of
2Ki 18:20 Now on whom *d'* thou trust, that
2Ch 6:26 their sin, when thou *d'* afflict them;
Ne 2: 4 For what *d'* thou make request?
Job 2: 9 *D'* thou still retain thine integrity?
7:21 *d'* thou not pardon my transgression
10: 8 round about; yet thou *d'* destroy
14: 3 And *d'* thou open thine eyes upon
16 *d'* thou not watch over my sin?
15: 8 *d'* thou restrain wisdom for thyself?
30:20 unto thee, and thou *d'* not hear me:
33:13 Why *d'* thou strive against him?
37:15 *D'* thou know when God disposed
16 *D'* thou know the balancings of the
Ps 39:11 thou with rebukes *d'* correct man for
43: 2 why *d'* thou cast me off? why go
44:12 and *d'* not increase thy wealth
99: 4 thou *d'* establish equity, thou executest
Pr 4: 8 to honour, when thou *d'* embrace her.
Ec 7:10 *d'* not enquire wisely concerning this.
Ca 5: 9 that thou *d'* so charge us?
Isa 26: 7 most upright, *d'* weigh the path of the
36: 5 now on whom *d'* thou trust, that thou
Jer 32: 3 Wherefore *d'* thou prophesy, and say,
40:14 *D'* thou certainly know that Baalis
48:18 daughter that *d'* inhabit Dibon,
La 5:20 Wherefore *d'* thou forget us for ever,
Eze 2: 6 and thou *d'* dwell among scorpions:
32:19 Whom *d'* thou pass in beauty?
33: 8 if thou *d'* not speak to warn the
Mic 4: 9 why *d'* thou cry out aloud? is there
Hab 1: 3 Why *d'* thou shew me iniquity, and
Lu 10:40 Lord, *d'* thou not care that my sister
23:40 *D'* not thou fear God, seeing thou art
Joh 6:30 believe thee? what *d'* thou work?
9:34 and *d'* thou teach us? And they cast
35 *D'* thou believe on the Son of God?
10:24 How long *d'* thou make us to doubt?
13: 6 Lord, *d'* thou wash my feet?
Ro 2:21 man should not steal, *d'* thou steal?
22 *d'* thou commit adultery? thou that
22 idols, *d'* thou commit sacrilege?
27 and circumcision *d'* transgress
14:10 But why *d'* thou judge thy brother?
10 or why *d'* thou set at nought thy
1Co 4: 7 why *d'* thou glory, as if thou hadst
Re 6:10 Lord, holy and true, *d'* thou not judge

dote See also DOTED; DOTING.
Jer 50:36 and they shall *d'*: a sword is upon

doted
Eze 23: 5 and she *d'* on her lovers, on the
7 with all on whom she *d'*: with all
9 of the Assyrians, upon whom she *d'*.
12 She *d'* upon the Assyrians her
16 she saw them with her eyes, she *d'*
20 For she *d'* upon their paramours,

doth See also DOETH.
Ge 3: 5 God *d'* know that in the day ye eat
27:42 Esau, as touching thee, *d'* comfort
45: 3 *d'* my father yet live?
Ex 11: 7 how that the Lord *d'* put a difference
31:13 am the Lord that *d'* sanctify you.
32:11 why *d'* thy wrath wax hot against thy
31 when they are dead, *d'* fall, it shall be
Le 11:32 *d'* touch them, when they be dead,
25:16 years of the fruits *d'* he sell unto thee.
Nu 5:21 the Lord *d'* make thy thigh to rot,
16: 7 the man whom the Lord *d'* choose,
36: 6 thing which the Lord *d'* command
De 1:20 Lord our God *d'* give unto us.
25 the Lord our God *d'* give us.
31 God bare thee, as a man *d'* bear his
5:24 this day that God *d'* talk with man,
8: 3 that man *d'* not live by bread only,
3 of the mouth of the Lord *d'* man live.
9: 4 the Lord *d'* drive them out from before
5 thy God *d'* drive them out from before
De 11:10 *d'* the Lord thy God require of thee,
18 He *d'* execute the judgment of the
16:19 a gift *d'* blind the eyes of the wise,
18:12 the Lord thy God *d'* drive them out
20:16 the Lord thy God *d'* give thee for
31: 6 thy God, he it is that *d'* go with thee;
8 Lord, he it is that *d'* go before thee;
Jos 1:18 Whosoever he be that *d'* rebel
20: 4 when he that *d'* flee unto one of
J'g 4:20 any man *d'* come and enquire of thee,
Ru 3:11 for all the city of my people *d'* know
1Sa 9:13 because he *d'* bless the sacrifice; and
23:19 *D'* not David hide himself with us
26: 1 *D'* not David hide himself in the hill
18 Wherefore *d'* my lord thus pursue
20 flea, as when one *d'* hunt a partridge
2Sa 10: 3 Thinkest thou that David *d'* honour
14:13 for the king *d'* speak this thing
13 in that the king *d'* not fetch home
14 *d'* God respect any person: yet *d'*
19: 8 Behold, the king *d'* sit in the gate.
20 servant *d'* know that I have sinned:
24: 3 but why *d'* my lord the king delight
24 that which *d'* cost me nothing.
1Ki 1:11 Adonijah the son of Haggith *d'* reign,
13 throne? why then *d'* Adonijah reign?
22: 8 *d'* not prophesy good concerning me,
2Ki 2:15 The spirit of Elijah *d'* rest on Elisha.
5: 7 this man *d'* send unto me to recover
1Ch 19: 3 thou that David *d'* honour thy father,
21: 3 then *d'* my lord require this thing?
2Ch 6:33 and fear thee, as *d'* thy people Israel,
32:11 *D'* not Hezekiah persuade you to give
Job 1: 9 said, *D'* Job fear God for nought?
4:21 *D'* not their excellency which is
5: 6 *d'* trouble spring out of the ground;
6: 5 *D'* the wild ass bray when he hath
25 but what *d'* your arguing reprove?
8: 3 *D'* God pervert judgment? or *d'* the
12:11 *D'* not the ear try words? and the
15:12 Why *d'* thine heart carry thee away?
16:13 my reins asunder, and *d'* not spare;
17: 2 *d'* not mine eye continue in their
22:13 How *d'* God know? can he judge
23: 9 On the left hand, where he *d'* work,
24:19 *d'* the grave those which have sinned.
25: 3 upon whom *d'* not his light arise?
31: 4 *D'* not he see my ways, and count all
35:16 *d'* Job open his mouth in vain;
36: 7 he *d'* establish them for ever, and
39:26 *D'* the hawk fly by thy wisdom, and
27 *D'* the eagle mount up at thy
41:18 By his neesings a light *d'* shine,
Ps 1: 2 and in his law *d'* he meditate day and
10: 2 his pride *d'* persecute the poor:
8 in the secret places *d'* he murder the
9 *d'* catch the poor, when he draweth
13 Wherefore *d'* the wicked contemn
11: 7 his countenance *d'* behold the
29: 9 in his temple *d'* every one speak
41:11 because mine enemy *d'* not triumph
54:*title* *D'* not David hide himself with us?
59: 7 their lips: for who, say they, *d'* hear?
68:33 lo, he *d'* send out his voice, and
73:11 How *d'* God know? and is there
74: 1 why *d'* thine anger smoke against
77: 8 *d'* his promise fail for evermore?
80:13 boar out of the wood *d'* waste it,
13 wild beast of the field *d'* devour it.
92: 6 neither *d'* a fool understand this.
119:129 therefore *d'* my soul keep them.
130: 5 *d'* wait, and in his word do I hope.
147: 2 The Lord *d'* build up Jerusalem:
Pr 6:16 These six things *d'* the Lord hate:
8: 1 *D'* not wisdom cry? and understanding
14:10 stranger *d'* not intermeddle with his
22: 5 *d'* keep his soul shall be far from
24:12 *d'* not he that pondereth the heart
12 keepeth thy soul, *d'* not he know it?
25:23 so *d'* an angry countenance a
26:14 upon his hinges, so *d'* the slothful
27: 9 so *d'* the sweetness of a man's friend
24 and *d'* the crown endure to every
29: 6 but the righteous *d'* sing and rejoice.
30:11 and *d'* not bless their mother.
31:11 husband *d'* safely trust in her,
Ec 10: 1 so *d'* a little folly him that is in
Ca 2: 6 and his right hand *d'* embrace me.
Isa 1: 3 but Israel *d'* not know,
3 my people *d'* not consider.
23 *d'* the cause of the widow come unto
3: 1 the Lord of hosts, *d'* take away from
9 shew of their countenance *d'* witness
10: 7 neither *d'* his heart think so;
28:24 *D'* the plowman plow all day to sow?
24 *d'* he open and break the clods of his
25 *d'* he not cast abroad the fitches,
26 *d'* instruct him to discretion, and *d'*
30:33 a stream of brimstone, *d'* kindle it.
42:11 the villages that Kedar *d'* inhabit:
44:14 an ash, and the rain *d'* nourish it.
52: 6 that day that I am he that *d'* speak:
59: 9 us, neither *d'* judgment overtake us:
Jer 2:11 glory for that which *d'* not profit.
10: 7 for to thee *d'* it appertain:
12: 1 *d'* the way of the wicked prosper?
14:10 therefore the Lord *d'* not accept them;
15:10 yet every one of them *d'* curse me.
23:14 none *d'* return from his wickedness:
30: 6 whether a man *d'* travail with child?
31:10 keep him, as a shepherd *d'* his flock.
49: 1 why then *d'* their king inherit Gad,
51:43 *d'* any son of man pass thereby.
La 1: 1 How *d'* the city sit solitary, that was
3:33 For he *d'* not afflict willingly nor
39 Wherefore *d'* a living man complain,

La 5: 8 *d'* deliver us out of their hand.
Eze 3:20 When a righteous man *d'* turn from
21 and he *d'* not sin, he shall surely live
18:19 Why? *d'* not the son bear the iniquity
20:49 me, *D'* he not speak in parables?
Ho 4:14 the people that *d'* not understand
5: 5 pride of Israel *d'* testify to his face:
Mic 6: 8 and what *d'* the Lord require of thee,
Hab 1: 4 and judgment *d'* never go forth: for
4 *d'* compass about the righteous;
Zep 3: 5 morning *d'* he bring his judgment
M't 6:19 where moth and rust *d'* corrupt,
20 neither moth nor rust *d'* corrupt,
12:24 This fellow *d'* not cast out devils,
17:24 *D'* not your master pay tribute?
18:12 *d'* he not leave the ninety and nine,
19: 9 is put away *d'* commit adultery.
22:43 then *d'* David in spirit call him Lord,
24:42 not what hour your Lord *d'* come.
26:46 he is at hand that *d'* betray me.
M'r 2: 7 *d'* this man thus speak blasphemies?
22 new wine *d'* burst the bottles,
8:12 *d'* this generation seek after a sign?
Lu 1:46 My soul *d'* magnify the Lord,
6:43 neither *d'* a corrupt tree bring
11:36 a candle *d'* give thee light.
13:15 Thou hypocrite, *d'* not each one of
34 a hen *d'* gather her brood under
14:27 And whosoever *d'* not bear his cross,
15: 4 if he lose one of them, *d'* not leave the
8 lose one piece, *d'* not light a candle,
17: 9 *D'* he thank that servant because he
22:26 that is chief, as he that *d'* serve.
Joh 2:10 beginning *d'* set forth good wine;
6:61 said unto them, *D'* this offend you?
7:51 *D'* our law judge any man, before
9:19 born blind? how then *d'* he now see?
10:17 Therefore *d'* my Father love me,
Ac 4:10 even by him *d'* this man stand here
8:36 what *d'* hinder me to be baptized?
22: 5 the high priest *d'* bear me witness,
26:24 much learning *d'* make thee mad.
Ro 8:24 seeth, why *d'* he yet hope for?
9:19 Why *d'* he yet find fault? For who
14: 6 to the Lord he *d'* not regard it.
1Co 9: 9 *D'* God take care for oxen?
11:14 *D'* not even nature itself teach you,
13: 5 *D'* not behave itself unseemly,
15:50 *d'* corruption inherit incorruption.
2Co 1:10 so great a death, and *d'* deliver:
3: 9 *d'* the ministration of righteousness
Eph 5:13 *d'* make manifest is light.
Col 1: 6 *d'* also in you, since the day ye heard
1Th 2:11 you, as a father *d'* his children.
2Th 2: 7 mystery of iniquity *d'* already work:
2Ti 2:17 their word will eat as *d'* a canker:
Heb 1:11 all shall wax old as *d'* a garment;
12: 1 the sin which *d'* so easily beset us,
Jas 2:14 What *d'* it profit, my brethren, though
16 to the body; what *d'* it profit?
3:11 *D'* a fountain send forth at the same
5: 6 killed the just; and he *d'* not resist
1Pe 3:21 even baptism *d'* also now save us,
5:13 you; and so *d'* Marcus my son.
1Jo 3: 2 and it *d'* not yet appear what we
9 is born of God *d'* not commit sin;
3Jo 1:10 *d'* he himself receive the brethren,
Re 19:11 righteousness he *d'* judge and make

Dothan (*do'-than*)
Ge 37:17 I heard them say, Let us go to *D'*.
17 his brethren, and found them in *D'*.
2Ki 6:13 him, saying, Behold, he is in *D'*.

doting
1Ti 6: 4 but *d'* about questions and strifes

double See also DOUBLED; DOUBLETONGUED.
Ge 43:12 take *d'* money in your hand;
15 they took *d'* money in their hand,
Ex 22: 4 or sheep; and he shall restore *d'*.
7 the thief be found, let him pay *d'*.
9 shall pay *d'* unto his neighbour.
26: 9 and shalt *d'* the sixth curtain in
39: 9 they made the breastplate *d'*: a
De 15:18 worth a *d'* hired servant to thee,
21:17 by giving him a *d'* portion of all
2Ki 2: 9 *d'* portion of thy spirit be upon me.
1Ch 12:33 they were not of *d'* heart.
Job 11: 6 of wisdom, that they are *d'*
41:13 who can come to him with his *d'*
Ps 12: 2 and with a *d'* heart do they speak.
Isa 40: 2 received of the Lord's hand *d'* for
61: 7 shall have *d'*; and for confusion
7 they shall possess the *d'*:
Jer 16:18 their iniquity and their sin *d'*;
17:18 destroy them with *d'* destruction.
Zec 9:12 that I will render *d'* unto thee;
1Ti 5:17 be counted worthy of *d'* honour,
Jas 1: 8 A *d'* minded man is unstable in all
4: 8 purify your hearts, ye *d'* minded.
Re 18: 6 rewarded you, and *d'* unto her
6 *d'* according to her works: *3588*.
6 which she hath filled fill to her *d'*.

doubled
Ge 41:32 for that the dream was *d'* unto
Ex 28:16 Foursquare it shall be being *d'*;
39: 9 the breadth thereof, being *d'*.
Eze 21:14 and let the sword be *d'* the third

double-minded See DOUBLE and MINDED.

doubletongued
1Ti 3: 8 not *d'*, not given to much wine,

doubt See also DOUBTED; DOUBTETH; DOUBTFUL; DOUBTING; DOUBTLESS; DOUBTS.
Ge 37:33 Joseph is without *d'* rent in pieces.
De 28:66 life shall hang in *d'* before thee:
Job 12: 2 No *d'* but ye are the people,
M't 14:31 faith, wherefore didst thou *d'*?
21:21 If ye have faith, and *d'* not, ye
M'r 11:23 shall not *d'* in his heart, but shall
Lu 11:20 no *d'* the kingdom of God is come
Joh 10:24 dost thou make us to *d'*?
Ac 2:12 were all amazed, and were in *d'*,
28: 4 No *d'* this man is a murderer,
1Co 9:10 our sakes, no *d'*, this is written:
Gal 4:20 voice; for I stand in *d'* of you.
1Jo 2:19 they would no *d'* have continued

doubted
M't 28:17 worshipped him: but some *d'*.
Ac 5:24 they *d'* of them whereunto this
10:17 while Peter *d'* in himself what
25:20 *d'* of such manner of questions,

doubteth
Ro 14:23 he that *d'* is damned if he eat,

doubtful
Lu 12:29 drink, neither be ye of *d'* mind.
Ro 14: 1 ye, but not to *d'* disputations.

doubting
Joh 13:22 on another, *d'* of whom we spake.
Ac 10:20 and go with them, *d'* nothing:
11:12 bade me go with them, nothing *d'*.
1Ti 2: 8 holy hands, without wrath and *d'*.

doubtless
Nu 14:30 *D'* ye shall not come into the
2Sa 5:19 I will *d'* deliver the Philistines
Ps 126: 6 *d'* come again with rejoicing,
Isa 63:16 *D'* thou art our Father, though
1Co 9: 2 unto others, yet *d'* I am to you:
2Co 12: 1 not expedient for me *d'* to glory.
Ph'p 3: 8 Yea *d'*, and I count all things

doubts
Da 5:12 and dissolving of *d'*, were found
16 interpretations, and dissolve *d'*:

dough
Ex 12:34 the people took their *d'* before it
39 baked unleavened cakes of the *d'*
Nu 15:20 a cake of the first of your *d'* for an
21 the first of your *d'* ye shall give
Ne 10:37 the firstfruits of your *d'*, and our
Jer 7:18 the women knead their *d'*, to
Eze 44:30 the first of your *d'*, that he may
Ho 7: 4 after he hath kneaded the *d'*,

dove See also DOVE'S; DOVES; TURTLEDOVE.
Ge 8: 8 he sent forth a *d'* from him, to
9 the *d'* found no rest for the sole of
10 again he sent forth the *d'* out of
11 *d'* came in to him in the evening;
12 seven days; and sent forth the *d'*;
Ps 55: 6 O that I had wings like a *d'*! for
68:13 ye be as the wings of a *d'* covered
Ca 2:14 O my *d'*, that art in the clefts of
5: 2 to me, my sister, my love, my *d'*,
6: 9 My *d'*, my undefiled is but one;
Isa 38:14 I did mourn as a *d'*: mine eyes fail
Jer 48:28 be like the *d'* that maketh her nest
Ho 7:11 Ephraim also is like a silly *d'*
11:11 as a *d'* out of the land of Assyria:
M't 3:16 Spirit of God descending like a *d'*,
M'r 1:10 and the Spirit like a *d'* descending
Lu 3:22 in a bodily shape like a *d'* upon
Joh 1:32 descending from heaven like a *d'*,

dove's
2Ki 6:25 fourth part of a cab of *d'* dung

doves See also DOVES'; TURTLEDOVES.
Ca 5:12 His eyes are as the eyes of *d'*
Isa 59:11 like bears, and mourn sore like *d'*:
60: 8 and as the *d'* to their windows?
Eze 7:16 shall be on the mountains like *d'*
Na 2: 7 lead her as with the voice of *d'*,
M't 10:16 as serpents, and harmless as *d'*.
21:12 the seats of them that sold *d'*,
M'r 11:15 the seats of them that sold *d'*;
Jo 2:14 that sold oxen and sheep and *d'*,
16 said unto them that sold *d'*, Take

doves'
Ca 1:15 thou art fair; thou hast *d'* eyes.
4: 1 thou hast *d'* eyes within thy locks:

down^ See also DOWNSITTING; DOWNWARD.
Ge 11: 5 the Lord came *d'* to see the city
7 Go to, let us go *d'*, and there
12:10 Abram went *d'* into Egypt to
15:11 fowls came *d'* upon the carcasses,
12 And when the sun was going *d'*,
17 to pass, that, when the sun went *d'*,
18:21 I will go *d'* now, and see whether
19: 4 But before they lay *d'*, the men
33, 35 perceived not when she lay *d'*,
21:16 and sat her *d'* over against him
23:12 And Abraham bowed *d'* himself
24:11 he made his camels to kneel *d'*
14 Let *d'* thy pitcher, I pray thee,
16 and she went *d'* to the well, and
18 let *d'* her pitcher upon her hand,
26 And the man bowed *d'* his head,
45 and she went *d'* unto the well, and
46 she let *d'* her pitcher from her
48 And I bowed *d'* my head, and
26: 2 Go not *d'* into Egypt; dwell in
27:29 thee, and nations bow *d'* to thee:
29 thy mother's sons bow *d'* to thee:
28:11 and lay *d'* in that place to sleep.
37:10 come to bow *d'* ourselves to thee
25 And they sat *d'* to eat bread: and
25 going to carry it *d'* to Egypt.
35 I will go *d'* into the grave unto my
38: 1 Judah went *d'* from his brethren,
39: 1 Joseph was brought *d'* to Egypt;
1 which had brought him *d'* thither.
Ge 42: 2 get you *d'* thither, and buy for us
3 Joseph's ten brethren went *d'* to
6 came, and bowed *d'* themselves
38 shall ye bring *d'* my gray hairs
43: 4 we will go *d'* and buy thee food:
5 not send him, we will not go *d'*:
7 would say, Bring your brother *d'*?
11 and carry *d'* the man a present,
15 and rose up, and went *d'* to Egypt,
20 came indeed *d'* at the first time
22 other money have we brought *d'*
28 And they bowed *d'* their heads,
44:11 they speedily took *d'* every man
21 Bring him *d'* unto me, that I may
23 your youngest brother come *d'* with
26 And we said, We cannot go *d'*: if
26 be with us, then will we go *d'*:
29 ye shall bring *d'* my gray hairs
31 shall bring *d'* the gray hairs of thy
45: 9 come *d'* unto me, tarry not:
13 and bring *d'* my father hither.
46: 3 fear not to go *d'* into Egypt; for I
4 I will go *d'* with thee into Egypt;
49: 6 selfwill they digged *d'* a wall.
8 children shall bow *d'* before thee.
9 stooped *d'*, he couched as a lion,
14 a strong ass couching *d'* between
50:18 went and fell *d'* before his face;
Ex 2: 5 daughter of Pharaoh came *d'* to
15 of Midian: and he sat *d'* by a well.
3: 8 I am come *d'* to deliver them out
7:10 cast *d'* his rod before Pharaoh,
12 they cast *d'* every man his rod,
9:19 the hail shall come *d'* upon them,
11: 8 servants shall come *d'* unto me,
8 and bow *d'* themselves unto me,
17:11 and when he let *d'* his hand,
12 steady until the going *d'* of the sun.
19:11 third day the Lord will come *d'* in
14 Moses went *d'* from the mount
20 Lord came *d'* upon mount Sinai,
21 Go *d'*, charge the people, lest they
24 Away, get thee *d'*, and thou shalt
25 So Moses went *d'* unto the people,
20: 5 shalt not bow *d'* thyself to them,
22:26 unto him by that the sun goeth *d'*:
23:24 shalt not bow *d'* to their gods,
24 and quite break *d'* their images.
32: 1 to come *d'* out of the mount,
6 people sat *d'* to eat and to drink,
7 said unto Moses, Go, get thee *d'*;
15 and went *d'* from the mount,
34:13 images, and cut *d'* their groves:
29 Moses came *d'* from mount Sinai
29 when he came *d'* from the mount,
Le 9:22 came *d'* from offering of the sin
11:35 for pots, they shall be broken *d'*:
14:45 And he shall break *d'* the house,
18:23 before a beast to lie *d'* thereto:
19:16 Thou shalt not go up and *d'* as a
20:16 unto any beast, and lie *d'* thereto,
22: 7 when the sun is *d'*, he shall be
26: 1 in your land, to bow *d'* unto it:
6 in the land, and ye shall lie *d'*,
30 places, and cut *d'* your images,
Nu 1:51 the Levites shall take it *d'*:
4: 5 shall take *d'* the covering vail,
10:17 And the tabernacle was taken *d'*;
11:17 I will come *d'* and talk with thee
25 And the Lord came *d'* in a cloud,
12: 5 came *d'* in the pillar of the cloud,
13:23 and cut *d'* from thence a branch
24 which the children of Israel cut *d'*
14:45 Amalekites came *d'*, and the
16:30 and they go *d'* quick into the pit;
33 went *d'* alive into the pit, and the
20:15 How our fathers went *d'* into Egypt,
28 And Moses and Eleazar came *d'*
21:15 brooks that goeth *d'* to the
22:27 of the Lord, she fell *d'* under
31 bowed *d'* his head, and fell flat
23:24 he shall not lie *d'* until he eat of
24: 9 He couched, he lay *d'* as a lion, and
25: 2 people did eat, and bowed *d'* to
33:52 and quite pluck *d'* all their high
34:11 And the coast shall go *d'* from
De 1:25 brought it *d'* unto us, and brought
5: 9 Thou shalt not bow *d'* thyself unto
6: 7 when thou liest *d'*, and when thou
7: 5 and break *d'* their images and
5 cut *d'* their groves, and
9: 3 he shall bring them *d'* before thy
12 Arise, get thee *d'* quickly from
15 I turned and came *d'* from the
18 I fell *d'* before the Lord, as at the
25 Thus I fell *d'* before the Lord forty
25 and forty nights, as I fell *d'* at the
10: 5 and came *d'* from the mount, and
22 Thy fathers went *d'* into Egypt
11:19 when thou liest *d'*, and when thou
30 way where the sun goeth *d'*,
12: 3 and ye shall hew *d'* the graven
16: 6 at the going *d'* of the sun, at the
19: 5 a stroke with the ax to cut *d'* the
20:19 and thou shalt not cut them *d'*
20 thou shalt destroy and cut them *d'*:
21: 4 elders of that city shall bring *d'*
22: 4 brother's ass or his ox fall *d'* by
23:11 when the sun is *d'*, he shall come
24:13 pledge again when the sun goeth *d'*,
15 neither shall the sun go *d'* upon it;
19 thou cuttest *d'* thine harvest
25: 2 shall cause him to lie *d'*, and to be
26: 4 and set it *d'* before the altar of the
5 and he went *d'* into Egypt, and
15 Look *d'* from thy holy habitation.

De 28:24 from heaven shall it come d' upon
43 and thou shalt come d' very low.
52 thy high and fenced walls come d',
33: 3 and they sat d' at thy feet;
28 his heavens shall drop d' dew.
Jos 1: 4 great sea toward the going d' of
2: 8 And before they were laid d',
15 Then she let them d' by a cord
18 window which thou didst let us d'
3:13 from the waters that come d' from
16 the waters which came d' from
16 and those that came d' toward the
4: 8 they lodged, and laid them d'
6: 5 walls of the city shall fall d' flat,
20 shout, that the wall fell d' flat,
7: 5 and smote them in the going d':
8:29 and as soon as the sun was d',
29 should take his carcase d' from
10:11 in the going d' to Beth-horon,
11 the Lord cast d' great stones from
13 hasted not to go d' about a whole day.
27 at the time of the going d' of the
27 and they took them d' off the trees,
15:10 and went d' to Beth-shemesh, and
16: 3 goeth d' westward to the coast of
7 And it went d' from Janohah to
17:15 and cut d' for thyself there in the
18 is a wood, and thou shalt cut it d':
18:16 border came d' to the end of the
18 northward, and went d' unto
24: 4 Jacob and his children went d'
J'g 1: 9 Judah went d' to fight against the
34 not suffer them to come d' to the
2: 2 ye shall throw d' their altars:
19 to serve them, and to bow d' unto
3:25 their lord was fallen d' dead on the
27 the children of Israel went d' with
28 And they went d' after him, and
4:14 Barak went d' from mount Tabor,
15 so that Sisera lighted d' off his
5:11 people of the Lord go d' to the
14 out of Machi came d' governors,
21 thou hast trodden d' strength.
27 feet he bowed, he fell, he lay d':
27 where he bowed, there he fell d'
6:25 and throw d' the altar of Baal that
25 hath, and cut d' the grove that is
26 the grove which thou shalt cut d'.
28 the altar of Baal was cast d',
28 and the grove was cut d' that was
30 because he hath cast d' the altar
30 and because he hath cut d' the
31 because one hath cast d' his altar.
32 because he hath thrown d' his altar.
7: 4 bring them d' unto the water, and
5 So he brought d' the people unto the
5 that boweth d' upon his knees to
6 all the rest of the people bowed d'
9 Arise, get thee d' unto the host;
10 But if thou fear to go d', go thou
10 with Phurah thy servant d' to the
11 hands be strengthened to go d'
11 Then went he d' with Phurah his
24 Come d' against the Midianites, and
8: 9 again in peace, I will break d' this
17 And he beat d' the tower of Penuel,
9:36 Behold, there come people d' from
37 See there come people d' by the
45 that was therein, and beat d' the
48 and cut d' a bough from the trees,
49 all the people likewise cut d' every
11:37 go up and d' upon the mountains,
14: 1 And Samson went d' to Timnath,
5 Then went Samson d', and his
7 And he went d', and talked with the
10 So his father went d' unto the
18 seventh day before the sun went d',
19 and he went d' to Ashkelon, and
15: 8 and he went d' and dwelt in the
12 We are come d' to bind thee, that
16:21 his eyes, and brought him d' to
31 the house of his fathers came d',
19: 6 And they sat d', and did eat and drink
14 and the sun went d' upon them when
15 he sat him d' in a street of the city:
26 and fell d' at the door of the man's
27 his concubine was fallen d' at the
20:21 of Gibeah, and destroyed d' to the
25 destroyed d' to the ground of the
32 They are smitten d' before us, as at
39 Surely they are smitten d' before us,
43 and trode them d' with ease over
Ru 3: 3 upon thee, and get thee d' to the
4 And it shall be, when he lieth d',
4 uncover his feet, and lay thee d';
6 And she went d' unto the floor,
7 he went to lie d' at the end of the
7 uncovered his feet, and laid her d'.
13 liveth: lie d' until the morning.
4: 1 up to the gate, and sat him d' there:
1 such a one! turn aside, sit d' here.
1 And he turned aside, and sat d'.
2 said, Sit ye d' here. And they sat d'.
1Sa 2: 6 he bringeth d' to the grave, and
3: 2 when Eli was laid d' in his place,
3 and Samuel was laid d' to sleep;
5 lie d' again. And he . . . lay d'.
6 I called not, my son; lie d' again.
9 Eli said unto Samuel, Go, lie d':
9 went and lay d' in his place.
6:15 And the Levites took d' the ark of
18 Abel, whereon they set d' the ark
21 the ark of the Lord; come ye d',
9:25 come d' from the high place into
27 were going d' to the end of the city,
10: 5 coming d' from the high place

1Sa 10: 8 shalt go d' before me to Gilgal;
8 behold, I will come d' unto thee,
13:12 The Philistines will come d' now
20 Israelites went d' to the Philistines,
14:16 went on beating d' one another.
36 Let us go d' after the Philistines
37 Shall I go d' after the Philistines?
15: 6 get you d' from among the
12 passed on, and gone d' to Gilgal.
16:11 we will not sit d' till he come hither.
17: 8 you, and let him come d' to me.
28 said, Why comest thou d' hither?
28 thou art come d' that thou mightest
52 Philistines fell d' by the way to
19:12 let David d' through a window:
24 lay d' naked all that day and all
20:19 then thou shalt go d' quickly,
24 the king sat him d' to eat meat.
21:13 his spittle fall d' upon his beard.
22: 1 it, they went d' thither to him.
23: 4 and said, Arise, go d' to Keilah;
6 came d' with an ephod in his hand.
8 to go d' to Keilah, to besiege David
11 And the Lord said, He will come d'
11 come d' as thy servant hath heard?
20 O king, come d' according to all
20 the desire of thy soul to come d';
25 wherefore he came d' into a rock,
25: 1 went d' to the wilderness of Paran.
20 that she came d' by the covert of
20 and his men came d' against her;
26: 2 Saul arose, and went d' to the
6 Who will go d' with me to Saul to
6 Abishai said, I will go d' with thee.
29: 4 let him not go d' with us to battle,
30:15 Canst thou bring me d' to this
15 will bring thee d' to this company.
16 And when he had brought him d',
24 part is that goeth d' to the battle,
31: 1 and fell d' slain in mount Gilboa.
2Sa 2:16 so they fell d' together: wherefore
13 the pool of Gibeon: and they sat d'
23 and he fell d' there, and died in
23 where Asahel fell d' and died stood
24 and the sun went d' when they were
3:35 or ought else, till the sun be d'.
5:17 of it, and went d' to the hold.
8: 2 with a line, casting them d' to the
11: 8 Go d' to thy house, and wash thy
9 lord, and went not d' to his house,
10 Uriah went not d' unto his house,
10 why then didst thou not go d' unto
13 servants of his lord, but went not d'
13: 5 Lay thee d' on thy bed, and make
6 So Amnon lay d' and made himself
8 Amnon's house; and he was laid d'.
15:20 make thee go up and d' with us?
24 and they set d' the ark of God;
17:18 court; whither they went d'.
18:28 he fell d' to the earth upon his
19:16 hasted and came d' with the men
18 Shimei the son of Gera fell d' before
20 of all the house of Joseph to go d'
24 Mephibosheth the son of Saul came d'
31 Gileadite came d' from Rogelim,
20:15 battered the wall, to throw it d'.
21:15 and David went d', and his
22:10 the heavens also, and came d';
28 that thou mayest bring them d'.
48 and that bringeth d' the people
23:13 of the thirty chief went d',
20 he went d' also and slew a lion in
21 but he went d' to him with a staff
1Ki 1:25 he is gone d' this day, and hath slain
33 mule, and bring him d' to Gihon;
38 and the Pelethites, went d', and
53 and they brought him d' from the
2: 6 let not his hoar head go d' to the
8 he came d' to meet me at Jordan,
9 his hoar head bring thou d' to the
19 and sat d' on his throne, and caused a
5: 9 shall bring them d' from Lebanon
8:33 When thy people Israel be smitten d'
17:23 and brought him d' out of the
18:30 altar of the lord that was broken d'.
40 Elijah brought them d' to the
42 he cast himself d' upon the earth,
44 and get thee d', that the rain stop
19: 4 and came and sat down under a
6 and drink, and laid him d' again
10 covenant, thrown d' thine altars,
14 thrown d' thine altars, and slain
21: 4 And he laid him d' upon his bed,
16 Ahab rose up to go d' to the
18 Arise, go d' to meet Ahab king of
18 whither he is gone d' to possess it.
22: 2 the king of Judah came d' to the
36 about the going d' of the sun,
2Ki 1: 2 And Ahaziah fell d' through a
4 Thou shalt not come d' from that
6 therefore thou shalt not come d'
9 God, the king hath said, Come d'.
10 let fire come d' from heaven, and
10 thy fifty. And there came d' fire
11 the king said, Come d' quickly.
12 let fire come d' from heaven, and
12 fifty. And the fire of God came d'
14 Behold, there came d' fire from
15 Go d' with him: be not afraid of
15 he arose, and went d' with him unto
16 thou shalt not come d' off that bed
2: 2 thee. So they went d' to Beth-el.
3:12 the king of Edom went d' to him.
25 And they beat d' the cities, and
5:14 went he d', and dipped himself
18 I bow d' myself in the house of

2Ki 5:21 he lighted d' from his chariot to
6: 4 to the Jordan they cut d' wood,
6 And he cut d' a stick, and cast it
9 thither the Syrians are come d'.
18 And when they came d' to him,
33 the messenger came d' unto him:
7:17 when the king came d' to him.
8:29 king of Judah went d' to see Joram'
9:16 Judah was come d' to see Joram.
24 and he sunk d' in his chariot.
33 Throw her d'. So...threw her d':
10:13 we go d' to salute the children of
27 they brake d' the image of Baal,
27 and brake d' the house of Baal,
11: 6 house, that it be not broken d'.
18 the house of Baal, and brake it d';
19 they brought d' the king from the
12:20 of Millo, which goeth d' to Silla.
13:14 king of Israel came d' unto him,
21 and when the man was let d', and
14: 9 in Lebanon, and trode d' the thistle.
13 brake d' the wall of Jerusalem
16:17 and took d' the sea from off the
18: 4 and cut d' the groves, and brake
19:16 Lord, bow d' thine ear, and hear:
23 and will cut d' the tall cedars
20:10 the shadow to go d' ten degrees:
11 by which it had gone d' in the
21:13 wiping it, and turning it upside d'.
23: 5 he put d' the idolatrous priests,
7 And he brake d' the houses of the
8 and brake d' the high places of
12 did the king beat d', and
12 and brake them d' from thence,
14 and cut d' the groves, and filled
15 and the high places he brake d',
25:10 brake d' the walls of Jerusalem
1Ch 5:22 For there fell d' many slain,
7:21 because they came d' to take
10: 1 and fell d' slain in mount Gilboa.
11:15 went d' to the rock to David, into
22 he went d' and slew a lion in a pit
23 and he went d' to him with a staff,
29:20 and bowed d' their heads, and
2Ch 6:13 kneeled d' upon his knees before
7: 1 the fire came d' from heaven,
3 of Israel saw how the fire came d',
13:17 so there fell d' slain of Israel five
14: 3 and brake d' the images,
3 and cut d' the groves:
15:16 Asa cut d' her idol, and stamped
18: 2 certain years he went d' to Ahab
34 time of the sun going d' he died.
20:16 To morrow go ye d' against them:
22: 6 Jehoram king of Judah went d' to
23:17 the house of Baal, and brake it d',
20 and brought d' the king from the
25: 8 power to help, and to cast d'.
12 cast them d' from the top of the rock,
14 and bowed d' himself before them,
18 Lebanon, and trode d' the thistle.
23 brake d' the wall of Jerusalem
26: 6 and brake d' the wall of Gath, and
31: 1 in pieces, and d' the groves, and
1 and threw d' the high places and
32:30 brought it straight d' to the west
33: 3 Hezekiah his father had broken d',
34: 4 brake d' the altars of Baalim in
4 on high above them, he cut d';
7 when he had broken d' the altars
7 powder, and cut d' all the idols
36: 3 the king of Egypt put him d' at
19 brake d' the wall of Jerusalem,
Ezr 6:11 be pulled d' from his house,
9: 3 of my beard, and sat d' astonied.
10: 1 weeping and casting himself d'
16 sat d' in the first day of the tenth
Ne 1: 3 of Jerusalem also is broken d',
4 I sat d' and wept, and mourned
2:13 Jerusalem, which were broken d',
3:15 the stairs that go d' from the city
4: 3 even break d' their stone wall.
6: 3 I cannot come d': why should the
3 I leave it, and come d' to you?
16 much cast d' in their own eyes:
9:13 camest d' also upon mount Sinai,
Es 3:15 the king and Haman sat d' to drink;
8: 3 fell d' at his feet, and besought
Job 1: 7 and from walking up and d' in it.
20 and fell d' upon the ground, and
2: 2 and from walking up and d' in it.
8 and he sat d' among the ashes.
13 they sat d' with him upon the ground
6:21 see my casting d' and are afraid
7: 4 When I lie d', I say, When shall I
9 so he that goeth d' to the grave
19 me alone till I swallow d' my spittle?
8:12 and not cut d', it withereth before
11:19 Also thou shalt lie d', and none
12:14 breaketh d', and it cannot be built
14: 2 forth as a flower, and is cut d':
7 is hope of a tree, if it be cut d',
12 So man lieth d', and riseth not:
17: 3 Lay d' now, put me in a surety
16 shall go d' to the bars of the pit,
18: 7 and his counsel shall cast him d'.
20:11 shall lie d' with him in the dust.
15 He hath swallowed d' riches, and he
18 shall not swallow it d': according
21:13 in a moment go d' to the grave.
26 They shall lie d' alike in the dust,
22:16 Which were cut d' out of time,
20 our substance is not cut d', but
29 When men are cast d', then thou
27:19 The rich man shall lie d', but he
29:24 my countenance they cast not d'.

Job 31:10 and let others bow d' upon her.
32:13 God thrusteth him d', not man.
33:24 him from going d' to the pit:
36:27 they pour d' rain according to the
40:12 and tread d' the wicked in their place.
41: 1 with a cord which thou lettest d'?
9 one be cast d' even at the sight
Ps 3: 5 I laid me d' and slept; I awaked;
4: 8 both lay me d' in peace, and sleep;
7: 5 yea, let him tread d' my life upon the
16 dealing shall come d' upon his
9:15 The heathen are sunk d' in the pit
14: 2 Lord looked d' from heaven upon
17:11 have set their eyes bowing d' to
13 disappoint him, cast him d':
18: 9 the heavens also, and came d':
27 but wilt bring d' high looks.
20: 8 They are brought d' and fallen:
22:29 that go d' to the dust shall bow
23: 2 me to lie d' in green pastures,
28: 1 like them that go d' into the pit.
30: 3 that I should not go d' to the pit.
9 in my blood, when I go d' to the pit?
31: 2 Bow d' thine ear to me; deliver
35:14 I bowed d' heavily, as one that
36:12 they are cast d', and shall not be
37: 2 For they shall soon be cut d' like
14 to cast d' the poor and needy, and
24 he shall not be utterly cast d': for
38: 6 I am bowed d' greatly; I go
42: 5 Why art thou cast d', O my soul?
6 God, my soul is cast d' within me:
11 Why art thou cast d', O my soul?
43: 5 Why art thou cast d', O my soul?
44: 5 thee will we push d' our enemies:
25 our soul is bowed d' to the dust:
50: 1 the sun unto the going d' thereof.
53: 2 God looked d' from heaven upon
55:15 let them go d' quick into hell:
23 shalt bring them d' into the pit of
56: 7 thine anger cast d' the people, O God.
57: 6 my soul is bowed d': they have
59:11 bring them d', O Lord our shield.
15 Let them wander up and d' for meat,
60:12 it is that shall tread d' our enemies.
62: 4 They only consult to cast him d'
72: 6 He shall come d' like rain upon
11 all kings shall fall d' before him:
73:18 castedst them d' into destruction.
74: 6 they break d' the carved work
7 by casting d' the dwellingplace
75: 7 he putteth d' one, and setteth up
78:16 caused waters to run d' like rivers.
24 And had rained d' manna upon them
31 smote d' the chosen men of Israel.
80:12 thou then broken d' her hedges,
14 look d' from heaven, and behold,
16 It is burned with fire, it is cut d':
85:11 shall look d' from heaven.
86: 1 Bow d' thine ear, O Lord, hear
88: 4 am counted with them that go d'
89:23 I will beat d' his foes before his
40 hast broken d' all his hedges;
44 cast his throne d' to the ground.
90: 6 in the evening it is cut d', and
95: 6 come, let us worship and bow d':
102:10 hast lifted me up, and cast me d'.
19 he hath looked d' from the height
104: 8 they go d' by the valleys unto
19 the sun knoweth his going d'.
22 and lay them d' in their dens.
107:12 brought d' their heart with labour;
12 they fell d', and there was none
23 that go d' to the sea in ships,
26 they go d' again to the depths:
108:13 he that shall tread d' our enemies.
109:23 am tossed up and d' as the locust.
113: 3 sun unto the going d' of the same
115:17 any that go d' into silence.
119:118 hast trodden d' all them that err
136 Rivers of waters run d' mine eyes,
133: 2 head, that ran d' upon the beard,
2 that went d' to the skirts of his
137: 1 rivers of Babylon, there we sat d',
139: 3 my path and my lying d'
143: 3 smitten my life d' to the ground;
7 unto them that go d' into the pit.
144: 5 thy heavens, O Lord, and come d':
145:14 up all those that be bowed d'.
146: 8 raiseth them that are bowed d':
9 the wicked he turneth upside d'.
147: 6 casteth the wicked d' to the
Pr 1:12 as those that go d' into the pit:
3:20 and the clouds drop d' the dew.
24 When thou liest d', thou shalt not
24 thou shalt lie d', and thy sleep
5: 5 Her feet go d' to death;
7:26 she hath cast d' many wounded:
27 to hell, going d' to the chambers
14: 1 plucketh it d' with her hands.
18: 8 go d' into the innermost parts of
21:22 and casteth d' the strength of the
22:17 Bow d' thine ear, and hear the
23:34 lieth d' in the midst of the sea,
24:31 stone wall thereof was broken d'.
25:26 A righteous man falling d' before
28 is like a city that is broken d',
26:22 go d' into the innermost parts of
Ec 1: 5 also ariseth, and the sun goeth d',
3: 3 a time to break d', and a time to
Ca 2: 3 I sat d' under his shadow with great
6: 2 beloved is gone d' into his garden,
11 I went d' into the garden of nuts
7: 9 that goeth d' sweetly, causing the
Isa 2: 9 And the mean man boweth d',
11 . . . shall be bowed d',

Isa 2:17 loftiness of man shall be bowed d',
5: 5 and break d' the wall thereof,
5 and it shall be trodden d':
15 mean man shall be brought d',
9:10 The bricks are fallen d', but we
10 the sycamores are cut d', but we
10: 4 Without me they shall bow d'
6 and to tread them d' like the mire
13 I have put d' the inhabitants like
33 ones of stature shall be hewn d',
34 And he shall cut d' the thickets
11: 6 leopard shall lie d' with the kid;
7 young ones shall lie d' together:
14: 8 Since thou art laid d', no feller is
11 pomp is brought d' to the grave,
12 art thou cut d' to the ground,
15 thou shalt be brought d' to hell,
19 that go d' to the stones of the pit;
30 the needy shall lie d' in safety:
16: 8 of the heathen have broken d'
17: 2 be for flocks, which shall lie d',
18: 2 a nation meted out and trodden d',
5 away and cut d' the branches.
21: 3 was bowed d' at the hearing of it;
22: 5 day of trouble, and of treading d',
5 breaking d' the walls, and of
10 and the houses have ye broken d'
19 from thy state shall he pull thee d'.
25 and be cut d', and fall;
24: 1 it waste, and turneth it upside d',
10 The city of confusion is broken d':
19 The earth is utterly broken d',
25: 5 bring d' the noise of strangers,
10 Moab shall be trodden d' under
10 straw is trodden d' for the dunghill.
11 and he shall bring d' their pride
12 fort of thy walls shall he bring d',
26: 5 bringeth d' them that dwell on
6 The foot shall tread it d',
27:10 and there shall he lie d',
28: 2 cast d' to the earth with the hand.
18 then ye shall be trodden d' by it.
29: 4 And thou shalt be brought d',
16 your turning of things upside d'
30: 2 That walk to go d' into Egypt,
30 show the lighting d' of his arm,
31 shall the Assyrian be beaten d',
31: 1 that go d' to Egypt for help;
3 he that is holpen shall fall d',
4 so shall the Lord of hosts come d'
32:19 hail, coming d' on the forest;
33: 9 Lebanon is ashamed and hewn d':
20 that shall not be taken d';
34: 4 and all their host shall fall d',
5 it shall come d' upon Idumea,
7 unicorn shall come d' with them,
37:24 will cut d' the tall cedars thereof,
38: 8 is gone d' in the sun dial of Ahaz,
8 by which degrees it was gone d'.
18 they that go d' into the pit cannot
42:10 ye that go d' to the sea, and all
43:14 have brought d' all their nobles,
17 they shall lie d' together, they shall
44:14 He heweth him d' cedars,
15 it a graven image, and falleth d'
17 falleth d' unto it, and worshippeth
19 fall d' to the stock of a tree?
45: 8 Drop d', ye heavens, from above,
8 the skies pour d' righteousness:
14 and they shall fall d' unto thee,
46: 1 Bel boweth d', Nebo stoopeth,
2 They stoop, they bow d' together;
6 they fall d', yea, they worship.
47: 1 Come d', and sit in the dust,
49:23 shall bow d' to thee with their
50:11 ye shall lie d' in sorrow.
51:23 Bow d', that we may go over:
52: 2 arise, and sit d', O Jerusalem:
4 went d' aforetime into Egypt
55:10 For as the rain cometh d', and the
56:10 sleeping, lying d', loving to
58: 5 to bow d' his head as a bulrush,
60:14 d' at the soles of thy feet;
20 Thy sun shall no more go d';
63: 6 And I will tread d' the people in
6 and I will bring d' their strength
14 a beast goeth d' into the valley,
15 Look d' from heaven,
18 our adversaries have trodden d' thy
64: 1 that thou wouldest come d',
1 the mountains might flow d' at
3 looked not for, thou camest d',
3 mountains flowed d' at thy
65:10 place for the herds to lie d' in,
12 shall all bow d' to the slaughter:
Jer 1:10 to root out, and to pull d', and to
10 throw d', to build, and to plant.
3:25 We lie d' in our shame,
4:26 the cities thereof were broken d'
6: 6 Hew ye d' trees, and cast a mount
15 they shall be cast d', saith the
8:12 they shall be cast d', saith the Lord.
9:18 our eyes may run d' with tears,
13:17 and run d' with tears, because
18 Humble yourselves, sit d': for
18 your principalities shall come d',
14:17 Let mine eyes run d' with tears
15: 9 sun is gone d' while it was yet day:
18: 2 and go d' to the potter's house,
3 Then I went d' to the potter's
7 and to pull d', and to destroy it;
21:13 Who shall come d' against us?
22: 1 Go d' to the house of the king
7 shall cut d' thy choice cedars,
24: 6 build them, and not pull them d';
25:37 cut d' because of the fierce anger

Jer 26:10 sat d' in the entry of the new gate
31:28 pluck up, and to break d', and
28 and to throw d', and to destroy
40 nor thrown d' any more for ever.
33: 4 are thrown d' by the mounts,
12 causing their flock to lie d'.
36:12 went d' into the king's house,
15 Sit d' now, and read it in our ears.
38: 6 they let d' Jeremiah with cords.
11 and let them d' by cords into the
39: 8 brake d' the walls of Jerusalem.
42:10 and not pull you d', and I will
45: 4 which I have built will I break d',
46: 5 their mighty ones are beaten d',
23 They shall cut d' her forest,
48: 2 thou shalt be cut d', O Madmen;
5 for in the going d' of Horonaim
15 men are gone d' to the slaughter,
18 come d' from thy glory, and sit in
20 it is broken d': howl and cry;
39 How is it broken d'! how hath
49:16 I will bring thee d' from thence,
50:15 her walls are thrown d': for it is
27 bullocks; let them go d' to the
51:25 and roll thee d' from the rocks, and
40 I will bring them d' like lambs to
52:14 brake d' all the walls of Jerusalem
La 1: 9 she came d' wonderfully:
16 mine eye runneth d' with water,
2: 1 and cast d' from heaven unto
2 he hath thrown d' in his wrath
2 brought them d' to the ground:
10 hang d' their heads to the ground.
17 thrown d', and hath not pitied:
18 tears run d' like a river day and night:
3:48 eye runneth d' with rivers of water
49 eye trickleth d', and ceaseth not,
50 Till the Lord look d', and behold
63 their sitting d', and their rising up;
Eze 1:13 it went up and d' among the living
24 they stood, they let d' their wings.
25 stood, and had let d' their wings.
6: 4 and I will cast d' your slain men
6 and your images may be cut d',
11:13 Then fell I d' upon my face, and
13:14 I break d' the wall that ye have
14 and bring it d' to the ground,
16:39 throw d' thine eminent place,
39 shall break d' thy high places:
17:24 have brought d' the high tree,
19: 2 thy mother? A lioness: she lay d'
6 went up and d' among the lions,
12 she was cast d' to the ground,
24:16 neither shall thy tears run d'.
26: 4 and break d' her towers: I will
9 axes he shall break d' thy towers.
11 shall he tread d' all thy streets: he
11 shall go d' to the ground.
12 and they shall break d' thy walls,
16 shall come d' from their thrones,
20 I shall bring thee d' with them
20 with them that go d' to the pit,
27:29 shall come d' from their ships,
28: 8 They shall bring thee d' to the pit,
14 thou hast walked up and d' in the
30: 4 her foundations shall be broken d'.
6 pride of her power shall come d':
25 the arms of Pharaoh shall fall d';
31:12 are gone d' from his shadow, and
14 with them that go d' to the pit.
15 day when he went d' to the grave
16 when I cast him d' to hell with
17 They also went d' into hell with
18 thou be brought d' with the trees
32:18 and cast them d', even her, and the
18 with them that go d' into the pit.
19 go d', and be thou laid with the
21 gone d', they lie uncircumcised,
24 are gone d' uncircumcised into
24 with them that go d' to the pit.
25 that go d' to the pit: he is put in
27 gone d' to hell with their weapons
29 with them that go d' to the pit.
30 which are gone d' with the slain;
30 with them that go d' to the pit.
34:15 them to lie d', saith the Lord God.
18 ye must tread d' with your feet the
26 I will cause the shower to come d'
37: 1 and set me d' in the midst of a valley
38:20 the mountains shall be thrown d',
39:10 cut d' any out of the forests; for
47: 1 came d' from under from the right
8 and go d' into the desert, and go
Da 3: 5 ye fall d' and worship the golden
6 falleth not d' and worshippeth
7 fell d' and worshipped the golden
10 shall fall d' and worship the golden
11 falleth not d' and worshippeth,
15 ye fall d' and worship the image
23 fell d' bound into the midst of the
4:13 an holy one came d' from heaven;
14 Hew d' the tree, and cut off his
23 one coming d' from heaven, and
23 Hew the tree d', and destroy it;
5:19 and whom he would he put d'.
6:14 till the going d' of the sun
7: 9 till the thrones were cast d', and
23 and shall tread it d' and break it
8: 7 but he cast him d' to the ground,
10 and it cast d' some of the host
11 place of his sanctuary was cast d'.
12 and it cast d' the truth to the
11:12 shall cast d' many ten thousands:
26 and many shall fall d' slain,
Ho 2:18 will make them to lie d' safely.
7:12 I will bring them d' as the fowls

Ho 10: 2 he shall break d' their altars, he
Joe 1:17 the barns are broken d'; for the
2:23 cause to come d' for you the rain,
3: 2 will bring them d' into the valley
11 mighty ones to come d', O Lord.
13 come, get you d'; for the press is
18 mountains shall drop d' new wine,
Am 2: 8 lay themselves d' upon clothes
3:11 and he shall bring d' thy strength
5:24 let judgment run d' as waters, and
6: 2 go d' to Gath of the Philistines:
8: 9 the sun to go d' at noon, and I will
9: 2 thence will I bring them d':
Ob 3 shall bring me d' to the ground?
4 I bring thee d', saith the Lord.
16 and they shall swallow d', and they
Jon 1: 3 went d' to Joppa; and he found
3 fare thereof, and went d' into it,
5 Jonah was gone d' into the sides
2: 6 I went d' to the bottoms of the
Mic 1: 3 and will come d', and tread upon
4 that are poured d' a steep place.
6 I will pour d' the stones thereof
12 but evil came d' from the Lord
3: 6 the sun shall go d' over the prophets,
5: 8 both treadeth d', and teareth in pieces,
11 and throw d' all thy strong holds:
6:14 and thy casting d' shall be in the
7:10 shall she be trodden d' as the mire
Na 1: 6 the rocks are thrown d' by him
12 thus shall they be cut d', when he
Zep 1:11 the merchant people are cut d';
2: 7 Ashkelon shall they lie d' in the
14 And flocks shall lie d' in the midst
15 a place for beasts to lie d' in!
3:13 they shall feed and lie d', and none
Hag 2:22 riders shall come d', every one
Zec 10: 5 which tread d' their enemies in the
11 Assyria shall be brought d', and
12 shall walk up and d' in his name,
11: 2 forest of the vintage is come d'.
Mal 1: 4 I will throw d'; and they shall
11 even unto the going d' of the same
4: 3 ye shall tread d' the wicked;
M't 2:11 and fell d', and worshipped him:
3:10 not forth good fruit is hewn d',
4: 6 the Son of God, cast thyself d':
9 if thou wilt fall d' and worship me.
7:19 is hewn d', and cast into the fire.
8: 1 When he was come d' from the
11 shall sit d' with Abraham, and
32 swine ran violently d' a steep place
9:10 and sinners came and sat d'
11:23 shall be brought d' to hell:
13:48 and sat d', and gathered the good
14:29 when Peter was come d' out of the
15:29 into a mountain, and sat d' there.
30 and cast them d' at Jesus' feet;
35 multitudes to sit d' on the ground.
17: 9 And as they came d' from the
14 kneeling d' to him, and saying,
18:26 The servant therefore fell d', and
29 And his fellow servant fell d' at his
21: 8 others cut d' branches from the
24: 2 that shall not be thrown d'.
17 housetop not come d' to take any
26:20 even was come, he sat d' with the
27: 5 And he cast d' the pieces of silver
19 he was set d' on the judgment
36 And sitting d' they watched him
40 If thou be the Son of God, come d'
42 let him now come d' from the cross,
M'r 1: 7 not worthy to stoop d' and unloose.
40 and kneeling d' to him, and saying
2: 4 they let d' the bed wherein the sick
3:11 fell d' before him, and cried,
22 the scribes which came d' from
5:13 the herd ran violently d' a steep
33 came and fell d' before him, and
6:39 to make all sit d' by companies
40 they sat d' in ranks, by hundreds,
8: 6 the people to sit d' on the ground:
9: 9 And as they came d' from the
35 he sat d', and called the twelve,
11: 8 and others cut d' branches off the
13: 2 that shall not be thrown d'.
15 on the housetop not go d' into
15:30 and come d' from the cross.
36 Elias will come to take him d'.
46 and took him d', and wrapped him
Lu 1:52 He hath put d' the mighty from
2:51 And he went d' with them, and
3: 9 good fruit is hewn d', and cast
4: 9 of God, cast thyself d' from hence:
20 again to the minister, and sat d'.
29 they might cast him d' headlong.
31 And came d' to Capernaum, a city
5: 3 he sat d', and taught the people
4 and let d' your nets for a draught.
5 at thy word will I let d' the net.
8 he fell d' at Jesus' knees, saying,
19 and let him d' through the tiling
29 of others that sat d' with them.
6:17 he came d' with them, and stood
38 good measure, pressed d', and shaken
7:36 the Pharisee's house, and sat d' to
8: 5 it was trodden d', and the fowls
23 and there came d' a storm of wind
28 he cried out, and fell d' before him,
33 herd ran violently d' a steep place
41 fell d' at Jesus' feet, and besought
47 and falling d' before him, she
9:14 Make them sit d' by fifties in a
15 and made them all sit d'.
37 when they were come d' from the
42 the devil threw him d', and tare
Lu 9:44 Let these sayings sink d' into
54 fire to come d' from heaven, and
10:15 to heaven, shalt be thrust d' to
30 A certain man went d' from
31 chance there came d' a certain
11:37 and he went in, and sat d' to meat.
12:18 I will pull d' my barns, and
37 them to sit d' to meat, and will
13: 7 cut it d'; why cumbereth it the
9 after that thou shalt cut it d'.
29 and shall sit d' in the kingdom
14: 8 sit not d' in the highest room;
10 go and sit d' in the lowest room;
28 sitteth not d' first, and counteth
31 sitteth not d' first, and consulteth
16: 6 thy bill, and sit d' quickly, and
17: 7 the field, Go and sit d' to meat?
16 And fell d' on his face at his feet,
31 him not come d' to take it away:
18:14 this man went d' to his house
19: 5 make haste, and come d'; for
6 And he made haste, and came d',
21 takest up that thou layedst not d',
22 taking up that I laid not d', and
21: 6 that shall not be thrown d'.
24 Jerusalem shall be trodden d' of the
22:14 he sat d', and the twelve apostles
41 a stone's cast, and kneeled d', and
44 drops of blood falling d' to the
55 and were set d' together,
55 Peter sat d' among them.
23:53 And he took it d', and wrapped it
24: 5 bowed d' their faces to the earth,
12 and stooping d', he beheld the
Joh 2:12 this he went d' to Capernaum,
3:13 but he that came d' from heaven;
4:47 he would come d', and heal his son:
49 Sir, come d' ere my child die,
51 as he was now going d', his servants
5: 4 angel went d' at a certain season
7 another steppeth d' before me,
6:10 Make the men sit d'. Now there
10 So the men sat d', in number
11 disciples to them that were set d';
16 his disciples went d' unto the sea,
33 which cometh d' from heaven,
38 For I came d' from heaven, not
41 bread which came d' from heaven.
42 he saith, I came d' from heaven?
50 which cometh d' from heaven, that
51 living bread which came d' from
58 bread which came d' from heaven:
8: 2 and he sat d', and taught them.
6 Jesus stooped d', and with his
8 And again he stooped d', and wrote
10:15 and I lay d' my life for the sheep.
17 because I lay d' my life, that I
18 I lay it d' of myself. I have power
18 to lay it d', and I have power to
11:32 she fell d' at his feet, saying unto
13:12 and was set d' again, he said unto
37 I will lay d' my life for thy sake.
38 Wilt thou lay d' thy life for my
15:13 that a man lay d' his life for his
19:13 and sat d' in the judgment seat in
20: 5 And he stooping d', and looking
11 she stooped d', and looked into
Ac 4:35 laid them d' at the apostles' feet:
5: 5 hearing these words fell d', and
10 Then fell she d' straightway at his
7:15 So Jacob went d' into Egypt, and
34 and am come d' to deliver them.
58 laid d' their clothes at a young
60 And he kneeled d', and cried with a
8: 5 Philip went d' to the city of
15 when they were come d', prayed
26 way that goeth d' from Jerusalem
38 and they went d' both into the water
9:25 and let him d' by the wall in a
30 they brought him d' to Cesarea,
32 he came d' also to the saints
40 and kneeled d', and prayed; and
10:11 corners, and let d' to the earth:
20 and get thee d', and go with them,
21 Then Peter went d' to the men
25 fell d' at his feet, and worshipped
11: 5 great sheet, let d' from heaven by
12:19 he went d' from Judæa to Cæsarea,
13:14 on the sabbath day, and sat d'.
29 they took him d' from the tree,
14:11 The gods are come d' to us in the
25 Perga, they went d' into Attalia:
15: 1 men which came d' from Judæa
16 of David, which is fallen d'; and
16: 8 passing by Mysia came d' to
13 and we sat d', and spake unto the
29 and fell d' before Paul and Silas,
17: 6 turned the world upside d' are
18:22 the church, he went d' to Antioch.
19:35 image which fell d' from Jupiter?
20: 9 he sunk d' with sleep, and
9 and fell d' from the third loft.
10 And Paul went d', and fell on him,
36 he kneeled d', and prayed with them
21: 5 and we kneeled d' on the shore, and
10 there came d' from Judæa a
32 and ran d' unto them: and when
22:30 and brought Paul d', and set him
23:10 commanded the soldiers to go d',
15 that he bring him d' unto you
20 thou wouldest bring d' Paul
24:22 chief captain shall come d', I
25: 5 you are able, go d' with me,
6 he went d' unto Cæsarea; and
7 which came d' from Jerusalem
27:27 as we were driven up and d' in
Ac 27:30 when they had let d' the boat into
28: 6 or fallen d' dead suddenly: but
Ro 10: 6 to bring Christ d' from above:)
11: 3 and digged d' thine altars; and
10 and bow d' their back alway.
16: 4 Who have for my life laid d' their
1Co 10: 7 The people sat d' to eat and drink,
14:25 and so falling d' on his face he
15:24 when he shall have put d' all rule
2Co 4: 9 cast d', but not destroyed;
7: 6 those that are cast d', comforted
10: 4 to the pulling d' of strong holds:)
5 Casting d' imaginations, and
11:33 a basket was I let d' by the wall,
Eph 2:14 and hath broken d' the middle wall of
4:26 let not the sun go d' upon your
Heb 1: 3 himself purged our sins, sat d' on
11:30 the walls of Jericho fell d',
12:12 which hang d', and the feeble
Jas 1:17 cometh d' from the Father of lights,
5: 4 labourers who have reaped d'
1Pe 1:12 Holy Ghost sent d' from heaven;
2Pe 2: 4 but cast them d' to hell,
1Joh 3:16 because he laid d' his life
16 we ought to lay d' our lives
Re 1:13 clothed with a garment d' to the foot,
3:12 Jerusalem, which cometh d' out
21 d' with my Father in his throne.
4:10 The four and twenty elders fall d'
5: 8 elders fell d' before the Lamb,
14 the four and twenty elders fell d'
10: 1 angel come d' from heaven,
12:10 accuser of our brethren is cast d',
12 for the devil is come d' unto you,
13:13 maketh fire come d' from heaven
18: 1 I saw another angel come d' from
21 great city Babylon be thrown d',
19: 4 and the four beasts fell d' and
20: 1 an angel come d' from heaven,
9 and fire came d' from God out of
21: 2 Jerusalem, coming d' from God out
22: 8 I fell d' to worship before the feet

downsitting
Ps 139: 2 Thou knowest my d' and mine

downward
2Ki 19:30 shall yet again take root d', and
Ec 3:21 the spirit of the beast that goeth d'
Isa 37:31 shall again take root d', and bear
Eze 1:27 appearance of his loins even d', I saw
8: 2 appearance of his loins even d', fire;

dowry
Ge 30:20 hath endued me with a good d';
34:12 Ask me never so much d' and gift,
Ex 22:17 pay money according to the d' of
1Sa 18:25 The king desireth not any d', but

drag See also DRAGGING.
Hab 1:15 net, and gather them in their d':
16 burn incense unto their d'; because

dragging
Joh 21: 8 cubits,) d' the net with fishes.

dragon See also DRAGONS.
Neh 2:13 even before the d' well, and
Ps 91:13 the young lion and the d' shalt
Isa 27: 1 he shall slay the d' that is in the
51: 9 cut Rahab, and wounded the d'?
Jer 51:34 hath swallowed me up like a d',
Eze 29: 3 the great d' that lieth in the midst
Rev 12: 3 behold a great red d', having
4 the d' stood before the woman
7 his angels fought against the d';
7 and the d' fought and his angels,
9 the great d' was cast out, that
13 when the d' saw that he was cast
16 the flood which the d' cast out
17 the d' was wroth with the woman,
13: 2 and the d' gave him his power,
4 they worshipped the d' which gave
11 like a lamb, and he spake as a d'.
16:13 out of the mouth of the d',
20: 2 he laid hold on the d', that old

dragons
De 32:33 Their wine is the poison of d',
Job 30:29 I am a brother to d', and a
Ps 44:19 sore broken us in the place of d',
74:13 thou breakest the heads of the d'
148: 7 the earth, ye d', and all deeps:
Isa 13:22 and d' in their pleasant palaces:
34:13 it shall be an habitation of d',
35: 7 in the habitation of d', where
43:20 honour me, the d' and the owls:
Jer 9:11 Jerusalem heaps, and a den of d';
10:22 Judah desolate, and a den of d'.
14: 6 they snuffed up the wind like d';
49:33 Hazor shall be a dwelling for d',
51:37 a dwellingplace for d', an
Mic 1: 8 make a wailing like the d', and
Mal 1: 3 waste for the d' of the wilderness.

dragon-well See DRAGON and WELL.

drams
1Ch 29: 7 talents and ten thousand d',
Ezr 2:69 and one thousand d' of gold,
8:27 of gold, of a thousand d'; and
Ne 7:70 thousand d' of gold, fifty basons,
71 twenty thousand d' of gold, and
72 gave was twenty thousand d'

drank
Ge 9:21 And he d' of the wine, and was
24:46 I d', and she made the camels drink
27:25 he brought him wine, and he d'.
43:34 they d', and were merry with him.
Nu 20:11 and the congregation d', and their
De 32:38 d' the wine of their drink offerings?

2Sa 12: 3 and *d'* of his own cup, and lay in
1Ki 13:19 bread in his house, and *d'* water.
17: 6 evening; and he *d'* of the brook.
Da 1: 5 and of the wine which he *d'*:
8 nor with the wine which he *d'*:
5: 1 and *d'* wine before the thousand.
3 his wives, and his concubines, *d'*
4 They *d'* wine, and praised the gods
M'r 14:23 it to them: and they all *d'* of it.
Lu 17:27 They did eat, they *d'*, they married
28 they did eat, they *d'*, they bought,
Joh 4:12 us the well, and *d'* thereof himself,
1Co 10: 4 for they *d'* of that spiritual Rock

draught
2Ki 10:27 made it *d'* house unto this day.
M't 15:17 and is cast out into the *d'*?
M'r 7:19 goeth out into the *d'*, purging
Lu 5: 4 and let down your nets for a *d'*.
9 at the *d'* of the fishes which they

draught-house See DRAUGHT and HOUSE.

drave See also DROVE.
Ex 14:25 that they *d'* them heavily: so that
Jos 16:10 they *d'* not out the Canaanites
24:12 *d'* them out from before you,
18 the Lord *d'* out from before us
J'g 1:19 he *d'* out the inhabitants of the
6: 9 and *d'* them out from before you,
1Sa 30:20 and the herds, which they *d'*
2Sa 6: 3 sons of Abinadab, *d'* the new cart.
2Ki 16: 6 and *d'* the Jews from Elath:
17:21 *d'* Israel from following the Lord,
1Ch 13: 7 and Uzza and Ahio *d'* the cart.
Ac 7:45 whom God *d'* out before the face
18:16 *d'* them from the judgment seat.

draw See also DRAWETH; DRAWING; DRAWN; DREW; WITHDRAW.
Ge 24:11 that women go out to *d'* water.
13 of the city come out to *d'* water:
19 I will *d'* water for thy camels also,
20 ran unto the well to *d'* water,
43 virgin cometh forth to *d'* water,
44 I will also *d'* for thy camels:
Ex 3: 5 *D'* not nigh hither: put off thy
12:21 *D'* out and take you a lamb
15: 9 I will *d'* my sword, mine hand
Le 26:33 and will *d'* out a sword after you:
J'g 3:22 he could not *d'* the dagger out
4: 6 and *d'* toward mount Tabor, and
7 And I will *d'* unto thee to the river
9:54 *D'* thy sword, and slay me, that
19:13 us *d'* near to one of these places
20:32 and *d'* them from the city unto
1Sa 9:11 maidens going out to *d'* water,
14:36 Let us *d'* near hither unto God.
38 *D'* ye near hither, all the chief of
31: 4 his armourbearer, *D'* thy sword,
2Sa 17:13 and we will *d'* it into the river,
1Ch 10: 4 *D'* thy sword, and thrust me
Job 21:33 and every man shall *d'* after him.
40:23 that he can *d'* up Jordan
41: 1 Canst thou *d'* out leviathan with
Ps 28: 3 *D'* me not away with the wicked,
35: 3 *D'* out also the spear, and stop
69:18 *D'* nigh unto my soul, and redeem
73:28 is good for me to *d'* near to God:
85: 5 wilt thou *d'* out thine anger to all
107:18 *d'* near unto the gates of death.
119:150 *d'* nigh that follow after mischief:
Pr 20: 5 of understanding will *d'* it out.
Ec 12: 1 *d'* nigh, when thou shalt say,
Ca 1: 4 *D'* me, we will run after thee:
Isa 5:18 *d'* iniquity with cords of vanity,
19 of the Holy One of Israel *d'* nigh
12: 3 Therefore with joy shall ye *d'*
29:13 people *d'* near me with their mouth,
45:20 *d'* near together, ye that are escaped
57: 3 But *d'* near hither, ye sons of the
4 mouth, and *d'* out the tongue?
58:10 *d'* out thy soul to the hungry,
66:19 *d'* the bow, to Tubal, and Javan,
Jer 30:21 and I will cause him to *d'* near,
46: 3 and shield, and *d'* near to battle.
49:20 shall *d'* them out: surely he shall
50:45 of the flock shall *d'* them out:
La 4: 3 sea monsters *d'* out the breast,
Eze 5: 2 in the wind; and I will *d'* out a
12 I will *d'* out a sword after them.
9: 1 charge over the city to *d'* near,
12:14 will *d'* out the sword after them.
21: 3 and will *d'* forth my sword out of
22: 4 thy days to *d'* near, and art
28: 7 *d'* their swords against the beauty
30:11 *d'* their swords against Egypt,
32:20 *d'* her and all her multitudes.
Joe 3: 9 let all the men of war *d'* near;
Na 3:14 *D'* thee waters for the siege,
Hag 2:16 press at for to *d'* out fifty vessels
Joh 2: 8 saith unto them, *D'* out now, and
4: 7 a woman of Samaria to *d'* water:
11 Sir, thou hast nothing to *d'* with,
15 not, neither come hither to *d'*.
6:44 Father which hath sent me *d'* him:
12:32 the earth, will *d'* all men unto me.
21: 6 now they were not able to *d'* it for
Ac 20:30 to *d'* away disciples after them.
Heb 7:19 by the which we *d'* nigh unto God.
10:22 Let us *d'* near with a true heart
38 but if any man *d'* back, my soul
39 we are not of them who *d'* back
Jas 2: 6 rich men oppress you, and *d'* you
4: 8 *D'* nigh to God, and he will *d'* nigh

drawer See also DRAWERS.
De 29:11 the hewer of thy wood unto the *d'*

drawers
Jos 9:21 hewers of wood and *d'* of water
23 *d'* of water for the house of my God.
27 *d'* of water for the congregation,

drawest See WITHDRAWEST.

draweth See also WITHDRAWETH.
De 25:11 and the wife of the one *d'* near
J'g 19: 9 the day *d'* toward evening,
Job 24:22 He *d'* also the mighty with his
33:22 his soul *d'* near unto the grave,
Ps 10: 9 when he *d'* him into his net.
88: 3 my life *d'* nigh unto the grave.
Isa 26:17 *d'* near the time of her delivery,
Eze 7:12 the day *d'* near: let not the
M't 15: 8 This people *d'* nigh unto me with
Lu 21: 8 the time *d'* near: go ye not
28 for your redemption *d'* nigh.
Jas 5: 8 the coming of the Lord *d'* nigh.

drawing
J'g 5:11 archers in the places of *d'* water,
Joh 6:19 the sea, and *d'* nigh unto the ship:

drawn See also WITHDRAWN.
Nu 22:23, 31 and his sword *d'* in his hand:
De 21: 3 which hath not *d'* in the yoke;
30:17 but shall be *d'* away, and worship
Jos 5:13 against him with his sword *d'*
8: 6 till we have *d'* them from the city;
16 and were *d'* away from the city.
15: 9 And the border was *d'* from the
9 and the border was *d'* to Baalah,
11 and the border was *d'* to Shicron,
18:14 And the border was *d'* thence,
17 And was *d'* from the north, and
J'g 20:31 were *d'* away from the city; and
Ru 2: 9 that which the young men have *d'*.
1Ch 21:16 having a *d'* sword in his hand
Job 20:25 It is *d'*, and cometh out of the
Ps 37:14 The wicked have *d'* out the sword,
55:21 than oil, yet were they *d'* swords.
Pr 24:11 them that are *d'* unto death,
Isa 21:15 the swords, from the *d'* sword,
28: 9 the milk, and *d'* from the breasts.
Jer 22:19 burial of an ass, *d'* and cast forth
31: 3 lovingkindness have I *d'* thee.
La 2: 3 he hath *d'* back his right hand
Eze 21: 5 I the Lord have *d'* forth my sword
28 The sword, the sword is *d'*: for
Ac 11:10 all were *d'* up again into heaven.
Jas 1:14 when he is *d'* away of his own lust,

dread See also DREADFUL.
Ge 9: 2 the fear of you and the *d'* of you
Ex 15:16 Fear and *d'* shall fall upon them;
De 1:29 *D'* not, neither be afraid of them.
2:25 the *d'* of thee and the fear of thee
11:25 and the *d'* of you upon all the land
1Ch 22:13 courage; *d'* not, nor be dismayed.
Job 13:11 afraid? and his *d'* fall upon you?
21 and let not thy *d'* make me afraid.
Isa 8:13 fear, and let him be your *d'*.

dreadful
Ge 28:17 How *d'* is this place! this is none
Job 15:21 A *d'* sound is in his ears:
Eze 1:18 were so high that they were *d'*;
Da 7: 7 a fourth beast, *d'* and terrible,
19 from all the others, exceeding *d'*,
9: 4 O Lord, the great and *d'* God,
Hab 1: 7 They are terrible and *d'*: their
Mal 1:14 name is *d'* among the heathen.
4: 5 the great and *d'* day of the Lord:

dream See also DREAMED; DREAMETH; DREAMS.
Ge 20: 3 to Abimelech in a *d'* by night,
6 And God said unto him in a *d'*,
31:10 and saw in a *d'*, and, behold, the
11 spake unto me in a *d'*, saying,
24 came to Laban the Syrian in a *d'*
37: 5 Joseph dreamed a *d'*, and he told
6 you, this *d'* which I have dreamed:
9 he dreamed yet another *d'*, and
9 Behold, I have dreamed a *d'*
10 What is this *d'* that thou hast
40: 5 they dreamed a *d'* both of them,
5 each man his *d'* in one night,
5 to the interpretation of his *d'*,
8 We have dreamed a *d'*, and there
9 chief butler told his *d'* to Joseph,
9 In my *d'*, behold, a vine was
16 I also was in my *d'*, and, behold, I
41: 7 awoke, and, behold, it was a *d'*.
8 Pharaoh told them his *d'*; but there
11 we dreamed a *d'* in one night, I and
11 to the interpretation of his *d'*.
12 to each man according to his *d'*
15 I have dreamed a *d'*, and there is
15 that thou canst understand a *d'*
17 In my *d'*, behold, I stood upon the
22 I saw in my *d'*, and, behold, seven
25 The *d'* of Pharaoh is one: God
26 ears are seven years: the *d'* is one.
32 for that the *d'* was doubled unto
Nu 12: 6 and will speak unto him in a *d'*.
J'g 7:13 a man that told a *d'* unto his fellow,
13 and said, Behold, I dreamed a *d'*,
15 Gideon heard the telling of the *d'*,
1Ki 3: 5 Lord appeared to Solomon in a *d'*
15 awoke; and, behold, it was a *d'*.
Job 20: 8 He shall fly away as a *d'*, and shall
33:15 In a *d'*, in a vision of the night,
Ps 73:20 As a *d'* when one awaketh;
126: 1 Zion, we were like them that *d'*.
Ec 5: 3 a *d'* cometh through the multitude
Isa 29: 7 shall be as a *d'* of a night vision.
Jer 23:28 The prophet that hath a *d'*, let him
28 let him tell a *d'*; and he that hath

Da 2: 3 I have dreamed a *d'*, and my spirit
3 was troubled to know the *d'*.
4 tell thy servants the *d'*, and we
5 not make known unto me the *d'*,
6 But if ye shew the *d'*, and the
6 honour: therefore shew me the *d'*,
7 the king tell his servants the *d'*,
9 not make known unto me the *d'*,
9 therefore tell me the *d'*, and I shall
26 able to make known unto me the *d'*
28 Thy *d'*, and the visions of thy head
36 This is the *d'*; and we will tell the
45 and the *d'* is certain, and the
4: 5 I saw a *d'* which made me afraid,
6 unto me the interpretation of the *d'*.
7 and I told the *d'* before them;
8 and before him I told the *d'*,
9 tell me the visions of my *d'* that I
18 This *d'* I king Nebuchadnezzar
19 let not the *d'*, or the interpretation
19 the *d'* be to them that hate thee,
7: 1 Daniel had a *d'* and visions of his
1 then he wrote the *d'*, and told the
Joe 2:28 your old men shall *d'* dreams, your
M't 1:20 Lord appeared unto him in a *d'*,
2:12 being warned of God in a *d'* that
13 Lord appeareth to Joseph in a *d'*,
19 Lord appeareth in a *d'* to Joseph
22 being warned of God in a *d'*, he
27:19 this day in a *d'* because of him.
Ac 2:17 and your old men shall *d'* dreams:

dreamed
Ge 28:12 And he *d'*, and behold a ladder set
37: 5 And Joseph *d'* a dream, and he told
6 you, this dream which I have *d'*:
9 And he *d'* yet another dream, and
9 Behold, I have *d'* a dream more;
10 is this dream that thou hast *d'*?
40: 5 And they *d'* a dream both of them,
8 We have *d'* a dream, and there is no
41: 1 of two full years, that Pharaoh *d'*:
5 he slept and *d'* the second time:
11 And we *d'* a dream in one night, I
11 we *d'* each man according to the
15 unto Joseph, I have *d'* a dream,
42: 9 the dreams which he *d'* of them,
J'g 7:13 said, Behold, I *d'* a dream, and,
Jer 23:25 name, saying, I have *d'*, I have *d'*.
29: 8 dreams, which ye cause to be *d'*.
Da 2: 1 Nebuchadnezzar *d'* dreams,
3 I have *d'* a dream, and my spirit

dreamer See also DREAMERS.
Ge 37:19 Behold, this *d'* cometh.
De 13: 1 you a prophet, or a *d'* of dreams,
3 that prophet, or that *d'* of dreams:
5 that prophet, or that *d'* of dreams,

dreamers
Jer 27: 9 nor to your *d'*, nor to your
Jude 8 Likewise also these filthy *d'* defile

dreameth
Isa 29: 8 as when an hungry man *d'*, and,
8 as when a thirsty man *d'*,

dreams
Ge 37: 8 hated him yet the more for his *d'*,
20 see what will become of his *d'*.
41:12 he interpreted to us our *d'*; to each
42: 9 Joseph remembered the *d'* which
De 13: 1 or a dreamer of *d'*, and giveth thee
3 that prophet, or that dreamer of *d'*:
5 that prophet, or that dreamer of *d'*,
1Sa 28: 6 neither by *d'*, nor by Urim, nor by
15 neither by prophets, nor by *d'*:
Job 7:14 Then thou scarest me with *d'*, and
Ec 5: 7 in the multitude of *d'* and many
Jer 23:27 to forget my name by their *d'*
32 against them that prophesy false *d'*,
29: 8 neither hearken to your *d'* which
Da 1:17 understanding in all visions and *d'*.
2: 1 Nebuchadnezzar dreamed *d'*,
2 for to shew the king his *d'*.
5:12 interpreting of *d'*, and shewing of
Joe 2:28 your old men shall dream *d'*, your
Zec 10: 2 seen a lie, and have told false *d'*;
Ac 2:17 and your old men shall dream *d'*:

dregs
Ps 75: 8 but the *d'* thereof, all the wicked
Isa 51:17 thou hast drunken the *d'* of the
22 even the *d'* of the cup of my fury;

dress See also DRESSED; DRESSETH.
Ge 2:15 of Eden to *d'* it and to keep it.
18: 7 young man; and he hasted to *d'* it.
De 28:39 shalt plant vineyards, and *d'* them,
2Sa 12: 4 to *d'* for the wayfaring man that
13: 5 meat, and *d'* the meat in my sight,
7 Amnon's house, and *d'* him meat.
1Ki 17:12 that I may go in and *d'* it for me
18:23 I will *d'* the other bullock, and lay
25 one bullock for yourselves, and *d'* it

dressed See also UNDRESSED.
Ge 18: 8 milk, and the calf which he had *d'*,
Le 7: 9 all that is *d'* in the fryingpan,
1Sa 25:18 and five sheep ready *d'*, and five
2Sa 12: 4 and *d'* it for the man that was come
19:24 had neither *d'* his feet, nor trimmed
1Ki 18:26 which was given them, and they *d'*
Heb 6: 7 for them by whom it is *d'*,

dresser See also DRESSERS.
Lu 13: 7 said he unto the *d'* of his vineyard,

dressers See also VINEDRESSERS.
2Ch 26:10 and vine *d'* in the mountains, and

dresseth
Ex 30: 7 when he *d'* the lamps, he shall

drew See also DREWEST; WITHDREW.
Ge 18:23 And Abraham *d'* near, and said,
24:45 down unto the well, and *d'* water:
37:28 and they *d'* and lifted up Joseph
38:29 to pass, as he *d'* back his hand,
47:29 time *d'* nigh that Israel must die:
Ex 2:10 Because I *d'* him out of the water.
16 they came and *d'* water, and filled
19 and also *d'* water enough for us,
14:10 when Pharaoh *d'* nigh, the
20:21 *d'* near unto the thick darkness
Le 9: 5 and all the congregation *d'* near
Jos 8:11 went up, and *d'* nigh, and came
26 Joshua *d'* not his hand back,
J'g 8:10 thousand men that *d'* sword.
20 But the youth *d'* not his sword:
20: 2 thousand footmen that *d'* sword.
15 six thousand men that *d'* sword,
17 thousand men that *d'* sword:
25, 35 men; all these *d'* the sword.
37 liers in wait *d'* themselves along,
46 thousand men that *d'* the sword;
Ru 4: 8 for thee. So he *d'* off his shoe.
1Sa 7: 6 together to Mizpeh, and *d'* water,
10 the Philistines *d'* near to battle
9:18 Saul *d'* near to Samuel in the gate,
17:16 the Philistine *d'* near morning
40 and he *d'* near to the Philistine.
41 Philistine came on and *d'* near
48 arose, and came and *d'* nigh
51 *d'* it out of the sheath thereof,
2Sa 10:13 And Joab *d'* nigh, and the people
18:25 And he came apace, and *d'* near.
22:17 he *d'* me out of many waters;
23:16 and *d'* water out of the well of
24: 9 valiant men that *d'* the sword;
1Ki 2: 1 Now the days of David *d'* nigh
8: 8 And they *d'* out the staves,
22:34 certain man *d'* a bow at a venture,
2Ki 3:26 hundred men that *d'* swords,
9:24 *d'* a bow with his full strength,
1Ch 11:18 of the Philistines, and *d'* water
19:14 people that were with him *d'* nigh
16 and *d'* forth the Syrians that were
21: 5 thousand men that *d'* swords:
5 ten thousand men that *d'* sword.
2Ch 5: 9 they *d'* out the staves of the ark,
14: 8 that bare shields and *d'* bows,
18:33 certain man *d'* a bow at a venture
Es 5: 2 So Esther *d'* near, and touched
9: 1 and his decree *d'* near to be put
Ps 18:16 he *d'* me out of many waters.
Isa 41: 5 the earth were afraid, *d'* near,
Jer 38:13 they *d'* up Jeremiah with cords,
Ho 11: 4 I *d'* them with cords of a man,*
Zep 3: 2 Lord; she *d'* not near to her God.
M't 13:48 they *d'* to shore, and sat down,
21: 1 they *d'* nigh unto Jerusalem,
34 when the time of the fruit *d'* near,
26:51 and *d'* his sword, and struck a
M'r 6:53 Gennesaret, and *d'* to the shore.
14:47 them that stood by *d'* a sword,
Lu 15: 1 Then *d'* near unto him all the
25 he came and *d'* nigh to the house,
22: 1 feast of unleavened bread *d'* nigh,
47 *d'* near unto Jesus to kiss him.
23:54 preparation, and the sabbath *d'* on.
24:15 Jesus himself *d'* near, and went
28 And they *d'* nigh unto the village,
Joh 2: 9 servants which *d'* the water knew;)
18:10 Peter having a sword *d'* it, and
21:11 Peter went up, and *d'* the net to
Ac 5:37 *d'* away much people after him:
7:17 the time of the promise *d'* nigh,
31 and as he *d'* near to behold it,
10: 9 and *d'* nigh unto the city, Peter
14:19 Paul, *d'* him out of the city,
16:19 Paul and Silas, and *d'* them into
27 he *d'* out his sword, and would
17: 6 *d'* Jason and certain brethren
19:33 *d'* Alexander out of the multitude,
21:30 and *d'* him out of the temple:
27:27 they *d'* near to some country;
Re 12: 4 *d'* the third part of the stars

drewest
La 3:57 Thou *d'* near in the day that I

dried See also DRIEDST.
Ge 8: 7 until the waters were *d'* up from
13 were *d'* up from off the earth:
14 of the month, was the earth *d'*.
Le 2:14 green ears of corn *d'* by the fire,
Nu 6: 3 nor eat moist grapes, or *d'*.
11: 6 now our soul is *d'* away: there
Jos 2:10 *d'* up the water of the Red sea
4:23 God *d'* up the waters of Jordan
23 which he *d'* up from before us,
5: 1 the Lord had *d'* up the waters of
J'g 16: 7 green withs that were never *d'*,
8 green withs which had not been *d'*,
1Ki 13: 4 he put forth against him, *d'* up,
17: 7 that the brook *d'* up, because
2Ki 19:24 with the sole of my feet have I *d'*
Job 18:16 His roots shall be *d'* up beneath,
28: 4 they are *d'* up, they are gone
Ps 22:15 strength is *d'* up like a potsherd;
69: 3 my throat is *d'*: mine eyes fail
106: 9 Red sea also, and it was *d'* up:
Isa 5:13 their multitude *d'* up with thirst.
19: 5 river shall be wasted and *d'* up.
6 shall be emptied and *d'* up:
37:25 the sole of my feet have I *d'*
51:10 thou not it which hath *d'* the sea,
Jer 23:10 of the wilderness are *d'* up.
50:38 waters: and they shall be *d'* up:
Eze 17:24 have *d'* up the green tree, and have
19:12 the east wind *d'* up her fruit:
37:11 they say, Our bones are *d'*, and
Ho 9:16 their root is *d'* up, they shall bear
13:15 and his fountain shall be *d'* up:
Joe 1:10 the new wine is *d'* up, the oil
12 The vine is *d'* up, and the fig tree
20 the rivers of waters are *d'* up, and
Zec 11:17 his arm shall be clean *d'* up, and
M'r 5:29 fountain of her blood was *d'* up;
11:20 the fig tree *d'* up from the roots.
Re 16:12 and the water thereof was *d'* up,

driedst
Ps 74:15 flood: thou *d'* up mighty rivers.

drieth
Job 14:11 the flood decayeth and *d'* up:
Pr 17:22 but a broken spirit *d'* the bones.
Na 1: 4 it dry, and *d'* up all the rivers:

drink See also DRANK; DRINKETH; DRINKING; DRINKS; DRUNK.
Ge 19:32 let us make our father *d'* wine,
33 And they made their father *d'* wine
34 make him *d'* wine this night also;
35 And they made their father *d'* wine
21:19 with water, and gave the lad *d'*.
24:14 pitcher, I pray thee, that I may *d'*;
14 and she shall say, *D'*, and I will
14 I will give thy camels *d'* also:
17 Let me, I pray thee, *d'* a little
18 And she said, *D'*, my lord: and
18 upon her hand, and gave him *d'*.
19 when she had done giving him *d'*,
43 a little water of thy pitcher to *d'*;
44 And she say to me, Both *d'* thou,
45 unto her, Let me *d'*, I pray thee.
46 from her shoulder, and said, *D'*,
46 I will give thy camels *d'* also:
46 and she made the camels *d'* also.
54 they did eat and *d'*, he and the
25:34 he did eat and *d'*, and rose up, and
26:30 a feast, and they did eat and *d'*.
30:38 when the flocks came to *d'*, that
38 conceive when they came to *d'*.
35:14 poured a *d'* offering thereon,
Ex 7:18 Egyptians shall lothe to *d'* of the
21 the Egyptians could not *d'* of the
24 about the river for water to *d'*;
24 for they could not *d'* of the water
15:23 they could not *d'* of the waters of
24 Moses, saying, What shall we *d'*?
17: 1 was no water for the people to *d'*.
2 Give us water that we may *d'*.
6 out of it, that the people may *d'*.
24:11 they saw God, and did eat and *d'*.
29:40 hin of wine for a *d'* offering.
41 according to the *d'* offering thereof,
30: 9 shall ye pour *d'* offering thereon.
32: 6 people sat down to eat and to *d'*,
20 and made the children of Israel *d'*
34:28 neither eat bread, nor *d'* water.
Le 10: 9 Do not *d'* wine nor strong
9 wine nor strong *d'*, thou, nor thy
11:34 all *d'* that may be drunk in
23:13 and the *d'* offering thereof
18 and their *d'* offerings, even an
37 a sacrifice, and *d'* offerings, every
Nu 5:24 cause the woman to *d'* the bitter
26 cause the woman to *d'* the water.
27 he hath made her to *d'* the water,
6: 3 himself from wine and strong *d'*,
3 and shall *d'* no vinegar of wine,
3 of wine, or vinegar of strong *d'*,
3 shall he *d'* any liquor of grapes
15 offering, and their *d'* offerings.
17 meat offering, and his *d'* offering.
20 that the Nazarite may *d'* wine.
15: 5 of an hin of wine for a *d'* offering
7 for a *d'* offering thou shalt offer
10 for a *d'* offering half an hin of wine,
24 and his *d'* offering, according to
20: 5 neither is there any water to *d'*.
8 congregation and their beasts *d'*.
17 neither will we *d'* of the water
19 if I and my cattle *d'* of thy water,
21:22 we will not *d'* of the waters
23:24 prey, and *d'* the blood of the slain.
28: 7 And the *d'* offering thereof shall
7 unto the Lord for a *d'* offering.
8 and as the *d'* offering thereof, thou
9 oil, and the *d'* offering thereof:
10 burnt offering, and his *d'* offering.
14 their *d'* offerings shall be half an
15, 24 offering, and his *d'* offering.
31 blemish) and their *d'* offerings.
29: 6 *d'* offerings, according unto their
11 offering of it, and their *d'* offerings.
16 meat offering, and his *d'* offering.
18 their *d'* offerings for the bullocks,
19 thereof, and their *d'* offerings.
21 meat offering and their *d'* offerings
22 meat offering, and his *d'* offering.
24 their *d'* offerings for the bullocks,
25 meat offering, and his *d'* offering.
27 meat offering and their *d'* offerings
28 meat offering, and his *d'* offering.
30 offering and their *d'* offerings
31 meat offering, and his *d'* offering.
33 their *d'* offerings for the bullocks,
34 meat offering, and his *d'* offering.
37 meat offering and their *d'* offerings
38 meat offering, and his *d'* offerings
39 and for your *d'* offerings, and for
33:14 was no water for the people to *d'*.
De 2: 6 them for money, that ye may *d'*.
28 water for money, that I may *d'*:
9: 9 neither did eat bread, nor *d'* water,
18 neither eat bread nor *d'* water,
14:26 for wine, or for strong *d'*, or for
28:39 but shalt neither *d'* of the wine,
29: 6 have ye drunk wine or strong *d'*:
32:14 *d'* the pure blood of the grape.
38 the wine of their *d'* offerings?
J'g 4:19 I pray thee, a little water to *d'*;
19 and gave him *d'*, and covered him.
7: 5 boweth down upon his knees to *d'*.
6 bowed down upon their knees to *d'*
9:27 eat and *d'*, and cursed Abimelech.
13: 4 and *d'* not wine nor strong
4 not wine nor strong *d'*, and eat
7 no wine nor strong *d'*, neither
7 and now *d'* no wine nor strong
14 neither let her *d'* wine or strong
14 wine or strong *d'*, nor eat any
19: 4 did eat and *d'*, and lodged there.
6 did eat and *d'* both of them
21 washed their feet, and did eat and *d'*.
Ru 2: 9 and *d'* of that which the young men
1Sa 1:15 drunk neither wine nor strong *d'*,
30:11 eat; and they made him *d'* water;
2Sa 11:11 to eat and to *d'*, and to lie with my
13 he did eat and *d'* before him;
16: 2 be faint in the wilderness may *d'*.
19:35 taste what I eat or what I *d'*?
23:15 one would give me *d'* of the water
16 he would not *d'* thereof, but
17 lives? therefore he would not *d'* it.
1Ki 1:25 they eat and *d'* before him, and say,
13: 8 neither will I eat bread nor *d'* water
9 Eat no bread, nor *d'* water,nor turn
16 will I eat bread nor *d'* water with
17 shalt eat no bread nor *d'* water
18 he may eat bread and *d'* water.
22 Eat no bread, and *d'* no water;
17: 4 be, that thou shalt *d'* of the brook;
10 water into a vessel, that I may *d'*.
18:41 unto Ahab, Get thee up, eat and *d'*;
42 Ahab went up to eat and to *d'*.
19: 6 he did eat and *d'*, and laid him
8 eat and *d'*, and went in the strength
2Ki 3:17 water, that ye may *d'*, both ye, and
6:22 that they may eat and *d'*, and go to
7: 8 into one tent, and did eat and *d'*,
9:34 was come in, he did eat and *d'*,
16:13 and poured his *d'* offering, and
15 offering, and their *d'* offerings;
18:27 and *d'* their own piss with you?
31 and *d'* ye every one the waters
1Ch 11:17 would give me *d'* of the water
18 David would not *d'* of it, but poured
19 shall I *d'* the blood of these men
19 it. Therefore he would not *d'* it.
29:21 lambs, with their *d'* offerings,
22 did eat and *d'* before the Lord
2Ch 28:15 and gave them to eat and to *d'*,
29:35 and the *d'* offerings for every
Ezr 3: 7 meat, and *d'*, and oil, unto them
7:17 their *d'* offerings, and offer them
10: 6 he did eat no bread, nor *d'* water:
Ne 8:10 eat the fat, and *d'* the sweet,
12 went their way to eat, and to *d'*,
Es 1: 7 gave them *d'* in vessels of gold,
3:15 king and Haman sat down to *d'*;
4:16 neither eat nor *d'* three days, night
Job 1: 4 sisters to eat and to *d'* with them.
21:20 *d'* of the wrath of the Almighty.
22: 7 not given water to the weary to *d'*,
Ps 16: 4 *d'* offerings of blood will I not
36: 8 thou shalt make them *d'* of the
50:13 of bulls, or *d'* the blood of goats?
60: 3 to *d'* the wine of astonishment.
69:21 thirst they gave me vinegar to *d'*.
75: 8 wring them out, and *d'* them.
78:15 gave them *d'* as out of the great
44 floods, that they could not *d'*.
80: 5 tears to *d'* in great measure.
102: 9 and mingled my *d'* with weeping,
104:11 give *d'* to every beast of the field:
110: 7 shall *d'* of the brook in the way:
Pr 4:17 and *d'* the wine of violence.
5:15 *D'* waters out of thine own cistern,
9: 5 eat of my bread, and *d'* of the wine
20: 1 is a mocker, strong *d'* is raging:
23: 7 Eat and *d'*, saith he to thee;
25:21 be thirsty, give him water to *d'*:
31: 4 it is not for kings to *d'* wine;
4 wine; nor for princes strong *d'*:
5 Lest they *d'*, and forget the law,
6 Give strong *d'* unto him that is
7 Let him *d'*, and forget his
Ec 2:24 that he should eat and *d'*, and
3:13 every man should eat and *d'*, and
5:18 comely for one to eat and to *d'*
8:15 to eat, and to *d'*, and to be merry:
9: 7 *d'* thy wine with a merry heart;
Ca 5: 1 eat, O friends; *d'*, yea,
5 yea, *d'* abundantly, O beloved.
8: 2 I would cause thee to *d'* of spiced
Isa 5:11 that they may follow strong *d'*;
22 them that are mighty to *d'* wine,
22 of strength to mingle strong *d'*:
21: 5 watch in the watchtower, eat, *d'*:
22:13 drinking wine: let us eat and *d'*;
24: 9 They shall not *d'* wine with a song;
9 strong *d'* shall be bitter to them
9 shall be bitter to them that *d'* it.
28: 7 strong *d'* are out of the way;
7 have erred through strong *d'*,
7 out of the way through strong *d'*;
29: 9 stagger, but not with strong *d'*.
32: 6 he will cause the *d'* of the thirsty
36:12 and *d'* their own piss with you?
16 *d'* ye every one the waters of his

Isa 43:20 desert, to give d' to my people,
51:22 thou shalt no more d' it again:
56:12 will fill ourselves with strong d';
57: 6 hast thou poured a d' offering,
62: 8 the stranger shall not d' thy wine,
9 d' it in the courts of my holiness.
65:11 d' offering unto that number.
13 shall d', but ye shall be thirsty:
Jer 2:18 to d' the waters of Sihor? or what
18 to d' the waters of the river?
7:18 d' offerings unto other gods, that
8:14 and given us water of gall to d'.
9:15 and give them water of gall to d'.
16: 7 them the cup of consolation to d'
8 to sit with them to eat and to d'.
19:13 have poured out d' offerings unto
22:15 did not thy father eat and d',
23:15 make them d' the water of gall:
25:15 to whom I send thee, to d' it.
16 And they shall d', and be moved,
17 and made all the nations to d',
26 of Sheshach shall d' after them.
27 D' ye, and be drunken, and spue,
28 take the cup at thine hand to d',
28 Lord of hosts; Ye shall certainly d'.
32:29 out d' offerings unto other gods,
35: 2 and give them wine to d'.
5 I said unto them, D' ye wine.
6 We will d' no wine: for Jonadab
6 Ye shall d' no wine, neither ye,
8 to d' no wine all our days,
14 commanded his sons not to d' wine,
14 for unto this day they d' none,
44:17, 18 pour out d' offerings unto her,
19 poured out d' offerings unto her,
19 and pour out d' offerings unto her,
25 to pour out d' offerings unto her:
49:12 whose judgment was not to d' of
12 but thou shalt surely d' of it.
Eze 4:11 shalt d' also water by measure,
11 from time to time shalt thou d'.
16 they shall d' water by measure,
12:18 and d' thy water with trembling
19 d' their water with astonishment,
20:28 poured out there their d' offerings.
23:32 Thou shalt d' of thy sister's cup
34 shalt even d' it and suck it out,
25: 4 fruit, and they shall d' thy milk.
31:14 in their height, all that d' water:
16 all that d' water, shall be comforted
34:19 they d' that which ye have fouled
39:17 that ye may eat flesh, and d' blood.
18 d' the blood of the princes of the
19 and d' blood till ye be drunken,
44:21 Neither shall any priest d' wine,
45:17 meat offerings, and d' offerings,
Da 1:10 appointed your meat and your d':
12 pulse to eat, and water to d'.
16 and the wine that they should d';
5: 2 his concubines, might d' therein.
Ho 2: 5 and my flax, mine oil and my d',
4:18 Their d' is sour: they have
Joe 1: 9 the d' offering is cut off from the
13 and the d' offering is withholden
2:14 a d' offering unto the Lord your
3: 3 girl for wine, that they might d'.
Am 2: 8 they d' the wine of the condemned
12 ye gave the Nazarites wine to d';
4: 1 masters, Bring, and let us d'.
8 unto one city, to d' water;
5:11 but ye shall not d' wine of them.
6: 6 That d' wine in bowls, and anoint
9:14 vineyards, and d' the wine thereof;
Ob 16 all the heathen d' continually,
16 yea, they shall d', and they
Jon 3: 7 let them not feed, nor d' water:
Mic 2:11 thee of wine and of strong d';
6:15 and sweet wine, but shalt not d'
Hab 2:15 him that giveth his neighbour d',
16 d' thou also, and let thy foreskin
Zep 1:13 but not d' the wine thereof.
Hag 1: 6 ye d', but ye are not filled
6 but ye are not filled with d';
Zec 7: 6 did eat, and when ye did d',
6 yourselves, and d' for yourselves?
9:15 they shall d', and make a noise
M't 6:25 ye shall eat, or what ye shall d';
31 What shall we d'? or, Wherewithal
10:42 whosoever shall give to d' unto
20:22 to d' of the cup that I shall d' of,
23 Ye shall d' indeed of my cup,
24:49 to eat and d' with the drunken;
25:35 I was thirsty, and ye gave me d':
37 or thirsty, and gave thee d'?
42 I was thirsty and ye gave me no d':
26:27 to them, saying, D' ye all of it;
29 I will not d' henceforth of this fruit
29 day when I d' it new with you
42 except I d' it, thy will be done.
27:34 vinegar to d' mingled with gall:
34 tasted thereof, he would not d'.
48 on a reed, and gave him to d'.
M'r 9:41 shall give you a cup of water to d'
10:38 can ye d' of the cup that I d' of?
39 indeed d' of the cup that I d' of;
14:25 I will d' no more of the fruit of the
25 vine, until that day that I d' it new
15:23 And they gave him to d' wine
36 gave him to d', saying, Let alone;
16:18 and if they d' any deadly thing,
Lu 1:15 shall d' neither wine nor strong
15 neither wine nor strong d';
5:30 do ye eat and d' with publicans
33 Pharisees; but thine eat and d'?
12:19 thine ease, eat, d', and be merry.
29 ye shall eat, or what ye shall d',
Lu 12:45 to eat and d', and to be drunken;
17: 8 afterward thou shalt eat and d'?
22:18 will not d' of the fruit of the vine,
30 That ye may eat and d' at my table
Joh 4: 7 Jesus saith unto her, Give me to d'.
9 askest d' of me, which am a woman
10 Give me to d'; thou wouldest
6:53 and d' his blood, ye have no life
55 and my blood is d' indeed.
7:37 let him come unto me, and d'.
18:11 hath given me, shall I not d' it?
Ac 9: 9 sight, and neither did eat nor d'.
10:41 who did eat and d' with him
23:12 they would neither eat nor d' till
21 they will neither eat nor d' till
Ro 12:20 if he thirst, give him d': for in so
14:17 of God is not meat and d';
21 nor to d' wine, nor any thing
1Co 9: 4 we not power to eat and to d'?
10: 4 And did all d' the same spiritual
4 same spiritual d': for they drank
7 The people sat down to eat and d',
21 Ye cannot d' the cup of the Lord,
31 Whether therefore ye eat, or d', or
11:22 ye not houses to eat and to d' in?
25 this do ye, as oft as ye d' it,
26 ye eat this bread, and d' this cup,
27 d' this cup of the Lord, unworthily,
28 of that bread, and d' of that cup.
12:13 all made to d' into one Spirit.
15:32 let us eat and d'; for to-morrow
Col 2:16 judge you in meat, or in d',
1Ti 5:23 D' no longer water, but use a
Re 14: 8 because she made all nations d'
10 The same shall d' of the wine
16: 6 thou hast given them blood to d';

drinkers
Joe 1: 5 howl, all ye d' of wine, because of

drinketh
Ge 44: 5 Is not this it in which my lord d',
De 11:11 d' water of the rain of heaven:
Job 6: 4 poison whereof d' up my spirit;
15:16 man, which d' iniquity like water?
34: 7 Job, who d' up scorning like water?
40:23 Behold, he d' up a river, and
Pr 26: 6 cutteth off the feet, and d' damage.
Isa 29: 8 behold, he d'; but he awaketh,
44:12 he d' no water, and is faint.
M'r 2:16 d' with publicans and sinners?
Joh 4:13 d' of this water shall thirst again:
14 But whosoever d' of the water that
6:54 and d' my blood, hath eternal life;
56 eateth my flesh, and d' my blood,
1Co 11:29 For he that eateth and d'
29 unworthily, eateth and d' damnation
Heb 6: 7 the earth which d' in the rain

drinking
Ge 24:19 also, until they have done d'.
22 to pass, as the camels had done d',
Ru 3: 3 he shall have done eating and d'.
1Sa 30:16 earth, eating and d', and dancing,
1Ki 4:20 eating and d', and making merry.
10:21 all king Solomon's d' vessels were
16: 9 in Tirzah, d' himself drunk in the
20:12 message, as he was d', he and the
16 Ben-hadad was d' himself drunk in
1Ch 12:39 David three days, eating and d':
2Ch 9:20 all the d' vessels of king Solomon
Es 1: 8 And the d' was according to the
Job 1:13 his daughters were eating and d'
18 thy daughters were eating and d'
Isa 22:13 sheep, eating flesh, and d' wine:
M't 11:18 John came neither eating nor d',
19 Son of man came eating and d',
24:38 they were eating and d', marrying
Lu 7:33 neither eating bread nor d' wine;
34 Son of man is come eating and d';
10: 7 eating and d' such things as they

drink-offering See DRINK and OFFERING.

drinks
Heb 9:10 Which stood only in meats and d',

drive See also DRAVE; DROVE; DRIVEN; DRIVETH; DRIVING; OVERDRIVE.
Ex 6: 1 with a strong hand shall he d' them
23:28 which shall d' out the Hivite, the
29 I will not d' them out from before
30 By little and little I will d' them
31 and thou shalt d' them out before
33: 2 and I will d' out the Canaanite, the
34:11 I d' out before thee the Amorite,
Nu 22: 6 and that I may d' them out of the
11 to overcome them, and d' them out.
33:52 ye shall d' out all the inhabitants
55 if ye will not d' out the inhabitants
De 4:38 To d' out nations from before thee
9: 3 so shalt thou d' them out, and
4 the Lord doth d' them out from
5 the Lord thy God doth d' them out
11:23 Then will the Lord d' out all these
18:12 the Lord thy God doth d' them out
Jos 3:10 and that he will without fail d' out
13: 6 them will I d' out from before the
14:12 then I shall be able to d' them out,
15:63 children of Judah could not d' them
17:12 children of Mannasseh could not d'
13 but did not utterly d' them out.
18 thou shalt d' out the Canaanites,
23: 5 and d' them from out of your sight;
13 your God will no more d' out any
J'g 1:19 could not d' out the inhabitants of
21 the children of Benjamin did not d'
27 Manasseh d' out the inhabitants of
28 and did not utterly d' them out.
29 did Ephraim d' out the Canaanites
J'g 1:30 did Zebulun d' out the inhabitants
31 did Asher d' out the inhabitants
32 land: for they did not d' them out.
33 did Naphtali d' out the inhabitants
2: 3 I will not d' them out from before
21 I also will not henceforth d' out
11:24 the Lord our God shall d' out
2Ki 4:24 D', and go forward; slack not thy
2Ch 20: 7 didst d' out the inhabitants of this
Job 18:11 side, and shall d' him to his feet.
24: 3 d' away the ass of the fatherless,
Ps 44: 2 thou didst d' out the heathen with
68: 2 is driven away, so d' them away:
Pr 22:15 the rod of correction shall d' it far
Isa 22:19 I will d' thee from thy station,
Jer 24: 9 all places whither I shall d' them.
27:10 that I should d' you out, and ye
15 that I might d' you out, and that
46:15 not, because the Lord did d' them.
Eze 4:13 Gentiles, whither I will d' them.
Da 4:25 they shall d' thee from men, and
32 And they shall d' thee from men,
Ho 9:15 I will d' them out of mine house,
Joe 2:20 and will d' him into a land barren
Zep 2: 4 they shall d' out Ashdod at the
Ac 27:15 up into the wind, we let her d'.

driven
Ge 4:14 thou hast d' me out this day from
Ex 10:11 they were d' out from Pharaoh's
22:10 die, or be hurt, or d' away, no man
Nu 32:21 until he hath d' out his enemies
De 4:19 shouldest be d' to worship them,
30: 1 whither the Lord thy God hath d'
4 If any of thine be d' out unto the
Jos 23: 9 the Lord hath d' out from before
1Sa 26:19 for they have d' me out this day
Job 6:13 and is wisdom d' quite from me?
13:25 thou break a leaf d' to and fro?
18:18 He shall be d' from light into
30: 5 They were d' forth from among
Ps 40:14 let them be d' backward and put
68: 2 As smoke is d' away, so drive
114: 3 it, and fled: Jordan was d' back.
5 thou Jordan, that thou wast d'
Pr 14:32 The wicked is d' away in his
Isa 8:22 they shall be d' to darkness.
19: 7 by the brooks, shall wither, be d'
41: 2 sword, and as d' stubble to his bow.
Jer 8: 3 the places whither I have d' them,
16:15 the lands whither he had d' them:
23: 2 scattered my flock, and d' them
3 all countries whither I have d' them.
8 all countries whither I had d' them:
23:12 they shall be d' on, and fall
29:14 all the places whither I have d'
18 the nations whither I have d' them:
32:37 all countries, whither I have d'
40:12 all places whither they were d',
43: 5 nations, whither they had been d',
46:28 the nations whither I have d' thee:
49: 5 and ye shall be d' out every man
50:17 the lions have d' him away:
Eze 31:11 have d' him out for his wickedness.
34: 4 brought again that which was d'
16 bring again that which was d' away,
Da 4:33 he was d' from men, and did eat
5:21 he was d' from the sons of men;
9: 7 countries whither thou hast d'
Ho 13: 3 chaff that is d' with the whirlwind
Mic 4: 6 I will gather her that is d' out,
Zep 3:19 and gather her that was d' out;
Lu 8:29 d' of the devil into the wilderness.)
Ac 27:17 strake sail, and so were d'.
27 we were d' up and down in Adria,
Jas 1: 6 the sea d' with the wind and tossed.
3: 4 are d' of fierce winds, yet are they

driver
1Ki 22:34 he said unto the d' of his chariot,
Job 39: 7 regardeth he the crying of the d'.

driveth
2Ki 9:20 son of Nimshi; for he d' furiously.
Ps 1: 4 the chaff which the wind d' away.
Pr 25:23 The north wind d' away rain: so
M'r 1:12 spirit d' him into the wilderness.

driving
J'g 2:23 without d' them out hastily;
2Ki 9:20 and the d' is like the d' of Jehu
1Ch 17:21 by d' out nations from before thy

dromedaries
1Ki 4:28 and d' brought they unto the
Es 8:10 mules, camels, and young d':
Isa 60: 6 the d' of Midian and Ephah;

dromedary See also DROMEDARIES.
Jer 2:23 a swift d' traversing her ways;

drop See also DROPPED; DROPPETH; DROPPING; DROPS.
De 32: 2 My doctrine shall d' as the rain,
33:28 also his heaven shall d' down dew.
Job 36:28 the clouds do d' and distil upon
Ps 65:11 goodness; and thy paths d' fatness.
12 They d' upon the pastures of the
Pr 3:20 and the clouds d' down the dew.
5: 3 woman d' as an honeycomb,
Ca 4:11 my spouse, d' as the honeycomb:
Isa 40:15 a d' of a bucket, and are counted
45: 8 D' down, ye heavens, from above,
Eze 20:46 and d' thy word toward the south,
21: 2 and d' thy word toward the holy
Joel 3:18 the mountains shall d' down new
Am 7:16 d' not thy word against the house
9:13 and the mountains shall d' sweet

dropped
J'g 5: 4 the heavens d', the clouds also d'

1Sa 14:26 behold, the honey d·; but no man
2Sa 21:10 until water d· upon them out of
Job 29:22 and my speech d· upon them.
Ps 68: 8 heavens also d· at the presence of
Ca 5: 5 my hands d· with myrrh, and my

droppeth
Ec 10:18 the hands the house d· through.

dropping
Pr 19:13 of a wife are a continual d·.
27:15 A continual d· in a very rainy day
Ca 5:13 lilies, d sweet smelling myrrh.

drops
Job 36:27 he maketh small the d· of water:
38:28 who hath begotten the d· of dew?
Ca 5: 2 my locks with the d· of the night.
Lu 22:44 as it were great d· of blood falling

dropsy
Lu 14: 2 man before him which had the d·.

dross
Ps 119:119 all the wicked of the earth like d·:
Pr 25: 4 Take away the d· from the silver,
26:23 a potsherd covered with silver d·.
Isa 1:22 Thy silver is become d·, thy wine
25 purely purge away thy d·, and take
Eze 22:18 house of Israel is to me become d·;
18 they are even the d· of silver.
19 all become d·, behold, therefore

drought
Ge 31:40 in the day the d· consumed me,
De 8:15 serpents, and scorpions, and d·,
Job 24:19 D and heat consume the snow
Ps 32: 4 is turned into the d· of summer.
Isa 58:11 and satisfy thy soul in d·, and
Jer 2: 6 through a land of d·, and of the
17: 8 not be careful in the year of d·,
50:38 A d· is upon her waters; and they
Hos 13: 5 wilderness, in the land of great d·.
Hag 1:11 I called for a d· upon the land,

drove See also DRAVE; DROVES.
Ge 3:24 So he d· out the man; and he
15:11 carcases, Abram d· them away.
32:16 every d· by themselves; and said
16 put a space betwixt d· and d·.
33: 8 What meanest thou by all this d·
Ex 2:17 came and d· them away: but
Nu 21:32 and d· out the Amorites that were
Jos 15:14 Caleb d· thence the three sons of
1Ch 8:13 who d· away the inhabitants of
Ps 34:*title* who d· him away, and he
Hab 3: 6 and d· asunder the nations; and
Joh 2:15 he d· them all out of the temple,

droves
Ge 32:19 all that followed the d·, saying,

drown See also DROWNED.
Ca 8: 7 neither can the floods d· it: if a
1Ti 6: 9 which d· men in destruction and

drowned
Ex 15: 4 his chosen captains also are d·
Am 8: 8 and it shall be cast out and d·, as
9: 5 and shall be d·, as by the flood of
M't 18: 6 he were d· in the depth of the sea.
Heb 11:29 Egyptians assaying to do were d·.

drowsiness
Pr 23:21 d· shall clothe a man with rags.

drunk See also DRUNKEN.
Le 11:34 all drink that may be d· in every
De 29: 6 neither have ye d· wine or strong
32:42 make mine arrows d· with blood,
J'g 15:19 and when he had d·, his spirit
Ru 3: 7 when Boaz had eaten and d·, and
1Sa 1: 9 in Shiloh, and after they had d·.
15 I have d· neither wine nor strong
30:12 eaten no bread, nor d· any water,
2Sa 11:13 and he made him d·: and at even
1Ki 13:22 and d· water in the place, of the
23 after he had d·, that he saddled
16: 9 drinking himself d· in the house of
20:16 drinking himself d· in the pavilions,
2Ki 6:23 when they had eaten and d·, he
19:24 digged and d· strange waters, and
Ca 5: 1 I have d· my wine with my milk:
Isa 37:25 I have digged, and d· water; and
51:17 which hast d· at the hand of the
63: 6 and make them d· in my fury,
Jer 46:10 and made d· with their blood:
51:57 And I will make d· her princes,
Eze 34:18 to have d· of the deep waters,
Da 5:23 have d· wine in them; and thou
Ob 16 have d· upon my holy mountain,
Lu 5:39 No man also having d· old wine
13:26 have eaten and d· in thy presence,
Joh 2:10 when men have well d·, then
Eph 5:18 And be not d· with wine, wherein
Re 17: 2 have been made d· with the wine
18: 3 all nations have d· of the wine

drunkard See also DRUNKARDS.
De 21:20 voice; he is a glutton, and a d·.
Pr 23:21 the d· and the glutton shall come
26: 9 goeth up into the hand of a d·,
Isa 24:20 shall reel to and fro like a d·,
1Co 5:11 railer, or a d·, or an extortioner;

drunkards
Ps 69:12 and I was the song of the d·. 8354.
Isa 28: 1 of pride, to the d· of Ephraim,
3 crown of pride, the d· of Ephraim,
Joe 1: 5 Awake, ye d·, and weep; and howl,
Na 1:10 while they are drunken as d·,
1Co 6:10 nor d·, nor revilers, nor

drunken
Ge 9:21 he drank of the wine, and was d·;
1Sa 1:13 Eli thought she had been d·.
1Sa 1:14 How long wilt thou be d·? put
25:36 within him, for he was very d·:
Job 12:25 them to stagger like a d· man.
Ps 107:27 and stagger like a d· man.
Isa 19:14 a d· man staggereth in his vomit.
29: 9 they are d·, but not with wine;
49:26 shall be d· with their own blood,
51:17 thou hast d· the dregs of the cup
21 and d·, but not with wine:
Jer 23: 9 I am like a d· man, and like a
25:27 Drink ye, and be d·, and spue,
48:26 Make ye him d·: for he magnified
49:12 of the cup have assuredly d·;
51: 7 that made all the earth d·:
7 the nations have d· of her wine;
39 feasts, and I will make them d·,
La 3:15 hath made me d· with wormwood.
4:21 thou shalt be d·, and shalt make
5: 4 We have d· our water for money;
Eze 39:19 and drink blood till ye be d·,
Na 1:10 while they are d· as drunkards,
3:11 Thou also shalt be d·: thou shalt
Hab 2:15 to him, and makest him d· also,
M't 24:49 and to eat and drink with the d·;
Lu 12:45 eat and drink, and to be d·;
17: 8 till I have eaten and d·; and
Ac 2:15 these are not d·, as ye suppose,
1Co 11:21 one is hungry, and another is d·.
1Th 5: 7 they that be d· are d· in the night.
Re 17: 6 d· with the blood of the saints,

drunkenness
De 29:19 mine heart, to add d· to thirst:
Ec 10:17 for strength, and not for d·!
Jer 13:13 inhabitants of Jerusalem, with d·.
Eze 23:33 shalt be filled with d· and sorrow,
Lu 21:34 and d·, and cares of this life,
Ro 13:13 rioting and d·, not in chambering
Ga 5:21 Envyings, murders, d·, revellings,

Drusilla (*dru-sil'-lah*)
Ac 24:24 when Felix came with his wife D·,

dry See also DRIED; DRIETH; DRYSHOD.
Ge 1: 9 let the d· land appear: and it was
10 And God called the d· land Earth;
7:22 of all that was in the d· land, died.
8:13 the face of the ground was d·.
Ex 4: 9 pour it upon the d· land: and the
9 become blood upon the d· land:
14:16 of Israel shall go on d· ground
21 the sea d· land, and the waters
22 of the sea upon the d· ground:
29 of Israel walked upon d· land
15:19 children of Israel went on d· land
Le 7:10 offering mingled with oil, and d·,
13:30 it is a d· scall, even a leprosy upon
Jos 3:17 stood firm on d· ground in the
17 Israelites passed over on d· ground,
4:18 were lifted up unto the d· land,
22 came over this Jordan on d· land.
9: 5 their provision was d· and mouldy.
12 behold, it is d·, and it is mouldy:
J'g 6:37 be d· upon all the earth beside,
39 it now be d· only upon the fleece,
40 for it was d· upon the fleece only,
2Ki 2: 8 they two went over on d· ground.
Ne 9:11 midst of the sea on the d· land;
Job 12:15 the waters, and they d· up: also
13:25 wilt thou pursue the d· stubble?
15:30 the flame shall d· up his branches,
Ps 63: 1 for thee in a d· and thirsty land,
66: 6 He turned the sea into d· land:
68: 6 the rebellious dwell in a d· land.
95: 5 and his hands formed the d· land.
105:41 ran in the d· places like a river.
107:33 the watersprings into d· ground;
35 and d· ground into watersprings.
Pr 17: 1 is a d· morsel, and quietness
Isa 25: 5 strangers, as the heat in a d· place;
32: 2 as rivers of water in a d· place,
41:18 and the d· land springs of water.
42:15 and d· up all their herbs; and I
15 islands, and I will d· up the pools.
44: 3 and floods upon the d· ground:
27 saith to the deep, Be d·,
27 and I will d· up thy rivers.
50: 2 at my rebuke I d· up the sea,
53: 2 as a root out of a d· ground:
56: 3 say, Behold, I am a d· tree.
Jer 4:11 A d· wind of the high places
50:12 a d· land, and a desert.
51:36 I will d· up her sea, and make
36 and make her springs d·.
43 a d· land, and a wilderness,
Eze 17:24 have made the d· tree to flourish:
19:13 in a d· and thirsty ground.
20:47 tree in thee, and every d· tree:
30:12 I will make the rivers d·, and sell
37: 2 valley; and, lo, they were very d·.
4 O ye d· bones, hear the word of
Ho 2: 3 set her like a d· land, and slay
9:14 miscarrying womb and d· breasts.
13:15 and his spring shall become d·,
Jon 1: 9 hath made the sea and the d· land.
2:10 vomited out Jonah upon the d· land.
Na 1: 4 rebuketh the sea, and maketh it d·,
10 be devoured as stubble fully d·.
Zep 2:13 desolation, and d· like a wilderness.
Hag 2: 6 and the sea, and the d· land;
Zec 10:11 the deeps of the river shall d· up:
M't 12:43 he walketh through d· places,
Lu 11:24 he walketh through d· places,
23:31 what shall be done in the d·?
Heb 11:29 through the Red sea as by d· land:

dry-ground See DRY and GROUND.

dry-land See DRY and LAND.

dryshod
Isa 11:15 streams, and make men go over d·.

due See also DUES.
Le 10:13 it is thy d·, and thy sons' d·,
14 they be thy d·, and thy sons d·,
26: 4 I will give thee rain in d· season,
Nu 28: 2 offer unto me in their d· season.
De 11:14 rain of your land in his d· season,
18: 3 be the priest's d· from the people,
32:35 their foot shall slide in d· time:
1Ch 15:13 sought him not after the d· order.
16:29 Give unto the Lord the glory d·
Ne 11:23 for the singers, d· for every day.
Ps 29: 2 Lord the glory d· unto his name;
96: 8 the Lord the glory d· unto his name:
104:27 give them their meat in d· season.
145:15 them their meat in d· season.
Pr 3:27 good from them to whom it is d·,
15:23 a word spoken in d· season, how
Ec 10:17 princes eat in d· season, for strength,
M't 18:34 pay all that was d· unto him.
24:45 to give them meat in d· season?
Lu 12:42 their portion of meat in d· season?
23:41 receive the d· reward of our deeds:
Ro 5: 6 in d· time Christ died for the ungodly.
13: 7 dues: tribute to whom tribute is d·;
1Co 7: 3 unto the wife d· benevolence:
15: 8 as of one born out of d· time.
Ga 6: 9 for in d· season we shall reap,
1Ti 2: 6 for all, to be testified in d· time.
Tit 1: 3 in d· time manifested his word
1Pe 5: 6 that he may exalt you in d· time:

dues
Ro 13: 7 Render therefore to all their d·:

dug See DIGGED.

duke See also DUKES.
Ge 36:15 d· Teman, d· Omar,
15 d· Zepho, d· Kenaz,
16 D· Korah, d· Gatam, and d· Amalek:
17 d· Nahath, d· Zerah,
17 d· Shammah, d· Mizzah:
18 d· Jeush, d· Jaalam, d· Korah:
29 d· Lotan, d· Shobal,
29 d· Zibeon, d· Anah,
30 D· Dishon, d· Ezer, d· Dishan:
40 d· Timnah, d· Alvah, d· Jetheth,
41 D· Aholibamah, d· Elah, d· Pinon,
42 D· Kenaz, d· Teman, d· Mibzar,
43 D· Magdiel, d·Iram:
1Ch 1:51 d· Timnah, d· Aliah, d· Jetheth,
52 D· Aholibamah, d· Elah, d· Pinon,
53 D· Kenaz, d· Teman, d· Mibzar,
54 D· Magdiel, d· Iram.

dukes
Ge 36:15 These were d· of the sons
16 are the d· that came of Eliphaz
17 are the d· that came of Reuel
18 the d· that came of Aholibamah
19 is Edom, and these are their d·.
21 these are the d· of the Horites,
29 the d· that came of the Horites;
30 are the d· that came of Hori,
30 among their d· in the land of Seir.
40 of the d· that came of Esau,
43 these be the d· of Edom,
Ex 15:15 the d· of Edom shall be amazed;
Jos 13:21 were d· of Sihon, dwelling in the
1Ch 1:51 And the d· of Edom were;
54 These are the d· of Edom.

dulcimer
Da 3: 5, 10, 15 d·, and all kinds of musick,

dull
M't 13:15 their ears are d· of hearing, and
Ac 28:27 their ears are d· of hearing, and
Heb 5:11 seeing ye are d· of hearing.

Dumah (*doo'-mah*)
Ge 25:14 Mishma, and D·, and Massa,
Jos 15:52 Arab, and D·, and Eshean,
1Ch 1:30 and D·, Massa, Hadad, and Tema,
Isa 21:11 The burden of D·. He calleth to

dumb
Ex 4:11 or who maketh the d·, or deaf,
Ps 38:13 and I was as a d· man that openeth
39: 2 I was d· with silence, I held my
9 I was d·, I opened not my mouth;
Pr 31: 8 Open thy mouth for the d· in the
Isa 35: 6 and the tongue of the d· sing:
53: 7 a sheep before her shearers is d·,
56:10 they are all d· dogs, they cannot
Eze 3:26 thou shalt be d·, and shalt not be
24:27 shalt speak, and be no more d·:
33:22 was opened, and I was no more d·.
Da 10:15 toward the ground, and I became d·.
Hab 2:18 trusteth therein, to make d· idols?
19 Awake; to the d· stone, Arise,
M't 9:32 brought to him a d· man possessed
33 devil was cast out, the d· spake:
12:22 with a devil, blind, and d·: and he
22 that the blind and d· both spake
15:30 blind, d·, maimed, and many others,
31 when they saw the d· to speak,
M'r 7:37 deaf to hear, and the d· to speak.
9:17 my son, which hath a d· spirit;
25 Thou d· and deaf spirit, I charge
Lu 1:20 shalt be d·, and not able to speak,
11:14 casting out a devil, and it was d·.
14 devil was gone out, the d· spake,
Ac 8:32 like a lamb d· before his shearer,
1Co 12: 2 carried away unto these d· idols,
2Pe 2:16 d· ass speaking with man's voice

dung See also DUNGHILL.
Ex 29:14 bullock, and his skin, and his d·,

Le 4:11 his legs, and his inwards, and his d',
8:17 and his hide, his flesh, and his d',
16:27 skins, their flesh, and their d'.
Nu 19: 5 flesh, and her blood, with her d',
1Ki 14:10 as a man taketh away d', till it be
2Ki 6:25 fourth part of a cab of dove's d'
9:37 Jezebel shall be as d' upon the face
18:27 they may eat their own d',
Ne 2:13 and to the d' port, and viewed the
3:13 cubits on the wall unto the d' gate.
14 But the d' gate repaired Malchiah
12:31 upon the wall toward the d' gate:
Job 20: 7 shall perish for ever like his own d':
Ps 83:10 they became as d' for the earth.
Isa 36:12 may eat their own d',
Jer 8: 2 they shall be for d' upon the face
9:22 shall fall as d' upon the open field,
16: 4 they shall be as d' upon the face of
25:33 they shall be d' upon the ground.
Eze 4:12 and thou shalt bake it with d' that
15 Lo, I have given thee cow's d'
15 for man's d', and thou shalt
Zep 1:17 as dust, and their flesh as the d'.
Mal 2: 3 spread d' upon your faces, even
3 even the d' of your solemn feasts;
Lu 13: 8 I shall dig about it, and d' it:
Ph'p 3: 8 and do count them but d', that I

dungeon
Ge 40:15 that they should put me into the d'.
41:14 brought him hastily out of the d':
Ex 12:29 the captive that was in the d';
Jer 37:16 was entered into the d',
38: 6 cast him into the d' of Malchiah the
6 And in the d' there was no water, but
7 they had put Jeremiah into the d';
9 whom they have cast into the d'; and
10 Jeremiah the prophet out of the d',
11 let them down by cords into the d' to
13 cords, and took him up out of the d':
La 3:53 They have cut off my life in the d',
55 thy name, O Lord, out of the low d'.

dung-gate See DUNG and GATE.

dunghill See also DUNGHILLS.
1Sa 2: 8 lifted up the beggar from the d',
Ezr 6:11 his house be made a d' for this.
Ps 113: 7 and lifteth the needy out of the d';
Isa 25:10 as straw is trodden down for the d'.
Da 2: 5 your houses shall be made a d'.
3:29 their houses shall be made a d':
Lu 14:35 for the land, nor yet for the d';

dunghills
La 4: 5 brought up in scarlet embrace d'.

Dura (*doo'-rah*)
Da 3: 1 he set it up in the plain of D', in the

durable
Pr 8:18 yea, d' riches and righteousness.
Isa 23:18 sufficiently, and for d' clothing.

dureth See also ENDURETH.
M't 13:21 root in himself, but d' for a while:

durst
Es 7: 5 that d' presume in his heart to do so?
Job 32: 6 and d' not shew you mine opinion.
M't 22:46 neither d' any man from that day
M'r 12:34 no man after that d' ask him any
Lu 20:40 they d' not ask him any question
Joh 21:12 none of the disciples d' ask him,
Ac 5:13 And of the rest d' no man join
7:32 Moses trembled, and d' not behold.
Jude 9 d' not bring against him a railing

dust
Ge 2: 7 Lord God formed man of the d' of
3:14 and d' shalt thou eat all the days of
19 wast thou taken; for d' thou art,
19 and unto d' shalt thou return.
13:16 as the d' of the earth: so that if a
16 man can number the d' of the earth,
18:27 Lord, which am but d' and ashes:
28:14 shall be as the d' of the earth,
Ex 8:16 smite the d' of the land, that it
17 and smote the d' of the earth,
17 in beast; all the d' of the land
9: 9 And it shall become small d' in all
Le 14:41 they shall pour out the d' that
17:13 blood thereof, and cover it with d'.
Nu 5:17 and of the d' that is in the floor of
23:10 Who can count the d' of Jacob,
De 9:21 until it was as small as d': and
21 I cast the d' thereof into the brook
28:24 the rain of thy land powder and d':
32:24 the poison of serpents of the d'.
Jos 7: 6 and put d' upon their heads.
1Sa 2: 8 raiseth up the poor out of the d',
2Sa 16:13 threw stones at him, and cast d'.
22:43 I beat them as small as the d' of
1Ki 16: 2 I exalted thee out of the d',
18:38 the wood, and the stones, and the d',
20:10 if the d' of Samaria shall suffice
2Ki 13: 7 and had made them like the d' by
23:12 cast the d' of them into the brook
2Ch 1: 9 people like the d' of the earth
34: 4 and made d' of them, and strowed
Job 2:12 sprinkled d' upon their heads
4:19 whose foundation is in the d',
5: 6 affliction cometh not forth of the d',
7: 5 with worms and with clods of d';
21 now shall I sleep in the d'; and
10: 9 wilt thou bring me into d' again?
14:19 grow out of the d' of the earth;
16:15 and defiled my horn in the d'.
17:16 our rest together is in the d',
20:11 shall lie down with him in the d'
21:26 They shall lie down alike in the d',
22:24 Then shalt thou lay up gold as d',
Job 27:16 Though he heap up silver as the d',
28: 6 sapphires: and it hath d' of gold.
30:19 I am become like d' and ashes.
34:15 man shall turn again unto d'.
38:38 When the d' groweth into hardness,
39:14 earth, and warmeth them in d',
40:13 Hide them in the d' together;
42: 6 and repent in d' and ashes.
Ps 7: 5 and lay mine honour in the d'.
18:42 I beat them small as the d' before
22:15 brought me into the d' of death.
29 they that go down to the d' shall
30: 9 Shall the d' praise thee? shall it
44:25 our soul is bowed down to the d':
72: 9 and his enemies shall lick the d'.
78:27 rained flesh also upon them as d',
102:14 stones, and favour the d' thereof.
103:14 he remembereth that we are d'.
104:29 they die, and return to their d'.
113: 7 raiseth up the poor out of the d',
119:25 My soul cleaveth unto the d':
Pr 8:26 highest part of the d' of the world.
Ec 3:20 all are of the d', and all turn to d'
12: 7 shall the d' return to the earth
Isa 2:10 and hide thee in the d', for fear of
5:24 their blossom shall go up as d':
25:12 to the ground, even to the d'.
26: 5 he bringeth it even to the d'.
19 and sing, ye that dwell in d':
29: 4 speech shall be low out of the d',
4 speech shall whisper out of the d'.
5 strangers shall be like small d',
34: 7 their d' made fat with fatness.
9 and the d' thereof into brimstone,
40:12 comprehended the d' of the earth
15 as the small d' of the balance:
41: 2 gave them as the d' to his sword,
47: 1 Come down, and sit in the d',
49:23 and lick up the d' of thy feet;
52: 2 Shake thyself from the d'; arise,
65:25 and d' shall be the serpent's meat.
La 2:10 have cast up d' upon their heads;
3:29 He putteth his mouth in the d';
Eze 24: 7 the ground, to cover it with d';
26: 4 I will also scrape her d' from her,
10 his horses their d' shall cover thee:
12 timber and thy d' in the midst of
27:30 shall cast up d' upon their heads,
Da 12: 2 many of them that sleep in the d'
Am 2: 7 that pant after the d' of the earth
Mic 1:10 of Aphrah roll thyself in the d'.
7:17 shall lick the d' like a serpent,
Na 1: 3 the clouds are the d' of his feet.
3:18 thy nobles shall dwell in the d':
Hab 1:10 they shall heap d', and take it.
Zep 1:17 blood shall be poured out as d',
Zec 9: 3 heaped up silver as the d', and fine
M't 10:14 city, shake off the d' of your feet.
M'r 6:11 shake off the d' under your feet
Lu 9: 5 shake off the very d' from your feet
10:11 Even the very d' of your city, which
Ac 13:51 they shook off the d' of their feet
22:23 clothes, and threw d' into the air,
Re 18:19 And they cast d' on their heads,

duty See also DUTIES.
Ex 21:10 and her d' of marriage, shall he not
De 25: 5 d' of an husband's brother unto her.
7 the d' of my husband's brother.
2Ch 8:14 as the d' of every day required:
Ezr 3: 4 as the d' of every day required;
Ec 12:13 for this is the whole d' of man.
Lu 17:10 done that which was our d' to do.
Ro 15:27 their d' is also to minister unto

dwarf
Le 21:20 crookbackt, or a d', or that hath

dwell See also DWELLED; DWELLEST; DWELLETH; DWELLING; DWELT.
Ge 4:20 the father of such as d' in tents,
9:27 he shall d' in the tents of Shem;
13: 6 that they might d' together: for
6 so that they could not d' together,
16:12 he shall d' in the presence of all
19:30 he feared to d' in Zoar: and he
20:15 thee: d' where it pleaseth thee.
24: 3 the Canaanites, among whom I d':
37 the Canaanites, in whose land I d':
26: 2 d' in the land which I shall tell
30:20 now will my husband d' with me,
34:10 And ye shall d' with us: and the
10 d' and trade ye therein, and get you
16 and we will d' with you, and we
21 therefore let them d' in the land,
22 consent unto us for to d' with us,
23 unto them, and they will d' with us.
35: 1 go up to Beth-el, and d' there: and
36: 7 than that they might d' together;
45:10 thou shalt d' in the land of Goshen,
46:34 ye may d' in the land of Goshen;
47: 4 servants d' in the land of Goshen.
6 make thy father and brethren to d';
6 in the land of Goshen let them d':
49:13 Zebulun shall d' at the haven of
Ex 2:21 Moses was content to d' with the
8:22 Goshen, in which my people d',
15:17 thou hast made for thee to d' in,
23:33 They shall not d' in thy land, lest
25: 8 that I may d' among them.
29:45 d' among the children of Israel,
46 that I may d' among them: I am
Le 13:46 he shall d' alone; without the camp
20:22 whither I bring you to d' therein,
23:42 Ye shall d' in booths seven days;
42 Israelites born shall d' in booths:
43 children of Israel to d' in booths,
25:18 ye shall d' in the land in safety.
Le 25:19 your fill, and d' therein in safety.
26: 5 the full, and d' in your land safely.
32 your enemies which d' therein
Nu 5: 3 camps, in the midst whereof I d'.
13:19 what the land is that they d' in,
19 that they d' in, whether in tents,
28 people be strong that d' in the land,
29 The Amalekites d' in the land of
29 the Amorites, d' in the mountains:
29 and the Canaanites d' by the sea,
14:30 make you d' therein, save Caleb
23: 9 the people shall d' alone, and shall
32:17 ones shall d' in the fenced cities
33:53 of the land, and d' therein: for I
55 vex you in the land wherein ye d'.
35: 2 of their possession cities to d' in;
3 the cities shall they have to d' in;
32 should come again to d' in the land,
34 ye shall inhabit, wherein I d': for
34 d' among the children of Israel.
De 2: 4 children of Esau, which d' in Seir;
29 children of Esau which d' in Seir,
29 and the Moabites which d' in Ar,
11:30 which d' in the champaign over
31 ye shall possess it, and d' therein.
12:10 and d' in the land which the Lord
10 round about, so that ye d' in safety;
11 to cause his name to d' there;
13:12 God hath given thee to d' there,
17:14 possess it, and shalt d' therein,
23:16 He shall d' with thee, even among
25: 5 If brethren d' together, and one of
28:30 and thou shalt not d' therein:
30:20 that thou mayest d' in the land
33:12 Lord shall d' in safety by him;
12 he shall d' between his shoulders.
28 Israel then shall d' in safety
Jos 9: 7 Peradventure ye d' among us;
22 from you; when ye d' among us?
10: 6 d' in the mountains are gathered
13:13 the Maachathites d' among the
14: 4 cities to d' in, with their suburbs
15:63 Jebusites d' with the children
16:10 but the Canaanites d' among the
17:12 Canaanites would d' in that land.
16 that d' in the land of the valley
20: 4 place, that he may d' among them.
6 And he shall d' in that city,
21: 2 of Moses to give us cities to d' in,
24:13 ye built not, and ye d' in them;
15 the Amorites, in whose land ye d':
J'g 1:21 Jebusites d' with the children
27 Canaanites would d' in that land.
35 Amorites would d' in mount Heres
6:10 in whose land ye d': but ye have
9:41 they should not d' in Shechem.
17:10 Micah said unto him, D' with me,
11 the Levite was content to d' with
18: 1 sought them an inheritance to d' in;
1Sa 12: 8 and made them d' in this place.
27: 5 country, that I may d' there: for
5 why should thy servant d' in the
2Sa 7: 2 I d' in an house of cedar, but the ark
5 build me an house for me to d' in?
10 that they may d' in a place of their
1Ki 2:36 house in Jerusalem, and d' there,
3:17 I and this woman d' in one house;
6:13 And I will d' among the children
8:12 The Lord said that he would d' in
13 built thee an house to d' in, a
27 will God indeed d' on the earth?
17: 9 belongeth to Zidon, and d' there:
2Ki 4:13 I d' among mine own people.
6: 1 the place where we d' with thee
2 a place there, where we may d'.
17:27 let them go and d' there,
25:24 d' in the land, and serve the king
1Ch 17: 1 I d' in an house of cedars,
4 not build me an house to d' in:
9 and they shall d' in their place,
23:25 may d' in Jerusalem for ever:
2Ch 2: 3 build him an house to d' therein,
6: 1 he would d' in the thick darkness.
18 will God in very deed d' with men
8: 2 the children of Israel to d' there.
11 shall not d' in the house of David
19:10 brethren that d' in their cities,
Ezr 4:17 companions that d' in Samaria,
6:12 hath caused his name to d' there
Ne 8:14 the children of Israel should d' in
11: 1 to d' in Jerusalem the holy city,
2 themselves to d' at Jerusalem.
Job 3: 5 stain it; let a cloud d' upon it;
4:19 in them that d' in houses of clay,
11:14 wickedness d' in thy tabernacles.
18:15 It shall d' in his tabernacle,
19:15 They that d' in mine house, and
30: 6 To d' in the cliffs of the valleys,
Ps 4: 8 Lord, only makest me d' in safety.
5: 4 neither shall evil d' with thee.
15: 1 who shall d' in thy holy hill?
23: 6 I will d' in the house of the Lord
24: 1 world, and they that d' therein.
25:13 His soul shall d' at ease; and his
27: 4 I may d' in the house of the Lord
37: 3 So shalt thou d' in the land, and
27 and do good; and d' for evermore.
29 inherit the land, and d' therein for
65: 4 that he may d' in thy courts:
8 They also that d' in the uttermost
68: 6 but the rebellious d' in a dry land.
16 hill which God desireth to d' in;
16 yea, the Lord will d' in it for ever.
18 Lord God might d' among them
69:25 and let none d' in their tents.
35 that they may d' there, and have

Ps 69:36 they that love his name shall *d*
72: 9 that *d* in the wilderness shall bow
78:55 made the tribes of Israel to *d*
84: 4 Blessed are they that *d* in thy
10 to *d* in the tents of wickedness.
85: 9 that glory may *d* in our land.
98: 7 world, and they that *d* therein.
101: 6 the land, that they may *d* with me:
7 shall not *d* within my house:
107: 4 way; they found no city to *d* in.
34 of them that *d* therein.
36 there he maketh the hungry to *d*,
120: 5 I *d* in the tents of Kedar!
132:14 here will I *d*; for I have desired it.
133: 1 brethren to *d* together in unity!
139: 9 and *d* in the uttermost parts of the
140:13 upright shall *d* in thy presence.
143: 3 he hath made me to *d* in darkness,
Pr 1:33 hearkeneth unto me shall *d*
2:21 the upright shall *d* in the land,
8:12 I wisdom *d* with prudence, and
21: 9 to *d* in the corner of the housetop,
19 It is better to *d* in the wilderness,
25:24 to *d* in the corner of the housetop.
Isa 6: 5 I *d* in the midst of a people of
9: 2 that *d* in the land of the shadow
11: 6 wolf also shall *d* with the lamb,
13:21 owls shall *d* there, and satyrs
16: 4 Let mine outcasts *d* with thee,
23:13 them that *d* in the wilderness:
18 them that *d* before the Lord, to
24: 6 they that *d* therein are desolate:
26: 5 down them that *d* on high; the
19 and sing, ye that *d* in dust: for
30:19 For the people shall *d* in Zion at
32:16 shall *d* in the wilderness, and
18 *d* in a peaceable habitation,
33:14 shall *d* with the devouring fire?
14 shall *d* with everlasting
16 He shall *d* on high: his place of
24 the people that *d* therein shall
34:11 the raven shall *d* in it: and he
17 generation shall they *d* therein.
40:22 them out as a tent to *d* in:
49:20 give place to me that I may *d*.
51: 6 *d* therein shall die in like manner:
57:15 I *d* in the high and holy place,
58:12 The restorer of paths to *d* in.
65: 9 and my servants shall *d* there.
Jer 4:29 forsaken, and not a man *d* therein.
7: 3 I will cause you to *d* in this place.
7 will I cause you to *d* in this place,
8:16 city, and those that *d* therein.
19 of them that *d* in a far country:
9:26 corners, that *d* in the wilderness:
12: 4 wickedness of them that *d* therein?
20: 6 all that *d* in thine house shall go
23: 6 Israel shall *d* safely: and this
8 they shall *d* in their own land.
24: 8 them that *d* in the land of Egypt:
25: 5 and *d* in the land that the Lord
24 people that *d* in the desert,
27:11 they shall till it, and *d* therein.
29: 5 Build ye houses, and *d* in them;
28 build ye houses, and *d* in them;
32 a man to *d* among his people;
31:24 And there shall *d* in Judah itself,
32:37 and I will cause them to *d* safely:
33:16 and Jerusalem shall *d* safely:
35: 7 all your days ye shall *d* in tents;
9 Nor to build houses for us to *d* in:
11 Syrians: so we *d* at Jerusalem.
15 and ye shall *d* in the land which
40: 5 and *d* with him among the people:
9 *d* in the land, and serve the king
10 for me, behold, I will *d* at Mizpah,
10 and *d* in your cities that ye have
42:13 We will not *d* in this land, neither
14 of bread: and there will we *d*:
43: 4 Lord, to *d* in the land of Judah.
5 driven, to *d* in the land of Judah;
44: 1 which *d* in the land of Egypt,
1 which *d* at Migdol, and at
8 whither ye be gone to *d*, that
13 I will punish them that *d* in the
14 have a desire to return to *d* there:
26 Judah that *d* in the land of Egypt;
47: 2 the city, and them that *d* therein:
48: 9 desolate, without any to *d* therein.
28 O ye that *d* in Moab, leave the
28 cities, and *d* in the rock, and be
49: 1 and his people *d* in his cities?
8 Flee ye, turn back, *d* deep, O
18 neither shall a son of man *d* in it.
30 Flee, get you far off, *d* deep, O ye
31 gates nor bars which *d* alone.
33 nor any son of man *d* in it.
50: 3 none shall *d* therein: they shall
39 beasts of the islands shall *d* there,
39 and the owls shall *d* therein: and
40 shall any son of man *d* therein.
51: 1 against them that *d* in the midst
Eze 2: 6 thou dost *d* among scorpions:
12:19 violence of all them that *d* therein.
16:46 daughters that *d* at thy left hand:
17:23 and under it shall *d* all fowl
23 the branches thereof shall they *d*.
28:25 then shall they *d* in their land
26 And they shall *d* safely therein,
26 yea, they shall *d* with confidence,
32:15 shall smite all them that *d* therein,
34:25 and they shall *d* safely in the
28 but they shall *d* safely, and none
36:28 And ye shall *d* in the land that
33 also cause you to *d* in the cities,
37:25 And they shall *d* in the land that

Eze 37:25 and they shall *d* therein, even they,
38: 8 and they shall *d* safely all of them.
11 that are at rest, that *d* safely,
12 that *d* in the midst of the land.
39: 6 among them that *d* carelessly
9 they that *d* in the cities of Israel
43: 7 where I will *d* in the midst of the
9 and I will *d* in the midst of them
Da 2:38 wheresoever the children of men *d*,
4: 1 that *d* in all the earth; Peace be
6:25 that *d* in all the earth; Peace be
Ho 9: 3 shall not *d* in the Lord's land;
12: 9 make thee to *d* in tabernacles,
14: 7 They that *d* under his shadow
Joe 3:20 Judah shall *d* for ever, and
Am 3:12 be taken out that *d* in Samaria
5:11 but ye shall not *d* in them;
9: 5 all that *d* therein shall mourn:
Mic 4:10 and thou shalt *d* in the field,
7:13 because of them that *d* therein,
14 which *d* solitarily in the wood,
Na 1: 5 the world, and all that *d* therein.
3:18 thy nobles shall *d* in the dust:
Hab 2: 8 the city, and of all that *d* therein.
17 city, and of all that *d* therein.
Zep 1:18 of all them that *d* in the land.
Hag 1: 4 to *d* in your cieled houses, and
Zec 2:10 I come, and I will *d* in the midst
11 people: and I will *d* in the midst
8: 3 will *d* in the midst of Jerusalem:
4 and old women *d* in the streets
8 shall *d* in the midst of Jerusalem:
9: 6 And a bastard shall *d* in Ashdod,
14:11 And men shall *d* in it, and there
M't 12:45 and they enter in and *d* there:
Lu 11:26 and they enter in, and *d* there:
21:35 all them that *d* on the face of the
Ac 1:20 and let no man *d* therein:
2:14 and all ye that *d* at Jerusalem,
4:16 to all them that *d* in Jerusalem;
7: 4 into this land, wherein ye now *d*.
13:27 For they that *d* at Jerusalem, and
17:26 to *d* on all the face of the earth,
28:16 Paul was suffered to *d* by himself
Ro 8: 9 that the Spirit of God *d* in you.
11 raised up Jesus from the dead *d*
1Co 7:12 and she be pleased to *d* with him,
13 if he be pleased to *d* with her,
2Co 6:16 God hath said, I will *d* in them,
Eph 3:17 That Christ may *d* in your hearts
Col 1:19 that in him should all fulness *d*;
3:16 Let the word of Christ *d* in you
1Pe 3: 7 husbands *d* with them according
1Jo 4:13 know we that we *d* in him,
Re 3:10 try them that *d* upon the earth.
6:10 blood on them that *d* on the earth?
7:15 the throne shall *d* among them.
11:10 they that *d* upon the earth shall
10 tormented them that *d* on the earth.
12:12 heavens, and ye that *d* in them.
13: 6 and them that *d* in heaven.
8 all that *d* upon the earth shall
12 which *d* therein to worship the
14 And deceiveth them that *d* on the
14 saying to them that *d* on the earth,
14: 6 to preach unto them that *d* on
17: 8 and they that *d* on the earth shall
21: 3 and he will *d* with them, and they

dwelled See also DWELT.
Ge 13: 7 the Perizzite *d* then in the land.
12 Abram *d* in the land of Canaan,
12 and Lot *d* in the cities of the plain,
20: 1 and *d* between Kadesh and Shur,
Ru 1: 4 and they *d* there about ten years.
1Sa 12:11 on every side, and ye *d* safe.

dwellers
Isa 18: 3 of the world, and *d* on the earth,
Ac 1:19 known unto all the *d* at Jerusalem;
2: 9 and the *d* in Mesopotamia, and in

dwellest
De 12:29 them, and *d* in their land;
19: 1 them, and *d* in their cities,
26: 1 and possessest it, and *d* therein;
2Ki 19:15 which *d* between the cherubims,
Ps 80: 1 that *d* between the cherubims,
123: 1 O thou that *d* in the heavens.
Ca 8:13 Thou that *d* in the gardens, the
Isa 10:24 O my people that *d* in Zion,
37:16 that *d* between the cherubims,
47: 8 to pleasures, that *d* carelessly,
Jer 49:16 O thou that *d* in the clefts of the
51:13 O thou that *d* upon many waters,
La 4:21 Edom, that *d* in the land of Uz;
Eze 7: 7 O thou that *d* in the land:
12: 2 thou *d* in the midst of a rebellious
Ob 3 that *d* in the clefts of the rock,
Zec 2: 7 *d* with the daughter of Babylon.
Joh 1:38 Master,) where *d* thou?
Re 2:13 and where thou *d*, even where

dwelleth
Le 19:34 the stranger that *d* with you
25:39 And if thy brother that *d* by thee
47 and thy brother that *d* by him
Nu 13:18 people that *d* therein, whether
De 33:20 he *d* as a lion, and teareth the arm
Jos 6:25 and she *d* in Israel even unto
22:19 wherein the Lord's tabernacle *d*,
1Sa 4: 4 which *d* between the cherubims:
27:11 while he *d* in the country of the
2Sa 6: 2 that *d* between the cherubims.
7: 2 the ark of God *d* within curtains.
1Ch 13: 6 that *d* between the cherubims,
Job 15:28 And he *d* in desolate cities, and
38:19 Where is the way where light *d*?

Job 39:28 She *d* and abideth on the rock,
Ps 9:11 to the Lord, which *d* in Zion:
26: 8 the place where thine honour *d*.
91: 1 He that *d* in the secret place of the
113: 5 the Lord our God, who *d* on high,
135:21 of Zion, which *d* at Jerusalem.
Pr 3:29 seeing he *d* securely by thee.
Isa 8:18 of hosts, which *d* in mount Zion.
33: 5 for he *d* on high: he hath filled
Jer 29:16 of all the people that *d* in this
44: 2 desolation, and no man *d* therein,
49:31 nation that *d* without care,
51:43 a land wherein no man *d*, neither
La 1: 3 she *d* among the heathen, she
Eze 16:46 that *d* at thy right hand, is Sodom
17:16 the place where the king *d* that
38:14 when my people of Israel *d* safely,
Da 2:22 darkness, and the light *d* with
Ho 4: 3 every one that *d* therein shall
Joe 3:21 cleansed: for the Lord *d* in Zion.
Am 8: 8 every one mourn that *d* therein?
M't 23:21 by it, and by him that *d* therein.
Joh 6:56 my blood, *d* in me, and I in him.
14:10 the Father that *d* in me, he doeth
17 for he *d* with you, and shall be
Ac 7:48 the most High *d* not in temples
17:24 of heaven and earth, *d* not in temples
Ro 7:17 that do it, but sin that *d* in me.
18 is, in my flesh,) *d* no good thing:
20 I that do it, but sin that *d* in me.
8:11 bodies by his Spirit that *d* in you.
1Co 3:16 and that the Spirit of God *d* in you?
Col 2: 9 in him *d* all the fulness of the
2Ti 1:14 the Holy Ghost which *d* in us.
Jas 4: 5 The spirit that *d* in us lusteth
2Pe 3:13 earth, wherein *d* righteousness.
1Jo 3:17 how *d* the love of God in him?
24 his commandments *d* in him,
4:12 God *d* in us, and his love is
15 God *d* in him, and he in God.
16 he that *d* in love *d* in God, and
2Jo 2 the truth's sake, which *d* in us,
Re 2:13 slain among you, where Satan *d*.

dwelling See also DWELLINGPLACE; DWELLINGS.
Ge 10:30 their *d* was from Mesha, as thou
25:27 Jacob was a plain man, *d* in tents.
27:39 thy *d* shall be the fatness of the
Le 25:29 if a man sell a *d* house in a walled
Nu 21:15 that goeth down to the *d* of Ar,
Jos 13:21 dukes of Sihon, *d* in the country.
1Ki 8:30 and hear thou in heaven thy *d*
39 Then hear thou in heaven thy *d*
43 Hear thou in heaven thy *d* place,
49 supplication in heaven thy *d* place.
21: 8 were in his city, *d* with Naboth.
2Ki 17:25 the beginning of their *d* there, that
1Ch 6:32 they ministered before the *d*
54 are their *d* places throughout
2Ch 6: 2 a place for thy *d* for ever.
21 hear thou from thy *d* place, even
30 hear thou from heaven thy *d* place,
33 even from thy *d* place, and do
39 even from thy *d* place, their prayer
30:27 came up to his holy *d* place,
36:15 his people, and on his *d* place:
Job 8:22 and the *d* place of the wicked
21:28 are the *d* places of the wicked?
Ps 49:11 their *d* places to all generations;
14 consume in the grave from their *d*.
52: 5 pluck thee out of thy *d* place,
74: 7 down the *d* place of thy name
76: 2 and his *d* place in Zion.
79: 7 Jacob, and laid waste his *d* place.
90: 1 Lord, thou hast been our *d* place
91:10 shall any plague come nigh thy *d*.
Pr 21:20 and oil in the *d* of the wise;
24:15 against the *d* of the righteous;
Isa 4: 5 every *d* place of mount Zion,
18: 4 I will consider in my *d* place
Jer 46:19 O thou daughter *d* in Egypt,
49:33 Hazor shall be a *d* for dragons,
Eze 38:11 all of them *d* without walls, and
48:15 the city, for *d*, and for suburbs:
Da 2:11 gods, whose *d* is not with flesh.
4:25, 32 thy *d* shall be with the beasts
5:21 and his *d* was with the wild asses:
Joe 3:17 the Lord your God *d* in Zion,
Na 2:11 Where is the *d* of the lions,
Zep 3: 7 so their *d* should not be cut off,
M'r 5: 3 Who had his *d* among the tombs;
Ac 2: 5 And there were *d* at Jerusalem
19:17 Greeks also *d* at Ephesus; and
1Ti 6:16 *d* in the light which no man can
Heb 11: 9 *d* in tabernacles with Isaac and
2Pe 2: 8 righteous man *d* among them.

dwelling-house See DWELLING and HOUSE.

dwellingplace See also DWELLING and PLACE; DWELLINGPLACES.
Nu 24:21 Strong is thy *d*, and thou puttest
Jer 51:37 Babylon shall become heaps, a *d*
1Co 4:11 are buffeted, have no certain *d*;

dwellingplaces
Jer 30:18 tents, and have mercy on his *d*;
51:30 women: they have burned her *d*;
Eze 6: 6 In all your *d* the cities shall be
37:23 I will save them out of all their *d*,
Hab 1: 6 possess the *d* that are not theirs.

dwellings
Ex 10:23 of Israel had light in their *d*.
Le 3:17 throughout all your *d*, that ye eat
7:26 fowl or of beast, in any of your *d*.
23: 3 sabbath of the Lord in all your *d*.
14 your generations in all your *d*.
21 for ever in all your *d* throughout

Le 23:31 your generations in all your *d'*.
Nu 35:29 your generations in all your *d'*.
Job 18:19 nor any remaining in his *d'*.
21 such are the *d'* of the wicked,
39: 6 and the barren land his *d'*.
Ps 55:15 wickedness is in their *d'*, and
87: 2 Zion more than all the *d'* of Jacob.
Isa 32:18 and in sure *d'*, and in quiet resting
Jer 9:19 because our *d'* have cast us out.
Eze 25: 4 thee, and to make their *d'* in thee:
Zep 2: 6 And the sea coast shall be *d'* and

dwelt^ See also DWELLED.
Ge 4:16 the Lord, and *d'* in the land of Nod,
11: 2 land of Shinar; and they *d'* there.
31 came unto Haran, and *d'* there.
13:18 and *d'* in the plain of Mamre,
14: 7 Amorites, that *d'* in Hazezon-tamar.
12 who *d'* in Sodom, and his goods,
13 for he *d'* in the plain of Mamre
16: 3 after Abram had *d'* ten years in
19:29 the cities in the which Lot *d'*.
30 and *d'* in the mountain, and his two
30 and he *d'* in a cave, he and his two
21:20 grew, and *d'* in the wilderness,
21 he *d'* in the wilderness of Paran:
22:19 and Abraham *d'* at Beer-sheba.
23:10 Ephron *d'* among the children of
24:62 for he *d'* in the south country.
25:11 Isaac *d'* by the well Lahai-roi.
18 they *d'* from Havilah unto Shur,
26: 6 And Isaac *d'* in Gerar:
17 the valley of Gerar, and *d'* there.
35:22 when Israel *d'* in that land, that
36: 8 Thus *d'* Esau in mount Seir:
37: 1 And Jacob *d'* in the land wherein
38:11 Tamar went and *d'* in her father's
47:27 And Israel *d'* in the land of Egypt,
50:22 And Joseph *d'* in Egypt, he, and his
Ex 2:15 and *d'* in the land of Midian:
12:40 of Israel, who *d'* in Egypt,
Le 18: 3 the land of Egypt, wherein ye *d'*,
26:35 sabbaths, when ye *d'* upon it.
Nu 14:25 the Canaanites *d'* in the valley.)
45 Canaanites which *d'* in that hill,
20:15 we have *d'* in Egypt a long time;
21: 1 which *d'* in the south, heard tell
25 and Israel *d'* in all the cities of the
31 Israel *d'* in the land of the Amorites.
34 Amorites, which *d'* at Heshbon.
31:10 all their cities wherein they *d'*,
32:40 Manasseh; and he *d'* therein.
33:40 which *d'* in the south in the land of
De 1: 4 which *d'* in Heshbon, and Og the
4 which *d'* at Astaroth in Edrei:
6 have *d'* long enough in this mount:
44 which *d'* in that mountain, came
2: 8 Esau, which *d'* in Seir, through
10 Emims *d'* therein in times past,
12 Horims also *d'* in Seir beforetime;
12 before them, and *d'* in their stead;
20 giants *d'* therein in old time;
21 them, and *d'* in their stead:
22 children of Esau, which *d'* in Seir,
22 and *d'* in their stead even unto
23 the Avims which *d'* in Hazerim,
23 them, and *d'* in their stead.)
3: 2 the Amorites, which *d'* at Heshbon.
4:46 who *d'* at Heshbon, whom Moses
8:12 built goodly houses, and *d'* therein;
29:16 we have *d'* in the land of Egypt;
33:16 will of him that *d'* in the bush:
Jos 2:15 and she *d'* upon the wall.
7: 7 and *d'* on the other side Jordan!
9:16 and that they *d'* among them.
12: 2 who *d'* in Heshbon, and ruled
4 that *d'* at Ashtaroth and at Edrei,
16:10 the Canaanites that *d'* in Gezer:
19:47 possessed it, and *d'* therein, and
50 he built the city, and *d'* therein.
21:43 they possessed it, and *d'* therein.
22:33 the children of Reuben and Gad *d'*.
24: 2 *d'* on the other side of the flood
7 *d'* in the wilderness a long season.
8 *d'* on the other side Jordan;
Jos 24:18 the Amorites which *d'* in the land:
J'g 1: 9 Canaanites, that *d'* in the mountain,
10 Canaanites that *d'* in Hebron:
16 they went and *d'* among the people.
29 the Canaanites that *d'* in Gezer;
29 but the Canaanites *d'* in Gezer
30 but the Canaanites *d'* among them,
32 Asherites *d'* among the Canaanites,
33 but he *d'* among the Canaanites,
3: 3 Hivites that *d'* in mount Lebanon,
5 of Israel *d'* among the Canaanites,
4: 2 *d'* in Harosheth of the Gentiles.
5 *d'* under the palm tree of Deborah
8:11 the way of them that *d'* in tents
29 Joash went and *d'* in his own
9:21 went to Beer, and *d'* there, for fear
41 And Abimelech *d'* at Arumah: and
10: 1 he *d'* in Shamir in mount Ephraim.
11: 3 and *d'* in the land of Tob:
26 Israel *d'* in Heshbon and her towns,
15: 8 and *d'* in the top of the rock Etam.
18: 7 they *d'* careless, after the manner
28 they built a city, and *d'* therein.
21:23 repaired the cities, and *d'* in them.
Ru 2:23 and *d'* with her mother in law.
1Sa 19:18 and Samuel went and *d'* in Naioth.
22: 4 and they *d'* with him all the while
23:29 and *d'* in strong holds at En-gedi.
27: 3 And David *d'* with Achish at Gath,
7 *d'* in the country of the Philistines
31: 7 Philistines came and *d'* in them.
2Sa 2: 3 and they *d'* in the cities of Hebron.
5: 9 David *d'* in the fort, and called it
7: 6 I have not *d'* in any house since
9:12 all that *d'* in the house of Ziba
13 Mephibosheth *d'* in Jerusalem:
14:28 So Absalom *d'* two full years in
1Ki 2:38 Shimei *d'* in Jerusalem many days.
4:25 And Judah and Israel *d'* safely,
7: 8 his house where he *d'* had another
9:16 the Canaanites that *d'* in the city,
11:24 went to Damascus, and *d'* therein,
12: 2 and Jeroboam *d'* in Egypt;
17 which *d'* in the cities of Judah,
25 in mount Ephraim, and *d'* therein;
13:11 there *d'* an old prophet in Beth-el;
25 the city where the old prophet *d'*.
15:18 of Syria, that *d'* at Damascus,
21 of Ramah, and *d'* in Tirzah.
17: 5 went and *d'* by the brook Cherith,
2Ki 13: 5 children of Israel *d'* in their tents,
15: 5 his death, and *d'* in a several house.
16: 6 Elath, and *d'* there unto this day.
17:24 Samaria, and *d'* in the cities thereof.
28 came and *d'* in Beth-el, and taught
29 in their cities wherein they *d'*.
19:36 and returned, and *d'* at Nineveh.
22:14 she *d'* in Jerusalem in the college;)
1Ch 2:55 of the scribes which *d'* at Jabez;
4:23 *d'* among plants and hedges:
23 there they *d'* with the king
28 *d'* at Beer-sheba, and Moladah,
40 they of Ham had *d'* there of old.
41 this day, and *d'* in their rooms:
43 escaped, and *d'* there unto this day.
5: 8 who *d'* in Aroer, even unto Nebo
10 they *d'* in their tents throughout
11 the children of Gad *d'* over against
16 And they *d'* in Gilead in Bashan,
22 *d'* in their steads until the captivity.
23 tribe of Manasseh *d'* in the land:
7:29 In these *d'* the children of Joseph
8:28 chief men. These *d'* in Jerusalem.
29 Gibeon *d'* the father of Gibeon;
32 *d'* with their brethren in Jerusalem,
9: 2 Now the first inhabitants that *d'*
3 in Jerusalem *d'* of the children of
16 that *d'* in the villages of the
34 generations; these *d'* at Jerusalem.
35 in Gibeon *d'* the father of Gibeon;
38 *d'* with their brethren at Jerusalem,
10: 7 Philistines came and *d'* in them.
11: 7 And David *d'* in the castle;
17: 5 I have not *d'* in an house since the
2Ch 10:17 that *d'* in the cities of Judah,
11: 5 And Rehoboam *d'* in Jerusalem,
16: 2 king of Syria, that *d'* at Damascus,
19: 4 And Jehoshaphat *d'* at Jerusalem:
20: 8 And they *d'* therein, and have built
26: 7 the Arabians that *d'* in Gur-baal,
21 *d'* in a several house, being a leper;
28:18 villages thereof: and they *d'* there.
30:25 of Israel, and that *d'* in Judah,
31: 4 the people that *d'* in Jerusalem to
6 that *d'* in the cities of Judah, they
34:22 she *d'* in Jerusalem in the college:)
Ezr 2:70 the Nethinims, *d'* in their cities,
Ne 3:26 the Nethinims *d'* in Ophel, unto the
4:12 the Jews which *d'* by them came,
7:73 all Israel, *d'* in their cities; and
11: 1 of the people *d'* at Jerusalem:
3 the province that *d'* in Jerusalem:
3 but in the cities of Judah *d'* every
4 at Jerusalem *d'* certain of the
6 sons of Perez that *d'* at Jerusalem
21 the Nethinims *d'* in Ophel: and
25 of Judah *d'* at Kirjath-arba,
30 they *d'* from Beer-sheba unto the
31 also of Benjamin from Geba *d'* at
13:16 There *d'* men of Tyre also therein,
Es 9:19 that *d'* in the unwalled towns,
Job 22: 8 and the honourable man *d'* in it.
29:25 and *d'* as a king in the army,
Ps 68:10 congregation hath *d'* therein:
74: 2 mount Zion, wherein thou hast *d'*.
94:17 my soul had almost *d'* in silence.
120: 6 My soul hath long *d'* with him
Isa 13:20 neither shall it be *d'* in from
29: 1 to Ariel, the city where David *d'*!
37:37 and returned, and *d'* at Nineveh.
Jer 35:10 But we have *d'* in tents, and have
39:14 home: so he *d'* among the peeple.
40: 6 and *d'* with him among the people
41:17 And they departed, and *d'* in the
44:15 all the people that *d'* in the land of
50:39 neither shall it be *d'* in from
Eze 3:15 that *d'* by the river of Chebar, and
31: 6 and under his shadow *d'* all great
17 that *d'* under his shadow in the
36:17 the house of Israel *d'* in their own
37:25 wherein your fathers have *d'*;
39:26 when they *d'* safely in their land,
Da 4:12 the fowls of the heaven *d'* in the
21 which the beasts of the field *d'*,
Zep 2:15 rejoicing city that *d'* carelessly,
M't 2:23 and *d'* in a city called Nazareth:
4:13 he came and *d'* in Capernaum,
Lu 1:65 on all that *d'* round about them:
13: 4 all men that *d'* in Jerusalem?
Joh 1:14 and *d'* among us, (and we beheld
39 They came and saw where he *d'*,
Ac 7: 2 Mesopotamia, before he *d'* in
4 Chaldeans, and *d'* in Charran:
9:22 the Jews which *d'* at Damascus,
32 to the saints which *d'* at Lydda.
35 all that *d'* at Lydda and Saron saw
11:29 the brethren which *d'* in Judæa:
13:17 when they *d'* as strangers in the
19:10 all they which *d'* in Asia heard
22:12 of all the Jews which *d'* there,
28:30 Paul *d'* two whole years in his
2Ti 1: 5 which *d'* first in thy grandmother

dyed
Ex 25: 5 rams' skins *d'* red, and badgers'
26:14 rams' skins *d'* red, and a covering
35: 7 rams' skins *d'* red, and badgers'
36:19 rams' skins *d'* red, and a covering
39:34 rams' skins *d'* red, and the covering
Isa 63: 1 with *d'* garments from Bozrah?
Eze 23:15 exceeding in *d'* attire upon their

dying
Nu 17:13 shall we be consumed with *d'*?
M'r 12:20 and the first took a wife, and *d'*
Lu 8:42 years of age, and she lay a *d'*.
2Co 4:10 bearing about in the body the *d'*
6: 9 known; as *d'*, and, behold, we live;
Heb 11:21 Jacob, when he was a *d'*, blessed

E.

each^
Ge 15:10 laid *e'* piece one against another;
34:25 took *e'* man his sword, and came
40: 5 them, *e'* man his dream in one night,
5 one night, *e'* man according to the
41:11 dreamed *e'* man according to the
12 to *e'* man according to his dream he
45:22 he gave *e'* man changes of raiment;
Ex 18: 7 asked *e'* other of their welfare;
30:34 of *e'* shall there be a like weight.
Nu 1:44 *e'* one was for the house of his
7: 3 of the princes, and for *e'* one an ox:
11 offer their offering, *e'* prince on his
85 *E'* charger of silver weighing an
85 thirty shekels, *e'* bowl seventy:
14:34 even forty days, *e'* day for a year,
16:17 and Aaron, *e'* of you his censer.
17: 6 him a rod apiece, for *e'* prince one,
29:14 two tenth deals to *e'* ram of the
15 a several tenth deal to *e'* lamb
Jos 18: 4 from among you three men for *e'*
22:14 with him ten princes, of *e'* chief
14 *e'* one was an head of the house
J'g 8:18 *e'* one resembled the children of a
21:22 not to *e'* man his wife in the war:
Ru 1: 8 return *e'* to her mother's house:
9 *e'* of you in the house of her husband.
1Ki 4: 7 *e'* man his month in a year made
6:23 two cherubims of olive tree, *e'* ten
22:10 sat *e'* on his throne, having put on
2Ki 9:21 *e'* in his chariot, and they went out
15:20 of *e'* man fifty shekels of silver,
1Ch 20: 6 six on *e'* hand, and six on *e'* foot:
2Ch 3:15 the top of *e'* of them was five cubits.
4:13 two rows of pomegranates on *e'*
9:18 stays on *e'* side of the sitting
Ne 13:24 according to the language of *e'* people.
Ps 85:10 and peace have kissed *e'* other.
Isa 2:20 they made *e'* one for himself to
6: 2 seraphims: *e'* one had six wings;
35: 7 of dragons, where *e'* lay, shall be
57: 2 *e'* one walking in his uprightness
Eze 4: 6 have appointed thee *e'* day for a year,
40:16 and upon *e'* post were palm trees.
48 and measured *e'* post of the porch,
Lu 13:15 doth not *e'* one of you on the
Ac 2: 3 fire, and it sat upon *e'* of them.
Ph'p 2: 3 let *e'* esteem other better than
2Th 1: 3 all toward *e'* other aboundeth;
Re 4: 8 And the four beasts had *e'* of them

eagle See also EAGLE'S; EAGLES.
Le 11:13 the *e'*, and the ossifrage, and the
18 and the pelican and the gier *e'*,
De 14:12 not eat: the *e'*, and the ossifrage,
17 the gier *e'*, and the cormorant,
28:49 the earth, as swift as the *e'* flieth;
32:11 As an *e'* stirreth up her nest,
Job 9:26 as the *e'* that hasteth to the prey.
39:27 Doth the *e'* mount up at thy
Pr 23: 5 fly away as an *e'* toward heaven.
30:19 The way of an *e'* in the air;
Jer 48:40 Behold, he shall fly as an *e'*,
49:16 make thy nest as high as the *e'*,
22 and fly as the *e'*, and spread his
Eze 1:10 they four also had the face of an *e'*.
10:14 and the fourth the face of an *e'*.
17: 3 A great *e'* with great wings, long
7 There was also another great *e'*
Ho 8: 1 He shall come as an *e'* against the
Ob 4 Though thou exalt thyself as the *e'*,
Mic 1:16 enlarge thy baldness as the *e'*;
Hab 1: 8 they shall fly as the *e'* that hasteth
Re 4: 7 the fourth beast was like a flying *e'*.
12:14 were given two wings of a great *e'*,

eagle's
Ps 103: 5 thy youth is renewed like the *e*.
Da 7: 4 was like a lion, and had *e* wings;
eagles See also EAGLES'.
2Sa 1:23 they were swifter than *e*, they
Pr 30:17 and the young *e* shall eat it.
Isa 40:31 shall mount up with wings as *e*;
Jer 4 :13 his horses are swifter than *e*.
La 4:19 swifter than the *e* of the heaven:
M't 24:28 is, there will the *e* be gathered
Lu 17:37 is, thither will the *e* be gathered
eagles'
Ex 19: 4 and how I bare you on *e* wings,
Da 4:33 his hairs were grown like *e*
ear See also EARED; EARING; EARRINGS; EARS; PLOW.
Ex 9:31 for the barley was in the *e*,
15:26 will give *e* to his commandments,
21: 6 his master shall bore his *e* through
29:20 upon the tip of the right *e* of Aaron,
20 upon the tip of the right *e* of his
Le 8:23 upon the tip of Aaron's right *e*,
24 upon the tip of their right *e*, and
14:14, 17, 25, 28 tip of the right *e* of him
De 1:45 to your voice, nor give *e* unto you.
15:17 it through his *e* unto the door,
32: 1 Give *e*, O ye heavens, and I will
J'g 5: 3 give *e*, O ye princes; I, even I, will
1Sa 8:12 and will set them to *e* his ground,
9:15 had told Samuel in his *e* a day
2Ki 19:16 Lord, bow down thine *e*, and hear:
2Ch 24:19 them: but they would not give *e*.
Ne 1: 6 Let thine *e* now be attentive, and
11 thine *e* be attentive to the prayer
9:30 yet would they not give *e*:
Job 4:12 mine *e* received a little thereof.
12:11 Doth not the *e* try words? and the
13: 1 mine *e* hath heard and understood
29:11 the *e* heard me, then it blessed me;
21 Unto me men gave *e*, and waited,
32:11 I gave *e* to your reasons, whilst
34: 2 give *e* unto me, ye that have
3 the *e* trieth words, as the mouth
36:10 openeth also their *e* to discipline,
42: 5 of thee by the hearing of the *e*:
Ps 5: 1 Give *e* to my words, O Lord,
10:17 thou wilt cause thine *e* to hear:
17: 1 my cry, give *e* unto my prayer,
6 incline thine *e* unto me, and hear
31: 2 Bow down thine *e* to me; deliver
39:12 give *e* unto my cry; hold not thy
45:10 and consider, and incline thine *e*;
49: 1 give *e*, all ye inhabitants of the
4 I will incline mine *e* to a parable:
54: 2 give *e* to the words of my mouth.
55: 1 Give *e* to my prayer, O God;
58: 4 deaf adder that stoppeth her *e*;
71: 2 incline thine *e* unto me, and save
77: 1 my voice; and he gave *e* unto me.
78: 1 Give *e*, O my people, to my law:
80: 1 Give *e*, O Shepherd of Israel,
84: 8 give *e*, O God of Jacob.
86: 1 down thine *e*, O Lord, hear me:
6 Give *e*, O Lord, unto my prayer;
88: 2 incline thine *e* unto my cry;
94: 9 planted the *e*, shall he not hear?
102: 2 trouble; incline thine *e* unto me:
116: 2 he hath inclined his *e* unto me,
141: 1 give *e* unto my voice, when I cry
143: 1 O Lord, give *e* to my supplications:
Pr 2: 2 thou incline thine *e* unto wisdom,
4:20 incline thine *e* unto my sayings.
5: 1 bow thine *e* to my understanding:
13 mine *e* to them that instructed me!
15:31 The *e* that heareth the reproof of
17: 4 liar giveth *e* to a naughty tongue.
18:15 *e* of the wise seeketh knowledge.
20:12 The hearing *e*, and the seeing eye,
22:17 Bow down thine *e*, and hear the
25:12 a wise reprover upon an obedient *e*.
28: 9 away his *e* from hearing the law,
Ec 1: 8 nor the *e* filled with hearing.
Isa 1: 2 O heavens, and give *e*, O earth:
10 give *e* unto the law of our God,
8: 9 and give *e*, all ye of far countries:
28:23 Give ye *e*, and hear my voice;
30:24 young asses that *e* the ground
32: 9 daughters; give *e* unto my speech.
37:17 Incline thine *e*, O Lord, and hear;
42:23 among you will give *e* to this?
48: 8 time that thine *e* was not opened:
50: 4 wakeneth mine *e* to hear as the
5 The Lord God hath opened mine *e*,
51: 4 give *e* unto me, O my nation:
55: 3 Incline your *e*, and come unto me:
59: 1 his *e* heavy, that it cannot hear:
64: 4 not heard, nor perceived by the *e*,
Jer 6:10 behold, their *e* is uncircumcised,
7:24 nor inclined their *e*, but walked in
26 nor inclined their *e*, but hardened
9:20 *e* receive the word of his mouth,
11: 8 nor inclined their *e*, but walked
13:15 ye, and give *e*; be not proud:
17:23 neither inclined their *e*, but made
25: 4 nor inclined your *e* to hear.
34:14 unto me, neither inclined their *e*.
35:15 but ye have not inclined your *e*,
44: 5 nor inclined their *e* to turn from
La 3:56 hide not thine *e* at my breathing,
Da 9:18 O my God, incline thine *e*, and hear;
Ho 5: 1 give ye *e*, O house of the king;
Joe 1: 2 Hear this, ye old men, and give *e*,
Am 3:12 two legs, or a piece of an *e*;
M't 10:27 what ye hear in the *e*, that preach
26:51 high priest's, and smote off his *e*.
M'r 4:28 first the blade, then the *e*, after
28 after that the full corn in the *e*.
14:47 high priest, and cut off his *e*.
Lu 12: 3 which ye have spoken in the *e*
22:50 high priest, and cut off his right *e*.
51 he touched his *e*, and healed him.
Joh 18:10 servant, and cut off his right *e*.
26 his kinsman whose *e* Peter cut off,
1Co 2: 9 nor *e* heard, neither have entered
12:16 And if the *e* shall say, Because I
Re 2: 7, 11, 17, 29 He that hath an *e*, let him
3: 6, 13, 22 He that hath an *e*, let him
13: 9 If any man have an *e*, let him hear.
eared See also PLOWED.
De 21: 4 which is neither *e* nor sown,
earing See also PLOWING.
Ge 45: 6 there neither be *e* nor harvest.
Ex 34:21 in *e* time and in harvest thou
early
Ge 19: 2 rise up *e*, and go on your ways.
27 Abraham gat up *e* in the morning
20: 8 Abimelech rose *e* in the morning,
21:14 Abraham rose up *e* in the morning,
22: 3 Abraham rose up *e* in the morning,
28:18 Jacob rose up *e* in the morning,
31:55 *e* in the morning Laban rose up,
Ex 8:20 Rise up *e* in the morning, and
9:13 Moses, Rise up *e* in the morning,
24: 4 and rose up *e* in the morning,
32: 6 And they rose up *e* on the morrow,
34: 4 Moses rose up *e* in the morning,
Nu 14:40 And they rose up *e* in the morning,
Jos 3: 1 And Joshua rose *e* in the morning;
6:12 And Joshua rose *e* in the morning,
15 *e* about the dawning of the day,
7:16 Joshua rose up *e* in the morning,
8:10 Joshua rose up *e* in the morning,
14 they hasted and rose up *e*, and the
J'g 6:28 when the men of the city arose *e*
38 for he rose up *e* on the morrow,
7: 1 Then Jerubbaal,...rose up *e*,
3 and depart *e* from mount Gilead.
9:33 rise *e*, and set upon the city:
19: 5 when they arose *e* in the morning,
8 And he arose *e* in the morning
9 to morrow get you *e* on your way,
21: 4 the morrow, that the people rose *e*,
1Sa 1:19 And they rose up in the morning *e*,
5: 3 they of Ashdod arose *e* on the
4 when they arose *e* on the morrow
9:26 they arose *e*: and it came to pass
15:12 when Samuel rose *e* to meet Saul
17:20 David rose up *e* in the morning,
29:10 now rise up *e* in the morning
10 and as soon as ye be up *e* in the
11 So David and his men rose up *e* to
2Sa 15: 2 And Absalom rose up *e*, and stood
2Ki 3:22 And they rose up *e* in the morning,
6:15 of the man of God was risen *e*,
19:35 when they arose *e* in the morning,
2Ch 20:20 And they rose *e* in the morning,
29:20 Then Hezekiah the king rose *e*,
Job 1: 5 and rose up *e* in the morning,
Ps 46: 5 shall help her, and that right *e*.
57: 8 I myself will awake *e*.
63: 1 art my God; *e* will I seek thee:
78:34 and enquired *e* after God.
90:14 satisfy us *e* with thy mercy;
101: 8 I will *e* destroy all the wicked of
108: 2 and harp: I myself will awake *e*.
127: 2 It is vain for you to rise up *e*,
Pr 1:28 they shall seek me *e*, but they
8:17 that seek me *e* shall find me.
27:14 voice, rising *e* in the morning,
Ca 7:12 Let us get up *e* to the vineyards;
Isa 5:11 Woe unto them that rise up *e*
26: 9 within me will I seek thee *e*:
37:36 they arose *e* in the morning,
Jer 7:13 you, rising up *e* and speaking,
25 rising up *e* and sending them:
11: 7 rising *e* and protesting, saying,
25: 3 unto you, rising *e* and speaking;
4 rising *e* and sending them;
26: 5 rising up *e*, and sending them,
29:19 rising up *e* and sending them;
32:33 rising up *e* and teaching them,
35:14 rising *e* and speaking; but ye
15 rising up *e* and sending them,
44: 4 rising *e* and sending them,
Da 6:19 king arose very *e* in the morning,
Ho 5:15 affliction they will seek me *e*.
6: 4 as the *e* dew it goeth away.
13: 3 as the *e* dew that passeth away,
Zep 3: 7 but they rose *e*, and corrupted all
M't 20: 1 went out *e* in the morning to
M'r 16: 2 And very *e* in the morning the
9 risen *e* the first day of the week,
Lu 21:38 the people came *e* in the morning
24: 1 very *e* in the morning, they came
22 which were *e* at the sepulchre;
Joh 8: 2 And *e* in the morning he came
18:28 it was *e*; and they themselves
20: 1 cometh Mary Magdalene *e*, when
Ac 5:21 *e* in the morning, and taught.
Jas 5: 7 he receive the *e* and latter rain.
earnest
Ro 8:19 the *e* expectation of the creature
2Co 1:22 the *e* of the Spirit in our hearts.
5: 5 given unto us the *e* of the Spirit.
7: 7 he told us your *e* desire, your
8:16 put the same *e* care into the heart
Eph 1:14 Which is the *e* of our inheritance
Ph'p 1:20 to my *e* expectation and my hope,
Heb 2: 1 we ought to give the more *e* heed
earnestly
Nu 22:37 Did I not *e* send unto thee to call thee?
1Sa 20: 6 say, David *e* asked leave of me that
28 David *e* asked leave of me to go to
Ne 3:20 the son of Zabbai *e* repaired
Job 7: 2 As a servant *e* desireth the shadow,
Jer 11: 7 For I *e* protested unto your fathers
31:20 him, I do *e* remember him still:
Mic 7: 3 may do evil with both hands *e*,
Lu 22:44 in an agony he prayed more *e*:
56 and *e* looked upon him, and said,
Ac 3:12 why look ye so *e* on us,
23: 1 Paul, *e* beholding the council,
1Co 12:31 But covet *e* the best gifts:
2Co 5: 2 *e* desiring to be clothed upon
Jas 5:17 prayed *e* that it might not rain:
Jude 3 ye should *e* contend for the faith
earneth
Hag 1: 6 he that *e* wages, *e* wages to put it
earring See also EARRINGS.
Ge 24:22 golden *e* of half a shekel weight,
30 came to pass, when he saw the *e*
47 I put the *e* upon her face,
Job 42:11 and every one an *e* of gold.
Pr 25:12 an *e* of gold, and an ornament of
earrings
Ge 35: 4 their *e* which were in their ears;
Ex 32: 2 Break off the golden *e*, which
3 people brake off the golden *e*
35:22 *e*, and rings, and tablets, all jewels
Nu 31:50 chains, and bracelets, rings, *e*,
J'g 8:24 me every man the *e* of his prey.
24 (For they had golden *e*, because they
25 every man the *e* of his prey.
26 And the weight of the golden *e*
Isa 3:20 and the tablets, and the *e*,
Eze 16:12 *e* in thine ears, and a beautiful
Ho 2:13 herself with her *e* and her jewels,
ears
Ge 20: 8 and told all these things in their *e*:
35: 4 earrings which were in their *e*;
41: 5 seven *e* of corn came up upon
6 seven thin *e* and blasted with the
7 And the seven thin *e* devoured the
7 devoured the seven rank and full *e*.
22 seven *e* came up in one stalk,
23 seven *e*, withered, thin, and
24 thin *e* devoured the seven good *e*:
26 the seven good *e* are seven years:
27 the seven empty *e* blasted with
44:18 speak a word in my lord's *e*,
50: 4 I pray you, in the *e* of Pharaoh,
Ex 10: 2 mayest tell in the *e* of thy son,
11: 2 Speak now in the *e* of the people,
17:14 rehearse it in the *e* of Joshua:
32: 2 which are in the *e* of your wives,
3 earrings which were in their *e*,
Le 2:14 of thy firstfruits green *e* of corn
14 even corn beaten out of full *e*.
23:14 nor parched corn, nor green *e*,
Nu 11:18 ye have wept in the *e* of the Lord,
14:28 as ye have spoken in mine *e*, so
De 5: 1 which I speak in your *e* this day,
23:25 pluck the *e* with thine hand;
29: 4 eyes to see, and *e* to hear, unto this
31:28 I may speak these words in their *e*,
30 Moses spake in the *e* of all the
32:44 this song in the *e* of the people,
Jos 20: 4 his cause in the *e* of the elders
J'g 7: 3 proclaim in the *e* of the people,
9: 2 Speak, I pray you, in the *e* of all
3 in the *e* of all the men of Shechem
17: 2 and spakest of also in mine *e*,
Ru 2: 2 and glean *e* of corn after him
1Sa 3:11 the *e* of every one that heareth
8:21 rehearse them in the *e* of the Lord.
11: 4 the tidings in the *e* of the people:
15:14 bleating of the sheep in mine *e*,
18:23 those words in the *e* of David.
2Sa 3:19 also spake in the *e* of Benjamin:
19 also to speak in the *e* of David
7:22 all that we have heard with our *e*.
22: 7 my cry did enter into his *e*.
2Ki 4:42 *e* of corn in the husk thereof.
18:26 in the *e* of the people that are on
19:28 tumult is come up into mine *e*,
21:12 of it, both his *e* shall tingle.
23: 2 read in their *e* all the words of the
1Ch 17:20 all that we have heard with our *e*.
2Ch 6:40 and let thine *e* be attent unto the
7:15 and mine *e* attent unto the prayer
34:30 read in their *e* all the words of the
Ne 8: 3 and the *e* of all the people were
Job 13:17 and my declaration with your *e*.
15:21 A dreadful sound is in his *e*:
24:24 off as the tops of the *e* of corn.
28:22 heard the fame thereof with our *e*.
33:16 Then he openeth the *e* of men,
36:15 openeth their *e* in oppression.
Ps 18: 6 came before him, even into his *e*.
34:15 and his *e* are open unto their cry.
40: 6 mine *e* hast thou opened:
44: 1 We have heard with our *e*, O God,
78: 1 incline your *e* to the words of my
92:11 mine *e* shall hear my desire of
115: 6 They have *e*, but they hear not:
130: 2 let thine *e* be attentive to the voice
135:17 They have *e*, but they hear not;
Pr 21:13 Whoso stoppeth his *e* at the cry
23: 9 Speak not in the *e* of a fool:
12 thine *e* to the words of knowledge.
26:17 one that taketh a dog by the *e*.
Isa 5: 9 In mine *e* said the Lord of hosts,
6:10 and make their *e* heavy, and shut

Isa 6:10 their eyes, and hear with their e',
11: 3 reprove after the hearing of his e':
17: 5 and reapeth the e' with his arm;
5 it shall be as he that gathereth e'
22:14 revealed in mine e' by the Lord
30:21 And thine e' shall hear a word
32: 3 e' of them that hear shall hearken.
33:15 stoppeth his e' from hearing of
35: 5 e' of the deaf shall be unstopped.
36:11 in the e' of the people that are on
37:29 tumult, is come up into mine e',
42:20 opening the e', but he heareth not.
43: 8 have eyes, and the deaf that have e'.
49:20 other, shall say again in thine e',
Jer 2: 2 Go and cry in the e' of Jerusalem,
5:21 which have e', and hear not:
19: 3 whosoever heareth, his e' shall
26:11 as ye have heard with your e'.
15 speak all these words in your e'.
28: 7 this word that I speak in thine e',
7 and in the e' of all the people;
29:29 this letter in the e' of Jeremiah
36: 6 in the e' of the people in the Lord's
6 in the e' of all Judah that come out
10 house, in the e' of all the people.
13 read the book in the e' of the people.
14 hast read in the e' of the people,
15 down now, and read it in our e'.
15 So Baruch read it in their e'.
20 all the words in the e' of the king.
21 Jehudi read it in the e' of the king,
21 and in the e' of all the princes
Eze 3:10 thine heart, and hear with thine e'.
8:18 cry in mine e' with a loud voice,
9: 1 cried also in mine e' with a loud
12: 2 they have e' to hear, and hear not:
16:12 and earrings in thine e', and a
23:25 take away thy nose and thine e';
24:26 cause thee to hear it with thine e'?
40: 4 thine eyes, and hear with thine e',
44: 5 and hear with thine e' all that I say
Mic 7:16 their mouth, their e' shall be deaf.
Zec 7:11 and stopped their e', that they
M't 11:15 He that hath e' to hear, let him
12: 1 and began to pluck the e' of corn,
13: 9 Who hath e' to hear, let him hear.
15 and their e' are dull of hearing,
15 their eyes, and hear with their e',
16 and your e', for they hear.
43 Who hath e' to hear, let him hear.
28:14 if this come to the governor's e',
M'r 2:23 went, to pluck the e' of corn.
4: 9 He that hath e' to hear, let him
23 If any man have e' to hear,
7:16 If any man have e' to hear, let
33 and put his fingers into his e',
35 straightway his e' were opened,
8:18 and having e', hear ye not?
Lu 1:44 thy salutation sounded in mine e',
4:21 this scripture fulfilled in your e'.
6: 1 disciples plucked the e' of corn,
8: 8 He that hath e' to hear, let him
9:44 sayings sink down into your e':
14:35 He that hath e' to hear, let him
Ac 7:51 and uncircumcised in heart and e',
57 and stopped their e', and ran upon
11:22 came unto the e' of the church
17:20 certain strange things to our e':
28:27 and their e' are dull of hearing,
27 their eyes, and hear with their e',
Ro 11: 8 and e' that they should not hear:)
2Ti 4: 3 teachers, having itching e';
4 turn away their e' from the truth,
Jas 5: 4 entered into the e' of the Lord
1Pe 3:12 his e' are open unto their prayers:

earth See also EARTHQUAKE.
Ge 1: 1 God created the heaven and the e'.
2 And the e' was without form, and
10 And God called the dry land E';
11 said, Let the e' bring forth grass,
11 whose seed is in itself, upon the e':
12 And the e' brought forth grass,
15 to give light upon the e': and it was
17 to give light upon the e',
20 and fowl that may fly above the e' in
22 and let fowl multiply in the e'.
24 Let the e' bring forth the living
24 and beast of the e' after his kind:
25 God made the beast of the e' after
25 thing that creepeth upon the e'
26 and over all the e', and over every
26 thing that creepeth upon the e'.
28 multiply, and replenish the e', and
28 living thing that moveth upon the e'.
29 which is upon the face of all the e',
30 to every beast of the e', and to
30 thing that creepeth upon the e',
2: 1 the heavens and the e' were finished
4 of the heavens and of the e' when
4 day that the Lord God made the e'
5 of the field before it was in the e',
5 had not caused it to rain upon the e',
6 there went up a mist from the e',
4:11 now art thou cursed from the e',
12 vagabond shalt thou be in the e'.
14 this day from the face of the e';
14 fugitive and a vagabond in the e';
6: 1 multiply upon the face of the e',
4 were giants in the e' in those days;
5 of man was great in the e', and that
6 that he had made man on the e',
7 created from the face of the e';
11 e' also was corrupt before God,
11 the e' was filled with violence.
12 God looked upon the e', and, behold,
12 had corrupted his way upon the e'.
Ge 6:13 for the e' is filled with violence
13 I will destroy them with the e'.
17 bring a flood of waters upon the e',
17 every thing that is in the e' shall die.
20 of every creeping thing of the e'
7: 3 seed alive upon the face of all the e'.
4 I will cause it to rain upon the e'
4 destroy from off the face of the e'.
6 the flood of waters was upon the e'.
8 thing that creepeth upon the e',
10 waters of the flood were upon the e'.
12 the rain was upon the e' forty days
14 creepeth upon the e' after his kind,
17 flood was forty days upon the e';
17 and it was lift up above the e'.
18 increased greatly upon the e';
19 prevailed exceedingly upon the e';
21 flesh died that moved upon the e',
21 thing that creepeth upon the e',
23 they were destroyed from the e':
24 the waters prevailed upon the e'
8: 1 God made a wind to pass over the e',
3 the waters returned from off the e'
7 were dried up from off the e':
9 were on the face of the whole e':
11 waters were abated from off the e'.
13 were dried up from off the e':
14 day of the month, was the e' dried.
17 thing that creepeth upon the e';
17 may breed abundantly in the e',
17 be fruitful, and multiply upon the e'.
19 whatsoever creepeth upon the e',
22 While the e' remaineth, seed time
9: 1 and multiply, and replenish the e'.
2 shall be upon every beast of the e',
2 upon all that moveth upon the e',
7 bring forth abundantly in the e',
10 of every beast of the e' with you;
10 of the ark, to every beast of the e'.
11 more be a flood to destroy the e'.
13 a covenant between me and the e'.
14 when I bring a cloud over the e',
16 of all flesh that is upon the e'.
17 and all flesh that is upon the e'.
19 then was the whole e' overspread.
10: 8 began to be a mighty one in the e'.
25 in his days was the e' divided;
32 were the nations divided in the e'
11: 1 the whole e' was of one language,
4 abroad upon the face of the whole e'.
8 thence upon the face of all the e':
9 confound the language of all the e':
9 abroad upon the face of all the e'.
12: 3 shall all families of the e' be blessed.
13:16 make thy seed as the dust of the e':
16 a man can number the dust of the e',
14:19 God, possessor of heaven and e':
22 God, the possessor of heaven and e',
18:18 the nations of the e' shall be blessed
25 not the Judge of all the e' do right?
19:23 The sun was risen upon the e' when
31 there is not a man in the e' to come
31 us after the manner of all the e':
22:18 all the nations of the e' be blessed;
24: 3 of heaven, and the God of the e',
52 the Lord, bowing himself to the e'.
26: 4 all the nations of the e' be blessed;
15 them, and filled them with e'.
27:28 the fatness of the e', and plenty of
39 shall be the fatness of the e', and of
28:12 behold a ladder set up on the e',
14 shall be as the dust of the e',
14 all the families of the e' be blessed.
37:10 down ourselves to thee to the e'?
41:47 the e' brought forth by handfuls.
56 was over all the face of the e':
42: 6 before him with their faces to the e'.
43:26 bowed themselves to him to the e'.
45: 7 to preserve you a posterity in the e',
48:12 himself with his face to the e',
16 a multitude in the midst of the e'.
Ex 8:17 and smote the dust of the e',
22 I am the Lord in the midst of the e'.
9:14 there is none like me in all the e'.
15 thou shalt be cut off from the e'.
16 be declared throughout all the e'.
29 know how that the e' is the Lord's.
33 the rain was not poured upon the e'.
10: 5 they shall cover the face of the e',
5 that one cannot be able to see the e':
6 the day that they were upon the e'
15 they covered the face of the whole e',
15:12 right hand, the e' swallowed them.
19: 5 all people: for all the e' is mine:
20: 4 or that is in the e' beneath, or
4 that is in the water under the e':
11 days the Lord made heaven and e',
24 An altar of e' thou shalt make unto
31:17 days the Lord made heaven and e',
32:12 them from the face of the e'?
33:16 that are upon the face of the e'.
34: 8 and bowed his head toward the e',
10 as have not been done in all the e',
Le 11: 2 all the beasts that are on the e'.
21 feet, to leap withal upon the e';
29 things that creep upon the e';
41 thing that creepeth upon the e'
42 things that creep upon the e',
44 thing that creepeth upon the e'.
46 creature that creepeth upon the e':
15:12 the vessel of e', that he toucheth
26:19 as iron, and your e' as brass:
Nu 11:31 cubits high upon the face of the e'.
12: 3 which were upon the face of the e'.)
14:21 the e' shall be filled with the glory
16:30 and the e' open her mouth, and
Nu 16:32 And the e' opened her mouth, and
33 and the e' closed upon them: and
34 Lest the e' swallow us up also.
22: 5 they cover the face of the e', and they
11 which covereth the face of the e':
26:10 And the e' opened her mouth, and
De 3:24 what God is there in heaven or in e',
4:10 that they shall live upon the e',
17 of any beast that is on the e', the
18 that is in the waters beneath the e':
26 I call heaven and e' to witness
32 that God created man upon the e',
36 upon e' he shewed thee his great fire;
39 above, and upon the e' beneath:
40 mayest prolong thy days upon the e'
5: 8 or that is in the e' beneath, or that
8 is in the waters beneath the e':
6:15 thee from off the face of the e'.
7: 6 that are upon the face of the e'.
10:14 the e' also, with all that therein is.
11: 6 now the e' opened her mouth, and
21 as the days of heaven upon the e'.
12: 1 all the days that ye live upon the e'.
16 ye shall pour it upon the e' as water,
19 as long as thou livest upon the e'.
24 thou shalt pour it upon the e' as
13: 7 from the one end of the e' even unto
7 even unto the other end of the e';
14: 2 all the nations that are upon the e'.
26: 2 the first of all the fruit of the e',
28: 1 on high above all nations of the e':
10 all people of the e' shall see that thou
23 and the e' that is under thee shall be
25 into all the kingdoms of the e'.
26 the air, and unto the beasts of the e',
49 from afar, from the end of the e',
64 end of the e' even unto the other;
30:19 call heaven and e' to record this day
31:28 and e' to record against them,
32: 1 hear, O e', the words of my mouth.
13 ride on the high places of the e',
22 consume the e' with her increase,
33:16 And for the precious things of the e'
17 people together to the ends of the e':
Jos 2:11 in heaven above, and in e' beneath.
3:11 the Lord of all the e' passeth over
13 Lord of all the e', shall rest in the
4:24 That all the people of the e' might
5:14 Joshua fell on his face to the e', and
7: 6 and fell to the e' upon his face before
9 cut off our name from the e':
21 they are hid in the e' in the midst
23:14 I am going the way of all the e':
J'g 3:25 lord was fallen down dead on the e'.
5: 4 the e' trembled, and the heavens
6: 4 destroyed the increase of the e',
37 it be dry upon all the e' beside,
18:10 no want of anything that is in the e'.
1Sa 2: 8 the pillars of the e' are the Lord's,
10 Lord shall judge the ends of the e';
4: 5 a great shout, so that the e' rang
12 rent, and with e' upon his head.
5: 3 was fallen upon his face to the e'
14:15 also trembled, and the e' quaked:
17:46 air, and to the wild beasts of the e';
46 that all the e' may know that there
49 and he fell upon his face to the e'.
20:15 every one from the face of the e'.
24: 8 stooped with his face to the e', and
25:41 bowed herself on her face to the e',
26: 8 the spear even to the e' at once,
20 let not my blood fall to the e' before
28:13 I saw gods ascending out of the e'.
20 fell straightway all along on the e',
23 So he rose from the e', and sat upon
30:16 were spread abroad upon all the e',
2Sa 1: 2 clothes rent, and e' upon his head:
2 he fell to the e', and did obeisance.
4:11 and take you away from the e'?
7: 9 of the great men that are in the e'.
23 nation in the e' is like thy people,
12:16 in, and lay all night upon the e'.
17 to him, to raise him up from the e':
20 Then David arose from the e', and
13:31 tare his garments, and lay on the e';
14: 7 name nor remainder upon the e'.
11 not one hair of thy son fall to the e'.
20 know all things that are in the e'.
15:32 his coat rent, and e' upon his head:
18: 9 up between the heaven and the e';
28 he fell down to the e' upon his face
22: 8 Then the e' shook and trembled;
43 them as small as the dust of the e',
23: 4 tender grass springing out of the e'
1Ki 1:31 bowed with her face to the e', and
40 the e' rent with the sound of them.
52 not an hair of him fall to the e':
2: 2 I go the way of all the e': be thou
4:34 from all kings of the e', which had
8:23 in heaven above, or on e' beneath,
27 will God indeed dwell on the e'?
43 that all people of the e' may know
53 from among all the people of the e',
60 all the people of the e' may know
10:23 exceeded all the kings of the e' for
24 And all the e' sought to Solomon,
13:34 destroy it from off the face of the e'.
17:14 the Lord sendeth rain upon the e'.
18: 1 and I will send rain upon the e'.
42 he cast himself down upon the e',
2Ki 5:15 that there is no God in all the e',
17 servant two mules' burden of e'?
10:10 there shall fall unto the e' nothing
19:15 alone, of all the kingdoms of the e';
15 thou hast made heaven and e'.
19 the kingdoms of the e' may know

1Ch 1:10 he began to be mighty upon the e'.
19 in his days the e' was divided:
16:14 God; his judgments are in all the e'.
23 Sing unto the Lord, all the e';
30 Fear before him, all the e': the
31 let the e' rejoice: and let men say
33 because he cometh to judge the e'.
17: 8 of the great men that are in the e'.
21 what one nation in the e' is like thy
21:16 stand between the e' and the heaven,
22: 8 hast shed much blood upon the e'
29:11 in the heaven and in the e' is thine;
15 our days on the e' are as a shadow,
2Ch 1: 9 like the dust of the e' in multitude.
2:12 that made heaven and e', who hath
6:14 thee in the heaven, nor in the e';
18 very deed dwell with men on the e'?
33 people of the e' may know thy name,
9:22 passed all the kings of the e' in
23 kings of the e' sought the presence
16: 9 and fro throughout the whole e',
20:24 were dead bodies fallen to the e',
32:19 the gods of the people of the e',
36:23 All the kingdoms of the e' hath the
Ezr 1: 2 given me all the kingdoms of the e';
5:11 of the God of heaven and e', and
Ne 9: 1 with sackclothes, and e' upon them.
6 e', and all things that are therein,
Job 1: 7 From going to and fro in the e',
8 that there is none like him in the e',
2: 2 From going to and fro in the e',
3 that there is none like him in the e',
3:14 With kings and counsellors of the e',
5:10 Who giveth rain upon the e', and
22 thou be afraid of the beasts of the e'.
25 offspring as the grass of the e'.
7: 1 an appointed time to man upon e'?
8: 9 our days upon e' are a shadow:)
19 and out of the e' shall others grow.
9: 6 shaketh the e' out of her place, and
24 The e' is given into the hand of the
11: 9 thereof is longer than the e', and
12: 8 Or speak to the e', and it shall
15 them out, and they overturn the e'.
24 of the chief of the people of the e',
14: 8 the root thereof wax old in the e',
19 which grow out of the dust of the e';
15:19 whom alone the e' was given,
29 the perfection thereof upon the e'.
16:18 O e', cover not thou my blood,
18: 4 shall the e' be forsaken for thee?
17 shall perish from the e', and he
19:25 stand at the latter day upon the e':
20: 4 since man was placed upon e',
27 and the e' shall rise up against him.
22: 8 for the mighty man, he had the e';
24: 4 the poor of the e' hide themselves
18 their portion is cursed in the e':
26: 7 and hangeth the e' upon nothing.
28: 2 Iron is taken out of the e',
5 for the e', out of it cometh bread:
24 For he looketh to the ends of the e',
30: 6 caves of the e', and in the rocks.
8 men: they were viler than the e'.
34:13 given him a charge over the e'?
35:11 us more than the beasts of the e',
37: 3 his lightning unto the ends of the e'.
6 saith to the snow, Be thou on the e';
12 upon the face of the world in the e'.
17 quieteth the e' by the south wind?
38: 4 when I laid the foundations of the e'?
13 might take hold of the ends of the e',
18 perceived the breadth of the e'?
24 scattereth the east wind upon the e'?
26 To cause it to rain on the e',
33 set the dominion thereof in the e'?
39:14 Which leaveth her eggs in the e',
41:33 Upon e' there is not his like,
Ps 2: 2 The kings of the e' set themselves,
8 parts of the e' for thy possession.
10 be instructed, ye judges of the e'.
7: 5 him tread down my life upon the e',
8: 1, 9 excellent is thy name in all the e'!
10:18 man of the e' may no more oppress.
12: 6 as silver tried in a furnace of e',
16: 3 But to the saints that are in the e',
17:11 their eyes bowing down to the e';
18: 7 Then the e' shook and trembled;
19: 4 line is gone out through all the e',
21:10 fruit shalt thou destroy from the e',
22:29 All they that be fat upon e' shall eat
24: 1 The e' is the Lord's, and the
25:13 and his seed shall inherit the e'.
33: 5 e' is full of the goodness of the Lord.
8 Let all the e' fear the Lord:
14 upon all the inhabitants of the e'.
34:16 remembrance of them from the e'.
37: 9 Lord, they shall inherit the e'.
11 But the meek shall inherit the e';
22 blessed of him shall inherit the e';
41: 2 he shall be blessed upon the e':
44:25 our belly cleaveth unto the e'.
45:16 mayest make princes in all the e'.
46: 2 we fear, though the e' be removed,
6 he uttered his voice, the e' melted.
8 desolations he hath made in the e'.
9 was to cease unto the end of the e';
10 am God: I will be exalted in the e'.
47: 2 he is a great King over all the e'.
7 For God is the King of all the e':
9 shields of the e' belong unto God:
48: 2 joy of the whole e', is mount Zion,
10 thy praise unto the ends of the e':
50: 1 the e' from the rising of the sun
4 heavens from above, and to the e',
57: 5, 11 let thy glory be above all the e'.
Ps 58: 2 violence of your hands in the e'.
11 he is a God that judgeth in the e'.
59:13 in Jacob unto the ends of the e'.
60: 2 hast made the e' to tremble;
61: 2 From the end of the e' will I cry
63: 9 go into the lower parts of the e'.
65: 5 confidence of all the ends of the e',
9 Thou visitest the e', and waterest it:
66: 4 All the e' shall worship thee, and
67: 2 That thy way may be known upon e',
4 and govern the nations upon e'.
6 Then shall the e' yield her increase;
7 all the ends of the e' shall fear him.
68: 8 The e' shook, the heavens also
32 unto God, ye kingdoms of the e';
69:34 Let the heaven and e' praise him,
71:20 up again from the depths of the e'.
72: 6 grass: as showers that water the e'.
8 the rivers unto the ends of the e'.
16 shall be an handful of corn in the e'
16 shall flourish like grass of the e'.
19 the whole e' be filled with his glory;
73: 9 their tongue walketh through the e'.
25 there is none upon e' that I desire
74:12 salvation in the midst of the e'.
17 hast set all the borders of the e':
20 the dark places of the e' are full of
75: 3 e' and all the inhabitants thereof
8 wicked of the e' shall wring them out,
76: 8 heaven; the e' feared, and was still.
9 to save all the meek of the e'.
12 he is terrible to the kings of the e'.
77:18 the world: the e' trembled and shook.
78:69 e' which he hath established forever.
79: 2 thy saints unto the beasts of the e'.
82: 5 all the foundations of the e' are out
8 Arise, O God, judge the e': for thou
83:10 they became as dung for the e'.
18 art the most high over all the e'.
85:11 Truth shall spring out of the e';
89:11 The heavens are thine, the e' also is
27 higher than the kings of the e'.
90: 2 or ever thou hadst formed the e'
94: 2 Lift up thyself, thou judge of the e':
95: 4 hand are the deep places of the e':
96: 1 sing unto the Lord, all the e'.
9 holiness: fear before him, all the e'.
11 rejoice, and let the e' be glad;
13 for he cometh to judge the e':
97: 1 let the e' rejoice; let the multitude
4 world: the e' saw, and trembled.
5 presence of the Lord of the whole e'.
9 thou, Lord, art high above all the e':
98: 3 all the ends of the e' have seen the
4 noise unto the Lord, all the e':
9 for he cometh to judge the e':
99: 1 the cherubims; let the e' be moved.
102:15 and all the kings of the e' thy glory.
19 heaven did the Lord behold the e';
25 thou laid the foundation of the e':
103:11 the heaven is high above the e',
104: 5 Who laid the foundations of the e',
9 they turn not again to cover the e'.
13 the e' is satisfied with the fruit of
14 may bring forth food out of the e';
24 the e' is full of thy riches.
30 thou renewest the face of the e'.
32 looketh on the e', and it trembleth:
35 sinners be cousumed out of the e',
105: 7 his judgments are in all the e'.
106:17 e' opened and swallowed up Dathan,
108: 5 and thy glory above all the e';
109:15 the memory of them from the e'.
112: 2 His seed shall be mighty upon e':
113: 6 that are in heaven, and in the e'!
114: 7 Tremble, thou e', at the presence
115:15 the Lord which made heaven and e'.
16 but the e' hath he given to the
119:19 I am a stranger in the e':
64 The e', O Lord, is full of thy mercy:
87 had almost consumed me upon e';
90 thou hast established the e', and it
119 puttest away all the wicked of the e'
121: 2 the Lord, which made heaven and e'.
124: 8 the Lord, who made heaven and e'.
134: 3 The Lord that made heaven and e'
135: 6 that did he in heaven, and in e',
7 to ascend from the ends of the e';
136: 6 To him that stretched out the e'
138: 4 All the kings of the e' shall praise
139:15 in the lowest parts of the e'.
140:11 speaker be established in the e':
141: 7 and cleaveth wood upon the e'.
146: 4 goeth forth, he returneth to his e';
6 Which made heaven, and e', the
147: 8 who prepareth rain for the e', who
15 forth his commandment upon e':
148: 7 Praise the Lord from the e',
11 Kings of the e', and all people;
11 princes, and all judges of the e':
13 his glory is above the e' and heaven.
Pr 2:22 wicked shall be cut off from the e',
3:19 by wisdom hath founded the e';
8:16 even all the judges of the e'.
23 the beginning, or ever the e' was.
26 as yet he had not made the e',
29 appointed the foundations of the e':
31 in the habitable part of his e';
10:30 the wicked shall not inhabit the e'.
11:31 shall be recompensed in the e':
17:24 of a fool are in the ends of the e'.
25: 3 for height, and the e' for depth,
30: 4 established all the ends of the e'?
14 to devour the poor from off the e',
16 the e' that is not filled with water;
21 For three things the e' is disquieted,
Pr 30:24 things which are little upon the e',
Ec 1: 4 but the e' abideth for ever.
3:21 that goeth downward to the e'?
5: 2 God is in heaven, and thou upon e':
9 the profit of the e' is for all:
7:20 there is not a just man upon e', that
8:14 a vanity which is done upon the e';
16 business that is done upon the e':
10: 7 walking as servants upon the e'.
11: 2 what evil shall be upon the e'.
3 they empty themselves upon the e':
12: 7 Then shall the dust return to the e'
Ca 2:12 The flowers appear on the e';
Isa 1: 2 Hear, O heavens, and give ear, O e':
2:19 rocks, and into the caves of the e',
19, 21 ariseth to shake terribly the e'.
4: 2 fruit of the e' shall be excellent
5: 8 placed alone in the midst of the e'!
26 unto them from the end of the e':
6: 3 the whole e' is full of his glory.
8:22 And they shall look unto the e';
10:14 are left, have I gathered all the e';
11: 4 with equity for the meek of the e':
4 and he shall smite the e' with the rod
9 the e' shall be full of the knowledge
12 from the four corners of the e'.
12: 5 things: this is known in all the e'.
13:13 and the e' shall remove out of her
14: 7 The whole e' is at rest, and is quiet:
9 even all the chief ones of the e';
16 the man that made the e' to tremble,
26 that is purposed upon the whole e':
18: 3 of the world, and dwellers on the e',
6 and to the beasts of the e': and the
6 all the beasts of the e' shall winter
23: 8 are the honourable of the e'?
9 contempt all the honourable of the e'.
17 the world upon the face of the e'.
24: 1 the Lord maketh the e' empty,
4 The e' mourneth and fadeth away,
4 haughty people of the e' do languish.
5 The e' also is defiled under the
6 hath the curse devoured the e',
6 the inhabitants of the e' are burned,
16 From the uttermost part of the e'
17 upon thee, O inhabitant of the e'.
18 the foundations of the e' do shake.
19 The e' is utterly broken down, the
19 e' is clean dissolved, the e' is moved
20 The e' shall reel to and fro like a
21 the kings of the e' upon the e'.
25: 8 he take away from off all the e':
26: 9 when thy judgments are in the e',
15 it far unto all the ends of the e'.
18 wrought any deliverance in the e';
19 and the e' shall cast out the dead.
21 to punish the inhabitants of the e'
21 the e' also shall disclose her blood,
28: 2 shall cast down to the e' with the
22 even determined upon the whole e'.
30:23 bread of the increase of the e',
33: 9 The e' mourneth and languisheth:
34: 1 let the e' hear, and all that is
37:16 alone, of all the kingdoms of the e':
16 thou hast made heaven and e'.
20 all the kingdoms of the e' may know
40:12 and comprehended the dust of the e'
21 from the foundations of the e'?
22 that sitteth upon the circle of the e',
23 he maketh the judges of the e' as
24 stock shall not take root in the e':
28 the Creator of the ends of the e',
41: 5 the ends of the e' were afraid,
9 have taken from the ends of the e',
42: 4 till he have set judgment in the e':
5 he that spread forth the e', and that
10 his praise from the end of the e',
43: 6 daughters from the ends of the e';
44:23 shout, ye lower parts of the e':
24 that spreadeth abroad the e' by
45: 8 let the e' open, and let them bring
9 strive with the potsherds of the e'.
12 I have made the e', and created
18 God himself that formed the e' and
19 secret, in a dark place of the e':
22 be ye saved, all the ends of the e':
48:13 hath laid the foundation of the e',
20 utter it even to the end of the e';
49: 6 my salvation unto the end of the e'.
8 to establish the e', to cause to
13 Sing, O heavens; and be joyful, O e';
23 with their face toward the e', and
51: 6 and look upon the e' beneath: for
6 the e' shall wax old like a garment,
13 and laid the foundations of the e';
16 and lay the foundations of the e',
52:10 all the ends of the e' shall see the
54: 5 The God of the whole e' shall he be
9 Noah should no more go over the e';
55: 9 the heavens are higher than the e',
10 but watereth the e', and maketh it
58:14 ride upon the high places of the e',
60: 2 the darkness shall cover the e',
61:11 as the e' bringeth forth her bud,
62: 7 make Jerusalem a praise in the e'.
63: 6 bring down their strength to the e'.
65:16 he who blesseth himself in the e'
16 and he that sweareth in the e' shall
17 I create new heavens and a new e':
66: 1 throne, and the e' is my footstool:
8 Shall the e' be made to bring forth
22 as the new heavens and the new e',
Jer 4:23 I beheld the e', and, lo, it was
28 For this shall the e' mourn, and the
6:19 Hear, O e': behold, I will bring evil
22 be raised from the sides of the e'.

Jer 7:33 heaven, and for the beasts of the e·;
8: 2 be for dung upon the face of the e·.
9: 3 valiant for the truth upon the e·:
24 and righteousness, in the e·;
10:10 at his wrath the e· shall tremble,
11 not made the heavens and the e·,
11 even they shall perish from the e·,
12 He hath made the e· by his power,
13 to ascend from the ends of the e·;
14: 4 for there was no rain in the e·,
15: 3 and the beasts of the e·, to devour
4 removed into all kingdoms of the e·,
10 a man of contention to the whole e·!
16: 4 as dung upon the face of the e·:
4 heaven, and for the beasts of the e·.
19 unto thee from the ends of the e·,
17:13 from me shall be written in the e·,
19: 7 heaven, and for the beasts of the e·.
22:29 O e·, e·, e·, hear the word of the Lord.
23: 5 judgment and justice in the e·.
24 Do not I fill heaven and e·? saith the
24: 9 into all the kingdoms of the e· for
25:26 which are upon the face of the e·:
29 upon all the inhabitants of the e·,
30 against all the inhabitants of the e·.
31 shall come even to the ends of the e·;
32 be raised from the coasts of the e·.
33 at that day from one end of the e·
33 even unto the other end of the e·:
26: 6 a curse to all the nations of the e·.
27: 5 I have made the e·, the man and the
28:16 cast thee from off the face of the e·:
29:18 to all the kingdoms of the e·,to be a
31: 8 them from the coasts of the e·,
22 hath created a new thing in the e·,
37 foundations of the e· searched out
32:17 made the heaven and the e· by thy
33: 9 before all the nations of the e·, which
25 the ordinances of heaven and e·;
34: 1 army, and all the kingdoms of the e·
17 into all the kingdoms of the e·.
20 heaven, and to the beasts of the e·.
44: 8 among all the nations of the e·?
46: 8 will go up, and will cover the e·;
49:21 The e· is moved at the noise of their
50:23 whole e· cut asunder and broken!
41 raised up from the coasts of the e·.
46 taking of Babylon the e· is moved,
51: 7 hand, that made all the e· drunken:
15 He hath made the e· by his power,
16 to ascend from the ends of the e·:
25 Lord, which destroyest all the e·:
41 the praise of the whole e· surprised!
48 Then the heaven and the e·, and all
49 shall fall the slain of all the e·.
La 2: 1 cast down from heaven unto the e·
11 my liver is poured upon the e·,
15 of beauty, The joy of the whole e·?
3:34 his feet all the prisoners of the e·,
4:12 The kings of the e·, and all the
Eze 1:15 behold one wheel upon the e· by the
19 creatures were lifted up from the e·,
21 those were lifted up from the e·,
7:21 to the wicked of the e· for a spoil;
8: 3 up between the e· and the heaven,
12 not; the Lord hath forsaken the e·.
9: 9 The Lord hath forsaken the e·, and
10:16 their wings to mount up from the e·,
19 mounted up from the e· in my sight:
26:20 set thee in the low parts of the e·,
27:33 thou didst enrich the kings of the e·
28:18 will bring thee to ashes upon the e·
31:12 all the people of the e· are gone
14 death, to the nether parts of the e·,
16 in the nether parts of the e·.
18 Eden unto the nether parts of the e·:
32: 4 the beasts of the whole e· with thee.
18 unto the nether parts of the e·, with
24 into the nether parts of the e·, which
34: 6 scattered upon all the face of the e·,
27 and the e· shall yield her increase,
35:14 When the whole e· rejoiceth, I will
38:20 things that creep upon the e·,
20 men that are upon the face of the e·,
39:14 remain upon the face of the e·,
18 the blood of the princes of the e·,
43: 2 and the e· shined with his glory.
Da 2:10 There is not a man upon the e·
35 mountain, and filled the whole e·.
39 which shall bear rule over all the e·.
4: 1 languages, that dwell in all the e·;
10 behold a tree in the midst of the e·,
11 sight thereof to the end of all the e·:
15 the stump of his roots in the e·,
15 the beasts in the grass of the e·:
20 and the sight thereof to all the e·;
22 thy dominion to the end of the e·.
23 stump of the roots thereof in the e·,
35 And all the inhabitants of the e·
35 among the inhabitants of the e·:
6:25 languages, that dwell in all the e·;
27 and wonders in heaven and in e·,
7: 4 and it was lifted up from the e·,
17 which shall arise out of the e·.
23 shall be the fourth kingdom upon e·,
23 and shall devour the whole e·, and
8: 5 west on the face of the whole e·,
12: 2 them that sleep in the dust of the e·
Ho 2:18 sword and the battle out of the e·,
21 heavens, and they shall hear the e·;
22 And the e· shall hear the corn,
23 I will sow her unto me in the e·;
6: 3 latter and former rain unto the e·.
Joe 2:10 The e· shall quake before them;
30 in the heavens and in the e·,
3:16 the heavens and the e· shall shake:

Am 2: 7 That pant after the dust of the e·
3: 2 known of all the families of the e·:
5 a bird fall in a snare upon the e·,
5 one take up a snare from the e·,
4:13 upon the high places of the e·,
5: 7 leave off righteousness in the e·,
8 them out upon the face of the e·:
8: 9 will darken the e· in the clear day:
9: 6 hath founded his troop in the e·;
6 them out upon the face of the e·:
8 destroy it from off the face of the e·;
9 not the least grain fall upon the e·.
Jon 2: 6 the e· with her bars was about me
Mic 1: 2 Hear, all ye people; hearken, O e·,
3 tread upon the high places of the e·.
4:13 unto the Lord of the whole e·.
5: 4 he be great unto the ends of the e·.
6: 2 ye strong foundations of the e·:
7: 2 good man is perished out of the e·:
17 of their holes like worms of the e·:
Na 1: 5 and the e· is burned at his presence,
2:13 I will cut off thy prey from the e·,
Hab 2:14 e· shall be filled with the knowledge
20 let all the e· keep silence before him.
3: 3 and the e· was full of his praise.
6 He stood, and measured the e·:
9 Thou didst cleave the e· with rivers.
Zep 2: 3 ye the Lord, all ye meek of the e·,
11 he will famish all the gods of the e·;
3: 8 the e· shall be devoured with the fire
20 praise among all people of the e·,
Hag 1:10 and the e· is stayed from her fruit.
2: 6 the heavens, and the e·, and the sea,
21 I will shake the heavens and the e·;
Zec 1:10 to walk to and fro through the e·.
11 walked to and fro through the e·,
11 all the e· sitteth still, and is at rest.
4:10 run to and fro through the whole e·.
14 stand by the Lord of the whole e·.
5: 3 forth over the face of the whole e·:
6 resemblance through all the e·.
9 ephah between the e· and the heaven.
6: 5 standing before the Lord of all the e·.
7 and fro through the e·: and he said,
7 hence, walk to and fro through the e·.
7 walked to and fro through the e·.
9:10 the river even to the ends of the e·.
12: 1 and layeth the foundation of the e·,
3 though all the people of the e· be
14: 9 Lord shall be king over all the e·:
17 families of the e· unto Jerusalem
Mal 4: 6 come and smite the e· with a curse.
M't 5: 5 meek: for they shall inherit the e·.
13 Ye are the salt of the e·: but if the
18 Till heaven and e· pass, one jot or
35 Nor by the e·; for it is his footstool:
6:10 will be done in e·, as it is in heaven.
19 for yourselves treasures upon e·,
9: 6 hath power on e· to forgive sins,
10:34 I am come to send peace on e·:
11:25 O Father, Lord of heaven and e·,
12:40 three nights in the heart of the e·.
42 uttermost parts of the e· to hear
13: 5 where they had not much e·:
5 because they had no deepness of e·:
16:19 whatsoever thou shalt bind on e·
19 whatsoever thou shalt loose on e·
17:25 whom doth the kings of the e· take
18:18 Whatsoever ye shall bind on e·
18 and whatsoever ye shall loose on e·
19 if two of you shall agree on e· as
23: 9 no man your father upon the e·:
35 righteous blood shed upon the e·,
24:30 shall the tribes of the e· mourn,
35 Heaven and e· shall pass away, but
25:18 one went and digged in the e·,
25 went and hid thy talent in the e·:
27:51 e· did quake, and the rocks rent;
28:18 given unto me in heaven and in e·.
M'r 2:10 Son of man hath power on e· to
4: 5 ground; where it had not much e·;
5 because it had no depth of e·:
28 e· bringeth forth fruit of herself;
31 it is sown in the e·, is less than
31 all the seeds that be in the e·:
9: 3 as no fuller on e· can white them.
13:27 from the uttermost part of the e·
31 Heaven and e· shall pass away:
Lu 2:14 on e· peace, good will toward men.
5:24 the Son of man hath power upon e·
6:49 built an house upon the e·;
10:21 O Father, Lord of heaven and e·,
11: 2 be done, as in heaven, so in e·.
31 from the utmost parts of the e· to
12:49 I am come to send fire on the e·;
51 that I am come to give peace on e·?
56 the face of the sky and of the e·;
16:17 is easier for heaven and e· to pass,
18: 8 shall he find faith on the e·?
21:25 and upon the e· distress of nations,
26 which are coming on the e·:
33 Heaven and e· shall pass away:
35 dwell on the face of the whole e·.
23:44 was a darkness over all the e·
24: 5 bowed down their faces to the e·,
Joh 3:31 he that is of the e· is earthly,
31 and speaketh of the e·:
12:32 if I be lifted up from the e·,
17: 4 I have glorified thee on the e·:
Ac 1: 8 unto the uttermost part of the e·.
2:19 and signs in the e· beneath; blood,
3:25 the kindreds of the e· be blessed.
4:24 which hast made heaven, and e·,
26 The kings of the e· stood up,
7:49 my throne, and e· is my footstool:
8:33 for his life is taken from the e·.

Ac 9: 4 he fell to the e·, and heard a voice
8 Saul arose from the e·; and when
10:11 corners, and let down to the e·:
12 of fourfooted beasts of the e·, and
11: 6 and saw fourfooted beasts of the e·,
13:47 salvation unto the ends of the e·.
14:15 God, which made heaven, and e·,
17:24 is Lord of heaven and e·, dwelleth
26 to dwell on all the face of the e·,
22:22 with such a fellow from the e·:
26:14 when we were all fallen to the e·,
Ro 9:17 be declared throughout all the e·.
28 will the Lord make upon the e·.
10:18 their sound went into all the e·,
1Co 8: 5 gods, whether in heaven or in e·,
10:26 For the e· is the Lord's, and the
28 for the e· is the Lord's, and the
15:47 The first man is of the e·, earthy:
Eph 1:10 are in heaven, and which are on e·;
3:15 family in heaven and e· is named,
4: 9 into the lower parts of the e·?
6: 3 thou mayest live long on the e·.
Ph'p 2:10 things in heaven, and things in e·,
10 and things under the e·;
Col 1:16 are in heaven, and that are in e·,
20 whether they be things in e·, or
3: 2 above, not on things on the e·.
5 members which are upon the e·;
2Ti 2:20 but also of wood and of e·; and
Heb 1:10 hast laid the foundation of the e·;
6: 7 the e· which drinketh in the rain
8: 4 For if he were on e·, he should not
11:13 strangers and pilgrims on the e·:
38 and in dens and caves of the e·.
12:25 who refused him that spake on e·,
26 Whose voice then shook the e·:
26 once more I shake not the e· only,
Jas 5: 5 Ye have lived in pleasure on the e·,
7 for the precious fruit of the e·,
12 neither by heaven, neither by the e·,
17 it rained not on the e· by the space
18 and the e· brought forth her fruit.
2Pe 3: 5 the e· standing out of the water
7 heavens and the e·, which are now,
10 the e· also and the works that are
13 look for new heavens and a new e·,
1Jo 5: 8 are three that bear witness in e·,
Re 1: 5 the prince of the kings of the e·.
7 all kindreds of the e· shall wail
3:10 to try them that dwell upon the e·.
5: 3 nor in e·, neither under the e·,
6 of God sent forth into all the e·.
10 and we shall reign on the e·.
13 and on the e·, and under the e·,
6: 4 thereon to take peace from the e·,
8 them over the fourth part of the e·,
8 death, and with the beasts of the e·.
10 blood on them that dwell on the e·?
13 the stars of heaven fell unto the e·,
15 kings of the e·, and the great men,
7: 1 on the four corners of the e·,
1 holding the four winds of the e·,
1 the wind should not blow on the e·,
2 to whom it was given to hurt the e·
3 Saying, Hurt not the e·, neither the
8: 5 altar, and cast it into the e·:
7 and they were cast upon the e·:
13 woe, to the inhabiters of the e· by
9: 1 a star fall from heaven unto the e·:
3 of the smoke locusts upon the e·:
3 the scorpions of the e· have power.
4 should not hurt the grass of the e·,
10: 2 the sea, and his left foot on the e·,
5 stand upon the sea and upon the e·
6 e·, and the things that therein are,
8 upon the sea and upon the e·.
11: 4 standing before the God of the e·.
6 to smite the e· with all plagues,
10 that dwell upon the e· shall rejoice
10 tormented them that dwelt on the e·
18 destroy them which destroy the e·.
12: 4 and did cast them to the e·:
9 he was cast out into the e·,
12 Woe to the inhabiters of the e· and
13 saw that he was cast unto the e·,
16 And the e· helped the woman,
16 and the e· opened her mouth,
13: 8 dwell upon the e· shall worship
11 beast coming up out of the e·;
12 causeth the e· and them which
13 heaven on the e· in the sight of men.
14 deceiveth them that dwell on the e·
14 saying to them that dwell on the e·,
14: 3 which were redeemed from the e·.
6 unto them that dwell on the e·,
7 him that made heaven, and e·,
15 for the harvest of the e· is ripe.
16 thrust in his sickle on the e·;
16 and the e· was reaped.
18 the clusters of the vine of the e·;
19 angel thrust his sickle into the e·,
19 and gathered the vine of the e·,
16: 1 the wrath of God upon the e·.
2 poured out his vial upon the e·;
14 of the e· and of the whole world,
18 not since men were upon the e·,
17: 2 With whom the kings of the e· have
2 of the e· have been made drunk
5 harlots and abominations of the e·
8 dwell upon the e· shall wonder,
18 reigneth over the kings of the e·.
18: 1 the e· was lightened with his glory.
3 the e· have committed fornication
3 merchants of the e· are waxed rich
9 kings of the e·, who have committed
11 the merchants of the e· shall weep

Re 18:23 were the great men of the e';
24 all that were slain upon the e'.
19: 2 corrupt the e' with her fornication,
19 the beast, and the kings of the e',
20: 8 in the four quarters of the e',
9 went up on the breadth of the e',
11 the e' and the heaven fled away;
21: 1 I saw a new heaven and a new e':
1 and first e' were passed away;
24 the kings of the e' do bring their

earthen See also EARTHY.
Le 6:28 the e' vessel wherein it is sodden
11:33 every e' vessel, whereinto any of
14: 5 birds be killed in an e' vessel
50 the one of the birds in an e' vessel
Nu 5:17 take holy water in an e' vessel;
2Sa 17:28 beds, and basons, and e' vessels,
Jer 19: 1 Go and get a potter's e' bottle,
32:14 and put them in an e' vessel,
La 4: 2 are they esteemed as e' pitchers,
2Co 4: 7 have this treasure in e' vessels,

earthly See also EARTHY.
Joh 3:12 If I have told you e' things,
31 that is of the earth is e',
2Co 5: 1 if our e' house of this tabernacle
Ph'p 3:19 their shame, who mind e' things.)
Jas 3:15 above, but is e', sensual, devilish.

earthquake See also EARTHQUAKES.
1Ki 19:11 and after the wind an e';
11 but the Lord was not in the e':
12 after the e' a fire; but the Lord
Isa 29: 6 and with e', and great noise,
Am 1: 1 two years before the e'.
Zec 14: 5 the e' in the days of Uzziah
M't 27:54 saw the e', and those things that
28: 2 behold, there was a great e':
Ac 16:26 And suddenly there was a great e',
Re 6:12 lo, there was a great e';
8: 5 and lightnings, and an e'.
11:13 same hour was there a great e',
13 and in the e' were slain of men
19 and an e', and great hail.
16:18 and there was a great e',
18 so mighty an e', and so great.

earthquakes
M't 24: 7 and e', in divers places.
M'r 13: 8 there shall be e' in divers places,
Lu 21:11 great e' shall be in divers places,

earthy See also EARTHEN; EARTHLY.
1Co 15:47 The first man is of the earth, e':
48 As is the e', such are they also
48 such are they also that are e':
49 we have born the image of the e',

ease See also EASED; DISEASE.
De 23:13 when thou wilt e' thyself abroad,
28:65 these nations shalt thou find no e',
J'g 20:43 and trode them down with e'
2Ch 10: 4 e' thou somewhat the grievous
9 E' somewhat the yoke that thy
Job 7:13 my couch shall e' my complaint;
12: 5 the thought of him that is at e'.
16:12 I was at e', but he hath broken
21:23 being wholly at e' and quiet.
Ps 25:13 His soul shall dwell at e'; and
123: 4 scorning of those that are at e',
Isa 1:24 will e' me of mine adversaries,
32: 9 Rise up, ye women that are at e';
11 Tremble, ye women that are at e';
Jer 46:27 and be in rest and at e',
48:11 Moab hath been at e' from his
Eze 23:42 a voice of a multitude being at e'
Am 6: 1 Woe to them that are at e' in Zion,
Zec 1:15 with the heathen that are at e':
Lu 12:19 take thine e', eat, drink, and be

eased See also DISEASED.
Job 16: 6 though I forbear, what am I e'?
2Co 8:13 I mean not that other men be e',

easier
Ex 18:22 so shall it be e' for thyself,
M't 9: 5 whether is e', to say, Thy sins be
19:24 It is e' for a camel to go through
M'r 2: 9 Whether it is e' to say to the sick
10:25 It is e' for a camel to go through
Lu 5:23 Whether is e', to say, Thy sins be
16:17 it is e' for heaven and earth to pass,
18:25 For it is e' for a camel to go through

easily
1Co 13: 5 not e' provoked, thinketh no evil;
Heb 12: 1 the sin which doth so e' beset us,

east See also EASTWARD.
Ge 2:14 goeth toward the e' of Assyria
3:24 at the e' of the garden of Eden
4:16 the land of Nod, on the e' of Eden.
10:30 was...Sephar a mount of the e'.
11: 2 pass, as they journeyed from the e',
12: 8 a mountain on the e' of Beth-el,
8 his tent, having...Hai on the e':
13:11 and Lot journeyed e': and they
25: 6 eastward, unto the e' country.
28:14 abroad to the west, and to the e',
29: 1 into the land of the people of the e'.
41: 6 ears and blasted with the e' wind
23 ears...blasted with the e' wind,
27 empty ears blasted with the e' wind
Ex 10:13 brought an e' wind upon the land
13 the e' wind brought the locusts.
14:21 to go back by a strong e' wind
27:13 breadth of the court on the e' side
38:13 for the e' side eastward fifty cubits.
Le 1:16 it beside the altar on the e' part,
Nu 2: 3 on the e' side toward the rising of
3:38 the tabernacle toward the e',

Nu 10: 5 the camps that lie on the e' parts
23: 7 out of the mountains of the e',
34:10 your e' border from Hazar-enan
11 to Riblah, on the e' side of Ain;
35: 5 from without the city on the e' side
Jos 4:19 Gilgal, in the e' border of Jericho.
7: 2 to Ai,....on the e' side of Beth-el,
11: 3 And to the Canaanite on the e'
12: 1 and all the plain on the e':
3 the sea of Chinneroth on the e',
3 even the salt sea on the e',
15: 5 the e' border was the salt sea,
16: 1 the water of Jericho on the e',
5 of their inheritance on the e' side
6 passed by it on the e' to Janohah;
17:10 north, and in Issachar on the e'.
18: 7 beyond Jordan on the e',
20 the border of it on the e' side.
19:13 passeth on along on the e'
J'g 6: 3 the children of the e',....came up
33 children of the e' were gathered
7:12 all the children of the e' lay along
8:10 the hosts of the children of the e':
11 them that dwelt in tents on the e'
11:18 came by the e' side of the land
21:19 on the e' side of the highway
1Ki 4:30 all the children of the e' country,
7:25 and three looking toward the e':
1Ch 4:39 unto the e' side of the valley,
5:10 tents throughout all the e' land
6:78 on the e' side of Jordan, were
9:24 the e', west, north, and south.
12:15 toward the e', and toward the west.
2Ch 4: 4 three looking toward the e': and
10 on the right side of the e' end,
5:12 stood at the e' end of the altar,
29: 4 them together into the e' street,
31:14 the porter toward the e', was
Ne 3:26 the water gate toward the e',
29 the keeper of the e' gate.
Job 1: 3 greatest of all the men of the e'.
15: 2 and fill his belly with the e' wind?
27:21 The e' wind carrieth him away,
38:24 which scattereth the e' wind upon
Ps 48: 7 ships of Tarshish with an e' wind.
75: 6 cometh neither from the e',
78:26 He caused an e' wind to blow in
103:12 far as the e' is from the west,
107: 3 from the e', and from the west,
Isa 2: 6 they be replenished from the e',
11:14 shall spoil them of the e' together:
27: 8 wind in the day of the e' wind.
41: 2 up the righteous man from the e',
43: 5 I will bring thy seed from the e',
46:11 Calling a ravenous bird from the e',
Jer 18:17 scatter them as with an e' wind
19: 2 is by the entry of the e' gate,
31:40 of the horse gate toward the e',
49:28 and spoil the men of the e'.
Eze 8:16 their faces toward the e'; and they
16 worshipped the sun toward the e'.
10:19 stood at the door of the e' gate
11: 1 brought me unto the e' gate
23 mountain which is on the e' side
17:10 when the e' wind toucheth it?
19:12 the e' wind dried up her fruit:
25: 4 deliver thee to the men of the e'
10 Unto the men of the e' with the
27:26 the e' wind hath broken thee in
39:11 passengers on the e' of the sea;
40: 6 gate which looketh toward the e',
22 the gate that looketh toward the e'
23 toward the north, and toward the e';
32 into the inner court toward the e':
44 at the side of the e' gate
41:14 the separate place toward the e',
42: 9 was the entry on the e' side,
10 the wall of the court toward the e',
12 before the wall toward the e',
15 whose prospect is toward the e',
16 He measured the e' side with the
43: 1 the gate that looketh toward the e':
2 came from the way of the e':
4 whose prospect is toward the e'.
17 his stairs shall look toward the e'.
44: 1 which looketh toward the e';
45: 7 and from the e' side eastward:
7 west border unto the e' border.
46: 1 court that looketh toward the e'
12 gate that looketh toward the e',
47: 1 of the house stood toward the e',
8 waters issue out toward the e'
18 the e' side ye shall measure from
18 from the border unto the e' sea.
18 And this is the e' side.
48: 1 these are his sides e' and west;
2 border of Dan, from the e' side
3 border of Asher, from the e' side
4 border of Naphtali, from the e' side
5 border of Manasseh, from the e'
6 border of Ephraim, from the e' side
7 border of Reuben, from the e' side
8 border of Judah, from the e' side
8 the e' side unto the west side:
10 and toward the e' ten thousand in
16 the e' side four thousand and five
17 the e' two hundred and fifty,
21 the oblation toward the e' border,
23 from the e' side unto the west side,
24 from the e' side unto the west
25 border of Simeon, from the e' side
26 border of Issachar, from the e' side
27 border of Zebulun, from the e' side
32 at the e' side four thousand and
Da 8: 9 the south ,and toward the e',
11:44 But tidings out of the e' and out

Ho 12: 1 and followeth after the e' wind:
13:15 an e' wind shall come, the wind
Joe 2:20 with his face toward the e' sea,
Am 8:12 from the north even to the e',
Jon 4: 5 and sat on the e' side of the city,
8 God prepared a vehement e' wind;
Hab 1: 9 faces shall sup up as the e' wind,
Zec 8: 7 save my people from the e'
14: 4 is before Jerusalem on the e',
4 the midst thereof toward the e'
M't 2: 1 men from the e' to Jerusalem,
2 we have seen his star in the e',
9 the star, which they saw in the e',
8:11 shall come from the e' and west,
24:27 the lightning cometh out of the e',
Lu 13:29 they shall come from the e', and
Rev 7: 2 angel ascending from the e',
16:12 the way of the kings of the e'
21:13 On the e' three gates; on the north

Easter
Ac 12: 4 intending after E' to bring him

east-side See EAST and SIDE.

eastward
Ge 2: 8 God planted a garden e' of Eden;
13:14 southward, and e', and westward:
25: 6 yet lived, e', unto the east country.
Ex 27:13 east side e' shall be fifty cubits.
38:13 the east side e' fifty cubits.
Le 16:14 his finger upon the mercy seat e';
Nu 3:38 e', shall be Moses, and Aaron
32:19 fallen to us on this side Jordan e'.
34: 3 outmost coast of the salt sea e':
11 side of the sea of Chinnereth e':
15 Jericho e', toward the sunrising.
De 3:17 sea, under Ashdoth-pisgah e'.
27 northward, and southward, and e',
4:49 the plain on this side Jordan e'.
Jos 11: 8 and unto the valley of Mizpeh e';
13: 8 gave them, beyond Jordan e',
27 on the other side Jordan e'.
32 other side Jordan, by Jericho, e'.
16: 6 about e' unto Taanath-shiloh,
19:12 from Sarid e' toward the sunrising
20: 8 other side Jordan by Jericho e',
1Sa 13: 5 in Michmash, e' from Beth-aven.
1Ki 7:39 on the right side of the house e',
17: 3 Get thee hence, and turn thee e',
2Ki 10:33 Jordan e', all...land of Gilead,
13:17 And he said, Open the window e'.
1Ch 5: 9 And e' he inhabited unto the
7:28 e' Naaran, and westward Gezer,
9:18 waited in the king's gate e':
26:14 the lot e' fell to Shelemiah.
17 E' were six Levites, northward four
Ne 12:37 even unto the water gate e'.
Eze 11: 1 Lord's house, which looketh e':
40:10 little chambers of the gate e' 1870,
19 hundred cubits e' and northward.
45: 7 and from the east side e':
47: 1 the threshold of the house e':
2 gate by the way that looketh e';
3 the line in his hand went forth e',
48:18 residue...shall be ten thousand e',

east-wind See EAST and WIND.

easy See also EASIER.
Pr 14: 6 knowledge is e' unto him that
M't 11:30 For my yoke is e', and my burden
1Co 14: 9 tongue words e' to be understood,
Jas 3:17 e' to be intreated, full of mercy

eat See also ATE; EATEN; EATEST; EATETH; EATING.
Ge 2:16 garden thou mayest freely e':
17 thou shalt not e' of it: for in the
3: 1 not e' of every tree of the garden?
2 We may e' of the fruit of the trees
3 God hath said, Ye shall not e' of it,
5 know that in the day ye e' thereof,
6 and did e', and gave also unto her
6 husband with her; and he did e'.
11 thee that thou shouldest not e'?
12 she gave me of the tree, and I did e'.
13 serpent beguiled me, and I did e'.
14 dust shalt thou e' all the days of thy
17 saying, Thou shalt not e' of it:
17 thou e' of it all the days of thy life;
18 thou shalt e' the herb of the field;
19 the sweat of thy face shalt thou e'
22 take also of the tree of life, and e',
9: 4 the blood thereof, shall ye not e'.
18: 8 under the tree, and they did e'.
19: 3 unleavened bread, and they did e'.
24:33 was set meat before him to e':
33 but he said, I will not e',
54 And they did e' and drink, he and
25:28 he did e' of his venison:
34 he did e' and drink, and rose up,
26:30 made them a feast, and they did e'
27: 4 bring it to me, that I may e';
7 me savoury meat, that I may e',
10 may e', and that he may bless thee
19 sit and e' of my venison, that thy
25 and I will e' of my son's venison,
25 it near to him, and he did e':
31 arise, and e' of his son's venison,
28:20 I go, and will give me bread to e',
31:46 and they did e' there upon the heap.
54 and called his brethren to e' bread,
54 did e' bread, and tarried all night
32:32 children of Israel e' not of the sinew
37:25 and they sat down to e' bread:
39: 6 save the bread which he did e'.
40:17 birds did e' them out of the basket
19 and the birds shall e' thy flesh

Ge 41: 4 did e' up the seven well favoured
20 the...kine did e' up the first seven
43:25 that they should e' bread there.
32 Egyptians, which did e' with him,
32 not e' bread with the Hebrews;
45:18 and ye shall e' the fat of the land.
47:22 and did e' their portion which
Ex 2:20 call him, that he may e' bread.
10: 5 and they shall e' the residue of
5 shall e' every tree which groweth
12 and e' every herb of the land,
15 they did e' every herb of the land,
12: 7 houses, wherein they shall e' it.
8 shall e' the flesh in that night
8 with bitter herbs they shall e' it.
9 E' not of it raw, nor sodden at all
11 And thus shall ye e' it; with your
11 and ye shall e' it in haste:
15 days shall ye e' unleavened bread;
16 save that which every man must e',
18 ye shall e' unleavened bread, until
20 Ye shall e' nothing leavened; in all
20 shall ye e' unleavened bread.
43 There shall no stranger e' thereof:
44 him, then shall he e' thereof.
45 an hired servant shall not e' thereof.
48 no uncircumcised person shall e'
13: 6 thou shalt e' unleavened bread,
16: 3 when we did e' bread to the full;
8 give you in the evening flesh to e',
12 At even ye shall e' flesh, and in the
15 which the Lord hath given you to e'.
25 And Moses said, E' that to day;
35 the children of Israel did e' manna
35 they did e' manna, until they came
18:12 e' bread with Moses' father in law
22:31 shall ye e' any flesh that is torn
23:11 that the poor of thy people may e':
11 the beasts of the field shall e'.
15 e' unleavened bread seven days,
24:11 they saw God, and did e' and drink.
29:32 And Aaron and his sons shall e'
33 And they shall e' those things
33 but a stranger shall not e' thereof,
32: 6 people sat down to e' and to drink,
34:15 and thou e' of his sacrifice;
18 thou shalt e' unleavened bread,
28 neither e' bread, nor drink water.
Le 3:17 that ye e' neither fat nor blood.
6:16 thereof shall Aaron and his sons e':
16 the congregation they shall e' it.
18 the children of Aaron shall e' of it.
26 that offereth it for sin shall e' it:
29 among the priests shall e' thereof:
7: 6 among the priests shall e' thereof:
19 all that be clean shall e' thereof.
21 and e' of the flesh of the sacrifice
23 Ye shall e' no manner of fat,
24 but ye shall in no wise e' of it.
26 ye shall e' no manner of blood,
8:31 and there e' it with the bread that is
31 Aaron and his sons shall e' it.
10:12 and e' it without leaven beside the
13 And ye shall e' it in the holy place,
14 and heave shoulder shall ye e'
11: 2 ye shall e' among all the beasts
3 among the beasts, that shall ye e'.
4 Nevertheless these shall ye not e'
8 Of their flesh shall ye not e',
9 ye e' of all that are in the waters:
9 and in the rivers, them shall ye e'.
11 ye shall not e' of their flesh,
21 Yet these may ye e' of every flying
22 even these of them ye may e';
39 any beast, of which ye may e',
42 them ye shall not e'; for they are
17:12 No soul of you shall e' blood,
12 any stranger...among you e' blood.
14 Ye shall e' the blood of no manner
19:25 fifth year shall ye e' of the fruit
26 not e' anything with the blood,
21:22 He shall e' the bread of his God,
22: 4 he shall not e' of the holy things,
6 and shall not e' of the holy things,
7 shall afterward e' the holy things;
8 he shall not e' to defile himself
10 no stranger e' of the holy thing:
10 shall not e' of the holy thing.
11 he shall e' of it, and he that is born
11 they shall e' of his meat.
12 she may not e' of an offering
13 she shall e' of her father's meat:
13 there shall no stranger e' thereof.
14 if a man e' of the holy thing
16 when they e' their holy things:
23: 6 days ye must e' unleavened bread.
14 And ye shall e' neither bread, nor
24: 9 they shall e' it in the holy place:
25:12 ye shall e' the increase thereof out
19 shall e' your fill, and dwell therein
20 What shall we e' the seventh year?
22 and e' yet of old fruit until the ninth
22 ye shall e' of the old store.
26: 5 ye shall e' your bread to the full,
10 ye shall e' old store, and bring forth
16 for your enemies shall e' it.
26 ye shall e', and not be satisfied.
29 ye shall e' the flesh of your sons,
29 flesh of your daughters shall ye e'.
38 land of your enemies shall e' you
Nu 6: 3 nor e' moist grapes, or dried.
4 shall he e' nothing that is made
9:11 and e' it with unleavened bread
11: 4 Who shall give us flesh to e'?
5 remember the fish, which we did e'
13 Give us flesh, that we may e'.

Nu 11:18 and ye shall e' flesh: for ye have
18 Who shall give us flesh to e'?
18 will give you flesh, and ye shall e'.
19 shall not e' one day, nor two days,
21 that they may e' a whole month.
15:19 when ye e' of the bread of the land,
18:10 most holy place shalt thou e' it;
10 every male shall e' it:
11 is clean in thy house shall e' of it.
13 is clean in thine house shall e' of it.
31 And ye shall e' it in every place,
23:24 not lie down until he e' of the prey,
24: 8 he shall e' up the nations
25: 2 the people did e', and bowed down
De 2: 6 of them for money, that ye may e';
28 me meat for money, that I may e';
4:28 see, nor hear, nor e', nor smell.
8: 9 A land wherein thou shalt e' bread
9: 9 did e' bread nor drink water:
18 neither e' bread, nor drink water,
11:15 that thou mayest e' and be full.
12: 7 there ye shall e' before the Lord
15 kill and e' flesh in all thy gates,
15 and the clean may e' thereof,
16 Only ye shall not e' the blood;
17 mayest not e' within thy gates
18 thou must e' them before the Lord
20 and thou shalt say, I will e' flesh,
20 because thy soul longeth to e' flesh;
20 thou mayest e' flesh, whatsoever
21 and thou shalt e' in thy gates
22 so thou shalt e' them: the unclean
22 and the clean shall e' of them alike.
23 be sure that thou e' not the blood:
23 mayest not e' the life with the flesh.
24 Thou shalt not e' it; thou shalt pour
25 Thou shalt not e' it; that it may go
27 and thou shalt e' the flesh.
14: 3 shalt not e' any abominable thing.
4 are the beasts which ye shall e':
6 among the beasts, that ye shall e'.
7 Nevertheless these ye shall not e':
8 ye shall not e' of their flesh,
9 shall e' of all that are in the waters:
9 that have fins and scales shall ye e':
10 not fins and scales ye may not e';
11 Of all clean birds ye shall e'.
12 are they of which ye shall not e':
20 But of all clean fowls ye may e'.
21 Ye shall not e' of anything that
21 is in thy gates, that he may e' it;
23 And thou shalt e' before the Lord
26 thou shalt e' there before the Lord
29 come, and shall e' and be satisfied;
15:20 Thou shalt e' it before the Lord
22 Thou shalt e' it within thy gates:
23 thou shalt not e' the blood thereof;
16: 3 shalt e' no leavened bread with it;
3 seven days shalt thou e' unleavened
7 And thou shalt roast and e' it
8 Six days shalt thou e' unleavened
18: 1 shall e' the offerings of the Lord
8 They shall have like portions to e',
20: 6 battle, and another man e' of it.
14 shalt e' the spoil of thine enemies,
19 for thou mayest e' of them, and
23:24 then thou mayest e' grapes thy fill
26:12 that they may e' within thy gates,
27: 7 e' there, and rejoice before the Lord
28:31 and thou shalt not e' thereof:
33 which thou knowest not e' up:
39 grapes; for the worms shall e' them.
51 he shall e' the fruit of thy cattle,
53 shalt e' the fruit of thine own body,
55 his children whom he shall e':
57 shall e' them for want of all things
32:13 might e' the increase of the fields;
38 did e' the fat of their sacrifices,
Jos 5:11 And they did e' of the old corn
12 but they did e' of the fruit of the
24:13 which ye planted not do ye e'.
J'g 9:27 e' and drink, and cursed Abimelech.
13: 4 and e' not any unclean thing:
7 drink, neither e' any unclean thing:
14 She may not e' of any thing that
14 nor e' any unclean thing: all that I
16 I will not e' of thy bread:
14: 9 he gave them, and they did e':
19: 4 did e' and drink, and lodged there.
6 they sat down, and did e' and drink
8 and they did e' both of them.
21 their feet, and did e' and drink.
Ru 2:14 e' of the bread, and dip thy morsel
14 and she did e', and was sufficed,
1Sa 1: 7 therefore she wept, and did not e'.
18 the woman went her way, and did e',
2:36 that I may e' a piece of bread.
9:13 he go up to the high place to e':
13 the people will not e' until he come,
13 afterwards they e' that be bidden.
19 for ye shall e' with me to day,
24 set it before thee, and e': for unto
24 So Saul did e' with Samuel that day.
14:32 people did e' them with the blood.
33 in that they e' with the blood.
34 slay them here, and e'; and sin not
20:24 the king sat him down to e' meat.
34 and did e' no meat the second day
28:22 e', that thou mayest have strength,
23 he refused, and said, I will not e'.
25 before his servants; and they did e'.
30:11 and gave him bread, and he did e';
2Sa 3:35 to cause David to e' meat while it
9: 7 thou shalt not e' bread at my table
10 master's son may have food to e':
10 thy master's son shall e' bread

2Sa 9:11 e' at my table, as one of the king's
13 he did e' continually at the king's
11:11 into mine house, to e' and to drink,
13 And...he did e' and drink before him;
12: 3 it did e' of his own meat,
17 neither did he e' bread with them.
20 set bread before him, and he did e'.
21 thou didst rise and e' bread.
13: 5 that I may see it, and e' it at her hand.
6 that I may e' at her hand.
9 before him; but he refused to e'.
10 that I may e' of thine hand.
11 had brought them unto him to e',
16: 2 fruit for the young men to e';
17:29 the people that were with him, to e':
19:28 them that did e' at thine own table.
35 taste what I e' or what I drink?
1Ki 1:25 they e' and drink before him,
2: 7 be of those that e' at thy table:
13: 8 neither will I e' bread nor drink
9 E' no bread, nor drink water, nor
15 Come home with me, and e' bread.
16 neither will I e' bread nor drink
17 Thou shalt e' no bread nor drink
18 he may e' bread and drink water.
19 and did e' bread in his house,
22 E' no bread, and drink no water;
14:11 in the city shall the dogs e'; and
11 the field shall the fowls of the air e':
16: 4 Baasha in the city shall the dogs e';
4 fields shall the fowls of the air e'.
17:12 that we may e' it, and die.
15 she, and he, and her house, did e'
18:19 hundred, which e' at Jezebel's table.
41 Get thee up, e' and drink; for there
42 Ahab went up to e' and to drink.
19: 5 and said unto him, Arise and e'.
6 did e' and drink, and laid him down
7 Arise and e'; because the journey is
8 he arose, and did e' and drink,
21 unto the people, and they did e'.
21: 4 his face, and would e' no bread.
7 arise, and e' bread, and let thine
23 dogs shall e' Jezebel by the wall
24 Ahab in the city the dogs shall e';
24 field shall the fowls of the air e'.
2Ki 4: 8 she constrained him to e' bread.
8 he turned in thither to e' bread.
40 they poured out for the men to e'.
40 And they could not e' thereof.
41 for the people, that they may e'.
42 unto the people, that they may e'.
43 Give the people, that they may e':
43 shall e', and shall leave thereof.
44 set it before them, and they did e',
6:22 e' and drink, and go to their master.
28 thy son, that we may e' him to day,
28 and we will e' my son to-morrow.
29 we boiled my son, and did e' him:
29 Give thy son, that we may e' him:
7: 2 thine eyes, but shalt not e' thereof.
8 into one tent, and did e' and drink,
19 thine eyes, but shalt not e' thereof.
9:10 dogs shall e' Jezebel in the portion
34 he did e' and drink, and said, Go,
36 the portion of Jezreel shall dogs e'
18:27 that they may e' their own dung,
31 e' ye every man of his own vine,
19:29 e' this year such things as grow
29 vineyards, and e' the fruits thereof.
23: 9 they did e' of the unleavened bread
25:29 did e' bread continually before him
1Ch 29:22 did e' and drink before the Lord
2Ch 28:15 and gave them to e' and to drink,
30:18 did they e' the passover otherwise
22 and they did e' throughout the feast
31:10 we have had enough to e', and
Ezr 2:63 should not e' of the most holy things,
6:21 seek the Lord God of Israel, did e',
9:12 and e' the good of the land,
10: 6 he did e' no bread, nor drink water:
Ne 5: 2 for them, that we may e', and live.
7:65 should not e' of the most holy things,
8:10 e' the fat, and drink the sweet,
12 the people went their way to e',
9:25 so they did e', and were filled,
36 our fathers to e' the fruit thereof
Es 4:16 neither e' nor drink three days,
Job 1: 4 to e' and to drink with them.
3:24 For my sighing cometh before I e',
31: 8 let me sow, and let another e';
42:11 did e' bread with him in his house:
Ps 14: 4 e' up my people as they e' bread,
22:26 The meek shall e' and be satisfied:
29 fat upon earth shall e' and worship:
27: 2 came upon me to e' up my flesh,
41: 9 I trusted, which did e' of my bread,
50:13 Will I e' the flesh of bulls, or drink
53: 4 e' up my people as they e' bread:
78:24 down manna upon them to e',
25 Man did e' angels' food: he sent
29 So they did e', and were well filled:
102: 4 so that I forget to e' my bread.
105:35 did e' up all the herbs in their land,
127: 2 up late, to e' the bread of sorrows:
128: 2 shalt e' the labour of thine hands:
141: 4 let me not e' of their dainties.
Pr 1:31 e' of the fruit of their own way,
4:17 they e' the bread of wickedness,
9: 5 Come, e' of my bread, and drink of
13: 2 e' good by the fruit of his mouth:
2 of the transgressors shall e' violence.
18:21 they that love it shall e' the fruit
23: 1 thou sittest to e' with a ruler,
6 E' thou not the bread of him that
7 E' and drink, said he to thee;

Pr 24:13 e· thou honey, because it is good;
25:16 e· so much as is sufficient for thee,
21 give him bread to e·; and if he be
27 It is not good to e· much honey:
27:18 fig tree shall e· the fruit thereof:
30:17 and the young eagles shall e· it.
Ec 2:24 than that he should e· and drink,
25 For who can e·, or who else can
3:13 that every man should e· and drink,
5:11 they are increased that e· them:
12 sweet, whether he e· little or much:
18 comely for one to e· and to drink,
19 hath given him power to e· thereof,
6: 2 God giveth him not power to e·
8:15 than to e·, and to drink,
9: 7 e· thy bread with joy, and drink
10:16 and thy princes e· in the morning!
17 and thy princes e· in due season,
Ca 4:16 garden, and e· his pleasant fruits.
5: 1 e·, O friends; drink, yea, drink
Isa 1:19 ye shall e· the good of the land:
3:10 shall e· the fruit of their doings.
4: 1 We will e· our own bread, and
5:17 of the fat ones shall strangers e·.
7:15 Butter and honey shall he e·, that
22 he shall e· butter: for butter
22 and honey shall every one e·
9:20 and he shall e· on the left hand,
20 they shall e· every man the flesh of
11: 7 the lion shall e· straw like the ox.
21: 5 watch in the watchtower, e·, drink:
22:13 drinking wine: let us e· and drink;
23:18 to e· sufficiently, and for durable
30:24 shall e· clean provender, which
36:12 that they may e· their own dung,
16 and e· ye every one of his vine,
37:30 shall e· this year such as groweth
30 vineyards, and e· the fruit thereof.
50: 9 the moth shall e· them up.
51: 8 For the moth shall e· them up like
8 the worm shall e· them like wool:
55: 1 come ye, buy, and e·; yea, come,
2 and e· ye that which is good,
61: 6 shall e· the riches of the Gentiles,
62: 9 that have gathered it shall e· it,
65: 4 which e· swine's flesh, and broth
13 Behold, my servants shall e·, but
21 vineyards, and e· the fruit of them.
22 they shall not plant, and another e·:
25 lion shall e· straw like the bullock:
Jer 2: 7 to e· the fruit thereof and the
5:17 And they shall e· up thine harvest
17 sons and thy daughters should e·:
17 e· up thy flocks and thine herds:
17 they shall e· up thy vines
7:21 unto your sacrifices, and e· flesh.
15:16 were found, and I did e· them;
16: 8 to sit with them to e· and to drink.
19: 9 I will cause them to e· the flesh of
9 they shall e· every one the flesh of
22:15 did not thy father e· and drink,
22 wind shall e· up all thy pastors,
29: 5 gardens, and e· the fruit of them;
28 and plant gardens, and e· the fruit
31: 5 shall e· them as common things.
41: 1 there they did e· bread together
52:33 and he did continually e· bread
La 2:20 Shall the women e· their fruit, and
Eze 2: 8 open thy mouth, and e· that I give
3: 1 Son of man, e· that thou findest;
1 e· this roll, and go speak
2 and he caused me to e· that roll.
3 Son of man, cause thy belly to e·,
3 did I e· it; and it was in my mouth
4: 9 days shalt thou e· thereof.
10 thy meat which thou shalt e· shall
10 from time to time shalt thou e· it.
12 thou shalt e· it as barley cakes,
13 thus shall the children of Israel e·
16 and they shall e· bread by weight,
5:10 the fathers shall e· the sons
10 and the sons shall e· their fathers;
12:18 man, e· thy bread with quaking,
19 e· their bread with carefulness,
16:13 thou didst e· fine flour, and honey,
22: 9 thee they e· upon the mountains:
24:17 and e· not the bread of men.
22 your lips, nor e· the bread of men.
25: 4 they shall e· thy fruit, and they
33:25 Ye e· with the blood, and lift up
34: 3 Ye e· the fat, and ye clothe you with
19 e· that which ye have trodden
39:17 ye may e· flesh, and drink blood.
18 shall e· the flesh of the mighty,
19 And ye shall e· fat till ye be full,
42:13 Lord shall e· the most holy things:
44: 3 he shall sit in it to e· bread
29 They shall e· the meat offering, and
31 The priests shall not e· of any thing
Da 1:12 let them give us pulse to e·,
13 e· of the portion of the king's meat:
15 did e· the portion of the king's meat.
4:25 they shall make thee to e· grass
32 make thee to e· grass as oxen,
33 and did e· grass as oxen, and his
Ho 2:12 the beasts of the field shall e· them.
4: 8 They e· up the sin of my people,
10 they shall e·, and not have enough:
8:13 of mine offerings, and e· it;
9: 3 shall e· unclean things in Assyria.
4 that e· thereof shall be polluted:
Joe 2:26 And ye shall e· in plenty, and be
Am 6: 4 and e· the lambs out of the flock,
7: 4 the great deep, and did e· up a part.
12 there e· bread, and prophesy there:
9:14 gardens, and e· the fruit of them.

Ob 1: 7 they that e· thy bread have laid a
Mic 3: 3 Who also e· the flesh of my people,
6:14 Thou shalt e·, but not be satisfied;
7: 1 vintage: there is no cluster to e·:
Na 3:15 e· thee up like the cankerworm:
Hab 1: 8 as the eagle that hasteth to e·.
Hag 1: 6 ye e·, but ye have not enough;
Zec 7: 6 when ye did e·, and when ye did
6 did not ye e· for yourselves, and
11: 9 e· every one the flesh of another.
16 he shall e· the flesh of the fat,
M't 6:25 what ye shall e·, or what ye shall
31 saying, What shall we e·? or, What
12: 1 pluck the ears of corn, and to e·.
4 and did e· the shewbread,
4 which was not lawful for him to e·,
14:16 not depart; give ye them to e·.
20 And they did all e·, and were filled:
15: 2 wash not their hands when they e·
20 but to e· with unwashen hands
27 the dogs e· of the crumbs which
32 three days, and have nothing to e·:
37 they did all e·, and were filled:
38 did e· were four thousand men,
24:49 to e· and drink with the drunken;
26:17 prepare for thee to e· the passover?
21 as they did e·, he said, Verily I say
26 said, Take, e·; this is my body.
M'r 1: 6 he did e· locusts and wild honey;
2:16 e· with publicans and sinners,
26 and did e· the shewbread, which is
26 not lawful to e· but for the priests,
3:20 could not so much as e· bread.
5:43 should be given her to e·.
6:31 had no leisure so much as to e·.
36 bread: for they have nothing to e·.
37 said unto them, Give ye them to e·.
37 of bread, and give them to e·?
42 And they did all e·, and were filled.
44 And they that did e· of the loaves
7: 2 saw some of his disciples e· bread
3 e· not, holding the tradition of
4 except they wash, they e· not.
5 but e· bread with unwashen hands?
28 yet the dogs under the table e· of
8: 1 having nothing to e·, Jesus called
2 days, and have nothing to e·:
8 So they did e·, and were filled:
11:14 No man e· fruit of thee hereafter
14:12 and prepare that thou mayest e·
14 where I shall e· the passover with
18 as they sat and did e·, Jesus said,
22 as they did e·, Jesus took bread,
22 said, Take, e·; this is my body.
Lu 4: 2 in those days he did e· nothing:
5:30 ye e· and drink with publicans
33 Pharisees; but thine e· and drink?
6: 1 and did e·, rubbing them in their
4 did take and e· the shewbread,
4 not lawful to e· but for the priests
7:36 him that he would e· with him.
9:13 unto them, Give ye them to e·.
17 And they did e·, and were all filled:
10: 8 e· such things as are set before
12:19 take thine ease, e·, drink, and be
22 for your life, what ye shall e·;
29 seek not ye what ye shall e·,
45 to e· and drink, and to be drunken;
14: 1 to e· bread on the sabbath day,
15 Blessed is he that shall e· bread in
15:16 the husks that the swine did e·:
23 and let us e·, and be merry:
17: 8 afterward thou shalt e· and drink?
27 They did e·, they drank, they
28 they did e·, they drank, they
22: 8 us the passover, that we may e·.
11 where I shall e· the passover with
15 I have desired to e· this passover
16 I will not any more e· thereof,
30 That ye may e· and drink at my
24:43 he took it, and did e· before them.
Joh 4:31 prayed him, saying, Master, e·.
32 I have meat to e· that ye know not
33 any man brought him ought to e·?
6: 5 we buy bread, that these may e·?
23 the place where they did e· bread,
26 but because ye did e· of the loaves,
31 Our fathers did e· manna in the
31 gave them bread from heaven to e·.
49 Your fathers did e· manna in the
50 that a man may e· thereof, and not
51 if any man e· of this bread,
52 can this man give us his flesh to e·?
53 Except ye e· the flesh of the Son of
58 not as your fathers did e· manna,
18:28 but that they might e· the passover.
Ac 2:46 did e· their meat with gladness
9: 9 sight, and neither did e· nor drink.
10:13 Rise, Peter; kill, and e·.
41 who did e· and drink with him
11: 3 uncircumcised, and didst e· with
7 Arise, Peter; slay and e·.
23:12 they would neither e· nor drink
14 we will e· nothing until we have
21 an oath, that they will neither e·
27:35 he had broken it, he began to e·.
Ro 14: 2 believeth that he may e· all things:
21 It is good neither to e· flesh, nor to
23 that doubteth is damned if he e·,
1Co 5:11 with such a one no not to e·.
8: 7 e· it as a thing offered unto an
8 neither, if we e·, are we the better;
8 if we e· not, are we the worse.
10 e· those things which are offered
13 I will e· no flesh while the world
9: 4 Have we not power to e· and to

1Co 10: 3 did all e· the same spiritual meat;
7 people sat down to e· and drink,
18 are they which e· of the sacrifices
25 is sold in the shambles, that e·,
27 whatsoever is set before you, e·,
28 e· not for his sake that shewed it,
31 Whether therefore ye e·, or drink,
11:20 this is not to e· the Lord's supper.
22 have ye not houses to e· and to
24 Take, e·; this is my body, which
26 as often as ye e· this bread,
27 whosoever shall e· this bread, and
28 and so let him e· of that bread,
33 when ye come together to e·, tarry
34 man hunger, let him e· at home;
15:32 let us e· and drink; for to-morrow
Ga 2:12 James, he did e· with the Gentiles:
2Th 3: 8 Neither did we e· any man's
10 not work, neither should he e·.
12 with quietness they work, and e·
2Ti 2:17 word will e· as doth a canker:
Heb 13:10 they have no right to e· which
Jas 5: 3 and shall e· your flesh as it were
Rev 2: 7 will I give to e· of the tree of life,
14 to e· things sacrificed unto idols,
17 will I give to e· of the hidden
20 to e· things sacrificed unto idols.
10: 9 Take it, and e· it up; and it shall
17:16 and shall e· her flesh, and burn her
19:18 That ye may e· the flesh of kings,

eaten

Ge 3:11 Hast thou e· of the tree, whereof I
17 hast e· of the tree, of which I
6:21 unto thee of all food that is e·,
14:24 that which the young men have e·,
27:33 I have e· of all before thou camest,
31:38 the rams of thy flock have I not e·.
41:21 when they had e· them
21 that they had e· them;
43: 2 when they had e· up the corn
Ex 12:46 In one house shall it be e·;
13: 3 there shall no leavened bread be e·.
7 Unleavened bread shall be e· seven
21:28 and his flesh shall not be e·;
22: 5 cause a field or vineyard to be e·,
29:34 it shall not be e·, because it is holy.
Le 6:16 with unleavened bread shall it be e·
23 be wholly burnt: it shall not be e·.
26 in the holy place shall it be e·,
30 no sin offering....shall be e·:
7: 6 it shall be e· in the holy place:
15 shall be e· the same day that it is
16 it shall be e· the same day that he
16 the remainder of it shall be e·:
18 his peace offerings be e· at all
19 any unclean thing shall not be e·;
10:17 Wherefore have ye not e· the sin
18 ye should indeed have e· it in the
19 and if I had e· the sin offering
11:13 they shall not be e·, they are an
34 Of all meat which may be e·,
41 an abomination; it shall not be e·.
47 between the beast that may be e·
47 and the beast that may not be e·.
17:13 any beast or fowl that may be e·;
19: 6 It shall be e· the same day ye offer
7 if it be e· at all on the third day,
23 it shall not be e· of.
22:30 On the same day it shall be e·
Nu 28:17 days shall unleavened bread be e·.
De 6:11 when thou shalt have e· and be
8:10 when thou hast e· and art full,
12 Lest when thou hast e· and art full,
12:22 the roebuck and the hart is e·,
14:19 unto you: they shall not be e·.
20: 6 vineyard, and hath not yet e· of it?
26:14 I have not e· thereof in my
29: 6 Ye have not e· bread, neither have
31:20 and they shall have e· and filled
Jos 5:12 after they had e· of the old corn
Ru 3: 7 when Boaz had e· and drunk, and
1 Sa 1: 9 Hannah rose up after they had e· in
14:30 if haply the people had e· freely
28:20 he had e· no bread all the day,
30:12 and when he had e·, his spirit came
12 for he had e· no bread, nor drunk
2 Sa 19:42 have we e· at all of the king's cost?
1Ki 13:22 and hast e· bread and drunk water
23 it came to pass, after he had e·
28 the lion had not e· the carcase,
2Ki 6:23 and when they had e· and drunk,
Ne 5:14 my brethren have not e· the bread
Job 6: 6 Can that which is unsavoury be e·
13:28 as a garment that is moth e·.
31:17 Or have e· my morsel myself alone,
17 the fatherless hath not e· thereof;
39 If I have e· the fruits thereof
Ps 69: 9 the zeal of thine house hath e· me
102: 9 For I have e· ashes like bread,
Pr 9:17 and bread e· in secret is pleasant.
23: 8 The morsel which thou hast e·
Ca 5: 1 I have e· my honeycomb with my
Isa 3:14 for ye have e· up the vineyard;
5: 5 hedge thereof, and it shall be e· up;
6:13 it shall return, and shall be e·:
44:19 I have roasted flesh, and e· it:
Jer 10:25 for they have e· up Jacob, and
24: 2 naughty figs, which could not be e·,
3 evil, very evil, that cannot be e·,
8 as the evil figs, which cannot be e·,
29:17 like vile figs, that cannot be e·.
31:29 The fathers have e· a sour grape,
Eze 4:14 have I not e· of that which dieth
18: 2 The fathers have e· sour grapes,
6 and hath not e· upon the mountains,
11 even hath e· upon the mountains.

Eze 18:15 hath not *e*· upon the mountains,
34:18 to have *e*· up the good pasture,
45:21 days; unleavened bread shall be *e*·.
Ho 10:13 ye have *e*· the fruit of lies:
Joe 1: 4 worm hath left hath the locust *e*·;
4 hath left hath the cankerworm *e*·;
4 hath left hath the caterpiller *e*·.
2:25 the years that the locust hath *e*·,
M't 14:21 And they that had *e*· were about
M'r 8: 9 And they that had *e*· were about
Lu 13:26 We have *e*· and drunk in thy
17: 8 till I have *e*· and drunken; and
Joh 2:17 zeal of thine house hath *e*· me up.
6:13 and above unto them that had *e*·.
Ac 10:10 very hungry, and would have *e*·:
14 for I have never *e*· anything that
12:23 and he was *e*· of worms,
20:11 had broken bread, and *e*·, and
27:38 when they had *e*· enough, they
Rev 10:10 as soon as I had *e*· it,

eater See also EATERS.
J'g 14:14 Out of the *e*· came forth meat,
Isa 55:10 to the sower, and bread to the *e*·:
Nah 3:12 even fall into the mouth of the *e*·.

eaters
Pro 23:20 among riotous *e*· of flesh:

eatest
Ge 2:17 the day that thou *e*· thereof thou
1Sa 1: 8 weepest thou? and why *e*· thou not?
1Ki 21: 5 spirit so sad, that thou *e*· no bread?

eateth
Ex 12:15 whosoever *e*· leavened bread from
19 whosoever *e*· that which is leavened,
Lev 7:18 the soul that *e*· of it shall bear his
20 But the soul that *e*· of the flesh
25 For whosoever *e*· the fat of the
25 even the soul that *e*· it shall be cut
27 Whatsoever soul it be that *e*· any
11:40 And he that *e*· of the carcase
14:47 and he that *e*· in the house shall
17:10 that *e*· any manner of blood; I will
10 against that soul that *e*· blood,
14 whosoever *e*· it shall be cut off.
15 every soul that *e*· that which died
19: 8 Therefore every one that *e*· it shall
Nu 13:32 *e*· up the inhabitants thereof; and
1Sa 14:24 the man that *e*· any food until
28 Cursed be the man that *e*· any food
Job 5: 5 the hungry *e*· up, and taketh it
21:25 soul, and never *e*· with pleasure.
40:15 he *e*· grass as an ox.
Ps 106:20 the similitude of an ox that *e*· grass.
Pr 13:25 The righteous *e*· to the satisfying of
30:20 she *e*·, and wipeth her mouth,
31:27 and *e*· not the bread of idleness.
Ec 4: 5 together, and *e*· his own flesh.
5:17 All his days also he *e*· in darkness,
6: 2 but a stranger *e*· it: this is vanity,
Isa 28: 4 it is yet in his hand he *e*· it up.
29: 8 man dreameth, and, behold, he *e*·;
44:16 with part thereof he *e*· flesh;
59: 5 he that *e*· of their eggs dieth,
Jer 31:30 every man that *e*· the sour grape,
M't 9:11 *e*· your Master with publicans
M'r 2:16 How is it that he *e*· and drinketh
14:18 you, One of you which *e*· with me
Lu 15: 2 receiveth sinners, and *e*· with them.
Joh 6:54 Whoso *e*· my flesh, and drinketh
56 He that *e*· my flesh, and drinketh
57 so he that *e*· me, even he shall live
58 he that *e*· of this bread shall live
13:18 He that *e*· bread with me hath lifted
Ro 14: 2 another, who is weak, *e*· herbs.
3 Let not him that *e*· despise him that
3 *e*· not; and let not him which *e*· not
3 not judge him that *e*·:
6 He that *e*·, *e*· to the Lord, for he
6 God thanks; and he that *e*· not,
6 not, to the Lord he *e*· not,
20 it is evil for that man who *e*· with
23 because he *e*· not of faith:
1Co 9: 7 and *e*· not of the fruit thereof?
7 and *e*· not of the milk of the flock?
11:29 he that *e*· and drinketh unworthily,
29 *e*· and drinketh damnation to

eating
Ex 12: 4 every man according to his *e*· shall
16:16 of it every man according to his *e*·,
18 every man according to his *e*·.
21 every man according to his *e*·: and
J'g 14: 9 went on *e*·, and came to his father
Ru 3: 3 until he shall have done *e*· and
1Sa 14:34 sin not against the Lord in *e*·
30:16 *e*· and drinking, and dancing,
1Ki 1:41 as they had made an end of *e*·.
4:20 *e*· and drinking, and making merry.
2Ki 4:40 as they were *e*· of the pottage,
1Ch 12:39 David three days, *e*· and drinking:
Job 1:13 his sons and his daughters were *e*·
18 thy sons and thy daughters were *e*·
20:23 rain it upon him while he is *e*·.
Isa 22:13 killing sheep, *e*· flesh, and drinking
66:17 *e*· swine's flesh, and the abomination,
Am 7: 2 when they had made an end of *e*·
M't 11:18 John came neither *e*· nor drinking,
19 Son of man came *e*· and drinking,
24:38 were *e*· and drinking, marrying
26:26 And as they were *e*·, Jesus took
Lu 7:33 the Baptist came neither *e*· bread
34 The Son of man is come *e*· and
10: 7 remain, *e*· and drinking such
1Co 8: 4 the *e*· of those things that are
11:21 For in *e*· every one taketh before

Ebal (*e'-bal*)
Ge 36:23 Alvan, and Manaheth, and *E*·,
De 11:29 and the curse upon mount *E*·.
27: 4 command you this day, in mount *E*·,
13 shall stand upon mount *E*· to curse;
Jos 8:30 Lord God of Israel in mount *E*·,
33 half of them over against mount *E*·;
1Ch 1:22 And *E*·, and Abimael, and Sheba,
40 Alian, and Manahath, and *E*·,

Ebed (*e'-bed*) See also EBED-MELECH.
J'g 9:26 Gaal the son of *E*· came with his
28 Gaal the son of *E*· said, Who is
30 the words of Gaal the son of *E*·, his
31 Behold, Gaal the son of *E*· and his
35 Gaal the son of *E*· went out, and
Ezr 8: 6 *E*· the son of Jonathan, and with

Ebed-melech (*e''-bed-me'-lek*)
Jer 38: 7 Now when *E*· the Ethiopian,
8 *E*· went forth out of the king's
10 Then the king commanded *E*· the
11 So *E*· took the men with him,
12 *E*· the Ethiopian said unto
39:16 Go and speak to *E*· the Ethiopian,

Eben-ezer (*eb-en-e'-zur*)
1Sa 4: 1 to battle, and pitched beside *E*·:
5: 1 and brought it from *E*· unto Ashdod.
7:12 and called the name of it *E*·,

Eber (*e'-bur*) See also HEBER.
Ge 10:21 the father of all the children of *E*·,
24 begat Salah; and Salah begat *E*·.
25 And unto *E*· were born two sons:
11:14 lived thirty years, and begat *E*·:
15 Salah lived after he begat *E*·
16 And *E*· lived four and thirty years,
17 And *E*· lived after he begat Peleg
Nu 24:24 shall afflict *E*·, and he also shall
1Ch 1:18 begat Shelah, and Shelah begat *E*·.
19 And unto *E*· were born two sons;
25 *E*·, Peleg, Reu,
8:12 *E*·, and Misham, and Shamed, who
Ne 12:20 of Sallai, Kallai; of Amok, *E*·;

Ebiasaph (*e-bi'-a-saf*) See also ABIASAPH.
1Ch 6:23 Elkanah his son, and *E*· his son,
37 the son of Assir, the son of *E*·,
9:19 the son of Kore, the son of *E*·,

ebony
Eze 27:15 a present horns of ivory and *e*·.

Ebronah (*eb-ro'-nah*)
Nu 33:34 Jotbathah, and encamped at *E*·.
35 And they departed from *E*·, and

Ed (*ed*)
Jos 22:34 children of Gad called the altar *E*·:

Edar (*e'-dar*) See also EDER.
Ge 35:21 his tent beyond the tower of *E*·.

Eden (*e'-dun*)
Ge 2: 8 planted a garden eastward in *E*·;
10 went out of *E*· to water the garden;
15 him into the garden of *E*· to dress it
3:23 him forth from the garden of *E*·,
24 east of the garden of *E*· Cherubims,
4:16 the land of Nod, on the east of *E*·.
2Ki 19:12 of *E*· which were in Thelasar?
2Ch 29:12 of Zimnah, and *E*· the son of Joah:
31:15 next him were *E*·, and Miniamin,
Isa 37:12 of *E*· which were in Telassar?
51: 3 will make her wilderness like *E*·,
Eze 27:23 Haran, and Canneh, and *E*·, the
28:13 hast been in *E*· the garden of God;
31: 9 trees of *E*·, that were in the garden
16 the trees of *E*·, the choice and best
18 greatness among the trees of *E*·?
18 brought down with the trees of *E*·
36:35 is become like the garden of *E*·;
Joe 2: 3 is as the garden of *E*· before them,
Am 1: 5 the sceptre from the house of *E*·:

Eder (*e'-dur*) See also EDAR.
Jos 15:21 were Kabzeel, and *E*·, and Jagur,
1Ch 23:23 Mahli, and *E*·, and Jeremoth, three.
24:30 Mahli, and *E*·, and Jerimoth.

edge See also EDGES; SELVEDGE; TWOEDGED.
Ge 34:26 with the *e*· of the sword,
Ex 13:20 Etham, in the *e*· of the wilderness
17:13 people with the *e*· of the sword.
26: 4 upon the *e*· of the one curtain
4 uttermost *e*· of another curtain,
5 thou make in the *e*· of the curtain
10 make fifty loops on the *e*· of the
10 fifty loops in the *e*· of the curtain
36:11 of blue on the *e*· of one curtain
12 made he in the *e*· of the curtain
17 the uttermost *e*· of the curtain
17 made he upon the *e*· of the curtain
Nu 21:24 smote him with the *e*· of the sword,
33: 6 Etham, which is in the *e*· of the
37 Hor, in the *e*· of the land of Edom.
De 13:15 that city with the *e*· of the sword,
15 thereof, with the *e*· of the sword.
20:13 thereof with the *e*· of the sword:
Jos 6:21 and ass, with the *e*· of the sword.
8:24 all fallen on the *e*· of the sword.
24 smote it with the *e*· of the sword.
10:28 smote it with the *e*· of the sword,
30 he smote it with the *e*· of the sword,
32, 35, 37 and smote it with the *e*· of
39 smote them with the *e*· of the sword,
11:11 therein with the *e*· of the sword,
12 smote them with the *e*· of the sword,
14 they smote with the *e*· of the sword.
13:27 the *e*· of the sea of Chinnereth
19:47 smote it with the *e*· of the sword,
J'g 1: 8 smitten it with the *e*· of the sword,
25 the city with the *e*· of the sword;
4:15 all his host, with the *e*· of the sword
16 Sisera fell upon the *e*· of the sword;
18:27 smote them with the *e*· of the sword,
20:37 the city with the *e*· of the sword.
48 smote them with the *e*· of the sword,
21:10 with the *e*· of the sword, with the
1Sa 15: 8 the people with the *e*· of the sword.
22:19 smote he with the *e*· of the sword,
19 and sheep, with the *e*· of the sword.
2Sa 15:14 the city with the *e*· of the sword.
2Ki 10:25 them with the *e*· of the sword;
Job 1:15 servants with the *e*· of the sword;
17 servants with the *e*· of the sword;
Ps 89:43 also turned the *e*· of his sword,
Ec 10:10 and he do not whet the *e*·,
Jer 21: 7 them with the *e*· of the sword;
31:29 the children's teeth are set on *e*·.
30 his teeth shall be set on *e*·.
Eze 18: 2 the children's teeth are set on *e*·?
Lu 21:24 shall fall by the *e*· of the sword,
Heb 11:34 escaped the *e*· of the sword, out of

edges
Ex 28: 7 joined at the two *e*· thereof;
39: 4 two *e*· was it coupled together.
J'g 3:16 a dagger which had two *e*·,
Re 2:12 hath the sharp sword with two *e*·;

edification
Ro 15: 2 his neighbour for his good to *e*·.
1Co 14: 3 speaketh unto men to *e*·,
2Co 10: 8 the Lord hath given us for *e*·,
13:10 the Lord hath given me to *e*·,

edified
Ac 9:31 the churches rest...and were *e*·;
1Co 14:17 thanks well, but the other is not *e*·.

edifieth
1Co 8: 1 puffeth up, but charity *e*·.
14: 4 an unknown tongue *e*· himself;
4 he that prophesieth *e*· the church.

edify See also EDIFIED; EDIFIETH; EDIFYING.
Ro 14:19 wherewith one may *e*· another.
1Co 10:23 lawful for me, but all things *e*· not.
1Th 5:11 each other, and *e*· one another,

edifying
1Co 14: 5 that the church may receive *e*·.
12 may excel to the *e*· of the church.
26 Let all things be done unto *e*·.
2Co 12:19 things, dearly beloved, for your *e*·.
Eph 4:12 for the *e*· of the body of Christ:
16 unto the *e*· of itself in love.
29 which is good to the use of *e*·,
1Ti 1: 4 than godly *e*· which is in faith:

Edom (*e'-dum*) See also EDOMITES; ESAU; IDUMEA; OBED-EDOM.
Ge 25:30 therefore was his name called *E*·.
32: 3 the land of Seir, the country of *E*·.
36: 1 the generations of Esau, who is *E*·.
8 Esau in mount Seir: Esau is *E*·.
16 came of Eliphaz in the land of *E*·;
17 came of Reuel in the land of *E*·;
19 are the sons of Esau, who is *E*·,
21 children of Seir in the land of *E*·.
31 kings that reigned in the land of *E*·,
32 Bela the son of Beor reigned in *E*·:
43 these be the dukes of *E*·,
Ex 15:15 the dukes of *E*· shall be amazed;
Nu 20:14 from Kadesh unto the king of *E*·,
18 *E*· said unto him, Thou shalt not
20 *E*· came out against him with much
21 *E*· refused to give Israel passage
23 by the coast of the land of *E*·,
21: 4 to compass the land of *E*·:
24:18 And *E*· shall be a possession,
33:37 in the edge of the land of *E*·.
34: 3 of Zin along by the coast of *E*·
Jos 15: 1 border of *E*· the wilderness of Zin
21 of Judah toward the coast of *E*·
J'g 5: 4 marchedst out of the field of *E*·,
11:17 sent messengers unto the king of *E*·,
17 but the king of *E*· would not hearken
18 and compassed the land of *E*·,
1Sa 14:47 against *E*·, and against the kings of
2Sa 8:14 And he put garrisons in *E*·;
14 throughout all *E*· put he garrisons,
14 they of *E*· became David's servants.
1Ki 9:26 of the Red sea, in the land of *E*·.
11:14 he was of the king's seed in *E*·.
15 came to pass, when David was in *E*·,
15 he had smitten every male in *E*·;
16 he had cut off every male in *E*·;
22:47 There was then no king in *E*·:
2Ki 3: 8 way through the wilderness of *E*·.
9 king of Judah, and the king of *E*·:
12 the king of *E*· went down to him.
20 there came water by the way of *E*·,
26 through even unto the king of *E*·:
8:20 *E*· revolted from under the hand of
22 Yet *E*· revolted from under the hand
14: 7 He slew of *E*· in the valley of salt
10 Thou hast indeed smitten *E*·,
1Ch 1:43 kings that reigned in the land of *E*·
51 the dukes of *E*· were; duke Timnah,
54 Iram. These are the dukes of *E*·.
18:11 from *E*·, and from Moab, and from
13 And he put garrisons in *E*·; and all
2Ch 8:17 at the sea side in the land of *E*·.
25:20 they sought after the gods of *E*·.
Ps 60:*title* smote in *E*· in the valley of salt
8 over *E*· will I cast out my shoe:
9 Who will lead me into *E*·?
83: 6 of *E*·, and the Ishmaelites;
108: 9 over *E*· will I cast out my shoe;
10 who will lead me into *E*·?
137: 7 the children of *E*· in the day of

Isa 11:14 lay their hand upon *E'* and Moab;
63: 1 Who is this that cometh from *E'*,
Jer 9:26 Egypt, and Judah, and *E'*, and the
25:21 *E'*, and Moab, and the children of
27: 3 And send them to the king of *E'*,
40:11 among the Ammonites, and in *E'*,
49: 7 concerning *E'*, thus saith the Lord
17 Also *E'* shall be a desolation:
20 that he hath taken against *E'*;
22 the heart of the mighty men of *E'*
La 4:21 and be glad, O daughter of *E'*,
22 thine iniquity, O daughter of *E'*;
Eze 25:12 *E'* hath dwelt against the house of
13 also stretch out mine hand upon *E'*,
14 I will lay my vengeance upon *E'*
14 do in *E'* according to mine anger
32:29 There is *E'*, her kings, and all her
Da 11:41 out of his hand, even *E'*, and Moab,
Joe 3:19 *E'* shall be a desolate wilderness,
Am 1: 6 captivity to deliver them up to *E'*:
9 up the whole captivity to *E'*, and
11 For three transgressions of *E'*, and
2: 1 burned the bones of the king of *E'*
9:12 they may possess the remnant of *E'*,
Ob 1 saith the Lord God concerning *E'*;
8 even destroy the wise men out of *E'*,
Mal 1: 4 *E'* saith, We are impoverished,

Edomite (*e'-dum-ite*) See also EDOMITES.
De 23: 7 Thou shalt not abhor an *E'*;
1Sa 21: 7 and his name was Doeg, an *E'*,
22: 9 Then answered Doeg the *E'*,
18 And Doeg the *E'* turned, and he fell
22 day, when Doeg the *E'* was there,
1Ki 11:14 unto Solomon, Hadad the *E'*:
Ps 52:*title* Doeg the *E'* came and told Saul,

Edomites (*e'-dum-ites*)
Ge 36: 9 Esau the father of the *E'* in mount
43 he is Esau the father of the *E'*.
1Ki 11: 1 *E'*, Zidonians, and Hittites;
17 Hadad fled, he and certain *E'*
2Ki 8:21 smote the *E'* which compassed him
1Ch 18:12 the son Zeruiah slew of the *E'*
13 all the *E'* became David's servants.
2Ch 21: 8 In his days the *E'* revolted from
9 smote the *E'* which compassed him
10 So the *E'* revolted from under the
25:14 come from the slaughter of the *E'*,
19 sayest, Lo, thou hast smitten the *E'*;
28:17 *E'* had come and smitten Judah,

Edrei (*ed'-re-i*)
Nu 21:33 all his people, to the battle at *E'*.
De 1: 4 which dwelt at Astaroth in *E'*:
3: 1 and all his people, to battle at *E'*.
10 all Bashan, unto Salchah and *E'*,
Jos 12: 4 that dwelt at Ashtaroth and at *E'*,
13:12 reigned in Ashtaroth and in *E'*,
31 half Gilead, and Ashtaroth, and *E'*,
19:37 And Kedesh, and *E'*, and En-hazor,

effect See also EFFECTED.
Nu 30: 8 shall make her vow...of none *e'*:
2Ch 34:22 and they spake to her to that *e'*.
Ps 33:10 devices of the people of none *e'*:
Isa 32:17 the *e'* of righteousness quietness
Jer 48:30 his lies shall not so *e'* it.
Eze 12:23 hand, and the *e'* of every vision.
M't 15: 6 commandment of God of none *e'*
M'r 7:13 the word of God of none *e'*
Ro 3: 3 make the faith of God without *e'*?
4:14 and the promise made of none *e'*:
9: 6 word of God hath taken none *e'*.
1Co 1:17 Christ should be made of none *e'*.
Gal 3:17 make the promise of none *e'*.
5: 4 Christ is become of no *e'* unto

effected
2Ch 7:11 own house, he prosperously *e'*.

effectual
1Co 16: 9 a great door and *e'* is opened
2Co 1: 6 which is *e'* in the enduring of the
Eph 3: 7 by the *e'* working of his power.
4:16 the *e'* working in the measure of
Ph'm 6 become *e'* by the acknowledging
Jas 5:16 *e'* fervent prayer of a righteous

effectually
Gal 2: 8 (For he that wrought *e'* in Peter
1Th 2:13 which *e'* worketh also in you

effeminate
1Co 6: 9 adulterers, nor *e'*, nor abusers of

egg See also EGGS.
Job 6: 6 any taste in the white of an *e'*?
Lu 11:12 Or if he shall ask an *e'*, will he

eggs
De 22: 6 whether they be young ones, or *e'*,
6 upon the young, or upon the *e'*,
Job 39:14 Which leaveth her *e'* in the earth,
Isa 10:14 as one gathereth *e'* that are left,
59: 5 They hatch cockatrice' *e'*, and
5 he that eateth of their *e'* dieth,
Jer 17:11 As the partridge sitteth on *e'*,

Eglah (*eg'-lah*) See also MICHAL.
2Sa 3: 5 Ithream, by *E'* David's wife.
1Ch 3: 3 the sixth, Ithream by *E'* his wife.

Eglaim (*eg'-la-im*) See also EN-EGLAIM.
Isa 15: 8 the howling thereof unto *E'*,

Eglon (*eg'-lon*)
Jos 10: 3 and unto Debir king of *E'*, saying,
5 the king of Lachish, the king of *E'*,
23 the king of Lachish, the king of *E'*.
34 Lachish Joshua passed unto *E'*,
36 And Joshua went up from *E'*,
37 to all that he had done to *E'*;
12:12 The king of *E'*, one; the king of
Jos 15:39 Lachish, Bozkath, and *E'*,
J'g 3:12 Lord strengthened *E'* the king of
14 children of Israel served *E'* the
15 Israel sent a present unto *E'* the
17 brought the present unto *E'* the
17 And *E'* was a very fat man.

Egypt (*e'-jipt*) See also EGYPTIAN; MIZRAIM
Ge 12:10 and Abram went down into *E'*
11 was come near to enter into *E'*,
14 when Abram was come into *E'*,
13: 1 Abram went up out of *E'*, he,
10 of the Lord, like the land of *E'*,
15:18 given this land, from the river of *E*
21:21 him a wife out of the land of *E'*.
25:18 *E'*, as thou goest toward Assyria:
26: 2 and said, Go not down into *E'*;
37:25 going to carry it down to *E'*.
28 and they brought Joseph into *E'*.
36 sold him into *E'* unto Potiphar,
39: 1 Joseph was brought down to *E'*;
40: 1 that the butler of the king of *E'*
1 offended their lord the king of *E'*.
5 the baker of the king of *E'*, which
41: 8 the magicians of *E'*, and all the
19 in all the land of *E'* for badness:
29 throughout all the land of *E'*:
30 be forgotten in the land of *E'*;
33 and set him over the land of *E'*.
34 up the fifth part of the land of *E'*
36 which shall be in the land of *E'*;
41 have set thee over all the land of *E'*.
43 him ruler over all the land of *E'*.
44 hand or foot in all the land of *E'*.
45 went out over all the land of *E'*.
46 he stood before Pharaoh king of *E'*.
46 went throughout all the land of *E'*.
48 which were in the land of *E'*, and
53 that was in the land of *E'*,
54 all the land of *E'* there was bread.
55 all the land of *E'* was famished,
56 famine waxed sore in the land of *E'*.
57 And all the countries came into *E'*
42: 1 saw that there was corn in *E'*,
2 heard that there is corn in *E'*:
3 went down to buy corn in *E'*.
43: 2 which they had brought out of *E'*,
15 and went down to *E'*, and stood
45: 4 your brother, whom ye sold into *E'*.
8 throughout all the land of *E'*.
9 God hath made me lord of all *E'*:
13 tell my father of all my glory in *E'*,
18 give you the good of the land of *E'*,
19 you wagons out of the land of *E'*
20 good of all the land of *E'* is yours.
23 laden with the good things of *E'*,
25 they went up out of *E'*, and came
26 governor over all the land of *E'*.
46: 3 fear not to go down into *E'*; for
4 I will go down with thee into *E'*;
6 and came into *E'*, Jacob, and all
7 seed brought he with him into *E'*.
8 of Israel, which came into *E'*,
20 unto Joseph in the land of *E'* were
26 that came with Jacob into *E'*,
27 Joseph, which were born him in *E'*,
27 which came into *E'*, were
47: 6 The land of *E'* is before thee; in
11 them a possession in the land of *E'*,
13 the land of *E'* and all the land of
14 that was found in the land of *E'*,
15 money failed in the land of *E'*,
20 all the land of *E'* for Pharaoh;
21 from one end of the borders of *E'*
26 made it a law over the land of *E'*
27 Israel dwelt in the land of *E'*,
28 And Jacob lived in the land of *E'*
29 bury me not, I pray thee, in *E'*:
30 thou shalt carry me out of *E'*,
48: 5 born unto thee in the land of *E'*
5 I came unto thee into *E'*, are mine
50: 7 and all the elders of the land of *E'*,
14 Joseph returned into *E'*, he, and
22 Joseph dwelt in *E'*, he, and his
26 and he was put in a coffin in *E'*.
Ex 1: 1 of Israel, which came into *E'*;
5 for Joseph was in *E'* already.
8 there arose up a new king over *E'*,
15 And the king of *E'* spake to the
17 and did not as the king of *E'*
18 And the king of *E'* called for the
2:23 of time, that the king of *E'* died:
3: 7 of my people which are in *E'*, and
10 the children of Israel out of *E'*.
11 the children of Israel out of *E'*?
12 brought forth the people out of *E'*,
16 that which is done to you in *E'*:
17 you up out of the affliction of *E'*
18 unto the king of *E'*, and ye shall
19 the king of *E'* will not let you go,
20 stretch out my hand, and smite *E'*
4:18 unto my brethren which are in *E'*,
19 in Midian, Go, return into *E'*:
20 and he returned to the land of *E'*:
21 return into *E'*, see that thou do all
5: 4 the king of *E'* said unto them,
12 throughout all the land of *E'* to
6:11 speak unto Pharaoh king of *E'*,
13 and unto Pharaoh king of *E'*,
13 of Israel out of the land of *E'*.
26 from the land of *E'* according to
27 spake to Pharaoh king of *E'*,
27 out the children of Israel from *E'*:
28 spake unto Moses in the land of *E'*.
29 thou unto Pharaoh king of *E'* all
7: 3 and my wonders in the land of *E'*.
4 lay my hand upon *E'*, and bring
Ex 7: 4 land of *E'* by great judgments.
5 stretch forth mine hand upon *E'*,
11 magicians of *E'*, they also did in
19 thine hand upon the waters of *E'*,
19 blood throughout all the land of *E'*,
21 blood throughout all the land of *E'*.
22 the magicians of *E'* did so with
8: 5 to come up upon the land of *E'*.
6 his hand over the waters of *E'*;
6 came up, and covered the land of *E'*.
7 up frogs upon the land of *E'*.
16 become lice throughout all...of *E'*.
17 became lice throughout all...of *E'*.
24 houses, and into all the land of *E'*:
9: 4 of Israel and the cattle of *E'*:
6 and all the cattle of *E'* died:
9 small dust in all the land of *E'*,
9 beast, throughout all the land of *E'*.
18 hail, such as hath not been in *E'*
22 may be hail in all the land of *E'*,
22 field, throughout the land of *E'*.
23 rained hail upon the land of *E'*.
24 none like it in all the land of *E'*
25 smote throughout all the land of *E'*
10: 2 what things I have wrought in *E'*,
7 thou not yet that *E'* is destroyed?
12 over the land of *E'* for the locusts,
12 may come up upon the land of *E'*,
13 forth his rod over the land of *E'*,
14 went up over all the land of *E'*,
14 and rested in all the coasts of *E'*:
15 field, through all the land of *E'*.
19 one locust in all the coasts of *E'*.
21 be darkness over the land of *E'*,
22 in all the land of *E'* three days:
11: 1 more upon Pharaoh, and upon *E'*;
3 was very great in the land of *E'*,
4 will I go out into the midst of *E'*:
5 firstborn in the land of *E'* shall die,
6 cry throughout all the land of *E'*,
9 be multiplied in the land of *E'*.
12: 1 Moses and Aaron in the land of *E'*,
12 through the land of *E'* this night,
12 all the firstborn in the land of *E'*,
12 gods of *E'* I will execute judgment.
13 you, when I smite the land of *E'*.
17 your armies out of the land of *E'*:
27 of the children of Israel in *E'*,
29 all the firstborn in the land of *E'*,
30 and there was a great cry in *E'*;
39 which they brought forth out of *E'*,
39 because they were thrust out of *E'*,
40 who dwelt in *E'*, was four hundred
41 Lord went out from the land of *E'*.
42 them out from the land of *E'*:
51 of Israel out of the land of *E'*
13: 3 day, in which ye came out from *E'*,
8 me when I came forth out of *E'*.
9 the Lord brought thee out of *E'*.
14 the Lord brought us out from *E'*,
15 in the land of *E'*, both the firstborn
16 the Lord brought us forth out of *E'*.
17 see war, and they return to *E'*:
18 harnessed out of the land of *E'*.
14: 5 the king of *E'* that the people fled:
7 the chariots of *E'*, and captains
8 the heart of Pharaoh king of *E'*,
11 Because there were no graves in *E'*,
11 us, to carry us forth out of *E'*?
12 that we did tell thee in *E'*, saying,
16: 1 departing out of the land of *E'*.
3 hand of the Lord in the land of *E'*,
6 you out from the land of *E'*:
32 you forth from the land of *E'*.
17: 3 thou hast brought us up out of *E'*,
18: 1 hath brought Israel out of *E'*;
19: 1 gone forth out of the land of *E'*,
20: 2 brought thee out of the land of *E*,
22:21 ye were strangers in the land of *E'*.
23: 9 ye were strangers in the land of *E'*.
15 in it thou camest out from *E'*:
29:46 out of the land of *E'*, that I may
32: 1 us up out of the land of *E'*,
4 thee up out of the land of *E'*.
7 broughtest out of the land of *E'*,
8 thee up out of the land of *E'*.
11 brought forth out of the land of *E'*
23 brought us up out of the land of *E'*,
33: 1 brought up out of the land of *E'*,
34:18 Abib thou camest out from *E'*.
Le 11:45 of the land of *E'*, to be your God:
18: 3 the land of *E'*, wherein ye dwelt,
19:34 strangers in the land of *E'*: I am
36 brought you out of the land of *E'*.
22:33 brought you out of the land of *E'*,
23:43 brought them out of the land of *E'*:
25:38 forth out of the land of *E'*, to give
42 forth out of the land of *E'*: they
55 forth out of the land of *E'*: I am
26:13 forth out of the land of *E'*, that ye
45 forth out of the land of *E'* in the
Nu 1: 1 come out of the land of *E'*, saying,
3:13 all the firstborn in the land of *E'*
8:17 of *E'* I sanctified them for myself.
9: 1 come out of the land *E'*, saying,
11: 5 fish, which we did eat in *E'* freely;
18 eat? for it was well with us in *E'*:
20 Why came we forth out of *E'*?
13:22 built seven years before Zoan in *E'*.)
14: 2 we had died in the land of *E'*!
3 not better for us to return into *E'*?
4 captain, and let us return into *E'*.
19 people, from *E'* even until now.
22 I did in *E'* and in the wilderness,
15:41 brought you out of the land of *E*,
20: 5 up out of *E'*, to bring us in unto

Nu 20:15 E', and we have dwelt in E' a long
16 hath brought us forth out of E':
21: 5 out of E' to die in the wilderness?
22: 5 is a people come out from E':
11 out of E', which covereth the face
23:22 God brought them out of E'; he
24: 8 God brought him forth out of E';
26: 4 went forth out of the land of E'.
59 her mother bare to Levi in E':
32:11 of the men that came up out of E',
33: 1 went forth out of the land of E'
38 the land of E', in the first day of
34: 5 from Azmon unto the river of E',
De 1:27 the land of E', to deliver us into
30 did for you in E' before your eyes;
4:20 of the iron furnace, even out of E';
34 Lord your God did for you in E'
37 with his mighty power out of E';
45 after they came forth out of E',
46 they were come forth out of E':
5: 6 brought thee out of the land of E',
15 wast a servant in the land of E',
6:12 thee forth out of the land of E',
21 We were Pharaoh's bondmen in E';
21 the Lord brought us out of E' with
22 wonders, great and sore, upon E',
7: 8 the hand of Pharaoh king of E'.
15 none of the evil diseases of E',
18 did unto Pharaoh, and unto all E';
8:14 thee forth out of the land of E',
9: 7 didst depart out of the land of E',
12 thou hast brought forth out of E'
26 out of E' with a mighty hand.
10:19 were strangers in the land of E'.
22 Thy fathers went down into E' with
11: 3 acts, which he did in the midst of E'
3 unto Pharaoh the king of E', and
4 what he did unto the army of E',
10 it, is not as the land of E', from
13: 5 brought you out of the land of E',
10 brought thee out of the land of E',
15:15 wast a bondman in the land of E',
16: 1 God brought thee forth out of E' by
3 forth out of the land of E' in haste:
3 out of the land of E' all the days of
6 that thou camest forth out of E'.
12 that thou wast a bondman in E':
17:16 cause the people to return to E',
20: 1 brought thee up out of the land of E'.
23: 4 way, when ye came forth out of E';
24: 9 that ye were come forth out of E'.
18 that thou wast a bondman in E',
22 wast a bondman in the land of E':
25:17 when ye were come forth out of E';
26: 5 and he went down into E', and
8 the Lord brought us forth out of E'
28:27 will smite thee with the botch of E',
60 upon thee all the diseases of E',
68 Lord shall bring thee into E' again
29: 2 before your eyes in the land of E'
16 we have dwelt in the land of E';
25 them forth out of the land of E':
34:11 sent him to do in the land of E'
Jos 2:10 for you, when ye came out of E';
5: 4 All the people that came out of E',
4 the way, after they came out of E'.
5 way as they came forth out of E',
6 men of war, which came out of E',
9 I rolled away the reproach of E'
9: 9 of him, and all that he did in E',
13: 3 From Sihor, which is before E',
15: 4 and went out unto the river of E';
47 her villages, unto the river of E',
24: 4 his children went down into E'.
5 and I plagued E', according to that
6 I brought your fathers out of E':
7 have seen what I have done in E':
14 other side of the flood, and in E';
17 our fathers out of the land of E',
32 of Israel brought up out of E',
J'g 2: 1 said, I made you to go up out of E',
12 brought them out of the land of E',
6: 8 Israel, I brought you up from E',
13 not the Lord bring us up from E'?
11:13 land, when they came up out of E',
16 When Israel came up from E',
19:30 came up out of the land of E' unto
1Sa 2:27 thy father, when they were in E'
8: 8 day that I brought them up out of E'
10:18 I brought up Israel out of E', and
12: 6 fathers up out of the land of E'.
8 When Jacob was come into E', and
8 brought forth your fathers out of E',
15: 2 the way, when he came up from E'.
6 when they came up out of E'.
7 to Shur, that is over against E'.
27: 8 to Shur, even unto the land of E'.
30:13 I am a young man of E', servant
2Sa 7: 6 up the children of Israel out of E',
23 thou redeemedst to thee from E',
1Ki 3: 1 affinity with Pharaoh king of E',
4:21 and unto the border of E': they
30 country, and all the wisdom of E'.
6: 1 were come out of the land of E',
8: 9 they came out of the land of E'.
16 my people Israel out of E', I chose
21 brought them out of the land of E'.
51 thou broughtest forth out of E',
53 broughtest our fathers out of E',
65 in of Hamath unto the river of E',
9: 9 their fathers out of the land of E',
16 For Pharaoh king of E' had gone
10:28 had horses brought out of E', and
29 and went out of E' for six hundred
11:17 servants with him, to go into E';
18 came to E', unto Pharaoh king of E';

1Ki 11:21 And when Hadad heard in E' that
40 fled into E', unto Shishak king of E',
40 and was in E' until the death of
12: 2 son of Nebat, who was yet in E',
2 Solomon, and Jeroboam dwelt in E';
28 brought thee up out of the land of E'.
14:25 that Shishak king of E' came up
2Ki 17: 4 sent messengers to So king of E',
7 them up out of the land of E',
7 the hand of Pharaoh king of E',
36 you up out of the land of E' with
18:21 of this bruised reed, even upon E',
21 is Pharaoh king of E' unto all that
24 put thy trust on E' for chariots and
21:15 their fathers came forth out of E',
23:29 Pharaoh-nechoh king of E' went up
34 and he came to E', and died there.
24: 7 And the king of E' came not again
7 had taken from the river of E' unto
7 all that pertained to the king of E'.
25:26 arose, and came to E': for they
1Ch 13: 5 Israel together, from Shihor of E'
17:21 whom thou hast redeemed out of E'?
2Ch 1:16 had horses brought out of E', and
17 and brought forth out of E' a
5:10 Israel, when they came out of E'.
6: 5 forth my people out of the land of E'
7: 8 in of Hamath unto the river of E'.
22 them forth out of the land of E',
9:26 Philistines, and to the border of E'.
28 unto Solomon horses out of E',
10: 2 the son of Nebat, who was in E',
2 that Jeroboam returned out of E'.
12: 2 king Rehoboam, Shishak king of E'
3 that came with him out of E';
9 Shishak king of E' came up against
20:10 they came out of the land of E',
26: 8 abroad even to the entering in of E';
35:20 Necho king of E' came up to fight
36: 3 And the king of E' put him down at
4 the king of E' made Eliakim his
4 his brother, and carried him to E'.
Ne 9: 9 the affliction of our fathers in E',
18 that brought thee up out of E',
Ps 68:31 Princes shall come out of E';
78:12 of their fathers, in the land of E',
43 he had wrought his signs in E', and
51 And smote all the firstborn in E';
80: 8 Thou hast brought a vine out of E':
81: 5 he went out through the land of E':
10 brought thee out of the land of E':
105:23 Israel also came into E'; and Jacob
38 E' was glad when they departed:
106: 7 understood not thy wonders in E';
21 which had done great things in E';
114: 1 When Israel went out of E', the
135: 8 Who smote the firstborn of E', both
9 into the midst of thee, O E',
136:10 that smote E' in their firstborn:
Pr 7:16 carved works, with fine linen of E'.
Isa 7:18 uttermost part of the rivers of E',
10:24 against thee, after the manner of E'.
26 he lift it up after the manner of E'.
11:11 and from E', and from Pathros, and
16 he came up out of the land of E'.
19: 1 The burden of E'. Behold, the Lord
1 swift cloud, and shall come into E':
1 and the idols of E' shall be moved
1 and the heart of E' shall melt in
3 And the spirit of E' shall fail in the
12 of hosts hath purposed upon E'.
13 they have also seduced E', even
14 and they have caused E' to err in
15 shall there be any work for E',
16 day shall E' be like unto women:
17 of Judah shall be a terror unto E',
18 five cities in the land of E' speak
19 Lord in the midst of the land of E',
20 the Lord of hosts in the land of E':
21 the Lord shall be known to E', and
22 And the Lord shall smite E': he
23 shall there be a highway out of E'
23 the Assyrian shall come into E', and
24 shall Israel be the third with E'
25 Blessed be E' my people, and
20: 3 for a sign and wonder upon E' and
4 uncovered, to the shame of E'.
5 expectation, and of E' their glory.
23: 5 As at the report concerning E', so
27:12 of the river unto the stream of E',
13 and the outcasts in the land of E',
30: 2 That walk to go down into E', and
2 and to trust in the shadow of E'!
3 the trust in the shadow of E' your
31: 1 that go down to E' for help; and
36: 6 the staff of this broken reed, on E';
6 so is Pharaoh king of E' to all that
9 servants, and put thy trust on E'
43: 3 I gave E' for thy ransom, Ethiopia
45:14 The labour of E', and merchandise
52: 4 people went down aforetime into E'
Jer 2: 6 brought us up out of the land of E',
18 hast thou to do in the way of E',
36 thou also shalt be ashamed of E',
7:22 brought them out of the land of E',
25 came forth out of the land of E'
9:26 E', and Judah, and Edom, and the
11: 4 them forth out of the land of E',
7 them up out of the land of E',
16:14 of Israel out of the land of E';
23: 7 of Israel out of the land of E';
24: 8 them that dwell in the land of E':
25:19 Pharaoh king of E', and his
26:21 afraid, and fled, and went into E';
22 the king sent men into E', namely,
22 and certain men with him into E'.

Jer 26:23 they fetched forth Urijah out of E',
31:32 bring them out of the land of E';
32:20 signs and wonders in the land of E',
21 people Israel out of the land of E'
34:13 them forth out of the land of E', out
37: 5 army was come forth out of E':
7 to help you, shall return to E' into
41:17 Bethlehem, to go to enter into E',
42:14 but we will go into the land of E',
15 set your faces to enter into E',
16 overtake you there in the land of E'
16 follow close after you there in E';
17 that set their faces to go into E'
18 you, when ye shall enter into E':
19 of Judah; Go ye not into E':
43: 2 sent thee to say, Go not into E' to
7 they came into the land of E': for
11 he shall smite the land of E',
12 fire in the houses of the gods of E';
12 array himself with the land of E',
13 that is in the land of E'; and the
44: 1 Jews which dwell in the land of E',
8 unto other gods in the land of E',
12 their faces to go into the land of E'
12 consumed, and fall in the land of E';
13 them that dwell in the land of E',
14 which are gone into the land of E'
15 people that dwelt in the land of E',
24 all Judah that are in the land of E':
26 Judah that dwell in the land of E';
26 man of Judah in all the land of E',
27 the land of E' shall be consumed by
28 shall return out of the land of E'
28 into the land of E' to sojourn there,
30 give Pharaoh-hophra king of E'
46: 2 Against E', against the army of
2 Pharaoh-necho king of E', which
8 E' riseth up like a flood, and his
11 balm, O virgin, the daughter of E':
13 come and smite the land of E'.
14 Declare ye in E', and publish in
17 Pharaoh king of E' is but a noise;
19 O thou daughter dwelling in E',
20 E' is like a very fair heifer, but
24 The daughter of E' shall be
25 of No, and Pharaoh, and E', with
Eze 17:15 sending his ambassadors into E',
19: 4 him with chains into the land of E'.
20: 5 known unto them in the land of E',
6 to bring them forth of the land of E'
7 not yourselves with the idols of E':
8 did they forsake the idols of E':
8 them in the midst of the land of E'.
9 them forth out of the land of E'.
10 to go forth out of the land of E',
36 in the wilderness of the land of E',
23: 3 they committed whoredoms in E';
8 her whoredoms brought from E':
19 played the harlot in the land of E'.
27 brought from the land of E':
27 them, nor remember E' any more.
27: 7 linen with broidered work from E'
29: 2 face against Pharaoh king of E',
2 against him, and against all E':
3 Pharaoh king of E', the great
6 E' shall know that I am the Lord,
9 the land of E' shall be desolate
10 make the land of E' utterly waste
12 I will make the land of E' desolate
14 will bring again the captivity of E',
19 I will give the land of E' unto
20 given him the land of E' for his
30: 4 And the sword shall come upon E',
4 when the slain shall fall in E',
6 They also that uphold E' shall fall;
8 when I have set a fire in E', and
9 upon them, as in the day of E':
10 make the multitude of E' to cease
11 shall draw their swords against E',
13 no more a prince of the land of E':
13 I will put a fear in the land of E'.
15 fury upon Sin, the strength of E';
16 And I will set fire in E': Sin shall
18 I shall break there the yokes of E:
19 will I execute judgments in E':
21 the arm of Pharaoh king of E';
22 I am against Pharaoh king of E',
25 stretch it out upon the land of E'.
31: 2 speak unto Pharaoh king of E',
32: 2 lamentation for Pharaoh king of E',
12 they shall spoil the pomp of E',
15 shall make the land of E' desolate,
16 shall lament for her, even for E',
18 man, wail for the multitude of E',
Da 9:15 people forth out of the land of E'
11: 8 carry captives into E' their gods,
42 and the land of E' shall not escape.
43 over all the precious things of E':
Ho 2:15 she came up out of the land of E';
7:11 without heart: they call to E',
16 be their derision in the land of E'.
8:13 their sins: they shall return to E'.
9: 3 Ephraim shall return to E', and
6 E' shall gather them up, Memphis
11: 1 him, and called my son out of E'.
5 shall not return into the land of E',
11 shall tremble as a bird out of E',
12: 1 and oil is carried into E'.
9 thy God from the land of E' will yet
13 the Lord brought Israel out of E',
13: 4 Lord thy God from the land of E',
Joe 3:19 E' shall be a desolation, and Edom
Am 2:10 up from the land of E', and led you
3: 1 up from the land of E', saying,
9 and in the palaces in the land of E',
4:10 pestilence after the manner of E':

Am 8: 8 and drowned, as by the flood of E'.
9: 5 be drowned, as by the flood of E'.
7 up Israel out of the land of E'?
Mic 6: 4 thee up out of the land of E',
7:15 of thy coming out of the land of E'
Na 3: 9 Ethiopa and E' were her strength,
Hag 2: 5 with you when ye came out of E',
Zec 10:10 them again also out of the land of E',
11 and the sceptre of E' shall depart
14:18 if the family of E' go not up, and
19 This shall be the punishment of E',
M't 2:13 flee into E', and be thou there
14 by night, and departed into E':
15 Out of E' have I called my son.
19 in a dream to Joseph in E',
Ac 2:10 in E', and in the parts of Libya
7: 9 with envy, sold Joseph into E':
10 the sight of Pharaoh king of E';
10 he made him governor over E'
11 came a dearth over all the land of E'
12 Jacob heard that there was corn in E',
15 Jacob went down into E', and died,
17 people grew and multiplied in E',
34 of my people which is in E',
34 now come, I will send thee into E'.
36 wonders and signs in the land of E',
39 hearts turned back again into E',
40 brought us out of the land of E',
13:17 as strangers in the land of E',
Heb 3:16 that came out of E' by Moses.
8: 9 to lead them out of the land of E';
11:26 riches than the treasures in E':
27 By faith he forsook E', not fearing
Jude 5 the people out of the land of E',
Re 11: 8 spiritually is called Sodom and E',

Egyptian (*e-jip'-shun*) See also EGYPTIAN'S; EGYPTIANS.
Ge 16: 1 an E', whose name was Hagar.
3 wife, took Hagar her maid the E',
21: 9 Sarah saw the son of Hagar the E',
25:12 Hagar the E', Sarah's handmaid,
39: 1 an E', bought him of the hands of
2 in the house of his master the E'.
Ex 1:19 women are not as the E' women;
2:11 he spied an E' smiting an Hebrew,
12 slew the E', and hid him in the sand.
14 to kill me, as thou killedst the E'?
19 An E' delivered us out of the hand
Le 24:10 woman, whose father was an E',
De 23: 7 thou shalt not abhor an E'; because
1Sa 30:11 And they found an E' in the field,
2Sa 23:21 And he slew an E', a goodly man:
21 the E' had a spear in his hand;
1Ch 2:34 And Sheshan had a servant, an E',
11:23 slew an E', a man of great stature,
Isa 11:15 destroy the tongue of the E' sea;
19:23 and the E' into Assyria, and
Ac 7:24 was oppressed, and smote the E':
28 as thou didst the E' yesterday?
21:38 Art not thou that E', which before

Egyptian's (*e-jip'-shuns*)
Ge 39: 5 the Lord blessed the E' house for
2Sa 23:21 plucked the spear out of the E'
1Ch 11:23 E' hand was a spear like a weaver's
23 out of the E' hand, and slew him

Egyptians (*e-jip'-shuns*)
Ge 12:12 when the E' shall see thee, that
14 Abram was come into Egypt, the E'
41:55 Pharaoh said unto all the E', Go
56 storehouses, and sold unto the E';
43:32 by themselves, and for the E',
32 the E' might not eat bread with the
32 is an abomination unto the E'.
45: 2 the E' and the house of Pharaoh
46:34 is an abomination unto the E'.
47:15 the E' came unto Joseph, and said,
20 for the E' sold every man his field,
50: 3 the E' mourned for him threescore
11 is a grievous mourning to the E':
Ex 1:13 the E' made the children of Israel
3: 8 them out of the hand of the E',
9 wherewith the E' oppress them.
21 people favour in the sight of the E':
22 and ye shall spoil the E'.
6: 5 whom the E' kept in bondage;
6 from under the burdens of the E',
7 from under the burdens of the E'.
7: 5 E' shall know that I am the Lord,
18 the E' shall lothe to drink of the
21 and the E' could not drink of
24 E' digged round about the river
8:21 the houses of the E' shall be full
26 abomination of the E' to the Lord
26 abomination of the E' before their
9:11 the magicians, and upon all the E'.
10: 6 and the houses of all the E';
11: 3 people favour in the sight of the E'.
7 a difference between the E' and
12:23 will pass through to smite the E';
27 when he smote the E', and
30 and all his servants, and all the E';
33 E' were urgent upon the people,
35 borrowed of the E' jewels of silver,
36 people favour in the sight of the E',
36 required. And they spoiled the E'.
14: 4 E' may know that I am the Lord.
9 But the E' pursued after them, all
10 the E' marched after them; and
12 alone, that we may serve the E'?
12 been better for us to serve the E',
13 the E' whom ye have seen to day,
17 I will harden the hearts of the E',
18 E' shall know that I am the Lord,
20 between the camp of the E' and
Ex 14:23 E' pursued, and went in after them
24 looked unto the host of the E'
24 and troubled the host of the E',
25 the E' said, Let us flee from the
25 fighteth for them against the E'.
26 waters may come again upon the E',
27 the E' fled against it; and the Lord
27 the E' in the midst of the sea.
30 day out of the hand of the E';
30 saw the E' dead upon the sea shore.
31 which the Lord did upon the E':
15:26 which I have brought upon the E':
18: 8 and to the E' for Israel's sake,
9 delivered out of the hand of the E'.
10 you out of the hand of the E',
10 from under the hand of the E'.
19: 4 have seen what I did unto the E',
32:12 Wherefore should the E' speak,
Nu 14:13 the Lord, Then the E' shall hear it,
20:15 the E' vexed us, and our fathers:
33: 3 high hand in the sight of all the E'.
4 the E' buried all their firstborn,
De 26: 6 E' evil entreated us, and afflicted
Jos 24: 6 E' pursued after your fathers
7 and the E', and brought the sea
J'g 6: 9 you out of the hand of the E',
10:11 Did not I deliver you from the E',
1Sa 4: 8 are the Gods that smote the E'
6: 6 do ye harden your hearts, as the E'
10:18 the E', and out of the hand of all
2Ki 7: 6 the Hittites, and the kings of the E',
Ezr 9: 1 Ammonites, the Moabites, the E',
Isa 19: 2 I will set the E' against the E':
4 And the E' will I give over into the
21 E' shall know the Lord in that day,
23 E' shall serve with the Assyrians.
20: 4 Assyria lead away...E' prisoners,
30: 7 the E' shall help in vain, and to
31: 3 the E' are men, and not God; and
Jer 43:13 the gods of the E' shall he burn
La 5: 6 to the E', and to the Assyrians,
Eze 16:26 committed fornication with the E'
23:21 in bruising thy teats by the E' for
29:12 scatter the E' among the nations,
13 of forty years will I gather the E'
30:23, 26 scatter the E' among the
Ac 7:22 in all the wisdom of the E',
Heb 11:29 E' assaying to do were drowned.

Ehi (*e'-hi*) See also AHARAH.
Ge 46:21 Gera, and Naaman, E', and Rosh,

Ehud (*e'-hud*)
J'g 3:15 raised them up a deliverer, E'
16 E' made him a dagger which had
20 And E' came unto him; and he was
20 E' said, I have a message from God
21 E' put forth his left hand, and took
23 E' went forth through the porch,
26 And E' escaped while they tarried,
4: 1 of the Lord, when E' was dead.
1Ch 7:10 Benjamin, and E', and Chenaanah,
8: 6 And these are the sons of E': these

eight See also EIGHTEEN.
Ge 5: 4 Seth were e' hundred years:
7 e' hundred and seven years, and
10 e' hundred and fifteen years,
13 e' hundred and forty years,
16 Jared e' hundred and thirty years,
17 e' hundred ninety and five years:
19 begat Enoch e' hundred years, and
17:12 is e' days old shall be circumcised
21: 4 his son Isaac being e' days old, as
22:23 these e' Milcah did bear to Nahor,
Ex 26: 2 shall be e' and twenty cubits,
25 And they shall be e' boards, and
36: 9 curtain was twenty and e' cubits,
30 And there were e' boards; and
Nu 2:24 and e' thousand and an hundred,
3:28 e' thousand and six hundred,
4:48 were e' thousand and five hundred
7: 8 four wagons and e' oxen he gave
29:29 on the sixth day e' bullocks,
35: 7 Levites shall be forty and e' cities:
De 2:14 Zered, was thirty and e' years;
Jos 21:41 forty and e' cities with their
J'g 3: 8 Chushan-rishathaim e' years.
12:14 and he judged Israel e' years.
1Sa 4:15 Eli was ninety and e' years old;
17:12 was Jesse; and he had e' sons:
2Sa 23: 8 against e' hundred, whom he slew
24: 9 e' hundred thousand valiant men
1Ki 7:10 of ten cubits, stones of e' cubits.
2Ki 8:17 he reigned e' years in Jerusalem.
10:36 Samaria was twenty and e' years.
22: 1 Josiah was e' years old when he
1Ch 12:24 six thousand and e' hundred,
30 twenty thousand and e' hundred,
35 and e' thousand and six hundred.
16:38 their brethren, three score and e';
23: 3 man, was thirty and e' thousand.
24: 4 and e' among the sons of Ithamar
25: 7 was two hundred fourscore and e'.
2Ch 11:21 begat twenty and e' sons, and
13: 3 e' hundred thousand chosen men,
21: 5 he reigned e' years in Jerusalem.
20 he reigned in Jerusalem e' years,
29:17 the house of the Lord in e' days;
34: 1 Josiah was e' years old when he
36: 9 Jehoiachin was e' years old when
Ezr 2: 6 thousand e' hundred and twelve.
16 Ater of Hezekiah, ninety and e'.
23 Anathoth, an hundred twenty and e'.
41 Asaph, an hundred twenty and e'.
8:11 and with him twenty and e' males.
Ne 7:11 and e' hundred and eighteen.
13 Zattu, e' hundred forty and five.
Ne 7:15 Binnui, six hundred forty and e'.
16 Bebai, six hundred twenty and e'.
21 Ater of Hezekiah, ninety and e'.
22 three hundred twenty and e'.
26 an hundred fourscore and e'.
27 an hundred twenty and e'.
44 of Asaph, an hundred forty and e'.
45 of Shobai, an hundred thirty and e'.
11: 6 threescore and e' valiant men.
8 Sallai, nine hundred twenty and e'.
12 were e' hundred twenty and two:
14 of valour an hundred twenty and e':
Ec 11: 2 a portion to seven, and also to e';
Jer 41:15 escaped from Johanan with e' men,
52:29 from Jerusalem e' hundred thirty
Eze 40: 9 he the porch of the gate, e' cubits;
31, 34, 37 going up to it had e' steps.
41 e' tables, whereupon they slew
Mic 5: 5 shepherds, and e' principal men.
Lu 2:21 when e' days were accomplished
9:28 an e' days after these sayings,
Joh 5: 5 an infirmity thirty and e' years.
20:26 after e' days again his disciples
Ac 9:33 which had kept his bed e' years,
1Pe 3:20 is, e' souls were saved by water.

eighteen
Ge 14:14 house, three hundred and e',
J'g 3:14 the king of Moab e' years.
10: 8 children of Israel: e' years,
20:25 Israel again e' thousand men;
44 Benjamin e' thousand men;
2Sa 8:13 salt, being e' thousand men.
1Ki 7:15 brass, e' cubits high apiece:
2Ki 24: 8 Jehoiachin was e' years old
25:17 of one pillar was e' cubits,
1Ch 12:31 tribe of Manasseh e' thousand,
18:12 the valley of salt e' thousand.
26: 9 and brethren, strong men, e'.
29: 7 of brass e' thousand talents,
2Ch 11:21 for he took e' wives, and
Ezr 8: 9 him two hundred and e' males.
18 his sons and his brethren, e';
Ne 7:11 eight hundred and e'.
Jer 52:21 of one pillar was e' cubits;
Eze 48:35 about e' thousand measures;
Lu 13: 4 Or those e', upon whom
11 spirit of infirmity e' years,
16 lo, these e' years, be

eighteenth
1Ki 15: 1 the e' year of king Jeroboam
2Ki 3: 1 Israel in Samaria the e' year
22: 3 in the e' year of king Josiah,
23:23 in the e' year of king Josiah,
1Ch 24:15 to Hezer, the e' to Aphses,
25:25 The e' to Hanani, he, his sons,
2Ch 13: 1 the e' year of king Jeroboam
34: 8 in the e' year of his reign,
35:19 e' year of the reign of Josiah
Jer 32: 1 the e' year of Nebuchadrezzar.
52:29 the e' year of Nebuchadrezzar

eighteen-thousand See EIGHTEEN and THOUSAND.

eighth
Ex 22:30 the e' day thou shalt give it me.
Le 9: 1 it came to pass on the e' day,
12: 3 the e' day the flesh of his foreskin
14:10 e' day he shall take two he lambs
23 he shall bring them on the e' day
15:14 e' day he shall take to him two
29 e' day she shall take unto her two
22:27 from the e' day and thenceforth
23:36 e' day shall be a holy convocation
39 on the e' day shall be a sabbath.
25:22 ye shall sow the e' year, and eat
Nu 6:10 e' day he shall bring two turtles,
7:54 the e' day offered Gamaliel the son
29:35 On the e' day ye shall have a
1Ki 6:38 month Bul, which is the e' month,
8:66 the e' day he sent the people away:
12:32 ordained a feast in the e' month,
33 the fifteenth day of the e' month,
16:29 in the thirty and e' year of Asa
2Ki 15: 8 the thirty and e' year of Azariah
24:12 took him in the e' year of his reign.
1Ch 12:12 Johanan the e', Elzabad the
24:10 to Hakkoz, the e' to Abijah,
25:15 The e' to Jeshaiah, he, his sons
26: 5 Peulthai the e': for God blessed
27:11 The e' captain for the e' month
2Ch 7: 9 e' day they made a solemn assembly:
29:17 and on the e' day of the month
34: 3 For in the e' year of his reign,
Ne 8:18 the e' day was a solemn assembly,
Eze 43:27 upon the e' day, and so forward,
Zec 1: 1 In the e' month, in the second year
Lu 1:59 e' day they came to circumcise
Ac 7: 8 and circumcised him the e' day;
Ph'p 3: 5 Circumcised the e' day, of the
2Pe 2: 5 but saved Noah the e' person,
Re 17:11 was, and is not, even he is the e',
21:20 the e', beryl; the ninth, a topaz;

eight-hundred See EIGHT and HUNDRED.

eightieth
1Ki 6: 1 in the four hundred and e' year

eight-thousand See EIGHT and THOUSAND.

eighty
Ge 5:25 an hundred e' and seven years,
26 seven hundred e' and two years,
28 lived an hundred e' and two years,

either See also NEITHER.
Ge 31:24 speak not to Jacob e' good or bad.
29 thou speak not to Jacob e' good or bad.
Le 10: 1 took e' of them his censer, and

Le 13:49 or in the skin, e' in the warp, or
51, 53 in the garment, e' in the warp,
57 still in the garment, e' in the warp,
58 And the garment, e' warp, or woof,
59 or linen, e' in the warp, or woof,
22:23 E' a bullock or a lamb that hath
25:49 E' his uncle, or his uncle's son,
Nu 6: 2 e' man or woman shall separate
22:26 no way to turn e' to the right hand
24:13 e' good or bad of mine own mind;
De 17: 3 e' the sun, or moon, or any of
28:51 also shall not leave thee e' corn,
J'g 9: 2 e' that all the sons of Jerubbaal,
1Sa 20: 2 will do nothing e' great or small,
25:31 e' that thou hast shed blood causeless,
30: 2 slew not any, e' great or small,
1Ki 7:15 did compass e' of them about.
10:19 and there were stays on e' side
18:27 e' he is talking, or he is pursuing,
1Ch 21:12 E' three years' famine; or three
2Ch 18: 9 king of Judah sat e' of them on
Ec 9: 1 man knoweth e' love or hatred
11: 6 not whether shall prosper, e' this
Isa 7:11 ask it e' in the depth, or in the
17: 8 e' the groves, or the images.
Eze 21:16 one way or other, e' on the right
M't 6:24 for e' he will hate the one, and
12:33 E' make the tree good, and his
Lu 6:42 E' how canst thou say to thy
15: 8 E' what woman having ten pieces
16:13 two masters: for e' he will hate
Joh 19:18 on e' side one, and Jesus in
Ac 17:21 but e' to tell, or to hear some
1Co 14: 6 shall speak to you e' by revelation,
Ph'p 3:12 attained, e' were already perfect:
Jas 3:12 bear olive berries? e' a vine, figs?
Re 22: 2 and on e' side of the river,

Eker (*e'-ker*)
1Ch 2:27 were, Maaz, and Jamin, and E'.

Ekron (*ec'-ron*) See also EKRONITES.
Jos 13: 3 Egypt, even unto the borders of E'
15:11 unto the side of E' northward:
45 E', with her towns and her villages:
46 From E' even unto the sea, all
19:43 Elon, and Thimnathah, and E',
J'g 1:18 with the coast thereof, and E'
1Sa 5:10 they sent the ark of God to E'.
10 pass, as the ark of God came to E',
6:16 had seen it, they returned to E'
17 one, for Gath one, for E' one;
7:14 to Israel, from E' even unto Gath;
17:52 the valley, and to the gates of E'.
52 even unto Gath, and unto E'.
2Ki 1: 2 enquire of Baal-zebub the god of E'
3, 6 of Baal-zebub the god of E'?
16 enquire of Baal-zebub the god of E',
Jer 25:20 and E', and the remnant of Ashdod,
Am 1: 8 I will turn mine hand against E':
Zep 2: 4 and E' shall be rooted up.
Zec 9: 5 and E'; for her expectation shall
7 in Judah, and E' as a Jebusite.

Ekronites (*ek'-ron-ites*)
Jos 13: 3 the Gittites, and the E'; also the
1Sa 5:10 that the E' cried out, saying, They

El See BETH-EL; EL-BETH-EL; EL-ELOHE-ISRAEL; EL-HARAN; JIPHTHAH-EL; MIGDAL-EL.

Eladah (*el'-a-dah*)
1Ch 7:20 E' his son, and Tahath his son,

Elah (*e'-lah*)
Ge 36:41 Duke Aholibamah, duke E', duke
1Sa 17: 2 and pitched by the valley of E',
19 were in the valley of E', fighting
21: 9 thou slewest in the valley of E',
1Ki 4:18 Shimei the son of E', in Benjamin.
16: 6 E' his son reigned in his stead.
8 E' the son of Baasha to reign
13 sins of Baasha, and the sins of E'
14 the rest of the acts of E', and all
2Ki 15:30 the son of E' made a conspiracy
17: 1 began Hoshea the son of E' to reign
18: 1 the third year of Hoshea son of E'
9 seventh year of Hoshea son of E'
1Ch 1:52 Duke Aholibamah, duke E', duke
4:15 Jephunneh; Iru, E', and Naam:
15 and the sons of E', even Kenaz.
9: 8 the son of Jeroham, and E'

Elam (*e'-lam*) See also ELAMITES; PERSIA.
Ge 10:22 children of Shem; E', and Ashur,
14: 1 Chedorlaomer king of E', and
9 With Chedorlaomer the king of E',
1Ch 1:17 The sons of Shem; E', and Asshur,
8:24 Hananiah, and E', and Antothijah,
26: 3 E' the fifth, Jehohanan the sixth,
Ezr 2: 7 The children of E', a thousand two
31 The children of the other E',
8: 7 And of the sons of E'; Jeshaiah
10: 2 son of Jehiel, one of the sons of E',
26 sons of E'; Mattaniah, Zechariah,
Ne 7:12 children of E', a thousand two
34 The children of the other E',
10:14 people; Parosh, Pahath-moab, E',
12:42 and Malchijah, and E', and Ezer.
Isa 11:11 and from Cush, and from E', and
21: 2 Go up, O E': besiege, O Media;
22: 6 E' bare the quiver with chariots
Jer 25:25 and all the kings of E', and all the
49:34 Jeremiah the prophet against E',
35 Behold, I will break the bow of E',
36 upon E' will I bring the four winds
36 the outcasts of E' shall not come.
37 For I will cause E' to be dismayed
38 And I will set my throne in E', and
39 bring again the captivity of E',
Eze 32:24 is E and all her multitude round
Da 8: 2 which is in the province of E';

Elamites (*e'-lam-ites*) See also PERSIANS.
Ezr 4: 9 the Dehavites, and the E',
Ac 2: 9 Parthians, and Medes, and E',

Elasah (*el'-a-sah*) See also ELEASAH.
Ezr 10:22 Nethaneel, Jozabad, E'.
Jer 29: 3 hand of E' the son of Shaphan,

Elath (*e'-lath*) See also ELOTH.
De 2: 8 the way of the plain from E',
2Ki 14:22 built E', and restored it to Judah,
16: 6 king of Syria recovered E' to Syria,
6 and drave the Jews from E':
6 Syrians came to E', and dwelt there

El-beth-el (*el-beth'-el*)
Ge 35: 7 an altar, and called the place E';

Eldaah (*el'-da-ah*)
Ge 25: 4 and Hanoch, and Abidah, and E'.
1Ch 1:33 and Henoch, and Abida, and E',

Eldad (*el'-dad*)
Nu 11:26 the name of the one was E',
27 E' and Medad do prophesy in the

elder See also ELDERS.
Ge 10:21 the brother of Japheth the e',
25:23 and the e' shall serve the younger.
27:42 these words of Esau her e' son
29:16 the name of the e' was Leah,
1Sa 18:17 Behold my e' daughter Merab,
1Ki 2:22 for he is mine e' brother;
Job 15:10 men, much e' than thy father.
32: 4 because they were e' than he.
Eze 16:46 thine e' sister is Samaria, she and
61 sisters, thine e' and thy younger:
23: 4 names of them were Aholah the e',
Lu 15:25 Now his e' son was in the field:
Ro 9:12 The e' shall serve the younger.
1Ti 5: 1 Rebuke not an e', but entreat him
2 e' women as mothers; the younger
19 an e' receive not an accusation,
1Pe 5: 1 I exhort, who am also an e',
5 submit yourselves unto the e'.
2Jo 1 The e' unto the elect lady and her
3Jo 1 The e' unto the well beloved Gaius,

elders
Ge 50: 7 of Pharaoh, the e' of his house,
7 all the e' of the land of Egypt,
Ex 3:16 Go, and gather the e' of Israel
18 come, thou and the e' of Israel,
4:29 gathered together all the e' of the
12:21 Moses called for all the e' of Israel,
17: 5 take with thee of the e' of Israel;
6 did so in the sight of the e' of
18:12 Aaron came, all the e' of Israel,
19: 7 called for the e' of the people,
24: 1 seventy of the e' of Israel; and
9 and seventy of the e' of Israel:
14 he said unto the e', Tarry ye here
Le 4:15 the e' of the congregation shall
9: 1 and his sons, and the e' of Israel;
Nu 11:16 seventy men of the e' of Israel,
16 knowest to be the e' of the people,
24 seventy men of the e' of the people,
25 and gave it unto the seventy e':
30 the camp, he and the e' of Israel.
16:25 and the e' of Israel followed him.
22: 4 Moab said unto the e' of Midian,
7 And the e' of Moab and the
7 and the e' of Midian departed
De 5:23 heads of your tribes, and your e';
19:12 Then the e' of his city shall send
21: 2 thy e' and thy judges shall come
3 e' of that city shall take an heifer,
4 And the e' of that city shall bring
6 And all the e' of that city,
19 him out unto the e' of his city,
20 shall say unto the e' of his city,
22:15 virginity unto the e' of the city
16 damsel's father shall say unto the e',
17 the cloth before the e' of the city.
18 And the e' of that city shall take
25: 7 go up to the gate unto the e',
8 the e' of his city shall call him,
9 unto him in the presence of the e',
27: 1 with the e' of Israel commanded
29:10 your e', and your officers, with all
31: 9 and unto all the e' of Israel.
28 Gather unto me all the e' of your
32: 7 thy e', and they will tell thee.
Jos 7: 6 eventide, he and the e' of Israel,
8:10 he and the e' of Israel, before the
33 all Israel, and their e', and officers,
9:11 our e' and all the inhabitants
20: 4 his cause in the ears of the e' of
23: 2 for their e', and for their heads,
24: 1 and called for the e' of Israel,
31 days of the e' that overlived Joshua,
J'g 2: 7 days of the e' that outlived Joshua,
8:14 and the e' thereof, even three score
16 And he took the e' of the city,
11: 5 the e' of Gilead went to fetch
7 Jephthah said unto the e' of Gilead,
8 e' of Gilead said unto Jephthah,
9 Jephthah said unto the e' of Gilead,
10 the e' of Gilead said unto Jephthah,
11 Jephthah went with the e' of Gilead,
21:16 the e' of the congregation said,
Ru 4: 2 took ten men of the e' of the city.
4 and before the e' of my people.
9 And Boaz said unto the e',
11 and the e', said, We are witnesses.
1Sa 4: 3 the e' of Israel said, Wherefore
8: 4 Then all the e' of Israel gathered
11: 3 the e' of Jabesh said unto him,
15:30 thee, before the e' of my people,
16: 4 the e' of the town trembled at his
30:26 he sent of the spoil unto the e' of
2Sa 3:17 communication with the e' of
5: 3 the e' of Israel came to the king
12:17 the e' of his house arose, and went
17: 4 Absalom well, and all the e' of
15 Absalom and the e' of Israel;
19:11 Speak unto the e' of Judah, saying,
1Ki 8: 1 Solomon assembled the e' of Israel,
3 And all the e' of Israel came,
20: 7 king of Israel called all the e' of
8 And all the e' and all the people
21: 8 and sent the letters unto the e' and
11 even the e' and the nobles who were
2Ki 6:32 and the e' sat with him;
32 came to him, he said to the e',
10: 1 unto the rulers of Jezreel, to the e',
5 the e' also, and the bringers up
19: 2 and the e' of the priests, covered
23: 1 gathered unto him all the e' of
1Ch 11: 3 Therefore came all the e' of Israel,
15:25 So David, and the e' of Israel,
21:16 Then David and the e' of Israel,
2Ch 5: 2 Then Solomon assembled the e' of
4 And all the e' of Israel came;
34:29 gathered together all the e' of
Ezr 5: 5 of their God was upon the e' of
9 Then asked we those e', and said
6: 7 and the e' of the Jews build this
8 what ye shall do to the e' of these
14 And the e' of the Jews builded,
10: 8 counsel of the princes and the e',
14 with them the e' of every city,
Ps 107:32 praise him in the assembly of the e'.
Pr 31:23 when he sitteth among the e' of the
Isa 37: 2 and the e' of the priests covered
Jer 26:17 Then rose up certain of the e' of
29: 1 Jerusalem unto the residue of the e'
La 1:19 my priests and mine e' gave up the
2:10 The e' of the daughter of Zion
4:16 priests, they favoured not the e'.
5:12 the faces of e' were not honoured.
14 The e' have ceased from the gate,
Eze 8: 1 and the e' of Judah sat before me,
14: 1 Then came certain of the e' of
20: 1 certain of the e' of Israel came to
3 of man speak unto the e' of Israel,
Joe 1:14 assembly, gather the e' and all the
2:16 congregation, assemble the e',
M't 15: 2 transgress the tradition of the e'?
16:21 suffer many things of the e' and
21:23 and the e' of the people came unto
26: 3 scribes, and the e' of the people,
47 chief priests and e' of the people.
57 scribes and the e' were assembled.
59 the chief priests, and e', and all
27: 1 chief priests and e' of the people
3 silver to the chief priests and e',
12 accused of the chief priests and e',
20 the chief priests and e' persuaded
41 with the scribes and e', said,
28:12 they were assembled with the e',
M'r 7: 3 holding the tradition of the e'.
5 according to the tradition of the e',
8:31 and be rejected of the e', and of the
11:27 priests, and the scribes, and the e',
14:43 priests and the scribes and the e'.
53 priests and the e' and the scribes.
15: 1 with the e' and scribes and the
Lu 7: 3 he sent unto him the e' of the Jews,
9:22 and be rejected of the e' and chief
20: 1 scribes came upon him with the e',
22:52 captains of the temple, and the e',
66 the e' of the people and the chief
Ac 4: 5 that their rulers, and e', and
8 of the people, and e' of Israel,
23 chief priests and e' had said unto
6:12 the people, and the e', and the
11:30 and sent it to the e' by the hands
14:23 ordained them e' in every church,
15: 2 unto the apostles and e' about this
4 and of the apostles and e', and they
6 And the apostles and e' came
22 Then pleased it the apostles and e',
23 The apostles and e' and brethren
16: 4 were ordained of the apostles and e'
20:17 and called the e' of the church.
21:18 and all the e' were present.
22: 5 and all the estate of the e':
23:14 came to the chief priests and e',
24: 1 high priest descended with the e',
25:15 the chief priests and the e' of the
1Ti 5:17 Let the e' that rule well be counted
Tit 1: 5 ordain e' in every city, as I had
Heb 11: 2 For by it the e' obtained a good
Jas 5:14 let him call for the e' of the church;
1Pe 5: 1 The e' which are among you I
Re 4: 4 I saw four and twenty e' sitting,
10 The four and twenty e' fall down
5: 5 And one of the e' saith unto me,
6 and in the midst of the e',
8 and four and twenty e' fell down
11 and the beasts and the e':
14 the four and twenty e' fell down
7:11 and about the e' and the four beasts,
13 And one of the e' answered, saying
11:16 the four and twenty e', which sat
14: 3 before the four beasts, and the e':
19: 4 the four and twenty e' and the four

eldest
Ge 24: 2 Abraham said unto his e' servant
27: 1 he called Esau his e' son, and
15 took goodly raiment of her e' son
44:12 began at the e', and left at the
Nu 1:20 children of Reuben, Israel's e' son.

Nu 26: 5 Reuben, the e' son of Israel: the
1Sa 17:13 And the three e' sons of Jesse
14 and the three e' followed Saul.
28 Eliab his e' brother heard when he
2Ki 3:27 Then he took his e' son that
2Ch 22: 1 of men . . . had slain all the e'.
Job 1:13, 18 wine in their e' brother's
Joh 8: 9 beginning at the e', even unto the

Elead (e'-le-ad)
1Ch 7:21 and Ezer, and E', whom the men

Elealeh (el-e-a'-leh)
Nu 32: 3 Heshbon, and E', and Shebam,
37 of Reuben built Heshbon, and E',
Isa 15: 4 And Heshbon shall cry, and E':
16: 9 with my tears, O Heshbon, and E':
Jer 48:34 the cry of Heshbon even unto E',

Eleasah (el-e'-a-sah) See also ELASAH.
1Ch 2:39 begat Helez, and Helez begat E',
40 E' begat Sisamai, and Sisamai
8:37 Rapha was his son, E' his son,
9:43 Rephaiah his son, E' his son,

Eleazar (el-e-a'-zar)
Ex 6:23 bare him Nadab, and Abihu, E',
25 E' Aaron's son took him one of the
28: 1 even Aaron, Nadab and Abihu, E'
Le 10: 6 Moses said unto Aaron, and unto E'
12 spake unto Aaron, and unto E'
16 and he was angry with E' and
Nu 3: 2 Nadab the firstborn, and Abihu, E',
4 E' and Ithamar ministered in the
32 E' the son of Aaron the priest shall
4:16 to the office of E' the son of Aaron
16:37 Speak unto E' the son of Aaron the
39 E' the priest took the brazen
19: 3 ye shall give her unto E' the priest,
4 E' the priest shall take of her blood
20:25 Take Aaron and E' his son, and
26, 28 garments, and put them upon E'
28 Moses and E' came down from the
25: 7 when Phinehas, the son of E', the
11 Phinehas, the son of E', the son of
26: 1 Lord spake unto Moses and unto E'
3 E' the priest spake with them in
60 was born Nadab, and Abihu, E',
63 Moses and E' the priest, who
27: 2 stood before Moses, and before E'
19 And set him before E' the priest,
21 he shall stand before E' the priest,
22 took Joshua, and set him before E'
31: 6 them and Phinehas the son of E'
12 and the spoil, unto Moses, and E'
13 Moses, and E' the priest, and all
21 E' the priest said unto the men of
26 thou, and E' the priest, and the
29 it of their half, and give it unto E'
31 Moses and E' the priest did as the
41 the Lord's heave offering, unto E'
51, 54 Moses and E' the priest took the
32: 2 E' the priest, and unto the princes
28 Moses commanded E' the priest,
34:17 E' the priest, and Joshua the son
De 10: 6 E' his son ministered in the priest's
Jos 14: 1 in the land of Canaan, which E' the
17: 4 they came near before E' the priest,
19:51 are the inheritances, which E' the
21: 1 the fathers of the Levites unto E'
22:13 of Gilead, Phinehas the son of E'
31 the son of E' the priest said unto
32 the son of E' the priest, and the
24:33 E' the son of Aaron died; and they
J'g 20:28 son of E', the son of Aaron, stood
1Sa 7: 1 sanctified E' his son to keep the ark
2Sa 23: 9 after him was E' the son of Dodo
1Ch 6: 3 of Aaron; Nadab, and Abihu, E',
4 E' begat Phinehas, Phinehas begat
50 these are the sons of Aaron. E' his
9:20 Phinehas the son of E' was the
11:12 after him was E' the son of Dodo,
23:21 The sons of Mahli; E', and Kish.
22 E' died, and had no sons,
24: 1 of Aaron; Nadab, and Abihu, E',
2 therefore E' and Ithamar executed
3 both Zadok of the sons of E', and
4 chief men found of the sons of E'
4 Among the sons of E' there were
5 were of the sons of E', and of the
6 household being taken for E',
28 Of Mahli came E', who had no sons.
Ezr 7: 5 the son of E', the son of Aaron the
8:33 and with him was E' the son of
10:25 Miamin, and E', and Malchijah,
Ne 12:42 Shemaiah, and E', and Uzzi,
M't 1:15 And Eliud begat E'; and E' begat

elect See also ELECTED; ELECT'S.
Isa 42: 1 e', in whom my soul delighteth;
45: 4 sake, and Israel mine e',
65: 9 mine e' shall inherit it, and my
22 mine e' shall long enjoy the work
M't 24:24 they shall deceive the very e'.
31 and shall gather together his e'
M'r 13:22 if it were possible, even the e'.
27 and shall gather together his e'
Lu 18: 7 shall not God avenge his own e',
Ro 8:33 any thing to the charge of God's e'?
Col 3:12 Put on therefore, as the e' of God,
1Ti 5:21 Lord Jesus Christ, and the e' angels,
Tit 1: 1 according to the faith of God's e',
1Pe 1: 2 E' according to the foreknowledge
2: 6 a chief corner stone, e', precious:
2Joh 1 The elder unto the e' lady and her
13 The children of thy e' sister greet

elected
1Pe 5:13 e' together with you, saluteth you;

election
Ro 9:11 the purpose of God according to e'
11: 5 according to the e' of grace.
7 the e' hath obtained it, and the rest
28 as touching the e', they are beloved
1Th 1: 4 brethren beloved, your e' of God.
2Pe 1:10 make your calling and e' sure:

elect's
M't 24:22 for the e' sake those days shall be
M'r 13:20 for the e' sake, whom he hath
2Ti 2:10 endure all things for the e' sakes,

El-elohe-Israel (el-el-o''-he-iz'-rah-el)
Ge 33:20 there an altar, and called it E'

elements
Ga 4: 3 in bondage under the e' of the
9 to the weak and beggarly e',
2Pe 3:10 the e' shall melt with fervent heat,
12 the e' shall melt with fervent heat?

Eleph (e'-lef)
Jos 18:28 And Zelah, E', and Jebusi which is

eleven
Ge 32:22 took....his e' sons, and passed
37: 9 and the moon and the e' stars
Ex 26: 7 e' curtains shalt thou make.
8 e' curtains shall be all of one
36:14 e' curtains he made them.
15 the e' curtains were of one
Nu 29:20 on the third day e' bullocks,
De 1: 2 e' days' journey from Horeb
Jos 15:51 e' cities with their villages.
J'g 16: 5 one of us e' hundred pieces of
17: 2 e' hundred shekels of silver
3 restored the e' hundred shekels
2Ki 23:36 reign; and he reigned e' years
24:18 reign, and he reigned e' years
2Ch 36: 5, 11 and he reigned e' years in
Jer 52: 1 reigned e' years in Jerusalem.
Eze 40:49 and the breadth e' cubits;
M't 28:16 Then the e' disciples went away
M'r 16:14 he appeared unto the e' as they
Lu 24: 9 told all these things unto the e',
33 found the e' gathered together,
Ac 1:26 was numbered with the e' apostles.
2:14 Peter, standing up with the e',

eleven-hundred See ELEVEN and HUNDRED.

eleventh
Nu 7:72 the e' day Pagiel...offered:
De 1: 3 in the fortieth year, in the e'
1Ki 6:38 in the e' year, in the month
2Ki 9:29 in the e' year of Joram the
25: 2 the e' year of king Zedekiah.
1Ch 12:13 the tenth, Machbanai the e'.
24:12 The e' to Eliashib, the twelfth
25:18 The e' to Azareel, he, his sons,
27:14 The e' captain for the e' month
Jer 1: 3 of the e' year of Zedekiah the
39: 2 in the e' year of Zedekiah, in
52: 5 was besieged unto the e' year
Eze 26: 1 in the e' year, in the first day
30:20 came to pass in the e' year,
31: 1 the e' year, in the third month,
Zec 1: 7 twentieth day of...e' month,
M't 20: 6 about the e' hour he went out,
9 that were hired about the e' hour,
Re 21:20 the e', a jacinth; the twelfth, an

Elhanan (el-ha'-nan)
2Sa 21:19 where E' the son of Jaare-oregim,
23:24 E' the son of Dodo of Bethlehem,
1Ch 11:26 brother of Joab, E' the son of Dodo
20: 5 E' the son of Jair slew Lahmi

Eli (e'-li) See also ELI'S; ELOI.
1Sa 1: 3 sons of E', Hophni and Phinehas,
9 now E' the priest sat upon a seat
12 Lord, that E' marked her mouth.
13 E' thought she had been drunken.
14 And E' said unto her, How long
17 Then E' answered and said, Go in
25 and brought the child to E'.
2:11 minister unto the Lord before E'
12 sons of E' were sons of Belial;
20 And E' blessed Elkanah and his
22 Now E' was very old, and heard
27 a man of God unto E', and said
3: 1 ministered unto the Lord before E'.
2 when E' was laid down in his place,
5 And he ran unto E', and said, Here
6 And Samuel arose and went to E',
8 he arose and went to E', and said,
8 And E' perceived that the Lord had
9 E' said unto Samuel, Go, lie down:
12 I will perform against E' all things
14 I have sworn unto the house of E',
15 Samuel feared to show E' the vision.
16 Then E' called Samuel, and said,
4: 4 sons of E', Hophni and Phinehas,
11 E', Hophni and Phinehas, were slain.
13 E' sat upon a seat by the wayside
14 E' heard the noise of the crying,
14 man came in hastily, and told E'.
15 Now E' was ninety and eight
16 And the man said unto E', I am he
14: 3 son of Phinehas, the son of E',
1Ki 2:27 spake concerning the house of E'
M't 27:46 E', E', lama sabachthani? that is

Eliab (e'-le-ab) See also ELIAB'S; ELIEL.
Nu 1: 9 Of Zebulun; E' the son of Helon.
2: 7 E' the son of Helon shall be captain
7:24 the third day E' the son of Helon,
29 the offering of E' the son of Helon.
10:16 of the children of Zebulun was E'
16: 1 Dathan and Abiram, the sons of E',
12 Dathan and Abiram, the sons of E':
Nu 26: 8 And the sons of Pallu; E'.
9 the sons of E'; Nemuel, and Dathan,
De 11: 6 the sons of E', the son of Reuben:
1Sa 16: 6 he looked on E', and said, Surely
17:13 were E' the firstborn, and next unto
28 E' his eldest brother heard when
1Ch 2:13 And Jesse begat his firstborn E',
6:27 E' his son, Jeroham his son,
12: 9 Obadiah the second, E' the third,
15:18 Jehiel, and Unni, E', and Benaiah,
20 Unni, and E', and Maaseiah,
16: 5 Mattithiah, and E', and Benaiah,
2Ch 11:18 Abihail the daughter of E' the son

Eliab's (e'-le-abs)
1Sa 17:28 E' anger was kindled against

Eliada (e-li'-a-dah) See also ELIADAH.
2Sa 5:16 Elishama, and E', and Eliphalet.
1Ch 3: 8 E', and Eliphelet, nine.
2Ch 17:17 E' a mighty man of valour,

Eliadah (e-li'-a-dah) See also ELIADA.
1Ki 11:23 Rezon the son of E', which fled

Eliah (e-li'-ah) See also ELIJAH.
1Ch 8:27 Jaresiah, and E', and Zichri,
Ezr 10:26 and Abdi, and Jeremoth, and E'.

Eliahba (e-li'-ah-bah)
2Sa 23:32 E' the Shaalbonite, of the sons of
1Ch 11:33 the Baharumite, E' the Shaalbonite,

Eliakim (e-li'-a-kim) See also JEHOIAKIM.
2Ki 18:18 there came out to them E' the son
26 Then said E' the son of Hilkiah,
37 Then came E' the son of Hilkiah,
19: 2 And he sent E', which was over the
23:34 Pharaoh-nechoh made E' the son of
2Ch 36: 4 of Egypt made E' his brother king
Ne 12:41 the priests; E', Maaseiah, Miniamin,
Isa 22:20 I will call my servant E' the son of
36: 3 Then came forth unto him E',
11 Then said E', and Shebna and Joah
22 Then came E', the son of Hilkiah,
37: 2 And he sent E', who was over the
M't 1:13 Abiud begat E'; and E' begat Azor;
Lu 3:30 Jonan, which was the son of E',

Eliam (e'-le-am)
2Sa 11: 3 Bath-sheba, the daughter of E',
23:34 E' the son of Ahithophel the

Elias (e-li'-as) See also ELIJAH.
M't 11:14 is Elias, which was for to come.
16:14 some, E'; and others, Jeremias,
17: 3 Moses and E' talking with him.
4 and one for Moses, and one for E'.
10 scribes that E' must first come?
11 E' truly shall first come, and
12 unto you, That E' is come already,
27:47 This man calleth for E'.
49 whether E' will come to save him.
M'r 6:15 Others said, That it is E'.
8:28 but some say, E'; and others,
9: 4 unto them E' with Moses:
5 and one for Moses, and one for E'.
11 that E' must first come?
12 E' verily cometh first, and
13 unto you, That E' is indeed come,
15:35 Behold, he calleth E'.
36 whether E' will come to take him
Lu 1:17 in the spirit and power of E',
4:25 were in Israel in the days of E',
26 But unto none of them was E'
9: 8 of some, that E' had appeared;
19 but some say, E'; and others say,
30 men, which were Moses and E':
33 and one for Moses, and one for E':
54 consume them, even as E' did?
Joh 1:21 What then? Art thou E'? And he
25 nor E', neither that prophet?
Ro 11: 2 what the scripture saith of E'?
Jas 5:17 E' was a man subject to like

Eliasaph (e-li'-a-saf)
Nu 1:14 Of Gad; E' the son of Deuel.
2:14 of the sons of Gad shall be E'
3:24 Gershonites shall be E' the son of
7:42 the sixth day E' the son of Deuel,
47 the offering of E' the son of Deuel.
10:20 tribe of the children of Gad was E'

Eliashib (e-li'-a-shib)
1Ch 3:24 Hodaiah, and E', and Pelaiah,
24:12 eleventh to E', the twelfth to Jakim,
Ezr 10: 6 chamber of Johanan the son of E':
24 Of the singers also; E':
27 Elioenai, E', Mattaniah,
36 Vaniah, Meremoth, E',
Ne 3: 1 Then E' the high priest rose up
20 unto the door of the house of E'
21 from the door of the house of E'
21 even to the end of the house of E'.
12:10 Joiakim also begat E',
10 and E' begat Joiada,
22 Levites in the days of E', Joiada,
23 the days of Johanan the son of E'.
13: 4 E' the priest, having the oversight
7 the evil that E' did for Tobiah,
28 the son of E' the high priest, was

Eliathah (e-li'-a-thah)
1Ch 25: 4 Hanani, E', Giddalti,
27 The twentieth to E', he, his sons,

Elidad (e-li'-dad)
Nu 34:21 of Benjamin, E' the son of Chislon.

Eliel (e'-le-el) See also ELIAB.
1Ch 5:24 Epher, and Ishi, and E', and Azriel,
6:34 the son of Jeroham, the son of E',
8:20 And Elienai, and Zilthai, and E',
22 And Ishpan, and Heber, and E',

1Ch 11:46 *E*· the Mahavite, and Jeribai
47 *E*·, and Obed, and Jasiel the
12:11 Attai the sixth, *E*· the seventh,
15: 9 *E*· the chief, and his brethren
11 Shemaiah, and *E*·, and Amminadab,
2Ch 31:13 Jozabad, and *E*·, and Ismachiah,

Elienai *(e-li-e'-nahee)*
1Ch 8:20 *E*·, and Zilthai, and Eliel,

Eliezer *(e-li-e'-zur)*
Ge 15: 2 the steward of my house is this *E*·
Ex 18: 4 the name of the other was *E*·;
1Ch 7: 8 Zemira, and Joash, and *E*·,
15:24 Benaiah, and *E*·, the priests, did
23:15 of Moses were, Gershom, and *E*·.
17 sons of *E*· were, Rehabiah the chief.
17 And *E*· had none other sons;
26:25 brethren by *E*·; Rehabiah his son,
27:16 the ruler of the Reubenites was *E*·
2Ch 20:37 Then *E*· the son of Dodavah of
Ezr 8:16 Then sent I for *E*·, for Ariel,
10:18 Maaseiah, and *E*·, and Jarib,
23 Pethahiah, Judah, and *E*·.
31 of the sons of Harim, *E*·, Ishijah,
Lu 3:29 which was the son of *E*·,

Elihoenai *(e-li-ho-e'-nahee)* See also ELIOENAI.
Ezr 8: 4 *E*· the son of Zerahiah, and with

Elihoreph *(e-li-ho'-ref)*
1Ki 4: 3 *E*· and Ahiah, the sons of Shisha,

Elihu *(e-li'-hew)*
1Sa 1: 1 the son of *E*·, the son of Tohu,
1Ch 12:20 Jozabad, and *E*·, and Zilthai,
26: 7 strong men, *E*·, and Semachiah,
27:18 *E*·, one of the brethren of David:
Job 32: 2 Then was kindled the wrath of *E*·
4 *E*· had waited till Job had spoken,
5 *E*· saw that there was no answer
6 *E*· the son of Barachel the Buzite
34: 1 *E*· answered and said,
35: 1 *E*· spake moreover, and said,
36: 1 *E*· also proceeded, and said,

Elijah *(e-li'-jah)* See also ELIAH; ELIAS.
1Ki 17: 1 *E*· the Tishbite, who was of the
13 *E*· said unto her, Fear not; go and
15 did according to the saying of *E*·:
16 of the Lord, which he spake by *E*·.
18 she said unto *E*·, What have I to do
22 the Lord heard the voice of *E*·; and
23 *E*· took the child, and brought him
23 and *E*· said, See, thy son liveth.
24 the woman said to *E*·, Now by this
18: 1 Lord came to *E*· in the third year,
2 *E*· went to shew himself unto Ahab.
7 was in the way, behold, *E*· met him:
7 Art thou that my lord *E*·?
8 go, tell thy lord, Behold, *E*· is here.
11 Go, tell thy lord, Behold, *E*· is here.
14 Go, tell thy lord, Behold, *E*· is here:
15 *E*· said, As the Lord of hosts liveth,
16 and Ahab went to meet *E*·.
17 it came to pass, when Ahab saw *E*·,
21 *E*· came unto all the people, and
22 Then said *E*· unto the people, I,
25 *E*· said unto the prophets of Baal,
27 *E*· mocked them, and said, Cry
30 *E*· said unto all the people, Come
31 *E*· took twelve stones, according to
36 *E*· the prophet came near, and said,
40 And *E*· said unto them, Take the
40 *E*· brought them down to the brook
41 *E*· said unto Ahab, Get thee up, eat
42 *E*· went up to the top of Carmel;
46 the hand of the Lord was on *E*·;
19: 1 told Jezebel all that *E*· had done,
2 Jezebel sent a messenger unto *E*·,
9 unto him, What doest thou here, *E*·?
13 it was so, when *E*· heard it, that he
13 and said, What doest thou here, *E*·?
19 and *E*· passed by him, and cast his
20 he left the oxen, and ran after *E*·,
21 Then he arose, and went after *E*·,
21:17 the Lord came to *E*· the Tishbite,
20 Ahab said to *E*·, Hast thou found
28 word of the Lord came to *E*· the
2Ki 1: 3 said to *E*· the Tishbite, Arise, go up
4 shalt surely die. And *E*· departed.
8 And he said, It is *E*· the Tishbite.
10 *E*· answered and said to the captain
12 *E*· answered and said unto them,
13 came and fell on his knees before *E*·,
15 the angel of the Lord said unto *E*·,
17 of the Lord which *E*· had spoken.
2: 1 Lord would take up *E*· into heaven
1 *E*· went with Elisha from Gilgal.
2 *E*· said unto Elisha, Tarry here, I
4 *E*· said unto him, Elisha, tarry here,
6 *E*· said unto him, Tarry, I pray thee,
8 *E*· took his mantle, and wrapped it
9 *E*· said unto Elisha, Ask what I
11 *E*· went up by a whirlwind into
13 He took up also the mantle of *E*·
14 And he took the mantle of *E*· that
14 Where is the Lord God of *E*·?
15 The spirit of *E*· doth rest on Elisha.
3:11 poured water on the hand of *E*·.
9:36 which he spake by his servant *E*· the
10:10 which he spake by his servant *E*·.
17 of the Lord, which he spake to *E*·.
2Ch 21:12 there came a writing to him from *E*·
Ezr 10:21 Maaseiah, and *E*·, and Shemaiah,
Mal 4: 5 I will send you *E*· the prophet

Elika *(e-li'-kah)*
2Sa 23:25 the Harodite, *E*· the Harodite,

Elim *(e'-lim)* See also BEER-ELIM.
Ex 15:27 they came to *E*·, where were twelve
16: 1 they took their journey from *E*·,
1 Sin, which is between *E*· and Sinai,
Nu 33: 9 from Marah, and came unto *E*·:
9 in *E*· were twelve fountains of water,
10 And they removed from *E*·, and

Elimelech *(e-lim'-e-lek)* See also ELIMELECH'S.
Ru 1: 2 And the name of the man was *E*·,
3 And *E*· Naomi's husband died;
2: 1 man of wealth, of the family of *E*·:
3 Boaz, who was of the kindred of *E*·.

Elimelech's *(e-lim'-e-leks)*
Ru 4: 3 of land, which was our brother *E*·:
9 that I have bought all that was *E*·,

Elioenai *(e-li-o-e'-nahee)* See also ELIHOENAI.
1Ch 3:23 sons of Neariah: *E*·, and Hezekiah,
24 the sons of *E*· were, Hodaiah, and
4:36 *E*·, and Jaakobah, and Jeshohaiah,
7: 8 Eliezer, and *E*·, and Omri,
26: 3 Jehohanan the sixth, *E*· the
Ezr 10:22 the sons of Pashur; *E*·, Maaseiah,
27 of the sons of Zattu; *E*·, Eliashib,
Ne 12:41 Michaiah, *E*·, Zechariah, and

Eliphal *(el'-i-fal)*
1Ch 11:35 Sacar the Hararite, *E*· the son of Ur,

Eliphalet *(e-lif'-a-let)* See also ELIPHELET; ELPALET.
2Sa 5:16 Elishama, and Eliada, and *E*·.
1Ch 14: 7 Elishama, and Beeliada, and *E*·.

Eliphaz *(el'-if-az)*
Ge 36: 4 And Adah bare to Esau *E*·;
10 *E*· the son of Adah the wife of Esau,
11 the sons of *E*· were Teman, Omar,
12 Timna was concubine to *E*· Esau's
12 and she bare to *E*· Amalek:
15 sons of *E*· the firstborn son of Esau;
16 these are the dukes that came of *E*·
1Ch 1:35 The sons of Esau; *E*·, Reuel,
36 The sons of *E*·; Teman, and Omar,
Job 2:11 *E*· the Temanite, and Bildad the
4: 1 *E*· the Temanite answered and said,
15: 1 Then answered *E*· the Temanite,
22: 1 *E*· the Temanite answered and said,
42: 7 the Lord said to *E*· the Temanite,
9 So *E*· the Temanite and Bildad the

Elipheleh *(e-lif'-e-leh)*
1Ch 15:18 Mattithiah, and *E*·, and Mikneiah,
21 *E*·, and Mikneiah, and Obed-edom,

Eliphelet *(e-lif'-e-let)* See also ELIPHALET.
2Sa 23:34 *E*· the son of Ahasbai, the son of
1Ch 3: 6 Ibhar also, and Elishama, and *E*·,
8 Elishama, and Eliada, and *E*·, nine.
8:39 Jehush the second, and *E*· the third.
Ezr 8:13 whose names are these, *E*·, Jeiel,
10:33 Zabad, *E*·, Jeremai, Manasseh,

Eli's *(e'-lize)*
1Sa 3:14 the iniquity of *E*· house shall not

Elisabeth *(e-liz'-a-beth)* See also ELISABETH'S.
Lu 1: 5 of Aaron, and her name was *E*·.
7 child, because that *E*· was barren,
13 thy wife *E*· shall bear thee a son,
24 those days his wife *E*· conceived,
36 behold, thy cousin *E*·, she hath also
40 house of Zacharias, and saluted *E*·.
41 *E*· heard the salutation of Mary,
41 *E*· was filled with the Holy Ghost:

Elisabeth's *(e-liz'-a-beths)*
Lu 1:57 Now *E*· full time came that she

Elisæus See ELISEUS.

Eliseus *(el-i-se'-us)* See also ELISHA.
Lu 4:27 in the time of *E*· the prophet;

Elisha *(e-li'-shah)* See also ELISEUS.
1Ki 19:16 *E*· the son Shaphat of Abel-meholah
17 from the sword of Jehu shall *E*· slay.
19 he departed thence, and found *E*·
2Ki 2: 1 Elijah went with *E*· from Gilgal.
2 Elijah said unto *E*·, Tarry here,
2 *E*· said unto him, As the Lord
3 were at Beth-el came forth to *E*·,
4 Elijah said unto him, *E*·, tarry here,
5 that were at Jericho came to *E*·,
9 Elijah said unto *E*·, Ask what I
9 *E*· said, I pray thee, let a double
12 *E*· saw it, and he cried, My father,
14 and thither: and *E*· went over.
15 The spirit of Elijah doth rest on *E*·.
19 the men of the city said unto *E*·,
22 to the saying of *E*· which he spake.
3:11 Here is *E*· the son of Shaphat,
13 *E*· said unto the king of Israel, What
14 *E*· said, As the Lord of hosts liveth,
4: 1 of the sons of the prophets unto *E*·,
2 *E*· said unto her, What shall I do
8 on a day, that *E*· passed to Shunem,
17 season that *E*· had said unto her,
32 when *E*· was come into the house,
38 *E*· came again to Gilgal: and there
5: 8 when *E*· the man of God had heard
9 stood at the door of the house of *E*·.
10 *E*· sent a messenger unto him,
20 Gehazi, the servant of *E*· the man
25 *E*· said unto him, Whence comest
6: 1 sons of the prophets said unto *E*·,
12 but *E*·, the prophet that is in Israel,
17 *E*· prayed, and said, Lord, I pray
17 and chariots of fire round about *E*·.
18 *E*· prayed unto the Lord, and said,
18 according to the word of *E*·.
19 *E*· said unto them, This is not the
20 *E*· said, Lord, open the eyes of these
2Ki 6:21 the king of Israel said unto *E*·,
31 the head of *E*· the son of Shaphat
32 *E*· sat in his house, and the elders
7: 1 *E*· said, Hear ye the word of the Lord;
8: 1 Then spake *E*· unto the woman,
4 the great things that *E*· hath done.
5 is her son, whom *E*· restored to life.
7 And *E*· came to Damascus; and
10 *E*· said unto him, Go, say unto him,
13 *E*· answered, The Lord hath shewed
14 So he departed from *E*·, and came
14 said to him, What said *E*· to thee?
9: 1 *E*· the prophet called one of the
13:14 *E*· was fallen sick of his sickness
15 *E*· said unto him, Take bow and
16 *E*· put his hands upon the king's
17 Then *E*· said, Shoot. And he shot.
20 And *E*· died, and they buried him.
21 the man into the sepulchre of *E*·:
21 down, and touched the bones of *E*·,

Elishah *(e-li'-shah)*
Ge 10: 4 the sons of Javan; *E*·, and Tarshish,
1Ch 1: 7 the sons of Javan; *E*·, and Tarshish,
Eze 27: 7 blue and purple from the isles of *E*·

Elishama *(e-lish'-a-mah)* See also ELISHUA.
Nu 1:10 Ephraim; *E*· the son of Ammihud:
2:18 of the sons of Ephraim shall be *E*·
7:48 seventh day *E*· the son of Ammihud,
53 this was the offering of *E*· the son of
10:22 over his host was *E*· the son of
2Sa 5:16 *E*·, and Eliada, and Eliphalet.
2Ki 25:25 the son of *E*·, of the seed royal,
1Ch 2:41 Jekamiah, and Jekamiah begat *E*·.
3: 6 Ibhar also, and *E*·, and Eliphalet,
8 *E*·, and Eliada, and Eliphelet, nine.
7:26 Ammihud his son, *E*· his son,
14: 7 *E*·, and Beeliada, and Eliphalet.
2Ch 17: 8 and with them *E*· and Jehoram,
Jer 36:12 even *E*· the scribe, and Delaiah
20 in the chamber of *E*· the scribe,
21 out of *E*· the scribe's chamber.
41: 1 the son of Nethaniah the son of *E*·.

Elishaphat *(e-lish'-a-fat)*
2Ch 23: 1 and *E*· the son of Zichri, into

Elisheba *(e-lish'-e-bah)*
Ex 6:23 Aaron took him *E*·, daughter of

Elishua *(e-lish'-oo-ah)* See also ELISHAMA.
2Sa 5:15 Ibhar also, and *E*·, and Nepheg,
1Ch 14: 5 And Ibhar, and *E*·, and Elpalet,

Elite See BETH-ELITE.

Eliud *(e-li'-ud)*
M't 1:14 begat Achim; and Achim begat *E*·;
15 And *E*· begat Eleazar; and

Elizabeth See ELISABETH.

Elizaphan *(e-liz'-a-fan)* See also ELZAPHAN.
Nu 3:30 of the Kohathites shall be *E*·
34:25 of Zebulun, *E*· the son of Parnach.
1Ch 15: 8 the sons of *E*·; Shemaiah the chief,
2Ch 29:13 of the sons of *E*·; Shimri, and Jeiel:

Elizur *(e-li'-zur)*
Nu 1: 5 of Reuben; *E*· the son of Shedeur.
2:10 the children of Reuben shall be *E*·
7:30 fourth day *E*· the son of Shedeur,
35 this was the offering of *E*· the son
10:18 host was *E*· the son of Shedeur.

Elkanah *(el-ka'-nah)*
Ex 6:24 the sons of Korah; Assir, and *E*·,
1Sa 1: 1 and his name was *E*·, the son of
4 when the time was that *E*· offered,
8 Then said *E*· her husband to her,
19 and *E*· knew Hannah his wife;
21 the man *E*·, and all his house, went
23 *E*· her husband said unto her, Do
2:11 And *E*· went to Ramah to his house.
20 And Eli blessed *E*· and his wife,
1Ch 6:23 *E*· his son, and Ebiasaph his son,
25 sons of *E*·; Amasai, and Ahimoth.
26 As for *E*·: the sons of *E*·; Zophai
27 Jeroham his son, *E*· his son.
34 The son of *E*·, the son of Jeroham,
35 The son of Zuph, the son of *E*·,
36 The son of *E*·, the son of Joel,
9:16 the son of *E*·, that dwelt in the
12: 6 *E*·, and Jesiah, and Azareel,
15:23 Berechiah and *E*· were door keepers
2Ch 28: 7 and *E*· that was next to the king

Elkoshite *(el'-ko-shite)*
Na 1: 1 book of the vision of Nahum the *E*·.

Ellasar *(el'-la-sar)*
Ge 14: 1 Arioch king of *E*·, Chedorlaomer
9 and Arioch king of *E*·; four kings

Elmodam *(el-mo'-dam)*
Lu 3:28 which was the son of *E*·, which

elms
Ho 4:13 under oaks and poplars and *e*·,

Elnaam *(el-na'-am)*
1Ch 11:46 and Joshaviah, the sons of *E*·,

Elnathan *(el-na'-than)*
2Ki 24: 8 the daughter of *E*· of Jerusalem.
Ezr 8:16 for *E*·, and for Jarib, and for *E*·,
16 and for *E*·, men of understanding.
Jer 26:22 *E*· the son of Achbor, and certain
36:12 *E*· the son of Achbor, and Gemariah
25 Nevertheless *E*· and Delaiah and

Elohe See EL-ELOHE-ISRAEL.

Eloi *(e-lo'-ee)* See also ELI.
M'r 15:34 *E*·, *E*·, lama sabachthani?

Elon *(e'-lon)* See also ELON-BETH-HANAN; ELONITES.
Ge 26:34 Bashemath the daughter of E' the
36: 2 Adah the daughter of E' the
46:14 sons of Zebulun; Sered, and E',
Nu 26:26 of E' the family of the Elonites:
Jos 19:43 E', and Thimnathah, and Ekron,
J'g 12:11 And after him E', a Zebulonite,
12 And E' the Zebulonite died, and was

Elon-beth-hanan *(e''-lon-beth-ha'-nan)*
1Ki 4: 9 and Beth-shemesh, and E':

Elonites *(e'-lon-ites)*
Nu 26:26 of Elon, the family of the E':

eloquent
Ex 4:10 O my Lord, I am not e',
Isa 3: 3 artificer, and the e' orator.
Ac 18:24 an e' man, and mighty in the

Eloth *(e'-loth)* See also ELATH.
1Ki 9:26 Ezion-geber, which is beside E',
2Ch 8:17 E', at the sea side in the land of
26: 2 He built E', and restored it to Judah,

Elpaal *(el-pa'-al)*
1Ch 8:11 Hushim he begat Abitub, and E'.
12 The sons of E'; Eber, and Misham,
18 Jezliah, and Jobab, the sons of E';

Elpalet^ *(el-pa'-let)* See also ELIPHALET.
1Ch 14: 5 Ibhar, and Elishua, and E',

El-paran *(el-pa'-ran)*
Ge 14: 6 unto E', which is by the wilderness.

else^
Ge 30: 1 Give me children, or e' I die.
42:16 or e' by the life of Pharaoh
Ex 8:21 E', if thou wilt not let my people
10: 4 E', if thou refuse to let my people
Nu 20:19 without doing anything e', go through
De 4:35 he is God; there is none e' beside
39 the earth beneath: there is none e'.
Jos 23:12 E' if ye do in any wise go back,
J'g 7:14 This is nothing e' save the sword
2Sa 3:35 if I taste bread, or ought e', till the
15:14 for we shall not e' escape from
1Ki 8:60 is God, and that there is none e'.
1Ch 21:12 or e' three days the sword of the
2Ch 23: 7 and whosoever e' cometh into the
Ne 2: 2 this is nothing e' but sorrow of
Ps 51:16 thou desirest not sacrifice; e' would I
Ec 2:25 or who e' can hasten hereunto,
Isa 45:5 am the Lord, and there is none e',
6 I am the Lord, and there is none e'.
14 and there is none e', there is no God.
18 I am the Lord; and there is none e'.
21 and there is no God e' beside me; a
22 for I am God, and there is none e'.
46: 9 I am God, and there is none e'; I
47: 8 I am, and none e' beside me; I shall
10 I am, and none e' beside me.
Jo 2:27 am the Lord your God, and none e':
M't 6:24 either he will hate the one, ... or e' he
9:17 e' the bottles break, and the wine
12:29 Or e' how can one enter into the
33 or e' make the tree corrupt, and
M'r 2:21 e' the new piece that filled it up
22 e' the new wine doth burst the bottles,
Lu 5:37 e' the new wine will burst the bottles,
14:32 Or e', while the other is yet a great
16:13 or e' he will hold to the one,
Joh 14:11 or e' believe me for the very works'
Ac 17:21 spent their time in nothing e', but
24:20 Or e' let these same here say,
Ro 2:15 accusing or e' excusing one
1Co 7:14 e' were your children unclean;
14:16 E' when thou shalt bless with the
15:29 E' what shall they do which are
Ph'p 1:27 come and see you, or e' be absent,
Re 2: 5 or e' I will come unto thee quickly,
16 Repent; or e' I will come unto thee

Eltekeh *(el'-te-keh)*
Jos 19:44 And E', and Gibbethon, and Baalath,
21:23 out of the tribe of Dan, E' with her

Eltekon *(el'-te-kon)*
Jos 15:59 Maarath, and Beth-anoth, and E';

Eltolad *(el-to'-lad)*
Jos 15:30 And E', and Chesil, and Hormah,
19: 4 And E', and Bethul, and Hormah,

Elul *(e'-lul)*
Ne 6:15 and fifth day of the month E',

Eluzai *(e-loo'-zahee)*
1Ch 12: 5 E', and Jerimoth, and Bealiah,

Elymas *(el'-i-mas)* See also BAR-JESUS.
Ac 13: 8 But E' the sorcerer (for so is his

Elzabad *(el'-za-bad)*
1Ch 12:12 Johanan the eighth, E' the ninth,
26: 7 E', whose brethren were strong

Elzaphan *(el'-za-fan)* See also ELIZAPHAN.
Ex 6:22 the sons of Uzziel; Mishael, and E',
Lev 10: 4 Moses called Mishael and E',

embalm See also EMBALMED.
Ge 50: 2 the physicians to e' his father:

embalmed
Ge 50: 2 and the physicians e' Israel.
3 the days of those which are e':
26 and they e' him, and he was put in

embassy See AMBASSAGE.

emboldened
1Co 8:10 of him which is weak be e' to eat

emboldeneth
Job 16: 3 what e' thee that thou answerest?

embrace See also EMBRACED; EMBRACING.
2Ki 4:16 time of life, thou shalt e' a son.
Job 24: 8 e' the rock for want of a shelter.
Pr 4: 8 to honour when thou dost e' her.
5:20 and e' the bosom of a stranger?
Ec 3: 5 a time to e', and a time to refrain
Ca 2: 6 and his right hand doth e' me.
8: 3 and his right hand should e' me.
La 4: 5 that were brought up in scarlet e'

embraced
Ge 29:13 he ran to meet him, and e' him,
33: 4 Esau ran to meet him, and e' him,
48:10 he kissed them, and e' them.
Ac 20: 1 unto him the disciples, and e'
He 11:13 e' them, and confessed that they

embracing
Ec 3: 5 a time to refrain from e';
Ac 20:10 and fell on him, and e' him said,

embroider
Ex 28:39 And thou shalt e' the coat of fine

embroiderer
Ex 35:35 manner of work, ... and of the e',
38:23 and an e' in blue, and in purple,

Emek See BETH-EMEK.

emerald See also EMERALDS.
Ex 28:18 And the second row shall be an e',
39:11 an e', a sapphire, and a diamond.
Eze 28:13 sapphire, the e', and the carbuncle,
Re 4: 3 in sight like unto an e'.
21:19 a chalcedony; the fourth, an e';

emeralds
Eze 27:16 they occupied in thy fairs with e',

emerods *(em'-e-rods)*
De 28:27 and with the e', and with the scab,
1Sa 5: 6 smote them with e', even Ashdod
9 they had e' in their secret parts.
12 died not were smitten with the e':
6: 4 Five golden e', and five golden
5 ye shall make images of your e',
11 and the images of their e'.
17 these are the golden e' which the

Emims *(e'-mims)*
Ge 14: 5 and the E' in Shaveh Kiriathaim,
De 2:10 E' dwelt therein in times past,
11 but the Moabites call them E'.

eminence See PRE-EMINENCE.

eminent
Eze 16:24 also built unto thee an e' place,
31 thou buildest thine e' place in the
39 shall throw down thine e' place,
17:22 upon an high mountain and e':

Emmanuel *(em-man'-uel)* See also IMMANUEL.
M't 1:23 they shall call his name E',

Emmaus *(em'-ma-us)*
Lu 24:13 to a village called E', which was

Emmor *(em'-mor)* See also HAMOR.
Ac 7:16 of the sons of E' the father of

empire
Es 1:20 published throughout all his e',

employ See also EMPLOYED; EMPLOYMENT.
De 20:19 to e' them in the siege:

employed
1Ch 9:33 for they were e' in that work day
Ezr 10:15 Tikvah were e' about this matter:

employment
Eze 39:14 shall sever out men of continual e',

emptied
Ge 24:20 she hasted, and e' her pitcher
42:35 to pass as they e' their sacks,
2Ch 24:11 officer came and e' the chest,
Ne 5:13 thus be he shaken out, and e'.
Isa 19: 6 defence shall be e' and dried up;
24: 3 The land shall be utterly e', and
Jer 48:11 hath not been e' from vessel to
Na 2: 2 for the emptiers have e' them out,

emptiers
Na 2: 2 for the e' have emptied them out,

emptiness
Isa 34:11 of confusion, and the stones of e'.

empty See also EMPTIED.
Ge 31:42 thou hadst sent me away now e'.
37:24 the pit was e'; there was no water
41:27 the seven e' ears blasted with the
Ex 3:21 when ye go, ye shall not go e':
23:15 and none shall appear before me e':)
34:20 And none shall appear before me e'.
Le 14:36 command that they e' the house,
De 15:13 thou shalt not let him go away e':
16:16 shall not appear before the Lord e':
J'g 7:16 e' pitchers, and lamps within the
Ru 1:21 hath brought me home again e':
3:17 Go not e' unto thy mother in law.
1Sa 6: 3 send it not e'; but in any wise
20:18 missed because thy seat will be e'.
25 side, and David's place was e'.
27 that David's place was e': and Saul
2Sa 1:22 the sword of Saul returned not e'.
2Ki 4: 3 borrow thee vessels...e' vessels;
Job 22: 9 Thou hast sent widows away e',
26: 7 out the north over the e' place,
Ec 11: 3 they e' themselves upon the earth:
Isa 24: 1 the Lord maketh the earth e',
29: 8 he awaketh, and his soul is e':
32: 6 to make e' the soul of the hungry,
Jer 14: 3 returned with their vessels e';
48:12 shall e' his vessels, and break
51: 2 shall fan her, and shall e' her land:
34 he hath made me an e' vessel,

Eze 24:11 set it e' upon the coals thereof
Ho 10: 1 Israel is an e' vine, he bringeth
Na 2:10 She is e', and void, and waste:
Hab 1:17 Shall they therefore e' their net,
Zec 4:12 through the two golden pipes e'
M't 12:44 he findeth it e', swept, and
M'r 12: 3 beat him, and sent him away e'.
Lu 1:53 the rich he hath sent e' away.
20:10 beat him, and sent him away e'.
11 shamefully, and sent him away e'.

emulation See also EMULATIONS.
Ro 11:14 I may provoke to e' them which

emulations
Ga 5:20 hatred, variance, e', wrath, strife,

En See EN-DOR; EN-EGLAIM; EN-GANNIM; EN-GEDI; EN-HADDAH; EN-HAKKORE; EN-HAZOR; EN-MISHPAT; EN-RIMMON; EN-ROGEL; EN-SHEMESH; EN-TAPPUAH.

enabled
1Ti 1:12 Jesus our Lord, who hath e' me,

Enam *(e'-nam)*
Jos 15:34 and En-gannim, Tappuah, and E',

Enan *(e'-nan)* See also HAZAR-ENAN.
Nu 1:15 Of Naphtali; Ahira the son of E'.
2:29 shall be Ahirah the son of E'.
7:78 the twelfth day Ahira the son of E',
83 the offering of Ahira the son of E'.
10:27 Naphtali was Ahira the son of E'.

encamp See also ENCAMPED; ENCAMPETH; ENCAMPING.
Ex 14: 2 turn and e' before Pi-hahiroth,
2 before it shall ye e' by the sea.
Nu 1:50 shall minister unto it, and shall e'
2:17 as they e', so shall they set forward,
27 And those that e' by him shall be
3:38 But those that e' before the
10:31 how we are to e' in the wilderness,
2Sa 12:28 and e' against the city, and take it:
Job 19:12 and e' round about my tabernacle.
Ps 27: 3 Though an host should e' against
Zec 9: 8 And I will e' about mine house

encamped
Ex 13:20 and e' in Etham, in the edge of the
15:27 and they e' there by the waters.
18: 5 where he e' at the mount of God:
Nu 33:10 and e' by the Red Sea.
11 and e' in the wilderness of Sin.
12 and e' in Dophkah.
13 and e' in Alush.
14 and e' at Rephidim, where was no
17 and e' at Hazeroth.
24 and e' in Haradah.
26 and e' at Tahath.
30 and e' at Moseroth.
32 and e' at Hor-hagidgad.
34 and e' at Ebronah.
35 and e' at Ezion-gaber.
46 and e' in Almon-diblathaim.
Jos 4:19 and e' in Gilgal, in the east border
5:10 And the children of Israel e' in
10: 5 and e' before Gibeon, and made war
31 and e' against it, and fought
34 and they e' against it, and fought
J'g 6: 4 And they e' against them, and
9:50 and e' against Thebez, and took it.
10:17 gathered together, and e' in Gilead.
17 together, and e' in Mizpeh.
20:19 morning, and e' against Gibeah.
1Sa 11: 1 and e' against Jabesh-gilead:
13:16 but the Philistines e' in Michmash.
2Sa 11:11 my lord, are e' in the open fields;
1Ki 16:15 And the people were e' against
16 the people that were e' heard say,
1Ch 11:15 the Philistines e' in the valley of
2Ch 32: 1 and e' against the fenced cities,

encampeth
Ps 34: 7 The angel of the Lord e' round
53: 5 the bones of him that e' against

encamping
Ex 14: 9 and overtook them e' by the sea,

enchanter See also ENCHANTERS.
De 18:10 spirits, or an e', or a witch,

enchanters
Jer 27: 9 your e', nor to your sorcerers,

enchantment See also ENCHANTMENTS.
Le 19:26 neither shall ye use e',
Nu 23:23 there is no e' against Jacob,
Ec 10:11 the serpent will bite without e';

enchantments
Ex 7:11 did in like manner with their e'.
22 of Egypt did so with their e':
8: 7 the magicians did so with their e',
18 did so with their e' to bring forth
Nu 24: 1 to seek for e', but he set his face
2Ki 17:17 and used divination and e', and
21: 6 and observed times, and used e',
2Ch 33: 6 also he observed times, and used e',
Isa 47: 9 the great abundance of thine e'.
12 Stand now with thine e', and with

enclose See INCLOSE.

encountered
Ac 17:18 and of the Stoicks, e' him.

encourage See also ENCOURAGED.
De 1:38 he shall go in thither: e' him:
3:28 charge Joshua, and e' him, and
2Sa 11:25 and overthrow it: and e' thou him.
Ps 64: 5 They e' themselves in an evil

encouraged
J'g 20:22 the men of Israel e' themselves,
1Sa 30: 6 but David e' himself in the Lord
2Ch 31: 4 that they might be e' in the law of

2Ch 35: 2 and e' them to the service of the
Isa 41: 7 So the carpenter e' the goldsmith,

end See also ENDED; ENDETH; ENDING; ENDLESS; ENDS.

Ge 6:13 The e' of all flesh is come before
8: 3 after the e' of the hundred and
6 came to pass at the e' of forty days,
23: 9 which is in the e' of his field;
27:30 as Isaac had made an e' of blessing
41: 1 it came to pass at the e' of two full
47:21 from one e' of the borders of Egypt
21 even to the other e' thereof.
49:33 And when Jacob had made an e' of
Ex 8:22 to the e' thou mayest know that I
12:41 at the e' of the four hundred and
23:16 in the e' of the year, when thou
25:19 one cherub on the one e', and the
19 the other cherub on the other e':
26:28 the boards shall reach from e' to e'.
31:18 choses, when he had made an e' of
34:22 of ingathering at the year's e'.
36:33 the boards from the one e' to the
37: 8 One cherub on the e' on this side,
8 and another cherub on the other e'
Le 8:33 of your consecration be at an e':
16:20 hath made an e' of reconciling
17: 5 To the e' that the children of
Nu 4:15 have made an e' of covering
16:31 as he had made an e' of speaking
23:10 and let my last e' be like his!
24:20 but his latter e' shall be that he perish
De 8:16 to do thee good at thy latter e';
9:11 at the e' of forty days and forty
11:12 even unto the e' of the year.
13: 7 from the one e' of the earth even
7 even unto the other e' of the earth,
14:28 At the e' of three years thou shalt
15: 1 At the e' of every seven years thou
17:16 to the e' that he should multiply
20 to the e' that he may prolong his
20: 9 officers have made an e' speaking
26:12 thou hast made an e' of tithing all
28:49 from the e' of the earth, as swift
64 from the one e' of the earth even
31:10 At the e' of every seven years,
24 Moses had made an e' of writing
32:20 I will see what their e' shall be:
29 they would consider their latter e'!
45 And Moses made an e' of speaking
Jos 8:24 Israel had made an e' of slaying
9:16 to pass at the e' of three days
10:20 Israel had made an e' of slaying
15: 5 sea, even unto the e' of Jordan.
8 at the e' of the valley of the giants
18:15 from the e' of Kirjath-jearim,
16 down to the e' of the mountain
19 salt sea at the south e' of Jordan:
19:49 they had made an e' of dividing
51 So they made an e' of dividing the
J'g 3:18 when he had made an e' to offer
6:21 Lord put forth the e' of the staff
11:39 to pass at the e' of two months,
15:17 he had made an e' of speaking,
19: 9 behold, the day groweth to an e',
Ru 2:23 unto the e' of barley harvest and
3: 7 at the e' of the heap of corn:
10 more kindness at the latter e' than
1Sa 3:12 I begin, I will also make an e'.
9:27 going down to the e' of the city,
10:13 he had made an e' of prophesying,
13:10 as he had made an e' of offering
14:27 he put forth the e' of the rod
43 a little honey with the e' of the rod
18: 1 he had made an e' of speaking
24:16 David had made an e' of speaking
2Sa 2:23 Abner with the hinder e' of the spear
26 it will be bitterness in the latter e'?
6:18 David had made an e' of offering
11:19 thou hast made an e' of telling
13:36 as he had made an e' of speaking,
14:26 every year's e' that he polled it:
24: 8 at the e' of nine months and twenty
1Ki 1:41 as they had made an e' of eating.
2:39 to pass at the e' of three years,
3: 1 he had made an e' of building
7:40 So Hiram made an e' of doing all
8:54 Solomon had made an e' of praying
9:10 to pass at the e' of twenty years,
2Ki 8: 3 came to pass at the seven years' e',
10:21 of Baal was full from one e' to
25 as he had made an e' of offering
18:10 at the e' of three years they took it:
21:16 Jerusalem from one e' to another;
1Ch 16: 2 David had made an e' of offering
2Ch 4:10 sea on the right side of the east e',
5:12 stood at the east e' of the altar,
7: 1 Solomon had made an e' of praying,
8: 1 to pass at the e' of twenty years,
20:16 find them at the e' of the brook,
23 had made an e' of the inhabitants
21:19 of time, after the e' of two years,
24:10 chest, until they had made an e'.
23 came to pass at the e' of the year,
29:17 sixteenth day...they made an e'.
29 they had made an e' of offering,
Ezr 9:11 filled it from one e' to another
10:17 they made an e' with all the men
Ne 3:21 to the e' of the house of Eliashib.
4: 2 will they make an e' in a day?
Job 6:11 and what is mine e', that I should
8: 7 thy latter e' should greatly increase.
16: 3 Shall vain words have an e'?
18: 2 ere ye make an e' of words?
26:10 the day and night come to an e'.
28: 3 He setteth an e' to darkness.
34:36 that Job may be tried unto the e'
Job 42:12 the Lord blessed the latter e' of Job
Ps 7: 9 of the wicked come to an e';
9: 6 are come to a perpetual e':
19: 4 their words to the e' of the world.
6 forth is from the e' of the heaven,
30:12 To the e' that my glory may sing
37:37 for the e' of that man is peace.
38 e' of the wicked shall be cut off.
39: 4 Lord, make me to know mine e',
46: 9 to cease unto the e' of the earth;
61: 2 From the e' of the earth will I cry
73:17 God; then understood I their e'.
102:27 and thy years shall have no e'.
107:27 man, and are at their wit's e'.
119:33 I shall keep it unto the e'.
96 have seen an e' of all perfection:
112 statutes alway, even unto the e'.
Pr 5: 4 But her e' is bitter as wormwood,
14:12 e' thereof are the ways of death.
13 the e' of that mirth is heaviness.
16:25 the e' thereof are the ways of death.
19:20 thou mayest be wise in thy latter e'.
20:21 the e' thereof shall not be blessed.
23:18 For surely there is an e'; and
25: 8 what to do in the e' thereof,
Ec 3:11 from the beginning to the e'.
4: 8 yet is there no e' of all his labour;
16 There is no e' of all the people,
7: 2 for that is the e' of all men;
8 Better is the e' of a thing than the
14 e' that man should find nothing
10:13 the e' of his talk is mischievous
12:12 making many books there is no e'
Isa 2: 7 is there any e' of their treasures;
7 is there any e' of their chariots:
5:26 unto them from the e' of the earth:
7: 3 at the e' of the conduit of the upper
9: 7 and peace there shall be no e',
13: 5 far country, from the e' of heaven,
16: 4 for the extortioner is at an e',
23:15 the e' of seventy years shall Tyre
17 pass after the e' of seventy years,
33: 1 make an e' to deal treacherously,
38:12, 13 wilt thou make an e' of me.
41:22 and know the latter e' of them;
42:10 his praise from the e' of the earth,
45:17 world without e'.
46:10 the e' from the beginning,
47: 7 didst remember the latter e' of it.
48:20 it even to the e' of the earth;
49: 6 salvation unto the e' of the earth.
62:11 proclaimed unto the e' of the world
Jer 1: 3 unto the e' of the eleventh year
3: 5 will he keep it to the e'?
4:27 yet will I not make a full e'.
5:10 but make not a full e': take away
18 I will not make a full e' with you.
31 what will ye do in the e' thereof?
12: 4 He shall not see our last e'.
12 from the one e' of the land
12 even to the other e' of the land:
17:11 and at his e' shall be a fool.
25:33 from one e' of the earth even
33 unto the other e' of the earth:
26: 8 had made an e' of speaking all
29:11 of evil, to give you an expected e'.
30:11 I make a full e' of all nations
11 yet will I not make a full e' of thee:
31:17 And there is hope in thine e',
34:14 At the e' of seven years let ye go
43: 1 had made an e' of speaking unto
44:27 until there be an e' of them.
46:28 will make a full e' of all the nations
28 I will not make a full e' of thee,
51:13 thine e' is come, and the measure
31 that his city is taken at one e',
63 made an e' of reading this book,
La 1: 9 she remembereth not her last e';
4:18 our e' is near, our days are fulfilled;
18 for our e' is come.
Eze 3:16 to pass at the e' of seven days,
7: 2 An e', the e' is come upon the four
3 Now is the e' come upon thee,
6 An e' is come, the e' is come:
11:13 God! wilt thou make a full e' of
20:17 neither did I make an e' of them
26 to the e' that they might know
21:25 when iniquity shall have an e',
29 their iniquity shall have an e'.
29:13 At the e' of forty years will I gather
31:14 To the e' that none of all the trees
35: 5 that their iniquity had an e':
39:14 after the e' of seven months shall
41:12 at the e' toward the west was
42:15 he had made an e' of measuring
43:23 hast made an e' of cleansing it,
48: 1 From the north e' to the coast of
Da 1: 5 at the e' thereof they might stand
15 And at the e' of ten days their
18 at the e' of the days that the king
4:11 thereof to the e' of all the earth:
22 thy dominion to the e' of the earth.
29 the e' of twelve months he walked
34 the e' of the days I Nebuchadnezzar
6:26 dominion shall be even unto the e'.
7:26 and to destroy it unto the e'.
28 Hitherto is the e' of the matter.
8:17 time of the e' shall be the vision.
19 in the last e' of the indignation:
19 the time appointed the e' shall be
9:24 and to make an e' of sins,
26 the e' thereof shall be with a flood,
26 and unto the e' of the war
11: 6 in the e' of years they shall join
27 the e' shall be at the time appointed.
35 even to the time of the e':
Da 11:40 at the time of the e' shall the king
45 yet he shall come to his e',
12: 4 book, even to the time of the e':
6 it be to the e' of these wonders?
8 shall be the e' of these things?
9 and sealed till the time of the e'.
13 go thou thy way till the e' be:
13 stand in thy lot at the e' of the days.
Am 3:15 the great houses shall have an e',
5:18 to what e' is it for you?
7: 2 they had made an e' of eating
8: 2 The e' is come upon my people
10 and the e' thereof as a bitter day.
Ob 9 to the e' that every one of the
Na 1: 8 will make an utter e' of the place
9 the Lord? he will make an utter e'
2: 9 for there is none e' of the store
3: 3 there is none e' of their corpses;
Hab 2: 3 but at the e' it shall speak,
M't 10:22 endureth to the e' shall be saved.
11: 1 when Jesus had made an e' of
13:39 the harvest is the e' of the world;
40 so shall it be in the e' of this world.
49 So shall it be at the e' of the world:
24: 3 and of the e' of the world?
6 come to pass, but the e' is not yet.
13 he that shall endure unto the e',
14 and then shall the e' come.
31 from one e' of heaven to the other.
26:58 with the servants to see the e'.
28: 1 the e' of the sabbath, as it began
20 even unto the e' of the world.
M'r 3:26 he cannot stand, but hath an e'.
13: 7 but the e' shall not be yet.
13 but he that shall endure unto the e',
Lu 1:33 of his kingdom there shall be no e'.
18: 1 a parable unto them to this e', that men
21: 9 but the e' is not by and by.
22:37 things concerning me have an e'.
Joh 13: 1 world, he loved them unto the e'.
18:37 To this e' was I born, and for this
Ac 7:19 to the e' they might not live.
Ro 1:11 to the e' ye may be established;
4:16 the e' the promise might be sure
6:21 for the e' of those things is death.
22 and the e' everlasting life.
10: 4 For Christ is the e' of the law
14: 9 to this e' Christ both died, and rose
1Co 1: 8 shall also confirm you unto the e',
15:24 Then cometh the e', when he shall
2Co 1:13 shall acknowledge even to the e';
2: 9 to this e' also did I write, that I might
3:13 the e' of that which is abolished:
11:15 e' shall be according to their works.
Eph 3:21 ages, world without e'.
Ph'p 3:19 Whose e' is destruction, whose God
1Th 3:13 To the e' he may stablish your
1Ti 1: 5 Now the e' of the commandment
Heb 3: 6 of the hope firm unto the e'.
14 our confidence stedfast unto the e';
6: 8 cursing; whose e' is to be burned.
11 full assurance of hope unto the e':
16 is to them an e' of all strife.
7: 3 beginning of days, nor e' of life;
9:26 e' of the world hath he appeared
13: 7 the e' of their conversation.
Jas 5:11 and have seen the e' of the Lord;
1Pe 1: 9 Receiving the e' of your faith,
13 and hope to the e' for the grace
4: 7 But the e' of all things is at hand:
17 what shall the e' be of them that
2Pe 2:20 the latter e' is worse with them
Re 2:26 and keepeth my works unto the e',
21: 6 the beginning and the e'. I will give
22:13 Omega, the beginning and the e',

endamage
Ezr 4:13 so thou shalt e' the revenue of

endanger See also ENDANGERED.
Da 1:10 then shall ye make me e' my head

endangered
Ec 10: 9 he that cleaveth wood shall be e'

endeavour See also ENDEAVOURED; ENDEAVOURING; ENDEAVOURS.
2Pe 1:15 I will e' that ye may be able after

endeavoured
Ac 16:10 we e' to go into Macedonia,
1Th 2:17 e' the more abundantly to see

endeavouring
Eph 4: 3 E' to keep the unity of the Spirit

endeavours
Ps 28: 4 to the wickedness of their e':

ended
Ge 2: 2 And on the seventh day God e'
41:53 years of plenteousness,...were e'.
47:18 When that year was e', they came
De 31:30 of this song, until they were e'.
34: 8 and mourning for Moses were e'.
Ru 2:21 until they have e' all my harvest.
2Sa 20:18 so they e' the matter.
1Ki 7:51 So was e' all the work that king
2Ch 29:34 till the work was e', and until the
Job 31:40 The words of Job are e'.
Ps 72:20 of David the son of Jesse are e'.
Isa 60:20 days of thy mourning shall be e'.
Jer 8:20 the summer is e', and we are not
Eze 4: 8 till thou hast e' the days of thy
M't 7:28 when Jesus had e' these sayings,
Lu 4: 2 and when they were e', he
13 And when the devil had e' all the
7: 1 when he had e' all his sayings
Joh 13: 2 supper being e', the devil having
Ac 19:21 After these things were e', Paul
21:27 the seven days were almost e',

endeth
Isa 24: 8 the noise of them that rejoice e'.
ending
Re 1: 8 Omega, the beginning and the e'.
endless
1Ti 1: 4 to fables and e' genealogies, which
Heb 7:16 but after the power of an e' life.
En-dor (en'-dor)
Jos 17:11 and the inhabitants of E' and her
1Sa 28: 7 that hath a familiar spirit at E'.
Ps 83:10 Which perished at E': they became
endow See also ENDUED.
Ex 22:16 he shall surely e' her to be his
ends
Ex 25:18 in the two e' of the mercy seat.
19 the cherubims on the two e' thereof.
28:14 two chains of pure gold at the e';
22 the e' of wreathen work of pure
23 on the two e' of the breastplate.
24 are on the e' of the breastplate
25 And the other two e' of the two
26 upon the two e' of the breastplate
37: 7 on the two e' of the mercy seat;
8 cherubims on the two e' thereof.
38: 5 four rings for the four e' of the
39:15 the breastplate chains at the e',
16 in the two e' of the breastplate.
17 rings on the e' of the breastplate.
18 two e' of the two wreathen chains
19 on the two e' of the breastplate,
De 33:17 together to the e' of the earth:
1Sa 2:10 Lord shall judge the e' of the earth:
1Ki 8: 8 the e' of the staves were seen out
2Ch 5: 9 the e' of the staves were seen from
Job 28:24 he looketh to the e' of the earth,
37: 3 lightning unto the e' of the earth.
38:13 take hold of the e' of the earth,
Ps 19: 6 and his circuit unto the e' of it:
22:27 All the e' of the world shall
48:10 thy praise unto the e' of the earth:
59:13 in Jacob unto the e' of the earth.
65: 5 confidence of all the e' of the earth,
67: 7 all the e' of the earth shall fear
72: 8 the river unto the e' of the earth.
98: 3 all the e' of the earth have seen the
135: 7 to ascend from the e' of the earth;
Pr 17:24 of a fool are in the e' of the earth.
30: 4 established all the e' of the earth?
Isa 26:15 far unto all the e' of the earth.
40:28 the Creator of the e' of the earth,
41: 5 the e' of the earth were afraid,
9 have taken from the e' of the earth,
43: 6 my daughters from the e' of the
45:22 saved, all the e' of the earth:
52:10 all the e' of the earth shall see the
Jer 10:13 vapours to ascend from the e' of
16:19 shall come unto thee from the e' of
25:31 come even to the e' of the earth;
51:16 vapours to ascend from the e' of the
Eze 15: 4 the fire devoureth both the e' of it,
Mic 5: 4 be great unto the e' of the earth.
Zec 9:10 the river even to the e' of the earth.
Ac 13:47 salvation unto the e' of the earth.
Ro 10:18 their words unto the e' of the world.
1Co 10:11 upon whom the e' of the world are
endued See also ENDOW.
Ge 30:20 God hath e' me with a good
2Ch 2:12 a wise son, e' with prudence and
13 man, e' with understanding,
Lu 24:49 until ye be e' with power from on
Jas 3:13 e' with knowledge among you?
endure See also ENDURED; ENDURETH; ENDURING.
Ge 33:14 me and the children be able to e',
Ex 18:23 then thou shalt be able to e',
Es 8: 6 how can I e' to see the evil that
6 how can I e' to see the destruction
Job 8:15 hold it fast, but it shall not e'.
31:23 of his highness I could not e'.
Ps 9: 7 But the Lord shall e' for ever:
30: 5 weeping may e' for a night, but
72: 5 as long as the sun and moon e',
17 His name shall e' for ever:
89:29 His seed also will I make to e' forever,
36 His seed shall e' for ever, and his
102:12 thou, O Lord, shalt e' for ever;
26 shall perish, but thou shalt e':
104:31 glory of the Lord shall e' for ever:
Pr 27:24 ever: and doth the crown e' to every
Eze 22:14 Can thine heart e', or can thine
M't 24:13 But he that shall e' unto the end,
M'r 4:17 and so e' but for a time:
13:13 but he that shall e' unto the end,
2Th 1: 4 and tribulations that ye e':
2Ti 2: 3 therefore e' hardness, as a good
10 Therefore I e' all things for the
4: 3 they will not e' sound doctrine;
5 e' afflictions, do the work of an
Heb 12: 7 If ye e' chastening, God dealeth
20 (For they could not e' that which
Jas 5:11 we count them happy which e'.
1Pe 2:19 conscience toward God e' grief,
endured
Ps 81:15 their time should have e' for ever.
Ro 9:22 e' with much longsuffering the
2Ti 3:11 what persecutions I e': but out of
Heb 6:15 And so, after he had patiently e',
10:32 ye e' a great fight of afflictions;
11:27 for he e', as seeing him who is
12: 2 e' the cross, despising the shame,
3 him that e' such contradiction
endureth See also DURETH.
1Ch 16:34 he is good; for his mercy e' for ever.

1Ch 16:41 Lord, because his mercy e' for ever;
2Ch 5:13 he is good; for his mercy e' for ever:
7: 3 he is good; for his mercy e' for ever.
6 Lord, because his mercy e' for ever,
20:21 the Lord; for his mercy e' for ever.
Ezr 3:11 his mercy e' for ever toward Israel.
Ps 30: 5 For his anger e' but a moment;
52: 1 the goodness of God e' continually.
72: 7 peace so long as the moon e'.
100: 5 and his truth e' to all generations.
106: 1 he is good: for his mercy e' for ever.
107: 1 he is good: for his mercy e' for ever.
111: 3 and his righteousness e' for ever.
10 commandments: his praise e' for
112: 3 and his righteousness e' for ever.
9 poor; his righteousness e' for ever;
117: 2 and the truth of the Lord e' for ever.
118: 1 is good: because his mercy e' for ever.
2 Israel now say, that his mercy e' for
3 Aaron now say, that his mercy e' for
4 Lord say, that his mercy e' for ever.
29 he is good: for his mercy e' for ever.
119:160 thy righteous judgments e' for ever.
135:13 Thy name, O Lord, e' for ever;
136: 1 he is good: for his mercy e' for ever.
2 of gods: for his mercy e' for ever.
3 of lords: for his mercy e' for ever.
4 wonders: for his mercy e' for ever.
5 heavens: for his mercy e' for ever.
6 the waters: for his mercy e' for ever.
7 lights: for his mercy e' for ever:
8 by day: for his mercy e' for ever:
9 by night: for his mercy e' for ever.
10 firstborn: for his mercy e' for ever,
11 among them: for his mercy e'
12 out arm: for his mercy e' for ever.
13 into parts: for his mercy e' for ever:
14 the midst of it: for his mercy e' for ever.
15 the Red sea: for his mercy e' for ever.
16 wilderness: for his mercy e' for ever.
17 great kings: for his mercy e' for ever.
18 famous kings: for his mercy e' for ever.
19 the Amorites: for his mercy e' for ever.
20 of Bashan: for his mercy e' for ever.
21 an heritage: for his mercy e' for ever.
22 his servant: for his mercy e' for ever.
23 low estate: for his mercy e' for ever:
24 our enemies: for his mercy e' for ever.
25 to all flesh: for his mercy e' for ever.
26 of heaven: for his mercy e' for ever.
138: 8 thy mercy, O Lord, e' for ever: forsake
145:13 and thy dominion e' throughout all
Jer 33:11 for his mercy e' for ever: and of them
M't 10:22 that e' to the end shall be saved.
Joh 6:27 which e' unto everlasting life,
1Co 13: 7 hopeth all things, e' all things.
Jas 1:12 is the man that e' temptation:
1Pe 1:25 the word of the Lord e' for ever.
enduring
Ps 19: 9 of the Lord is clean, e' for ever:
2Co 1: 6 is effectual in the e' of the same
Heb 10:34 a better and an e' substance.
Eneas See ÆNEAS.
En-eglaim (en-eg'-la-im)
Eze 47:10 from Engedi even unto E';
enemies See also ENEMIES'.
Ge 14:20 delivered thine e' into thy hand.
22:17 seed shall possess the gate of his e';
49: 8 hand shall be in the neck of thine e';
Ex 1:10 they join also unto our e', and
23:22 I will be an enemy unto thine e',
27 make all thine e' turn their backs
32:25 unto their shame among their e':)
Le 26: 7 And ye shall chase your e',
8 and your e' shall fall before you
16 seed in vain, for your e' shall eat it.
17 ye shall be slain before your e':
32 your e' which dwell therein shall be
36 their hearts in the lands of their e';
37 no power to stand before your e'.
38 the land of your e' shall eat you up.
41 them into the land of their e';
44 when they be in the land of their e',
Nu 10: 9 ye shall be saved from your e'.
35 Lord, and let thine e' be scattered;
14:42 ye be not smitten before your e'.
23:11 I took thee to curse mine e',
24: 8 he shall eat up the nations his e',
10 I called thee to curse mine e',
18 also shall be a possession for his e';
32:21 driven out his e' from before him,
De 1:42 lest ye be smitten before your e'.
6:19 out all thine e' from before thee,
12:10 he giveth you rest from all your e'
20: 1 goest out to battle against thine e',
3 this day unto battle against your e':
4 to fight for you against your e',
14 thou shalt eat the spoil of thine e',
21:10 goest forth to war against thine e',
23: 9 host goeth forth against thine e',
14 to give up thine e' before thee;
25:19 given thee rest from all thine e',
28: 7 Lord shall cause thine e' that rise
25 thee to be smitten before thine e':
31 sheep shall be given unto thine e',
48 Therefore shalt thou serve thine e'
53 wherewith thine e' shall distress
55 thine e' shall distress thee in all
68 ye shall be sold unto your e' for
30: 7 put all these curses upon thine e',
32:31 our e' themselves being judges.
41 will render vengeance to mine e',
33: 7 be thou an help to him from his e';
29 thine e' shall be found liars unto

Jos 7: 8 turneth their backs before their e'!
12 Israel could not stand before their e',
12 turned their backs before their e',
13 thou canst not stand before thine e',
10:13 avenged themselves upon their e'.
19 but pursue after your e', and smite
25 thus shall the Lord do to all your e'
21:44 stood not a man of all their e' before
44 delivered all their e' into their hand.
22: 8 divide the spoil of your e' with your
23: 1 rest unto Israel from all their e'
J'g 2:14 sold them into the hands of their e'
14 any longer stand before their e'.
18 out of the hand of their e' all the
3:28 for the Lord hath delivered your e'
5:31 So let all thine e' perish,
8:34 out of the hands of all their e' on
11:36 taken vengeance for thee of thine e',
1Sa 2: 1 my mouth is enlarged over mine e';
4: 3 save us out of the hand of our e'.
12:10 deliver us out of the hand of our e',
11 out of the hand of your e' on every
14:24 that I may be avenged on mine e'.
30 spoil of their e' which they found?
47 against all his e' on every side,
18:25 to be avenged of the king's e'.
20:15 Lord hath cut off the e' of David
16 require it at the hand of David's e'.
25:22 also do God unto the e' of David,
26 let thine e', and they that seek evil
29 souls of thine e', them shall he sling
29: 8 go fight against the e' of my lord
30:26 the spoil of the e' of the Lord;
2Sa 3:18 out of the hand of all their e'.
5:20 hath broken forth upon mine e'
7: 1 rest round about from all his e';
9 cut off all thine e' out of thy sight,
11 caused thee to rest from all thine e'.
12:14 great occasion to the e' of the Lord
18:19 the Lord hath avenged him of his e'.
32 The e' of my lord the king, and all
19: 6 thine e', and hatest thy friends.
9 saved us out of the hand of our e',
22: 1 him out of the hand of all his e', and
4 so shall I be saved from mine e'.
38 I have pursued mine e', and
41 also given me the necks of mine e',
49 bringeth me forth from mine e':
24:13 flee three months before thine e',
1Ki 3:11 nor hast asked the life of thine e';
8:48 their soul, in the land of their e',
2Ki 17:39 you out of the hand of all your e'.
21:14 them into the hand of their e';
14 a prey and a spoil to all their e';
1Ch 12:17 be come to betray me to mine e',
14:11 God hath broken in upon mine e'
17: 8 and have cut off all thine e' from
10 Moreover I will subdue all thine e'.
21:12 while that the sword of thine e'
22: 9 I will give him rest from all his e'
2Ch 1:11 or honour, nor the life of thine e',
6:28 their e' besiege them in the cities
34 go out to war against their e' by the
36 deliver them over before their e',
20:27 made them to rejoice over their e'.
29 fought against the e' of Israel,
25:20 deliver them into the hands of their e',
Ne 4:15 our e' heard that it was known
5: 9 the reproach of the heathen our e'?
6: 1 the Arabian, and the rest of our e',
16 that when all our e' heard thereof,
9:27 them into the hand of their e',
27 saved out of the hand of their e'.
28 thou them in the hand of their e',
Es 8:13 to avenge themselves on their e'.
9: 1 the day that the e' of the Jews hoped
5 Thus the Jews smote all their e'
16 and had rest from their e', and slew
22 the Jews rested from their e',
Job 19:11 me unto him as one of his e'.
Ps 3: 7 thou hast smitten all mine e'
5: 8 because of mine e'; make thy way
6: 7 waxeth old because of all mine e'.
10 Let all mine e' be ashamed and
7: 6 because of the rage of mine e':
8: 2 strength because of thine e', that
9: 3 When mine e' are turned back,
10: 5 for all his e', he puffeth at them.
17: 9 from my deadly e', who compass me
18:title him from the hand of all his e',
3 so shall I be saved from mine e'.
37 I have pursued mine e', and
40 also given me the necks of mine e';
48 He delivereth me from mine e':
21: 8 Thine hand shall find out all thine e':
23: 5 me in the presence of mine e':
25: 2 let not mine e' triumph over me.
19 consider mine e'; for they are many;
27: 2 even mine e' and my foes, came
6 head be lfted up above mine e':
11 a plain path, because of mine e'.
12 not over unto the will of mine e':
31:11 was a reproach among all mine e',
15 me from the hand of mine e',
35:19 Let not them that are mine e'
37:20 and the e' of the Lord shall be as
38:19 But mine e' are lively, and they
41: 2 deliver him unto the will of his e'.
5 Mine e' speak evil of me, When
42:10 mine e' reproach me; while they
44: 5 thee will we push down our e':
7 thou hast saved us from our e',
45: 5 in the heart of the king's e';
54: 5 He shall reward evil unto mine e':
7 hath seen his desire upon mine e'.
56: 2 Mine e' would daily swallow me

Ps 56: 9 then shall mine *e'* turn back:
59: 1 Deliver me from mine *e'*, O my God:
10 me see my desire upon mine *e'*.
60:12 it is that shall tread down our *e'*.
66: 3 shall thine *e'* submit themselves
68: 1 God arise, let his *e'* be scattered:
21 God shall wound the head of his *e'*,
23 be dipped in the blood of thine *e'*,
69: 4 being mine *e'* wrongfully, are mighty:
18 deliver me because of mine *e'*.
71:10 For mine *e'* speak against me;
72: 9 and his *e'* shall lick the dust.
74: 4 Thine *e'* roar in the midst of thy
23 Forget not the voice of thine *e'*:
78:53 but the sea overwhelmed their *e'*.
66 smote his *e'* in the hinder parts:
80: 6 our *e'* laugh among themselves.
81:14 I should soon have subdued their *e'*,
83: 2 For, lo, thine *e'* make a tumult:
89:10 scattered thine *e'* with thy strong
42 thou hast made all his *e'* to rejoice.
51 Wherewith thine *e'* have reproached,
92: 9 For, lo, thine *e'*, O Lord,
9 for, lo, thine *e'* shall perish;
11 shall see my desire on mine *e'*,
97: 3 burneth up his *e'* round about.
102: 8 Mine *e'* reproach me all the day;
105:24 made them stronger than their *e'*.
106:11 And the waters covered their *e'*:
42 Their *e'* also oppressed them, and
108:13 it is that shall tread down our *e'*.
110: 1 until I make thine *e'* thy footstool.
2 rule thou in the midst of thine *e'*.
112: 8 he see his desire upon his *e'*.
119:98 hast made me wiser than mine *e'*:
139 mine *e'* have forgotten thy words.
157 are my persecutors and mine *e'*;
127: 5 but they shall speak with the *e'*
132:18 His *e'* will I clothe with shame:
136:24 hath redeemed us from our *e'*:
138: 7 hand against the wrath of mine *e'*,
139:20 thine *e'* take thy name in vain.
22 hatred: I count them mine *e'*.
143: 9 Deliver me, O Lord, from mine *e'*:
12 And of thy mercy cut off mine *e'*,
Pr 16: 7 maketh even his *e'* to be at peace
Isa 1:24 and avenge me of mine *e'*:
9:11 and join his *e'* together;
26:11 of thine *e'* shall devour them.
42:13 he shall prevail against his *e'*.
59:18 adversaries, recompence to his *e'*;
62: 8 thy corn to be meat for thine *e'*;
66: 6 rendereth recompence to his *e'*.
14 and his indignation toward his *e'*.
Jer 12: 7 my soul into the hand of her *e'*.
15: 9 deliver to the sword before their *e'*,
14 make thee to pass with thine *e'*
17: 4 I will cause thee to serve thine *e'*
19: 7 to fall by the sword before their *e'*,
9 and straitness, wherewith their *e'*,
20: 4 shall fall by the sword of their *e'*,
5 I give into the hand of their *e'*,
21: 7 and into the hand of their *e'*,
34:20 give them into the hand of their *e'*,
21 I give into the hand of their *e'*,
44:30 king of Egypt into the hand of his *e'*,
48: 5 *e'* have heard a cry of destruction.
49:37 Elam to be dismayed before their *e'*,
La 1: 2 with her, they are become her *e'*.
5 are the chief, her *e'* prosper;
21 mine *e'* have heard of my trouble;
2:16 thine *e'* have opened their mouth
3:46 All our *e'* have opened their mouths
52 Mine *e'* chased me sore, like a bird,
Eze 39:23 them into the hand of their *e'*;
Da 4:19 interpretation thereof to thine *e'*.
Am 9: 4 go into captivity before their *e'*,
Mic 4:10 thee from the hand of thine *e'*.
5: 9 all thine *e'* shall be cut off.
7: 6 a man's *e'* are the men of his own
Na 1: 2 he reserveth wrath for his *e'*.
8 and darkness shall pursue his *e'*.
3:13 be set wide open unto thine *e'*:
Zec 10: 5 which tread down their *e'* in the
M't 5:44 Love your *e'*, bless them that curse
22:44 till I make thine *e'* thy footstool?
M'r 12:36 till I make thine *e'* thy footstool.
Lu 1:71 That we should be saved from our *e'*,
74 delivered out of the hand of our *e'*
6:27 Love your *e'*, do good to them that
35 love ye your *e'*, and do good,
19:27 But those mine *e'*, which would not
43 thine *e'* shall cast a trench about
20:43 Till I make thine *e'* thy footstool.
Ro 5:10 when we were *e'*, we were reconciled
11:28 they are *e'* for your sakes:
1Co 15:25 till he hath put all *e'* under his feet.
Ph'p 3:18 that they are the *e'* of the cross of
Col 1:21 *e'* in your mind by wicked works,
Heb 1:13 until I make thine *e'* thy footstool?
10:13 till his *e'* be made his footstool.
Re 11: 5 their mouth and devoureth their *e'*:
12 and their *e'* beheld them.

enemies'
Le 26:34 and ye be in your *e'* land;
39 their iniquity in your *e'* lands;
Eze 39:27 gathered them out of their *e'* lands,

enemy See also ENEMIES; ENEMY'S.
Ex 15: 6 Lord hath dashed in pieces the *e'*.
9 The *e'* said, I will pursue, I will
23:22 I will be an *e'* unto thine enemies,
Le 26:25 delivered into the hand of the *e'*.
Nu 10: 9 the *e'* that oppresseth you, then
35:23 that he die, and was not his *e'*,
De 28:57 wherewith thine *e'* shall distress
De 32:27 not that I feared the wrath of the *e'*,
42 beginning of revenges upon the *e'*.
33:27 he shall thrust out the *e'* from
J'g 16:23 hath delivered Samson our *e'* into
24 hath delivered into our hands our *e'*,
1Sa 2:32 shalt see an *e'* in my habitation,
18:29 Saul became David's *e'* continually.
19:17 and sent away mine *e'*, that he is
24: 4 will deliver thine *e'* into thine hand,
19 For if a man find his *e'*, will he let
26: 8 hath delivered thine *e'* into thine
28:16 thee, and is become thine *e'*?
2Sa 4: 8 the son of Saul thine *e'*, which
22:18 He delivered me from my strong *e'*,
1Ki 8:33 Israel be smitten down before the *e'*,
37 if their *e'* besiege them in the land
44 go out to battle against their *e'*,
46 them, and deliver them to the *e'*,
46 captives unto the land of the *e'*,
21:20 Hast thou found me, O mine *e'*?
2Ch 6:24 be put to the worse before the *e'*,
25: 8 shall make thee fall before the *e'*:
26:13 to help the king against the *e'*.
Ezr 8:22 help us against the *e'* in the way:
31 delivered us from the hand of the *e'*,
Es 3:10 the Agagite, the Jews' *e'*.
7: 4 the *e'* could not countervail the
6 and *e'* is this wicked Haman.
8: 1 Haman the Jews' *e'* unto Esther
9:10 Hammedatha, the *e'* of the Jews,
24 the Agagite, the *e'* of all the Jews,
Job 13:24 and holdest me for thine *e'*?
16: 9 mine *e'* sharpeneth his eyes upon
27: 7 Let mine *e'* be as the wicked,
33:10 he counteth me for his *e'*,
Ps 7: 4 that without cause is mine *e'*:)
5 Let the *e'* persecute my soul,
8: 2 that thou mightest still the *e'* and
9: 6 O thou *e'*, destructions are come
13: 2 how long shall mine *e'* be exalted
4 Lest mine *e'* say, I have prevailed
18:17 He delivered me from my strong *e'*,
31: 8 shut me up into the hand of the *e'*:
41:11 mine *e'* doth not triumph over me.
42: 9 because of the oppression of the *e'*?
43: 2 because of the oppression of the *e'*?
44:10 us to turn back from the *e'*:
16 by reason of the *e'* and avenger.
55: 3 Because of the voice of the *e'*,
12 For it was not an *e'* that reproached
61: 3 and a strong tower from the *e'*.
64: 1 preserve my life from fear of the *e'*.
74: 3 all that the *e'* hath done wickedly
10 shall the *e'* blaspheme thy name
18 this, that the *e'* hath reproached,
78:42 he delivered them from the *e'*.
89:22 The *e'* shall not exact upon him;
106:10 them from the hand of the *e'*.
107: 2 redeemed from the hand of the *e'*;
143: 3 the *e'* hath persecuted my soul;
Pr 24:17 Rejoice not when thine *e'* falleth,
25:21 If thine *e'* be hungry, give him
27: 6 the kisses of an *e'* are deceitful.
Isa 59:19 the *e'* shall come in like a flood,
63:10 he was turned to be their *e'*,
Jer 6:25 for the sword of the *e'* and fear is on
15:11 I will cause the *e'* to entreat thee
18:17 as with an east wind before the *e'*;
30:14 thee with the wound of an *e'*,
31:16 come again from the land of the *e'*.
44:30 king of Babylon, his *e'*, and that
La 1: 5 gone into captivity before the *e'*.
7 people fell into the hand of the *e'*,
9 for the *e'* hath magnified himself.
16 desolate, because the *e'* prevailed.
2: 3 his right hand from before the *e'*,
4 He hath bent his bow like an *e'*:
5 The Lord was as an *e'*: he hath
7 hath given up into the hand of the *e'*
17 he hath caused thine *e'* to rejoice
22 brought up hath mine *e'* consumed.
4:12 and the *e'* should have entered into
Eze 36: 2 Because the *e'* hath said against you,
Ho 8: 3 is good: the *e'* shall pursue him.
Mic 2: 8 my people is risen up as an *e'*:
7: 8 Rejoice not against me, O mine *e'*:
10 Then she that is mine *e'* shall see it,
Na 3:11 seek strength because of the *e'*.
Zep 3:15 he hath cast out thine *e'*:
M't 5:43 thy neighbour, and hate thine *e'*.
13:25 his *e'* came and sowed tares among
28 unto them, An *e'* hath done this.
39 The *e'* that sowed them is the devil;
Lu 10:19 and over all the power of the *e'*:
Ac 13:10 devil, thou *e'* of all righteousness,
Ro 12:20 Therefore if thine *e'* hunger, feed
1Co 15:26 The last *e'* that shall be destroyed
Gal 4:16 Am I therefore become your *e'*,
2Th 3:15 Yet count him not as an *e'*,
Jas 4: 4 friend of the world is the *e'* of God.

enemy's
Ex 23: 4 If thou meet thine *e'* ox or his ass
Job 6:23 Deliver me from the *e'* hand?
Ps 78:61 and his glory into the *e'* hand.

enflaming See also INFLAME.
Isa 57: 5 *E'* yourselves with idols under

engaged
Jer 30:21 for who is this that *e'* his heart to

En-gannim (*en-gan'-nim*)
Jos 15:34 And Zanoah, and *E'*, Tappuah,
19:21 Remeth, and *E'*, and En-haddah,
21:29 Jarmuth with her suburbs, *E'* with

En-gedi (*en-ghe'-di*) See also HAZAZON-TAMAR.
Jos 15:62 and the city of Salt, and *E'*;
1Sa 23:29 and dwelt in strong holds at *E'*.
24: 1 David is in the wilderness of *E'*.
2Ch 20: 2 be in Hazazon-tamar, which is *E'*.
Ca 1:14 camphire in the vineyards of *E'*.
Eze 47:10 fishers shall stand upon it from *E'*

engines
2Ch 26:15 And he made in Jerusalem *e'*,
Eze 26: 9 he shall set *e'* of war against thy

engrafted See also GRAFFED.
Jas 1:21 with meekness the *e'* word, which

engrave See also ENGRAVEN; ENGRAVINGS.
Ex 28:11 shalt thou *e'* the two stones with
Zec 3: 9 behold, I will *e'* the graving thereof,

engraven
2Co 3: 7 written and *e'* in stones, was

engraver
Ex 28:11 With the work of an *e'* in stone,
35:35 all manner of work, of the *e'*,
38:23 an *e'*, and a cunning workman,

engravings
Ex 28:11 in stone, like the *e'* of a signet,
21 names, like the *e'* of a signet;
36 upon it, like the *e'* of a signet,
39:14 names, like the *e'* of a signet,
30 writing, like to the *e'* of a signet,

En-haddah (*en-had'-dah*)
Jos 19:21 and *E'*, and Beth-pazzez;

En-hakkore (*en-hak'-ko-re*)
J'g 15:19 he called the name thereof *E'*,

En-hazor (*en-ha'-zor*)
Jos 19:37 And Kedesh, and Edrei, and *E'*,

enjoin See also ENJOINED.
Ph'm 8 much bold in Christ to *e'* thee

enjoined
Es 9:31 and Esther the queen had *e'* them,
Job 36:23 Who hath *e'* him his way? who
Heb 9:20 which God hath *e'* unto you.

enjoy See also ENJOYED.
Le 26:34 shall the land *e'* her sabbaths,
34 the land rest, and *e'* her sabbaths.
43 shall *e'* her sabbaths, while she
Nu 36: 8 children of Israel may *e'* every
De 28:41 daughters, but thou shalt not *e'*
Jos 1:15 land of your possession, and *e'* it,
Ec 2: 1 with mirth, therefore *e'* pleasure:
24 he should make his soul *e'* good in
3:13 and *e'* the good of all his labour,
5:18 eat and to drink, and to *e'* the good
Isa 65:22 long *e'* the work of their hands.
Ac 24: 2 Seeing that by thee we *e'* great
1Ti 6:17 giveth us richly all things to *e'*;
Heb 11:25 than to *e'* the pleasures of sin

enjoyed
2Ch 36:21 until the land had *e'* her sabbaths:

enlarge See also ENLARGED; ENLARGETH; ENLARGING.
Ge 9:27 God shall *e'* Japheth, and he shall
Ex 34:24 before thee, and *e'* thy borders:
De 12:20 When the Lord thy God shall *e'* thy
19: 8 if the Lord thy God *e'* thy coast,
1Ch 4:10 wouldest bless....and *e'* my coast,
Ps 119:32 when thou shalt *e'* my heart.
Isa 54: 2 *E'* the place of thy tent, and let
Am 1:13 that they might *e'* their border:
Mic 1:16 *e'* thy baldness as the eagle for;
M't 23: 5 *e'* the borders of their garments,

enlarged
1Sa 2: 1 my mouth is *e'* over mine enemies;
2Sa 22:37 Thou hast *e'* my steps under me;
Ps 4: 1 thou hast *e'* me when I was in
18:36 Thou hast *e'* my steps under me,
25:17 The troubles of my heart are *e'*:
Isa 5:14 Therefore hell hath *e'* herself,
57: 8 gone up; thou hast *e'* thy bed,
60: 5 thine heart shall fear, and be *e'*;
2Co 6:11 is open unto you, our heart is *e'*.
13 unto my children,) be ye also *e'*.
10:15 that we shall be *e'* by you

enlargement
Es 4:14 shall there *e'* and deliverance

enlargeth
De 33:20 Blessed be he that *e'* Gad:
Job 12:23 he *e'* the nations, and straiteneth
Hab 2: 5 who *e'* his desire as hell, and is

enlarging
Eze 41: 7 there was an *e'*, and a winding

enlighten See also ENLIGHTENED; ENLIGHTENING.
Ps 18:28 Lord my God will *e'* my darkness.

enlightened
1Sa 14:27 his mouth; and his eyes were *e'*.
29 mine eyes have been *e'*, because
Job 33:30 to be *e'* with the light of the living.
Ps 97: 4 His lightnings *e'* the world:
Eph 1:18 of your understanding being *e'*;
Heb 6: 4 those who were once *e'*, and have

enlightening
Ps 19: 8 of the Lord is pure, *e'* the eyes.

En-mishpat (*en-mish'-pat*) See also KADESH.
Ge 14: 7 they returned, and came to *E'*,

enmity
Ge 3:15 put *e'* between thee and the woman,
Nu 35:21 Or in *e'* smite him with his hand,
22 thrust him suddenly without *e'*,
Lu 23:12 were at *e'* between themselves.
Ro 8: 7 the carnal mind is *e'* against God:

Eph 2:15 abolished in his flesh the e',
16 having slain the e' thereby:
Jas 4: 4 friendship of the world is e' with

Enoch (e'-nok) See also HENOCH.
Ge 4:17 and she conceived, and bare E':
17 after the name of his son, E'.
18 unto E' was born Irad: and Irad
5:18 and two years, and he begat E':
19 Jared lived after he begat E' eight
21 And E' lived sixty and five years,
22 E' walked with God after he begat
23 the days of E' were three hundred
24 E' walked with God: and he was not;
Lu 3:37 which was the son of E', which
Heb 11: 5 By faith E' was translated that he
Jude 14 E' also, the seventh from Adam,

Enon. See ÆNON.

Enos (e'-nos) See also ENOSH.
Ge 4:26 called his name E': then began
5: 6 and five years, and begat E':
7 And Seth lived after he begat E'
9 E' lived ninety years, and begat
10 E' lived after he begat Cainan
11 the days of E' were nine hundred
Lu 3:38 Which was the son of E', which

Enosh (e'-nosh) See also ENOS.
1Ch 1: 1 Adam, Sheth, E',

enough
Ge 24:25 have both straw and provender e'
33: 9 Esau said, I have e', my brother;
11 with me, and because I have e'.
34:21 behold, it is large e' for them;
45:28 Israel said, It is e'; Joseph my
Ex 2:19 and also drew water e' for us,
9:28 Intreat the Lord (for it is e') that
36: 5 much more than e' for the service
De 1: 6 Ye have dwelt long e' in this mount;
2: 3 compassed this mountain long e':
Jos 17:16 The hill is not e' for us:
2Sa 24:16 It is e': stay now thine hand. And
1Ki 19: 4 It is e'; now, O Lord, take away
1Ch 21:15 It is e', stay now thine hand. And
2Ch 31:10 we have had e' to eat, and have
Pr 27:27 have goats' milk e' for thy food,
28:19 persons shall have poverty e'.
30:15 yea, four things say not, It is e':
16 and the fire that saith not, It is e'.
Isa 56:11 dogs which can never have e',
Jer 49: 9 they will destroy till they have e'.
Ho 4:10 they shall eat, and not have e':
Ob 5 not have stolen till they had e'?
Na 2:12 did tear in pieces e' for his whelps,
Hag 1: 6 little; ye eat, but ye have not e';
Mal 3:10 that there shall not be room e'
M't 10:25 It is e' for the disciple that he be
25: 9 lest there be not e' for us and you:
M'r 14:41 your rest: it is e', the hour is come;
Lu 15:17 have bread e' and to spare, and I
22:38 he said unto them, It is e'.
Ac 27:38 they had eaten e', they lightened

enquire See also ENQUIRED; ENQUIREST; ENQUIRY.
Ge 24:57 We will call the damsel, and e' at
25:22 And she went to e' of the Lord.
Ex 18:15 people come unto me to e' of God:
De 12:30 that thou e' not after their gods,
13:14 shalt thou e', and make search,
17: 9 and e'; and they shall shew thee
J'g 4:20 man doth come and e' of thee,
1Sa 9: 9 when a man went to e' of God,
17:56 E' thou whose son the stripling is.
22:15 Did I then begin to e' of God for
28: 7 that I may go to her, and e' of her.
1Ki 22: 5 E', I pray thee, at the word of the
7 besides, that we might e' of him?
8 by whom we may e' of the Lord:
2Ki 1: 2 e' of Baal-zebub the god of Ekron
3 that ye go to e' of Baal-zebub
6 thou sendest to e' of Baal-zebub
16 e' of Baal-zebub the god of Ekron,
16 no God in Israel to e' of his word?
3:11 that we may e' of the Lord by him?
8: 8 and e' of the Lord by him,
16:15 altar shall be for me to e' by.
22:13 Go ye, e' of the Lord for me,
18 which sent you to e' of the Lord,
1Ch 10:13 had a familiar spirit, to e' of it;
18:10 his son to king David, to e' of his
21:30 could not go before it to e' of God:
2Ch 18: 4 E', I pray thee, at the word of the
6 besides, that we might e' of him?
7 by whom we may e' of the Lord:
32:31 sent unto him to e' of the wonder
34:21 Go, e' of the Lord for me, and for
26 who sent you to e' of the Lord,
Ezr 7:14 to e' concerning Judah and
Job 8: 8 e', I pray thee, of the former age,
Ps 27: 4 the Lord, and to e' in his temple.
Ec 7:10 dost not e' wisely concerning this.
Isa 21:12 if ye will e', e' ye: return, come,
Jer 21: 2 E', I pray thee, of the Lord for us;
37: 7 that sent you unto me to e' of me;
Eze 14: 7 prophet to e' of him concerning
20: 1 of Israel came to e' of the Lord,
3 Are ye come to e' of me?
M't 10:11 e' who in it is worthy; and there
Lu 22:23 began to e' among themselves,
Joh 16:19 Do ye e' among yourselves of that
Ac 9:11 e' in the house of Judas for one
19:39 But if ye e' any thing concerning
23:15 as though ye would e' something
20 as though they would e' somewhat
2Co 8:23 Whether any do e' of Titus, he is

enquired
De 17: 4 e' diligently, and, behold, it be
J'g 6:29 And when they e' and asked,
8:14 a young man..., and e' of him:
20:27 children of Israel e' of the Lord,
1Sa 10:22 they e' of the Lord further, if the
22:10 And he e' of the Lord for him,
13 and hast e' of God for him,
23: 2 Therefore David e' of the Lord,
4 David e' of the Lord yet again.
28: 6 And when Saul e' of the Lord,
30: 8 And David e' at the Lord, saying,
2Sa 2: 1 that David e' of the Lord, saying,
5:19 And David e' of the Lord, saying,
23 when David e' of the Lord, he said,
11: 3 David sent and e' after the woman.
16:23 as if a man had e' at the oracle
21: 1 year; and David e' of the Lord.
1Ch 10:14 And e' not of the Lord: therefore
13: 3 we e' not at it in the days of Saul.
14:10 And David e' of God, saying,
14 Therefore David e' again of God;
Ps 78:34 returned and e' early after God.
Eze 14: 3 should I be e' of at all by them?
20: 3 Lord God, I will not be e' of by you.
31 and shall I be e' of by you, O house
31 Lord God, I will not be e' of by you.
36:37 I will yet for this be e' of by the
Da 1:20 king e' of them, he found them
Zep 1: 6 sought the Lord, nor e' for him.
M't 2: 7 e' of them diligently what time the
16 had diligently e' of the wise men.
Joh 4:52 Then e' he of them the hour
2Co 8:23 or our brethren be e' of, they
1Pe 1:10 have e' and searched diligently,

enquirest
Job 10: 6 That thou e' after mine iniquity,

enquiry
Pr 20:25 and after vows to make e'.
Ac 10:17 had made e' for Simon's house,

enrich See also ENRICHED; ENRICHEST.
1Sa 17:25 king will e' him with great riches,
Eze 27:33 thou didst e' the kings of the earth

enriched
1Co 1: 5 in every thing ye are e' by him,
2Co 9:11 e' in every thing to all bountifulness,

enrichest
Ps 65: 9 greatly e' it with the river of God,

En-rimmon (en-rim'-mon) See also AIN and RIMMON.
Ne 11:29 And at E', and at Zareah, and at

En-rogel (en-ro'-ghel)
Jos 15: 7 the goings out thereof were at E':
18:16 on the south, and descended to E',
2Sa 17:17 and Ahimaaz stayed by E';
1Ki 1: 9 stone of Zoheleth, which is by E',

ensample See also ENSAMPLES; EXAMPLE.
Ph'p 3:17 walk as ye have us for an e'.
2Th 3: 9 to make ourselves an e' unto you
2Pe 2: 6 making them an e' unto those

ensamples
1Co 10:11 things happened unto them for e':
1Th 1: 7 that ye were e' to all that believe
1Pe 5: 3 but being e' to the flock.

En-shemesh (en-she'-mesh)
Jos 15: 7 passed toward the waters of E',
18:17 and went forth to E', and went

ensign See also ENSIGNS.
Nu 2: 2 the e' of their father's house:
Isa 5:26 he will lift up an e' to the nations
11:10 shall stand for an e' of the people;
12 he shall set up an e' for the nations,
18: 3 lifteth up an e' on the mountains;
30:17 and as an e' on an hill.
31: 9 his princes shall be afraid of the e'.
Zec 9:16 lifted up as an e' upon his land.

ensigns
Ps 74: 4 they set up their e' for signs.

ensnared
Job 34:30 reign not, lest the people be e'.

ensue See also PURSUE.
1Pe 3:11 let him seek peace, and e' it.

entangle See also ENTANGLED; ENTANGLETH.
M't 22:15 how they might e' him in his talk.

entangled
Ex 14: 3 of Israel, They are e' in the land,
Ga 5: 1 e' again with the yoke of bondage,
2Pe 2:20 they are again e' therein, and

entangleth
2Ti 2: 4 e' himself with the affairs of this

En-tappuah (en-tap'-poo-ah)
Jos 17: 7 hand, unto the inhabitants of E'.

enter See also ENTERED; ENTERETH; ENTERING.
Ge 12:11 he was come near to e' into Egypt,
Ex 40:35 Moses was not able to e' into the
Nu 4: 3 that e' into the host, to do the work
23 all that e' in to perform service,
5:24, 27 causeth the curse shall e' into
20:24 for he shall not e' into the land
De 23: 1 member cut off, shall not e' into the
2 A bastard shall not e' into the
2 generation shall he not e' into the
3 or Moabite shall not e' into the
3 generation shall they not e' into the
8 begotten of them shall not e' into the
29:12 thou shouldest e' into covenant

Jos 10:19 them not to e' into their cities:
J'g 18: 9 and to e' to possess the land.
2Sa 22: 7 and my cry did e' into his ears.
1Ki 14:12 when thy feet e' into the city,
22:30 myself, and e' into the battle:
2Ki 7: 4 If we say, We will e' into the city,
11: 5 that e' in on the sabbath shall
19:23 e' into the lodgings of his borders,
2Ch 7: 2 priests could not e' into the house
23:19 unclean in any thing should e' in.
30: 8 and e' into his sanctuary, which he
Ne 2: 8 for the house that I shall e' into.
Es 4: 2 none might e' into the king's gate
Job 22: 4 he e' with thee into judgment?
34:23 that he should e' into judgment
Ps 37:15 sword shall e' into their own heart,
45:15 they shall e' into the king's palace.
95:11 that they should not e' into my rest.
100: 4 E' into his gates with thanksgiving,
118:20 into which the righteous shall e'.
143: 2 And e' not into judgment with thy
Pr 4:14 E' not into the path of the wicked,
18: 6 A fool's lips e' into contention,
23:10 and e' not into the fields of the
Isa 2:10 E' into the rock, and hide thee in
3:14 The Lord will e' into judgment with
26: 2 which keepeth the truth may e' in.
20 people, e' thou into thy chambers,
37:24 will e' into the height of his border,
57: 2 shall e' into peace: they shall rest
59:14 in the street, and equity cannot e'.
Jer 7: 2 that e' in at these gates to worship
8:14 and let us e' into the defenced cities,
14:18 if I e' into the city, then behold
16: 5 E' not into the house of mourning,
17:20 Jerusalem, that e' in by these gates:
25 Then shall there e' into the gates
21:13 who shall e' into our habitations?
22: 2 thy people that e' in by these gates:
4 then shall there e' in by the gates
41:17 Bethlehem, to go to e' into Egypt,
42:15 set your faces to e' into Egypt,
18 when ye shall e' into Egypt:
La 1:10 should not e' into thy congregation.
3:13 caused the arrows of his quiver to e'
Eze 7:22 for the robbers shall e' into it.
13: 9 they e' into the land of Israel;
20:38 shall not e' into the land of Israel:
26:10 when he shall e' into thy gates,
10 as men e' into a city wherein is
37: 5 I will cause breath to e' into you,
42:14 When the priests e' therein, then
44: 2 and no man shall e' in by it;
3 he shall e' by the way of the porch
9 in flesh, shall e' into my sanctuary,
16 They shall e' into my sanctuary,
17 when they e' in at the gates of the
21 when they e' into the inner court.
46: 2 And the prince shall e' by the way
8 And when the prince shall e', he
Da 11: 7 army, and shall e' into the fortress
17 He shall also set his face to e'
24 He shall e' peaceably even upon
40 and he shall e' into the countries,
41 shall e' also into the glorious land,
Ho 11: 9 and I will not e' into the city.
Joe 2: 9 they shall e' in at the windows
Am 5: 5 seek not Bethel, nor e' into Gilgal,
Jon 3: 4 And Jonah began to e' into the city
Zec 5: 4 and it shall e' into the house of the
M't 5:20 e' into the kingdom of heaven.
6: 6 thou prayest, e' into thy closet,
7:13 E' ye in at the strait gate:
21 Lord, shall e' into the kingdom of
10: 5 city of the Samaritans e' ye not:
11 whatsoever city or town ye shall e',
12:29 one e' into a strong man's house,
45 and they e' in and dwell there:
18: 3 not e' into the kingdom of heaven.
8 thee to e' into life halt or maimed,
9 for thee to e' into life with one eye,
19:17 if thou wilt e' into life, keep the
23 shall hardly e' into the kingdom of
24 to e' into the kingdom of God.
25:21, 23 e' thou into the joy of thy lord.
26:41 that ye e' not into temptation:
M'r 1:45 no more openly e' into the city,
3:27 can e' into a strong man's house,
5:12 swine, that we may e' into them.
6:10 place soever ye e' into an house,
9:25 of him, and e' no more into him.
43 for thee to e' into life maimed,
45 better for thee to e' halt into life,
47 thee to e' into the kingdom of God
10:15 little child, he shall not e' therein.
23 shall...e' into the kingdom of God!
24 riches to e' into the kingdom of God!
25 man to e' into the kingdom of God.
13:15 neither e' therein, to take any
14:38 pray, lest ye e' into temptation.
Lu 7: 6 thou shouldest e' under my roof:
8:16 they which e' in may see the light.
32 would suffer them to e' into them.
9: 4 house ye e' into, there abide,
10: 5 whatsoever house ye e', first say,
8 into whatsoever city ye e', and
10 But into whatsoever city ye e',
11:26 and they e' in, and dwell there:
13:24 Strive to e' in at the strait gate:
24 seek to e' in, and shall not be able.
18:17 child shall in no wise e' therein.
24 riches e' into the kingdom of God!
25 man to e' into the kingdom of God.
21:21 are in the countries e' thereinto.
22:40 that ye e' not into temptation.

Lu 22:46 pray, lest ye *e* into temptation.
24:26 things, and to *e* into his glory?
Joh 3: 4 can he *e* the second time into his
5 cannot *e* into the kingdom of God.
10: 9 if any man *e* in, he shall be saved,
Ac 14:22 *e* into the kingdom of God.
20:29 grievous wolves *e* in among you,
Heb 3:11 They shall not *e* into my rest.)
18 that they should not *e* into his rest,
19 that they could not *e* in because
4: 3 which have believed do *e* into rest,
3 wrath, if they shall *e* into my rest:
5 again, If they shall *e* into my rest.
6 that some must *e* therein, and they
11 therefore to *e* into that rest, lest
10:19 boldness to *e* into the holiest by
Re 15: 8 was able to *e* into the temple,
21:27 there shall in no wise *e* into it
22:14 *e* in through the gates into the city.

entered
Ge 7:13 In the selfsame day *e* Noah, and
19: 3 unto him, and *e* into his house;
23 the earth when Lot *e* into Zoar.
31:33 Leah's tent, and *e* into Rachel's
43:30 and he *e* into his chamber, and
Ex 33: 9 as Moses *e* into the tabernacle,
Jos 2: 3 which are *e* into thine house: for
8:19 and they *e* into the city, and took it,
10:20 of them *e* into fenced cities.
J'g 6: 5 they *e* into the land to destroy it,
9:46 they *e* into an hold of the house
2Sa 10:14 Abishai, and *e* into the city.
2Ki 7: 8 again, and *e* into another tent,
9:31 as Jehu *e* in at the gate,
1Ch 19:15 and *e* into the city. Then Joab
2Ch 12:11 king *e* into the house of the Lord,
15:12 *e* into a covenant to seek the Lord
27: 2 howbeit he *e* not into the temple
32: 1 and *e* into Judah, and encamped
Ne 2:15 and *e* by the gate of the valley,
10:29 *e* into a curse, and into an oath,
Job 38:16 Hast thou *e* into the springs of the
22 Hast thou *e* into the treasures of
Jer 2: 7 but when ye *e*, ye defiled my land,
9:21 and is *e* into our palaces, to cut off
34:10 which had *e* into the covenant,
37:16 was *e* into the dungeon, and into
La 1:10 the heathen *e* into her sanctuary.
4:12 should have *e* into the gates
Eze 2: 2 the spirit *e* into me when he spake
3:24 Then the spirit *e* into me, and set
16: 8 and *e* into a covenant with thee,
36:20 when they *e* unto the heathen,
41: 6 and they entered into the wall
44: 2 the God of Israel, hath *e* in by it,
Ob 11 and foreigners *e* into his gates,
13 shouldest not have *e* into the gate
Hab 3:16 rottenness *e* into my bones, and I
M't 8: 5 when Jesus was *e* into Capernaum,
23 when he was *e* into a ship,
9: 1 he *e* into a ship, and passed over,
12: 4 How he *e* into the house of God,
24:38 the day that Noe *e* into the ark,
M'r 1:21 he *e* into the synagogue, and
29 they *e* into the house of Simon
2: 1 again he *e* into Capernaum after
3: 1 he *e* again into the synagogue;
4: 1 he *e* into a ship, and sat in the sea;
5:13 went out, and *e* into the swine:
6:56 whithersoever he *e*, into villages,
7:17 when he was *e* into the house
24 *e* into an house, and would have
8:10 he *e* into a ship with his disciples.
11: 2 as soon as ye be *e* into it,
11 Jesus *e* into Jerusalem, and into
Lu 1:40 And *e* into the house of Zacharias,
4:38 synagogue, and *e* into Simon's
5: 3 he *e* into one of the ships, which
6: 6 *e* into the synagogue and taught:
7: 1 people, he *e* into Capernaum.
44 I *e* into thine house, thou gavest
8:30 many devils were *e* into him.
33 *e* into the swine: and the herd ran
9:34 feared as they *e* into the cloud.
52 they went, and *e* into a village
10:38 that he *e* into a certain village:
11:52 ye *e* not in yourselves, and them
17:12 as he *e* into a certain village,
27 day that Noe *e* into the ark,
19: 1 Jesus *e* and passed through
22: 3 Then *e* Satan into Judas surnamed
10 when ye are *e* into the city, there
24: 3 they *e* in, and found not the body
Joh 4:38 and ye are *e* into their labours.
6:17 *e* into a ship, and went over the
22 whereinto his disciples were *e*,
13:27 after the sop Satan *e* into him.
18: 1 was a garden, into the which he *e*,
33 Then Pilate *e* into the judgment
21: 3 They went forth, and *e* into a ship
Ac 3: 2 ask alms of them that *e* into the
8 and *e* with them into the temple,
5:21 they *e* into the temple early in the
9:17 went his way, and *e* into the house;
10:24 And the morrow after they *e* into
11: 8 hath at any time *e* into my mouth.
12 and we *e* into the man's house:
16:40 and *e* into the house of Lydia:
18: 7 and *e* into a certain man's house,
19 *e* the synagogue, and reasoned
19:30 Paul would have *e* in unto the
21: 8 we *e* into the house of Philip
26 with them *e* into the temple, to
23:16 *e* into the castle, and told Paul.
25:23 and was *e* into the place of hearing,
Ac 28: 8 to whom Paul *e* in, and prayed,
Ro 5:12 sin *e* into the world, and death by
20 Moreover the law *e*, that the
1Co 2: 9 neither have *e* into the heart of
Heb 4: 6 *e* not in because of unbelief:
10 For he that is *e* into his rest, he
6:20 Whither the forerunner is for us *e*,
9:12 he *e* in once into the holy place,
24 For Christ is not *e* into the holy
Jas 5: 4 are *e* into the ears of the Lord
2Jo 7 deceivers are *e* into the world,
Re 11:11 spirit of life from God *e* into them,

entereth
Nu 4:30 that *e* into the service, to do the
35, 39, 43 that *e* into the service, for
2Ch 31:16 every one that *e* into the house of
Pr 2:10 When wisdom *e* into thine heart,
17:10 A reproof *e* more into a wise man
Eze 21:14 which *e* into their privy chambers.
42:12 toward the east, as one *e* into them.
46: 9 he that *e* in by the way of the north
9 he that *e* by the way of the south
M't 15:17 whatsoever *e* in at the mouth
M'r 5:40 *e* in where the damsel was lying.
7:18 from without *e* into the man,
19 Because it *e* not into his heart,
Lu 22:10 him into the house where he *e* in.
Joh 10: 1 He that *e* not by the door into the
2 But he that *e* in by the door is
Heb 6:19 which *e* into that within the veil;
9:25 as the high priest *e* into the holy

entering See also ENTRANCE.
Ex 35:15 at the *e* in of the tabernacle.
Jos 8:29 at the *e* of the gate of the city,
13: 5 unto the *e* into Hamath.
20: 4 at the *e* of the gate of the city,
J'g 3: 3 unto the *e* in of Hamath.
9:35 in the *e* of the gate of the city:
40 even unto the *e* of the gate.
44 in the *e* of the gate of the city:
18:16 Dan, stood by the *e* of the gate.
17 priest stood in the *e* of the gate
2Sa 10: 8 in array at the *e* in of the gate:
11:23 them even unto the *e* of the gate.
1Ki 6:31 And for the *e* of the oracle he made
8:65 from the *e* in of Hamath unto the
19:13 and stood in the *e* in of the cave.
2Ki 7: 3 leprous men at the *e* in of the gate;
10: 8 two heaps at the *e* in of the gate
23: 8 in the *e* in of the gate of Joshua
11 at the *e* in of the house of the
1Ch 5: 9 unto the *e* in of the wilderness
13: 5 Egypt even unto the *e* of Hemath,
2Ch 7: 8 from the *e* in of Hamath unto the
18: 9 void place at the *e* in of the gate
23: 4 part of you *e* on the sabbath
13 king stood at his pillar at the *e*
15 when she was come to the *e* of
26: 8 abroad even to the *e* in of Egypt;
33:14 even to the *e* in at the fish gate.
Isa 23: 1 so that there is no house, no *e* in:
Jer 1:15 at the *e* of the gates of Jerusalem,
17:27 *e* in at the gates of Jerusalem
Eze 44: 5 mark well the *e* in of the house,
Am 6:14 afflict you from the *e* in of Hemath
M't 23:13 suffer ye them that are *e* to go in.
M'r 4:19 the lusts of other things *e* in,
7:15 that *e* into him can defile him;
8:13 *e* into the ship again departed
16: 5 *e* into the sepulchre, they saw a
Lu 11:52 them that were *e* in ye hindered.
19:30 in the which at your *e* ye shall
Ac 8: 3 As for Saul, . . . *e* into every house,
27: 2 *e* into a ship of Adramyttium,
1Th 1: 9 what manner of *e* in we had unto
Heb 4: 1 being left us of *e* into his rest,

enterprise
Job 5:12 hands cannot perform their *e*.

entertain See also ENTERTAINED.
Heb 13: 2 Be not forgetful to *e* strangers:

entertained
Heb 13: 2 some have *e* angels unawares.

entice See also ENTICED; ENTICETH.
Ex 22:16 if a man *e* a maid that is not
De 13: 6 *e* thee secretly, saying, Let us go
J'g 14:15 *E* thy husband, that he may
16: 5 *E* him, and see wherein his great
2Ch 18:19 Who shall *e* Ahab king of Israel,
20 before the Lord, and said, I will *e*
21 Thou shalt *e* him, and thou shalt
Pr 1:10 My son, if sinners *e* thee, consent

enticed
Job 31:27 my heart hath been secretly *e*,
Jer 20:10 Peradventure he will be *e*, and
Jas 1:14 drawn away of his own lust, and *e*.

enticeth
Pr 16:29 A violent man *e* his neighbour,

enticing
1Co 2: 4 with *e* words of man's wisdom,
Col 2: 4 should beguile you with *e* words,

entire
Jas 1: 4 that ye may be perfect and *e*,

entrance See also ENTERING; ENTRANCES; ENTRY.
Nu 34: 8 border unto the *e* of Hamath;
J'g 1:24 Shew us. . . the *e* into the city,
25 when he shewed them the *e* into
1Ki 18:46 ran before Ahab to the *e* of Jezreel.
22:10 in the *e* of the gate of Samaria;
1Ch 4:39 they went to the *e* of Gedor,
2Ch 12:10 that kept the *e* of the king's
Ps 119:130 The *e* of thy words giveth light;
Eze 40:15 the face of the gate of the *e*
1Th 2: 1 know our *e* in unto you, that it
2Pe 1:11 an *e* shall be ministered unto you

entrances
Mic 5: 6 land of Nimrod in the *e* thereof:

entreat See also ENTREATED; ENTREATETH; INTREAT.
Jer 15:11 cause the enemy to *e* thee well
Ac 7: 6 and *e* them evil four hundred

entreated See also INTREATED.
Ge 12:16 he *e* Abram well for her sake:
Ex 5:22 hast thou so evil *e* this people?
De 26: 6 And the Egyptians evil *e* us,
M't 22: 6 *e* them spitefully, and slew them.
Lu 18:32 shall be mocked, and spitefully *e*.
20:11 *e* him shamefully, and sent him
Ac 7:19 evil *e* our fathers, so that they
27: 3 Julius courteously *e* Paul, and
1Th 2: 2 before, and were shamefully *e*.

entreateth
Job 24:21 He evil *e* the barren that beareth

entreaty See INTREATY.

entries
Eze 40:38 the chambers and the *e* thereof

entry See also ENTERING; ENTRANCE; ENTRIES.
2Ki 16:18 king's *e* without, turned he from
1Ch 9:19 of the Lord, were keepers of the *e*.
2Ch 4:22 *e* of the house, the inner doors
Pr 8: 3 at the *e* of the city, at the coming
Jer 19: 2 which is by the *e* of the east gate,
26:10 sat down in the *e* of the new gate
36:10 court, at the *e* of the new gate
38:14 prophet unto him into the third *e*
43: 9 is at the *e* of Pharaoh's house
Eze 8: 5 this image of jealousy in the *e*.
27: 3 art situate at the *e* of the sea,
40:11 the breadth of the *e* of the gate,
40 goeth up to the *e* of the north gate,
42: 9 was the *e* on the east side,
46:19 he brought me through the *e*,

envied
Ge 26:14 and the Philistines *e* him.
30: 1 no children, Rachel *e* her sister;
37:11 his brethren *e* him; but his father
Ps 106:16 They *e* Moses also in the camp,
Ec 4: 4 this a man is *e* of his neighbour.
Eze 31: 9 that all the trees of Eden,... *e* him.

envies
1Pe 2: 1 guile, and hypocrisies, and *e*, and

enviest
Nu 11:29 unto him, *E* thou for my sake?

envieth
1Co 13: 4 charity *e* not; charity vaunteth

envious
Ps 37: 1 neither be thou *e* against the
73: 3 For I was *e* at the foolish, when
Pr 24: 1 Be not thou *e* against evil men,
19 neither be thou *e* at the wicked;

environ
Jos 7: 9 shall *e* us round, and cut off our

envy See also ENVIABLE; ENVIED; ENVIES; ENVIEST; ENVYING.
Job 5: 2 and *e* slayeth the silly one.
Pr 3:31 *E* thou not the oppressor, and
14:30 but *e* the rottenness of the bones.
23:17 Let not thine heart *e* sinners: but
27: 4 who is able to stand before *e*?
Ec 9: 6 their hatred, and their *e*, is now
Isa 11:13 The *e* also of Ephraim shall depart,
13 Ephraim shall not *e* Judah, and
26:11 for their *e* at the people; yea,
Eze 35:11 according to thine *e* which thou
M't 27:18 that for *e* they had delivered him.
M'r 15:10 priests had delivered him for *e*.
Ac 7: 9 patriarchs, moved with *e*, sold
13:45 were filled with *e*, and spake
17: 5 which believed not, moved with *e*
Ro 1:29 full of *e*, murder, debate, deceit,
Ph'p 1:15 preach Christ even of *e* and strife;
1Ti 6: 4 whereof cometh *e*, strife, railings,
Tit 3: 3 living in malice and *e*, hateful,
Jas 4: 5 that dwelleth in us lusteth to *e*?

envying See also ENVYINGS.
Ro 13:13 wantonness, not in strife and *e*.
1Co 3: 3 *e*, and strife, and divisions, are
Ga 5:26 one another, *e* one another.
Jas 3:14 But if ye have bitter *e* and strife
16 For where *e* and strife is, there

envyings
2Co 12:20 *e*, wraths, strifes, backbitings,
Ga 5:21 *E*, murders, drunkenness,

Epænetus (*ep-en'-e-tus*)
Ro 16: 5 Salute my well beloved *E*, who

Epaphras (*ep'-a-fras*)
Col 1: 7 As ye also learned of *E* our dear
4:12 *E*, who is one of you, a servant of
Ph'm 23 salute thee *E*, my fellowprisoner

Epaphroditus (*e-paf-ro-di'-tus*)
Ph'p 2:25 it necessary to send to you *E*,
4:18 having received of *E* the things
subscr. the Philippians from Rome by *E*.

Epenetus See EPAENETUS.

ephah (*e'-fah*)
Ex 16:36 an omer is the tenth part of an *e*.
Le 5:11 the tenth part of an *e* of fine flour
6:20 the tenth part of an *e* of fine flour
19:36 just weights, a just *e*, and a just
Nu 5:15 tenth part of an *e* of barley meal;

Nu 28: 5 And a tenth part of an e' of flour
J'g 6:19 unleavened cakes of an e' of flour:
Ru 2:17 and it was about an e' of barley.
1Sa 1:24 one e' of flour, and a bottle of wine,
17:17 brethren an e' of this parched corn,
Isa 5:10 seed of an homer shall yield an e'.
Eze 45:10 and a just e', and a just bath.
11 The e' and the bath shall be of one
11 the e' the tenth part of an homer
13 part of an e' of an homer of wheat,
13 part of an e' of an homer of barley:
24 an e' for a bullock, and an e' for a
24 a ram, and an hin of oil for an e'.
46: 5 offering shall be an e' for a ram,
5 to give, and an hin of oil to an e'.
7 an e' for a bullock, and an e' for a
7 unto, and an hin of oil to an e'.
11 an e' to a bullock, and an e' to a ram
11 to give, and an hin of oil to an e'.
14 morning, the sixth part of an e',
Am 8: 5 making the e' small, and the shekel
Zec 5: 6 This is an e' that goeth forth.
7 sitteth in the midst of the e'.
8 he cast it into the midst of the e';
9 they lifted up the e' between the
10 Whither do these bear the e'?

Ephah (*e'-fah*)
Ge 25: 4 And the sons of Midian; E', and
1Ch 1:33 E', and Epher, and Henoch, and
2:46 E', Caleb's concubine, bare Haran,
47 And Pelet, and E', and Shaaph.
Isa 60: 6 the dromedaries of Midian and E';

Ephai (*e'-fahee*)
Jer 40: 8 the sons of E' the Netophathite,

Epher (*e'-fur*)
Ge 25: 4 sons of Midian; Ephah, and E',
1Ch 1:33 Ephah, and E', and Henoch, and
4:17 were, Jether, and Mered, and E',
5:24 the house of their fathers, even E',

Ephes-dammim (*e''-fes-dam'-mim*) See also PAS-DAMMIM.
1Sa 17: 1 Shochoh and Azekah, in E'.

Ephesian (*e-fe'-zheun*) See also EPHESIANS.
Ac 21:29 him in the city Trophimus an E',

Ephesians (*e-fe'-zheuns*)
Ac 19:28 saying, Great is Diana of the E'.
34 cried out, Great is Diana of the E'.
35 the city of the E' is a worshipper
Eph *subs.* Written from Rome unto the E'
2Ti *subs.* first bishop of the church of the E',

Ephesus (*ef'-e-sus*) See also EPHESIAN.
Ac 18:19 And he came to E', and left them
21 God will. And he sailed from E'.
24 mighty in the scriptures, came to E'.
19: 1 through the upper coasts came to E':
17 and Greeks also dwelling at E';
26 that not alone at E', but almost
35 Ye men of E', what man is there
20:16 Paul had determined to sail by E',
17 And from Miletus he sent to E',
1Co 15:32 I have fought with beasts at E',
16: 8 I will tarry at E' until Pentecost.
Eph 1: 1 to the saints which are at E',
1Ti 1: 3 besought thee to abide still at E',
2Ti 1:18 he ministered unto me at E',
4:12 And Tychicus have I sent to E'.
Re 1:11 unto E', and unto Smyrna, and
2: 1 angel of the church of E' write;

Ephlal (*ef'-lal*)
1Ch 2:37 Zabad begat E', and E' begat

ephod (*e'-fod*)
Ex 25: 7 and stones to be set in the e',
28: 4 a breastplate, and an e', and a robe,
6 they shall make the e' of gold,
8 And the curious girdle of the e',
12 upon the shoulders of the e' for
15 after the work of the e' thou shalt
25 shoulderpieces of the e' before it.
26 is in the side of the e' inward.
27 the two sides of the e' underneath,
27 above the curious girdle of the e'.
28 rings thereof unto the rings of the e'
28 above the curious girdle of the e',
28 breastplate be not loosed from the e'.
31 make the robe of the e' all of blue.
29: 5 and the robe of the e', and the e',
5 with the curious girdle of the e':
35: 9, 27 and stones to be set for the e',
39: 2 he made the e' of gold, blue,
5 And the curious girdle of his e',
7 them on the shoulders of the e',
8 like the work of the e'; of gold,
18 shoulderpieces of the e', before it.
19 was on the side of the e' inward.
20 the two sides of the e' underneath,
20 above the curious girdle of the e'.
21 his rings unto the rings of the e' with
21 above the curious girdle of the e',
21 it might not be loosed from the e';
22 And he made the robe of the e' of
Le 8: 7 put the e' upon him, and he girded
7 with the curious girdle of the e',
J'g 8:27 And Gideon made an e' thereof,
17: 5 made an e', and teraphim, and
18:14 there is in these houses an e',
17 took the graven image, and the e',
18 fetched the carved image, the e',
20 he took the e', and the teraphim,
1Sa 2:18 being a child, girded with a linen e'.
28 to wear an e' before me? and did
14: 3 priest in Shiloh, wearing an e'.
21: 9 wrapped in a cloth behind the e':
1Sa 22:18 persons that did wear a linen e'.
23: 6 came down with an e' in his hand.
9 the priest, Bring hither the e'.
30: 7 I pray thee, bring me hither the e'.
7 And Abiathar brought thither the e'
2Sa 6:14 David was girded with a linen e'.
1Ch 15:27 David also had upon him an e' of
Ho 3: 4 without an e', and without teraphim:

Ephod (*e'-fod*)
Nu 34:23 Manasseh, Hanniel the son of E'.

Ephphatha (*ef'-fath-ah*)
M'r 7:34 unto him, E', that is, Be opened.

Ephraim (*e'-fra-im*) See also EPHRAIMITE; EPHRAIM'S; EPHRAIN.
Ge 41:52 name of the second called he E':
46:20 were born Manasseh and E', which
48: 1 him his two sons, Manasseh and E'.
5 now thy two sons, E' and Manasseh,
13 E' in his right hand toward Israel's
17 his right hand upon the head of E',
20 God make thee as E' and as
20 and he set E' before Manasseh.
Nu 1:10 of E'; Elishama the son of Ammihud:
32 namely, of the children of E',
33 even of the tribe of E', were forty
2:18 be the standard of the camp of E'
18 the captain of the sons of E' shall
24 were numbered of the camp of E'
7:48 prince of the children of E', offered:
10:22 of the camp of the children of E'
13: 8 Of the tribe of E', Oshea the son
26:28 families were Manasseh and E'.
35 the sons of E' after their families:
37 are the families of the sons of E'
34:24 of the tribe of the children of E',
De 33:17 they are the ten thousands of E',
34: 2 all Naphtali, and the land of E',
Jos 14: 4 were two tribes, Manasseh and E':
16: 4 Manasseh and E', took their
5 the border of the children of E'
8 of the tribe of the children of E'
9 separate cities for the children of E'
17: 8 belonged to the children of E';
9 these cities of E' are among the cities
15 if mount E' be too narrow for thee.
17 the house of Joseph, even to E'
19:50 Even Timnath-serah in mount E':
20: 7 and Shechem in mount E',
21: 5 of the families of the tribe of E',
20 of their lot out of the tribe of E'.
21 with her suburbs in mount E',
24:30 Timnath-serah, ... is in mount E',
33 which was given him in mount E'.
J'g 1:29 did E' drive out the Canaanites
2: 9 in the mount of E', on the north side
3:27 a trumpet in the mountain of E',
4: 5 Ramah and Bethel in mount E':
5:14 Out of E' was there a root of them
7:24 throughout all mount E', saying,
24 the men of E' gathered themselves
8: 1 the men of E' said unto him, Why
2 the gleaning of the grapes of E'
10: 1 he dwelt in Shamir in mount E'.
9 and against the house of E';
12: 1 men of E' gathered themselves
4 of Gilead, and fought with E':
4 and the men of Gilead smote E',
4 Ye Gileadites are fugitives of E'
15 in Pirathon in the land of E',
17: 1 there was a man of mount E',
8 to mount E' to the house of Micah,
18: 2 who when they came to mount E',
13 they passed thence unto mount E',
19: 1 sojourning on the side of mount E',
16 which was also of mount E'; and
18 toward the side of mount E';
1Sa 1: 1 Ramathaim-zophim, of mount E',
9: 4 he passed through mount E', and
14:22 had hid themselves in mount E',
2Sa 2: 9 and over E', and over Benjamin,
13:23 in Baal-hazor, which is beside E':
18: 6 and the battle was in the wood of E';
20:21 but a man of mount E', Sheba the
1Ki 4: 8 The son of Hur, in mount E':
12:25 built Shechem in mount E',
2Ki 5:22 there be come to me from mount E'
14:13 from the gate of E' unto the corner
1Ch 6:66 of their coasts out of the tribe of E'.
67 Shechem in mount E' with her
7:20 sons of E'; Shuthelah, and Bered
22 E' their father mourned many days,
9: 3 of the children of E', and Manasseh;
12:30 the children of E' twenty thousand
27:10 the Pelonite, of the children of E':
14 Pirathonite, of the children of E':
20 Of the children of E', Hoshea the
2Ch 13: 4 Zemaraim, which is in mount E',
15: 8 which he had taken from mount E',
9 the strangers with them out of E'
17: 2 and in the cities of E', which Asa
19: 4 people from Beer-sheba to mount E',
25: 7 to wit, with all the children of E'.
10 that was come to him out of E',
23 from the gate of E' to the corner
28: 7 Zichri, a mighty man of E', slew
12 of the heads of the children of E',
30: 1 and wrote letters also to E' and
10 to city through the country of E'
18 of people, even many of E',
31: 1 in E' also and Manasseh, until they
34: 6 and E', and Simeon, even unto
9 and E', and of all the remnant of
Ne 8:16 in the street of the gate of E'
12:39 And from above the gate of E',
Ps 60: 7 E' also is the strength of mine head;
78: 9 The children of E', being armed,
67 and chose not the tribe of E':
80: 2 E' and Benjamin and Manasseh
108: 8 E' also is the strength of mine head;
Isa 7: 2 saying, Syria is confederate with E'.
5 Syria, E', and the son of Remaliah,
8 and five years shall E' be broken,
9 And the head of E' is Samaria,
17 day that E' departed from Judah;
9: 9 all the people shall know, even E'
21 Manasseh, E'; and E', Manasseh:
11:13 The envy also of E' shall depart,
13 E' shall not envy Judah,
13 and Judah shall not vex E'.
17: 3 fortress also shall cease from E',
28: 1 to the drunkards of E', whose
3 the drunkards of E', shall be trodden
Jer 4:15 publisheth affliction from mount E'.
7:15 brethren, even the whole seed of E'.
31: 6 the watchmen upon the mount E'
9 to Israel, and E' is my firstborn.
18 surely heard E' bemoaning himself
20 Is E' my dear son? is he a pleasant
50:19 shall be satisfied upon mount E'
Eze 37:16 For Joseph, the stick of E',
19 which is in the hand of E', and the
48: 5 unto the west side, a portion for E'.
6 by the border of E', from the east
Ho 4:17 E' is joined to idols: let him alone.
5: 3 I know E', and Israel is not hid
3 for now, O E', thou committest
5 therefore shall Israel and E' fall
9 E' shall be desolate in the day of
11 E' is oppressed and broken in
12 will I be unto E' as a moth,
13 E' saw his sickness, and Judah
13 then went E' to the Assyrian, and
14 I will be unto E' as a lion,
6: 4 O E', what shall I do unto thee?
10 there is the whoredom of E',
7: 1 the iniquity of E' was discovered,
8 E', he hath mixed himself among
8 E' is a cake not turned.
11 E' also is like a silly dove without
8: 9 E' hath hired lovers.
11 E' hath made many altars to sin,
9: 3 but E' shall return to Egypt,
8 watchman of E' was with my God:
11 As for E', their glory shall fly away
13 E', as I saw Tyrus, is planted in
13 E' shall bring forth his children
16 E' is smitten, their root is dried up,
10: 6 E' shall receive shame, and Israel
11 E' is as an heifer that is taught,
11 I will make E' to ride; Judah shall
11: 3 I taught E' also to go, taking them
8 How shall I give thee up, E'?
9 I will not return to destroy E':
12 E' compasseth me about with lies,
12: 1 E' feedeth on wind, and followeth
8 E' said, Yet I am become rich,
14 E' provoked him to anger most
13: 1 When E' spake trembling, he
12 The iniquity of E' is bound up;
14: 8 E' shall say, What have I to do any
Ob 1:19 they shall possess the fields of E',
Zec 9:10 I will cut off the chariot from E',
13 filled the bow with E', and raised
10: 7 And they of E' shall be like a mighty
Joh 11:54 into a city called E', and there

Ephraimite (*e'-fra-im-ite*) See also EPHRAIMITES.
J'g 12: 5 said unto him, Art thou an E'?

Ephraimites (*e'-fra-im-ites*)
Jos 16:10 Canaanites dwell among the E'
J'g 12: 4 fugitives of Ephraim among the E',
5 passages of Jordan before the E':
5 those E' which were escaped said,
6 there fell at that time of the E'

Ephraim's (*e'-fra-ims*)
Ge 48:14 and laid it upon E' head, who was
17 to remove it from E' head unto
50:23 Joseph saw E' children of the third
Jos 17:10 Southward it was E', and northward

Ephrain (*e'-fra-in*) See also EPHRAIM; EPHRON.
2Ch 13:19 and E' with the towns thereof.

Ephratah (*ef'-rat-ah*) See also BETHLEHEM; CALEB-EPHRATAH; EPHRATH; EPHRATHITE.
Ru 4:11 and do thou worthily in E',
1Ch 2:50 the son of Hur, the firstborn of E';
4: 4 E', the father of Beth-lehem.
Ps 132: 6 Lo, we heard of it at E': we found
Mic 5: 2 But thou Beth-lehem E', though

Ephrath (*e'-frath*) See also EPHRATAH.
Ge 35:16 was but a little way to come to E':
19 and was buried in the way to E',
48: 7 but a little way to come unto E':
7 I buried her there in the way of E';
1Ch 2:19 Caleb took unto him E', which bare

Ephrathite (*ef'-rath-ite*) See also EPHRATHITES.
1Sa 1: 1 of John, the son of Zuph, an E':
17:12 Now David was the son of that E'
1Ki 11:26 Jeroboam the son of Nebat, an E'

Ephrathites (*ef'-rath-ites*)
Ru 1: 2 E' of Beth-lehem-judah.

Ephron (*e'-fron*) See also EPHRAIM; EPHRAIN.
Ge 23: 8 for me to E' the son of Zohar,
10 And E' dwelt among the children
10 E' the Hittite answered Abraham
13 he spake unto E' in the audience
14 And E' answered Abraham, saying

Ge 23:16 And Abraham hearkened unto E·;
16 Abraham weighed to E· the silver,
17 of E·, which was in Machpelah,
25: 9 of E· the son of Zohar the Hittite,
49:29 that is in the field of E· the Hittite,
30 with the field of E· the Hittite for a
50:13 of a burying place of E· the Hittite,
Jos 15: 9 went out to the cities of mount E·;

Epicureans (*ep-i-cu-re'-ans*)
Ac 17:18 certain philosophers of the E·.

epistle See also EPISTLES.
Ac 15:30 together, they delivered the e·:
23:33 delivered the e· to the governor,
Ro 16:22 I Tertius, who wrote this e·,
1Co 5: 9 I wrote unto you in an e·
subscr. The first e· to the Corinthians was
2Co 3: 2 are our e· written in our hearts,
3 the e· of Christ ministered by us,
7: 8 I perceive that the same e· hath
subscr. The second e· to the Corinthians
Col 4: 16 when this e· is read among you,
16 that ye likewise read the e· from
1Th 5:27 this e· be read unto all the holy
subscr. The first e· unto the Thessalonians
2Th 2:15 whether my word, or our e·.
3:14 our word by this e·, note that man,
17 which is the token in every e·:
subscr. The second e· to the Thessalonians
2Ti *subscr.* The second e· unto Timotheus,
2Pe 3: 1 second e·, beloved, I now write

epistles
2Co 3: 1 e· of commendation to you, or
2Pe 3:16 As also in all his e·, speaking in

equal See also EQUALS; UNEQUAL.
Job 28:17 gold and the crystal cannot e· it:
19 topaz of Ethiopia shall not e· it,
Ps 17: 2 behold the things that are e·.
55:13 it was thou, a man mine e·,
Pr 26: 7 The legs of the lame are not e·:
Isa 40:25 will ye liken me, or shall I be e·?
46: 5 will ye liken me, and make me e·,
La 2:13 what shall I e· to thee, that I may
Eze 18:25 The way of the Lord is not e·.
25 house of Israel; Is not my way e·?
29 The way of the Lord is not e·. O
29 of Israel, are not my ways e·?
33:17 The way of the Lord is not e·: but
17 as for them, their way is not e·.
20 The way of the Lord is not e·.
M't 20:12 thou hast made them e· unto us,
Lu 20:36 for they are e· unto the angels;
Joh 5:18 making himself e· with God.
Ph'p 2: 6 it not robbery to be e· with God:
Col 4: 1 servants that which is just and e·;
Re 21:16 breadth and the height of it are e·.

equality
2Co 8:14 But by an e·, that now at this time
14 your want: that there may be e·:

equally See also UNEQUALLY.
Ex 36:22 e· distant one from another:

equals
Ga 1:14 many my e· in mine own nation,

equity See also INIQUITY.
Ps 98: 9 the world, and the people with e·.
99: 4 dost establish e·, thou executest
Pr 1: 3 justice, and judgment, and e·;
2: 9 and judgment, and e·; yea, every
17:26 good, nor to strike princes for e·.
Ec 2:21 and in knowledge, and in e·;
Isa 11: 4 with e· for the meek of the earth:
59:14 in the street, and e· cannot enter.
Mic 3: 9 abhor judgment, pervert all e·.
Mal 2: 6 walked with me in peace and e·,

Er (*ur*)
Ge 38: 3 a son; and he called his name E·.
6 And Judah took a wife for E· his
7 E·, Judah's firstborn, was wicked
46:12 the sons of Judah; E·, and Onan,
12 but E· and Onan died in the land
Nu 26:19 sons of Judah were E·, and Onan:
19 and E· and Onan died in the land
1Ch 2: 3 The sons of Judah; E·, and Onan,
3 And E·, the firstborn of Judah,
4:21 son of Judah were, E· the father
Lu 3:28 Elmodam, which was the son of E·.

Eran (*e'-ran*) See also ERANITES.
Nu 26:36 of E·, the family of the Eranites.

Eranites (*e'-ran-ites*)
Nu 26:36 of Eran, the family of the E·.

Erastus (*e-ras'-tus*)
Ac 19:22 Timotheus and E·; but he himself
Ro 16:23 E· the chamberlain of the city
2Ti 4:20 E· abode at Corinth: but Trophimus

ere
Ex 1:19 delivered e· the midwives come
Nu 11:33 their teeth, e· it was chewed,
14:11 how long will it be e· they believe
1Sa 3: 3 And e· the lamp of God went out
2Sa 2:26 it be then, e· thou bid the people
2Ki 6:32 but e· the messenger came to him.
Job 18: 2 How long will it be e· ye make an
Jer 47: 6 how long will it be e· thou be quiet?
Ho 8: 5 how long will it be e· they attain
Joh 4:49 Sir, come down e· my child die.

Erech (*e'-rek*) See also ARCHEVITES.
Ge 10:10 Babel, and E·, and Accad, and

erected
Ge 33:20 And he e· there an altar,

Eri (*e'-ri*) See also ERITES.
Ge 46:16 Ezbon, E·, and Arodi, and Areli.
Nu 26:16 of E·, the family of the Erites:

Erites (*e'-rites*)
Nu 26:16 of Eri, the family of the E·:

err See also ERRED; ERRETH.
2Ch 33: 9 So Manasseh made Judah....to e·,
Ps 95:10 is a people that do e· in their heart.
119:21 rebuked the proud... which do e·
118 hast trodden down all them that e·
Pr 14:22 Do they not e· that devise evil?
19:27 the instruction that causeth to e·
Isa 3:12 which lead thee cause thee to e·,
9:16 of this people cause them to e·;
19:14 they have caused Egypt to e· in
28: 7 they e· in vision, they stumble in
30:28 of the people, causing them to e·.
35: 8 men, though fools, shall not e·
63:17 why hast thou made us to e· from
Jer 23:13 and caused my people Israel to e·.
32 cause my people to e· by their lies,
Ho 4:12 whoredoms hath caused them to e·,
Am 2: 4 and their lies caused them to e·,
Mic 3: 5 prophets that make my people e·,
M't 22:29 Ye do e·, not knowing the
M'r 12:24 Do ye not therefore e·, because ye
27 ye therefore do greatly e·.
Heb 3:10 They do alway e· in their heart;
Jas 1:16 Do not e·, my beloved brethren.
5:19 Brethren, if any of you do e· from

errand
Ge 24:33 not eat, until I have told mine e·.
J'g 3:19 I have a secret e· unto thee,
2Ki 9: 5 I have an e· to thee, O captain.

erred
Le 5:18 his ignorance wherein he e· and
Nu 15:22 if ye have e·, and not observed all
1Sa 26:21 the fool, and have e· exceedingly.
Job 6:24 me to understand wherein I have e·.
19: 4 And be it indeed that I have e·,
Ps 119:110 I have e· not from thy precepts.
Isa 28: 7 they also have e· through wine,
7 priest and the prophet have e·
29:24 They also that e· in spirit shall
1Ti 6:10 they have e· from the faith, and
21 have e· concerning the faith.
2Ti 2:18 Who concerning the truth have e·,

erreth
Pr 10:17 but he that refuseth reproof e·.
Eze 45:20 every one that e·, and for him that

error See also ERRORS.
2Sa 6: 7 God smote him there for his e·;
Job 19: 4 mine e· remaineth with myself.
Ec 5: 6 neither say thou...it was an e·:
10: 5 as an e· which proceedeth from the
Isa 32: 6 and to utter e· against the Lord,
Da 6: 4 neither was there any e· or fault
M't 27:64 so the last e· shall be worse than
Ro 1:27 that recompence of their e· which
Jas 5:20 the sinner from the e· of his way
2Pe 2:18 escape from them who live in e·.
3:17 being led away with the e· of the
1Jo 4: 6 spirit of truth, and the spirit of e·.
Jude 11 ran greedily after the e· of Balaam

errors
Ps 19:12 Who can understand his e·?
Jer 10:15 are vanity, and the work of e·:
51:18 They are vanity, the work of e·:
Heb 9: 7 himself, and for the e· of the people:

Esaias (*e-sah'-yas*) See also ISAIAH.
M't 3: 3 spoken of by the prophet E·,
4:14 was spoken by E· the prophet,
8:17 fulfilled which was spoken by E·
12:17 fulfilled which was spoken by E·
13:14 fulfilled the prophecy of E·,
15: 7 hypocrites, well did E· prophesy
M'r 7: 6 Well hath E· prophesied of you
Lu 3: 4 in the book of the words of E·
4:17 him the book of the prophet E·.
Joh 1:23 the Lord, as said the prophet E·.
12:38 That the saying of E· the prophet
39 could not believe, because that E·
41 These things said E·, when he
Ac 8:28 sitting in his chariot read E· the
30 heard him read the prophet E·,
28:25 Well spake the Holy Ghost by E·
Ro 9:27 E· also crieth concerning Israel,
29 and as E· said before, Except the
10:16 E· saith, Lord, who hath believed
20 But E· is very bold, and saith, I
15:12 And again, E· saith, There shall

Esar-haddon (*e''-zar-had'-dun*)
2Ki 19:37 E· his son reigned in his stead.
Ezr 4: 2 since the days of E· king of Assur,
Isa 37:38 E· his son reigned in his stead.

Esau (*e'-saw*) See also EDOM; ESAU'S.
Ge 25:25 they called his name E·.
27 E· was a cunning hunter, a man of
28 Isaac loved E·, because he did eat
29 E· came from the field, and he was
30 E· said to Jacob, Feed me, I pray
32 E· said, Behold, I am at the point
34 Then Jacob gave E· bread and
34 Thus E· despised his birthright.
26:34 And E· was forty years old when he
27: 1 he called E· his eldest son, and said
5 heard when Isaac spake to E·
5 And E· went to the field to hunt for
6 I heard thy father speak unto E·
11 Behold, E· my brother is a hairy
15 goodly raiment of her eldest son E·,
19 Jacob said unto his father, I am E·

Ge 27:21 whether thou be my very son E· or
22 but the hands are the hands of E·.
24 he said, Art thou my very son E·?
30 that E· his brother came in from
32 said, I am thy son, thy firstborn E·.
34 when E· heard the words of his
37 Isaac answered and said unto E·,
38 E· said unto his father, Hast thou
38 E· lifted up his voice, and wept.
41 And E· hated Jacob because of the
41 E· said in his heart, The days of
42 these words of E· her elder son
42 Behold, thy brother E·, as touching
28: 6 When E· saw that Isaac had blessed
8 And E· seeing that the daughters of
9 Then went E· unto Ishmael, and
32: 3 sent messengers before him to E·
4 shall ye speak unto my lord E·;
6 We came to thy brother E·, and
8 If E· come to the one company,
11 of my brother, from the hand of E·:
13 hand a present for E· his brother;
17 When E· my brother meeteth thee,
18 sent unto my lord E·: and, behold,
19 this manner shall ye speak unto E·,
33: 1 and, behold, E· came, and with him
4 And E· ran to meet him, and
9 E· said, I have enough, my brother;
15 And E· said, Let me now leave
16 So E· returned that day on his way
35: 1 from the face of E· thy brother.
29 his sons E· and Jacob buried him.
36: 1 generations of E·, who is Edom.
2 E· took his wives of the daughters
4 And Adah bare to E· Eliphaz;
5 these are the sons of E·, which
6 And E· took his wives, and his sons,
8 dwelt E· in Mount Seir: E· is Edom.
9 of E· the father of the Edomites in
10 the son of Adah the wife of E·,
10 son of Bashemath the wife of E·.
14 she bare to E· Jeush, and Jaalam,
15 were dukes of the sons of E·:
15 of Eliphaz, the firstborn son of E·;
19 are the sons of E·, who is Edom,
40 of the dukes that came of E·,
43 he is E· the father of the Edomites.
De 2: 4 children of E·, which dwell in Seir;
5 Seir unto E· for a possession.
8 children of E·, which dwelt in Seir,
12 the children of E· succeeded them,
22 As he did to the children of E·,
29 children of E· which dwelt in Seir,
Jos 24: 4 I gave unto Isaac Jacob and E·:
4 and I gave unto E· mount Seir,
1Ch 1:34 The sons of Isaac; E· and Israel.
35 The sons of E·; Eliphaz, Reuel,
Jer 49: 8 bring the calamity of E· upon him,
10 But I have made E· bare, I have
Ob 6 are the things of E· searched out!
8 the wise men out of the mount of E·?
9 every one of the mount of E· may
18 and the house of E· for stubble,
18 any remaining of the house of E·;
19 shall possess the mount of E·;
21 Zion to judge the mount of E·;
Mal 1: 2 Was not E· Jacob's brother? saith
3 I hated E·, and laid his mountains
Ro 9:13 I loved, but E· have I hated.
Heb 11:20 By faith Isaac blessed Jacob and E·
12:16 fornicator, or profane person, as E·,

Esau's (*e'-saws*)
Ge 25:26 his hand took hold on E· heel;
27:23 hairy, as his brother E· hands:
28: 5 Rebekah, Jacob's and E· mother.
36:10 are the names of E· sons; Eliphaz
12 was concubine to Eliphaz E· son;
12 were the sons of Adah E· wife.
13 the sons of Bashemath E· wife.
14 of Zibeon, E· wife: and she bare
17 these are the sons of Reuel E· son;
17 are the sons of Bashemath E· wife.
18 the sons of Aholibamah E· wife;
18 the daughter of Anah, E· wife.

escape See also ESCAPED; ESCAPETH; ESCAPING.
Ge 19:17 E· for thy life; look not behind
17 e· to the mountain, lest thou be
19 I cannot e· to the mountain, lest
20 Oh, let me e· thither, (is it not
22 Haste thee, e· thither; for I can not
32: 8 company which is left shall e·.
Jos 8:22 let none of them remain or e·.
1Sa 27: 1 I should speedily e· into the land
1 so shall I e· out of his hand.
2Sa 15:14 we shall not else e· from Absalom:
20: 6 lest he get him fenced cities, and e·
1Ki 18:40 let not one of them e·. And they
2Ki 9:15 then let none go forth nor e·
10:24 If any of the men...e·,
19:31 and they that e· out of mount Zion:
Ezr 9: 8 to leave us a remnant to e·,
Es 4:13 thou shalt e· in the king's house.
Job 11:20 they shall not e·, and their hope
Ps 55: 8 my e· from the windy storm and
56: 7 Shall they e· by iniquity? in thine
71: 2 cause me to e·: incline thine ear
141:10 own nets, whilst that I withal e·.
Pr 19: 5 he that speaketh lies shall not e·.
Ec 7:26 pleaseth God shall e· from her;
Isa 20: 6 of Assyria: and how shall we e·?
37:32 and they that e· out of mount Zion:
66:19 I will send those that e· of them
Jer 11:11 they shall not be able to e·;
25:35 nor the principal of the flock to e·.
32: 4 shall not e· out of the hand of the

Jer 34: 3 thou shalt not e· out of his hand,
38:18, 23 shalt not e· out of their hand.
42:17 none of them shall remain or e·
44:14 of Egypt to sojourn there, shall e·
14 shall return but such as shall e·.
28 a small number that e· the sword
46: 6 flee away, nor the mighty man e·;
48: 8 no city shall e·: the valley also
50:28 The voice of them that flee and e·
29 let none thereof e·: recompense
Eze 6: 8 ye may have some that shall e·
9 they that e· of you shall remember
7:16 But they that e· of them shall
16 But they that...of them shall e·,
17:15 shall he e· that doeth such things?
18 all these things, he shall not e·.
Da 11:41 But these shall e· out of his hand,
42 and the land of Egypt shall not e·.
Joe 2: 3 yea, and nothing shall e· them.
Ob 14 to cut off those of his that did e·;
M't 23:33 ye e· the damnation of hell?
Lu 21:36 worthy to e· all these things
Ac 27:42 of them should swim out, and e·.
Ro 2: 3 thou shalt e· the judgment of God?
1Co 10:13 temptation also make a way to e·,
1Th 5: 3 with child; and they shall not e·.
Heb 2: 3 How shall we e·, if we neglect so
12:25 earth, much more shall not we e·,

escaped
Ge 14:13 And there came one that had e·,
Ex 10: 5 the residue of that which is e·,
Nu 21:29 he hath given his sons that e·,
De 23:15 servant which is e· from his master
J'g 3:26 Ehud e· while they tarried, and
26 quarries, and e· unto Seirath.
29 of valour; and there e· not a man.
12: 5 those Ephraimites which were e·
21:17 for them that be e· of Benjamin,
1Sa 14:41 were taken: but the people e·.
19:10 and David fled, and e· that night.
12 and he went, and fled, and e·.
17 away mine enemy, that he is e?
18 David fled, and e·, and came to
22: 1 thence, and e· to the cave Adullam:
20 sons of Ahimelech...e·, and fled
23:13 that David was e· from Keilah;
30:17 and there e· not a man of them,
2Sa 1: 3 Out of the camp of Israel am I e·.
4: 6 Rechab and Baanah his brother e·.
1Ki 20:20 Ben-hadad the king of Syria e·
2Ki 19:30 that is e· of the house of Judah
37 they e· into the land of Armenia.
1Ch 4:43 of the Amalekites that were e·,
2Ch 16: 7 the host of the king of Syria e·
20:24 fallen to the earth, and none e·.
30: 6 the remnant of you, that are e·
36:20 them that had e· from the sword
Ezr 9:15 we remain yet e·, as it is this day:
Ne 1: 2 concerning the Jews that had e·,
Job 1:15, 16, 17, 19 I only am e· alone to tell
19:20 I am e· with the skin of my teeth.
Ps 124: 7 Our soul is e· as a bird out of the
7 the snare is broken, and we are e·.
Isa 4: 2 for them that are e· of Israel.
10:20 such as are e· of the house of Jacob.
37:31 that is e· of the house of Judah
38 and they e· into the land of
45:20 ye that are e· of the nations:
Jer 41:15 Ishmael the son of Nethaniah e·
51:50 Ye that have e· the sword,
La 2:22 the day of the Lord's anger none e·
Eze 24:27 mouth be opened to him which is e·,
33:21 one that had e· out of Jerusalem
22 evening, afore he that was e· came;
Joh 10:39 him: but he e· out of their hand,
Ac 27:44 pass, that they e· all safe to land.
28: 1 when they were e·, then they knew
4 whom, though he hath e· the sea,
2Co 11:33 was I let down by the wall, and e·
Heb 11:34 of fire, e· the edge of the sword,
12:25 For if they e· not who refused him
2Pe 1: 4 having e· the corruption that is in
2:18 those that were clean e· from them
20 For if after they have e· the

escapeth
1Ki 19:17 him that e· the sword of Hazael
17 him that e· from the sword of Jehu
Isa 15: 9 lions upon him that e· of Moab,
Jer 48:19 him that fleeth, and her that e·,
Eze 24:26 he that e· in that day shall come
Am 9: 1 he that e· of them shall not be

escaping
Ezr 9:14 should be no remnant nor e·?

eschew See also ESCHEWED; ESCHEWETH.
1Pe 3:11 Let him e· evil, and do good;

eschewed
Job 1: 1 one that feared God, and e· evil.

escheweth
Job 1: 8 one that feareth God and e· evil?
2: 3 one that feareth God, and e· evil?

Esek (*e'-sek*)
Ge 26:20 he called the name of the well E·;

Esh-baal (*esh'-ba-al*) See also ISH-BOSHETH.
1Ch 8:33 Malchi-shua, and Abinadab, and E·.
9:39 Malchi-shua, and Abinadab, and E·.

Esh-ban (*esh'-ban*)
Ge 36:26 Hemdan, and E·, and Ithran,
1Ch 1:41 Amram, and E·, and Ithran.

Eshcol (*esh'-col*)
Ge 14:13 brother of E·, and brother of Aner:
24 men which went with me, Aner, E·,
Nu 13:23 they came unto the brook of E·,
24 The place was called the brook E·,
32: 9 they went up unto the valley of E·,
De 1:24 came unto the valley of E·, and

Eshean (*esh'-e-an*)
Jos 15:52 Arab, and Dumah, and E·,

Eshek (*e'-shek*)
1Ch 8:39 And the sons of E· his brother

Eshkalonites (*esh'-ka-lon-ites*)
Jos 13: 3 Ashdothites, the E·, the Gittites,

Eshtaol (*esh'-ta-ol*) See also ESHTAULITES.
Jos 15:33 in the valley, E·, and Zoreah,
19:41 Zorah, and E·, and Ir-shemesh,
J'g 13:25 camp of Dan between Zorah and E·.
16:31 buried him between Zorah and E·
18: 2 of valour, from Zorah, and from E·,
8 unto their brethren to Zorah and E·:
11 out of Zorah and out of E·,

Eshtaulites (*esh'-ta-u-lites*)
1Ch 2:53 the Zareathites, and the E·.

Eshtemoa (*esh-te-mo'-ah*) See also ESHTEMOH.
Jos 21:14 and E· with her suburbs,
1Sa 30:28 and to them which were in E·,
1Ch 4:17 and Ishbah the father of E·.
19 Garmite, and E· the Maachathite.
6:57 Jattir, and E·, with their suburbs,

Eshtemoh (*esh'-te-moh*) See also ESHTEMOA.
Jos 15:50 Anab, and E·, and Anim,

Eshton (*esh'-ton*)
1Ch 4:11 Mehir, which was the father of E·.
12 E· begat Beth-rapha, and Paseah,

Esli (*es'-li*)
Lu 3:25 which was the son of E·, which

especially
Ps 31:11 but e· among my neighbours,
Ac 26: 3 E· because I know thee to be
Ga 6:10 men, e· unto them who are of the
1Ti 5:17 e· they who labour in the word and
2Ti 4:13 the books, but e· the parchments.

espied
Ge 42:27 of them opened his sack . . . he e·
Eze 20: 6 into a land that I had e· for them,

espousals
Ca 3:11 crowned him in the day of his e·,
Jer 2: 2 of thy youth, the love of thine e·,

espoused
2Sa 3:14 my wife Michal, which I e· to me
M't 1:18 When as his mother Mary was e·
Lu 1:27 To a virgin e· to a man whose
2: 5 To be taxed with Mary his e· wife,
2Co 11: 2 For I have e· you to one husband,

espy See also ESPIED; SPY.
Jos 14: 7 sent...from Kadesh-barnea to e·
Jer 48:19 stand by the way, and e·; ask him

Esrom (*es'-rom*) See also HEZRON.
M't 1: 3 Phares begat E·; and E· begat
Lu 3:33 which was the son of E·, which

essay See ASSAY.

establish See also ESTABLISHED; ESTABLISHETH; STABLISH.
Ge 6:18 with thee will I e· my covenant;
9: 9 behold, I e· my covenant with you,
11 And I will e· my covenant with you;
17: 7 And I will e· my covenant between
19 and I will e· my covenant with him
21 my covenant will I e· with Isaac,
Le 26: 9 you, and e· my covenant with you.
Nu 30:13 her husband may e· it, or her
De 8:18 that he may e· his covenant which
28: 9 The Lord shall e· thee an holy people
29:13 That he may e· thee to day
1Sa 1:23 only the Lord e· his word. So the
2Sa 7:12 and I will e· his kingdom.
25 concerning his house, e· it for
1Ki 9: 5 Then I will e· the throne of thy
15: 4 after him, and to e· Jerusalem.
1Ch 17:11 and I will e· his kingdom.
22:10 and I will e· the throne of his
28: 7 Moreover I will e· his kingdom
2Ch 9: 8 loved Israel, to e· them for ever,
Job 36: 7 yea, he doth e· them for ever,
Ps 7: 9 but e· the just: for the righteous
48: 8 God will e· it for ever. Selah.
87: 5 and the highest himself shall e· her.
89: 2 thy faithfulness shalt thou e· in the
4 Thy seed will I e· for ever,
90:17 and e· thou the work of our hands
17 the work of our hands e· thou it.
99: 4 thou dost e· equity, thou executest
Pr 15:25 he will e· the border of the widow.
Isa 9: 7 and to e· it with judgment and
49: 8 of the people, to e· the earth, to
62: 7 And give him no rest, till he e·,
Jer 33: 2 the Lord that formed it, to e· it;
Eze 16:60 I will e· unto thee an everlasting
62 And I will e· my covenant with thee;
Da 6: 7 together to e· a royal statute,
8 Now, O king, e· the decree,
11:14 exalt themselves to e· the vision.
Am 5:15 and e· judgment in the gate:
Ro 3:31 God forbid: yea, we e· the law.
10: 3 about to e· their own righteousness,
1Th 3: 2 to e· you, and to comfort you
Heb 10: 9 the first, that he may e· the second.

established See also STABLISHED.
Ge 9:17 the covenant, which I have e·
41:32 because the thing is e· by God,
Ex 6: 4 I have also e· my covenant with
15:17 O Lord, which thy hands have e·.
Le 25:30 then the house . . . shall be e·
De 19:15 witnesses, shall the matter be e·.
32: 6 hath he not made thee, and e· thee?
1Sa 3:20 knew that Samuel was e· to be a
13:13 the Lord have e· thy kingdom
20:31 shalt not be e·, nor thy kingdom.
24:20 the kingdom of Israel shall be e·
2Sa 5:12 Lord had e· him king over Israel,
7:16 thy kingdom shall be e· for ever.
16 thy throne shall be e· for ever.
26 house of thy servant David be e·
1Ki 2:12 and his kingdom was e· greatly.
24 the Lord liveth, which hath e· me,
45 throne of David shall be e· before
46 the kingdom was e· in the hand of
1Ch 17:14 his throne shall be e· for evermore.
23 let the thing . . . be e· for ever,
24 Let it even be e·, that thy name be
24 let the house of David . . . be e·
2Ch 1: 9 unto David my father be e·:
12: 1 when Rehoboam had e· the
20:20 so shall ye be e·; believe his
25: 3 when the kingdom was e· to him,
30: 5 So they e· a decree to make
Job 21: 8 Their seed is e· in their sight
22:28 and it shall be e· unto thee:
Ps 24: 2 and e· it upon the floods.
40: 2 feet upon a rock, and e· my goings.
78: 5 For he e· a testimony in Jacob,
69 earth which he hath e· for ever·
89:21 with whom my hand shall be e·:
37 It shall be e· for ever as the moon,
93: 2 Thy throne is e· of old: thou art
96:10 the world also shall be e· that it
102:28 their seed shall be e· before thee.
112: 8 His heart is e·, he shall not be
119:90 thou hast e· the earth, and it
140:11 Let not an evil speaker be e·
Pr 3:19 by understanding hath he e· the
4:26 and let all thy ways be e·.
8:28 when he e· the clouds above:
12: 3 man shall not be e· by wickedness:
19 The lip of truth shall be e· for ever:
15:22 of counsellors they are e·.
16: 3 and thy thoughts shall be e·.
12 the throne is e· by righteousness.
20:18 Every purpose is e· by counsel:
24: 3 and by understanding it is e·:
25: 5 and his throne shall be e· in
29:14 his throne shall be e· for ever.
30: 4 hath e· all the ends of the earth?
Isa 2: 2 of the Lord's house shall be e·
7: 9 believe, surely ye shall not be e·.
16: 5 in mercy shall the throne be e·:
45:18 he hath e· it, he created it
54:14 In righteousness shalt thou be e·:
Jer 10:12 hath e· the world by his wisdom,
30:20 their congregation shall be e·
51:15 by his power, he hath e· the world
Da 4:36 I was e· in my kingdom,
Mic 4: 1 be e· in the top of the mountains,
Hab 1:12 thou hast e· them for correction.
Zec 5:11 and it shall be e·, and set there
M't 18:16 witnesses every word may be e·.
Ac 16: 5 were the churches e· in the faith,
Ro 1:11 to the end ye may be e·;
2Co 13: 1 witnesses shall every word be e·.
Heb 8: 6 was e· upon better promises.
13: 9 that the heart be e· with grace;
2Pe 1:12 and be e· in the present truth.

establisheth
Nu 30:14 then he e· all her vows, or all her
Pr 29: 4 The king by judgment e· the land:
Da 6:15 nor statute which the king e·

establishment
2Ch 32: 1 After these things, and the e·

estate See also ESTATES; STATE.
1Ch 17:17 regarded me according to the e·
Es 1:19 give give her royal e· unto another
Ps 136:23 Who remembered us in our low e·:
Ec 1:16 Lo, I am come to great e·,
3:18 concerning the e· of the sons of
Eze 16:55, 55 shall return to their former e·,
55 shall return to your former e·.
Da 11: 7 shall one stand up in his e·,
20 Then shall stand up in his e·
21 And in his e· shall stand up a vile
38 in his e· shall he honour the God
Ac 22: 5 and all the e· of the elders:
Lu 1:48 the low e· of his handmaiden:
Ro 12:16 condescend to men of low e·.
Col 4: 8 he might know your e·, and
Jude 6 which kept not their first e·,

estates
Eze 36:11 I will settle you after your old e·,
M'r 6:21 captains, and chief e· of Galilee;

esteem See also ESTEEMED; ESTEEMETH; ESTEEMING.
Job 36:19 Will he e· thy riches? no, not
Ps 119:128 I e· all thy precepts...to be right;
Isa 53: 4 yet we did e· him stricken,
Ph'p 2: 3 e· other better than themselves.
1Th 5:13 And to e· them very highly in love

esteemed
De 32:15 lightly e· the Rock of his salvation.
1Sa 2:30 despise me shall be lightly e·.
18:23 I am a poor man, and lightly e·?
Job 23:12 I have e· the words of his mouth
Pr 17:28 shutteth his lips is e· a man of
Isa 29:16 shall be e· as the potter's clay
17 fruitful field shall be e· as a forest?
53: 3 was despised, and we e· him not.

La 4: 2 are they e' as earthern pitchers,
Lu 16:15 which is highly e' among men
1Co 6: 4 them to judge who are least e'

esteemeth
Job 41:27 He e' iron as straw, and brass
Ro 14: 5 One man e' one day above another:
5 another e' every day alike.
14 but to him that e' any thing to be

esteeming
Heb 11:26 E' the reproach of Christ greater

Esther (*es'-thur*) See also ESTHER'S; HADASSAH.
Es 2: 7 brought up Hadassah, that is, E',
8 E' was brought also unto the king's
10 E' had not shewed her people nor
11 to know how E' did, and what
15 Now when the turn of E', the
15 E' obtained favour in the sight of
16 E' was taken unto king Ahasuerus
17 king loved E' above all the women,
20 E' had not yet shewed her kindred
20 E' did the commandment of
22 who told it unto E' the queen;
22 and E' certified the king thereof
4: 5 Then called E' for Hatach, one of
8 to shew it unto E', and to declare
9 Hatach came and told E' the words
10 Again E' spake unto Hatach, and
13 Mordecai commanded to answer E',
15 E' bade them return Mordecai this
17 to all that E' had commanded
5: 1 that E' put on her royal apparel,
2 when the king saw E' the queen
2 held out to E' the golden sceptre
2 E' drew near, and touched the top
3 What wilt thou queen E'?
4 E' answered, If it seem good unto
5 that he may do as E' had said.
5 the banquet that E' had prepared.
6 said unto E' at the banquet of wine,
7 Then answered E', and said, My
12 E' the queen did let no man come
6:14 the banquet that E' had prepared.
7: 1 came to banquet with E' the queen.
2 the king said again unto E' on the
2 What is thy petition, queen E'?
3 E' the queen answered and said,
5 answered and said unto E' the
6 E' said, The adversary and enemy
7 to make request for his life to E'
8 upon the bed whereon E' was.
8: 1 the Jews' enemy unto E' the queen.
1 E' had told what he was unto her.
2 E' set Mordecai over the house of
3 E' spake yet again before the king,
4 out the golden sceptre toward E'.
4 E' arose, and stood before the king,
7 Ahasuerus said unto E' the queen
7 have given E' the house of Haman,
9:12 the king said unto E' the queen,
13 Then said E', If it please the king,
25 when E' came before the king,
29 Then E' the queen, the daughter of
31 E' the queen had enjoined them,
32 the decree of E' confirmed these

Esther's (*es'-thurs*)
Es 2:18 and his servants, even E' feast;
4: 4 E' maids and her chamberlains
12 they told to Mordecai E' words.

estimate
Le 27:14 then the priest shall e' it, whether
14 as the priest shall e' it, so shall

estimation See also ESTIMATIONS.
Le 5:15 with thy e' by shekels of silver,
18 with thy e', for a trespass offering,
6: 6 with thy e', for a trespass offering,
27: 2 shall be for the Lord by thy e'.
3 And thy e' shall be of the male
3 thy e' shall be fifty shekels of silver,
4 thy e' shall be thirty shekels.
5 then thy e' shall be of the male
6 e' shall be of the male five shekels
6 for the female thy e' shall be three
7 thy e' shall be fifteen shekels.
8 But if he be poorer than thy e',
13 add a fifth part thereof unto thy e'.
15 part of the money of thy e' unto it,
16 e' shall be according to the seed
17 year of jubile, according to thy e'
18 and it shall be abated from thy e'.
19 part of the money of thy e' unto it,
23 unto him the worth of thy e', even
23 he shall give thine e' in that day,
27 redeem it according to thine e',
27 it shall be sold according to thy e'.
Nu 18:16 according to thine e', for the money

estimations
Le 27:25 thy e' shall be according to the

estranged
Job 19:13 mine acquaintance are verily e'
Ps 58: 3 The wicked are e' from the womb:
78:30 They were not e' from their lust.
Jer 19: 4 and have e' this place, and have
Eze 14: 5 they are all e' from me through

Etam (*e'-tam*)
J'g 15: 8 dwelt in the top of the rock E'.
11 went to the top of the rock E', and
1Ch 4: 3 And these were of the father of E';
32 their villages were, E' and Ain,
2Ch 11: 6 He built even Bethlehem, and E',

eternal
De 33:27 The e' God is thy refuge, and
Isa 60:15 I will make thee an e' excellency,
M't 19:16 shall I do, that I may have e' life?
25:46 but the righteous into life e'.
M'r 3:29 in danger of e' damnation:
10:17 I do that I may inherit e' life?
30 and in the world to come e' life.
Lu 10:25 what shall I do to inherit e' life?
18:18 what shall I do to inherit e' life?
Joh 3:15 should not perish, but have e' life.
4:36 and gathereth fruit unto life e':
5:39 for in them ye think ye have e' life:
6:54 and drinketh my blood, hath e' life;
68 thou hast the words of e' life.
10:28 And I give unto them e' life;
12:25 this world shall keep it unto life e'.
17: 2 he should give e' life to as many as
3 this is life e', that they might know
Ac 13:48 many as were ordained to e' life
Ro 1:20 even his e' power and Godhead;
2: 7 and honour and immortality, e' life:
5:21 through righteousness unto e' life
6:23 but the gift of God is e' life through
2Co 4:17 exceeding and e' weight of glory;
18 the things which are not seen are e'.
5: 1 made with hands, e' in the heavens.
Eph 3:11 According the e' purpose which
1Ti 1:17 Now unto the King e', immortal,
6:12 lay hold on e' life, whereunto thou
19 that they may lay hold on e' life.
2Ti 2:10 is in Christ Jesus with e' glory.
Tit 1: 2 In hope of e' life, which God, that
3: 7 according to the hope of e' life.
Heb 5: 9 became the author of e' salvation
6: 2 of the dead, and of e' judgment.
9:12 having obtained e' redemption
14 who through the e' Spirit offered
15 the promise of e' inheritance.
1Pe 5:10 who hath called us unto his e' glory
1Jo 1: 2 shew unto you that e' life, which
2:25 he hath promised us, even e' life.
3:15 no murderer hath e' life abiding in
5:11 that God hath given to us e' life,
13 ye may know that ye have e' life,
20 This is the true God, and e' life.
Jude 7 suffering the vengeance of e' fire.
21 of our Lord Jesus Christ unto e' life.

eternity
Isa 57:15 and lofty One that inhabiteth e',

Etham (*e'-tham*)
Ex 13:20 and encamped in E', in the edge of
Nu 33: 6 and pitched in E', which is in the
7 they removed from E', and turned
8 journey in the wilderness of E',

Ethan (*e'-than*)
1Ki 4:31 than E' the Ezrahite, and Heman,
1Ch 2: 6 And the sons of Zera; Zimri, and E',
8 And the sons of E'; Azariah.
6:42 The son of E', the son of Zimmah,
44 E' the son of Kishi, the son of Abdi,
15:17 of Merari their brethren, E' the son
19 the singers, Heman, Asaph, and E',
Ps 89:*title* Maschil of E' the Ezrahite.

Ethanim (*eth'-a-nim*) See also TISRI.
1Ki 8: 2 at the feast in the month E',

Ethbaal (*eth'-ba-al*)
1Ki 16:31 to wife Jezebel the daughter of E'

Ether (*e'-ther*)
Jos 15:42 Libnah, and E', and Ashan,
19: 7 Ain, Remmon, and E', and Ashan;

Ethiopia (*e-the-o'-pe-ah*) See also CUSH; ETHIOPIAN.
Ge 2:13 compasseth the whole land of E'
2Ki 19: 9 heard say of Tirhakah king of E',
Es 1: 1 reigned from India even unto E',
8: 9 which are from India unto E',
Job 28:19 The topaz of E' shall not equal it,
Ps 68:31 E' shall soon stretch out her hands
87: 4 behold Philistia, and Tyre, with E';
Isa 18: 1 which is beyond the rivers of E':
20: 3 wonder upon Egypt and upon E';
5 afraid and ashamed of E' their
37: 9 concerning Tirhakah king of E',
43: 3 thy ransom, E' and Seba for thee.
45:14 of Egypt, and merchandise of E'
Eze 29:10 even unto the borders of E'.
30: 4 and great pain shall be in E',
5 E', and Libya, and Lydia, and all
38: 5 Persia, E', and Libya with them;
Na 3: 9 E' and Egypt were her strength,
Zep 3:10 From beyond the rivers of E' my
Ac 8:27 and, behold, a man of E',

Ethiopian See also ETHIOPIANS.
Nu 12: 1 against Moses because of the E'
1 for he had married an E' woman.
2Ch 14: 9 out against them Zerah the E'
Jer 13:23 Can the E' change his skin, or the
38: 7 Now when Ebed-melech the E',
10 commanded Ebed-melech the E',
12 Ebed-melech the E' said unto
39:16 and speak to Ebed-melech the E',

Ethiopians
2Ch 12: 3 Lubims, the Sukkiims, and the E'.
14:12 the Lord smote the E' before Asa,
12 before Judah; and the E' fled.
13 and the E' were overthrown,
16: 8 Were not the E' and the Lubims
21:16 Arabians, that were near the E':
Isa 20: 4 Egyptians prisoners, and the E'
Jer 46: 9 E' and the Libyans, that handle
Eze 30: 9 to make the careless E' afraid,
Da 11:43 and the E' shall be at his steps.
Am 9: 7 not as children of the E' unto me,
Zep 2:12 Ye E' also, ye shall be slain
Ac 8:27 under Candace queen of the E',

Ethnan (*eth'-nan*)
1Ch 4: 7 Zereth, and Jezoar, and E'.

Ethni (*eth'-ni*) See also JEATERAI.
1Ch 6:41 The son of E', the son of Zerah,

Eubulus (*yu-bu'-lus*)
2Ti 4:21 E' greeteth thee, and Pudens, and

Eunice (*yu-ni'-see*)
2Ti 1: 5 Lois, and thy mother E'; and I am

eunuch See also EUNUCHS.
Isa 56: 3 neither let the e' say, Behold, I
Jer 52:25 e', which had the charge of the
Ac 8:27 an e' of great authority under
34 the e' answered Philip, and said,
36 the e' said, See, here is water;
38 the water, both Philip and the e';
39 that the e' saw him no more:

eunuchs
2Ki 9:32 looked out to him two or three e'.
20:18 and they shall be e' in the palace
Isa 39: 7 and they shall be e' in the palace
56: 4 thus saith the Lord unto the e'
Jer 29: 2 and the queen, and the e', the
34:19 the princes of Jerusalem, the e',
38: 7 Ethiopian, one of the e' which
41:16 the children, and the e', whom
Da 1: 3 Ashpenaz the master of his e',
7 the prince of the e' gave names:
8 requested of the prince of the e'
9 love with the prince of the e'.
10 prince of the e' said unto Daniel,
11 prince of the e'...set over Daniel,
18 prince of the e' brought them in
M't 19:12 For there are some e', which were
12 and there are some e', which
12 which were made e' of men:
12 and there be e', which have made
12 have made themselves e' for the

Euodias (*yu-o'-de-as*)
Ph'p 4: 2 beseech E', and beseech Syntyche,

Euphrates (*yu-fra'-teze*)
Ge 2:14 Assyria. And the fourth river is E'.
15:18 unto the great river, the river E':
De 1: 7 unto the great river, the river E'.
11:24 from the river, the river E', even
Jos 1: 4 unto the great river, the river E',
2Sa 8: 3 recover his border at the river E'.
2Ki 23:29 the king of Assyria to the river E':
24: 7 river of Egypt unto the river E'
1Ch 5: 9 the wilderness from the river E':
18: 3 his dominion by the river E'.
2Ch 35:20 to fight against Carchemish by E':
Jer 13: 4 upon thy loins, and arise, go to E',
5 went, and hid it by E', as the Lord
6 Arise, go to E', and take the girdle
7 Then I went to E', and digged, and
46: 2 of Egypt, which was by the river E'
6 towards the north by the river E'.
10 the north country by the river E'.
51:63 it, and cast it into the midst of E':
Re 9:14 are bound in the great river E'.
16:12 his vial upon the great river E';

Euroclydon (*yu-roc'-lid-on*)
Ac 27:14 a tempestuous wind, called E'.

Eutychus (*yu'-tik-us*)
Ac 20: 9 a certain young man named E',

evangelist See also EVANGELISTS.
Ac 21: 8 entered the house of Philip the e',
2Ti 4: 5 afflictions, do the work of an e',

evangelists
Eph 4:11 and some, e'; and some, pastors

Eve (*eev*)
Ge 3:20 Adam called his wife's name E';
4: 1 And Adam knew E' his wife; and
2Co 11: 3 the serpent beguiled E' through
1Ti 2:13 Adam was first formed, then E'.

even See also EVENING; EVENTIDE.
Ge 6:17 behold, I, e' I, do bring a flood
9: 3 e' as the green herb have I given
10: 9 E' as Nimrod the mighty hunter
19 and Zeboim, e' unto Lasha.
21 e' to him were children born.
13: 3 from the south e' to Bethel,
10 e' as the garden of the Lord,
14:23 from a thread e' to a shoelatchet,
19: 1 came two angels to Sodom at e';
4 men of the city, e' the men of Sodom,
9 pressed sore upon the man, e' Lot,
20: 5 she, e' she herself said, He is my
21:10 be heir with my son, e' with Isaac.
24:11 e' the time that women go to draw
26:28 e' betwixt us and thee, and let us
27:34 Bless me, e' me also, O my father.
38 bless me, e' me also, O my father.
34:29 spoiled e' all that was in the house
35:14 with him, e' a pillar of stone:
37:18 e' before he came unto them,
44:18 servant: for thou art e' as Pharaoh.
46:18 she bare unto Jacob, e' sixteen souls.
34 our youth e' until now, both we,
47: 2 some of his brethren, e' five men
21 of the borders of Egypt e' to the other
49:22 Joseph is..., e' a fruitful bough
25 E' by the God of thy father, who
Ex 3: 1 mountain of God, e' to Horeb.
4:16 e' he shall be to thee instead of
22 Israel is my son, e' my firstborn:
23 will slay thy son, e' thy firstborn.
9:18 foundation thereof e' until now.
10:12 eat every herb of the land, e' all

Ex 10:21 e' darkness that may be felt.
11: 5 e' unto the firstborn of the
12:15 e' the first day ye shall put away
18 fourteenth day of the month at e',
18 twentieth day of the month at e'.
19 e' that soul shall be cut off from
38 flocks, and herds, e' very much cattle.
41 e' the selfsame day it came to pass,
14:23 the sea, e' all Pharaoh's horses,
16: 6 At e', then ye shall know that the
12 At e' ye shall eat flesh, and in the
13 that at e' the quails came up, and
18:14 by thee from morning unto e'?
23:31 e' unto the sea of the Philistines,
25: 9 instruments thereof, e' so shall ye
19 e' of the mercy seat shall ye make
27: 5 be e' to the midst of the altar.
28: 1 e' Aaron, Nadab and Abihu, Eleazar
8 e' of gold, of blue, and purple,
17 of stones, e' four rows of stones:
42 from the loins e' unto the thighs
29:27 e' of that which is for Aaron, and of
28 e' their heave offering unto the Lord.
39 other lamb thou shalt offer at e':
41 other lamb thou shalt offer at e',
30: 8 Aaron lighteth the lamps at e',
21 e' to him and to his seed throughout
23 so much, e' two hundred shekels,
33 upon a stranger, shall e' be cut off
38 to smell thereto, shall e' be cut off
32:29 e' every man upon his son, and
35:35 e' of them that do any work, and of
36: 2 e' every one whose heart stirred
37: 3 e' two rings upon the one side of it,
9 e' to the mercy seatward were
38:21 of the tabernacle, e' of the tabernacle
24 e' the gold of the offering, was twenty
39:37 e' with the lamps to be set in order,
43 Lord had commanded, e' so had they
Le 1: 2 offering of the cattle, e' of the herd,
2:14 corn dried by the fire, e' corn
3:14 his offering, e' an offering made by
4:12 E' the whole bullock shall he carry
17 before the Lord e' before the vail.
5:12 of it, e' a memorial thereof, and
6: 5 shall e' restore it in the principal,
15 e' the memorial of it, unto the
7: 8 e' the priest shall have to himself
20 upon him, e' that soul shall be cut
21 the Lord, e' that soul shall be cut
25 e' the soul that eateth it shall be
27 of blood, e' that soul shall be cut
8: 9 mitre, e' upon his forefront, did
11:11 They shall be e' an abomination
22 E' these of them ye may eat; the
24 shall be unclean until the e'.
25 clothes, and be unclean until the e'.
27 carcase shall be unclean until the e'.
28 clothes, and be unclean until the e':
31 dead, shall be unclean until the e'.
32 and it shall be unclean until the e';
39 thereof shall be unclean until the e'.
40 clothes, and be unclean until the e':
40 and be unclean until the e'.
13:12 from his head e' to his foot,
18 e' in the skin thereof, was a boil,
30 it is a dry scall, e' a leprosy upon
38 bright spots, e' white bright spots;
14: 9 e' all his hair he shall shave off: and
31 E' such as he is able to get, the one
46 up shall be unclean until the e'.
15: 5, 6, 7, 8 and be unclean until the e'.
10 him shall be unclean until the e':
10, 11, 16, 17, 18 unclean until the e'.
19 her shall be unclean until the e'.
21, 22 and be unclean until the e'.
23 he shall be unclean until the e'.
27 water, and be unclean until the e'.
16:32 linen clothes, e' the holy garments:
17: 5 e' that they may bring them unto
9 e' that man shall be cut off from
10 I will e' set my face against that
13 e' pour out the blood thereof,
15 and be unclean until the e':
18: 9, 10 e' their nakedness thou shalt not
29 e' the souls that commit them shall
19:21 e' a ram for a trespass offering.
20:10 e' he that committeth adultery with
22: 6 such shall be unclean until e',
23: 2 convocations, e' these are my feasts.
4 of the Lord, e' holy convocations,
5 day of the first month at e'
16 E' unto the morrow after the
18 e' an offering made by fire, of sweet
32 the ninth day of the month at e',
32 from e' unto e', shall ye celebrate
24: 7 e' an offering made by fire unto the
26:16 I will e' appoint over you terror,
28 I, e' I, will chastise you seven
34 e' then shall the land rest, and enjoy
43 because, e' because they despised
27: 3 twenty years old e' unto sixty
3 e' thy estimation shall be fifty
5 years old e' unto twenty years old,
6 a month old e' unto five years old,
18 the years that remain, e' unto
23 e' unto the year of the jubilee:
24 e' to him to whom the possession of
32 e' of whatsoever passeth under
Nu 1:21 e' of the tribe of Reuben, were
23 e' of the tribe of Simeon, were
25 e' of the tribe of Gad, were forty
27 e' of the tribe of Judah, were
29 e' of the tribe of Issachar, were
31 e' of the tribe of Zebulun, were
33 e' of the tribe of Ephraim, were
Nu 1:35 e' of the tribe of Manasseh, were
37 e' of the tribe of Benjamin, were
39 e' of the tribe of Dan, were
41 e' of the tribe of Asher, were
43 e' of the tribe of Naphtali, were
46 E' all they that were numbered were
3:22 e' those that were numbered of them
38 e' before the tabernacle of the
47 shalt e' take five shekels apiece
4: 3 e' until fifty years old, all that
14 e' the censers, the fleshhooks,
30 e' unto fifty years old shalt thou
35 years old and upward e' unto fifty
39 and upward e' unto fifty years old,
40 E' those that were numbered of them,
43 e' unto fifty years old, every one
44 E' those that were numbered of them
47 e' unto fifty years old, every one
48 E' those that were numbered of them,
5: 8 unto the Lord, e' to the priest;
26 e' the memorial thereof, and burn
6: 4 from the kernels e' to the husk.
7:10 e' the princes offered their offering
8: 8 e' fine flour mingled with oil,
16 e' instead of the firstborn of all the
9: 3 fourteenth day of this month, at e',
5 day of the first month at e' in the
11 day of the second month at e' they
13 e' the same soul shall be cut off
15 and at e' there was upon the
21 abode from e' unto the morning,
11:20 But e' a whole month, until it
12: 8 mouth to mouth, e' apparently,
14:19 from Egypt e' until now.
34 e' forty days, each day for a year,
34 e' forty years, and ye shall know
37 E' those men that did bring up the
45 discomfited them, e' unto Hormah.
15:23 E' all that the Lord hath commanded
16: 5 E' to morrow the Lord will shew
5 e' him whom he hath chosen will
17: 6 fathers' houses, e' twelve rods:
18:21 e' the service of the tabernacle of
26 e' a tenth part of the tithe.
29 e' the hallowed part thereof out of it.
19: 7 shall be unclean until the e'.
8 and shall be unclean until the e'.
10 and be unclean until the e':
19 in water, shall be clean at e'.
21 shall be unclean until e'.
22 it shall be unclean until e'.
20: 1 e' the whole congregation, into the
22 e' the whole congregation, journeyed
29 e' all the house of Israel.
21:24 e' unto the children of Ammon:
26 out of his hand, e' unto Arnon.
30 is perished e' unto Dibon, and
30 laid them waste e' unto Nophah,
25:13 e' the covenant of an everlasting
14 e' that was slain with the
27:21 with him, e' all the congregation.
28: 4 other lamb shalt thou offer at e';
8 other lamb shalt thou offer at e':
31:47 E' of the children of Israel's half,
51 them, e' all wrought jewels.
32: 4 E' the country which the Lord
33 them, e' to the children of Gad,
33 e' the cities of the country round
33:49 from Beth-jesimoth e' unto
34: 2 e' the land of Canaan with the
6 e' have the great sea for a border:
36:10 E' as the Lord commanded Moses,
De 1:44 you in Seir, e' unto Hormah.
2:22 in their stead e' unto this day:
23 e' unto Azzah, the Caphtorims,
36 e' unto Gilead, there was not one
3:16 from Gilead e' unto the river Jabbok,
16 the border e' unto the river Jabbok,
17 from Chinnereth e' unto the sea
17 the sea, e' the salt sea, under
4: 5 e' as the Lord my God commanded
13 to perform, e' ten commandments;
19 stars, e' all the host of heaven,
20 e' out of Egypt, to be unto him a
24 consuming fire, e' a jealous God.
30 e' in the latter days, if thou turn
48 e' unto mount Sion, which is Hermon,
49 e' unto the sea of the plain,
5: 3 but with us, e' us, who are all of
23 e' all the heads of your tribes,
9: 9 e' the tables of the covenant which
11 e' the tables of the covenant.
21 e' until it was as small as dust:
10:15 e' you above all people, as it is this
11:12 the year e' unto the end of the
24 e' unto the uttermost sea shall
12: 5 e' unto his habitation shall you
22 E' as the roebuck and the hart
30 e' so will I do likewise.
31 for e' their sons and their
13: 7 the earth, e' unto the other end
16: 3 bread therewith, e' the bread of
4 first day at e', remain all night
6 sacrifice the passover at e',
17: 5 e' that man or that woman, and
18:20 e' that prophet shall die.
20:14 e' all the spoil thereof, shalt thou
21: 3 e' the elders of that city shall take
22:26 e' so is this matter:
23: 2 e' to his tenth generation shall
3 e' to their tenth generation shall
16 e' among you, in that place
18 for e' both these are abomination
23 e' a freewill offering, according
25:18 e' all that were feeble behind
26: 9 e' a land that floweth with
De 28:59 e' great plagues, and of long
64 of the earth e' unto the other;
64 have known, e' wood and stone.
67 Would God it were e'! and at e'
29:24 E' all nations shall say,
31:21 e' now, before I have brought
32:31 e' our enemies themselves being
39 that I, e' I, am he, and there is
33: 4 e' the inheritance of the
Jos 1: 2 e' to the children of Israel.
4 e' unto the great river, the river
2: 1 Go view the land, e' Jericho.
24 for e' all the inhabitants of the
3:16 of the plain, e' the salt sea, failed,
5: 4 e' all the men of war, died in the
10 fourteenth day of the month at e'
6:17 e' it, and all that are therein, to the
25 in Israel e' unto this day;
7: 5 before the gate e' unto Shebarim,
11 e' taken of the accursed thing,
11 put it e' among their own stuff.
8: 4 the city, e' behind the city:
11 e' the people of war that were with
13 e' all the host that was on the north
25 e' all the men of Ai.
28 e' a desolation unto this day.
9:20 we will e' let them live, lest
27 e' unto this day, in the place
10:41 Kadesh-barnea e' unto Gaza,
41 country of Goshen, e' unto Gibeon.
11: 4 e' as the sand that is upon the sea
17 E' from the mount Halak,
17 e' unto Baal-gad in the valley of
12: 2 Gilead, e' unto the river Jabbok,
3 e' the salt sea on the east,
7 e' unto the mount Halak,
13: 3 e' unto the borders of Ekron
8 e' as Moses the servant of the Lord
24 e' unto the children of Gad
27 e' unto the edge of the sea of
31 e' to the one half of the children
14:10 e' since the Lord spake this word
11 e' so is my strength now, for
15: 1 e' to the border of Edom the
5 e' unto the end of Jordan.
13 e' the city of Arba the father of
46 From Ekron e' unto the sea,
16: 5 e' the border of their inheritance
17:11 and her towns, e' three countries.
17 e' to Ephraim and to Manasseh,
19: 1 e' for the tribe of the children of
28 and Kanah, e' unto great Zidon;
32 e' for the children of Naphtali
50 e' Timnath-serah in mount
21:20 e' they had the cities of their lot
23: 4 e' unto the great sea westward.
12 e' these that remain among you,
24: 2 e' Terah, the father of Abraham,
12 e' the two kings of the Amorites;
18 e' the Amorites which dwelt in the
J'g 3: 1 e' as many of Israel as had not
9 e' Othniel the son of Kenaz,
4:13 e' nine hundred chariots of iron,
5: 3 I, e' I, will sing unto the Lord;
5 e' that Sinai from before the Lord
11 e' the righteous acts toward the
15 e' Issachar, and also Barak:
6: 3 the east, e' they came up against
25 e' the second bullock of seven years
7:22 fellow, e' throughout all the host:
8:14 e' threescore and seventeen men.
19 e' the sons of my mother:
27 put it in his city, e' in Ophrah:
9:40 e' unto the entering of the gate.
11:13 of Egypt, from Arnon e' unto Jabbok,
22 Amorites, from Arnon e' unto Jabbok,
22 the wilderness e' unto Jordan.
33 e' till thou come to Minnith,
33 e' twenty cities, and unto the plain
36 e' of the children of Ammon.
18:15 e' unto the house of Micah, and
19:16 there came an old man . . . at e',
20: 1 from Dan e' to Beer-sheba,
2 e' of all the tribes of Israel,
23 wept before the Lord until e',
26 and fasted that day until e',
33 e' out of the meadows of Gibeah.
21: 2 abode there till e' before God,
Ru 2: 7 continued e' from the morning
15 her glean e' among the sheaves,
17 she gleaned in the field until e',
1Sa 3:20 from Dan e' to Beer-sheba knew
5: 6 e' Ashdod and the coasts thereof.
6:18 e' unto the great stone of Abel,
19 e' he smote of the people fifty
7:14 from Ekron e' unto Gath;
8: 8 e' unto this day, wherewith they
14 e' the best of them, and give them
14:21 e' they also turned to be with
22 e' they also followed hard after
17:40 in a shepherd's bag...e' in a scrip;
52 e' unto Gath, and unto Ekron.
18: 4 e' to his sword, and to his bow,
11 smite David e' to the wall with it.
19:10 David e' to the wall with the javelin;
20: 4 I will e' do it for thee.
5 the field unto the third day at e'.
16 Lord e' require it at the hand of
25 set...e' upon a seat by the wall:
25:25 regard this man of Belial, e' Nabal:
27 it e' be given unto the young men
26: 8 him...e' to the earth at once,
27: 3 e' David with his two wives,
8 e' unto the land of Egypt.
28: 3 him in Ramah, e' in his own city.
17 it to thy neighbour, e' to David:

1Sa 30:17 the twilight e' unto the evening
26 the elders of Judah, e' to his friends,
2Sa 1: 2 It came e' to pass on the third day,
12 and fasted until e', for Saul, and
2: 5 unto your Lord, e' unto Saul,
3: 9 to David, e' so I do to him;
10 from Dan e' to Beer-sheba.
15 e' from Phaltiel the son of Laish.
6: 5 e' on harps, and on psalteries,
19 e' among the whole multitude of
7: 6 out of Egypt, e' to this day,
23 like thy people, e' like Israel,
8: 2 e' with two lines measured he to
10: 4 their garments...e' to their buttocks,
11:13 at e' he went out to lie on his bed
23 were upon them e' unto the entering
14:25 his foot e' to the crown of his head
15:12 from his city, e' from Giloh,
21 e' there also will thy servant be.
17:11 from Dan e' to Beer-sheba,
18: 5 with the young man, e' with Absalom.
19:11 come to the king, e' to his house.
14 e' as the heart of one man;
32 very aged man, e' fourscore years
20: 2 from Jordan e' to Jerusalem.
21 against the king, e' against David:
22:42 e' unto the Lord, but he answered
23: 4 e' a morning without clouds;
24: 2 from Dan e' to Beer-sheba,
7 south of Judah, e' to Beer-sheba.
15 e' to the time appointed:
15 Dan e' to Beer-sheba seventy
1Ki 1:26 But me, e' me thy servant,
30 E' as I sware unto thee by the
30 e' so will I certainly do this day,
37 e' so be he with Solomon, and
48 mine eyes e' seeing it.
2:22 e' for him, and for Abiathar the priest,
4:12 e' unto the place that is beyond
24 from Tiphsah e' to Azzah,
25 from Dan e' to Beer-sheba,
29 e' as the sand that is on the sea shore.
33 e' unto the hyssop that springeth
6:16 he e' built them for it within,
16 e' for the oracle, e' for the most holy
7: 7 e' the porch of judgment:
9 e' from the foundation unto the coping.
10 costly stones, e' great stones,
42 e' two rows of pomegranates for
51 e' the silver; and the gold,
8: 4 e' those did the priests and the Levites
6 e' under the wings of the cherubims.
29 e' toward the place of which thou
39 for thou, e' thou only, knowest the
65 and seven days, e' fourteen days.
11:26 Jeroboam...e' he lifted up his
35 will give it unto thee, e' ten tribes.
12:27 e' unto Rehoboam king of Judah,
30 went to worship... e' unto Dan.
33 e' in the month which he had devised
13:34 e' to cut it off, and to destroy it
14:14 that day: but what? e' now.
15:13 Maachah...e' her he removed
28 E' in the third year of Asa king of
16: 7 e' for all the evil that he did in
18:22 I, e' I only, remain a prophet of the
26 from morning e' until noon,
19:10, 14 and I, e' I only, am left; and they
20: 3 children, e' the goodliest, are mine.
14 E' by the young men of the
15 people, e' all the children of Israel,
21:11 e' the elders and the nobles who were
13 against him, e' against Naboth, in the
19 shall dogs lick thy blood, e' thine.
22:35 was stayed up...and died at e':
2Ki 3:24 Moabites, e' in their own country.
26 e' unto the king of Edom:
4: 3 of thy neighbours, e' empty vessels;
5:22 Behold, e' now there be come...two
7: 6 of horses, e' the noise of a great host:
7 e' the camp as it was, and fled for
13 they are e' as all the multitude of
8: 6 she left the land, e' until now.
9 a present...e' of every good thing
9: 4 e' the young man the prophet, went
6 anointed thee king...e' over Israel.
20 saying, He came e' unto them, and
10: 3 Look e' out the best and meetest
14 e' two and forty men;
33 e' Gilead and Bashan.
11: 2 they hid him, e' him and his nurse,
5 shall e' be keepers of the watch
7 e' they shall keep the watch of the
12: 4 e' the money of every one that
14:10 e' thou, and Judah with thee?
29 e' with the kings of Israel;
15:20 e' of all the mighty men of wealth,
17:16 molten images, e' two calves,
18: 8 e' unto Gaza, and the borders
10 e' in the sixth year of Hezekiah,
21 e' upon Egypt, on which if a man
19:15 thou art the God, e' thou alone,
19 thou art the Lord God, e' thou only.
22 e' against the Holy One of Israel.
20:14 from a far country, e' from Babylon.
21:15 out of Egypt, e' unto this day.
22:16 e' all the words of the book which
24:14 e' ten thousand captives, and all the
16 the men of might, e' seven thousand,
16 e' them the king of Babylon brought
25:22 e' over them he made Gedaliah . . .
23 e' Ishmael the son of Nethaniah, and
1Ch 2:23 the towns thereof, e' threescore cities.
4:15 and the sons of Elah, e' Kenaz.
39 e' unto the east side of the valley,
42 e' of the sons of Simeon, five hundred
1Ch 5: 8 e' unto Nebo and Baal-meon
24 e' Epher, and Ishi, and Eliel, and
26 e' the Reubenites, and the Gadites,
6:39 e' Asaph the son of Berachiah,
10:13 e' against the word of the Lord,
11: 2 time past, e' when Saul was king,
12: 2 e' of Saul's brethren of Benjamin.
40 e' unto Issachar and Zebulun and
13: 5 from Shihor of Egypt e' unto the
14:16 smote the host . . . from Gibeon e'
16:16 E' of the covenant which he made
19 When ye were but few, e' a few,
17: 7 from the sheepcote, e' from
24 Let it e' be established,
24 Lord of hosts is . . . e' a God to Israel:
20: 3 E' so dealt David with all the
21: 2 Israel from Beer-sheba e' unto Dan;
12 e' the pestilence, in the land, and the
17 e' I it is that have sinned and done evil
23:24 e' the chief of the fathers, as they were
30 morning . . . and likewise at e';
24:31 e' the principal fathers over against
25: 7 e' all that were cunning, was two
26:12 divisions of the porters, e' among
21 e' of Laadan the Gershonite,
31 e' among the Hebronites, according to
28:15 E' the weight for the candlesticks
19 e' all the works of this pattern.
20 the Lord God, e' my God, will be with
21 e' they shall be with thee for all
29: 4 E' three thousand talents of gold,
21 e' a thousand bullocks, a thousand
2Ch 2: 3 As thou didst deal with David . . . e' so
9 E' to prepare me timber in abundance:
5: 7 e' under the wings of the cherubims:
13 It came e' to pass, as the trumpeters
13 was filled with a cloud, e' the house of
6:21 dwelling place, e' from heaven; and
33 e' from thy dwelling place, and do
39 e' from thy dwelling place, their prayer
8:10 chief of king Solomon's officers, e' two
13 E' after a certain rate every day,
13 e' in the feast of unleavened bread,
9:26 from the river e' unto the land of
11: 6 He built e' Beth-lehem, and Etam, and
13: 3 e' four hundred thousand chosen men:
5 e' to him and to his sons by a covenant
17: 7 to his princes, e' to Ben-hail, and to
8 he sent Levites, e' Shemaiah, and
18:13 e' what my God saith, that will
21 prevail: go out, and do e' so.
34 against the Syrians until the e':
19:10 ye shall e' warn them that they
20: 4 e' out of all the cities of Judah
24:14 e' vessels to minister, and to offer
25:13 from Samaria e' unto Beth-horon,
19 thou shouldest fall, e' thou, and Judah
26: 8 spread abroad e' to the entering in
19 leprosy e' rose up in his forehead
28:10 are there not with you, e' with you,
27 buried him in the city, e' in
30: 5 from Beer-sheba e' to Dan,
10 and Manasseh e' unto Zebulun:
18 e' many of Ephraim, and Manasseh,
27 to his holy dwelling place, e' unto
31:16 e' unto every one that entereth into
33:14 e' to the entering in at the fish gate,
34: 6 and Simeon, e' unto Naphtali,
11 E' to the artificers and builders gave
24 e' all the curses that are written in the
27 I have e' heard thee also, saith
33 e' to serve the Lord their God.
Ezr 1: 8 E' those did Cyrus king of Persia
3: 3 e' burnt offerings morning and evening.
4: 5 e' until the reign of Darius king
11 sent unto him, e' unto Artaxerxes
5: 1 unto the Jews . . . e' unto them,
16 since that time e' until now
6: 8 of the king's goods, e' of the tribute
7:11 e' a scribe of the words of the
21 And I, e' I Artaxerxes the king,
8:25 e' the offering of the house of our God,
26 I e' weighed unto their hand six
9: 1 e' of the Canaanites, the Hittites,
Ne 2:13 e' before the dragon well,
3: 1 e' unto the tower of Meah they
10 e' over against his house.
21 e' to the end of the house of
24 of the wall, e' unto the corner,
27 e' unto the wall of Ophel.
4: 3 E' that which they build,
3 he shall e' break down their stone
13 e' set the people after their families
Ne 5: 8 and will ye e' sell your brethren?
11 Restore...e' this day, their lands, their
13 e' thus be he shaken out, and
14 twentieth year e' unto the two and
15 yea, e' their servants bare rule
8:13 e' to understand the words of the law.
9: 6 Thou, e' thou, art Lord alone;
12:23 e' until the days of Johanan the son
37 e' unto the water gate eastward.
38 tower of the furnaces e' unto the broad
39 e' unto the sheep gate:
43 Jerusalem was heard e' afar off.
13:26 e' him did outlandish women
Es 1: 1 from India e' unto Ethiopia,
4 e' an hundred and fourscore days.
2:18 made a great feast...e' Esther's
3: 6 e' the people of Mordecai.
13 e' upon the thirteenth day of the
4: 2 came e' before the king's gate:
5: 3 it shall be e' given thee to the half
6 e' to the half of the kingdom it
6:10 and do e' so to Mordecai the Jew,
7: 2 e' to the half of the kingdom.
Job 4: 8 E' as I have seen, they that plow
21 they die, e' without wisdom.
5: 5 and taketh it e' out of the thorns,
6: 9 E' that it would please God to destroy
10:21 e' to the land of darkness and the
15:26 runneth upon him, e' on his neck,
17: 5 e' the eyes of his children shall fail.
11 e' the thoughts of my heart.
18:13 e' the firstborn of death shall
21: 6 E' when I remember I am afraid,
23: 2 E' to day is my complaint bitter:
3 that I might come e' to his seat!
13 his soul desireth, e' that he doeth.
24:17 them e' as the shadow of death:
25: 5 Behold e' to the moon, and it
28: 4 e' the waters forgotten of the
31: 6 me be weighed in an e' balance,
34:17 Shall e' he that hateth right govern?
36:16 E' so would he have removed
41: 9 cast down e' at the sight of him?
42:16 his son's sons, e' four generations.
Ps 18: 6 before him, e' into his ears.
41 e' unto the Lord, but he answered
21: 4 e' length of days for ever and ever.
24: 9 e' lift them up, ye everlasting
26:12 My foot standeth in an e' place:
27: 2 wicked, e' mine enemies and my foes,
35:23 to my judgment, e' unto my cause,
39:*title* the chief Musician, e' to Jeduthun,
2 I held my peace, e' from good;
40: 3 in my mouth, e' praise unto our God:
45:12 e' the rich among the people shall
47: 9 e' the people of the God of
48:14 he will be our guide e' unto death.
50: 1 The mighty God, e' the Lord,
7 I am God, e' thy God.
55:19 e' he that abideth of old.
57: 4 I lie e' among them that are set
4 e the sons of men, whose teeth are
59:12 let them e' be taken in their pride:
64: 3 to shoot their arrows, e' bitter words:
65: 4 thy house, e' thy holy temple.
67: 6 God, e' our own God, shall bless us.
68: 8 e' Sinai itself was moved at the
17 thousand, e' thousands of angels:
19 loadeth...with benefits, e' the God of
24 e' the goings of my God, my King,
26 e' the Lord, from the fountain of
71:16 thy righteousness, e' of thine only.
22 e' thy truth, O my God:
73: 1 e' to such as are of a clean heart.
74: 3 e' all that the enemy hath done
11 thy hand, e' thy right hand?
76: 7 Thou, e' thou, art to be feared:
77: 1 e' unto God with my voice;
78: 6 know them, e' the children which
54 e' to this mountain, which his right
84: 2 yea, e' fainteth for the courts of
3 e' thine altars, O Lord of hosts, my
90: 2 e' from everlasting to everlasting.
11 e' according to thy fear, so is thy
91: 9 e' the most High, thy habitation;
105:17 e' Joseph, who was sold for a
20 e' the ruler of the people, and let
106: 7 him at the sea, e' at the Red sea.
38 blood, e' the blood of their sons
107:43 e' they shall understand the
108: 1 and give praise, e' with my glory.
109:16 might e' slay the broken in heart.
113: 8 e' with the princes of his people.
115:16 e' the heavens, are the Lord's:
118:27 e' unto the horns of the altar.
119:41 e' thy salvation, according to thy
112 thy statutes alway, e' unto the end.
121: 8 time forth, and e' for evermore.
125: 2 from henceforth e' for ever.
131: 2 my soul is e' as a weaned child.
133: 2 down upon the beard, e' Aaron's beard:
3 the blessing, e' life for evermore.
136:22 E' an heritage unto Israel his servant:
137: 7 it, e' to the foundation thereof.
139:10 E' there shall thy hand lead me,
11 e' the night shall be light about
146:10 e' thy God, O Zion, unto all
148:14 e' of the children of Israel, a people
Pr 2:16 e' from the stranger which flattereth
3:12 e' as a father the son in whom he
8:16 e' all the judges of the earth.
14:13 E' in laughter the heart is
20 is hated e' of his own neighbour:
16: 4 e' the wicked for the day of evil.
7 he maketh e' his enemies to be at
17:15 e' they both are abomination to
28 E' a fool, when he holdeth his
20:11 E' a child is known by his doings,
12 Lord hath made e' both of them.
22:19 known to thee this day, e' to thee.
23:15 my heart shall rejoice, e' mine.
28: 9 e' his prayer shall be abomination.
30: 1 of Jakeh, e' the prophecy:
1 spake unto Ithiel, e' unto Ithiel
Ec 2:12 e' that which hath been already
15 so it happeneth e' to me;
3:19 e' one thing befalleth them:
4:16 e' of all that have been before them:
7:25 of folly, e' of foolishness and
9: 1 in my heart e' to declare all this,
11: 5 e' so thou knowest not the works
12:10 was upright, e' words of truth.
Ca 4: 2 flock of sheep that are e' shorn,
Isa 1: 6 soul of the foot e' unto the head
13 iniquity, e' the solemn meeting.
4: 3 be called holy, e' every one that is
5: 9 shall be desolate, e' great and fair,
7: 6 in the midst...e' the son of Tabeal:
17 e' the king of Assyria.

Isa 7:23 it shall e' be for briers and thorns.
8: 7 and many, e' the king of Assyria,
8 he shall reach e' to the neck;
9: 7 justice from henceforth e' for ever.
9 all the people...e' Ephraim and the
10:21 shall return, e' the remnant of Jacob,
23 e' determined, in the midst of all
13: 3 e' them that rejoice in my highness.
5 e' the Lord, and the weapons of his
12 precious than fine gold; e' a man
14: 9 e' all the chief ones of the earth;
18 kings...e' all of them, lie in glory,
15: 4 shall be heard e' unto Jahaz:
16: 6 e' of his haughtiness, and his pride,
8 they are come e' unto Jazer, they
18: 2 e' in vessels of bulrushes upon the
19:13 e' they that are the stay of the
22 they shall return e' to the Lord,
24 e' a blessing in the midst of the
20: 4 e' with their buttocks uncovered,
22:15 unto this treasurer, e' unto Shebna,
24 e' to all the vessels of flagons.
23: 4 spoken, e' the strength of the sea,
24:15 e' the name of the Lord God of
16 songs, e' glory to the righteous.
25: 5 e' the heat with the shadow of a
10 e' as straw is trodden down for the
12 to the ground, e' to the dust.
26: 5 he layeth it low, e' to the ground;
5 he bringeth it e' to the dust.
6 tread it down, e' the feet of the poor,
27: 1 e' leviathan that crooked
28:22 e' determined upon the whole
29: 7 fight against Ariel, e' all that fight
8 It shall e' be as when an hungry
14 e' a marvellous work and a wonder:
32: 7 e' when the needy speaketh right.
35: 2 rejoice e' with joy and singing:
4 e' God with a recompence;
37:16 thou art the God, e' thou alone,
20 thou art the Lord, e' thou only.
23 e' against the Holy One of Israel.
38:11 I shall not see the Lord, e' the Lord,
12 sickness: from day e' to night wilt
13 my bones: from day e' to night wilt
39: 3 country unto me, e' from Babylon.
40:30 E' the youths shall faint and be weary,
41: 3 e' by the way that he had not gone
12 e' them that contended with thee:
28 e' among them, and there was no
43: 7 E' every one that is called by my
11 I, e' I, am the Lord;
19 e' make a way in the wilderness,
25 I, e' I, am he that blotteth out
44: 8 ye are e' my witnesses.
17 maketh a god, e' his graven image:
28 e' saying to Jerusalem, Thou shalt be
45: 4 have e' called thee by thy name:
12 I, e' my hands, have stretched out
24 e' to him shall men come;
46: 4 And e' to your old age I am he;
4 e' to hoar hairs will I carry you:
4 e' I will carry, and will deliver
47:15 e' thy merchants, from thy youth:
48: 5 I have e' from the beginning
6 have showed you new...e' hidden
7 e' before the day when thou
11 For mine own sake, e' for mine
15 I, e' I, have spoken;
20 utter it e' to the end of the earth;
49:10 e' by the springs of water shall he
19 of thy destruction shall e' now be
25 E' the captives of the mighty
51:12 I, e' I, am he that comforteth you:
22 e' the dregs of the cup of my fury;
55: 3 e' the sure mercies of David.
56: 5 E' unto them will I give in mine
7 E' them will I bring to my holy
57: 6 e' to them hast thou poured a
7 e' thither wentest thou up to offer
9 didst debase thyself e' unto hell.
11 have not I held my peace e' of old,
65: 6 e' recompense into their bosom,
66: 2 e' to him that is poor and of a contrite
Jer 3:25 from your youth e' unto this day,
4:12 E' a full wind from those places
6:11 e' the husband with the wife
13 the least of them e' unto the greatest
13 from the prophet e' unto the priest
19 e' the fruit of their thoughts,
7:11 Behold, e' I have seen it,
15 e' the whole seed of Ephraim.
25 unto this day I have e' sent
8:10 from the least e' unto the greatest
10 from the prophet e' unto the priest
9:15 will feed them, e' this people, with
22 E' the carcases of men shall fall
10:11 e' they shall perish from the
11: 7 e' unto this day, rising early and
13 e' altars to burn incense unto Baal.
23 e' the year of their visitation.
12: 6 For e' thy brethren, and the house
6 of thy father, e' they have dealt
12 from the one end of the land e' to
13:10 to worship them, shall e' be as this
13 inhabitants of this land, e' the kings
14 one against another, e' the fathers
18 shall come down, e' the crown of your
15:13 for all thy sins, e' in all thy borders.
16: 5 e' lovingkindness and mercies.
17: 4 And thou, e' thyself, shalt discontinue
10 I try the reins, e' to give every man
27 not to bear a burden, e' entering
19:11 E' so will I break this people,
12 and e' make this city as Tophet:
21: 5 with a strong arm, e' in anger,

Jer 22:25 whose face thou fearest, e' into the
23:12 e' the year of their visitation,
19 in fury, e' a grievous whirlwind:
33 I will e' forsake you,
34 I will e' punish that man
39 behold, I, e' I, will utterly forget
24: 2 very good figs, e' like the figs
25: 3 Amon king of Judah, e' unto this day,
13 e' all that is written in this book.
31 noise shall come e' to the ends of
33 one end of the earth e' unto the other
28: 6 E' the prophet Jeremiah said,
11 E' so will I break the yoke
29:23 I have not commanded them; e' I
30: 7 none is like it: it is e' the time
31: 2 grace in the wilderness; e' Israel,
19 I was ashamed, yea, e' confounded,
21 heart toward the highway, e' the way
32: 9 weighed him the money, e' seventeen
20 land of Egypt, e' unto this day,
31 they built it e' unto this day,
33:10 beast, e' in the cities of Judah,
24 he hath e' cast them off?
34:20 I will e' give them into the hand
36: 2 the days of Josiah, e' unto this day.
12 all the princes sat there e' Elishama
39: 3 in the middle gate, e' Nergal-sharezer,
12 do unto him e' as he shall say
14 E' they sent and took Jeremiah,
40: 7 in the fields, e' they and their men,
8 to Mizpah, e' Ishmael the son
12 E' all the Jews returned out
41: 1 the princes of the king, e' ten men
3 that were with him, e' with Gedaliah,
5 and from Samaria, e' fourscore men,
10 that were in Mizpah, e' the king's
16 son of Ahikam, e' mighty men
42: 1 from the least e' unto the greatest,
2 Lord thy God, e' for all this remnant;
5 if we do not e' according to all
8 from the least e' to the greatest,
43: 1 him to them, e' all these words,
6 E' men, and women, and children,
7 thus came they e' to Tahpanhes.
44:10 are not humbled e' unto this day,
12 they shall e' be consumed.
12 from the least e' unto the greatest,
15 a great multitude, e' all the people
45: 4 I will pluck up, e' this whole land.
46:25 and their kings; e' Pharaoh,
48:32 they reach e' to the sea of Jazer:
34 the cry of Heshbon e' unto Elealeh,
34 Elealeh, and e' unto Jahaz,
34 from Zoar e' unto Horonaim,
44 I will bring upon it, e' upon Moab,
49:37 evil upon them, e' my fierce anger,
50: 7 the habitation of justice, e' the Lord,
21 land of Merathaim, e' against it,
51: 9 and is lifted up e' to the skies.
56 is come upon her, e' upon Babylon,
60 come upon Babylon, e' all these
La 4: 3 E' the sea monsters draw out
Eze 1:27 of his loins e' upward,
27 of his loins e' downward,
2: 3 against me, e' unto this very day.
4: 1 upon it the city, e' Jerusalem:
13 said, E' thus shall the children
14 from my youth up e' till now
5: 8 Behold, I, e' I, am against thee,
6: 3 Behold, I, e' I, will bring a sword
7:14 the trumpet, e' to make all ready;
8: 2 of his loins e' downward,
2 from his loins e' upward,
9: 1 to draw near, e' every man
10: 2 the wheels, e' under the cherub,
5 was heard e' to the outer court,
12 full of eyes round about, e' the wheels
11:15 thy brethren, e' thy brethren,
17 e' gather you from the people,
12: 4 thou shalt go forth at e' in their
7 in the e' I digged through the wall
13:10 Because, e' because they have seduced
13 I will e' rend it with a stormy wind
20 will let the souls go, e' the souls that
14:10 prophet shall be e' as the punishment
22 e' concerning all that I have brought
16:19 thou hast e' set it before them
37 e' gather them round about against
59 I will e' deal with thee as thou hast
17: 9 e' without great power or many
16 whose covenant he brake, e' with him
19 hath broken, e' it will I recompense
18:11 but e' hath eaten upon the
18 lo, e' he shall die in his iniquity.
20:11 13, 21 he shall e' live in them.
31 all your idols, e' unto this day:
21:13 if the sword contemn e' the rod?
28 concerning their reproach; e' say
22: 4 art come e' unto thy years:
18 they are e' the dross of silver.
23:34 Thou shalt e' drink it and suck it out,
24: 2 the name of the day, e' this same
4 pieces thereof into it, e' every good
9 will e' make the pile for fire great.
18 and at e' my wife died;
29:10 tower of Syene e' unto the border
30: 3 the day is near, e' the day of the Lord
32: 6 thou swimmest, e' to the mountains;
16 shall lament for her, e' for Egypt,
18 cast them down, e' her,
31 all his multitude, e' Pharaoh
32 are slain with the sword, e' Pharaoh
33:18 he shall e' die thereby.
34:11 Behold, I, e' I, will both search
20 Behold, I, e' I, will judge between the
23 shall feed them, e' my servant

Eze 34:30 and they, e' the house of Israel,
35: 6 e' blood shall pursue thee.
11 I will e' do according to thine
15 and all Idumea, e' all of it:
36: 2 Aha, e' the ancient high places
10 the house of Israel, e' all of it:
12 to walk upon you, e' my people
37:19 put them with him, e' with the stick
25 they shall dwell therein, e' they,
38: 4 of armour, e' a great company
39:17 sacrifice for you, e' a great sacrifice
40:14 e' unto the post of the court
41:17 the door, e' unto the inner house,
42:12 the head of the way, e' the way
43: 1 e' the gate that looketh toward the
3 I saw, e' according to the vision
8 have e' defiled my holy name
13 e' the bottom shall be a cubit,
14 upon the ground e' to the lower
14 settle e' to the greater settle
44: 6 rebellious, e' to the house of Israel,
7 to pollute it, e' my house,
10 they shall e' bear their iniquity.
19 into the utter court, e' into the utter
47:10 from En-gedi e' unto En-eglaim;
19 from Tamar e' to the waters of
48: 3, 6 from the east side e' unto the west
10 for them, e' for the priests,
28 the border shall be e' from Tamar
Da 1:21 Daniel continued e' unto the first
2:43 e' as iron is not mixed with clay.
4:15 roots in the earth, e' with a band
23 e' with a band of iron and brass,
5:14 I have e' heard of thee,
6:26 dominion shall be e' unto the end
7:11 I beheld e' till the beast was slain,
18 the kingdom for ever, e' for ever
20 before whom three fell; e' of that horn
8: 1 appeared unto me, e' unto me Daniel,
10 it waxed great, e' to the host of heaven;
11 magnified himself e' to the prince of
15 when I, e' I Daniel, had seen
9: 5 have rebelled, e' by departing
11 transgressed thy law, e' by departing
21 I was speaking in prayer, e' the man
25 the wall, e' in troublous times
27 e' until the consummation,
11: 1 Darius the Mede, e' I, stood to
4 shall be plucked up, e' for others
10 be stirred up, e' to his fortress,
11 fight with him, e' with the king
24 enter peaceably e' upon the fattest
24 the strong holds, e' for a time.
30 he shall e' return, and have
35 make them white, e' to the time
41 escape out of his hand, e' Edom,
12: 1 was a nation e' to that same time:
4 the book e' to the time of the end:
Ho 2:20 I will e' betroth thee unto me
5:14 I, e' I, will tear and go away;
9:16 will I slay e' the beloved fruit of
12: 5 E' the Lord God of hosts;
Joe 1: 2 in your days, or e' in the days
12 and the apple tree, e' all the trees
2: 2 after it, e' to the years of many
12 ye e' to me with all your heart,
14 e' a meat offering and a drink offering
Am 2:11 Is it not e' thus, O ye children
3:11 then shall be e' round about the land;
5: 1 up against you, e' a lamentation,
20 not light? e' very dark, and no
8: 4 e' to make the poor of the land to
12 from the north e' to the east,
14 e' they shall fall and never rise
Ob 7 brought thee e' to the border:
8 e' destroy the wise men out of
11 cast lots upon Jerusalem, e' thou
20 Canaanites, e' unto Zarephath;
Jon 2: 5 compassed me about, e' to the soul:
3: 5 greatest of them e' to the least
4: 9 do well to be angry, e' unto death.
Mic 1: 9 gate of my people, e' to Jerusalem.
2: 2 oppress a man in his house, e' a man
8 E' of late my people is risen
10 you e' with a sore destruction.
11 shall e' be the prophet of this people.
3: 4 he will e' hide his face from them
5 they e' prepare war against him.
4: 7 from henceforth, e' for ever.
8 it come, e' the first dominion;
10 thou shalt go e' to Babylon;
7:12 he shall come e' to thee
12 from the fortress e' to the river,
Na 2:11 where the lion, e' the old lion,
3:12 they shall e' fall into the mouth
Hab 1: 2 e' cry out unto thee of violence,
3: 9 oaths of the tribes, e' thy word.
13 e' for the salvation with thine
Zep 1:14 e' the voice of the day of the Lord:
18 shall make e' a speedy riddance
2: 5 I will e' destroy thee,
9 e' the breeding of nettles,
11 from his place, e' all the isles
3: 8 mine indignation, e' all my fierce
10 my suppliants, e' the daughter
15 the king of Israel, e' the Lord,
20 bring you again, e' in the time
Hag 2:18 the ninth month, e' from the day
Zec 3: 2 O Satan; e' the Lord that hath
6:10 of the captivity, e' of Heldai,
13 E' he shall build the temple
7: 1 the ninth month, e' in Chisleu;
5 and seventh month, e' those seventy
5 did ye at all fast unto me, e' to me?
8:23 e' shall take hold of the skirt of him
9: 7 he that remaineth, e' he, shall be

Zec 9:10 dominion shall be from sea e' to
10 and from the river e' to the ends
12 e' to day do I declare that I will
11: 7 flock of slaughter, e' you, O poor
10 I took my staff, e' Beauty,
14 asunder mine other staff, e' Bands,
12: 6 in her own place, e' in Jerusalem.
14:16 shall e' go up from year to year
17 the Lord of hosts, e' upon them
Mal 1:10 Who is there e' among you
11 rising of the sun e' unto the going
12 the fruit thereof, e' his meat,
2: 2 I will e' send a curse upon you,
3 your faces, e' the dung of your
3: 1 to his temple, e' the messenger
7 E' from the days of your fathers
9 ye have robbed me, e' this whole
15 that tempt God are e' delivered.
M't 5:46 do not e' the publicans the same?
47 do not e' publicans so?
48 perfect, e' as your Father
6:29 That e' Solomon in his glory was
7:12 do ye e' so to them: for this is
17 E' so every good tree bringeth
8:16 When the e' was come, they
27 that e' the winds and the sea
9:18 My daughter is e' now dead: but
11:26 E' so, Father: for so it seemed
12: 8 Son of man is Lord e' of the
45 E' so shall it be also unto this
13:12 taken away e' that he hath.
15:28 be it unto thee e' as thou wilt.
18:14 E' so it is not the will of your
33 on thy fellowservant, e' as I had
20: 8 So when e' was come, the lord of
14 unto this last, e' as unto thee.
28 E' as the Son of man came not
23: 8 one is your Master, e' Christ;
10 one is your Master, e' Christ.
28 E' so ye also outwardly appear
37 e' as a hen gathereth her
24:27 and shineth e' unto the west;
33 that it is near, e' at the doors.
25:29 taken away e' that which he hath.
26:20 Now when the e' was come, he sat
38 is exceedingly sorrowful, e' unto
27:57 e' was come, there came a rich
28:20 e' unto the end of the world.
M'r 1:27 commandeth he e' the unclean
32 at e', when the sun did set,
4:25 shall be taken e' that which he
35 when the e' was come, he saith
36 took him e' as he was in the ship.
41 of man is this, that e' the wind
6: 2 e' such mighty works are wrought
47 And when e' was come, the ship
10:45 For e' the son of man came not
11: 6 them e' as Jesus had commanded:
19 when e' was come, he went out
12:44 all that she had, e' all her living.
13:22 if it were possible, e' the elect.
29 know that it is nigh, e' at the doors.
35 at e', or at midnight, or at the
14:30 thee, That this day, e' in this night,
54 e' into the palace of the high priest:
15:42 And now when the e' was come,
Lu 1: 2 E' as they delivered them unto us,
15 Ghost, e' from his mother's womb.
2:15 Let us now go e' unto Bethlehem,
6:33 for sinners also do e' the same.
8:18 be taken e' that which he seemeth
25 he commandeth e' the winds and
9:54 consume them, e' as Elias did?
10:11 E' the very dust of your city,
17 saying, Lord, e' the devils are
21 e' so, Father; for so it seemed
12: 7 But e' the very hairs of your head
41 this parable unto us, or e' to all?
57 and why e' of yourselves judge
17:30 E' thus shall it be in the days
18:11 or e' as this publican.
19:26 him that hath not, e' that he hath
32 e' as he had said unto them.
37 when he was come nigh, e' now
42 If thou hadst known, e' thou,
44 shall lay thee e' with the ground,
20:37 are raised, e' Moses shewed at
24:24 found it e' as the woman had said:
Joh 1:12 to become the sons of God, e' to them
3:13 came down from heaven, e' the Son
14 e' so must the Son of man be lifted
5:21 e' so the Son quickeneth whom he
23 honour the Son, e' as they honour
45 that accuseth you, e' Moses,
6:16 And when e' was now come,
57 he that eateth me, e' he shall live
8: 9 beginning at the eldest, e' unto the
25 E' the same that I said unto you
41 we have one Father, e' God.
43 e' because ye can not hear my word.
10:15 e' so know I the Father: and I lay
11:22 But I know, that e' now,
37 have caused that e' this man
12:50 e' as the Father said unto me,
14:17 E' the Spirit of truth;
31 gave me commandment, e' so I do.
15:10 e' as I have kept my Father's
26 from the Father, e' the Spirit of truth,
17:14 e' as I am not of the world.
16 They are not of the world, e' as I
18 e' so have I also sent them
22 they may be one e' as we are one:
20:21 hath sent me, e' so send I you.
21:25 e' the world itself could not
Ac 2:39 are afar off, e' as many as
4:10 e' by him doth this man stand
Ac 5:37 and all, e' as many as obeyed him,
39 be found e' to fight against God.
9:17 the Lord, e' Jesus, hath appeared
10:41 chosen before of God, e' to us,
11: 5 by four corners; and it came e' to
12:15 constantly affirmed that it was e' so.
15: 8 Holy Ghost, e' as he did unto us.
11 we shall be saved, e' as they.
20:11 talked a long while, e' till break
22:17 e' while I prayed in the temple
26:11 I persecuted them e' unto strange
27:25 it shall be e' as it was told me.
Ro 1:13 fruit among you also, e' as among
20 e' his eternal power and Godhead:
26 for e' their women did change the
28 e' as they did not like to retain God
3:22 E' the righteousness of God
4: 6 E' as David also describeth the
17 whom he believed, e' God,
5: 7 peradventure some would e' dare to die.
14 from Adam to Moses, e' over them
18 e' so by the righteousness of one
21 e' so might grace reign through
6: 4 e' so we also should walk in
19 e' so now yield your members
7: 4 married to another, e' to him who
8:23 e' we ourselves groan within
34 who is e' at the right hand of God,
9:10 conceived by one, e' by our father
17 unto Pharaoh, E' for this same
24 E' us, whom he hath called,
30 e' the righteousness which is of
10: 8 word is nigh thee, e' in thy mouth
11: 5 E' so then at this present time
31 E' so have these also now not
15: 3 For e' Christ pleased not himself;
6 glorify God, e' the Father of our
1Co 1: 6 E' as the testimony of Christ was
2: 7 in a mystery, e' the hidden wisdom,
11 e' so the things of God knoweth no
3: 1 as unto carnal, e' as unto babes
5 e' as the Lord gave to every man?
4:11 E' unto this present hour we both
5: 7 For e' Christ our passover is
7: 7 I would that all men were e' as I
8 good for them if they abide e' as I.
9:14 E' so hath the Lord ordained
10:33 E' as I please all men in all things,
11: 1 e' as I also am of Christ.
5 that is e' all one as she were
12 e' so is the man also by the woman;
14 Doth not e' nature itself teach you,
12: 2 these dumb idols, e' as ye were
13:12 shall I know e' as also I am known
14: 7 And e' things without life giveth
12 E' so ye, forasmuch as ye are
15:22 e' so in Christ shall all be made
24 the kingdom of God, e' the Father,
16: 1 churches of Galatia e' so do ye.
2Co 1: 3 Blessed be God, e' the Father of
8 that we despaired e' of life:
13 shall acknowledge e' to the end;
14 e' as ye also are ours in the day
19 preached among you by us, e' by me
3:10 For e' that which was made
15 But e' unto this day, when Moses
18 from glory to glory, e' as by the Spirit
7:14 e' so our boasting, which I made
10: 7 is Christ's, e' so are we Christ's.
13 a measure to reach e' unto you.
11:12 they may be found e' as we.
13: 9 this also we wish e' your perfection.
Ga 2:16 e' we have believed in Jesus
3: 6 E' as Abraham believed God, and
4: 3 E' so we, when we were children,
14 as an angel of God, e' as Christ Jesus.
29 after the Spirit, e' so it is now.
5:12 I would they were e' cut off
14 law is fulfilled in one word, e' in this:
Eph 2: 3 children of wrath, e' as others.
5 E' when we were dead in sins,
15 in his flesh the enmity, e' the law of
4: 4 one Spirit, e' as ye are called
15 which is the head, e' Christ:
32 forgiving one another, e' as God
5:12 it is a shame e' to speak of those
23 the wife, e' as Christ is the head
25 love your wives, e' as Christ also
29 cherisheth it, e' as the Lord the
33 so love his wife e' as himself.
Ph'p 1: 7 E' as it is meet for me to think this
15 preach Christ e' of envy
2: 8 obedient unto death, e' the death
3:15 God shall reveal e' this unto you.
18 now tell you e' weeping,
21 he is able e' to subdue all things
4:16 For e' Thessalonica ye sent once
Col 1:14 e' the forgiveness of sins:
26 E' the mystery which hath
3:13 e' as Christ forgave you, so also do
1Th 1:10 whom he raised from the dead, e' Jesus,
2: 2 But e' after that we had suffered
4 e' so we speak; not as pleasing
7 gentle among you: e' as a nurse
14 e' as they have of the Jews:
18 e' I Paul, once and again; but
19 Are not e' ye in the presence
3: 4 suffer tribulation; e' as it came to
12 toward all men, e' as we do toward
13 holiness before God, e' our Father,
4: 3 will of God, e' your sanctification
5 concupiscence, e' as the Gentiles
13 that ye sorrow not, e' as others
14 e' so them also which sleep in
5:11 e' as also ye do.
2Th 2: 9 E' him, whose coming is after
2Th 2:16 and God, e' our Father,
3: 1 be glorified, e' as it is with you:
10 For e' when we were with you,
1Ti 3:11 E' so must their wives be grave,
6: 3 wholesome words, e' the words
2Ti 2: 9 as an evil doer, e' unto bonds;
Tit 1:12 One of themselves, e' a prophet
15 e' their mind and conscience is
Ph'm 19 thou owest unto me e' thine own
Heb 1: 9 God, e' thy God, hath anointed
4:12 e' to the dividing asunder of soul
5:14 of full age, e' those who by reason
6:20 for us entered, e' Jesus made
7: 4 whom e' the patriarch Abraham
11:12 sprang there e' of one,
19 to raise him up, e' from the dead;
Jas 2:17 E' so faith, if it hath not works,
3: 5 E' so the tongue is a little member
9 bless we God, e' the Father;
4: 1 come they not hence, e' of your lusts
14 It is e' a vapour, that appeareth
1Pe 1: 9 end of your faith, e' the salvation
2: 8 rock of offence, e' to them which
21 e' hereunto were ye called:
3: 4 not corruptible, e' the ornament
6 E' as Sara obeyed Abraham,
21 whereunto e' baptism doth also
4:10 received the gift, e' so minister
2Pe 1:14 e' as our Lord Jesus Christ
2: 1 among the people, e' as there shall
1 damnable heresies, e' denying the
3:15 e' as our beloved brother Paul also
1Jo 2: 6 so to walk, e' as he walked.
9 is in darkness e' until now.
18 antichrist shall come, e' now are
25 he hath promised us, e' eternal life.
27 e' as it hath taught you, ye shall
3: 3 purifieth himself, e' as he is pure.
7 is righteous, e' as he is righteous.
4: 3 it should come; and e' now
5: 4 overcometh the world, e' our faith.
6 by water and blood, e' Jesus Christ;
3Jo 2 health, e' as thy soul prospereth.
3 e' as thou walkest in the truth.
Jude 7 E' as Sodom and Gomorrha, and
23 hating e' the garment spotted
Re 1: 7 because of him. E' so, Amen.
2:13 thou dwellest, e' where Satan's
13 denied my faith, e' in those days
27 e' as I received of my father.
3: 4 hast a few names e' in Sardis
21 e' as I also overcame, and am set
6:13 fell unto the earth, e' as a fig tree
14:20 e' unto the horse bridles,
16: 7 E' so, Lord God Almighty, true
17:11 e' he is the eighth,
18: 6 Reward her e' as she rewarded you,
21:11 e' like a jasper stone, clear as
22:20 E' so, come, Lord Jesus.

evening See also EVEN; EVENINGS; EVENTIDE.
Ge 1: 5 e' and the morning were the first
8 e' and the morning were the second
13 e' and the morning were the third
19 e' and the morning were the fourth
23 e' and the morning were the fifth
31 e' and the morning were the sixth
8:11 the dove came in to him in the e';
24:11 at the time of the e', even the time
29:23 it came to pass in the e',
30:16 Jacob came out of the field in the e',
Ex 12: 6 Israel shall kill it in the e'.
16: 8 shall give you in the e' flesh to eat,
18:13 Moses from the morning unto the e'.
27:21 shall order it from e' to morning
Le 24: 3 e' unto the morning before the Lord
De 23:11 when e' cometh on, he shall wash
Jos 10:26 hanging upon the trees until the e'.
J'g 19: 9 now the day draweth toward e',
1Sa 14:24 man that eateth any food until e',
17:16 drew near morning and e',
30:17 unto the e' of the next day:
1Ki 17: 6 and bread and flesh in the e';
18:29, 36 the offering of the e' sacrifice,
2Ki 16:15 e' meat offering, and the king's
1Ch 16:40 continually morning and e',
2Ch 2: 4 burnt offerings morning and e',
13:11 Lord every morning and every e'
11 the lamps thereof, to burn every e':
31: 3 the morning and e' burnt offerings,
Ezr 3: 3 burnt offerings morning and e'.
9: 4 I sat astonied until the e' sacrifice.
5 at the e' sacrifice I arose up from
Es 2:14 e' she went, and on the morrow
Job 4:20 are destroyed from morning to e':
Ps 55:17 E', and morning, and at noon,
59: 6 They return at e': they make a
14 at e' let them return; and let them
65: 8 the morning and e' to rejoice.
90: 6 the e' it is cut down, and withereth.
104:23 forth unto his work...until the e'.
141: 2 up of my hands as the e' sacrifice.
Pr 7: 9 in the e', in the black and dark
Ec 11: 6 in the e' withhold not thine hand:
Jer 6: 4 shadows of the e' are stretched out.
Eze 33:22 of the Lord was upon me in the e',
46: 2 gate shall not be shut until the e'.
Da 8:26 vision of the e' and the morning
9:21 about the time of the e' oblation.
Hab 1: 8 are more fierce than the e' wolves:
Zep 2: 7 shall they lie down in the e':
3: 3 judges are e' wolves; they gnaw
Zec 14: 7 at e' time it shall be light.
M't 14:15 when it was e', his disciples came
23 e' was come, he was there alone.
16: 2 When it is e', ye say, it will be fair
M'r 14:17 in the e' he cometh with the twelve,

Lu 24:29 toward e·, and the day is far spent.
Joh 20:19 same day at e·, being the first
Ac 28:23 the prophets, from morning till e·.

evenings
Jer 5: 6 a wolf of the e· shall spoil them,

eveningtide See also EVENTIDE.
2Sa 11: 2 it came to pass in an e·,
Isa 17:14 And behold at e· trouble;

event
Ec 2:14 one e· happeneth to them all.
9: 2 one e· to the righteous, and to the
3 that there is one e· unto all:

eventide See also EVENINGTIDE.
Ge 24:63 Isaac went out...at the e·:
Jos 7: 6 the ark of the Lord until the e·,
8:29 he hanged on a tree until e·:
M'r 11:11 and now the e· was come,
Ac 4: 3 the next day: for it was now e·.

ever See also EVERLASTING; EVERMORE; NEVER; SOEVER.
Ge 3:22 life, and eat, and live for e·:
13:15 I give it, and to thy seed for e·.
43: 9 let me bear the blame for e·:
44:32 the blame to my father for e·.
Ex 3:15 this is my name for e·, and
12:14 a feast by an ordinance for e·.
17 by an ordinance for e·.
24 to thee and to thy sons for e·.
14:13 them again no more for e·.
15:18 Lord shall reign for e· and e·
19: 9 thee, and believe thee for e·.
21: 6 and he shall serve him for e·.
27:21 it shall be a statute for e· unto
28:43 it shall be a statute for e· unto him
29:28 for e· from the children of Israel;
30:21 it shall be a statute for e· to them,
31:17 the children of Israel for e·.
32:13 and they shall inherit it for e·.
Le 6:13 e· be burning upon the altar;
18 statute for e· in your generations
22 a statute for e· unto the Lord;
7:34 for e· from among the children
36 for e· throughout their generations.
10: 9 for e· throughout your generations:
15 a statute for e·; as the Lord hath
16:29 shall be a statute for e· unto you:
31 afflict your souls, by a statute for e·.
17: 7 shall be a statute for e· unto them
23:14 for e· throughout your generations
21 statute for e· in all your dwellings
31 for e· throughout your generations
41 statute for e· in your generations:
24: 3 statute for e· in your generations.
25:23 The land shall not be sold for e·:
30 shall be established for e· to him
46 shall be your bondmen for e·:
Nu 10: 8 for e· throughout your generations.
15:15 for e· in your generations:
18: 8 to thy sons, by an ordinance for e·.
11, 19 with thee, by a statute for e·:
19 of salt for e· before the Lord
23 for e· throughout your generations,
19:10 among them, for a statute for e·.
22:30 which thou hast ridden e· since
30 was I e· wont to do so unto thee?
24:20 end shall be that he perish for e·.
24 and he also shall perish for e·.
De 4:33 Did e· people hear the voice of God
40 thy God giveth thee, for e·.
5:29 and with their children for e·!
12:28 with thy children after thee for e·,
13:16 it shall be a heap for e·;
15:17 and he shall be thy servant for e·.
18: 5 Lord, him and his sons for e·.
19: 9 and to walk e· in his ways;
23: 3 congregation of the Lord for e·:
6 prosperity all thy days for e·.
28:46 wonder, and upon thy seed for e·.
29:29 unto us and to our children for e·,
32:40 and say, I live for e·.
Jos 4: 7 unto the children of Israel for e·.
24 fear the Lord your God for e·.
8:28 Ai, and made it an heap for e·.
14: 9 and thy children's for e·,
J'g 11:25 did he e· strive against Israel,
25 or did he e· fight against them,
1Sa 1:22 the Lord, and there abide for e·.
2:30 should walk before me for e·:
32 old man in thine house for e·.
35 before mine anointed for e·.
3:13 I will judge his house for e·
14 with sacrifice nor offering for e·.
13:13 thy kingdom upon Israel for e·.
20:15 thy kindness from my house for e·:
23 Lord between thee and me for e·.
42 my seed and thy seed for e·.
27:12 he shall be my servant for e·.
28: 2 keeper of mine head for e·.
2Sa 2:26 Shall the sword devour for e·?
3:28 guiltless before the Lord for e·
7:13 the throne of his kingdom for e·.
16 established for e· before thee:
16 throne shall be established for e·.
24 to be a people unto thee for e·:
25 his house, establish it for e·,
26 let thy name be magnified for e·,
29 continue for e· before thee:
29 thy servant be blessed for e·.
1Ki 1:31 lord king David live for e·.
2:33 the head of his seed for e·:
33 be peace for e· from the Lord.
45 established before the Lord for e·.
5: 1 Hiram was e· a lover of David.
8:13 place for thee to abide in for e·.

1Ki 9: 3 to put my name there for e·;
5 kingdom upon Israel for e·,
10: 9 the Lord loved Israel for e·,
11:39 seed of David, but not for e·.
12: 7 they will be thy servants for e·.
2Ki 5:27 thee, and unto thy seed for e·.
21: 7 will I put my name for e·:
1Ch 15: 2 and to minister unto him for e·.
16:34 for his mercy endureth for e·.
36 the Lord God of Israel for e·
36 Lord God of Israel...and e·,
41 for his mercy endureth for e·;
17:12 I will stablish his throne for e·.
14 house and in my kingdom for e·:
22 thou make thine own people for e·;
23 his house be established for e·,
24 thy name may be magnified for e·,
27 it may be before thee for e·:
27 and it shall be blessed for e·.
22:10 of his kingdom over Israel for e·.
23:13 he and his sons for e·, to burn
13 to bless in his name for e·.
25 dwell in Jerusalem for e·:
28: 4 to be king over Israel for e·:
7 establish his kingdom for e·,
8 for your children after you for e·.
9 he will cast thee off for e·.
29:10 Lord God of Israel our father, for e·.
10 of Israel our father,...and e·.
18 for e· in the imagination of
2Ch 2: 4 an ordinance for e· to Israel.
5:13 for his mercy endureth for e·:
6: 2 a place for thy dwelling for e·.
7: 3 for his mercy endureth for e·.
6 because his mercy endureth for e·,
16 that my name may be there for e·:
9: 8 to establish them for e·,
10: 7 will be thy servants for e·.
13: 5 over Israel to David for e·,
20: 7 of Abraham thy friend for e·?
21 for his mercy endureth for e·.
21: 7 to him and to his sons for e·.
30: 8 he hath sanctified for e·:
33: 4 shall my name be for e·.
7 will I put my name for e·:
Ezr 3:11 for his mercy endureth for e·
9:12 their peace or their wealth for e·:
12 inheritance to your children for e·.
Ne 2: 3 king, Let the king live for e·:
9: 5 the Lord your God for e· and e·:
13: 1 the congregation of God for e·;
Job 4: 7 who e· perished, being innocent? or
20 they perish for e· without any
14:20 Thou prevailest for e· against him,
19:24 pen and lead in the rock for e·!
20: 7 he shall perish for e· like his own
23: 7 so should I be delivered for e· from
36: 7 yea, he doth establish them for e·,
41: 4 take him for a servant for e·?
Ps 5:11 let them e· shout for joy, because
9: 5 thou hast put out their name for e·.
5 hast put out their name...and e·.
7 the Lord shall endure for e·:
18 of the poor shall not perish for e·.
10:16 The Lord is King for e·
16 The Lord is King...and e·.
12: 7 from this generation for e·,
13: 1 thou forget me, O Lord? for e·?
19: 9 the Lord is clean, enduring for e·:
21: 4 even length of days for e·
4 even length of days...and e·.
6 made him most blessed for e·:
22:26 him: your heart shall live for e·.
23: 6 the house of the Lord for e·.
25: 6 for they have been e· of old.
15 Mine eyes are e· toward the Lord;
28: 9 them also, and lift them up for e·.
29:10 the Lord sitteth King for e·.
30:12 give thanks unto thee for e·.
33:11 counsel of the Lord standeth for e·,
37:18 and their inheritance shall be for e·.
26 is e· merciful, and lendeth;
28 they are preserved for e·:
29 the land, and dwell therein for e·.
41:12 settest me before thy face for e·.
44: 8 and praise thy name for e·.
23 Lord? arise, cast us not off for e·.
45: 2 God hath blessed thee for e·.
6 Thy throne, O God, is for e·
6 Thy throne, O God, is...and e·:
17 shall the people praise thee for e·
17 the people praise thee...and e·.
48: 8 God will establish it for e·.
14 God is our God for e· and e·:
49: 8 precious, and it ceaseth for e·:)
9 That he should still live for e·
11 their houses shall continue for e·,
51: 3 and my sin is e· before me.
52: 5 shall likewise destroy thee for e·,
8 trust in the mercy of God for e·
8 trust in the mercy of God...and e.·
9 will praise thee for e·, because
61: 4 will abide in thy tabernacle for e·:
7 He shall abide before God for e·:
8 I sing praise unto thy name for e·,
66: 7 He ruleth by his power for e·;
68:16 the Lord will dwell in it for e·.
72:17 name shall endure for e·:
19 be his glorious name for e·:
73:26 heart, and my portion for e·.
74: 1 why hast thou cast us off for e·?
10 enemy blaspheme thy name for e·?
19 the congregation of thy poor for e·.
75: 9 I will declare for e·; I will
77: 7 Will the Lord cast off for e·?
8 Is his mercy clean gone for e·?

Ps 78:69 he hath established for e·.
79: 5 Lord? wilt thou be angry for e·?
13 will give thee thanks for e·:
81:15 should have endured for e·.
83:17 be confounded and troubled for e·;
85: 5 thou be angry with us for e·?
89: 1 of the mercies of the Lord for e·:
2 Mercy shall be built up for e·:
4 Thy seed will I establish for e·,
29 also will I make to endure for e·,
36 His seed shall endure for e·,
37 It shall be established for e· as
46 Lord? wilt thou hide thyself for e·?
90: 2 or e· thou hadst formed the earth
92: 7 that they shall be destroyed for e·:
93: 5 thine house, O Lord, for e·.
102:12 thou O Lord, shalt endure for e·;
103: 9 neither will he keep his anger for e·.
104: 5 should not be removed for e·.
31 glory of the Lord...endure for e·:
105: 8 remembered his covenant for e·,
106: 1 for his mercy endureth for e·.
107: 1 for his mercy endureth for e·.
110: 4 Thou art a priest for e· after the
111: 3 his righteousness endureth for e·.
5 will e· be mindful of his covenant.
8 They stand fast for e·
8 They stand fast...and e·,
9 remembered his covenant for e·:
10 his praise endureth for e·.
112: 3 his righteousness endureth for e·.
6 he shall not be moved for e·:
9 his righteousness endureth for e·;
117: 2 truth of the Lord endureth for e·.
118: 1 because his mercy endureth for e·.
2, 3, 4 that his mercy endureth for e·.
29 for his mercy endureth for e·.
119:44 I keep thy law continually for e·
44 I keep thy law continually...and e·.
89 For e·, O Lord, thy word is settled
98 enemies: for they are e· with me.
111 have I taken as a heritage for e·:
152 thou hast founded them for e·.
160 judgments endureth for e·.
125: 1 be removed, but abideth for e·.
2 people from henceforth even for e·.
131: 3 Lord from henceforth and for e·.
132:14 This is my rest for e·: here will I
135:13 Thy name, O Lord, endureth for e·;
136: 1, 2, 3, 4, 5, 6 his mercy endureth for e·.
7, 8, 10, 11 his mercy endureth for e·
9, 12, 15, 16 his mercy endureth for e·.
13, 14, 17, 18, 19, 20, 21, 23 for his mercy endureth for e.:
22, 24, 25, 26 his mercy endureth for e·.
138: 8 thy mercy, O Lord, endureth for e·:
145: 1 and I will bless thy name for e·
1 and I will bless thy name...and e·.
2 and I will praise thy name for e·
2 and I will praise thy name...and e·.
21 all flesh bless his holy name for e·
21 flesh bless his holy name...and e·.
146: 6 which keepeth truth for e·:
10 The Lord shall reign for e·,
148: 6 hath also stablished them for e·
6 hath also stablished them...and e·.
Pr 8:23 the beginning, or e· the earth
12:19 truth shall be established for e·:
27:24 for riches are not for e·:
29:14 throne shall be established for e·.
Ec 1: 4 but the earth abideth for e·.
2:16 more than of the fool for e·;
3:14 God doeth, it shall be for e·:
9: 6 they any more a portion for e·
12: 6 Or e· the silver cord be loosed,
Ca 6:12 Or e· I was aware, my soul made
Isa 9: 7 from henceforth even for e·.
26: 4 Trust ye in the Lord for e·:
28:28 because he will not e· be threshing
30: 8 may be for the time to come for e·
8 be for the time to come... and e·:
32:14 and towers shall be for dens for e·,
17 quietness and assurance for e·.
33:20 thereof shall e· be removed,
34:10 smoke thereof shall go up for e·:
10 none shall pass through it for e·
17 they shall possess it for e·, from
40: 8 word of our God shall stand for e·
47: 7 saidst, I shall be a lady for e·:
51: 6 but my salvation shall be for e·,
8 but my righteousness shall be for e·,
57:16 For I will not contend for e·,
59:21 Lord, from henceforth and for e·.
60:21 they shall inherit the land for e·,
64: 9 neither remember iniquity for e·:
65:18 But be ye glad and rejoice for e·
Jer 3: 5 Will he reserve his anger for e·?
12 and I will not keep anger for e·.
7: 7 gave to your fathers, for e· and e·
17: 4 anger, which shall burn for e·.
25 and this city shall remain for e·.
25: 5 and to your fathers for e· and e·:
31:36 a nation before me for e·.
40 nor thrown down any more for e·.
32:39 that they may fear me for e·,
33:11 for his mercy endureth for e·:
35: 6 neither ye, nor your sons for e·:
19 man to stand before me for e·.
49:33 dragons, and a desolation for e·:
50:39 shall be no more inhabited for e·;
51:26 but thou shalt be desolate for e·,
62 but that it shall be desolate for e·.
La 3:31 For the Lord will not cast off for e·:
5:19 Thou O Lord, remainest for e·;
20 dost thou forget us for e·,
Eze 37:25 and their children's children for e·:

Eze 37:25 David shall be their prince for e'.
43: 7 midst of the children of Israel for e',
9 will dwell in the midst of them for e'.
Da 2: 4 O king, live for e': tell thy servants
20 Blessed be...of God for e' and e':
44 kingdoms, and it shall stand for e'.
3: 9 Nebuchadnezzar, O king, live for e'.
4:34 and honoured him that liveth for e',
5:10 O king, live for e': let not thy
6: 6 unto him, King Darius, live for e'.
21 unto the king, O king, live for e'.
24 all their bones in pieces or e' they
26 the living God, and stedfast for e',
7:18 kingdom for e', even for e' and e'.
12: 3 righteousness as the stars for e'
3 righteousness as the stars...and e'.
7 and sware by him that liveth for e',
Ho 2:19 I will betroth thee unto me for e';
Joe 2: 2 there hath not been e' the like,
3:20 But Judah shall dwell for e',
Am 1:11 and he kept his wrath for e':
Ob 10 thou shalt be cut off for e'.
Jon 2: 6 with her bars was about me for e':
Mic 2: 9 have ye taken away my glory for e'.
4: 5 name of the Lord our God for e'
5 name of the Lord our God...and e'.
7 Zion from henceforth, even for e'.
7:18 he retaineth not his anger for e',
Zec 1: 5 prophets, do they live for e'?
Mal 1: 4 the Lord hath indignation for e'.
M't 6:13 power, and the glory, for e'.
21:19 on thee henceforward for e'.
24:21 world to this time, no, nor e' shall
M'r 11:14 fruit of thee hereafter for e'.
15: 8 as he had e' done unto them.
Lu 1:33 over the house of Jacob for e';
55 Abraham, and to his seed for e'.
15:31 Son, thou art e' with me, and all
Joh 4:29 told me all things that e' I did:
39 testified, He told me all that e' I did.
6:51 this bread, he shall live for e':
58 of this bread shall live for e'.
8:35 abideth not in the house for e':
35 but the Son abideth for e'.
10: 8 All that e' came before me are
12:34 law that Christ abideth for e':
14:16 he may abide with you for e';
18:20 I e' taught in the synagogue, and
Ac 23:15 and we, or e' he come near, are
Ro 1:25 Creator, who is blessed for e'.
9: 5 is over all, God blessed for e'.
11:36 To whom be glory for e'. Amen.
16:27 through Jesus Christ for e'.
2Co 9: 9 his righteousness remaineth for e'.
Ga 1: 5 To whom be glory for e' and e'.
Eph 5:29 For no man e' yet hated his own
Ph'p 4:20 Father be glory for e' and e'.
1Th 4:17 and so shall we e' be with the
5:15 but e' follow that which is good,
1Ti 1:17 honour and glory for e' and e'.
2Ti 3: 7 E' learning, and never able to
4:18 to whom be glory for e' and e'.
Ph'm 15 thou shouldest receive him for e';
Heb 1: 8 thy throne, O God, is for e' and e':
5: 6 Thou art a priest for e' after the
6:20 made an high priest for e' after the
7:17, 21 Thou art a priest for e' after the
24 this man, because he continueth e',
25 he e' liveth to make intercession
10:12 for e' sat down on the right
14 he hath perfected for e' them
13: 8 yesterday, and to day, and for e'.
21 whom be glory for e' and e'.
1Pe 1:23 which liveth and abideth for e'.
25 the word of the Lord endureth for e'.
4:11 praise and dominion for e' and e'.
5:11 glory and dominion for e' and e'.
2Pe 2:17 of darkness is reserved for e'.
3:18 be glory both now and for e'.
1Jo 2:17 doeth the will of God abideth for e'.
2Jo 2 and shall be with us for e'.
Jude 13 the blackness of darkness for e'.
25 and power, both now and for e'.
Re 1: 6 be glory and dominion for e' and e'.
4: 9 throne, who liveth for e' and e',
10 worship him that liveth for e' and e',
5:13 and unto the Lamb for e' and e'.
14 him that liveth for e' and e'.
7:12 be unto our God for e' and e'.
10: 6 by him that liveth for e' and e',
11:15 and he shall reign for e' and e'.
14:11 torment ascendeth up for e' and e':
15: 7 God, who liveth for e' and e'.
19: 3 her smoke rose up for e' and e'.
20:10 tormented day and night for e' and e'.
22: 5 and they shall reign for e' and e'.

everlasting
Ge 9:16 I may remember the e' covenant
17: 7 an e' covenant, to be a God unto
8 for an e' possession; and I will be
13 be in your flesh for an e' covenant.
19 with him for an e' covenant,
21:33 name of the Lord, the e' God.
48: 4 after thee for an e' possession.
49:26 the utmost bound of the e' hills:
Ex 40:15 an e' priesthood throughout their
Le 16:34 this shall be an e' statute unto you,
24: 8 of Israel by an e' covenant.
Nu 25:13 the covenant of an e' priesthood;
De 33:27 and underneath are the e' arms:
2Sa 23: 5 hath made with me an e' covenant,
1Ch 16:17 and to Israel for an e' covenant,
Ps 24: 7 be ye lift up, ye e' doors;
9 even lift them up, ye e' doors;
41:13 Lord God of Israel from e', and to e'.
90: 2 even from e' to e', thou art God.
93: 2 established of old; thou art from e'.
100: 5 the Lord is good; his mercy is e';
103:17 mercy of the Lord is from e' to e'
105:10 and to Israel for an e' covenant:
106:48 the Lord God of Israel from e' to e':
112: 6 shall be in e' remembrance.
119:142 Thy righteousness is an e'
144 of thy testimonies is e':
139:24 and lead me in the way e'.
145:13 Thy kingdom is an e' kingdom,
Pr 8:23 I was set up from e', from the
10:25 the righteous is an e' foundation.
Isa 9: 6 The e' Father, The Prince of Peace.
24: 5 ordinance, broken the e' covenant.
26: 4 in the Lord Jehovah is e' strength:
33:14 us shall dwell with e' burnings?
35:10 and e' joy upon their heads:
40:28 not heard, that the e' God, the Lord,
45:17 in the Lord with an e' salvation:
51:11 e' joy shall be upon their head:
54: 8 with e' kindness will I have mercy
55: 3 I will make an e' covenant with you,
13 an e' sign that shall not be cut off.
56: 5 I will give them an e' name,
60:19 Lord shall be unto thee an e' light,
20 the Lord shall be thine e' light,
61: 7 e' joy shall be unto them.
8 I will make an e' covenant with
63:12 to make himself an e' name?
16 redeemer; thy name is from e'.
Jer 10:10 the living God, and an e' king:
20:11 their e' confusion shall never be
23:40 I will bring an e' reproach upon
31: 3 I have loved thee with an e' love:
32:40 I will make an e' covenant with
Eze 16:60 establish unto thee an e' covenant.
37:26 shall be an e' covenant with them:
Da 4: 3 his kingdom is an e' kingdom,
34 whose dominion is an e' dominion,
7:14 his dominion is an e' dominion,
27 whose kingdom is an e' kingdom,
9:24 and to bring in e' righteousness,
12: 2 some to e' life, and some to shame
2 to shame and e' contempt.
Mic 5: 2 forth have been from of old, from e'.
Hab 1:12 Art thou not from e', O Lord
3: 6 the e' mountains were scattered,
6 hills did bow: his ways are e'.
M't 18: 8 or two feet to be cast into e' fire.
19:29 and shall inherit e' life.
25:41 from me, ye cursed, into e' fire,
46 shall go away into e' punishment:
Lu 16: 9 receive you into e' habitations.
18:30 and in the world to come life e'.
Joh 3:16 should not perish, but have e' life.
36 believeth on the Son hath e' life;
4:14 of water springing up into e' life.
5:24 on him that sent me, hath e' life,
6:27 meat which endureth unto e' life,
40 on him, may have e' life:
47 believeth on me hath e' life.
12:50 that his commandment is life e':
Ac 13:46 yourselves unworthy of e' life, lo,
Ro 6:22 unto holiness, and the end e' life.
16:26 the commandment of the e' God,
Ga 6: 8 shall of the spirit reap life e'.
2Th 1: 9 be punished with e' destruction
2:16 and hath given us e' consolation
1Ti 1:16 believe on him to life e'.
6:16 to whom be honour and power e'.
Heb 13:20 the blood of the e' covenant,
2Pe 1:11 to the e' kingdom of our Lord and
Jude 6 he hath reserved in e' chains
Re 14: 6 having the e' gospel to preach

evermore
De 28:29 oppressed and spoiled e',
2Sa 22:51 unto David, and to his seed for e'.
2Ki 17:37 ye shall observe to do for e';
1Ch 17:14 throne shall be established for e'.
Ps 16:11 hand there are pleasures for e'.
18:50 David, and to his seed for e'.
37:27 and do good; and dwell for e'.
77: 8 doth his promise fail for e'?
86:12 I will glorify thy name for e'.
89:28 My mercy will I keep for him for e',
52 Blessed be the Lord for e'. Amen.
92: 8 thou, Lord, art most high for e'.
105: 4 and his strength: seek his face e'.
106:31 unto all generations for e'.
113: 2 from this time forth and for e'.
115:18 from this time forth and for e'.
121: 8 from this time forth, and even for e'
132:12 shall also sit upon thy throne for e'.
133: 3 the blessing, even life for e'.
Eze 37:26 in the midst of them for e'.
28 shall be in the midst of them for e'.
Joh 6:34 Lord, e' give us this bread.
2Co 11:31 Christ, which is blessed for e',
1Th 5:16 Rejoice e'.
Heb 7:28 Son, who is consecrated for e'.
Re 1:18 I am alive for e',

every^
Ge 1:21 and e' living creature that
21 and e' winged fowl after his kind:
25 e' thing that creepeth upon the
26 over e' creeping thing that creepeth
28 e' living thing that moveth upon
29 given you e' herb bearing seed,
29 and e' tree, in the which is the
30 e' beast of the earth, and to e' fowl
30 and to e' thing that creepeth
30 I have given e' green herb for meat:
31 God saw e' thing that he had made,
2: 5 And e' plant of the field before
5 and e' herb of the field before
9 to grow e' tree that is pleasant
16 e' tree of the garden thou mayest
19 God formed e' beast of the field,
19 and e' fowl of the air;
20 and to e' beast of the field;
3: 1 not eat of e' tree of the garden?
14 cattle, and above e' beast of the field;
24 flaming sword which turned e' way,
4:14 e' one that findeth me shall slay
22 instructor of e' artificer in brass
6: 5 e' imagination of the thoughts
17 e' thing that is in the earth shall
19 And of e' living thing of all flesh,
19 two of e' sort shalt thou bring
20 of e' creeping thing of the earth
20 two of e' sort shall come unto thee,
7: 2 Of e' clean beast thou shalt take
4 e' living substance that I have
8 and of e' thing that creepeth
14 They, and e' beast after his kind,
14 and e' creeping thing that creepeth
14 and e' fowl after his kind
14 e' bird of e' sort.
21 and of e' creeping thing that
21 upon the earth, and e' man.
23 And e' living substance was
8: 1 Noah, and e' living thing, and all
17 Bring forth with thee e' living thing
17 and of e' creeping thing that
19 E' beast, e' creeping thing, and e'
20 and took of e' clean beast,
20 and of e' clean fowl,
21 smite any more e' thing living,
9: 2 upon e' beast of the earth,
3 E' moving thing that liveth
5 at the hand of e' man's brother
10 And with e' living creature that
10 and of e' beast of the earth
12 e' living creature that is with you,
15 e' living creature of all flesh;
16 e' living creature of all flesh that
10: 5 e' one after his tongue, after their
13:10 it was well watered e' where,
16:12 his hand will be against e' man,
12 and e' man's hand against him;
17:10 E' man child among you shall be
12 e' man child in your generations,
23 e' male among the men of
20:13 at e' place whither we shall come,
27:29 cursed be e' one that curseth thee,
30:33 e' one that is not speckled and
35 e' one that had some white in it,
32:16 e' drove by themselves;
34:15 e' male of you be circumcised;
22 e' male among us be circumcised,
23 and e' beast of theirs be ours?
24 e' male was circumcised,
41:48 which was round about e' city,
42:25 e' man's money into his sack,
35 e' man's bundle of money was
43:21 behold, e' man's money was in
44: 1 and put e' man's money in his
11 took down e' man his sack
11 opened e' man his sack.
13 laded e' man his ass,
45: 1 Cause e' man to go out from me.
46:34 for e' shepherd is an abomination
47:20 Egyptians sold e' man his field,
49:28 e' one according to his blessing
Ex 1: 1 e' man and his household came
22 E' son that is born ye shall cast
22 e' daughter ye shall save alive.
3:22 But e' woman shall borrow of her
7:12 they cast down e' man his rod,
9:19 upon e' man and beast which
22 and upon e' herb of the field,
25 hail smote e' herb of the field,
25 break e' tree of the field.
10: 5 shall eat e' tree which groweth
12 eat e' herb of the land,
15 did eat e' herb of the land,
11: 2 let e' man borrow of his neighbour,
2 e' woman of her neighbour,
12: 3 shall take to them e' man a lamb,
4 e' man according to his eating
16 save that which e' man must eat,
13:12 e' firstling that cometh of a
13 And e' firstling of an ass
14: 7 captains over e' one of them.
16: 4 gather a certain rate e' day,
16 Gather of it e' man according to
16 an omer for e' man, according to
16 take ye e' man for them which are
18 gathered e' man according to his
21 And they gathered it e' morning,
21 morning, e' man according to his
29 e' man in his place, let no man go
18:22 e' great matter they shall bring
22 e' small matter they shall judge:
26 e' small matter they judged
25: 2 of e' man that giveth it willingly
26: 2 e' one of the curtains shall have
28:21 e' one with his name shall they be
29:36 And thou shalt offer e' day
30: 7 thereon sweet incense e' morning:
12 give e' man a ransom for his soul
13 e' one that passeth among them
14 E' one that passeth among them
31:14 e' one that defileth it shall surely
32:27 Put e' man his sword by his side,
27 slay e' man his brother,
27 and e' man his companion,
27 and e' man his neighbour.
29 e' man upon his son, and upon his
33: 7 e' one which sought the Lord
8 e' man at his tent door, and looked

Ex 33:10 worshipped, e' man in his tent door.
34:19 e' firstling among thy cattle,
35:10 And e' wise hearted among you
21 they came, e' one whose heart
21 e' one whom his spirit made
22 and e' man that offered offered
23 And e' man, with whom was
24 E' one that did offer an offering
24 e' man, with whom was found
29 unto the Lord, e' man and woman,
36: 1 and e' wise hearted man, in whom
2 and e' wise hearted man, in whose
2 e' one whose heart stirred him
3 free offerings e' morning.
4 came e' man from his work
8 And e' wise hearted man among
30 silver, under e' board two sockets.
38:26 for e' man, that is, half a shekel,
26 e' one that went to be numbered.
39:14 e' one with his name, according to
Le 2:13 And e' oblation of thy meat
6:12 burn wood on it e' morning,
18 e' one that toucheth them shall
23 For e' meat offering for the priest
7: 6 E' male among the priests shall
10 And e' meat offering, mingled
11:21 ye eat of e' flying creeping thing
26 The carcases of e' beast which
26 e' one that toucheth them shall be
33 And e' earthen vessel, whereinto
34 may be drunk in e' such vessel
35 And e' thing whereupon any part
41 e' creeping thing that creepeth
46 of e' living creature that moveth
46 and of e' creature that creepeth
15: 4 E' bed, whereon he lieth that hath
12 e' vessel of wood shall be rinsed
17 And e' garment, and e' skin,
20 And e' thing that she lieth upon
20 e' thing also that she sitteth upon
26 E' bed whereon she lieth
17:15 e' soul that eateth that which died
19: 3 Ye shall fear e' man his mother,
8 Therefore e' one that eateth it
10 gather e' grape of thy vineyard;
20: 9 e' one that curseth his father or
23:37 e' thing upon his day:
24: 8 E' sabbath he shall set it in order
25:10 return e' man unto his possession,
10 shall return e' man unto his family.
13 return e' man unto his possession.
27:28 e' devoted thing is most holy
Nu 1: 2 e' male by their polls;
4 a man of e' tribe
4 e' one head of the house of his
20, 22 e' male from twenty years old
52 e' man by his own camp,
52 and e' man by his own standard,
2: 2 E' man of the children of Israel
17 e' man in his place by their
34 e' one after their families, according
3:15 e' male from a month old
4:19 appoint them e' one to his service
30, 35, 39, 43 e' one that entereth into
47 e' one that came to do the service
49 e' one according to his service, and
5: 2 e' leper, and e' one that hath an
9 e' offering of all the holy things
10 And e' man's hallowed things
7: 5 to e' man according to his service.
8:16 instead of such as open e' womb,
17 I smote e' firstborn in the land
11:10 e' man in the door of his tent:
13: 2 e' tribe of their fathers shall ye
2 a man, e' one a ruler among them.
15:12 so shall ye do to e' one according
16: 3 congregation are holy, e' one of
17 take e' man his censer, and put
17 before the Lord e' man his censer,
18 And they took e' man his censer,
27 the tabernacle of Korah,...on e' side:
17: 2 and take of e' one of them a rod
2 write thou e' man's name upon
6 e' one of their princes gave him
9 looked, and took e' man his rod.
18: 7 office for e' thing of the altar,
9 e' oblation of theirs,
9 e' meat offering
9 e' sin offering of theirs, e' trespass
10 e' male shall eat it:
11 e' one that is clean in thy house
13 e' one that is clean in thine house
14 E' thing devoted in Israel shall be
15 E' thing that openeth the matrix
29 ye shall offer e' heave offering
31 ye shall eat it in e' place,
19:15 And e' open vessel, which hath no
21: 8 E' one that is bitten,
23: 2 Balaam offered on e' altar a bullock
4 I have offered upon e' altar a bullock
14, 30 a bullock and a ram on e' altar.
25: 5 Slay ye e' one his men that
26:54 to e' one shall his inheritance be
28:10 is the burnt offering of e' sabbath,
14 burnt offering for e' month
21 deal shalt thou offer for e' lamb,
29:14 three tenth deals unto e' bullock
30: 4 and e' bond wherewith she hath
9 But e' vow of a widow, and of her
11 e' bond wherewith she bound
13 E' vow, and e' binding oath
31: 4 Of e' tribe a thousand, throughout
5 of Israel, a thousand of e' tribe,
6 to the war, a thousand of e' tribe,
17 Now therefore kill e' male among
17 and kill e' woman that hath known
Nu 31:23 E' thing that may abide the fire,
50 what e' man hath gotten, of jewels
53 had taken spoil, e' man for himself.)
32:18 inherited e' man his inheritance.
27 pass over, e' man armed for war,
29 Jordan, e' man armed to battle,
33:54 e' man's inheritance shall be in
34:18 take one prince of e' tribe,
35: 8 e' one shall give of his cities
15 e' one that killeth any person
36: 7 e' one of the children of Israel
8 may enjoy e' man the inheritance
9 but e' one of the tribes of the
De 1:16 between e' man and his brother,
22 came near unto me e' one of you,
41 on e' man his weapons of war,
2:34 of e' city, we left none to remain:
3: 6 and children, of e' city.
20 return e' man, unto his possession,
4: 4 are alive e' one of you this day.
8: 3 but by e' word that proceedeth
11:24 E' place whereon the soles of your
12: 2 and under e' green tree:
8 e' man whatsoever is right in his
13 offerings in e' place that thou
31 for e' abomination to the Lord,
13:16 and all the spoil thereof e' whit,
14: 6 And e' beast that parteth the hoof,
14 And e' raven after his kind,
19 And e' creeping thing that flieth
15: 1 end of e' seven years thou shalt
2 E' creditor that lendeth ought
16:17 E' man shall give as he is able,
19: 3 that e' slayer may flee thither.
20:13 thou shalt smite e' male thereof
21: 5 shall e' controversy and e' stroke
23: 9 keep thee from e' wicked thing.
24:16 e' man shall be put to death
26:11 shalt rejoice in e' good thing
28:61 Also e' sickness, and e' plague
30: 9 plenteous in e' work
31:10 At the end of e' seven years,
33: 3 e' one shall receive of thy words.
Jos 1: 3 E' place that the sole of your foot
3:12 of Israel, out of e' tribe a man.
4: 2 the people, out of e' tribe a man,
4 of Israel, out of e' tribe a man:
5 take you up e' man of you a stone
10 until e' thing was finished that
6: 5 shall ascend up e' man straight
20 e' man straight before him, and
11:14 e' man they smote with the edge
21:42 were e' one with their suburbs round
24:28 e' man unto his inheritance.
J'g 2: 6 e' man unto his inheritance to
5:30 to e' man a damsel or two;
7: 5 E' one that lappeth of the water
5 e' one that boweth down upon his
7 people go e' man unto his place.
8 of Israel e' man unto his tent,
16 a trumpet in e' man's hand,
18 on e' side of all the camp,
21 and they stood e' man in his place
22 e' man's sword against his fellow,
8:24 me e' man the earrings of his prey.
25 cast therein e' man the earrings of
34 of all their enemies on e' side:
9:49 cut down e' man his bough,
55 they departed e' man unto his place.
16: 5 e' one of us eleven hundred pieces
17: 6 e' man did that which was right
20:16 e' one could sling stones at an
48 as well the men of e' city,
21:11 destroy e' male, and e' woman
21 and catch you e' man his wife
24 e' man to his tribe and to his family,
24 thence e' man to his inheritance.
25 e' man did that which was right in
1Sa 2:36 e' one that is left in thine house
3:11 ears of e' one that heareth it shall
18 Samuel told him e' whit,
4:10 fled e' man into his tent:
8:22 Go ye e' man unto his city.
10:25 people away, e' man to his house.
12:11 your enemies on e' side, and ye
13: 2 he sent e' man to his tent.
20 to sharpen e' man his share, and
14:20 e' man's sword was against his
34 Bring me hither e' man his ox,
34 and e' man his sheep,
34 e' man his ox with him that night,
47 against all his enemies on e' side,
15: 9 but e' thing that was vile
20:15 And e' one from the face of the earth.
22: 2 and e' one that was in distress,
2 and e' one that was in debt,
2 and e' one that was discontented,
7 son of Jesse give e' one of you
23:14 And Saul sought him e' day,
25:10 away e' man from his master.
13 Gird ye on e' man his sword.
13 they girded on e' man his sword;
26:23 The Lord render to e' man his
27: 3 e' man with his household, even
30: 6 e' man for his sons and for his
22 e' man his wife and his children,
2Sa 2: 3 e' man with his household: and
16 e' one his fellow by the head,
27 e' one from following his brother.
6:19 to e' one a cake of bread, and a
19 people departed e' one to his house.
13: 9 And they went out e' man from him.
29 e' man gat him up upon his mule,
37 David mourned for his son e' day.
14:26 was at e' year's end that he polled it:
15: 4 e' man which hath any suit or
2Sa 15:30 covered e' man his head, and they
36 send unto me e' thing that ye can
18:17 all Israel fled e' one to his tent.
19: 8 Israel had fled e' man to his tent.
20: 1 e' man to his tents, O Israel.
2 e' man of Israel went up from
12 saw that e' one that came by him
22 from the city, e' man to his tent.
21:20 had on e' hand six fingers,
20 on e' foot six toes,
1Ki 1:49 rose up, and went e' man his way.
4:25 e' man under his vine and under
27 e' man in his month: they lacked
28 e' man according to his charge.
5: 3 which were about him on e' side,
4 God hath given me rest on e' side,
7:30 e' base had four brasen wheels,
30 at the side of e' addition.
36 the proportion of e' one, and
38 and e' laver was four cubits:
38 and upon e' one of the ten bases
8:38 which shall know e' man the plague
39 to e' man according to his ways,
9: 8 e' one that passeth by it shall be
10:25 they brought e' man his present,
11:15 had smitten e' male in Edom;
16 until he cut off e' male in Edom:
12:24 return e' man to his house; for
14:23 groves, on e' high hill,
23 and under e' green tree.
19:18 and e' mouth which hath not
20:20 And they slew e' one his man:
24 e' man out of his place, and put
22:17 let them return e' man to his house
28 Hearken, O people, e' one of you.
36 E' man to his city, and
36 e' man to his own country.
2Ki 3:19 smite e' fenced city, and e' choice
19 and shall fell e' good tree,
19 mar e' good piece of land
25 on e' good piece of land
25 cast e' man his stone,
6: 2 and take thence e' man a beam,
8: 9 of e' good thing of Damascus,
9:13 took e' man his garment, and put
11: 8 e' man with his weapons in his
9 they took e' man his men that were
11 guard stood, e' man with weapons
12: 4 the money of e' one that passeth
4 the money that e' man is set at,
5 them, e' man of his acquaintance:
14: 6 but e' man shall be put to death
12 and they fled e' man to their tents.
16: 4 the hills, and under e' green tree.
17:10 in e' high hill, and under e' green
29 Howbeit e' nation made gods
29 e' nation in their cities wherein
18:31 eat ye e' man of his own vine, and
31 e' one of his fig...and drink ye e' one
23:35 e' one according to his taxation,
25: 9 e' great man's house burnt he
30 a daily rate for e' day, all the days
1Ch 9:27 the opening thereof e' morning
32 shewbread, to prepare it e' sabbath.
13: 1 hundreds, and with e' leader.
2 send abroad our brethren e' where,
16: 3 dealt to e' one of Israel, both man
3 man and woman, to e' one a loaf
37 before the ark continually, as e' day's
43 departed e' man to his house:
22:15 men for e' manner of work.
18 he not given you rest on e' side?
23:30 And to stand e' morning to thank
26:13 cast lots...for e' gate.
32 for e' matter pertaining to God,
27: 1 of e' course were twenty and four
28:14 instruments of e' kind of service:
15 by weight for e' candlestick,
15 according to the use of e' candlestick.
28:16 tables of shewbread, for e' table;
17 he gave gold by weight for e' bason;
21 workmanship e' willing skilful
2Ch 2:14 to find out e' device which
6:29 e' one shall know his own sore
30 e' man according unto all his ways,
7:21 an astonishment to e' one that
8:13 Even after a certain rate e' day,
14 as the duty of e' day required:
9:21 e' three years once came the ships
24 they brought e' man his present,
10:16 e' man to your tents, O Israel:
11: 4 return e' man to his house; for this
12 And in e' special city he put
23 Benjamin, unto e' fenced city:
13:11 e' morning and e' evening burnt
11 lamps thereof, to burn e' evening:
14: 7 he hath given us rest on e' side.
18:16 therefore e' man to his house
20:23 e' one helped to destroy another.
27 they returned, e' man of Judah
23: 7 e' man with his weapons in his
8 e' man his men that were to come
10 e' man having his weapon in his
25: 4 but e' man shall die for his own sin.
22 and they fled e' man to his tent.
28: 4 the hills, and under e' green tree.
24 altars in e' corner of Jerusalem.
25 And in e' several city of Judah
29:35 drink offerings for e' burnt offering.
30:17 for e' one that was not clean,
18 The good Lord pardon e' one
31: 1 e' man to his possession, into their
2 e' man according to his service,
16 even unto e' one that entereth
19 in e' several city, the men that
21 And in e' work that he began

2Ch 32:22 and guided them on e· side.
35:15 and the porters waited at e· gate;
Ezr 2: 1 and Judah, e· one unto his city;
3: 4 as the duty of e· day required;
5 of e· one that willingly offered
6: 5 at Jerusalem, e· one to his place,
8:34 and by weight of e· one:
9: 4 assembled unto me e· one that
10:14 with them the elders of e· city,
Ne 3:28 e· one over against his house.
4:15 to the wall, e· one unto his work.
17 e· one with one of his hands
18 e· one had his sword girded by his
22 Let e· one with his servant lodge
23 e· one put them off for washing.
5: 7 exact usury, e· one of his brother.
13 shake out e· man from his house,
7: 3 e· one in his watch, and e· one to be
6 and to Judah, e· one unto his city;
8:16 e· one upon the roof of his house,
10:28 e· one having knowledge, and
31 and the exaction of e· debt.
11: 3 e· one in his possession in their
20 of Judah, e· one in his inheritance.
23 be for the singers, due for e· day.
12:47 the singers and the porters, e· day
13:10 were fled e· one to his field.
30 the Levites, e· one in his business;
Es 1: 8 do according to e· man's pleasure.
22 king's provinces, into e· province
22 to e· people after their language,
22 that e· man should bear rule in
22 to the language of e· people.
2:11 Mordecai walked e· day before the
12 Now when e· maid's turn was come
13 came e· maiden unto the king;
3:12 governors that were over e· province,
12 rulers of e· people of e· province
12 to e· people after their language;
14 to be given in e· province
4: 3 And in e· province, whithersoever
6:13 e· thing that had befallen him.
8: 9 unto e· province according to
9 and unto e· people after their
11 Jews which were in e· city to
13 to be given in e· province was
17 And in e· province, and in e· city,
9:27 their appointed time e· year;
28 e· [3605] generation, e· family,
28 e· province, and e· city;
Job 1: 4 their houses, e· one his day;
10 about all that he hath on e· side?
2:11 came e· one from his own place;
12 and they rent e· one his mantle,
7:18 visit him e· morning, and try him e·
12:10 the soul of e· living thing,
18:11 shall make him afraid on e· side,
19:10 He hath destroyed me on e· side,
20:22 e· hand of the wicked shall come
21:33 and e· man shall draw after him,
24: 6 They reap e· one his corn
28:10 his eye seeth e· precious thing.
34:11 and cause e· man to find according
36:25 E· man may see it;
37: 7 sealeth up the hand of e· man;
39: 8 he searcheth after e· green thing.
40:11 behold e· one that is proud,
12 Look on e· one that is proud,
42: 2 thou canst do e· thing,
11 e· man also gave him a piece of
11 and e· one an earring
Ps 7:11 angry with the wicked e· day.
12: 2 vanity e· one with his neighbour:
8 The wicked walk on e· side,
29: 9 doth e· one speak of his glory.
31:13 fear was on e· side:
32: 6 For this shall e· one that is godly
39: 5 e· man at his best state is altogether
6 e· man walketh in a vain shew:
11 surely e· man is vanity. Selah.
50:10 For e· beast of the forest is mine,
53: 3 E· one of them is gone back:
56: 5 E· day they wrest my words:
58: 8 let e· one of them pass away:
62:12 to e· man according to his work.
63:11 e· one that sweareth by him shall
64: 6 inward thought of e· one of them,
65:12 the little hills rejoice on e· side.
68:30 till e· one submit himself with
69:34 the seas, and e· thing that moveth
71:18 thy power to e· one that is to come.
21 and comfort me on e· side.
73:14 plagued, and chastened e· morning.
84: 7 e· one of them in Zion appeareth
92: 2 and thy faithfulness e· night,
104:11 drink to e· beast of the field:
115: 8 so is e· one that trusteth in them.
119:101 my feet from e· evil way,
104 therefore I hate e· false way.
128 and I hate e· false way.
160 e· one of thy righteous judgments
128: 1 Blessed is e· one that feareth
135:18 so is e· one that trusteth in them.
145: 2 E· day I will bless thee;
16 the desire of e· living thing.
150: 6 Let e· thing that hath breath
Pr 1:19 the ways of e· one that is greedy
2: 9 yea, e· good path.
3:18 happy is e· one that retaineth her.
7:12 and lieth in wait at e· corner.)
13:16 E· prudent man dealeth with
14: 1 E· wise woman buildeth her house:
15 The simple believeth e· word:
15: 3 The eyes of the Lord are in e· place,
16: 5 E· one that is proud in heart
19: 6 e· man that is a friend to him

Pr 20: 3 but e· fool will be meddling.
6 e· one his own goodness: but a
18 E· purpose is established by counsel:
21: 2 E· way of a man is right in his
5 of e· one that is hasty only to want.
24:12 to e· man according to his works?
26 E· man shall kiss his lips
27: 7 soul e· bitter thing is sweet.
24 crown endure to e· generation?
29:26 e· man's judgment cometh from
30: 5 E· word of God is pure:
Ec 3: 1 To e· thing there is a season,
1 to e· purpose under the heaven:
11 e· thing beautiful in his time:
13 that e· man should eat and drink,
17 for e· purpose and for e· work.
4: 4 all travail, and e· right work,
5:19 E· man also to whom God hath
8: 6 Because to e· purpose there is
9 unto e· work that is done under
10: 3 he saith to e· one that he is a fool.
15 wearieth e· one of them,
12:14 God shall bring e· work into
14 with e· secret thing, whether it be
Ca 3: 8 e· man hath his sword upon his
4: 2 whereof e· one bear twins,
6: 6 whereof e· one beareth twins,
8: 11 e· one for the fruit thereof was to
Isa 1:23 e· one loveth gifts, and followeth
2:12 be upon e· one that is proud
12 and upon e· one that is lifted up;
15 e· high tower, and upon e· fenced
3: 5 be oppressed, e· one by another,
5 and e· one by his neighbour:
4: 3 even e· one that is written among
5 create upon e· dwelling place
7:22 honey shall e· one eat that is
23 that e· place shall be, where
9: 5 For e· battle of the warrior is
17 e· one is an hypocrite and an
17 and e· mouth speaketh folly,
20 eat e· man the flesh of his own
13: 7 e· man's heart shall melt:
14 e· man turn to his own people, and
14 flee e· one into his own land.
15 E· one that is found shall be
15 and e· one that is joined unto
14:18 in glory, e one in his own house.
15: 2 and e· beard cut off.
3 in their streets, e· one shall howl,
16: 7 for Moab, e· one shall howl:
19: 2 e· one against his brother,
2 and e· one against his neighbour:
7 and e· thing sown by the brooks
14 Egypt to err in e· work thereof,
17 e· one that maketh mention
24:10 e· house is shut up,
27: 3 I will water it e· moment:
25 and upon e· high mountain
30:25 and upon e· high hill,
32 And in e· place where the grounded
31: 7 e· man shall cast away his idols
33: 2 be thou their arm e· morning,
34:15 be gathered, e· one with her mate.
36:16 eat ye e· one of his vine, and e· one
16 drink ye e· one the waters of his
40: 4 E· valley shall be exalted
4 e· mountain and hill shall be made
41: 6 helped e· one his neighbour;
6 and e· one said to his brother,
43: 7 e· one that is called by my name:
44:23 O forest, and e· tree therein:
45:23 unto me e· knee shall bow,
23 e· tongue shall swear.
47:15 they shall wander e· one to his
51:13 feared continually e· day because
52: 5 continually e· day is blasphemed.
53: 6 we have turned e· one to his own
54:17 e· tongue that shall rise against
55: 1 Ho, e· one that thirsteth,
56: 6 e· one that keepeth the sabbath
11 e· one for his gain, from his quarter.
57: 5 with idols under e· green tree,
58: 6 that ye break e· yoke?
Jer 1:15 shall set e· one his throne at the
2:20 when upon e· high hill and under
20 under e· green tree thou wanderest,
3: 6 gone up upon e· high mountain and
6 and under e· green tree, and there
13 to the strangers under e· green tree,
4:29 e· city shall be forsaken,
5: 8 e· one neighed after his neighbour's
6: 3 they shall feed e· one in his place.
13 e· one is given to covetousness;
13 unto the priest e· one dealeth
25 the enemy and fear is on e· side.
8: 6 e· one turned to his course,
10 for e· one from the least even unto
10 the priest e· one dealeth falsely.
9: 4 ye heed e· one of his neighbour,
4 for e· brother will utterly supplant
4 e· neighbour will walk with slanders.
5 deceive e· one his neighbour,
20 e· one her neighbour lamentation.
10:14 E· man is brutish in his
14 e· founder is confounded by the
11: 8 walked e· one in the imagination
12: 4 and the herbs of e· field wither,
15 e· man to his heritage, and e· man
13:12 E· bottle shall be filled with wine:
12 know that e· bottle shall be filled
15:10 e· one of them doth curse me.
16:12 e· one after the imagination of his
16 from e· mountain, and from e· hill,
17:10 give e· man according to his ways,
18:11 return ye now e· one from his evil

Jer 18:12 we will e· one do the imagination
16 e· one that passeth thereby shall
19: 8 e· one that passeth thereby shall be
9 and they shall eat e· one the flesh
20: 7 daily, e· one mocketh me.
10 defaming of many, fear on e· side.
22: 7 thee, e· one with his weapons;
8 shall say e· man to his neighbour,
23:17 they say unto e· one that walketh
27 they tell e· man to his neighbour,
30 my words e· one from his neighbour.
35 ye say e· one to his neighbour, and
35 and e· one to his brother,
36 e· man's word shall be his burden;
25: 5 Turn ye again now e· one from his
26: 3 and turn e· man from his evil way,
29:26 for e· man that is mad, and maketh
30: 6 I see e· man with his hands on his
16 e· one of them, shall go into
31:25 replenished e· sorrowful soul.
30 e· one shall die for his own iniquity:
34 teach no more e· man his neighbour,
34 and e· man his brother,
32:19 to give e· one according to his ways
34: 9 e· man should let his manservant,
9 and e· man his maidservant,
10 e· one should let his manservant,
10 and e· one his maidservant, go free,
14 let ye go e· man his brother
15 proclaiming liberty e· man to his
16 e· man his servant, and e· man his
17 e· one to his brother, and e· man to
35:15 Return ye now e· man from his evil
36: 3 return e· man from his evil way;
7 return e· one from his evil way:
37:10 rise up e· man in his tent,
43: 6 and e· person that Nebuzar-adan
47: 4 from Tyrus and Zidon e· helper
48: 8 spoiler shall come upon e· city,
37 For e· head shall be bald,
37 and e· beard clipped:
49: 5 ye shall be driven out e· man
17 e· one that goeth by it shall be
29 cry unto them, Fear is on e· side.
50:13 e· one that goeth by Babylon shall
16 shall turn e· one to his people, and
16 and they shall flee e· one
42 e· one put in array, like a man to the
51: 6 and deliver e· man his soul:
9 go e· one into his own country:
17 E· man is brutish by his
17 e· founder is confounded by the
29 for e· purpose of the Lord shall be
45 and deliver ye e· man his soul
56 men are taken, e· one of their
52:34 e· day a portion until the day of his
La 2:19 for hunger in the top of e· street.
3:23 They are new e· morning: great is
4: 1 poured out in the top of e· street.
Eze 1: 6 e· one had four faces, and e· one
9 went e· one straight forward.
11 two wings of e· one were joined
12 they went e· one straight forward:
23 e· one had two, which covered on
23 this side, and e· one had two,
6:13 upon e· high hill,...under e· green
13 and under e· thick oak, the place
7:16 all of them mourning, e· one for his
8:10 and behold e· form of creeping
11 with e· man his censer in his hand;
12 e· man in the chambers of his
9: 1 even e· man with his destroying
2 and e· man a slaughter weapon
10:14 And e· one had four faces:
19 and e· one stood at the door
21 E· one had four faces apiece, and
21 and e· one four wings;
22 they went e· one straight forward.
11: 5 into your mind, e· one of them,
12:14 And I will scatter toward e· wind
22 The days are prolonged, and e·
23 at hand, and the effect of e· vision.
13:18 kerchiefs upon the head of e· stature
14: 4 E· man of the house of Israel
7 e· one of the house of Israel,
16:15 thy fornications on e· one that
24 made thee an high place in e· street.
25 built thy high place at e· head of
25 opened thy feet to e· one that
31 eminent place in the head of e· way,
31 makest thine high place in e· street;
33 may come unto thee on e· side
44 Behold, e· one that useth proverbs
17:23 under it shall dwell all fowl of e·
18:30 e· one according to his ways, saith
19: 8 the nations set against him on e·
20: 7 Cast ye away e· man the
8 they did not e· man cast away
28 then they saw e· high hill, and all
39 Go ye, serve ye e· one his idols,
47 e· green tree in thee, and e· dry
21: 7 and e· heart shall melt, and all
7 and e· spirit shall faint,
10 the rod of my son, as e· tree.
22: 6 e· one were in thee to their power
23:22 bring them against thee on e· side;
24: 4 even e· good piece, the thigh, and
26:16 and shall tremble at e· moment, and
28:13 e· precious stone was thy covering
23 by the sword upon her on e· side;
29:18 e· head was made bald, and
18 and e· shoulder was peeled;
32:10 and they shall tremble at e· moment,
10 e· man for his own life, in the day
33:20 I will judge you e· one after his ways
26 and ye defile e· one his neighbour's

Eze 33:30 e' one to his brother, saying,
34: 6 the mountains, and upon e' high
8 my flock became meat to e' beast
36: 3 and swallowed you up on e' side,
37:21 and will gather them on e' side,
38:20 and e' wall shall fall to the ground
21 e' man's sword shall be against
39: 4 unto the ravenous birds of e' sort,
17 Speak unto e' feathered fowl, and
17 and to e' beast of the field,
17 gather yourselves on e' side to
40: 7 e' little chamber was one reed long,
41: 5 and the breadth of e' side chamber,
5 round about the house on e' side.
10 round about the house on e' side.
18 and e' cherub had two faces;
43:25 shalt thou prepare e' day a goat for a
44: 5 e' going forth of the sanctuary.
29 and e' dedicated thing in Israel
30 fruits of all things, and e' oblation
30 of e' sort of your oblations,
45:20 for e' one that erreth, and for him
46:13 thou shalt prepare it e' morning.
14 a meat offering for it e' morning,
15 e' offering, and the oil, e' morning
18 e' man from his possession.
21 in e' corner of the court there was a
47: 9 come to pass, that e' thing that
9 and e' thing shall live whither the
Da 3:10 that e' man that shall hear the
29 e' people, nation, and language,
6:12 that e' man that shall ask a petition
26 in e' dominion of my kingdom
11:36 and magnify himself above e' god,
12: 1 e' one shall be found written in
Ho 4: 3 e' one that dwelleth therein shall
9: 1 thou hast loved a reward upon e'
Joe 2: 7 and they shall march e' one on his
8 they shall walk e' one in his path:
Am 2: 8 clothes laid to pledge by e' altar,
4: 3 e' cow at that which is before her;
4 bring your sacrifices e' morning,
8: 3 be many dead bodies in e' place;
8 e' one mourn that dwelleth therein?
10 all loins, and baldness upon e' head;
Ob 9 e' one of the mount of Esau
Jon 1: 5 and cried e' man unto his god,
7 and they said e' one to his fellow,
3: 8 them turn e' one from his evil way,
Mic 4: 4 sit e' man under his vine and under
5 walk e' one in the name of his god,
7: 2 hunt e' man his brother with a net.
Hab 1:10 they shall divide e' stronghold; for
Zep 2:11 e' one from his place, even all the
15 e' one that passeth by her shall
3: 5 e' morning doth he bring his judgment
19 fame in e' land where they have
Hag 1: 9 ye run e' man unto his own house.
2:14 and so is e' work of their hands;
22 e' one by the sword of his brother.
Zec 3:10 call e' man his neighbour under
5: 3 e' one that stealeth shall be cut
3 e' one that sweareth shall be cut
7: 9 compassions e' man to his brother:
8: 4 e' man with his staff in his hand
10 men e' one against his neighbour.
16 e' man the truth to his neighbour;
10: 1 to e' one grass in the field.
4 out of him e' oppressor together.
11: 6 e' one into his neighbour's hand,
9 rest eat e' one the flesh of another.
12: 4 smite e' horse with astonishment,
4 e' horse of the people with blindness.
12 the land shall mourn, e' family apart;
14 families that remain, e' family apart,
13: 4 be ashamed e' one of his vision.
14:13 e' one on the hand of his neighbour,
16 e' one that is left of all the nations
21 e' pot in Jerusalem and in Judah
Mal 1:11 in e' place incense shall be offered
2:10 do we deal treacherously e' man
17 E' one that doeth evil is good in
M't 3:10 e' tree which bringeth not forth
4: 4 but by e' word that proceedeth out
7: 8 For e' one that asketh receiveth;
17 so e' good tree bringeth forth good
19 E' tree that bringeth not forth good
21 Not e' one that saith unto me,
26 e' one that heareth these sayings
8:33 e' thing, and what was befallen
9:35 healing e' sickness and e' disease
12:25 E' kingdom divided against
25 e' city or house divided against
36 e' idle word that men shall speak
13:47 the sea, and gathered of e' kind:
52 e' scribe which is instructed
15:13 E' plant, which my heavenly Father
16:27 e' man according to his works.
18:16 e' word may be established.
35 e' one his brother their trespasses.
19: 3 put away his wife for e' cause?
29 e' one that hath forsaken houses,
20: 9 they received e' man a penny.
10 likewise received e' man a penny.
25:15 e' man according to his several
29 e' one that hath shall be given,
26:22 e' one of them to say unto him,
M'r 1:45 they came to him from e' quarter.
7:14 Hearken unto me e' one of you,
8:25 restored, and saw e' man clearly.
9:49 e' one shall be salted with fire,
49 and e' sacrifice shall be salted
13:34 and to e' man his work, and
15:24 them, what e' man should take.
16:15 preach the gospel to e' creature.
20 went forth, and preached e' where

Lu 2: 3 to be taxed, e' one into his own city.
23 E' male that openeth the womb
41 e' year at the feast of the passover.
3: 5 E' valley shall be filled,
5 and e' mountain and hill shall be
9 e' tree therefore which bringeth not
4: 4 but by e' word of God.
37 fame of him went out into e' place
40 laid his hands on e' one of them,
5:17 come out of e' town of Galilee,
6:30 Give to e' man that asketh of thee;
40 but e' one that is perfect shall be as
44 e' tree is known by his own fruit.
8: 1 that he went throughout e' city
4 were come to him out of e' city,
9: 6 the gospel, and healing e' where.
43 they wondered e' one at all things
10: 1 into e' city and place, whither he
11: 4 forgive e' one that is indebted to
10 For e' one that asketh receiveth;
17 E' kingdom divided against itself
16: 5 called e' one of his lord's debtors
16 and e' man presseth into it.
19 and fared sumptuously e' day:
18:14 e' one that exalteth himself shall
19:15 how much e' man had gained
26 e' one which hath shall be given;
43 and keep thee in on e' side,
Joh 1: 9 lighteth e' man that cometh into
2:10 E' man at the beginning doth set
3: 8 e' one that is born of the Spirit.
20 e' one that doeth evil hateth the
6: 7 e' one of them may take a little.
40 e' one which seeth the Son, and
45 E' man therefore that hath heard,
7:23 I have made a man e' whit whole
53 e' man went unto his own house.
13:10 but is clean e' whit: and ye are
15: 2 E' branch in me that beareth not
2 and e' branch that beareth fruit,
16:32 be scattered, e' man to his own,
18:37 E' one that is of the truth heareth
19:23 four parts, to e' soldier a part;
21:25 if they should be written e' one,
Ac 2: 5 out of e' nation under heaven.
6 e' man heard them speak in his
8 hear we e' man in our own tongue,
38 and be baptized e' one of you
43 fear came upon e' soul: and many
45 all men, as e' man had need.
3:23 shall come to pass, that e' soul,
26 in turning away e' one of you
4:35 e' man according as he had need.
5:16 and they were healed e' one.
42 and in e' house, they ceased not
8: 3 entering into e' house, and haling
4 e' where preaching the word.
10:35 in e' nation he that feareth him,
11:29 e' man according to his ability,
13:27 which are read e' sabbath day,
14:23 ordained them elders in e' church,
15:21 in e' city them that preach him,
21 in the synagogues e' sabbath day.
36 and visit our brethren in e' city
16:26 and e' one's bands were loosed.
17:27 he be not far from e' one of us:
30 commandeth all men e' where to
18: 4 in the synagogue e' sabbath,
20:23 Holy Ghost witnesseth in e' city,
31 to warn e' one night and day
21:26 be offered for e' one of them.
28 that teacheth all men e' where
22:19 beat in e' synagogue them that
26:11 them oft in e' synagogue,
28: 2 and received us e' one, because
22 e' where it is spoken against.
Ro 1:16 salvation to e' one that believeth;
2: 6 to e' man according to his deeds:
9 e' soul of man that doeth evil,
10 to e' man that worketh good, to the
3: 2 Much e' way: chiefly, because that
4 but e' man a liar; as it is written,
19 that e' mouth may be stopped, and
10: 4 to e' one that believeth.
12: 3 to e' man that is among you, not
3 as God hath dealt to e' man
5 and e' one members one of
13: 1 e' soul be subject unto the higher
14: 5 another esteemeth e' day alike.
5 Let e' man be fully persuaded
11 e' knee shall bow to me,
11 and e' tongue shall confess to God.
12 e' one of us shall give account
15: 2 e' one of us please his neighbour
1Co 1: 2 with all that in e' place call upon
5 That in e' thing ye are enriched
12 e' one of you saith, I am of Paul;
3: 5 as the Lord gave to e' man?
8 e' man shall receive his own
10 let e' man take heed how he
13 E' man's work shall be made
13 the fire shall try e' man's work
4: 5 shall e' man have praise of God.
17 as I teach e' where in
17 as I teach...in e' church.
6:18 E' sin that a man doeth is without
7: 2 let e' man have his own wife,
2 and let e' woman have her own
7 e' man hath his proper gift of
17 distributed to e' man, as the Lord
17 as the Lord hath called e' one, so
20 e' man abide in the same calling
24 let e' man, wherein he is called,
8: 7 Howbeit there is not in e' man
9:25 And e' man that striveth for the
10:24 but e' man another's wealth.

1Co 11: 3 the head of e' man is Christ;
4 E' man praying or prophesying,
5 But e' woman that prayeth or
21 in eating e' one taketh before
12: 7 given to e' man to profit withal.
11 to e' man severally as he will.
18 e' one of them in the body,
14:26 e' one of you hath a psalm,
15:23 But e' man in his own order:
30 stand we in jeopardy e' hour?
38 and to e' seed his own body.
16: 2 e' one of you lay by him in store,
16 and to e' one that helpeth with us,
2Co 2:14 his knowledge by us in e' place.
4: 2 to e' man's conscience in the sight
8 We are troubled on e' side,
5:10 e' one may receive the things
7: 5 but we were troubled on e' side;
8: 7 as ye abound in e' thing,
9: 7 E' man according as he
8 may abound to e' good work:
11 in e' thing to all bountifulness,
10: 5 e' high thing that exalteth itself
5 e' thought to the obedience of
13: 1 shall e' word be established.
Ga 3:10 e' one that continueth not in all
13 is e' one that hangeth on a tree:
5: 3 For I testify again to e' man that
6: 4 let e' man prove his own work,
5 e' man shall bear his own burden.
Eph 1:21 and e' name that is named, not
4: 7 unto e' one of us is given grace
14 about with e' wind of doctrine,
16 by that which e' joint supplieth,
16 in the measure of e' part,
25 e' man truth with his neighbour:
5:24 to their own husbands in e' thing.
33 let e' one of you in particular
Ph'p 1: 3 upon e' remembrance of you,
4 in e' prayer of mine for you all
18 notwithstanding, e' way, whether
2: 4 not e' man on his own things,
4 but e' man also on the things of
9 a name which is above e' name:
10 name of Jesus e' knee should bow,
11 And that e' tongue should confess
4: 6 e' thing by prayer and supplication
12 e' where and in all things I am
21 Salute e' saint in Christ Jesus.
Col 1:10 being fruitful in e' good work,
15 God, the firstborn of e' creature:
23 to e' creature which is under
28 warning e' man, and teaching e' man
28 that we may present e' man
4: 6 ye ought to answer e' man.
1Th 1: 8 in e' place your faith to God-ward
2:11 and charged e' one of you,
4: 4 That e' one of you should know
5:18 In e' thing give thanks: for this
2Th 1: 3 the charity of e' one of you all
2:17 stablish you in e' good word and
3: 6 e' brother that walketh disorderly,
17 which is the token in e' epistle:
1Ti 2: 8 that men pray e' where,
4: 4 For e' creature of God is good,
5:10 diligently followed e' good work.
2Ti 2:19 Let e' one that nameth the name
21 and prepared unto e' good work.
4:18 shall deliver me from e' evil work,
Tit 1: 5 and ordain elders in e' city, as I
16 and unto e' good work reprobate.
3: 1 to be ready to e' good work,
Ph'm 6 the acknowledging of e' good thing
Heb 2: 2 e' transgression and disobedience
9 God should taste death for e' man.
3: 4 For e' house is builded by some
5: 1 For e' high priest taken from among
13 For e' one that useth milk is
6:11 desire that e' one of you do shew
8: 3 For e' high priest is ordained to
11 e' man his neighbour, and e' man
9: 7 high priest alone once e' year,
19 spoken e' precept to all the people
25 the high priest entereth...e' year
10: 3 again made of sins e' year.
11 And e' priest standeth daily
12: 1 let us lay aside e' weight, and the
6 and scourgeth e' son whom he
13:21 in e' good work to do his will,
Jas 1:14 e' man is tempted, when he is
17 E' good gift and e' perfect gift
19 let e' man be swift to hear, slow to
3: 7 For e' kind of beasts, and of birds,
16 there is confusion and e' evil work.
1Pe 1:17 according to e' man's work,
2:13 yourself to e' ordinance of man
3:15 answer to e' man that asketh you
4:10 As e' man hath received the gift,
1Jo 2:29 e' one that doeth righteousness is
3: 3 And e' man that hath this hope
4: 1 believe not e' spirit, but try the
2 E' spirit that confesseth that Jesus
3 And e' spirit that confesseth not
7 e' one that loveth is born of God,
5: 1 e' one that loveth him that begat,
Re 1: 7 e' eye shall see him, and they also
2:23 I will give unto e' one of you
5: 8 having e' one of them harps, and
9 out of e' kindred, and tongue,
13 And e' creature which is in heaven,
6:11 were given unto e' one of them;
14 e' mountain and island were
15 e' bondman, and e' free man, hid
14: 6 e' nation, and kindred, and tongue,
16: 3 and e' living soul died in the sea.
20 And e' island fled away, and the

Re 16:21 e' stone about the weight of a
18: 2 the hold of e' foul spirit, and a cage
2 of e' unclean and hateful bird.
17 e' shipmaster, and all the company
20:13 were judged e' man according to
21:21 e' several gate was of one pearl:
22: 2 yielded her fruit e' month:
12 to give e' man according as his
18 I testify unto e' man that heareth

everyone See EVERY and ONE.
everything See EVERY and THING.
everywhere See EVERY and WHERE.

Evi (*e'-vi*)
Nu 31: 8 namely, *E'*, and Rekem, and Zur,
Jos 13:21 with the princes of Midian, *E'*, and

evidence See also EVIDENCES.
Jer 32:10 I subscribed the e', and sealed it,
11 So I took the e' of the purchase,
12 And I gave the e' of the purchase
14 this e' of the purchase,
14 and this e' which is open;
16 delivered the e' of the purchase
Heb 11: 1 the e' of things not seen.

evidences
Jer 32:14 Take these e', this evidence of the
44 and subscribe e', and seal them,

evident
Job 6:28 for it is e' unto you if I lie.
Ga 3:11 in the sight of God, it is e': for,
Ph'p 1:28 is to them an e' token of perdition,
Heb 7:14 For it is e' that our Lord sprang
15 And it is yet far more e': for that

evidently
Ac 10: 3 He saw in a vision e', about the
Ga 3: 1 Jesus Christ hath been e' set forth,

evil See also EVILDOER; EVILFAVOUREDNESS; EVILS.
Ge 2: 9 tree of knowledge of good and e'.
17 of the knowledge of good and e',
3: 5 be as gods, knowing good and e'.
22 as one of us, to know good and e':
6: 5 of his heart was only e' continually.
8:21 imagination of man's heart is e'
19:19 lest some e' take me, and I die:
37: 2 unto his father their e' report.
20 Some e' beast hath devoured him:
33 an e' beast hath devoured him;
44: 4 have ye rewarded e' for good?
5 ye have done e' in so doing.
34 lest...I see the e' that shall come
47: 9 few and e' have the days of the
48:16 which redeemed me from all e',
50:15 the e' which we did unto him.
17 their sin; for they did unto thee e':
20 for you, ye thought e' against me;
Ex 5:19 Israel did see they were in e' case,
22 hast thou so e' entreated this
23 he hath done e' to this people;
10:10 look to it; for e' is before you.
23: 2 not follow a multitude to do e';
32:12 repent of this e' against thy people.
14 e' which he thought to do unto his
33: 4 the people heard these e' tidings,
Le 5: 4 pronouncing with his lips to do e',
26: 6 I will rid e' beasts out of the land,
Nu 13:32 they brought up an e' report of
14:27 I bear with this e' congregation,
35 do it unto all this e' congregation,
37 that did bring up the e' report
20: 5 to bring us in unto this e' place?
32:13 the generation, that had done e' in
De 1:35 these men of this e' generation see
39 knowledge between good and e',
4:25 do e' in the sight of the Lord
7:15 none of the e' diseases of Egypt,
13: 5 So shalt thou put the e' away
15: 9 thine eye be e' against thy poor
17: 7 put the e' away from among you.
12 shalt put away the e' from Israel.
19:19 put the e' away from among you.
20 commit no more any such e' among
21:21 so shalt thou put e' away from
22:14 and bring up an e' name upon her,
19 brought up an e' name upon a
21 thou put e' away from among you.
22 shalt thou put away e' from Israel.
24 thou shalt put away e' from among
24: 7 shalt put e' away from among you.
26: 6 the Egyptians e' entreated us,
28:54 eye shall be e' toward his brother,
56 her eye shall be e' toward the
29:21 Lord shall separate him unto e'
30:15 life and good, and death and e';
31:29 e' will befall you in the latter days;
29 will do e' in the sight of the Lord,
Jos 23:15 Lord bring upon you all e' things,
24:15 if it seem e' unto you to serve the
J'g 2:11 children of Israel did e' in the
15 the Lord was against them for e',
3: 7 did e' in the sight of the Lord,
12 did e' again in the sight of the Lord:
12 they had done e' in the sight of the
4: 1 the children of Israel again did e'
6: 1 children of Israel did e' in the sight
9:23 God sent an e' spirit between
57 all the e' of the men of Shechem
10: 6 did e' again in the sight of the Lord,
13: 1 did e' again in the sight of the Lord;
20:13 death, and put away e' from Israel.
34 but they knew not that e' was near
41 saw that e' was come upon them.
1Sa 2:23 I hear of your e' dealings by all this
6: 9 he hath done us this great e':

1Sa 12:19 have added unto all our sins this e'.
15:19 didst e' in the sight of the Lord?
16:14 an e' spirit from the Lord troubled
15 e' spirit from God troubleth thee.
16 the e' spirit from God is upon thee,
23 it came to pass, when the e' spirit
23 the e' spirit departed from him.
18:10 e' spirit from God came upon Saul,
19: 9 e' spirit from the Lord was upon
20: 7 sure that e' is determined by him.
9 certainly that e' were determined
13 if it please my father to do thee e',
24:11 e' nor transgression in mine hand,
17 whereas I have rewarded thee e'.
25: 3 was churlish and e' in his doings;
17 e' is determined against our master,
21 he hath requited me e' for good.
26 they that seek e' to my lord,
28 and e' hath not been found in thee
39 and hath kept his servant from e':
26:18 or what e' is in mine hand?
29: 6 I have not found e' in thee
2Sa 3:39 reward the doer of e' according
12: 9 the Lord to do e' in his sight?
11 I will raise up e' against thee
13:16 e' in sending me away is greater
15:14 us suddenly, and bring e' upon us,
17:14 Lord might bring e' upon Absalom.
19: 7 than all the e' that befell thee
35 I discern between good and e'?
24:16 the Lord repented him of the e'.
1Ki 5: 4 neither adversary nor e' occurrent.
9: 9 Lord brought upon them all this e'.
11: 6 Solomon did e' in the sight of the
13:33 Jeroboam returned not from his e'
14: 9 done e' above all that were before
10 e' upon the house of Jeroboam,
22 Judah did e' in the sight of the Lord,
15:26, 34 did e' in the sight of the Lord,
16: 7 e' that he did in the sight of the Lord,
19 in doing e' in the sight of the Lord,
25 Omri wrought e' in the eyes of the
30 Ahab the son of Omri did e' in the
17:20 also brought e' upon the widow
21:20 thou hast sold thyself to work e'
21 Behold, I will bring e' upon thee,
29 I will not bring the e' in his days:
29 in his son's days will I bring the e'
22: 8 doth not prophesy good...but e'.
18 he would prophesy no good...but e'?
23 Lord hath spoken e' concerning
52 he did e' in the sight of the Lord,
2Ki 3: 2 wrought e' in the sight of the Lord;
6:33 Behold, this e' is of the Lord;
8:12 I know the e' that thou wilt do
18 he did e' in the sight of the Lord.
27 and did e' in the sight of the Lord,
13: 2 was e' in the sight of the Lord,
11 did that which was e' in the sight
14:24 And he did that which was e' in the
15: 9, 18, 24, 28 was e' in the sight of the
17: 2 was e' in the sight of the Lord,
13 Turn ye from your e' ways, and
17 to do e' in the sight of the Lord,
21: 2 was e' in the sight of the Lord,
9 seduced them to do more e' than
12 bringing such e' upon Jerusalem
15 done that which was e' in my sight,
16 doing that which was e' in the sight
20 did that which was e' in the sight
22:16 I will bring e' upon this place,
20 all the e' which I will bring upon
23:32, 37 he did that which was e' in the
24: 9, 19 that which was e' in the sight
1Ch 2: 3 Er, the firstborn of Judah, was e'
4:10 thou wouldest keep me from e',
7:23 because it went e' with his house.
21:15 and he repented him of the e',
17 is that have sinned and done e'
2Ch 7:22 he brought all this e' upon them.
12:14 he did e', because he prepared
18: 7 good unto me, but always e':
17 prophesy good unto me, but e'?
22 Lord hath spoken e' against thee.
20: 9 e' cometh upon us, as the sword,
21: 6 was e' in the eyes of the Lord,
22: 4 he did e' in the sight of the Lord
29: 6 done that which was e' in the eyes
33: 2 was e' in the sight of the Lord,
6 much e' in the sight of the Lord,
22 did that which was e' in the sight
34:24 I will bring e' upon this place,
28 e' that I will bring upon this place,
36: 5 e' in the sight of the Lord his God.
9 was e' in the sight of the Lord.
12 he did that which was e' in the
Ezr 9:13 is come upon us for our e' deeds,
Ne 6:13 might have matter for an e' report,
9:28 they did e' again before thee:
13: 7 understood of the e' that Eliashib
17 What e' thing is this that ye do,
18 our God bring all this e' upon us,
27 to do all this great e', to transgress
Es 7: 7 there was e' determined against
8: 6 e' that shall come unto my people?
Job 1: 1 that feared God, and eschewed e'.
8 that feareth God, and escheweth e'?
2: 3 that feareth God, and escheweth e'?
10 God, and shall we not receive e'?
11 this e' that was come upon him,
5:19 seven there shall no e' touch thee.
8:20 neither will he help the e' doers:
24:21 He e' entreateth the barren that
28:28 depart from e' is understanding.
30:26 for good, then e' came upon me:
31:29 lifted up myself when e' found him:

Job 35:12 because of the pride of e' men.
42:11 the e' that the Lord had brought
Ps 5: 4 neither shall e' dwell with thee.
7: 4 If I have rewarded e' unto him
10:15 arm of the wicked and the e' man:
15: 3 nor doeth e' to his neighbour, nor
21:11 For they intended e' against thee:
23: 4 I will fear no e': for thou art
34:13 Keep thy tongue from e', and thy
14 Depart from e', and do good; seek
16 the Lord is against them that do e',
21 *E'* shall slay the wicked: and they
35:12 They rewarded me e' for good to
36: 4 is not good; he abhorreth not e'.
37: 8 not thyself in any wise to do e'.
19 not be ashamed in the e' time:
27 Depart from e', and do good; and
38:20 They also that render e' for good
40:14 backward...that wish me e'.
41: 5 Mine enemies speak e' of me,
8 An e' disease, say they, cleaveth
49: 5 should I fear in the days of e',
50:19 Thou givest thy mouth to e', and
51: 4 and done this e' in thy sight:
52: 3 Thou lovest e' more than good;
54: 5 shall reward e' unto mine enemies:
56: 5 their thoughts are against me for e'.
64: 5 encourage themselves in an e'
78:49 by sending e' angels among them.
90:15 the years wherein we have seen e'.
91:10 There shall no e' befall thee,
97:10 Ye that love the Lord, hate e':
109: 5 have rewarded me e' for good,
20 that speak e' against my soul.
112: 7 He shall not be afraid of e' tidings:
119:101 refrained my feet from every e'
121: 7 Lord shall preserve thee from all e':
140: 1 Deliver me, O Lord, from the e'
11 an e' speaker be established
11 e' shall hunt the violent man to
141: 4 not my heart to any e' thing,
Pr 1:16 their feet run to e', and make haste
33 and shall be quiet from fear of e'.
2:12 me from the way of the e' man,
14 Who rejoice to do e', and delight
3: 7 fear the Lord, and depart from e'.
29 not e' against thy neighbour,
4:14 go not in the way of e' men.
27 to the left: remove thy foot from e'.
5:14 I was almost in all e' in the midst
6:24 To keep thee from the e' woman,
8:13 The fear of the Lord is to hate e':
13 pride, and arrogancy, and the e'
11:19 e' pursueth it to his own death.
12:12 wicked desireth the net of e' men:
20 the heart of them that imagine e':
21 shall no e' happen to the just:
13:19 to fools to depart from e'.
21 *E'* pursueth sinners: but to the
14:16 man feareth, and departeth from e':
19 The e' bow before the good;
22 Do they not err that devise e'?
15: 3 eyes of the Lord...beholding the e'
15 All the days of the afflicted are e':
28 the wicked poureth out e' things.
16: 4 even the wicked for the day of e'.
6 of the Lord men depart from e'.
17 of the upright is to depart from e':
27 An ungodly man diggeth up e':
30 his lips he bringeth e' to pass.
17:11 An e' man seeketh only rebellion:
13 Whoso rewardeth e' for good,
13 e' shall not depart from his house.
19:23 he shall not be visited with e'.
20: 8 A king...scattereth away all e' with
22 Say not thou I will recompense e';
30 of a wound cleanseth away e':
21:10 The soul of the wicked desireth e':
22: 3 A prudent man foreseeth the e',
23: 6 bread of him that hath an e' eye,
24: 1 Be not thou envious against e' men,
8 He that deviseth to do e' shall be
19 Fret not thyself because of e' men.
20 shall be no reward to the e' man;
27:12 A prudent man foreseeth the e',
28: 5 *E'* men understand not judgment:
10 righteous to go astray in an e' way,
22 hasteth to be rich hath an e' eye,
29: 6 the transgression of an e' man
30:32 or if thou hast thought e', lay thine
31:12 She will do him good and not e'
Ec 2:21 This also is vanity and a great e'.
4: 3 e' work that is done under the sun.
5: 1 they consider not that they do e'.
13 a sore e' which I have seen
14 riches perish by e' travail: and he
16 this also is a sore e', that in all
6: 1 e' which I have seen under the sun,
2 and it is an e' disease.
8: 3 stand not in an e' thing; for he
5 the commandment shall feel no e'
11 sentence against an e' work is not
11 men is fully set in them to do e'.
12 a sinner do e' an hundred times,
9: 3 e' among all things that are done
3 heart of the sons of men is full of e',
12 fishes that are taken in an e' net,
12 sons of men snared in an e' time,
10: 5 e' which I have seen under the sun,
11: 2 not what e' shall be upon the earth.
10 and put away e' from thy flesh:
12: 1 while the e' days come not, nor the
14 it be good, or whether it be e'.
Isa 1:16 put away the e' of your doings
16 before mine eyes, cease to do e';
3: 9 rewarded e' unto themselves.

Isa 5:20 them that call e' good, and good e';
7: 5 taken e' counsel against thee,
15 that he may know to refuse the e',
16 child shall know to refuse the e',
13:11 will punish the world for their e',
31: 2 he also is wise, and will bring e',
32: 7 instruments also of the churl are e':
33:15 shutteth his eyes from seeing e';
41:23 do good, or do e', that we may be
45: 7 I make peace, and create e': I
47:11 Therefore shall e' come upon thee;
56: 2 his hand from doing any e'.
57: 1 righteous is taken away from the e'
59: 7 Their feet run to e', and they
15 he that departeth from e' maketh
65:12 hear; but did e' before mine eyes,
66: 4 but they did e' before mine eyes,
Jer 1:14 an e' shall break forth upon all the
2: 3 e' shall come upon them, saith the
19 it is an e' thing and bitter,
3: 5 hast spoken and done e' things
17 the imagination of their e' heart.
4: 4 because of the e' of your doings.
6 I will bring e' from the north,
22 they are wise to do e', but to
5:12 neither shall e' come upon us;
6: 1 for e' appeareth out of the north,
19 I will bring e' upon this people,
7:24 in the imagination of their e' heart,
30 Judah have done e' in my sight,
8: 3 them that remain of this e' family,
9: 3 they proceed from e' to e', and
10: 5 they cannot do e', neither also
11: 8 the imagination of their e' heart:
11 Behold, I will bring e' upon them,
15 thou doest e', then thou rejoicest.
17 hath pronounced e' against thee,
17 for the e' of the house of Israel,
23 e' upon the men of Anathoth,
12:14 all mine e' neighbours, that touch
13:10 e' people, which refuse to hear
23 ye...that are accustomed to do e'.
15:11 entreat thee well in the time of e'
16:10 all this great e' against us?
12 the imagination of his e' heart,
17:17 thou art my hope in the day of e'.
18 bring upon them the day of e',
18: 8 If that nation,...turn from their e',
8 I will repent of the e' that I thought
10 If it do e' in my sight, that it
11 I frame e' against you, and devise
11 ye now every one from his e' way,
12 do the imagination of his e' heart.
20 Shall e' be recompensed for good?
19: 3 I will bring e' upon this place,
15 will bring upon this city...all the e'
21:10 set my face against the city for e',
12 because of the e' of your doings.
23: 2 visit upon you the e' of your doings,
10 their course is e', and their force
12 I will bring e' upon them, even
17 No e' shall come upon you.
22 turned them from their e' way,
22 and from the e' of their doings.
24: 3 the e',very e',that cannot be eaten,
3 cannot be eaten, they are so e'.
8 the e' figs, which cannot be eaten,
8 cannot be eaten, they are so e';
25: 5 ye now every one from his e' way,
5 and from the e' of your doings,
29 I begin to bring e' on the city
32 e' shall go forth from nation to
26: 3 turn every man from his e' way,
3 that I may repent me of the e',
3 because of the e'of their doings.
13 the Lord will repent him of the e'
19 the Lord repented him of the e'
19 procure great e' against our souls,
28: 8 war, and of e', and of pestilence.
29:11 thoughts of peace, and not of e',
17 cannot be eaten, they are so e'.
32:23 all this e' to come upon them:
30 have only done e' before me from
32 the e' of the children of Israel
42 all this great e' upon this people,
35:15 now every man from his e' way,
17 all the e' that I have pronounced
36: 3 all the e' which I purpose to do
3 return every man from his e' way;
7 return every one from his e' way:
31 all the e' that I have pronounced
38: 9 these men have done e' in all
39:16 my words upon this city for e',
40: 2 pronounced this e' upon this place.
41:11 the e' that Ishmael...had done,
42: 6 it be good, or whether it be e',
10 I repent me of the e' that I have
17 escape from the e' that I will bring
44: 2 seen all the e' that I have brought
7 Wherefore commit ye this great e'
11 will set my face against you for e',
17 and were well, and saw no e'.
22 because of the e' of your doings,
23 this e' is happened unto you,
27 I will watch over them for e',
29 words shall surely stand...for e':
45: 5 I will bring e' upon all flesh,
48: 2 they have devised e' against it;
49:23 for they have heard e' tidings:
37 and I will bring e' upon them,
51:24 their e' that they have done in Zion
60 e' that should come upon Babylon,
64 the e' that I will bring upon her:
52: 2 which was e' in the eyes of the Lord,
La 3:38 High proceedeth not e' and good?
Eze 5:16 upon them the e' arrows of famine,

Eze 5:17 upon you famine and e' beasts,
6:10 said in vain that I would do this e'
11 all the e' abominations of the house
7: 5 An e', an only e', behold, is come.
14:22 the e' that I have brought upon
33:11 turn ye from your e' ways; for
34:25 will cause the e' beasts to cease
36:31 ye remember your own e' ways,
38:10 thou shalt think an e' thought:
Da 9:12 by bringing upon us a great e':
13 all this e' is come upon us:
14 hath the Lord watched upon the e',
Joel 2:13 and repenteth him of the e'.
Am 3: 6 shall there be e' in a city,
5:13 that time; for it is an e' time.
14 Seek good, and not e', that ye may
15 Hate the e', and love the good,
6: 3 Ye that put far away the e' day,
9: 4 will set mine eyes upon them for e',
10 The e' shall not overtake...us.
Jo 1: 7, 8 for whose cause that e' is upon us.
3: 8 turn every one from his e' way,
10 that they turned from their e' way;
10 God repented of the e', that he had
4: 2 and repentest thee of the e'.
Mic 1:12 e' came down from the Lord unto
2: 1 and work e' upon their beds!
3 against this family do I devise an e',
3 go haughtily: for this time is e'.
3: 2 Who hate the good, and love the e';
11 none e' can come upon us.
7: 3 they may do e' with both hands
Na 1:11 that imagineth e' against the Lord,
Hab 1:13 art of purer eyes than to behold e',
2: 9 that coveteth an e' covetousness
9 delivered from the powers of e'!
Zep 1:12 not do good, neither will he do e'.
3:15 thou shalt not see e' any more.
Zec 1: 4 Turn ye now from your e' ways,
4 and from your e' doings:
7:10 none of you imagine e' against his
8:17 let none of you imagine e' in your
Mal 1: 8 blind for the sacrifice, is it not e'?
8 offer the lame and sick, is it not e'?
2:17 Every one that doeth e' is good
M't 5:11 and shall say all manner of e'
37 is more than these cometh of e'.
39 unto you, That ye resist not e':
45 maketh his sun to rise on the e'
6:13 but deliver us from e':
23 if thine eye be e', thy whole body
34 Sufficient unto the day is the e'
7:11 If ye then, being e', know how to
17 corrupt tree bringeth forth e' fruit.
18 good tree cannot bring forth e' fruit,
9: 4 Wherefore think ye e' in your
12:34 how can ye, being e', speak good
35 an e' man out of the e' treasure
35 bringeth forth e' things.
39 An e' and adulterous generation
15:19 of the heart proceed e' thoughts,
20:15 Is thine eye e', because I am good?
24:48 and if that e' servant shall say
27:23 Why, what e' hath he done?
M'r 3: 4 on the sabbath day, or to do e'?
7:21 e' thoughts, adulteries,
22 lasciviousness, an e' eye,
23 these e' things come from within,
9:39 that can lightly speak e' of me.
15:14 Why, what e' hath he done?
Lu 6: 9 to do good, or to do e'?
22 and cast out your name as e',
35 unto the unthankful and to the e'.
45 and an e' man out of the e' treasure
45 bringeth forth that which is e':
7:21 and plagues, and of e' spirits;
8: 2 healed of e' spirits and infirmities,
11: 4 but deliver us from e'.
13 If ye then, being e', know how to
29 This is an e' generation: they seek
34 when thine eye is e', thy body also
16:25 likewise Lazarus e' things: but
23:22 Why, what e' hath he done?
Joh 3:19 light, because their deeds were e'.
20 every one that doeth e' hateth the
5:29 they that hath done e', unto the
7: 7 of it, that the works thereof are e'.
17:15 should keep them from the e'.
18:23 answered him, If I have spoken e',
23 bear witness of the e': but if well,
Ac 7: 6 entreat them e' four hundred
19 e' entreated our fathers, so that
9:13 of this man, how much e' he hath
14: 2 made their minds e' affected
19: 9 but spake e' of that way before the
12 the e' spirits went out of them.
13 call over them which had e' spirits
15 the e' spirit answered and said,
16 the man in whom the e' spirit was
23: 5 Thou shalt not speak e' of the ruler
9 We find no e' in this man:
24:20 have found any e' doing in me,
Ro 1:30 inventors of e' things, disobedient
2: 9 every soul of man that doeth e',
3: 8 that we say,) Let us do e', that good
7:19 but the e' which I would not,
21 do good, e' is present with me.
9:11 having done any good or e',
12: 9 Abhor that which is e'; cleave to
17 Recompense to no man e' for e'.
21 Be not overcome of e', but
21 but overcome e' with good.
13: 3 terror to good works, but to the e'.
4 But if thou do that which is e',
4 wrath upon him that doeth e'.
14:16 Let not then your good be e' spoken of:

Ro 14:20 but it is e' for that man who eateth
16:19 is good, and simple concerning e'.
1Co 10: 6 we should not lust after e' things,
30 why am I e' spoken of for that for
13: 5 easily provoked, thinketh no e';
15:33 e' communications corrupt good
2Co 6: 8 by e' report and good report:
13: 7 I pray to God that ye do no e';
Ga 1: 4 deliver us from this present e'
Eph 4:31 clamour, and e' speaking, be put
5:16 the time, because the days are e'.
6:13 be able to withstand in the e' day,
Ph'p 3: 2 of dogs, beware of e' workers,
Co 3: 5 e' concupiscence, and covetousness,
1Th 5:15 See that none render e' for e'
22 Abstain from all appearance of e'.
2Th 3: 3 stablish you, and keep you from e'.
1Ti 6: 4 envy, strife, railings, e' surmisings,
10 love of money is the root of all e':
2Ti 2: 9 as an e' doer, even unto bonds:
3:13 But e' men and seducers shall wax
4:14 the coppersmith did me much e':
18 deliver me from every e' work,
Tit 1:12 e' beasts, slow bellies.
2: 8 having no e' thing to say of you.
3: 2 speak e' of no man, to be no
Heb 3:12 any of you an e' heart of unbelief,
5:14 to discern both good and e'.
10:22 sprinkled from an e' conscience,
Jas 1:13 God cannot be tempted with e',
2: 4 are become judges of e' thoughts?
3: 8 an unruly e', full of deadly poison.
16 is confusion and every e' work.
4:11 Speak not e' one of another,
11 that speaketh e' of his brother,
11 speaketh e' of the law, and
16 boastings: all such rejoicing is e'.
1Pe 2: 1 and envies, and all e' speakings,
3: 9 Not rendering e' for e', or railing
10 refrain his tongue from e',
11 Let him eschew e', and do good;
12 Lord is against them that do e'.
16 speak e' of you, as of evildoers,
17 for well doing, than for e' doing.
4: 4 excess of riot, speaking e' of you:
14 on their part he is e' spoken of,
2Pe 2: 2 of truth shall be e' spoken of.
10 not afraid to speak e' of dignities
12 speak e' of the things that they
1Jo 3:12 Because his own works were e',
2Jo 11 is partaker of his e' deeds.
3Jo 11 follow not that which is e', but
11 that doeth e' hath not seen God.
Jude 8 despise dominion, and speak e' of
10 these speak e' of those things
Re 2: 2 canst not bear them which are e':

evil-affected See EVIL and AFFECTED.

evildoer See also EVIL and DOER; EVILDOERS.
Isa 9:17 every one is a hypocrite and an e'
1Pe 4:15 or as an e', or as a busybody

evildoers
Ps 37: 1 Fret not thyself because of e',
9 e' shall be cut off: but those that
94:16 will rise up for me against the e'?
119:115 Depart from me, ye e': for I will
Isa 1: 4 a seed of e', children that are
14:20 seed of e' shall never be renowned.
31: 2 arise against the house of the e',
Jer 20:13 soul of the poor from the hand of e'.
23:14 strengthen also the hands of e',
1Pe 2:12 they speak against you as e',
14 by him for the punishment of e',
3:16 speak evil of you, as of e',

evil-doing See EVIL and DOING.

evilfavouredness
De 17: 1 wherein is blemish,or any e':

Evil-merodach (*e''-vil-mer'-o-dak*)
2Ki 25:27 that E' king of Babylon in the year
Jer 52:31 E' king of Babylon in the first year

evils
De 31:17 e' and troubles shall befall them;
17 Are not these e' come upon us,
18 e' which they shall have wrought,
21 e' and troubles are befallen them,
Ps 40:12 innumerable e' have compassed me
Jer 2:13 my people have committed two e';
Eze 6: 9 the e' which they have committed
20:43 all your e' that ye have committed.
Lu 3:19 all the e' which Herod had done,

evil-speaking See EVIL and SPEAKING.

ewe See also EWES.
Ge 21:28 Abraham set seven e' lambs of
29 What mean these seven e' lambs
30 seven e' lambs shalt thou take
Le 14:10 and one e' lamb of the first year
22:28 cow or e', ye shall not kill it and
Nu 6:14 and one e' lamb of the first year
2Sa 12: 3 one little e' lamb, which he had

ewe-lamb See EWE and LAMB.

ewes
Ge 31:38 thy e' and thy she goats have not
32:14 two hundred e', and twenty rams,
Ps 78:71 following the e' great with young

exact See also EXACTED; EXACTETH.
De 15: 2 shall not e' it of his neighbour,
3 foreigner thou mayest e' it again:
Ne 5: 7 Ye e' usury, every one of his
10 and my brethren, . . .might e'
11 the corn,. . .that ye e' of them.
Ps 89:22 The enemy shall not e' upon him;
Isa 58: 3 pleasure, and e' all your labours.
Lu 3:13 E' no more than that which is

exacted
2Ki 15:20 Menahem e' the money of Israel,
23:35 he e' the silver and the gold of

exacteth
Job 11: 6 God e' of thee less than thine

exaction See also EXACTIONS.
Ne 10:31 year, and the e' of every debt.

exactions
Eze 45: 9 take away your e' from my people.

exactors
Isa 60:17 peace, and thine e' righteousness.

exalt See also EXALTED; EXALTEST; EXALTETH.
Ex 15: 2 my father's God, and I will e' him.
1Sa 2:10 and e' the horn of his anointed.
Job 17: 4 therefore shalt thou not e' them.
Ps 34: 3 and let us e' his name together.
37:34 shall e' thee to inherit the land:
66: 7 let not the rebellious e' themselves.
92:10 But my horn shalt thou e' like the
99: 5 E' ye the Lord our God, and
9 E' the Lord our God, and worship
107:32 e' him also in the congregation
118:28 thou art my God, I will e' thee.
140: 8 device; lest they e' themselves.
Pr 4: 8 E' her, and she shall promote thee:
Isa 13: 2 e' the voice unto them, shake
14:13 I will e' my throne above the stars
25: 1 thou art my God; I will e' thee,
Eze 21:26 e' him that is low, and abase him
29:15 neither shall it e' itself any more
31:14 e' themselves for their height,
Da 11:14 the robbers of thy people shall e'
36 shall e' himself, and magnify
Ho 11: 7 most High, none at all would e' him.
Ob 4 Though thou e' thyself as the
M't 23:12 And whosoever shall e' himself
2Co 11:20 a man e' himself, if a man smite
1Pe 5: 6 that he may e' you in due time:

exalted
Nu 24: 7 and his kingdom shall be e'.
1Sa 2: 1 mine horn is e' in the Lord:
2Sa 5:12 had e' his kingdom for his people
22:47 and e' be the God of the rock of
1Ki 1: 5 the son of Haggith e' himself,
14: 7 I e' thee from among the people,
16: 2 Forasmuch as I e' thee out of the
2Ki 19:22 against whom hast thou e' thy
1Ch 29:11 thou art e' as head above all.
Ne 9: 5 name, which is e' above all
Job 5:11 which mourn may be e' to safety.
24:24 They are e' for a little while,
36: 7 them forever, and they are e'.
Ps 12: 8 when the vilest men are e'.
13: 2 how long shall mine enemy be e'
18:46 let the God of my salvation be e'.
21:13 Be thou e', Lord, in thine own
46:10 I will be e' among the heathen,
10 I will be e' in the earth.
47: 9 belong unto God: he is greatly e'.
57: 5 thou e', O God, above the heavens;
11 thou e', O God, above the heavens:
75:10 horns of the righteous shall be e'.
89:16 thy righteousness shall they be e'.
17 in thy favour our horn shall be e'.
19 e' one chosen out of the people.
24 in my name shall his horn be e'.
97: 9 thou art e' far above all gods.
108: 5 thou e', O God, above the heavens:
112: 9 his horn shall be e' with honour.
118:16 The right hand of the Lord is e':
Pr 11:11 of the upright the city is e':
Isa 2: 2 and shall be e' above the hills;
11, 17 Lord alone shall be e' in that
5:16 But the Lord of hosts shall be e'
12: 4 make mention that his name is e'.
30:18 and therefore he will be e',
33: 5 The Lord is e', for he dwelleth on
10 now will I be e'; now will I lift up
37:23 against whom hast thou e' thy voice,
40: 4 Every valley shall be e', and every
49:11 and my highways shall be e'.
52:13 he shall be e' and extolled, and be
Eze 17:24 have e' the low tree, have dried
19:11 was e' among the thick branches,
31: 5 Therefore his height was e' above
Ho 13: 1 Ephraim e' himself in Israel;
6 filled, and their heart was e';
Mic 4: 1 and it shall be e' above the hills;
M't 11:23 which art e' unto heaven, shalt be
23:12 shall humble himself, shalt be e'.
Lu 1:52 seats, and e' them of low degree.
10:15 which art e' to heaven, shalt be
14:11 that humbleth himself shall be e'.
18:14 that humbleth himself shall be e'.
Ac 2:33 being by the right hand of God e',
5:31 Him hath God e' with his right
13:17 e' the people when they dwelt as
2Co 11: 7 abasing myself that ye might be e',
12: 7 lest I should be e' above measure
7 lest I should be e' above measure.
Ph'p 2: 9 God also hath highly e' him,
Jas 1: 9 low degree rejoice in that he is e':

exaltest
Ex 9:17 e' thou thyself against my people,

exalteth
Job 36:22 Behold, God e' by his power:
Ps 148:14 also e' the horn of his people,
Pr 14:29 he that is hasty of spirit e' folly.
34 Righteousness e' a nation: but sin
17:19 e' his gate seeketh destruction.
Lu 14:11 e' himself shall be abased;
18:14 one that e' himself shall be abased;
2Co 10: 5 every high thing that e' itself
2Th 2: 4 Who opposeth and e' himself

examination
Ac 25:26 that, after e' had, I might have

examine See also EXAMINED; EXAMINING.
Ezr 10:16 the tenth month to e' the matter.
Ps 26: 2 E' me, O Lord, and prove me;
1Co 9: 3 to them that do e' me in this,
11:28 let a man e' himself, and so let
2Co 13: 5 E' yourselves, whether ye be in

examined
Lu 23:14 I, having e' him before you,
Ac 4: 9 If we this day be e' of the good deed
12:19 found him not, he e' the keepers,
22:24 he should be e' by scourging;
29 him which should have e' him:
28:18 Who, when they had e' me,

examining
Ac 24: 8 e' of whom thyself mayest take

example See also ENSAMPLE; EXAMPLES.
M't 1:19 make her a public e', was minded
Joh 13:15 For I have given you an e', that
1Ti 4:12 be thou an e' of the believers,
Heb 4:11 after the same e' of unbelief.
8: 5 serve unto the e' and shadow
Jas 5:10 for an e' of suffering affliction,
1Pe 2:21 leaving us an e', that ye should
Jude 7 for an e', suffering the vengeance

examples
1Co 10: 6 Now these things were our e',

exceed See also EXCEEDED; EXCEEDEST; EXCEEDETH; EXCEEDING.
De 25: 3 he may give him, and not e':
3 lest, if he should e', and beat him
M't 5:20 your righteousness shall e' the
2Co 3: 9 of righteousness e' in glory.

exceeded
1Sa 20:41 one with another, until David e'.
1Ki 10:23 So king Solomon e' all the kings
Job 36: 9 transgressions that they have e'.

exceedest
2Ch 9: 6 thou e' the fame that I heard.

exceedeth
1Ki 10: 7 thy wisdom and prosperity e' the

exceeding See also EXCEEDINGLY.
Ge 15: 1 shield, and thy e' great reward.
17: 6 And I will make thee e' fruitful,
27:34 with a great and e' bitter cry,
Ex 1: 7 multiplied, and waxed e' mighty;
19:16 the voice of the trumpet e' loud;
Nu 14: 7 to search it, is an e' good land.
1Sa 2: 3 Talk no more so e' proudly;
2Sa 8: 8 king David took e' much brass.
12: 2 The rich man had e' many flocks
1Ki 4:29 wisdom and understanding e' much,
7:47 because they were e' many:
1Ch 20: 2 also e' much spoil out of the city.
22: 5 the Lord must be e' magnifical,
2Ch 11:12 and made them e' strong,
14:14 for there was e' much spoil in
16:12 until his disease was e' great:
32:27 Hezekiah had e' much riches and
Ps 21: 6 him e' glad with thy countenance.
43: 4 altar of God, unto God my e' joy:
119:96 thy commandment is e' broad.
Pr 30:24 the earth, but they are e' wise:
Ec 7:24 That which is far off, and e' deep,
Jer 48:29 pride of Moab, (he is e' proud)
Eze 9: 9 Israel and Judah is e' great,
16:13 and thou wast e' beautiful, and
23:15 e' in dyed attire upon their heads,
37:10 upon their feet, an e' great army.
47:10 fish of the great sea, e' many.
Da 3:22 and the furnace e' hot, the flame
6:23 was the king e' glad for him,
7:19 e' dreadful, whose teeth were of
8: 9 waxed e' great, toward the south,
Jon 3: 3 Nineveh was an e' great city
4: 6 Jonah was e' glad of the gourd.
M't 2:10 they rejoiced with e' great joy.
16 of the wise men, was e' wroth,
4: 8 him up into an e' high mountain,
5:12 Rejoice, and be e' glad: for great
8:28 coming out of the tombs, e' fierce,
17:23 And they were e' sorry.
26:22 And they were e' sorrowful, and
38 soul is e' sorrowful, even unto
M'r 6:26 And the king was e' sorry; yet for
9: 3 became shining, e' white as snow;
14:34 soul is e' sorrowful unto death:
Lu 23: 8 Herod saw Jesus he was e' glad:
Ac 7:20 and was e' fair, and nourished
Ro 7:13 sin...might become e' sinful.
2Co 4:17 a far more e' and eternal
7: 4 am e' joyful in all our tribulation.
9:14 for the e' grace of God in you.
Eph 1:19 And what is the e' greatness of
2: 7 shew the e' riches of his grace
3:20 e' abundantly above all that we
1Ti 1:14 Lord was e' abundant with faith
1Pe 4:13 ye may be glad also with e' joy.
2Pe 1: 4 us e' great and precious promises:
Jude 24 the presence of his glory with e' joy,
Re 16:21 the plague thereof was e' great.

exceedingly See also EXCEEDING.
Ge 7:19 prevailed e' upon the earth;
13:13 and sinners before the Lord e'.
16:10 I will multiply thy seed e',
17: 2 and thee, and will multiply thee e'.
20 multiply him e'; twelve princes
27:33 And Isaac trembled very e',
30:43 And the man increased e', and
47:27 and grew, and multiplied e'.
1Sa 26:21 the fool, and have erred e'.
2Sa 13:15 Then Amnon hated her e';
2Ki 10: 4 But they were e' afraid, and said,
1Ch 29:25 the Lord magnified Solomon e'
2Ch 1: 1 was with him, and magnified him e'.
17:12 great e'; and he built in Judah
26: 8 for he strengthened himself e'.
Ne 2:10 it grieved them e' that there was
Es 4: 4 Then was the queen e' grieved:
Job 3:22 Which rejoice e', and are glad,
Ps 68: 3 yea, let them e' rejoice.
106:14 But lusted e' in the wilderness,
119:167 testimonies; and I love them e'.
123: 3 for we are e' filled with contempt.
4 soul is e' filled with the scorning
Isa 24:19 dissolved, the earth is moved e'.
Da 7: 7 strong e'; and it had great iron
Jon 1:10 Then were the men e' afraid, and
16 Then the men feared the Lord e',
4: 1 it displeased Jonah e', and he was
M't 19:25 they were e' amazed, saying, Who
M'r 4:41 they feared e', and said one
15:14 they cried out the more e', Crucify
Ac 16:20 being Jews, do e' trouble our city,
26:11 and being e' mad against them,
27:18 we being e' tossed with a tempest,
2Co 7:13 e' the more joyed we for the joy of
Ga 1:14 more e' zealous of the traditions
1Th 3:10 Night and day praying e'
2Th 1: 3 your faith groweth e', and the charity
Heb 12:21 Moses said, I e' fear and quake:)

excel See also EXCELLED; EXCELLEST; EXCELLETH.
Ge 49: 4 as water, thou shalt not e';
1Ch 15:21 with harps on the Sheminith to e'.
Ps 103:20 that e' in strength, that do his
Isa 10:10 whose graven images did e' them of
1Co 14:12 that ye may e' to the edifying of

excelled
1Ki 4:30 Solomon's wisdom e' the wisdom

excellency
Ge 49: 3 e' of dignity, and the e' of power:
Ex 15: 7 the greatness of thine e' thou hast
De 33:26 and in his e' on the sky.
29 and who is the sword of thy e'!
Job 4:21 Doth not their e' which is in them
13:11 Shall not his e' make you afraid?
20: 6 Though his e' mount up to the
37: 4 with the voice of his e'; and he will
40:10 thyself now with majesty and e';
Ps 47: 4 the e' of Jacob whom he loved.
62: 4 to cast him down from his e':
68:34 his e' is over Israel, and his
Ec 7:12 but the e' of knowledge is, that
Isa 13:19 the beauty of the Chaldees' e',
35: 2 the e' of Carmel and Sharon,
2 of the Lord, and the e' of our God.
60:15 I will make thee an eternal e',
Eze 24:21 the e' of your strength, the desire
Am 6: 8 I abhor the e' of Jacob, and hate
8: 7 hath sworn by the e' of Jacob,
Na 2: 2 turned away the e' of Jacob,
2 as the e' of Israel:
1Co 2: 1 you, came not with e' of speech
2Co 4: 7 the e' of the power may be of God,
Ph'p 3: 8 the e' of the knowledge of Christ

excellent
Es 1: 4 and the honour of his e' majesty
Job 37:23 he is e' in power, and in judgment,
Ps 8: 1, 9 e' is thy name in all the earth!
16: 3 to the e', in whom is all my delight.
36: 7 e' is thy loving kindness, O God!
76: 4 Thou art more glorious and e' than
141: 5 it shall be an e' oil, which shall
148:13 his name alone is e'; his glory is
150: 2 him according to his e' greatness.
Pr 8: 6 for I will speak of e' things;
12:26 The righteous is more e' than his
17: 7 E' speech becometh not a fool;
27 of understanding is of an e' spirit.
22:20 not I written to thee e' things in
Ca 5:15 Lebanon, e' as the cedars.
Isa 4: 2 the fruit of the earth shall be e'
12: 5 for he hath done e' things:
28:29 in counsel, and e' in working.
Eze 16: 7 thou art come to e' ornaments:
Da 2:31 image, whose brightness was e',
4:36 and e' majesty was added unto me,
5:12 Forasmuch as an e' spirit, and
14 and e' wisdom is found in thee.
6: 3 because an e' spirit was in him;
Lu 1: 3 in order, most e' Theophilus,
Ac 23:26 unto the most e' governor Felix
Ro 2:18 the things that are more e', being
1Co 12:31 shew I unto you a more e' way.
Ph'p 1:10 ye may approve things that are e';
Heb 1: 4 obtained a more e' name than they.
8: 6 hath he obtained a more e' ministry,
11: 4 a more e' sacrifice than Cain,
2Pe 1:17 a voice to him from the e' glory,

excellest
Pr 31:29 virtuously, but thou e' them all.

excelleth
Ec 2:13 Then I saw that wisdom e' folly,
13 as far as light e' darkness.
2Co 3:10 by reason of the glory that e'.

except See also EXCEPTED.
Ge 31:42 E' the God of my father, the God
32:26 let thee go, e' thou bless me.
42:15 e' your youngest brother come
43: 3 e' your brother be with you.

Ge 43: 5 not see my face, e' your brother
10 e' we had lingered, surely now we
44:23 E' your youngest brother
26 e' our youngest brother be with
47:26 e' the land of the priests only,
Nu 16:13 e' thou make thyself altogether
De 32:30 e' their Rock had sold
Jos 7:12 e' ye destroy the accursed
1Sa 25:34 e' thou hadst hasted and
2Sa 3: 9 God to Abner, and more also, e',
13 not see my face, e' thou first
5: 6 E' thou take away the blind
2Ki 4:24 not thy riding for me, e' I bid
Es 2:14 e' the king delighted in her,
4:11 e' such to whom the king shall
Ps 127: 1 E' the Lord build the house,
1 e' the Lord keep the city, the
Pr 4:16 sleep not, e' they have done
Isa 1: 9 E' the Lord of hosts had left unto
Da 2:11 e' the gods, whose dwelling is not
3:28 nor any god, e' their own God.
6: 5 Daniel, e' we find it against him
Am 3: 3 walk together, e' they be agreed?
M't 5:20 e' your righteousness shall exceed
12:29 e' he first bind the strong man?
18: 3 E' ye be converted, and become as
19: 9 e' it be for fornication, and shall
24:22 e' those days should be shortened,
26:42 e' I drink it, thy will be done.
M'r 3:27 e' he will first bind the strong man;
7: 3 e' they wash their hands oft,
4 e' they wash, they eat not.
13:20 e' that the Lord had shortened
Lu 9:13 e' we should go and buy meat for
13: 3, 5 e' ye repent, ye shall all likewise
Joh 3: 2 that thou doest, e' God be with him.
3 E' a man be born again, he cannot
5 E' a man be born of water and of
27 e' it be given him from heaven.
4:48 E' ye see signs and wonders, ye
6:44 e' the Father which hath sent me
53 E' ye eat the flesh of the Son of
65 e' it were given unto him of my
12:24 E' a corn of wheat fall into the
15: 4 e' it abide in the vine; no more can
4 no more can ye, e' ye abide in me.
19:11 e' it were given thee from above:
20:25 E' I shall see in his hands the print
Ac 8: 1 were all scattered...e' the apostles.
31 How can I, e' some man should
15: 1 E' ye be circumcised after the
24:21 E' it be for this one voice, that I
26:29 such as I am, e' these bonds.
27:31 E' these abide in the ship, ye
Ro 7: 7 e' the law had said, Thou shalt not
9:29 E' the Lord of Sabaoth had left us
10:15 e' they be sent, as it is written,
1Co 7: 5 e' it be with consent for a time,
14: 5 tongues, e' he interpret, that
6 e' I shall speak to you either by
7 e' they give a distinction in the
9 e' ye utter by the tongue words
15:36 sowest is not quickened, e' it die:
2Co 12:13 e' it be that I myself was not
13: 5 is in you, e' ye be reprobates?
2Th 2: 3 e' there come a falling away first,
2Ti 2: 5 not crowned, e' he strive lawfully.
Re 2: 5 out of his place, e' thou repent.
22 e' they repent of their deeds.

excepted
1Co 15:27 that he is e', which did put

excess
M't 23:25 they are full of extortion and e'.
Eph 5:18 drunk with wine, wherein is e';
1Pe 4: 3 e' of wine, revellings,
4 e' of riot, speaking evil of you:

exchange
Ge 47:17 them bread in e' for horses, and
Le 27:10 and the e' thereof shall be holy.
Job 28:17 and the e' of it shall not be
Eze 48:14 e', nor alienate the first fruits
M't 16:26 shall a man give in e' for his soul?
M'r 8:37 shall a man give in e' for his soul?

exchangers
M't 25:27 to have put my money to the e',

exclude See also EXCLUDED.
Ga 4:17 yea, they would e' you, that ye

excluded
Ro 3:27 Where is boasting then? It is e'.

excusable See INEXCUSABLE.

excuse See also EXCUSED; EXCUSING.
Lu 14:18 with one consent began to make e'.
Ro 1:20 so that they are without e':
2Co 12:19 that we e' ourselves unto you?

excused
Lu 14:18 and see it: I pray thee have me e'.
19 prove them: I pray thee have me e'.

excusing
Ro 2:15 accusing or else e' one another;)

execration
Jer 42:18 be an e', and an astonishment,
44:12 shall be an e', and an astonishment,

execute See also EXECUTED; EXECUTEST; EXECUTETH; EXECUTING.
Ex 12:12 will e' judgment: I am the Lord.
Nu 5:30 priest shall e' upon her all this law.
8:11 may e' the service of the Lord.
De 10:18 e' the judgment of the fatherless
1Ki 6:12 and e' my judgments, and keep all
Ps 119:84 when wilt thou e' judgment on
149: 7 To e' vengeance upon the heathen,
9 To e' upon them the judgment
Isa 16: 3 Take counsel, e' judgment; make
Jer 7: 5 thoroughly e' judgment between
21:12 E' judgment in the morning, and
22: 3 saith the Lord; E' ye judgment
23: 5 and prosper, and shall e' judgment
33:15 and he shall e' judgment and
Eze 5: 8 and will e' judgments in the midst
10 and I will e' judgments in thee,
15 when I shall e' judgment in thee
11: 9 and will e' judgments among you.
16:41 and e' judgments upon thee in the
25:11 I will e' judgments upon Moab;
17 will e' great vengeance upon them
30:14 and will e' judgments in No.
19 Thus will I e' judgments in Egypt:
45: 9 e' judgment and justice, take away
Ho 11: 9 not e' the fierceness of mine anger
Mic 5:15 And I will e' vengeance in anger
7: 9 my cause, and e' judgment for me:
Zec 7: 9 E' true judgment, and shew
8:16 e' the judgment of truth and peace
Joh 5:27 authority to e' judgment also,
Ro 13: 4 a revenger to e' wrath upon him
Jude 15 To e' judgment upon all, and to

executed See also EXECUTEDST.
Nu 33: 4 gods also the Lord e' judgments
De 33:21 he e' the justice of the Lord,
2Sa 8:15 David e' judgment and justice
1Ch 6:10 (he it is that e' the priest's office in the
18:14 e' judgment and justice among
24: 2 and Ithamar e' the priest's office,
2Ch 24:24 they e' judgment against Joash.
Ezr 7:26 judgment be e' speedily upon him,
Ps 106:30 stood up Phinehas, and e' judgment:
Ec 8:11 an evil work is not e' speedily,
Jer 23:20 until he have e', and till he have
Eze 11:12 neither e' my judgments, but have
18: 8 hath e' true judgment between
17 hath e' my judgments, hath walked
20:24 they had not e' my judgments,
23:10 for they had e' judgment upon her.
28:22 I shall have e' judgments in her,
26 when I have e' judgments upon all
39:21 see my judgment that I have e',
Lu 1: 8 that while he e' the priest's office

executedst
1Sa 28:18 e' his fierce wrath upon Amalek,

executest
Ps 99: 4 e' judgment and righteousness in

executeth
Ps 9:16 by the judgment which he e':
103: 6 The Lord e' righteousness and
146: 7 e' judgment for the oppressed:
Isa 46:11 the man that e' my counsel from
Jer 5: 1 if there be any that e' judgment,
Joe 2:11 for he is strong that e' his word:

executing
2Ki 10:30 thou hast done well in e' that
2Ch 11:14 them off from e' the priest's office
22: 8 when Jehu was e' judgment upon

execution
Es 9: 1 decree drew near to be put in e',

executioner
M'r 6:27 king sent an e', and commanded

exempted
1Ki 15:22 none was e': and they took away

exercise See also EXERCISED; EXERCISETH.
Ps 131: 1 do I e' myself in great matters,
Jer 9:24 the Lord which e' lovingkindness,
M't 20:25 Gentiles e' dominion over them,
25 are great e' authority upon them.
M'r 10:42 the Gentiles e' lordship over them;
42 great ones e' authority upon them.
Lu 22:25 kings of the earth e' lordship
25 they that e' authority upon them
Ac 24:16 herein do I e' myself, to have alway
1Ti 4: 7 e' thyself rather unto godliness.
8 For bodily e' profiteth little: but

exercised
Ec 1:13 sons of man to be e' therewith.
3:10 to the sons of men to be e' in it.
Eze 22:29 and e' robbery, and have vexed
Heb 5:14 e' to discern both good and evil.
12:11 unto them which are e' thereby.
2Pe 2:14 have e' with covetous practices;

exerciseth
Re 13:12 e' all the power of the first beast

exhort See also EXHORTED; EXHORTETH; EXHORTING.
Ac 2:40 did he testify and e', saying, Save
27:22 now I e' you to be of good cheer:
2Co 9: 5 it necessary to e' the brethren,
1Th 4: 1 and e' you by the Lord Jesus,
5:14 we e' you, brethren, warn them
2Th 3:12 and e' by our Lord Jesus Christ,
1Ti 2: 1 I e' therefore, that, first of all,
6: 2 These things teach and e'.
2Ti 4: 2 rebuke, e' with all long suffering
Tit 1: 9 to e' and to convince the gainsayers.
2: 6 likewise e' to be sober minded.
9 E' servants to be obedient unto their
15 speak, and e', and rebuke with all
Heb 3:13 But e' one another daily, while it
1Pe 5: 1 I e', who am also an elder,
Jude 3 me to write unto you, and e' you

exhortation
Lu 3:18 e' preached he unto the people.
Ac 13:15 any word of e' for the people,
20: 2 and had given them much e',
Ro 12: 8 Or he that exhorteth, on e':
1Co 14: 3 edification, and e', and comfort.
2Co 8:17 For indeed he accepted the e';
1Th 2: 3 For our e' was not of deceit,
1Ti 4:13 to reading, to e', to doctrine.
Heb 12: 5 forgotten the e' which speaketh
13:22 brethren, suffer the word of e':

exhorted
Ac 11:23 and e' them all, that with purpose
15:32 e' the brethren with many words,
1Th 2:11 As ye know how we e' and

exhorteth
Ro 12: 8 Or he that e', on exhortation:

exhorting
Ac 14:22 e' them to continue in the faith,
18:27 e' the disciples to receive him:
Heb 10:25 but e' one another: and so much
1Pe 5:12 written briefly, e', and testifying

exile
2Sa 15:19 art a stranger, and also an e'.
Isa 51:14 The captive e' hasteneth that he

exorcists
Ac 19:13 vagabond Jews, e', took upon them

expectation
Ps 9:18 the e' of the poor shall not perish
62: 5 my e' is from him.
Pr 10:28 the e' of the wicked shall perish.
11: 7 man dieth, his e' shall perish:
23 the e' of the wicked is wrath.
23:18 and thine e' shall not be cut off.
24:14 and thy e' shall not be cut off.
Isa 20: 5 Ethiopia their e', and of Egypt
6 such is our e' whither we flee
Zec 9: 5 Ekron; for her e' shall be ashamed;
Lu 3:15 as the people were in e',
Ac 12:11 all the e' of the people of the Jews.
Ro 8:19 the earnest e' of the creature
Ph'p 1:20 to my earnest e' and my hope,

expected
Jer 29:11 not of evil, to give you an e' end.

expecting
Ac 3: 5 e' to receive something of them.
Heb 10:13 e' till his enemies be made his

expedient
Joh 11:50 Nor consider that it is e' for us,
16: 7 It is e' for you that I go away:
18:14 it was e' that one man should die
1Co 6:12 unto me, but all things are not e':
10:23 but all things are not e':
2Co 8:10 this is e' of you, who have begun
12: 1 not e' for me doubtless to glory.

expel See also EXPELLED.
Jos 23: 5 shall e' them from before you,
J'g 11: 7 Did not ye hate me, and e' me

expelled
Jos 13:13 of Israel e' not the Geshurites, *
J'g 1:20 e' thence the three sons of Anak.
2Sa 14:14 his banished be not e' from him.
Ac 13:50 and e' them out of their coasts.

expences
Ezr 6: 4 and let the e' be given out of the
8 forthwith e' be given unto these

expense See EXPENCES.

experience
Ge 30:27 by e' that the Lord hath blessed
Ec 1:16 my heart had great e' of wisdom
Ro 5: 4 And patience, e'; and e', hope:

experiment
2Co 9:13 by the e' of this ministration

expert
1Ch 12:33 e' in war, with all instruments of
35 of the Danites e' in war twenty
36 battle, e' in war, forty thousand.
Ca 3: 8 being e' in war: every man hath
Jer 50: 9 shall be as of a mighty e' man;
Ac 26: 3 be e' in all customs and questions

expired
1Sa 18:26 and the days were not e'.
2Sa 11: 1 after the year was e', at the time
1Ch 17:11 when thy days be e' that thou
20: 1 after the year was e', at the time
2Ch 36:10 was e', king Nebuchadnezzar
Es 1: 5 And when these days were e',
Eze 43:27 these days are e', it shall be,
Ac 7:30 And when forty years were e',
Re 20: 7 when the thousand years are e',

exploits
Da 11:28 and he shall do e', and return to
32 God shall be strong, and do e'.

expound See also EXPOUNDED.
J'g 14:14 they could not in three days e'

expounded
J'g 14:19 unto them which e' the riddle.
M'r 4:34 he e' all things to his disciples.
Lu 24:27 he e' unto them in all the
Ac 11: 4 e' it by order unto them, saying,
18:26 and e' unto him the way of God
28:23 to whom he e' and testified the

express See also EXPRESSED.
Heb 1: 3 and the e' image of his person,

expressed
Nu 1:17 men which are e' by their names:
1Ch 12:31 which were e' by name, to come
16:41 were e' by name, to give thanks
2Ch 28:15 which were e' by name rose up,
31:19 the men that were e' by name, to
Ezr 8:20 all of them were e' by name.

expressly
1Sa 20:21 If I e' say unto the lad, Behold,
Eze 1: 3 word of the Lord came e' unto Ezekiel
1Ti 4: 1 Now the Spirit speaketh e',
extend See also EXTENDED; EXTENDETH.
Ps 109:12 Let there be none to e' mercy
Isa 66:12 I will e' peace to her like a river,
extended
Ezr 7:28 e' mercy unto me before the king,
9: 9 hath e' mercy unto us in the sight
extendeth
Ps 16: 2 my goodness e' not to thee;
extinct
Job 17: 1 breath is corrupt, my days are e',
Isa 43:17 they are e', they are quenched as
extol See also EXTOLLED.
Ps 30: 1 I will e' thee, O Lord; for thou
68: 4 e' him that rideth upon the
145: 1 I will e' thee, my God, O king;
Da 4:37 I Nebuchadnezzar praise and e'
extolled
Ps 66:17 and he was e' with my tongue.
Isa 52:13 he shall be exalted and e', and be
extortion
Eze 22:12 gained of thy neighbours by e',
M't 23:25 they are full of e' and excess.
extortioner See also EXTORTIONERS.
Ps 109:11 Let the e' catch all that he hath;
Isa 16: 4 the e' is at an end, the spoiler
1Co 5:11 a railer, or a drunkard, or an e';
extortioners
Lu 18:11 not as other men are, e', unjust,
1Co 5:10 covetous, or e', or with idolaters;
6:10 revilers, nor e', shall inherit the
extreme
De 28:22 an e' burning, and with the sword,
extremity
Job 35:15 he knoweth it not in great e':
eye See also EYEBROWS; EYED; EYELIDS; EYE'S EYES; EYESALVE; EYESERVICE; EYESIGHT; EYE-WITNESSES.
Ex 21:24 E' for e', tooth for tooth, hand for
26 if a man smite the e' of his servant,
26 or the e' of his maid, that it perish;
Le 21:20 or that hath a blemish in his e',
24:20 e' for e', tooth for tooth: as he
De 7:16 e' shall have no pity upon them:
13: 8 neither shall thine e' pity him,
15: 9 thine e' be evil against thy poor
19:13 Thine e' shall not pity him, but
21 And thine e' shall not pity;
21 but life shall go for life, e' for e',
25:12 hand, thine e' shall not pity her.
28:54 e' shall be evil toward his brother,
56 e' shall be evil toward the husband
32:10 he kept him as the apple of his e'.
34: 7 his e' was not dim, nor his natural
1Sa 24:10 but mine e' spared thee; and I
2Sa 22:25 to my cleanness in his e' sight.
Ezr 5: 5 e' of their God was upon the elders
Job 7: 7 mine e' shall no more see good.
8 The e' of him that hath seen me
10:18 the ghost, and no e' had seen me!
13: 1 Lo, mine e' hath seen all this,
16:20 mine e' poureth out tears unto God.
17: 2 e' continue in their provocation?
7 e' also is dim by reason of sorrow,
20: 9 The e' also which saw him shall see
24:15 The e' also of the adulterer
15 twilight, saying, No e' shall see me:
28: 7 the vulture's e' hath not seen:
10 his e' seeth every precious thing.
29:11 and when the e' saw me, it gave
42: 5 but now mine e' seeth thee.
Ps 6: 7 e' is consumed because of grief;
17: 8 Keep me as the apple of the e',
31: 9 mine e' is consumed with grief,
32: 8 I will guide thee with mine e'.
33:18 the e' of the Lord is upon them
35:19 neither let them wink with the e'
21 Aha, aha, our e' hath seen it.
54: 7 and mine e' hath seen his desire
88: 9 e' mourneth by reason of affliction:
92:11 Mine e' also shall see my desire
94: 9 he that formed the e', shall he not
Pr 7: 2 my law as the apple of thine e'.
10:10 that winketh with the e' causeth
20:12 The hearing ear, and the seeing e',
22: 9 He that hath a bountiful e' shall
23: 6 bread of him that hath an evil e',
28:22 hasteth to be rich hath an evil e',
30:17 The e' that mocketh at his father,
Ec 1: 8 the e' is not satisfied with seeing,
4: 8 is his e' satisfied with riches;
Isa 13:18 their e' shall not spare children.
52: 8 they shall see e' to e', when the
64: 4 neither hath the e' seen, O God,
Jer 13:17 mine e' shall weep sore, and run
La 1:16 mine e', mine e' runneth down with
2: 4 slew all that were pleasant to the e'
18 let not the apple of thine e' cease.
3:48 Mine e' runneth down with rivers of
49 Mine e' trickleth down, and ceaseth
51 Mine e' affecteth mine heart
Eze 5:11 neither shall mine e' spare, neither
7: 4 And mine e' shall not spare thee,
9 And mine e' shall not spare, neither
8:18 mine e' shall not spare, neither
9: 5 let not your e' spare, neither have
10 for me also, mine e' shall not spare,
16: 5 None e' pitied thee, to do any of
Eze 20:17 e' spared them from destroying
Mic 4:11 and let our e' look upon Zion.
Zec 2: 8 you toucheth the apple of his e'.
11:17 his arm, and upon his right e':
17 right e' shall be utterly darkened.
M't 5:29 if thy right e' offend thee, pluck it
38 e' for an e', and a tooth for a tooth:
6:22 The light of the body is the e':
22 if therefore thine e' be single,
23 But if thine e' be evil, thy whole
7: 3 mote that is in thy brother's e',
3 the beam that is in thine own e'?
4 me pull out the mote out of thine e';
4 behold, a beam is in thine own e'?
5 out the beam out of thine own e';
5 out the mote out of thy brother's e'.
18: 9 if thine e' offend thee, pluck it out,
9 thee to enter into life with one e',
19:24 to go through the e' of a needle,
20:15 Is thine e' evil, because I am good?
M'r 7:22 an evil e', blasphemy, pride,
9:47 if thine e' offend thee, pluck it out,
47 the kingdom of God with one e',
10:25 to go through the e' of a needle,
Lu 6:41 the mote that is in thy brother's e',
41 the beam that is in thine own e'?
42 out the mote that is in thine e',
42 the beam that is in thine own e'?
42 first the beam out of thine own e',
42 the mote that is in thy brother's e'.
11:34 The light of the body is the e':
34 therefore when thine e' is single,
34 but when thine e' is evil, thy
18:25 camel to go through a needle's e',
1Co 2: 9 E' hath not seen, nor ear heard,
12:16 Because I am not the e', I am not
17 If the whole body were an e', where
21 the e' cannot say unto the hand,
15:52 in the twinkling of an e', at the
Re 1: 7 every e' shall see him, and they
eyebrows
Le 14: 9 and his e', even all his hair
eyed
Ge 29:17 Leah was tender e'; but Rachel
1Sa 18: 9 Saul e' David from that day
eyelids
Job 16:16 on my e' is the shadow of death;
41:18 eyes are like the e' of the morning.
Ps 11: 4 his e' try, the children of men.
132: 4 mine eyes, or slumber to mine e',
Pr 4:25 thine e' look straight before thee.
6: 4 thine eyes, nor slumber to thine e'.
25 neither let her take thee with her e'.
30:13 and their e' are lifted up.
Jer 9:18 and our e' gush out with waters.
eye's
Ex 21:26 let him go free for his e' sake.
eyes
Ge 3: 5 then your e' shall be opened, and
6 and that it was pleasant to the e',
7 the e' of them both were opened,
6: 8 found grace in the e' of the Lord.
13:10 Lot lifted up his e', and beheld
14 Lift up now thine e', and look
16: 4 her mistress was despised in her e'.
5 I was despised in her e'; the Lord
18: 2 And he lifted up his e' and looked,
19: 8 do ye to them as is good in your e':
20:16 he is to thee a covering of the e',
21:19 God opened her e', and she saw a
22: 4 Abraham lifted up his e', and saw
13 Abraham lifted up his e', and looked
24:63 and he lifted up his e', and saw,
64 Rebekah lifted up her e', and when
27: 1 Isaac was old, and his e' were dim,
30:27 if I have found favour in thine e',
41 the rods before the e' of the cattle
31:10 I lifted up mine e', and saw in a
12 Lift up now thine e', and see,
40 my sleep departed from mine e'.
33: 1 Jacob lifted up his e', and looked,
5 lifted up his e', and saw the women
34:11 Let me find grace in your e',
37:25 they lifted up their e' and looked,
39: 7 his master's wife cast her e' upon
41:37 was good in the e' of Pharaoh,
37 and in the e' of all his servants.
42:24 and bound him before their e'.
43:29 lifted up his e', and saw his brother
44:21 that I may set mine e' upon him.
45:12 your e' see, and the e' of my brother
46: 4 shall put his hand upon thine e'.
47:19 shall we die before thine e', both
48:10 the e' of Israel were dim for age,
49:12 His e' shall be red with wine,
50: 4 now I have found grace in your e',
Ex 5:21 be abhorred in the e' of Pharaoh,
21 and in the e' of his servants,
8:26 of the Egyptians before their e',
13: 9 for a memorial between thine e',
16 and for frontlets between thine e':
14:10 children of Israel lifted up their e',
24:17 in the e' of the children of Israel.
Le 4:13 be hid from the e' of the assembly,
20: 4 the land do any ways hide their e'
26:16 ague, that shall consume the e',
Nu 5:13 be hid from the e' of her husband,
10:31 thou mayest be to us instead of e'.
11: 6 beside this manna, before our e'.
15:39 your own heart and your own e',
16:14 thou put out the e' of these men?
20: 8 ye unto the rock before their e':
12 sanctify me in the e' of the children
Nu 22:31 the Lord opened the e' of Balaam,
24: 2 Balaam lifted up his e', and he saw
3 man whose e' are open hath said:
4 a trance, but having his e' open:
15 man whose e' are open hath said:
16 a trance, but having his e' open:
27:14 me at the water before their e':
33:55 of them shall be pricks in your e',
De 1:30 did for you in Egypt before your e';
3:21 Thine e' have seen all that the Lord
27 and lift up thine e' westward, and
27 and behold it with thine e':
4: 3 Your e' have seen what the Lord
9 things which thine e' have seen,
19 And lest thou lift up thine e' unto
34 did for you in Egypt before your e'?
6: 8 be as frontlets between thine e'.
22 all his household, before our e':
7:19 temptations which thine e' saw,
9:17 and brake them before your e'.
10:21 things, which thine e' have seen.
11: 7 your e' have seen all the great acts
12 the e' of the Lord thy God are
18 be as frontlets between your e'.
12: 8 whatsoever is right in his own e'.
13:18 which is right in the e' of the Lord
14: 1 make any baldness between your e'
16:19 a gift doth blind the e' of the wise,
21: 7 neither have our e' seen it.
24: 1 that she find no favour in his e',
28:31 ox shall be slain before thine e',
32 and thine e' shall look, and fail with
34 be mad for the sight of thine e'
65 a trembling heart, and failing of e',
67 of thine e' which thou shalt see.
29: 2 all that the Lord did before your e'
3 temptations which thine e' have
4 a heart to perceive, and e' to see,
34: 4 caused thee to see it with thine e',
Jos 5:13 he lifted up his e' and looked,
23:13 thorns in your e', until ye perish
24: 7 your e' have seen what I have done
J'g 16:21 took him, and put out his e',
28 of the Philistines for my two e'.
17: 6 that which was right in his own e'.
19:17 when he had lifted up his e', he saw
21:25 that which was right in his own e'.
Ru 2: 9 Let thine e' be on the field that
10 have I found grace in thine e',
1Sa 2:33 shall be to consume thine e', and
3: 2 and his e' began to wax dim,
4:15 his e' were dim, that he could not
6:13 lifted up their e', and saw the ark,
11: 2 I may thrust out all your right e',
12: 3 bribe to blind mine e' therewith?
16 the Lord will do before your e'.
14:27 and his e' were enlightened.
29 how mine e' have been enlightened,
20: 3 I have found grace in thine e';
29 if I have found favour in thine e',
24:10 thine e' have seen how that the Lord
25: 8 young men find favour in thine e':
26:21 my soul was precious in thine e'
24 much set by this day in mine e',
24 much set by in the e' of the Lord,
27: 5 I have now found grace in thine e',
2Sa 6:20 to day in the e' of the handmaids
12:11 I will take thy wives before thine e',
13:34 that kept the watch lifted up his e',
15:25 find favour in the e' of the Lord,
18:24 and lifted up his e', and looked,
19:27 therefore what is good in thine e'.
22:28 thine e' are upon the haughty,
24: 3 the e' of my lord the king may see
1Ki 1:20 O king, the e' of all Israel are upon
48 this day, mine e' even seeing it.
8:29 e' may be open toward this house
52 That thine e' may be open unto the
9: 3 e' and mine heart shall be there
10: 7 mine e' had seen it: and, behold,
11:33 do that which is right in mine e',
14: 4 Ahijah could not see; for his e'
8 only which was right in mine e';
15: 5 was right in the e' of the Lord,
11 that which was right in the e' of
16:25 Omri wrought evil in the e' of
20: 6 whatsoever is pleasant in thine e',
22:43 was right in the e' of the Lord:
2Ki 4:34 and his e' upon his e', and his hands
35 times, and the child opened his e'.
6:17 Lord, I pray thee, open his e',
17 opened the e' of the young man;
20 Lord, open the e' of these men,
20 And the Lord opened their e',
7: 2, 19 thou shalt see it with thine e',
10: 5 thou that which is good in thine e'.
30 that which is right in mine e',
19:16 open, Lord, thine e', and see:
22 and lifted up thine e' on high?
22:20 thine e' shall not see all the evil
25: 7 the sons of Zedekiah before his e',
7 and put out the e' of Zedekiah,
1Ch 13: 4 was right in the e' of all the people.
17:17 this was a small thing in thine e',
21:16 And David lifted up his e', and saw
23 do that which is good in his e':
2Ch 6:20 e' may be open upon this house
40 let, I beseech thee, thine e' be open,
7:15 Now mine e' shall be open, and
16 mine e' and mine heart shall be
9: 6 mine e' had seen it: and, behold,
14: 2 good and right in the e' of the Lord
16: 9 the e' of the Lord run to and fro
20:12 but our e' are upon thee.
21: 6 was evil in the e' of the Lord.

2Ch 29: 6 evil in the e' of the Lord our God,
8 to hissing, as ye see with your e'.
34:28 neither shall thine e' see all the evil
Ezr 3:12 house was laid before their e',
9: 8 that our God may lighten our e',
Ne 1: 6 e' open, that thou mayest hear
6:16 much cast down in their own e':
Es 1:17 despise their husbands in their e',
8: 5 the king, and I be pleasing in his e',
Job 2:12 they lifted up their e' afar off,
3:10 nor hid sorrow from mine e'.
4:16 an image was before mine e',
7: 8 thine e' are upon me, and I am not.
10: 4 Hast thou e' of flesh? or seest the
11: 4 and I am clean in thine e'.
20 But the e' of the wicked shall fail,
14: 3 open thine e' upon such an one,
15:12 and what do thy e' wink at,
16: 9 enemy sharpeneth his e' upon me.
17: 5 even the e' of his children shall fail.
19:27 and mine e' shall behold, and not
21: 8 and their offspring before their e'.
20 His e' shall see his destruction,
24:23 yet his e' are upon their ways.
27:19 he openeth his e', and he is not.
28:21 it is hid from the e' of all living,
29:15 I was e' to the blind, and feet was I
31: 1 I made a covenant with mine e';
7 mine heart walked after mine e',
16 caused the e' of the widow to fail;
32: 1 he was righteous in his own e'.
34:21 his e' are upon the ways of man,
36: 7 not his e' from the righteous:
39:29 prey, and her e' behold afar off.
40:24 He taketh it with his e': his nose
41:18 and his e' are like the eyelids of the
Ps 10: 8 e' are privily set against the poor.
11: 4 his e' behold, his eyelids try,
13: 3 lighten mine e', lest I sleep
15: 4 whose e' a vile person is contemned;
17: 2 e' behold the things that are equal.
11 they have set their e' bowing down
19: 8 Lord is pure, enlightening the e'.
25:15 Mine e' are ever toward the Lord;
26: 3 lovingkindness is before mine e':
31:22 I am cut off from before thine e':
34:15 The e' of the Lord are upon the
36: 1 there is no fear of God before his e'.
2 he flattereth himself in his own e',
38:10 the light of mine e', it also is gone
50:21 set them in order before thine e'.
66: 7 his e' behold the nations: let not
69: 3 mine e' fail while I wait for my God.
23 e' be darkened, that they see not;
73: 7 Their e' stand out with fatness:
77: 4 Thou holdest mine e' waking: I
91: 8 Only with thine e' shalt thou behold
101: 3 set no wicked thing before mine e':
6 Mine e' shall be upon the faithful
115: 5 e' have they, but they see not:
116: 8 soul from death, mine e' from tears,
118:23 doing; it is marvellous in our e'.
119:18 Open thou mine e', that I may
37 mine e' from beholding vanity;
82 Mine e' fail for thy word, saying,
123 Mine e' fail for thy salvation, and
136 Rivers of waters run down mine e',
148 Mine e' prevent the night watches,
121: 1 I will lift up mine e' unto the hills,
123: 1 Unto thee lift I up mine e', O thou
2 as the e' of servants look unto the
2 as the e' of a maiden unto the hand
2 our e' wait upon the Lord our God,
131: 1 is not haughty, nor mine e' lofty:
132: 4 I will not give sleep to mine e',
135:16 e' have they, but they see not;
139:16 Thine e' did see my substance, yet
141: 8 But mine e' are unto thee, O God
145:15 The e' of all wait upon thee;
146: 8 The Lord openeth the e' of the blind:
Pr 3: 7 Be not wise in thine own e':
21 let not them depart from thine e':
4:21 Let them not depart from thine e';
25 Let thine e' look right on, and let
5:21 man are before the e' of the Lord,
6: 4 Give not sleep to thine e', nor
13 winketh with his e', he speaketh
10:26 smoke to the e', so is the sluggard
12:15 way of a fool is right in his own e':
15: 3 e' of the Lord are in every place,
30 light of the e' rejoiceth the heart:
16: 2 of a man are clean in his own e';
30 shutteth his e' to devise froward
17: 8 as a precious stone in the e' of him
24 but the e' of a fool are in the ends
20: 8 scattereth away all evil with his e'.
13 open thine e', and thou shalt be
21: 2 way of a man is right in his own e':
10 findeth no favour in his e'.
22:12 The e' of the Lord preserve
23: 5 thine e' upon that which is not?
26 and let thine e' observe my ways.
29 cause? who hath redness of e'?
33 Thine e' shall behold strange
25: 7 prince whom thine e' have seen.
27:20 so the e' of man are never satisfied.
28:27 his e' shall have many a curse.
29:13 the Lord lighteneth both their e'.
30:12 that are pure in their own e',
13 O how lofty are their e'!
Ec 2:10 e' desired I kept not from them,
14 The wise man's e' are in his head;
5:11 beholding of them with their e'?
6: 9 Better is the sight of the e' than
8:16 nor night seeth sleep with his e':)
11: 7 thing it is for the e' to behold the
Ec 11: 9 heart, and in the sight of thine e':
Ca 1:15 thou art fair; thou hast doves' e'.
4: 1 thou art fair; thou hast doves' e'
9 my heart with one of thine e',
5:12 His e' are as the e' of doves
6: 5 Turn away thine e' from me, for
7: 4 e' like the fishpools in Heshbon:
8:10 in his e' as one that found favour.
Isa 1:15 I will hide mine e' from you: yea,
16 of your doings from before mine e';
3: 8 Lord, to provoke the e' of his glory.
16 stretched forth necks and wanton e',
5:15 the e' of the lofty shall be humbled:
21 them that are wise in their own e',
6: 5 for mine e' have seen the King,
10 their ears heavy, and shut their e';
10 lest they see with their e',
11: 3 not judge after the sight of his e',
13:16 be dashed to pieces before their e';
17: 7 and his e' shall have respect to the
29:10 sleep, and hath closed your e':
18 the e' of the blind shall see out of
30:20 but thine e' shall see thy teachers:
32: 3 e' of them that see shall not be dim,
33:15 and shutteth his e' from seeing evil;
17 e' shall see the King in his beauty:
20 thine e' shall see Jerusalem a quiet
35: 5 the e' of the blind shall be opened,
37:17 open thine e', O Lord, and see:
23 and lifted up thine e' on high?
38:14 mine e' fail with looking upward:
40:26 Lift up your e' on high, and behold
42: 7 To open the blind e', to bring out
43: 8 forth the blind people that have e',
44:18 he hath shut their e', that they
49: 5 I be glorious in the e' of the Lord,
18 Lift up thine e' round about, and
51: 6 Lift up your e' to the heavens,
52:10 made bare his holy arm in the e'
59:10 we grope as if we had no e':
60: 4 Lift up thine e' round about, and
65:12 but did evil before mine e', and did
16 because they are hid from mine e'.
66: 4 but they did evil before mine e',
Jer 3: 2 up thine e' unto the high places,
5: 3 are not thine e' upon the truth?
21 which have e', and see not;
7:11 become a den of robbers in your e'?
9: 1 and mine e' a fountain of tears,
18 that our e' may run down with tears,
13:20 Lift up your e', and behold them
14: 6 their e' did fail, because there was
17 Let mine e' run down with tears
16: 9 cease out of this place in your e',
17 mine e' are upon all their ways:
17 is their iniquity hid from mine e'.
20: 4 and thine e' shall behold it: and
22:17 thine e' and thine heart are not
24: 6 set mine e' upon them for good,
29:21 he shall slay them before your e';
31:16 weeping, and thine e' from tears:
32: 4 and his e' shall behold his e';
19 thine e' are open upon all the ways
34: 3 thine e' shall behold the e' of the
39: 6 Zedekiah in Riblah before his e':
7 Moreover he put out Zedekiah's e',
42: 2 few of many, as thine e' do behold
52: 2 was evil in the e' of the Lord,
10 the sons of Zedekiah before his e':
11 Then he put out the e' of Zedekiah;
La 2:11 Mine e' do fail with tears,
4:17 e' as yet failed for our vain help:
5:17 for these things our e' are dim.
Eze 1:18 rings were full of e' round about
6: 9 their e', which go a whoring after
8: 5 Son of man, lift up thine e' now
5 So I lifted up mine e'...the north,
10:12 wheels, were full of e' round about,
12: 2 a rebellious house, which have e'
12 he see not the ground with his e'.
18: 6 neither hath lifted up his e' to the
12 and hath lifted up his e' to the idols
15 neither hath lifted up his e' to the
20: 7 man the abominations of his e',
8 away the abominations of their e',
24 e' were after their fathers' idols.
21: 6 with bitterness sigh before their e'.
22:26 hid their e' from my sabbaths,
23:16 soon as she saw them with her e',
27 thou shalt not lift up thine e' unto
40 didst wash thyself, paintedst thy e',
24:16 from thee the desire of thine e'
21 the desire of your e', and that which
25 their glory, the desire of their e',
33:25 lift up your e' toward your idols,
36:23 be sanctified in you before their e'.
37:20 be in thine hand before their e'.
38:16 in thee, O Gog, before their e'.
23 known in the e' of many nations,
40: 4 Son of man, behold with thine e',
44: 5 mark well, and behold with thine e',
Da 4:34 Nebuchadnezzar lifted up mine e'
7: 8 this horn were e' like the e' of man,
20 even of that horn that had e',
8: 3 Then I lifted up mine e', and saw,
5 had a notable horn between his e'.
21 great horn that is between his e'
9:18 thine e', and behold our desolations,
10: 5 I lifted up mine e', and looked,
6 his e' as lamps of fire, and his arms
Ho 13:14 shall be hid from mine e'.
Joe 1:16 not the meat cut off before our e',
Am 9: 4 will set mine e' upon them for evil,
8 the e' of the Lord God are upon
Mic 7:10 mine e' shall behold her: now shall
Hab 1:13 Thou art of purer e' than to behold
Zep 3:20 back your captivity before your e',
Hag 2: 3 not in your e' in comparison of it
Zec 1:18 Then lifted I up mine e', and saw,
2: 1 I lifted up mine e' again, and looked,
3: 9 upon one stone shall be seven e':
4:10 they are the e' of the Lord, which
5: 1 I turned, and lifted up mine e',
5 Lift up now thine e', and see
9 lifted I up mine e', and looked,
6: 1 Then I turned, and lifted up mine e',
8: 6 marvellous in the e' of the remnant
6 it also be marvellous in mine e'?
9: 1 the e' of man, as of all the tribes
8 for now have I seen with mine e'.
12: 4 mine e' upon the house of Judah,
14:12 their e' shall consume away in
Mal 1: 5 your e' shall see, and ye shall say,
M't 9:29 Then touched he their e', saying,
30 their e' were opened; and Jesus
13:15 and their e' they have closed;
15 time they should see with their e',
16 blessed are your e', for they see:
17: 8 when they had lifted up their e',
18: 9 rather than having two e' to be
20:33 Lord, that our e' may be opened.
34 on them, and touched their e':
34 their e' received sight, and they
21:42 and it is marvellous in our e'?
26:43 for their e' were heavy.
M'r 8:18 Having e', see ye not? having ears,
23 and when he had spit on his e',
25 put his hands again upon his e',
9:47 having two e' to be cast into hell
12:11 and it is marvellous in our e'?
14:40 (for their e' were heavy,) neither
Lu 2:30 For mine e' have seen thy salvation,
4:20 And the e' of all them that were
6:20 he lifted up his e' on his disciples,
10:23 Blessed are the e' which see the
16:23 And in hell he lifted up his e',
18:13 up so much as his e' unto heaven,
19:42 but now they are hid from thine e'.
24:16 e' were holden that they should
31 And their e' were opened, and they
Joh 4:35 Lift up your e', and look on the
6: 5 Jesus then lifted up his e', and saw
9: 6 he anointed the e' of the blind man
10 him, How were thine e' opened?
11 and anointed mine e', and said
14 made the clay, and opened his e'.
15 He put clay upon mine e', and I
17 him, that he hath opened thine e'?
21 who hath opened his e', we know
26 thee? how opened he thine e'?
30 and yet he hath opened mine e'.
32 that any man opened the e' of one
10:21 Can a devil open the e' of the blind?
11:37 which opened the e' of the blind,
41 Jesus lifted up his e', and said,
12:40 He hath blinded their e', and
40 they should not see with their e',
17: 1 and lifted up his e' to heaven, and
Ac 3: 4 Peter, fastening his e' upon him with
9: 8 his e' were opened, he saw no man:
18 from his e' as it had been scales:
40 And she opened her e': and when
11: 6 when I had fastened mine e', I
13: 9 the Holy Ghost, set his e' on him,
26:18 To open their e', and to turn them
28:27 and their e' have they closed;
27 lest they should see with their e',
Ro 3:18 is no fear of God before their e'.
11: 8 e' that they should not see, and
10 Let their e' be darkened, that they
Ga 3: 1 before whose e' Jesus Christ hath
4:15 have plucked out your own e',
Eph 1:18 The e' of your understanding being
Heb 4:13 and opened unto the e' of him with
1Pe 3:12 For the e' of the Lord are over the
2Pe 2:14 Having e' full of adultery, and that
1Jo 1: 1 which we have seen with our e',
2:11 that darkness hath blinded his e'.
16 lust of the e', and the pride of life,
Re 1:14 and his e' were as a flame of fire;
2:18 hath his e' like unto a flame of fire,
3:18 and anoint thine e' with eyesalve,
4: 6 there four beasts full of e' before
8 and they were full of e' within:
5: 6 seven e', which are the seven spirits
7:17 wipe away all tears from their e'.
19:12 His e' were as a flame of fire,
21: 4 wipe away all tears from their e';

eyesalve
Re 3:18 and anoint thine eyes with e', that

eyeservice
Eph 6: 6 Not with e', as menpleasers; but as
Col 3:22 not with e', as menpleasers; but in

eyesight See also EYE and SIGHT.
Ps 18:24 cleanness of my hands in his e'.

eyewitnesses
Lu 1: 2 which from the beginning were e',
2Pe 1:16 but were e' of his majesty.

Ezar (*e'-zar*) See also EZER.
1Ch 1:38 and Dishon, and E', and Dishan.

Ezbai (*ez'-bahee*)
1Ch 11:37 Carmelite, Naarai the son of E',

Ezbon (*ez'-bon*)
Ge 46:16 Haggi, Shuni, and E', Eri,
1Ch 7: 7 the sons of Bela; E', and Uzzi,

Ezekias (*ez-e-ki'-as*) See also HEZEKIAH.
M't 1: 9 Achaz; and Achaz begat E';
10 And E' begat Manasses; and

Ezekiel^ (*e-zeke'-yel*)
Eze 1: 3 the Lord came expressly unto *E'*
24:24 Thus *E'* is unto you a sign:

Ezel (*e'-zel*) See also BETH-EZEL.
1Sa 20:19 and shalt remain by the stone *E'*.

Ezem (*e'-zem*) See also AZEM.
1Ch 4:29 Bilhah, and at *E'*, and at Tolad,

Ezer (*e'-zur*) See also ABI-EZER; EBEN-EZER; EZAR; ROMAMTI-EZER.
Ge 36:21 And Dishon, and *E'*, and Dishan:
27 The children of *E'* are these; Bilhan,
30 Dishon, duke *E'*, duke Dishan:
1Ch 1:42 The sons of *E'*; Bilhan, and Zavan,
4: 4 and *E'* the father of Hushah.
7:21 and *E'*, and Elead, whom the men
12: 9 *E'* the first, Obadiah the second,
Ne 3:19 next to him repaired *E'* the son of
12:42 and Malchijah, and Elam, and *E'*.

Ezion-gaber (*e''-ze-on-ga'-bur*) See also EZION-GEBER.
Nu 33:35 Ebronah, and encamped at *E'*.
36 And they removed from *E'*, and
De 2: 8 from *E'*, we turned and passed
2Ch 20:36 and they made the ships in *E'*.

Ezion-geber (*e''-ze-on-ghe'-bur*) See also EZION-GABER.
1Ki 9:26 made a navy of ships in *E'*,
22:48 for the ships were broken at *E'*.
2Ch 8:17 went Solomon to *E'*, and to Eloth,

Eznite (*ez'-nite*)
2Sa 23: 8 the same was Adino the *E'*: he

Ezra^ (*ez'-rah*) See also AZARIAH; EZRAHITE.
1Ch 4:17 of *E'* were, Jether, and Mered,
Ezr 7: 1 *E'* the son of Seraiah, the son of
6 This *E'* went up from Babylon;
10 *E'* had prepared his heart to seek
11 Artaxerxes gave unto *E'* the priest,
12 king of kings, Unto *E'* the priest,
21 whatsoever *E'* the priest, the scribe
25 *E'*, after the wisdom of thy God,
10: 1 Now when *E'* had prayed, and
2 said unto *E'*, We have trespassed
5 Then arose *E'*, and made the chief
Ezr 10: 6 *E'* rose up from before the house
10 *E'* the priest stood up, and said
16 And *E'* the priest, with certain chief
Ne 8: 1 and they spake unto *E'* the scribe
2 And *E'* the priest brought the law
4 *E'* the scribe stood upon a pulpit
5 *E'* opened the book in the sight of
6 *E'* blessed the Lord, the great God.
9 and *E'* the priest the scribe, and the
13 Levites, unto *E'* the scribe, even to
12: 1 Seraiah, Jeremiah, *E'*,
13 Of *E'*, Meshullam; of Amariah,
26 and of *E'* the priest, the scribe.
33 And Azariah, *E'*, Meshullam,
36 of God, and *E'* the scribe before

Ezrahite (*ez'-rah-hite*)
1Ki 4:31 than Ethan the *E'*, and Heman,
Ps 88:*title* Maschil of Heman the *E'*.
89:*title* Maschil of Ethan the *E'*.

Ezri (*ez'-ri*)
1Ch 27:26 ground was *E'* the son of Chelub:

Ezrite See ABI-EZRITE.

F.

fables
1Ti 1: 4 Neither give heed to *f'* and endless
4: 7 refuse profane and old wives' *f'*,
2Ti 4: 4 and shall be turned unto *f'*.
Tit 1:14 Not giving heed to Jewish *f'*, and
2Pe 1:16 not followed cunningly devised *f'*,

face See also FACES.
Ge 1: 2 darkness was upon the *f'* of the
2 Spirit of God moved upon the *f'* of
29 which is upon the *f'* of all the earth,
2: 6 watered the whole *f'* of the ground.
3:19 In the sweat of thy *f'* shalt thou eat
4:14 driven me out this day from the *f'*
14 of the earth; and from thy *f'* shall I
6: 1 to multiply on the *f'* of the earth,
7 destroy...from the *f'* of the earth;
7: 3 seed alive upon the *f'* of all the earth.
4 destroy from off the *f'* of the earth.
18 ark went upon the *f'* of the waters.
23 was upon the *f'* of the ground,
8: 8 abated from off the *f'* of the ground;
9 were on the *f'* of the whole earth:
13 behold, the *f'* of the ground was dry.
11: 4 upon the *f'* of the whole earth.
8 thence upon the *f'* of all the earth:
9 abroad upon the *f'* of all the earth.
16: 6 hardly with her, she fled from her *f'*.
8 I flee from the *f'* of my mistress
17: 3 And Abram fell on his *f'*:
17 Then Abraham fell upon his *f'*,
19: 1 with his *f'* toward the ground;
13 great before the *f'* of the Lord;
24:47 and I put the earring upon her *f'*,
30:33 come for my hire before thy *f'*:
31:21 set his *f'* toward the mount Gilead.
32:20 and afterward I will see his *f'*;
30 for I have seen God *f'* to *f'*,
33:10 I have seen thy *f'*, as though I had
10 though I had seen the *f'* of God,
35: 1 thou fleddest from the *f'* of Esau
7 he fled from the *f'* of his brother.
36: 6 from the *f'* of his brother Jacob.
38:15 because she had covered her *f'*.
41:56 was over all the *f'* of the earth:
43: 3 Ye shall not see my *f'*, except your
5 unto us, Ye shall not see my *f'*,
31 he washed his *f'*, and went out,
44:23 with you, ye shall see my *f'* no more.
26 for we may not see the man's *f'*,
46:28 him unto Joseph, to direct his *f'*
30 let me die, since I have seen thy *f'*,
48:11 I had not thought to see thy *f'*:
12 bowed himself with his *f'* to the
50: 1 Joseph fell upon his father's *f'*,
18 went and fell down before his *f'*;
Ex 2:15 Moses fled from the *f'* of Pharaoh,
3: 6 Moses hid his *f'*; for he was afraid
10: 5 they shall cover the *f'* of the earth,
15 covered the *f'* of the whole earth,
28 see my *f'* no more; for in that day
28 thou seest my *f'* thou shalt die.
29 I will see thy *f'* again no more.
14:19 cloud went from before their *f'*,
25 Let us flee from the *f'* of Israel;
16:14 upon the *f'* of the wilderness there
32:12 to consume them from the *f'* of the
33:11 the Lord spake unto Moses *f'* to *f'*,
16 that are upon the *f'* of the earth.
20 he said, Thou canst not see my *f'*:
23 but my *f'* shall not be seen.
34:29 wist not that the skin of his *f'* shone
30 behold, the skin of his *f'* shone;
33 he put a vail on his *f'*.
35 saw the *f'* of Moses, that the skin of
35 the skin of Moses' *f'* shone:
35 and Moses put the vail upon his *f'*
Le 13:41 the part of his head toward his *f'*,
17:10 I will even set my *f'* against that
19:32 and honour the *f'* of the old man,
20: 3, 5 I will set my *f'* against that man,
6 I will even set my *f'* against that
26:17 And I will set my *f'* against you,
Nu 6:25 Lord make his *f'* shine upon thee,
11:31 cubits high upon the *f'* of the earth.
12: 3 which were upon the *f'* of the earth.)
14 If her father had but spit in her *f'*,
Nu 14:14 that thou Lord art seen *f'* to *f'*,
16: 4 Moses heard it, he fell upon his *f'*:
19: 3 and one shall slay her before his *f'*:
22: 5 they cover the *f'* of the earth,
11 which covereth the *f'* of the earth:
31 and fell flat on his *f'*.
24: 1 set his *f'* toward the wilderness.
De 1:17 shall not be afraid of the *f'* of man;
5: 4 Lord talked with you *f'* to *f'* in the
6:15 thee from off the *f'* of the earth.
7: 6 that are upon the *f'* of the earth.
10 them that hate him to their *f'*,
10 he will repay him to his *f'*.
8:20 Lord destroyeth before your *f'*,
9: 3 bring them down before thy *f'*:
25: 2 and to be beaten before his *f'*,
9 and spit in his *f'*, and shall answer
28: 7 to be smitten before thy *f'*:
31 taken away from before thy *f'*,
31: 5 shall give them up before your *f'*,
17 and I will hide my *f'* from them,
18 I will surely hide my *f'* in that day
32:20 said, I will hide my *f'* from them,
34:10 whom the Lord knew *f'* to *f'*,
Jos 5:14 Joshua fell on his *f'* to the earth,
7: 6 fell to the ear th upon his *f'* before
10 liest thou thus upon thy *f'*?
J'g 6:22 seen an angel of the Lord *f'* to *f'*.
Ru 2:10 Then she fell on her *f'*, and bowed
1Sa 5: 3 was fallen upon his *f'* to the earth
4 was fallen upon his *f'* to the ground
17:49 he fell upon his *f'* to the earth.
20:15 every one from the *f'* of the earth.
41 and fell on his *f'* to the ground,
24: 8 David stooped with his *f'* to the
25:23 and fell before David on her *f'*,
41 bowed herself on her *f'* to the earth,
26:20 earth before the *f'* of the Lord:
28:14 stooped with his *f'* to the ground,
2Sa 2:22 how then should I hold up my *f'*
3:13 Thou shalt not see my *f'*, except
13 when thou comest to see my *f'*.
9: 6 he fell on his *f'*, and did reverence.
14: 4 she fell on her *f'* to the ground,
22 Joab fell to the ground on his *f'*,
24 and let him not see my *f'*.
24 house, and saw not the king's *f'*.
28 and saw not the king's *f'*.
32 therefore let me see the king's *f'*;
33 himself on his *f'* to the ground
18: 8 over the *f'* of all the country:
28 his *f'* before the king, and said,
19: 4 But the king covered his *f'*,
24:20 king on his *f'* upon the ground.
1Ki 1:23 the king with his *f'* to the ground.
31 bowed with her *f'* to the earth,
8:14 And the king turned his *f'* about,
13: 6 Intreat now the *f'* of the Lord
34 destroy it from off the *f'* of the earth.
18: 7 he knew him, and fell on his *f'*,
42 and put his *f'* between his knees.
19:13 he wrapped his *f'* in his mantle,
20:38 himself with ashes upon his *f'*.
41 took the ashes away from his *f'*;
21: 4 turned away his *f'*, and would eat
2Ki 4:29 lay my staff upon the *f'* of the child.
31 the staff upon the *f'* of the child;
8:15 spread it on his *f'*, so that he died:
9:30 she painted her *f'*, and tired her
32 he lifted up his *f'* to the window,
37 as dung upon the *f'* of the field
12:17 set his *f'* to go up to Jerusalem.
13:14 and wept over his *f'*, and said,
14: 8 let us look one another in the *f'*.
11 Judah looked one another in the *f'*
18:24 thou turn away the *f'* of one captain
20: 2 he turned his *f'* to the wall,
1Ch 16:11 strength, seek his *f'* continually.
21:21 to David with his *f'* to the ground.
2Ch 6: 3 And the king turned his *f'*, and
42 not away the *f'* of thine anointed:
7:14 and pray, and seek my *f'*,
20:18 head with his *f'* to the ground:
25:17 let us see one another in the *f'*.
21 they saw one another in the *f'*,
30: 9 will not turn away his *f'* from you,
2Ch 32:21 with shame of *f'* to his own land.
35:22 Josiah would not turn his *f'* from
Ezr 9: 6 and blush to lift up my *f'* to thee,
7 to a spoil, and to confusion of *f'*,
Es 1:14 and Media, which saw the king's *f'*,
7: 8 mouth, they covered Haman's *f'*.
Job 1:11 and he will curse thee to thy *f'*.
2: 5 and he will curse thee to thy *f'*.
4:15 Then a spirit passed before my *f'*;
11:15 For then shalt thou lift up thy *f'*
13:24 Wherefore hidest thou thy *f'*, and
15:27 he covereth his *f'* with his fatness,
16: 8 in me beareth witness to my *f'*.
16 My *f'* is foul with weeping,
21:31 Who shall declare his way to his *f'*?
22:26 shalt lift up thy *f'* unto God.
23:17 covered the darkness from my *f'*.
24:15 see me: and disguiseth his *f'*.
26: 9 holdeth back the *f'* of his throne,
30:10 and spare not to spit in my *f'*.
33:26 he shall see his *f'* with joy;
34:29 and when he hideth his *f'*, who
37:12 the *f'* of the world in the earth.
38:30 and the *f'* of the deep is frozen.
41:13 discover the *f'* of his garment?
14 Who can open the doors of his *f'*?
Ps 5: 8 thy way straight before my *f'*.
10:11 hideth his *f'*; he will never see it.
13: 1 how long wilt thou hide thy *f'*
17:15 will behold thy *f'* in righteousness:
21:12 thy strings against the *f'* of them.
22:24 hath he hid his *f'* from him;
24: 6 that seek thy *f'*, O Jacob. Selah.
27: 8 Seek ye my *f'*; my heart said unto
8 Thy *f'*, Lord, will I seek.
9 Hide not thy *f'* far from me;
30: 7 hide thy *f'*, and I was troubled.
31:16 thy *f'* to shine upon thy servant:
34:16 The *f'* of the Lord is against them
41:12 settest me before thy *f'* for ever.
44:15 shame of my *f'* hath covered me,
24 Wherefore hidest thou thy *f'*, and
51: 9 Hide thy *f'* from my sins,
67: 1 and cause his *f'* to shine upon us;
69: 7 shame hath covered my *f'*.
17 hide not thy *f'* from thy servant;
80: 3 O God, and cause thy *f'* to shine;
7 of hosts, and cause thy *f'* to shine;
19 of hosts, cause thy *f'* to shine;
84: 9 look upon the *f'* of thine anointed.
88:14 why hidest thou thy *f'* from me?
89:14 and truth shall go before thy *f'*.
23 beat down his foes before his *f'*,
102: 2 Hide not thy *f'* from me in the day
104:15 and oil to make his *f'* to shine,
29 hidest thy *f'*, they are troubled:
30 thou renewest the *f'* of the earth.
105: 4 strength: seek his *f'* evermore.
119:135 Make thy *f'* to shine upon thy
132:10 not away the *f'* of thine anointed.
143: 7 faileth: hide not thy *f'* from me,
Pr 7:13 with an impudent *f'* said unto him,
15 thee, diligently to seek thy *f'*,
8:27 compass upon the *f'* of the depth:
21:29 A wicked man hardeneth his *f'*:
24:31 nettles had covered the *f'* thereof,
27:19 As in water *f'* answereth to *f'*, so
Ec 8: 1 wisdom maketh his *f'* to shine,
1 boldness of his *f'* shall be changed.
Isa 6: 2 with twain he covered his *f'*,
8:17 his *f'* from the house of Jacob,
14:21 fill the *f'* of the world with cities.
16: 4 to them from the *f'* of the spoiler:
23:17 the world upon the *f'* of the earth.
25: 7 the *f'* of the covering cast over all
27: 6 fill the *f'* of the world with fruit.
28:25 he hath made plain the *f'* thereof,
29:22 neither shall his *f'* now wax pale.
36: 9 turn away the *f'* of one captain
38: 2 Hezekiah turned his *f'* toward the
49:23 with their *f'* toward the earth,
50: 6 my *f'* from shame and spitting.
7 have I set my *f'* like a flint,
54: 8 hid my *f'* from thee for a moment;
59: 2 your sins have hid his *f'* from you,
64: 7 thou hast hid thy *f'* from us,

Isa 65: 3 me to anger continually to my *f*;
Jer 1:13 the *f* thereof is toward the north.
2:27 their back unto me, and not their *f*:
4:30 thou rentest thy *f* with painting,
8: 2 for dung upon the *f* of the earth.
13:26 I discover thy skirts upon thy *f*,
16: 4 as dung upon the *f* of the earth:
17 ways: they are not hid from my *f*,
18:17 shew them the back, and not the *f*,
21:10 I have set my *f* against this city
22:25 of them whose *f* thou fearest,
25:26 which are upon the *f* of the earth:
28:16 thee from off the *f* of the earth:
32:31 should remove it from before my *f*,
33 unto me the back, and not the *f*:
33: 5 I have hid my *f* from this city.
44:11 I will set my *f* against you
La 2:19 like water before the *f* of the Lord:
3:35 before the *f* of the most High,
Eze 1:10 the *f* of a man, and the *f* of a lion,
10 had the *f* of an ox on the left side;
10 four also had the *f* of an eagle.
28 fell upon my *f*, and I heard a voice
3: 8 thy *f* strong against their faces,
23 of Chebar: and I fell on my *f*.
4: 3 and set thy *f* against it, and it shall
7 shalt set thy *f* toward the siege
6: 2 set thy *f* toward the mountains
7:22 My *f* will I turn also from them,
9: 8 I fell upon my *f*, and cried,
10:14 the first *f* was the *f* of a cherub,
14 the second *f* was the *f* of a man,
14 and the third the *f* of a lion,
14 and the fourth the *f* of an eagle.
11:13 Then fell I down upon my *f*,
12: 6 shalt cover thy *f*, that thou see not
12 shall cover his *f*, that he see not
13:17 set thy *f* against the daughters of
14: 3 of their iniquity before their *f*:
4, 7 of his iniquity before his *f*, and
8 I will set my *f* against that man,
15: 7 I will set my *f* against them;
7 when I set my *f* against them.
20:35 there will I plead with you *f* to *f*.
46 man, set thy *f* toward the south,
21: 2 man, set thy *f* toward Jerusalem,
16 left, whithersoever thy *f* is set.
25: 2 set thy *f* against the Ammonites,
28:21 of man, set thy *f* against Zidon,
29: 2 of man, set thy *f* against Pharaoh
34: 6 upon all the *f* of the earth,
35: 2 man, set thy *f* against mount Seir,
38: 2 Son of man, set thy *f* against Gog,
18 my fury shall come up in my *f*.
20 that are upon the *f* of the earth,
39:14 remain upon the *f* of the earth,
23 therefore hid I my *f* from them,
24 and hid my *f* from them.
29 Neither will I hide my *f* any more
40:15 And from the *f* of the gate of the
15 entrance unto the *f* of the porch
41:14 the breadth of the *f* of the house,
19 *f* of a man was toward the palm
19 *f* of a young lion toward the palm
21 and the *f* of the sanctuary;
25 upon the *f* of the porch without.
43: 3 of Chebar; and I fell upon my *f*.
44: 4 the Lord: and I fell upon my *f*.
Da 2:46 Nebuchadnezzar fell upon his *f*,
8: 5 on the *f* of the whole earth,
17 I was afraid, and fell upon my *f*:
18 I was in a deep sleep on my *f*
9: 3 I set my *f* unto the Lord God,
8 to us belongeth confusion of *f*,
17 thy *f* to shine upon thy sanctuary
10: 6 *f* as the appearance of lightning,
9 then was I in a deep sleep on my *f*,
9 and my *f* toward the ground.
15 I set my *f* toward the ground,
11:17 He shall also set his *f* to enter
18 shall he turn his *f* unto the isles,
19 he shall turn his *f* toward the fort
Ho 5: 5 pride of Israel doth testify to his *f*:
15 their offence, and seek my *f*:
7: 2 about: they are before my *f*.
10 pride of Israel testifieth to his *f*:
Joe 2: 6 Before their *f* the people shall be
20 with his *f* toward the east sea,
Am 5: 8 them out upon the *f* of the earth:
9: 6 them out upon the *f* of the earth:
8 destroy it from off the *f* of the earth;
Mic 3: 4 he will even hide his *f* from them
Na 2: 1 in pieces is come up before thy *f*:
3: 5 discover thy skirts upon thy *f*,
Zec 5: 3 over the *f* of the whole earth:
M't 6:17 anoint thine head, and wash thy *f*;
11:10 I send my messenger before thy *f*,
16: 3 ye can discern the *f* of the sky;
17: 2 and his *f* did shine as the sun,
6 on their *f*, and were sore afraid.
18:10 always behold the *f* of my Father
26:39 and fell on his *f*, and prayed,
67 Then did they spit in his *f*,
M'r 1: 2 I send my messenger before thy *f*,
14:65 to cover his *f*, and to buffet him,
Lu 1:76 shalt go before the *f* of the Lord
2:31 prepared before the *f* of all people;
5:12 who seeing Jesus fell on his *f*,
7:27 I send my messenger before thy *f*,
9:51 set his *f* to go to Jerusalem,
52 And sent messengers before his *f*:
53 because his *f* was as though he
10: 1 sent them two and two before his *f*
12:56 ye can discern the *f* of the sky
17:16 And fell down on his *f* at his feet,
Lu 21:35 dwell on the *f* of the whole earth.
22:64 struck him on the *f*, and asked
Joh 11:44 *f* was bound about with a napkin.
Ac 2:25 the Lord always before my *f*, for
6:15 saw his *f* as it had been the *f* of
7:45 out before the *f* of our fathers,
17:26 to dwell on all the *f* of the earth,
20:25 shall see my *f* no more.
38 that they should see his *f* no more.
25:16 have the accusers *f* to *f*,
1Co 13:12 a glass, darkly; but then *f* to *f*:
14:25 and so falling down on his *f*
2Co 3: 7 stedfastly behold the *f* of Moses
13 which put a vail over his *f*,
18 with open *f* beholding as in a glass
4: 6 of God in the *f* of Jesus Christ.
11:20 if a man smite you on the *f*.
Ga 1:22 unknown by *f* unto the churches
2:11 I withstood him to the *f*,
Col 2: 1 as have not seen my *f* in the flesh;
1Th 2:17 to see your *f* with great desire.
3:10 that we might see your *f*,
Jas 1:23 beholding his natural *f* in a glass:
1Pe 3:12 the *f* of the Lord is against them
2Jo 12 and speak *f* to *f*, that our joy may
3Jo 14 see thee, and we shall speak *f* to *f*.
Re 4: 7 the third beast had a *f* as a man,
6:16 hide us from the *f* of him that
10: 1 and his *f* was as it were the sun,
12:14 a time, from the *f* of the serpent.
20:11 from whose *f* the earth and the
22: 4 And they shall see his *f*;

faced See SHAMEFACEDNESS.

faces
Ge 9:23 and their *f* were backward, and
18:22 their *f* from thence, and went
30:40 and set the *f* of the flocks
42: 6 with their *f* to the earth.
Ex 19: 7 before their *f* all these words
20:20 his fear may be before your *f*,
25:20 their *f* shall look one to another;
20 shall the *f* of the cherubims be.
37: 9 with their *f* one to another; even
9 were the *f* of the cherubims.
Le 9:24 they shouted, and fell on their *f*.
Nu 14: 5 Moses and Aaron fell on their *f*
16:22 they fell upon their *f*, and said,
45 And they fell upon their *f*.
20: 6 they fell upon their *f*: and the
J'g 13:20 and fell on their *f* to the ground.
18:23 turned their *f*, and said unto Micah,
2Sa 19: 5 this day the *f* of all thy servants,
1Ki 2:15 all Israel set their *f* on me,
18:39 they fell on their *f*: and they said,
1Ch 12: 8 whose *f* were like the *f* of lions,
21:16 in sackcloth, fell upon their *f*.
2Ch 3:13 feet, and their *f* were inward.
7: 3 with their *f* to the ground upon the
29: 6 have turned away their *f* from
Ne 8: 6 Lord with their *f* to the ground.
Job 9:24 he covereth the *f* of the judges
40:13 and bind their *f* in secret.
Ps 34: 5 and their *f* were not ashamed.
83:16 Fill their *f* with shame; that they
Isa 3:15 and grind the *f* of the poor?
13: 8 their *f* shall be as flames.
25: 8 wipe away tears from off all *f*;
53: 3 we hid as it were our *f* from him;
Jer 1: 8 Be not afraid of their *f*: for I am
17 be not dismayed at their *f*,
5: 3 made their *f* harder than a rock;
7:19 to the confusion of their own *f*?
30: 6 all *f* are turned into paleness?
42:15 If ye wholly set your *f* to enter
17 all the men that set their *f* to
44:12 that have set their *f* to go into
50: 5 to Zion with their *f* thitherward,
51:51 shame hath covered our *f*: for
La 5:12 *f* of elders were not honoured.
Eze 1: 6 And every one had four *f*,
8 four had their *f* and their wings.
10 As for the likeness of their *f*,
11 Thus were their *f*: and their wings
15 living creatures, with his four *f*.
3: 8 thy face strong against their *f*,
7:18 and shame shall be upon all *f*,
8:16 and their *f* toward the east;
10:14 And every one had four *f*:
21 Every one had four *f* apiece,
22 And the likeness of their *f* was
22 was the same *f* which I saw
14: 6 *f* from all your abominations.
20:47 all *f* from the south to the north
41:18 and every cherub had two *f*;
Da 1:10 why should he see your *f* worse
9: 7 us confusion of *f*, as at this day;
Joe 2: 6 all *f* shall gather blackness.
Na 2:10 *f* of them shall gather blackness.
Hab 1: 9 *f* shall sup up as the east wind,
Mal 2: 3 and spread dung upon your *f*,
M't 6:16 for they disfigure their *f*, that
Lu 24: 5 bowed down their *f* to the earth,
Re 7:11 fell before the throne on their *f*,
9: 7 and their *f* were as the *f* of men.
11:16 upon their *f*, and worshipped God,

fade See also FADETH; FADING.
2Sa 22:46 Strangers shall *f* away, and they
Ps 18:45 strangers shall *f* away, and be
Isa 64: 6 and we all do *f* as a leaf;
Jer 8:13 the fig tree, and the leaf shall *f*;
Eze 47:12 whose leaf shall not *f*, neither
Jas 1:11 so also shall the rich man *f* away

fadeth
Isa 1:30 shall be as an oak whose leaf *f*,
Isa 24: 4 The earth mourneth and *f* away,
4 the world languisheth and *f* away,
40: 7 the flower *f*: because the spirit
8 the flower *f*: but the word of
1Pe 1: 4 undefiled, and that *f* not away,
5: 4 a crown of glory that *f* not away.

fading
Isa 28: 1 glorious beauty is a *f* flower,
4 shall be a *f* flower, and as the

fail See also FAILED; FAILETH; FAILING.
Ge 47:16 you for your cattle, if money *f*.
De 28:32 thine eyes shall look, and *f* with
31: 6 he will not *f* thee, nor forsake
8 he will not *f* thee, neither forsake
Jos 1: 5 I will not *f* thee, nor forsake thee.
3:10 that he will without *f* drive out from
J'g 11:30 without *f* deliver the children
1Sa 2:16 Let them not *f* to burn the fat
17:32 no man's heart *f* because of him;
20: 5 *f* to sit with the king at meat:
30: 8 overtake them, and without *f* recover
2Sa 3:29 not *f* from the house of Joab
1Ki 2: 4 there shall not *f* thee (said he)
8:25 There shall not *f* thee a man in
9: 5 There shall not *f* thee a man upon
17:14 neither shall the cruse of oil *f*,
16 neither did the cruse of oil *f*,
1Ch 28:20 will not *f* thee, nor forsake thee,
2Ch 6:16 There shall not *f* thee a man in
7:18 There shall not *f* thee a man to be
Ezr 4:22 now that ye *f* not to do this:
6: 9 given them day by day without *f*:
Es 6:10 let nothing *f* of all that thou
9:27 so as it should not *f*, that they
28 should not *f* from among the Jews,
Job 11:20 the eyes of the wicked shall *f*,
14:11 As the waters *f* from the sea,
17: 5 the eyes of his children shall *f*.
31:16 caused the eyes of the widow to *f*:
Ps 12: 1 *f* from among the children of men.
69: 3 eyes *f* while I wait for my God.
77: 8 doth his promise *f* for evermore?
89:33 nor suffer my faithfulness to *f*.
119:82 Mine eyes *f* for thy word,
123 Mine eyes *f* for thy salvation,
Pr 22: 8 and the rod of his anger shall *f*.
Ec 12: 5 and desire shall *f*: because man
Isa 19: 3 And the spirit of Egypt shall *f*
5 the waters shall *f* from the sea,
21:16 and all the glory of Kedar shall *f*:
31: 3 and they shall *f* together.
32: 6 cause the drink of the thirsty to *f*.
10 the vintage shall *f*, the gathering
34:16 no one of these shall *f*, none
38:14 mine eyes *f* with looking upward:
42: 4 shall not *f* nor be discouraged,
51:14 nor that his bread should *f*.
57:16 the spirit should *f* before me,
58:11 spring of water, whose waters *f*
Jer 14: 6 their eyes did *f*, because there
15:18 and as waters that *f*?
48:33 and I have caused wine to *f* from
La 2:11 Mine eyes do *f* with tears, my
3:22 because his compassions *f* not.
Ho 9: 2 and the new wine shall *f* in her.
Am 8: 4 to make the poor of the land to *f*,
Hab 3:17 the labour of the olive shall *f*,
Lu 16: 9 when ye *f*, they may receive you
17 than one tittle of the law to *f*.
22:32 for thee, that thy faith *f* not:
1Co 13: 8 there be prophecies, they shall *f*;
Heb 1:12 same, and thy years shall not *f*.
11:32 time would *f* me to tell of Gedeon,
12:15 any man *f* of the grace of God;

failed
Ge 42:28 and their heart *f* them, and they
47:15 And when money *f* in the land
Jos 3:16 the plain, even the salt sea, *f*,
21:45 *f* not ought of any good thing
23:14 thing hath *f* of all the good things
14 and not one thing hath *f* thereof.
1Ki 8:56 there hath not *f* one word of all his
Job 19:14 My kinsfolk have *f*, and my
Ps 142: 4 refuge *f* me; no man cared for my
Ca 5: 6 my soul *f* when he spake:
Jer 51:30 their might hath *f*; they became
La 4:17 eyes as yet *f* for our vain help:

faileth
Ge 47:15 thy presence? for the money *f*.
Job 21:10 Their bull gendereth, and *f* not;
Ps 31:10 my strength *f* because of mine
38:10 heart panteth, my strength *f* me:
40:12 therefore my heart *f* me.
71: 9 me not when my strength *f*.
73:26 My flesh and my heart *f*:
109:24 and my flesh *f* of fatness.
143: 7 O Lord; my spirit *f*: hide not
Ec 10: 3 his wisdom *f* him, and he saith
Isa 15: 6 grass *f*, there is no green thing.
40:26 he is strong in power; not one *f*.
41:17 and their tongue *f* for thirst, I the
44:12 he is hungry, and his strength *f*:
59:15 truth *f*; and he that departeth
Eze 12:22 prolonged, and every vision *f*?
Zep 3: 5 his judgment to light, he *f* not;
Lu 12:33 treasure in the heavens that *f* not,
1Co 13: 8 Charity never *f*: but whether

failing
De 28:65 a trembling heart, and *f* of eyes,
Lu 21:26 Men's hearts *f* them for fear,

fain
Job 27:22 he would *f* flee out of his hand.
Lu 15:16 he would *f* have filled his belly

faint See also FAINTED; FAINTEST; FAINTETH; FAINTHEARTED.
Ge 25:29 came from the field, and he was *f*:
30 that same red pottage; for I am *f*:
De 20: 3 let not your hearts *f*, fear not,
8 lest his brethren's heart *f* as well
25:18 when thou wast *f* and weary;
Jos 2: 9 inhabitants of the land *f* because
24 inhabitants of the country do *f*
J'g 8: 4 men that were with him, *f*, yet
5 that follow me; for they be *f*,
1Sa 14:28 And the people were *f*.
31 and the people were very *f*.
30:10 were so *f* that they could not go
21 two hundred men, which were so *f*
2Sa 16: 2 such as be *f* in the wilderness
21:15 Philistines: and David waxed *f*.
Pr 24:10 If thou *f* in the day of adversity,
Isa 1: 5 is sick, and the whole heart *f*.
13: 7 Therefore shall all hands be *f*,
29: 8 he awaketh, and, behold, he is *f*,
40:29 He giveth power to the *f*;
30 Even the youths shall *f* and be
31 and they shall walk, and not *f*.
44:12 he drinketh no water, and is *f*.
Jer 8:18 sorrow, my heart is *f* in me.
51:46 lest your heart *f*, and ye fear
La 1:13 me desolate and *f* all the day.
22 sighs are many, and my heart is *f*.
2:19 young children, that *f* for hunger
5:17 For this our heart is *f*; for these
Eze 21: 7 and every spirit shall *f*, and all
15 that their heart may *f*, and their
Am 8:13 the fair virgins and young men *f*
M't 15:32 lest they *f* in the way.
M'r 8: 3 they will *f* by the way:
Lu 18: 1 always to pray, and not to *f*;
2Co 4: 1 we have received mercy, we *f* not;
16 For which cause we *f* not; but
Gal 6: 9 we shall reap, if we *f* not.
Eph 3:13 Wherefore I desire that ye *f* not
Heb 12: 3 be wearied and *f* in your minds.
5 *f* when thou art rebuked of him:

fainted
Ge 45:26 Jacob's heart *f*, for he believed
47:13 all the land of Canaan *f* by reason
Ps 27:13 I had *f*, unless I had believed
107: 5 thirsty, their soul *f* in them.
Isa 51:20 Thy sons have *f*, they lie at the
Jer 45: 3 I *f* in my sighing, and I find no
Eze 31:15 the trees of the field *f* for him.
Da 8:27 And I Daniel *f*, and was sick
Jon 2: 7 When my soul *f* within me I
4: 8 upon the head of Jonah, that he *f*,
M't 9:36 they *f*, and were scattered
Re 2: 3 hast laboured, and hast not *f*.

faintest
Job 4: 5 it is come upon thee, and thou *f*;

fainteth
Ps 84: 2 My soul longeth, yea, even *f* for
119:81 My soul *f* for thy salvation:
Isa 10:18 be as when a standardbearer *f*.
40:28 of the ends of the earth, *f* not,

fainthearted
De 20: 8 there that is fearful and *f*?
Isa 7: 4 quiet; fear not, neither be *f*
Jer 49:23 they are *f*; there is sorrow on the

faintness
Le 26:36 I will send a *f* into their hearts

fair See also FAIRER; FAIREST; FAIRS.
Ge 6: 2 daughters of men that they were *f*;
12:11 I know that thou art a *f* woman
14 the woman that she was very *f*.
24:16 damsel was very *f* to look upon,
26: 7 because she was *f* to look upon.
1Sa 17:42 ruddy, and of a *f* countenance.
2Sa 13: 1 the son of David had a *f* sister,
14:27 was a woman of a *f* countenance.
1Ki 1: 3 So they sought for a *f* damsel
4 damsel was very *f*, and cherished
Es 1:11 for she was *f* to look on.
2: 2 *f* young virgins sought for
3 together all the *f* young virgins
7 maid was *f* and beautiful;
Job 37:22 *F* weather cometh out of the
42:15 so *f* as the daughters of Job:
Pr 7:21 With her much *f* speech she
11:22 so is a *f* woman which is without
26:25 When he speaketh *f*, believe him
Ca 1:15 Behold, thou art *f*, my love:
15 behold, thou art *f*; thou hast dove's
16 Behold, thou art *f*, my beloved,
2:10 Rise up, my love, my *f* one,
13 my love, my *f* one, and come
4: 1 Behold, thou art *f*, my love;
1 behold, thou art *f*; thou hast dove's
7 Thou art all *f*, my love;
10 How *f* is thy love, my sister,
6:10 *f* as the moon, clear as the sun,
7: 6 How *f* and how pleasant art thou,
Isa 5: 9 be desolate, even great and *f*,
54:11 will lay thy stones with *f* colours,
Jer 4:30 in vain shalt thou make thyself *f*;
11:16 olive tree, *f*, and of goodly fruit:
12: 6 they speak *f* words unto thee.
46:20 Egypt is like a very *f* heifer,
Eze 16:17 Thou hast also taken thy *f* jewels
39 and shall take thy *f* jewels, and
23:26 and take away thy *f* jewels.
31: 3 cedar in Lebanon with *f* branches,
7 Thus was he *f* in his greatness,
9 made him *f* by the multitude
Da 4:12 The leaves thereof were *f*, and
21 Whose leaves were *f*, and the fruit
Ho 10:11 passed over upon her *f* neck:
Am 8:13 In that day shall the *f* virgins
Zec 3: 5 them set a *f* mitre upon his head.
5 they set a *f* mitre upon his head,
M't 16: 2 ye say, It will be *f* weather:
Ac 7:20 was born, and was exceeding *f*,
27: 8 which is called The *f* havens;
Ro 16:18 by good words and *f* speeches
Gal 6:12 to make a *f* shew in the flesh,

fairer
J'g 15: 2 her younger sister *f* than she?
Ps 45: 2 art *f* than the children of men:
Da 1:15 appeared *f* and fatter in flesh

fairest
Ca 1: 8 O thou *f* among women, go thy
5: 9 thou *f* among women? what is thy
6: 1 O thou *f* among women? whither

fair-havens See FAIR and HAVENS.

fairs
Eze 27:12 and lead, they traded in thy *f*.
14 of Togarmah traded in thy *f*
16 occupied in thy *f* with emeralds,
19 going to an fro occupied in thy *f*:
22 in thy *f* with chief of all spices,
27 and thy *f*, thy merchandise,

faith See also FAITHFUL; FAITHLESS.
De 32:20 children in whom is no *f*.
Hab 2: 4 but the just shall live by his *f*.
M't 6:30 more clothe you, O ye of little *f*?
8:10 I have not found so great *f*, no, not
26 are ye fearful, O ye of little *f*?
9: 2 Jesus seeing their *f* said unto the
22 thy *f* hath made thee whole.
29 According to your *f* be it unto you.
14:31 O thou of little *f*, wherefore didst
15:28 O woman, great is thy *f*:
16: 8 O ye of little *f*, why reason ye
17:20 If ye have *f* as a grain of mustard
21:21 If ye have *f*, and doubt not,
23:23 the law, judgment, mercy, and *f*:
M'r 2: 5 When Jesus saw their *f*, he said
4:40 how is it that ye have no *f*?
5:34 Daughter, thy *f* hath made thee
10:52 way; thy *f* hath made thee whole.
11:22 saith unto them, Have *f* in God.
Lu 5:20 when he saw their *f*, he said unto
7: 9 I have not found so great *f*, no, not
50 Thy *f* hath saved thee; go in peace.
8:25 Where is your *f*? And they being
48 thy *f* hath made thee whole; go in
12:28 will he clothe you, O ye of little *f*?
17: 5 unto the Lord, Increase our *f*.
6 If ye had *f* as a grain of mustard
19 way: thy *f* hath made thee whole.
18: 8 shall he find *f* on the earth?
42 thy sight: thy *f* hath saved thee.
22:32 prayed for thee, that thy *f* fail not:
Ac 3:16 his name through *f* in his name
16 yea, the *f* which is by him
6: 5 a man full of *f* and of the Holy
7 the priests were obedient to the *f*.
8 Stephen, full of *f* and power,
11:24 full of the Holy Ghost and of *f*:
13: 8 to turn away the deputy from the *f*.
14: 9 that he had *f* to be healed,
22 exhorting them to continue in the *f*,
27 how he had opened the door of *f*
15: 9 purifying their hearts by *f*.
16: 5 the churches established in the *f*,
20:21 and *f* toward our Lord Jesus Christ.
24:24 him concerning the *f* in Christ.
26:18 are sanctified by *f* that is in me.
Ro 1: 5 for obedience to the *f* among all
8 that your *f* is spoken of throughout
12 by the mutual *f* both of you and me.
17 God revealed from *f* to *f*: as it is
17 written, The just shall live by *f*.
3: 3 make the *f* of God without effect?
22 which is by *f* of Jesus Christ unto
25 propitiation through *f* in his blood,
27 of works? Nay: but by the law of *f*.
28 a man is justified by *f* without the
30 justify the circumcision by *f*, and
30 and uncircumcision through *f*.
31 make void the law through *f*?
4: 5 his *f* is counted for righteousness.
9 for we say that *f* was reckoned to
11 seal of the righteousness of the *f*
12 walk in the steps of that *f* of our
13 through the righteousness of *f*.
14 *f* is made void, and the promise
16 Therefore it is of *f*, that it might
16 which is of the *f* of Abraham;
19 being not weak in *f*, he considered
20 but was strong in *f*, giving glory
5: 1 being justified by *f*, we have peace
2 we have access by *f* into this grace
9:30 the righteousness which is of *f*.
32 Because they sought it not by *f*,
10: 6 But the righteousness which is of *f*
8 is, the word of *f*, which we preach;
17 So then *f* cometh by hearing,
11:20 broken off, and thou standest by *f*.
12: 3 to every man the measure of *f*.
6 according to the proportion of *f*;
14: 1 Him that is weak in the *f* receive
22 Hast thou *f*? have it to thyself
23 because he eateth not of *f*: for
23 whatsoever is not of *f* is sin.
16:26 all nations for the obedience of *f*:
1Co 2: 5 That your *f* should not stand in
12: 9 To another *f* by the same Spirit;
13: 2 though I have all *f*, so that I could
13 And now abideth *f*, hope, charity,
1Co 15:14 and your *f* is also vain.
17 your *f* is vain; ye are yet in your
16:13 Watch ye, stand fast in the *f*,
2Co 1:24 that we have dominion over your *f*,
24 of your joy: for by *f* ye stand.
4:13 We having the same spirit of *f*,
5: 7 (For we walk by *f*, not by sight:)
8: 7 in *f*, and utterance, and knowledge,
10:15 hope, when your *f* is increased,
13: 5 yourselves, whether ye be in the *f*;
Ga 1:23 now preacheth the *f* which once
2:16 but by the *f* of Jesus Christ,
16 be justified by the *f* of Christ,
20 I live by the *f* of the Son of God,
3: 2, 5 the law, or by the hearing of *f*?
7 they which are of *f*, the same are
8 justify the heathen through *f*,
9 they which be of *f* are blessed
11 for, The just shall live by *f*.
12 And the law is not of *f*:
14 promise of the Spirit through *f*.
22 the promise by *f* of Jesus Christ
23 But before *f* came, we were kept
23 shut up unto the *f*, which should
24 that we might be justified by *f*.
25 But after that *f* is come,
26 children of God by *f* in Christ
5: 5 the hope of righteousness by *f*.
6 but *f* which worketh by love.
22 gentleness, goodness, *f*,
6:10 who are of the household of *f*.
Eph 1:15 after I heard of your *f* in the Lord
2: 8 by grace are ye saved through *f*;
3:12 with confidence by the *f* of him.
17 may dwell in your hearts by *f*;
4: 5 One Lord, one *f*, one baptism,
13 we all come in the unity of the *f*,
6:16 Above all, taking the shield of *f*,
23 and love with *f*, from God the
Ph'p 1:25 for your furtherance and joy of *f*;
27 together for the *f* of the gospel;
2:17 the sacrifice and service of your *f*,
3: 9 which is through the *f* of Christ,
9 righteousness which is of God by *f*:
Col 1: 4 Since we heard of your *f* in Christ
23 If ye continue in the *f* grounded
2: 5 the stedfastness of your *f* in Christ.
7 stablished in the *f*, as ye have been
12 through the *f* of the operation of
1Th 1: 3 your work of *f*, and labour of love,
8 *f* to God-ward is spread abroad;
3: 2 to comfort you concerning your *f*:
5 forbear, I sent to know your *f*,
6 good tidings of your *f* and charity,
7 affliction and distress by your *f*:
10 that which is lacking in your *f*?
5: 8 the breastplate of *f* and love;
2Th 1: 3 your *f* groweth exceedingly, and
4 for your patience and *f* in all your
11 and the work of *f* with power:
3: 2 for all men have not *f*.
1Ti 1: 2 Timothy, my own son in the *f*:
4 than godly edifying which is in *f*:
5 conscience, and of *f* unfeigned:
14 with *f* and love which is in Christ
19 Holding *f*, and a good conscience;
19 concerning *f* have made shipwreck:
2: 7 of the Gentiles in *f* and verity.
15 if they continue in *f* and charity
3: 9 Holding the mystery of the *f* in a
13 great boldness in the *f* which is in
4: 1 some shall depart from the *f*,
6 words of *f* and of good doctrine,
12 in charity, in spirit, in *f*, in purity.
5: 8 he hath denied the *f*, and is worse
12 they have cast off their first *f*.
6:10 they have erred from the *f*,
11 godliness, *f*, love, patience,
12 Fight the good fight of *f*, lay hold
21 have erred concerning the *f*.
2Ti 1: 5 the unfeigned *f* that is in thee,
13 in *f* and love which is in Christ
2:18 and overthrow the *f* of some.
22 follow righteousness, *f*, charity,
3: 8 minds, reprobate concerning the *f*.
10 *f*, longsuffering, charity, patience,
15 through *f* which is in Christ Jesus.
4: 7 my course, I have kept the *f*:
Tit 1: 1 according to the *f* of God's elect,
4 mine own son after the common *f*:
13 that they may be sound in the *f*;
2: 2 sound in *f*, in charity, in patience.
3:15 Greet them that love us in the *f*.
Ph'm 5 Hearing of thy love and *f*,
6 the communication of thy *f* may
Heb 4: 2 not being mixed with *f* in them
6: 1 dead works, and of *f* toward God,
12 who through *f* and patience inherit
10:22 a true heart in full assurance of *f*,
23 hold fast the profession of our *f*
38 Now the just shall live by *f*:
11: 1 Now *f* is the substance of things
3 Through *f* we understand that the
4 By *f* Abel offered unto God a more
5 By *f* Enoch was translated that he
6 without *f* it is impossible to please
7 By *f* Noah, being warned of God
7 of the righteousness which is by *f*.
8 By *f* Abraham, when he was called
9 By *f* he sojourned in the land of
11 Through *f*... Sara herself received
13 These all died in *f*, not having
17 By *f* Abraham, when he was tried,
20 By *f* Isaac blessed Jacob and Esau
21 By *f* Jacob, when he was a dying,
22 By *f* Joseph, when he died, made

Heb 11:23 By f Moses, when he was born,
24 By f Moses, when he was come to
27 By f he forsook Egypt, not fearing
28 Through f he kept the passover,
29 By f he passed through the Red
30 By f the walls of Jericho fell down,
31 By f the harlot Rahab perished not
33 Who through f subdued kingdoms,
39 obtained a good report through f,
12: 2 the author and finisher of our f;
13: 7 whose f follow, considering the
Jas 1: 3 trying of your f worketh patience.
6 let him ask in f, nothing wavering.
2: 1 My brethren, have not the f of our
5 rich in f and heirs of the kingdom
14 though a man say he hath f, and
14 have not works? can f save him?
17 Even so f, if it hath not works, is
18 Thou hast f, and I have works:
18 shew me thy f without thy works,
18 I will shew thee my f by my works.
20 that f without works is dead?
22 Seest thou how f wrought with his
22 and by works was f made perfect?
24 man is justified, and not by f only.
26 so f without works is dead also.
5:15 the prayer of f shall save the sick,
1Pe 1: 5 through f unto salvation ready to
7 That the trial of your f, being much
9 Receiving the end of your f,
21 your f and hope might be in God.
5: 9 Whom resist stedfast in the f,
2Pe 1: 1 obtained like precious f with us
5 add to your f virtue: and to virtue
1Jo 5: 4 overcometh the world, even our f.
Jude 3 for the f which was once delivered
20 up yourselves on your most holy f,
Re 2:13 and hast not denied my f,
19 and charity, and service, and f,
13:10 the patience and the f of the saints.
14:12 of God, and the f of Jesus.

faithful See also UNFAITHFUL.
Nu 12: 7 who is f in all mine house.
De 7: 9 thy God, he is God, the f God,
1Sa 2:35 I will raise me up a f priest,
22:14 who is so f among all thy servants
2Sa 20:19 that are peaceable and f in Israel:
Ne 7: 2 he was a f man, and feared God
9: 8 foundest his heart f before thee,
13:13 for they were counted f, and their
Ps 12: 1 the f fail from among the children
31:23 for the Lord preserveth the f,
89:37 and as a f witness in heaven.
101: 6 eyes shall be upon the f of the land
119:86 All thy commandments are f:
138 are righteous and very f.
Pr 11:13 he that is of a f spirit concealeth
13:17 but a f ambassador is health.
14: 5 A f witness will not lie: but a false
20: 6 but a f man who can find?
25:13 is a f messenger to them that send
27: 6 F are the wounds of a friend;
28:20 A f man shall abound with
Isa 1:21 How is the f city become an harlot!
26 city of righteousness, the f city.
8: 2 And I took unto me f witnesses to
49: 7 because of the Lord that is f,
Jer 42: 5 a true and f witness between us,
Da 6: 4 forasmuch as he was f, neither
Ho 11:12 and is f with the saints.
M't 24:45 Who then is a f and wise servant,
25:21 done, thou good and f servant:
21 thou hast been f over a few things,
23 Well done, good and f servant;
23 thou hast been f over a few things,
Lu 12:42 then is that f and wise steward,
16:10 He that is f in that which is
10 is least is f also in much:
11 f in the unrighteous mammon,
12 And if ye have not been f in that
19:17 thou hast been f in a very little,
Ac 16:15 have judged me to be f to the Lord,
1Co 1: 9 God is f, by whom ye were called
4: 2 stewards, that a man be found f.
17 my beloved son, and f in the Lord,
7:25 mercy of the Lord to be f.
10:13 but God is f, who will not suffer
Ga 3: 9 faith are blessed with f Abraham.
Eph 1: 1 and to the f in Christ Jesus:
6:21 and f minister in the Lord,
Col 1: 2 saints and f brethren in Christ
7 is for you a f minister in Christ;
4: 7 a f minister and fellowservant in
9 Onesimus, a f and beloved brother,
1Th 5:24 F is he that calleth you,
2Th 3: 3 Lord is f, who shall stablish you,
1Ti 1:12 for that he counted me f,
15 This is a f saying, and worthy of all
3:11 slanderers, sober, f in all things.
4: 9 This is a f saying and worthy of all
6: 2 because they are f and beloved,
2Ti 2: 2 the same commit thou to f men,
11 It is a f saying: For if we be dead
13 yet he abideth f: he cannot deny
Tit 1: 6 having f children not accused
9 the f word as he hath been taught,
3: 8 This is a f saying, and these things
Heb 2:17 be a merciful and f high priest in
3: 2 was f to him that appointed him,
2 also Moses was f in all his house.
5 Moses verily was f in all his
10:23 (for he is f that promised;)
11:11 judged him f who had promised.
1Pe 4:19 in well doing, as unto a f Creator.
5:12 By Silvanus, a f brother unto you,
1Jo 1: 9 he is f and just to forgive us our
Re 1: 5 Jesus Christ who is the f witness,
2:10 be thou f unto death, and I will
13 Antipas was my f martyr, who was
3:14 the Amen, the f and true witness,
17:14 him are called, and chosen, and f.
19:11 upon him was called F and True,
21: 5 for these words are true and f.
22: 6 These sayings are f and true:

faithfully See also UNFAITHFULLY.
2Ki 12:15 on workmen: for they dealt f.
22: 7 their hand, because they dealt f.
2Ch 19: 9 Lord, f, and with a perfect heart.
31:12 tithes and the dedicated things f:
34:12 And the men did the work f:
Pr 29:14 The king that f judgeth the poor,
Jer 23:28 let him speak my word f.
3Jo 5 doest f whatsoever thou doest

faithfulness
1Sa 26:23 man his righteousness and his f:
Ps 5: 9 there is no f in their mouth;
36: 5 thy f reacheth unto the clouds.
40:10 declared thy f and thy salvation:
88:11 the grave? or thy f in destruction?
89: 1 mouth will I make known thy f to all
2 thy f shalt thou establish in the very
5 thy f also in the congregation of the
8 or to thy f round about thee?
24 But my f and my mercy shall be with
33 nor suffer my f to fail.
92: 2 and thy f every night,
119:75 that thou in f hast afflicted me.
90 Thy f is unto all generations:
143: 1 in thy f answer me, and in thy
Isa 11: 5 and f the girdle of his reins.
25: 1 counsels of old are f and truth.
La 3:23 every morning: great is thy f.
Ho 2:20 will even betroth thee unto me in f:

faithless
M't 17:17 said, O f and perverse generation,
M'r 9:19 saith, O f generation, how long shall
Lu 9:41 said, O f and perverse generation,
Joh 20:27 and be not f, but believing.

fall See also BEFALL; FALLEN; FALLEST; FALLETH; FALLING; FELL.
Ge 2:21 a deep sleep to f upon Adam,
43:18 occasion against us, and f upon us,
45:24 See that ye f not out by the way.
49:17 that his rider shall f backward.
Ex 5: 3 lest he f upon us with pestilence,
15:16 and dread shall f upon them;
21:33 and an ox or an ass f therein;
Le 11:32 them, when they are dead, doth f,
37 if any part of their carcase f upon
38 any part of their carcase f thereon,
19:29 lest the land f to whoredom,
26: 7 and they shall f before you by the
8 your enemies shall f before you by
36 they shall f when none pursueth.
37 they shall f one upon another,
Nu 11:31 and let them f by the camp,
14: 3 unto this land, to f by the sword,
29 carcases shall f in this wilderness;
32 they shall f in this wilderness.
43 and ye shall f by the sword:
34: 2 is the land that shall f unto you for
De 22: 4 thy brother's ass or his ox f down
8 if any man f from thence.
Jos 6: 5 the wall of the city shall f down
J'g 8:21 Rise thou, and f upon us:
15:12 unto me that ye will not f upon me
18 thirst, and f into the hand of the
Ru 2:16 let f also some of the handfuls
3:18 thou know how the matter will f:
1Sa 3:19 and did let none of his words f to
14:45 shall not one hair of his head f to
18:25 Saul thought to make David f by
21:13 his spittle f down upon his beard.
22:17 their hand to f upon the priests
18 Turn thou, and f upon the priests.
26:20 let not my blood f to the earth
2Sa 1:15 said, Go near, and f upon him.
14:11 shall not one hair of thy son f to
24:14 us f now into the hand of the Lord;
14 let me not f into the hand of man.
1Ki 1:52 there shall not an hair of him f to
2:29 Jehoiada, saying, Go, f upon him,
31 as he hath said, and f upon him,
22:20 go up and f at Ramoth-gilead?
2Ki 7: 4 us f unto the host of the Syrians:
10:10 shall f unto the earth nothing
14:10 shouldest f, even thou, and Judah
19: 7 will cause him to f by the sword
1Ch 12:19 He will f to his master Saul
21:13 f now into the hand of the Lord;
13 let me not f into the hand of man.
2Ch 18:19 that he may go up and f at
21:15 until thy bowels f out by reason
25: 8 God shall make thee f before
19 shouldest f, even thou, and Judah
Es 6:13 before whom thou hast began to f,
13 but shalt surely f before him.
Job 13:11 afraid? and his dread f upon you?
31:22 arm f from my shoulder blade,
Ps 5:10 let them f by their own counsels:
9: 3 they shall f and perish at thy
10:10 the poor may f by his strong ones.
35: 8 into that very destruction let him f.
37:24 Though he f, he shall not be
45: 5 whereby the people f under thee.
63:10 They shall f by the sword: they
64: 8 make their own tongue to f upon
72:11 kings shall f down before him:
78:28 let it f in the midst of their camp,
Ps 82: 7 and f like one of the princes.
91: 7 A thousand shall f at thy side,
118:13 thrust sore at me that I might f:
140:10 Let burning coals f upon them:
141:10 the wicked f into their own nets,
145:14 The Lord upholdeth all that f,
Pr 4:16 unless they cause some to f.
10: 8 but a prating fool shall f.
10 sorrow: but a prating fool shall f.
11: 5 shall f by his own wickedness.
14 Where no counsel is, the people f:
28 that trusteth in his riches shall f:
16:18 and an haughty spirit before a f.
22:14 of the Lord shall f therein.
24:16 the wicked shall f into mischief.
26:27 diggeth a pit shall f therein:
28:10 he shall f himself into his own pit:
14 that hardeneth his heart shall f
18 is perverse in his ways shall f at
29:16 the righteous shall see their f.
Ec 4:10 For if they f, the one will lift up
10: 8 that diggeth a pit shall f into it;
11: 3 if the tree f toward the south,
Isa 3:25 Thy men shall f by the sword,
8:15 among them shall stumble, and f,
10: 4 and they shall f under the slain.
34 Lebanon shall f by a mighty one.
13:15 unto them shall f by the sword.
22:25 removed, and be cut down, and f;
24:18 noise of the fear shall f into the pit;
20 and it shall f, and not rise again.
28:13 they might go, and f backward,
30:13 as a breach ready to f, swelling
25 slaughter, when the towers f.
31: 3 both he that helpeth shall f, and
3 he that is holpen shall f down,
8 the Assyrian f with the sword,
34: 4 all their host shall f down, as
37: 7 will cause him to f by the sword
40:30 the young men shall utterly f:
44:19 I f down to the stock of a tree?
45:14 they shall f down unto thee,
46: 6 they f down, yea, they worship.
47:11 and mischief shall f upon thee;
54:15 together against thee shall f for thy
Jer 3:12 not cause mine anger to f upon
6:15 they shall f among them that f:
21 the sons together shall f upon
8: 4 Shall they f, and not arise? shall
12 shall they f among them that f:
9:22 Even the carcases of men shall f as
15: 8 I have caused him to f upon it
19: 7 and I will cause them to f by the
20: 4 and they shall f by the sword
23:12 shall be driven on, and f therein:
19 shall f grievously upon the head
25:27 be drunken, and spue, and f,
34 ye shall f like a pleasant vessel,
30:23 shall f with pain upon the head
37:14 I f not away to the Chaldeans.
39:18 thou shalt not f by the sword,
44:12 and f in the land of Egypt,
46: 6 and f toward the north by the
16 made many to f, yea, one fell
48:44 fleeth from the fear shall f into
49:21 is moved at the noise of their f,
26 young men shall f in her streets,
50:30 shall her young men f in the
32 most proud shall stumble and f,
51: 4 Thus the slain shall f in the land
44 yea, the wall of Babylon shall f.
47 all her slain shall f in the midst
49 hath caused the slain of Israel to f,
49 so at Babylon shall f the slain of
La 1:14 he hath made my strength to f,
Eze 5:12 a third part shall f by the sword
6: 7 the slain shall f in the midst of you,
11 for they shall f by the sword,
12 that is near shall f by the sword;
11:10 Ye shall f by the sword; I will
13:11 morter, that it shall f:
11 ye, O great hailstones, shall f;
14 and it shall f, and ye shall be
17:21 fugitives with all his bands shall f
23:25 remnant shall fall by the sword:
24: 6 piece by piece; let no lot f upon it.
21 daughters whom ye have left shall f
25:13 they of Dedan shall f by the sword.
26:15 isles shake at the sound of thy f,
18 isles tremble in the day of thy f;
27:27 is in the midst of thee, shall f into
34 in the midst of thee shall f.
29: 5 thou shalt f upon the open fields;
30: 4 when the slain shall f in Egypt,
5 land that is in league, shall f with
6 also that uphold Egypt shall f;
6 shall they f in it by the sword,
17 of Pi-beseth shall f by the sword.
22 I will cause the sword to f out of
25 the arms of Pharaoh shall f down;
31:16 to shake at the sound of his f,
32:10 his own life, in the day of thy f.
12 will I cause thy multitude to f,
20 They shall f in the midst of them
33:12 he shall not f thereby in the day
27 the wastes shall f by the sword,
35: 8 rivers, shall they f that are slain
36:15 shalt thou cause thy nations to f.
38:20 and the steep places shall f,
20 every wall shall f to the ground.
39: 3 will cause thine arrows to f out of
4 Thou shalt f upon the mountains
5 Thou shalt f upon the open field:
44:12 house of Israel to f into iniquity;
47:14 and this land shall f unto you

Da 3: 5 ye f down and worship the golden
10 shall f down and worship the golden
15 ye f down and worship the golden
11:14 establish...vision; but they shall f.
19 stumble and f, and not be found.
26 overflow: and many shall f down
33 yet they shall f by the sword,
34 Now when they shall f, they shall
35 of them of understanding shall f,
Ho 4: 5 Therefore shalt thou f in the day,
5 and the prophet also shall f with
14 that doth not understand shall f.
5: 5 shall Israel and Ephraim f in
5 Judah also shall f with them.
7:16 their princes shall f by the sword
10: 8 and to the hills, F on us.
13:16 they shall f by the sword: their
14: 9 the transgressors shall f therein.
Joe 2: 8 when they f upon the sword,
Am 3: 5 Can a bird f in a snare upon the
14 be cut off, and f to the ground.
7:17 sons and thy daughters shall f by
8:14 they shall f, and never rise up
9: 9 yet shall not the least grain f upon
Mic 7: 8 enemy: when I f, I shall arise;
Na 3:12 they shall even f into the mouth of
M't 4: 9 wilt f down and worship me.
7:27 and great was the f of it.
10:29 them shall not f on the ground
12:11 if it f into the pit on the sabbath
15:14 blind, both shall f into the ditch.
27 which f from their masters' table.
21:44 whosoever shall f on this stone
44 on whomsoever it shall f, it will
24:29 and the stars shall f from heaven,
M'r 13:25 And the stars of heaven shall f,
Lu 2:34 child is set for the f and rising
6:39 shall they not both f into the ditch?
8:13 and in time of temptation f away.
10:18 as lightning f from heaven.
20:18 Whosoever shall f upon that
18 but on whomsoever it shall f,
21:24 shall f by the edge of the sword,
23:30 F on us; and to the hills, Cover us.
Joh 12:24 wheat f into the ground and die,
Ac 27:17 should f into the quicksands,
32 ropes of the boat, and let her f off.
34 shall not an hair f from the head
Ro 11:11 they stumbled that they should f?
11 through their f salvation is come
12 Now if the f of them be the riches
14:13 occasion to f in his brother's way.
1Co 10:12 he standeth take heed lest he f.
1Ti 3: 6 pride he f into the condemnation
7 he f into reproach and the snare
6: 9 rich f into temptation and a snare,
Heb 4:11 lest any man f after the same
6: 6 If they shall f away, to renew
10:31 to f into the hands of the living
Jas 1: 2 when ye f into divers temptations;
5:12 nay; lest ye f into condemnation.
2Pe 1:10 do these things, ye shall never f:
3:17 f from your own stedfastness,
Re 4:10 four and twenty elders f down
6:16 mountains and rocks, F on us,
9: 1 and I saw a star f from heaven

fallen See also BEFALLEN.
Ge 4: 6 and why is thy countenance f?
Le 13:40 the man whose hair is f off
41 he that hath his hair f off
25:35 and f in decay with thee;
Nu 32:19 because our inheritance is f to us
Jos 2: 9 and that your terror is f upon us,
8:24 were all f on the edge of the sword,
J'g 3:25 their lord was f down dead on the
18: 1 inheritance had not f unto them
19:27 concubine was f down at the door
1Sa 5: 3 was f upon his face to the earth
4 was f upon his face to the ground
26:12 from the Lord was f upon them.
31: 8 found Saul and his three sons f in
2Sa 1: 4 many of the people also are f and
10 could not live after that he was f:
12 because they were f by the sword.
19 high places: how are the mighty f!
25 How are the mighty f in the midst
27 How are the mighty f, and the
3:38 there is a prince and a great man f
22:39 yea, they are f under my feet.
2Ki 13:14 Now Elisha was f sick of his sickness
1Ch 10: 8 they found Saul and his sons f in
2Ch 20:24 were dead bodies f to the earth,
29: 9 our fathers have f by the sword,
Es 7: 8 Haman was f upon the bed where
Job 1:16 The fire of God is f from heaven,
Ps 7:15 is f into the ditch which he made.
16: 6 are f unto me in pleasant places:
18:38 they are f under my feet.
20: 8 They are brought down and f:
36:12 There are the workers of iniquity f:
55: 4 the terrors of death are f upon me.
57: 6 whereof they are f themselves.
69: 9 reproached thee are f upon me.
Isa 3: 8 is ruined, and Judah is f:
9:10 The bricks are f down, but we will
14:12 How art thou f from heaven,
16: 9 fruits and for thy harvest is f.
21: 9 and said, Babylon is f, is f;
26:18 have the inhabitants of the world f.
59:14 truth is f in the street, and equity
Jer 38:19 Jews that are f to the Chaldeans,
46:12 mighty, they are f both together.
48:32 the spoiler is f upon thy summer
50:15 her foundations are f, her walls
51: 8 Babylon is suddenly f and
La 2:21 my young men are f by the sword;
5:16 The crown is f from our head:
Eze 13:12 the wall is f, shall it not be said
31:12 all the valleys his branches are f,
32:22 all of them slain, f by the sword:
23, 24 all of them slain, f by the sword,
27 that are f of the uncircumcised,
Ho 7: 7 all their kings are f: there is none
14: 1 for thou hast f by thine iniquity.
Am 5: 2 The virgin of Israel is f; she
9:11 the tabernacle of David that is f,
Zec 11: 2 Howl, fir tree; for the cedar is f;
Lu 14: 5 have an ass or an ox f into a pit,
Ac 8:16 yet he was f upon none of them:
15:16 of David, which is f down,
20: 9 being f into a deep sleep:
26:14 when we were all f to the earth,
27:29 lest we should have f upon rocks,
28: 6 should have swollen, or f down
1Co 15: 6 but some are f asleep.
18 also which are f asleep in Christ
Ga 5: 4 by the law; ye are f from grace.
Ph'p 1:12 happened unto me have f out
Re 2: 5 from whence thou art f,
14: 8 Babylon is f, is f, that great city,
17:10 five are f, and one is, and the
18: 2 Babylon the great is f, is f,

fallest
Jer 37:13 Thou f away to the Chaldeans.

falleth See also BEFALLETH.
Ex 1:10 when there f out any war,
Le 11:33 vessel, whereinto any of them f,
35 any part of their carcase f shall be
Nu 33:54 in the place where his lot f;
2Sa 3:29 or that f on the sword, or that
34 as a man f before wicked men,
17:12 as the dew f on the ground:
Job 4:13 when deep sleep f on men,
33:15 when deep sleep f upon men,
Pr 13:17 wicked messenger f into mischief:
17:20 that hath a perverse tongue f into
24:16 For a just man f seven times,
17 Rejoice not when thine enemy f,
Ec 4:10 to him that is alone when he f;
9:12 when it f suddenly upon them.
11: 3 in the place where the tree f,
Isa 34: 4 as the leaf f off from the vine,
44:15 image, and f down thereto.
17 he f down unto it, and worshippeth
Jer 21: 9 f to the Chaldeans that besiege
Da 3: 6 f not down and worshippeth shall
11 whoso f not down and worshippeth,
M't 17:15 for ofttimes he f into the fire,
Lu 11:17 a house divided against a house f.
15:12 the portion of goods that f to me.
Ro 14: 4 his own master he standeth or f.
Jas 1:11 the grass, and the flower thereof f,
1Pe 1:24 and the flower thereof f away:

fallible See INFALLIBLE.

falling
Nu 24: 4, 16 f into a trance, but having his
Job 4: 4 have upholden him that was f,
14:18 mountain f cometh to nought,
Ps 56:13 not thou deliver my feet from f,
116: 8 from tears, and my feet from f.
Pr 25:26 A righteous man f down before
Isa 34: 4 as a f fig from the fig tree.
Lu 8:47 trembling, and f down before him,
22:44 of blood f down to the ground.
Ac 1:18 f headlong, he burst asunder
27:41 And f into a place where two
1Co 14:25 and so f down on his face he will
2Th 2: 3 except there come a f away first,
Jude 24 that is able to keep you from f,

fallow See also FALLOWDEER.
De 14: 5 and the roebuck and the f deer,
Jer 4: 3 Break up your f ground, and sow
Ho 10:12 break up your f ground: for it is

fallowdeer See also FALLOW and DEER.
1Ki 4:23 harts, and roebucks, and f,

fallow-ground See FALLOW and GROUND.

false See also FALSEHOOD; FALSIFYING.
Ex 20:16 Thou shalt not bear f witness
23: 1 Thou shalt not raise a f report:
7 Keep thee far from a f matter;
De 5:20 Neither shalt thou bear f witness
19:16 If a f witness rise up against any
18 if the witness be a f witness,
2Ki 9:12 they said, It is f: tell us now.
Job 36: 4 truly my words shall not be f:
Ps 27:12 f witnesses are risen up against
35:11 F witnesses did rise up; they
119:104 therefore I hate every f way.
128 and I hate every f way.
120: 3 done unto thee, thou f tongue?
Pr 6:19 A f witness that speaketh lies,
11: 1 A f balance is abomination to
12:17 but a f witness deceit.
14: 5 but a f witness will utter lies.
17: 4 doer giveth heed to f lips;
19: 5, 9 A f witness shall not be
20:23 and a f balance is not good.
21:28 A f witness shall perish: but the
25:14 boasteth himself of a f gift is
18 A man that beareth f witness
Jer 14:14 you a f vision and divination,
23:32 them that prophesy f dreams,
37:14 Then said Jeremiah, It is f;
La 2:14 have seen for thee f burdens and
Eze 21:23 as a f divination in their sight,
Zec 8:17 and love no f oath: for all these
10: 2 a lie, and have told f dreams;
Mal 3: 5 and against f swearers, and
M't 7:15 Beware of f prophets, which come
15:19 thefts, f witness, blasphemies:
19:18 Thou shalt not bear f witness,
24:11 And many f prophets shall rise,
24 For there shall arise f Christs,
24 and f prophets, and shall shew
26:59 sought f witness against Jesus,
60 though many f witnesses came,
60 At the last came two f witnesses,
M'r 10:19 Do not bear f witness, Defraud
13:22 For f Christs...shall rise, and shall
22 and f prophets shall rise, and shall
14:56 For many bare f witness against
57 and bare f witness against him.
Lu 6:26 their fathers to the f prophets.
18:20 Do not bear f witness, Honour
19: 8 from any man by f accusation,
Ac 6:13 set up f witnesses, which said,
13: 6 sorcerer, a f prophet, a Jew,
Ro 13: 9 Thou shalt not bear f witness,
1Co 15:15 we are found f witnesses of God;
2Co 11:13 For such are f apostles, deceitful
26 sea, in perils among f brethren;
Ga 2: 4 because of f brethren unawares
2Ti 3: 3 trucebreakers, f accusers,
Tit 2: 3 not f accusers, not given to much
2Pe 2: 1 there were f prophets also among
1 there shall be f teachers among
1Jo 4: 1 because many f prophets are gone
Re 16:13 out of the mouth of the f prophet.
19:20 f prophet that wrought miracles
20:10 the beast and the f prophet are,

false-accusation See FALSE and ACCUSATION.

false-apostles See FALSE and APOSTLES.

false-brethren See FALSE and BRETHREN.

false-christs See FALSE and CHRISTS.

falsehood
2Sa 18:13 wrought f against mine own life:
Job 21:34 your answers there remaineth f?
Ps 7:14 mischief, and brought forth f.
119:118 thy statutes: for their deceit is f.
144: 8 their right hand is a right hand of f.
11 their right hand is a right hand of f:
Isa 28:15 under f have we hid ourselves:
57: 4 of transgression, a seed of f,
59:13 uttering from the heart words of f.
Jer 10:14 for his molten image is f, and
13:25 hast forgotten me, and trusted in f.
51:17 for his molten image is f, and
Ho 7: 1 for they commit f; and the thief
Mic 2:11 walking in the spirit and f do lie,

falsely
Ge 21:23 that thou wilt not deal f with me,
Le 6: 3 it, and sweareth f;
5 that about which he hath sworn f:
19:11 Ye shall not steal, neither deal f,
12 ye shall not swear by my name f,
De 19:18 hath testified f against his brother;
Ps 44:17 neither have we dealt f in thy
Jer 5: 2 Lord liveth; surely they swear f.
31 prophets prophesy f, and the
6:13 unto the priest every one dealeth f.
7: 9 and commit adultery, and swear f,
8:10 unto the priest every one dealeth f.
29: 9 prophesy f unto you in my name:
40:16 for thou speakest f of Ishmael.
43: 2 unto Jeremiah, Thou speakest f:
Hos 10: 4 swearing f in making a covenant:
Zec 5: 4 the house of him that sweareth f
M't 5:11 all manner of evil against you f,
Lu 3:14 neither accuse any f; and be
1Ti 6:20 oppositions of science f so called:
1Pe 3:16 ashamed that f accuse your

false-prophet See FALSE and PROPHET.

false-teacher See FALSE and TEACHER.

false-witness See FALSE and WITNESS.

falsifying
Am 8: 5 and f the balances by deceit?

fame See also DEFAME.
Ge 45:16 f thereof was heard in Pharaoh's
Nu 14:15 which have heard the f of thee
Jos 6:27 his f was noised throughout all
9: 9 for we have heard the f of him,
1Ki 4:31 his f was in all nations round
10: 1 of Sheba heard of the f of Solomon
7 exceedeth the f which I heard.
1Ch 14:17 the f of David went out into all
22: 5 magnifical, of f and of glory
2Ch 9: 1 Sheba heard of the f of Solomon,
6 thou exceedest the f that I heard.
Es 9: 4 his f went out throughout all the
Job 28:22 We have heard the f thereof with
Isa 66:19 afar off, that have not heard my f,
Jer 6:24 We have heard the f thereof: our
Zep 3:19 I will get them praise and f in
M't 4:24 his f went throughout all Syria:
9:26 the f hereof went abroad into all
31 spread abroad his f in all that
14: 1 tetrarch heard of the f of Jesus,
M'r 1:28 immediately his f spread abroad
Lu 4:14 and there went out a f of him
37 the f of him went out into every
5:15 went there a f abroad of him:

familiar See also FAMILIARS.
Le 19:31 not them that have f spirits,
20: 6 turneth after such as have f spirits,
27 also or woman that hath a f spirit,
De 18:11 or a consulter with f spirits, or a
1Sa 28: 3 put away those that had f spirits,

1Sa 28: 7 me a woman that hath a *f* spirit,
7 woman that hath a *f* spirit at En-dor.
8 divine unto me by the *f* spirit, and
9 hath cut off those that have *f* spirits,
2Ki 21: 6 and dealt with *f* spirits and wizards:
23:24 the workers with *f* spirits, and the
1Ch 10:13 counsel of one that had a *f* spirit,
2Ch 33: 6 and dealt with a *f* spirit, and with
Job 19:14 my *f* friends have forgotten me.
Ps 41: 9 Yea, mine own *f* friend, in whom
Isa 8:19 unto them that have *f* spirits, and
19: 3 and to them that have *f* spirits, and
29: 4 as of one that hath a *f* spirit,

familiars
Jer 20:10 all my *f* watched for my halting.

familiar-spirit See FAMILIAR and SPIRIT.

families
Ge 10: 5 after their *f*, in their nations.
18 were the *f* of the Canaanites
20 are the sons of Ham, after their *f*,
31 are the sons of Shem, after their *f*,
32 These are the *f* of the sons of Noah,
12: 3 shall all *f* of the earth be blessed.
28:14 all the *f* of the earth be blessed.
36:40 of Esau according to their *f*,
47:12 with bread, according to their *f*.
Ex 6:14 Carmi: these be the *f* of Reuben.
15 women: these are the *f* of Simeon.
17 and Shimi, according to their *f*.
19 these are the *f* of Levi according
24 these are the *f* of the Korhites.
25 of the Levites according to their *f*.
12:21 you a lamb according to your *f*,
Le 25:45 and of their *f* that are with you,
Nu 1: 2 the children of Israel, after their *f*,
18 their pedigrees after their *f*,
20, 22, 24, 26, 28, 30, 32, 34, 36, 38, 40 by
their generations, after their *f*,
42 their generations, after their *f*, by
2:34 forward, every one after their *f*,
3:15 children of Levi,...after their *f*:
18 the sons of Gershon by their *f*;
19 the sons of Kohath by their *f*;
20 the sons of Merari by their *f*;
20 These are the *f* of the Levites
21 these are the *f* of the Gershonites.
23 The *f* of the Gershonites shall
27 these are the *f* of the Kohathites.
29 The *f* of the sons of Kohath
30 father of the *f* of the Kohathites
33 these are the *f* of Merari.
35 of the *f* of Merari was Zuriel
39 throughout their *f*, all the males
4: 2 the sons of Levi, after their *f*,
18 tribe of the *f* of the Kohathites
22 houses of their fathers, by their *f*;
24 service of the *f* of the Gershonites,
28 of the *f* of the sons of Gershon in
29 shalt number them after their *f*,
33 of the *f* of the sons of Merari,
34 sons of the Kohathites after their *f*,
36 were numbered of them by their *f*
37 of the *f* of the Kohathites, all that
38 of Gershon, throughout their *f*,
40 throughout their *f*, by the house of
41 of the *f* of the sons of Gershon,
42 of the *f* of the sons of Merari,
42 throughout their *f*, by the house of
44 numbered of them after their *f*,
45 of the *f* of the sons of Merari,
46 of Israel, numbered after their *f*,
11:10 people weep throughout their *f*,
26: 7 These are the *f* of the Reubenites:
12 The sons of Simeon after their *f*:
14 These are the *f* of the Simeonites,
15 The children of Gad after their *f*:
18 These are the *f* of the children of
20 sons of Judah after their *f* were;
22 These are the *f* of Judah
23 the sons of Issachar after their *f*:
25 These are the *f* of Issachar
26 the sons of Zebulun after their *f*:
27 These are the *f* of the Zebulunites
28 The sons of Joseph after their *f*
34 These are the *f* of Manasseh, after
35 the sons of Ephraim after their *f*:
37 are the *f* of the sons of Ephraim
37 are the sons of Joseph after their *f*.
38 The sons of Benjamin after their *f*:
41 the sons of Benjamin after their *f*:
42 are the sons of Dan after their *f*;
42 These are the *f* of Dan after their *f*.
43 All the *f* of the Shuhamites,
44 the children of Asher after their *f*:
47 These are the *f* of the sons of Asher
48 Of the sons of Naphtali after their *f*:
50 *f* of Naphtali according to their *f*:
57 of the Levites after their *f*:
58 These are the *f* of the Levites:
27: 1 of the *f* of Manasseh the son of
33:54 for an inheritance among your *f*:
36: 1 the *f* of the children of Gilead,
1 of the *f* of the sons of Joseph,
12 married into the *f* of the sons of
Jos 7:14 according to the *f* thereof; and
13:15 inheritance according to their *f*.
23 children of Reuben after their *f*,
24 of Gad according to their *f*.
28 the children of Gad after their *f*,
29 children of Manasseh by their *f*.
31 the children of Machir by their *f*.
15: 1 the children of Judah by their *f*;
12 round about according to their *f*.
20 of Judah according to their *f*.

Jos 16: 5 of Ephraim according to their *f*
8 the children of Ephraim by their *f*.
17: 2 children of Manasseh by their *f*;
2 the son of Joseph by their *f*.
18:11 came up according to their *f*:
20 round about, according to their *f*.
21 of Benjamin according to their *f*
28 of Benjamin according to their *f*.
19: 1 of Simeon according to their *f*:
8 of Simeon according to their *f*.
10 of Zebulun according to their *f*:
16 of Zebulun according to their *f*,
17 of Issachar according to their *f*.
23 of Issachar according to their *f*,
24 of Asher according to their *f*.
31 of Asher according to their *f*,
32 of Naphtali according to their *f*.
39 of Naphtali according to their *f*,
40 of Dan according to their *f*.
48 of Dan according to their *f*,
21: 4 for the *f* of the Kohathites:
5 of the *f* of the tribe of Ephraim,
6 of the *f* of the tribe of Issachar,
7 The children of Merari by their *f*
10 being of the *f* of the Kohathites,
20 And the *f* of the children of Kohath,
26 for the *f* of the children of Kohath
27 of Gershon, of the *f* of the Levites,
33 according to their *f* were thirteen
34 unto the *f* of the children of Merari,
40 the children of Merari by their *f*,
40 remaining of the *f* of the Levites,
1Sa 9:21 and my family the least of all the *f*
10:21 Benjamin to come near by their *f*,
1Ch 2:53 And the *f* of Kirjath-jearim; the
55 the *f* of the scribes which dwelt
4: 2 These are the *f* of the Zorathites.
8 the *f* of Aharhel the son of Harum.
21 and the *f* of the house of them
38 names were princes in their *f*:
5: 7 And his brethren by their *f*,
6:19 And these are the *f* of the Levites
54 Aaron, of the *f* of the Kohathites:
60 All their cities throughout their *f*
62 of Gershom throughout their *f*
63 given by lot, throughout their *f*,
66 of the *f* of the sons of Kohath had
7: 5 among all the *f* of Issachar were
2Ch 35: 5 divisions of the *f* of the fathers
5 division of the *f* of the Levites.
12 divisions of the *f* of the people,
Ne 4:13 after their *f* with their swords,
Job 31:34 did the contempt of *f* terrify me,
Ps 68: 6 God setteth the solitary in *f*:
107:41 and maketh him *f* like a flock.
Jer 1:15 will call all the *f* of the kingdoms
2: 4 all the *f* of the house of Israel:
10:25 the *f* that call not on thy name:
25: 9 and take all the *f* of the north,
31: 1 the God of all the *f* of Israel,
33:24 two *f* which the Lord hath chosen,
Eze 20:32 as the *f* of the countries, to serve
Am 3: 2 I known of all the *f* of the earth:
Na 3: 4 and *f* through her witchcrafts.
Zec 12:14 *f* that remain, every family apart,
14:17 come up of all the *f* of the earth

family See also FAMILIES.
Le 20: 5 that man, and against his *f*,
25:10 shall return every man unto his *f*.
41 and shall return unto his own *f*,
47 or to the stock of the stranger's *f*:
49 is nigh of kin unto him of his *f*
Nu 3:21 Gershon was the *f* of the Libnites,
21 and the *f* of the Shimites:
27 Kohath was the *f* of the Amramites
27 and the *f* of the Izeharites,
27 and the *f* of the Hebronites,
27 and the *f* of the Uzzielites:
33 Merari was the *f* of the Mahlites,
33 and the *f* of the Mushites:
26: 5 cometh the *f* of the Hanochites:
5 of Pallu, the *f* of the Palluites:
6 Of Hezron, the *f* of the Hezronites:
6 of Carmi, the *f* of the Carmites.
12 Nemuel, the *f* of the Nemuelites:
12 of Jamin, the *f* of the Jaminites:
12 of Jachin, the *f* of the Jachinites:
13 Of Zerah, the *f* of the Zarhites:
13 of Shaul, the *f* of the Shaulites.
15 of Zephon, the *f* of the Zephonites:
15 of Haggi, the *f* of the Haggites:
15 of Shuni, the *f* of the Shunites:
16 Of Ozni, the *f* of the Oznites:
16 of Eri, the *f* of the Erites:
17 Of Arod, the *f* of the Arodites:
17 of Areli, the *f* of the Arelites.
20 of Shelah, the *f* of the Shelanites:
20 of Pharez, the *f* of the Pharzites:
20 of Zerah, the *f* of the Zarhites.
21 of Hezron, the *f* of the Hezronites:
21 of Hamul, the *f* of the Hamulites.
23 of Tola, the *f* of the Tolaites:
23 of Pua, the *f* of the Punites:
24 Of Jashub, the *f* of the Jashubites:
24 Shimron, the *f* of the Shimronites.
26 of Sered, the *f* of the Sardites:
26 of Elon, the *f* of the Elonites:
26 of Jahleel, the *f* of the Jahleelites.
29 of Machir, the *f* of the Machirites:
29 Gilead come the *f* of the Gileadites.
30 of Jeezer, the *f* of the Jeezerites:
30 of Helek, the *f* of the Helekites:
31 of Asriel, the *f* of the Asrielites:
31 Shechem, the *f* of the Shechemites:
32 Shemida, the *f* of the Shemidaites:

Nu 26:32 Hepher, the *f* of the Hepherites.
35 Shuthelah, the *f* of the Shuthalhites:
35 of Becher, the *f* of the Bachrites:
35 of Tahan, the *f* of the Tahahamites,
36 of Eran, the *f* of the Eranites.
38 of Bela, the *f* of the Belaites:
38 of Ashbel, the *f* of the Ashbelites:
38 of Ahiram, the *f* of the Ahiramites:
39 Shupham, the *f* of the Shuphamites:
39 Hupham, the *f* of the Huphamites.
40 of Ard, the *f* of the Ardites:
40 of Naaman, the *f* of the Naamites.
42 Shuham, the *f* of the Shuhamites.
44 of Jimna, the *f* of the Jimnites:
44 of Jesui, the *f* of the Jesuites:
44 of Beriah, the *f* of the Beriites.
45 of Heber, the *f* of the Heberites:
45 Malchiel, the *f* of the Malchielites.
48 Jahzeel, the *f* of the Jahzeelites:
48 of Guni, the *f* of the Gunites:
49 of Jezer, the *f* of the Jezerites:
49 of Shillem, the *f* of the Shillemites.
57 Gershon, the *f* of the Gershonites:
57 Kohath, the *f* of the Kohathites:
57 of Merari, the *f* of the Merarites.
58 of the Levites: the *f* of the Libnites,
58 the *f* of the Hebronites,
58 the *f* of the Mahlites,
58 the *f* of the Mushites,
58 the *f* of the Korathites.
27: 4 be done away from among his *f*,
11 that is next to him of his *f*,
36: 6 only to the *f* of the tribe of their
8 wife unto one of the *f* of the tribe
12 or the tribe of the *f* of their father.
De 29:18 in *f*, or tribe, whose heart turneth
Jos 7:14 the *f* which the Lord shall take
17 And he brought the *f* of Judah;
17 and he took the *f* of the Zarhites:
17 he brought the *f* of the Zarhites
J'g 1:25 they let go the man and all his *f*.
6:15 behold, my *f* is poor in Manasseh,
9: 1 and with all the *f* of the house of
13: 2 of Zorah, of the *f* of the Danites,
17: 7 of Judah, who was a Levite,
18: 2 of Dan sent of their *f* five men
11 from thence of the *f* of the Danites,
19 unto a tribe and a *f* in Israel?
21:24 every man to his tribe and to his *f*,
Ru 2: 1 of wealth, of the *f* of Elimelech;
1Sa 9:21 my *f* the least of all the families
10:21 the *f* of Matri was taken,
18:18 my life, or my father's *f* in Israel,
20: 6 yearly sacrifice there for all the *f*.
29 for our *f* hath a sacrifice in the city,
2Sa 14: 7 *f* is risen against thine handmaid,
16: 5 a man of the *f* of the house of Saul,
1Ch 4:27 neither did all their *f* multiply, like
6:61 were left of the *f* of that tribe,
70 the *f* of the remnant of the sons
71 given out of the *f* of the half tribe
13:14 ark of God remained with the *f* of
Es 9:28 every *f*, every province, and every
Jer 3:14 one of a city, and two of a *f*,
8: 3 of them that remain of this evil *f*,
Am 3: 1 the whole *f* which I brought up
Mic 2: 3 against this *f* do I devise an evil,
Zec 12:12 shall mourn, every *f* apart;
12 the *f* of the house of David apart,
12 the *f* of the house of Nathan apart,
13 The *f* of the house of Levi apart,
13 the *f* of Shimei apart, and their
14 families that remain, every *f* apart,
14:18 if the *f* of Egypt go not up,
Eph 3:15 *f* in heaven and earth is named,

famine See also FAMINES.
Ge 12:10 And there was a *f* in the land:
10 for the *f* was grievous in the land.
26: 1 And there was a *f* in the land,
1 beside the first *f* that was in the
41:27 east wind shall be seven years of *f*.
30 arise after them seven years of *f*;
30 and the *f* shall consume the land;
31 in the land by reason of that *f*
36 against the seven years of *f*, which
36 the land perish not through the *f*.
50 before the years of *f* came,
56 And the *f* was over all the face of
56 and the *f* waxed sore in the land of
57 that the *f* was so sore in all lands.
42: 5 the *f* was in the land of Canaan.
19 corn for the *f* of your houses:
33 food for the *f* of your households,
43: 1 And the *f* was sore in the land.
45: 6 years hath the *f* been in the land:
11 yet there are five years of *f*;
47: 4 the *f* is sore in the land of Canaan:
13 for the *f* was very sore, so that the
13 Canaan fainted by reason of the *f*.
20 because the *f* prevailed over them:
Ru 1: 1 that there was a *f* in the land.
2Sa 21: 1 there was a *f* in the days of David
24:13 Shall seven years of *f* come unto
1Ki 8:37 If there be in the land *f*,
18: 2 And there was a sore *f* in Samaria.
2Ki 6:25 there was a great *f* in Samaria:
7: 4 then the *f* is in the city,
8: 1 the Lord hath called for a *f*;
25: 3 month the *f* prevailed in the city,
1Ch 21:12 Either three years' *f*; or three
2Ch 20: 9 judgment, or pestilence, or *f*,
32:11 to die by *f* and by thirst,
Job 5:20 In *f* he shall redeem thee from
22 At destruction and *f* thou shalt
30: 3 For want and *f* they were solitary;

Ps 33:19 and to keep them alive in *f*.
37:19 days of *f* they shall be satisfied.
105:16 he called for a *f* upon the land:
Isa 14:30 I will kill thy root with *f*,
51:19 and the *f*, and the sword:
Jer 5:12 neither shall we see sword nor *f*:
11:22 and their daughters shall die by *f*:
14:12 them by the sword, and by the *f*,
13 the sword, neither shall ye have *f*;
15 and *f* shall not be in this land;
15 *f* shall those prophets be consumed.
16 because of the *f* and the sword;
18 behold them that are sick with *f*!
15: 2 such as are for the *f*, to the *f*;
16: 4 consumed by the sword, and by *f*;
18:21 deliver up their children to the *f*,
21: 7 from the sword, and from the *f*,
9 die by the sword, and by the *f*,
24:10 I will send the sword, the *f*,
27: 8 with the sword, and with the *f*,
13 thy people, by the sword, by the *f*,
29:17 send upon them the sword, the *f*,
18 them with the sword, with the *f*,
32:24 because of the sword, and of the *f*,
36 Babylon by the sword, and by the *f*,
34:17 to the pestilence, and to the *f*;
38: 2 shall die by the sword, by the *f*,
42:16 and the *f*, whereof ye were afraid,
17 shall die by the sword, by the *f*,
22 ye shall die by the sword, by the *f*,
44:12, 12 by the sword and by the *f*:
13 Jerusalem, by the sword, by the *f*,
18 by the sword and by the *f*,
27 by the sword and by the *f*, until
52: 6 month the *f* was sore in the city,
La 5:10 an oven because of the terrible *f*.
Eze 5:12 and with *f* shall they be consumed
16 upon them the evil arrows of *f*,
16 and I will increase the *f* upon you,
17 So will I send upon you *f* and evil
6:11 they shall fall by the sword, by the *f*,
12 and is besieged shall die by the *f*:
7:15 the pestilence and the *f* within:
15 *f* and pestilence shall devour him.
12:16 them from the sword, from the *f*,
14:13 and will send *f* upon it,
21 and the *f*, and the noisome beast,
36:29 and lay no *f* upon you.
30 shall receive no more reproach of *f*
Am 8:11 that I will send a *f* in the land,
11 not a *f* of bread, nor a thirst of
Lu 4:25 when great *f* was throughout all
15:14 there arose a mighty *f* in that land;
Ro 8:35 or *f*, or nakedness, or peril, or
Re 18: 8 day, death, and mourning, and *f*;

famines
M't 24: 7 there shall be *f*, and pestilences,
M'r 13: 8 and there shall be *f* and troubles:
Lu 21:11 and *f*, and pestilences: and fearful

famish See also FAMISHED.
Pr 10: 3 the soul of the righteous to *f*:
Zep 2:11 will *f* all the gods of the earth;

famished
Ge 41:55 when all the land of Egypt was *f*,
Isa 5:13 and their honourable men are *f*,

famous See also INFAMOUS.
Nu 16: 2 assembly, *f* in the congregation,
26: 9 which were *f* in the congregation,
Ru 4:11 Ephratah...*f* in Beth-lehem:
14 that his name may be *f* in Israel.
1Ch 5:24 mighty men of valour, *f* men,
12:30 *f* throughout the house of their
Ps 74: 5 A man was *f* according as he had
136:18 And slew *f* kings: for his
Eze 23:10 she became *f* among women,
32:18 the daughters of the *f* nations,

fan
Isa 30:24 with the shovel and with the *f*.
41:16 Thou shalt *f* them, and the wind
Jer 4:11 not to *f*, nor to cleanse,
15: 7 And I will *f* them...in the gates
7 And I will...with a *f* in the gates
51: 2 Babylon fanners, that shall *f* her,
M't 3:12 Whose *f* is in his hand, and he
Lu 3:17 Whose *f* is in his hand, and he will

fanners
Jer 51: 2 Babylon *f*, that shall fan her,

far See also AFAR; FARTHER.
Ge 18:25 That be *f* from thee to do after
25 as the wicked, that be *f* from thee:
44: 4 and not yet *f* off, Joseph said
Ex 8:28 ye shall not go very *f* away:
23: 7 Keep thee *f* from a false matter;
Nu 2: 2 *f* off about the tabernacle of the
De 12:21 name there be too *f* from thee,
13: 7 nigh unto thee, or *f* off from thee,
14:24 if the place be too *f* from thee,
20:15 the cities which are very *f* off
28:49 bring a nation against thee from *f*,
29:22 that shall come from a *f* land,
30:11 from thee, neither is it *f* off.
Jos 3:16 heap very *f* from the city Adam,
8: 4 go not very *f* from the city,
9: 6 We be come from a *f* country:
9 *f* country thy servants are come
22 We are very *f* from you; when ye
J'g 9:17 and adventured his life *f*, and
18: 7 they were *f* from the Zidonians,
28 it was *f* from Zidon, and they had
19:11 by Jebus, the day was *f* spent;
1Sa 2:30 the Lord saith, Be it *f* from me;
20: 9 Jonathan said, *F* be it from thee:
22:15 be it *f* from me: let not the king
2Sa 15:17 in a place that was *f* off.
20:20 said, *F* be it, *f* be it from me,
23:17 he said, Be it *f* from me,
1Ki 8:41 cometh out of a *f* country for thy
46 the land of the enemy, *f* or near;
2Ki 20:14 They are come from a *f* country,
2Ch 6:32 but is come from a *f* country
36 unto a land *f* off or near;
26:15 And his name spread *f* abroad;
Ezr 6: 6 the river, be ye *f* from thence:
Ne 4:19 the wall, one *f* from another.
Es 9:20 king Ahasuerus, both nigh and *f*,
Job 5: 4 His children are *f* from safety,
11:14 be in thine hand, put it *f* away,
13:21 Withdraw thine hand *f* from me:
19:13 hath put my brethren *f* from me,
21:16 counsel of the wicked is *f* from me,
22:18 but the counsel of the wicked is *f*
23 shalt put away iniquity *f* from thy
30:10 abhor me, they flee *f* from me,
34:10 *f* be it from God, that he should
Ps 10: 5 are *f* above out of his sight:
22: 1 art thou so *f* from helping me,
11 Be not *f* from me; for trouble is
19 be not thou *f* from me, O Lord:
27: 9 Hide not thy face *f* from me;
35:22 O Lord, be not *f* from me.
38:21 O my God, be not *f* from me.
55: 7 Lo, then would I wander *f* off,
71:12 O God, be not *f* from me:
73:27 that are *f* from thee shall perish:
88: 8 put away mine acquaintance *f*
18 and friend hast thou put *f* from me,
97: 9 thou art exalted *f* above all gods.
103:12 As *f* as the east is from the west,
12 so *f* hath he removed our
109:17 so let it be *f* from him.
119:150 they are *f* from thy law.
155 Salvation is *f* from the wicked:
Pr 4:24 and perverse lips put *f* from thee.
5: 8 Remove thy way *f* from her,
15:29 The Lord is *f* from the wicked:
19: 7 do his friends go *f* from him?
22: 5 keep his soul shall be *f* from them.
15 rod of correction shall drive it *f*
25:25 is good news from a *f* country.
27:10 that is near than a brother *f* off.
30: 8 Remove *f* from me vanity and
31:10 for her price is *f* above rubies.
Ec 7:23 be wise; but it was *f* from me.
24 That which is *f* off, and exceeding
Isa 5:26 an ensign to the nations from *f*,
6:12 Lord have removed men *f* away,
8: 9 give ear, all ye of *f* countries:
10: 3 which shall come from *f*?
13: 5 They come from a *f* country, from
17:13 they shall flee *f* off, and shall
19: 6 they shall turn the rivers *f* away;
22: 3 together, which have fled from *f*.
26:15 removed it *f* unto all the ends of
29:13 removed their heart *f* from me
30:27 name of the Lord cometh from *f*,
33:13 Hear, ye that are *f* off, what I
17 behold the land that is very *f* off.
39: 3 They are come from a *f* country
43: 6 not back; bring my sons from *f*,
46:11 my counsel from a *f* country:
12 that are *f* from righteousness:
13 righteousness; it shall not be *f* off,
49: 1 and hearken, ye people, from *f*;
12 Behold, these shall come from *f*:
19 swallowed thee up shall be *f* away.
54:14 thou shalt be *f* from oppression;
57: 9 didst send thy messengers *f* off,
19 Peace, peace to him that is *f* off,
59: 9 Therefore is judgment *f* from us,
11 salvation, but it is *f* off from us.
60: 4 thy sons shall come from *f*, and
9 to bring thy sons from *f*, their
Jer 2: 5 that they are gone *f* from me,
4:16 watchers come from a *f* country,
5:15 bring a nation upon you from *f*,
6:20 the sweet cane from a *f* country?
8:19 of them that dwell in a *f* country;
12: 2 mouth, and *f* from their reins.
25:26 the kings of the north, *f* and near,
27:10 to remove you *f* from your land;
48:24 of the land of Moab, *f* or near.
47 Thus *f* is the judgment of Moab.
49:30 Flee, get you *f* off, dwell deep,
51:64 Thus *f* are the words of Jeremiah.
La 1:16 relieve my soul is *f* from me:
3:17 thou hast removed my soul *f* off
Eze 6:12 He that is *f* off shall die
7:20 therefore have I set it *f* from
8: 6 go *f* off from my sanctuary?
11:15 Get you *f* from the Lord:
16 I have cast them *f* off among the
12:27 of the times that are *f* off.
22: 5 and those that be *f* from thee,
23:40 sent for men to come from *f*,
43: 9 carcases of their kings, *f* from me,
44:10 Levites that are gone away *f* from
Da 9: 7 that are near, and that are *f* off,
11: 2 fourth shall be *f* richer than they
Joe 2:20 I will remove *f* off from you the
3: 6 remove them *f* from their border.
8 the Sabeans, to a people *f* off:
Am 6: 3 Ye that put *f* away the evil day,
Mic 4: 7 her that was cast *f* off a strong nation:
7:11 shall the decree be *f* removed.
Hab 1: 8 their horsemen shall come from *f*;
Zec 6:15 they that are *f* off shall come
10: 9 shall remember me in *f* countries;
M't 15: 8 but their heart is *f* from me.
16:22 Be it *f* from thee, Lord:
21:33 and went into a *f* country:
25:14 man travelling into a *f* country,
M'r 6:35 when the day was now *f* spent,
35 and now the time is *f* passed:
7: 6 but their heart is *f* from me.
8: 3 for divers of them came from *f*.
12: 1 and went into a *f* country.
34 not *f* from the kingdom of God.
13:34 as a man taking a *f* journey,
Lu 7: 6 was now not *f* from the house,
15:13 his journey into a *f* country,
19:12 went into a *f* country to receive
20: 9 went into a *f* country for a long time.
22:51 and said, Suffer ye thus *f*.
24:29 and the day is *f* spent.
50 them out as *f* as to Bethany,
Joh 21: 8 for they were not *f* from land,
Ac 11:19 Stephen travelled as *f* as Phenice,
22 that he should go as *f* as Antioch.
17:27 he be not *f* from every one
22:21 I will send thee *f* hence unto the
28:15 to meet us as *f* as Appii forum,
Ro 13:12 night is *f* spent, the day is at hand:
2Co 4:17 for us a *f* more exceeding
10:14 we are come as *f* as to you also in
Eph 1:21 *F* above all principality, and
2:13 ye who sometimes were *f* off are
4:10 ascended up *f* above all heavens,
Ph'p 1:23 Christ; which is *f* better:
Heb 7:15 And it is yet *f* more evident:

fare See also FARED; FAREWELL; SEAFARING; WARFARE; WAYFARING; WELFARE.
1Sa 17:18 and look how thy brethren *f*,
Jon 1: 3 he paid the *f* thereof, and went
Ac 15:29 ye shall do well. *F* ye well.

fared
Lu 16:19 and *f* sumptuously every day:

farewell See also FARE and WELL.
Lu 9:61 but let me first go bid them *f*,
Ac 18:21 But bade them *f*, saying, I must
23:30 what they had against him. *F*.
2Co 13:11 Finally, brethren, *f*. Be perfect,

faring See SEAFARING; WAYFARING.

farm
M't 22: 5 and went their ways, one to his *f*,

far-off See FAR and OFF.

farther See also FURTHER.
Ec 8:17 yea *f*; though a wise man think
M't 26:39 And he went a little *f*, and fell
M'r 1:19 And when he had gone a little *f*
10: 1 by the *f* side of Jordan:

farthing See also FARTHINGS.
M't 5:26 thou hast paid the uttermost *f*.
10:29 not two sparrows sold for a *f*?
M'r 12:42 in two mites, which make a *f*.

farthings
Lu 12: 6 not five sparrows sold for two *f*,

fashion See also FASHIONED; FASHIONETH; FASHIONING; FASHIONS.
Ge 6:15 *f* which thou shalt make it of:
Ex 26:30 according to the *f* thereof which
37:19 made after the *f* of almonds
1Ki 6:38 according to all the *f* of it.
2Ki 16:10 the *f* of the altar, and the pattern
Job 31:15 did not one *f* us in the womb?
Eze 43:11 the house, and the *f* thereof,
M'r 2:12 We never saw it on this *f*.
Lu 9:29 the *f* of his countenance was
Ac 7:44 to the *f* that he had seen.
1Co 7:31 for the *f* of this world passeth
Ph'p 2: 8 And being found in *f* as a man,
Jas 1:11 the grace of the *f* of it perisheth:

fashioned
Ex 32: 4 and *f* it with a graving tool,
Job 10: 8 hands have made me and *f* me
Ps 119:73 hands have made me and *f* me:
139:16 which in continuance were *f*,
Isa 22:11 had respect unto him that *f* it
Eze 16: 7 thy breasts are *f*, and thine hair
Ph'p 3:21 be *f* like unto his glorious body,

fashioneth
Ps 33:15 He *f* their hearts alike; he
Isa 44:12 the coals, and *f* it with hammers,
45: 9 Shall the clay say to him that *f* it,

fashioning
1Pe 1:14 not *f* yourselves according to the

fashions
Eze 42:11 out were both according to their *f*,

fast See also FASTED; FASTING; STEDFAST.
Ge 20:18 Lord had *f* closed up all the wombs
J'g 4:21 for he was *f* asleep and weary.
15:13 No, but we will bind thee *f*,
16:11 they bind me *f* with new ropes
Ru 2: 8 but abide here *f* by my maidens:
21 Thou shalt keep *f* by my young men,
23 So she kept *f* by the maidens of Boaz
2Sa 12:21 didst *f* and weep for the child,
23 he is dead, wherefore should I *f*?
1Ki 21: 9 Proclaim a *f*, and set Naboth
12 proclaimed a *f*, and set Naboth
2Ki 6:32 and hold him *f* at the door:
2Ch 20: 3 proclaimed a *f* throughout all
Ezr 5: 8 and this work goeth *f* on,
8:21 Then I proclaimed a *f* there,
Es 4:16 and *f* ye for me, and neither eat
16 and my maidens will *f* likewise;
Job 2: 3 and still he holdeth *f* his integrity,
8:15 he shall hold it *f*, but it shall not
27: 6 My righteousness I hold *f*, and will
38:38 and the clods cleave *f* together?

Ps 33: 9 he commanded, and it stood *f*.
38: 2 For thine arrows stick *f* in me,
41: 8 disease, say they, cleaveth *f* unto him:
65: 6 his strength setteth *f* the mountains:
89:28 my covenant shall stand *f* with him.
111: 8 They stand *f* for ever and ever,
Pr 4:13 Take *f* hold of instruction; let her not
Isa 58: 3 Behold, in the day of your *f* ye
4 ye *f* for strife and debate,
4 ye shall not *f* as ye do this day,
5 Is it such a *f* that I have chosen?
5 wilt thou call this a *f*, and an
6 not this the *f* that I have chosen?
Jer 8: 5 they hold *f* deceit, they refuse to
14:12 When they *f*, I will not hear their
36: 9 proclaimed a *f* before the Lord
46:14 Stand *f*, and prepare thee; for
48:16 and his affliction hasteth *f*.
50:33 took them captives held them *f*;
Joe 1:14 Sanctify ye a *f*, call a solemn
2:15 sanctify a *f*, call a solemn assembly:
Jon 1: 5 and he lay, and was *f* asleep.
3: 5 and proclaimed a *f*, and put on
Zec 7: 5 did ye all *f* unto me, even to me?
8:19 The *f* of the fourth month,
19 and the *f* of the fifth,
19 and the *f* of the seventh,
19 and the *f* of the tenth,
M't 6:16 Moreover when ye *f*, be not, as
16 they may appear unto men to *f*.
18 thou appear not unto men to *f*,
9:14 Why do we and the Pharisees *f* oft,
14 but thy disciples *f* not?
15 from them, and then shall they *f*.
26:48 that same is he: hold him *f*.
M'r 2:18 of the Pharisees used to *f*:
18 of John and of the Pharisees *f*,
18 but thy disciples *f* not?
19 children of the bridechamber *f*.
19 bridegroom with..., they cannot *f*.
20 then shall they *f* in those days.
Lu 5:33 do the disciples of John *f* often,
34 children of the bridechamber *f*,
35 then shall they *f* in those days.
18:12 I *f* twice in the week,
Ac 16:24 made their feet *f* in the stocks.
27: 9 because the *f* was now already
41 forepart stuck *f*, and remained
1Co 16:13 Watch ye, stand *f* in the faith, quit
Ga 5: 1 Stand *f* therefore in the liberty
Ph'p 1:27 that ye stand *f* in one spirit, with one
4: 1 so stand *f* in the Lord, my dearly
1Th 3: 8 now we live, if ye stand *f* in the Lord.
5:21 hold *f* that which is good.
2Th 2:15 brethren, stand *f*, and hold the
2Ti 1:13 Hold *f* the form of sound words,
Tit 1: 9 Holding *f* the faithful word as he
Heb 3: 6 if we hold *f* the confidence and
4:14 let us hold *f* our profession.
10:23 Let us hold *f* the profession of our
Re 2:13 and thou holdest *f* my name,
25 ye have already, hold *f* till I come.
3: 3 and hold *f*, and repent.
11 hold that *f* which thou hast, that no

fasted
J'g 20:26 *f* that day until even, and offered
1Sa 7: 6 and *f* on that day, and said there,
31:13 tree at Jabesh, and *f* seven days.
2Sa 1:12 and *f* until even, for Saul,
12:16 and David *f*, and went in,
22 child was yet alive, I *f* and wept:
1Ki 21:27 and *f*, and lay in sackcloth,
1Ch 10:12 oak in Jabesh, and *f* seven days.
Ezr 8:23 So we *f* and besought our God
Ne 1: 4 and *f*, and prayed before the God of
Isa 58: 3 Wherefore have we *f*, say they,
Zec 7: 5 When ye *f* and mourned in the
M't 4: 2 when he had *f* forty days
Ac 13: 2 they ministered to the Lord, and *f*,
3 when they had *f* and prayed,

fasten See also FASTENED; FASTENING.
Ex 28:14 and *f* the wreathen chains to the
25 thou shalt *f* in the two ouches,
39:31 to *f* it on high upon the mitre;
Isa 22:23 And I will *f* him as a nail
Jer 10: 4 they *f* it with nails and with

fastened
Ex 39:18 chains they *f* in the two ouches,
40:18 and *f* his sockets, and set up the
J'g 4:21 and *f* it into the ground:
16:14 And she *f* it with the pin,
1Sa 31:10 and they *f* his body to the wall of
2Sa 20: 8 with a sword *f* upon his loins in
1Ki 6: 6 beams should not be *f* in the
1Ch 10:10 and *f* his head in the temple of
2Ch 9:18 which were *f* to the throne,
Es 1: 6 *f* with cords of fine linen and purple
Job 38: 6 are the foundations thereof *f*?
Ec 12:11 *f* by the masters of assemblies,
Isa 22:25 shall the nail that is *f* in the sure
41: 7 *f* it with nails, that it should not
Eze 40:43 a hand broad, *f* round about:
Lu 4:20 in the synagogue were *f* on him.
Ac 11: 6 which when I had *f* mine eyes, I
28: 3 out of the heat, and *f* on his hand.

fastening
Ac 3: 4 Peter, *f* his eyes upon him with

fastest
M't 6:17 when thou *f*, anoint thine head,

fasting See also FASTINGS.
Ne 9: 1 of Israel were assembled with *f*,
Es 4: 3 and *f*, and weeping, and wailing;
Ps 35:13 I humbled my soul with *f*;
69:10 and chastened my soul with *f*,
109:24 My knees are weak through *f*;
Jer 36: 6 the Lord's house upon the *f* day:
Da 6:18 palace, and passed the night *f*:
9: 3 with *f*, and sackcloth, and ashes:
Joe 2:12 and with *f*, and with weeping, and
M't 15:32 I will not send them away *f*, lest
17:21 not out but by prayer and *f*.
M'r 8: 3 And if I send them away *f* to their
9:29 by nothing, but by prayer and *f*.
Ac 10:30 Four days ago I was *f* until this
14:23 prayed with *f*, they commended
27:33 ye have tarried and continued *f*,
1Co 7: 5 give yourselves to *f* and prayer;

fastings
Es 9:31 the matters of the *f* and their cry.
Lu 2:37 with *f* and prayers night and day.
2Co 6: 5 in labours, in watchings, in *f*;
11:27 in *f* often, in cold and nakedness.

fastness See STEDFASTNESS.

fat See also FATFLESHED; FATLING; FATS; FATTED; FATTER; FATTEST; PRESSFAT; WINEFAT.
Ge 4: 4 his flock and of the *f* thereof.
41: 4 seven well favoured and *f* kine.
20 did eat up the first seven *f* kine:
45:18 ye shall eat the *f* of the land.
49:20 Out of Asher his bread shall be *f*,
Ex 23:18 shall the *f* of my sacrifice remain
29:13 shalt take all the *f* that covereth
13 kidneys, and the *f* that is upon
22 thou shalt take of the ram the *f*
22 the *f* that covereth the inwards,
22 and the *f* that is upon them,
Le 1: 8 the head, and the *f*, in order upon
12 his pieces, with his head and his *f*:
3: 3 the *f* that covereth the inwards,
3 all the *f* that is upon the inwards,
4 and the *f* that is on them,
9 the *f* thereof, and the whole rump,
9 the *f* that covereth the inwards,
9 all the *f* that is upon the inwards,
10 the *f* that is upon them, which is
14 the *f* that covereth the inwards,
14 all the *f* that is upon the inwards,
15 and the *f* that is upon them,
16 savour: all the *f* is the Lord's.
17 that ye eat neither *f* nor blood.
4: 8 shall take off from it all the *f* of the
8 the *f* that covereth the inwards,
8 and the *f* that is upon the inwards,
9 and the *f* that is upon them,
19 he shall take all his *f* from him,
26 he shall burn all his *f* upon the
26 as the *f* of the sacrifice of
31 shall take away all the *f* thereof,
31 as the *f* is taken away from off
35 shall take away all the *f* thereof,
35 as the *f* of the lamb is taken away
6:12 he shall burn thereon the *f* of the
7: 3 offer of it all the *f* thereof;
3 the *f* that covereth the inwards,
4 and the *f* that is on them,
23 Ye shall eat no manner of *f*,
24 And the *f* of the beast that dieth
24 and the *f* of that which is torn
25 whosoever eateth the *f* of the beast,
30 *f* with the breast, it shall he bring,
31 And the priest shall burn the *f*
33 the peace offerings, and the *f*,
8:16 the *f* that was upon the inwards,
16 the two kidneys, and their *f*, and
20 head, and the pieces, and the *f*.
25 he took the *f*, and the rump, and
25 the *f* that was upon the inwards,
25 the two kidneys, and their *f*, and
26 and put them on the *f*, and upon
9:10 But the *f*, and the kidneys, and
19 And the *f* of the bullock and of the
20 they put the *f* upon the breasts,
20 and he burnt the *f* upon the altar:
24 altar the burnt offering and the *f*:
10:15 the offerings made by fire of the *f*,
16:25 And the *f* of the sin offering shall
17: 6 and burn the *f* for a sweet savour
Nu 13:20 land is, whether it be *f* or lean,
18:17 shalt burn their *f* for an offering
De 31:20 filled themselves, and waxen *f*;
32:14 with *f* of lambs, and rams of the
14 with the *f* of kidneys of wheat;
15 Jeshurun waxed *f*, and kicked:
15 art waxen *f*, thou art grown thick,
38 did eat the *f* of their sacrifices,
J'g 3:17 and Eglon was a very *f* man.
22 and the *f* closed upon the blade,
1Sa 2:15 Also before they burnt the *f*,
16 Let them not fail to burn the *f*
29 yourselves *f* with the chiefest of
15:22 and to hearken than the *f* of rams.
28:24 And the woman had a *f* calf
2Sa 1:22 from the *f* of the mighty, the bow
1Ki 1: 9 slew sheep and oxen and *f* cattle
19 he hath slain oxen and *f* cattle
25 slain oxen and *f* cattle and sheep
4:23 Ten *f* oxen, and twenty oxen out
8:64 and the *f* of the peace offerings:
64 and the *f* of the peace offerings.
1Ch 4:40 they found *f* pasture and good,
2Ch 7: 7 and the *f* of the peace offerings,
7 the meat offerings, and the *f*.
29:35 with the *f* of the peace offerings,
35:14 offerings and the *f* until night;
Ne 8:10 eat the *f*, and drink the sweet,
9:25 took strong cities, and a *f* land,
25 and were filled, and became *f*, and
Ne 9:35 and in the large and *f* land which
Job 15:27 maketh collops of *f* on his flanks.
Ps 17:10 They are inclosed in their own *f*:
22:29 All they that be *f* upon earth shall
37:20 Lord shall be as the *f* of lambs:
92:14 they shall be *f* and flourishing;
119:70 Their heart is as *f* as grease;
Pr 11:25 The liberal soul shall be made *f*:
13: 4 soul of the diligent shall be made *f*.
15:30 a good report maketh the bones *f*.
28:25 trust in the Lord shall be made *f*.
Isa 1:11 rams, and the *f* of fed beasts;
5:17 the waste places of the *f* ones
6:10 Make the heart of this people *f*,
10:16 send among his *f* ones leanness;
25: 6 unto all people a feast of *f* things,
6 of *f* things full of marrow,
28: 1 are on the head of the *f* valleys of
4 which is on the head of the *f* valley,
30:23 and it shall be *f* and plenteous:
34: 6 it is made *f* with fatness,
6 with the *f* of the kidneys of rams:
7 their dust made *f* with fatness.
43:24 hast thou filled me with the *f* of
58:11 drought, and make *f* thy bones:
Jer 5:28 They are waxen *f*, they shine:
50:11 ye are grown *f* as the heifer
Eze 34: 3 Ye eat the *f*, and ye clothe you
14 in a *f* pasture shall they feed
16 will destroy the *f* and the strong;
20 I will judge between the *f* cattle
39:19 And ye shall eat *f* till ye be full,
44: 7 my bread, the *f* and the blood,
15 offer unto me the *f* and the blood,
45:15 out of the *f* pastures of Israel:
Am 5:22 peace offerings of your *f* beasts.
Hab 1:16 by them their portion is *f*,
Zec 11:16 but he shall eat the flesh of the *f*,

fatfleshed
Ge 41: 2 seven well favoured kine and *f*;
18 seven kine, *f* and well favoured;

father See also FATHERLESS; FATHER'S; FATHERS.
Ge 2:24 a man leave his *f* and his mother,
4:20 was the *f* of such as dwell in tents,
21 the *f* of all such as handle the harp
9:18 and Ham is the *f* of Canaan.
22 And Ham, the *f* of Canaan, saw the
22 saw the nakedness of his *f*,
23 and covered the nakedness of their *f*;
10:21 Shem also, the *f* of all the children
11:28 And Haran died before his *f* Terah
29 the *f* of Milcah, and the *f* of Iscah.
17: 4 thou shalt be a *f* of many nations.
5 *f* of many nations have I made thee.
19:31 Our *f* is old, and there is not a man
32 Come, let us make our *f* drink wine,
32 that we may preserve seed of our *f*.
33 made their *f* drink wine that night:
33 firstborn went in, and lay with her *f*;
34 Behold, I lay yesternight with my *f*:
34 that we may preserve seed of our *f*.
35 And they made their *f* drink wine
36 of Lot with child by their *f*.
37 the same is the *f* of the Moabites
38 is the *f* of the children of Ammon
20:12 she is the daughter of my *f*, but not
22: 7 Abraham his *f*, and said, My *f*:
21 and Kemuel the *f* of Aram,
26: 3 which I swear unto Abraham thy *f*;
15 digged in the days of Abraham his *f*,
18 digged in the days of Abraham his *f*;
18 by which his *f* had called them.
24 I am the God of Abraham thy *f*:
27: 6 I heard thy *f* speak unto Esau thy
9 make them savoury meat for thy *f*,
10 And thou shalt bring it to thy *f*,
12 My *f* peradventure will feel me,
14 savoury meat, such as his *f* loved.
18 came unto his *f*, and said, My *f*:
19 And Jacob said unto his *f*, I am Esau
22 Jacob went near unto Isaac his *f*;
26 And his *f* Isaac said unto him, Come
30 out from the presence of Isaac his *f*,
31 and brought it unto his *f*, and said
31 and said unto his *f*, Let my *f* arise,
32 And Isaac his *f* said unto him, Who
34 when Esau heard the words of his *f*,
34 and said unto his *f*, Bless me, even
34 Bless me, even me also, O my *f*.
38 Esau said unto his *f*, Hast thou but
38 but one blessing, my *f*? bless me,
38 bless me, even me also, O my *f*.
39 And Isaac his *f* answered and said
41 the blessing wherewith his *f* blessed
41 the days of mourning for my *f* are at
28: 2 the house of Bethuel thy mother's *f*
7 Jacob obeyed his *f* and his mother,
8 of Canaan pleased not Isaac his *f*;
13 am the Lord God of Abraham thy *f*,
29:12 and she ran and told her *f*.
31: 5 the God of my *f* hath been with me.
6 all my power I have served your *f*.
7 And your *f* hath deceived me, and
9 hath taken away the cattle of your *f*,
16 which God hath taken from our *f*,
18 for to go to Isaac his *f* in the land
29 but the God of your *f* spake unto me
35 And she said to her *f*, Let it not
42 Except the God of my *f*, the God of
53 the God of their *f*, judge betwixt us.
53 sware by the fear of his *f* Isaac.
32: 9 Jacob said, O God of my *f* Abraham
9 and God of my *f* Isaac, the Lord

Ge 33:19 children of Hamor, Shechem's *f*.
34: 4 Shechem spake unto his *f* Hamor,
6 Hamor the *f* of Shechem went out
11 Shechem said unto her *f* and unto
13 answered Shechem and Hamor his *f*
19 than all the house of his *f*.
35:18 but his *f* called him Benjamin.
27 Jacob came unto Isaac his *f* unto
36: 9 of Esau the *f* of the Edomites in
24 as he fed the asses of Zibeon his *f*.
43 he is Esau the *f* of the Edomites.
37: 1 wherein his *f* was a stranger,
2 brought unto his *f* their evil report.
4 saw that their *f* loved him more than
10 And he told it to his *f*, and to his
10 and his *f* rebuked him, and said
11 but his *f* observed the saying.
22 to deliver him to his *f* again.
32 they brought it to their *f*; and said,
35 Thus his *f* wept for him.
38:13 thy *f* in law goeth up to Timnath
25 she sent to her *f* in law, saying,
42:13 the youngest is this day with our *f*,
29 And they came unto Jacob their *f*
32 be twelve brethren, sons of our *f*;
32 the youngest is this day with our *f*
35 they and their *f* saw the bundles
36 And Jacob their *f* said unto them,
37 Reuben spake unto his *f*, saying,
43: 2 their *f* said unto them, Go again,
7 Is your *f* yet alive? have ye another
8 And Judah said unto Israel his *f*,
11 And their *f* Israel said unto them.
23 the God of your *f*, hath given you
27 and said, Is your *f* well, the old man
28 Thy servant our *f* is in good health,
44:17 get you up in peace unto your *f*.
19 saying, Have ye a *f*, or a brother?
20 my lord, We have a *f*, an old man,
20 his mother, and his *f* loveth him.
22 The lad cannot leave his *f*:
22 for if he should leave his *f*,
22 his *f* would die.
24 we came up unto thy servant my *f*,
25 And our *f* said, Go again, and buy
27 thy servant my *f* said unto us,
30 when I come to thy servant my *f*,
31 the gray hairs of thy servant our *f*
32 became surety for the lad unto my *f*,
32 then I shall bear the blame to my *f*
34 For how shall I go up to my *f*,
34 see the evil that shall come on my *f*.
45: 3 I am Joseph; doth my *f* yet live?
8 he hath made me a *f* to Pharaoh,
9 Haste ye, and go up to my *f*,
13 tell my *f* of all my glory in Egypt,
13 haste and bring down my *f* hither.
18 take your *f* and your households,
19 and bring your *f*, and come.
23 to his *f* he sent after his manner;
23 and meat for his *f* by the way.
25 land of Canaan unto Jacob their *f*,
27 the spirit of Jacob their *f* revived:
46: 1 sacrifices unto the God of his *f* Isaac.
3 I am God, the God of thy *f*:
5 carried Jacob their *f*, and their
29 and went up to meet Israel his *f*,
47: 1 and said, My *f* and my brethren, and
5 Thy *f* and thy brethren are come
6 make thy *f* and brethren to dwell;
7 And Joseph brought in Jacob his *f*,
11 placed his *f* and his brethren, and
12 nourished his *f*, and his brethren,
48: 1 told Joseph, Behold, thy *f* is sick:
9 Joseph said unto his *f*, They are
17 Joseph saw that his *f* laid his right
18 said unto his *f*, Not so, my *f*: for
19 his *f* refused, and said, I know it,
49: 2 and hearken unto Israel your *f*.
25 Even by the God of thy *f*, who shall
26 The blessings of thy *f* have prevailed
28 is it that their *f* spake unto them,
50: 2 the physicians to embalm his *f*:
5 My *f* made me swear, saying, Lo,
5 go up, I pray thee, and bury my *f*,
6 Pharaoh said, Go up, and bury thy *f*,
7 And Joseph went up to bury his *f*:
10 a mourning for his *f* seven days.
14 went up with him to bury his *f*,
14 after he had buried his *f*.
15 brethren saw that their *f* was dead,
16 Thy *f* did command before he died,
17 the servants of the God of thy *f*.
Ex 2:18 when they came to Reuel their *f*,
3: 1 the flock of Jethro his *f* in law,
6 I am the God of thy *f*,
4:18 returned to Jethro his *f* in law,
18: 1 priest of Midian, Moses' *f* in law,
2 Then Jethro, Moses' *f* in law, took
4 God of my *f*, said he, was mine help,
5 Jethro, Moses' *f* in law, came with
6 I thy *f* in law Jethro am come unto
7 went out to meet his *f* in law,
8 And Moses told his *f* in law all that
12 And Jethro, Moses' *f* in law, took a
12 to eat bread with Moses' *f* in law
14 when Moses' *f* in law saw that he
15 And Moses said unto his *f* in law,
17 And Moses' *f* in law said unto him,
24 hearkened to the voice of his *f* in
27 And Moses let his *f* in law depart;
20:12 Honour thy *f* and thy mother:
21:15 he that smiteth his *f*, or his mother
17 he that curseth his *f*, or his mother
22:17 If her *f* utterly refuse to give her
40:15 as thou didst anoint their *f*,
Le 18: 7 The nakedness of thy *f*, or the
9 thy sister, the daughter of thy *f*,
11 begotten of thy *f*, she is thy sister,
19: 3 every man his mother, and his *f*,
20: 9 For every man that curseth his *f*
9 he hath cursed his *f* or his mother;
21: 2 for his mother, and for his *f*,
9 she profaneth her *f*: she shall be
11 nor defile himself for his *f*,
24:10 whose *f* was an Egyptian,
Nu 3: 4 office in the sight of Aaron their *f*.
24 chief of the house of the *f* of the
30 *f* of the families of the Kohathites
35 the *f* of the families of Merari
6: 7 not make himself unclean for his *f*.
10:29 the Midianite, Moses' *f* in law,
11:12 nursing *f* beareth the sucking child,
12:14 If her *f* had but spit in her face,
18: 2 the tribe of Levi, the tribe of thy *f*,
27: 3 Our *f* died in the wilderness,
4 the name of our *f* be done away
4 among the brethren of our *f*.
7 inheritance of their *f* to pass unto
11 And if his *f* have no brethren,
30: 4 her *f* hear her vow, and her bond
4 her *f* shall hold his peace at her:
5 if her *f* disallow her in the day
5 because her *f* disallowed her.
16 between the *f* and his daughter,
36: 6 the tribe of their *f* shall they marry.
8 the family of the tribe of her *f*,
12 the tribe of the family of their *f*.
De 5:16 Honour thy *f* and thy mother,
21:13 and bewail her *f* and her mother
18 will not obey the voice of his *f*,
19 shall his *f* and his mother lay hold
22:15 Then shall the *f* of the damsel,
16 And the damsel's *f* shall say
19 give them unto the *f* of the damsel,
29 shall give unto the damsel's *f* fifty
26: 5 A Syrian ready to perish was my *f*,
27:16 be he that setteth light by his *f*
22 with his sister, the daughter of his *f*,
32: 6 is not he thy *f* that hath bought thee?
7 ask thy *f*, and he will shew thee;
33: 9 Who said unto his *f* and to his mother,
Jos 2:13 that ye will save alive my *f*,
18 shalt bring thy *f*, and thy mother,
6:23 brought out Rahab, and her *f*, and
15:13 the city of Arba the *f* of Anak,
18 she moved him to ask of her *f* a field:
17: 1 of Manasseh, the *f* of Gilead:
4 among the brethren of their *f*.
19:47 after the name of Dan their *f*.
21:11 the city of Arba the *f* of Anak,
24: 2 Terah, the *f* of Abraham, and the *f*
3 took your *f* Abraham from the other
32 the sons of Hamor the *f* of Shechem
J'g 1:14 she moved him to ask of her *f* a field:
16 Moses' *f* in law, went up out of
4:11 Hobab the *f* in law of Moses,
6:25 the altar of Baal that thy *f* hath,
8:32 Joash his *f*, in Ophrah of the
9: 1 of the house of his mother's *f*,
17 my *f* fought for you, and adventured
28 the men of Hamor the *f* of Shechem:
56 Abimelech, which he did unto his *f*,
11:36 And she said unto him, My *f*, if thou
37 she said unto her *f*, Let this thing
39 she returned unto her *f*, who did
14: 2 up, and told his *f* and his mother,
3 his *f* and his mother said unto him,
3 Samson said unto his *f*, Get her for
4 But his *f* and his mother knew not
5 went Samson down, and his *f* and
6 he told not his *f* or his mother
9 came to his *f* and mother, and he
10 So his *f* went down unto the woman:
16 have not told it my *f* nor my mother,
15: 1 her *f* would not suffer him to go in.
2 And her *f* said, I verily thought
6 and burnt her and her *f* with fire.
16:31 brethren and all the house of his *f*
31 the burying-place of Manoah his *f*.
17:10 and be unto me a *f* and a priest,
18:19 and be to us a *f* and a priest:
29 after the name of Dan their *f*,
19: 3 when the *f* of the damsel saw him,
4 And his *f* in law,...retained him;
4 law, the damsel's *f*, retained him;
5 damsel's *f* said unto his son in law,
6 damsel's *f* had said unto the man,
7 his *f* in law urged him: therefore
8 damsel's *f* said, Comfort thine heart,
9 his *f* in law,...said unto him, Behold
9 law, the damsel's *f*, said unto him,
Ru 2:11 thou hast left thy *f* and thy mother,
4:17 he is the *f* of Jesse, the *f* of David.
1Sa 2:25 not unto the voice of their *f*,
27 appear unto the house of thy *f*,
28 did I give unto the house of thy *f*
30 thy house, and the house of thy *f*,
4:19 that her *f* in law and her husband
21 of her *f* in law and her husband.
9: 3 the asses of Kish Saul's *f* were lost.
5 lest my *f* leave caring for the asses,
10: 2 thy *f* hath left the care of the asses,
12 and said, But who is their *f*?
14: 1 But he told not his *f*.
27 But Jonathan heard not when his *f*
28 Thy *f* straightly charged the people
29 My *f* hath troubled the land:
51 Kish was the *f* of Saul; and Ner the
51 the *f* of Abner was the son of Abiel.
19: 2 Saul my *f* seeketh to kill thee:
3 stand beside my *f* in the field
1Sa 19: 3 I will commune with my *f* of thee;
4 spake good of David unto Saul his *f*,
20: 1 and what is my sin before thy *f*,
2 behold, my *f* will do nothing either
2 and why should my *f* hide this thing
3 Thy *f* certainly knoweth that I have
6 If thy *f* at all miss me, then say,
8 shouldest thou bring me to thy *f*?
9 determined by my *f* to come upon
10 what if thy *f* answer thee roughly?
12 when I have sounded my *f* about
13 but if it please my *f* to do thee evil,
13 as he hath been with my *f*.
32 Jonathan answered Saul his *f*, and
33 it was determined of his *f* to slay
34 because his *f* had done him shame.
22: 3 Let my *f* and my mother, I pray
15 nor to all the house of my *f*:
23:17 the hand of Saul my *f* shall not find
17 and that also Saul my *f* knoweth.
24:11 Moreover, my *f*, see, yea, see the
2Sa 2:32 buried him in the sepulchre of his *f*,
3: 8 this day unto the house of Saul thy *f*,
6:21 Lord, which chose me before thy *f*,
7:14 I will be his *f*, and he shall be my
9: 7 thee all the land of Saul thy *f*;
10: 2 as his *f* shewed kindness unto me.
2 by the hand of his servants for his *f*.
3 thou that David doth honour thy *f*,
13: 5 and when thy *f* cometh to see thee,
16: 3 restore me the kingdom of my *f*.
21 that thou art abhorred of thy *f*:
17: 8 thou knowest thy *f* and his men,
8 and thy *f* is a man of war, and will
10 knoweth that thy *f* is a mighty man,
23 was buried in the sepulchre of his *f*.
19:37 and be buried by the grave of my *f*
21:14 in the sepulchre of Kish his *f*:
1Ki 1: 6 his *f* had not displeased him at any
2:12 upon the throne of David his *f*;
24 set me on the throne of David my *f*,
26 ark of the Lord before David my *f*,
26 in all wherein my *f* was afflicted.
31 me, and from the house of my *f*.
32 my *f* David not knowing thereof,
44 that thou didst to David my *f*:
3: 3 in the statutes of David his *f*:
6 shewed unto thy servant David my *f*
7 servant king instead of David my *f*:
14 as thy *f* David did walk, then I will
5: 1 him king in the room of his *f*:
3 Thou knowest how that David my *f*
5 the Lord spake unto David my *f*,
6:12 which I spake unto David thy *f*:
7:14 and his *f* was a man of Tyre,
51 which David his *f* had dedicated;
8:15 with his mouth unto David my *f*,
17 And it was in the heart of David my *f*
18 and the Lord said unto David my *f*,
20 risen up in the room of David my *f*,
24 kept with thy servant David my *f*
25 keep with thy servant David my *f*
26 thou unto thy servant David my *f*.
9: 4 before me, as David thy *f* walked,
5 as I promised to David thy *f*,
11: 4 as was the heart of David his *f*.
6 after the Lord, as did David his *f*.
27 breaches of the city of David his *f*.
33 my judgments, as did David his *f*.
43 was buried in the city of David his *f*
12: 4 Thy *f* made our yoke grievous:
4 thou the grievous service of thy *f*,
6 that stood before Solomon his *f*
9 yoke which thy *f* did put upon us
10 saying, Thy *f* made our yoke heavy,
11 whereas my *f* did lade you with
11 my *f* hath chastised you with whips
14 My *f* made your yoke heavy, and
14 my *f* also chastised you with whips,
13:11 them they told also to their *f*.
12 their *f* said unto them, What way
15: 3 he walked in all the sins of his *f*,
3 his God, as the heart of David his *f*.
11 eyes of the Lord, as did David his *f*.
15 things which his *f* had dedicated,
19 thee, and between my *f* and thy *f*:
24 fathers in the city of David his *f*;
26 and walked in the way of his *f*,
19:20 thee, kiss my *f* and my mother,
20:34 cities, which my *f* took from thy *f*,
34 Damascus, as my *f* made in Samaria.
22:43 walked in the ways of Asa his *f*;
46 which remained in the days of his *f*
50 fathers in the city of David his *f*:
52 and walked in the way of his *f*,
53 according to all that is *f* had done.
2Ki 2:12 My *f*, my *f*, the chariot of Israel,
3: 2 not like his *f*, and like his mother:
2 image of Baal that his *f* had made.
13 get thee to the prophets of thy *f*,
4:18 he went out to his *f* to the reapers.
19 he said unto his *f*, My head, my head.
5:13 My *f*, if the prophet had bid thee do
6:21 My *f*, shall I smite them? shall I
9:25 thou rode together after Ahab his *f*,
13:14 and said, O my *f*, my *f*, the chariot
25 the hand of Jehoahaz his *f* by war.
14: 3 yet not like David his *f*:
3 to all things as Joash his *f* did.
5 which had slain the king his *f*.
21 him king instead of his *f* Amaziah.
15: 3 to all that his *f* Amaziah had done;
34 to all that his *f* Uzziah had done.
38 fathers in the city of David his *f*:
16: 2 Lord his God, like David his *f*.
18: 3 according to all that David his *f* did.

2Ki 20: 5 the Lord, the God of David thy *f*,
21: 3 which Hezekiah his *f* had destroyed:
20 of the Lord, as his *f* Manasseh did.
21 all the way that his *f* walked in,
21 served the idols that his *f* served,
22: 2 walked in all the way of David his *f*,
23:34 king in the room of Josiah his *f*,
24: 9 according to all that his *f* had done.
1Ch 2:17 and the *f* of Amasa was Jether
21 daughter of Machir the *f* of Gilead,
23 the sons of Machir the *f* of Gilead.
24 bare him Ashur the *f* of Tekoa.
42 which was the *f* of Ziph; and the
42 sons of Mareshah the *f* of Hebron.
44 begat Raham, the *f* of Jorkoam:
45 and Maon was the *f* of Beth-zur.
49 Shaaph the *f* of Madmannah,
49 Sheva the *f* of Machbenah,
49 and the *f* of Gibea:
50 Shobal the *f* of Kirjath-jearim,
51 Salma the *f* of Beth-lehem,
51 Hareph the *f* of Beth-gader.
52 Shobal the *f* of Kirjath-jearim had
55 the *f* of the house of Rechab.
4: 3 And these were of the *f* of Etam;
4 Penuel the *f* of Gedor,
4 and Ezer the *f* of Hushah.
4 of Ephratah, the *f* of Beth-lehem.
5 Ashur the *f* of Tekoa had two wives
11 Mehir, which was the *f* of Eshton.
12 and Tehinnah the *f* of Ir-nahash.
14 Joab the *f* of the valley of Charashim,
17 and Ishbah the *f* of Eshtemoa.
18 bare Jered the *f* of Gedor,
18 and Heber the *f* of Socho,
18 and Jekuthiel the *f* of Zanoah.
19 of Naham, the *f* of Keilah the
21 were, Er the *f* of Lecah,
21 and Laadah the *f* of Mareshah,
7:14 bare Machir the *f* of Gilead:
22 Ephraim their *f* mourned many
31 Malchiel, who is the *f* of Birzavith.
8:29 at Gibeon dwelt the *f* of Gibeon
9:19 the house of his *f*, the Korahites,
35 in Gibeon dwelt the *f* of Gibeon,
17:13 will be his *f*, and he shall be my son:
19: 2 because his *f* shewed kindness to me.
2 to comfort him concerning his *f*.
3 thou that David doth honour thy *f*,
22:10 be my son, and I will be his *f*;
24: 2 Nadab and Abihu died before their *f*,
19 their manner, under Aaron their *f*,
25: 3 under the hands of their *f* Jeduthun,
6 were under the hands of their *f*
26: 6 throughout the house of their *f*:
10 yet his *f* made him the chief;)
28: 4 me before all the house of my *f*
4 house of Judah, the house of my *f*;
4 among the sons of my *f* he liked me
6 him to be my son, and I will be his *f*.
9 my son, know thou the God of thy *f*,
29:10 of Israel our *f*, for ever and ever.
23 as king instead of David his *f*,
2Ch 1: 8 great mercy unto David my *f*,
9 unto David my *f* be established:
2: 3 As thou didst deal with David my *f*,
7 whom David my *f* did provide.
14 and his *f* was a man of Tyre,
14 cunning men of my lord David thy *f*.
17 David his *f* had numbered them;
3: 1 the Lord appeared unto David his *f*,
4:16 instruments did Huram his *f* make
5: 1 that David his *f* had dedicated;
6: 4 with his mouth to my *f* David,
7 Now it was in the heart of David my *f*
8 But the Lord said to David my *f*,
10 risen up in the room of David my *f*,
15 kept with thy servant David my *f*
16 keep with thy servant David my *f*
7:17 before me as David thy *f* walked,
18 I have covenanted with David thy *f*,
8:14 to the order of David his *f*,
9:31 was buried in the city of David his *f*:
10: 4 Thy *f* made our yoke grievous:
4 the grievous servitude of thy *f*,
6 had stood before Solomon his *f*
9 yoke that thy *f* did put upon us?
10 Thy *f* made our yoke heavy, but
11 my *f* put a heavy yoke upon you,
11 my *f* chastised you with whips, but I
14 My *f* made your yoke heavy, but I
14 my *f* chastised you with whips, but I
15:18 the things that his *f* had dedicated,
16: 3 there was between my *f* and thy *f*:
17: 2 Ephraim, which Asa his *f* had taken.
3 in the first ways of his *f* David,
4 sought to the Lord God of his *f*,
20:32 he walked in the way of Asa his *f*,
21: 3 And their *f* gave them great gifts of
4 risen up to the kingdom of his *f*,
12 the Lord God of David thy *f*,
12 in the ways of Jehoshaphat thy *f*,
22: 4 death of his *f* to his destruction,
24:22 Jehoiada his *f* had done to him,
25: 3 that had killed the king his *f*.
26: 1 king in the room of his *f* Amaziah.
4 according to all that his *f* Amaziah
27: 2 according to all that his *f* Uzziah
28: 1 sight of the Lord, like David his *f*:
29: 2 to all that David his *f* had done.
33: 3 Hezekiah his *f* had broken down,
22 as did Manasseh his *f*; for Amon
22 which Manasseh his *f* had made,
23 as Manasseh his *f* had humbled
34: 2 walked in the ways of David his *f*,
3 to seek after the God of David his *f*:

Es 2: 7 for she had neither *f* nor mother,
7 when her *f* and mother were dead,
Job 15:10 aged men, much elder than thy *f*.
17:14 said to corruption, Thou art my *f*:
29:16 I was a *f* to the poor: and the cause
31:18 was brought up with me, as with a *f*,
38:28 Hath the rain a *f*? or who hath
42:15 and their *f* gave them inheritance
Ps 27:10 my *f* and my mother forsake me,
68: 5 A *f* of the fatherless, and a judge of
89:26 He shall cry unto me, Thou art my *f*,
103:13 Like as a *f* pitieth his children, so
Pr 1: 8 My son, hear the instruction of thy *f*,
3:12 as a *f* the son in whom he delighteth.
4: 1 ye children, the instruction of a *f*,
10: 1 A wise son maketh a glad *f*: but a
15:20 A wise son maketh a glad *f*: but a
17:21 and the *f* of a fool hath no joy.
25 A foolish son is a grief to his *f*, and
19:13 foolish son is the calamity of his *f*:
26 that wasteth his *f*, and chaseth
20:20 Whoso curseth his *f* or his mother,
23:22 Hearken unto thy *f* that begat thee,
24 The *f* of the righteous shall greatly
25 Thy *f* and thy mother shall be glad,
28: 7 of riotous men shameth his *f*.
24 Whoso robbeth his *f* or his mother,
29: 3 loveth wisdom rejoiceth his *f*: but he
30:11 is a generation that curseth their *f*,
17 The eye that mocketh at his *f*, and
Isa 3: 6 of his brother of the house of his *f*,
8: 4 to cry, My *f*, and my mother,
9: 6 everlasting *F*, The Prince of Peace.
22:21 and he shall be a *f* to the inhabitants
38: 5 the Lord, the God of David thy *f*,
19 *f* to the children shall make known
43:27 Thy first *f* hath sinned, and thy
45:10 Woe unto him that saith unto his *f*,
51: 2 Look unto Abraham your *f*, and
58:14 with the heritage of Jacob thy *f*:
63:16 Doubtless thou art our *f*, though
16 thou, O Lord, art our *f*, our
64: 8 But now, O Lord, thou art our *f*;
Jer 2:27 Saying to a stock, Thou art my *f*;
3: 4 My *f*, thou art the guide of my youth?
19 I said, Thou shalt call me, My *f*;
12: 6 thy brethren, and the house of thy *f*,
16: 7 drink for their *f* or for their mother.
20:15 man who brought tidings to my *f*,
22:11 which reigned instead of Josiah his *f*,
15 did not thy *f* eat and drink, and do
31: 9 for I am a *f* to Israel, and Ephraim
35: 6 our *f* commanded us, saying, Ye shall
8 for Jonadab the son of Rechab our *f*
10 that Jonadab our *f* commanded us.
16 the commandment of their *f*,
18 commandment of Jonadab your *f*,
Eze 16: 3 thy *f* was an Amorite, and thy mother
45 an Hittite, and your *f* an Amorite.
18: 4 souls are mine; as the soul of the *f*,
17 shall not die for the iniquity of his *f*,
18 As for his *f*, because he cruelly
19 the son bear the iniquity of the *f*?
20 shall not bear the iniquity of the *f*,
20 neither shall the *f* bear the iniquity
22: 7 have they set light by *f* and mother:
44:25 but for *f*, or for mother, or for son,
Da 5: 2 golden and silver vessels which his *f*
11 and in the days of thy *f* light and
11 the king Nebuchadnezzar thy *f*,
11 the king, I say, thy *f*, made master
13 the king my *f* brought out of Jewry?
18 God gave Nebuchadnezzar thy *f* a
Am 2: 7 a man and his *f* will go in unto the
Mic 7: 6 For the son dishonoureth the *f*, the
Zec 13: 3 then his *f* and his mother that begat
3 and his *f* and his mother that begat
Mal 1: 6 A son honoureth his *f*, and a servant
6 then I be a *f*, where is mine honour?
2:10 Have we not all one *f*? hath not one
M't 2:22 Judæa in the room of his *f* Herod,
3: 9 We have Abraham to our *f*: for I
4:21 in a ship with Zebedee their *f*,
22 left the ship and their *f*, and
5:16 glorify your *F* which is in heaven.
45 ye may be the children of your *F*
48 even as your *F* which is in heaven
6: 1 of your *F* which is in heaven.
4 and thy *F* which seeth in secret
6 pray to thy *F* which is in secret;
6 and thy *F* which seeth in secret
8 your *F* knoweth what things ye
9 *F* which art in heaven, Hallowed
14 your heavenly *F* will also forgive
15 neither will your *F* forgive your
18 but unto thy *F* which is in secret:
18 and thy *F*, which seeth in secret,
26 yet your heavenly *F* feedeth them.
32 for your heavenly *F* knoweth that
7:11 how much more shall your *F* which
21 he that doeth the will of my *F*
8:21 suffer me first to go and bury my *f*.
10:20 Spirit of your *F* which speaketh
21 the *f* the child: and the children
29 fall on the ground without your *F*.
32 will I confess also before my *F*
33 him will I also deny before my *F*
35 set a man at variance against his *f*,
37 He that loveth *f* or mother more
11:25 I thank thee, O *F*, Lord of heaven
26 Even so, *F*: for so it seemed good
27 delivered unto me of my *F*: and no
27 man knoweth the Son, but the *F*;
27 neither knoweth any man the *F*,
12:50 whosoever shall do the will of my *F*
13:43 the sun in the kingdom of their *F*.

M't 15: 4 Honour thy *f* and mother: and,
4 He that curseth *f* or mother, let him
5 Whosoever shall say to his *f* or his
6 And honour not his *f* or his mother,
13 my heavenly *F* hath not planted,
16:17 but my *F* which is in heaven.
27 shall come in the glory of his *F*
18:10 do always behold the face of my *F*
14 Even so it is not the will of your *F*
19 it shall be done for them of my *F*
35 shall my heavenly *F* do also unto
19: 5 shall a man leave *f* and mother,
19 Honour thy *f* and thy mother:
29 or brethren, or sisters, or *f*, or
20:23 for whom it is prepared of my *F*.
21:31 them twain did the will of his *f*?
23: 9 call no man your *f* upon the earth:
9 one is your *F*, which is in heaven.
24:36 angels in heaven, but my *F* only.
25:34 Come, ye blessed of my *F*, inherit
26:39 O my *F*, if it be possible, let this
42 O my *F*, if this cup may not pass
53 that I cannot now pray to my *F*,
28:19 baptizing them in the name of the *F*,
M'r 1:20 they left their *f* Zebedee in the ship
5:40 he taketh the *f* and the mother of
7:10 Honour thy *f* and thy mother; and
10 Whoso curseth *f* or mother, let him
11 If a man shall say to his *f* or mother,
12 him no more to do ought for his *f*
8:38 cometh in the glory of his *F* with the
9:21 he asked his *f*, How long is it ago
24 And straightway the *f* of the child
10: 7 this cause shall a man leave his *f*
19 not, Honour thy *f* and mother.
29 brethren, or sisters, or *f*, or mother,
11:10 be the kingdom of our *f* David,
25 that your *F* also which is in heaven
26 neither will your *F* which is in
13:12 and the *f* the son; and the children
32 neither the Son, but the *F*.
14:36 he said, Abba, *F*, all things are
15:21 *f* of Alexander and Rufus, to bear
Lu 1:32 unto him the throne of his *f* David:
59 Zacharias, after the name of his *f*.
62 And they made signs to his *f*, how
67 his *f* Zacharias was filled with the
73 which he sware to our *f* Abraham,
2:48 behold, thy *f* and I have sought thee
3: 8 We have Abraham to our *f*: for I
6:36 merciful, as your *F* also is merciful.
8:51 *f* and the mother of the maiden.
9:42 and delivered him again to his *f*.
59 suffer me first to go and bury my *f*.
10:21 I thank thee, O *F*, Lord of heaven
21 even so, *F*; for so it seemed good
22 things are delivered to me of my *F*:
22 but the *F*; and who the *F* is, but
11: 2 say, Our *F* which art in heaven,
11 bread of any of you that is a *f*,
13 much more shall your heavenly *F*
12:30 your *F* knoweth that ye have need
53 The *f* shall be divided against the
53 son, and the son against the *f*;
14:26 and hate not his *f*, and mother,
15:12 of them said to his *f*, *F*, give me
18 I will arise and go to my *f*, and
18 say unto him, *F*, I have sinned
20 And he arose, and came to his *f*.
20 his *f* saw him, and had compassion,
21 *F*, I have sinned against heaven,
22 But the *f* said to his servants,
27 and thy *f* hath killed the fatted calf,
28 therefore came his *f* out, and
29 said to his *f*, Lo, these many years
16:24 And he cried and said, *F* Abraham,
27 I pray thee therefore, *f*, that thou
30 And he said, Nay, *f* Abraham, but
18:20 Honour thy *f* and thy mother.
22:29 as my *F* hath appointed unto me;
42 Saying, *F*, if thou be willing,
23:34 *F*, forgive them; for they know
46 *F*, into thy hands I commend my
24:49 I send the promise of my *F* upon
Joh 1:14 as of the only begotten of the *F*,)
18 in the bosom of the *F*, he hath
3:35 The *F* loveth the Son, and hath
4:12 Art thou greater than our *f* Jacob,
21 nor yet at Jerusalem, worship the *F*.
23 shall worship the *F* in spirit and
23 in truth: for the *F* seeketh such to
53 So the *f* knew that it was at the
5:17 My *F* worketh hitherto, and I work.
18 but said also that God was his *F*,
19 but what he seeth the *F* do: for
20 For the *F* loveth the Son, and
21 For as the *F* raiseth up the dead,
22 For the *F* judgeth no man, but
23 Son, even as they honour the *F*.
23 honoureth not the *F* which hath
26 For as the *F* hath life in himself;
30 but the will of the *F* which hath
36 the works which the *F* hath given
36 bear witness of me, that the *F* hath
37 And the *F* himself, which hath sent
45 that I will accuse you to the *F*:
6:27 for him hath God the *F* sealed.
32 but my *F* giveth you the true bread
37 All that the *F* giveth me shall come
42 whose *f* and mother we know?
44 except the *F* which hath sent me
45 hath learned of the *F*, cometh unto
46 Not that any man hath seen the *F*,
46 which is of God, he hath seen the *F*.
57 As the living *F* hath sent me, and
57 and I live by the *F*: so he that

Joh 6:65 it were given unto him of my F.
8:16 but I and the F that sent me.
18 and the F that sent me beareth
19 they unto him, Where is thy F?
19 ye neither know me, nor my F:
19 ye should have known my F also.
27 not that he spake to them of the F.
28 as my F hath taught me, I speak
29 the F hath not left me alone;
38 which I have seen with my F:
38 which ye have seen with your f.
39 said unto him, Abraham is our f.
41 Ye do the deeds of your f.
41 we have one F, even God.
42 If God were your F, ye would love
44 Ye are of your f the devil, and the
44 and the lusts of your f ye will do:
44 for he is a liar, and the f of it.
49 but I honour my F, and ye do
53 Art thou greater than our f
54 it is my F that honoureth me;
56 Your f Abraham rejoiced to see my
10:15 As the F knoweth me, even so
15 even so know I the F:
17 Therefore doth my F love me,
18 have I received of my F.
29 My F which gave them me, is
30 I and my F are one.
32 have I shewed you from my F;
36 him, whom the F hath sanctified,
37 not the works of my F, believe me
38 that the F is in me, and I in him.
11:41 F, I thank thee that thou hast
12:26 serve me, him will my F honour.
27 F, save me from this hour: but
28 F, glorify thy name. Then came
49 but the F which sent me, he gave
50 even as the F said unto me, so I
13: 1 depart out of this world unto the F,
3 that the F had given all things into
14: 6 cometh unto the F, but by me.
7 ye should have known my F also:
8 Lord, shew us the F, and it
9 hath seen the F; and how sayest
9 thou then, Shew us the F?
10 I am in the F, and the F in me?
10 but the F that dwelleth in me, he
11 Believe me that I am in the F,
11 and the F in me: or else believe
12 shall he do; because I go unto my F.
13 that the F may be glorified in the
16 And I will pray the F, and he shall
20 that I am in my F, and ye in me,
21 loveth me shall be loved of my F,
23 and my F will love him, and we
26 whom the F will send in my name,
28 because I said, I go unto the F:
28 for my F is greater than I.
31 may know that I love the F; and as
31 as the F gave me commandment,
15: 1 and my F is the husbandman.
8 Herein is my F glorified, that ye
9 As the F hath loved me, so have I
15 things that I have heard of my F
16 ye shall ask of the F in my name,
23 that hateth me hateth my F also.
24 have they hated both me and my F.
26 I will send unto you from the F,
26 which proceedeth from the F,
16: 3 they have not known the F, nor me.
10 because I go to my F, and ye see
15 things that the F hath are mine:
16 shall see me, because I go to the F.
17 and, Because I go to the F?
23 ye shall ask the F in my name,
25 shall shew you plainly of the F.
26 that I will pray the F for you:
27 For the F himself loveth you,
28 I came forth from the F, and am
28 leave the world, and go to the F.
32 alone, because the F is with me.
17: 1 F, the hour is come; glorify thy
5 And now, O F, glorify thou me
11 Holy F, keep through thine own
21 as thou, F, art in me, and I in thee,
24 F, I will that they also, whom thou
25 O righteous F, the world hath not
18:11 cup which my F hath given me,
13 for he was f in law to Caiphas,
20:17 I am not yet ascended to my F:
17 I ascend unto my F, and your F,
21 as my F hath sent me, even so
Ac 1: 4 but wait for the promise of the F,
7 the F hath put in his own power.
2:33 received of the F the promise of
7: 2 appeared unto our f Abraham,
4 when his f was dead, he removed
14 and called his f Jacob to him,
16 sons of Emmor the f of Sychem.
16: 1 but his f was a Greek:
3 knew all that his f was a Greek.
28: 8 that the f of Publius lay sick of a
Ro 1: 7 and peace from God our F, and the
4: 1 our f, as pertaining to the flesh,
11 be the f of all them that believe,
12 And the f of circumcision to them
12 of that faith of our f Abraham,
16 Abraham, who is the f of us all,
17 I have made thee a f of many
18 become the f of many nations,
6: 4 the dead by the glory of the F,
8:15 adoption, whereby we cry, Abba, F.
9:10 by one, even by our f Isaac;
15: 6 God, even the F of our Lord Jesus
1Co 1: 3 and peace, from God our F, and
8: 6 one God, the F, of whom are all

1Co 15:24 the kingdom to God, even the F;
2Co 1: 2 from God our F, and from the
3 even the F of our Lord Jesus
3 the F of mercies, and the God of
6:18 And will be a F unto you, and ye
11:31 The God and F of our Lord Jesus
Gal 1: 1 and God the F, who raised him
3 peace from God the F, and from
4 to the will of God and our F:
4: 2 until the time appointed of the f.
6 unto your hearts, crying, Abba, F.
Eph 1: 2 from God and our F, and from
3 be the God and F of our Lord
17 the F of glory, may give unto you
2:18 access by one Spirit unto the F.
3:14 my knees unto the F of our Lord
4: 6 One God and F of all, who is above
5:20 unto God and the F in the name
31 a man leave his f and mother,
6: 2 Honour thy f and mother; which
23 from God the F and the Lord Jesus
Ph'p 1: 2 from God our F, and from the Lord
2:11 to the glory of God the F.
22 as a son with the f, he hath served
4:20 Now unto God and our F be glory
Col 1: 2 and peace, from God our F and
3 God and the F of our Lord Jesus
12 Giving thanks unto the F, which
19 For it pleased the F that in him
2: 2 and of the F, and of Christ;
3:17 thanks to God and the F by him.
1Th 1: 1 in God the F and in the Lord
1 and peace, from God our F, and
3 in the sight of God and our F;
2:11 of you, as a f doth his children,
3:11 Now God himself and our F, and
13 holiness before God, even our F,
2Th 1: 1 in God our F and the Lord Jesus
2 and peace, from God our F and the
2:16 and God, even our F, which hath
1Ti 1: 2 peace, from God our F and Jesus
5: 1 an elder, but intreat him as a f;
2Ti 1: 2 peace, from God the F and Christ
Tit 1: 4 and peace, from God the F and the
Ph'm 3 and peace, from God our F and the
Heb 1: 5 And again, I will be to him a F,
7: 3 Without f, without mother,
10 he was yet in the loins of his f,
12: 7 for what son is he whom the f
9 unto the F of spirits, and live?
Jas 1:17 cometh down from the F of lights,
27 undefiled before God and the F is
2:21 Was not Abraham our f justified
3: 9 bless we God, even the F; and
1Pe 1: 2 the foreknowledge of God the F,
3 Blessed be the God and F of our
17 And if ye call on the F, who
2Pe 1:17 For he received from God the F
1Jo 1: 2 eternal life, which was with the F,
3 our fellowship is with the F, and
2: 1 we have an advocate with the F,
13 because ye have known the F.
15 the love of the F is not in him.
16 is not of the F, but is of the world.
22 that denieth the F and the Son.
23 the Son, the same hath not the F:
23 acknowledgeth the Son hath the F
24 continue in the Son, and in the F.
3: 1 of love the F hath bestowed upon
4:14 F sent the Son to be the Saviour
5: 7 F, the Word, and the Holy Ghost:
2Jo 3 and peace from God the F, and from
3 the Son of the F, in truth and love.
4 a commandment from the F.
9 he hath both the F and the Son.
Jude 1 that are sanctified by God the F,
Re 1: 6 and priests unto God and his F;
2:27 even as I received of my F.
3: 5 confess his name before my F,
21 set down with my F in his throne.

father-in-law See FATHER and LAW.

fatherless
Ex 22:22 not afflict any widow, or f child.
24 be widows, and your children f.
De 10:18 the judgment of the f and widow,
14:29 and the stranger, and the f, and
16:11 and the stranger, and the f, and
14 the stranger, and the f, and the
24:17 of the stranger, nor of the f;
19, 20, 21 for the stranger, for the f,
26:12 Levite, the stranger, the f, and the
13 and unto the stranger, to the f, and
27:19 judgment of the stranger, f, and
Job 6:27 overwhelm the f, and ye dig a pit
22: 9 arms of the f have been broken.
24: 3 They drive away the ass of the f,
9 They pluck the f from the breast,
29:12 the poor that cried, and the f, and
31:17 and the f hath not eaten thereof;
21 lifted up my hand against the f,
Ps 10:14 thou art the helper of the f.
18 to judge the f and the oppressed,
68: 5 A father of the f, and a judge of
82: 3 Defend the poor and f: do justice
94: 6 the stranger, and murder the f.
109: 9 Let his children be f, and his wife
12 be any to favour his f children.
146: 9 he relieveth the f and widow: but
Pr 23:10 enter not into the fields of the f:
Isa 1:17 judge the f, plead for the widow.
23 they judge not the f, neither doth
9:17 neither shall have mercy on their f
10: 2 and that they may rob the f!
Jer 5:28 not the cause, the cause of the f,
7: 6 oppress not the stranger, the f, and

Jer 22: 3 no violence to the stranger, the f,
49:11 Leave thy f children, I will preserve
La 5: 3 We are orphans and f, our
Eze 22: 7 in thee have they vexed the f and
Ho 14: 3 for in thee the f findeth mercy.
Zec 7:10 oppress not the widow, nor the f,
Mal 3: 5 in his wages, the widow, and the f,
Jas 1:27 To visit the f and widows in their

father's^
Ge 9:23 and they saw not their f nakedness.
12: 1 thy kindred, and from thy f house,
20:13 me to wander from my f house,
24: 7 which took me from my f house,
23 is there room in thy f house for us to
38 But thou shalt go unto my f house,
40 of my kindred, and of my f house:
26:15 which his f servants had digged in
28:21 So that I come again to my f house
29: 9 Rachel came with her f sheep: for
12 told Rachel that he was her f brother,
31: 1 taken away all that was our f; and
1 that which was our f hath he gotten
5 I see your f countenance, that it is
14 inheritance for us in our f house?
19 stolen the images that were her f.
30 thou sore longedst after thy f house,
35:22 and lay with Bilhah his f concubine:
37: 2 with the sons of Zilpah, his f wives:
12 brethren went to feed their f flock
38:11 Remain a widow at thy f house,
11 Tamar went and dwelt in her f house.
41:51 forget all my toil, and all my f house.
46:31 his brethren, and unto his f house,
31 My brethren, and my f house,
47:12 brethren, and all his f household,
48:17 and he held up his f hand,
49: 4 thou wentest up to thy f bed;
8 thy f children shall bow down before
50: 1 And Joseph fell upon his f face,
8 and his brethren, and his f house:
22 dwelt in Egypt, he, and his f house:
Ex 2:16 the troughs to water their f flock.
6:20 him Jochebed his f sister to wife;
15: 2 my f God, and I will exalt him
Le 16:32 in the priest's office in his f stead,
18: 8 The nakedness of thy f wife shalt
8 not uncover: it is thy f nakedness.
11 nakedness of thy f wife's daughter,
12 uncover the nakedness of thy f sister:
12 she is thy f near kinswoman.
14 the nakedness of thy f brother,
20:11 the man that lieth with his f wife
11 hath uncovered his f nakedness:
17 shall take his sister, his f daughter,
19 mother's sister, nor of thy f sister:
22:13 and is returned unto her f house,
13 she shall eat of her f meat:
Nu 2: 2 with the ensign of their f house:
18: 1 and thy sons and thy f house
27: 7 inheritance among their f brethren;
10 his inheritance unto his f brethren.
30: 3 being in her f house in her youth;
16 yet in her youth in her f house.
36:11 unto their f brothers' sons:
De 22:21 damsel to the door of her f house,
21 to play the whore in her f house:
30 A man shall not take his f wife,
30 nor discover his f skirt.
27:20 be he that lieth with his f wife;
20 because he uncovereth his f skirt.
Jos 2:12 shew kindness unto my f house,
18 all thy f household, home unto thee.
6:25 the harlot alive, and her f household,
J'g 6:15 and I am the least in my f house.
25 Take thy f young bullock, even the
27 because he feared his f household,
9: 5 he went unto his f house at Ophrah,
18 ye are risen up against my f house
11: 2 Thou shalt not inherit our f house;
7 and expel me out of my f house?
14:15 lest we burn thee and thy f house
19 and he went up to his f house.
19: 2 away from him unto her f house
3 she brought him into her f house:
1Sa 2:31 thine arm, and the arm of thy f house,
9:20 not on thee, and on all thy f house?
17:15 to feed his f sheep at Beth-lehem.
25 and make his f house free in Israel.
34 Thy servant kept his f sheep,
18: 2 him go no more home to his f house.
18 is my life, or my f family in Israel,
22: 1 when his brethren and all his f house
11 son of Ahitub, and all his f house,
16 Ahimelech, thou, and all thy f house.
22 of all the persons of thy f house.
24:21 destroy my name out of my f house.
2Sa 3: 7 thou gone in unto my f concubine?
29 head of Joab, and on all his f house;
9: 7 kindness for Jonathan thy f sake,
14: 9 be on me, and on my f house:
15:34 as I have been thy f servant hitherto,
16:19 as I have served in thy f presence,
21 Go in unto thy f concubines, which
22 went in unto his f concubines in the
19:28 of my f house were but dead men
24:17 against me, and against my f house.
1Ki 11:12 will not do it for David thy f sake:
17 certain Edomites of his f servants
12:10 shall be thicker than my f loins.
18:18 Israel; but thou and thy f house,
2Ki 10: 3 and set him on his f throne,
23:30 and made him king in his f stead.
24:17 made Mattaniah his f brother
1Ch 5: 1 forasmuch as he defiled his f bed,
7: 2 Shemuel, heads of their f house,

1Ch 7:40 heads of their *f'* house, choice and
12:28 his *f'* house twenty and two captains.
21:17 be on me, and on my *f'* house;
23:11 according to their *f'* house.
2Ch 2:13 understanding, of Huram my *f*,
10:10 shall be thicker than my *f'* loins.
21:13 slain thy brethren of thy *f'* house,
36: 1 made him king in his *f'* stead in
Ezr 2:59 they could not shew their *f'* house,
Ne 1: 6 both I and my *f'* house have sinned.
Es 4:14 and thy *f'* house shall be destroyed:
Ps 45:10 thine own people, and thy *f'* house;
Pr 4: 3 I was my *f'* son, tender and only
6:20 My son, keep thy *f'* commandment,
13: 1 A wise son heareth his *f'* instruction:
15: 5 A fool despiseth his *f'* instruction:
27:10 and thy *f'* friend forsake not:
Isa 7:17 thy people, and upon thy *f'* house,
22:23 for a glorious throne to his *f'* house.
24 upon him all the glory of his *f'* house,
Jer 35:14 but obey their *f'* commandment:
Eze 18:14 a son, that seeth all his *f'* sins which
22:11 humbled his sister, his *f'* daughter.
M't 26:29 new with you in my *F'* kingdom.
Lu 2:49 I must be about my *F'* business?
9:26 in his *F'*, and of the holy angels.
12:32 it is your *F'* good pleasure to give
15:17 hired servants of my *f'* have bread
16:27 wouldest send him to my *f'* house:
Joh 2:16 make not my *F'* house an house of
5:43 I am come in my *F'* name, and ye
6:39 And this is the *F'* will which hath
10:25 that I do in my *F'* name, they bear
29 to pluck them out of my *F'* hand.
14: 2 In my *F'* house are many mansions:
24 not mine, but the *F'* which sent me.
15:10 I have kept my *F'* commandments,
Ac 7:20 was nourished up in his *f'* house
1 Co 5: 1 that one should have his *f'* wife.
Re 14: 1 having his *F'* name written in

fathers ^ See also FATHERS'; FOREFATHERS.
Ge 15:15 And thou shalt go to thy *f* in peace;
31: 3 Return unto the land of thy *f*,
46:34 until now, both we, and also our *f*:
47: 3 shepherds, both we, and also our *f*.
9 of the years of the life of my *f* in the
30 But I will lie with my *f*, and thou
48:15 my *f* Abraham and Isaac did walk,
16 name of my *f* Abraham and Isaac;
21 you again unto the land of your *f*.
49:29 bury me with my *f* in the cave that is
Ex 3:13 The God of your *f* hath sent me unto
15 of Israel, the Lord God of your *f*,
16 unto them, The Lord God of your *f*,
4: 5 believe that the Lord God of their *f*,
6:25 the heads of the *f* of the Levites
10: 6 thy *f*, nor thy fathers' *f* have seen,
12: 3 according to the house of their *f*,
13: 5 he sware unto thy *f* to give thee,
11 as he sware unto thee and to thy *f*,
20: 5 visiting the iniquity of the *f* upon the
34: 7 visiting the iniquity of the *f* upon the
Le 25:41 possession of his *f* shall he return.
26:39 iniquities of their *f* shall they pine
40 and the iniquity of their *f*, with their
Nu 1: 2 families, by the house of their *f*,
4 one head of the house of his *f*.
16 princes of the tribes of their *f*,
18, 20 house of their *f*, according
22 by the house of their *f*, those that
24, 26, 28, 30, 32, 34, 36, 38, 40, 42 by
the house of their *f*, according to
44 eachone was for the house of his *f*.
45 the house of their *f*, from twenty
47 Levites after the tribe of their *f* were
2:32 of Israel by the house of their *f*:
34 according to the house of their *f*.
3:15 of Levi after the house of their *f*,
20 according to the house of their *f*.
4: 2 families, by the house of their *f*,
22 throughout the houses of their *f*,
29 families by the house of their *f*;
34 and after the house of their *f*,
38 and by the house of their *f*,
40 by the house of their *f*, were two
42 families, by the house of their *f*,
46 and after the house of their *f*,
7: 2 heads of the house of their *f*,
11:12 which thou swarest unto their *f*?
13: 2 every tribe of their *f* shall ye send
14:18 visiting the iniquity of the *f* upon
23 the land which I sware unto their *f*,
17: 2 according to the house of their *f*,
2 according to the house of their *f*
3 the head of the house of their *f*.
20:15 How our *f* went down into Egypt,
15 the Egyptians vexed us, and our *f*:
26:55 the names of the tribes of their *f*
31:26 the chief *f* of the congregation:
32: 8 Thus did your *f*, when I sent them
28 and the chief *f* of the tribes of the
33:54 according to the tribes of your *f*
34:14 Reuben according to...of their *f*,
14 Gad according to the...of their *f*,
36: 1 And the chief *f* of the families of
1 the chief *f* of the children of Israel:
3 taken from the inheritance of our *f*,
4 the inheritance of the tribe of our *f*.
7 the inheritance of the tribe of his *f*.
8 every man the inheritance of his *f*.
De 1: 8 which the Lord sware unto your *f*,
11 (The Lord God of your *f* make you
21 the Lord God of thy *f* hath said
35 which I sware to give unto your *f*,
4: 1 which the Lord God of your *f* giveth
31 nor forget the covenant of thy *f* which

De 4:37 because he loved thy *f*, therefore he
5: 3 made not this covenant with our *f*,
9 visiting the iniquity of the *f* upon the
6: 3 the Lord God of thy *f* hath promised
10 the land which he sware unto thy *f*,
18 which the Lord sware unto thy *f*,
23 the land which he sware unto our *f*.
7: 8 oath, which he had sworn unto your *f*,
12 the mercy which he sware unto thy *f*:
13 the land which he sware unto thy *f*
8: 1 which the Lord sware unto your *f*.
3 knewest not, neither did thy *f* know;
16 with manna, which thy *f* knew not,
18 covenant which he sware unto thy *f*,
9: 5 word which the Lord sware unto thy *f*,
10:11 the land, which I sware unto their *f*
15 the Lord had a delight in thy *f*
22 Thy *f* went down into Egypt with
11: 9 which the Lord sware unto your *f*
21 which the Lord sware unto your *f*
12: 1 the land, which the Lord God of thy *f*
13: 6 thou hast not known, thou, nor thy *f*;
17 as he hath sworn unto thy *f*;
19: 8 coast, as he hath sworn unto thy *f*,
8 which he promised to give unto thy *f*;
24:16 The *f* shall not be put to death for
16 children be put to death for the *f*:
26: 3 which the Lord sware unto our *f* for
7 we cried unto the Lord God of our *f*,
15 given us, as thou swarest unto our *f*,
27: 3 as the Lord God of thy *f* hath
28:11 Lord sware unto thy *f* to give thee.
36 neither thou nor thy *f* have known;
64 neither thou nor thy *f* have known,
29:13 as he hath sworn unto thy *f*,
25 covenant of the Lord God of their *f*,
30: 5 into the land which thy *f* possessed,
5 and multiply thee above thy *f*.
9 as he rejoiced over thy *f*:
20 which the Lord sware unto thy *f*,
31: 7 the Lord hath sworn unto their *f*
16 Behold, thou shalt sleep with thy *f*;
20 the land which I sware unto their *f*,
32:17 newly up, whom your *f* feared not.
Jos 1: 6 I sware unto their *f* to give them.
4: 6 children ask their *f* in time to
21 children shall ask their *f* in time to
5: 6 which the Lord sware unto their *f*
14: 1 the heads of the *f* of the tribes
18: 3 land which the Lord God of your *f*
19:51 the heads of the *f* of the tribes
21: 1 the heads of the *f* of the Levites
1 unto the heads of the *f* of the tribes
43 which he sware to give unto their *f*;
44 all that he sware unto their *f*:
22:14 an head of the house of their *f*
28 altar of the Lord, which our *f* made,
24: 2 Your *f* dwelt on the other side of the
6 And I brought your *f* out of Egypt:
6 the Egyptians pursued after your *f*
14 the gods which your *f* served on the
15 gods which your *f* served that were
17 brought us up and our *f* out of the
J'g 2: 1 the land which I sware unto your *f*;
10 were gathered unto their *f*: and there
12 they forsook the Lord God of their *f*,
17 the way which their *f* walked in,
19 themselves more than their *f*,
20 covenant which I commanded their *f*,
22 as their *f* did keep it, or not.
3: 4 which he commanded their *f* by the
6:13 his miracles which our *f* told us of,
21:22 when their *f* or their brethren come
1Sa 12: 6 brought your *f* up out of the land
7 which he did to you and to your *f*.
8 and your *f* cried unto the Lord,
8 brought forth your *f* out of Egypt,
15 against you, as it was against your *f*.
2Sa 7:12 and thou shalt sleep with thy *f*,
1Ki 1:21 lord the king shall sleep with his *f*,
2:10 David slept with his *f*, and was buried
8: 1 the chief of the *f* of the children
21 the Lord, which he made with our *f*,
34 land which thou gavest unto their *f*.
40 land which thou gavest unto our *f*.
48 land, which thou gavest unto their *f*,
53 thou broughtest our *f* out of Egypt,
57 be with us, as he was with our *f*:
58 which he commanded our *f*.
9: 9 brought forth their *f* out of the land
11:21 in Egypt that David slept with his *f*,
43 Solomon slept with his *f*, and was
13:22 come unto the sepulchre of thy *f*.
14:15 good land, which he gave to their *f*,
20 he slept with his *f*, and Nadab his
22 above all that their *f* had done.
31 And Rehoboam slept with his *f*,
31 and was buried with his *f* in the city
15: 8 Abijam slept with his *f*; and they
12 all the idols that his *f* had made.
24 Asa slept with his *f*, and was buried
24 with his *f* in the city of David his
16: 6 Baasha slept with his *f*, and was
28 Omri slept with his *f*, and was buried
19: 4 for I am not better than my *f*.
21: 3 should give the inheritance of my *f*
4 not give thee the inheritance of my *f*.
22:40 Ahab slept with his *f*; and Ahaziah
50 And Jehoshaphat slept with his *f*,
50 and was buried with his *f* in the city
2Ki 8:24 And Joram slept with his *f*,
24 and was buried with his *f* in the city
9:28 in his sepulchre with his *f* in the city
10:35 And Jehu slept with his *f*: and they
12:18 his *f*, kings of Judah, had dedicated,
21 and they buried him with his *f* in the

2Ki 13: 9 Jehoahaz slept with his *f*; and they
13 And Joash slept with his *f*; and
14: 6 The *f* shall not be put to death for
6 children be put to death for the *f*;
16 Jehoash slept with his *f*, and was
20 was buried at Jerusalem with his *f*
22 after that the king slept with his *f*,
29 Jeroboam slept with his *f*, even with
15: 7 So Azariah slept with his *f*; and they
7 buried him with his *f* in the city of
9 as his *f* had done: he departed not
22 And Menahem slept with his *f*; and
38 And Jotham slept with his *f*,
38 and was buried with his *f* in the city
16:20 And Ahaz slept with his *f*,
20 and was buried with his *f* in the city
17:13 the law which I commanded your *f*,
14 like to the neck of their *f*,
15 covenant that he made with their *f*,
41 as did their *f*, so do they unto this
19:12 them which my *f* have destroyed;
20:17 that which thy *f* have laid up in
21 And Hezekiah slept with his *f*: and
21: 8 the land which I gave their *f*;
15 since the day their *f* came forth
18 Manasseh slept with his *f*, and was
22 he forsook the Lord God of his *f*,
22:13 our *f* have not hearkened unto the
20 I will gather thee unto thy *f*,
23:32, 37 according to all that his *f* had
24: 6 So Jehoiakim slept with his *f*:
1Ch 4:38 house of their *f* increased greatly
5:13 brethren of the house of their *f*
15 chief of the house of their *f*.
24 the heads of the house of their *f*,
24 and heads of the house of their *f*.
25 trespassed against the God of their *f*,
6:19 the Levites according to their *f*.
7: 4 after the house of their *f*, were
7, 9 heads of the house of their *f*,
11 by the heads of their *f*, mighty
8: 6 these are the heads of the *f* of
10 were his sons, heads of the *f*.
13 who were heads of the *f* of the
28 These were heads of the *f*,
9: 9 of the *f* in the house of their *f*.
13 heads of the house of their *f*,
19 and their *f*, being over the host
33 chief of the *f* of the Levites,
34 These chief *f* of the Levites were
12:17 the God of our *f* look thereon, and
30 throughout the house of their *f*.
15:12 chief of the *f* of the Levites:
17:11 that thou must go to be with thy *f*,
23: 9 the chief of the *f* of Laadan.
24 Levi after the house of their *f*;
24 the chief of the *f*, as they were
24: 4 chief men of the house of their *f*,
4 according to the house of their *f*.
6 before the chief of the *f* of the
30 Levites after the house of their *f*.
31 the chief of the *f* of the priests
31 and Levites, even the principal *f*
26:13 according to the house of their *f*,
21 the Gershonite Laadan, chief *f*,
26 David the king, and the chief *f*,
31 to the generations of his *f*.
32 and seven hundred chief *f*,
27: 1 chief *f* and captains of thousands
29: 6 the chief of the *f* and princes
15 and sojourners, as were all our *f*:
18 Abraham, Isaac, and of Israel, our *f*,
20 blessed the Lord God of their *f*,
2Ch 1: 2 in all Israel, the chief of the *f*.
5: 2 chief of the *f* of the children of
6:25 thou gavest to them and to their *f*.
31 land which thou gavest unto our *f*.
38 land, which thou gavest unto their *f*,
7:22 they forsook the Lord God of their *f*,
9:31 Solomon slept with his *f*, and he
11:16 unto the Lord God of their *f*.
12:16 Rehoboam slept with his *f*, and was
13:12 not against the Lord God of your *f*;
18 relied upon the Lord God of their *f*.
14: 1 Abijah slept with his *f*, and they
4 to seek the Lord God of their *f*, and
15:12 to seek the Lord God of their *f* with
16:13 And Asa slept with his *f*, and died
17:14 according to the house of their *f*:
19: 4 back unto the Lord God of their *f*.
8 and of the chief of the *f* of Israel,
20: 6 And said, O Lord God of our *f*,
33 their hearts unto the God of their *f*.
21: 1 Now Jehoshaphat slept with his *f*,
1 and was buried with his *f* in the city
10 had forsaken the Lord God of his *f*.
19 for him, like the burning of his *f*.
23: 2 and the chief of the *f* of Israel,
24:18 house of the Lord God of their *f*,
24 forsaken the Lord God of their *f*.
25: 4 The *f* shall not die for the children,
4 shall the children die for the *f*,
5 according to the houses of their *f*,
28 buried him with his *f* in the city
26: 2 after that the king slept with his *f*.
12 whole number of the chief of the *f*
23 So Uzziah slept with his *f*, and they
23 buried him with his *f* in the field
27: 9 Jotham slept with his *f*, and they
28: 6 forsaken the Lord God of their *f*.
9 because the Lord God of your *f* was
25 to anger the Lord God of his *f*.
27 And Ahaz slept with his *f*, and they
29: 5 the house of the Lord God of your *f*,
6 for our *f* have trespassed, and done
9 lo, our *f* have fallen by the sword,

2Ch 30: 7 And be not ye like your f,
7 against the Lord God of their f,
8 be ye not stiffnecked, as your f were,
19 to seek God, the Lord God of his f,
22 confession to the Lord God of their f.
31:17 priests by the house of their f,
32:13 what I and my f have done unto all
14 nations that my f utterly destroyed,
15 hand, and out of the hand of my f:
33 Hezekiah slept with his f, and they
33: 8 which I have appointed for your f;
12 greatly before the God of his f,
20 So Manasseh slept with his f,
34:21 because our f have not kept the word
28 Behold, I will gather thee to thy f,
32 covenant of God, the God of their f.
33 following the Lord, the God of their f.
35: 4 by the houses of your f, after
5 of the f of your brethren
24 in one of the sepulchres of his f.
36:15 the Lord God of their f sent to them
Ezr 1: 5 Then rose up the chief of the f
2:68 And some of the chief of the f,
3:12 Levites and chief of the f, who
4: 2 and to the chief of the f, and said,
3 of the chiefs of the f of Israel,
15 in the book of the records of thy f:
5:12 f had provoked the God of heaven
7:27 Blessed be the Lord God of our f,
8: 1 These are now the chief of their f,
28 offering unto the Lord God of your f.
29 and chief of the f of Israel,
9: 7 Since the days of our f have we
10:11 unto the Lord God of your f, and do
16 the f, after the house of their f,
Ne 7:70 of the f gave unto the work.
71 of the f gave to the treasure
8:13 together the chief of the f
9: 2 sins, and the iniquities of their f.
9 didst see the affliction of our f
16 But they and our f dealt proudly,
23 which thou hadst promised to their f,
32 and on our f, and on all thy people,
34 our priests, nor our f, kept thy law,
36 the land that thou gavest unto our f
10:34 after the houses of our f, at times
11:13 And his brethren, chief of the f,
12:12 were priests, the chief of the f:
22 were recorded chief of the f:
23 the chief of the f, were written
13:18 Did not your f thus, and did not
Job 8: 8 thyself to the search of their f:
15:18 wise men have told from their f,
30: 1 whose f I would have disdained to
Ps 22: 4 Our f trusted in thee: they trusted,
39:12 and a sojourner, as all my f were.
44: 1 O God, our f have told us, what
45:16 Instead of thy f shall be thy children,
49:19 shall go to the generation of his f;
78: 3 and known, and our f have told us.
5 Israel, which he commanded our f,
8 And might not be as their f,
12 things did he in the sight of their f,
57 and dealt unfaithfully like their f:
95: 9 When your f tempted me, proved
106: 6 We have sinned with our f, we have
7 Our f understood not thy wonders
109:14 the iniquity of his f be remembered
Pr 17: 6 and the glory of children are their f.
19:14 and riches are the inheritance of f:
22:28 landmark, which thy f have set.
Isa 14:21 children for the iniquity of their f;
37:12 which my f have destroyed, as Gozan,
39: 6 that which thy f have laid up in
49:23 And kings shall be thy nursing f,
64:11 house, where our f praised thee,
65: 7 the iniquities of your f together,
Jer 2: 5 iniquity have your f found in me,
3:18 given for an inheritance unto your f.
24 hath devoured the labour of our f
25 the Lord our God, we and our f,
6:21 the f and the sons together shall fall
7: 7 the land that I gave to your f,
14 which I gave to you and to your f,
18 and the f kindle the fire, and the
22 For I spake unto your f,
25 Since the day that your f came forth
26 they did worse than their f.
9:14 Baalim, which their f taught them:
16 neither they nor their f have known:
11: 4 Which I commanded your f in the
5 oath which I have sworn unto your f,
7 I earnestly protested unto your f
10 covenant which I made with their f.
13:14 even the f and the sons together,
14:20 wickedness, and the iniquity of our f:
16: 3 concerning their f that begat them
11 Because your f have forsaken me,
12 ye have done worse than your f;
13 ye know not, neither ye nor your f;
15 their land that I gave unto their f.
19 Surely our f have inherited lies,
17:22 sabbath day, as I commanded your f.
19: 4 neither they nor their f have known,
23:27 as their f have forgotten my name
39 the city that I gave you and your f,
24:10 that I gave unto them and to their f.
25: 5 hath given unto you and to your f
30: 3 to the land that I gave to their f,
31:29 The f have eaten a sour grape,
32 covenant that I made with their f
32:18 recompensest the iniquity of the f
22 land, which thou didst swear to their f
34: 5 and with the burnings of thy f, the
13 I made a covenant with your f in the
14 but your f hearkened not unto me,

Jer 35:15 I have given to you and to your f:
44: 3 not, neither they, ye, nor your f.
9 forgotten the wickedness of your f,
10 I set before you, and before your f.
17 as we have done, we, and our f,
21 ye, and your f, your kings, and your
47: 3 the f shall not look back to their
50: 7 even the Lord, the hope of their f.
La 5: 7 Our f have sinned, and are not;
Eze 2: 3 their f have transgressed against
5:10 Therefore the f shall eat the sons in
10 and the sons shall eat their f;
18: 2 saying, The f have eaten sour grapes,
20: 4 to know the abominations of their f.
18 Walk ye not in the statutes of your f,
27 Yet in this your f have blasphemed
30 polluted after the manner of your f?
36 Like as I pleaded with your f in the
42 up mine hand to give it to your f.
36:28 the land that I gave to your f;
37:25 wherein your f have dwelt; and they
47:14 up mine hand to give it unto your f:
Da 2:23 praise thee, O thou God of my f,
9: 6 our princes, and our f, and to all
8 to our princes, and to our f, because
16 and for the iniquities of our f,
11:24 f have not done, nor his fathers' f;
37 shall he regard the God of his f, nor
38 and a god whom his f knew not shall
Ho 9:10 I saw your f as the firstripe in the fig
Joe 1: 2 or even in the days of your f?
Am 2: 4 after the which their f have walked:
Mic 7:20 hast sworn unto our f from the days
Zec 1: 2 been sore displeased with your f.
4 Be ye not as your f, unto whom the
5 Your f where are they? and the
6 did they not take hold of your f?
8:14 when your f provoked me to wrath,
Mal 2:10 by profaning the covenant of our f?
3: 7 Even from the days of your f ye are
4: 6 the heart of the f to the children,
6 the heart of the children to their f,
M't 23:30 we had been in the days of our f,
32 ye up then the measure of your f.
Lu 1:17 to turn the hearts of the f to the
55 As he spake to our f, to Abraham,
72 the mercy promised to our f,
6:23 did their f unto the prophets.
26 so did their f to the false prophets.
11:47 prophets, and your f killed them.
48 that ye allow the deeds of your f:
Joh 4:20 f worshipped in this mountain;
6:31 Our f did eat manna in the desert;
49 f did eat manna in the wilderness,
58 not as your f did eat manna,
7:22 because it is of Moses, but of the f;)
Ac 3:13 God of our f, hath glorified his Son
22 For Moses truly said unto the f,
25 which God made with our f,
5:30 The God of our f raised up Jesus,
7: 2 Men, brethren, and f, hearken;
11 and our f found no sustenance.
12 Egypt, he sent out our f first.
15 Egypt, and died, he, and our f,
19 evil entreated our f, so that they
32 Saying, I am the God of thy f,
38 the mount Sina, and with our f:
39 To whom our f would not obey,
44 f had the tabernacle of witness
45 Which also our f that came after
45 drave out before the face of our f,
51 as your f did, so do ye.
52 have not your f persecuted?
13:17 chose our f, and exalted the people
32 which was made unto the f,
36 and was laid unto his f, and saw
15:10 our f nor we were able to bear?
22: 1 Men, brethren, and f, hear ye
3 manner of the law of the f,
14 God of our f hath chosen thee,
24:14 so worship I the God of my f,
26: 6 promise made of God unto our f:
28:17 the people, or customs of our f,
25 Esaias the prophet unto our f,
Ro 9: 5 Whose are the f, and of whom
15: 8 the promises made unto the f:
1Co 4:15 yet have ye not many f:
10: 1 all our f were under the cloud,
Ga 1:14 zealous of the traditions of my f.
Eph 6: 4 ye f, provoke not your children to
Col 3:21 F, provoke not your children to
1Ti 1: 9 for murderers of f and murderers
Heb 1: 1 spake in time past unto the f by
3: 9 When your f tempted me, proved
8: 9 that I made with their f in the day
12: 9 Furthermore we have had f of our
1Pe 1:18 received by tradition from your f;
2Pe 3: 4 since the f fell asleep, all things
1Jo 2:13 I write unto you, f, because ye
14 I have written unto you, f, because

fathers'
Ex 6:14 These be the heads of their f houses:
10: 6 fathers, nor thy f fathers have seen,
Nu 17: 6 according to their f houses, even
26: 2 upward, throughout their f house,
32:14 ye are risen up in your f stead, an
Ne 2: 3 the place of my f sepulchres, lieth
5 the city of my f sepulchres, that I
Eze 20:24 their eyes were after their f idols.
22:10 they discovered their f nakedness:
Ro 11:28 they are beloved for the f sakes.

fathoms
Ac 27:28 sounded, and found it twenty f:
28 again, and found it fifteen f.

fatling See also FATLINGS.
Isa 11: 6 young lion and the f together;

fatlings
1Sa 15: 9 and of the f, and the lambs,
2Sa 6:13 he sacrificed oxen and f.
Ps 66:15 unto thee burnt sacrifices of f,
Eze 39:18 bullocks, all of them f of Bashan.
M't 22: 4 my oxen and my f are killed,

fatness
Ge 27:28 of heaven, and the f of the earth,
39 dwelling shall be the f of the earth,
De 32:15 thick, thou art covered with f;
J'g 9: 9 Should I leave my f, wherewith
Job 15:27 he covereth his face with his f,
36:16 thy table should be full of f.
Ps 36: 8 satisfied with the f of thy house;
63: 5 be satisfied as with marrow and f;
65:11 goodness; and thy paths drop f.
73: 7 Their eyes stand out with f:
109:24 and my flesh faileth of f.
Isa 17: 4 the f of his flesh shall wax lean.
34: 6 it is made fat with f, and with the
7 and their dust made fat with f.
55: 2 let your soul delight itself in f.
Jer 31:14 the soul of the priests with f,
Ro 11:17 the root and f of the olive tree;

fats
Joe 2:24 the f shall overflow with wine
3:13 the press is full, the f overflow;

fatted
1Ki 4:23 and fallowdeer, and f fowl.
Jer 46:21 the midst of her like f bullocks;
Lu 15:23 And bring hither the f calf, and
27 thy father hath killed the f calf,
30 thou hast killed for him the f calf.

fatter
Da 1:15 appeared fairer and f in flesh

fattest
Ps 78:31 upon them, and slew the f of them,
Da 11:24 upon the f places of the province;

fault See also FAULTS; FAULTLESS.
Ex 5:16 but the f is in thine own people.
De 25: 2 before his face, according to his f,
1Sa 29: 3 I have found no f in him since
2Sa 3: 8 with a f concerning this woman?
Ps 59: 4 prepare themselves without my f:
Da 6: 4 could find none occasion nor f;
4 there any error or f found in him.
M't 18:15 and tell him his f between thee
M'r 7: 2 unwashen, hands, they found f
Lu 23: 4 I find no f in this man.
14 have found no f in this man
Joh 18:38 I find in him no f at all.
19: 4 know that I find no f in him.
6 for I find no f in him.
Ro 9:19 Why doth he yet find f? For who
1Co 6: 7 there is utterly a f among you,
Ga 6: 1 if a man be overtaken in a f,
Heb 8: 8 For finding f with them, he saith,
Re 14: 5 are without f before the throne

faultless
Heb 8: 7 if that first covenant had been f,
Jude 24 and to present you f before the

faults
Ge 41: 9 I do remember my f this day:
Ps 19:12 cleanse thou me from secret f.
Jas 5:16 Confess your f one to another,
1Pe 2:20 if, when ye be buffeted for your f,

faulty
2Sa 14:13 this thing as one which is f,
Ho 10: 2 now shall they be found f:

favour See also FAVOURABLE; FAVOURED; FAVOUREST; FAVOURETH.
Ge 18: 3 now I have found f in thy sight,
30:27 if I have found f in thine eyes,
39:21 him f in the sight of the keeper
Ex 3:21 will give this people f in the sight
11: 3 And the Lord gave the people f in
12:36 Lord gave the people f in the sight
Nu 11:11 have I not found f in thy sight,
15 if I have found f in thy sight;
De 24: 1 pass that she find no f in his eyes,
28:50 the old, nor shew f to the young:
33:23 O Naphtali, satisfied with f, and
Jos 11:20 and that they might have no f,
Ru 2:13 Let me find f in thy sight,
1Sa 2:26 and was in f both with the Lord,
16:22 for he hath found f in my sight.
20:29 if I have found f in thine eyes,
25: 8 young men find f in thine eyes:
29: 6 the lords f thee not.
2Sa 15:25 if I shall find f in the eyes of the
1Ki 11:19 Hadad found great f in the sight
Ne 2: 5 if thy servant have found f in thy
Es 2:15 Esther obtained f in the sight of
17 she obtained grace and f in his
5: 2 that she obtained f in his sight:
8 If I have found f in the sight of the
7: 3 If I have found f in thy sight, O
8: 5 and if I have found f in his sight,
Job 10:12 Thou hast granted me life and f,
Ps 5:12 with f wilt thou compass him as
30: 5 his f is life: weeping may endure
7 f thou hast made my mountain
35:27 glad, that f my righteous cause:
44: 3 because thou hadst a f unto them.
45:12 the people shall intreat thy f.
89:17 thy f our horn shall be exalted.
102:13 for the time to f her, yea, the set
14 stones, and f the dust thereof.
106: 4 with the f that thou bearest unto
109:12 neither let there be any to f his

Ps 112: 5 man sheweth f, and lendeth:
119:58 I intreated thy f with my whole
Pr 3: 4 So shalt thou find f and good
8:35 and shall obtain f of the Lord.
11:27 seeketh good procureth f: but
12: 2 good man obtaineth f of the Lord
13:15 Good understanding giveth f:
14: 9 among the righteous there is f.
35 king's f is toward a wise servant:
16:15 f is as a cloud of the latter rain.
18:22 thing, and obtaineth f of the Lord.
19: 6 will intreat the f of the prince:
12 his f is as dew upon the grass.
21:10 neighbour findeth no f in his eyes.
22: 1 f rather than silver and gold.
28:23 find more f than he that flattereth
29:26 Many seek the ruler's f;
31:30 F is deceitful, and beauty is vain:
Ec 9:11 nor yet f to men of skill;
Ca 8:10 I in his eyes as one that found f.
Isa 26:10 Let f be shewed to the wicked,
27:11 formed them will shew them no f.
60:10 but in my f have I had mercy on
Jer 16:13 where I will not shew you f.
Da 1: 9 God had brought Daniel into f
Lu 1:30 for thou hast found f with God.
2:52 and in f with God and man.
Ac 2:47 and having f with all the people.
7:10 him f and wisdom in the sight of
46 Who found f before God, and
25: 3 And desired f against him, that

favourable
J'g 21:22 Be f unto them for our sakes:
Job 33:26 and he will be f unto him:
Ps 77: 7 and will he be f no more?
85: 1 thou hast been f unto thy land:

favoured See also EVILFAVOUREDNESS.
Ge 29:17 Rachel was beautiful and well f.
39: 6 was a goodly person, and well f.
41: 2 out of the river seven well f kine
3 seven other kine...ill f and
4 the ill f...kine did eat up the seven
4 kine did eat up the seven well f
18 kine, fatfleshed and well f;
19 poor and very ill f and leanfleshed,
20 the lean and the ill f kine did eat
21 were still ill f, as at the beginning.
27 And the seven thin and ill f kine
La 4:16 priests, they f not the elders.
Da 1: 4 was no blemish, but well f,
Lu 1:28 Hail, thou that art highly f,

favourest
Ps 41:11 By this I know that thou f me,

favoureth
2Sa 20:11 He that f Joab, and he that is for

fear See also FEARED; FEAREST; FEARETH; FEARFUL; FEARING; FEARS.
Ge 9: 2 the f of you and the dread of you
15: 1 F not, Abram: I am thy shield,
20:11 the f of God is not in this place;
21:17 What aileth thee, Hagar? f not;
26:24 f not, for I am with thee, and will
31:42 and the f of Isaac, had been with
53 Jacob sware by the f of his father
32:11 I f him, lest he will come and
35:17 F not; thou shalt have this son
42:18 This do, and live; for I f God:
43:23 he said, Peace be to you, f not:
46: 3 f not to go down into Egypt;
50:19 Joseph said unto them, F not:
21 Now therefore f ye not: I will
Ex 9:30 I know that ye will not yet f the
14:13 F ye not, stand still, and see the
15:16 F and dread shall fall upon them;
18:21 people able men, such as f God,
20:20 Moses said unto the people, F not:
20 that his f may be before your
23:27 I will send my f before thee,
Le 19: 3 Ye shall f every man his mother,
14 but shalt f thy God: I am the
32 face of the old man, and f thy God:
25:17 but thou shalt f thy God: for I am
36 but f thy God; that thy brother
43 with rigour; but shalt f thy God.
Nu 14: 9 neither f ye the people of the land;
9 the Lord is with us; f them not.
21:34 Lord said unto Moses, F him not:
De 1:21 said unto thee; f not, neither be
2:25 the dread of thee and the f of thee
3: 2 Lord said unto me, F him not:
22 Ye shall not f them: for the Lord
4:10 that they may learn to f me
5:29 that they would f me, and keep all
6: 2 That thou mightest f the Lord thy
13 Thou shalt f the Lord thy God,
24 to f the Lord our God, for our
8: 6 to walk in his ways, and to f him.
10:12 but to f the Lord thy God,
20 Thou shalt f the Lord thy God;
11:25 the f of you and the dread of you
13: 4 the Lord your God, and f him,
11 And all Israel shall hear, and f,
14:23 thou mayest learn to f the Lord
17:13 all the people shall hear, and f,
19 that he may learn to f the Lord
19:20 which remain shall hear, and f,
20: 3 f not, and do not tremble, neither
21:21 and all Israel shall hear, and f.
28:58 that thou mayest f this glorious
66 and thou shalt f day and night,
67 for the f of thine heart wherewith
67 heart wherewith thou shalt f,
31: 6 f not, nor be afraid of them:
8 f not, neither be dismayed.
De 31:12 they may learn, and f the Lord
13 and learn to f the Lord your God,
Jos 4:24 that ye might f the Lord your God
8: 1 F not, neither be thou dismayed:
10: 8 Lord said unto Joshua, F them not:
25 Joshua said unto them, F not, nor
22:24 rather done it for f of this thing,
24:14 Now therefore f the Lord, and
J'g 4:18 my lord, turn in to me; f not.
6:10 f not the gods of the Amorites,
23 Peace be unto thee; f not: thou
7:10 if thou f to go down, go thou
9:21 dwelt there, for f of Abimelech
Ru 3:11 my daughter, f not; I will do to
1Sa 4:20 F not; for thou hast born a son.
11: 7 And the f of the Lord fell on the
12:14 If ye will f the Lord, and serve
20 Samuel said unto the people, F not:
24 Only f the Lord, and serve him in
21:10 and fled that day for f of Saul,
22:23 Abide thou with me, f not:
23:17 And he said unto him, F not:
26 haste to get away for f of Saul;
2Sa 9: 7 And David said unto him, F not:
13:28 Amnon; then kill him, f not:
23: 3 be just, ruling in the f of God.
1Ki 8:40 That they may f thee all the days
43 to f thee, as do thy people Israel;
17:13 Elijah said unto her, F not;
18:12 I thy servant f the Lord from my
2Ki 4: 1 that thy servant did f the Lord:
6:16 he answered, F not: for they
17:28 taught them how they should f the
34 manners: they f not the Lord,
35 saying, Ye shall not f other gods,
36 him shall ye f, and him shall ye
37 and ye shall not f other gods.
38 neither shall ye f other gods.
39 the Lord your God ye shall f;
25:24 F not to be the servants of the
1Ch 14:17 the Lord brought the f of him
16:30 F before him, all the earth:
28:20 do it: f not, nor be dismayed:
2Ch 6:31 That they may f thee, to walk in
33 and f thee, as doth thy people
14:14 the f of the Lord came upon them:
17:10 the f of the Lord fell upon all the
19: 7 let the f of the Lord be upon you;
9 Thus shall ye do in the f of the
20:17 f not, nor be dismayed;
29 And the f of God was on all the
Ezr 3: 3 f was upon them because of the
Ne 1:11 thy servants, who desire to f thy
5: 9 ought ye not to walk in the f of
15 so did not I, because of the f of
6:14 that would have put me in f.
19 Tobiah sent letters to put me in f.
Es 8:17 the f of the Jews fell upon them.
9: 2 the f of them fell upon all people.
3 the f of Mordecai fell upon them.
Job 1: 9 said, Doth Job f God for nought?
4: 6 Is not this thy f, thy confidence,
14 F came upon me, and trembling,
6:14 but he forsaketh the f of the
9:34 and let not his f terrify me:
35 Then would I speak, and not f him;
11:15 shalt be stedfast, and shalt not f:
15: 4 thou castest off f, and restrainest
21: 9 Their houses are safe from f,
22: 4 Will he reprove thee for f of thee?
10 and sudden f troubleth thee;
25: 2 Dominion and f are with him,
28:28 the f of the Lord, that is wisdom;
31:34 Did I f a great multitude, or
37:24 Men do therefore f him: he
39:16 her labour is in vain without f;
22 He mocketh at f, and is not
41:33 his like, who is made without f.
Ps 2:11 Serve the Lord with f, and rejoice
5: 7 and in thy f will I worship toward
9:20 Put them in f, O Lord: that the
14: 5 There were they in great f: for
15: 4 honoureth them that f the Lord,
19: 9 The f of the Lord is clean,
22:23 Ye that f the Lord, praise him;
23 and f him, all ye the seed of
25 my vows before them that f him.
23: 4 I will f no evil: for thou art with
25:14 the Lord is with them that f him;
27: 1 whom shall I f? the Lord is the
3 my heart shall not f: though war
31:11 and a f to mine acquaintance:
13 f was on every side: while they
19 hast laid up for them that f thee;
33: 8 Let all the earth f the Lord:
18 the Lord is upon them that f him;
34: 7 round about them that f him,
9 O f the Lord, ye his saints:
9 is no want to them that f him.
11 I will teach you the f of the Lord.
36: 1 is no f of God before his eyes.
40: 3 many shall see it, and f, and shall
46: 2 Therefore will not we f, though
48: 6 F took hold upon them there,
49: 5 should I f in the days of evil,
52: 6 The righteous also shall see, and f,
53: 5 There were they in great f,
5 There were...where no f was:
55:19 therefore they f not God.
56: 4 I will not f what flesh can do unto
60: 4 a banner to them that f thee,
61: 5 heritage of those that f thy name.
64: 1 preserve my life from f of the
4 do they shoot at him, and f not.
9 all men shall f, and shall declare
66:16 Come and hear, all ye that f God,
Ps 67: 7 the ends of the earth shall f him.
72: 5 They shall f thee as long as the
85: 9 salvation is nigh them that f him;
86:11 unite my heart to f thy name.
90:11 even according to thy f, so is thy
96: 9 f before him, all the earth.
102:15 shall f the name of the Lord,
103:11 mercy toward them that f him.
13 the Lord pitieth them that f him.
17 everlasting upon them that f him,
105:38 for the f of them fell upon them.
111: 5 given meat unto them that f him:
10 The f of the Lord is the beginning
115:11 Ye that f the Lord, trust in the
13 He will bless them that f the Lord,
118: 4 Let them now that f the Lord say,
6 Lord is on my side; I will not f:
119:38 servant, who is devoted to thy f.
39 away my reproach which I f:
63 companion of all them that f thee,
74 They that f thee will be glad
79 those that f thee turn unto me,
120 My flesh trembleth for f of thee;
135:20 ye that f the Lord, bless the Lord.
145:19 the desire of them that f him:
147:11 taketh pleasure in them that f him,
Pr 1: 7 The f of the Lord is the beginning
26 will mock when your f cometh;
27 When your f cometh as desolation,
29 did not chose the f of the Lord:
33 and shall be quiet from f of evil.
2: 5 thou understand the f of the Lord,
3: 7 f the Lord, and depart from evil.
25 Be not afraid of sudden f,
8:13 The f of the Lord is to hate evil:
9:10 The f of the Lord is the beginning
10:24 The f of the wicked, it shall come
27 f of the Lord prolongeth days:
14:26 In the f of the Lord is strong
27 f of the Lord is a fountain of life,
15:16 Better is little with the f of the
33 The f of the Lord is the instruction
16: 6 by the f of the Lord men depart
19:23 The f of the Lord tendeth to life:
20: 2 The f of the king is as the roaring
22: 4 humility and the f of the Lord
23:17 be thou in the f of the Lord
24:21 f thou the Lord and the king:
29:25 The f of man bringeth a snare:
Ec 3:14 God doeth it, that men should f
5: 7 divers vanities: but f thou God.
8:12 shall be well with them that f God,
12 with them...which f before him:
12:13 matter: F God, and keep his
Ca 3: 8 because of f in the night.
Isa 2:10 in the dust, for f of the Lord,
19 of the earth, for f of the Lord,
21 ragged rocks, for f of the Lord,
7: 4 Take heed, and be quiet; f not,
25 thither the f of briers and thorns:
8:12 neither f ye...nor be afraid.
12 neither...their f, nor be afraid.
13 let him be your f, and let him be
11: 2 knowledge and of the f of the
3 understanding in the f of the
14: 3 from thy sorrow and from thy f,
19:16 and f because of the shaking of
21: 4 pleasure hath he turned into f
24:17 F, and the pit, and the snare,
18 who fleeth from the noise of the f
25: 3 the terrible nations shall f thee.
29:13 their f toward me is taught by
23 and shall f the God of Israel.
31: 9 pass over to his strong hold for f,
33: 6 the f of the Lord is his treasure.
35: 4 Be strong, f not: behold, your
41:10 F thou not; for I am with thee:
13 thee, F not; I will help thee.
14 F not, thou worm Jacob, and ye
43: 1 F not: for I have redeemed thee,
5 F not: for I am with thee: I will
44: 2 F not, O Jacob, my servant;
8 F ye not, neither be afraid: have
11 yet they shall f, and they shall be
51: 7 f ye not the reproach of men,
54: 4 F not; for thou shalt not be
14 oppression; for thou shalt not f:
59:19 shall they f the name of the Lord
60: 5 and thine heart shall f, and be
63:17 hardened our heart from thy f?
Jer 2:19 that my f is not in thee,
5:22 F ye not me? saith the Lord:
24 Let us now f the Lord our God,
6:25 enemy, and f is on every side.
10: 7 Who would not f thee, O King
20:10 of many, f on every side.
23: 4 and they shall f no more, nor be
26:19 did he not f the Lord, and
30: 5 a voice of trembling, of f, and
10 f thou not, O my servant Jacob,
32:39 that they may f me for ever,
40 I will put my f in their hearts,
33: 9 and they shall f and tremble
35:11 for f of the army of the Chaldeans,
11 for f of the army of the Syrians:
37:11 for f of Pharaoh's army,
40: 9 F not to serve the Chaldeans:
41: 9 for f of Baasha king of Israel:
46: 5 f was round about, saith the
27 f not thou, O my servant Jacob,
28 F thou not, O Jacob my servant,
48:43 F, and the pit, and the snare,
44 He that fleeth from the f shall fall
49: 5 I will bring a f upon thee, saith
24 to flee, and f hath seized on her:
29 unto them, F is on every side.

Jer 50:16 for *f* of the oppressing sword they
51:46 lest your heart faint, and ye *f* for
La 3:47 *F* and a snare is come upon us,
57 upon thee: thou saidst, *F* not.
Eze 3: 9 *f* them not, neither be dismayed
30:13 will put a *f* in the land of Egypt.
Da 1:10 I *f* my lord the king, who hath
6:26 and *f* before the God of Daniel:
10:12 Then said he unto me, *F* not,
19 O man greatly beloved, *f* not:
Ho 3: 5 shall *f* the Lord and his goodness
10: 5 inhabitants of Samaria shall *f*
Joe 2:21 *F* not, O land; be glad and
Am 3: 8 lion hath roared, who will not *f*?
Jon 1: 9 I *f* the Lord, the God of heaven,
Mic 7:17 God, and shall *f* because of thee.
Zep 3: 7 I said, Surely thou wilt *f* me,
16 be said to Jerusalem, *F* thou not:
Hag 1:12 the people did *f* before the Lord.
2: 5 remaineth among you: *f* ye not.
Zec 8:13 *f* not, but let your hands be strong.
15 the house of Judah: *f* ye not.
9: 5 Ashkelon shall see it, and *f*; Gaza
Mal 1: 6 if I be a master, where is my *f*?
2: 5 the *f* wherewith he feared me,
3: 5 and *f* not me, saith the Lord
4: 2 But unto you that *f* my name
M't 1:20 *f* not to take unto thee Mary
10:26 *F* them not therefore: for there is
28 *f* not them which kill the body,
28 *f* him which is able to destroy both
31 *F* ye not therefore, ye are of more
14:26 a spirit; and they cried out for *f*.
21:26 we *f* the people; for all hold John
28: 4 for *f* of him the keepers did shake,
5 *F* not ye: for I know that ye seek
8 sepulchre with *f* and great joy;
Lu 1:12 was troubled, and *f* fell upon him.
13 *F* not, Zacharias: for thy prayer
30 *F* not, Mary: for thou hast found
50 his mercy is on them that *f* him
65 *f* came on all that dwelt round
74 enemies might serve him without *f*,
2:10 *F* not: for, behold, I bring you
5:10 And Jesus said unto Simon, *F* not;
26 were filled with *f*, saying, We have
7:16 came a *f* on all: and they glorified
8:37 for they were taken with great *f*:
50 *F* not: believe only, and she shall
12: 5 whom ye shall *f*: *F* him, which
5 yea, I say unto you, *F* him.
7 *F* not therefore: ye are of more
32 *F* not, little flock; for it is your
18: 4 I *f* not God, nor regard man;
21:26 Men's hearts failing them for *f*,
23:40 Dost not thou *f* God, seeing thou
Joh 7:13 openly of him for *f* of the Jews.
12:15 *F* not, daughter of Sion: behold,
19:38 but secretly for *f* of the Jews,
20:19 assembled for *f* of the Jews, came
Ac 2:43 *f* came upon every soul: and many
5: 5 great *f* came on all them that heard
11 great *f* came upon all the church,
9:31 and walking in the *f* of the Lord,
13:16 and ye that *f* God, give audience.
19:17 *f* fell on them all, and the name
27:24 *F* not, Paul; thou must be brought
Ro 3:18 There is no *f* of God before their
8:15 the spirit of bondage again to *f*;
11:20 faith. Be not highminded, but *f*:
13: 7 *f* to whom *f*; honour to whom
1Co 2: 3 and in *f*, and in much trembling.
16:10 he may be with you without *f*:
2Co 7: 1 perfecting holiness in the *f* of God.
11 what indignation, yea, what *f*, yea,
15 with *f* and trembling ye received
11: 3 But I *f*, lest by any means, as the
12:20 For I *f*, lest, when I come, I shall
Eph 5:21 one to another in the *f* of God.
6: 5 with *f* and trembling, in singleness
Ph'p 1:14 bold to speak the word without *f*.
2:12 salvation with *f* and trembling.
1Ti 5:20 all, that others also may *f*.
2Ti 1: 7 hath not given us the spirit of *f*;
Heb 2:15 who through *f* of death were all
4: 1 Let us therefore *f*, lest, a promise
11: 7 moved with *f*, prepared an ark
12:21 I exceedingly *f* and quake:)
28 with reverence and godly *f*:
13: 6 I will not *f* what man shall do unto
1Pe 1:17 time of your sojourning here in *f*:
2:17 *F* God. Honour the king.
18 subject to your masters with all *f*;
3: 2 chaste conversation coupled with *f*.
15 is in you with meekness and *f*:
1Jo 4:18 There is no *f* in love; but perfect
18 love casteth out *f*: because *f* hath
Jude 12 feeding themselves without *f*:
23 others save with *f*, pulling them
Re 1:17 saying unto me, *F* not; I am the
2:10 *F* none of those things which thou
11:11 great *f* fell upon them which saw
18 saints, and them that *f* thy name,
14: 7 *F* God, and give glory to him;
15: 4 Who shall not *f* thee, O Lord,
18:10, 15 afar off for the *f* of her torment,
19: 5 that *f* him, both small and great.

feared

Ge 19:30 for he *f* to dwell in Zoar:
26: 7 for he *f* to say, She is my wife;
Ex 1:17 the midwives *f* God, and did not as
21 the midwives *f* God, that he made
2:14 And Moses *f*, and said, Surely this
9:20 He that *f* the word of the Lord
14:31 people *f* the Lord, and believed
De 25:18 and he *f* not God.
32:17 up, whom your fathers *f* not.
27 that I *f* the wrath of the enemy,
Jos 4:14 sight of all Israel; and they *f* him,
14 they *f* Moses, all the days of his life.
10: 2 they *f* greatly, because Gibeon was
J'g 6:27 because he *f* his father's household,
8:20 he *f*, because he was yet a youth.
1Sa 3:15 Samuel *f* to shew Eli the vision.
12:18 all the people greatly *f* the Lord
14:26 mouth: for the people *f* the oath.
15:24 because I *f* the people, and obeyed
2Sa 3:11 a word again, because he *f* him.
10:19 the Syrians *f* to help the children
12:18 And the servants of David *f* to tell
1Ki 1:50 Adonijah *f* because of Solomon,
3:28 they *f* the king: for they saw that
18: 3 Obadiah *f* the Lord greatly:
2Ki 17: 7 and had *f* other gods,
25 they *f* not the Lord: therefore the
32 they *f* the Lord, and made unto
33 *f* the Lord, and served their own
41 nations *f* the Lord, and served
1Ch 16:25 he also is to be *f* above all gods.
2Ch 20: 3 Jehoshaphat *f*, and set himself to
Ne 7: 2 man, and *f* God above many.
Job 1: 1 and one that *f* God, and eschewed
3:25 thing which I greatly *f* is come
Ps 76: 7 Thou, even thou, art to be *f*:
8 the earth *f*, and was still,
11 unto him that ought to be *f*.
78:53 them on safely so that they *f* not:
89: 7 God is greatly to be *f* in the
96: 4 he is to be *f* above all gods.
130: 4 with thee, that thou mayest be *f*.
Isa 41: 5 The isles saw it, and *f*; the ends of
51:13 and hast *f* continually every day
57:11 whom hast thou been afraid or *f*,
Jer 3: 8 her treacherous sister Judah *f* not,
42:16 sword, which ye *f*, shall overtake
44:10 they *f*, nor walked in my law,
Eze 11: 8 Ye have *f* the sword; and I will
Da 5:19 languages, trembled and *f* before
Ho 10: 3 because we *f* not the Lord; what
Jon 1:16 the men *f* the Lord exceedingly,
Mal 2: 5 fear wherewith he *f* me, and was
3:16 they that *f* the Lord spake often
16 before him for them that *f* the Lord,
M't 14: 5 he *f* the multitude, because they
21:46 they *f* the multitude, because they
27:54 *f* greatly, saying, Truly this was
M'r 4:41 they *f* exceedingly, and said
6:20 For Herod *f* John, knowing that
11:18 they *f* him, because all the people
32 Of men; they *f* the people:
12:12 lay hold on him, but *f* the people:
Lu 9:34 *f* as they entered into the cloud.
45 they *f* to ask him of that saying.
18: 2 judge, which *f* not God, neither
19:21 For I *f* thee, because thou art an
20:19 and they *f* the people: for they
22: 2 kill him; for they *f* the people.
Joh 9:22 because they *f* the Jews: for the
Ac 5:26 for they *f* the people, lest they
10: 2 one that *f* God with all his house,
16:38 they *f*, when they heard that they
Heb 5: 7 and was heard in that he *f*;

fearest

Ge 22:12 now I know that thou *f* God,
Isa 57:11 even of old, and thou *f* me not?
Jer 22:25 hand of them whose face thou *f*,

feareth

1Ki 1:51 Behold, Adonijah *f* king Solomon:
Job 1: 8 an upright man, one that *f* God,
2: 3 an upright man, one that *f* God,
Ps 25:12 What man is he that *f* the Lord?
112: 1 Blessed is the man that *f* the
128: 1 is every one that *f* the Lord;
4 shall the man be blessed that *f* the
Pr 13:13 but he that *f* the commandment
14: 2 in his uprightness *f* the Lord:
16 A wise man *f*, and departeth from
28:14 Happy is the man that *f* alway:
31:30 but a woman that *f* the Lord,
Ec 7:18 he that *f* God shall come forth
8:13 because he *f* not before God.
9: 2 as he that *f* an oath.
Isa 50:10 Who is among you that *f* the Lord,
Ac 10:22 a just man, and one that *f* God,
35 But in every nation he that *f* him,
13:26 whosoever among you *f* God,
1Jo 4:18 He that *f* is not made perfect in

fearful

Ex 15:11 *f* in praises, doing wonders?
De 20: 8 What man is there that is *f* and
28:58 fear this glorious and *f* name,
J'g 7: 3 Whosoever is *f* and afraid, let
Isa 35: 4 Say to them that are of a *f* heart,
M't 8:26 Why are ye *f*, O ye of little faith?
M'r 4:40 said unto them, Why are ye so *f*?
Lu 21:11 *f* sights and great signs shall
Heb 10:27 certain *f* looking for of judgment
31 It is a *f* thing to fall into the hands
Re 21: 8 the *f*, and unbelieving, and the

fearfully

Ps 139:14 I am *f* and wonderfully made:

fearfulness

Ps 55: 5 *F* and trembling are come upon
Isa 21: 4 heart panted, *f* affrighted me:
33:14 *f* hath surprised the hypocrites.

fearing

Jos 22:25 children cease from *f* the Lord.
M'r 5:33 But the woman *f* and trembling,
Ac 23:10 the chief captain, *f* lest Paul
27:17 and, *f* lest they should fall into
Ac 27:29 *f* lest we should have fallen upon
Ga 2:12 himself, *f* them which were of the
Col 3:22 but in singleness of heart, *f* God:
Heb 11:27 not *f* the wrath of the king:

fears

Ps 34: 4 and delivered me from all my *f*.
Ec 12: 5 and *f* shall be in the way,
Isa 66: 4 and will bring their *f* upon them;
2Co 7: 5 were fightings, within were *f*.

feast See also FEASTED; FEASTING; FEASTS.

Ge 19: 3 he made them a *f*, and did bake
21: 8 Abraham made a great *f* the same
26:30 he made them a *f*, and they did eat
29:22 men of the place, and made a *f*.
40:20 he made a *f* unto all his servants:
Ex 5: 1 that they may hold a *f* unto me
10: 9 we must hold a *f* unto the Lord.
12:14 ye shall keep it a *f* to the Lord
14 shall keep it a *f* by an ordinance
17 observe the *f* of unleavened bread:
13: 6 in the seventh day shall be a *f* to
23:14 Three times thou shalt keep a *f*
15 keep the *f* of unleavened bread:
16 And the *f* of harvest, the firstfruits
16 and the *f* of ingathering, which is
32: 5 To morrow is a *f* to the Lord.
34:18 The *f* of unleavened bread shalt
22 thou shalt observe the *f* of weeks,
22 *f* of ingathering at the year's end.
25 sacrifice of the *f* of the passover
Le 23: 6 the *f* of unleavened bread unto the
34 the *f* of tabernacles for seven days
39 ye shall keep a *f* unto the Lord
41 ye shall keep it a *f* unto the Lord
Nu 28:17 fifteenth day of this month is the *f*:
29:12 ye shall keep a *f* unto the Lord
De 16:10 thou shalt keep the *f* of weeks
13 shalt observe the *f* of tabernacles
14 And thou shalt rejoice in thy *f*,
15 days shalt thou keep a solemn *f*
16 in the *f* of unleavened bread, and
16 in the *f* of weeks, and in the *f* of
31:10 of release, in the *f* of tabernacles,
J'g 14:10 Samson made there a *f*; for so
12 within the seven days of the *f*,
17 seven days, while their *f* lasted:
21:19 Behold, there is a *f* of the Lord
1Sa 25:36 behold he held a *f* in his house,
36 like the *f* of a king; and Nabal's
2Sa 3:20 the men that were with him a *f*.
1Ki 3:15 and made a *f* to all his servants.
8: 2 at the *f* in the month Ethanim,
65 at that time Solomon held a *f*,
12:32 Jeroboam ordained a *f* in the
32 like unto the *f* that is in Judah,
33 a *f* unto the children of Israel;
2Ch 5: 3 themselves unto the king in the *f*
7: 8 Solomon kept the *f* seven days,
9 seven days, and the *f* seven days.
8:13 even in the *f* of unleavened bread,
13 and in the *f* of weeks,
13 and in the *f* of tabernacles.
30:13 to keep the *f* of unleavened bread
21 kept the *f* of unleavened bread
22 eat throughout the *f* seven days,
35:17 kept...the *f* of unleavened bread
Ezr 3: 4 They kept also the *f* of tabernacles,
6:22 kept the *f* of unleavened bread
Ne 8:14 should dwell in booths in the *f* of
18 And they kept the *f* seven days;
Es 1: 3 he made a *f* unto all his princes
5 king made a *f* unto all the people
9 Vashti the queen made a *f* for the
2:18 Then the king made a great *f* unto
18 and his servants, even Esther's *f*;
8:17 and gladness, a *f* and a good day.
Ps 81: 3 appointed, on our solemn *f* day.
Pr 15:15 a merry heart hath a continual *f*.
Ec 10:19 A *f* is made for laughter, and
Isa 25: 6 unto all people a *f* of fat things,
6 a *f* of wines on the lees,
La 2: 7 as in the day of a solemn *f*.
Eze 45:21 the passover, a *f* of seven days;
23 seven days of the *f* he shall prepare
25 shall he do the like in the *f* of the
Da 5: 1 the king made a great *f* to a
Ho 2:11 her *f* days, her new moons, and
9: 5 in the day of the *f* of the Lord?
12: 9 as in the days of the solemn *f*.
Am 5:21 I hate, I despise your *f* days,
Zec 14:16 and to keep the *f* of tabernacles.
18, 19 that come not up to keep the *f*
M't 26: 2 two days is the *f* of the passover,
5 But they said, Not on the *f* day,
17 day of the *f* of unleavened bread
27:15 at that *f* the governor was wont
M'r 14: 1 two days was the *f* of the passover,
2 But they said, Not on the *f* day,
15: 6 Now at that *f* he released unto
Lu 2:41 every year at the *f* of the passover.
42 Jerusalem after the custom of the *f*.
5:29 Levi made him a great *f* in his
14:13 when thou makest a *f*, call the
22: 1 the *f* of unleavened bread drew
23:17 release one unto them at the *f*.
Joh 2: 8 bear unto the governor of the *f*.
9 When the ruler of the *f* had tasted
9 the governor of the *f* called the
23 at the passover, in the *f* day,
4:45 that he did at Jerusalem at the *f*:
45 for they also went unto the *f*.
5: 1 After this there was a *f* of the Jews;
6: 4 a *f* of the Jews, was nigh.
7: 2 the Jews' *f* of tabernacles was at
8 Go ye up unto this *f*:

Joh 7: 8 I go not up yet unto this *f*:
10 then went he also up unto the *f*,
11 Then the Jews sought him at the *f*,
14 Now about the midst of the *f* Jesus
37 last day, that great day of the *f*,
10:22 Jerusalem the *f* of the dedication,
11:56 that he will not come to the *f*?
12:12 people that were come to the *f*,
20 that came up to worship at the *f*:
13: 1 Now before the *f* of the passover,
29 we have need of against the *f*;
Ac 18:21 I must by all means keep this *f*
1Co 5: 8 Therefore let us keep the *f*,
10:27 them that believe not bid you to a *f*,
2Pe 2:13 deceivings while they *f* with you;
Jude 12 of charity, when they *f* with you,

feast-day See FEAST and DAY.

feasted
Job 1: 4 his sons went and *f* in their

feasting
Es 9:17, 18 and made it a day of *f* and
19 Adar a day of gladness and *f*,
22 they should make them days of *f*
Job 1: 5 when the days of their *f* were
Ec 7: 2 than to go to the house of *f*:
Jer 16: 8 not also go into the house of *f*,

feasts
Le 23: 2 Concerning the *f* of the Lord,
2 convocations, even these are my *f*.
4 These are the *f* of the Lord, even
37 These are the *f* of the Lord, which
44 of Israel the *f* of the Lord.
Nu 15: 3 in your solemn *f*, to make a sweet
29:39 do unto the Lord in your set *f*,
1Ch 23:31 and on the set *f*, by number,
2Ch 2: 4 and on the solemn *f* of the Lord
8:13 new moons, and on the solemn *f*
31: 3 the new moons, and for the set *f*,
Ezr 3: 5 and of all the set *f* of the Lord
Ne 10:33 the set *f*, and for the holy things,
Ps 35:16 With hypocritical mockers in *f*,
Isa 1:14 your appointed *f* my soul hateth:
5:12 and pipe and wine, are in their *f*:
Jer 51:39 In their heat I will make their *f*,
La 1: 4 none come to the solemn *f*:
2: 6 caused the solemn *f* and sabbaths
Eze 36:38 of Jerusalem in her solemn *f*;
45:17 to give drink...offerings, in the *f*,
46: 9 before the Lord in the solemn *f*,
11 And in the *f* and in the solemnities
Ho 2:11 sabbaths, and all her solemn *f*.
Am 8:10 I will turn your *f* into mourning,
Na 1:15 keep thy solemn *f*, perform thy
Zec 8:19 joy and gladness, and cheerful *f*;
Mal 2: 3 even the dung of your solemn *f*;
M't 23: 6 love the uppermost rooms at *f*,
M'r 12:39 and the uppermost rooms at *f*:
Lu 20:46 and the chief rooms at *f*;
Jude 12 are spots in your *f* of charity,

feathered
Ps 78:27 and *f* fowls like as the sand
Eze 39:17 Speak unto every *f* fowl, and to

feathers
Le 1:16 pluck away his crop with his *f*,
Job 39:13 wings and *f* unto the ostrich?
Ps 68:13 and her *f* with yellow gold.
91: 4 He shall cover thee with his *f*,
Eze 17: 3 great wings, long winged, full of *f*,
7 with great wings and many *f*:
Da 4:33 hairs were grown like eagles' *f*,

fed
Ge 30:36 Jacob *f* the rest of Laban's flocks
36:24 as he *f* the asses of Zibeon his
41: 2 fatfleshed; and they *f* in a meadow.
18 favoured; and they *f* in a meadow:
47:17 and he *f* them with bread for all
48:15 the God which *f* me all my life
Ex 16:32 I have *f* you in the wilderness,
De 8: 3 to hunger, and *f* thee with manna,
16 Who *f* thee in the wilderness with
2Sa 20: 3 put them in ward, and *f* them,
1Ki 18: 4 and *f* them with bread and water.)
13 and *f* them with bread and water?
1Ch 27:29 over the herds that *f* in Sharon
Ps 37: 3 and verily thou shalt be *f*.
78:72 *f* them according to the integrity
81:16 He should have *f* them also with
Isa 1:11 of rams, and the fat of *f* beasts;
Jer 5: 7 when I had *f* them to the full,
8 They were as *f* horses in the
Eze 16:19 and honey, wherewith I *f* thee,
34: 3 ye kill them that are *f*: but ye
8 but the shepherds *f* themselves,
8 and *f* not my flock;
Da 4:12 and all flesh was *f* of it.
5:21 they *f* him with grass like oxen,
Zec 11: 7 called Bands; and I *f* the flock.
M't 25:37 thee an hungered, and *f* thee?
M'r 5:14 they that *f* the swine fled, and
Lu 8:34 they that *f* them saw what was
16:21 desiring to be *f* with the crumbs
1Co 3: 2 I have *f* you with milk, and not

feeble See also FEEBLEMINDED; FEEBLER.
Ge 30:42 But when the cattle were *f*, he
De 25:18 even all that were *f* behind thee,
1Sa 2: 5 hath many children is waxed *f*.
2Sa 4: 1 his hands were *f*, and all the
2Ch 28:15 and carried all the *f* of them upon
Ne 4: 2 What do these *f* Jews? will they
Job 4: 4 hast strengthened the *f* knees,
Ps 38: 8 I am *f* and sore broken:
105:37 and there was not one *f* person
Pr 30:26 The conies are but a *f* folk,
Isa 16:14 the remnant shall be very
35: 3 hands, and confirm the *f* knees.
Jer 6:24 our hands wax *f*: anguish hath
49:24 Damascus is waxed *f*, and turneth
50:43 and his hands waxed *f*: anguish
Eze 7:17 All hands shall be *f*, and all knees
21: 7 and all hands shall be *f*,
Zec 12: 8 and he that is *f* among them at
1Co 12:22 which seem to be more *f*, are
Heb 12:12 hang down, and the *f* knees.

feebleminded
1Th 5:14 comfort the *f*, support the weak,

feebleness
Jer 47: 3 to their children for *f* of hands;

feebler
Ge 30:42 so the *f* were Laban's, and the

feed See also FED; FEEDEST; FEEDETH; FEEDING.
Ge 25:30 *F* me, I pray thee, with that same
29: 7 ye the sheep, and go and *f* them.
30:31 I will again *f* and keep thy flock:
37:12 went to *f* their father's flock in
13 Do not thy brethren *f* the flock in
16 tell me, I pray thee, where they *f*
46:32 their trade hath been to *f* cattle;
Ex 22: 5 shall *f* in another man's field;
34: 3 neither let the flocks nor herds *f*
1Sa 17:15 from Saul to *f* his father's sheep
2Sa 5: 2 Thou shalt *f* my people Israel,
7: 7 to *f* my people Israel, saying,
19:33 and I will *f* thee with me in
1Ki 17: 4 commanded the ravens to *f* thee
22:27 and *f* him with bread of affliction
1Ch 11: 2 Thou shalt *f* my people Israel,
17: 6 I commanded to *f* my people,
2Ch 18:26 and *f* him with bread of affliction
Job 24: 2 take away flocks, and *f* thereof.
20 the worm shall *f* sweetly on him;
Ps 28: 9 *f* them also, and lift them up
49:14 death shall *f* on them; and the
78:71 brought him to *f* Jacob his people,
Pr 10:21 The lips of the righteous *f* many:
30: 8 *f* me with food convenient for me:
Ca 1: 8 *f* thy kids beside the shepherds'
4: 5 twins, which *f* among the lilies.
6: 2 bed of spices, to *f* in the gardens,
Isa 5:17 the lambs *f* after their manner,
11: 7 And the cow and the bear shall *f*;
14:30 And the firstborn of the poor shall *f*,
27:10 there shall the calf *f*, and there
30:23 shall thy cattle *f* in large pastures.
40:11 shall *f* his flock like a shepherd:
49: 9 They shall *f* in the ways, and their
26 I will *f* them that oppress thee
58:14 *f* thee with the heritage of Jacob
61: 5 strangers shall stand and *f* your
65:25 wolf and the lamb shall *f* together,
Jer 3:15 which shall *f* you with knowledge
6: 3 they shall *f* every one in his place.
9:15 I will *f* them, even this people,
23: 2 the pastors that *f* my people;
4 over them which shall *f* them:
15 I will *f* them with wormwood, and
50:19 he shall *f* on Carmel and Bashan,
La 4: 5 They that did *f* delicately are
Eze 34: 2 the shepherds of Israel that do *f*
2 not the shepherds *f* the flocks?
3 that are fed; but ye *f* not the flock.
10 shall the shepherds *f* themselves
13 and *f* them upon the mountains of
14 I will *f* them in a good pasture,
14 in a fat pasture they shall *f* upon
15 I will *f* my flock, and I will cause
16 I will *f* them with judgment.
23 he shall *f* them, even my servant
23 he shall *f* them, and he shall be
Da 11:26 that *f* of the portion of his meat
Ho 4:16 the Lord will *f* them as a lamb
9: 2 and the winepress shall not *f* them,
Jon 3: 7 let them not *f*, nor drink water:
Mic 5: 4 and *f* in the strength of the Lord,
7:14 *F* thy people with thy rod, the
14 let them *f* in Bashan and Gilead,
Zep 2: 7 they shall *f* thereupon: in the
3:13 for they shall *f* and lie down,
Zec 11: 4 *F* the flock of the slaughter;
7 And I will *f* the flock of slaughter,
9 Then said I, I will not *f* you:
16 nor *f* that that standeth still:
Lu 15:15 him into his fields to *f* swine.
Joh 21:15 He saith unto him, *F* my lambs.
16 He saith unto him, *F* my sheep.
17 Jesus saith unto him, *F* my sheep.
Ac 20:28 overseers, to *f* the church of God,
Ro 12:20 if thine enemy hunger, *f* him; if
1Co 13: 3 bestow all my goods to *f* the poor,
1Pe 5: 2 *F* the flock of God which is
Re 7:17 midst of the throne shall *f* them,
12: 6 that they should *f* her there a

feedest
Ps 80: 5 *f* them with the bread of tears;
Ca 1: 7 my soul loveth, where thou *f*,

feedeth
Pr 15:14 mouth of fools *f* on foolishness.
Ca 2:16 I am his: he *f* among the lilies.
6: 3 is mine: he *f* among the lilies.
Isa 44:20 He *f* on ashes: a deceived heart
Ho 12: 1 Ephraim *f* on wind, and followeth
M't 6:26 yet your heavenly Father *f* them.
Lu 12:24 and God *f* them: how much more
1Co 9: 7 who *f* a flock, and eateth not

feeding See also FEEDINGPLACE.
Ge 37: 2 was *f* the flock with his brethren;
Job 1:14 oxen were plowing, and the asses *f*
Eze 34:10 them to cease from *f* the flock;
M't 8:30 them an herd of many swine *f*.
M'r 5:11 mountains a great herd of swine *f*.
Lu 8:32 many swine *f* on the mountain:
17: 7 a servant plowing or *f* cattle,
Jude 12 you, *f* themselves without fear:

feedingplace
Na 2:11 and the *f* of the young lions,

feel See also FEELING; FELT.
Ge 27:12 will *f* me, and I shall seem to him
21 I pray thee, that I may *f* thee,
J'g 16:26 Suffer me that I may *f* the pillars
Job 20:20 shall not *f* quietness in his belly,
Ps 58: 9 Before your pots can *f* the thorns,
Ec 8: 5 the commandment shall *f* no evil
Ac 17:27 if haply they might *f* after him,

feeling
Eph 4:19 Who being past *f* have given
Heb 4:15 cannot be touched with the *f* of our

feet
Ge 18: 4 wash your *f*, and rest yourselves
19: 2 tarry all night, and wash your *f*,
24:32 and water to wash his *f*, and the
32 and the men's *f* that were with him.
43:24 water, and they washed their *f*;
49:10 nor a lawgiver from between his *f*,
33 he gathered up his *f* into the bed,
Ex 3: 5 put off thy shoes from off thy *f*,
4:25 of her son, and cast it at his *f*,
12:11 your shoes on your *f*, and your
24:10 under his *f* as it were a paved work
25:26 that are on the four *f* thereof.
30:19 shall wash their hands and their *f*
21 shall wash their hands and their *f*,
37:13 that were in the four *f* thereof.
40:31 washed their hands and their *f*
Le 8:24 the great toes of their right *f*:
11:21 which have legs above their *f*, to
23 creeping things, which have four *f*,
42 more *f* among all creeping things
Nu 20:19 anything else, go through on my *f*.
De 2:28 only I will pass through on my *f*;
11:24 the soles of your *f* shall tread
28:57 cometh out from between her *f*,
33: 3 and they sat down at thy *f*;
Jos 3:13 of the *f* of the priests that bear
15 and the *f* of the priests that bare
4: 3 where the priests' *f* stood firm,
9 where the *f* of the priests which
18 soles of the priests' *f* were lifted
9: 5 old shoes and clouted upon their *f*,
10:24 put your *f* upon the necks of these
24 put their *f* upon the necks of them.
14: 9 land whereon thy *f* have trodden
J'g 3:24 he covereth his *f* in his summer
4:10 with ten thousand men at his *f*:
15 chariot, and fled away on his *f*.
17 fled away on his *f* to the tent
5:27 At her *f* he bowed, he fell, he lay
27 at her *f* he bowed, he fell: where
19:21 they washed their *f*, and did eat
Ru 3: 4 uncover his *f*, and lay thee down;
7 came softly, and uncovered his *f*,
8 behold, a woman lay at his *f*.
14 she lay at his *f* until the morning:
1Sa 2: 9 He will keep the *f* of his saints,
14:13 upon his hands and upon his *f*,
24: 3 and Saul went in to cover his *f*:
25:24 And fell at his *f*, and said,
41 to wash the *f* of the servants of
2Sa 3:34 nor thy *f* put into fetters: as a
4: 4 had a son that was lame of his *f*.
12 cut off their hands and their *f*,
9: 3 yet a son, which is lame on his *f*.
13 and was lame on both his *f*.
11: 8 to thy house, and wash thy *f*,
19:24 had neither dressed his *f*, nor
22:10 and darkness was under his *f*.
34 He maketh my *f* like hind's *f*:
37 so that my *f* did not slip.
39 yea, they are fallen under my *f*.
1Ki 2: 5 in his shoes that were on his *f*.
5: 3 put them under the soles of his *f*.
14: 6 Ahijah heard the sound of her *f*,
12 when thy *f* enter into the city,
15:23 old age he was diseased in his *f*.
2Ki 4:27 she caught him by the *f*: but
37 she went in, and fell at his *f*,
6:32 sound of his master's *f* behind
9:35 the skull, and the *f*, and the palms
13:21 he revived, and stood up on his *f*.
19:24 the sole of my *f* have I dried up
21: 8 Neither will I make the *f* of Israel
1Ch 28: 2 David the king stood up upon his *f*,
2Ch 3:13 they stood on their *f*, and their
16:12 was diseased in his *f*, until his
Neh 9:21 not old, and their *f* swelled not.
Es 8: 3 fell down at his *f*, and besought
Job 12: 5 He that is ready to slip with his *f*
13:27 puttest my *f* also in the stocks,
27 a print upon the heels of my *f*.
18: 8 is cast into a net by his own *f*,
11 and shall drive him to his *f*.
29:15 and *f* was I to the lame.
30:12 they push away my *f*, and they
33:11 He putteth my *f* in the stocks,
Ps 8: 6 hast put all things under his *f*:
18: 9 and darkness was under his *f*.
33 He maketh my *f* like hinds' *f*,
36 under me, that my *f* did not slip.
38 they are fallen under my *f*.
22:16 they pierced my hands and my *f*.
25:15 he shall pluck my *f* out of the net.
31: 8 thou hast set my *f* in a large room.

Ps 40: 2 and set my *f* upon a rock.
47: 3 and the nations under our *f*.
56:13 not thou deliver my *f* from falling
58:10 he shall wash his *f* in the blood
66: 9 suffereth not our *f* to be moved.
73: 2 for me, my *f* were almost gone;
74: 3 *f* unto the perpetual desolations;
91:13 dragon shalt thou trample under *f*.
105:18 Whose *f* they hurt with fetters:
115: 7 *f* have they, but they walk not:
116: 8 from tears, and my *f* from falling.
119:59 turned my *f* unto thy testimonies.
101 refrained my *f* from every evil way
105 Thy word is a lamp unto my *f*,
122: 2 Our *f* shall stand within thy gates,
Pr 1:16 their *f* run to evil, and make haste
4:26 Ponder the path of thy *f*, and let
5: 5 Her *f* go down to death; her steps
6:13 speaketh with his *f*, he teacheth
18 *f* that be swift in running to
28 coals, and his *f* not be burned?
7:11 her *f* abide not in her house:
19: 2 he that hasteth with his *f* sinneth.
26: 6 the hand of a fool cutteth off the *f*,
29: 5 spreadeth a net for his *f*.
Ca 5: 3 I have washed my *f*; how shall
7: 1 How beautiful are thy *f* with
Isa 3:16 making a tinkling with their *f*:
18 tinkling ornaments about their *f*
6: 2 with twain he covered his *f*, and
7:20 the head, and the hair of the *f*:
14:19 as a carcase trodden under *f*.
23: 7 her own *f* shall carry her afar off
26: 6 it down, even the *f* of the poor,
28: 3 Ephraim, shall be trodden under *f*:
32:20 thither the *f* of the ox and the ass.
37:25 the sole of my *f* have I dried up
41: 3 that he had not gone with his *f*.
49:23 and lick up the dust of thy *f*;
52: 7 the *f* of him that bringeth good
59: 7 Their *f* run to evil, and they make
60:13 make the place of my *f* glorious.
14 down at the soles of thy *f*;
Jer 13:16 your *f* stumble upon the dark
14:10 they have not refrained their *f*,
18:22 and hid snares for my *f*.
38:22 thy *f* are sunk in the mire, and they
La 1:13 he hath spread a net for my *f*,
3:34 under his *f* all the prisoners
Eze 1: 7 And their *f* were straight *f*;
7 and the sole of their *f* was like
2: 1 Son of man, stand upon thy *f*,
2 unto me, and set me upon my *f*,
3:24 into me, and set me upon my *f*,
16:25 opened thy *f* to every one that
24:17 and put on thy shoes upon thy *f*,
23 and your shoes upon your *f*: ye
25: 6 hands, and stamped with the *f*,
32: 2 troubledst the waters with thy *f*,
34:18 down with your *f* the residue of
18 must foul the residue with your *f*?
19 which ye have trodden with your *f*;
19 which ye have fouled with your *f*.
37:10 lived, and stood up upon their *f*,
43: 7 and the place of the soles of my *f*,
Da 2:33 his *f* part of iron and part of clay.
34 smote the image upon his *f*
41 *f* and toes, part of potters' clay,
42 And as the toes of the *f*
7: 4 made stand upon the *f* as a man,
7 stamped the residue with the *f* of
19 stamped the residue with his *f*;
10: 6 his arms and his *f* like in colour
Na 1: 3 the clouds are the dust of his *f*.
15 the *f* of him that bringeth good
Hab 3: 5 burning coals went forth at his *f*.
19 he will make my *f* like hinds' *f*,
Zec 14: 4 And his *f* shall stand in that day
12 while they stand upon their *f*,
Mal 4: 3 ashes under the soles of your *f*
M't 7: 6 they trample them under their *f*,
10:14 city, shake off the dust of your *f*.
15:30 and cast them down at Jesus' *f*;
18: 8 than having two hands or two *f*
29 fellowservant fell down at his *f*,
28: 9 they came and held him by the *f*,
M'r 5:22 when he saw him, he fell at his *f*,
6:11 dust under your *f* for a testimony
7:25 and came and fell at his *f*:
9:45 having two *f* to be cast into hell,
Lu 1:79 guide our *f* into the way of peace.
7:38 stood at his *f* behind him weeping,
38 and began to wash his *f* with tears,
38 kissed his *f*, and anointed them
44 thou gavest me no water for my *f*:
44 she hath washed my *f* with tears,
45 hath not ceased to kiss my *f*.
46 hath anointed my *f* with ointment.
8:35 sitting at the *f* of Jesus, clothed,
41 fell down at Jesus' *f*, and besought
9: 5 off the very dust from your *f* for a
10:39 which also sat at Jesus' *f*, and
15:22 on his hand, and shoes on his *f*:
17:16 And fell down on his face at his *f*,
24:39 Behold my hands and my *f*,
40 shewed them his hands and his *f*.
Joh 11: 2 and wiped his *f* with her hair,
32 she fell down at his *f*, saying unto
12: 3 and anointed the *f* of Jesus,
3 and wiped his *f* with her hair:
13: 5 and began to wash the disciples' *f*,
6 Lord, dost thou wash my *f*?
8 Thou shalt never wash my *f*.
9 Lord, not my *f* only, but also my
10 needeth not save to wash his *f*,
12 So after he had washed their *f*,
Joh 13:14 and Master, have washed your *f*;
14 also ought to wash one another's *f*.
20:12 at the head, and the other at the *f*,
Ac 3: 7 his *f* and ancle bones received
4:35 laid them down at the apostles' *f*:
37 money, and laid it at the apostles' *f*.
5: 2 part, and laid it at the apostles' *f*.
9 the *f* of them which have buried
10 fell she down straightway at his *f*,
7:33 Put off thy shoes from thy *f*:
58 their clothes at a young man's *f*,
10:25 met him, and fell down at his *f*,
13:25 of his *f* I am not worthy to loose.
51 they shook off the dust of their *f*
14: 8 impotent in his *f*, being a cripple
10 loud voice, Stand upright on thy *f*.
16:24 and made their *f* fast in the stocks.
21:11 and bound his own hands and *f*,
22: 3 in this city at the *f* of Gamaliel,
26:16 But rise, and stand upon thy *f*:
Ro 3:15 Their *f* are swift to shed blood:
10:15 How beautiful are the *f* of them
16:20 bruise Satan under your *f* shortly.
1Co 12:21 nor again the head to the *f*,
15:25 hath put all enemies under his *f*.
27 he hath put all things under his *f*.
Eph 1:22 And hath put all things under his *f*,
6:15 your *f* shod with the preparation
1Ti 5:10 if she have washed the saints' *f*,
Heb 2: 8 all things in subjection under his *f*.
12:13 And make straight paths for your *f*,
Re 1:15 And his *f* like unto fine brass,
17 I saw him, I fell at his *f* as dead.
2:18 and his *f* are like fine brass;
3: 9 to come and worship before thy *f*,
10: 1 and his *f* as pillars of fire:
11:11 and they stood upon their *f*; and
12: 1 the sun, and the moon under her *f*,
13: 2 and his *f* were as the *f* of a bear,
19:10 I fell at his *f* to worship him.
22: 8 before the *f* of the angel which

feign See also FEIGNED; FEIGNEST.
2Sa 14: 2 thee, *f* thyself to be a mourner,
1Ki 14: 5 *f* herself to be another woman.
Lu 20:20 sent forth spies which would *f*

feigned See also UNFEIGNED.
1Sa 21:13 and *f* himself mad in their hands,
Ps 17: 1 that goeth not out of *f* lips.
2Pe 2: 3 with *f* words make merchandise

feignedly
Jer 3:10 me with her whole heart, but *f*,

feignest
1Ki 14: 6 why *f* thou thyself to be another?
Ne 6: 8 thou *f* them out of thine own heart.

Felix (*fe'-lix*) See also FELIX'.
Ac 23:24 him safe unto *F* the governor.
26 unto the most excellent governor *F*
24: 3 and in all places, most noble *F*,
22 And when *F* heard these things,
24 *F* came with his wife Drusilla,
25 *F* trembled, and answered, Go thy
27 and *F*, willing to shew the Jews a
25:14 a certain man left in bonds by *F*:

Felix' (*fe'-lix*)
Ac 24:27 Porcius Festus came into *F* room:

fell See also BEFELL; FELLED; FELLEST; FELLING.
Ge 4: 5 very wroth, and his countenance *f*.
14:10 and Gomorrah fled, and *f* there;
15:12 a deep sleep *f* upon Abram; and,
12 an horror of great darkness *f* upon
17: 3 And Abram *f* on his face: and God
17 Then Abraham *f* upon his face,
33: 4 and *f* on his neck, and kissed him:
44:14 they *f* before him on the ground.
45:14 he *f* upon his brother Benjamin's
46:29 and he *f* on his neck, and wept
50: 1 Joseph *f* upon his father's face,
18 his brethren also went and *f* down
Ex 32:28 and there *f* of the people that day
Le 9:24 they shouted, and *f* on their faces.
16: 9 goat upon which the Lord's lot *f*,
10 the goat, on which the lot *f* to be the
Nu 11: 4 that was among them *f* a lusting:
9 when the dew *f* upon the camp
9 in the night, the manna *f* upon it.
14: 5 Moses and Aaron *f* on their faces
16: 4 Moses heard it, he *f* upon his face:
22 they *f* upon their faces, and said,
45 And they *f* upon their faces.
20: 6 and they *f* upon their faces: and
22:27 angel of the Lord, she *f* down
31 bowed down his head, and *f* flat
De 9:18 And I *f* down before the Lord,
25 Thus I *f* down before the Lord
25 forty nights, as I *f* down at the first;
Jos 5:14 Joshua *f* on his face to the earth,
6:20 shout, that the wall *f* down flat,
7: 6 and *f* to the earth upon his face
8:25 so it was, that all that *f* that day,
11: 7 suddenly; and they *f* upon them.
16: 1 of Joseph, *f* from Jordan by
17: 5 there *f* ten portions to Manasseh,
22:20 wrath *f* on all the congregation
J'g 4:16 and all the host of Sisera *f* upon
5:27 feet he bowed, he *f*, he lay down:
27 her feet he bowed, he *f*: where he
27 bowed, there he *f* down dead.
7:13 unto a tent, and smote it that it *f*,
8:10 *f* an hundred and twenty thousand
12: 6 *f* at that time of the Ephraimites
13:20 and *f* on their faces to the ground.
16:30 and the house *f* upon the lords,
19:26 *f* down at the door of the man's
J'g 20:44 *f* of Benjamin eighteen thousand
46 So that all which *f* that day of
Ru 2:10 Then she *f* on her face, and bowed
1Sa 4:10 there *f* of Israel thirty thousand
18 he *f* from off the seat backward
11: 7 fear of the Lord *f* on the people,
14:13 and they *f* before Jonathan; and
17:49 and he *f* upon his face to the earth.
52 the wounded of the Philistines *f*
20:41 and *f* on his face to the ground,
22:18 he *f* upon the priests, and slew
25:23 and *f* before David on her face,
24 And *f* at his feet, and said,
28:20 Then Saul *f* straightway all along
29: 3 found no fault in him since he *f*
30:13 because three days agone I *f* sick.
31: 1 *f* down slain in mount Gilboa.
4 Saul took a sword, and *f* upon it.
5 he *f* likewise upon his sword, and
2Sa 1: 2 *f* to the earth, and did obeisance.
2:16 they *f* down together: wherefore
23 and he *f* down there, and died
23 Asahel *f* down and died stood still.
4: 4 as she made haste to flee, that he *f*,
9: 6 he *f* on his face, and did reverence.
11:17 and there *f* some of the people
13: 2 that he *f* sick for his sister Tamar;
14: 4 to the king, she *f* on her face
22 Joab *f* to the ground on his face,
18:28 And he *f* down to the earth
19:18 Shimei the son of Gera *f* down
20: 8 and as he went forth it *f* out.
21: 9 and they *f* all seven together,
22 and *f* by the hand of David,
1Ki 2:25 and he *f* upon him that he died.
32 *f* upon two men more righteous
34 and *f* upon him, and slew him:
46 and *f* upon him, that he died.
14: 1 Abijah the son of Jeroboam *f* sick.
17:17 the mistress of the house, *f* sick;
18: 7 he knew him, and *f* on his face,
38 Then the fire of the Lord *f*,
39 people saw it, they *f* on their faces:
20:30 *f* upon twenty and seven thousand
2Ki 1: 2 Ahaziah *f* down through a lattice
13 and *f* on his knees before Elijah,
2:13 mantle of Elijah that *f* from him,
14 mantle of Elijah that *f* from him,
3:19 and shall *f* every good tree,
4: 8 And it *f* on a day, that Elisha
11 it *f* on a day, that he came thither
18 the child was grown, it *f* on a day,
37 she went in, and *f* at his feet,
6: 5 the axe head *f* into the water:
6 Where *f* it? And he shewed him
7:20 And so it *f* out unto him: for the
25:11 fugitives that *f* away to the king
1Ch 5:10 Hagarites, who *f* by their hand:
22 there *f* down many slain, because
10: 1 and *f* down slain in mount Gilboa.
4 Saul took a sword, and *f* upon it.
5 *f* likewise on the sword, and died.
12:19 there *f* some of Manasseh to David,
20 there *f* to him of Manasseh, Adnah,
20: 8 and they *f* by the hand of David,
21:14 there *f* of Israel seventy thousand
16 in sackcloth, *f* upon their faces,
26:14 the lot eastward *f* to Shelemiah.
27:24 *f* wrath for it against Israel;
2Ch 13:17 so there *f* down slain of Israel
15: 9 they *f* to him out of Israel
17:10 And the fear of the Lord *f* upon
20:18 inhabitants of Jerusalem *f* before
21:19 *f* out by reason of his sickness:
25:13 *f* upon the cities of Judah, from
Ezr 9: 5 I *f* upon my knees, and spread
Es 8: 3 *f* down at his *f*, and besought
17 the fear of the Jews *f* upon them.
9: 2 fear of them *f* upon all people.
3 the fear of Mordecai *f* upon them.
Job 1:15 And the Sabeans *f* upon them,
17 bands, and *f* upon the camels,
19 and it *f* upon the young men,
20 and *f* down upon the ground, and
Ps 27: 2 up my flesh, they stumbled and *f*.
78:64 Their priests *f* by the sword; and
105:38 the fear of them *f* upon them.
107:12 they *f* down, and there was none
Jer 39: 9 those that *f* away, that *f* to him,
46:16 one *f* upon another: and they said,
52:15 that *f* away, that *f* to the king
La 1: 7 people *f* into the hand of the enemy,
5:13 the children *f* under the wood.
Eze 1:28 when I saw it, I *f* upon my face,
3:23 of Chebar: and I *f* on my face.
8: 1 of the Lord God *f* there upon me.
9: 8 that I *f* upon my face, and cried,
11: 5 the Spirit of the Lord *f* upon me,
13 Then *f* I down upon my face,
39:23 so *f* they all by the sword.
43: 3 river Chebar; and I *f* upon my face.
44: 4 of the Lord: and I *f* upon my face.
Da 2:46 Nebuchadnezzar *f* upon his face,
3: 7 *f* down and worshipped the golden
23 *f* down bound into the midst of the
4:31 there *f* a voice from heaven, saying,
7:20 came up, and before whom three *f*;
8:17 I was afraid, and *f* upon my face:
10: 7 but a great quaking *f* upon them,
Jon 1: 7 lots, and the lot *f* upon Jonah.
M't 2:11 and *f* down, and worshipped him:
7:25 and it *f* not: for it was founded
27 and it *f*: and great was the fall of it.
13: 4 some seeds *f* by the way side, and
5 Some *f* upon stony places, where
7 And some *f* among thorns; and

M't 13: 8 But other *f* into good ground, and
17: 6 they *f* on their face, and were sore
18:26 therefore *f* down, and worshipped
29 fellowservant *f* down at his feet.
26:39 and *f* on his face, and prayed,
M'r 3:11 they saw him, *f* down before him,
4: 4 some *f* by the way side, and the
5 And some *f* on stony ground, where
7 And some *f* among thorns, and the
8 And other *f* on good ground, and
5:22 when he saw him, he *f* at his feet,
33 came and *f* down before him, and
7:25 and came and *f* at his feet:
9:20 he *f* on the ground, and wallowed
14:35 and *f* on the ground, and prayed
Lu 1:12 troubled, and fear *f* upon him.
5: 8 he *f* down at Jesus' knees, saying,
12 *f* on his face, and besought him,
6:49 immediately it *f*; and the ruin
8: 5 he sowed, some *f* by the way side;
6 And some *f* upon a rock; and as
7 And some *f* among thorns; and the
8 And other *f* on good ground, and
14 which *f* among thorns are they,
23 as they sailed he *f* asleep: and there
28 cried out, and *f* down before him,
41 he *f* down at Jesus' feet, and
10:30 *f* among thieves, which stripped
36 him that *f* among the thieves?
13: 4 upon whom the tower in Siloam *f*,
15:20 and ran, and *f* on his neck,
16:21 which *f* from the rich man's table:
17:16 *f* down on his face at his feet,
Joh 11:32 *f* down at his feet, saying unto him,
18: 6 backward, and *f* to the ground.
Ac 1:25 from which Judas by transgression *f*,
26 and the lot *f* upon Matthias;
5: 5 *f* down, and gave up the ghost:
10 Then *f* she down straightway at
7:60 when he had said this, he *f* asleep.
9: 4 *f* to the earth, and heard a voice
18 there *f* from his eyes as it had been
10:10 made ready, he *f* into a trance,
25 and *f* down at his feet, and
44 the Holy Ghost *f* on all them which
11:15 the Holy Ghost *f* on them, as on us
12: 7 his chains *f* off from his hands.
13:11 *f* on him a mist and a darkness;
36 *f* on sleep, and was laid unto his
16:29 and *f* down before Paul and Silas,
19:17 and fear *f* on them all, and the
35 which *f* down from Jupiter?
20: 9 and *f* down from the third loft,
10 Paul went down, and *f* on him,
37 *f* on Paul's neck, and kissed him,
22: 7 I *f* unto the ground, and heard
Ro 11:22 on them which *f*, severity; but
15: 3 that reproached thee *f* on me.
1Co 10: 8 and *f* in one day three and twenty
Heb 3:17 carcasses *f* in the wilderness?
11:30 faith the walls of Jericho *f* down,
2Pe 3: 4 since the fathers *f* asleep, all things
Re 1:17 I saw him, I *f* at his feet as dead.
5: 8 elders *f* down before the Lamb,
14 *f* down and worshipped him that
6:13 stars of heaven *f* unto the earth,
7:11 *f* before the throne on their faces,
8:10 there *f* a great star from heaven,
10 *f* upon the third part of the rivers,
11:11 fear *f* upon them which saw them.
13 and the tenth part of the city *f*,
16 *f* upon their faces, and worshipped
16: 2 *f* a noisome and grievous sore
19 and the cities of the nations *f*:
21 there *f* upon men a great hail
19: 4 and the four beasts *f* down and
10 And I *f* at his feet to worship
22: 8 I *f* down to worship before the feet

felled
2Ki 3:25 and *f* all the good trees: only in

feller
Isa 14: 8 no *f* is come up against us.

fellest
2Sa 3:34 before wicked men, so *f* thou.

felling
2Ki 6: 5 But as one was *f* a beam,

felloes
1Ki 7:33 and their *f*, and their spokes,

fellow^ See also FELLOWCITIZENS; FELLOWDISCIPLES; FELLOWHEIRS; FELLOWHELPER; FELLOWLABOURER; FELLOWPRISONER; FELLOW'S; FELLOWS; FELLOWSERVANT; FELLOWSHIP; FELLOWSOLDIER; FELLOWWORKERS; WORKFELLOW; YOKEFELLOW.
Ex 2:13 Wherefore smitest thou thy *f*?
J'g 7:13 man that told a dream unto his *f*,
14 his *f* answered and said, This is
22 every man's sword against his *f*,
1Sa 14:20 man's sword was against his *f*,
21:15 have brought this *f* to play the mad
15 shall this *f* come into my house?
25:21 in vain I have kept all that this *f* hath
29: 4 Make this *f* return, that he may
2Sa 2:16 caught every one his *f* by the head,
1Ki 22:27 Put this *f* in the prison, and feed him
2Ki 9:11 wherefore came this mad *f* to thee?
2Ch 18:26 Put this *f* in the prison, and feed him
Ec 4:10 the one will lift up his *f*:
Isa 34:14 and the satyr shall cry to his *f*;
Jon 1: 7 And they said every one to his *f*,
Zec 13: 7 and against the man that is my *f*,
M't 12:24 This *f* doth not cast out devils,
26:61 This *f* said, I am able to destroy
71 This *f* was also with Jesus of
Lu 22:59 a truth this *f* also was with him:
23: 2 We found this *f* perverting the
Joh 9:29 as for this *f*, we know not from
Ac 18:13 Saying, This *f* persuadeth men
22:22 Away with such a *f* from the
24: 5 found this man a pestilent *f*, and

fellowcitizens
Eph 2:19 but *f* with the saints, and of the

fellowdisciples
Joh 11:16 Didymus, unto his *f*, Let us also

fellowheirs
Eph 3: 6 That the Gentiles should be *f*,

fellowhelper See also FELLOWHELPERS.
2Co 8:23 partner and *f* concerning you:

fellowhelpers
3Jo 8 that we might be *f* to the truth.

fellowlabourer See also FELLOWLABOURERS.
1Th 3: 2 our *f* in the gospel of Christ,
Ph'm 1 our dearly beloved, and *f*,

fellowlabourers
Ph'p 4: 3 also, and with other my *f*,
Ph'm 24 Demas, Lucas, my *f*.

fellowprisoner See also FELLOWPRISONERS.
Col 4:10 Aristarchus my *f* saluteth you,
Ph'm 23 Epaphras, my *f* in Christ Jesus;

fellowprisoners
Ro 16: 7 and Junia, my kinsmen, and my *f*,

fellow's
2Sa 2:16 thrust his sword in his *f* side;

fellows
J'g 11:37 bewail my virginity, I and my *f*.
18:25 lest angry *f* run upon thee, and
2Sa 6:20 as one of the vain *f* shamelessly
Ps 45: 7 the oil of gladness above thy *f*.
Isa 44:11 Behold, all his *f* shall be ashamed:
Eze 37:19 and the tribes of Israel his *f*,
Da 2:13 they sought Daniel and his *f*
18 that Daniel and his *f* should not
7:20 look was more stout than his *f*.
Zec 3: 8 the high priest, thou, and thy *f*
M't 11:16 markets, and calling unto their *f*,
Ac 17: 5 certain lewd *f* of the baser sort,
Heb 1: 9 the oil of gladness above thy *f*.

fellowservant See also FELLOWSERVANTS.
M't 18:29 And his *f* fell down at his feet,
33 also have had compassion on thy *f*,
Col 1: 7 Epaphras our dear *f*, who is for
4: 7 minister and *f* in the Lord:
Re 19:10 do it not: I am thy *f*, and of thy
22: 9 do it not: for I am thy *f*, and of thy

fellowservants
M't 18:28 went out, and found one of his *f*,
31 So when his *f* saw what was done,
24:49 And shall begin to smite his *f*,
Re 6:11 their *f* also and their brethren,

fellowship
Le 6: 2 or in *f*, or in a thing taken
Ps 94:20 of iniquity have *f* with thee,
Ac 2:42 and *f*, and in breaking of bread,
1Co 1: 9 were called unto the *f* of his Son
10:20 that ye should have *f* with devils.
2Co 6:14 what *f* hath righteousness with
8: 4 upon us the *f* of the ministering
Ga 2: 9 and Barnabas the right hand of *f*;
Eph 3: 9 see what is the *f* of the mystery,
5:11 And have no *f* with the unfruitful
Ph'p 1: 5 your *f* in the gospel from the first
2: 1 of love, if any *f* of the Spirit,
3:10 and the *f* of his sufferings,
1Jo 1: 3 ye also may have *f* with us: and
3 truly our *f* is with the Father,
6 If we say that we have *f* with him,
7 light, we have *f* one with another,

fellowsoldier
Ph'p 2:25 and companion in labour, and *f*,
Ph'm 2 and Archippus our *f*, and to the

fellowworkers
Col 4:11 only are my *f* unto the kingdom

felt
Ge 27:22 and he *f* him, and said, The voice
Ex 10:21 even darkness which may be *f*.
Pr 23:35 I *f* it not: when shall I awake?
M'r 5:29 *f* in her body that she was healed
Ac 28: 5 beast into the fire, and *f* no harm.

female^
Ge 1:27 him; male and *f* created he them.
5: 2 Male and *f* created he them: and
6:19 with thee; they shall be male and *f*.
7: 2 thee by sevens, the male and his *f*:
2 clean by two, the male and his *f*.
3 air by sevens, the male and the *f*;
9 into the ark, the male and the *f*,
16 went in male and *f* of all flesh,
Le 3: 1 whether it be a male or *f*, he shall
6 flock; male or *f*, he shall offer it
4:28 of the goats, a *f* without blemish,
32 shall bring it a *f* without blemish.
5: 6 a *f* from the flock, a lamb or a kid
12: 7 her that hath born a male or a *f*.
27: 4 if it be a *f*, then thy estimation
5 and for the *f* ten shekels.
6 and for the *f* thy estimation shall
7 and for the *f* ten shekels.
Nu 5: 3 Both male and *f* shall ye put out,
De 4:16 the likeness of male or *f*,
M't 19: 4 beginning made them male and *f*,
M'r 10: 6 God made them male and *f*.
Gal 3:28 there is neither male nor *f*: for

fence See also DEFENCE; FENCED; OFFENCE.
Ps 62: 3 shall ye be, and as a tottering *f*.

fenced See also DEFENCED.
Nu 32:17 ones shall dwell in the *f* cities
36 *f* cities: and folds for sheep.
De 3: 5 cities were *f* with high walls,
9: 1 cities great and *f* up to heaven,
28:52 thy high and *f* walls come down,
Jos 10:20 of them entered into *f* cities.
14:12 that the cities were great and *f*:
19:35 the *f* cities are Ziddim, Zer, and
1Sa 6:18 *f* cities, and of country villages,
2Sa 20: 6 he get him *f* cities, and escape
23: 7 that shall touch them must be *f*
2Ki 3:19 And ye shall smite every *f* city,
10: 2 a *f* city also, and armour;
17: 9 of the watchmen to the *f* city.
18: 8 of the watchmen to the *f* city.
13 come up against all the *f* cities
19:25 shouldest be to lay waste *f* cities
2Ch 8: 5 *f* cities, with walls, gates, and
11:10 Judah and in Benjamin *f* cities.
23 unto every *f* city: and he gave
12: 4 *f* cities which pertained to Judah,
14: 6 And he built *f* cities in Judah:
17: 2 placed forces in all the *f* cities
19 whom the king put in the *f* cities
19: 5 all the *f* cities of Judah, city by
21: 3 things, with *f* cities in Judah:
32: 1 encamped against the *f* cities,
33:14 war in all the *f* cities of Judah.
Job 10:11 *f* me with bones and sinews.
19: 8 *f* up my way that I cannot pass,
Isa 2:15 tower, and upon every *f* wall,
5: 2 And he *f* it, and gathered out
Jer 5:17 shall impoverish thy *f* cities,
15:20 unto this people a *f* brasen wall:
Eze 36:35 and ruined cities are become *f*,
Da 11:15 and take the most *f* cities: and
Ho 8:14 Judah had multiplied *f* cities:
Zep 1:16 and alarm against the *f* cities,

fenced-city See FENCED and CITY.

fenced-wall See FENCED and WALL.

fens
Job 40:21 in the covert of the reed, and *f*.

ferret
Le 11:30 And the *f*, and the chameleon,

ferry
2Sa 19:18 And there went over a *f* boat to

ferry-boat See FERRY and BOAT.

fervent
Ac 18:25 being *f* in the spirit, he spake
Ro 12:11 *f* in spirit; serving the Lord;
2Co 7: 7 your *f* mind toward me; so that
Jas 5:16 *f* prayer of a righteous man
1Pe 4: 8 have *f* charity among yourselves:
2Pe 3:10 the elements shall melt with *f* heat,
12 the elements shall melt with *f* heat?

fervently
Col 4:12 labouring *f* for you in prayers,
1Pe 1:22 one another with a pure heart *f*:

Festus (*fes'-tus*) See also FESTUS'.
Ac 24:27 Porcius *F* came into Felix' room:
25: 1 *F* was come into the province,
4 But *F* answered, that Paul should
9 But *F*, willing to do the Jews a
12 Then *F*, when he had conferred
13 came unto Cæsarea to salute *F*.
14 *F* declared Paul's cause unto the
22 Then Agrippa said unto *F*, I would
24 and *F* said, King Agrippa, and all
26:24 *F* said with a loud voice, Paul,
25 I am not mad, most noble *F*;
32 Then said Agrippa unto *F*, This

Festus' (*fes'-tus*)
Ac 25:23 at *F* commandment Paul was

fetch See FETCHED; FETCHETH; FETCHT.
Ge 18: 5 And I will *f* a morsel of bread,
27: 9 *f* me from thence two good kids
13 obey my voice, and go *f* me them.
45 will send, and *f* thee from thence:
42:16 and let him *f* your brother, and ye
Ex 2: 5 she sent her maid to *f* it.
Nu 20:10 we *f* you water out of this rock?
34: 5 the border shall *f* a compass
De 19:12 of his city shall send and *f* him
24:10 into his house to *f* his pledge.
19 thou shalt not go again to *f* it:
30: 4 and from thence will he *f* thee:
J'g 11: 5 elders of Gilead went to *f* Jephthah
20:10 to *f* victual for the people, that
1Sa 4: 3 Let us *f* the ark of the covenant
6:21 come ye down, and *f* it up to you.
16:11 Send and *f* him: for we will not
20:31 now send and *f* him unto me, for
26:22 the young men come over and *f* it.
2Sa 5:23 but *f* a compass behind them,
14:13 the king doth not *f* home again
20 To *f* about this form of speech
1Ki 17:10 *F* me, I pray thee, a little water
11 And as she was going to *f* it,
2Ki 6:13 that I may send and *f* him.
2Ch 18: 8 *F* quickly Micaiah the son of Imla.
Ne 8:15 and *f* olive branches, and pine
Job 36: 3 I will *f* my knowledge from afar,
Isa 56:12 I will *f* wine, and we will fill
Jer 36:21 the king sent Jehudi to *f* the roll:
Ac 16:37 come themselves and *f* us out.

fetched See also FETCHT.
Ge 18: 4 Let a little water, I pray you, be *f*,
27:14 he went, and *f*, and brought them

Jos 15: 3 and *f* a compass to Karkaa
J'g 18:18 *f* the carved image, the ephod,
1Sa 7: 1 and *f* up the ark of the Lord,
10:23 And they ran and *f* him thence:
2Sa 4: 6 though they would have *f* wheat;
9: 5 king David sent, and *f* him out of
11:27 sent and *f* her to his house,
14: 2 and *f* thence a wise woman, and
1Ki 7:13 king Solomon sent and *f* Hiram
9:28 to Ophir, and *f* from thence gold.
2Ki 3: 9 they *f* a compass of seven days'
11: 4 Jehoiada sent and *f* the rulers
2Ch 1:17 And they *f* up, and brought forth
12:11 the guard came and *f* them, and *
Jer 26:23 they *f* forth Urijah out of Egypt,
Ac 28:13 from thence we *f* a compass, and

fetcheth
De 19: 5 his hand *f* a stroke with the axe

fetcht See also FETCHED.
Ge 18: 7 and *f* a calf tender and good,

fetters
J'g 16:21 and bound him with *f* of brass;
2Sa 3:34 not bound, nor thy feet put into *f*:
2Ki 25: 7 and bound him with *f* of brass,
2Ch 33:11 and bound him with *f*, and carried
36: 6 and bound him in *f*, to carry him
Job 36: 8 And if they be bound in *f*,
Ps 105:18 Whose feet they hurt with *f*: he
149: 8 and their nobles with *f* of iron;
M'r 5: 4 often bound with *f* and chains,
4 and the *f* broken in pieces:
Lu 8:29 kept bound with chains and in *f*;

fever
De 28:22 with a consumption, and with a *f*,
M't 8:14 wife's mother laid, and sick of a *f*.
15 and the *f* left her: and she arose,
M'r 1:30 wife's mother lay sick of a *f*,
31 and immediately the *f* left her,
Lu 4:38 mother was taken with a great *f*;
39 and rebuked the *f*; and it left her:
Joh 4:52 at the seventh hour the *f* left him.
Ac 28: 8 lay sick of a *f* and of a bloody flux:

few See also FEWER; FEWEST.
Ge 24:55 the damsel abide with us a *f* days
27:44 And tarry with him a *f* days,
29:20 they seemed unto him but a *f* days,
34:30 I being *f* in number, they shall
47: 9 *f* and evil have the days of the
Le 25:52 if there remain but *f* years unto
26:22 and make you *f* in number;
Nu 9:20 when the cloud was a *f* days upon
13:18 be strong or weak, *f* or many;
26:54 and to *f* thou shalt give the less
56 be divided between many and *f*.
35: 8 but from them that have *f*
8 ye shall give *f*: every one
De 4:27 and ye shall be left *f* in number
26: 5 and sojourned there with a *f*, and
28:62 And ye shall be left *f* in number,
33: 6 and let not his men be *f*.
Jos 7: 3 labour thither; for they are but *f*.
1Sa 14: 6 to save by many or by *f*.
17:28 with whom hast thou left those *f*
2Ki 4: 3 empty vessels; borrow not a *f*.
1Ch 16:19 When ye were but *f*, even
19 even a *f*, and strangers in it,
2Ch 29:34 But the priests were too *f*, so
Ne 2:12 I and some *f* men with me;
7: 4 but the people were *f* therein, and
Job 10:20 Are not my days *f*? cease then,
14: 1 that is born of woman is of *f* days,
16:22 When a *f* years are come, then I
Ps 105:12 When they were but a *f* men in
12 yea, very *f*, and strangers in it.
109: 8 Let his days be *f*: and let another
Ec 5: 2 therefore let thy words be *f*.
9:14 a little city and *f* men within it;
12: 3 grinders cease because they are *f*,
Isa 10: 7 and cut off nations not a *f*.
19 the trees of his forest shall be *f*,
24: 6 earth are burned, and *f* men left.
Jer 30:19 them, and they shall not be *f*;
42: 2 we are left but a *f* of many,
Eze 5: 3 also take thereof a *f* in number,
12:16 I will leave a *f* men of them
Da 11:20 *f* days he shall be destroyed,
M't 7:14 and *f* there be that find it.
9:37 but the labourers are *f*;
15:34 Seven, and a *f* little fishes.
20:16 for many be called, but *f* chosen.
22:14 many are called, but *f* are chosen.
25:21, 23 thou hast been faithful over a *f*
M'r 6: 5 he laid hands upon a *f* sick folk,
8: 7 And they had a *f* small fishes:
Lu 10: 2 is great, but the labourers are *f*:
12:48 shall be beaten with *f* stripes.
13:23 Lord, are there *f* that be saved?
Ac 17: 4 and of the chief women not a *f*.
12 were Greeks, and of men, not a *f*.
24: 4 us of thy clemency a *f* words.
Eph 3: 3 (as I wrote afore in *f* words,
Heb 12:10 verily for a *f* days chastened us
13:22 a letter unto you in *f* words.
1Pe 3:20 wherein *f*, that is, eight souls
Re 2:14 But I have a *f* things against thee,
20 I have a *f* things against thee,
3: 4 Thou hast a *f* names even in Sardis

fewer
Nu 33:54 and to the *f* ye shall give the less

fewest
De 7: 7 ye were the *f* of all people:

fewness
Le 25:16 according to the *f* of years thou

fidelity
Tit 2:10 but shewing all good *f*; that they

field See also FIELDS.
Ge 2: 5 every plant of the *f* before it was
5 every herb of the *f* before it grew:
19 God formed every beast of the *f*,
20 and to every beast of the *f*;
3: 1 than any beast of the *f* which the
14 and above every beast of the *f*;
18 and thou shalt eat the herb of the *f*;
4: 8 to pass, when they were in the *f*,
23: 9 which is in the end of his *f*;
11 the *f* give I thee, and the cave
13 I will give thee money for the *f*;
17 And the *f* of Ephron, which was in
17 the *f*, and the cave which was
17 and all the trees that were in the *f*,
19 the cave of the *f* of Machpelah
20 the *f*, and the cave that is therein,
24:63 went out to meditate in the *f* at the
65 man is this that walketh in the *f* to
25: 9 the *f* of Ephron the son of Zohar
10 The *f* which Abraham purchased
27 a cunning hunter, a man of the *f*;
29 and Esau came from the *f*, and he
27: 3 and go out to the *f* and take me
5 And Esau went to the *f* to hunt
27 my son is as the smell of a *f* which
29: 2 and behold a well in the *f*,
30:14 found mandrakes in the *f*, and
16 Jacob came out of the *f* in the
31: 4 called Rachel and Leah to the *f*
33:19 he bought a parcel of a *f*,
34: 5 sons were with his cattle in the *f*:
7 sons of Jacob came out of the *f*
28 and that which was in the *f*,
36:35 smote Midian in the *f* of Moab,
37: 7 we were binding sheaves in the *f*,
15 behold, he was wandering in the *f*:
39: 5 he had in the house, and in the *f*.
41:48 the food of the *f*, which was round
47:20 Egyptians sold every man his *f*,
24 seed of the *f*, and for your food,
49:29 in the *f* of Ephron the Hittite,
30 In the cave that is in the *f* of
30 with the *f* of Ephron the Hittite
32 purchase of the *f* and of the cave
50:13 the cave of the *f* of Machpelah,
13 which Abraham bought with the *f*
Ex 1:14 in all manner of service in the *f*:
9: 3 thy cattle which is in the *f*,
19 all that thou hast in the *f*;
19 which shall be found in the *f*,
21 servants and his cattle in the *f*.
22 and upon every herb of the *f*,
25 all that was in the *f*, both man and
25 the hail smote every herb of the *f*,
25 and brake every tree of the *f*.
10: 5 which groweth for you out of the *f*:
15 or in the herbs of the *f*,
16:25 ye shall not find it in the *f*.
22: 5 If a man shall cause a *f* or
5 shall feed in another man's *f*;
5 of the best of his own *f*,
6 corn, or the *f* be consumed
31 flesh that is torn of beasts in the *f*;
23:11 the beasts of the *f* shall eat.
16 which thou hast sown in the *f*:
16 in thy labours out of the *f*.
29 the beast of the *f* multiply against
Le 14: 7 living bird loose into the open *f*,
17: 5 which they offer in the open *f*,
19: 9 wholly reap the corners of thy *f*,
19 not sow thy *f* with mingled seed:
23:22 riddance of the corners of thy *f*
25: 3 Six years thou shalt sow thy *f*,
4 thou shalt neither sow thy *f*, nor
12 the increase thereof out of the *f*.
34 the *f* of the suburbs of their cities
26: 4 and the trees of the *f* shall yield
27:16 unto the Lord some part of a *f* of
17 his *f* from the year of jubile,
18 he sanctify his *f* after the jubile
19 he that sanctified the *f* will in any
20 And if he will not redeem the *f*,
20 or if he have sold the *f* to another
21 But the *f*, when it goeth out in the
21 unto the Lord, as a *f* devoted;
22 a man sanctify unto the Lord a *f*
24 the *f* shall return unto him of
28 and of the *f* of his possession,
Nu 22: 4 ox licketh up the grass of the *f*.
23 of the way, and went into the *f*:
23:14 brought him into the *f* of Zophim,
De 5:21 house, his *f*, or his manservant,
7:22 lest the beasts of the *f* increase
14:22 the *f* bringeth forth year by year.
20:19 the tree of the *f* is man's life)
21: 1 lying in the *f*, and it be not known
22:25 find a betrothed damsel in the *f*,
27 For he found her in the *f*,
24:19 cuttest down thine harvest in thy *f*,
19 and hast forgot a sheaf in the *f*,
28: 3 blessed shalt thou be in the *f*.
16 cursed shalt thou be in the *f*.
38 carry much seed out into the *f*,
Jos 8:24 all the inhabitants of Ai in the *f*,
15:18 moved him to ask of her father a *f*:
J'g 1:14 moved him to ask of her father a *f*:
5: 4 marchedst out of the *f* of Edom,
18 in the high places of the *f*.
9:32 and lie in wait in the *f*:
42 the people went out into the *f*;
43 laid wait in the *f*, and looked,
13: 9 the woman as she sat in the *f*:
J'g 19:16 old man from his work out of the *f*
20:31 the other to Gibeah in the *f*,
Ru 2: 2 Let me now go to the *f*, and glean
3 gleaned in the *f* after the reapers:
3 part of the *f* belonging unto Boaz,
8 Go not to glean in another *f*,
9 be on the *f* that they do reap,
17 she gleaned in the *f* until even,
22 they meet thee not in any other *f*.
4: 5 buyest the *f* of the hand of Naomi,
1Sa 4: 2 they slew of the army in the *f*
6:14 the *f* of Joshua, a Beth-shemite,
18 remaineth unto this day in the *f*
11: 5 came after the herd out of the *f*;
14:15 trembling in the host, in the *f*,
17:44 the air, and to the beasts of the *f*.
19: 3 stand beside my father in the *f*
20: 5 that I may hide myself in the *f*
11 Come, and let us go out into the *f*.
11 went out both of them into the *f*.
24 So David hid himself in the *f*:
35 that Jonathan went out into the *f*
30:11 they found an Egyptian in the *f*,
2Sa 10: 8 were by themselves in the *f*.
11:23 and came out unto us into the *f*,
14: 6 they two strove together in the *f*,
30 See, Joab's *f* is near mine, and he
30 Absalom's servants set the *f* on fire.
31 have thy servants set my *f* on fire?
17: 8 bear robbed of her whelps in the *f*:
18: 6 So the people went out into the *f*
20:12 out of the highway into the *f*,
21:10 nor the beasts of the *f* by night.
1Ki 11:29 and they two were alone in the *f*:
14:11 and him that dieth in the *f* shall the
21:24 and him that dieth in the *f* shall the
2Ki 4:39 went out into the *f* to gather herbs,
7:12 to hide themselves in the *f*, saying,
8: 6 and all the fruits of the *f* since the
9:25 in the portion of the *f* of Naboth
37 the *f* in the portion of Jezreel;
18:17 in the highway of the fuller's *f*.
19:26 they were as the grass of the *f*,
1Ch 1:46 smote Midian in the *f* of Moab,
19: 9 come were by themselves in the *f*.
27:26 them that did the work of the *f*
2Ch 26:23 the *f* of the burial which belonged
31: 5 and of all the increase of the *f*;
Ne 13:10 were fled every one to his *f*.
Job 5:23 in league with the stones of the *f*:
23 beasts of the *f* shall be at peace
24: 6 reap every one his corn in the *f*:
40:20 where all the beasts of the *f* play.
Ps 8: 7 yea, and the beasts of the *f*;
50:11 the wild beasts of the *f* are mine.
78:12 the land of Egypt, in the *f* of Zoan.
43 and his wonders in the *f* of Zoan:
80:13 the wild beast of the *f* doth devour
96:12 Let the *f* be joyful, and all that is
103:15 flower of the *f*, so he flourisheth.
104:11 drink to every beast of the *f*:
Pr 24:27 and make it fit for thyself in the *f*;
30 I went by the *f* of the slothful,
27:26 and the goats are the price of the *f*.
31:16 She considereth a *f*, and buyeth it:
Ec 5: 9 the king himself is served by the *f*.
Ca 2: 7 and by the hinds of the *f*, that ye
3: 5 and by the hinds of the *f*, that ye
7:11 beloved, let us go forth into the *f*;
Isa 5: 8 join house to house, that lay *f* to *f*,
7: 3 in the highway of the fuller's *f*;
10:18 of his forest, and of his fruitful *f*,
16:10 and joy out of the plentiful *f*;
29:17 shall be turned into a fruitful *f*,
17 and the fruitful *f* shall be esteemed
32:15 and the wilderness be a fruitful *f*,
15 the fruitful *f* be counted for a forest.
16 righteousness remain in the fruitful *f*.
36: 2 in the highway of the fuller's *f*.
37:27 they were as the grass of the *f*,
40: 6 thereof is as the flower of the *f*:
43:20 The beast of the *f* shall honour me,
55:12 and all the trees of the *f* shall clap
56: 9 ye beasts of the *f*, come to devour,
Jer 4:17 As keepers of a *f*, are they against
6:25 Go not forth into the *f*, nor walk
7:20 and upon the trees of the *f*,
9:22 fall as dung upon the open *f*,
12: 4 and the herbs of every *f* wither,
9 assemble all the beasts of the *f*,
14: 5 the hind also calved in the *f*,
18 If I go forth into the *f*, then behold
17: 3 O my mountain in the *f*, I will give
18:14 cometh from the rock of the *f*?
26:18 Zion shall be plowed like a *f*,
27: 6 the beasts of the *f* have I given
28:14 have given him the beasts of the *f*
32: 7 Buy thee my *f* that is in Anathoth:
8 Buy my *f*, I pray thee, that is in
9 And I bought the *f* of Hanameel
25 Buy thee the *f* for money, and
35: 9 have we vineyard, nor *f*, nor seed:
41: 8 for we have treasures in the *f*, of
48:33 gladness is taken from the plentiful *f*,
La 4: 9 for want of the fruits of the *f*.
Eze 7:15 he that is in the *f* shall die with the
16: 5 but thou wast cast out in the open *f*,
7 to multiply as the bud of the *f*,
17: 5 and planted it in a fruitful *f*;
24 all the trees of the *f* shall know
20:46 against the forest of the south *f*,
26: 6 her daughters which are in the *f*
8 the sword thy daughters in the *f*:
29: 5 beasts of the *f* and to the fowls
31: 4 rivers unto all the trees of the *f*.
5 exalted above all the trees of the *f*,

Eze 31: 6 beasts of the f bring forth their
13 beasts of the f shall be upon his
15 all the trees of the f fainted for him.
32: 4 cast thee forth upon the open f,
33:27 him that is in the open f will I
34: 5 meat to all the beasts of the f, when
8 meat to every beast of the f, because
27 tree of the f shall yield her fruit,
36:30 the increase of the f, that ye shall
38:20 heaven, and the beasts of the f,
39: 4 beasts of the field to be devoured,
5 Thou shalt fall upon the open f:
10 shall take no wood out of the f,
17 and to every beast of the f,
Da 2:38 the beasts of the f and the fowls
4:12 the beasts of the f had shadow
15 in the tender grass of the f: and let
21 which the beasts of the f dwelt,
23 in the tender grass of the f, and let
23 portion be with the beasts of the f,
25 shall be with the beasts of the f,
32 shall be with the beasts of the f:
Ho 2:12 beasts of the f shall eat them.
18 with the beasts of the f, and with
4: 3 languish, with the beasts of the f,
10: 4 hemlock in the furrows of the f.
Joe 1:10 f is wasted, the land mourneth;
11 the harvest of the f is perished.
12 all the trees of the f, are withered:
19 hath burned all the trees of the f.
20 beasts of the f cry also unto thee:
2:22 Be not afraid, ye beasts of the f:
Mic 1: 6 make Samaria as an heap of the f,
3:12 Zion for your sake be plowed as a f,
4:10 and thou shalt dwell in the f,
Zec 10: 1 of rain, to every one grass in the f.
Mal 3:11 her fruit before the time in the f,
M't 6:28 Consider the lilies of the f, how they
30 so clothe the grass of the f, which
13:24 which sowed good seed in his f:
27 not thou sow good seed in thy f?
31 a man took, and sowed in his f:
36 us the parable of the tares of the f.
38 The f is the world; the good seed
44 is like unto treasure hid in a f;
44 all that he hath, and buyeth that f.
24:18 Neither let him which is in the f
40 Then shall two be in the f;
27: 7 bought with them the potter's f,
8 that f was called, The f of blood,
10 And gave them for the potter's f,
M'r 13:16 him that is in the f not turn back
Lu 2: 8 shepherds abiding in the f, keeping
12:28 is to day in the f, and to-morrow
15:25 Now his elder son was in the f:
17: 7 and by, when he is come from the f,
31 he that is in the f, let him likewise
36 Two men shall be in the f;
Ac 1:18 purchased a f with the reward of
19 f is called in their proper tongue,
19 that is to say, The f of blood.

fields
Ex 8:13 of the villages, and out of the f.
Le 14:53 out of the city into the open f,
25:31 counted as the f of the country:
27:22 is not of the f of his possession;
Nu 16:14 us inheritance of f and vineyards:
19:16 slain with a sword in the open f,
20:17 we will not pass through the f,
21:22 we will not turn into the f, or into
De 11:15 I will send grass in thy f
32:13 might eat the increase of the f;
32 Sodom, and of the f of Gomorrah:
Jos 21:12 the f of the city, and the villages
J'g 9:27 And they went out into the f,
44 the people that were in the f,
1Sa 8:14 take your f, and your vineyards,
22: 7 Jesse give every one of you good f
25:15 with them, when we were in the f:
2Sa 1:21 rain, upon you, nor f of offerings:
11:11 encamped in the open f; shall I
1Ki 2:26 to Anathoth, unto thine own f;
16: 4 and him that dieth of his in the f
2Ki 23: 4 Jerusalem in the f of Kidron,
1Ch 6:56 the f of the city, and the villages
16:32 let the f rejoice, and all that is
27:25 storehouses in the f, in the cities,
2Ch 31:19 which were in the f of the suburbs
Ne 11:25 And for the villages, with their f,
30 Lachish, and the f thereof, at
12:29 of the f of Geba and Azmaveth:
44 into them out of the f of the cities
Job 5:10 and sendeth waters upon the f:
Ps 107:37 sow the f, and plant vineyards,
132: 6 we found it in the f of the wood.
Pr 8:26 had not made the earth, nor the f,
23:10 not into the f of the fatherless:
Isa 16: 8 For the f of Heshbon languish,
32:12 for the teats, for the pleasant f,
Jer 6:12 with their f and wives together:
8:10 their f to them that shall inherit
13:27 abominations on the hills in the f.
31:40 the f unto the brook of Kidron,
32:15 Houses and f and vineyards shall
43 And f shall be bought in this land,
44 Men shall buy f for money, and
39:10 vineyards and f at the same time.
40: 7 of the forces which were in the f,
13 of the forces that were in the f,
Eze 29: 5 thou shalt fall upon the open f;
Ho 12:11 heaps in the furrows of the f.
Ob 19 f of Ephraim, and the f of Samaria:
Mic 2: 2 covet f, and take them by violence;
4 turning away he hath divided our f.
Hab 3:17 and the f shall yield no meat;

M'r 2:23 that he went through the corn f on
Lu 6: 1 that he went through the corn f; and
15:15 sent him into his f to feed swine.
Joh 4:35 look on the f; for they are white
Jas 5: 4 who have reaped down your f,

fierce See also FIERCER.
Ge 49: 7 Cursed be their anger, for it was f;
Ex 32:12 Turn from thy f wrath, and repent
Nu 25: 4 f anger of the Lord may be turned
32:14 augment yet the f anger of the
De 28:50 A nation of f countenance, which
1Sa 20:34 arose from the table in f anger,
28:18 nor executedst his f wrath upon
2Ch 28:11 f wrath of the Lord is upon you.
13 and there is f wrath against Israel.
29:10 that his f wrath may turn away
Ezr 10:14 until the f wrath of our God for this
Job 4:10 voice of the f lion, and the teeth
10:16 Thou huntest me as a f lion:
28: 8 nor the f lion passed by it.
41:10 None is so f that dare stir him up:
Ps 88:16 Thy f wrath goeth over me; thy
Isa 7: 4 the f anger of Rezin with Syria,
13: 9 with wrath and f anger, to lay
13 and in the day of his f anger.
19: 4 and a f king shall rule over them,
33:19 Thou shalt not see a f people,
Jer 4: 8 f anger of the Lord is not turned
26 of the Lord, and by his f anger.
12:13 revenues because of the f anger of
25:37 cut down because of the f anger of
38 and because of his f anger.
30:24 The f anger of the Lord shall not
49:37 evil upon them, even my f anger,
51:45 man his soul from the f anger of
La 1:12 me in the day of his f anger.
2: 3 He hath cut off in his f anger all
4:11 he hath poured out his f anger,
Da 8:23 a king of f countenance, and
Jon 3: 9 and turn away from his f anger,
Hab 1: 8 more f than the evening wolves:
Zep 2: 2 the f anger of the Lord come upon
3: 8 indignation, even all my f anger:
M't 8:28 exceeding f, so that no man might
Lu 23: 5 they were the more f, saying,
2Ti 3: 3 false accusers, incontinent, f,
Jas 3: 4 driven of f winds, yet are they

fierceness
De 13:17 turn from the f of his anger,
Jos 7:26 turned from the f of his anger.
2Ki 23:26 not from the f of his great wrath,
2Ch 30: 8 the f of his wrath may turn away
Job 39:24 He swalloweth the ground with f
Ps 78:49 cast upon them the f of his anger,
85: 3 thyself from the f of thine anger.
Jer 25:38 because of the f of the oppressor,
Ho 11: 9 not execute the f of mine anger,
Na 1: 6 can abide in the f of his anger?
Re 16:19 of the wine of the f of his wrath.
19:15 the f and wrath of Almighty God.

fiercer
2Sa 19:43 words of the men of Judah were f

fiery
Nu 21: 6 the Lord sent f serpents among
8 a f serpent, and set it upon a pole:
De 8:15 were f serpents, and scorpions,
33: 2 right hand went a f law for them.
Ps 21: 9 Thou shalt make them as a f oven
Isa 14:29 fruit shall be a f flying serpent.
30: 6 the viper and f flying serpent,
Da 3: 6, 11 midst of a burning f furnace.
15 the midst of a burning f furnace;
17 us from the burning f furnace,
20 to cast them into the burning f
21, 23 into the midst of the burning f
26 the mouth of the burning f furnace,
7: 9 his throne was like the f flame,
10 A f stream issued and came forth
Eph 6:16 all the f darts of the wicked.
Heb 10:27 and f indignation, which shall
1Pe 4:12 the f trial which is to try you,

fifteen
Ge 5:10 eight hundred and f years,
7:20 F cubits upward did the
25: 7 an hundred threescore and f
Ex 27:14 of the gate shall be f cubits:
15 shall be hangings f cubits:
38:14 side of the gate were f cubits;
15 were hangings of f cubits;
25 threescore and f shekels,
Le 27: 7 estimation shall be f shekels,
Nu 31:37 and threescore and f,
J'g 8:10 about f thousand men, all
2Sa 9:10 Ziba had f sons and twenty
19:17 house of Saul, and his f sons
1Ki 7: 3 forty five pillars, f in a row.
2Ki 14:17 Jehoahaz king of Israel f years.
20: 6 will add unto thy days f years;
2Ch 25:25 Jehoahaz king of Israel f years.
Isa 38: 5 will add unto thy days f years.
Eze 45:12 f shekels, shall be your
Ho 3: 2 to me for f pieces of silver.
Joh 11:18 unto Jerusalem, about f furlongs
Ac 7:14 threescore and f souls.
27:28 again, and found it f fathoms.
Ga 1:18 Peter, and abode with him f days.

fifteenth
Ex 16: 1 f day of the second month
Le 23: 6 the f day of the same month
34 f day of this seventh month
39 the f day of the seventh month,
Nu 28:17 in the f day of this month is
29:12 f day of the seventh month ye

Nu 33: 3 the f day of the first month;
1Ki 12:32 the eighth month, on the f day
33 the f day of the eighth month,
2Ki 14:23 In the f year of Amaziah the
1Ch 24:14 The f to Bilgah, the sixteenth
25:22 f to Jeremoth, he, his sons,
2Ch 15:10 the f year of the reign of Asa.
Es 9:18 f day of the same they rested,
21 and the f day of the same,
Eze 32:17 in the f day of the month,
45:25 seventh month, in the f day
Lu 3: 1 Now in the f year of the reign

fifth
Ge 1:23 and the morning were the f day.
30:17 conceived, and bare Jacob the f
41:34 and take up the f part of the land
47:24 that ye shall give the f part unto
26 that Pharaoh should have the f
Le 5:16 and shall add the f part thereto,
6: 5 add the f part more thereto, and
19:25 And in the f year shall ye eat of the
22:14 then he shall put the f part thereof
27:13 then he shall add a f part thereof
15, 19 shall add the f part of the money
27 and shall add a f part of it thereto:
31 shall add thereto the f part thereof.
Nu 5: 7 and add unto it the f part thereof,
7:36 On the f day Shelumiel the son of
29:26 And on the f day nine bullocks,
33:38 in the first day of the f month.
Jos 19:24 the f lot came out for the tribe
J'g 19: 8 morning on the f day to depart:
2Sa 2:23 spear smote him under the f rib,
3: 4 and the f, Shephatiah the son of
27 smote him there under the f rib,
4: 6 they smote him under the f rib:
20:10 smote him therewith in the f rib,
1Ki 6:31 lintel and side posts were a f part
14:25 in the f year of king Rehoboam,
2Ki 8:16 in the f year of Joram the son of
25: 8 the f month, on the seventh day
1Ch 2:14 Nethaneel the fourth, Raddai the f,
3: 3 The f, Shephatiah of Abital: the
8: 2 Nohah the fourth, and Rapha the f.
12:10 the fourth, Jeremiah the f,
24: 9 The f to Malchijah, the sixth to
25:12 The f to Nethaniah, he, his sons,
26: 3 Elam the f, Jehohanan the sixth,
4 Sacar the fourth, Nethaneel the f,
27: 8 The f captain for the f month
2Ch 12: 2 in the f year of king Rehoboam
Ezr 7: 8 came to Jerusalem in the f month,
9 on the first day of the f month
Ne 6: 5 the f time with an open letter
15 finished in the twenty and f day
Jer 1: 3 Jerusalem captive in the f month.
28: 1 fourth year, and in the f month,
36: 9 to pass in the f year of Jehoiakim
52:12 in the f month, in the tenth day
Eze 1: 1 in the f day of the month, as I was
2 In the f day of the month, which
2 the f year of king Jehoiachin's
8: 1 in the f day of the month, as I sat
20: 1 the seventh year, in the f month,
33:21 in the f day of the month, that one
Zec 7: 3 Should I weep in the f month,
5 mourned in the f and seventh
8:19 of the f, and the fast of the seventh,
Re 6: 9 when he had opened the f seal,
9: 1 And the f angel sounded, and I saw
16:10 And the f angel poured out his vial
21:20 The f, sardonyx; the sixth, sardius;

fifties
Ex 18:21 rulers of f, and rulers of tens:
25 rulers of hundreds, rulers of f,
De 1:15 captains over f, and captains over
1Sa 8:12 captains over f; and will set them
2Ki 1:14 captains of...former f [*] with...f:
M'r 6:40 in ranks, by hundreds, and by f.
Lu 9:14 them sit down by f in a company.

fiftieth
Le 25:10 And ye shall hallow the f year,
11 A jubile shall that f year be unto
2Ki 15:23 In the f year of Azariah king of
27 In the two and f year of Azariah

fifty See also FIFTIES.
Ge 6:15 the breadth of it f cubits, and
7:24 the earth an hundred and f days.
8: 3 the end of the hundred and f days
9:28 flood three hundred and f years.
29 of Noah were nine hundred and f
18:24 Peradventure there be f righteous
24 spare the place for the f righteous
26 said, If I find in Sodom f righteous
28 there shall lack five of the f
Ex 26: 5 F loops shalt thou make in the
5 one curtain, and f loops shalt thou
6 thou shalt make f taches of gold,
10 shalt make f loops on the edge of
10 and f loops in the edge of the
11 thou shalt make f taches of brass,
27:12 side shall be hangings of f cubits:
13 side eastward shall be f cubits.
18 and the breadth f every where,
30:23 even two hundred and f shekels,
23 two hundred and f shekels,
36:12 F loops made he in one curtain,
12 and f loops made he in the edge
13 And he made f taches of gold,
17 f loops upon the uttermost edge
17 and f loops made he upon the edge
18 And he made f taches of brass
38:12 side were hangings of f cubits,

Ex 38:13 the east side eastward f cubits.
26 and five hundred and f men.
Le 23:16 sabbath shall ye number f days;
27: 3 thy estimation shall be f shekels
16 be valued at f shekels of silver.
Nu 1:23 f and nine thousand and three
25 five thousand six hundred and f.
29 were f and four thousand and four
31 were f and seven thousand and four
43 were f and three thousand and four
46 thousand and five hundred and f.
2: 6 were f and four thousand and four
8 were f and seven thousand and four
13 were f and nine thousand and three
15 thousand and six hundred and f.
16 an hundred thousand and f and
16 thousand and four hundred and f.
30 were f and three thousand and four
31 an hundred thousand and f and
32 thousand and five hundred and f.
4: 3 even until f years old, all that
23 until f years old shalt thou number
30 even unto f years old shalt thou
35 upward even unto f years old,
36 two thousand seven hundred and f.
39, 43, 47 upward even unto f years
8:25 the age of f years they shall cease
16: 2 two hundred and f princes of the
17 censer, two hundred and f censers;
35 consumed the two hundred and f
26:10 devoured two hundred and f men:
34 them, f and two thousand and seven
47 were f and three thousand and four
31:30 thou shalt take one portion of f,
47 Moses took one portion of f, both
52 thousand seven hundred and f
De 22:29 unto the damsel's father f shekels
Jos 7:21 and a wedge of gold of f shekels
1Sa 6:19 he smote of the people f thousand
2Sa 15: 1 and f men to run before him.
24:24 and the oxen for f shekels of silver.
1Ki 1: 5 and f men to run before him.
7: 2 and the breadth thereof f cubits,
6 the length thereof was f cubits,
9:23 five hundred and f, which bare rule
10:29 and an horse for an hundred and f:
18: 4 and hid them by f in a cave,
13 the Lord's prophets by f in a cave,
19 prophets of Baal four hundred and f.
22 prophets are four hundred and f
2Ki 1: 9 unto him a captain of f with his f.
10 and said to the captain of f,
10 and consume thee and thy f.
10 and consumed him and his f.
11 him another captain of f with his f.
12 and consume thee and thy f.
12 and consumed him and his f.
13 a captain of the third f with his f.
13 And the third captain of f went
13 the life of these f thy servants,
2: 7 f men of the sons of the prophets
16 be with thy servants f strong men;
17 They sent therefore f men: and
13: 7 people to Jehoahaz but f horsemen,
15: 2 and he reigned two and f years in
20 of each man f shekels of silver,
25 with him f men of the Gileadites:
21: 1 and reigned f and five years in
1Ch 5:21 of their camels f thousand, and
21 two hundred and f thousand,
8:40 and sons' sons, an hundred and f.
9: 9 nine hundred and f and six.
12:33 instruments of war, f thousand,
2Ch 1:17 an horse for an hundred and f:
2:17 an hundred and f thousand and
3: 9 of the nails was f shekels of gold.
8:10 two hundred and f, that bare rule
18 four hundred and f talents of gold,
26: 3 and he reigned f and two years in
33: 1 and he reigned f and five years in
Ezr 2: 7 thousand two hundred f and four.
14 of Bigvai, two thousand f and six.
15 of Adin, four hundred f and four.
22 The men of Netophah, f and six.
29 The children of Nebo, f and two.
30 of Magbish, an hundred f and six.
31 thousand two hundred f and four.
37 of Immer, a thousand f and two.
60 of Nekoda, six hundred f and two.
8: 3 of the males an hundred and f.
6 Jonathan, and with him f males.
26 six hundred and f talents of silver,
Ne 5:17 an hundred and f of the Jews and
6:15 the month Elul, in f and two days.
7:10 of Arah, six hundred f and two.
12 thousand two hundred f and four.
20 of Adin, six hundred f and five.
33 of the other Nebo, f and two.
34 thousand two hundred f and four.
40 of Immer, a thousand f and two.
70 f basons, five hundred and thirty
Es 5:14 gallows be made of f cubits high,
7: 9 also, the gallows f cubits high,
Isa 3: 3 captain of f, and the honourable
Eze 40:15 of the inner gate were f cubits.
21 the length thereof was f cubits,
25 the length was f cubits, and the
29, 33 it was f cubits long, and five
36 the length was f cubits, and the
42: 2 and the breadth was f cubits.
7 the length thereof was f cubits.
8 in the utter court was f cubits:
45: 2 and f cubits round about for the
48:17 the north two hundred and f,
17 the south two hundred and f,
17 toward the east two hundred and f,
Eze 48:17 the west two hundred and f.
Hag 2:16 draw out f vessels out of the press,
Lu 7:41 hundred pence, and the other f.
16: 6 and sit down quickly, and write f.
Joh 8:57 Thou art not yet f years old,
21:11 an hundred and f and three:
Ac 13:20 of four hundred and f years,
19:19 found it f thousand pieces of

fig See also FIGS.
Ge 3: 7 and they sewed f leaves together,
De 8: 8 barley, and vines, and f trees,
J'g 9:10 the trees said to the f tree,
11 But the f tree said unto them,
1Ki 4:25 his vine and under his f tree,
2Ki 18:31 and every one of his f tree,
Ps 105:33 their vines also and their f trees;
Pr 27:18 Whoso keepeth the f tree shall eat
Ca 2:13 f tree putteth forth her green figs,
Isa 34: 4 as a falling f [] from the f tree
36:16 vine, and every one of his f tree,
Jer 5:17 eat up thy vines and thy f trees:
8:13 nor figs on the f tree, and the leaf
Ho 2:12 destroy her vines and her f trees,
9:10 as the firstripe in the f tree
Joe 1: 7 vine waste, and barked my f tree,
12 and the f tree languisheth; the
2:22 the f tree and the vine do yield
Am 4: 9 your vineyards and your f trees
Mic 4: 4 under his f tree; and none shall
Na 3:12 strong holds shall be like f trees
Hab 3:17 the f tree shall not blossom,
Hag 2:19 as yet the vine, and the f tree,
Zec 3:10 the vine and under the f tree.
M't 21:19 when he saw a f tree in the way,
19 presently the f tree withered away.
20 soon is the f tree withered away!
21 do this which is done to the f tree,
24:32 learn a parable of the f tree;
M'r 11:13 a f tree afar off having leaves,
20 they saw the f tree dried up
21 the f tree which thou cursedst
13:28 learn a parable of the f tree;
Lu 13: 6 A certain man had a f tree planted
7 come seeking fruit on this f tree,
21:29 Behold the f tree, and all the trees;
Joh 1:48 when thou wast under the f tree,
50 I saw thee under the f tree,
Jas 3:12 Can the f tree, my brethren, bear
Re 6:13 a f tree casteth her untimely figs,

fight See also FIGHTETH; FIGHTING; FOUGHT.
Ex 1:10 also unto our enemies, and f
14:14 The Lord shall f for you, and ye
17: 9 go out, f with Amalek: tomorrow
De 1:30 he shall f for you, according to all
41 we will go up and f, according to
42 Go not up, neither f; for I am
2:32 out he and all his people, to f
3:22 your God he shall f for you.
20: 4 to f for you against your enemies,
10 thou comest nigh unto a city to f
Jos 9: 2 to f with Joshua and with Israel,
10:25 your enemies against whom ye f.
11: 5 of Merom, to f against Israel.
19:47 children of Dan went up to f
J'g 1: 1 Canaanites first, to f against them?
3 we may f against the Canaanites;
9 down to f against the Canaanites,
8: 1 us not, when thou wentest to f
9:38 out, I pray now, and f with them.
10: 9 to f also against Judah, and
18 is he that will begin to f against
11: 6 that we may f with the children
8 f against the children of Ammon,
9 to f against the children of Ammon,
12 come against me to f in my land?
25 or did he ever f against them,
32 the children of Ammon to f against
12: 1 Wherefore passedst thou over to f
3 unto me this day, to f against me?
20:20 put themselves in array to f
1Sa 4: 9 quit yourselves like men, and f.
8:20 go out before us, and f our battles.
13: 5 gathered themselves together to f
15:18 and f against them until they be
17: 9 If he be able to f with me,
10 man, that we may f together.
20 the host was going forth to the f,
32 go and f with this Philistine.
33 to go against this Philistine to f
18:17 for me, and f the Lord's battles.
23: 1 the Philistines f against Keilah,
28: 1 for warfare to f with Israel.
29: 8 may not go f against the enemies
2Sa 11:20 nigh unto the city when ye did f?
1Ki 12:21 to f against the house of Israel,
24 nor f against your brethren the
20:23 us f against them in the plain,
25 will f against them in the plain,
26 up to Aphek, to f against Israel.
22:31 F neither with small nor great,
32 turned aside to f against him:
2Ki 3:21 the kings were come up to f
10: 3 and f for your master's house.
19: 9 he is come out to f against thee:
2Ch 11: 1 to f against Israel, that he might
4 nor f against your brethren:
13:12 f ye not against the Lord God
18:30 F ye not with small or great,
31 they compassed about him to f:
20:17 shall not need to f in this battle:
32: 2 purposed to f against Jerusalem,
8 to help us, and to f our battles.
35:20 Necho king of Egypt came up to f
22 might f with him, and hearkened
22 came to f in the valley of Megiddo.
Ne 4: 8 to f against Jerusalem, and to
14 and f for your brethren, your
20 our God shall f for us.
Ps 35: 1 f against them that f against me.
56: 2 they be many that f against me,
144: 1 to war, and my fingers to f:
Isa 19: 2 and they shall f every one against
29: 7 the nations that f against Ariel,
7 even all that f against her and her
8 be, that f against mount Zion.
30:32 in battles of shaking will he f
31: 4 to f for mount Zion, and for the
Jer 1:19 they shall f against thee; but
15:20 and they shall f against thee;
21: 4 ye f against the king of Babylon,
5 And I myself will f against you
32: 5 though ye f with the Chaldeans,
24 of the Chaldeans, that f against it,
29 Chaldeans, that f against this city,
33: 5 They come to f with the Chaldeans,
34:22 and they shall f against it, and
37: 8 again, and f against this city,
10 army of the Chaldeans that f
41:12 to f with Ishmael the son of
51:30 men of Babylon have forborn to f,
Da 10:20 will I return to f with the prince
11:11 shall come forth and f with him,
Zec 10: 5 and they shall f, because the Lord
14: 3 forth, and f against those nations,
14 Judah also shall f at Jerusalem;
Joh 18:36 then would my servants f,
Ac 5:39 be found even to f against God.
23: 9 let us not f against God.
1Co 9:26 so f I, not as one that beateth
1Ti 6:12 F the good...of faith, lay hold on
12 the good f of faith, lay hold on
2Ti 4: 7 a good f, I have finished my course,
Heb 10:32 endured a great f of afflictions;
11:34 waxed valiant in f, turned to
Jas 4: 2 ye f and war, yet ye have not,
Re 2:16 f against them with the sword

fighteth
Ex 14:25 the Lord f for them against the
Jos 23:10 he it is that f for you, as he hath
1Sa 25:28 my lord f the battles of the Lord,

fighting See also FIGHTINGS.
1Sa 17:19 of Elah, f with the Philistines.
2Ch 26:11 host of f men, that went
Ps 56: 1 me up; he f daily oppresseth me.

fightings
2Co 7: 5 without were f, within were fears.
Jas 4: 1 come wars and f among you?

fig-leaves See FIG and LEAVES.

figs
Nu 13:23 the pomegranates, and of the f.
20: 5 it is no place of seed, or of f,
1Sa 25:18 two hundred cakes of f, and laid
30:12 they gave him a piece of a cake of f.
2Ki 20: 7 Isaiah said, Take a lump of f.
1Ch 12:40 oxen, and meat, meal, cakes of f,
Ne 13:15 also wine, grapes, and f,
Ca 2:13 fig tree putteth forth her green f,
Isa 38:21 Let them take a lump of f,
Jer 8:13 nor f on the fig tree, and the leaf
24: 1 two baskets of f were set before
2 One basket had very good f,
2 even like the f that are first ripe:
2 other basket had very naughty f,
3 I said, F; the good f, very good;
5 Like these good f, so will I
8 the evil, f which cannot be eaten,
29:17 I will make them like vile f,
Na 3:12 like fig trees with the firstripe f:
M't 7:16 grapes of thorns, or f of thistles?
M'r 11:13 for the time of f was not yet.
Lu 6:44 of thorns men do not gather f,
Jas 3:12 either a vine, f? so can no fountain
Re 6:13 a fig tree casteth her untimely f,

fig-tree See FIG and TREE.

figure See also DISFIGURE; FIGURES; TRANSFIGURED.
De 4:16 image, the similitude of any f,
Isa 44:13 maketh it after the f of a man,
Ro 5:14 is the f of him that was to come.
1Co 4: 6 I have in a f transferred to myself
Heb 9: 9 was a f for the time then present,
11:19 also he received him in a f.
1Pe 3:21 like f whereunto even baptism

figures
1Ki 6:29 carved f of cherubims and palm
Ac 7:43 f which ye made to worship
Heb 9:24 which are the f of the true;

file
1Sa 13:21 had a f for the mattocks,

fill See also FILLED; FILLEST; FILLETH; FILLING; FULFIL.
Ge 1:22 and f the waters in the seas,
42:25 Joseph commanded to f their sacks
44: 1 F the men's sacks with food, as
Ex 10: 6 And they shall f thy houses,
16:32 F an omer of it to be kept
Le 25:19 eat your f, and dwell therein
De 23:24 thou mayest eat grapes thy f at
1Sa 16: 1 f thine horn with oil, and go,
1Ki 18:33 F four barrels with water, and
Job 8:21 Till he f thy mouth with laughing,
15: 2 and f his belly with the east wind?
20:23 When he is about to f his belly,
23: 4 and f my mouth with arguments.
38:39 f the appetite of the young lions,
41: 7 thou f his skin with barbed irons?

Ps 81:10 thy mouth wide, and I will *f* it.
83:16 *F* their faces with shame; that
110: 6 he shall *f* the places with the dead
Pr 1:13 we shall *f* our houses with spoil:
7:18 Come, let us take our *f* of love
8:21 and I will *f* their treasures.
Isa 8: 8 shall *f* the breadth of thy land,
14:21 *f* the face of the world with cities.
27: 6 *f* the face of the world with fruit.
56:12 *f* ourselves with strong drink;
Jer 13:13 I will *f* all the inhabitants of
23:24 Do not I *f* heaven and earth?
33: 5 is to *f* them with the dead bodies
51:14 Surely I will *f* thee with men,
Eze 3: 3 and *f* thy bowels with this roll
7:19 their souls, neither *f* their bowels:
9: 7 and *f* the courts with the slain:
10: 2 *f* thine hand with coals of fire
24: 4 *f* it with the choice bones.
30:11 and *f* the land with the slain.
32: 4 *f* the beasts of the whole earth
5 and *f* the valleys with thy height.
35: 8 and I will *f* his mountains with
Zep 1: 9 which *f* their masters' houses
Hag 2: 7 and I will *f* this house with glory,
M't 9:16 which is put in to *f* it up taketh
15:33 as to *f* so great a multitude?
23:32 *F* ye up then the measure of
Joh 2: 7 *F* the water pots with water.
Ro 15:13 *f* you with all joy and peace in
Eph 4:10 that he might *f* all things.)
Col 1:24 *f* up that which is behind of the
1Th 2:16 to *f* up their sins alway: for the
Re 18: 6 she hath filled *f* to her double.

filled See also FILLEDST; FULFILLED.
Ge 6:11 the earth was *f* with violence.
13 for the earth is *f* with violence
21:19 went, and *f* the bottle with water,
24:16 and *f* her pitcher, and came up.
26:15 them, and *f* them with earth.
Ex 1: 7 and the land was *f* with them.
2:16 and *f* the troughs to water their
16:12 morning ye shall be *f* with bread;
28: 3 whom I have *f* with the spirit
31: 3 And I have *f* him with the spirit
35:31 And he hath *f* him with the spirit
35 hath he *f* with wisdom of heart,
40:34, 35 and the glory of the Lord *f* the
Nu 14:21 the earth shall be *f* with the glory
De 26:12 eat within thy gates, and be *f*;
31:20 shall have eaten and *f* themselves
Jos 9:13 these bottles of wine, which we *f*,
1Ki 7:14 and he was *f* with wisdom, and
8:10 the cloud *f* the house of the Lord,
11 glory of the Lord had *f* the house
18:35 he *f* the trench also with water.
20:27 but the Syrians *f* the country.
2Ki 3:17 that valley shall be *f* with water,
20 and the country was *f* with water.
25 cast every man his stone, and *f* it;
21:16 till he had *f* Jerusalem from one
23:14 and *f* their places with the bones
24: 4 for he *f* Jerusalem with innocent
2Ch 5:13 the house was *f* with a cloud,
14 glory of the Lord had *f* the house
7: 1 the glory of the Lord *f* the house.
2 glory of the Lord had *f* the Lord's
16:14 which was *f* with sweet odours
Ezr 9:11 have *f* it from one end to another
Ne 9:25 so they did eat, and were *f*,
Job 3:15 who *f* their houses with silver:
16: 8 thou hast *f* me with wrinkles,
22:18 *f* their houses with good things:
Ps 38: 7 are *f* with a loathsome disease:
71: 8 Let my mouth be *f* with thy praise
72:19 the whole earth be *f* with his glory;
78:29 they did eat, and were well *f*:
80: 9 take deep root, and it *f* the land.
104:28 thy hand, they are *f* with good.
123: 3 are exceedingly *f* with contempt.
4 exceedingly *f* with the scorning
126: 2 was our mouth *f* with laughter,
Pr 1:31 fruit of their own way, and be *f*
3:10 shall thy barns be *f* with plenty,
5:10 strangers be *f* with thy wealth;
12:21 wicked shall be *f* with mischief.
14:14 backslider in heart shall be *f*
18:20 increase of his lips shall he be *f*.
20:17 his mouth shall be *f* with gravel.
24: 4 shall the chambers be *f* with all
25:16 thou be *f* therewith, and vomit
30:16 the earth that is not *f* with water;
22 a fool when he is *f* with meat;
Ec 1: 8 nor the ear *f* with hearing.
6: 3 his soul be not *f* with good,
7 and yet the appetite is not *f*.
Ca 5: 2 head is *f* with dew, and my locks
Isa 6: 1 up, and his train *f* the temple.
4 and the house was *f* with smoke.
21: 3 Therefore are my loins *f* with
33: 5 he hath *f* Zion with judgment
34: 6 sword of the Lord is *f* with blood,
43:24 neither hast thou *f* me with the
65:20 old man that hath not *f* his days:
Jer 13:12 Every bottle shall be *f* with wine:
12 every bottle shall be *f* with wine?
15:17 thou hast *f* me with indignation.
16:18 they have *f* mine inheritance with
19: 4 have *f* this place with the blood
41: 9 Ishmael the son of Nethaniah *f* it
46:12 and the cry hath *f* the land:
51: 5 though their land was *f* with sin
34 hath *f* his belly with my delicates,
La 3:15 He hath *f* me with bitterness,
30 he is *f* full with reproach.
Eze 8:17 have *f* the land with violence,
10: 3 and the cloud *f* the inner court.
4 the house was *f* with the cloud,
11: 6 and ye have *f* the streets thereof
23:33 Thou shalt be *f* with drunkenness
28:16 *f* the midst of thee with violence,
36:38 the waste cities be *f* with flocks
39:20 Thus ye shall be *f* at my table
43: 5 the glory of the Lord *f* the house.
44: 4 the Lord *f* the house of the Lord:
Da 2:35 mountain, and *f* the whole earth.
Ho 13: 6 to their pasture, so were they *f*;
6 they were *f*, and their heart was
Na 2:12 and *f* his holes with prey, and his
Hab 2:14 shall be *f* with the knowledge
16 Thou art *f* with shame for glory:
Hag 1: 6 but ye are not *f* with drink;
Zec 9:13 *f* the bow with Ephraim, and
15 and they shall be *f* like bowls,
M't 5: 6 righteousness: for they shall be *f*.
14:20 And they did all eat, and were *f*:
15:37 And they did all eat, and were *f*:
27:48 a spunge, and *f* it with vinegar,
M'r 2:21 the new piece that *f* it up
6:42 And they did all eat, and were *f*.
7:27 Let the children first be *f*:
8: 8 So they did eat, and were *f*:
15:36 and *f* a spunge full of vinegar,
Lu 1:15 he shall be *f* with the Holy Ghost,
41 Elisabeth was *f* with the Holy
53 He hath *f* the hungry with good
67 Zacharias was *f* with the Holy
2:40 strong in spirit, *f* with wisdom:
3: 5 Every valley shall be *f*, and every
4:28 these things, were *f* with wrath,
5: 7 they came and *f* both the ships,
26 and were *f* with fear, saying,
6:11 And they were *f* with madness;
21 hunger now: for ye shall be *f*.
8:23 and they were *f* with water,
9:17 And they did eat, and were all *f*:
14:23 come in, that my house may be *f*:
15:16 And he would fain have *f* his
Joh 2: 7 And they *f* them up to the brim.
6:12 When they were *f*, he said unto
13 and *f* twelve baskets with the
26 ye did eat of the loaves, and were *f*.
12: 3 the house was *f* with the odour
16: 6 sorrow hath *f* your heart.
19:29 and they *f* a spunge with vinegar,
Ac 2: 2 *f* all the house where they were
4 were all *f* with the Holy Ghost,
3:10 and they were *f* with wonder and
4: 8 Then Peter, *f* with the Holy Ghost,
31 were all *f* with the Holy Ghost,
5: 3 hath Satan *f* thine heart to lie
17 and were *f* with indignation,
28 and, behold, ye have *f* Jerusalem
9:17 and be *f* with the Holy Ghost.
13: 9 Paul,) *f* with the Holy Ghost, set
45 they were *f* with envy, and spake
52 And the disciples were *f* with joy,
19:29 whole city was *f* with confusion:
Ro 1:29 Being *f* with all unrighteousness,
15:14 *f* with all knowledge, able also to
24 somewhat *f* with your company.
2Co 7: 4 *f* with comfort, I am exceeding
Eph 3:19 might be *f* with all the fulness of
5:18 but be *f* with the Spirit;
Ph'p 1:11 *f* with the fruits of righteousness,
Col 1: 9 might be *f* with the knowledge
2Ti 1: 4 that I may be *f* with joy;
Jas 2:16 in peace, be ye warmed and *f*;
Re 8: 5 *f* it with fire of the altar, and cast
15: 1 in them is *f* up the wrath of God.
8 the temple was *f* with smoke
18: 6 she hath *f* fill to her double.
19:21 the fowls were *f* with their flesh.

filledst
De 6:11 all good things, which thou *f* not,
Eze 27:33 thou *f* many people: thou didst

fillest
Ps 17:14 whose belly thou *f* with thy hid

fillet See also FILLETED; FILLETS.
Jer 52:21 *f* of twelve cubits did compass it;

filleted
Ex 27:17 round about the court shall be *f*
38:17 all the pillars of the court were *f*
28 overlaid their chapiters, and *f*

filleth
Job 9:18 but *f* me with bitterness.
Ps 84: 6 the rain also *f* the pools.
107: 9 *f* the hungry soul with goodness.
129: 7 Wherewith the mower *f* not his
147:14 *f* thee with the finest of the wheat.
Eph 1:23 the fulness of him that *f* all in all.

fillets
Ex 27:10 and their *f* shall be of silver.
11 the pillars and their *f* of silver.
36:38 chapiters and their *f* with gold.
38:10 and their *f* were of silver.
11 and their *f* were of silver.
12 of the pillars and their *f* of silver.
17 of the pillars and their *f* of silver;
19 their chapiters and their *f* of silver.

filling See also FULFILLING.
Ac 14:17 *f* our hearts with food and

filth
Isa 4: 4 the *f* of the daughters of Zion,
Na 3: 6 I will cast abominable *f* upon thee,
1Co 4:13 are made as the *f* of the world,
1Pe 3:21 putting away of the *f* of the flesh,

filthiness
2Ch 29: 5 forth the *f* out of the holy place.
Ezr 6:21 them from the *f* of the heathen of
9:11 an unclean land with the *f* of the
Pr 30:12 yet is not washed from their *f*.
Isa 28: 8 all tables are full of vomit and *f*,
La 1: 9 Her *f* is in her skirts; she
Eze 16:36 Because thy *f* was poured out,
22:15 will consume thy *f* out of thee.
24:11 that the *f* of it may be molten in it,
13 In thy *f* is lewdness: because I
13 shalt not be purged from thy *f*
36:25 ye shall be clean: from all your *f*.
2Co 7: 1 from all *f* of the flesh and spirit,
Eph 5: 4 Neither *f*, nor foolish talking, nor
Jas 1:21 lay apart all *f* and superfluity
Re 17: 4 full of abominations and *f* of her

filthy
Job 15:16 more abominable and *f* is man,
Ps 14: 3 aside, they are altogether become *f*:
53: 3 back: they are altogether become *f*:
Isa 64: 6 righteousnesses are as *f* rags;
Zep 3: 1 Woe to her that is *f* and polluted,
Zec 3: 3 was clothed with *f* garments,
4 Take away the *f* garments from
Col 3: 8 *f* communication out of your
1Ti 3: 3 no striker, not greedy of *f* lucre;
8 much wine, not greedy of *f* lucre;
Tit 1: 7 no striker, not given to *f* lucre;
11 they ought not, for *f* lucre's sake.
1Pe 5: 2 not for *f* lucre, but of a ready mind;
2Pe 2: 7 vexed with the *f* conversation of
Jude 8 also these *f* dreamers defile
Re 22:11 he which is *f*, let him be *f* still:

finally
2Co 13:11 *F*, brethren, farewell. Be perfect,
Eph 6:10 *F*, my brethren, be strong in the
Ph'p 3: 1 *F*, my brethren, rejoice in the Lord.
4: 8 *F*, brethren, whatsoever things are
2Th 3: 1 *F*, brethren, pray for us, that the
1Pe 3: 8 *F*, be ye all of one mind, having

find See also FINDEST; FINDETH; FINDING; FOUND.
Ge 18:26 If I *f* in Sodom fifty righteous
28 If I *f* there forty and five,
30 I will not do it, if I *f* thirty there.
19:11 wearied themselves to *f* the door.
32: 5 that I may *f* grace in thy sight.
19 speak unto Esau, when ye *f* him.
33: 8 to *f* grace in the sight of my lord.
15 me *f* grace in the sight of my lord.
34:11 Let me *f* grace in your eyes,
38:22 I cannot *f* her; and also the men
41:38 Can we *f* such a one as this is,
47:25 us *f* grace in the sight of my lord.
Ex 5:11 get you straw where ye can *f* it:
16:25 ye shall not *f* it in the field.
33:13 that I may *f* grace in thy sight:
Nu 32:23 be sure your sin will *f* you out.
35:27 And the revenger of blood *f* him
De 4:29 thou shalt *f* him, if thou seek him
22:23 and a man *f* her in the city,
25 if a man *f* a betrothed damsel
28 a man *f* a damsel that is a virgin,
24: 1 that she *f* no favour in his eyes,
28:65 these nations shalt thou *f* no ease,
J'g 9:33 to them as thou shalt *f* occasion.
14:12 and *f* it out, then I will give you
17: 8 sojourn where he could *f* a place;
9 to sojourn where I may *f* a place.
Ru 1: 9 that ye may *f* rest, each of you
2: 2 in whose sight I shall *f* grace.
13 Let me *f* favour in thy sight,
1Sa 1:18 handmaid *f* grace in thy sight.
9:13 ye shall straightway *f* him,
13 about this time we shall *f* him.
10: 2 *f* two men by Rachel's sepulchre
20:21 saying, Go *f* out the arrows.
36 *f* out now the arrows which I shoot.
23:17 of Saul my father shall not *f* thee;
24:19 a man *f* his enemy, will he let him
25: 8 let the young men *f* favour in thine
2Sa 15:25 if I shall *f* favour in the eyes
16: 4 that I may *f* grace in thy sight
17:20 had sought and could not *f* them,
1Ki 18: 5 peradventure we may *f* grass to
12 he cannot *f* thee, he shall slay me:
2Ch 2:14 and to *f* out every device which
20:16 and ye shall *f* them at the end
30: 9 your children shall *f* compassion
32: 4 Assyria come, and *f* much water?
Ezr 4:15 thou *f* in the book of the records,
7:16 thou canst *f* in all the province
Job 3:22 glad, when they can *f* the grave?
11: 7 Canst thou by searching *f* out God?
7 canst thou *f* out the Almighty
17:10 cannot *f* one wise man among you.
23: 3 that I knew where I might *f* him!
34:11 man to *f* according to his ways.
37:23 Almighty we cannot *f* him out:
Ps 10:15 out his wickedness till thou *f* none.
17: 3 tried me, and shalt *f* nothing;
21: 8 Thine hand shall *f* out all thine
8 thy right hand shall *f* out those
132: 5 Until I *f* out a place for the Lord,
Pr 1:13 We shall *f* all precious substance,
28 me early, but they shall not *f* me:
2: 5 Lord, and *f* the knowledge of God.
3: 4 *f* favour and good understanding
4:22 are life unto those that *f* them,
8: 9 right to them that *f* knowledge,
12 and *f* out knowledge of witty
17 that seek me early shall *f* me.
16:20 a matter wisely shall *f* good;

Pr 19: 8 keepeth understanding shall *f*
20: 6 but a faithful man who can *f*?
28:23 shall *f* more favour than he that
31:10 Who can *f* a virtuous woman?
Ec 3:11 no man can *f* out the work that God
7:14 man should *f* nothing after him.
24 exceeding deep, who can *f* it out?
26 I *f* more bitter than death the
27 one by one, to *f* out the account:
28 yet my soul seeketh, but I *f* not:
8:17 that a man cannot *f* out the work
17 yet he shall not *f* it: yea, farther;
17 yet shall he not be able to *f* it.
11: 1 for thou shalt *f* it after many days.
12:10 sought to *f* out acceptable words:
Ca 5: 6 but I could not *f* him; I called him,
8 if ye *f* my beloved, that ye tell him,
8: 1 should *f* thee without, I would kiss
Isa 34:14 and *f* for herself a place of rest.
41:12 seek them, and shalt not *f* them,
58: 3 day of your fast ye *f* pleasure,
Jer 2:24 in her month they shall *f* her.
5: 1 if ye can *f* a man, if there be any
6:16 and ye shall *f* rest for your souls.
10:18 distress them, that they may *f* it
29:13 And ye shall seek me, and *f* me,
45: 3 in my sighing, and I *f* no rest,
La 1: 6 like harts that *f* no pasture,
2: 9 also *f* no vision from the Lord.
Da 6: 4 to *f* occasion against Daniel
4 but they could *f* none occasion
5 not *f* occasion against this Daniel,
5 Daniel, except we *f* it against him
Ho 2: 6 that she shall not *f* her paths.
7 seek them, but shall not *f* them:
5: 6 they shall not *f* him; he hath
12: 8 they shall *f* none iniquity in me
Am 8:12 of the Lord, and shall not *f* it.
M't 7: 7 seek, and ye shall *f*; knock, and
14 and few there be that *f* it.
10:39 loseth his life for my sake shall *f* it.
11:29 ye shall *f* rest unto your souls.
16:25 lose his life for my sake shall *f* it.
17:27 thou shalt *f* a piece of money:
18:13 if so be that he *f* it, verily I say
21: 2 ye shall *f* an ass tied, and a colt
22: 9 as many as ye shall *f*, bid to the
24:46 when he cometh shall *f* so doing.
M'r 11: 2 ye shall *f* a colt tied, whereon
13 he might *f* any thing thereon:
13:36 coming suddenly he *f* you sleeping.
Lu 2:12 Ye shall *f* the babe wrapped in
5:19 they could not *f* by what way
6: 7 might *f* an accusation against him.
11: 9 given you; seek, and ye shall *f*;
12:37 when he cometh shall *f* watching:
38 and *f* them so, blessed are those
43 when he cometh shall *f* so doing.
13: 7 fruit on this fig tree, and *f* none:
15: 4 that which is lost, until he *f* it?
8 and seek diligently till she *f* it?
18: 8 shall he *f* faith on the earth?
19:30 your entering ye shall *f* a colt tied,
48 could not *f* what they might do:
23: 4 I *f* no fault in this man.
Joh 7:34 shall seek me, and shall not *f* me:
35 we shall not *f* him? will he go
36 and shall not *f* me: and where I
10: 9 shall go in and out, and *f* pasture.
18:38 I *f* in him no fault at all.
19: 4 may know that I *f* no fault in him.
6 for I *f* no fault in him.
21: 6 side of the ship, and ye shall *f*.
Ac 7:46 to *f* a tabernacle for the God of
17:27 might feel after him, and *f* him,
23: 9 We *f* no evil in this man:
Ro 7:18 that which is good I *f* not.
21 I *f* then a law, that, when I would
9:19 Why doth he yet *f* fault? For who
2Co 9: 4 with me, and *f* you unprepared,
12:20 I shall not *f* you such as I would,
2Ti 1:18 that he may *f* mercy of the Lord
Heb 4:16 we may obtain mercy, and *f* grace
Re 9: 6 seek death, and shall not *f* it;
18:14 thou shalt *f* them no more at all.

findest
Ge 31:32 with whomsoever thou *f* thy gods,
Eze 3: 1 Son of man, eat that thou *f*;

findeth^
Ge 4:14 every one that *f* me shall slay me.
Job 33:10 Behold, he *f* occasions against me,
Ps 119:162 thy word as one that *f* great spoil.
Pr 3:13 Happy is the man that *f* wisdom,
8:35 whoso *f* me, *f* life, and shall
17:20 hath a froward heart *f* no good:
18:22 Whoso *f* a wife *f* a good thing,
21:10 neighbour *f* no favour in his eyes.
21 righteousness and mercy *f* life,
Ec 9:10 Whatsoever thy hand *f* to do, do it
La 1: 3 she *f* no rest: all her persecutors
Ho 14: 3 in thee the fatherless *f* mercy.
M't 7: 8 he that seeketh *f*; and to him
10:39 He that *f* his life shall lose it:
12:43 places, seeking rest, and *f* none.
44 is come he *f* it empty, swept, and
26:40 *f* them asleep, and saith unto
M'r 14:37 he cometh, and *f* them sleeping,
Lu 11:10 receiveth; and he that seeketh *f*;
25 he *f* it swept and garnished.
Joh 1:41 He first *f* his own brother Simon,
43 and *f* Philip, and saith unto him,
45 Philip *f* Nathanael, and saith unto
5:14 Jesus *f* him in the temple, and

finding
Ge 4:15 lest any *f* him should kill him.
Job 9:10 doeth great things past *f* out;
Isa 58:13 nor *f* thine own pleasure, nor
Lu 11:24 and *f* none, he saith, I will return
Ac 4:21 *f* nothing how they might punish
19: 1 and *f* certain disciples,
21: 2 And *f* a ship sailing over unto
4 *f* disciples, we tarried there seven
Ro 11:33 and his ways past *f* out!
Heb 8: 8 For *f* fault with them, he saith

fine^ See also FINEST; FINING; REFINE.
Ge 41:42 and arrayed him in vestures of *f* linen,
Ex 25: 4 scarlet, and *f* linen, and goats' hair,
26: 1 with ten curtains of *f* twined linen,
31 and *f* twined linen of cunning work:
36 and *f* twined linen, wrought with
27: 9 for the court of *f* twined linen of an
16 purple and scarlet, and *f* twined linen,
18 the height five cubits of *f* twined linen,
28: 5 and purple, and scarlet, and *f* linen.
6 purple, of scarlet, and *f* twined linen,
8 purple, and scarlet, and *f* twined linen.
15 of *f* twined linen, shalt thou make it.
39 shalt embroider the coat of *f* linen,
39 thou shalt make the mitre of *f* linen,
35: 6, 23 scarlet, and *f* linen, and goats' hair,
25 purple, and of scarlet, and of *f* linen.
35 in purple, in scarlet, and in *f* linen,
36: 8 made ten curtains of *f* twined linen,
35 and purple, and scarlet, and *f* twined
37 and *f* twined linen, of needlework;
38: 9 of the court were of *f* twined linen, an
16 round about were of *f* twined linen.
18 purple, and scarlet, and *f* twined linen:
23 in purple, and in scarlet, and *f* linen.
39: 2 purple, and scarlet, and *f* twined linen,
3 and in the scarlet, and in the *f* linen,
5 purple, and scarlet, and *f* twined linen;
8 purple, and scarlet, and *f* twined linen.
27 made coats of *f* linen of woven work
28 And a mitre of *f* linen, and goodly
28 and goodly bonnets of *f* linen, and
28 and linen breeches of *f* twined linen,
29 And a girdle of *f* twined linen, and
Le 2: 1 his offering shall be of *f* flour; and
4 shall be unleavened cakes of *f* flour
5 it shall be of *f* flour unleavened,
7 it shall be made of *f* flour with oil,
5:11 the tenth part of an ephah of *f* flour
6:20 the tenth part of an ephah of *f* flour
7:12 and cakes mingled with oil, of *f* flour,
14:10 and three tenth deals of *f* flour for
21 and one tenth deal of *f* flour mingled
23:13 two tenth deals of *f* flour mingled
17 tenth deals: they shall be of *f* flour;
24: 5 And thou shalt take *f* flour, and bake
Nu 6:15 cakes of *f* flour mingled with oil,
7:13, 19, 25, 31, 37, 43, 49, 55, 61, 67, 73 both
of them were full of *f* flour
79 both of them full of *f* flour mingled
8: 8 even *f* flour mingled with oil,
1Ki 4:22 was thirty measures of *f* flour,
2Ki 7: 1 measure of *f* flour be sold for a shekel,
16 So a measure of *f* flour was sold
18 a measure of *f* flour for a shekel,
1Ch 4:21 house of them that wrought *f* linen,
9:29 the *f* flour, and the wine, and the oil,
15:27 was clothed with a robe of *f* linen,
23:29 and for the *f* flour for meat offering,
2Ch 2:14 in blue, and in *f* linen, and in crimson;
3: 5 which he overlaid with *f* gold,
8 and he overlaid it with *f* gold,
14 purple, and crimson, and *f* linen,
Ezr 8:27 two vessels of *f* copper, precious
Es 1: 6 fastened with cords of *f* linen and
8:15 and with a garment of *f* linen and
Job 28: 1 place for gold where they *f* it.
17 of it shall not be for jewels of *f* gold.
31:24 or have said to the *f* gold, Thou art my
Ps 19:10 yea, than much *f* gold: sweeter also
119:127 above gold; yea, above *f* gold.
Pr 3:14 and the gain thereof than *f* gold.
7:16 works, with *f* linen of Egypt.
8:19 is better than gold, yea, than *f* gold;
25:12 and an ornament of *f* gold, so is a wise
31:24 She maketh *f* linen, and selleth
Ca 5:11 His head is as the most *f* gold,
15 marble, set upon sockets of *f* gold:
Isa 3:23 The glasses, and the *f* linen, and the
13:12 a man more precious than *f* gold;
19: 9 Moreover they that work in *f* flax,
La 4: 1 how is the most *f* gold changed!
2 sons of Zion, comparable to *f* gold,
Eze 16:10 and I girded thee about with *f* linen,
13 and thy raiment was of *f* linen,
13 thou didst eat *f* flour, and honey,
19 thee, *f* flour, and oil, and honey, and
27: 7 *F* linen with broidered work from
16 and *f* linen, and coral, and agate.
46:14 of oil, to temper with the *f* flour;
Da 2:32 This image's head was of *f* gold,
10: 5 were girded with *f* gold of Uphaz:
Zec 9: 3 and *f* gold as the mire of the streets.
M'r 15:46 And he bought *f* linen, and took
Lu 16:19 was clothed in purple and *f* linen,
Re 1:15 And his feet like unto *f* brass,
2:18 and his feet are like *f* brass;
18:12 and of pearls, and *f* linen, and purple,
13 and *f* flour, and wheat, and
16 great city, that was clothed in *f* linen,
19: 8 that she should be arrayed in *f* linen,
8 the *f* linen is the righteousness of
14 clothed in *f* linen, white and clean.

finer
Pr 25: 4 come forth a vessel for the *f*.

finest
Ps 81:16 them also with the *f* of the wheat:
147:14 filleth thee with the *f* of the wheat.

finger See also FINGERS.
Ex 8:19 Pharaoh, This is the *f* of God:
29:12 the horns of the altar with thy *f*,
31:18 stone, written with the *f* of God.
Le 4: 6 priest shall dip his *f* in the blood,
17 the priest shall dip his *f* in some
25 blood of the sin offering with his *f*,
30 take of the blood thereof with his *f*,
34 blood of the sin offering with his *f*,
8:15 of the altar round about with his *f*,
9: 9 he dipped his *f* in the blood,
14:16 the priest shall dip his right *f* in
16 sprinkle of the oil with his *f* seven
27 shall sprinkle with his right *f* some
16:14 and sprinkle it with his *f* seven
14 of the blood with his *f* seven times.
19 blood upon it with his *f* seven times,
Nu 19: 4 shall take of her blood with his *f*,
De 9:10 them was written with the *f* of God;
1Ki 12:10 My little *f* shall be thicker than
2Ch 10:10 My little *f* shall be thicker than
Isa 58: 9 the putting forth of the *f*, and
Lu 11:20 with the *f* of God cast out devils,
16:24 may dip the tip of his *f* in water,
Joh 8: 6 with his *f* wrote on the ground,
20:25 put my *f* into the print of the nails,
27 Reach hither thy *f*, and behold my

fingers
2Sa 21:20 that had on every hand six *f*,
1Ch 20: 6 *f* and toes were four and twenty,
Ps 8: 3 thy heavens, the work of thy *f*,
144: 1 my hands to war, and my *f* to fight:
Pr 6:13 his feet, he teacheth with his *f*;
7: 3 Bind them upon thy *f*, write them
Ca 5: 5 my *f* with sweet smelling myrrh,
Isa 2: 8 that which their own *f* have made:
17: 8 that which his *f* have made,
59: 3 and your *f* with iniquity; your lips
Jer 52:21 the thickness thereof was four *f*:
Da 5: 5 In the same hour came forth *f* of a
M't 23: 4 move them with one of their *f*.
M'r 7:33 put his *f* into his ears, and he spit,
Lu 11:46 the burdens with one of your *f*.

fining
Pr 17: 3 The *f* pot is for silver, and the
27:21 As the *f* pot for silver, and the

fining-pot See FINING and POT.

finish See also FINISHED.
Ge 6:16 in a cubit shalt thou *f* it above;
Da 9:24 to *f* the transgresssion, and to
Zec 4: 9 his hands shall also *f* it;
Lu 14:28 whether he have sufficient to *f* it?
29 foundation, and is not able to *f* it,
30 to build, and was not able to *f*.
Joh 4:34 that sent me, and to *f* his work.
5:36 the Father hath given me to *f*,
Ac 20:24 I might *f* my course with joy,
Ro 9:28 will *f* the work, and cut it short
2Co 8: 6 he would also *f* in you the same

finished
Ge 2: 1 the heavens and the earth were *f*,
Ex 39:32 of the tent of the congregation *f*:
40:33 So Moses *f* the work.
De 31:24 law in a book, until they were *f*,
Jos 4:10 until every thing was *f* that the
Ru 3:18 until he have *f* the thing this day.
1Ki 6: 9 he built the house, and *f* it;
14 Solomon built the house, and *f* it.
22 until he had *f* all the house:
38 eighth month, was the house *f*
7: 1 and he *f* all his house.
22 so was the work of the pillars *f*.
9: 1 when Solomon had *f* the building
25 the Lord. So he *f* the house.
1Ch 27:24 Zeruiah began to number, but he *f*
28:20 until thou hast *f* all the work for
2Ch 4:11 Huram *f* the work that he was
5: 1 for the house of the Lord was *f*:
7:11 Solomon *f* the house of the Lord,
8:16 of the Lord, and until it was *f*.
24:14 when they had *f* it, they brought
29:28 until the burnt offering was *f*.
31: 1 Now when all this was *f*, all Israel
7 and *f* them in the seventh month.
Ezr 5:16 building, and yet it is not *f*.
6:14 And they builded, and *f* it,
15 this house was *f* on the third day
Ne 6:15 So the wall was *f* in the twenty
Da 5:26 numbered thy kingdom, and *f* it.
12: 7 all these things shall be *f*.
M't 13:53 when Jesus had *f* these parables,
19: 1 when Jesus had *f* these sayings,
26: 1 when Jesus had *f* all these sayings,
Joh 17: 4 I have *f* the work which thou
19:30 he said, It is *f*: and he bowed
Ac 21: 7 And when we had *f* our course
2Ti 4: 7 I have *f* my course, I have kept
Heb 4: 3 works were *f* from the foundation
Jas 1:15 sin, when it is *f*, bringeth forth
Re 10: 7 the mystery of God should be *f*,
11: 7 they shall have *f* their testimony,
20: 5 until the thousand years were *f*.

finisher
Heb 12: 2 Jesus the author and *f* of our

finite See INFINITE.

fins
Le 11: 9 hath *f* and scales in the waters,
10 have not *f* and scales in the seas,
12 Whatsoever hath no *f* nor scales

De 14: 9 have f and scales shall ye eat:
10 not f and scales ye may not eat;

fir
2Sa 6: 5 of instruments made of f wood,
1Ki 5: 8 and concerning timber of f.
10 gave Solomon cedar trees and f
6:15 of the house with planks of f.
34 the two doors were of f tree:
9:11 with cedar trees and f trees, and
2Ki 19:23 and the choice f trees thereof:
2Ch 2: 8 Send me also cedar trees, f trees,
3: 5 greater house he cieled with f tree,
Ps 104:17 stork, the f trees are her house.
Ca 1:17 are cedar, and our rafters of f.
Isa 14: 8 Yea, the f trees rejoice at thee,
37:24 and the choice f trees thereof:
41:19 I will set in the desert the f tree,
55:13 the thorn shall come up the f tree,
60:13 f tree, the pine tree, and the box
Eze 27: 5 thy ship boards of f trees of Senir:
31: 8 f trees were not like his boughs,
Ho 14: 8 I am like a green f tree.
Na 2: 3 f trees shall be terribly shaken.
Zec 11: 2 f tree; for the cedar is fallen;

fire^ See also FIREBRAND; FIREPANS; FIRES.
Ge 19:24 brimstone and f from the Lord out
22: 6 and he took the f in his hand, and a
7 Behold, the f and the wood:
Ex 3: 2 appeared unto him in a flame of f
2 behold, the bush burned with f,
9:23 the f ran along upon the ground;
24 and f mingled with the hail, very
12: 8 roast with f, and unleavened bread;
9 but with f; his head with his legs,
10 the morning ye shall burn with f.
13:21 and by night in a pillar of f,
22 nor the pillar of f by night,
14:24 the pillar of f and of the cloud,
19:18 the Lord descended upon it in f:
22: 6 If f break out, and catch in thorns,
6 that kindled the f shall surely
24:17 like devouring f on the top of the
29:14 his dung, shalt thou burn with f
18, 25 offering made by f unto the Lord.
34 shalt burn the remainder with f:
41 an offering made by f unto the Lord.
30:20 an offering made by f unto the Lord:
32:20 burnt it in the f, and ground it
24 then I cast it into the f,
35: 3 Ye shall kindle no f throughout
40:38 and f was on it by night,
Le 1: 7 the priest shall put f upon the altar,
7 and lay the wood in order upon the f:
8 upon the wood that is on the f
9 burnt sacrifice, an offering made by f,
12 upon the wood that is on the f
13 offering made by f, of a sweet savour
17 upon the wood that is upon the f:
17 offering made by f, of a sweet savour
2: 2 offering made by f, of sweet savour
3 the offerings of the Lord made by f.
9 offering made by f, of sweet savour
10 the offerings of the Lord made by f.
11 any offering of the Lord made by f.
14 green ears of corn dried by the f,
16 an offering made by f unto the Lord.
3: 3 an offering made by f unto the Lord:
5 upon the wood that is on the f:
5 offering made by f, of a sweet savour
9 an offering made by f unto the Lord;
11 the offering made by f unto the Lord.
14 an offering made by f unto the Lord.
16 offering made by f of a sweet savour
4:12 burn him on the wood with f:
35 the offerings made by f unto the Lord:
5:12 offerings made by f unto the Lord:
6: 9 the f of the altar shall be burning
10 ashes which the f hath consumed
12 f upon the altar shall be burning in
13 The f shall ever be burning upon
17 portion of my offerings made by f;
18 the offerings of the Lord made by f:
30 it shall be burnt in the f.
7: 5 an offering made by f unto the Lord:
17 third day shall be burnt with f.
19 be with f: and as for the flesh,
25 an offering made by f unto the Lord:
30 the offerings of the Lord made by f,
35 the offerings of the Lord made by f,
8:17 be burnt with f without the camp;
21 an offering made by f unto the Lord;
28 an offering made by f unto the Lord.
32 the bread shall ye burn with f.
9:11 he burnt with f without the camp.
24 came a f out from before the Lord,
10: 1 them his censer, and put f therein,
1 offered strange f before the Lord,
2 there went out f from the Lord,
12 the offerings of the Lord made by f,
13 the sacrifices of the Lord made by f:
15 the offerings made by f of the fat,
13:52 it shall be burnt in the f.
55 thou shalt burn it in the f;
57 that wherein the plague is with f.
16:12 a censer full of burning coals of f
13 he shall put the incense upon the f
27 they shall burn in the f their skins,
18:21 seed pass through the f to Molech,
19: 6 it shall be burnt in the f.
20:14 be burnt with f, both he and they;
21: 6 the offerings of the Lord made by f,
9 she shall be burnt with f.
21 the offerings of the Lord made by f:
22:22 nor make an offering by f of them
27 an offering made by f unto the Lord.
Le 23: 8 ye shall offer an offering made by f
13 an offering made by f unto the Lord
18 an offering made by f, of sweet savour
25 ye shall offer an offering made by f
27 and offer an offering made by f
36 ye shall offer an offering made by f
36 ye shall offer an offering made by f
37 to offer an offering made by f
24: 7 an offering made by f unto the Lord.
9 the offerings of the Lord made by f
Nu 3: 4 offered strange f before the Lord,
6:18 put it in the f which is under the
9:15 as it were the appearance of f,
16 and the appearance of f by night.
11: 1 f of the Lord burnt among them,
2 unto the Lord, the f was quenched.
3 because the f of the Lord burnt
14:14 and in a a pillar of f by night.
15: 3 And will make an offering by f
10 of wine, for an offering made by f.
13 in offering an offering made by f,
14 offering made by f, of a sweet savour
25 a sacrifice made by f unto the Lord,
16: 7 put f therein, and put incense
18 and put f in them, and laid incense
35 there came out a f from the Lord,
37 scatter thou the f yonder; for they
46 put f therein from off the altar,
18: 9 holy things, reserved from the f:
17 offering made by f, for a sweet savour
21:28 there is a f gone out of Heshbon,
26:10 time the f devoured two hundred
61 offered strange f before the Lord.
28: 2 bread for my sacrifices made by f,
3 This is the offering made by f
6 a sacrifice made by f unto the Lord.
8 a sacrifice made by f, of a sweet
13 a sacrifice made by f unto the Lord.
19 ye shall offer a sacrifice made by f
24 the meat of the sacrifice made by f,
29: 6 a sacrifice made by f unto the Lord.
13, 36 a sacrifice made by f, of a sweet
31:10 and all their goodly castles, with f.
23 Every thing that may abide the f,
23 ye shall make it go through the f,
23 abideth not the f ye shall make go
De 1:33 in f by night, to shew you by what
4:11 the mountain burned with f unto
12 unto you out of the midst of the f:
15 Horeb out of the midst of the f;
24 the Lord thy God is a consuming f,
33 speaking out of the midst of the f,
36 earth he shewed thee his great f;
36 his words out of the midst of the f.
5: 4 mount out of the midst of the f,
5 ye were afraid by reason of the f,
22 the mount out of the midst of the f,
23 (for the mountain did burn with f,)
24 his voice out of the midst of the f:
25 for this great f will consume us:
26 speaking out of the midst of the f,
7: 5 burn their graven images with f.
25 of their gods shall ye burn with f:
9: 3 as a consuming f he shall destroy
10 the mount out of the midst of the f
15 and the mount burned with f:
21 burnt it with f, and stamped it,
10: 4 the mount out of the midst of the f
12: 3 and burn their groves with f;
31 have burnt in the f to their gods.
13:16 and shalt burn with f the city,
18: 1 offerings of the Lord made by f,
10 his daughter to pass through the f,
16 neither let me see this great f
32:22 For a f is kindled in mine anger,
22 set on f the foundations of the
Jos 6:24 And they burnt the city with f,
7:15 accursed thing shall be burnt with f,
25 and burned them with f, after they
8: 8 that ye shall set the city on f:
19 and hasted and set the city on f.
11: 6 and burn their chariots with f.
9 and burnt their chariots with f.
11 and he burnt Hazor with f.
13:14 sacrifices of the Lord...made by f
J'g 1: 8 of the sword, and set the city on f.
6:21 there rose up f out of the rock,
9:15 let f come out of the bramble,
20 let f come out from Abimelech,
20 and let f come out from the men of
49 and set the hold on f upon them;
52 of the tower to burn it with f.
12: 1 burn thine house upon thee with f.
14:15 thee and thy father's house with f:
15: 5 when he had set the brands on f,
6 burnt her and her father with f.
14 as flax that was burnt with f,
16: 9 tow is broken when it toucheth the f.
18:27 and burnt the city with f.
20:48 also they set on f all the cities
1Sa 2:28 offerings made by f of the children
30: 1 Ziklag, and burned it with f;
3 behold, it was burned with f;
14 and we burned Ziklag with f.
2Sa 14:30 hath barley there; go and set it on f.
30 servants set the field on f.
31 have thy servants set my field on f?
22: 9 and f out of his mouth devoured:
13 before him were coals of f kindled.
23: 7 they shall be utterly burned with f
1Ki 9:16 taken Gezer, and burned it with f,
16:18 the king's house over him with f,
18:23 lay it on wood, and put no f under:
23 lay it on wood, and put no f under:
24 and the God that answereth by f,
25 of your gods, but put no f under.
1Ki 18:38 Then the f of the Lord fell,
19:12 a f; but the Lord was not in the f
12 and after the f a still small voice.
2Ki 1:10 then let f come down from heaven,
10 there came down f from heaven,
12 let f come down from heaven,
12 f of God came down from heaven,
14 there came f down from heaven,
2:11 a chariot of f, and horses of f, and
6:17 was full of horses and chariots of f
8:12 their strong holds wilt thou set on f,
16: 3 made his son to pass through the f,
17:17 daughters to pass through the f,
31 burnt their children in f to
19:18 And have cast their gods into the f:
21: 6 he made his son pass through the f,
23:10 to pass through the f to Molech.
11 the chariots of the sun with f.
25: 9 great man's house burnt he with f.
1Ch 14:12 and they were burned with f.
21:26 he answered him from heaven by f
2Ch 7: 1 the f came down from heaven,
3 Israel saw how the f came down,
28: 3 and burnt his children in the f,
33: 6 his children to pass through the f
35:13 they roasted the passover with f
36:19 burnt all the palaces thereof with f,
Ne 1: 3 the gates thereof are burned with f.
2: 3 gates thereof are consumed with f?
13 gates thereof were consumed with f.
17 the gates thereof are burned with f:
9:12 and in the night by a pillar of f,
19 neither the pillar of f by night,
Job 1:16 The f of God is fallen from heaven,
15:34 f shall consume the tabernacles of
18: 5 the spark of his f shall not shine.
20:26 a f not blown shall consume him:
22:20 remnant of them the f consumeth.
28: 5 it is turned up as it were f.
31:12 For it is a f that consumeth to
41:19 and sparks of f leap out.
Ps 11: 6 f and brimstone, and an horrible
18: 8 and f out of his mouth devoured:
12 passed, hail stones and coals of f.
13 his voice; hail stones and coals of f.
21: 9 wrath, and the f shall devour them.
29: 7 the Lord divideth the flames of f.
39: 3 while I was musing the f burned:
46: 9 he burneth the chariot in the f.
50: 3 a f shall devour before him,
57: 4 even among them that are set on f,
66:12 through f and through water:
68: 2 as wax melteth before the f, so let
74: 7 They have cast f into thy sanctuary,
78:14 and all the night with a light of f.
21 so a f was kindled against Jacob,
63 The f consumed their young men;
79: 5 shall thy jealousy burn like f?
80:16 It is burned with f, it is cut down:
83:14 As the f burneth a wood, and as
14 flame setteth the mountains on f;
89:46 shall thy wrath burn like f?
97: 3 A f goeth before him, and burneth
104: 4 spirits; his ministers a flaming f:
105:32 rain, and flaming f in their land.
39 and f to give light in the night.
106:18 a f was kindled in their company;
118:12 are quenched as the f of thorns:
140:10 let them be cast into the f;
148: 8 F, and hail; snow, and vapours;
Pr 6:27 Can a man take f in his bosom,
16:27 in his lips there is as a burning f.
25:22 shalt heap coals of f upon his head,
26:20 no wood is, there the f goeth out:
21 to burning coals, and wood to f;
30:16 and the f that saith not, It is
Ca 8: 6 the coals thereof are coals of f,
Isa 1: 7 your cities are burned with f:
4: 5 the shining of a flaming f by night:
5:24 as the f devoureth the stubble,
9: 5 shall be with burning and fuel of f.
18 For wickedness burneth as the f:
19 people shall be as the fuel of the f:
10:16 a burning like the burning of a f.
17 the light of Israel shall be for a f,
26:11 the f of thine enemies shall devour
27:11 women come, and set them on f
29: 6 and the flame of devouring f.
30:14 a sherd to take f from the hearth,
27 and his tongue as a devouring f:
30 the flame of a devouring f, with
33 pile thereof is f and much wood;
31: 9 saith the Lord, whose f is in Zion,
33:11 your breath, as f, shall devour you.
12 cut up shall they be burned in the f.
14 shall dwell with the devouring f?
37:19 And have cast their gods into the f:
42:25 it hath set him on f round about,
43: 2 when thou walkest through the f,
44:16 He burneth part thereof in the f;
16 I am warm, I have seen the f:
19 I have burned part of it in the f;
47:14 as stubble; the f shall burn them;
14 to warm at, nor f to sit before it.
50:11 Behold, all ye that kindle a f,
11 walk in the light of your f, and in
54:16 that bloweth the coals in the f,
64: 2 As when the melting f burneth,
2 the f causeth the waters to boil,
11 praised thee, is burned up with f:
65: 5 a f that burneth all the day.
66:15 behold, the Lord will come with f,
15 and his rebuke with flames of f.
16 For by f and by his sword will the
24 neither shall their f be quenched;
Jer 4: 4 lest my fury come forth like f,

Jer 5:14 make my words in thy mouth *f*,
6: 1 up a sign of *f* in Beth-haccerem:
29 the lead is consumed of the *f*;
7:18 and the fathers kindle the *f*,
31 sons and their daughters in the *f*;
11:16 he hath kindled *f* upon it, and the
15:14 for a *f* is kindled in mine anger,
17: 4 ye have kindled a *f* in mine anger,
27 then will I kindle a *f* in the gates
19: 5 to burn their sons with *f* for burnt
20: 9 as a burning *f* shut up in my bones,
21:10 and he shall burn it with *f*.
12 lest my fury go out like *f*,
14 and I will kindle a *f* in the forest
22: 7 cedars, and cast them into the *f*.
23:29 Is not my word like as a *f*?
29:22 king of Babylon roasted in the *f*;
32:29 shall come and set *f* on this city,
34: 2 and he shall burn it with *f*:
22 and take it, and burn it with *f*:
36:22 and there was a *f* on the hearth
23 into the *f* that was on the hearth,
23 all the roll was consumed in the *f*
32 king of Judah had burned in the *f*:
37: 8 and take it, and burn it with *f*.
10 tent, and burn this city with *f*.
38:17 this city shall not be burnt with *f*;
18 and they shall burn it with *f*,
23 cause this city to be burned with *f*.
39: 8 the houses of the people, with *f*,
43:12 And I will kindle a *f* in the houses
13 Egyptians shall he burn with *f*.
48:45 *f* shall come forth out of Heshbon,
49: 2 daughters shall be burned with *f*:
27 And I will kindle a *f* in the wall of
50:32 and I will kindle a *f* in his cities,
51:32 the reeds they have burned with *f*,
58 high gates shall be burned with *f*;
58 and the folk in the *f*, and they shall
52:13 of the great men, burned he with *f*:
La 1:13 above hath he sent *f* into my bones,
2: 3 against Jacob like a flaming *f*,
4 he poured out his fury like *f*.
4:11 and hath kindled a *f* in Zion,
Eze 1: 4 *f* infolding itself, and a brightness
4 amber, out of the midst of the *f*.
13 was like burning coals of *f*,
13 the *f* was bright, and out of the *f*
27 as the appearance of *f* round about
27 as it were the appearance of *f*,
5: 2 Thou shalt burn with *f* a third part
4 cast them into the midst of the *f*,
4 and burn them in the *f*;
4 for thereof shall a *f* come forth into
8: 2 a likeness as the appearance of *f*:
2 downward, *f*; and from his loins
10: 2 fill thine hand with coals of *f* from
6 Take *f* from between the wheels,
7 *f* that was between the cherubims,
15: 4 into the *f* for fuel; the *f* devoureth
5 when the *f* hath devoured it,
6 which I have given to the *f* for fuel,
7 they shall go out from one *f*,
7 and another *f* shall devour them;
16:21 them to pass through the *f* for them?
41 they shall burn thine houses with *f*,
19:12 withered; the *f* consumed them.
14 And *f* is gone out of a rod of her
20:26 through the *f* all that openeth the
31 your sons to pass through the *f*,
47 Behold, I will kindle a *f* in thee,
21:31 against thee in the *f* of my wrath,
32 Thou shalt be for fuel to the *f*;
22:20 to blow the *f* upon it, to melt it;
21 blow upon you in the *f* of my wrath,
31 them with the *f* of my wrath:
23:25 residue shall be devoured by the *f*.
37 to pass for them through the *f*, to
47 and burn up their houses with *f*.
24: 9 even make the pile for *f* great.
10 Heap on wood, kindle the *f*,
12 her scum shall be in the *f*.
28:14 down in the midst of the stones of *f*.
16 from the midst of the stones of *f*.
18 therefore will I bring forth a *f* from
30: 8 when I have set a *f* in Egypt,
14 will set *f* in Zoan, and will execute
16 And I will set *f* in Egypt:
36: 5 Surely in the *f* of my jealousy have
38:19 in the *f* of my wrath have I spoken,
22 great hailstones, *f*, and brimstone.
39: 6 And I will send a *f* on Magog,
9 and shall set on *f* and burn the
9 burn them with *f* seven years:
10 shall burn the weapons with *f*:
Da 3:22 the flame of the *f* slew those men
24 bound into the midst of the *f*?
25 loose, walking in the midst of the *f*,
26 came forth of the midst of the *f*.
27 whose bodies the *f* had no power,
27 the smell of *f* had passed on them.
7: 9 and his wheels as burning *f*.
10: 6 and his eyes as lamps of *f*,
Ho 7: 6 morning it burneth as a flaming *f*.
8:14 but I will send a *f* upon his cities,
Joe 1:19 for the *f* hath devoured the pastures
20 the *f* hath devoured the pastures
2: 3 A *f* devoureth before them; and
5 like the noise of a flame of *f* that
30 blood, and *f*, and pillars of smoke.
Am 1: 4 I will send a *f* into the house of
7 I will send a *f* on the wall of Gaza,
10 I will send a *f* on the wall of Tyrus,
12 I will send a *f* upon Teman,
14 will kindle a *f* in the wall of Rabbah,
2: 2 I will send a *f* upon Moab,

Am 2: 5 I will send a *f* upon Judah,
5: 6 lest he break out like *f* in the house
7: 4 Lord God called to contend by *f*,
Ob 18 And the house of Jacob shall be a *f*,
Mic 1: 4 wax before the *f*, and as the waters
7 thereof shall be burned with the *f*.
Na 1: 6 his fury is poured out like *f*,
3:13 the *f* shall devour thy bars.
15 There shall the *f* devour thee;
Hab 2:13 people shall labour in the very *f*,
Zep 1:18 land shall be devoured by the *f* of
3: 8 earth shall be devoured with the *f*
Zec 2: 5 will be unto her a wall of *f* round
3: 2 this a brand plucked out of the *f*?
9: 4 and she shall be devoured with *f*.
11: 1 that the *f* may devour thy cedars.
12: 6 like an hearth of *f* among the wood,
6 and like a torch of *f* in a sheaf;
13: 9 bring the third part through the *f*,
Mal 1:10 neither do ye kindle *f* on mine altar
3: 2 for he is like a refiner's *f*,
M't 3:10 is hewn down, and cast into the *f*.
11 with the Holy Ghost, and with *f*:
12 up the chaff with unquenchable *f*.
5:22 fool, shall be in danger of hell *f*.
7:19 is hewn down, and cast into the *f*.
13:40 are gathered and burned in the *f*;
42 shall cast them into a furnace of *f*:
50 cast them into the furnace of *f*:
17:15 for ofttimes he falleth into the *f*,
18: 8 feet to be cast into everlasting *f*.
9 two eyes to be cast into hell *f*.
25:41 into everlasting *f*, prepared for the
M'r 9:22 it hath cast him into the *f*,
43 the *f* that never shall be quenched:
44 not, and the *f* is not quenched.
45 the *f* that never shall be quenched:
46 not, and the *f* is not quenched.
47 two eyes to be cast into hell *f*:
48 not, and the *f* is not quenched.
49 every one shall be salted with *f*,
14:54 and warmed himself at the *f*.
Lu 3: 9 is hewn down, and cast into the *f*.
16 with the Holy Ghost and with *f*:
17 he will burn with *f* unquenchable.
9:54 that we command *f* to come down
12:49 I am come to send *f* on the earth;
17:29 it rained *f* and brimstone from
22:55 And when they had kindled a *f*
56 beheld him as he sat by the *f*,
Joh 15: 6 them, and cast them into the *f*,
18:18 had made a *f* of coals; for it was cold:
21: 9 they saw a *f* of coals there, and fish
Ac 2: 3 them cloven tongues like as of *f*,
19 blood, and *f*, and vapour of smoke:
7:30 the Lord in a flame of *f* in a bush.
28: 2 they kindled a *f*, and received us
3 of sticks, and laid them on the *f*,
5 he shook off the beast into the *f*,
Ro 12:20 shalt heap coals of *f* on his head.
1Co 3:13 shall be revealed by *f*; and the *f*
15 shall be saved; yet so as by *f*.
2Th 1: 8 In flaming *f* taking vengeance on
Heb 1: 7 and his ministers a flame of *f*.
11:34 Quenched the violence of *f*,
12:18 and that burned with *f*, nor unto
29 For our God is a consuming *f*.
Jas 3: 5 great a matter a little *f* kindleth!
6 tongue is a *f*, a world of iniquity:
6 setteth on *f* the course of nature;
6 and it is set on *f* of hell.
5: 3 shall eat your flesh as it were *f*.
1Pe 1: 7 though it be tried with *f*, might
2Pe 3: 7 reserved unto *f* against the day of
12 being on *f* shall be dissolved,
Jude 7 the vengeance of eternal *f*.
23 fear, pulling them out of the *f*;
Re 1:14 and his eyes were as a flame of *f*;
2:18 hath his eyes like unto a flame of *f*,
3:18 to buy of me gold tried in the *f*,
4: 5 seven lamps of *f* burning before
8: 5 and filled it with *f* of the altar,
7 hail and *f* mingled with blood,
8 a great mountain burning with *f*
9:17 having breastplates of *f*, and of
17 out of their mouths issued *f* and
18 killed, by the *f*, and by the smoke,
10: 1 and his feet as pillars of *f*:
11: 5 *f* proceedeth out of their mouth,
13:13 maketh *f* come down from heaven
14:10 tormented with *f* and brimstone
18 which had power over *f*; and cried
15: 2 were a sea of glass mingled with *f*:
16: 8 unto him to scorch men with *f*.
17:16 eat her flesh, and burn her with *f*.
18: 8 she shall be utterly burned with *f*:
19:12 His eyes were as a flame of *f*,
20 lake of *f* burning with brimstone.
20: 9 and *f* came down from God out of
10 into the lake of *f* and brimstone,
14 hell were cast into the lake of *f*.
15 of life was cast into the lake of *f*.
21: 8 burneth with *f* and brimstone:

firebrand See also FIREBRANDS.
J'g 15: 4 turned tail to tail, and put a *f*
Am 4:11 ye were as a *f* plucked out of the

firebrands
J'g 15: 4 and took *f* and turned tail to tail,
Pro 26:18 As a mad man who casteth *f*,
Isa 7: 4 for the two tails of these smoking *f*,

firepans
Ex 27: 3 and his fleshhooks, and his *f*:
38: 3 and the fleshhooks, and the *f*:
2Ki 25:15 And the *f*, and the bowls, and such
Jer 52:19 the basons, and the *f*, and the bowls,

fires
Isa 24:15 glorify ye the Lord in the *f*, even

firkins
Joh 2: 6 containing two or three *f* apiece.

firm See also AFFIRM; CONFIRM.
Jos 3:17 the covenant of the Lord stood *f*
4: 3 where the priests' feet stood *f*,
Job 41:23 they are *f* in themselves; they
24 His heart is as *f* as a stone; they
Ps 73: 4 but their strength is *f*.
Dan 6: 7 and to make a *f* decree,
Heb 3: 6 rejoicing of the hope *f* unto the end.

firmament
Gen 1: 6 Let there be a *f* in the midst of
7 God made the *f*, and divided the
7 which were under the *f* from the
7 the waters which were above the *f*:
8 And God called the *f* Heaven.
14 Let there be lights in the *f* of the
15 for lights in the *f* of heaven to give
17 God set them in the *f* of heaven to
20 earth in the open *f* of heaven.
Ps 19: 1 and the *f* sheweth his handywork.
150: 1 praise him in the *f* of his power.
Eze 1:22 the likeness of the *f* upon the heads
23 And under the *f* were their wings
25 And there was a voice from the *f*
26 And above the *f* that was over their
10: 1 in the *f* that was above the head
Dan 12: 3 shine as the brightness of the *f*;

first^ See also FIRSTBORN; FIRSTBEGOTTEN; FIRSTFRUIT; FIRSTLING; FIRSTRIPE.
Gen 1: 5 and the morning were the *f* day.
2:11 The name of the *f* is Pison:
8: 5 on the *f* day of the month, were
13 in the six hundredth and *f* year, in
13 the *f* [7223] month, the *f* day of the
13: 4 which he had made there at the *f*:
25:25 And the *f* came out red, all over
26: 1 the *f* famine that was in the days
28:19 that city was called Luz at the *f*.
38:28 saying, This came out *f*.
41:20 did eat up the *f* seven fat kine:
43:18 in our sacks at the *f* time are we
20 we came indeed down at the *f* time
Ex 4: 8 hearken to the voice of the *f* sign,
12: 2 be the *f* month of the year to you.
5 blemish, a male of the *f* year;
15 the *f* day ye shall put away leaven
15 from the *f* day until the seventh
16 in the *f* day there shall be an holy
18 In the *f* month, on the fourteenth
22:29 to offer the *f* of thy ripe fruits,
23:19 The *f* of the firstfruits of thy land
28:17 the *f* row shall be a sardius, a
17 carbuncle: this shall be the *f* row.
29:38 two lambs of the *f* year day by
34: 1 tables of stone like unto the *f*:
1 the words that were in the *f* tables,
4 two tables of stone like unto the *f*:
26 The *f* of the firstfruits of thy land
39:10 the *f* row was a sardius, a topaz,
10 a carbuncle: this was the *f* row.
40: 2 On the *f* day of the...month shalt
2 On the...day of the *f* month shalt
17 the *f* month in the second year,
17 on the *f* day of the month, that the
Le 4:21 and burn him as he burned the *f*
5: 8 that which is for the sin offering *f*,
9: 3 and a lamb, both of the *f* year,
15 and offered it for sin, as the *f*.
12: 6 shall bring a lamb of the *f* year
14:10 and one ewe lamb of the *f* year
23: 5 the fourteenth day of the *f* month
7 In the *f* day ye shall have an holy
12 lamb without blemish of the *f*
18 lambs without blemish of the *f*
19 two lambs of the *f* year for a
24 In the seventh month, in the *f* day
35 On the *f* day shall be an holy
39 on the *f* day shall be a sabbath,
40 take you on the *f* day the boughs
Nu 1: 1, 18 the *f* day of the second month,
2: 9 armies. These shall *f* set forth.
6:12 shall bring a lamb of the *f* year
14 Lord, one he lamb of the *f* year
14 and one ewe lamb of the *f* year
7:12 he that offered his offering the *f*
15 one ram, one lamb of the *f* year,
17 goats, five lambs of the *f* year:
21 one lamb of the *f* year, for a
23 five lambs of the *f* year: this
27 one lamb of the *f* year, for a
29 goats, five lambs of the *f* year:
33 one ram, one lamb of the *f* year,
35 five lambs of the *f* year: this
39 one lamb of the *f* year, for a
41 five lambs of the *f* year: this
45 one ram, one lamb of the *f* year,
47 goats, five lambs of the *f* year:
51 one ram, one lamb of the *f* year,
53 goats, five lambs of the *f* year:
57 one ram, one lamb of the *f* year,
59 goats, five lambs of the *f* year:
63 one ram, one lamb of the *f* year,
65 goats, five lambs of the *f* year:
69 one ram, one lamb of the *f* year,
71 goats, five lambs of the *f* year:
75 one ram, one lamb of the *f* year,
77 goats, five lambs of the *f* year:
81 one ram, one lamb of the *f* year,
83 goats, five lambs of the *f* year:
87 the lambs of the *f* year twelve,

Nu 7:88 the lambs of the f year sixty.
9: 1 in the f month of the second year
5 f month at even in the wilderness
10:13 they f took their journey according
14 In the f place went the standard
15:20 up a cake of the f of your dough
21 Of the f of your dough ye shall give
27 bring a she goat of the f year
18:13 whatsoever is f ripe in the land,
20: 1 the desert of Zin in the f month:
24:20 Amalek was the f of the nations;
28: 3, 9 lambs of the f year without
11 seven lambs of the f year without
16 fourteenth day of the f month
18 f day shall be an holy convocation;
19 and seven lambs of the f year:
27 ram, seven lambs of the f year;
29: 1 in the seventh month, on the f day
2 seven lambs of the f year without
8 and seven lambs of the f year
13 and fourteen lambs of the f year;
17, 20 fourteen lambs of the f year
23, 26, 29, 32 two rams, and fourteen
lambs of the f year without
36 ram, seven lambs of the f year
33: 3 from Rameses in the f month,
3 on the fifteenth day of the f month;
38 in the f day of the fifth month.
De 1: 3 the f day of the month, that Moses
9:18 down before the Lord, as at the f,
25 as I fell down at the f; because
10: 1 two tables of stone like unto the f,
2 the words that were in the f tables
3 two tables of stone like unto the f,
4 according to the f writing, the ten
10 mount, according to the f time,
11:14 the f rain and the latter rain,
13: 9 thine hand shall be f upon him
16: 4 thou sacrificedst the f day at even,
17: 7 hands of the witnesses shall be f
18: 4 f fleece of the fleece of thy sheep,
26: 2 thou shalt take of the f of all the
33:21 he provided the f part for himself.
Jos 4:19 on the tenth day of the f month,
8: 5 come out against us, as at the f,
6 They flee before us, as at the f:
21:10 Levi, had: for their's was the f lot.
J'g 1: 1 for us against the Canaanites f,
18:29 name of the city was Laish at the f.
20:18 Which of us shall go up f to the
18 Lord said, Judah shall go up f.
22 themselves in array the f day.
32 smitten down before us, as at the f.
39 down before us, as in the f battle.
1Sa 14:14 that f slaughter, which Jonathan
35 same was the f altar that he built
2Sa 3:13 f bring Michael Saul's daughter,
17: 9 of them be overthrown at the f,
19:20 I am come the f this day of all the
43 that our advice should not be f
21: 9 the days of harvest, in the f days,
23:19 he attained not unto the f three.
23 but he attained not unto the f three.
1Ki 16:23 In the thirty and f year of Asa
17:13 make me thereof a little cake f,
18:25 for yourselves, and dress it f;
20: 9 send for to thy servant at the f
17 princes of the provinces went out f;
1Ch 9: 2 f inhabitants that dwelt in their
11: 6 Whosoever smiteth the Jebusites f
6 Joab the son of Zeruiah went f up,
21 howbeit he attained not to the f three.
25 but attained not to the f three:
12: 9 Ezer the f, Obadiah the second,
15 went over Jordan in the f month,
15:13 because ye did it not at the f,
16: 7 David delivered f this psalm to
23:19 Jeriah the f, Amariah the second,
20 Micah the f, and Jesiah the
24: 7 the f lot came forth to Jehoiarib,
21 of Rehabiah, the f was Isshiah.
23 Jeriah the f, Amariah the second,
25: 9 the f lot came forth for Asaph
27: 2 Over the f course for the f month
3 captains of the host for the f month.
29:29 acts of David the king, f and last,
2Ch 3: 3 f measure was threescore cubits,
9:29 the acts of Solomon, f and last,
12:15 the acts of Rehoboam, f and last,
16:11 the acts of Asa, f and last,
17: 3 in the f ways of his father David,
20:34 the acts of Jehoshaphat, f and last,
25:26 the acts of Amaziah, f and last,
26:22 the acts of Uzziah, f and last,
28:26 acts and of all his ways, f and last,
29: 3 He in the f year of his reign,
3 in the f month, opened the doors of
17 on the f day of the f month to
17 in the sixteenth day of the f month
35: 1 the fourteenth day of the f month.
27 And his deeds, f and last, behold,
36:22 the f year of Cyrus king of Persia,
Ezr 1: 1 the f year of Cyrus king of Persia,
3: 6 From the f day of the seventh month
12 men, that had seen the f house,
5:13 But in the f year of Cyrus the king
6: 3 In the f year of Cyrus the king
19 the fourteenth day of the f month.
7: 9 For upon the f day of the...month
9 day of the f month began he to go
9 and on the f day of the fifth month
8:31 on the twelfth day of the f month,
10:16 in the f day of the tenth month to
17 wives by the f day of the...month.
17 wives by the...day of the f month.
Ne 7: 5 of them which came up at the f,

Ne 8: 2 the f day of the seventh month.
18 from the f day unto the last day,
Es 1:14 which sat the f in the kingdom;)
3: 7 In the f month, that is, the month
12 the thirteenth day of the f month,
Job 15: 7 Art thou the f man that was born?
42:14 And he called the name of the f,
Pr 18:17 He that is f in his own cause
Isa 1:26 will restore thy judges as at the f,
9: 1 when at the f he lightly afflicted
41: 4 the Lord, the f, and with the last;
27 The f shall say to Zion, Behold,
43:27 Thy f father hath sinned, and thy
44: 6 I am the f, and I am the last; and
48:12 he; I am the f, I also am the last.
60: 9 the ships of Tarshish f, to bring
Jer 4:31 that bringeth forth her f child,
7:12 where I set my name at the f,
16:18 f I will recompense their iniquity
24: 2 even like the figs that are f ripe:
25: 1 was the f year of Nebuchadrezzar
33: 7 and will build them, as at the f.
11 the captivity of the land, as at the f,
36:28 words that were in the f roll,
50:17 away: f the king of Assyria hath
52:31 f year of his reign lifted up the head
Eze 10:14 the f face was the face of a cherub,
26: 1 in the f day of the month, that the
29:17 in the f month, in the...day of the
17 in the f day of the month, the word
30:20 the f month, in the seventh day
31: 1 in the f day of the month, that the
32: 1 in the f day of the month, that the
40:21 were the measure of the f gate:
44:30 And the f of all the firstfruits
30 unto the priest the f of your dough,
45:18 In the f month, in the...day of the
18 in the f day of the month, thou shalt
21 In the f month, in the fourteenth
46:13 of a lamb of the f year without
Da 1:21 even unto the f year of king Cyrus.
6: 2 presidents of whom Daniel was f:
7: 1 In the f year of Belshazzar king
4 The f was like a lion, and had
8 three of the f horns plucked up
24 he shall be diverse from the f,
8: 1 which appeared unto me at the f.
21 between his eyes is the f king.
9: 1 In the f year of Darius the son of
2 In the f year of his reign I Daniel
10: 4 and twentieth day of the f month,
12 from the f day that thou didst set
11: 1 Also I in the f year of Darius the
Ho 2: 7 go and return to my f husband;
9:10 in the fig tree at her f time: but
Joe 2:23 and the latter rain in the f month.
Am 6: 7 captive with the f that go captive,
Mic 4: 8 the f dominion; the kingdom
Hag 1: 1 in the f day of the month, came the
2: 3 saw this house in her f glory?
Zec 6: 2 In the f chariot were red horses;
12: 7 also shall save the tents of Judah f,
14:10 gate unto the place of the f gate,
M't 5:24 f be reconciled to thy brother,
6:33 But seek ye f the kingdom of God,
7: 5 f cast out the beam out of thine
8:21 suffer me f to go and bury my
10: 2 The f, Simon, who is called Peter,
12:29 except he f bind the strong man?
45 of that man is worse than the f.
13:30 Gather ye together f the tares,
17:10 scribes that Elias must f come?
11 Elias truly shall f come, and
27 take up the fish that f cometh up;
19:30 But many that are f shall be last;
30 shall be last; and the last shall be f.
20: 8 beginning from the last unto the f.
10 when the f came, they supposed
16 the last shall be f, and the f last:
21:28 and he came to the f, and said,
31 They say unto him, The f.
36 other servants more than the f:
22:25 and the f, when he had married a
38 is the f and great commandment.
23:26 cleanse f that which is within the
26:17 Now the f day of the feast of
27:64 last error shall be worse than the f.
28: 1 toward the f day of the week,
M'r 3:27 he will f bind the strong man;
4:28 f the blade, then the ear, after that
7:27 Let the children f be filled: for it
9:11 the scribes that Elias must f come?
12 Elias verily cometh f, and restoreth
35 man desire to be f, the same shall
10:31 But many that are f shall be last;
31 shall be last; and the last f.
12:20 f took a wife, and dying left no
28 Which is the f commandment of
29 The f of all the commandments is,
30 this is the f commandment.
13:10 the gospel must f be published
14:12 the f day of unleavened bread,
16: 2 morning the f day of the week,
9 early the f day of the week,
9 he appeared f to Mary Magdalene,
Lu 1: 3 of all things from the very f,
2: 2 taxing was f made when Cyrenius
6: 1 the second sabbath after the f,
42 hypocrite, cast out f the beam
9:59 suffer me f to go and bury my
61 but let me f go bid them farewell,
10: 5 f say, Peace be to this house.
11:26 of that man is worse than the f.
38 had not f washed before dinner.
12: 1 to say unto his disciples f of all,
13:30 shall be f, and there are f which

Lu 14:18 f said unto him, I have bought
28 sitteth not down f, and counteth
31 sitteth not down f, and consulteth
16: 5 and said unto the f, How much
17:25 But f must he suffer many things,
19:16 Then came the f, saying, Lord,
20:29 and the f took a wife, and died
21: 9 these things must f come to pass;
24: 1 Now upon the f day of the week,
Joh 1:41 f findeth his own brother Simon,
5: 4 then f after the troubling of the
8: 7 let him f cast a stone at her.
10:40 place where John at f baptized;
12:16 not his disciples at the f: but when
18:13 And led him away to Annas f; for
19:32 and brake the legs of the f, and of
39 at the f came to Jesus by night,
20: 1 f day of the week cometh Mary
4 Peter, and came f to the sepulchre.
8 which came f to the sepulchre, and
19 being the f day of the week,
Ac 3:26 Unto you f God, having raised up
7:12 Egypt, he sent out our fathers f.
11:26 were called Christians f in Antioch.
12:10 past the f and the second ward,
13:24 When John had f preached before his
46 should f have been spoken to you:
15:14 how God at the f did visit the
20: 7 And upon the f day of the week,
18 know, from the f day that I came
26: 4 at the f among mine own nation
20 shewed f unto them of Damascus
23 should be the f that should rise
27:43 cast themselves f into the sea,
Ro 1: 8 F, I thank my God through Jesus
16 to the Jew f, and also to the Greek.
2: 9 the Jew f, and also of the Gentile;
10 the Jew f, and also to the Gentile:
10:19 F Moses saith, I will provoke you
11:35 Or who hath f given to him,
15:24 if f I be somewhat filled with your
1Co 11:18 For f of all, when ye come
12:28 f apostles, secondarily prophets,
14:30 sitteth by, let the f hold his peace.
15: 3 I delivered unto you f of all
45 f man Adam was made a living
46 that was not f which is spiritual,
47 The f man is of the earth, earthy:
16: 2 Upon the f day of the week let
subscr. The f epistle to the Corinthians
2Co 8: 5 f gave their own selves to the
12 if there be f a willing mind,
Ga 4:13 the gospel unto you at the f.
Eph 1:12 who f trusted in Christ.
4: 9 also descended f into the lower
6: 2 f commandment with promise;
Ph'p 1: 5 gospel from the f day until now;
1Th 4:16 the dead in Christ shall rise f:
subscr. f epistle unto the Thessalonians
2Th 2: 3 except there come a falling away f,
1Ti 1:16 in me f Jesus Christ might shew
2: 1 f of all, supplications, prayers,
13 Adam was f formed, then Eve.
3:10 And let these also f be proved;
5: 4 let them learn f to shew piety
12 they have cast off their f faith.
subscr. The f to Timothy was written for
2Ti 1: 5 which dwelt f in thy grandmother
2: 6 must be f partaker of the fruits.
4:16 At my f answer no man stood with
subscr. Timotheus, ordained the f bishop
Tit 3:10 after the f and second admonition
subscr. Titus, ordained the f bishop of
Heb 2: 3 which at the f began to be spoken
4: 6 they to whom it was f preached
5:12 f principles of the oracles of God;
7: 2 f being by interpretation King of
27 f for his own sins, and then for
8: 7 that f covenant had been faultless,
13 covenant, he hath made the f old.
9: 1 Then verily the f covenant had
2 the f, wherein was the candlestick,
6 went always into the f tabernacle,
8 while as the f tabernacle was yet
15 that were under the f testament,
18 the f testament was dedicated
10: 9 He taketh away the f, that he may
Jas 3:17 is f pure, then peaceable, gentle,
1Pe 4:17 and if it f begin at us, what shall
2Pe 1:20 Knowing this f, that no prophecy
3: 3 Knowing this f, that there shall
1Jo 4:19 love him, because he f loved us.
Jude 6 which kept not their f estate,
Re 1: 5 and the f begotten of the dead,
11 Alpha and Omega, the f and the
17 Fear not; I am the f and the last:
2: 4 because thou hast left thy f love.
5 and do the f works; or else I will
8 saith the f and the last, which was
19 and the last to be more than the f.
4: 1 and the f voice which I heard was
7 And the f beast was like a lion,
8: 7 The f angel sounded, and there
13:12 all the power of the f beast before
12 therein to worship the f beast,
16: 2 the f went, and poured out his vial
20: 5 This is the f resurrection.
6 hath part in the f resurrection:
21: 1 the f heaven and the f earth were
19 the f foundation was jasper; the
22:13 and the end, the f and the last.

firstbegotten See also FIRST and BEGOTTEN.
Heb 1: 6 bringeth in the f into the world,

firstborn
Ge 10:15 Canaan begat Sidon his f, and

Ge 19:31 And the f said unto the younger,
33 f went in, and lay with her father,
34 f said unto the younger, Behold,
37 f bare a son, and called his name
22:21 Huz his f, and Buz his brother,
25:13 f of Ishmael, Nebajoth; and Kedar,
27:19 I am Esau thy f; I have done
32 he said, I am thy son, thy f Esau.
29:26 to give the younger before the f.
35:23 Reuben, Jacob's f, and Simeon,
36:15 sons of Eliphaz the f son of Esau;
38: 6 And Judah took a wife for Er his f,
7 Er, Judah's f, was wicked in the
41:51 called the name of the f Manasseh:
43:33 the f according to his birthright,
46: 8 and his sons: Reuben, Jacob's f.
48:14 for Manasseh was the f.
18 Not so, my father: for this is the f;
49: 3 Reuben, thou art my f, my might,
Ex 4:22 Israel is my son, even my f:
23 I will slay thy son, even thy f.
6:14 the f of Israel; Hanoch and Pallu,
11: 5 all the f in the land of Egypt shall
5 die, from the f of Pharaoh that
5 unto the f of the maidservant that
5 the mill; and all the f of beasts.
12:12 and will smite all the f in the land
29 Lord smote all the f in the land of
29 from the f of Pharaoh that sat on
29 unto the f of the captive that was
29 dungeon; and all the f of cattle.
13: 2 Sanctify unto me all the f,
13 the f of man among thy children
15 the Lord slew all the f in the land
15 of Egypt, both the f of man, and
15 of man, and the f of beast:
15 all the f of my children I redeem.
22:29 the f of thy sons shalt thou give
34:20 the f of thy sons thou shalt redeem,
Nu 3: 2 Nadab the f, and Abihu, Eleazar,
12 all the f that openeth the matrix
13 Because all the f are mine; for on
13 on the day that I smote all the f of
13 I hallowed unto me all the f in
40 Number all the f of the males of the
41 instead of all the f among the
42 all the f among the children of
43 And all the f males by the number
45 Take the Levites instead of all the f
46 of the f of the children of Israel,
50 Of the f of the children of Israel
8:16 even instead the f of all the children
17 For all the f of the children of Israel
17 day that I smote every f in the land
18 have taken the Levites for all the f
18:15 f of man shalt thou surely redeem,
33: 4 the Egyptians buried all their f,
De 21:15 the f son be hers that was hated:
16 not make the son of the beloved f
16 of the hated, which is indeed the f:
17 the son of the hated for the f,
17 strength; the right of the f is his.
25: 6 f which she beareth shall succeed
Jos 6:26 lay the foundation thereof in his f,
17: 1 for he was the f of Joseph;
1 for Machir the f of Manasseh,
J'g 8:20 And he said unto Jether his f,
1Sa 8: 2 Now the name of his f was Joel;
14:49 the name of the f Merab,
17:13 Eliab the f, and next unto him
2Sa 3: 2 and his f was Amnon, of Ahinoam
1Ki 16:34 foundation thereof in Abiram his f,
1Ch 1:13 And Canaan begat Zidon his f, and
29 The f of Ishmael, Nebaioth; then
2: 3 And Er, the f of Judah, was evil
13 begat his f Eliab, and Abinadab
25 the f of Hezron were, Ram the f,
27 the sons of Ram the f of Jerahmeel
42 of Jerahmeel were, Mesha his f,
50 Hur, the f of Ephratah; Shobal the
3: 1 the f Amnon, of Ahinoam the
15 f Johanan, the second Jehoiakim,
4: 4 the sons of Hur, the f of Ephratah,
5: 1 the sons of Reuben the f of Israel,
1 (for he was the f; but, forasmuch
3 I say, of Reuben the f of Israel were,
6:28 the sons of Samuel; the f Vashni,
8: 1 Now Benjamin begat Bela his f,
30 And his f son Abdon, and Zur, and
39 Ulam his f, Jehush the second,
9: 5 Asaiah the f, and his sons.
31 who was the f of Shallum the
36 And his f son Abdon, then Zur, and
26: 2 Zechariah the f, Jediael the second,
4 were, Shemiah the f, Jehozabad the
10 not the f, yet his father made him
2Ch 21: 3 to Jehoram; because he was the f.
Ne 10:36 Also the f of our sons, and of our
Job 18:13 the f of death shall devour his
Ps 78:51 And smote all the f in Egypt;
89:27 Also I will make him my f,
105:36 smote also all the f in their land,
135: 8 Who smote the f of Egypt,
136:10 him that smote Egypt in their f:
Isa 14:30 And the f of the poor shall feed,
Jer 31: 9 to Israel, and Ephraim is my f.
Mic 6: 7 I give my f for my transgression,
Zec 12:10 as one that is in bitterness for his f.
M't 1:25 she had brought forth her f son:
Lu 2: 7 And she brought forth her f son,
Ro 8:29 be the f among many brethren.
Col 1:15 God, the f of every creature:
18 the beginning, the f from the dead;
Heb 11:28 destroyed the f shall touch them.
12:23 assembly and church of the f,

firstfruit See also FIRSTFRUITS.
De 18: 4 f also of thy corn, of thy wine,
Ro 11:16 if the f be holy, the lump is also

firstfruits
Ex 23:16 the f of thy labours, which thou
19 The first of the f of thy land thou
34:22 f of wheat harvest, and the feast
26 first of the f of thy land thou shalt
Le 2:12 the oblation of the f, ye shall offer
14 offer a meat offering of thy f
14 offer for the meat offering of thy f
23:10 ye shall bring a sheaf of the f of
17 they are the f unto the Lord.
20 wave them with the bread of the f
Nu 18:12 f of them which they shall offer
28:26 Also in the day of the f, when ye
De 26:10 I have brought the f of the land,
2Ki 4:42 bread of the f, twenty loaves of
2Ch 31: 5 the f of corn, wine, and oil, and
Ne 10:35 And to bring the f of our ground,
35 and the f of all fruit trees, yearly
37 should bring the f of our dough,
12:44 for the f, and for the tithes, to
13:31 at times appointed, and for the f.
Pr 3: 9 with the f of all thine increase:
Jer 2: 3 the Lord, and the f of his increase:
Eze 20:40 and the f of your oblations,
44:30 the first of all the f of all things,
48:14 nor alienate the f of the land:
Ro 8:23 which have the f of the Spirit,
16: 5 who is the f of Achaia unto Christ.
1Co 15:20 and become the f of them that slept,
23 Christ the f; afterward they that
16:15 Stephanas, that it is the f of Achaia,
Jas 1:18 be a kind of f of his creatures,
Re 14: 4 the f unto God and to the Lamb.

firstling See also FIRSTLINGS.
Ex 13:12 every f that cometh of a beast
13 every f of an ass thou shalt redeem
34:19 and every f among thy cattle,
20 the f of an ass thou shalt redeem
Le 27:26 Only the f of the beasts, which
26 which should be the Lord's f, no
Nu 18:15 the f of unclean beasts shall thou
17 But the f of a cow, or the f of a
17 a sheep, or the f of a goat, thou
De 15:19 All the f males that come of thy
19 no work with the f of thy bullock,
19 nor shear the f of thy sheep.
33:17 glory is like the f of his bullock,

firstlings
Ge 4: 4 also brought of the f of his flock
Nu 3:41 instead of all the f among the
De 12: 6 and the f of your herds
17 the f of thy herds or of thy flock,
14:23 the f of your herds and of your
Ne 10:36 f of our herds and of our flocks,

firstripe See also FIRST and RIPE.
Nu 13:20 was the time of the f grapes.
Ho 9:10 I saw your fathers as the f in the
Mic 7: 1 eat: my soul desired the f fruit.
Na 3:12 be like fig trees with the f figs:

fir-tree See FIR and TREE.

fir-wood See FIR and WOOD.

fish See also FISHERMEN; FISHER'S; FISHERS; FISHES; FISHHOOKS; FISHING; FISHPOOLS; FISH'S.
Ge 1:26, 28, dominion over the f of the sea,
Ex 7:18 And the f that is in the river shall
21 And the f that was in the river died,
Nu 11: 5 remember the f, which we did eat
22 or shall all the f of the sea be
De 4:18 of any f that is in the waters
2Ch 33:14 the entering in at the f gate,
Ne 3: 3 f gate did the sons of Hassenaah
12:39 above the f gate, and the tower
13:16 which brought f, and all manner
Job 41: 7 irons? or his head with f spears?
Ps 8: 8 the f of the sea, and whatsoever
105:29 into blood, and slew their f.
Isa 19:10 make sluices and ponds for f.
50: 2 their f stinketh, because there is
Jer 16:16 and they shall f them; and after
Eze 29: 4 I will cause the f of thy rivers to
4 all the f of thy rivers shall stick
5 thee and all the f of thy rivers:
47: 9 be a very great multitude of f,
10 f shall be according to their kinds,
10 as the f of the great sea,
Jon 1:17 the Lord had prepared a great f
17 Jonah was in the belly of the f
2:10 And the Lord spake unto the f,
Zep 1:10 the noise of a cry from the f gate,
M't 7:10 Or if he ask a f, will he give him
17:27 take up the f that first cometh up;
Lu 11:11 or if he ask a f, will he for a f give
24:42 gave him a piece of a broiled f,
Joh 21: 9 and f laid thereon, and bread.
10 the f which ye have now caught.
13 and giveth them, and f likewise.

fishermen
Lu 5: 2 but the f were gone out of them,

fisher's
Joh 21: 7 he girt his f coat unto him, (for

fishers
Isa 19: 8 The f also shall mourn, and all
Jer 16:16 Behold, I will send for many f,
Eze 47:10 that the f shall stand upon it
M't 4:18 a net into the sea: for they were f.
19 I will make you f of men.
M'r 1:16 a net into the sea: for they were f.
17 I will make you to become f of men.

fishes
Ge 9: 2 shall be upon all the f of the sea;
1Ki 4:33 and of creeping things, and of f.
Job 12: 8 the f of the sea shall declare unto
Ec 9:12 the f that are taken in an evil net,
Eze 38:20 So that the f of the sea, and the
Ho 4: 3 the f of the sea also shall be taken
Hab 1:14 makest men as the f of the sea,
Zep 1: 3 and the f of the sea, and the
M't 14:17 here but five loaves, and two f.
19 took the five loaves, and the two f,
15:34 said, Seven, and a few little f.
36 took the seven loaves and the f,
M'r 6:38 they say, Five, and two f.
41 taken the five loaves and the two f,
41 the two f divided he among them
43 full of the fragments, and of the f.
8: 7 And they had a few small f:
Lu 5: 6 inclosed a great multitude of f:
9 draught of the f which they had
9:13 no more but five loaves and two f;
16 took the five loaves and the two f,
Joh 6: 9 barley loaves, and two small f:
11 and likewise of the f as much as
21: 6 to draw it for the multitude of f.
8 dragging the net with f.
11 drew the net to land full of great f,
1Co 15:39 another of f, and another of birds.

fish-gate See FISH and GATE.

fishhooks
Am 4: 2 and your posterity with f.

fishing
Joh 21: 3 Peter saith unto them, I go a f.

fishpools
Ca 7: 4 thine eyes like the f in Heshbon

fish's
Jon 2: 1 Lord his God out of the f belly,

fist See also FISTS.
Ex 21:18 or with his f, and he die not,
Isa 58: 4 to smite with the f of wickedness:

fists
Pr 30: 4 hath gathered the wind in his f?

fit See also FITTED; FITTETH.
Le 16:21 by the hand of a f man into the
1Ch 7:11 soldiers, f to go out for war
12: 8 and men of war f for the battle,
Job 34:18 Is it f to say to a king, Thou art
Pr 24:27 make it f for thyself in the field:
Lu 9:62 back, is f for the kingdom of God.
14:35 It is neither f for the land, nor yet
Ac 22:22 it is not f that he should live.
Col 3:18 husbands, as it is f in the Lord.

fitches
Isa 28:25 cast abroad the f, and scatter the
27 For the f are not threshed with a
27 the f are beaten out with a staff,
Eze 4: 9 and lentiles, and millet, and f,

fitly
Pr 25:11 word f spoken is like apples,
Ca 5:12 washed with milk, and f set.
Eph 2:21 all the building f framed together
4:16 the whole body f joined together

fitted
1Ki 6:35 with gold f upon the carved work.
Pr 22:18 they shall withal be f in thy lips.
Ro 9:22 vessels of wrath f to destruction:

fitteth
Isa 44:13 he f it with planes, and he

five
Ge 5: 6 lived an hundred and f years,
11 nine hundred and f years: and
15 Mahalaleel lived sixty and f years,
17 eight hundred ninety and f years:
21 Enoch lived sixty and f years,
23 three hundred sixty and f years:
30 f hundred ninety and f years,
32 Noah was f hundred years old:
11:11 f hundred years, and begat sons
12 Arphaxad lived f and thirty years,
32 were two hundred and f years:
12: 4 Abram was seventy and f years old
14: 9 of Ellasar; four kings with f.
18:28 Peradventure there shall lack f of
28 destroy all the city for lack of f?
28 If I find there forty and f, I will
43:34 Benjamin's mess was f times so
45: 6 and yet there are f years, in the
11 yet there are f years of famine;
22 silver, and f changes of raiment.
47: 2 some of his brethren, even f men,
Ex 22: 1 he shall restore f oxen for an ox,
26: 3 The f curtains shall be coupled
3 other f curtains shall be coupled
9 couple f curtains by themselves,
26 f for the boards of the one side
27 f bars for the boards of the other
27 f bars for the boards of the side of
37 make for the hanging f pillars
37 thou shalt cast f sockets of brass
27: 1 f cubits long, and f cubits broad;
18 the height f cubits of fine twined
30:23 of pure myrrh f hundred shekels,
24 And of cassia f hundred shekels,
36:10 the f curtains one unto another:
10 the other f curtains he coupled
16 coupled f curtains by themselves,
31 f for the boards of the one side of
32 f bars for the boards of the other
32 and f bars for the boards of the
38 f pillars of it with their hooks:

Ex 36:38 but their f sockets were of brass
38: 1 f cubits was the length thereof,
1 and f cubits the breadth thereof;
18 height in the breadth was f cubits,
26 three thousand and f hundred
28 hundred seventy and f shekels
Le 26: 8 f of you shall chase an hundred,
27: 5 from f years old even unto twenty
6 a month old even unto f years old,
6 of the male f shekels of silver,
Nu 1:21 and six thousand and f hundred.
25 forty and f thousand six hundred
33 forty thousand and f hundred.
37 and f thousand and four hundred.
41 and one thousand and f hundred.
46 thousand and f hundred and fifty.
2:11 and six thousand and f hundred.
15 f thousand and six hundred and
19 forty thousand and f hundred.
23 and f thousand and four hundred.
28 and one thousand and f hundred.
32 thousand and f hundred and fifty.
3:22 seven thousand and f hundred.
47 shalt even take f shekels apiece
50 and threescore and f shekels,
4:48 and f hundred and fourscore.
7:17, 23, 29, 35, 41, 47, 53, 59, 65, 71, 77, 83 f
rams, f he goats, f lambs of the
8:24 from twenty and f years old and
11:19 two days, nor f days, neither ten
18:16 for the money of f shekels, after
26:18 forty thousand and f hundred.
22 sixteen thousand and f hundred.
27 threescore thousand and f hundred
37 and two thousand and f hundred.
41 and f thousand and six hundred.
50 and f thousand and four hundred.
31: 8 f kings of Midian: Balaam also
28 one soul of f hundred, both of the
32 thousand and f thousand sheep,
36 thirty thousand and f hundred
39 thirty thousand and f hundred;
43 seven thousand and f hundred
45 thousand asses and f hundred,
Jos 8:12 he took about f thousand men,
10: 5 the f kings of the Amorites,
16 But these f kings fled, and hid
17 f kings are found hid in a cave
22 bring out those f kings unto me
23 brought forth those f kings unto
26 and hanged them on f trees:
13: 3 f lords of the Philistines; the
14:10 these forty and f years, even since
10 day fourscore and f years old.
J'g 3: 3 f lords of the Philistines,
18: 2 Dan sent of their family f men
7 Then the f men departed, and
14 answered the f men that went
17 the f men that went to spy
20:35 twenty and f thousand and an
45 in the highways f thousand men;
46 twenty and f thousand men that
1Sa 6: 4 F golden emerods, and f golden
16 when the f lords of the Philistines
18 Philistines belonging to the f
17: 5 was f thousand shekels of brass.
40 f smooth stones out of the brook,
21: 3 give me f loaves of bread
22:18 fourscore and f persons that did
25:18 and f sheep ready dressed,
18 and f measures of parched corn,
42 with f damsels of hers that went
2Sa 4: 4 He was f years old when the
21: 8 f sons of Michal the daughter of
24: 9 were f hundred thousand men.
1Ki 4:32 his songs were a thousand and f.
6: 6 chamber was f cubits broad,
10 against all the house, f cubits
24 And f cubits was the one wing
24 and f cubits the other wing
7: 3 on forty f pillars, f in a row.
16 one chapiter was f cubits, and the
16 height of the other chapiter was f
23 and his height was f cubits: and
39 put f bases on the right side of the
39 f on the left side of the house:
49 f on the right side,
49 and f on the left,
9:23 Solomon's work, f hundred and
22:42 Jehoshaphat was thirty and f
42 and he reigned twenty and f years
2Ki 6:25 a cab of dove's dung for f pieces
7:13 f of the horses that remain,
13:19 have smitten f or six times;
14: 2 twenty and f years old when he
15:33 F and twenty years old was he
18: 2 Twenty and f years old was he
19:35 hundred fourscore and f thousand:
21: 1 reigned fifty and f years in
23:36 twenty and f years old when he
25:19 and f men of them that were in
1Ch 2: 4 All the sons of Judah were f.
6 and Dara, f of them in all.
3:20 Hasadiah, Jushab-hesed, f.
4:32 and Tochen, and Ashan, f cities:
42 sons of Simeon, f hundred men,
7: 3 and Ishiah, f: all of them chief
7 and Jerimoth, and Iri, f; heads of
11:23 of great stature, f cubits high;
29: 7 f thousand talents and ten
2Ch 3:11 one wing of the one cherub was f
11 other wing was likewise f cubits
12 of the other cherub was f cubits,
12 the other wing was f cubits also,
15 two pillars of thirty and f cubits
15 top of each of them was f cubits.
2Ch 4: 2 and f cubits the height thereof;
6 lavers, and put f on the right hand,
6 and f on the left, to wash in them:
7 in the temple, f on the right hand,
7 right hand, and f on the left.
8 in the temple, f on the right side,
8 right side, and f on the left.
6:13 brasen scaffold, of f cubits long,
13 and f cubits broad, and three cubits
13:17 slain of Israel f hundred thousand
15:19 f and thirtieth year of the reign
20:31 thirty and f years old when he
31 and he reigned twenty and f years
25: 1 Amaziah was twenty and f years
26:13 and seven thousand and f hundred,
27: 1 Jotham was twenty and f years old
8 He was f and twenty years old
29: 1 when he was f and twenty years old,
33: 1 and he reigned fifty and f years in
35: 9 f thousand small cattle, and
9 small cattle, and f hundred oxen.
36: 5 Jehoiakim was twenty and f years
Ezr 1:11 were f thousand and four hundred.
2: 5 Arah, seven hundred seventy and f.
8 of Zattu, nine hundred forty and f.
20 children of Gibbar, ninety and f.
33 Ono, seven hundred twenty and f.
34 Jericho, three hundred forty and f.
66 mules, two hundred forty and f;
67 camels, four hundred thirty and f;
69 and f thousand pound of silver,
Ne 7:13 of Zattu, eight hundred forty and f.
20 of Adin, six hundred fifty and f.
25 children of Gibeon, ninety and f.
36 Jericho, three hundred forty and f.
67 hundred forty and f singing men
68 mules, two hundred forty and f:
69 camels, four hundred thirty and f:
70 f hundred and thirty priests'
Es 9: 6 slew and destroyed f hundred men.
12 and destroyed f hundred men in
16 their foes seventy and f thousand,
Job 1: 3 camels, and f hundred yoke of oxen,
3 of oxen, and f hundred she asses,
Isa 7: 8 and within threescore and f years
17: 6 four or f in the outmost fruitful
19:18 that day shall f cities in the land
30:17 at the rebuke of f shall ye flee:
37:36 and fourscore and f thousand:
Jer 52:22 of one chapiter was f cubits,
30 seven hundred forty and f persons:
31 in the f and twentieth day of the
Eze 8:16 were about f and twenty men,
11: 1 door of the gate f and twenty men;
40: 1 In the f and twentieth year of our
7 the little chambers were f cubits;
13 breadth was f and twenty cubits,
21, 25 the breadth f and twenty cubits.
29 and f and twenty cubits broad.
30 were f and twenty cubits long,
30 long, and f cubits broad.
33 and f and twenty cubits broad.
36 the breadth f and twenty cubits.
48 the porch, f cubits on this side,
48 this side, and f cubits on that side:
41: 2 the sides of the door were f cubits
2 and f cubits on that side:
9 chamber without, was f cubits:
11 was left was f cubits round about.
12 was f cubits thick round about,
42:16 reed, f hundred reeds, with the
17 the north side, f hundred reeds,
18 the south side, f hundred reeds,
19 and measured f hundred reeds
20 round about, f hundred reeds long,
20 and f hundred broad, to make
45: 1 length of f and twenty thousand
2 sanctuary f hundred in length,
2 with f hundred in breadth, square
3 length of f and twenty thousand,
5 f and twenty thousand of length,
6 of the city f thousand broad,
6 and f and twenty thousand long,
12 f and twenty shekels, fifteen
48: 8 offer of f and twenty thousand
9 shall be of f and twenty thousand
10 the north f and twenty thousand
10 the south f and twenty thousand
13 shall have f and twenty thousand
13 shall be f and twenty thousand,
15 And the f thousand, that are left
15 against the f and twenty thousand
16 north side four...and f hundred,
16 south side four...and f hundred,
16 east side four...and f hundred,
16 west side four...and f hundred.
20 f and twenty thousand by f and
21 city, over against the f and twenty
21 westward over against the f and
30 the north side, four thousand and f
32 the east side four thousand and f
33 the south side four thousand and f
34 the west side four thousand and f
Da 12:12 hundred and f and thirty days.
M't 14:17 here but f loaves, and two fishes.
19 the f loaves, and the two fishes,
21 were about f thousand men,
16: 9 neither remember the f loaves of
9 of the f thousand, and how many
25: 2 And f of them were wise,
2 were wise, and f were foolish.
15 And unto one he gave f talents,
16 he that had received the f talents
16 and made them other f talents.
20 so he that had received f talents
20 came and brought other f talents,
M't 25:20 thou deliveredst unto me f talents:
20 gained beside them f talents more.
M'r 6:38 they say, F, and two fishes.
41 when he had taken the f loaves
44 loaves were about f thousand men.
8:19 When I brake the f loaves among
19 loaves among the f thousand, how
Lu 1:24 hid herself f months, saying,
7:41 one owed f hundred pence, and
9:13 more but f loaves and two fishes;
14 For they were about f thousand
16 the f loaves and the two fishes,
12: 6 f sparrows sold for two farthings,
52 there shall be f in one house
14:19 I have bought f yoke of oxen,
16:28 For I have f brethren; that he
19:18 thy pound hath gained f pounds.
19 Be thou also over f cities.
Joh 4:18 For thou hast had f husbands; and
5: 2 tongue Bethesda, having f porches.
6: 9 which hath f barley loaves, and two
10 in number about f thousand.
13 fragments of the f barley loaves,
19 rowed about f and twenty or thirty
Ac 4: 4 of the men was about f thousand.
20: 6 came unto them to Troas in f days;
24: 1 And after f days Ananias the
1Co 14:19 church I had rather speak f words
15: 6 seen of above f hundred brethren
2Co 11:24 f times received I forty stripes
Rev 9: 5 should be tormented f months:
10 power was to hurt men f months.
17:10 f are fallen, and one is, and the

five-hundred See FIVE and HUNDRED.

five-thousand See FIVE and THOUSAND.

five-times See FIVE and TIMES.

fixed
Ps 57: 7 My heart is f, O God, my heart
7 O God, my heart is f: I will sing
108: 1 O God, my heart is f; I will sing
112: 7 his heart is f, trusting in the Lord.
Lu 16:26 us and you there is a great gulf f:

flag See also FLAGS.
Job 8:11 can the f grow without water?

flagon See also FLAGONS.
2Sa 6:19 piece of flesh, and a f of wine.
1Ch 16: 3 piece of flesh, and a f of wine.

flagons
Ca 2: 5 Stay me with f, comfort me with
Isa 22:24 even to all the vessels of f.
Hos 3: 1 to other gods, and love f of wine.

flags
Ex 2: 3 laid it in the f by the river's brink.
5 when she saw the ark among the f,
Isa 19: 6 the reeds and f shall wither.

flakes
Job 41:23 f of his flesh are joined together:

flame See also FLAMES; FLAMING; INFLAME.
Ex 3: 2 the Lord appeared unto him in a f
Nu 21:28 a f from the city of Sihon:
J'g 13:20 when the f went up toward heaven
20 of the Lord ascended in the f of
20:38 make a great f with smoke rise
40 But when the f began to rise
40 the f of the city ascended up
Job 15:30 the f shall dry up his branches,
41:21 and a f goeth out of his mouth.
Ps 83:14 as the f setteth the mountains
106:18 the f burned up the wicked.
Ca 8: 6 which hath a most vehement f.
Isa 5:24 and the f consumeth the chaff, so
10:17 and his Holy One for a f:
29: 6 and the f of devouring fire.
30:30 and with the f of a devouring fire,
Isa 43: 2 neither shall the f kindle upon
47:14 themselves from the power of the f
Jer 48:45 a f from the midst of Sihon,
Eze 20:47 flaming f shall not be quenched,
Da 3:22 the f of the fire slew those men
7: 9 his throne was like the fiery f
11 and given to the burning f.
11:33 shall fall by the sword, and by f,
Joe 1:19 the f hath burned all the trees
2: 3 and behind them a f burneth:
5 like the noise of a f of fire
Ob 18 and the house of Joseph a f,
Lu 16:24 for I am tormented in this f.
Ac 7:30 in a f of fire in a bush.
Heb 1: 7 and his ministers a f of fire.
Re 1:14 and his eyes were as a f of fire;
2:18 hath his eyes like unto a f of fire,
19:12 His eyes were as a f of fire,

flames
Ps 29: 7 voice of the Lord divideth the f
Isa 13: 8 their faces shall be as f.
66:15 and his rebuke with f of fire.

flaming See also ENFLAMING.
Ge 3:24 f sword which turned every way,
Ps 104: 4 and his ministers a f fire:
105:32 and f fire in their land.
Isa 4: 5 the shining of a f fire by night:
La 2: 3 burned against Jacob like a f fire,
Eze 20:47 the f flame shall not be quenched,
Ho 7: 6 the morning it burneth as a f fire.
Na 2: 3 shall be with f torches in the day
2Th 1: 8 In f fire taking vengeance on

flanks
Le 3: 4 is on them, which is by the f,
10, 15 upon them which is by the f,
4: 9 is upon them, which is by the f,

Le 7: 4 is on them, which is by the *f*.
Job 15:27 maketh collops of fat on his *f*.

flash
Eze 1:14 the appearance of a *f* of lightning.

flat
Le 21:18 or he that hath a *f* nose,
Nu 22:31 bowed down his head, and fell *f*.
Jos 6: 5 wall of the city shall fall down *f*,
20 that the wall fell down *f*, so that

flatter See also FLATTERETH; FLATTERING.
Ps 5: 9 they *f* with their tongue.
78:36 Nevertheless they did *f* him with

flattereth
Ps 36: 2 For he *f* himself in his own eyes,
Pr 2:16 stranger which *f* with her words;
7: 5 stranger which *f* with her words.
20:19 meddle not with him that *f*
28:23 than he that *f* with the tongue.
29: 5 A man that *f* his neighbour

flatteries
Da 11:21 and obtain the kingdom by *f*.
32 covenant shall he corrupt by *f*:
34 many shall cleave to them with *f*.

flattering
Job 32:21 let me give *f* titles unto man.
22 I know not to give *f* titles;
Ps 12: 2 *f* lips and with a double heart
3 The Lord shall cut off all *f* lips,
Pr 7:21 the *f* of her lips she forced him.
26:28 and a *f* mouth worketh ruin.
Eze 12:24 any vain vision nor *f* divination
1Th 2: 5 used we *f* words, as ye know,

flattery See also FLATTERIES.
Job 17: 5 that speaketh *f* to his friends,
Pr 6:24 from the *f* of the tongue of a

flax
Ex 9:31 the *f* and the barley was smitten:
31 in the ear, and the *f* was bolled
Jos 2: 6 and hid them with the stalks of *f*
J'g 15:14 were upon his arms became of *f*
Pr 31:13 seeketh wool, and *f*, and worketh
Isa 19: 9 Moreover they that work in fine *f*,
42: 3 smoking *f* shall he not quench:
Eze 40: 3 with a line of *f* in his hand,
Ho 2: 5 my wool and my *f*, mine oil and
9 wool and my *f* given to cover her
M't 12:20 smoking *f* shall he not quench,

flay See also FLAYED.
Le 1: 6 And he shall *f* the burnt offering,
2Ch 29:34 could not *f* all the burnt offerings:
Mic 3: 3 and *f* their skin from off them;

flayed
2Ch 35:11 hands, and the Levites *f* them.

flea
1Sa 24:14 after a dead dog, after a *f*.
26:20 of Israel is come out to seek a *f*,

fled See also FLEDDEST.
Ge 14:10 kings of Sodom and Gomorrah *f*,
10 that remained *f* to the mountain.
16: 6 Sarai dealt hardly with her, she *f*
31:20 in that he told him not that he *f*.
21 So he *f* with all that he had;
22 on the third day that Jacob was *f*.
35: 7 he *f* from the face of his brother.
39:12 his garment in her hand, and *f*,
13 his garment in her hand, and was *f*
15 with me and *f*, and got him out.
18 left his garment with me, and *f*.
Ex 2:15 Moses *f* from the face of Pharaoh,
4: 3 and Moses *f* from before it.
14: 5 king of Egypt that the people *f*:
27 appeared; and the Egyptians *f*
Nu 16:34 that were round about them *f*
35:25 of his refuge, whither he was *f*:
26 of his refuge, whither he was *f*;
32 for him that is *f* to the city of his
Jos 7: 4 and they *f* before the men of Ai.
8:15 and *f* by the way of the wilderness.
20 the people that *f* to the wilderness.
10:11 pass, as they *f* from before Israel,
16 But these five kings *f*, and hid
20: 6 unto the city from whence he *f*.
J'g 1: 6 Adoni-bezek *f*; and they pursued
4:15 his chariot, and *f* away on his feet.
17 Sisera *f* away on his feet to the
7:21 the host ran, and cried, and *f*.
22 and the host *f* to Beth-shittah
8:12 And when Zebah and Zalmunna *f*,
9:21 Jotham ran away, and *f*, and went
40 and he *f* before him, and many
51 thither *f* all the men and women,
11: 3 Jephthah *f* from his brethren,
20:45 and *f* toward the wilderness
47 But six hundred men turned and *f*
1Sa 4:10 and they *f* every man into his tent:
16 and I *f* to day out of the army.
17 Israel is *f* before the Philistines,
14:22 they heard that the Philistines *f*,
17:24 *f* from him, and were sore afraid.
51 their champion was dead, they *f*.
19: 8 slaughter; and they *f* from him.
10 David *f*, and escaped that night.
12 and he went, and *f*, and escaped.
18 So David *f*, and escaped, and came
20: 1 David *f* from Naioth in Ramah,
21:10 and *f* that day for fear of Saul,
22:17 and because they knew when he *f*,
20 escaped, and *f* after David.
23: 6 Abiathar the son of Ahimelech *f*
27: 4 it was told Saul that David was *f*
30:17 which rode upon camels, and *f*.
31: 1 the men of Israel *f* from before
1Sa 31: 7 saw that the men of Israel *f*, and
7 they forsook the cities, and *f*;
2Sa 1: 4 the people are *f* from the battle,
4: 3 And the Beerothites *f* to Gittaim,
4 and his nurse took him up, and *f*:
10:13 Syrians: and they *f* before him.
14 saw that the Syrians were *f*,
14 then *f* they also before Abishai,
18 And the Syrians *f* before Israel;
13:29 gat him up upon his mule, and *f*.
34 Absalom *f*. And the young man
37 Absalom *f*, and went to Talmai,
38 So Absalom *f*, and went to Geshur,
18:17 all Israel *f* every one to his tent.
19: 8 Israel had *f* every man to his tent.
9 and now he is *f* out of the land
23:11 the people *f* from the Philistines.
1Ki 2: 7 *f* because of Absalom thy brother.
28 And Joab *f* unto the tabernacle
29 told king Solomon that Joab was *f*
11:17 That Hadad *f*, he and certain
23 which *f* from his lord Hadadezer
40 Jeroboam arose, and *f* into Egypt,
12: 2 he was *f* from the presence of king
20:20 the Syrians *f*; and Israel pursued
30 the rest *f* to Aphek, into the city;
30 Ben-hadad *f*, and came into the
2Ki 3:24 so that they *f* before them:
7: 7 they arose and *f* in the twilight,
7 camp as it was, and *f* for their life.
8:21 and the people *f* into their tents.
9:10 And he opened the door, and *f*.
23 Joram turned his hands, and *f*,
27 *f* by the way of the garden house.
27 he *f* to Megiddo, and died there.
14:12 they *f* every man to their tents.
19 and he *f* to Lachish; but they sent
25: 4 and all the men of war *f* by night
1Ch 10: 1 the men of Israel *f* from before
7 were in the valley saw that they *f*,
7 they forsook their cities, and *f*:
11:13 *f* from before the Philistines.
19:14 the battle; and they *f* before him.
15 saw that the Syrians were *f*, they
15 they likewise *f* before Abishai his
18 But the Syrians *f* before Israel;
2Ch 10: 2 *f* from the presence of Solomon
13:16 children of Israel *f* before Judah:
14:12 Judah; and the Ethiopians *f*.
25:22 and they *f* every man to his tent.
27 and he *f* to Lachish: but they sent
Ne 13:10 singers, that did the work, were *f*
Ps 3 *title* he *f* from Absalom his son.
31:11 they that did see me without *f*
57 *title* he *f* from Saul in the cave.
104: 7 At thy rebuke they *f*; at the voice
114: 3 the sea saw it, and *f*: Jordan was
Isa 10:29 is afraid; Gibeah of Saul is *f*.
21:14 with their bread him that *f*.
15 For they *f* from the swords, from
22: 3 All thy rulers are *f* together,
3 together, which have *f* from far.
33: 3 noise of the tumult the people *f*;
Jer 4:25 all the birds of the heavens were *f*.
9:10 the heavens and the beast are *f*;
26:21 afraid and *f*, and went into Egypt;
39: 4 then they *f*, and went forth out of
46: 5 are beaten down, and are *f* apace,
21 back, and are *f* away together:
48:45 They that *f* stood under the shadow
52: 7 all the men of war *f*, and went
La 4:15 when they *f* away and wandered,
Da 10: 7 so that they *f* to hide themselves.
Ho 7:13 them! for they have *f* from me:
12:12 Jacob *f* into the country of Syria,
Jon 1:10 knew that he *f* from the presence
4: 2 I *f* before unto Tarshish:
Zec 14: 5 ye *f* from before the earthquake
M't 8:33 And they that kept them *f*, and
26:56 the disciples forsook him, and *f*.
M'r 5:14 And they that fed the swine *f*, and
14:50 And they all forsook him, and *f*.
52 cloth, and *f* from them naked.
16: 8 quickly, and *f* from the sepulchre;
Lu 8:34 they *f* and went and told it in the
Ac 7:29 Then *f* Moses at this saying, and
14: 6 and *f* unto Lystra and Derbe,
16:27 that the prisoners had been *f*.
19:16 they *f* out of that house naked
Heb 6:18 who have *f* for refuge to lay hold
Re 12: 6 the woman *f* into the wilderness,
16:20 And every island *f* away, and the
20:11 the earth and the heaven *f* away;

fleddest
Ge 35: 1 when thou *f* from the face of Esau
Ps 114: 5 ailed thee, O thou sea, that thou *f*?

flee See also FLED; FLEETH; FLEEING.
Ge 16: 8 *f* from the face of my mistress
19:20 now this city is near to *f* unto,
27:43 arise, *f* thou to Laban my brother
31:27 Wherefore didst thou *f* away
Ex 9:20 made his servants and his cattle *f*
14:25 Let us *f* from the face of Israel;
21:13 thee a place wither he shall *f*.
Le 26:17 and ye shall *f* when none pursueth
36 and they shall *f*, as fleeing from a
Nu 10:35 and let them that hate thee *f*
24:11 Therefore now *f* thou to thy place:
35: 6 that he may *f* thither: and to
11 that the slayer may *f* thither,
15 killeth any person unawares may *f*
De 4:42 That the slayer might *f* thither,
19: 3 that every slayer may *f* thither
4 the slayer, which shall *f* thither,
5 he shall *f* unto one of those cities.
De 28: 7 and *f* before thee seven ways.
25 and *f* seven ways before them:
Jos 8: 5 first, that we will *f* before them,
6 They *f* before us, as at the first:
6 therefore we will *f* before them.
20 they had no power to *f* this way
20: 3 unawares and unwittingly may *f*
4 And when he that doth *f* unto one
9 any person at unawares might *f*
J'g 20:32 Let us *f*, and draw them from the
2Sa 4: 4 as she made haste to *f*, that he fell,
15:14 and let us *f*: for we shall not else
17: 2 people that are with him shall *f*;
18: 3 for if we *f* away, they will not
19: 3 steal away when they *f* in battle.
24:13 or wilt thou *f* three months before
1Ki 12:18 up to his chariot, to *f* to Jerusalem.
2Ki 9: 3 open the door, and *f*, and tarry not.
2Ch 10:18 to his chariot, to *f* to Jerusalem.
Ne 6:11 Should such a man as I *f*?
Job 9:25 they *f* away, they see no good.
20:24 He shall *f* from the iron weapon,
27:22 he would fain *f* out of his hand.
30:10 abhor me, they *f* far from me,
41:28 The arrow cannot make him *f*:
Ps 11: 1 *F* as a bird to your mountain?
64: 8 all that see them shall *f* away.
68: 1 them also that hate him *f* before
12 Kings of armies did *f* apace:
139: 7 shall I *f* from thy presence?
143: 9 enemies: I *f* unto thee to hide me.
Pr 28: 1 wicked *f* when no man pursueth:
17 of any person shall *f* to the pit;
Ca 2:17 and the shadows *f* away, turn, my
4: 6 and the shadows *f* away, I will
Isa 10: 3 whom will ye *f* for help? and where
31 of Gebim gather themselves to *f*.
13:14 *f* every one into his own land.
15: 5 his fugitives shall *f* unto Zoar, an
17:13 and they shall *f* far off, and shall
20: 6 we *f* for help to be delivered
30:16 *f* upon horses; therefore shall ye *f*:
17 thousand shall *f* at the rebuke of one;
17 at the rebuke of five shall ye *f*:
31: 8 but he shall *f* from the sword,
35:10 sorrow and sighing shall *f* away.
48:20 *f* ye from the Chaldeans, with a
51:11 sorrow and mourning shall *f*
Jer 4:29 whole city shall *f* for the noise
6: 1 gather yourselves to *f* out of the
25:35 shepherds shall have no way to *f*,
46: 6 the swift *f* away, nor the mighty
48: 6 *F*, save your lives, and be like the
9 Moab, that it may *f* and get away:
49: 8 *F* ye, turn back, dwell deep,
24 feeble, and turneth herself to *f*,
30 *F*, get you far off, dwell deep,
50:16 they shall *f* every one to his own
28 voice of them that *f* and escape
51: 6 *F* out of the midst of Babylon,
Am 2:16 the mighty shall *f* away naked
5:19 As if a man did *f* from a lion,
7:12 go, *f* thee away into the land of
9: 1 fleeth of them shall not *f* away,
Jon 1: 3 Jonah rose up to *f* unto Tarshish
Na 2: 8 yet they shall *f* away. Stand,
3: 7 they that look upon thee shall *f*
17 when the sun ariseth they *f* away,
Zec 2: 6 and *f* from the land of the north,
14: 5 And ye shall *f* to the valley of the
5 yea, ye shall *f*, like as ye fled from
M't 2:13 *f* into Egypt, and be thou there
3: 7 you to *f* from the wrath to come?
10:23 *f* ye into another: for verily I say
24:16 them which be in Judæa *f* into the
M'r 13:14 them that be in Judæa *f* to the
Lu 3: 7 you to *f* from the wrath to come?
21:21 them which are in Judæa *f* to the
Joh 10: 5 will *f* from him: for they know not
Ac 27:30 were about to *f* out of the ship,
1Co 6:18 *F* fornication. Every sin that a
10:14 my dearly beloved, *f* from idolatry.
1Ti 6:11 O man of God, *f* these things;
2Ti 2:22 *F* also youthful lusts: but follow
Jas 4: 7 the devil, and he will *f* from you.
Re 9: 6 and death shall *f* from them.

fleece
De 18: 4 the first of the *f* of thy sheep,
J'g 6:37 I will put a *f* of wool in the floor;
37 and if the dew be on the *f* only,
38 thrust the *f* together, and wringed
38 and wringed the dew out of the *f*,
39 I pray thee, but this once with the *f*;
39 let it now be dry only upon the *f*,
40 for it was dry upon the *f* only,
Job 31:20 if he were not warmed with the *f*

fleeing
Le 26:36 they shall flee, as *f* from a sword;
De 4:42 and that *f* unto one of these cities
Job 30: 3 *f* into the wilderness in former

fleeth
De 19:11 and *f* into one of these cities:
Job 14: 2 he *f* also as a shadow, and
Isa 24:18 who *f* from the noise of the fear
Jer 48:19 ask him that *f*, and her that
44 he that *f* from the fear shall fall
Am 9: 1 he that *f* of them shall not flee
Na 3:16 cankerworm spoileth, and *f* away.
Joh 10:12 leaveth the sheep, and *f*: and the
13 The hireling *f*, because he is an

flesh See also FATFLESHED; FLESHHOOK; LEAN-FLESHED.
Ge 2:21 closed up the *f* instead thereof;
23 bone of my bones, and *f* of my *f*:

Ge 2:24 and they shall be one f.
6: 3 with man, for that he also is f:
12 for all f had corrupted his way
13 The end of all f is come before me;
17 destroy all f, wherein is the breath
19 And of every living thing of all f,
7:15 two of all f, wherein is the breath
16 went in male and female of all f,
21 all f died that moved upon the
8:17 of all f, both of fowl, and of cattle,
9: 4 But f with the life thereof, which is
11 neither shall all f be cut off any
15 and every living creature of all f;
15 become a flood to destroy all f.
16every living creature of all f that is
17 established between me and all f
17:11 circumcise the f of your foreskin;
13 my covenant shall be in your f for
14 whose f of his foreskin is not
23 circumcised the f of their foreskin
24, 25 circumcised in the f of his
29:14 Surely thou art my bone and my f.
37:27 for he is our brother and our f.
40:19 and the birds shall eat thy f from
Ex 4: 7 it was turned again as his other f.
12: 8 they shall eat the f in that night,
46 carry forth ought of the f abroad
16: 3 when we sat by the f pots,
8 give you in the evening f to eat,
12 At even ye shall eat f, and in the
21:28 and his f shall not be eaten;
22:31 shall ye eat any f that is torn of
29:14 the f of the bullock, and his skin,
31 and seethe his f in the holy place.
32 his sons shall eat the f of the ram,
34 ought of the f of the consecrations,
30:32 Upon man's f shall it not be poured,
Le 4:11 all his f, with his head, and with
6:10 breeches shall he put upon his f,
27 Whatsoever shall touch the f
7:15 And the f of the sacrifice of his
17 remainder of the f of the sacrifice
18 And if any of the f of the sacrifice
19 f that toucheth any unclean thing
19 as for the f, all that be clean shall
20 But the soul that eateth of the f
21 and eat of the f of the sacrifice of
8:17 the bullock, and his hide, his f,
31 Boil the f at the door of the
32 And that which remaineth of the f
9:11 And the f and the hide he burnt
11: 8 Of their f shall ye not eat, and their
11 ye shall not eat of their f, but ye
12: 3 the eighth day the f of his foreskin
13: 2 man shall have in the skin of his f
2 and it be in the skin of his f like
3 on the plague in the skin of his f:
3 be deeper than the skin of his f,
4 spot be white in the skin of his f,
10 there be quick raw f in the rising;
11 an old leprosy in the skin of his f,
13 the leprosy have covered all his f,
14 But when raw f appeareth in him,
15 And the priest shall see the raw f,
15 the raw f is unclean: it is a leprosy.
16 Or if the raw f turn again,
18 The f also, in which, even in the
24 there be any f, in the skin whereof
24 and the quick f that burneth have a
38 in the skin of their f bright spots,
39 bright spots in the skin of their f
43 appeareth in the skin of the f;
14: 9 also he shall wash his f in water,
15: 2 hath a running issue out of his f,
3 whether his f run with his issue,
3 or his f be stopped from his issue,
7 And he that toucheth the f of him
13 and bathe his f in running water,
16 then he shall wash all his f in
19 and her issue in her f be blood,
16: 4 have the linen breeches upon his f,
4 shall he wash his f in water, and so
24 And he shall wash his f with water
26 bathe his f in water, and afterward
27 their skins, and their f, and their
28 clothes, and bathe his f in water,
17:11 For the life of the f is in the blood;
14 For it is the life of all f;
14 eat the blood of no manner of f:
14 for the life of all f is the blood
16 nor bathe his f; then he shall bear
19:28 not make any cuttings in your f
21: 5 nor make any cuttings in their f.
22: 6 unless he wash his f with water.
26:29 And ye shall eat the f of your sons,
29 and the f of your daughters shall
Nu 8: 7 and let them shave all their f,
11: 4 said, Who shall give us f to eat?
13 Whence should I have f to give unto
13 saying, Give us f, that we may eat.
18 to-morrow, and ye shall eat f: for
18 saying, Who shall give us f to eat?
18 therefore the Lord will give you f,
21 thou hast said, I will give them f,
33 And while the f was yet between
12:12 of whom the f is half consumed
16:22 the God of the spirits of all f,
18:15 that openeth the matrix in all f,
18 And the f of them shall be thine,
19: 5 her skin, and her f, and her blood,
7 and he shall bathe his f in water,
8 and bathe his f in water, and shall
27:16 the God of the spirits of all f,
De 5:26 For who is there of all f, that hath
12:15 kill and eat f in all thy gates,
20 and thou shalt say, I will eat f,
De 12:20 because thy soul longeth to eat f;
20 thou mayest eat f, whatsoever
23 mayest not eat the life with the f.
27 the f and the blood, upon the altar
27 thy God, and thou shalt eat the f.
14: 8 ye shall not eat of their f, nor
16: 4 shall there any thing of the f,
28:53 f of thy sons and of thy daughters,
55 f of his children whom he shall eat:
32:42 and my sword shall devour f;
J'g 6:19 the f he put in a basket, and he put
20 Take the f and the unleavened
21 touched the f and the unleavened
21 consumed the f and the unleavened
8: 7 I will tear your f with the thorns
9: 2 that I am your bone and your f.
1Sa 2:13 came, while the f was in seething,
15 Give f to roast for the priest; for
15 he will not have sodden f of thee;
17:44 and I will give thy f unto the fowls
25:11 and my f that I have killed for my
2Sa 5: 1 Behold, we are thy bone and thy f.
6:19 and a good piece of f, and a flagon
19:12 ye are my bones and my f:
13 thou not of my bone, and of my f?
1Ki 17: 6 him bread and f in the morning,
6 and bread and f in the evening;
19:21 boiled their f with the instruments
21:27 sackcloth upon his f, and fasted,
2Ki 4:34 and the f of the child waxed warm
5:10 and thy f shall come again to thee,
14 his f came again like unto the f of
6:30 had sackcloth within upon his f.
9:36 shall dogs eat the f of Jezebel:
1Ch 11: 1 Behold, we are thy bone and thy f.
16: 3 a good piece of f, and a flagon of
2Ch 32: 8 With him is an arm of f;
Ne 5: 5 Yet now our f is as the f of our
Job 2: 5 now, and touch his bone and his f,
4:15 my face; the hair of my f stood up:
6:12 of stones? or is my f of brass?
7: 5 My f is clothed with worms and
10: 4 Hast thou eyes of f? or seest thou
11 hast clothed me with skin and f,
13:14 Wherefore do I take my f in my
14:22 his f upon him shall have pain,
19:20 cleaveth to my skin and to my f,
22 and are not satisfied with my f?
26 yet in my f shall I see God:
21: 6 and trembling taketh hold on my f
31:31 said not, Oh that we had of his f!
33:21 His f is consumed away, that it
25 His f shall be fresher than a
34:15 All f shall perish together, and
41:23 The flakes of his f are joined
Ps 16: 9 my f also shall rest in hope.
27: 2 came upon me to eat up my f,
38: 3 There is no soundness in my f
7 and there is no soundness in my f.
50:13 Will I eat the f of bulls, or drink
56: 4 I will not fear what f can do unto
63: 1 my f longeth for thee in a dry and
65: 2 unto thee shall all f come.
73:26 My f and my heart faileth: but
78:20 can he provide f for his people?
27 rained f also upon them as dust,
39 remembered that they were but f;
79: 2 the f of thy saints unto the beasts
84: 2 my heart and my f crieth out for
109:24 fasting, and my f faileth of fatness.
119:120 My f trembleth for fear of thee;
136:25 Who giveth food to all f: for his
145:21 and let all f bless his holy name
Pr 4:22 find them, and health to all their f.
5:11 thy f and thy body are consumed,
11:17 that is cruel troubleth his own f.
14:30 a sound heart is the life of the f:
23:20 among riotous eaters of f:
Ec 4: 5 together, and eateth his own f.
5: 6 not thy mouth to cause thy f to sin;
11:10 and put away evil from thy f:
12:12 much study is a weariness of the f.
Isa 9:20 every man the f of his own arm:
17: 4 the fatness of his f shall wax lean.
22:13 eating f, and drinking wine:
31: 3 and their horses f, and not spirit.
40: 5 and all f shall see it together:
6 What shall I cry? All f is grass,
44:16 with part thereof he eateth f; he
19 I have roasted f, and eaten it:
49:26 that oppress thee with their own f;
26 and all f shall know that I the Lord
58: 7 hide not thyself from thine own f?
65: 4 which eat swine's f, and broth of
66:16 will the Lord plead with all f:
17 the midst, eating swine's f, and the
23 all f come to worship before me,
24 shall be an abhorring unto all f.
Jer 7:21 unto your sacrifices, and eat f.
11:15 and the holy f is passed from thee?
12:12 the land: no f shall have peace.
17: 5 in man, and maketh f his arm,
19: 9 cause them to eat the f of their sons
9 and the f of their daughters,
9 eat every one the f of his friend in
25:31 he will plead with all f; he will
32:27 I am the Lord, the God of all f:
45: 5 behold, I will bring evil upon all f,
51:35 violence done to me and to my f
La 3: 4 My f and my skin hath he made
Eze 4:14 there abominable f into my mouth
11: 3 is the caldron, and we be the f.
7 they are the f, and this city is the
11 neither shall ye be the f in the midst
19 take the stony heart out of their f,
19 and will give them an heart of f:
Eze 16:26 thy neighbours, great of f; and
20:48 And all f shall see that I the Lord
21: 4 forth out of his sheath against all f,
5 That all f may know that I the Lord
23:20 whose f is as the f of asses,
24:10 consume the f, and spice it well,
32: 5 will lay thy f upon the mountains,
36:26 away the stony heart out of your f,
26 and I will give you an heart of f.
37: 6 and will bring up f upon you,
8 lo, the sinews and the f came up
39:17 that ye may eat f, and drink blood.
18 Ye shall eat the f of the mighty,
40:43 and upon the tables was the f of the
44: 7 and uncircumcised in f, to be in my
9 nor uncircumcised in f, shall enter
Da 1:15 appeared fairer and fatter in f
2:11 gods, whose dwelling is not with f.
4:12 and all f was fed of it.
7: 5 thus unto it, Arise, devour much f.
10: 3 came f nor wine in my mouth,
Ho 8:13 They sacrifice f for the sacrifices
Joe 2:28 will pour out my spirit upon all f;
Mic 3: 2 and their f from off their bones;
3 Who also eat the f of my people,
3 and as f within the caldron.
Zep 1:17 as dust, and their f as the dung.
Hag 2:12 If one bear holy f in the skirt of
Zec 2:13 Be silent, O all f, before the Lord:
11: 9 rest eat every one the f of another.
16 but he shall eat the f of the fat,
14:12 Their f shall consume away while
M't 16:17 f and blood hath not revealed it
19: 5 and they twain shall be one f?
6 they are no more twain, but one f.
24:22 there should no f be saved: but
26:41 indeed is willing, but the f is weak.
M'r 10: 8 And they twain shall be one f:
8 they are no more twain, but one f.
13:20 no f should be saved: but for the
14:38 truly is ready, but the f is weak.
Lu 3: 6 And all f shall see the salvation of
24:39 for a spirit hath not f and bones,
Joh 1:13 nor of the will of the f, nor of the
14 And the Word was made f, and
3: 6 That which is born of the f is f;
6:51 the bread that I will give is my f,
52 can this man give us his f to eat?
53 Except ye eat the f of the Son of
54 Whoso eateth my f, and drinketh
55 For my f is meat indeed, and my
56 He that eateth my f, and drinketh
63 quickeneth; the f profiteth nothing:
8:15 judge after the f; I judge no man.
17: 2 hast given him power over all f,
Ac 2:17 pour out of my Spirit upon all f:
26 also my f shall rest in hope:
30 fruit of his loins, according to the f,
31 neither his f did see corruption.
Ro 1: 3 seed of David according to the f;
2:28 which is outward in the f:
3:20 shall no f be justified in his sight:
4: 1 as pertaining to the f, hath found?
6:19 because of the infirmity of your f:
7: 5 For when we were in the f,
18 in me, (that is, in my f,)
25 but with the f the law of sin.
8: 1 after the f, but after the Spirit.
3 in that it was weak through the f,
3 Son in the likeness of sinful f, and
3 for sin, condemned sin in the f:
4 in us, who walk not after the f,
5 For they that are after the f do
5 do mind the things of the f;
8 that are in the f cannot please God.
9 But ye are not in the f, but in the
12 we are debtors, not to the f,
12 to live after the f.
13 For if ye live after the f, ye shall
9: 3 my kinsmen according to the f:
5 as concerning the f Christ came,
8 which are the children of the f,
11:14 emulation them which are my f,
13:14 and make not provision for the f,
14:21 It is good neither to eat f, nor to
1Co 1:26 not many wise men after the f,
29 no f should glory in his presence.
5: 5 Satan for the destruction of the f,
6:16 for two, saith he, shall be one f.
7:28 such shall have trouble in the f:
8:13 eat no f while the world standeth,
10:18 Behold Israel after the f: are not
15:39 All f is not the same f: but there
39 but there is one kind of f of men,
39 another f of beasts, another of
50 that f and blood cannot inherit the
2Co 1:17 do I purpose according to the f,
4:11 be made manifest in our mortal f.
5:16 know we no man after the f: yea,
16 we have known Christ after the f,
7: 1 all filthiness of the f and spirit,
5 f had no rest, but we were troubled
10: 2 as if we walked according to the f.
3 in the f, we do not war after the f:
11:18 Seeing that many glory after the f,
12: 7 a thorn in the f, the messenger of
Ga 1:16 I conferred not with f and blood:
2:16 of the law shall no f be justified.
20 the life which I now live in the f
3: 3 are ye now made perfect by the f?
4:13 infirmity of the f I preached
14 my temptation which was in my f
23 bondwoman was born after the f;
29 as then he that was born after the f
5:13 not liberty for an occasion to the f,
16 ye shall not fulfil the lust of the f.

Ga 5:17 the f' lusteth against the Spirit,
17 and the Spirit against the f':
19 the works of the f' are manifest,
24 crucified the f' with the affections
6: 8 soweth to his f' shall of the f' reap
12 desire to make a fair show in the f',
13 that they may glory in your f'.
Eph 2: 3 in the lusts of our f', fulfilling the
3 desires of the f' and of the mind;
11 being in time past Gentiles in the f',
11 is called the Circumcision in the f'
15 Having abolished in his f' the
5:29 no man ever yet hated his own f';
30 his body, of his f', and of his bones.
31 and they two shall be one f'.
6: 5 your masters according to the f',
12 we wrestle not against f' and blood,
Ph'p 1:22 if I live in the f', this is the fruit of
24 Nevertheless to abide in the f' is
3: 3 and have no confidence in the f'.
4 might also have confidence in the f'.
4 whereof he might trust in the f',
Col 1:22 In the body of his f' through death,
24 in my f' for his body's sake, which
2: 1 as have not seen my face in the f';
5 For though I be absent in the f',
11 off the body of the sins of the f' by
13 and the uncircumcision of your f',
23 honour to the satisfying of the f'.
3:22 your masters according to the f';
1Ti 3:16 God was manifest in the f', justified
Ph'm 16 both in the f' and in the Lord?
Heb 2:14 the children are partakers of f' and
5: 7 Who in the days of his f', when he
9:13 sanctifieth to the purifying of the f':
10:20 the veil, that is to say, his f';
12: 9 we have had fathers of our f' which
Jas 5: 3 and shall eat your f' as it were fire.
1Pe 1:24 For all f' is grass, and all the glory
3:18 to death in the f', but quickened
21 putting away of the filth of the f',
4: 1 Christ hath suffered for us in the f',
1 he that hath suffered in the f' hath
2 live the rest of his time in the f' to
6 be judged according to men in the f',
2Pe 2:10 that walk after the f' in the lust of
18 allure through the lusts of the f',
1Jo 2:16 the lust of the f', and the lust of the
4: 2 that Jesus Christ is come in the f'
3 not that...Christ is come in the f'
2Jo 7 that Jesus Christ is come in the f'.
Jude 7 going after strange f', are set forth
8 these filthy dreamers defile the f',
23 even the garment spotted by the f'.
Re 17:16 and shall eat her f', and burn her
19:18 f' of kings, and the f' of captains,
18 captains, and the f' of mighty men,
18 men, and the f' of horses, and of
18 and the f' of all men, both free and
21 the fowls were filled with their f'.

fleshhook See also FLESHHOOKS.
1Sa 2:13 with a f' of three teeth in his hand;
14 all that the f' brought up the priest

fleshhooks
Ex 27: 3 and his f', and his firepans: all the
38: 3 and the f', and the firepans: all the
Nu 4:14 the censers, the f', and the shovels,
1Ch 28:17 pure gold for the f', and the bowls,
2Ch 4:16 and the shovels, and the f', and all

fleshly
2Co 1:12 not with f' wisdom, but by the
Col 2:18 vainly puffed up by his f' mind,
1Pe 2:11 abstain from f' lusts, which war

flesh-pots See FLESH and POTS.

fleshy
2Co 3: 3 but in f' tables of the heart.

flew
1Sa 14:32 And the people f' upon the spoil,
Isa 6: 6 Then f' one of the seraphims unto

flies
Ex 8:21 I will send swarms of f' upon thee, and
21 shall be full of swarms of f', and also
22 that no swarms of f' shall be there;
24 there came a grievous swarm of f' into
24 corrupted by reason of the swarm of f'.
29 that the swarms of f' may depart from
31 and he removed the swarms of f' from
Ps 78:45 He sent divers sorts of f' among
105:31 there came divers sorts of f', and
Ec 10: 1 Dead f' cause the ointment of the

flieth
De 4:17 likeness of any winged fowl that f'
14:19 creeping thing that f' is unclean
28:49 the earth as swift as the eagle f';
Ps 91: 5 nor for the arrow that f' by day;

flight
Le 26: 8 you shall put ten thousand to f':
De 32:30 and two put ten thousand to f',
1Ch 12:15 and they put to f' all them of the
Isa 52:12 not go out with haste, nor go by f':
Am 2:14 the f' shall perish from the swift,
M't 24:20 But pray ye that your f' be not in
M'r 13:18 And pray ye that your f' be not in
Heb 11:34 turned to f' the armies of the aliens.

flint
De 8:15 forth water out of the rock of f';
Ps 114: 8 the f' into a fountain of waters.
Isa 5:28 hoofs shall be counted like f',
50: 7 have I set my face like a f',
Eze 3: 9 As an adamant harder than f' have

flinty
De 32:13 and oil out of the f' rock;

floats See also FLOTES.
1Ki 5: 9 and I will convey them by sea in f'

flock See also FLOCKS.
Ge 4: 4 the firstlings of his f' and the fat
21:28 ewe lambs of the f' by themselves.
27: 9 Go now to the f', and fetch me two
29:10 and watered the f' of Laban his
30:31 I will again feed and keep thy f'.
32 I will pass through all thy f' to day,
40 all the brown in the f' of Laban;
31: 4 and Leah to the field unto his f',
38 rams of thy f' have I not eaten.
33:13 them one day, all the f' will die.
37: 2 years old was feeding the f' with his
12 went to feed their father's f' in
13 Do not thy brethren feed the f' in
38:17 I will send thee a kid from the f'.
Ex 2:16 troughs to water their father's f'.
17 helped them, and watered their f'.
19 enough for us, and watered the f'.
3: 1 kept the f' of Jethro his father in
1 the f' to the backside of the desert,
Le 1: 2 even of the herd, and of the f'.
3: 6 be of the f'; male or female, he
5: 6 female from the f', a lamb or a kid
18 ram without blemish out of the f',
6: 6 ram without blemish out of the f',
27:32 the tithe of the herd, or of the f',
Nu 15: 3 the Lord, of the herd, or of the f':
De 12:17 firstlings of thy herds or of thy f',
21 shalt kill of thy herd and of thy f',
15:14 out of thy f', and out of thy floor,
19 that come of thy herd and of thy f'
16: 2 of the f' and the herd, in the place
1Sa 17:34 and took a lamb out of the f':
2Sa 12: 4 he spared to take of his own f' and
2Ch 35: 7 Josiah gave to the people, of the f',
Ezr 10:19 they offered a ram of the f' for their
Job 21:11 send forth their little ones like a f',
30: 1 to have set with the dogs of my f'.
Ps 77:20 Thou leddest thy people like a f' by
78:52 them in the wilderness like a f'.
80: 1 thou that leadest Joseph like a f';
107:41 and maketh him families like a f'.
Ca 1: 7 thou makest thy f' to rest at noon:
8 way forth by the footsteps of the f',
4: 1 thy hair is as a f' of goats, that
2 Thy teeth are like a f' of sheep
6: 5 thy hair is as a f' of goats that
6 Thy teeth are as a f' of sheep which
Isa 40:11 He shall feed his f' like a shepherd:
63:11 sea with the shepherd of his f'?
Jer 13:17 Lord's f' is carried away captive.
20 where is the f' that was given thee,
20 was given thee, thy beautiful f'?
23: 2 have scattered my f', and driven
3 I will gather the remnant of my f'
25:34 in the ashes, ye principal of the f':
35 nor the principal of the f' to escape.
36 howling of the principal of the f',
31:10 him, as a shepherd doth his f'.
12 young of the f' and of the herd:
49:20 the least of the f' shall draw them
50:45 the least of the f' shall draw them
51:23 with thee the shepherd and his f';
Eze 24: 5 Take the choice of the f', and
34: 3 are fed: but ye feed not the f'.
6 my f' was scattered upon all the
8 because my f' became a prey,
8 and my f' became meat to every
8 did my shepherds search for my f',
8 fed themselves, and fed not my f';
10 I will require my f' at their hand,
10 them to cease from feeding the f';
10 I will deliver my f' from their
12 As a shepherd seeketh out his f'
15 I will feed my f', and I will cause
17 And as for you, O my f', thus saith
19 And as for my f', they eat that
22 Therefore will I save my f', and
31 And ye my f', the f' of my pasture,
36:37 increase them with men like a f'.
38 the holy f', as the f' of Jerusalem
43:23, 25 a ram out of the f' without
45:15 And one lamb out of the f', out of
Am 6: 4 and eat the lambs out of the f', and
7:15 Lord took me as I followed the f',
Jon 3: 7 beast, herd nor f', taste anything:
Mic 2:12 as the f' in the midst of their fold:
4: 8 And thou, O tower of the f', the
7:14 thy rod, the f' of thine heritage,
Hab 3:17 the f' shall be cut off from the fold,
Zec 9:16 in that day as the f' of his people:
10: 2 they went their way as a f', they
3 Lord of hosts hath visited his f'
11: 4 Feed the f' of the slaughter;
7 And I will feed the f' of slaughter,
7 even you, O poor of the f'.
7 I called Bands; and I fed the f'.
11 poor of the f' that waited upon me
17 idol shepherd that leaveth the f'!
Mal 1:14 which hath in his f' a male, and
M't 26:31 sheep of the f' shall be scattered
Lu 2: 8 watch over their f' by night.
12:32 Fear not, little f'; for it is your
Ac 20:28 unto yourselves, and to all the f',
29 in among you, not sparing the f'.
1Co 9: 7 who feedeth a f', and eateth not of
7 eateth not of the milk of the f'?
1Pe 5: 2 the f' of God which is among you,
3 but being ensamples to the f'.

flocks
Ge 13: 5 with Abram, had f', and herds,
24:35 he hath given him f', and herds,
26:14 possession of f', and possession of
29: 2 were three f' of sheep lying by it;
2 out of that well they watered the f':
3 And thither were all the f' gathered:
8 until all the f' be gathered together,
30:36 Jacob fed the rest of Laban's f'.
38 which he had pilled before the f'
38 when the f' came to drink,
39 the f' conceived before the rods,
40 of the f' toward the ringstraked,
40 he put his own f' by themselves,
32: 5 and asses, f', and menservants,
7 the f', and herds, and the camels,
33:13 and the f' and herds with young
37:14 brethren, and well with the f':
16 thee, where they feed their f'.
45:10 and thy f', and thy herds, and all
46:32 and they have brought their f',
47: 1 my brethren, and their f', and their
4 have no pasture for their f'; for the
17 exchange for horses, and for the f',
50: 8 only their little ones, and their f',
Ex 10: 9 with our f' and with our herds will
24 your f' and your herds be stayed:
12:32 Also take your f' and your herds,
38 and f', and herds, even very much
34: 3 neither let the f' nor herds feed
Le 1:10 And if his offering be of the f',
5:15 ram without blemish out of the f',
Nu 11:22 Shall the f' and the herds be slain
31: 9 and all their f', and all their goods.
30 of the asses, and of the f', of all
32:26 Our little ones, our wives, our f',
De 7:13 and the f' of thy sheep, in the
8:13 thy herds and thy f' multiply,
12: 6 of your herds and of your f':
14:23 of thy herds and of thy f';
28: 4, 18 kine and the f' of thy sheep.
51 of thy kine, or f' of thy sheep,
J'g 5:16 to hear the bleatings of the f'?
1Sa 30:20 David took all the f' and the herds,
2Sa 12: 2 had exceeding many f' and herds:
1Ki 20:27 them like two little f' of kids;
1Ch 4:39 valley, to seek pasture for their f'.
41 there was pasture there for their f'.
27:31 over the f' was Jaziz the Hagerite.
2Ch 17:11 the Arabians brought him f', seven
32:28 manner of beasts, and cotes for f'.
29 and possessions of f' and herds
Ne 10:36 firstlings of our herds and of our f',
Job 24: 2 they violently take away f', and
Ps 65:13 The pastures are clothed with f';
78:48 and their f' to hot thunderbolts.
Pr 27:23 to know the state of thy f', and
Ca 1: 7 as one that turneth aside by the f'
Isa 17: 2 they shall be for f', which shall
32:14 a joy of wild asses, a pasture of f';
60: 7 the f' of Kedar shall be gathered
61: 5 shall stand and feed your f', and the
65:10 And Sharon shall be a fold of f',
Jer 3:24 their f' and their herds, their sons
5:17 shall eat up thy f' and thine herds:
6: 3 shepherds with their f' shall come
10:21 and all their f' shall be scattered.
31:24 and they that go forth with f'.
33:12 shepherds causing their f' to lie
13 the cities of Judah, shall the f' pass
49:29 tents and their f' shall they take
50: 8 as the he goats before the f'.
Eze 25: 5 Ammonites a couchingplace for f';
34: 2 not the shepherds feed the f'?
36:38 waste cities be filled with f' of men;
Ho 5: 6 with their f' and with their herds
Joe 1:18 the f' of sheep are made desolate.
Mic 5: 8 young lion among the f' of sheep:
Zep 2: 6 for shepherds, and folds for f'.
14 And f' shall lie down in the midst

flood See also FLOODS; WATERFLOOD.
Ge 6:17 I do bring a f' of waters upon the
7: 6 the f' of waters was upon the earth.
7 because of the waters of the f'.
10 waters of the f' were upon the earth.
17 f' was forty days upon the earth;
9:11 off any more by the waters of a f';
11 neither shall there any more be a f'
15 waters shall no more become a f'
28 And Noah lived after the f' three
10: 1 them were sons born after the f'.
32 divided in the earth after the f'.
11:10 Arphaxad two years after the f':
Jos 24: 2 dwelt on the other side of the f'
3 from the other side of the f',
14 served on the other side of the f',
15 were on the other side of the f',
Job 14:11 and the f' decayeth and drieth up:
22:16 was overflown with a f':
28: 4 The f' breaketh out from the
Ps 29:10 The Lord sitteth upon the f'; yea,
66: 6 they went through the f' on foot:
74:15 cleave the fountain and the f':
90: 5 carriest them away as with a f';
Isa 28: 2 f' of mighty waters overflowing,
59:19 the enemy shall come in like a f',
Jer 46: 7 Who is this that cometh up as a f',
8 Egypt riseth up like a f', and his
47: 2 and shall be an overflowing f',
Dan 9:26 The end thereof shall be with a f',
11:22 with the arms of a f' shall they be
Am 8: 8 and it shall rise up wholly as a f';
8 drowned, as by the f' of Egypt.
9: 5 it shall rise up wholly like a f';
5 be drowned, as by the f' of Egypt.
Na 1: 8 But with an overrunning f' he will
M't 24:38 f' they were eating and drinking,
39 until the f' came, and took them all
Lu 6:48 when the f' arose, the stream beat

Lu 17:27 the f came, and destroyed them
2Pe 2: 5 bringing in the f upon the world
Re 12:15 cast out of his mouth water as a f
15 her to be carried away of the f.
16 mouth, and swallowed up the f

floods
Ex 15: 8 the f stood upright as an heap,
2Sa 22: 5 f of ungodly men made me afraid:
Job 20:17 He shall not see the rivers, the f,
28:11 bindeth the f from overflowing;
Ps 18: 4 f of ungodly men made me afraid.
24: 2 and established it upon the f.
32: 6 surely in the f of great waters
69: 2 waters, where the f overflow me.
78:44 rivers into blood; and their f,
93: 3 The f have lifted up, O Lord,
3 the f have lifted up their voice;
3 the f lift up their waves.
98: 8 the f clap their hands: let the hills
Ca 8: 7 neither can the f drown it: if a
Isa 44: 3 and f upon the dry ground:
Eze 31:15 f thereof, and the great waters
Jon 2: 3 and the f compassed me about:
M't 7:25, 27 and the f came, and the winds

floor See also BARNFLOOR; CORNFLOOR; FLOORS; THRESHINGFLOOR.
Ge 50:11 the mourning in the f of Atad,
Nu 5:17 of the dust that is in the f of the
De 15:14 out of thy flock, and out of thy f,
J'g 6:37 will put a fleece of wool in the f;
Ru 3: 3 and get thee down to the f:
6 And she went down unto the f,
14 that a woman came unto the f.
1Ki 6:15 the f of the house, and the walls
15 covered the f of the house with
16 the f and the walls with boards
30 And the f of the house he overlaid
7: 7 from one side of the f to the other.
2Ch 34:11 to f the houses which the kings
Isa 21:10 threshing, and the corn of my f:
Ho 9: 2 The f and the winepress shall
13: 3 with the whirlwind out of the f,
Mic 4:12 them as the sheaves into the f.
M't 3:12 and he will throughly purge his f,
Lu 3:17 and he will throughly purge his f,

floors See also THRESHINGFLOORS.
Joe 2:24 And the f shall be full of wheat,

flotes See also FLOATS.
2Ch 2:16 and we will bring it to thee in f by

flour
Ex 29: 2 wheaten f shalt thou make them.
40 tenth deal of f mingled with the
Le 2: 1 his offering shall be of fine f;
2 his handful of the f thereof,
4 shall be unleavened cakes of fine f
5 it shall be of fine f unleavened,
7 it shall be made of fine f with oil.
5:11 the tenth part of an ephah of fine f
6:15 take of it his handful, of the f
20 the tenth part of an ephah of fine f
7:12 cakes mingled with oil, of fine f,
14:10 and three tenth deals of fine f
21 and one tenth deal of fine f
23:13 shall be two tenth deals of fine f
17 tenth deals: they shall be of fine f;
24: 5 thou shalt take fine f, and bake
Nu 6:15 cakes of fine f mingled with oil,
7:13 both of them were full of fine f
19, 25, 31, 37, 43, 49, 55, 61, 67, 73, 79 full of fine f mingled with oil for a
8: 8 even fine f mingled with oil,
15: 4 meat offering of a tenth deal of f
6 offering two tenth deals of f
9 offering of three tenth deals of f
28: 5 an ephah of f for a meat offering,
9 two tenth deals of fine f for a
12 three tenth deals of f for a meat
12 two tenth deals of f for a meat
13 And a several tenth deal of f
20 shall be of f mingled with oil:
28 their meat offering of f mingled
29: 3 shall be of f mingled with oil,
9 shall be of f mingled with oil,
14 shall be of f mingled with oil,
J'g 6:19 cakes of an ephah of f:
1Sa 1:24 bullocks, and one ephah of f,
28:24 and took f, and kneaded it,
2Sa 13: 8 And she took f, and kneaded it,
17:28 wheat, and barley, and f, and
1Ki 4:22 was thirty measures of fine f,
2Ki 7: 1 a measure of fine f be sold for a
16 So a measure of fine f was sold for
18 a measure of fine f for a shekel,
1Ch 9:29 the fine f, and the wine, and the
23:29 for the fine f for meat offering,
Eze 16:13 thou didst eat fine f, and honey,
19 gave thee fine f, and oil, and honey,
46:14 to temper with the fine f;
Re 18:13 fine f, and wheat, and beasts,

flourish See also FLOURISHED; FLOURISHETH; FLOURISHING.
Ps 72: 7 In his days shall the righteous f;
16 and they of the city shall f like
92: 7 all the workers of iniquity do f;
12 The righteous shall f like the
13 shall f in the courts of our God.
132:18 upon himself shall his crown f.
Pr 11:28 the righteous shall f as a branch,
14:11 tabernacle of the upright shall f.
Ec 12: 5 and the almond tree shall f,
Ca 7:12 let us see if the vine f,
Isa 17:11 shalt thou make thy seed to f:
66:14 your bones shall f like an herb:
Eze 17:24 and have made the dry tree to f:

flourished
Ca 6:11 and to see whether the vine f,
Ph'p 4:10 your care of me hath f again;

flourisheth
Ps 90: 6 In the morning it f, and groweth
103:15 as a flower of the field, so he f.

flourishing
Ps 92:14 they shall be fat and f;
Da 4: 4 mine house, and f in my palace:

flow See also FLOWED; FLOWETH; FLOWING; OVERFLOW.
Job 20:28 his goods shall f away in the day
Ps 147:18 wind to blow, and the waters f.
Ca 4:16 that the spices thereof may f out.
Isa 2: 2 and all nations shall f unto it.
48:21 the waters to f out of the rock
60: 5 thou shalt see, and f together,
64: 1 might f down at thy presence,
Jer 31:12 shall f together to the goodness
51:44 the nations shall not f together
Joe 3:18 the hills shall f with milk, and
18 all the rivers of Judah shall f with
Mic 4: 1 and people shall f unto it.
Joh 7:38 belly shall f rivers of living water

flowed See also OVERFLOWED.
Jos 4:18 and f over all his banks, as they
Isa 64: 3 mountains f down at thy presence.
La 3:54 Waters f over mine head; then

flower See also FLOWERS.
Ex 25:33 a knop and a f in one branch;
33 other branch, with a knop and a f:
37:19 in one branch, a knop and a f;
19 another branch, a knop and a f:
1Sa 2:33 shall die in the f of their age.
Job 14: 2 He cometh forth like a f, and is cut
15:33 shall cast off his f as the olive.
Ps 103:15 a f of the field, so he flourisheth.
Isa 18: 5 sour grape is ripening in the f,
28: 1 glorious beauty is a fading f,
4 shall be a fading f, and as the
40: 6 thereof is as the f of the field:
7 the f fadeth: because the spirit
8 f fadeth: but the word of our God
Na 1: 4 the f of Lebanon languisheth.
1Co 7:36 if she pass the f of her age,
Jas 1:10 because as the f of the grass
11 the grass, and the f thereof falleth,
1Pe 1:24 the glory of man as the f of grass.
24 and the f thereof falleth away:

flowers
Ex 25:31 his bowls, his knops, and his f,
34 with their knops and their f.
37:17 and his f were of the same:
20 like almonds, his knops, and his f:
Le 15:24 her f be upon him, he shall be
33 And of her that is sick of her f,
Nu 8: 4 the f thereof, was beaten work:
1Ki 6:18 knops and open f: all was cedar;
29 palm trees and open f, within and
32 palm trees and open f, and overlaid
35 palm trees and open f: and covered
7:26 the brim of a cup, with f of lilies:
49 with the f, and the lamps, and the
2Ch 4: 5 brim of a cup, with f of lilies;
21 And the f, and the lamps, and the
Ca 2:12 The f appear on the earth;
5:13 as a bed of spices, as sweet f:

floweth See also OVERFLOWETH.
Le 20:24 land that f with milk and honey:
Nu 13:27 surely it f with milk and honey;
14: 8 land which f with milk and honey.
16:13, 14 that f with milk and honey,
De 6: 3 land that f with milk and honey.
11: 9 land that f with milk and honey.
26: 9, 15 that f with milk and honey.
27: 3 land that f with milk and honey;
31:20 land that f with milk and honey;
Jos 5: 6 land that f with milk and honey.

flowing See also OVERFLOWING.
Ex 3: 8 a land f with milk and honey;
17 unto a land f with milk and honey.
13: 5 thee, a land f with milk and honey,
33: 3 Unto a land f with milk and
Pr 18: 4 wellspring of wisdom as a f brook.
Isa 66:12 the glory of the Gentiles like a f
Jer 11: 5 to give them a land f with milk
18:14 the cold f waters that come from
32:22 a land f with milk and honey;
49: 4 f valley, O backsliding daughter?
Eze 20: 6 f with milk and honey, which is
15 them, f with milk and honey,

flown See OVERFLOWN.

flute
Da 3: 5 ye hear the sound of the cornet, f,
7 heard the sound of the cornet, f,
10 hear the sound of the cornet, f,
15 ye hear the sound of the cornet, f,

fluttereth
De 32:11 up her nest, f over her young,

flux
Ac 28: 8 sick of a fever and of a bloody f:

fly See also FLEW; FLIES; FLIETH; FLYING.
Ge 1:20 fowl that may f above the earth
1Sa 15:19 but didst f upon the spoil, and
2Sa 22:11 he rode upon a cherub, and did f:
Job 5: 7 trouble, as the sparks f upward.
20: 8 He shall f away as a dream,
39:26 Doth the hawk f by thy wisdom,
Ps 18:10 rode upon a cherub, and did f:
10 yea, he did f upon the wings
55: 6 would I f away, and be at rest.
90:10 it is soon cut off, and we f away.
Pr 23: 5 they f away as an eagle toward
Isa 6: 2 his feet, and with twain he did f.
7:18 shall hiss for the f that is in the
11:14 they shall f upon the shoulders
60: 8 Who are these that f as a cloud,
Jer 48:40 Behold, he shall f as an eagle,
49:22 shall come up and f as the eagle,
Eze 13:20 hunt the souls to make them f,
20 souls that ye hunt to make them f.
Da 9:21 being caused to f swiftly, touched
Ho 9:11 glory shall f away like a bird
Hab 1: 8 shall f as the eagle that hasteth
Re 12:14 she might f into the wilderness,
14: 6 saw another angel f in the midst
19:17 to all the fowls that f in the midst

flying
Le 11:21 ye eat of every f creeping thing
23 But all other f creeping things,
Ps 148:10 creeping things, and f fowl:
Pr 26: 2 as the swallow by f, so the curse
Isa 14:29 his fruit shall be a fiery f serpent.
30: 6 the viper and fiery f serpent,
31: 5 birds f, so will the Lord of hosts
Zec 5: 1 and looked, and behold a f roll.
2 And I answered, I see a f roll;
Re 4: 7 fourth beast was like a f eagle.
8:13 f through the midst of heaven,

foal See also FOALS.
Ge 49:11 Binding his f unto the vine, and
Zec 9: 9 and upon a colt the f of an ass.
M't 21: 5 and a colt the f of an ass.

foals
Ge 32:15 bulls, twenty she asses, and ten f.

foam See also FOAMETH; FOAMING.
Ho 10: 7 cut off as the f upon the water.

foameth
M'r 9:18 he f, and gnasheth with his teeth,
Lu 9:39 and it teareth him that he f again,

foaming
M'r 9:20 on the ground, and wallowed f.
Jude 13 of the sea, f out their own shame;

fodder
Job 6: 5 or loweth the ox over his f?

foes
1Ch 21:12 to be destroyed before thy f,
Es 9:16 their f seventy and five thousand,
Ps 27: 2 even mine enemies and my f,
30: 1 and hast not made my f to rejoice
89:23 beat down his f before his face,
M't 10:36 And a man's f shall be they of his
Ac 2:35 Until I make thy f thy footstool.

fold See also BLINDFOLD; FOLDEN; FOLDETH; FOLDING; FOLDS; FOURFOLD; HUNDREDFOLD; INFOLDING; MANIFOLD; SEVENFOLD; SHEEPFOLD; SIXTYFOLD; TENFOLD; THIRTYFOLD; THREEFOLD; TWOFOLD.
Isa 13:20 shall the shepherds make their f
65:10 And Sharon shall be a f of flocks,
Eze 34:14 mountains of Israel shall their f
14 there shall they lie in a good f,
Mic 2:12 the flock in the midst of their f:
Hab 3:17 flock shall be cut off from the f,
Joh 10:16 I have, which are not of this f:
16 shall be one f, and one shepherd.
Heb 1:12 as a vesture shalt thou f them up,

folden
Na 1:10 they be f together as thorns,

foldeth
Ec 4: 5 The fool f his hands together,

folding See also INFOLDING.
1Ki 6:34 two leaves of the one door were f,
34 two leaves of the other door were f.
Pr 6:10 a little f of the hands to sleep:
24:33 a little f of the hands to sleep:

folds See also SHEEPFOLDS.
Nu 32:24 and f for your sheep; and do that
36 fenced cities: and f for sheep.
Ps 50: 9 nor he goats out of thy f.
Jer 23: 3 will bring them again to their f;
Zep 2: 6 for shepherds, and f for flocks.

folk See also FOLKS; KINSFOLK.
Ge 33:15 now leave with thee some of the f
Pr 30:26 The conies are but a feeble f,
Jer 51:58 and the f in the fire, and they
M'r 6: 5 laid his hands upon a few sick f
Joh 5: 3 a great multitude of impotent f,

folks See also KINSFOLKS.
Ac 5:16 bringing sick f, and them which

follow See also FOLLOWED; FOLLOWETH; FOLLOWING.
Ge 24: 5 will not be willing to f me unto
8 will not be willing to f thee, then
39 the woman will not f me.
44: 4 Up, f after the men; and when
Ex 11: 8 and all the people that f thee:
14: 4 that he shall f after them;
17 and they shall f them: and
21:22 and yet no mischief f: he shall
23 And if any mischief f, then thou
23: 2 not f a multitude to do evil;
De 16:20 is altogether just shalt thou f,
18:22 if the thing f not, nor come to
J'g 3:28 he said unto them, F after me:
8: 5 bread unto the people that f me;
9: 3 hearts inclined to f Abimelech:
1Sa 25:27 young men that f my lord.
30:21 so faint that they could not f
2Sa 17: 9 among the people that f Absalom.
1Ki 18:21 God, f him: but if Baal, then f
19:20 mother, and then I will f thee.
20:10 for all the people that f me.

2Ki 6:19 f me, and I will bring you
Ps 23: 6 goodness and mercy shall f me
38:20 I f the thing that good is.
45:14 virgins her companions that f her
94:15 all the upright in heart shall f it.
119:150 draw nigh that f after mischief:
Isa 5:11 that they may f strong drink;
51: 1 me, ye that f after righteousness,
Jer 17:16 from being a pastor to f thee:
42:16 f close after you there in Egypt;
Eze 13: 3 foolish prophets, that f their
Ho 2: 7 And she shall f after her lovers,
6: 3 if we f on to know the Lord:
M't 4:19 he saith unto them, F me,
8:19 I will f thee whithersoever thou
22 And Jesus said unto him, F me;
9: 9 and he saith unto him, F me.
16:24 and take up his cross, and f me.
19:21 in heaven: and come and f me.
M'r 2:14 and said unto him, F me. And he
5:37 And he suffered no man to f him,
6: 1 country; and his disciples f him.
8:34 and take up his cross, and f me.
10:21 come, take up the cross, and f me.
14:13 bearing a pitcher of water: f him.
16:17 And these signs shall f them that
Lu 5:27 and he said unto him, F me.
9:23 take up his cross daily, and f me.
57 I will f thee whithersoever thou
59 And he said unto another, F me.
61 also said, Lord, I will f thee;
17:23 go not after them, nor f them.
18:22 treasure in heaven: and come, f me.
22:10 f him into the house where he
49 were about him saw what would f,
Joh 1:43 Philip, and saith unto him, F me.
10: 4 before them, and the sheep f him:
5 And a stranger will they not f,
27 and I know them, and they f me:
12:26 If any man serve me, let him f me;
13:36 not f me now; but thou shalt f me
37 why cannot I f thee now?
21:19 he saith unto him, F me.
22 what is that to thee? f thou me.
Ac 3:24 Samuel and those that f after,
12: 8 thy garment about thee, and f me.
Ro 14:19 therefore f after the things which
1Co 14: 1 F after charity, and desire
Ph'p 3:12 I f after, if that I may apprehend
1Th 5:15 but ever f that which is good,
2Th 3: 7 know how ye ought to f us:
9 an ensample unto you to f us.
1Ti 5:24 and some men they f after.
6:11 f after righteousness, godliness,
2Ti 2:22 f righteousness, faith, charity,
Heb 12:14 F peace with all men, and
13: 7 whose faith f, considering the
1Pe 1:11 and the glory that should f.
2:21 example, that ye should f his steps:
2Pe 2: 2 And many shall f their pernicious
3Jo 11 Beloved, f not that which is evil,
Re 14: 4 These are they which f the Lamb
13 and their works do f them.

followed See also FOLLOWEDST.
Ge 24:61 f the man: and the servant
32:19 all that f the droves, saying,
Nu 14:24 hath f me fully, him will I bring
16:25 and the elders of Israel f him.
32:11 because they have not wholly f me:
12 for they have wholly f the Lord.
De 1:36 because he hath wholly f the Lord.
4: 3 all the men that f Baal-peor,
Jos 6: 8 the covenant of the Lord f them.
14: 8 but I wholly f the Lord my God.
9 because thou hast wholly f the Lord
14 he wholly f the Lord God of Israel,
J'g 2:12 and f other gods, of the gods
9: 4 and light persons, which f him.
49 his bough, and f Abimelech,
1Sa 13: 7 and all the people f him trembling.
14:22 even they also f hard after them
17:13 and f Saul to the battle:
14 and the three eldest f Saul.
31: 2 the Philistines f hard upon Saul
2Sa 1: 6 chariots and horsemen f hard after
2:10 the house of Judah f David.
3:31 And king David himself f the
11: 8 and there f him a mess of meat
17:23 saw that his counsel was not f, he
20: 2 up from after David, and f Sheba
1Ki 12:20 none that f the house of David,
14: 8 who f me with all his heart,
16:21 half of the people f Tibni
21 make him king; and half f Omri.
22 the people that f Omri prevailed
22 against the people that f Tibni
18:18 Lord, and thou hast f Baalim.
20:19 and the army which f them.
2Ki 3: 9 and for the cattle that f them.
4:30 And he arose, and f her.
5:21 So Gehazi f after Naaman.
9:27 And Jehu f after him, and said,
13: 2 and f the sins of Jeroboam the
17:15 they f vanity, and became vain
1Ch 10: 2 And the Philistines f hard after
Ne 4:23 nor the men of the guard which f
Ps 68:25 the players on instruments f after;
Eze 10:11 the head looked they f it;
Am 7:15 the Lord took me as I f the flock,
M't 4:20 straightway left their nets, and f
22 the ship and their father, and f him.
25 f him great multitudes of people
8: 1 mountain, great multitudes f him.
10 and said to them that f, Verily I say
23 into a ship, his disciples f him.
M't 9: 9 Follow me. And he arose, and f
19 And Jesus arose, and f him,
27 two blind men f him, crying, and
12:15 great multitudes f him, and he
14:13 they f him on foot out of the cities.
19: 2 great multitudes f him; and he
27 we have forsaken all, and f thee;
28 That ye which have f me, in the
20:29 Jericho, a great multitude f him.
34 received sight, and they f him.
21: 9 that went before, and that f,
26:58 Peter f him afar off unto the high
27:55 f Jesus from Galilee, ministering
62 day, that f the day of the
M'r 1:18 they forsook their nets, and f him.
36 they that were with him f after
2:14 Follow me. And he arose and f him.
15 there were many, and they f him.
3: 7 great multitude from Galilee f him,
5:24 with him; and much people f him;
10:28 have left all, and have f thee.
32 and as they f, they were afraid.
52 he received his sight, and f Jesus
11: 9 that went before, and they that f,
14:51 there f him a certain young man,
54 Peter f him afar off, even into the
15:41 when he was in Galilee, f him, and
Lu 5:11 they forsook all, and f him.
28 And he left all, rose up, and f him.
7: 9 and said unto the people that f him,
9:11 people, when they knew it, f him:
18:28 we have left all, and f thee.
43 he received his sight, and f him,
22:39 and his disciples also f him.
54 priest's house. And Peter f afar off.
23:27 And there f him a great company of
49 and the women that f him from
55 f after, and beheld the sepulchre,
Joh 1:37 heard him speak, and they f Jesus.
40 which heard John speak, and f him,
6: 2 And a great multitude f him,
11:31 rose up hastily and went out, f her,
18:15 And Simon Peter f Jesus, and so did
Ac 12: 9 And he went out, and f him;
13:43 proselytes f Paul and Barnabas:
16:17 same f Paul and us, and cried,
21:36 the multitude of the people f after,
Ro 9:30 which f not after righteousness,
31 Israel, which f after the law of
1Co 10: 4 of that spiritual Rock that f them:
1Ti 5:10 have diligently f every good work.
2Pe 1:16 we have not f cunningly devised
Re 6: 8 was Death, and Hell f with him.
8: 7 there f hail and fire mingled with
14: 8 and there f another angel, saying,
9 And the third angel f them, saying
19:14 armies which were in heaven f him

followedst
Ru 3:10 as thou f not young men,

followers
1Co 4:16 I beseech you, be ye f of me.
11: 1 Be ye f of me, even as I also am
Eph 5: 1 Be ye therefore f of God,
Ph'p 3:17 be f together of me, and mark
1Th 1: 6 became f of us, and of the Lord,
2:14 became f of the churches of God
Heb 6:12 but f of them who through faith
1Pe 3:13 if ye be f of that which is good?

followeth
2Ki 11:15 that f her kill with the sword.
2Ch 23:14 whoso f her, let him be slain
Ps 63: 8 My soul f hard after thee:
Pr 12:11 but he that f vain persons is void
15: 9 him that f after righteousness.
21:21 He that f after righteousness and
28:19 but he that f after vain persons
Isa 1:23 loveth gifts, and f after rewards:
Eze 16:34 none f thee to commit whoredoms:
Ho 12: 1 and f after the east wind: he
M't 10:38 and f after me, is not worthy of
M'r 9:38 in thy name, and he f not us:
38 we forbad him, because he f not
Lu 9:49 we forbad him, because he f not
Joh 8:12 he that f me shall not walk in

following
Ge 41:31 by reason of that famine f;
De 7: 4 will turn away thy son from f me.
12:30 thou be not snared by f them,
Jos 22:16 to turn away this day from f the
18 must turn away this day from f the
23 an altar to turn from f the Lord,
29 to turn this day from f the Lord,
J'g 2:19 in f other gods to serve them,
Ru 1:16 or to return from f after thee:
1Sa 12:14 continue f the Lord your God:
20 yet turn not aside from f the Lord,
14:46 went up from f the Philistines:
15:11 for he is turned back from f me,
24: 1 returned from f the Philistines,
2Sa 2:19 hand nor to the left from f Abner.
21 would not turn aside from f of him.
22 Asahel, Turn thee aside from f me:
26 return from f their brethren?
27 up every one from f his brother.
30 And Joab returned from f Abner:
7: 8 from f the sheep, to be ruler over
1Ki 1: 7 and they f Adonijah helped him.
9: 6 if ye shall at all turn from f me,
21:26 very abominably in f idols,
2Ki 17:21 drave Israel from f the Lord,
18: 6 departed not from f him, but kept
1Ch 17: 7 sheepcote, even from f the sheep,
2Ch 25:27 did turn away from f the Lord
34:33 they departed not from f the Lord,
Ps 48:13 ye may tell it to the generation f.
78:71 From f the ewes great with young
109:13 in the generation f let their name
M'r 16:20 confirming the word with signs f.
Lu 13:33 and tomorrow, and the day f:
Joh 1:38 Jesus turned, and saw them f,
43 The day f Jesus would go forth
6:22 The day f, when the people
20: 6 Then cometh Simon Peter f him,
21:20 the disciple whom Jesus loved f;
Ac 21: 1 and the day f unto Rhodes, and
18 the day f Paul went in with us
23:11 And the night f the Lord stood
2Pe 2:15 f the way of Balaam the son of

folly
Ge 34: 7 he had wrought f in Israel
De 22:21 she hath wrought f in Israel,
Jos 7:15 and because he hath wrought f
J'g 19:23 come into mine house, do not this f.
20: 6 committed lewdness and f in
10 f that they have wrought in Israel.
1Sa 25:25 Nabal is his name, and f is with
2Sa 13:12 done in Israel: do not thou this f.
Job 4:18 his angels he charged with f:
24:12 yet God layeth not f to them.
42: 8 lest I deal with you after your f.
Ps 49:13 This their way is their f:
85: 8 but let them not turn again to f.
Pr 5:23 in the greatness of his f he shall
13:16 but a fool layeth open his f.
14: 8 but the f of fools is deceit.
18 The simple inherit f: but the
24 but the foolishness of fools is f.
29 he that is hasty of spirit exalteth f.
15:21 F is joy to him that is destitute of
16:22 but the instruction of fools is f.
17:12 rather than a fool in his f.
18:13 matter before he heareth it, it is f
26: 4 Answer not a fool according to his f,
5 Answer a fool according to his f,
11 so a fool returneth to his f.
Ec 1:17 and to know madness and f:
2: 3 to lay hold on f, till I might see
12 wisdom, and madness, and f:
13 I saw that wisdom excelleth f,
7:25 and to know the wickedness of f,
10: 1 so doth a little f him that is in
6 F is set in great dignity, and the
Isa 9:17 and every mouth speaketh f.
Jer 23:13 I have seen f in the prophets
2Co 11: 1 bear with me a little in my f:
2Ti 3: 9 their f shall be manifest unto all

food
Ge 2: 9 to the sight, and good for f;
3: 6 saw that the tree was good for f,
6:21 unto thee of all f that is eaten,
21 and it shall be for f for thee,
41:35 And let them gather all the f
35 and let them keep f in the cities.
36 And that f shall be for store to the
48 And he gathered up all the f of the
48 laid up the f in the cities: the f of
42: 7 From the land of Canaan to buy f.
10 but to buy f are thy servants come.
33 and take f for the famine of your
43: 2 Go again, buy us a little f.
4 we will go down and buy thee f:
20 down at the first time to buy f:
22 down in our hands to buy f:
44: 1 Fill the men's sacks with f,
25 Go again, and buy us a little f.
47:24 seed of the field, and for your f,
24 and for f for your little ones.
Ex 21:10 her f, her raiment, and her duty
Le 3:11, 16 it is the f of the offering made
19:23 planted all manner of trees for f,
22: 7 holy things; because it is his f.
De 10:18 in giving him f and raiment.
1Sa 14:24 be the man that eateth any f until
24 So none of the people tasted any f
28 be the man that eateth any f this
2Sa 9:10 master's son may have f to eat:
1Ki 5: 9 desire, in giving f for my household.
11 thousand measures of wheat for f
Job 23:12 mouth more than my necessary f.
24: 5 wilderness yieldeth f for them
38:41 provideth for the raven his f?
40:20 the mountains bring him forth f.
Ps 78:25 Man did eat angels' f: he sent
104:14 bring forth f out of the earth;
136:25 Who giveth f to all flesh: for his
146: 7 which giveth f to the hungry.
147: 9 He giveth to the beast his f,
Pr 6: 8 gathereth her f in the harvest.
13:23 Much f is in the tillage of the poor:
27:27 have goats' milk enough for thy f,
27 for the f of thy household, and for
28: 3 sweeping rain which leaveth no f.
30: 8 feed me with f convenient for me:
31:14 she bringeth her f from afar.
Eze 16:27 and have diminished thine ordinary f
48:18 f unto them that serve the city.
Ac 14:17 our hearts with f and gladness.
2Co 9:10 both minister bread for your f,
1Ti 6: 8 having f and raiment let us be
Jas 2:15 be naked, and destitute of daily f,

fool See also FOOL'S; FOOLS.
1Sa 26:21 behold, I have played the f, and
2Sa 3:33 said, Died Abner as a f dieth?
Ps 14: 1 The f hath said in his heart,
49:10 the f and the brutish person
53: 1 The f hath said in his heart,
92: 6 neither doth a f understand this.

Pr 7:22 *f* to the correction of the stocks:
10: 8 commandments: but a prating *f*
10 sorrow: but a prating *f* shall fall.
18 he that uttereth a slander, is a *f*.
23 It is as sport to a *f* to do mischief:
11:29 *f* shall be servant to the wise
12:15 of a *f* is right in his own eyes:
13:16 but a *f* layeth open his folly.
14:16 but the *f* rageth, and is confident.
15: 5 *f* despiseth his father's instruction:
17: 7 speech becometh not a *f*:
10 than an hundred stripes into a *f*.
12 rather than a *f* in his folly.
16 in the hand of a *f* to get wisdom,
21 He that begetteth a *f* doeth it to his
21 and the father of a *f* hath no joy.
24 the eyes of a *f* are in the ends of
28 a *f*, when he holdeth his peace,
18: 2 A *f* hath no delight in
19: 1 is perverse in his lips, and is a *f*.
10 Delight is not seemly for a *f*;
20: 3 but every *f* will be meddling.
23: 9 Speak not in the ears of a *f*:
24: 7 Wisdom is too high for a *f*:
26: 1 So honour is not seemly for a *f*.
4 Answer not a *f* according to his
5 Answer a *f* according to his folly,
6 a message by the hand of a *f*
8 so is he that giveth honour to a *f*.
10 rewardeth the *f*, and rewardeth
11 so a *f* returneth to his folly.
12 is more hope of a *f* than of him.
27:22 Though thou shouldest bray a *f* in
28:26 trusteth in his own heart is a *f*:
29:11 A *f* uttereth all his mind:
20 is more hope of a *f* than of him.
30:22 a *f* when he is filled with meat;
Ec 2:14 but the *f* walketh in darkness:
15 As it happeneth to the *f*, so it
16 of the wise more than of the *f*
16 how dieth the wise man? as the *f*.
19 he shall be a wise man or a *f*?
4: 5 The *f* foldeth his hands together,
6: 8 hath the wise more than the *f*?
7: 6 so is the laughter of the *f*:
10: 3 he that is a *f* walketh by the way,
3 he saith to every one that he is a *f*.
12 but the lips of a *f* will swallow up
14 A *f* also is full of words:
Jer 17:11 and at his end shall be a *f*.
Ho 9: 7 the prophet is a *f*, the spiritual
M't 5:22 but whosoever shall say, Thou *f*,
Lu 12:20 Thou *f*, this night thy soul shall
1Co 3:18 become a *f*, that he may be wise.
15:36 Thou *f*, that which thou sowest
2Co 11:16 Let no man think me a *f*;
16 yet as a *f* receive me,
23 (I speak as a *f*) I am more;
12: 6 I shall not be a *f*; for I will say
11 I am become a *f* in glorying;

foolish
De 32: 6 O *f* people and unwise? is not he
21 them to anger with a *f* nation.
Job 2:10 speakest as one of the *f* women
5: 2 For wrath killeth the *f* man,
3 I have seen the *f* taking root:
Ps 5: 5 The *f* shall not stand in thy
39: 8 me not the reproach of the *f*.
73: 3 For I was envious at the *f*,
22 So *f* was I, and ignorant: I was
74:18 the *f* people have blasphemed
22 the *f* man reproacheth thee daily.
Pr 9: 6 Forsake the *f*, and live; and go
13 A *f* woman is clamorous: she is
10: 1 a *f* son is the heaviness of his
14 mouth of the *f* is near destruction.
14: 1 but the *f* plucketh it down with
3 In the mouth of the *f* is a rod of
7 Go from the presence of a *f* man,
15: 7 but the heart of the *f* doeth not so.
20 but a *f* man despiseth his mother.
17:25 A *f* son is a grief to his father,
19:13 A *f* son is the calamity of his
21:20 but a *f* man spendeth it up.
29: 9 wise man contendeth with a *f* man.
Ec 4:13 an old and *f* king, who will no
7:17 neither be thou *f*: why shouldest
10:15 The labour of the *f* wearieth
Isa 44:25 and maketh their knowledge *f*;
Jer 4:22 For my people is *f*, they have not
5: 4 they are *f*: for they know not
21 Hear now this, O *f* people,
10: 8 they are altogether brutish and *f*:
La 2:14 seen vain and *f* things for thee:
Eze 13: 3 Woe unto the *f* prophets, that
Zec 11:15 the instruments of a *f* shepherd.
M't 7:26 shall be likened unto a *f* man,
25: 2 them were wise, and five were *f*.
3 They that were *f* took their lamps,
8 And the *f* said unto the wise,
Ro 1:21 and their *f* heart was darkened.
2:20 An instructor of the *f*, a teacher
10:19 by a *f* nation I will anger you.
1Co 1:20 hath not God made *f* the wisdom
27 God hath chosen the *f* things of
Gal 3: 1 O *f* Galatians, who hath bewitched
3 Are ye so *f*? having begun in the
Eph 5: 4 nor *f* talking, nor jesting,
1Ti 6: 9 into many *f* and hurtful lusts,
2Ti 2:23 *f* and unlearned questions avoid,
Tit 3: 3 ourselves also were sometimes *f*,
9 *f* questions, and genealogies,
1Pe 2:15 to silence the ignorance of *f* men:

foolishly
Ge 31:28 thou hast now done *f* in so doing.
Nu 12:11 wherein we have done *f*, and
2Sa 24:10 servant; for I have done very *f*
1Ch 21: 8 thy servant; for I have done very *f*.
2Ch 16: 9 Herein thou hast done *f*:
Job 1:22 sinned not, nor charged God *f*.
Ps 75: 4 Deal not *f*: and to the wicked,
Pr 14:17 He that is soon angry dealeth *f*:
30:32 If thou hast done *f* in lifting up
2Co 11:17 but as it were *f*, in this
21 (I speak *f*,) I am bold also.

foolishness
2Sa 15:31 the counsel of Ahithophel into *f*.
Ps 38: 5 and are corrupt because of my *f*.
69: 5 O God, thou knowest my *f*;
Pr 12:23 the heart of fools proclaimeth *f*.
14:24 but the *f* of fools is folly.
15: 2 mouth of fools poureth out *f*.
14 the mouth of fools feedeth on *f*.
19: 3 The *f* of man perverteth his way:
22:15 *F* is bound in the heart of a child;
24: 9 The thought of *f* is sin:
27:22 yet will not his *f* depart from him.
Ec 7:25 of folly, even of *f* and madness:
10:13 of the words of his mouth is *f*:
M'r 7:22 an evil eye, blasphemy, pride, *f*:
1Co 1:18 the cross is to them that perish, *f*;
21 the *f* of preaching to save them
23 and unto the Greeks *f*;
25 the *f* of God is wiser than men;
2:14 for they are *f* unto him:
3:19 wisdom of this world is *f* with God.

fool's
Pr 12:16 A *f* wrath is presently known: but
18: 6 A *f* lips enter into contention,
7 A *f* mouth is his destruction,
26: 3 the ass, and a rod for the *f* back.
27: 3 a *f* wrath is heavier than them
Ec 5: 3 a *f* voice is known by multitude
10: 2 but a *f* heart at his left.

fools
2Sa 13:13 shalt be as one of the *f* in Israel.
Job 12:17 and maketh the judges *f*.
30: 8 They were children of *f*, yea,
Ps 75: 4 I said unto the *f*, Deal not
94: 8 and ye *f*, when will ye be wise?
107:17 *F*, because of their transgression,
Pr 1: 7 *f* despise wisdom and instruction.
22 and *f* hate knowledge?
32 prosperity of *f* shall destroy them.
3:35 shame shall be the promotion of *f*.
8: 5 ye *f*, be ye of an understanding
10:21 but *f* die for want of wisdom.
12:23 but the heart of *f* proclaimeth
13:19 it is abomination to *f* to depart
20 companion of *f* shall be destroyed.
14: 8 but the folly of *f* is deceit.
9 *F* make a mock at sin: but
24 but the foolishness of *f* is folly.
33 that which is in the midst of *f*
15: 2 mouth of *f* poureth out foolishness
14 mouth of *f* feedeth on foolishness.
16:22 but the instruction of *f* is folly.
19:29 and stripes for the back of *f*.
26: 7, 9 is a parable in the mouth of *f*.
Ec 5: 1 than to give the sacrifice of *f*:
4 for he hath no pleasure in *f*:
7: 4 but the heart of *f* is in the house of
5 for a man to hear the song of *f*.
9 for anger resteth in the bosom of *f*.
9:17 the cry of him that ruleth among *f*.
Isa 19:11 Surely the princes of Zoan are *f*,
13 The princes of Zoan are become *f*,
35: 8 wayfaring men, though *f*, shall not
M't 23:17 Ye *f* and blind: for whether is
19 Ye *f* and blind: for whether is
Lu 11:40 Ye *f*, did not he that made that
24:25 O *f*, and slow of heart to believe
Ro 1:22 to be wise, they became *f*,
1Co 4:10 We are *f* for Christ's sake, but ye
2Co 11:19 For ye suffer *f* gladly, seeing ye
Eph 5:15 circumspectly, not as *f*, but as

foot See also AFOOT; BAREFOOT; BROKENFOOTED; CLOVENFOOTED; FEET; FOOTMEN; FOOTSTEPS; FOOTSTOOL; FOURFOOTED.
Ge 8: 9 found no rest for the sole of her *f*,
41:44 shall no man lift up his hand or *f*
Ex 12:37 about six hundred thousand on *f*
21:24 for tooth, hand for hand, *f* for *f*,
29:20 upon the great toe of their right *f*
30:18 a laver of brass, and his *f* also
28 vessels, and the laver and his *f*.
31: 9 furniture, and the laver and his *f*,
35:16 his vessels, the laver and his *f*,
38: 8 the laver of brass, and the *f* of it
39:39 his vessels, the laver and his *f*,
40:11 laver and his *f*, and sanctify it.
Le 8:11 laver and his *f*, to sanctify them.
23 upon the great toe of his right *f*.
13:12 from his head even to his *f*,
14:14 upon the great toe of his right *f*:
17 upon the great toe of his right *f*,
25 upon the great toe of his right *f*:
28 upon the great toe of his right *f*,
Nu 22:25 crushed Balaam's *f* against the
De 2: 5 no, not so much as a *f* breadth:
8: 4 did thy *f* swell, these forty years.
11:10 wateredst it with thy *f*, as a garden
19:21 for tooth, hand for hand, *f* for *f*,
25: 9 and loose his shoe from off his *f*,
28:35 from the sole of thy *f* unto the top
56 the sole of her *f* upon the ground
65 shall the sole of thy *f* have rest:
29: 5 shoe is not waxen old upon thy *f*.
32:35 their *f* shall slide in due time:
33:24 and let him dip his *f* in oil.
Jos 1: 3 the sole of your *f* shall tread upon,
5:15 Loose thy shoe from off thy *f*;
J'g 5:15 he was sent on *f* into the valley.
2Sa 2:18 was as light of *f* as a wild roe.
14:25 the sole of his *f* even to the crown
21:20 and on every *f* six toes, four and
1Ch 20: 6 on each hand, and six on each *f*:
2Ch 33: 8 any more remove the *f* of Israel
Job 2: 7 the sole of his *f* unto his crown.
23:11 My *f* hath held his steps, his way
28: 4 the waters forgotten of the *f*:
31: 5 if my *f* hath hasted to deceit;
39:15 forgetteth that the *f* may crush
Ps 9:15 which they hid is their own *f* taken.
26:12 My *f* standeth in an even place:
36:11 Let not the *f* of pride come against
38:16 when my *f* slippeth, they magnify
66: 6 they went through the flood on *f*:
68:23 thy *f* may be dipped in the blood of
91:12 thou dash thy *f* against a stone.
94:18 I said, My *f* slippeth; thy mercy,
121: 3 will not suffer thy *f* to be moved:
Pr 1:15 refrain thy *f* from their path:
3:23 and thy *f* shall not stumble.
26 shall keep thy *f* from being taken.
4:27 to the left: remove thy *f* from evil.
25:17 thy *f* from thy neighbour's house;
19 broken tooth, and a *f* out of joint.
Ec 5: 1 Keep thy *f* when thou goest to the
Isa 1: 6 From the sole of the *f* even unto
14:25 my mountains tread him under *f*:
18: 7 meted out and trodden under *f*,
20: 2 and put off thy shoe from thy *f*.
26: 6 The *f* shall tread it down, even the
41: 2 from the east, called him to his *f*,
58:13 turn away thy *f* from the sabbath,
Jer 2:25 Withhold thy *f* from being unshod,
12:10 have trodden my portion under *f*,
La 1:15 Lord hath trodden under *f* all
Eze 1: 7 was like the sole of a calf's *f*:
6:11 and stamp with thy *f*, and say,
29:11 No *f* of man shall pass through it,
11 nor *f* of beast shall pass through it,
32:13 shall the *f* of man trouble them
Da 8:13 the host to be trodden under *f*?
Am 2:15 that is swift of *f* shall not deliver
M't 4: 6 lest at any time thou dash thy *f*
5:13 and to be trodden under *f* of men.
14:13 followed him on *f* out of the cities.
18: 8 if thy hand or thy *f* offend thee,
22:13 Bind him hand and *f*, and take him
M'r 9:45 And if thy *f* offend thee, cut it off:
Lu 4:11 thou dash thy *f* against a stone.
Joh 11:44 hand and *f* with graveclothes:
Ac 7: 5 not so much as to set his *f* on:
1Co 12:15 If the *f* shall say, Because I am not
Heb 10:29 trodden under *f* the Son of God,
Re 1:13 with a garment down to the *f*,
10: 2 and he set his right *f* upon the
2 sea, and his left *f* on the earth,
11: 2 the holy city shall they tread under *f*.

foot-breadth See FOOT and BREADTH.

footmen
Nu 11:21 are six hundred thousand *f*; and
J'g 20: 2 thousand *f* that drew sword.
1Sa 4:10 fell of Israel thirty thousand *f*.
15: 4 two hundred thousand *f*, and ten
22:17 king said unto the *f* that stood
2Sa 8: 4 and twenty thousand *f*: and
10: 6 twenty thousand *f*, and of king
1Ki 20:29 hundred thousand *f* in one day.
2Ki 13: 7 and ten thousand *f*; for the king
1Ch 18: 4 and twenty thousand *f*:
19:18 forty thousand *f*, and killed
Jer 12: 5 If thou hast run with the *f*,

footsteps
Ps 17: 5 in thy paths, that my *f* slip not.
77:19 and thy *f* are not known.
89:51 reproached the *f* of thine anointed.
Ca 1: 8 thy way forth by the *f* of the flock,

footstool
1Ch 28: 2 and for the *f* of our God,
2Ch 9:18 to the throne, with a *f* of gold.
Ps 99: 5 and worship at his *f*; for he
110: 1 I make thine enemies thy *f*.
132: 7 we will worship at his *f*.
Isa 66: 1 and the earth is my *f*: where
La 2: 1 remembered not his *f* in the
M't 5:35 earth; for it is his *f*:
22:44 thine enemies thy *f*?
M'r 12:36 thine enemies thy *f*.
Lu. 20:43 thine enemies thy *f*.
Ac 2:35 make thy foes thy *f*.
7:49 and earth is my *f*:
Heb 1:13 thine enemies thy *f*?
10:13 enemies be made his *f*.
Jas 2: 3 or sit here under my *f*:

forasmuch See also FORSOMUCH.
Ge 41:39 *F* as God hath shewed thee all
Nu 10:31 *f* as thou knowest how
De 12:12 *f* as he hath no part nor
17:16 *f* as the Lord hath said unto you, Ye
Jos 17:14 *f* as the Lord hath blessed me
J'g 11:36 *f* as the Lord hath taken
1Sa 20:42 *f* as we have sworn both of
24:18 *f* as when the Lord had
2Sa 19:30 *f* as my lord the ki
1Ki 11:11 unto Solomon
13:21 *F* as thou
14: 7 *F* as

1Ki 16: 2 *F* as I exalted thee out of the3282.
2Ki 1:16 *F* as thou hast sent messengers"
1Ch 5: 1 *f* as he defiled his father's bed,
2Ch 6: 8 *F* as it was in thine heart to
Ezr 7:14 *F* as thou art sent of
Isa 8: 6 *F* as this people refuseth the
29:13 *F* as this people draw near me
Jer 10: 6 *F* as there is none like unto thee,
7 *f* as among all the wise men of the
Da 2:40 *f* as iron breaketh in
41 *f* as thou sawest the iron
45 *F* as thou sawest that
4:18 *f* as all the wise men of
5:12 *F* as an excellent spirit,
6: 4 *f* as he was faithful,
22 *f* as before him...was
Am 5:11 *F* therefore as your treading is
M't 18:25 But *f* as he had not to pay,
Lu 1: 1 *F* as many have taken in hand
Ac 9:38 And *f* as Lydda was nigh to
11:17 *F* then as God gave them the
15:24 *F* as we have heard, that certain
17:29 *F* then as we are the offspring of
24:10 *F* as I know that thou hast been of
1Co 11: 7 *f* as he is the image and glory of God:
14:12 *f* as ye are zealous of spiritual
15:58 *f* as ye know that your labour is not in
2Co 3: 3 *F* as ye are manifestly declared
Heb 2:14 *F* then as the children are
1Pe 1:18 *F* as ye know that ye were not
4: 1 *F* then as Christ hath suffered for us

forbad
De 2:37 the Lord our God *f* us.
M't 3:14 John *f* him, saying, I have need
M'r 9:38 we *f* him, because he followeth
Lu 9:49 we *f* him, because he followeth
2Pe 2:16 *f* the madness of the prophet.

forbare
1Sa 23:13 and he *f* to go forth.
2Ch 25:16 Then the prophet *f*, and said, I
Jer 41: 8 So he *f*, and slew them not among

forbear See also FORBARE; FORBEARETH; FORBEARING; FORBORN.
Ex 23: 5 and wouldest *f* to help him,
De 23:22 But if thou shalt *f* to vow,
1Ki 22: 6 battle, or shall I *f*? And they said,
15 or shall we *f*? And he answered
2Ch 18: 5 or shall I *f*? And they said,
14 to battle, or shall I *f*? And he said,
25:16 *f*; why shouldest thou be smitten?
35:21 *f* thee from meddling with God,
Ne 9:30 many years didst thou *f* them,
Job 16: 6 and though I *f*, what am I eased?
Pr 24:11 If thou *f* to deliver them that are
Jer 40: 4 to come with me into Babylon, *f*:
Eze 2: 5 will hear, or whether they will *f*,
7 will hear, or whether they will *f*:
3:11 will hear, or whether they will *f*.
27 he that forbeareth, let him *f*:
24:17 *F* to cry, make no mourning
Zec 11:12 and if not, *f*. So they weighed
1Co 9: 6 have not we power to *f* working?
2Co 12: 6 I *f*, lest any man should think of
1Th 3: 1 when we could no longer *f*, we
5 when I could no longer *f*, I went

forbearance
Ro 2: 4 the riches of his goodness and *f*
3:25 that are past, through the *f* of God;

forbeareth
Nu 9:13 and *f* to keep the passover, even
Eze 3:27 and he that *f*, let him forbear:

forbearing
Pr 25:15 by long *f* is a prince persuaded,
Jer 20: 9 I was weary with *f*, and I could
Eph 4: 2 *f* one another in love;
6: 9 things unto them, *f* threatening:
Col 3:13 *F* one another, and forgiving one

forbid See also FORBAD; FORBIDDEN; FORBIDDETH; FORBIDDING.
Ge 44: 7 God *f* that thy servants should
17 God *f* that I should do so:
Nu 11:28 said, My lord Moses, *f* them.
Jos 22:29 God *f* that we should rebel
24:16 God *f* that we should forsake the
1Sa 12:23 God *f* that I should sin against
14:45 God *f*: as the Lord liveth,
20: 2 And he said unto him, God *f*;
24: 6 he said unto his men, The Lord *f*
26:11 The Lord *f* that I should stretch
1Ki 21: 3 The Lord *f* it me, that I should
1Ch 11:19 And said, My God *f* it me,
Job 27: 5 God *f* that I should justify you:
M't 19:14 and *f* them not, to come unto me:
M'r 9:39 But Jesus said, *F* him not:
10:14 to come unto me, and *f* them not:
Lu 6:29 *f* not to take thy coat also.
9:50 *F* him not: for he that is not
18:16 and *f* them not: for of such is the
20:16 heard it, they said, God *f*.
Ac 10:47 Can any man *f* water, that these
24:23 and that he should *f* none of his
Ro 3: 4 God *f*: let God be true, but
6 God *f*: for then how shall God
31 God *f*: yea, we establish the
6: 2 God *f*. How shall we, that are
15 law, but under grace? God *f*.
7: 7 Is the law sin? God *f*. Nay, I
13 made death unto me? God *f*.
9:14 unrighteousness...God? God *f*.
11: 1 cast away his people? God *f*.
11 that they should fall? God *f*:
6:15 members of an harlot? God *f*.
f not to speak with tongues.

Ga 2:17 the ministers of sin? God *f*.
3:21 the promises of God? God *f*:
6:14 God *f* that I should glory,

forbidden
Le 5:17 things which are *f* to be done by
De 4:23 the Lord thy God hath *f* thee.
Ac 16: 6 *f* of the Holy Ghost to preach

forbiddeth
3Jo 10 *f* them that would, and casteth

forbidding
Lu 23: 2 *f* to give tribute to Cæsar, saying
Ac 28:31 all confidence, no man *f* him.
1Th 2:16 *F* us to speak to the Gentiles
1Ti 4: 3 *F* to marry, and commanding to

forbore See FORBARE.

forborn
Jer 51:30 men of Babylon have *f* to fight,

forborne See FORBORN.

force See also FORCED; FORCES; FORCIBLE; FORCING.
Ge 31:31 wouldest take by *f* thy daughters
De 22:25 the man *f* her, and lie with her:
34: 7 not dim, nor his natural *f* abated.
1Sa 2:16 and if not, I will take it by *f*.
2Sa 13:12 Nay, my brother, do not *f* me;
Ezr 4:23 them to cease by *f* and power.
Es 7: 8 he *f* the queen also before me
Job 30:18 By the great *f* of my disease
40:16 and his *f* is in the navel of his
Jer 18:21 their blood by the *f* of the sword
23:10 is evil, and their *f* is not right.
48:45 of Heshbon because of the *f*:
Eze 34: 4 but with *f* and with cruelty have
35: 5 by the *f* of the sword in the time
Am 2:14 strong shall not strengthen his *f*,
M't 11:12 and the violent take it by *f*.
Joh 6:15 take him by *f*, to make him a king
Ac 23:10 to take him by *f* from among them,
Heb 9:17 a testament is of *f* after men are

forced
J'g 1:34 Amorites *f* the children of Dan
20: 5 have they *f*, that she is dead.
1Sa 13:12 I *f* myself therefore, and offered a
2Sa 13:14 than she, *f* her, and lay with her.
22 because he had *f* his sister
32 from the day that he *f* his sister
Pr 7:21 the flattering of her lips she *f* him.

forces
2Ch 17: 2 he placed *f* in all the fenced cities
Job 36:19 nor all the *f* of strength.
Isa 60: 5 the *f* of the Gentiles shall come
11 unto thee the *f* of the Gentiles,
Jer 40: 7 when all the captains of the *f* which
13 and all the captains of the *f* that
41:11, 13, 16 the *f* that were with him,
42: 1 Then all the captains of the *f*, and
8 the *f* which were with him, and all
43: 4 captains of the *f*, and all the people,
5 all the captains of the *f*, took all
Da 11:10 assemble a multitude of great *f*:
38 shall he honour the God of *f*:
Ob 11 carried away captive his *f*, and

forcible
Job 6:25 How *f* are right words! but what

forcing
De 20:19 destroy the trees thereof by *f* an
Pr 30:33 *f* of wrath bringeth forth strife.

ford See also FORDS.
Ge 32:22 and passed over the *f* Jabbok.

fords
Jos 2: 7 the way to Jordan unto the *f*:
J'g 3:28 the *f* of Jordan toward Moab,
Isa 16: 2 Moab shall be at the *f* of Arnon.

fore See AFORE; BEFORE; FORECAST; FOREFATHERS; FOREFRONT; FOREHEAD; FOREKNOW; FOREKNOWLEDGE; FOREMEN; FOREMOST; FOREPART; FOREORDAINED; FORERUNNER; FORESAW; FORESEETH; FORESEEING; FORESHIP; FORESKIN; FORETELL; FORWARD; FOREWARN; HERETOFORE; THERETOFORE; WHEREFORE.

forecast
Da 11:24 *f* his devices against the strong
25 they shall *f* devices against him.

forefathers
Jer 11:10 back to the iniquities of their *f*,
2Ti 1: 3 whom I serve from my *f* with pure

forefront
Ex 26: 9 in the *f* of the tabernacle.
28:37 upon the *f* of the mitre it shall
Le 8: 9 upon his *f*, did he put the
1Sa 14: 5 The *f* of the one was situate
2Sa 11:15 in the *f* of the hottest battle,
2Ki 16:14 the *f* of the house, from between
2Ch 20:27 Jehoshaphat in the *f* of them,
Eze 40:19 from the *f* of the lower gate unto
19 the *f* of the inner court without
47: 1 *f* of the house stood toward the

forehead See also FOREHEADS.
Ex 28:38 And it shall be upon Aaron's *f*,
38 and it shall be always upon his *f*,
Le 13:41 he is *f* bald: yet is he clean.
42 or bald *f*, a white reddish sore;
42 in his bald head, or his bald *f*.
43 or in his bald *f*, as the leprosy
1Sa 17:49 and smote the Philistine in his *f*,
49 that the stone sunk into his *f*;
2Ch 26:19 the leprosy even rose up in his *f*
20 behold, he was leprous in his *f*,
Jer 3: 3 and thou hadst a whore's *f*,

Eze 3: 8 *f* strong against their foreheads.
9 harder than flint have I made thy *f*.
16:12 And I put a jewel on thy *f*,
Re 14: 9 and receive his mark in his *f*,
17: 5 upon her *f* was a name written,

foreheads
Eze 3: 8 forehead strong against their *f*.
9: 4 set a mark upon the *f* of the men
Re 7: 3 servants of our God in their *f*.
9: 4 have not the seal of God in their *f*.
13:16 in their right hand, or in their *f*:
14: 1 Father's name written in their *f*.
20: 4 received his mark upon their *f*,
22: 4 and his name shall be in their *f*.

foreigner See also FOREIGNERS.
Ex 12:45 A *f* and an hired servant shall
De 15: 3 Of a *f* thou mayest exact it again:

foreigners
Ob 11 and *f* entered into his gates, and
Eph 2:19 ye are no more strangers and *f*,

foreknew
Ro 11: 2 cast away his people which he *f*.

foreknow See also FOREKNEW.
Ro 8:29 For whom he did *f*, he also did

foreknowledge
Ac 2:23 and *f* of God, ye have taken, and
1Pe 1: 2 Elect according to the *f* of God

foremost
Ge 32:17 And he commanded the *f*, saying,
33: 2 handmaids and their children *f*,
2Sa 18:27 the running of the *f* is like the

foreordained
1Pe 1:20 Who verily was *f* before the

forepart
Ex 28:27 toward the *f* thereof, over against
39:20 ephod underneath, toward the *f*
1Ki 6:20 oracle in the *f* was twenty cubits
Eze 42: 7 court on the *f* of the chambers,
Ac 27:41 the *f* stuck fast, and remained

forerunner
Heb 6:20 Whither the *f* is for us entered,

foresaw
Ac 2:25 I *f* the Lord always before my

foreseeing
Ga 3: 8 the scripture, *f* that God would

foreseeth
Pr 22: 3 A prudent man *f* the evil, and
27:12 A prudent man *f* the evil, and

foreship
Ac 27:30 have cast anchors out of the *f*,

foreskin See also FORESKINS.
Ge 17:11 circumcise the flesh of your *f*;
14 flesh of his *f* is not circumcised,
23 circumcised the flesh of their *f*
24, 25 circumcised in the flesh of his *f*.
Ex 4:25 stone, and cut off the *f* of her son,
Le 12: 3 flesh of his *f* shall be circumcised.
De 10:16 Circumcise therefore the *f* of your
Hab 2:16 and let thy *f* be uncovered:

foreskins
Jos 5: 3 of Israel at the hill of the *f*.
1Sa 18:25 an hundred *f* of the Philistines,
27 David brought their *f*, and they
2Sa 3:14 an hundred *f* of the Philistines.
Jer 4: 4 and take away the *f* of your heart,

forest See also FORESTS.
1Sa 22: 5 and came into the *f* of Hareth.
1Ki 7: 2 also the house of the *f* of Lebanon;
10:17 in the house of the *f* of Lebanon.
21 of the house of the *f* of Lebanon
2Ki 19:23 and into the *f* of his Carmel.
2Ch 9:16 in the house of the *f* of Lebanon
20 of the house of the *f* of Lebanon
Ne 2: 8 Asaph the keeper of the king's *f*,
Ps 50:10 For every beast of the *f* is mine,
104:20 all the beasts of the *f* do creep
Isa 9:18 kindle in the thickets of the *f*,
10:18 shall consume the glory of his *f*,
19 And the trees of his *f* shall be few,
34 shall cut down the thickets of the *f*
21:13 In the *f* in Arabia shall ye lodge,
22: 8 the armour of the house of the *f*.
29:17 field shall be esteemed as a *f*?
32:15 fruitful field be counted for a *f*
19 shall hail, coming down on the *f*;
37:24 border, and the *f* of his Carmel.
44:14 himself among the trees of the *f*;
23 O *f*, and every tree therein:
56: 9 yea, all ye beasts in the *f*.
Jer 5: 6 a lion out of the *f* shall slay them,
10: 3 one cutteth a tree out of the *f*,
12: 8 is unto me as a lion in the *f*;
21:14 I will kindle a fire in the *f* thereof,
26:18 the house as the high places of a *f*.
46:23 They shall cut down her *f*, saith
Eze 15: 2 which is among the trees of the *f*?
6 vine tree among the trees of the *f*,
20:46 prophesy against the *f* of the south
47 And say to the *f* of the south,
Ho 2:12 and I will make them a *f*,
Am 3: 4 Will a lion roar in the *f*, when he
Mic 3:12 the house as the high places of the *f*.
5: 8 as a lion among the beasts of the *f*,
Zec 11: 2 the *f* of the vintage is come down.

forests
2Ch 27: 4 and in the *f* he built castles and
Ps 29: 9 to calve, and discovereth the *f*:
Eze 39:10 neither cut down any out of the *f*;

foretell See also FORETOLD.
2Co 13: 2 and f you, as if I were present,

foretold
M'r 13:23 behold, I have f you all things.
Ac 3:24 have likewise f of these days.

forever See EVER.

forewarn See also FORWARNED.
Lu 12: 5 I will f you whom ye shall fear:

forewarned
1Th 4: 6 all such as we also have f you and

forfeited
Ezr 10: 8 all his substance should be f, and

forgat See also FORGOT.
Ge 40:23 remember Joseph, but f him.
J'g 3: 7 and f the Lord their God, and
1Sa 12: 9 when they f the Lord their God,
Ps 78:11 And f his works, and his wonders
106:13 They soon f his works; they
21 They f God their saviour, which
La 3:17 far off from peace: I f prosperity.
Ho 2:13 went after her lovers, and f me,

forgave See also FORGAVEST.
Ps 78:38 f their iniquity, and destroyed
M't 18:27 loosed him, and f him the debt.
32 I f thee all that debt, because thou
Lu 7:42 to pay, he frankly f them both.
43 that he, to whom he f most.
2Co 2:10 if I f any thing, to whom I f it,
10 for your sakes f I it in the person
Col 3:13 even as Christ f you, so also do ye.

forgavest
Ps 32: 5 and thou f the iniquity of my sin.
99: 8 thou wast a God that f them,

forged
Ps 119:69 the proud have f a lie against me:

forgers
Job 13: 4 But ye are f of lies, ye are all

forget See also FORGAT; FORGETFUL; FORGETTEST; FORGETTETH; FORGETTING; FORGOT; FORGOTTEN.
Ge 27:45 and he f that which thou hast
41:51 hath made me f all my toil,
De 4: 9 lest thou f the things which thine
23 lest ye f the covenant of the Lord
31 nor f the covenant of thy fathers
6:12 Then beware lest thou f the Lord,
8:11 Beware that thou f not the Lord
14 and thou f the Lord thy God,
19 if thou do at all f the Lord thy God,
9: 7 Remember, and f not, how thou
25:19 under heaven; thou shalt not f it.
1Sa 1:11 and not f thine handmaid, but
2Ki 17:38 have made with you ye shall not f;
Job 8:13 So are the paths of all that f God;
9:27 If I say, I will f my complaint,
11:16 Because thou shalt f thy misery,
24:20 The womb shall f him; the worm
Ps 9:17 and all the nations that f God.
10:12 thine hand: f not the humble.
13: 1 How long wilt thou f me, O Lord?
45:10 f also thine own people, and thy
50:22 ye that f God, lest I tear you in
59:11 slay them not, lest my people f:
74:19 f not the congregation of thy poor
23 F not the voice of thine enemies:
78: 7 and not f the works of God,
102: 4 so that I f to eat my bread.
103: 2 my soul, and f not all his benefits:
119:16 thy statutes: I will not f thy word.
83 yet do I not f thy statutes.
93 I will never f thy precepts: for
109 in my hand: yet do I not f thy law.
141 yet do not I f thy precepts.
153 deliver me: for I do not f thy law.
176 I do not f thy commandments.
137: 5 If I f thee, O Jerusalem,
5 let my right hand f her cunning.
Pr 3: 1 My son, f not my law; but let thine
4: 5 get understanding: f it not;
31: 5 Lest they drink, and f the law,
7 Let him drink, and f his poverty,
Isa 49:15 Can a woman f her sucking child,
15 son of her womb? yea, they may f,
15 yet will I not f thee.
54: 4 shalt f the shame of thy youth,
65:11 forsake the Lord, that f my holy
Jer 2:32 Can a maid f her ornaments,
23:27 to cause my people to f my name
39 I, even I, will utterly f you,
La 5:20 Wherefore dost thou f us for ever,
Ho 4: 6 thy God, I will also f thy children.
Am 8: 7 I will never f any of their works.
Heb 6:10 to f your work and labour of love,
13:16 do good and to communicate f not:

forgetful
He 13: 2 Be not f to entertain strangers:
Jas 1:25 being not a f hearer, but a doer

forgetfulness
Ps 88:12 righteousness in the land of f?

forgettest
Ps 44:24 and f our affliction and our
Isa 51:13 And f the Lord thy maker, that

forgetteth
Job 39:15 And f that the foot may crush
Ps 9:12 he f not the cry of the humble.
Pr 2:17 and f the covenant of her God.
Jas 1:24 f what manner of man he was.

forgetting
Ph'p 3:13 f those things which are behind,

forgive See also FORGAVE; FORGIVEN; FORGIVETH; FORGIVING.
Ge 50:17 F, I pray thee now the trespass,
17 f the trespass of the servants of the
Ex 10:17 Now therefore f, I pray thee, my
32:32 Yet now, if thou wilt f their sin—;
Nu 30: 5 the Lord shall f her, because her
8 effect: and the Lord shall f her.
12 void; and the Lord shall f her.
Jos 24:19 he will not f your transgressions
1Sa 25:28 I pray thee, f the trespass of thine
1Ki 8:30 and when thou hearest, f.
34 and f the sin of thy people Israel,
36 and f the sin of thy servants,
39 heaven thy dwelling place, and f,
50 And f thy people that have sinned
2Ch 6:21 heaven; and when thou hearest, f.
25 hear thou from the heavens, and f
27 hear thou from heaven, and f
30 heaven, thy dwelling place, and f,
39 and f thy people which have
7:14 and will f their sin, and will heal
Ps 25:18 my pain; and f all my sins.
86: 5 Lord, art good and ready to f;
Isa 2: 9 himself: therefore f them not.
Jer 18:23 f not their iniquity, neither blot
31:34 I will f their iniquity, and I will
36: 3 that I may f their iniquity and
Da 9:19 O Lord, hear; O Lord, f;
Am 7: 2 O Lord God, f, I beseech thee:
M't 6:12 f us our debts, as we f our
14 For if ye f men their trespasses,
14 your heavenly Father will also f
15 if ye f not men their trespasses,
15 will your Father f your trespasses.
9: 6 hath power on earth to f sins,
18:21 my brother sin against me and I f
35 f not every one his brother their
M'r 2: 7 who can f sins but God only?
10 man hath power on earth to f sins,
11:25 f, if ye have ought against any:
25 may f you your trespasses.
26 if ye do not f, neither will your
26 in heaven f your trespasses.
Lu 5:21 Who can f sins, but God alone?
24 hath power upon earth to f sins,
6:37 f, and ye shall be forgiven:
11: 4 f us our sins; for we also f every
17: 3 and if he repent, f him.
4 saying, I repent; thou shalt f him.
23:34 Then said Jesus, Father, f them;
2Co 2: 7 ought rather to f him, and comfort
10 To whom ye f any thing, I f also:
12:13 to you? f me this wrong.
1Jo 1: 9 faithful and just to f us our sins,

forgiven
Le 4:20 for them, and it shall be f them.
26 concerning his sin, and it shall be f
31 for him, and it shall be f him.
35 committed, and it shall be f him.
5:10 hath sinned, and it shall be f him.
13 of these, and it shall be f him:
16 offering, and it shall be f him.
18 it not, and it shall be forgiven him.
6: 7 shall be f him for any thing of all
19:22 which he hath done shall be f him.
Nu 14:19 and as thou hast f this people,
15:25 and it shall be f them; for it is
26 it shall be f all the congregation
28 for him; and it shall be f him.
De 21: 8 And the blood shall be f them.
Ps 32: 1 is he whose transgression is f,
85: 2 Thou hast f the iniquity of thy
Isa 33:24 that dwell therein shall be f their
M't 9: 2 be of good cheer; thy sins be f
5 to say, Thy sins be f thee;
12:31 and blasphemy shall be f unto
31 the Holy Ghost shall not be f unto
32 the Son of man, it shall be f him:
32 Holy Ghost, it shall not be f him,
M'r 2: 5 the palsy, Son, thy sins be f thee.
9 Thy sins be f thee; or to say, Arise,
3:28 All sins shall be f unto the sons of
4:12 and their sins should be f them.
Lu 5:20 unto him, Man, thy sins are f thee.
23 Thy sins be f thee; or to say, Rise
6:37 forgive, and ye shall be f:
7:47 Her sins, which are many, are f;
47 to whom little is f, the same loveth
48 he said unto her, Thy sins are f.
12:10 the Son of man, it shall be f him;
10 the Holy Ghost it shall not be f.
Ac 8:22 thought of thine heart may be f thee.
Ro 4: 7 are they whose iniquities are f,
Eph 4:32 God for Christ's sake hath f you.
Col 2:13 him, having f you all trespasses;
Jas 5:15 sins, they shall be f him.
1Jo 2:12 because your sins are f you for

forgiveness See also FORGIVENESSES.
Ps 130: 4 But there is f with thee, that thou
M'r 3:29 the Holy Ghost hath never f,
Ac 5:31 repentance to Israel, and f of
13:38 preached unto you the f of sins:
26:18 that they may receive f of sins,
Eph 1: 7 the f of sins, according to the
Col 1:14 through his blood, even the f of sins:

forgivenesses
Da 9: 9 to... God belong mercies and f,

forgiveth
Ps 103: 3 Who f all thine iniquities; who
Lu 7:49 Who is this that f sins also?

forgiving
Ex 34: 7 for thousands, f iniquity and
Nu 14:18 of great mercy, f iniquity and
Eph 4:32 f one another, even as God for
Col 3:13 and f one another, if any man

forgot See also FORGAT; FORGOTTEN.
De 24:19 and hast f a sheaf in the field,

forgotten
Ge 41:30 and all the plenty shall be f in
De 26:13 neither have I f them:
31:21 for it shall not be f out of the
32:18 and hast f God that formed thee.
Job 19:14 and my familiar friends have f me.
28: 4 even the waters f of the foot:
Ps 9:18 the needy shall not always be f:
10:11 hath said in his heart, God hath f:
31:12 I am f as a dead man out of
42: 9 Why hast thou f me? why go I
44:17 yet have we not f thee, neither
20 If we have f the name of our God,
77: 9 Hath God f to be gracious? hath
119:61 but I have not f thy law.
139 because mine enemies have f thy
Ec 2:16 in the days to come shall all be f.
8:10 and they were f in the city where
9: 5 for the memory of them is f.
Isa 17:10 Because thou hast f the God of thy
23:15 that Tyre shall be f seventy years,
16 thou harlot that hast been f;
44:21 Israel, thou shalt not be f of me.
49:14 and my Lord hath f me.
65:16 because the former troubles are f,
Jer 2:32 yet my people have f me days
3:21 they have f the Lord their God.
13:25 because thou hast f me, and
18:15 my people hath f me, they have
20:11 their...confusion shall never be f.
23:27 their fathers have f my name
40 shame, which shall not be f.
30:14 All thy lovers have f thee;
44: 9 f the wickedness of your fathers,
50: 5 covenant that shall not be f.
6 they have f their restingplace.
La 2: 6 solemn feasts and sabbaths to be f
Eze 22:12 and hast f me, saith the Lord God.
23:35 Because thou hast f me, and cast
Ho 4: 6 thou hast f the law of thy God,
8:14 For Israel hath f his Maker,
13: 6 therefore have they f me.
M't 16: 5 side, they had f to take bread.
M'r 8:14 disciples had f to take bread,
Lu 12: 6 not one of them is f before God?
Heb 12: 5 And ye have f the exhortation
2Pe 1: 9 hath f that he was purged

forks
1Sa 13:21 the coulters, and for the f,

form See also FORMED; FORMETH; FORMS; INFORM; PERFORM; REFORM; TRANSFORM.
Ge 1: 2 And the earth was without f,
1Sa 28:14 said unto her, What f is he of?
2Sa 14:20 To fetch about this f of speech
2Ch 4: 7 of gold according to their f, and
Job 4:16 I could not discern the f thereof:
Isa 45: 7 I f the light, and create darkness:
52:14 his f more than the sons of men:
53: 2 he hath no f nor comeliness;
Jer 4:23 earth, and, lo, it was without f,
Eze 8: 3 he put forth the f of an hand,
10 behold every f of creeping things,
10: 8 the f of a man's hand under their
43:11 shew them the f of the house,
11 may keep the whole f thereof,
Da 2:31 and the f thereof was terrible.
3:19 the f of his visage was changed
25 f of the fourth is like the Son of
M'r 16:12 he appeared in another f unto
Ro 2:20 which hast the f of knowledge
6:17 that f of doctrine which was
Ph'p 2: 6 Who, being in the f of God,
7 took upon him the f of a servant,
2Ti 1:13 Hold fast the f of sound words,
3: 5 Having a f of godliness, but

formed See also CONFORMED; DEFORMED; REFORMED; TRANSFORMED.
Ge 2: 7 And the Lord God f man of the
8 he put the man whom he had f.
19 the ground the Lord f every beast
De 32:18 hast forgotten God that f thee.
2Ki 19:25 of ancient times that I have f it?
Job 26: 5 Dead things are f from under
13 hand hath f the crooked serpent.
33: 6 I also am f out of the clay.
Ps 90: 2 or ever thou hadst f the earth
94: 9 that f the eye, shall he not see?
95: 5 and his hands f the dry land.
Pr 26:10 The great God that f all things
Isa 27:11 he that f them will shew them
37:26 of ancient times, that I have f it?
43: 1 and he that f thee, O Israel,
7 I have f him; yea, I have made
10 before me there was no God f,
21 This people have I f for myself;
44: 2 and f thee from the womb,
10 Who hath f a god, or molten a
21 have f thee; thou art my servant:
24 and he that f thee from the womb,
45:18 God himself that f the earth and
18 he f it to be inhabited: I am the
49: 5 the Lord that f me from the womb
54:17 No weapon that is f against thee
Jer 1: 5 Before I f thee in the belly
33: 2 the Lord that f it, to establish it;
Am 7: 1 f grasshoppers in the beginning
Ro 9:20 the thing f say to him that f it,
Gal 4:19 until Christ be f in you,
1Ti 2:13 Adam was first f, then Eve.

former
Ge 40:13 after the f manner when thou
Nu 21:26 fought against the f king of Moab.
De 24: 4 Her f husband, which sent her
Ru 4: 7 this was the manner in f time
1Sa 17:30 answered him again after the f
2Ki 1:14 two captains of the f fifties with
17:34 they do after the f manners:
40 but they did after their f manner.
Ne 5:15 the f governors that had been
Job 8: 8 enquire, I pray thee, of the f age.
30: 3 in f time desolate and waste.
Ps 79: 8 not against us f iniquities:
89:49 where are thy f lovingkindnesses,
Ec 1:11 is no remembrance of f things;
7:10 the f days were better than these?
Isa 41:22 let them shew the f things, what
42: 9 the f things are come to pass,
43: 9 declare this, and shew us f things?
18 Remember ye not the f things,
46: 9 Remember the f things of old:
48: 3 I have declared the f things from
61: 4 shall raise up the f desolations,
65: 7 will I measure their f work into
16 the f troubles are forgotten,
17 and the f shall not be remembered,
Jer 5:24 rain, both the f and the latter,
10:16 for he is the f of all things:
34: 5 f kings which were before thee,
36:28 f words that were in the first roll,
51:19 for he is the f of all things:
Eze 16:55 shall return to their f estate, and
55 shall return to their f estate, then
55 shall return to your f estate.
Da 11:13 a multitude greater than the f,
29 but it shall not be as the f,
Hos 6: 3 latter and f rain unto the earth.
Joe 2:23 given you the f rain moderately,
23 the f rain, and the latter rain
Hag 2: 9 shall be greater than of the f,
Zec 1: 4 unto whom the f prophets have
7: 7 Lord hath cried by the f prophets,
12 sent in his spirit by the f prophets:
8:11 of this people as in the f days,
14: 8 half of them toward the f sea.
Mal 3: 4 the days of old, and as in f years.
Ac 1: 1 The f treatise have I made, O
Eph 4:22 concerning the f conversation
Heb 10:32 call to remembrance the f days,
1Pe 1:14 according to the f lusts in your
Re 21: 4 for the f things are passed away.

formeth See also PERFORMETH.
Am 4:13 For, lo, he that f the mountains,
Zec 12: 1 and f the spirit of man within him.

forming See PERFORMING; TRANSFORMING.

forms
Eze 43:11 f thereof, and all the ordinances
11 all the f thereof, and all the laws

fornication See also FORNICATIONS.
2Ch 21:11 of Jerusalem to commit f, and
Isa 23:17 and shall commit f with all the
Eze 16:26 Thou hast also committed f with
29 hast moreover multiplied thy f
M't 5:32 his wife, saving for the cause of f,
19: 9 away his wife, except it be for f,
Joh 8:41 We be not born of f; we have one
Ac 15:20 from f, and from things strangled
29 from things strangled, and from f:
21:25 and from strangled, and from f.
Ro 1:29 f, wickedness, covetousness,
1Co 5: 1 that there is f among you, and
1 such f as is not so much as
6:13 Now the body is not for f,
18 Flee f. Every sin that a man doeth
18 but he that committeth f sinneth
7: 2 to avoid f, let every man have
10: 8 Neither let us commit f, as some
2Co 12:21 and f and lasciviousness which
Ga 5:19 Adultery, f, uncleanness,
Eph 5: 3 But f, and all uncleanness, or
Col 3: 5 f, uncleanness, inordinate
1Th 4: 3 that ye should abstain from f:
Jude 7 giving themselves over to f,
Re 2:14 unto idols, and to commit f.
20 to commit f, and to eat things
21 gave her space to repent of her f;
9:21 nor of their f, nor of their thefts.
14: 8 the wine of the wrath of her f.
17: 2 of the earth have committed f,
2 drunk with the wine of her f.
4 and filthiness of her f:
18: 3 of the wine of the wrath of her f,
3 have committed f with her, and
9 who have committed f and lived
19: 2 did corrupt the earth with her f,

fornications
Eze 16:15 pouredst out thy f on every one
M't 15:19 thoughts, murders, adulteries, f,
M'r 7:21 evil thoughts, adulteries, f,

fornicator See also FORNICATORS.
1Co 5:11 Man that is called a brother be a f,
Heb 12:16 Lest there be any f, or profane

fornicators
1Co 5: 9 an epistle not to company with f:
10 altogether with the f of this world.
6: 9 neither f, nor idolaters, nor

forsake See FORSAKEN; FORSAKETH; FORSAKING; FORSOOK.
De 4:31 he will not f thee, neither destroy
12:19 heed to thyself that thou f not
14:27 thou shalt not f him; for he hath
31: 6 he will not fail thee, nor f thee.
8 will not fail thee, neither f thee:
De 31:16 will f me, and break my covenant
17 and I will f them, and I will hide
Jos 1: 5 I will not fail thee, nor f thee.
24:16 forbid that we should f the Lord,
20 If ye f the Lord, and serve strange
J'g 9:11 Should I f my sweetness, and my
1Sa 12:22 the Lord will not f his people for
1Ki 6:13 and will not f my people Israel.
8:57 let him not leave us, nor f us:
2Ki 21:14 And I will f the remnant of mine
1Ch 28: 9 if thou f him, he will cast thee off
20 he will not fail thee, nor f thee,
2Ch 7:19 if ye turn away, and f my statutes
15: 2 but if ye f him, he will f you.
Ezr 8:22 is against all them that f him.
Ne 9:31 utterly consume them, nor f them;
10:39 we will not f the house of our
Job 20:13 Though he spare it, and f it not;
Ps 27: 9 leave me not, neither f me, O God
10 my father and my mother f me,
37: 8 Cease from anger, and f wrath:
38:21 F me not, O Lord: O my God,
71: 9 f me not when my strength faileth
18 O God, f me not; until I have
89:30 If his children f my law, and walk
94:14 neither will he f his inheritance.
119: 8 will keep thy statutes: O f me not
53 of the wicked that f thy law.
138: 8 f not the works of thine own
Pr 1: 8 and f not the law of thy mother:
3: 3 Let not mercy and truth f thee:
4: 2 good doctrine, f ye not my law.
6 F her not, and she shall preserve
6:20 and f not the law of thy mother:
9: 6 F the foolish, and live; and go
27:10 and thy father's friend, f not;
28: 4 that f the law praise the wicked:
Isa 1:28 that f the Lord shall be consumed.
41:17 the God of Israel will not f them.
42:16 I do unto them, and not f them.
55: 7 Let the wicked f his way, and the
65:11 But ye are they that f the Lord,
Jer 17:13 all that f thee shall be ashamed,
23:33 I will even f you, saith the Lord.
39 and I will f you, and the city
51: 9 but she is not healed: f her,
La 5:20 thou forget us for ever, and f us
Eze 20: 8 did they f the idols of Egypt:
Da 11:30 them that f the holy covenant.
Jon 2: 8 lying vanities f their own mercy.
Ac 21:21 among the Gentiles to f Moses,
Heb 13: 5 I will never leave thee, nor f thee.

forsaken
De 28:20 doings, whereby thou hast f me.
29:25 they have f the covenant of the
J'g 6:13 but now the Lord hath f us,
10:10 have f our God, and also served
13 have f me, and served other gods:
1Sa 8: 8 have f me, and served other gods,
12:10 have f the Lord, and have served
1Ki 11:33 have f me, and have worshipped
18:18 f the commandments of the Lord,
19:10, 14 of Israel have f thy covenant,
2Ki 22:17 Because they have f me, and have
2Ch 12: 5 Thus saith the Lord, Ye have f me,
13:10 our God, and we have not f him;
11 Lord our God, but ye have f him.
21:10 had f the Lord God of his fathers.
24:20 have f the Lord, he hath also f you.
24 hand, because they had f the Lord
28: 6 men; because they had f the Lord
29: 6 have f him, and have turned away
34:25 f me, and have burned incense
Ezr 9: 9 yet our God hath not f us
10 for we have f thy commandments,
Ne 13:11 Why is the house of God f?
Job 18: 4 shall the earth be f for thee?
20:19 oppressed and hath f the poor;
Ps 9:10 hast not f them that seek thee.
22: 1 my God, why hast thou f me?
37:25 have I not seen the righteous f,
71:11 God hath f him: persecute and
Isa 1: 4 they have f the Lord, they have
2: 6 thou hast f thy people the house
7:16 that thou abhorrest shall be f of
17: 2 The cities of Aroer are f: they
9 his strong cities be as a f bough,
27:10 the habitation f, and left like a
32:14 palaces shall be f; the multitude
49:14 Zion said, The Lord hath f me,
54: 6 hath called thee as a woman f and
7 For a small moment have I f thee;
60:15 thou hast been f and hated,
62: 4 Thou shalt no more be termed F;
12 called, Sought out, A city not f.
Jer 1:16 who have f me, and have burned
2:13 have f me the fountain of living
17 in that thou hast f the Lord thy
19 that thou hast f the Lord thy God,
4:29 every city shall be f, and not a man
5: 7 thy children have f me, and sworn
19 Like as ye have f me, and served
7:29 and f the generation of his wrath.
9:13 they have f my law which I set
19 we have f the land, because our
12: 7 I have f mine house, I have left
15: 6 Thou hast f me, saith the Lord,
16:11 fathers have f me, saith the Lord,
11 and have f me, and have not kept
17:13 they have f the Lord, the fountain
18:14 come from another place be f?
19: 4 have f me, and have estranged
22: 9 have f the covenant of the Lord
25:38 He hath f his covert, as the lion;
51: 5 Israel hath not been f, nor Judah
Eze 8:12 not; the Lord hath f the earth.
Eze 9: 9 say, The Lord hath f the earth.
36: 4 the cities that are f, which became
Am 5: 2 she is f upon her land; there is
Zep 2: 4 Gaza shall be f, and Ashkelon
M't 19:27 we have f all, and followed thee;
29 every one that hath f houses,
27:46 my God, why hast thou f me?
M'r 15:34 God, my God, why hast thou f me?
2Co 4: 9 Persecuted, but not f; cast down,
2Ti 4:10 Demas hath f me, having loved
2Pe 2:15 Which have f the right way, and

forsaketh
Job 6:14 he f the fear of the Almighty.
Ps 37:28 judgment, and f not his saints;
Pr 2:17 Which f the guide of her youth,
15:10 is grievous unto him that f the way:
28:13 confesseth and f them shall have
Lu 14:33 of you that f not all that he hath,

forsaking
Isa 6:12 there be a great f in the midst
Heb 10:25 Not f the assembling of ourselves

forsomuch See also FORASMUCH; INASMUCH.
Lu 19: 9 f as he also is a son of Abraham.

forsook See also FORSOOKEST.
De 32:15 then he f God which made him,
J'g 2:12 f the Lord God of their fathers,
13 they f the Lord, and served Baal
10: 6 f the Lord, and served not him.
1Sa 31: 7 they f the cities, and fled; and the
1Ki 9: 9 Because they f the Lord their God,
12: 8 he f the counsel of the old men,
13 and f the old men's counsel that
2Ki 21:22 he f the Lord God of his fathers,
1Ch 10: 7 then they f their cities, and fled;
2Ch 7:22 they f the Lord God of their fathers,
10: 8 he f the counsel which the old men
13 Rehoboam f the counsel of the old.
12: 1 he f the law of the Lord, and all
Ps 78:60 he f the tabernacle of Shiloh,
119:87 earth; but I f not thy precepts.
Isa 58: 2 f not the ordinance of their God;
Jer 14: 5 also calved in the field, and f it,
M't 26:56 all the disciples f him, and fled.
M'r 1:18 they f their nets, and followed
14:50 And they all f him, and fled.
Lu 5:11 land, they f all, and followed him.
2Ti 4:16 stood with me, but all men f me;
Heb 11:27 By faith he f Egypt, not fearing

forsookest
Ne 9:17 great kindness, and f them not.
19 thy manifold mercies f them not.

forswear
M't 5:33 Thou shalt not f thyself, but shalt

fort See also FORTS.
2Sa 5: 9 David dwelt in the f, and called
Isa 25:12 fortress of the high f of thy walls
Eze 4: 2 and build a f against it, and cast
21:22 to cast a mount, and to build a f.
26: 8 he shall make a f against thee,
Da 11:19 shall turn his face toward the f

forth^ See also FORTHWITH; HENCEFORTH.
Ge 1:11 said, Let the earth bring f grass,
12 And the earth brought f grass,
20 God said, Let the waters bring f
21 the waters brought f abundantly,
24 earth bring f the living creature
3:16 thou shalt bring f children; and
18 thistles shall it bring f to thee;
22 lest he put f his hand, and take
23 God sent him f from the garden
8: 7 and he sent f a raven, which went
7 a raven, which went f to and fro,
8 also he sent f a dove from him, to
9 put f his hand, and took her,
10 he sent f his dove out of the ark;
12 sent f the dove; which returned not
16 Go f of the ark, thou, and thy wife,
17 Bring f with thee every living
18 And Noah went f, and his sons,
19 their kinds, went f out of the ark.
9: 7 bring f abundantly in the earth,
18 of Noah, that went f of the ark,
10:11 Out of that land went f Asshur,
11:31 they went f with them from Ur of
12: 5 and they went f to go into the land
14:18 king of Salem brought f bread
15: 4 come f out of thine own bowels,
5 he brought him f abroad, and said,
19:10 But the men put f their hand,
16 they brought him f, and set him
17 when they had brought f abroad,
22:10 Abraham stretched f his hand, and
24:43 virgin cometh f to draw water,
45 Rebekah came f with her pitcher
53 servant brought f jewels of silver,
30:39 brought f cattle ringstraked,
38:24 And Judah said, Bring her f, and
25 When she was brought f, she sent
29 said, How hast thou broken f?
39:13 in her hand, and was fled f,
40:10 budded, and her blossoms shot f;
10 thereof brought f ripe grapes:
41:47 the earth brought f by handfuls.
42:15 Pharaoh ye shall not go f hence,
Ex 3:10 that thou mayest bring f my people
11 should bring f the children of Israel
12 thou hast brought f the people
4: 4 Put f thine hand and take it by
4 he put f his hand and caught it
14 behold, he cometh f to meet thee:
5:20 as they came f from Pharaoh:
7: 4 and bring f mine armies, and my
5 stretch f mine hand upon Egypt,

Ex 8: 3 shall bring f frogs abundantly,
5 Stretch f thine hand with thy rod over
18 their enchantment to bring f lice,
20 lo, he cometh f to the water;
9: 9 be a boil breaking f with blains
10 a boil breaking f with blains
22 Stretch f thine hand toward heaven,
23 And Moses stretched f his rod toward
10:13 Moses stretched f his rod over the land
22 Moses stretched f his hand toward
12:31 get you f from among my people,
39 which they brought f out of Egypt,
46 shalt not carry f ought of the flesh
13: 8 unto me when I came f out of Egypt.
16 the Lord brought us f out of Egypt.
14:11 with us, to carry us f out of Egypt?
27 stretched f his hand over the sea,
15: 7 sentest f thy wrath, which consumed
13 in thy mercy hast led f the people
16: 3 brought us f into this wilderness,
32 when I brought you f from the land
19: 1 Israel were gone f out of the land
17 Moses brought f the people out of
22 lest the Lord break f upon them.
24 unto the Lord lest he break f upon
25:20 cherubims shall stretch f their
29:46 that brought them f out of the land
32:11 which thou hast brought f out of
Le 4:12 shall he carry f without the camp
21 carry f the bullock without the
6:11 carry f the ashes without the camp
14: 3 priest shall go f out of the camp;
45 shall carry them f out of the city
16:24 come f, and offer his burnt offering,
27 one carry f without the camp;
22:27 or a sheep, or a goat, is brought f,
24:14 Bring f him that hath cursed
23 should bring f him that cursed
25:21 shall bring f fruit for three years.
38 brought you f out of the land of
42 which I brought f out of the land
55 whom I brought f out of the land
26:10 bring f the old because of the new.
13 which brought you f out of the land
45 whom I brought f out of the land
Nu 1: 3 are able to go f to war in Israel:
20, 22, 24, 26, 28, 30, 32, 34, 36, 38, 40, 42,
all that were able to go f to war;
45 were able to go f to war in Israel;
2: 9 armies. These shall first set f.
16 they shall set f in the second rank.
11:20 Why came we f out of Egypt?
31 there went f a wind from the Lord,
17: 8 was budded, and brought f buds,
19: 3 may bring her f without the camp,
20: 8 rock, and it shall give f his water,
8 thou shalt bring f to them water
16 hath brought us f out of Egypt;
24: 6 As the valley are they spread f,
8 God brought him f out of Egypt;
26: 4 went f out of the land of Egypt.
31:13 went f to meet them without the
33: 1 went f out of the land of Egypt
34: 4 the going f thereof shall be from
8 goings f of the border shall be to
De 1:27 hath brought us f out of the land
2:23 which came f out of Caphtor,
4:20 and brought you f out of the iron
45 after they came f out of Egypt,
46 they were come f out of Egypt:
6:12 brought thee f out of the land of
8:14 brought thee f out of the land of
15 brought thee f out of the rock of
9:12, 26 hast brought f out of the land
14:22 the field bringeth f year by year.
28 shalt bring f all the tithe of thine
16: 1 brought thee f out of the land of
3 for thou comest f out of the land
3 when thou camest f out of the land
6 that thou camest f out of Egypt.
17: 5 then shalt thou bring f that man or
21: 2 elders and thy judges shall come f,
10 thou goest f to war against thine
22:15 bring f the tokens of the damsel's
23: 4 way, when ye came f out of Egypt;
9 host goeth f against thine enemies,
12 whither thou shalt go f abroad:
24: 9 that we were come f out of Egypt.
25:11 putteth f her hand, and taketh
17 when ye were come f out of Egypt;
26: 8 Lord brought us f out of Egypt
29:25 he brought them f out of the land
33: 2 he shined f from Mount Paran, and
14 fruits brought f by the sun,
14 things put f by the moon.
Jos 2: 3 Bring f the men that are come to
5: 5 as they came f out of Egypt, them
8: 9 Joshua therefore sent them f; and
9:12 day we came f to go unto you;
10:23 so, and brought f those five kings
18:11 coast of their lot came f between
17 went f to En-shemesh, and went f
19: 1 the second lot came f to Simeon,
J'g 1:24 spies saw a man come f out of the
3:21 Ehud put f his left hand, and took
23 Ehud went f through the porch,
5:25 brought f water in a lordly dish.
31 sun when he goeth f in his might.
6: 8 brought you f out of the house of
18 unto thee, and bring f my present,
21 the Lord put f the end of the staff
9: 8 went f on a time to anoint a king
43 were come f out of the city;
11:31 whatsoever cometh f of the doors
14:12 I will now put f a riddle unto you:
13 Put f thy riddle, that we may hear

J'g 14:14 Out of the eater came f meat,
14 out of the strong came f sweetness.
16 thou hast put f a riddle unto the
15:15 of an ass, and put f his hand,
19:22 Bring f the man that came into
25 and brought her f unto them;
20:21 children of Benjamin came f out
25 And Benjamin went f against
33 the liers in wait of Israel came f
Ru 1: 7 Wherefore she went f out of the
2:18 she brought f, and gave to her
1Sa 11: 7 Whosoever cometh not f after
12: 8 brought f your fathers up out
14:11 Hebrews come f out of the holes
27 wherefore he put f the end of the
17:20 the host was going f to the fight,
55 And when Saul saw David go f
18:30 princes of the Philistines went f:
30 came to pass, after they went f,
22: 3 I pray thee, come f, and be with
17 would not put f their hand to fall
23:13 Keilah; and he forbare to go f.
24: 6 to stretch f mine hand against him,
10 will not put f mine hand against
26: 9 for who can stretch f his hand against
11 that I should stretch f mine hand
23 but I would not stretch f mine hand
30:21 and they went f to meet David,
2Sa 1:14 thou not afraid to stretch f thine hand
5:20 The Lord hath broken f upon
6: 6 Uzzah put f his hand to the ark
11: 1 at the time when kings go f to
12:30 And he brought f the spoil of the
31 And he brought f the people that
13:39 king David longed to go f unto
15: 5 he put f his hand, and took him,
16 And the king went f and all his
17 And the king went f, and all the
16: 5 he came f, and cursed still as he
11 son, which came f of my bowels,
18: 2 And David sent f a third part of the
2 I will surely go f with you myself
3 Thou shalt not go f: for if we flee
12 yet would I not put f mine hand
19: 7 Now, therefore arise, go f, and
7 swear by the Lord, if thou go not f,
20: 8 and as he went f it fell out.
22:20 He brought me f also into a large
49 and that bringeth me f from mine
1Ki 2:30 Thus saith the king, Come f.
36 and go not f thence any whither.
6:27 and they stretched f the wings of
8: 7 For the cherubims spread f their
19 thy son that shall come f out of
22 spread f his hands toward heaven:
38 spread f his hands toward this house:
51 thou broughtest f out of Egypt,
9: 9 who brought f their fathers out of
13: 4 that he put f his hand from the
4 And his hand which he put f
19:11 And he said, Go f, and stand upon
20:33 Then Ben-hadad came f to him;
21:13 They carried him f out of the city,
22:21 there came f a spirit and stood
22 I will go f and I will be a lying
22 and prevail also; go f, and do so.
2Ki 2: 3 were at Beth-el came f to Elisha,
21 And he went f unto the spring of
23 there came f little children out of
24 And there came f two she bears
6:15 was risen early, and gone f,
8: 3 and she went f to cry unto the
9:11 Then Jehu came f to the servants
15 let none go f nor escape out of the
10:22 Bring f vestments for all the
22 And he brought them f vestments.
25 and slay them; let none come f.
26 And they brought f the images out
11: 7 of all you that go f on the sabbath,
12 And he brought f the king's son,
15 her f without the ranges;
18: 7 whithersoever he went f:
19: 3 there is no strength to bring f.
31 Jerusalem shall go f a remnant,
21:15 their fathers came f out of Egypt,
23: 4 to bring f out of the temple of the
1Ch 12:33, 36 such as went f to battle,
13: 9 Uzzah put f his hand to hold the
14:11 like the breaking f of waters:
15 for God is gone f before thee to
16:23 shew f from day to day his
19:16 and drew f the Syrians that were
20: 1 Joab led f the power of the army,
24: 7 the first lot came f to Jehoiarib,
25: 9 Now the first lot came f for Asaph
26:16 and Hosah the lot came f
2Ch 1:17 they fetched up, and brought f
3:13 cherubims spread themselves f
5: 8 For the cherubims spread f their
6: 5 Since the day that I brought f my
9 but thy son which shall come f out
12 of Israel, and spread f his hands:
13 of Israel, and spread f his hands
29 shall spread f his hands in this
7:22 brought them f out of the land
20:20 early in the morning, and went f
20 and as they went f, Jehoshaphat
21: 9 Then Jehoram went f with his
23:14 Have her f of the ranges;
25: 5 able to go f to war, that could
11 and led f his people, and went to
26: 6 And he went f and warred against
29: 5 and carry f the filthiness out of
23 And they brought f the he goats
32:21 that came f of his own bowels
Ezr 1: 7 Also Cyrus the king brought f

Ezr 1: 7 Nebuchadnezzer had brought f
8 did Cyrus king of Persia bring f
6: 5 took f out of the temple which is
Ne 4:16 came to pass from that time f, that
8:15 Go f unto the mount, and fetch
16 So the people went f, and brought
9: 7 and broughtest him f out of Ur of
15 broughtest f water for them out
13: 8 I cast f all the household stuff
21 From that time f came they no more
Es 4: 6 So Hatach went f to Mordecai
5: 9 went Haman f that day joyful and
Job 1:11 But put f thine hand now, and
12 upon himself put not f thine hand.
12 went f from the presence of the
2: 5 But put f thine hand now, and
7 went Satan f from the presence
5: 6 affliction cometh not f of the dust,
8:16 and his branch shooteth f in his
10:18 hast thou brought me f out of the
11:17 thou shalt shine f, thou shalt be
14: 2 He cometh f like a flower, and is
9 it will bud, and bring f boughs
15:35 and bring f vanity, and their belly
21:11 They send f their little ones like a
30 they shall be brought f to the day
23:10 he hath tried me, I shall come f
24: 5 wild asses in the desert, go they f
28: 9 He putteth f his hand upon the
11 that is hid bringeth he f to light.
30: 5 They were driven f from among
38: 8 when it brake f, as if it had issued
27 of the tender herb to spring f?
32 Canst thou bring f Mazzaroth in
39: 1 when the wild goats bring f? or
2 thou the time when they bring f?
3 they bring f their young ones,
4 they go f, and return not unto
40:20 the mountains bring him f food,
Ps 1: 3 that bringeth f his fruit in his
7:14 mischief, and brought f falsehood.
9: 1 I will shew f all thy marvellous
14 that I may shew f all thy praise
17: 2 Let my sentence come f from
18:19 He brought me f also into a large
19: 6 His going f is from the end of the
37: 6 shall bring f thy righteousness
44: 9 and goest not f with our armies.
51:15 and my mouth shall shew f thy
55:20 He hath put f his hands against
57: 3 God shall send f his mercy and his
66: 2 Sing f the honour of his name: make
68: 7 when thou wentest f before thy
71:15 shall shew f thy righteousness
78:52 But made his own people to go f
79:13 we will shew f thy praise to all
80: 1 between the cherubims, shine f.
88: 8 am shut up, and I cannot come f.
90: 2 the mountains were brought f,
92: 2 To shew f thy lovingkindness
14 still bring f fruit in old age;
96: 2 shew f his salvation from day to
104:14 that he may bring f food out of
20 all the beasts of the forest do creep f,
23 Man goeth f unto his work and
30 Thou sendest f thy spirit, they are
105:30 brought f frogs in abundance,
37 brought them f also with silver
43 he brought f his people with joy,
106: 2 who can shew f all his praise?
107: 7 he led them f by the right way,
108:11 thou, O God, go f with our hosts?
113: 2 from this time f and for evermore.
115:18 from this time f and for evermore.
121: 8 thy coming in from this time f,
125: 3 the righteous put f their hands
5 the Lord shall lead them f with
126: 6 He that goeth f and weepeth,
138: 7 thou shalt stretch f thine hand against
141: 2 be set f before thee as incense;
143: 6 I stretch f my hands unto thee:
144: 6 Cast f lightning, and scatter them:
13 our sheep may bring f thousands
146: 4 His breath goeth f, he returneth
147:15 He sendeth f his commandment
17 He casteth f his ice like morsels:
Pr 7:15 Therefore came I f to meet thee,
8: 1 understanding put f her voice?
24 were no depths, I was brought f;
25 before the hills was I brought f:
9: 3 She hath sent f her maidens:
10:31 of the just bringeth f wisdom;
12:17 truth sheweth f righteousness:
25: 4 shall come f a vessel for the finer.
6 Put not f thyself in the presence
8 Go not f hastily to strive, lest thou
27: 1 not what a day may bring f.
30:27 go they f all of them by bands;
33 churning of milk bringeth f butter,
33 of the nose bringeth f blood:
33 forcing of wrath bringeth f strife.
31:20 yea, she reacheth f her hands to
Ec 2: 6 the wood that bringeth f trees:
5:15 he came f of his mother's womb,
7:18 God shall come f of them all.
10: 1 apothecary to send f a stinking
Ca 1: 3 thy name is as ointment poured f,
8 go thy way f by the footsteps
12 spikenard sendeth f the smell
2: 9 he looketh f at the windows,
13 fig tree putteth f her green figs,
3:11 Go f, O ye daughters of Zion,
6:10 that looketh f as the morning,
7:11 let us go f into the field;
12 and the pomegranates bud f:
8: 5 there thy mother brought thee f;

Ca 8: 5 she brought thee f that bare thee.
Isa 1:15 And when ye spread f your hands,
2: 3 for out of Zion shall go f the law,
3:16 and walk with stretched f necks
5: 2 that it should bring f grapes,
2 and it brought f wild grapes.
4 that it should bring f grapes,
4 brought it f wild grapes?
25 and he hath stretched f his hand
7: 3 Go f now to meet Ahaz, thou,
25 shall be for the sending f of oxen,
11: 1 And there shall come f a rod
13:10 shall be darkened in his going f,
14: 7 they break f into singing.
29 root shall come f a cockatrice,
23: 4 travail not, nor bring f children,
25:11 And he shall spread f his hands in
11 as he that swimmeth spreadeth f his
26:18 have as it were brought f wind;
27: 8 In measure, when it shooteth f,
28:19 from the time that it goeth f
29 cometh f from the Lord of hosts,
31: 4 multitude of shepherds is called f
32:20 that send f thither the feet of the ox
33:11 chaff, ye shall bring f stubble:
34: 1 and all things that come f of it.
36: 3 Then came f unto him Eliakim,
37: 3 there is not strength to bring f.
9 come f to make war with thee.
32 For out of Jerusalem shall go f
36 Then the angel of the Lord went f.
41:21 bring f your strong reasons,
22 Let them bring them f, and shew
42: 1 he shall bring f judgment to the
3 bring f judgment unto truth.
5 he that spread f the earth,
9 before they spring f I tell you
13 Lord shall go f as a mighty man,
43: 8 Bring f the blind people that have
9 let them bring f their witnesses,
17 bringeth f the chariot and horse,
19 now it shall spring f;
21 they shall shew f my praise.
44:23 break f into singing, ye
24 that stretcheth f the heavens alone:
45: 8 and let them bring f salvation,
10 What hast thou brought f?
48: 1 come f out of the waters of Judah,
3 and they went f out of my mouth,
20 Go ye f of Babylon, flee ye from
49: 9 mayest say to the prisoners, Go f;
13 and break f into singing,
17 made thee waste shall go f of thee.
51: 5 my salvation is gone f, and mine
13 that hath stretched f the heavens,
18 sons whom she hath brought f;
52: 9 Break f into joy, sing together,
54: 1 break f into singing, and cry
2 and let them stretch f the curtains
3 shalt break f on the right hand
16 that bringeth f an instrument
55:10 and maketh it bring f and bud,
11 So shall my word be that goeth f
12 and be led f with peace:
12 and the hills shall break f
58: 8 Then shall the light break f as
8 health shall spring f speedily:
9 the putting f of the finger, and
59: 4 mischief, and bring f iniquity.
60: 6 shew f the praises of the Lord.
61:11 as the earth bringeth f her bud,
11 that are sown in it to spring f;
11 and praise to spring f before all
62: 1 the righteousness thereof go f
65: 9 I will bring f a seed out of Jacob,
23 nor bring f for trouble:
66: 7 she travailed, she brought f;
8 be made to bring f in one day?
8 she brought f her children.
9 and not cause to bring f? saith
9 shall I cause to bring f, and shut
24 And they shall go f, and look
Jer 1: 5 and before thou camest f out of
9 Then the Lord put f his hand,
14 the north an evil shall break f
2:27 stone, Thou hast brought me f:
37 Yea, thou shalt go f from him,
4: 4 lest my fury come f like fire,
7 is gone f from his place to make
31 anguish as of her that bringeth f
6:25 Go not f into the field, nor walk
7:25 day that your fathers came f out
10:13 and bringeth f the wind out of his
20 my children are gone f of me,
20 there is none to stretch f my tent
11: 4 I brought them f out of the land
12: 2 they grow, yea, they bring f fruit:
14:18 If I go f into the field, then
15: 1 out of my sight, and, let them go f.
2 Whither shall ye go f? then thou
19 and if thou take f the precious
17:22 carry f a burden out of your houses
19: 2 And go f unto the valley of the son
20: 3 Pashur brought f Jeremiah out of
18 Wherefore came I f out of the
22:11 which went f out of this place;
19 cast f beyond the gates of Jerusalem.
23:15 profaneness gone f into all the
19 the Lord is gone f in fury, even
25:32 shall go f from nation to nation,
26:23 they fetched f Urijah out of Egypt,
29:16 not gone f with you into captivity;
30:23 the Lord goeth f with fury, a
31: 4 shalt go f in the dances of them
24 and they that go f with flocks.
39 shall yet go f over against it

Jer 32:21 brought f thy people Israel out of
34:13 I brought them f out of the land
37: 5 Pharaoh's army was come f out of
7 which is come f to help you, shall
12 Jeremiah went f out of Jerusalem
38: 2 he that goeth f to the Chaldeans
8 Ebed-melech went f out of the
17 wilt assuredly go f unto the king
18 if thou wilt not go f to the king
21 But if thou refuse to go f, this is
22 Judah's house shall be brought f
39: 4 and went f out of the city by night,
41: 6 went f from Mizpah to meet them,
42:18 my fury hath been poured f upon
18 shall my fury be poured f upon you,
43:12 shall go f from thence in peace.
44: 6 fury and mine anger was poured f,
17 every thing goeth f out of our
46: 4 and stand f with your helmets;
9 and let the mighty men come f;
48: 7 Chemosh shall go f into captivity
45 fire shall come f out of Heshbon,
49: 5 driven out every man right f;
50: 8 and go f out of the land of the
25 and hath brought f the weapons of
51:10 The Lord hath brought f our
16 and bringeth f the wind out of his
44 and I will bring f out of his mouth
52: 7 and went f out of the city by night
31 and brought him f out of prison,
La 1:17 Zion spreadeth f her hands, and
Eze 1:13 out of the fire went f lightning.
22 the terrible crystal, stretched f over
3:22 Arise, go f into the plain, and I
23 and went f into the plain: and,
5: 4 come f into all the house of Israel.
7:10 the morning is gone f; the rod hath
8: 3 And he put f the form of an hand,
9: 7 go ye f. And they went f, and
10: 7 cherub stretched f his hand from
11: 7 bring you f out of the midst of it.
12: 4 Thou shalt bring f thy stuff by
4 shalt go f at even in their sight,
4 as they that go f into captivity.
6 and carry it f in the twilight:
7 I brought f my stuff by day, as
7 I brought it f in the twilight, and
12 in the twilight, and shall go f:
14:22 shall be brought f, both sons and
22 they shall come f unto you, and ye
16:14 And thy renown went f among the
17: 2 Son of man, put f a riddle, and
6 a vine and brought f branches,
6 branches, and shot f sprigs.
7 and shot f her branches toward him,
8 that it might bring f branches,
23 and it shall bring f boughs, and
18: 8 He that hath not given f upon usury,
13 Hath given f upon usury, and hath
20: 6 bring them f of the land of Egypt
9 in bringing them f out of the land
10 Wherefore I caused them to go f
22 in whose sight I brought them f.
38 bring them f out of the country
21: 3 and will draw f my sword out of
4 shall my sword go f out of his
5 have drawn f my sword out of his
19 twain shall come f out of one land:
24:12 great scum went not f out of her:
27: 7 which thou spreadest f to be thy
10 they set f thy comeliness.
33 thy wares went f out of the seas,
28:18 therefore will I bring f a fire from
29:21 house of Israel bud f, and I will
30: 9 shall messengers go f from me
31: 5 multitude of waters, when he shot f.
6 of the field bring f their young,
32: 2 and thou camest f with thy rivers,
4 will cast thee f upon the open field,
33:30 that cometh f from the Lord.
36: 8 ye shall shoot f your branches, and
20 and are gone f out of his land.
38: 4 I will bring thee f, and all thine
8 it is brought f out of the nations,
39: 9 cities of Israel shall go f, and shall
42: 1 he brought me f into the utter
15 he brought me f toward the gate
44: 5 every going f of the sanctuary.
19 they go f into the utter court,
46: 2 then he shall go f: but the gate
8 he shall go f by the way thereof.
9 go f by the way of the north gate:
9 but shall go f over against it.
10 and when they go f, shall go f.
12 then he shall go f; and after his
12 after his going f one shall shut the
21 Then he brought me f into the
47: 3 line in his hand went f eastward,
8 which being brought f into the sea,
10 shall be a place to spread f nets;
12 it shall bring f new fruit according
Da 2:13 decree went f that the wise men
14 which was gone f to slay the wise
3:26 come f, and come hither.
26 and Abed-nego, came f of the
5: 5 In the same hour came f fingers
7:10 stream issued and came f from
8: 9 out of one of them came f a little
9:15 brought thy people f out of the
22 I am now come f to give thee skill
23 the commandment came f, and I
25 going f of the commandment
10:20 and when I am gone f, lo, the
11:11 shall come f and fight with him,
11 shall set f a great multitude;
13 and shall set f a multitude greater

Da 11:42 He shall stretch f his hand also upon
44 therefore he shall go f with great
Ho 6: 3 his going f is prepared as the
5 are as the light that goeth f.
9:13 shall bring f his children to the
16 though they bring f, yet will I
10: 1 he bringeth f fruit unto himself:
13:13 of the breaking f of children.
14: 5 and cast f his roots as Lebanon.
Joe 2:16 bridegroom go f of his chamber
3:18 fountain shall come f of the house
Am 5: 3 which went f by an hundred shall
7:17 go into captivity f of his land.
8: 3 shall cast them f with silence.
5 that we may set f wheat, making
Jon 1: 5 cast f the wares that were in the
12 and cast me f into the sea: so
15 cast him f into the sea: and the sea
Mic 1: 3 Lord cometh f out of his place,
11 Zaanan came not f in the morning
4: 2 for the law shall go f of Zion, and
10 labour to bring f, O daughter of
10 go f out of the city, and thou
5: 2 shall he come f unto me that is to
2 be ruler in Israel; whose goings f
3 which travaileth hath brought f:
7: 9 he will bring me f to the light,
Hab 1: 4 and judgment doth never go f: for
3: 5 burning coals went f at his feet.
13 Thou wentest f for the salvation
Zep 2: 2 Before the decree bring f, before
Hag 1:11 that which the ground bringeth f
2:19 the olive tree, hath not brought f:
Zec 1:16 shall be stretched f upon Jerusalem.
2: 3 angel that talked with me went f,
6 Ho, ho, come f, and flee from the
3: 8 bring f my servant the Branch.
4: 7 and he shall bring f the headstone
5: 3 curse that goeth f over the face of
4 I will bring it f, saith the Lord of
5 angel that talked with me went f,
5 and see what is this that goeth f.
6 This is an ephah that goeth f.
6: 5 which go f from standing before
6 therein go f into the north country;
6 and the white go f after them;
6 the grisled go f toward the south
7 the bay went f, and sought to go
9:11 I have sent f thy prisoners out of
14 arrow shall go f as the lightning:
10: 4 Out of him came f the corner,
12: 1 which stretcheth f the heavens,
14: 2 the city shall go f into captivity,
3 Then shall the Lord go f, and fight
Mal 4: 2 and ye shall go f, and grow up
M't 1:21 And she shall bring f a son, and
23 and shall bring f a son, and they
25 till she had brought f her firstborn
2:16 sent f, and slew all the children
3: 8 Bring f therefore fruits, meet for
10 which bringeth not f good fruit
7:17 good tree bringeth f good fruit;
17 corrupt tree bringeth f evil fruit.
18 good tree cannot bring f evil fruit,
18 neither can a corrupt tree bring f
19 tree that bringeth not f good fruit
8: 3 And Jesus put f his hand,
9: 9 as Jesus passed f from thence
25 But when the people were put f,
38 that he will send f labourers
10: 5 These twelve Jesus sent f, and
16 Behold, I send you f as sheep
12:13 Stretch f thine hand.
13 And he stretched it f;
20 till he send f judgment unto
35 of the heart bringeth f good things:
35 treasure bringeth f evil things.
49 And he stretched f his hand
13: 3 Behold a sower went f to sow;
8 good ground, and brought f fruit,
23 beareth fruit, and bringeth f,
24 Another parable put he f unto
26 sprung up, and brought f fruit,
31 Another parable put he f unto
41 The son of man shall send f his
43 Then shall the righteous shine f
49 the angels shall come f,
52 bringeth f out of his treasure
14: 2 therefore mighty works do shew f
14 And Jesus went f, and saw
31 immediately Jesus stretched f
15:18 mouth come f from the heart;
16:21 From that time f began Jesus to
21:43 to a nation bringing f the fruits
22: 3 sent f his servants to call them
4 he sent f other servants, saying,
7 sent f his armies, and destroyed
46 from that day f ask him any more
24:26 go not f: behold, he is in the secret
32 and putteth f leaves, ye know that
25: 1 went f to meet the bridegroom,
M'r 1:38 there also: for therefore came I f.
41 put f his hand, and touched him,
2:12 and went f before them all:
13 And he went f again by the sea side
3: 3 he saith... Stand f.
5 the man, Stretch f thine hand.
6 And the Pharisees went f, and
14 he might send them f to preach,
4: 8 brought f, some thirty, and some
20 and bring f fruit, some thirtyfold,
28 earth bringeth f fruit of herself;
29 fruit is brought f, immediately he
6: 7 to send them f by two and two;
14 mighty works do shew f
17 Herod himself had sent f and laid

M'r 6:24 And she went *f* and said unto her
7:26 he would cast *f* the devil out of
8:11 the Pharisees came *f*, and began
9:29 This kind can come *f* by nothing,
10:17 when he was gone *f* into the way,
11: 1 sendeth *f* two of his disciples,
13:28 and putteth *f* leaves, ye know that
14:13 he sendeth *f* two of his disciples,
16 his disciples went *f*, and came
16:20 they went *f*, and preached every
Lu 1: 1 to set *f* in order a declaration
31 bring *f* a son, and shalt call his
57 be delivered; and she brought *f*
2: 7 she brought *f* her firstborn son,
3: 7 that came *f* to be baptized of
8 Bring *f* therefore fruits worthy of
9 which bringeth not *f* good fruit
5:13 he put *f* his hand, and touched
27 after these things he went *f*, and
6: 8 Rise up, and stand *f* in the midst.
8 And he arose and stood *f*.
10 unto the man, Stretch *f* thy hand.
43 bringeth not *f* corrupt fruit;
43 a corrupt tree bring *f* good fruit.
45 bringeth *f* that which is good;
45 treasure of his heart bringeth *f*
7:17 of him went *f* throughout all
8:14 when they have heard, go *f*, and
15 and bring *f* fruit with patience.
22 of the lake. And they launched *f*.
27 And when he went *f* to land,
10: 2 that he would send *f* labourers
3 I send you *f* as lambs among
12:16 rich man brought *f* plentifully;
37 and will come *f* and serve them.
14: 7 put *f* a parable to those which
15:22 Bring *f* the best robe, and put it
20: 9 and let it *f* to husbandmen, and
20 sent *f* spies, which should feign
21:30 When they now shoot *f*, ye see
22:53 ye stretched *f* no hands against
Joh 1:43 Jesus would go *f* into Galilee,
2:10 doth set *f* good wine; and when
11 and manifested *f* his glory;
5:29 And shall come *f*; they that have
8:42 I proceeded *f* and came from God;
10: 4 when he putteth *f* his own sheep,
11:43 a loud voice, Lazarus, come *f*.
44 he that was dead came *f*, bound
53 from that day *f* they took counsel
12:13 went *f* to meet him, and cried,
24 if it die, it bringeth *f* much fruit.
15: 2 that it may bring *f* more fruit,
5 the same bringeth *f* much fruit:
6 he is cast *f* as a branch, and is
16 should go and bring *f* fruit, and
16:28 I came *f* from the Father, and
30 that thou camest *f* from God.
18: 1 *f* with his disciples over the brook
4 went *f*, and said unto them, Whom
19: 4 Pilate therefore went *f* again,
4 unto them, Behold, I bring him *f*
5 came Jesus *f*, wearing the crown
13 he brought Jesus *f*, and sat down
17 went *f* into a place called the
20: 3 Peter therefore went *f*, and that
21: 3 went *f*, and entered into a ship
18 thou shalt stretch *f* thy hands,
Ac 1:26 And they gave *f* their lots; and
2:33 he hath shed *f* this, which ye now
4:30 By stretching *f* thine hand to heal;
5:10 and, carrying her *f*, buried her by
15 brought *f* the sick into the streets,
19 and brought them *f*, and said,
34 put the apostles *f* a little space;
7: 7 shall they come *f*, and serve me
9:30 Cæsarea, and sent him *f* to Tarsus.
40 Peter put them all *f*, and kneeled
11:22 they sent *f* Barnabas, that he
12: 1 the king stretched *f* his hands to
4 Easter to bring him *f* to the people.
6 Herod would have brought him *f*,
13: 4 being sent *f* by the Holy Ghost,
16: 3 would Paul have to go *f* with him;
17:18 to be a setter *f* of strange gods:
21: 2 we went aboard, and set *f*.
23:28 brought him *f* into their council:
24: 2 he was called *f*, Tertullus began
25:17 the man to be brought *f*.
23 Paul was brought *f*.
26 have brought him *f* before you,
26: 1 Then Paul stretched *f* the hand,
25 but speak *f* the words of truth and
27:21 Paul stood *f* in the midst of them,
Ro 3:25 Whom God hath set *f* to be a
7: 4 that we should bring *f* fruit unto
5 our members to bring *f* fruit unto
10:21 I have stretched *f* my hands unto
1Co 4: 9 God hath set *f* us the apostles
16:11 but conduct him *f* in peace, that
Ga 3: 1 Christ hath been evidently set *f*,
4: 4 God sent *f* his son, made of a
6 God hath sent *f* the Spirit of his
27 *f* and cry, thou that travailest
Ph'p 2:16 Holding *f* the word of life; that I
3:13 and reaching *f* unto those things
Col 1: 6 and bringeth *f* fruit, as it doth
1Ti 1:16 Jesus Christ might shew *f* all
Heb 6: 7 bringeth *f* herbs meet for them
13:13 Let us go *f* therefore unto him
Jas 1:15 lust hath conceived, it bringeth *f*
15 it is finished, bringeth *f* death.
3:11 Doth a fountain send *f* at the same
5:18 and the earth brought *f* her fruit.
1Pe 2: 9 that ye should shew *f* the praises
3Jo 7 for his name's sake they went *f*,
Jude 7 are set *f* for an example, suffering
Re 5: 6 seven spirits of God sent *f* into
6: 2 went *f* conquering, and to conquer.
12: 5 And she brought *f* a man child,
13 woman which brought *f* the man
16:14 go *f* unto the kings of the earth

forthwith
Ezr 6: 8 *f* expences be given unto these
M't 13: 5 *f* they sprung up, because they
26:49 *f* he came to Jesus, and said,
M'r 1:29 *f*, when they were come out of
43 charged him, and *f* sent him away,
5:13 And *f* Jesus gave them leave.
Joh 19:34 *f* came thereout blood and water.
Ac 9:18 he received sight *f*, and arose,
12:10 *f* the angel departed from him.
21:30 and *f* the doors were shut.

fortieth
Nu 33:38 and died there, in the *f* year after
De 1: 3 and it came to pass in the *f* year,
1Ch 26:31 In the *f* year of the reign of David
2Ch 16:13 and died in the one and *f* year of

fortified
2Ch 11:11 And he *f* the strong holds, and
26: 9 turning of the wall, and *f* them.
Ne 3: 8 *f* Jerusalem unto the broad wall.
Mic 7:12 Assyria, and from the *f* cities,

fortify See also FORTIFIED.
J'g 9:31 they *f* the city against thee.
Ne 4: 2 Jews? will they *f* themselves?
Isa 22:10 ye broken down to *f* the wall.
Jer 51:53 should *f* the height of her strength,
Na 2: 1 loins strong, *f* thy power mightily.
3:14 *f* thy strong holds: go into clay,

fortress See also FORTRESSES.
2Sa 22: 2 The Lord is my rock, and my *f*,
Ps 18: 2 rock, and my *f*, and my deliverer;
31: 3 For thou art my rock and my *f*;
71: 3 for thou art my rock and my *f*.
91: 2 He is my refuge and my *f*:
144: 2 My goodness, and my *f*; my high
Isa 17: 3 *f* also shall cease from Ephraim,
25:12 And the *f* of the high fort of thy
Jer 6:27 a tower and a *f* among my people,
10:17 the land, O inhabitant of the *f*.
16:19 O Lord, my strength, and my *f*,
Da 11: 7 shall enter into the *f* of the king
10 and be stirred up, even to his *f*.
Am 5: 9 spoiled shall come against the *f*.
Mic 7:12 and from the *f* even to the river,

fortresses
Isa 34:13 and brambles in the *f* thereof:
Ho 10:14 and all thy *f* shall be spoiled,

forts
2Ki 25: 1 they built *f* against it round about.
Isa 29: 3 and I will raise *f* against thee.
32:14 *f* and towers shall be for dens
Jer 52: 4 and built *f* against it round about.
Eze 17:17 casting up mounts, and building *f*,
33:27 that be in the *f* and in the caves

Fortunatus (*for-chu-na'-tus*)
1Co 16:17 the coming of Stephanas and *F*
subscr. Philippi by Stephanas, and *F*.

forty See also FORTY'S.
Ge 5:13 Mahalaleel eight hundred and *f*
7: 4 upon the earth *f* days and *f* nights;
17 flood was *f* days upon the earth;
8: 6 it came to pass at the end of *f* days,
18:28 he said, If I find there *f* and five,
29 there shall be *f* found there.
25:20 Isaac was *f* years old when he took
26:34 Esau was *f* years old when he took
32:15 *f* kine, and ten bulls, twenty she
47:28 Jacob was an hundred *f* and seven
50: 3 And *f* days were fulfilled for him;
Ex 16:35 of Israel did eat manna *f* years,
24:18 in the mount *f* days and *f* nights.
26:19 thou shalt make *f* sockets of silver
21 And their *f* sockets of silver; two
34:28 with the Lord *f* days and *f* nights;
36:24 And *f* sockets of silver he made
26 And their *f* sockets of silver;
Le 25: 8 shall be unto thee *f* and nine years.
Nu 1:21 *f* and six thousand and five hundred.
25 *f* and five thousand six hundred
33 were *f* thousand and five hundred.
41 *f* and one thousand and five hundred.
2:11 *f* and six thousand and five hundred.
15 *f* and five thousand and six hundred
19 were *f* thousand and five hundred.
28 *f* and one thousand and five hundred.
13:25 searching of the land after *f* days.
14:33 wander in the wilderness *f* years,
34 searched the land, even *f* days,
34 bear your iniquities, even *f* years,
26: 7 numbered of them were *f* and three
18 them, *f* thousand and five hundred.
41 *f* and five thousand and six hundred.
50 were *f* and five thousand and four
32:13 wander in the wilderness *f* years,
35: 6 them ye shall add *f* and two cities.
7 Levites shall be *f* and eight cities:
De 2: 7 these *f* years the Lord thy God
8: 2 these *f* years in the wilderness,
4 did thy foot swell, these *f* years.
9: 9 in the mount *f* days and *f* nights.
11 at the end of *f* days and *f* nights,
18 at the first, *f* days and *f* nights:
25 before the Lord *f* days and *f* nights,
10:10 the first time, *f* days and *f* nights;
25: 3 *F* stripes he may give him, and
29: 5 led you *f* years in the wilderness:
Jos 4:13 About *f* thousand prepared for war
5: 6 walked *f* years in the wilderness,
14: 7 *F* years old was I when Moses the
10 as he said these *f* and five years,
21:41 were *f* and eight cities with their
J'g 3:11 And the land had rest *f* years.
5: 8 seen among *f* thousand in Israel?
31 And the land had rest *f* years.
8:28 country was in quietness *f* years
12: 6 Ephraimites *f* and two thousand.
14 he had *f* sons and thirty nephews,
13: 1 the hand of the Philistines *f* years.
1Sa 4:18 And he had judged Israel *f* years.
17:16 and presented himself *f* days.
2Sa 2:10 Ish-bosheth Saul's son was *f* years
5: 4 to reign, and he reigned *f* years.
10:18 and *f* thousand horsemen, and
15: 7 And it came to pass after *f* years,
1Ki 2:11 reigned over Israel were *f* years:
4:26 Solomon had *f* thousand stalls of
6:17 temple before it, was *f* cubits long.
7: 3 that lay on *f* five pillars, fifteen in
38 one layer contained *f* baths:
11:42 over all Israel was *f* years.
14:21 Rehoboam was *f* and one years old
15:10 And *f* and one years reigned he in
19: 8 of that meat *f* days and *f* nights
2Ki 2:24 tare *f* and two children of them.
8: 9 of Damascus, *f* camels' burden,
10:14 even two and *f* men; neither left he
12: 1 *f* years reigned he in Jerusalem.
14:23 and reigned *f* and one years.
1Ch 5:18 were four and *f* thousand seven
12:36 to battle, expert in war, *f* thousand.
19:18 chariots, and *f* thousand footmen,
29:27 he reigned over Israel was *f* years;
2Ch 9:30 in Jerusalem over all Israel *f* years.
12:13 Rehoboam was one and *f* years old
22: 2 *F* and two years old was Ahaziah
24: 1 he reigned *f* years in Jerusalem.
Ezr 2: 8 of Zattu, nine hundred *f* and five.
10 of Bani, six hundred *f* and two.
24 children of Azmaveth, *f* and two.
25 seven hundred and *f* and three.
34 of Jericho, three hundred *f* and five.
38 thousand two hundred *f* and seven.
64 together was *f* and two
66 mules, two hundred *f* and five;
Ne 5:15 wine, beside *f* shekels of silver;
7:13 of Zattu, eight hundred *f* and five.
15 of Binnui, six hundred *f* and eight.
28 men of Beth-azmaveth, *f* and two.
29 and Beeroth, seven hundred *f* and
36 Jericho, three hundred *f* and five.
41 thousand two hundred *f* and seven.
44 of Asaph, an hundred *f* and eight.
62 of Nekoda, six hundred *f* and two.
66 was *f* and two thousand three
67 two hundred *f* and five singing
68 mules, two hundred *f* and five:
9:21 Yea, *f* years didst thou sustain them
11:13 the fathers, two hundred *f* and two:
Job 42:16 lived Job an hundred and *f* years,
Ps 95:10 *F* years long was I grieved with
Jer 52:30 seven hundred *f* and five persons:
Eze 4: 6 of the house of Judah *f* days:
29:11 neither shall it be inhabited *f* years.
12 waste shall be desolate *f* years:
13 At the end of *f* years will I gather
41: 2 the length thereof, *f* cubits: and the
46:22 were courts joined of *f* cubits long
Am 2:10 you *f* years through the wilderness,
5:25 offerings in the wilderness *f* years,
Jon 3: 4 Yet *f* days, and Nineveh shall be
M't 4: 2 he had fasted *f* days and *f* nights,
M'r 1:13 was there in the wilderness *f* days,
Lu 4: 2 Being *f* days tempted of the devil.
Joh 2:20 *F* and six years was this temple
Ac 1: 3 proofs, being seen of them *f* days,
4:22 For the man was above *f* years old,
7:23 And when he was full *f* years old,
30 And when *f* years were expired,
36 sea, and in the wilderness *f* years.
42 space of *f* years in the wilderness?
13:18 And about the time of *f* years
21 Benjamin, by the space of *f* years.
23:13 were more than *f* which had made
21 for him of them more than *f* men,
2Co 11:24 times received I *f* stripes save one.
Heb 3: 9 me, and saw my works *f* years.
17 with whom was he grieved *f* years?
Re 7: 4 sealed an hundred and *f* and four
11: 2 tread under foot *f* and two months.
13: 5 him to continue *f* and two months.
14: 1 with him an hundred *f* and four
3 but the hundred and *f* and four
21:17 an hundred and *f* and four cubits,

forty's
Ge 18:29 he said, I will not do it for *f* sake.

forty-thousand See FORTY and THOUSAND.

forum
Ac 28:15 came to meet us as far as Appii *f*,

forward See also HENCEFORWARD.
Ge 26:13 the man waxed great, and went *f*,
Ex 14:15 children of Israel, that they go *f*:
Nu 1:51 And when the tabernacle setteth *f*,
2:17 of the congregation shall set *f*
17 so shall they set *f*, every man in
24 they shall go *f* in the third rank.
34 and so they set *f*, every one after
4: 5 And when the camp setteth *f*,
15 as the camp is to set *f*; after that,
10: 5 lie on the east parts shall go *f*.
17 and the sons of Merari set *f*,

Nu 10:18 of the camp of Reuben set f
21 And the Kohathites set f, bearing
22 of the children of Ephraim set f
25 camp of the children of Dan set f,
28 to their armies, when they set f.
35 when the ark set f, that Moses
21:10 And the children of Israel set f,
22: 1 And the children of Israel set f,
32:19 them on yonder side Jordan, or f;
J'g 9:44 that was with him, rushed f, and
1Sa 10: 3 Then shalt thou go on f from
16:13 upon David from that day f.
18: 9 eyed David from that day and f.
30:25 And it was so from that day f,
2Ki 3:24 but they went f smiting the Moabites,
4:24 Drive, and go f; slack not thy riding
20: 9 shall the shadow go f ten degrees,
1Ch 23: 4 to set f the work of the house
2Ch 34:12 to set it f; and other of the Levites
Ezr 3: 8 to set f the work of the house
9 set f the workmen in the house
Job 23: 8 I go f, but he is not there;
30:13 they set f my calamity, they have
Jer 7:24 and went backward, and not f.
Eze 1: 9 they went every one straight f.
12 they went every one straight f:
10:22 they went every one straight f
39:22 their God from that day and f.
43:27 and so f, the priests shall make
Zec 1:15 and they helped f the affliction.
M'r 14:35 And he went f a little, and fell on
Ac 19:33 the Jews putting him f.
2Co 8:10 but also to be f a year ago.
17 but being more f, of his own
Gal 2:10 the same which I also was f to do.
3Jo 6 if thou bring f on their journey

forwardness
2Co 8: 8 by occasion of the f of others,
9: 2 For I know the f of your mind,

fought
Ex 17: 8 came Amalek, and f with Israel
10 said to him, and f with Amalek:
Nu 21: 1 then he f against Israel, and took
23 to Jahaz, and f against Israel.
26 who had f against the former king
Jos 10:14 the Lord f for Israel.
29 for f against Libnah:
31, 34 against it, and f against it:
36 unto Hebron; and they f against it:
38 to Debir; and f against it:
42 the Lord God of Israel f for Israel.
23: 3 your God is he that hath f for you.
24: 8 and they f with you: and I gave
11 the men of Jericho f against you,
J'g 1: 5 they f against him, and they slew
8 Now the children of Judah had f
5:19 kings came and f, then f the kings
20 They f from heaven;
20 the stars in their courses f against
9:17 (For my father f for you, and
39 Shechem, and f with Abimelech.
45 Abimelech f against the city all
52 and f against it, and went hard
11:20 in Jahaz, and f against Israel.
12: 4 and f with Ephraim: and the men
1Sa 4:10 And the Philistines f, and Israel
12: 9 Moab, and they f against them.
14:47 and f against all his enemies on
19: 8 went out, and f with the Philistines,
23: 5 Keilah, and f with the Philistines,
31: 1 the Philistines f against Israel:
2Sa 2:28 no more neither f they any more.
8:10 he had f against Hadadezer, and
10:17 in array against David, and f with
11:17 the men of the city went out, and f
12:26 And Joab f against Rabbah of the
27 I have f against Rabbah, and have
29 and f against it, and took it,
21:15 and f against the Philistines.
2Ki 8:29 he f against Hazael king of Syria.
9:15 he f with Hazael king of Syria.)
12:17 Syria went up, and f against Gath,
13:12 f against Amaziah king of Judah,
14:15 he f with Amaziah king of Judah,
1Ch 10: 1 the Philistines f against Israel;
18:10 he had f against Hadarezer, and
19:17 the Syrians, they f with him.
18 seven thousand men which f in
2Ch 20:29 the Lord f against the enemies
22: 6 when he f with Hazeal king of Syria.
27: 5 He f also with the king of the
Ps 109: 3 and f against me without a cause.
Isa 20: 1 and f against Ashdod, and took it;
63:10 enemy, and he f against them.
Jer 34: 1 the people, f against Jerusalem,
7 king of Babylon's army f against
Zec 14: 3 as when he f in the day of battle.
12 that have f against Jerusalem;
1Co 15:32 I have f with beasts at Ephesus,
2Ti 4: 7 I have f a good fight, I have
Re 12: 7 his angels f against the dragon;
7 and the dragon f and his angels.

foul See also FOULED.
Job 16:16 My face is f with weeping, and
Eze 34:18 ye must f the residue with your
M't 16: 3 It will be f weather to day: for
M'r 9:25 he rebuked the f spirit, saying
Re 18: 2 hold of every f spirit, and a cage

fouled See also FOULEDST.
Eze 34:19 they drink that which ye have f

fouledst
Eze 32: 2 with thy feet, and f their rivers.

found See also CONFOUND; FOUNDED; FOUNDEST.
Ge 2:20 there was not f an help meet
6: 8 Noah f grace in the eyes of the
8: 9 f no rest for the sole of her foot,
11: 2 that they f a plain in the land of
16: 7 And the angel of the Lord f her
18: 3 now I have f favour in thy sight,
29 Peradventure there shall be forty f
30 Peradventure there shall thirty be f
31 there shall be twenty f there.
32 Peradventure ten shall be f there.
19:19 servant hath f grace in thy sight,
26:19 f there a well of springing water.
32 said unto him, We have f water.
27:20 How is it that thou hast f it so
30:14 and f mandrakes in the field,
27 if I have f favour in thine eyes,
31:33 tents, but he f them not
34 all the tent, but f them not.
35 he searched, but f not the images.
37 hast thou f of all thy household
33:10 if now I have f grace in thy sight,
36:24 had f the mules in the wilderness,
37:15 And a certain man f him, and,
17 brethren, and f them in Dothan.
32 This have we f: know now
38:20 woman's hand: but he f her not.
23 this kid, and thou hast not f her.
39: 4 And Joseph f grace in his sight,
44: 8 which we f in our sacks' mouths,
9 of thy servants it be f, both let him
10 he with whom it is f shall be my
12 the cup was f in Benjamin's sack.
16 God hath f out the iniquity of thy
16 he also with whom the cup is f.
17 man in whose hand the cup is f,
47:14 the money that was f in the land
29 If now I have f grace in thy sight,
50: 4 If now I have f grace in your eyes,
Ex 9:19 man and beast which shall be f in
12:19 days shall there be no leaven f in
15:22 in the wilderness, and f no water.
16:27 for to gather, and they f none.
21:16 or if he be f in his hand, he shall
22: 2 If a thief be f breaking up, and be
4 If the theft be certainly f in his
7 if the thief be f, let him pay
8 If the thief be not f, then the
33:12 thou hast also f grace in my sight.
13 if I have f grace in thy sight,
16 people have f grace in thy sight?
17 thou hast f grace in my sight,
34: 9 now I have f grace in thy sight,
35:23 with whom was f blue, and purple,
24 was f shittim wood for any work
Le 6: 3 Or have f that which was lost,
4 or the lost thing which he f,
Nu 11:11 have I not f favour in thy sight,
15 if I have f favour in thy sight;
15:32 they f a man that gathered sticks
33 they that f him gathering sticks
32: 5 if we have f grace in thy sight,
De 17: 2 If there be f among you, within
18:10 There shall not be f among you
20:11 all the people that is f therein
21: 1 If one be f slain in the land which
22: 3 which he hath lost, and thou hast f,
14 I came to her, I f her not a maid:
17 I f not thy daughter a maid;
20 virginity be not f for the damsel;
22 If a man be f lying with a woman
27 For he f her in the field, and the
28 and lie with her, and they be f;
24: 1 hath f some uncleanness in her:
7 If a man be f stealing any of his
32:10 He f him in a desert land,
33:29 thine enemies shall be f liars
Jos 2:22 all the way, but f them not.
10:17 The five kings are f hid in a cave
J'g 1: 5 And they f Adoni-bezek in Bezek:
6:17 If now I have f grace in thy sight,
14:18 ye had not f out my riddle.
15:15 he f a new jawbone of an ass,
21:12 And they f among the inhabitants
Ru 2:10 Why have I f grace in thine eyes,
1Sa 9: 4 Shalisha, but they f them not:
4 Benjamites, but they f them not.
11 they f young maidens going out
20 thy mind on them; for they are f.
10: 2 which thou wentest to seek are f:
16 us plainly that the asses were f.
21 they sought him, he could not be f.
12: 5 ye have not f ought in my hand.
13:19 smith f throughout all the land
22 was neither sword nor spear f in
22 with Jonathan his son was there f.
14:30 of their enemies which they f?
16:22 for he hath f favour in my sight.
20: 3 that I have f grace in thine eyes;
29 if I have f favour in thine eyes,
25:28 and evil hath not been f in thee all
27: 5 If I have now f grace in thine eyes,
29: 3 and I have f no fault in him since
6 for I have not f evil in thee since
8 what hast thou f in thy servant
30:11 they f an Egyptian in the field,
31: 8 that they f Saul and his three sons
2Sa 7:27 hath thy servant f in his heart
14:22 that I have f grace in thy sight,
17:12 some place where he shall be f,
13 be not one small stone f there.
1Ki 1: 3 and f Abishag a Shunammite, and
52 if wickedness shall be f in him,
7:47 was the weight of the brass f out.
11:19 Hadad f great favour in the sight
29 the Shilonite f him in the way;
1Ki 13:14 and f him sitting under an oak:
28 he went and f his carcase cast in
14:13 in him there is f some good thing
18:10 and nation, that they f thee not.
19:19 and f Elisha the son of Shaphat,
20:36 him, a lion f him, and slew him.
37 Then he f another man, and said,
21:20 Hast thou f me, O mine enemy?
20 I have f thee: because thou hast
2Ki 2:17 sought three days, but f him not.
4:39 and f a wild vine, and gathered
9:35 f no more of her than the skull,
12: 5 wheresoever any breach shall be f.
10 the money that was f in the house
18 gold that was f in the treasures
14:14 vessels that were f in the house
16: 8 the silver and gold that was f in the
17: 4 the king of Assyria f conspiracy
18:15 the silver that was f in the house
19: 8 and f the king of Assyria warring
20:13 and all that was f in his treasures:
22: 8 I have f the book of the law in the
9 the money that was f in the house,
13 the words of this book that is f:
23: 2 book of the covenant which was f
24 the book that Hilkiah the priest f
25:19 which were f in the city, and the
19 of the land that were f in the city:
1Ch 4:40 And they f fat pasture and good,
41 the habitations that were f there,
10: 8 they f Saul and his sons fallen
17:25 thy servant hath f in his heart to
20: 2 and f it to weigh a talent of gold,
24: 4 And there were more chief men f
26:31 were f among them mighty men
28: 9 thou seek him, he will be f of thee;
29: 8 with whom precious stones were f
2Ch 2:17 and they were f an hundred and
4:18 the brass could not be f out.
15: 2 ye seek him, he will be f of you;
4 and sought him, he was f of them.
15 desire; and he was f of them:
19: 3 there are good things f in thee,
20:25 they f among them in abundance
21:17 that was f in the king's house,
22: 8 and f the princes of Judah, and
25: 5 and f them three hundred...men,
24 vessels that were f in the house
29:16 they f in the temple of the Lord
34:14 Hilkiah the priest f a book of the
15 I have f the book of the law in the
17 the money that was f in the house
21 the words of the book that is f:
30 book of the covenant that was f in
36: 8 and that which was f in him,
Ezr 2:62 genealogy, but they were not f:
4:19 and it is f that this city of old
6: 2 And there was f at Achmetha, in
8:15 f there none of the sons of Levi.
10:18 priests there were f that had taken
Ne 2: 5 and if thy servant have f favour in
5: 8 peace, and f nothing to answer.
7: 5 And I f a register of the genealogy
5 at the first, and f written therein,
64 by genealogy, but it was not f:
8:14 And they f written in the law
13: 1 and therein was f written, that the
Es 2:23 made of the matter, it was f out;
5: 8 If I have f favour in the sight of
6: 2 it was f written, that Mordecai
7: 3 If I have f favour in thy sight,
8: 5 if I have f favour in his sight,
Job 19:28 the root of the matter is f in me?
20: 8 as a dream, and shall not be f:
28:12 But where shall wisdom be f? and
13 neither is it f in the land of the
31:29 lifted up myself when evil f him:
32: 3 because they had f no answer, and
13 should say, We have f out wisdom:
33:24 down to the pit: I have f a ransom.
42:15 were no women f so fair as the
Ps 32: 6 in a time when thou mayest be f:
36: 2 his iniquity be f to be hateful.
37:36 sought him, but he could not be f.
69:20 and for comforters, but I f none.
76: 5 men of might have f their hands.
84: 3 yea, the sparrow hath f an house,
89:20 I have f David my servant; with
107: 4 way; they f no city to dwell in.
116: 3 upon me: I f trouble and sorrow.
132: 6 we f it in the fields of the wood.
Pr 6:31 But if he be f, he shall restore
7:15 to seek thy face, and I have f thee.
10:13 hath understanding wisdom is f:
16:31 it be f in the way of righteousness.
24:14 when thou hast f it, then there
25:16 Hast thou f honey? eat so much
30: 6 he reprove thee, and thou be f a liar.
10 curse thee, and thou be f guilty.
Ec 7:27 this have I f, saith the preacher,
28 man among a thousand have I f;
28 among all those have I not f.
29 this only have I f, that God hath
9:15 Now there was f in it a poor wise
Ca 3: 1, 2 I sought him, but I f him not.
3 watchmen that go about the city f
4 but I f him whom my soul loveth:
5: 7 that went about the city f me,
8:10 I in his eyes as one that f favour.
Isa 10:10 As my hand hath f the kingdoms
14 And my hand hath f as a nest the
13:15 Every one that is f shall be thrust
22: 3 all that are f in thee are bound
30:14 there shall not be f in the bursting
35: 9 it shall not be f there; but the
37: 8 and f the king of Assyria warring

Isa 39: 2 and all that was *f* in his treasures:
51: 3 joy and gladness shall be *f* therein,
55: 6 ye the Lord while he may be *f*,
57:10 thou hast *f* the life of thine hand;
65: 1 I am *f* of them that sought me not:
8 As the new wine is *f* in the cluster,
Jer 2: 5 What iniquity have your fathers *f*
26 the thief is ashamed when he is *f*,
34 in thy skirts is *f* the blood of the
34 I have not *f* it by secret search,
5:26 among my people are *f* wicked
11: 9 A conspiracy is *f* among the men
14: 3 came to the pits, and *f* no water;
15:16 Thy words were *f*, and I did eat
23:11 have I *f* their wickedness, saith
29:14 And I will be *f* of you, saith the
31: 2 were left of the sword *f* grace in
41: 3 the Chaldeans that were *f* there,
8 But ten men were *f* among them
12 and *f* him by the great waters that
48:27 was he *f* among thieves? for since
50: 7 that *f* them have devoured them:
20 shall not be *f*: for I will pardon
24 art *f*, and also caught, because
52:25 which were *f* in the city; and the
25 that were *f* in the midst of the city.
La 2:16 for; we have *f*, we have seen it.
Eze 22:30 not destroy it: but I *f* none.
26:21 yet shalt thou never be *f* again,
28:15 created, till iniquity was *f* in thee.
Da 1:19 them all was *f* none like Daniel,
20 he *f* them ten times better than all
2:25 I have *f* a man of the captives of
35 that no place was *f* for them:
5:11 wisdom of the gods, was *f* in him;
12 doubts, were *f* in the same Daniel,
14 and excellent wisdom is *f* in thee.
27 in the balances, and art *f* wanting.
6: 4 was there any error or fault *f* in
11 and *f* Daniel praying and making
22 before him innocency was *f* in me;
23 no manner of hurt was *f* upon him,
11:19 stumble and fall, and not be *f*.
12: 1 every one that shall be *f* written
Ho 9:10 I *f* Israel like grapes in the
10: 2 now shall they be *f* faulty:
12: 4 he *f* him in Beth-el, and there he
8 I have *f* me out substance: in all
14: 8 From me is thy fruit *f*.
Jon 1: 3 and he *f* a ship going to Tarshish:
Mic 1:13 the transgressions of Israel were *f*
Zep 3:13 shall a deceitful tongue be *f* in
Zec 10:10 and place shall not be *f* for them.
Mal 2: 6 and iniquity was not *f* in his lips
M't 1:18 she was *f* with child of the Holy
2: 8 child; and when ye have *f* him,
8:10 I have not *f* so great faith, no, not
13:44 when a man hath *f*, he hideth,
46 he had *f* one pearl of great price,
18:28 and *f* one of his fellowservants,
20: 6 and *f* others standing idle, and
21:19 *f* nothing thereon, but leaves only,
22:10 all as many as they *f*, both bad
26:43 he came and *f* them asleep again:
60 But *f* none: yea, though many
60 witnesses came, yet *f* they none.
27:32 they *f* a man of Cyrene, Simon by
M'r 1:37 And when they had *f* him, they
7: 2 unwashen, hands, they *f* fault.
30 she *f* the devil gone out, and her
11: 4 and *f* the colt tied by the door
13 to it, he *f* nothing but leaves;
14:16 and *f* as he had said unto them:
40 returned, he *f* them asleep again,
55 to put him to death; and *f* none.
Lu 1:30 Mary: for thou hast *f* favour
2:16 came with haste, and *f* Mary, and
45 And when they *f* him not, they
46 they *f* him in the temple, sitting
4:17 *f* the place where it was written,
7: 9 I have not *f* so great faith, no, not
10 *f* the servant whole that had been
8:35 and *f* the man, out of whom the
9:36 voice was past, Jesus was *f* alone.
13: 6 sought fruit thereon, and *f* none.
15: 5 when he hath *f* it, he layeth it on
6 I have *f* my sheep which was lost.
9 when she hath *f* it, she calleth
9 for I have *f* the piece which I had
24 alive again; he was lost, and is *f*.
32 alive again; and was lost, and is *f*.
17:18 There are not *f* that returned to
19:32 and *f* even as he had said unto
22:13 and *f* as he had said unto them:
45 he *f* them sleeping for sorrow,
23: 2 We *f* this fellow perverting the
14 you, have *f* no fault in this man
22 I have *f* no cause of death in him:
24: 2 And they *f* the stone rolled away
3 and *f* not the body of the Lord
23 And when they *f* not his body, they
24 and *f* it even so as the women had
33 and *f* the eleven gathered together,
Joh 1:41 We have *f* the Messias, which is,
45 saith unto him, We have *f* him,
2:14 And *f* in the temple those that sold
6:25 And when they had *f* him on the
9:35 and when he had *f* him, he said
11:17 he *f* that he had lain in the grave
12:14 he had *f* a young ass, sat thereon;
Ac 5:10 young men came in, and *f* her dead,
22 officers came, and *f* them not in
23 prison truly *f* we shut in all safety,
23 had opened, we *f* no man within.
39 ye be *f* even to fight against God.
7:11 and our fathers *f* no sustenance.

Ac 7:46 Who *f* favour before God, and
8:40 But Philip was *f* at Azotus:
9: 2 that if he *f* any of this way,
33 And there he *f* a certain man
10:27 *f* many that were come together.
11:26 when he had *f* him, he brought
12:19 *f* him not, he examined the keepers
13: 6 *f* a certain sorcerer, a false prophet,
22 I have *f* David the son of Jesse,
28 though they *f* no cause of death
17: 6 when they *f* them not, they drew
23 I *f* an altar with this inscription,
18: 2 And *f* a certain Jew named Aquila,
19:19 *f* it fifty thousand pieces of silver.
24: 5 we have *f* this man a pestilent
12 they neither *f* me in the temple
18 Jews from Asia *f* me purified in
20 if they have *f* any evil doing in
25:25 when I *f* that he had committed
27: 6 And there the centurion *f* a ship
28 sounded, and *f* it twenty fathoms:
28 again, and *f* it fifteen fathoms.
28:14 Where we *f* brethren, and were
Ro 4: 1 as pertaining to the flesh, hath *f*?
7:10 to life, I *f* to be unto death.
10:20 was *f* of them that sought me not;
1Co 4: 2 stewards, that a man be *f* faithful.
15:15 Yea, and we are *f* false witnesses
2Co 2:13 because I *f* not Titus my brother:
5: 3 clothed we shall not be *f* naked.
7:14 made before Titus, is *f* a truth,
11:12 they may be *f* even as we.
12:20 and that I shall be *f* unto you such
Ga 2:17 we ourselves also are *f* sinners,
Ph'p 2: 8 And being *f* in fashion as a man,
3: 9 And be *f* in him, not having mine
1Ti 3:10 of a deacon, being *f* blameless.
2Ti 1:17 me out very diligently, and *f* me.
Heb 11: 5 and was not *f*, because God had
12:17 for he *f* no place of repentance,
1Pe 1: 7 might be *f* unto praise and honour
2:22 neither was guile *f* in his mouth:
2Pe 3:14 that ye may be *f* of him in peace,
2 Joh 4 *f* of thy children walking in truth,
Re 2: 2 and are not, and hast *f* them liars:
3: 2 for I have not *f* thy works perfect
5: 4 no man was *f* worthy to open and
12: 8 neither was their place *f* any more
14: 5 And in their mouth was *f* no guile:
16:20 and the mountains were not *f*.
18:21 and shall be *f* no more at all.
22 he be, shall be *f* any more in thee;
24 in her was *f* the blood of prophets,
20:11 and there was *f* no place for them.
15 And whosoever was not *f* written

foundation See also FOUNDATIONS.
Ex 9:18 the *f* thereof even until now.
Jos 6:26 he shall lay the *f* thereof in his
1Ki 5:17 stones, to lay the *f* of the house.
6:37 In the fourth year was the *f* of the
7: 9 even from the *f* unto the coping,
10 And the *f* was of costly stones,
16:34 he laid the *f* thereof in Abiram his
2Ch 8:16 unto the day of the *f* of the house
23: 5 a third part at the gate of the *f*:
31: 7 began to lay the *f* of the heaps,
Ezr 3: 6 *f* of the temple of the Lord was not
10 when the builders laid the *f* of the
11 the *f* of the house of the Lord was
12 when the *f* of the house was laid
5:16 and laid the *f* of the house of God
Job 4:19 whose *f* is in the dust, which are
22:16 whose *f* was overflown with a flood:
Ps 87: 1 His *f* is in the holy mountains.
102:25 Of old hast thou laid the *f* of the
137: 7 rase it, even to the *f* thereof.
Pr 10:25 the righteous is an everlasting *f*.
Isa 28:16 I lay in Zion for a *f* a stone,
16 a precious corner stone, a sure *f*:
44:28 to the temple, Thy *f* shall be laid.
48:13 Mine hand also hath laid the *f* of
Eze 13:14 the *f* thereof shall be discovered,
Hab 3:13 discovering the *f* unto the neck.
Hag 2:18 *f* of the Lord's temple was laid.
Zec 4: 9 have laid the *f* of this house;
8: 9 the day that the *f* of the house
12: 1 and layeth the *f* of the earth,
M't 13:35 secret from the *f* of the world.
25:34 for you from the *f* of the world:
Lu 6:48 deep, and laid the *f* on a rock:
49 without a *f* built an house upon the
11:50 shed from the *f* of the world,
14:29 after he hath laid the *f*, and is not
Joh 17:24 lovest me before the *f* of the world,
Ro 15:20 build upon another man's *f*:
1Co 3:10 I have laid the *f*, and another
11 For other *f* can no man lay than
12 upon this *f* gold, silver, precious
Eph 1: 4 in him before the *f* of the world,
2:20 built upon the *f* of the apostles
1Ti 6:19 for themselves a good *f* against
2Ti 2:19 the *f* of God standeth sure, having
He 1:10 hast laid the *f* of the earth;
4: 3 finished from the *f* of the world.
6: 1 laying again the *f* of repentance
9:26 suffered since the *f* of the world:
1Pe 1:20 before the *f* of the world, but was
Re 13: 8 Lamb slain from the *f* of the world.
17: 8 of life from the *f* of the world,
21:19 The first *f* was jasper; the second,

foundations
De 32:22 on fire the *f* of the mountains.
2Sa 22: 8 the *f* of heaven moved and shook,
16 the *f* of the world were discovered,
Ezr 4:12 the wall thereof, and joined the *f*,

Ezr 6: 3 let the *f* thereof be strongly laid;
Job 38: 4 thou when I laid the *f* of the earth?
6 are the *f* thereof fastened? or who
Ps 11: 3 If the *f* be destroyed, what can the
18: 7 the *f* also of the hills moved and
15 the *f* of the world were discovered
82: 5 all of the *f* of the earth are out of
104: 5 Who laid the *f* of the earth,
Pr 8:29 he appointed the *f* of the earth:
Isa 16: 7 *f* of Kir-hareseth shall ye mourn;
24:18 and the *f* of the earth do shake.
40:21 understood from the *f* of the earth?
51:13 and laid the *f* of the earth;
16 and lay the *f* of the earth,
54:11 and lay thy *f* with sapphires.
58:12 up the *f* of many generations;
Jer 31:37 and the *f* of the earth searched out
50:15 her *f* are fallen, her walls are
51:26 thee a corner, nor a stone for *f*;
La 4:11 and it hath devoured the *f* thereof.
Eze 30: 4 and her *f* shall be broken down.
41: 8 *f* of the side chambers were a full
Mic 1: 6 and I will discover the *f* thereof.
6: 2 and ye strong *f* of the earth:
Ac 16:26 the *f* of the prison were shaken:
He 11:10 he looked for a city which hath *f*,
Re 21:14 the wall of the city had twelve *f*,
19 And the *f* of the wall of the city

founded See also CONFOUNDED.
Ps 24: 2 For he hath *f* it upon the seas,
89:11 fulness thereof, thou hast *f* them.
104: 8 place which thou hast *f* for them.
119:152 that thou hast *f* them for ever.
Pro 3:19 Lord by wisdom hath *f* the earth;
Isa 14:32 the Lord hath *f* Zion, and the poor
23:13 Assyrian *f* it for them that dwell
Am 9: 6 and hath *f* his troop in the earth;
M't 7:25 fell not: for it was *f* upon a rock.
Lu 6:48 shake it: for it was *f* upon a rock

founder
J'g 17: 4 and gave them to the *f*, who made
Jer 6:29 *f* melteth in vain: for the wicked
10: 9 hands of the *f*: blue and purple
14 every *f* is confounded by the
51:17 every *f* is confounded by the

foundest
Ne 9: 8 *f* his heart faithful before thee,

fountain See also FOUNTAINS.
Ge 16: 7 found her by a *f* of water in the
7 by the *f* in the way to Shur.
Le 11:36 Nevertheless a *f* or pit, wherein
20:18 he hath discovered her *f*, and she
18 she hath uncovered the *f* of her
De 33:28 *f* of Jacob shall be upon a land
Jos 15: 9 the *f* of the water of Nephtoah,
1Sa 29: 1 Israelites pitched by a *f* which
Ne 2:14 I went on to the gate of the *f*,
3:15 the gate of the *f* repaired Shallun
12:37 And at the *f* gate, which was over
Ps 36: 9 For with thee is the *f* of life:
68:26 the Lord, from the *f* of Israel.
74:15 Thou didst cleave the *f* and the
114: 8 water, the flint into a *f* of waters.
Pr 5:18 Let thy *f* be blessed: and rejoice
13:14 The law of the wise is a *f* of life,
14:27 The fear of the Lord is a *f* of life,
25:26 troubled *f*, and a corrupt spring.
Ec 12: 6 or the pitcher be broken at the *f*,
Ca 4:12 a spring shut up, a *f* sealed.
15 a *f* of gardens, a well of living
Jer 2:13 forsaken me the *f* of living waters,
6: 7 As a *f* casteth out her waters,
9: 1 waters, and mine eyes a *f* of tears,
17:13 forsaken the Lord, the *f* of living
Ho 13:15 and his *f* shall be dried up:
Joel 3:18 a *f* shall come forth of the house
Zec 13: 1 that day there shall be a *f* opened
M'r 5:29 straightway the *f* of her blood
Jas 3:11 Doth a *f* send forth at the same
12 so can no *f* both yield salt water
Re 21: 6 that is athirst of the *f* of the water

fountains
Ge 7:11 were all the *f* of the great deep
8: 2 *f* also of the deep and the windows
Nu 33: 9 in Elim were twelve *f* of water,
De 8: 7 of *f* and depths that spring out of
1Ki 18: 5 unto all *f* of water, and unto all
2Ch 32: 3 to stop the waters of the *f* which
4 stopped all the *f*, and the brook
Pr 5:16 Let thy *f* be dispersed abroad,
8:24 when there were no *f* abounding
28 he strengthened the *f* of the deep:
Isa 41:18 and *f* in the midst of the valleys:
Re 7:17 shall lead them unto living *f* of
8:10 rivers, and upon the *f* of waters;
14: 7 the sea, and the *f* of waters.
16: 4 upon the rivers and *f* of waters:

four See also FOURFOLD; FOURSCORE; FOURSQUARE; FOURTEEN.
Ge 2:10 parted, and became into *f* heads.
11:13 after he begat Salah *f* hundred and
15 after he begat Eber *f* hundred
16 And Eber lived *f* and thirty years,
17 after he begat Peleg *f* hundred
14: 9 king of Ellasar; *f* kings with five.
15:13 shall afflict them *f* hundred years;
23:15 worth *f* hundred shekels of silver;
16 Heth, *f* hundred shekels of silver,
32: 6 and *f* hundred men with him.
33: 1 and with him *f* hundred men.
47:24 and *f* parts shall be your own,
Ex 12:40 was *f* hundred and thirty years.
41 the *f* hundred and thirty years,
22: 1 an ox, and *f* sheep for a sheep.

Ex 25:12 thou shalt cast *f* rings of gold for it,
12 and put them in the *f* corners
26 shalt make for it *f* rings of gold,
26 and put the rings in the *f* corners
26 that are on the *f* feet thereof.
34 *f* bowls made like unto almonds,
26: 2, 8 breadth of one curtain *f* cubits,
32 *f* pillars of shittim wood overlaid
32 gold, upon the *f* sockets of silver.
27: 2 horns of it upon the *f* corners
4 net shalt thou make *f* brasen rings
4 rings in the *f* corners thereof.
16 and their pillars shall be *f*,
16 and their sockets *f*.
28:17 even *f* rows of stones: the first row
36: 9 the breadth of one curtain *f* cubits:
15 *f* cubits was the breadth of one
36 *f* pillars of shittim wood, and
36 he cast for them *f* sockets of silver.
37: 3 And he cast for it *f* rings of gold,
3 to be set by the *f* corners of it;
13 And he cast for it *f* rings of gold,
13 and put the rings upon the *f* corners
13 that were in the *f* feet thereof.
20 were *f* bowls made like almonds,
38: 2 the horns thereof on the *f* corners
5 And he cast *f* rings for the *f* ends
19 And their pillars were *f*,
19 and their sockets of brass *f*;
29 thousand and *f* hundred shekels.
39:10 they set in it *f* rows of stones:
Le 11:20 fowls that creep, going upon all *f*,
21 creeping thing that goeth upon all *f*,
23 creeping things, which have *f* feet,
27 manner of beasts that go on all *f*,
42 and whatsoever goeth upon all *f*,
Nu 1:29 fifty and *f* thousand and *f* hundred.
31 and seven thousand and *f* hundred.
37 and five thousand and *f* hundred.
43 and three thousand and *f* hundred
2: 6 fifty and *f* thousand and *f* hundred.
8 and seven thousand and *f* hundred.
9 and six thousand and *f* hundred,
16 thousand and *f* hundred and fifty,
23 and five thousand and *f* hundred.
30 and three thousand and *f* hundred.
7: 7 Two wagons and *f* oxen he gave
8 *f* wagons and eight oxen he gave
85 thousand and *f* hundred shekels,
88 were twenty and *f* bullocks, the
25: 9 plague were twenty and *f* thousand.
26:25 threescore and *f* thousand and
43 and *f* thousand and *f* hundred.
47 and three thousand and *f* hundred.
50 and five thousand and *f* hundred.
De 3:11 and *f* cubits the breadth of it,
22:12 upon the *f* quarters of thy vesture,
Jos 19: 7 Ashan; *f* cities and their villages:
21:18 Almon with her suburbs; *f* cities.
22 Beth-horon with her suburbs; *f*
24 Gath-rimmon with her suburbs; *f*
29 En-gannim with her suburbs; *f*
31 Rehob with her suburbs; *f* cities.
35 Nahalal with her suburbs; *f* cities.
37 Mephaath with her suburbs; *f*
39 with her suburbs; *f* cities in all.
J'g 9:34 against Shechem in *f* companies.
11:40 of Jephthah the Gileadite *f* days
19: 2 and was there *f* whole months.
20: 2 *f* hundred thousand footmen that
17 *f* hundred thousand men that drew
47 in the rock Rimmon *f* months.
21:12 *f* hundred young virgins, that had
1Sa 4: 2 in the field about *f* thousand men.
22: 2 with him about *f* hundred men.
25:13 after David about *f* hundred men;
27: 7 was a full year and *f* months.
30:10 David pursued, he and *f* hundred
17 save *f* hundred young men, which
2Sa 21:20 six toes, *f* and twenty in number;
22 These *f* were born to the giant in
1Ki 6: 1 in the *f* hundred and eightieth year
7: 2 upon *f* rows of cedar pillars, with
19 lily work in the porch, *f* cubits.
27 *f* cubits was the length of one base,
27 and *f* cubits the breadth thereof,
30 every base had *f* brasen wheels,
30 *f* corners thereof had undersetters:
32 under the borders were *f* wheels;
34 *f* undersetters to the *f* corners of
38 and every layer was *f* cubits: and
42 *f* hundred pomegranates for the
9:28 gold, *f* hundred and twenty talents,
10:26 thousand and *f* hundred chariots,
15:33 in Tirzah twenty and *f* years.
18:19 the prophets of Baal *f* hundred and
19 prophets of the groves *f* hundred,
22 Baal's prophets are *f* hundred and
33 Fill *f* barrels with water, and pour
22: 6 together, about *f* hundred men, and
2Ki 7: 3 And there were *f* leprous men at
14:13 unto the corner gate, *f* hundred
1Ch 3: 5 and Nathan, and Solomon, *f*,
5:18 *f* and forty thousand seven hundred
7: 1 and Pua, Jashub, and Shimrom, *f*.
7 and two thousand and thirty and *f*.
9:24 In *f* quarters were the porters,
26 the *f* chief porters, were in their set
12:26 Levi *f* thousand and six hundred.
20: 6 whose fingers and toes were *f* and
21: 5 *f* hundred threescore and ten
20 his *f* sons with him hid themselves.
23: 4 twenty and *f* thousand were to set
5 Moreover *f* thousand were porters;
5 and *f* thousand praised the Lord
10 These *f* were the sons of Shimei.

1Ch 23:12 Izhar, Hebron, and Uzziel, *f*.
24:18 the *f* and twentieth to Maaziah.
25:31 *f* and twentieth to Romamti-ezer,
26:17 northward *f* a day, southward *f* a
18 *f* at the causeway, and two at
27: 1 of every course were...*f* thousand
2 in his course were... *f* thousand.
4 likewise were...and *f* thousand.
5, 7, 8, 9, 10, 11, 12, 13, 14, 15 and in
his course were twenty and *f* thousand.
2Ch 1:14 a thousand and *f* hundred chariots,
4:13 *f* hundred pomegranates on the
8:18 *f* hundred and fifty talents of gold,
9:25 Solomon had *f* thousand stalls for
13: 3 even *f* hundred thousand chosen
18: 5 of prophets *f* hundred men, and
25:23 the corner gate, *f* hundred cubits.
Ezr 1:10 basons of a second sort *f* hundred.
11 were five thousand and *f* hundred
2: 7 a thousand two hundred fifty and *f*.
15 of Adin, *f* hundred fifty and *f*.
31 a thousand two hundred fifty and *f*
40 children of Hodaviah, seventy and *f*.
67 Their camels, *f* hundred thirty and
6:17 hundred rams, *f* hundred lambs;
Ne 6: 4 Yet they sent unto me *f* times
7:12 thousand two hundred fifty and *f*.
23 Bezai, three hundred twenty and *f*.
34 thousand two hundred fifty and *f*.
43 children of Hodevah, seventy and *f*.
69 Their camels, *f* hundred thirty
11: 6 *f* hundred three score and eight
18 were two hundred fourscore and *f*.
Job 1:19 smote the *f* corners of the house,
42:16 his sons' sons, even *f* generations.
Pr 30:15 *f* things say not, It is enough:
18 yea, *f* which I know not:
21 and for *f* which it cannot bear:
24 *f* things which are little upon the
29 yea, *f* are comely in going:
Isa 11:12 from the *f* corners of the earth.
17: 6 *f* or five in the outmost fruitful
Jer 15: 3 I will appoint over them *f* kinds,
36:23 Jehudi had read three or *f* leaves,
49:36 the *f* winds from the *f* quarters
52:21 thickness thereof was *f* fingers:
30 persons were *f* thousand and six
Eze 1: 5 the likeness of *f* living creatures.
6 And every one had *f* faces,
6 and every one had *f* wings.
8 *f* sides; and they *f* had their faces
10 they *f* had the face of a man,
10 and they *f* had the face of an ox on
10 they *f* also had the face of an eagle.
15 living creatures, with his *f* faces.
16 they *f* had one likeness: and their
17 went, they went upon their *f* sides:
18 full of eyes round about them *f*.
7: 2 upon the *f* corners of the land.
10: 9 the *f* wheels by the cherubims,
10 they *f* had one likeness, as if a
11 went, they went upon their *f* sides;
12 even the wheels that they *f* had.
14 And every one had *f* faces: the
21 Every one had *f* faces apiece,
21 and every one *f* wings;
14:21 when I send my *f* sore judgments
37: 9 Come from the *f* winds, O breath,
40:41 *F* tables were on this side,
41 and *f* tables on that side,
42 And the *f* tables were of hewn
41: 5 of every side chamber, *f* cubits
42:20 He measured it by the *f* sides:
43:14 the greater settle shall be *f* cubits,
15 So the altar shall be *f* cubits;
15 altar and upward shall be *f* horns.
16 square in the *f* squares thereof.
17 fourteen broad in the *f* squares
20 *f* horns of it, and on the *f* corners
45:19 upon the *f* corners of the settle
46:21 pass by the *f* corners of the court;
22 In the *f* corners of the court were
22 *f* corners were of one measure.
23 in them round about them *f*, and
48:16 the north side *f* thousand and five
16 the south side *f* thousand and five
16 the east side *f* thousand and five
16 the west side *f* thousand and five
30 on the north side, *f* thousand and
32 at the east side, *f* thousand and
33 at the side *f* thousand and
34 At the west side *f* thousand and
Da 1:17 these *f* children, God gave them
3:25 Lo, I see *f* men loose, walking
7: 2 the *f* winds of the heaven strove
3 And *f* great beasts came up from
6 upon the back of it *f* wings of a
6 the beast had also *f* heads;
17 beasts, which are *f*, are *f* kings,
8: 8 and for it came up *f* notable ones
8 toward the *f* winds of heaven.
22 *f* stood up for it, *f* kingdoms shall
10: 4 in the *f* and twentieth day of the
11: 4 be divided toward the *f* winds of
Am 1: 3 of Damascus, and for *f*, I will not
6 of Gaza, and for *f*, I will not turn
9 transgressions of Tyrus, and for *f*,
11 of Edom, and for *f*, I will not turn
13 Ammon, and for *f*, I will not turn
2: 1 of Moab, and for *f*, I will not turn
4 of Judah, and for *f*, I will not turn
6 of Israel, and for *f*, I will not turn
Hag 1:15 In the *f* and twentieth day of the
2:10 In the *f* and twentieth day of the
18 from the *f* and twentieth day of

Hag 2:20 in the *f* and twentieth day of the
Zec 1: 7 Upon the *f* and twentieth day of
18 and saw, and behold *f* horns.
20 the Lord shewed me *f* carpenters.
2: 6 as the *f* winds of the heaven,
6: 1 there came *f* chariots out from
5 are the *f* spirits of the heavens,
M't 15:38 *f* thousand men, beside women
16:10 the seven loaves of the *f* thousand,
24:31 together his elect from the *f*
M'r 2: 3 of the palsy, which was borne of *f*
8: 9 eaten were about *f* thousand:
20 when the seven among *f* thousand,
13:27 his elect from the *f* winds,
Lu 2:37 of about fourscore and *f* years,
Joh 4:35 not ye, There are yet *f* months,
11:17 lain in the grave *f* days already.
39 for he hath been dead *f* days.
19:23 *f* parts, to every soldier a part;
Ac 5:36 number of men, about *f* hundred,
7: 6 entreat them evil *f* hundred years.
10:11 great sheet knit at the *f* corners,
30 *F* days ago I was fasting until
11: 5 down from heaven by *f* corners;
12: 4 and delivered him to *f* quaternions
13:20 the space of *f* hundred and fifty
21: 9 the same man had *f* daughters,
23 We have *f* men which have a vow
38 wilderness *f* thousand men that
27:29 they cast *f* anchors out of the
Ga 3:17 *f* hundred and thirty years after,
Re 4: 4 throne were *f* and twenty seats:
4 I saw *f* and twenty elders sitting,
6 *f* beasts full of eyes before and
8 And the *f* beasts had each of them
10 The *f* and twenty elders fall down
5: 6 of the throne and of the *f* beasts,
8 *f* beasts and *f* and twenty elders
14 And the *f* beasts said, Amen.
14 *f* and twenty elders fell down
6: 1 one of the *f* beasts saying, Come
6 in the midst of the *f* beasts say,
7: 1 after these things I saw *f* angels
1 on the *f* corners of the earth,
1 holding the *f* winds of the earth,
2 with a loud voice to the *f* angels,
4 hundred and forty and *f* thousand
11 about the elders and the *f* beasts,
9:13 I heard a voice from the *f* horns
14 Loose the *f* angels which are
15 And the *f* angels were loosed,
11:16 the *f* and twenty elders, which sat
14: 1 an hundred forty and *f* thousand,
3 and before the *f* beasts, and the
3 hundred and forty and *f* thousand
15: 7 And one of the *f* beasts gave
19: 4 the *f* and twenty elders and the *f*
20: 8 are in the *f* quarters of the earth,
21:17 an hundred and forty and *f* cubits,

fourfold
2Sa 12: 6 And he shall restore the lamb *f*,
Lu 19: 8 false accusation, I restore him *f*.

fourfooted
Ac 10:12 manner of *f* beasts of the earth,
11: 6 and saw *f* beasts of the earth,
Ro 1:23 *f* beasts, and creeping things.

four-hundred See FOUR and HUNDRED.

fourscore
Ge 16:16 Abram was *f* and six years old,
35:28 of Isaac were an hundred and *f*
Ex 7: 7 And Moses was *f* years old,
7 and Aaron *f* and three years old,
Nu 2: 9 hundred thousand and *f* thousand
4:48 thousand and five hundred and *f*.
Jos 14:10 I am this day *f* and five years old.
J'g 3:30 And the land had rest *f* years.
1Sa 22:18 slew on that day *f* and five persons
2Sa 19:32 a very aged man, even *f* years old:
35 I am this day *f* years old: and can
1Ki 5:15 and *f* thousand hewers in the
12:21 an hundred and *f* thousand chosen
2Ki 6:25 an ass's head was sold for *f* pieces
10:24 Jehu appointed *f* men without,
19:35 an hundred *f* and five thousand:
1Ch 7: 5 genealogies *f* and seven thousand.
15: 9 Eliel the chief, and his brethren *f*:
25: 7 was two hundred *f* and eight.
2Ch 2: 2 and *f* thousand to hew in the
18 and *f* thousand to be hewers in the
11: 1 an hundred and *f* thousand chosen
14: 8 two hundred and *f* thousand: all
17:15 him two hundred and *f* thousand.
18 an hundred and *f* thousand ready
26:17 and with him *f* priests of the Lord,
Ezr 8: 8 Michael, and with him *f* males.
Ne 7:26 Netopha, an hundred *f* and eight.
11:18 city were two hundred *f* and four.
Es 1: 4 days, even an hundred and *f* days.
Ps 90:10 if by reason of strength they be *f*
Ca 6: 8 queens, and *f* concubines, and
Isa 37:36 a hundred and *f* and five thousand:
Jer 41: 5 and from Samaria, even *f* men,
Lu 2:37 widow of about *f* and four years.
16: 7 Take thy bill, and write *f*.

fourscore-thousand See FOURSCORE and THOUSAND.

foursquare
Ex 27: 1 the altar shall be *f*: and the height
28:16 *F* it shall be being doubled; a span
30: 2 *f* shall it be: and two cubits shall
37:25 it was *f*; and two cubits was the
38: 1 it was *f*; and three cubits the
39: 9 It was *f*; they made the

1Ki 7:31 with their borders, *f*, not round.
Eze 40:47 an hundred cubits broad, *f*;
48:20 ye shall offer the holy oblation *f*,
Re 21:16 And the city lieth *f*, and the length

fourteen
Ge 31:41 I served thee *f* years for thy
46:22 Jacob: all the souls were *f*.
Nu 1:27 *f* thousand and six hundred.
2: 4 *f* thousand and six hundred.
16:49 were *f* thousand and seven
29:13 and *f* lambs of the first year:
15 to each lamb of the *f* lambs:
17, 20 *f* lambs of the first year
23, 26, 29, 32 and *f* lambs of the
Jos 15:36 *f* cities with their villages.
18:28 *f* cities with their villages.
1Ki 8:65 and seven days, even *f* days.
1Ch 25: 5 And God gave to Heman *f* sons
2Ch 13:21 mighty, and married *f* wives,
Job 42:12 for he had *f* thousand sheep,
Eze 43:17 settle shall be *f* cubits long
17 *f* broad in the four squares
M't 1:17 Abraham to David are *f* generations
17 into Babylon are *f* generations;
17 unto Christ are *f* generations.
2Co 12: 2 a man in Christ above *f* years ago,
Ga 2: 1 *f* years after I went up again to

fourteenth
Ge 14: 5 *f* year came Chedorlaomer,
Ex 12: 6 shall keep it up until the *f* day
18 on the *f* day of the month at
Le 23: 5 In the *f* day of the first month
Nu 9: 3 In the *f* day of this month, at
5 the passover on the *f* day of
11 *f* day of the second month at
28:16 in the *f* day of the first month
Jos 5:10 the passover on the *f* day of
2Ki 18:13 in the *f* year of king Hezekiah
1Ch 24:13 Huppah, the *f* to Jeshebeab,
25:21 *f* to Mattithiah, he, his sons,
2Ch 30:15 the passover on the *f* day of
35: 1 on the *f* day of the first month.
Ezr 6:19 the passover upon the *f* day
Es 9:15 on the *f* day also of the month
17 and on the *f* day of the same
18 and on the *f* thereof;
19 the *f* day of the month Adar
21 they should keep the *f* day of
Isa 36: 1 in the *f* year of king Hezekiah,
Eze 40: 1 the *f* year after that the city
45:21 first month, in the *f* day of the
Ac 27:27 But when the *f* night was come,
33 is the *f* day that ye have tarried

fourteen-thousand See FOURTEEN and THOUSAND.

fourth^
Ge 1:19 and the morning were the *f* day.
2:14 And the *f* river is Euphrates.
15:16 the *f* generation they shall come
Ex 20: 5 unto the third and *f* generation
28:20 the *f* row a beryl, and an onyx,
29:40 the *f* part of an hin of beaten oil;
40 and the *f* part of an hin of wine
34: 7 the third and to the *f* generation.
39:13 the *f* row, a beryl, an onyx,
Le 19:24 in the *f* year all the fruit thereof
23:13 of wine, the *f* part of an hin.
Nu 7:30 On the *f* day Elizur the son of
14:18 unto the third and *f* generation.
15: 4 with the *f* part of an hin of oil.
5 And the *f* part of an hin of wine
23:10 the number of the *f* part of Israel?
28: 5 the *f* part of an hin of beaten oil.
7 the *f* part of an hin for the one
14 and a *f* part of an hin unto a lamb:
29:23 And on the *f* day ten bullocks,
De 5: 9 unto the third and *f* generation
Jos 19:17 the *f* lot came out to Issachar,
J'g 19: 5 And it came to pass on the *f* day,
1Sa 9: 8 the *f* part of a shekel of silver:
2Sa 3: 4 And the *f*, Adonijah the son of
1Ki 6: 1 in the *f* year of Solomon's reign
33 olive tree, a *f* part of the wall.
37 In the *f* year was the foundation
22:41 the *f* year of Ahab king of Israel.
2Ki 6:25 the *f* part of a cab of dove's dung
10:30 children of the *f* generation shall
15:12 of Israel unto the *f* generation.
18: 9 in the *f* year of king Hezekiah,
25: 3 of the *f* month the famine prevailed
1Ch 2:14 Nethaneel the *f*, Raddai the fifth,
3: 2 the *f*, Adonijah the son of Haggith:
15 the third Zedekiah, the *f* Shallum.
8: 2 Nohah the *f*, and Rapha the fifth.
12:10 Mishmannah the *f*, Jeremiah the
23:19 the third, Jekameam the *f*.
24: 8 third to Harim, the *f* to Seorim,
23 the third, Jekameam the *f*.
25:11 The *f* to Izri, he, his sons,
26: 2 the third, Jathniel the *f*,
4 Joah the third, Sacar the *f*, and
11 the third, Zechariah the *f*:
27: 7 The *f* captain for the *f* month was
2Ch 3: 2 month, in the *f* year of his reign.
20:26 And on the *f* day they assembled
Ezr 8:33 Now on the *f* day was the silver
Ne 9: 1 Now in the twenty and *f* day
3 their God one *f* part of the day; of
3 and another *f* part they confessed,
Jer 25: 1 Judah in the *f* year of Jehoiakim
28: 1 the *f* year, and in the fifth month,
36: 1 pass in the *f* year of Jehoiakim
39: 2 the *f* month, the ninth day of the
45: 1 the *f* year of Jehoiakim the son of
46: 2 smote in the *f* year of Jehoiakim
51:59 Babylon in the *f* year of his reign.
52: 6 And in the *f* month, in the ninth day
Eze 1: 1 in the *f* month, in the fifth day of
10:14 and the *f* the face of an eagle.
Da 2:40 And the *f* kingdom shall be strong
3:25 the form of the *f* is like the Son of
7: 7 and behold a *f* beast, dreadful and
19 know the truth of the *f* beast,
23 The *f* beast shall be the *f* kingdom
11: 2 *f* shall be far richer than they all:
Zec 6: 3 the *f* chariot grisled and bay horses.
7: 1 pass in the *f* year of king Darius,
1 in the *f* day of the ninth month,
8:19 The fast of the *f* month, and the
M't 14:25 And in the *f* watch of the night
M'r 6:48 and about the *f* watch of the night
Re 4: 7 the *f* beast was like a flying eagle.
6: 7 And when he had opened the *f* seal,
7 I heard the voice of the *f* beast
8 them over the *f* part of the earth,
8:12 And the *f* angel sounded, and the
16: 8 And the *f* angel poured out his vial
21:19 a chalcedony; the *f*, an emerald;

four-thousand See FOUR and THOUSAND.

fowl^ See also FOWLS.
Ge 1:20 and *f* that may fly above the earth
21 and every winged *f* after his kind:
22 and let *f* multiply in the earth.
26 of the sea, and over the *f* of the air,
30 of the earth, and to every *f* of the air,
2:19 and every *f* of the air; and brought
20 and to the *f* of the air, and to every
7:14 every *f* after his kind, every bird
21 both of *f*, and of cattle, and of
23 the *f* of the heaven; and they were
8:17 both of *f*, and of cattle, and of
19 every creeping thing, and every *f*,
20 clean beast, and of every clean *f*,
9: 2 and upon every *f* of the air,
10 creature that is with you, of the *f*,
Le 7:26 manner of blood, whether it be of *f*
11:46 the law of the beasts, and of the *f*,
17:13 hunteth and catcheth any beast or *f*
20:25 souls abominable by beast, or by *f*,
De 4:17 the likeness of any winged *f* that
1Ki 4:23 and fallowdeer, and fatted *f*.
33 he spake also of beasts, and of *f*,
Job 28: 7 is a path which no *f* knoweth,
Ps 8: 8 The *f* of the air, and the fish of the
148:10 creeping things, and flying *f*:
Jer 9:10 both the *f* of the heavens and the
Eze 17:23 shall dwell all *f* of every wing;
39:17 feathered *f*, and to every beast
44:31 or torn, whether it be *f* or beast.
Da 7: 6 the back of it four wings of a *f*;

fowler See also FOWLERS.
Ps 91: 3 thee from the snare of the *f*, and
Pr 6: 5 as a bird from the hand of the *f*,
Ho 9: 8 but the prophet is a snare of a *f*

fowlers
Ps 124: 7 as a bird out of the snare of the *f*:

fowls
Ge 6: 7 thing, and the *f* of the air; for it
20 *f* after their kind, and of cattle
7: 3 Of *f* also of the air by sevens,
8 *f*, and of every thing that creepeth
15:11 *f* came down upon the carcases,
Le 1:14 his offering to the Lord be of *f*,
11:13 have in abomination among the *f*;
20 All *f* that creep, going upon all
20:25 between unclean *f* and clean:
De 14:20 But of all clean *f* ye may eat.
28:26 carcase shall be meat unto all *f* of
1Sa 17:44 and I will give thy flesh unto the *f*
46 the Philistines this day unto the *f*
1Ki 14:11 the field shall the *f* of the air eat:
16: 4 the fields shall the *f* of the air eat.
21:24 the field shall the *f* of the air eat.
Ne 5:18 also *f* were prepared for me, and
Job 12: 7 and the *f* of the air, and they shall
28:21 kept close from the *f* of the air.
35:11 us wiser than the *f* of heaven?
Ps 50:11 I know all the *f* of the mountains:
78:27 and feathered *f* like as the sand
79: 2 meat unto the *f* of the heaven,
104:12 By them shall the *f* of the heaven
Isa 18: 6 unto the *f* of the mountains,
6 the *f* shall summer upon them,
Jer 7:33 people shall be meat for the *f* of
15: 3 the *f* of the heaven, and the beasts
16: 4 shall be meat for the *f* of heaven,
19: 7 to be meat for the *f* of the heaven,
34:20 shall be for meat unto the *f* of the
Eze 29: 5 field and to the *f* of the heaven.
31: 6 the *f* of heaven made their nests
13 all the *f* of the heaven remain,
32: 4 all the *f* of the heaven to remain
38:20 the sea and the *f* of the heaven,
Da 2:38 and the *f* of the heaven hath he
4:12 and the *f* of the heaven dwelt in
14 it, and the *f* from his branches:
21 the *f* of the heaven had their
Ho 2:18 with the *f* of heaven, and with the
4: 3 and with the *f* of heaven; yea, the
7:12 them down as the *f* of heaven; I
Zep 1: 3 I will consume the *f* of the heaven,
M't 6:26 Behold, the *f* of the air: for they
13: 4 the *f* came and devoured them
M'r 4: 4 and the *f* of the air came and
32 the *f* of the air may lodge under
Lu 8: 5 and the *f* of the air devoured it.
12:24 more are ye better than the *f*?
13:19 and the *f* of the air lodged in the
Ac 10:12 creeping things, and *f* of the air.
11: 6 creeping things, and *f* of the air.
Re 19:17 saying to all the *f* that fly in the
21 the *f* were filled with their flesh.

fox See also FOXES.
Ne 4: 3 if a *f* go up, he shall even break
Lu 13:32 Go ye, and tell that *f*, Behold, I

foxes
J'g 15: 4 went and caught three hundred *f*,
Ps 63:10 they shall be a portion for *f*.
Ca 2:15 Take us the *f*, the little *f*, that
La 5:18 is desolate, the *f* walk upon it.
Eze 13: 4 are like the *f* in the deserts.
M't 8:20 The *f* have holes, and the birds of
Lu 9:58 *F* have holes, and birds of the air

fragments
M't 14:20 took up of the *f* that remained
M'r 6:43 up twelve baskets full of the *f*,
8:19, 20 baskets full of *f* took ye up?
Lu 9:17 taken up of *f* that remained to
Joh 6:12 Gather up the *f* that remain,
13 filled twelve baskets with the *f*

frail
Ps 39: 4 that I may know how *f* I am.

frame See also FRAMED; FRAMETH.
J'g 12: 6 could not *f* to pronounce it right.
Ps 103:14 For he knoweth our *f*; he
Jer 18:11 I *f* evil against you, and devise
Eze 40: 2 by which was as the *f* of a city on
Ho 5: 4 They will not *f* their doings to

framed
Isa 29:16 or shall the thing *f* say of him
16 say of him that *f* it, He had no
Eph 2:21 In whom all the building fitly *f*
Heb 11: 3 the worlds were *f* by the word of

frameth
Ps 50:19 evil, and thy tongue *f* deceit.
94:20 which *f* mischief by a law?

frankincense
Ex 30:34 these sweet spices with pure *f*:
Le 2: 1 oil upon it, and put *f* thereon:
2 with all the *f* thereof; and the
15 and lay *f* thereon: it is a meat
16 with all the *f* thereof: it is an
5:11 neither shall he put any *f* thereon:
6:15 all the *f* which is upon the meat
24: 7 shalt put pure *f* upon each row,
Nu 5:15 put *f* thereon; for it is an offering
1Ch 9:29 the oil, and the *f*, and the spices.
Ne 13: 5 the *f*, and the vessels, and the
9 with the meat offering and the *f*.
Ca 3: 6 perfumed with myrrh and *f*, with
4: 6 of myrrh, and to the hill of *f*.
14 with all trees of *f*; myrrh and
M't 2:11 gifts; gold, and *f*, and myrrh.
Re 18:13 *f*, and wine, and oil, and fine flour,

frankly
Lu 7:42 to pay, he *f* forgave them both.

fraud See also DEFRAUD.
Ps 10: 7 full of cursing and deceit and *f*:
Jas 5: 4 which is of you kept back by *f*,

fray
De 28:26 and no man shall *f* them away.
Jer 7:33 and none shall *f* them away.
Zec 1:21 but these are come to *f* them,

freckled
Le 13:39 it is a *f* spot that groweth in the

free^ See also FREED; FREEMAN; FREEWILL; FREEWOMAN.
Ex 21: 2 in the seventh he shall go out *f*
5 my children; I will not go out *f*:
11 shall she go out *f* without money.
26 let him go *f* for his eye's sake.
27 let him go *f* for his tooth's sake.
36: 3 brought yet unto him *f* offerings
Le 19:20 to death, because she was not *f*.
Nu 5:19 be thou *f* from this bitter water
28 then she shall be *f*, and shall
De 15:12 thou shalt let him go *f* from thee.
13 thou sendest him out *f* from thee,
18 sendest him away *f* from thee;
24: 5 he shall be *f* at home one year,
1Sa 17:25 his father's house *f* in Israel.
1Ch 9:33 in the chambers were *f*: for they
2Ch 29:31 and as many as were of a *f* heart*
Job 3:19 the servant is *f* from his master.
39: 5 Who hath sent out the wild ass *f*?
Ps 51:12 and uphold me with thy *f* spirit.
88: 5 *F* among the dead, like the slain
105:20 of the people, and let him go *f*.
Isa 58: 6 and to let the oppressed go *f*,
Jer 34: 9 an Hebrew or an Hebrewess, go *f*;
10 every one his maidservant, go *f*,
11 whom they had let go *f*, to return,
14 thou shalt let him go *f* from thee:
M't 15: 6 or his mother, he shall be *f*.
17:26 unto him, Then are the children *f*
M'r 7:11 be profited by me; he shall be *f*.
Joh 8:32 and the truth shall make you *f*.
33 sayest thou, Ye shall be made *f*?
36 Son therefore shall make you *f*,
36 ye shall be *f* indeed.
Ac 22:28 And Paul said, But I was *f* born.
Ro 5:15 the offence, so also is the *f* gift.
16 but the *f* gift is of many offences
18 the *f* gift came upon all men unto
6:18 Being then made *f* from sin, ye
20 ye were *f* from righteousness.
22 But now being made *f* from sin,

Ro 7: 3 she is *f* from that law; so that
8: 2 hath made me *f* from the law of
1Co 7:21 if thou mayest be made *f*, use it
22 that is called, being *f*, is Christ's
9: 1 Am I not an apostle? am I not *f*?
19 For though I be *f* from all men,
12:13 whether we be bond or *f*; and have
Gal 3:28 Greek, there is neither bond nor *f*,
4:26 But Jerusalem which is above is *f*,
31 of the bondwoman, but of the *f*.
5: 1 wherewith Christ hath made us *f*,
Eph 6: 8 whether he be bond or *f*.
Col 3:11 Barbarian, Scythian, bond nor *f*:
2Th 3: 1 of the Lord may have *f* course,
1Pe 2:16 As *f*, and not using your liberty
Re 6:15 every bondman, and every *f* man,
13:16 rich and poor, *f* and bond, to
19:18 all men, both *f* and bond, both

free-born See FREE and BORN.

freed
Jos 9:23 there shall none of you be *f* from
Ro 6: 7 For he that is dead is *f* from sin.

freedom
Le 19:20 at all redeemed, nor *f* given her;
Ac 22:28 a great sum obtained I this *f*.

freely
Ge 2:16 tree of the garden thou mayest *f* eat:
Nu 11: 5 which we did eat in Egypt *f*;
1Sa 14:30 if haply the people had eaten *f* to day
Ezr 2:68 offered *f* for the house of God to
7:15 and his counsellors have *f* offered unto
Ps 54: 6 I will *f* sacrifice unto thee: I
Ho 14: 4 I will love them *f*: for mine anger
M't 10: 8 *f* ye have received, *f* give.
Ac 2:29 let me *f* speak unto you of
26:26 before whom also I speak *f*:
Ro 3:24 Being justified *f* by his grace
8:32 shall he not with him also *f* give us
1Co 2:12 we might know the things that are *f*
2Co 11: 7 to you the gospel of God *f*?
Re 21: 6 the fountain of the water of life *f*.
22:17 let him take the water of life *f*.

freeman
1Co 7:22 being a servant, is the Lord's *f*:

freewill See also FREE and WILL.
Le 22:18 all his *f* offerings, which they
21 a *f* offering in beeves or sheep,
23 mayest thou offer for a *f* offering;
23:38 all your *f* offerings, which ye give
Nu 15: 3 a vow, or in a *f* offering, or in your
29:39 your vows, and your *f* offerings, for
De 12: 6 your vows, and your *f* offerings, and
17 thy *f* offerings, or heave offering of
16:10 of a *f* offering of thine hand, which
23:23 a *f* offering, according as thou hast
2Ch 31:14 the *f* offerings of God, to distribute
Ezr 1: 4 the *f* offering for the house of God
3: 5 offered a *f* offering unto the Lord.
7:13 which are minded of their own *f*
16 with the *f* offering of the people,
8:28 a *f* offering unto the Lord God of
Ps 119:108 the *f* offerings of my mouth, O

freewoman
Gal 4:22 by a bondmaid, the other by a *f*.
23 but he of the *f* was by promise.
30 not be heir with the son of the *f*.

freeze See FROZEN.

frequent
2Co 11:23 in prisons more *f*, in deaths oft.

fresh See also AFRESH; FRESHER; REFRESH.
Nu 11: 8 taste of it was as the taste of *f* oil.
Job 29:20 My glory was *f* in me, and my
Ps 92:10 I shall be anointed with *f* oil.
Jas 3:12 both yield salt water and *f*.

fresher
Job 33:25 His flesh shall be *f* than a child's:

fret See also FRETTED; FRETTETH; FRETTING.
Le 13:55 burn it in the fire; it is *f* inward,
1Sa 1: 6 sore, for to make her *f*, because
Ps 37: 1 *F* not thyself because of
7 *f* not thyself because of him who
8 *f* not thyself in any wise to do evil
Pr 24:19 *F* not thyself because of evil men,
Isa 8:21 hungry, they shall *f* themselves,

fretted
Eze 16:43 hast *f* me in all these things; but

fretteth
Pr 19: 3 and his heart *f* against the Lord.

fretting
Le 13:51 the plague is a *f* leprosy; it is
52 it is a *f* leprosy; it shall be burnt
14:44 it is a *f* leprosy in the house: it is

fried
Le 7:12 mingled with oil, of fine flour, *f*.
1Ch 23:29 and for that which is *f*, and for

friend See also FRIENDS; FRIENDSHIP.
Ge 38:12 and his *f* Hirah the Adullamite.
20 sent the kid by the hand of his *f*
Ex 33:11 face, as a man speaketh unto his *f*.
De 13: 6 or the wife of thy bosom, or thy *f*,
J'g 14:20 whom he had used as his *f*.
2Sa 13: 3 Amnon had a *f*, whose name was
15:37 Hushai David's *f*, came into
16:16 Hushai the Archite, David's *f*
17 Is this thy kindness to thy *f*?
17 why wentest thou not with thy *f*?
1Ki 4: 5 principal officer, and the king's *f*:
2Ch 20: 7 seed of Abraham thy *f* for ever?
Job 6:14 pity should be shewed from his *f*;
27 and ye dig a pit for your *f*.
Ps 35:14 as though he had been my *f* or
41: 9 mine own familiar *f*, in whom I trusted
88:18 Lover and *f* hast thou put far
Pr 6: 1 son, if thou be surety for thy *f*,
3 art come into the hand of thy *f*;
3 thyself, and make sure thy *f*.
17:17 A *f* loveth at all times, and a
18 surety in the presence of his *f*.
18:24 and there is a *f* that sticketh closer
19: 6 man is a *f* to him that giveth gifts.
22:11 of his lips the king shall be his *f*.
27: 6 Faithful are the wounds of a *f*;
9 doth the sweetness of a man's *f* by
10 Thine own *f*, and thy father's *f*,
14 blesseth his *f* with a loud voice,
17 a man... the countenance of his *f*.
Ca 5:16 my *f*, O daughters of Jerusalem.
Isa 41: 8 chosen, the seed of Abraham my *f*.
Jer 6:21 neighbour and his *f* shall perish.
19: 9 eat every one the flesh of his *f* in
Ho 3: 1 yet, love a woman beloved of her *f*,
Mic 7: 5 Trust ye not in a *f*, put ye not
M't 11:19 a *f* of publicans and sinners.
20:13 *F*, I do thee no wrong: didst not
22:12 *F*, how camest thou in hither not
26:50 *F*, wherefore art thou come?
Lu 7:34 a *f* of publicans and sinners!
11: 5 Which of you shall have a *f*, and
5 unto him, *F*, lend me three loaves;
6 For a *f* of mine in his journey is
8 and give him, because he is his *f*,
14:10 *F*, go up higher: then shalt thou
Joh 3:29 but the *f* of the bridegroom, which
11:11 Our *f* Lazarus sleepeth; but I go,
19:12 thou art not Cæsar's *f*: whosoever
Ac 12:20 and having made Blastus their *f*,
Jas 2:23 and he was called the *F* of God.
4: 4 *f* of the world is the enemy of God.

friendly
J'g 19: 3 to speak *f* unto her, and to bring
Ru 2:13 spoken *f* unto thine handmaid,
Pr 18:24 friends must shew himself *f*:

friends
Ge 26:26 and Ahuzzath one of his *f*, and
1Sa 30:26 to his *f*, saying, Behold a present
2Sa 3: 8 to his brethren, and to his *f*, and
19: 6 thine enemies, and hatest thy *f*.
1Ki 16:11 of his kinsfolks, nor of his *f*. and
Es 5:10 he sent and called for his *f*,
14 said Zeresh his wife and all his *f*
6:13 told Zeresh his wife and all his *f*
Job 2:11 when Job's three *f* heard of all
16:20 My *f* scorn me: but mine eye
17: 5 He that speaketh flattery to his *f*,
19:14 and my familiar *f* have forgotten me.
19 All my inward *f* abhorred me:
21 have pity upon me, O ye my *f*;
32: 3 against his three *f* was his wrath
42: 7 thee, and against thy two *f*: for ye
10 when he prayed for his *f*: also the
Ps 38:11 My lovers and my *f* stand aloof
Pr 14:20 but the rich hath many *f*.
16:28 and a whisperer separateth chief *f*.
17: 9 he that...a matter separateth very *f*.
18:24 A man that hath *f* must shew
19: 4 Wealth maketh many *f*; but the
7 more do his *f* go far from him?
Ca 5: 1 eat, O *f*; drink, yea, drink
Jer 20: 4 terror to thyself, and to all thy *f*:
6 be buried there, thou, and all thy *f*,
38:22 say, Thy *f* have set thee on,
La 1: 2 her *f* have dealt treacherously
Zec 13: 6 was wounded in the house of my *f*
M'r 3:21 when his *f* heard of it, they
5:19 Go home to thy *f*, and tell them
Lu 7: 6 centurion sent *f* to him, saying,
12: 4 And I say unto you my *f*, Be not
14:12 call not thy *f*, nor thy brethren.
15: 6 he calleth together his *f* and
9 calleth her *f* and her neighbours
29 I might make merry with my *f*:
16: 9 to yourselves *f* of the mammon of
21:16 brethren, and kinsfolks, and *f*;
23:12 day Pilate and Herod were made *f*
Joh 15:13 a man lay down his life for his *f*.
14 Ye are my *f*, if ye do whatsoever
15 I have called you *f*; for all things
Ac 10:24 together his kinsmen and near *f*.
19:31 the chief of Asia, which were his *f*,
27: 3 to go unto his *f* to refresh himself.
3Jo 14 Our *f* salute thee.
14 Greet the *f* by name.

friendship
Pr 22:24 Make no *f* with an angry man;
Jas 4: 4 *f* of the world is enmity with God?

fright See AFFRIGHT.

fringe See also FRINGES.
Nu 15:38 put upon the *f* of the borders a
39 And it shall be unto you for a *f*,

fringes
Nu 15:38 may make them *f* in the borders
De 22:12 thee *f* upon the four quarters

fro See also FROWARD.
Ge 8: 7 raven, which went forth to and *f*,
2 Ki 4:35 walked in the house to and *f*;
2 Ch 16: 9 the eyes of the Lord run to and *f*
Job 1: 7 From going to and *f* in the earth,
2: 2 From going to and *f* in the earth,
7: 4 I am full of tossings to and *f*
13:25 break a leaf driven to and *f*?
Ps 107:27 They reel to and *f*, and stagger
Pr 21: 6 a vanity tossed to and *f* of them
Isa 24:20 shall reel to and *f* like a drunkard,
33: 4 as the running to and *f* of locusts
49:21 a captive, and removing to and *f*?
Jer 5: 1 ye to and *f* through the streets
49: 3 and run to and *f* by the hedges;
Eze 27:19 Dan also and Javan going to and *f*
Da 12: 4 many shall run to and *f*, and
Joe 2: 9 shall run to and *f* in the city;
Am 8:12 they shall run to and *f* to seek the
Zec 1:10 to walk to and *f* through the earth.
11 We have walked to and *f* through the
4:10 of the Lord, which run to and *f*
6: 7 might walk to and *f* through the earth:
7 Get you hence, walk to and *f* through
7 So they walked to and *f* through the
Eph 4:14 tossed to and *f*, and carried about

frogs
Ex 8: 2 will smite all thy borders with *f*:
3 And the river shall bring forth *f*
4 the *f* shall come up both on thee,
5 and cause *f* to come upon the land
6 the *f* came up, and covered the land
7 and brought up *f* upon the land of
8 that he may take away the *f* from
9 the *f* from thee and thy houses,
11 And the *f* shall depart from thee,
12 of the *f* which he had brought
13 and the *f* died out of the houses,
Ps 78:45 and *f*, which destroyed them.
105:30 land brought forth *f* in abundance,
Re 16:13 I saw three unclean spirits like *f*

front See also FOREFRONT.
2Sa 10: 9 Joab saw that the *f* of the battle
2Ch 3: 4 that was in the *f* of the house,

frontiers
Eze 25: 9 from his cities which are on his *f*,

frontlets
Ex 13:16 and for *f* between thine eyes:
De 6: 8 shall be as *f* between thine eyes.
11:18 they may be as *f* between your eyes.

frost See also HOARFROST.
Ge 31:40 consumed me, and the *f* by night;
Ex 16:14 small as the hoar *f* on the ground.
Job 37:10 By the breath of God *f* is given:
38:29 and the hoary *f* of heaven, who
Ps 78:47 and their sycamore trees with *f*.
Jer 36:30 the heat, and in the night to the *f*.

froward
De 32:20 for they are a very *f* generation,
2 Sa 22:27 with the *f* thou wilt shew thyself
Job 5:13 counsel of the *f* is carried
Ps 18:26 and with the *f* thou wilt shew
26 with...thou wilt show thyself *f*.
101: 4 A *f* heart shall depart from me:
Pr 2:12 the man that speaketh *f* things;
15 and they *f* in their paths:
3:32 the *f* is abomination to the Lord:
4:24 Put away from thee a *f* mouth,
6:12 man, walketh with a *f* mouth,
8: 8 nothing *f* or perverse in them.
13 and the *f* mouth, do I hate.
10:31 but the *f* tongue shall be cut out.
11:20 are of a *f* heart are abomination
16:28 A *f* man soweth strife: and a
30 his eyes to devise *f* things:
17:20 hath a *f* heart findeth no good:
21: 8 way of man is *f* and strange:
22: 5 snares are in the way of the *f*:
1Pe 2:18 good and gentle, but also to the *f*.

frowardly
Isa 57:17 he went on *f* in the way of his

frowardness
Pro 2:14 delight in the *f* of the wicked;
6:14 *F* is in his heart, he deviseth
10:32 mouth of the wicked speaketh *f*.

frozen
Job 38:30 and the face of the deep is *f*.

fruit See also FIRSTFRUIT; FRUITFUL; FRUITS.
Ge 1:11 *f* tree yielding *f* after his kind,
12 yielding *f*, whose seed was in itself,
29 is the *f* of a tree yielding seed;
3: 2 the *f* of the trees of the garden:
3 *f* of the tree which is in the midst
6 took of the *f* thereof, and did eat,
4: 3 Cain brought of the *f* of the ground
30: 2 from thee the *f* of the womb?
Ex 10:15 *f* of the trees which the hail had
21:22 so that her *f* depart from her,
Le 19:23 the *f* thereof as uncircumcised:
24 year all the *f* thereof shall be holy
25 year shall ye eat of the *f* thereof,
23:39 have gathered in the *f* of the land,
25: 3 and gather in the *f* thereof;
19 And the land shall yield her *f*,
21 and it shall bring forth *f* for three
22 yet of old *f* until the ninth year;
26: 4 trees of the field shall yield their *f*.
27:30 the *f* of the tree, is the Lord's:
Nu 13:20 and bring of the *f* of the land.
26 and shewed them the *f* of the land.
27 and honey; and this is the *f* of it.
De 1:25 And they took of the *f* of the land
7:13 *f* of thy womb, and the *f* of thy
11:17 that the land yield not her *f*;
22: 9 lest the *f* of thy seed
9 the *f* of thy vineyard, be defiled.
26: 2 the first of all the *f* of the earth,
28: 4 the *f* of thy body, and the *f* of thy
4 ground, and the *f* of thy cattle,
11 in the *f* of thy body, and in the *f* of
11 cattle, and in the *f* of thy ground,
18 *f* of thy body, and the *f* of thy land,

De 28:33 f of thy land, and all thy labours,
40 oil; for thine olive shall cast his f.
42 All thy trees and f of thy land
51 the f of thy cattle, and the f of thy
53 shall eat the f of thine own body,
30: 9 in the f of thy body, and in the f of
9 thy cattle, and in the f of thy land,
Jos 5:12 they did eat of the f of the land
J'g 9:11 my sweetness, and my good f,
2Sa 16: 2 bread and summer f for the young
2Ki 19:30 downward, and bear f upward.
Ne 9:25 and f trees in abundance:
36 to eat the f thereof and the good
10:35 the firstfruits of all f of all trees,
37 and the f of all manner of trees,
Ps 1: 3 bringeth forth his f in his season;
21:10 Their f shalt thou destroy from
72:16 f thereof shall shake like Lebanon:
92:14 shall still bring forth f in old age;
104:13 satisfied with the f of thy works.
105:35 devoured the f of their ground.
127: 3 the f of the womb is his reward.
132:11 Of the f of thy body will I set upon
Pr 1:31 they eat of the f of their own way,
8:19 My f is better than gold, yea, than
10:16 the f of the wicked to sin.
11:30 The f of the righteous is a tree
12:12 the root of the righteous yieldeth f.
14 with good by the f of his mouth:
13: 2 shall eat good by the f of his mouth:
18:20 satisfied with the f of his mouth;
21 that love it shall eat the f thereof.
27:18 the fig tree shall eat the f thereof:
31:16 the f of her hands she planteth
31 Give her of the f of her hands;
Ca 2: 3 and his f was sweet to my taste.
8:11 every one for the f thereof was to
12 those that keep the f thereof two
Isa 3:10 they shall eat the f of their doings.
4: 2 the f of the earth shall be excellent
10:12 the f of the stout heart of the king
13:18 have no pity on the f of the womb;
14:29 his f shall be a fiery flying serpent.
27: 6 fill the face of the world with f.
9 is all the f to take away his sin;
28: 4 the hasty f before the summer;
37:30 plant vineyards, and eat the f
31 downward, and bear f upward:
57:19 I create the f of the lips;
65:21 plant vineyards, and eat the f of
Jer 2: 7 eat the f thereof and the goodness
6:19 f of their thoughts, because they
7:20 and upon the f of the ground;
11:16 olive tree, fair, and of goodly f:
19 Let us destroy the tree with the f
12: 2 they grow, yea, they bring forth f:
17: 8 neither shall cease from yielding f.
10 according to the f of his doings.
21:14 according to the f of your doings,
29: 5, 28 plant gardens, and eat the f of
32:19 according to the f of his doings:
La 2:20 Shall the women eat their f, and
Eze 17: 8 that it might bear f, that it might
9 cut off the f thereof, that it wither?
23 bring forth boughs, and bear f;
19:12 and the east wind dried up her f:
14 which hath devoured her f,
25: 4 they shall eat thy f, and they shall
34:27 tree of the field shall yield her f,
36: 8 and yield your f to my people
11 they shall increase and bring f:
30 I will multiply the f of the tree,
47:12 the f thereof be consumed:
12 it shall bring forth new f
12 and the f thereof shall be for meat,
Da 4:12 the f thereof much, and it was meat
14 off his leaves, and scatter his f:
21 f thereof much, and in it was meat
Ho 9:16 they shall bear no f: yea, though
16 yet will I slay even the beloved f
10: 1 bringeth forth f unto himself:
1 according to the multitude of his f
13 ye have eaten the f of lies:
14: 8 From me is thy f found.
Joe 2:22 the tree beareth her f, the fig tree
Am 2: 9 I destroyed his f from above,
6:12 f of righteousness unto hemlock:
7:14 and a gatherer of sycomore f:
8: 1 and behold a basket of summer f.
2 And I said, A basket of summer f.
9:14 make gardens, and eat the f of
Mic 6: 7 f of my body for the sin of my soul?
7: 1 my soul desired the first ripe f.
13 therein, for the f of their doings.
Hab 3:17 neither shall f be in the vines;
Hag 1:10 the earth is stayed from her f.
Zec 8:12 vine shall give her f, and the
Mal 1:12 and the f thereof, even his meat,
3:11 your vine cast her f before the
M't 3:10 which bringeth not forth good f
7:17 good tree bringeth forth good f;
17 corrupt tree bringeth forth evil f.
18 good tree cannot bring forth evil f,
18 a corrupt tree bring forth good f.
19 tree that bringeth not forth good f
12:33 the tree good, and his f good;
33 the tree corrupt, and his f corrupt:
33 for the tree is known by his f.
13: 8 and brought forth f, some an
23 also beareth f, and bringeth forth,
26 sprung up, and brought forth f,
21:19 no f grow on thee henceforward
34 when the time of the f drew near,
26:29 henceforth of this f of the vine,
M'r 4: 7 and choked it, and it yielded no f.
8 and did yield f that sprang up

M'r 4:20 and bring forth f, some thirtyfold,
28 earth bringeth forth f of herself;
29 But when the f is brought forth,
11:14 No man eat f of thee hereafter
12: 2 from the husbandmen of the f of
14:25 drink no more of the f of the vine,
Lu 1:42 blessed is the f of thy womb.
3: 9 bringeth forth not good f is hewn
6:43 tree bringeth not forth corrupt f;
43 a corrupt tree bring forth good f.
44 every tree is known by his own f.
8: 8 up, and bare f an hundredfold.
14 and bring no f to perfection.
15 and bring forth f with patience.
13: 6 he came and sought f thereon,
7 these three years I come seeking f
9 And if it bear f, well: and if not,
20:10 that they should give him of the f
22:18 will not drink of the f of the vine,
Joh 4:36 and gathereth f unto life eternal:
12:24 if it die, it bringeth forth much f.
15: 2 that beareth not f he taketh away:
2 that beareth f, he purgeth it,
2 that it may bring forth more f.
4 the branch cannot bear f of itself,
5 the same bringeth forth much f:
8 glorified, that ye bear much f;
16 ye should go and bring forth f,
16 and that your f should remain:
Ac 2:30 that of the f of his loins, he would
Ro 1:13 I might have some f among you
6:21 What f had ye then in those things
22 ye have your f unto holiness,
7: 4 we should bring forth f unto God.
5 to bring forth f unto death.
15:28 and have sealed to them this f,
1Co 9: 7 and eateth not of the f thereof?
Ga 5:22 But the f of the Spirit is love,
Eph 5: 9 f of the Spirit is in all goodness
Ph'p 1:22 this is the f of my labour:
4:17 but I desire f that may abound
Col 1: 6 bringeth forth f, as it doth also
Heb 12:11 it yieldeth the peaceable f of
13:15 the f of our lips giving thanks
Jas 3:18 And the f of righteousness is sown
5: 7 for the precious f of the earth,
18 and the earth brought forth her f.
Jude 12 tree whose f withereth,
12 without f, twice dead,
Re 22: 2 and yielded her f every month:

fruitful See also UNFRUITFUL.
Ge 1:22 Be f, and multiply, and fill the
28 Be f, and multiply, and replenish
8:17 be f, and multiply upon the earth.
9: 1 Be f, and multiply, and replenish
7 be ye f, and multiply; bring forth
17: 6 And I will make thee exceeding f,
20 will make him f, and will multiply
26:22 and we shall be f in the land.
28: 3 bless thee, and make thee f,
35:11 be f and multiply; a nation
41:52 God hath caused me to be f
48: 4 Behold, I will make thee f, and
49:22 Joseph is a f bough, even a f
Ex 1: 7 the children of Israel were f, and
Le 26: 9 respect unto you, and make you f,
Ps 107:34 A f land into barrenness, for the
128: 3 Thy wife shall be as a f vine
148: 9 all hills; f trees, and all cedars;
Isa 5: 1 a vineyard in a very f hill:
10:18 of his forest, and of his f field,
17: 6 the outmost f branches thereof,
29:17 Lebanon shall be turned into a f
17 field, and the f field shall be
32:12 the pleasant fields, for the f vine.
15 wilderness be a f field, and the
15 f field be counted for a forest.
16 righteousness remain in the f field.
Jer 4:26 lo, the f place was a wilderness,
23: 3 and they shall be f and increase.
Eze 17: 5 and planted it in a f field;
19:10 she was f and full of branches
Ho 13:15 he be f among his brethren,
Ac 14:17 and f seasons, filling our hearts
Col 1:10 being f in every good work,

fruits
Ge 43:11 take of the best f in the land
Ex 22:29 the first of thy ripe f, and of thy
23:10 shalt gather in the f thereof:
Le 25:15 the f he shall sell unto thee:
16 the f doth he sell unto thee.
22 until her f come in ye shall eat
26:20 trees of the land yield their f.
De 33:14 for the precious f brought forth
2Sa 9:10 bring in the f, that thy master's son
16: 1 hundred of summer f, and a bottle
2Ki 8: 6 all the f of the field since the day
19:29 vineyards, and eat the f thereof.
Job 31:39 If I have eaten the f thereof
Ps 107:37 which may yield f of increase.
Ec 2: 5 trees in them of all kind of f:
Ca 4:13 with pleasant f; camphire, with
16 his garden, and eat his pleasant f.
6:11 to see the f of the valley,
7:13 are all manner of pleasant f,
Isa 16: 9 for the shouting for thy summer f
33: 9 and Carmel shake off their f.
Jer 40:10 gather ye wine, and summer f, and
12 gathered wine and summer f very
48:32 spoiler is fallen upon thy summer f
La 4: 9 for want of the f of the field.
Mic 7: 1 they have gathered the summer f,
Mal 3:11 not destroy the f of your ground;
M't 3: 8 therefore f meet for repentance:
7:16 Ye shall know them by their f.

M't 7:20 by their f ye shall know them.
21:34 they might receive the f of it.
41 render him the f in their seasons.
43 bringeth forth the f thereof.
Lu 3: 8 therefore f worthy of repentance;
12:17 no room where to bestow my f?
18 I bestow all my f and my goods,
2Co 9:10 the f of your righteousness;
Ph'p 1:11 with the f of righteousness,
2Ti 2: 6 must be first partaker of the f.
Jas 3:17 full of mercy and good f,
Re 18:14 the f that thy soul lusted after
22: 2 which bare twelve manner of f,

fruit-tree See FRUIT and TREE.

frustrate See also FRUSTRATETH.
Ezr 4: 5 to f their purpose, all the days
Ga 2:21 I do not f the grace of God:

frustrateth
Isa 44:25 That f the tokens of the liars,

fryingpan
Le 2: 7 a meat offering baken in the f,
7: 9 all that is dressed in the f,

fuel
Isa 9: 5 be with burning and f of fire.
19 shall be as the f of the fire:
Eze 15: 4 it is cast into the fire for f;
6 I have given to the fire for f,
21:32 Thou shalt be for f to the fire;

fugitive See also FUGITIVES.
Ge 4:12 a f and a vagabond shalt thou be
14 I shall be a f and a vagabond

fugitives
J'g 12: 4 Ye Gileadites are f of Ephraim
2Ki 25:11 the f that fell away to the king
Isa 15: 5 his f shall flee unto Zoar, an
Eze 17:21 his f with all his bands shall fall

fulfil See also FULFILLED; FULFILLING.
Ge 29:27 F her week, and we will give thee
Ex 5:13 F your works, your daily tasks,
23:26 the number of thy days I will f.
1Ki 2:27 he might f the word of the Lord,
1Ch 22:13 takest heed to f the statutes
2Ch 36:21 To f the word of the Lord by the
21 to f threescore and ten years.
Job 39: 2 number the months that they f?
Ps 20: 4 and f all thy counsel.
5 the Lord f all thy petitions.
145:19 He will f the desire of them that
M't 3:15 us to f all righteousness.
5:17 I am not come to destroy, but to f.
Ac 13:22 heart, which shall f all my will.
Ro 2:27 if it f the law, judge thee,
13:14 provision for the flesh, to f the lusts
Ga 5:16 shall not f the lust of the flesh.
6: 2 and so f the law of Christ.
Ph'p 2: 2 F ye my joy, that ye be
Col 1:25 for you, to f the word of God;
4:17 in the Lord, that thou f it.
2Th 1:11 and f all the good pleasure of his
Jas 2: 8 If ye f the royal law according to
Re 17:17 to f his will, and to agree, and

fulfilled
Ge 25:24 her days to be delivered were f,
29:21 my days are f, that I may go
28 Jacob did so, and f her week:
50: 3 And forty days were f for him;
3 for so are f the days of those
Ex 5:14 Wherefore have ye not f your
7:25 And seven days were f, after that
Le 12: 4 until the days of her purifying be f.
6 the days of her purifying are f,
Nu 6: 5 until the days be f, in the which
13 the days of his separation are f:
2Sa 7:12 when thy days be f, and thou shalt
14:22 hath f the request of his servant.
1Ki 8:15 hath with his hand f it, saying,
24 and hast f it with thine hand,
2Ch 6: 4 who hath with his hands f
15 and hast f it with thine hand,
Ezr 1: 1 mouth of Jeremiah might be f,
Job 36:17 f the judgment of the wicked:
Jer 44:25 spoken with your mouths, and f
La 2:17 he hath f his word that he had
4:18 our end is near, our days are f;
Eze 5: 2 when the days of the siege are f:
Da 4:33 The same hour was the thing f
10: 3 till three whole weeks were f.
M't 1:22 this was done, that it might be f
2:15 it might be f which was spoken
17 Then was f that which was spoken
23 that it might be f which was
4:14 it might be f which was spoken
5:18 from the law, till all be f.
8:17 it might be f which was spoken
12:17 be f which was spoken by Esaias
13:14 And in them is f the prophecy
35 That it might be f which was
21: 4 it might be f which was spoken by
24:34 pass, till all these things be f.
26:54 then shall the scriptures be f,
56 of the prophets might be f.
27: 9 was f that which was spoken
35 it might be f which was spoken
M'r 1:15 The time is f, and the kingdom
13: 4 when all these things shall be f?
14:49 but the scriptures must be f.
15:28 the scripture was f, which saith,
Lu 1:20 which shall be f in their season.
2:43 And when they had f the days,
4:21 day is this scripture f in your ears.
21:22 things which are written may be f.
24 until the times of the Gentiles be f.
32 shall not pass away, till all be f.

Lu 22:16 until it be f in the kingdom
24:44 must be f, which were written
Joh 3:29 this my joy therefore is f.
12:38 might be f, which he spake, Lord,
13:18 but that the scripture may be f,
15:25 word might be f that is written
17:12 that the scripture might be f.
13 that they might have my joy f
18: 9 saying might be f, which he spake,
32 the saying of Jesus might be f,
19:24 scripture might be f, which saith,
28 that the scripture might be f,
36 the scripture should be f, A bone
Ac 1:16 scripture must needs have been f,
3:18 should suffer, he hath so f.
9:23 And after that many days were f,
12:25 when they had f their ministry,
13:25 as John f his course, he said,
27 have f them in condemning him.
29 f all that was written of him,
33 God hath f the same unto us
14:26 for the work which they f.
Ro 8: 4 of the law might be f in us,
13: 8 loveth another hath f the law.
2Co 10: 6 when your obedience is f.
Ga 5:14 all the law is f in one word,
Jas 2:23 the scripture was f which saith,
Re 6:11 killed as they were, should be f.
15: 8 of the seven angels were f.
17:17 until the words of God shall be f.
20: 3 the thousand years should be f:

fulfilling
Ps 148: 8 vapours; stormy wind f his word:
Ro 13:10 therefore love is the f of the law.
Eph 2: 3 f the desires of the flesh and of

full^ See also BEAUTIFUL; BOUNTIFUL; CHEERFUL; DECEITFUL; DESPITEFUL; DOUBTFUL; DREADFUL; FAITHFUL; FEARFUL; FORGETFUL; FRUITFUL; FULFIL; HANDFUL; HARMFUL; HATEFUL; HURTFUL; JOYFUL; LAWFUL; MERCIFUL; MINDFUL; MOURNFULLY; NEEDFUL; PAINFUL; PITIFUL; PLENTIFUL; POWERFUL; REPROACHFULLY; SCORNFUL; SHAMEFUL; SINFUL; SKILFUL; SLOTHFUL; SORROWFUL; THANKFUL; WATCHFUL; WILFULLY; WOEFUL; WONDERFUL; WRATHFUL; YOUTHFUL.
Ge 15:16 of the Amorites is not yet f.
25: 8 an old man, and f of years;
35:29 old and f of days: and his sons
41: 1 at the end of two f years,
7 the seven rank and f ears.
22 came up in one stalk, f and good:
43:21 money in f weight: and we have
Ex 8:21 of the Egyptians shall be f
16: 3 when we did eat bread to the f;
8 in the morning bread to the f;
33 put an omer f of manna therein,
22: 3 he should make f restitution;
Le 2:14 even corn beaten out of f ears.
16:12 shall take a censer f of burning
12 f of sweet incense beaten small,
19:29 the land become f of wickedness.
25:29 within a f year may he redeem it.
30 within the space of a f year,
26: 5 ye shall eat your bread to the f,
Nu 7:13 both of them were f of fine flour.
14 of ten shekels of gold, f of incense
19 f of fine flour mingled with oil
20 of gold of ten shekels, f of incense:
25 f of fine flour mingled with oil
26 spoon of ten shekels, f of incense
31 both of them f of fine flour
32 spoon of ten shekels, f of incense:
37 f of fine flour mingled with oil
38 spoon of ten shekels, f of incense
43 both of them f of fine flour
44 spoon of ten shekels, f of incense
49 both of them f of fine flour
50 spoon of ten shekels, f of incense:
55 f of fine flour mingled with oil
56 spoon of ten shekels, f of incense:
61 f of fine flour mingled with oil
62 spoon of ten shekels, f of incense:
67 f of fine flour mingled with oil
68 spoon of ten shekels, f of incense:
73 f of fine flour mingled with oil
74 spoon of ten shekels, f of incense:
79 f of fine flour mingled with oil for
80 spoon of ten shekels, f of incense:
86 spoons were twelve, f of incense,
22:18 give me his house f of silver
24:13 give me his house f of silver
De 6:11 houses f of all good things,
11 thou shalt have eaten and be f;
8:10 When thou hast eaten and art f,
12 when thou hast eaten and art f,
11:15 that thou mayest eat and be f.
21:13 father and her mother a f month:
33:23 f with the blessing of the Lord:
34: 9 Nun was f of the spirit of wisdom;
J'g 6:38 of the fleece, a bowl f of water.
16:27 house was f of men and women;
Ru 1:21 went out f, and the Lord hath
2:12 and a f reward be given thee
1Sa 2: 5 They that were f have hired out
18:27 gave them in f tale to the king,
27: 7 of the Philistines was a f year
2Sa 8: 2 and with one f line to keep alive.
13:23 it came to pass after two f years,
14:28 Absalom dwelt two f years in
23:11 a piece of ground f of lentiles:
2Ki 3:16 Lord, Make this valley f of ditches.
4: 4 shalt set aside that which is f.
6 when the vessels were f, that she
39 thereof wild gourds his lap f,
2Ki 4:42 and f ears of corn in the husk
6:17 the mountain was f of horses
7:15 was f of garments and vessels,
9:24 drew a bow with his f strength,
10:21 of Baal was f from one end
15:13 reigned a f month in Samaria.
1Ch 11:13 a parcel of ground f of barley;
21:22 grant it me for the f price:
24 I will verily buy it for the f price:
23: 1 David was old and f of days,
29:28 f of days, riches, and honour:
2Ch 24:15 and was f of days when he died;
Ne 9:25 possessed houses f of all goods,
Es 3: 5 then was Haman f of wrath.
5: 9 he was f of indignation against
Job 5:26 shalt come to thy grave in a f age,
7: 4 and I am f of tossings to and fro
10:15 I am f of confusion; therefore see
11: 2 should a man f of talk be justified?
14: 1 is of few days, and f of trouble.
20:11 His bones are f of the sin of his
21:23 One dieth in his f strength, being
24 His breasts are f of milk, and
32:18 I am f of matter, the spirit within
36:16 thy table should be f of fatness.
42:17 Job died, being old and f of days.
Ps 10: 7 His mouth is f of cursing and
17:14 they are f of children, and leave
26:10 their right hand is f of bribes.
29: 4 voice of the Lord is f of majesty.
33: 5 the earth is f of the goodness of
48:10 right hand is f of righteousness.
65: 9 river of God, which is f of water:
69:20 and I am f of heaviness: and I looked
73:10 waters of a f cup are wrung out
74:20 the earth are f of the habitations
75: 8 it is f of mixture; and he poureth
78:25 he sent them meat to the f.
38 he, being f of compassion, forgave
86:15 a God f of compassion, and gracious,
88: 3 For my soul is f of troubles:
104:16 trees of the Lord are f of sap;
24 the earth is f of thy riches.
111: 4 Lord is gracious and f of compassion.
112: 4 he is gracious, and f of compassion,
119:64 earth, O Lord, is f of thy mercy:
127: 5 that hath his quiver f of them:
144:13 That our garners may be f,
145: 8 Lord is gracious, and f of compassion;
Pr 17: 1 than an house f of sacrifices
27: 7 f soul loatheth an honeycomb;
20 Hell and destruction are never f;
30: 9 Lest I be f, and deny thee, and
Ec 1: 7 yet the sea is not f; unto the
8 All things are f of labour; man
4: 6 both the hands f with travail
9: 3 of the sons of men is f of evil,
10:14 A fool also is f of words:
11: 3 If the clouds be f of rain, they
Isa 1:11 I am f of the burnt offerings of
15 hear: your hands are f of blood.
21 it was f of judgment;
2: 7 land also is f of silver and gold,
7 their land is also f of horses,
8 Their land also is f of idols;
6: 3 the whole earth is f of his glory.
11: 9 earth shall be f of the knowledge
13:21 shall be f of doleful creatures;
15: 9 of Dimon shall be f of blood:
22: 2 art f of stirs, a tumultuous city,
7 valleys shall be f of chariots,
25: 6 fat things f of marrow, of wines
28: 8 are f of vomit and filthiness,
30:27 his lips are f of indignation, and
51:20 they are f of the fury of the Lord,
Jer 4:12 a f wind from those places shall
27 yet will I not make a f end.
5: 7 when I had fed them to the f,
10 but make not a f end: take away
18 I will not make a f end with you.
27 As a cage is f of birds,
27 so are their houses f of deceit:
6:11 I am f of the fury of the Lord;
11 aged with him that is f of days.
23:10 For the land is f of adulterers;
28: 3 two f years will I bring again
11 within the space of two f years.
30:11 though I make a f end of all nations
11 yet will I not make a f end of thee:
35: 5 pots f of wine, and cups, and I
46:28 I will make a f end of all the nations
28 I will not make a f end of thee,
La 1: 1 solitary, that was f of people!
3:30 he is filled f with reproach.
Eze 1:18 their rings were f of eyes round
7:23 the land is f of bloody crimes,
23 and the city is f of violence.
9: 9 and the land is f of blood,
9 and the city f of perverseness:
10: 4 the court was f of the brightness
12 were f of eyes round about,
11:13 Lord God! wilt thou make a f end
17: 3 longwinged, f of feathers, which
19:10 she was fruitful and f of branches
28:12 f of wisdom, and perfect in
32: 6 and the rivers shall be f of thee.
15 destitute of that whereof it was f,
37: 1 the valley which was f of bones,
39:19 ye shall eat fat till ye be f,
41: 8 the side chambers were a f reed
Da 3:19 was Nebuchadnezzar f of fury,
8:23 transgressors are come to the f,
10: 2 was mourning three f weeks
Joe 2:24 And the floors shall be f of wheat,
3:13 the press is f, the fats overflow;
Am 2:13 is pressed that is f of sheaves.
Mic 3: 8 I am f of power by the spirit
6:12 rich men thereof are f of violence,
Na 3: 1 it is all f of lies and robbery;
Hab 3: 3 the earth was f of his praise.
Zec 8: 5 the city shall be f of boys and girls
M't 6:22 the whole body shall be f of light.
23 whole body shall be f of darkness.
13:48 Which, when it was f, they drew
14:20 that remained twelve baskets f.
15:37 that was left seven baskets f.
23:25 within they are f of extortion
27 are within f of dead men's bones,
28 are f of hypocrisy and iniquity.
M'r 4:28 after that the f corn in the ear.
37 the ship, so that it was now f.
6:43 baskets f of the fragments,
7: 9 F well ye reject the commandment
8:19 many baskets f of fragments
20 how many baskets f of fragments
15:36 And one ran and filled a spunge f
Lu 1:57 Elisabeth's f time came that she
4: 1 Jesus being f of the Holy Ghost
5:12 behold a man f of leprosy: who
6:25 Woe unto you that are f! for ye
11:34 the whole body also is f of light;
34 thy body also is f of darkness.
36 whole body therefore be f of light,
36 the whole shall be f of light, as
39 your inward part is f of ravening
16:20 laid at his gate f of sores,
Joh 1:14 the Father,) f of grace and truth.
7: 8 my time is not yet f come.
15:11 and that your joy might be f.
16:24 receive, that your joy may be f.
19:29 was set a vessel f of vinegar:
21:11 f of great fishes, an hundred and
Ac 2:13 These men are f of new wine.
28 thou shalt make me f of joy with
6: 3 f of the Holy Ghost and wisdom,
5 f of faith and of the Holy Ghost,
8 Stephen, f of faith and power,
7:23 when he was f forty years old,
55 he, being f of the Holy Ghost,
9:36 this woman was f of good works
11:24 f of the Holy Ghost and of faith:
13:10 O f of all subtilty and all mischief,
19:28 they were f of wrath, and cried
Ro 1:29 f of envy, murder, debate, deceit,
3:14 is f of cursing and bitterness:
15:14 that ye are also f of goodness,
1Co 4: 8 Now ye are f, now ye are rich,
Ph'p 2:26 you all, and was f of heaviness,
4:12 both to be f and to be hungry,
18 I am f, having received of
Col 2: 2 the f assurance of understanding,
2Ti 4: 5 of an evangelist, make f proof of
Heb 5:14 belongeth to them that are of f
6:11 f assurance of hope unto the end:
10:22 in f assurance of faith, having
Jas 3: 8 an unruly evil, f of deadly poison.
17 f of mercy and good fruits, without
1Pe 1: 8 with joy unspeakable and f of glory:
2Pe 2:14 Having eyes f of adultery, and that
1Jo 1: 4 you, that your joy may be f.
2Jo 8 but that we receive a f reward.
12 to face, that our joy may be f.
Re 4: 6 f of eyes before and behind.
8 they were f of eyes within: and
5: 8 harps, and golden vials f of odours,
15: 7 f of the wrath of God, who liveth
16:10 his kingdom was f of darkness;
17: 3 f of names of blasphemy, having
4 cup in her hand f of abominations
21: 9 vials f of the seven last plagues,

fuller See also FULLER'S; FULLERS'.
M'r 9: 3 as no f on earth can white them.

fuller's
2Ki 18:17 is in the highway of the f field.
Isa 7: 3 pool in the highway of the f field;
36: 2 pool in the highway of the f field.

fullers'
Mal 3: 2 like a refiner's fire, and like f sope.

fully See also MOURNFULLY; REPROACHFULLY; SHAMEFULLY; SKILFULLY; WILFULLY; WONDERFULLY.
Nu 7: 1 had f set up the tabernacle,
14:24 and hath followed me f, him will
Ru 2:11 It hath f been shewed me, all
1Ki 11: 6 went not f after the Lord, as did
Ec 8:11 heart of the sons of men is f set
Na 1:10 be devoured as stubble f dry.
Ac 2: 1 the day of Pentecost was f come,
Ro 4:21 And being f persuaded that, what
14: 5 Let every man be f persuaded
15:19 I have f preached the gospel of
2Ti 3:10 thou hast f known my doctrine,
4:17 the preaching might be f known,
Re 14:18 for her grapes are f ripe.

fulness See also SKILFULNESS; SLOTHFULNESS; THANKFULNESS.
Nu 18:27 and as the f of the winepress.
De 33:16 things of the earth and f thereof,
1Ch 16:32 Let the sea roar, and the f thereof:
Job 20:22 In the f of his sufficiency he shall
Ps 16:11 in thy presence is f of joy;
24: 1 is the Lord's, and the f thereof;
50:12 world is mine, and the f thereof.
89:11 the world and the f thereof, thou
96:11 let the sea roar, and the f thereof.
98: 7 Let the sea roar, and the f thereof;
Eze 16:49 f of bread, and abundance of
19: 7 was desolate, and the f thereof.
Joh 1:16 of his f have all we received,
Ro 11:12 Gentiles; how much more their f?

Ro 11:25 the f of the Gentiles be come
15:29 come in the f of the blessing
1Co 10:26 is the Lord's, and the f thereof.
28 is the Lord's, and the f thereof:
Gal 4: 4 when the f of the time was come
Eph 1:10 dispensation of the f of times
23 the f of him that filleth all in all.
3:19 be filled with all the f of God.
4:13 the stature of the f of Christ:
Col 1:19 that in him should all f dwell;
2: 9 all the f of the Godhead bodily.

furbish See also FURBISHED.
Jer 46: 4 f the spears, and put on the

furbished
Eze 21: 9 sword is sharpened, and also f:
10 it is f that it may glitter:
11 he hath given it to be f,
11 and it is f, to give it into the hand
28 the slaughter it is f, to consume

furious
Pr 22:24 with a f man thou shalt not go:
29:22 and a f man aboundeth in
Eze 5:15 and in fury, and in f rebukes.
25:17 upon them with f rebukes;
Da 2:12 the king was angry and very f,
Na 1: 2 Lord revengeth, and is f;

furiously
2Ki 9:20 son of Nimshi; for he driveth f.
Eze 23:25 and they shall deal f with thee:

furlongs
Lu 24:13 Jerusalem about threescore f.
Joh 6:19 about five and twenty or thirty f,
11:18 unto Jerusalem, about fifteen f off:
Re 14:20 a thousand and six hundred f.
21:16 the reed, twelve thousand f.

furnace See also FURNACES.
Ge 15:17 behold a smoking f, and a
19:28 went up as the smoke of a f.
Ex 9: 8 to you handfuls of ashes of the f,
10 And they took ashes of the f,
19:18 ascended as the smoke of a f,
De 4:20 you forth out of the iron f,
1Ki 8:51 from the midst of the f of iron:
Ps 12: 6 as silver tried in a f of earth,
Pr 17: 3 and the f for gold: but the Lord
27:21 and the f for gold; so is a man
Isa 31: 9 and his f in Jerusalem.
48:10 I have chosen thee in the f of
Jer 11: 4 from the iron f, saying, Obey
Eze 22:18 and lead, in the midst of the f;
20 into the midst of the f,
22 is melted in the midst of the f,
Da 3: 6, 11 the midst of a burning fiery f.
15 into the midst of a burning fiery f;
17 deliver us from the burning fiery f,
19 heat the f one seven times more
20 cast them into the burning fiery f.
21 the midst of the burning fiery f.
22 and the f exceeding hot, the flame
23 the midst of the burning fiery f.
26 to the mouth of the burning fiery f.
M't 13:42 shall cast them into a f of fire:
50 shall cast them into the f of fire:
Re 1:15 as if they burned in a f;
9: 2 as the smoke of a great f;

furnaces
Ne 3:11 other piece, and the tower of the f.
12:38 of the f even unto the broad wall;

furnish See also FURNISHED.
De 15:14 f him liberally out of thy flock,
Ps 78:19 God f a table in the wilderness?
Isa 65:11 f the drink offering unto that
Jer 46:19 f thyself to go into captivity:

furnished
1 Ki 9:11 Hiram the king of Tyre had f
Pr 9: 2 she hath also f her table.
M't 22:10 the wedding was f with guests.
M'r 14:15 large upper room f and prepared
Lu 22:12 shew you a large upper room f:
2Ti 3:17 throughly f unto all good works.

furniture
Ge 31:34 the camel's f, and sat upon them.
Ex 31: 7 and all the f of the tabernacle,
8 the table and his f, and the
8 pure candlestick with all his f,
9 of burnt offering with all his f,
35:14 also for the light, and his f,
39:33 all his f, his taches, his boards,
Na 2: 9 glory out of all the pleasant f.

furrow See also FURROWS.
Job 39:10 unicorn with his band in the f?

furrows
Job 31:38 the f likewise thereof complain;
Ps 65:10 settlest the f thereof: thou makest
129: 3 they made long their f.
Eze 17: 7 it by the f of her plantation.
10 wither in the f where it grew.
Ho 10: 4 as hemlock in the f of the field.
10 bind themselves in their two f.
12:11 are as heaps in the f of the fields.

further: See also FARTHER; FURTHERED; FURTHERMORE.
Nu 22:26 the angel of the Lord went f,
De 20: 8 shall speak f unto the people,
1Sa 10:22 enquired of the Lord f, if the man
Es 9:12 is thy request f? and it shall be
Job 38:11 shalt thou come, but no f:
40: 5 yea, twice; but I will proceed no f.
Ps 140: 8 f not his wicked device; lest they
Ec 12:12 And f, by these, my son, be
M't 26:65 what f need have we of witnesses?
M'r 5:35 troublest thou the Master any f.?
14:63 What need we any f witnesses?
Lu 22:71 What need we any f witness?
24:28 as though he would have gone f.
Ac 4:17 spread no f among the people,
21 when they had f threatened them,
12: 3 he proceeded f to take Peter also.
21:28 f brought Greeks also into the
24: 4 I be not f tedious unto thee,
27:28 when they had gone a little f,
2Ti 3: 9 proceed no f: for their folly,
He 7:11 f need was there that another

furtherance
Ph'p 1:12 rather unto the f of the gospel;
25 for your f and joy of faith;

furthered
Ezr 8:36 they f the people, and the house

furthermore
Ex 4: 6 And the Lord said f unto him,
De 4:21 F the Lord was angry with me
9:13 F the Lord spake unto me,
1Sa 26:10 David said f, As the Lord liveth,
1Ch 17:10 F I tell thee that the Lord will
27:16 F over the tribes of Israel: the
29: 1 F David the king said unto
2Ch 4: 9 F he made the court of the
Job 34: 1 F Elihu answered and said,
Eze 8: 6 He said f unto me, Son of man,
23:40 And f, that ye have sent for men
2Co 2:12 F, when I came to Troas to
1Th 4: 1 F then we beseech you, brethren,
He 12: 9 F we have had fathers of our

fury
Ge 27:44 until thy brother's f turn away;
Le 26:28 walk contrary unto you also in f;
Job 20:23 God shall cast the f of his wrath
Isa 27: 4 F is not in me: who would set
34: 2 and his f upon all their armies:
42:25 upon him the f of his anger,
51:13 because of the f of the oppressor,
13 where is the f of the oppressor?
17 of the Lord the cup of his f;
20 they are full of the f of the Lord,
22 the dregs of the cup of my f;
59:18 f to his adversaries, recompence
63: 3 anger, and trample them in my f;
5 and my f, it upheld me.
6 and make them drunk in my f,
66:15 to render his anger with f, and
Jer 4: 4 lest my f come forth like fire,
6:11 I am full of the f of the Lord;
7:20 mine anger and my f shall be
10:25 Pour out thy f upon the heathen
21: 5 and in f, and in great wrath.
12 my f go out like fire, and burn
23:19 the Lord is gone forth in f,
25:15 Take the wine cup of this f at my
30:23 of the Lord goeth forth with f,
32:31 of mine anger and of my f
37 and in my f, and in great wrath;
33: 5 in mine anger and in my f,
36: 7 f that the Lord hath pronounced
42:18 and my f hath been poured forth
18 my f be poured forth upon you,
44: 6 f and mine anger was poured
La 2: 4 he poured out his f like fire.
4:11 Lord hath accomplished his f;
Eze 5:13 cause my f to rest upon them,
13 have accomplished my f in them.
15 in f and in furious rebukes.
6:12 I accomplish my f upon them.
7: 8 Now will I shortly pour out my f
8:18 Therefore will I also deal in f:
9: 8 in thy pouring out of thy f
13:13 with a stormy wind in my f;
13 hailstones in my f to consume it.
14:19 pour out my f upon it in blood,
16:38 I will give thee blood in f
42 I make my f toward thee to rest,
19:12 plucked up in f, she was cast
20: 8 I will pour out my f upon them,
13 I would pour out my f upon them
21 would pour out my f upon them,
33 and with f poured out, will I rule
34 stretched out arm, and with f
21:17 and I will cause my f to rest:
22:20 in mine anger and in my f,
22 have poured out my f upon you,
24: 8 That it might cause f to come up
13 caused my f to rest upon thee.
25:14 anger and according to my f;
30:15 I will pour my f upon Sin,
36: 6 in my jealousy and in my f,
18 my f upon them for the blood
38:18 my f shall come up in my face.
Da 3:13 rage and f commanded to bring
19 Then was Nebuchadnezzar full of f,
8: 6 unto him in the f of his power.
9:16 thine anger and thy f be turned
11:44 go forth with great f to destroy,
Mic 5:15 in anger and f upon the heathen,
Na 1: 6 f is poured out like fire, and the
Zec 8: 2 I was jealous for her with great f.

G.

Gaal (*ga'-al*)
J'g 9:26 And G' the son of Ebed came with
28 G' the son of Ebed said, Who is
30 words of G' the son of Ebed, his
31 Behold, G' the son of Ebed and his
35 G' the son of Ebed went out, and
36 G' saw the people, he said to Zebul,
37 G' spake again and said, See,
39 G' went out before the men of
41 thrust out G' and his brethren,

Gaash (*ga'-ash*)
Jos 24:30 on the north side of the hill of G'.
J'g 2: 9 on the north side of the hill G'.
2Sa 23:30 Hiddai of the brooks of G',
1Ch 11:32 Hurai of the brooks of G', Abiel the

Gaba (*ga'-bah*) See also GEBA.
Jos 18:24 and Ophni, and G'; twelve cities
Ezr 2:26 The children of Ramah and G',
Ne 7:30 The men of Ramah and G',

Gabbai (*gab'-bahee*)
Ne 11: 8 And after him G', Sallai, nine

Gabbatha (*gab'-ba-thah*)
Joh 19:13 but in the Hebrew, G'.

Gaber See EZION-GABER.

Gabriel (*ga'-bre-el*)
Da 8:16 G', make this man to understand
9:21 even the man G', whom I had seen
Lu 1:19 I am G', that stand in the
26 sixth month the angel G' was sent

gad See GADDEST.

Gad (*gad*) See also BAAL-GAD; DIBON-GAD; GADITE; MIGDAL-GAD.
Ge 30:11 and she called his name G'.
35:26 Leah's handmaid; G', and Asher:
46:16 And the sons of G'; Ziphion, and
49:19 G', a troop shall overcome him:
Ex 1: 4 Dan, and Naphtali, G', and Asher.
Nu 1:14 Of G'; Eliasaph the son of Deuel.
24 Of the children of G', by their
25 even of the tribe of G', were forty
2:14 Then the tribe of G': and the
14 captain of the sons of G' shall be
7:42 of the children of G', offered:
10:20 of the children of G' was Eliasaph
13:15 Of the tribe of G', Geuel the son of
26:15 The children of G' after their
18 families of the children of G'
32: 1 and the children of G' had a very
2 The children of G' and the
6 Moses said unto the children of G'
25 And the children of G' and the
29 If the children of G' and the
31 And the children of G' and the
33 even to the children of G', and to
34 And the children of G' built Dibon,
34:14 tribe of the children of G' according
De 27:13 Reuben, G', and Asher, and
33:20 And of G' he said, Blessed be
20 Blessed be he that enlargeth G':
Jos 4:12 and the children of G', and half
13:24 of G', even unto the children of G'
28 children of G' after their families,
18: 7 and G', and Reuben, and half the
20: 8 out of the tribe of G', and Golan
Jos 21: 7 out of the tribe of G', and out of
38 And out of the tribe of G', Ramoth
22: 9, 10, 11, 13, 15, 21 children of G' and the
25 of Reuben and children of G';
30 children of G' and the children of
31 children of G', and to the children of
32 children of G', out of the land of
33 children of Reuben and G' dwelt.
34 children of G' called the altar Ed:
1Sa 13: 7 Jordan to the land of G' and Gilead.
22: 5 prophet G' said unto David, Abide
2Sa 24: 5 the river of G', and toward Jazer:
11 unto the prophet G', David's seer,
13 So G' came to David, and told him,
14 David said unto G', I am in a great
18 And G' came that day to David,
19 according to the saying of G', went
1Ch 2: 2 Benjamin, Naphtali, G', and Asher.
5:11 And the children of G' dwelt over
6:63 out of the tribe of G', and out of the
80 And out of the tribe of G'; Ramoth
12:14 sons of G', captains of the host:
21: 9 And the Lord spake unto G',
11 So G' came to David, and said unto
13 David said unto G', I am in a great
18 Lord commanded G' to say to
19 David went up at the saying of G',
29:29 and in the book of G' the seer,
2Ch 29:25 of David, and of G' the king's seer,
Jer 49: 1 why then doth their king inherit G',
Eze 48:27 unto the west side, G' a portion.
28 And by the border of G', at the
34 one gate of G', one gate of Asher,
Re 7: 5 Of the tribe of G' were sealed

Gadarenes *(gad-a-renes')*
M'r 5: 1 sea, into the country of the *G'*.
Lu 8:26 arrived at the country of the *G'*,
37 of the country of the *G'* round

Gaddah See HAZAR-GADDAH.

gaddest
Jer 2:36 Why *g'* thou about so much to

Gaddi *(gad'-di)*
Nu 13:11 tribe of Manasseh, *G'* the son of

Gaddiel *(gad'-de-el)*
Nu 13:10 of Zebulun, *G'* the son of Sodi.

Gader See BETH-GADER.

Gadi *(ga'-di)*
2Ki 15:14 Menahem the son of *G'* went up
17 Menahem the son of *G'* to reign

Gadite *(gad'-ite)* See also GADITES.
2Sa 23:36 of Zobah, Bani the *G'*,

Gadites *(gad'-ites)*
De 3:12 the Reubenites and to the *G'*.
16 unto the *G'* I gave from Gilead even
4:43 Gilead, of the *G'*; and Golan in
29: 8 and to the *G'*, and to the half tribe
Jos 1:12 and to the *G'*, and to half the tribe
12: 6 unto the Reubenites, and the *G'*,
13: 8 the Reubenites and the *G'* have
22: 1 and the *G'*, and the half tribe of
2Ki 10:33 land of Gilead, the *G'*, and the
1Ch 5:18 and the *G'*, and half the tribe of
26 and the *G'*, and the half tribe of
12: 8 And of the *G'* there separated
37 and the *G'*, and of the half tribe of
26:32 the *G'*, and the half tribe of

Gaham *(ga'-ham)*
Ge 22:24 bare also Tebah, and *G'*, and

Gahar *(ga'-har)*
Ezr 2:47 of Giddel, the children of *G'*, the
Ne 7:49 of Giddel, the children of *G'*,

gain See also AGAIN; GAINED; GAINS; GAINSAY.
J'g 5:19 they took no *g'* of money.
Job 22: 3 or is it *g'* to him, that thou makest
Pr 1:19 every one that is greedy of *g'*;
3:14 and the *g'* thereof than fine gold.
15:27 He that is greedy of *g'* troubleth
28: 8 by usury and unjust *g'* increaseth
Isa 33:15 despiseth the *g'* of oppressions,
56:11 one for his *g'*, from his quarter.
Eze 22:13 mine hand at thy dishonest *g'*
27 destroy souls, to get dishonest *g'*.
Da 2: 8 certainty that ye would *g'* the time.
11:39 and shall divide the land for *g'*.
Mic 4:13 consecrate their *g'* unto the Lord,
M't 16:26 if he shall *g'* the whole world, and
M'r 8:36 if he shall *g'* the whole world, and
Lu 9:25 if he *g'* the whole world, and lose
Ac 16:16 brought her masters much *g'* by
19:24 brought no small *g'* unto the
1Co 9:19 unto all, that I might *g'* the more.
20 that I might *g'* the Jews;
20 that I might *g'* them that are under
21 might *g'* them that are without law.
22 that I might *g'* the weak:
2Co 12:17 Did I make a *g'* of you by any
18 Did Titus make a *g'* of you?
Ph'p 1:21 to live is Christ, and to die is *g'*.
3: 7 But what things were *g'* to me,
1Ti 6: 5 supposing that *g'* is godliness:
6 with contentment is great *g'*.
Jas 4:13 and buy and sell, and get *g'*:

gained
Job 27: 8 though he hath *g'*, when God
Eze 22:12 and thou hast greedily *g'* of thy
M't 18:15 thee, thou hast *g'* thy brother.
25:17 received two, he also *g'* other two.
20 I have *g'* beside them five talents
22 *g'* two other talents beside them.
Lu 19:15 every man had *g'* by trading.
16 thy pound hath *g'* ten pounds.
18 thy pound hath *g'* five pounds.
Ac 27:21 to have *g'* this harm and loss.

gains
Ac 16:19 the hope of their *g'* was gone,

gainsay See also GAINSAYING.
Lu 21:15 shall not be able to *g'* nor resist.

gainsayers
Tit 1: 9 to exhort and to convince the *g'*.

gainsaying
Ac 10:29 came I unto you without *g'*,
Ro 10:21 a disobedient and *g'* people.
Jude 11 and perished in the *g'* of Core.

Gaius *(gah'-yus)*
Ac 19:29 caught *G'* and Aristarchus,
20: 4 and *G'* of Derbe, and Timotheus;
Ro 16:23 *G'* mine host, and of the whole
1Co 1:14 none of you, but Crispus and *G'*;
3Jo 1 The elder unto the wellbeloved *G'*,

Galal *(ga'-lal)*
1Ch 9:15 Heresh, and *G'*, and Mattaniah
16 the son of *G'*, the son of Jeduthun,
Ne 11:17 Shammua, the son of *G'*, the son of

Galatia *(ga-la'-she-ah)* See also GALATIANS.
Ac 16: 6 Phrygia and the region of *G'*,
18:23 country of *G'* and Phrygia in order,
1Co 16: 1 given order to the churches of *G'*,
Ga 1: 2 with me unto the churches of *G'*:
2Ti 4:10 Crescens to *G'*, Titus unto
1Pe 1: 1 Pontus, *G'*, Cappadocia, Asia,

Galatians^ *(ga-la'-she-uns)*
Ga 3: 1 O foolish *G'*. who hath bewitched
subscr. Unto the *G'* written from Rome.

galbanum *(gal'-ba-num)*
Ex 30:34 onycha, and *g'*; these sweet spices

Galeed *(ga'-le-ed)* See also JAGAR-SAHADUTHA.
Ge 31:47 but Jacob called it *G'*.
48 was the name of it called *G'*;

Galilæan *(gal-i-le'-un)* See also GALILÆANS.
M'r 14:70 for thou art a *G'*, and thy speech
Lu 22:59 also was with him: for he is a *G'*.
23: 6 asked whether the man were a *G'*.

Galilæans *(gal-i-le'-uns)*
Lu 13: 1 some that told him of the *G'*,
2 Suppose ye that these *G'* were
2 sinners above all the *G'*,
Joh 4:45 the *G'* received him, having seen
Ac 2: 7 are not all these which speak *G'*?

Galilee *(gal'-i-lee)* See also GALILÆAN.
Jos 20: 7 Kedesh in *G'* in mount Naphtali,
21:32 Kedesh in *G'* with her suburbs,
1Ki 9:11 twenty cities in the land of *G'*.
2Ki 15:29 Hazor, and Gilead, and *G'*, all the
1Ch 6:76 Kedesh in *G'* with her suburbs,
Isa 9: 1 beyond Jordan, in *G'* of the nations.
M't 2:22 he turned aside in the parts of *G'*:
3:13 cometh Jesus from *G'* to Jordan
4:12 into prison, he departed into *G'*;
15 beyond Jordan, *G'* of the Gentiles;
18 Jesus, walking by the sea of *G'*,
23 And Jesus went about all *G'*,
25 great multitudes of people from *G'*.
15:29 came nigh unto the sea of *G'*;
17:22 while they abode in *G'*, Jesus said
19: 1 he departed from *G'*, and came
21:11 the prophet of Nazareth of *G'*.
26:32 I will go before you into *G'*.
69 Thou also wast with Jesus of *G'*.
27:55 which followed Jesus from *G'*,
28: 7 he goeth before you into *G'*;
10 that they go into *G'*, and there
16 eleven disciples went away into *G'*,
M'r 1: 9 Jesus came from Nazareth of *G'*,
14 Jesus came into *G'*, preaching the
16 Now as he walked by the sea of *G'*,
28 all the region round about *G'*.
39 synagogues throughout all *G'*,
3: 7 multitude from *G'* followed him,
6:21 captains, and chief estates of *G'*;
7:31 he came unto the sea of *G'*,
9:30 thence, and passed through *G'*;
14:28 I will go before you into *G'*.
15:41 when he was in *G'*, followed him,
16: 7 that he goeth before you into *G'*:
Lu 1:26 unto a city of *G'*, named Nazareth,
2: 4 And Joseph also went up from *G'*,
39 they returned into *G'*, to their own
3: 1 and Herod being tetrarch of *G'*,
4:14 in the power of the Spirit into *G'*:
31 down to Capernaum, a city of *G'*,
44 preached in the synagogues of *G'*.
5:17 were come out of every town of *G'*,
8:26 which is over against *G'*.
17:11 the midst of Samaria and *G'*.
23: 5 beginning from *G'* to this place.
6 When Pilate heard of *G'*, he asked
49 women that followed him from *G'*,
55 which came with him from *G'*,
24: 6 unto you when he was yet in *G'*,
Joh 1:43 Jesus would go forth into *G'*,
2: 1 there was a marriage in Cana of *G'*;
11 miracles did Jesus in Cana of *G'*,
4: 3 Judæa, and departed again into *G'*.
43 departed thence, and went into *G'*.
45 Then when he was come into *G'*,
46 Jesus came again into Cana of *G'*,
47 was come out of Judæa into *G'*, he
54 he was come out of Judæa into *G'*.
6: 1 Jesus went over the sea of *G'*,
7: 1 these things Jesus walked in *G'*:
9 unto them, he abode still in *G'*.
41 said, Shall Christ come out of *G'*?
52 Art thou also of *G'*? Search, and
52 for out of *G'* ariseth no prophet.
12:21 which was of Bethsaida of *G'*,
21: 2 and Nathanael of Cana in *G'*,
Ac 1:11 Ye men of *G'*, why stand ye gazing
5:37 After this man rose up Judas of *G'*
9:31 all Judæa and *G'* and Samaria,
10:37 began from *G'*, after the baptism
13:31 which came up with him from *G'*

gall
De 29:18 that beareth *g'* and wormwood;
32:32 their grapes are grapes of *g'*,
Job 16:13 out my *g'* upon the ground.
20:14 it is the *g'* of asps within him.
25 sword cometh out of his *g'*:
Ps 69:21 gave me also *g'* for my meat;
Jer 8:14 given us water of *g'* to drink,
9:15 give them water of *g'* to drink.
23:15 make them drink the water of *g'*:
La 3: 5 compassed me with *g'* and travel.
19 misery, the wormwood and the *g'*.
Am 6:12 ye have turned judgment into *g'*,
M't 27:34 vinegar to drink mingled with *g'*:
Ac 8:23 thou art in the *g'* of bitterness,

gallant
Isa 33:21 neither shall *g'* ship pass thereby.

galleries
Ca 7: 5 the king is held in the *g'*.
Eze 41:15 and the *g'* thereof on the one side
41:16 windows, and the *g'* round about
42: 5 for the *g'* were higher than these,

gallery See also GALLERIES.
Eze 42: 3 *g'* against *g'* in three stories.

galley
Isa 33:21 wherein shall go no *g'* with oars,

Gallim *(gal'-lim)*
1Sa 25:44 son of Laish, which was of *G'*.
Isa 10:30 Lift up thy voice, O daughter of *G'*:

Gallio *(gal'-le-o)*
Ac 18:12 *G'* was the deputy of Achaia,
14 *G'* said unto the Jews, If it were a
17 And *G'* cared for none of those

gallows
Es 5:14 a *g'* be made of fifty cubits high,
14 he caused the *g'* to be made.
6: 4 to hang Mordecai on the *g'* that he
7: 9 Behold also, the *g'* fifty cubits high,
10 So they hanged Haman on the *g'*
8: 7 they have hanged upon the *g'*,
9:13 ten sons be hanged upon the *g'*.
25 his sons should be hanged on the *g'*.

Gamaliel *(gam-a'-le-el)*
Nu 1:10 Manasseh; *G'* the son of Pedahzur.
2:20 of Manasseh shall be *G'* the son of
7:54 offered *G'* the son of Pedahzur
59 this was the offering of *G'* the son
10:23 of the children of Manasseh was *G'*
Ac 5:34 a Pharisee, named *G'*, a doctor of
22: 3 in this city at the feet of *G'*,

Gammadims *(gam'-ma-dims)*
Eze 27:11 and the *G'* were in thy towers:

Gamul *(ga'-mul)* See also BETH-GAMUL.
1Ch 24:17 the two and twentieth to *G'*,

Gannim See EN-GANNIM.

gaoler See JAILER.

gap See also GAPED; GAPS.
Eze 22:30 and stand in the *g'* before me

gaped
Job 16:10 *g'* upon me with their mouth;
Ps 22:13 *g'* upon me with their mouths,

gaps
Eze 13: 5 Ye have not gone up into the *g'*,

garden See also GARDENS.
Ge 2: 8 And the Lord God planted a *g'*
9 also in the midst of the *g'*,
10 out of Eden to water the *g'*;
15 put him into the *g'* of Eden
16 of the *g'* thou mayest freely eat:
3: 1 shall not eat of every tree of the *g'*?
2 the fruit of the trees of the *g'*:
3 which is in the midst of the *g'*,
8 the Lord God walking in the *g'*
8 amongst the trees of the *g'*.
10 I heard thy voice in the *g'*,
23 sent him forth from the *g'* of Eden,
24 at the east of the *g'* of Eden
13:10 even as the *g'* of the Lord,
De 11:10 with thy foot, as a *g'* of herbs:
1Ki 21: 2 that I may have it for a *g'* of herbs,
2Ki 9:27 he fled by the way of the *g'* house.
21:18 buried in the *g'* of his own house,
18 in the *g'* of Uzza: and Amon his
26 his sepulchre in the *g'* of Uzza:
25: 4 which is by the king's *g'*:
Ne 3:15 the pool of Siloah by the king's *g'*,
Es 1: 5 court of the *g'* of the king's palace;
7: 7 his wrath went into the palace *g'*:
8 king returned out of the palace *g'*
Job 8:16 his branch shooteth forth in his *g'*.
Ca 4:12 A *g'* inclosed is my sister, my
16 thou south; blow upon my *g'*,
16 Let my beloved come into his *g'*,
5: 1 I am come into my *g'*, my sister,
6: 2 beloved is gone down into his *g'*,
11 I went down into the *g'* of nuts
Isa 1: 8 as a lodge in a *g'* of cucumbers,
30 and as a *g'* that hath no water.
51: 3 her desert like the *g'* of the Lord;
58:11 thou shalt be like a watered *g'*,
61:11 and as the *g'* causeth the things
Jer 31:12 their soul shall be as a watered *g'*;
39: 4 by the way of the king's *g'*,
52: 7 walls, which was by the king's *g'*;
La 2: 6 as if it were of a *g'*:
Eze 28:13 been in Eden the *g'* of God;
31: 8 The cedars in the *g'* of God
8 nor any tree in the *g'* of God
9 that were in the *g'* of God,
36:35 is become like the *g'* of Eden;
Joe 2: 3 the land is as the *g'* of Eden
Lu 13:19 a man took, and cast into his *g'*;
Joh 18: 1 where was a *g'*, into the which
26 Did not I see thee in the *g'*
19:41 a *g'*; and in the *g'* a new sepulchre,

gardener
Joh 20:15 She, supposing him to be the *g'*,

garden-house See GARDEN and HOUSE.

gardens
Nu 24: 6 forth, as *g'* by the river's side,
Ec 2: 5 I made me *g'* and orchards,
Ca 4:15 of *g'*, a well of living waters,
6: 2 in the *g'*, and to gather lilies.
8:13 Thou that dwellest in the *g'*,
Isa 1:29 for the *g'* that ye have chosen.
65: 3 that sacrificeth in *g'*, and burneth
66:17 the *g'* behind one tree in the midst,
Jer 29: 5 plant *g'*, and eat the fruit of them;

Jer 29:28 plant g', and eat the fruit of them.
Am 4: 9 when your g' and your vineyards
9:14 make g', and eat the fruit of them.

Gareb (*ga'-reb*)
2 Sa 23:38 Ira an Ithrite, G' an Ithrite,
1 Ch 11:40 Ira the Ithrite, G' the Ithrite,
Jer 31:39 upon the hill G', and shall compass

garlands
Ac 14:13 brought oxen and g' unto the gates,

garlick
Nu 11: 5 leeks, and the onions, and the g':

garment See also GARMENTS.
Ge 9:23 And Shem and Japheth took a g',
25:25 red, all over like an hairy g';
39:12 she caught him by his g', saying,
12 he left his g' in her hand,
13 she saw that he had left his g'
15 that he left his g' with me,
16 she laid up his g' by her,
18 he left his g' with me, and fled
Le 6:10 the priest shall put on his linen g',
27 of the blood thereof upon any g',
13:47 g' also that the plague of leprosy
47 it be a woollen g', or a linen g';
49 be greenish or reddish in the g',
51 plague be spread in the g',
52 He shall therefore burn that g',
53 be not spread in the g',
56 he shall rend it out of the g',
57 if it appear still in the g',
58 And the g', either warp, or woof,
59 in a g' of woollen or linen,
14:55 And for the leprosy of a g',
15:17 And every g', and every skin,
19:19 neither shall a g' mingled of linen
De 22: 5 shall a man put on a woman's g':
11 g' of divers sorts, as of woollen
Jos 7:21 Babylonish g', and two hundred
24 silver, and the g', and the wedge
J'g 8:25 they spread a g', and did cast
2 Sa 13:18 she had a g' of divers colours
19 and rent her g' of divers colours
20: 8 Joab's g' that he had put on
1 Ki 11:29 he had clad himself with a new g';
30 caught the new g' that was on him,
2 Ki 9:13 hasted, and took every man his g',
Ezr 9: 3 I rent my g' and my mantle,
5 having rent my g' and my mantle,
Es 8:15 and with a g' of fine linen
Job 13:28 as a g' that is moth eaten.
30:18 of my disease is my g' changed:
38: 9 I made the cloud the g' thereof,
14 and they stand as a g'.
41:13 Who can discover the face of his g'?
Ps 69:11 I made sackcloth also my g';
73: 6 violence covereth them as a g'.
102:26 all of them shall wax old like a g';
104: 2 thyself with light as with a g':
6 with the deep as with a g':
109:18 with cursing like as with his g',
19 Let it be unto him as the g'
Pr 20:16 his g' that is surety for a stranger:
25:20 As he that taketh away a g'
27:13 Take his g' that is surety
30: 4 who hath bound the waters in a g'?
Isa 50: 9 they all shall wax old as a g';
51: 6 the earth shall wax old like a g',
8 shall eat them up like a g',
61: 3 the g' of praise for the spirit of
Jer 43:12 as a shepherd putteth on his g';
Eze 18: 7 hath covered the naked with a g';
16 hath covered the naked with a g',
Da 7: 9 whose g' was white as snow,
Mic 2: 8 ye pull off the robe with the g'
Hag 2:12 holy flesh in the skirt of his g',
Zec 13: 4 wear a rough g' to deceive:
Mal 2:16 one covereth violence with his g',
M't 9:16 piece of new cloth unto an old g',
16 to fill it up taketh from the g',
20 and touched the hem of his g':
21 If I may but touch his g',
14:36 only touch the hem of his g':
22:11 which had not on a wedding g':
12 in hither not having a wedding g'?
M'r 2:21 piece of new cloth on an old g':
5:27 press behind, and touched his g'.
6:56 it were but the border of his g':
10:50 And he, casting away his g', rose,
13:16 back again for to take up his g'.
16: 5 clothed in a long white g'; and
Lu 5:36 a piece of a new g' upon an old;
8:44 and touched the border of his g':
22:36 let him sell his g', and buy one.
Ac 12: 8 Cast thy g' about thee,
He 1:11 all shall wax old as doth a g';
Jude 23 hating even the g' spotted by the
Re 1:13 clothed with a g' down to the foot,

garments
Ge 35: 2 change your g':
38:14 she put her widow's g' off from
19 put on the g' of her widowhood.
49:11 he washed his g' in wine, and his
Ex 28: 2 thou shalt make holy g' for Aaron
3 that they may make Aaron's g'
4 these are the g' which they shall
4 they shall make holy g' for Aaron
29: 5 thou shalt take the g', and put upon
21 and upon his g' and upon his sons,
21 and upon the g' of his sons with him:
21 he shall be hallowed, and his g', and
21 his sons, and his sons' g' with him.
29 And the holy g' of Aaron shall be
31:10 the holy g' for Aaron the priest,
Ex 31:10 the g' of his sons, to minister in
35:19 the holy g' for Aaron the priest,
19 the g' of his sons, to minister in
21 service, and for the holy g'.
39: 1 and made the holy g' for Aaron;
41 the holy g' for Aaron the priest,
41 and his sons, g', to minister in the
40:13 put upon Aaron the holy g',
Le 6:11 put off his g', and put on other g',
8: 2 the g', and the anointing oil,
30 upon Aaron, and upon his g', and
30 and upon his sons' g' with him;
30 Aaron, and his g', and his sons,
30 and his sons' g' with him.
16: 4 these are holy g'; therefore shall
23 and shall put off the linen g',
24 put on his g', and come forth,
32 the linen clothes, even the holy g':
21:10 is consecrated to put on the g',
Nu 15:38 fringes in the borders of their g'
20:26 strip Aaron of his g', and put them
28 And Moses stripped Aaron of his g',
Jos 9: 5 and old g' upon them; and all the
13 these our g' and our shoes
J'g 14:12 and thirty changes of g':
13 sheets and thirty change of g':
19 gave change of g' unto them
1Sa 18: 4 and his g', even to his sword,
2Sa 10: 4 cut off their g' in the middle,
13:31 the king arose, and tare his g',
1Ki 10:25 vessels of gold, and g', and
2Ki 5:22 of silver, and two changes of g'.
23 two bags, with two changes of g',
26 and to receive g', and oliveyards,
7:15 all the way was full of g'
25:29 And changed his prison g': and he
1Ch 19: 4 and cut off their g' in the midst
Ezr 2:69 and one hundred priests' g'.
Ne 7:70 five hundred and thirty priests' g'.
72 threescore and seven priests' g'.
Job 37:17 How thy g' are warm, when he
Ps 22:18 They part my g' among them,
45: 8 All thy g' smell of myrrh, and aloes,
133: 2 went down to the skirts of his g';
Ec 9: 8 Let thy g' be always white;
Ca 4:11 the smell of thy g' is like the smell
Isa 9: 5 noise, and g' rolled in blood;
52: 1 on thy beautiful g', O Jerusalem,
59: 6 Their webs shall not become g',
17 he put on the g' of vengeance
61:10 clothed me with the g' of salvation,
63: 1 Edom, with dyed g' from Bozrah?
2 and thy g' like him that treadeth
3 shall be sprinkled upon my g',
Jer 36:24 were not afraid, nor rent their g',
52:33 And changed his prison g': and he
La 4:14 that men could not touch their g'.
Eze 16:16 And of thy g' thou didst take,
18 And tookest thy broidered g',
26:16 robes, and put off their broidered g':
42:14 but there they shall lay their g'
14 and shall put on other g',
44:17 they shall be clothed with linen g';
19 they shall put off their g' wherein
19 and they shall put on other g';
19 sanctify the people with their g'.
Da 3:21 and their other g', and were cast
Joe 2:13 rend your heart, and not your g',
Zec 3: 3 Joshua was clothed with filthy g',
4 Take away the filthy g' from him.
5 his head, and clothed him with g'.
M't 21: 8 spread their g' in the way;
23: 5 enlarge the borders of their g',
27:35 and parted his g', casting lots:
35 They parted my g' among them,
M'r 11: 7 and cast their g' on him; and he
8 many spread their g' in the way;
15:24 they parted his g', casting lots
Lu 19:35 they cast their g' upon the colt,
24: 4 men stood by them in shining g':
Joh 13: 4 from supper, and laid aside his g';
12 and had taken his g', and was set
19:23 took his g' and made four parts,
Ac 9:39 shewing the coats and g' which
Jas 5: 2 and your g' are motheaten.
Re 3: 4 which have not defiled their g';
16:15 that watcheth, and keepeth his g',

Garmite (*gar'-mite*)
1Ch 4:19 Keilah the G', and Eshtemoa the

garner See also GARNERS.
M't 3:12 and gather his wheat into the g';
Lu 3:17 will gather the wheat into his g';

garners
Ps 144:13 That our g' may be full, affording
Joe 1:17 the g' are laid desolate, the barns

garnish See also GARNISHED.
M't 23:29 and g' the sepulchres of the

garnished
2Ch 3: 6 And he g' the house with precious
Job 26:13 his spirit he hath g' the heavens;
M't 12:44 he findeth it empty, swept, and g'.
Lu 11:25 he findeth it swept and g'.
Re 21:19 of the wall of the city were g'

garrison See also GARRISONS.
1Sa 10: 5 where is the g' of the Philistines:
13: 3 Jonathan smote the g' of the
4 had smitten a g' of the Philistines,
23 the g' of the Philistines went out
14: 1 let us go over to the Philistines' g',
4 to go over unto the Philistines' g',
6 Come, and let us go over unto the g'
11 unto the g' of the Philistines; and
12 men of the g' answered Jonathan
1Sa 14:15 people, the g', and the spoilers,
2Sa 23:14 and the g' of the Philistines was
1Ch 11:16 the Philistines' g' was then at
2Co 11:32 king kept the city of...with a g',

garrisons
2Sa 8: 6 Then David put g' in Syria of
14 And he put g' in Edom;
14 throughout all Edom put he g',
1Ch 18: 6 Then David put g' in Syria-damascus;
13 And he put g' in Edom; and all
2Ch 17: 2 and set g' in the land of Judah,
Eze 26:11 and thy strong g' shall go down

Gashmu (*gash'-mu*) See also GESHEM.
Ne 6: 6 and G' saith it, that thou and the

gat See also BEGAT; FORGAT; GOT.
Ge 19:27 And Abraham g' up early in the
Ex 24:18 and g' him up into the mount:
Nu 11:30 And Moses g' him into the camp,
14:40 and g' them up into the top of the
16:27 so they g' up from the tabernacle
J'g 9:48 Abimelech g' him up to mount
51 and g' them up to the top of the
19:28 the man rose up, and g' him unto
1Sa 13:15 And Samuel arose, and g' him up
24:22 David and his men g' them up unto
26:12 and they g' them away, and no
2Sa 4: 7 and g' them away through the
8:13 And David g' him a name when
13:29 every man g' him up upon his
17:23 and g' him home to his house,
19: 3 And the people g' them by stealth
1Ki 1: 1 him with clothes, but he g' no heat.
Ps 116: 3 the pains of hell g' hold upon me:
Ec 2: 8 I g' me men singers and women
La 5: 9 We g' our bread with the peril of

Gatam (*ga'-tam*)
Ge 36:11 Omar, Zepho, and G', and Kenaz.
16 Duke Korah, duke G', and duke
1Ch 1:36 Omar, Zephi, and G', Kenaz, and

gate^ See also GATES.
Ge 19: 1 Lot sat in the gate of Sodom:
22:17 possess the g' of his enemies;
23:10 all that went in at the g' of his city,
18 that went in at the g' of his city.
24:60 let thy seed possess the g' of those
28:17 and this is the g' of heaven.
34:20 came unto the g' of their city,
24 went out of the g' of his city;
24 that went out of the g' of his city.
Ex 27:14 The hangings of one side of the g'
16 And for the g' of the court
32:26 Moses stood in the g' of the camp,
27 from g' to g' throughout the camp,
38:14 The hangings of the one side of the g'
38:15 for the other side of the court g',
18 the hanging for the g' of the court
31 and the sockets of the court g',
39:40 and the hanging for the court g',
40: 8 hang up the hanging at the court g'.
33 set up the hanging of the court g'.
Nu 4:26 the hanging for the door of the g'
De 21:19 and unto the g' of his place;
22:15 unto the elders of the city in the g':
24 bring them both out unto the g'
25: 7 go up to the g' unto the elders,
Jos 2: 5 about the time of shutting of the g',
7 were gone out, they shut the g'.
7: 5 chased them from before the g'
8:29 cast it at the entering of the g'
20: 4 stand at the entering of the g'
J'g 9:35 stood in the entering of the g'
40 even unto the entering of the g'.
44 stood in the entering of the g'
16: 2 laid wait for him all night in the g'
3 took the doors of the g' of the city,
18:16 stood by the entering of the g'.
17 stood in the entering of the g'
Ru 4: 1 Then went Boaz up to the g',
10 and from the g' of his place:
11 all the people that were in the g',
1Sa 4:18 seat backward by the side of the g',
9:18 Saul drew near to Samuel in the g',
21:13 scrabbled on the doors of the g',
2Sa 3:27 Joab took him aside in the g'
10: 8 at the entering in of the g':
11:23 even unto the entering of the g'.
15: 2 stood beside the way of the g':
18: 4 the king stood by the g' side,
24 went up to the roof over the g'
33 up to the chamber over the g',
19: 8 the king arose, and sat in the g'.
8 the king doth sit in the g'.
23:15 of Beth-lehem, which is by the g'!
16 that was by the g', and took it,
1Ki 17:10 when he came to the g' of the city,
22:10 the entrance of the g' of Samaria;
2Ki 7: 1 a shekel, in the g' of Samaria.
3 at the entering of the g':
17 to have the charge of the g':
17 the people trode upon him in the g',
18 about this time in the g' of Samaria:
20 the people trode upon him in the g',
9:31 as Jehu entered in at the g',
10: 8 entering in of the g' until the
11: 6 third part shall be at the g' of Sur;
6 part at the g' behind the guard:
19 the way of the g' of the guard
14:13 of Ephraim unto the corner g',
15:35 built the higher g' of the house
23: 8 the g' of Joshua the governor of
8 left hand at the g' of the city,
25: 4 way of the g' between two walls,

1Ch 9:18 hitherto waited in the king's g'
11:17 well of Beth-lehem, that is at the g'!
18 that was by the g', and took it,
19: 9 array before the g' of the city:
26:13 house of their fathers, for every g'.
16 with the g' Shallecheth, by the
2Ch 8:14 also by their courses at every g':
18: 9 the entering in of the g' of Samaria;
23: 5 part at the g' of the foundation:
15 to the entering of the horse g'
20 and they came through the high g'
24: 8 set it without at the g' of the house
25:23 the g' of Ephraim to the corner g',
26: 9 the corner g', and at the valley g',
27: 3 He built the high g' of the house
32: 6 the street of the g' of the city,
33:14 the entering in at the fish g',
35:15 and the porters waited at every g';
Ne 2:13 by night by the g' of the valley,
14 I went on to the g' of the fountain,
15 entered by the g' of the valley,
3: 1 they builded the sheep g'; they
3 fish g' did the sons of Hassenaah
6 the old g' repaired Jehoiada
13 The valley g' repaired Hanun,
13 on the wall unto the dung g'.
14 the dung g' repaired Malchiah
15 g' of the fountain repaired Shallun
26 place over against the water g'
28 the horse g' repaired the priests,
29 the keeper of the east g'.
31 over against the g' Miphkad,
32 unto the sheep g' repaired the
8: 1 street that was before the water g';
3 street that was before the water g'
16 and in the street of the water g',
16 in the street of the g' of Ephraim.
12:31 upon the wall toward the dung g':
37 And at the fountain g', which was
37 even unto the water g' eastward.
39 from above the g' of Ephraim,
39 the old g', and above the fish g',
39 even unto the sheep g':
39 they stood still in the prison g'.
Es 2:19 then Mordecai sat in the king's g'.
21 while Mordecai sat in the king's g'.
3: 2 servants, that were in the king's g',
3 which were in the king's g',
4: 2 And came even before the king's g':
2 more might enter into the king's g'
6 which was before the king's g'.
5: 1 over against the g' of the house.
9 saw Mordecai in the king's g',
13 the Jew sitting at the king's g'.
6:10 Jew, that sitteth at the king's g':
12 came again to the king's g'.
Job 5: 4 and they are crushed in the g',
29: 7 When I went out to the g'
31:21 when I saw my help in the g':
Ps 69:12 They that sit in the g' speak
118:20 This g' of the Lord, into which the
127: 5 speak with the enemies in the g'.
Pr 17:19 he that exalteth his g' seeketh
22:22 oppress the afflicted in the g':
24: 7 he openeth not his mouth in the g'.
Ca 7: 4 Heshbon, by the g' of Bath-rabbim:
Isa 14:31 Howl, O g'; cry, O city; thou,
22: 7 set themselves in array at the g'.
24:12 the g' is smitten with destruction.
28: 6 them that turn the battle to the g'.
29:21 for him that reproveth in the g',
Jer 7: 2 Stand in the g' of the Lord's house,
17:19 and stand in the g' of the children
19: 2 which is by the entry of the east g',
20: 2 were in the high g' of Benjamin,
26:10 down in the entry of the new g'
31:38 Hananeel unto the g' of the corner.
40 unto the corner of the horse g'
36:10 at the entry of the new g' of the
37:13 he was in the g' of Benjamin,
38: 7 the king then sitting in the g'
39: 3 came in, and sat in the middle g',
4 by the g' betwixt the two walls:
52: 7 of the g' between the two walls,
La 5:14 elders have ceased from the g',
Eze 8: 3 to the door of the inner g' that
5 at the g' of the altar this image
14 brought me to the door of the g' of
9: 2 from the way of the higher g',
10:19 stood at the door of the east g'
11: 1 unto the east g' of the Lord's house,
1 behold at the door of the g'
40: 3 seed; he stood in the g'.
6 Then came he unto the g' which
6 measured the threshold of the g',
6 and the other threshold of the g',
7 and the threshold of the g' by the
7 by the porch of the g' within was
8 measured also the porch of the g'
9 measured he the porch of the g',
9 the porch of the g' was inward.
10 little chambers of the g' eastward
11 breadth of the entry of the g', ten
11 and the length of the g', thirteen
13 measured then the g' from the roof
14 post of the court round about the g'.
15 the face of the g' of the entrance
15 porch of the inner g' were fifty
16 posts within the g' round about,
19 from the forefront of the lower g'
20 And the g' of the outward court
21 after the measure of the first g':
22 the measure of the g' that looketh
23 And the g' of the inner court was
23 against the g' toward the north,
23 from g' to g' an hundred cubits.

Eze 40:24 behold a g' toward the south:
27 there was a g' in the inner court
27 he measured from g' to g' toward
28 to the inner court by the south g':
28 and he measured the south g'
32 he measured the g' according to
35 And he brought me to the north g',
39 And in the porch of the g' were two
40 up to the entry of the north g',
40 at the porch of the g', were two
41 by the side of the g'; eight tables,
44 And without the inner g' were the
44 was at the side of the north g';
44 one at the side of the east g' having
48 and the breadth of the g' was three
42:15 forth toward the g' whose prospect
43: 1 to the g', even the g' that looketh
4 the house by the way of the g'
44: 1 the way of the g' whose prospect
2 This g' shall be shut, it shall not
3 by the way of the porch of that g',
4 brought...the way of the north g'
45:19 posts of the g' of the inner court.
46: 1 g' of the inner court that looketh
2 way of the porch of that g' without,
2 and shall stand by the post of the g',
2 worship at the threshold of the g':
2 but the g' shall not be shut until
3 shall worship at the door of this g'
8 by the way of the porch of that g',
9 the way of the north g' to worship
9 go out by the way of the south g';
9 entereth by the way of the south g'
9 go forth by the way of the north g':
9 shall not return by the way of the g'
12 the g' that looketh toward the east,
12 going forth one shall shut the g'.
19 which was at the side of the g',
47: 2 he me out of the way of the g'
2 the way without unto the utter g'
48:31 gates northward; one g' of Reuben,
31 one g' of Judah, one g' of Levi.
32 and three gates; one g' of Joseph,
32 one g' of Benjamin, one g' of Dan.
33 and three gates: one g' of Simeon,
33 g' of Issachar, one g' of Zebulun.
34 their three gates; one g' of Gad,
34 g' of Asher, one g' of Naphtali.
Da 2:49 Daniel sat in the g' of the king.
Am 5:10 hate him that rebuketh in the g',
12 they turn aside the poor in the g'
15 and establish judgment in the g':
Ob 13 not have entered into the g' of
Mic 1: 9 he is come unto the g' of my people,
12 the Lord unto the g' of Jerusalem.
2:13 have passed through the g', and are
Zep 1:10 the noise of a cry from the fish g',
Zec 14:10 from Benjamin's g' unto the place
10 of the first g', unto the corner g',
M't 7:13 Enter ye in at the strait g':
13 for wide is the g', and broad is the
14 Because strait is the g', and narrow
Lu 7:12 he came nigh to the g' of the city,
13:24 Strive to enter in at the strait g':
16:20 which was laid at his g', full of
Ac 3: 2 the g' of the temple which is called
10 at the Beautiful g' of the temple:
10:17 house, and stood before the g',
12:10 they came unto the iron g' that
13 knocked at the door of the g',
14 she opened not the g' for gladness,
14 told how Peter stood before the g'.
Heb 13:12 own blood, suffered without the g'.
gates
Ex 20:10 thy stranger that is within thy g':
De 3: 5 with high walls, g', and bars;
5:14 thy stranger that is within thy g';
6: 9 posts of thy house, and on thy g'.
11:20 of thine house, and upon thy g':
12:12 the Levite that is within your g';
15 kill and eat flesh in all thy g',
17 Thou mayest not eat within thy g'
18 and the Levite that is within thy g':
21 and thou shalt eat in thy g'
14:21 unto the stranger that is in thy g',
27 the Levite that is within thy g';
28 and shalt lay it up within thy g':
29 which are within thy g', shall come,
15: 7 of thy brethren within any of thy g'
22 Thou shalt eat it within thy g':
16: 5 the passover within any of thy g',
11 and the Levite that is within thy g',
14 widow, that are within thy g'.
18 shalt thou make thee in all thy g',
17: 2 among you, within any of thy g'
5 that wicked thing, unto thy g',
8 of controversy within thy g':
18: 6 if a Levite come from any of thy g'
23:16 he shall choose in one of thy g',
24:14 that are in thy land within thy g':
26:12 that they may eat within thy g',
28:52 he shall besiege thee in all thy g',
55 shall distress thee in all thy g'.
57 enemy shall distress thee in thy g'.
31:12 thy stranger that is within thy g',
Jos 6:26 son shall he set up the g' of it.
J'g 5: 8 then was war in the g': was there
11 people of the Lord go down to the g'.
1Sa 17:52 the valley, and to the g' of Ekron.
23: 7 into a town that hath g' and bars.
2Sa 18:24 David sat between the two g': and
1Ki 16:34 up the g' thereof in his youngest
2Ki 23: 8 down the high places of the g'
1Ch 9:19 keepers of the g' of the tabernacle:
22 were chosen to be porters in the g'
23 oversight of the g' of the house

1Ch 22: 3 for the nails for the doors of the g',
2Ch 8: 5 cities, with walls, g', and bars;
14: 7 walls, and towers, g', and bars,
23:19 And he set the porters at the g'
31: 2 to praise in the g' of the tents
Ne 1: 3 the g' thereof are burned with fire.
2: 3 g' thereof are consumed with fire?
8 beams for the g' of the palace
13 g' thereof were consumed with fire.
17 the g' thereof are burned with fire:
6: 1 not set up the doors upon the g';)
7: 3 Let not the g' of Jerusalem be
11:19 and their brethren that kept the g',
12:25 ward at the thresholds of the g'.
30 the people, and the g', and the wall.
13:19 when the g' of Jerusalem began to
19 that the g' should be shut,
19 some of my servants set I at the g',
22 they should come and keep the g',
Job 38:17 Have the g' of death been opened
Ps 9:13 liftest me up from the g' of death:
14 in the g' of the daughter of Zion:
24: 7 your heads, O ye g'; and be ye lift up
9 your heads, O ye g'; even lift them
87: 2 The Lord loveth the g' of Zion
100: 4 Enter into his g' with thanksgiving,
107:16 he hath broken the g' of brass,
18 draw near unto the g' of death.
118:19 Open to me the g' of righteousness:
122: 2 Our feet shall stand within thy g',
147:13 strengthened the bars of thy g';
Pr 1:21 in the openings of the g': in the
8: 3 She crieth at the g', at the entry of
34 watching daily at my g', waiting
14:19 wicked at the g' of the righteous.
31:23 Her husband is known in the g',
31 her own works praise her in the g'
Ca 7:13 our g' are all manner of pleasant
Isa 3:26 her g' shall lament and mourn;
13: 2 go into the g' of the nobles.
26: 2 Open ye the g', that the righteous
38:10 I shall go to the g' of the grave:
45: 1 before him the two-leaved g';
1 and the g' shall not be shut;
2 break in pieces the g' of brass,
54:12 and thy g' of carbuncles, and all
60:11 thy g' shall be open continually;
18 walls Salvation, and thy g' Praise.
62:10 through the g'; prepare ye the way
Jer 1:15 the entering of the g' of Jerusalem,
7: 2 that enter in at these g' to worship
14: 2 Judah mourneth, and the g' thereof
15: 7 I will fan them with a fan in the g'
17:19 and in all the g' of Jerusalem;
20 that enter in by these g':
21 bring it in by the g' of Jerusalem;
24 bring in no burden through the g'
25 Then shall there enter into the g'
27 entering in at the g' of Jerusalem
27 I kindle a fire in the g' thereof,
22: 2 thy people that enter in by these g':
4 enter in by the g' of this house
19 forth beyond the g' of Jerusalem.
49:31 which have neither g' nor bars
51:58 and her high g' shall be burned
La 1: 4 g' are desolate: her priests sigh,
2: 9 Her g' are sunk into the ground;
4:12 entered into the g' of Jerusalem.
Eze 21:15 the sword against all their g',
22 battering rams against the g',
26: 2 that was the g' of the people:
10 when he shall enter into thy g',
38:11 and having neither bars nor g',
40:18 pavement by the side of the g' over
18 over against the length of the g'
38 thereof were by the posts of the g',
44:11 charge at the g' of the house,
17 in at the g' of the inner court,
17 they minister in the g' of the inner
48:31 And the g' of the city shall be
31 g' northward; one gate of Reuben,
32 three g'; and one gate of Joseph,
33 three g'; and one gate of Simeon,
34 their three g'; and one gate of Gad,
Ob 11 foreigners entered into his g',
Na 2: 6 g' of the rivers shall be opened,
3:13 g' of thy land shall be set wide open
Zec 8:16 truth and peace in your g':
M't 16:18 the g' of hell shall not prevail
Ac 9:24 they watched the g' day and night
14:13 oxen and garlands unto the g',
Re 21:12 and had twelve g',
12 and at the g' twelve angels,
13 On the east three g';
13 on the north three g';
13 on the south three g';
13 and on the west three g',
15 and the g' thereof, and the wall
21 the twelve g' were twelve pearls;
25 And the g' of it shall not be shut
22:14 enter in through the g' into the city,
Gath (*gath*) See also GATH-HEPHER; GATH-RIMMON; GITTITE; MORESHETH-GATH.
Jos 11:22 only in Gaza, in G', and Ashdod,
1Sa 5: 8 of Israel be carried about unto G'.
6:17 Ashkelon one, for G' one, for Ekron
7:14 to Israel, from Ekron even unto G':
17: 4 Goliath, of G', whose height was
23 Philistine of G', Goliath by name,
52 Shaaraim, even unto G', and unto
21:10 and went to Achish the king of G'.
12 afraid of Achish the king of G'.
27: 2 Achish, the son of Maoch, king of G'.
3 David dwelt with Achish at G', he
4 told Saul that David was fled to G':
11 woman alive, to bring tidings to G',

2Sa 1:20 Tell it not in *G*', publish it not in
15:18 men which came after him from *G*',
21:20 was yet a battle in *G*', where was a
22 four were born to the giant in *G*',
1Ki 2:39 Achish son of Maachah king of *G*'.
39 Behold, thy servants be in *G*'.
40 saddled his ass, and went to *G*' to
40 and brought his servants from *G*'.
41 had gone from Jerusalem to *G*', and
2Ki 12:17 went up, and fought against *G*',
1Ch 7:21 and Elead, whom the men of *G*' that
8:13 drove away the inhabitants of *G*':
18: 1 subdued them, and took *G*' and
20: 6 war at *G*', where was a man of
8 were born unto the giant in *G*';
2Ch 11: 8 And *G*', and Mareshah, and Ziph,
26: 6 and brake down the wall of *G*', and
Ps 56:*title* the Philistines took him in *G*'.
Am 6: 2 go down to *G*' of the Philistines:
Mi 1:10 Declare ye it not at *G*', weep ye not

gather See also GATHERED; GATHEREST; GATHERETH; GATHERING; TOGETHER.
Ge 6:21 and thou shalt *g*' it to thee;
31:46 said unto his brethren, *G*' stones;
34:30 *g*' themselves together against me,
41:35 And let them *g*' all the food
49: 1 *G*' yourselves together, that I may
2 *G*' yourselves together, and hear,
Ex 3:16 Go, and *g*' the elders of Israel
5: 7 and *g*' straw for themselves,
12 to *g*' stubble instead of straw.
9:19 therefore now, and *g*' thy cattle,
16: 4 the people shall go out and *g*'
5 twice as much as they *g*' daily.
16 *G*' of it every man according to his
26 Six days ye shall *g*' it; but on the
27 on the seventh day for to *g*',
23:10 shall *g*' in the fruits thereof:
Le 8: 3 *g*' thou all the congregation
19: 9 shalt thou *g*' the gleanings
10 neither shalt thou *g*' every grape
23:22 neither shalt thou *g*' any gleaning
25: 3 prune thy vineyard, and *g*' in the
5 neither *g*' the grapes of thy vine
11 nor *g*' the grapes in it of thy vine
20 not sow, nor *g*' in our increase:
Nu 8: 9 shalt *g*' the whole assembly of the
10: 4 of Israel, shall *g*' themselves
11:16 *G*' unto me seventy men of the
19: 9 And a man that is clean shall *g*'
20: 8 *g*' thou the assembly together,
21:16 *G*' the people together, and I will
De 4:10 *G*' me the people together, and I
11:14 that thou mayest *g*' in thy corn,
13:16 thou shalt *g*' all the spoil of it
28:30 shalt not *g*' the grapes thereof.
38 shalt *g*' but little in; for the locust
39 nor *g*' the grapes; for the worm
30: 3 and *g*' thee from all the nations,
4 will the Lord thy God *g*' thee,
31:12 *G*' the people together, men, and
28 *G*' unto me all the elders of your
Ru 2: 7 me glean and *g*' after the reapers
1Sa 7: 5 said, *G*' all Israel to Mizpeh,
2Sa 3:21 and will *g*' all Israel unto my lord
12:28 *g*' the rest of the people together,
1Ki 18:19 *g*' to me all Israel unto mount
2Ki 4:39 went out into the field to *g*' herbs,
22:20 I will *g*' thee unto thy fathers,
1Ch 13: 2 they may *g*' themselves unto us:
16:35 and *g*' us together, and deliver us
22: 2 David commanded to *g*' together
2Ch 24: 5 *g*' of all Israel money to repair
34:28 I will *g*' thee to thy fathers,
Ezr 10: 7 they should *g*' themselves together
Ne 1: 9 yet will I *g*' them from thence,
7: 5 to *g*' together the nobles, and the
12:44 to *g*' into them out of the fields
Es 2: 3 may *g*' together all the fair young
4:16 *g*' together all the Jews that are
8:11 to *g*' themselves together, and to
Job 11:10 and shut up, or *g*' together,
24: 6 they *g*' the vintage of the wicked.
34:14 if he *g*' unto himself his spirit
39:12 thy seed, and *g*' it into thy barn?
Ps 26: 9 *G*' not my soul with sinners,
39: 6 and knoweth not who shall *g*' them.
50: 5 *G*' my saints together unto me;
56: 6 They *g*' themselves together,
94:21 *g*' themselves together against
104:22 they *g*' themselves together, and
28 That thou givest them they *g*':
106:47 *g*' us from among the heathen,
Pr 28: 8 *g*' it for him that will pity the poor.
Ec 2:26 to *g*' and to heap up, that he may
3: 5 and a time to *g*' stones together;
Ca 6: 2 in the gardens, and to *g*' lilies.
Isa 10:31 the inhabitants of Gebim *g*'
11:12 *g*' together the dispersed of Judah
34:15 hatch, and *g*' under her shadow:
40:11 shall *g*' the lambs with his arm,
43: 5 and *g*' thee from the west;
49:18 all these *g*' themselves together,
54: 7 with great mercies will I *g*' thee.
15 they shall surely *g*' together,
15 whosoever shall *g*' together against
56: 8 Yet will I *g*' others to him,
60: 4 all they *g*' themselves together,
62:10 *g*' out the stones; lift up a
66:18 I will *g*' all nations and tongues;
Jer 4: 5 the trumpet in the land: cry, *g*'
6: 1 ye children of Benjamin, *g*'
7:18 children *g*' wood, and the fathers
9:22 and none shall *g*' them.
10:17 *G*' up thy wares out of the land,
Jer 23: 3 I will *g*' the remnant of my flock
29:14 I will *g*' you from all the nations,
31: 8 *g*' them from the coasts of the earth,
10 He that scattered Israel will *g*' him,
32:37 I will *g*' them out of all countries,
40:10 ye, *g*' ye wine, and summer fruits,
49: 5 shall *g*' up him that wandereth.
14 *G*' ye together, and come against
51:11 the arrows; *g*' the shields:
Eze 11:17 I will even *g*' you from the people,
16:37 therefore I will *g*' all thy lovers,
37 will even *g*' them round about
20:34 and will *g*' you out of the countries
41 and *g*' you out of the countries
22:19 *g*' you into the midst of Jerusalem.
20 they *g*' silver, and brass, and iron,
20 so will I *g*' you in mine anger
21 Yea, I will *g*' you, and blow upon
24: 4 *G*' the pieces thereof into it,
29:13 At the end of forty years will I *g*'
34:13 and *g*' them from the countries,
36:24 and *g*' you out of all countries,
37:21 and will *g*' them on every side,
39:17 *g*' yourselves on every side to my
Da 3: 2 sent to *g*' together the princes,
Ho 8:10 now will I *g*' them, and they shall
9: 6 Egypt shall *g*' them up, Memphis
Joe 1:14 *g*' the elders and all the
2: 6 all faces shall *g*' blackness.
16 *G*' the people, sanctify the
16 assemble the elders, *g*' the children,
3: 2 I will also *g*' all nations, and will
11 *g*' yourselves together round about:
Mic 2:12 surely *g*' the remnant of Israel;
4: 6 I will *g*' her that is driven out,
12 for he shall *g*' them as the sheaves
5: 1 *g*' thyself in troops, O daughter
Na 2:10 the faces of them all *g*' blackness.
Hab 1: 9 shall *g*' the captivity as the sand.
15 and *g*' them in their drag:
Zep 2: 1 *G*' yourselves together, yea,
1 *g*' together, O nation not desired;
3: 8 to *g*' the nations, that I may
18 I will *g*' them that are sorrowful
19 and *g*' her that was driven out;
20 even in the time that I *g*' you:
Zec 10: 8 and *g*' them; for I have redeemed
10 and *g*' them out of Assyria; and I
14: 2 *g*' all nations against Jerusalem
M't 3:12 and *g*' his wheat into the garner;
6:26 do they reap, nor *g*' into barns;
7:16 Do men *g*' grapes of thorns,
13:28 that we go and *g*' them up?
29 Nay; lest while ye *g*' up the tares,
30 *G*' ye together first the tares,
30 but *g*' the wheat into my barn.
41 they shall *g*' out of his kingdom
24:31 they shall *g*' together his elect
25:26 and *g*' where I have not strawed:
M'r 13:27 and shall *g*' together his elect
Lu 3:17 will *g*' the wheat into his garner;
6:44 of thorns men do not *g*' figs,
44 of a bramble bush *g*' they grapes.
13:34 as a hen doth *g*' her brood under
Joh 6:12 *G*' up the fragments that remain,
11:52 also he should *g*' together in one
15: 6 and men *g*' them, and cast them
Eph 1:10 he might *g*' together in one all
Re 14:18 *g*' the clusters of the vine of the
16:14 to *g*' them to battle of that great
19:17 Come and *g*' yourselves together
20: 8 to *g*' them together to battle:

gathered
Ge 1: 9 be *g*' together unto one place,
12: 5 their substance that they had *g*',
25: 8 of years; and was *g*' to his people.
17 died; and was *g*' unto his people.
29: 3 And thither were all the flocks *g*':
7 the cattle should be *g*' together:
8 until all the flocks be *g*' together,
22 And Laban *g*' together all the men
35:29 died, and was *g*' unto his people,
41:48 he *g*' up all the food of the seven
49 And Joseph *g*' corn as the sand
47:14 And Joseph *g*' up all the money
49:29 I am to be *g*' unto my people:
33 he *g*' up his feet into the bed,
33 and was *g*' unto his people.
Ex 4:29 *g*' together all the elders of Israel:
8:14 *g*' them together upon heaps:
15: 8 the waters were *g*' together, the
16:17 and *g*', some more, some less.
18 he that *g*' much had nothing over,
18 and he that *g*' little had no lack;
18 they *g*' every man according to his
21 they *g*' it every morning, every man
22 the sixth day they *g*' twice as much
23:16 when thou hast *g*' in thy labours
32: 1 *g*' themselves together unto Aaron,
26 *g*' themselves together unto him.
35: 1 Moses *g*' all the congregation
Le 8: 4 and the assembly was *g*' together
23:39 ye have *g*' in the fruit of the land,
26:25 and when ye are *g*' together within
Nu 10: 7 congregation is to be *g*' together,
11: 8 the people went about, and *g*' it,
22 all the fish of the sea be *g*' together
24 and *g*' the seventy men of the elders
32 and they *g*' the quails:
32 he that *g*' least...ten homers:
32 he that...least *g*' ten homers:
14:35 that are *g*' together against me:
15:32 they found a man that *g*' sticks
16: 3 And they *g*' themselves together
11 are *g*' together against the Lord:
Nu 16:19 And Korah *g*' all the congregation
42 the congregation was *g*' against
20: 2 And they *g*' themselves together
10 And Moses and Aaron *g*' the
24 Aaron shall be *g*' unto his people:
26 Aaron shall be *g*' unto his people,
21:23 but Sihon *g*' all his people together,
27: 3 them that *g*' themselves together
13 also shalt be *g*' unto thy people,
13 as Aaron thy brother was *g*'.
31: 2 shalt thou be *g*' unto thy people.
De 16:13 after that thou hast *g*' in thy corn
32:50 and be *g*' unto thy people; as Aaron
50 and was *g*' unto his people:
33: 5 the tribes of Israel were *g*' together.
Jos 9: 2 That they *g*' themselves together,
10: 5 *g*' themselves together, and went
6 in the mountains are *g*' together
22:12 *g*' themselves together at Shiloh,
24: 1 Joshua *g*' all the tribes of Israel
J'g 1: 7 *g*' their meat under my table:
2:10 were *g*' unto their fathers:
3:13 And he *g*' unto him the children
4:13 Sisera *g*' together all his chariots,
6:33 were *g*' together, and went over,
34 and Abi-ezer was *g*' after him.
35 Manasseh; who also was *g*' after
7:23 the men of Israel *g*' themselves
24 of Ephraim *g*' themselves together.
9: 6 the men of Shechem *g*' together,
27 and *g*' their vineyards, and trode
47 of Shechem were *g*' together.
10:17 the children of Ammon were *g*'
11: 3 were *g*' vain men to Jephthah,
20 Sihon *g*' all his people together,
12: 1 the men of Ephraim *g*' themselves
4 Jephthah *g*' together all the men
16:23 of the Philistines *g*' them together
18:22 to Micah's house were *g*' together,
20: 1 the congregation was *g*' together
11 So all the men of Israel were *g*'
14 children of Benjamin *g*' themselves
1Sa 5: 8 sent therefore and *g*' all the lords
11 sent and *g*' together all the lords
7: 6 And they *g*' together to Mizpeh,
7 children of Israel were *g*' together
8: 4 of Israel *g*' themselves together,
13: 5 Philistines *g*' themselves together
11 Philistines *g*' themselves together
14:48 And he *g*' an host, and smote the
15: 4 And Saul *g*' the people together,
17: 1 Philistines *g*' together their armies
1 and were *g*' together at Shochoh,
2 the men of Israel were *g*' together,
20:38 Jonathan's lad *g*' up the arrows,
22: 2 was discontented, *g*' themselves
25: 1 all the Israelites were *g*' together,
28: 1 that the Philistines *g*' their armies
4 Philistines *g*' themselves together,
4 and Saul *g*' all Israel together, and
29: 1 Now the Philistines *g*' together all
2Sa 2:25 And the children of Benjamin *g*'
30 he had *g*' all the people together,
6: 1 David *g*' together all the chosen
10:15 were smitten before Israel, they *g*'
17 told David, he *g*' all Israel together,
12:29 And David *g*' all the people together,
14:14 which cannot be *g*' up again;
17:11 all Israel be generally *g*' unto thee,
20:14 and they were *g*' together, and
21:13 and they *g*' the bones of them
23: 9 that were there *g*' together to battle,
11 the Philistines were *g*' together into
1Ki 10:26 And Solomon *g*' together chariots
11:24 he *g*' men unto him, and became
18:20 and *g*' the prophets together unto
20: 1 of Syria *g*' all his host together:
22: 6 of Israel *g*' the prophets together,
2Ki 3:21 they *g*' all that were able to put on
4:39 and *g*' thereof wild gourds his lap
6:24 Ben-hadad king of Syria *g*' all his
10:18 And Jehu *g*' all the people together,
22: 4 of the door have *g*' of the people:
9 Thy servants have *g*' the money
20 and thou shalt be *g*' into thy grave
23: 1 and they *g*' unto him all the elders
1Ch 11: 1 all Israel *g*' themselves to David
13 the Philistines were *g*' together to
13: 5 So David *g*' all Israel together,
15: 3 And David *g*' all Israel together
19: 7 of Ammon *g*' themselves together
17 and he *g*' all Israel, and passed over
23: 2 And he *g*' together all the princes
2Ch 1:14 And Solomon *g*' chariots and
11: 1 he *g*' of the house of Judah and
12: 5 that were *g*' together to Jerusalem
13: 7 there are *g*' unto him vain men,
15: 9 And he *g*' all Judah and Benjamin,
10 So they *g*' themselves together at
18: 5 Therefore the king of Israel *g*'
20: 4 And Judah *g*' themselves together,
23: 2 *g*' the Levites out of all the cities
24: 5 And he *g*' together the priests
11 day, and *g*' money in abundance.
25: 5 Amaziah *g*' Judah together, and
28:24 And Ahaz *g*' together the vessels
29: 4 *g*' them together into the east street,
15 And they *g*' their brethren, and
20 and *g*' the rulers of the city,
30: 3 the people *g*' themselves together
32: 4 was *g*' much people together,
6 and *g*' them together to him in the
34: 9 had *g*' of the hand of Manasseh
17 they have *g*' together the money
28 and thou shalt be *g*' to thy grave

2Ch 34:29 the king sent and g' together all the
Ezr 3: 1 the people g' themselves together
7:28 and I g' together out of Israel
8:15 And I g' them together to the river
10: 9 the men of Judah and Benjamin g'
Ne 5:16 all my servants were g' thither
8: 1 the people g' themselves together
13 on the second day were g' together
12:28 the singers g' themselves together,
13:11 I g' them together, and set them
Es 2: 8 and when many maidens were g'
19 when the virgins were g' together
9: 2 The Jews g' themselves together
15 the Jews that were in Shushan g'
16 g' themselves together, and stood
Job 16:10 they have g' themselves together
27:19 lie down, but he shall not be g':
30: 7 the nettles they were g' together.
Ps 35:15 and g' themselves together: yea,
15 the abjects g' themselves together
47: 9 The princes of the people are g'
59: 3 the mighty are g' against me;
102:22 When the people are g' together,
107: 3 And g' them out of the lands,
140: 2 are they g' together for war.
Pr 27:25 and herbs of the mountains are g'.
30: 4 who hath g' the winds in his fists?
Ec 2: 8 I g' me also silver and gold,
Ca 5: 1 I have g' my myrrh with my spice;
Isa 5: 2 it, and g' out the stones thereof,
10:14 are left, have I g' all the earth;
13: 4 kingdoms of nations g' together:
22: 9 and ye g' together the waters
24:22 And they shall be g' together,
22 as prisoners are g' in the pit,
27:12 ye shall be g' one by one,
33: 4 spoil shall be g' like the gathering
34:15 there shall the vultures also be g',
16 and his spirit it hath g' them.
43: 9 Let all the nations be g' together,
44:11 let them all be g' together, let them
49: 5 Though Israel be not g', yet shall
56: 8 beside those that are g' unto him.
60: 7 All the flocks of Kedar shall be g'
62: 9 they that have g' it shall eat it,
Jer 3:17 all the nations shall be g' unto it,
8: 2 they shall not be g', nor be buried;
25:33 shall not be lamented, neither g',
26: 9 people were g' against Jeremiah
40:12 and g' wine and summer fruits
15 g' unto thee should be scattered,
Eze 28:25 I shall have g' the house of Israel
29: 5 not be brought together, nor g':
38: 8 and is g' out of many people,
12 upon the people that are g' out
13 g' thy company to take a prey?
39:27 and g' them out of their enemies'
28 have g' them unto their own land,
Da 3: 3 g' together unto the dedication
27 being g' together, saw these men,
Ho 1:11 and the children of Israel be g'
10:10 people shall be g' against them,
Mic 1: 7 she g' it of the hire of an harlot,
4:11 many nations are g' against thee,
7: 1 they have g' the summer fruits,
Zec 12: 3 people of the earth be g' together
14:14 round about shall be g' together,
M't 2: 4 he had g' all the chief priests
13: 2 great multitudes were g' together
40 As therefore the tares are g' and
47 into the sea, and g' of every kind:
48 and g' the good into vessels,
18:20 three are g' together in my name,
22:10 and g' together all as many as they
34 to silence, they were g' together.
41 the Pharisees were g' together,
23:37 often would I have g' thy children
24:28 will the eagles be g' together.
25:32 before him shall be g' all nations:
27:17 they were g' together, Pilate said
27 and g' unto him the whole band
M'r 1:33 city was g' together at the door.
2: 2 many were g' together, insomuch
4: 1 was g' unto him a great multitude,
5:21 much people g' unto him: and he
6:30 the apostles g' themselves together
Lu 8: 4 much people were g' together,
11:29 people were g' thick together,
12: 1 when there were g' together an
13:34 how often would I have g' thy
15:13 the younger son g' all together
17:37 will the eagles be g' together.
24:33 and found the eleven g' together.
Joh 6:13 Therefore they g' them together,
11:47 Then g' the chief priests and the
Ac 4: 6 were g' together at Jerusalem.
26 rulers were g' together against the
27 and the people of Israel, were g'
12:12 many were g' together praying.
14:27 and had g' the church together,
15:30 had g' the multitude together,
17: 5 g' a company, and set all the city
20: 8 where there they were g' together.
28: 3 And when Paul had g' a bundle
1Co 5: 4 when ye are g' together, and my
2Co 8:15 He that had g' much had nothing
15 and he that had g' little had no lack.
Re 14:19 and g' the vine of the earth,
16:16 And he g' them together into a
19:19 and their armies, g' together to

gatherer
Am 7:14 and a g' of sycomore fruit:

gatherest
De 24:21 When thou g' the grapes of thy

gathereth
Nu 19:10 he that g' the ashes of the heifer
Ps 33: 7 he g' the waters of the sea
41: 6 his heart g' iniquity to itself;
147: 2 g' together the outcasts of Israel.
Pr 6: 8 and g' her food in the harvest.
10: 5 He that g' in summer is a wise son:
13:11 but he that g' by labour shall
Isa 10:14 and as one g' eggs that are left,
17: 5 when the harvestman g' the corn,
5 as he that g' ears in the valley
56: 8 which g' the outcasts of Israel
Na 3:18 mountains, and no man g' them.
Hab 2: 5 but g' unto him all nations,
M't 12:30 he that g' not with me scattereth
23:37 even as a hen g' her chickens
Lu 11:23 he that g' not with me scattereth.
Joh 4:36 and g' fruit unto life eternal:

gathering See also GATHERINGS.
Ge 1:10 and the g' together of the waters
49:10 him shall the g' of the people be.
Nu 15:33 they that found him g' sticks
1Ki 17:10 widow woman was there g' of sticks:
12 and, behold, I am g' two sticks,
2Ch 20:25 were three days in g' of the spoil,
Isa 32:10 shall fail, the g' shall not come.
33: 4 the gathering of the caterpiller:
M't 25:24 g' where thou hast not strawed:
Ac 16:10 assuredly g' that the Lord had
2Th 2: 1 by our g' together unto him,

gatherings
1Co 16: 2 that there be no g' when I come.

Gath-hepher (*gath-he'-fer*) See also GITTAH-HEPHER.
2Ki 14:25 the prophet, which was of G'.

Gath-rimmon (*gath-rim'-mon*)
Jos 19:45 Jehud, and Bene-berak, and G',
21:24 her suburbs, G' with her suburbs;
25 suburbs, and G' with her suburbs;
1Ch 6:69 suburbs, and G' with her suburbs:

gave See also FORGAVE; GAVEST.
Ge 2:20 And Adam g' names to all cattle,
3: 6 and g' also unto her husband
12 to be with me, she g' me of the tree,
14:20 And he g' him tithes of all.
16: 3 g' her to her husband Abram to be
18: 7 and g' it unto a young man; and he
20:14 and g' them unto Abraham, and
21:14 and g' it unto Hagar, putting it on
19 with water, and g' the lad drink.
27 and g' them unto Abimelech; and
24:18 upon her hand, and g' him drink.
32 and g' straw and provender for
53 and g' them to Rebekah: he g' also
25: 5 And Abraham g' all that he had
6 Abraham g' gifts, and sent them
8 Then Abraham g' up the ghost, and
17 and he g' up the ghost and died;
34 Jacob g' Esau bread and pottage
27:17 And she g' the savoury meat and
28: 4 which God g' unto Abraham.
6 he g' him a charge, saying, Thou
29:24 And Laban g' unto his daughter
28 and he g' him Rachel his daughter
29 Laban g' to Rachel his daughter
30: 4 she g' him Bilhah her handmaid
9 and g' her Jacob to wife.
35 and g' them into the hand of his
35: 4 And they g' unto Jacob all the
12 the land which I g' Abraham and
29 And Isaac g' up the ghost, and died,
38:18 And he g' it her, and came in unto
26 I g' her not to Shelah my son.
39:21 and g' him favour in the sight of
40:11 and I g' the cup into Pharaoh's
21 and he g' the cup into Pharaoh's
41:45 and he g' him to wife Asenath the
43:24 g' them water, and they washed
24 their feet; and he g' their asses
45:21 Joseph g' them wagons, according
21 and g' them provision for the way.
22 he g' each man changes of raiment;
22 to Benjamin he g' three hundred
46:18 Zilpah, whom Laban g' to Leah
25 Bilhah, which Laban g' unto
47:11 and g' them a possession in the
17 Joseph g' them bread in exchange
22 eat their portion which Pharaoh g'
Ex 2:21 and he g' Moses Zipporah his
6:13 and g' them a charge unto the
11: 3 And the Lord g' the people favour
12:36 the Lord g' the people favour in
14:20 but it g' light by night to these:
31:18 And he g' unto Moses, when he
32:24 So they g' it me: then I cast it
34:32 and he g' them in commandment
36: 6 And Moses g' commandment, and
Nu 3:51 And Moses g' the money of them
7: 6 and g' them unto the Levites.
7 four oxen he g' unto the sons of
8 eight oxen he g' unto the sons of
9 unto the sons of Kohath he g' none:
11:25 and g' it unto the seventy elders:
17: 6 every one of their princes g' him a
27:23 and g' him a charge, as the Lord
31:41 And Moses g' the tribute, which
47 and g' them unto the Levites,
32:33 And Moses g' unto them, even to
38 and g' other names unto the cities
40 And Moses g' Gilead unto Machir
De 2:12 his possession, which the Lord g'
3:12 the cities thereof, g' I unto the
13 the kingdom of Og, g' I unto the
De 3:15 And I g' Gilead unto Machir.
16 g' from Gilead even unto the river
9:11 the Lord g' me the two tables
10: 4 and the Lord g' them unto me.
22:16 I g' my daughter unto this man
29: 8 and g' it for an inheritance unto
31:23 And he g' Joshua the son of Nun charge,
Jos 1:14 the land which Moses g' you on
15 which Moses the Lord's servant g'
11:23 and Joshua g' it for an inheritance
12: 6 Moses the servant of the Lord g'
7 which Joshua g' unto the tribes
13: 8 their inheritance, which Moses g'
8 Moses the servant of the Lord g'
14 tribe of Levi he g' none inheritance;
15 And Moses g' unto the tribe of the
24 g' inheritance unto the tribe of Gad,
29 g' inheritance unto the half tribe of
33 the tribe of Levi Moses g' not any
14: 3 but unto the Levites he g' none
4 they g' no part unto the Levites
13 and g' unto Caleb the son of
15:13 Caleb, the son of Jephunneh he g'
17 and he g' him Achsah his daughter
19 And he g' her the upper springs,
17: 4 he g' them an inheritance among
18: 7 the servant of the Lord g' them.
19:49 children of Israel g' an inheritance
50 they g' him the city which he asked,
21: 3 of Israel g' unto the Levites out of
8 And the children of Israel g' by lot
9 And they g' out of the tribe of the
11 And they g' them the city of Arba
12 villages thereof, g' they to Caleb
13 they g' to the children of Aaron
21 For they g' them Shechem with her
27 tribe of Manasseh they g' Golan in
43 And the Lord g' unto Israel all
44 Lord g' them rest round about,
22: 4 the servant of the Lord g' you
7 g' Joshua among their brethren on
24: 3 his seed, and g' him Isaac.
4 I g' unto Isaac Jacob and Esau:
4 and I g' unto Esau mount Seir,
8 and I g' them into your hand,
J'g 1:13 and he g' him Achsah his daughter
15 And Caleb g' her the upper springs
20 And they g' Hebron unto Caleb, as
3: 6 and g' their daughters to their sons,
4:19 bottle of milk, and g' him drink,
5:25 water, and she g' him milk;
6: 9 and g' you their land;
9: 4 g' him threescore and ten pieces
14: 9 and he g' them, and they did eat:
19 g' change of garments unto them
15: 2 I g' her to thy companion:
17: 4 and g' them to the founder, who
19:21 and g' provender unto the asses: and
20:36 for the men of Israel g' place to
21:14 and they g' them wives which they
Ru 2:18 and g' to her that she had reserved
3:17 six measures of barley g' he me;
4: 7 his shoe, and g' it to his neighbour:
13 her, the Lord g' her conception,
17 her neighbours g' it a name,
1Sa 1: 4 he g' to Peninnah his wife, and to
5 Hannah he g' a worthy portion;
23 and g' her son suck until she weaned
9:23 Bring the portion which I g' thee,
10: 9 Samuel, God g' him another heart:
18: 4 that was upon him, and g' it
27 and they g' them in full tale to the king
27 Saul g' him Michal his daughter
20:40 And Jonathan g' his artillery unto
21: 6 the priest g' him hallowed bread:
22:10 g' him victuals, and g' him the
27: 6 Achish g' him Ziklag that day:
30:11 and g' him bread, and he did eat;
12 they g' him a piece of a cake of figs,
2Sa 12: 8 And I g' thee thy master's house,
8 and g' thee the house of Israel
18: 5 the king g' all the captains charge
24: 9 And Joab g' up the sum of the
1Ki 4:29 And God g' Solomon wisdom and
5:10 Hiram g' Solomon cedar trees and
11 And Solomon g' Hiram twenty
11 g' Solomon to Hiram year by year.
12 the Lord g' Solomon wisdom, as
9:11 Solomon g' Hiram twenty cities
10:10 And she g' the king an hundred
10 queen of Sheba g' to king Solomon.
13 king Solomon g' unto the queen of
13 Solomon g' her of his royal bounty.
11:18 of Egypt; which g' him an house,
18 him victuals, and g' him land.
19 that he g' him to wife the sister
12:13 men's counsel that they g' him;
13: 3 And he g' a sign the same day,
14: 8 the house of David, and g' it thee:
15 land which he g' to their fathers,
19:21 and g' unto the people, and they
2Ki 10:15 And he g' him his hand; and he
11:12 upon him, and g' him the testimony;
12:11 And they g' the money, being told,
14 But they g' that to the workmen,
13: 5 (And the Lord g' Israel a saviour,
15:19 and Menahem g' Pul a thousand
17: 3 his servant, and g' him presents.
18:15 And Hezekiah g' him all the silver
16 and g' it to the king of Assyria.
21: 8 land which I g' their fathers;
22: 8 Hilkiah g' the book to Shaphan,
23:35 Jehoiakim g' the silver and the
25: 6 and they g' judgment upon him.
1Ch 2:35 Sheshan g' his daughter to Jarha

1Ch 6:55 they g' them Hebron in the land
56 they g' to Caleb the son of
57 Aaron they g' the cities of Judah,
64 of Israel g' to the Levites
65 And they g' by lot out of the tribe
67 And they g' unto them, of the cities
67 g' also Gezer with her suburbs,
14:12 David g' a commandment, and they
21: 5 Joab g' the sum of the number
25 So David g' to Ornan for the place
25: 5 God g' to Heman fourteen sons
28:11 Then David g' to Solomon his son
14 He g' of gold by weight for things
16 he g' gold for the tables of
17 for the gold basons he g' gold by
29: 7 g' for the service of the house
8 precious stones were found g' them
2Ch 9: 9 And she g' the king an hundred
9 queen of Sheba g' king Solomon.
12 Solomon g' to the queen of Sheba
10: 8 counsel which the old men g' him,
11:23 he g' them victual in abundance.
13: 5 God of Israel g' the kingdom over
15 Then the men of Judah g' a shout:
15:15 and the Lord g' them rest round about.
20:30 for his God g' him rest round about.
21: 3 their father g' them great gifts
3 but the kingdom g' he to Jehoram;
23:11 the crown, and g' him the testimony,
24:12 And the king and Jehoiada g' it
26: 8 the Ammonites g' gifts to Uzziah:
27: 5 And the children of Ammon g' him
28:15 and g' them to eat and to drink,
21 and g' it unto the king of Assyria:
30: 7 therefore g' them up to desolation,
24 the princes g' to the congregation
32:24 unto him, and he g' him a sign.
34:10 and they g' it to the workmen
11 artificers and builders g' they it,
35: 7 And Josiah g' to the people, of the
8 g' willingly unto the people,
8 g' unto the priests for the passover
9 of the Levites, g' unto the Levites
36:17 he g' them all into his hand.
Ezr 2:69 They g' after their ability unto
3: 7 g' money also unto the masons,
5:12 he g' them into the hand of
7:11 the king Artaxerxes g' unto Ezra
10:19 And they g' their hands that they
Ne 2: 1 I took up the wine, and g' it
9 river, and g' them the king's letters.
7: 2 That I g' my brother Hanani,...charge
70 of the fathers g' unto the work.
70 The Tirshatha g' to the treasure
71 the chief of the fathers g' to the
72 which the rest of the people g'
8: 8 God distinctly, and g' the sense,
12:31 companies of them that g' thanks,
38 other company of them that g' thanks
40 companies of them that g' thanks
47 g' the portions of the singers
Es 1: 7 And they g' them drink in vessels of
2: 9 and he speedily g' her things for
18 and g' gifts, according to the state
3:10 his hand, and g' it unto Haman
4: 5 and g' him a commandment to
8 he g' him the copy of the writing
10 and g' him commandment unto
8: 2 Haman, and g' it unto Mordecai.
Job 1:21 Lord g', and the Lord hath taken
19:16 servant, and he g' me no answer;
29:11 the eye saw me, it g' witness to me:
21 Unto me men g' ear, and waited,
32:11 I g' ear to your reasons, whilst
42:10 also the Lord g' Job twice as much
11 man also g' him a piece of money,
15 their father g' them inheritance
Ps 18:13 and the Highest g' his voice;
68:11 The Lord g' the word: great was
69:21 They g' me also gall for my meat;
21 in my thirst they g' me vinegar to drink.
77: 1 and he g' ear unto me.
78:15 and g' them drink as out of the great
29 for he g' them their own desire;
46 He g' also their increase unto the
48 g' up their cattle also to the hail,
50 g' their life over to the pestilence;
62 g' his people over also unto the
81:12 So I g' them up unto their own
99: 7 the ordinance that he g' them.
105:32 g' them hail for rain, and flaming
44 g' them the lands of the heathen:
106:15 And he g' them their request;
41 he g' them into the hand of the
135:12 And g' their land for an heritage,
136:21 And g' their land for an heritage:
Pr 8:29 When he g' to the sea his decree,
Ec 1:13 g' my heart to seek and search
17 I g' my heart to know wisdom,
12: 7 spirit shall return unto God who g'
9 yea, he g' good heed, and sought
Ca 5: 6 him, but he g' me no answer.
Isa 41: 2 g' the nations before him, and
2 g' them as the dust to his sword,
42:24 Who g' Jacob for a spoil, and
43: 3 I g' Egypt for thy ransom,
50: 6 I g' my back to the smiters,
Jer 7: 7 the land that I g' to your fathers,
14 the place which I g' to you and to
16:15 land that I g' unto their fathers.
17: 4 from thine heritage that I g' thee;
23:39 that I g' you and your fathers,
24:10 the land that I g' unto them and to
30: 3 the land that I g' to their fathers,
32:12 I g' the evidence of the purchase
36:32 and g' it to Baruch the scribe,
Jer 39: 5 where he g' judgment upon him.
10 and g' them vineyards and fields
11 king of Babylon g' charge
40: 5 the captain of the guard g' him
44:30 as I g' Zedekiah king of Judah
52: 9 where he g' judgment upon him.
La 1:19 and mine elders g' up the ghost
Eze 16:19 My meat also which I g' thee,
20:11 And I g' them my statutes, and
12 also I g' them my sabbaths,
25 Wherefore I g' them also statutes
36:28 the land that I g' to your fathers;
39:23 and g' them into the hand of their
Da 1: 2 And the Lord g' Jehoiakim king of
7 prince of the eunuchs g' names:
7 for he g' unto Daniel the name
16 should drink; and g' them pulse.
17 God g' them knowledge and skill
2:48 and g' him many great gifts, and
5:18 most high God g' Nebuchadnezzar
19 for the majesty that he g' him,
6:10 and g' thanks before his God, as he did
Ho 2: 8 I g' her corn, and wine, and oil,
13:11 I g' thee a king in mine anger,
Am 2:12 ye g' the Nazarites wine to drink;
Mal 2: 5 and I g' them to him for the fear
M't 8:18 he g' commandment to depart
10: 1 g' them power against unclean
14:19 and g' the loaves to his disciples,
15:36 and g' thanks, and brake them,
36 and g' to his disciples,
21:23 who g' thee this authority?
25:15 unto one he g' five talents, to
35 an hungred, and ye g' me meat:
35 was thirsty, and ye g' me drink:
37 or thirsty, and g' thee drink?
42 an hungred, and ye g' me no meat:
42 thirsty, and ye g' me no drink:
26:26 brake it, and g' it to the disciples,
27 g' thanks, and g' it to them, saying,
48 that betrayed him g' them a sign,
27:10 and g' them for the potter's field,
34 g' him vinegar to drink mingled
48 on a reed, and g' him to drink.
28:12 g' large money unto the soldiers,
M'r 2:26 g' also to them which were with
5:13 forthwith Jesus g' them leave.
6: 7 and g' them power over unclean
28 a charger, and g' it to the damsel:
28 and the damsel g' it to her mother.
41 g' them to his disciples to set
8: 6 loaves and g' thanks, and brake,
6 and g' to his disciples to set before
11:28 who g' thee this authority to do
13:34 and g' authority to his servants,
14:22 brake it, and g' to them, and said,
23 had given thanks, he g' it to them:
15:23 And they g' him to drink wine
36 and g' him to drink, saying, Let
37 with a loud voice, and g' up the ghost,
39 so cried out, and g' up the ghost,
45 he g' the body to Joseph.
Lu 2:38 g' thanks likewise unto the Lord,
4:20 he g' it again to the minister, and
6: 4 g' also to them that were with him:
7:21 many that were blind he g' sight.
9: 1 g' them power and authority over
16 g' to the disciples to set before the
10:35 two pence, and g' them to the host,
15:16 and no man g' unto him.
18:43 they saw it, g' praise unto God.
20: 2 who is he that g' thee this authority?
22:17 g' thanks, and said, Take this,
19 and g' thanks, and brake it,
19 and g' unto them, saying, This is
23:24 Pilate g' sentence that it should be
29 and the paps which never g' suck.
46 having said thus, he g' up the ghost.
24:30 blessed it, and brake and g' to them,
42 they g' him a piece of a broiled fish,
Joh 1:12 g' he power to become the sons
3:16 that he g' his only begotten Son,
4: 5 that Jacob g' to his son Joseph.
12 Father Jacob, which g' us the well,
6:31 g' them bread from heaven to eat.
32 Moses g' you not that bread from
7:22 Moses...g' unto you circumcision;
10:29 Father, which g' them me, is
12:49 he g' me a commandment, what I
13:26 the sop, he g' it to Judas Iscariot,
14:31 Father g' me commandment, even
18:14 Caiaphas was he, which g' counsel
19: 9 thou? But Jesus g' him no answer.
30 his head, and g' up the ghost.
38 and Pilate g' him leave. He came
Ac 1:26 they g' forth their lots; and the lot
2: 4 as the Spirit g' them utterance.
3: 5 he g' heed unto them, expecting to
4:33 g' the apostles witness of the
5: 5 fell down, and g' up the ghost:
7: 5 he g' him none inheritance in it,
8 g' him the covenant of circumcision:
10 g' him favour and wisdom in the
42 g' them up to worship the host of
8: 6 g' heed unto these things which
10 To whom they all g' heed, from the
9:41 he g' her his hand, and lifted her
10: 2 which g' much alms to the people,
11:17 God g' them the like gift as he did
12:22 And the people g' a shout, saying,
23 because he g' not God the glory:
23 eaten of worms, and g' up the ghost
13:20 after that he g' unto them judges
21 God g' unto them Saul the son of
22 to whom also he g' testimony, and
14: 3 which g' testimony unto the word
Ac 14:17 and g' us rain from heaven, and
15:12 g' audience to Barnabas and
24 we g' no such commandment:
22:22 g' him audience unto this word,
23:30 g' commandment to his accusers
26:10 I g' my voice against them.
27: 3 g' him liberty to go unto his
35 g' thanks to God in presence of them
Ro 1:24 Wherefore God also g' them up to
26 g' them up unto vile affections:
28 God g' them over to a reprobate
1Co 3: 5 even as the Lord g' to every man?
6 but God g' the increase.
2Co 8: 5 g' their own selves to the Lord,
Ga 1: 4 Who g' himself for our sins, that
2: 5 whom we g' place by subjection,
9 g' to me and Barnabas the right
20 loved me, and g' himself for me.
3:18 God g' it to Abraham by promise.
Eph 1:22 g' him to be the head over all
4: 8 captive, and g' gifts unto men.
11 he g' some, apostles; and some,
5:25 the church, and g' himself for it;
1Th 4: 2 we g' you by the Lord Jesus.
1Ti 2: 6 Who g' himself a ransom for all,
Tit 2:14 Who g' himself for us, that he might
Heb 7: 2 Abraham g' a tenth part of all;
4 Abraham g' the tenth of the spoils.
13 no man g' attendance at the altar,
11:22 g' commandment concerning his
12: 9 we g' them reverence: shall we not
Jas 5:18 the heaven g' rain, and the earth
1Pe 1:21 from the dead, and g' him glory;
1Jo 3:23 another as he g' us commandment.
5:10 the record that God g' of his Son.
Jude 3 when I g' all diligence to write
Re 1: 1 which God g' unto him, to shew
2:21 I g' her space to repent of her
11:13 and g' glory to the God of heaven.
13: 2 the dragon g' him his power,
4 which g' power unto the beast:
15: 7 g' unto the seven angels seven
20:13 sea g' up the dead which were in it;

gavest See also FORGAVEST.
Ge 3:12 woman whom thou g' to be with
1Ki 8:34 unto the land which thou g' unto
40 in the land which thou g' unto our
48 their land, which thou g' unto their
2Ch 6:25 the land which thou g' to them
31 in the land which thou g' unto our
38 toward their land, which thou g'
20: 7 and g' it to the seed of Abraham
Ne 9: 7 and g' him the name of Abraham;
13 g' them right judgments, and true
15 g' them bread from heaven for
20 g' also thy good spirit to instruct
20 and g' them water for their thirst.
22 thou g' them kingdoms and nations,
24 g' them into their hands, with their
27 g' them saviours, who saved them
30 therefore g' thou them into the hand
35 great goodness that thou g' them,
35 fat land which thou g' before them.
36 land that thou g' unto our fathers
Job 39:13 G' thou the goodly wings unto
Ps 21: 4 life of thee, and thou g' it him,
74:14 g' him to be meat to the people
Lu 7:44 g' me no water for my feet:
45 Thou g' me no kiss: but this woman
15:29 and yet thou never g' me a kid,
19:23 Wherefore then g' thou not my
Joh 17: 4 the work which thou g' me to do.
6 which thou g' me out of the world:
6 they were, and thou g' them me:
8 them the words which thou g' me:
12 those that thou g' me I have kept,
22 glory which thou g' me I have
18: 9 which thou g' me have I lost none.

gay
Jas 2: 3 the g' clothing, and say unto him,

Gaza (*ga'-zah*) See also AZZAH; GAZITES.
Ge 10:19 as thou comest to Gerar, unto G';
Jos 10:41 from Kadesh-barnea even unto G',
11:22 only in G', in Gath, and in Ashdod,
15:47 G' with her towns and her villages,
J'g 1:18 Also Judah took G' with the coast
6: 4 till thou come unto G', and left no
16: 1 Then went Samson to G', and saw
21 and brought him down to G', and
1Sa 6:17 for Ashdod one, for G' one, for
2Ki 18: 8 the Philistines, even unto G',
1Ch 7:28 unto G' and the towns thereof:
Jer 47: 1 before that Pharaoh smote G'.
5 is come upon G'; Ashkelon is cut
Am 1: 6 transgressions of G', and for four,
7 will send a fire on the wall of G',
Zep 2: 4 For G' shall be forsaken, and
Zec 9: 5 G' also shall see it, and be very
5 and the king shall perish from G',
Ac 8:26 down from Jerusalem unto G'.

Gazathites (*ga'-zath-ites*) See also GAZITES.
Jos 13: 3 lords of the Philistines; the G',

gaze See also GAZING.
Ex 19:21 break through unto the Lord to g',

Gazer (*ga'-zur*) See also GEZER.
2Sa 5:25 from Geba until thou come to G'.
1Ch 14:16 Philistines from Gibeon even to G'.

gazers See STARGAZERS.

Gazez (*ga'-zez*)
1Ch 2:46 Moza, and G': and Haran begat G'.

gazing See also GAZINGSTOCK.
Ac 1:11 why stand ye g' up into heaven?

gazingstock
Na 3: 6 and will set thee as a g·.
Heb 10:33 whilst ye were made a g· both by
Gazites *(ga'-zites)* See also GAZATHITES.
J'g 16: 2 it was told the G·, saying, Samson
Gazzam *(gaz'-zam)*
Ezr 2:48 of Nekoda, the children of G·,
Ne 7:51 The children of G·, the children of
Geba *(ghe'-bah)* See also GABA; GIBEAH; GIBEON.
Jos 21:17 her suburbs, G· with her suburbs,
1Sa 13: 3 of the Philistines that was in G·,
2Sa 5:25 Philistines from G· until thou come
1Ki 15:22 built with them G· of Benjamin,
2Ki 23: 8 incense, from G· to Beer-sheba, and
1Ch 6:60 Benjamin; G· with her suburbs,
8: 6 fathers of the inhabitants of G·,
2Ch 16: 6 he built therewith G· and Mizpah.
Ne 11:31 of Benjamin from G· dwelt at
12:29 Gilgal, and out of the fields of G·
Isa 10:29 have taken up their lodging at G·;
Zec 14:10 turned as a plain from G· to
Gebal *(ghe'-bal)* See also GIBLITES.
Ps 83: 7 G·, and Ammon, and Amalek; the
Eze 27: 9 The ancients of G· and the wise
Geber See also EZION-GEBER.
1Ki 4: 13 The son of G·, in Ramoth-gilead;
19 G· the son Uri was in the country
Gebim *(ghe'-bim)*
Isa 10:31 the inhabitants of G· gather
Gedaliah *(ghed-a-li'-ah)*
2Ki 25:22 G· the son of Ahikam, the son of
23 G· governor, there came to G· to
24 G· sware to them, and to their men,
25 smote G·, that he died, and the
1Ch 25: 3 sons of Jeduthun; G·, and Zeri,
9 the second to G·, who with his
Ezr 10:18 and Eliezer, and Jarib, and G·.
Jer 38: 1 G· the son of Pashur, and Jucal the
39:14 committed him unto G· the son of
40: 5 Go back to G· the son of Ahikam
6 G· the son of Ahikam to Mizpah;
7 had made G· the son of Ahikam
8 came to G· to Mizpah, even Ishmael
9 And G· the son of Ahikam the son
11 over them G· the son of Ahikam
12 Judah, to G·, unto Mizpah, and
13 that were in the fields, came to G·
14 But G· the son of Ahikam believed
15 spake to G· in Mizpah secretly,
16 G· the son of Ahikam said unto
41: 1 ten men with him, came unto G· the
2 smote G· the son of Ahikam the
3 even with G·, at Mizpah, and the
4 second day after he had slain G·,
6 unto them, Come to G· the son of
9 had slain because of G·, was it
10 committed to G· the son of Ahikam
16 slain G· the son of Ahikam, even
18 of Nehemiah had slain G· the son of
43: 6 guard had left with G· the son of
Zep 1: 1 Cushi, the son of G·, the son of
Gedeon *(ghed'-e-on)* See also GIDEON.
Heb 11:32 time would fail me to tell of G·,
Geder *(ghe'-dur)* See also BETH-GADER; GEDERITE; GEDOR.
Jos 12:13 Debir, one; the king of G·, one;
Gederah *(ghed'-e-rah)* See also GEDERATHITE.
Jos 15:36 and Adithaim, and G·, and
Gederathite *(ghed'-e-rath-ite)*
1Ch 12: 4 Johanan, and Josabad the G·,
Gederite *(ghed'-e-rite)*
1Ch 27:28 low plains was Baal-hanan the G·:
Gederoth *(ghed'-e-roth)*
Jos 15:41 And G·, Beth-dagon, and Naamah,
2Ch 28:18 Ajalon, and G·, and Shocho with the
Gederothaim *(ghed-e-ro-tha'-im)*
Jos 15:36 Adithaim, and Gederah, and G·;
Gedi See EN-GEDI.
Gedor *(ghe'-dor)* See also GEDER.
Jos 15:58 Halhul, Beth-zur, and G·,
1Ch 4: 4 Penuel the father of G·, Ezer the
18 Jered the father of G·, and Heber
39 entrance of G·, even unto the east
8:31 And G·, and Ahio, and Zacher.
9:37 G·, and Ahio, and Zechariah, and
12: 7 the sons of Jeroham of G·.
Gehazi *(ghe-ha'-zi)*
2Ki 4:12 said to G· his servant, Call this
14 G· answered, Verily she hath no
25 to G· his servant, Behold, yonder is
27 G· came near to thrust her away.
29 said to G·, Gird up thy loins, and
31 And G· passed on before them,
36 And he called G·, and said, Call
5:20 But G·, the servant of Elisha the
21 So G· followed after Naaman.
25 Whence comest thou, G·? And he
8: 4 G· the servant of the man of God,
5 G· said, My lord, O king, this is the
Geliloth *(ghel'-il-oth)*
Jos 18:17 went forth toward G·, which is
Gemalli *(ghe-mal'-li)*
Nu 13:12 of Dan, Ammiel the son of G·.
Gemariah *(ghem-a-ri'-ah)*
Jer 29: 3 and G· the son of Hilkiah, (whom
36:10 in the chamber of G· the son of
11 Michaiah the son of G·, the son of
12 Elnathan the son of Achbor, and G·
25 Elnathan and Delaiah and G· had

gender See also GENDERED; GENDERETH.
Le 19:19 Thou shalt not let thy cattle g·
2Ti 2:23 knowing that they do g· strifes.
gendered
Job 38:29 frost of heaven, who hath g· it?
gendereth
Job 21:10 Their bull g·, and faileth not;
Ga 4:24 g· to bondage, which is Agar.
genealogies
1Ch 5:17 All these were reckoned by g· in
7: 5 reckoned in all by their g·
7 and were reckoned by their g·
9: 1 all Israel were reckoned by g·;
2Ch 12:15 and of Iddo the seer concerning g·?
31:19 to all that were reckoned by g·
1Ti 1: 4 give heed to fables and endless g·,
Tit 3: 9 But avoid foolish questions, and g·,
genealogy See also GENEALOGIES.
1Ch 4:33 their habitations, and their g·.
5: 1 and the g· is not to be reckoned
7 when the g· of their generations
7: 9 after their g· by their generations,
40 throughout the g· of them that
9:22 These were reckoned by their g· in
2Ch 31:16 Beside their g· of males, from three
17 the g· of the priests by the house
18 And to the g· of all their little ones,
Ezr 2:62 those that were reckoned by g·,
8: 1 and this is the g· of them that went
3 were reckoned by g· of the males
Ne 7: 5 that they might be reckoned by g·.
5 And I found a register of the g. of
64 those that were reckoned by g·,
general^
1Ch 27:34 and the g· of the king's army
Heb 12:23 To the g· assembly and church of
generally
2Sa 17:11 that all Israel be g· gathered
Jer 48:38 There shall be lamentation g·
generation See also GENERATIONS.
Ge 7: 1 righteous before me in this g·.
15:16 But in the fourth g· they shall come
50:23 Ephraim's children of the third g·:
Ex 1: 6 and all his brethren, and all that g·.
17:16 war with Amalek from g· to g·.
20: 5 unto the third and fourth g· of them
34: 7 unto the third and to the fourth g·.
Nu 14:18 children unto the third and fourth g·.
32:13 until all the g·, that had done evil
De 1:35 one of these men of this evil g·
2:14 all the g· of the men of war
5: 9 unto the third and fourth g· of them
23: 2 even to his tenth g· shall he not
3 even to their tenth g· shall they not
8 of the Lord in their third g·.
29:22 So that the g· to come of your
32: 5 they are a perverse and crooked g·.
20 for they are a very froward g·,
J'g 2:10 also all that g· were gathered unto
10 there arose another g· after them,
2Ki 10:30 thy children of the fourth g· shall sit
15:12 throne of Israel unto the fourth g·.
Es 9:28 kept throughout every g·, every
Ps 12: 7 preserve them from this g· for ever.
14: 5 God is in the g· of the righteous.
22:30 be accounted to the Lord for a g·.
24: 6 is the g· of them that seek him,
48:13 ye may tell it to the g· following.
49:19 He shall go to the g· of his fathers;
71:18 shewed thy strength unto this g·,
73:15 against the g· of thy children.
78: 4 shewing to the g· to come the
6 That the g· to come might know
8 a stubborn and rebellious g·;
8 a g· that set not their heart aright,
95:10 long was I grieved with this g·,
102:18 shall be written for the g· to come:
109:13 in the g· following let their name
112: 2 g· of the upright shall be blessed.
145: 4 One g· shall praise thy works to
Pr 27:24 doth the crown endure to every g·?
30:11 is a g· that curseth their father,
12 a g· that are pure in their own eyes,
13 is a g·, O how lofty are their eyes!
14 is a g·, whose teeth are as swords,
Ec 1: 4 One g· passeth away, and another g·
Isa 13:20 it shall be dwelt in from g· to g·:
34:10 from g· to g· it shall lie waste;
17 from g· to g· shall they dwell therein.
51: 8 my salvation from g· to g·.
53: 8 and who shall declare his g·? for he
Jer 2:31 O g·, see ye the word of the Lord.
7:29 and forsaken the g· of his wrath.
50:39 shall it be dwelt in from g· to g·.
La 5:19 thy throne from g· to g·.
Da 4: 3 his dominion is from g· to g·.
34 his kingdom is from g· to g·:
Joe 1: 3 and their children another g·.
3:20 and Jerusalem from g· to g·.
M't 1: 1 the book of the g· of Jesus Christ,
3: 7 O g· of vipers, who hath warned
11:16 whereunto shall I liken this g·?
12:34 O g· of vipers, how can ye,
39 An evil and adulterous g· seeketh
41 shall rise in judgment with this g·,
42 rise up in the judgment with this g·,
45 shall it be also unto this wicked g·.
16: 4 wicked and adulterous g· seeketh
17:17 O faithless and perverse g·, how
23:33 Ye serpents, ye g· of vipers, how
36 things shall come upon this g·.
24:34 This g· shall not pass, till all these

M'r 8:12 Why doth this g· seek after a sign?
12 shall no sign be given unto this g·.
38 in this adulterous and sinful g·;
9:19 O faithless g·, how long shall I be
13:30 that this g· shall not pass, till all
Lu 1:50 on them that fear him from g· to g·.
3: 7 O g· of vipers, who hath warned
7:31 shall I liken the men of this g·?
9:41 O faithless and perverse g·, how
11:29 he began to say, This is an evil g·:
30 also the Son of man be to this g·.
31 the men of this g·, and condemn
32 with this g·, and shall condemn it:
50 may be required of this g·;
51 It shall be required of this g·.
16: 8 in their g· wiser than the children
17:25 and be rejected of this g·.
21:32 This g· shall not pass away, till
Ac 2:40 yourselves from this untoward g·.
8:33 who shall declare his g·? for his
13:36 had served his own g· by the
Heb 3:10 I was grieved with that g·,
1Pe 2: 9 a chosen g·, a royal priesthood,
generations
Ge 2: 4 These are the g· of the heavens
5: 1 This is the book of the g· of Adam.
6: 9 These are the g· of Noah: Noah was
9 a just man and perfect in his g·,
9:12 is with you, for perpetual g·:
10: 1 These are the g· of the sons of
32 after their g·, in their nations:
11:10 These are the g· of Shem: Shem was
27 Now these are the g· of Terah:
17: 7 thy seed after thee in their g· for
9 and thy seed after thee in their g·.
12 every man child in your g·, he that
25:12 Now these are the g· of Ishmael,
13 their names, according to their g·:
19 And these are the g· of Isaac,
36: 1 Now these are the g· of Esau, who
9 And these are the g· of Esau the
37: 2 These are the g· of Jacob.
Ex 3:15 this is my memorial unto all g·.
6:16 sons of Levi according to their g·;
19 families of Levi according to their g·.
12:14 throughout your g·; ye shall keep
17 ye observe this day in your g·
42 the children of Israel in their g·.
16:32 to be kept for your g·; that they
33 the Lord, to be kept for your g·.
27:21 a statute for ever unto their g·
29:42 burnt offering throughout your g·
30: 8 before the Lord throughout your g·.
10 upon it throughout your g·:
21 to his seed throughout their g·.
31 oil unto me throughout your g·.
31:13 me and you throughout your g·;
16 the sabbath throughout their g·,
40:15 priesthood throughout their g·.
Le 3:17 perpetual statute for your g·
6:18 a statute for ever in your g·
7:36 for ever throughout their g·.
10: 9 for ever throughout your g·:
17: 7 unto them throughout their g·.
21:17 he be of thy seed in their g·
22: 3 all your seed among your g·,
23:14 for ever throughout your g· in all
21 your dwellings throughout your g·.
31 for ever throughout your g·
41 a statute for ever in your g·:
43 That your g· may know that I
24: 3 a statute for ever in your g·.
25:30 that bought it throughout his g·:
Nu 1:20 Israel's eldest son, by their g·,
22 children of Simeon, by their g·, after
24 children of Gad, by their g·, after
26 children of Judah, by their g·, after
28 children of Assachar, by their g·,
30 children of Zebulun, by their g·,
32 children of Joseph, by their g·, by
34 children of Manasseh, by their g·,
36 children of Benjamin, by their g·,
38 children of Dan, by their g·, after
40 children of Asher, by their g·, after
42 Naphtali, throughout their g·, after
3: 1 These also are the g· of Aaron
10: 8 for ever throughout your g·.
15:14 be among you in your g·,
15 an ordinance for ever in your g·:
21 Lord an heave offering in your g·.
23 and henceforward among your g·;
38 garments throughout their g·,
18:23 for ever throughout your g·,
35:29 throughout your g· in all your
De 7: 9 commandments to a thousand g·;
32: 7 consider the years of many g·:
Jos 22:27 us, and you, and our g· after us,
28 to us or to our g· in time to come,
J'g 3: 2 Only that the g· of the children
Ru 4:18 Now these are the g· of Pharez:
1Ch 1:29 These are their g·: The firstborn
5: 7 genealogy of their g· was reckoned,
7: 2 valiant men of might in their g·;
4 And with them, by their g·, after
9 after their genealogy by their g·,
8:28 the fathers, by their g·, chief men.
9: 9 brethren, according to their g·,
34 were chief throughout their g·;
16:15 he commanded to a thousand g·;
26:31 according to the g· of his fathers.
Job 42:16 and his sons' sons, even four g·.
Ps 33:11 the thoughts of his heart to all g·.
45:17 name to be remembered in all g·:
49:11 and their dwelling places to all g·;
61: 6 and his years as many g·.
72: 5 moon endure, throughout all g·.

Ps 79:13 will shew forth thy praise to all g'.
85: 5 draw out thine anger to all g'?
89: 1 known thy faithfulness to all g'.
4 and build up thy throne to all g'.
90: 1 been our dwelling place in all g'.
100: 5 and his truth endureth to all g'.
102:12 and thy remembrance unto all g'.
24 thy years are throughout all g'.
105: 8 he commanded to a thousand g'.
106:31 him for righteousness unto all g'
119:90 Thy faithfulness is unto all g':
135:13 memorial, O Lord, throughout all g'.
145:13 endureth throughout all g'.
146:10 thy God, O Zion, unto all g'.
Isa 41: 4 calling the g' from the beginning?
51: 9 in the ancient days, in the g' of old.
58:12 up the foundations of many g';
60:15 excellency, a joy of many g'.
61: 4 cities, the desolations of many g'.
Joe 2: 2 even to the years of many g'.
M't 1:17 So all the g' from Abraham to
17 Abraham to David are fourteen g';
17 away into Babylon are fourteen g';
17 Babylon unto Christ are fourteen g'.
Lu 1:48 all g' shall call me blessed.
Col 1:26 hid from ages and from g',

Gennesaret (*ghen-nes'-a-ret*) See also CHINNERETH.
M't 14:34 they came into the land of G'.
M'r 6:53 into the land of G', and drew to
Lu 5: 1 he stood by the lake of G',

Gentile (*jen'-tile*) See also GENTILES.
Ro 2: 9 the Jew first, and also of the G';
10 the Jew first, and also to the G':

Gentiles (*jen'-tiles*)
Ge 10: 5 By these were the isles of the G'
J'g 4: 2 dwelt in Harosheth of the G'.
13 from Harosheth of the G' unto the
16 the host, unto Harosheth of the G':
Isa 11:10 to it shall the G' seek: and his
42: 1 bring forth judgment to the G'.
6 of the people, for a light of the G';
49: 6 give thee for a light to the G',
22 I will lift up mine hand to the G',
54: 3 and thy seed shall inherit the G',
60: 3 the G' shall come to thy light,
5 the forces of the G' shall come
11 unto thee the forces of the G',
16 shalt also suck the milk of the G',
61: 6 ye shall eat the riches of the G',
9 shall be known among the G',
62: 2 G' shall see thy righteousness,
66:12 of the G' like a flowing stream:
19 declare my glory among the G'.
Jer 4: 7 destroyer of the G' is on his way;
14:22 among the vanities of the G'
16:19 the G' shall come unto thee
46: 1 the prophet against the G';
La 2: 9 her princes are among the G':
Eze 4:13 their defiled bread among the G',
Ho 8: 8 shall they be among the G' as a
Joe 3: 9 Proclaim ye this among the G';
Mic 5: 8 of Jacob shall be among the G'
Zec 1:21 to cast out the horns of the G',
Mal 1:11 name shall be great among the G';
M't 4:15 beyond Jordan, Galilee of the G';
6:32 all these things do the G' seek:)
10: 5 Go not into the way of the G',
18 testimony against them and the G'.
12:18 he shall shew judgment to the G'.
21 in his name shall the G' trust.
20:19 they shall deliver him to the G'
25 the princes of the G' exercise
M'r 10:33 and shall deliver him to the G':
42 are accounted to rule over the G'
Lu 2:32 A light to lighten the G', and the
18:32 he shall be delivered unto the G',
21:24 shall be trodden down of the G',
24 the times of the G' be fulfilled.
22:25 kings of the G' exercise lordship
Joh 7:35 the dispersed among the G',
35 and teach the G'?
Ac 4:27 the G', and the people of Israel,
7:45 into the possession of the G',
9:15 to bear my name before the G',
10:45 on the G' also was poured out
11: 1 the G' had also received the word
18 hath God also to the G' granted
13:42 the G' besought that these words
46 lo, we turn to the G'.
47 set thee to be a light of the G',
48 the G' heard this, they were glad,
14: 2 Jews stirred up the G',
5 of the G', and also of the Jews
27 the door of faith unto the G'.
15: 3 declaring the conversion of the G':
7 the G' by my mouth should hear
12 wrought among the G' by them.
14 did visit the G', to take out of them
17 all the G', upon whom my name
19 from among the G' are turned
23 the brethren which are of the G'
18: 6 henceforth I will go unto the G'.
21:11 him into the hands of the G'.
19 God had wrought among the G'
21 the Jews which are among the G'
25 As touching the G' which believe,
22:21 send thee far hence unto the G'.
26:17 from the people, and from the G',
20 to the G', that they should repent
23 light unto the people, and to the G'.
28:28 salvation of God is sent unto the G',
Ro 1:13 you also, even as among other G'.
2:14 the G', which have not the law,
24 God is blasphemed among the G'
3: 9 before proved both Jews and G',
29 of the G'? Yes, of the G' also:
9:24 the Jews only, but also of the G'?
30 That the G', which followed not
11:11 salvation is come unto the G',
12 of them the riches of the G';
13 For I speak to you G', inasmuch as
13 I am the apostle of the G',
25 until the fulness of the G' be come
15: 9 And that the G' might glorify God
9 I will confess to thee among the G',
10 he saith, Rejoice, ye G', with his
11 Praise the Lord, all ye G'; and
12 shall rise to reign over the G';
12 in him shall the G' trust.
16 minister of Jesus Christ to the G',
16 the offering up of the G' might be
18 to make the G' obedient, by word
27 if the G' have been made partakers
16: 4 but also all the churches of the G'.
1Co 5: 1 so much as named among the G',
10:20 the things which the G' sacrifice,
32 neither to the Jews, nor to the G',
12: 2 Ye know that ye were G', carried
13 whether we be Jews or G',
Ga 2: 2 which I preach among the G',
8 was mighty in me toward the G':)
12 he did eat with the G': but when
14 livest after the manner of G',
14 the G' to live as do the Jews?
15 nature, and not sinners of the G',
3:14 come on the G' through Jesus
Eph 2:11 being in time past G' in the flesh,
3: 1 prisoner of Jesus Christ for you G',
6 That the G' should be fellowheirs,
8 that I should preach among the G'
4:17 walk not as other G' walk, in the
Col 1:27 of this mystery among the G';
1Th 2:16 Forbidding us to speak to the G'
4: 5 as the G' which know not God:
1Ti 2: 7 a teacher of the G' in faith and
3:16 preached unto the G', believed
2Ti 1:11 apostle, and a teacher of the G'.
4:17 and that all the G' might hear:
1Pe 2:12 conversation honest among the G':
4: 3 to have wrought the will of the G',
3Jo 7 forth, taking nothing of the G'.
Re 11: 2 for it is given unto the G':

gentle
1Th 2: 7 But we were g' among you, even
2Ti 2:24 not strive; but be g' unto all men,
Tit 3: 2 to be no brawlers, but g', shewing
Jas 3:17 g', and easy to be intreated,
1Pe 2:18 not only to the good and g', but also

gentleness
2Sa 22:36 and thy g' hath made me great.
Ps 18:35 and thy g' hath made me great.
2Co 10: 1 by the meekness and g' of Christ,
Ga 5:22 longsuffering, g', goodness, faith,

gently
2Sa 18: 5 Deal g' for my sake with the
Isa 40:11 g' lead those that are with young.

Genubath (*ghen'-u-bath*)
1Ki 11:20 Tahpenes bare him G' his son,
20 and G' was in Pharaoh's household

Gera (*ghe'-rah*)
Ge 46:21 and Becher, and Ashbel, G', and
J'g 3:15 Ehud the son of G', a Benjamite,
2Sa 16: 5 name was Shimei, the son of G':
19:16 Shimei the son of G', a Benjamite,
18 Shimei the son of G' fell down
1Ki 2: 8 hast with thee Shimei the son of G',
1Ch 8: 3 Addar, and G', and Abihud,
5 G', and Shephuphan, and Huram.
7 Ahiah, and G', he removed them,

gerahs (*ghe'-rahs*)
Ex 30:13 shekel is twenty g':) an half shekel
Le 27:25 twenty g' shall be the shekel.
Nu 3:47 take them: (the shekel is twenty g':)
18:16 the sanctuary, which is twenty g'.
Eze 45:12 the shekel shall be twenty g':

Gerar (*ghe'-rar*)
Ge 10:19 as thou comest to G', unto Gaza;
20: 1 and Shur, and sojourned in G'.
2 and Abimelech king of G' sent,
26: 1 king of the Philistines unto G'.
6 And Isaac dwelt in G':
17 pitched his tent in the valley of G',
20 herdmen of G' did strive with
26 Abimelech went to him from G',
2Ch 14:13 with him pursued them unto G':
14 smote all the cities round about G';

Gergesenes (*ghur''-ghes-enes'*)
M't 8:28 side into the country of the G',

Gerizim (*gher'-iz-im*)
De 11:29 put the blessing upon mount G',
27:12 upon mount G' to bless the people,
Jos 8:33 against mount G', and half of them
J'g 9: 7 in the top of mount G', and lifted

Gershom (*ghur'-shom*) See also GERSHON.
Ex 2:22 son, and he called his name G':
18: 3 which the name of the one was G';
J'g 18:30 and Jonathan, the son of G', the
1Ch 6:16 The sons of Levi; G', Kohath, and
17 the sons of G'; Libni, and Shimei.
20 G'; Libni his son, Jahath his son,
43 The son of Jahath, the son of G',
62 of G' throughout their families
71 the sons of G' were given out of
15: 7 Of the sons of G'; Joel the chief,
23:15 sons of Moses were, G', and Eliezer.
16 sons of G', Shebuel was the chief.
1Ch 26:24 And Shebuel the son of G', the son
Ezr 8: 2 Of the sons of Phinehas; G': of the

Gershon (*ghur'-shon*) See also GERSHOM; GERSHONITE.
Ge 46:11 sons of Levi; G', Kohath, and
Ex 6:16 G', and Kohath, and Merari: and
17 sons of G', Libni, and Shimi,
Nu 3:17 by their names; G', and Kohath,
18 the sons of G' by their families;
21 Of G was the family of the Libnites,
25 charge of the sons of G' in the
4:22 sum of the sons of G', throughout
28 the sons of G' in the tabernacle
38 were numbered of the sons of G',
41 of the families of the sons of G',
7: 7 oxen he gave unto the sons of G',
10:17 sons of G' and the sons of Merari
26:57 G', the family of the Gershonites:
Jos 21: 6 G' had by lot out of the families
27 unto the children of G', of the
1Ch 6: 1 The sons of Levi; G', Kohath, and
23: 6 sons of Levi, namely G', Kohath,

Gershonite (*ghur'-shon-ite*) See also GERSHONITES.
1Ch 26:21 the sons of the G' Laadam, chief
21 even of Laadan the G', were
29: 8 Lord, by the hand of Jehiel the G'.

Gershonites (*ghur'-shon-ites*)
Nu 3:21 these are the families of the G'.
23 The families of the G' shall pitch
3:24 father of the G' shall be Eliasaph
4:24 service of the families of the G',
27 service of the sons of the G', in all
26:57 of Gershon, the family of the G':
Jos 21:33 the cities of the G' according to
1Ch 23: 7 Of the G' were, Laadan, and
2Ch 29:12 and of the G'; Joah the son of

Gesham (*ghe'-sham*)
1Ch 2:47 Regem, and Jotham, and G', and

Geshem (*ghe'-shem*) See also GASHMU.
Ne 2:19 and G' the Arabian, heard it,
6: 1 Tobiah, and G' the Arabian, and
2 Sanballat and G' sent unto me,

Geshur (*ghe'-shur*) See also GESHURITES.
2Sa 3: 3 the daughter of Talmai king of G';
13:37 the son of Ammihud, king of G'.
38 Absalom fled, and went to G',
14:23 Joab arose and went to G', and
32 Wherefore am I come from G'?
15: 8 vow while I abode at G' in Syria,
1Ch 2:23 And he took G', and Aram, with
3: 2 daughter of Talmai king of G':

Geshuri (*ghesh'-u-ri*) See also GESHURITES.
De 3:14 the coasts of G' and Maachathi;
Jos 13: 2 of the Philistines, and all G',

Geshurites (*ghesh'-u-rites*)
Jos 12: 5 of the G' and the Maachathites,
13:11 border of the G' and Maachathites,
13 Israel expelled not the G', nor the
13 the G' and the Maachathites dwell
1Sa 27: 8 invaded the G', and the Gezrites,

get See also BEGET; FORGET; GAT; GETTETH; GETTING; GOT.
Ge 12: 1 G' thee out of thy county, and
19:14 said, Up, g' you out of this place;
22: 2 g' thee into the land of Moriah;
31:13 g' thee out from this land, and
34: 4 saying, G' me this damsel to wife.
10 therein, and g' you possessions therein.
42: 2 g' you down thither, and buy for
44:17 g' you up in peace unto your
45:17 g' you unto the land of Canaan;
Ex 1:10 and so g' them up out of the land.
5: 4 g' you unto your burdens.
11 g' you straw where ye can find it:
7:15 G' thee unto Pharaoh in the
10:28 G' thee from me, take heed to
11: 8 G' thee out, and all the people
12:31 g' you forth from among my people,
14:17 I will g' me honour upon Pharaoh,
19:24 Away, g' thee down, and thou
32: 7 Go, g' thee down; for thy people,
Le 14:21 he be poor, and cannot g' so much;
22 such as he is able to g';
30 young pigeons, such as he can g';
31 Even such as he is able to g',
32 whose hand is not able to g' that
Nu 6:21 that that his hand shall g':
13:17 G' you up this way southward,
14:25 and g' you into the wilderness by
16:24 G' you up from about the
45 G' you up from among this
22:13 G' you into your land: for the
34 I will g' me back again.
27:12 G' thee up into this mount
De 2:13 and g' you over the brook Zered.
3:27 G' thee up into the top of Pisgah,
5:30 G' you into your tents again.
8:18 that giveth the power to g' wealth,
9:12 g' thee down quickly from hence;
17: 8 and get thee up into the place
28:43 is within thee shall g' up above
32:49 G' thee up into this mountain
Jos 2:16 G' you to the mountain, lest the
7:10 G' thee up; wherefore liest thou
17:15 g' thee up to the wood country,
22: 4 and g' you unto your tents, and
J'g 7: 9 Arise, g' thee down unto the host;
14: 2 therefore g' her for me to wife.
3 G' her for me; for she pleaseth me
19: 9 to morrow g' you early on your way,
Ru 3: 3 and g' thee down to the floor:
1Sa 9:13 Now therefore g' you up; for
15: 6 g' you down from among the

1Sa 20:29 let me g' away, I pray thee, and
22: 5 and g' thee into the land of Judah.
23:26 David made haste to g' away for
25: 5 G' you up to Carmel, and go to
2Sa 20: 6 lest he g' him fenced cities, and
1Ki 1: 2 that my lord the king may g' heat.
13 Go and g' thee in unto king David,
2:26 G' thee to Anathoth, unto thine
12:18 Rehoboam made speed to g' him
14: 2 g' thee to Shiloh: behold, there is
12 Arise thou therefore, g' thee to
17: 3 G' thee hence, and turn the
9 Arise, g' thee to Zarephath, which
18:41 G' thee up, eat and drink; for
44 Prepare thy chariot, and g' thee
2Ki 3:13 g' thee to the prophets of thy
7:12 shall catch them alive, and g' into
2Ch 10:18 Rehoboam made speed to g' him
Ne 9:10 So didst thou g' thee a name, as it
Ps 119:104 thy precepts I g' understanding:
Pr 4: 5 G' wisdom, g' understanding:
7 therefore g' wisdom: and with all
7 thy getting g' understanding.
6:33 wound and dishonour shall he g';
16:16 better is it to g' wisdom than gold!
16 to g' understanding rather to be
17:16 the hand of a fool to g' wisdom,
22:25 learn his ways, and g' a snare to
Ec 3: 6 A time to g', and a time to lose;
Ca 4: 6 I will g' me to the mountain of
7:12 Let us g' up early to the vineyards;
Isa 22:15 Go, g' thee unto this treasurer,
30:11 G' you out of the way, turn aside
22 shalt say unto it, G' thee hence.
40: 9 g' thee up into the high mountain;
47: 5 g' thee into darkness, O daughter
Jer 5: 5 I will g' me unto the great men,
13: 1 Go and g' thee a linen girdle,
19: 1 and g' a potter's earthen bottle,
46: 4 g' up, ye horsemen, and stand
48: 9 that it may flee and g' away: for
49:30 Flee, g' you far off, dwell deep,
31 Arise, g' you up unto the wealthy
La 3: 7 me about, that I cannot g' out:
Eze 3: 4 go, g' thee unto the house of Israel,
11 go, g' thee to them of the captivity,
11:15 G' you far from the Lord: unto us
22:27 to destroy souls, to g' dishonest
Da 4:14 let the beasts g' away from under
Joe 3:13 come, g' you down; for the press
Zep 3:19 and I will g' them praise and
Zec 6: 7 G' you hence, walk to and fro
M't 4:10 G' thee hence, Satan: for it is
14:22 his disciples to g' into a ship,
16:23 unto Peter, G' thee behind me,
M'r 6:45 his disciples to g' into the ship,
8:33 G' thee behind me, Satan: for
Lu 4: 8 G' thee behind me, Satan: for it
9:12 and lodge, and g' victuals: for we
13:31 G' thee out, and depart hence:
Ac 7: 3 G' thee out of thy country, and
10:20 g' thee down, and go with them,
22:18 g' thee quickly out of Jerusalem:
27:43 first into the sea, and g' to land:
2Co 2:11 Lest Satan should g' an advantage
Jas 4:13 and buy and sell, and g' gain:

Gether (*ghe'-ther*)
Ge 10:23 of Aram; Uz, and Hul, and G',
1Ch 1:17 Aram, and Uz, and Hul, and G'.

Gethsemane (*gheth-sem'-a-ne*)
M't 26:36 with them unto a place called G',
M'r 14:32 to a place which was named G':

getteth See also BEGETTETH; FORGETTETH.
2Sa 5: 8 Whosoever g' up to the gutter,
Pr 3:13 the man that g' understanding.
9: 7 a scorner g' to himself shame:
7 rebuketh a wicked man g' himself a
15:32 heareth reproof g' understanding.
18:15 heart of the prudent g' knowledge;
19: 8 He that g' wisdom loveth his own
Jer 17:11 he that g' riches, and not by right,
48:44 and he that g' up out of the pit

getting See also FORGETTING.
Ge 31:18 the cattle of his g', which he had
Pr 4: 7 with all thy g' get understanding.
21: 6 g' of treasures by a lying tongue

Geuel (*ghe-u'-el*)
Nu 13:15 Of the tribe of Gad, G' the son of

Gezer (*ghe'-zur*) See also GAZER; GEZRITES.
Jos 10:33 Horam king of G' came up to
12:12 Eglon, one; the king of G', one;
16: 3 Beth-horon the nether, and to G':
10 Canaanites that dwelt in G': but
21:21 of refuge for the slayer; and G'
J'g 1:29 G'; but the Canaanites dwelt in G'
1Ki 9:15 and Hazor, and Megiddo, and G'.
16 gone up, and taken G', and burnt
17 Solomon built G', and Beth-horon
1Ch 6:67 they gave also G' with her suburbs,
7:28 eastward Naaran, and westward G',
20: 4 a war at G' with the Philistines;

Gezrites (*ghez'-rites*)
1Sa 27: 8 Geshurites, and the G', and the

ghost [or GHOST]
Ge 25: 8 Then Abraham gave up the g',
17 and he gave up the g' and died;
35:29 And Isaac gave up the g', and died,
49:33 and yielded up the g', and was
Job 3:11 why did I not give up the g' when
10:18 Oh that I had given up the g',
11:20 shall be as the giving up of the g'
13:19 tongue, I shall give up the g'.
14:10 yea, man giveth up the g', and
Jer 15: 9 she hath given up the g'; her sun
La 1:19 mine elders gave up the g' in the
M't 1:18 found with child of the Holy G'.
20 in her is of the Holy G'.
3:11 with the Holy G', and with fire:
12:31 blasphemy against the Holy G'
32 speaketh against the Holy G',
27:50 yielded up the g'.
28:19 of the Son, and of the Holy G':
M'r 1: 8 baptize you with the Holy G'.
3:29 blaspheme against the Holy G'
12:36 himself said by the Holy G',
13:11 ye that speak, but the Holy G'.
15:37 a loud voice, and gave up the g'.
39 so cried out, and gave up the g',
Lu 1:15 be filled with the Holy G',
35 Holy G' shall come upon thee,
41 was filled with the Holy G':
67 was filled with the Holy G',
2:25 and the Holy G' was upon him,
26 unto him by the Holy G',
3:16 baptize you with the Holy G'
22 And the Holy G' descended in
4: 1 Jesus being full of the Holy G'
12:10 against the Holy G'
12 For the Holy G' shall teach
23:46 said thus, he gave up the g'.
Joh 1:33 baptizeth with the Holy G'.
7:39 for the Holy G' was not yet
14:26 Holy G', whom the Father
19:30 his head, and gave up the g'.
20:22 them, Receive ye the Holy G':
Ac 1: 2 he through the Holy G' had
5 be baptized with the Holy G'
8 after that the Holy G' is come
16 which the Holy G' by the mouth
2: 4 were all filled with the Holy G',
33 the promise of the Holy G',
38 receive the gift of the Holy G'.
4: 8 Peter, filled with the Holy G',
31 were all filled with the Holy G',
5: 3 to lie to the Holy G', and to keep
5 fell down, and gave up the g':
10 at his feet and yielded up the g':
32 and so is also the Holy G',
6: 3 full of the Holy G' and wisdom,
5 of faith and of the Holy G',
7:51 do always resist the Holy G':
55 he, being full of the Holy G',
8:15 they might receive the Holy G':
17 they received the Holy G'.
18 Holy G' was given, he offered
19 he may receive the Holy G'.
9:17 and be filled with the Holy G'.
31 in the comfort of the Holy G',
10:38 the Holy G' and with power:
44 the Holy G' fell on all them
45 out the gift of the Holy G'.
47 have received the Holy G' as
11:15 the Holy G' fell on them, as on
16 be baptized with the Holy G'.
24 man, and full of the Holy G'
12:23 of worms and gave up the g'.
13: 2 the Holy G' said, Separate me
4 being sent forth by the Holy G',
9 Paul,) filled with the Holy G',
52 with joy, and with the Holy G'.
15: 8 giving them the Holy G', even
28 it seemed good to the Holy G',
16: 6 were forbidden of the Holy G'
19: 2 Have ye received the Holy G'
2 whether there be any Holy G'.
6 the Holy G' came on them; and
20:23 that the Holy G' witnesseth
28 Holy G' hath made you overseers,
21:11 Thus saith the Holy G', So
28:25 spake the Holy G' by Esaias
Ro 5: 5 by the Holy G' which is given
9: 1 me witness in the Holy G',
14:17 peace, and joy in the Holy G'.
15:13 the power of the Holy G'.
16 being sanctified by the Holy G'.
1Co 2:13 the Holy G' teacheth;
6:19 the temple of the Holy G'
12: 3 the Lord, but by the Holy G'.
2Co 6: 6 the Holy G', by love unfeigned,
13:14 the communion of the Holy G',
1Th 1: 5 in power, and in the Holy G',
6 with joy of the Holy G':
2Ti 1:14 by the Holy G' which dwelleth
Tit 3: 5 and renewing of the Holy G';
Heb 2: 4 gifts of the Holy G', according
3: 7 (as the Holy G' saith, To day if
6: 4 made partakers of the Holy G',
9: 8 The Holy G' this signifying,
10:15 Holy G' also is a witness to us:
1Pe 1:12 Holy G' sent down from heaven;
2Pe 1:21 were moved by the Holy G'.
1Jo 5: 7 Holy G': and these three are one.
Jude 20 praying in the Holy G',

Giah (*ghi'-ah*)
2Sa 2:24 G' by the way of the wilderness

giant See also GIANTS.
2Sa 21:16 which was of the sons of the g',
18 which was of the sons of the g'.
20 and he also was born to the g'.
22 four were born to the g' in Gath,
1Ch 20: 4 that was of the children of the g':
6 and he also was the son of the g'.
8 were born unto the g' in Gath;
Job 16:14 he runneth upon me like a g'.

giants
Ge 6: 4 were g' in the earth in those days;
Nu 13:33 And there we saw the g', the sons
13:33 of Anak, which come of the g':
De 2:11 accounted g', as the Anakims;
20 accounted a land of g': g' dwelt
3:11 remained of the remnant of g';
13 which was called the land of g'.
Jos 12: 4 was of the remnant of the g',
13:12 remained of the remnant of the g':
15: 8 at the end of the valley of the g'
17:15 of the Perizzites and of the g',
18:16 which is in the valley of the g'

Gibbar (*ghib'-bar*) See also GIBEON.
Ezr 2:20 children of G', ninety and five.

Gibbethon (*ghib'-be-thon*)
Jos 19:44 Eltekeh, and G', and Baalath,
21:23 Eltekeh with her suburbs, G' with
1Ki 15:27 and Baasha smote him at G',
27 and all Israel laid siege to G'.
16:15 encamped against G', which
17 Omri went up from G', and all

Gibea (*ghib'-e-ah*) See also GIBEAH.
1Ch 2:49 Machbenah, and the father of G':

Gibeah (*ghib'-e-ah*) See also GIBEA; GIBEATH; GIBEON.
Jos 15:57 Cain, G', and Timnah; ten cities
J'g 19:12 of Israel; we will pass over to G'.
13 lodge all night, in G', or in Ramah.
14 G', which belongeth to Benjamin.
15 thither, to go in and to lodge in G':
16 he sojourned in G': but the men
20: 4 answered and said, I came into G'
5 And the men of G' rose against me,
9 the thing which we will do to G';
10 when they come to G' of Benjamin,
13 of Belial, which are in G', that we
14 out of the cities unto G', to go out
15 beside the inhabitants of G',
19 morning, and encamped against G'.
20 array to fight against them at G'.
21 Benjamin came forth out of G',
25 at G' the second day, and destroyed
29 set liers in wait round about G'.
30 put themselves in array against G',
31 God, and the other to G' in the field,
33 even out of the meadows of G'.
34 came against G' ten thousand
36 wait which they had set beside G'.
37 wait hasted, and rushed upon G';
43 down with ease over against G'
1Sa 10:26 Saul also went home to G'; and
11: 4 came the messengers to G' of Saul,
13: 2 thousand were with Jonathan in G'
15 and gat him up from Gilgal unto G'
16 them, abode in G' of Benjamin:
14: 2 tarried in the uttermost part of G'
5 other southward over against G'.
16 of Saul in G' of Benjamin looked;
15:34 went up to his house to G' of Saul.
22: 6 in G' under a tree in Ramah,
23:19 came up the Ziphites to Saul to G',
26: 1 the Ziphites came unto Saul to G',
2Sa 6: 3 of Abinadab that was in G':
4 of Abinadab which was at G',
21: 6 unto the Lord in G' of Saul, whom
23:29 of G' of the children of Benjamin,
1Ch 11:31 Ithai the son of Ribai of G', that
2Ch 13: 2 the daughter of Uriel of G'.
Isa 10:29 Ramah is afraid; G' of Saul is fled.
Ho 5: 8 Blow ye the cornet in G', and the
9: 9 themselves, as in the days of G':
10: 9 hast sinned from the days of G':
9 battle in G' against the children of

Gibeath (*ghib'-e-ath*) See also GIBEAH; GIBEATHITE.
Jos 18:28 Jebusi, which is in Jerusalem, G',

Gibeathite (*ghib'-e-ath-ite*)
1Ch 12: 3 of Shemaah the G'; and Jeziel,

Gibeon (*ghib'-e-on*) See also GEBA; GIBEAH; GIBEONITE.
Jos 9: 3 G' heard what Joshua had done
17 cities were G', and Chephirah,
10: 1 inhabitants of G' had made peace
2 because G' was a great city, as
4 help me, that we may smite G':
5 and encamped before G', and made
6 men of G' sent unto Joshua to the
10 great slaughter at G', and chased
12 Sun, stand thou still upon G'; and
41 country of Goshen, even unto G'.
11:19 the Hivites the inhabitants of G':
18:25 G', and Ramah, and Beeroth,
21:17 of Benjamin, G' with her suburbs,
2Sa 2:12 went out from Mahanaim to G'.
13 and met together by the pool of G':
16 Helkath-hazzurim, which is in G'.
24 by the way of the wilderness of G'.
3:30 brother Asahel at G' in the battle.
20: 8 at the great stone which is in G',
1Ki 3: 4 king went to G' to sacrifice there;
5 In G' the Lord appeared to
9: 2 as he had appeared unto him at G'.
1Ch 8:29 And at G' dwelt the father...whose
29 And at...dwelt the father of G'; whose
9:35 And in G' dwelt...Jehiel, whose
35 And...dwelt the father of G', Jehiel,
14:16 Philistines from G' even to Gazer.
16:39 in the high place that was at G',
21:29 that season in the high place at G'.
2Ch 1: 3 to the high place that was at G';
13 from...the high place that was at G'
Ne 3: 7 the men of G', and of Mizpah, unto
7:25 The children of G', ninety and five.
Isa 28:21 shall be wroth as in the valley of G',
Jer 28: 1 Azur the prophet, which was of G',

Jer 41:12 by the great waters that are in *G*.
16 he had brought again from *G*:

Gibeonite (*ghib'-e-on-ite*) See also GIBEONITES.
1Ch 12: 4 Ismaiah the *G*, a mighty man
Ne 3: 7 Melatiah the *G*, and Jadon the

Gibeonites (*ghib'-e-on-ites*)
2Sa 21: 1 house, because he slew the *G*.
2 *G* and said unto them; (now the *G*
3 David said unto the *G*, What shall
4 the *G* said unto him, We will have
9 them into the hands of the *G*,

Giblites (*ghib'-lites*)
Jos 13: 5 And the land of the *G*,

Giddalti (*ghid-dal'-ti*)
1Ch 25: 4 Hanani, Eliathah, *G*, and
29 and twentieth to *G*, he, his sons,

Giddel (*ghid'-del*)
Ezr 2:47 The children of *G*, the children
56 of Darkon, the children of *G*,
Ne 7:49 of Hanan, the children of *G*, the
58 of Darkon, the children of *G*,

Gideon (*ghid'-e-on*) See also GEDEON; JERUBBAAL.
J'g 6:11 his son *G* threshed wheat by the
13 *G* said unto him, O my Lord, if the
19 *G* went in, and made ready a kid,
22 *G* perceived that he was an angel
22 *G* said, Alas, O Lord God! for
24 *G* built an altar there unto the
27 *G* took ten men of his servants,
29 *G* the son of Joash hath done this
34 Spirit of the Lord came upon *G*,
36 *G* said unto God, If thou wilt save
39 *G* said unto God, Let not thine
7: 1 who is *G*, and all the people that
2 said unto *G*, The people that are
4 said unto *G*, The people are yet
5 said unto *G*, Every one that
7 said unto *G*, By the three hundred
13 when *G* was come, behold, there
14 save the sword of *G* the son of
15 *G* heard the telling of the dream,
18 The sword of the Lord, and of *G*.
19 So *G*, and the hundred men that
20 The sword of the Lord, and of *G*.
24 *G* sent messengers throughout all
25 to *G* on the other side Jordan.
8: 4 *G* came to Jordan, and passed
7 *G* said, Therefore when the Lord
11 And *G* went up by the way of them
13 *G* the son of Joash returned from
21 *G* arose, and slew Zebah and
22 Israel said unto *G*, Rule thou over
23 *G* said unto them, I will not rule
24 *G* said unto them, I would desire
27 *G* made an ephod thereof, and put
27 thing became a snare unto *G*, and
28 forty years in the days of *G*.
30 *G* had threescore and ten sons of
32 *G* the son of Joash died in a good
33 as *G* was dead, that the children of
35 house of Jerubbaal, namely, *G*,

Gideoni (*ghid-e-o'-ni*)
Nu 1:11 Benjamin; Abidan, the son of *G*.
2:22 shall be Abidan the son of *G*.
7:60 Abidan the son of *G*, prince of the
65 offering of Abidan the son of *G*.
10:24 Benjamin was Abidan the son of *G*

Gidom (*ghi'-dom*)
J'g 20:45 pursued hard after them unto *G*,

gier (*jeer*)
Le 11:18 the pelican, and the *g* eagle,
De 14:17 the pelican, and the *g* eagle, and

gier-eagle See GIER and EAGLE.

gift See also GIFTS.
Ge 34:12 me never so much dowry and *g*,
Ex 23: 8 And thou shalt take no *g*:
8 for the *g* blindeth the wise,
Nu 8:19 I have given the Levites as a *g*
18: 6 are given as a *g* for the Lord,
7 office unto you as a service of *g*:
11 the heave offering of their *g*,
De 16:19 neither take a *g*: for a *g* doth
2Sa 19:42 or hath he given us any *g*?
Ps 45:12 of Tyre shall be there with a *g*;
Pr 17: 8 A *g* is as a precious stone in the
23 A wicked man taketh a *g* out of
18:16 A man's *g* maketh room for him,
21:14 A *g* in secret pacifieth anger:
25:14 boasteth himself of a false *g*
Ec 3:13 of all his labour, it is the *g* of God.
5:19 in his labour; this is the *g* of God.
7: 7 a *g* destroyeth the heart.
Eze 46:16 prince give a *g* unto any of his sons,
17 if he give a *g* of his inheritance
M't 5:23 if thou bring thy *g* to the altar,
24 Leave there thy *g* before the altar,
24 and then come and offer thy *g*.
8: 4 offer the *g* that Moses commanded.
15: 5 It is a *g*, by whatsoever thou
23:18 sweareth by the *g* that is upon it,
19 for whether is greater, the *g*, or
19 or the altar that sanctifieth the *g*?
M'r 7:11 Corban, that is to say, a *g*, by
Joh 4:10 If thou knewest the *g* of God,
Ac 2:38 receive the *g* of the Holy Ghost.
8:20 hast thought that the *g* of God
10:45 poured out the *g* of the Holy Ghost.
11:17 God gave them the like *g* as he did
Ro 1:11 impart unto you some spiritual *g*,
5:15 as the offence, so also is the free *g*.

Ro 5:15 grace of God, and the *g* by grace,
16 by one that sinned, so is the *g*:
16 the free *g* is of many offences
17 the *g* of righteousness shall reign
18 the free *g* came upon all men unto
6:23 but the *g* of God is eternal life
1Co 1: 7 So that ye come behind in no *g*;
7: 7 every man hath his proper *g* of God,
13: 2 though I have the *g* of prophecy,
2Co 1:11 for the *g* bestowed upon us by
8: 4 that we would receive the *g*, and
9:15 unto God for his unspeakable *g*.
Eph 2: 8 of yourselves: it is the *g* of God:
3: 7 according to the *g* of the grace of
4: 7 the measure of the *g* of Christ.
Ph'p 4:17 Not because I desire a *g*: but I
1Ti 4:14 Neglect not the *g* that is in thee,
2Ti 1: 6 stir up the *g* of God, which is in
Heb 6: 4 have tasted of the heavenly *g*,
Jas 1:17 Every good *g* and every perfect *g*
1Pe 4:10 As every man hath received the *g*,

gifts
Ge 25: 6 Abraham gave *g*, and sent them
Ex 28:38 Israel shall hallow all their holy *g*;
Le 23:38 beside your *g*, and beside all your
Nu 18:29 Out of all your *g* ye shall offer
2Sa 8: 2 David's servants, and brought *g*.
6 to David, and brought *g*.
1Ch 18: 2, 6 servants and brought *g*.
2Ch 19: 7 of persons, nor taking of *g*.
21: 3 their father gave them great *g*
26: 8 Ammonites gave *g* to Uzziah:
32:23 many brought *g* unto the Lord
Es 2:18 to the provinces, and gave *g*,
9:22 portions one to another, and *g*
Ps 68:18 thou hast received *g* for men;
72:10 of Sheba and Seba shall offer *g*.
Pr 6:35 though thou givest many *g*.
15:27 but he that hateth *g* shall live.
19: 6 is a friend to him that giveth *g*.
29: 4 that receiveth *g* overthroweth it.
Isa 1:23 every one loveth *g*, and followeth
Eze 16:33 They give *g* to all whores:
33 but thou givest thy *g* to all thy
20:26 I polluted them in their own *g*,
31 when ye offer your *g*, when ye
39 holy name no more with your *g*,
22:12 have they taken *g* to shed blood;
Da 2: 6 shall receive of me *g* and rewards
48 and gave him many great *g*, and
5:17 Let thy *g* be to thyself, and give
M't 2:11 they presented unto him *g*; gold,
7:11 give good *g* unto your children,
Lu 11:13 give good *g* unto your children:
21: 1 casting their *g* into the treasury.
5 with goodly stones and *g*,
Ro 11:29 For the *g* and calling of God are
12: 6 Having then *g* differing according
1Co 12: 1 concerning spiritual *g*, brethren,
4 there are diversities of *g*, but the
9 to another the *g* of healing by the
28 *g* of healings, helps, governments,
30 Have all the *g* of healing? do all
31 covet earnestly the best *g*: and
14: 1 desire spiritual *g*, but rather that
12 as ye are zealous of spiritual *g*,
Eph 4: 8 captive, and gave *g* unto men.
Heb 2: 4 miracles, and *g* of the Holy Ghost,
5: 1 may offer both *g* and sacrifices
8: 3 ordained to offer *g* and sacrifices:
4 that there are priests that offer *g*
9: 9 were offered both *g* and sacrifices,
11: 4 God testifying of his *g*: and by it
Re 11:10 shall send *g* one to another;

Gihon (*ghi'-hon*)
Ge 2:13 the name of the second river is *G*:
1Ki 1:33 mule, and bring him down to *G*:
38 mule, and brought him to *G*.
45 have anointed him king in *G*:
2Ch 32:30 the upper watercourse of *G*,
33:14 of David, on the west side of *G*,

Gilalai (*ghil'-a-lahee*)
Ne 12:36 Milalai, *G*, Maai, Nethaneel, and

Gilboa (*ghil-bo'-ah*)
1Sa 28: 4 together, and they pitched in *G*.
31: 1 and fell down slain in mount *G*.
8 his three sons fallen in mount *G*.
2Sa 1: 6 happened by chance upon mount *G*,
21 Ye mountains of *G*, let there be no
21:12 Philistines had slain Saul in *G*:
1Ch 10: 1 and fell down slain in mount *G*.
8 and his sons fallen in mount *G*.

Gilead (*ghil'-e-ad*) See also GILEADITE; GILEAD'S; JABESH-GILEAD; RAMOTH-GILEAD.
Ge 31:21 set his face toward the mount *G*.
23 they overtook him in the mount *G*.
25 brethren pitched in the mount of *G*.
37:25 of Ishmaelites came from *G*
Nu 26:29 Machir begat *G*: of *G* come the
30 These are the sons of *G*: of Jeezer,
27: 1 Hepher, the son of *G*, the son of
32: 1 and the land of *G*, that, behold,
26 shall be there in the cities of *G*:
29 ye shall give them the land of *G*
39 son of Manasseh went to *G*, and
40 Moses gave *G* unto Machir the son
36: 1 families of the children of *G*,
De 2:36 by the river, even unto *G*, there
3:10 cities of the plain, and all *G*, and
12 and half mount *G*, and the cities
13 rest of *G*, and all Bashan, being
15 And I gave *G* unto Machir.
16 Gadites I gave from *G* even unto
4:43 and Ramoth in *G*, of the Gadites;

De 34: 1 shewed him all the land of *G*,
Jos 12: 2 and from half *G*, even unto the
5 and half *G*, the border of Sihon
13:11 and *G*, and the border of the
25 and all the cities of *G*, and half
31 half *G*, and Ashtaroth, and Edrei,
17: 1 the father of *G*: because he
1 therefore he had *G* and Bashan.
3 the son of *G*, the son of Machir,
5 besides the land of *G* and Bashan,
6 Manasseh's sons had the land of *G*.
20: 8 Ramoth in *G* out of the tribe of
21:38 Ramoth in *G* with her suburbs,
22: 9 to go into the country of *G*, to the
13 the land of *G*, Phinehas the son
15 unto the land of *G*, and they spake
32 Gad, out of the land of *G*, unto the
J'g 5:17 *G* abode beyond Jordan: and why
7: 3 depart early from mount *G*.
10: 4 day, which are in the land of *G*.
8 of the Amorites, which is in *G*.
17 together, and encamped in *G*.
18 princes of *G* said to one another,
18 head over all the inhabitants of *G*.
11: 1 and *G* begat Jephthah.
5 elders of *G* went to fetch Jephthah
7 Jephthah said unto the elders of *G*
8 elders of *G* said unto Jephthah,
8 head over all the inhabitants of *G*.
9 Jephthah said unto the elders of *G*,
10 the elders of *G* said unto Jephthah,
11 with the elders of *G*, and the people
29 he passed over *G*, and Manasseh,
29 and passed over Mizpeh of *G*,
29 and from Mizpeh of *G* he passed
12: 4 gathered together all the men of *G*,
4 and the men of *G* smote Ephraim,
5 that the men of *G* said unto him,
7 buried in one of the cities of *G*.
20: 1 with the land of *G*, unto the Lord
1Sa 13: 7 Jordan to the land of Gad and *G*.
2Sa 2: 9 made him king over *G*, and over
17:26 Absalom pitched in the land of *G*.
24: 6 they came to *G*, and to the land of
1Ki 4:13 son of Manasseh, which are in *G*;
19 son of Uri was in the country of *G*,
17: 1 who was of the inhabitants of *G*,
22: 3 Know ye that Ramoth in *G* is
2Ki 10:33 all the land of *G*, the Gadites,
33 river Arnon, even *G* and Bashan.
15:29 and Hazor, and *G*, and Galilee,
1Ch 2:21 the father of *G*, whom he married
22 and twenty cities in the land of *G*,
23 sons of Machir the father of *G*.
5: 9 were multiplied in the land of *G*.
10 throughout all the east land of *G*.
14 the son Jaroah, the son of *G*, the
16 and they dwelt in *G*, in Bashan,
6:80 Ramoth in *G* with her suburbs,
7:14 bare Machir the father of *G*:
17 the sons of *G*, the son of Machir,
26:31 men of valour at Jazer of *G*.
27:21 tribe of Manasseh in *G*, Iddo the
Ps 60: 7 *G* is mine, and Manasseh is mine;
108: 8 *G* is mine, Manasseh is mine;
Ca 4: 1 goats, that appear from mount *G*:
6: 5 of goats that appear from *G*:
Jer 8:22 Is there no balm in *G*; is there no
22: 6 Thou art *G* unto me, and the head
46:11 Go up into *G*, and take balm,
50:19 upon mount Ephraim and *G*.
Eze 47:18 and from Damascus, and from *G*,
Ho 6: 8 *G* is a city of them that work
12:11 Is there iniquity in *G*? surely
Am 1: 3 because they have threshed *G*
13 the women with child of *G*,
Ob 1:19 and Benjamin shall possess *G*.
Mic 7:14 in Bashan and *G*, as in the days of
Zec 10:10 into the land of *G* and Lebanon:

Gileadite (*ghil'-e-ad-ite*) See also GILEADITES.
J'g 10: 3 after him arose Jair, a *G*, and
11: 1 Jephthah the *G* was a mighty
40 the daughter of Jephthah the *G*
12: 7 Then died Jephthah the *G*, and
2Sa 17:27 and Barzillai the *G* of Rogelim,
19:31 And Barzillai the *G* came down
1Ki 2: 7 of Barzillai the *G*, and let them be
Ezr 2:61 daughters of Barzillai the *G*, and
Ne 7:63 daughters of Barzillai the *G* to

Gileadites (*ghil'-e-ad-ites*)
Nu 26:29 Gilead come the family of the *G*.
J'g 12: 4 Ye *G* are fugitives of Ephraim
5 the *G* took the passages of Jordan
2Ki 15:25 and with him fifty men of the *G*:

Gilead's (*ghil'-e-ads*)
J'g 11: 2 And *G* wife bare him sons;

Gilgal (*ghil'-gal*)
De 11:30 the champaign over against *G*,
Jos 4:19 and encamped in *G*, in the east
20 of Jordan, did Joshua pitch in *G*.
5: 9 place is called *G* unto this day.
10 Israel encamped in *G*, and kept
9: 6 to Joshua unto the camp at *G*,
10: 6 to the camp to *G*, saying, Slack
7 Joshua ascended from *G*, he, and
9 and went up from *G* all night.
15, 43 with him, unto the camp to *G*.
12:23 the king of the nations of *G*, one;
14: 6 came unto Joshua in *G*: and
15: 7 looking toward *G*, that is before
J'g 2: 1 Lord came up from *G* to Bochim.
3:19 quarries that were by *G*, and said,
1Sa 7:16 year in circuit to Beth-el, and *G*,
10: 8 shalt go down before me to *G*;

1Sa 11:14 Come, and let us go to G·, and
15 And all the people went to G·;
15 Saul king before the Lord in G·;
13: 4 called together after Saul to G·.
7 As for Saul, he was yet in G·, and
8 but Samuel came not to G·; and
12 come down now upon me to G·,
15 gat him up from G· unto Gibeah of
15:12 passed on, and gone down to G·.
21 unto the Lord thy God in G·.
33 in pieces before the Lord in G·.
2Sa 19:15 And Judah came to G·, to go to
40 king went on to G·, and Chimham
2Ki 2: 1 Elijah went with Elisha from G·.
4:38 And Elisha came again to G·: and
Ne 12:29 Also from the house of G·, and out
Ho 4:15 and come not ye unto G·, neither
9:15 All their wickedness is in G·: for
12:11 they sacrifice bullocks in G·; yea,
Am 4: 4 at G· multiply transgression;
5: 5 nor enter into G·, and pass not to
5 G· shall surely go into captivity,
Mic 6: 5 him, from Shittim unto G·.

Giloh (*ghi'-loh*) See also GILONITE.
Jos 15:51 Goshen, and Holon, and G·;
2Sa 15:12 city, even from G·, while he offered

Gilonite (*ghi'-lo-nite*)
2Sa 15:12 Ahithophel the G·, David's
23:34 Eliam the son of Ahithophel the G·,

Gimzo (*ghim'-zo*)
2Ch 28:18 G· also and the villages thereof:

gin See also GINS.
Job 18: 9 The g· shall take him by the heel,
Isa 8:14 for a g· and for a snare to the
Am 3: 5 where no g· is for him? shall

Ginath (*ghi'-nath*)
1Ki 16:21 Tibni the son of G·, to make him
22 Tibni the son of G·: so Tibni died,

Ginnetho (*ghin'-ne-tho*) See also GINNETHON.
Ne 12: 4 Iddo, G·, Abijah,

Ginnethon (*ghin'-ne-thon*) See also GINNETHO.
Ne 10: 6 Daniel, G·, Baruch,
12:16 Iddo, Zechariah; of G·, Meshullam;

gins
Ps 140: 5 wayside; they have set g· for me.
141: 9 the g· of the workers of iniquity.

gird See also GIRDED; GIRDETH; GIRDING; GIRT.
Ex 29: 5 and g· him with the curious girdle
9 thou shalt g· them with girdles,
J'g 3:16 he did g· it under his raiment
1Sa 25:13 G· ye on every man his sword.
2Sa 3:31 g· you with sackcloth, and mourn
2Ki 4:29 G· up thy loins, and take my staff
9: 1 G· up thy loins, and take this box
Job 38: 3 G· up now thy loins like a man;
40: 7 G· up thy loins now like a man:
Ps 45: 3 G· thy sword upon thy thigh, O
Isa 8: 9, 9 g· yourselves, and ye shall be
15: 3 g· themselves with sackcloth:
32:11 and g· sackcloth upon your loins.
Jer 1:17 Thou therefore g· up thy loins,
4: 8 For this g· you with sackcloth,
6:26 g· thee with sackcloth, and wallow
49: 3 g· you with sackcloth; lament, and
Eze 7:18 They shall also g· themselves
27:31 and g· them with sackcloth, and
44:18 they shall not g· themselves with
Joe 1:13 G· yourselves, and lament, ye
Lu 12:37 that he shall g· himself, and make
17: 8 and g· thyself, and serve me, till
Joh 21:18 another shall g· thee, and carry
Ac 12: 8 G· thyself, and bind on thy
1Pe 1:13 Wherefore g· up the loins of your

girded See also GIRDEDST; GIRT; UNGIRDED.
Ex 12:11 shall ye eat it; with your loins g·,
Le 8: 7 and g· him with the girdle, and
7 he g· him with the curious girdle
13 them, and g· them with girdles,
16: 4 and shall be g· with a linen girdle,
De 1:41 And when ye had g· on every man
1Sa 2: 4 stumbled are g· with strength.
18 a child, g· with a linen ephod.
17:39 And David g· his sword upon his
25:13 they g· on every man his sword;
13 and David also g· on his sword:
2Sa 6:14 David was g· with a linen ephod.
20: 8 garment that he had put on was g·
21:16 he being g· with a new sword,
22:40 For thou hast g· me with strength
1Ki 18:46 and he g· up his loins, and ran
20:32 So they g· sackcloth on their loins,
Ne 4:18 one had his sword g· by his side,
Ps 18:39 For thou hast g· me with strength
30:11 sackcloth, and g· me with gladness;
65: 6 mountains; being g· with power:
93: 1 wherewith he hath g· himself:
109:19 wherewith he is g· continually.
Isa 45: 5 I g· thee, though thou hast not
La 2:10 they have g· themselves with
Eze 16:10 and I g· thee about with fine linen,
23:15 G· with girdles upon their loins,
Da 10: 5 whose loins were g· with fine gold
Joe 1: 8 like a virgin g· with sackcloth
Lu 12:35 Let your loins be g· about,
Joh 13: 4 and took a towel, and g· himself.
5 the towel wherewith he was g·.
Re 15: 6 breasts g· with golden girdles.

girdedst
Joh 21:18 thou wast young, thou g· thyself

girdeth
1Ki 20:11 Let not him that g· on his harness
Job 12:18 and g· their loins with a girdle.
Ps 18:32 It is God that g· me with strength,
Pr 31:17 She g· her loins with strength,

girding See also UNDERGIRDING.
Isa 3:24 of a stomacher a g· of sackcloth;
22:12 baldness, and to g· with sackcloth

girdle See also GIRDLES.
Ex 28: 4 broidered coat, a mitre, and a g·:
8 And the curious g· of the ephod,
27 above the curious g· of the ephod.
28 above the curious g· of the ephod,
39 shalt make the g· of needlework.
29: 5 with the curious g· of the ephod:
39: 5 And the curious g· of his ephod,
20 above the curious g· of the ephod.
21 above the curious g· of the ephod,
29 a g· of fine twined linen, and blue,
Le 8: 7 and girded him with the g·, and
7 with the curious g· of the ephod,
16: 4 and shall be girded with a linen g·,
1Sa 18: 4 sword, and to his bow, and to his g·
2Sa 18:11 ten shekels of silver, and a g·.
20: 8 upon it a g· with a sword fastened
1Ki 2: 5 put the blood of war upon his g·
2Ki 1: 8 girt with a g· of leather about his
Job 12:18 and girdeth their loins with a g·.
Ps 109:19 and for a g· wherewith he is girded
Isa 3:24 and instead of a g· a rent; and
5:27 shall the g· of their loins be loosed,
11: 5 righteousness shall be the g· of his
5 loins, and faithfulness the g· of his
22:21 strengthen him with thy g·, and I
Jer 13: 1 Go and get thee a linen g·, and put
2 So I got a g· according to the word
4 Take the g· that thou hast got,
6 take the g· from thence, which I
7 took the g· from the place where I
7 g· was marred, it was profitable for
10 even be as this g·, which is good for
11 For as the g· cleaveth to the loins
M't 3: 4 and a leathern g· about his loins;
M'r 1: 6 with a g· of a skin about his loins;
Ac 21:11 he took Paul's g·, and bound his
11 bind the man that owneth this g·,
Re 1:13 about the paps with a golden g·.

girdles
Ex 28:40 shalt make for them g·, and bonnets
29: 9 And thou shalt gird them with g·,
Le 8:13 girded them with g·, and put
Pr 31:24 delivereth g· unto the merchant.
Eze 23:15 with g· upon their loins, exceeding
Re 15: 6 breasts girded with golden g·.

Girgashite (*ghur'-gash-ite*) See also GIRGASHITES; GIRGASITE.
1Ch 1:14 also, and the Amorite, and the G·,

Girgashites (*ghur'-gash-ites*)
Ge 15:21 the Canaanites, and the G·, and
De 7: 1 the Hittites, and the G·, and the
Jos 3:10 the Perizzites, and the G·, and
24:11 and the G·, the Hivites, and the
Ne 9: 8 Jebusites, and the G·, to give it, I

Girgasite (*ghur'-ga-site*) See also GIRGASHITE.
Ge 10:16 and the Amorite, and the G·,

girl See also GIRLS.
Joe 3: 3 and sold a g· for wine, that they

girls
Zec 8: 5 boys and g· playing in the streets

girt See also GIRDED.
2Ki 1: 8 and g· with a girdle of leather about
Joh 21: 7 he g· his fisher's coat unto him,
Eph 6:14 your loins g· about with truth,
Re 1:13 and g· about the paps with a golden

Gispa (*ghis'-pah*)
Ne 11:21 and Ziha and G· were over the

Gittah-hepher (*ghit''-tah-he'-fer*) See also GATH-HEPHER.
Jos 19:13 on the east to G·, to Ittah-kazin,

Gittaim (*ghit-ta'-im*)
2Sa 4: 3 Beerothites fled to G·, and were
Ne 11:33 Hazor, Ramah, G·,

Gittite (*ghit'-tite*) See also GITTITES; GITTITH.
2Sa 6:10 the house of Obed-edom the G·.
11 house of Obed-edom the G· three
15:19 the king to Ittai the G·, Wherefore
22 Ittai the G· passed over, and all his
18: 2 under the hand of Ittai the G·.
21:19 slew the brother of Goliath the G·,
1Ch 13:13 the house of Obed-edom the G·.
20: 5 the brother of Goliath the G·,

Gittites (*ghit'-tites*)
Jos 13: 3 the G·, and the Ekronites; also the
2Sa 15:18 and all the G·, six hundred men

Gittith (*ghit'-tith*)
Ps 8:*title* To the chief Musician upon G·,
81:*title* To the chief Musician upon G·,
84:*title* To the chief Musician upon G·,

give See also FORGIVE; GAVE; GIVEN; GIVEST; GIVETH; GIVING.
Ge 1:15, 17 heaven to g· light upon the earth,
12: 7 Unto thy seed will I g· this land;
13:15 to thee will I g· it, and to thy seed
17 for will I g· it unto thee.
14:21 G· me the persons, and take the
15: 2 what wilt thou g· me, seeing I go
7 to g· thee this land to inherit it.
17: 8 will g· unto thee, and to thy seed
16 I will bless her, and g· thee a son
23: 4 g· me a possession of a...with you,
9 may g· me the cave of Machpelah,
Ge 23: 9 he shall g· it me for a possession
11 the field g· I thee, and the cave
11 that is therein, I g· it thee; in the
11 sons of my people g· I it thee:
13 But if thou wilt g· it, I pray thee,
13 I will g· thee money for the field;
24: 7 Unto thy seed will I g· this land;
14 I will g· thy camels drink also:
41 if they g· not thee one, thou shalt
43 G· me, I pray thee, a little...to drink;
46 I will g· thy camels drink also:
26: 3 seed, I will g· all these countries,
4 g· unto thy seed all these countries;
27:28 God g· thee of the dew of heaven,
28: 4 g· thee the blessing of Abraham,
13 to thee will I g· it, and to thy seed;
20 and will g· me bread to eat, and
22 and of all that thou shalt g· me
22 I will surely g· the tenth unto thee.
29:19 better that I g· her to thee, than
19 I should g· her to another man:
21 G· me my wife, for my days are
26 g· the younger before the firstborn.
27 and we will g· thee this also for.
30: 1 G· me children, or else I die.
14 G· me, I pray thee, of thy son's
26 G· me my wives and my children,
28 me thy wages, and I will g· it.
31 And he said, What shall I g· thee?
31 Thou shalt not g· me any thing:
34: 8 I pray you g· her him to wife.
9 g· your daughters unto us, and
11 what ye shall say unto me I will g·.
12 I will g· according as ye shall say
12 but g· me the damsel to wife.
14 to g· our sister to one that is
16 will we g· our daughters unto you,
21 and let us g· them our daughters.
35:12 Isaac, to thee will I g· it, and to thy
12 seed after thee will I g· the land.
38: 9 he should g· seed to his brother.
16 What wilt thou g· me, that thou
17 Wilt thou g· me a pledge, till thou
18 What pledge shall I g· thee? And
41:16 God shall g· Pharaoh an answer of
42:25 to g· them provision for the way:
27 to g· his ass provender in the inn,
43:14 God Almighty g· you mercy before
45:18 I will g· you the good of the land
47:15 Joseph, and said, G· us bread:
16 And Joseph said, G· your cattle;
16 I will g· you for your cattle,
19 and g· us seed, that we may live,
24 shall g· the fifth part unto Pharaoh,
48: 4 and will g· this land to thy seed
Ex 2: 9 and I will g· thee thy wages.
3:21 g· this people favour in the sight
5: 7 shall no more g· the people straw
10 Pharaoh, I will not g· you straw.
6: 4 to g· them the land of Canaan,
8 to g· it to Abraham, to Isaac, and
8 and I will g· it you for an heritage:
10:25 Thou must g· us also sacrifices
12:25 the land which the Lord will g· you,
13: 5 sware unto thy fathers to g· thee,
11 to thy fathers, and shall g· it thee,
21 a pillar of fire, to g· them light;
15:26 and wilt g· ear to his commandments,
16: 8 Lord shall g· you in the evening
17: 2 G· us water that we may drink.
18:19 I will g· thee counsel, and God shall
21:23 then thou shalt g· life for life,
30 then he shall g· for the ransom
32 g· unto their master thirty shekels
34 shall make it good, and g· money
22:17 utterly refuse to g· her unto him,
29 thy sons shalt thou g· unto me.
30 the eighth day thou shalt g· it me.
24:12 and I will g· thee tables of stone,
25:16 the testimony which I shall g· thee.
21 the testimony that I shall g· thee.
22 I will g· thee in commandment unto
37 that they may g· light over against it.
30:12 shall they g· every man a ransom
13 This they shall g·, every one that
14 shall g· an offering unto the Lord.
15 The rich shall not g· more,
15 shall not g· less than half a shekel,
15 when they g· an offering unto the
32:13 will I g· unto your seed, and they
33: 1 Unto thy seed will I g· it:
14 go with thee, and I will g· thee rest.
Le 5:16 thereto, and g· it unto the priest:
6: 5 g· it unto him to whom it
7:32 shoulder shall ye g· unto the priest
14:34 land of Canaan, which I g· to you
15:14 and g· them unto the priest:
20:24 I will g· it unto you to possess it,
22:14 and shall g· it unto the priest
23:10 the land which I g· unto you,
38 offerings, which ye g· unto the Lord.
25: 2 come into the land which I g· you,
37 Thou shalt not g· him thy money
38 to g· you the land of Canaan,
51 shall g· again the price of his
52 years shall he g· him again the
26: 4 I will g· you rain in due season,
6 And I will g· peace in the land,
27:23 and he shall g· thine estimation
Nu 3: 9 shalt g· the Levites unto Aaron
48 And thou shalt g· the money,
5: 7 and g· it unto him against whom he
6:26 upon thee, and g· thee peace.
7: 5 shalt g· them unto the Levites,
8: 2 the seven lamps shall g· light over
10:29 the Lord said, I will g· it you:

Nu 11: 4 Who shall g' us flesh to eat?
13 flesh to g' unto all this people?
13 G' us flesh, that we may eat.
18 Who shall g' us flesh to eat?
18 therefore the Lord will g' you flesh,
21 will g' them flesh, that they may eat
13: 2 the land of Canaan, which I g' unto
14: 8 bring us into this land, and g' it us;
15: 2 habitations, which I g' unto you,
21 the first of your dough ye shall g'
18:28 and ye shall g' thereof the Lord's
19: 3 And ye shall g' her unto Eleazar
20: 8 and it shall g' forth his water,
8 thou shalt g' the congregation...drink.
21 Thus Edom refused to g' Israel
21:16 I will g' them water.
22:13 the Lord refuseth to g' me leave
18 If Balak would g' me his house full
24:13 If Balak would g' me his house full
25:12 I g' unto him my covenant of peace:
26:54 thou shalt g' the more inheritance,
54 thou shalt g' the less inheritance:
27: 4 G' unto us therefore a possession?
7 shalt surely g' them a possession
9, 10, 11 ye shall g' his inheritance
19 and g' him a charge in their sight.
31:29 and g' it unto Eleazar the priest,
30 and g' them unto the Levites,
32:29 ye shall g' them the land of Gilead
33:54 more ye shall g' the more inheritance,
54 fewer ye shall g' the less inheritance:
34:13 to g' unto the nine tribes, and to
35: 2 that they g' unto the Levites of the
2 ye shall g' also unto the Levites
4, 6 which ye shall g' unto the Levites
7 which ye shall g' to the Levites
7 them shall ye g' with their suburbs.
8 shall g' shall be of the possession
8 that have many ye shall g' many;
8 that have few ye shall g' few:
8 every one shall g' of his cities
13 cities which ye shall g' six cities
14 Ye shall g' three cities on this side
14 three cities shall ye g' in the land
36: 2 to g' the land for an inheritance
2 to g' the inheritance of Zelophehad
De. 1: 8 to g' unto them and to their seed
20 Lord our God doth g' unto us.
25 the Lord our God doth g' us.
35 I sware to g' unto your fathers,
36 to him will I g' the land that he
39 unto them will I g' it, and they shall
45 to your voice, nor g' ear unto you.
2: 5 I will not g' you of their land,
9 I will not g' thee of their land
19 I will not g' thee of the land of the
28 g' me water for money, that I may
31 Behold, I have begun to g' Sihon
4:38 to g' thee their land for an
5:31 the land which I g' them to possess
6:10 to g' thee great and goodly cities,
23 to g' us the land which he sware
7: 3 thy daughter thou shalt not g' unto
13 he sware unto thy fathers to g'
10:11 I sware unto their fathers to g'
11: 9 to g' unto them and to their seed,
14 I will g' you the rain of your land
21 Lord sware unto your fathers to g'
14:21 thou shalt g' it unto the stranger
15:10 Thou shalt surely g' him, and thine
14 blessed thee thou shalt g' unto him.
16:10 shalt g' unto the Lord thy God,
17 Every man shall g' as he is able,
18: 3 g' unto the priest the shoulder,
4 fleece of thy sheep, shalt thou g'
19: 8 and g' thee all the land which
8 the land which he promised to g'
20:16 the Lord thy God doth g' thee
22:14 g' occasions of speech against
19 and g' them unto the father of the
29 shall g' unto the damsel's father
23:14 to g' up thine enemies before thee;
24: 1 her a bill of divorcement, and g' it
15 his day thou shalt g' him his hire,
25: 3 Forty stripes he may g' him, and
26: 3 sware unto our fathers for to g'
28:11 Lord sware unto thy fathers to g'
12 g' the rain unto thy land in his
55 So that he will not g' to any of them
65 but the Lord shall g' thee there a
30:20 to Isaac, and to Jacob, to g' them.
31: 5 And the Lord shall g' them up
7 hath sworn unto their fathers to g'
14 that I may g' him a charge.
32: 1 G' ear, O ye heavens, and I will speak;
49 the land of Canaan, which I g'
52 which I g' the children of Israel.
34: 4 I will g' it unto thy seed: I have
Jos 1: 2 the land which I do g' to them,
6 I sware unto their fathers to g'
2:12 and g' me a true token:
5: 6 unto their fathers that he would g'
7:19 g', I pray thee, glory to the Lord
8:18 for I will g' it into thine hand.
9:24 Moses to g' you all the land, and
14:12 g' me this mountain, whereof the
15:16 I g' Achsah my daughter to wife.
19 G' me a blessing; for thou hast
19 g' me also springs of water.
17: 4 to g' us an inheritance among our
18: 4 G' out from among you three
20: 4 and g' him a place, that he may
21: 2 to g' us cities to dwell in, with the
43 the land which he sware to g'
J'g 1:12 him will I g' Achsah my daughter
15 G' me a blessing: for thou hast

J'g 1:15 land; g' me also springs of water.
4:19 G' me, I pray thee, a little...to drink;
5: 3 g' ear, O ye princes; I, even I,
7: 2 for me to g' the Midianites into
8: 5 G', I pray you, loaves of bread
6 should g' bread unto thine army?
15 we should g' bread unto thy men
24 that ye would g' me every man the
25 We will willingly g' them.
14:12 then I will g' you thirty sheets and
13 then shall ye g' me thirty sheets
16: 5 we will g' thee every one of us
17:10 I will g' thee ten shekels of silver
20: 7 g' here your advice and counsel.
21: 1 shall not any of us g' his daughter
7 will not g' them of our daughters
18 g' them wives of our daughters:
22 ye did not g' unto them at this time
Ru 4:12 seed which the Lord shall g' thee
1Sa 1:11 wilt g' unto thine handmaid a man
11 then I will g' him unto the Lord
2:10 he shall g' strength unto his king,
15 G' flesh to roast for the priest;
16 but thou shalt g' it me now:
20 Lord g' thee seed of this woman
28 I g' unto the house of thy father
32 wealth which God shall g' Israel:
6: 5 g' glory unto the God of Israel:
8: 6 said, G' us a king to judge us.
14 them, and g' them to his servants.
15 and g' to his officers, and to his
9: 8 that will I g' to the man of God,
10: 4 and g' thee two loaves of bread;
11: 3 G' us seven days' respite, that we
14:41 G' a perfect lot. And Saul and
17:10 g' me a man, that we may fight
25 will g' him his daughter, and make
44 I will g' thy flesh unto the fowls
46 I will g' the carcases of the host
47 and he will g' you into our hands.
18:17 Merab, her will I g' thee to wife:
21 g' him her, that she may be a snare
21: 3 g' me five loaves of bread in mine
9 There is none like that; g' it me.
22: 7 will the son of Jesse g' every one
25: 8 g', I pray thee, whatsoever cometh
11 and g' it unto men, whom I know
27: 5 them g' me a place in some town
30:22 will not g' them ought of the spoil
2Sa 12:11 wives before thine eyes, and g' them
13: 5 come, and g' me meat, and dress
14: 8 and I will g' charge concerning thee.
16:20 G' counsel among you what we
21: 6 And the king said, I will g' them.
22:50 Therefore I will g' thanks unto thee,
23:15 one would g' me drink of the water
24:23 things did Araunah, as a king, g'
1Ki 1:12 let me, I pray thee, g' thee counsel,
2:17 he g' me Abishag the Shunammite
3: 5 God said, Ask what I shall g' thee.
9 G' therefore thy servant an
21 in the morning to g' my child suck,
25 and g' half to the one, and half to
26 g' her the living child, and in no
27 G' her the living child, and in no
5: 6 thee will I g' hire for thy servants
8:32 to g' him according to his
36 g' rain upon thy land, which thou
39 g' to every man according to his
50 g' them compassion before them
11:11 and will g' it to thy servant.
13 g' one tribe to thy son for David
31 and will g' ten tribes to thee:
35 will g' it unto thee, even ten tribes.
36 unto his son will I g' one tribe,
38 and will g' Israel unto thee.
12: 9 counsel g' ye that we may answer
13: 7 and I will g' thee a reward.
8 If thou wilt g' me half thine house,
14:16 g' Israel up because of the sins
15: 4 did the Lord his God g' him a lamp
17:19 he said unto her, G' me thy son.
18:23 them therefore g' us two bullocks;
21: 2 G' me thy vineyard, that I may
2 will g' thee for it a better vineyard
2 g' thee the worth of it in money.
3 g' the inheritance of my fathers
4 I will not g' thee the inheritance
6 G' me thy vineyard for money; or
6 I will g' thee another vineyard
6 I will not g' thee my vineyard.
7 will g' thee the vineyard of Naboth
15 he refused to g' thee for money;
2Ki 4:42 G' unto the people, that they may
43 G' the people, that they may eat:
5:22 g' them, I pray thee, a talent of
6:28 G' thy son, that we may eat him to
29 G' thy son, that we may eat him:
8:19 to g' him alway a light, and to his
10:15 g' me thine hand. And he gave
11:10 over hundreds did the priest g'
14: 9 G' thy daughter to my son to wife:
15:20 silver, to g' to the king of Assyria.
18:23 g' pledges to my lord the king of
22: 5 and let them g' it to the doers of
23:35 to g' the money according to the
35 to g' it unto Pharaoh-nechoh.
1Ch 11:17 Oh that one would g' me drink of the
16: 8 G' thanks unto the Lord, call upon
18 thee will I g' the land of Canaan,
28 G' unto the Lord, ye kindreds of
28 g' unto the Lord glory and strength.
29 G' unto the Lord the glory due
34 O g' thanks unto the Lord; for he is
35 that we may g' thanks to thy holy
41 to g' thanks to the Lord, because his

1Ch 21:23 I g' thee the oxen also for burnt
23 for the meat offering; I g' it all.
22: 9 g' him rest from all his enemies
9 and I will g' peace and quietness
12 the Lord g' thee wisdom and
12 g' thee charge concerning Israel,
25: 3 g' thanks and to praise the Lord.
29:12 make great, and to g' strength unto all.
19 g' unto Solomon my son a perfect
2Ch 1: 7 Ask what I shall g' thee.
10 G' me now wisdom and knowledge
12 I will g' thee riches, and wealth,
2:10 I will g' to thy servants, the hewers
10: 6 What counsel g' ye me to return
9 What advice g' ye that we may return
21: 7 to g' a light to him and to his sons
24:19 them: but they would not g' ear.
25: 9 The Lord is able to g' thee much
18 G' thy daughter to my son to wife:
30:12 to g' them one heart to do the
24 Hezekiah king of Judah did g' to
31: 2 to minister, and to g' thanks, and to
4 to g' the portion of the priests
15 to g' to their brethren by courses,
19 to g' portions to all the males
32:11 g' over yourselves to die by famine
35:12 that they might g' according to
Ezr 4:21 G' ye now commandment
9: 8 to g' us a nail in his holy place,
8 and g' us a little reviving in our
9 to g' us a reviving, to set up the
9 and to g' us a wall in Judah
12 g' not your daughters unto their
Ne 2: 8 may g' me timber to make beams
4: 4 and g' them for a prey in the land
9: 8 to g' the land of the Canaanites,
8 to g' it, I say, to his seed,
12 fire, to g' them light in the way
15 thou hadst sworn to g' them.
30 yet would they not g' ear:
10:30 we would not g' our daughters
12:24 to praise and to g' thanks, according
13:25 Ye shall not g' your daughters
Es 1:19 and let the king g' her royal estate
20 the wives shall g' to their husbands
8: 1 that day did the king Ahasuerus g'
Job 2: 4 all that a man hath will he g' for
3:11 why did I not g' up the ghost
6:22 G' a reward for me of your substance?
13:19 tongue, I shall g' up the ghost.
32:21 neither let me g' flattering titles
22 For I know not to g' flattering titles;
34: 2 and g' ear unto me, ye that have
Ps 2: 8 and I shall g' thee the heathen for
5: 1 G' ear to my words, O Lord,
6: 5 in the grave who shall g' thee thanks?
17: 1 g' ear unto my prayer, that goeth
18:49 Therefore will I g' thanks unto thee,
28: 4 G' them according to their deeds,
4 g' them after the work of their
29: 1 G' unto the Lord, O ye mighty,
1 g' unto the Lord glory and strength.
2 G' unto the Lord the glory due
11 The Lord will g' strength unto his
30: 4 and g' thanks at the remembrance
12 I will g' thanks unto thee for ever.
35:18 I will g' thee thanks in the great
37: 4 and he shall g' thee the desires of
39:12 g' ear unto my cry; hold not thy
49: 1 g' ear, all ye inhabitants of the
7 nor g' to God a ransom for him:
51:16 not sacrifice; else would I g' it:
54: 2 g' ear to the words of my mouth.
55: 1 G' ear to my prayer, O God;
57: 7 I will sing and g' praise.
60:11 G' us help from trouble: for vain
72: 1 G' the king thy judgments, O God,
75: 1 Unto thee, O God, do we g' thanks,
1 unto thee do we g' thanks:
78: 1 G' ear, O my people, to my law:
20 he g' bread also? can he provide
79:13 pasture will g' thee thanks for ever:
80: 1 G' ear, O Shepherd of Israel,
84: 8 g' ear, O God of Jacob. Selah.
11 the Lord will g' grace and glory:
85:12 Lord shall g' that which is good;
86: 6 G' ear, O Lord, unto my prayer;
16 g' thy strength unto thy servant,
91:11 he shall g' his angels charge over
92: 1 It is a good thing to g' thanks
94:13 That thou mayest g' him rest
96: 7 G' unto the Lord, O ye kindreds
7 g' unto the Lord glory and strength.
8 G' unto the Lord the glory due
97:12 and g' thanks at the remembrance of
104:11 g' drink to every beast of the field:
27 that thou mayest g' them their
105: 1 g' thanks unto the Lord; call upon
11 Unto thee will I g' the land of
39 and fire to g' light in the night.
106: 1 O g' thanks unto the Lord; for he is
47 to g' thanks unto thy holy name, and
107: 1 g' thanks unto the Lord; for he is
108: 1 I will sing and g' praise, even
12 G' us help from trouble: for vain
109: 4 but I g' myself unto prayer.
111: 6 that he may g' them the heritage
115: 1 but unto thy name g' glory, for thy
118: 1, 29 O g' thanks unto the Lord; for he
119:34 G' me understanding, and I shall keep
62 I will rise to g' thanks unto thee
73 g' me understanding, that I may learn
125 g' me understanding, that I may know
144 g' me understanding, and I shall live.
169 g' me understanding according to thy
122: 4 g' thanks unto the name of the Lord,

Ps 132: 4 I will not g' sleep to mine eyes,
136: 1 O g' thanks unto the Lord; for he is
2 O g' thanks unto the God of gods:
3 O g' thanks to the Lord of lords:
26 O g' thanks unto the God of heaven:
140:13 Surely the righteous shall g' thanks
141: 1 g' ear unto my voice, when I cry
143: 1 g' ear to my supplications: in thy
Pr 1: 4 To g' subtilty to the simple, and
3:28 to morrow I will g'; when thou hast
4: 2 I g' you good doctrine, forsake ye
9 shall g' to thine head an ornament
5: 9 thou g' thine honour unto others,
6: 4 G' not sleep to thine eyes, nor
31 he shall g' all the substance of his
9: 9 G' instruction to a wise man and
23:26 My son, g' me thine heart, and let
25:21 enemy be hungry, g' him bread to
21 if he be thirsty, g' him water to drink:
29:15 The rod and reproof g' wisdom:
17 correct thy son, and he shall g' thee
17 he shall g' delight unto thy soul.
30: 8 g' me neither poverty nor riches;
15 hath two daughters, crying, G', g'.
31: 3 G' not thy strength unto women,
6 G' strong drink unto him that is
31 G' her of the fruit of her hands;
Ec 2: 3 heart to g' myself unto wine,
26 that he may g' to him that is good
5: 1 to hear, than to g' the sacrifice of
11: 2 G' a portion to seven, and also to
Ca 2:13 the tender grape g' a good smell.
7:12 there will I g' thee my loves.
13 The mandrakes g' a smell, and at
8: 7 if a man would g' all the substance
Isa 1: 2 Hear, O heavens, and g' ear, O earth;
10 g' ear unto the law of our God,
3: 4 And I will g' children to be their
7:14 Lord himself shall g' you a sign,
22 of milk that they shall g',
8: 9 and g' ear, all ye of far countries:
10: 6 of my wrath will I g' him a charge,
13:10 thereof shall not g' their light:
14: 3 day that the Lord shall g' thee rest
19: 4 And the Egyptians will I g' over
28:23 G' ye ear, and hear my voice;
30:20 the Lord g' you the bread of
23 Then shall he g' the rain of thy
32: 9 daughters; g' ear unto my speech.
36: 8 g' pledges, I pray thee, to my
8 and I will g' thee two thousand
41:27 g' to Jerusalem one that bringeth
42: 6 and g' thee for a covenant of the
8 my glory will I not g' to another,
12 Let them g' glory unto the Lord,
23 Who among you will g' ear to this?
43: 4 therefore will I g' men for thee,
6 I will say to the north, G' up;
20 I g' waters in the wilderness, and
20 desert, to g' drink to my people,
45: 3 And I will g' thee the treasures of
48:11 I will not g' my glory unto another.
49: 6 I will also g' thee for a light
8 and g' thee for a covenant of the
20 g' place to me that I may dwell.
51: 4 g' ear unto me, O my nation: for a
55:10 that it may g' seed to the sower,
56: 5 Even unto them will I g' in mine
5 I will g' them an everlasting name,
60:19 shall the moon g' light unto thee:
61: 3 to g' unto them beauty for ashes,
62: 7 And g' him no rest, till he establish,
8 I will no more g' thy corn to be
Jer 3:15 And I will g' you pastors according
19 and g' thee a pleasant land, a
4:12 will I g' sentence against them.
16 and g' out their voice against
6:10 shall I speak, and g' warning,
8:10 Therefore will I g' their wives
9:15 and g' them water of gall to drink.
11: 5 to g' them a land flowing with
13:15 Hear ye, and g' ear; be not proud:
16 G' glory to the Lord your God,
14:13 I will g' you assured peace in this
22 or can the heavens g' showers?
15:13 thy treasures will I g' to the spoil
16: 7 shall men g' them the cup...to drink
17: 3 I will g' thy substance and all thy
10 g' every man according to his ways,
18:18 let us not g' heed to any of his words.
19 G' heed to me, O Lord, and hearken
19: 7 their carcases will I g' to be meat
20: 4 I will g' all Judah into the hand
5 the kings of Judah will I g' into
22:25 And I will g' thee into the hand of
24: 7 will g' them an heart to know me,
8 I g' Zedekiah the king of Judah,
25:30 he shall g' a shout, as they that tread
31 he will g' them that are wicked
26:24 should not g' him into the hand
29: 6 g' your daughters to husbands,
11 of evil, to g' you an expected end.
30:16 upon thee will I g' for a prey.
32: 3 Behold, I will g' this city into the
19 to g' every one according to his
22 to g' them, a land flowing with milk
28 the Lord; Behold, I will g' this city
39 And I will g' them one heart, and
34: 2 I will g' this city into the hand of
18 g' the men that have transgressed
20 I will even g' them into the hand
21 Judah and his princes will I g' into
35: 2 and g' them wine to drink.
37:21 g' him daily a piece of bread out
38:15 if I g' thee counsel, wilt thou not
16 neither will I g' thee into the

Jer 44:30 I will g' Pharaoh-hophra king of
45: 5 life will I g' unto thee for a prey
48: 9 G' wings unto Moab, that it may
50:34 that he may g' rest to the land,
La 2:18 g' thyself no rest; let not the
3:65 G' them sorrow of heart, thy
4: 3 they g' suck to their young ones: the
Eze 2: 8 thy mouth, and eat that I g' thee.
3: 3 bowels with this roll that I g' thee.
17 and g' them warning from me.
7:21 And I will g' it into the hands of
11: 2 and g' wicked counsel in this city:
17 I will g' you the land of Israel.
19 And I will g' them one heart,
19 and will g' them an heart of flesh:
15: 6 fuel, so will I g' the inhabitants of
16:33 They g' gifts to all whores: but
36 which thou didst g' unto them;
38 and I will g' thee blood in fury
39 I will also g' thee into their hand,
41 also shalt g' no hire any more.
61 g' them unto thee for daughters,
17:15 that they might g' him horses and
20:28 lifted up mine hand to g' it to them,
42 mine hand to g' it to your fathers.
21:11 to g' it into the hand of the slayer.
27 right it is; and I will g' it him.
23:31 will I g' her cup into thine hand.
46 and will g' them to be removed
25:10 and will g' them in possession,
29:19 I will g' the land of Egypt unto
21 g' thee the opening of the mouth
32: 7 the moon shall not g' her light.
33:15 g' again that he had robbed, walk
27 open field will I g' to the beasts
36:26 A new heart also will I g' you,
26 and I will g' you an heart of flesh.
39: 4 will g' thee unto the ravenous birds
11 I will g' unto Gog a place there
43:19 shalt g' to the priests the Levites
44:28 g' them no possession in Israel:
30 ye shall also g' unto the priest the
45: 8 the rest of the land shall they g'
13 ye shall g' the sixth part of an ephah
16 land shall g' this oblation
17 prince's part to g' burnt offerings
46: 5 the lambs as he shall be able to g',
11 and to the lambs as he is able to g',
16 If the prince g' a gift unto any of
17 if he g' a gift of his inheritance
18 he shall g' his sons inheritance out of
47:14 hand to g' it unto your fathers:
23 shall ye g' him his inheritance,
Da 1:12 let them g' us pulse to eat, and
2:16 king that he would g' him time,
5:17 and g' thy rewards to another;
6: 2 might g' accounts unto them,
8:13 to g' both the sanctuary and the
9:22 g' thee skill and understanding.
11:17 g' him the daughter of women,
21 they shall not g' the honour of the
Ho 2: 5 g' me my bread and my water,
15 And I will g' her her vineyards
4:18 rulers with shame do love, G' ye.
5: 1 g' ye ear, O house of the king;
9:14 G' them, O Lord:
14 what wilt thou g'?
14 g' them a miscarrying womb
11: 8 How shall I g' thee up, Ephraim?
13:10 saidst, G' me a king and princes?
Joe 1: 2 Hear this, ye old men, and g' ear,
2:17 g' not thine heritage to reproach,
Mic 1:14 g' presents to Moresheth-gath:
5: 3 Therefore will he g' them up,
6: 7 shall I g' my firstborn for my
14 which thou deliverest will I g' up
Hag 2: 9 will I g' peace, saith the Lord
Zec 3: 7 and I will g' thee places to walk
8:12 the vine shall g' her fruit, and the
12 ground shall g' her increase, and
12 the heavens shall g' their dew;
10: 1 and g' them showers of rain, to
11:12 If ye think good, g' me my price;
Mal 2: 2 to g' glory unto my name, saith
M't 4: 6 He shall g' his angels charge
9 All these things will I g' thee,
5:31 g' her a writing of divorcement:
42 G' to him that asketh thee, and
6:11 G' us this day our daily bread.
7: 6 G' not that which is holy unto the
9 ask bread, will he g' him a stone?
10 a fish, will he g' him a serpent?
11 g' good gifts unto your children,
11 Father which is in heaven g' good
9:24 He said unto them, G' place: for the
10: 8 freely ye have received, freely g'.
42 whosoever shall g' to drink unto
11:28 heavy laden, and I will g' you rest.
12:36 shall g' account thereof in the day
14: 7 g' her whatsoever she would ask.
8 G' me here John Baptist's head in
16 need not depart; g' ye them to eat.
16:19 I will g' unto thee the keys of the
26 a man g' in exchange for his soul?
17:27 and g' unto them for me and thee.
19: 7 to g' a writing of divorcement,
21 g' to the poor, and thou shalt have
20: 4 whatsoever is right I will g' you.
8 labourers, and g' them their hire,
14 g' unto this last, even as unto thee.
23 and on my left, is not mine to g',
28 to g' his life a ransom for many.
22:17 Is it lawful to g' tribute unto
24:19 them that g' suck in those days!
29 the moon shall not g' her light,
45 to g' them meat in due season?

M't 25: 8 G' us of your oil; for our lamps
28 g' it unto him which hath ten
26:15 said unto them, What will ye g' me,
53 he shall presently g' me more
M'r 6:22 whatsoever thou wilt, and I will g'
23 I will g' it thee, unto the half
25 I will that thou g' me by and by
37 G' ye them to eat. And they say
37 of bread, and g' them to eat?
8:37 Or what shall a man g' in exchange
9:41 g' you a cup of water to drink
10:21 g' to the poor, and thou shalt have
40 on my left hand is not mine to g';
45 to g' his life a ransom for many.
12: 9 will g' the vineyard unto others.
14 Is it lawful to g' tribute to Cæsar,
15 Shall we g', or shall we not g'?
13:17 to them that g' suck in those days!
24 the moon shall not g' her light,
14:11 and promised to g' him money.
Lu 1:32 the Lord God shall g' unto him the
77 To g' knowledge of salvation unto
79 To g' light to them that sit in
4: 6 All this power will I g' thee,
6 and to whomsoever I will I g' it.
10 shall g' his angels charge over thee.
6:30 G' to every man that asketh of
38 G', and it shall be given unto you;
38 shall men g' into your bosom.
8:55 he commanded to g' her meat.
9:13 said unto them, G' ye them to eat.
10: 7 drinking such things as they g':
19 I g' unto you power to tread on
11: 3 G' us day by day our daily bread.
7 I cannot rise and g' thee.
8 Though he will not rise and g' him,
8 he will rise and g' him as many
11 will he g' him a stone? or if he ask
11 will he for a fish g' him a serpent?
13 g' good gifts unto your children:
13 your heavenly Father g' the Holy
36 of a candle doth g' thee light.
41 g' alms of such things as ye have;
12:32 Father's good pleasure to g' you
33 Sell that ye have, and g' alms;
42 to g' them their portion of meat
51 I am come to g' peace on earth?
58 g' diligence that thou mayest be
14: 9 say to thee, G' this man place;
15:12 Father, g' me the portion of goods
16: 2 g' an account of thy stewardship;
12 g' you that which is your own?
17:18 that returned to g' glory to God,
18:12 I g' tithes of all that I possess.
19: 8 half of my goods I g' to the poor;
24 g' it to him that hath ten pounds.
20:10 they should g' him of the fruit
16 and shall g' the vineyard to others.
22 Is it lawful for us to g' tribute
21:15 I will g' you a mouth and wisdom,
23 to them that g' suck, in those days!
22: 5 covenanted to g' him money.
23: 2 forbidding to g' tribute to Cæsar,
Joh 1:22 g' an answer to them that sent us.
4: 7 saith unto her, G' me to drink.
10 saith to thee, G' me to drink;
14 the water that I shall g' him shall
14 water that I shall g' him shall be in
15 g' me this water, that I thirst not,
6:27 the Son of man shall g' unto you:
34 Lord, evermore g' us this bread.
51 bread that I will g' is my flesh,
51 I will g' for the life of the world.
52 How can this man g' us his flesh
7:19 Did not Moses g' you the law,
9:24 said unto him, G' God the praise:
10:28 And I g' unto them eternal life;
11:22 ask of God, God will g' it thee.
13:26 to whom I shall g' a sop, when I
29 should g' something to the poor.
34 A new commandment I g' unto you,
14:16 he shall g' you another Comforter,
27 my peace I g' unto you: not as the
27 as the world giveth, g' I unto you.
15:16 in my name, he may g' it you.
16:23 in my name, he will g' it you.
17: 2 he should g' eternal life to as many
Ac 3: 6 but such as I have g' I thee: In the
5:31 for to g' repentance to Israel, and
6: 4 g' ourselves continually to prayer,
7: 5 promised that he would g' it to
38 the lively oracles to g' unto us:
8:19 Saying, G' me also this power, that
10:43 g' all the prophets witness, that
13:16 and ye that fear God, g' audience.
34 g' you the sure mercies of David.
19:40 g' an account of this concourse.
20:32 to g' you an inheritance among all
35 more blessed to g' than to receive.
Ro 8:32 him also freely g' us all things?
12:19 but rather g' place unto wrath:
20 if he thirst, g' him drink: for in so
14:12 shall g' account of himself to God.
16: 4 I g' thanks, but also all the churches
1Co 7: 5 ye may g' yourselves to fasting
25 yet I g' my judgment, as one that
10:30 for that for which I g' thanks?
32 G' none offence, neither to the
12: 3 I g' you to understand, that no man
13: 3 though I g' my body to be burned,
14: 7 they g' a distinction in the sounds,
8 the trumpet g' an uncertain sound,
2Co 4: 6 shined in our hearts, to g' the light
5:12 g' you occasion to glory on our
8:10 herein I g' my advice: for this is
9: 7 in his heart, so let him g'; not

Eph 1:16 Cease not to *g*˙ thanks for you,
17 *g*˙ unto you the spirit of wisdom
4:27 Neither *g*˙ place to the devil.
28 have to *g*˙ to him that needeth.
5:14 and Christ shall *g*˙ thee light.
Col 1: 3 We *g*˙ thanks to God and the Father
4: 1 *g*˙ unto your servants that which
1Th 1: 2 We *g*˙ thanks to God always for
5:18 In everything *g*˙ thanks: for this is the
2Th 2:13 bound to *g*˙ thanks alway to God
3:16 *g*˙ you peace always by all means.
1Ti 1: 4 Neither *g*˙ heed to fables and endless
4:13 I come, *g*˙ attendance to reading, to
15 things; *g*˙ thyself wholly to them;
5: 7 these things *g*˙ in charge, that
14 *g*˙ none occasion to the adversary
6:13 *g*˙ thee charge in the sight of God,
2Ti 1:16 the Lord *g*˙ mercy unto the house
2: 7 Lord *g*˙ thee understanding in all
25 if God peradventure will *g*˙ them
4: 8 judge, shall *g*˙ me at that day:
Heb 2: 1 to *g*˙ the more earnest heed to the
13:17 they that must *g*˙ account, that
Jas 2:16 notwithstanding ye *g*˙ them not
1Pe 3:15 be ready always to *g*˙ an answer
4: 5 Who shall *g*˙ account to him that is
2Pe 1:10 *g*˙ diligence to make your calling
1Jo 5:16 he shall *g*˙ him life for them that
Re 2: 7 will I *g*˙ to eat of the tree of life,
10 and I will *g*˙ thee a crown of life.
17 him that overcometh will I *g*˙ to eat
17 and will *g*˙ him a white stone,
23 and I will *g*˙ unto every one of you
26 to him will I *g*˙ power over the
28 And I will *g*˙ him the morning star.
4: 9 those beasts *g*˙ glory and honour
10: 9 said unto him, *G*˙ me the little book.
11: 3 will *g*˙ power unto my two witnesses,
17 We *g*˙ thee thanks, O Lord God
18 *g*˙ reward unto thy servants the
13:15 *g*˙ life unto the image of the beast,
14: 7 Fear God, and *g*˙ glory to him;
16: 9 they repented not to *g*˙ him glory.
19 to *g*˙ unto her the cup of the wine
17:13 *g*˙ their power and strength unto
17 *g*˙ their kingdom unto the beast,
18: 7 much torment and sorrow *g*˙ her:
19: 7 and rejoice, and *g*˙ honour to him:
21: 6 I will *g*˙ unto him that is athirst
22:12 *g*˙ every man according as his work

given See also FORGIVEN.
Ge 1:29 *g*˙ you every herb bearing seed,
30 I have *g*˙ every green herb for meat:
9: 3 as the green herb have I *g*˙ you
15: 3 Behold, to me thou hast *g*˙ no seed:
18 Unto thy seed have I *g*˙ this land,
16: 5 I have *g*˙ my maid into thy bosom;
20:16 I have *g*˙ thy brother a thousand
21: 7 should have *g*˙ children suck?
24:35 he hath *g*˙ him flocks, and herds,
36 and unto him hath he *g*˙ all
27:37 all his brethren have I *g*˙ to him
29:33 he hath therefore *g*˙ me this son
30: 6 and hath *g*˙ me a son: therefore
18 God hath *g*˙ me my hire,
18 because I have *g*˙ my maiden
31: 9 cattle of your father, and *g*˙ them
33: 5 hath graciously *g*˙ thy servant.
38:14 she was not *g*˙ unto him to wife.
43:23 the God of your father, hath *g*˙ you
48: 9 my sons, whom God hath *g*˙ me
22 I have *g*˙ to thee one portion above
Ex 5:16 is no straw *g*˙ unto thy servants,
18 for there shall no straw be *g*˙ you,
16:15 bread which the Lord hath *g*˙ you
29 the Lord hath *g*˙ you the sabbath,
21: 4 If his master have *g*˙ him a wife,
31: 6 I have *g*˙ with him Aholiab,
Le 6:17 *g*˙ it unto them for their portion
7:34 have *g*˙ them unto Aaron the priest
36 the Lord commanded to be *g*˙ them
10:14 are *g*˙ out of the sacrifices of peace
17 God hath *g*˙ it you to bear the
17:11 I have *g*˙ it to you upon the altar
19:20 not at all redeemed, nor freedom *g*˙
20: 3 he hath *g*˙ of his seed unto Molech,
Nu 3: 9 they are wholly *g*˙ unto him out of
8:16 they are wholly *g*˙ unto me from
19 And I have *g*˙ the Levites as a gift
16:14 or *g*˙ us inheritance of fields and
18: 6 they are *g*˙ as a gift for the Lord,
7 *g*˙ your priest's office unto you
8 also have *g*˙ thee the charge of mine
8 unto thee have I *g*˙ them by reason
11 I have *g*˙ them unto thee, and to thy
12 unto the Lord, them have I *g*˙ thee.
19 have I *g*˙ thee, and thy sons and
21 I have *g*˙ the children of Levi all
24 I have *g*˙ to the Levites to inherit:
26 the tithes which I have *g*˙ you from
20:12 the land which I have *g*˙ them.
24 which I have *g*˙ unto the children
21:29 he hath *g*˙ his sons that escaped,
26:54 every one shall his inheritance be *g*
62 there was no inheritance *g*˙ them
27:12 the land which I have *g*˙ unto the
32: 5 this land be *g*˙ unto thy servants
7 land which the Lord hath *g*˙ them?
9 land which the Lord had *g*˙ them.
33:53 I have *g*˙ you the land to possess it.
De 1: 3 Lord had *g*˙ him in commandment
2: 5 I have *g*˙ mount Seir unto Esau
9 have *g*˙ Ar unto the children of Lot
19 I have *g*˙ it unto the children of Lot
24 I have *g*˙ into thine hand Sihon
3:18 Lord your God hath *g*˙ you this

De 3:19 your cities which I have *g*˙ you;
20 have *g*˙ rest unto your brethren,
20 the Lord your God hath *g*˙ them
20 possession, which I have *g*˙ you.
8:10 good land which he hath *g*˙ thee.
9:23 the land which I have *g*˙ you;
12:15 blessing...which he hath *g*˙ thee:
21 flock, which the Lord hath *g*˙ thee,
13:12 God hath *g*˙ thee to dwell there,
16:17 blessing...which he hath *g*˙ thee.
20:14 the spoil...thy God hath *g*˙ thee.
22:17 *g*˙ occasions of speech against
25:19 the Lord thy God hath *g*˙ thee rest
26: 9 hath *g*˙ us this land, even a land
10 which thou, O Lord, hast *g*˙ me.
11 the Lord thy God hath *g*˙ unto thee,
12 and hast *g*˙ it unto the Levite,
13 also have *g*˙ them unto the Levite,
14 nor *g*˙ ought thereof for the dead:
15 the land which thou hast *g*˙ us,
28:31 shall be *g*˙ unto thine enemies,
32 daughters shall be *g*˙ unto another
52 land...Lord thy God hath *g*˙ thee.
53 daughters...thy God hath *g*˙ thee,
29: 4 the Lord hath not *g*˙ you an heart
26 whom he had not *g*˙ unto them:
Jos 1: 3 that have I *g*˙ unto you, as I said
13 Lord your God hath *g*˙ you rest,
13 and hath *g*˙ you this land.
15 the Lord have *g*˙ your brethren
15 rest, as he hath *g*˙ you,
2: 9 the Lord hath *g*˙ you the land,
14 when the Lord hath *g*˙ us the land,
6: 2 I have *g*˙ into thine hand Jericho,
16 the Lord hath *g*˙ you the city.
8: 1 *g*˙ into thy hand the king of Ai,
14: 3 Moses had *g*˙ the inheritance of two
15:19 thou hast *g*˙ me a south land;
17:14 Why hast thou *g*˙ me but one lot
18: 3 Lord God of your fathers hath *g*˙
22: 4 the Lord your God hath *g*˙ rest
7 had *g*˙ possession in Bashan:
23: 1 the Lord had *g*˙ rest unto Israel
13, 15 the Lord your God hath *g*˙ you.
16 land which he hath *g*˙ unto you.
24:13 And I have *g*˙ you a land for
33 was *g*˙ him in mount Ephraim.
J'g 1:15 for thou hast *g*˙ me a south land;
14:20 Samson's wife was *g*˙ to his companion,
15: 6 wife, and *g*˙ her to his companion.
18 Thou hast *g*˙ this great deliverance
18:10 God hath *g*˙ it into your hands;
Ru 2:12 full reward be *g*˙ thee of the Lord
1Sa 1:27 the Lord hath *g*˙ me my petition
15:28 hath *g*˙ it to a neighbour of thine,
18:19 Saul's daughter should have been *g*˙
19 David, that she was *g*˙ unto Adriel
22:13 in that thou hast *g*˙ him bread,
25:27 it even be *g*˙ unto the young men
44 Saul had *g*˙ Michal his daughter,
28:17 and *g*˙ it to thy neighbour, even to
30:23 that which the Lord hath *g*˙ us,
2Sa 4:10 I would have *g*˙ him a reward
7: 1 Lord had *g*˙ him rest round about
9: 9 I have *g*˙ unto thy master's son
12: 8 would moreover have *g*˙ unto thee
14 hast *g*˙ great occasion to the enemies
17: 7 Ahithophel hath *g*˙ is not good
18:11 I would have *g*˙ thee ten shekels
19:42 or hath he *g*˙ us any gift?
22:36 Thou hast also *g*˙ me the shield
41 *g*˙ me the necks of mine enemies,
1Ki 1:48 hath *g*˙ one to sit on my throne
2:21 Let Abishag the Shunammite be *g*˙
3: 6 *g*˙ him a son to sit on his throne,
12 I have *g*˙ thee a wise and an
13 also *g*˙ thee that which thou hast
5: 4 the Lord my God hath *g*˙ me rest
7 day, which hath *g*˙ unto David
8:36 thy land, which thou hast *g*˙ to thy
56 the Lord, that hath *g*˙ rest unto his
9: 7 out of the land which I have *g*˙
12 cities which Solomon had *g*˙ him;
13 cities are these which thou hast *g*˙
16 and *g*˙ it for a present unto his
12: 8 old men, which they had *g*˙ him,
13: 5 sign which the man of God had *g*˙
18:26 the bullock which was *g*˙ them,
2Ki 5: 1 had *g*˙ deliverance unto Syria:
17 I pray thee, be *g*˙ to thy servant
8:29 wounds which the Syrians had *g*˙
9:15 wounds which the Syrians had *g*˙
23:11 kings of Judah had *g*˙ to the sun,
25:30 allowance *g*˙ him of the king,
1Ch 5: 1 was *g*˙ unto the sons of Joseph
6:61 cities *g*˙ out of the half tribe,
63 Unto the sons of Merari were *g*˙ by
71 Unto the sons of Gershom were *g*˙
77 the children of Merari were *g*˙ out of
78 *g*˙ them out of the tribe of Reuben,
22:18 he not *g*˙ you rest on every side?
18 for he hath *g*˙ of the inhabitants
23:25 The Lord God of Israel hath *g*˙ rest
28: 5 the Lord hath *g*˙ me many sons,)
29: 3 gold and silver, which I have *g*˙
14 and of thine own have we *g*˙ thee.
2Ch 2:12 *g*˙ to David the king a wise son,
6:27 upon thy land, which thou hast *g*˙
7:20 out of my land which I have *g*˙
14: 6 because the Lord had *g*˙ him rest.
7 he hath *g*˙ us rest on every side.
20:11 which thou hast *g*˙ us to inherit.
22: 6 the wounds which were *g*˙ him at
25: 9 hundred talents which I have *g*˙
32:29 God had *g*˙ him substance very
34:14 the law of the Lord *g*˙ by Moses.

2Ch 34:18 the priest hath *g*˙ me a book.
36:23 hath the Lord God of heaven *g*˙ me;
Ezr 1: 2 The Lord God of heaven hath *g*˙ me
4:21 commandment shall be *g*˙ from
6: 4 expences be *g*˙ out of the king's
8 expences be *g*˙ unto these men,
9 be *g*˙ them day by day without fail:
7: 6 the Lord God of Israel had *g*˙:
19 The vessels also that are *g*˙ thee
9:13 *g*˙ us such deliverance as this;
Ne 2: 7 letters be *g*˙ me to the governors
10:29 God's law, which was *g*˙ by Moses
13: 5 commanded to be *g*˙ to the Levites,
10 the Levites had not been *g*˙ them.
Es 2: 3 their things for purification be *g*˙
9 which were meet to be *g*˙ her,
13 whatsoever she desired was *g*˙ her
3:11 silver is *g*˙ to thee, the people also,
14 a commandment to be *g*˙ in every
15 was *g*˙ in Shushan the palace.
4: 8 the decree that was *g*˙ at Shushan
5: 3 it shall be even *g*˙ thee to the half
7: 3 let my life be *g*˙ me at my petition,
8: 7 have *g*˙ Esther the house of Haman,
13 a commandment to be *g*˙ in every
14 was *g*˙ at Shushan the palace.
9:14 and the decree was *g*˙ at Shushan;
Job 3:20 is light *g*˙ to him that is in misery,
23 Why is light *g*˙ to a man whose way
9:24 is *g*˙ into the hand of the wicked:
10:18 O that I had *g*˙ up the ghost,
15:19 unto whom alone the earth was *g*˙,
22: 7 not *g*˙ water to the weary to drink,
24:23 Though it be *g*˙ him to be in safety,
33: 4 of the Almighty hath *g*˙ me life.
34:13 *g*˙ him a charge over the earth?
37:10 By the breath of God frost is *g*˙:
38:36 *g*˙ understanding to the heart?
39:19 Hast thou *g*˙ the horse strength?
Ps 16: 7 the Lord, who hath *g*˙ me counsel:
18:35 Thou hast also *g*˙ me the shield
40 *g*˙ me the necks of mine enemies;
21: 2 hast *g*˙ him his heart's desire,
44:11 *g*˙ us like sheep appointed for
60: 4 hast *g*˙ a banner to them that fear
61: 5 thou hast *g*˙ me the heritage of
71: 3 hast *g*˙ commandment to save me;
72:15 and to him shall be *g*˙ of the gold
78:24 had *g*˙ them of the corn of heaven.
63 maidens were not *g*˙ to marriage.
79: 2 bodies of thy servants have they *g*˙
111: 5 *g*˙ meat unto them that fear him:
112: 9 *g*˙ to the poor; his righteousness
115:16 earth hath he *g*˙ to the children
118:18 he hath not *g*˙ me over unto death.
120: 3 What shall be *g*˙ unto thee? or what
124: 6 who hath not *g*˙ us as a prey
Pr 19:17 that which he hath *g*˙ will he pay
23: 2 if thou be a man *g*˙ to appetite.
24:21 not with them that are *g*˙ to change:
Ec 1:13 sore travail hath God *g*˙ to the sons
3:10 travail, which God hath *g*˙ to the
5:19 to whom God hath *g*˙ riches and
19 and hath *g*˙ him power to eat
6: 2 man to whom God hath *g*˙ riches,
8: 8 deliver those that are *g*˙ to it.
9: 9 thy vanity, which he hath *g*˙ thee
12:11 which are *g*˙ from one shepherd.
Isa 3:11 reward of his hands shall be *g*˙ him.
8:18 children whom the Lord hath *g*˙
9: 6 a child is born, unto us a son is *g*˙:
23:11 the Lord hath *g*˙ a commandment
33:16 bread shall be *g*˙ him; his waters
35: 2 glory of Lebanon shall be *g*˙ unto
37:10 Jerusalem shall not be *g*˙ into the
43:28 and have *g*˙ Jacob to the curse,
47: 6 and *g*˙ them into thine hand:
8 thou that art *g*˙ to pleasures, that
50: 4 Lord God hath *g*˙ me the tongue
55: 4 Behold, I have *g*˙ him for a witness
Jer 3: 8 away, and *g*˙ her a bill of divorce;
18 I have *g*˙ for an inheritance unto your
6:13 every one is *g*˙ to covetousness;
8:10 the greatest is *g*˙ to covetousness,
13 the things that I have *g*˙ them
14 and *g*˙ us water of gall to drink,
11:18 the Lord hath *g*˙ me knowledge
12: 7 *g*˙ the dearly beloved of my soul
13:20 where is the flock that was *g*˙ thee,
15: 9 she hath *g*˙ up the ghost; her sun
21:10 shall be *g*˙ into the hand of the king
25: 5 land that the Lord hath *g*˙ unto you
27: 5 *g*˙ it unto whom it seemed meet
6 now have I *g*˙ all these lands
6 beasts of the field have I *g*˙ him
28:14 *g*˙ him the beasts of the field also.
32:22 *g*˙ them this land, which thou didst
24 and the city is *g*˙ into the hand of
25 for the city is *g*˙ into the hand of the
43 it is *g*˙ into the hand of the
35:15 the land which I have *g*˙ to you
38: 3 This city shall surely be *g*˙ into the
18 shall this city be *g*˙ into the hand
39:17 thou shalt not be *g*˙ into the hand
44:20 people which had *g*˙ him that answer,
47: 7 the Lord hath *g*˙ it a charge against
50:15 hath *g*˙ her hand: her foundations
52:34 continual diet *g*˙ him of the king
La 1:11 *g*˙ their pleasant things for meat
2: 7 *g*˙ up into the hand of the enemy
5: 6 have *g*˙ the hand to the Egyptians,
Eze 3:20 because thou hast not *g*˙ him warning,
4:15 *g*˙ thee cow's dung for man's dung,
11:15 unto us is this land *g*˙ in possession.
15: 6 which I have *g*˙ to the fire for fuel,
16:17 of my silver, which I had *g*˙ thee,

Eze 16:34 and no reward is g' unto thee.
17:18 he had g' his hand, and hath done
18: 7 hath g' his bread to the hungry,
8 that hath not g' forth upon usury,
13 Hath g' forth upon usury, and hath
16 hath g' his bread to the hungry,
20:15 into the land which I had g' them,
21:11 And he hath g' it to be furbished,
28:25 land that I have g' to my servant
29: 5 have g' thee for meat to the beasts
20 I have g' him the land of Egypt
33:24 the land is g' us for inheritance.
35:12 desolate, they are g' us to consume.
37:25 the land that I have g' unto Jacob
47:11 they shall be g' to salt.
Da 2:23 who hast g' me wisdom and might,
37 for the God of heaven hath g' thee
38 heaven hath he g' into thine hand,
4:16 let a beast's heart be g' unto him;
5:28 and g' to the Medes and Persians.
7: 4 and a man's heart was g' to it.
6 and dominion was g' to it.
11 and g' to the burning flame.
14 And there was g' him dominion,
22 and judgment was g' to the saints
25 and they shall be g' into his hand
27 be g' to the people of the saints of
8:12 host was g' him against the daily
11: 6 she shall be g' up, and they that
11 multitude shall be g' into his hand.
Ho 2: 9 flax g' to cover her nakedness.
12 rewards that my lovers have g' me:
Joe 2:23 he hath g' you the former rain
3: 3 and have g' a boy for an harlot,
Am 4: 6 have g' you cleanness of teeth
9:15 their land which I have g' them,
Na 1:14 And the Lord hath g' a commandment
M't 7: 7 Ask, and it shall be g' you: seek,
9: 8 glorified God, which had g' such
10:19 it shall be g' you in that same hour
12:39 and there shall no sign be g' to it,
13:11 g' unto you to know the mysteries
11 but to them it is not g'.
12 whosoever hath, to him shall be g',
14: 9 he commanded it to be g' her.
11 in a charger, and g' to the damsel:
16: 4 there shall no sign be g' unto it,
19:11 save they to whom it is g'.
20:23 it shall be g' to them for whom it
21:43 taken from you, and g' to a nation
22:30 marry, nor are g' in marriage,
25:29 every one that hath shall be g',
26: 9 sold for much, and g' to the poor.
28:18 All power is g' unto me in heaven
M'r 4:11 you it is g' to know the mystery
24 you that hear shall more be g'.
25 he that hath, to him shall be g':
5:43 something should be g' her to eat.
6: 2 this which is g' unto him, that even
8:12 no sign be g' unto this generation.
10:40 but it shall be g' to them for whom
12:25 neither marry, nor are g' in marriage;
13:11 shall be g' you in that hour,
14: 5 and have been g' to the poor.
23 cup, and when he had g' thanks,
44 him had g' them a token, saying,
Lu 6:38 Give, and it shall be g' unto you;
8:10 you it is g' to know the mysteries
18 whosoever hath, to him shall be g'
11: 9 Ask, and it shall be g' you; seek,
29 there shall no sign be g' it, but the
12:48 unto whomsoever much is g', of
17:27 they were g' in marriage, until the day
19:15 whom he had g' the money, that
26 every one which hath shall be g';
20:34 marry, and are g' in marriage; but
35 neither marry, nor are g' in marriage:
22:19 This is my body which is g' for you:
Joh 1:17 law was g' by Moses, but grace
3:27 except it be g' him from heaven.
35 hath g' all things into his hand.
4:10 he would have g' thee living water.
5:26 so hath he g' to the Son to have
27 hath g' him authority to execute
36 which the Father hath g' me
6:11 when he had g' thanks, he distributed
23 after that the Lord had g' thanks:)
39 that of all which he hath g' me
65 it were g' unto him of my Father.
7:39 for the Holy Ghost was not yet g';
11:57 Pharisees had g' a commandment,
12: 5 hundred pence, and g' to the poor?
13: 3 the Father had g' all things into his
15 For I have g' you an example,
17: 2 thou hast g' him power over all
2 to as many as thou hast g' him.
7 whatsoever thou hast g' me are of
8 have g' unto them the words which
9 for them which thou hast g' me;
11 those whom thou hast g' me, that
14 I have g' them thy word; and the
22 thou gavest me I have g' them; that
24 they also, whom thou hast g' me,
24 my glory, which thou hast g' me:
18:11 cup which my Father hath g' me,
19:11 except it were g' thee from above:
Ac 1: 2 Holy Ghost had g' commandments
3:16 hath g' him this perfect soundness
4:12 name under heaven g' among men,
5:32 whom God hath g' to them that
8:18 the Holy Ghost was g', he offered
17:16 saw the city wholly g' to idolatry.
31 whereof he hath g' assurance unto
20: 2 and had g' them much exhortation,
21:40 And when he had g' him licence, Paul
24:26 money should have been g' him of

Ac 27:24 God hath g' thee all them that
Ro 5: 5 by the Holy Ghost which is g' unto
11: 8 hath g' them the spirit of slumber,
35 Or who hath first g' to him, and it
12: 3 say through the grace g' unto me,
6 the grace that is g' to us, whether
13 necessity of saints; g' to hospitality.
15:15 the grace that is g' to me of God,
1Co 1: 4 the grace of God which is g' you by
2:12 know the things that are freely g'
3:10 the grace of God which is g' unto
11:15 for her hair is g' her for a covering.
24 And when he had g' thanks, he
12: 7 manifestation of the Spirit is g'
8 to one is g' by the Spirit the word
24 having g' more abundant honour
16: 1 as I have g' order to the churches
2Co 1:11 thanks may be g' by many on our
22 and g' the earnest of the Spirit
5: 5 also hath g' unto us the earnest of
18 and hath g' to us the ministry
9: 9 g' to the poor: his righteousness
10: 8 the Lord hath g' us for edification,
12: 7 there was g' to me a thorn in the
13:10 power which the Lord hath g' me
Ga 2: 9 the grace that was g' unto me, they
3:21 for if there had been a law g'
21 which could have g' life,
22 might be g' to them that believe.
4:15 own eyes, and have g' them to me.
Eph 3: 2 which is g' me to you-ward:
7 the grace of God g' unto me by the
8 is this grace g', that I should preach
4: 7 unto every one of us is g' grace
19 past feeling have g' themselves
5: 2 hath loved us, and hath g' himself
6:19 that utterance may be g' unto me,
Ph'p 1:29 you it is g' in the behalf of Christ,
2: 9 and g' him a name which is above
Col 1:25 of God which is g' to me for you,
1Th 4: 8 also g' unto us his holy Spirit.
2Th 2:16 hath g' us everlasting consolation
1Ti 3: 2 g' to hospitality, apt to teach;
3 g' to wine, no striker, not greedy
8 not g' to much wine, not greedy
4:14 which was g' thee by prophecy,
2Ti 1: 7 For God hath not g' us the spirit
9 grace, which was g' us in Christ
3:16 All scripture is g' by inspiration
Tit 1: 7 not soon angry, not g' to wine,
7 not g' to filthy lucre;
2: 3 not g' to much wine, teachers of
Ph'm 22 prayers I shall be g' unto you.
Heb 2:13 the children which God hath g'
4: 8 For if Jesus had g' them rest, then
Jas 1: 5 upbraideth not; and it shall be g'
2Pe 1: 3 power hath g' unto us all things
4 Whereby are g' unto us exceeding
3:15 according to the wisdom g' unto
1Jo 3:24 by the Spirit which he hath g' us.
4:13 because he hath g' us of his Spirit.
5:11 that God hath g' to us eternal life,
20 and hath g' us an understanding,
Re 6: 2 and a crown was g' unto him:
4 power was g' to him that sat thereon
4 and there was g' unto him a great
8 power was g' unto them over the
11 white robes were g' unto every one
7: 2 to whom it was g' to hurt the earth
8: 2 to them were g' seven trumpets.
3 there was g' unto him much incense,
9: 1 was g' the key of the bottomless pit.
3 unto them was g' power, as the
5 to them it was g' that they should
10: 9 unto him, G' me the little book.
11: 1 there was g' me a reed like unto a
2 for it is g' unto the Gentiles:
12:14 to the woman were g' two wings
13: 5 there was g' unto him a mouth
5 power was g' unto him to continue
7 it was g' unto him to make war
7 power was g' him over all kindreds,
16: 6 thou hast g' them blood to drink;
8 power was g' unto him to scorch
20: 4 and judgment was g' unto them:

giver See also LAWGIVER.
Isa 24: 2 so with the g' of usury to him.
2Co 9: 7 for God loveth a cheerful g'.

givest
De 15: 9 thou g' him nought; and he cry
10 grieved when thou g' unto him:
Job 35: 7 what g' thou him? or what
Ps 50:19 Thou g' thy mouth to evil, and
80: 5 and g' them tears to drink in great
104:28 That thou g' them they gather:
145:15 thou g' them their meat in due
Pr 6:35 content, though thou g' many gifts.
Eze 3:18 thou g' him not warning, nor speakest
16:33 thou g' thy gifts to all thy lovers,
34 in that thou g' a reward, and no
1Co 14:17 For thou verily g' thanks well,

giveth See also FORGIVETH.
Ge 49:21 hind let loose: he g' goodly words.
Ex 16:29 therefore he g' you on the sixth
20:12 the land which the Lord thy God g'
25: 2 every man that g' it willingly
Le 20: 2 g' any of his seed unto Molech;
4 when he g' of his seed unto Molech,
27: 9 all that any man g' such unto the
Nu 5:10 whatsoever any man g' the priest,
De 2:29 the land which the Lord our God g'
4: 1 the Lord God of your fathers g'
21 the Lord thy God g' thee for an
40 the land which the Lord thy God g'

De 5:16 the land which the Lord thy God g'
8:18 it is he that g' thee power to get
9: 6 Lord thy God g' thee not this land
11:17 the good land which the Lord g'
31 land which the Lord your God g'
12: 1 God of thy fathers g' thee to
9 which the Lord your God g' you.
10 Lord your God g' you to inherit,
10 and when he g' you rest from all
13: 1 and g' thee a sign or a wonder,
15: 4 which the Lord thy God g' thee
7 God g' thee, thou shalt not harden
16: 5 which the Lord thy God g' thee:
18 thy God g' thee, throughout thy
20 the land which the Lord thy God g'
17: 2 the Lord thy God g' thee, man or
14 which the Lord thy God g' thee,
18: 9 which the Lord thy God g' thee,
19: 1 whose land the Lord thy God g'
2 which the Lord thy God g' thee to
3 God g' thee to inherit, into three
10 thy God g' thee for an inheritance,
14 Lord thy God g' thee to possess
21: 1 which the Lord thy God g' thee to
23 the Lord thy God g' thee for an
24: 3 a bill of divorcement, and g' it
4 which the Lord thy God g' thee for
25:15 which the Lord thy God g' thee.
19 the land which the Lord thy God g'
26: 1 thy God g' thee for an inheritance,
2 that the Lord thy God g' thee, and
27: 2 the Lord thy God g' thee, that thou
3 thy God g' thee, a land that floweth
28: 8 which the Lord thy God g' thee.
Jos 1:11 which the Lord your God g' you
15 which the Lord your God g' them:
J'g 11:24 Chemosh thy god g' thee to possess?
21:18 Cursed be he that g' a wife to
Job 5:10 Who g' rain upon the earth, and
14:10 yea, man g' up the ghost, and
32: 8 the Almighty g' them understanding.
33:13 g' not account of any of his matters.
34:29 When he g' quietness, who then
35:10 who g' songs in the night;
12 There they cry, but none g' answer.
36: 6 but g' right to the poor.
31 he g' meat in abundance.
Ps 18:50 Great deliverance g' he to his king:
37:21 righteous sheweth mercy, and g'.
68:35 he that g' strength and power
119:130 The entrance of thy words g' light;
130 it g' understanding unto the simple.
127: 2 for so he g' his beloved sleep.
136:25 Who g' food to all flesh: for his
144:10 is he that g' salvation unto kings:
146: 7 which g' food to the hungry.
147: 9 He g' to the beast his food,
16 He g' snow like wool: he
Pr 2: 6 For the Lord g' wisdom: out of his
3:34 but he g' grace unto the lowly.
13:15 Good understanding g' favour:
17: 4 A wicked doer g' heed to false lips;
4 and a liar g' ear to a naughty tongue.
19: 6 is a friend to him that g' gifts.
21:26 the righteous g' and spareth not.
22: 9 he g' of his bread to the poor.
16 he that g' to the rich, shall surely
23:31 when it g' his colour in the cup,
24:26 kiss his lips that g' a right answer.
26: 8 so is he that g' honour to a fool.
28:27 that g' unto the poor shall not lack:
31:15 and g' meat to her household, and
Ec 2:26 For God g' to a man that is good
26 but to the sinner he g' travail, to
5:18 days of his life, which God g' him:
6: 2 God g' him not power to eat thereof,
7:12 wisdom g' life to them that have
8:15 which God g' him under the sun.
Isa 40:29 He g' power to the faint; and to
42: 5 that g' breath unto the people
Jer 5:24 the Lord our God, that g' rain,
22:13 and g' him not for his work;
31:35 Lord, which g' the sun for a light
La 3:30 g' his cheek to him that smiteth
Da 2:21 he g' wisdom unto the wise, and
4:17 and g' it to whomsoever he will,
25, 32 and g' it to whomsoever he will.
Hab 2:15 him that g' his neighbour drink,
M't 5:15 and it g' light unto all that are in
Joh 3:34 God g' not the Spirit by measure
6:32 my Father g' you the true bread
33 and g' life unto the world.
37 All that the Father g' me shall
10:11 good shepherd g' his life for the
14:27 not as the world g', give I unto you.
21:13 taketh bread, and g' them, and fish
Ac 17:25 seeing he g' to all life, and breath,
Ro 12: 8 he that g', let him do it with
14: 6 for he g' God thanks; and he that
6 eateth not, and g' God thanks.
1Co 3: 7 but God that g' the increase.
7:38 he that g' her in marriage doeth well;
38 but he that g' her not in marriage
15:38 God g' it a body as it hath pleased
57 God which g' us the victory through
2Co 3: 6 killeth, but the Spirit g' life.
1Ti 6:17 g' us richly all things to enjoy;
Jas 1: 5 ask of God, that g' to all men
4: 6 But he g' more grace. Wherefore
6 but g' grace unto the humble.
1Pe 4:11 it as of the ability which God g':
5: 5 proud, and g' grace to the humble.
Re 22: 5 for the Lord God g' them light:

giving See also FORGIVING; THANKSGIVING.
Ge 24:19 when she had done g' him drink,

De 10:18 in g' him food and raiment.
21:17 by g' him a double portion of all
Ru 1: 6 visited his people in g' them bread.
1Ki 5: 9 in g' food for my household.
2Ch 6:23 by g' him according to his
Ezr 3:11 praising and g' thanks unto the Lord;
Job 11:20 shall be as the g' up of the ghost.
M't 24:38 marrying and g' in marriage,
Lu 17:16 at his feet, g' him thanks: and he was
Ac 8: 9 g' out that himself was some
15: 8 g' them the Holy Ghost, even as
Ro 4:20 strong in faith, g' glory to God;
9: 4 covenants, and the g' of the law,
1Co 14: 7 even things without life g' sound,
16 say Amen at thy g' of thanks,
2Co 6: 3 G' no offence in any thing, that
Eph 5: 4 but rather g' of thanks.
20 G' thanks always for all things
Ph'p 4:15 concerning g' and receiving, but
Col 1:12 G' thanks unto the Father, which
3:17 g' thanks to God and the Father
1Ti 2: 1 intercessions, and g' of thanks,
4: 1 g' heed to seducing spirits, and
Tit 1:14 Not g' heed to Jewish fables, and
Heb 13:15 of our lips g' thanks to his name.
1Pe 3: 7 g' honour unto the wife, as unto
2Pe 1: 5 g' all diligence, add to your faith
Jude 7 g' themselves over to fornication.

Gizonite (*ghi'-zo-nite*)
1Ch 11:34 sons of Hashem the G', Jonathan

glad^
Ex 4:14 thee, he will be g' in his heart.
J'g 18:20 And the priest's heart was g',
1Sa 11: 9 men of Jabesh; and they were g'.
1Ki 8:66 joyful and g' of heart for all the
1Ch 16:31 Let the heavens be g', and let
2Ch 7:10 g' and merry in heart for the
Es 5: 9 day joyful and with a g' heart:
8:15 of Shushan rejoiced and was g'.
Job 3:22 rejoice exceedingly, and are g',
22:19 The righteous see it, and are g':
Ps 9: 2 I will be g' and rejoice in thee:
14: 7 rejoice, and Israel shall be g'.
16: 9 heart is g', and my glory rejoiceth:
21: 6 thou hast made him exceeding g'
31: 7 be g' and rejoice in thy mercy:
32:11 Be g' in the Lord, and rejoice,
34: 2 shall hear thereof, and be g'.
35:27 Let them shout for joy, and be g',
45: 8 whereby they have made thee g'.
46: 4 shall make g' the city of God,
48:11 let the daughters of Judah be g',
53: 6 rejoice, and Israel shall be g'.
64:10 righteous shall be g' in the Lord,
67: 4 O let the nations be g' and sing
68: 3 But let the righteous be g'; let
69:32 humble shall see this, and be g':
70: 4 seek thee rejoice and be g' in thee:
90:14 that we may rejoice and be g' all
15 Make us g' according to the days
92: 4 hast made me g' through thy work:
96:11 and let the earth be g'; let the sea
97: 1 let the multitude of isles be g'
8 Zion heard, and was g'; and the
104:15 wine that maketh g' the heart of
34 I will be g' in the Lord.
105:38 Egypt was g' when they departed:
107:30 Then are they g' because they be
118:24 we will rejoice and be g' in it.
119:74 They that fear thee will be g'
122: 1 I was g' when they said unto me,
126: 3 things for us; whereof we are g'.
Pr 10: 1 A wise son maketh a g' father:
12:25 but a good word maketh it g'.
15:20 A wise son maketh a g' father:
17: 5 and he that is g' at calamities
23:25 father and thy mother shall be g',
24:17 let not thine heart be g' when he
27:11 be wise, and make my heart g',
Ca 1: 4 we will be g' and rejoice in thee,
Isa 25: 9 we will be g' and rejoice in his
35: 1 solitary place shall be g' for them;
39: 2 And Hezekiah was g' of them,
65:18 be ye g' and rejoice for ever
66:10 and be g' with her, all ye that love
Jer 20:15 unto thee; making him very g'.
41:13 were with him, then they were g'.
50:11 Because ye were g', because ye
La 1:21 they are g' that thou hast done it:
4:21 Rejoice and be g', O daughter of
Da 6:23 was the king exceeding g' for him,
Ho 7: 3 They make the king g' with their
Joe 2:21 Fear not, O land; be g' and rejoice:
23 Be g' then, ye children of Zion,
Jon 4: 6 So Jonah was exceeding g' of the
Hab 1:15 therefore they rejoice and are g'.
Zep 3:14 be g' and rejoice with all the
Zec 10: 7 shall see it, and be g'; their heart
M't 5:12 Rejoice, and be exceeding g': for
M'r 14:11 when they heard it, they were g',
Lu 1:19 to shew thee these g' tidings.
8: 1 the g' tidings of the kingdom
15:32 we should make merry, and be g':
22: 5 And they were g', and covenanted
23: 8 saw Jesus, he was exceeding g':
Joh 8:56 and he saw it, and was g'.
11:15 And I am g' for your sakes that
20:20 Then were the disciples g', when
Ac 2:26 rejoice, and my tongue was g';
11:23 was g', and exhorted them all,
13:32 we declare unto you g' tidings,
48 Gentiles heard this, they were g',
Ro 10:15 of peace, and bring g' tidings
16:19 I am g' therefore on your behalf:
1Co 16:17 am g' of the coming of Stephanas
2Co 2: 2 who is he then that maketh me g',
13: 9 For we are g', when we are weak,
1Pe 4:13 be g' also with exceeding joy.
Re 19: 7 Let us be g' and rejoice, and we

gladly
M'r 6:20 many things, and heard him g'.
12:37 the common people heard him g'.
Lu 8:40 the people g' received him:
Ac 2:41 they that g' received his word
21:17 the brethren received us g'.
2Co 11:19 For ye suffer fools g', seeing ye
12: 9 Most g' therefore will I rather
15 I will very g' spend and be spent

gladness
Nu 10:10 Also in the day of your g',
De 28:47 joyfulness, and with g' of heart,
2Sa 6:12 into the city of David with g'.
1Ch 16:27 strength and g' are in his place.
29:22 Lord on that day with great g'.
2Ch 29:30 they sang praises with g', and
30:21 bread seven days with great g':
23 kept other seven days with g'.
Ne 8:17 And there was very great g'.
12:27 to keep the dedication with g',
Es 8:16 The Jews had light, and g', and joy,
17 Jews had joy and g', a feast
9:17, 18 made it a day of feasting and g'.
19 day of the month Adar a day of g'
Ps 4: 7 Thou hast put g' in my heart,
30:11 sackcloth, and girded me with g';
45: 7 anointed thee with the oil of g'
15 With g' and rejoicing shall they
51: 8 Make me to hear joy and g';
97:11 and g' for the upright in heart.
100: 2 Serve the Lord with g': come
105:43 joy, and his chosen with g':
106: 5 rejoice in the g' of thy nation,
Pr 10:28 hope of the righteous shall be g':
Ca 3:11 in the day of the g' of his heart.
Isa 16:10 And g' is taken away, and joy out
22:13 behold joy and g', slaying oxen,
30:29 and g' of heart, as when one goeth
35:10 they shall obtain joy and g', and
51: 3 joy and g' shall be found therein,
11 they shall obtain g' and joy; and
Jer 7:34 voice of mirth, and the voice of g',
16: 9 voice of mirth, and the voice of g',
25:10 voice of mirth, and the voice of g',
31: 7 Sing with g' for Jacob, and shout
33:11 The voice of joy, and the voice of g'
48:33 And joy and g' is taken from the
Joe 1:16 and g' from the house of our God?
Zec 8:19 to the house of Judah joy and g',
M'r 4:16 immediately receive it with g';
Lu 1:14 And thou shalt have joy and g';
Ac 2:46 with g' and singleness of heart,
12:14 she opened not the gate for g',
14:17 filling our hearts with food and g'.
Ph'p 2:29 therefore in the Lord with all g';
Heb 1: 9 hath anointed thee with the oil of g'

glass See also GLASSES.
Job 37:18 and as a molten looking g'?
1Co 13:12 now we see through a g' darkly;
2Co 3:18 beholding as in a g' the glory of
Jas 1:23 beholding his natural face in a g':
Re 4: 6 was a sea of g' like unto crystal:
15: 2 a sea of g' mingled with fire:
2 sea of g', having the harps of God.
21:18 was pure gold, like unto clear g'.
21 gold, as it were transparent g'.

glasses See also LOOKINGGLASSES.
Isa 3:23 The g', and the fine linen, and

glean See also GLEANED; GLEANING.
Le 19:10 thou shalt not g' thy vineyard,
De 24:21 thou shalt not g' it afterward:
Ru 2: 2 and g' ears of corn after him
7 let me g' and gather after the
8 Go not to g' in another field,
15 when she was risen up to g',
15 Let her g' even among the sheaves,
16 that she may g' them, and rebuke
23 to g' unto the end of barley harvest
Jer 6: 9 shall thoroughly g' the remnant

gleaned
J'g 20:45 they g' of them in the highways
Ru 2: 3 g' in the field after the reapers:
17 So she g' in the field until even,
17 and beat out that she had g':
18 mother in law saw what she had g':
19 Where hast thou g' to day?

gleaning See also GLEANINGS.
Le 23:22 shalt thou gather any g' of thy
J'g 8: 2 the g' of the grapes of Ephraim
Isa 17: 6 Yet g' grapes shall be left in it,
24:13 as the g' grapes when the vintage
Jer 49: 9 they not leave some g' grapes?

gleaning-grapes See GLEANING and GRAPES.

gleanings
Le 19: 9 shalt thou gather the g' of thy

glede
De 14:13 And the g', and the kite, and the

glistering See also GLITTERING.
1Ch 29: 2 g' stones, and of divers colours,
Lu 9:29 his raiment was white and g'.

glitter See also GLITTERING.
Eze 21:10 it is furbished that it may g':

glittering See also GLISTERING.
De 32:41 If I whet my g' sword, and mine
Job 20:25 yea, the g' sword cometh out of
39:23 the g' spear and the shield.
Eze 21:28 to consume because of the g':
Na 3: 3 the bright sword and the g' spear:
Hab 3:11 at the shining of thy g' spear.

gloominess
Joe 2: 2 A day of darkness and of g', a day
Zep 1:15 a day of darkness and g', a day of

gloriest
Jer 49: 4 Wherefore g' thou in the valleys,

glorieth
Jer 9:24 But let him that g' glory in this,
1Co 1:31 that g', let him glory in the Lord.
2Co 10:17 that g', let him glory in the Lord.

glorified
Le 10: 3 before all the people I will be g'.
Isa 26:15 increased the nation: thou art g':
44:23 Jacob, and g' himself in Israel.
49: 3 O Israel, in whom I will be g'.
55: 5 One of Israel; for he hath g' thee.
60: 9 of Israel, because he hath g' thee.
21 of my hands, that I may be g'.
61: 3 of the Lord, that he might be g'.
66: 5 Let the Lord be g': but he shall
Eze 28:22 I will be g' in the midst of thee:
39:13 that I shall be g', saith the Lord
Da 5:23 are all thy ways, hast thou not g':
Hag 1: 8 and I will be g', saith the Lord.
M't 9: 8 they marvelled, and g' God, which
15:31 and they g' the God of Israel.
M'r 2:12 then were all amazed, and g' God,
Lu 4:15 their synagogues, being g' of all.
5:26 were all amazed, and they g' God,
7:16 they g' God, saying, That a great
13:13 she was made straight, and g' God.
17:15 and with a loud voice g' God.
23:47 saw what was done, he g' God,
Joh 7:39 because that Jesus was not yet g'.)
11: 4 Son of God might be g' thereby.
12:16 but when Jesus was g', then
23 that the Son of man should be g'.
28 I have both g' it, and will glorify
13:31 Now is the Son of man g',
31 and God is g' in him.
32 If God be g' in him, God shall
14:13 the Father may be g' in the Son.
15: 8 Herein is my Father g', that ye bear
17: 4 I have g' thee on the earth: I
10 and am g' in them.
Ac 3:13 hath g' his Son Jesus;
4:21 for all men g' God for that which
11:18 they held their peace, and g' God,
13:48 and g' the word of the Lord: and
21:20 they g' the Lord, and said unto him,
Ro 1:21 they g' him not as God, neither
8:17 that we may be also g' together.
30 whom he justified, them he also g'.
Ga 1:24 And they g' God in me.
2Th 1:10 shall come to be g' in his saints,
12 of our Lord Jesus Christ may be g'
3: 1 may have free course and be g',
Heb 5: 5 Christ g' not himself to be made
1Pe 4:11 may be g' through Jesus Christ,
14 but on your part he is g'.
Re 18: 7 How much she hath g' herself,

glorifieth
Ps 50:23 Whoso offereth praise g' me: and

glorify See also GLORIFIED; GLORIFIETH; GLORIFYING.
Ps 22:23 all ye the seed of Jacob, g' him;
50:15 deliver thee, and thou shalt g' me.
86: 9 O Lord; and shall g' thy name.
12 I will g' thy name for evermore.
Isa 24:15 Wherefore g' ye the Lord in the
25: 3 shall the strong people g' thee,
60: 7 I will g' the house of my glory.
Jer 30:19 I will also g' them, and they shall
M't 5:16 see your good works, and g' your
Joh 12:28 Father, g' thy name. Then came
28 have both glorified it, and will g' it
13:32 God shall also g' him in himself,
32 and shall straightway g' him.
16:14 He shall g' me: for he shall receive
17: 1 g' thy Son, that thy Son also
1 that thy Son also may g' thee:
5 O Father, g' thou me with thine
21:19 by what death he should g' God.
Ro 15: 6 one mind and one mouth g' God.
9 the Gentiles might g' God for his
1Co 6:20 therefore g' God in your body,
2Co 9:13 they g' God for your professed
1Pe 2:12 g' God in the day of visitation.
4:16 let him g' God on this behalf.
Re 15: 4 fear thee, O Lord, and g' thy name?

glorifying
Lu 2:20 g' and praising God for all things
5:25 departed to his own house, g' God.
18:43 and followed him, g' God:

glorious
Ex 15: 6 O Lord, is become g' in power:
11 who is like thee, g' in holiness,
De 28:58 fear this g' and fearful name,
2Sa 6:20 How g' was the king of Israel to day,
1Ch 29:13 thank thee, and praise thy g' name.
Ne 9: 5 blessed be thy g' name, which is
Es 1: 4 shewed the riches of his g' kingdom
Ps 45:13 king's daughter is all g' within:
66: 2 of his name: make his praise g'.
72:19 And blessed be his g' name for ever:
76: 4 Thou art more g' and excellent
87: 3 G' things are spoken of thee, O
111: 3 His work is honourable and g':
145: 5 I will speak of the g' honour of thy
12 and the g' majesty of his kingdom.

Isa 4: 2 of the Lord be beautiful and g'.
11:10 and his rest shall be g'.
22:23 and he shall be for a g' throne
28: 1 whose g' beauty is a fading flower,
4 the g' beauty, which is on the head
30:30 the Lord shall cause his g' voice
33:21 But there the g' Lord will be
49: 5 I be g' in the eyes of the Lord,
60:13 I will make the place of my feet g'.
63: 1 g' in his apparel, travelling in the
12 with his g' arm, dividing the water
14 people, to make thyself a g' name.
Jer 17:12 A g' high throne from the
Eze 27:25 wast replenished, and made very g'
Da 11:16 and he shall stand in the g' land,
41 He shall enter also into the g' land,
45 the seas in the g' holy mountain;
Lu 13:17 g' things that were done by him.
Ro 8:21 g' liberty of the children of God.
2Co 3: 7 engraven in stones, was g',
8 of the spirit be rather g'?
10 which was made g' had no glory
11 which is done away was g',
11 that which remaineth is g'.
4: 4 the light of the g' gospel of Christ,
Eph 5:27 present it to himself a g' church,
Ph'p 3:21 fashioned like unto his g' body,
Col 1:11 according to his g' power, unto
1Ti 1:11 the g' gospel of the blessed God,
Tit 2:13 the g' appearing of the great God

gloriously
Ex 15: 1 the Lord, for he hath triumphed g':
21 to the Lord, for he hath triumphed g':
Isa 24:23 and before his ancients g'.

glory See also GLORIEST; GLORIETH; GLORYING; VAINGLORY.
Ge 31: 1 hath he gotten all this g'.
45:13 ye shall tell my father of all my g'
Ex 8: 9 Moses said unto Pharaoh, G' over
16: 7 ye shall see the g' of the Lord;
10 g' of the Lord appeared in a cloud.
24:16 g' of the Lord abode upon mount
17 g' of the Lord was like devouring
28: 2 thy brother for g' and for beauty.
40 for them, for g' and for beauty.
29:43 shall be sanctified by my g'.
33:18 I beseech thee, shew me thy g'.
22 while my g' passeth by, I will put
40:34, 35 g' of the...filled the tabernacle.
Le 9: 6 g' of the Lord shall appear unto you.
23 the g' of the Lord appeared unto all
Nu 14:10 the g' of the Lord appeared in the
21 be filled with the g' of the Lord.
22 those men which have seen my g',
16:19 the g' of the Lord appeared unto all
42 and the g' of the Lord appeared.
20: 6 g' of the Lord appeared unto them.
De 5:24 Lord our God hath shewed us his g'
33:17 His g' is like the firstling of his
Jos 7:19 thee, g' to the Lord God of Israel,
1Sa 2: 8 make them inherit the throne of g':
4:21, 22 The g' is departed from Israel:
6: 5 shall give g' unto the God of Israel:
1Ki 8:11 g' of the Lord had filled the house
2Ki 14:10 g' of this, and tarry at home:
1Ch 16:10 G' ye in his holy name: let the
24 Declare his g' among the heathen;
27 G' and honour are in his presence;
28 give unto the Lord g' and strength.
29 the Lord the g' due unto his name:
35 holy name, and g' in thy praise.
22: 5 and of g' throughout all countries:
29:11 and the power, and the g',
2Ch 5:14 g' of the Lord had filled the house
7: 1 the g' of the Lord filled the house.
2 g' of the Lord had filled the Lord's
3 the g' of the Lord upon the house,
Es 5:11 Haman told them of the g' of his
Job 19: 9 He hath stripped me of my g',
29:20 My g' was fresh in me, and my
39:20 the g' of his nostrils is terrible.
40:10 array thyself with g' and beauty.
Ps 3: 3 my g', and the lifter up of mine
4: 2 long will ye turn my g' into shame?
8: 1 hast set thy g' above the heavens.
5 crowned him with g' and honour.
16: 9 and my g' rejoiceth: my flesh also
19: 1 The heavens declare the g' of God;
21: 5 His g' is great in thy salvation:
24: 7 and the King of g' shall come in.
8 Who is this King of g'? The Lord
9 and the King of g' shall come in.
10 Who is this King of g'? The Lord
10 of hosts, he is the King of g'.
29: 1 give unto the Lord g' and strength.
2 the Lord the g' due unto his name;
3 the God of g' thundereth: the Lord
9 doth every one speak of his g'.
30:12 that my g' may sing praise to thee,
45: 3 with thy g' and thy majesty.
49:16 the g' of his house is increased;
17 his g' shall not descend after him.
57: 5 let thy g' be above all the earth.
8 Awake up, my g'; awake, psaltery
11 let thy g' be above all the earth.
62: 7 In God is my salvation and my g':
63: 2 To see thy power and thy g',
11 one that sweareth by him shall g':
64:10 all the upright in heart shall g'.
72:19 whole earth be filled with his g';
73:24 and afterward receive me to g'.
78:61 and his g' into the enemy's hand.
79: 9 Help us...for the g' of thy name:
84:11 the Lord will give grace and g':
85: 9 that g' may dwell in our land.

Ps 89:17 thou art the g' of their strength:
44 Thou hast made his g' to cease,
90:16 and thy g' unto their children.
96: 3 Declare his g' among the heathen,
7 give unto the Lord g' and strength.
8 the Lord the g' due unto his name:
97: 6 and all the people see his g'.
102:15 and all the kings of the earth thy g'.
16 he shall appear in his g'.
104:31 g' of the Lord shall endure for ever:
105: 3 G' ye in his holy name: let the
106: 5 I may g' with thine inheritance.
20 Thus they changed their g' into
108: 1 and give praise, even with my g'.
5 and thy g' above all the earth;
113: 4 and his g' above the heavens.
115: 1 but unto thy name give g', for thy
138: 5 for great is the g' of the Lord.
145:11 speak of the g' of thy kingdom,
148:13 g' is above the earth and heaven.
149: 5 Let the saints be joyful in g':
Pr 3:35 The wise shall inherit g': but
4: 9 a crown of g' shall she deliver
16:31 The hoary head is a crown of g',
17: 6 the g' of children are their fathers.
19:11 his g' to pass over a transgression.
20:29 g' of young men is their strength:
25: 2 g' of God to conceal a thing:
27 to search their own g' is not g'.
28:12 men do rejoice, there is great g':
Isa 2:10 and for the g' of his majesty.
19, 21 and for the g' of his majesty,
3: 8 to provoke the eyes of his g'.
4: 5 upon all the g' shall be a defence.
5:14 and their g', and their multitude,
6: 3 the whole earth is full of his g'.
8: 7 the king of Assyria, and all his g':
10: 3 and where will ye leave your g'?
12 and the g' of his high looks.
16 and under his g' he shall kindle
18 shall consume the g' of his forest,
13:19 Babylon, the g' of kingdoms, the
14:18 nations, even all of them, lie in g',
16:14 the g' of Moab shall be contemned,
17: 3 shall be as the g' of the children
4 the g' of Jacob shall be made thin,
20: 5 expectation, and of Egypt their g'.
21:16 and all the g' of Kedar shall fail:
22:18 the chariots of thy g' shall be the
24 him all the g' of his father's house,
23: 9 to stain the pride of all g', and to
24:16 songs, even g' to the righteous.
28: 5 Lord of hosts be for a crown of g',
35: 2 g' of Lebanon shall be given unto
2 they shall see the g' of the Lord,
40: 5 the g' of the Lord shall be revealed,
41:16 shalt g' in the Holy One of Israel.
42: 8 my g' will I not give to another,
12 Let them give g' unto the Lord,
43: 7 for I have created him for my g',
45:25 of Israel be justified, and shall g'.
46:13 salvation in Zion for Israel my g'.
48:11 I will not give my g' unto another.
58: 8 g' of the...shall be thy rereward.
59:19 his g' from the rising of the sun.
60: 1 and the g' of the Lord is risen upon
2 and his g' shall be seen upon thee.
7 I will glorify the house of my g'.
13 The g' of Lebanon shall come
19 light, and thy God thy g'.
61: 6 and in their g' shall ye boast
62: 2 and all kings thy g': and thou shalt
3 Thou shalt also be a crown of g'
63:15 of thy holiness and of thy g':
66:11 with the abundance of her g'.
12 the g' of the Gentiles like a flowing
18 they shall come, and see my g'.
19 neither have seen my g'; and they
19 declare my g' among the Gentiles.
Jer 2:11 my people have changed their g'
4: 2 and in him shall they g'.
9:23 Let not the wise man g' in his
23 let the mighty man g' in his might,
23 let not the rich man g' in his riches:
24 But let him that glorieth g' in this,
13:11 and for a praise, and for a g':
16 Give g' to the Lord your God,
18 down, even the crown of your g'.
14:21 not disgrace the throne of thy g':
22:18 saying, Ah Lord! or, Ah his g'!
48:18 come down from thy g', and sit in
Eze 1:28 the likeness of the g' of the Lord.
3:12 Blessed be the g' of the Lord from
23 the g' of the Lord stood there,
23 as the g' which I saw by the river
8: 4 the g' of the God of Israel was there,
9: 3 the g' of the God of Israel was gone
10: 4 the g' of the Lord went up from the
4 of the brightness of the Lord's g'.
18 the g' of the Lord departed from off
19 the g' of the God of Israel was over
11:22 the g' of the God of Israel was over
23 the g' of the Lord went up from the
20: 6 honey, which is the g' of all lands:
15 honey, which is the g' of all lands;
24:25 the joy of their g', the desire of
25: 9 his frontiers, the g' of the country,
26:20 I shall set g' in the land of the
31:18 To whom art thou thus like in g'
39:21 I will set my g' among the heathen,
43: 2 g' of the God of Israel came from
2 and the earth shined with his g'.
4 And the g' of the Lord came into
5 the g' of the Lord filled the house.
44: 4 the g' of the Lord filled the house
Da 2:37 power, and strength, and g'.

Da 4:36 and for the g' of my kingdom,
5:18 a kingdom, and majesty, and g',
20 and they took his g' from him:
7:14 was given him dominion, and g',
11:20 of taxes in the g' of the kingdom:
39 acknowledge and increase with g':
Hos 4: 7 therefore will I change their g'
9:11 their g' shall fly away like a bird,
10: 5 that rejoiced in it, for the g' thereof,
Mic 1:15 come unto Adullam the g' of Israel.
2: 9 have ye taken away my g' for ever.
Na 2: 9 is none end of the store and g'
Hab 2:14 with the knowledge of the g' of the
16 Thou art filled with shame for g':
16 shameful spewing shall be on thy g'.
3: 3 His g' covered the heavens, and
Hag 2: 3 that saw this house in her first g'?
7 I will fill this house with g', saith
9 The g' of this latter house shall be
Zec 2: 5 will be the g' in the midst of her.
8 After the g' hath he sent me unto
6:13 he shall bear the g', and shall sit
11: 3 for their g' is spoiled: a voice of
12: 7 that the g' of the house of David
7 and the g' of the inhabitants of
Mal 2: 2 give g' unto my name, saith the
M't 4: 8 of the world, and the g' of them;
6: 2 that they may have g' of men.
13 the power, and the g', for ever.
29 even Solomon in all his g' was not
16:27 come in the g' of his Father with his
19:28 also shall sit in the throne of his g',
24:30 with power and great g'.
25:31 the Son of man shall come in his g',
31 shall he sit upon the throne of his g':
M'r 8:38 cometh in the g' of his Father with
10:37 other on thy left hand, in thy g'.
13:26 the clouds with great power and g'.
Lu 2: 9 and the g' of the Lord shone round
14 G' to God in the highest, and on
32 and the g' of thy people Israel.
4: 6 will I give thee, and the g' of them:
9:26 when he shall come in his own g',
31 Who appeared in g', and spake of
32 they saw his g', and the two men
12:27 that Solomon in all his g' was not
17:18 returned to give g' to God, save
19:38 peace in heaven, and g' in the
21:27 in a cloud with power and great g'.
24:26 things, and to enter into his g'?
Joh 1:14 we beheld his g', the g' as of the
2:11 and manifested forth his g';
7:18 of himself seeketh his own g': but
18 he that seeketh his g' that sent him,
8:50 I seek not mine own g': there is
11: 4 but for the g' of God, that the Son
40 thou shouldest see the g' of God?
12:41 said Esaias, when he saw his g',
17: 5 with the g' which I had with thee
22 And the g' which thou gavest me
24 that they may behold my g',
Ac 7: 2 The God of g' appeared unto our
55 and saw the g' of God, and Jesus
12:23 because he gave not God the g':
22:11 could not see for the g' of that light,
Ro 1:23 the g' of the uncorruptible God into
2: 7 well doing seek for g' and honour
10 g', honour, and peace, to every man
3: 7 through my lie unto his g';
23 and come short of the g' of God;
4: 2 he hath whereof to g': but not
20 strong in faith, giving g' to God;
5: 2 and rejoice in hope of the g' of God.
3 but we g' in tribulations also:
6: 4 the dead by the g' of the Father,
8:18 the g' which shall be revealed in us.
9: 4 the adoption, and the g', and the
23 make known the riches of his g' on
23 he had afore prepared unto g',
11:36 to whom be g' for ever. Amen.
15: 7 also received us to the g' of God.
17 I have therefore whereof I may g'
16:27 To God only wise, be g' through
1Co 1:29 no flesh should g' in his presence.
31 that glorieth, let him g' in the Lord.
2: 7 before the world unto our g':
8 not have crucified the Lord of g'.
3:21 Therefore let no man g' in men.
4: 7 why dost thou g', as if thou hadst
9:16 I have nothing to g' of: for
10:31 ye do, do all to the g' of God.
11: 7 as he is the image and g' of God:
7 but the woman is the g' of the man.
15 have long hair, it is a g' to her:
15:40 but the g' of the celestial is one,
40 the g' of the terrestial is another.
41 There is one g' of the sun, and
41 and another g' of the moon, and
41 and another g' of the stars: for
41 differeth from another star in g'.
43 sown in dishonour; it is raised in g':
2Co 1:20 Amen, unto the g' of God by us.
3: 7 g' of his countenance; which g' was
9 ministration of condemnation be g',
9 of righteousness exceed in g'.
10 which was made glorious had no g'
10 by reason of the g' that excelleth.
18 as in a glass the g' of the Lord,
18 into the same image from g' to g',
4: 6 the knowledge of the g' of God
15 of many redound to the g' of God.
17 exceeding and eternal weight of g';
5:12 you occasion to g' on our behalf,
12 them which g' in appearance,
8:19 by us to the g' of the same Lord,
23 the churches, and the g' of Christ.

2Co 10:17 glorieth, let him g' in the Lord.
11:12 that wherein they g', they may be
18 Seeing that many g' after the flesh,
18 after the flesh, I will g' also.
30 If I must needs g', I will g' of the
12: 1 expedient for me doubtless to g'.
5 Of such an one will I g':
5 yet of myself I will not g',
6 For though I would desire to g',
9 will I rather g' in my infirmities,
Ga 1: 5 To whom be g' for ever and ever.
5:26 Let us not be desirous of vain g',
6:13 that they may g' in your flesh.
14 But God forbid that I should g',
Eph 1: 6 To the praise of the g' of his grace,
12 should be to the praise of his g',
14 possession unto the praise of his g'.
17 the Father of g', may give unto you
18 riches of the g' of his inheritance
3:13 tribulations for you, which is your g'.
16 according to the riches of his g',
21 Unto him be g' in the church by
Ph'p 1:11 unto the g' and praise of God.
2:11 is Lord, to the g' of God the Father.
3:19 and whose g' is in their shame,
4:19 to his riches in g' by Christ Jesus.
20 our Father be g' for ever and ever.
Col 1:27 the riches of the g' of this mystery
27 is Christ in you, the hope of g':
3: 4 shall ye also appear with him in g'.
1Th 2: 6 Nor of men sought we g', neither
12 called you unto his kingdom and g'.
20 For ye are our g' and joy.
2Th 1: 4 So that we ourselves g' in you
9 and from the g' of his power;
2:14 of the g' of our Lord Jesus Christ.
1Ti 1:17 be honour and g' for ever and ever.
3:16 in the world, received up into g'.
2Ti 2:10 is in Christ Jesus with eternal g'.
4:18 to whom be g' for ever and ever.
Heb 1: 3 Who being the brightness of his g',
2: 7 crownedst him with g' and honour,
9 suffering of death, crowned with g'
10 in bringing many sons unto g',
3: 3 worthy of more g' than Moses,
9: 5 it the cherubims of g' shadowing
13:21 to whom be g' for ever and ever.
Jas 2: 1 Lord Jesus Christ, the Lord of g',
3:14 g' not, and lie not against the
1Pe 1: 7 honour and g' at the appearing of
8 joy unspeakable and full of g':
11 and the g' that should follow.
21 up from the dead, and gave him g';
24 the g' of man as the flower of grass.
2:20 For what g' is it, if, when ye be
4:13 when his g' shall be revealed,
14 the spirit of g' and of God resteth
5: 1 a partaker of the g' that shall be
4 ye shall receive a crown of g' that
10 hath called us unto his eternal g'
11 him be g' and dominion for ever
2Pe 1: 3 that hath called us to g' and virtue:
17 from God the Father honour and g',
17 voice to him from the excellent g',
3:18 To him be g' both now and for ever.
Jude 24 before the presence of his g' with
25 our Saviour, be g' and majesty,
Re 1: 6 to him be g' and dominion for ever
4: 9 those beasts give g' and honour
11 receive g' and honour and power:
5:12 and honour, and g', and blessing.
13 Blessing, and honour, and g', and
7:12 Saying, Amen: Blessing, and g',
11:13 and gave g' to the God of heaven.
14: 7 Fear God, and give g' to him;
15: 8 with smoke from the g' of God,
16: 9 they repented not to give him g'.
18: 1 the earth was lightened with his g'.
19: 1 Salvation, and g', and honour, and
21:11 Having the g' of God: and her light
23 for the g' of God did lighten it, and
24 bring their g' and honour into it.
26 they shall bring the g' and honour

glorying
1Co 5: 6 Your g' is not good. Know ye not
9:15 any man should make my g' void.
2Co 7: 4 great is my g' of you:
12:11 I am become a fool in g'; ye have

glutton
De 21:20 he is a g', and a drunkard.
Pr 23:21 the drunkard and the g' shall come

gluttonous
M't 11:19 a man g', and a winebibber, a
Lu 7:34 Behold a g' man, and a winebibber,

gnash See also GNASHED; GNASHETH; GNASHING.
Ps 112:10 he shall g' with his teeth, and
La 2:16 they hiss and g' the teeth: they

gnashed
Ps 35:16 they g' upon me with their teeth.
Ac 7:54 they g' on him with their teeth.

gnasheth
Job 16: 9 he g' upon me with his teeth;
Ps 37:12 and g' upon him with his teeth.
M'r 9:18 foameth, and g' with his teeth,

gnashing
M't 8:12 shall be weeping and g' of teeth.
13:42, 50 shall be wailing and g' of teeth.
22:13 shall be weeping and g' of teeth.
24:51 shall be weeping and g' of teeth.
25:30 shall be weeping and g' of teeth.
Lu 13:28 shall be weeping and g' of teeth,

gnat
M't 23:24 which strain at a g', and swallow

gnaw See also GNAWED.
Zep 3: 3 they g' not the bones till the

gnawed
Re 16:10 and they g' their tongues for pain,

go^ See also AGO; GOEST; GOETH; GOING; GONE; WENT.
Ge 3:14 upon thy belly shalt thou g', and
8:16 G' forth of the ark, thou, and thy
9:10 g' out of the ark, to every beast
11: 3 G' to, let us make brick, and burn
4 G' to, let us build us a city and a
7 G' to, let us...down, and there
7 let us g' down, and there confound
31 to g' into the land of Canaan;
12: 5 forth to g' into the land of Canaan;
19 thy wife, take her, and g' thy way.
13: 9 then I will g' to the right; or if thou
9 right hand, then I will g' to the left.
15: 2 seeing I g' childless, and the
15 shalt g' to thy fathers in peace;
16: 2 I pray thee, g' in unto my maid;
8 whither wilt thou g'? And she
18:21 I will g' down now, and see
19: 2 rise up early, and g' on your ways.
34 and g' thou in, and lie with him,
22: 5 I and the lad will g' yonder and
24: 4 But thou shalt g' unto my country,
11 that women g' out to draw water.
38 shalt g' unto my father's house,
42 do prosper my way which I g':
51 is before thee, take her, and g',
55 at least ten; after that she shall g'.
56 away that I may g' to my master.
58 Wilt thou g' with this man?
58 And she said, I will g'.
26: 2 G' not down into Egypt; dwell in
16 said unto Isaac, G' from us;
27: 3 and g' out to the field, and take
9 G' now to the flock, and fetch me
13 my voice, and g' fetch me them.
28: 2 Arise, g' to Padan-aram, to the
20 in this way that I g', and will give
29: 7 ye the sheep, and g' and feed
21 that I may g' in unto her.
30: 3 g' in unto her; and she shall bear
25 I may g' unto mine own place,
26 I have served thee, and let me g':
31:18 for to g' to Isaac his father in the
32:26 And he said, Let me g', for the day
26 let thee g', except thou bless me.
33:12 take our journey, and let us g',
12 and I will g' before thee.
35: 1 unto Jacob, Arise, g' up to Beth-el,
3 let us arise, and g' up to Beth-el;
37:14 he said to him, G', I pray thee,
17 Let us g' to Dothan. And Joseph
30 is not; and I, whither shall I g'?
35 I will g' down into the grave unto
38: 8 G' in unto thy brother's wife, and
16 G' to, I pray thee, let me come in
41:55 said unto all the Egyptians, G'
42:15 ye shall not g' forth hence, except
19 g' ye, carry corn for the famine
38 My son shall not g' down with you;
38 the way in which ye g',
43: 2 father said unto them, G' again,
4 will g' down and buy thee food:
5 not send him, we will not g' down:
8 we will arise and g'; that we may
13 your brother, and arise, g' again
44:25 our father said, G' again, and buy
26 And we said, We cannot g' down:
26 be with us, then will we g' down:
33 the lad g' up with his brethren.
34 For how shall I g' up to my father,
45: 1 Cause every man to g' out from
9 Haste ye, and g' up to my father,
17 and g', get you unto the land of
28 I will g' and see him before I die.
46: 3 fear not to g' down into Egypt;
4 I will g' down with thee into Egypt;
31 I will g' up, and shew Pharaoh,
50: 5 let me g' up, I pray thee, and bury
6 said, G' up, and bury thy father,
Ex 2: 7 Shall I g' and call to thee a nurse
8 Pharaoh's daughter said to her, G'.
3:11 am I, that I should g' unto Pharaoh,
16 G', and gather the elders of Israel
18 now let us g', we beseech thee,
19 king of Egypt will not let you g',
20 and after that he will let you g'.
21 come to pass, that when ye g',
21 ye shall not g' empty:
4:12 Now therefore g', and I will be with
18 Let me g', I pray thee, and return
18 Jethro said to Moses, G' in peace.
19 G', return into Egypt: for all the
21 that he shall not let the people g'.
23 Let my son g', that he may serve
23 if thou refuse to let him g', behold,
26 So he let him g': then she said,
27 G' into the wilderness to meet
5: 1 Let my people g', that they may
2 obey his voice to let Israel g'?
2 neither will I let Israel g'.
3 let us g', we pray thee, three days'
7 g' and gather straw for themselves.
8 Let us g' and sacrifice to our God.
11 G' ye, get you straw where ye can
17 us g' and do sacrifice to the Lord.
18 G' therefore now, and work; for
6: 1 a strong hand shall he let them g',
Ex 6:11 G' in, speak unto Pharaoh king of
11 that he let the children of Israel g'
7:14 he refuseth to let the people g'.
16 unto thee, saying, Let my people g',
8: 1 G' unto Pharaoh, and say unto
1 Let my people g', that they may
2 if thou refuse to let them g',
3 g' up and come into thine house,
8 and I will let the people g', that
20 Let my people g', that they may
21 if thou wilt not let my people g',
25 G' ye, sacrifice to your God in the
27 We will g' three days' journey into
28 said, I will let you g', that ye may
28 only ye shall not g' very far away:
29 Behold, I g' out from thee, and I
29 letting the people g' to sacrifice
32 neither would he let the people g'.
9: 1 G' in unto Pharaoh, and tell him,
1 Let my people g', that they may
2 For if thou refuse to let them g',
7 and he did not let the people g'.
13 Let my people g', that they may
28 and I will let you g', and ye shall
35 he let the children of Israel g';
10: 1 G' in unto Pharaoh, for I have
3 let my people g', that they may
4 if thou refuse to let my people g',
7 let the men g', that they may serve
8 G', serve the Lord your God:
8 but who are they that shall g'?
9 We will g' with our young and
9 and with our herds will we g';
10 as I will let you g', and your little
11 g' now ye that are men, and serve
20 not let the children of Israel g'.
24 G' ye, serve the Lord; and let
24 let your little ones also g' with you.
26 Our cattle also shall g' with us;
27 and he would not let them g'.
11: 1 afterwards he will let you g' hence:
1 when he shall let you g', he shall
4 About midnight will I g' out into
8 after that I will g' out. And he
10 not let the children of Israel g'
12:22 none of you shall g' out at the
31 and g', serve the Lord, as ye have
13:15 Pharaoh would hardly let us g',
17 Pharaoh had let the people g',
21 light; to g' by day and night:
14: 5 that we have let Israel g' from
15 of Israel, that they g' forward:
16 children of Israel shall g' on dry
21 Lord caused the sea to g' back
16: 4 the people shall g' out and gather
29 let no man g' of his place on the
17: 5 G' on before the people, and
5 take in thine hand, and g'.
9 Choose us out men, and g' out,
18:23 all this people shall also g' to
19:10 G' unto the people, and sanctify
12 that ye g' not up into the mount,
21 G' down, charge the people, lest
20:26 Neither shalt thou g' up by steps
21: 2 he shall g' out free for nothing.
3 he shall g' out by himself: if he
3 then his wife shall g' out with him.
4 and he shall g' out by himself.
5 my children; I will not g' out free:
7 not g' out as the menservants do.
11 then shall she g' out free without
26 let him g' free for his eye's sake.
27 he shall let him g' free for his
23:23 mine Angel shall g' before thee,
24: 2 shall the people g' up with him.
30:20 When they g' into the tabernacle
32: 1 us gods, which shall g' before us;
7 said unto Moses, G', get thee down:
23 us gods, which shall g' before us:
27 his sword by his side, and g' in
30 now I will g' up unto the Lord;
34 Therefore now g', lead the people
34 mine Angel shall g' before thee:
33: 1 unto Moses, Depart, and g' up
3 I will not g' up in the midst of thee;
14 My presence shall g' with thee,
15 If thy presence g' not with me,
34: 9 Lord, I pray thee, g' among us;
15 g' a whoring after their gods,
16 their daughters g' a whoring
16 and make thy sons g' a whoring
24 when thou shalt g' up to appear
Le 6:13 on the altar; it shall never g' out.
8:33 ye shall not g' out of the door
9: 7 G' unto the altar, and offer thy
10: 7 ye shall not g' out from the door
9 when ye g' into the tabernacle of
11:27 that g' on all four, those are
14: 3 And the priest shall g' forth out
36 before the priest g' into it to see
36 the priest shall g' in to see the house:
38 priest shall g' out of the house
53 But he shall let g' the living bird
15:16 man's seed of copulation g' out
16:10 to let him g' for a scapegoat
18 And he shall g' out unto the altar
22 and he shall let g' the goat in the
26 he that let g' the goat for the
19:16 g' up and down as a talebearer
20: 5 all that g' a whoring after him,
6 wizards, to g' a whoring after
21:11 shall he g' in to any dead body,
12 shall he g' out of the sanctuary,
23 he shall not g' in unto the vail,
25:28 and in the jubile it shall g' out,
30 it shall not g' out in the jubile.

Le 25:31 and they shall *g'* out in the jubile.
33 shall *g'* out in the year of jubile:
54 he shall *g'* out in the year of jubile,
26: 6 the sword *g'* through your land.
13 yoke, and made you *g'* upright.
Nu 1: 3 all that are able to *g'* forth to war
20, 22, 24, 26, 30, 32, 34, 36, 38, 40, 42 all
that were able to *g'* forth to war;
45 all that were able to *g'* forth to war
2:24 shall *g'* forward in the third rank.
31 *g'* hindmost with their standards.
4:19 Aaron and his sons shall *g'* in,
20 But they shall not *g'* in to see when
5:12 man's wife *g'* aside, and commit a
22 causeth the curse shall *g'* into thy
8:15 the Levites *g'* in to do the service
24 shall *g'* in to wait upon the service
10: 5 the east parts shall *g'* forward.
9 And if ye *g'* to war in your land
30 he said unto him, I will not *g'*; but
32 if thou *g'* with us, yea, it shall be,
13:17 and *g'* up into the mountain:
30 Let us *g'* up at once, and possess it;
31 We be not able to *g'* up against the
14:40 *g'* up unto the place which the Lord
42 *G'* not up, for the Lord is not among
44 presumed to *g'* up unto the hill top:
15:39 which ye use to *g'* a whoring:
16:30 they *g'* down quick into the pit;
46 *g'* quickly unto the congregation,
20:17 we will *g'* by the king's high way,
19 him, We will *g'* by the high way:
19 doing anything else, *g'* through
20 said, Thou shalt not *g'* through.
21:22 *g'* along by the king's high way,
22:12 Thou shalt not *g'* with them; thou
13 to give me leave to *g'* with you.
18 cannot *g'* beyond the word of the
20 thee, rise up, and *g'* with them;
35 *G'* with the men: but only the word
23: 3 by thy burnt offering, and I will *g'*:
16 *G'* again unto Balak, and say thus.
24:13 *g'* beyond the commandment of
14 now, behold, I *g'* unto my people:
26: 2 all that are able to *g'* to war in
27:17 Which may *g'* out before them,
17 which may *g'* in before them,
21 at his word shall they *g'* out, and
31: 3 let them *g'* against the Midianites,
23 shall make it *g'* through the fire,
23 ye shall make *g'* through the water.
32: 6 Shall your brethren *g'* to war,
9 that they should not *g'* into the land
17 ourselves will *g'* ready armed before
20 if ye will *g'* armed before the Lord
21 *g'* all of you armed over Jordan
34: 4 and shall *g'* on to Hazar-addar,
9 the border shall *g'* on to Ziphron,
11 coast shall *g'* down from Shepham,
12 the border shall *g'* down to Jordan,
De 1: 7 *g'* to the mount of the Amorites,
8 *g'* in and possess the land which
21 before thee: *g'* up and possess it,
22 by what way we must *g'* up, and
26 ye would not *g'* up, but rebelled
28 Whither shall we *g'* up? our
33 you by what way ye should *g'*,
37 Thou also shalt not *g'* in thither.
38 he shall *g'* in thither: encourage
39 they shall *g'* in thither, and unto
41 we will *g'* up and fight, according
41 ye were ready to *g'* up into the hill.
42 *G'* not up, neither fight; for I am
2:27 I will *g'* along by the high way,
3:25 I pray thee, let me *g'* over, and
27 thou shalt not *g'* over this Jordan.
28 he shall *g'* over before this people,
4: 1 and *g'* in and possess the land
5 the land whither ye *g'* to possess it.
14 them in the land whither ye *g'* over
21 that I should not *g'* over Jordan,
21 and that I should not *g'* in unto that
22 land, I must not *g'* over Jordan:
22 but ye shall *g'* over, and possess
26 ye *g'* over Jordan to possess it;
34 hath God assayed to *g'* and take him
40 that it may *g'* well with thee, and with
5:16 that it may *g'* well with thee, in the
27 *G'* thou near, and hear all that
30 *G'* say to them, Get you into your
6: 1 the land whither ye *g'* to possess
14 Ye shall not *g'* after other gods,
18 that thou mayest *g'* in and possess
8: 1 and *g'* in and possess the land which
9: 1 to *g'* in to possess nations greater
5 dost thou *g'* to possess their land;
23 *G'* up and possess the land which
10:11 may *g'* in and possess the land,
11: 8 and *g'* in and possess the land
8 land, whither ye *g'* to possess it;
10 whither thou goest in to possess it,
28 to *g'* after other gods, which ye
31 Jordan to *g'* in to possess the land
12:10 when ye *g'* over Jordan, and dwell
25 that it may *g'* well with thee, and with
26 *g'* unto the place which the Lord
28 that it may *g'* well with thee, and with
13: 2 Let us *g'* after other gods, which
6 *g'* and serve other gods, which thou
13 *g'* and serve other gods, which ye
14:25 *g'* unto the place which the Lord
15:12 shalt let him *g'* free from thee.
13 shalt not let him *g'* away empty:
16 I will not *g'* away from thee;
16: 7 morning, and *g'* unto thy tents.
19:13 that it may *g'* well with thee.

De 19:21 life shall *g'* for life, eye for eye, tooth
20: 5 let him *g'* and return to his house,
6 also *g'* and return unto his house,
7, 8 him *g'* and return unto his house,
21:13 after that thou shalt *g'* in unto her,
14 shalt let her *g'* whither she will;
22: 1 brother's ox or his sheep *g'* astray,
7 shalt in any wise let the dam *g'*,
13 and *g'* in unto her, and hate her,
23:10 shall he *g'* abroad out of the camp,
12 whither thou shalt *g'* forth abroad:
24: 2 out of his house, she may *g'* and be
5 he shall not *g'* out to war, neither
10 thou shalt not *g'* into his house
15 shall the sun *g'* down upon it;
19 thou shalt not *g'* again to fetch it:
20 shalt not *g'* over the boughs again:
25: 5 brother shall *g'* in unto her, and
7 then let his brother's wife *g'* up
26: 2 and shalt *g'* unto the place which
3 And thou shalt *g'* unto the priest
27: 3 that thou mayest *g'* in unto the land
28:14 thou shalt not *g'* aside from any
14 *g'* after other gods to serve them.
25 shalt *g'* out one way against them,
41 for they shall *g'* into captivity.
29:18 to *g'* and serve the gods of these
30:12 Who shall *g'* up for us to heaven,
13 Who shall *g'* over the sea for us,
18 over Jordan to *g'* to possess it.
31: 2 I can no more *g'* out and come in:
2 Thou shalt not *g'* over this Jordan.
3 he will *g'* over before thee, and he
3 Joshua, he shall *g'* over before thee,
6 he it is that doth *g'* with thee;
7 for thou must *g'* with this people
8 he it is that doth *g'* before thee;
13 ye *g'* over Jordan to possess it.
16 and *g'* a whoring after the gods
16 whither they *g'* to be among them,
21 imagination which they *g'* about,
32:47 ye *g'* over Jordan to possess it.
52 but thou shalt not *g'* thither unto
34: 4 but thou shalt not *g'* over thither.
Jos 1: 2 therefore arise, *g'* over this Jordan,
11 to *g'* in to possess the land, which
16 thou sendest us, we will *g'*.
2: 1 *G'* view the land, even Jericho.
16 afterward may ye *g'* your way.
19 that whosoever shall *g'* out of the
3: 3 from your place, and *g'* after it.
4 the way by which ye must *g'*:
6: 3 and *g'* round about the city once.
22 *G'* into the harlot's house, and
7: 2 *G'* up and view the country.
3 Let not all the people *g'* up; but let
3 about two or three thousand *g'* up
8: 1 *g'* up to Ai: see, I have given into
3 people of war, to *g'* up against Ai:
4 *g'* not very far from the city,
9:11 and *g'* to meet them, and say unto
12 day we came forth to *g'* unto you;
10:13 hasted not to *g'* down about a
14:11 both to *g'* out, and to come in.
18: 3 ye slack to *g'* to possess the land,
4 rise, and *g'* through the land,
8 *G'* and walk through the land,
22: 9 to *g'* unto the country of Gilead,
12 to *g'* up to war against them.
33 not intend to *g'* up against them
23:12 if ye do in any wise *g'* back, and
12 *g'* in unto them, and they to you:
J'g 1: 1 Who shall *g'* up for us against
2 the Lord said, Judah shall *g'* up:
3 will *g'* with thee into thy lot.
25 let *g'* the man and all his family.
2: 1 I made you to *g'* up out of Egypt,
6 Joshua had let the people *g'*,
4: 6 *G'* and draw toward mount Tabor,
8 unto her, If thou wilt *g'* with me,
8 then I will *g'*: but if thou
8 but if thou wilt not *g'* with me,
8 with me, then I will not *g'*.
9 she said, I will surely *g'* with thee:
5:11 the people of the Lord *g'* down
6:14 *G'* in this thy might, and thou
7: 3 *g'* to, proclaim in the ears of the
4 unto thee, This shall *g'* with thee,
4 the same shall *g'* with thee;
4 thee, This shall not *g'* with thee,
4 with thee, the same shall not *g'*.
7 all the other people *g'* every man
10 But if thou fear to *g'* down,
10 *g'* thou with Phurah...down to
11 hands be strengthened to *g'* down
9: 9, 11, 13 *g'* to be promoted over the
38 *g'* out, I pray now, and fight with
10:14 *G'* and cry unto the gods which
11: 8 that thou mayest *g'* with us, and
35 and I cannot *g'* back.
37 two months, that I may *g'* up
38 And he said, *G'*. And he sent her
12: 1 didst not call us to *g'* with thee?
5 escaped said, Let me *g'* over;
15: 1 *g'* in to my wife into the chamber.
1 father would not suffer him to *g'* in.
5 the brands on fire, he let them *g'*
16:17 then my strength will *g'* from me,
20 *g'* out as at other times before,
17: 9 I *g'* to sojourn where I may find
18: 2 *G'*, search the land: who when
5 which we *g'* shall be prosperous.
6 said unto them, *G'* in peace:
6 Lord is your way wherein ye *g'*.
9 that we may *g'* up against them:
9 be not slothful to *g'*, and to enter

J'g 18:10 ye *g'*, ye shall come unto a people
19 *g'* with us, and be to us a father
19: 5 and afterward *g'* your way.
9 way, that thou mayest *g'* home.
15 to *g'* in and to lodge in Gibeah:
25 began to spring, they let her *g'*.
27 went out to *g'* his way: and,
20: 8 We will not any of us *g'* to his tent.
14 to *g'* out to battle against the
18 of us shall *g'* up first to the battle
23 Shall I *g'* up again to battle
23 And the Lord, *G'* up against him.)
28 Shall I yet again *g'* out to battle
28 And the Lord said, *G'* up; for to
21:10 *G'* and smite the inhabitants of
20 *G'* and lie in wait in the vineyards:
21 and *g'* to the land of Benjamin.
Ru 1: 8 *G'*, return each to her mother's
11 why will ye *g'* with me? are there
12 again, my daughters, *g'* your way;
16 for whither thou goest, I will *g'*;
18 stedfastly minded to *g'* with her,
2: 2 Let me now *g'* to the field,
2 she said unto her, *G'*, my daughter.
8 *G'* not to glean in another field,
8 neither *g'* from hence, but abide
9 and *g'* thou after them: have I not
9 art athirst, *g'* unto the vessels,
22 that thou *g'* out with his maidens,
3: 4 shalt *g'* in, and uncover his feet,
17 *G'* not empty unto thy mother in
1Sa 1:17 Eli answered and said, *G'* in peace:
22 I will not *g'* up until the child be
3: 9 Eli said unto Samuel, *G'*, lie down:
5:11 let it *g'* again to his own place,
6: 6 did they not let the people *g'*,
8 and send it away, that it may *g'*.
20 to whom shall he *g'* up from us?
8:20 *g'* out before us, and fight our
22 *G'* ye every man unto his city.
9: 3 and arise, *g'* seek the asses.
6 let us *g'* thither; peradventure he
6 shew us our way that we should *g'*.
7 we *g'*, what shall we bring the man?
9 Come, and let us *g'* to the seer:
10 Well said; come, let us *g'*. So they
13 he *g'* up to the high place to eat:
14 for to *g'* up to the high place.
19 *g'* up before me unto the high place:
19 and to morrow I will let thee *g'*,
10: 3 thou *g'* on forward from thence,
8 shalt *g'* down before me to Gilgal;
9 turned his back to *g'* from Samuel,
11:14 Come, and let us *g'* to Gilgal,
14: 1 let us *g'* over to the Philistines,
4 Jonathan sought to *g'* over unto the
6 and let us *g'* over unto the garrison
9 still in our place, and will not *g'* up
10 up unto us; then we will *g'* up:
36 Let us *g'* down after the Philistines
37 I *g'* down after the Philistines?
15: 3 Now *g'* and smite Amalek, and
6 *G'*, depart, get you down from
18 *G'* and utterly destroy the sinners
27 Samuel turned about to *g'* away,
16: 1 fill thine horn with oil, and *g'*,
2 And Samuel said, How can I *g'*?
17:32 *g'* and fight with this Philistine.
33 not able to *g'* against this Philistine
37 Saul said unto David, *G'*, and the
39 he assayed to *g'*; for he had not
39 I cannot *g'* with these; for I have
55 Saul saw David *g'* forth against
18: 2 *g'* no more home to his father's
19: 3 *g'* out and stand beside my father
17 He said unto me, Let me *g'*;
20: 5 but let me *g'*, that I may hide
11 and let us *g'* out into the field.
13 that thou mayest *g'* in peace: and
19 thou shalt *g'* down quickly,
21 saying, *G'*, find out the arrows.
22 *g'* thy way: for the Lord hath sent
28 asked leave of me to *g'* to Bethlehem:
29 he said, Let me *g'*, I pray thee;
40 him, *G'*, carry them to the city.
42 Jonathan said to David, *G'* in peace,
23: 2 I *g'* and smite these Philistines?
2 *G'*, and smite the Philistines, and
4 Arise, *g'* down to Keilah; for I will
8 people together to war, to *g'* down
13 went whithersoever they could *g'*.
13 he forbare to *g'* forth.
22 *G'*, I pray you, prepare yet, and
23 I will *g'* with you: and it shall
24:19 will he let him *g'* well away?
25: 5 *g'* to Nabal, and greet him
19 her servants, *G'* on before me;
35 *G'* up in peace to thine house;
26: 6 will *g'* down with me to Saul to
6 And Abishai said, I will *g'* down
11 the cruse of water, and let us *g'*.
19 saying, *G'*, serve other gods.
28: 1 shalt *g'* out with me to battle,
7 I may *g'* to her, and enquire of her.
29: 4 that he may *g'* again to his place
4 him not *g'* down with us to battle,
7 now return, and *g'* in peace,
8 not *g'* fight against the enemies
9 not *g'* up with us to the battle.
30:10 they could not *g'* over the brook
2Sa 1:15 *G'* near, and fall upon him.
2: 1 Shall I *g'* up into any of the cities
1 And the Lord said unto him, *G'* up.
1 David said, Whither shall I *g'* up?
3:16 said Abner unto him, *G'*, return.
21 I will arise and *g'*, and will gather

2Sa 5:19 Shall I g· up to the Philistines?
19 Lord said unto David, G· up: for
23 Thou shalt not g· up; but fetch a
24 shall the Lord g· out before thee,
7: 3 G·, do all that is in thine heart;
5 G· and tell thy servant David,
11: 1 time when kings g· forth to battle,
8 G· down to thy house, and wash
10 not g· down unto thine house?
11 shall I then g· into mine house,
12:23 I shall g· to him, but he shall not
13: 7 G· now to thy brother Amnon's
13 shall I cause my shame to g·?
24 his servants g· with thy servant.
25 Nay, my son, let us not all now g·,
25 he would not g·, but blessed him.
26 let my brother Amnon g· with us.
26 Why should he g· with thee?
27 Amnon and all the king's sons g·
39 longed to g· forth unto Absalom:
14: 8 unto the woman, G· to thine house,
21 g· therefore, bring the young man
30 g· and set it on fire. And Absalom's
15: 7 let me g· and pay my vow,
9 the king said unto him, G· in peace.
20 should I this day make thee g· up
20 seeing I g· whither I may,
22 David said to Ittai, G· and pass
16: 9 let me g· over, I pray thee, and
21 G· in unto thy father's concubines,
17:11 that thou g· to battle in thine own
18: 2 surely g· forth with you myself
3 Thou shalt not g· forth: for if we
21 G· tell the king what thou hast
19: 7 Now therefore arise, g· forth, and
7 by the Lord, if thou g· not forth,
15 to g· to meet the king, to conduct
20 g· down to meet my lord the king.
26 and g· to the king; because thy
34 that I should g· up with the king
36 servant will g· a little way over
37 servant Chimham; let him g· over
38 Chimham shall g· over with me,
20:11 that is for David, let him g· after
21:17 Thou shalt g· no more out with
24: 1 G·, number Israel and Judah.
2 G· now through all the tribes of
12 G· and say unto David, Thus saith
18 G· up, rear an altar unto the Lord
1Ki 1:13 G· and get thee in unto king
53 Solomon said unto him, G· to thine
2: 2 I g· the way of all the earth;
6 let not his hoar head g· down to
29 saying, G·, fall upon him.
36 g· not forth thence any whither.
3: 7 know not how to g· out or come in.
8:44 If thy people g· out to battle
9: 6 but g· and serve other gods,
11: 2 Ye shall not g· in to them, neither
10 that he should not g· after other
17 servants with him, to g· into Egypt;
21 that I may g· to mine own country.
22 thou seekest to g· to thine own
22 Nothing: howbeit let me g· in any
12:24 saith the Lord, Ye shall not g· up,
27 this people g· up to do sacrifice
28 much for you to g· up to Jerusalem:
13: 8 I will not g· in with thee, neither
16 nor g· in with thee: neither will I
17 turn again to g· by the way that
14: 3 and g· to him: he shall tell thee
7 G·, tell Jeroboam, Thus saith the
15:17 he might not suffer any to g· out
17:12 that I may g· in and dress it for
13 Fear not; g· and do as thou hast
18: 1 G·, show thyself unto Ahab; and
5 G· into the land, unto all fountains
8 I am: g·, tell thy lord, Behold, Elijah
11, 14 sayest, G·, tell thy lord, Behold,
43 G· up now, look toward the sea.
43 he said, G· again seven times.
44 G· up, say unto Ahab, Prepare
19:11 G· forth, and stand upon the
15 G·, return on thy way to the
20 he said unto him, G· back again:
20:22 G·, strengthen thyself, and mark,
31 and g· out to the king of Israel:
33 Then he said, G· ye, bring him.
42 Because thou hast let g· out of
42 therefore thy life shall g· for his
21:16 Ahab rose up to g· down to the
18 Arise, g· down to meet Ahab king
22: 4 Wilt thou g· with me to battle to
6 Shall I g· against Ramoth-gilead
6 G· up; for the Lord shall deliver it
12 G· up to Ramoth-gilead, and
15 shall we g· against Ramoth-gilead
15 G·, and prosper: for the Lord
20 persuade Ahab, that he may g· up
22 will g· forth, and I will be a lying
22 and prevail also: g· forth, and do
25 when thou shalt g· into an inner
48 ships of Tharshish to g· to Ophir
49 my servants g· with thy servants
2Ki 1: 2 G·, enquire of Baal-zebub the god
3 g· up to meet the messengers of
3 ye g· to enquire of Baal-zebub
6 G·, turn again unto the king that
15 G· down with him: be not afraid
2:16 let them g·, we pray thee, and seek
18 Did I not say unto you, G· not?
23 G· up, thou bald head; g· up, thou
3: 7 wilt thou g· with me against Moab
7 And he said, I will g· up: I am as
8 Which way shall we g· up? And he
4: 3 he said, G·, borrow thee vessels
2Ki 4: 7 G·, sell the oil, and pay thy debt,
23 Wherefore wilt thou g· to him
24 Drive, and g· forward; slack not
29 take my staff in thine hand, and g·
5: 5 And the king of Syria said, G· to,
5 g·, and I will send a letter
10 G· and wash in Jordan seven
19 And he said unto him, G· in peace.
24 and he let the men g·, and they
6: 2 us g·, we pray thee, unto Jordan,
2 And he answered, G· ye.
3 I pray thee, and g· with thy servants.
3 And he answered, I will g·.
13 he said, G· and spy where he is,
22 and drink, and g· to their master.
7: 5 g· unto the camp of the Syrians:
9 that we may g· and tell the king's
14 the Syrians, saying, G· and see.
8: 1 and g· thou and thine household,
8 and g·, meet the man of God, and
10 G·, say unto him, Thou mayest
9: 1 thine hand and g· to Ramoth-gilead:
2 and g· in, and make him arise up
15 let none g· forth nor escape out
15 of the city, to g· to tell it in Jezreel.
34 G·, see now this cursed woman,
10:13 and we g· down to salute the
24 he that letteth him g·, his life shall be
25 G· in, and slay them; let none
11: 7 you that g· forth on the sabbath,
9 that should g· out on the sabbath,
12:17 Hazael set his face to g· up to
17:27 and let them g· and dwell there,
18:21 a man lean, it will g· into his hand,
25 said to me, G· up against this land,
19:31 shall g· forth a remnant, and they
20: 5 on the third day thou shalt g· up
8 shall g· into the house of the Lord
9 shall the shadow g· forward ten
9 degrees, or g· back ten degrees?
10 shadow to g· down ten degrees:
22: 4 G· up to Hilkiah the high priest,
13 G· ye, enquire of the Lord for me,
1Ch 7:11 fit to g· out for war and battle.
14:10 I g· up against the Philistines?
10 the Lord said unto him, G· up;
14 God said unto him, G· not up after
15 then thou shalt g· out to battle:
17: 4 G· and tell David my servant,
11 must g· to be with thy fathers,
20: 1 time that kings g· out to battle,
21: 2 G·, number Israel from Beer-sheba
10 G· and tell David, saying, Thus
18 that David should g· up, and set
30 David could not g· before it to
2Ch 1:10 that I may g· out and come in
6:34 If thy people g· out to war against
7:19 and shall g· and serve other gods,
11: 4 Ye shall not g· up, nor fight against
14:11 we g· against this multitude.
16: 1 he might let none g· out or come in
3 g·, break thy league with Baasha
18: 2 persuaded him to g· up with him
3 g· with me to Ramoth-gilead?
5 Shall we g· to Ramoth-gilead to
5 G· up; for God will deliver it into
11 G· up to Ramoth-gilead, and
14 Shall we g· to Ramoth-gilead to
14 G· ye up, and prosper, and they
19 that he may g· up and fall at
21 I will g· out, and be a lying spirit
21 also prevail: g· out, and do even so.
24 that day when thou shalt g· into
29 and will g· to the battle; but put
20:16 morrow g· ye down against them:
17 to morrow g· out against them:
27 to g· again to Jerusalem with joy;
36 to make ships to g· to Tarshish:
37 were not able to g· to Tarshish.
21:13 of Jerusalem to g· a whoring,
23: 6 shall g· in, for they are holy:
8 were to g· out on the sabbath:
24: 5 G· out unto the cities of Judah,
25: 5 able to g· forth to war, that could
7 the army of Israel g· with thee;
8 But if thou wilt g·, do it, be strong
10 out of Ephraim, to g· home again:
13 should not g· with him to battle,
26:18 g· out of the sanctuary; for thou
20 yea, himself hasted also to g· out,
34:21 G·, enquire of the Lord for me,
36:23 be with him, and let him g· up.
Ezr 1: 3 be with him, and let him g· up to
5 to g· up to build the house of the
5:15 g·, carry them into the temple
7: 9 the first month began he to g· up
13 to g· to Jerusalem, g· with thee.
28 chief men to g· up with me.
8:31 to g· unto Jerusalem: and the
9:11 unto which ye g· to possess it,
Ne 3:15 stairs that g· down from the city
4: 3 if a fox g· up, he shall even break
6:11 g· into the temple to save his life?
11 to save his life? I will not g· in.
8:10 G· your way, eat the fat, and drink
15 G· forth unto the mount, and
9:12 the way wherein they should g·.
15 they should g· in to possess the land
19 the way wherein they should g·.
23 that they should g· in to possess it.
Es 1:19 let there g· a royal commandment
2:12 maid's turn was come to g· into
13 was given her to g· with her out
15 was come to g· in unto the king,
4: 8 that she should g· in unto the king,
16 G·, gather together all the Jews
Es 4:16 and so will I g· in unto the king,
5:14 g· thou in merrily with the king
Job 4:21 which is in them g· away? they
6:18 they g· to nothing, and perish.
10:21 I g· whence I shall not return,
15:13 such words g· out of thy mouth?
30 of his mouth shall he g· away.
16:22 then I shall g· the way whence
17:16 They shall g· down to the bars of
20:26 it shall g· ill with him that is left
21:13 in a moment g· down to the grave.
29 asked them that g· by the way?
23: 8 Behold, I g· forward, but he is
24: 5 asses in the desert, g· they forth
10 They cause him to g· naked
27: 6 hold fast, and will not let it g·:
31:37 prince would I g· near unto him.
37: 8 Then the beasts g· into dens, and
38:35 send lightnings, that they may g·,
39: 4 they g· forth, and return not
41:19 of his mouth g· burning lamps,
42: 8 and g· to my servant Job, and
Ps 22:29 all they that g· down to the dust
26: 4 will I g· in with dissemblers.
28: 1 them that g· down into the pit.
30: 3 that I should not g· down to the pit.
9 when I g· down to the pit? shall
32: 8 the way which thou shalt g·:
38: 6 I g· mourning all the day long.
39:13 before I g· hence, and be no more.
42: 9 why g· I mourning because of the
43: 2 why g· I mourning because of the
4 will I g· unto the altar of God,
48:12 Zion, and g· round about her:
49:19 He shall g· to the generation of
55:10 Day and night they g· about it
15 let them g· down quick into hell:
58: 3 they g· astray as soon as they be
59: 6, 14 and g· round about the city.
60:10 didst not g· out with our armies?
63: 9 shall g· into the lower parts of the
66:13 I will g· into thy house with
71:16 I will g· in the strength of the
73:27 that g· a whoring from thee.
78:52 made his own people to g· forth
80:18 So will not we g· back from thee:
84: 7 They g· from strength to strength,
85:13 Righteousness shall g· before him;
88: 4 them that g· down into the pit:
89:14 and truth shall g· before thy face.
104: 8 They g· up by the mountains;
8 they g· down by the valleys
26 There g· the ships: there is that
105:20 of the people, and let him g· free.
107: 7 that they might g· to a city of
23 They that g· down to the sea in
26 they g· down again to the depths:
108:11 wilt not thou, O God, g· forth with
115:17 any that g· down into silence.
118:19 I will g· into them, and I will
119:35 Make me to g· in the path of thy
122: 1 Let us g· into the house of the
4 Whither the tribes g· up, the
129: 8 Neither do they which g· by say,
132: 3 my house, nor g· up into my bed;
7 We will g· into his tabernacles:
139: 7 Whither shall I g· from thy spirit?
143: 7 them that g· down into the pit.
Pr 1:12 as those that g· down into the pit:
2:19 None that g· unto her return again,
3:28 Say not unto thy neighbour, G·,
4:13 hold of instruction; let her not g·:
14 g· not in the way of evil men.
5: 5 Her feet g· down to death; her
23 of his folly he shall g· astray.
6: 3 g·, humble thyself, and make sure
6 G· to the ant, thou sluggard;
28 Can one g· upon hot coals, and
7:25 g· not astray in her paths.
9: 6 g· in the way of understanding.
15 To call passengers who g· right on
14: 7 G· from the presence of a foolish
15:12 neither will he g· unto the wise.
18: 8 they g· down into the innermost
19: 7 do his friends g· far from him?
22: 6 a child in the way he should g·:
10 and contention shall g· out; yea,
24 a furious man thou shalt not g·:
23:30 they that g· to seek mixed wine.
25: 8 G· not forth hastily to strive,
26:22 they g· down into the innermost
27:10 neither g· into thy brother's house
28:10 causeth the righteous to g· astray
30:27 yet g· they forth all of them by
29 three things which g· well, yea,
Ec 2: 1 I said in mine heart, G· to now,
3:20 All g· unto one place; all are of
5:15 shall he return to g· as he came,
16 so shall he g·: and what profit hath
6: 6 do not all g· to one place?
7: 2 to g· to the house of mourning,
2 than to g· to the house of feasting:
8: 3 Be not hasty to g· out of his sight:
9: 3 and after that they g· to the dead.
7 G· thy way, eat thy bread with
10:15 knoweth not how to g· to the city.
12: 5 the mourners g· about the streets:
Ca 1: 8 g· thy way forth by the footsteps
3: 2 I will rise now, and g· about the
3 watchmen that g· about the city
4 him, and would not let him g·,
11 G· forth, O ye daughters of Zion,
6: 6 as a flock of sheep which g· up
7: 8 said, I will g· up to the palm tree,
11 let us g· forth into the field; let
Isa 2: 3 And many people shall g· and say,

Isa 2: 3 and let us g' up to the mountain
3 out of Zion shall g' forth the law,
19 And they shall g' into the holes
21 To g' into the clefts of the rocks,
3:16 walking and mincing as they g',
5: 5 And now g' to; I will tell you what
24 their blossom shall g' up as dust:
6: 8 who will g' for us? Then said I,
9 he said, G', and tell this people,
7: 3 G' forth now to meet Ahaz, thou,
6 Let us g' up against Judah, and
8: 6 waters of Shiloah that g' softly,
7 channels, and g' over all his banks:
8 he shall overflow and g' over,
11:15 and make men g' over dryshod.
13: 2 that they may g' into the gates
14:19 g' down to the stones of the pit;
15: 5 with weeping shall they g' it up;
18: 2 G', ye swift messengers, to a
20: 2 G' and loose the sackcloth from off
21: 2 G' up, O Elam: besiege, O Media;
6 G', set a watchman, let him
22:15 G', get thee unto this treasurer,
23:16 Take an harp, g' about the city,
27: 4 I would g' through them, I would
28:13 they might g', and fall backward,
30: 2 That walk to g' down into Egypt,
8 g', write it before them in a table,
31: 1 to them that g' down to Egypt
33:21 shall g' no galley with oars,
34:10 smoke thereof shall g' up for ever:
35: 9 ravenous beast shall g' up thereon,
36: 6 man lean, it will g' into his hand,
10 G' up against this land, and
37:32 out of Jerusalem shall g' forth a
38: 5 G', and say to Hezekiah, Thus
10 shall g' to the gates of the grave:
15 I shall g' softly all my years in
18 they that g' down into the pit
22 What is the sign that I shall g' up
42:10 ye that g' down to the sea, and all
13 Lord shall g' forth as a mighty
45: 2 I will g' before thee, and make
13 he shall let g' my captives, not
16 shall g' to confusion together
48:17 by the way that thou shouldest g'.
20 G' ye forth of Babylon, flee ye
49: 9 say to the prisoners, G' forth;
17 that made thee waste shall g' forth
51:23 Bow down, that we may g' over:
52:11 g' ye out from thence, touch no
11 g' ye out of the midst of her;
12 ye shall not g' out with haste,
12 with haste, nor g' by flight:
12 for the Lord will g' before you;
54: 9 should no more g' over the earth;
55:12 For ye shall g' out with joy, and
58: 6 and to let the oppressed g' free,
8 righteousness shall g' before thee;
60:20 Thy sun shall no more g' down;
62: 1 thereof g' forth as brightness,
10 G' through, g' through the gates;
66:24 And they shall g' forth, and look
Jer 1: 7 shalt g' to all that I shall send
2: 2 G' and cry in the ears of
25 strangers, and after them will I g'.
37 Yea, thou shalt g' forth from him,
3: 1 and she g' from him, and become
12 G' and proclaim these words
4: 5 let us g' into the defenced cities.
29 shall g' into thickets, and climb up
5:10 G' ye up upon her walls, and
6: 4 arise, and let us g' up at noon.
5 Arise, and let us g' by night,
25 G' not forth into the field, nor
7:12 g' ye now unto my place which
9: 2 and g' from them! for they be all
10: 5 be borne, because they cannot g'.
11:12 and inhabitants of Jerusalem g',
13: 1 G' and get thee a linen girdle,
4 and arise, g' to Euphrates, and
6 Arise, g' to Euphrates, and take
14:18 If I g' forth into the field, then
18 the prophet and the priest g' about
15: 1 my sight, and let them g' forth.
2 Whither shall we g' forth? then
5 g' aside to ask how thou doest?
16: 5 g' to lament nor bemoan them:
8 also g' into the house of feasting,
17:19 G' and stand in the gate of the
19 by the which they g' out, and in
18: 2 Arise, and g' down to the potter's
11 g' to, speak to the men of Judah,
19: 1 G' and get a potter's earthen
2 g' forth unto the valley of the son
10 sight of the men that g' with thee,
20: 6 that dwell in thine house shall g'
21: 2 that he may g' up from us.
12 lest my fury g' out like fire, and
22: 1 G' down to the house of the king
20 G' up to Lebanon, and cry; and
22 thy lovers shall g' into captivity:
25: 6 g' not after other gods to serve
32 evil shall g' forth from nation to
27:18 at Jerusalem, g' not to Babylon.
28:13 G' and tell Hananiah, saying,
29:12 and ye shall g' and pray unto me,
30:16 of them, shall g' into captivity;
31: 4 and shalt g' forth in the dances of
6 Arise ye, and let us g' up to Zion
22 How long wilt thou g' about, O
24 and they that g' forth with flocks.
39 measuring line shall yet g' forth
34: 2 G' and speak to Zedekiah king of
3 thou shalt g' to Babylon.
9 an Hebrewess, g' free; that none

Jer 34:10 every one his maidservant, g' free;
10 then they obeyed, and let them g'.
11 whom they had let g' free, to return,
14 let ye g' every man his brother an
14 thou shalt let him g' free from
35: 2 G' unto the house of the
11 and let us g' to Jerusalem for fear
13 G' and tell the men of Judah and
15 g' not after other gods to serve
36: 5 I cannot g' into the house of the
6 Therefore g' thou, and read in the
19 G', hide thee, thou and Jeremiah;
37:12 to g' into the land of Benjamin,
38:17 thou wilt assuredly g' forth unto
18 if thou wilt not g' forth to the king
21 if thou refuse to g' forth, this is the
39:16 G' and speak to Ebed-melech the
40: 1 guard had let him g' from Ramah,
4 convenient for thee to g', thither g'.
5 G' back also to Gedaliah the son
5 or g' wheresoever it seemeth
5 convenient unto thee to g'.
5 and a reward, and let him g'.
15 Let me g', I pray thee, and I will
41:10 and departed to g' over to the
17 to g' to enter into Egypt,
42:14 we will g' into the land of Egypt,
15 into Egypt, and g' to sojourn there;
17 that set their faces to g' into Egypt
19 G' ye not into Egypt: know
22 the place whither ye desire to g'
43: 2 G' not into Egypt to sojourn there:
12 and he shall g' forth from thence
44:12 have set their faces to g' into the
46: 8 and he saith, I will g' up, and
11 G' up into Gilead, and take balm,
16 let us g' again to our own people,
22 The voice thereof shall g' like a
48: 5 continual weeping shall g' up;
7 and Chemosh shall g' forth into
49: 3 their king shall g' into captivity,
12 that shall altogether g' unpunished?
28 g' up to Kedar, and spoil the men
50: 4 they shall g', and seek the Lord
6 have caused them to g' astray,
8 g' forth out of the land of the
21 G' up against the land of
27 them g' down to the slaughter:
33 fast; they refused to let them g'.
51: 9 and let us g' every one into his
45 people, g' ye out of the midst of
50 have escaped the sword, g' away,
La 4:18 that we cannot g' in our streets:
Eze 1:12 whither the spirit was to g', they
20 Whithersoever the spirit was to g',
20 thither was their spirit to g';
3: 1 g' speak unto the house of Israel.
4 of man, g', get thee unto the house
11 And g', get thee to them of the
22 Arise, g' forth into the plain,
24 G', shut thyself within thine house.
25 and thou shalt not g' out among
6: 9 g' a whoring after their idols:
8: 6 that I should g' far off from my
9 G' in, and behold the wicked
9: 4 G' through the midst of the city,
5 G' ye after him through the city,
7 g' ye forth. And they went forth,
10: 2 G' in between the wheels, even
12: 4 thou shalt g' forth at even in their
4 as they that g' forth into captivity.
11 shall remove and g' into captivity.
12 and shall g' forth: they shall dig
13:20 and will let the souls g', even the
14:11 Israel may g' no more astray from
17 Sword, g' through the land; so
15: 7 they shall g' out from one fire,
20:10 I caused them to g' forth out of the
29 is the high place whereunto ye g'?
39 G' ye, serve ye every one his idols,
21: 4 therefore shall my sword g' forth
16 G' thee one way or other, either on
23:44 as they g' in unto a woman that
24:14 I will not g' back, neither will I
26:11 thy strong garrisons shall g' down
20 with them that g' down to the pit,
30: 9 that day shall messengers g' forth
17 these cities shall g' into captivity.
18 daughters shall g' into captivity.
31:14 with them that g' down to the pit.
32:18 with them that g' down into the pit.
19 g' down, and be thou laid with the
24 with them that g' down to the pit.
25 with them that g' down to the pit:
29, 30 them that g' down to the pit.
38:11 I will g' up to the land of unwalled
11 I will g' to them that are at rest,
39: 9 the cities of Israel shall g' forth,
40:26 there were seven steps to g' up to
42:14 shall they not g' out of the holy
44: 3 shall g' out by the way of the same.
19 And when they g' forth into the
46: 2 then he shall g' forth; but the gate
8 shall g' in by the way of the porch
8 shall g' forth by the way thereof.
9 g' out by the way of the south gate;
9 shall g' forth by the way of the
9 but he shall g' forth over against it.
10 when they g' in, shall g' in;
10 when they g' forth, shall g' forth.
12 then he shall g' forth; and after
47: 8 and g' down into the desert,
8 and g' into the sea: which being
15 of Hethlon, as men g' to Zedad;
Da 11:44 therefore he shall g' forth with
12: 9 he said, G' thy way, Daniel: for

Da 12:13 g' thou thy way till the end be:
Ho 1: 2 G' take unto thee a wife of
2: 5 I will g' after my lovers, that give
7 g' and return to my first husband;
3: 1 G' yet, love a woman beloved of
4:15 neither g' ye up to Beth-aven, nor
5: 6 They shall g' with their flocks
14 I, even I, will tear and g' away;
15 I will g' and return to my place,
7:11 call to Egypt, they g' to Assyria.
12 When they shall g', I will spread
11: 3 taught Ephraim also to g', taking
Joe 2:16 let the bridegroom g' forth of his
Am 1: 5 people of Syria shall g' into captivity
15 their king shall g' into captivity,
2: 7 his father will g' in unto the same
4: 3 ye shall g' out at the breaches,
5: 5 Gilgal shall surely g' into captivity,
27 will I cause you to g' into captivity
6: 2 and from thence g' ye to Hamath
2 then g' down to Gath of the
7 Therefore now shall they g' captive
7 with the first that g' captive, and the
7:12 g', flee thee away into the land of
15 G', prophesy unto my people Israel.
17 Israel shall surely g' into captivity
8: 9 cause the sun to g' down at noon
9: 4 though they g' into captivity
Jon 1: 2 Arise, g' to Nineveh, that great city,
3 to g' with them unto Tarshish
3: 2 Arise, g' unto Nineveh, that great
Mic 1: 8 I will g' stripped and naked: I will
2: 3 neither shall ye g' haughtily: for
3: 6 and the sun shall g' down over the
4: 2 and let us g' up to the mountain
2 the law shall g' forth of Zion,
10 now shalt thou g' forth out of the
10 and thou shalt g' even to Babylon;
5: 8 if he g' through, both treadeth
Na 3:14 g' into clay, and tread the morter,
Hab 1: 4 judgment doth never g' forth: for
Hag 1: 8 G' up to the mountain, and bring
Zec 6: 5 which g' forth from standing
6 g' forth into the north country;
6 white g' forth after them; and
6 grisled g' forth toward the south
7 bay went forth, and sought to g'
8 that g' toward the north country
10 thou the same day, and g' into the
8:21 inhabitants of one city shall g'
21 Let us g' speedily to pray before
21 the Lord of hosts: I will g' also.
23 We will g' with you: for we have
9:14 and his arrow shall g' forth as the
14 and shall g' with whirlwinds of
14: 2 and half of the city shall g' forth
3 Then shall the Lord g' forth, and
8 that living waters shall g' out from
16 shall even g' up from year to year
18 if the family of Egypt g' not up,
Mal 4: 2 and ye shall g' forth, and grow up
M't 2: 8 G' and search diligently for the
20 and g' into the land of Israel: for
22 he was afraid to g' thither:
5:24 before the altar, and g' thy way;
41 shall compel thee to g' a mile,
41 a mile, g' with him twain.
7:13 there be which g' in thereat:
8: 4 but g' thy way, shew thyself to
9 I say to this man, G' and he goeth;
13 G' thy way; and as thou hast
21 suffer me first to g' and bury my
31 suffer us to g' away into the herd
32 And he said unto them, G'. And
9: 6 thy bed, and g' unto thine house.
13 But g' ye and learn what that
10: 5 G' not into the way of the Gentiles,
6 But g' rather to the lost sheep
7 And as ye g', preach, saying,
11 and there abide till ye g' thence.
11: 4 G' and shew John again those
13:28 that we g' and gather them up?
14:15 that they may g' into the villages,
22 g' before him unto the other side,
29 on the water, to g' to Jesus.
16:21 that he must g' unto Jerusalem,
17:27 g' thou to the sea, and cast an
18:15 g' and tell him his fault between
19:21 g' and sell that thou hast, and give
24 for a camel to g' through the eye
20: 4 G' ye also into the vineyard, and
7 G' ye also into the vineyard; and
14 Take that thine is, and g' thy way:
18 Behold, we g' up to Jerusalem;
21: 2 G' into the village over against
28 g' work to day in my vineyard.
30 And he answered and said I g', sir:
31 g' into the kingdom of God before
22: 9 G' ye therefore into the highways.
23:13 ye neither g' in yourselves,
13 ye them that are entering to g' in.
24:26 he is in the desert; g' not forth:
25: 6 cometh; g' ye out to meet him.
9 but g' ye rather to them that sell,
46 these shall g' away into everlasting
26:18 G' into the city to such a man,
32 I will g' before you into Galilee.
36 here, while I g' and pray yonder.
27:65 g' your way, make it as sure as ye
28: 7 g' quickly, and tell his disciples
10 Be not afraid: g' tell my brethren
10 brethren that they g' into Galilee,
19 G' ye therefore, and teach all
M'r 1:38 Let us g' into the next towns,
44 but g' thy way, shew thyself to
2:11 and g' thy way into thine house,

M'r 5:19 G· home to thy friends, and tell
34 g· in peace, and be whole of thy
6:36 that they may g· into the country
37 Shall we g· and buy two hundred
38 many loaves have ye? g· and see.
45 to g· to the other side before unto
7:29 For this saying g· thy way; the
8:26 Neither g· into the town, nor
9:43 having two hands to g· into hell,
10:21 g· thy way, sell whatsoever thou
25 to g· through the eye of a needle,
33 Behold, we g· up to Jerusalem;
52 G· thy way; thy faith hath made
11: 2 G· your way into the village over
6 commanded: and they let them g·.
12:38 which love to g· in long clothing,
13:15 not g· down into the house,
14:12 wilt thou that we g· and prepare
13 G· ye into the city, and there
14 wheresoever he shall g· in, say
28 I will g· before you into Galilee.
42 Rise up, let us g·: lo, he that
16: 7 But g· your way, tell his disciples
15 he said unto them, G· ye into all
Lu 1:17 shall g· before him in the spirit
76 g· before the face of the Lord
2:15 us now g· even unto Bethlehem,
5:14 g·, and shew thyself to the priest,
24 couch, and g· unto thine house.
7: 8 I say unto one, G·, and he goeth;
22 G· your way, and tell John what
50 faith hath saved thee; g· in peace.
8:14 g· forth, and are choked with cares
22 Let us g· over unto the other side
31 them to g· out into the deep.
48 made thee whole; g· in peace.
51 he suffered no man to g· in, save
9: 5 when ye g· out of that city,
12 that they may g· into the towns
13 except we should g· and buy meat
51 set his face to g· to Jerusalem,
53 though he would g· to Jerusalem.
59 me first to g· and bury my father.
60 g· thou and preach the kingdom
61 let me first g· bid them farewell,
10: 3 G· your ways; Behold, I send you
7 G· not from house to house.
10 g· your ways out into the streets
37 unto him, G·, and do thou likewise.
11: 5 and shall g· unto him at midnight,
13:32 G· ye, and tell that fox, Behold, I
14: 4 and healed him, and let him g·;
10 g· and sit down in the lowest
10 Friend, g· up higher: then shalt
18 and I must needs g· and see it:
19 I g· to prove them: I pray thee
21 G· out quickly into the streets
23 G· out into the highways and
15: 4 and g· after that which is lost,
18 I will arise and g· to my father,
28 was angry, and would not g· in:
17: 7 G· and sit down to meat?
14 G· shew yourselves unto the
19 Arise, g· thy way: thy faith hath
23 g· not after them, nor follow them.
18:25 camel to g· through a needle's eye,
31 we g· up to Jerusalem, and all
19:30 G· ye into the village over against
21: 8 g· ye not therefore after them.
22: 8 G· and prepare us the passover,
33 am ready to g· with thee, both
68 not answer me, nor let me g·.
23:22 chastise him, and let him g·.
Joh 1:43 Jesus would g· forth into Galilee,
4: 4 must needs g· through Samaria.
16 G·, call thy husband, and come
50 G· thy way; thy son liveth. And
6:67 Will ye also g· away?
68 Lord, to whom shall we g·? thou
7: 3 Depart hence, and g· into Judæa,
8 G· ye up unto this feast: I g· not up
19 Why g· ye about to kill me?
33 then I g· unto him that sent me.
35 Whither will he g·, that we shall
35 will he g· unto the dispersed
8:11 do I condemn thee: g·, and sin no
14 whence I came, and whither I g·;
14 whence I come, and whither I g·.
21 I g· my way, and ye shall seek me,
21 whither I g·, ye cannot come.
22 Whither I g·, ye cannot come.
9: 7 G·, wash in the pool of Siloam,
11 G· to the pool of Siloam, and wash:
10: 9 be saved, and shall g· in and
11: 7 Let us g· into Judæa again.
11 but I g·, that I may awake him
15 nevertheless let us g· unto him.
16 Let us also g·, that we may die with
44 them, Loose him, and let him g·.
13:33 Whither I g·, ye cannot come; so
36 Whither I g·, thou canst not follow
14: 2 I g· to prepare a place for you.
3 if I g· and prepare a place for you,
4 whither I g· ye know, and the way
12 do; because I g· unto my Father.
28 I g· away, and come again unto
28 I said, I g· unto the Father:
31 even so I do. Arise, let us g· hence.
15:16 ye should g· and bring forth fruit,
16: 5 I g· my way to him that sent me;
7 expedient for you that I g· away:
7 for if I g· not away, the Comforter
10 because I g· to my Father, and ye
16 see me, because I g· to my Father.
17 and, Because I g· to the F·?
28 the world, and g· to the Father.

Joh 18: 8 ye seek me, let these g· their way:
19:12 thou let this man g·, thou art not
20:17 but g· to my brethren, and say
21: 3 Peter saith unto them, I g· a fishing.
3 unto him, We also g· with thee.
Ac 1:11 ye have seen him g· into heaven.
25 that he might g· to his own place.
3: 3 Peter and John about to g· into
13 he was determined to let him g·.
4:15 commanded them to g· aside out
21 they let them g·, finding nothing
23 And being let g·, they went to their
5:20 G·, stand and speak in the temple
40 name of Jesus, and let them g·.
7:40 Make us gods to g· before us: for
8:26 Arise, and g· toward the south
29 G· near, and join thyself to this
9: 6 Arise, and g· into the city, and it
11 Arise, and g· into the street which
15 G· thy way: for he is a chosen
10:20 get thee down, and g· with them,
11:12 the spirit bade me g· with them,
22 he should g· as far as Antioch.
12:17 he said, G· shew these things
15: 2 should g· up to Jerusalem unto the
33 let g· in peace from the brethren
36 g· again and visit our brethren
16: 3 Paul have to g· forth with him;
7 they assayed to g· into Bithynia:
10 endeavoured to g· into Macedonia,
35 serjeants, saying, Let those men g·.
36 sent to let you g·: now therefore
36 therefore depart, and g· in peace.
17: 9 and of the other, they let them g·.
14 Paul to g· as it were to the sea:
18: 6 I will g· unto the Gentiles.
19:21 to g· to Jerusalem, saying, After I
20: 1 departed for to g· into Macedonia.
13 appointed, minding himself to g· afoot.
22 behold, I g· bound in the spirit
21: 4 he should not g· up to Jerusalem.
12 besought him not to g· up to
22:10 Arise, and g· into Damascus; and
23:10 commanded the soldiers to g·
23 hundred soldiers to g· to Cæsarea,
32 left the horsemen to g· with him,
24:25 G· thy way for this time; when I
25: 5 g· down with me, and accuse this
9 said, Wilt thou g· up to Jerusalem,
12 Cæsar? unto Cæsar shalt thou g·.
20 whether he would g· to Jerusalem,
27: 3 him liberty to g· unto his friends
28:18 would have let me g·, because
26 G· unto this people, and say,
Ro 15:25 now I g· unto Jerusalem to minister
1Co 5:10 must ye needs g· out of the world.
6: 1 another, g· to law before the unjust,
7 ye g· to law one with another.
10:27 ye be disposed to g·; whatsoever
16: 4 it be meet that I g· also, they shall g·
6 on my journey whithersoever I g·.
2Co 9: 5 they would g· before unto you,
Ga 2: 9 that we should g· unto the heathen,
Eph 4:26 let not the sun g· down upon your
Ph'p 2:23 I shall see how it will g· with me.
1Th 4: 6 no man g· beyond and defraud
Heb 6: 1 let us g· on unto perfection; not
11: 8 he was called to g· out into a place
13:13 Let us g· forth therefore unto him
Jas 4:13 G· to now, ye that say, To day or
13 we will g· into such a city,
5: 1 G· to now, ye rich men, weep and
Re 3:12 and he shall g· no more out:
10: 8 G· and take the little book which
13:10 captivity shall g· into captivity:
16: 1 G· your ways, and pour out the vials
14 g· forth unto the kings of the earth
17: 8 pit, and g· into perdition:
20: 8 shall g· out to deceive the nations

goad See also GOADS.
J'g 3:31 six hundred men with an ox g·:

goads
1Sa 13:21 for the axes, and to sharpen the g·.
Ec 12:11 The words of the wise are as g·,

goat See also GOATS; GOATSKINS; SCAPEGOAT.
Ge 15: 9 and a she g· of three years old,
Le 3:12 if his offering be a g·, then he shall
4:24 his hand upon the head of the g·,
7:23 fat, of ox, or of sheep, or of g·.
9:15 and took the g·, which was the sin
10:16 Moses diligently sought the g· of
16: 9 Aaron shall bring the g· upon which
10 But the g·, on which the lot fell to be
15 Then shall he kill the g· of the sin
18 and of the blood of the g·, and put it
20 he shall bring the live g·:
21 hands upon the head of the live g·,
21 putting them upon the head of the g·,
22 the g· shall bear upon him all their
22 shall let go the g· in the wilderness.
26 that let go the g· for the scapegoat
27 and the g· for the sin offering,
17: 3 that killeth an ox, or lamb, or g·,
22:27 When a bullock, or a sheep, or a g·,
Nu 15:27 he shall bring a she g· of the first
18:17 or the firstling of a g·, thou shalt
28:22 And one g· for a sin offering, to
29:22, 28, 31, 34, 38 one g· for a sin
De 14: 4 eat: the ox, the sheep, and the g·,
5 and the wild g·, and the pygarg,
Pr 30:31 A greyhound; an he g· also; and
Eze 43:25 every day a g· for a sin offering:
Da 8: 5 an he g· came from the west
5 and the g· had a notable horn
8 Therefore the he g· waxed very

Da 8:21 the rough g· is the king of Grecia:

Goath (go'-ath)
Jer 31:39 and shall compass about to G·.

goats See also GOATS'.
Ge 27: 9 thence two good kids of the g·;
16 put the skins of the kids of the g·
30:32 spotted and speckled among the g·:
33 speckled and spotted among the g·.
35 he removed that day the he g·
35 the she g· that were speckled and
31:38 thy ewes and thy she g· have not
32:14 Two hundred she g·, and twenty
14 and twenty he g·, two hundred
37:31 killed a kid of the g·, and dipped
Ex 12: 5 out from the sheep, or from the g·:
Le 1:10 of the sheep, or of the g·,
4:23, 28 his offering, a kid of the g·,
5: 6 a lamb or a kid of the g·, for a sin
9: 3 Take ye a kid of the g· for a sin
16: 5 two kids of the g· for a sin offering,
7 shall take the two g·, and present
8 shall cast lots upon the two g·;
22:19 beeves, of the sheep, or of the g·.
23:19 kid of the g· for a sin offering,
Nu 7:16 One kid of the g· for a sin offering:
17 five rams, five he g·, five lambs of
22 One kid of the g· for a sin offering:
23 five he g·, five lambs of the first
28 One kid of the g· for a sin offering:
29 five he g·, five lambs of the first
34 One kid of the g· for a sin offering:
35 five he g·, five lambs of the first
40 One kid of the g· for a sin offering:
41 five he g·, five lambs of the first
46 One kid of the g· for a sin offering.
47 five he g·, five lambs of the first
52 One kid of the g· for a sin offering:
53 five he g·, five lambs of the first
58 One kid of the g· for a sin offering:
59 five he g·, five lambs of the first
64 One kid of the g· for a sin offering:
65 five he g·, five lambs of the first
70 One kid of the g· for a sin offering:
71 five he g·, five lambs of the first
76 One kid of the g· for a sin offering:
77 five he g·, five lambs of the first
82 One kid of the g· for a sin offering:
83 five he g·, five lambs of the first
87 the kids of the g· for sin offering
88 the rams sixty, the he g· sixty,
15:24 one kid of the g· for a sin offering.
28:15 one kid of the g· for a sin offering
30 And one kid of the g·, to make
29: 5 one kid of the g· for a sin offering,
11 One the g· for a sin offering;
16, 19, 25 And one kid of the g· for a
De 32:14 of the breed of Bashan, and g·,
1Sa 24: 2 men upon the rocks of the wild g·.
25: 2 sheep, and a thousand g·:
2Ch 17:11 thousand and seven hundred he g·.
29:21 seven lambs, and seven he g·,
23 they brought forth the he g· for
Ezr 6:17 offering for all Israel, twelve he g·,
8:35 twelve he g· for a sin offering:
Job 39: 1 wild g· of the rock bring forth?
Ps 50: 9 house, nor he g· out of thy folds.
13 of bulls, or drink the blood of g·?
66:15 I will offer bullocks with g·.
104:18 hills are a refuge for the wild g·.
Pr 27:26 and the g· are the price of the field.
Ca 4: 1 thy hair is as a flock of g·, that
6: 5 thy hair is as a flock of g· that
Isa 1:11 the blood of bullocks,...or of he g·.
34: 6 and with the blood of lambs and g·,
Jer 50: 8 as the he g· before the flocks.
51:40 slaughter like rams with he g·.
Eze 27:21 thee in lambs, and rams, and g·:
34:17 between the rams and the he g·.
39:18 of rams, of lambs, and of g·, of
43:22 shalt offer a kid of the g· without
45:23 a kid of the g· daily for a sin
Zec 10: 3 I punished the g·: for the Lord
M't 25:32 divideth his sheep from the g·:
33 right hand, but the g· on the left.
Heb 9:12 Neither by the blood of g· and
13 For if the blood of bulls and of g·,
19 took the blood of calves and of g·,
10: 4 that the blood of bulls and of g·

goats'
Ex 25: 4 scarlet, and fine linen, and g· hair,
26: 7 thou shalt make curtains of g· hair
35: 6,23 scarlet, and fine linen, and g· hair,
26 them up in wisdom spun g· hair.
36:14 he made curtains of g· hair
Nu 31:20 all work of g· hair, and all things
1Sa 19:13 put a pillow of g· hair for his bolster.
16 with a pillow of g· hair for his bolster,
Pr 27:27 thou shalt have g· milk enough for

goats'-hair See GOATS' and HAIR.

goatskins
Heb 11:37 about in sheepskins and g·;

Gob (gob)
2Sa 21:18 a battle with the Philistines at G·:
19 a battle in G· with the Philistines,

goblet
Ca 7: 2 Thy navel is like a round g·,

God [or GOD]^ See also GODDESS; GODHEAD; GOD'S; GODS; GOD-WARD.
Ge 1: 1 G· created the heaven and the
2 Spirit of G· moved upon the face
3 And G· said, Let there be light:
4 And G· saw the light, that it was

Ge 1: 4 and G· divided the light from the
5 And G· called the light Day, and the
6 G· said, Let there be a firmament
7 G· made the firmament, and divided
8 G· called the firmament Heaven.
9 G· said, Let the waters under the
10 And G· called the dry land Earth;
10 and G· saw that it was good.
11 G· said, Let the earth bring forth
12 and G· saw that it was good.
14 And G· said, Let there be lights
16 And G· made two great lights: the
17 And G· set them in the firmament
18 and G· saw that it was good.
20 G· said, Let the waters bring forth
21 G· created great whales, and every
21 and G· saw that it was good.
22 And G· blessed them, saying, Be
24 G· said, Let the earth bring forth
25 G· made the beast of the earth after
25 and G· saw that it was good.
26 And G· said, Let us make man in
27 G· created man in his own image,
27 in the image of G· created he him;
28 G· blessed them, and G· said unto
29 And G· said, Behold, I have given
31 And G· saw everything that he had
2: 2 the seventh day G· ended his work
3 And G· blessed the seventh day, and
3 his work which G· created and made.
4 day that the Lord G· made the earth
5 for the Lord G· had not caused it to
7 the Lord G· formed man of the dust
8 Lord G· planted a garden eastward
9 the Lord G· to grow every tree that
15 Lord G· took the man, and put him
16 the Lord G· commanded the man,
18 And the Lord G· said, It is not good
19 the Lord G· formed every beast of
21 the Lord G· caused a deep sleep to
22 the Lord G· had taken from man,
3: 1 field which the Lord G· had made.
1 hath G· said, Ye shall not eat of every
3 G· hath said, Ye shall not eat of it,
5 For G· doth know that in the day
8 they heard the voice of the Lord G·
8 from the presence of the Lord G·
9 And the Lord G· called unto Adam,
13 the Lord G· said unto the woman,
14 the Lord G· said unto the serpent,
21 did the Lord G· make coats of skins,
22 Lord G· said, Behold, the man is
23 Therefore the Lord G· sent him forth
4:25 For G·, said she, hath appointed me
5: 1 In the day that G· created man,
1 in the likeness of G· made he him.
22 And Enoch walked with G·, after he
24 And Enoch walked with G·: and he
24 And he was not; for G· took him.
6: 2 the sons of G· saw the daughters
4 when the sons of G· came in unto
5 And G· saw that the wickedness
9 and Noah walked with G·.
11 earth also was corrupt before G·,
12 And G· looked upon the earth, and,
13 G· said unto Noah, The end of all
22 according to all that G· commanded
7: 9 female, as G· had commanded Noah.
16 as G· had commanded him: and the
8: 1 And G· remembered Noah, and every
1 and G· made a wind to pass over the
15 And G· spake unto Noah, saying,
9: 1 and G· blessed Noah and his sons,
6 in the image of G· made he man.
8 G· spake unto Noah, and to his sons
12 And G· said, This is the token of
16 between G· and every living creature
17 G· said unto Noah, This is the token
26 Blessed be the Lord G· of Shem;
27 G· shall enlarge Japheth, and he
14:18 was the priest of the most high G·.
19 Blessed be Abram of the most high G·,
20 blessed be the most high G·, which
22 unto the Lord, the most high G·,
15: 2 Abram said, Lord G·, what wilt
8 he said, Lord G·, whereby shall I
16:13 Thou G· seest me: for she said,
17: 1 I am the Almighty G·; walk before
3 and G· talked with him, saying,
7 to be a G· unto thee, and to thy seed
8 possession; and I will be their G·.
9 G· said unto Abraham, Thou shalt
15 G· said unto Abraham, As for Sarai
18 And Abraham said unto G·, O that
19 G· said, Sarah thy wife shall bear
22 and G· went up from Abraham.
23 selfsame day, as G· had said unto
19:29 when G· destroyed the cities of the
29 that G· remembered Abraham,
20: 3 G· came to Abimelech in a dream
6 And G· said unto him in a dream,
11 the fear of G· is not in this place;
13 G· caused me to wander from my
17 So Abraham prayed unto G·: and G·
21: 2 time of which G· had spoken to him.
4 old, as G· had commanded him.
6 G· hath made me to laugh, so that
12 G· said unto Abraham, Let it not be
17 And G· heard the voice of the lad;
17 and the angel of G· called to Hagar
17 G· hath heard the voice of the lad
19 G· opened her eyes, and she saw
20 G· was with the lad; and he grew,
22 G· is with thee in all that thou doest:
23 therefore swear unto me here by G·
33 of the Lord, the everlasting G·.

Ge 22: 1 G· did tempt Abraham, and said
3 the place of which G· had told him.
8 G· will provide himself a lamb for a
9 to the place which G· had told him of
12 now I know that thou fearest G·,
24: 3 G· of heaven, and the G· of the earth,
7 Lord G· of heaven, which took me
12 O Lord G· of my master Abraham,
27 the Lord G· of my master Abraham,
42 O Lord G· of my master Abraham,
48 the Lord G· of my master Abraham,
25:11 G· blessed his son Isaac; and Isaac
26:24 I am the G· of Abraham thy father:
27:20 the Lord thy G· brought it to me.
28 G· give thee of the dew of heaven,
28: 3 G· Almighty bless thee, and make
4 which G· gave unto Abraham.
12 the angels of G· ascending and
13 said, I am the Lord G· of Abraham
13 thy father, and the G· of Isaac:
17 is none other but the house of G·,
20 If G· will be with me, and will keep
21 then shall the Lord be my G·:
30: 6 Rachel said, G· hath judged me, and
17 G· hearkened unto Leah, and she
18 G· hath given me my hire, because
20 G· hath endued me with a good
22 G· remembered...and G· hearkened
23 G· hath taken away my reproach:
31: 5 but the G· of my father hath been
7 G· suffered him not to hurt me.
9 Thus G· hath taken away the cattle
11 the angel of G· spake unto me in a
13 I am the G· of Beth-el, where thou
16 all the riches which G· hath taken
16 whatsoever G· hath said unto thee,
24 G· came to Laban the Syrian in a
29 the G· of your father spake unto me
42 G· of my father, the G· of Abraham,
42 G· hath seen mine affliction and the
50 G· is witness betwixt me and thee.
53 The G· of Abraham, and the G· of
53 Nahor, the G· of their father,
32: 1 and the angels of G· met him.
9 O G· of my father Abraham,
9 and G· of my father Isaac,
28 as a prince hast thou power with G·
30 for I have seen G· face to face,
33: 5 which G· hath graciously given
10 as though I had seen the face of G·,
11 G· hath dealt graciously with me,
35: 1 G· said unto Jacob, Arise, go up to
1 and make there an altar unto G·,
3 I will make there an altar unto G·,
5 terror of G· was upon the cities
7 there G· appeared unto him,
9 And G· appeared unto Jacob again
10 And G· said unto him, Thy name is
11 G· said unto him, I am...Almighty:
11 said unto him, I am G· Almighty:
13 G· went up from him in the place
15 the place where G· spake with him,
39: 9 wickedness, and sin against G·?
40: 8 Do not interpretations belong to G·?
41:16 G· shall give Pharaoh an answer of
25 G· hath shewed Pharaoh what he is
28 What G· is about to do he sheweth
32 the thing is established by G·,
32 and G· will shortly bring it to pass.
38 a man in whom the Spirit of G· is?
39 as G· hath shewed thee all this,
51 the firstborn Manasseh: For G·,
52 G· hath caused me to be fruitful
42:18 This do, and live; for I fear G·:
28 What is this that G· hath done
43:14 And G· Almighty give you mercy
23 your G·, and the G· of your father,
29 G· be gracious unto thee, my son.
44: 7 G· forbid that thy servants should
16 G· hath found out the iniquity of
17 G· forbid that I should so:
45: 5 for G· did send me before you to
7 G· sent me before you to preserve
8 not you that sent me hither, but G·:
9 G· hath made me lord of all Egypt:
46: 1 unto the G· of his father Isaac.
2 G· spake unto Israel in the visions
3 And he said, I am G·,
3 the G· of thy father: fear not to
48: 3 G· Almighty appeared unto me at
9 G· hath given me in this place.
11 G· hath shewed me also thy seed.
15 G·, before whom my fathers
15 G· which fed me all my life long
20 G· make thee as Ephraim and
21 but G· shall be with you, and bring
49:24 by the hands of the mighty G·
25 Even by the G· of thy father,
50:17 the servants of the G· of thy father.
19 for am I in the place of G·?
20 G· meant it unto good, to bring to
24 and G· will surely visit you, and
25 saying, G· will surely visit you, and
Ex 1:17 But the midwives feared G·, and did
20 G· dealt well with the midwives:
21 because the midwives feared G·,
2:23 their cry came up unto G· by reason
24 And G· heard their groaning, and
24 and G· remembered his covenant
25 And G· looked upon the children of
25 and G· had respect unto them.
3: 1 the mountain of G·, even to Horeb.
4 G· called unto him out of the midst
6 I am the G· of thy father,
6 the G· of Abraham, the G· of Isaac,
6 and the G· of Jacob.

Ex 3: 6 for he was afraid to look upon G·.
11 And Moses said unto G·, Who am I;
12 shall serve G· upon this mountain.
13 Moses said unto G·, Behold, when
13 The G· of your fathers hath sent me
14 G· said unto Moses, I Am that I Am:
15 And G· said moreover unto Moses,
15 The Lord G· of your fathers,
15 the G· of Abraham, the G· of Isaac,
15 and the G· of Jacob,
16 The Lord G· of your fathers,
16 the G· of Abraham, of Isaac, and
18 The Lord G· of the Hebrews hath
18 we may sacrifice to the Lord our G·.
4: 5 the Lord G· of their fathers,
5 the G· of Abraham, the G· of Isaac,
5 and the G· of Jacob, hath appeared
16 thou shalt be to him instead of G·.
20 Moses took the rod of G· in his hand.
27 in the mount of G·, and kissed him.
5: 1 Thus saith the Lord G· of Israel,
3 G· of the Hebrews hath met with us:
3 and sacrifice unto the Lord our G·;
8 Let us go and sacrifice to our G·.
6: 2 G· spake unto Moses, and said
3 by the name of G· Almighty, but
7 and I will be to you a G·:
7 know that I am the Lord your G·,
7: 1 I have made thee a g· to Pharaoh:
16 Lord G· of the Hebrews hath sent
8:10 none like unto the Lord our G·.
19 This is the finger of G·: and
25 sacrifice to your G· in the land.
26 of the Egyptians to the Lord our G·:
27 sacrifice to the Lord our G·, as he
28 sacrifice to the Lord your G· in the
9: 1, 13 saith the Lord G· of the Hebrews,
30 ye will not yet fear the Lord G·.
10: 3 saith the Lord G· of the Hebrews,
7 they may serve the Lord their G·:
8 Go, serve the Lord your G·: but who
16 sinned against the Lord your G·,
17 intreat the Lord your G·, that he
25 may sacrifice unto the Lord our G·.
26 we take to serve the Lord our G·;
13:17 G· led them not through the way
17 G· said, Lest peradventure the
18 But G· led the people about,
19 G· will surely visit you; and ye
14:19 the angel of G·, which went before
15: 2 become my salvation: he is my G·,
2 father's G·, and I will exalt him.
26 to the voice of the Lord thy G·,
16: 3 Would to G· we had died by the hand of
12 know that I am the Lord your G·.
17: 9 with the rod of G· in mine hand.
18: 1 of all that G· had done for Moses,
4 for the G· of my father, said he,
5 he encamped at the mount of G·:
12 burnt offering and sacrifices for G·:
12 with Moses' father in law before G·.
15 come unto me to enquire of G·:
16 make them know the statutes of G·,
19 counsel, and G· shall be with thee:
19 mayest bring the causes unto G·:
21 able men, such as fear G·, men of
23 this thing, and G· command thee so,
19: 3 Moses went up unto G·, and the
17 out of the camp to meet with G·;
19 and G· answered him by a voice.
20: 1 G· spake all these words, saying,
2 I am the Lord thy G·, which have
5 serve them: for I the Lord thy G·
5 a jealous G·, visiting the iniquity
7 name of the Lord thy G· in vain;
10 is the sabbath of the Lord thy G·:
12 which the Lord thy G· giveth thee.
19 let not G· speak with us, lest we die.
20 G· is come to prove you, and that
21 the thick darkness where G· was.
21:13 but G· deliver him into his hand;
22:20 He that sacrificeth unto any g·,
23:17 shall appear before the Lord G·.
19 into the house of the Lord thy G·.
25 ye shall serve the Lord your G·,
24:10 they saw the G· of Israel: and there
11 they saw G·, and did eat and drink.
13 Moses went up into the mount of G·.
29:45 of Israel, and will be their G·.
46 know that I am the Lord their G·,
46 among them: I am the Lord their G·.
31: 3 have filled him with the spirit of G·,
18 stone, written with the finger of G·.
32:11 Moses besought the Lord his G·,
16 And the tables were the work of G·,
16 the writing was the writing of G·,
27 Thus saith the Lord G· of Israel,
34: 6 Lord G·, merciful and gracious,
14 For thou shalt worship no other g·:
14 name is Jealous, is a jealous G·:
23 appear before the Lord G·,
23 appear before...the G· of Israel,
24 appear before the Lord thy G·
26 unto the house of the Lord thy G·,
35:31 hath filled him with the spirit of G·
Le 2:13 the salt of the covenant of thy G·
4:22 commandments of the Lord his G·
10:17 G· hath given it you to bear
11:44 For I am the Lord your G·:
45 of the land of Egypt, to be your G·:
18: 2 unto them I am the Lord your G·.
4 therein: I am the Lord your G·.
21 thou profane the name of thy G·:
30 therein: I am the Lord your G·.
19: 2 for I the Lord your G· am holy.
3 am the Lord your G·.

Le 19: 4 molten gods, I am the Lord your G'.
10 stranger: I am the Lord your G'.
12 thou profane the name of thy G':
14 shalt fear thy G': I am the Lord.
25 thereof: I am the Lord your G'.
31 by them: I am the Lord your G'.
32 and fear thy G': I am the Lord.
34 of Egypt: I am the Lord your G'.
36 the Lord your G', which brought
20: 7 be ye holy, for I am the Lord your G'.
24 I am the Lord your G', which have
21: 6 They shall be holy unto their G',
6 not profane the name of their G':
6 the bread of their G', they do offer:
7 for he is holy unto his G'.
8 for he offereth the bread of thy G':
12 profane the sanctuary of his G'; for
12 of the anointing oil of his G' is upon
17 approach to offer the bread of his G'.
21 nigh to offer the bread of his G'.
22 He shall eat the bread of his G',
22:25 shall ye offer the bread of your G'
33 the land of Egypt, to be your G':
23:14 brought an offering unto your G':
22 the stranger: I am the Lord your G'.
28 for you before the Lord your G'.
40 rejoice before the Lord your G'
43 land of Egypt: I am the Lord your G'.
24:15 Whosoever curseth his G' shall
22 country: for I am the Lord your G'.
25:17 but thou shalt fear thy G':
17 for I am the Lord your G'.
36 but fear thy G'; that thy brother
38 I am the Lord your G', which
38 land of Canaan, and to be your G'.
43 with rigour; but shalt fear thy G'.
55 land of Egypt; I am the Lord your G'.
26: 1 down into it: I am the Lord your G'.
12 among you, and will be your G',
13 am the Lord your G', which brought
44 them: for I am the Lord their G'.
45 that I might be their G': I am the
Nu 6: 7 consecration of his G' is upon his
10: 9 remembered before...Lord your G',
10 you for a memorial before your G':
10 I am the Lord your G'.
11:29 would G' that all the Lord's people
12:13 Heal her now, O G', I beseech thee.
14: 2 Would G' that we had died in
2 would G' we had died in this
15:40 and be holy unto your G'.
41 am the Lord your G', which brought
41 the land of Egypt, to be your G':
41 I am the Lord your G'.
16: 9 the G' of Israel hath separated
22 upon their faces, and said, O G',
22 the G' of the spirits of all flesh,
20: 3 Would G' that we had died when
21: 5 the people spake against G', and
22: 9 G' came unto Baalam, and said,
10 Balaam said unto G', Balak the
12 G' said unto Balaam, Thou shalt
18 beyond the word of the Lord my G',
20 G' came unto Balaam at night,
38 word that G' putteth in my mouth,
23: 4 And G' met Balaam: and he said
8 How shall I curse, whom G' hath
19 G' is not a man, that he should
21 the Lord his G' is with him, and
22 G' brought them out of Egypt; he
23 What hath G' wrought!
27 peradventure it will please G'
24: 2 the spirit of G' came upon him.
4 which heard the words of G', which
8 G' brought him forth out of Egypt;
16 which heard the words of G', and
23 who shall live when G' doeth this!
25:13 because he was zealous for his G',
27:16 the G' of the spirits of all flesh,
De 1: 6 The Lord our G' spake unto us
10 Lord your G' hath multiplied you,
11 Lord G' of your fathers make you
19 as the Lord our G' commanded us;
20 the Lord our G' doth give unto us.
21 the Lord thy G' hath set the land
21 Lord G' of thy fathers hath said
25 which the Lord our G' doth give us.
26 commandment of the Lord your G';
30 Lord your G' which goeth before
31 the Lord thy G' bare thee, as a man
32 ye did not believe the Lord your G',
41 that the Lord our G' commanded us.
2: 7 the Lord thy G' hath blessed thee
7 Lord thy G' hath been with thee;
29 which the Lord our G' giveth us.
30 the Lord thy G' hardened his spirit,
33 our G' delivered him before us;
36 Lord our G' delivered all unto us:
37 whatsoever the Lord our G' forbad
3: 3 So the Lord our G' delivered into
18 The Lord your G' hath given you
20 the Lord your G' hath given them
21 that the Lord your G' hath done
22 Lord your G' he shall fight for you.
24 O Lord G', thou hast begun to
24 G' is there in heaven or in earth,
4: 1 which the Lord G' of your fathers
2 commandments of the Lord your G'
3 Lord thy G' hath destroyed them
4 did cleave unto the Lord your G'
5 as the Lord my G' commanded me,
7 who hath G' so nigh unto them,
7 as the Lord our G' is in all things
10 before the Lord thy G' in Horeb,
19 which the Lord thy G' hath divided
21 which the Lord thy G' giveth thee

De 4:23 the covenant of the Lord your G',
23 the Lord thy G' hath forbidden thee.
24 the Lord thy G' is a consuming fire,
24 consuming fire, even a jealous G'.
25 evil in the sight of the Lord thy G',
29 thou shalt seek the Lord thy G',
30 days, if thou turn to the Lord thy G',
31 (For the Lord thy G' is a merciful
31 (For the Lord...is a merciful G';)
32 since the day that G' created man
33 Did ever people hear the voice of G'
34 hath G' assayed to go and take him
34 all that the Lord your G' did for you
35 know that the Lord he is G'; there
39 the Lord he is G' in heaven above,
40 which the Lord thy G' giveth thee,
5: 2 The Lord our G' made a covenant
6 am the Lord thy G', which brought
9 for I the Lord thy G' am a jealous
9 a jealous G', visiting the iniquity
11 the name of the Lord thy G' in vain:
12 as the Lord thy G' hath commanded
14 is the sabbath of the Lord thy G':
15 the Lord thy G' brought thee out
15 the Lord thy G' commanded thee
16 Lord thy G' hath commanded thee,
16 which the Lord thy G' giveth thee.
24 the Lord our G' hath shewed us his
24 that G' doth talk with man, and he
25 we hear the voice of the Lord our G'
26 hath heard the voice of the living G'
27 all that the Lord our G' shall say;
27 all that the Lord our G' shall speak
32 Lord your G' hath commanded you:
33 Lord your G' hath commanded you,
6: 1 Lord your G' commanded to teach
2 thou mightest fear the Lord thy G',
3 G' of thy fathers hath promised thee,
4 The Lord our G' is one Lord:
5 And thou shalt love the Lord thy G'
10 when the Lord thy G' shall have into
13 Thou shalt fear the Lord thy G',
15 (For the Lord thy G' is a jealous
15 Lord...is a jealous G' among you)
15 lest the anger of the Lord thy G'
16 Ye shall not tempt the Lord your G',
17 commandments of the Lord your G',
20 Lord our G' hath commanded you?
24 to fear the Lord our G', for our good
25 before the Lord our G', as he hath
7: 1 When the Lord thy G' shall bring
2 the Lord thy G' shall deliver them
6 holy people unto the Lord thy G':
6 the Lord thy G' hath chosen thee
9 that the Lord thy G', he is G',
9 the faithful G', which keepeth
12 Lord thy G' shall keep unto thee
16 the Lord thy G' shall deliver thee;
18 the Lord thy G' did unto Pharaoh,
19 the Lord thy G' brought thee out:
19 so shall the Lord thy G' do unto all
20 Lord thy G' will send the hornet
21 for the Lord thy G' is among you,
21 you, a mighty G' and terrible.
22 the Lord thy G' will put out those
23 the Lord thy G' shall deliver them
25 an abomination to the Lord thy G'.
8: 2 way which the Lord thy G' led thee
5 so the Lord thy G' chasteneth thee.
6 commandments of the Lord thy G',
7 Lord thy G' bringeth thee into a
10 thou shalt bless the Lord thy G' for
11 that thou forget not the Lord thy G',
14 up, and thou forget the Lord thy G',
18 shalt remember the Lord thy G':
19 at all forget the Lord thy G', and
20 unto the voice of the Lord your G'.
9: 3 Lord thy G' is he which goeth over
4 that the Lord thy G' hath cast them
5 the Lord thy G' doth drive them out
6 the Lord thy G' giveth thee not this
7 thou provokedst the Lord thy G' to
21 stone written with the finger of G';
16 had sinned against the Lord your G',
23 commandment of the Lord your G',
26 O Lord G', destroy not thy people
10: 9 as the Lord thy G' promised him.
12 what doth the Lord thy G' require
12 of thee, but to fear the Lord thy G',
12 and to serve the Lord thy G' with all
14 of heavens is the Lord's thy G', the
17 For the Lord your G', is G' of gods,
17 a great G', and mighty, and a
20 Thou shalt fear the Lord thy G';
21 He is thy praise, and he is thy G',
22 Lord thy G' hath made thee as the
11: 1 thou shalt love the Lord thy G', and
2 chastisement of the Lord your G',
12 which the Lord thy G' careth for:
12 eyes of the Lord thy G' are always
13 to love the Lord your G', and to
22 to love the Lord your G', to walk
25 the Lord your G' shall lay the fear
27 if ye obey the...of the Lord your G',
28 not obey the...of the Lord your G',
29 when the Lord thy G' hath brought
31 land which the Lord your G' giveth
12: 1 land which the Lord G' of thy fathers
4 shall not do so unto the Lord your G'.
5 the place which the Lord your G'
7 ye shall eat before the Lord your G',
7 the Lord thy G' hath blessed thee.
9 inheritance...Lord your G' giveth
10 land which the Lord your G' giveth
11 Lord your G' shall choose to cause
12 shall rejoice before the Lord your G',

De 12:15 to the blessing of the Lord thy G'
18 must eat them before the Lord thy G'
18 in the place which the Lord thy G'
18 shalt rejoice before the Lord thy G'
20 When the Lord thy G' shall enlarge
21 which the Lord thy G' hath chosen
27 upon the altar of the Lord thy G':
27 upon the altar of the Lord thy G',
28 right in the sight of the Lord thy G'.
29 Lord thy G' shall cut off the nations
31 shall not do so unto the Lord thy G':
13: 3 for the Lord your G' proveth you,
3 whether ye love the Lord your G'
4 shall walk after the Lord your G',
5 you away from the Lord your G',
5 which the Lord thy G' commanded
10 thee away from the Lord thy G',
12 which the Lord thy G' hath given
16 every whit, for the Lord thy G':
18 to the voice of the Lord thy G',
18 right in the eyes of the Lord thy G'.
14: 1 are the children of the Lord your G'.
2 an holy people unto the Lord thy G',
21 an holy people unto the Lord thy G'.
23 shalt eat before the Lord thy G',
23 mayest learn to fear the Lord thy G'
24 which the Lord thy G' shall choose
24 when the Lord thy G' hath blessed
25 which the Lord thy G' shall choose:
26 eat there before the Lord thy G',
29 that the Lord thy G' may bless thee
15: 4 which the Lord thy G' giveth thee
5 unto the voice of the Lord thy G',
6 For the Lord thy G' blesseth thee,
7 land which the Lord thy G' giveth
10 the Lord thy G' shall bless thee in
14 the Lord thy G' hath blessed thee
15 and the Lord thy G' redeemed thee:
18 and the Lord thy G' shall bless thee.
19 shalt sanctify unto the Lord thy G':
20 shalt eat it before the Lord thy G'
21 not sacrifice it unto the Lord thy G'.
16: 1 the passover unto the Lord thy G':
1 the Lord thy G' brought thee forth
2 the passover unto the Lord thy G',
5 which the Lord thy G' giveth thee:
6 which the Lord thy G' shall choose
7 which the Lord thy G' shall choose:
8 solemn assembly to the Lord thy G':
10 feast of weeks unto the Lord thy G'
10 shalt give unto the Lord thy G',
10 according as the Lord thy G' hath
11 shalt rejoice before the Lord thy G',
11 which the Lord thy G' hath chosen
15 a solemn feast unto the Lord thy G'
15 the Lord thy G' shall bless thee in
16 appear before the Lord thy G' in the
17 to the blessing of the Lord thy G'
18 gates, which the Lord thy G' giveth
20 land which the Lord thy G' giveth
21 unto the altar of the Lord thy G',
22 which the Lord thy G' hateth.
17: 1 not sacrifice unto the Lord thy G'
1 abomination unto the Lord thy G'.
2 gates which the Lord thy G' giveth
2 in the sight of the Lord thy G', in
8 which the Lord thy G' shall choose;
12 minister...before the Lord thy G',
14 land which the Lord thy G' giveth
15 whom the Lord thy G' shall choose:
19 may learn to fear the Lord his G',
18: 5 the Lord thy G' hath chosen him
7 in the name of the Lord his G',
9 land which the Lord thy G' giveth
12 the Lord thy G' doth drive them out
13 shalt be perfect with the Lord thy G'.
14 the Lord thy G' hath not suffered
15 The Lord thy G' will raise up unto
16 thou desiredst of the Lord thy G' in
16 again the voice of the Lord my G',
19: 1 When the Lord thy G' hath cut off
1 whose land the Lord thy G' giveth
2 Lord thy G' giveth thee to possess
3 Lord thy G' giveth thee to inherit
8 if the Lord thy G' enlarge thy
9 to love the Lord thy G', and to
10 land, which the Lord thy G' giveth
14 land that the Lord thy G' giveth
20: 1 for the Lord thy G' is with thee,
4 the Lord your G' is he that goeth
13 the Lord thy G' hath delivered it
14 which the Lord thy G' hath given
16 land which the Lord thy G' doth give
17 the Lord thy G' hath commanded
18 ye sin against the Lord your G'.
21: 1 land which the Lord thy G' giveth
5 them the Lord thy G' hath chosen
10 Lord thy G' hath delivered them
23 he that is hanged is accursed of G';)
23 which the Lord thy G' giveth thee
22: 5 abomination unto the Lord thy G'.
23: 5 Nevertheless the Lord thy G' would
5 but the Lord thy G' turned the curse
5 because the Lord thy G' loved thee.
14 For the Lord thy G' walketh in the
18 into the house of the Lord thy G' for
18 abomination unto the Lord thy G'.
20 that the Lord thy G' may bless thee
21 vow a vow unto the Lord thy G',
21 the Lord thy G' will surely require
23 hast vowed unto the Lord thy G',
24: 4 which the Lord thy G' giveth thee
9 Remember what the Lord thy G' did
13 unto thee before the Lord thy G'.
18 and the Lord thy G' redeemed thee
19 that the Lord thy G' may bless thee

De **25:**15 land which the Lord thy *G·* giveth
16 abomination unto the Lord thy *G·*.
18 and he feared not *G·*.
19 Lord thy *G·* hath given thee rest
19 land which the Lord thy *G·* giveth
26: 1 land which the Lord thy *G* giveth
2 land that the Lord thy *G·* giveth
2 the Lord thy *G·* shall choose to place
3 this day unto the Lord thy *G·*, that
4 before the altar of the Lord thy *G·*.
5 say before the Lord thy *G·*, A Syrian
7 unto the Lord *G·* of our fathers,
10 shalt set it before the Lord thy *G·*,
10 and worship before the Lord thy *G·*:
11 thing which the Lord thy *G·* hath
13 say before the Lord thy *G·*, I have
14 to the voice of the Lord my *G·*, and
16 Lord thy *G·* hath commanded thee
17 the Lord this day to be thy *G·*,
19 an holy people unto the Lord thy *G·*,
27: 2 Lord thy *G·* giveth thee, that thou
3 Lord thy *G·* giveth thee, a land that
3 Lord *G·* of thy fathers hath promised
5 build an altar unto the Lord thy *G·*,
6 build the altar of the Lord thy *G·* of
6 thereon unto the Lord thy *G·*:
7 and rejoice before the Lord thy *G·*.
9 the people of the Lord thy *G·*.
10 obey the voice of the Lord thy *G·*,
28: 1 unto the voice of the Lord thy *G·*,
1 Lord thy *G·* will set thee on high
2 unto the voice of the Lord thy *G·*.
8 land which the Lord thy *G·* giveth
9 shalt keep the...of the Lord thy *G·*,
13 hearken unto the...of the Lord thy *G·*,
15 unto the voice of the Lord thy *G·*, to
45 unto the voice of the Lord thy *G·*,
47 thou servedst not the Lord thy *G·*
52 which the Lord thy *G·* hath given
53 daughters...the Lord thy *G·* hath
58 fearful name, The Lord thy *G·*;
62 obey the voice of the Lord thy *G·*.
67 shalt say, Would *G·* it were even!
67 shalt say, Would *G·* it were morning!
29: 6 know that I am the Lord your *G·*.
10 all of you before the Lord your *G·*;
12 covenant with the Lord thy *G·*,
12 the Lord thy *G·* maketh with thee
13 and that he may be unto thee a *G·*,
15 us this day before the Lord our *G·*,
18 away this day from the Lord our *G·*,
25 of the Lord *G·* of their fathers,
29 things belong unto the Lord our *G·*:
30: 1 the Lord thy *G·* hath driven thee,
2 shalt return unto the Lord thy *G·*,
3 Lord thy *G·* will turn thy captivity
3 the Lord thy *G·* hath scattered thee.
4 will the Lord thy *G·* gather thee,
5 the Lord thy *G·* will bring thee into
6 Lord thy *G·* will circumcise thine
6 love the Lord thy *G·* with all thine
7 the Lord thy *G·* will put all these
9 the Lord thy *G·* will make thee
10 unto the voice of the Lord thy *G·*,
10 if thou turn unto the Lord thy *G·*,
16 to love the Lord thy *G·*, to walk in
16 and the Lord thy *G·* shall bless thee
20 thou mayest love the Lord thy *G·*,
31: 3 The Lord thy *G·*, he will go before
6 Lord thy *G·*, he it is that doth go
11 to appear before the Lord thy *G·*
12 learn, and fear the Lord your *G·*,
13 and learn to fear the Lord your *G·*,
17 because our *G·* is not among us?
26 the covenant of the Lord your *G·*,
32: 3 ascribe ye greatness unto our *G·*.
4 a *G·* of truth and without iniquity,
12 there was no strange *g·* with him.
15 he forsook *G·* which made him,
17 sacrificed unto devils, not to *G·*;
18 hast forgotten *G·* that formed thee.
21 jealousy with that which is not *G·*;
39 and there is no *g·* with me:
33: 1 Moses the man of *G·* blessed the
26 none like unto the *G·* of Jeshurun,
27 The eternal *G·* is thy refuge, and
Jos **1:** 9 for the Lord thy *G·* is with thee
11 land, which the Lord your *G·* giveth
13 Lord your *G·* hath given you rest,
15 land which the Lord your *G·* giveth
17 the Lord thy *G·* be with thee,
2:11 the Lord your *G·*, he is *G·* in heaven
3: 3 the covenant of the Lord your *G·*,
9 hear the words of the Lord your *G·*.
10 know that the living *G·* is among
4: 5 before the ark of the Lord your *G·*
23 Lord your *G·* dried up the waters
23 Lord your *G·* did to the Red sea,
24 fear the Lord your *G·* for ever.
7: 7 Joshua said, Alas, O Lord *G·*,
7 would to *G·* we had been content.
13 thus saith the Lord *G·* of Israel,
19 glory to the Lord *G·* of Israel,
20 sinned against the Lord *G·* of Israel,
8: 7 the Lord your *G·* will deliver it into
30 Lord *G·* of Israel in mount Ebal,
9: 9 of the name of the Lord thy *G·*: for
18 had sworn unto them by the Lord *G·*
19 sworn unto them by the Lord *G·* of
23 of water for the house of my *G·*.
24 that the Lord thy *G·* commanded
10:19 Lord your *G·* hath delivered them
40 the Lord *G·* of Israel commanded.
42 Lord *G·* of Israel fought for Israel.
13:14 sacrifices of the Lord *G·* of Israel
33 the Lord *G·* of Israel was their

Jos **14:** 6 Lord said unto Moses the man of *G·*
8 I wholly followed the Lord my *G·*.
9 wholly followed the Lord my *G·*.
14 he wholly followed the Lord *G·* of
18: 3 land, which the Lord *G·* of your
6 for you here before the Lord our *G·*.
22: 3 commandment of the Lord your *G·*.
4 now the Lord your *G·* hath given
5 love the Lord your *G·*, and to walk
16 committed against the *G·* of Israel,
19 beside the altar of the Lord our *G·*.
22 Lord *G·* of gods, the Lord *G·* of
24 to do with the Lord *G·* of Israel?
29 *G·* forbid that we should rebel
29 beside the altar of the Lord our *G·*
33 the children of Israel blessed *G·*,
34 between us that the Lord is *G·*.
23: 3 that the Lord your *G·* hath done
3 for the Lord your *G·* is he that hath
5 And the Lord your *G·*, he shall expel
5 as the Lord your *G·* hath promised
8 But cleave unto the Lord your *G*,
10 for the Lord your *G·*, he it is that
11 that ye love the Lord your *G·*.
13 Lord your *G·* will no more drive
13 the Lord your *G·* hath given you.
14 things which the Lord your *G·* spake
15 the Lord your *G·* promised you;
15 the Lord your *G·* hath given you.
16 the covenant of the Lord your *G·*,
24: 1 presented themselves before *G·*.
2 Thus saith the Lord *G·* of Israel,
16 *G·* forbid that we should forsake
17 For the Lord our *G·*, he it is that
18 also serve the Lord; for he is our *G·*.
19 the Lord: for he is an holy *G·*;
19 he is a jealous *G·*; he will forgive
23 heart unto the Lord *G·* of Israel.
24 The Lord our *G·* will we serve,
26 words in the book of the law of *G·*,
27 unto you, lest ye deny your *G·*.
J'g **1:** 7 have done, so *G·* had requited me.
2:12 forsook the Lord *G·* of their fathers,
3: 7 forgat the Lord their *G·*, and served
20 have a message from *G·* unto thee.
4: 6 the Lord *G·* of Israel commanded
23 So *G·* subdued on that day Jabin
5: 3 sing praise to the Lord *G·* of Israel.
5 from before the Lord *G·* of Israel.
6: 8 Thus saith the Lord *G·* of Israel,
10 I am the Lord your *G·*; fear not
20 And the angel of *G·* said unto him,
22 Gideon said, Alas, O Lord *G·*! for
26 build an altar unto the Lord thy *G·*
31 if he be a *g·*, let him plead for
36 Gideon said unto *G·*, If thou wilt
39 Gideon said unto *G·*, Let not thine
40 *G·* did so that night: for it was dry
7:14 his hand hath *G·* delivered Midian,
8: 3 *G·* hath delivered into your hands
33 and made Baal-berith their *g·*.
34 remembered not the Lord their *G·*,
9: 7 that *G·* may hearken unto you.
9 by me they honour *G·* and man,
13 which cheereth *G·* and man, and go
23 Then *G·* sent an evil spirit between
27 and went into the house of their *g·*,
29 would to *G·* this people were under my
46 hold of the house of the *g·* Berith.
56 *G·* rendered the wickedness of
57 did *G·* render upon their heads:
10:10 because we have forsaken our *G·*,
11:21 Lord *G·* of Israel delivered Sihon
23 So now the Lord *G·* of Israel hath
24 which Chemosh thy *g·* giveth thee to
24 the Lord our *G·* shall drive out from
13: 5 a Nazarite unto *G·* from the womb:
6 A man of *G·* came unto me,
6 the countenance of an angel of *G·*,
7 be a Nazarite to *G·* from the womb
8 the man of *G·* which thou didst send
9 *G·* hearkened to the voice of Manoah;
9 and the angel of *G·* came again unto
22 surely die, because we have seen *G·*.
15:19 *G·* clave an hollow place that was
16:17 Nazarite unto *G·* from my mother's
23 great sacrifice unto Dagon their *g·*,
23 Our *g·* hath delivered Samson our
24 praised their *g·*: for they said, Our *g·*
28 O Lord *G·*, remember me, I pray
28 only this once, O *G·* that I may,
18: 5 Ask counsel, we pray thee, of *G·*,
10 *G·* hath given it into your hands;
31 all the time that the house of *G·* was
20: 2 in the assembly of the people of *G·*,
18 and went up to the house of *G·*,
18 and asked counsel of *G·*, and said
26 came into the house of *G·*, and
27 the ark of the covenant of *G·*
31 one goeth up to the house of *G·*,
21: 2 people came to the house of *G·*,
2 and abode there till even before *G·*,
3 And said, O Lord *G·* of Israel,
Ru **1:**16 my people, and thy *G·* my *G·*:
2:12 given thee of the Lord *G·* of Israel,
1Sa **1:**17 *G·* of Israel grant thee thy petition
2: 2 neither is there any rock like our *G·*.
3 the Lord is a *G·* of knowledge,
27 there came a man of *G·* unto Eli,
30 Wherefore the Lord *G·* of Israel
32 the wealth which *G·* shall give Israel:
3: 3 And ere the lamp of *G·* went out in
3 Lord, where the ark of *G·* was, and
17 *G·* do so to thee, and more also,
4: 4 with the ark of the covenant of *G·*.
7 they said, *G·* is come into the camp.

1Sa **4:**11 And the ark of *G·* was taken; and
13 his heart trembled for the ark of *G·*.
17 are dead, and the ark of *G·* is taken.
18 he made mention of the ark of *G·*,
19 that the ark of *G·* was taken, and
21 because the ask of *G·* was taken,
22 for the ark of *G·* is taken.
5: 1, 2 the Philistines took the ark of *G·*,
7 The ark of the *G·* of Israel shall not
7 upon us, and upon Dagon our *g·*.
8 with the ark of the *G·* of Israel?
8 Let the ark of the *G·* of Israel be
8 carried the ark of the *G·* of Israel
10 they sent the ark of *G·* to Ekron.
10 as the ark of *G·* came to Ekron,
10 brought about the ark of the *G·* of
11 Send away the ark of the *G·* of Israel,
11 hand of *G·* was very heavy there.
6: 3 send away the ark of the *G·* of Israel
5 give glory unto the *G·* of Israel:
20 to stand before this holy Lord *G·*?
7: 8 to cry unto the Lord our *G·* for us,
9: 6 now, there is in this city a man of *G·*,
7 present to bring to the man of *G·*:
8 that will I give to the man of *G·*,
9 when a man went to inquire of *G·*,
10 the city where the man of *G·* was.
27 I may shew thee the word of *G·*.
10: 3 meet thee three men going up to *G·*
5 thou shalt come to the hill of *G·*,
7 serve thee, for *G·* is with thee.
9 *G·* gave him another heart: and all
10 and the Spirit of *G·* came upon him,
18 Thus saith the Lord *G·* of Israel,
19 ye have this day rejected your *G·*,
24 and said, *G·* save the king.
26 men, whose hearts *G·* had touched.
11: 6 And the Spirit of *G·* came upon Saul
12: 9 when they forgat the Lord their *G·*,
12 the Lord your *G·* was your king.
14 continue following the Lord your *G·*:
19 thy servants unto the Lord thy *G·*,
23 *G·* forbid that I should sin against
13:13 commandment of the Lord thy *G·*,
14:18 Bring hither the ark of *G·*.
18 For the ark of *G·* was at that time
36 Let us draw near hither unto *G·*.
37 And Saul asked counsel of *G·*,
41 Saul said unto the Lord *G·* of Israel,
44 *G·* do so and more also: for thou
45 *G·* forbid: as the Lord liveth,
45 he hath wrought with *G·* this day.
15:15 sacrifice unto the Lord thy *G·*;
21 sacrifice unto the Lord thy *G·* in
30 that I may worship the Lord thy *G·*.
16:15 evil spirit from *G·* troubleth thee.
16 when the evil spirit from *G·* is upon
23 evil spirit from *G·* was upon Saul,
17:26 defy the armies of the living *G·*?
36 defied the armies of the living *G·*.
45 the *G·* of the armies of Israel, whom
46 know that there is a *G·* in Israel.
18:10 evil spirit from *G·* came upon Saul,
19:20 Spirit of *G·* was upon the messengers
23 the Spirit of *G·* was upon him also,
20: 2 he said unto him, *G·* forbid; thou
12 O Lord *G·* of Israel, when I have
22: 3 till I know what *G·* will do for me.
13 and hast enquired of *G·* for him,
15 then begin to enquire of *G·* for him?
23: 7 *G·* hath delivered him into mine
10 Then said David, O Lord *G·* of Israel,
11 O Lord *G·* of Israel, I beseech thee,
14 *G·* delivered him not into his hand.
16 and strengthened his hand in *G·*.
25:22 do *G·* unto the enemies of David,
29 bundle of life with the Lord thy *G·*;
32 Blessed be the Lord *G·* of Israel,
34 Lord *G·* of Israel liveth, which hath
26: 8 *G·* hath delivered thine enemy into
28:15 and *G·* is departed from me, and
29: 9 good in my sight, as an angel of *G·*:
30: 6 himself in the Lord his *G·*.
15 Swear unto me by *G·*, that thou wilt
2Sa **2:**27 Joab said, As *G·* liveth, unless thou
3: 9 So do *G·* to Abner, and more also,
35 So do *G·* to me, and more also,
5:10 the Lord *G·* of hosts was with him.
6: 2 bring up from thence the ark of *G·*,
3 set the ark of *G·* upon a new cart
4 accompanying the ark of *G·*: and
6 put forth his hand to the ark of *G·*,
7 *G·* smote him there for his error;
7 and there he died by the ark of *G·*.
12 unto him, because of the ark of *G·*.
12 and went and brought up the ark of *G·*
7: 2 ark of *G·* dwelleth within curtains.
18 he said, Who am I, O Lord *G·*?
19 thing in thy sight, O Lord *G·*;
19 the manner of man, O Lord *G·*?
20 Lord *G·*, knowest thy servant.
22 thou art great, O Lord *G·*: for there
22 neither is there any *G·* beside thee,
23 *G·* went to redeem for a people to
24 and thou, Lord, art become their *G·*.
25 Lord *G·*, the word that thou hast
26 Lord of hosts is the *G·* over Israel:
27 thou, O Lord of hosts, *G·* of Israel,
28 And now O Lord *G·*, thou art
28 thou art that *G·*, and thou hast
29 thou, O Lord *G·*, hast spoken it:
9: 3 shew the kindness of *G·* unto him?
10:12 people, and for the cities of our *G·*:
12: 7 Thus saith the Lord *G·* of Israel,
16 David therefore besought *G·* for the
22 whether *G·* will be gracious to

2Sa 14:11 king remember the Lord thy G',
13 a thing against the people of G'?
14 neither doth G' respect any person:
16 out of the inheritance of G'.
17 for as an angel of G', so is my lord
17 therefore the Lord thy G' will be
20 to the wisdom of an angel of G',
15:24 the ark of the covenant of G':
24 and they set down the ark of G';
25 back the ark of G' into the city:
29 carried the ark of G' again to
32 the mount, where he worshipped G',
16:16 G' save the king, G' save the
23 had enquired at the oracle of G':
18:28 Blessed be the Lord thy G',
33 would G' I...died for thee, O Absalom,
19:13 G' do so to me, and more also, if
27 my lord the king is as an angel of G':
21:14 that G' was intreated for the land.
22: 3 G' of my rock; in him will I trust:
7 and cried to my G': and he did hear
22 not wickedly departed from my G'.
30 by my G' have I leaped over a wall.
31 As for G', his way is perfect;
32 For who is G', save the Lord?
32 and who is a rock, save our G'?
33 G' is my strength and power:
47 the G' of the rock of my salvation.
48 It is G' that avengeth me, and
23: 1 the anointed of the G' of Jacob,
3 The G' of Israel said, the Rock of
3 must be just, ruling in the fear of G'.
5 my house be not so with G'; yet
24: 3 Now the Lord thy G' add unto the
23 The Lord thy G' accept thee.
24 burnt offerings unto the Lord my G'
1Ki 1:17 thou swarest by the Lord thy G'
25 and say, G' save king Adonijah.
30 unto thee by the Lord G' of Israel,
34 and say, G' save king Solomon.
36 the Lord G' of my lord the king
39 said, G' save king Solomon.
47 G' make the name of Solomon
48 Blessed be the Lord G' of Israel,
2: 3 keep the charge of the Lord thy G',
23 G' do so to me, and more also, if
26 thou barest the ark of the Lord G'
3: 5 G' said, Ask what I shall give thee.
7 O Lord my G', thou hast made thy
11 And G' said unto him, Because thou
28 that the wisdom of G' was in him,
4:29 And G' gave Solomon wisdom and
5: 3 unto the name of the Lord his G'
4 But now the Lord my G' hath given
5 unto the name of the Lord my G',
8:15 Blessed be the Lord G' of Israel,
17 the name of the Lord G' of Israel.
23 And he said, Lord G' of Israel,
23 there is no G' like thee, in heaven
25 now, Lord G' of Israel, keep with thy
26 And now, O G' of Israel, let thy word
27 will G' indeed dwell on the earth?
28 to his supplication, O Lord my G',
53 fathers out of Egypt, O Lord G'.
57 The Lord our G' be with us,
59 be nigh unto the Lord our G' by day
60 earth may know that the Lord is G',
61 be perfect with the Lord our G', to
65 before the Lord our G', seven days
9: 9 they forsook the Lord their G', who
10: 9 Blessed be the Lord thy G', which
24 which G' had put in his heart.
11: 4 was not perfect with the Lord his G',
9 turned from the Lord G' of Israel,
23 G' stirred him up another adversary,
31 thus saith the Lord, the G' of Israel,
33 Chemosh the g' of the Moabites,
33 and Milcom the g' of the children
12:22 But the word of G' came unto
22 unto Shemaiah the man of G',
13: 1 there came a man of G' out of Judah
4 heard the saying of the man of G',
5 which the man of G' had given by
6 and said unto the man of G', Intreat
6 now the face of the Lord thy G',
6 the man of G' besought the Lord,
7 the king said unto the man of G',
8 the man of G' said unto the king,
11 works that the man of G' had done
12 seen what way the man of G' went,
14 And went after the man of G',
14 man of G' that camest from Judah?
21 And he cried unto the man of G'
21 which the Lord thy G' commanded
26 he said, It is the man of G', who
29 up the carcase of the man of G',
31 wherein the man of G' is buried;
14: 7 Thus saith the Lord G' of Israel,
13 the Lord G' of Israel in the house
15: 3 not perfect with the Lord his G',
4 for David's sake did the Lord his G
30 he provoked the Lord G' of Israel
16:13 in provoking the Lord G' of Israel
26, 33 to provoke the Lord G' of Israel
17: 1 As the Lord G' of Israel liveth,
12 she said, As the Lord thy G' liveth,
14 thus saith the Lord G' of Israel,
18 to do with thee, O thou man of G'?
20 the Lord, and said, O Lord my G',
21 said, O Lord my G', I pray thee,
24 I know that thou art a man of G',
18:10 the Lord thy G' liveth, there is no
21 If the Lord be G', follow him: but
24 and the G' that answereth by fire,
24 answereth by fire, let him be G'.
27 and said, Cry aloud: for he is a g';

1Ki 18:36 Lord G' of Abraham, Isaac, and of
36 be known this day that thou art G'
37 know that thou art the Lord G',
39 they said, The Lord, he is the G';
39 the Lord, he is the G'.
19: 8 nights unto Horeb the mount of G'.
10, 14 jealous for the Lord G' of hosts:
20:28 there came a man of G', and spake
28 said, The Lord is G' of the hills,
28 but he is not G' of the valleys,
21:10 didst blaspheme G' and the king.
13 did blaspheme G' and the king.
22:53 provoked to anger the Lord G' of
2Ki 1: 2 of Baal-zebub the g' of Ekron
3 is not a G' in Israel, that ye go to
3 of Baal-zebub the g' of Ekron?
6 not a G' in Israel, that thou sendest
6 to enquire of Baal-zebub the g' of
9 he spake unto him, Thou man of G',
10 If I be a man of G', then let the fire
11 and said unto him, O man of G',
12 If I be a man of G', let fire come
12 fire of G' came down from heaven,
13 and said unto him, O man of G',
16 of Baal-zebub the g' of Ekron, is it
16 not because there is no G' in Israel
2:14 Where is the Lord G' of Elijah?
4: 7 she came and told the man of G'.
9 that this is an holy man of G', which
16 Nay, my lord, thou man of G', do not
21 laid him on the bed of the man of G',
22 that I may run to the man of G',
25 unto the man of G' to mount Carmel.
25 when the man of G' saw her afar off,
27 when she came to the man of G'
27 the man of G' said, Let her alone;
40 O thou man of G', there is death
42 and brought the man of G' bread
5: 3 Would G' my lord were with the
7 Am I G', to kill and to make alive,
8 Elisha the man of G' had heard
11 call on the name of the Lord his G',
14 to the saying of the man of G':
15 And he returned to the man of G',
15 now I know that there is no G' in
20 the servant of Elisha the man of G',
6: 6 the man of G' said, Where fell it?
9 the man of G' sent unto the king
10 place which the man of G' told him
15 servant of the man of G' was risen
31 G' do so and more also to me, if
7: 2 answered the man of G', and said,
17 he died, as the man of G' had said,
18 as the man of G' had spoken to
19 answered the man of G', and said,
8: 2 after the saying of the man of G':
4 servant of the man of G', saying
7 The man of G' is come hither.
8 meet the man of G', and enquire
11 and the man of G' wept.
9: 6 Thus saith the Lord G' of Israel,
10:31 in the law of the Lord G' of Israel
11:12 hands, and said, G' save the king.
13:19 the man of G' was wroth with him,
14:25 to the word of the Lord G' of Israel,
16: 2 right in the sight of the Lord his G',
17: 7 sinned against the Lord their G',
9 not right against the Lord their G',
14 did not believe in the Lord their G'.
16 left all the...of the Lord their G',
19 kept not the...of the Lord their G',
26 not the manner of the G' of the land:
26 not the manner of the G' of the land.
27 the manner of the G' of the land.
39 But the Lord your G' ye shall fear;
18: 5 He trusted in the Lord G' of Israel;
12 not the voice of the Lord their G',
22 We trust in the Lord our G':
19: 4 It may be the Lord thy G' will hear
4 hath sent to reproach the living G';
4 words which the Lord thy G' hath
10 not thy G' in whom thou trustest
15 O Lord G' of Israel, which dwellest
15 thou art the G', even thou alone,
16 sent him to reproach the living G'.
19 Now therefore, O Lord our G',
19 thou art the Lord G', even thou only.
20 Thus saith the Lord G' of Israel,
37 in the house or Nisroch his g',
20: 5 Lord, the G' of David thy father,
21:12 thus saith the Lord G' of Israel,
22 forsook the Lord G' of his fathers,
22:15 unto them, Thus saith the Lord G'
18 say to him, Thus saith the Lord G'
23:16 which the man of G' proclaimed,
17 It is the sepulchre of the man of G',
21 the passover unto the Lord your G',
1Ch 4:10 Jabez called on the G' of Israel,
10 And G' granted him that which he
5:20 for they cried to G' in the battle,
22 slain, because the war was of G'.
25 against the G' of their fathers, and
25 whom G' destroyed before them.
26 the G' of Israel stirred up the spirit
6:48 the tabernacle of the house of G'.
49 the servant of G' had commanded.
9:11 the ruler of the house of G';
13 of the service of the house of G'.
26 and treasuries of the house of G'.
27 lodged round about the house of G',
11: 2 and the Lord thy G' said unto thee,
19 My G' forbid it me, that I should
12:17 the G' of our fathers look thereon,
18 helpers; for thy G' helpeth thee.
22 was a great host, like the host of G'.
13: 2 and that it be of the Lord our G',

1Ch 13: 3 let us bring again the ark of our G'
5 the ark of G' from Kirjath-jearim.
6 up thence the ark of G' the Lord,
7 they carried the ark of G' in a new
8 all Israel played before G' with
10 and there he died before G'.
12 David was afraid of G' that day,
12 How shall I bring the ark of G'
14 ark of G' remained with the family
14:10 And David enquired of G', saying,
11 said, G' hath broken in upon mine
14 David enquired again of G'; and G'
15 for G' is gone forth before thee to
16 therefore did as G' commanded
15: 1 prepared a place for the ark of G',
2 None ought to carry the ark of G'
2 Lord chosen to carry the ark of G',
12 up the ark of the Lord G' of Israel
13 Lord our G' made a breach upon us,
14 up the ark of the Lord G' of Israel.
15 the Levites bare the ark of G' upon
24 the trumpets before the ark of G':
26 when G' helped the Levites that
16: 1 So they brought the ark of G',
1 and peace offerings before G'.
4 and praise the Lord G' of Israel:
6 before the ark of the covenant of G'.
14 is the Lord our G'; his judgments
35 Save us, O G' of our salvation,
36 Blessed be the Lord G' of Israel
42 and with musical instruments of G'.
17: 2 thine heart; for G' is with thee.
3 that the word of G' came to Nathan,
16 Who am I, O Lord G', and what is
17 a small thing in thine eyes, O G';
17 a man of high degree, O Lord G'.
20 neither is there any G' beside thee,
21 whom G' went to redeem to be his
22 and thou, Lord, becamest their G'.
24 The Lord of hosts is the G' of Israel
24 even a G' to Israel: and let the
25 For thou, O my G', hast told thy
26 And now, Lord, thou art G',
19:13 people, and for the cities of our G':
21: 7 G' was displeased with this thing;
8 David said unto G', I have sinned
15 G' sent an angel unto Jerusalem to
17 And David said unto G', Is it not I
17 O Lord my G', be on me, and on my
30 not go before it to enquire of G':
22: 1 This is the house of the Lord G',
2 stones to build the house of G'.
6 an house for the Lord G' of Israel.
7 unto the name of the Lord my G':
11 build the house of the Lord thy G',
12 keep the law of the Lord thy G'.
18 Is not the Lord your G' with you?
19 your soul to seek the Lord your G';
19 ye the sanctuary of the Lord G',
19 holy vessels of G', into the house
23:14 concerning Moses the man of G',
25 The Lord G' of Israel hath given
28 of the service of the house of G';
24: 5 and governors of the house of G',
19 Lord G' of Israel had commanded
25: 5 the king's seer in the words of G',
5 G' gave to Heman fourteen sons
6 for the service of the house of G',
26: 5 the eighth; for G' blessed him.
20 over the treasures of the house of G',
32 for every matter pertaining to G',
28: 2 and for the footstool of our G',
3 But G' said unto me, Thou shalt
4 Howbeit the Lord G' of Israel chose
8 and in the audience of our G', keep
8 commandments of the Lord your G':
9 know thou the G' of thy father,
12 of the treasuries of the house of G',
20 nor be dismayed: for the Lord G',
20 even my G', will be with thee;
21 for all the service of the house of G':
29: 1 my son, whom alone G' hath chosen,
1 not for man, but for the Lord G'.
2 all my might for the house of my G'
3 my affection to the house of my G',
3 I have given to the house of my G',
7 for the service of the house of G'
10 Blessed be thou, Lord G' of Israel
13 Now therefore, our G', we thank
16 O Lord our G', all this store that
17 I know also, my G', that thou triest
18 O Lord G' of Abraham, Isaac, and
20 Now bless the Lord your G'. And
20 blessed the Lord G' of their fathers,
2Ch 1: 1 and the Lord his G' was with him,
3 tabernacle of the congregation of G',
4 the ark of G' had David brought
7 In that night did G' appear unto
8 Solomon said unto G', Thou hast
9 Lord G', let thy promise unto David
11 G' said to Solomon, Because this
2: 4 to the name of the Lord my G',
4 solemn feasts of the Lord our G'.
5 for great is our G' above all gods.
12 Blessed be the Lord G' of Israel,
3: 3 for the building of the house of G'.
4:11 king Solomon for the house of G';
19 vessels that were for the house of G',
5: 1 the treasures of the house of G'.
14 the Lord had filled the house of G'.
6: 4 Blessed be the Lord G' of Israel,
7, 10 name of the Lord G' of Israel.
14 G' of Israel, there is no G' like thee
16 Now therefore, O Lord G' of Israel,
17 Now then, O Lord G' of Israel,
18 But will G' in very deed dwell with

2Ch 6:19 to his supplication, O Lord my G',
40 Now, my G', let, I beseech thee,
41 Now therefore arise, O Lord G',
41 thy priests, O Lord G', be clothed
42 O Lord G', turn not away the face
7: 5 people dedicated the house of G'.
22 Because they forsook the Lord G'
8:14 David the man of G' commanded.
9: 8 Blessed be the Lord thy G', which
8 Lord thy G': because thy G' loved
23 wisdom, that G' had put in his heart.
10:15 for the cause was of G', that the
11: 2 to Shemaiah the man of G', saying
16 hearts to seek the Lord G' of Israel
16 unto the Lord G' of their fathers.
13: 5 to know that the Lord G' of Israel
10 But as for us, the Lord is our G',
11 keep the charge of the Lord our G';
12 G' himself is with us for our captain,
12 fight ye not against the Lord G' of
15 to pass, that G' smote Jeroboam
16 G' delivered them into their hand.
18 they relied upon the Lord G' of
14: 2 right in the eyes of the Lord his G':
4 to seek the Lord G' of their fathers,
7 we have sought the Lord our G',
11 And Asa cried unto the Lord his G',
11 help us, O Lord our G'; for we rest
11 O Lord, thou art our G'; let not
15: 1 the Spirit of G' came upon Azariah
3 Israel hath been without the true G',
4 did turn unto the Lord G' of Israel,
6 G' did vex them with all adversity.
9 that the Lord his G' was with him.
12 a covenant to seek the Lord G' of
13 would not seek the Lord G' of Israel
18 And he brought into the house of G'
16: 7 and not relied on the Lord thy G',
17: 4 sought to the Lord G' of his father,
18: 5 for G' will deliver it into the king's
13 even what my G' saith, that will I
31 G' moved them to depart from him.
19: 3 hast prepared thine heart to seek G'.
4 unto the Lord G' of their fathers.
7 is no iniquity with the Lord our G',
20: 6 And said, O Lord G' of our fathers,
6 art not thou G' in heaven?
7 Art not thou our G', who didst drive
12 O our G', wilt thou not judge them?
19 to praise the Lord G' of Israel with
20 Believe in the Lord your G', so shall
29 fear of G' was on all the kingdoms
30 his G' gave him rest round about.
33 hearts unto the G' of their fathers.
21:10 forsaken the Lord G' of his fathers.
12 Thus saith the Lord G' of David thy
22: 7 destruction of Ahaziah was of G' by
12 was hid in the house of G' six years:
23: 3 with the king in the house of G'.
9 which were in the house of G'.
11 him, and said, G' save the king.
24: 5 repair the house of your G' from
7 had broken up the house of G';
9 Moses the servant of G' laid upon
13 they set the house of G' in his state,
16 toward G', and toward his house.
18 house of the Lord G' of their fathers,
20 Spirit of G' came upon Zechariah
20 Thus saith G', Why transgress ye
24 had forsaken the Lord G' of their
27 and the repairing of the house of G',
25: 7 But there came a man of G' to him,
8 G' shall make thee fall before the
8 for G' hath power to help, and to
9 And Amaziah said to the man of G',
9 the man of G' answered, The Lord
16 I know that G' hath determined to
20 would not hear; for it came of G',
24 the house of G' with Obed-edom,
26: 5 sought G' in the days of Zechariah,
5 understanding in the visions of G':
5 the Lord, G' made him to prosper.
7 And G' helped him against the
16 against the Lord his G', and went
18 for thine honour from the Lord G'.
27: 6 his ways before the Lord his G'.
28: 5 the Lord his G' delivered him into
6 had forsaken the Lord G' of their
9 because the Lord G' of your fathers
10 you, sins against the Lord your G'?
24 the vessels of the house of G', and
24 pieces the vessels of the house of G',
25 provoked to anger the Lord G' of
29: 5 house of the Lord G' of your fathers,
6 evil in the eyes of the Lord our G',
7 holy place unto the G' of Israel.
10 covenant with the Lord G' of Israel,
36 that G' had prepared the people:
30: 1 passover unto the Lord G' of Israel.
5 passover unto the Lord G' of Israel
6 again unto the Lord G' of Abraham,
7 against the Lord G' of their fathers,
8 serve the Lord your G', that the
9 for the Lord your G' is gracious and
12 the hand of G' was to give them one
16 to the law of Moses the man of G':
19 That prepareth his heart to seek G',
19 the Lord G' of his fathers, though he
22 to the Lord G' of their fathers.
31: 6 consecrated unto the Lord their G',
13 Azariah the ruler of the house of G'.
14 was over the freewill offerings of G',
20 and truth before the Lord his G'.
21 in the service of the house of G',
21 the commandments, to seek his G',
32: 8 but with us is the Lord our G' to

2Ch 32:11 The Lord our G' shall deliver us
14 your G' should be able to deliver
15 for no g' of any nation or kingdom
15 much less shall your G' deliver
16 spake yet more against the Lord G',
17 to rail on the Lord G' of Israel,
17 so shall not the G' of Hezekiah
19 spake against the G' of Jerusalem,
21 he was come to the house of his g',
29 for G' had given him substance
31 G' left him, to try him, that he
33: 7 in the house of G', of which G' had
12 he besought the Lord his G', and
12 greatly before the G' of his fathers,
13 knew that the Lord he was G'.
16 Judah to serve the Lord G' of Israel.
17 yet unto the Lord their G' only.
18 and his prayer unto his G', and the
18 the name of the Lord G' of Israel,
19 and how G' was intreated of him,
34: 3 began to seek after the G' of David
8 repair the house of the Lord his G'.
9 was brought into the house of G',
23 Thus saith the Lord G' of Israel,
26 Thus saith the Lord G' of Israel
27 thou didst humble thyself before G',
32 according to the covenant of G',
32 the G' of their fathers.
33 even to serve the Lord their G'.
33 following the Lord, the G' of their
35: 3 serve now the Lord your G', and
8 rulers of the house of G', gave unto
21 G' commanded me to make haste:
21 forbear thee from meddling with G',
22 words of Necho from the mouth of G',
36: 5 evil in the sight of the Lord his G'.
12 evil in the sight of the Lord his G',
13 who had made him swear by G':
13 turning unto the Lord G' of Israel.
15 the Lord G' of their fathers sent
16 they mocked the messengers of G',
18 all the vessels of the house of G',
19 And they burnt the house of G',
23 hath the Lord G' of heaven given me;
23 The Lord his G' be with him,
Ezr 1: 2 The Lord G' of heaven hath given
3 his G' be with him, and let him go
3 the house of the Lord G' of Israel,
3 (he is the G',) which is in
4 freewill offering for the house of G'
5 them whose spirit G' hath raised,
2:68 offered freely for the house of G' to
3: 2 builded the altar of the G' of Israel,
2 in the law of Moses the man of G'.
8 their coming unto the house of G'
9 the workmen in the house of G':
4: 1 temple unto the Lord G' of Israel;
2 for we seek your G', as ye do;
3 to build an house unto our G';
3 will build unto the Lord G' of Israel,
24 ceased the work of the house of G'
5: 1 in the name of the G' of Israel,
2 and began to build the house of G'
2 with them were the prophets of G'
5 But the eye of their G' was upon
8 to the house of the great G', which
11 are the servants of the G' of heaven
12 had provoked the G' of heaven unto
13 a decree to build this house of G'.
14 gold and silver of the house of G',
15 and let the house of G' be builded
16 the foundation of the house of G'
17 build this house of G' at Jerusalem,
6: 3 the house of G' at Jerusalem, Let
5 and silver vessels of the house of G',
5 and place them in the house of G'.
7 the work of this house of G' alone;
7 build this house of G' in his place.
8 for the building of this house of G':
9 burnt offerings of the G' of heaven,
10 savours unto the G' of heaven,
12 the G' that hath caused his name
12 to destroy this house of G' which is
14 commandment of the G' of Israel,
16 dedication of this house of G' with
17 at the dedication of this house of G'
18 for the service of G', which is at
21 to seek the Lord G' of Israel, did
22 of the house of G', the G' of Israel.
7: 6 the Lord G' of Israel had given:
6 to the hand of the Lord his G' upon
9 according to the good hand of his G'
12 of the law of the G' of heaven,
14 according to the law of thy G' which
15 freely offered unto the G' of Israel,
16 willingly for the house of their G'
17 the altar of the house of your G'
18 that do after the will of your G'.
19 the service of the house of thy G',
19 those deliver thou before the G' of
20 be needful for the house of thy G',
21 scribe of the law of the G' of heaven,
23 commanded by the G' of heaven,
23 for the house of the G' of heaven:
24 or ministers of this house of G',
25 Ezra, after the wisdom of thy G',
25 such as know the laws of thy G';
26 will not do the law of thy G', and
27 Blessed be the Lord G' of our
28 as the hand of the Lord my G' was
8:17 ministers for the house of our G'.
18 And by the good hand of our G' upon
21 might afflict ourselves before our G',
22 The hand of our G' is upon all them
23 fasted and besought our G' for this:
25 the offering of the house of our G',

Ezr 8:28 unto the Lord G' of your fathers.
30 unto the house of our G'.
31 and the hand of our G' was upon us,
33 weighed in the house of our G' by
35 burnt offerings unto the G' of
36 the people, and the house of G'.
9: 4 at the words of the G' of Israel,
5 my hands unto the Lord my G',
6 O my G', I am ashamed and blush
6 to lift up my face to thee, my G':
8 been shewed from the Lord our G',
8 that our G' may lighten our eyes,
9 yet our G' hath not forsaken us
9 to set up the house of our G', and
10 our G', what shall we say after this?
13 seeing that thou our G' hast
15 O Lord G' of Israel, thou art
10: 1 down before the house of G', there
2 We have trespassed against our G',
3 make a covenant with our G' to put
3 at the commandment of our G';
6 before the house of G', and went
9 sat in the street of the house of G',
11 make confession unto the Lord G'
14 until the fierce wrath of our G' for
Ne 1: 4 and prayed before the G' of heaven,
5 I beseech thee, O Lord G' of heaven,
5 the great and terrible G', that
2: 4 So I prayed to the G' of heaven.
8 to the good hand of my G' upon me.
12 what my G' had put in my heart
18 I told them of the hand of my G' to
20 The G' of heaven, he will prosper us;
4: 4 Hear, O our G'; for we are despised:
9 we made our prayer unto our G',
15 and G' had brought their counsel to
20 unto us: our G' shall fight for us.
5: 9 walk in the fear of our G' because
13 So G' shake out every man from
15 did not I, because of the fear of G'.
19 Think upon me, my G', for good,
6: 9 therefore, O G', strengthen my hands.
10 meet together in the house of G',
12 perceived that G' had not sent him;
14 My G', think thou upon Tobiah and
16 this work was wrought of our G'.
7: 2 a faithful man, and feared G' above
5 G' put into mine heart to gather
8: 6 Ezra blessed the Lord, the great G'.
8 they read in the book in the law of G'
9 day is holy unto the Lord your G';
16 and in the courts of the house of G',
18 he read in the book of the law of G'.
9: 3 book of the law of the Lord their G'
3 and worshipped the Lord their G'.
4 a loud voice unto the Lord their G'.
5 and bless the Lord your G' for ever
7 Thou art the Lord the G', who didst
17 but thou art a G' ready to pardon,
18 This is thy G' that brought thee up
31 thou art a gracious and merciful G'.
32 our G', the great, the mighty, and
32 terrible G', who keepest covenant
10:28 of the lands unto the law of G',
29 given by Moses the servant of G',
32 the service of the house of our G';
33 all the work of the house of our G'.
34 bring it into the house of our G',
34 upon the altar of the Lord our G',
36 to bring to the house of our G',
36 that minister in the house of our G':
37 chambers of the house of our G';
38 the tithes unto the house of our G'.
39 will not forsake the house of our G'.
11:11 was the ruler of the house of G'.
16 outward business of the house of G'.
22 over the business of the house of G'.
12:24 of David the man of G', ward
36 instruments of David the man of G',
40 that gave thanks in the house of G',
43 for G' had made them rejoice with
45 porters kept the ward of their G',
46 praise and thanksgiving unto G'.
13: 1 the congregation of G' for ever;
2 howbeit our G' turned the curse
4 the chamber of the house of our G',
7 in the courts of the house of G'.
9 again the vessels of the house of G',
11 Why is the house of G' forsaken?
14 Remember me, O my G', concerning
14 I have done for the house of my G',
18 did not our G' bring all this evil
22 Remember me, O my G', concerning
25 made them swear by G', saying,
26 like him, who was beloved of his G',
26 and G' made him king over all
27 to transgress against our G' in
29 Remember them, O my G', because
31 Remember me, O my G', for good.
Job 1: 1 that feared G', and eschewed evil.
5 and cursed G' in their hearts.
6 when the sons of G' came to present
8 that feareth G', and escheweth evil?
9 said, Doth Job fear G' for nought?
16 The fire of G' is fallen from heaven,
22 sinned not, nor charged G' foolishly.
2: 1 a day when the sons of G' came
3 upright man, one that feareth G',
9 retain thine integrity? curse G',
10 we receive good at the hand of G',
3: 4 let not G' regard it from above,
23 and whom G' hath hedged in?
4: 9 By the blast of G' they perish,
17 mortal man be more just than G'?
5: 8 I would seek unto G', and unto
8 and unto G' would I commit my

Job 5:17 is the man whom G' correcteth:
6: 4 the terrors of G' do set themselves
8 that G' would grant me the thing
9 that it would please G' to destroy
8: 3 Doth G' pervert judgment? or doth
5 thou wouldest seek unto G' betimes,
13 are the paths of all that forget G';
20 G' will not cast away a perfect man,
9: 2 how should man be just with G'?
13 G' will not withdraw his anger,
10: 2 I will say unto G', Do not condemn
11: 5 But oh that G' would speak, and
6 Know therefore that G' exacteth of
7 Canst thou by searching find out G'?
12: 4 who calleth upon G', and he
6 they that provoke G' are secure;
6 into whose hand G' bringeth
13: 3 and I desire to reason with G'.
7 Will ye speak wickedly for G'?
8 will ye contend for G'?
15: 4 and restrainest prayer before G'.
8 Hast thou heard the secret of G'?
11 consolations of G' small with thee?
13 thou turnest thy spirit against G',
25 stretcheth out his hand against G',
16:11 G' hath delivered me to the ungodly,
20 eye poureth out tears unto G'.
21 one might plead for a man with G',
18:21 place of him that knoweth not G'.
19: 6 now that G' hath overthrown me,
21 the hand of G' hath touched me.
22 Why do ye persecute me as G',
26 yet in my flesh shall I see G':
20:15 G' shall cast them out of his belly.
23 G' shall cast the fury of his wrath upon
29 portion of a wicked man from G',
29 heritage appointed unto him by G'.
21: 9 neither is the rod of G' upon them.
14 Therefore they say unto G',
17 G' distributeth sorrows in his anger.
19 G' layeth up his iniquity for his
22 Shall any teach G' knowledge?
22: 2 Can a man be profitable unto G',
12 Is not G' in the height of heaven?
13 thou sayest, How doth G' know?
17 said unto G', Depart from us:
26 and shalt lift up thy face unto G'.
23:16 For G' maketh my heart soft, and
24:12 yet G' layeth not folly to them.
25: 4 then can man be justified with G'?
27: 2 As G' liveth, who hath taken away
3 the spirit of G' is in my nostrils;
5 G' forbid that I should justify
8 when G' taketh away his soul?
9 Will G' hear his cry when trouble
10 will he always call upon G'?
11 I will teach you by the hand of G':
13 the portion of a wicked man with G',
22 For G' shall cast upon him, and not
28:23 G' understandeth the way thereof,
29: 2 in the days when G' preserved me;
4 when the secret of G' was upon my
31: 2 portion of G' is there from above?
6 that G' may know mine integrity.
14 then shall I do when G' riseth up?
23 destruction from G' was a terror
28 have denied the G' that is above.
32: 2 he justified himself rather than G'.
13 G' thrusteth him down, not man.
33: 4 The Spirit of G' hath made me,
12 thee, that G' is greater than man.
14 For G' speaketh once, yea twice,
26 He shall pray unto G', and he will
29 worketh G' oftentimes with man,
34: 5 G' hath taken away my judgment.
9 he should delight himself with G'.
10 far be it from G', that he should do
12 Yea, surely G' will not do wickedly,
23 should enter into judgment with G'.
31 Surely it is meet to be said unto G',
37 multiplieth his words against G'.
35:10 Where is G' my maker, who giveth
13 Surely G' will not hear vanity,
36: 5 G' is mighty, and despiseth not any:
22 Behold, G' exalteth by his power:
26 G' is great, and we know him not,
37: 5 G' thundereth marvellously with
10 By the breath of G' frost is given:
14 consider the wondrous works of G'.
15 thou know when G' disposed them,
22 with G' is terrible majesty.
38: 7 all the sons of G' shouted for joy?
41 when his young ones cry unto G',
39:17 G' hath deprived her of wisdom,
40: 2 that reproveth G', let him answer
9 Hast thou an arm like G'? or canst
19 He is the chief of the ways of G':
Ps 3: 2 There is no help for him in G'.
7 Arise, O Lord; save me, O my G':
4: 1 O G' of my righteousness: thou
5: 2 my King, and my G': for unto thee
4 art not a G' that hath pleasure in
10 Destroy thou them, O G'; let them
7: 1 my G', in thee do I put my trust;
3 O Lord my G', if I have done this;
9 the righteous G' trieth the hearts
10 My defence is of G', which saveth
11 G' judgeth the righteous,
11 and G' is angry with the wicked
9:17 and all the nations that forget G'.
10: 4 countenance, will not seek after G':
4 G' is not in all his thoughts.
11 in his heart, G' hath forgotten:
12 O G', lift up thine hand: forget not
13 doth the wicked contemn G'? he
13: 3 and hear me, O Lord my G':

Ps 14: 1 said in his heart, There is no G'.
2 that did understand, and seek G'.
5 for G' is in the generation of the
16: 1 Preserve me, O G': for in thee do
4 that hasten after another g': their
17: 6 for thou wilt hear me, O G':
18: 2 my G', my strength, in whom I will
6 and cried unto my G': he heard my
21 not wickedly departed from my G'.
28 my G' will enlighten my darkness.
29 and by my G' have I leaped over a
30 As for G', his way is perfect:
31 For who is G' save the Lord?
31 or who is a rock save our G'?
32 G' that girdeth me with strength,
46 the G' of my salvation be exalted.
47 It is G' that avengeth me, and
19: 1 heavens declare the glory of G';
20: 1 of the G' of Jacob defend thee;
5 in the name of our G' we will set
7 the name of the Lord our G'.
22: 1 My G', my G', why hast thou
2 O my G', I cry in the daytime,
10 art my G' from my mother's belly.
24: 5 from the G' of his salvation.
25: 2 O my G', I trust in thee: let me not
5 for thou art the G' of my salvation;
22 Israel, O G', out of all his troubles.
27: 9 forsake me, O G' of my salvation.
29: 3 G' of glory thundereth: the Lord
30: 2 O Lord my G', I cried unto thee,
12 O Lord my G', I will give thanks
31: 5 redeemed me, O Lord G' of truth.
14 I said, Thou art my G'.
33:12 is the nation whose G' is the Lord;
35:23 unto my cause, my G' and my Lord.
24 Judge me, O Lord my G', according
36: 1 is no fear of G' before his eyes.
7 is thy lovingkindness, O G'!
37:31 The law of his G' is in his heart;
38:15 thou wilt hear, O Lord my G'.
21 O my G', be not far from me.
40: 3 even praise unto our G': many shall
5 O Lord my G', are thy wonderful
8 I delight to do thy will, O my G':
17 make no tarrying, O my G'.
41:13 Blessed be the Lord G' of Israel
42: 1 so panteth my soul after thee, O G'.
2 My soul thirsteth for G',
2 for the living G': when shall
2 I come and appear before G'?
3 say unto me, Where is thy G'?
4 I went with them to the house of G',
5 hope thou in G': for I shall yet
6 O my G', my soul is cast down
8 my prayer unto the G' of my life.
9 I will say unto G' my rock, Why
10 daily unto me, Where is thy G'?
11 hope thou in G': for I shall yet
11 of my countenance, and my G'.
43: 1 Judge me, O G', and plead my
2 For thou art the G' of my strength:
4 Then will I go unto the altar of G',
4 unto G' my exceeding joy:
4 will I praise thee, O G' my G'.
5 hope in G': for I shall yet praise
5 of my countenance, and my G'.
44: 1 We have heard with our ears, O G',
4 Thou art my King, O G': command
8 In G' we boast all the day long,
20 have forgotten the name of our G',
20 out our hands to a strange g':
21 Shall not G' search this out?
45: 2 therefore G' hath blessed thee for
6 Thy throne, O G', is for ever and
7 therefore G', thy G', hath anointed
46: 1 G' is our refuge and strength, a
4 shall make glad the city of G',
5 G' is in the midst of her; she shall
5 not be moved: G' shall help her,
7 the G' of Jacob is our refuge.
10 and know that I am G': I will be
11 the G' of Jacob is our refuge.
47: 1 unto G' with the voice of triumph.
5 G' is gone up with a shout, the
6 Sing praises to G', sing praises:
7 G' is the King of all the earth:
8 G' reigneth over the heathen:
8 G' sitteth upon the throne of his
9 the people of the G' of Abraham:
9 shields of the earth belong unto G':
48: 1 the city of our G', in the mountain
3 G' is known in her palaces for a
8 Lord of hosts, in the city of our G':
8 G' will establish it for ever.
9 lovingkindness, O G', in the midst
10 According to thy name, O G', so is
14 this G' is our G' for ever and ever:
49: 7 nor give to G' a ransom for him:
15 But G' will redeem my soul from
50: 1 The mighty G', even the Lord,
2 perfection of beauty, G' hath shined.
3 Our G' shall come, and shall not
6 for G' is judge himself. Selah.
7 I am G', even thy G'.
14 Offer unto G' thanksgiving; and
16 But unto the wicked G' saith, What
22 ye that forget G', lest I tear you
23 will I shew the salvation of G'.
51: 1 Have mercy upon me, O G',
10 Create in me a clean heart, O G';
14 me from bloodguiltiness, O G',
14 thou G' of my salvation:
17 sacrifices of G' are a broken spirit:
17 a broken and a contrite heart, O G',
52: 1 of G' endureth continually.

Ps 52: 5 G' shall likewise destroy thee for
7 man that made not G' his strength;
8 green olive tree in the house of G':
8 I trust in the mercy of G' for ever
53: 1 said in his heart, There is no G'.
2 G' looked down from heaven upon
2 did understand, that did seek G'.
4 they have not called upon G'.
5 G' hath scattered the bones of him
5 because G' hath despised them.
6 G' bringeth back the captivity of
54: 1 Save me, O G', by thy name,
2 Hear my prayer, O G'; give ear
3 they have not set G' before them.
4 Behold, G' is mine helper: the Lord
55: 1 Give ear to my prayer, O G';
14 unto the house of G' in company.
16 As for me, I will call upon G';
19 G' shall hear, and afflict them,
19 therefore they fear not G'.
23 But thou, O G', shalt bring them
56: 1 Be merciful unto me, O G': for man
4 In G' I will praise his word,
4 in G' I have put my trust;
7 anger cast down the people, O G'.
9 this I know; for G' is for me.
10 In G' will I praise his word:
11 In G' have I put my trust:
12 Thy vows are upon me, O G':
13 I may walk before G' in the light
57: 1 Be merciful unto me, O G', be
2 I will cry unto G' most high;
2 unto G' that performeth all
3 G' shall send forth his mercy and
5 exalted, O G', above the heavens;
7 My heart is fixed, O G', my heart is
11 Be thou exalted, O G', above
58: 6 Break their teeth, O G', in their
11 he is a G' that judgeth in the earth.
59: 1 me from mine enemies, O my G':
5 Thou therefore, O Lord G' of hosts,
5 the G' of Israel, awake to visit
9 upon thee: for G' is my defence.
10 The G' of my mercy shall prevent
10 G' shall let me see my desire
13 them know that G' ruleth in Jacob
17 will I sing: for G' is my defence,
17 my defence, and the G' of my mercy.
60: 1 O G', thou hast cast us off,
6 G' hath spoke in his holiness;
10 Wilt not thou, O G', which hadst
10 and thou, O G', which didst not go
12 Through G' we shall do valiantly:
61: 1 Hear my cry, O G'; attend unto my
5 For thou, O G', hast heard my vows:
7 He shall abide before G' for ever:
62: 1 Truly my soul waiteth upon G':
5 My soul, wait thou only upon G';
7 In G' is my salvation and my glory:
7 strength, and my refuge, is in G'.
8 before him: G' is a refuge for us.
11 G' hath spoken once; twice have I
11 that power belongeth unto G'.
63: 1 O G', thou art my...; early will I
1 thou art my G'; early will I
11 But the king shall rejoice in G';
64: 1 Hear my voice, O G', in my prayer:
7 But G' shall shoot at them with an
9 and shall declare the work of G';
65: 1 waiteth for thee, O G', in Sion:
5 answer us, O G' of our salvation;
9 enrichest it with the river of G',
66: 1 Make a joyful noise unto G', all ye
3 Say unto G', How terrible art thou
5 Come and see the works of G':
8 O bless our G', ye people, and make
10 For thou, O G', hast proved us:
16 Come and hear, all ye that fear G',
19 But verily G' hath heard me;
20 Blessed be G', which hath not
67: 1 G' be merciful unto us, and bless
3, 5 Let the people praise thee, O G';
6 G', even our own G', shall bless us.
7 G' shall bless us; and all the ends
68: 1 Let G' arise, let his enemies be
2 wicked perish at the presence of G'.
3 let them rejoice before G': yea,
4 Sing unto G', sing praises to his
5 widows, is G' in his holy habitation.
6 G' setteth the solitary in families:
7 O G', when thou wentest forth
8 dropped at the presence of G':
8 the presence of G', the G' of Israel.
9 O G', didst send a plentiful rain,
10 thou, O G', hast prepared of thy
15 hill of G' is as the hill of Bashan;
16 the hill which G' desireth to dwell
17 The chariots of G' are twenty
18 Lord G' might dwell among them.
19 even the G' of our salvation.
20 that is our G' is the G' of salvation;
20 G' the Lord belong the issues
21 G' shall wound the head of his
24 They have seen thy goings, O G';
24 even the goings of my G', my
26 Bless ye G' in the congregations,
28 G' hath commanded thy strength:
28 strengthen, O G', that which thou
31 soon stretch out her hands unto G'.
32 Sing unto G', ye kingdoms of the
34 Ascribe ye strength unto G':
35 O G', thou art terrible out of thy
35 the G' of Israel is he that giveth
35 unto his people. Blessed be G'.
69: 1 Save me, O G'; for the waters are
3 eyes fail while I wait for my G'.

Ps 69: 5 O G', thou knowest my foolishness;
6 wait on thee, O Lord G' of hosts,
6 for my sake, O G' of Israel.
13 O G', in the multitude of thy mercy
29 thy salvation, O G', set me up on
30 I will praise the name of G'
32 your heart shall live that seek G'.
35 For G' will save Zion, and will build
70: 1 Make haste, O G', to deliver me;
4 continually, Let G' be magnified.
5 make haste unto me, O G': thou
71: 4 Deliver me, O my G', out of the
5 thou art my hope, O Lord G':
11 Saying, G' hath forsaken him:
12 O G', be not far from me: O my G',
16 go in the strength of the Lord G':
17 O G', thou hast taught me from
18 O G', forsake me not; until I have
19 Thy righteousness also, O G', is
19 O G', who is like unto thee!
22 even thy truth, O my G': unto thee
72: 1 Give the king thy judgments, O G',
18 be the Lord G', the G' of Israel,
73: 1 Truly G' is good to Israel,
11 they say, How doth G' know?
17 I went into the sanctuary of G';
26 but G' is the strength of my heart,
28 is good for me to draw near to G':
28 have put my trust in the Lord G',
74: 1 O G', why hast thou cast us off
8 burned up all the synagogues of G'
10 O G', how long shall the adversary
12 For G' is my King of old, working
22 Arise, O G', plead thine own cause:
75: 1 Unto thee, O G', do we give thanks,
7 But G' is the judge: he putteth
9 will sing praises to the G' of Jacob.
76: 1 In Judah is G' known: his name is
6 At thy rebuke, O G' of Jacob,
9 When G' arose to judgment, to save
11 and pay unto the Lord your G':
77: 1 G' with my voice, even unto G' with
3 I remembered G', and was troubled:
9 Hath G' forgotten to be gracious?
13 Thy way, O G', is in the sanctuary:
13 sanctuary: who is so great a G' as
13 who is so great...as our G'?
14 Thou art the G' that doest wonders:
16 waters saw thee, O G', the waters
78: 7 they might set their hope in G',
7 and not forget the works of G',
8 whose spirit was not stedfast with G'.
10 They kept not the covenant of G',
18 they tempted G' in their heart by
19 Yea, they spake against G';
19 they said, Can G' furnish a table
22 Because they believed not in G',
31 The wrath of G' came upon them,
34 and enquired early after G'.
35 they remembered that G' was their
35 and the high G' their redeemer.
41 they turned back and tempted G',
56 and provoked the most high G',
59 When G' heard this, he was wroth,
79: 1 O G', the heathen are come into
9 Help us, O G' of our salvation,
10 the heathen say, Where is their G'?
80: 3 Turn us again, O G', and cause thy
4 O Lord G' of hosts, how long wilt
7 Turn us again, O G' of hosts,
14 Return, we beseech thee, O G' of
19 Turn us again, O Lord G' of hosts,
81: 1 Sing aloud unto G' our strength:
1 make a joyful noise unto the G' of
4 and a law of the G' of Jacob.
9 There shall no strange g' be in thee:
9 shalt thou worship any strange g'.
10 am the Lord thy G', which brought
82: 1 G' standeth in the congregation of
8 Arise, O G', judge the earth: for
83: 1 Keep not thou silence, O G':
1 not thy peace, and be not still, O G'.
12 the houses of G' in possession.
13 O my G', make them like a wheel;
84: 2 flesh crieth out for the living G'.
3 Lord of hosts, my King, and my G'.
7 them in Zion appeareth before G'.
8 O Lord G' of hosts, hear my prayer:
8 give ear, O G' of Jacob.
9 Behold, O G' our shield, and look
10 doorkeeper in the house of my G',
11 For the Lord G' is a sun and shield:
85: 4 Turn us, O G' of our salvation,
8 I will hear what G' the Lord will
86: 2 O thou my G', save thy servant
10 wondrous things: thou art G' alone.
12 I will praise thee, O Lord my G',
14 O G', the proud are risen against
15 O Lord, art a G' full of compassion,
87: 3 are spoken of thee, O city of G'.
88: 1 O Lord G' of my salvation, I have
89: 7 G' is greatly to be feared in the
8 O Lord G' of hosts, who is a strong
26 Thou art my father, my G', and
90:*title* Prayer of Moses the man of G'.
2 to everlasting, thou art G'.
17 let the beauty of the Lord our G'
91: 2 fortress: my G'; in him will I trust.
92:13 shall flourish in the courts of our G',
94: 1 O Lord G', to whom vengeance
1 O G', to whom vengeance belongeth,
7 neither shall the G' of Jacob regard
22 and my G' is the rock of my refuge.
23 the Lord our G' shall cut them off.
95: 3 For the Lord is a great G', and a
7 For he is our G'; and we are the

Ps 98: 3 have seen the salvation of our G'.
99: 5 exalt ye the Lord our G', and
8 answeredst them, O Lord our G':
8 thou wast a G' that forgavest them,
9 the Lord our G', and worship at
9 hill; for the Lord our G' is holy.
100: 3 Know ye that the Lord he is G':
102:24 O my G', take me not away in the
104: 1 O Lord my G', thou art very great;
21 and seek their meat from G'.
33 I will sing praise to my G' while I
105: 7 He is the Lord our G': his
106:14 and tempted G' in the desert.
21 They forgat G' their saviour, which
47 Save us, O Lord our G', and gather
48 Blessed be the Lord G' of Israel
107:11 rebelled against the words of G',
108: 1 O G', my heart is fixed; I will sing
5 Be thou exalted, O G', above the
7 G' hath spoken in his holiness;
11 O G', who hast cast us off? and
11 wilt not thou, O G', go forth with
13 Through G' we shall do valiantly:
109: 1 Hold not thy peace, O G' of my
21 But do thou for me, O G' the Lord,
26 Help me, O Lord my G': O save
113: 5 Who is like unto the Lord our G',
114: 7 at the presence of the G' of Jacob;
115: 2 heathen say, Where is now their G'?
3 But our G' is in the heavens: he
116: 5 yea, our G' is merciful.
118:27 G' is the Lord, which hath shewed
28 art my G' and I will praise thee:
28 thou art my G', I will exalt thee.
119:115 keep the commandments of my G'.
122: 9 of the house of the Lord our G' I
123: 2 our eyes wait upon the Lord our G',
132: 2 unto the mighty G' of Jacob;
5 for the mighty G' of Jacob.
135: 2 the courts of the house of our G',
136: 2 unto the G' of Gods: for his mercy
26 give thanks unto the G' of heaven:
139:17 are thy thoughts unto me, O G'!
19 thou wilt slay the wicked, O G':
23 Search me, O G', and know my
140: 6 unto the Lord, Thou art my G':
141: 8 eyes are unto thee, O G' the Lord:
143:10 for thou art my G': thy spirit
144: 9 sing a new song unto thee, O G':
15 that people whose G' is the Lord.
145: 1 I will extol thee, my G', O king;
146: 2 I will sing praises unto my G' while
5 Happy is he that hath the G' of
5 whose hope is in the Lord his G':
10 thy G', O Zion, unto all generations.
147: 1 good to sing praises unto our G';
7 praise upon the harp unto our G':
12 Jerusalem; praise thy G', O Zion.
149: 6 the high praises of G' be in their
150: 1 Praise G' in his sanctuary: praise
Pr 2: 5 and find the knowledge of G'.
17 forgetteth the covenant of her G'.
3: 4 understanding in the sight of G' and
21:12 but G' overthroweth the wicked
25: 2 the glory of G' to conceal a thing:
26:10 great G' that formed all things
30: 5 Every word of G' is pure: he is a
9 take the name of my G' in vain.
Ec 1:13 this sore travail hath G' given to
2:24 that it was from the hand of G'.
26 For G' giveth to a man that is good in
26 to him that is good before G'.
3:10 G' hath given to the sons of men
11 find out the work that G' maketh
13 all his labour, it is the gift of G'.
14 whatsoever G' doeth, it shall be for
14 G' doeth it, that men should fear
15 and G' requireth that which is past.
17 G' shall judge the righteous and the
18 that G' might manifest them, and
5: 1 when thou goest to the house of G',
2 utter anything before G': for G' is
4 When thou vowest a vow unto G',
6 wherefore should G' be angry at
7 vanities: but fear thou G'.
18 of his life, which G' giveth him:
19 to whom G' hath given riches and
19 his labour; this is the gift of G'.
20 G' answereth him in the joy of his
6: 2 man to whom G' hath given riches,
2 yet G' giveth him not power to eat
7:13 Consider the work of G': for who
14 G' also hath set the one over
18 he that feareth G' shall come forth
26 pleaseth G' shall escape from her;
29 that G' hath made man upright;
8: 2 and that in regard of the oath of G'.
12 shall be well with them that fear G',
13 because he feareth not before G'.
15 which G' giveth him under the sun.
17 Then I beheld all the work of G',
9: 1 their works, are in the hand of G':
7 for G' now accepteth thy works.
11: 5 thou knowest not the works of G'
9 G' will bring thee into judgment.
12: 7 shall return unto G' who gave it.
13 matter: Fear G', and keep his
14 For G' shall bring every work into
Isa 1:10 give ear unto the law of our G',
2: 3 to the house of the G' of Jacob;
3:15 of the poor? saith the Lord G'
5:16 G' that is holy shall be sanctified
7: 7 Thus saith the Lord G', It shall
11 Ask thee a sign of the Lord thy G';
13 but will ye weary my G' also?
8:10 it shall not stand: for G' is with us.

Isa 8:19 not a people seek unto their G'?
21 and curse their king and their G',
9: 6 The mighty G', The everlasting
10:21 of Jacob, unto the mighty G'.
23 the Lord G' of hosts shall make
24 saith the Lord G' of hosts, O my
12: 2 Behold, G' is my salvation: I will
13:19 be as when G' overthrew Sodom
14:13 my throne above the stars of G':
17: 6 thereof, saith the Lord G' of Israel.
10 forgotten the G' of thy salvation,
13 but G' shall rebuke them, and
21:10 the Lord of hosts, the G' of Israel,
17 the Lord G' of Israel hath spoken
22: 5 by the Lord G' of hosts in the
12 day did the Lord G' of hosts call
14 you till ye die, saith the Lord G'
15 saith the Lord G' of hosts, Go,
24:15 the name of the Lord G' of Israel
25: 1 O Lord, thou art my G'; I will exalt
8 the Lord G' will wipe away tears
9 in that day, Lo, this is our G';
26: 1 salvation will G' appoint for
13 O Lord our G', other lords beside
28:16 the Lord G', Behold, I lay in Zion
22 heard from the Lord G' of hosts
26 G' doth instruct him to discretion,
29:23 and shall fear the G' of Israel.
30:15 saith the Lord G', the Holy One
18 for the Lord is a G' of judgment:
31: 3 Egyptians are men, and not G';
35: 2 and the excellency of our G'.
4 your G' will come with vengeance,
4 even G' with a recompence;
36: 7 We trust in the Lord our G': is it
37: 4 It may be the Lord thy G' will hear
4 hath sent to reproach the living G',
4 which the Lord thy G' hath heard:
10 Let not thy G', in whom thou
16 O Lord of hosts, G' of Israel,
16 thou art the G', even thou alone,
17 hath sent to reproach the living G'.
20 Now therefore, O Lord our G', save
21 Thus saith the Lord G' of Israel,
38 in the house of Nisroch his g',
38: 5 the G' of David thy father, I have
40: 1 comfort ye my people, saith your G'.
3 in the desert a highway for our G'.
8 but the word of our G' shall stand
9 the cities of Judah, Behold your G'!
10 Lord G' will come with strong
18 To whom then will ye liken G'?
27 is passed over from my G'?
28 G', the Lord, the Creator
41:10 be not dismayed; for I am thy G':
13 I the Lord thy G' will hold thy
17 the G' of Israel will not forsake
42: 5 Thus saith G' the Lord, he that
43: 3 For I am the Lord thy G', the Holy
10 before me there was no G' formed,
12 there was no strange g' among you:
12 saith the Lord, that I am G'.
44: 6 and beside me there is no G'.
8 Is there a G' beside me? yea,
8 there is no G'; I know not any.
10 Who hath formed a g', or molten
15 he maketh a g', and worshippeth it;
17 the residue thereof he maketh a g',
17 Deliver me; for thou art my g'.
45: 3 by thy name, am the G' of Israel.
5 there is no G' beside me: I girded
14 Surely G' is in thee; and there is
14 there is none else, there is no G'.
15 Verily thou art a G' that hidest
15 thyself, O G' of Israel, the Saviour.
18 G' himself that formed the earth
20 pray unto a g' that cannot save.
21 there is no G' else beside me;
21 a just G' and a Saviour;
22 for I am G', and there is none else.
46: 6 he maketh it a g': they fall down
9 for I am G', and there is none else;
9 I am G', and there is none like me,
48: 1 make mention of the G' of Israel,
2 themselves upon the G' of Israel;
16 now the Lord G', and his Spirit,
17 I am the Lord thy G' which
49: 4 and my work with my G'.
5 and my G' shall be my strength.
22 saith the Lord G', Behold, I will
50: 4 The Lord G' hath given me the
5 Lord G' hath opened mine ear,
7 the Lord G' will help me;
9 the Lord G' will help me; who is
10 and stay upon his G'.
51:15 But I am the Lord thy G',
20 of the Lord, the rebuke of thy G'.
22 and thy G' that pleadeth the cause
52: 4 saith the Lord G', My people
7 saith unto Zion, Thy G' reigneth!
10 shall see the salvation of our G'.
12 and the G' of Israel will be your
53: 4 stricken, smitten of G', and afflicted
54: 5 The G' of the whole earth shall he
6 thou wast refused, saith thy G'.
55: 5 because of the Lord thy G', and for
7 and to our G', for he will abundantly
56: 8 The Lord G' which gathereth
57:21 peace, saith my G', to the wicked.
58: 2 not the ordinance of their G':
2 take delight in approaching to G'.
59: 2 separated between you and your G',
13 and departing away from our G',
60: 9 unto the name of the Lord thy G',
19 and thy G' thy glory.
61: 1 Spirit of the Lord G' is upon me;

Isa 61: 2 the day of vengeance of our G';
6 call you the Ministers of our G':
10 my soul shall be joyful in my G';
11 Lord G' will cause righteousness
62: 3 royal diadem in the hand of thy G'.
5 so shall thy G' rejoice over thee.
64: 4 neither hath the eye seen, O G',
65:13 saith the Lord G', Behold, my
15 the Lord G' shall slay thee, and
16 bless himself in the G' of truth;
16 shall swear by the G' of truth;
66: 9 and shut the womb? saith thy G'.
Jer 1: 6 Lord G'! behold, I cannot speak:
2:17 forsaken the Lord thy G', when
19 hast forsaken the Lord thy G',
19 is not in thee, saith the Lord G',
22 before me, saith the Lord G'.
3:13 against the Lord thy G',
21 have forgotten the Lord their G'.
22 for thou art the Lord our G'.
23 our G' is the salvation of Israel.
25 sinned against the Lord our G',
25 the voice of the Lord our G'.
4:10 Then said I, Ah, Lord G'!
5: 4 nor the judgment of their G'.
5 and the judgment of their G': but
14 thus saith the Lord G' of hosts,
19 Wherefore doeth the Lord our G'
24 Let us now fear the Lord our G',
7: 3 the Lord of hosts, the G' of Israel,
20 saith the Lord G'; Behold, mine
21 the Lord of hosts, the G' of Israel;
23 my voice, and I will be your G',
28 not the voice of the Lord their G',
8:14 for the Lord our G' hath put us
9:15 the Lord of hosts, the G' of Israel;
10:10 But the Lord is the true G',
10 he is the living G', and an
11: 3 saith the Lord G' of Israel; Cursed
4 my people, and I will be your G':
13:12 saith the Lord G' of Israel, Every
16 Give glory to the Lord your G',
14:13 Ah, Lord G'! behold, the prophets
22 art not thou he, O Lord our G'?
15:16 by thy name, O Lord G' of hosts.
16: 9 the Lord of hosts, the G' of Israel;
10 committed against the Lord our G'?
19: 3, 15 Lord of hosts, the G' of Israel;
21: 4 saith the Lord G' of Israel; Behold,
22: 9 the covenant of the Lord their G',
23: 2 saith the Lord G' of Israel against
23 Am I a G' at hand, saith the Lord,
23 and not a G' afar off?
36 perverted the words of the living G',
36 of the Lord of hosts our G'.
24: 5 saith the Lord, the G' of Israel; Like
7 and I will be their G': for they shall
25:15 saith the Lord, G' of Israel unto me;
27 the Lord of hosts, the G' of Israel;
26:13 obey the voice of the Lord your G';
16 in the name of the Lord our G'.
27: 4 the Lord of hosts, the G' of Israel;
21 the Lord of hosts, the G' of Israel,
28: 2 speaketh the Lord of hosts, the G'
14 the Lord of hosts, the G' of Israel;
29: 4 the Lord of hosts, the G' of Israel,
8 the Lord of hosts, the G' of Israel;
21 the Lord of hosts, the G' of Israel,
25 speaketh the Lord of hosts, the G'
30: 2 speaketh the Lord G' of Israel,
9 they shall serve the Lord their G',
22 my people, and I will be your G'.
31: 1 will I be the G' of all the families
6 up to Zion unto the Lord our G'.
18 for thou art the Lord my G'.
23 the Lord of hosts, the G' of Israel;
33 and will be their G', and they shall
32:14 the Lord of hosts, the G' of Israel;
15 the Lord of hosts, the G' of Israel;
17 Ah, Lord G'! behold, thou hast
18 the Great, the Mighty G', the Lord
25 hast said unto me, O Lord G',
27 I am the Lord, the G' of all flesh:
36 thus saith the Lord, the G' of Israel,
38 my people, and I will be their G':
33: 4 thus saith the Lord, the G' of Israel,
34: 2 saith the Lord, the G' of Israel; Go
13 saith the Lord, the G' of Israel; I
35: 4 the son of Igdaliah, a man of G',
13 the Lord of hosts, the G' of Israel;
17 thus saith the Lord G' of hosts,
17 the G' of Israel; Behold, I will
18, 19 Lord of hosts, the G' of Israel;
37: 3 Pray now unto the Lord our G' for
7 the Lord, the G' of Israel; Thus
38:17 thus saith the Lord, the G' of hosts,
17 the G' of Israel; If thou wilt
39:16 the Lord of hosts, the G' of Israel;
40: 2 The Lord thy G' hath pronounced
42: 2 pray for us unto the Lord thy G',
3 That the Lord thy G' may shew us
4 I will pray unto the Lord your G'
5 the Lord thy G' shall send thee
6 obey the voice of the Lord our G',
6 obey the voice of the Lord our G'.
9 saith the Lord, the G' of Israel, unto
13 obey the voice of the Lord your G',
15, 18 Lord of hosts, the G' of Israel;
20 ye sent me unto the Lord your G',
20 Pray for us unto the Lord our G';
20 unto all that the Lord our G' shall
21 the voice of the Lord your G',
43: 1 all the words of the Lord their G',
1 the Lord their G' had sent him to
2 the Lord our G' hath not sent thee
10 the Lord of hosts, the G' of Israel;

Jer 44: 2 the Lord of hosts, the G' of Israel;
7 thus saith the Lord, the G' of hosts,
7 the G' of Israel; Wherefore
11 the Lord of hosts, the G' of Israel;
25 the Lord of hosts, the G' of Israel,
26 Egypt, saying, The Lord G' liveth.
45: 2 Lord, the G' of Israel, unto thee,
46:10 the day of the Lord G' of hosts,
10 for the Lord G' of hosts hath a
25 The Lord of hosts, the G' of Israel,
48: 1 the Lord of hosts, the G' of Israel;
49: 5 upon thee, saith the Lord G' of
50: 4 go, and seek the Lord their G'.
18 the Lord of hosts, the G' of Israel;
25 work of the Lord G' of hosts,
28 vengeance of the Lord our G',
31 most proud, saith the Lord G' of
40 As G' overthrew Sodom and
51: 5 nor Judah of his G', of the Lord of
10 Zion the work of the Lord our G'.
33 the Lord of hosts, the G' of Israel;
56 for the Lord G' of recompences
La 3:41 our heart with our hands unto G'
Eze 1: 1 opened, and I saw visions of G'.
2: 4 them, Thus saith the Lord G'.
3:11 saith the Lord G'; whether they
27 saith the Lord G'; He that
4:14 Ah Lord G'! behold, my soul
5: 5 saith the Lord G'; This is
7 saith the Lord G'; Because ye
8 saith the Lord G'; Behold, I,
11 as I live, saith the Lord G';
6: 3 hear the word of the Lord G';
3 Thus saith the Lord G' to the
11 saith the Lord G'; Smite with
7: 2 of man, thus saith the Lord G'
5 saith the Lord G'; An evil, an
8: 1 the hand of the Lord G' fell there
3 in the visions of G' to Jerusalem,
4 glory of the G' of Israel was there,
9: 3 glory of the G' of Israel was gone
8 Ah Lord G'! wilt thou destroy
10: 5 as the voice of the Almighty G'
19 glory of the G' of Israel was over
20 I saw under the G' of Israel by the
11: 7 saith the Lord G'; Your slain
8 sword upon you, saith the Lord G'.
13 loud voice, and said, Ah Lord G'!
16 saith the Lord G'; Although I
17 saith the Lord G'; I will even
20 my people, and I will be their G'.
21 own heads, saith the Lord G'.
22 the glory of the G' of Israel
24 in a vision by the Spirit of G'
12:10 saith the Lord G'; This burden
19 the Lord G' of the inhabitants of
23 saith the Lord G'; I will make
25 will perform it, saith the Lord G'.
28 saith the Lord G'; There shall
28 shall be done, saith the Lord G'.
13: 3 said the Lord G'; Woe unto the
8 saith the Lord G'; Because ye
8 against you, saith the Lord G'.
9 shall know that I am the Lord G'.
13 saith the Lord G'; I will even
16 is no peace, saith the Lord G'.
18 saith the Lord G'; Woe to the
20 saith the Lord G'; Behold, I am
14: 4 saith the Lord G'; Every man of
6 saith the Lord G'; Repent, and
11 I may be their G', saith the Lord
11 may be their..., saith the Lord G'.
14 righteousness, saith the Lord G'.
16 saith the Lord G', they shall
18 as I live, saith the Lord G', they
20 in it, as I live, saith the Lord G',
21 saith the Lord G'; How much
23 have done in it, saith the Lord G'.
15: 6 saith the Lord G'; As the vine
8 a trespass, saith the Lord G'.
16: 3 saith the Lord G' unto Jerusalem;
8 saith the Lord G', and thou
14 put upon thee, saith the Lord G'.
19 thus it was, saith the Lord G'.
23 woe unto thee! saith the Lord G';)
30 is thine heart, saith the Lord G',
36 saith the Lord G'; Because thy
43 thine head, saith the Lord G':
48 saith the Lord G', Sodom thy
59 saith the Lord G'; I will even deal
63 thou hast done, saith the Lord G'.
17: 3 saith the Lord G'; A great eagle
9 saith the Lord G'; Shall it prosper?
16 saith the Lord G', surely in the
19 saith the Lord G'; As I live,
22 saith the Lord G'; I will also
18: 3 saith the Lord G', ye shall not
9 surely live, saith the Lord G'.
23 should die? saith the Lord G':
30 to his ways, saith the Lord G'.
32 that dieth, saith the Lord G':
20: 3 saith the Lord G'; Are ye come
3 saith the Lord G', I will not be
5 saith the Lord G'; In the day
5 saying, I am the Lord your G';
7 of Egypt: I am the Lord your G'.
19 I am the Lord your G'; walk in my
20 know that I am the Lord your G'.
27 saith the Lord G'; Yet in this
30 saith the Lord G'; Are ye polluted
31 As I live, saith the Lord G', I will
33 saith the Lord G', surely with a
36 plead with you, saith the Lord G'.
39 saith the Lord G'; Go ye, serve
40 height of Israel, saith the Lord G',
44 house of Israel, saith the Lord G'.

Eze 20:47 saith the Lord G'; Behold, I will
49 Ah Lord G'! they say of me, Doth
21: 7 to pass: saith the Lord G'.
13 be no more, saith the Lord G'.
24 saith the Lord G'; Because ye
26 saith the Lord G'; Remove the
28 saith the Lord G' concerning the
22: 3 saith the Lord G', The city
12 forgotten me, saith the Lord G'.
19 saith the Lord G'; Because ye are
28 saith the Lord G', when the Lord
31 their heads, saith the Lord G'.
23:22, 28 saith the Lord G'; Behold, I
32 saith the Lord G'; Thou shalt
34 have spoken it, saith the Lord G'.
35 saith the Lord G'; Because thou
46 saith the Lord G'; I will bring up
49 shall know that I am the Lord G'.
24: 3 saith the Lord G'; Set on a pot,
6, 9 saith the Lord G'; Woe to the
14 judge thee, saith the Lord G'.
21 saith the Lord G'; Behold, I will
24 shall know that I am the Lord G'.
25: 3 Hear the word of the Lord G';
3 the Lord G'; Because thou saidst,
6 the Lord G'; Because thou hast
8 the Lord G'; Because that Moab
12 the Lord G'; Because that Edom
13 saith the Lord G'; I will also
14 my vengeance, saith the Lord G'.
15 saith the Lord G'; Because the
16 saith the Lord G'; Behold, I will
26: 3 saith the Lord G'; Behold, I am
5 have spoken it, saith the Lord G';
7 saith the Lord G'; Behold, I will
14 have spoken it, saith the Lord G'.
15 saith the Lord G' to Tyrus; Shall
19 saith the Lord G'; When I shall
21 found again, saith the Lord G'.
27: 3 saith the Lord G'; O Tyrus, thou
28: 2 saith the Lord G'; Because thine
2 and thou hast said, I am a G',
2 I sit in the seat of G', in the midst
2 thou art a man, and not G', though
2 set thine heart as the heart of G':
6 saith the Lord G'; Because thou
6 set thine heart as the heart of G';
9 him that slayeth thee, I am G'?
9 but thou shalt be a man, and no G',
10 have spoken it, saith the Lord G'
12 said the Lord G'; Thou sealest
13 been in Eden the garden of G';
14 wast upon the holy mountain of G';
16 profane out of the mountain of G':
22 saith the Lord G'; Behold, I am
24 shall know that I am the Lord G'.
25 saith the Lord G'; When I shall
26 know that I am the Lord their G'.
29: 3 saith the Lord G'; Behold, I am
8 saith the Lord G'; Behold, I will
13 saith the Lord G'; At the end of
16 shall know that I am the Lord G'.
19 saith the Lord G'; Behold, I will
20 wrought for me, saith the Lord G'.
30: 2 saith the Lord G'; Howl ye, Woe
6 by the sword, saith the Lord G'.
10 the Lord G'; I will also make
13 the Lord G'; I will also destroy
22 saith the Lord G'; Behold, I am
31: 8 The cedars in the garden of G'
8 nor any tree in the garden of G'
9 that were in the garden of G',
10 said the Lord G'; Because thou
15 saith the Lord G'; In the day
18 his multitude, saith the Lord G'.
32: 3 Thus saith the Lord G'; I will
8 upon thy land, saith the Lord G'.
11 saith the Lord G'; The sword of
14 to run like oil, saith the Lord G'.
16 her multitude, saith the Lord G'.
31 by the sword, saith the Lord G'.
32 his multitude, saith the Lord G'.
33:11 As I live, saith the Lord G', I
25 thus saith the Lord G'; Ye eat
27 saith the Lord G'; As I live,
34: 2 the Lord G' unto the shepherds;
8 As I live, saith the Lord G', surely
10 Lord G'; Behold, I am against
11 the Lord G'; Behold, I, even I,
15 to lie down, saith the Lord G'.
17 saith the Lord G'; Behold, I judge
20 saith the Lord G' unto them;
24 And I the Lord will be their G',
30 they know that I the Lord their G'
30 are my people, saith the Lord G',
31 are men, and I am your G',
31 and I am...saith the Lord G'.
35: 3 saith the Lord G'; Behold, O
6 saith the Lord G', I will prepare
11 saith the Lord G', I will even do
14 saith the Lord G'; When the
36: 2 saith the Lord G'; Because the
3 saith the Lord G'; Because they
4 hear the word of the Lord G';
4 the Lord G' to the mountains
5 saith the Lord G'; Surely in the
6 saith the Lord G'; Behold, I have
7 saith the Lord G'; I have lifted
13 saith the Lord G'; Because they
14 nations...more, saith the Lord G'.
15 fall any more, saith the Lord G'.
22 saith the Lord G'; I do not this
23 am the Lord, saith the Lord G',
28 my people, and I will be your G'.
32 sakes do I this, saith the Lord G',
33 saith the Lord G'; In the day

Eze 36:37 saith the Lord G·; I will yet
37: 3 And I answered, O Lord G·,
5 the Lord G· unto these bones;
9 saith the Lord G·; Come from
12 saith the Lord G·; Behold, O
19 saith the Lord G·; Behold, I will
21 saith the Lord G·; Behold, I will
23 my people, and I will be their G·.
27 I will be their G·, and they shall be
38: 3 saith the Lord G·; Behold, I am
10 saith the Lord G·; It shall also
14 saith the Lord G·; In that day
17 saith the Lord G·; Art thou he
18 land of Israel, saith the Lord G·,
21 my mountains, saith the Lord G·:
39: 1 saith the Lord G·; Behold I am
5 have spoken it, saith the Lord G·.
8 and it is done, saith the Lord G·;
10 robbed them, saith the Lord G·.
13 be glorified, saith the Lord G·.
17 saith the Lord G·; Speak unto
20 all men of war, saith the Lord G·.
22 I am the Lord their G· from that
25 saith the Lord G·; Now will I
28 I am the Lord their G·, which
29 house of Israel, saith the Lord G·.
40: 2 In the visions of G· brought he me
43: 2 glory of the G· of Israel came from
18 saith the Lord G·; These are the
19 minister unto me, saith the Lord G·
27 accept you, saith the Lord G·.
44: 2 because the Lord, the G· of Israel,
6 saith the Lord G·; O ye house of
9 saith the Lord G·; No stranger,
12 against them, saith the Lord G·,
15 and the blood, saith the Lord G·:
27 sin offering, saith the Lord G·.
45: 9 saith the Lord G·; Let it suffice
9 my people, saith the Lord G·.
15 for them, saith the Lord G·.
18 saith the Lord G·; In the first
46: 1 saith the Lord G·; The gate of
16 saith the Lord G·; If the prince
47:13 saith the Lord G·; This shall be
23 inheritance, saith the Lord G·.
48:29 their portions, saith the Lord G·.
Da 1: 2 the vessels of the house of G·:
2 of Shinar to the house of his g·;
2 into the treasure house of his g·.
9 G· had brought Daniel into favour
17 G· gave them knowledge and skill
2:18 desire mercies of the G· of heaven
19 Daniel blessed the G· of heaven.
20 Blessed be the name of G· for ever
23 O thou G· of my fathers, who hast
28 is a G· in heaven that revealeth
37 the G· of heaven hath given thee
44 the G· of heaven set up a kingdom,
45 G· hath made known to the king
47 that your G· is a G· of gods,
3:15 who is that G· that shall deliver you
17 G· whom we serve is able to deliver
25 the fourth is like the Son of G·.
26 ye servants of the most high G·,
28 Blessed be the G· of Shadrach,
28 worship any g·, except their own G·.
29 against the G· of Shadrach,
29 is no other G· that can deliver
4: 2 and wonders that the high G· hath
8 according to the name of my g·, and
5: 3 of the temple of the house of G·
18 most high G· gave Nebuchadnezzar
21 knew that the most high G· ruled
23 the G· in whose hand thy breath is,
26 G· hath numbered thy kingdom,
6: 5 concerning the law of his G·.
7 shall ask a petition of any G· or
10 gave thanks before his G·, as he did
11 making supplication before his G·.
12 that shall ask a petition of any G·
16 G· whom thou servest continually,
20 servant of the living G·, is thy G·,
22 My G· hath sent his angel, and
23 him, because he believed in his G·.
26 and fear before the G· of Daniel:
26 for he is the living G·, and stedfast
9: 3 And I set my face unto the Lord G·,
4 I prayed unto the Lord my G·,
4 O Lord, the great and dreadful G·,
9 To the Lord our G· belong mercies
10 obeyed the voice of the Lord our G·,
11 law of Moses the servant of G·,
13 prayer before the Lord our G·,
14 for the Lord our G· is righteous
15 now, O Lord our G·, thou hast
17 Now therefore, O our G·, hear
18 O my G·, incline thine ear, and hear
19 for thine own sake, O my G·:
20 supplication before the Lord my G·
20 for the holy mountain of my G·;
10:12 to chasten thyself before thy G·,
11:32 do know their G· shall be strong,
36 magnify himself above every g·,
36 things against the G· of gods,
37 he regard the G· of his fathers,
37 nor regard any g·: for he shall
38 the G· of forces: and a g· whom his
39 most strong holds with a strange g·,
Ho 1: 6 And G· said unto him, Call her
7 save them by the Lord their G·,
9 said G·, Call his name Lo-ammi:
9 my people, and I will not be your G·.
10 Ye are the sons of the living G·.
2:23 they shall say, Thou art my G·.
3: 5 seek the Lord their G·, and David
4: 1 nor knowledge of G· in the land.

Ho 4: 6 hast forgotten the law of thy G·,
12 a whoring from under their G·.
5: 4 doings to turn unto their G·:
6: 6 the knowledge of G· more than
7:10 return to the Lord their G·,
8: 2 Israel shall cry unto me, My G·,
6 therefore it is not G·: but the calf
9: 1 hast gone a whoring from thy G·,
8 of Ephraim was with my G·: but
8 and hatred in the house of his G·.
17 My G· will cast them away, because
11: 9 for I am G·, and not man;
12 but Judah yet ruleth with G·, and
12: 3 his strength he had power with G·:
5 Even the Lord G· of hosts; the Lord
6 therefore turn thou to thy G·: keep
6 and wait on thy G· continually.
9 And I that am the Lord thy G· from
13: 4 Yet I am the Lord thy G· from the
4 and thou shalt know no g· but me:
16 she hath rebelled against her G·:
14: 1 return unto the Lord thy G·; for
Joe 1:13 ye ministers of my G·: for the meat
13 withholden from the house of your G·.
14 into the house of the Lord your G·,
16 gladness from the house of our G·?
2:13 and turn unto the Lord your G·:
14 offering unto the Lord your G·?
17 the people, Where is their G·?
23 and rejoice in the Lord your G·:
26 praise the name of the Lord your G·,
27 am the Lord your G·, and none else:
3:17 I am the Lord your G· dwelling
Am 1: 8 shall perish, saith the Lord G·.
2: 8 condemned in the house of their g·.
3: 7 the Lord G· will do nothing, but
8 the Lord G· hath spoken, who
11 saith the Lord G·; An adversary
13 of Jacob, saith the Lord G·,
13 saith the...the G· of hosts,
4: 2 The Lord G· hath sworn by his
5 of Israel, saith the Lord G·.
11 as G· overthrew Sodom and
12 prepare to meet thy G·, O Israel.
13 The G· of hosts, is his name.
5: 3 saith the Lord G·; The city that
14 the G· of hosts, shall be with you,
15 Lord G· of hosts will be gracious
16 Therefore the Lord, the G· of hosts,
26 the star of your g·, which ye made
27 whose name is The G· of hosts.
6: 8 Lord G· hath sworn by himself,
8 saith the Lord the G· of hosts,
14 saith the Lord the G· of hosts;
7: 1 the Lord G· shewed unto me;
2 then I said, O Lord G·, forgive,
4 the Lord G· shewed unto me:
4 the Lord G· called to contend by
5 Then said I, O Lord G·, cease,
6 shall not be, saith the Lord G·.
8: 1 the Lord G· shewed unto me:
3 that day, saith the Lord G·: there
9 that day, saith the Lord G·, that
11 days come, saith the Lord G·,
14 and say, Thy g·, O Dan, liveth;
9: 5 the Lord G· of hosts is he that
8 the eyes of the Lord G· are upon
15 given them, saith the Lord thy G·.
Ob 1 the Lord G· concerning Edom;
Jon 1: 5 cried every man unto his g·,
6 call upon thy G·, if so be that G·
9 I fear the Lord, the G· of heaven,
2: 1 Jonah prayed unto the Lord his G·
6 from corruption, O Lord my G·.
3: 5 the people of Nineveh believed G·,
8 cry mightily unto G·: yea,
9 Who can tell if G· will turn and
10 G· saw their works, that they
10 G· repented of the evil, that he
4: 2 I knew that thou art a gracious G·,
6 the Lord G· prepared a gourd,
7 But G· prepared a worm when the
8 G· prepared a vehement east wind;
9 G· said to Jonah, Doest thou well
Mic 1: 2 Lord G· be witness against you,
3: 7 for there is no answer of G·.
4: 2 to the house of the G· of Jacob;
5 of the name of his g·, and we will
5 in the name of the Lord our G·
5: 4 of the name of the Lord his G·;
6: 6 and bow myself before the high G·?
8 and to walk humbly with thy G·?
7: 7 will wait for the G· of my salvation:
7 salvation: my G· will hear me.
10 Where is the Lord thy G·? mine
17 shall be afraid of the Lord our G·,
18 Who is a G· like unto thee, that
Na 1: 2 G· is jealous, and the Lord
Hab 1:11 imputing this his power unto his g·.
12 from everlasting, O Lord my G·,
12 mighty G·, thou hast established
3: 3 G· came from Teman, and the
18 joy in the G· of my salvation.
19 The Lord G· is my strength, and
Zep 1: 7 at the presence of the Lord G·:
2: 7 the Lord their G· shall visit them,
9 the Lord of hosts, the G· of Israel,
3: 2 she drew not near to her G·.
17 The Lord thy G· in the midst of thee
Hag 1:12 the voice of the Lord their G·,
12 as the Lord their G· had sent him,
14 house of the Lord of hosts, their G·,
Zec 6:15 obey the voice of the Lord your G·.
7: 2 unto the house of G· Sherezer
8: 8 I will be their G·, in truth
23 we have heard that G· is with you.

Zec 9: 7 even he, shall be for our G·,
14 Lord G· shall blow the trumpet,
16 the Lord their G· shall save them
10: 6 for I am the Lord their G·, and will
11: 4 Thus saith the Lord my G·; Feed
12: 5 strength in the Lord of hosts their G·.
8 the house of David shall be as G·,
13: 9 they shall say, The Lord is my G·.
14: 5 and the Lord my G· shall come,
Mal 1: 9 beseech G· that he will be gracious
2:10 hath not one G· created us? why
11 married the daughter of a strange g·.
16 For the Lord, the G· of Israel, saith
17 Where is the G· of judgment?
3: 8 Will a man rob G·? Yet ye have
14 It is vain to serve G·: and what
15 that tempt G· are even delivered.
18 between him that serveth G· and
M't 1:23 being interpreted is, G· with us.
2:12 being warned of G· in a dream that
22 warned of G· in a dream, he turned
3: 9 G· is able of these stones to raise
16 he saw the Spirit of G· descending
4: 3 If thou be the Son of G·, command
4 proceedeth out of the mouth of G·.
6 If thou be the Son of G·, cast
7 shalt not tempt the Lord thy G·.
10 Thou shalt worship the Lord thy G·,
5: 8 pure in heart: for they shall see G·.
9 shall be called the children of G·.
6:24 Ye cannot serve G· and mammon.
30 G· so clothe the grass of the field,
33 seek ye first the kingdom of G·,
8:29 Jesus, thou Son of G·? art thou
9: 8 and glorified G·, which had given
12: 4 he entered into the house of G·,
28 cast out devils by the Spirit of G·,
28 the kingdom of G· is come unto
14:33 Of a truth thou art the Son of G·.
15: 3 the commandment of G· by your
4 For G· commanded, saying, Honour
6 the commandment of G· of none
31 and they glorified the G· of Israel.
16:16 Christ, the Son of the living G·.
23 not the things that be of G·,
19: 6 therefore G· hath joined together,
17 none good but one, that is, G·:
24 to enter into the kingdom of G·.
26 but with G· all things are possible.
21:12 into the temple of G·, and cast out
31 into the kingdom of G· before you.
43 The kingdom of G· shall be taken
22:16 and teachest the way of G· in truth,
21 and unto G· the things that are
29 the scriptures, nor the power of G·.
30 but are as the angels of G· in
31 which was spoken unto you by G·,
32 I am the G· of Abraham,
32 the G· of Isaac, and the G· of Jacob?
32 G· is not the G· of the dead,
37 Thou shalt love the Lord thy G·
23:22 sweareth by the throne of G·, and
26:61 to destroy the temple of G·, and to
63 I adjure thee by the living G·,
63 thou be the Christ, the Son of G·.
27:40 thou be the Son of G·, come down
43 He trusted in G·; let him deliver
43 for he said, I am the Son of G·.
46 My G·, my G·, why hast thou
54 Truly this was the Son of G·.
M'r 1: 1 of Jesus Christ, the Son of G·;
14 the gospel of the kingdom of G·,
15 the kingdom of G· is at hand:
24 who thou art, the Holy One of G·.
2: 7 who can forgive sins but G· only?
12 and glorified G·, saying, We never
26 he went into the house of G·
3:11 saying, Thou art the Son of G·.
35 shall do the will of G·, the same
4:11 the mystery of the kingdom of G·:
26 So is the kingdom of G·, as if
30 shall we liken the kingdom of G·?
5: 7 thou Son of the most high G·?
7 adjure thee by G·, that thou torment
7: 8 aside the commandment of G·,
9 ye reject the commandment of G·,
13 Making the word of G· of none
8:33 not the things that be of G·, but
9: 1 they have seen the kingdom of G·
47 to enter into the kingdom of G·
10: 6 G· made them male and female.
9 therefore G· hath joined together,
14 for of such is the kingdom of G·.
15 shall not receive the kingdom of G·
18 is none good but one, that is, G·.
23 riches enter into the kingdom of G·!
24 to enter into the kingdom of G·!
25 to enter into the kingdom of G·.
27 impossible, but not with G·:
27 for with G· all things are possible.
11:22 saith unto them, Have faith in G·.
12:14 teachest the way of G· in truth:
17 and to G· the things that are God's.
24 scriptures, neither the power of G·?
26 how in the bush, G· spake unto him,
26 saying, I am the G· of Abraham,
26 the G· of Isaac, and the G· of Jacob?
27 He is not the G· of the dead,
27 but the G· of the living:
29 The Lord our G· is one Lord:
30 thou shalt love the Lord thy G·
32 for there is one G·; and there is
34 not far from the kingdom of G·.
13:19 which G· created unto this time,
14:25 drink it new in the kingdom of G·.
15:34 My G·, my G·, why hast thou

M'r 15:39 Truly this man was the Son of G'.
43 also waited for the kingdom of G'.
16:19 and sat on the right hand of G'.
Lu 1: 6 they were both righteous before G',
8 before G' in the order of his course,
16 shall he turn to the Lord their G'.
19 that stand in the presence of G';
26 Gabriel was sent from G' unto a
30 for thou hast found favour with G'.
32 the Lord G' shall give unto him
35 of thee shall be called the Son of G'.
37 G' nothing shall be impossible.
47 hath rejoiced in G' my Saviour.
64 and he spake, and praised G'.
68 Blessed be the Lord G' of Israel;
78 the tender mercy of our G';
2:13 of the heavenly host praising G',
14 Glory to G' in the highest, and on
20 and praising G' for all the things
28 arms, and blessed G', and said,
37 G' with fastings and prayers
40 and the grace of G' was upon him.
52 and in favour with G' and man.
3: 2 the word of G' came unto John
6 flesh shall see the salvation of G'.
8 G' is able of these stones to raise
38 of Adam, which was the son of G'.
4: 3 If thou be the Son of G', command
4 alone, but by every word of G'.
8 Thou shalt worship the Lord thy G',
9 thou be the Son of G', cast thyself
12 shalt not tempt the Lord thy G'.
34 who thou art, the Holy One of G'.
41 Thou art Christ the Son of G'.
43 kingdom of G' to other cities also:
5: 1 upon him to hear the word of G',
21 Who can forgive sins, but G' alone?
25 to his own house, glorifying G'.
26 and they glorified G', and were filled
6: 4 How he went into the house of G',
12 continued all night in prayer to G'.
20 for yours is the kingdom of G'.
7:16 and they glorified G', saying, That
16 G' hath visited his people.
28 in the kingdom of G' is greater
29 justified G', being baptized with
30 council of G' against themselves,
8: 1 glad tidings of the kingdom of G':
10 the mysteries of the kingdom of G':
11 The seed is the word of G'.
21 which hear the word of G', and do
28 Son of G' most high? I beseech
39 how great things G' hath done unto
9: 2 to preach the kingdom of G', and
11 unto them of the kingdom of G',
20 answering said, The Christ of G'.
27 till they see the kingdom of G'.
43 amazed at the mighty power of G'.
60 thou and preach the kingdom of G'.
62 back, is fit for the kingdom of G'.
10: 9 The kingdom of G' is come nigh
11 that the kingdom of G' is come nigh
27 Thou shalt love the Lord thy G'
11:20 But if I with the finger of G' cast
20 no doubt the kingdom of G' is come
28 are they that hear the word of G',
42 judgment and the love of G':
49 said the wisdom of G', I will send
12: 6 one of them is forgotten before G'?
8 also confess before the angels of G':
9 be denied before the angels of G'.
20 But G' said unto him, Thou fool,
21 and is not rich toward G'.
24 G' feedeth them: how much more
28 G' so clothed the grass, which is
31 rather seek ye the kingdom of G';
13:13 was made straight, and glorified G'.
18 what is the kingdom of G' like?
20 shall I liken the kingdom of G'?
28 the prophets, in the kingdom of G',
29 shall sit down in the kingdom of G'.
14:15 eat bread in the kingdom of G'.
15:10 in the presence of the angels of G'
16:13 Ye cannot serve G' and mammon.
15 but G' knoweth your hearts: for
15 is abomination in the sight of G'.
16 the kingdom of G' is preached, and
17:15 and with a loud voice glorified G',
18 give glory to G', save this stranger.
20 when the kingdom of G' should
20 kingdom of G' cometh not with
21 the kingdom of G' is within you.
18: 2 feared not G', neither regarded
4 Though I fear not G', nor regard
7 And shall not G' avenge his own
11 G', I thank thee, that I am not as
13 G' be merciful to me a sinner.
16 for of such is the kingdom of G'.
17 shall not receive the kingdom of G'
19 None is good, save one, that is, G'.
24 riches enter into the kingdom of G'!
25 man to enter into the kingdom of G'.
27 with men are possible with G'.
43 followed him, glorifying G': and all
43 they saw it, gave praise unto G'.
19:11 kingdom of G' should immediately
37 and praise G' with a loud voice for
20:16 heard it, they said, G' forbid.
21 but teachest the way of G' truly:
25 and unto G' the things which be
36 and are the children of G', being
37 calleth the Lord the G' of Abraham,
37 the G' of Isaac, and the G' of Jacob.
38 For he is not a G' of the dead, but
21: 4 cast in unto the offerings of G':
31 the kingdom of G' is nigh at hand.

Lu 22:16 be fulfilled in the kingdom of G'.
18 until the kingdom of G' shall come.
69 the right hand of the power of G'.
70 Art thou then the Son of G'?
23:35 if he be Christ, the chosen of G'.
40 Dost not thou fear G', seeing thou
47 he glorified G', saying, Certainly
51 waited for the kingdom of G'.
24:19 word before G' and all the people:
53 temple, praising and blessing G'.
Joh 1: 1 was with G', and the Word was G'.
2 same was in the beginning with G'.
6 There was a man sent from G',
12 power to become the sons of G',
13 nor of the will of man, but of G'.
18 No man hath seen G' at any time;
29 and saith, Behold the Lamb of G',
34 record that this is the Son of G'.
36 he saith, Behold the Lamb of G'!
49 Rabbi, thou art the Son of G';
51 and the angels of G' ascending and
3: 2 thou art a teacher, come from G':
2 thou doest, except G' be with him.
3 he cannot see the kingdom of G'.
5 cannot enter into the kingdom of G'.
16 G' so loved the world, that he gave
17 G' sent not his Son into the world
18 name of the only begotten Son of G'.
21 that they are wrought in G'.
33 hath set to his seal that G' is true.
34 For he whom G' hath sent speaketh
34 words of G': for G' giveth not the
36 the wrath of G' abideth on him.
4:10 If thou knewest the gift of G', and
24 G' is a Spirit: and they that worship
5:18 said also that G' was his Father,
18 making himself equal with G'.
25 shall hear the voice of the Son of G':
42 ye have not the love of G' in you.
44 honour that cometh from G' only?
6:27 for him hath G' the Father sealed.
28 we might work the works of G'?
29 This is the work of G', that ye
33 For the bread of G' is he which
45 And they shall be all taught of G'.
46 save he which is of G', he hath seen
69 that Christ, the Son of the living G'.
7:17 whether it be of G', or whether I
8:40 the truth which I have heard of G':
41 we have one Father, even G'.
42 If G' were your Father, ye would
42 proceeded forth, and came from G';
47 that is of G' heareth God's words:
47 them not, because ye are not of G'.
54 of whom ye say, that he is your G':
9: 3 that the works of G' should be made
16 This man is not of G', because he
24 Give G' the praise: we know that
29 know that G' spake unto Moses:
31 know that G' heareth not sinners:
31 if any man be a worshipper of G',
33 If this man were not of G', he
35 Dost thou believe on the Son of G'?
10:33 being a man, makest thyself G'.
35 unto whom the word of G' came,
36 because I said, I am the Son of G'?
11: 4 unto death, but for the glory of G',
4 the Son of G' might be glorified
22 whatsoever thou wilt ask of G',
22 G' will give it thee.
27 thou art the Christ, the Son of G',
40 thou shouldest see the glory of G'?
52 children of G' that were scattered
12:43 of men more than the praise of G'.
13: 3 was come from G', and went to G';
31 glorified, and G' is glorified in him.
32 If G' be glorified in him,
32 G' shall also glorify him in
14: 1 ye believe in G', believe also in me.
16: 2 think that he doeth G' service.
27 believed that I came out from G'.
30 that thou camest forth from G'.
17: 3 might know thee the only true G',
19: 7 he made himself the Son of G'.
20:17 and to my G', and your G'.
28 said unto him, My Lord and my G'.
31 Jesus is the Christ, the Son of G';
21:19 by what death he should glorify G'.
Ac 1: 3 pertaining to the kingdom of G':
2:11 tongue the wonderful works of G'.
17 saith G', I will pour out of my
22 a man approved of G' among you
22 G' did by him in the midst of you,
23 counsel and foreknowledge of G',
24 Whom G' hath raised up, having
30 G' had sworn with an oath to him,
32 This Jesus hath G' raised up,
33 by the right hand of G' exalted
36 that G' hath made that same Jesus,
39 many as the Lord our G' shall call.
47 Praising G', and having favour
3: 8 and leaping, and praising G'.
9 saw him walking and praising G'.
13 The G' of Abraham, and of Isaac,
13 and of Jacob, the G' of our fathers,
15 whom G' hath raised from the dead;
18 things, which G' before had shewed
21 which G' hath spoken by the mouth
22 the Lord your G' raise up unto you
25 covenant which G' made with our
26 G', having raised up his Son Jesus,
4:10 whom G' raised from the dead,
19 right in the sight of G' to hearken
19 unto you more than unto G',
21 all men glorified G' for that which
24 they lifted up their voice to G'

Ac 4:24 art G', which hast made heaven,
31 they spake the word of G' with
5: 4 not lied unto men, but unto G'.
29 ought to obey G' rather than men.
30 The G' of our fathers raised up
31 Him hath G' exalted with his
32 G' hath given to them that obey
39 But if it be of G', ye cannot
39 be found even to fight against G'.
6: 2 we should leave the word of G',
7 And the word of G' increased; and
11 against Moses, and against G'.
7: 2 The G' of glory appeared unto our
6 And G' spake on this wise, That
7 in bondage will I judge, said G':
9 into Egypt; but G' was with him,
17 which G' had sworn to Abraham,
25 how that G' by his hand would
32 Saying, I am the G' of thy fathers,
32 thy fathers, the G' of Abraham,
32 G' of Isaac, and the G' of Jacob.
35 the same did G' send to be a ruler
37 the Lord your G' raise up unto you
42 Then G' turned, and gave them up
43 and the star of your g' Remphan,
45 whom G' drave out before the face
46 favour before G', and desired to
46 a tabernacle for the G' of Jacob.
55 and saw the glory of G', and Jesus
55 standing on the right hand of G',
56 standing on the right hand of G'.
59 stoned Stephen calling upon G',
8:10 This man is the great power of G'.
12 concerning the kingdom of G',
14 had received the word of G',
20 hast thought that the gift of G' may
21 heart is not right in the sight of G'.
22 pray G', if perhaps the thought
37 that Jesus Christ is the Son of G'.
9:20 synagogues, that he is the Son of G'.
10: 2 that feared G' with all his house,
2 people, and prayed to G' alway.
3 an angel of G' coming in to him,
4 come up for a memorial before G'.
15 What G hath cleansed, that call not
22 and one that feareth G', and of good
22 was warned from G. by an holy angel
28 G' hath shewed me that I should
31 in remembrance in the sight of G'.
33 are we all here present before G',
33 that are commanded thee of G'.
34 that G' is no respecter of persons:
36 The word which G' sent unto the
38 G' anointed Jesus of Nazareth
38 of the devil; for G' was with him.
40 Him G' raised up the third day,
41 witnesses chosen before of G', even
42 was ordained of G' to be the Judge
46 speak with tongues, and magnify G'.
11: 1 had also received the word of G'.
9 What G' hath cleansed, that call
17 G' gave them the like gift as he did
17 was I, that I could withstand G'?
18 and glorified G', saying, then hath
18 G' also to the Gentiles granted
23 had seen the grace of G', was glad,
12: 5 of the church unto G' for him.
22 the voice of a g', and not of a man.
23 because he gave not G' the glory:
24 word of G' grew and multiplied.
13: 5 they preached the word of G' in the
7 and desired to hear the word of G'.
16 ye that fear G', give audience.
17 The G' of this people of Israel
21 G' gave unto them Saul the son of
23 this man's seed hath G' according
26 whosoever among you feareth G',
30 But G' raised him from the dead:
33 G' hath fulfilled the same unto us
36 by the will of G', fell on sleep, and
37 But he, whom G' raised again, saw
43 to continue in the grace of G'.
44 together to hear the word of G'.
46 the word of G' should first have
14:15 unto the living G', which made
22 enter into the kingdom of G'.
26 to the grace of G' for the work
27 all that G' had done with them,
15: 4 things that G' had done with them.
7 G' made choice among us, that the
8 And G', which knoweth the hearts,
10 Now therefore why tempt ye G',
12 miracles and wonders G' had
14 how G' at the first did visit the
18 Known unto G' are all his works
19 the Gentiles are turned to G':
40 brethren unto the grace of G'.
16:14 which worshipped G', heard us:
17 the servants of the most high G',
25 and sang praises unto G': and
34 believing in G' with all his house.
17:13 word of G' was preached of Paul
23 To The Unknown G'. Whom
24 G' that made the world and all
29 then as we are the offspring of G',
30 ignorance G' winked at; but now
18: 7 one that worshipped G', whose
11 the word of G' among them.
13 to worship G' contrary to the law.
21 return again unto you, if G' will.
26 him the way of G' more perfectly.
19: 8 concerning the kingdom of G'.
11 G' wrought special miracles by the
20 mightily grew the word of G' and
20:21 repentance toward G', and faith
24 the gospel of the grace of G'.

Ac 20:25 preaching the kingdom of *G*.
27 unto you all the counsel of *G*.
28 to feed the church of *G*, which
32 I commend you to *G*, and to
21:19 things *G* had wrought among the
22: 3 and was zealous toward *G*, as ye
14 *G* of our fathers hath chosen thee,
23: 1 in all good conscience before *G*
3 *G* shall smite thee, thou whited
9 let us not fight against *G*.
24:14 worship I the *G* of my fathers,
15 And have hope toward *G*, which
16 void of offence toward *G*,
26: 6 made of *G* unto our fathers:
7 instantly serving *G* day and night,
8 that *G* should raise the dead?
18 from the power of Satan unto *G*,
20 repent and turn to *G*, and do
22 therefore obtained help of *G*, I
29 I would to *G*, that not only thou,
27:23 the angel of *G*, whose I am, and
24 *G* hath given thee all them that
25 for I believe *G*, that it shall be
35 and gave thanks to *G* in presence
28: 6 minds, and said that he was a *g*.
15 he thanked *G*, and took courage.
23 and testified the kingdom of *G*,
28 the salvation of *G* is sent unto
31 Preaching the kingdom of *G*, and
Ro 1: 1 separated unto the gospel of *G*,
4 And declared to be the Son of *G*
7 be in Rome, beloved of *G*, called
7 from *G* our Father, and the Lord
8 thank my *G* through Jesus Christ
9 For *G* is my witness, whom I serve
10 by the will of *G* to come unto you.
16 for it is the power of *G* unto
17 therein is the righteousness of *G*
18 For the wrath of *G* is revealed
19 may be known of *G* is manifest
19 for *G* hath shewed it unto them.
21 Because that, when they knew *G*,
21 they glorified him not as *G*,
23 the glory of the uncorruptible *G*
24 Wherefore *G* also gave them up to
25 changed the truth of *G* into a lie,
26 cause *G* gave them up unto vile
28 to retain *G* in their knowledge,
28 *G* gave them over to a reprobate
30 haters of *G*, despiteful, proud,
32 Who knowing the judgment of *G*,
2: 2 the judgment of *G* is according
3 shalt escape the judgment of *G*?
4 the goodness of *G* leadeth thee to
5 of the righteous judgment of *G*;
11 is no respect of persons with *G*.
13 are just before *G*, but the doers
16 *G* shall judge the secrets of men
17 and makest thy boast of *G*,
23 the law dishonourest thou *G*?
24 For the name of *G* is blasphemed
29 praise is not of men, but of *G*.
3: 2 were committed the oracles of *G*.
3 the faith of *G* without effect?
4 *G* forbid: yea, let
4 let *G* be true, but every man a
5 commend the righteousness of *G*,
5 Is *G* unrighteous who taketh
6 *G* forbid: for then
6 how shall *G* judge the world?
7 truth of *G* hath more abounded
11 there is none that seeketh after *G*.
18 is no fear of *G* before their eyes.
19 may become guilty before *G*.
21 righteousness of *G* without the law
22 Even the righteousness of *G* which
23 and come short of the glory of *G*;
25 Whom *G* hath set forth to be a
25 through the forbearance of *G*;
29 Is he the *G* of the Jews only?
30 Seeing it is one *G*, which shall
31 *G* forbid: yea, we establish
4: 2 to glory; but not before *G*.
3 Abraham believed *G*, and it was
6 whom *G* imputeth righteousness
17 even *G*, who quickeneth the dead,
20 promise of *G* through unbelief;
20 strong in faith, giving glory to *G*;
5: 1 we have peace with *G* through our
2 rejoice in hope of the glory of *G*.
5 the love of *G* is shed abroad in our
8 *G* commendeth his love toward us,
10 were reconciled to *G* by the death
11 we also joy in *G* through our Lord
15 much more the grace of *G*, and the
6: 2 *G* forbid. How shall we,
10 that he liveth, he liveth unto *G*.
11 alive unto *G* through Jesus Christ
13 yield yourselves unto *G*, as those
13 of righteousness unto *G*.
15 but under grace? *G* forbid.
17 But *G* be thanked, that ye were
22 and become servants to *G*, ye have
23 but the gift of *G* is eternal life
7: 4 should bring forth fruit unto *G*.
7 *G* forbid. Nay, I had not
13 *G* forbid. But sin, that it
22 For I delight in the law of *G*
25 I thank *G* through Jesus Christ
25 then I myself serve the law of *G*;
8: 3 *G* sending his own Son in the
7 carnal mind is enmity against *G*:
7 for it is not subject to the law of *G*,
8 are in the flesh cannot please *G*.
9 if so be that the Spirit of *G* dwell
14 many as are led by the Spirit of *G*:

Ro 8:14 they are the sons of *G*.
16 that we are the children of *G*:
17 heirs of *G*, and joint-heirs with
19 the manifestation of the sons of *G*.
21 liberty of the children of *G*.
27 saints according to the will of *G*.
28 for good to them that love *G*, to
31 If *G* be for us, who can be against
33 God's elect? It is *G* that justifieth.
34 who is even at the right hand of *G*,
39 to separate us from the love of *G*,
9: 4 the service of *G*, and the promises;
5 who is over all, *G* blessed forever.
6 word of *G* hath taken none effect,
8 these are not the children of *G*:
11 purpose of *G* according to election
14 Is there unrighteousness with *G*?
14 unrighteousness...? *G* forbid.
16 but of *G* that sheweth mercy.
20 art thou that repliest against *G*?
22 if *G*, willing to shew his wrath,
26 called the children of the living *G*.
10: 1 and prayer to *G* for Israel is, that
2 have a zeal of *G*, but not according
3 unto the righteousness of *G*.
9 *G* hath raised him from the dead,
17 and hearing by the word of *G*.
11: 1 Hath *G* cast away his people?
1 away his people? *G* forbid.
2 *G* hath not cast away his people
2 how he maketh intercession to *G*
4 what saith the answer of *G* unto him?
8 *G* hath given them the spirit of
11 they should fall? *G* forbid.
21 For if *G* spared not the natural
22 the goodness and severity of *G*:
23 for *G* is able to graff them in
29 For the gifts and calling of *G*
30 times past have not believed *G*,
32 For *G* hath concluded them all in
33 the wisdom and knowledge of *G*!
12: 1 the mercies of *G*, that ye present
1 acceptable unto *G*, which is your
2 acceptable, and perfect, will of *G*.
3 according as *G* hath dealt to every
13: 1 For there is no power but of *G*:
1 powers that be are ordained of *G*.
2 resisteth the ordinance of *G*: and
4 For he is the minister of *G* to thee
4 for he is the minister of *G*,
14: 3 for *G* hath received him.
4 for *G* is able to make him stand.
6 the Lord, for he giveth *G* thanks:
6 eateth not, and giveth *G* thanks.
11 every tongue shall confess to *G*.
12 shall give account of himself to *G*.
17 For the kingdom of *G* is not meat
18 serveth Christ is acceptable to *G*,
20 meat destroy not the work of *G*.
22 faith? have it to thyself before *G*.
15: 5 the *G* of patience and consolation
6 mind and one mouth glorify *G*,
7 also received us to the glory of *G*.
8 for the truth of *G*, to confirm the
9 Gentiles might glorify *G* for his
13 Now the *G* of hope fill you with
15 the grace that is given to me of *G*,
16 ministering the gospel of *G*, that
17 in those things which pertain to *G*.
19 by the power of the Spirit of *G*;
30 in your prayers to *G* for me;
32 unto you with joy by the will of *G*,
33 Now the *G* of peace be with you
16:20 And the *G* of peace shall bruise
26 of the everlasting *G*, made known
27 To *G* only wise, be glory through
1Co 1: 1 apostle...through the will of *G*,
2 Unto the church of *G* which is at
3 and peace, from *G* our Father, and
4 I thank my *G* always on your
4 behalf, for the grace of *G* which
9 *G* is faithful, by whom ye were
14 I thank *G* that I baptized none of
18 are saved it is the power of *G*.
20 not *G* made foolish the wisdom
21 For after that in the wisdom of *G*
21 the world by wisdom knew not *G*,
21 it pleased *G* by the foolishness
24 power of *G*, and the wisdom of *G*.
25 the foolishness of *G* is wiser than
25 men; and the weakness of *G* is
27 *G* hath chosen the foolish things
27 *G* hath chosen the weak things
28 are despised, hath *G* chosen,
30 who of *G* is made unto us wisdom,
2: 1 unto you the testimony of *G*.
5 of men, but in the power of *G*.
7 the wisdom of *G* in a mystery,
7 *G* ordained before the world unto
9 which *G* hath prepared for them
10 But *G* hath revealed them unto us
10 things, yea, the deep things of *G*.
11 even so the things of *G* knoweth
11 no man, but the Spirit of *G*.
12 but the spirit which is of *G*; that
12 that are freely given to us of *G*.
14 not the things of the Spirit of *G*:
3: 6 watered; but *G* gave the increase.
7 but *G* that giveth the increase.
9 are labourers together with *G*:
10 According to the grace of *G* which
16 that ye are the temple of *G*, and
16 that the Spirit of *G* dwelleth in
17 If any man defile the temple of *G*,
17 him shall *G* destroy;
17 for the temple of *G* is holy, which

1Co 3:19 this world is foolishness with *G*.
4: 1 stewards of the mysteries of *G*.
5 shall every man have praise of *G*.
8 and I would to *G* ye did reign,
9 *G* hath set forth us the apostles
20 the kingdom of *G* is not in word,
5:13 them that are without *G* judgeth.
6: 9 not inherit the kingdom of *G*?
10 shall inherit the kingdom of *G*.
11 Jesus, and by the Spirit of our *G*.
13 *G* shall destroy both it and them.
14 *G* hath both raised up the Lord,
15 of an harlot? *G* forbid.
19 which ye have of *G*, and ye are
20 therefore glorify *G* in your body,
7: 7 man hath his proper gift of *G*,
15 but *G* hath called us to peace.
17 *G* hath distributed to every man,
19 of the commandments of *G*.
24 he is called, therein abide with *G*.
40 also that I have the Spirit of *G*.
8: 3 But if any man love *G*, the same
4 there is none other *G* but one.
6 there is but one *G*, the Father,
8 meat commendeth us not to *G*:
9: 9 Doth *G* take care of oxen?
21 (being not without law to *G*, but
10: 5 of them *G* was not well pleased:
13 *G* is faithful, who will not suffer
20 sacrifice to devils, and not to *G*:
31 ye do, do all to the glory of *G*.
32 Gentiles, nor to the church of *G*:
11: 3 and the head of Christ is *G*.
7 as he is the image and glory of *G*:
12 by the woman; but all things of *G*.
13 woman pray unto *G* uncovered?
16 custom, neither the churches of *G*.
22 or despise ye the church of *G*, and
12: 3 speaking by the Spirit of *G* calleth
6 it is the same *G* which worketh
18 But now hath *G* set the members
24 but *G* hath tempered the body
28 *G* hath set some in the church,
14: 2 not unto men, but unto *G*:
18 thank my *G*, I speak with tongues
25 he will worship *G*, and report
25 report that *G* is in you of a truth.
28 let him speak to himself, and to *G*.
33 *G* is not the author of confusion,
36 came the word of *G* out from you?
15: 9 I persecuted the church of *G*.
10 But by the grace of *G* I am what
10 but the grace of *G* which was
15 are found false witnesses of *G*;
15 have testified of *G* that he raised
24 delivered up the kingdom to *G*,
28 that *G* may be all in all.
34 some have not the knowledge of *G*:
38 But *G* giveth it a body as it hath
50 cannot inherit the kingdom of *G*;
57 But thanks be to *G*, which giveth
16: 2 in store, as *G* has prospered him,
2Co 1: 1 an apostle...by the will of *G*, and
1 unto the church of *G* which is at
2 and peace from *G* our Father, and
3 Blessed be *G*, even the Father
3 and the *G* of all comfort;
4 we ourselves are comforted of *G*.
9 but in *G* which raiseth the dead:
12 but by the grace of *G*, we have
18 But as *G* is true, our word toward
19 For the Son of *G*, Jesus Christ,
20 For all the promises of *G* in him
20 unto the glory of *G* by us.
21 and hath anointed us, is *G*;
23 call *G* for a record upon my soul,
2:14 Now thanks be unto *G*, which
15 we are unto *G* a sweet savour of
17 many, which corrupt the word of *G*:
17 but as of *G*, in the sight of *G*
3: 3 with the Spirit of the living *G*;
5 but our sufficiency is of *G*;
4: 2 handling the word of *G* deceitfully;
2 man's conscience in the sight of *G*.
4 the *g* of this world hath blinded
4 who is the image of *G*, should
6 For, *G*, who commanded the light
6 of the knowledge of the glory of *G*
7 of the power may be of *G*, and not
15 many redound to the glory of *G*.
5: 1 we have a building of *G*, an house
5 us for the selfsame thing is *G*,
11 but we are made manifest unto *G*;
13 we be beside ourselves, it is to *G*:
18 And all things are of *G*, who hath
19 To wit, that *G* was in Christ,
20 though *G* did beseech you by us:
20 Christ's stead, be ye reconciled to *G*.
21 the righteousness of *G* in him.
6: 1 receive not the grace of *G* in vain.
4 ourselves as the ministers of *G*,
7 by the power of *G*, by the armour
16 hath the temple of *G* with idols?
16 ye are the temple of the living *G*;
16 as *G* hath said, I will be their *G*,
7: 1 perfecting holiness in the fear of *G*.
6 *G*, that comforteth those that are
12 care for you in the sight of *G*
8: 1 of the grace of *G* bestowed on the
5 and unto us by the will of *G*.
16 But thanks be to *G*, which put the
9: 7 for *G* loveth a cheerful giver.
8 And *G* is able to make all grace
11 through us thanksgiving to *G*.
12 by many thanksgivings unto *G*;
13 they glorify *G* for your professed

2Co 9:14 the exceeding grace of G' in you.
15 Thanks be unto G' for his...gift.
10: 4 mighty through G' to the pulling
5 itself against the knowledge of G',
13 G' hath distributed to us, a
11: 1 Would to G' ye could bear with
7 preached to you the gospel of G'
11 I love you not? G' knoweth.
31 G' and Father of our Lord Jesus
12: 2 I cannot tell: G' knoweth;) such
3 I cannot tell: G' knoweth;)
19 we speak before G' in Christ: but
21 my G' will humble me among you,
13: 4 yet he liveth by the power of G'.
4 him by the power of G' toward you.
7 Now I pray to G' that ye do no evil;
11 and the G' of love and peace shall
14 the love of G', and the communion
Ga 1: 1 and G' the Father, who raised him
3 and peace from G' the Father, and
4 according to the will of G' and our
10 For do I now persuade men, or G'?
13 I persecuted the church of G',
15 when it pleased G', who separated
20 behold, before G', I lie not.
24 And they glorified G' in me.
2: 6 G' accepteth no man's person:)
17 minister of sin? G' forbid.
19 the law, that I might live unto G'.
20 live by the faith of the Son of G',
21 I do not frustrate the grace of G':
3: 6 Even as Abraham believed G', and
8 that G' would justify the heathen
11 by the law in the sight of G', it is
17 that was confirmed before of G' in
18 G' gave it to Abraham by promise.
20 not a mediator of one, but G' is one.
21 law then against the promises of G'?
21 G' forbid: for if there had
26 For ye are all the children of G'
4: 4 G' sent forth his Son, made of a
6 G' hath sent forth the Spirit of his
7 then an heir of G' through Christ.
8 Howbeit then, when ye knew not G',
9 now, after that ye have known G',
9 or rather are known of G',
14 but received me as an angel of G',
5:21 shall not inherit the kingdom of G'.
6: 7 G' is not mocked: for whatsoever
14 But G' forbid that I should
16 and upon the Israel of G'.
Eph 1: 1 an apostle ... by the will of G', to
2 and peace from G' our Father, and
3 Blessed be the G' and Father of
17 the G' of our Lord Jesus Christ,
2: 4 But G', who is rich in mercy, for his
8 of yourselves: it is the gift of G':
10 which G' hath before ordained that
12 hope, and without G' in the world:
16 unto G' in one body by the cross,
19 saints, and of the household of G';
22 for an habitation of G' through the
3: 2 of the grace of G' which is given me
7 gift of the grace of G' given unto me
9 of the world hath been hid in G',
10 church the manifold wisdom of G',
19 be filled with all the fulness of G'.
4: 6 One G' and Father of all, who is
13 of the knowledge of the Son of G',
18 alienated from the life of G' through
24 after G' is created in righteousness
30 And grieve not the holy Spirit of G',
32 even as G' for Christ's sake hath
5: 1 followers of G', as dear children;
2 sacrifice to G' for a sweetsmelling
5 in the kingdom of Christ and of G'.
6 cometh the wrath of G' upon the
20 thanks...unto G' and the Father
21 one to another in the fear of G'.
6: 6 the will of G' from the heart;
11 Put on the whole armour of G',
13 unto you the whole armour of G',
17 the Spirit which is the word of G':
23 from G' the Father and the Lord
Ph'p 1: 2 and peace, from G' our Father, and
3 I thank my G' upon every
8 For G' is my record, how greatly I
11 unto the glory and praise of G'.
28 you of salvation, and that of G'.
2: 6 Who, being in the form of G',
6 it not robbery to be equal with G':
9 G' also hath highly exalted him,
11 to the glory of G' the Father.
13 For it is G' which worketh in you
15 the sons of G', without rebuke,
27 but G' had mercy on him; and not
3: 3 which worship G' in the spirit, and
9 the righteousness which is of G' by
14 the prize of the high calling of G'
15 G' shall reveal even this unto you.
19 whose G' is their belly, and whose
4: 6 requests be made known unto G'.
7 And the peace of G', which passeth
9 and the G' of peace shall be with
18 acceptable, wellpleasing to G'.
19 my G' shall supply all your need
20 unto G' and our Father be glory
Col 1: 1 an apostle...by the will of G', and
2 and peace, from G' our Father and
3 give thanks to G' and the Father
6 and knew the grace of G' in truth:
10 increasing in the knowledge of G';
15 is the image of the invisible G',
25 dispensation of G' which is given
25 for you, to fulfil the word of G';
27 G' would make known what is the

Col 2: 2 mystery of G', and of the Father,
12 of G', who hath raised him from the
19 increaseth with the increase of G'.
3: 1 sitteth on the right hand of G'.
3 your life is hid with Christ in G'.
6 wrath of G' cometh on the children
12 as the elect of G', holy and beloved,
15 And let the peace of G' rule in
17 giving thanks to G' and the Father
22 in singleness of heart, fearing G':
4: 3 that G' would open unto us a door
11 unto the kingdom of G', which
12 and complete in all the will of G'.
1Th 1: 1 which is in G' the Father and in the
1 and peace, from G' our Father,
2 We give thanks to G' always for
3 in the sight of G' and our Father;
4 knowing...your election of G'.
9 and how ye turned to G' from idols
9 to serve the living and true G';
2: 2 were bold in our G' to speak unto
2 to speak unto you the gospel of G'
4 we were allowed of G' to be put
4 not as pleasing men, but G', which
5 of covetousness; G' is witness:
8 gospel of G' only, but also our own
9 preached unto you the gospel of G'.
10 Ye are witnesses, and G' also,
12 That ye would walk worthy of G',
13 also thank we G' without ceasing,
13 the word of G' which ye heard of
13 but as it is in truth, the word of G',
14 the churches of G' which in Judæa
15 please not G', and are contrary
3: 2 and minister of G', and our
9 can we render to G' again for you,
9 joy for your sakes before our G';
11 Now G' himself and our Father,
13 in holiness before G', even our
4: 1 ought to walk and to please G',
3 For this is the will of G', even
5 as the Gentiles which know not G':
7 For G' hath not called us unto
8 despiseth not man, but G', who
9 are taught of G' to love one
14 which sleep in Jesus will G' bring
16 and with the trump of G': and the
5: 9 G' hath not appointed us to wrath,
18 for this is the will of G' in Christ
23 the very G' of peace sanctify you
23 and I pray G' your whole spirit
2Th 1: 1 church...in G' our Father and the
2 peace, from G' our Father and the
3 We are bound to thank G' always
4 churches of G' for your patience
5 of the righteous judgment of G',
5 worthy of the kingdom of G', for
6 it is a righteous thing with G' to
8 on them that know not G',
11 our G' would count you worthy of
12 according to the grace of our G'
2: 4 is called G', or that is worshipped;
4 he as G' sitteth in the temple of G',
4 shewing himself that he is G'.
11 G' shall send them strong delusion,
13 to give thanks alway to G' for you,
13 G' hath from the beginning chosen
16 G', even our Father, which hath
3: 5 into the love of G', and into the
1Ti 1: 1 commandment of G' our Saviour,
2 peace, from G' our Father and Jesus
11 glorious gospel of the blessed G',
17 the only wise G', be honour and
2: 3 in the sight of G' our Saviour;
5 For there is one G', and one
5 one mediator between G' and men,
3: 5 he take care of the church of G'?)
15 behave thyself in the house of G',
15 which is the church of the living G',
16 G' was manifest in the flesh,
4: 3 G' hath created to be received with
4 For every creature of G' is good,
5 sanctified by the word of G' and
10 because we trust in the living G',
5: 4 is good and acceptable before G'.
5 trusteth in G', and continueth in
21 I charge thee before G', and the
6: 1 the name of G' and his doctrine
11 But thou, O man of G', flee these
13 give thee charge in the sight of G',
17 but in the living G', who giveth us
2Ti 1: 1 an apostle ... by the will of G',
2 peace, from G' the Father and Christ
3 I thank G', whom I serve from my
6 that thou stir up the gift of G',
7 For G' hath not given us the spirit
8 according to the power of G';
2: 9 but the word of G' is not bound.
15 to shew thyself approved unto G',
19 the foundation of G' standeth sure,
25 if G' peradventure will give them
3: 4 of pleasure more than lovers of G';
16 is given by inspiration of G',
17 That the man of G' may be perfect,
4: 1 G', and the Lord Jesus Christ,
16 I pray G' that it may not be laid
Tit 1: 1 Paul, a servant of G', and an
2 which G', that cannot lie, promised
3 commandment of G' our Saviour;
4 peace, from G' the Father and the
7 blameless, as the steward of G';
16 They profess that they know G';
2: 5 the word of G' be not blasphemed.
10 the doctrine of G' our Saviour
11 For the grace of G' that bringeth
13 appearing of the great G' and our

Tit 3: 4 kindness and love of G' our Saviour
8 they which have believed in G'
Ph'm 3 peace, from G' our Father and the
4 I thank my G', making mention of
Heb 1: 1 G', who at sundry times and in
6 all the angels of G' worship him.
8 Thy throne, O G', is for ever and
9 G', even thy G', hath anointed thee
2: 4 G' also bearing them witness, both
9 that he by the grace of G' should
13 children which G' hath given me.
17 in things pertaining to G', to make
3: 4 but he that built all things is G'.
12 in departing from the living G'.
4: 4 G' did rest the seventh day from
9 therefore a rest to the people of G'.
10 his own works, as G' did from his.
12 For the word of G' is quick, and
14 high priest...Jesus the Son of G',
5: 1 in things pertaining to G', that he
4 that is called of G', as was Aaron.
10 called of G' an high priest after
12 be principles of the oracles of G';
6: 1 dead works, and of faith toward G',
3 And this will we do, if G' permit.
5 have tasted the good word of G',
6 to themselves the Son of G' afresh,
7 receiveth blessing from G':
10 For G' is not unrighteous to forget
13 when G' made promise to Abraham,
17 Wherein G', willing more
18 it was impossible for G' to lie,
7: 1 priest of the most high G', who
3 but made like unto the Son of G';
19 the which we draw nigh unto G'.
25 that come unto G' by him, seeing
8: 5 as Moses was admonished of G'
10 I will be to them a G', and they
9: 6 accomplishing the service of G'.
14 without spot to G', purge your
14 dead works to serve the living G'?
20 G' hath enjoined unto you.
24 appear in the presence of G' for us:
10: 7 written of one,) to do thy will, O G'.
9 Lo, I come to do thy will, O G'.
12 sat down on the right hand of G';
21 high priest over the house of G';
29 trodden under foot the Son of G',
31 fall into the hands of the living G'.
36 after ye have done the will of G',
11: 3 were framed by the word of G',
4 faith Abel offered unto G' a more
4 righteous, G' testifying of his gifts:
5 G' had translated him: for before
5 this testimony, that he pleased G'.
6 he that cometh to G' must believe
7 Noah, being warned of G' of things
10 whose builder and maker is G'.
16 wherefore G' is not ashamed to be
16 ashamed to be called their G':
19 G' was able to raise him up, even
25 affliction with the people of G',
40 G' having provided some better
12: 2 the right hand of the throne of G'.
7 G' dealeth with you as with sons;
15 any man fail of the grace of G';
22 and unto the city of the living G',
23 and to G' the Judge of all, and to
28 serve G' acceptably with reverence
29 for our G' is a consuming fire.
13: 4 and adulterers G' will judge.
7 spoken unto you the word of G':
15 sacrifice of praise to G' continually,
16 such sacrifices G' is well pleased.
20 Now the G' of peace, that brought
Jas 1: 1 James, a servant of G' and of the
5 let him ask of G', that giveth to all
13 he is tempted, I am tempted of G':
13 for G' cannot be tempted with evil,
20 worketh not the righteousness of G'.
27 religion and undefiled before G'
2: 5 Hath not G' chosen the poor of this
19 Thou believest that there is one G';
23 Abraham believed G', and it was
23 and he was called the Friend of G'.
3: 9 Therewith bless we G', even the
9 are made after the similitude of G'.
4: 4 of the world is enmity with G'?
4 of the world is the enemy of G'.
6 G' resisteth the proud, but giveth
7 Submit yourselves therefore to G'.
8 Draw nigh to G', and he will draw
1Pe 1: 2 foreknowledge of G' the Father,
3 Blessed be the G' and Father of
5 Who are kept by the power of G'
21 do believe in G', that raised him
21 your faith and hope might be in G'.
23 by the word of G', which liveth and
2: 4 but chosen of G', and precious,
5 acceptable to G' by Jesus Christ.
10 but are now the people of G':
12 glorify G' in the day of visitation.
15 For so is the will of G', that with
16 but as the servants of G'.
17 Fear G'. Honour the king.
19 if a man for conscience toward G'
20 patiently, this is acceptable with G'.
3: 4 is in the sight of G' of great price.
5 holy women also, who trusted in G',
15 the Lord G' in your hearts: and
17 it is better, if the will of G' be so,
18 that he might bring us to G', being
20 the longsuffering of G' waited in
21 of a good conscience toward G',)
22 and is on the right hand of G';
4: 2 lusts of men, but to the will of G'.

1Pe 4: 6 live according to G' in the spirit.
10 of the manifold grace of G'.
11 let him speak as the oracles of G';
11 as of the ability which G' giveth:
11 G' in all things may be glorified
14 the spirit of glory and of G' resteth
16 let him glorify G' on this behalf.
17 must begin at the house of G':
17 that obey not the gospel of G'?
19 according to the will of G' commit
5: 2 Feed the flock of G' which is among
5 G' resisteth the proud, and giveth
6 under the mighty hand of G',
10 But the G' of all grace, who hath
12 the true grace of G' wherein ye
2Pe 1: 1 through the righteousness of G'
2 through the knowledge of G', and of
17 For he received from G' the Father
21 holy men of G' spake as they were
2: 4 For if G' spared not the angels that
3: 5 that by the word of G' the heavens
12 unto the coming of the day of G',
1Jo 1: 5 that G' is light, and in him is no
2: 5 verily is the love of G' perfected:
14 and the word of G' abideth in you,
17 doeth the will of G' abideth for ever.
3: 1 should be called the sons of G':
2 now are we the sons of G', and
8 Son of G' was manifested, that he
9 is born of G' doth not commit sin;
9 sin, because he is born of G'.
10 the children of G' are manifest,
10 doeth not righteousness is not of G',
16 Hereby perceive we the love of G',
17 how dwelleth the love of G' in him?
20 G' is greater than our heart, and
21 then have we confidence toward G'.
4: 1 the Spirits whether they are of G':
2 Hereby know ye the Spirit of G':
2 Christ is come in the flesh is of G':
3 is come in the flesh is not of G':
4 Ye are of G', little children, and
6 We are of G': he that knoweth G'
6 he that is not of G' heareth not us.
7 for love is of G'; and every one that
7 loveth is born of G', and knoweth G'.
8 knoweth not G'; for G' is love.
9 manifested the love of G' toward us,
9 G' sent his only begotten Son into
10 not that we loved G', but that he
11 if G' so loved us, we ought also to
12 No man hath seen G' at any time.
12 G' dwelleth in us, and his love is
15 that Jesus Christ is the Son of G',
15 G' dwelleth in him, and he in G'.
16 love that G' hath to us. G' is love;
16 dwelleth in G', and G' in him.
20 If a man say, I love G', and hateth
20 G' whom he hath not seen?
21 he who loveth G' love his brother
5: 1 Jesus is the Christ is born of G':
2 the children of G', when we love G',
3 For this is the love of G', that
4 is born of G' overcometh the world:
5 that Jesus is the Son of G'?
9 men, the witness of G' is greater:
9 for this is the witness of G' which
10 He that believeth on the Son of G'
10 he that believeth not G' hath made
10 the record that G' gave of his Son.
11 G' hath given to us eternal life,
12 hath not the Son of G' hath not life.
13 on the name of the Son of G';
13 believe on the name of the Son of G'.
18 whosoever is born of G' sinneth
18 but he that is begotten of G'
19 And we know that we are of G', and
20 we know that the Son of G' is come,
20 This is the true G', and eternal life.
2Jo 3 peace, from G' the Father, and from
9 the doctrine of Christ, hath not G'.
10 house, neither bid him G' speed:
11 he that biddeth him G' speed is
3Jo 11 He that doeth good is of G': but
11 he that doeth evil hath not seen G'.
Jude 1 that are sanctified by G' the Father,
4 grace of our G' into lasciviousness,
4 and denying the only Lord G',
21 Keep yourselves in the love of G',
25 To the only wise G' our Saviour,
Re 1: 1 which G' gave unto him, to shew
2 Who bare record the word of G', and
6 made us kings and priests unto G'
9 for the word of G', and for the
2: 7 in the midst of the paradise of G'.
18 These things saith the Son of G',
3: 1 that hath the seven Spirits of G',
2 found thy works perfect before G'.
12 a pillar in the temple of my G', and
12 write upon him the name of my G',
12 and the name of the city of my G',
12 down out of heaven from my G':
14 the beginning of the creation of G';
4: 5 which are the seven Spirits of G'.
8 Lord G' Almighty, which was, and
5: 6 the seven Spirits of G' sent forth
9 and hast redeemed us to G' by thy
10 hast made us unto our G' kings
6: 9 that were slain for the word of G',
7: 2 having the seal of the living G':
3 sealed the servants of our G' in
10 Salvation to our G' which sitteth
11 on their faces, and worshipped G',
12 and might, be unto our G' for ever
15 are they before the throne of G',
Re 7:17 G' shall wipe away all tears from
8: 2 seven angels which stood before G';
4 before G' out of the angel's hand.
9: 4 not the seal of G' in their foreheads.
13 the golden altar which is before G',
10: 7 mystery of G' should be finished.
11: 1 and measure the temple of G', and
4 standing before the G' of the
11 the Spirit of life from G' entered
13 and gave glory to the G' of heaven.
16 which sat before G' on their seats
16 their faces, and worshipped G',
17 O Lord G' Almighty, which art, and
19 temple of G' was opened in heaven,
12: 5 was caught up unto G', and to his
6 she hath a place prepared of G',
10 kingdom of our G', and the power
10 accused them before our G' day
17 keep the commandments of G',
13: 6 mouth in blasphemy against G',
14: 4 firstfruits unto G' and to the Lamb.
5 fault before the throne of G'.
7 Fear G', and give glory to him;
10 drink of the wine of the wrath of G',
12 that keep the commandments of G',
19 great winepress of the wrath of G'.
15: 1 in them is filled up the wrath of G'.
2 sea of glass, having the harps of G'.
3 the song of Moses the servant of G',
3 are thy works, Lord G' Almighty;
7 vials full of the wrath of G', who
8 smoke from the glory of G', and
16: 1 out the vials of the wrath of G'
7 say, Even so, Lord G' Almighty,
9 and blasphemed the name of G',
11 And blasphemed the G' of heaven
14 of that great day of G' Almighty.
19 came in remembrance before G',
21 men blasphemed G' because of the
17:17 For G' hath put in their hearts
17 the words of G' shall be fulfilled.
18: 5 G' hath remembered her iniquities.
8 is the Lord G' who judgeth her.
20 for G' hath avenged you on her.
19: 1 and power, unto the Lord our G':
4 and worshipped G' that sat on the
5 Praise our G', all ye his servants,
6 the Lord G' omnipotent reigneth.
9 These are the true sayings of G'.
10 worship G': for the testimony of
13 his name is called The Word of G'.
15 fierceness and wrath of Almighty G'.
17 unto the supper of the great G';
20: 4 and for the word of G', and which
6 shall be priests of G' and of Christ,
9 came down from G' out of heaven,
12 small and great, stand before G';
21: 2 coming down from G' out of heaven,
3 the tabernacle of G' is with men,
3 and G' himself shall be with them,
3 be with them, and be their G'.
4 And G' shall wipe away all tears
7 and I will be his G', and he shall be
10 descending out of heaven from G',
11 Having the glory of G': and her
22 Lord G' Almighty and the Lamb
23 for the glory of G' did lighten it,
22: 1 the throne of G' and of the Lamb.
3 the throne of G' and of the Lamb
5 for the Lord G' giveth them light:
6 the Lord G' of the holy prophets
9 sayings of this book: worship G'.
18 G' shall add unto him the plagues
19 G' shall take away his part out of

goddess
1Ki 11: 5 went after Ashtoreth the g'
33 Ashtoreth the g' of the Zidonians,
Ac 19:27 the temple of the great g' Diana
35 worshipper of the great g' Diana,
37 nor yet blasphemers of your g'.

Godhead
Ac 17:29 think that the G' is like unto gold,
Ro 1:20 even his eternal power and G';
Col 2: 9 all the fulness of the G' bodily.

godliness See also UNGODLINESS.
1Ti 2: 2 life in all g' and honesty.
10 becometh women professing g')
3:16 great is the mystery of g': God
4: 7 and exercise thyself rather unto g'.
8 but g' is profitable unto all things,
6: 3 doctrine which is according to g';
5 supposing that gain is g': from such
6 g' with contentment is great gain.
11 follow after righteousness, g', faith,
2Ti 3: 5 Having a form of g', but denying
Tit 1: 1 of the truth which is after g';
2Pe 1: 3 pertain unto life and g', through
6 patience; and to patience g';
7 And to g' brotherly kindness;
3:11 in all holy conversation and g',

godly See also UNGODLY.
Ps 4: 3 apart him that is g' for himself:
12: 1 Help, Lord; for the g' man ceaseth;
32: 6 this shall every one that is g' pray
Mal 2:15 That he might seek a g' seed.
2Co 1:12 simplicity and g' sincerity, not
7: 9 made sorry after a g' manner,
10 g' sorrow worketh repentance
11 that ye sorrowed after a g' sort,
11: 2 jealous over you with g' jealousy:
1Ti 1: 4 questions, rather than g' edifying
2Ti 3:12 all that will live g' in Christ Jesus
Tit 2:12 live soberly, righteously, and g',
Heb 12:28 with reverence and g' fear:
2Pe 2: 9 knoweth how to deliver the g' out
3Jo 6 their journey after a g' sort,

God's
Ge 28:22 set for a pillar, shall be G' house:
30: 2 I in G' stead, who hath withheld
32: 2 he said, This is G' host: and he
Nu 22:22 And G' anger was kindled because
De 1:17 the judgment is G': and the cause
2Ch 20:15 for the battle is not your's, but G'.
Ne 10:29 to walk in G' law, which was given
Job 33: 6 according to thy wish in G' stead:
35: 2 My righteousness is more than G'?
36: 2 I have yet to speak on G' behalf.
M't 5:34 by heaven; for it is G' throne:
22:21 unto God the things that are G'.
M'r 12:17 and to God the things that are G'.
Lu 18:29 for the kingdom of G' sake,
20:25 unto God the things which be G'.
Joh 8:47 that is of God heareth G' words:
Ac 23: 4 said, Revilest thou G' high priest?
Ro 8:33 thing to the charge of G' elect?
10: 3 being ignorant of G' righteousness,
13: 6 they are G' ministers, attending
1Co 3: 9 Ye are G' husbandry,
9 ye are G' building.
23 ye are Christ's; and Christ is G'.
6:20 and in your spirit, which are G'.
Tit 1: 1 according to the faith of G' elect,
1Pe 5: 3 as being lords over G' heritage,

Gods [or GODS]
Ge 3: 5 ye shall be as g', knowing good
31:30 wherefore hast thou stolen my g'?
32 whomsoever thou findest thy g',
35: 2 the strange g' that are among you,
4 gave unto Jacob all the strange g'
Ex 12:12 all the g' of Egypt I will execute
15:11 unto thee, O Lord, among the g'?
18:11 the Lord is greater than all g':
20: 3 shalt have no other g' before me.
23 not make with me g' of silver,
23 shall ye make unto you g' of gold.
22:28 Thou shalt not revile the g', nor
23:13 mention of the name of other g',
24 Thou shalt not bow down to their g',
32 with them, nor with their g'.
33 if thou serve their g', it will surely
32: 1 make us g', which shall go before us;
4 be thy g', O Israel, which brought
8 be thy g', O Israel, which have
23 Make us g', which shall go before
31 and have made them g' of gold.
34:15 and they go a whoring after their g',
15 and do sacrifice unto their g',
16 and they go a whoring after their g',
16 thy sons go a whoring after their g'.
17 Thou shalt make thee no molten g'.
Le 19: 4 nor make to yourselves molten g':
Nu 25: 2 unto the sacrifices of their g':
2 did eat, and bowed down to their g'.
33: 4 upon their g' also the Lord executed
De 4:28 there ye shall serve g', the work of
5: 7 Thou shalt have none other g' before
6:14 Ye shall not go after other g', of the
14 the g' of the people which are round
7: 4 that they may serve other g':
16 neither shalt thou serve their g';
25 The graven images of their g' shall
8:19 walk after other g', and serve them,
10:17 is God of g', and Lord of lords,
11:16 and serve other g', and worship
28 to go after other g', which ye have
12: 2 ye shall possess served their g',
3 down the graven images of their g',
30 enquire not after their g', saying,
30 did these nations serve their g'?
31 hateth, have they done unto their g';
31 have burnt in the fire to their g'.
13: 2 Let us go after other g', which thou
6 Let us go and serve other g', which
7 the g' of the people which are round
13 Let us go and serve other g', which
17: 3 And hath gone and served other g',
18:20 shall speak in the name of other g',
20:18 which they have done unto their g';
28:14 to go after other g' to serve them.
36 there shalt thou serve other g', wood
64 there thou shalt serve other g', which
29:18 go and serve the g' of these nations;
26 For they went and served other g',
26 them, g' whom they knew not, and
30:17 drawn away, and worship other g',
31:16 whoring after the g' of the strangers
18 they are turned unto other g'.
20 then will they turn unto other g',
32:16 him to jealousy with strange g',
17 to g' whom they knew not,
17 to new g' that came newly up,
37 he shall say, Where are their g',
Jos 22:22 Lord God of g', the Lord God of g',
23: 7 make mention of the name of their g',
16 and have gone and served other g',
24: 2 and they served other g'.
14 put away the g' which your fathers
15 whether the g' which your fathers
15 or the g' of the Amorites, in whose
16 forsake the Lord, to serve other g';
20 and serve strange g', then he will
23 strange g' which are among you,
J'g 2: 3 their g' shall be a snare unto you.
12 and followed other g', of the g' of the
17 they went a whoring after other g',
19 in following other g' to serve them,

J'g 3: 6 their sons, and served their g'.
5: 8 They chose new g'; then was war
6:10 fear not the g' of the Amorites,
10: 6 the g' of Syria, and the g' of Zidon,
6 and the g' of Moab, and the g' of the
6 Ammon, and the g' of the Philistines,
13 forsaken me, and served other g':
14 unto the g' which ye have chosen;
16 And they put away the strange g'
17: 5 the man Micah had an house of g',
18:24 taken away my g' which I made,
Ru 1:15 unto her people, and unto her g':
1Sa 4: 8 out of the hand of these mighty G'?
8 these are the G' that smote the
6: 5 from off you, and from off your g',
7: 3 away the strange g' and Ashtaroth
8: 8 forsaken me, and served other g',
17:43 Philistine cursed David by his g'.
26:19 saying, Go, serve other g'.
28:13 saw g' ascending out of the earth.
2Sa 7:23 from the nations and their g'?
1Ki 9: 6 go and serve other g', and worship
9 and have taken hold upon other g',
11: 2 turn away your heart after their g':
4 turned away his heart after other g':
8 incense and sacrificed unto their g'.
10 that he should not go after other g':
12:28 behold thy g', O Israel, which
14: 9 hast gone and made thee other g',
18:24 call ye on the name of your g',
25 and call on the name of your g',
19: 2 So let the g' do to me, and more
20:10 The g' do so unto me, and more
23 Their g' are g' of the hills;
2Ki 5:17 nor sacrifice unto other g', but unto
17: 7 and had feared other g',
29 every nation made g' of their own,
31 Anammelech, the g' of Sepharvaim.
33 served their own g', after the manner
35 Ye shall not fear other g', nor bow
37 and ye shall not fear other g'
38 neither shall ye fear other g'.
18:33 Hath any of the g' of the nations
34 Where are the g' of Hamath, and of
34 where are the g' of Sepharvaim,
35 among all the g' of the countries,
19:12 Have the g' of the nations delivered
18 And have cast their g' into the fire:
18 for they were no g', but the work
22:17 have burned incense unto other g',
1Ch 5:25 a whoring after the g' of the people
10:10 his armour in the house of their g',
14:12 And when they had left their g' there,
16:25 he also is to be feared above all g'.
26 For all the g' of the people are idols:
2Ch 2: 5 for great is our God above all g'.
7:19 go and serve other g', and worship
22 and laid hold on other g', and
13: 8 which Jeroboam made you for g'.
9 be a priest of them that are no g'.
14: 3 away the altars of the strange g',
25:14 he brought the g' of the children of
14 Seir, and set them up to be his g',
15 thou soughtafter the g' of the people,
20 they sought after the g' of Edom.
28:23 sacrificed unto the g' of Damascus,
23 g' of the kings of Syria help them,
25 to burn incense unto other g', and
32:13 were the g' of the nations of those
14 Who was there among all the g' of
17 the g' of the nations of other lands
19 as against the g' of the people of the
33:15 And he took away the strange g',
34:25 have burned incense unto other g',
Ez 1: 7 had put them in the house of his g';
Ps 82: 1 mighty; he judgeth among the g'.
6 I have said, Ye are g'; and all of you
86: 8 Among the g' there is none like unto
95: 3 and a great King above all g'.
96: 4 he is to be feared above all g'.
5 all the g' of the nations are idols:
97: 7 worship him, all ye g'.
9 thou art exalted far above all g'.
135: 5 and that our Lord is above all g'.
136: 2 O give thanks unto the God of g':
138: 1 before the g' will I sing praise unto
Isa 21: 9 images of her g' he hath broken unto
36:18 Hath any of the g' of the nations
19 Where are the g' of Hamath and
19 where are the g' of Sepharvaim?
20 they among all the g' of these lands,
37:12 Have the g' of the nations delivered
19 And have cast their g' into the fire:
19 for they were no g',
41:23 that we may know that ye are g':
42:17 the molten images, Ye are our g'.
Jer 1:16 have burned incense unto other g',
2:11 changed their g', which are yet no g'?
28 But where are thy g' that thou hast
28 the number of thy cities are thy g'.
5: 7 and sworn by them that are no g':
19 and served strange g' in your land,
7: 6 walk after other g' to your hurt:
9 after other g' whom ye know not;
18 pour out... offerings unto other g',
10:11 g' that have not made the heavens
11:10 went after other g' to serve them:
12 go, and cry unto the g' unto whom
13 the number of thy cities were thy g',
13:10 and walk after other g', to serve
16:11 and have walked after other g', and
13 there shall ye serve other g' day and
20 Shall a man make g' unto himself,
20 unto himself, and they are no g'?
19: 4 burned incense in it unto other g',

Jer 19:13 out drink offerings unto other g'.
22: 9 and worshipped other g', and served
25: 6 And go not after other g' to serve
32:29 out drink offerings unto other g',
35:15 and go not after other g' to serve
43:12 in the houses of the g' of Egypt;
13 the houses of the g' of the Egyptians
44: 3 and to serve other g', whom they
5 to burn no incense unto other g'.
8 burning incense unto other g' in the
15 had burned incense unto other g',
46:25 Pharaoh, and Egypt, with their g',
48:35 him that burneth incense to his g'.
Da 2:11 except the g', whose dwelling is not
47 your God is a God of g', and a Lord
3:12 they serve not thy g', nor worship
14 do not ye serve my g', nor worship
18 we will not serve thy g', nor worship
4: 8 in whom is the spirit of the holy g':
9 the spirit of the holy g' is in thee,
18 the spirit of the holy g' is in thee.
5: 4 praised the g' of gold, and of silver,
11 in whom is the spirit of the holy g';
11 like the wisdom of the g', was found
14 that the spirit of the g' is in thee,
23 thou hast praised the g' of silver,
11: 8 carry captives into Egypt their g',
36 things against the God of g', and
Hos 3: 1 look to other g', and love flagons
14: 3 work of our hands, Ye are our g':
Na 1:14 out of the house of thy g' will I
Zep 2:11 will famish all the g' of the earth;
Joh 10:34 in your law, I said, Ye are g'?
35 If he called them g', unto whom
Ac 7:40 Make us g' to go before us: for as
14:11 The g' are come down to us in the
17:18 to be a setter forth of strange g':
19:26 that they be no g', which are made
1Co 8: 5 though there be that are called g',
5 (as there be g' many, and lords
Ga 4: 8 them which by nature are no g'.

God-ward

Ex 18:19 Be thou for the people to G'.
2Co 3: 4 have we through Christ to G':
1Th 1: 8 your faith to G' is spread

goest^

Ge 10:19 Gaza; as thou g', unto Sodom,
30 as thou g', unto Sephar a mount
25:18 as thou g' toward Assyria: and he
28:15 thee in all places whither thou g',
32:17 Whose art thou? and whither g'
Ex 4:21 When thou g' to return into Egypt,
33:16 is it not in that thou g' with us?
34:12 the land whither thou g', lest it be
Nu 14:14 and that thou g' before them,
De 7: 1 land whither thou g' to possess it,
11:10 land, whither thou g' in to possess
29 land whither thou g' to possess it,
12:29 before thee, whither thou g' to
20: 1 When thou g' out to battle against
21:10 When thou g' forth to war against
23:20 land whither thou g' to possess it.
28: 6 shalt thou be when thou g' out.
19 shalt thou be when thou g' out.
21 land, whither thou g' to possess it.
63 land whither thou g' to possess it.
30:16 land whither thou g' to possess it.
32:50 in the mount whither thou g' up,
Jos 1: 7 prosper whithersoever thou g'.
9 with thee whithersoever thou g'.
J'g 14: 3 that thou g' to take a wife of the
19:17 old man said, Whither g' thou?
Ru 1:16 for whither thou g', I will go;
1Sa 27: 8 as thou g' to Shur, even unto the
28:22 strength, when thou g' on thy way.
2Sa 15:19 Wherefore g' thou also with us?
1Ki 2:37 the day thou g' out, and passest
42 the day thou g' out, and walkest
Ps 44: 9 and g' not forth with our armies.
Pr 4:12 When thou g', thy steps shall not
6:22 When thou g', it shall lead thee;
Ec 5: 1 when thou g' to the house of God,
9:10 in the grave, whither thou g'.
Jer 45: 5 prey in all places whither thou g'.
Zec 2: 2 Whither g' thou? And he said
Lu 9:57 follow thee whithersoever thou g'.
12:58 When thou g' with thine adversary
Joh 11: 8 and g' thou thither again?
13:36 Lord, whither g' thou? Jesus
14: 5 Lord, we know not whither thou g';
16: 5 you asketh me, Whither g' thou?

goeth

Ge 2:14 is it which g' toward the east of
32:20 with the present that g' before me,
33:14 as the cattle that g' before me
38:13 father in law g' up to Timnath
Ex 7:15 he g' out unto the water; and thou
22:26 him by that the sun g' down:
28:29 when he g' in unto the holy place,
30 when he g' in before the Lord:
35 when he g' in unto the holy place
Le 11:21 that g' upon all four, which
27 And whatsoever g' upon his paws,
42 Whatsoever g' upon the belly, and
42 and whatsoever g' upon all four,
14:46 that g' into the house all the while
15:32 of him whose seed g' from him,
16:17 he g' in to make an atonement
22: 3 that g' unto the holy things,
4 a man whose seed g' from him;
27:21 when it g' out in the jubile,
Nu 5:29 when a wife g' aside to another

Nu 21:15 stream of the brooks that g' down
De 1:30 your God which g' before you,
9: 3 is he which g' over before thee;
11:30 where the sun g' down, in the
19: 5 As when a man g' into the wood
20: 4 God is he that g' with you, to
23: 9 When the host g' forth against
24:13 when the sun g' down, that he may
Jos 10:10 way that g' up to Beth-horon,
11:17 mount Halak, that g' up to Seir,
12: 7 mount Halak, that g' up to Seir;
16: 1 wilderness... g' up from Jericho
2 And g' out from Beth-el to Luz,
3 g' down westward to the coast
19:12 and then g' out to Daberath,
12 and g' up to Japhia,
13 and g' out to Remmon-methoar
27 and g' out to Cabul on the left
34 g' out from thence to Hukkok,
J'g 5:31 sun when he g' forth in his might.
20:31 one g' up to the house of God,
21:19 highway that g' up from Beth-el
1Sa 6: 9 it g' up by the way of his own coast
22:14 in law, and g' at thy bidding,
30:24 part is that g' down to the battle,
2Ki 5:18 when my master g' into the house
11: 8 be ye with the king as he g' out
12:20 of Millo, which g' down to Silla.
2Ch 23: 7 he cometh in, and when he g' out.
Ezr 5: 8 and this work g' fast on, and
Job 7: 9 so he that g' down to the grave
9:11 Lo, he g' by me, and I see him
34: 8 g' in company with the workers of
37: 2 the sound that g' out of his mouth.
39:21 he g' on to meet the armed men.
41:20 Out of his nostrils g' smoke, as out
21 and a flame g' out of his mouth.
Ps 17: 1 prayer, that g' not out of feigned
41: 6 when he g' abroad, he telleth it.
68:21 such an one as g' on still in his
88:16 Thy fierce wrath g' over me;
97: 3 A fire g' before him, and burneth
104:23 Man g' forth unto his work and to
126: 6 He that g' forth and weepeth,
146: 4 His breath g' forth, he returneth
Pr 6:29 that g' in to his neighbour's wife;
7:22 He g' after her straightway,
22 as an ox g' to the slaughter,
11:10 When it g' well with the righteous,
16:18 Pride g' before destruction, and an
20:19 He that g' about as a talebearer
26: 9 g' up into the hand of a drunkard,
20 no wood is, there the fire g' out:
31:18 her candle g' not out by night.
Ec 1: 5 and the sun g' down, and hasteth
6 The wind g' toward the south, and
3:21 the spirit of man that g' upward,
21 of the beast that g' downward
12: 5 because man g' to his long home,
Ca 7: 9 that g' down sweetly, causing the
Isa 28:19 From the time that it g' forth
30:29 as when one g' with a pipe to
55:11 So shall my word be that g' forth
59: 8 whosoever g' therein shall not
63:14 a beast g' down into the valley,
Jer 5: 6 every one that g' out thence shall
6: 4 the day g' away, for the shadows
21: 9 but he that g' out, and falleth to
22:10 weep sore for him that g' away:
30:23 whirlwind of the Lord g' forth
38: 2 he that g' forth to the Chaldeans
44:17 whatsoever thing g' forth out of
49:17 every one that g' by it shall be
50:13 every one that g' by Babylon shall
Eze 7:14 but none g' to the battle: for my
33:31 heart g' after their covetousness.
40:40 one g' up to the entry of the north
42: 9 as one g' into them from the utter
44:27 in the day that he g' into the
48: 1 one g' to Hamath, Hazar-enan,
Hos 6: 4 as the early dew it g' away.
5 are as the light that g' forth.
Zec 5: 3 This is the curse that g' forth
5 see what is this that g' forth.
6 This is an ephah that g' forth.
M't 8: 9 say to this man; Go, and he g';
12:45 Then g' he, and taketh with himself
13:44 and for joy thereof g' and selleth
15:11 that which g' into the mouth
17 g' into the belly, and is cast out
17:21 this kind g' not out but by prayer
18:12 and g' into the mountains, and
26:24 The Son of man g' as it is written
28: 7 he g' before you into Galilee;
M'r 3:13 And he g' up into a mountain, and
7:19 g' out into the draught, purging
14:21 The Son of man indeed g', as it is
45 he g' straightway to him, and
16: 7 that he g' before you into Galilee:
Lu 7: 8 I say unto one, Go, and he g';
11:26 Then g' he, and taketh to him seven
22:22 the Son of man g', as it was
Joh 3: 8 it cometh, and whither it g':
7:20 devil: who g' about to kill thee?
10: 4 he g' before them, and the sheep
11:31 She g' unto the grave to weep
12:35 knoweth not whither he g'.
Ac 8:26 unto the way that g' down from
1Co 6: 6 But brother g' to law with brother,
9: 7 Who g' a warfare at any time at
Jas 1:24 beholdeth himself, and g' his way,
1Jo 2:11 and knoweth not whither he g'.
Re 14: 4 the Lamb whithersoever he g'.
17:11 and g' into perdition.
19:15 his mouth g' a sharp sword,

Gog See also HAMON-GOG; MAGOG.
1Ch 5: 4 Shemaiah his son, G' his son,
Eze 38: 2 Son of man, set thy face against G',
3 I am against thee, O G', the chief
14 prophesy and say unto G', Thus
16 I shall be sanctified in thee, O G',
18 G' shall come against the land
39: 1 prophesy against G', and say,
1 I am against thee, O G', the chief
11 that I will give unto G' a place
11 and there shall they bury G' and
Re 20: 8 G' and Magog, to gather them

going See also GOINGS.
Ge 12: 9 Abram journeyed, g' on ... toward
15:12 And when the sun was g' down,
37:25 g' to carry it down to Egypt.
Ex 17:12 until the g' down of the sun.
23: 4 enemy's ox or his ass g' astray,
37:18 six branches g' out of the sides
19 branches g' out of the candlestick.
21 to the six branches g' out of it.
Le 11:20 that creep, g' upon all four,
Nu 32: 7 children of Israel from g' over
34: 4 the g' forth thereof shall be from
De 16: 6 at the g' down of the sun, at the
33:18 Rejoice, Zebulun, in thy g' out;
Jos 1: 4 toward the g' down of the sun,
6: 9 after the ark, the priests g' on,
11 g' about it once: and they came
13 the priests g' on, and blowing
7: 5 and smote them in the g' down:
10:11 were in the g' down to Beth-horon,
27 the time of the g' down of the sun,
15: 7 is before the g' up to Adummim,
18:17 against the g' up of Adummim,
23:14 I am g' the way of all the earth:
J'g 1:36 from the g' up to Akrabbim,
19:18 now g' to the house of the Lord;
28 said unto her, Up, and let us be g'.
1Sa 9:11 they found young maidens g' out
27 were g' down to the end of the city,
10: 3 meet thee three men g' up to God
17:20 the host was g' forth to the fight,
29: 6 thy g' out and thy coming in with
2Sa 2:19 in g' he turned not to the right
3:25 know thy g' out and thy coming in,
5:24 thou hearest the sound of a g'
1Ki 17:11 as she was g' to fetch it, he called
22:36 about the g' down of the sun,
2Ki 2:23 as he was g' up by the way,
9:27 at the g' up to Gur, which is by
19:27 I know thy abode, and thy g' out,
1Ch 14:15 thou shalt hear a sound of g'
26:16 by the causeway of the g' up,
2Ch 11: 4 from g' against Jeroboam.
18:34 the time of the sun g' down he
Ne 3:19 against the g' up to the armoury
31 to the g' up of the corner.
32 g' up of the corner unto the sheep
12:37 at the g' up of the wall, above the
Job 1: 7 From g' to and fro in the earth,
2: 2 From g' to and fro in the earth, and
33:24 Deliver him from g' down to the
28 his soul from g' into the pit,
Ps 19: 6 His g' forth is from the end of
50: 1 the sun unto the g' down thereof.
104:19 the sun knoweth his g' down.
113: 3 unto the g' down of the same
121: 8 The Lord shall preserve thy g' out
144:14 there be no breaking in, nor g' out;
Pr 7:27 g' down to the chambers of death.
14:15 man looketh well to his g'.
30:29 four are comely in g':
Isa 13:10 shall be darkened in his g' forth,
37:28 I know thy abode, and thy g' out,
Jer 48: 5 in the g' up of Luhith continual
5 in the g' down of Horonaim the
50: 4 g' and weeping: they shall go,
Eze 27:19 and Javan g' to and fro occupied
40:31, 34, 37 g' up to it had eight steps.
44: 5 every g' forth of the sanctuary.
46:12 after his g' forth one shall shut
Da 6:14 laboured till the g' down of the sun
9:25 the g' forth of the commandment
Ho 6: 3 his g' forth is prepared as the
Jon 1: 3 he found a ship g' to Tarshish:
Mal 1:11 unto the g' down of the same
M't 4:21 And g' on from thence, he saw
20:17 Jesus g' up to Jerusalem took the
26:46 Rise, let us be g': behold, he
28:11 Now when they were g', behold
M'r 6:31 there were many coming and g',
10:32 in the way g' up to Jerusalem;
Lu 14:31 g' to make war against another
Joh 4:51 And as he was now g' down,
8:59 g' through the midst of them,
Ac 9:28 coming in and g' out at Jerusalem.
20: 5 These g' before tarried for us at
Ro 10: 3 and g' about to establish their
1Ti 5:24 g' before to judgment; and some
Heb 7:18 of the commandment g' before
1Pe 2:25 ye were as sheep g' astray;
Jude 7 g' after strange flesh, are set

goings See also OUTGOINGS.
Nu 33: 2 And Moses wrote their g' out
2 journeys according to their g' out,
34: 5 g' out of it shall be at the sea.
8 the g' forth of the border shall be
9 g' out of it shall be at Hazar-enan:
12 g' out of it shall be at the salt sea:
Jos 15: 4 the g' out of that coast were at the
7 the g' out thereof were at En-rogel:
11 the g' out of the border were at the
16: 3 the g' out thereof are at the sea.
8 the g' out thereof were at the sea.
Jos 18:12 g' out...at the wilderness
14 g' out...at Kirjath-baal,
Job 34:21 man; and he seeth all his g'.
Ps 17: 5 Hold up my g' in thy paths,
40: 2 a rock, and established my g'.
68:24 They have seen thy g', O God;
24 even the g' of my God, my King,
140: 4 purposed to overthrow my g'.
Pr 5:21 and he pondereth all his g'.
20:24 Man's g' are of the Lord; how
Isa 59: 8 there is no judgment in their g':
Eze 42:11 their g' out were both according
43:11 thereof, and the g' out thereof,
48:30 these are the g' out of the city
Mic 5: 2 whose g' forth have been from of

Golan (*go'-lan*)
De 4:43 G' in Bashan of the Manassites.
Jos 20: 8 G' in Bashan out of the tribe of
21:27 of Manasseh they gave G' in
1Ch 6:71 Manasseh, G' in Bashan with her

gold See also GOLDSMITH.
Ge 2:11 land of Havilah, where there is g';
12 And the g' of that land is good:
13: 2 in cattle, in silver, and in g'.
24:22 hands of ten shekels weight of g';
35 flocks, and herds, and silver, and g',
53 jewels of silver, and jewels of g',
41:42 put a g' chain about his neck;
44: 8 out of thy lord's house silver or g'?
Ex 3:22 jewels of silver, and jewels of g',
11: 2 jewels of silver, and jewels of g',
12:35 jewels of silver, and jewels of g',
20:23 shall ye make unto you gods of g'.
25: 3 take of them; g', and silver, and
11 overlay it with pure g', within and
11 make upon it a crown of g' round
12 thou shalt cast four rings of g'
13 wood, and overlay them with g'.
17 make a mercy seat of pure g':
18 cherubims of g', of beaten work
24 thou shalt overlay it with pure g',
24 and make thereto a crown of g'
26 shalt make for it four rings of g',
28 overlay them with g', that the table
29 of pure g' shalt thou make them.
31 shalt make a candlestick of pure g':
36 shall be one beaten work of pure g'.
38 thereof, shall be of pure g'.
39 talent of pure g' shall he make it,
26: 6 thou shalt make fifty taches of g',
29 shalt overlay the boards with g',
29 and make their rings of g'
29 thou shalt overlay the bars with g'.
32 of shittim wood overlaid with g':
32 their hooks shall be of g', upon the
37 and overlay them with g',
37 and their hooks shall be of g':
28: 5 shall take g', and blue, and purple,
6 they shall make the ephod of g',
8 g', of blue, and purple, and scarlet,
11 them to be set in ouches of g'.
13 thou shalt make ouches of g';
14 two chains of pure g' at the ends;
15 even of g', of blue, and of purple,
20 they shall be set in g' in their
22 ends of wreathen work of pure g'.
23 upon the breastplate two rings of g',
24 put the two wreathen chains of g'
26 And thou shalt make two rings of g',
27 And two other rings of g' thou shalt
33 and bells of g' between them round
36 thou shalt make a plate of pure g',
30: 3 thou shalt overlay it with pure g',
3 make unto it a crown of g' round
5 and overlay them with g'.
31: 4 to work in g', and in silver, and in
32:24 Whosoever hath any g', let them
31 and have made them gods of g'.
35: 5 offering of the Lord; g', and silver,
22 rings, and tablets, all jewels of g':
22 an offering of g' unto the Lord.
32 to work in g', and in silver, and in
36:13 And he made fifty taches of g',
34 And he overlaid the boards with g',
34 and made their rings of g'
34 and overlaid the bars with g'.
36 and overlaid them with g':
36 their hooks were of g'; and he cast
38 chapiters and their fillets with g':
37: 2 he overlaid it with pure g' within
2 and made a crown of g' to it round
3 And he cast for it four rings of g',
4 and overlaid them with g'.
6 he made the mercy seat of pure g':
7 And he made two cherubims of g',
11 And he overlaid it with pure g',
11 and made thereunto a crown of g'
12 made a crown of g' for the border
13 And he cast for it four rings of g',
15 and overlaid them with g', to bear
16 covers to cover withal, of pure g'.
17 he made the candlestick of pure g':
22 it was one beaten work of pure g'.
23 and his snuffdishes of pure g'.
24 Of a talent of pure g' made he it,
26 And he overlaid it with pure g',
26 also he made unto it a crown of g'
27 And he made two rings of g' for it
28 and overlaid them with g'.
38:24 g' that was occupied for the work
24 the g' of the offering, was twenty
39: 2 And he made the ephod of g', blue,
3 they did beat the g' into thin plates,
5 of g', blue, and purple, and scarlet,
6 inclosed in ouches of g', graven, as
Ex 39: 8 the ephod; of g', blue, and purple,
13 inclosed in ouches of g', in their
15 ends, of wreathen work of pure g'.
16 two ouches of g', and two g' rings,
17 put the two wreathen chains of g'
19 they made two rings of g', and put
25 and they made bells of pure g', and
30 of the holy crown of pure g',
40: 5 thou shalt set the altar of g' for
Nu 7:14 One spoon of ten shekels of g',
20 One spoon of g' of ten shekels,
84 silver bowls, twelve spoons of g':
86 g' of the spoons was an hundred
8: 4 the candlestick was of beaten g',
22:18 me his house full of silver and g',
24:13 me his house full of silver and g',
31:22 Only the g', and the silver, the
50 gotten of jewels of g', chains, and
51 Eleazar the priest took the g' of
52 all the g' of the offering that they
54 priest took the g' of the captains
De 7:25 shalt not desire the silver or g' that
8:13 thy silver and thy g' is multiplied,
17:17 multiply to himself silver and g'.
29:17 idols, wood and stone, silver and g',
Jos 6:19 all the silver, and g', and vessels
24 only the silver, and the g', and the
7:21 and a wedge of g' of fifty shekels
24 the garment, and the wedge of g',
22: 8 silver, and with g', and with brass,
J'g 8:26 and seven hundred shekels of g';
1Sa 6: 8 the jewels of g', which ye return
11 and the coffer with the mice of g'
15 wherein the jewels of g' were, and
2Sa 1:24 ornaments of g' upon your apparel.
8: 7 And David took the shields of g'
10 vessels of g', and vessels of brass:
11 silver and g' that he had dedicated
12:30 weight whereof was a talent of g'
21: 4 We will have no silver nor g' of
1Ki 6:20 and he overlaid it with pure g';
21 the house within with pure g':
21 the chains of g' before the oracle;
21 and he overlaid it with g'.
22 he overlaid with g', until he had
22 oracle he overlaid with g'.
28 he overlaid the cherubims with g'.
30 of the house he overlaid with g',
32 and overlaid them with g', and
32 and spread g' upon the cherubims,
35 and covered them with g' fitted
7:48 the altar of g', and the table of g',
49 the candlesticks of pure g', five on
49 the lamps, and the tongs of g',
50 spoons, and the censers of pure g';
50 and the hinges of g', both for the
51 silver, and the g', and the vessels,
9:11 trees and fir trees, and with g',
14 to the king sixscore talents of g'.
28 from thence g', four hundred and
10: 2 that bare spices, and very much g',
10 hundred and twenty talents of g',
11 that brought g' from Ophir, brought
14 weight of g' that came to Solomon
14 threescore and six talents of g',
16 two hundred targets of beaten g':
16 six hundred shekels of g' went to
17 three hundred shields of beaten g';
17 three pound of g' went to one shield:
18 and overlaid it with the best g'.
21 drinking vessels were of g', and all
21 forest of Lebanon were of pure g';
22 the navy of Tharshish, bringing g',
25 vessels of silver, and vessels of g',
12:28 made two calves of g', and said
14:26 he took away all the shields of g'
15:15 Lord, silver, and g', and vessels.
18 Asa took all the silver and the g'
19 thee a present of silver and g';
20: 3 Thy silver and thy g' is mine; thy
5 silver, and thy g', and thy wives,
7 and for my silver, and for my g';
22:48 of Tharshish to go to Ophir for g':
2Ki 5: 5 six thousand pieces of g', and ten
7: 8 thence silver, and g', and raiment,
12:13 vessels of g', or vessels of silver.
18 g' that was found in the treasures
14:14 And he took all the g' and silver,
16: 8 Ahaz took the silver and g' that
18:14 of silver and thirty talents of g'.
16 Hezekiah cut off the g' from the
20:13 silver, and the g', and the spices,
23:33 talents of silver, and a talent of g'.
35 the silver, and the g' to Pharaoh;
35 he exacted the silver and the g'
24:13 cut in pieces all the vessels of g'
25:15 such things as were of g', in g',
1Ch 18: 7 And David took the shields of g'
10 manner of vessels of g' and silver
11 and the g' that he brought from all
20: 2 and found it to weigh a talent of g',
21:25 hundred shekels of g' by weight.
22:14 an hundred thousand talents of g',
16 Of the g', the silver, and the brass,
28:14 He gave of g' by weight for things
14 by weight for things of g', for all
15 weight for the candlesticks of g',
15 and for their lamps of g',
16 by weight he gave g' for the tables
17 Also pure g' for the fleshhooks,
17 for the golden basons he gave g'
18 the altar of incense refined g'
18 g' for the pattern of the chariot
29: 2 the g' for things to be made of g',
3 own proper good, of g' and silver,
4 Even three thousand talents of g',

1Ch 29: 4 of the g' of Ophir, and seven
5 The g' for things of g', and the silver
7 of g' five thousand talents and ten
2Ch 1:15 made silver and g' at Jerusalem
2: 7 a man cunning to work in g', and in
14 skilful to work in g', and in silver,
3: 4 he overlaid it within with pure g'.
5 which he overlaid with fine g', and
6 and the g' was g' of Parvaim.
7 and the doors thereof, with g'; and
8 and overlaid it with fine g',
9 of the nails was fifty shekels of g'.
9 the upper chambers with g'.
10 and overlaid them with g'.
4: 7 And he made ten candlesticks of g'
8 he made an hundred basons of g'.
20 before the oracle, of pure g';
21 made he of g', and that perfect g';
22 spoons, and the censers, of pure g':
22 the house of the temple, were of g'.
5: 1 the silver, and the g', and all the
8:18 four hundred and fifty talents of g',
9: 1 bare spices, and g' in abundance,
9 hundred and twenty talents of g',
10 which brought g' from Ophir,
13 Now the weight of g' that came
13 threescore and six talents of g';
14 brought g' and silver to Solomon.
15 two hundred targets of beaten g':
15 six hundred shekels of beaten g'
16 shields made he of beaten g':
16 three hundred shekels of g' went
17 ivory, and overlaid it with pure g'.
18 with a footstool of g', which were
20 vessels of king Solomon were of g',
20 forest of Lebanon were of pure g':
21 bringing g', and silver, ivory,
24 vessels of silver, and vessels of g',
12: 9 carried away also the shields of g'
13:11 candlestick of g' with the lamps
15:18 himself had dedicated, silver, and g',
16: 2 Then Asa brought out silver and g'
3 I have sent thee silver and g'; go
21: 3 them great gifts of silver, and of g',
24:14 spoons, and vessels of g' and silver.
25:24 he took all the g' and the silver,
32:27 treasuries for silver, and for g',
36: 3 talents of silver and a talent of g'.
Ezr 1: 4 help him with silver, and with g',
6 hands with vessels of silver, with g',
9 thirty chargers of g', a thousand
10 Thirty basons of g', silver basons
11 All the vessels of g' and of silver
2:69 and one thousand drams of g',
5:14 the vessels also of g' and silver
7:15 And to carry the silver and g',
16 silver and g' that thou canst find
18 the rest of the silver and the g',
8:25 unto them the silver, and the g',
26 and of g' an hundred talents;
27 Also twenty basons of g', of a
27 vessels of fine copper, precious as g'.
28 the silver and the g' are a freewill
30 silver, and the g', and the vessels,
33 and the g' and the vessels weighed
Ne 7:70 thousand drams of g', fifty basons,
71 twenty thousand drams of g', and
72 was twenty thousand drams of g',
Es 1: 6 the beds were of g' and silver,
7 gave them drink in vessels of g',
8:15 with a great crown of g', and with
Job 3:15 Or with princes that had g', who
22:24 Then shalt thou lay up g' as dust,
24 and the g' of Ophir as the stones
23:10 tried me, I shall come forth as g'.
28: 1 a place for g' where they fine it.
6 sapphires: and it hath dust of g'.
15 It cannot be gotten for g',
16 be valued with the g' of Ophir,
17 g' and the crystal cannot equal it:
17 shall not be for jewels of fine g'.
19 shall it be valued with pure g'.
31:24 If I have made g' my hope,
24 or have said to the fine g', Thou
36:19 no, not g', nor all the forces of
42:11 and every one an earring of g'.
Ps 19:10 More to be desired are they than g',
10 yea, than much fine g':
21: 3 thou settest a crown of pure g' on
45: 9 did stand the queen in g' of Ophir.
13 her clothing is of wrought g'.
68:13 and her feathers with yellow g'.
72:15 shall be given of the g' of Sheba:
105:37 them forth also with silver and g':
115: 4 Their idols are silver and g', the
119:72 better unto me than thousands of g'
127 love thy commandments above g';
127 yea, above fine g'.
135:15 of the heathen are silver and g',
Pr 3:14 and the gain thereof than fine g'.
8:10 knowledge rather than choice g'.
19 My fruit is better than g';
19 yea, than fine g'; and my
11:22 a jewel of g' in a swine's snout,
16:16 better is it to get wisdom than g'!
17: 3 the furnace for g': but the Lord
20:15 There is g', and a multitude of
22: 1 favour rather than silver and g'.
25:11 apples of g' in pictures of silver.
12 As an earring of g', and
12 an ornament of fine g', so is a
27:21 the furnace for g'; so is a man
Ec 2: 8 I gathered me also silver and g',
Ca 1:10 jewels, thy neck with chains of g'.
11 We will make thee borders of g'
3:10 bottom thereof of g', the covering
Ca 5:11 His head is as the most fine g',
14 are as g' rings set with the beryl:
15 marble, set upon sockets of fine g':
Isa 2: 7 land also is full of silver and g',
20 his idols of g', which they made
13:12 a man more precious than fine g';
17 as for g', they shall not delight
30:22 of thy molten images of g':
31: 7 idols of silver, and his idols of g',
39: 2 silver, and the g', and the spices,
40:19 spreadeth it over with g', and
46: 6 They lavish g' out of the bag,
60: 6 they shall bring g' and incense;
9 their silver and their g' with them,
17 For brass I will bring g', and for
Jer 4:30 deckest thee with ornaments of g',
10: 4 They deck it with silver and with g';
9 and g' from Uphaz, the work of the
52:19 cups; that which was of g' in g',
La 4: 1 How is the g' become dim!
1 how is the most fine g' changed!
2 sons of Zion, comparable to fine g',
Eze 7:19 and their g' shall be removed:
19 their silver and their g' shall not
16:13 wast thou decked with g' and silver;
17 fair jewels of my g' and of my silver,
27:22 with all precious stones, and g'.
28: 4 g' and silver into thy treasures:
13 emerald, and the carbuncle, and g':
38:13 to carry away silver and g', to take
Da 2:32 This image's head was of fine g',
35 the brass, the silver, and the g',
38 Thou art this head of g'.
45 brass, the clay, the silver, and the g';
3: 1 the king made an image of g', whose
5: 4 and praised the gods of g', and of
7 have a chain of g' about his neck,
16 have a chain of g' about thy neck,
23 praised the gods of silver, and g',
29 and put a chain of g' about his neck,
10: 5 were girded with fine g' of Uphaz:
11: 8 precious vessels of silver and of g';
38 shall he honour with g', and silver,
43 have power over the treasures of g'
Hos 2: 8 multiplied her silver and g', which
8: 4 their silver and their g' have they
Joe 3: 5 ye have taken my silver and my g',
Na 2: 9 take the spoil of g': for there is
Hab 2:19 it is laid over with g' and silver,
Zep 1:18 Neither their silver nor their g'
Hag 2: 8 The silver is mine, and the g',
Zec 4: 2 a candlestick all of g', with a bowl
6:11 Then take silver and g', and make
9: 3 fine g' as the mire of the streets.
13: 9 and will try them as g' is tried:
14:14 shall be gathered together, g', and
Mal 3: 3 and purge them as g' and silver,
M't 2:11 him gifts; g', and frankincense,
10: 9 Provide neither g', nor silver, nor
23:16 shall swear by the g' of the temple,
17 whether is greater, the g', or the
17 temple that sanctifieth the g'?
Ac 3: 6 said, Silver and g' have I none;
17:29 that the Godhead is like unto g',
20:33 have coveted no man's silver, or g',
1Co 3:12 upon this foundation g', silver,
1Ti 2: 9 not with broidered hair, or g', or
2Ti 2:20 not only vessels of g' and of silver,
Heb 9: 4 overlaid round about with g',
Jas 2: 2 with a g' ring, in goodly apparel,
5: 3 Your g' and silver is cankered;
1Pet 1: 7 much more precious than of g'
18 corruptible things, as silver and g',
3: 3 the hair, and of wearing of g',
Re 3:18 to buy of me g' tried in the fire,
4: 4 had on their heads crowns of g'.
9: 7 were as it were crowns like g',
20 devils, and idols of g', and
17: 4 decked with g' and precious
18:12 The merchandise of g', and silver,
16 decked with g', and precious stones,
21:18 and the city was pure g', like unto
21 the street of the city was pure g',

golden
Ge 24:22 the man took a g' earring of half a
Ex 25:25 thou shalt make a g' crown to the
28:34 g' bell and a pomegranate, a g' bell
30: 4 And two g' rings shalt thou make
32: 2 Break off the g' earrings, which are
3 the people brake off the g' earrings
39:20 And they made two other g' rings,
38 the g' altar, and the anointing oil,
40:26 he put the g' altar in the tent
Lev 8: 9 did he put the g' plate, the holy
Nu 4:11 upon the g' altar they shall spread
7:26, 32, 38, 44, 50, 56, 62, 68, 74, 80 One
g' spoon of ten shekels, full of
86 The g' spoons were twelve, full of
J'g 8:24 (For they had g' earrings, because
26 the weight of the g' earrings that he
1Sa 6: 4 Five g' emerods, and five g' mice,
17 these are the g' emerods which the
18 And the g' mice, according to the
2Ki 10:29 the g' calves that were in Beth-el,
1Ch 28:17 and for the g' basons he gave gold
2Ch 4:19 the g' altar also, and the tables
13: 8 and there are with you g' calves,
Ezr 6: 5 also let the g' and silver vessels
Es 4:11 king shall hold out the g' sceptre,
5: 2 held out to Esther the g' sceptre
8: 4 out the g' sceptre toward Esther.
Ec 12: 6 or the g' bowl be broken, or the
Isa 13:12 a man than the g' wedge of Ophir.
14: 4 the oppressed ceased! the g' city
Jer 51: 7 Babylon hath been a g' cup in the
Da 3: 5 down and worship the g' image
Da 3: 7 down and worshipped the g' image
10 fall down and worship the g' image:
12 worship the g' image which thou
14 nor worship the g' image which I
18 worship the g' image which thou
5: 2 commanded to bring the g' and
3 they brought the g' vessels that
Zec 4:12 which through the two g' pipes
12 empty the g' oil ... of themselves?
Heb 9: 4 Which had the g' censer, and the
4 wherein was the g' pot that had
Re 1:12 turned, I saw seven g' candlesticks;
13 about the paps with a g' girdle.
20 and the seven g' candlesticks.
2: 1 midst of the seven g' candlesticks;
5: 8 harps, and g' vials full of odours,
8: 3 having a g' censer; and there was
3 upon the g' altar which was before
9:13 from the four horns of the g' altar
14:14 having on his head a g' crown,
15: 6 their breasts girded with g' girdles.
7 seven g' vials full of the wrath of
17: 4 having a g' cup in her hand full
21:15 had a g' reed to measure the city,

goldsmith See also GOLDSMITH'S; GOLDSMITHS.
Isa 40:19 and the g' spreadeth it over with
41: 7 the carpenter encouraged the g',
46: 6 and hire a g'; and he maketh it

goldsmith's
Ne 3:31 repaired Malchiah the g' son unto

goldsmiths
Ne 3: 8 the son of Harhaiah, of the g'.
32 repaired the g' and the merchants.

Golgotha (*gol'-go-thah*) See also CALVARY.
M't 27:33 were come unto a place called G',
M'r 15:22 they bring him unto the place G',
Joh 19:17 which is called in the Hebrew G':

Goliath (*go-li'-ath*)
1Sa 17: 4 named G', of Gath, whose height
23 Gath, G' by name, out of the armies
21: 9 sword of G' the Philistine, whom
22:10 and g' him the sword of G' the
2Sa 21:19 slew the brother of G' the Gittite,
1Ch 20: 5 slew...the brother of G' the Gittite,

Gomer (*go'-mer*)
Ge 10: 2 sons of Japheth; G', and Magog,
3 And the sons of G'; Ashkenaz,
1Ch 1: 5 sons of Japheth; G', and Magog,
6 the sons of G'; Ashchenaz, and
Eze 38: 6 G', and all his bands; the house of
Hos 1: 3 went and took G' the daughter of

Gomorrah (*go-mor'-rah*) See also GOMORRHA.
Ge 10:19 thou goest, unto Sodom, and G',
13:10 the Lord destroyed Sodom and G',
14: 2 and with Birsha king of G', Shinab
8 and the king of G', and the king of
10 and the kings of Sodom and G' fled,
11 took all the goods of Sodom and G',
18:20 Because the cry of Sodom and G' is
19:24 rained upon Sodom and upon G',
28 he looked toward Sodom and G',
De 29:23 like the overthrow of Sodom, and G',
32:32 of Sodom, and of the fields of G':
Isa 1: 9 we should have been like unto G'.
10 the law of our God, ye people of G'.
13:19 when God overthrew Sodom and G'.
Jer 23:14 and the inhabitants thereof as G'.
49:18 in the overthrow of Sodom and G',
50:40 As God overthrew Sodom and G'
Am 4:11 as God overthrew Sodom and G',
Zep 2: 9 and the children of Ammon as G',

Gomorrha (*go-mor'-rah*) See also GOMORRAH.
M't 10:15 for the land of Sodom and G' in
M'r 6:11 more tolerable for Sodom and G'
Ro 9:29 and been made like unto G'.
2Pe 2: 6 turning the cities of ... and G'
Jude 7 Even as Sodom and G', and the

gone See also AGONE.
Ge 27:30 Jacob was yet scarce g' out from
28: 7 and was g' to Padan-aram;
31:30 though thou wouldest needs be g',
34:17 our daughter, and we will be g',
42:33 of your households, and be g':
44: 4 when they were g' out of the city,
49: 9 the prey, my son, thou art g' up:
Ex 9:29 As soon as I am g' out of the city,
12:32 herds, as ye have said, and be g':
16:14 when the dew that lay was g' up,
19: 1 the children of Israel were g' forth
33: 8 until he was g' into the tabernacle.
Le 17: 7 whom they have g' a whoring.
Nu 5:19 hast not g' aside to uncleanness
20 if thou hast g' aside to another
7:89 And when Moses was g' into the
13:32 land, through which we have g'
16:46 is wrath g' out from the Lord;
21:28 there is a fire g' out of Heshbon,
De 9: 9 When I was g' up into the mount
13:13 the children of Belial, are g' out
17: 3 hath g' and served other gods,
23:23 That which is g' out of thy lips
27: 4 when ye be g' over Jordan, that
32:36 he seeth that their power is g',
Jos 2: 7 pursued after them were g' out,
4:23 before us, until we were g' over:
23:16 have g' and served other gods,
J'g 3:24 When he was g' out, his servants
4:12 the son of Abinoam was g' up
14 is not the Lord g' out before thee?
18:24 and ye are g' away: and what
20: 3 the children of Israel were g' up

Ru 1:13 hand of the Lord is g' out against
15 thy sister in law is g' back unto
1Sa 14: 3 knew not that Jonathan was g'.
17 now, and see who is g' from us.
15:12 him up a place, and is g' about,
12 passed on, and g' down to Gilgal.
20 g' the way which the Lord sent
20:41 And as soon as the lad was g',
25:37 when the wine was g' out of Nabal,
2Sa 2:27 the people had g' up every one
3: 7 Wherefore hast thou g' in unto
22 him away, and he was g' in peace.
23 him away, and he is g' in peace.
24 sent him away, and he is quite g'?
6:13 bare the ark of the Lord had g' six
13:15 Amnon said unto her, Arise, be g'.
17:20 They be g' over the brook of water.
22 one of them that was not g' over
23: 9 the men of Israel were g' away:
24: 8 So when they had g' through all
1Ki 1:25 he is g' down this day, and hath
2:41 Shimei had g' from Jerusalem to
9:16 Pharaoh king of Egypt had g' up,
11:15 the captain of the host was g' up
13:24 when he was g', a lion met him
14: 9 for thou hast g' and made thee
10 taketh away dung, till it be all g'.
18:12 as soon as I am g' from thee,
20:40 was busy here and there, he was g'.
21:18 whither he is g' down to possess it.
22:13 the messenger that was g' to call
2Ki 1: 4, 6, 16 bed on which thou art g' up,
2: 9 when they were g' over, that Elijah
5: 2 Syrians had g' out by companies,
6:15 God was risen early, and g' forth,
7:12 therefore are they g' out of the
20: 4 afore Isaiah was g' out into the
11 had g' down in the dial of Ahaz.
1Ch 14:15 God is g' forth before thee to smite
17: 5 but have g' from tent to tent, and
Job 1: 5 the days of their feasting were g'
7: 4 shall I arise, and the night be g'?
19:10 and I am g': and mine hope hath
23:12 Neither have I g' back from the
24:24 but are g' and brought low;
28: 4 they are g' away from men.
Ps 14: 3 They are all g' aside, they are
19: 4 line is g' out through all the earth,
38: 4 mine iniquities are g' over mine
10 mine eyes, it also is g' from me.
42: 4 I had g' with the multitude,
7 and thy billows are g' over me.
47: 5 God is g' up with a shout, the Lord
51:*title* after he had g' in to Bath-sheba.
53: 3 Every one of them is g' back: they
73: 2 as for me, my feet were almost g';
77: 8 Is his mercy clean g' for ever?
89:34 nor alter the thing that is g' out
103:16 wind passeth over it, and it is g';
109:23 I am g' like the shadow when it
119:176 I have g' astray like a lost sheep;
124: 4 the stream had g' over our soul:
5 proud waters had g' over our soul.
Pr 7:19 he is g' a long journey:
20:14 but when he is g' his way, then he
Ec 8:10 and g' from the place of the holy,
Ca 2:11 is past, the rain is over and g';
5: 6 withdrawn himself, and was g':
6: 1 Whither is thy beloved g', O thou
2 beloved is g' down into his garden,
Isa 1: 4 they are g' away backward.
5:13 my people are g' into captivity,
10:29 They are g' over the passage: they
15: 2 He is g' up to Bajith, and to Dibon,
8 cry is g' round about the borders
16: 8 they are g' over the sea.
22: 1 art wholly g' up to the housetops?
24:11 the mirth of the land is g'.
38: 8 is g' down in the sun dial of Ahaz,
8 by which degrees it was g' down.
41: 3 that he had not g' with his feet.
45:23 the word is g' out of my mouth
46: 2 themselves are g' into captivity.
51: 5 my salvation is g' forth, and mine
53: 6 All we like sheep have g' astray;
57: 8 to another than me, and art g' up;
Jer 2: 5 they are g' far from me, and have
23 I have not g' after Baalim? see
3: 6 is g' up upon every high mountain
4: 7 is g' forth from his place to make
5:23 they are revolted and g'.
9:10 and the beast are fled; they are g'.
10:20 my children are g' forth of me,
14: 2 and the cry of Jerusalem is g' up.
15: 6 thou art g' backward: therefore
9 her sun is g' down while it was
23:15 Jerusalem is profaneness g' forth
19 a whirlwind of the Lord is g' forth
29:16 your brethren that are not g' forth
34:21 army, which are g' up from you.
40: 5 while he was not yet g' back, he
44: 8 land of Egypt, whither ye be g'
14 which are g' into the land of Egypt
28 that are g' into the land of Egypt
48:11 neither hath he g' into captivity:
15 Moab is spoiled, and g' up out of
15 his chosen young men are g' down
32 thy plants are g' over the sea,
50: 6 have g' from mountain to hill,
La 1: 3 Judah is g' into captivity because
5 her children are g' into captivity
6 and they are g' without strength
18 young men are g' into captivity.
Eze 7:10 the morning is g' forth; the rod
9: 3 glory of the God of Israel was g'
13: 5 Ye have not g' up into the gaps,

Eze 19:14 And fire is g' out of a rod of her
23:30 because thou hast g' a whoring
24: 6 and whose scum is not g' out of it!
31:12 people of the earth are g' down
32:21 g' down, they lie uncircumcised,
24 which are g' down uncircumcised
27 g' down to hell with their weapons
30 which are g' down with the slain;
36:20 and are g' forth out of his land.
37:21 whither they be g', and will
44:10 the Levites that are g' away far
Da 2: 5 The thing is g' from me: if ye will
8 ye see the thing is g' from me.
14 which was g' forth to slay the wise
10:20 when I am g' forth, lo, the prince
Ho 4:12 and they have g' a whoring from
8: 9 For they are g' up to Assyria,
9: 1 for thou hast g' a whoring from
6 they are g' because of destruction:
Am 8: 5 When will the new moon be g',
Jon 1: 5 Jonah was g' down into the sides
Mic 1:16 for they are g' into captivity from thee.
2:13 the gate, and are g' out by it:
Mal 3: 7 g' away from mine ordinances,
M't 10:23 shall not have g' over the cities
12:43 unclean spirit is g' out of a man,
14:34 when they were g' over, they
18:12 and one of them be g' astray,
12 seeketh that which is g' astray?
25: 8 oil; for our lamps are g' out.
26:71 when he was g' out into the porch,
M'r 1:19 he had g' a little farther thence,
5:30 that virtue had g' out of him,
7:29 the devil is g' out of thy daughter.
30 she found the devil g' out, and her
10:17 when he was g' forth ... the way,
Lu 2:15 as the angels were g' away from
5: 2 the fishermen were g' out of them,
8:46 that virtue is g' out of me.
11:14 when the devil was g' out, the
24 the unclean spirit is g' out of a man,
19: 7 he was g' to be guest with a man
24:28 though he would have g' further.
Joh 4: 8 For his disciples were g' away unto
6:22 that his disciples were g' away
7:10 when his brethren were g' up, then
12:19 behold, the world is g' after him.
13:31 Therefore, when he was g' out,
Ac 13: 6 when they had g' through the isle
42 were g' out of the synagogue,
16: 6 when they had g' through Phrygia
19 the hope of their gains was g',
18:22 landed at Cæsarea, and g' up,
20: 2 when he had g' over those parts,
25 among whom I have g' preaching
24: 6 Who also hath g' about to profane
26:31 when they were g' aside, they
27:28 when they had g' a little further,
Ro 3:12 They are all g' out of the way,
1Pe 3:22 Who is g' into heaven, and is on
2Pe 2:15 and are g' astray, following the
1Jo 4: 1 false prophets are g' out into the
Jude 11 they have g' in the way of Cain,

good^A See also BEST; BETTER; GOODMAN; GOODS.
Ge 1: 4 God saw the light, that it was g':
10, 12, 18, 21, 25 God saw that it was g'.
31 made, and, behold, it was very g'.
2: 9 pleasant to the sight and g' for food;
9 tree of knowledge of g' and evil.
12 And the gold of that land is g':
17 tree of the knowledge of g' and evil,
18 not g' that the man should be alone;
3: 5 be as gods, knowing g' and evil.
6 saw that the tree was g' for food,
22 to know g' and evil: and now, lest
15:15 shalt be buried in a g' old age.
18: 7 fetcht a calf tender and g', and
19: 8 do ye to them as is g' in your eyes:
21:16 down over against him a g' way
24:12 thee, send me g' speed this day,
50 cannot speak unto thee bad or g'.
25: 8 died in a g' old age, an old man,
26:29 done unto thee nothing but g',
27: 9 fetch me from thence two g' kids
46 what g' shall my life do me?
30:20 endued me with a g' dowry;
31:24, 29 not to Jacob either g' or bad.
32:12 saidst, I will surely do thee g',
40:16 that the interpretation was g',
41: 5 up upon one stalk, rank and g'.
22 came up in one stalk, full and g':
24 thin ears devoured the seven g'
26 The seven g' kine are seven years;
26 and the seven g' ears are seven
35 food of those g' years that come,
37 was g' in the eyes of Pharaoh,
43:28 servant our father is in g' health,
44: 4 have ye rewarded evil for g'?
45:18 I will give you the g' of the land
20 for the g' of all the land of Egypt
23 laden with the g' things of Egypt,
46:29 and wept on his neck a g' while.
49:15 he saw that rest was g', and the
50:20 God meant it unto g', to bring to
Ex 3: 8 unto a g' land and a large, unto
18:17 The thing that thou doest is not g'.
21:34 owner of the pit shall make it g',
22:11 and he shall not make it g'.
13 not make g' that which was torn.
14 he shall surely make it g'.
15 he shall not make it g':
Le 5: 4 to do evil, or to do g', whatsoever
24:18 killeth a beast shall make it g';
27:10 nor change it, a g' for a bad,
10 or a bad for a g':

Le 27:12 value it, whether it be g' or bad:
14 estimate it, whether it be g' or bad:
33 not search whether it be g' or bad,
Nu 10:29 with us, and we will do thee g':
29 for the Lord hath spoken g'
13:19 whether it be g' or bad; and what
20 And be ye of g' courage, and bring
14: 7 search it, is an exceeding g' land.
23:19 and shall he not make it g'?
24:13 to do either g' or bad of mine own
De 1:14 thing which thou hast spoken is g'
25 a g' land which the Lord our God
35 evil generation see that g' land,
39 no knowledge between g' and evil,
2: 4 take ye g' heed unto yourselves
3:25 the g' land that is beyond Jordan,
4:15 therefore g' heed unto yourselves;
21 should not go in unto that g' land,
22 go over, and possess that g' land.
6:11 And houses full of all g' things,
18 and g' in the sight of the Lord:
18 possess the g' land which the Lord
24 for our g' always, that he might
8: 7 God bringeth thee into a g' land,
10 for the g' land which he hath given
16 to do thee g' at thy latter end;
9: 6 God giveth thee not this g' land
10:13 command thee this day for thy g'?
11:17 perish quickly from off the g' land
12:28 doest that which is g' and right
26:11 And thou shalt rejoice in every g'
28:12 open unto thee his g' treasure,
63 rejoiced over you to do you g',
30: 5 he will do thee g', and multiply
9 in the fruit of thy land, for g':
9 again rejoice over thee for g',
15 before thee this day life and g',
31: 6 Be strong and of a g' courage, fear not
7, 23 Be strong and of a g' courage: for
33:16 for the g' will of him that dwelt
Jos 1: 6 Be strong and of a g' courage: for unto
8 then thou shalt have g' success.
9 Be strong and of g' courage; be not
18 only be strong, and of a g' courage;
9:25 it seemeth g' and right unto thee
10:25 be strong and of g' courage: for thus
21:45 failed not ought of any g' thing
23:11 Take g' heed therefore unto
13 perish from off this g' land which
14 hath failed of all the g' things
15 as all g' things are come upon you,
15 destroyed you from off this g' land
16 perish quickly from off the g' land
24:20 after that he hath done you g'.
J'g 8:32 died in a g' old age, and was
9:11 my sweetness, and my g' fruit,
10:15 whatsoever seemeth g' unto thee:
17:13 I that the Lord will do me g',
18: 9 the land, and, behold, it is very g':
22 a g' way from the house of Micah,
19:24 them what seemeth g' unto you:
Ru 2:22 It is g', my daughter, that thou go
1Sa 1:23 Do what seemeth thee g'; tarry
2:24 for it is no g' report that I hear:
3:18 let him do what seemeth him g'.
11:10 all that seemeth g' unto you.
12:23 teach you the g' and the right way:
14:36 whatsoever seemeth g' unto thee.
40 Do what seemeth g' unto thee.
15: 9 all that was g', and would not
19: 4 Jonathan spake g' of David unto
4 have been to thee-ward very g':
20:12 behold, if there be g' toward David,
24: 4 do to him as it shall seem g'
17 for thou hast rewarded me g',
19 the Lord reward thee g' for that
25: 3 was a woman of g' understanding,
8 for we come in a g' day: give, I
15 But the men were very g' unto us,
21 and he hath requited me evil for g'.
30 according to all the g' that he hath
26:16 This thing is not g' that thou hast
29: 6 coming in with me in the host is g'
9 know that thou art g' in my sight,
2Sa 3:19 all that seemed g' to Israel,
19 that seemed g' to the whole house
4:10 to have brought g' tidings,
6:19 a g' piece of flesh, and a flagon
10:12 Be of g' courage, and let us play
12 do that which seemeth him g'.
13:22 brother Amnon neither g' nor bad:
14:17 the king to discern g' and bad:
32 been g' for me to have been there
15: 3 See, thy matters are g' and right;
26 let him do to me as seemeth g'
16:12 will requite me g' for his cursing
17: 7 Ahithophel hath given is not g'
14 appointed to defeat the g' counsel
18:27 He is a g' man, and cometh with g'
19:18 and to do what he thought g'.
27 do therefore what is g' in thine
35 can I discern between g' and evil?
37 what shall seem g' unto thee.
38 that which shall seem g' unto thee:
24:22 offer up what seemeth g' unto him:
1Ki 1:42 man, and bringest g' tidings.
2:38 The saying is g': as my lord the
42 The word that I have heard is g'.
3: 9 may discern between g' and bad:
8:36 teach them the g' way wherein they
56 one word of all his g' promise,
12: 7 and speak g' words to them, then
14:13 him there is found some g' thing
15 root up Israel out of this g' land,
21: 2 than it; or, if it seem g' to thee,
22: 8 not prophesy g' concerning me,

1Ki 22:13 prophets declare g' unto the king
13 and speak that which is g'.
18 prophesy no g' concerning me,
2Ki 3:19 and shall fell every g' tree, and stop
19 and mar every g' piece of land with
25 on every g' piece of land cast every
25 and felled all the g' trees: only in
7: 9 this day is a day of g' tidings, and
8: 9 of every g' thing of Damascus,
10: 5 that which is g' in thine eyes.
20: 3 have done that which is g' in thy
19 G' is the word of the Lord which
19 And he said, Is it not g', if peace
1Ch 4:40 they found fat pasture and g',
13: 2 If it seem g' unto you, and that it
16: 3 of bread, and a g' piece of flesh,
34 thanks unto the Lord; for he is g';
19:13 Be of g' courage, and let us behave
13 do that which is g' in his sight.
21:23 do that which is g' in his eyes:
22:13 be strong, and of g' courage; dread not
28: 8 that ye may possess this g' land,
20 Be strong, and of g' courage; and do it:
29: 3 I have of mine own proper g',
28 died in a g' old age, full of days,
2Ch 5:13 For he is g'; for his mercy endureth
6:27 thou hast taught them the g' way,
7: 3 For he is g'; for his mercy endureth
10: 7 speak g' words to them, they will
14: 2 And Asa did that which was g' and
18: 7 for he never prophesied g' unto me,
12 prophets declare g' to the king
12 one of theirs, and speak thou g'.
17 he would not prophesy g' unto me,
19: 3 there are g' things found in thee,
11 and the Lord shall be with the g'.
24:16 because he had done g' in Israel,
30:18 The g' Lord pardon every one
22 that taught the g' knowledge of
31:20 wrought that which was g' and right
Ezr 3:11 because he is g', for his mercy
5:17 therefore, if it seem g' to the king,
7: 9 according to the g' hand of his God
18 whatsoever shall seem g' to thee,
8:18 And by the g' hand of our God
22 all them for g' that seek him;
9:12 eat the g' of the land, and leave it
10: 4 be of g' courage, and do it.
Ne 2: 8 to the g' hand of my God upon me.
18 my God which was g' upon me;
18 their hands for this g' work.
5: 9 I said, It is not g' that ye do:
19 Think upon me, my God, for g',
6:19 reported his g' deeds before me,
9:13 g' statutes and commandments:
20 Thou gavest also thy g' spirit to
36 fruit thereof and the g' thereof,
13:14 and wipe not out my g' deeds
31 Remember me, O my God, for g'.
Es 3:11 do with them as it seemeth g'
5: 4 If it seem g' unto the king,
7: 9 who had spoken g' for the king,
8:17 gladness, a feast and a g' day.
9:19 gladness and feasting, and a g' day,
22 and from mourning into a g' day:
Job 2:10 we receive g' at the hand of God,
5:27 hear it, and know thou it for thy g'.
7: 7 mine eye shall no more see g'.
9:25 they flee away, they see no g'.
10: 3 Is it g' unto thee that thou shouldest
13: 9 g' that he should search you out?
15: 3 wherewith he can do no g'?
21:16 their g' is not in their hand:
22:18 filled their house with g' things:
21 thereby g' shall come unto thee.
24:21 and doeth not g' to the widow.
30:26 I looked for g', then evil came
34: 4 know among ourselves what is g'.
39: 4 Their young ones are in g' liking,
Ps 4: 6 Who will shew us any g'? Lord,
14: 1 works, there is none that doeth g'.
3 filthy: there is none that doeth g'.
25: 8 G' and upright is the Lord:
27:14 be of g' courage, and he shall
31:24 Be of g' courage, and he shall
34: 8 taste and see that the Lord is g':
10 Lord shall not want any g' thing.
12 many days, that he may see g'?
14 Depart from evil, and do g'; seek
35:12 They rewarded me evil for g' to the
36: 3 hath left off to be wise, and to do g'.
4 himself in a way that is not g';
37: 3 Trust in the Lord, and do g';
23 The steps of a g' man are ordered
27 Depart from evil, and do g'; and
38:20 They also that render evil for g'
20 because I follow the thing that g' is.
39: 2 I held my peace, even from g';
45: 1 My heart is inditing a g' matter:
51:18 Do g' in thy...pleasure unto Zion:
18 Do...in thy g' pleasure unto Zion:
52: 3 Thou lovest evil more than g';
9 for it is g' before thy saints.
53: 1 iniquity: there is none that doeth g'.
3 filthy; there is none that doeth g'.
54: 6 thy name, O Lord; for it is g'.
69:16 Lord; for thy lovingkindness is g':
73: 1 Truly God is g' to Israel,
28 But it is g' for me to draw near
84:11 no g' thing will he withhold from
85:12 Lord shall give that which is g';
86: 5 For thou, Lord, art g', and ready to
17 Shew me a token for g'; that they
92: 1 It is a g' thing to give thanks
100: 5 For the Lord is g'; his mercy is
103: 5 thy mouth with g' things; so that
Ps 104:28 thine hand, they are filled with g'.
106: 1 for he is g': for his mercy endureth
5 That I may see the g' of thy chosen,
107: 1 for he is g': for his mercy endureth
109: 5 have rewarded me evil for g',
21 because thy mercy is g', deliver thou
111:10 a g' understanding have all they
112: 5 a g' man sheweth favour, and
118: 1 for he is g': because his mercy
29 for he is g': for his mercy endureth
119:39 I fear: for thy judgments are g'.
66 Teach me g' judgment and
68 Thou art g', and doest
68 Thou art..., and doest g';
71 It is g' for me that I have been
122 Be surety for thy servant for g':
122: 9 the Lord our God I will seek thy g'.
125: 4 Do g', O Lord, unto those that be
4 unto those that be g', and to them
128: 5 thou shalt see the g' of Jerusalem
133: 1 how g' and how pleasant it is for
135: 3 for the Lord is g': sing praises unto
136: 1 for he is g': for his mercy endureth
143:10 thy spirit is g'; lead me into the
145: 9 The Lord is g' to all: and his tender
147: 1 for it is g' to sing praises unto our
Pr 2: 9 and equity; yea, every g' path.
20 mayest walk in the way of g' men,
3: 4 find favour and g' understanding
27 Withhold not g' from them to
4: 2 For I give you g' doctrine,
11:17 The merciful man doeth g' to his
23 desire of the righteous is only g':
27 diligently seeketh g' procureth
12: 2 A g' man obtaineth favour of the
14 A man shall be satisfied with g'
25 but a g' word maketh it glad.
13: 2 A man shall eat g' by the fruit
15 G' understanding giveth favour:
21 to the righteous g' shall be repayed.
22 A g' man leaveth an inheritance
14:14 and a g' man shall be satisfied
19 The evil bow before the g'; and the
22 shall be to them that devise g'.
15: 3 beholding the evil and the g'.
23 word spoken in due season, how g'
30 a g' report maketh the bones fat.
16:20 a matter wisely shall find g':
29 him into the way that is not g'.
17:13 Whoso rewardeth evil for g', evil
20 hath a froward heart findeth no g':
22 A merry heart doeth g' like a
26 Also to punish the just is not g',
18: 5 It is not g' to accept the person of
22 findeth a wife findeth a g' thing,
19: 2 without knowledge, it is not g';
8 keepeth understanding shall find g'.
20:18 and with g' advice make war.
23 and a false balance is not g'.
22: 1 g' name is rather to be chosen than
24:13 eat thou honey, because it is g';
23 It is not g' to have respect of
25 a g' blessing shall come upon them.
25:25 so is g' news from a far country.
27 It is not g' to eat much honey:
28:21 To have respect of persons is not g':
31:12 She will do him g' and not evil
18 that her merchandise is g':
Ec 2: 3 was that g' for the sons of men,
24 he should make his soul enjoy g'
26 God giveth to a man that is g' in
26 he may give to him that is g'
3:12 I know that there is no g' in them,
12 rejoice, and to do g' in his life.
13 and enjoy the g' of all his labour,
4: 8 and bereave my soul of g'?
9 have a g' reward for their labour.
5:11 what g' is there to the owners
18 it is g' and comely for one to eat
18 to enjoy the g' of all his labour
6: 3 and his soul be not filled with g',
6 yet hath he seen no g': do not all go
12 who knoweth what is g' for man
7: 1 a g' name is better than precious
11 Wisdom is g' with an inheritance:
18 is g' that thou shouldest take hold
20 just man upon earth, that doeth g',
9: 2 to the g' and to the clean, and to the
2 as is the g', so is the sinner;
18 but one sinner destroyeth much g'.
11: 6 whether they both shall be alike g'.
12: 9 yea, he gave g' heed, and sought
14 whether it be g', or whether it be
Ca 1: 3 of the savour of thy g' ointments
2:13 tender grape give a g' smell.
Isa 1:19 ye shall eat the g' of the land:
5:20 them that call evil g', and g' evil;
7:15 to refuse the evil, and choose the g'.
16 to refuse the evil, and choose the g',
38: 3 and have done that which is g'
39: 8 G' is the word of the Lord which
40: 9 O Zion, that bringest g' tidings, get
9 Jerusalem, that bringest g' tidings,
41: 6 said to his brother, Be of g' courage.
23 do g', or do evil, that we may be
27 one that bringeth g' tidings.
52: 7 feet of him that bringeth g' tidings,
7 him that bringeth...tidings of g',
55: 2 and eat ye that which is g',
61: 1 preach g' tidings unto the meek;
65: 2 walketh in a way that was not g',
Jer 4:22 to do g' they have no knowledge.
5:25 withholden g' things from you.
6:16 is the g' way, and walk therein,
8:15 looked for peace, but no g' came;
10: 5 neither also is it in them to do g'.
Jer 13:10 this girdle, which is g' for nothing.
23 then may ye also do g', that are
14:11 not for this people for their g'.
19 and there is no g'; and for the time
17: 6 and shall not see when g' cometh;
18: 4 seemed g' to the potter to make it.
10 I will repent of the g', wherewith
11 your ways and your doings g'.
20 Shall evil be recompensed for g'?
20 I stood before thee to speak g'
21:10 this city for evil, and not for g',
24: 2 One basket had very g' figs, even
3 I said, Figs; the g' figs, very g';
5 these g' figs, so will I acknowledge
5 land of the Chaldeans for their g'.
6 will set mine eyes upon them for g',
26:14 as seemeth g' and meet unto you.
29:10 perform my g' word toward you,
32 shall he behold the g' that I will do
32:39 the g' of them, and of their children
40 away from them, to do them g';
41 rejoice over them to do them g',
42 bring upon them all the g' that I
33: 9 hear all the g' that I do unto them:
11 for the Lord is g'; for his mercy
14 I will perform that g' thing which
39:16 this city for evil, and not for g';
40: 4 If it seem g' unto thee to come
4 whither it seemeth g' and
42: 6 Whether it be g', or whether it be
44:27 over them for evil, and not for g':
La 3:25 The Lord is g' unto them that wait
26 It is g' that a man should both hope
27 It is g' for a man that he bear the
38 High proceedeth not evil and g'?
Ez 16:50 I took them away as I saw g'.
17: 8 was planted in a g' soil by great
18:18 and did that which is not g' among
20:25 them also statutes that were not g',
24: 4 even every g' piece, the thigh, and
34:14 I will feed them in a g' pasture,
14 there shall they lie in a g' fold,
18 to have eaten up the g' pasture,
36:31 your doings that were not g',
Da 4: 2 I thought it g' to shew the signs
Ho 4:13 because the shadow thereof is g':
8: 3 cast off the thing that is g':
Am 5:14 Seek g', and not evil, that ye may
15 Hate the evil, and love the g',
9: 4 upon them for evil, and not for g'.
Mic 1:12 Maroth waited carefully for g':
2: 7 do not my words do g' to him
3: 2 Who hate the g', and love the evil;
6: 8 shewed thee, O man, what is g';
7: 2 The g' man is perished out of the
Na 1: 7 The Lord is g', a strong hold
15 of him that bringeth g' tidings,
Zep 1:12 heart, The Lord will not do g',
Zec 1:13 g' words and comfortable words.
11:12 If ye think g', give me my price;
Mal 2:13 or receiveth it with g' will
17 Every one that doeth evil is g' in
M't 3:10 which bringeth not forth g' fruit
5:13 it is henceforth g' for nothing,
16 that they may see your g' works,
44 do g' to them that hate you, and
45 sun to rise on the evil and on the g',
7:11 to give g' gifts unto your children,
11 which is in heaven give g' things
17 Even so every g' tree bringeth forth
17 tree bringeth forth g' fruit; but a
18 A g' tree cannot bring forth evil
18 a corrupt tree bring forth g' fruit.
19 that bringeth not forth g' fruit
8:30 there was a g' way off from them
9: 2 be of g' cheer; thy sins be forgiven
22 Daughter, be of g' comfort; thy faith
11:26 for so it seemed g' in thy sight.
12:33 make the tree g', and his fruit g';
34 can ye, being evil, speak g' things?
35 A g' man out of the g' treasure of
35 the heart bringeth forth g' things:
13: 8 fell into g' ground, and brought
23 received seed into the g' ground
24 a man which sowed g' seed in his
27 Sir, didst thou not sow g' seed in
37 He that soweth the g' seed is the
38 the g' seed are the children of the
48 and gathered the g' into vessels,
14:27 of g' cheer; it is I; be not afraid.
17: 4 Lord, it is g' for us to be here:
19:10 with his wife, it is not g' to marry.
16 G' Master, what...thing shall I do,
16 what g' thing shall I do, that I may
17 callest thou me g'? there is none g'
20:15 Is thine eye evil, because I am g'?
22:10 many as they found, both bad and g':
25:21 done, thou g' and faithful servant:
23 Well done, g' and faithful servant:
26:10 she hath wrought a g' work upon
24 it had been g' for that man if he had
M'r 3: 4 to do g' on the sabbath days, or to
4: 8 And other fell on g' ground, and
20 they which are sown on g' ground;
6:50 Be of g' cheer: it is I; be not afraid.
9: 5 Master, it is g' for us to be here:
50 Salt is g': but if the salt have lost
10:17 G' Master, what shall I do that I
18 callest thou me g'? there is none g'
49 Be of g' comfort, rise; he calleth thee.
14: 6 hath wrought a g' work on me.
7 ye will ye may do them g': but
21 g' were it for that man if he had
Lu 1: 3 It seemed g' to me also, having had
53 He hath filled the hungry with g'
2:10 bring you g' tidings of great joy,

Lu 2:14 earth peace, g' will toward men.
3: 9 not forth g' fruit is hewn down.
6: 9 on the sabbath days to do g', or to
27 do g' to them which hate you,
33 ye do g' to them which do g' to you,
35 do g', and lend, hoping for nothing
38 g' measure, pressed down, and
43 For a g' tree bringeth not forth
43 a corrupt tree bring forth g' fruit.
45 A g' man out of the g' treasure of
45 heart bringeth forth that which is g';
8: 8 And other fell on g' ground, and
15 But that on the g' ground are they
15 which in an honest and g' heart,
48 Daughter, be of g' comfort: thy
9:33 it is g' for us to be here: and let
10:21 for so it seemed g' in thy sight.
42 and Mary hath chosen that g' part,
11:13 know how to give g' gifts unto your
12:32 your Father's g' pleasure to give you
14:34 Salt is g': but if the salt have lost
16:25 thy lifetime receivedst thy g' things,
18:18 G' Master, what shall I do to inherit
19 Why callest thou me g'? none is g',
19:17 Well, thou g' servant: because thou
23:50 and he was a g' man, and a just:
Joh 1:46 Can there any g' thing come out
2:10 doth set forth g' wine; and when
10 but thou hast kept the g' wine
5:29 they that have done g', unto the
7:12 some said, He is a g' man: others
10:11 the g' shepherd: the g' shepherd
14 I am the g' shepherd, and know
32 Many g' works have I shewed you
33 For a g' work we stone thee not;
16:33 but be of g' cheer; I have overcome
Ac 4: 9 g' deed done to the impotent man,
9:36 this woman was full of g' works
10:22 of g' report among all the nation
38 went about doing g', and healing
11:24 For he was a g' man, and full of the
14:17 in that he did g', and gave us
15: 7 that a g' while ago God made choice
25 It seemed g' unto us, being assembled
28 For it seemed g' to the Holy Ghost,
38 Paul thought not g' to take him
18:18 this tarried there yet a g' while,
22:12 having a g' report of all the Jews
23: 1 I have lived in all g' conscience until
11 Be of g' cheer, Paul: for as thou hast
27:22 And now I exhort you to be of g' cheer:
25 Wherefore, sirs, be of g' cheer: for I
36 Then were they all of g' cheer, and
2:10 peace to every man the worketh g',
3: 8 Let us do evil, that g' may come?
12 there is none that doeth g', no, not
5: 7 for a g' man some would even dare
7:12 commandment holy, and just, and g'.
13 Was then that which is g' made
13 death in me by that which is g';
16 I consent unto the law that it is g'.
18 in my flesh,) dwelleth no g' thing:
18 how to perform that which is g' I
19 For the g' that I would I do not:
21 a law, that when I would do g',
8:28 all things work together for g' to
9:11 neither having done any g' or evil,
10:15 and bring glad tidings of g' things!
11:24 contrary to nature into a g' olive
12: 2 that ye may prove what is that g',
9 is evil; cleave to that which is g'.
21 of evil, but overcome evil with g'.
13: 3 rulers are not a terror to g' works,
3 do that which is g', and thou shalt
4 the minister of God to thee for g'.
14:16 Let not then your g' be evil spoken
21 It is g' neither to eat flesh, nor to
15: 2 please his neighbour for his g' to
16:18 by g' words and fair speeches
19 have you wise unto that which is g',
1Co 5: 6 Your glorying is not g'. Know ye
7: 1 It is g' for a man not to touch a
8 It is g' for them if they abide even as
26 that this is g' for the present
26 that it is g' for a man so to be.
15:33 evil communications corrupt g'
2Co 5:10 hath done, whether it be g' or bad.
6: 8 by evil report and g' report: as
9: 8 may abound to every g' work:
13:11 Be perfect, be of g' comfort, be
Ga 4:18 But it is g' to be zealously
18 affected always in a g' thing,
6: 6 him that teacheth in all g' things.
10 let us do g' unto all men, especially
Eph 1: 5 according to the g' pleasure of his
9 according to his g' pleasure which
2:10 created in Christ Jesus unto g'
4:28 his hands the thing which is g',
29 but that which is g' to the use of
6: 7 With g' will doing service, as to
8 whatsoever g' thing any man doeth,
Ph'p 1: 6 he which hath begun a g' work in
15 and some also of g' will:
2:13 to will and to do of his g' pleasure.
19 that I also may be of g' comfort,
4: 8 whatsoever things are of g' report;
Col 1:10 being fruitful in every g' work.
1Th 3: 1 thought it g' to be left at Athens
6 brought us g' tidings of your faith
6 have g' remembrance of us always,
5:15 but ever follow that which is g',
21 things; hold fast that which is g'.
2Th 1:11 the g' pleasure of his goodness,
2:16 and g' hope through grace,
17 you in every g' word and work.
1Ti 1: 5 a pure heart, and of a g' conscience,
1Ti 1: 8 But we know that the law is g',
18 them mightest war a g' warfare;
19 Holding faith, and a g' conscience;
2: 3 For this is g' and acceptable in
10 professing godliness) with g' works.
3: 1 of a bishop, he desireth a g' work.
2 vigilant, sober, of g' behaviour,
7 he must have a g' report of them
13 purchase to themselves a g' degree,
4: 4 For every creature of God is g',
6 thou shalt be a g' minister of Jesus
6 of faith and of g' doctrine,
5: 4 for that is g' and acceptable
10 Well reported of for g' works;
10 diligently followed every g' work.
25 the g' works of some are manifest
6:12 Fight the g' fight of faith, lay hold
12 and hast professed a g' profession
13 Pilate witnessed a g' confession;
18 That they do g', that they be
18 that they be rich in g' works,
19 a g' foundation against the time
2Ti 1:14 That g' thing which was committed
2: 3 as a g' soldier of Jesus Christ.
21 and prepared unto every g' work.
3: 3 despisers of those that are g',
17 furnished unto all g' works.
4: 7 I have fought a g' fight, I have
Tit 1: 8 of hospitality, a lover of g' men,
16 and unto every g' work reprobate.
2: 3 much wine, teachers of g' things;
5 keepers at home, g', obedient to
7 thyself a pattern of g' works:
10 shewing all g' fidelity; that they
14 peculiar people, zealous of g'
3: 1 to be ready to every g' work,
8 be careful to maintain g' works.
8 These things are g' and profitable
14 also learn to maintain g' works for
Ph'm 6 the acknowledging of every g' thing
Heb 5:14 to discern both g' and evil.
6: 5 And have tasted the g' word
9:11 an high priest of g' things to come,
10: 1 a shadow of g' things to come,
24 provoke unto love and to g' works:
11: 2 the elders obtained a g' report.
12 of one, and him as g' as dead,
39 a g' report through faith,
13: 9 it is a g' thing that the heart be
16 But to do g' and to communicate
18 we trust we have a g' conscience,
21 Make you perfect in every g' work
Jas 1:17 Every g' gift and every perfect gift
2: 3 Sit thou here in a g' place;
3:13 out of a g' conversation his works
17 full of mercy and g' fruits,
4:17 to him that knoweth to do g',
1Pe 2:12 they may by your g' works, which
18 not only to the g' and gentle, but
3:10 he that will love life, and see g' days,
11 Let him eschew evil, and do g';
13 be followers of that which is g'?
16 Having a g' conscience; that,
16 falsely accuse your g' conversation
21 answer of a g' conscience toward
4:10 as g' stewards of the manifold
1Jo 3:17 whoso hath this world's g', and
3Jo 11 which is evil, but that which is g'.
11 He that doeth g' is of God:
12 hath g' report of all men, and of

goodlier
1Sa 9: 2 of Israel a g' person than he: from

goodliest
1Sa 8:16 your g' young men, and your asses,
1Ki 20: 3 thy children, even the g', are mine.

goodliness
Isa 40: 6 all the g' thereof is as the flower

goodly See also GOODLIER; GOODLIEST.
Ge 27:15 Rebekah took g' raiment of her
39: 6 Joseph was a g' person,
49:21 hind let loose; he giveth g' words.
Ex 2: 2 saw him that he was a g' child,
39:28 and g' bonnets of fine linen, and
Le 23:40 the boughs of g' trees, branches
Nu 24: 5 How g' are thy tents, O Jacob,
31:10 and all their g' castles, with fire.
De 3:25 that g' mountain, and Lebanon.
6:10 to give thee great and g' cities,
8:12 and hast built g' houses, and dwelt
Jos 7:21 among the spoils a g' Babylonish
1Sa 9: 2 a choice young man, and a g':
16:12 countenance, and g' to look to.
2Sa 23:21 he slew an Egyptian, a g' man:
1Ki 1: 6 he also was a very g' man;
2Ch 36:10 with the g' vessels of the house
19 destroyed all the g' vessels thereof.
Job 39:13 the g' wings unto the peacocks?
Ps 16: 6 yea, I have a g' heritage.
80:10 thereof were like the g' cedars.
Jer 3:19 a g' heritage of the hosts of
11:16 fair, and of g' fruit: with
Eze 17: 8 that it might be a g' vine.
23 and bear fruit, and be a g' cedar:
Ho 10: 1 land they have made g' images.
Joe 3: 5 temples my g' pleasant things:
Zec 10: 3 as his g' horse in the battle.
11:13 a g' price that I was prised at of
M't 13:45 merchant man, seeking g' pearls:
Lu 21: 5 adorned with g' stones and gifts,
Jas 2: 2 in g' apparel, and there come
Re 18:14 were dainty and g' are departed

goodman
Pr 7:19 For the g' is not at home,
M't 20:11 against the g' of the house,
24:43 if the g' of the house had known
M'r 14:14 say ye to the g' of the house,
Lu 12:39 g' of the house had known what
22:11 shall say unto the g' of the house,

goodness See also GOODNESS'.
Ex 18: 9 And Jethro rejoiced for all the g'
33:19 make all my g' pass before thee,
34: 6 and abundant in g' and truth,
Nu 10:32 g' the Lord shall do unto us,
J'g 8:35 all the g' which he had shewed
2Sa 7:28 promised this g' unto thy servant:
1Ki 8:66 and glad of heart for all the g' that
1Ch 17:26 promised this g' unto thy servant;
2Ch 6:41 and let thy saints rejoice in g',
7:10 glad and merry in heart for the g'
32:32 the acts of Hezekiah, and his g',
35:26 the acts of Josiah, and his g',
Ne 9:25 themselves in thy great g'.
35 and in thy great g' that thou gavest
Ps 16: 2 my g' extendeth not to thee;
21: 3 him with the blessings of g': thou
23: 6 Surely g' and mercy shall follow me
27:13 see the g' of the Lord in the land
31:19 how great is thy g', which thou
33: 5 earth is full of the g' of the Lord.
52: 1 g' of God endureth continually.
65: 4 satisfied with the g' of thy house,
11 crownest the year with thy g';
68:10 hast prepared of thy g' for the poor.
107: 8 would praise the Lord for his g',
9 filleth the hungry soul with g'.
15, 21, 31 praise the Lord for his g',
144: 2 My g', and my fortress; my high
145: 7 utter the memory of thy great g',
Pr 20: 6 proclaim every one his own g':
Isa 63: 7 great g' toward the house of Israel,
Jer 2: 7 the fruit thereof and the g' thereof;
31:12 flow together to the g' of the Lord,
14 people shall be satisfied with my g',
33: 9 fear and tremble for all the g'
Ho 3: 5 fear the Lord and his g' in the
6: 4 your g' is as a morning cloud,
10: 1 according to the g' of his land
Zec 9:17 For how great is his g', and how
Ro 2: 4 despisest thou the riches of his g'
4 not knowing that the g' of God
11:22 the g' and severity of God:
22 but toward thee, g', if thou
22 if thou continue in his g':
15:14 ye also are full of g', filled with all
Ga 5:22 longsuffering, gentleness, g', faith,
Eph 5: 9 the fruit of the Spirit is in all g'
2Th 1:11 all the good pleasure of his g',

goodness'
Ps 25: 7 remember thou me for thy g' sake,

goods
Ge 14:11 they took all the g' of Sodom
12 Sodom, and his g', and departed.
16 he brought back all the g', and also
16 again his brother Lot, and his g',
21 persons, and take the g' to thyself.
24:10 g' of his master were in his hand:
31:18 all his g' which he had gotten,
46: 6 they took their cattle, and their g',
Ex 22: 8 his hand unto his neighbour's g'.
11 his hand unto his neighbour's g';
Nu 16:32 unto Korah, and all their g'.
31: 9 all their flocks, and all their g'.
35: 3 for their cattle, and for their g',
De 28:11 thee plenteous in g', in the fruit
2Ch 21:14 and thy wives, and all thy g':
Ezr 1: 4 silver, and with gold, and with g',
6 vessels of silver, with gold, with g',
6: 8 the king's g', even of the tribute
7:26 or to confiscation of g', or to
Ne 9:25 houses full of all g', wells digged,
Job 20:10 his hands shall restore their g'.
21 shall no man look for his g'.
28 and his g' shall flow away in the
Ec 5:11 g' increase, they are increased
Eze 38:12 which have gotten cattle and g',
13 to take away cattle and g', to take
Zep 1:13 their g' shall become a booty,
M't 12:29 and spoil his g', except he first
24:47 make him ruler over all his g'.
25:14 and delivered unto them his g'.
M'r 3:27 and spoil his g', except he will first
Lu 6:30 away thy g' ask them not again.
11:21 his palace, his g' are in peace:
12:18 I bestow all my fruits and my g'.
19 thou hast much g' laid up for many
15:12 me the portion of g' that falleth
16: 1 unto him that he had wasted his g'.
19: 8 Lord, the half of my g' I give to the
Ac 2:45 And sold their possessions and g',
1Co 13: 3 though I bestow all my g' to feed
Heb 10:34 joyfully the spoiling of your g',
Re 3:17 I am rich, and increased with g',

gopher
Ge 6:14 Make thee an ark of g' wood;

gopher-wood See GOPHER and WOOD.

gore See also GORED.
Ex 21:28 If an ox g' a man or a woman,

gored
Ex 21:31 Whether he have g' a son,
31 or have g' a daughter,

gorgeous
Lu 23:11 arrayed him in a g' robe, and sent

gorgeously
Eze 23:12 and rulers clothed most g',
Lu 7:25 they which are g' apparelled,

Goshen (*go'-shen*)
Ge 45:10 dwell in the land of G', and thou
46:28 Joseph, to direct his face unto G';
28 and they came into the land of G'.
29 meet Israel his father, to G', and
34 that ye may dwell in the land of G';
47: 1 behold, they are in the land of G'.
4 servants dwell in the land of G'.
6 in the land of G' let them dwell:
27 land of Egypt, in the country of G';
50: 8 herds, they left in the land of G'.
Ex 8:22 sever in that day the land of G', in
9:26 Only in the land of G', where the
Jos 10:41 and all the country of G', even
11:16 and all the land of G', and the
15:51 And G', and Holon, and Giloh;

gospel See also GOSPEL'S.
M't 4:23 preaching the g' of the kingdom,
9:35 preaching the g' of the kingdom,
11: 5 have the g' preached to them.
24:14 this g' of the kingdom shall be
26:13 Wheresoever this g' shall be
M'r 1: 1 beginning of the g' of Jesus Christ,
14 preaching the g' of the kingdom of
15 repent ye, and believe the g'.
13:10 the g' must first be published
14: 9 this g' shall be preached throughout
16:15 preach the g' to every creature.
Lu 4:18 to preach the g' to the poor;
7:22 to the poor the g' is preached.
9: 6 preaching the g', and healing every
20: 1 in the temple, and preached the g',
Ac 8:25 preached the g' in many villages
14: 7 And there they preached the g'.
21 And when they had preached the g'
15: 7 should hear the word of the g',
16:10 to preach the g' unto them.
20:24 testify the g' of the grace of God.
Ro 1: 1 separated unto the g' of God,
9 my spirit in the g' of his Son,
15 to preach the g' to you that are
16 For I am not ashamed of the g'
2:16 by Jesus Christ according to my g'.
10:15 them that preach the g' of peace,
16 they have not all obeyed the g'.
11:28 As concerning the g', they are
15:16 ministering the g' of God, that the
19 have fully preached the g' of Christ.
20 have I strived to preach the g',
29 of the blessing of the g' of Christ.
16:25 stablish you according to my g',
1Co 1:17 but I preach the g': not with
4:15 have begotten you through the g'.
9:12 we should hinder the g' of Christ.
14 that they which preach the g'
14 should live of the g'.
16 For though I preach the g', I have
16 is unto me, if I preach not the g'!
17 a dispensation of the g' is
18 that, when I preach the g', I may
18 I may make the g' of Christ of no
18 that I abuse not my power in the g'.
15: 1 the g' which I preached unto you,
2Co 2:12 to preach Christ's g', and a door
4: 3 But if our g' be hid, it is hid to them
4 lest the light of the glorious g' of
8:18 whose praise is in the g'
9:13 subjection unto the g' of Christ,
10:14 in preaching the g' of Christ:
16 To preach the g' in the regions
11: 4 or another g', which ye have not
7 have preached to you the g' of God
Ga 1: 6 grace of Christ unto another g':
7 and would pervert the g' of Christ.
8 preach any other g' unto you than
9 if any man preach any other g'
11 that the g' which was preached
2: 2 communicated unto them that g'
5 the truth of the g' might continue
7 the g' of the uncircumcision was
7 as the g' of the circumcision was
14 according to the truth of the g',
3: 8 before the g' unto Abraham,
4:13 I preached the g' unto you
Eph 1:13 of truth the g' of your salvation:
3: 6 promise in Christ by the g':
6:15 the preparation of the g' of peace;
19 make known the mystery of the g',
Ph'p 1: 5 For your fellowship in the g'
7 and confirmation of the g', ye all
12 unto the furtherance of the g';
17 I am set for the defence of the g'.
27 be as it becometh the g' of Christ:
27 together for the faith of the g';
2:22 he hath served with me in the g'.
4: 3 which laboured with me in the g',
15 that in the beginning of the g',
Col 1: 5 in the word of the truth of the g';
23 away from the hope of the g',
1Th 1: 5 For our g' came not unto you
2: 2 to speak unto you the g' of God
4 to be put in trust with the g',
8 not the g' of God only, but also our
9 we preached unto you the g' of God.
3: 2 fellowlabourer in the g' of Christ,
2Th 1: 8 and that obey not the g' of our
2:14 he called you by our g', to the
1Ti 1:11 According to the glorious g' of the
2Ti 1: 8 partaker of the afflictions of the g'
10 immortality to light through the g':
2: 8 from the dead according to my g':
Ph'm 13 unto me in the bonds of the g':
Heb 4: 2 For unto us was the g' preached,
1Pe 1:12 by them that have preached the g'
25 by the g' is preached unto you
1Pe 4: 6 was the g' preached also to them
17 them that obey not the g' of God?
Re 14: 6 the everlasting g' to preach

gospel's
M'r 8:35 his life for my sake and the g',
10:29 or lands, for my sake, and the g',
1Co 9:23 And this I do for the g' sake,

got See also FORGOT; GAT; GOTTEN.
Ge 36: 6 which he had g' in the land
39:12 her hand, and fled, and g' him out.
15 with me, and fled, and g' him out.
Ps 44: 3 they g' not the land in possession
Ec 2: 7 I g' me servants and maidens,
Jer 13: 2 So I g' a girdle according to the
4 Take the girdle that thou hast g',

gotten See also BEGOTTEN; FORGOTTEN; GOT.
Ge 4: 1 I have g' a man from the Lord.
12: 5 souls that they had g' in Haran;
31: 1 our father's hath he g' all this glory.
18 all his goods which he had g',
18 of his getting, which he had g'
46: 6 their goods, which they had g'
Ex 14:18 when I have g' me honour upon
Le 6: 4 thing which he hath deceitfully g',
Nu 31:50 what every man hath g', of
De 8:17 mine hand hath g' me this
2Sa 17:13 Moreover, if he be g' into a city,
Job 28:15 It cannot be g' for gold, neither
31:25 because mine hand hath g' much;
Ps 98: 1 arm, hath g' him the victory.
Pr 13:11 Wealth g' by vanity shall be
20:21 inheritance may be g' hastily
Ec 1:16 and have g' more wisdom than
Isa 15: 7 the abundance they have g',
Jer 48:36 riches that he hath g' are perished.
Eze 28: 4 thou hast g' thee riches,
4 and hast g' gold and silver
38:12 which have g' cattle and goods,
Da 9:15 and hast g' thee renown, as at this
Ac 21: 1 after we were g' from them,
Re 15: 2 them that had g' the victory

gourd See also GOURDS.
Jon 4: 6 And the Lord God prepared a g',
6 Jonah was exceeding glad of the g'.
7 it smote the g' that it withered.
9 thou well to be angry for the g'?
10 Thou hast had pity on the g',

gourds
2Ki 4:39 gathered thereof wild g' his lap

govern
1Ki 21: 7 Dost thou now g' the kingdom
Job 34:17 Shall even he that hateth right g'?
Ps 67: 4 and g' the nations upon earth.

government See also GOVERNMENTS.
Isa 9: 6 the g' shall be upon his shoulder:
7 Of the increase of his g' and peace
22:21 and I will commit thy g' into his
2Pe 2:10 of uncleanness, and despise g'.

governments
1Co 12:28 helps, g', diversities of tongues.

governor See also GOVERNOR'S; GOVERNORS.
Ge 42: 6 Joseph was the g' over the land,
45:26 he is g' over all the land
1Ki 18: 3 Obadiah, which was g' of the
22:26 Amon the g' of the city, and to
2Ki 23: 8 gate of Joshua the g' of the city,
25:23 of Babylon had made Gedaliah g',
1Ch 29:22 unto the Lord to be the chief g',
2Ch 1: 2 every g' in all Israel, the chief
18:25 back to Amon the g' of the city,
28: 7 and Azrikam the g' of the house,
34: 8 Maaseiah the g' of the city,
Ezr 5: 3 them Tatnai, g' on this side the
6 that Tatnai, g' on this side the
14 Sheshbazzar, whom he had made g';
6: 6 Tatnai, g' beyond the river,
7 the g' of the Jews and the elders
13 Tatnai, g' on this side the river,
Ne 3: 7 the throne of the g' on this side
5:14 I was appointed to be their g'
14 have not eaten the bread of the g'.
18 required not I the bread of the g',
12:26 in the days of Nehemiah the g',
Ps 22:28 he is the g' among the nations.
Jer 20: 1 chief g' in the house of the Lord,
30:21 and their g' shall proceed from
40: 5 made g' over the cities of Judah,
7 has made Gedaliah...g' in the land,
41: 2 Babylon had made g' over the land.
18 of Babylon made g' in the land.
Hag 1: 1, 14 son of Shealtiel, g' of Judah,
2: 2, 21 the son of Shealtiel, g' of Judah,
Zec 9: 7 he shall be as a g' in Judah,
Mal 1: 8 offer it now unto thy g'; will he
M't 2: 6 shall come a G', that shall rule
27: 2 him to Pontius Pilate the g'.
11 And Jesus stood before the g':
11 and the g' asked him, saying,
14 that the g' marvelled greatly.
15 the g' was wont to release unto
21 g' answered and said unto them,
23 And the g' said, Why, what evil
27 the soldiers of the g' took Jesus
Lu 2: 2 when Cyrenius was g' of Syria.)
3: 1 Pontius Pilate being g' of Judæa,
20:20 the power and authority of the g'.
Joh 2: 8 And bear unto the g' of the feast.
9 the g' of the feast called the
Ac 7:10 and he made him g' over Egypt
23:24 bring him safe unto Felix the g'.
26 unto the most excellent g' Felix
33 and delivered the epistle to the g',
Ac 23:34 when the g' had read the letter,
24: 1 who informed the g' against Paul.
10 after that the g' had beckoned unto
26:30 the king rose up, and the g',
2Co 11:32 the g' under Aretas the king kept
Jas 3: 4 whithersoever the g' listeth.

governor's
M't 28:14 And if this come to the g' ears,

governors
J'g 5: 9 My heart is toward the g' of Israel,
14 out of Machir came down g',
1Ki 10:15 and of the g' of the country.
1Ch 24: 5 the g' of the sanctuary, and g' of
2Ch 9:14 g' of the country brought gold
23:20 and the g' of the people, and all the
Ezr 8:36 and to the g' on this side the river:
Ne 2: 7 given me to the g' beyond the river,
9 Then I came to the g' beyond the
5:15 But the former g' that had been
Es 3:12 and to the g' that were over every
Da 2:48 and chief of the g' over all the
3: 2 gather together the princes, the g',
3 Then the princes, the g', and
27 And the princes, g', and captains,
6: 7 kingdom, the g' and the princes, the
Zec 12: 5 And the g' of Judah shall say in
6 day will I make the g' of Judah
M't 10:18 And ye shall be brought before g'
Gal 4: 2 But is under tutors and g' until
1Pe 2:14 Or unto g', as unto them that are

Gozan (*go'-zan*)
2Ki 17: 6 and in Habor by the river of G',
18:11 and in Habor by the river of G',
19:12 my fathers have destroyed; as G',
1Ch 5:26 and Hara, and to the river G',
Isa 37:12 my fathers have destroyed, as G',

grace See also DISGRACE.
Ge 6: 8 Noah found g' in the eyes of
19:19 now, thy servant hath found g' in
32: 5 that I may find g' in thy sight.
33: 8 to find g' in the sight of my lord.
10 now I have found g' in thy sight,
15 let me find g' in the sight of my
34:11 Let me find g' in your eyes,
39: 4 And Joseph found g' in his sight,
47:25 us find g' in the sight of my lord,
29 now I have found g' in thy sight,
50: 4 now I have found g' in your eyes,
Ex 33:12 hast also found g' in my sight.
13 if I have found g' in thy sight,
13 that I may find g' in thy sight:
16 people have found g' in thy sight?
17 thou hast found g' in my sight,
34: 9 now I have found g' in thy sight,
Nu 32: 5 if we have found g' in thy sight,
J'g 6:17 now I have found g' in thy sight,
Ru 2: 2 him in whose sight I shall find g'.
10 Why have I found g' in thine eyes,
1Sa 1:18 handmaid find g' in thy sight.
20: 3 knoweth that I have found g' in
27: 5 I have now found g' in thine eyes,
2Sa 14:22 knoweth that I have found g' in
16: 4 that I may find g' in thy sight, my
Ezr 9: 8 a little space g' hath been shewed
Es 2:17 she obtained g' and favour in his
Ps 45: 2 men: g' is poured into thy lips:
84:11 the Lord will give g' and glory:
Pr 1: 9 an ornament of g' unto thy head,
3:22 unto thy soul, and g' to thy neck.
34 but he giveth g' unto the lowly.
4: 9 to thine head an ornament of g':
22:11 for the g' of his lips the king shall
Jer 31: 2 found g' in the wilderness;
Zec 4: 7 shoutings, crying, G', g' unto it.
12:10 spirit of g' and of supplications:
Lu 2:40 and the g' of God was upon him.
Joh 1:14 of the Father,) full of g' and truth.
16 have all we received, and g' for g'.
17 g' and truth came by Jesus Christ.
Ac 4:33 and great g' was upon them all.
11:23 had seen the g' of God, was glad,
13:43 them to continue in the g' of God.
14: 3 testimony unto the word of his g',
26 recommended to the g' of God for
15:11 through the g' of the Lord Jesus
40 by the brethren unto the g' of God.
18:27 which had believed through g':
20:24 testify the gospel of the g' of God.
32 to God, and to the word of his g',
Ro 1: 5 By whom we have received g' and
7 G' to you and peace from God our
3:24 Being justified freely by his g'
4: 4 not reckoned of g', but of debt.
16 of faith, that it might be by g';
5: 2 faith into this g' wherein we stand,
15 the g' of God, and the gift by g',
17 they which receive abundance of g'
20 g' did much more abound:
21 even so might g' reign through
6: 1 continue in sin, that g' may abound?
14 are not under the law, but under g'.
15 not under the law, but under g'?
11: 5 according to the election of g'.
6 if by g', then is it no more of works:
6 otherwise g' is no more g'.
6 of works, then it is no more g':
12: 3 through the g' given unto me, to
6 according to the g' that is given to
15:15 because of the g' that is given to
16:20 The g' of our Lord Jesus Christ be
24 The g' of our Lord Jesus Christ
1Co 1: 3 G' be unto you, and peace, from
4 for the g' of God which is given you
3:10 According to the g' of God which

1Co 10:30 For if I by g' be a partaker, why am
15:10 by the g' of God I am what I am:
10 and his g' which was bestowed upon
10 the g' of God which was with me.
16:23 The g' of our Lord Jesus Christ be
2Co 1: 2 G' be to you and peace from God
12 by the g' of God, we have had our
4:15 the abundant g' might through the
6: 1 ye receive not the g' of God in vain.
8: 1 you to wit of the g' of God bestowed
6 also finish in you the same g' also.
7 see that ye abound in this g' also.
9 ye know the g' of our Lord Jesus
19 to travel with us with this g', which
9: 8 God is able to make all g' abound
14 for the exceeding g' of God in you.
12: 9 My g' is sufficient for thee: for my
13:14 The g' of the Lord Jesus Christ,
Ga 1: 3 G' be to you and peace from God
6 that called you into the g' of Christ
15 womb, and called me by his g',
2: 9 perceived the g' that was given unto
21 I do not frustrate the g' of God:
5: 4 by the law; ye are fallen from g'.
6:18 the g' of our Lord Jesus Christ be
Eph 1: 2 G' be to you, and peace, from God
6 To the praise of the glory of his g',
7 according to the riches of his g';
2: 5 with Christ, (by g' ye are saved;)
7 the exceeding riches of his g'
8 by g' are ye saved through faith;
3: 2 the dispensation of the g' of God
7 according to the gift of the g' of God
8 is this g' given, that I should preach
4: 7 unto every one of us is given g'
29 it may minister g' unto the hearers.
6:24 G' be with all them that love our
Ph'p 1: 2 G' be unto you, and peace, from
7 ye all are partakers of my g'.
4:23 The g' of our Lord Jesus Christ be
Col 1: 2 G' be unto you, and peace, from
6 and knew the g' of God in truth:
3:16 singing with g' in your hearts to
4: 6 your speech be always with g',
18 my bonds. G' be with you. Amen.
1Th 1: 1 G' be unto you, and peace, from
5:28 The g' of our Lord Jesus Christ be
2Th 1: 2 G' unto you, and peace, from God
12 according to the g' of our God and
2:16 and good hope through g',
3:18 The g' of our Lord Jesus Christ be
1Ti 1: 2 G', mercy, and peace, from God
14 the g' of our Lord was exceeding
6:21 the faith. G' be with thee. Amen.
2Ti 1: 2 G', mercy, and peace, from God the
9 to his own purpose and g',
2: 1 be strong in the g' that is in Christ
4:22 thy spirit. G' be with you. Amen.
Tit 1: 4 G', mercy, and peace, from God the
2:11 For the g' of God that bringeth
3: 7 That being justified by his g', we
15 faith. G' be with you all. Amen.
Ph'm 3 G' to you, and peace, from God our
25 The g' of our Lord Jesus Christ be
Heb 2: 9 he by the g' of God should taste
4:16 come boldly unto the throne of g',
16 and find g' to help in time of need.
10:29 done despite unto the Spirit of g'?
12:15 lest any man fail of the g' of God;
28 let us have g', whereby we may
13: 9 the heart be established with g';
25 G' be with you all. Amen.
Jas 1:11 g' of the fashion of it perisheth:
4: 6 But he giveth more g'. Wherefore
6 but giveth g' unto the humble.
1Pe 1: 2 G' unto you, and peace, be
10 the g' that should come unto you:
13 for the g' that is to be brought
3: 7 heirs together of the g' of life;
4:10 stewards of the manifold g' of God.
5: 5 proud, and giveth g' to the humble.
10 But the God of all g', who hath
12 true g' of God wherein ye stand.
2Pe 1: 2 G' and peace be multiplied unto
3:18 grow in g', and in the knowledge
2Jo 3 G' be with you, mercy, and peace,
Jude 4 turning the g' of our God into
Re 1: 4 G' be unto you, and peace, from
22:21 The g' of our Lord Jesus Christ be

gracious
Ge 43:29 God be g' unto thee, my son.
Ex 22:27 that I will hear; for I am g'.
33:19 g' to whom I will be g', and will
34: 6 The Lord God, merciful and g',
Nu 6:25 upon thee, and be g' unto thee:
2Sa 12:22 God will be g' to me, that the child
2Ki 13:23 And the Lord was g' unto them,
2Ch 30: 9 Lord your God is g' and merciful,
Ne 9:17 ready to pardon, g' and merciful,
31 thou art a g' and merciful God.
Job 33:24 Then he is g' unto him, and saith,
Ps 77: 9 Hath God forgotten to be g'?
86:15 a God full of compassion, and g',
103: 8 the Lord is merciful and g', slow to
111: 4 Lord is g' and full of compassion.
112: 4 he is g', and full of compassion,
116: 5 G' is the Lord, and righteous; yea,
145: 8 Lord is g', and full of compassion;
Pr 11:16 A g' woman retaineth honour:
Ec 10:12 of a wise man's mouth are g';
Isa 30:18 that he may be g' unto you, and
19 he will be very g' unto thee at the
33: 2 O Lord, be g' unto us; we have
Jer 22:23 g' shall thou be when pangs come
Joe 2:13 is g' and merciful, slow to anger,
Am 5:15 the Lord God of hosts will be g'
Jon 4: 2 I knew that thou art a g' God,
Mal 1: 9 God that he will be g' unto us:
Lu 4:22 wondered at the g' words which
1Pe 2: 3 ye have tasted that the Lord is g'.

graciously
Ge 33: 5 God hath g' given thy servant.
11 God hath dealt g' with me, and
Ps 119:29 lying: and grant me thy law g'.
Ho 14: 2 receive us g': so will we render

graff
Ro 11:23 God is able to g' them in again.

graffed See also UNGRAFFED.
Ro 11:17 wert g' in among them, and with
19 broken off, that I might be g' in.
23 not still in unbelief, shall be g' in:
24 and wert g' contrary to nature
24 be g' into their own olive tree?

graft See GRAFF.

grain
Am 9: 9 yet shall not the least g' fall
M't 13:31 like to a g' of mustard seed, which
17:20 faith as a g' of mustard seed, ye
M'r 4:31 It is like a g' of mustard seed,
Lu 13:19 It is like a g' of mustard seed,
17: 6 faith as a g' of mustard seed, ye
1Co 15:37 body that shall be, but bare g',
37 of wheat, or of some other g':

grandmother
2Ti 1: 5 which dwelt first in thy g' Lois,

grant See also GRANTED.
Le 25:24 shall g' a redemption for the land.
Ru 1: 9 Lord g' you that ye may find rest,
1Sa 1:17 God of Israel g' thee thy petition
1Ch 21:22 G' me the place of this
22 shalt g' it me for the full price:
2Ch 12: 7 I will g' them some deliverance;
Ezr 3: 7 according to the g' that they had
Ne 1:11 and g' him mercy in the sight of
Es 5: 8 it please the king to g' my petition,
Job 6: 8 and that God would g' me the thing
Ps 20: 4 G' thee according to thine own
85: 7 O Lord, and g' us thy salvation.
119:29 and g' me thy law graciously.
140: 8 G' not, O Lord, the desires of the
M't 20:21 G' that these my two sons may
M'r 10:37 G' unto us that we may sit, one
Lu 1:74 That he would g' unto us, that we
Ac 4:29 g' unto thy servants, that with all
Ro 15: 5 g' you to be likeminded one toward
Eph 3:16 That he would g' you, according to
2Ti 1:18 Lord g' unto him that he may find
Re 3:21 that overcometh will I g' to sit

granted
1Ch 4:10 And God g' him that which he
2Ch 1:12 and knowledge is g' unto thee;
Ezr 7: 6 and the king g' him all his request,
Ne 2: 8 And the king g' me, according to
Es 5: 6 petition? and it shall be g' thee:
7: 2 Esther? and it shall be g' thee:
8:11 the king g' the Jews which were in
9:12 petition? and it shall be g' thee:
13 let it be g' to the Jews which are in
Job 10:12 Thou hast g' me life and favour,
Pr 10:24 desire of the righteous shall be g'.
Ac 3:14 a murderer to be g' unto you;
11:18 Gentiles g' repentance unto life.
14: 3 g' signs and wonders to be done
Re 19: 8 to her was g' that she should

grape See also GRAPEGATHERER; GRAPEGLEANINGS; GRAPES.
Le 19:10 neither shalt thou gather every g'
De 32:14 drink the pure blood of the g'.
Job 15:33 He shall shake off his unripe g'
Ca 2:13 the vines with the tender g' give
7:12 whether the tender g' appear,
Isa 18: 5 and the sour g' is ripening in
Jer 31:29 The fathers have eaten a sour g',
30 every man that eateth the sour g',

grapegatherer See also GRAPEGATHERERS.
Jer 6: 9 turn back thine hand as a g' into

grapegatherers
Jer 49: 9 If g' come to thee, would they not
Ob 5 if the g' came to thee, would they

grapegleanings
Mic 7: 1 as the g' of the vintage:

grapes
Ge 40:10 thereof brought forth ripe g':
11 and I took the g', and pressed them
49:11 and his clothes in the blood of g':
Le 25: 5 neither gather the g' of thy vine
11 nor gather the g' in it of thy vine
Nu 6: 3 shall he drink any liquor of g',
3 nor eat moist g', or dried.
13:20 was the time of the firstripe g'.
23 a branch with one cluster of g',
24 because of the cluster of g'
De 23:24 thou mayest eat g' thy fill at thine
24:21 When thou gatherest the g' of thy
28:30 shalt not gather the g' thereof.
39 nor gather the g': for the worms
32:32 their g' are g' of gall, their clusters
J'g 8: 2 the gleaning of the g' of Ephraim
9:27 and trode the g', and made merry,
Ne 13:15 also wine, g', and figs, and all
Ca 2:15 for our vines have tender g'.
7: 7 and thy breasts to clusters of g'.
Isa 5: 2 that it should bring forth g', and
2 it brought forth wild g'.
4 looked that it should bring forth g',
4 brought it forth wild g'?
17: 6 gleaning g' shall be left in it, as
24:13 the gleaning g' when the vintage
Jer 8:13 there shall be no g' on the vine,
25:30 as they that tread the g', against
49: 9 they not leave some gleaning g'?
Eze 18: 2 The fathers have eaten sour g',
Ho 9:10 Israel like g' in the wilderness;
Am 9:13 the treader of g' him that soweth
Ob 5 would they not leave some g'?
M't 7:16 Do men gather g' of thorns, or figs
Lu 6:44 of a bramble bush gather they g'.
Re 14:18 the earth; for her g' are fully ripe.

grass See also GRASSHOPPER.
Ge 1:11 Let the earth bring forth g', the
12 earth brought forth g', and herb
Nu 22: 4 ox licketh up the g' of the field.
De 11:15 I will send g' in thy fields
29:23 nor any g' groweth therein, like
32: 2 and as the showers upon the g':
2Sa 23: 4 g' springing out of the earth by
1Ki 18: 5 peradventure we may find g' to
2Ki 19:26 they were as the g' of the field,
26 herb, as the g' on the house tops,
Job 5:25 offspring as the g' of the earth.
6: 5 the wild ass bray when he hath g'?
40:15 with thee; he eateth g' as an ox.
Ps 37: 2 shall soon be cut down like the g',
72: 6 upon the mown g': as showers that
16 of the city shall flourish like g' of
90: 5 in the morning they are like g'
92: 7 When the wicked spring as the g',
102: 4 is smitten, and withered like g';
11 and I am withered like g'.
103:15 As for man, his days are as g':
104:14 the g' to grow for the cattle,
106:20 similitude of an ox that eateth g'.
129: 6 as the g' upon the housetops,
147: 8 g' to grow upon the mountains.
Pr 19:12 his favour is as dew upon the g'.
27:25 the tender g' sheweth itself, and
Isa 15: 6 the g' faileth, there is no green
35: 7 shall be g' with reeds and rushes.
37:27 they were as the g' of the field,
27 as the g' on the housetops, and as
40: 6 What shall I cry? All flesh is g',
7 The g' withereth, the flower fadeth:
7 upon it: surely the people is g'.
8 The g' withereth, the flower fadeth:
44: 4 shall spring up as among the g',
51:12 man which shall be made as g';
Jer 14: 5 forsook it, because there was no g'.
6 did fail, because there was no g'.
50:11 as the heifer at g', and bellow
Da 4:15 in the tender g' of the field; and
15 the beasts in the g' of the earth:
23 brass, in the tender g' of the field;
25 and they shall make thee to eat g'
32 they shall make thee to eat g' as
33 did eat g' as oxen, and his body
5:21 they fed him with g' like oxen,
Am 7: 2 make an end of eating the g' of
Mic 5: 7 as the showers upon the g', that
Zec 10: 1 of rain, to every one g' in the field.
M't 6:30 God so clothe the g' of the field,
14:19 to sit down on the g', and took
M'r 6:39 by companies upon the green g'.
Lu 12:28 If then God so clothe the g',
Joh 6:10 there was much g' in the place.
Jas 1:10 as the flower of the g' he shall pass
11 it withereth the g', and the flower
1Pe 1:24 For all flesh is as g', and all the
24 glory of man as the flower of g'.
24 The g' withereth, and the flower
Re 8: 7 and all green g' was burnt up.
9: 4 should not hurt the g' of the earth,

grasshopper See also GRASSHOPPERS.
Le 11:22 kind, and the g' after his kind.
Job 39:20 thou make him afraid as a g'?
Ec 12: 5 the g' shall be a burden, and desire

grasshoppers
Nu 13:33 we were in our own sight as g'.
J'g 6: 5 they came as g' for multitude;
7:12 lay along in the valley like g'
Isa 40:22 the inhabitants thereof are as g';
Jer 46:23 because they are more than the g',
Am 7: 1 he formed g' in the beginning of
Na 3:17 as the great g', which camp in the

grate
Ex 27: 4 shalt make for it a g' of network
35:16 with his brasen g', his staves,
38: 4 he made for the altar a brasen g'
5 the four ends of the g' of brass,
30 and the brasen g' for it, and all
39:39 brasen altar, and his g' of brass,

grave See also ENGRAVE; GRAVECLOTHES; GRAVED; GRAVEN; GRAVE'S; GRAVES; GRAVETH; GRAVING.
Ge 35:20 Jacob set a pillar upon her g':
20 that is the pillar of Rachel's g'
37:35 go down into the g' unto my son
42:38 gray hairs with sorrow to the g'.
44:29 gray hairs with sorrow to the g'.
31 our father with sorrow to the g'.
50: 5 Lo, I die: in my g' which I have
Ex 28: 9 and g' on them the names of
36 and g' upon it, like the engravings
Nu 19:16 a g', shall be unclean seven days.
18 or one slain, or one dead, or a g':
1Sa 2: 6 he bringeth down to the g', and

2Sa 3:32 and wept at the g' of Abner:
19:37 be buried by the g' of my father
1Ki 2: 6 head go down to the g' in peace.
9 head bring thou down to the g'
13:30 he laid his carcase in his own g';
14:13 of Jeroboam shall come to the g',
2Ki 22:20 thou shalt be gathered into thy g'
2Ch 2: 7 to g' with the cunning men that
14 also to g' any manner of graving,
34:28 be gathered to thy g' in peace,
Job 3:22 are glad, when they can find the g'?
5:26 Thou shalt come to thy g' in a full
7: 9 goeth down to the g' shall come
10:19 carried from the womb to the g'.
14:13 wouldest hide me in the g', that
17:13 g' is mine house: I have made
21:13 in a moment go down to the g'.
32 he be brought to the g', and shall
24:19 so doth the g' those which have
30:24 stretch out his hand to the g',
33:22 soul draweth near unto the g',
Ps 6: 5 in the g' who shall give thee
30: 3 brought up my soul from the g':
31:17 let them be silent in the g'.
49:14 sheep they are laid in the g';
14 beauty shall consume in the g'
15 my soul from the power of the g':
88: 3 my life draweth nigh unto the g'.
5 like the slain that lie in the g',
11 be declared in the g'? or thy
89:48 his soul from the hand of the g'?
Pr 1:12 swallow them up alive as the g';
30:16 The g'; and the barren womb;
Ec 9:10 knowledge, nor wisdom, in the g',
Ca 8: 6 death; jealousy is cruel as the g':
Isa 14:11 pomp is brought down to the g',
19 thou art cast out of thy g' like an
38:10 I shall go to the gates of the g':
18 the g' cannot praise thee, death
53: 9 he made his g' with the wicked,
Jer 20:17 my mother might have been my g',
Eze 31:15 when he went down to the g' I
32:23 company is round about her g':
24 her mulitude round about her g',
Ho 13:14 them from the power of the g';
14 O g', I will be thy destruction:
Na 1:14 make thy g'; for thou art vile.
Joh 11:17 he had lain in the g' four days
31 She goeth unto the g' to weep
38 in himself cometh to the g'.
12:17 he called Lazarus out of his g',
1Co 15:55 sting? O g', where is thy victory?
1Ti 3: 8 Likewise must the deacons be g',
11 Even so must their wives be g',
Tit 2: 2 aged men be sober, g', temperate,

graveclothes
Joh 11:44 bound hand and foot with g':

graved See also GRAVEN.
1Ki 7:36 he g' cherubims, lions, and palm
2Ch 3: 7 and g' cherubims on the walls.

gravel
Pr 20:17 his mouth shall be filled with g'.
Isa 48:19 offspring of thy bowels like the g'
La 3:16 broken my teeth with g' stones,

graven See also GRAVED; ENGRAVEN.
Ex 20: 4 not make unto thee any g' image,
32:16 of God, g' upon the tables.
39: 6 g', as signets are g', with the
Le 26: 1 make you no idols nor g' image,
De 4:16 and make you a g' image,
23 you, and make you a g' image, or
25 yourselves, and make a g' image,
5: 8 shalt not make thee any g' image,
7: 5 burn their g' images with fire.
25 The g' images of their gods shall
12: 3 ye shall hew down the g' images
27:15 maketh any g' or molten image,
J'g 17: 3 to make a g' image and a molten
4 who made thereof a g' image and
18:14 and teraphim, and a g' image, and
17 took the g' image, and the ephod,
20 the teraphim, and the g' image,
30 children of Dan set up the g' image:
31 they set them up Micah's g' image,
2Ki 17:41 and served their g' images, both
21: 7 he set a g' image of the grove
2Ch 33:19 up groves and g' images, before
34: 7 and had beaten the g' images into
Job 19:24 they were g' with an iron pen
Ps 78:58 to jealousy with their g' images.
97: 7 they that serve g' images, that
Isa 10:10 and whose g' images did excel
21: 9 all the g' images of her gods
30:22 the covering of thy g' images of
40:19 workman melteth a g' image,
20 to prepare a g' image, that shall
42: 8 neither my praise to g' images.
17 that trust in g' images, that say
44: 9 They that make a g' image are all
10 or molten a g' image that is
15 maketh it a g' image, and falleth
17 maketh a god, even his g' image:
45:20 the wood of their g' image, and
48: 5 done them, and my g' image, and
49:16 I have g' thee upon the palms
Jer 8:19 me to anger with their g' images,
10:14 is confounded by the g' image:
17: 1 g' upon the table of their heart,
50:38 the land of g' images, and they
51:17 is confounded by the g' image:
47 the g' images of Babylon: and her
52 do judgment upon her g' images:
Ho 11: 2 and burned incense to g' images.
Mic 1: 7 all the g' images thereof shall be
5:13 Thy g' images also will I cut off,
Na 1:14 will I cut off the g' image and the
Hab 2:18 What profiteth the g' image that
18 the maker thereof hath g' it;
Ac 17:29 stone, g' by art and man's device.

grave's
Ps 141: 7 are scattered at the g' mouth,

graves
Ex 14:11 Because there were no g' in Egypt,
2Ki 23: 6 the powder thereof upon the g' of
2Ch 34: 4 strowed it upon the g' of them
Job 17: 1 extinct, the g' are ready for me.
Isa 65: 4 Which remain among the g', and
Jer 8: 1 of Jerusalem, out of their g':
26:23 cast his dead body into the g' of
Eze 32:22 company: his g' are about him:
23 Whose g' are set in the sides of the
25, 26 her g' are round about him:
37:12 I will open your g', and cause you
12 you to come up out of your g',
13 when I have opened your g', O my
13 and brought you up out of your g',
39:11 give unto Gog a place there of g'
M't 27:52 the g' were opened; and many
53 And came out of the g' after his
Lu 11:44 for ye are as g' which appear not,
Joh 5:28 that are in the g' shall hear his
Re 11: 9 their dead bodies to be put in g'.

graveth
Isa 22:16 and that g' an habitation for

graving See also GRAVINGS.
Ex 32: 4 fashioned it with a g' tool,
2Ch 2:14 also to grave any manner of g',
Zec 3: 9 I will engrave the g' thereof,

gravings
1Ki 7:31 also upon the mouth of it were g'

graving-tool See GRAVING and TOOL.

gravity
1Ti 3: 4 children in subjection with all g';
Tit 2: 7 uncorruptness, g', sincerity,

gray^ See also GRAYHEADED; GREY.
Ge 42:38 down my g' hairs with sorrow
44:29 bring down my g' hairs with sorrow
31 g' hairs of thy servant our father
De 32:25 also with the man of g' hairs.
Ho 7: 9 g' hairs are here and there upon

grayheaded See also GREYHEADED.
1Sa 12: 2 I am old and g'; and, behold, my
Job 15:10 the g' and very aged men, much
Ps 71:18 Now also when I am old and g',

grease
Ps 119:70 Their heart is as fat as g';

great^ See also GREATER; GREATEST.
Ge 1:16 And God made two g' lights; the
21 God created g' whales, and every
6: 5 that the wickedness of man was g'
7:11 fountains of the g' deep broken up,
10:12 and Calah: the same is a g' city.
12: 2 I will make of thee a g' nation, and
2 bless thee, and make thy name g';
17 with g' plagues because of Sarai
13: 6 for their substance was g', so that
15: 1 and thy exceeding g' reward.
12 horror of g' darkness fell upon
14 they come out with g' substance.
18 the g' river, the river Euphrates:
17:20 and I will make him a g' nation.
18:18 become a g' and mighty nation,
20 cry of Sodom and Gomorrah is g',
19:11 with blindness, both small and g':
13 the cry of them is waxen g' before
20: 9 and on my kingdom a g' sin?
21: 8 Abraham made a g' feast the same
18 for I will make him a g' nation.
24:35 and he is become g': and he hath
26:13 And the man waxed g', and
13 and grew until he became very g':
14 of herds, and g' store of servants:
27:34 a g' and exceeding bitter cry, and
29: 2 g' stone was upon the well's mouth.
30: 8 g' wrestlings have I wrestled
39: 9 then can I do this g' wickedness,
41:29 years of g' plenty throughout
45: 7 save your lives by a g' deliverance.
46: 3 will there make of thee a g' nation:
48:19 and he also shall be g': but truly
50: 9 and it was a very g' company.
10 a g' and very sore lamentation:
Ex 3: 3 and see this g' sight, why the bush
6: 6 out arm, and with g' judgments:
7: 4 the land of Egypt by g' judgments.
11: 3 the man Moses was very g' in the
6 there shall be a g' cry throughout
8 out from Pharaoh in a g' anger.
12:30 and there was a g' cry in Egypt;
14:31 Israel saw that g' work which the
18:22 every g' matter they shall bring
29:20 and upon the g' toe of their right foot,
32:10 I will make of thee a g' nation.
11 of Egypt with g' power, and with
21 brought so g' a sin upon them?
30 Ye have sinned a g' sin: and now
31 this people have sinned a g' sin,
Le 8:23 upon the g' toe of his right foot.
24 upon the g' toes of their right feet:
11:17 and the cormorant, and the g' owl,
14:14 upon the g' toe of his right foot:
17 his right hand, and upon the g' toe
25 upon the g' toe of his right foot:
28 upon the g' toe of his right foot,
Nu 11:33 the people with a very g' plague.
13:28 walled, and very g': and moreover
32 we saw in it are men of a g' stature.
14:17 let the power of my Lord be g',
18 of g' mercy, forgiving iniquity
22:17 promote thee unto very g' honour,
23:24 people shall rise up as a g' lion,
24: 9 down as a lion, and as a g' lion:
11 to promote thee unto g' honour;
32: 1 of Gad had a very g' multitude
34: 6 have the g' sea for a border:
7 from the g' sea ye shall point
De 1: 7 the g' river, the river Euphrates.
17 hear the small as well as the g';
19 all that g' and terrible wilderness,
28 the cities are g' and walled up to
2: 7 walking through this g' wilderness:
10 a people g', and many, and tall,
21 A people g', and many, and tall,
3: 5 beside unwalled towns a g' many.
4: 6 Surely this g' nation is a wise and
7 For what nation is there so g', who
8 And what nation is there so g', that
32 any such thing as this g' thing is,
34 and by g' terrors, according to all
36 earth he shewed thee his g' fire;
5:22 with a g' voice: and he added no
25 for this g' fire will consume us: if
6:10 to give thee g' and goodly cities,
22 wonders, g' and sore, upon Egypt,
7:19 g' temptations which thine eyes
8:15 that g' and terrible wilderness,
9: 1 cities g' and fenced up to heaven,
2 A people g' and tall, the children
10:17 a g' God, a mighty, and a terrible,
21 thee these g' and terrible things,
11: 7 eyes have seen all the g' acts of the
14:16 and the g' owl, and the swan,
18:16 let me see this g' fire any more
25:13 bag divers weights, a g' and a small.
14 divers measures, a g' and a small.
26: 5 nation, g', mighty, and populous:
8 with g' terribleness, and with signs,
27: 2 thou shalt set thee up g' stones,
28:59 even g' plagues, and of long
29: 3 The g' temptations which thine
3 the signs, and those g' miracles:
24 meaneth the heat of this g' anger?
28 and in g' indignation, and cast
34:12 in all the g' terror which Moses
Jos 1: 4 even unto the g' river, the river
4 unto the g' sea toward the going
6: 5 people shall shout with a g' shout;
20 people shouted with a g' shout,
7: 9 what wilt thou do unto thy g' name?
26 raised over him a g' heap of stones
8:29 raise thereon a g' heap of stones,
9: 1 the g' sea over against Lebanon,
10: 2 Gibeon was a g' city, as one of
10 slew them with a g' slaughter at
11 the Lord cast down g' stones from
18 Roll g' stones upon the mouth of
20 them with a very g' slaughter,
27 laid g' stones in the cave's mouth,
11: 8 chased them unto g' Zidon, and
14:12 that the cities were g' and fenced:
15 a g' man among the Anakims.
15:12 border was to the g' sea, and the
47 and the g' sea, and the border
17:14 I am a g' people, forasmuch as
15 If thou be a g' people, then get thee
17 saying, Thou art a g' people,
17 and hast g' power: thou shalt not
19:28 and Kanah, even unto g' Zidon;
22:10 by Jordan, a g' altar to see to.
23: 4 even unto the g' sea westward.
9 before you g' nations and strong:
24:17 which did those g' signs in our
26 and took a g' stone, and set it up
J'g 1: 6 cut off his thumbs and his g' toes.
7 their thumbs and their g' toes cut
2: 7 who had seen all the g' works of
5:15 there were g' thoughts of heart.
16 there were g' searchings of heart.
11:33 vineyards, with a very g' slaughter.
12: 2 I and my people were at g' strife
15: 8 hip and thigh with a g' slaughter:
18 hast given this g' deliverance into
16: 5 see wherein his g' strength lieth,
6 thee, wherein thy g' strength lieth,
15 me wherein thy g' strength lieth.
23 to offer a g' sacrifice unto Dagon
20:38 that they should make a g' flame
21: 5 For they had made a g' oath
1Sa 2:17 men was very g' before the Lord:
4: 5 all Israel shouted with a g' shout,
6 the noise of this g' shout in the
10 and there was a very g' slaughter;
17 there hath been also a g' slaughter
5: 9 city with a very g' destruction:
9 of the city, both small and g',
6: 9 then he hath done us this g' evil:
14 where there was a g' stone: and
15 and put them on the g' stone: and
18 even unto the g' stone of Abel,
19 of the people with a g' slaughter.
7:10 Lord thundered with a g' thunder
12:16 stand and see this g' thing, which
17 see that your wickedness is g',
22 his people for his g' name's sake:
24 how g' things he hath done for you.
14:15 so it was a very g' trembling.
20 there was a very g' discomfiture.
33 roll a g' stone unto me this day.
45 who hath wrought this g' salvation
15:22 Hath the Lord as g' delight in burnt

1Sa 17:25 king will enrich him with g' riches.
19: 5 Lord wrought a g' salvation for all
8 and slew them with a g' slaughter;
22 came to a g' well that is in Sechu:
20: 2 will do nothing either g' or small,
23: 5 and smote them with a g' slaughter.
25: 2 and the man was very g', and he had
26:13 a g' space being between them:
25 thou shalt both do g' things, and
30: 2 slew not any, either g' or small,
16 because of all the g' spoil that they
19 to them, neither small nor g',
2Sa 3:22 brought in a g' spoil with them:
38 and a g' man fallen this day in
5:10 David went on, and grew g', and
7: 9 and have made thee a g' name, like
9 like unto the name of the g' men
19 house for a g' while to come.
21 hast done all these g' things, to
22 Wherefore thou art g', O Lord
23 to do for you g' things and terrible,
12:14 thou hast given g' occasion to the
30 spoil of the city in g' abundance.
18: 7 and there was there a g' slaughter
9 under the thick boughs of a g' oak,
17 cast him into a g' pit in the wood,
17 and laid a very g' heap of stones
29 I saw a g' tumult, but I knew not
19:32 for he was a very g' man.
20: 8 they were at the g' stone which is
21:20 Gath, where was a man of g' stature,
22:36 thy gentleness hath made me g'.
23:10 wrought a g' victory that day;
12 and the Lord wrought a g' victory.
24:14 I am in a g' strait: let us all
14 for his mercies are g': and let me
1Ki 1:40 and rejoiced with g' joy, so that
3: 4 for that was the g' high place:
6 servant David my father g' mercy,
6 hast kept for him this g' kindness,
8 a g' people, that cannot be
9 to judge this thy so g' a people?
4:13 threescore g' cities with walls and
5: 7 a wise son over this g' people.
17 and they brought g' stones, costly
7: 9 on the outside toward the g' court.
10 even g' stones, stones of ten cubits,
12 the g' court round about was with
8:42 they shall hear of thy g' name,
65 with him, a g' congregation, from
10: 2 to Jerusalem with a very g' train,
10 and of spices very g' store, and
11 in from Ophir g' plenty of almug
18 king made a g' throne of ivory,
11:19 And Hadad found g' favour in the
18:32 g' as would contain two measures
45 and wind, and there was a g' rain.
19: 7 the journey is too g' for thee.
11 and a g' and strong wind rent the
20:13 thou seen all this g' multitude?
21 slew the Syrians with a g' slaughter.
28 deliver all this g' multitude into
22:31 Fight neither with small nor g',
2Ki 3:27 was g' indignation against Israel:
4: 8 where was a g' woman; and she
38 Set on the g' pot, and seethe
5: 1 was a g' man with his master, and
13 had bid thee do some g' thing,
6:14 and chariots, and a g' host: and
23 And he prepared g' provision for
25 there was a g' famine in Samaria:
7: 6 horses, even the noise of a g' host:
8: 4 the g' things that Elisha hath done.
13 that he should do this g' thing?
10: 6 were with the g' men of the city,
11 all his g' men, and his kinsfolks,
19 I have a g' sacrifice to do to Baal;
16:15 Upon the g' altar burn the morning
17:21 Lord, and made them sin a g' sin.
36 of the land of Egypt with g' power
18:17 with a g' host against Jerusalem.
19 Thus saith the g' king, the king
28 Hear the word of the g' king,
22:13 for g' is the wrath of the Lord
23: 2 all the people, both small and g':
26 from the fierceness of his g' wrath,
25: 9 every g' man's house burnt he
26 all the people, both small and g',
1Ch 11:14 saved them by a g' deliverance.
23 slew an Egyptian, a man of g' stature,
12:22 until it was a g' host, like the
16:25 For g' is the Lord, and greatly to be
17: 8 like the name of the g' men that
17 house for a g' while to come,
19 making known all these g' things.
20: 6 where was a man of g' stature,
21:13 I am in a g' strait: let me fall
13 Lord; for very g' are his mercies:
22: 8 hast made g' wars: thou shalt not
25: 8 ward, as well the small as the g',
26:13 lots, as well the small as the g',
29: 1 and the work is g': for the palace is
9 the king also rejoiced with g' joy.
12 and in thine hand it is to make g',
22 Lord on that day with g' gladness.
2Ch 1: 8 hast shewed g' mercy unto David
10 this thy people, that is so g'?
2: 5 the house which I build is g':
5 for g' is our God above all gods.
9 about to build shall be wonderful g'.
4: 9 and the g' court, and doors for the
18 all these vessels in g' abundance:
6:32 for thy g' name's sake, and thy
7: 8 a very g' congregation, from the
9: 1 with a very g' company, and
9 and of spices g' abundance, and

2Ch 9:17 the king made a g' throne of ivory,
13: 8 and ye be a g' multitude, and there
17 slew them with a g' slaughter:
15: 5 but g' vexations were upon all the
13 put to death, whether small or g',
16:12 until his disease was exceeding g':
14 made a very g' burning for him.
17:12 And Jehoshaphat waxed g'
18:30 Fight ye not with small or g',
20:12 this g' company that cometh
15 by reason of this g' multitude; for
21: 3 their father gave them g' gifts of
14 a g' plague will the Lord smite
15 shalt have g' sickness by disease
24:24 the Lord delivered a very g' host
25 (for they left him in g' diseases,)
25:10 they returned home in g' anger.
26:15 shoot arrows and g' stones withal.
28: 5 a g' multitude of them captives,
5 who smote him with a g' slaughter.
13 for our trespass is g', and there is
30:13 month, a very g' congregation.
21 bread seven days with g' gladness:
24 and a g' number of priests
26 So there was g' joy in Jerusalem:
31:10 and that which is left is this g' store.
15 as well to the g' as to the small:
33:14 and raised it up a very g' height, and
34:21 for g' is the wrath of the Lord
30 all the people, g' and small: and
36:18 g' and small, and the treasures of
Ezr 3:11 the people shouted with a g' shout,
4:10 the g' and noble Asnapper brought
5: 8 to the house of the g' God, which
8 which is builded with g' stones,
11 which a g' king of Israel builded
6: 4 With three rows of g' stones, and
9: 7 in a g' trespass unto this day;
13 and for our g' trespass, seeing that
10: 1 a very g' congregation of men and
9 of this matter, and for the g' rain.
Ne 1: 3 are in g' affliction and reproach:
5 the g' and terrible God, that keepeth
10 thou hast redeemed by thy g' power,
3:27 against the g' tower that lieth out,
4: 1 took g' indignation, and mocked
14 the Lord, which is g' and terrible,
19 The work is g' and large, and we
5: 1 there was a g' cry of the people
7 I set a g' assembly against them.
6: 3 I am doing a g' work, so that I
7: 4 Now the city was large and g':
8: 6 Ezra blessed the Lord, the g' God.
12 to make g' mirth, because they had
17 And there was very g' gladness.
9:17 slow to anger, and of g' kindness,
18 and had wrought g' provocations;
25 themselves in thy g' goodness.
26 and they wrought g' provocations.
31 thy g' mercies' sake thou didst
32 our God, the g', the mighty, and
35 and in thy g' goodness that thou
37 pleasure, and we are in g' distress.
11:14 the son of one of the g' men.
12:31 appointed two g' companies of
43 they offered g' sacrifices, and
43 God made them rejoice with g' joy:
13: 5 had prepared for him a g' chamber,
27 to do all this g' evil, to transgress
Es 1: 5 the palace, both unto g' and small,
20 all his empire, (for it is g',) all the
20 honour, both to g' and small.
2:18 the king made a g' feast unto all
4: 3 was g' mourning among the Jews,
8:15 with the g' crown of gold, and with
9: 4 g' in the king's house, and his fame
10: 3 g' among the Jews, and accepted
Job 1: 3 a very g' household; so that this
19 a g' wind from the wilderness,
2:13 saw that his grief was very g'.
3:19 The small and g' are there; and
5: 9 doeth g' things and unsearchable;
25 also that thy seed shall be g', and
9:10 Which doeth g' things past
22: 5 Is not thy wickedness g'? and
23: 6 against me with his g' power?
30:18 By the g' force of my disease
31:25 because my wealth was g',
34 Did I fear a g' multitude, or did
32: 9 G' men are not always wise:
35:15 knoweth it not in g' extremity:
36:18 a g' ransom cannot deliver thee.
26 God is g', and we know him not,
37: 5 g' things doeth he, which we
6 small rain, and of the g' rain of
38:21 the number of thy days is g'?
39:11 him, because his strength is g'?
Ps 14: 5 There were they in g' fear: for God
18:35 thy gentleness hath made me g'
50 G' deliverance giveth he to his
19:11 keeping of them there is g' reward.
13 innocent from the g' transgression.
21: 5 His glory is g' in thy salvation:
22:25 be of thee in the g' congregation:
25:11 pardon mine iniquity; for it is g'.
31:19 how g' is thy goodness, which thou
32: 6 in the floods of g' waters they shall
33:17 he deliver any by his g' strength.
35:18 thee thanks in the g' congregation:
36: 6 is like the g' mountains;
6 thy judgments are a g' deep:
37:35 have seen the wicked in g' power,
40: 9 preached righteousness in the g'
10 thy truth from the g' congregation.
47: 2 he is a g' king over all the earth.
48: 1 G' is the Lord, and greatly to be

Ps 48: 2 the north, the city of the g' King.
53: 5 were they in g' fear, where no fear was:
57:10 thy mercy is g' unto the heavens,
58: 6 break out the g' teeth of the young
68:11 g' was the company of those that
71:19 who hast done g' things: O God,
20 shewed me g' and sore troubles,
76: 1 known: his name is g' in Israel.
77:13 who is so g' a God as our God?
19 the sea, thy path in the g' waters.
78:15 drink as out of the g' depths.
71 following the ewes g' with young
80: 5 tears to drink in g' measure.
86:10 thou art g', and doest wondrous
13 g' is thy mercy toward me: and
92: 5 how g' are thy works! and thy
95: 3 the Lord is a g' God, and a g' King
96: 4 the Lord is g', and greatly to be
99: 2 The Lord is g' in Zion; and he is
3 praise thy g' and terrible name;
103:11 g' is his mercy toward them that
104: 1 thou art very g'; thou art clothed
25 So is this g' and wide sea, wherein
25 innumerable, both small and g'
106:21 which had done g' things in Egypt:
107:23 that do business in g' waters;
108: 4 thy mercy is g' above the heavens:
111: 2 The works of the Lord are g',
115:13 fear the Lord, both small and g'.
117: 2 merciful kindness is g' toward us:
119:156 G' are thy tender mercies, O
162 word, as one that findeth g' spoil.
165 G' peace have they which love thy
126: 2 Lord hath done g' things for them.
3 Lord hath done g' things for us;
131: 1 do I exercise myself in g' matters,
135: 5 I know that the Lord is g', and
10 Who smote g' nations, and slew
136: 4 him who alone doeth g' wonders:
7 To him that made g' lights: for his
17 To him which smote g' kings: for
138: 5 for g' is the glory of the Lord.
139:17 O God! how g' is the sum of them!
144: 7 deliver me out of g' waters, from
145: 3 G' is the Lord, and greatly to be
7 memory of thy g' goodness, and
8 slow to anger, and of g' mercy.
147: 5 G' is our Lord, and of...power:
5 is our Lord, and of g' power: his
Pr 13: 7 himself poor, yet hath g' riches.
14:29 to wrath is of g' understanding:
15:16 Lord than g' treasure and trouble
16: 8 than g' revenues without right.
18: 9 brother to him that is a g' waster.
16 and bringeth him before g' men.
19:19 A man of g' wrath shall suffer
22: 1 rather to be chosen than g' riches,
25: 6 stand not in the place of g' men:
26:10 The g' God that formed all things
28:12 men do rejoice, there is g' glory:
16 is also a g' oppressor: but he that
Ec 1:16 I am come to g' estate, and have
16 heart had g' experience of wisdom
2: 4 I made me g' works; I builded me
7 house; also I had g' possessions of
7 possessions of g' and small cattle
9 I was g', and increased more than
21 This also is vanity and a g' evil
8: 6 the misery of man is g' upon him.
9:13 the sun, and it seemed g' unto me:
14 there came a g' king against it, and
14 and built g' bulwarks against it:
10: 4 for yielding pacifieth g' offences.
6 Folly is set in g' dignity, and the
Ca 2: 3 down under his shadow with g' delight.
Isa 2: 9 and the g' man humbleth himself:
5: 9 g' and fair, without inhabitant:
6:12 and there be a g' forsaking in the
8: 1 Take thee a g' roll, and write in it
9: 2 in darkness have seen a g' light:
12: 6 for g' is the Holy One of Israel
13: 4 mountains, like as of a g' people;
16:14 with all that g' multitude; and the
19:20 send them a saviour, and a g' one,
23: 3 And by g' waters the seed of Sihor,
27: 1 his sore and g' and strong sword
13 that the g' trumpet shall be blown,
29: 6 and with earthquake, and g' noise,
30:25 in the day of the g' slaughter,
32: 2 the shadow of a g' rock in a weary
33:23 is the prey of a g' spoil divided;
34: 6 g' slaughter in the land of Idumea.
15 shall the g' owl make her nest,
36: 2 King Hezekiah with a g' army.
4 the g' king, the king of Assyria,
13 Hear ye the words of the g' king,
38:17 for peace I had g' bitterness:
47: 9 for the g' abundance of thine
51:10 the sea, the waters of the g' deep;
53:12 divide him a portion with the g',
54: 7 with g' mercies will I gather thee.
13 and g' shall be the peace of thy
63: 7 the g' goodness toward the house
Jer 4: 6 the north, and a g' destruction.
5: 5 me unto the g' men, and will speak
27 therefore they are become g', and
6: 1 of the north, and g' destruction.
22 and a g' nation shall be raised
10: 6 Lord; thou art g', and thy name is g'
22 and a g' commotion out of the north
11:16 with the noise of a g' tumult he
13: 9 and the g' pride of Jerusalem.
14:17 people is broken with a g' breach,
16: 6 the g' and the small shall die in
10 pronounced all this g' evil against
20:17 womb to be always g' with me.

Jer 21: 5 and in fury, and in g' wrath.
6 they shall die of a g' pestilence.
22: 8 Lord done thus unto this g' city?
25:14 g' kings shall serve themselves of
32 a g' whirlwind shall be raised up
26:19 procure g' evil against our souls.
27: 5 g' power and by my outstretched
7 many nations and g' kings shall
28: 8 against g' kingdoms, of war, and of
30: 7 Alas! for that day is g', so that
31: 8 a g' company shall return thither.
32:17 heaven and the earth by thy g'
18 the G', the Mighty God, the Lord
19 G' in counsel, and mighty in work:
21 out arm, and with g' terror;
37 and in my fury, and in g' wrath;
42 all this g' evil upon this people,
33: 3 shew thee g' and mighty things,
36: 7 for g' is the anger and the fury
41:12 the g' waters that are in Gibeon.
43: 9 Take g' stones in thine hand, and
44: 7 ye this g' evil against your souls,
15 a g' multitude, even all the people
26 I have sworn by my g' name, saith
45: 5 seekest thou g' things for thyself?
48: 3 spoiling and g' destruction.
50: 9 an assembly of g' nations from the
22 in the land, and of g' destruction.
41 and a g' nation, and many kings
51:54 g' destruction from the land of the
55 destroyed out of her the g' voice;
55 her waves do roar like g' waters,
52:13 all the houses of the g' men,
La 1: 1 that was g' among the nations,
3 and because of g' servitude:
2:13 thy breach is g' like the sea: who
3:23 morning: g' is thy faithfulness.
Eze 1: 4 came out of the north, a g' cloud,
24 like the noise of g' waters, as the
3:12 behind me a voice of a g' rushing,
13 them, and a noise of a g' rushing.
8: 6 the g' abominations that the house
9: 9 Judah is exceeding g', and the land
13:11 O g' hailstones, shall fall; and a
13 g' hailstones in my fury to consume
16: 7 thou hast increased and waxen g',
26 thy neighbours, g' of flesh; and
17: 3 saith the Lord God; A g' eagle
3 eagle with g' wings, full of
5 he placed it by g' waters, and set
7 There was also another g' eagle
7 with g' wings and many feathers,
8 in a good soil by g' waters, that
9 even without g' power or many
17 mighty army and g' company
21:14 it is the sword of the g' men that
23:23 g' lords and renowned, all of them
24: 9 will even make the pile for fire g'.
12 her g' scum went not forth out of
25:17 I will execute g' vengeance upon
26:19 and g' waters shall cover thee;
27:26 have brought thee into g' waters:
28: 5 By thy g' wisdom and by thy
29: 3 g' dragon that lieth in the midst
18 to serve a g' service against Tyrus:
30: 4 g' pain shall be in Ethiopia, when
9 g' pain shall come upon them, as
16 Sin shall have g' pain, and No
31: 4 The waters made him g', the
6 his shadow dwelt all g' nations.
7 for his root was by g' waters.
15 the g' waters were stayed: and I
32:13 from beside the g' waters;
36:23 I will sanctify my g' name, which
37:10 their feet, an exceeding g' army.
38: 4 a g' company with bucklers and
13 and goods, to take a g' spoil?
15 a g' company, and a mighty army:
19 there shall be a g' shaking in the
22 g' hailstones, fire, and brimstone.
39:17 a g' sacrifice upon the mountains
41: 8 were a full reed of six g' cubits.
47: 9 shall be a very g' multitude of fish,
10 as the fish of the g' sea, exceeding
15 from the g' sea, the way of Hethlon,
19 in Kadesh, the river to the g' sea.
20 the g' sea from the border, till a
48:28 and to the river toward the g' sea.
Da 2: 6 and rewards and g' honour:
31 and behold a g' image.
31 This g' image, whose brightness
35 became a g' mountain, and filled
45 the g' God hath made known to
48 the king made Daniel a g' man,
48 and gave him many g' gifts,
4: 3 How g' are his signs! and how
10 and the height thereof was g'.
30 Is not this g' Babylon, that I
5: 1 the king made a g' feast to a
7: 2 the heavens strove upon the g' sea.
3 And four g' beasts came up from
7 and it had g' iron teeth:
8 and a mouth speaking g' things.
11 because of the voice of the g' words
17 These g' beasts, which are four,
20 a mouth that spake very g' things,
25 And he shall speak g' words
8: 4 to his will, and became g'.
8 the he goat waxed very g': and
8 the g' horn was broken;
9 exceeding g', toward the south,
10 And it waxed g', even to the host
21 the g' horn that is between his
9: 4 the g' and dreadful God, keeping
12 by bringing upon us a g' evil:
18 but for thy g' mercies.

Da 10: 4 I was by the side of the g' river,
7 a g' quaking fell upon them, so
8 this g' vision, and there remained
11: 3 that shall rule with g' dominion,
5 dominion shall be a g' dominion.
10 a multitude of g' forces: and one
11 he shall set forth a g' multitude;
13 with a g' army and with much
25 with a g' army; and the king of the
25 with a very g' and mighty army;
28 return into his land with g' riches;
44 go forth with g' fury to destroy,
12: 1 the g' prince which standeth for
Ho 1: 2 hath committed g' whoredom,
11 for g' shall be the day of Jezreel.
8:12 written to him the g' things of
9: 7 thine iniquity, and the g' hatred.
10:15 because of your g' wickedness:
13: 5 in the land of g' drought.
Joe 1: 6 hath the cheek teeth of a g' lion.
2: 2 a g' people and a strong; there
11 for his camp is very g': for he is
11 of the Lord is g' and very terrible;
13 to anger, and of g' kindness,
20 because he hath done g' things.
21 for the Lord will do g' things.
25 g' army which I sent among you.
31 the g' and the terrible day of the
3:13 for their wickedness is g'.
Am 3: 9 g' tumults in the midst thereof,
15 the g' houses shall have an end,
6: 2 go ye to Hamath the g': then go
11 and he will smite the g' house
7: 4 it devoured the g' deep, and did
8: 5 and the shekel g', and falsifying
Jon 1: 2 go to Nineveh, that g' city, and cry
4 the Lord sent out a g' wind into
12 this g' tempest is upon you.
17 prepared a g' fish to swallow up
3: 2 go unto Nineveh, that g' city, and
3 g' city of three days' journey.
4: 2 to anger, and of g' kindness,
11 spare Nineveh, that g' city,
Mic 2:12 they shall make g' noise by reason of
5: 4 now shall he be g' unto the ends
7: 3 and the g' man, he uttereth his
Na 1: 3 and g' in power, and will not
3: 3 and a g' number of carcases; and
10 her g' men were bound in chains.
17 as the g' grasshoppers, which
Hab 3:15 through the heap of g' waters.
Zep 1:10 and a g' crashing from the hills.
14 The g' day of the Lord is near,
Zec 1:14 and for Zion with a g' jealousy.
4: 7 Who art thou, O g' mountain?
7:12 came a g' wrath from the Lord
8: 2 for Zion with g' jealousy, and I
2 I was jealous for her with g' fury.
9:17 how g' is his goodness, and how g' is
12:11 In that day shall there be a g'
14: 4 a very g' valley; and half of the
13 a g' tumult from the Lord shall
14 and apparel, in g' abundance.
Mal 1:11 shall be g' among the Gentiles;
11 shall be g' among the heathen,
14 for I am a g' King, saith the Lord
4: 5 coming of the g' and dreadful day
M't 2:10 rejoiced with exceeding g' joy.
18 and g' mourning, Rachel weeping
4:16 which sat in darkness saw g' light;
25 him g' multitudes of people from
5:12 for g' is your reward in heaven:
19 shall be called g' in the kingdom
35 for it is the city of the g' King.
6:23 how g' is that darkness!
7:27 and g' was the fall of it.
8: 1 g' multitudes followed him.
10 I have not found so g' faith, no,
18 Jesus saw g' multitudes about
24 arose a g' tempest in the sea,
26 the sea; and there was a g' calm.
12:15 and g' multitudes followed him,
13: 2 And g' multitudes were gathered
46 found one pearl of g' price, went
14:14 and saw a g' multitude, and was
15:28 O woman, g' is thy faith: be it
30 And g' multitudes came unto him,
33 as to fill so g' a multitude?
19: 2 And g' multitudes followed him;
22 sorrowful: for he had g' possessions.
20:25 that are g' exercise authority
26 whosoever will be g' among you,
29 a g' multitude followed him.
21: 8 And a very g' multitude spread
22:36 which is the g' commandment in
38 is the first and g' commandment.
24:21 then shall be g' tribulation, such
24 shall shew g' signs and wonders;
30 of heaven with power and g' glory.
31 with a g' sound of a trumpet, and
26:47 and with him a g' multitude with
27:60 he rolled a g' stone to the door
28: 2 there was a g' earthquake: for the
8 with fear and g' joy; and did run
M'r 1:35 rising up a g' while before day,
3: 7 and a g' multitude from Galilee
8 a g' multitude, when they had
8 heard what g' things he did
4: 1 gathered unto him a g' multitude,
32 and shooteth out g' branches; so
37 there arose a g' storm of wind,
39 ceased; and there was a g' calm.
5:11 a g' herd of swine feeding.
19 tell them how g' things the Lord
20 how g' things Jesus had done for
42 astonished with a g' astonishment.

M'r 7:36 so much the more a g' deal they
8: 1 the multitude being very g', and
9:14 saw a g' multitude about them,
10:22 grieved: for he had g' possessions.
42 their g' ones exercise authority
43 whosoever will be g' among you,
46 his disciples and a g' number of
48 but he cried the more a g' deal,
13: 2 Seest thou these g' buildings?
26 clouds with g' power and glory.
14:43 and with him a g' multitude
16: 4 rolled away: for it was very g'.
Lu 1:15 For he shall be g' in the sight of
32 He shall be g', and shall be called
49 hath done to me g' things; and
58 had shewed g' mercy upon her;
2: 5 his espoused wife, being g' with child.
10 I bring you good tidings of g' joy,
36 she was of a g' age, and had lived
4:25 when g' famine was throughout
38 was taken with a g' fever; and
5: 6 inclosed a g' multitude of fishes:
15 and g' multitudes came together
29 Levi made him a g' feast in his
29 and there was a g' company
6:17 a g' multitude of people out of all
23 your reward is g' in heaven: for
35 and your reward shall be g', and
49 and the ruin of that house was g'.
7: 9 I have not found so g' faith, no,
16 That a g' prophet is risen up
8:37 they were taken with g' fear: and
39 how g' things God hath done
39 how g' things Jesus had done unto
9:48 you all, the same shall be g'.
10: 2 The harvest truly is g', but the
13 they had a g' while ago repented
13:19 and waxed a g' tree; and the
14:16 A certain man made a g' supper,
25 there went g' multitudes with him:
32 while the other is yet a g' way off,
15:20 when he was yet a g' way off,
16:26 there is a g' gulf fixed: so that
21:11 g' earthquakes shall be in divers
11 and g' signs shall there be
23 shall be g' distress in the land,
27 cloud with power and g' glory.
22:44 as it were g' drops of blood
23:27 a g' company of people, and of
24:52 to Jerusalem with g' joy:
Joh 5: 3 a g' multitude of impotent folk,
6: 2 And a g' multitude followed him,
5 saw a g' company come unto him,
18 by reason of a g' wind that blew.
7:37 that g' day of the feast, Jesus
21:11 the net to land full of g' fishes,
Ac 2:20 before that g' and notable day of
4:33 with g' power gave the apostles
33 and g' grace was upon them all.
5: 5 and g' fear came on all them that
11 And g' fear came upon all the
6: 7 and a g' company of the priests
8 g' wonders and miracles among
7:11 and Chanaan, and g' affliction: and
8: 1 there was a g' persecution against
2 and made g' lamentation over him.
8 And there was g' joy in that city.
9 that himself was some g' one:
10 This man is the g' power of God.
27 an eunuch of g' authority under
9:16 how g' things he must suffer for
10:11 as it had been a g' sheet knit at
11: 5 as it had been a g' sheet, let down
21 and a g' number believed, and
28 that there should be g' dearth
14: 1 a g' multitude both of the Jews
15: 3 they caused g' joy unto all the
16:26 there was a g' earthquake, so that
17: 4 devout Greeks a g' multitude, and
19:27 of the g' goddess Diana should be
28 G' is Diana of the Ephesians.
34 out, G' is Diana of the Ephesians.
35 of the g' goddess Diana, and of the
21:40 there was made a g' silence, he
22: 6 shone from heaven a g' light round
28 With a g' sum obtained I this
23: 9 And there arose a g' cry: and the
10 there arose a g' dissension, the
14 bound ourselves under a g' curse,
24: 2 by thee we enjoy g' quietness,
7 with g' violence took him away
25:23 and Bernice, with g' pomp, and
26:22 witnessing both to small and g',
28: 6 after they had looked a g' while,
29 g' reasoning among themselves.
Ro 9: 2 That I have g' heaviness and
15:23 a g' desire these many years
1Co 9:11 it is a g' thing if we shall reap
16: 9 a g' door and effectual is opened
2Co 1:10 delivered us from so g' a death,
3:12 we use g' plainness of speech:
7: 4 G' is my boldness of speech toward
4 you, g' is my glorying of you:
8: 2 How that in a g' trial of affliction
22 diligent, upon the g' confidence
11:15 it is no g' thing if his ministers
Eph 2: 4 for his g' love wherewith he loved
5:32 This is a g' mystery: but I speak
Col 2: 1 ye knew what g' conflict I have
4:13 that he hath a g' zeal for you,
1Th 2:17 to see your face with g' desire.
1Ti 3:13 and g' boldness in the faith which
16 g' is the mystery of godliness:
6: 6 with contentment is g' gain.
2Ti 2:20 But in a g' house there are not
Tit 2:13 glorious appearing of the g' God

Ph'm 7 have g' joy and consolation in
Heb 2: 3 if we neglect so g' salvation;
4:14 that we have a g' high priest,
7: 4 consider how g' this man was,
10:32 ye endured a g' fight of afflictions;
35 hath g' recompence of reward.
12: 1 with so g' a cloud of witnesses,
13:20 that g' shepherd of the sheep,
Jas 3: 4 which though they be so g', and
5 member, and boasteth g' things.
5 g' a matter a little fire kindleth!
1Pe 3: 4 in the sight of God of g' price.
2Pe 1: 4 g' and precious promises:
2:18 speak g' swelling words of vanity,
3:10 shall pass away with a g' noise,
Jude 6 unto the judgment of the g' day.
16 mouth speaketh g' swelling words,
Re 1:10 and heard behind me a g' voice,
2:22 into g' tribulation, except they
6: 4 was given unto him a g' sword.
12 and, lo, there was a g' earthquake;
15 kings of the earth, and the g' men,
17 the g' day of his wrath is come;
7: 9 and, lo, a g' multitude, which no
14 which came out of g' tribulation,
8: 8 as it were a g' mountain burning
10 there fell a g' star from heaven,
9: 2 as the smoke of a g' furnace; and
14 are bound in the g' river Euphrates.
11: 8 in the street of the g' city, which
11 g' fear fell upon them which saw
12 they heard a g' voice from heaven
13 hour was there a g' earthquake,
15 there were g' voices in heaven,
17 hast taken to thee thy g' power,
18 that fear thy name, small and g';
19 and an earthquake, and g' hail.
12: 1 a g' wonder in heaven; a woman
3 g' red dragon, having seven heads
9 And the g' dragon was cast out,
12 having g' wrath, because he
14 two wings of a g' eagle, that she
13: 2 and his seat, and g' authority.
5 a mouth speaking g' things and
13 he doeth g' wonders, so that he
16 he causeth all, both small and g',
14: 2 as the voice of a g' thunder:
8 that g' city, because she made
19 into the g' winepress of the wrath
15: 1 g' and marvellous, seven angels
3 G' and marvelous are thy works,
16: 1 I heard a g' voice out of the temple
9 men were scorched with g' heat,
12 vial upon the g' river Euphrates;
14 of that g' day of God Almighty.
17 came a g' voice out of the temple
18 there was a g' earthquake, such as
18 mighty an earthquake, and so g'.
19 the g' city was divided into three
19 g' Babylon came in remembrance
21 upon men a g' hail out of heaven,
21 plague thereof was exceeding g'.
17: 1 judgment of the g' whore that
5 Mystery, Babylon The G', The
6 I wondered with g' admiration.
18 is that g' city, which reigneth over
18: 1 from heaven, having g' power;
2 Babylon the g' is fallen, is fallen,
10 Alas, alas that g' city Babylon, that
16 Alas, alas that g' city, that was
17 so g' riches is come to nought.
18 What city is like unto this g'
19 Alas, alas that g' city, wherein
21 took up a stone like a g' millstone,
21 shall that g' city Babylon be thrown
23 thy merchants were the g' men
19: 1 I heard a g' voice of much people
2 hath judged the g' whore, which
5 that fear him, both small and g'.
6 the voice of a g' multitude, and
17 unto the supper of the g' God;
18 free and bond, both small and g'.
20: 1 and a g' chain in his hand.
11 I saw a g' white throne, and him
12 I saw the dead, small and g',
21: 3 I heard a g' voice out of heaven
10 spirit to a g' and high mountain,
10 and shewed me that g' city,
12 had a wall g' and high, and had

greater
Ge 1:16 the g' light to rule the day, and
4:13 punishment is g' than I can bear.
39: 9 none g' in this house than I;
41:40 throne will I be g' than thou.
48:19 shall be g' than he, and his seed
Ex 18:11 the Lord is g' than all gods:
Nu 14:12 make of thee a g' nation and
De 1:28 The people is g' and taller than
4:38 thee g' and mightier than thou art,
7: 1 seven nations g' and mightier
9: 1 nations g' and mightier than
14 nation mightier and g' than they.
11:23 ye shall possess g' nations and
Jos 10: 2 because it was g' than Ai, and all
1Sa 14:30 not been now a much g' slaughter
2Sa 13:15 g' than the love wherewith he had
16 g' than the other that thou didst
1Ki 1:37 and make his throne g' than thee
47 and make his throne g' than thy
1Ch 11: 9 So David waxed g' and...: for the
9 and g'; for the Lord of hosts was
2Ch 3: 5 And the g' house he cieled with
Es 9: 4 this man Mordecai waxed g' and
4 this man Mordecai waxed...and g'.
Job 33:12 thee, that God is g' than man.
La 4: 6 people is g' than the punishment
Eze 8: 6 thou shalt see g' abominations.
13 shalt see g' abominations that
15 shalt see g' abominations than
43:14 lesser settle even to the g' settle
Da 11:13 a multitude g' than the former,
Am 6: 2 their border g' than your border?
Hag 2: 9 house shall be g' than the former,
M't 11:11 hath not risen a g' than John the
11 kingdom of heaven is g' than he.
12: 6 place is one g' than the temple.
41 behold, a g' than Jonas is here.
42 behold, a g' than Solomon is here.
23:14 ye shall receive the g' damnation.
17 for whether is g', the gold, or the
19 whether is g', the gift, or the
M'r 4:32 becometh g' than all herbs, and
12:31 none other commandment g' than
40 these shall receive g' damnation.
Lu 7:28 there is not a g' prophet than
28 is g' than he.
11:31 behold, a g' than Solomon is here.
32 and, behold, a g' than Jonas is here.
12:18 pull down my barns, and build g';
20:47 same shall receive g' damnation.
22:27 For whether is g', he that sitteth
Joh 1:50 thou shalt see g' things than these.
4:12 Art thou g' than our father Jacob,
5:20 g' works than these, that ye may
36 But I have g' witness than that
8:53 thou g' than our father Abraham,
10:29 gave them me, is g' than all; and no
13:16 The servant is not g' than his lord;
16 neither he that is sent g' than he
14:12 g' works than these shall he do;
28 for my Father is g' than I.
15:13 G' love hath no man than this,
20 The servant is not g' than his
19:11 me unto thee hath the g' sin.
Ac 15:28 to lay upon you no g' burden than
1Co 14: 5 for g' is he that prophesieth than
15: 6 g' part remain unto this present,
Heb 6:13 could swear by no g', he sware by
16 for men verily swear by the g':
9:11 a g' and more perfect tabernacle,
11:26 reproach of Christ g' riches than
Jas 3: 1 shall receive the g' condemnation.
2Pe 2:11 which are g' in power and might,
1Jo 3:20 God is g' than our heart, and
4: 4 because g' is he that is in you, than
5: 9 of men, the witness of God is g':
3Jo 4 I have no g' joy than to hear that

greatest
1Ch 12:14 an hundred, and the g' over a
29 the g' part of them had kept the
Job 1: 3 was the g' of all the men of the
Jer 6:13 the least even unto the g' of them
8:10 the least even unto the g' is given
31:34 least of them unto the g' of them,
42: 1 the least even unto the g', came
8 people from the least even to the g'.
44:12 the least even unto the g', by the
Jon 3: 5 the g' of them even to the least of
M't 13:32 g' among herbs, and becometh
18: 1 Who is the g' in the kingdom of
4 the same is g' in the kingdom of
23:11 But he that is g' among you shall
M'r 9:34 themselves, who should be the g'.
Lu 9:46 which of them should be g'.
22:24 of them should be accounted the g'.
26 but he that is g' among you, let
Ac 8:10 heed, from the least to the g',
1Co 13:13 but the g' of these is charity.
Heb 8:11 know me, from the least to the g'.

greatly^
Ge 3:16 I will g' multiply thy sorrow and
7:18 were increased g' upon the earth;
19: 3 pressed upon them g'; and they
24:35 Lord hath blessed my master g';
32: 7 Jacob was g' afraid and distressed:
Ex 19:18 and the whole mount quaked g'.
Nu 11:10 anger of the Lord was kindled g';
14:39 Israel: and the people mourned g'.
De 15: 4 for the Lord shall g' bless thee
17:17 neither shall he g' multiply to
Jos 10: 2 they feared g', because Gibeon
J'g 2:15 and they were g' distressed.
6: 6 And Israel was g' impoverished
1Sa 11: 6 and his anger was kindled g'.
15 all the men of Israel rejoiced g'.
12:18 all the people g' feared the Lord
16:21 he loved him g'; and he became
17:11 they were dismayed, and g' afraid.
28: 5 afraid, and his heart g' trembled.
30: 6 And David was g' distressed; for
2Sa 10: 5 because the men were g' ashamed:
12: 5 anger was g' kindled against the
24:10 have sinned g' in that I have done:
1Ki 2:12 his kingdom was established g'.
5: 7 of Solomon, that he rejoiced g',
18: 3 (Now Obadiah feared the Lord g':
1Ch 4:38 house of their fathers increased g'.
16:25 and g' to be praised: he also is
19: 5 for the men were g' ashamed.
21: 8 said unto God, I have sinned g',
2Ch 25:10 was g' kindled against Judah, and
33:12 and humbled himself g' before the
Job 3:25 thing which I g' feared is come
8: 7 thy latter end should g' increase.
Ps 21: 1 salvation how g' shall he rejoice!
28: 7 therefore my heart g' rejoiceth; and
38: 6 I am bowed down g'; I go
45:11 So shall the king g' desire thy
47: 9 belong unto God: he is g' exalted.
Ps 48: 1 and g' to be praised in the city
62: 2 defence; I shall not be g' moved.
65: 9 thou g' enrichest it with the
71:23 My lips shall g' rejoice when I
78:59 wroth, and g' abhorred Israel:
89: 7 God is g' to be feared in the
96: 4 and g' to be praised: he is to
105:24 And he increased his people g';
107:38 so that they are multiplied g';
109:30 I will g' praise the Lord with my
112: 1 delighteth g' in his commandments.
116:10 have I spoken: I was g' afflicted:
119:51 have had me g' in derision: yet
145: 3 the Lord, and g' to be praised;
Pr 23:24 father of the righteous shall g' rejoice:
Isa 42:17 they shall be g' ashamed, that
Jer 3: 1 shall not that land be g' polluted?
4:10 surely thou hast g' deceived this
9:19 we are g' confounded, because we
20:11 they shall be g' ashamed; for
Eze 20:13 and my sabbaths they g' polluted:
25:12 vengeance, and hath g' offended,
Da 5: 9 was king Belshazzar g' troubled,
9:23 for thou art g' beloved: therefore
10:11 man g' beloved, understand the word
19 O man g' beloved, fear not:
Ob 2 the heathen: thou art g' despised.
Zep 1:14 it is near, and hasteth g', even
Zec 9: 9 Rejoice g', O daughter of Zion;
M't 27:14 that the governor marvelled g'.
54 they feared g', saying, Truly this
M'r 5:23 And besought him g', saying, My
38 and them that wept and wailed g'.
9:15 were g' amazed, and running to
12:27 the living: ye therefore do g' err.
Joh 3:29 rejoiceth g' because of the
Ac 3:11 is called Solomon's, g' wondering.
6: 7 multiplied in Jerusalem g';
1Co 16:12 g' desired him to come unto you
Ph'p 1: 8 how g' I long after you all in the
4:10 I rejoiced in the Lord g', that now
1Th 3: 6 desiring g' to see us, as we also
2Ti 1: 4 G' desiring to see thee, being
4:15 he hath g' withstood our words.
1Pe 1: 6 Wherein ye g' rejoice, though now for
2Jo 4 I rejoiced g' that I found of thy
3Jo 3 I rejoiced g', when the brethren

greatness
Ex 15: 7 And in the g' of thine excellency
16 by the g' of thine arm they
Nu 14:19 unto the g' of thy mercy.
De 3:24 shew thy servant thy g', and thy
5:24 his glory and his g', and we
9:26 redeemed through thy g', which
11: 2 his g', his mighty hand, and his
32: 3 Lord: ascribe ye g' unto our God.
1Ch 17:19 hast thou done all this g', in
21 a name of g' and terribleness,
29:11 Thine, O Lord, is the g', and
2Ch 9: 6 the g' of thy wisdom was not
24:27 and the g' of the burdens laid
Ne 13:22 according to the g' of thy mercy.
Es 10: 2 the g' of Mordecai, whereunto the
Ps 66: 3 through the g' of thy power shall
71:21 Thou shalt increase my g', and
79:11 according to the g' of thy power
145: 3 and his g' is unsearchable.
6 acts: and I will declare thy g'.
150: 2 according to his excellent g'.
Pr 5:23 and in the g' of his folly he shall
Isa 40:26 by the g' of his might, for that
57:10 wearied in the g' of thy way;
63: 1 travelling in the g' of his strength?
Jer 13:22 For the g' of thine iniquity are
Eze 31: 2 Whom art thou like in thy g'?
7 Thus was he fair in his g', in the
18 in glory and in g' among the trees
Da 4:22 for thy g' is grown, and reacheth
7:27 and the g' of the kingdom under
Eph 1:19 g' of his power to us-ward who

great-owl See GREAT and OWL.

greaves
1Sa 17: 6 he had g' of brass upon his legs.

Grecia See also GRECIANS; GREECE.
Da 8:21 the rough goat is the king of G':
10:20 forth, lo, the prince of G' shall
11: 2 stir up all against the realm of G'.

Grecians See also GREEKS.
Joe 3: 6 have ye sold unto the G', that
Ac 6: 1 arose a murmuring of the G'
9:29 disputed against the G': but
11:20 spake unto the G', preaching

Greece See also GRECIA.
Zec 9:13 O Zion, against thy sons, O G',
Ac 20: 2 exhortation, he came into G',

greedily
Pr 21:26 He coveteth g' all the day long:
Eze 22:12 and thou hast g' gained of thy
Jude 11 ran g' after the error of Balaam

greediness
Eph 4:19 to work all uncleanness with g'.

greedy
Ps 17:12 as a lion that is g' of his prey,
Pr 1:19 every one that is g' of gain;
15:27 He that is g' of gain troubleth his
Isa 56:11 they are g' dogs which can
1Ti 3: 3 no striker, not g' of filthy lucre;
8 much wine, not g' of filthy lucre;

Greek See also GREEKS.
M'r 7:26 woman was a G', a Syrophenician

Lu 23:38 of *G*', and Latin, and Hebrew.
Joh 19:20 in Hebrew, and *G*', and Latin.
Ac 16: 1 believed; but his father was a *G*':
3 knew all that his father was a *G*'.
21:37 Who said, Canst thou speak *G*'?
Ro 1:16 the Jew first, and also to the *G*'.
10:12 between the Jew and the *G*': for
Ga 2: 3 who was with me, being a *G*',
3:28 There is neither Jew nor *G*', there
Col 3:11 there is neither *G*' nor Jew,
Re 9:11 in the *G*' tongue hath his name

Greeks See also GRECIANS.
Joh 12:20 there were certain *G*' among
Ac 14: 1 Jews and also of the *G*' believed.
17: 4 the devout *G*' a great multitude,
12 women which were *G*', and of
18: 4 persuaded the Jews and the *G*'.
17 the *G*' took Sosthenes, the chief
19:10 the Lord Jesus, both Jews and *G*'.
17 known to all the Jews and *G*' also
20:21 to the Jews, and also to the *G*',
21:28 brought *G*' also into the temple,
Ro 1:14 I am debtor both to the *G*', and to
1Co 1:22 and the *G*' seek after wisdom:
23 and unto the *G*' foolishness;
24 which are called, both Jews and *G*',

green See also GREENISH.
Ge 1:30 have given every *g*' herb for meat:
9: 3 even as the *g*' herb have I given
30:37 Jacob took him rods of *g*' poplar,
Ex 10:15 there remained not any *g*' thing
Le 2:14 of thy firstfruits *g*' ears of corn
23:14 parched corn, nor *g*' ears, until
De 12: 2 the hills, and under every *g*' tree:
J'g 16: 7 seven *g*' withs that were never
8 seven *g*' withs which had not been
1Ki 14:23 high hill, and under every *g*' tree.
2Ki 16: 4 the hills, and under every *g*' tree.
17:10 high hill, and under every *g*' tree:
19:26 and as the *g*' herb, as the grass on
2Ch 28: 4 the hills, and under every *g*' tree.
Es 1: 6 white, *g*', and blue, hangings,
Job 8:16 He is *g*' before the sun, and his
15:32 and his branch shall not be *g*'.
39: 8 he searcheth after every *g*' thing.
Ps 23: 2 me to lie down in *g*' pastures:
37: 2 grass, and wither as the *g*' herb.
35 himself like a *g*' bay tree.
52: 8 am like a *g*' olive tree in the house
Ca 1:16 yea, pleasant: also our bed is *g*'.
2:13 fig tree putteth forth her *g*' figs,
Isa 15: 6 grass faileth, there is no *g*' thing.
37:27 and as the *g*' herb, as the grass
57: 5 under every *g*' tree, slaying the
Jer 2:20 under every *g*' tree thou wanderest,
3: 6 under every *g*' tree, and there hath
13 under every *g*' tree, and ye have
11:16 A *g*' olive tree, fair, and of goodly
17: 2 the *g*' trees upon the high hills.
8 cometh, but her leaf shall be *g*';
Eze 6:13 under every *g*' tree, and under
17:24 have dried up the *g*' tree, and
20:47 shall devour every *g*' tree in thee,
Ho 14: 8 him: I am like a *g*' fir tree.
M'r 6:39 by companies upon the *g*' grass.
Lu 23:31 they do these things in a *g*' tree,
Re 8: 7 and all *g*' grass was burnt up.
9: 4 neither any *g*' thing, neither any

greenish
Le 13:49 if the plague be *g*' or reddish in
14:37 hollow strakes, *g*' or reddish, which

greenness
Job 8:12 Whilst it is yet in his *g*', and not cut

greet See also GREETETH; GREETING.
1Sa 25: 5 go to Nabal, and *g*' him in
Ro 16: 3 *G*' Priscilla and Aquila my
5 Likewise *g*' the church that is in
6 *G*' Mary; who bestowed much
8 *G*' Amplias my beloved in the
11 *G*' them that be of the household
1Co 16:20 All the brethren *g*' you. *G*' ye
2Co 13:12 *G*' one another with an holy kiss.
Ph'p 4:21 which are with me *g*' you.
Col 4:14 physician, and Demas, *g*' you.
1Th 5:26 *G*' all the brethren with an holy
Tit 3:15 *G*' them that love us in the faith.
1Pe 5:14 *G*' ye one another with a kiss of
2Jo 13 of thy elect sister *g*' thee.
3Jo 14 thee. *G*' the friends by name.

greeteth
2Ti 4:21 Eubulus *g*' thee, and Pudens,

greeting See also GREETINGS.
Ac 15:23 send *g*' unto the brethren which
23:26 excellent governor Felix sendeth *g*'.
Jas 1: 1 which are scattered abroad, *g*'.

greetings
M't 23: 7 And *g*' in the markets, and to be
Lu 11:43 synagogues and *g*' in the markets.
20:46 love *g*' in the markets, and the

grew
Ge 2: 5 herb of the field before it *g*':
19:25 that which *g*' upon the ground.
21: 8 the child *g*', and was weaned:
20 God was with the lad; and he *g*',
25:27 And the boys *g*': and Esau was
26:13 *g*' until he became very great:
47:27 had possession therein, and *g*',
Ex 1:12 the more they multiplied and *g*'.
2:10 And the child *g*', and she brought
J'g 11: 2 and his wife's sons *g*' up, and they
13:24 and the child *g*', and the Lord
1Sa 2:21 child Samuel *g*' before the Lord.
26 the child Samuel *g*' on, and was
3:19 And Samuel *g*', and the Lord was
2Sa 5:10 And David went on and *g*' great,
12: 3 it *g*' up together with him, and
Eze 17: 6 *g*', and became a spreading vine
10 wither in the furrows where it *g*'.
Da 4:11 The tree *g*', and was strong, and
20 tree that thou sawest, which *g*',
M'r 4: 7 thorns *g*' up, and choked it, and it
5:26 bettered, but rather *g*' worse,
Lu 1:80 And the child *g*', and waxed strong
2:40 And the child *g*', and waxed strong
13:19 it *g*', and waxed a great tree;
Ac 7:17 people *g*' and multiplied in Egypt,
12:24 the word of God *g*' and multiplied.
19:20 So mightily *g*' the word of God

grey [*so most editions here*] See also GRAY; GREYHEADED; GREYHOUND.
Pr 20:29 beauty of old men is the *g*' head.

greyheaded [*so most editions here*]
Ps 71:18 Now also when I am old and *g*',

greyhound
Pr 30:31 A *g*'; an he goat also; and a

grief See also GRIEFS.
Ge 26:35 Which were a *g*' of mind unto Isaac
1Sa 1:16 complaint and *g*' have I spoken
25:31 this shall be no *g*' unto thee, nor
2Ch 6:29 his own sore and his own *g*',
Job 2:13 saw that his *g*' was very great.
6: 2 my *g*' were thoroughly weighed,
16: 5 of my lips should asswage your *g*'.
6 I speak, my *g*' is not asswaged:
Ps 6: 7 eye is consumed because of *g*';
31: 9 mine eye is consumed with *g*', yea,
10 For my life is spent with *g*',
69:26 they talk to the *g*' of those whom
Pr 17:25 A foolish son is a *g*' to his father,
Ec 1:18 For in much wisdom is much *g*':
2:23 days are sorrows, and his travail *g*';
Isa 17:11 shall be a heap in the day of *g*'
53: 3 sorrows, and acquainted with *g*':
10 he hath put him to *g*': when thou
Jer 6: 7 before me continually is *g*' and
10:19 Truly this is a *g*', and I must bear
45: 3 Lord hath added *g*' to my sorrow;
La 3:32 though he cause *g*', yet will he
Jon 4: 6 head, to deliver him from his *g*'.
2Co 2: 5 if any have caused *g*', he hath
Heb 13:17 do it with joy, and not with *g*':
1Pe 2:19 conscience toward God endure *g*',

griefs
Isa 53: 4 hath borne our *g*', and carried our

grievance
Hab 1: 3 and cause me to behold *g*'?

grieve See also GRIEVED; GRIEVETH; GRIEVING.
1Sa 2:33 thine eyes, and to *g*' thine heart:
1Ch 4:10 from evil, that it may not *g*' me!
Ps 78:40 wilderness, and *g*' him in the desert!
La 3:33 willingly nor *g*' the children of
Eph 4:30 And *g*' not the holy spirit of God,

grieved
Ge 6: 6 and it *g*' him at his heart,
34: 7 and the men were *g*', and they were
45: 5 be not *g*', nor angry with yourselves,
49:23 The archers have sorely *g*' him,
Ex 1:12 And they were *g*' because of the
De 15:10 thine heart shall not be *g*' when
J'g 10:16 soul was *g*' for the misery of Israel.
1Sa 1: 8 thou not? and why is thy heart *g*'?
15:11 it *g*' Samuel; and he cried unto
20: 3 Jonathan know this, lest he be *g*':
34 was *g*' for David, because his father
30: 6 the soul of all the people was *g*',
2Sa 19: 2 the king was *g*' for his son.
Ne 2:10 it *g*' them exceedingly that there
8:11 the day is holy; neither be ye *g*'.
13: 8 And it *g*' me sore: therefore I cast
Es 4: 4 was the queen exceedingly *g*';
Job 4: 2 with thee, wilt thou be *g*'?
30:25 was not my soul *g*' for the poor?
Ps 73:21 Thus my heart was *g*', and I was
95:10 Forty years long was I *g*' with
112:10 The wicked shall see it, and be *g*';
119:158 the transgressors, and was *g*';
139:21 am not I *g*' with those that rise up
Isa 54: 6 thee as a woman forsaken and *g*'
57:10 hand; therefore thou wast not *g*'.
Jer 5: 3 have not *g*'; thou hast consumed
Da 7:15 I Daniel was *g*' in my spirit
11:30 he shall be *g*', and return,
Am 6: 6 they are not *g*' for the affliction
M'r 3: 5 *g*' for the hardness of their hearts,
10:22 at that saying, and went away *g*':
Joh 21:17 Peter was *g*' because he said unto
Ac 4: 2 *g*' that they taught the people,
16:18 Paul, being *g*', turned and said to
Ro 14:15 if thy brother be *g*' with thy meat,
2Co 2: 4 not that ye should be *g*', but that
5 he hath not *g*' me, but in part:
Heb 3:10 I was *g*' with that generation,
17 with whom was he *g*' forty years?

grieveth
Ru 1:13 for it *g*' me much for your sakes
Pr 26:15 it *g*' him to bring it again to his

grieving
Eze 28:24 nor any *g*' thorn of all that are

grievous
Ge 12:10 the famine was *g*' in the land.
18:20 and because their sin is very *g*';
21:11 the thing was very *g*' in Abraham's
12 Let it not be *g*' in thy sight because
41:31 following; for it shall be very *g*'.
50:11 is a *g*' mourning to the Egyptians:
Ex 8:24 there came a *g*' swarm of flies
9: 3 there shall be a very *g*' murrain.
18 will cause it to rain a very *g*' hail,
24 fire mingled with the hail, very *g*',
10:14 coasts of Egypt: very *g*' were they;
1Ki 2: 8 cursed me with a *g*' curse in the
12: 4 Thy father made our yoke *g*':
4 thou the *g*' service of thy father,
2Ch 10: 4 Thy father made our yoke *g*': now
4 the *g*' servitude of thy father,
Ps 10: 5 His ways are always *g*'; thy
31:18 be put to silence; which speak *g*'
Pr 15: 1 wrath: but *g*' words stir up anger.
10 Correction is *g*' unto him that
Ec 2:17 under the sun is *g*' unto me: for
Isa 15: 4 out; his life shall be *g*' unto him.
21: 2 A *g*' vision is declared unto me;
Jer 6:28 They are all *g*' revolters,
10:19 for my hurt! my wound is *g*':
14:17 a great breach, with a very *g*' blow
16: 4 They shall die of *g*' deaths; they
23:19 in fury, even a *g*' whirlwind:
30:12 incurable, and thy wound is *g*'.
Na 3:19 thy wound is *g*': all that hear
M't 23: 4 heavy burdens and *g*' to be borne,
Lu 11:46 with burdens *g*' to be borne, and ye
Ac 20:29 shall *g*' wolves enter in among you,
25: 7 and *g*' complaints against Paul,
Ph'p 3: 1 to me indeed is not *g*', but for
Heb 12:11 seemeth to be joyous, but *g*':
1Jo 5: 3 and his commandments are not *g*'.
Re 16: 2 noisome and *g*' sore upon the men

grievously
Isa 9: 1 afterward did more *g*' afflict her
Jer 23:19 whirlwind: it shall fall *g*' upon
La 1: 8 Jerusalem hath *g*' sinned;
20 for I have *g*' rebelled: abroad the
Eze 14:13 against me by trespassing *g*',
M't 8: 6 sick of the palsy, *g*' tormented.
15:22 daughter is *g*' vexed with a devil.

grievousness
Isa 10: 1 that write *g*' which they have
21:15 bent bow, and from the *g*' of war.

grind See also GRINDING; GROUND.
J'g 16:21 and he did *g*' in the prison house.
Job 31:10 Then let my wife *g*' unto another,
Isa 3:15 pieces, and *g*' the faces of the poor?
47: 2 Take the millstones, and *g*' meal:
La 5:13 They took the young men to *g*',
M't 21:44 shall fall, it will *g*' him to powder.
Lu 20:18 shall fall, it will *g*' him to powder.

grinders
Ec 12: 3 the *g*' cease because they are few,

grinding
Ec 12: 4 when the sound of the *g*' is low,
M't 24:41 Two women shall be *g*' at the mill;
Lu 17:35 Two women shall be *g*' together;

grisled
Ge 31:10 ringstraked, speckled, and *g*'.
12 are ringstraked, speckled, and *g*';
Zec 6: 3 fourth chariot *g*' and bay horses.
6 the *g*' go forth toward the south

groan See also GROANED; GROANETH; GROANING.
Job 24:12 Men *g*' from out of the city,
Jer 51:52 all her land the wounded shall *g*'.
Eze 30:24 he shall *g*' before him with the
Joe 1:18 How do the beasts *g*'! the herds
Ro 8:23 we ourselves *g*' within ourselves,
2Co 5: 2 in this we *g*', earnestly desiring to
4 we that are in this tabernacle do *g*',

groaned
Joh 11:33 *g*' in the spirit, and was troubled,

groaneth
Ro 8:22 *g*' and travaileth in pain together

groaning See also GROANINGS.
Ex 2:24 And God heard their *g*', and God
6: 5 And I have also heard the *g*' of the
Job 23: 2 my stroke is heavier than my *g*'.
Ps 6: 6 I am weary with my *g*'; all the
38: 9 and my *g*' is not hid from thee.
102: 5 By reason of the voice of my *g*' my
20 To hear the *g*' of the prisoner;
Joh 11:38 therefore again *g*' in himself
Ac 7:34 and I have heard their *g*', and

groanings
J'g 2:18 because of their *g*' by reason of
Eze 30:24 the *g*' of a deadly wounded man.
Ro 8:26 with *g*' which cannot be uttered.

grope See also GROPETH.
De 28:29 thou shalt *g*' at noonday, as the
Job 5:14 *g*' in the noonday as in the night.
12:25 They *g*' in the dark without light,
Isa 59:10 We *g*' for the wall like the blind,
10 and we *g*' as if we had no eyes:

gropeth
De 28:29 as the blind *g*' in darkness, and

gross
Isa 60: 2 earth, and *g*' darkness the people:
Jer 13:16 of death, and make it *g*' darkness.
M't 13:15 For this people's heart is waxed *g*',
Ac 28:27 the heart of this people is waxed *g*',

ground See also AGROUND; GROUNDED.
Ge 2: 5 there was not a man to till the *g*'.
6 and watered the whole face of the *g*'.

Ge 2: 7 formed man of the dust of the *g*.
9 out of the *g* made the Lord God to
19 out of the *g* the Lord God formed
3:17 cursed is the *g* for thy sake;
19 bread, till thou return unto the *g*;
23 to till the *g* from whence he was
4: 2 but Cain was a tiller of the *g*.
3 Cain brought of the fruit of the *g*
10 blood crieth unto me from the *g*.
12 When thou tillest the *g*, it shall
5:29 the *g* which the Lord hath cursed.
7:23 which was upon the face of the *g*,
8: 8 abated from off the face of the *g*;
13 behold, the face of the *g* was dry.
21 I will not again curse the *g* any
18: 2 and bowed himself toward the *g*,
19: 1 with his face toward the *g*,
25 and that which grew upon the *g*.
33: 3 himself to the *g* seven times,
38: 9 he spilled it on the *g*, lest that he
44:11 down every man his sack to the *g*,
14 and they fell before him on the *g*.
Ex 3: 5 whereon thou standest is holy *g*.
4: 3 And he said, Cast it on the *g*.
3 And he cast it on the *g*,
8:21 and also the *g* whereon they are.
9:23 the fire ran along upon the *g*;
14:16 shall go on dry *g* through the
22 midst of the sea upon the dry *g*
16:14 as small as the hoar frost on the *g*.
32:20 the fire, and *g* it to powder,
Le 20:25 that creepeth on the *g*, which I
Nu 11: 8 gathered it, and *g* it in mills,
16:31 *g* clave asunder that was under
De 4:18 anything that creepeth on the *g*,
9:21 *g* it very small, even until it was
15:23 shalt pour it upon the *g* as water.
22: 6 in any tree, or on the *g*, whether
28: 4 the fruit of thy *g*, and the fruit
11 the fruit of thy *g*, in the land
56 the sole of her foot upon the *g*
Jos 3:17 stood firm on dry *g* in the midst
17 Israelites passed over on dry *g*,
24:32 a parcel of *g* which Jacob bought
J'g 4:21 fastened it into the *g*: for he was
6:39 and upon all the *g* let there be dew.
40 and there was dew on all the *g*.
13:20 and fell on their faces to the *g*.
20:21 Gibeah, and destroyed down to the *g*
25 day, and destroyed down to the *g*
Ru 2:10 bowed herself to the *g*, and said
1Sa 3:19 let none of his words fall to the *g*.
5: 4 was fallen upon his face to the *g*
8:12 and will set them to ear his *g*,
14:25 and there was honey upon the *g*.
32 calves, and slew them on the *g*:
45 one hair of his head fall to the *g*;
20:31 the son of Jesse liveth upon the *g*,
41 fell on his face to the *g*, and bowed
25:23 face, and bowed herself to the *g*,
26: 7 and his spear stuck in the *g* at his
28:14 and stooped with his face to the *g*,
2Sa 2:22 should I smite thee to the *g*?
8: 2 casting them down to the *g*; even
14: 4 she fell on her face to the *g*, and did
14 water spilt on the *g*, which cannot
22 Joab fell to the *g* on his face,
33 bowed himself on his face to the *g*
17:12 as the dew falleth on the *g*:
19 and spread *g* corn thereon;
18:11 thou not smite him there to the *g*?
20:10 and shed out his bowels to the *g*,
23:11 a piece of *g* full of lentiles: and
12 stood in the midst of the *g*, and
24:20 the king on his face upon the *g*.
1Ki 1:23 the king with his face to the *g*.
7:46 cast them, in the clay *g* between
2Ki 2: 8 so that they two went over on dry *g*.
15 themselves to the *g* before him.
19 is naught, and the *g* barren.
4:37 bowed herself to the *g*, and took
9:26 and cast him into the plat of *g*,
13:18 Smite upon the *g*. And he smote
1Ch 11:13 was a parcel of *g* full of barley;
21:21 to David with his face to the *g*.
27:26 the field for tillage of the *g* was
2Ch 4:17 king cast them, in the clay *g*
7: 3 with their faces to the *g* upon the
20:18 his head with his face to the *g*:
Ne 8: 6 the Lord with their faces to the *g*.
10:35 to bring the firstfruits of our *g*,
37 the tithes of our *g* unto the Levites,
Job 1:20 down upon the *g*, and worshipped,
2:13 they sat down with him upon the *g*
5: 6 doth trouble spring out of the *g*;
14: 8 the stock thereof die in the *g*;
16:13 poureth out my gall upon the *g*.
18:10 The snare is laid for him in the *g*,
38:27 To satisfy the desolate and waste *g*;
39:24 swalloweth the *g* with fierceness
Ps 74: 7 dwelling place of thy name to the *g*.
89:39 his crown by casting it to the *g*.
44 cast his throne down to the *g*.
105:35 and devoured the fruit of their *g*.
107:33 and the watersprings into dry *g*;
35 and dry *g* into watersprings.
143: 3 hath smitten my life down to the *g*;
147: 6 casteth the wicked down to the *g*.
Isa 3:26 being desolate shall sit upon the *g*.
14:12 how art thou cut down to the *g*,
21: 9 her gods he hath broken unto the *g*.
25:12 bring to the *g*, even to the dust.
26: 5 he layeth it low, even to the *g*;
28:24 and break the clods of his *g*?
29: 4 shalt speak out of the *g*, and thy

Isa 29: 4 familiar spirit, out of the *g*, and
30:23 thou shalt sow the *g* withal;
24 young asses that ear the *g* shall eat
35: 7 parched *g* shall become a pool,
44: 3 and floods upon the dry *g*:
47: 1 sit on the *g*: there is no throne,
51:23 thou hast laid thy body as the *g*,
53: 2 plant, and as a root out of a dry *g*:
Jer 4: 3 Break up your fallow *g*, and sow
7:20 and upon the fruit of the *g*;
14: 2 they are black unto the *g*;
4 Because the *g* is chapt, for there
25:33 they shall be dung upon the *g*.
27: 5 the beast that are upon the *g*,
La 2: 2 hath brought them down to the *g*:
9 Her gates are sunk into the *g*;
10 sit upon the *g*, and keep silence:
10 hang down their heads to the *g*.
21 the old lie on the *g* in the streets:
Eze 12: 6 thy face, that thou see not the *g*:
12 that he see not the *g* with his eyes.
13:14 bring it down to the *g*, so that
19:12 she was cast down to the *g*, and the
13 wilderness, in a dry and thirsty *g*.
24: 7 she poured it not upon the *g*,
26:11 garrisons shall go down to the *g*.
16 they shall sit upon the *g*, and
28:17 I will cast thee to the *g*,
38:20 every wall shall fall to the *g*.
41:16 and from the *g* up to the windows,
20 From the *g* unto above the door
42: 6 and the middlemost from the *g*.
43:14 from the bottom upon the *g* even
Da 8: 5 earth, and touched not the *g*:
7 he cast him down to the *g*, and
10 the host and of the stars to the *g*,
12 it cast down the truth to the *g*;
18 sleep on my face toward the *g*:
10: 9 my face, and my face toward the *g*.
15 I set my face toward the *g*,
Ho 2:18 with the creeping things of the *g*:
10:12 mercy; break up your fallow *g*:
Am 3:14 be cut off, and fall to the *g*.
Ob 3 shall bring me down to the *g*?
Hag 1:11 upon that which the *g* bringeth
Zec 8:12 and the *g* shall give her increase,
Mal 3:11 not destroy the fruits of your *g*;
M't 10:29 shall not fall on the *g* without
13: 8 But other fell into good *g*, and
23 received seed into the good *g* is he
15:35 multitude to sit down on the *g*.
M'r 4: 5 And some fell on stony *g*, where it
8 other fell on good *g*, and did
16 which are sown on stony *g*, who,
20 they which are sown on good *g*;
26 man should cast seed into the *g*;
8: 6 people to sit down on the *g*:
9:20 he fell on the *g*, and wallowed
14:35 fell on the *g*, and prayed that, if it
Lu 8: 8 other fell on good *g*, and sprang
15 But that on the good *g* are they,
12:16 *g* of a certain rich man brought
13: 7 down; why cumbereth it the *g*?
14:18 I have bought a piece of *g*, and I,
19:44 shall lay thee even with the *g*,
22:44 of blood falling down to the *g*.
Joh 4: 5 near to the parcel of *g* that Jacob
8: 6 with his finger wrote on the *g*,
8 stooped down, and wrote on the *g*.
9: 6 he spat on the *g*, and made clay
12:24 a corn of wheat fall into the *g*
18: 6 went backward, and fell to the *g*.
Ac 7:33 where thou standest is holy *g*.
22: 7 I fell unto the *g*, and heard
1Ti 3:15 the pillar and *g* of the truth.

grounded
Isa 30:32 every place where the *g* staff
Eph 3:17 ye, being rooted and *g* in love,
Col 1:23 continue in the faith *g* and settled,

grove See also GROVES.
Ge 21:33 And Abraham planted a *g* in
De 16:21 Thou shalt not plant thee a *g*
J'g 6:25 cut down the *g* that is by it:
26 the wood of the *g* which thou
28 the *g* was cut down that was
30 he hath cut down the *g* that was
1Ki 15:13 she had made an idol in a *g*;
16:33 Ahab made a *g*; and Ahab did
2Ki 13: 6 remained the *g* also in Samaria.)
17:16 even two calves, and made a *g*,
21: 3 and made a *g*, as did Ahab king
7 set a graven image of the *g* that
23: 4 for Baal, and for the *g*, and for
6 he brought out the *g* from the
7 women wove hangings for the *g*.
15 to powder, and burned the *g*.
2Ch 15:16 she had made an idol in a *g*:

groves
Ex 34:13 images, and cut down their *g*:
De 7: 5 images, and cut down their *g*,
12: 3 and burn their *g* with fire;
J'g 3: 7 and served Baalim and the *g*.
1Ki 14:15 because they have made their *g*,
23 and *g*, on every high hill, and
18:19 prophets of the *g* four hundred
2Ki 17:10 and *g* in every high hill, and
18: 4 the images, and cut down the *g*,
23:14 the images, and cut down the *g*,
2Ch 14: 3 the images, and cut down the *g*:
17: 6 took away the high places,and *g*
19: 3 thou hast taken away the *g*
24:18 fathers, and served *g* and idols:
31: 1 in pieces, and cut down the *g*,
33: 3 and made *g*, and worshipped all

2Ch 33:19 and set up *g* and graven images,
34: 3, 4 the *g*, and the carved images,
7 altars and the *g*, and had beaten
Isa 17: 8 either the *g*, or the images.
27: 9 the *g* and images shall not stand
Jer 17: 2 their altars and their *g* by the
Mic 5:14 I will pluck up thy *g* out of the

grow^ See also GREW; GROWETH; GROWN.
Ge 2: 9 the Lord God to *g* every tree
48:16 and let them *g* into a multitude
Nu 6: 5 locks of the hair of his head *g*.
J'g 16:22 the hair of his head began to *g*
2Sa 23: 5 although he make it not to *g*.
2Ki 19:29 such things as *g* of themselves,
Ezr 4:22 why should damage *g* to the hurt
Job 8:11 Can the rush *g* up without mire?
19 out of the earth shall others *g*.
14:19 washest away the things which *g*
31:40 Let thistles *g* instead of wheat,
39: 4 good liking, they *g* up with corn;
Ps 92:12 shall *g* like a cedar in Lebanon.
104:14 causeth the grass to *g* for the
147: 8 who maketh grass to *g* upon the
Ec 11: 5 how the bones do *g* in the womb of her
Isa 11: 1 Branch shall *g* out of his roots:
17:11 shalt thou make thy plant to *g*,
53: 2 For he shall *g* up before him
Jer 12: 2 they have taken root: they *g*, yea,
33:15 Branch of righteousness to *g* up
Eze 44:20 nor suffer their locks to *g* long;
47:12 this side and on that side, shall *g*
Ho 14: 5 he shall *g* as the lily, and cast
7 as the corn, and *g* as the vine:
Jon 4:10 neither madest it *g*; which came
Zec 6:12 he shall *g* up out of his place,
Mal 4: 2 and *g* up as calves of the stall.
M't 6:28 the lilies of the field, how they *g*;
13:30 both *g* together until the harvest:
21:19 no fruit *g* on thee henceforward
M'r 4:27 the seed should spring and *g* up,
Lu 12:27 Consider the lilies how they *g*:
Ac 5:24 of them whereunto this would *g*.
Eph 4:15 may *g* up into him in all things,
1Pe 2: 2 the word, that ye may *g* thereby:
2Pe 3:18 *g* in grace, and in the knowledge

groweth
Ex 10: 5 every tree which *g* for you out of
Le 13:39 freckled spot that *g* in the skin;
25: 5 That which *g* of its own accord
11 reap that which *g* of itself in it,
De 29:23 beareth, nor any grass *g* therein,
J'g 19: 9 the day *g* to an end, lodge here,
Job 38:38 When the dust *g* into hardness,
Ps 90: 5 they are like grass which *g* up.
6 morning it flourisheth, and *g* up;
129: 6 which withereth afore it *g* up:
Isa 37:30 eat this year such as *g* of itself;
M'r 4:32 when it is sown, it *g* up, and
Eph 2:21 *g* unto an holy temple in the Lord:
2Th 1: 3 that your faith *g* exceedingly,

grown
Ge 38:11 house, till Shelah my son be *g*:
14 she saw that Shelah was *g*, and
Ex 2:11 when Moses was *g*, that he went
9:32 smitten: for they were not *g* up.
Le 13:37 there is black hair *g* up therein;
De 32:15 thou art waxen fat, thou art *g* thick,
Ru 1:13 tarry for them till they were *g*?
2Sa 10: 5 until your beards be *g*, and then
1Ki 12: 8 that were *g* up with him, and
10 that were *g* up with him spake
2Ki 4:18 And when the child was *g*, it fell
19:26 as corn blasted before it be *g* up.
1Ch 19: 5 at Jericho until your beards be *g*,
Ezr 9: 6 our trespass is *g* up unto the
Ps 144:12 as plants *g* up in their youth;
Pr 24:31 it was all *g* over with thorns,
Isa 37:27 as corn blasted before it be *g* up.
Jer 50:11 are *g* fat as the heifer at grass,
Eze 16: 7 are fashioned, and thine hair is *g*,
Da 4:22 that are *g* and become strong:
22 for thy greatness is *g*,
33 till his hairs were *g* like eagles'
M't 13:32 when it is *g*, it is the greatest

growth
Am 7: 1 the shooting up of the latter *g*;
1 and, lo, it was the latter *g* after

grudge See also GRUDGING.
Le 19:18 bear any *g* against the children
Ps 59:15 and *g* if they be not satisfied.
Jas 5: 9 *G* not one against another,

grudging
1Pe 4: 9 one to another without *g*.

grudgingly
2Co 9: 7 not *g*, or of necessity:

guard See also GUARDS; SAFEGUARD.
Ge 37:36 Pharaoh's, and captain of the *g*.
39: 1 of Pharaoh, captain of the *g*, an
40: 3 the house of the captain of the *g*,
4 the *g* charged Joseph with them,
41:12 servant to the captain of the *g*;
2Sa 23:23 And David set him over his *g*.
1Ki 14:27 the hands of the chief of the *g*,
28 that the *g* bare them, and brought
28 them back into the *g* chamber.
2Ki 10:25 that Jehu said to the *g* and to the
25 the *g* and the captains cast them
11: 4 with the captains and the *g*, and
6 third part at the gate behind the *g*:
11 And the *g* stood, every man with
13 Athaliah heard the noise of the *g*

2Ki 11:19 the captains, and the g', and all
19 gate of the g' to the king's house.
25: 8 Nebuzar-adan, captain of the g',
10 that were with the captain of the g',
11 the captain of the g' carry away.
12 the captain of the g' left of the poor
15 the captain of the g' took away.
18 the captain of the g' took Seraiah
20 captain of the g' took these, and
1Ch 11:25 and David set him over his g',
2Ch 12:10 the chief of the g', that kept the
11 the g' came and fetched them,
11 them again into the g' chamber.
Ne 4:22 in the night they may be a g' to us,
23 men of the g' which followed me,
Jer 39: 9 the captain of the g' carried away
10 the captain of the g' left of the poor
11 Nebuzar-adan the captain of the g',
13 the captain of the g' sent, and
40: 1 the captain of the g' had let him go
2 the captain of the g' took Jeremiah,
5 captain of the g' gave him victuals
41:10 captain of the g' had committed
43: 6 the captain of the g' had left with
52:12 the captain of the g', which served
14 the captain of the g', brake down
15 the captain of the g' carried away
16 the captain of the g' left certain of
19 took the captain of the g' away.
24 the captain of the g' took Seraiah
26 the captain of the g' took them,
30 the captain of the g' carried away
Eze 38: 7 thee, and be thou a g' unto them
Da 2:14 Arioch the captain of the king's g',
Ac 28:16 prisoners to the captain of the g':

guard's
Ge 41:10 in the captain of the g' house,

Gudgodah (*gud-go'-dah*) See also HOR-HAGIDGAD.
De 10: 7 unto G'; and from G' to Jotbath,

guest See also GUESTCHAMBER; GUESTS.
Lu 19: 7 gone to be g' with a man that is

guestchamber
M'r 14:14 The Master saith, Where is the g',
Lu 22:11 saith unto thee, Where is the g',

guests
1Ki 1:41 Adonijah and all the g' that were
49 the g' that were with Adonijah
Pr 9:18 her g' are in the depths of hell.
Zep 1: 7 a sacrifice, he hath bid his g'.
M't 22:10 the wedding was furnished with g'.
11 when the king came to see the g',

guide See also GUIDED; GUIDES; GUIDING.
Job 38:32 canst thou g' Arcturus with his
Ps 25: 9 The meek will he g' in judgment:
31: 3 name's sake lead me, and g' me.
32: 8 I will g' thee with mine eye.
48:14 he will be our g' even unto death.
55:13 my g', and mine acquaintance.
73:24 Thou shalt g' me with thy counsel.
112: 5 will g' his affairs with discretion.
Pr 2:17 forsaketh the g' of her youth,
6: 7 having no g', overseer, or ruler,
11: 3 of the upright shall g' them:
23:19 and g' thine heart in the way.
Isa 49:10 springs of water shall he g' them.
51:18 There is none to g' her among all
58:11 And the Lord shall g' thee
Jer 3: 4 thou art the g' of my youth?
Mic 7: 5 put ye not confidence in a g':
Lu 1:79 g' our feet into the way of peace.
Joh 16:13 he will g' you into all truth:
Ac 1:16 was g' to them that took Jesus.
8:31 except some man should g' me?
Ro 2:19 art a g' of the blind, a light of
1Ti 5:14 g' the house, give none occasion

guided
Ex 15:13 thou hast g' them in thy strength
2Ch 32:22 other, and g' them on every side.
Job 31:18 a father, and I have g' her from
Ps 78:52 and g' them in the wilderness
72 g' them by the skilfulness of his

guides
M't 23:16 Woe unto you, ye blind g', which
24 Ye blind g', which strain at a gnat

guiding
Ge 48:14 Manasseh's head, g' his hands

guile See also BEGUILE.
Ex 21:14 to slay him with g'; thou shalt
Ps 32: 2 in whose spirit there is no g'.
34:13 and thy lips from speaking g'.
55:11 deceit and g' depart not from her
Joh 1:47 Israelite indeed, in whom is no g'!
2Co 12:16 being crafty, I caught you with g'.
1Th 2: 3 nor of uncleanness, nor in g':
1Pe 2: 1 laying aside all malice, and all g',
22 neither was g' found in his mouth:
3:10 his lips that they speak no g':
Re 14: 5 in their mouth was found no g':

guilt See also GUILTLESS.
De 19:13 shalt put away the g' of innocent
21: 9 put away the g' of innocent blood

guiltiness See also BLOODGUILTINESS.
Ge 26:10 shouldest have brought g' upon us.

guiltless
Ex 20: 7 the Lord will not hold him g'
Nu 5:31 the man be g' from iniquity,
32:22 be g' before the Lord, and before
De 5:11 the Lord will not hold him g'
Jos 2:19 upon his head, and we will be g':
1Sa 26: 9 the Lord's anointed, and be g'?
2Sa 3:28 I and my kingdom are g'
14: 9 the king and his throne be g'.
1Ki 2: 9 hold him not g': for thou art
M't 12: 7 would not have condemned the g'.

guilty^
Ge 42:21 verily g' concerning our brother,
Le 4:13 should not be done, and are g';
22 should not be done, and is g';
27 ought not to be done, and be g';
5: 2 he also shall be unclean, and g'.
3 knoweth of it, then he shall be g'.
4 then he shall be g' in one of these.
5 he shall be g' in one of these things,
17 he wist it not, yet is he g',
6: 4 he hath sinned, and is g', that he
Nu 5: 6 the Lord, and that person be g';
14:18 and by no means clearing the g',
35:27 he shall not be g' of blood;
31 a murderer, which is g' of death:
J'g 21:22 at this time, that ye should be g'.
Ezr 10:19 wives; and being g', they offered
Pr 30:10 curse thee, and thou be found g'.
Eze 22: 4 Thou art become g' in thy blood.
Zec 11: 5 hold themselves not g': and they
M't 23:18 gift that is upon it, he is g'.
26:66 and said, He is g' of death.
M'r 14:64 condemned him to be g' of death.
Ro 3:19 world may become g' before God.
1Co 11:27 shall be g' of the body and blood
Jas 2:10 offend in one point, he is g' of all.

gulf
Lu 16:26 and you there is a great g' fixed:

Guni (*gu'-ni*) See also GUNITES.
Ge 46:24 Jahzeel, and G', and Jezer, and
Nu 26:48 of G', the family of the Gunites:
1Ch 5:15 the son of G', chief of the house of
7:13 Jahziel, and G', and Jezer, and

Gunites (*gu'-nites*)
Nu 26:48 of Guni, the family of the G':

Gur (*gur*) See also GUR-BAAL.
2Ki 9:27 they did so at the going up to G',

Gur-baal (*gur-ba'-al*)
2Ch 26: 7 the Arabians that dwelt in G',

gush See also GUSHED.
Jer 9:18 our eyelids g' out with waters.

gushed
1Ki 18:28 till the blood g' out upon them.
Ps 78:20 that the waters g' out, and the
105:41 and the waters g' out; they ran in
Isa 48:21 rock also, and the waters g' out.
Ac 1:18 midst, and all his bowels g' out.

gutter See also GUTTERS.
2Sa 5: 8 Whosoever getteth up to the g',

gutters
Ge 30:38 pilled before the flocks in the g'
41 the eyes of the cattle in the g',

H.

ha See also AHA.
Job 39:25 H', h.; and he smelleth the

Haahashtari (*ha-a-hash'-te-ri*)
1Ch 4: 6 Hepher, and Temeni, and H'.

Haammonai See CHEPHAR-HAAMMONAI.

Habaiah (*hab-ah'-yah*)
Ezr 2:61 the children of H', the children of
Ne 7:63 the children of H', the children of

Habakkuk^ (*hab'-ak-kuk*)
Hab 1: 1 The burden which H' the prophet
3: 1 A prayer of H' the prophet upon

Habaziniah (*hab-az-in-i'-ah*)
Jer 35: 3 Jeremiah, the son of H', and his

habergeon See also HABERGEONS.
Ex 28:32 as it were the hole of an h',
39:23 robe, as the hole of an h',
Job 41:26 the spear, the dart, nor the h'.

habergeons
2Ch 26:14 helmets, and h', and bows, and
Ne 4:16 shields, and the bows, and the h';

habitable
Pr 8:31 in the h' part of his earth;

habitation See also HABITATIONS.
Ex 15: 2 and I will prepare him an h';
13 in thy strength unto thy holy h'.
Le 13:46 without the camp shall his h' be.
De 12: 5 even unto his h' shall ye seek,
26:15 Look down from thy holy h',
1Sa 2:29 I have commanded in my h';
32 shalt see an enemy in my h',
2Sa 15:25 shew me both it, and his h':
2Ch 6: 2 have built an house of h' for thee,
29: 6 their faces from the h' of the Lord,
Ez 7:15 Israel, whose h' is in Jerusalem,
Job 5: 3 root: but suddenly I cursed his h'.
24 thou shalt visit thy h', and shalt
8: 6 h' of thy righteousness prosperous.
18:15 shall be scattered upon his h'.
Ps 26: 8 I have loved the h' of thy house,
33:14 From the place of his h' he looketh
68: 5 the widows, is God in his holy h'.
69:25 Let their h' be desolate; and let
71: 3 Be thou my strong h', whereunto
89:14 judgment...the h' of thy throne:
91: 9 refuge, even the most High, thy h';
97: 2 judgment are the h' of his throne.
104:12 fowls of the heaven have their h',
107: 7 that they might go to a city of h',
36 that they may prepare a city for h';
132: 5 h' for the mighty God of Jacob.
13 he hath desired it for his h'.
Pr 3:33 but he blesseth the h' of the just.
Isa 22:16 graveth an h' for himself in a rock?
27:10 and the h' forsaken, and left like
32:18 people shall dwell in a peaceable h',
33:20 eyes shall see Jerusalem a quiet h',
34:13 and it shall be an h' of dragons,
35: 7 in the h' of dragons, where each
63:15 behold from the h' of thy holiness
Jer 9: 6 Thine h' is in the midst of deceit;
10:25 and have made his h' desolate.
25:30 utter his voice from his holy h';
30 shall mightily roar upon his h';
31:23 O h' of justice, and mountain of
33:12 an h' of shepherds causing their
41:17 dwelt in the h' of Chimham,
49:19 against the h' of the strong:
50: 7 the h' of justice, even the Lord,
19 I will bring Israel again to his h',
44 Jordan unto the h' of the strong;
45 he shall make their h' desolate
Eze 29:14 Pathros, into the land of their h';
Da 4:21 fowls of the heaven had their h':
Ob 3 whose h' is high; that saith in his
Hab 3:11 and moon stood still in their h':
Zec 2:13 is raised up out of his holy h'.
Ac 1:20 Let his h' be desolate, and let no
17:26 and the bounds of their h';
Eph 2:22 for an h' of God through the
Jude 6 but left their own h', he hath
Re 18: 2 and is become the h' of devils,

habitations
Ge 36:43 according to their h' in the land of
49: 5 of cruelty are in their h'.
Ex 12:20 in all your h' shall ye eat
35: 3 kindle no fire throughout your h'
Le 23:17 Ye shall bring out of your h' two
Nu 15: 2 the land of your h', which I give
1Ch 4:33 These were their h', and their
41 the h' that were found there,
7:28 possessions and h' were, Beth-el
Ps 74:20 are full of the h' of cruelty.
78:28 their camp, round about their h'.
Isa 54: 2 forth the curtains of thine h':
Jer 9:10 and for the h' of the wilderness
21:13 or who shall enter into our h'?
25:37 the peaceable h' are cut down
49:20 he shall make their h' desolate
La 2: 2 swallowed up all the h' of Jacob,
Eze 6:14 toward Diblath, in all their h':
Am 1: 2 h' of the shepherds shall mourn,
Lu 16: 9 receive you into everlasting h'.

Habor (*Ha'-bor*)
2Ki 17: 6 placed him in Halah and in H'
18:11 put them in Halah and in H' by
1Ch 5:26 brought them unto Halah, and H',

Haccerem See BETH-HACCEREM.

Hachaliah (*hak-a-li'-ah*)
Ne 1: 1 words of Nehemiah the son of H'.
10: 1 the Tirshatha, the son of H',

Hachilah (*hak'-i-lah*)
1Sa 23:19 in the hill of H', which is on the
26: 1 David hide himself in the hill of H',
3 Saul pitched in the hill of H',

Hachmoni (*hak'-mo-ni*) See also HACHMONITE.
1Ch 27:32 of H' was with the king's sons;

Hachmonite (*hak'-mo-nite*) See also TACHMONITE.
1Ch 11:11 Jashobeam, an H', the chief of

had^ See also HADST.
Ge 1:31 every thing that he h' made, and
2: 2 ended his work which he h' made;
2 from all his work which he h' made.
3 in it he h' rested from all his work
5 the Lord God h' not caused it to rain
8 put the man whom he h' formed
22 which the Lord God h' taken from
3: 1 which the Lord God h' made.
4: 4 And the Lord h' respect unto Abel
5 Cain and his offering he h' not respect.
5: 4 after he h' begotten Seth were
6: 6 that he h' made man on the earth,
12 for all flesh h' corrupted his way upon
7: 9 and the female, as God h' commanded
16 of all flesh, as God had commanded
8: 6 window of the ark which he h' made:
9:24 what his younger son h' done unto
11: 3 h' brick for stone, and slime h'
30 But Sarai was barren; she h' no child.

Ge 12: 1 Now the Lord *h*· said unto Abram,
4 departed, as the Lord *h*· spoken unto
5 their substance that they *h*· gathered
5 and all the souls that they *h*· gotten
16 and he *h*· sheep, and oxen, and
20 away, and his wife, and all that he *h*·.
13: 1 and all that he *h*·, and Lot with him,
3 his tent *h*· been at the beginning,
4 the altar, which he *h*· made there at
5 And Lot also,...*h*· flocks,and herds,
14:13 there came one that *h*· escaped,
16: 1 and she *h*· an handmaid, an Egyptian,
3 after Abram *h*· dwelt ten years in the
4, 5 when she saw that she *h*· conceived,
17:23 selfsame day, as God *h*· said unto him.
18: 8 and the calf which he *h*· dressed, and
33 as soon as he *h*· left communing with
19:17 when they *h*· brought them forth
20: 4 But Abimelech *h*· not come near
18 For the Lord God *h*· fast closed up all
21: 1 Lord visited Sarah as he *h*· said, and
1 Lord did unto Sarah as he *h*· spoken.
2 the set time of which God *h*· spoken
4 days old, as God *h*· commanded him.
9 which she *h*· born unto Abraham,
25 which Abimelech's servants *h*· violently
22: 3 the place of which God *h*· told him.
9 to the place which God *h*· told him of;
23:16 the silver which he *h*· named in the
24: 1 and the Lord *h*· blessed Abraham in
2 house, that ruled over all that he *h*·,
15 before he *h*· done speaking, that,
16 virgin, neither *h*· any man known her;
19 And when she *h*· done giving him
21 whether the Lord *h*· made his journey
22 as the camels *h*· done drinking, that
29 And Rebekah *h*· a brother, and his
45 And before I *h*· done speaking in
48 which *h*· led me in the right way to
65 For she *h*· said unto the servant,
65 the servant *h*· said, It is my master
66 told Isaac all things that he *h*· done.
25: 5 Abraham gave all that he *h*· unto Isaac.
6 of the concubines, which Abraham *h*·,
26: 8 when he *h*· been there a long time,
14 For he *h*· possession of flocks, and
15 his father's servants *h*· digged in the
15 Philistines *h*· stopped them, and filled
18 which they *h*· digged in the days of
18 names by which his father *h*· called
32 concerning the well which they *h*·
27:17 and the bread, which she *h*· prepared,
30 as soon as Isaac *h*· made an end of
31 And he also *h*· made savoury meat,
28: 6 Esau saw that Isaac *h*· blessed Jacob,
9 unto the wives which he *h*·, Mahalath
18 took the stone that he *h*· put for his
29:16 Laban *h*· two daughters: the name of
20 a few days, for the love he *h*· to her.
30: 9 Leah saw that she *h*· left bearing,
25 Rachel *h*· borne Joseph, that Jacob said
35 and every one that *h*· some white in it,
38 which he *h*· pilled before the flocks
43 exceedingly, and *h*· much cattle,
31:18 all his goods which he *h*· gotten,
18 which he *h*· gotten in Padan-aram,
19 Rachel *h*· stolen the images that
21 he fled with all that he *h*·; and he rose
25 Jacob *h*· pitched his tent in the mount:
32 knew not that Rachel *h*· stolen them.
34 Now Rachel had taken the images,
42 fear of Isaac, *h*· been with me, surely
32:23 the brook, and sent over that he *h*·.
33:10 though I *h*· seen the face of God,
19 a field, where he *h*· spread his tent,
34: 5 Jacob heard that he *h*· defiled Dinah
7 because he *h*· wrought folly in Israel
13 and said, because he *h*· defiled Dinah
19 thing, because he *h*· delight in Jacob's
27 spoiled the city, because they *h*· defiled
35:16 Rachel travailed, and she *h*· hard
36: 6 his substance, which he *h*· got in the
38:15 to be an harlot, because she *h*· covered
30 his brother, that *h*· the scarlet thread
39: 1 the Ishmeelites, which *h*· brought him
4 all that he *h*· he put into his hand.
5 the time he *h*· made him overseer
5 his house, and over all that he *h*·,
5 the Lord was upon all that he *h*· in
6 he left all that he *h*· in Joseph's hand;
6 he knew not ought he *h*·, save the
13 saw that he *h*· left his garment in her
40: 1 and his baker *h*· offended their lord
16 I *h*· three white baskets on my
22 as Joseph *h*· interpreted to them.
41:21 And when they *h*· eaten them up, it
21 not be known that they *h*· eaten them;
43 ride in the second chariot which he *h*·;
54 to come, according as Joseph *h*· said:
43: 2 when they *h*· eaten up the corn which
2 *h*· brought out of Egypt, their father
6 the man whether ye *h*· yet a brother?
10 *h*· lingered, surely now we *h*· returned
23 in your sacks: I *h*· your money.
44: 2 to the word that Joseph *h*· spoken.
45:27 the words of Joseph, which he *h*· said
27 wagons which Joseph *h*· sent to carry
46: 1 took his journey with all that he *h*·,
5 wagons which Pharaoh *h*· sent to
6 their goods which they *h*· gotten in
47:11 Rameses, as Pharaoh *h*· commanded.
22 the priests *h*· a portion assigned them
27 *h*· possessions therein, and grew,
48:11 I *h*· not thought to see thy face:
49:33 when Jacob *h*· made an end of
50:14 returned...after he *h*· buried his

Ex 2: 6 And she *h*· compassion on him, and
16 priest of Midian *h*· seven daughters:
25 children of Israel, and God *h*· respect
4:28 words of the Lord who *h*· sent him,
28 signs which he *h*· commanded him.
30 all the words which the Lord *h*· spoken
31 they heard that the Lord *h*· visited the
31 that he *h*· looked upon their affliction,
5:14 Pharaoh's taskmasters *h*· set over
7:10 they did so as the Lord *h*· commanded:
13 hearkened not,... as the Lord *h*· said.
22 hearken unto them; as the Lord *h*· said.
25 after that the Lord *h*· smitten the river.
8:12 of the frogs which he *h*· brought
15 hearkened not...as the Lord *h*· said.
19 hearkened not...as the Lord *h*· said.
9:12 hearkened not...as the Lord *h*· spoken
35 as the Lord *h*· spoken by Moses.
10:15 fruit of the trees which the hail *h*· left:
23 children of Israel *h*· light in their
12:28 as the Lord *h*· commanded Moses
39 *h*· they prepared for themselves any
13:17 when Pharaoh *h*· let the people go,
19 for he *h*· straitly sworn the children
14:12 it *h*· been better for us to serve
15:25 when he *h*· cast into the waters,
16: 3 would to God we *h*· died by the hand
18 that gathered much *h*· nothing over,
18 he that gathered little *h*· no lack; they
17:10 Joshua did as Moses *h*· said to him,
18: 1 Jethro...heard of all that God *h*· done
1 that the Lord *h*· brought Israel out of
2 after he *h*· sent her back, and her
8 all that the Lord *h*· done unto Pharaoh
8 all the travail that *h*· come upon them
9 the goodness which the Lord *h*· done
9 whom he *h*· delivered out of the hand
24 hearkened...and did all that he *h*· said.
19: 2 desert of Sinai, and *h*· pitched in
31:18 Moses, when he *h*· made an end of
32: 4 a graving tool, after he *h*· made
20 he took the calf which they *h*· made,
25 (for Aaron *h*· made them naked
29 For Moses *h*· said, Consecrate
33: 5 the Lord *h*· said unto Moses, Say
34: 4 Sinai, as the Lord *h*· commanded
32 all that the Lord *h*· spoken with him
33 And till Moses *h*· done speaking with
35:25 and brought that which they *h*· spun,
29 the Lord *h*· commanded to be made
36: 1 to all that the Lord *h*· commanded.
2 heart the Lord *h*· put wisdom, even
3 the children of Israel *h*· brought for
7 stuff they *h*· was sufficient for all
22 board *h*· two tenons, equally distant
39:43 *h*· done it as the Lord *h*· commanded,
43 so *h*· they done it: and Moses blessed
40:23 the Lord; as the Lord *h*· commanded
Le 10: 5 out of the camp; as Moses *h*· said,
19 if I *h*· eaten the sin offering to day,
21: 3 unto him, which *h*· no husband;
24:23 bring forth him that *h*· cursed out of
Nu 1:48 the Lord *h*· spoken unto Moses:
3: 4 of Sinai, and they *h*· no children:
7: 1 on the day that Moses *h*· fully set up
1 and *h*· anointed them, and sanctified
8: 4 the pattern which the Lord *h*· shewed
22 as the Lord *h*· commanded Moses
12: 1 Ethiopian woman whom he *h*· married:
1 for he *h*· married an Ethiopian woman.
14 If her father *h*· but spit in her face,
13:32 of the land which they *h*· searched
14: 2 Would God that we *h*· died in the
2 would God we *h*· died in this
24 he *h*· another spirit with him,
16:31 as he *h*· made an end of speaking
39 they that were burnt *h*· offered;
20: 3 Would God that we *h*· died when our
21: 9 if a serpent *h*· bitten any man,
26 who *h*· fought against the former king
22: 2 saw all that Israel *h*· done to the
33 unless she *h*· turned from me, surely
33 now also I *h*· slain thee, and saved
23 2 Balak did as Balaam *h*· spoken;
30 did as Balaam *h*· said, and offered
26:33 the son of Hepher *h*· no sons,
65 For the Lord *h*· said of them, They
27: 3 in his own sin, and *h*· no sons.
31:32 which the men of war *h*· caught,
35 that *h*· not known man by lying
53 (For the men of war *h*· taken spoil,
32: 1 the children of Gad *h*· a very great
9 land which the Lord *h*· given them.
13 all the generation, that *h*· done evil
33: 4 firstborn, which the Lord *h*· smitten
De 1: 3 all that the Lord *h*· given him in
4 After he *h*· slain Sihon the king
39 *h*· no knowledge between good
41 when ye *h*· girded on every man
2:12 when they *h*· destroyed them
7: 8 the oath which he *h*· sworn unto
9:16 behold, ye *h*· sinned against the Lord
16 and *h*· made you a molten calf:
10: 5 tables in the ark which I *h*· made;
15 the Lord *h*· a delight in thy fathers
19:19 as he *h*· thought to have done unto
29:26 whom he *h*· not given unto them:
31:24 Moses *h*· made an end of writing
32:30 except their Rock *h*· sold them,
30 and the Lord *h*· shut them up?
34: 9 Moses *h*· laid his hands upon him:
Jos 2: 6 she *h*· brought them up to the roof
6 she *h*· laid in order upon the roof.
11 as soon as we *h*· heard these things,
4: 4 twelve men, whom he *h*· prepared of
5: 1 Lord *h*· dried up the waters of Jordan

Jos 5: 5 them they *h*· not circumcised.
7 because they *h*· not circumcised
8 when they *h*· done circumcising all
12 after they *h*· eaten of the old corn
12 neither *h*· the children of Israel
6: 8 Joshua *h*· spoken unto the people,
10 And Joshua *h*· commanded the people,
22 Joshua *h*· said unto the two men
22 that *h*· spied out the country, Go into
23 and her brethren, and all that she *h*·;
25 father's household, and all that she *h*·;
7: 7 we *h*· been content, and dwelt on the
24 and his tent, and all that he *h*·:
25 they *h*· stoned them with stones.
8:13 And when they *h*· set the people,
18 stretched out the spear that he *h*·
19 soon as he *h*· stretched out his hand:
20 and they *h*· no power to flee this way
21 that the ambush *h*· taken the city,
24 Israel *h*· made an end of slaying
26 until he *h*· utterly destroyed all the
33 as Moses...*h*· commanded before.
9: 3 Joshua *h*· done unto Jericho and to Ai,
4 made as if they *h*· been ambassadors,
16 they *h*· made a league with them,
18 *h*· sworn unto them by the Lord God
21 as the princes *h*· promised them.
10: 1 *h*· heard how Joshua *h*· taken Ai,
13 the people *h*· avenged themselves
20 children of Israel *h*· made an end of
27 the cave wherein they *h*· been hid,
32 all that he *h*· done to Libnah.
33 until he *h*· left none remaining.
35 to all which he *h*· done to Lachish.
37 to all that he *h*· done to Eglon;
39 as he *h*· done to Hebron, so he did to
39 as he *h*· done also to Libnah, and to
11: 1 Jabin king of Hazor *h*· heard those
14 until they *h*· destroyed them, neither
14: 3 For Moses *h*· given the inheritance of
15 And the land *h*· rest from war.
17: 1 man of war, therefore he *h*· Gilead
3 the son of Manasseh, *h*· no sons,
6 daughters of Manasseh *h*·...inheritance
6 of Manasseh's sons *h*· the land
8 Manasseh *h*· the...of Tappuah:
11 Manasseh *h*· in Issachar and in
18: 2 seven tribes, which *h*· not yet received
19: 2 *h*· in their inheritance Beer-sheba,
9 of Simeon *h*· their inheritance
49 they *h*· made an end of dividing
21: 4 *h*· by lot out of the tribe of Judah,
5 children of Kohath *h*· by lot out of
6 And the children of Gershon *h*· by lot
7 Merari by their families *h*· out of the
10 were of the children of Levi, *h*·:
20 of Kohath, even they *h*· the cities
45 the Lord *h*· spoken unto the house of
22: 7 Moses *h*· given possession in Bashan:
23: 1 the Lord *h*· given rest unto Israel
24:31 *h*· known all the works of the Lord,
31 Lord, that he *h*· done for Israel.
J'g 1: 8 children of Judah *h*· fought
8 Jerusalem, and *h*· taken it, and
19 because they *h*· chariots of iron.
2: 6 And when Joshua *h*· let the people go,
7 who *h*· seen all the great works of the
10 the works which he *h*· done for Israel.
15 Lord *h*· said, and as the Lord *h*· sworn
3: 1 as *h*· not known all the wars of
11 And the land *h*· rest forty years.
12 because they *h*· done evil in the sight
16 him a dagger which *h*· two edges,
18 And when he *h*· made an end to
20 a summer parlour, which he *h*·
30 And the land *h*· rest fourscore years.
4: 3 he *h*· nine hundred chariots of iron;
11 *h*· severed himself from the Kenites
18 when he *h*· turned in unto her
24 until they *h*· destroyed Jabin king of
5:26 When she *h*· pierced and stricken
31 And the land *h*· rest forty years.
6: 3 Israel *h*· sown, that the Midianites
27 and did as the Lord *h*· said unto him:
7:19 and they *h*· but newly set the watch:
8: 3 abated toward him, when he *h*· said
8 the men of Succoth *h*· answered him.
19 if ye *h*· saved them alive, I would not
24 (For they *h*· golden earrings, because
30 Gideon *h*· threescore and ten sons of
30 begotten: for he *h*· many wives.
34 their God, who *h*· delivered them out
35 which he *h*· shewed unto Israel.
9:22 Abimelech *h*· reigned three years
10: 4 And he *h*· thirty sons that rode on
4 and they *h*· thirty cities, which are
11:34 her he *h*· neither son nor daughter.
39 to his vow which he *h*· vowed:
12: 9 And he *h*· thirty sons, and thirty
14 *h*· forty sons, and thirty nephews,
14: 4 Philistines *h*· dominion over Israel.
6 a kid, and he *h*· nothing in his hand:
6 father or his mother what he *h*· done.
9 that he *h*· taken the honey out of the
18 *h*· not plowed with my heifer,
18 ye *h*· not found out my riddle.
20 whom he *h*· used as his friend.
15: 5 And when he *h*· set the brands on fire,
6 because he *h*· taken his wife, and
17 when he *h*· made an end of speaking,
19 and when he *h*· drunk, his spirit came
16: 8 which *h*· not been dried, and she
18 saw that he *h*· told her all his heart,
17: 3 he *h*· restored the eleven hundred
3 I *h*· wholly dedicated the silver
5 the man Micah *h*· an house of gods,

Jg 18: 1 all their inheritance h' not fallen
7 Zidonians, and h' no business with any
27 took the things which Micah h' made,
27 and the priest which he h',
28 they h' no business with any man;
19: 6 damsel's father h' said unto the man,
17 And when he h' lifted up his eyes,
20:36 liers in wait which they h' set beside
21: 1 men of Israel h' sworn in Mizpeh,
5 they h' made a great oath concerning
12 virgins that h' known no man by lying
14 they h' saved alive of the women
15 because that the Lord h' made a breach
Ru 1: 6 she h' heard in the country of Moab
6 Lord h' visited his people in giving
2: 1 Naomi h' a kinsman of her husband's,
17 beat out that she h' gleaned:
18 in law saw what she h' gleaned:
18 she h' reserved after she was sufficed.
19 with whom she h' wrought, and said,
3: 7 And when Boaz h' eaten and drunk,
16 all that the man h' done to her.
1Sa 1: 2 he h' two wives; the name of the one
2 Peninnah h' children, but Hannah
2 children, but Hannah h' no children.
5 but the Lord h' shut up her womb.
6 because the Lord h' shut up her womb.
9 rose up after they h' eaten in Shiloh,
9 and after they h' drunk.
13 Eli thought she h' been drunken.
20 after Hannah h' conceived, that she
24 And when she h' weaned him, she
3: 8 that the Lord h' called the child.
4:18 And he h' judged Israel forty years.
5: 9 after they h' carried it about, the
9 they h' emerods in their secret parts.
6: 6 he h' wrought wonderfully among
16 lords of the Philistines h' seen it,
19 because they h' looked into the ark
19 because the Lord h' smitten many of
7:14 cities which the Philistines h' taken
9: 2 he h' a son, whose name was Saul,
15 Now the Lord h' told Samuel in his
10: 9 when he h' turned his back to go
13 And when he h' made an end of
20 Samuel h' caused all the tribes
21 he h' caused the tribe of Benjamin
26 of men, whose hearts God h' touched.
13: 1 and when he h' reigned two years
4 that Saul h' smitten a garrison of
4 that Israel also was h' in abomination
8 set time that Samuel h' appointed:
10 soon as he h' made an end of offering
21 Yet they h' a file for the mattocks,
14:11 out of the holes where they h' hid,
17 And when they h' numbered, behold
22 which h' hid themselves in mount
24 Saul h' adjured the people, saying,
30 the people h' eaten freely to day
30 for h' there not been now a much
17: 5 he h' an helmet of brass upon his head,
6 And he h' greaves of brass upon his
12 name was Jesse; and he h' eight sons:
20 and went, as Jesse h' commanded him;
21 the Philistines h' put the battle in
39 assayed to go; for he h' not proved it.
40 in a shepherd's bag which he h', even
18: 1 when he h' made an end of speaking
19:18 told him all that Saul h' done to him.
20:34 because his father h' done him shame.
37 of the arrow which Jonathan h' shot,
22:21 that Saul h' slain the Lord's priests.
24: 5 because he h' cut off Saul's skirt.
10 the Lord h' delivered thee to day into
16 when David h' made an end of speaking
18 when the Lord h' delivered me into
25: 2 great, and he h' three thousand sheep,
34 there h' not been left unto Nabal
35 received...that which she h' brought
37 and his wife h' told him these things,
44 But Saul h' given Michal his daughter,
26: 5 to the place where Saul h' pitched:
28: 3 was dead, and all Israel h' lamented
3 And Saul h' put away those that
3 those that h' familiar spirits,
20 for he h' eaten no bread all the day,
24 And the woman h' a fat calf in the
30: 1 the Amalekites h' invaded the land
2 And h' taken the women captives, that
4 wept, until they h' no more power to
12 and when he h' eaten, his spirit came
12 for he h' eaten no bread, nor drunk
16 And when he h' brought him down,
16 spoil that they h' taken out of the land
18 that the Amalekites h' carried away:
19 any thing that they h' taken to them:
21 whom they h' made also to abide at the
31:11 which the Philistines h' done to Saul;
2Sa 1: 1 and David h' abode two days in Ziklag;
21 as though he h' not been anointed
2:27 the people h' gone up every one from
30 and when he h' gathered all the people
31 servants of David h' smitten of
3: 7 And Saul h' a concubine, whose name
17 And Abner h' communication with
22 for he h' sent him away, and he was
30 because he h' slain their brother
4: 2 And Saul's son h' two men that
4 Saul's son, h' a son that was lame of
5:12 that the Lord h' established him king
12 and that he h' exalted his kingdom for
17 heard that they h' anointed David
25 so, as the Lord h' commanded him;
6: 8 because the Lord h' made a breach
13 the ark of the Lord h' gone six paces,
17 the tabernacle that David h' pitched

2Sa 6:18 as David h' made an end of offering
22 of them shall I be h' in honour.
23 the daughter of Saul h' no child unto
7: 1 and the Lord h' given him rest round
8:10 because he h' fought against
10 for Hadadezer h' wars with Toi.
11 silver and gold that he h' dedicated
9: 2 And when they h' called him unto
10 Now Ziba h' fifteen sons and twenty
12 And Mephibosheth h' a young son,
11:10 And when they h' told David, saying,
13 And when David h' called him, he did
22 David all that Joab h' sent him for.
27 that David h' done displeased the
12: 2 The rich man h' exceeding many
3 But the poor man h' nothing, save one
6 this thing, and because he h' no pity.
8 if that h' been too little, I would
13: 1 the son of David h' a fair sister
3 But Amnon h' a friend, whose name
10 took the cakes which she h' made,
11 And when she h' brought them unto
15 the love wherewith he h' loved her.
18 And she h' a garment of divers colours
22 because he h' forced his sister Tamar.
23 that Absalom h' sheepshearers in
28 Now Absalom h' commanded his
29 Amnon as Absalom h' commanded.
36 as he h' made an end of speaking,
14: 2 woman that h' a long time mourned
6 and thy handmaid h' two sons, and
32 it h' been good for me to have been
33 and when he h' called for Absalom,
15: 2 any man that h' a controversy
24 until all the people h' done passing
30 and h' his head covered, and he went
16:23 as if a man h' enquired at the oracle
17:14 For the Lord h' appointed to defeat
18 which h' a well in his court; whither
20 And when they h' sought and could
18:18 Absalom...h' taken and reared up
33 would God I h' died for thee, O
19: 6 perceive, that if Absalom h' lived,
6 and all we h' died this day,
6 then it h' pleased thee well.
8 for Israel h' fled every man to his tent.
24 and h' neither dressed his feet, nor
32 and he h' provided the king of
43 our advice should not be first h' in
20: 3 whom he h' left to keep the house,
5 the set time which he h' appointed
8 garment that he h' put on was girded
21: 2 children of Israel h' sworn unto them;
11 Aiah, the concubine of Saul, h' done.
12 which h' stolen them from the street
12 where the Philistines h' hanged them,
15 the Philistines h' yet war again
20 that h' on every hand six fingers, and
22: 1 the day that the Lord h' delivered him
38 turned not again until I h' consumed
23: 8 the mighty men whom David h': the
18 and slew them, and h' the name among
20 who h' done many acts, he slew two
21 the Egyptian h' a spear in his hand;
22 and h' the name among three mighty
24: 8 So when they h' gone through all the
10 after that he h' numbered the people,
1Ki 1: 6 And his father h' not displeased him
41 heard it as they h' made an end of
2:28 for Joab h' turned after Adonijah,
41 that Shimei h' gone from Jerusalem to
3: 1 until he h' made an end of building
10 Pleased...that Solomon h' asked this
21 but when I h' considered it in the
28 judgment which the king h' judged;
4: 2 these were the princes which he h':
7 And Solomon h' twelve officers over
11 which h' Taphath the daughter of
14 the son of Iddo h' Mahanaim:
24 For he h' dominion over all the region
24 and he h' peace on all sides
26 And Solomon h' forty thousand stalls
34 earth which h' heard of his wisdom.
5:15 And Solomon h' three score and
7: 8 house where he dwelt h' another
20 pillars h' pomegranates also above,
28 they h' borders, and the borders were
30 And every base h' four brazen wheels,
30 four corners thereof h' undersetters
37 all of them h' one casting, one
51 which David his father h' dedicated,
8:11 glory of the Lord h' filled the house
54 Solomon h' made an end of praying
66 that the Lord h' done for David his
9: 1 when Solomon h' finished the building
2 as he h' appeared unto him at Gibeon.
10 when Solomon h' built two houses, the
11 Hiram...h' furnished Solomon with
12 see the cities which Solomon h' given
16 Pharaoh...h' gone up, and taken
19 the cities of stone that Solomon h',
24 her house which Solomon h' built for
27 shipmen that h' knowledge of the sea,
10: 4 when the queen of Sheba h' seen all
4 and the house that he h' built,
7 until I came, and mine eyes h' seen it;
15 Beside... he h' of the merchantmen,
19 The throne h' six steps, and the
22 For the king h' at sea a navy of
24 wisdom, which God h' put in his heart
26 and he h' a thousand and four
28 And Solomon h' horses brought out of
11: 3 And he h' seven hundred wives,
9 God of Israel, which h' appeared unto
10 And h' commanded him concerning
15 after he h' smitten every male in

1Ki 11:16 until he h' cut off every male in
29 h' clad himself with a new garment;
12: 8 counsel...which they h' given him
12 as the king h' appointed, saying,
32 unto the calves that he h' made:
32 the high places which he h' made.
33 upon the altar which he h' made in
33 the month which he h' devised of his
13: 4 which h' cried against the altar in
5 the sign which the man of God h' given
11 the man of God h' done that day in
11 the words which he h' spoken unto the
12 For his sons h' seen what way the man
23 came to pass, after he h' eaten bread,
23 and after he h' drunk, that he saddled
28 the lion h' not eaten the carcase, nor
31 after he h' buried him, that he spake
14:22 with their sins... they h' committed,
22 above all that their fathers h' done.
26 shields of gold... Solomon h' made.
15: 3 which he h' done before him: and his
12 the idols that his fathers h' made.
13 because she h' made an idol in a
15 things which his father h' dedicated,
15 which himself h' dedicated, into the
20 the captains of the hosts which he h'
22 timber... wherewith Baasha h' built;
29 until he h' destroyed him, according
16:31 as if it h' been a light thing for him
32 house of Baal, which he h' built in
17: 7 because there h' been no rain in
19: 1 told Jezebel all that Elijah h' done,
1 how he h' slain all the prophets
21: 1 Naboth the Jezreelite h' a vineyard
4 which Naboth...h' spoken to him:
4 for he h' said, I will not give thee the
11 did as Jezebel h' sent unto them, and
11 the letters which she h' sent unto them.
22:31 that h' rule over his chariots, saying,
53 according to all that his father h' done.
2Ki 1:17 word of the Lord... Elijah h' spoken.
17 of Judah; because he h' no son.
2:14 when he also h' smitten the waters,
3: 2 image of Baal that his father h' made.
4:12, 15 when he h' called her, she stood
17 season that Elijah h' said unto her,
20 And when he h' taken him,
5: 2 the Syrians h' gone out by companies,
2 and h' brought away captive out of the
7 king of Israel h' read the letter,
8 Elisha the man of God h' heard
8 that the king of Israel h' rent his
13 if the prophet h' bid thee do some
6:23 when they h' eaten and drunk,
30 he h' sackcloth upon his flesh.
7: 6 For the Lord h' made the host
15 which the Syrians h' cast away
17 as the man of God h' said,
18 as the man of God h' spoken
8: 1 woman, whose son he h' restored
5 how he h' restored a dead body
5 whose son he h' restored to life,
29 wounds which the Syrians h' given him
9:14 Now Joram h' kept Ramoth-gilead,
15 wounds which the Syrians h' given him,
31 she said, H' Zimri peace, who slew his
10: 1 And Ahab h' seventy sons in Samaria,
17 till he h' destroyed him, according to
25 soon as he h' made an end of offering
11:15 For the priest h' said, Let her not
12: 6 the priests h' not repaired the
11 that h' the oversight of the house of
18 his fathers, kings of Judah, h' dedicated,
13: 7 king of Syria h' destroyed them,
7 and h' made them like the dust
23 and h' compassion on them, and
23 h' respect unto them, because of his
25 which he h' taken out of the hand
14: 5 servants which h' slain the king
15: 3 his father Amaziah h' done;
9 as his fathers h' done:
34 that his father Uzziah h' done.
16:11 that king Ahaz h' sent from Damascus
18 that they h' built in the house,
17: 4 for he h' sent messengers to So king
4 as he h' done year by year:
7 children of Israel h' sinned against
7 which h' brought them up out of
7 and h' feared other gods,
8 which they h' made.
12 whereof the Lord h' said unto them,
15 concerning whom the Lord h' charged
20 until he h' cast them out
23 as he h' said by all his servants
28 priests whom they h' carried away
29 which the Samaritans h' made,
35 the Lord h' made a covenant,
18: 4 serpent that Moses h' made:
16 Hezekiah king of Judah h' overlaid,
18 when they h' called to the king,
19: 8 for he h' heard that he was departed
20:11 by which it h' gone down in the dial
12 for he h' heard that Hezekiah
12 heard that Hezekiah h' been sick.
21: 3 Hezekiah his father h' destroyed;
7 of the grove that he h' made
16 till he h' filled Jerusalem
24 slew all them that h' conspired
22:11 when the king h' heard the words of
23: 5 whom the kings of Judah h' ordained
8 where the priests h' burned incense,
11 kings of Judah h' given to the sun,
12 which the kings of Judah h' made,
12 altars which Manasseh h' made
13 Solomon... king of Israel h' builded
15 Nebat, who made Israel to sin, h' made,

2Ki 23: 19 kings of Israel *h*' made to provoke
19 acts that he *h*' done in Beth-el,
26 Manasseh *h*' provoked him
29 slew him...when he *h*' seen him.
32, 37 all that his fathers *h*' done.
24: 7 king of Babylon *h*' taken from the
9 all that his father *h*' done.
13 Solomon king of Israel *h*' made
13 As the Lord *h*' said.
19 all that Jehoiakim *h*' done,
20 until he *h*' cast them out
25: 16 bases which Solomon *h*' made
17 and like unto these *h*' the second pillar
22 king of Babylon *h*' left,
23 king of Babylon *h*' made Gedaliah
1Ch 2: 22 begat Jair, who *h*' three and
26 Jerahmeel *h*' also another wife, whose
34 Now Sheshan *h*' no sons, but
34 Sheshan *h*' a servant, an Egyptian,
52 Kirjath-jearim *h*' sons; Haroeh, and
4: 5 Ashur the father of Tekoa *h*' two
22 and Saraph, who *h*' the dominion in
27 And Shimei *h*' sixteen sons and six
27 but his brethren *h*' not many children,
40 they of Ham *h*' dwelt there of old.
6: 31 the Lord, after that the ark *h*' rest.
32 until Solomon *h*' built the house
49 the servant of God *h*' commanded.
66 the sons of Kohath *h*' cities of
7: 4 for they *h*' many wives and sons.
15 and Zelophehad *h*' daughters.
8: 8 after he *h*' sent them away;
38 And Azel *h*' six sons, whose names are
40 and *h*' many sons, and sons' sons, an
9: 23 they and their children *h*' the
28 And certain of them *h*' the charge of
31 the Korahite, *h*' the set office over the
44 And Azel *h*' six sons, whose names are
10: 9 when they *h*' stripped him,
11 Philistines *h*' done to Saul,
13 counsel of one that *h*' a familiar
11: 10 mighty men whom David *h*', who
11 the mighty men whom David *h*';
20 he slew them, and *h*' a name
22 who *h*' done many acts;
24 and *h*' the name among the three
12: 15 when it *h*' overflown all his banks;
29 greatest part of them *h*' kept the ward
32 were men that *h*' understanding of
39 their brethren *h*' prepared for them.
13: 11 because the Lord *h*' made a breach
14 house of Obed-edom, and all that he *h*'.
14: 2 that the Lord *h*' confirmed him
4 his children which he *h*' in
12 when they *h*' left their gods
15: 3 which he *h*' prepared for it.
27 David also *h*' upon him an ephod of
16: 1 that David *h*' pitched for it:
2 when David *h*' made an end
18: 9 how David *h*' smitten all
10 because he *h*' fought against
10 (for Hadarezer *h*' war with Tou;)
19: 6 they *h*' made themselves odious
17 when David *h*' put the battle
21: 28 Lord *h*' answered him
23: 11 but Jeush and Beriah *h*' not many
17 And Eliezer *h*' none other sons;
22 And Eliezer died, and *h*' no sons,
24: 2 died before their father, and *h*' no
19 God of Israel *h*' commanded him.
28 Of Mahli came Eleazar, who *h*' no
26: 9 And Meshelemiah *h*' sons and
10 of the children of Merari, *h*' sons;
26 captain of the host, *h*' dedicated.
28 Joab the son of Zeruiah, *h*' dedicated;
28 and whosoever *h*' dedicated
27: 23 because the Lord *h*' said
28: 2 As for me, I *h*' in mine heart to
2 and *h*' made ready for the building:
12 of all that he *h*' by the spirit, of the
29: 25 majesty as *h*' not been on any
2Ch 1: 3 servant of the Lord *h*' made
4 ark of God *h*' David brought
4 place which David *h*' prepared
4 for he *h*' pitched a tent
5 the son of Hur, *h*' made,
12 such as none of the kings have *h*'
14 and he *h*' a thousand and four
16 Solomon *h*' horses brought
2: 17 David his father *h*' numbered
3: 1 that David *h*' prepared
5: 1 David his father *h*' dedicated;
14 glory of the Lord *h*' filled
6: 13 Solomon *h*' made a brasen
13 and *h*' set it in the midst
7: 2 glory of the Lord *h*' filled
6 the king *h*' made to praise
7 altar which Solomon *h*' made
10 the Lord *h*' shewed unto David,
8: 1 wherein Solomon *h*' built
2 which Huram *h*' restored
6 store cities that Solomon *h*',
11 house that he *h*' built for her:
12 which he *h*' built before the porch,
14 for so *h*' David the man of God
18 ships, and servants that *h*' knowledge
9: 3 queen of Sheba *h*' seen the wisdom
3 and the house that he *h*' built,
6 and mine eyes *h*' seen it:
12 which she *h*' brought unto the king
23 that God *h*' put into his heart.
25 And Solomon *h*' four thousand
10: 2 whither he *h*' fled from
6 the old men that *h*' stood before
11: 14 his sons *h*' cast them off
15 calves which he *h*' made.

2Ch 12: 1 when Rehoboam *h*' established
1 the kingdom, and *h*' strengthened
2 they *h*' transgressed against the Lord,
9 which Solomon *h*' made.
13 city which the Lord *h*' chosen
14: 6 for the land *h*' rest, and
6 he *h*' no war in those years;
6 because the Lord *h*' given him rest.
8 And Asa *h*' an army of men that
15: 8 which he *h*' taken from mount
11 spoil which they *h*' brought,
15 for they *h*' sworn with all their hearts
16 she *h*' made an idol in a grove:
18 things that his father *h*' dedicated,
18 and that he himself *h*' dedicated,
16: 14 which he *h*' made for himself
17: 2 which Asa his father *h*' taken.
5 and he *h*' riches and honour in
9 taught in Judah, and *h*' the book
13 And he *h*' much business in the
18: 1 Now Jehoshaphat *h*' riches and
2 and for the people that he *h*' with
10 son of Chenaanah *h*' made him horns
30 king of Syria *h*' commanded
20: 21 when he *h*' consulted with
23 when they *h*' made an end
27 the Lord *h*' made them to rejoice
29 when they *h*' heard that the Lord
33 the people *h*' not prepared
21: 2 And he *h*' brethren the sons of
6 for he *h*' the daughter of Ahab to
7 that he *h*' made with David,
10 because he *h*' forsaken the Lord
22: 1 to the camp *h*' slain all the eldest.
7 whom the Lord *h*' anointed to cut
9 and when they *h*' slain him,
9 So the house of Ahaziah *h*' no power
23: 8 Jehoiada the priest *h*' commanded,
9 that *h*' been king David's,
23: 18 whom David *h*' distributed in the
21 that they *h*' slain Athaliah
24: 7 wicked woman, *h*' broken up
10 until they *h*' made an end.
14 And when they *h*' finished it,
16 because he *h*' done good in Israel,
22 his father *h*' done to him,
24 because they *h*' forsaken the Lord
25: 3 servants that *h*' killed the king
26: 5 Zechariah, who *h*' understanding
10 for he *h*' much cattle, both in the
11 Moreover Uzziah *h*' an host of fighting
19 and *h*' a censer in his hand to burn
20 because the Lord *h*' smitten him.
28: 3 whom the Lord *h*' cast out
6 they *h*' forsaken the Lord God
17 the Edomites *h*' come and smitten
18 Philistines also *h*' invaded
18 and *h*' taken Beth-shemesh,
29: 2 that David his father *h*' done.
22 when they *h*' killed the rams,
29 when they *h*' made an end
34 other priests *h*' sanctified themselves:
36 that God *h*' prepared the people:
30: 2 for the king *h*' taken counsel,
3 the priests *h*' not sanctified
3 neither *h*' the people gathered
5 for they *h*' not done it of a long
17 therefore the Levites *h*' the charge of
18 Zebulun, *h*' not cleansed themselves,
31: 1 until they *h*' utterly destroyed
10 we have *h*' enough to eat, and have
32: 27 And Hezekiah *h*' exceeding much
29 for God *h*' given him substance
33: 2 whom the Lord *h*' cast out
3 his father *h*' broken down,
4 whereof the Lord *h*' said,
7 the idol which he *h*' made,
7 of which God *h*' said to David,
9 whom the Lord *h*' destroyed
15 altars that he *h*' built in the mount
22 Manasseh his father *h*' made,
23 Manasseh his father *h*' humbled
25 all them that *h*' conspired against
34: 4 that *h*' sacrificed unto them.
7 when he *h*' broken down the altars
7 and *h*' beaten the graven images
8 when he *h*' purged the land,
9 Levites that kept the doors *h*' gathered
10 the workmen that *h*' the oversight of
11 kings of Judah *h*' destroyed.
19 when the king *h*' heard the words
22 they that the king *h*' appointed,
35: 20 when Josiah *h*' prepared the temple,
24 in the second chariot that he *h*';
36: 13 who *h*' made him swear
14 the Lord which he *h*' hallowed
15 because he *h*' compassion on his people,
17 and *h*' no compassion upon young man
20 And them that *h*' escaped from
21 until the land *h*' enjoyed
Ezr 1: 5 whose spirit God *h*' raised,
7 which Nebuchadnezzar *h*' brought
7 and *h*' put them in the house
2: 1 those which *h*' been carried away,
1 king of Babylon *h*' carried away
3: 7 the grant that they *h*' of Cyrus king of
12 that *h*' seen the first house,
5: 12 our fathers *h*' provoked the God
14 whom he *h*' made governor;
6: 13 which Darius the king *h*' sent,
21 all such as *h*' separated themselves
22 the Lord *h*' made them joyful,
7: 6 Lord God of Israel *h*' given:
10 For Ezra *h*' prepared his heart
20 the princes *h*' appointed for the
22 because we *h*' spoken unto the

Ezr 8: 25 all Israel there present, *h*' offered:
35 of those that *h*' been carried away,
9: 4 of those that *h*' been carried away;
10: 1 Now when Ezra *h*' prayed,
1 and when he *h*' confessed,
6 of them that *h*' been carried away.
8 of those that *h*' been carried away.
17 the men that *h*' taken strange
18 were found that *h*' taken strange
44 All these *h*' taken strange wives:
44 and some of them *h*' wives
44 by whom they *h*' children.
Ne 1: 2 the Jews that *h*' escaped,
2: 1 Now I *h*' not been beforetime
9 Now the king *h*' sent captains
12 what my God *h*' put in my heart
16 neither *h*' I as yet told it
18 words that he *h*' spoken unto me.
4: 6 for the people *h*' a mind to work.
15 and God *h*' brought their counsel
18 every one *h*' his sword girded by
5: 15 governors that *h*' been before me
15 and *h*' taken of them bread and
6: 1 heard that I *h*' builded the wall,
1 at that time I *h*' not set up the doors
12 that God *h*' not sent him;
12 and Sanballat *h*' hired him.
18 Johanan *h*' taken the daughter
7: 1 and I *h*' set up the doors,
6 of those that *h*' been carried away,
6 king of Babylon *h*' carried away,
67 and they *h*' two hundred forty and five
8: 1 which the Lord *h*' commanded
4 which they *h*' made for the purpose;
12 because they *h*' understood
14 law which the Lord *h*' commanded
17 unto that day *h*' not the children
9: 18 when they *h*' made them a molten
18 and *h*' wrought great provocations;
28 But after they *h*' rest, they did evil
28 so that they *h*' the dominion over them:
11: 16 the Levites, *h*' the oversight of the
12: 29 the singers *h*' builded them
43 for God *h*' made them rejoice
13: 3 when they *h*' heard the law,
5 And he *h*' prepared for him
10 of the Levites *h*' not been given
23 Jews that *h*' married wives
Es 1: 8 for so the king *h*' appointed
2: 1 and what she *h*' done,
6 Who *h*' been carried away from
6 which *h*' been carried away
6 king of Babylon *h*' carried away.
7 for she *h*' neither father nor mother,
10 Esther *h*' not shewed her people
10 Mordecai *h*' charged her that she
12 After that she *h*' been twelve months,
15 who *h*' taken her for his daughter,
20 Esther *h*' not yet shewed her
20 as Mordecai *h*' charged her:
3: 2 for the king *h*' so commanded
4 for he *h*' told them that he was
6 for they *h*' shewed him the people
12 to all that Haman *h*' commanded
4: 5 whom he *h*' appointed to attend
7 of all that *h*' happened unto him,
7 that Haman *h*' promised to pay
17 to all that Esther *h*' commanded
5: 5 that Esther *h*' prepared.
11 wherein the king *h*' promoted him,
11 and how he *h*' advanced him
12 that she *h*' prepared but myself;
6: 2 that Mordecai *h*' told of Bigthana
4 gallows that he *h*' prepared for him.
13 every thing that *h*' befallen him.
14 banquet that Esther *h*' prepared.
7: 4 But if we *h*' been sold for bondmen
4 I *h*' held my tongue,
9 which Haman *h*' made for
9 Mordecai, who *h*' spoken good
10 that he *h*' prepared for Mordecai.
8: 1 for Esther *h*' told what he was unto
2 which he *h*' taken from Haman,
3 that he *h*' devised against the Jews.
16 the Jews *h*' light, and gladness, and
17 the Jews *h*' joy and gladness, a feast
9: 1 that the Jews *h*' rule over them that
16 stood for their lives, and *h*' rest from
23 to do as they *h*' begun,
23 as Mordecai *h*' written unto them;
24 all the Jews, *h*' devised against
24 and *h*' cast Pur, that is, the lot,
26 which they *h*' seen concerning
26 and which *h*' come unto them,
31 Esther the queen *h*' enjoined them,
31 and as they *h*' decreed for themselves
Job 2: 11 for they *h*' made an appointment
3: 13 then *h*' I been at rest,
15 Or with princes that *h*' gold, who
16 untimely birth I *h*' not been;
26 neither *h*' I rest, neither was I quiet;
6: 20 confounded because they *h*' hoped;
9: 16 If I *h*' called, and he *h*' answered me;
16 that he *h*' hearkened unto my voice.
10: 18 Oh that I *h*' given up the ghost,
18 and no eye *h*' seen me!
19 as though I *h*' not been;
22: 8 as for the mighty man, he *h*' the earth;
24: 16 which they *h*' marked for
29: 12 and him that *h*' none to help him.
31: 25 because mine hand *h*' gotten
31 Oh that we *h*' of his flesh! we cannot
35 mine adversary *h*' written a book.
32: 3 because they *h*' found no answer,
3 and yet *h*' condemned Job.
4 Now Elihu *h*' waited

Job 32: 4 till Job h' spoken,
16 When I h' waited,
38: 8 as if it h' issued out of the womb?
42: 7 after the Lord h' spoken these words
10 gave Job twice as much as he h' before.
11 they that h' been of his acquaintance
11 that the Lord h' brought upon him:
12 for he h' fourteen thousand sheep,
13 He h' also seven sons and three
Ps 27: 13 I h' fainted, unless I h' believed to see
35: 14 as though he h' been my friend
42: 4 for I h' gone with the multitude,
55: 6 Oh that I h' wings like a dove! for then
73: 2 my steps h' well nigh slipped.
74: 5 according as he h' lifted up
78: 11 wonders that he h' shewed them.
23 Though he h' commanded the
24 And h' rained down manna
24 and h' given them of the corn
43 How he h' wrought his signs
44 And h' turned their rivers into
54 which his right hand h' purchased.
81: 13 that my people h' hearkened unto me,
13 and Israel h' walked in my ways?
84: 10 I h' rather be a doorkeeper in the
89: 7 and to be h' in reverence of all them
94: 17 Unless the Lord h' been my help,
17 my soul h' almost dwelt in silence.
105: 26 and Aaron whom he h' chosen.
106: 21 which h' done great things
23 destroy them, h' not Moses his
119: 51 The proud have h' me greatly in
56 This I h', because I kept thy
87 They h' almost consumed me
92 Unless thy law h' been my delights,
124: 1 If it h' not been the Lord
2 If it h' not been the Lord
3 Then they h' swallowed us up
4 Then the waters h' overwhelmed us,
4 the stream h' gone over our soul:
5 Then the proud waters h'
Pr 8: 26 While as yet he h' not made
24: 31 and nettles h' covered the face
Ec 1: 16 yea, my heart h' great experience of
2: 7 and h' servants born in my house;
7 also I h' great possessions of
11 that my hands h' wrought,
11 labour that I h' laboured to do:
18 which I h' taken under the sun:
4: 1 and they h' no comforter;
1 but they h' no comforter.
8: 10 who h' come and gone from
10 city where they h' so done:
Ca 3: 4 until I h' brought him
5: 6 but my beloved h' withdrawn
8: 11 Solomon h' a vineyard at
Isa 1: 9 Except the Lord of hosts h' left unto
6: 2 each one h' six wings;
6 which he h' taken with the tongs
22: 11 neither h' respect unto him that
26: 13 lords beside thee have h' dominion
29: 16 He h' no understanding?
37: 8 for he h' heard that he was
38: 9 when he h' been sick,
17 Behold, for peace I h' great bitterness:
21 For Isaiah h' said, Let them take
22 Hezekiah also h' said,
39: 1 for he h' heard that he
1 h' been sick, and was recovered.
41: 3 way that he h' not gone with
48: 18 then h' thy peace been as a river,
19 Thy seed also h' been as the
49: 21 these, where h' they been?
52: 15 for that which h' not been told
15 and that which they h' not heard
53: 9 because he h' done no violence,
59: 10 and we grope as if we h' no eyes:
60: 10 but in my favour have I h' mercy on
Jer 2: 21 Yet I h' planted thee a noble
3: 7 after she h' done all these things,
8 adultery I h' put her away,
4: 23 and the heavens, and they h' no light.
5: 7 when I h' fed them to the full,
6: 15 ashamed when they h' committed
8: 12 ashamed when they h' committed
9: 2 Oh that I h' in the wilderness a lodging
11: 19 I knew not that they h' devised
13: 7 the place where I h' hid it:
16: 15 the lands whither he h' driven them:
19: 14 whither the Lord h' sent him
23: 8 whither I h' driven them;
22 But if they h' stood in my counsel,
22 and h' caused my people to hear my
24: 1 king of Babylon h' carried away
1 from Jerusalem, and h' brought them
2 One basket h' very good figs, even like
2 the other basket h' very naughty figs,
25: 17 unto whom the Lord h' sent me:
26: 8 when Jeremiah h' made an end
8 all that the Lord h' commanded
19 evil which he h' pronounced
28: 12 the prophet h' broken the yoke
29: 1 Nebuchadnezzar h' carried away
32: 3 king of Judah h' shut him up,
16 Now when I h' delivered the evidence
34: 8 king Zedekiah h' made a covenant
10 which h' entered into the covenant,
11 whom they h' let go free,
15 turned, and h' done right in my
15 and ye h' made a covenant
16 whom he h' set at liberty
18 which they h' made before me,
36: 4 which he h' spoken unto him,
11 the son of Shaphan, h' heard out
13 all the words that he h' heard,
16 when they h' heard all the words,
Jer 36: 23 Jehudi h' read three or four leaves,
25 and Gemariah h' made intercession
27 after that the king h' burned the
32 king of Judah h' burned in the fire:
37: 4 for they h' not put him into prison.
10 though ye h' smitten the whole
15 for they h' made that the prison.
16 Jeremiah h' remained there
38: 1 that Jeremiah h' spoken unto all
7 that they h' put Jeremiah in the
27 that the king h' commanded.
39: 5 when they h' taken him,
10 poor of the people, which h' nothing,
40: 1 of the guard h' let him go from
1 Ramah, when he h' taken him
7 king of Babylon h' made Gedaliah
7 and h' committed unto him
11 king of Babylon h' left a remnant
11 and that he h' set over them
41: 2 king of Babylon h' made governor
4 after he h' slain Gedaliah,
9 wherein Ishmael h' cast all the dead
9 whom he h' slain because
10 captain of the guard h' committed
11 the son of Nethaniah h' done,
14 that Ishmael h' carried away captive
16 whom he h' recovered from
16 after that he h' slain Gedaliah
16 whom he h' brought again
18 son of Nethaniah h' slain Gedaliah
43: 1 when Jeremiah h' made an end
5 whither they h' been driven,
6 of the guard h' left with Gedaliah
44: 15 that their wives h' burned incense
17 for then h' we plenty of victuals,
20 which h' given him that answer,
45: 1 when he h' written these words
52: 2 to all that Jehoiakim h' done.
3 till he h' cast them out from
20 which king Solomon h' made
La 1: 7 pleasant things that she h' in the
9 wonderfully: she h' no comforter.
2: 17 that which he h' devised;
17 his word that he h' commanded
Eze 1: 5 they h' the likeness of a man.
6 And every one h' four faces,
6 and every one h' four wings.
8 And they h' the hands of a man under
8 and they four h' their faces and their
10 they four h' the face of a man, and the
10 they four h' the face of an ox on the
10 they four also h' the face of an eagle
16 and they four h' one likeness: and
23 every one h' two, which covered on this
23 every one h' two, which covered on that
25 when they stood, and h' let down
27 and it h' brightness round about.
3: 6 Surely, h' I sent thee to them,
8: 8 and when I h' digged in the wall,
9: 3 which h' the writer's inkhorn by his
11 which h' the inkhorn by his side,
10: 6 when he h' commanded the man
10 they four h' one likeness, as if a
10 as if a wheel h' been in the midst
12 even the wheels that the four h'.
14 and every one h' four faces: the first
21 Every one h' four faces apiece, and
11: 24 vision that I h' seen went up
25 things that the Lord h' shewed me.
16: 14 which I h' put upon thee,
17 which I h' given thee,
17: 3 full of feathers, which h' divers colours,
18 lo, he h' given his hand,
19: 5 she saw that she h' waited,
11 And she h' strong rods for the
20: 6 a land that I h' espied for them,
15 which I h' given them, flowing
24 they h' not executed my judgments,
24 but h' despised my statutes,
24 and h' polluted my sabbaths,
28 when I h' brought them into
23: 10 for they h' executed judgment
19 wherein she h' played the harlot
32 laughed to scorn and h' in derision;
39 when they h' slain their children
29: 18 yet h' he no wages, nor his army,
18 service that he h' served against
33: 15 give again that he h' robbed,
21 that one that h' escaped out of
22 and h' opened my mouth,
35: 5 Because thou hast h' a perpetual
5 their iniquity h' an end:
36: 18 the blood that they h' shed
18 wherewith they h' polluted it:
21 But I h' pity for mine holy name,
21 house of Israel h' profaned
40: 10 and the posts h' one measure on this
26 and it h' palm trees, one on this side,
31, 34, 37, the going up to it h' eight steps.
41: 6 but they h' not hold in the wall
18 and every cherub h' two faces;
23 and the sanctuary h' two doors.
24 And the doors h' two leaves apiece,
42: 6 but h' not pillars as the pillars of the
15 Now when he h' made an end of
20 it h' a wall round about, five hundred
44: 22 a widow that h' a priest before.
25 for sister that hath h' no husband,
47: 3 the man that h' the line in his hand
7 Now when I h' returned, behold,
Da 1: 4 and such as h' ability in them to
9 Now God h' brought Daniel into
11 prince of the eunuchs h' set over
17 Daniel h' understanding in all visions
18 the king h' said he should bring
2: 24 whom the king h' ordained to
Da 3: 2 Nebuchadnezzar the king h' set up.
3 Nebuchadnezzar the king h' set up;
3 image that Nebuchadnezzar h' set up.
7 Nebuchadnezzar the king h' set up:
27 upon whose bodies the fire h' no power,
27 smell of fire h' passed on them.
4: 12 the beasts of the field h' shadow under
21 fowls of the heaven h' their habitation;
5: 2 Nebuchadnezzar h' taken out
6: 24 those men which h' accused Daniel,
24 and the lions h' the mastery of them
7: 1 Daniel h' a dream and visions of
4 and h' eagle's wings: I beheld till
5 and it h' three ribs in the mouth
6 which h' upon the back of it four
6 the beast h' also four heads;
7 and it h' great iron teeth:
7 and it h' ten horns.
12 they h' their dominion taken away:
20 even of that horn that h' eyes, and a
8: 3 a ram which h' two horns: and the
5 and the goat h' a notable horn
6 to the ram that h' two horns
6 which I h' seen standing before
15 even I Daniel, h' seen the vision,
9: 21 whom I h' seen in the vision
10: 1 and h' understanding of the vision.
11 And when he h' spoken this word
15 And when he h' spoken such words
19 And when he h' spoken unto me,
Ho 1: 8 when she h' weaned Lo-ruhamah,
2: 23 upon her that h' not obtained
12: 3 his strength he h' power with God:
4 Yea, he h' power over the angel,
Am 7: 2 when they h' made an end
Ob 5 have stolen till they h' enough?
16 as though they h' not been.
Jon 1: 10 because he h' told them.
17 the Lord h' prepared a great fish
3: 10 that he h' said that he would
4: 10 Thou hast h' pity on the gourd, for
Na 3: 8 the rivers, that h' the waters round
Hab 3: 4 he h' horns coming out of his
Hag 1: 12 their God h' sent him,
Zec 1: 12 against which thou hast h' indignation
5: 9 for they h' wings like the wings of a
7: 2 When they h' sent unto the
10: 6 as though I h' not cast them off:
11: 10 which I h' made with all the people
Mal 2: 15 Yet h' he the residue of the spirit.
M't 1: 6 Solomon of her that h' been the wife
24 angel of the Lord h' bidden him,
25 till she h' brought forth her firstborn
2: 3 Herod the king h' heard these things,
4 when he h' gathered all the chief
7 when he h' privily called the wise
9 When they h' heard the king,
11 when they h' opened their treasures,
16 time which he h' diligently enquired
3: 4 And the same John h' his raiment
4: 2 when he h' fasted forty days
12 when Jesus h' heard that John
24 lunatick, and those that h' the palsy;
7: 28 when Jesus h' ended these sayings,
9: 8 which h' given such power
10: 1 And when he h' called unto him
11: 1 when Jesus h' made an end
2 Now when John h' heard in the prison
21 done in you, h' been done in Tyre
23 done in thee, h' been done in Sodom,
12: 7 But if ye h' known what this
10 a man which h' his hand withered.
13: 5 where they h' not much earth:
5 they h' no deepness of earth:
6 they h' no root, they withered
46 when he h' found one pearl
46 sold all that he h', and bought
53 when Jesus h' finished these
14: 3 For Herod h' laid hold on John,
13 when the people h' heard thereof,
21 And they that h' eaten were about
23 And when he h' sent the multitudes
35 the men of that place h' knowledge
16: 5 they h' forgotten to take bread.
17: 8 when they h' lifted up their eyes,
18: 24 And when he h' begun to reckon,
25 forasmuch as he h' not to pay, his
25 and children, and all that he h',
32 after that he h' called him,
33 not thou also have h' compassion
33 fellowservant, even as I h' pity on thee?
19: 1 when Jesus h' finished these sayings,
22 sorrowful: for he h' great
20: 2 And when he h' agreed with the
11 when they h' received it,
34 So Jesus h' compassion on them, and
21: 28 A certain man h' two sons; and he
32 when ye h' seen it,
45 and Pharisees h' heard his parables,
22: 11 a man which h' not on a wedding
22 When they h' heard these words,
25 when he h' married a wife,
28 be of the seven? for they all h' her.
34 But when the Pharisees h' heard
34 that he h' put the Sadducees to silence,
23: 30 If we h' been in the days of our
24: 43 of the house h' known in what hour
25: 16 Then he that h' received the five
17 likewise he that h' received two,
18 But he that h' received one went
20 so he that h' received five talents,
22 He also that h' received two
24 Then he that h' received the one
26: 1 when Jesus h' finished all these
8 they h' indignation, saying, To what
19 as Jesus h' appointed them;

M't 26: 24 it h' been good for that man
24 if he h' not been born.
30 And when they h' sung an hymn,
57 they that h' laid hold on Jesus led
27: 2 And when they h' bound him,
3 Then Judas, which h' betrayed him,
16 they h' then a notable prisoner,
18 that for envy they h' delivered him.
26 when he h' scourged Jesus,
29 they h' platted a crown of thorns,
31 after that they h' mocked him,
34 and when he h' tasted thereof,
50 Jesus, when he h' cried again
59 when Joseph h' taken the body,
60 which he h' hewn out in the rock:
28: 12 with the elders, and h' taken counsel,
16 a mountain where Jesus h' appointed
M'r 1: 19 when he h' gone a little farther
22 as one that h' authority, and not
26 when the unclean spirit h' torn him,
37 And when they h' found him,
42 as soon as he h' spoken,
2: 4 and when they h' broken it up,
25 what David did, when he h' need,
3: 1 a man there which h' a withered
3 the man which h' the withered
5 And when he h' looked round
10 For he h' healed many;
10 touch him, as many as h' plagues.
4: 5 where it h' not much earth; and
5 sprang up, because it h' no depth
6 because it h' no root, it withered
36 when they h' sent away the
5: 3 Who h' his dwelling among the
4 Because that he h' been often bound
4 and the chains h' been plucked
15 with the devil, and h' the legion,
18 he that h' been possessed with the
19 and hath h' compassion on thee.
20 how great things Jesus h' done for
25 h' an issue of blood twelve years,
26 And h' suffered many things
26 of many physicians, and h' spent
26 all that she h', and was nothing
27 When she h' heard of Jesus,
30 that virtue h' gone out of him,
32 to see her that h' done this thing.
40 But when he h' put them all out,
6: 17 Herod himself h' sent forth
17 for he h' married her.
18 For John h' said unto Herod,
19 Therefore Herodias h' a quarrel
30 both what they h' done,
30 and what they h' taught.
31 and they h' no leisure so much as to
41 when he h' taken the five loaves
46 And when he h' sent them away,
49 they supposed it h' been a spirit,
53 And when they h' passed over,
7: 14 when he h' called all the people
25 whose young daughter h' an
32 that was deaf, and h' an impediment
8: 7 And they h' a few small fishes:
9 they that h' eaten were about four
14 Now the disciples h' forgotten to
14 neither h' they in the ship with
23 and when he h' spit on his eyes,
33 But when he h' turned about
34 and when he h' called the people
9: 8 when they h' looked round about,
9 tell no man what things they h' seen,
34 they h' disputed among themselves,
36 and when he h' taken him in his
10: 22 away grieved: for he h' great
11: 6 even as Jesus h' commanded:
11 and when he h' looked round about
12: 12 knew that he h' spoken the parable
22 And the seven h' her, and left no
23 for the seven h' her to wife.
28 perceiving that he h' answered
44 all that she h', even all her living.
13: 20 except that the Lord h' shortened
14: 4 there were some that h' indignation
16 and found as he h' said unto them:
21 if he h' never been born.
23 and when he h' given thanks,
26 And when they h' sung an hymn,
44 he that betrayed him h' given them
15: 7 with them that h' made insurrection
7 who h' committed murder in
8 to do as he h' ever done unto them.
10 chief priests h' delivered him
15 when he h' scourged him,
20 And when they h' mocked him,
24 And when they h' crucified him,
44 whether he h' been any while dead.
16: 1 and Salome h' bought sweet spices,
9 out of whom he h' cast seven devils.
10 told them that h' been with him,
11 when they h' heard that he was alive,
11 and h' been seen of her,
14 believed not them which h' seen him
19 after the Lord h' spoken unto them,
Lu 1: 3 having h' perfect understanding
7 And they h' no child, because that
22 that he h' seen a vision in the temple:
58 how the Lord h' shewed great mercy
2: 17 And when they h' seen it,
20 things that they h' heard and seen,
26 before he h' seen the Lord's Christ.
36 great age, and h' lived with an
39 when they h' performed all things
43 when they h' fulfilled the days,
3: 19 evils which Herod h' done,
4: 13 when the devil h' ended all the
16 where he h' been brought up:

Lu 4: 17 And when he h' opened the book,
33 a man, which h' a spirit of an
35 when the devil h' thrown him
40 all they that h' any sick with
5: 4 Now when he h' left speaking,
6 And when they h' this done,
9 of the fishes which they h' taken:
11 And when they h' brought their ships
6: 8 the man which h' the withered
7: 1 Now when he h' ended all his
10 servant whole that h' been sick.
13 saw her, he h' compassion on her, and
39 which h' bidden him saw it,
41 a certain creditor which h' two
42 And when they h' nothing to pay,
8: 2 certain women, which h' been healed
8 And when he h' said these things,
27 which h' devils long time, and
29 For he h' commanded the unclean
29 For oftentimes it h' caught him:
39 how great things Jesus h' done unto
42 For he h' one only daughter,
43 which h' spent all her living
47 for what cause she h' touched him,
9: 8 some, that Elias h' appeared;
10 told him what they h' done.
11 and healed them that h' need of
36 any of those things which they h' seen.
10: 13 if the mighty works h' been done
13 they h' a great while ago repented,
33 he saw him, he h' compassion
39 And she h' a sister called Mary,
11: 38 marvelled that he h' not first washed
13: 1 whose blood Pilate h' mingled with
6 A certain man h' a fig tree
11 a woman which h' a spirit of
14 because that Jesus h' healed on the
17 And when he h' said these things,
14: 2 before him which h' the dropsy.
15: 9 found the piece which I h' lost.
11 And he said, A certain man h' two
14 And when he h' spent all,
20 father saw him, and h' compassion
16: 1 rich man, which h' a steward;
1 that he h' wasted his goods.
8 because he h' done wisely:
17: 6 If ye h' faith as a grain of mustard
19: 15 to whom he h' given the money,
15 how much every man h' gained
28 And when he h' thus spoken,
32 and found even as he h' said
37 the mighty works that they h' seen;
20: 19 that he h' spoken this parable
33 of them is she? for seven h' her
21: 4 cash in all the living that she h'.
22: 13 and found as he h' said unto them:
55 And when they h' kindled a fire
61 how he h' said unto him,
64 And when they h' blindfolded him,
23: 8 because he h' heard many things
13 when he h' called together the
25 whom they h' desired;
46 And when Jesus h' cried with a loud
51 The same h' not consented to the
24: 1 the spices which they h' prepared,
14 all these things which h happened.
21 we trusted that it h' been he
23 they h' also seen a vision of angels,
24 even so as the women h' said:
37 supposed that they h' seen a spirit.
40 And when he h' thus spoken,
Joh 2: 9 ruler of the feast h' tasted the
15 And when he h' made a scourge
22 remembered that he h' said this
22 and the word which Jesus h' said.
4: 1 how the Pharisees h' heard
18 For thou hast h' five husbands;
50 the word that Jesus h' spoken
5: 4 whole of whatsoever disease he h'.
5 which h' an infirmity thirty and
6 and knew that he h' been now
13 for Jesus h' conveyed himself away,
15 was Jesus, which h' made him whole.
16 because he h' done these things
18 he not only h' broken the sabbath,
46 For h' ye believed Moses, ye
6: 11 and when he h' given thanks,
13 unto them that h' eaten.
14 when they h' seen the miracle
19 So when they h' rowed about
23 after that the Lord h' given thanks:
25 And when they h' found him
60 when they h' heard this, said,
7: 9 When he h' said these words
8: 3 when they h' set her in the midst,
10 When Jesus h' lifted up himself,
19 if ye h' known me, ye should
9: 6 When he h' thus spoken,
8 they which before h' seen him
15 asked him how he h' received his
18 that he h' been blind,
18 that h' received his sight.
22 for the Jews h' agreed already,
35 that they h' cast him out;
35 and when he h' found him,
11: 6 When he h' heard therefore
13 they thought that he h' spoken
17 that he h' lain in the grave
21 my brother h' not died.
28 And when she h' so said,
32 my brother h' not died.
43 And when he thus h' spoken,
45 came to Mary, and h' seen the
46 what things Jesus h' done.
57 and the Pharisees h' given a
12: 1 Lazarus was which h' been dead,

Joh 12: 6 he was a thief, and h' the bag,
9 whom he h' raised from the dead.
14 when he h' found a young ass,
16 that they h' done these things
18 that he h' done this miracle.
37 But though he h' done so many
13: 3 the Father h' given all things into
12 So after he h' washed their feet,
12 and h' taken his garments,
21 When Jesus h' thus said,
26 And when he h' dipped the sop,
29 because Judas h' the bag, that
29 that Jesus h' said unto him,
14: 7 If ye h' known me, ye should
15: 22 If I h' not come and spoken
22 they h' not...sin, but now they
22 they...not h' sin: but now they
24 If I h' not done among them
24 they h' not...sin, but now have
24 they...not h' sin: but now have
17: 5 the glory which I h' with thee
18: 1 When Jesus h' spoken these words,
6 as he h' said unto them,
18 who h' made a fire of coals;
22 And when he h' thus spoken,
24 Now Annas h' sent him bound
38 And when he h' said this,
19: 23 when they h' crucified Jesus,
30 When Jesus therefore h' received the
20: 12 where the body of Jesus h' lain.
14 And when she h' thus said,
18 that she h' seen the Lord,
18 and that he h' spoken these things
20 And when he h' so said,
22 And when he h' said this,
21: 15 So when they h' dined, Jesus
19 And when he h' spoken this,
Ac 1: 2 Holy Ghost h' given commandments
2 unto the apostles whom he h' chosen:
9 And when he h' spoken these things,
17 and h' obtained part of this ministry.
2: 30 and knowing that God h' sworn
44 were together, and h' all things
45 to all men, as every man h' need.
3: 10 at that which h' happened
12 or holiness we h' made this man
18 which God before h' shewed
4: 7 And when they h' set them in the
13 that they h' been with Jesus.
15 But when they h' commanded
21 when they h' further threatened
23 and elders h' said unto them.
31 And when they h' prayed,
32 but they h' all things common.
35 every man according as he h' need.
5: 23 but when we h' opened, we found
27 And when they h' brought them,
34 a doctor of the law, h' in reputation
40 when they h' called the apostles,
6: 6 and when they h' prayed,
15 As it h' been the face of an angel.
7: 5 when as yet he h' no child.
17 which God h' sworn to Abraham,
36 after that he h' shewed wonders
44 Our fathers h' the tabernacle of
44 as he h' appointed, speaking
44 to the fashion that he h' seen.
60 And when he h' said this,
8: 11 And to him they h' regard,
11 that of long time he h' bewitched them
14 heard that Samaria h' received the
25 when they h' testified and preached
27 who h' the charge of all her treasure,
27 and h' come to Jerusalem ... to worship.
9: 18 fell from his eyes as it h' been scales:
19 And when he h' received meat,
27 how he h' seen the Lord in the way,
27 and that he h' spoken to him,
27 and how he h' preached boldly
31 Then h' the churches rest
33 which h' kept his bed eight years,
37 whom when they h' washed,
38 the disciples h' heard that Peter
41 and when he h' called the saints
10: 8 when he h' declared all these things
11 as it h' been a great sheet
17 which he h' seen should mean
24 and h' called together his
31 and thine alms are h' in remembrance
11: 1 the Gentiles h' also received
5 as it h' been a great sheet,
6 when I h' fastened mine eyes,
13 how he h' seen an angel
23 and h' seen the grace of God,
26 And when he h' found him,
12: 4 And when he h' apprehended him,
12 And when he h' considered the thing,
16 and when they h' opened the door,
17 how the Lord h' brought him out
19 And when Herod h' sought for him,
25 when they h' fulfilled their ministry,
13: 1 which h' been brought up with
3 And when they h' fasted and
5 and they h' also John to their
6 when they h' gone through
19 when he h' destroyed seven nations
22 And when he h' removed him,
24 When John h' first preached
29 And when they h' fulfilled all that
36 after he h' served his own
14: 8 who never h' walked:
9 perceiving that he h' faith to be
11 people saw what Paul h' done,
18 that they h' not done sacrifice
19 supposing he h' been dead.
21 when they h' preached the gospel

Ac 14:21 to that city, and h' taught many,
23 when they h' ordained them elders
23 in every church, and h' prayed
24 And after they h' passed throughout
25 And when they h' preached
26 from whence they h' been
27 and h' gathered the church
27 all that God h' done with them,
27 and how he h' opened the door
15: 2 Paul and Barnabas h' no small
4 that God h' done with them.
7 when there h' been much disputing,
12 God h' wrought among the Gentiles
13 And after they h' held their peace.
30 and when they h' gathered the
31 Which when they h' read,
33 And after they h' tarried there
16: 6 Now when they h' gone throughout
10 And after he h' seen the vision,
10 that the Lord h' called us for to
23 when they h' laid many stripes
27 that the prisoners h' been fled.
34 when he h' brought them into
40 and when they h' seen the brethren,
17: 1 when they h' passed through
9 when they h' taken security of Jason,
13 Jews of Thessalonica h' knowledge
18: 2 Claudius h' commanded all
18 in Cenchrea: for he h' a vow.
22 when he h' landed at Cæsarea,
23 after he h' spent some time there,
26 Aquila and Priscilla h' heard,
27 which h' believed through grace:
19: 6 when Paul h' laid his hands
13 over them which h' evil spirits
21 when he h' passed through
35 townclerk h' appeased the people,
41 And when he h' thus spoken,
20: 2 when he h' gone over those parts,
2 and h' given them much
11 come up again, and h' broken bread,
13 for so he h' appointed,
16 For Paul h' determined to sail
36 And when he h' thus spoken,
21: 1 gotten from them, and h' launched,
3 when we h' discovered Cyprus,
5 when we h' accomplished those
6 when we h' taken our leave
7 when we h' finished our course
9 the same man h' four daughters,
19 And when he h' saluted them,
19 what things God h' wrought among
29 For they h' seen before with him
29 supposed that Paul h' brought into
33 who he was, and what he h' done.
40 And when he h' given him licence,
22:29 and because he h' bound him.
23: 7 And when he h' so said, there arose a
12 eat nor drink till they h' killed Paul.
13 than forty which h' made this
30 say before thee what they h' against
34 And when the governor h' read the
24:10 after that the governor h' beckoned
19 and object, if they h' ought
25: 6 And when he h' tarried among them
12 Festus, when he h' conferred with the
14 And when they h' been there many
19 But h' certain questions against
21 But when Paul h' appealed to be
25 when I found that he h' committed
26 after examination h', I might
26:30 And when he h' thus spoken,
32 if he h' not appealed unto Cæsar.
27: 4 And when we h' launched from
5 And when we h' sailed over the sea
7 And when we h' sailed slowly many
13 supposing that they h' obtained their
16 we h' much work to come by the
17 Which when they h' taken up, they
28 and when they h' gone a little further,
30 when they h' let down the boat into
35 And when he h' thus spoken,
35 and when he h' broken it, he began
38 And when they h' eaten enough,
40 And when they h' taken up the
28: 3 And when Paul h' gathered a bundle
6 but after they h' looked a great while,
9 others also, which h' diseases in
11 which h' wintered in the isle,
18 Who, when they h' examined me,
19 not that I h' ought to accuse my
23 And when they h' appointed him a
25 after that Paul h' spoken one word,
29 And when he h' said these words,
29 and h' great reasoning among
Ro 1: 2 Which he h' promised afore by his
4:11 faith which he h' yet being
12 which he h' being yet uncircumcised.
21 persuaded that, what he h' promised,
5:14 even over them that h' not sinned
6:21 What fruit h' ye then in those
7: 7 Nay, I h' not known sin, but by the
7 for I h' not known lust, except the
7 law h' said, Thou shalt not covet.
9:10 but when Rebecca also h' conceived
23 which he h' afore prepared unto glory,
29 Except the Lord of Sabaoth h' left us
29 we h' been as Sodoma,
1Co 1:15 say that I h' baptized in mine own
2: 8 for h' they known it, they would not
7:29 be as though they h' none; and
11:24 And when he h' given thanks, he brake
25 took the cup, when he h' supped,
14:19 Yet in the church I h' rather speak five
2Co 1: 9 But we h' the sentence of death in
12 we have h' our conversation in the

2Co 2:13 I h' no rest in my spirit, because
3:10 which was made glorious h' no glory
7: 5 our flesh h' no rest, but we were
12 for his cause that h' done the wrong,
8: 6 we desired Titus, that as he h' begun
15 He that h' gathered
15 much h' nothing over;
15 and he that h' gathered
15 gathered little h' no lack.
9: 5 whereof ye h' notice before, that the
11:21 reproach, as though we h' been weak,
Ga 1:23 But they h' heard only, That he which
2: 2 by any means I should run, or h' run,
3:21 for if there h' been a law given which
4:15 that, if it h' been possible, ye would
22 Abraham h' two sons, the one by
Eph 2: 3 Among whom also we all h' our
Ph'p 2:26 because that ye h' heard
26 that he h' been sick.
27 but God h' mercy on him; and not on
3:12 Not as though I h' already attained
1Th 1: 9 what manner of entering in we h'
2: 2 even after that we h' suffered before,
2Th 2:12 believed not the truth, but h' pleasure
Tit 1: 5 elders in every city, as I h' appointed
Heb 1: 3 when he h' by himself purged our sins,
2:14 he might destroy him that h' the
3:16 For some, when they h' heard, did
17 was it not with them that h' sinned,
4: 8 For if Jesus h' given them rest,
5: 7 when he h' offered up prayers and
6:15 And so, after he h' patiently endured,
7: 6 blessed him that h' the promises.
8: 7 if that first covenant h' been faultless.
9: 1 verily the first covenant h' also
4 Which h' the golden censer, and
4 the golden pot that h' manna,
19 when Moses h' spoken every precept
10: 2 once purged should have h' no
6 sacrifices for sin thou hast h' no
12 But this man, after he h' offered one
15 for after that he h' said before,
34 ye h' compassion of me in my bonds,
11: 5 because God h' translated him:
5 before his translation he h' this
11 judged him faithful who h' promised.
15 if they h' been mindful of that country
15 they might have h' opportunity
17 and he that h' received the promises
26 for he h' respect unto the recompence
31 she h' received the spies with peace.
36 others h' trial of cruel mockings
12: 9 we have h' fathers of our flesh
Jas 2:21 when he h' offered Isaac his son
25 when she h' received the messengers,
25 and h' sent them out another way?
1Pe 2:10 people of God: which h' not obtained
2Pe 2:21 For it h' been better for them not
1Jo 2: 7 an old commandment which ye h'
19 for if they h' been of us, they would
2Jo 5 but that which we h' from the
3Jo 13 I h' many things to write, but I
Re 1:16 And he h' in his right hand seven
4: 4 and they h' on their heads crowns
7 and the third beast h' a face as a
8 And the four beasts h' each of
5: 6 stood a Lamb as it h' been slain,
8 and when he h' taken the book,
6: 2 and he that sat on him h' a bow;
3 And when he h' opened the second
5 And when he h' opened the third
5 and he that sat on him h' a pair
7 And when he h' opened the fourth
9 And when he h' opened the fifth seal,
12 And I beheld when he h' opened the
8: 1 And when he h' opened the seventh
6 seven angels which h' the seven
9 were in the sea, and h' life, died;
9: 8 And they h' hair as the hair of
9 And they h' breastplates, as it
10 they h' tails like unto scorpions,
11 And they h' a king over them,
14 the sixth angel which h' the
19 like unto serpents, and h' heads,
10: 2 And he h' in his hand a little book
3 when he h' cried, seven thunders
4 when the seven thunders h' uttered
10 as soon as I h' eaten it, my belly was
13:11 and he h' two horns like a lamb,
14 miracles which he h' power to do
14 the beast, which h' the wound
15 And he h' power to give life unto
17 save he that h' the mark, or the
14:18 another angel...which h' power
18 with a cry to him that h' the sharp
15: 2 them that h' gotten the victory over
16: 2 the men which h' the mark of
17: 1 of the seven angels which h' the
18:19 were made rich all that h' ships in
19:12 and he h' a name written, that no
20 he deceived them that h' received
20: 4 and which h' not worshipped the
4 neither h' received his mark
21: 9 seven angels which h' the seven
12 And h' a wall great and high
12 and h' twelve gates, and at the
14 And the wall of the city h' twelve
15 And he that talked with me h' a
23 And the city h' no need of the sun
22: 8 And when I h' heard and seen,

Hadad (*ha'-dad*) See also Ben-hadad; Hadadezer; Hadadrimmon; Hadar.
Ge 36:35 and H' the son of Bedad...reigned
36 And H' died, and Samlah of
1Ki 11:14 an adversary unto Solomon, H'
17 That H' fled, he and certain
1Ki 11:17 H' being yet a little child.
19 H' found great favour in the sight
21 when H' heard in Egypt that
21 H' said to Pharaoh, Let me depart,
25 besides the mischief that H' did:
1Ch 1:30 Mishma, and Dumah, Massa, H',
46 H' the son of Bedad, which smote
47 when H' was dead, Samlah of
50 Baal-hanan was dead, H' reigned
51 H' died also. And the dukes of

Hadadezer (*had-a-de'-zer*) See also Hadarezer.
2Sa 8: 3 David smote also H', the son of
5 came to succour H' king of Zobah,
7 that were on the servants of H',
8 Betah, and...Berothai, cities of H',
9 had smitten all the host of H',
10 because he had fought against H',
10 for H' had wars with Toi.
12 and of the spoil of H', son of
1Ki 11:23 which fled from his lord H'

Hadadrimmon (*ha''-dad-rim'-mon*)
Zec 12:11 as the mourning of H' in the

Hadar (*ha'-dar*) See also Hadad.
Ge 25:15 H', and Tema, Jetur, Naphish,
36:39 and H' reigned in his stead:

Hadarezer (*had-a-re'-zer*) See also Hadadezer.
2Sa 10:16 And H' sent, and brought out
16 the captain of the host of H'
19 the kings that were servants to H'
1Ch 18: 3 David smote H' king of Zobah
5 came to help H' king of Zobah,
7 that were on the servants of H',
8 and from Chun, cities of H',
9 had smitten all the host of H'
10 because he had fought against H',
10 for H' had war with Tou;
19:16 the captain of the host of H'
19 when the servants of H' saw that

Hadashah (*had'-a-shah*)
Jos 15:37 Zenan, and H', and Migdal-gad,

Hadassah (*ha-das'-sah*) See also Esther.
Es 2: 7 he brought up H', that is, Esther,

Hadattah (*ha-dat'-tah*) See also Hazor-hadattah.
Jos 15:25 Hazor, H', and Kerioth,

Haddah See En-haddah.

Haddon See Esar-haddon.

Hadid (*ha'-did*)
Ezr 2:33 The children of Lod, H', and Ono,
Ne 7:37 of Lod, H', and Ono, seven
11:34 H', Zeboim, Neballat,

Hadlai (*had'-la-i*)
2Ch 28:12 and Amasa the son of H', stood

Hadoram (*ha-do'-ram*) See also Adoram.
Ge 10:27 And H', and Uzal, and Diklah,
1Ch 1:21 H' also, and Uzal, and Diklah,
18:10 He sent H' his son to king David,
2Ch 10:18 Then king Rehoboam sent H'

Hadrach (*ha'-drak*)
Zec 9: 1 word of the Lord in the land of H',

hadst
Ge 30:30 For it was little which thou h' before I
31:42 with me, surely thou h' sent me away
J'g 15: 2 thought that thou h' utterly hated
1Sa 25:34 except thou h' hasted and come to
2Sa 2:27 As God liveth, unless thou h' spoken,
2Ki 13:19 then h' thou smitten Syria till thou h',
Ezr 9:14 be angry with us till thou h' consumed
Ne 9:15 land which thou h' sworn to give them.
23 concerning which thou h' promised
Ps 44: 3 because thou h' a favour unto them.
60:10 O God, which h' cast us off?
90: 2 or ever thou h' formed the earth
Isa 26:15 thou h' removed it far unto all the
48:18 O that thou h' hearkened to my
Jer 3: 3 and thou h' a whore's forehead,
Jon 2: 3 For thou h' cast me into the deep,
Lu 19:42 Saying, If thou h' known, even thou
Joh 11:21 unto Jesus, Lord, if thou h' been here
32 unto him, Lord, if thou h' been here,
1Co 4: 7 glory, as if thou h' not received it?
Heb 10: 8 not, neither h' pleasure therein;

haft See also handle.
J'g 3:22 the h' also went in after the blade;

Hagab (*ha'-gab*) See also Hagaba.
Ezr 2:46 The children of H', the children

Hagaba (*hag'-a-bah*) See also Hagab; Hagabah.
Ne 7:48 the children of H', the children of

Hagabah (*hag'-a-bah*) See also Hagaba.
Ezr 2:45 the children of H', the children of

Hagar (*ha'-gar*) See also Agar; Hagarites.
Ge 16: 1 an Egyptian, whose name was H'.
3 Sarai, Abram's wife, took H' her
4 he went in unto H', and she
8 he said, H', Sarai's maid, whence
15 H' bare Abram a son: and Abram
15 called his son's name, which H' bare,
16 when H' bare Ishmael to Abram.
21: 9 Sarah saw the son of H' the
14 and gave it unto H', putting it
17 and the angel of God called to H'
17 unto her, What aileth thee, H'?
25:12 Ishmael, Abraham's son, whom H'

Hagarenes (*hag-a-renes'*) See also Hagarites.
Ps 83: 6 Ishmaelites; of Moab, and the H';

Hagarites (*hag'-a-rites*) See also Hagarenes; Hagerite.
1Ch 5:10 they made war with the H', who

1Ch 5:19 they made war with the *H*˙, with
20 and the *H*˙ were delivered into

Hagerite (*hag'-e-rite*) See also HAGARITES; HAGERI.
1Ch 27:31 over the flocks was Jaziz the *H*˙.

Haggai (*hag'-ga-i*)
Ezr 5: 1 the prophets, *H*˙ the prophet, and
6:14 through the prophesying of *H*˙ the
Hag 1: 1 the Lord by *H*˙ the prophet unto
3 the Lord by *H*˙ the prophet, saying,
12 and the words of *H*˙ the prophet, as
13 Then spake *H*˙ the Lord's
2: 1, 10 of the Lord by the prophet *H*˙,
13 Then said *H*˙, If one that is unclean
14 Then answered *H*˙, and said, So is
20 came unto *H*˙ in the four and

Haggeri (*hag'-gher-i*) See also HAGERITE.
1Ch 11:38 Mibhar the son of *H*˙,

Haggi (*hag'-ghi*) See also HAGGITES.
Ge 46:16 Ziphion, and *H*˙, Shuni, and
Nu 26:15 of *H*˙, the family of the Haggites:

Haggiah (*hag-ghi'-ah*)
1Ch 6:30 Shimea his son, *H*˙ his son,

Haggites (*hag'-ghites*) See also HAGGI.
Nu 26:15 of Haggi, the family of the *H*˙:

Haggith (*hag'-ghith*)
2Sa 3: 4 fourth, Adonijah the son of *H*˙;
1Ki 1: 5 Adonijah the son of *H*˙ exalted
11 the son of *H*˙ doth reign, and
2:13 the son of *H*˙ came to Bath-sheba
1Ch 3: 2 the fourth, Adonijah the son of *H*˙:

Hahiroth See PI-HAHIROTH.

Hai (*ha'-i*) See also AI.
Ge 12: 8 Beth-el on the west, and *H*˙ on
13: 3 between Beth-el and *H*˙;

hail See also HAILSTONES.
Ex 9:18 to rain a very grievous *h*˙, such as
19 the *h*˙ shall come down upon them,
22 that there may be *h*˙ in all the
23 the Lord sent thunder and *h*˙, and
23 rained *h*˙ upon the land of Egypt.
24 was *h*˙, and fire mingled with the *h*˙,
25 the *h*˙ smote throughout all the
25 the *h*˙ smote every herb of the field,
26 of Israel were, was there no *h*˙.
28 more mighty thunderings and *h*˙;
29 neither shall there be any more *h*˙;
33 the thunders and *h*˙ ceased, and
34 saw that the rain and the *h*˙ and
10: 5 remaineth unto to you from the *h*˙,
12 even all that the *h*˙ hath left.
15 of the trees which the *h*˙ had left:
Job 38:22 thou seen the treasures of the *h*˙,
Ps 18:12 thick clouds passed, *h*˙ stones and
13 his voice; *h*˙ stones and coals of
78:47 He destroyed their vines with *h*˙,
48 He gave up their cattle...to the *h*˙,
105:32 He gave them *h*˙ for rain, and
148: 8 Fire, and *h*˙; snow, and vapours;
Isa 28: 2 as a tempest of *h*˙ and a destroying
17 the *h*˙ shall sweep away the refuge
32:19 When it shall *h*˙, coming down on
Hag 2:17 with mildew and with *h*˙ in all the
M't 26:49 and said, *H*˙, master; and kissed
27:29 mocked him, saying, *H*˙, King of the
28: 9 Jesus met them, saying, All *h*˙.
M'r 15:18 salute him, *H*˙, King of the Jews!
Lu 1:28 *H*˙, thou that art highly favoured,
Joh 19: 3 And said, *H*˙, King of the Jews!
Re 8: 7 followed *h*˙ and fire mingled with
11:19 and an earthquake, and great *h*˙.
16:21 there fell upon men a great *h*˙ out
21 because of the plague of the *h*˙;

Hail See BEN-HAIL.

hailstones See also HAIL and STONES.
Jos 10:11 more which died with *h*˙ than
Isa 30:30 scattering, and tempest, and *h*˙.
Eze 13:11 ye, O great *h*˙, shall fall; and a
13 and great *h*˙ in my fury to
38:22 and great *h*˙, fire, and brimstone.

hair See also HAIRS.
Ex 25: 4 scarlet, and fine linen, and goats' *h*˙,
26: 7 shalt make curtains of goats' *h*˙ to
35: 6 scarlet, and fine linen, and goats *h*˙,
23 and goats' *h*˙, and red skins of rams,
26 them up in wisdom spun goats' *h*˙.
36:14 And he made curtains of goats' *h*˙
Le 13: 3 and when the *h*˙ in the plague is
4 and the *h*˙ thereof be not turned
10 it have turned the *h*˙ white, and
20 and the *h*˙ thereof be turned white;
25 the *h*˙ in the bright spot be turned
26 no white *h*˙ in the bright spot,
30 there be in it a yellow thin *h*˙;
31 and that there is no black *h*˙
32 there be in it no yellow *h*˙,
36 priest shall not seek for yellow *h*˙;
37 and that there is black *h*˙ grown up
40 whose *h*˙ is fallen off his head, he
41 he that hath his *h*˙ fallen off from
14: 8 shave off all his *h*˙, and wash
9 he shall shave all his *h*˙ off his head
9 eyebrows, even all his *h*˙ he shall
Nu 6: 5 let the locks of the *h*˙ of his head
18 shall take the *h*˙ of the head
19 of the Nazarite, after the *h*˙ of his
31:20 of goats' *h*˙, and all things made of
J'g 16:22 the *h*˙ of his head began to grow
20:16 could sling stones at an *h*˙ breadth,
1Sa 14:45 there shall not one *h*˙ of his head
19:13 put a pillow of goats' *h*˙ for his bolster,
1Sa 19:16 a pillow of goats' *h*˙ for his bolster.
2Sa 14:11 there shall not one *h*˙ of thy son
26 because the *h*˙ was heavy on him,
26 he weighed the *h*˙ of his head
1Ki 1:52 there shall not an *h*˙ of him fall
Ezr 9: 3 plucked off the *h*˙ of my head
Ne 13:25 and plucked off their *h*˙, and made
Job 4:15 the *h*˙ of my flesh stood up:
Ca 4: 1 thy *h*˙ is as a flock of goats,
6: 5 thy *h*˙ is as a flock of goats
7: 5 and the *h*˙ of thine head like
Isa 3:24 instead of well set *h*˙ baldness;
7:20 head, and the *h*˙ of the feet:
50: 6 to them that plucked off the *h*˙:
Jer 7:29 Cut off thine *h*˙, O Jerusalem, and
Eze 5: 1 balances to weigh and divide the *h*˙.
16: 7 and thine *h*˙ is grown, whereas
Da 3:27 nor was an *h*˙ of their head singed,
7: 9 and the *h*˙ of his head like the pure
M't 3: 4 John had his raiment of camel's *h*˙,
5:36 canst not make one *h*˙ white or
M'r 1: 6 John was clothed with camel's *h*˙,
Lu 21:18 But there shall not an *h*˙ of your
Joh 11: 2 and wiped his feet with her *h*˙,
12: 3 wiped his feet with her *h*˙:
Ac 27:34 an *h*˙ fall from the head
1Co 11:14 if a man have long *h*˙, it is a
15 But if a woman have long *h*˙, it is a
15 for her *h*˙ is given her for a
1Ti 2: 9 not with broided *h*˙, or gold, or
1Pet 3: 3 of plaiting the *h*˙, and of wearing
Re 6:12 black as sackcloth of *h*˙,
9: 8 And they had *h*˙ as the *h*˙ of

hair-breadth See HAIR and BREADTH.

hairs
Ge 42:38 bring down my gray *h*˙ with sorrow
44:29 bring down my gray *h*˙ with sorrow
31 the gray *h*˙ of thy servant our father
Le 13:21 no white *h*˙ therein, and if it be
De 32:25 suckling also with the man of gray *h*˙.
Ps 40:12 they are more than the *h*˙ of mine
69: 4 cause are more than the *h*˙ of mine
Isa 46: 4 even to hoar *h*˙ will I carry you:
Da 4:33 his *h*˙ were grown like eagles'
Ho 7: 9 gray *h*˙ are here and there upon him,
M't 10:30 the very *h*˙ of your head are all
Lu 7:38 wipe them with the *h*˙ of her head,
44 wiped them with the *h*˙ of her head.
12: 7 But even the very *h*˙ of your head
Re 1:14 His head and his *h*˙ were white

hairy
Ge 25:25 red, all over like an *h*˙ garment;
27:11 Esau my brother is a *h*˙ man, and
23 becaus his hands were *h*˙, as his
2Ki 1: 8 answered him, He was an *h*˙ 1167,
Ps 68:21 the *h*˙ scalp of such an one as goeth

Hakkatan (*hak'-ka-tan*)
Ezr 8:12 Johannan the son of *H*˙, and with

Hakkore See EN-HAKKORE.

Hakkoz (*hak'-koz*) See also KOZ.
1Ch 24:10 The seventh to *H*˙, the eighth to

Hakupha (*ha-ku'-fah*)
Ezr 2:51 the children of *H*˙, the children of
Ne 7:53 the children of *H*˙, the children of

Halah (*ha'-lah*)
2Ki 17: 6 and placed them in *H*˙ and in
18:11 and put them in *H*˙ and in Habor
1Ch 5:26 and brought them unto *H*˙, and

Halak (*ha'-lak*)
Jos 11:17 mount *H*˙, that goeth up to Seir,
12: 7 mount *H*˙, that goeth up to Seir;

hale See also HALING.
Lu 12:58 lest he *h*˙ thee to the judge,

half See also BEHALF.
Ge 24:22 a golden earring of *h*˙ a shekel
Ex 24: 6 Moses took *h*˙ of the blood, and
6 and *h*˙ of the blood he sprinkled
25:10 two cubits and a *h*˙ shall be the
10 and a cubit and a *h*˙ the breadth
10 thereof, and a cubit and a *h*˙
10 cubit and a *h*˙ the height
17 two cubits and a *h*˙ shall be the
17 thereof, and a cubit and a *h*˙
23 cubit and a *h*˙ the height thereof.
26:12 the *h*˙ curtain that remaineth, shall
16 a cubit and a *h*˙ shall be the
30:13 *h*˙ a shekel after the shekel of the
13 an *h*˙ shekel shall be the offering
15 give less than *h*˙ a shekel,
23 sweet cinnamon *h*˙ so much, even
36:21 a board one cubit and a *h*˙.
37: 1 two cubits and a *h*˙ was the length
1 and a cubit and a *h*˙ the breadth of
1 and a cubit and a *h*˙ the height of
6 two cubits and a *h*˙ was the length
6 one cubit and a *h*˙ the breadth
10 a cubit and a *h*˙ the height thereof:
38:26 *h*˙ a shekel, after the shekel of
Le 6:20 *h*˙ of it in the morning, and *h*˙
Nu 12:12 of whom the flesh is *h*˙ consumed
15: 9 mingled with *h*˙ an hin of oil.
10 for a drink offering *h*˙ an hin
28:14 their drink offerings shall be *h*˙ an
31:29 Take it of their *h*˙, and give it unto
30 And of the children of Israel's *h*˙,
36 the *h*˙, which was the portion
42 And of the children of Israel's *h*˙,
43 the *h*˙ that pertained unto the
47 Even of the children of Israel's *h*˙,
32:33 and unto *h*˙ the tribe of Manasseh
34:13 nine tribes, and to the *h*˙ tribe:
14 and *h*˙ the tribe of Manasseh have
Nu 34:15 The two tribes and the *h*˙ tribe
De 3:12 *h*˙ mount Gilead, and the cities
13 gave I unto the *h*˙ tribe of
16 unto the river Arnon *h*˙ the
29: 8 and to the *h*˙ tribe of Manasseh.
Jos 1:12 and to *h*˙ the tribe of Manasseh,
4:12 and *h*˙ the tribe of Manasseh,
8:33 *h*˙ of them over against mount
33 Gerizim, and *h*˙ of them over
12: 2 and from *h*˙ Gilead, even unto the
5 Maachathites, and *h*˙ Gilead, the
6 Gadites, and the *h*˙ tribe of
13: 7 nine tribes, and the *h*˙ tribe of
25 and *h*˙ the land of the children
29 unto the *h*˙ tribe of Manasseh: and
29 was the possession of the *h*˙ tribe
31 And *h*˙ Gilead, and Ashtaroth, and
31 to the one *h*˙ of the children of
14: 2 nine tribes, and for the *h*˙ tribe.
3 two tribes and an *h*˙ tribe on the
18: 7 Reuben, and *h*˙ the tribe of
21: 5 and out of the *h*˙ tribe of Manasseh,
6 and out of the *h*˙ tribe of Manasseh
25 And out of the *h*˙ tribe of
27 out of the other *h*˙ tribe of
22: 1 the Gadites, and the *h*˙ tribe of
7 Now to the one *h*˙ of the tribe of
7 but unto the other *h*˙ thereof gave
9 the children of Gad and the *h*˙ tribe
10 Gad and the *h*˙ tribe of Manasseh
11 the children of Gad and the *h*˙ tribe
13, 15, and to the *h*˙ tribe of Manasseh,
21 and the *h*˙ tribe of Manasseh
1Sa 14:14 within as it were an *h*˙ acre of land,
2Sa 10: 4 shaved off the one *h*˙ of their beards,
18: 3 neither if *h*˙ of us die, will they
19:40 and also *h*˙ the people of Israel.
1Ki 3:25 give *h*˙ to the one, and *h*˙ to the
7:31 a cubit and an *h*˙: and also upon
32 a wheel was a cubit and *h*˙ a cubit.
35 a round compass of *h*˙ a cubit high:
10: 7 the *h*˙ was not told me: thy wisdom
13: 8 If thou wilt give me *h*˙ thine house,
16: 9 Zimri, captain of *h*˙ his chariots,
21 *h*˙ of the people followed Tibni
21 and *h*˙ followed Omri.
1Ch 2:52 Haroeh, and *h*˙ of the Manahethites.
54 Joab, and *h*˙ of the Manahethites,
5:18 and *h*˙ the tribe of Manasseh, of
23 the children of the *h*˙ tribe of
26 and the *h*˙ tribe of Manasseh, and
6:61 out of the *h*˙ tribe, namely, out
61 of the *h*˙ tribe of Manasseh,
70 out of the *h*˙ tribe of Manasseh;
71 the *h*˙ tribe of Manasseh, Golan in
12:31 And of the *h*˙ tribe of Manasseh
37 and of the *h*˙ tribe of Manasseh,
26:32 and the *h*˙ tribe of Manasseh, for
27:20 of the *h*˙ tribe of Manasseh, Joel
21 Of the *h*˙ tribe of Manasseh in
2Ch 9: 6 the one *h*˙ of the greatness of thy
Ne 3: 9 ruler of the *h*˙ part of Jerusalem.
12 ruler of the *h*˙ part of Jerusalem,
16 the ruler of the *h*˙ part of Beth-zur,
17 the ruler of the *h*˙ part of Keilah,
18 the ruler of the *h*˙ part of Keilah.
4: 6 joined together unto the *h*˙ thereof:
16 the *h*˙ of my servants wrought in
16 and the other *h*˙ of them held
21 *h*˙ of them held the spears
12:32 and *h*˙ of the princes of Judah.
38 and the *h*˙ of the people upon the
40 I, and the *h*˙ of the rulers with me:
13:24 their children spake *h*˙ in the
Es 5: 3 given thee to the *h*˙ of the kingdom.
6 the *h*˙ of the kingdom it shall be
7: 2 even to the *h*˙ of the kingdom.
Ps 55:23 shall not live out *h*˙ their days;
Eze 16:51 Neither hath Samaria committed *h*˙
40:42 a cubit and an *h*˙ long, and
42 a cubit and an *h*˙ broad,
43:17 border about it shall be *h*˙ a cubit;
Da 12: 7 for a time, times, and an *h*˙; and
Ho 3: 2 of barley, and an *h*˙ homer of
Zec 14: 2 *h*˙ of the city shall go forth into
4 *h*˙ of the mountain shall remove
4 and *h*˙ of it toward the south.
8 *h*˙ of them toward the former sea,
8 *h*˙ of them toward the hinder sea:
M'r 6:23 it thee, unto the *h*˙ of my kingdom.
Lu 10:30 departed, leaving him *h*˙ dead.
19: 8 the *h*˙ of my goods I give to the
Re 8: 1 about the space of *h*˙ an hour.
11: 9 three days and an *h*˙, and shall not
11 three days and an *h*˙ the Spirit of life
12:14 a time, and times, and *h*˙ a time,

half-dead See HALF and DEAD.

half-homer See HALF and HOMER.

Halhul (*hal'-hul*)
Jos 15:58 *H*˙, Beth-zur, and Gedor,

Hali (*ha'-li*)
Jos 19:25 their border was Helkath, and *H*˙,

haling
Ac 8: 3 *h*˙ men and women committed

hall
M't 27:27 took Jesus into the common *h*˙,
M'r 15:16 led him away into the *h*˙,
Lu 22:55 a fire in the midst of the *h*˙, and
Joh 18:28 led...unto the *h*˙ of judgment:
28 went not into the judgment *h*˙,
33 Pilate entered...the judgment *h*˙
19: 9 went again into the judgment *h*˙,
Ac 23:35 to be kept in Herod's judgment *h*˙.

Hallelujah See ALLELUIA.
Hallohesh (*hal-lo'-hesh*) See also HALOHESH.
Ne 10:24 *H*·, Pileha, Shobek,
hallow See also HALLOWED.
Ex 28:38 the children of Israel shall *h*· in
29: 1 to *h*· them, to minister unto me
40: 9 and shalt *h*· it, and all the vessels
Le 16:19 cleanse it, and *h*· it from the
22: 2 those things which they *h*· unto me:
3 which the children of Israel *h*· unto
32 I am the Lord which *h*· you,
25:10 And ye shall *h*· the fiftieth year,
Nu 6:11 and shall *h*· his head that same day.
1Ki 8:64 same day did the king *h*· the middle
Jer 17:22 but *h*· ye the sabbath day, as I
24 but *h*· the sabbath day, to do no
27 to *h*· the sabbath day, and not to
Eze 20:20 *h*· my sabbaths; and they shall be
44:24 and they shall *h*· my sabbaths.
hallowed
Ex 20:11 blessed the sabbath day, and *h*· it.
29:21 and he shall be *h*·, and his garments,
Le 12: 4 she shall touch no *h*· thing, nor
19: 8 profaned the *h*· thing of the Lord:
22:32 I will be *h*· among the children
Nu 3:13 I *h*· unto me all the firstborn
5:10 every man's *h*· things shall be his:
16:37 the fire yonder; for they are *h*·.
38 therefore they are *h*·: and they
18: 8 all the *h*· things of the children of
29 even the *h*· part thereof out of it.
De 26:13 I have brought away the *h*· things
1Sa 21: 4 there is *h*· bread; if the young
6 the priest gave him *h*· bread: for
1Ki 9: 3 I have *h*· this house, which thou
7 which I have *h*· for my name,
2Ki 12:18 all the *h*· things that Jehoshaphat,
18 and his own *h*· things, and all
2Ch 7: 7 Moreover Solomon *h*· the middle
36:14 of the Lord which he had *h*· in
M't 6: 9 in heaven, *H*· be thy name.
Lu 11: 2 in heaven, *H*· be thy name.
Halohesh (*ha-lo'-hesh*) See also HALLOHESH.
Ne 3:12 repaired Shallum the son of *H*·,
halt See also HALTED; HALTETH; HALTING.
1Ki 18:21 How long *h*· ye between two
Ps 38:17 I am ready to *h*·, and my sorrow
M't 18: 8 to enter into life *h*· or maimed,
M'r 9:45 better for thee to enter *h*· into life,
Lu 14:21 the maimed, and the *h*·, and the
Joh 5: 3 of blind, *h*·, withered, waiting for
halted
Ge 32:31 him, and he *h*· upon his thigh.
Mic 4: 7 I will make her that *h*· a remnant,
halteth
Mic 4: 6 will I assemble her that *h*·, and
Zep 3:19 I will save her that *h*·, and gather
halting
Jer 20:10 my familiars watched for my *h*·.
Ham (*ham*)
Ge 5:32 Noah begat Shem, *H*·, and
6:10 Noah begat three sons, Shem, *H*·,
7:13 Noah, and Shem, and *H*·, and
9:18 were Shem, and *H*·, and Japheth:
18 and *H*· is the father of Caanan.
22 And *H*·, the father of Caanan, saw
10: 1 Shem, *H*·, and Japheth: and unto
6 the sons of *H*·; Cush, and Mizraim,
20 These are the sons of *H*·, after their
14: 5 and the Zuzims in *H*·, and the
1Ch 1: 4 Noah, Shem, *H*·, and Japheth.
8 The sons of *H*·; Cush, and
4:40 for they of *H*· had dwelt there of
Ps 78:51 strength in the tabernacles of *H*·:
105:23 Jacob sojourned in the land of *H*·.
27 and wonders in the land of *H*·.
106:22 Wondrous works in the land of *H*·.
Haman (*ha'-man*) See also HAMAN'S.
Es 3: 1 *H*· the son of Hammedatha
2 bowed, and reverenced *H*·: for the
4 they told *H*·, to see whether
5 when *H*· saw that Mordecai bowed
5 then was *H*· full of wrath.
6 wherefore *H*· sought to destroy all
7 that is, the lot, before *H*· from day
8 *H*· said unto king Ahasuerus,
10 and gave it unto *H*· the son of
11 the king said unto *H*·, The silver
12 according to all that *H*· had
15 the king and *H*· sat down to drink;
4: 7 of the money that *H*· had promised
5: 4 let the king and *H*· come this day
5 Cause *H*· to make haste, that he
5 So the king and *H*· came to the
8 let the king and *H*· come to the
9 Then went *H*· forth that day joyful
9 but when *H*· saw Mordecai in the
10 Nevertheless *H*· refrained himself:
11 *H*· told them of the glory of his
12 *H*· said moreover, Yea, Esther the
14 And the thing pleased *H*·; and he
6: 4 Now *H*· was come into the outward
5 Behold, *H*· standeth in the court.
6 So *H*· came in. And the king
6 Now *H*· thought in his heart, To
7 *H*· answered the king, For the
10 Then the king said to *H*·, Make
11 Then took *H*· the apparel and the
12 But *H*· hasted to his house
13 And *H*· told Zeresh his wife
14 And hasted to bring *H*· unto the
7: 1 So the king and *H*· came to
6 and enemy is this wicked *H*·.

Es 7: 6 Then *H*· was afraid
7 and *H*· stood up to make request
8 and *H*· was fallen upon the bed
9 which *H*· had made for Mordecai,
9 standeth in the house of *H*·. Then
10 So they hanged *H*· on the gallows
8: 1 give the house of *H*· the Jews'
2 which he had taken from *H*·, and
2 Mordecai over the house of *H*·.
3 to put away the mischief of *H*· the
5 to reverse the letters devised by *H*·,
7 I have given Esther...house of *H*·,
9:10 The ten sons of *H*· the son of
12 the palace, and the ten sons of *H*·;
24 Because *H*· the son of
Haman's (*Ha'-mans*)
Es 7: 8 they covered *H*· face.
9:13 and let *H*· ten sons be hanged
14 and they hanged *H*· ten sons.
Hamath (*ha'-math*) See also HAMATHITE; HAMATH-ZOBAH; HEMATH.
Nu 13:21 unto Rehob, as men come to *H*·.
34: 8 your border unto...entrance of *H*·;
Jos 13: 5 Hermon unto the entering into *H*·.
J'g 3: 3 Baal-hermon...entering in of *H*·.
2 Sa 8: 9 When Toi king of *H*· heard that
1 Ki 8:65 from the entering in of *H*· unto the
2 Ki 14:25 from the entering of *H*· unto the
28 and *H*·, which belonged to Judah,
17:24 and from *H*·, and from Sepharvaim,
30 and the men of *H*· made Ashima,
18:34 Where are the gods of *H*·, and of
19:13 Where is the king of *H*·, and the
23:33 at Riblah in the land of *H*·, that he
25:21 slew them at Riblah...land of *H*·.
1Ch18: 3 Hadarezer king of Zobak unto *H*·,
9 when Tou king of *H*· heard how
2Ch 7: 8 of *H*· unto the river of Egypt.
8: 4 store cities, which he built in *H*·.
Isa 10: 9 is not *H*· as Arpad? is not
11:11 from *H*·, and from the islands
36:19 Where are the gods of *H*· and
37:13 Where is the king of *H*·, and the
Jer 39: 5 *H*·, where he gave judgment upon
49:23 *H*· is confounded, and Arpad:
52: 9 to Riblah in the land of *H*·;
27 to death in Riblah in the land of *H*·.
Eze 47:16 *H*·, Berothah, Sibraim, which is
16 of Damascus and the border of *H*·;
17 northward, and the border of *H*·.
20 till a man come over against *H*·.
48: 1 of Hethlon, as one goeth to *H*·,
1 Damascus northward...coast of *H*·;
Am 6: 2 from thence go ye to *H*· the great
Zec 9: 2 *H*· also shall border thereby;
Hamathite (*ham'-a-thite*)
Ge 10:18 the Zemarite, and the *H*·: and
1 Ch 1:16 the Zemarite, and the *H*·.
Hamath-zobah (*ha''-math-zo'-bah*)
2 Ch 8: 3 And Solomon went to *H*·, and
Hammahlekoth See SELA-HAMMAHLEKOTH.
Hammath (*ham'-math*)
Jos 19:35 and *H*·, Rakkath, and
Hammedatha (*ham-med'-a-thah*)
Es 3: 1 the son of *H*· the Agagite,
10 Haman the son of *H*· the Agagite,
8: 5 by Haman the son of *H*· the
9:10 sons of Haman the son of *H*·, the
24 son of *H*·, the Agagite, the enemy
Hammelech (*ham'-me-lek*)
Jer 36:26 Jerahmeel the son of *H*·, and
38: 6 Malchiah the son of *H*·, that was
hammer See also HAMMERS.
J'g 4:21 took an *h*· in her hand, and went
5:26 right hand to the workmen's *h*·;
26 and with the *h*· she smote
1 Ki 6: 7 neither *h*· nor axe nor any tool of
Isa 41: 7 he that smootheth with the *h*·
Jer 23:29 and like a *h*· that breaketh
50:23 the *h*· of the whole earth
hammers.
Ps 74: 6 work...at once with axes and *h*·.
Isa 44:12 and fashioneth it with *h*·, and
Jer 10: 4 fasten it with nails and with *h*·.
Hammoleketh (*ham-mol'-e-keth*)
1 Ch 7:18 And his sister *H*· bare Ishod,
Hammon (*ham'-mon*)
Jos 19:28 Hebron, and Rehob, and *H*·,
1 Ch 6:76 and *H*· with her suburbs, and
Hammoth-dor (*ham''-moth-dor'*)
Jos 21:32 and *H*· with her suburbs,
Hamon See BAAL-HAMON; HAMON-GOG.
Hamonah (*ha-mo'-nah*)
Eze 39:16 the name of the city shall be *H*·.
Hamon-gog (*ha''-mon-gog'*)
Eze 39:11 shall call it The valley of *H*·.
15 have buried it in the valley of *H*·.
Hamor (*ha'-mor*) See also EMMOR; HAMOR'S.
Ge 33:19 at the hand of the children of *H*·,
34: 2 when Shechem the son of *H*· the
4 Shechem spake unto his father *H*·,
6 *H*· the father of Shechem went
8 And *H*· communed with them,
13 answered Shechem and *H*· his
18 And their words pleased *H*·
20 *H*· and Shechem his son came
24 And unto *H*· and unto Shechem
26 they slew *H*· and Shechem his son
Jos 24:32 Jacob bought of the sons of *H*·
J'g 9:28 serve the men of *H*· the father of

Hamor's (*ha'-mors*)
Ge 34:18 and Shechem *H*· son.
Hamuel (*ha-mu'-el*)
1 Ch 4:26 *H*· his son, Zacchur his son,
Hamul (*ha'-mul*) See also HAMULITES.
Gen46:12 sons of Pharez...Hezron and *H*·.
Nu 26:21 of *H*·, the family of the Hamulites.
1 Ch 2: 5 sons of Pharez; Hezron, and *H*·
Hamulites (*ha'-mu-lites*)
Nu 26:21 of Hamul, the family of the *H*·.
Hamutal (*ha-mu'-tal*)
2 Ki 23:31 his mother's name was *H*·,
24:18 *H*·, the daughter of Jeremiah
Jer 52: 1 his mother's name was *H*·
Hanameel (*ha-nam'-e-el*)
Jer 32: 7 Behold, *H*· the son of Shallum
8 So *H*· mine uncle's son came
9 And I bought the field of *H*·
12 in the sight of *H*· mine uncle's
Hanan (*ha'-nan*) See also BAAL-HANAN; BEN-HANAN; ELON-BETH-HANAN.
1 Ch 8:23 And Abdon, and Zichri, and *H*·,
38 Sheariah, and Obadiah, and *H*·.
9:44 Obadiah, and *H*·: these were the
11:43 *H*· the son of Maachah, and
Ezr 2:46 of Shalmai, the children of *H*·,
Ne 7:49 The children of *H*·, the children
8: 7 Azariah, Jozabad, *H*·, Pelaiah,
10:10 Kelita, Pelaiah, *H*·,
22 Pelatiah, *H*·, Anaiah,
26 And Ahijah, *H*·, Anan,
13:13 and next to them was *H*· the son
Jer 35: 4 into the chamber of the sons of *H*·,
Hananeel (*ha-nan'-e-el*)
Ne 3: 1 sanctified it unto the tower of *H*·.
12:39 the tower of *H*·, and the tower of
Jer 31:38 the tower of *H*· unto the gate
Zec 14:10 the tower of *H*· unto the king's
Hanani (*ha-na'-ni*)
1 Ki 16: 1 came to Jehu the son of *H*·
7 of the prophet Jehu, the son of *H*·
1Ch 25: 4 Hananiah, *H*·, Eliathah, Giddalti,
25 The eighteenth to *H*·, he, his sons,
2Ch 16: 7 at that time *H*· the seer came to
19: 2 Jehu the son of *H*· the seer went
20:34 in the book of Jehu the son of *H*·,
Ezr 10:20 of the sons of Immer; *H*·, and
Ne 1: 2 That *H*·, one of my brethren,
7: 2 That I gave my brother *H*·, and
12:36 and Judah, *H*·, with the musical
Hananiah (*han-a-ni'-ah*) See also SHADRACH.
1 Ch 3:19 Meshullam, and *H*·, and
21 the sons of *H*·; Pelatiah, and
8:24 *H*·, and Elam, and Antothijah,
25: 4 Jerimoth, *H*·, Hanani,
25:23 The sixteenth to *H*·, he, his sons,
2Ch 26:11 *H*·, one of the king's captains.
Ezr 10:28 Jehohanan, *H*·, Zabbai,
Ne 3: 8 repaired *H*· the son of one of the
30 repaired *H*·, the son of Shelemiah,
7: 2 and *H*· the ruler of the palace,
10:23 Hoshea, *H*·, Hashub,
12:12 of Jeremiah, *H*·;
41 Zechariah, and *H*·, with trumpets;
Jer 28: 1 *H*· the son of Azur the prophet,
5 Jeremiah said unto the prophet *H*·
10 Then *H*· the prophet took the
11 *H*· spake in the presence of all the
12 after that *H*· the prophet had
13 Go and tell *H*·, saying, Thus saith
15 Then said...Jeremiah unto *H*·
15 the prophet, Hear now, *H*·;
17 So *H*· the prophet died the same
36:12 and Zedekiah the son of *H*·, and
37:13 Shelemiah the son of *H*·; and he
Da 1: 6 Daniel, *H*·, Mishael, and Azariah:
7 and to *H*·, of Shadrach; and to
11 over Daniel, *H*·, Mishael, and
19 none like Daniel, *H*·, Mishael,
2:17 and made the thing known to *H*·,
hand^ See also AFOREHAND; BEFOREHAND; HANDBREADTH; HANDED; HANDFUL; HANDKERCHIEFS; HANDMAID; HANDS; HANDSTAVES; HANDWRITING; HANDYWORK
Ge 3:22 now, lest he put forth his *h*·, and
4:11 thy brother's blood from thy *h*·;
8: 9 then he put forth his *h*·, and took
9: 2 fishes of the sea; into your *h*· are
5 at the *h*· of every beast will I
5 require it, and at the *h*· of man;
5 at the *h*· of every man's
13: 9 if thou wilt take the left *h*·,
9 or if thou depart to the right *h*·,
14:15 which is on the left *h*· of Damascus.
20 thine enemies into thy *h*·.
22 I have lift up mine *h*· unto the
16: 6 Behold, thy maid is in thy *h*·;
12 his *h*· will be against every man,
12 and every man's *h*· against him;
19:10 the men put forth their *h*·, and
16 the men laid hold upon his *h*·, and
16 upon the *h*· of his wife, and upon
16 the *h*· of his two daughters;
21:18 hold him in thine *h*·; for I will
30 lambs shalt thou take of my *h*·,
22: 6 he took the fire in his *h*·, and a
10 Abraham stretched forth his *h*·,
12 Lay not thine *h*· upon the lad,
24: 2 Put, I pray thee, thy *h*· under my
9 the servant put his *h*· under the
10 goods of his master were in his *h*·:
18 let down her pitcher upon her *h*·,
49 that I may turn to the right *h*·,

Ge 25:26 and his h' took hold on Esau's heel:
27:17 into the h' of her son Jacob.
41 mourning for my father are at h';
30: 35 gave them into the h' of his sons.
31:29 It is in the power of my h' to do
39 of my h' didst thou require it,
32:11 Deliver me, I pray thee, from the h'
11 of my brother, from the h' of Esau:
13 that which came to his h' a present
16 delivered them into the h' of his
33:10 then receive my present at my h':
19 at the h' of the children of Hamor,
35: 4 strange gods which were in their h',
37:22 and lay no h' upon him; that he
27 and let not our h' be upon him;
38:18 thy staff that is in thine h'.
20 sent the kid by the h' of his friend
20 his pledge from the woman's h':
28 put out his h': and the midwife
28 took and bound upon his h' a
29 as he drew back his h', that,
30 had the scarlet thread upon his h':
39: 3 that he did to prosper in his h'.
4 all that he had he put into his h'.
6 left all that he had in Joseph's h';
8 committed all that he hath to my h';
12 left his garment in her h', and fled,
13 he had left his garment in her h',
22 committed to Joseph's h' all the
23 any thing that was under his h';
40:11 Pharaoh's cup was in my h': and I
11 I gave the cup into Pharaoh's h'.
13 deliver Pharaoh's cup into his h',
21 he gave the cup into Pharaoh's h':
41:35 lay up corn under the h' of
42 took off his ring from his h', and
42 put it upon Joseph's h', and
44 shall no man lift up his h'
42:37 deliver him into my h', and I will
43: 9 of my h' shalt thou require him:
12 take double money in your h'; and
12 sacks, carry it again in your h';
15 they took double money in their h',
21 have brought it again in our h'.
26 present which was in their h' into
44:17 in whose h' the cup is found, he
46: 4 Joseph shall put his h' upon thine
47:29 put, I pray thee, thy h' under my
48:13 them both, Ephraim in his right h'
13 toward Israel's left h',
13 and Manasseh in his left h'
13 toward Israel's right h',
14 Israel stretched out his right h',
14 his left h' upon Manasseh's head,
17 laid his right h' upon the head
17 he held up his father's h', to remove
18 put thy right h' upon his head.
22 which I took out of the h' of the
49: 8 thy h' shall be in the neck of thine
Ex 2:19 delivered us out of the h' of the
3: 8 deliver them out of the h' of the
19 let you go, no, not by a mighty h'.
20 I will stretch out my h', and smite
4: 2 What is that in thine h'? And he
4 Put forth thine h', and take it by
4 And he put forth his h', and
4 it became a rod in his h':
6 Put now thine h' into thy bosom.
6 And he put his h' into his bosom:
6 behold, his h' was leprous as snow.
7 Put thine h' into thy bosom again.
7 And he put his h' into his bosom
13 send, I pray thee, by the h' of him
17 shalt take this rod in thine h',
20 took the rod of God in his h'.
21 which I have put in thine h':
5:21 to put a sword in their h' to slay us.
6: 1 for with a strong h' shall he let
1 and with a strong h' shall he drive
7: 4 that I may lay my h' upon Egypt,
5 when I stretch forth mine h' upon
15 serpent shalt thou take in thine h'.
17 with the rod that is in mine h'
19 stretch out thine h' upon the
8: 5 Stretch forth thine h' with thy rod
6 Aaron stretched out his h' over the
17 Aaron stretched out his h' with his
9: 3 the h' of the Lord is upon thy
15 now I will stretch out my h', that I
22 Stretch forth thine h' toward
10:12 Stretch out thine h' over the land
21 Stretch out thine h' toward heaven,
22 Moses stretched forth his h'
12:11 your staff in your h'; and ye
13: 3 for by strength of h' the Lord
9 a sign unto thee upon thine h',
9 for with a strong h' hath the Lord
14 By strength of h' the Lord brought
16 for a token upon thine h', and for
16 for by strength of h' the Lord
14: 8 of Israel went out with an high h'.
16 stretch out thine h' over the sea,
21 Moses stretched out his h' over the
22 on their right h', and on their left.
26 Stretch out thine h' over the sea,
27 Moses stretched forth his h' over
29 a wall unto them on their right h',
30 saved Israel that day out of the h'
15: 6 Thy right h', O Lord, is become
6 thy right h', O Lord, hath dashed
9 my sword, my h' shall destroy
12 Thou stretchedst out thy right h',
20 took a timbrel in her h'; and all
16: 3 we had died by the h' of the Lord
17: 5 the river, take in thine h', and go.
9 with the rod of God in mine h'.

Ex 17:11 Moses held up his h', that Israel
11 and when he let down his h',
18: 9 delivered out of the h' of the
10 delivered you out of the h' of the
10 and out of the h' of Pharaoh,
10 from under the h' of the Egyptians.
19:13 There shall not an h' touch it,
21:13 God deliver him into his h'; then I
16 him, or if he be found in his h',
20 and he die under his h'; he shall be
24 tooth for tooth, h' for h', foot
22: 4 the theft be certainly found in his h'
8 put his h' unto his neighbour's
11 he hath not put his h' unto his
23: 1 put not thine h' with the wicked
31 inhabitants of the land into your h';
24:11 of Israel he laid not his h':
25:25 a border of an h' breadth
29:20 upon the thumb of their right h',
32: 4 he received them at their h', and
11 great power, and with a mighty h'?
15 of the testimony were in his h':
33:22 and will cover thee with my h'
23 And I will take away mine h',
34: 4 took in his h' the two tables of
29 tables of testimony in Moses' h',
35:29 commanded to be made by the h'
38:15 court gate, on this h' and that h',
21 by the h' of Ithamar, son to Aaron
Le 1: 4 he shall put his h' upon the head
3: 2, 8, 13 shall lay his h' upon the head
4: 4 shall lay his h' upon the bullock's
24 lay his h' upon the head of the goat
29, 33 lay his h' upon the...sin
8:23 upon the thumb of his right h',
36 the Lord commanded by the h' of
9:22 Aaron lifted up his h' toward the
10:11 spoken unto them by the h' of
14:14 upon the thumb of his right h',
15 it into the palm of his own left h':
16 the oil that is in his left h', and
17 the rest of the oil that is in his h'
17 upon the thumb of his right h',
18 the oil that is in the priest's h'
25 upon the thumb of his right h',
26 oil into the palm of his own left h':
27 the oil that is in his left h' seven
28 the oil that is in his h' upon the
28 upon the thumb of his right h',
29 the oil that is in the priest's h' he
32 leprosy, whose h' is not able to get
16:21 send him away by the h' of a fit
22:25 Neither from a stranger's h' shall
25:14 ought of thy neighbour's h',
28 shall remain in the h' of him that
26:25 ye shall be delivered into the h' of
46 in mount Sinai by the h' of Moses.
Nu 4:28 charge shall be under the h' of
33 congregation, under the h' of
37 commandment...by the h' of Moses.
45 word of...by the h' of Moses.
49 were numbered by the h' of Moses,
5:18 and the priest shall have in his h'
25 offering out of the woman's h',
6:21 beside that that his h' shall get:
7: 8 under the h' of Ithamar the son of
9:23 of the Lord by the h' of Moses.
10:13 of the Lord by the h' of Moses.
11:15 kill me, I pray thee, out of h',
23 Is the Lord's h' waxed short?
15:23 by the h' of Moses, from the day
16:40 Lord said to him by the h' of Moses.
20:11 Moses lifted up his h', and with
17 we will not turn to the right h' nor
20 much people, and with a strong h'.
21: 2 deliver this people into my h', then
26 taken all his land out of his h',
34 I have delivered him into thy h',
22: 7 rewards of divination in their h';
23 his sword drawn in his h': and
26 to the right h' or to the left.
29 there were a sword in mine h',
31 sword drawn in his h': and he
25: 7 and took a javelin in his h';
27:18 spirit, and lay thine h' upon him;
23 commanded by the h' of Moses.
31: 6 the trumpets to blow in his h'.
33: 1 under the h' of Moses and Aaron.
3 of Israel went out with an high h'
35:18 if he smite him with an h' weapon
21 in enmity smite him with his h',
25 out of the h' of the revenger of
36:13 by the h' of Moses unto the
De 1:27 deliver us into the hand of the
2: 7 the works of thy h': he knoweth
15 the h' of the Lord was against
24 I have given into thine h' Sihon
27 I will neither turn unto the right h'
30 deliver him into thy h', as
3: 2 and his land, into thy h'; and thou
8 out of the h' of the two kings of the
24 thy mighty h': for what God
4:34 and by a mighty h', and by a
5:15 through a mighty h' and by a
32 turn aside to the right h' or to the
6: 8 a sign upon thine h', and they
21 out of Egypt with a mighty h':
7: 8 you out with a mighty h', and
8 from the h' of Pharaoh king of
19 and the mighty h', and the
24 deliver their kings into thine h',
8:17 the might of mine h' hath gotten
9:26 out of Egypt, with a mighty h'.
10: 3 having the two tables in mine h'.
11: 2 his mighty h', and his stretched
18 a sign upon your h', that they may

De 12: 6 heave offerings of your h', and
7 all that ye put your h' unto, ye
11 the heave offering of your h',
17 or heave offering of thine h':
13: 9 thine h' shall be first upon him to
9 and afterwards the h' of all the
17 the cursed thing to thine h': that
14:25 bind up the money in thine h',
29 the work of thine h' which thou
15: 3 thy brother thine h' shall release;
7 nor shut thine h' from thy poor
8 thou shalt open thine h' wide unto
9 the year of release, is at h';
10 all that thou puttest thine h' unto.
11 Thou shalt open thine h' wide unto
16:10 a freewill offering of thine h',
17:11 to the right h', nor to the left.
20 to the right h', or to the left: to the
19: 5 his h' fetcheth a stroke with the
12 into the h' of the avenger of blood,
21 for tooth, h' for h', foot for foot.
23:20 all that thou settest thine h' to in
25 pluck the ears with thine h';
24: 1 give it in her h', and send her
3 giveth it in her h', and sendeth
25:11 out of the h' of him that smiteth
11 and putteth forth her h',
12 Then thou shalt cut off her h',
26: 4 take the basket out of thine h',
8 with a mighty h', and with
28: 8 all that thou settest thine h' unto;
12 bless all the work of thine h':
14 to the right h', or to the left,
20 all that thou settest thine h' unto
32 shall be no might in thine h'.
30: 9 every work of thine h', in the
32:27 Our h' is high, and the Lord
35 the day of their calamity is at h',
39 that can deliver out of my h'.
40 I lift up my h' to heaven, and say,
41 mine h' take hold on judgment;
33: 2 from his right h' went a fiery law
3 all his saints are in thy h': and
34:12 in all that mighty h', and in all
Jos 1: 7 to the right h' or to the left,
2:19 our head, if any h' be upon him.
4:24 the h' of the Lord, that it is
5:13 his sword drawn in his h': and
6: 2 I have given into thine h' Jericho,
7: 7 into the h' of the Amorites, to
8: 1 I have given into thy h' the king
7 God will deliver it into your h'.
18 the spear that is in thy h' toward
18 for I will give it into thine h'.
18 the spear that he had in his h'
19 he had stretched out his h': and
26 Joshua drew not his h' back,
9:25 we are in thine h': as it
26 out of the h' of the children of
10: 6 Slack not thy h' from thy servants;
8 delivered them into thine h';
19 hath delivered them into your h'.
30 the king thereof, into the h' of
32 Lachish into the h' of Israel, which
11: 8 Lord delivered them into the h'
14: 2 by the h' of Moses, for the nine
17: 7 border went along on the right h'
19:27 goeth out to Cabul on the left h',
20: 2 I spake unto you by the h' of Moses:
5 deliver the slayer up into his h';
9 by the h' of the avenger of blood,
21: 2 by the h' of Moses to give us
8 commanded by the h' of Moses.
44 all their enemies into their h'.
22: 9 of the Lord by the h' of Moses.
31 out of the h' of the Lord.
23: 6 turn not aside...to the right h'
24: 8 I gave them into your h', that ye
10 I delivered you out of his h'.
11 and I delivered them into your h'.
J'g 1: 2 I have delivered the land into his h'.
4 the Perizzites into their h': and
35 the h' of the house of Joseph
2:15 the h' of the Lord was against them
16 out of the h' of those that spoiled
18 out of the h' of their enemies all
23 them into the h' of Joshua.
3: 4 their fathers by the h' of Moses.
8 into the h' of Chushan-rishathaim
10 into his h'; and his h' prevailed
21 Ehud put forth his left h', and took
28 enemies the Moabites into your h'.
30 that day under the h' of Israel.
4: 2 Lord sold them into the h' of Jabin
7 I will deliver him into thine h'.
9 Sisera into the h' of a woman.
14 hath delivered Sisera into thine h':
21 took an hammer in her h', and
24 the h' of the children of Israel
5:26 She put her h' to the nail,
26 and her right h' to the workmen's
6: 1 Lord delivered them into the h' of
2 the h' of Midian prevailed against
9 out of the h' of the Egyptians,
9 out of the h' of all that oppressed
14 from the h' of the Midianites:
21 the staff that was in his h',
36 If thou wilt save Israel by mine h',
37 thou wilt save Israel by mine h',
7: 2 Mine own h' hath saved me.
6 putting their h' to their mouth,
7 deliver the Midianites into thine h':
8 the people took victuals in their h',
9 I have delivered it into thine h'.
14 into his h' hath God delivered
15 Lord hath delivered into your h'

J'g 7:16 put a trumpet in every man's h',
8: 6 and Zalmunna now in thine h',
7 and Zalmunna into mine h', then
15 and Zalmunna now in thine h',
22 thou hast delivered us from the h'
9:17 delivered you out of the h' of
29 this people were under my h'! then
48 Abimelech took an axe in his h',
10:12 I delivered you out of their h'.
11:21 into the h' of Israel, and they
12: 3 the Lord delivered them into my h'
13: 1 delivered them into the h' of
5 out of the h' of the Philistines.
14: 6 he had nothing in his h':
15:12 deliver thee into the h' of the
13 deliver thee into their h': but
15 put forth his h', and took it,
17 cast away the jawbone out of his h',
18 into the h' of thy servant: and now
18 into the h' of the uncircumcised?
16:18 and brought money in their h'.
23 Samson our enemy into our h'.
26 the lad that held him by the h',
29 the one with his right h', and of the
17: 3 from my h' for my son, to make
18:19 lay thine h' upon thy mouth, and
20:28 I will deliver them into thine h'.
48 all that came to h': also they
Ru 1:13 the h' of the Lord is gone out
4: 5 thou buyest the field of the h' of
9 and Mahlon's, of the h' of Naomi.
1Sa 2:13 a fleshhook of three teeth in his h'
4: 3 out of the h' of our enemies.
8 out of the h' of these mighty Gods?
5: 6 the h' of the Lord was heavy upon
7 his h' is sore upon us, and upon
9 the h' of the Lord was against the
11 h' of God was very heavy there.
6: 3 why his h' is not removed from
5 peradventure he will lighten his h
9 we shall know that it is not his h'
12 turned not aside to the right h'
7: 3 he will deliver you out of the h' of
8 he will save us out of the h' of the
13 the h' of the Lord was against the
9: 8 I have here at h' the fourth part
16 out of the h' of the Philistines:
10:18 the h' of the Egyptians, and...the h'
12: 3 or of whose h' have I received any
4 taken ought of any man's h'.
5 ye have not found ought in my h'.
9 he sold them into the h' of Sisera,
9 and into the h' of the Philistines,
9 and into the h' of the king of Moab,
10 deliver us out of the h' of our
11 delivered you out of the h' of your
15 then shall the h' of the Lord be
13:22 in the h' of any of the people
14:10 hath delivered them into our h':
12 hath delivered them into the h' of
19 unto the priest; Withdraw thine h'.
26 no man put his h' to his mouth:
27 rod that was in his h', and dipped
27 and put his h' to his mouth;
37 wilt thou deliver them into the h'
43 the rod that was in mine h',
16:16 he shall play with his h', and thou
23 took an harp, and played with his h'
17:22 David left his carriage in the h' of
37 me out of the h' of this Philistine.
40 took his staff in his h', and
40 his sling was in his h':
46 the Lord deliver thee into mine h';
49 David put his h' in his bag, and
50 there was no sword in the h' of
57 the head of the Philistine in his h'.
18:10 David played with his h', as at
10 there was a javelin in Saul's h'.
17 Let not mine h' be upon him, but
17 the h' of the Philistines be upon
21 that the h' of the Philistines may be
25 fall by the h' of the Philistines.
19: 5 he did put his life in his h', and
9 with his javelin in his h':
9 and David played with his h'.
20:16 at the h' of David's enemies.
19 when the business was in h', and
21: 3 what is under thine h'? give me
3 five loaves of bread in mine h',
4 no common bread under mine h',
8 is there not here under thine h'
22: 6 having his spear in his h', and all
17 their h' also is with David, and
17 king would not put forth their h'
23: 4 deliver the Philistines into thine h.
6 came down with an ephod in his h'.
7 hath delivered him into mine h';
11 Keilah deliver me up into his h'?
12 me and my men into the h' of Saul?
14 God delivered him not into his h'.
16 and strengthened his h' in God.
17 h' of Saul my father shall not find
20 to deliver him into the king's h'.
24: 4 deliver thine enemy into thine h',
6 to stretch forth mine h' against
10 delivered thee to day into mine h'
10 I will not put forth mine h'
11 see the skirt of thy robe in my h':
11 nor transgression in mine h',
12, 13 mine h' shall not be upon thee.
15 and deliver me out of thine h'.
18 had delivered me into thine h',
20 shall be established in thine h'.
25: 8 whatsoever cometh to thine h'
26 avenging thyself with thine own h'
33 avenging myself with mine own h'.

1Sa 25:35 David received of her h' that which
39 cause of my reproach from the h'
26: 8 thine enemy into thine h' this day:
9 can stretch forth his h' against
11 that I should stretch forth mine h'
18 or what evil is in mine h'?
23 delivered thee into my h' to day,
23 I would not stretch forth mine h'
27: 1 perish one day by the h' of Saul:
1 so shall I escape out of his h'.
28:17 rent the kingdom out of thine h',
19 into the h' of the Philistines:
19 Israel into the h' of the Philistines.
21 I have put my life in my h',
30:23 that came against us into our h'.
2Sa 1:14 not afraid to stretch forth thine h'
2:19 he turned not to the right h'
21 Turn thee aside to thy right h'
3: 8 not delivered thee into the h' of
12 behold, my h' shall be with thee,
18 By the h' of my servant David I
18 save my people Israel out of the h'
18 Philistines, and out of the h' of all
4:11 require his blood of your h', and
5:19 thou deliver them into mine h'?
19 deliver the Philistines into thine h'.
6: 6 Uzzah put forth his h' to the ark
8: 1 out of the h' of the Philistines.
10: 2 to comfort him by the h' of his
10 he delivered into the h' of Abishai
11:14 sent it by the h' of Uriah.
12: 7 I delivered thee out of the h' of
25 he sent by the h' of Nathan the
13: 5 I may see it, and eat it at her h'.
6 my sight, that I may eat at her h'.
10 chamber, that I may eat of thine h'.
19 laid her h' on her head, and went
14:16 out of the h' of the man that
19 Is not the h' of Joab with thee
19 none can turn to the right h'
15: 5 he put forth his h', and took him,
16: 6 mighty men were on his right h'
8 into the h' of Absalom thy son:
18: 2 under the h' of Joab, and a third
2 under the h' of Abishai the son of
2 third part under the h' of Ittai
12 shekels of silver in mine h',
12 yet would I not put forth mine h'
28 that lifted up their h' against my
19: 9 out of the h' of our enemies, and
9 he delivered us out of the h' of the
20: 9 by the beard with the right h'
10 the sword that was in Joab's h':
21 hath lifted up his h' against the
21:20 that had on every h' six fingers,
22 the h' of David, and by the h' of his
22: 1 out of the h' of all his enemies,
1 enemies, and out of the h' of Saul:
23:10 smote the Philistines until his h'
10 was weary, and his h' clave unto
21 the Egyptian had a spear in his h';
21 the spear out of the Egyptian's h',
24:14 fall now into the h' of the Lord;
14 let me not fall into the h' of man.
16 the angel stretched out his h'
16 It is enough: stay now thine h'.
17 let thine h', I pray thee, be against
1Ki 2:19 and she sat on his right h'.
25 king Solomon sent by the h' of
46 kingdom was established in the h'
7:26 it was an h' breadth thick, and
8:15 and hath with his h' fulfilled it,
24 and hast fulfilled it with thine h',
42 thy strong h', and of thy stretched
53 by the h' of Moses thy servant,
56 by the h' of Moses his servant.
11:12 I will rend it out of the h' of thy
26 he lifted up his h' against the king.
27 the cause that he lifted up his h'
31 rend the kingdom out of the h' of
34 the whole kingdom out of his h':
35 the kingdom out of his son's h',
13: 4 he put forth his h' from the altar,
4 And his h', which he put forth
6 that my h' may be restored me
6 the king's h' was restored him
14:18 by the h' of his servant Ahijah
15:18 delivered them into the h' of his
16: 7 by the h' of the prophet Jehu
17:11 a morsel of bread in thine h'.
18: 9 deliver thy servant into the h' of
44 out of the sea, like a man's h'.
46 the h' of the Lord was on Elijah;
20: 6 they shall put it in their h',
13 I will deliver it into thine h'
28 this great multitude into thine h',
42 thou hast let go out of thy h'
22: 3 take it not out of the h' of the king
6 deliver it into the h' of the king.
12 shall deliver it into the king's h'.
15 deliver it into the h' of the king.
19 on his right h' and on his left.
34 Turn thine h', and carry me out
2Ki 3:10 deliver them into the h' of Moab!
13 to deliver them into the h' of
15 the h' of the Lord came upon him.
18 the Moabites also into your h'.
4:29 take my staff in thine h', and go
5:11 strike his h' over the place, and
18 he leaneth on my h', and I bow
24 he took them from their h',
6: 7 he put out his h', and took it.
7: 2 a lord on whose h' the king leaned
17 the lord on whose h' he leaned
8: 8 Take a present in thine h', and go,
20 under the h' of Judah, and made a

2Ki 8:22 revolted from under the h' of Judah
9: 1 take this box of oil in thine h',
7 the Lord, at the h' of Jezebel.
10:15 If it be, give me thine h'.
15 And he gave him his h';
11: 8 his weapons in his h': and he that
12:15 into whose h' they delivered the
13: 3 into the h' of Hazael king of Syria,
3 and into the h' of Ben-hadad
5 from under the h' of the Syrians:
16 Put thine h' upon the bow.
16 And he put his h' upon it: and
25 took again out of the h' of
25 which he had taken out of the h' of
14: 5 kingdom was confirmed in his h',
25 by the h' of his servant Jonah,
27 by the h' of Jeroboam the son of
15:19 that his h' might be with him to
19 confirm the kingdom in his h'.
16: 7 out of the h' of the king of Syria,
7 out of the h' of the king of Israel,
17: 7 from under the h' of Pharaoh,
20 delivered them into the h' of
39 out of the h' of all your enemies.
18:21 if a man lean, it will go into his h',
29 to deliver you out of his h':
30 delivered into the h' of the king
33 out of the h' of the king of Assyria
34 delivered Samaria out of mine h'?
35 their country out of mine h', that
35 deliver Jerusalem out of mine h'?
19:10 delivered into the h' of the king
14 letter of the h' of the messengers,
19 save thou us out of his h',
20: 6 thee and this city out of the h' of
21:14 into the h' of their enemies;
22: 2 turned not aside to the right h'
5 let them deliver it into the h' of
7 them into their h', because they
9 the h' of them that do the work,
23:13 on the right h' of the mount
1Ch 4:10 that thine h' might be with me,
5:10 who fell by their h': and they
20 were delivered into their h',
6:15 and Jerusalem by the h' of
39 who stood on his right h', even
44 sons of Merari stood on the left h':
11:23 in the Egyptian's h' was a spear
23 the spear out of the Egyptian's h',
12: 2 could use both the right h' and the
13: 9 Uzza put forth his h' to hold the
10 because he put his h' to the ark:
14:10 wilt thou deliver them into mine h'?
10 I will deliver them into thine h'.
11 by mine h' like the breaking forth
16: 7 into the h' of Asaph and his
18: 1 out of the h' of the Philistines.
19:11 delivered unto the h' of Abishai his
20: 6 six on each h', and six on each foot:
8 they fell by the h' of David, and
8 and by the h' of his servants.
21:13 me fall now into the h' of the Lord;
13 but let me not fall into the h' of man.
15 It is enough, stay now thine h'.
16 having a drawn sword in his h'
17 let thine h', I pray thee, O Lord my
22:18 inhabitants of the land into mine h';
26:28 it was under the h' of Shelomith,
28:19 in writing by his h' upon me,
29: 8 by the h' of Jehiel the Gershonite.
12 and in thine h' is power and might;
12 and in thine h' it is to make great,
16 cometh of thine h', and is all thine
2Ch 3:17 one on the right h', and the other
17 the name of that on the right h'
4: 5 thickness of it was an h' breadth,
6 put five on the right h', and five
7 in the temple, five on the right h',
6:15 and hast fulfilled it with thine h',
32 and thy mighty h', and thy
10:15 he spake by the h' of Ahijah
12: 5 I also left you in the h' of Shishak.
7 upon Jerusalem by the h' of
13: 8 in the h' of the sons of David;
16 God delivered them into their h'.
16: 7 the king...escaped out of thine h'.
8 he delivered them into thine h'.
17: 5 stablished the kingdom in his h';
18: 5 God will deliver it into the king's h'.
11 the Lord shall deliver it into the h'
14 they shall be delivered into your h'.
18 of heaven standing on his right h'
33 Turn thine h', that thou mayest
20: 6 and in thine h' is there not power
21:10 from under the h' of Judah unto
10 Libnah revolt from under his h';
23: 7 man with his weapons in his h';
10 man having his weapon in his h',
18 by the h' of the priests the Levites,
24:11 by the h' of the Levites, and when
24 a very great host into their h',
25:15 their own people out of thine h'?
20 into the h' of their enemies,
26:11 by the h' of Jeiel the scribe
11 under the h' of Hananiah, one of
13 under their h' was an army, three
19 and had a censer in his h'
28: 5 into the h' of the king of Syria;
5 into the h' of the king of Israel,
9 he hath delivered them into your h',
30: 6 of the h' of the kings of Assyria.
12 the h' of God was to give them
16 they received of the h' of the
31:13 under the h' of Cononiah and
32:11 out of the h' of the king of
13 deliver their lands out of mine h'?

2Ch 32: 14 deliver his people out of mine *h'*.
14 able to deliver you out of mine *h'*?
15 deliver his people out of mine *h'*,
15 and out of the *h'* of my fathers:
15 God deliver you out of mine *h'*?
17 delivered their people out of mine *h'*,
17 deliver his people out of mine *h'*.
22 from the *h'* of Sennacherib the
22 and from the *h'* of all other,
33: 8 the ordinances by the *h'* of Moses.
34: 2 to the right *h'*, nor to the left.
9 gathered of the *h'* of Manasseh
10 put it in the *h'* of the workmen
17 into the *h'* of the overseers, and
17 to the *h'* of the workmen.
35: 6 word of the Lord by the *h'* of Moses.
36: 17 he gave them all into his *h'*.
Ezr 1: 8 by the *h'* of Mithredath the
5: 12 he gave them into the *h'* of
6: 12 that shall put to their *h'* to alter
7: 6 according to the *h'* of the Lord
9 according to the good *h'* of his God
14 of thy God which is in thine *h'*;
25 of thy God, that is in thine *h'*,
28 as the *h'* of the Lord my God was
8: 18 by the good *h'* of our God upon us
22 The *h'* of our God is upon all
26 I even weighed unto their *h'* six
31 and the *h'* of our God was upon us,
31 and he delivered us from the *h'* of
33 by the *h'* of Meremoth the son of
9: 2 yea, the *h'* of the princes and
7 into the *h'* of the kings of the lands,
Ne 1: 10 great power, and by thy strong *h'*.
2: 8 according to the good *h'* of my God
18 Then I told them of the *h'* of my
4: 17 and with the other *h'* held a weapon.
6: 5 with an open letter in his *h'*;
8: 4 Hilkiah, and Maaseiah...right *h'*;
4 and on his left *h'*, Pedaiah, and
9: 14 by the *h'* of Moses thy servant:
27 into the *h'* of their enemies, who
27 out of the *h'* of their enemies.
28 in the *h'* of their enemies, so that
30 into the *h'* of the people of the
11: 24 son of Judah, was at the king's *h'*
12: 31 one went on the right *h'* upon the
Es 2: 21 sought to lay *h'* on the king
3: 10 the king took his ring from his *h'*,
5: 2 golden sceptre that was in his *h'*.
6: 2 who sought to lay *h'* on the king
9 the *h'* of one of the king's most
8: 7 he laid his *h'* upon the Jews.
9: 2 to lay *h'* on such as sought their
10 on the spoil laid they not their *h'*.
15 on the prey they laid not their *h'*.
Job 1: 11 put forth thine *h'* now, and touch
2: 5 put forth thine *h'* now, and touch
6 Behold, he is in thine *h'*; but save
10 we receive good at the *h'* of God,
5: 15 and from the *h'* of the mighty.
6: 9 that he would let loose his *h'*,
23 Deliver me from the enemy's *h'*? or,
23 Redeem me from the *h'* of the
9: 24 The earth is given into the *h'* of
33 that might lay his *h'* upon us both.
10: 7 none that can deliver out of thine *h'*.
11: 14 If iniquity be in thine *h'*, put it far
12: 6 into whose *h'* God bringeth
9 the *h'* of the Lord hath wrought
10 In whose *h'* is the soul of every
13: 14 and put my life in mine *h'*?
21 Withdraw thine *h'* far from me:
15: 23 day of darkness is ready at his *h'*.
25 stretcheth out his *h'* against God,
19: 21 the *h'* of God hath touched me.
20: 22 every *h'* of the wicked shall come
21: 5 lay your *h'* upon your mouth.
16 their good is not in their *h'*:
23: 9 the left *h'*, where he doth work,
9 he hideth himself on the right *h'*,
26: 13 his *h'* hath formed the crooked
27: 11 I will teach you by the *h'* of God:
22 he would fain flee out of his *h'*.
28: 9 He putteth forth his *h'* upon the
29: 9 and laid their *h'* on their mouth.
20 and my bow was renewed in my *h'*.
30: 12 Upon my right *h'* rise the youth;
21 with thy strong *h'* thou opposest
24 not stretch out his *h'* to the grave,
31: 21 have lifted up my *h'* against the
25 and because mine *h'* had gotten
27 or my mouth hath kissed my *h'*:
33: 7 neither shall my *h'* be heavy upon
34: 20 shall be taken away without *h'*.
35: 7 or what receiveth he of thine *h'*?
37: 7 He sealeth up the *h'* of every man;
40: 4 I will lay mine *h'* upon my mouth.
14 thine own right *h'* can save thee.
41: 8 Lay thine *h'* upon him, remember
Ps 10: 12 O God, lift up thine *h'*: forget not
14 spite, to requite it with thy *h'*:
16: 8 he is at my right *h'*, I shall not be
11 at thy right *h'* there are pleasures
17: 7 O thou that savest by thy right *h'*
14 From men which are thy *h'*, O
18: *title* delivered him from the *h'* of all
title enemies, and from the *h'* of Saul:
35 and thy right *h'* hath holden me
20: 6 the saving strength of his right *h'*.
21: 8 Thine *h'* shall find out all thine
8 thy right *h'* shall find out those
26: 10 and their right *h'* is full of bribes.
31: 5 Into thine *h'* I commit my spirit:
8 me up into the *h'* of the enemy:
15 My times are in thy *h'*: deliver me

Ps 31: 15 from the *h'* of mine enemies,
32: 4 day and night thy *h'* was heavy
36: 11 and let not the *h'* of the wicked
37: 24 Lord upholdeth him with his *h'*.
33 The Lord will not leave him in his *h'*,
38: 2 in me, and thy *h'* presseth me sore.
39: 10 consumed by the blow of thine *h'*.
44: 2 drive out the heathen with thy *h'*,
3 but thy right *h'*, and thine arm,
45: 4 thy right *h'* shall teach thee terrible
9 upon thy right *h'* did stand the
48: 10 thy right *h'* is full of righteousness.
60: 5 save with thy right *h'*, and hear me.
63: 8 thee: thy right *h'* upholdeth me.
71: 4 God, out of the *h'* of the wicked,
4 out of the *h'* of the unrighteous
73: 23 hast holden me by my right *h'*.
74: 11 Why withdrawest thou thy *h'*,
11 even thy right *h'*? pluck it out
75: 8 in the *h'* of the Lord there is a
77: 10 the right *h'* of the most High.
20 by the *h'* of Moses and Aaron.
78: 42 They remembered not his *h'*, nor
54 mountain, which his right *h'* had
61 his glory into the enemy's *h'*.
80: 15 which thy right *h'* hath planted,
17 Let thy *h'* be upon the man of thy
17 upon the man of thy right *h'*,
81: 14 turned my *h'* against their
82: 4 rid them out of the *h'* of the wicked.
88: 5 they are cut off from thy *h'*.
89: 13 mighty arm: strong is thy *h'*,
13 and high is thy right *h'*.
21 my *h'* shall be established: mine
25 I will set his *h'* also in the sea,
25 and his right *h'* in the rivers.
42 Thou hast set up the right *h'* of his
48 his soul from the *h'* of the grave?
91: 7 ten thousand at thy right *h'*; but
95: 4 In his *h'* are the deep places
7 pasture, and the sheep of his *h'*.
97: 10 them out of the *h'* of the wicked.
98: 1 his right *h'*, and his holy arm,
104: 28 thou openest thine *h'*, they are
106: 10 from the *h'* of him that hated them,
10 and redeemed them from the *h'* of
26 he lifted up his *h'* against them,
41 into the *h'* of the heathen; and
42 into subjection under their *h'*.
107: 2 redeemed from the *h'* of the enemy;
108: 6 save with thy right *h'*, and answer
109: 6 let Satan stand at his right *h'*.
27 know that this is thy *h'*; that thou,
31 at the right *h'* of the poor, to save
110: 1 Sit thou at my right *h'*, until I make
5 The Lord at thy right *h'* shall strike
118: 15 right *h'* of the Lord doeth valiantly.
16 The right *h'* of the Lord is exalted:
16 right *h'* of the Lord doeth valiantly.
119: 109 My soul is continually in my *h'*:
173 Let thine *h'* help me; for I have
121: 5 Lord is thy shade upon thy right *h'*.
123: 2 the *h'* of their masters, and as the
2 eyes of a maiden unto the *h'* of her
127: 4 As arrows are in the *h'* of a mighty
129: 7 the mower filleth not his *h'*;
136: 12 With a strong *h'*, and with a
137: 5 let my right *h'* forget her cunning.
138: 7 stretch forth thine *h'* against the
7 thy right *h'* shall save me.
139: 5 and before, and laid thine *h'* upon
10 there shall thy *h'* lead me, and
10 thy right *h'* shall hold me.
142: 4 I looked on my right *h'*, and
144: 7 Send thine *h'* from above; rid me,
7 from the *h'* of strange children;
8 and their right *h'* is a right *h'* of
11 from the *h'* of strange children;
11 and their right *h'* is a right *h'* of
145: 16 Thou openest thine *h'*, and
149: 6 a twoedged sword in their *h'*;
Pr 1: 24 I have stretched out my *h'*, and no
3: 16 Length of days is in her right *h'*;
16 in her left *h'* riches and honour.
27 the power of thine *h'* to do it.
4: 27 Turn not to the right *h'* nor to the
6: 1 thou hast stricken thine *h'* with
3 art come into the *h'* of thy friend;
5 as a roe from the *h'* of the hunter,
5 and as a bird from the *h'* of the
10: 4 poor that dealeth with a slack *h'*:
4 but the *h'* of the diligent maketh
11: 21 Though *h'* join in *h'*, the wicked
12: 24 The *h'* of the diligent shall bear
16: 5 though *h'* join in *h'*, he shall not
17: 16 is there a price in the *h'* of a fool
19: 24 A slothful man hideth his *h'* in his
21: 1 The king's heart is in the *h'* of the
26: 6 a message by the *h'* of a fool
9 into the *h'* of a drunkard, so is a
15 The slothful hideth his *h'* in his
27: 16 and the ointment of his right *h'*,
30: 32 lay thine *h'* upon thy mouth.
31: 20 She stretcheth out her *h'* to the
Ec 2: 24 that it was from the *h'* of God.
5: 14 and there is nothing in his *h'*.
15 which he may carry away in his *h'*.
7: 18 from this withdraw not thine *h'*:
9: 1 their works, are in the *h'* of God:
10 Whatsoever thy *h'* findeth to do,
10: 2 wise man's heart is at his right *h'*;
11: 6 evening withhold not thine *h'*:
Ca 2: 6 His left *h'* is under my head,
6 and his right *h'* doth embrace me.
5: 4 My beloved put in his *h'* by the
8: 3 His left *h'* should be under my

Ca 8: 3 his right *h'* should embrace me.
Isa 1: 12 who hath required this at your *h'*,
25 I will turn my *h'* upon thee,
3: 6 let this ruin be under thy *h'*:
5: 25 he hath stretched forth his *h'*
25 but his *h'* is stretched out still.
6: 6 having a live coal in his *h'*,
8: 11 with a strong *h'*, and instructed me
9: 12, 17 but his *h'* is stretched out still.
20 he shall snatch on the right *h'*,
20 and he shall eat on the left *h'*,
21 but his *h'* is stretched out still.
10: 4 but his *h'* is stretched out still.
5 the staff in their *h'* is mine
10 my *h'* hath found the kingdoms
13 the strength of mine *h'* I have done
14 my *h'* hath found as a nest
32 he shall shake his *h'* against the
11: 8 put his *h'* on the cockatrice' den.
11 the Lord shall set his *h'* again
14 they shall lay their *h'* upon Edom
15 shall he shake his *h'* over the river,
13: 2 shake the *h'*, that they may go
6 the day of the Lord is at *h'*;
14: 26 this is the *h'* that is stretched out
27 and his *h'* is stretched out, and who
19: 4 into the *h'* of a cruel lord;
16 the shaking of the *h'* of the Lord
22: 21 commit thy government into his *h'*:
23: 11 He stretched out his *h'* over the sea,
25: 10 mountain shall the *h'* of the Lord
26: 11 when thy *h'* is lifted up, they will
28: 2 cast down to the earth with the *h'*.
4 while it is yet in his *h'* he eateth it
31: 3 the Lord shall stretch out his *h'*,
34: 17 and his *h'* hath divided it unto
36: 6 it will go into his *h'*, and pierce
15 into the *h'* of the king of Assyria.
18 out of the *h'* of the king of Assyria?
19 delivered Samaria out of my *h'*?
20 delivered their land out of my *h'*,
20 deliver Jerusalem out of my *h'*?
37: 10 into the *h'* of the king of Assyria.
14 from the *h'* of the messengers,
20 save us from his *h'*, that all the
38: 6 thee and this city out of the *h'*
40: 2 received of the Lord's *h'* double
10 Lord God will come with strong *h'*,
12 the waters in the hollow of his *h'*,
41: 10 right *h'* of my righteousness.
13 thy God will hold thy right *h'*,
20 the *h'* of the Lord hath done this,
42: 6 will hold thine *h'*, and will keep
43: 13 none that can deliver out of my *h'*:
44: 5 another shall subscribe with his *h'*
20 Is there not a lie in my right *h'*?
45: 1 whose right *h'* I have holden, to
47: 6 and given them into thine *h'*:
48: 13 Mine *h'* also hath laid the
13 and my right *h'* hath spanned the
49: 2 in the shadow of his *h'* hath he
22 I will lift up mine *h'* to the
50: 2 Is my *h'* shortened at all, that it
11 This shall ye have of my *h'*; ye
51: 16 the shadow of mine *h'*, that I may
17 hast drunk at the *h'* of the Lord
18 that taketh her by the *h'* of all the
22 I have taken out of thine *h'* the cup
23 into the *h'* of them that afflict
53: 10 of the Lord shall prosper in his *h'*.
54: 3 shalt break forth on the right *h'*
56: 2 keepeth his *h'* from doing...evil,
57: 10 thou hast found...life of thine *h'*;
59: 1 the Lord's *h'* is not shortened,
62: 3 crown of glory in the *h'* of the Lord,
3 royal diadem in the *h'* of thy God.
8 Lord hath sworn by his right *h'*,
63: 12 That led them by the right *h'* of
64: 8 we all are the work of thy *h'*.
66: 2 all those things hath mine *h'*
14 the *h'* of the Lord shall be known
Jer 1: 9 the Lord put forth his *h'*, and
6: 9 turn back thine *h'* as a
12 I will stretch out my *h'* upon the
11: 21 that thou die not by our *h'*:
12: 7 soul into the *h'* of her enemies.
15: 6 therefore will I stretch out my *h'*
17 I sat alone because of thy *h'*:
21 thee out of the *h'* of the wicked,
21 thee out of the *h'* of the terrible.
16: 21 I will cause them to know mine *h'*
18: 4 marred in the *h'* of the potter:
6 as the clay is in the potter's *h'*,
6 so are ye in mine *h'*, O house
20: 4 into the *h'* of the king of Babylon,
5 into the *h'* of their enemies, which
13 the poor from the *h'* of evildoers.
21: 5 with an outstretched *h'* and with a
7 into the *h'* of Nebuchadrezzar
7 and into the *h'* of their enemies,
7 *h'* of those that seek their life:
10 into the *h'* of the king of Babylon,
12 out of the *h'* of the oppressor,
22: 3 out of the *h'* of the oppressor:
24 the signet upon my right *h'*, yet
25 the *h'* of them that seek thy life,
25 *h'* of them whose face thou fearest,
25 even into the *h'* of Nebuchadrezzar
25 and into the *h'* of the Chaldeans
23: 23 Am I a God at *h'*, saith the Lord,
25: 15 the wine cup of this fury at my *h'*,
17 the cup at the Lord's *h'*, and made
28 take the cup at thine *h'* to drink,
26: 14 I am in your *h'*: do with me
24 the *h'* of Ahikam the son of
24 give him into the *h'* of the people

Jer 27: 3 by the h' of the messengers which
6 into the h' of Nebuchadnezzar the
8 I have consumed them by his h'.
29: 3 By the h' of Elasah the son of
21 into the h' of Nebuchadrezzar king
31: 11 the h' of him that was stronger
32 the day that I took them by the h'
32: 3 into the h' of the king of Babylon,
4 out of the h' of the Chaldeans,
4 into the h' of the king of Babylon,
21 and with a strong h', and with a
24 and the city is given into the h' of
25 for the city is given into the h' of
28 h' of the Chaldeans, and into the h'
36 It shall be delivered into the h' of
43 it is given into the h' of the
34: 2 into the h' of the king of Babylon,
3 thou shalt not escape out of his h',
3 and delivered into his h';
20 into the h' of their enemies, and
20 the h' of them that seek their life:
21 give into the h' of their enemies,
21 h' of them that seek their life,
21 and into the h' of the king of
36: 14 Take in thine h' the roll wherein
14 took the roll in his h', and came
37: 17 into the h' of the king of Babylon.
38: 3 into the h' of the king of Babylon's
5 he is in your h': for the king is not
16 into the h' of these men that seek
18 into the h' of the Chaldeans, and
18 shalt not escape out of their h'.
19 lest they deliver me into their h',
23 not escape out of their h',
23 shalt be taken by the h' of the king
39: 17 into the h' of the men of whom
40: 4 the chains...were upon thine h'.
41: 5 offerings and incense in their h',
42: 11 and to deliver you from his h'.
43: 3 into the h' of the Chaldeans,
9 Take great stones in thine h', and
44: 25 and fulfilled with your h', saying,
30 into the h' of his enemies,
30 the h' of them that seek his life;
30 into the h' of Nebuchadrezzar king
46: 24 into the h' of the people of the north.
26 the h' of those that seek their lives,
26 into the h' of Nebuchadrezzar king
26 and into the h' of his servants:
50: 15 she hath given her h': her
51: 7 a golden cup in the Lord's h',
25 I will stretch out mine h' upon
La 1: 7 her people fell into the h' of the
10 The adversary...spread out his h'
14 transgressions is bound by his h'
2: 3 he hath drawn back his right h'
4 stood with his right h' as an
7 into the h' of the enemy the walls
8 he hath not withdrawn his h' from
3: 3 he turneth his h' against me all
5: 6 We have given the h' to the
8 that doth deliver us out of their h'.
12 Princes are hanged up by their h':
Eze 1: 3 the h' of the Lord was there upon
2: 9 an h' was sent unto me; and, lo,
3: 14 but the h' of the Lord was strong
18, 20 blood will I require at thine h'.
22 the h' of the Lord was there upon
6: 11 Smite with thine h', and stamp
14 So will I stretch out my h' upon
8: 1 the h' of the Lord God fell there
3 he put forth the form of an h',
11 every man his censer in his h';
9: 1 his destroying weapon in his h'.
2 a slaughter weapon in his h';
10: 2 fill thine h' with coals of fire
7 one cherub stretched forth his h'
8 the form of a man's h' under their
12: 7 I digged...the wall with mine h';
23 The days are at h', and the effect
13: 9 mine h' shall be upon the prophets
21 deliver my people out of your h',
21 and they...be no more in your h'
23 deliver my people out of your h':
14: 9 I will stretch out my h' upon him,
13 will I stretch out mine h' upon it,
16: 27 I have stretched out my h' over
39 I will also give thee into their h',
46 daughters that dwell at thy left h':
46 sister that dwelleth at thy right h',
49 neither did she strengthen the h'
17: 18 he had given his h', and hath
18: 8 hath withdrawn his h' from
17 hath taken off his h' from the poor,
20: 5 and lifted up mine h' unto the seed
5 when I lifted up mine h' unto them,
6 that I lifted up mine h' unto them,
15 also I lifted up my h' unto them in
22 I withdrew mine h', and wrought
23 I lifted up mine h' unto them also in
28 for the which I lifted up mine h' to
33 a mighty h', and with a stretched
34 ye are scattered, with a mighty h',
42 for the which I lifted up mine h' to
21: 11 to give it into the h' of the slayer.
16 either on the right h', or on...left,
22 At his right h' was the divination
24 ye shall be taken with the h'.
31 deliver thee into the h' of brutish
22: 13 I have smitten mine h' at thy
23: 9 I have delivered her into the h'
9 of her lovers, into the h' of the
28 the h' of them whom thou hatest,
28 h' of them from whom thy mind
31 will I give her cup into thine h'.
25: 7 I will stretch out mine h' upon
Eze 25: 13 I will also stretch out mine h' upon
14 by the h' of my people Israel:
16 I will stretch out mine h' upon
27: 15 the merchandise of thine h': they
28: 9 in the h' of him that slayeth thee.
10 by the h' of strangers: for I have
29: 7 they took hold of thee by thy h',
30: 10 by the h' of Nebuchadrezzar king
12 the land into the h' of the wicked:
12 is therein, by the h' of strangers:
22 the sword to fall out of his h'.
24 and put my sword in his h':
25 into the h' of the king of Babylon,
31: 11 into the h' of the mighty one
33: 6 will I require at the watchman's h'.
8 his blood will I require at thine h'.
22 Now the h' of the Lord was upon
34: 10 I will require my flock at their h',
27 out of the h' of those that served
35: 3 I will stretch out mine h' against
36: 7 I have lifted up mine h', Surely the
8 Israel; for they are at h' to come.
37: 1 The h' of the Lord was upon me,
17 they shall become one in thine h'.
19 which is in the h' of Ephraim, and
19 they shall be one in mine h'.
20 writest shall be in thine h' before
38: 12 turn thine h' upon the desolate
39: 3 smite the bow out of thy left h',
3 thine arrows to fall out of...right h'.
21 my h' that I have laid upon them.
23 them into the h' of their enemies:
40: 1 the h' of the Lord was upon me,
3 a line of flax in his h', and a
5 and in the man's h' a measuring
5 by the cubit and an h' breath
43 hooks, an h' broad, fastened
43: 13 cubit is a cubit and an h' breadth;
44: 12 I lifted up mine h' against them,
46: 7 according as his h' shall attain
47: 3 man that had the line in his h'
14 I lifted up mine h' to give it unto
Da 1: 2 into his h', with part of the vessels
2: 38 hath he given into thine h', and
3: 17 he will deliver us out of thine h',
4: 35 none can stay his h', or say
5: 5 came forth fingers of a man's h',
5 saw the part of the h' that wrote.
23 and the God in whose h' thy breath
24 Then was the part of the h' sent
7: 25 and they shall be given into his h'
8: 4 that could deliver out of his h';
7 deliver the ram out of his h'.
25 cause craft to prosper in his h';
25 but he shall be broken without h'.
9: 15 land of Egypt with a mighty h',
10: 10 an h' touched me, which set me
11: 11 multitude shall be given into his h'.
16 which by his h' shall be consumed.
41 escape out of his h', even Edom,
42 He shall stretch forth his h' also
12: 7 he held up his right h'
7 and his left h' unto heaven,
Ho 2: 10 shall deliver her out of mine h'.
7: 5 stretched out his h' with scorners.
12: 7 the balances of deceit are in his h':
Joe 1: 15 the day of the Lord is at h',
2: 1 the day of the Lord...is nigh at h';
3: 8 into the h' of the children of
Am 1: 8 I will turn mine h' against Ekron:
5: 19 leaned his h' on the wall, and a
7: 7 with a plumbline in his h'.
9: 2 hell, thence shall mine h' take
Jon 4: 11 cannot discern between...right h'
11 between their right...and...left h'.
Mic 2: 1 it is in the power of their h'.
4: 10 thee from the h' of thine enemies.
5: 9 Thine h' shall be lifted up upon
12 cut off witchcrafts out of thine h';
7: 16 lay their h' upon their mouth,
Hab 2: 16 the Lord's right h' shall be turned
3: 4 he had horns coming out of his h':
Zep 1: 4 I will also stretch out mine h'
7 the day of the Lord is at h':
2: 13 he will stretch out his h' against
15 by her shall hiss, and wag his h'.
Zec 2: 1 with a measuring line in his h'.
9 I will shake mine h' upon them,
3: 1 Satan standing at his right h' to
4: 10 plummet in the h' of Zerubbabel
8: 4 his staff in his h' for very age.
11: 6 every one into his neighbour's h',
6 and into the h' of his king:
6 out of their h' I will not deliver
12: 6 on the right h' and on the left:
13: 7 I will turn mine h' upon the little
14: 13 shall lay hold every one on the h'
13 of his neighbour, and...h' shall rise
13 up against the h' of his neighbour.
Mal 1: 10 should I accept an offering at your h'.
13 should I accept this of your h'?
2: 13 receiveth it with good will at your h'.
M't 3: 2 for the kingdom of heaven is at h'.
12 Whose fan is in his h', and he will
4: 17 for the kingdom of heaven is at h'.
5: 30 if thy right h' offend thee, cut it
6: 3 doest alms, let not thy left h'
3 know what thy right h' doeth.
8: 3 Jesus put forth his h', and touched
15 he touched her h', and the fever
9: 18 lay thy h' upon her, and she shall
25 took her by the h', and the maid
10: 7 The kingdom of heaven is at h'.
12: 10 a man which had his h' withered.
13 to the man, Stretch forth thine h'.
49 he stretched forth his h' toward his
M't 14: 31 Jesus stretched forth his h', and
18: 8 if thy h' or thy foot offend thee,
20: 21 may sit, the one on thy right h', and
23 to sit on my right h', and on my
22: 13 Bind him h' and foot, and take
44 Sit thou on my right h', till I make
25: 33 shall set the sheep on his right h',
34 say unto them on his right h', Come
41 unto them on the left h', Depart
26: 18 The Master saith, My time is at h';
23 He that dippeth his h' with me
45 behold, the hour is at h', and the
46 he is at h' that doth betray me.
51 stretched out his h', and drew his
64 sitting on the right h' of power,
27: 29 his head, and a reed in his right h':
38 one on the right h', and another on
M'r 1: 15 the kingdom of God is at h':
31 and took her by the h', and lifted
41 put forth his h', and touched
3: 1 man there which had a withered h'.
3 had the withered h', Stand forth.
5 Stretch forth thine h'. And he
5 and his h' was restored whole as the
5: 41 took the damsel by the h', and said
7: 32 beseech him to put his h' upon
8: 23 he took the blind man by the h',
9: 27 took him by the h', and lifted him
43 if thy h' offend thee, cut it off:
10: 37 we may sit, one on thy right h', and
37 the other on thy left h', in thy glory.
40 to sit on my right h' and on my left h',
12: 36 Sit thou on my right h', till I make
14: 42 lo, he that betrayeth me is at h'.
62 sitting on the right h' of power, and
15: 27 the one on his right h', and the other
16: 19 and sat on the right h' of God.
Lu 1: 1 many have taken in h' to set
66 And the h' of the Lord was with
71 and from the h' of all that hate us;
74 being delivered out of the h' of our
3: 17 Whose fan is in his h', and he will
5: 13 he put forth his h', and touched
6: 6 man whose right h' was withered.
8 which had the withered h', Rise up,
10 Stretch forth thy h'. And he did so.
10 his h' was restored whole as...other
8: 54 and took her by the h', and called,
9: 62 No man, having put his h' to the
15: 22 and put a ring on his h', and shoes
20: 42 my Lord, Sit thou on my right h',
21: 30 that summer is now nigh at h'.
31 kingdom of God is nigh at h'.
22: 21 the h' of him that betrayeth me
69 sit on the right h' of the power of
23: 33 one on the right h', and the other on
Joh 2: 13 the Jews' passover was at h', and
3: 35 hath given all things into his h'.
7: 2 feast of tabernacles was at h'.
10: 28 any man pluck them out of my h'.
29 to pluck them out of my Father's h'.
39 him: but he escaped out of their h',
11: 44 h' and foot with graveclothes:
55 Jews' passover was nigh at h': and
18: 22 struck Jesus with the palm of his h',
19: 42 for the sepulchre was nigh at h'.
20: 25 and thrust my h' into his side, I
27 and reach hither thy h', and thrust
Ac 2: 25 for he is on my right h', that
33 being by the right h' of God exalted,
34 my Lord, Sit thou on my right h',
3: 7 took him by the right h', and
4: 28 whatsoever thy h' and thy counsel
30 stretching forth thine h' to heal;
5: 31 hath God exalted with his right h'
7: 25 God by his h' would deliver them:
35 by the h' of the angel which
50 Hath not my h' made all these
55 Jesus standing on the right h' of God,
56 man standing on the right h' of God.
9: 8 they led him by the h', and
12 coming in, and putting his h' on
41 he gave her his h', and lifted
11: 21 And the h' of the Lord was with
12: 11 delivered me out of the h' of Herod,
17 beckoning unto them with the h' to
13: 11 behold, the h' of the Lord is upon
11 seeking some to lead him by the h'.
16 beckoning with his h' said, Men of
19: 33 Alexander beckoned with the h',
21: 3 Cyprus, we left it on the left h',
40 beckoned with the h' unto the
22: 11 being led by the h' of them that
23: 19 captain took him by the h', and
26: 1 Paul stretched forth the h', and
28: 3 of the heat, and fastened on his h'.
4 beast hang on his h', they said
Ro 8: 34 even at the right h' of God, who also
13: 12 night is far spent, the day is at h':
1Co 12: 15 Because I am not the h', I am not
21 And the eye cannot say unto the h',
16: 21 of me Paul with mine own h'.
2Co 6: 7 on the right h' and on the left,
10: 16 of things made ready to our h'.
Ga 3: 19 by angels in the h' of a mediator.
6: 11 written unto you with mine own h'.
Eph 1: 20 set him at his own right h' in the
Ph'p 4: 5 unto all men. The Lord is at h'.
Col 3: 1 Christ sitteth on the right h' of God,
4: 18 salutation by the h' of me Paul.
2Th 2: 2 as that the day of Christ is at h'.
3: 17 of Paul with mine own h',
2Ti 4: 6 the time of my departure is at h'.
Ph'm 19 written it with mine own h',
Heb 1: 3 the right h' of the Majesty on high;
13 Sit on my right h', until I make

Heb 8: 1 set on the right *h*· of the throne
9 when I took them by the *h*· to lead
10:12 sat down on the right *h*· of God;
12: 2 is set down at the right *h*· of the
1Pet 3:22 is on the right *h*· of God; angels, and
4: 7 the end of all things is at *h*·:
5: 6 under the mighty *h*· of God, that
Re 1: 3 therein: for the time is at *h*·.
16 he had in his right *h*· seven stars:
17 he laid his right *h*· upon me,
20 which thou sawest in my right *h*·, and
2: 1 the seven stars in his right *h*·,
5: 1 I saw in the right *h*· of him that sat
7 took the book out of the right *h*·
6: 5 him had a pair of balances in his *h*·.
8: 4 up before God out of the angel's *h*·.
10: 2 he had in his *h*· a little book
5 the earth lifted up his *h*· to heaven,
8 which is open in the *h*· of the angel
10 book out of the angel's *h*·, and ate
13:16 to receive a mark in their right *h*·,
14: 9 mark in his forehead, or in his *h*·,
14 and in his *h*· a sharp sickle.
17: 4 having a golden cup in her *h*· full of
19: 2 the blood of his servants at her *h*·.
20: 1 pit and a great chain in his *h*·.
22:10 of this book: for the time is at *h*·.

handbreadth See also HAND and BREADTH.
Ex 37:12 a border of an *h*· round about;
2Ch 4: 5 And the thickness of it was an *h*·,
Ps 39: 5 thou hast made my days as an *h*·;

handed See also BROKENHANDED; LEFTHANDED.
2Sa 17: 2 he is weary and weak *h*·, and will

handful See also HANDFULS.
Le 2: 2 shall take thereout his *h*· of
5:12 priest shall take his *h*· of it,
6:15 shall take of it his *h*·, of the flour
9:17 took an *h*· thereof, and burnt
Nu 5:26 And the priest shall take an *h*·
1Ki 17:12 an *h*· of meal in a barrel,
Ps 72:16 There shall be an *h*· of corn
Ec 4: 6 Better is an *h*· with quietness,
Jer 9:22 as the *h*· after the harvestman,

handfuls
Ge 41:47 the earth brought forth by *h*·.
Ex 9: 8 Take to you *h*· of ashes of
Ru 2:16 let fall also some of the *h*·
1Ki 20:10 Samaria shall suffice for *h*· for all
Eze 13:19 my people for *h*· of barley and for

handiwork See HANDYWORK.

handkerchiefs
Ac 19:12 brought unto the sick *h*· or aprons,

handle See also HAFT; HANDLED; HANDLES; HANDLETH; HANDLING.
Ge 4:21 father of all such as *h*· the harp
J'g 5:14 they that *h*· the pen of the writer.
1Ch 12: 8 that could *h*· shield and buckler,
2Ch 25: 5 that could *h*· spear and shield.
Ps 115: 7 They have hands, but they *h*· not:
Jer 2: 8 and they that *h*· the law knew
46: 9 the Libyans, that *h*· the shield; and
9 the Lydians, that *h*· and bend the
Eze 27:29 all that *h*· the oar, the mariners,
Lu 24:39 *h*· me, and see; for a spirit
Col 2:21 touch not; taste not; *h*· not;

handled
Eze 21:11 furbished, that it may be *h*·:
M'r 12: 4 and sent him away shamefully *h*·.
1Jo 1: 1 looked upon, and...hands have *h*·,

handles
Ca 5: 5 upon the *h*· of the lock.

handleth
Pr 16:20 He that *h*· a matter wisely shall
Jer 50:16 and him that *h*· the sickle
Am 2:15 shall he stand that *h*· the brow;

handling
Eze 38: 4 shields, all of them *h*· swords:
2Co 4: 2 *h*· the word of God deceitfully;

handmaid See also HANDMAIDEN; HANDMAIDS.
Ge 16: 1 she had an *h*·, an Egyptian,
25:12 the Egyptian, Sarah's *h*·, bare unto
29:24 Leah Zilpah his maid for an *h*·.
29 Bilhah his *h*· to be her maid.
30: 4 she gave him Bilhah her *h*· to wife
35:25 the sons of Bilhah, Rachel's *h*·;
26 And the sons of Zilpah, Leah's *h*·;
Ex 23:12 the son of thy *h*·, and the stranger,
J'g 19:19 also for me, and for thy *h*·,
Ru 2:13 spoken friendly unto thine *h*·,
3: 9 I am Ruth thine *h*·: spread
9 therefore thy skirt over thine *h*·;
1Sa 1:11 the affliction of thine *h*·, and
11 me, and not forget thine *h*·,
11 but wilt give unto thine *h*·
16 Count not thine *h*· for a daughter
18 Let thine *h*· find grace in thy sight.
25:24 let thine *h*·, I pray thee, speak in
24 and hear the words of thine *h*·.
25 but I thine *h*· saw not the young
27 which thine *h*· hath brought unto
28 forgive the trespass of thine *h*·:
31 my lord, then remember thine *h*·.
41 let thine *h*· be a servant
28:21 thine *h*· hath obeyed thy voice,
22 also unto the voice of thine *h*·,
2Sa 14: 6 And thy *h*· had two sons, and they
7 family is risen against thine *h*·,
12 woman said, Let thine *h*·, I pray
15 and thy *h*· said, I will now speak
15 perform the request of his *h*·.
16 to deliver his *h*· out of the hand
17 Then thine *h*· said, The word of
2Sa 14:19 words in the mouth of thine *h*·:
20:17 Hear the words of thine *h*·. And
1Ki 1:13 O king, swear unto thine *h*·,
17 the Lord thy God unto thine *h*·,
3:20 while thine *h*· slept, and laid it
2Ki 4: 2 Thine *h*· hath not any thing in the
16 man of God, do not lie unto thine *h*·.
Ps 86:16 and save the son of thine *h*·.
116:16 servant, and the son of thine *h*·:
Pr 30:23 and an *h*· that is heir to her
Jer 34:16 every man his *h*·, whom he had
Lu 1:38 Behold the *h*· of the Lord; be it

handmaiden See also HANDMAIDENS.
Lu 1:48 regarded the low estate of his *h*·:

handmaidens
Ge 33: 6 Then the *h*· came near, they and
Ru 2:13 like unto one of thine *h*·.
Ac 2:18 on my servants and on my *h*·

handmaids
Ge 33: 1 Rachel, and unto the two *h*·.
2 he put the *h*· and their children
2 Sa 6:20 eyes of the *h*· of his servants,
Isa 14: 2 them...for servants and *h*·: and
Jer 34:11 the servants and the *h*·, whom
11 subjection for servants and for *h*·.
16 you for servants and for *h*·.
Joe 2:29 upon the *h*· in those days will I

hands
Ge 5:29 our work and toil of our *h*·,
16: 9 and submit thyself under her *h*·.
20: 5 innocency of my *h*· have I done
24:22 two bracelets for her *h*· of ten
30 bracelets upon his sister's *h*·, and
47 and the bracelets upon her *h*·.
27:16 of the kids of the goats upon his *h*·,
22 but the *h*· are the *h*· of Esau.
23 him not, because his *h*· were hairy
23 hairy, as his brother Esau's *h*·:
31:42 the labour of my *h*·, and rebuked
37:21 delivered him out of their *h*·;
22 rid him out of their *h*·, to deliver
39: 1 bought him out of the *h*· of the
43:22 have we brought down in our *h*·
48:14 guiding his *h*· wittingly; for
49:24 the arms of his *h*· were made
24 strong by the *h*· of the mighty God
Ex 9:29 I will spread abroad my *h*·
33 spread abroad his *h*· unto the
15:17 Sanctuary, O Lord, which thy *h*·
17:12 But Moses' *h*· were heavy; and
12 Hur stayed up his *h*·, the one on the
12 his *h*· were steady until the going
29:10 *h*· upon the head of the bullock.
15, 19 *h*· upon the head of the ram.
24 the *h*· of Aaron, and in the *h*· of
25 shalt receive them of their *h*·,
30:19 sons shall wash their *h*· and their
21 they shall wash their *h*· and their
32:19 he cast the tables out of his *h*·,
35:25 did spin with their *h*·, and brought
40:31 washed their *h*· and their feet
Le 4:15 lay their *h*· upon the head of the
7:30 His own *h*· shall bring the offerings
8:14 their *h*· upon the head of the
18 laid their *h*· upon...of the bullock
22 laid their *h*· upon the...of the ram.
24 upon the thumbs of their right *h*·,
27 he put all upon Aaron's *h*·, and
27 and upon his sons' *h*·, and
28 Moses took them from off their *h*·,
15:11 and hath not rinsed his *h*· in water,
16:12 his *h*· full of sweet incense beaten
21 Aaron shall lay both his *h*· upon
24:14 lay their *h*· upon his head, and let
Nu 5:18 the offering of memorial in her *h*·,
6:19 upon the *h*· of the Nazarite, after
8:10 put their *h*· upon the Levites:
12 the Levites shall lay their *h*· upon
24:10 he smote his *h*· together: and
27:23 he laid his *h*· upon him, and gave
De 1:25 of the fruit of the land in their *h*·,
3: 3 God delivered into our *h*· Og also,
4:28 the work of men's *h*·, wood and
9:15 of the covenant were in my two *h*·.
17 cast them out of my two *h*·,
12:18 in all that thou puttest thine *h*·
16:15 all the works of thine *h*·, therefore
17: 7 The *h*· of the witnesses shall be
7 afterward the *h*· of all the people.
20:13 delivered it into thine *h*·, thou
21: 6 shall wash their *h*· over the
7 Our *h*· have not shed this blood,
10 delivered them into thine *h*·,
24:19 bless thee in all the work of thine *h*·.
27:15 work of the *h*· of the craftsman,
31:29 anger through the work of your *h*·.
33: 7 let his *h*· be sufficient for him;
11 accept the work of his *h*·: smite
34: 9 Moses had laid his *h*· upon him:
Jos 2:24 the Lord hath delivered into our *h*·
J'g 2:14 he delivered them into the *h*· of
14 sold them into the *h*· of their
6:13 us into the *h*· of the Midianites.
7: 2 give the Midianites into their *h*·,
11 shall thine *h*· be strengthened to go
19 the pitchers that were in their *h*·.
20 held the lamps in their left *h*·, and
20 the trumpets in their right *h*·
8: 3 God hath delivered into your *h*·
6, 15 said, Are the *h*· of Zebah and
34 out of the *h*· of all their enemies
9:16 according to...deserving of his *h*·:
10: 7 into the *h*· of the Philistines, and
7 into the *h*· of the children of
11:30 children of Ammon into mine *h*·,
J'g 11:32 Lord delivered them into his *h*·.
12: 2 ye delivered me not out of their *h*·.
3 I put my life in my *h*·, and
13:23 a meat offering at our *h*·, neither
14: 9 he took thereof in his *h*·, and
15:14 his bands loosed from off his *h*·.
16:24 hath delivered into our *h*· our
18:10 hath given it into your *h*·; a
19:27 her *h*· were upon the threshold.
1Sa 5: 4 both the palms of his *h*· were cut
7:14 out of the *h*· of the Philistines.
10: 4 thou shalt receive of their *h*·.
11: 7 by the *h*· of messengers, saying,
14:13 Jonathan climbed up upon his *h*·
48 out of the *h*· of them that spoiled
17:47 and he will give you into our *h*·.
21:13 feigned himself mad in their *h*·,
30:15 deliver me into the *h*· of my master,
2Sa 2: 7 now let your *h*· be strengthened,
3:34 Thy *h*· were not bound, nor thy
4: 1 his *h*· were feeble, and all the
12 cut off their *h*· and their feet,
16:21 the *h*· of all that are with thee
21: 9 he delivered them into the *h*· of
22:21 the cleanness of my *h*· hath he
35 He teacheth my *h*· to war; so that
23: 6 they cannot be taken with *h*·:
1Ki 8:22 spread forth his *h*· toward heaven:
38 spread forth his *h*· toward this
54 with his *h*· spread up to heaven.
14:27 the *h*· of the chief of the guard,
16: 7 the work of his *h*·, in being like
2Ki 3:11 poured water on the *h*· of Elijah.
4:34 and his *h*· upon his *h*·:
5:20 in not receiving at his *h*· that
9:23 Joram turned his *h*·, and fled, and
35 the feet, and the palms of her *h*·.
10:24 whom I have brought into your *h*·
11:12 they clapped their *h*·, and said,
16 they laid *h*· on her; and she went
12:11 the *h*· of them that did the work,
13:16 put his *h*· upon the king's *h*·.
19:18 the work of men's *h*·, wood and
22:17 the works of their *h*·; therefore
1Ch 12:17 there is no wrong in mine *h*·, the
25: 2 under the *h*· of Asaph, which
3 under the *h*· of their father
6 the *h*· of their father for song in
29: 5 to be made by the *h*· of artificers.
2Ch 6: 4 who hath with his *h*· fulfilled that
12 of Israel, and spread forth his *h*·:
13 and spread forth his *h*· toward
29 and shall spread forth his *h*· in
8:18 by the *h*· of his servants ships,
12:10 the *h*· of the chief of the guard,
15: 7 let not your *h*· be weak: for your
23:15 they laid *h*· on her; and when
29:23 they laid their *h*· upon them:
32:19 which were the work of the *h*· of
34:25 the works of their *h*·; therefore
35:11 sprinkled the blood from their *h*·,
Ezr 1: 6 about them strengthened their *h*·
4: 4 weakened the *h*· of the people of
5: 8 and prospereth in their *h*·.
6:22 to strengthen their *h*· in the
9: 5 and spread out my *h*· unto the
10:19 gave their *h*· that they would
Ne 2:18 they strengthened their *h*· for
4:17 one of his *h*· wrought in the work,
6: 9 Their *h*· shall be weakened from
9 O God, strengthen my *h*·.
8: 6 with lifting up their *h*·: and they
9:24 and gavest them into their *h*·,
13:21 ye do so again, I will lay *h*· on you.
Es 3: 6 he thought scorn to lay *h*· on
9 the *h*· of those that have the charge
9:16 but they laid not their *h*· on the
Job 1:10 hast blessed the work of his *h*·,
4: 3 hast strengthened the weak *h*·.
5:12 their *h*· cannot perform their
18 woundeth, and his *h*· make whole.
9:30 and make my *h*· never so clean;
10: 3 despise the work of thine *h*·, and
8 Thine *h*· have made me and
11:13 stretch out thine *h*· toward him;
14:15 desire to the work of thine *h*·.
16:11 me over into the *h*· of the wicked.
17 any injustice in mine *h*·: also
17: 3 who is he that will strike *h*·
9 he that hath clean *h*· shall be
20:10 and his *h*· shall restore their
22:30 by the pureness of thine *h*·.
27:23 Men shall clap their *h*· at him,
30: 2 the strength of their *h*· profit me,
31: 7 if any blot hath cleaved to mine *h*·;
34:19 they all are the work of his *h*·.
37 he clappeth his *h*· among us, and
Ps 7: 3 if there be iniquity in my *h*·;
8: 6 over the works of thy *h*·;
9:16 snared in the work of his own *h*·.
18:20 the cleanness of my *h*· hath he
24 the cleanness of my *h*· in his
34 He teacheth my *h*· to war, so that
22:16 they pierced my *h*· and my feet.
24: 4 He that hath clean *h*·, and a pure
26: 6 I will wash mine *h*· in innocency:
10 In whose *h*· is mischief, and their
28: 2 when I lift up my *h*· toward thy
4 them after the work of their *h*·;
5 the operation of his *h*·, he shall
44:20 stretched out our *h*· to a strange
47: 1 O clap your *h*·, all ye people;
55:20 He hath put forth his *h*· against
58: 2 the violence of your *h*· in the earth.
63: 4 I will lift up my *h*· in thy name.
68:31 Ethiopia shall...stretch out her *h*·

Ps 73:13 and washed my h' in innocency,
76: 5 men of might have found their h'.
78:72 them by the skilfulness of his h'.
81: 6 his h' were delivered from the
88: 9 I have stretched out my h' unto
90:17 the work of our h' upon us; yea,
17 the work of our h' establish thou
91:12 shall bear thee up in their h',
92: 4 triumph in the works of thy h'.
95: 5 his h' formed the dry land.
98: 8 Let the floods clap their h': let
102:25 heavens are the work of thy h'.
111: 7 The works of his h' are verity
115: 4 and gold, the work of men's h'.
7 They have h', but they handle not:
119:48 My h' also will I lift up unto thy
73 Thy h' have made me and
125: 3 the righteous put forth their h'
128: 2 shalt eat the labour of thine h':
134: 2 Lift up your h' in the sanctuary,
135:15 and gold, the work of men's h'.
138: 8 not the works of thine own h'.
140: 4 Lord, from the h' of the wicked;
141: 2 the lifting up of my h' as the
143: 5 I muse on the work of thy h'.
6 I stretch forth my h' unto thee:
144: 1 teacheth my h' to war, and my
Pr 6:10 a little folding of the h' to sleep:
17 and h' that shed innocent blood,
12:14 the recompence of a man's h' shall
14: 1 plucketh it down with her h'.
17:18 void of understanding striketh h',
21:25 him; for his h' refuse to labour.
22:26 one of them that strike h', or of
24:33 a little folding of the h' to sleep:
30:28 The spider taketh hold with her h',
31:13 worketh willingly with her h'.
16 the fruit of her h' she planteth
19 She layeth her h' to the spindle,
19 and her h' hold the distaff.
20 reacheth forth her h' to the needy.
31 Give her of the fruit of her h';
Ec 2:11 the works that my h' had wrought,
4: 5 The fool foldeth his h' together,
6 than both the h' full with travail
5: 6 destroy the work of thine h'?
7:26 her h' as bands: whoso pleaseth
10:18 through idleness of the h' the
Ca 5: 5 and my h' dropped with myrrh,
14 His h' are as gold rings set with
7: 1 the work of the h' of a cunning
Isa 1:15 when ye spread forth your h', I
15 your h' are full of blood.
2: 8 worship the work of their own h',
3:11 the reward of his h' shall be given
5:12 consider the operation of his h'.
13: 7 Therefore shall all h' be faint, and
17: 8 the work of his h', neither shall
19:25 and Assyria the work of my h',
25:11 And he shall spread forth his h'
11 swimmeth spreadeth forth his h':
11 together with the spoils of their h'.
29:23 the work of mine h', in the midst
31: 7 your own h' have made unto you
33:15 shaketh his h' from holding of
35: 3 Strengthen ye the weak h', and
37:19 the work of men's h', wood and
45: 9 or thy work, He hath no h'?
11 the work of my h' command ye me.
12 I, even my h', have stretched out
49:16 thee upon the palms of my h';
55:12 of the field shall clap their h'.
59: 3 your h' are defiled with blood, and
6 the act of violence is in their h'.
60:21 the work of my h', that I may
65: 2 I have spread out my h' all the
22 long enjoy the work of their h'.
Jer 1:16 the works of their own h'.
2:37 and thine h' upon thine head: for
4:31 that spreadeth her h', saying,
6:24 our h' wax feeble: anguish hath
10: 3 the work of the h' of the workman,
9 and of the h' of the founder:
19: 7 and by the h' of them that seek*
21: 4 weapons of war that are in your h',
23:14 they strengthen also the h' of
25: 6 anger with the works of your h';
7 works of your h' to your own hurt.
14 the works of their own h'.
30: 6 his h' on his loins, as a woman
32:30 the work of their h', saith the Lord.
33:13 the h' of him that telleth them,
38: 4 he weakeneth the h' of the men
4 and the h' of all the people,
44: 8 the works of your h', burning
47: 3 their children for feebleness of h';
48:37 upon all the h' shall be cuttings,
50:43 his h' waxed feeble: anguish took
La 1:14 hath delivered me into their h',
17 Zion spreadeth forth her h', and
2:15 All that pass by clap their h'
19 lift up thy h' toward him for the
3:41 lift up our heart with our h'
64 according to the work of their h'.
4: 2 the work of the h' of the potter!
6 moment, and no h' stayed on her.
10 The h' of the pitiful women have
Eze 1: 8 And they had the h' of a man
7:17 All h' shall be feeble, and all knees
21 into the h' of the strangers for a
27 and the h' of the people of the
10: 7 and put it into the h' of him
12 and their h', and their wings,
21 h' of a man was under their wings.
11: 9 into the h' of strangers, and will
13:22 strengthened the h' of the wicked,
Eze 16:11 I put bracelets upon thy h', and
21: 7 all h' shall be feeble, and every
14 smite thine h' together, and let
17 I will also smite mine h' together,
22:14 can thine h' be strong, in the days
23:37 blood is in their h', and with
42 which put bracelets upon their h',
45 adulteresses, and blood is in her h'.
25: 6 thou hast clapped thine h', and
Da 2:34 a stone was cut out without h',
45 cut out of the mountain without h',
3:15 that shall deliver you out of my h'?
10:10 and upon the palms of my h'.
Hos 14: 3 any more to the work of our h',
Ob 13 laid h' on their substance in the
Jon 3: 8 the violence that is in their h'.
Mic 5:13 worship the work of thine h'.
7: 3 they may do evil with both h'
Na 3:19 thee shall clap the h' over thee:
Hab 3:10 and lifted up his h' on high.
Zep 3:16 Zion, Let not thine h' be slack.
Hag 1:11 upon all the labour of the h'.
2:14 so is every work of their h';
17 in all the labours of your h';
Zec 4: 9 The h' of Zerubbabel have laid
9 his h' shall also finish it;
8: 9 Let your h' be strong, ye that
13 fear not, but let your h' be strong.
13: 6 are these wounds in thine h'?
M't 4: 6 in their h' they shall bear thee up,
15: 2 for they wash not their h' when
20 but to eat with unwashen h'
17:22 shall be betrayed into the h' of
18: 8 rather than having two h' or two
28 and he laid h' on him, and took
19:13 should put his h' on them, and
15 he laid his h' on them, and
21:46 when they sought to lay h' on
26:45 is betrayed into the h' of sinners.
50 laid h' on Jesus, and took him.
67 smote him with the palms of their h',
27:24 washed his h' before the multitude,
M'r 5:23 come and lay thy h' on her, that
6: 2 works are wrought by his h'?
5 laid his h' upon a few sick folk,
7: 2 with unwashen, h', they found
3 except they wash their h' oft, eat
5 but eat bread with unwashen h'?
8:23 his eyes, and put his h' upon him,
25 he put his h' again upon his eyes,
9:31 is delivered into the h' of men,
43 than having two h' to go into hell,
10:16 in his arms, put his h' upon them,
14:41 is betrayed into the h' of sinners.
46 laid their h' on him, and took him.
58 this temple that is made with h',
58 will build another made without h'.
65 strike him with the palms of their h'.
16:18 they shall lay h' on the sick, and
Lu 4:11 And in their h' they shall bear thee
40 laid his h' on every one of them,
6: 1 did eat, rubbing them in their h'.
9:44 shall be delivered into the h' of
13:13 And he laid his h' on her:
20:19 hour sought to lay h' on him;
21:12 they shall lay their h' on you,
22:53 ye stretched forth no h' against me:
23:46 into thy h' I commend my spirit:
24: 7 be delivered into the h' of sinful
39 Behold my h' and my feet, that it
40 he shewed them his h' and his
50 he lifted up his h', and blessed
Joh 7:30 but no man laid h' on him, because
44 him; but no man laid h' on him.
8:20 and no man laid h' on him; for
13: 3 given all things into his h', and
9 but also my h' and my head.
19: 3 and they smote him with their h'.
20:20 shewed unto them his h' and his
25 I shall see in his h' the print of the
27 hither thy finger, and behold my h';
21:18 thou shalt stretch forth thy h',
Ac 2:23 by wicked h' have crucified and
4: 3 they laid h' on them, and put
5:12 by the h' of the apostles were
18 laid their h' on the apostles, and
6: 6 prayed, they laid their h' on them.
7:41 in the works of their own h'.
48 not in temples made with h';
8:17 Then laid they their h' on them,
18 laying on of the apostles' h'
19 that on whomsoever I lay h', he
9:17 and putting his h' on him said,
11:30 by the h' of Barnabas and Saul.
12: 1 the king stretched forth his h' to
7 And his chains fell off from his h'.
13: 3 prayed, and laid their h' on them,
14: 3 and wonders to be done by their h'.
17:24 not in temples made with h';
25 is worshipped with men's h',
19: 6 when Paul had laid his h' upon
11 special miracles by the h' of Paul:
26 no gods, which are made with h':
20:34 these h' have ministered unto my
21:11 bound his own h' and feet,
11 shall deliver him into the h' of the
27 all the people, and laid h' on him,
24: 7 took him away out of our h',
27:19 out with our own h' the tackling
28: 8 laid his h' on him, and healed him.
17 into the h' of the Romans.
Ro 10:21 I have stretched forth my h' unto
1Co 4:12 labour, working with our own h':
2Co 5: 1 an house not made with h', eternal
11:33 by the wall, and escaped his h'.
Ga 2: 9 the right h' of fellowship; that
Eph 2:11 Circumcision in...flesh made by h';
4:28 working with his h' the thing
Col 2:11 the circumcision made without h',
1Th 4:11 and to work with your own h',
1Ti 2: 8 lifting up holy h', without wrath
4:14 with the laying on of the h' of the
5:22 Lay h' suddenly on no man, neither
2Ti 1: 6 in thee by the putting on of my h'.
Heb 1:10 heavens are the works of thine h':
2: 7 set him over the works of thy h':
6: 2 of baptisms, and of laying on of h',
9:11 tabernacle, not made with h', that
24 into the holy places made with h',
10:31 to fall into the h' of the living God.
12:12 lift up the h' which hang down,
Jas 4: 8 Cleanse your h', ye sinners; and
1Jo 1: 1 and our h' have handled, of the
Re 7: 9 white robes, and palms in their h';
9:20 not of the works of their h', that
20: 4 upon their foreheads, or in their h';

handstaves
Eze 39: 9 the arrows, and the h', and

hand-weapon See HAND and WEAPON.

handwriting
Col 2:14 Blotting out the h' of ordinances

handywork
Ps 19: 1 firmament sheweth his h'.

Hanes (*ha'-nees*) See also TAHPANES.
Isa 30: 4 and his ambassadors came to H'.

hang See also HANGED; HANGETH; HANGING.
Ge 40:19 and shall h' thee on a tree;
Ex 26:12 shall h' over the backside of the
13 it shall h' over the sides of the 1961,
32 And thou shalt h' it upon four
33 And thou shalt h' up the vail under
40: 8 and h' up the hanging at the
Nu 25: 4 and h' them up before the Lord
De 21:22 and thou h' him on a tree:
28:66 thy life shall h' in doubt before
2Sa 21: 6 and we will h' them up unto the
Es 6: 4 to h' Mordecai on the gallows
7: 9 Then the king said, H' him thereon.
Ca 4: 4 whereon there h' a thousand
Isa 22:24 And they shall h' upon him all the
La 2:10 the virgins of Jerusalem h' down
Eze 15: 3 will men take a pin of it to h'
M't 22:40 h' all the law and the prophets.
Ac 28: 4 venomous beast h' on his hand,
Heb 12:12 lift up the hands which h' down,

hanged See also HUNG.
Ge 40:22 But he h' the chief baker:
41:13 unto mine office, and him he h'.
De 21:23 he that is h' is accursed of God;
Jos 8:29 the king of Ai he h' on a tree
10:26 them: and h' them on five trees:
2Sa 4:12 and h' them up over the pool
17:23 and h' himself, and died, and was
18:10 I saw Absalom h' in an oak.
21: 9 and they h' them in the hill
12 where the Philistines had h' them,
13 the bones of them that were h'.
Ezr 6:11 let him be h' thereon; and let his
Es 2:23 therefore they were both h' on a
5:14 king that Mordecai may be h'
7:10 So they h' Haman on the gallows
8: 7 him they have h' upon the gallows,
9:13 let Haman's ten sons be h' upon
14 and they h' Haman's ten sons.
25 that he and his sons should be h'
Ps 137: 2 We h' our harps upon the willows
La 5:12 Princes are h' up by their hand:
Eze 27:10 they h' the shield and helmet in
11 they h' their shields upon thy walls
M't 18: 6 that a millstone were h' about his
27: 5 departed, and went and h' himself.
M'r 9:42 that a millstone were h' about his
Lu 17: 2 that a millstone were h' about his
23:39 of the malefactors which were h'
Ac 5:30 whom ye slew and h' on a tree.
10:39 whom they slew and h' on a tree:

hangeth
Job 26: 7 and h' the earth upon nothing.
Ga 3:13 Cursed is every one that h' on a

hanging See also HANGINGS.
Ex 26:36 shalt make an h' for the door
37 thou shalt make for the h' five
27:16 gate of the court shall be an h'
35:15 and the h' for the door at the
17 the h' for the door of the court,
36:37 he made an h' for the tabernacle
38:18 And the h' for the gate of the court
39:38 and the h' for the tabernacle door,
40 the h' for the court gate, his cords,
40: 5 the h' of the door to the tabernacle.
8 hang up the h' at the court gate.
28 he set up the h' at the door of the
33 and set up the h' of the court gate.
Nu 3:25 h' for the door of the tabernacle
31 and the h', and all the service
4:25 h' for the door of the tabernacle
26 and the h' for the door of the gate
Jos 10:26 they were h' upon the trees until

hangings
Ex 27: 9 side southward there shall be h'
11 side in length there shall be h'
12 west side shall be h' of fifty
14 The h' of one side of the gate
15 on the other side shall be h'
35:17 The h' of the court, his pillars,
38: 9 the h' of the court were of fine
11 side the h' were an hundred cubits.
12 for the west side were h'
14 The h' of the one side of the gate

Ex 38:15 that hand, were h' of fifteen cubits:
16 All the h' of the court round about
18 answerable to the h' of the court.
39:40 The h' of the court, his pillars,
Nu 3:26 And the h' of the court, and the
4:26 And the h' of the court, and the
2Ki 23: 7 where the women wove h' for the
Es 1: 6 were white, green, and blue, h',

Haniel (ha'-ne-el) See also HANNIEL.
1Ch 7:39 sons of Ulla; Arah, and H'.

Hannah (han'-nah)
1Sa 1: 2 the name of the one was H'.
2 but H' had no children.
5 unto H' he gave a worthy portion;
5 for he loved H': but the Lord
8 H', why weepest thou? and why
9 So H' rose up after they had eaten
13 Now H', she spake in her heart;
15 H' answered and said, No, my lord,
19 and Elkanah knew H' his wife;
20 about after H' had conceived,
22 But H' went not up; for she said
2: 1 H' prayed, and said, My heart
21 the Lord visited H', so that she

Hannathon (han'-na-thon)
Jos 19:14 it on the north side to H':

Hanniel (han'-ne-el) See also HANIEL.
Nu 34:23 Manasseh, H' the son of Ephod.

Hanoch (ha'-nok) See also HANOCHITES; HENOCH.
Ge 25: 4 Ephah, and Epher, and H', and
46: 9 of Reuben; H', and Phallu, and
Ex 6:14 H', and Pallu, Hezron, and Carmi:
Nu 26: 5 H', of whom cometh the family of
1Ch 5: 3 H', and Pallu, Hezron, and Carmi.

Hanochites (ha'-nok-ites)
Nu 26: 5 cometh the family of the H':

Hanun (ha'-nun)
2Sa 10: 1 H' his son reigned in his stead.
2 I will shew kindness unto H' the
3 of Ammon said unto H' their lord,
4 Wherefore H' took David's
1Ch 19: 2 said, I will shew kindness unto H'
2 of the children of Ammon to H',
3 said to H', Thinkest thou that
4 H' took David's servants, and
6 H' and the children of Ammon
Ne 3:13 The valley gate repaired H', and
30 and H' the sixth son of Zalaph,

hap See also PERHAPS.
Ru 2: 3 her h' was to light on a part of

Haphraim (haf-ra'-im)
Jos 19:19 And H', and Shihon, and

haply
1Sa 14:30 if h' the people had eaten freely
M'r 11:13 if h' he might find any thing
Lu 14:29 Lest h', after he hath laid the
Ac 5:39 lest h' ye be found even to fight
17:27 if h' they might feel after him,
2Co 9: 4 Lest h' if they of Macedonia come

happen See also HAPPENED; HAPPENETH.
1Sa 28:10 there shall no punishment h' to
Pr 12:21 There shall no evil h' to the just:
Isa 41:22 shew us what shall h': let them
M'r 10:32 what things should h' unto him,

happened
1Sa 6: 9 it was a chance that h' to us.
2Sa 1: 6 As I h' by chance upon mount
20: 1 there h' to be there a man of
Es 4: 7 all that had h' unto him, and of
Jer 44:23 therefore this evil is h' unto you,
Lu 24:14 of all these things which had h'.
Ac 3:10 at that which had h' unto him.
Ro 11:25 blindness in part is h' to Israel,
1Co 10:11 all these things h' unto them for
Ph'p 1:12 that the things which h' unto me
1Pe 4:12 as though some strange thing h'
2Pe 2:22 But it is h' unto them according to

happeneth
Ec 2:14 that one event h' to them all.
15 As it h' to the fool,
15 so it h' even to me:
8:14 men, unto whom it h' according
14 wicked men, to whom it h'
9:11 time and chance h' to them all.

happier
1Co 7:40 But she is h' if she so abide,

Happuch See KEREN-HAPPUCH.

happy See also HAPPIER.
Ge 30:13 Leah said, H' am I, for the
De 33:29 H' art thou, O Israel: who is like
1Ki 10: 8 H' are thy men, h' are these thy
2Ch 9: 7 H' are thy men, and h' are these
Job 5:17 h' is the man whom God correcteth:
Ps 127: 5 H' is the man that hath his quiver
128: 2 h' shalt thou be, and it shall be
137: 8 h' shall he be, that rewardeth thee
9 H' shall he be, that taketh and
144:15 H' is that people, that is in such a
15 h' is that people, whose God is the
146: 5 H' is he that hath the God
Pr 3:13 H' is the man that findeth wisdom,
18 h' is every one that retaineth her.
14:21 hath mercy on the poor, h' is he.
16:20 trusteth in the Lord, h' is he.
28:14 H' is the man that feareth alway:
29:18 he that keepeth the law, h' is he.
Jer 12: 1 are all they h' that deal very
Mal 3:15 And now we call the proud h';
Joh 13:17 h' are ye if you do them.
Ac 26: 2 I think myself h', king Agrippa,
Ro 14:22 H' is he that condemneth not
Jas 5:11 we count them h' which endure.
1Pe 3:14 for righteousness' sake, h' are ye:
4:14 for the name of Christ, h' are ye;

Hara (ha'-rah)
1Ch 5:26 Habor, and H', and to the river

Haradah (har'-a-dah)
Nu 33:24 Shapher, and encamped in H'.
25 And they removed from H', and

Haran (ha'-ran) See also BETH-HARAN; CHARRAN.
Ge 11:26 begat Abram, Nahor, and H'.
27 Nahor, and H'; and H' begat
28 H' died before his father Terah
29 Milcah, the daughter of H', the
31 Lot the son of H' his son's son,
31 they came unto H', and dwelt
32 five years: and Terah died in H'.
12: 4 when he departed out of H'.
5 souls that they had gotten in H';
27:43 thou to Laban my brother to H';
28:10 Beer-sheba, and went toward H'.
29: 4 And they said, Of H' are we.
2Ki 19:12 as Gozan, and H', and Rezeph,
1Ch 2:46 Caleb's concubine, bare H', and
46 and Gazez: and H' begat Gazez.
23: 9 Shelomith, and Haziel, and H',
Isa 37:12 H', and Rezeph, and the children
Eze 27:23 H', and Canneh, and Eden, the

Hararite (har'-a-rite)
2Sa 23:11 Shammah the son of Agee the H'.
33 Shammah the H', Ahiam the son of
33 Ahiam the son of Sharar the H',
1Ch 11:34 Jonathan the son of Shage the H',
35 Ahiam the son of Sacar the H',

Harbona (har-bo'-nah) See also HARBONAH.
Es 1:10 Biztha, H', Bigtha, and Abagtha,

Harbonah (har-bo'-nah) See also HARBONA.
Es 7: 9 H', one of the chamberlains,

hard See also HARDER; HARDHEARTED.
Ge 18:14 Is any thing too h' for the Lord?
35:16 travailed, and she had h' labour.
17 when she was in h' labour, that
Ex 1:14 their lives bitter with h' bondage,
18:26 the h' causes they brought unto
Lev 3: 9 he take off h' by the backbone;
De 1:17 the cause that is too h' for you,
15:18 It shall not seem h' unto thee,
17: 8 If there arise a matter too h' for
26: 6 us, and laid upon us h' bondage:
J'g 9:52 and went h' unto the door of the
20:45 and pursued h' after them unto
1Sa 14:22 even they also followed h' after
31: 2 the Philistines followed h' upon
2Sa 1: 6 and horsemen followed h' after
3:39 the sons of Zeruiah be too h' for
13: 2 and Amnon thought it h' for him
1Ki 10: 1 to prove him with h' questions.
21: 1 h' by the palace of Ahab king of
2Ki 2:10 Thou hast asked a h' thing:
1Ch 10: 2 the Philistines followed h' after
19: 4 in the midst h' by their buttocks,
2Ch 9: 1 prove Solomon with h' questions
Job 41:24 h' as a piece of the nether
Ps 60: 3 hast shewed thy people h' things:
63: 8 My soul followeth h' after thee:
88: 7 Thy wrath lieth h' upon me, and
94: 4 they utter and speak h' things?
Pr 13:15 the way of transgressors is h'.
Isa 14: 3 the h' bondage wherein thou
Jer 32:17 and there is nothing too h' for thee:
27 is there any thing too h' for me?
Eze 3: 5 and of an h' language, but to the
6 and of an h' language, whose words
Da 5:12 and shewing of h' sentences, and
Jon 1:13 men rowed h' to bring it to the land;
M't 25:24 that thou art an h' man, reaping
M'r 10:24 how h' is it for them that trust
Joh 6:60 This is an h' saying; who can
Ac 9: 5 h' for thee to kick against the
18: 7 house joined h' to the synagogue.
26:14 it is h' for thee to kick against
Heb 5:11 things to say, and h' to be uttered,
2Pe 3:16 some things h' to be understood,
Jude 15 and of all their h' speeches which

harden See also HARDENED.
Ex 4:21 but I will h' his heart, that he
7: 3 I will h' Pharaoh's heart, and
14: 4 I will h' Pharaoh's heart, that he
17 will h' the hearts of the Egyptians,
De 15: 7 thou shalt not h' thine heart, nor
Jos 11:20 was of the Lord to h' their hearts,
1Sa 6: 6 Wherefore then do ye h' your
Job 6:10 yea, I would h' myself in sorrow:
Ps 95: 8 H' not your heart, as in the
Heb 3: 8 H' not your hearts, as in the
15 voice, h' not your hearts, as in the
4: 7 his voice, h' not your hearts.

hardened
Ex 7:13 And he h' Pharaoh's heart, that
14 Pharaoh's heart is h', he refuseth
22 Pharaoh's heart was h', neither
8:15 he h' his heart, and hearkened not
19 and Pharaoh's heart was h', and
32 And Pharaoh h' his heart at this
9: 7 And the heart of Pharaoh was h',
12 the Lord h' the heart of Pharaoh,
34 sinned yet more, and h' his heart,
35 And the heart of Pharaoh was h',
10: 1 I have h' his heart, and the heart
20 the Lord h' Pharaoh's heart, so
27 the Lord h' Pharaoh's heart, and
11:10 the Lord h' Pharaoh's heart, so
Ex 14: 8 the Lord h' the heart of Pharaoh
De 2:30 the Lord thy God h' his spirit,
1Sa 6: 6 and Pharaoh h' their hearts?
2Ki 17:14 would not hear, but h' their necks,
2Ch 36:13 and h' his heart from turning
Ne 9:16 h' their necks, and hearkened not
17 but h' their necks, and in their
29 h' their neck, and would not hear.
Job 9: 4 who hath h' himself against him,
39:16 She is h' against her young
Isa 63:17 from thy ways, and h' our heart
Jer 7:26 but h' their neck: they did worse
19:15 they have h' their necks, that
Dan 5:20 up, and his mind h' in pride,
M'r 6:52 loaves: for their heart was h'.
8:17 have ye your heart yet h'?
Joh 12:40 blinded their eyes, and h' their
Ac 19: 9 But when divers were h', and
Heb 3:13 h' through the deceitfulness of sin.

hardeneth
Pr 21:29 A wicked man h' his face: but as
28:14 but he that h' his heart shall fall
29: 1 being often reproved h' his neck,
Rom 9:18 mercy, and whom he will he h'.

harder
Pr 18:19 A brother offended is h' to be won
Jer 5: 3 made their faces h' than a rock;
Eze 3: 9 As an adamant h' than flint

hardhearted
Eze 3: 7 Israel are impudent and h'.

hardly
Ge 16: 6 And when Sarai dealt h' with her,
Ex 13:15 Pharaoh would h' let us go,
Isa 8:21 through it, h' bestead and hungry:
M't 19:23 a rich man shall h' enter into
M'r 10:23 How h' shall they that have riches
Lu 9:39 bruising him h' departeth from
18:24 How h' shall they that have riches
Ac 27: 8 And, h' passing it, came unto a

hardness
Job 38:38 the dust groweth into h', and
M't 19: 8 because of the h' of your hearts
M'r 3: 5 grieved for the h' of their hearts,
10: 5 For the h' of your heart he wrote
16:14 their unbelief and h' of heart,
Ro 2: 5 thy h' and impenitent heart
2Ti 2: 3 therefore endure h', as a good

hare
Le 11: 6 the h', because he cheweth the cud,
De 14: 7 the camel, and the h', and the

Hareph (ha'-ref)
1Ch 2:51 H' the father of Beth-gader.

Haresha See TEL-HARESHA.

Hareth (ha'-reth)
1Sa 22: 5 and came into the forest of H'.

Harhaiah (har-ha-i'-ah)
Ne 3: 8 the son of H', of the goldsmiths.

Harhas (har'-has) See also HASRAH.
2Ki 22:14 the son of H', keeper of the

Harhur (har'-hur)
Ezr 2:51 of Hakupha, the children of H',
Ne 7:53 of Hakupha, the children of H',

Harim (ha'-rim)
1Ch 24: 8 The third to H', the fourth to
Ezr 2:32 The children of H', three hundred
39 The children of H', a thousand and
10:21 the sons of H'; Maaseiah, and
31 of the sons of H'; Eliezer, Ishijah,
Ne 3:11 Malchijah the son of H', and
7:35 The children of H', three hundred
42 The children of H', a thousand
10: 5 H', Meremoth, Obadiah,
27 Malluch, H', Baanah.
12:15 Of H', Adna; of Meraioth, Helkai;

Hariph (ha'-rif) See also JORAH.
Ne 7:24 The children of H', an hundred
10:19 H', Anathoth, Nebai,

harlot See also HARLOT'S; HARLOTS.
Ge 34:31 with our sister as with an h'?
38:15 he thought her to be an h';
21 Where is the h', that was openly
21 There was no h' in this place.
22 there was no h' in this place.
24 daughter in law hath played the h';
Le 21:14 or profane, or an h', these shall
Jos 6:17 only Rahab the h' shall live, she
25 Joshua saved Rahab the h' alive,
J'g 11: 1 he was the son of an h':
16: 1 saw there an h', and went
Pr 7:10 a woman with the attire of an h',
Isa 1:21 the faithful city become an h'!
23:15 years shall Tyre sing as an h'.
16 thou h' that hast been forgotten;
Jer 2:20 tree thou wanderest, playing the h'.
3: 1 played the h' with many lovers;
6 tree, and there hath played the h'.
8 but went and played the h' also.
Eze 16:15 and playedst the h' because of thy
16 and playedst the h' thereupon:
28 yea, thou hast played the h' with
31 hast not been as an h', in that thou
35 O h', hear the word of the Lord:
41 thee to cease from playing the h',
23: 5 And Aholah played the h' when she
19 wherein she had played the h' in
44 unto a woman that playeth the h':
Hos 2: 5 their mother hath played the h':
3: 3 thou shalt not play the h', and
4:15 Though thou, Israel, play the h',
Joe 3: 3 have given a boy for an h',
Am 7:17 Thy wife shall be an h' in the city,

Mic 1: 7 she gathered it of the hire of an h',
7 shall return to the hire of an h'.
Na 3: 4 of the wellfavoured h', the mistress
1Co 6:15 make them the members of an h'?
16 is joined to an h' is one body?
Heb 11:31 By faith the h' Rahab perished not
Jas 2:25 was not Rahab the h' justified by

harlot's
Jos 2: 1 came into an h' house, named
6:22 Go into the h' house, and bring

harlots See also HARLOTS'.
1Ki 3:16 two women, that were h', unto the
Pr 29: 3 he that keepeth company with h'
Ho 4:14 they sacrifice with h': therefore
M't 21:31 and the h' go into the kingdom
32 and the h' believed him: and ye,
Lu 15:30 devoured thy living with h', thou
Re 17: 5 mother of h' and abominations

harlots'
Jer 5: 7 by troops in the h' houses.

harm See also HARMFUL.
Ge 31:52 and this pillar unto me, for h'.
Le 5:16 for the h' that he hath done in
Nu 35:23 his enemy, neither sought his h':
1Sa 26:21 I will no more do thee h',
2Sa 20: 6 the son of Bichri do us more h'
2Ki 4:41 there was no h' in the pot.
1Ch 16:22 and do my prophets no h'.
Ps 105:15 and do my prophets no h'.
Pr 3:30 if he have done thee no h'.
Jer 39:12 look well to him, and do him no h';
Ac 16:28 Do thyself no h': for we are all
27:21 to have gained this h' and loss.
28: 5 into the fire, and felt no h'.
6 saw no h' come to him, they
21 shewed or spake any h' of thee.
1Pe 3:13 who is he that will h' you,

harmless
M't 10:16 wise as serpents, and h' as doves.
Ph'p 2:15 That ye may be blameless and h',
Heb 7:26 who is holy, h', undefiled,

Harnepher (*har-ne'-fur*)
1Ch 7:36 Suah, and H', and Shual,

harness See also HARNESSED.
1Ki 20:11 him that girdeth on his h' boast
22:34 between the joints of the h':
2Ch 9:24 raiment, h', and spices, horses,
18:33 between the joints of the h':
Jer 46: 4 H' the horses; and get up, ye

harnessed
Ex 13:18 the children of Israel went up h'

Harod (*ha'-rod*) See also HARODITE.
J'g 7: 1 and pitched beside the well of H':

Harodite (*ha'-ro-dite*) See also HARORITE.
2Sa 23:25 Shammah the H', Elika the H',

Haroeh (*ha-ro'-eh*) See also REAIAH.
1Ch 2:52 H', and half of the Manahethites.

Harorite (*ha'-ro-rite*) See also HARODITE.
1Ch 11:27 Shammoth the H', Helez the

Harosheth (*har'-o-sheth*)
J'g 4: 2 which dwelt in H' of the Gentiles.
13 from H' of the Gentiles unto the
16 the host, unto H' of the Gentiles:

harp See also HARPED; HARPING; HARPS.
Ge 4:21 such as handle the h' and organ.
31:27 songs, with tabret, and with h'?
1Sa 10: 5 a pipe, and a h', before them:
16:16 a cunning player on an h':
23 David took an h', and played
1Ch 25: 3 who prophesied with a h', to give
Job 21:12 They take the timbrel and h', and
30:31 My h' also is turned to mourning,
Ps 33: 2 Praise the Lord with h': sing unto
43: 4 upon the h' will I praise thee,
49: 4 open my dark saying upon the h'.
57: 8 awake, psaltery and h': I myself
71:22 unto thee will I sing with the h',
81: 2 the pleasant h' with the psaltery.
92: 3 upon the h' with a solemn sound.
98: 5 Sing unto the Lord with the h';
5 with the h', and the voice of a
108: 2 Awake, psaltery and h': I myself
147: 7 sing praise upon the h' unto our
149: 3 unto him with the timbrel and h'.
150: 3 praise him with the psaltery and h'.
Isa 5:12 the h', and the viol, the tabret, and
16:11 my bowels shall sound like an h'
23:16 Take an h', go about the city,
24: 8 endeth, the joy of the h' ceaseth.
Da 3: 5, 7, 10, 15 flute, h', sackbut,
1Co 14: 7 giving sound, whether pipe or h',

harped
1Co 14: 7 be known what is piped or h'?

harpers
Re 14: 2 I heard the voice of h' harping
18:22 And the voice of h', and musicians,

harping
Re 14: 2 voice of harpers h' with their

harps
2Sa 6: 5 even on h', and on psalteries, and
1Ki 10:12 h' also and psalteries for singers:
1Ch 13: 8 and with h', and with psalteries,
15:16 psalteries and h' and cymbals
21 with h' on the Sheminith
28 a noise with psalteries and h'.
16: 5 Jeiel with psalteries and with h';
25: 1 who should prophesy with h', with
6 with cymbals, psalteries, and h', for
2Ch 5:12 cymbals and psalteries and h',
9:11 and h' and psalteries for singers:
20:28 with psalteries and h' and
29:25 with psalteries, and with h',
Ne 12:27 cymbals, psalteries, and with h'.
Ps 137: 2 We hanged our h' upon the willows
Isa 30:32 it shall be with tabrets and h':
Eze 26:13 sound of thy h' shall no more be
Re 5: 8 having every one of them h',
14: 2 of harpers harping with their h':
15: 2 sea of glass, having the h' of God.

harrow See also HARROWS.
Job 39:10 will he h' the valleys after thee?

harrows
2Sa 12:31 saws, and under h' of iron, and
1Ch 20: 3 and with h' of iron, and with axes

Harsa See TEL-HARSA.

Harsha (*har'-shah*)
Ezr 2:52 of Mehida, the children of H',
Ne 7:54 of Mehida, the children of H',

hart See also HARTS.
De 12:15 the roebuck, and as of the h'.
22 as the roebuck and the h' is eaten,
14: 5 The h', and the roebuck, and the
15:22 as the roebuck, and as the h'.
Ps 42: 1 As the h' panteth after the water
Ca 2: 9 is like a roe or a young h':
17 or a young h' upon the mountains
8:14 to a young h' upon the mountains
Isa 35: 6 shall the lame man leap as an h',

harts
1Ki 4:23 an hundred sheep, beside h',
La 1: 6 her princes are become like h'

Harum (*ha'-rum*)
1Ch 4: 8 families of Aharhel the son of H'.

Harumaph (*ha-ru'-maf*)
Ne 3:10 repaired Jedaiah the son of H',

Haruphite (*ha'-ru-fite*)
1Ch 12: 5 Shemariah, and Shephatiah the H',

Haruz (*ha'-ruz*)
2Ki 21:19 Meshullemeth, the daughter of H'

harvest See also HARVESTMAN.
Ge 8:22 seedtime and h', and cold and
30:14 in the days of wheat h', and found
45: 6 there shall neither be earing nor h'.
Ex 23:16 the feast of h', the firstfruits of
34:21 in earing time and in h' thou shalt
22 the firstfruits of wheat h', and the
Le 19: 9 when ye reap the h' of your land,
9 thou gather the gleanings of thy h'.
23:10 shall reap the h' thereof, then ye
10 a sheaf of the firstfruits of your h'
22 when ye reap the h' of your land,
22 thou gather any gleaning of thy h':
25: 5 groweth of its own accord of thy h'
De 24:19 When thou cuttest down thine h'
Jos 3:15 all his banks all the time of h',
J'g 15: 1 in the time of wheat h',
Ru 1:22 in the beginning of barley h'.
2:21 until they have ended all my h'.
23 end of barley h' and of wheat h';
1Sa 6:13 their wheat h' in the valley:
8:12 to reap his h', and to make his
12:17 Is it not wheat h' to day?
2Sa 21: 9 were put to death in the days of h',
9 in the beginning of barley h'.
10 from the beginning of h' until
23:13 came to David in the h' time
Job 5: 5 Whose h' the hungry eateth up,
Pr 6: 8 and gathereth her food in the h'.
10: 5 he that sleepeth in h' is a son
20: 4 therefore shall he beg in h', and
25:13 the cold of snow in the time of h',
26: 1 as rain in h', so honour is not
Isa 9: 3 according to the joy in h', and as
16: 9 thy summer fruits and for thy h'
17:11 the h' shall be a heap in the day of
18: 4 like a cloud of dew in the heat of h'.
5 For afore the h', when the bud is
23: 3 the h' of the river, is her revenue;
Jer 5:17 they shall eat up thine h', and thy
24 us the appointed weeks of the h'.
8:20 The h' is past, the summer is
50:16 the sickle in the time of h':
51:33 the time of her h' shall come.
Ho 6:11 he hath set an h' for thee,
Joe 1:11 the h' of the field is perished.
3:13 the sickle, for the h' is ripe:
Am 4: 7 were yet three months to the h':
M't 9:37 The h' truly is plenteous, but the
38 Lord of the h', that he will send
38 send forth labourers into his h'.
13:30 both grow together until the h':
30 and in the time of h' I will say
39 the h' is the end of the world;
M'r 4:29 the sickle, because the h' is come.
Lu 10: 2 The h' truly is great, but the
2 ye therefore the Lord of the h',
2 send forth labourers into his h'.
Joh 4:35 four months, and then cometh h'?
35 for they are white already to h'.
Re 14:15 the h' of the earth is ripe.

harvestman
Isa 17: 5 when the h' gathereth the corn,
Jer 9:22 as the handful after the h',

has See HATH.

Hasadiah (*has-a-di'-ah*)
1Ch 3:20 and H', Jushab-hesed, five.

Hasenuah (*has-e-nu'-ah*) See also SENUAH.
1Ch 9: 7 son of Hodaviah, the son of H',

Hash See MAHER-SHALAL-HASH-BAZ.

Hashabiah (*hash-a-bi'-ah*)
1Ch 6:45 The son of H', the son of Amaziah,
9:14 son of H', of the sons of Merari;
25: 3 Jeshaiah, H', and Mattithiah,
19 The twelfth, to H', he, his sons,
26:30 Hebronites, H' and his brethren,
27:17 Of the Levites, H' the son of
2Ch 35: 9 his brethren, and H' and Jeiel
Ezr 8:19 H', and with him Jeshaiah of
24 H' and ten of their brethren
Ne 3:17 Next unto him repaired H',
10:11 Micha, Rehob, H',
11:15 the son of H', the son of Bunni;
22 the son of Bani, the son of H',
12:21 Of Hilkiah, H'; of Jedaiah,
24 chief of the Levites: H', Sherebiah,

Hashabnah (*hash-ab'-nah*)
Ne 10:25 Rehum, H', Maaseiah,

Hashabniah (*hash-ab-ni'-ah*)
Ne 3:10 repaired Hattush the son of H'.
9: 5 Bani, H', Sherebiah, Hadijah,

Hashbadana (*hash-bad'-a-nah*)
Ne 8: 4 Hashum, and H', Zechariah,

Hashem (*ha'-shem*)
1Ch 11:34 The sons of H' the Gizonite,

Hashmonah (*hash-mo'-nah*)
Nu 33:29 from Mithcah, and pitched in H'.
30 And they departed from H', and

Hashub (*ha'-shub*) See also HASSHUB.
Ne 3:11 and H' the son of Pahath-moab,
23 him repaired Benjamin and H'
10:23 Hoshea, Hananiah, H',
11:15 Shemaiah the son of H', the son

Hashubah (*hash-u'-bah*)
1Ch 3:20 H', and Ohel, and Berechiah,

Hashum (*ha'-shum*)
Ezr 2:19 The children of H', two hundred
10:33 Of the sons of H'; Mattenai,
Ne 7:22 The children of H', three hundred
8: 4 and Malchiah, and H', and
10:18 Hodijah, H', Bezai,

Hashupha (*hash-u'-fah*) See also HASUPHA.
Ne 7:46 the children of H', the children

Hasrah (*has'-rah*) See also HARHAS.
2Ch 34:22 the son of H' keeper of the

Hassenaah (*has-se-na'-ah*) See also SENAAH.
Ne 3: 3 fish gate did the sons of H' build,

Hasshub (*hash'-ub*) See also HASHUB.
1Ch 9:14 Shemaiah the son of H', the son

hast^
Ge 3:11 H' thou eaten of the tree,
13 What is this that thou h' done?
14 Because thou h' done this, thou art
17 Because thou h' hearkened unto the
17 and h' eaten of the tree, of which I
4:10 And he said, What h' thou done?
14 Behold, thou h' driven me out this
12:18 What is this that thou h' done unto
15: 3 Behold, to me thou h' given no seed:
18: 5 And they said, so do, as thou h' said.
19:12 unto Lot, H' thou here any besides?
12 whatsoever thou h' in the city, bring
19 and thou h' magnified thy mercy,
19 which thou h' shewed unto me in
21 this city, for the which thou h' spoken.
20: 3 woman which thou h' taken; for she
9 and said unto him, What h' thou done
9 that thou h' brought on me and my
9 thou h' done deeds unto me that ought
10 What sawest thou, that thou h' done
21:23 the land wherein thou h' sojourned.
29 ewe lambs which thou h' set by
22:12 seeing thou h' not withheld thy son,
16 for because thou h' done this thing,
16 and h' not withheld thy son, thine
18 because thou h' obeyed my voice.
24:14 same be she that thou h' appointed
14 I know that thou h' shewed kindness
26:10 What is this thou h' done unto us?
27:20 How is it that thou h' found it so
36 H' thou not reserved a blessing for
38 H' thou but one blessing, my father?
45 forget that which thou h' done to
29:25 What is this that thou h' done unto
25 wherefore then h' thou beguiled me?
30:15 Is it a small matter that thou h' taken
31:26 said to Jacob, What h' thou done,
26 that thou h' stolen away unawares to
28 And h' not suffered me to kiss my
28 thou h' now done foolishly in so doing,
30 yet wherefore h' thou stolen my gods?
36 my sin, that thou h' so hotly pursued
37 Whereas thou h' searched all my stuff,
37 what h' thou found of all thy
41 and thou h' changed my wages ten
32:10 which thou h' shewed unto thy
28 for as a prince h' thou power with
28 God and with men, and h' prevailed,
33: 9 my brother; keep that thou h' unto
37:10 is this dream that thou h' dreamed?
38:23 this kid, and thou h' not found her.
29 she said, How h' thou broken forth?
39:17 servant, which thou h' brought
45:10 and thy herds, and all that thou h':
11 and thy household, and all that thou h'.
47:25 And they said, Thou h' saved our lives:
30 And he said, I will do as thou h' said.
Ex 3:12 When thou h' brought forth the people
4:10 nor since thou h' spoken unto thy
5:22 h' thou so evil entreated this
22 why is it that thou h' sent me?

Ex 5:23 neither *h'* thou delivered thy people
9:19 gather thy cattle, and all that thou *h'*
10:29 And Moses said, Thou *h'* spoken well,
12:44 when thou *h'* circumcised him, then
13:12 cometh of a beast which thou *h'*;
14:11 *h'* thou taken us away to die in the
11 wherefore *h'* thou dealt thus
15: 7 thou *h'* overthrown them that rose
13 Thou in thy mercy *h'* led forth the
13 the people which thou *h'* redeemed:
13 thou *h'* guided them in thy strength
16 pass over, which thou *h'* purchased.
17 O Lord, which thou *h'* made for
17: 3 this that thou *h'* brought us up
20:25 thy tool upon it, thou *h'* polluted it.
23:16 thy labours, which thou *h'* sown
16 when thou *h'* gathered in thy
29:36 when thou *h'* made an atonement
32:11 which thou *h'* brought forth out of the
21 that thou *h'* brought so great a sin
32 of thy book which thou *h'* written.
33: 1 people which thou *h'* brought up
12 and thou *h'* not let me know whom
12 Yet thou *h'* said, I know thee by
12 and thou *h'* also found grace in my
17 this thing also that thou *h'* spoken:
17 for thou *h'* found grace in my sight,
Nu 5:19 and if thou *h'* not gone aside to
20 But if thou *h'* gone aside to another
11:11 Wherefore *h'* thou afflicted thy
21 and thou *h'* said, I will give them
14:17 be great, according as thou *h'* spoken,
19 and as thou *h'* forgiven this people,
16:13 a small thing that thou *h'* brought us
14 Moreover thou *h'* not brought us into
22:28 that thou *h'* smitten me these three
29 Because thou *h'* mocked me: I would
30 thine ass, upon which thou *h'* ridden
32 Wherefore *h'* thou smitten thine ass
23:11 What *h'* thou done unto me? I took
11 and, behold, thou *h'* blessed them
24:10 thou *h'* altogether blessed them these
27:13 And when thou *h'* seen it, thou also
De 1:14 The thing...thou *h'* spoken is good
31 where thou *h'* seen how that the Lord
2: 7 with thee; thou *h'* lacked nothing.
3:24 O Lord God, thou *h'* begun to shew thy
4:33 the midst of the fire, as thou *h'* heard,
8:10 When thou *h'* eaten and art full,
12 Lest when thou *h'* eaten and art full,
12 and *h'* built goodly houses, and dwelt
13 and all that thou *h'* is multiplied;
9: 2 thou *h'* heard say, Who can stand
12 for thy people which thou *h'* brought
26 inheritance, which thou *h'* redeemed:
26 which thou *h'* brought forth out of
12:26 Only thy holy things which thou *h'*,
13: 2 which thou *h'* not known, and let us
6 which thou *h'* not known, thou, nor
16:13 after that thou *h'* gathered in thy corn
17: 4 and thou *h'* heard of it, and enquired
21: 8 people Israel, whom thou *h'* redeemed,
10 and thou *h'* taken them captive,
11 a beautiful woman, and *h'* a desire
14 of her, because thou *h'* humbled her.
22: 3 which he hath lost, and thou *h'* found,
9 fruit of thy seed which thou *h'* sown,
23:23 according as thou *h'* vowed unto the
23 which thou *h'* promised with thy
24:19 harvest in thy field, and *h'* forgot a
26:10 land, which thou, O Lord, *h'* given me.
12 When thou *h'* made an end of tithing
12 and *h'* given it unto the Levite, the
13 which thou *h'* commanded me:
14 to all that thou *h'* commanded me.
15 the land which thou *h'* given us, as
17 Thou *h'* avouched the Lord this day
28:20 doings, whereby thou *h'* forsaken me:
32:18 art unmindful, and *h'* forgotten God
Jos 2:17 this thine oath...*h'* made us swear.
20 of thine oath...*h'* made us to swear.
7: 7 wherefore *h'* thou at all brought
19 and tell me now what thou *h'* done;
25 And Joshua said, Why *h'* thou troubled
14: 9 because thou *h'* wholly followed the
15:19 for thou *h'* given me a south land;
17:14 Why *h'* thou given me but one lot and
17 Thou art a great people, and *h'* great
J'g 1:15 Give me a blessing: for thou *h'* given
5:21 O my soul, thou *h'* trodden down
6:36 Israel by mine hand, as thou *h'* said,
37 Israel by mine hand, as thou *h'* said.
8: 1 said unto him, Why *h'* thou served us
22 for thou *h'* delivered us from the hand
9:38 the people that thou *h'* despised?
11:12 saying, What *h'* thou to do with me,
35 Alas, my daughter! thou *h'* brought
36 My father, if thou *h'* opened thy mouth
14:16 thou *h'* put forth a riddle unto the
16 children of my people, and *h'* not told
15:11 what is this that thou *h'* done unto
18 Thou *h'* given this great deliverance
16:10 Behold, thou *h'* mocked me, and told
13 Hitherto thou *h'* mocked me, and
15 thou *h'* mocked me these three times,
15 and *h'* not told me wherein thy great
18: 3 in this place? and what *h'* thou here?
Ru 2:11 thou *h'* done unto thy mother in
11 and how thou *h'* left thy father and
13 for that thou *h'* comforted me, and
19 Where *h'* thou gleaned to-day?
3:10 for thou *h'* shewed more kindness
15 Bring the vail that thou *h'* upon thee,
1Sa 1:17 thy petition that thou *h'* asked of him.
4:20 fear not; for thou *h'* born a son.
12: 4 And they said, Thou *h'* not defrauded

1Sa 12: 4 neither *h'* thou taken ought of any
13:11 And Samuel said, What *h'* thou done?
13 said to Saul, Thou *h'* done foolishly:
13 thou *h'* not kept the commandment
14 because thou *h'* not kept that...the Lord
14:43 Tell me what thou *h'* done. And
15:23 Because thou *h'* rejected the word of
26 for thou *h'* rejected the word of the
17:28 and with whom *h'* thou left those few
45 armies of Israel, whom thou *h'* defied.
20: 8 for thou *h'* brought thy servant into a
19 And when thou *h'* stayed three days,
30 do not I know that thou *h'* chosen the
22:13 in that thou *h'* given him bread, and a
13 and a sword, and *h'* enquired of God
24:17 for thou *h'* rewarded me good,
18 And thou *h'* shewed this day how
18 how that thou *h'* dealt well with me:
19 good for that thou *h'* done unto me
25: 6 and peace be upon all that thou *h'*.
7 I have heard that thou *h'* shearers:
31 either that thou *h'* shed blood
33 be thou which *h'* kept me this day
26:15 wherefore then *h'* thou not kept thy
16 thing is not good that thou *h'* done
28:12 Why *h'* thou deceived me? for thou
15 Why *h'* thou disquieted me, to bring
29: 4 place which thou *h'* appointed him,
6 as the Lord liveth, thou *h'* been
8 and what *h'* thou found in thy servant
2Sa 1:26 very pleasant *h'* thou been unto me:
3: 7 Wherefore *h'* thou gone in unto my
24 the king, and said, What *h'* thou done?
24 why is it that thou *h'* sent him away,
6:22 maidservants which thou *h'* spoken of,
7:18 my house, that thou *h'* brought me
19 but thou *h'* spoken also of thy
21 to thine own heart, *h'* thou done all
24 For thou *h'* confirmed to thyself thy
25 the word that thou *h'* spoken
25 it forever, and do as thou *h'* said.
27 God of Israel, *h'* revealed to thy
28 and thou *h'* promised this goodness
29 for thou, O Lord God, *h'* spoken it:
11:19 When thou *h'* made an end of telling
12: 9 Wherefore *h'* thou despised the
9 thou *h'* killed Uriah the Hittite with
9 and *h'* taken his wife to be thy wife,
9 and *h'* slain him with the sword of
10 because thou *h'* despised me,
10 and *h'* slain with the sword of the
14 by this deed thou *h'* given great
21 What thing is this that thou *h'* done?
14:13 Wherefore then *h'* thou thought such
15:35 And *h'* thou not there with thee Zadok
16: 8 Saul, in whose stead thou *h'* reigned:
10 say, Wherefore *h'* thou done so?
18:21 Go tell the king what thou *h'* seen.
22 son, seeing that thou *h'* no tidings
19: 5 Thou *h'* shamed this day the faces of
6 For thou *h'* declared this day, that
22:36 Thou *h'* also given me the shield of
37 Thou *h'* enlarged my steps under me;
40 for thou *h'* girded me with strength to
40 rose up against me *h'* thou subdued
41 Thou *h'* also given me the necks of
44 Thou also *h'* delivered me from the
44 thou *h'* kept me to be the head of the
49 thou also *h'* lifted me up on high
49 thou *h'* delivered me from the violent
1Ki 1:11 *H'* thou not heard that Adonijah the
24 my Lord, O king, *h'* thou said,
27 and thou *h'* not shewed it unto thy
2: 8 And behold, thou *h'* with thee
26 and because thou *h'* been afflicted in
43 Why then *h'* thou not kept the oath of
3: 6 Thou *h'* shewed unto thy servant
6 and thou *h'* kept for him this great
6 that thou *h'* given him a son to sit on
7 O Lord my God, thou *h'* made thy
8 thy people which thou *h'* chosen,
11 Because thou *h'* asked this thing, and
11 and *h'* not asked for thyself long life;
11 neither *h'* asked riches for thyself,
11 nor *h'* asked the life of thine enemies;
11 but *h'* asked for thyself understanding
13 which thou *h'* not asked, both riches,
8:24 Who *h'* kept with thy servant David
24 and *h'* fulfilled it with thine hand,
25 walk before me as thou *h'* walked
29 the place of which thou *h'* said, My
36 which thou *h'* given to thy people for
44 toward the city which thou *h'* chosen,
48 the city which thou *h'* chosen, and the
9: 3 thy supplication, that thou *h'* made
3 this house, which thou *h'* built, to put
13 cities are these which thou *h'* given
11:11 and thou *h'* not kept my covenant and
22 But what *h'* thou lacked with me,
13:21 forasmuch as thou *h'* disobeyed the
21 and *h'* not kept the commandment
22 But camest back, and *h'* eaten bread
14: 8 and yet thou *h'* not been as my
9 But *h'* done evil above all that were
9 for thou *h'* gone and made thee other
9 to provoke me to anger, and *h'* cast
16: 2 and thou *h'* walked in the way of
2 and *h'* made my people Israel to sin,
17:13 Fear not; go and do as thou *h'* said:
20 *h'* thou also brought evil upon the
18:18 of the Lord, and thou *h'* followed
37 and that thou *h'* turned their heart
20:13 *H'* thou seen all this great multitude?
25 like the army that thou *h'* lost, horse
36 Because thou *h'* not obeyed the voice
40 judgment be; thyself *h'* decided it.

1Ki 20:42 Because thou *h'* let go out of thy hand
21:19 *H'* thou killed, and also taken
20 said to Elijah, *H'* thou found me, O
20 because thou *h'* sold thyself to work
22 wherewith thou *h'* provoked me to
2Ki 1:16 Forasmuch as thou *h'* sent messengers
2:10 Thou *h'* asked a hard thing:
4: 2 tell me, what *h'* thou in the house?
13 thou *h'* been careful for us with all
5: 8 Wherefore *h'* thou rent thy clothes?
6:22 smite those whom thou *h'* taken
9:18 said, What *h'* thou to do with peace?
19 answered, What *h'* thou to do with
10:30 Because thou *h'* done well in
30 and *h'* done unto the house of Ahab
14:10 Thou *h'* indeed smitten Edom, and
17:26 The nations which thou *h'* removed,
19: 6 of the words which thou *h'* heard,
11 Behold, thou *h'* heard what the kings
15 thou *h'* made heaven and earth.
20 That which thou *h'* prayed to me
22 Whom *h'* thou reproached and
22 and against whom *h'* thou exalted thy
23 By thy messengers thou *h'* reproached
23 and *h'* said, With the multitude of my
25 *H'* thou not heard long ago how I
20:19 word of the Lord which thou *h'* spoken.
22:18 the words which thou *h'* heard;
19 and thou *h'* humbled thyself
19 and *h'* rent thy clothes, and wept
23:17 that thou *h'* done against the altar of
1Ch 17: 8 thee whithersoever thou *h'* walked,
16 that thou *h'* brought me hitherto?
17 for thou *h'* also spoken of thy servant's
17 and *h'* regarded me according to the
19 to thine own heart, *h'* thou done all
21 thy people, whom thou *h'* redeemed
23 let the thing that thou *h'* spoken
23 forever, and do as thou *h'* said.
25 For thou, O my God, *h'* told thy
26 Lord, thou art God, and *h'* promised
22: 8 saying, Thou *h'* shed blood
8 and *h'* made great wars: thou shalt
8 because thou *h'* shed much blood
28: 3 because thou *h'* been a man of war,
3 a man of war, and *h'* shed blood.
20 until thou *h'* finished all the work
29:17 triest the heart, and *h'* pleasure in
2Ch 1: 8 Thou *h'* shewed great mercy unto
8 and *h'* made me to reign in his stead.
9 for thou *h'* made me king over a
11 and thou *h'* not asked riches, wealth,
11 neither yet *h'* asked long life;
11 but *h'* asked wisdom and knowledge
6:15 Thou which *h'* kept with thy servant
15 that which thou *h'* promised him;
15 and *h'* fulfilled it with thine hand
16 that which thou *h'* promised him,
16 walk in my law, as thou *h'* walked
17 which thou *h'* spoken unto thy
20 the place whereof thou *h'* said that
27 when thou *h'* taught them the good
27 which thou *h'* given unto thy people
34 this city which thou *h'* chosen, and
38 the city which thou *h'* chosen, and
16: 7 Because thou *h'* relied on the king of
9 Herein thou *h'* done foolishly:
19: 3 in that thou *h'* taken away the groves
3 and *h'* prepared thine heart to seek
20:11 which thou *h'* given us to inherit.
37 Because thou *h'* joined thyself with
21:12 Because thou *h'* not walked in the
13 But *h'* walked in the way of the kings
13 and *h'* made Judah...to go a whoring,
13 and also *h'* slain thy brethren of thy
24: 6 Why *h'* thou not required of the
25:15 Why *h'* thou sought after the gods of
16 destroy thee, because thou *h'* done
16 and *h'* not hearkened unto my counsel.
19 Thou sayest, Lo, thou *h'* smitten the
26:18 sanctuary; for thou *h'* trespassed;
34:26 the words which thou *h'* heard;
Ezr 9:11 Which thou *h'* commanded by thy
13 that thou our God *h'* punished us
13 and *h'* given us such deliverance as
10:12 As thou *h'* said, so must we do.
Ne 1:10 whom thou *h'* redeemed by thy great
6: 7 And thou *h'* also appointed prophets
9: 6 thou *h'* made heaven, the heaven of
8 to his seed, and *h'* performed thy
33 for thou *h'* done right, but we have
37 whom thou *h'* set over us because of
Es 6:10 and the horse, as thou *h'* said,
10 nothing fail of all that thou *h'* spoken.
13 before whom thou *h'* begun to fall,
Job 1: 8 *H'* thou considered my servant Job,
10 *H'* not thou made an hedge about
10 thou *h'* blessed the work of his hands,
2: 3 *H'* thou considered my servant Job,
4: 3 Behold, thou *h'* instructed many, and
3 and thou *h'* strengthened the weak
4 and thou *h'* strengthened the feeble
7:20 why *h'* thou set me as a mark against
10: 4 *H'* thou eyes of flesh? or seest thou as
9 that thou *h'* made me as the clay;
10 *H'* thou not poured me out as milk,
11 Thou *h'* clothed me with skin and
11 and *h'* fenced me with bones and
12 Thou *h'* granted me life and favour,
13 And these things *h'* thou hid in
18 Wherefore then *h'* thou brought me
11: 4 For thou *h'* said, My doctrine is
14: 5 thou *h'* appointed his bounds that he
15: 8 *H'* thou heard the secret of God?
16: 7 thou *h'* made desolate all my
8 And thou *h'* filled me with wrinkles.

Job 17: 4 For thou h' hid their heart from
22: 6 For thou h' taken a pledge from thy
7 Thou h' not given water to the weary
7 and thou h' withholden bread from
9 Thou h' sent widows away empty,
15 H' thou marked the old way which
26: 2 How h' thou helped him that is
3 How h' thou counselled him that hath
3 and how h' thou plentifully declared
4 To whom h' thou uttered words? and
33: 32 If thou h' anything to say, answer
34: 16 If now thou h' understanding, hear
36: 17 But thou h' fulfilled the judgment of
21 for this h' thou chosen rather than
23 can say, Thou h' wrought iniquity?
37: 18 H' thou with him spread out the sky,
38: 4 declare if thou h' understanding.
12 H' thou commanded the morning
16 H' thou entered into the springs of
16 or h' thou walked in the search of the
17 h' thou seen the doors of the shadow
18 H' thou perceived the breadth of the
22 H' thou entered into the treasures of
22 h' thou seen the treasures of the hail,
39: 19 H' thou given the horse strength?
19 h' thou clothed his neck with
40: 9 H' thou an arm like God? or canst
Ps 3: 7 for thou h' smitten all mine enemies
4: 1 thou h' enlarged me when I was in
7 Thou h' put gladness in my heart,
7: 6 judgment that thou h' commanded.
8: 1 who h' set thy glory above the heavens.
2 babes and sucklings h' thou ordained
3 the stars, which thou h' ordained;
5 For thou h' made him a little lower
5 and h' crowned him with glory and
6 thou h' put all things under his feet:
9: 4 For thou h' maintained my right and
5 Thou h' rebuked the heathen,
5 thou h' destroyed the wicked,
5 thou h' put out their name for ever
6 end: and thou h' destroyed cities;
10 for thou, Lord, h' not forsaken them
10: 14 Thou h' seen it; for thou beholdest
17 Lord, thou h' heard the desire of the
16: 2 O my soul, thou h' said unto the Lord,
17: 3 Thou h' proved mine heart; thou
3 mine heart; thou h' visited me in the
3 thou h' tried me, and shalt find
18: 35 Thou h' also given me the shield of
36 Thou h' enlarged my steps under me,
39 For thou h' girded me with strength
39 thou h' subdued under me those that
40 Thou h' also given me the necks of
43 Thou h' delivered me from the
43 and thou h' made me the head of the
48 thou h' delivered me from the
21: 2 Thou h' given him his heart's desire,
2 and h' not withholden the request of
5 honour and majesty h' thou laid upon
6 For thou h' made him most blessed
6 thou h' made him exceeding glad with
22: 1 My God, my God, why h' thou forsaken
15 and thou h' brought me into the dust
21 for thou h' heard me from the horns
27: 9 thou h' been my help; leave me
30: 1 O Lord, for thou h' lifted me up,
1 and h' not made my foes to rejoice
2 I cried unto thee, and thou h' healed
3 thou h' brought up my soul from the
3 thou h' kept me alive, that I should not
7 thou h' made my mountain to stand
11 Thou h' turned for me my mourning
11 thou h' put off my sackcloth, and
31: 5 thou h' redeemed me, O Lord God of
7 in thy mercy: for thou h' considered
7 thou h' known my soul in adversities;
19 which thou h' laid up for them that
19 which thou h' wrought for them that
35: 22 This thou h' seen, O Lord: keep not
39: 5 Behold, thou h' made my days as an
40: 5 wonderful works which thou h' done,
6 desire; mine ears h' thou opened:
6 and sin-offering h' thou not required.
42: 9 Why h' thou forgotten me? why go I
44: 7 But thou h' saved us from our enemies,
7 and h' put them to shame that hated
9 But thou h' cast off, and put us to
11 Thou h' given us like sheep appointed
11 and h' scattered us among the
19 Though thou h' sore broken us in the
50: 16 What h' thou to do to declare my
18 and h' been partaker with adulterers.
21 These things h' thou done and I kept
51: 8 that the bones which thou h' broken
52: 9 because thou h' done it: and I will
53: 5 thou h' put them to shame, because
56: 13 For thou h' delivered my soul from
59: 16 for thou h' been my defence and
60: 1 O God, thou h' cast us off, thou
1 cast us off, thou h' scattered us, thou
1 thou h' been displeased; O turn
2 Thou h' made the earth to tremble;
2 thou h' broken it: heal the breaches
3 Thou h' shewed thy people hard
3 thou h' made us to drink the wine of
4 Thou h' given a banner to them that
61: 3 For thou h' been a shelter for me,
5 For thou, O God, h' heard my vows:
5 thou h' given me the heritage of those
63: 7 Because thou h' been my help,
65: 9 them corn, when thou h' so provided
66: 10 For thou, O God, h' proved us: thou
10 thou h' tried us as silver is tried.
12 Thou h' caused men to ride over our
68: 10 thou, O God, h' prepared of thy

Ps 68: 18 Thou h' ascended on high, thou
18 on high, thou h' led captivity captive:
18 thou h' received gifts for men; yea,
28 that which thou h' wrought for us.
69: 19 Thou h' known my reproach, and my
26 persecute him whom thou h' smitten;
26 grief of those whom thou h' wounded.
71: 3 thou h' given commandment to save
17 O God, thou h' taught me from my
19 is very high, who h' done great things:
20 Thou, which h' shewed me great
23 and my soul, which thou h' redeemed.
73: 23 thou h' holden me by my right hand.
27 thou h' destroyed all them that go a
74: 1 O God, why h' thou cast us off for ever?
2 which thou h' purchased of old; the
2 inheritance, which thou h' redeemed;
2 mount Zion, wherein thou h' dwelt.
16 thou h' prepared the light and the sun.
17 Thou h' set all the borders of the
17 thou h' made summer and winter.
77: 14 thou h' declared thy strength among
15 Thou h' with thine arm redeemed thy
80: 8 Thou h' brought a vine out of Egypt:
8 thou h' cast out the heathen and
12 Why h' thou then broken down her
85: 1 Lord, thou h' been favourable unto thy
1 thou h' brought back the captivity of
2 Thou h' forgiven the iniquity of thy
2 people, thou h' covered all their sins.
3 Thou h' taken away all thy wrath: thou
3 thou h' turned thyself from the
86: 9 All nations whom thou h' made shall
13 and thou h' delivered my soul from
17 because thou, O Lord, h' holpen me,
88: 6 Thou h' laid me in the lowest pit,
7 thou h' afflicted me with all thy waves.
8 Thou h' put away mine acquaintance
8 thou h' made me an abomination
18 Lover and friend h' thou put far from
89: 10 Thou h' broken Rahab in pieces, as
10 thou h' scattered thine enemies with
11 the fulness thereof, thou h' founded
12 north and the south thou h' created
13 Thou h' a mighty arm: strong is thy
38 But thou h' cast off and abhorred,
38 thou h' been wroth with thine
39 Thou h' made void the covenant of thy
39 thou h' profaned his crown by casting
40 Thou h' broken down all his hedges;
40 thou h' brought his strong holds to
42 Thou h' set up the right hand of his
42 thou h' made all his enemies to rejoice.
43 Thou h' also turned the edge of his
43 and h' not made him to stand in the
44 Thou h' made his glory to cease, and
45 days of his youth h' thou shortened:
45 thou h' covered him with shame.
47 wherefore h' thou made...men in vain?
90: 1 thou h' been our dwelling place
8 Thou h' set our iniquities before thee,
15 wherein thou h' afflicted us, and the
91: 9 Because thou h' made the Lord, which
92: 4 For thou, Lord, h' made me glad
102: 10 for thou h' lifted me up, and cast me
25 Of old h' thou laid the foundation of
104: 8 the place which thou h' founded for
9 Thou h' set a bound that they may not
24 in wisdom h' thou made them all:
26 whom thou h' made to play therein.
108: 11 Wilt not thou, O God, who h' cast us
109: 27 thy hand; that thou, Lord, h' done it.
110: 3 morning: thou h' the dew of thy youth.
116: 8 For thou h' delivered my soul from
16 handmaid: thou h' loosed my bonds.
118: 13 Thou h' thrust sore at me that I might
21 for thou h' heard me, and art become
119: 4 Thou h' commanded us to keep thy
21 Thou h' rebuked the proud that are
49 upon which thou h' caused me to hope.
65 Thou h' dealt well with thy servant,
75 thou in faithfulness h' afflicted me.
90 thou h' established the earth, and it
93 for with them thou h' quickened me.
98 commandments h' made me wiser
102 judgments: for thou h' taught me.
118 Thou h' trodden down all them that
138 testimonies that thou h' commanded
152 that thou h' founded them for ever.
171 when thou h' taught me thy statutes.
137: 8 rewardeth thee as thou h' served us.
138: 2 for thou h' magnified thy word above
139: 1 O Lord, thou h' searched me, and
5 Thou h' beset me behind and before,
13 For thou h' possessed my reins: thou
13 thou h' covered me in my mother's
140: 7 thou h' covered my head in the day of
Pr 3: 28 will give; when thou h' it by thee.
6: 1 if thou h' stricken thy hand with a
22: 27 If thou h' nothing to pay, why should
23: 8 The morsel which thou h' eaten shalt
24: 14 when thou h' found it; then there shall
25: 16 H' thou found honey? eat so much as
30: 32 If thou h' done foolishly in lifting up
32 or if thou h' thought evil, lay thine
Ec 5: 4 pay that which thou h' vowed.
7: 22 that thou thyself likewise h' cursed
Ca 1: 15 thou art fair; thou h' doves' eyes.
4: 1 thou h' doves' eyes within thy locks:
9 Thou h' ravished my heart, my sister,
9 thou h' ravished my heart with one of
Isa 2: 6 Therefore thou h' forsaken thy people
3: 6 Thou h' clothing, be thou our ruler,
9: 3 Thou h' multiplied the nation, and
4 For thou h' broken the yoke of his
14: 13 For thou h' said in thine heart, I will

Isa 14: 20 because thou h' destroyed thy land,
17: 10 Because thou h' forgotten the God of
10 and h' not been mindful of the rock
22: 16 What h' thou here? and whom
16 here? and whom h' thou here, that
16 that thou h' hewed thee out a
23: 16 thou harlot that h' been forgotten;
25: 1 for thou h' done wonderful things; thy
2 For thou h' made of a city an heap; of
4 For thou h' been a strength to the
26: 12 for thou also h' wrought all our works
14 therefore h' thou visited and destroyed
15 Thou h' increased the nation, O Lord,
15 O Lord, thou h' increased the nation:
37: 6 words that thou h' heard, wherewith
11 Behold, thou h' heard what the kings
16 thou h' made heaven and earth.
21 Israel, Whereas thou h' prayed to me
23 Whom h' thou reproached and
23 and against whom h' thou exalted thy
24 By thy servants h' thou reproached
24 and h' said, By the multitude of my
26 H' thou not heard long ago, how I
38: 17 but thou h' in love to my soul
17 for thou h' cast all my sins behind
39: 8 of the Lord which thou h' spoken.
40: 28 H' thou not known? h' thou not heard,
43: 4 thou h' been honourable, and I have
22 But thou h' not called upon me, O
22 but thou h' been weary of me, O Israel.
23 Thou h' not brought me the small
23 neither h' thou honoured me with thy
24 Thou h' bought me no sweet cane with
24 neither h' thou filled me with the fat
24 but thou h' made me to serve with
24 thou h' wearied me with thine
45: 4 thee, though thou h' not known me.
5 thee, though thou h' not known me:
10 woman, What h' thou brought forth?
47: 6 upon the ancient h' thou very heavily
10 For thou h' trusted in thy wickedness:
10 thou h' said, None seeth me. Thy
10 and thou h' said in thine heart, I am,
12 wherein thou h' laboured from thy
15 with whom thou h' laboured, even thy
48: 6 Thou h' heard, see all this; and will
49: 20 after thou h' lost the other, shall say
51: 13 and h' feared continually every day
17 which h' drunk at the hand of the Lord
17 thou h' drunken the dregs of the cup
23 and thou h' laid thy body as the
57: 6 even to them h' thou poured a drink
6 offering, thou h' offered a meat offering.
7 and high mountain h' thou set thy bed:
8 h' thou set up thy remembrance:
8 for thou h' discovered thyself to
8 thou h' enlarged thy bed, and made
10 thou h' found the life of thine hand;
11 and of whom h' thou been afraid or
11 afraid or feared, that thou h' lied,
11 and h' not remembered me, nor laid
60: 15 Whereas thou h' been forsaken
62: 8 for the which thou h' laboured:
63: 17 O Lord, why h' thou made us to err
64: 7 for thou h' hid thy face from us,
7 and h' consumed us, because of our
Jer 1: 12 Thou h' well seen: for I will hasten
2: 17 H' thou not procured this unto thyself,
17 in that thou h' forsaken the Lord thy
18 h' thou to do in the way of Egypt,
18 h' thou to do in the way of Assyria,
19 that thou h' forsaken the Lord thy God,
23 know what thou h' done: thou art a
27 Thou h' brought me forth: for they
28 are thy gods that thou h' made thee?
33 therefore h' thou also taught the
3: 1 but thou h' played the harlot with
2 and see where thou h' not been lien
2 In the ways h' thou sat for them,
2 and thou h' polluted the land with
5 Behold, thou h' spoken and done evil
6 H' thou seen that which backsliding
13 that thou h' transgressed against the
13 and h' scattered thy ways to the
4: 10 surely thou h' greatly deceived this
19 because thou h' heard, O my soul, the
5: 3 thou h' stricken them, but they have
3 thou h' consumed them, but they have
12: 2 Thou h' planted them, yea, they have
3 thou h' seen me, and tried mine heart
5 If thou h' run with the footmen,
13: 4 Take the girdle that thou h' got,
21 thou h' taught them to be captains,
25 because thou h' forgotten me, and
14: 19 H' thou utterly rejected Judah? hath
19 why h' thou smitten us, and there is
22 for thou h' made all these things.
15: 6 Thou h' forsaken me, saith the Lord,
10 thou h' borne me a man of strife
17 for thou h' filled me with indignation.
20: 6 friends, to whom thou h' prophesied
7 O Lord, thou h' deceived me, and I
7 art stronger than I, and h' prevailed:
26: 9 Why h' thou prophesied in the name
28: 6 thy words which thou h' prophesied,
13 Thou h' broken the yokes of wood; but
16 because thou h' taught rebellion
29: 25 Because thou h' sent letters in thy
27 therefore why h' thou not reproved
30: 13 thou h' no healing medicines.
31: 18 Thou h' chastised me, and I was
32: 17 thou h' made the heaven and the earth
20 Which h' set signs and wonders in
20 and h' made thee a name, as at this
21 And h' brought forth thy people Israel
22 And h' given them this land, which

Jer 32:23 therefore thou *h'* caused all this evil
24 and what thou *h'* spoken is come to
25 And thou *h'* said unto me, O Lord
36: 6 which thou *h'* written from my mouth,
14 wherein thou *h'* read in the ears of
29 Thus saith the Lord; Thou *h'* burned
29 Why *h'* thou written therein, saying,
38:25 now what thou *h'* said unto the king,
39:18 because thou *h'* put thy trust in me,
44:16 As for the word that thou *h'* spoken
48: 7 For because thou *h'* trusted in thy
50:24 caught, because thou *h'* striven
51:62 O Lord, thou *h'* spoken against this
63 when thou *h'* made an end of reading
La 1:21 they are glad that thou *h'* done it:
21 the day that thou *h'* called, and
22 unto them, as thou *h'* done unto me
2:20 and consider to whom thou *h'* done
21 thou *h'* slain them in the day of thine
21 thine anger; thou *h'* killed, and not
22 Thou *h'* called as in the solemn day
3:17 And thou *h'* removed my soul far off
42 have rebelled: thou *h'* not pardoned.
43 Thou *h'* covered with anger, and
43 thou *h'* slain, thou *h'* not pitied.
44 Thou *h'* covered thyself with a cloud,
45 Thou *h'* made us as the offscouring
56 Thou *h'* heard my voice: hide not
58 O Lord, thou *h'* pleaded the causes of
58 of my soul; thou *h'* redeemed my life.
59 O Lord, thou *h'* seen my wrong:
60 Thou *h'* seen all their vengeance and
61 Thou *h'* heard their reproach, O Lord,
5:22 But thou *h'* utterly rejected us; thou
Eze 3:19 but thou *h'* delivered thy soul.
20 thou *h'* not given him warning,
21 also thou *h'* delivered thy soul.
4: 6 And when thou *h'* accomplished them,
8 till thou *h'* ended the days of thy
5:11 because thou *h'* defiled my sanctuary
8:12 Son of man, *h'* thou seen what the
15, 17 *H'* thou seen this, O son of man?
9:11 I have done as thou *h'* commanded
16: 7 and thou *h'* increased and waxen
17 Thou *h'* also taken thy fair jewels of
18 and thou *h'* set mine oil and mine
19 I fed thee, thou *h'* even set it before
20 Moreover thou *h'* taken thy sons and
20 whom thou *h'* borne unto me, and
20 and these *h'* thou sacrificed unto
21 That thou *h'* slain my children and
22 whoredoms thou *h'* not remembered
24 That thou *h'* also built unto thee an
25 Thou *h'* built thy high place at every
25 and *h'* made thy beauty to be
25 and *h'* opened thy feet to every one
26 Thou *h'* also committed fornication
26 and *h'* increased thy whoredoms, to
28 Thou *h'* played the whore also with
28 yea, thou *h'* played the harlot with
29 Thou *h'* moreover multiplied thy
31 and *h'* not been as an harlot, in
37 with whom thou *h'* taken pleasure,
37 and all them that thou *h'* loved, with
37 with all them that thou *h'* hated; I
43 Because thou *h'* not remembered the
43 but *h'* fretted me in all these things;
47 Yet *h'* thou not walked after their
48 as thou *h'* done, thou and thy
51 thou *h'* multiplied thine abominations
51 and *h'* justified thy sisters in all
51 abominations which thou *h'* done.
52 Thou also, which *h'* judged thy sisters,
52 that thou *h'* committed more
52 in that thou *h'* justified thy sisters.
54 all that thou *h'* done, in that thou art
58 Thou *h'* borne thy lewdness and
59 even deal with thee as thou *h'* done,
59 which *h'* despised the oath in
63 for all that thou *h'* done, saith the Lord
22: 4 guilty in thy blood that thou *h'* shed;
4 and *h'* defiled thyself in thine idols
4 thine idols which thou *h'* made; and
4 and thou *h'* caused thy days to draw
8 Thou *h'* despised mine holy things,
8 and *h'* profaned my sabbaths.
12 to shed blood; thou *h'* taken usury
12 and thou *h'* greedily gained of thy
12 and *h'* forgotten me, saith the Lord
13 gain which thou *h'* made, and at thy
23:30 because thou *h'* gone a whoring after
31 Thou *h'* walked in the way of thy
35 Because thou *h'* forgotten me, and
41 whereupon thou *h'* set mine incense
25: 6 Because thou *h'* clapped thine hands,
27: 3 O Tyrus, thou *h'* said, I am of perfect
28: 2 and thou *h'* said, I am a god, I sit in
4 understanding thou *h'* gotten thee
4 and *h'* gotten gold and silver into thy
5 and by thy traffick *h'* thou increased
6 Because thou *h'* set thine heart as
13 Thou *h'* been in Eden the garden
14 thou *h'* walked up and down in the
16 and thou *h'* sinned: therefore I will
17 thou *h'* corrupted thy wisdom by
18 Thou *h'* defiled thy sanctuaries by the
31:10 Because thou *h'* lifted up thyself in
32: 9 countries which thou *h'* not known.
33: 9 but thou *h'* delivered thy soul.
35: 5 Because thou *h'* had a perpetual
5 and *h'* shed the blood of the children
6 thou *h'* not hated blood, even blood
10 Because thou *h'* said, These two
11 which thou *h'* used out of thy hatred
12 which thou *h'* spoken against the
36:13 up men, and *h'* bereaved thy nations;
Eze 38:13 *h'* thou gathered thy company to take
43:23 When thou *h'* made an end of cleansing
47: 6 Son of man, *h'* thou seen this? Then
Da 2:23 my fathers, who *h'* given me wisdom
23 and *h'* made known unto me now
23 for thou *h'* now made known unto
3:10 Thou, O king, *h'* made a decree, that
12 certain Jews whom thou *h'* set over
12, 18 golden image which thou *h'* set up.
5:22 *h'* not humbled thine heart, though
23 But *h'* lifted up thyself against the
23 and thou *h'* praised the gods of silver,
6:12 *H'* thou not signed a decree, that
13 the decree that thou *h'* signed, but
9: 7 whither thou *h'* driven them, because
15 that *h'* brought thy people forth out
15 and *h'* gotten thee renown, as at this
10:19 speak; for thou *h'* strengthened me.
Ho 4: 6 because thou *h'* rejected knowledge,
6 seeing thou *h'* forgotten the law of
9: 1 for thou *h'* gone a whoring from thy
1 thou *h'* loved a reward upon every
10: 9 O Israel, thou *h'* sinned from the
13: 9 O Israel, thou *h'* destroyed thyself;
14: 1 thy God; for thou *h'* fallen by thine
Ob 15 as thou *h'* done, it shall be done unto
Jon 1:10 Why *h'* thou done this? For the men
14 for thou, O Lord, *h'* done as it pleased
2: 6 yet *h'* thou brought up my life from
4:10 Then said the Lord, Thou *h'* had pity
10 for the which thou *h'* not laboured,
Mic 7:20 which thou *h'* sworn unto our fathers
Na 3:16 Thou *h'* multiplied thy merchants
Hab 1:12 O Lord, thou *h'* ordained him for
2: 8 Because thou *h'* spoiled many nations,
10 Thou *h'* consulted shame to thy house
Zep 3:11 thou *h'* transgressed against me: for
Zec 1:12 thou *h'* had indignation these
Mal 1: 2 Wherein *h'* thou loved us? Was not
2:14 against whom thou *h'* dealt
M't 5:26 thou *h'* paid the uttermost farthing.
6: 6 and when thou *h'* shut thy door, pray
8:13 and as thou *h'* believed, so be it done
11:25 because thou *h'* hid these things
25 and *h'* revealed them unto babes.
17:27 and when thou *h'* opened his mouth
18:15 if he shall hear thee thou *h'* gained
19:21 go and sell that thou *h'*, and give
20:12 and thou *h'* made them equal unto us,
21:16 babes and sucklings thou *h'* perfected
25:21, 23 thou *h'* been faithful over a few
24 reaping where thou *h'* not sown,
24 gathering where thou *h'* not strawed:
25 lo, there thou *h'* that is thine.
26:25 He said unto him, Thou *h'* said.
64 Jesus saith unto him, Thou *h'* said:
27:46 my God, why *h'* thou forsaken me?
M'k 10:21 sell whatsoever thou *h'*, and give
12:32 Well, Master, thou *h'* said the truth:
15:34 my God, why *h'* thou forsaken me?
Lu 1: 4 wherein thou *h'* been instructed.
30 Fear not, Mary: for thou *h'* found
2:31 Which thou *h'* prepared before the
48 Son, why *h'* thou thus dealt with us?
7:43 unto him, Thou *h'* rightly judged.
10:21 earth, that thou *h'* hid these things
21 and *h'* revealed them unto babes:
28 Thou *h'* answered right: this do,
11:27 and the paps which thou *h'* sucked.
12:19 Soul, thou *h'* much goods laid up
20 things be, which thou *h'* provided?
59 thence, till thou *h'* paid the very last
13:26 and thou *h'* taught in our streets.
14:22 it is done as thou *h'* commanded, and
15:30 thou *h'* killed for him the fatted calf,
18:22 sell all that thou *h'*, and distribute
19:17 because thou *h'* been faithful in a
20:39 said, Master, thou *h'* well said.
24:18 and *h'* not known the things which
Joh 2:10 but thou *h'* kept the good wine until
4:11 Sir, thou *h'* nothing to draw with,
11 from whence then *h'* thou that
17 Thou *h'* well said, I have no
18 For thou *h'* had five husbands;
6:68 thou *h'* the words of eternal life.
7:20 Thou *h'* a devil: who goeth about
8:48 art a Samaritan, and *h'* a devil?
52 Now we know that thou *h'* a devil.
57 years old, and *h'* thou seen Abraham?
9:37 Thou *h'* both seen him, and it is he
11:41 I thank thee that thou *h'* heard me.
42 may believe that thou *h'* sent me.
13: 8 If I wash thee not, thou *h'* no part
38 crow, till thou *h'* denied me thrice.
14: 9 and yet *h'* thou not known me,
17: 2 As thou *h'* given him power over all
2 life to as many as thou *h'* given him.
3 and Jesus Christ, whom thou *h'* sent.
7 whatsoever thou *h'* given me are of
9 but for them which thou *h'* given me;
11 name those whom thou *h'* given me,
18 As thou *h'* sent me into the world,
21 world may believe that thou *h'* sent
23 world may know that thou *h'* sent me,
23 *h'* loved them, as thou *h'* loved me.
24 whom thou *h'* given me, be with me
24 glory which thou *h'* given me: for
25 these have known that thou *h'* sent
26 thou *h'* loved me may be in them, and
18:35 thee unto me: what *h'* thou done?
20:15 tell me where thou *h'* laid him, and I
29 Thomas, because thou *h'* seen me,
29 thou *h'* believed: blessed are they that
Ac 1:24 whether of these two thou *h'* chosen,
2:28 Thou *h'* made known to me the ways
4:24 which *h'* made heaven, and earth,
Ac 4:25 by the mouth of David *h'* said, Why
27 child Jesus whom thou *h'* anointed,
5: 4 why *h'* thou conceived this thing in
4 thou *h'* not lied unto men, but unto
8:20 because thou *h'* thought that the gift
21 Thou *h'* neither part nor lot in this
10:33 and thou *h'* well done that thou art
22:15 unto all men of what thou *h'* seen and
23:11 for as thou *h'* testified of me in
19 What is that thou *h'* to tell me?
24:10 I know that thou *h'* been of many
25:12 *H'* thou appealed unto Cæsar? unto
26:16 of these things which thou *h'* seen,
Ro 2:20 which *h'* the form of knowledge
9:20 formed it, Why *h'* thou made me thus?
14:22 *H'* thou faith? have it to thyself
1Co 4: 7 and what *h'* thou that thou didst
7:28 and if thou marry, thou *h'* not sinned;
8:10 see thee which *h'* knowledge sit
Col 4:17 the ministry which thou *h'* received
1Ti 4: 6 doctrine, whereunto thou *h'* attained.
6:12 and *h'* professed a good profession
2Ti 1:13 which thou *h'* heard of me, in faith and
2: 2 And the things that thou *h'* heard of
3:10 But thou *h'* fully known my doctrine,
14 in the things which thou *h'* learned
14 learned and *h'* been assured of,
14 knowing of whom thou *h'* learned
15 And that from a child thou *h'* known
Ph'm 5 which thou *h'* toward the Lord
Heb 1: 9 Thou *h'* loved righteousness, and
10 Thou, Lord, in the beginning *h'* laid
2: 8 Thou *h'* put all things in subjection
10: 5 not, but a body *h'* thou prepared me:
6 for sin thou *h'* had no pleasure.
Jas 2:18 Thou *h'* faith, and I have works:
Re 1:19 Write the things which thou *h'* seen,
2: 2 thou *h'* tried them which say they are
2 and are not, and *h'* found them liars:
3 And *h'* borne, and...patience,
3 borne, and *h'* patience, and hast
3 and for my name's sake *h'* laboured,
3 laboured, and *h'* not fainted.
4 thee, because thou *h'* left thy first
6 But this thou *h'*, that thou hatest
13 and *h'* not denied my faith, even in
14 because thou *h'* there them that
15 So *h'* thou also them that hold the
3: 1 that thou *h'* a name that thou
3 therefore how thou *h'* received
4 Thou *h'* a few names even in
8 for thou *h'* a little strength,
8 strength, and *h'* kept my word
8 my word, and *h'* not denied my name.
10 Because thou *h'* kept the word of my
11 hold that fast which thou *h'*, that
4:11 for thou *h'* created all things, and
5: 9 for thou wast slain, and *h'* redeemed
10 And *h'* made us unto our God kings
11:17 because thou *h'* taken to thee thy
17 thee thy great power, and *h'* reigned.
16: 5 shalt be, because thou *h'* judged thus.
6 thou *h'* given them blood to drink;

haste See also HASTED; HASTETH; HASTING.
Ge 19:22 *H'* thee, escape thither; for I
24:46 And she made *h'*, and let down her
43:30 And Joseph made *h'*; for his
45: 9 *H'* ye, and go up to my father,
13 and ye shall *h'* and bring down
Ex 10:16 called for Moses and Aaron in *h'*;
12:11 ye shall eat it in *h'*: it is the
33 send them out of the land in *h'*;
34: 8 And Moses made *h'*, and bowed
De 16: 3 out of the land of Egypt in *h'*:
32:35 shall come upon them make *h'*.
J'g 9:48 make *h'*, and do as I have done.
13:10 And the woman made *h'*, and ran,
1Sa 9:12 make *h'* now, for he came to day
20:38 Make speed, *h'*, stay not. And
21: 8 the king's business required *h'*.
23:26 David made *h'* to get away for
27 *H'* thee, and come; for the
25:18 Then Abigail made *h'*, and took
2Sa 4: 4 as she made *h'* to flee, that he
2Ki 7:15 Syrians had cast away in their *h'*.
2Ch 35:21 God commanded me to make *h'*;
Ezr 4:23 they went up in *h'* to Jerusalem
Es 5: 5 Cause Haman to make *h'*, that
6:10 Make *h'*, and take the apparel
Job 20: 2 answer, and for this I make *h'*.
Ps 22:19 my strength, *h'* thee to help me.
31:22 For I said in my *h'*, I am cut
38:22 Make *h'* to help me, O Lord
40:13 O Lord, make *h'* to help me.
70: 1 Make *h'*, O God, to deliver me;
1 make *h'* to help me, O Lord.
5 make *h'* unto me, O God: thou
71:12 my God, make *h'* for my help.
116:11 I said in my *h'*, All men are liars.
119:60 I made *h'*, and delayed not to keep
141: 1 I cry unto thee: make *h'* unto me;
Pr 1:16 evil, and make *h'* to shed blood.
28:20 but he that maketh *h'* to be rich
Ca 8:14 Make *h'*, my beloved, and be
Isa 28:16 that believeth shall not make *h'*.
49:17 Thy children shall make *h'*; thy
52:12 ye shall not go out with *h'*,
59: 7 they make *h'* to shed innocent
Jer 9:18 And let them make *h'*, and take
Da 2:25 in Daniel before the king in *h'*,
3:24 was astonied, and rose up in *h'*,
6:19 and went in *h'* unto the den of lions.
Na 2: 5 they shall make *h'* to the wall
M'r 6:25 she came in straightway with *h'*
Lu 1:39 went into the hill country with *h'*,
2:16 And they came with *h'*, and found

Lu 19: 5 Zacchæus, make h·, and come
6 And he made h·, and came down,
Ac 22:18 Make h·, and get thee quickly out
hasted See also HASTENED.
Ge 18: 7 young man; and he h· to dress it.
24:18 and she h·, and let down her
20 And she h·, and emptied her
Ex 5:13 the taskmasters h· them, saying,
Jos 4:10 and the people h· and passed over.
8:14 that they h· and rose up early,
19 and h· and set the city on fire.
10:13 h· not to go down about a whole
J'g 20:37 the liers in wait h·, and rushed
1Sa 17:48 that David h·, and ran toward
25:23 when Abigail saw David, she h·,
34 except thou hadst h· and come to
42 And Abigail h·, and arose, and
28:24 and she h·, and killed it, and took
2Sa 19:16 was of Bahurim, h· and came
1Ki 20:41 And he h·, and took the ashes
2Ki 9:13 Then they h·, and took every man
2Ch 26:20 himself h· also to go out, because
Es 6:12 h· to his house mourning, and
14 and h· to bring Haman unto the
Job 31: 5 or if my foot hath h· to deceit;
Ps 48: 5 they were troubled, and h· away.
104: 7 voice of thy thunder they h· away.
Ac 20:16 for he h·, if it were possible for
hasten See also HASTENED; HASTENETH.
1Ki 22: 9 H· hither Micaiah the son of
2Ch 24: 5 and see that ye h· the matter.
Ps 16: 4 be multiplied that h· after
55: 8 I would h· my escape from the
Ec 2:25 or who else can h· hereunto, more
Isa 5:19 Let him make speed, and h·
60:22 I the Lord will h· it in his time.
Jer 1:12 I will h· my word to perform it.
hastened See also HASTED.
Ge 18: 6 And Abraham h· into the tent
19:15 then the angels h· Lot, saying,
2Ch 24: 5 Howbeit the Levites h· it not.
Es 3:15 The posts went out, being h·
8:14 being h· and pressed on by the
Jer 17:16 I have not h· from being a pastor
hasteneth See also HASTETH.
Isa 51:14 The captive exile h· that he may
hasteth See also HASTENETH.
Job 9:26 as the eagle that h· to the prey.
40:23 drinketh up a river, and h· not:
Pr 7:23 as a bird h· to the snare,
19: 2 and he that h· with his feet sinneth.
28:22 He that h· to be rich hath an evil
Ec 1: 5 the sun goeth down, and h· to his
Jer 48:16 to come, and his affliction h· fast.
Hab 1: 8 fly as the eagle that h· to eat.
Zep 1:14 is near, it is near, and h· greatly,
hastily
Ge 41:14 and they brought him h· out of
J'g 2:23 without driving them out h·;
9:54 he called h· unto the young man
1Sa 4:14 And the man came in h·, and told
1Ki 20:33 and did h· catch it: and they said,
Pr 20:21 inheritance may be gotten h· at
25: 8 Go not forth h· to strive, lest thou
Joh 11:31 that she rose up h· and went out,
hasting
Isa 16: 5 judgment, and h· righteousness.
2Pe 3:12 h· unto the coming of the day of
hasty
Pr 14:29 but he that is h· of spirit exalteth
21: 5 every one that is h· only to want.
29:20 Seest thou a man that is h· in his
Ec 5: 2 let not thine heart be h· to utter
7: 9 Be not h· in thy spirit to be
8: 3 Be not h· to go out of his sight:
Isa 28: 4 the h· fruit before the summer;
Dan 2:15 Why is the decree so h· from the
Hab 1: 6 that bitter and h· nation, which
Hasupha (*has-u'-fah*) See also HASHUPHA.
Ezr 2:43 the children of H·, the children
Hatach (*ha'-tak*)
Es 4: 5 called Esther for H·, one of the
6 So H· went forth to Mordecai unto
9 And H· came and told Esther the
10 Esther spake unto H·, and gave
hatch See also HATCHETH.
Isa 34:15 make her nest, and lay, and h·,
59: 5 They h· cockatrice' eggs, and
hatcheth
Jer 17:11 partridge sitteth on eggs, and h·
hate See also HATED; HATEFUL; HATEST; HATETH; HATING.
Ge 24:60 the gate of those which h· them.
26:27 come ye to me, seeing ye h· me,
50:15 Joseph will peradventure h· us,
Ex 20: 5 fourth generation of them that h·
Le 19:17 Thou shalt not h· thy brother in
26:17 they that h· you shall reign over
Nu 10:35 let them that h· thee flee before
De 5: 9 fourth generation of them that h·
7:10 repayeth them that h· him to their
15 them upon all them that h· thee.
19:11 But if any man h· his neighbour,
22:13 go in unto her, and h· her,
24: 3 And if the latter husband h· her,
30: 7 on them that h· thee, which
32:41 and will reward them that h· me.
33:11 and of them that h· him, that they
J'g 11: 7 Did not ye h· me, and expel me out
14:16 Thou dost but h· me, and lovest me
2Sa 22:41 that I might destroy them that h·
1Ki 22: 8 but I h· him; for he doth not
2Ch 18: 7 but I h· him; for he never
19: 2 and love them that h· the Lord?
Job 8:22 They that h· thee shall be clothed
Ps 9:13 of them that h· me, thou that liftest
18:40 that I might destroy them that h·
21: 8 shall find out those that h· thee.
25:19 they h· me with cruel hatred.
34:21 and they that h· the righteous
35:19 eye that h· me without a cause.
38:19 they that h· me wrongfully are
41: 7 All that h· me whisper together
44:10 and they which h· us spoil for
55: 3 me, and in wrath they h· me.
68: 1 let them also that h· him flee
69: 4 They that h· me without a cause
14 delivered from them that h· me,
83: 2 and they that h· thee have lifted up
86:17 that they which h· me may see
89:23 face, and plague them that h· him.
97:10 Ye that love the Lord, h· evil:
101: 3 I h· the work of them that turn
105:25 turned their heart to h· his people,
118: 7 see my desire upon them that h·
119:104 therefore I h· every false way.
113 I h· vain thoughts: but thy law
128 right; and I h· every false way.
163 I h· and abhor lying: but thy law
129: 5 and turned back that h· Zion.
139:21 I h· them, O Lord, that h· thee?
22 I h· them with perfect hatred:
Pr 1:22 scorning, and fools h· knowledge?
6:16 These six things doth the Lord h·:
8:13 The fear of the Lord is to h· evil:
13 and the froward mouth, do I h·.
36 all they that h· me love death.
9: 8 Reprove not a scorner, lest he h·
19: 7 the brethren of the poor do h· him:
25:17 he be weary of thee, and so h· thee.
29:10 The bloodthirsty h· the upright:
Ec 3: 8 A time to love, and a time to h·;
Isa 61: 8 I h· robbery for burnt offering; and
Jer 44: 4 this abominable thing that I h·.
Eze 16:27 unto the will of them that h· thee,
Da 4:19 the dream be to them that h· thee,
Am 5:10 They h· him that rebuketh in the
15 H· the evil, and love the good,
21 I h·, I despise your feast days,
6: 8 and h· his palaces: therefore will I
Mic 3: 2 Who h· the good, and love the evil;
Zec 8:17 for all these are things that I h·,
M't 5:43 shalt love thy neighbour, and h·
44 do good to them that h· you,
6:24 for either he will h· the one,
24:10 another, and shall h· one another.
Lu 1:71 from the hand of all that h· us;
6:22 when men shall h· you, and when
27 enemies, do good to them which h·
14:26 and h· not his father, and mother,
16:13 either he will h· the one, and love
Joh 7: 7 cannot h· you; but me it hateth,
15:18 If the world h· you, ye know that
Ro 7:15 do I not; but what I h·, that do I.
1Jo 3:13 my brethren, if the world h· you.
Re 2: 6 of the Nicolaitanes, which I also h·.
15 the Nicolaitanes, which thing I h·.
17:16 these shall h· the whore, and shall
hated
Ge 27:41 And Esau h· Jacob because of the
29:31 the Lord saw that Leah was h·,
33 the Lord hath heard that I was h·,
37: 4 than all his brethren, they h· him,
5 and they h· him yet the more.
8 they h· him yet the more for his
49:23 and shot at him, and h· him:
De 1:27 Because the Lord h· us, he hath
4:42 h· him not in times past;
9:28 and because he h· them, he hath
19: 4 whom he h· not in times past;
6 as he h· him not in time past,
21:15 one beloved, and another h·, and
15 both the beloved and the h·;
15 firstborn son be her's that was h·:
16 firstborn before the son of the h·,
17 acknowledge the son of the h· for
Jos 20: 5 neighbour unwittingly, and h· him
J'g 15: 2 thought that thou hadst utterly h·
2Sa 5: 8 that are h· of David's soul, he shall
13:15 Then Amnon h· her exceedingly; so
15 the hatred wherewith he h· her was
22 for Absalom h· Amnon, because he
22:18 enemy, and from them that h· me:
Es 9: 1 Jews had rule over them that h·
5 what they would unto those that h·
Job 31:29 the destruction of him that h· me,
Ps 18:17 enemy, and from them which h· me
26: 5 I have h· the congregation of evil
31: 6 I have h· them that regard lying
44: 7 hast put them to shame that h· us.
55:12 neither was it he that h· me that
Pr 1:29 For that they h· knowledge, and
5:12 How have I h· instruction, and my
14:17 a man of wicked devices is h·.
20 The poor is h· even of his own
Ec 2:17 Therefore I h· life; because the
18 Yea, I h· all my labour which I had
Isa 60:15 thou hast been forsaken and h·, so
66: 5 Your brethren that h· you, that
Jer 12: 8 against me: therefore have I h· it.
Eze 16:37 with all them that thou hast h·;
35: 6 sith thou hast not h· blood, even
Ho 9:15 for there I h· them: for the
Mal 1: 3 I h· Esau, and laid his mountains
M't 10:22 ye shall be h· of all men for my
24: 9 and ye shall be h· of all nations for
M'r 13:13 And ye shall be h· of all men for my
Lu 19:14 But his citizens h· him, and sent a
Lu 21:17 And ye shall be h· of all men for my
Joh 15:18 ye know that it h· me before it
18 me before it h· you.
24 they both seen and h· both me
25 They h· me without a cause.
17:14 the world hath h· them, because
Ro 9:13 I loved, but Esau have I h·.
Eph 5:29 no man ever yet h· his own flesh;
Heb 1: 9 loved righteousness, and h· iniquity;
hateful
Ps 36: 2 his iniquity be found to be h·.
Tit 3: 3 envy, h·, and hating one another.
Re 18: 2 of every unclean and h· bird.
hatefully
Eze 23:29 they shall deal with thee h·,
haters
Ps 81:15 The h· of the Lord should have
Ro 1:30 h· of God, despiteful, proud,
hatest
2Sa 19: 6 thine enemies, and h· thy friends.
Ps 5: 5 thou h· all workers of iniquity.
45: 7 righteousness, and h· wickedness:
50:17 Seeing thou h· instruction, and
Eze 23:28 the hand of them whom thou h·,
Re 2: 6 thou h· the deeds of...Nicolaitanes,
hateth
Ex 23: 5 see the ass of him that h· thee
De 7:10 will not be slack to him that h· him,
12:31 which he h·, have they done unto
16:22 image; which the Lord thy God h·.
22:16 unto this man to wife, and he h· her;
Job 16: 9 teareth me in his wrath, who h· me:
34:17 even he that h· right govern?
Ps 11: 5 him that loveth violence his soul h·.
120: 6 long dwelt with him that h· peace.
Pr 11:15 and he that h· suretiship is sure.
12: 1 but he that h· reproof is brutish.
13: 5 A righteous man h· lying: but a
24 He that spareth his rod h· his son:
15:10 and he that h· reproof shall die.
27 but he that h· gifts shall live.
26:24 He that h· dissembleth with his lips,
28 A lying tongue h· those that are
28:16 he that h· covetousness shall
29:24 partner with a thief h· his own soul:
Isa 1:14 your appointed feasts my soul h·:
Mal 2:16 saith that he h· putting away:
Joh 3:20 h· the light, neither cometh to the
7: 7 cannot hate you; but me it h·,
12:25 he that h· his life in this world
15:19 world, therefore the world h· you.
23 He that h· me h· my Father also.
1Jo 2: 9 is in the light, and h· his brother,
11 But he that h· his brother is in
3:15 Whosoever h· his brother, is a
4:20 and h· his brother, he is a liar:
hath^A
Ge 1:20 the moving creature that h· life,
3: 1 Yea, h· God said, Ye shall not eat of
3 God h· said, Ye shall not eat of it,
4:11 earth, which h· opened her mouth to
25 For God, said she, h· appointed me
5:29 ground which the Lord h· cursed.
14:20 the most high God, which h· delivered
16: 2 Behold now, the Lord h· restrained
11 because the Lord h· heard thy
17:14 people; he h· broken my covenant.
18:19 Abraham that which he h· spoken
19:13 and the Lord h· sent us to destroy it.
19 thy servant h· found grace in thy
21: 6 Sarah said, God h· made me to laugh,
12 in all that Sarah h· said unto thee,
17 for God h· heard the voice of the lad
26 I wot not who h· done this thing:
22:20 Behold, Milcah, she h· also born
23: 9 me the cave of Machpelah, which he h·,
24:27 who h· not left destitute my master
35 And the Lord h· blessed my master
35 and he h· given him flocks,
36 unto him h· he given all that he h·.
44 woman whom the Lord h· appointed
51 son's wife, as the Lord h· spoken
56 seeing the Lord h· prospered my way;
26:22 For now the Lord h· made room for
27:27 of a field which the Lord h· blessed:
33 where is he that h· taken venison,
35 came with subtilty, and h· taken
36 for he h· supplanted me these two
36 behold, now he h· taken away my
29:32 Surely the Lord h· looked upon my
33 Because the Lord h· heard that I was
33 he h· therefore given me this son
30: 2 who h· withheld from thee the fruit
6 And Rachel said, God h· judged me,
6 and h· also heard my voice, and
6 voice, and h· given me a son:
18 Leah said, God h· given me my hire,
20 God h· endued me with a good dowry;
23 and said, God h· taken away my
27 the Lord h· blessed me for thy sake.
30 and the Lord h· blessed thee since
31: 1 saying, Jacob h· taken away all that
1 which was our father's h· he gotten
5 the God of my father h· been with me.
7 And your father h· deceived me,
9 Thus God h· taken away the cattle of
15 of him strangers? for he h· sold us,
15 and h· quite devoured also our
16 riches which God h· taken from
16 whatsoever God h· said unto thee,
42 God h· seen mine affliction and the
33: 5 which God h· graciously given thy
11 because God h· dealt graciously with
37:20 Some evil beast h· devoured him:

Ge 37:33 an evil beast h' devoured him;
38:24 Tamar thy daughter in law h' played
26 She h' been more righteous than I;
39: 8 me in the house, and he h' committed
8 all that he h' to my hands;
9 neither h' he kept back any thing from
14 See, he h' brought in an Hebrew unto
41:25 God h' shewed Pharaoh what he is
39 Forasmuch as God h' shewed thee all
51 For God, said he, h' made me forget
52 For God h' caused me to be fruitful
42:28 What is this that God h' done unto us?
43:23 God of your father, h' given you
44:16 God h' found out the iniquity of thy
45: 6 For these two years h' the famine been
8 but God: and he h' made me a father
9 God h' made me lord of all Egypt:
46:32 their trade h' been to feed cattle;
34 Thy servants' trade h' been about
47:18 my lord also h' our herds of cattle;
48: 9 my sons, whom God h' given me
11 and, lo, God h' shewed me also thy
Ex 3:13 The God of your fathers h' sent me
14 I Am h' sent me unto you.
15 the God of Jacob, h' sent me unto you:
18 The Lord God of the Hebrews h' met
4: 1 The Lord h' not appeared unto thee.
5 the God of Jacob, h' appeared unto
11 unto him, Who h' made man's mouth?
5: 3 The God of the Hebrews h' met with
23 to speak in thy name, he h' done evil
7:16 Lord God of the Hebrews h' sent me
9:18 hail, such as h' not been in Egypt
10:12 even all that the hail h' left.
12:25 give you, according as he h' promised,
13: 9 strong hand h' the Lord brought thee
14: 3 the wilderness h' shut them in.
15: 1 unto the Lord, for he h' triumphed
1 the horse and his rider h' he thrown
4 and his host h' he cast into the sea:
6 thy right hand, O Lord, h' dashed in
21 ye to the Lord, for he h' triumphed
21 the horse and his rider h' he thrown
16: 6 that the Lord h' brought you out
9 for he h' heard your murmurings.
15 bread which the Lord h' given you to
16 thing which the Lord h' commanded,
23 This is that which the Lord h' said,
29 See, for that the Lord h' given you the
17:16 Because the Lord h' sworn that
18:10 who h' delivered you out of the hand of
10 who h' delivered the people from under
19: 8 All that the Lord h' spoken we will do.
21: 8 her master, who h' betrothed her to
8 seeing he h' dealt deceitfully with
29 and it h' been testified to his owner,
29 and he h' not kept him in, but
29 that he h' killed a man or a woman;
36 that the ox h' used to push in time
36 and his owner h' not kept him in;
22:11 that he h' not put his hand unto his
24: 3 All the words which the Lord h' said
7 All that the Lord h' said will we do,
8 which the Lord h' made with you
32:24 Whosoever h' any gold, let them
33 Whosoever h' sinned against me,
35: 1 words which the Lord h' commanded,
10 make all that the Lord h' commanded;
30 See, the Lord h' called by name
31 And he h' filled him with the spirit
34 And he h' put in his heart that he
35 Them h' he filled with wisdom of
Le 4: 3 bring for his sin, which he h' sinned,
22 When a ruler h' sinned, and done
23 Or if his sin, wherein he h' sinned,
28 Or if his sin, which he h' sinned
28 blemish, for his sin which he h' sinned.
35 for his sin which he h' committed,
5: 1 whether he h' seen or known of it;
5 shall confess that he h' sinned in
6 Lord for his sin which he h' sinned,
7 his trespass, which he h' committed,
10 for him for his sin which he h' sinned,
13 that he h' sinned in one of these,
16 the harm that he h' done in the holy
19 he h' certainly trespassed against
6: 2 or h' oppressed his neighbour;
4 Then it shall be, because he h' sinned,
4 thing which he h' deceitfully gotten,
5 all that about which he h' sworn
7 for any thing of all that he h' done
10 the ashes which the fire h' consumed
7: 8 the burnt-offering which he h' offered.
8:34 As he h' done this day, so the Lord
34 h' commanded to do, to make an
10: 6 burning which the Lord h' kindled.
11 statutes which the Lord h' spoken
15 for ever; as the Lord h' commanded.
17 and God h' given it you to bear the
11: 9 whatsoever h' fins and scales in the
12 Whatsoever h' no fins nor scales in
42 whatsoever h' more feet among all
12: 7 the law for her that h' born a male
13: 4 shut up him that h' the plague seven
7 after that he h' been seen of the
12 skin of him that h' the plague from
13 him clean that h' the plague: it is
17 him clean that h' the plague: he is
31 shall shut up him that h' the plague
33 shall shut up him that h' the scall
41 And he that h' his hair fallen off
50 shut up it that h' the plague seven
14:43 after that he h' taken away the stones,
43 and after he h' scraped the house,
48 behold, the plague h' not spread in
15: 2 When any man h' a running issue

Le 15:4 bed, whereon he lieth that h' the issue,
6 whereon he sat that h' the issue
7 the flesh of him that h' the issue
8 And if he that h' the issue spit upon
9 he rideth upon that h' the issue
11 he toucheth that h' the issue,
11 and h' not rinsed his hands in water,
12 that he toucheth which h' the issue,
13 And when he that h' an issue is
32 This is the law of him that h' an issue,
33 and of him that h' an issue, of the
16:20 when he h' made an end of reconciling
17: 2 thing which the Lord h' commanded,
4 unto that man; he h' shed blood;
19: 8 because he h' profaned the hallowed
22 for his sin which he h' done:
22 and the sin which he h' done shall be
20: 3 because he h' given of his seed unto
9 he h' cursed his father or his mother;
11 with his father's wife h' uncovered
17 he h' uncovered his sister's nakedness;
18 he h' discovered her fountain,
18 and she h' uncovered the fountain
20 he h' uncovered his uncle's nakedness:
21 he h' uncovered his brother's
27 also or woman that h' a familiar
21: 3 him, which h' had no husband;
17 generations that h' any blemish,
18 man he be that h' a blemish,
18 or a lame, or that he h' a flat nose,
20 or a dwarf, or that h' a blemish in his
20 or scabbed, or h' his stones broken;
21 No man that h' a blemish of the seed
21 he h' a blemish; he shall not come
23 unto the altar, because he h' a blemish;
22: 4 is a leper, or h' a running issue;
5 whatsoever uncleanness he h';
6 The soul which h' touched any such
20 But whatsoever h' a blemish, that
23 bullock or a lamb that h' any thing
24:14 Bring forth him that h' cursed
19 as he h' done, so shall it be done
20 as he h' caused a blemish in a man,
25:25 brother be waxen poor, and h' sold
28 hand of him that h' bought it until
27:22 the Lord a field which he h' bought,
28 devote unto the Lord of all that he h',
Nu 5: 2 leper, and every one that h' an issue,
7 him against whom he h' trespassed.
27 And when he h' made her to drink
6: 9 and he h' defiled the head of his
21 law of the Nazarite who h' vowed,
10:29 the Lord h' spoken good concerning
12: 2 H' the Lord indeed spoken only by
2 h' he not spoken also by us?
14: 3 And wherefore h' the Lord brought
16 therefore he h' slain them in the
24 and h' followed me fully, him will
40 the place which the Lord h' promised:
15:22 which the Lord h' spoken unto
23 Even all that the Lord h' commanded
31 Because he h' despised the word of the
31 and h' broken his commandment,
16: 5 whom he h' chosen will he cause to
9 that the God of Israel h' separated
10 And he h' brought thee near to him,
28 shall know that the Lord h' sent me
29 then the Lord h' not sent me.
19: 2 law which the Lord h' commanded,
15 open vessel, which h' no covering
20 because he h' defiled the sanctuary
20 of separation h' not been sprinkled
20: 14 all the travel that h' befallen us;
16 and h' brought us forth out of Egypt:
21:28 it h' consumed Ar of Moab, and
29 he h' given his sons that escaped,
22:10 king of Moab, h' sent unto me, saying,
23: 7 Balak the king of Moab h' brought me
8 I curse, whom God h' not cursed?
8 whom the Lord h' not defied?
12 that which the Lord h' put in my
17 him, What h' the Lord spoken?
19 h' he said, and shall he not do it?
19 or h' he spoken, and shall he not
20 and he h' blessed; and I cannot
21 He h' not beheld iniquity in Jacob,
21 neither h' he seen perverseness in
22 he h' as it were the strength of an
23 and of Israel, What h' God wrought!
24: 3 said, Balaam the son of Beor h' said,
3 man whose eyes are open h' said:
4 He h' said, which heard the words of
6 aloes which the Lord h' planted,
8 he h' as it were the strength of an
11 the Lord h' kept thee back from
15 Balaam the son of Beor h' said,
15 man whose eyes are open h' said:
16 He h' said, which heard the words of
25:11 son of Aaron the priest, h' turned my
27: 4 his family, because he h' no son?
30: 1 thing which the Lord h' commanded.
4 her bond wherewith she h' bound
4 every bond wherewith she h' bound
5 her bonds wherewith she h' bound
12 if her husband h' utterly made them
12 her husband h' made them void;
15 them void after that he h' heard them;
31:17 kill every woman that h' known man
19 whosoever h' killed any person,
19 and whosoever h' touched any slain,
50 what every man h' gotten, of jewels
32: 7 the land which the Lord h' given
21 until he h' driven out his enemies
24 that which h' proceeded out of your
31 As the Lord h' said unto thy servants,
36: 5 of the sons of Joseph h' said well.

De 1:10 The Lord your God h' multiplied you,
11 and bless you, as he h' promised you!
21 the Lord thy God h' set the land
21 as the Lord God of thy fathers h' said
27 hated us, he h' brought us forth
36 I give the land that he h' trodden
36 because he h' wholly followed the
2: 7 For the Lord thy God h' blessed thee
7 the Lord thy God h' been with thee;
3:18 The Lord your God h' given you this
20 the Lord your God h' given them
21 all that the Lord your God h' done
4: 3 the Lord thy God h' destroyed them
7 great, who h' God so nigh unto them,
8 that h' statutes and judgments
19 which the Lord thy God h' divided
20 But the Lord h' taken you, and
23 which the Lord thy God h' forbidden
32 whether there h' been any such thing
32 as this great thing is, or h' been heard
34 Or h' God assayed to go and take him
5:12 as the Lord...God h' commanded thee.
16 as the Lord...God h' commanded thee;
24 Lord our God h' shewed us his glory
26 of all flesh, that h' heard the voice
32 as the Lord...God h' commanded you:
33 which the Lord...God h' commanded
6: 3 Lord God of thy fathers h' promised
17 his statutes, which he h' commanded
19 before thee, as the Lord h' spoken.
20 the Lord our God h' commanded
25 as he h' commanded us.
7: 1 and h' cast out many nations before
6 the Lord thy God h' chosen thee to be
8 unto your fathers, h' the Lord brought
8:10 for the good land which he h' given
17 the might of mine hand h' gotten me
9: 3 them quickly, as the Lord h' said
4 after that the Lord thy God h' cast
4 the Lord h' brought me in to possess
28 he h' brought them out to slay them
10: 9 Levi h' no part nor inheritance
21 he is thy God, that h' done for thee
22 now the Lord thy God h' made thee as
11: 4 and how the Lord h' destroyed them
25 ye shall tread upon, as he h' said unto
29 when the Lord thy God h' brought
12: 7 wherein the Lord thy God h' blessed
12 forasmuch as he h' no part nor
15 of the Lord thy God which he h' given
20 enlarge thy border, as he h' promised
21 the Lord thy God h' chosen to put
13: 5 because he h' spoken to turn you
10 because he h' sought to thrust thee
12 which the Lord thy God h' given thee
17 as he h' sworn unto thy fathers;
14: 2 and the Lord h' chosen thee to be a
10 And whatsoever h' not fins and scales
24 when the Lord thy God h' blessed
27 he h' no part nor inheritance with
29 And the Levite, (because he h' no part
15:14 wherewith the Lord thy God h' blessed
18 for he h' been worth a double hired
16:10 as the Lord thy God h' blessed thee:
11 which the Lord thy God h' chosen to
17 of the Lord thy God which he h' given
17: 2 man or woman, that h' wrought
3 And h' gone and served other gods,
16 forasmuch as the Lord h' said unto
18: 2 is their inheritance, as he h' said unto
5 For the Lord thy God h' chosen him
14 the Lord thy God h' not suffered thee
21 word which the Lord h' not spoken?
22 thing which the Lord h' not spoken,
22 but the prophet h' spoken it
19: 1 When the Lord thy God h' cut off the
8 enlarge thy coast, as he h' sworn unto
18 a false witness, and h' testified falsely
20: 5 What man is there that h' built a new
5 house, and h' not dedicated it?
6 what man is he that h' planted a
6 vineyard, and h' not yet eaten of it?
7 what man is there that h' betrothed
7 a wife, and h' not taken her?
13 when the Lord thy God h' delivered it
14 which the Lord thy God h' given thee.
17 as the Lord thy God h' commanded
21: 1 and it be not known who h' slain him:
3 which h' not been wrought with,
3 and which h' not drawn in the yoke;
5 the Lord thy God h' chosen to minister
10 the Lord thy God h' delivered them
16 sons to inherit that which he h',
17 a double portion of all that he h':
22: 3 which he h' lost, and thou hast found,
17 And, lo, he h' given occasions of
19 because he h' brought up an evil
21 because she h' wrought folly in Israel,
24 because he h' humbled his neighbour's
29 because he h' humbled her, he may
23: 1 or h' his privy member cut off, shall
24: 1 When a man h' taken a wife,
1 because he h' found some uncleanness
5 When a man h' taken a new wife,
5 cheer up his wife which he h' taken.
25:10 house of him that h' his shoe loosed.
19 when the Lord thy God h' given thee
26: 9 And he h' brought us into this place,
9 and h' given us this land,
11 which the Lord thy God h' given unto
16 day the Lord thy God h' commanded
18 And the Lord h' avouched thee this
18 peculiar people, as he h' promised
19 above all nations which he h' made,
19 the Lord thy God, as he h' spoken.
27: 3 Lord God of thy fathers h' promised

De 28: 9 people unto himself, as he h' sworn
52 which the Lord thy God h' given thee.
53 which the Lord thy God h' given thee,
55 because he h' nothing left him in the
29: 4 Yet the Lord h' not given you an
13 be unto thee a God, as he h' said unto
13 and as he h' sworn unto thy fathers,
22 sicknesses which the Lord h' laid
24 Wherefore h' the Lord done thus
30: 1 whither the Lord thy God h' driven
3 whither the Lord thy God h' scattered
31: 2 also the Lord h' said unto me, Thou
3 go before thee, as the Lord h' said.
7 land which the Lord h' sworn unto
32: 6 is not he thy father that h' bought
6 h' he not made thee, and established
27 and the Lord h' not done all this.
Jos 1:13 The Lord your God h' given you rest,
13 and h' given you this land.
15 your brethren rest, as he h' given you,
2: 9 I know that the Lord h' given you the
14 it shall be, when the Lord h' given us
24 Truly the Lord h' delivered into our
6:16 Shout; for the Lord h' given you the
22 thence the woman, and all that she h',
7:11 Israel h' sinned, and they have also
15 burnt with fire, he and all that he h':
15 because he h' transgressed the
15 and because he h' wrought folly in
8:31 over which no man h' lift up any iron:
10: 4 for it h' made peace with Joshua
19 the Lord your God h' delivered them
14:10 behold, the Lord h' kept me alive,
17:14 forasmuch as the Lord h' blessed me
18: 3 the Lord God of your fathers h' given
22: 4 now the Lord your God h' given rest
25 For the Lord h' made Jordan a border
23: 3 all that the Lord your God h' done
3 the Lord your God is he that h' fought
5 as the Lord your God h' promised
9 For the Lord h' driven out from before
9 but as for you, no man h' been able to
10 fighteth for you as he h' promised
13 which the Lord your God h' given you.
14 that not one thing h' failed of all the
14 and not one thing h' failed thereof.
15 which the Lord your God h' given you.
16 off the good land which he h' given
24:20 after that he h' done you good.
27 for it h' heard all the words of the
J'g 1: 7 as I have done, so God h' requited me.
2:20 that this people h' transgressed
3:28 for the Lord h' delivered your enemies
4: 6 said unto him, H' not the Lord God of
14 day in which the Lord h' delivered
6:13 but now the Lord h' forsaken us,
25 the altar of Baal that thy father h',
29 to another, Who h' done this thing?
29 Gideon the son of Joash h' done this
30 because he h' cast down the altar of
30 and because he h' cut down the grove
31 because one h' cast down his altar.
32 because he h' thrown down his altar.
7: 2 saying, Mine own hand h' saved me.
14 into his hand h' God delivered Midian,
15 for the Lord h' delivered into your
8: 3 God h' delivered into your hands
7 Therefore when the Lord h' delivered
11:23 the Lord God of Israel h' dispossessed
36 according to that which h' proceeded
36 as the Lord h' taken vengeance
13:10 Behold, the man h' appeared unto me,
15: 6 the Philistines said, Who h' done this?
10 up, to do to him as he h' done to us.
16:17 There h' not come a razor upon mine
18 for he h' shewed me all his heart.
23 Our god h' delivered Samson our
24 Our god h' delivered into our hands
18: 4 Micah with me, and h' hired me,
10 for God h' given it into your hands;
21:11 and every woman that h' lain by man.
Ru 1:20 for the Almighty h' dealt very bitterly
21 and the Lord h' brought me home
21 seeing the Lord h' testified against
21 and the Almighty h' afflicted me?
2: 7 so she came, and h' continued even
11 unto her, It h' fully been shewed me,
20 Blessed be he of the Lord, who h' not
4:14 Blessed be the Lord, which h' not left
15 to thee than seven sons, h' born him.
1Sa 1:27 and the Lord h' given me my petition
2: 5 so that the barren h' born seven;
5 she that h' many children is waxed
8 and he h' set the world upon them.
3:17 the thing that the Lord h' said unto
4: 3 Wherefore h' the Lord smitten us
7 for there h' not been such a thing
17 and there h' been also a great
6: 7 on which there h' come no yoke,
9 then he h' done us this great evil:
7:12 saying, Hitherto h' the Lord helped
9:24 for unto this time h' it been kept
10: 1 Is it not because the Lord h' anointed
2 lo, thy father h' left the care of
22 Behold, he h' hid himself among the
24 See ye him whom the Lord h' chosen,
11:13 to day the Lord h' wrought salvation
12:13 behold, the Lord h' set a king over you.
22 because it h' pleased the Lord to make
24 consider how great things he h' done
13:14 the Lord h' sought him a man after
14 and the Lord h' commanded him
14:10 the Lord h' delivered them into our
12 the Lord h' delivered them into the
29 My father h' troubled the land: see
38 and see wherein this sin h' been

1Sa 14:45 Shall Jonathan die, who h' wrought
45 for he h' wrought with God this day.
15:11 h' not performed my commandments.
16 I will tell thee what the Lord h' said
22 said, H' the Lord as great delight
23 he h' also rejected thee from being
26 the Lord h' rejected thee from being
28 the Lord h' rent the kingdom of
28 and h' given it to a neighbour of
33 As thy sword h' made women
16: 8, 9 Neither h' the Lord chosen this.
10 Jesse, The Lord h' not chosen these.
22 for he h' found favour in my sight.
17:36 seeing he h' defied the armies of the
18: 7 Saul h' slain his thousands, and David
22 Behold, the king h' delight in thee,
19: 4 because he h' not sinned against thee,
20:13 as he h' been with my father.
15 not when the Lord h' cut off the
22 go thy way: for the Lord h' sent thee
26 for he thought, Something h' befallen
29 for our family h' a sacrifice in the city;
29 my brother, he h' commanded me
32 shall he be slain? what h' he done?
21: 2 The king h' commanded me a
2 and h' said unto me, Let no man
11 Saul h' slain his thousands, and David
22: 8 my son h' made a league with the
8 that my son h' stirred up my
23: 7 God h' delivered him into mine hand;
7 entering into a town that h' gates and
10 thy servant h' certainly heard that
11 come down, as thy servant h' heard?
22 where his haunt is, and who h' seen
25:21 all that this fellow h' in the wilderness,
26 seeing the Lord h' withholden thee
27 thine handmaid h' brought unto my
28 and evil h' not been found in thee
30 all the good that he h' spoken
31 or that my lord h' avenged himself:
34 which h' kept me back from hurting
39 the Lord, that h' pleaded the cause of
39 and h' kept his servant from evil:
26: 8 God h' delivered thine enemy into
27:12 saying, He h' made his people Israel
28: 7 a woman that h' a familiar spirit,
7 a woman that h' a familiar spirit
9 thou knowest what Saul h' done,
9 how he h' cut off those that have
17 And the Lord h' done to him, as he
17 for the Lord h' rent the kingdom
18 therefore h' the Lord done this thing
21 Behold thine handmaid h' obeyed thy
29: 3 which h' been with me these days,
30:23 with that which the Lord h' given us,
23 who h' preserved us and delivered
2Sa 1:16 for thy mouth h' testified against thee,
3: 9 as the Lord h' sworn to David, even so
18 for the Lord h' spoken of David,
23 and he h' sent him away, and he is
29 one that h' an issue, or that is a leper,
4: 8 and the Lord h' avenged my lord the
9 As the Lord liveth, who h' redeemed
5:20 The Lord h' broken forth upon mine
6:12 The Lord h' blessed the house of
7:27 therefore h' thy servant found in his
9: 3 Jonathan h' yet a son, which is lame
11 that my lord the king h' commanded
10: 3 that he h' sent comforters unto thee?
3 h' not David rather sent his servants
12: 5 the man that h' done this thing
13 The Lord also h' put away thy sin;
13:20 H' Amnon thy brother been with
24 thy servant h' sheepshearers; let the
32 of Absalom this h' been determined
14:19 that my lord the king h' spoken:
20 h' thy servant Joab done this thing:
22 in that the king h' fulfilled the request
30 field is near mine, and he h' barley
15: 4 that every man which h' any suit or
16: 8 The Lord h' returned upon thee all the
8 and the Lord h' delivered the
10 because the Lord h' said unto him,
11 let him curse; for the Lord h' bidden
21 which he h' left to keep the house;
17: 6 Ahithophel h' spoken after this
7 that Ahithophel h' given is not good
21 for thus h' Ahithophel counselled
18:19 how that the Lord h' avenged him of
28 the Lord thy God, which h' delivered
31 for the Lord h' avenged thee this day
19:27 And he h' slandered thy servant unto
42 or h' he given us any gift?
20:21 Bichri by name, h' lifted up his hand
22:21 of my hands h' he recompensed me.
25 Therefore the Lord h' recompensed
36 and thy gentleness h' made me great.
23: 5 yet he h' made with me an everlasting
1Ki 1:19 And he h' slain oxen and fat cattle
19 and h' called all the sons of the king,
19 Solomon thy servant h' he not called.
25 gone down this day, and h' slain oxen
25 and h' called all the king's sons,
26 thy servant Solomon, h' he not called.
29 As the Lord liveth, that h' redeemed
37 As the Lord h' been with my lord
43 lord king David h' made Solomon king.
44 And the king h' sent with him Zadok
48 which h' given one to sit on my throne
51 lo, he h' caught hold on the horns of
2:24 the Lord liveth, which h' established
24 and who h' made me an house,
31 Do as he h' said, and fall upon him,
38 as my lord the king h' said, so will
5: 4 the Lord my God h' given me rest
7 the Lord this day, which h' given unto

1Ki 8:15 and h' with his hand fulfilled it,
20 And the Lord h' performed his word
56 Blessed be the Lord, that h' given rest
56 there h' not failed one word of all his
9: 8 Why h' the Lord done thus unto this
9 therefore h' the Lord brought upon
12:11 father h' chastised you with whips,
13: 3 is the sign which the Lord h' spoken;
26 therefore the Lord h' delivered him
26 unto the lion, which h' torn him,
14:11 the air eat: for the Lord h' spoken it.
16:16 Zimri h' conspired, and h' also slain
18:10 whither my Lord h' not sent to seek
19:18 and every mouth which h' not kissed
22:23 behold, the Lord h' put a lying spirit
23 and the Lord h' spoken evil concerning
28 the Lord h' not spoken by me.
2Ki 1: 9 Thou man of God, the king h' said,
11 O man of God, thus h' the king said,
2: 2 for the Lord h' sent me to Beth-el.
4 for the Lord h' sent me to Jericho.
6 for the Lord h' sent me to Jordan.
16 the Spirit of the Lord h' taken him up,
3: 7 The king of Moab h' rebelled against
10 that the Lord h' called these three
13 for the Lord h' called these three
4: 2 Thine handmaid h' not any thing in
14 Verily she h' no child, and her
27 and the Lord h' hid it from me,
27 hid it from me, and h' not told me.
5:20 Behold, my master h' spared Naaman
22 My master h' sent me, saying,
6:29 eat him: and she h' hid her son.
32 this son of a murderer h' sent to take
7: 6 Lo, the king of Israel h' hired against
8: 1 for the Lord h' called for a famine;
4 the great things that Elisha h' done.
9 king of Syria h' sent me to thee,
10 the Lord h' shewed me that he shall
13 The Lord h' shewed me that thou shalt
10:10 for the Lord h' done that which he
14:10 and thine heart h' lifted thee up:
17:26 therefore he h' sent lions among
18:22 and whose altars Hezekiah h' taken
22 and h' said to Judah and Jerusalem,
27 H' my master sent me to thy master,
27 h' he not sent me to the men which
33 H' any of the gods of the nations
19: 4 king of Assyria his master h' sent to
4 which the Lord thy God h' heard:
16 which h' sent him to reproach the
21 the word that the Lord h' spoken
21 the daughter of Zion h' despised thee,
21 the daughter of Jerusalem h' shaken
20: 9 will do the thing that he h' spoken:
21:11 Manasseh king of Judah h' done these
11 abominations, and h' done wickedly
11 and h' made Judah also to sin
22:10 Hilkiah the priest h' delivered
16 book which the king of Judah h' read:
1Ch 14:11 God h' broken in upon mine enemies
15: 2 for them h' the Lord chosen to carry
16:12 his marvellous works that he h' done,
17 And h' confirmed the same to Jacob
17:25 therefore thy servant h' found in his
19: 3 that he h' sent comforters unto thee?
22:11 house of the Lord thy God, as he h' said
18 and h' he not given you rest on every
18 for he h' given the inhabitants of the
23:25 The Lord God of Israel h' given rest
28: 4 for he h' chosen Judah to be the ruler;
5 for the Lord h' given me many sons,
5 he h' chosen Solomon my son to sit
10 for the Lord h' chosen thee to build an
29: 1 whom alone God h' chosen, is yet
2Ch 2:11 Because the Lord h' loved his people,
11 he h' made thee king over them.
12 who h' given to David the king a wise
15 which my lord h' spoken of, let him
6: 1 The Lord h' said that he would dwell
4 who h' with his hands fulfilled that
10 The Lord therefore h' performed his
10 that he h' spoken: for I am risen
7:21 Why h' the Lord done thus unto this
22 therefore h' he brought all this evil
8:11 the ark of the Lord h' come.
13: 6 is risen up, and h' rebelled against
14: 7 we have sought him, and he h' given
15: 3 long season Israel h' been without
18:22 the Lord h' put a lying spirit in the
22 and the Lord h' spoken evil against
27 in peace, then h' not the Lord spoken
20:37 the Lord h' broken thy works.
23: 3 as the Lord h' said of the sons of
24:20 forsaken the Lord, he h' also forsaken
25: 8 for God h' power to help, and to
16 I know that God h' determined to
28: 9 he h' delivered them into your hand,
29: 8 and he h' delivered them to trouble,
11 for the Lord h' chosen you to stand
30: 8 his sanctuary, which he h' sanctified
31:10 for the Lord h' blessed his people;
32:12 H' not the same Hezekiah taken
34:18 Hilkiah the priest h' given me a book.
36:23 kingdoms of the earth h' the Lord
23 heaven given me; and he h' charged
Ezr 1: 2 The Lord God of heaven h' given me
2 and he h' charged me to build him
4: 3 the king of Persia h' commanded us.
18 ye sent unto us h' been plainly read
19 commanded, and search h' been made,
19 this city of old time h' made
5: 3 Who h' commanded you to build this
16 even until now h' it been in building
6:12 the God that h' caused his name to
7:27 which h' put such a thing as this in

Ezr 7:28 And h' extended mercy unto me
9: 2 princes and rulers h' been chief
8 little space grace h' been shewed
9 yet our God h' not forsaken us in our
9 but h' extended mercy unto us in the
Es 1:15 because she h' not performed the
16 Vashti the queen h' not done wrong
5: 5 that he may do as Esther h' said.
8 will do to morrow as the king h' said.
6: 3 What honour and dignity h' been done
Job 1:10 about all that he h' on every side?
11 touch all that he h', and he will curse
12 all that he h' is in thy power; only
16 and h' burned up the sheep, and the
21 the Lord gave, and the Lord h' taken
2: 4 all that a man h' will he give for his
3:23 and whom God h' hedged in?
5:16 So the poor h' hope, and iniquity
6: 5 the wild ass bray when he h' grass?
7: 8 The eye of him that h' seen me shall
9: 4 who h' hardened himself against him,
4 against him and h' prospered?
10:12 and thy visitation h' preserved my
12: 9 the hand of the Lord h' wrought this?
13 and strength, he h' counsel and
13: 1 Lo, mine eye h' seen all this,
12 mine ear h' heard and understood it.
16: 7 But now he h' made me weary:
12 I was at ease, but he h' broken me:
12 he h' also taken me by my neck,
17: 6 He h' made me also a byword of the
9 and he that h' clean hands shall
19: 6 Know now that God h' overthrown
6 and h' compassed me with his net.
8 He h' fenced up my way that I cannot
8 pass, and he h' set darkness in my
9 He h' stripped me of my glory,
10 He h' destroyed me on every side,
10 and mine hope h' he removed like a
11 He h' also kindled his wrath against
13 He h' put my brethren far from me,
21 for the hand of the Lord h' touched
20:15 He h' swallowed down riches, and
19 Because he h' oppressed and
19 oppressed and h' forsaken the poor;
19 he h' violently taken away an house,
21:21 For what pleasure h' he in his house
31 shall repay him what he h' done?
23:10 when he h' tried me, I shall come
11 My foot h' held his steps, his way
17 neither h' he covered the darkness
26: 2 the arm that h' no strength?
3 counselled him that h' no wisdom?
6 and destruction h' no covering.
10 He h' compassed the waters with
13 By his spirit he h' garnished the
13 his hand h' formed the crooked
27: 2 As God liveth, who h' taken away my
2 the Almighty, who h' vexed my soul;
8 the hypocrite, though he h' gained,
28: 6 of sapphires: and it h' dust of gold.
7 which the vulture's eye h' not seen:
30:11 Because he h' loosed my cord, and
19 He h' cast me into the mire, and I
31: 5 or my foot h' hasted to deceit;
7 If my step h' turned out of the way,
7 and if any blot h' cleaved to mine
17 the fatherless h' not eaten thereof;
27 my heart h' been secretly enticed,
27 or my mouth h' kissed my hand:
32:14 Now he h' not directed his words
19 my belly is as wine which h' no vent;
33: 2 my tongue h' spoken in my mouth.
4 The Spirit of God h' made me,
4 breath of the Almighty h' given me
34: 5 For Job h' said, I am righteous:
5 and God h' taken away my judgment.
9 For he h' said, It profiteth a man
13 Who h' given him a charge over the
13 or who h' disposed the whole world?
35 Job h' spoken without knowledge,
35:15 it is not so, he h' visited in his anger;
36:23 Who h' enjoined him his way?
38: 5 Who h' laid the measures thereof,
5 or who h' stretched the line upon it?
25 Who h' divided a watercourse for the
28 H' the rain a father? or who
28 h' begotten the drops of dew?
29 hoary frost of heaven, who h' gendered
36 Who h' put wisdom in the inward
36 or who h' given understanding to the
39: 5 Who h' sent out the wild ass free?
5 or who h' loosed the bands of the
17 Because God h' deprived her of
17 neither h' he imparted to her
41:11 Who h' prevented me, that I should
42: 7 that is right as my servant Job h'.
Ps 2: 7 the Lord h' said unto me, Thou art
4: 3 know that the Lord h' set apart him
5: 4 thou art not a God that h' pleasure in
6: 8 for the Lord h' heard the voice of my
9 The Lord h' heard my supplication;
7:12 he h' bent his bow, and made it ready.
13 He h' also prepared for him the
14 iniquity, and h' conceived mischief,
9: 7 he h' prepared his throne for
10: 6 He h' said in his heart, I shall not
11 He h' said in his heart, God
11 said in his heart, God h' forgotten:
13 he h' said in his heart, Thou wilt
13: 6 because he h' dealt bountifully with
14: 1 The fool h' said in his heart, There is
16: 7 bless the Lord, who h' given me
18:20 of my hands h' he recompensed me.
24 Therefore h' the Lord recompensed
35 and thy right hand h' holden me

Ps 18:35 and thy gentleness h' made me great.
19: 4 In them h' he set a tabernacle for the
22:24 For he h' not despised nor abhorred
24 neither h' he hid his face from him;
31 shall be born, that he h' done this.
24: 2 For he h' founded it upon the seas,
4 He that h' clean hands, and a pure
4 who h' not lifted up his soul unto
28: 6 because he h' heard the voice
31:21 for he h' shewed me his marvellous
33:12 and the people whom he h' chosen
35: 8 let his net that he h' hid catch
21 Aha, aha, our eye h' seen it.
27 which h' pleasure in the prosperity
36: 3 he h' left off to be wise, and to do
37:16 little that a righteous man h' is better
40: 3 And he h' put a new song in my
41: 9 which did eat of my bread, h' lifted up
44:15 and the shame of my face h' covered
45: 2 therefore God h' blessed thee for ever.
7 thy God, h' anointed thee with the oil
46: 8 what desolations he h' made in the
50: 1 even the Lord, h' spoken, and called
2 perfection of beauty, God h' shined.
53: 1 The fool h' said in his heart, There is
5 for God h' scattered the bones of
5 because God h' despised them.
54: 7 For he h' delivered me out of all my
7 and mine eye h' seen his desire upon
55: 5 and horror h' overwhelmed me.
18 He h' delivered my soul in peace
20 He h' put forth his hands against
20 with him: he h' broken his covenant.
60: 6 God h' spoken in his holiness;
62:11 God h' spoken once; twice have I
66:14 have uttered, and my mouth h' spoken,
16 I will declare what he h' done for my
19 But verily God h' heard me;
19 he h' attended to the voice of my
20 Blessed be God, which h' not turned
68:10 Thy congregation h' dwelt therein:
28 Thy God h' commanded thy strength:
69: 7 borne reproach; shame h' covered my
9 zeal of thine house h' eaten me up;
20 Reproach h' broken my heart; and I
31 an ox or bullock that h' horns and
71:11 saying, God h' forsaken him:
72:12 poor also, and him that h' no helper.
74: 3 all that the enemy h' done wickedly
18 that the enemy h' reproached, O Lord,
77: 9 H' God forgotten to be gracious?
9 h' he in anger shut up his tender
78: 4 his wonderful works that he h' done.
69 like the earth which he h' established
80:15 which thy right hand h' planted,
84: 3 Yea, the sparrow h' found an house,
88: 4 I am as a man that h' no strength:
91:14 Because he h' set his love upon me,
93: 1 wherewith he h' girded himself: the
98: 1 for he h' done marvellous things: his
1 his holy arm, h' gotten him the victory.
2 The Lord h' made known his
2 his righteousness h' he openly shewed
3 He h' remembered his mercy and his
100: 3 it is he that h' made us, and not we
101: 5 him that h' an high look and a proud
102:19 For he h' looked down from the
103:10 He h' not dealt with us after our sins;
12 far h' he removed our transgressions
19 The Lord h' prepared his throne in
104:16 of Lebanon, which he h' planted;
105: 5 his marvellous works that he h' done;
8 He h' remembered his covenant
107: 2 whom he h' redeemed from the hand
16 For he h' broken the gates of brass,
108: 7 God h' spoken in his holiness;
109:11 Let the extortioner catch all that he h';
110: 4 The Lord h' sworn, and will not
111: 4 He h' made his wonderful works to be
5 He h' given meat unto them that fear
6 He h' shewed his people the power
9 he h' commanded his covenant
112: 9 He h' dispersed, he h' given to the
115: 3 God is in the heavens: he h' done
3 done whatsoever he h' pleased.
12 The Lord h' been mindful of us:
16 but the earth h' he given to the
116: 1 I love the Lord, because he h' heard ‡
2 Because he h' inclined his ear unto
7 for the Lord h' dealt bountifully with
118:18 The Lord h' chastened me sore:
18 but he h' not given me over unto
24 is the day which the Lord h' made;
27 God is the Lord, which h' shewed us
119:20 the longing that it h' unto thy
50 for thy word h' quickened me.
53 Horror h' taken hold upon me because
139 My zeal h' consumed me, because
167 My soul h' kept thy testimonies;
120: 6 My soul h' long dwelt with him that
124: 6 who h' not given us as a prey to their
126: 2 Lord h' done great things for them.
3 The Lord h' done great things for us;
127: 5 Happy is the man that h' his quiver
129: 4 he h' cut asunder the cords of the
132:11 The Lord h' sworn in truth unto
135: 4 For the Lord h' chosen Jacob unto
136:24 And h' redeemed us from our
138: 6 Lord be high, yet h' he respect unto
143: 3 For the enemy h' persecuted my soul;
3 he h' smitten my life down to the
3 he h' made me to dwell in darkness,
146: 5 Happy is he that h' the God of Jacob
147:13 For he h' strengthened the bars of thy
13 he h' blessed thy children within thee.
20 He h' not dealt so with any nation:

Ps 148: 6 He h' also stablished them for ever
6 he h' made a decree which shall not
150: 6 Let every thing that h' breath praise
Pr 3:19 The Lord by wisdom h' founded the
19 by understanding h' he established
7:20 He h' taken a bag of money with him,
26 For she h' cast down many wounded:
9: 1 Wisdom h' builded her house,
1 she h' hewn out her seven pillars:
2 She h' killed her beasts;
2 she h' mingled her wine;
2 she h' also furnished her table.
3 She h' sent forth her maidens:
10:13 the lips of him that h' understanding
23 a man of understanding h' wisdom.
12: 9 He that is despised, and h' a servant,
13: 4 the sluggard desireth, and h' nothing:
7 maketh himself rich, yet h' nothing:
7 himself poor, yet h' great riches.
14:20 but the rich h' many friends.
21 but he that h' mercy on the poor,
31 but he that honoureth him h' mercy on
32 but the righteous h' hope in his death.
33 heart of him that h' understanding:
15:14 the heart of him that h' understanding
15 a merry heart h' a continual feast.
23 A man h' joy by the answer of his
16: 4 The Lord h' made all things for
22 of life unto him that h' it.
17: 8 stone in the eyes of him that h' it:
16 seeing he h' no heart to it?
20 He that h' a froward heart findeth no
20 and he that h' a perverse tongue
21 and the father of a fool h' no joy.
24 is before him that h' understanding;
27 He that h' knowledge spareth his 3045
18: 2 A fool h' no delight in understanding,
24 A man that h' friends must shew
19:17 He that h' pity upon the poor lendeth
17 that which he h' given will he pay
23 and he that h' it shall abide satisfied;
25 reprove one that h' understanding,
20:12 the Lord h' made even both of them.
22: 9 He that h' a bountiful eye shall be
23: 6 the bread of him that h' an evil eye,
29 Who h' woe? who h' sorrow?
29 who h' contentions? who h' babbling?
29 who h' wounds without cause?
29 who h' redness of eyes?
24:29 I will do so to him as he h' done to me:
25: 8 thy neighbour h' put thee to shame.
28 He that h' no rule over his own
28:11 but the poor that h' understanding
22 He that hasteth to be rich h' an evil
30: 4 Who h' ascended up into heaven, or
15 The horseleach h' two daughters,
Ec 1: 3 What profit h' a man of all his labour
9 The thing that h' been, it is that which
10 it h' been already of old time,
13 this sore travail h' God given to the
2:12 even that which h' been already done.
21 yet to a man that h' not laboured
22 For what h' man of all his labour,
22 he h' laboured under the sun?
3: 9 What profit h' he that worketh in that
10 the travail, which God h' given to the
11 He h' made every thing beautiful in
11 also he h' set the world in their heart,
15 That which h' been is now; and
15 that which is to be h' already been;
19 so that a man h' no preeminence
4: 3 both they, which h' not yet been,
3 who h' not seen the evil work that
8 yea, he h' neither child nor brother:
10 for he h' not another to help him up.
5:16 so shall he go: and what profit h' he
16 he that h' laboured for the wind?
17 and he h' much sorrow and wrath
19 to whom God h' given riches and
19 and h' given him power to eat thereof,
6: 2 A man to whom God h' given riches,
5 Moreover he h' not seen the sun,
5 this h' more rest than the other.
6 years twice told, yet h' he seen no
8 For what h' the wise more than the
8 what h' the poor, that knoweth to
10 That which h' been is named
7:13 straight, which he h' made crooked?
14 God also h' set the one over against
29 found, that God h' made man upright;
8: 8 There is no man that h' power over the
8 neither h' he power in the day of
15 because a man h' no better thing
9: 9 which he h' given thee under the sun,
10:20 and that which h' wings shall tell
Ca 1: 4 the king h' brought me into his
6 because the sun h' looked upon me:
3: 8 every man h' his sword upon his
8: 6 which h' a most vehement flame.
8 little sister, and she h' no breasts:
Isa 1: 2 O earth: for the Lord h' spoken, I
12 who h' required this at your hand,
20 for the mouth of the Lord h' spoken it.
30 and as a garden that h' no water.
5: 1 My wellbeloved h' a vineyard in a
14 Therefore hell h' enlarged herself,
25 and he h' stretched forth his hand
25 them, and h' smitten them:
6: 7 and said, Lo, this h' touched thy lips;
8:18 children whom the Lord h' given me
9: 2 death, upon them h' the light shined.
8 word into Jacob, and it h' lighted upon
10:10 As my hand h' found the kingdoms of
12 when the Lord h' performed his whole
14 And my hand h' found as a nest the
28 at Michmash he h' laid up his

Isa 12: 5 the Lord: for he h' done excellent
14: 5 The Lord h' broken the staff of the
9 it h' raised up from their thrones all
24 The Lord of hosts h' sworn, saying,
27 For the Lord of hosts h' purposed, and
32 That the Lord h' founded Zion,
16:13 the word that the Lord h' spoken
14 But now the Lord h' spoken, saying,
19:12 what the Lord of hosts h' purposed
14 The Lord h' mingled a perverse spirit
17 which he h' determined against it.
20: 3 Like as my servant Isaiah h' walked
21: 4 the night of my pleasure h' he turned
6 For thus h' the Lord said unto me, Go,
9 images of her gods he h' broken unto
16 For thus h' the Lord said unto me,
17 for the Lord God of Israel h' spoken it.
22:25 shall be cut off: for the Lord h' spoken
23: 4 O Zidon: for the sea h' spoken,
8 Who h' taken this counsel against
9 The Lord of hosts h' purposed it, to
11 the Lord h' given a commandment
24: 3 for the Lord h' spoken this word.
6 Therefore h' the curse devoured the
25: 8 all the earth: for the Lord h' spoken it.
27: 7 H' he smitten him, as he smote those
28: 2 the Lord h' a mighty and strong one,
25 When he h' made plain the face
29: 4 as of one that h' a familiar spirit,
8 he is faint, and his soul h' appetite:
10 For the Lord h' poured out upon you
10 of deep sleep, and h' closed your eyes:
10 your rulers, the seers h' he covered.
30:24 which h' been winnowed with the
33 it is prepared; he h' made it deep and
31: 4 For thus h' the Lord spoken unto me,
33: 5 he h' filled Zion with judgment and
8 he h' broken the covenant,
8 he h' despised the cities, he regardeth
14 fearfulness h' surprised the
34: 2 he h' utterly destroyed them,
2 he h' delivered them to the slaughter.
6 for the Lord h' a sacrifice in Bozrah,
16 for my mouth it h' commanded, and
16 his spirit it h' gathered them.
17 And he h' cast the lot for them, and
17 his hand h' divided it unto them by
36: 7 whose altars Hezekiah h' taken away,
12 said, H' my master sent me to thy
12 h' he not sent me to the men that sit
18 H' any of the gods of the nations
37: 4 his master h' sent to reproach the
4 which the Lord thy God h' heard:
17 which h' sent to reproach the living
22 the word which the Lord h' spoken
22 the daughter of Zion, h' despised thee,
22 the daughter of Jerusalem h' shaken
38: 7 will do this thing that he h' spoken;
15 he h' both spoken unto me,
15 and himself h' done it: I shall go
40: 2 for she h' received of the Lord's hand
5 for the mouth of the Lord h' spoken
12 Who h' measured the waters in the
13 Who h' directed the Spirit of the Lord,
13 or being his counsellor h' taught him?
20 impoverished that he h' no oblation
21 h' it not been told you from the
26 and behold who h' created these
41: 4 Who h' wrought and done it, calling
20 the hand of the Lord h' done this, and
20 the Holy One of Israel h' created it.
26 Who h' declared from the beginning,
42:25 Therefore he h' poured upon him the
25 and it h' set him on fire round about,
43:27 Thy first father h' sinned, and thy
44:10 who h' formed a god, or molten a
18 for he h' shut their eyes, that they
20 a deceived heart h' turned him aside,
23 O ye heavens; for the Lord h' done it:
23 for the Lord h' redeemed Jacob, and
45: 9 or thy work, He h' no hands?
18 he h' established it, he created it not
21 counsel together: who h' declared this
21 from ancient time? who h' told it
47:10 thy knowledge, it h' perverted thee;
48: 5 Mine idol h' done them, and my
5 molten image, h' commanded
13 Mine hand also h' laid the foundation
13 and my right hand h' spanned the
14 which among them h' declared these
14 The Lord h' loved him: he will do
16 the Lord God, and his Spirit, h' sent
20 The Lord h' redeemed his servant
49: 1 The Lord h' called me from the womb;
1 of my mother h' he made mention of
2 And he h' made my mouth like a sharp
2 in the shadow of his hand h' he hid
2 in his quiver h' he hid me;
10 for he that h' mercy on them shall
13 for the Lord h' comforted his people,
14 But Zion said, The Lord h' forsaken
14 and my Lord h' forgotten me.
21 Who h' begotten me these, seeing I
21 and who h' brought up these?
50: 4 The Lord God h' given me the tongue
5 The Lord God h' opened mine ear,
10 walketh in darkness, and h' no light?
51: 9 Art thou not it that h' cut Rahab,
10 Art thou not it which h' dried the sea,
10 that h' made the depths of the sea
13 that h' stretched forth the heavens,
18 all the sons whom she h' brought forth;
18 of all the sons that she h' brought up.
52: 9 for the Lord h' comforted his people,
9 he h' redeemed Jerusalem.
10 The Lord h' made bare his holy arm

Isa 53: 1 Who h' believed our report?
2 he h' no form nor comeliness;
4 Surely he h' borne our griefs, and
6 and the Lord h' laid on him the
10 bruise him; he h' put him to grief:
12 because he h' poured out his soul
54: 6 For the Lord h' called thee as a
10 saith the Lord that h' mercy on thee.
55: 1 the waters, and he that h' no money;
5 Holy One of Israel; for he h' glorified
56: 3 stranger, that h' joined himself to
3 The Lord h' utterly separated me
58:14 for the mouth of the Lord h' spoken it.
59: 3 your tongue h' muttered perverseness.
60: 9 because he h' glorified thee.
61: 1 because the Lord h' anointed me to
1 he h' sent me to bind up the
9 the seed which the Lord h' blessed.
10 for he h' clothed me with the garments
10 he h' covered me with the robe of
62: 8 The Lord h' sworn by his right hand,
11 Behold, the Lord h' proclaimed unto
63: 7 to all that the Lord h' bestowed on us,
7 which he h' bestowed on them
64: 4 by the ear, neither h' the eye seen,
4 beside thee, what he h' prepared for
65:20 nor an old man that h' not filled his
66: 2 all those things h' mine hand made,
8 Who h' heard such a thing?
8 who h' seen such things?
Jer 2:11 H' a nation changed their gods,
30 your own sword h' devoured your
37 the Lord h' rejected thy confidences,
3: 3 and there h' been no latter rain;
6 which backsliding Israel h' done?
6 and there h' played the harlot.
10 Judah h' not turned unto me with
11 backsliding Israel h' justified herself
24 For shame h' devoured the labour of
4:17 because she h' been rebellious against
27 For thus h' the Lord said, The whole
5:23 But this people h' a revolting and a
6: 6 For thus h' the Lord of hosts said,
24 anguish h' taken hold of us, and pain,
30 because the Lord h' rejected them.
7:29 for the Lord h' rejected and forsaken
8:14 the Lord our God h' put us to silence,
21 astonishment h' taken hold on me.
9:12 whom the mouth of the Lord h' spoken,
10:12 He h' made the earth by his power,
12 he h' established the world by his
12 and h' stretched out the heavens by
11:15 What h' my beloved to do in mine
15 seeing she h' wrought lewdness
16 of a great tumult he h' kindled fire
17 that planted thee, h' pronounced evil
18 And the Lord h' given me knowledge
13:15 not proud: for the Lord h' spoken.
14:19 Judah? h' thy soul lothed Zion?
15: 9 She that h' borne seven languisheth:
9 she h' given up the ghost;
9 she h' been ashamed and confounded:
16:10 Wherefore h' the Lord pronounced all
18:13 heathen, who h' heard such things:
13 of Israel h' done a very horrible thing.
15 Because my people h' forgotten me,
20: 3 The Lord h' not called thy name
13 for he h' delivered the soul of the poor
22: 8 Wherefore h' the Lord done thus unto
21 This h' been thy manner from thy
23: 9 like a man whom wine h' overcome,
17 The Lord h' said, Ye shall have peace;
18 For who h' stood in the counsel of the
18 and h' perceived and heard his word?
18 who h' marked his word, and heard it?
28 The prophet that h' a dream, let him
28 a dream; and he that h' my word, let
35 What h' the Lord answered?
35 and, What h' the Lord spoken?
37 What h' the Lord answered thee?
37 and, What h' the Lord spoken?
25: 3 the word of the Lord h' come unto me,
4 And the Lord h' sent unto you all
5 in the land that the Lord h' given
13 Jeremiah h' prophesied against all
31 for the Lord h' a controversy with the
36 for the Lord h' spoiled their pasture.
38 He h' forsaken his covert, as the lion:
26:11 for he h' prophesied against this city,
13 him of the evil that he h' pronounced
15 for of a truth the Lord h' sent me
16 for he h' spoken to us in the name of
27:13 as the Lord h' spoken against the
28: 9 that the Lord h' truly sent him.
15 The Lord h' not sent thee; but thou
29:15 The Lord h' raised us up prophets in
26 The Lord h' made thee priest in the
31 Because that Shemaiah h' prophesied
32 because he h' taught rebellion
31: 3 The Lord h' appeared of old unto me,
11 For the Lord h' redeemed Jacob,
22 for the Lord h' created a new thing in
32:31 For this city h' been to me as a
33:24 families which the Lord h' chosen,
24 he h' even cast them off?
34:14 an Hebrew, which h' been sold unto
14 and when he h' served thee six years,
35: 8 our father in all that he h' charged us,
16 but this people h' not hearkened unto
18 unto all that he h' commanded you:
36: 7 the Lord h' pronounced against this
28 Jehoiakim the king of Judah h' burned.
38:21 the word that the Lord h' shewed me:
40: 2 The Lord thy God h' pronounced this
3 Now the Lord h' brought it, and done
3 done according as he h' said:

Jer 40: 5 the king of Babylon h' made governor
14 king of the Ammonites h' sent Ishmael
42:18 anger and my fury h' been poured
19 The Lord h' said concerning you,
21 for the which he h' sent me unto you.
43: 2 the Lord our God h' not sent thee to
45: 3 for the Lord h' added grief to my
46:10 God of hosts h' a sacrifice in the north
12 and thy cry h' filled the land:
12 for the mighty man h' stumbled
17 he h' passed the time appointed.
47: 7 seeing the Lord h' given it a charge
7 the sea shore? there h' he appointed
48: 8 be destroyed, as the Lord h' spoken.
11 Moab h' been at ease from his youth,
36 because the riches that he h' gotten
39 how h' Moab turned the back with
42 because he h' magnified himself
49: 1 H' Israel no sons? h' he no heir?
16 Thy terribleness h' deceived thee,
20 that he h' taken against Edom;
20 and his purposes, that he h' purposed
24 to flee, and fear h' seized on her:
30 king of Babylon h' taken counsel
30 you, and h' conceived a purpose
50: 6 My people h' been lost sheep:
14 for she h' sinned against the Lord.
15 she h' given her hand: her foundations
15 as she h' done, do unto her.
17 king of Assyria h' devoured him;
17 king of Babylon h' broken his bones.
25 The Lord h' opened his armoury,
25 and h' brought forth the weapons
29 according to all that she h' done, do
29 she h' been proud against the Lord,
43 The king of Babylon h' heard the
45 the Lord, that he h' taken against
45 and his purposes, that he h' purposed
51: 5 For Israel h' not been forsaken,
7 Babylon h' been a golden cup in the
10 The Lord h' brought forth our
11 the Lord h' raised up the spirit of the
12 for the Lord h' both devised and done
14 The Lord of hosts h' sworn by himself,
15 He h' made the earth by his power,
15 he h' established the world by his
15 and h' stretched out the heaven by his
30 their might h' failed; they became as
34 the king of Babylon h' devoured me,
34 he h' crushed me,
34 he h' made me an empty vessel,
34 he h' swallowed me up like a dragon,
34 he h' filled his belly with my delicates,
34 he h' cast me out.
44 that which he h' swallowed up:
49 As Babylon h' caused the slain of
51 shame h' covered our faces:
55 Because the Lord h' spoiled Babylon,
La 1: 2 among all her lovers she h' none to
8 Jerusalem h' grievously sinned;
9 for the enemy h' magnified himself.
10 The adversary h' spread out his hand
10 she h' seen that the heathen entered
12 the Lord h' afflicted me in the day
13 From above h' he sent fire into my
13 he h' spread a net for my feet,
13 he h' turned me back:
13 he h' made me desolate and faint all
14 he h' made my strength to fall,
15 The Lord h' trodden under foot all my
15 he h' called an assembly against me
15 the Lord h' trodden the virgin, the
17 Lord h' commanded concerning Jacob,
2: 1 How h' the Lord covered the daughter
2 The Lord h' swallowed up all the
2 of Jacob, and h' not pitied:
2 he h' thrown down in his wrath the
2 h' brought them down to the ground:
2 he h' polluted the kingdom and
3 He h' cut off in his fierce anger all the
3 he h' drawn back his right hand
4 He h' bent his bow like an enemy:
5 an enemy: he h' swallowed up Israel,
5 he h' swallowed up all her palaces:
5 he h' destroyed his strong holds,
5 and h' increased in the daughter of
6 and he h' violently taken away his
6 he h' destroyed his places of the
6 the Lord h' caused the solemn feasts
6 and h' despised in the indignation of
7 The Lord h' cast off his altar,
7 he h' abhorred his sanctuary,
7 he h' given up into the hand of the
8 The Lord h' purposed to destroy the
8 he h' stretched out a line,
8 he h' not withdrawn his hand from
9 he h' destroyed and broken her bars:
17 The Lord h' done that which he had
17 he h' fulfilled his word that he had
17 he h' thrown down, and h' not pitied:
17 and he h' caused thine enemy to
17 he h' set up the horn of thine
22 up h' mine enemy consumed.
3: 1 I am the man that h' seen affliction by
2 He h' led me, and brought me into
4 My flesh and my skin h' he made old;
4 he h' broken my bones.
5 He h' builded against me, and
6 He h' set me in dark places,
7 He h' hedged me about, that I cannot
7 he h' made my chain heavy.
9 He h' inclosed my ways with hewn
9 he h' made my paths crooked.
11 He h' turned aside my ways,
11 he h' made me desolate.
12 He h' bent his bow, and set me as

La 3:13 He h· caused the arrows of his quiver
15 He h· filled me with bitterness,
15 he h· made me drunken with
16 He h· also broken my teeth with gravel
16 he h· covered me with ashes.
20 My soul h· them still in remembrance,
28 because he h· borne it upon him.
4:11 The Lord h· accomplished his fury;
11 he h· poured out his fierce anger,
11 and h· kindled a fire in Zion,
11 and it h· devoured the foundations
16 The anger of the Lord h· divided them;
Eze 2: 3 to a rebellious nation that h· rebelled
5 that there h· been a prophet
3:20 his righteousness which he h· done
4:14 behold, my soul h· not been polluted:
5: 6 And she h· changed my judgments
6: 9 whorish heart, which h· departed
7:10 the rod h· blossomed, pride h· budded.
8:12 not; the Lord h· forsaken the earth.
9: 9 The Lord h· forsaken the earth, and
12: 9 h· not the house of Israel...said
13: 6 and the Lord h· not sent them:
14: 9 be deceived when he h· spoken a
15: 5 when the fire h· devoured it, and it is
16:48 Sodom thy sister h· not done, she nor
51 Neither h· Samaria committed half
17:12 come to Jerusalem, and h· taken the
13 And h· taken of the king's seed,
13 and h· taken an oath of him:
13 he h· also taken the mighty of the
18 given his hand, and h· done all these
19 surely mine oath that he h· despised,
19 and my covenant that he h· broken,
20 his trespass that he h· trespassed
18: 6 And h· not eaten upon the mountains,
6 neither h· lifted up his eyes to the idols
6 neither h· defiled his neighbour's wife
6 neither h· come near to a menstruous
7 And h· not oppressed any,
7 but h· restored to the debtor his
7 h· spoiled none by violence,
7 h· given his bread to the hungry,
7 and h· covered the naked with a
8 He that h· not given forth upon usury,
8 neither h· taken any increase,
8 that h· withdrawn his hand from
8 h· executed true judgment between
9 H· walked in my statutes,
9 and h· kept my judgments, to deal
11 but even h· eaten upon the mountains,
12 H· oppressed the poor and needy,
12 h· spoiled by violence,
12 h· not restored the pledge, and
12 h· not lifted up his eyes to the idols
12 h· committed abomination,
13 H· given forth upon usury,
13 and h· taken increase:
13 he h· done all these abominations;
14 all his father's sins which he h· done,
15 That h· not eaten upon the mountains,
15 neither h· lifted up his eyes to the idols
15 h· not defiled his neighbour's wife,
16 Neither h· oppressed any,
16 h· not withholden the pledge,
16 neither h· spoiled by violence,
16 but h· given his bread to the hungry,
16 h· covered the naked with a garment,
17 That h· taken off his hand from the
17 That h· not received usury nor increase,
17 h· executed my judgments,
17 h· walked in my statutes;
19 When the son h· done that which is
19 and right, and h· kept all my statutes,
19 and h· done them, he shall surely live.
21 from all his sins that he h· committed,
22 transgressions that he h· committed,
22 in his righteousness that he h· done
24 righteousness that he h· done shall not
24 in his trespass that he h· trespassed,
24 and in his sin that he h· sinned,
26 for his iniquity that he h· done shall
27 his wickedness that he h· committed,
28 transgressions that he h· committed,
19:14 her branches, which h· devoured her
14 so that she h· no strong rod to be a
21:11 And he h· given it to be furbished,
22:11 And one h· committed abomination
11 and another h· lewdly defiled his
11 and another in thee h· humbled his
13 thy blood which h· been in the midst
28 God, when the Lord h· not spoken.
24:12 She h· wearied herself with lies,
24 according to all that he h· done shall
25:12 Because that Edom h· dealt against
12 and h· greatly offended, and revenged
26: 2 because that Tyrus h· said against
27:26 east wind h· broken thee in the midst
29: 3 which h· said, My river is mine own,
9 because he h· said, The river is mine,
31:10 and he h· shot up his top among the
33:13 for his iniquity that he h· committed,
16 sins that he h· committed shall be
16 he h· done that which is lawful and
32 song of one that h· a pleasant voice,
33 a prophet h· been among them
36: 2 Because the enemy h· said against
44: 2 the God of Israel, h· entered in by it,
25 or for sister that h· had no husband,
Da 1:10 who h· appointed your meat and your
2:27 secret which the king h· demanded
37 for the God of heaven h· given thee a
38 fowls of the heaven h· he given into
38 hand, and h· made thee ruler over
45 the great God h· made known to the
3: 5 Nebuchadnezzar the king h· set up:

Da 3:28 who h· sent his angel, and delivered
4: 2 that the high God h· wrought toward
5:26 God h· numbered thy kingdom, and
6:22 My God h· sent his angel, and
22 h· shut the lions' mouths,
27 who h· delivered Daniel from the
9:12 And he h· confirmed his words, which
12 the whole heaven h· not been done
12 as h· been done upon Jerusalem.
14 Therefore h· the Lord watched upon
11:12 And when he h· taken away the
Ho 1: 2 for the land h· committed great
2: 5 For their mother h· played the harlot:
5 conceived them h· done shamefully:
12 whereof she h· said, These are my
4: 1 for the Lord h· a controversy with the
12 for the spirit of whoredoms h· caused
19 The wind h· bound her up in her
5: 6 he h· withdrawn himself from them.
6: 1 for he h· torn, and he will heal us;
1 he h· smitten, and he will bind us up.
11 Also, O Judah, he h· sent an harvest
7: 4 after he h· kneaded the dough, until
8 Ephraim, he h· mixed himself among
12 them, as their congregation h· heard.
8: 3 Israel h· cast off the thing that is good:
5 Thy calf, O Samaria, h· cast thee off;
7 it h· no stalk: the bud shall yield no
9 alone by himself: Ephraim h· hired
11 Because Ephraim h· made many altars
14 For Israel h· forgotten his Maker,
14 and Judah h· multiplied fenced cities:
10: 1 multitude of his fruit he h· increased
12: 2 The Lord h· also a controversy with
13:16 for she h· rebelled against her God:
Joe 1: 2 H· this been in your days, or
4 That which the palmerworm h· left
4 h· the locust eaten; and that
4 and that which the locust h· left
4 left h· the cankerworm eaten;
4 and that which the cankerworm h· left
4 left h· the caterpiller eaten.
6 and he h· the cheek teeth of a great
7 He h· laid my vine waste, and barked
7 he h· made it clean bare, and cast it
19 for the fire h· devoured the pastures
19 and the flame h· burned all the trees
20 and the fire h· devoured the pastures
2: 2 there h· not been ever the like,
20 because he h· done great things.
23 for he h· given you the former rain
25 you the years that the locust h· eaten,
26 that h· dealt wondrously with you:
32 as the Lord h· said, and in the
3: 8 people far off: for the Lord h· spoken
Am 3: 1 word that the Lord h· spoken against
4 when he h· no prey? will a young lion
6 evil in a city, and the Lord h· not done
8 The lion h· roared, who will not fear?
8 the Lord God h· spoken, who can but
4: 2 The Lord God h· sworn by his holiness,
6: 8 The Lord God h· sworn by himself,
7:1,4 Thus h· the Lord God shewed unto
10 Amos h· conspired against thee in
8: 1 Thus h· the Lord God shewed unto
7 The Lord h· sworn by the excellency
9: 6 and h· founded his troop in the
Ob 3 The pride of thine heart h· deceived
18 house of Esau; for the Lord h· spoken
Jon 1: 9 which h· made the sea and the dry
Mic 2: 4 he h· changed the portion of my
4 how h· he removed it from me!
4 turning away he h· divided our fields.
4: 4 mouth of the Lord of hosts h· spoken
5: 1 daughter of troops: he h· laid siege
3 which travaileth h· brought forth:
6: 2 for the Lord h· a controversy with his
8 He h· shewed thee, O man, what is
9 ye the rod, and who h· appointed it.
Na 1: 3 the Lord h· his way in the whirlwind
14 the Lord h· given a commandment
2: 2 For the Lord h· turned away the
3:19 whom h· not thy wickedness passed
Hab 2:18 that the maker thereof h· graven it;
Zep 1: 7 for the Lord h· prepared a sacrifice,
7 he h· bid his guests.
3:15 Lord h· taken away thy judgments,
15 he h· cast out thine enemy:
Hag 2:19 the olive tree, h· not brought forth:
Zec 1: 2 The Lord h· been sore displeased
6 according to our doings, so h· he dealt
10 they whom the Lord h· sent to walk to
2: 8 After the glory h· he sent me unto the
9 that the Lord of hosts h· sent me.
11 the Lord of hosts h· sent me unto thee.
3: 2 the Lord that h· chosen Jerusalem
4: 9 the Lord of hosts h· sent me unto you.
10 For who h· despised the day of small
6:15 the Lord of hosts h· sent me unto you.
7: 7 words which the Lord h· cried by the
12 which the Lord of hosts h· sent in his
10: 3 the Lord of hosts h· visited his flock
3 and h· made them as his goodly horse
13: 4 of his vision, when he h· prophesied;
Mal 1: 4 against whom the Lord h· indignation
9 this h· been by your means: will
14 the deceiver, which h· in his flock
2:10 all one father? h· not one God created
11 Judah h· dealt treacherously, and an
11 Judah h· profaned the holiness of the
11 and h· married the daughter of a
14 Because the Lord h· been witness
M't 3: 7 who h· warned you to flee from the
5:23 that thy brother h· ought against
28 to lust after her h· committed
31 It h· been said, Whosoever shall put

M't 5:33 ye have heard that it h· been said by
38, 43 Ye have heard that it h· been said,
8:20 the Son of man h· not where to lay
9: 6 the Son of man h· power on earth
22 comfort; thy faith h· made thee whole.
11:11 born of women there h· not risen a
15 He that h· ears to hear, let him
18 and they say, He h· a devil.
13: 9 Who h· ears to hear, let him hear.
12 For whosoever h·, to him shall be
12 but whosoever h· not, from him
12 shall be taken away even that he h·.
21 Yet h· he not root in himself, but
27 from whence then h· it tares?
28 unto them, An enemy h· done this.
43 Who h· ears to hear, let him hear.
44 the which when a man h· found,
44 goeth and selleth all that he h·,
54 Whence h· this man this wisdom,
56 Whence then h· this man all these
16:17 for flesh and blood h· not revealed it
19: 6 What therefore God h· joined together,
29 And every one that h· forsaken houses,
20: 7 Because no man h· hired us.
21: 3 ye shall say, The Lord h· need of
24:45 whom his lord h· made ruler over his
25:28 unto him which h· ten talents.
29 every one that h· shall be given,
29 from him that h· not shall be
29 taken away even that which he h·.
26:10 for she h· wrought a good work upon
12 For in that she h· poured this
13 that this woman h· done, be told
65 saying, He h· spoken blasphemy;
27:23 Why, what evil h· he done?
M'r 2:10 the Son of man h· power on earth
3:22 He h· Beelzebub, and by the prince
26 he cannot stand, but h· an end.
29 Holy Ghost h· never forgiveness,
30 they said, He h· an unclean spirit.
4: 9 He that h· ears to hear, let him
25 he that h·, to him shall be given:
25 and he that h· not, from him shall
25 be taken even that which he h·.
5:19 great things the Lord h· done for thee,
19 and h· had compassion on thee.
34 thy faith h· made thee whole;
6: 2 From whence h· this man these
7: 6 Well h· Esaias prophesied of you
37 He h· done all things well: he maketh
9:17 my son, which h· a dumb spirit;
22 And ofttimes it h· cast him into the
10: 9 What therefore God h· joined together,
29 There is no man that h· left house,
52 thy way; thy faith h· made thee whole.
11: 3 ye that the Lord h· need of him;
12:43 That this poor widow h· cast more in,
13:20 the elect's sake, whom he h· chosen,
20 he h· shortened the days.
14: 6 she h· wrought a good work on me.
8 She h· done what she could: she is
9 this also that she h· done shall be
15:14 Why, what evil h· he done?
Lu 1:25 Thus h· the Lord dealt with me
36 she h· also conceived a son in her old
47 And my spirit h· rejoiced in God my
48 For he h· regarded the low estate of
49 he that is mighty h· done to me great
51 He h· shewed strength with his arm;
51 he h· scattered the proud in the
52 He h· put down the mighty from
53 He h· filled the hungry with good
53 and the rich he h· sent empty away.
54 He h· holpen his servant Israel,
68 for he h· visited and redeemed his
69 And h· raised up an horn of salvation
78 the dayspring from on high h· visited
2:15 the Lord h· made known unto us.
3: 7 who h· warned you to flee from the
11 He that h· two coats, let him
11 impart to him that h· none;
11 and he that h· meat, let him do
4:18 because he h· anointed me to preach
18 h· sent me to heal the brokenhearted,
5:24 Son of man h· power upon earth
7: 5 and he h· built us a synagogue.
16 That God h· visited his people.
20 they said, John Baptist h· sent us unto
33 wine; and ye say, He h· a devil.
44 but she h· washed my feet with tears,
45 the time I came in h· not ceased to
46 but this woman h· anointed my feet
50 Thy faith h· saved thee; go in peace.
8: 8 He that h· ears to hear, let him
16 No man, when he h· lighted a candle,
18 whosoever h·, to him shall be
18 and whosoever h· not, from him
39 great things God h· done unto thee.
46 said, Somebody h· touched me:
48 thy faith h· made thee whole;
9:58 the Son of man h· not where to
10:40 that my sister h· left me to serve
42 and Mary h· chosen that good part,
12: 5 Fear him, which after he h· killed
5 h· power to cast into hell;
44 make him ruler over all that he h·.
13:16 of Abraham, whom Satan h· bound,
25 is risen up, and h· shut to the door,
14:29 after he h· laid the foundation,
33 that forsaketh not all that he h·,
35 He that h· ears to hear, let him
15: 5 And when he h· found it, he layeth it
9 And when she h· found it, she calleth
27 and thy father h· killed the fatted
27 because he h· received him safe and
30 which h· devoured thy living with

Lu 17:19 way: thy faith h· made thee whole.
18:29 no man that h· left house, or parents,
42 thy sight: thy faith h· saved thee.
19:16 Lord, thy pound h· gained ten pounds.
18 Lord, thy pound h· gained five pounds.
24 give it to him that h· ten pounds.
25 unto him, Lord, he h· ten pounds.
26 every one which h· shall be given;
26 from him that h· not, even that
26 he h· shall be taken away from
31 Because the Lord h· need of him.
34 they said, The Lord h· need of him.
20:24 image and superscription h· it?
21: 3 this poor widow h· cast in more than
4 of her penury h· cast in all the
22:29 as my Father h· appointed unto me;
31 behold, Satan h· desired to have you,
36 he that h· a purse, let him take it,
36 his scrip: and he that h· no sword,
23:22 Why, what evil h· he done?
41 but this man h· done nothing amiss.
24:34 is risen indeed, and h· appeared to
39 for a spirit h· not flesh and bones,
Joh 1:18 No man h· seen God at any time;
18 of the Father, he h· declared him.
2:17 zeal of thine house h· eaten me up.
3:13 And no man h· ascended up to heaven,
18 because he h· not believed in the
29 He that h· the bride is the
32 And what he h· seen and heard,
33 He that h· received his testimony
33 h· set to his seal that God is true.
34 For he whom God h· sent speaketh
35 and h· given all things into his hand.
36 believeth on the Son h· everlasting
4:33 H· any man brought him ought to
44 a prophet h· no honour in his own
5:22 judgeth no man, but h· committed
23 not the Father which h· sent him.
24 him that sent me, h· everlasting
26 For as the Father h· life in himself;
26 so h· he given to the Son to have life
27 And h· given him authority to
30 will of the Father which h· sent me.
36 the Father h· given me to finish,
36 of me, that the Father h· sent me.
37 the Father himself, which h· sent me,
37 h· borne witness of me.
38 whom he h· sent, him ye believe not.
6: 9 here, which h· five barley loaves,
27 for him h· God the Father sealed.
29 ye believe on him whom he h· sent.
39 the Father's will which h· sent me,
39 that of all which he h· given me
44 except the Father which h· sent me
45 Every man therefore that h· heard,
45 and h· learned of the Father, cometh
46 Not that any man h· seen the Father,
46 he which is of God, he h· seen the
47 believeth on me h· everlasting
54 and drinketh my blood, h· eternal
57 As the living Father h· sent me,
7:29 for I am from him, and he h· sent me.
31 than these which this man h· done?
38 on me as the scripture h· said,
42 H· not the scripture said, That Christ
8:10 accusers? h· no man condemned
28 but as my Father h· taught me, I
29 the Father h· not left me alone; for I
37 because my word h· no place in you.
40 a man that h· told you the truth,
9: 3 Neither h· this man sinned, nor his
17 that he h· opened thine eyes?
21 or who h· opened his eyes, we know
30 whence he is, and yet he h· opened
10:20 He h· a devil, and is mad;
21 not the words of him that h· a devil.
36 whom the Father h· sanctified, and
11:39 for he h· been dead four days.
12: 7 the day of my burying h· she kept
38 Lord, who h· believed our report?
38 and to whom h· the arm of the Lord
40 He h· blinded their eyes, and
48 not my words, h· one that judgeth
13:18 eateth bread with me h· lifted up his
14: 9 Philip? he that h· seen me
9 seen me h· seen the Father;
21 He that h· my commandments,
30 of this world cometh, and h· nothing
15: 9 As the Father h· loved me, so have I
13 Greater love h· no man than this,
16: 6 unto you, sorrow h· filled your heart.
15 All things that the Father h· are
21 when she is in travail h· sorrow,
17:14 and the world h· hated them,
25 Father, the world h· not known thee:
18:11 the cup which my Father h· given me,
19:11 me unto thee h· the greater sin.
20:21 as my Father h· sent me, even so send
Ac 1: 7 which the Father h· put in his own
2:24 Whom God h· raised up, having
32 This Jesus h· God raised up, whereof
33 he h· shed forth this, which ye now
36 that God h· made that same Jesus,
3:13 God of our fathers, h· glorified his Son
15 whom God h· raised from the dead;
16 in his name h· made this man strong,
16 faith which is by him h· given him
18 should suffer, he h· so fulfilled.
21 which God h· spoken by the mouth of
4:16 a notable miracle h· been done by
5: 3 why h· Satan filled thine heart to lie
31 Him h· God exalted with his right
32 whom God h· given to them that obey
7:50 H· not my hand made all these
9:12 And h· seen in a vision a man named

Ac 9:13 much evil he h· done to thy saints
14 And here he h· authority from
17 way as thou camest, h· sent me,
10:15 What God h· cleansed, that call not
28 but God h· shewed me that I should
11: 8 or unclean h· at any time entered
9 What God h· cleansed, that call not
18 h· God also to the Gentiles granted
12:11 that the Lord h· sent his angel,
11 and h· delivered me out of the hand
13:23 Of this man's seed h· God...raised
33 God h· fulfilled the same unto us
33 in that he h· raised up Jesus again;
47 For so h· the Lord commanded us,
15:14 Simeon h· declared how God at the
21 For Moses of old time h· in every
17: 7 Whom Jason h· received: and these
26 And h· made of one blood all nations
26 face of the earth, and h· determined
31 Because he h· appointed a day, in
31 by that man whom he h· ordained;
31 whereof he h· given assurance unto
31 in that he h· raised him from the
19:26 this Paul h· persuaded and turned
20:28 the Holy Ghost h· made you overseers,
28 which he h· purchased with his own
21:28 and h· polluted this holy place.
22:14 The God of our fathers h· chosen
23: 9 but if a spirit or an angel h· spoken to
17 he h· a certain thing to tell him.
18 who h· something to say unto thee.
25:25 and that he himself h· appealed to
27:24 lo, God h· given thee all them that sail
28: 4 whom, though he h· escaped the sea,
Ro 1:19 for God h· shewed it unto them.
3: 1 What advantage then h· the Jew?
7 if the truth of God h· more abounded
25 Whom God h· set forth to be
4: 1 as pertaining to the flesh, h· found?
2 he h· whereof to glory; but not
5:15 Jesus Christ, h· abounded unto many.
21 That as sin h· reigned unto death,
6: 9 death h· no more dominion over him.
7: 1 how that the law h· dominion over a
2 the woman which h· an husband
8: 2 in Christ Jesus h· made me free
20 of him who h· subjected the same in
9: 6 the word of God h· taken none effect.
18 Therefore h· he mercy on whom he
19 For who h· resisted his will?
21 H· not the potter power over the
24 Even us, whom he h· called, not of
31 of righteousness, h· not attained to
10: 9 that God h· raised him from the dead,
16 Lord, who h· believed our report?
11: 1 H· God cast away his people?
2 God h· not cast away his people.
7 Israel h· not obtained that which
7 but the election h· obtained it,
8 God h· given them the spirit of
32 For God h· concluded them all in
34 For who h· known the mind of the
34 or who h· been his counsellor?
35 Or who h· first given to him,
12: 3 according as God h· dealt to every
13: 8 for he that loveth another h· fulfilled
14: 3 that eateth: for God h· received him.
15:18 things which Christ h· not wrought
26 For it h· pleased them of Macedonia
27 It h· pleased them verily; and their
16: 2 whatsoever business she h· need of
2 for she h· been a succourer of many,
1Co 1:11 For it h· been declared unto me of
20 h· not God made foolish the wisdom
27 But God h· chosen the foolish things
27 and God h· chosen the weak things
28 which are despised, h· God chosen,
2: 9 But as it is written, Eye h· not seen,
9 the things which God h· prepared for
10 But God h· revealed them unto us by
16 For who h· known the mind of the
3:14 man's work abide which he h· built
4: 9 I think that God h· set forth us the
5: 2 that he that h· done this deed might
3 concerning him that h· so done this
6:14 And God h· both raised up the Lord,
7: 4 The wife h· not power of her own
4 also the husband h· not power of
7 But every man h· his proper gift
12 If any brother h· a wife that
13 the woman which h· an husband
15 but God h· called us to peace.
17 But as God h· distributed to every
17 as the Lord h· called every one, so let
25 as one that h· obtained mercy of the
28 if a virgin marry, she h· not sinned.
37 no necessity, but h· power over his
37 and h· so decreed in his heart that he
9:14 Even so h· the Lord ordained that
10:13 There h· no temptation taken you but
12:12 body is one, and h· many members,
18 But now h· God set the members every
18 in the body, as it h· pleased him.
24 but God h· tempered the body
28 And God h· set some in the church,
14:26 one of you h· a psalm, h· a doctrine,
26 h· a tongue, h· a revelation,
26 h· an interpretation. Let all things
15:25 he must reign, till he h· put all
27 he h· put all things under his feet.
38 God giveth it a body as it h· pleased
16: 2 as God h· prospered him, that there
2Co 1:21 you in Christ, and h· anointed us,
22 Who h· also sealed us, and given the
2: 5 he h· not grieved me, but in part:
3: 6 Who also h· made us able ministers

2Co 4: 4 the god of this world h· blinded the
6 out of darkness, h· shined in our
5: 5 Now he that h· wrought us for the
5 who also h· given unto us the earnest
10 according to that he h· done, whether
18 are of God, who h· reconciled us to
18 by Jesus Christ, and h· given to us
19 and h· committed unto us the word
21 For he h· made him to be sin for us,
6:14 fellowship h· righteousness with
14 communion h· light with darkness?
15 concord h· Christ with Belial?
15 h· he that believeth with an infidel?
16 And what agreement h· the temple of
16 as God h· said, I will dwell in them,
7: 8 that the same epistle h· made you
8:12 according to that a man h·, and
12 not according to that he h· not.
9: 2 and your zeal h· provoked very many.
9 As it is written, He h· dispersed
9 he h· given to the poor:
10: 8 which the Lord h· given us for
13 of the rule which God h· distributed
13:10 power which the Lord h· given me to
Ga 3: 1 foolish Galatians, who h· bewitched
1 Christ h· been evidently set forth,
13 Christ h· redeemed us from the curse
22 But the scripture h· concluded all
4: 6 God h· sent forth the Spirit of his Son
27 for the desolate h· many more
27 than she which h· an husband.
5: 1 liberty wherewith Christ h· made us
Eph 1: 3 who h· blessed us with all spiritual
4 According as he h· chosen us in him
6 wherein he h· made us accepted
8 Wherein he h· abounded toward us
9 good pleasure which he h· purposed
22 And h· put all things under his feet,
2: 1 And you h· he quickened, who were
5 dead in sins, h· quickened us together
6 And h· raised us up together, and
10 which God h· before ordained that we
14 he is our peace, who h· made both
14 one, and h· broken down the middle
3: 9 beginning of the world h· been hid in
4:32 as God for Christ's sake h· forgiven
5: 2 as Christ also h· loved us, and
2 h· given himself for us an offering
5 an idolater, h· any inheritance
Ph'p 1: 6 that he which h· begun a good work
2: 9 God also h· highly exalted him; and
22 he h· served with me in the gospel.
3: 4 thinketh that he h· whereof he might
4:10 last your care of me h· flourished
Col 1:12 the Father, which h· made us meet
13 Who h· delivered us from the power
13 of darkness, and h· translated us
21 works, yet now h· he reconciled
26 Even the mystery which h· been hid
2:12 who h· raised him from the dead.
13 h· he quickened together with him,
18 into those things which he h· not seen,
3:25 for the wrong which he h· done:
4:13 I bear him record, that he h· a zeal
1Th 2:12 who h· called you unto his kingdom
4: 7 For God h· not called us unto
8 but God, who h· also given unto us
5: 9 For God h· not appointed us to wrath,
2Th 2:13 God h· from the beginning chosen
16 even our Father, which h· loved us,
16 and h· given us everlasting
1Ti 1:12 Jesus our Lord, who h· enabled me,
4: 3 which God h· created to be received
5: 8 those of his own house, he h· denied
6:16 Who only h· immortality, dwelling
16 whom no man h· seen, nor can see:
2Ti 1: 7 For God h· not given us the spirit of
9 Who h· saved us, and called us with
10 Jesus Christ, who h· abolished
10 and h· brought life and immortality
2: 4 may please him who h· chosen him
4:10 For Demas h· forsaken me, having
15 for he h· greatly withstood our words.
Tit 1: 3 But h· in due times manifested
9 faithful word as he h· been taught,
2:11 that bringeth salvation h· appeared
Ph'm 18 If he h· wronged thee, or oweth thee
Heb 1: 2 H· in these last days spoken unto
2 whom he h· appointed heir of all
4 as he h· by inheritance obtained a
9 even thy God, h· anointed thee with
2: 5 unto the angels h· he not put in
13 the children which God h· given me.
18 in that he himself h· suffered being
3: 3 as he who h· builded the house
3 h· more honour than the house.
4:10 he also h· ceased from his own works.
7:24 h· an unchangeable priesthood.
8: 6 But now h· he obtained a more
13 new covenant, he h· made the first old.
9:20 testament which God h· enjoined
26 end of the world h· he appeared to put
10:14 by one offering he h· perfected for
20 living way, which he h· consecrated
29 who h· trodden under foot the Son of
29 and h· counted the blood of the
29 and h· done despite unto the Spirit
30 we know him that h· said, Vengeance
35 which h· great recompence of
11:10 for a city which h· foundations,
16 for he h· prepared for them a city.
12:26 but now he h· promised, saying,
13: 5 for he h· said, I will never leave thee,
Jas 1:12 which the Lord h· promised to them
15 Then when lust h· conceived, it
2: 5 H· not God chosen the poor of this

Jas 2: 5 of the kingdom which he h' promised
13 without mercy, that h' shewed no
14 though a man say he h' faith, and
17 faith, if it h' not works, is dead,
3: 7 is tamed, and h' been tamed of
5: 7 of the earth, and h' long patience
1Pe 1: 3 to his abundant mercy h' begotten
15 But as he which h' called you is holy,
2: 9 the praises of him who h' called you
3: 18 For Christ also h' once suffered for
4: 1 Forasmuch then as Christ h' suffered
1 for he that h' suffered in the flesh
1 in the flesh h' ceased from sin;
10 As every man h' received the gift,
5: 10 who h' called us unto his eternal glory
2Pe 1: 3 as his divine power h' given unto us
3 knowledge of him that h' called us to
9 and h' forgotten that he was purged
14 our Lord Jesus Christ h' shewed me.
3: 15 wisdom given unto him h' written
1Jo 2: 11 because that darkness h' blinded
23 Son, the same h' not the Father:
23 acknowledgeth the Son h' the Father
25 is the promise that he h' promised
27 as it h' taught you, ye shall abide
3: 1 of love the Father h' bestowed upon
3 every man that h' this hope in
6 whosoever sinneth h' not seen him,
15 no murderer h' eternal life
17 But whoso h' this world's good, and
24 by the Spirit which he h' given us.
4: 12 No man h' seen God at any time.
13 because he h' given us of his Spirit.
16 believed the love that God h' to us.
18 out fear: because fear h' torment.
20 his brother whom he h' seen, how
20 can he love God whom he h' not seen?
5: 9 witness of God which he h' testified of
10 on the Son of God h' the witness
10 believeth not God h' made him a liar;
11 that God h' given to us eternal life,
12 He that h' the Son h' life; and he
12 that h' not the Son of God h' not life.
20 and h' given us an understanding, that
2Jo 9 the doctrine of Christ, h' not God.
9 of Christ, he h' both the Father
3Jo 11 he that doeth evil h' not seen God.
12 Demetrius h' good report of all men,
Jude 6 he h' reserved in everlasting chains
Re 1: 6 And h' made us kings and priests
2: 7, 11 He that h' an ear, let him hear
12 saith he which h' the sharp sword
17 He that h' an ear, let him hear
18 who h' his eyes like unto a flame of
29 He that h' an ear, let him hear
3: 1 saith he that h' the seven Spirits
6 He that h' an ear, let him hear
7 he that is true, he that h' the key of
13, 22 He that h' an ear, let him hear
5: 5 the Root of David, h' prevailed to open
9: 11 in the Greek tongue h' his name
10: 7 as he h' declared to his servants the
12: 6 where she h' a place prepared of
12 knoweth that he h' but a short
13: 18 Let him that h' understanding
16: 9 the name of God, which h' power
17: 7 which h' the seven heads and ten
9 here is the mind which h' wisdom.
17 For God h' put in their hearts to fulfil
18: 5 and God h' remembered her iniquities.
6 in the cup which she h' filled fill to
7 How much she h' glorified herself,
20 for God h' avenged you on her.
19: 2 for he h' judged the great whore,
2 and h' avenged the blood of his
7 and his wife h' made herself ready.
16 And he h' on his vesture and on
20: 6 Blessed and holy is he that h' part
6 such the second death h' no power,

Hathath (*ha'-thath*)
1Ch 4: 13 and the sons of Othniel; H'.

hating
Ex 18: 21 men of truth, h' covetousness;
Tit 3: 3 envy, hateful, and h' one another.
Jude 23 h' even the garment spotted by the

Hatipha (*hat'-if-ah*)
Ezr 2: 54 of Neziah, the children of H'.
Ne 7: 56 of Neziah, the children of H'.

Hatita (*hat'-it-ah*)
Ezr 2: 42 the children of H', the children
Ne 7: 45 the children of H', the children

hatred
Nu 35: 20 But if he thrust him of h',
2Sa 13: 15 that the h' wherewith he hated her
Ps 25: 19 and they hate me with cruel h'.
109: 3 me about also with words of h';
5 for good, and h' for my love.
139: 22 I hate them with perfect h':
Pr 10: 12 H' stirreth up strifes: but love
18 He that hideth h' with lying lips,
15: 17 than a stalled ox and h' therewith.
26: 26 Whose h' is covered by deceit, his
Ec 9: 1 no man knoweth either love or h'
6 Also their love, and their h', and
Eze 25: 15 to destroy it for the old h';
35: 5 thou hast had a perpetual h', and
11 which thou hast used out of thy h'
Ho 9: 7 thine iniquity, and the great h'.
8 h' in the house of his God.
Ga 5: 20 h', variance, emulations, wrath,

hats
Da 3: 21 their hosen, and their h', and

Hattaavah See KIBROTH-HATTAAVAH.

Hatticon See HAZAR-HATTICON.

Hattil (*hat'-til*)
Ezr 2: 57 the children of H', the children
Ne 7: 59 of Shephatiah, the children of H'.

Hattush (*hat'-tush*)
1Ch 3: 22 H', and Igeal, and Bariah, and
Ezr 8: 2 Daniel: of the sons of David; H'.
Ne 3: 10 And next unto him repaired H' the
10: 4 H', Shebaniah, Malluch,
12: 2 Amariah, Malluch, H',

haughtily
Mic 2: 3 necks; neither shall ye go h':

haughtiness
Isa 2: 11 the h' of men shall be bowed
17 the h' of men shall be made low:
13: 11 will lay low the h' of the terrible
16: 6 his h', and his pride, and his
Jer 48: 29 and the h' of his heart.

haughty
2Sa 22: 28 thine eyes are upon the h', that
Ps 131: 1 my heart is not h', nor mine eyes
Pr 16: 18 and an h' spirit before a fall.
18: 12 destruction the heart of man is h',
21: 24 Proud and h' scorner is his name,
Isa 3: 16 the daughters of Zion are h',
10: 33 and the h' shall be humbled.
24: 4 h' people of the earth do languish.
Eze 16: 50 And they were h', and committed
Zep 3: 11 shalt no more be h' because of my

haul See HALE.

haunt
1Sa 23: 22 his place where his h' is, and
30: 31 and his men were wont to h'.
Eze 26: 17 terror to be on all that h' it!

Hauran (*haw'-ran*)
Eze 47: 16 which is by the coast of H'.
18 ye shall measure from H', and

have^ See also HAD; HAST; HATH; HAVING.
Ge 1: 26 let them h' dominion over the fish
28 and h' dominion over the fish of
29 And God said, Behold, I h' given you
30 I h' given every green herb for meat:
4: 20 in tents, and of such as h' cattle.
23 for I h' slain a man to my wounding,
6: 7 whom I h' created from the face of
7 it repenteth me that I h' made
7: 1 for thee h' I seen righteous before me
4 that I h' made will I destroy from
8: 21 more every thing living, as I h' done.
9: 3 as the green herb h' I given you
17 which I h' established between me
11: 6 and they h' all one language; and
6 from them, which they h' imagined
12: 19 so I might h' taken her to me to
14: 22 I h' lift up mine hand unto the Lord,
23 shouldest say, I h' made Abram rich:
24 the young men h' eaten, and the
15: 18 Unto thy seed h' I given this land,
16: 5 I h' given my maid into thy bosom;
13 H' I also here looked after him that
17: 5 father of many nations h' I made
20 as for Ishmael, I h' heard thee:
18: 3 My Lord, if now I h' found favour in
10 and lo, Sarah thy wife shall h' a son.
12 am waxed old shall I h' pleasure,
14 time of life, and Sarah shall h' a son.
21 they h' done altogether according to
27 Behold now, I h' taken upon me to
31 now, I h' taken upon me to speak unto
19: 8 Behold now, I h' two daughters
8 which h' not known man; let me, I
21 See, I h' accepted thee concerning
20: 5 and innocency of my hands h' I done
9 and what h' I offended thee, that
16 Behold, I h' given thy brother a
21: 7 And she said, Who would h' said unto
7 that Sarah should h' given children
23 kindness that I h' done unto thee,
30 witness unto me, that I h' digged this
22: 16 By myself h' I sworn, saith the Lord,
24: 19 also, until they h' done drinking.
25 We h' both straw and provender
31 for I h' prepared the house, and
33 I will not eat, until I h' told mine
26: 10 might lightly h' lien with thy wife,
27 seeing ye hate me, and h' sent me
29 do us no hurt, as we h' not touched
29 and as we h' done unto thee nothing
32 said unto him, We h' found water.
27: 19 I h' done according as thou badest
33 and I h' eaten of all before thou
37 Behold, I h' made him thy lord, and
37 all his brethren h' I given to him
37 and with corn and wine h' I sustained
40 when thou shalt h' the dominion,
28: 15 I will not leave thee, until I h' done
15 that which I h' spoken to thee of.
22 And this stone, which I h' set for a
29: 34 because I h' born him three sons:
30: 3 that I may also h' children by her.
8 with my sister, and I h' prevailed:
16 for surely I h' hired thee with my
18 because I h' given my maiden to my
20 because I h' born him six sons: and
26 for whom I h' served thee, and let me
26 knowest my service which I h' done
27 if I h' found favour in thine eyes,
27 I h' learned by experience that the
29 Thou knowest how I h' served thee,
31: 6 with all my power I h' served your
12 for I h' seen all that Laban doeth unto
27 that I might h' sent thee away with
38 This twenty years h' I been with thee;
38 ewes and thy she goats h' not cast
Ge 31: 38 the rams of thy flock h' I not eaten.
41 Thus h' I been twenty years in thy
43 their children which they h' born?
51 which I h' cast betwixt me and thee;
32: 4 I h' sojourned with Laban and
5 And I h' oxen, and asses, flocks,
30 for I h' seen God face to face, and my
33: 9 And Esau said, I h' enough, my
10 if now I h' found grace in thy sight,
10 for therefore I h' seen thy face, as
11 and because I h' enough. And he
34: 30 Ye h' troubled me to make me to
35: 17 Fear not; thou shalt h' this son also.
37: 6 you, this dream which I h' dreamed:
8 or shalt thou indeed h' dominion
9 Behold, I h' dreamed a dream more;
32 and said, This h' we found: know
40: 8 We h' dreamed a dream, and there is
15 and here also h' I done nothing that
41: 15 I h' dreamed a dream, and there is
15 and I h' heard say of thee, that thou
28 This is the thing which I h' spoken
41 See, I h' set thee over all the land
42: 2 I h' heard that there is corn in Egypt:
36 Me h' ye bereaved of my children:
43: 7 yet alive? h' ye another brother?
21 and we h' brought it again in our
22 And other money h' we brought
44: 4 Wherefore h' ye rewarded evil for
5 indeed he divineth? ye h' done evil
15 What deed is this that ye h' done?
19 saying, H' ye a father, or a
20 We h' a father, an old man, and a
45: 13 and of all that ye h' seen; and ye
46: 30 let me die, since I h' seen thy face,
32 and they h' brought their flocks, and
47: 1 and all that they h', are come out of
4 for thy servants h' no pasture for
9 evil h' the days of the years of my life
9 and h' not attained unto the days of
23 Behold, I h' bought you this day and
26 that Pharaoh should h' the fifth part;
29 If now I h' found grace in thy sight,
48: 22 Moreover I h' given to thee one
49: 18 I h' waited for thy salvation, O Lord.
23 The archers h' sorely grieved him,
26 blessings of thy father h' prevailed
50: 4 If now I h' found grace in your eyes,
5 in my grave which I h' digged for
Ex 1: 18 and said unto them, Why h' ye done
18 and h' saved the men children alive?
2: 20 why is it that ye h' left the man?
22 he said, I h' been a stranger
3: 7 I h' surely seen the affliction of my
7 and h' heard their cry by reason of
9 and I h' also seen the oppression
12 that I h' sent thee: When thou hast
16 I h' surely visited you, and seen that
17 And I h' said, I will bring you up out
4: 11 or the seeing, or the blind? h' not I
21 which I h' put in thine hand: but I
5: 14 Wherefore h' ye not fulfilled your
21 ye h' made our savour to be abhorred
6: 4 And I h' also established my
5 And I h' also heard the groaning of
5 and I h' remembered my covenant.
12 the children of Israel h' not hearkened
7: 1 See, I h' made thee a god to Pharaoh:
9: 16 for this cause h' I raised thee up,
27 I h' sinned this time: the Lord is
10: 1 for I h' hardened his heart, and the
2 what things I h' wrought in Egypt,
2 and my signs which I h' done among
6 nor thy fathers' fathers h' seen, since
16 I h' sinned against the Lord your
12: 17 for in this selfsame day h' I brought
31 and go, serve the Lord, as ye h' said.
32 and your herds, as ye h' said, and be
14: 5 and they said, Why h' we done this,
5 that we h' let Israel go from serving
13 whom ye h' seen to day, ye shall see
18 when I h' gotten me honour upon
15: 5 The depths h' covered them: they
17 which thy hands h' established.
26 which I h' brought upon the
16: 3 for ye h' brought us forth into this
12 I h' heard the murmurings of the
32 I h' fed you in the wilderness, when
17: 16 sworn that the Lord will h' war
18: 3 I h' been an alien in a strange
16 When they h' a matter, they come
19: 4 Ye h' seen what I did unto the
20: 2 which h' brought thee out of the land
3 Thou shalt h' no other gods before
22 unto the children of Israel, Ye h' seen
22 that I h' talked with you from heaven.
21: 4 If his master h' given him a wife, and
4 she h' born him sons or daughters;
8 he shall h' no power, seeing he
9 And if he h' betrothed her unto his
31 Whether he h' gored a son, or
31 or h' gored a daughter, according to
22: 3 if he h' nothing, then he shall be
8 he h' put his hand unto his neighbour's
23: 13 And in all things that I h' said unto
20 into the place which I h' prepared.
24: 12 commandments which I h' written;
14 if any man h' any matters to do, let
26: 2 every one of the curtains shall h' one
28: 3 whom I h' filled with the spirit of
7 It shall h' the two shoulderpieces
32 shall h' a binding of woven work
29: 35 to all things which I h' commanded
31: 2 See, I h' called by name Bezaleel the
3 And I h' filled him with the spirit
6 And I, behold, I h' given with him

Ex 31: 6 that are wise hearted I *h'* put wisdom,
6 may make all that I *h'* commanded
11 according to all that I *h'* commanded
32: 7 of Egypt, *h'* corrupted themselves.
8 They *h'* turned aside quickly out of
8 they *h'* made them a molten calf,
8 a molten calf, and *h'* worshipped it,
8 and *h'* sacrificed thereunto, and
8 which *h'* brought thee up out of the
9 I *h'* seen this people, and, behold, it is
13 and all this land that I *h'* spoken of
30 Ye *h'* sinned a great sin: and now I
31 and said, Oh, this people *h'* sinned a
31 a great sin, and *h'* made them gods
34 the place of which I *h'* spoken unto
33: 13 if I *h'* found grace in thy sight,
16 I and thy people *h'* found grace in thy
34: 9 If now I *h'* found grace in thy sight,
10 do marvels, such as *h'* not been done
27 I *h'* made a covenant with thee and
Le 4: 13 and they *h'* done somewhat against
14 When the sin, which they *h'* sinned
6: 3 Or *h'* found that which was lost, and
17 I *h'* given it unto them for their
7: 7 atonement therewith shall *h'* it.
8 even the priest shall *h'* to himself
10 shall all the sons of Aaron *h'*, one
33 fat, shall *h'* the right shoulder
34 and the heave shoulder *h'* I taken of
34 and *h'* given them unto Aaron the
10: 17 Wherefore *h'* ye not eaten the sin
18 ye should indeed *h'* eaten it in the
19 Behold, this day *h'* they offered their
19 and such things *h'* befallen me:
19 should it *h'* been accepted in the
11: 10 And all that *h'* not fins and scales in
11 shall *h'* their carcases in abomination.
13 which ye shall *h'* in abomination
21 which *h'* legs above their feet, to leap
23 which *h'* four feet, shall be an
12: 2 If a woman *h'* conceived seed, and
13: 2 When a man shall *h'* in the skin
10 and it *h'* turned the hair white, and
13 if the leprosy *h'* covered all his flesh,
24 burneth *h'* a white bright spot,
29 If a man or a woman *h'* a plague
38 If a man also or a woman *h'* in
55 if the plague *h'* not changed his
15: 19 And if a woman *h'* an issue, and
25 And if a woman *h'* an issue of her
16: 4 and he shall *h'* the linen breeches
17: 7 after whom they *h'* gone a whoring.
11 and I *h'* given it to you upon the
18: 27 abominations *h'* the men of the land
19: 23 and shall *h'* planted all manner of
31 Regard not them that *h'* familiar
36 ephah, and a just hin, shall ye *h'*:
20: 6 after such as *h'* familiar spirits, and
12 they *h'* wrought confusion; their
13 both of them *h'* committed an
24 But I *h'* said unto you, Ye shall
24 which *h'* separated you from other
25 on the ground, which I *h'* separated
26 Lord am holy, and *h'* severed you
22: 13 and *h'* no child, and is returned unto
23: 7 ye shall *h'* an holy convocation:
14 the selfsame day that ye *h'* brought
24 shall ye *h'* a sabbath, a memorial
39 when ye *h'* gathered in the fruit of
24: 22 Ye shall *h'* one manner of law, as
25: 26 And if the man *h'* none to redeem
31 the villages which *h'* no wall round
44 bondmaids, which thou shalt *h'*,
26: 9 For I will *h'* respect unto you, and
13 and I *h'* broken the bands of your
26 And when I *h'* broken the staff of your
37 and ye shall *h'* no power to stand
40 and that also they *h'* walked contrary
41 And that I also *h'* walked contrary
41 and *h'* brought them into the land of
27: 20 or if he *h'* sold the field to another
Nu 3: 12 And I, behold, I *h'* taken the Levites
32 and *h'* the oversight of them that
4: 15 Aaron and his sons *h'* made an
5: 7 confess their sin which they *h'* done:
8 But if the man *h'* no kinsman to
18 the priest shall *h'* in his hand
19 If no man *h'* lain with thee, and if
20 and some man *h'* lain with thee
27 and *h'* done trespass against her
8: 16 of Israel, *h'* I taken them unto me.
18 And I *h'* taken the Levites for all the
19 And I *h'* given the Levites as a gift to
9: 14 ye shall *h'* one ordinance, both for
11: 11 and wherefore *h'* I not found favour
12 *H'* I conceived all this people?
12 *h'* I begotten them, that thou
13 Whence should I *h'* flesh to give unto
15 if I *h'* found favour in thy sight; and
18 for ye *h'* wept in the ears of the Lord,
20 because that ye *h'* despised the Lord
20 and *h'* wept before him, saying, Why
12: 11 us, wherein we *h'* done foolishly,
11 foolishly, and wherein we *h'* sinned.
13: 32 The land, through which we *h'* gone
14: 11 for all the signs which I *h'* shewed
14 for they *h'* heard that thou Lord art
15 then the nations which *h'* heard the
22 Because all those men which *h'* seen
22 in the wilderness, and *h'* tempted me
22 these ten times, and *h'* not hearkened
27 I *h'* heard the murmurings of the
28 as ye *h'* spoken in mine ears, so will I
29 and upward, which *h'* murmured
31 know the land which ye *h'* despised.
35 I the Lord *h'* said, I will surely do it
Nu 14: 40 Lord hath promised: for we *h'* sinned.
15: 22 And if ye *h'* erred, and not observed
29 Ye shall *h'* one law for him that
16: 15 I *h'* not taken one ass from them,
15 from them, neither *h'* I hurt one of
28 for I *h'* not done them of mine own
30 that these men *h'* provoked the Lord.
41 saying, Ye *h'* killed the people of the
18: 6 And I, behold, I *h'* taken your
7 I *h'* given your priest's office unto you
8 Behold, I also *h'* given thee the charge
8 unto thee *h'* I given them by reason of
11 I *h'* given them unto thee, and to thy
12 offer unto the Lord, them *h'* I given
19 unto the Lord, *h'* I given thee, and
20 Thou shalt *h'* no inheritance in their
20 neither shalt thou *h'* any part
21 And, behold, I *h'* given the children of
23 of Israel they *h'* no inheritance.
24 I *h'* given to the Levites to inherit:
24 therefore I *h'* said unto them, Among
26 which I *h'* given you from them for
30 When ye *h'* heaved the best thereof
32 when ye *h'* heaved from it the best of
20: 4 And why *h'* ye brought up the
5 And wherefore *h'* ye made us to come
12 into the land which I *h'* given them.
15 and we *h'* dwelt in Egypt a long time;
17 nor to the left, until we *h'* passed thy
24 into the land which I *h'* given unto
21: 5 Wherefore *h'* ye brought us up out of
7 came to Moses, and said, We *h'* sinned,
7 we *h'* spoken against the Lord, and
30 We *h'* shot at them; Heshbon is
30 and we *h'* laid them waste even unto
34 Fear him not: for I *h'* delivered him
22: 28 What *h'* I done unto thee, that thou
34 I *h'* sinned; for I knew not that thou
38 *h'* I now any power at all to say
23: 4 him, I *h'* prepared seven altars,
4 and I *h'* offered upon every altar a
20 Behold, I *h'* received commandment
24: 19 come he that shall *h'* dominion,
25: 13 And he shall *h'* it, and his seed
18 they *h'* beguiled you in the matter of
27: 8 If a man die, and *h'* no son, then ye
9 And if he *h'* no daughter, then ye
10 And if he *h'* no brethren, then ye
11 And if his father *h'* no brethren, then
12 which I *h'* given unto the children of
17 be not as sheep which *h'* no shepherd.
28: 25, 26 ye shall *h'* an holy convocation;
29: 1 ye shall *h'* an holy convocation;
7 And ye shall *h'* on the tenth day
12 ye shall *h'* an holy convocation;
35 ye shall *h'* a solemn assembly:
30: 9 they *h'* bound their souls, shall stand
31: 15 him, *H'* ye saved all the women alive?
18 children, that *h'* not known a man
49 Thy servants *h'* taken the sum of the
50 We *h'* therefore brought an oblation
32: 4 for cattle, and thy servants *h'* cattle:
5 if we *h'* found grace in thy sight, let
11 because they *h'* not wholly followed
12 for they *h'* wholly followed the Lord.
17 until we *h'* brought them unto their
18 until the children of Israel *h'* inherited
23 behold, ye *h'* sinned against the Lord:
30 they shall *h'* possessions among
33: 53 for I *h'* given you the land to possess
34: 6 ye shall even *h'* the great sea for
14 fathers, *h'* received their inheritance;
14 Manasseh *h'* received...inheritance:
15 half tribe *h'* received their inheritance
35: 8 from them that *h'* many ye shall
8 but from them that *h'* few ye shall
13 six cities shall ye *h'* for refuge.
22 or *h'* cast upon him any thing without
28 Because he should *h'* remained in the
De 1: 6 in Horeb, saying, Ye *h'* dwelt long
8 Behold, I *h'* set the land before you:
28 our brethren *h'* discouraged our
28 and moreover we *h'* seen the sons of
41 We *h'* sinned against the Lord, we
2: 3 Ye *h'* compassed this mountain long
5 because I *h'* given mount Seir unto
9 because I *h'* given Ar unto the
19 because I *h'* given it unto the
24 behold, I *h'* given into thine hand
31 Behold, I *h'* begun to give Sihon and
3: 19 (for I know that ye *h'* much cattle,)
19 in your cities which I *h'* given you;
20 Until the Lord *h'* given rest unto your
20 his possession, which I *h'* given you.
21 Thine eyes *h'* seen all that the Lord
4: 3 Your eyes *h'* seen what the Lord did
5 Behold, I *h'* taught you statutes and
9 things which thine eyes *h'* seen,
25 and ye shall *h'* remained long in the
5: 7 Thou shalt *h'* none other gods
24 and we *h'* heard his voice out of the
24 we *h'* seen this day that God doth talk
26 out of the midst of the fire, as we *h'*,
28 and the Lord said unto me, I *h'* heard
28 of this people, which they *h'* spoken
28 spoken unto thee: they *h'* well said
28 well said all that they *h'* spoken.
6: 10 Lord thy God shall *h'* brought thee
11 when thou shalt *h'* eaten and be full;
7: 16 thine eye shall *h'* no pity upon
24 thee, until thou *h'* destroyed them.
9: 7 ye *h'* been rebellious against the
8 angry with you to *h'* destroyed you.
12 forth out of Egypt *h'* corrupted
12 they *h'* made them a molten image.
13 I *h'* seen this people, and, behold, it is
De 9: 20 very angry with Aaron to *h'* destroyed
23 which I *h'* given you; then ye rebelled
24 Ye *h'* been rebellious against the
10: 21 things, which thine eyes *h'* seen.
11: 2 your children which *h'* not known,
2 *h'* not seen the chastisement
7 But your eyes *h'* seen all the great
28 other gods, which ye *h'* not known.
12: 21 as I *h'* commanded thee, and thou
31 which he hateth, *h'* they done unto
31 they *h'* burnt in the fire to their gods.
13: 13 and *h'* withdrawn the inhabitants of
13 other gods, which ye *h'* not known;
17 and *h'* compassion upon thee, and
14: 9 all that *h'* fins and scales shall ye
15: 21 or *h'* any ill blemish, thou shalt not
17: 3 heaven, which I *h'* not commanded;
5 woman which *h'* committed that
18: 1 the tribe of Levi, shall *h'* no part
2 Therefore shall...*h'* no inheritance
8 They shall *h'* like portions to eat,
17 said unto me, They *h'* well spoken
17 well spoken that which they *h'* spoken.
20 which I *h'* not commanded him to
19: 14 which they of old time *h'* set in thine
19 as he had thought to *h'* done unto his
20: 9 when the officers *h'* made an end of
18 which they *h'* done unto their gods;
21: 7 and say, Our hands *h'* not shed this
7 this blood, neither *h'* our eyes seen it.
11 that thou wouldest *h'* her to thy
14 And it shall be, if thou *h'* no delight in
15 If a man *h'* two wives, one beloved,
15 and they *h'* born him children, both
18 If a man *h'* a stubborn and
18 and that, when they *h'* chastened him,
22 And if a man *h'* committed a sin
23: 12 Thou shalt *h'* a place also without
13 And thou shalt *h'* a paddle upon thy
25: 5 and one of them die, and *h'* no child,
13 Thou shalt not *h'* in thy bag divers
14 Thou shalt not *h'* in thine house
15 But thou shalt *h'* a perfect and just
15 and just measure shalt thou *h'*:
26: 10 And now, behold, I *h'* brought the
13 before the Lord thy God, I *h'* brought
13 out of mine house, and also *h'* given
13 me: I *h'* not transgressed thy
13 neither *h'* I forgotten them:
14 I *h'* not eaten thereof in my mourning,
14 neither *h'* I taken away ought thereof
14 but I *h'* hearkened to the voice of
14 and *h'* done according to all that thou
28: 21 until he *h'* consumed thee from off the
31 and thou shalt *h'* none to rescue them.
36 thou nor thy fathers *h'* known;
51 of thy sheep, until he *h'* destroyed
64 nor thy fathers *h'* known, even wood
65 shall the sole of thy foot *h'* rest:
66 and shalt *h'* none assurance of thy life:
29: 2 Ye *h'* seen all that the Lord did before
3 which thine eyes *h'* seen, the
5 And I *h'* led you forty years in the
6 Ye *h'* not eaten bread, neither
6 *h'* ye drunk wine or strong drink: that
16 For ye know how we *h'* dwelt in the
17 And ye *h'* seen their abominations, and
19 I shall *h'* peace, though I walk in the
25 Because they *h'* forsaken the covenant
30: 1 curse, which I *h'* set before thee,
3 and *h'* compassion upon thee, and
15 See, I *h'* set before thee this day life
19 that I *h'* set before you life and death,
31: 5 which I *h'* commanded you.
13 which *h'* not known any thing, may
16 break my covenant which I *h'* made
18 which they shall *h'* wrought, in that
20 For when I shall *h'* brought them into
20 and they shall *h'* eaten and filled
21 I *h'* brought them into the land which
27 ye *h'* been rebellious against the
29 the way which I *h'* commanded you;
32: 5 They *h'* corrupted themselves, their
21 They *h'* moved me to jealousy with
21 they *h'* provoked me to anger with
33: 9 I *h'* not seen him; neither did he
9 for they *h'* observed thy word, and
34: 4 I *h'* caused thee to see it with thine
Jos 1: 3 that *h'* I given unto you, as I said unto
8 and then thou shalt *h'* good success.
9 *H'* not I commanded thee? Be strong
15 Until the Lord *h'* given your brethren
15 and they also *h'* possessed the land
2: 10 For we *h'* heard how the Lord dried
12 since I *h'* shewed you kindness, that
13 and all that they *h'*, and deliver our
3: 4 for ye *h'* not passed this way
5: 9 This day *h'* I rolled away the reproach
6: 2 I *h'* given into thine hand Jericho, and
7: 11 and they *h'* also transgressed my
11 for they *h'* even taken of the accursed
11 and *h'* also stolen, and dissembled
11 and they *h'* put it even among their
20 Indeed I *h'* sinned against the Lord
20 of Israel, and thus and thus *h'* I done:
8: 1 see, I *h'* given into thy hand the
6 till we *h'* drawn them from the city;
8 And it shall be, when ye *h'* taken the
8 shall ye do. See, I *h'* commanded you.
9: 9 for we *h'* heard the fame of him, and
19 We *h'* sworn unto them by the Lord
22 Wherefore *h'* ye beguiled us, saying,
24 lives because of you, and *h'* done this
10: 8 Fear them not: for I *h'* delivered them
11: 20 and that they might *h'* no favour,
13: 6 for an inheritance, as I *h'* commanded

Jos 13: 8 and the Gadites h' received their
14: 9 land whereon thy feet h' trodden
17: 16 in the land of the valley h' chariots of
17 thou shalt not h' one lot only:
18 though they h' iron chariots, and
18: 7 But the Levites h' no part among you;
22: 2 And said unto them, Ye h' kept all
2 and h' obeyed my voice in all that I
3 Ye h' not left your brethren these
3 but h' kept the charge of the
11 tribe of Manasseh h' built an altar
16 trespass is this that ye h' committed
16 in that ye h' builded you an altar, that
23 That we h' built us an altar to turn
24 And if we h' not rather done it for fear
25 ye h' no part in the Lord: so shall
27 in time to come, Ye h' no part in the
31 because ye h' not committed this
31 now ye h' delivered the children of
23: 3 And ye h' seen all that the Lord your
4 Behold, I h' divided unto you by lot
4 with all the nations that I h' cut off,
8 your God, as ye h' done unto this day.
15 until he h' destroyed you from off this
16 When ye h' transgressed the
16 and h' gone and served other gods,
24: 7 them; and your eyes h' seen
7 what I h' done in Egypt: and ye dwelt
13 And I h' given you a land for which
22 that ye h' chosen you the Lord, to
J'g 1: 2 behold, I h' delivered the land into his
7 as I h' done, so God hath requited me.
2: 1 and h' brought you unto the land
2 but ye h' not obeyed my voice:
2 my voice: why h' ye done this?
20 their fathers, and h' not hearkened
3: 19 and said, I h' a secret errand unto
20 And Ehud said, I h' a message from
5: 13 that remaineth h' dominion
13 the Lord made me h' dominion
30 H' they not sped?
30 h' they not divided the prey; to every
6: 10 but ye h' not obeyed my voice.
14 of the Midianites: h' not I sent thee?
17 If now I h' found grace in thy sight,
22 for because I h' seen an angel of the
7: 9 unto the host; for I h' delivered it into
8: 2 What h' I done now in comparison of
9: 16 Now therefore, if ye h' done truly and
16 in that ye h' made Abimelech king,
16 and if ye h' dealt well with Jerubbaal
16 and h' done unto him according to the
18 and h' slain his sons, threescore and
18 and h' made Abimelech, the son of his
19 If ye then h' dealt truly and sincerely
48 What ye h' seen me do, make haste,
48 me do, make haste, and do as I h' done.
10: 10 unto the Lord, saying, We h' sinned
10 because we h' forsaken our God, and
13 Yet ye h' forsaken me, and served
14 unto the gods which ye h' chosen;
15 We h' sinned: do thou unto us
11: 27 Wherefore I h' not sinned against
35 for I h' opened my mouth unto the
13: 15 until we shall h' made ready a kid for
22 surely die, because we h' seen God.
23 he would not h' received a burnt
23 neither would he h' shewed us all
23 nor would as at this time h' told us
14: 2 and said, I h' seen a woman in
6 and he rent him as he would h' rent a
15 house with fire: h' ye called us to
15 ye called us to take that we h'? is it
16 Behold, I h' not told it my father nor
15: 7 Though ye h' done this, yet will I be
11 As they did unto me, so h' I done unto
16 with the jaw of an ass h' I slain a
16: 17 for I h' been a Nazarite unto God from
17: 13 good, seeing I h' a Levite to my
18: 9 for we h' seen the land, and, behold, it
14 therefore consider what ye h' to do.
24 And he said, Ye h' taken away my gods
24 are gone away: and what h' I more?
20: 5 night, and thought to h' slain me:
5 and my concubine h' they forced,
6 for they h' committed lewdness and
10 all the folly that they h' wrought in
21: 7 seeing we h' sworn by the Lord that
18 for the children of Israel h' sworn,
Ru 1: 8 as ye h' dealt with the dead, and with
12 for I am too old to h' an husband.
12 If I should say, I h' hope,
12 if I should h' an husband also to night,
2: 9 h' I not charged the young men that
9 which the young men h' drawn.
10 Why h' I found grace in thine eyes,
21 until they h' ended all my harvest.
3: 3 until he shall h' done eating and
18 until he h' finished the thing this day.
4: 9 witnesses this day, that I h' bought all
10 the wife of Mahlon, h' I purchased to
1Sa 1: 15 I h' drunk neither wine nor strong
15 but h' poured out my soul before the
16 of my complaint and grief h' I spoken
20 Because I h' asked him of the Lord.
23 tarry until thou h' weaned him; only
28 Therefore also I h' lent him to the
2: 5 They that were full h' hired out
15 he will not h' sodden flesh of thee,
29 mine offering, which I h' commanded
3: 12 all things which I h' spoken concerning
13 For I h' told him that I will judge his
14 And therefore I h' sworn unto the
4: 9 as they h' been to you: quit yourselves
5: 10 They h' brought about the ark of the
6: 21 The Philistines h' brought again the

1Sa 7: 6 We h' sinned against the Lord. And
8: 7 thee: for they h' not rejected thee,
7 but they h' rejected me, that I should
8 all the works which they h' done since
8 wherewith they h' forsaken me, and
18 your king which ye shall h' chosen
19 Nay; but we will h' a king over us;
9: 7 bring...the man of God: what h' we?
8 Behold, I h' here at hand the
16 for I h' looked upon my people,
24 I h' invited the people. So Saul did
10: 19 And ye h' this day rejected your God,
19 and ye h' said unto him, Nay, but set a
12: 1 Israel, Behold, I h' hearkened unto
1 me, and h' made a king over you.
2 and I h' walked before you from my
3 his anointed: whose ox h' I taken?
3 I taken? or whose ass h' I taken?
3 I taken? or whom h' I defrauded?
3 I defrauded? whom h' I oppressed?
3 whose hand h' I received any bribe
5 that ye h' not found ought in my hand.
10 unto the Lord, and said, We h' sinned,
10 because we h' forsaken the Lord,
10 and h' served Baalim and Ashtaroth:
13 behold the king whom ye h' chosen,
13 and whom ye h' desired! and, behold,
17 which ye h' done in the sight of the
19 for we h' added unto all our sins this
20 Fear not: ye h' done all this
13: 12 and I h' not made supplication unto
13 for now would the Lord h' established
14: 29 how mine eyes h' been enlightened,
33 And he said, Ye h' transgressed:
15: 3 destroy all that they h', and spare
11 repenteth me that I h' set up Saul to
13 I h' performed the commandment of
15 Saul said, They h' brought them from
15 and the rest we h' utterly destroyed.
20 I h' obeyed the voice of the Lord,
20 and h' gone the way which the Lord
20 and h' brought Agag the king of
20 and h' utterly destroyed the
21 should h' been utterly destroyed
24 Saul said unto Samuel, I h' sinned:
24 I h' transgressed the commandment
30 Then he said, I h' sinned: yet honour
16: 1 for Saul, seeing I h' rejected him
1 for I h' provided me a king among
7 because I h' refused him: for the
18 Behold, I h' seen a son of Jesse the
17: 25 men of Israel said, H' ye seen this
29 David said, What h' I now done? Is
39 these; for I h' not proved them.
18: 8 They h' ascribed unto David ten
8 and to me they h' ascribed but
19 should h' been given to David, that
20: 1 What h' I done? what is mine
7 is well; thy servant shall h' peace:
12 when I h' sounded my father about
23 thou and I h' spoken of, behold, the
29 and now, if I h' found favour in thine
42 forasmuch as we h' sworn both of us
21: 2 thee, and what I h' commanded thee:
2 I h' appointed my servants to such
4 if the young men h' kept themselves
5 Of a truth women h' been kept from
8 for I h' neither brought my sword
14 wherefore then h' ye brought him
15 H' I need of mad men, that ye
15 that ye h' brought this fellow to play
22: 8 That all of you h' conspired against
13 Why h' ye conspired against me, thou
22 I h' occasioned the death of all the
23: 21 Lord; for ye h' compassion on me.
27 for the Philistines h' invaded the
24: 10 Behold, this day thine eyes h' seen
11 and I h' not sinned against thee; yet
17 me good, whereas I h' rewarded
25: 7 And now I h' heard that thou hast
11 and my flesh that I h' killed for my
21 Surely in vain h' I kept all that this
30 when the Lord shall h' done to my
30 and shall h' appointed thee ruler over
31 when the Lord shall h' dealt well with
35 see, I h' harkened to thy voice,
35 thy voice, and h' accepted thy person.
26: 16 because ye h' not kept your master,
18 for what h' I done? or what evil is in
19 If the Lord h' stirred thee up against
19 for they h' driven me out this day
21 Then said Saul, I h' sinned: return,
21 this day: behold, I h' played the fool,
21 the fool, and h' erred exceedingly.
27: 5 If I h' now found grace in thine
10 Whither h' ye made a road to day?
28: 9 cut off those that h' familiar spirits,
15 therefore I h' called thee, that thou
21 obeyed thy voice, and I h' put my life
21 and h' hearkened unto thy words
22 eat, that thou mayest h' strength,
29: 3 and I h' found no fault in him since
6 for I h' not found evil in thee since
8 But what h' I done? and what hast
8 I h' been with thee unto this day,
9 the Philistines h' said, He shall not
10 up early in the morning, and h' light,
30: 22 of the spoil that we h' recovered, save
2Sa 1: 10 was on his arm, and h' brought them
16 against thee, saying, I h' slain the
2: 5 that ye h' shewed this kindness unto
5 even unto Saul, and h' buried him.
6 because ye h' done this thing.
7 also the house of Judah h' anointed
3: 8 and h' not delivered thee into the
4: 6 as though they would h' fetched

2Sa 4: 10 Saul is dead, thinking to h' brought
10 who thought that I would h' given
11 much more, when wicked men h' slain
7: 6 Whereas I h' not dwelt in any house
6 but h' walked in a tent and in a
7 all the places wherein I h' walked
9 and h' cut off all thine enemies out
9 and h' made thee a great name, like
11 and h' caused thee to rest from all
22 according to all that we h' heard
9: 9 I h' given unto thy master's son all
10 that thy master's son may h' food
12: 8 I would moreover h' given unto thee
13 David said unto Nathan, I h' sinned
27 to David, and said, I h' fought against
27 against Rabbah, and h' taken the city
13: 9 And Amnon said, H' out all men
28 h' not I commanded you? be
32 not my lord suppose that they h' slain
14: 15 because the people h' made me afraid:
21 Behold now, I h' done this thing: go
22 that I h' found grace in thy sight, my
29 to h' sent him to the king; but he
31 h' thy servants set my field on fire?
32 good for me to h' been there still:
15: 7 pay my vow, which I h' vowed unto
26 But if he thus say, I h' no delight in
34 as I h' been thy father's servant
36 Behold, they h' there with them their
16: 10 What h' I to do with you, ye sons of
19 as I h' served in thy father's presence,
17: 15 and thus and thus h' I counselled.
18: 11 and I would h' given thee ten shekels
13 Otherwise I should h' wrought
13 thyself wouldest h' set thyself against
18 I h' no son to keep my name in
19: 5 this day h' saved thy life, and the
20 I h' sinned: therefore, behold, I am
22 What h' I to do with you, ye sons of
28 What right therefore h' I yet to
29 I h' said, Thou and Ziba divide the
34 How long h' I to live, that I should
41 Why h' our brethren...stolen thee
41 and h' brought the king, and his
42 h' we eaten at all of the king's cost?
43 said, We h' ten parts in the king,
43 and we h' also more right in David
20: 1 and said, We h' no part in David,
1 neither h' we inheritance in the son
21: 4 We will h' no silver nor gold of Saul,
16 sword, thought to h' slain David.
22: 22 for I h' kept the ways of the Lord,
22 and h' not wickedly departed from
24 h' kept myself from mine iniquity.
30 for by thee I h' run through a troop:
30 by my God h' I leaped over a wall.
38 I h' pursued mine enemies, and
39 And I h' consumed them, and
24: 10 David said unto the Lord, I h' sinned
10 sinned greatly in that I h' done:
10 servant; for I h' done very foolishly.
17 the people, and said, Lo, I h' sinned,
17 and I h' done wickedly: but these
17 what h' they done? let thine hand,
1Ki 1: 35 and I h' appointed him to be ruler
44 and they h' caused him to ride upon
45 h' annointed him king in Gihon:
2: 14 said moreover, I h' somewhat to say
23 if Adonijah h' not spoken this word
42 The word that I h' heard is good.
43 commandment that I h' charged thee
3: 12 Behold, I h' done according to thy
12 lo, I h' given thee a wise and
13 And I h' also given thee that which
5: 8 I h' considered the things which thou
8: 13 I h' surely built thee an house to
20 and h' built an house for the name
21 And I h' set there a place for the ark,
27 less this house that I h' builded?
28 Yet h' thou respect unto the prayer
33 because they h' sinned against thee,
35 because they h' sinned against thee;
43 this house, which I h' builded, is
44 and toward the house that I h' built
47 them captives, saying, We h' sinned,
47 sinned, and h' done perversely, we
47 we h' committed wickedness;
48 the house which I h' built for thy
50 And forgive thy people that h' sinned
50 wherein they h' transgressed against
50 that they may h' compassion on
59 wherewith I h' made supplication
9: 3 I h' heard thy prayer and thy
3 I h' hallowed this house, which thou
4 to all that I h' commanded thee, and
6 my statutes which I h' set before you,
7 out of the land which I h' given them;
7 and this house, which I h' hallowed for
9 and h' taken hold on other gods,
9 and h' worshipped them, and served
11: 11 my statutes, which I h' commanded
13 for Jerusalem's sake which I h' chosen.
32 But he shall h' one tribe for my
32 the city which I h' chosen out of all
33 Because that they h' forsaken me,
33 and h' worshipped Ashtoreth the
33 and h' not walked in my ways, to do
36 the city which I h' chosen me to put
12: 9 people, who h' spoken to me, saying,
16 saying, What portion h' we in David?
16 neither h' we inheritance in the son
14: 15 because they h' made their groves,
15: 19 behold, I h' sent unto thee a present
17: 4 and I h' commanded the ravens to
9 I h' commanded a widow woman
12 thy God liveth, I h' not a cake,

1Ki 17:18 What *h'* I to do with thee, O thou man
18: 9 And he said, What *h'* I sinned, that
18 answered, I *h'* not troubled Israel;
18 ye *h'* forsaken the commandments
36 and that I *h'* done all these things at
19:10 And he said, I *h'* been very jealous
10 for the children of Israel *h'* forsaken
14 And he said, I *h'* been very jealous
14 the children of Israel *h'* forsaken
18 Yet I *h'* left me seven thousand in
18 all the knees which *h'* not bowed
20 Go back again: for what *h'* I done to
20: 4 saying, I am thine, and all that I *h'*.
5 Although I *h'* sent unto thee, saying,
28 Because the Syrians *h'* said, The
31 Behold now, we *h'* heard that the
21: 2 thy vineyard, that I may *h'* it for
20 he answered, I *h'* found thee: because
22:11 Syrians, until thou *h'* consumed them.
17 as sheep that *h'* not a shepherd:
17 These *h'* no master: let them return
2Ki 2:21 Thus saith the Lord, I *h'* healed these
3:13 What *h'* I to do with thee? get thee to
23 and they *h'* smitten one another: now
27 eldest son that should *h'* reigned in
5: 6 behold, I *h'* therewith sent Naaman
13 wouldest thou not *h'* done it? how
7:12 shew you what the Syrians *h'* done to
17 whose hand he leaned to *h'* the charge
9: 3 I *h'* anointed thee king over Israel.
5 and he said, I *h'* an errand to thee, O
6 I *h'* anointed thee king over the
12 saith the Lord, I *h'* anointed thee king
26 Surely I *h'* seen yesterday the blood
10: 8 They *h'* brought the heads of the
19 wanting: for I *h'* a great sacrifice to
24 any of the men whom I *h'* brought
11:15 *H'* her forth without the ranges:
13:17 in Aphek, till thou *h'* consumed
19 Thou shouldest *h'* smitten five or six
17:38 And the covenant that I *h'* made with
18:14 saying, I *h'* offended; return from me:
20 I *h'* counsel and strength for the war.
34 *h'* they delivered Samaria out of
35 that *h'* delivered their country out of
19: 6 of the king of Assyria *h'* blasphemed
11 the kings of Assyria *h'* done to all
12 *H'* the gods of the nations delivered
12 which my fathers *h'* destroyed; as
17 the kings of Assyria *h'* destroyed the
18 And *h'* cast their gods into the fire:
18 and stone: therefore they *h'* destroyed
20 Sennacherib king of Assyria I *h'* heard.
24 *h'* digged and drunk strange waters,
24 and with the sole of my feet *h'* I dried
25 not heard long ago how I *h'* done it,
25 of ancient times that I *h'* formed it?
25 now *h'* I brought it to pass, that
20: 3 remember now how I *h'* walked before
3 and *h'* done that which is good in
5 thy father, I *h'* heard thy prayer,
5 I *h'* seen thy tears: behold, I will heal
9 This sign shalt thou *h'* of the Lord,
15 And he said, What *h'* they seen in
15 that are in mine house *h'* they seen:
15 my treasures that I *h'* not shewed
17 and that which thy fathers *h'* laid up
21: 7 and in Jerusalem, which I *h'* chosen
8 according to all that I *h'* commanded
15 Because they *h'* done that which was
15 and *h'* provoked me to anger, since the
22: 4 keepers of the door *h'* gathered of the
5 that *h'* the oversight of the house of
8 I *h'* found the book of the law in the
9 Thy servants *h'* gathered the money
9 and *h'* delivered it into the hand of
9 that *h'* the oversight of the house of
13 because our fathers *h'* not hearkened
17 Because they *h'* forsaken me, and
17 and *h'* burned incense unto other
19 I also *h'* heard thee, saith the Lord.
23:27 as I *h'* removed Israel, and will cast
27 city Jerusalem which I *h'* chosen,
1Ch 11:19 blood of these men that *h'* put their
15:12 unto the place that I *h'* prepared for
17: 5 For I *h'* not dwelt in an house since the
5 but *h'* gone from tent to tent, and
6 Wheresoever I *h'* walked with all
6 Why *h'* ye not built me an house of
8 I *h'* been with thee whithersoever
8 and *h'* cut off all thine enemies from
8 and *h'* made thee a name like the
20 to all that we *h'* heard with our ears.
21: 8 And David said unto God, I *h'* sinned
8 because I *h'* done this thing: but now,
8 servant; for I *h'* done very foolishly.
17 even I it is that *h'* sinned and done
17 as for these sheep, what *h'* they done?
22:14 behold, in my trouble I *h'* prepared
14 and stone *h'* I prepared; and thou
28: 6 for I *h'* chosen him to be my son, and
29: 2 Now I *h'* prepared with all my might
3 because I *h'* set my affection to thee
3 I *h'* of mine own proper good, of
3 I *h'* given to the house of my God,
3 all that I *h'* prepared for the holy
14 and of thine own *h'* we given thee.
16 all this store that we *h'* prepared to
17 I *h'* willingly offered all these things:
17 and now *h'* I seen with joy thy people,
19 for the which I *h'* made provision.
2Ch 1:11 over whom I *h'* made thee king:
12 such as none of the kings *h'* had
12 that *h'* been before thee, either shall
12 there any after thee *h'* the like.
2:13 And now I *h'* sent a cunning man,

2Ch 6: 2 But I *h'* built an house of habitation
6 But I *h'* chosen Jerusalem, that my
6 and *h'* chosen David to be over my
10 and *h'* built the house for the name of
11 And in it *h'* I put the ark, wherein is
18 much less this house which I *h'* built!
19 *H'* respect therefore to the prayer of
24, 26 because they *h'* sinned against thee;
33 this house which I *h'* built is called by
34 the house which I *h'* built for thy
37 their captivity, saying, We *h'* sinned,
37 sinned, we *h'* done amiss, and
37 done amiss, and *h'* dealt wickedly;
38 whither they *h'* carried them captives,
38 and toward the house which I *h'* built
39 forgive thy people which *h'* sinned
7:12 and said unto him, I *h'* heard thy
12 and *h'* chosen this place to myself for
16 For now I *h'* chosen and sanctified
17 according to all that I *h'* commanded
18 according as I *h'* covenanted with
19 which I *h'* set before you, and shall go
20 out of my land which I *h'* given them;
20 and this house, which I *h'* sanctified
10: 9 answer to this people, that *h'* spoken
16 saying, What portion *h'* we in David?
16 and we *h'* none inheritance in the son
12: 5 saith the Lord, Ye *h'* forsaken me,
5 and therefore *h'* I also left you in
7 They *h'* humbled themselves:
13: 7 *h'* strengthened themselves against
9 *H'* ye not cast out the priests of the
9 and *h'* made you priests after the
10 our God, and we *h'* not forsaken him;
11 our God; but ye *h'* forsaken him.
14: 7 because we *h'* sought the Lord our
7 we *h'* sought him, and he hath given
11 or with them that *h'* no power: help
16: 3 behold, I *h'* sent thee silver and gold;
9 henceforth thou shalt *h'* wars.
18:16 as sheep that *h'* no shepherd:
16 and the Lord said, These *h'* no master;
20: 8 they dwelt therein, and *h'* built thee
12 for we *h'* no might against this great
21:15 And thou shalt *h'* great sickness by
23:14 them, *H'* her forth of the ranges:
24:20 because ye *h'* forsaken the Lord, he
25: 9 hundred talents which I *h'* given to
28: 9 and ye *h'* slain them in a rage that
11 which ye *h'* taken captive of your
13 for whereas we *h'* offended against
29: 6 For our fathers *h'* trespassed, and
6 Lord our God, and *h'* forsaken him,
6 and *h'* turned away their faces from
7 Also they *h'* shut up the doors of the
7 and *h'* not burned incense nor offered
9 For, lo, our fathers *h'* fallen by the
18 We *h'* cleansed all the house of the
19 *h'* we prepared and sanctified
31 Now ye *h'* consecrated yourselves unto
31:10 of the Lord, we *h'* had enough to eat,
10 and *h'* left plenty: for the Lord hath
32:13 what I and my fathers *h'* done unto all
17 *h'* not delivered their people out of
33: 7 which I *h'* chosen before all the tribes
8 land which I *h'* appointed for your
8 to do all that I *h'* commanded them,
34:15 I *h'* found the book of the law in the
17 And they *h'* gathered together the
17 and *h'* delivered it into the hand of the
21 because our fathers *h'* not kept the
24 book which they *h'* read before the
25 Because they *h'* forsaken me, and
25 and *h'* burned incense unto other gods,
27 I *h'* even heard thee also, saith the
35:21 What *h'* I to do with thee, thou king of
21 against the house wherewith I *h'* war:
23 *H'* me away; for I am sore
Ezr 4: 3 Ye *h'* nothing to do with us to build
12 and *h'* set up the walls thereof, and
14 Now because we *h'* maintenance
15 and that they *h'* moved sedition within
16 thou shalt *h'* no portion on this
19 rebellion and sedition *h'* been made
20 There *h'* been mighty kings also
20 which *h'* ruled over all countries
6: 9 And that which they *h'* need of, both
11 Also I *h'* made a decree, that whosoever
12 I Darius *h'* made a decree; let it be
7:15 and his counsellors *h'* freely offered
20 which thou shalt *h'* occasion to bestow,
9: 1 and the Levites, *h'* not separated
2 For they *h'* taken of their daughters
2 so that the holy seed *h'* mingled
7 *h'* we been in a great trespass
7 iniquities *h'* we...been delivered
10 for we *h'* forsaken thy commandments,
11 which *h'* filled it from one end to
10: 2 said unto Ezra, We *h'* trespassed
2 and *h'* taken strange wives of the
10 said unto them, Ye *h'* transgressed,
10 and *h'* taken strange wives, to increase
13 we are many that *h'* transgressed in
14 let all them which *h'* taken strange
Ne 1: 6 which we *h'* sinned against thee: both
6 I and my father's house *h'* sinned.
7 We *h'* dealt very corruptly against
7 and *h'* not kept the commandments,
9 the place that I *h'* chosen to set my
2: 5 and if thy servant *h'* found favour in
20 but ye *h'* no portion, nor right, nor
4: 5 for they *h'* provoked thee to anger
5: 3 We *h'* mortgaged our lands,
4 We *h'* borrowed money for the king's
5 for other men *h'* our lands and
8 after our ability *h'* redeemed our

Ne 5:14 I and my brethren *h'* not eaten the
19 according to all that I *h'* done for
6:13 and that they might *h'* matter for
14 the prophets, that would *h'* put me in
9:33 thou hast done right, but we *h'* done
34 Neither *h'* our kings...kept thy law,
35 For they *h'* not served thee in their
37 also they *h'* dominion over our bodies,
10:37 same Levites might *h'* the tithes
13:14 that I *h'* done for the house of my God,
29 because they *h'* defiled the priesthood,
Es 1:18 which *h'* heard of the deed of the
3: 9 of those that *h'* the charge of the
4:11 but I *h'* not been called to come in
5: 4 the banquet that I *h'* prepared for
8 If I *h'* found favour in the sight of the
7: 3 If I *h'* found favour in thy sight, O
8: 5 and if I *h'* found favour in his sight
7 Behold, I *h'* given Esther the house of
7 and him they *h'* hanged upon the
9: 1 enemies of the Jews hoped to *h'* power
12 The Jews *h'* slain and destroyed five
12 what *h'* they done in the rest of the
Job 1: 5 It may be that my sons *h'* sinned, and
15 yea, they *h'* slain the servants with
17 fell upon the camels, and *h'* carried
3: 9 let it look for light, but *h'* none;
13 For now should I *h'* lain still and
13 I should *h'* slept: then had I been at
4: 4 Thy words *h'* upholden him that was
8 Even as I *h'* seen, that they plow
5: 3 I *h'* seen the foolish taking root: but
27 Lo this, we *h'* searched it, so it is;
6: 8 Oh that I might *h'* my request;
10 Then should I yet *h'* comfort;
10 for I *h'* not concealed the words of
15 My brethren *h'* dealt deceitfully as a
24 me to understand wherein I *h'* erred.
7:20 I *h'* sinned; what shall I do unto
8: 4 If thy children *h'* sinned against him,
4 and he *h'* cast them away for their
18 deny him, saying, I *h'* not seen thee.
10: 8 Thine hands *h'* made me and
19 I should *h'* been as though I had
19 I should *h'* been carried from the
12: 3 But I *h'* understanding as well as
14:15 thou wilt *h'* a desire to the work
22 his flesh upon him shall *h'* pain,
15:17 and that which I *h'* seen I will
18 Which wise men *h'* told from their
18 from their fathers, and *h'* not hid it:
16: 2 I *h'* heard many such things:
3 Shall vain words *h'* an end? or what
10 They *h'* gaped upon me with their
10 they *h'* smitten me upon the cheek
10 they *h'* gathered themselves together
15 I *h'* sewed sackcloth upon my skin,
18 blood, and let my cry *h'* no place.
17:13 I *h'* made my bed in the darkness.
14 I *h'* said to corruption, Thou art my
18:17 the earth, and he shall *h'* no name in
19 He shall neither *h'* son nor nephew
19: 3 These ten times *h'* ye reproached me:
4 And be it indeed that I *h'* erred, mine
14 my kinsfolk *h'* failed, and my
14 and my familiar friends *h'* forgotten
21 *H'* pity upon me, *h'* pity upon me,
20: 3 I *h'* heard the check of my reproach,
7 they which *h'* seen him shall say,
21: 3 and after that I *h'* spoken, mock on.
15 what profit should we *h'*, if we pray
29 *H'* ye not asked them that go by the
22: 9 of the fatherless *h'* been broken.
15 way which wicked men *h'* trodden?
25 and thou shalt *h'* plenty of silver.
26 then shalt thou *h'* thy delight in the
23:11 hath held his steps, his way *h'* I kept,
12 Neither *h'* I gone back from the
12 I *h'* esteemed the words of his mouth
24: 7 clothing, that they *h'* no covering
19 the grave those which *h'* sinned.
27:12 Behold, all ye yourselves *h'* seen it;
28: 8 The lion's whelps *h'* not trodden it,
22 We *h'* heard the fame thereof with
30: 1 are younger than I *h'* me in derision,
1 whose fathers I would *h'* disdained
1 to *h'* set with the dogs of my flock.
13 my calamity, they *h'* no helper.
16 the days of affliction *h'* taken hold
31: 5 If I *h'* walked with vanity, or if my
9 If mine heart *h'* been deceived by a
9 or if I *h'* laid wait at my neighbour's
16 If I *h'* withheld the poor from their
16 or *h'* caused the eyes of the widow to
17 Or *h'* eaten my morsel myself alone,
18 and I *h'* guided her from my mother's
19 If I *h'* seen any perish for want of
20 If his loins *h'* not blessed me, and if
21 If I *h'* lifted up my hand against the
24 If I *h'* made gold my hope, or
24 or *h'* said to the fine gold, Thou art
28 for I should *h'* denied the God that is
30 Neither *h'* I suffered my mouth to
39 If I *h'* eaten the fruits thereof without
39 or *h'* caused the owners thereof to
32:13 should say, We *h'* found out wisdom:
33: 2 Behold, now I *h'* opened my mouth,
8 and I *h'* heard the voice of thy words,
24 to the pit: I *h'* found a ransom.
27 and if any say, I *h'* sinned, and
34: 2 ear unto me, ye that *h'* knowledge.
31 I *h'* borne chastisement, I will not
32 if I *h'* done iniquity, I will do no more.
35: 3 What profit shall I *h'*, if I be cleansed
36: 2 that I *h'* yet to speak on God's behalf.
9 transgressions that they *h'* exceeded.

Job 36:16 Even so would he h' removed thee out
38:17 H' the gates of death been opened
23 Which I h' reserved against the time
39: 6 Whose house I h' made the wilderness,
40: 5 Once h' I spoken; but I will not
42: 3 therefore h' I uttered that I
5 I h' heard of thee by the hearing of
7 for ye h' not spoken of me the thing
8 in that ye h' not spoken of me the thing
Ps 2: 4 the Lord shall h' them in derision.
6 Yet h' I set my king upon my holy
7 art my Son; this day h' I begotten
3: 6 that h' set themselves against me
4: 1 h' mercy upon me, and hear my
5:10 transgressions; for they h' rebelled
6: 2 H' mercy upon me, O Lord; for I
7: 3 O Lord my God, if I h' done this; if
4 If I h' rewarded evil unto him that
4 yea, I h' delivered him that without
8: 6 madest him to h' dominion over
9:13 H' mercy upon me, O Lord;
10: 2 in the devices that they h' imagined.
12: 4 Who h' said, With our tongue will we
13: 4 Lest mine enemy say, I h' prevailed
5 But I h' trusted in thy mercy; my
14: 1 they h' done abominable works,
4 H' all...of iniquity no knowledge?
6 Ye h' shamed the counsel of the
16: 6 places; yea, I h' a goodly heritage.
8 I h' set the Lord always before me:
17: 4 I h' kept me from the paths of the
6 I h' called upon thee, for thou wilt
11 They h' now compassed us in our
11 they h' set their eyes bowing down
14 which h' their portion in this life.
18:21 For I h' kept the ways of the Lord,
21 and h' not wickedly departed from
29 For by thee I h' run through a troop;
29 and by my God h' I leaped over a
37 I h' pursued mine enemies, and
38 I h' wounded them that they were
43 a people whom I h' not known shall
19:13 let them not h' dominion over me:
22:12 Many bulls h' compassed me: strong
12 strong bulls of Bashan h' beset me
16 For dogs h' compassed me: the
16 assembly of the wicked h' inclosed
25: 6 for they h' been ever of old.
16 thee unto me, and h' mercy upon
26: 1 Judge me, O Lord; for I h' walked in
1 I h' trusted also in the Lord;
3 before mine eyes: and I h' walked in
4 I h' not sat with vain persons, neither
5 I h' hated the congregation of evil
8 Lord, I h' loved the habitation of thy
27: 4 One thing h' I desired of the Lord,
7 h' mercy also upon me, and
30:10 Hear, O Lord, and h' mercy upon
31: 4 me out of the net that they h' laid
6 I h' hated them that regard lying
9 H' mercy upon me, O Lord, for I
13 For I h' heard the slander of many:
17 for I h' called upon thee: let the
32: 5 thee, and mine iniquity h' I not hid.
9 the mule, which h' no understanding:
33: 21 because we h' trusted in his holy
35: 7 For without cause h' they hid for me
7 without cause they h' digged for my
25 Ah, so would we h' it: let them not
25 say, We h' swallowed him up.
37:14 The wicked h' drawn out the sword,
14 and h' bent their bow, to cast down
25 I h' been young, and now am old;
25 yet h' I not seen the righteous
35 I h' seen the wicked in great power,
38: 8 I h' roared by reason of...disquietness
40: 9 I h' preached righteousness in the
9 lo, I h' not refrained my lips, O Lord,
10 I h' not hid thy righteousness within
10 I h' declared thy faithfulness and thy
10 I h' not concealed thy lovingkindness
12 For innumerable evils h' compassed
12 mine iniquities h' taken hold upon
41: 4 heal my soul; for I h' sinned against
42: 3 My tears h' been my meat day
44: 1 We h' heard with our ears, O God, our
1 our fathers h' told us, what work
17 come upon us; yet h' we not forgotten
17 neither h' we dealt falsely in thy
18 neither h' our steps declined from
20 If we h' forgotten the name of our
45: 1 which I h' made touching the king:
8 whereby they h' made thee glad.
48: 8 As we h' heard, so h' we seen in the
9 We h' thought of thy lovingkindness,
49:14 the upright shall h' dominion
50: 5 those that h' made a covenant with
8 to h' been continually before me.
51: 1 H' mercy upon me, O God,
4 Against thee, thee only, h' I sinned,
53: 1 and h' done abominable iniquity:
4 H' the...of iniquity no knowledge?
4 as they eat bread: they h' not called
54: 3 after my soul: they h' not set God
55: 9 for I h' seen violence and strife in the
12 then I could h' borne it: neither was it
12 against me; then I would h' hid
19 Because they h' no changes, therefore
56: 4 in God I h' put my trust; I will not fear
11 In God h' I put my trust: I will not be
57: 6 They h' prepared a net for my steps;
6 they h' digged a pit before me, into
59: 8 shalt h' all the heathen in derision.
62: 11 hath spoken once; twice h' I heard
63: 2 thy glory, so as I h' seen thee in the
66: 14 Which my lips h' uttered, and my

Ps 68:13 Though ye h' lien among the pots,
24 They h' seen thy goings, O God;
69: 7 for thy sake I h' borne reproach;
22 should h' been for their welfare,
35 there, and h' it in possession.
71: 6 By thee h' I been holden up from the
17 and hitherto h' I declared thy
18 until I h' shewed thy strength unto
72: 8 He shall h' dominion also from sea to
73: 7 with fatness: they h' more than heart
13 Verily I h' cleansed my heart in vain,
14 For all the day long h' I been plagued,
25 Whom h' I in heaven but thee? and
28 I h' put my trust in the Lord God, that
74: 7 They h' cast fire into thy sanctuary,
7 they h' defiled by casting down the
8 they h' burned up all the synagogues
18 that the foolish people h' blasphemed
20 H' respect unto the covenant: for the
76: 5 are spoiled, they h' slept their sleep:
5 none of the men of might h' found
77: 5 I h' considered the days of old, the
78: 3 Which we h' heard and known, and
3 known, and our fathers h' told us.
79: 1 thy holy temple h' they defiled;
1 they h' laid Jerusalem on heaps.
2 thy servants h' they given to be meat
3 Their blood h' they shed like water
6 the heathen that h' not known thee,
6 the kingdoms that h' not called upon
7 For they h' devoured Jacob, and laid
12 wherewith they h' reproached thee,
81:14 I should soon h' subdued their
15 of the Lord should h' submitted
15 but their time should h' endured
16 He should h' fed them also with the
16 the rock should I h' satisfied thee.
82: 6 I h' said, Ye are gods; and all of you
83: 2 and they that hate thee h' lifted up
3 They h' taken crafty counsel against
4 They h' said, Come, and let us cut
5 For they h' consulted together with
8 they h' holpen the children of Lot.
85:10 righteousness and peace h' kissed
86:14 of violent men h' sought after my
14 and h' not set thee before them.
16 O turn unto me, and h' mercy
88: 1 I h' cried day and night before thee:
9 Lord, I h' called daily upon thee, I
9 I h' stretched out my hands unto thee.
13 But unto thee h' I cried, O Lord; and
16 over me; thy terrors h' cut me off.
89: 2 For I h' said, Mercy shall be built up
3 I h' made a covenant with my chosen,
3 I h' sworn unto David my servant,
19 I h' laid help upon one that is mighty;
19 I h' exalted one chosen out of the
20 I h' found David my servant; with my
20 with my holy oil h' I anointed him:
35 Once h' I sworn by my holiness that
51 thine enemies h' reproached, O
51 wherewith they h' reproached the
90:15 and the years wherein we h' seen evil.
93: 3 The floods h' lifted up, O Lord, the
3 the floods h' lifted up their voice;
94:20 the throne of iniquity h' fellowship
95:10 and they h' not known my ways:
98: 3 all the ends of the earth h' seen the
102: 9 For I h' eaten ashes like bread, and
13 Thou shalt arise, and h' mercy
27 same, and thy years shall h' no end.
104:12 fowls of the heaven h' their habitation,
33 praise to my God while I h' my being.
106: 6 We h' sinned with our fathers, we
6 we h' committed iniquity, we
6 iniquity, we h' done wickedly.
109: 2 they h' spoken against me with a
5 And they h' rewarded me evil for
111: 2 sought out of all them that h' pleasure
10 a good understanding h' all they that
115: 5 They h' mouths, but they speak not:
5 eyes h' they, but they see not:
6 They h' ears, but they hear not: noses
6 noses h' they, but they smell not:
7 They h' hands, but they handle not:
7 feet h' they, but they walk not:
116:10 I believed, therefore h' I spoken: I
118:26 we h' blessed you out of the house of
119: 6 when I h' respect unto all thy
7 when I shall h' learned thy righteous
10 With my whole heart h' I sought thee:
11 Thy word h' I hid in mine heart, that
13 With my lips h' I declared all the
14 I h' rejoiced in the way of thy
15 and h' respect unto thy ways.
22 for I h' kept thy testimonies.
26 I h' declared my ways, and thou
30 I h' chosen the way of truth: thy
30 thy judgments h' I laid before me.
31 I h' stuck unto thy testimonies: O
40 Behold, I h' longed after thy precepts:
42 So shall I h' wherewith to answer him
43 for I h' hoped in thy judgments.
47 in thy commandments,...I h' loved.
48 unto thy commandments,...I h' loved;
51 proud h' had me greatly in derision:
51 yet h' I not declined from thy law.
52 O Lord; and h' comforted myself.
54 Thy statutes h' been my songs in
55 I h' remembered thy name, O Lord, in
55 in the night, and h' kept thy law.
57 I h' said that I would keep thy words.
61 The bands of the wicked h' robbed me:
61 but I h' not forgotten thy law.
66 for I h' believed thy commandments.
67 astray: but now h' I kept thy word.

Ps 119:69 The proud h' forged a lie against me:
71 good for me that I h' been afflicted;
73 Thy hands h' made me and fashioned
74 me; because I h' hoped in thy word.
79 that h' known thy testimonies.
85 The proud h' digged pits for me,
92 I should then h' perished in mine
94 me; for I h' sought thy precepts.
95 The wicked h' waited for me to
96 I h' seen an end of all perfection:
99 I h' more understanding than all my
101 I h' refrained my feet from every evil
102 I h' not departed from thy judgments:
106 I h' sworn, and I will perform it, that
110 The wicked h' laid a snare for me:
111 Thy testimonies h' I taken as an
112 I h' inclined mine heart to perform
117 and I will h' respect unto thy statutes
121 I h' done judgment and justice:
126 work: for they h' made void thy law.
133 let not any iniquity h' dominion
139 mine enemies h' forgotten thy words.
143 Trouble and anguish h' taken hold on
152 I h' known of old that thou hast
161 Princes h' persecuted me without a
165 Great peace h' they which love thy
166 Lord, I h' hoped for thy salvation,
168 I h' kept thy precepts and thy
173 help me; for I h' chosen thy precepts.
174 I h' longed for thy salvation, O Lord;
176 I h' gone astray like a lost sheep;
123: 2 until that he h' mercy upon us.
3 H' mercy upon us, O Lord, h' mercy
129: 1,2 Many a time h' they afflicted me
2 yet they h' not prevailed against me.
130: 1 Out of the depths h' I cried unto thee
131: 2 Surely I h' behaved and quieted
132:14 here will I dwell; for I h' desired it.
17 I h' ordained a lamp for mine
135:16 They h' mouths, but they speak not;
16 eyes h' they, but they see not;
17 They h' ears, but they hear not;
140: 3 They h' sharpened their tongues like
4 who h' purposed to overthrow my
5 The proud h' hid a snare for me, and
5 they h' spread a net by the wayside;
5 wayside; they h' set gins for me.
141: 9 the snares which they h' laid for me,
142: 3 I walked h' they privily laid a snare
143: 3 as those that h' been long dead.
146: 2 unto my God while I h' any being.
147:20 judgments, they h' not known them.
149: 9 this honour h' all his saints. Praise
Pr 1:14 among us; let us all h' one purse:
24 Because I h' called, and ye refused;
24 I h' stretched out my hand, and no
25 But ye h' set at nought all my counsel,
3:30 cause, if he h' done thee no harm.
4:11 I h' taught thee in the way of wisdom;
11 of wisdom; I h' led thee in right paths.
16 sleep not, except they h' done mischief;
5:12 And say, How h' I hated instruction,
13 And h' not obeyed the voice of my
7:14 I h' peace offerings with me; this day
14 with me; this day h' I paid my vows.
15 to seek thy face, and I h' found thee.
16 I h' decked my bed with coverings of
17 I h' perfumed my bed with myrrh,
26 yea, many strong men h' been slain
8:14 I am understanding; I h' strength.
9: 5 drink of the wine which I h' mingled.
13: 3 wide his lips shall h' destruction.
14:26 his children shall h' a place of
17: 2 A wise servant shall h' rule over a son
2 shall h' part of the inheritance
19:10 much less for a servant to h' rule over
20: 4 shall he beg in harvest, and h' nothing.
9 Who can say, I h' made my heart clean,
22:19 I h' made known to thee this day, even
20 H' not I written to thee excellent
28 landmark, which thy fathers h' set.
23:24 begetteth a wise child shall h' joy
35 They h' stricken me, shalt thou say,
24:23 It is not good to h' respect of persons
25: 7 of the prince whom thine eyes h' seen.
27:27 And thou shalt h' goats' milk
28:10 but the upright shall h' good things
13 forsaketh them shall h' mercy.
19 tilleth his land shall h' plenty of
19 after vain persons shall h' poverty
21 To h' respect of persons is not good:
27 hideth his eyes shall h' many a curse.
29:21 shall h' him become his son at the
30: 2 h' not the understanding of a man.
3 wisdom, nor h' the knowledge of
7 Two things h' I required of thee; deny
20 and saith, I h' done no wickedness.
27 The locusts h' no king, yet go they
31:11 so that he shall h' no need of spoil.
29 Many daughters h' done virtuously,
Ec 1:14 I h' seen all the works that are done
16 and h' gotten more wisdom than all
16 that h' been before me in Jerusalem:
2:19 yet shall he h' rule over all my
19 all my labour wherein I h' laboured,
19 and wherein I h' shewed myself wise
3:10 I h' seen the travail, which God hath
19 yea, they h' all one breath; so that a
4: 9 because they h' a good reward for
11 if two lie together, then they h' heat:
16 even of all that h' been before them:
5:13 There is a sore evil which I h' seen
18 Behold that which I h' seen: it is good
6: 1 There is an evil which I h' seen under
3 and also that he h' no burial; I
7:12 giveth life to them that h' it.

Ec 7:15 All things h' I seen in the days of my
23 All this h' I proved by wisdom: I
27 Behold, this h' I found, saith the
28 one man among a thousand h' I found;
28 among all those h' I not found.
29 Lo, this only h' I found, that God hath
29 they h' sought out many inventions.
8: 9 All this h' I seen, and applied my heart
9: 5 neither h' they any more a reward;
6 neither h' they any more a portion for
13 This wisdom h' I seen also under the
10: 5 There is an evil which I h' seen under
7 I h' seen servants upon horses, and
12: 1 when thou shalt say, I h' no pleasure
Ca 1: 6 but mine own vineyard h' I not kept.
9 I h' compared thee, O my love, to a
2:15 for our vines h' tender grapes.
5: 1 I h' gathered my myrrh with my spice;
1 I h' eaten my honeycomb with my
1 I h' drunk my wine with my milk:
3 I h' put off my coat; how shall I
3 I h' washed my feet; how shall I
6: 5 for they h' overcome me: thy hair is
7:13 which I h' laid up for thee, O my
8: 8 We h' a little sister, and she hath no
12 thou, O Solomon, must h' a thousand,
Isa 1: 2 I h' nourished and brought up
2 children, and they h' rebelled against
4 that are corrupters: they h' forsaken
4 they h' provoked the Holy One of
6 they h' not been closed, neither
9 remnant, we should h' been as
9 we should h' been like unto Gomorrah.
29 of the oaks which ye h' desired,
29 for the gardens that ye h' chosen.
2: 8 that which their own fingers h' made:
3: 9 for they h' rewarded evil unto
14 for ye h' eaten up the vineyard; the
4: 4 When the Lord shall h' washed away
4 and shall h' purged the blood of
5: 4 What could h' been done more to my
4 that I h' not done in it? wherefore
13 because they h' no knowledge: and
24 because they h' cast away the law of
6: 5 for mine eyes h' seen the King, the
12 the Lord h' removed men far away,
7: 5 h' taken evil counsel against thee,
17 days that h' not come, from the day
8: 4 the child shall h' knowledge
19 unto them that h' familiar spirits,
9: 2 walked in darkness h' seen a great
17 the Lord shall h' no joy in their
17 neither shall h' mercy on their
10: 1 which they h' prescribed;
11 Shall I not, as I h' done unto Samaria
13 the strength of my hand I h' done it,
13 and I h' removed the bounds of the
13 people, and h' robbed their treasures,
13 and I h' put down the inhabitants
14 that are left, h' I gathered all the
29 they h' taken up their lodging at
13: 3 I h' commanded my sanctified ones,
3 I h' also called my mighty ones for
18 and they shall h' no pity on the fruit
14: 1 For the Lord will h' mercy on
24 Surely as I h' thought, so shall it
15: 7 the abundance they h' gotten, and
7 and that which they h' laid up, shall
16: 6 We h' heard of the pride of Moab; he
8 lords of the heathen h' broken down
10 I h' made their vintage shouting to
17: 7 and his eyes shall h' respect to the
8 which his fingers h' made, either the
18: 2 whose land the rivers h' spoiled!
7 whose land the rivers h' spoiled, to
19: 3 to them that h' familiar spirits, and
13 they h' also seduced Egypt, even they
14 and they h' caused Egypt to err in
21: 2 the sighing thereof h' I made to cease.
3 pangs h' taken hold upon me, as the
10 that which I h' heard of the Lord of
10 of Israel, h' I declared unto you.
22: 3 are bound together, which h' fled
9 Ye h' seen also the breaches of the
10 And ye h' numbered the houses of
10 and the houses h' ye broken down to
11 but ye h' not looked unto the maker
23: 2 that pass over the sea, h' replenished.
12 there also shalt thou h' no rest.
24: 5 because they h' transgressed
16 part of the earth h' we heard songs,
16 me! the treacherous dealers h' dealt
16 yea, the treacherous dealers h' dealt
25: 9 we h' waited for him, and he will save
9 we h' waited for him, we will be glad
26: 1 We h' a strong city; salvation will
8 O Lord, h' we waited for thee; the
9 With my soul h' I desired thee in the
13 lords beside thee h' had dominion
16 Lord, in trouble h' they visited thee,
17 so h' we been in thy sight, O Lord.
18 We h' been with child, we
18 with child, we h' been in pain, we
18 we h' as it were brought forth wind;
18 we h' not wrought any deliverance in
18 h' the inhabitants of the world fallen.
27: 11 made them will not h' mercy on
28: 7 But they also h' erred through wine,
7 the priest and the prophet h' erred
15 ye h' said, We h' made a covenant
15 for we h' made lies our refuge, and
15 under falsehood h' we hid ourselves:
22 I h' heard from the Lord God of hosts
29: 13 but h' removed their heart far from
30: 2 and h' not asked at my mouth; to
7 therefore h' I cried concerning this,

Isa 30:18 that he may h' mercy upon you:
29 Ye shall h' a song, as in the night
31: 6 children of Israel h' deeply revolted.
7 which your own hands h' made unto
33: 2 unto us; we h' waited for thee:
13 ye that are far off, what I h' done;
36: 5 I h' counsel and strength for war:
19 and h' they delivered Samaria out of
20 that h' delivered their land out of my
37: 6 the king of Assyria h' blasphemed me.
11 the kings of Assyria h' done to all
12 H' the gods of the nations delivered
12 my fathers h' destroyed, as Gozan,
18 the kings of Assyria h' laid waste all
19 And h' cast their gods into the fire:
19 and stone: therefore they h' destroyed
25 I h' digged, and drunk water; and
25 the sole of my feet h' I dried up all
26 heard long ago, how I h' done it;
26 of ancient times, that I h' formed it?
26 now h' I brought it to pass, that thou
38: 3 I beseech thee, how I h' walked before
3 and h' done that which is good in thy
5 thy father, I h' heard thy prayer,
5 I h' seen thy tears: behold, I will add
12 I h' cut off like a weaver my life: he
39: 4 Then said he, What h' they seen in
4 All that is in mine house h' they seen:
4 treasures that I h' not shewed them.
6 and that which thy fathers h' laid up
40: 21 H' ye not known? h' ye not heard?
21 h' ye not understood from the
29 to them that h' no might he increaseth
41: 8 Jacob whom I h' chosen, the seed of
9 Thou whom I h' taken from the ends
9 I h' chosen thee, and not cast thee
25 I h' raised up one from the north, and
42: 1 I h' put my spirit upon him: he shall
4 till he h' set judgment in the earth:
6 I the Lord h' called thee in
14 I h' long time holden my peace; I
14 I h' been still, and refrained myself:
16 in paths that they h' not known:
24 he against whom we h' sinned? for
43: 1 O Israel, Fear not: for I h' redeemed
1 I h' called thee by thy name; thou art
4 and I h' loved thee: therefore will I
7 by my name: for I h' created him
7 for my glory, I h' formed him;
7 formed him; yea, I h' made him.
8 the blind people that h' eyes,
8 eyes, and the deaf that h' ears.
12 I h' declared, and h' saved, and I
12 and I h' shewed them, when there was
14 For your sake I h' sent to Babylon,
14 and h' brought down all their nobles,
21 This people h' I formed for myself;
23 I h' not caused thee to serve with an
27 and thy teachers h' transgressed
28 Therefore I h' profaned the princes
28 and h' given Jacob to the curse, and
44: 1 servant; and Israel, whom I h' chosen:
2 thou, Jesurun, whom I h' chosen.
8 h' not I told thee from that time,
8 and h' declared it? ye are even my
16 Aha, I am warm, I h' seen the fire:
18 They h' not known nor understood:
19 to say, I h' burned part of it in the
19 yea, also I h' baked bread upon the
19 I h' roasted flesh, and eaten it: and
21 I h' formed thee; thou art my
22 I h' blotted out, as a thick cloud, thy
22 return unto me; for I h' redeemed
45: 1 whose right hand I h' holden, to
4 I h' even called thee by thy name: I
4 I h' surnamed thee, though thou hast
8 up together; I the Lord h' created it.
12 I h' made the earth, and created man
12 I, even my hands, h' stretched out the
12 all their host h' I commanded.
13 I h' raised him up in righteousness,
19 I h' not spoken in secret, in a dark
20 they h' no knowledge that set up
21 h' not I the Lord? and there is no
23 I h' sworn by myself, the word is gone
24 in the Lord h' I righteousness and
46: 4 I h' made, and I will bear; even I will
11 yea, I h' spoken it, I will also bring it
11 I h' purposed it, I will also do it.
47: 6 I h' polluted mine inheritance, and
48: 3 I h' declared the former things from
5 h' even from the beginning declared
6 I h' shewed thee new things from this
10 Behold, I h' refined thee, but not with
10 I h' chosen thee in the furnace of
15 I, even I, h' spoken; yea, I h' called
15 I h' brought him, and he shall make
16 I h' not spoken in secret from the
19 his name should not h' been cut off
49: 4 Then I said, I h' laboured in vain,
4 I h' spent my strength for nought,
8 In an acceptable time h' I heard thee,
8 and in a day of salvation h' I helped
13 will h' mercy upon his afflicted.
15 that she should not h' compassion
16 Behold, I h' graven thee upon the
20 children which thou shalt h', after
50: 1 whom I h' put away? or which of
1 creditors is it to whom I h' sold you?
1 Behold, for your iniquities h' ye sold
2 or h' I no power to deliver? behold,
7 therefore h' I set my face like a flint,
11 and in the sparks that ye h' kindled.
11 This shall ye h' of mine hand; ye
51: 16 And I h' put my words in thy mouth,
16 and I h' covered thee in the shadow

Isa 51:20 Thy sons h' fainted, they lie at the
22 Behold, I h' taken out of thine hand
23 which h' said to thy soul, Bow down,
52: 3 Ye h' sold yourselves for nought;
5 Now therefore, what h' I here, saith
53: 6 All we like sheep h' gone astray; we
6 we h' turned every one to his own
54: 7 For a small moment h' I forsaken
8 kindness will I h' mercy on thee,
9 for as I h' sworn that the waters of
9 so h' I sworn that I would not be
16 Behold, I h' created the smith that
16 and I h' created the waster to destroy.
55: 4 Behold, I h' given him for a witness
7 and he will h' mercy upon him;
56: 11 dogs which can never h' enough,
57: 11 h' not I held my peace even of old,
18 I h' seen his ways, and will heal him:
58: 3 Wherefore h' we fasted, say they, and
3 wherefore h' we afflicted our soul,
5 Is it such a fast that I h' chosen?
6 Is not this the fast that I h' chosen?
59: 2 But your iniquities h' separated
2 and your sins h' hid his face from
3 your lips h' spoken lies, your tongue
8 they h' made them crooked paths:
21 and my words which I h' put in thy
60: 10 but in my favour h' I had mercy
61: 7 For your shame ye shall h' double;
62: 6 I h' set watchmen upon thy walls, O
9 But they that h' gathered it shall eat
9 and they that h' brought it together
63: 3 I h' trodden the winepress alone;
18 of thy holiness h' possessed it
18 our adversaries h' trodden down thy
64: 4 men h' not heard, nor perceived by
5 for we h' sinned: in those is
6 iniquities, like the wind, h' taken us
65: 2 I h' spread out my hands all the day
7 which h' burned incense upon the
10 in, for my people that h' sought me.
66: 2 all those things h' been, saith
3 Yea, they h' chosen their own ways,
19 afar off, that h' not heard my fame,
19 neither h' seen my glory; and they
24 of the men that h' transgressed
Jer 1: 9 Behold, I h' put my words in thy
10 See, I h' this day set thee over the
16 all their wickedness, who h' forsaken
16 and h' burned incense unto other
18 For, behold, I h' made thee this day a
2: 5 What iniquity h' your fathers found in
5 and h' walked after vanity, and are
11 but my people h' changed their glory
13 For my people h' committed two evils;
13 they h' forsaken me the fountain of
16 and Tahapanes h' broken the crown
20 For of old time I h' broken thy yoke,
23 I am not polluted, I h' not gone after
25 for I h' loved strangers, and after
27 for they h' turned their back unto me,
29 ye all h' transgressed against me,
30 In vain h' I smitten your children;
31 H' I been a wilderness unto
32 yet my people h' forgotten me days
34 I h' not found it by secret search,
35 because thou sayest, I h' not sinned.
3: 3 the showers h' been withholden,
13 and ye h' not obeyed my voice, saith
18 I h' given for an inheritance unto
20 so h' ye dealt treacherously with me,
21 of Israel: for they h' perverted their
21 and they h' forgotten the Lord their
25 for we h' sinned against the Lord our
25 and h' not obeyed the voice of the
4: 10 Ye shall h' peace; whereas the
18 Thy way and thy doings h' procured
22 is foolish, they h' not known me;
22 and they h' none understanding: they
22 to do good they h' no knowledge.
28 be black: because I h' spoken it, I
28 I h' purposed it, and will not repent,
31 For I h' heard a voice as of a woman
5: 3 them, but they h' not grieved;
3 but they h' refused to receive
3 they h' made their faces harder than
3 than a rock; they h' refused to return.
5 for they h' known the way of the Lord
5 but these h' altogether broken the
7 thy children h' forsaken me, and
11 and the house of Judah h' dealt very
12 They h' belied the Lord, and said, It
19 Like as ye h' forsaken me, and served
21 which h' eyes, and see not;
21 see not; which h' ears, and hear not:
22 which h' placed the sand for the
25 Your iniquities h' turned away these
25 and your sins h' withholden good
31 and my people love to h' it so: and
6: 2 I h' likened the daughter of Zion to
10 they h' no delight in it.
14 They h' healed also the hurt of the
19 because they h' not hearkened unto
23 they are cruel, and h' no mercy;
24 We h' heard the fame thereof: our
27 I h' set thee for a tower and a fortress
7: 11 Behold, even I h' seen it, saith the
13 And now, because ye h' done all these
14 and to your fathers, as I h' done to
15 as I h' cast out all your brethren, even
23 in all the ways that I h' commanded
25 unto this day I h' even sent unto you
30 For the children of Judah h' done evil
30 they h' set their abominations in the
31 And they h' built the high places of
8: 2 host of heaven, whom they h' loved,

Jer 8: 2 loved, and whom they h' served, and
2 and after whom they h' walked, and
2 walked, and whom they h' sought, and
2 and whom they h' worshipped: they
3 whither I h' driven them, saith the
6 What h' I done? every one turned to
9 lo, they h' rejected the word of the
11 For they h' healed the hurt of the
13 and the things that I h' given them
14 because we h' sinned against the
16 for they are come, and h' devoured the
19 Why h' they provoked me to anger
9: 5 they h' taught their tongue to speak
13 Because they h' forsaken my law
13 and h' not obeyed my voice, neither
14 But h' walked after the imagination
16 they nor their fathers h' known:
16 sword after them, till I h' consumed
19 confounded, because we h' forsaken
19 land, because our dwellings h' cast us
10: 11 The gods that h' not made the heavens
21 are become brutish, and h' not sought
25 for they h' eaten up Jacob, and
25 and h' made his habitation desolate.
11: 5 which I h' sworn unto your fathers,
10 and the house of Judah h' broken my
13 streets of Jerusalem h' ye set up altars
17 which they h' done against themselves
20 for unto thee h' I revealed my cause.
12: 2 yea, they h' taken root: they grow,
5 and they h' wearied thee, then how
6 even they h' dealt treacherously with
6 yea, they h' called a multitude after
7 I h' forsaken mine house, I h' left
7 I h' given the dearly beloved of my
8 out against me: therefore h' I hated it.
10 Many pastors h' destroyed my
10 they h' trodden my portion under foot,
10 they h' made my pleasant portion a
11 They h' made it desolate, and being
12 end of the land: no flesh shall h' peace.
13 They h' sown wheat, but shall reap
13 they h' put themselves to pain, but
14 inheritance which I h' caused my
15 after that I h' plucked them out I will
15 and h' compassion on them, and
13: 11 so h' I caused to cleave unto me the
14 pity, nor spare, nor h' mercy,
27 I h' seen thine adulteries, and thy
14: 3 And their nobles h' sent their little
7 are many; we h' sinned against thee.
10 people, Thus h' they loved to wander,
10 they h' not refrained their feet,
14 not, neither h' I commanded them,
16 and they shall h' none to bury them,
20 our fathers: for we h' sinned against
15: 5 For who shall h' pity upon thee,
8 I h' brought upon them against the
8 h' caused him to fall upon it suddenly,
10 I h' neither lent on usury, nor men
10 nor men h' lent to me on usury; yet
15 for thy sake I h' suffered rebuke.
16: 2 neither shalt thou h' sons or
5 for I h' taken away my peace from this
10 what is our sin that we h' committed
11 Because your fathers h' forsaken me,
11 Lord, and h' walked after other gods,
11 after other gods, and h' served them,
11 served them, and h' worshipped them,
11 worshipped them, and h' forsaken me,
11 forsaken me, and h' not kept my law;
12 And ye h' done worse than your
18 sin double; because they h' defiled my
18 they h' filled mine inheritance with
19 Surely our fathers h' inherited lies,
17: 4 for ye h' kindled a fire in mine anger,
13 because they h' forsaken the Lord, the
16 As for me, I h' not hastened from
16 neither h' I desired the woeful day;
18: 8 nation, against whom I h' pronounced,
15 hath forgotten me, they h' burned
15 and they h' caused them to stumble in
20 for they h' digged a pit for my soul.
22 for they h' digged a pit to take me,
19: 4 Because they h' forsaken me, and
4 me, and h' estranged this place, and
4 and h' burned incense in it unto other
4 they nor their fathers h' known
4 and h' filled this place with the blood
5 They h' built also the high places of
13 upon whose roofs they h' burned
13 and h' poured out drink offerings
15 all the evil that I h' pronounced
15 because they h' hardened their necks,
20: 12 for unto thee h' I opened my cause.
17 mother might h' been my grave,
21: 7 neither h' pity, nor h' mercy.
10 For I h' set my face against this city
22: 9 Because they h' forsaken the covenant
12 in the place whither they h' led him
23: 2 Ye h' scattered my flock, and driven
2 them away, and h' not visited them:
3 whither I h' driven them, and will
11 yea, in my house h' I found their
13 And I h' seen folly in the prophets of
14 I h' seen also in the prophets of
17 Ye shall h' peace; and they say
20 shall not return, until he h' executed,
20 and till he h' performed the thoughts
21 I h' not sent these prophets, yet they
21 I h' not spoken to them, yet they
22 then they should h' turned them from
25 I h' heard what the prophets said,
25 saying, I h' dreamed, I h' dreamed.
27 as their fathers h' forgotten my name
36 for ye h' perverted the words of the

Jer 23: 38 and I h' sent unto you, saying, Ye shall
24: 5 whom I h' sent out of this place into
25: 3 and I h' spoken unto you, rising
3 and speaking; but ye h' not hearkened.
4 but ye h' not hearkened, nor inclined
7 Yet ye h' not hearkened unto me, saith
8 Because ye h' not heard my words,
13 my words which I h' pronounced
26: 4 to walk in my law, which I h' set before
5 them, but ye h' not hearkened;
11 this city, as ye h' heard with your ears.
12 this city all the words that ye h' heard.
27: 5 I h' made the earth, the man and the
5 and h' given it unto whom it seemed
6 And now h' I given all these lands
6 and the beasts of the field h' I given
8 until I h' consumed them by his hand.
15 For I h' not sent them, saith the Lord,
28: 2 I h' broken the yoke of the king of
8 The prophets that h' been before me
14 I h' put a yoke of iron upon the neck
14 and I h' given him the beasts of the
29: 4 whom I h' caused to be carried away
7 I h' caused you to be carried away
9 I h' not sent them, saith the Lord.
14 whither I h' driven you, saith the
15 Because ye h' said, The Lord hath
18 the nations whither I h' driven them:
19 Because they h' not hearkened to my
20 whom I h' sent from Jerusalem to
23 Because they h' committed villany in
23 and h' committed adultery with their
23 and h' spoken lying words in my
23 which I h' not commanded them;
32 shall not h' a man to dwell among
30: 2 the words that I h' spoken unto thee
5 We h' heard a voice of trembling, of
14 All thy lovers h' forgotten thee; they
14 for I h' wounded thee with the wound
15 increased, I h' done these things unto
18 and h' mercy on his dwellingplaces;
24 shall not return, until he h' done it,
24 and until he h' performed the intents
31: 3 Yea, I h' loved thee with an
3 with lovingkindness h' I drawn thee.
18 I h' surely heard Ephraim bemoaning
20 I will surely h' mercy upon him,
25 For I h' satiated the weary soul, and
25 and I h' replenished every sorrowful
28 that like as I h' watched over them,
29 The fathers h' eaten a sour grape,
37 for all that they h' done, saith the
32: 23 they h' done nothing of all that thou
29 upon whose roofs they h' offered
30 children of Judah h' only done evil
30 children of Israel h' only provoked
32 which they h' done to provoke me to
33 And they h' turned unto me the back,
33 yet they h' not hearkened to receive
37 whither I h' driven them in mine
42 Like as I h' brought all this great
42 all the good that I h' promised them.
33: 5 whom I h' slain in mine anger and in
5 wickedness I h' hid my face from this
8 whereby they h' sinned against
8 iniquities, whereby they h' sinned,
8 whereby they h' transgressed against
14 which I h' promised unto the house
21 he should not h' a son to reign
24 thou not what this people h' spoken,
24 thus they h' despised my people, that
25 if I h' not appointed the ordinances
26 to return, and h' mercy on them.
34: 5 for I h' pronounced the word, saith
17 Ye h' not hearkened unto me, in
18 will give the men that h' transgressed
18 which h' not performed the words of
35: 7 seed, nor plant vineyard, nor h' any:
8 Thus h' we obeyed the voice of
9 neither h' we vineyard, nor field,
10 we h' dwelt in tents, and h' obeyed,
14 notwithstanding I h' spoken unto
15 I h' sent also unto you all my
15 which I h' given to you and to your
15 but ye h' not inclined your ear, nor
16 the son of Rechab h' performed the
17 all the evil that I h' pronounced
17 because I h' spoken unto them, but
17 unto them, but they h' not heard;
17 and I h' called unto them, but they
17 unto them, but they h' not answered.
18 ye h' obeyed the commandment
36: 2 all the words that I h' spoken unto
30 He shall h' none to sit upon the
31 all the evil that I h' pronounced
37: 18 What h' I offended against thee, or
18 people, that ye h' put me in prison?
38: 2 for he shall h' his life for a prey,
9 lord the king, these men h' done evil
9 in all that they h' done to Jeremiah
9 whom they h' cast into the dungeon;
22 shall say, Thy friends h' set thee on,
22 set thee on, and h' prevailed against
25 the princes hear that I h' talked
40: 3 because ye h' sinned against the
3 and h' not obeyed his voice, therefore
10 dwell in your cities that ye h' taken.
41: 8 Slay us not: for we h' treasures
42: 4 prophet said unto them, I h' heard
10 repent me of the evil that I h' done
12 that he may h' mercy upon you,
14 the trumpet, nor h' hunger of bread
19 know certainly that I h' admonished
21 And now I h' this day declared it to
21 but ye h' not obeyed the voice of the
43: 10 throne upon these stones that I h' hid;

Jer 44: 2 God of Israel; Ye h' seen all the evil
2 that I h' brought upon Jerusalem,
3 they h' committed to provoke me to
9 H' ye forgotten the wickedness of
9 which they h' committed in the land
10 neither h' they feared, nor walked in
12 that h' set their faces to go into the
13 as I h' punished Jerusalem, by the
14 they h' a desire to return
17 as we h' done, we, and our fathers,
18 unto her, we h' wanted all things,
18 and h' been consumed by the sword
22 abominations which you h' committed;
23 Because ye h' burned incense, and
23 because ye h' sinned against the
23 and h' not obeyed the voice of the
25 Ye and your wives h' both spoken
25 perform our vows that we h' vowed,
26 Behold, I h' sworn by my great name,
45: 4 Behold, that which I h' built will I
4 and that which I h' planted I will
46: 5 Wherefore h' I seen them dismayed
12 The nations h' heard of thy shame,
28 the nations whither I h' driven thee:
48: 2 in Heshbon they h' devised evil
5 the enemies h' heard a cry of
29 We h' heard the pride of Moab,
33 and I h' caused wine to fail from the
34 Jahaz, h' they uttered their voice,
38 for I h' broken Moab like a vessel
49: 9 they will destroy till they h' enough.
10 I h' made Esau bare, I h' uncovered
12 drink of the cup h' assuredly drunken;
13 For I h' sworn by myself, saith the
14 I h' heard a rumour from the Lord,
23 for they h' heard evil tidings: they are
24 anguish and sorrows h' taken her, as
31 which h' neither gates nor bars
37 sword after them, till I h' consumed
50: 6 their shepherds h' caused them to go
6 they h' turned them away on the
6 they h' gone from mountain to hill,
6 they h' forgotten their restingplace.
7 that found them h' devoured them:
7 because they h' sinned against the
17 the lions h' driven him away: first
18 as I h' punished the king of Assyria.
21 to all that I h' commanded thee.
24 I h' laid a snare for thee, and thou
51: 7 the nations h' drunken of her wine;
9 We would h' healed Babylon, but she
24 their evil that they h' done in Zion
30 mighty men of Babylon h' foreborn to
30 they h' remained in their holds:
30 they h' burned her dwellingplaces;
32 the reeds they h' burned with fire,
50 Ye that h' escaped the sword, go
51 because we h' heard reproach:
La 1: 2 all her friends h' dealt treacherously
8 because they h' seen her nakedness:
11 they h' given their pleasant things
18 for I h' rebelled against his
20 for I h' grievously rebelled: abroad
21 They h' heard that I sigh: there is
21 all mine enemies h' heard of my
2: 7 they h' made a noise in the house of
10 they h' cast up dust upon their heads;
10 they h' girded themselves with
14 Thy prophets h' seen vain and foolish
14 and they h' not discovered thine
14 but h' seen for thee false burdens and
16 All thine enemies h' opened their
16 We h' swallowed her up: certainly
16 looked for; we h' found, we h' seen it.
22 those that I h' swaddled and brought
3: 21 recall to my mind, therefore h' I hope.
32 yet will he h' compassion according
42 We h' transgressed and h' rebelled:
46 All our enemies h' opened their
53 They h' cut off my life in the dungeon,
4: 10 the pitiful women h' sodden their own
12 would not h' believed that the
12 the enemy should h' entered into
13 that h' shed the blood of the just in
14 They h' wandered as blind men in
14 they h' polluted themselves with
17 in our watching we h' watched for a
5: 4 We h' drunken our water for money;
5 persecution: we labour, and h' no rest.
6 We h' given the hand to the Egyptians,
7 Our fathers h' sinned, and are not;
7 and we h' borne their iniquities.
8 Servants h' ruled over us: there is
14 The elders h' ceased from the gate,
16 woe unto us, that we h' sinned!
Eze 2: 3 they and their fathers h' transgressed
3: 6 they would h' hearkened unto thee.
8 Behold, I h' made thy face strong
9 adamant harder than flint h' I made
17 Son of man, I h' made thee a
4: 5 For I h' laid upon thee the years of
6 I h' appointed thee each day for a
14 till now h' I not eaten of that which
15 Lo, I h' given thee cow's dung for
5: 5 I h' set it in the midst of the nations
6 for they h' refused my judgments and
6 statutes, they h' not walked in them.
7 and h' not walked in my statutes,
7 neither h' kept my judgments,
7 neither h' done according to the
9 do in thee that which I h' not done,
11 eye spare, neither will I h' any pity.
13 that I the Lord h' spoken it in my
13 when I h' accomplished my fury in
15 furious rebukes. I the Lord h' spoken
17 upon thee. I the Lord h' spoken it.

Eze 6: 8 that ye may h' some that shall
9 for the evils which they h' committed
10 that I h' not said in vain that I would
7: 4 neither will I h' pity: but I will
9 will I h' pity: I will recompense thee
14 They h' blown the trumpet, even to
20 therefore h' I set far from them.
8: 17 they h' filled the land with violence,
17 and h' returned to provoke me to
18 neither will I h' pity: and though
9: 1 Cause them that h' charge over
5 your eye spare, neither h' ye pity:
10 neither will I h' pity, but I will
11 saying, I h' done as thou hast
11: 5 Thus h' ye said, O house of Israel:
6 Ye h' multiplied your slain in this
6 ye h' filled the streets thereof with the
7 Your slain whom ye h' laid in the
8 Ye h' feared the sword; and I will
12 for ye h' not walked in my statutes,
12 but h' done after the manners of the
15 of Jerusalem h' said, Get you far from
16 I h' cast them far off among the
16 and although I h' scattered them
17 countries where ye h' been scattered,
12: 2 which h' eyes to see, and see not;
2 they h' ears to hear, and hear not:
6 for I h' set thee for a sign unto the
11 like as I h' done, so shall it be done
22 proverb that ye h' in the land of
28 but the word which I h' spoken shall
13: 3 their own spirit, and h' seen nothing!
5 Ye h' not gone up into the gaps,
6 They h' seen vanity and lying
6 and they h' made others to hope that
7 H' ye not seen a vain vision, and
7 h' ye not spoken a lying divination,
7 Lord saith it; albeit I h' not spoken?
8 Because ye h' spoken vanity, and
10 because they h' seduced my people,
12 the daubing wherewith ye h' daubed
14 the wall that ye h' daubed with
15 and upon them that h' daubed it with
22 ye h' made the heart of the righteous
22 sad, whom I h' not made sad;
14: 3 Son of man, these men h' set up their
9 I the Lord h' deceived that prophet,
22 the evil that I h' brought upon
22 even concerning all that I h' brought
23 and ye shall know that I h' not done
23 all that I h' done in it, saith the Lord
15: 6 which I h' given to the fire for fuel,
8 because they h' committed a trespass,
16: 5 to h' compassion upon thee; but thou
7 I h' caused thee to multiply as the
27 Behold, therefore I h' stretched out
27 and h' diminished thine ordinary food,
17: 21 know that I the Lord h' spoken it.
24 I the Lord h' brought down the high
24 high tree, h' exalted the low tree,
24 h' dried up the green tree, and
24 and h' made the dry tree to flourish:
24 I the Lord h' spoken and h' done it.
18: 2 The fathers h' eaten sour grapes, and
3 ye shall not h' occasion any more to
23 H' I any pleasure at all that the
31 whereby ye h' transgressed; and
32 For I h' no pleasure in the death
20: 27 Yet in this your fathers h' blasphemed
27 in that they h' committed a trespass
41 wherein ye h' been scattered; and I
43 doings, wherein ye h' been defiled;
43 for all your evils that ye h' committed.
44 when I h' wrought with you for my
48 I the Lord h' kindled it: it shall not
21: 5 that I the Lord h' drawn forth my
15 I h' set the point of the sword against
17 fury to rest: I the Lord h' said it.
23 to them that h' sworn oaths: but he
24 Because ye h' made your iniquity to
25 when iniquity shall h' an end,
29 when their iniquity shall h' an end.
32 for I the Lord h' spoken it.
22: 4 therefore h' I made thee a reproach
7 In thee h' they set light by father
7 in the midst of thee h' they dealt by
7 in thee h' they vexed the fatherless
10 In thee h' they discovered their
10 in thee h' they humbled her that was
12 In thee h' they taken gifts to shed
13 Behold, therefore I h' smitten mine
14 I the Lord h' spoken it, and will do it.
22 that I the Lord h' poured out my
25 the prey; they h' devoured souls;
25 they h' taken the treasure and
25 they h' made her many widows in
26 Her priests h' violated my law, and
26 law, and h' profaned mine holy things:
26 they h' put no difference between the
26 neither h' they shewed difference
26 and h' hid their eyes from my
28 And her prophets h' daubed them
29 The people of the land h' used
29 and h' vexed the poor and needy:
29 yea, they h' oppressed the stranger
31 Therefore h' I poured out mine
31 I h' consumed them with the fire of
31 their own way h' I recompensed upon
23: 9 Wherefore I h' delivered her into the
37 That they h' committed adultery, and
37 and with their idols h' they committed
37 h' also caused their sons...to pass
38 Moreover this they h' done unto me:
38 they h' defiled my sanctuary in the
38 day, and h' profaned my sabbaths.
39 thus h' they done in the midst of

Eze 23: 40 furthermore, that ye h' sent for men
24: 8 I h' set her blood upon the top of a
13 because I h' purged thee, and thou
13 till I h' caused my fury to rest upon
14 I the Lord h' spoken it: it shall come
21 whom ye h' left shall fall by the
22 And ye shall do as I h' done: ye shall
25: 15 Because the Philistines h' dealt by
15 and h' taken vengeance with a
26: 5 for I h' spoken it, saith the Lord God:
14 for I the Lord h' spoken it, saith the
27: 4 thy builders h' perfected thy beauty.
5 They h' made all thy ship boards of
5 they h' taken cedars from Lebanon
6 Of the oaks of Bashan h' they made
6 the company of the Ashurites h' made
11 they h' made thy beauty perfect.
26 Thy rowers h' brought thee into great
28: 10 strangers: for I h' spoken it, saith the
14 and I h' set thee so: thou wast upon
16 merchandise they h' filled the midst
22 when I shall h' executed judgments
25 When I shall h' gathered the house of
25 land that I h' given to my servant
29: 3 own, and I h' made it for myself.
5 I h' given thee for meat to the beasts
6 because they h' been a staff of reed to
9 The river is mine, and I h' made it.
20 I h' given him the land of Egypt for
30: 8 when I h' set a fire in Egypt, and
12 strangers: I the Lord h' spoken it.
16 Sin shall h' great pain, and No shall
16 and Noph shall h' distresses daily.
21 Son of man, I h' broken the arm of
31: 9 I h' made him fair by the multitude
11 I h' therefore delivered him into the
11 I h' driven him out for his wickedness.
12 h' cut him off, and h' left him:
12 from his shadow, and h' left him.
32: 24 yet h' they borne their shame with
25 They h' set her a bed in the midst of
25 yet h' they borne their shame with
27 and they h' laid their swords under
32 For I h' caused my terror in the land
33: 7 I h' set thee a watchman unto the
11 I h' no pleasure in the death of
29 when I h' laid the land most desolate
29 abominations...they h' committed.
34: 4 The diseased h' ye not strengthened,
4 neither h' ye healed that which was
4 neither h' ye bound up that which
4 neither h' ye brought again that
4 neither h' ye sought that which was
4 and with cruelty h' ye ruled them.
12 they h' been scattered in the cloudy
18 to h' eaten up the good pasture,
18 and to h' drunk of the deep waters,
19 they eat that which ye h' trodden
19 drink that which ye h' fouled with
21 Because ye h' thrust with side and
21 with your horns, till ye h' scattered
24 among them; I the Lord h' spoken it.
27 when I h' broken the bands of their
35: 11 among them, when I h' judged thee.
12 and that I h' heard all thy blasphemies
13 your mouth ye h' boasted against me,
13 and h' multiplied your words against
13 words against me: I h' heard them.
36: 3 Because they h' made you desolate,
5 of my jealousy h' I spoken against
5 which h' appointed my land into
6 Behold, I h' spoken in my jealousy
6 because ye h' borne the shame of the
7 I h' lifted up mine hand, Surely the
22 which ye h' profaned among the
23 which ye h' profaned in the midst of
33 In the day that I shall h' cleansed
36 I the Lord h' spoken it, and I will
37: 13 when I h' opened your graves, O my
14 that I the Lord h' spoken it, and
23 wherein they h' sinned, and will
24 and they all shall h' one shepherd:
25 land that I h' given unto Jacob my
25 wherein your fathers h' dwelt; and
38: 8 which h' been always waste: but it is
12 which h' gotten cattle and goods,
17 Art thou he of whom I h' spoken in
19 in the fire of my wrath h' I spoken,
39: 5 the open field: for I h' spoken it,
8 this is the day whereof I h' spoken.
15 till the buriers h' buried it in the
19 sacrifice which I h' sacrificed for
21 see my judgment that I h' executed,
21 and my hand that I h' laid upon
24 their transgressions h' I done unto
25 and h' mercy upon the whole
26 After that they h' borne their shame,
26 they h' trespassed against me, when
27 When I h' brought them again from
28 but I h' gathered them unto their
28 and h' left none of them any more
41: 6 that they might h' hold, but they
43: 8 they h' even defiled my holy name by
8 abominations that they h' committed:
8 wherefore I h' consumed them in
11 ashamed of all that they h' done,
44: 7 In that ye h' brought into my
7 and they h' broken my covenant
8 And ye h' not kept the charge of
8 but ye h' set keepers of my charge in
12 therefore h' I lifted up mine hand
13 abominations...they h' committed.
18 They shall h' linen bonnets upon
18 and shall h' linen breeches upon
45: 5 house, h' for themselves, for a
10 Ye shall h' just balances, and a just

Eze 45: 21 ye shall h' the passover, a feast of
47: 13 Israel: Joseph shall h' two portions.
22 they shall h' inheritance with you
48: 11 which h' kept my charge, which went
13 the Levites shall h' five and twenty
23 side, Benjamin shall h' a portion.
24 west side, Simeon shall h' a portion.
Da 2: 3 I h' dreamed a dream, and my spirit
9 for ye h' prepared lying and corrupt
25 I h' found a man of the captives of
26 unto me the dream which I h' seen,
30 that I h' more than any living,
3: 12 these men, O king, h' not regarded
14 the golden image which I h' set up?
15 worship the image which I h' made;
25 of the fire, and they h' no hurt;
28 and h' changed the king's word,
4: 9 my dream that I h' seen, and the
18 dream I king Nebuchadnezzar h' seen.
26 after that thou shalt h' known that
30 that I h' built for the house of the
5: 7 and h' a chain of gold about his neck,
14 I h' even heard of thee, that the spirit
15 the astrologers, h' been brought in
16 And I h' heard of thee, that thou canst
16 and h' a chain of gold about thy neck,
23 and they h' brought the vessels of his
23 and thy concubines, h' drunk wine in
6: 2 the king should h' no damage.
7 and the captains, h' consulted
22 mouths, that they h' not hurt me:
22 before thee, O king, h' I done no hurt.
9: 5 We h' sinned, and h' committed
5 and h' done wickedly, and h' rebelled,
6 Neither h' we hearkened unto thy
7 trespass that they h' trespassed
8 to our fathers, because we h' sinned
9 forgivenesses, though we h' rebelled
10 Neither h' we obeyed the voice of the
11 Yea, all Israel h' transgressed thy law,
11 of God, because we h' sinned against
15 we h' sinned, we h' done wickedly.
10: 16 me, and I h' retained no strength.
11: 5 and h' dominion; his dominion shall
24 his fathers h' not done, nor his fathers'
30 and h' indignation against the
30 and h' intelligence with them that
43 he shall h' power over the treasures
12: 7 and when he shall h' accomplished to
Ho 1: 6 for I will no more h' mercy upon
7 But I will h' mercy upon the house
2: 4 And I will not h' mercy upon her
12 rewards that my lovers h' given me:
23 and I will h' mercy upon her that
4: 10 For they shall eat, and not h' enough:
10 because they h' left off to take heed to
12 they h' gone a whoring from under
18 they h' committed whoredom
5: 1 because ye h' been a snare on Mizpah,
2 though I h' been a rebuker of them
4 and they h' not known the Lord.
7 They h' dealt treacherously against
7 for they h' begotten strange children:
9 the tribes of Israel h' I made known
6: 5 Therefore h' I hewed them by the
5 I h' slain them by the words of my
7 But they like men h' transgressed the
7 there h' they dealt treacherously
10 I h' seen an horrible thing in the
7: 1 When I would h' healed Israel, then
2 now their own doings h' beset them
5 the princes h' made him sick with
6 For they h' made ready their heart
7 and h' devoured their judges;
9 Strangers h' devoured his strength,
13 Woe unto them! for they h' fled from
13 because they h' transgressed against
13 though I h' redeemed them, yet they
13 yet they h' spoken lies against me.
14 And they h' not cried unto me with
15 Though I h' bound and strengthened
8: 1 because they h' transgressed my
4 They h' set up kings, but not by me:
4 they h' made princes, and I knew it not;
4 their gold h' they made them idols,
7 For they h' sown the wind, and they
10 Yea, though they h' hired among the
12 I h' written to him the great things of
9: 9 They h' deeply corrupted themselves,
10: 1 of his land they h' made goodly images.
3 We h' no king, because we feared not
4 They h' spoken words, swearing
13 Ye h' plowed wickedness, ye h' reaped
13 ye h' eaten the fruit of lies: because
12: 8 rich, I h' found me out substance:
10 I h' also spoken by the prophets, and
10 and I h' multiplied visions, and used
13: 2 and h' made them molten images of
6 therefore h' they forgotten me.
14: 8 What h' I to do any more with idols?
8 I h' heard him, and observed him: I
Joe 1: 18 because they h' no pasture;
3: 2 whom they h' scattered among the
3 And they h' cast lots for my people;
3 and h' given a boy for an harlot, and
4 Yea, and what h' ye to do with me,
5 Because ye h' taken my silver and
5 and h' carried into your temples my
6 Jerusalem h' ye sold unto the Grecians,
7 out of the place whither ye h' sold
19 because they h' shed innocent blood
21 their blood that I h' not cleansed:
Am 1: 3 because they h' threshed Gilead with
13 because they h' ripped up the women
2: 4 because they h' despised the law of
4 and h' not kept his commandments,

Am 2: 4 the which their fathers h· walked:
3: 2 You only h· I known of all the families
4 out of his den, if he h· taken nothing?
5 from the earth, and h· taken nothing
15 great houses shall h· an end, saith
4: 6 And I also h· given you cleanness of
6 yet h· ye not returned unto me, saith
7 And also I h· withholden the rain
8 yet h· ye not returned unto me, saith
9 I h· smitten you with blasting and
9 yet h· ye not returned unto me, saith
10 I h· sent among you the pestilence
10 your young men h· I slain with sword,
10 and h· taken away your horses; and
10 I h· made the stink of your camps to
10 yet h· ye not returned unto me, saith
11 I h· overthrown some of you, as God
11 yet h· ye not returned unto me, saith
5: 11 ye h· built houses of hewn stone, but
11 ye h· planted pleasant vineyards, but
14 shall be with you, as ye h· spoken.
25 H· ye offered unto me sacrifices and
26 But ye h· borne the tabernacle of
6: 12 for ye h· turned judgment into gall,
13 H· we not taken to us horns by our
9: 7 H· not I brought up Israel out of the
15 of their land which I h· given them,
Ob 1 We h· heard a rumour from the Lord,
2 Behold, I h· made thee small among
5 would they not h· stolen till they had
7 thy confederacy h· brought thee even
7 h· deceived thee, and prevailed
12 thou shouldest not h· looked on the
12 neither shouldest thou h· rejoiced
12 thou h· spoken proudly in the day of
13 Thou shouldest not h· entered into
13 thou shouldest not h· looked on their
13 nor h· laid hands on their substance
14 Neither shouldest thou h· stood in
14 thou h· delivered up those of his that
16 For as ye h· drunk upon my holy
Jon 2: 9 I will pay that that I h· vowed.
Mic 2: 5 Therefore thou shalt h· none that
9 The women of my people h· ye cast
9 from their children h· ye taken away
13 up before them: they h· broken up,
13 and h· passed through the gate, and
3: 4 as they h· behaved themselves ill in
6 that ye shall not h· a vision; and it
4: 6 driven out, and her that I h· afflicted;
9 for pangs h· taken thee as a woman in
5: 2 whose goings forth h· been from of
12 shalt h· no more soothsayers:
15 heathen, such as they h· not heard.
6: 3 O my people, what h· I done unto
3 and wherein h· I wearied thee? testify
12 and the inhabitants thereof h· spoken
7: 1 for I am as when they h· gathered the
9 because I h· sinned against him, until
19 he will h· compassion upon us;
Na 1: 12 Though I h· afflicted thee, I will afflict
2: 2 for the emptiers h· emptied them out,
Hab 1: 14 creeping things, that h· no ruler over
3: 2 O Lord, I h· heard thy speech, and
Zep 1: 6 and those that h· not sought the
17 because they h· sinned against the
2: 3 which h· wrought his judgment;
8 I h· heard the reproach of Moab,
8 whereby they h· reproached my people,
10 This shall they h· for their pride,
10 because they h· reproached and
3: 4 her priests h· polluted the sanctuary,
4 they h· done violence to the law.
6 I h· cut off the nations: their towers
19 every land where they h· been put to
Hag 1: 6 Ye h· sown much, and bring in little;
6 ye eat, but ye h· not enough; ye drink,
Zec 1: 4 former prophets h· cried, saying,
11 We h· walked to and fro through the
12 how long wilt thou not h· mercy
19 These are the horns which h· scattered
21 These are the horns which h· scattered
2: 6 for I h· spread you abroad as the four
3: 4 I h· caused thine iniquity to pass
9 For behold the stone that I h· laid
4: 2 I h· looked, and behold a candlestick
9 h· laid the foundations of this house;
6: 8 toward the north country h· quieted
7: 3 as I h· done these so many years?
8: 15 So again h· I thought in these days
23 for we h· heard that God is with you.
9: 8 any more: for now h· I seen with
11 I h· sent forth thy prisoners out of the
13 When I h· bent Judah for me, filled
10: 2 For the idols h· spoken vanity, and the
2 vanity, and the diviners h· seen a lie,
2 and h· told false dreams; they comfort
6 for I h· mercy upon them: and
8 gather them; for I h· redeemed them:
8 shall increase as they h· increased.
12: 10 look upon me whom they h· pierced,
14: 12 will smite all the people that h· fought
18 and come not, that h· no rain; there
Mal 1: 2 I h· loved you, saith the Lord. Yet ye
6 And ye say, Wherein h· we despised
7 and ye say, Wherein h· we polluted
10 I h· no pleasure in you, saith the Lord
12 But ye h· profaned it, in that ye say,
13 and ye h· snuffed at it, saith the
2: 2 yea, I h· cursed them already, because
4 And ye shall know that I h· sent this
8 ye h· caused many to stumble at the
8 ye h· corrupted the covenant of Levi,
9 Therefore h· I also made you
9 according as ye h· not kept my ways,
9 ways, but h· been partial in the law.
Mal 2: 10 H· we not all one father? hath not one
13 And this h· ye done again, covering
17 Ye h· wearied the Lord with your
17 Yet ye say, Wherein h· we wearied
3: 7 ordinances, and h· not kept them.
8 man rob God? Yet ye h· robbed me.
8 ye say, Wherein h· we robbed thee?
9 for ye h· robbed me, even this whole
13 Your words h· been stout against me,
13 What h· we spoken so much against
14 Ye h· said, It is vain to serve God:
14 and what profit is it that we h· kept
14 and that we h· walked mournfully
M't 2: 2 for we h· seen his star in the east,
8 and when ye h· found him, bring me
15 Out of Egypt h· I called my son.
3: 9 We h· Abraham to our father: for
14 I h· need to be baptized of thee,
5: 13 but if the salt h· lost his savour,
21, 27 Ye h· heard that it was said by
33 Again, ye h· heard that it hath been
38 Ye h· heard that it hath been said,
40 thy coat, let him h· thy cloke also.
43 Ye h· heard that it hath been said,
46 what reward h· ye? do not even
6: 1 otherwise ye h· no reward of your
2 that they may h· glory of men.
2, 5 unto you, They h· their reward.
8 what things ye h· need of, before
16 unto you, They h· their reward.
32 knoweth that ye h· need of all these
7: 22 Lord, h· we not prophesied in thy
22 and in thy name h· cast out devils?
8: 10 I h· not found so great faith, no, not in
20 unto him, The foxes h· holes,
20 and the birds of the air h· nests; but
29 What h· we to do with thee,
9: 13 I will h· mercy, and not sacrifice:
27 Thou son of David, h· mercy on us.
10: 8 freely ye h· received, freely give.
23 Ye shall not h· gone over the cities
25 If they h· called the master of the house
11: 5 and the poor h· the gospel preached
17 We h· piped unto you, and ye
17 piped unto you, and ye h· not danced;
17 we h· mourned unto you, and ye
17 unto you, and ye h· not lamented.
21 they would h· repented long ago in
23 mighty works, which h· been done in
23 it would h· remained until this day.
12: 3 H· ye not read what David did, when
5 Or h· ye not read in the law, how that
7 meaneth, I will h· mercy, and not
7 ye would not h· condemned the
11 that shall h· one sheep, and if it fall
18 Behold my servant, whom I h· chosen;
13: 12 and he shall h· more abundance: but
15 and their eyes they h· closed; lest at
17 righteous men h· desired to see
17 which ye see, and h· not seen them;
35 things which h· been kept secret
51 H· ye understood all these things?
14: 4 It is not lawful for thee to h· her.
5 when he would h· put him to death,
17 We h· here but five loaves, and two
15: 6 Thus h· ye made the commandment
22 H· mercy on me, O Lord, thou son
32 I h· compassion on the multitude,
32 three days, and h· nothing to eat:
33 Whence should we h· so much bread
34 How many loaves h· ye? And they
16: 7 It is because we h· taken no bread.
8 because ye h· brought no bread?
17: 12 but h· done unto him whatsoever they
15 Lord, h· mercy on my son: for he is
20 If ye h· faith as a grain of mustard
18: 12 if a man h· an hundred sheep, and
26 Lord, h· patience with me, and I will
29 H· patience with me, and I will pay
33 not thou also h· had compassion.
19: 4 H· ye not read, that he which made
12 which h· made themselves eunuchs
16 shall I do, that I may h· eternal
20 All these things h· I kept from my
21 and thou shalt h· treasure in
27 Behold, we h· forsaken all, and followed
27 thee; what shall we h· therefore?
28 That ye which h· followed me, in the
20: 10 that they should h· received more;
12 These last h· wrought but one hour,
12 which h· borne the burden and heat of
30 cried out saying, H· mercy on us,
31 cried the more, saying, H· mercy on
21: 13 but ye h· made it a den of thieves.
16 h· ye never read, Out of the mouth
21 If ye h· faith, and doubt not, ye
22: 4 I h· prepared my dinner: my oxen and
31 h· ye not read that which was spoken
23: 23 and h· omitted the weightier matters of
23 these ought ye to h· done, and not to
30 we would not h· been partakers with
37 how often would I h· gathered thy
24: 25 Behold, I h· told you before.
43 would come, he would h· watched,
43 and would not h· suffered his house
25: 20 I h· gained beside them five talents
22 I h· gained two other talents beside
26 and gather where I h· not strawed:
27 to h· put my money to the exchangers,
27 I should h· received mine own with
29 and he shall h· abundance: but from
40 Inasmuch as ye h· done it unto one of
40 my brethren, ye h· done it unto me.
26: 9 For this ointment might h· been sold
11 For ye h· the poor always with you;
11 with you; but me ye h· not always.
M't 26: 65 further need h· we of witnesses?
65 behold, now ye h· heard his blasphemy.
27: 4 Saying, I h· sinned in that I
4 that I h· betrayed the innocent blood.
19 H· thou nothing to do with that just
19 for I h· suffered many things this day
43 deliver him now, if he will h· him:
65 said unto them, Ye h· a watch:
28: 7 there shall ye see him: lo, I h· told you.
20 whatsoever I h· commanded you:
M'r 1: 8 I indeed h· baptized you with water:
24 what h· we to do with thee,
2: 17 They that are whole h· no need
19 as long as they h· the bridegroom
25 H· ye never read what David did,
3: 15 And to h· power to heal sicknesses,
4: 15 but when they h· heard, Satan cometh
16 who, when they h· heard the word,
17 And h· no root in themselves, and
23 If any man h· ears to hear, let him
40 how is it that ye h· no faith?
5: 7 What h· I to do with thee,
6: 18 for thee to h· thy brother's wife,
19 and would h· killed him; but she
36 for they h· nothing to eat.
38 How many loaves h· ye? go and see.
48 the sea, and would h· passed by them.
7: 4 which they h· received to hold, as the
13 tradition, which ye h· delivered: and
16 If any man h· ears to hear, let
24 and would h· no man know it: but he
8: 2 I h· compassion on the multitude,
2 because they h· now been with me
2 three days, and h· nothing to eat:
5 How many loaves h· ye? And they
16 It is because we h· no bread.
17 reason ye, because ye h· no bread?
17 h· ye your heart yet hardened?
9: 1 till they h· seen the kingdom of God
13 and they h· done unto him whatsoever
17 Master, I h· brought unto thee my son,
22 h· compassion on us, and help us.
50 but if the salt h· lost his saltness,
50 ye season it? H· salt in yourselves
50 and h· peace with one another.
10: 20 Master, all these h· I observed from
21 and thou shalt h· treasure in
23 How hardly shall they that h· riches
28 we h· left all, and h· followed thee.
47 Jesus, thou son of David, h· mercy
48 Thou son of David, h· mercy on me.
11: 17 but ye h· made it a den of thieves.
22 saith unto them, H· faith in God.
23 he shall h· whatsoever he saith.
24 receive them, and ye shall h· them.
25 forgive, if ye h· ought against any:
12: 10 And h· ye not read this scripture; The
26 h· ye not read in the book of Moses,
43 than all they which h· cast into the
13: 23 But take ye heed: behold, I h· foretold
14: 5 For it might h· been sold for more
5 and h· been given to the poor. And
7 For ye h· the poor with you
7 good: but me ye h· not always.
64 Ye h· heard the blasphemy: what
Lu 1: 1 Forasmuch as many h· taken in hand
14 And thou shalt h· joy and gladness;
62 father, how he would h· him called.
70 holy prophets, which h· been since the
2: 30 For mine eyes h· seen thy salvation,
44 they, supposing him to h· been in the
48 and I h· sought thee sorrowing.
3: 8 We h· Abraham to our father:
4: 23 whatsoever we h· heard done in
34 What h· we to do with thee,
5: 5 Master, we h· toiled all the night, and
5 and h· taken nothing: nevertheless
26 saying, We h· seen strange things
6: 3 H· ye not read so much as this, what
24 for ye h· received your consolation.
32 which love you, what thank h· ye?
33 do good to you, what thank h· ye?
34 hope to receive, what thank h· ye?
7: 9 I h· not found so great faith, no, not
22 tell John what things ye h· seen and
32 and saying, We h· piped unto you,
32 unto you, and ye h· not danced;
32 danced; we h· mourned to you,
32 mourned to you, and ye h· not wept.
39 would h· known who and what manner
40 I h· somewhat to say unto thee.
8: 13 and these h· no root, which for a
14 when they h· heard, go forth, and are
18 even that which he seemeth to h·.
28 What h· I to do with thee,
9: 3 neither h· two coats apiece.
9 And Herod said, John h· I beheaded:
13 We h· no more but five loaves
58 said unto him, Foxes h· holes,
58 and birds of the air h· nests; but
10: 13 which h· been done in you, they had
24 many prophets and kings h· desired
24 which ye see, and h· not seen them;
24 ye hear, and h· not heard them.
11: 5 Which of you shall h· a friend,
6 and I h· nothing to set before him?
41 give alms of such things as ye h·;
42 these ought ye to h· done, and not to
52 for ye h· taken away the key of
12: 3 Therefore whatsoever ye h· spoken in
3 and that which ye h· spoken in the
4 that h· no more that they can do.
17 because I h· no room where to
24 which neither h· storehouse nor
30 knoweth that ye h· need of these
33 Sell that ye h·, and give alms;

Lu 12:39 would h' watched, and not h' suffered
48 to whom men h' committed much,
50 But I h' a baptism to be baptized
13:26 h' eaten and drunk in thy presence,
34 how often would I h' gathered thy
14: 5 Which of you shall h' an ass or an ox
10 then shalt thou h' worship in the
18 him, I h' bought a piece of ground,
18 see it: I pray thee h' me excused.
19 And another said, I h' bought five yoke
19 them: I pray thee h' me excused.
20 And another said, I h' married a wife,
28 the cost, whether he h' sufficient
34 Salt is good: but if the salt h' lost
15: 6 for I h' found my sheep which was
9 for I h' found the piece which I
16 And he would fain h' filled his belly
17 h' bread enough and to spare, and I
18 Father, I h' sinned against heaven,
21 I h' sinned against heaven, and in
31 with me, and all that I h' is thine.
16:11 If therefore ye h' not been faithful in
12 And if ye h' not been faithful in that
24 Father Abraham, h' mercy on me,
28 For I h' five brethren; that he
29 They h' Moses and the prophets;
17: 8 serve me, till I h' eaten and drunken;
10 when ye shall h' done all those things
10 we h' done that which was our duty to
13 and said, Jesus, Master, h' mercy
18:21 And he said, All these h' I kept from
22 thou shalt h' treasure in heaven:
24 hardly shall they that h' riches
28 Then Peter said, Lo, we h' left all, and
38 Jesus, thou son of David, h' mercy
39 Thou son of David, h' mercy on
19: 8 and if I h' taken any thing from any
14 We will not h' this man to reign over
17 h' thou authority over ten cities.
20 here is thy pound, which I h' kept
23 I might h' required mine own with
46 but ye h' made it a den of thieves.
21: 4 all these h' of their abundance cast
22:15 With desire I h' desired to eat this
28 Ye are they which h' continued
31 Satan hath desired to h' you, that he
32 But I h' prayed for thee, that thy
37 things concerning me h' an end.
71 for we ourselves h' have heard of his
23: 8 and he hoped to h' seen some miracle
14 Ye h' brought this man unto me, as
14 h' found no fault in this man
22 I h' found no cause of death in him:
24:17 that ye h' one to another, as ye
20 condemned to death, and h' crucified
21 he which should h' redeemed Israel:
25 believe all that the prophets h' spoken:
26 Ought not Christ to h' suffered these
28 made as though he would h' gone
39 flesh and bones, as ye see me h'.
41 unto them, H' ye here any meat?
Joh 1:16 And of his fulness h' all we received,
41 We h' found the Messias, which is,
45 We h' found him, of whom Moses in
2: 3 saith unto him, They h' no wine.
4 Woman, what h' I to do with thee?
10 and when men h' well drunk, then
3:11 and testify that we h' seen; and ye
12 If I h' told you earthly things, and ye
15 not perish, but h' eternal life.
16 not perish, but h' everlasting life.
4: 9 the Jews h' no dealings with the
10 drink; thou wouldest h' asked of him,
10 and he would h' given thee living
17 and said, I h' no husband.
17 hast well said, I h' no husband.
32 I h' meat to eat that ye know not
42 for we h' heard him ourselves, and
5: 7 Sir, I h' no man, when the water
26 given to the Son to h' life in himself;
29 they that h' done good, unto the
29 they that h' done evil, unto the
36 But I h' greater witness than that
37 Ye h' neither heard his voice at any
38 And ye h' not his word abiding in
39 in them ye think ye h' eternal life:
40 come to me, that ye might h' life.
42 that ye h' not the love of God in
46 Moses, ye would h' believed me:
6:36 ye also h' seen me, and believe not.
40 may h' everlasting life: and I will
53 drink his blood, ye h' no life in you.
70 H' not I chosen you twelve, and one
7:21 I h' done one work, and ye all marvel.
23 because I h' made a man every whit
44 some of them would h' taken him;
45 them, Why h' ye not brought him.
48 H' any of the rulers...believed on him?
8: 6 that they might h' to accuse him.
12 but shall h' the light of life.
19 ye should h' known my Father also.
26 I h' many things to say and to
26 those things which I h' heard of him.
28 When ye h' lifted up the Son of man,
38 I speak that which I h' seen with
38 that which ye h' seen with your
40 the truth, which I h' heard of God:
41 we h' one Father, even God.
49 Jesus answered, I h' not a devil;
55 Yet ye h' not known him; but I know
9:27 He answered them, I h' told you
41 were blind, ye should h' no sin:
10:10 I am come that they might h' life,
10 and that they might h' it more
16 And other sheep I h', which are not
18 I h' power to lay it down, and I

Joh 10:18 and I h' power to take it again.
18 This commandment h' I received of
32 Many good works h' I shewed you
11:34 And said, Where h' ye laid him? They
37 blind, h' caused that even this man
37 even this man should not h' died.
12: 8 the poor always ye h' with you;
8 you; but me ye h' not always.
28 I h' both glorified it, and will glorify
34 We h' heard out of the law that
35 Walk while ye h' the light, lest
36 While ye h' light, believe in the
48 the word that I h' spoken, the same
49 For I h' not spoken of myself; but
13:12 them, Know ye what I h' done to you?
14 Lord and Master, h' washed your feet;
15 For I h' given you an example, that ye
15 that ye should do as I h' done to you.
18 I know whom I h' chosen: but that
26 I shall give a sop, when I h' dipped it.
29 Buy those things that we h' need
34 as I h' loved you, that ye also love
35 ye are my disciples, if ye h' love
14: 2 if it were not so, I would h' told you.
7 ye should h' known my Father also:
7 henceforth ye know him, and h' seen
9 H' I been so long time with you, and
25 These things h' I spoken unto you,
26 remembrance, whatsoever I h' said
28 Ye h' heard how I said unto you, I
29 And now I h' told you before it come
15: 3 the word which I h' spoken unto
9 so h' I loved you: continue ye in my
10 even as I h' kept my Father's
11 These things h' I spoken unto you,
12 love one another, as I h' loved you.
15 doeth: but I h' called you friends.
15 for all things that I h' heard of my
15 Father I h' made known to you.
16 h' not chosen me, but I h' chosen you,
19 but I h' chosen you out of the world,
20 If they h' persecuted me, they will
20 if they h' kept my saying, they will
22 now they h' no cloke for their sin.
24 but now h' they both seen and hated
27 because ye h' been with me from the
16: 1 These things h' I spoken unto you,
3 because they h' not known the Father,
4 But these things h' I told you, that
6 But because I h' said these things unto
12 I h' yet many things to say unto
22 And ye now therefore h' sorrow:
24 Hitherto h' ye asked nothing in my
25 These things h' I spoken unto you,
27 because ye h' loved me, and h' believed
33 These things I h' spoken unto you
33 you, that in me ye might h' peace.
33 In the world ye shall h' tribulation:
33 good cheer; I h' overcome the world.
17: 4 I h' glorified thee on the earth:
4 I h' finished the work which thou
6 I h' manifested thy name unto the
6 them me; and they h' kept thy word.
7 Now they h' known that all things
8 For I h' given unto them the words
8 they h' received them, and h' known
8 and they h' believed that thou didst
12 those that thou gavest me I h' kept,
13 that they might h' my joy fulfilled
14 I h' given them thy word; and the
18 even so h' I also sent them into
22 which thou gavest me I h' given them;
25 I h' known thee, and these h' known
26 And I h' declared unto them thy name,
18: 8 Jesus answered, I h' told you that I
9 which thou gavest me h' I lost none.
20 and in secret h' I said nothing.
21 them which heard me, what I h' said
23 If I h' spoken evil, bear witness of the
30 we would not h' delivered him up unto
35 chief priests h' delivered thee unto
39 But ye h' a custom, that I should
19: 7 We h' a law, and by our law he
10 knowest thou not that I h' power
10 crucify thee, and h' power to
11 Thou couldest h' no power at all
15 answered, we h' no king but Cæsar.
22 What I h' written I h' written.
20: 2 They h' taken away the Lord out of the
2 and we know not where they h' laid
13 Because they h' taken away my Lord,
13 I know not where they h' laid him.
15 if thou h' borne him hence, tell me
25 said unto him, We h' seen the Lord.
29 that h' not seen, and yet h' believed.
31 that believing ye might h' life
21: 5 Children, h' ye any meat? They
10 of the fish which ye h' now caught.
Ac 1: 1 The former treatise h' I made, O
4 which, saith he, ye h' heard of me.
11 come in like manner as ye h' seen him
16 must needs h' been fulfilled,
21 men which h' companied with us all
2:23 Him, being delivered...ye h' taken,
23 by wicked hands h' crucified and
36 whom ye h' crucified, both Lord and
3: 6 silver and gold h' I none;
6 but such as I h' give I thee:
24 follow after, as many as h' spoken,
24 h' likewise foretold of these days.
4: 7 or by what name h' ye done this?
20 speak the things which we h' seen
5: 9 How is it that ye h' agreed together
9 the feet of them which h' buried thy
21 sent to the prison to h' them brought.
26 lest they should h' been stoned.

Ac 5:28 and, behold, ye h' filled Jerusalem
6:11 We h' heard him speak blasphemous
14 For we h' heard him say, that this
7:25 his brethren would h' understood
26 and would h' set them at one again,
34 I h' seen, I...the affliction of my
34 I h' seen the affliction of my people
34 and I h' heard their groaning, and am
42 h' ye offered to me slain beasts and
52 h' not your fathers persecuted?
52 and they h' slain them which shewed
52 of whom ye h' been now the betrayers
53 Who h' received the law by the
53 disposition of angels, and h' not kept
8:24 these things which ye h' spoken come
9: 6 said, Lord, what wilt thou h' me to
13 Lord, I h' heard by many of this man,
10:10 very hungry, and would h' eaten:
14 for I h' never eaten any thing that is
20 doubting nothing: for I h' sent them.
29 for what intent ye h' sent for me?
47 which h' received the Holy Ghost as
12: 6 And when Herod would h' brought
13: 2 Saul for the work whereunto I h' called
15 if ye h' any word of exhortation
22 I h' found David the son of Jesse, a
27 they h' fulfilled them in condemning
33 Thou art my Son, this day h' I begotten
46 should first h' been spoken to you:
47 I h' set thee to be a light of the Gentiles,
14:13 and would h' done sacrifice with the
15:24 Forasmuch as we h' heard, that certain
24 out from us h' troubled you with words,
26 Men that h' hazarded their lives for the
27 We h' sent therefore Judas and Silas,
36 in every city where we h' preached
16: 3 Him would Paul h' to go forth with
15 If ye h' judged me to be faithful to the
27 and would h' killed himself,
36 The magistrates h' sent to let you go:
37 h' beaten us openly uncondemned,
37 Romans, and h' cast us into prison;
17: 3 that Christ must needs h' suffered,
6 These that h' turned the world upside
28 we live, and move, and h' our being;
18:10 for I h' much people in this city.
19: 2 H' ye received the Holy Ghost since
2 We h' not so much as heard whether
21 After I h' been there, I must also see
25 by this craft we h' our wealth.
30 And when Paul would h' entered in
33 and would h' made his defence unto
37 For ye h' brought hither these men,
38 h' a matter against any man, the
20:18 after what manner I h' been with you
20 but h' shewed you, and h' taught
24 which I h' received of the Lord Jesus,
25 among whom I h' gone preaching the
27 For I h' not shunned to declare
33 I h' coveted no man's silver, or gold,
34 that these hands h' ministered unto
35 I h' shewed you all things, how
21:23 We say to thee, We h' four men
23 four men which h' a vow on them;
25 we h' written and concluded that they
22:29 from him which should h' examined
30 he would h' known the certainty
23: 1 I h' lived in all good conscience before
10 Paul should h' been pulled in pieces
14 We h' bound ourselves under a great
14 eat nothing until we h' slain Paul.
20 The Jews h' agreed to desire thee that
21 which h' bound themselves with an
21 neither eat nor drink till they h' killed
27 and should h' been killed of them:
28 when I would h' known the cause
29 to h' nothing laid to his charge
24: 5 For we h' found this man a pestilent
6 and would h' judged according to
15 And h' hope toward God, which
16 to h' always a conscience void of
19 Who ought to h' been here before thee,
20 if they h' found any evil doing in me,
23 and to let him h' liberty, and
25 when I h' a convenient season,
26 that money should h' been given
25: 8 against Cæsar, h' I offended any thing
10 to the Jews h' I done no wrong, as
11 For if I be an offender, or h' committed
15 desiring to h' judgment against him.
16 h' the accusers face to face,
16 and h' licence to answer for himself
24 multitude of the Jews h' dealt with me,
25 to Augustus, I h' determined to send
26 Of whom I h' no certain thing to
26 I h' brought him forth before you,
26 had, I might h' somewhat to write.
26:16 for I h' appeared unto thee for this
32 This man might h' been set at liberty,
27:21 Sirs, ye should h' hearkened unto me,
21 unto me, and not h' loosed from Crete,
21 and to h' gained this harm and loss.
29 lest we should h' fallen upon rocks,
30 they would h' cast anchors out of the
33 that ye h' tarried and continued
28: 6 when he should h' swollen, or fallen
17 I h' committed nothing against
18 would h' let me go, because there
20 For this cause therefore h' I called
27 and their eyes h' they closed; lest
Ro 1: 5 By whom we h' received grace and
10 I might h' a prosperous journey by
13 Now I would not h' you ignorant,
13 that I might h' some fruit among
32 h' pleasure in them that do them.
2:12 For as many as h' sinned without law

Ro 2:12 and as many as h' sinned in the law
14 the Gentiles, which h' not the law;
3: 9 for we h' before proved both Jews
13 with their tongues they h' used deceit;
17 the way of peace h' they not known:
23 For all h' sinned, and come short of
4:17 I h' made thee a father of many
5: 1 we h' peace with God through
2 By whom also we h' access by faith
11 by whom we h' now received the
12 upon all men, for that all h' sinned:
6: 5 For if we h' been planted together in
14 For sin shall not h' dominion over you:
17 but ye h' obeyed from the heart
19 for as ye h' yielded your members
22 ye h' your fruit unto holiness,
8: 9 if any man h' not the Spirit of
15 For ye h' not received the spirit of
15 ye h' received the Spirit of adoption,
23 which h' the firstfruits of the
9: 2 That I h' great heaviness and
9 I come, and Sarah shall h' a son.
13 Jacob h' I loved, but Esau h' I hated.
15 saith to Moses, I will h' mercy on whom
15 mercy on whom I will h' mercy, and
15 and I will h' compassion on whom
15 on whom I will h' compassion.
17 for this same purpose h' I raised thee
18 mercy on whom he will h' mercy,
30 h' attained to righteousness, even
10: 2 record that they h' a zeal of God,
3 h' not submitted themselves unto the
14 on him in whom they h' not believed?
14 in him of whom they h' not heard?
16 But they h' not all obeyed the gospel.
18 But I say, H' they not heard? Yes
21 All day long I h' stretched forth
11: 3 Lord, they h' killed thy prophets, and
4 I h' reserved to myself seven thousand
4 who h' not bowed the knee to the
11 I say then, H' they stumbled that
30 in times past h' not believed God,
30 yet h' now obtained mercy through
31 so h' these also now not believed,
32 that he might h' mercy upon all.
12: 4 For as we h' many members in
4 members h' not the same office:
13: 3 thou shalt h' praise of the same:
14:22 Hast thou faith? h' it to thyself
15: 4 of the scriptures might h' hope.
15 I h' written the more boldly unto you
17 I h' therefore whereof I may glory
19 I h' fully preached the gospel of Christ.
20 Yea, so I h' strived to preach the
21 and they that h' not heard shall
22 I h' been much hindered from coming
27 if the Gentiles h' been made partakers
28 I h' performed this, and h' sealed to
31 my service which I h' for Jerusalem
16: 4 Who h' for my life laid down their
17 to the doctrine which ye h' learned;
19 but yet I would h' you wise unto that
1Co 2: 8 they would not h' crucified the Lord of
9 neither h' entered into the heart of
12 Now we h' received, not the spirit of
16 But we h' the mind of Christ.
3: 2 I h' fed you with milk, and not with
6 I h' planted, Apollos watered; but
10 I h' laid the foundation, and another
4: 5 shall every man h' praise of God.
6 I h' in a figure transferred to myself
8 ye h' reigned as kings without us:
11 and h' no certain dwellingplace;
15 ye h' ten thousand instructors in
15 yet h' ye not many fathers: for in
17 For this cause h' I sent unto you
5: 1 one should h' his father's wife.
2 puffed up, and h' not rather mourned,
3 h' judged already, as though I were
11 But now I h' written unto you not to
12 For what h' I to do to judge them also
6: 4 If then ye h' judgments of things
19 which ye h' of God, and ye are not
7: 2 let every man h' his own wife,
2 every woman h' her own husband.
25 virgins I h' no commandment of
28 Nevertheless such shall h' trouble
29 that both they that h' wives be as
32 I would h' you without carefulness.
40 I think also that I h' the Spirit
8: 1 we know that we all h' knowledge.
9: 1 h' I not seen Jesus Christ our Lord?
4 H' we not power to eat and to
5 H' we not power to lead about a
6 h' we not power to forbear
11 If we h' sown unto you spiritual
12 we h' not used this power;
15 But I h' used none of these things:
15 neither h' I written these things,
16 gospel, I h' nothing to glory of:
17 thing willingly, I h' a reward:
19 yet h' I made myself servant unto
27 when I h' preached to others, I
10:20 that ye should h' fellowship with
11: 3 But I would h' you know, that the
10 to h' power on her head because
14 if a man h' long hair, it is a shame
15 But if a woman h' long hair, it is a
16 we h' no such custom, neither the
22 h' ye not houses to eat and to
22 and shame them that h' not?
23 For I h' received of the Lord that
12: 1 I would not h' you ignorant.
13 and h' been all made to drink into
21 unto the hand, I h' no need of thee:
21 to the feet, I h' no need of you.

1Co 12:23 parts h' more abundant comeliness.
24 For our comely parts h' no need:
25 members should h' the same care
30 H' all the gifts of healing? do all
13: 1 and of angels, and h' not charity
2 though I h' the gift of prophecy,
2 and though I h' all faith, so that
2 mountains, and h' not charity,
3 to be burned, and h' not charity,
15: 1 which also ye h' received, and wherein
2 unto you, unless ye h' believed in vain.
15 because we h' testified of God that
19 If in this life only we h' hope in
24 when he shall h' delivered up the
24 when he shall h' put down all rule
31 which I h' in Christ Jesus our
32 I h' fought with beasts at Ephesus,
34 for some h' not the knowledge of
49 And as we h' borne the image of the
54 this corruptible shall h' put on
54 and this mortal shall h' put on
16: 1 as I h' given order to the churches of
12 when he shall h' convenient time.
15 and that they h' addicted themselves
17 lacking on your part they h' supplied.
18 For they h' refreshed my spirit and
2Co 1: 8 h' you ignorant of our trouble which
12 we h' had our conversation in the
14 As also ye h' acknowledged us in
15 that ye might h' a second benefit;
24 Not for that we h' dominion over
2: 3 I should h' sorrow from them of
4 the love which I h' more
5 But if any h' caused grief, he hath
3: 4 And such trust h' we through
12 Seeing then that we h' such hope,
4: 1 Therefore seeing we h' this
1 as we h' received mercy, we faint
2 But h' renounced the hidden things
7 But we h' this treasure in earthen
13 and therefore h' I spoken; we
5: 1 we h' a building of God, an house
12 that ye may h' somewhat to answer
16 yea, though we h' known Christ after
6: 2 For he saith, I h' heard thee in a
2 of salvation h' I succoured thee:
7: 2 we h' wronged no man,
2 we h' corrupted no man,
2 we h' defrauded no man.
3 for I h' said before, that ye are in
11 things ye h' approved yourselves
14 For if I h' boasted any thing to him
16 rejoice therefore that I h' confidence
8:10 who h' begun before, not only to do,
11 also out of that which ye h'.
18 And we h' sent with him the brother,
22 And we h' sent with him our brother,
22 whom we h' oftentimes proved
22 great confidence which I h' in you.
9: 3 Yet h' I sent the brethren, lest our
11: 2 I h' espoused you to one husband,
4 Christ, whom we h' not preached,
4 spirit, which ye h' not received,
4 gospel, which ye h' not accepted,
6 h' been thoroughly made manifest
7 H' I committed an offence in abasing
7 because I h' preached to you the
9 and in all things I h' kept myself
25 and a day I h' been in the deep;
12:11 in glorifying; ye h' compelled me:
11 for I ought to h' been commended
21 many which h' sinned already,
21 h' not repented of the uncleanness
21 which they h' committed.
13: 2 which heretofore h' sinned, and to
Ga 1: 8 than that which we h' preached unto
9 than that ye h' received, let him be
13 For ye h' heard of my conversation
2: 4 liberty which we h' in Christ
16 even we h' believed in Jesus Christ,
3: 4 H' ye suffered so many things in
21 a law given which could h' given life,
21 righteousness should h' been by the
27 as many of you as h' been baptized
27 into Christ h' put on Christ.
4: 9 But now, after that ye h' known God,
11 I am afraid of you, lest I h' bestowed
12 for I am as ye are: ye h' not injured
15 would h' plucked out your own eyes,
15 own eyes, and h' given them to me.
5:10 I h' confidence in you through the
13 For, brethren, ye h' been called unto
21 as I h' also told you in time past,
24 And they that are Christ's h' crucified
6: 4 and then shall he h' rejoicing in
10 As we h' therefore opportunity, let
11 Ye see how large a letter I h' written
13 but desire to h' you circumcised, that
Eph 1: 7 In whom we h' redemption
11 In whom also we h' obtained an
2:18 For through him we both h' access
3: 2 If ye h' heard of the dispensation of
12 In whom we h' boldness and
4:19 past feeling h' given themselves
20 But ye h' not so learned Christ;
21 ye h' heard him, and h' been taught
28 that he may h' to give to him
5:11 And h' no fellowship with the
6:22 Whom I h' sent unto you for the
Ph'p 1: 7 because I h' you in my heart;
12 which happened unto me h' fallen out
2:12 as ye h' always obeyed, not as in my
16 that I h' not run in vain, neither
20 For I h' no man likeminded, who
27 lest I should h' sorrow upon
3: 3 and h' no confidence in the flesh.

Ph'p 3:4 Though I might also h' confidence
8 for whom I h' suffered the loss of all
13 I count not myself to h' apprehended:
16 whereto we h' already attained, let
17 so as ye h' us for an ensample.
18 of whom I h' told you often, and now
4: 9 things, which ye h' both learned, and
11 for I h' learned, in whatsoever state
14 ye h' well done, that ye did
18 But I h' all, and abound: I am full,
Col 1: 4 and of the love which ye h' to all the
14 In whom we h' redemption
18 things he might h' the preeminence.
23 gospel, which ye h' heard, and which
2: 1 what great conflict I h' for you,
1 and for as many as h' not seen my
6 As ye h' therefore received Christ
7 in the faith, as ye h' been taught,
23 Which things h' indeed a shew
3: 9 seeing that ye h' put off the old man
10 And h' put on the new man, which is
13 if any man h' a quarrel against
4: 1 that ye also h' a Master in heaven.
8 Whom I h' sent unto you for the
11 of God, which h' been a comfort unto
1Th 2: 6 when we might h' been burdensome,
8 we were willing to h' imparted unto
14 for ye also h' suffered like things of
14 even as they h' of the Jews:
15 and h' persecuted us; and they
18 Wherefore we would h' come unto
3: 5 the tempter h' tempted you, and our
6 and that ye h' good remembrance
4: 1 that as ye h' received of us how ye
6 as we also h' forewarned you and
12 and that ye may h' lack of nothing.
13 But I would not h' you to be ignorant,
13 even as others which h' no hope.
5: 1 brethren, ye h' no need that I write
2Th 2:15 traditions which ye h' been taught,
3: 1 word of the Lord may h' free course,
2 wicked men: for all men h' not faith.
4 And we h' confidence in the Lord
9 Not because we h' not power, but
14 and h' no company with him, that
1Ti 1: 6 some having swerved h' turned aside
19 concerning faith h' made shipwreck:
20 whom I h' delivered unto Satan, that
2: 4 Who will h' all men to be saved, and
3: 7 he must h' a good report of them
13 For they that h' used the office of a
5: 4 But if any widow h' children or
10 if she h' brought up children,
10 if she h' lodged strangers,
10 if she h' washed the saints' feet,
10 if she h' relieved the afflicted,
10 if she h' diligently followed every
11 for when they h' begun to wax
12 because they h' cast off their first
16 woman that believeth h' widows,
6: 2 And they that h' believing masters,
10 after, they h' erred from the faith,
21 Which some professing h' erred
2Ti 1: 3 ceasing I h' remembrance
12 for I know whom I h' believed, and
12 keep that which I h' committed unto
2:18 Who concerning the truth h' erred,
4: 7 I h' fought a good fight, I h' finished
7 finished my course, I h' kept the faith:
12 And Tychicus h' I sent to Ephesus.
20 but Trophimus h' I left at Miletum
Tit 3: 5 righteousness which we h' done,
8 that they which h' believed in God
12 for I h' determined there to winter.
Ph'm 7 we h' great joy and consolation
10 Onesimus, whom I h' begotten in my
12 Whom I h' sent again: thou therefore
13 Whom I would h' retained with me,
13 in thy stead he might h' ministered
19 I Paul h' written it with mine own
20 Yea, brother, let me h' joy of thee in
Heb 1: 5 my Son, this day h' I begotten thee?
2: 1 to the things which we h' heard,
3:10 and they h' not known my ways.
4: 3 For we which h' believed do enter
3 As I h' sworn in my wrath, if they
8 he not afterward h' spoken of
13 eyes of him with whom we h' to do.
14 that we h' a great high priest,
15 For we h' not an high priest which
5: 2 Who can h' compassion on the
5 Thou art my Son, to day h' I begotten
11 Of whom we h' many things to say,
12 ye h' need that one teach you
12 and are become such as h' need of
14 of use h' their senses exercised to
6: 4 and h' tasted of the heavenly gift,
5 And h' tasted the good word of God,
10 labour of love, which ye h' shewed
10 in that ye h' ministered to the saints,
18 we might h' a strong consolation,
18 who h' fled for refuge to lay hold
19 Which hope we h' as an anchor of
7: 5 h' a commandment to take tithes
28 high priests which h' infirmity;
8: 1 the things which we h' spoken
1 We h' such an high priest, who is
3 that this man h' somewhat also to
7 then should no place h' been sought
9:26 For then must he often h' suffered
10: 2 For then would they not h' ceased
2 should h' had no more conscience
26 that we h' received the knowledge
34 that ye h' in heaven a better and
36 For ye h' need of patience,
36 that, after ye h' done the will of God,

Heb10:38 my soul shall *h'* no pleasure
11:15 they might *h'* had opportunity
15 opportunity to *h'* returned.
12: 4 Ye *h'* not yet resisted unto blood,
5 And ye *h'* forgotten the exhortation
9 Furthermore we *h'* had fathers
17 when he would *h'* inherited the
28 let us *h'* grace, whereby we may
13: 2 for thereby some *h'* entertained
5 content with such things as ye *h'*:
7 Remember them which *h'* the rule
7 who *h'* spoken unto you the word of
9 not with meats, which *h'* not profited
9 them that *h'* been occupied therein.
10 We *h'* an altar, whereof they
10 they *h'* no right to eat which serve
14 For here we *h'* no continuing city,
17 Obey them that *h'* the rule over you,
18 trust we *h'* a good conscience,
22 for I *h'* written a letter unto you in
24 Salute all them that *h'* the rule over
Jas 1: 4 But let patience *h'* her perfect
2: 1 My brethren, *h'* not the faith of
3 ye *h'* respect to him that weareth
6 But ye *h'* despised the poor. Do not
9 But if ye *h'* respect to persons, ye
13 For he shall *h'* judgment without
14 he hath faith, and *h'* not works?
18 Thou hast faith, and I *h'* works: shew
3:14 But if ye *h'* bitter envying and
4: 2 Ye lust, and *h'* not: ye kill, and
2 desire to *h'*, and cannot obtain:
2 ye fight and war, yet ye *h'* not,
5: 3 Ye *h'* heaped treasure together for the
4 hire of the labourers who *h'* reaped
4 the cries of them which *h'* reaped
5 Ye *h'* lived in pleasure on the earth,
5 ye *h'* nourished your hearts, as in a
6 Ye *h'* condemned and killed the just;
10 *h'* spoken in the name of the Lord,
11 Ye *h'* heard of the patience of Job,
11 and *h'* seen the end of the Lord; that
15 and if he *h'* committed sins, they shall
1Pe 1:10 prophets *h'* enquired and searched
12 by them that *h'* preached the gospel
22 Seeing ye *h'* purified your souls in
2: 3 If so be ye *h'* tasted that the Lord is
10 mercy, but now *h'* obtained mercy.
4: 3 may suffice us to *h'* wrought the will
8 all things *h'* fervent charity
5:10 after that ye *h'* suffered a while, make
12 as I suppose, I *h'* written briefly,
2Pe 1: 1 to them that *h'* obtained like precious
15 to *h'* these things in remembrance.
16 For we *h'* not followed cunningly
19 We *h'* also a more sure word of
2:14 an heart they *h'* exercised with
15 Which *h'* forsaken the right way, and
20 For if after they *h'* escaped the
21 better for them not to *h'* known the
21 than, after they *h'* known it, to turn
1Jo 1: 1 which we *h'* heard, which we *h'* seen
1 which we *h'* looked upon, and
1 our hands *h'* handled of the Word
2 and we *h'* seen it, and bear witness,
3 That which we *h'* seen and heard
3 that ye also may *h'* fellowship
5 message which we *h'* heard of him,
6 If we say that we *h'* fellowship
7 as he is in the light, we *h'* fellowship
8 If we say that we *h'* no sin, we
10 we say that we *h'* not sinned, we
2: 1 any man sin, we *h'* an advocate
7 the word which ye *h'* heard from the
13 because ye *h'* known him that is from
13 because ye *h'* overcome the wicked
13 because ye *h'* known the Father.
14 I *h'* written unto you, fathers, because
14 because ye *h'* known him that is from
14 I *h'* written unto you, young men,
14 and ye *h'* overcome the wicked one.
18 and as ye *h'* heard that antichrist
19 they would no doubt *h'* continued
20 But ye *h'* an unction from the Holy
21 I *h'* not written unto you because ye
24 which ye *h'* heard from the beginning.
24 If that which ye *h'* heard from the
26 These things *h'* I written unto you
27 the anointing which ye *h'* received
28 we may *h'* confidence, and not be
3:14 We know that we *h'* passed from
17 and seeth his brother *h'* need,
21 then *h'* we confidence toward God.
4: 3 whereof ye *h'* heard that it should
4 and *h'* overcome them: because
14 And we *h'* seen and do testify that the
16 And we *h'* known and believed the
17 that we may *h'* boldness in the
21 this commandment *h'* we from him,
5:13 These things *h'* I written unto you
13 may know that ye *h'* eternal life,
14 the confidence that we *h'* in him,
15 we know that we *h'* the petitions
2Jo 1 also all they that *h'* known the truth;
4 as we *h'* received a commandment
6 That, as ye *h'* heard from the
8 those things which we *h'* wrought,
3Jo 4 I *h'* no greater joy than to hear
6 Which *h'* borne witness of thy charity
9 who loveth to *h'* the preeminence
Jude 11 for they *h'* gone in the way of Cain,
15 which they *h'* ungodly committed, and
15 which ungodly sinners *h'* spoken
22 And of some *h'* compassion, making a
Re 1:18 Amen; and *h'* the keys of hell and
2: 4 Nevertheless I *h'* somewhat against

Re 2:10 and ye shall *h'* tribulation ten days:
14 But I *h'* a few things against thee,
20 I *h'* a few things against thee,
24 as many as *h'* not this doctrine,
24 and which *h'* not known the depths
25 But that which ye *h'* already hold
3: 2 for I *h'* not found thy works perfect
4 in Sardis which *h'* not defiled their
8 behold, I *h'* set before thee an open
9 and to know that I *h'* loved thee.
17 goods, and *h'* need of nothing;
7: 3 till we *h'* sealed the servants of our
14 and *h'* washed their robes, and made
9: 3 scorpions of the earth *h'* power.
4 men which *h'* not the seal of God
11: 6 These *h'* power to shut heaven,
6 and *h'* power over waters to turn
7 And when they shall *h'* finished their
12:17 and *h'* the testimony of Jesus
13: 9 If any man *h'* an ear, let him hear.
14:11 and they *h'* no rest day nor night,
16: 6 For they *h'* shed the blood of saints
17: 2 the earth *h'* committed fornication,
2 the earth *h'* been made drunk with
12 which *h'* received no kingdom as yet;
13 These *h'* one mind, and shall give
18: 3 For all nations *h'* drunk of the wine
3 the earth *h'* committed fornication,
5 For her sins *h'* reached unto heaven,
9 who *h'* committed fornication and
19:10 brethren that *h'* the testimony
21: 8 shall *h'* their part in the lake which
22:14 that they may *h'* right to the tree
16 I Jesus *h'* sent mine angel to testify

haven See also HAVENS.
Ge 49:13 shall dwell at the *h'* of the sea
13 and he shall be for an *h'* of ships;
Ps 107:30 them unto their desired *h'*.
Ac 27:12 the *h'* was not commodious
12 which is an *h'* at Crete, and lieth

havens
Ac 27: 8 place which is called The fair *h'*;

Havilah (*hav'-il-ah*)
Ge 2:11 compasseth the whole land of *H'*,
10: 7 of Cush; Seba, and *H'*, and Sabtah,
29 Ophir, and *H'*, and Jobab: all these
25:18 they dwelt from *H'* unto Shur, that
1Sa 15: 7 from *H'* until thou comest to
1Ch 1: 9 Cush; Seba, and *H'*, and Sabta,
23 And Ophir, and *H'*, and Jobab. All

having^
Ge 12: 8 and pitched his tent, *h'* Bethel on the
Le 7:20 *h'* his uncleanness upon him, even
20:18 lie with a woman *h'* her sickness,
22: 3 the Lord, *h'* his uncleanness upon
22 or maimed, or *h'* a wen, or scurvy,
Nu 24: 4, 16 a trance, but *h'* his eyes open:
De 10: 3 the mount, *h'* the two tables in mine
J'g 1: 7 *h'* their thumbs and their toes cut off,
19: 3 *h'* his servant with him, and a couple
Ru 1:13 ye stay for them from *h'* husbands?
1Sa 22: 6 in Ramah, *h'* his spear in his hand,
26: 2 of Ziph, *h'* three thousand chosen men
1Ki 22:10 on his throne, *h'* put on their robes,
1Ch 4:42 *h'* for their captains Pelatiah, and
21:16 and the heaven, *h'* a drawn sword in
26:12 men, *h'* wards one against another,
2Ch 5:12 *h'* cymbals and psalteries and harps,
11:12 *h'* Judah and Benjamin on his
23:10 every man *h'* his weapon in his hand,
Ezr 9: 5 and *h'* rent my garment and my
Ne 10:28 *h'* knowledge, and *h'* understanding;
13: 4 the priest, *h'* the oversight of
Es 6:12 mourning, and *h'* his head covered.
Ps 13: 2 in my soul, *h'* sorrow in my heart
Pr 6: 7 Which *h'* no guide, overseer, or ruler,
18: 1 desire a man, *h'* separated himself,
Isa 6: 6 *h'* a live coal in his hand,
41:15 threshing instrument *h'* teeth:
Jer 41: 5 *h'* their beards shaven, and their
5 and *h'* cut themselves, with offerings
Eze 38:11 and *h'* neither bars nor gates,
40:44 the east gate *h'* the prospect toward
44:11 my sanctuary, *h'* charge at the gates
Da 8:20 which thou sawest *h'* two horns
Mic 1:11 of Saphir, *h'* thy shame naked:
Zec 9: 9 he is just, and *h'* salvation;
M't 7:29 them as one *h'* authority,
8: 9 authority, *h'* soldiers under me:
9:36 as sheep *h'* no shepherd.
15:30 *h'* with them those that were lame,
18: 8 rather than *h'* two hands or two
9 rather than *h'* two eyes to be cast
22:12 in hither not *h'* a wedding garment?
24 If a man die, *h'* no children, his
25 deceased, and, *h'* no issue, left his
26: 7 a woman *h'* an alabaster box of
M'r 6:34 were as sheep not *h'* a shepherd:
8: 1 and *h'* nothing to eat, Jesus called
18 *H'* eyes, see ye not? and *h'* ears,
9:43 than *h'* two hands to go into hell,
45 than *h'* two feet to be cast into hell,
47 than *h'* two eyes to be cast into hell
11:13 a fig tree afar off *h'* leaves, he came,
12: 6 *H'* yet therefore one son, his
28 *h'* heard them reasoning together,
14: 3 a woman *h'* an alabaster box of
51 young man, *h'* a linen cloth cast about
Lu 1: 3 *h'* had perfect understanding of all
5:39 No man also *h'* drunk old wine
7: 8 authority, *h'* under me soldiers,
8:15 heart, *h'* heard the word, keep it,
43 a woman *h'* an issue of blood
9:62 No man, *h'* put his hand to the plough,
11:36 full of light, *h'* no part dark, the

Lu 15: 4 man of you, *h'* an hundred sheep,
8 what woman *h'* ten pieces of silver,
17: 7 *h'* a servant plowing or feeding
19:15 returned, *h'* received the kingdom,
20:28 If any man's brother die, *h'* a wife,
23:14 *h'* examined him before you, have
46 and *h'* said thus, he gave up the ghost.
Joh 4:45 *h'* seen all the things that he did at
5: 2 tongue Bethesda, *h'* five porches.
7:15 this man letters, *h'* never learned?
13: 1 *h'* loved his own which were in the
2 the devil now *h'* put into the heart of
30 He then *h'* received the sop went
18: 3 Judas then, *h'* received a band of men
10 Simon Peter *h'* a sword drew it,
Ac 2:24 raised up, *h'* loosed the pains of death
33 *h'* received of the Father the promise
47 and *h'* favour with all the people,
3:26 God, *h'* raised up his Son Jesus, sent
4:37 *H'* land, sold it, and brought
12:20 *h'* made Blastus...their friend,
14:19 *h'* stoned Paul, drew him out of the
16:24 Who, *h'* received such a charge,
18:18 *h'* shorn his head in Cenchrea: for he
19: 1 Paul *h'* passed through the upper
29 and *h'* caught Gaius and Aristarchus,
22:12 *h'* a good report of all the Jews
23:27 *h'* understood that he was a Roman.
24:22 *h'* more perfect knowledge of that
26:10 *h'* received authority from the chief
22 *H'* therefore obtained help of God, I
27:33 continued fasting, *h'* taken nothing.
Ro 2:14 *h'* not the law, are a law unto
9:11 neither *h'* done any good or evil, that
12: 6 *H'* then gifts differing according
15:23 But now *h'* no more place in these
1Co 6: 1 *h'* a matter against another, go
7:37 *h'* no necessity, but hath power
11: 4 prophesying, *h'* his head covered,
12:24 *h'* given more abundant honour to
2Co 2: 3 *h'* confidence in you all, that my joy
4:13 We *h'* the same spirit of faith,
6:10 as *h'* nothing, and yet possessing
7: 1 *H'* therefore these promises,
9: 8 that ye, always *h'* all sufficiency
10: 6 And *h'* in a readiness to revenge
15 but *h'* hope, when your faith is
Ga 3: 3 *h'* begun in the Spirit, are ye now
Eph 1: 5 *H'* predestinated us unto the
9 *H'* made known unto us the mystery
2:12 *h'* no hope, and without God in
15 *H'* abolished in his flesh the enmity,
16 cross, *h'* slain the enmity thereby:
4:18 *H'* the understanding darkened,
5:27 not *h'* spot, or wrinkle, or any
6:13 the evil day, and *h'* done all, to stand.
14 Stand therefore, *h'* your loins girt
14 and *h'* on the breastplate of
Ph'p 1:23 *h'* a desire to depart, and to be
25 And *h'* this confidence, I know that I
30 *H'* the same conflict which ye
2: 2 *h'* the same love, being of one
3: 9 not *h'* mine own righteousness,
4:18 *h'* received of Epaphroditus the
Col 1:20 *h'* made peace through the blood of
2:13 him, *h'* forgiven you all trespasses;
15 *h'* spoiled principalities and powers,
19 body *h'*... nourishment ministered,
1Th 1: 6 *h'* received the word in much
1Ti 1: 6 From which some *h'* swerved have
19 some *h'* put away concerning faith
3: 4 *h'* his children in subjection with
4: 2 *h'* their conscience seared with a hot
8 *h'* promise of the life that now is,
5: 9 years old, *h'* been the wife of one man,
12 *H'* damnation, because they have
6: 8 And *h'* food and raiment let us be
2Ti 2:19 of God standeth sure, *h'* this seal,
3: 5 *H'* a form of godliness, but
4: 3 themselves teachers, *h'* itching ears;
10 *h'* loved this present world, and is
Tit 1: 6 *h'* faithful children not accused
2: 8 *h'* no evil thing to say of you.
Ph'm 21 *H'* confidence in thy obedience I
Heb 7: 3 *h'* neither beginning of days, nor
9:12 *h'* obtained eternal redemption for us.
10: 1 For the law *h'* a shadow of good
19 *H'* therefore, brethren, boldness to
21 And *h'* an high priest over the house
22 *h'* our hearts sprinkled from an evil
11:13 not *h'* received the promises, but
39 all, *h'* obtained a good report through
40 God *h'* provided some better thing for
1Pe 1: 8 Whom *h'* not seen, ye love;
2:12 *H'* your conversation honest
3: 8 *h'* compassion one of another,
16 *H'* a good conscience; that,
2Pe 1: 4 *h'* escaped the corruption that is in
2:14 *H'* eyes full of adultery, and that
2Jo 12 *H'* many things to write unto you,
Jude 5 *h'* saved the people out of the land of
16 *h'* men's persons in admiration
19 sensual, *h'* not the Spirit.
Re 5: 6 *h'* seven horns and seven eyes,
8 *h'* every one of them harps, and
7: 2 *h'* the seal of the living God:
8: 3 at the altar, *h'* a golden censer;
9:17 *h'* breastplates of fire, and of
12: 3 *h'* seven heads and ten horns, and
12 down unto you, *h'* great wrath,
13: 1 *h'* seven heads and ten horns, and
14: 1 *h'* his Father's name written in
6 *h'* the everlasting gospel to preach
14 *h'* on his head a golden crown, and
17 heaven, he also *h'* a sharp sickle.
15: 1 angels *h'* the seven last plagues;

Re 15: 2 sea of glass, h' the harps of God.
6 the temple, h' the seven plagues,
6 h' their breasts girded with
17: 3 h' seven heads and ten horns.
4 h' a golden cup in her hand full of
18: 1 from heaven, h' great power;
20: 1 h' the key of the bottomless pit
21: 11 H' the glory of God: and her light

havock
Ac 8: 3 Saul, he made h' of the church.

Havoth-jair *(ha''-voth-ja'-ir)* See also BASHAN-HAVOTH.
Nu 32: 41 thereof, and called them H'.
J'g 10: 4 which are called H' unto this day.

hawk
Le 11: 16 the owl, and the night h', and the
16 cuckow, and the h' after his kind.
De 14: 15 the owl, and the night h', and the
15 cuckow, and the h' after his kind,
Job 39: 26 Doth the h' fly by thy wisdom,

hay
Pr 27: 25 The h' appeareth, and the tender
Isa 15: 6 for the h' is withered away, the
1Co 3: 12 silver, precious stones, wood, h',

Hazael *(ha'-za-el)*
1Ki 19: 15 anoint H' to be king over Syria:
17 that escapeth the sword of H' shall
2Ki 8: 8 the king said unto H', Take a
9 So H' went to meet him, and took
12 And H' said, Why weepeth my
13 And H' said, But what, is thy
15 and H' reigned in his stead.
28 of Ahab to war against H' king of
29 Ramah, when he fought against H'
9: 14 and all Israel, because of H' king
15 when he fought with H' king of
10: 32 and H' smote them in all the
12: 17 Then H' king of Syria went up,
17 and H' set his face to go up to
18 and sent it to H' king of Syria:
13: 3 into the hand of H' king of Syria,
3 hand of Ben-hadad the son of H',
22 But H' king of Syria oppressed
24 So H' king of Syria died; and
25 hand of Ben-hadad the son of H'
2Ch 22: 5 to war against H' king of Syria
6 Ramah, when he fought with H'
Am 1: 4 send a fire into the house of H',

Hazaiah *(ha-za-i'-ah)*
Ne 11: 5 Col-hozeh, the son of H', the son

Hazar See HAZAR-ADDAR; HAZAR-ENAN; HAZAR-GADDAH; HAZAR-HATTICON; HAZAR-SHUAL; HAZAR-SUSAH; HAZAR-SUSIM.

Hazar-addar *(ha''-zar-ad'-dar)* See also ADDAR.
Nu 34: 4 and shall go on to H', and pass

hazarded
Ac 15: 26 Men that have h' their lives for

Hazar-enan *(ha''-zar-e'-nan)*
Nu 34: 9 goings out of it shall be at H':
10 east border from H' to Shepham:
Eze 47: 17 border from the sea shall be H',
48: 1 as one goeth to Hamath, H',

Hazar-gaddah *(ha''-zar-gad'-dah)*
Jos 15: 27 H', and Heshmon, and Beth-palet,

Hazar-hatticon *(ha''-zar-hat'-ti-con)*
Eze 47: 16 H', which is by the coast of

Hazarmaveth *(ha-zar-ma'-veth)*
Ge 10: 26 Sheleph, and H', and Jerah,
1Ch 1: 20 Sheleph, and H', and Jerah,

Hazar-shual *(ha''-zar-shoo'-al)*
Jos 15: 28 And H', and Beer-sheba, and
19: 3 H', and Balah, and Azem,
1Ch 4: 28 Beer-sheba, and Moladah, and H',
Ne 11: 27 at H', and at Beer-sheba, and in

Hazar-susah *(ha''-zar-soo'-sah)* See also HAZAR-SUSIM.
Jos 19: 5 and Beth-marcaboth, and H',

Hazar-susim *(ha''-zar-soo'-sim)* See also HAZAR-SUSAH.
1Ch 4: 31 at Beth-marcaboth, and H',

Hazazon-tamar *(haz''-a-zon-ta'-mar)* See also HAZEZON-TAMAR.
2Ch 20: 2 they be in H', which is Engedi.

hazel
Ge 30: 37 and of the h' and chestnut tree;

Hazelelponi *(haz-el-el-po'-ni)*
1Ch 4: 3 the name of their sister was H':

Hazerim *(haz'-e-rim)*
De 2: 23 the Avims which dwelt in H',

Hazeroth *(haz'-e-roth)*
Nu 11: 35 from Kibroth-hattaavah unto H';
35 and abode at H'.
12: 16 the people removed from H',
33: 17 and encamped at H'.
18 And they departed from H', and
De 1: 1 Laban, and H', and Dizahab.

Hazezon-tamar *(haz''-e-zon-ta'-mar)* See also EN-GEDI; HAZAZON-TAMAR.
Ge 14: 7 the Amorites, that dwelt in H'.

Haziel *(ha'-ze-el)*
1Ch 23: 9 Shelomith, and H', and Haran,

Hazo *(ha'-zo)*
Ge 22: 22 Chesed, and H', and Pildash,

Hazor *(ha'-zor)* See also BAAL-HAZOR; EN-HAZOR; HEZRON.
Jos 11: 1 when Jabin king of H' had heard
10 and took H', and smote the king
10 for H' beforetime was the head
Jos 11: 11 and he burnt H' with fire.
13 Israel burned none of them, save H'
12: 19 Madon, one; the king of H', one;
15: 23 And Kedesh, and H', and Ithnan,
25 And H', Hadattah, and
25 Kerioth, and Hezron, which is H',
19: 36 And Adamah, and Ramah, and H',
J'g 4: 2 king of Canaan, that reigned in H';
17 peace between Jabin the king of H'
1Sa 12: 9 of Sisera, captain of the host of H',
1Ki 9: 15 and H', and Megiddo, and Gezer.
2Ki 15: 29 Kedesh, and H', and Gilead,
Ne 11: 33 H', Ramah, Gittaim,
Jer 49: 28 and concerning the kingdoms of H',
30 dwell deep, O ye inhabitants of H',
33 H' shall be a dwelling for dragons,

Hazor-hadattah See HAZOR and HADATTAH.

Hazzurim See HELKATH-HAZZURIM.

head See also BEHEADED; FOREHEAD; GODHEAD; GRAYHEADED; HEADBANDS; HEADLONG; HEADS; HEADSTONE.
Ge 3: 15 it shall bruise thy h', and thou
24: 26 And the man bowed down his h', and
48 And I bowed down my h', and
40: 13 shall Pharaoh lift up thine h', and
16 I had three white baskets on my h':
17 them out of the basket upon my h'.
19 shall Pharaoh lift up thy h' from off
20 he lifted up the h' of the chief
47: 31 bowed himself upon the bed's h'.
48: 14 laid it upon Ephraim's h', who was
14 his left hand upon Manasseh's h',
17 hand upon the h' of Ephraim,
17 Ephraim's h' unto Manasseh's h'.
18 put thy right hand upon his h'.
49: 26 they shall be on the h' of Joseph,
26 and on the crown of the h' of him
Ex 12: 9 his h' with his legs, and with the
27 And the people bowed the h' and
26: 24 coupled together above the h' of
29: 6 put the mitre upon his h', and put
7 oil, and pour it upon his h', and
10 hands upon the h' of the bullock.
15 their hands upon the h' of the ram.
17 unto his pieces, and unto his h'.
19 their hands upon the h' of the ram.
34: 8 Moses made haste, and bowed his h'
36: 29 coupled together at the h' thereof,
Le 1: 4 upon the h' of the burnt offering;
8 the parts, the h', and the fat,
12 pieces, with his h' and his fat:
15 wring off his h', and burn it on the
3: 2, 8 hand upon the h' of his offering,
13 lay his hand upon the h' of it,
4: 4 lay his hand upon the bullock's h',
11 with his h', and with his legs,
15 hands upon the h' of the bullock
24 his hand upon the h' of the goat,
29, 33 upon the h' of the sin offering,
5: 8 wring off his h' from his neck,
8: 9 And he put the mitre upon his h';
12 the anointing oil upon Aaron's h',
14 upon the h' of the bullock for the
18 their hands upon the h' of the ram.
20 Moses burnt the h', and the pieces,
22 hands upon the h' of the ram.
9: 13 with the pieces thereof, and the h':
13: 12 plague from his h' even to his foot,
29 a plague upon the h' or the beard;
30 a leprosy upon the h' or beard.
40 whose hair is fallen off his h',
41 the part of his h' toward his face,
42 if there be in the bald h', or bald
42 leprosy sprung up in his bald h',
43 sore be white reddish in his bald h',
44 unclean; his plague is in his h'.
45 shall be rent, and his h' bare,
14: 9 shall shave all his hair off his h'
18 the h' of him that is to be cleansed:
29 the h' of him that is to be cleansed,
16: 21 hands upon the h' of the live goat,
21 them upon the h' of the goat,
19: 32 rise up before the hoary h', and
21: 5 not make baldness upon their h',
10 upon whose h' the anointing oil
10 shall not uncover his h', nor rend
24: 14 lay their hands upon his h', and
Nu 1: 4 one h' of the house of his fathers.
5: 18 uncover the woman's h', and put
6: 5 shall no rasor come upon his h':
5 the locks of the hair of his h' grow.
7 of his God is upon his h'.
9 defiled the h' of his consecration;
9 shall shave his h' in the day
11 and shall hallow his h' that same
18 Nazarite shall shave the h' of his
18 the hair of the h' of his separation,
17: 3 h' of the house of their fathers.
22: 31 and he bowed down his h', and fell
25: 15 he was h' over a people, and of a
De 19: 5 the h' slippeth from the helve, and
21: 12 she shall shave her h', and pare
28: 13 the Lord shall make thee the h',
23 thy heaven that is over thy h'
35 of thy foot unto the top of thy h'.
44 he shall be the h', and thou shalt
33: 16 come upon the h' of Joseph,
16 and upon the top of the h' of him
20 the arm with the crown of the h'.
Jos 2: 19 his blood shall be upon his h',
19 his blood shall be on our h',
11: 10 was the h' of all those kingdoms.
22: 14 each one was an h' of the house of
J'g 5: 26 Sisera, she smote off his h',
J'g 9: 53 of a millstone upon Abimelech's h',
10: 18 h' over all the inhabitants of
11: 8 be our h' over all the inhabitants
9 before me, shall I be your h'?
11 the people made him h' and captain
13: 5 no rasor shall come on his h':
16: 13 weavest the seven locks of my h'
17 hath not come a rasor upon mine h';
19 shave off the seven locks of his h';
22 the hair of his h' began to grow
1Sa 1: 11 shall no rasor come upon his h'.
4: 12 rent, and with earth upon his h'.
5: 4 and the h' of Dagon and both the
10: 1 vial of oil, and poured it upon his h',
14: 45 one hair of his h' fall to the ground;
15: 17 made the h' of the tribes of Israel,
17: 5 had an helmet of brass upon his h',
7 and his spear's h' weighed six
38 an helmet of brass upon his h';
46 take thine h' from thee; and I will
51 him, and cut off his h' therewith.
54 David took the h' of the Philistine,
57 with the h' of the Philistine in his
25: 39 of Nabal upon his own h'.
28: 2 thee keeper of mine h' for ever.
31: 9 they cut off his h', and stripped off
2Sa 1: 2 rent, and earth upon his h'; and so
10 the crown that was upon his h',
16 Thy blood be upon thy h'; for
2: 16 every one his fellow by the h',
3: 8 Am I a dog's h', which against
29 Let it rest on the h' of Joab
4: 7 beheaded him, and took his h',
8 they brought the h' of Ish-bosheth
8 Behold the h' of Ish-bosheth the
12 they took the h' of Ish-bosheth,
12: 30 their king's crown from off his h',
30 and it was set on David's h'.
13: 19 Tamar put ashes on her h', and
19 laid her hand on her h', and went
14: 25 his foot even to the crown of his h'
26 And when he polled his h', (for it
26 he weighed the hair of his h' at two
15: 30 and had his h' covered, and he
30 covered every man his h', and they
32 coat rent, and earth upon his h':
16: 9 I pray thee, and take off his h'.
18: 9 and his h' caught hold of the oak,
20: 21 his h' shall be thrown to thee over
22 they cut off the h' of Sheba
22: 44 kept me to be h' of the heathen:
1Ki 2: 6 let not his hoar h' go down to the grave
9 his hoar h' bring thou down to the
32 return his blood upon his own h',
33 return upon the h' of Joab, and
33 and upon the h' of his seed for ever:
37 blood shall be upon thine own h'.
44 thy wickedness upon thine own h';
8: 32 to bring his way upon his h';
19: 6 and a cruse of water at his h'.
2Ki 2: 3, 5 thy master from thy h' to-day?
23 thou bald h'; go up, thou bald h'.
4: 19 said unto his father, My h', my h'.
6: 5 the axe h' fell into the water:
25 an ass's h' was sold for fourscore
31 the h' of Elisha the son of Shaphat
32 hath sent to take away mine h'?
9: 3 the box of oil, and pour it on his h',
6 he poured the oil on his h',
30 painted her face, and tired her h',
19: 21 Jerusalem hath shaken her h' at
25: 27 did lift up the h' of Jehoiachin
1Ch 10: 9 they took his h', and his armour,
10 fastened his h' in the temple of
20: 2 crown of their king from off his h',
2 and it was set upon David's h':
29: 11 thou art exalted as h' above all.
2Ch 6: 23 his way upon his own h';
20: 18 And Jehoshaphat bowed his h' with
Ezr 9: 3 plucked off the hair of my h' and
6 iniquities are increased over our h',
Ne 4: 4 their reproach upon their own h',
Es 2: 17 he set the royal crown upon her h',
6: 8 royal which is set upon his h':
12 and having his h' covered.
9: 25 should return upon his own h',
Job 1: 20 rent his mantle, and shaved his h',
10: 15 yet will I not lift up my h'.
16: 4 you, and shake mine h' at you.
19: 9 and taken the crown from my h'.
20: 6 and his h' reach unto the clouds;
29: 3 When his candle shined upon my h',
41: 7 irons? or his h' with fish spears?
Ps 3: 3 glory, and the lifter up of mine h'.
7: 16 shall return upon his own h',
18: 43 made me the h' of the heathen;
21: 3 a crown of pure gold on his h'.
22: 7 the lip, they shake the h', saying,
23: 5 thou anointest my h' with oil;
27: 6 now shall mine h' be lifted up
38: 4 iniquities are gone over mine h':
40: 12 more than the hairs of mine h':
44: 14 shaking of the h' among the people.
60: 7 also is the strength of mine h';
68: 21 shall wound the h' of his enemies,
69: 4 more than the hairs of mine h':
83: 2 that hate thee have lifted up the h'.
108: 8 also is the strength of mine h';
110: 7 therefore shall he lift up the h'.
118: 22 become the h' stone of the corner.
133: 2 the precious ointment upon the h',
140: 7 covered my h' in the day of battle.
9 the h' of those that compass me
141: 5 oil, which shall not break my h':
Pr 1: 9 an ornament of grace unto thy h',
4: 9 shall give to thine h' an ornament

Pr 10: 6 Blessings are upon the h' of the
11: 26 blessing shall be upon the h' of him
16: 31 The hoary h' is a crown of glory,
20: 29 the beauty of old men is the gray h'.
25: 22 heap coals of fire upon his h',
Ec 2: 14 The wise man's eyes are in his h';
9: 8 and let thy h' lack no ointment.
Ca 2: 6 His left hand is under my h',
5: 2 for my h' is filled with dew,
11 His h' is as the most fine gold,
7: 5 Thine h' upon thee is like Carmel,
5 and the hair of thine h' like purple;
8: 3 left hand should be under my h',
Isa 1: 5 the whole h' is sick, and the whole
6 the sole of the foot even unto the h'
3: 17 with a scab the crown of the h' of
7: 8 the h' of Syria is Damascus, and
8 the h' of Damascus is Rezin;
9 And the h' of Ephraim is Samaria,
9 the h' of Samaria is Remaliah's son.
20 the h', and the hair of the feet:
9: 14 will cut off from Israel h' and tail,
15 ancient and honourable, he is the h';
19: 15 the h' or tail, branch or rush,
28: 1 are on the h' of the fat valleys
4 which is on the h' of the fat valley,
37: 22 of Jerusalem hath shaken her h'
51: 11 joy shall be upon their h':
20 they lie at the h' of all the streets,
58: 5 to bow down his h' as a bulrush,
59: 17 an helmet of salvation upon his h':
Jer 2: 16 have broken the crown of thy h'.
37 and thine hands upon thine h':
9: 1 Oh that my h' were waters,
18: 16 shall be astonished, and wag his h'.
22: 6 unto me, and the h' of Lebanon:
23: 19 grievously upon the h' of the wicked.
30: 23 with pain upon the h' of the wicked.
48: 37 every h' shall be bald, and every
45 of the h' of the tumultuous ones.
52: 31 h' of Jehoiachin king of Judah,
La 2: 15 they hiss and wag their h' at the
3: 54 Waters flowed over mine h'; then I
5: 16 The crown is fallen from our h':
Eze 5: 1 upon thine h' and upon thy beard:
8: 3 took me by a lock of mine h';
9: 10 recompense their way upon their h'.
10: 1 above the h' of the cherubims there
11 whither the h' looked they followed
13: 18 upon the h' of every stature to hunt
16: 12 a beautiful crown upon thine h'.
25 high place at every h' of the way,
31 eminent place the h' of every way,
43 recompense thy way upon thine h',
17: 19 will I recompense upon his own h'.
21: 19 at the h' of the way to the city.
21 at the h' of the two ways,
24: 17 bind the tire of thine h' upon thee,
29: 18 every h' was made bald, and every
33: 4 his blood shall be upon his own h'.
42: 12 was a door in the h' of the way.
Da 1: 10 me endanger my h' to the king.
2: 28 the visions of thy h' upon thy bed
32 This image's h' was of fine gold,
38 Thou art this h' of gold.
3: 27 nor was an hair of their h' singed,
4: 5 the visions of my h' troubled me.
10 the visions of mine h' in my bed;
13 I saw in the visions of my h' upon
7: 1 and visions of his h' upon his bed:
9 hair of his h' like the pure wool:
15 the visions of my h' troubled me.
20 of the ten horns that were in his h',
Ho 1: 11 and appoint themselves one h',
Joe 3: 4 recompence upon your own h';
7 your recompence upon your own h':
Am 2: 7 of the earth on the h' of the poor,
8: 10 loins, and baldness upon every h';
9: 1 cut them in the h', all of them:
Ob 15 shall return upon thine own h'.
Jon 2: 5 weeds were wrapped about my h'.
4: 6 a shadow over his h', to deliver
8 the sun beat upon the h' of Jonah,
Mic 2: 13 and the Lord on the h' of them.
Hab 3: 13 woundedst the h' out of the house
14 his staves the h' of his villages:
Zec 1: 21 so that no man did lift up his h':
3: 5 men set a fair mitre upon his h'.
5 they set a fair mitre upon his h',
6: 11 set them upon the h' of Joshua
M't 5: 36 Neither shalt thou swear by thy h',
6: 17 when thou fastest, anoint thine h',
8: 20 hath not where to lay his h'.
10: 30 hairs of your h' are all numbered.
14: 8 Give me here John Baptist's h' in
11 And his h' was brought in a
21: 42 is become the h' of the corner:
26: 7 ointment, and poured it on his h',
27: 29 of thorns, they put it upon his h',
30 the reed, and smote him on the h'.
37 set up over his h' his accusation
M'r 6: 24 she said, The h' of John the Baptist.
25 in a charger the h' of John the
27 commanded his h' to be brought:
28 brought his h' in a charger, and
12: 4 and wounded him in the h', and
10 is become the h' of the corner:
14: 3 the box, and poured it on his h'.
15: 17 thorns, and put it about his h',
19 they smote him on the h' with a
Lu 7: 38 wipe them with the hairs of her h',
44 wiped them with the hairs of her h'.
46 My h' with oil thou didst not
9: 58 hath not where to lay his h'.
12: 7 hairs of your h' are all numbered.
20: 17 is become the h' of the corner?

Lu 21: 18 shall not an hair of your h' perish.
Jo 13: 9 but also my hands and my h'.
19: 2 of thorns, and put it on his h', and
30 and he bowed his h', and gave up
20: 7 the napkin, that was about his h',
12 the one at the h', and the other
Ac 4: 11 is become the h' of the corner.
18: 18 having shorn his h' in Cenchrea:
27: 34 shall not an hair fall from the h' of
Ro 12: 20 shalt heap coals of fire on his h'.
1Co 11: 3 the h' of every man is Christ; and
3 the h' of the woman is the man;
3 and the h' of Christ is God.
4 prophesying, having his h' covered,
4 covered, dishonoureth his h'.
5 prophesieth with her h' uncovered
5 uncovered dishonoureth her h':
7 indeed ought not to cover his h',
10 woman to have power on her h'
12: 21 nor again the h' to the feet, I have
Eph 1: 22 gave him to be h' over all things
4: 15 which is the h', even Christ:
5: 23 the husband is the h' of the wife,
23 as Christ is the h' of the church:
Col 1: 18 he is the h' of the body, the church:
2: 10 the h' of all principality and power:
19 And not holding the H', from
1Pe 2: 7 same is made the h' of the corner,
Re 1: 14 His h' and his hairs were white
10: 1 and a rainbow was upon his h',
12: 1 her h' a crown of twelve stars:
14: 14 having on his h' a golden crown,
19: 12 and on his h' were many crowns;

headbands
Isa 3: 20 and the h', and the tablets, and

headed See BEHEADED; GRAYHEADED.

headlong
Job 5: 13 counsel of the froward is carried h'.
Lu 4: 29 that they might cast him down h'.
Ac 1: 18 of iniquity; and falling h', he burst

heads
Ge 2: 10 parted, and became into four h'.
43: 28 And they bowed down their h', and
Ex 4: 31 then they bowed their h' and
6: 14 the h' of their fathers' houses:
25 the h' of the fathers of the Levites
18: 25 and made them h' over the people,
Le 10: 6 Uncover not your h', neither rend
19: 27 not round the corners of your h',
Nu 1: 16 fathers, h' of thousands in Israel.
7: 2 h' of the house of their fathers,
8: 12 hands upon the h' of the bullocks:
10: 4 are h' of the thousands of Israel,
13: 3 were h' of the children of Israel.
25: 4 Take all the h' of the people,
30: 1 spake unto the h' of the tribes
De 1: 15 and made them h' over you,
5: 23 even all the h' of your tribes, and
33: 5 when the h' of the people and the
21 he came with the h' of the people,
Jos 7: 6 Israel, and put dust upon their h'.
14: 1 the h' of the fathers of the tribes
19: 51 the h' of the fathers of the tribes
21: 1 the h' of the fathers of the Levites
1 the h' of the fathers of the tribes
22: 21 the h' of the thousands of Israel,
30 and h' of the thousands of Israel
23: 2 for their h', and for their judges,
24: 1 for their h', and for their judges,
J'g 7: 25 brought the h' of Oreb and Zeeb to
8: 28 they lifted up their h' no more.
9: 57 did God render upon their h':
1Sa 29: 4 it not be with the h' of these men?
1Ki 8: 1 all the h' of the tribes, the chief of
20: 31 on our loins, and ropes upon our h',
32 and put ropes on their h', and came
2Ki 10: 6 take ye the h' of the men your
7 put their h' in baskets, and sent
8 have brought the h' of the king's
1 Ch 5: 24 h' of the house of their fathers,
7: 2 h' of their father's house, to wit, of
7, 9 h' of the house of their fathers,
11 by the h' of their fathers, mighty
40 h' of their father's house, choice
8: 6 the h' of the fathers of the
10 were his sons, h' of the fathers.
13 h' of the fathers of the inhabitants
28 These were h' of the fathers, by
9: 13 h' of the house of their fathers,
12: 19 Saul to the jeopardy of our h'.
32 the h' of them were two hundred;
29: 20 and bowed down their h', and
2 Ch 3: 16 put them on the h' of the pillars;
5: 2 all the h' of the tribes, the chief of
28: 12 the h' of the children of Ephraim,
29: 30 bowed their h' and worshipped.
Ne 8: 6 bowed their h', and worshipped
Job 2: 12 sprinkled dust upon their h'
Ps 24: 7 Lift up your h', O ye gates; and
9 Lift up your h', O ye gates; even
66: 12 caused men to ride over our h';
74: 13 thou brakest the h' of the dragons
14 Thou brakest the h' of leviathan
109: 25 upon me they shaked their h'.
110: 6 wound the h' over many countries.
Isa 15: 2 on all their h' shall be baldness,
35: 10 and everlasting joy upon their h':
Jer 14: 3 confounded, and covered their h'.
4 ashamed, they covered their h'.
La 2: 10 have cast up dust upon their h';
10 of Jerusalem hang down their h'
Eze 1: 22 upon the h' of the living creature
22 stretched forth over their h' above.
25 firmament that was over their h',
26 firmament that was over their h'

Eze 7: 18 and baldness upon all their h'.
11: 21 their way upon their own h', saith
22: 31 have I recompensed upon their h',
23: 15 in dyed attire upon their h', all of
42 beautiful crowns upon their h'.
24: 23 your tires shall be upon your h',
27: 30 shall cast up dust upon their h',
32: 27 laid their swords under their h',
44: 18 have linen bonnets upon their h',
20 Neither shall they shave their h',
20 they shall only poll their h'.
Da 7: 6 the beast had also four h'; and
Mic 3: 1 Hear, I pray you, O h' of Jacob,
9 ye h' of the house of Jacob,
11 The h' thereof judge for reward,
M't 27: 39 by reviled him, wagging their h',
M'r 15: 29 railed on him, wagging their h',
Lu 21: 28 look up, and lift up your h';
Ac 18: 6 Your blood be upon your own h';
21: 24 that they may shave their h':
Re 4: 4 they had on their h' crowns of gold.
9: 7 on their h' were as it were crowns
17 and the h' of the horses were as the
17 horses were as the h' of lions;
19 like unto serpents, and had h',
12: 3 having seven h' and ten horns, and
3 and seven crowns upon his h'.
13: 1 having seven h' and ten horns,
1 upon his h' the name of blasphemy.
3 And I saw one of his h' as it were
17: 3 having seven h' and ten horns.
7 hath the seven h' and ten horns.
9 The seven h' are seven mountains,
18: 19 they cast dust on their h', and cried,

headstone See also HEAD and STONE.
Zec 4: 7 he shall bring forth the h'

heady
2 Ti 3: 4 Traitors, h', highminded, lovers

heal See also HEALED; HEALETH; HEALING.
Nu 12: 13 H' her now, O God, I beseech
De 32: 39 I make alive; I wound, and I h':
2 Ki 20: 5 I will h' thee: on the third day
8 the sign that the Lord will h' me,
2 Ch 7: 14 their sin, and will h' their land.
Ps 6: 2 O Lord, h' me; for my bones are
41: 4 be merciful unto me: h' my soul;
60: 2 h' the breaches thereof; for it
Ec 3: 3 A time to kill, and a time to h';
Isa 19: 22 he shall smite and h' it: and they
22 of them, and shall h' them.
57: 18 I have seen his ways, and will h'
19 saith the Lord; and I will h' him.
Jer 3: 22 and I will h' your backslidings.
17: 14 H' me, O Lord, and I shall be
30: 17 I will h' thee of thy wounds,
La 2: 13 great like the sea: who can h' thee?
Ho 5: 13 yet could he not h' you, nor cure
6: 1 he hath torn, and he will h' us; he
14: 4 I will h' their backsliding, I will
Zec 11: 16 nor h' that that is broken,
M't 8: 7 unto him, I will come and h' him.
10: 1 and to h' all manner of sickness
8 H' the sick, cleanse the lepers,
12: 10 lawful to h' on the sabbath days?
13: 15 converted, and I should h' them.
M'r 3: 2 he would h' on the sabbath day;
15 to have power to h' sicknesses,
Lu 4: 18 sent me to h' the brokenhearted,
23 proverb, Physician, h' thyself:
5: 17 the Lord was present to h' them.
6: 7 he would h' on the sabbath day;
7: 3 would come and h' his servant.
9: 2 of God, and to h' the sick.
10: 9 h' the sick that are therein, and
14: 3 lawful to h' on the sabbath day?
Jo 4: 47 would come down, and h' his son:
12: 40 be converted, and I should h' them.
Ac 4: 30 stretching forth thine hand to h';
28: 27 be converted, and I should h' them.

healed
Ge 20: 17 and God h' Abimelech, and his
Ex 21: 19 cause him to be thoroughly h'.
Le 13: 18 skin thereof, was a boil, and is h',
37 the scall is h', he is clean:
14: 3 if the plague of leprosy be h' in
48 clean, because the plague is h'.
De 28: 27 itch, whereof thou canst not be h'.
35 a sore botch that cannot be h',
1 Sa 6: 3 then ye shall be h', and it shall be
2 Ki 2: 21 the Lord, I have h' these waters;
22 So the waters were h' unto this
8: 29 king Joram went back to be h' in
9: 15 king Joram was returned to be h'
2Ch 22: 6 he returned to be h' in Jezreel
30: 20 to Hezekiah, and h' the people.
Ps 30: 2 cried unto thee, and thou hast h' me.
107: 20 He sent his word, and h' them,
Isa 6: 10 their heart, and convert, and be h'.
53: 5 and with his stripes we are h'.
Jer 6: 14 They have h' also the hurt of the
8: 11 For they have h' the hurt of the
15: 18 incurable, which refuseth to be h'?
17: 14 Heal me, O Lord, and I shall be h';
51: 8 her pain, if so be she may be h'.
9 We would have h' Babylon,
9 Babylon, but she is not h':
Eze 30: 21 not be bound up to be h',
34: 4 have ye h' that which was sick,
47: 8 the sea, the waters shall be h'.
9 for they shall be h'; and every
11 marishes thereof shall not be h';
Ho 7: 1 When I would have h' Israel, then
11: 3 they knew not that I h' them.
M't 4: 24 had the palsy; and he h' them.
8: 8 only, and my servant shall be h'.

M't 8:13 servant was h' in the selfsame
16 his word, and h' all that were sick:
12:15 followed him, and he h' them all;
22 blind, and dumb: and he h' him,
14:14 toward them, and he h' their sick.
15:30 at Jesus' feet; and he h' them:
19: 2 followed him; and he h' them there.
21:14 him in the temple; add he h' them.
M'r 1:34 he h' many that were sick of
3:10 For he had h' many; insomuch
5:23 hands on her, that she may be h';
29 that she was h' of that plague.
6: 5 upon a few sick folk, and h' them.
13 many that were sick, and h' them.
Lu 4:40 on every one of them, and h' them.
5:15 hear, and to be h' by him of their
6:17 and to be h' of their diseases;
18 unclean spirits: and they were h'.
19 virtue out of him, and h' them all.
7: 7 word, and my servant shall be h'.
8: 2 women, which had been h' of evil
36 possessed of the devils was h'.
43 neither could be h' of any,
47 and how she was h' immediately.
9:11 h' them that had need of healing.
42 and h' the child, and delivered
13:14 Jesus had h' on the sabbath day,
14 in them therefore come and be h',
14: 4 him, and h' him, and let him go;
17:15 when he saw that he was h',
22:51 he touched his ear, and h' him.
Joh 5:13 And he that was h' wist not who
Ac 3:11 man which was h' held Peter and
4:14 beholding the man which was h'
5:16 and they were h' every one.
8: 7 and that were lame, were h'.
14: 9 that he had faith to be h',
28: 8 his hands on him and h' him.
9 in the island, came, and were h':
Heb 12:13 the way; but let it rather be h'.
Jas 5:16 one for another, that ye may be h'.
1Pe 2:24 by whose stripes ye were h'.
Re 13: 3 his deadly wound was h': and all
12 beast, whose deadly wound was h'.

healer
Isa 3: 7 swear, saying, I will not be an h';

healeth
Ex 15:26 for I am the Lord that h' thee.
Ps 103: 3 iniquities; who h' all thy diseases;
147: 3 He h' the broken in heart, and
Isa 30:26 and h' the stroke of their wound.

healing See also HEALINGS.
Jer 14:19 us, and there is no h' for us?
19 and for the time of h', and behold
30:13 up: thou hast no h' medicines.
Na 3:19 There is no h' of thy bruise;
Mal 4: 2 arise with h' in his wings;
M't 4:23 h' all manner of sickness and all
9:35 h' every sickness and every disease
Lu 9: 6 the gospel, and h' every where.
11 healed them that had need of h'.
Ac 4:22 this miracle of h' was shewed.
10:38 and h' all that were oppressed of
1Co 12: 9 gifts of h' by the same Spirit;
30 Have all the gifts of h'? do all
Re 22: 2 were for the h' of the nations.

healings
1Co 12:28 miracles, then gift of h', helps,

health
Ge 43:28 servant our father is in good h',
2Sa 20: 9 Art thou in h', my brother?
Ps 42:11 who is the h' of my countenance,
43: 5 who is the h' of my countenance,
67: 2 thy saving h' among all nations.
Pr 3: 8 It shall be h' to thy navel, and
4:22 find them, and h' to all their flesh.
12:18 but the tongue of the wise is h'.
13:17 but a faithful ambassador is h'.
16:24 the soul, and h' to the bones.
Isa 58: 8 and thine h' shall spring forth
Jer 8:15 and for a time of h', and behold
22 the h' of the daughter of my
30:17 For I will restore h' unto thee,
33: 6 I will bring it h' and cure, and I
Ac 27:34 some meat: for this is for your h':
3Jo 2 thou mayest prosper and be in h',

heap See also HEAPED; HEAPETH; HEAPS.
Ge 31:46 they took stones, and made an h':
46 they did eat there upon the h'.
48 This h' is a witness between me
51 Behold this h', and behold this
52 This h' be witness, and this pillar
52 I will not pass over this h' to thee,
52 thou shalt not pass over this h' and
Ex 15: 8 the floods stood upright as an h',
De 13:16 and it shall be an h' for ever;
32:23 I will h' mischiefs upon them;
Jos 3:13 and they shall stand upon an h'.
16 rose up upon an h' very far from
7:26 over him a great h' of stones
8:28 Ai, and made it an h' for ever, even
29 raise thereon a great h' of stones,
Ru 3: 7 down at the end of the h' of corn:
2Sa 18:17 very great h' of stones upon him:
Job 8:17 roots are wrapped about the h',
16: 4 I could h' up words against you,
27:16 Though he h' up silver as the dust,
36:13 hypocrites in heart h' up wrath:
Ps 33: 7 waters of the sea together as an h':
78:13 made the waters to stand as an h'.
Pr 25:22 shalt h' coals of fire upon his head,
Ec 2:26 gather and to h' up, that he may
Ca 7: 2 thy belly is like an h' of wheat
Isa 17: 1 city, and it shall be a ruinous h'.
Isa 17:11 the harvest shall be a h' in the day
25: 2 thou hast made of a city an h';
Jer 30:18 shall be builded on her own h',
49: 2 it shall be a desolate h', and her
Eze 24:10 H' on wood, kindle the fire,
Mic 1: 6 make Samaria as an h' of the field,
Hab 1:10 for they shall h' dust, and take it.
3:15 through the h' of great waters.
Hag 2:16 came to an h' of twenty measures,
Ro 12:20 shalt h' coals of fire on his head.
2Ti 4: 3 they h' to themselves teachers,

heaped
Zec 9: 3 and h' up silver as the dust, and
Jas 5: 3 Ye have h' treasures together for

heapeth
Ps 39: 6 he h' up riches, and knoweth not
Hab 2: 5 and h' unto him all people:

heaps
Ex 8:14 gathered them together upon h':
J'g 15:16 the jawbone of an ass, h' upon h',
2Ki 10: 8 Lay ye them in two h' at the
19:25 waste fenced cities into ruinous h'.
2Ch 31: 6 their God, and laid them by h'.
7 to lay the foundation of the h',
8 the princes came and saw the h',
9 and the Levites concerning the h'.
Ne 4: 2 stones out of the h' of the rubbish
Job 15:28 which are ready to become h'.
Ps 79: 1 they have laid Jerusalem on h'.
Isa 37:26 defenced cities into ruinous h'.
Jer 9:11 I will make Jerusalem h', and a
26:18 Jerusalem shall become h', and
31:21 up waymarks, make thee high h':
50:26 cast her up as h', and destroy her
51:37 And Babylon shall become h', a
Ho 12:11 their altars are as h' in the furrows
Mic 3:12 Jerusalem shall become h', and

hear See also HEARD; HEAREST; HEARETH; HEARING.
Ge 4:23 H' my voice; ye wives of Lamech,
21: 6 that all that h' will laugh with me.
23: 6 H' us, my lord: thou art a mighty
8 h' me, and intreat for me to Ephron
11 Nay, my lord, h' me: the field give
13 I pray thee, h' me: I will give thee
37: 6 H', I pray you, this dream which
42:21 besought us, and we would not h';
22 the child; and ye would not h'?
49: 2 together, and h', ye sons of Jacob;
Ex 6:12 how then shall Pharaoh h' me,
7:16 hitherto thou wouldest not h'.
15:14 The people shall h', and be afraid:
19: 9 the people may h' when I speak
20:19 Speak thou with us, and we will h':
22:23 unto me, I will surely h' their cry;
27 he crieth unto me, that I will h';
32:18 the noise of them that sing do I h'.
Le 5: 1 sin and h' the voice of swearing,
Nu 9: 8 h' what the Lord will command
12: 6 H' now my words: If there be a
14:13 Then the Egyptians shall h' it,
16: 8 H', I pray you, ye sons of Levi:
20:10 said unto them, H' now, ye rebels;
23:18 Rise up, Balak, and h'; hearken
30: 4 And her father h' her vow, and
De 1:16 H' the causes between your
17 ye shall h' the small as well as the
17 bring it unto me, and I will h' it.
43 and ye would not h', but rebelled
2:25 who shall h' report of thee, and
3:26 your sakes, and would not h' me:
4: 6 which shall h' all these statutes,
10 and I will make them h' my words,
28 which neither see, nor h', nor eat,
33 Did ever people h' the voice of God
36 of heaven he made thee to h' his
5: 1 H', O Israel, the statutes and
25 if we h' the voice of the Lord our
27 and h' all that the Lord our God
27 thee; and we will h' it, and do it.
6: 3 H' therefore, O Israel, and observe
4 H', O Israel: The Lord our God is
9: 1 H', O Israel: Thou art to pass over
12:28 Observe and h' all these words
13:11 all Israel shall h', and fear, and
12 shalt h' say in one of thy cities,
17:13 all the people shall h', and fear,
18:16 Let me not h' again the voice of
19:20 which remain shall h', and fear,
20: 3 H', O Israel, ye approach this day
21:21 and all Israel shall h', and fear.
29: 4 eyes to see, and ears to h', unto this
30:12, 13 that we may h' it, and do it?
17 turn away, so that thou wilt not h',
31:12 that they may h', and that they may
13 may h', and learn to fear the
32: 1 and h', O earth, the words of my
33: 7 said, H', Lord, the voice of Judah,
Jos 3: 9 hither, and h' the words of the Lord
6: 5 ye h' the sound of the trumpet,
7: 9 inhabitants of the land shall h' of
J'g 5: 3 H', O ye kings; give ear, O ye
16 to h' the bleatings of the flocks?
7:11 And thou shalt h' what they say;
14:13 forth thy riddle, that we may h' it.
1Sa 2:23 I h' of your evil dealings by all
24 for it is no good report that I h':
8:18 the Lord will not h' you in that
13: 3 land, saying, Let the Hebrews h'.
15:14 the lowing of the oxen which I h'?
16: 2 can I go? if Saul h' it, he will kill me.
22: 7 H' now, ye Benjamites; will the
12 said, H' now, thou son of Ahitub.
25:24 h' the words of thine handmaid.
26:19 let my lord the king h' the words
2Sa 14:16 For the king will h', to deliver his
15: 3 man deputed of the king to h' thee.
10 as ye h' the sound of the trumpet,
35 thing soever thou shalt h' out of the
36 unto me every thing that ye can h'.
16:21 shall h' that thou art abhorred of
17: 5 let us h' likewise what he saith.
19:35 I h' any more the voice of singing
20:16 H', h'; say, I pray you, unto Joab,
17 H' the words of thine handmaid.
17 And he answered, I do h'.
22: 7 did h' my voice out of his temple,
45 as soon as they h', they shall be
1Ki 4:34 people to h' the wisdom of Solomon,
8:30 and h' thou in heaven thy dwelling
32 Then h' thou in heaven, and do,
34, 36 h' thou in heaven, and forgive
39 Then h' thou in heaven thy
42 For they shall h' of thy great name,
43 H' thou in heaven thy dwelling
45 h' thou in heaven their prayer
49 Then h' thou their prayer and
10: 8 before thee, and that h' thy wisdom.
24 sought to Solomon, to h' his wisdom,
18:26 O Baal, h' us. But there was no
37 H' me, O Lord, h' me, that this
22:19 H' thou therefore the word of
2Ki 7: 1 said, H' ye the word of the Lord;
6 Syrians to h' a noise of chariots,
14:11 But Amaziah would not h'.
17:14 they would not h', but hardened
18:12 would not h' them, nor do them.
28 H' the word of the great king, the
19: 4 thy God will h' all the words of
7 and he shall h' a rumour, and shall
16 Lord, bow down thine ear, and h':
16 and h' the words of Sennacherib,
20:16 Hezekiah, H' the word of the Lord.
1Ch 14:15 thou shalt h' a sound of going
28: 2 H' me, my brethren, and my
2Ch 6:21 h' thou from thy dwelling place,
23 Then h' thou from heaven, and
25 Then h' thou from the heavens,
27 Then h' thou from heaven, and
30 Then h' thou from heaven thy
33 Then h' thou from the heavens,
35 Then h' thou from the heavens
39 Then h' thou from the heavens,
7:14 then will I h' from heaven, and
9: 7 before thee, and h' thy wisdom.
23 Solomon, to h' his wisdom, that
13: 4 H' me, thou Jeroboam, and all
15: 2 H' ye me, Asa, and all Judah and
18:18 Therefore h' the word of the Lord;
20: 9 then thou wilt h' and help.
20 and said, H' me, O Judah, and ye
25:20 But Amaziah would not h'; for it
28:11 Now h' me therefore, and deliver
29: 5 H' me, ye Levites, sanctify now
Ne 1: 6 that thou mayest h' the prayer of
4: 4 H', O our God: for we are despised:
20 ye h' the sound of the trumpet,
8: 2 that could h' with understanding,
9:29 their neck, and would not h'.
Job 3:18 h' not the voice of the oppressor.
5:27 h' it, and know thou it for thy good.
13: 6 H' now my reasoning, and hearken
17 H' diligently my speech, and my
15:17 I will shew thee, h' me; and that
21: 2 H' diligently my speech, and let
22:27 prayer unto him, and he shall h'
27: 9 Will God h' his cry when trouble
30:20 thee, and thou dost not h' me:
31:35 Oh that one would h' me! behold
33: 1 Job, I pray thee, h' my speeches,
34: 2 H' my words, O ye wise men;
16 thou hast understanding, h' this:
35:13 God will not h' vanity, neither will
37: 2 H' attentively the noise of his
42: 4 H', I beseech thee, and I will speak:
Ps 4: 1 H' me when I call, O God of my
1 mercy upon me, and h' my prayer.
3 the Lord will h' when I call unto
5: 3 voice shalt thou h' in the morning,
10:17 thou wilt cause thine ear to h':
13: 3 Consider and h' me, O Lord my
17: 1 H' the right, O Lord, attend unto
6 for thou wilt h' me, O God:
6 ear unto me, and h' my speech.
18:44 As soon as they h' of me, they
20: 1 h' thee in the day of trouble;
6 will h' him from his holy heaven
9 let the king h' us when we call.
27: 7 H', O Lord, when I cry with my
28: 2 H' the voice of my supplications,
30:10 H', O Lord, and have mercy upon
34: 2 the humble shall h' thereof, and be
38:15 thou wilt h', O Lord my God.
16 For I said, H' me, lest otherwise
39:12 H' my prayer, O Lord, and give
49: 1 H' this, all ye people; give ear,
50: 7 H', O my people, and I will speak;
51: 8 Make me to h' joy and gladness;
54: 2 H' my prayer, O God; give ear to
55: 2 Attend unto me, and h' me:
17 aloud: and he shall h' my voice.
19 God shall h', and afflict them, even
59: 7 lips: for who, say they, doth h'?
60: 5 with thy right hand, and h' me.
61: 1 H' my cry, O God; attend unto my
64: 1 H' my voice, O God, in my prayer:
66:16 Come and h', all ye that fear God,
18 in my heart, the Lord will not h' me:
69:13 the multitude of thy mercy h' me,
16 H' me, O Lord; for thy
17 I am in trouble: h' me speedily.

Ps 81: 8 H', O my people, and I will testify.
84: 8 O Lord God of hosts, h' my prayer:
85: 8 h' what God the Lord will speak:
86: 1 down thine ear, O Lord, h' me:
92: 11 shall h' my desire of the wicked
94: 9 planted the ear, shall he not h'?
95: 7 To day if ye will h' his voice,
102: 1 H' my prayer, O Lord, and let my
20 To h' the groaning of the prisoner;
115: 6 They have ears, but they h' not:
119: 145 my whole heart; h' me, O Lord:
149 H' my voice according unto thy
130: 2 Lord, h' my voice: let thine ears
135: 17 They have ears, but they h' not;
138: 4 they h' the words of thy mouth.
140: 6 h' the voice of my supplications,
141: 6 h' my words; for they are sweet.
143: 1 H' my prayer, O Lord, give ear to
7 H' me speedily, O Lord: my
8 Cause me to h' thy lovingkindness
145: 19 he also will h' their cry, and will
Pr 1: 5 wise man will h', and will increase
8 h' the instruction of thy father,
4: 1 H', ye children, the instruction of a
10 H', O my son, and receive my
5: 7 H' me now therefore, O ye
8: 6 H'; for I will speak of excellent
33 H' instruction, and be wise, and
19: 20 H' counsel, and receive instruction,
27 Cease, my son, to h' the instruction
22: 17 ear, and h' the words of the wise,
23: 19 H' thou, my son, and be wise,
Ec 5: 1 be more ready to h', than to give
7: 5 better to h' the rebuke of the wise,
5 for a man to h' the song of fools.
21 lest thou h' thy servant curse thee:
12: 13 us h' the conclusion of the whole
Ca 2: 14 let me h' thy voice; for sweet is thy
8: 13 to thy voice: cause me to h' it.
Isa 1: 2 H', O heavens, and give ear, O
10 H' the word of the Lord, ye rulers
15 make many prayers, I will not h':
6: 9 H' ye indeed, but understand not;
10 h' with their ears, and understand
7: 13 said, H' ye now, O house of David;
18: 3 when he bloweth a trumpet, h' ye.
28: 12 refreshing: yet they would not h'.
14 h' the word of the Lord, ye scornful
23 Give ye ear, and h' my voice;
23 voice; hearken, and h' my speech.
29: 18 And in that day shall the deaf h' the
30: 9 children that will not h' the law of
19 when he shall h' it, he will answer
21 ears shall h' a word behind thee,
32: 3 ears of them that h' shall hearken.
9 h' my voice, ye careless daughters;
33: 13 H', ye that are far off, what I have
34: 1 Come near, ye nations, to h'; and
1 the earth h', and all that is therein;
36: 13 H' ye the words of the great king,
37: 4 the Lord thy God will h' the words
7 and he shall h' a rumour, and
17 Incline thine ear, O Lord, and h';
17 and h' all the words of Sennacherib,
39: 5 H' the word of the Lord of hosts:
41: 17 I the Lord will h' them, I the God
42: 18 H', ye deaf; and look, ye blind,
23 and h' for the time to come?
43: 9 or let them h', and say, It is truth.
44: 1 Yet now h', O Jacob my servant;
47: 8 Therefore h' now this, thou that art
48: 1 H' ye this, O house of Jacob, which
14 All ye, assemble yourselves, and h';
16 Come ye near unto me, h' ye this;
50: 4 mine ear to h' as the learned.
51: 21 Therefore h' now this, thou afflicted,
55: 3 h', and your soul shall live; and I
59: 1 his ear heavy, that it cannot h':
2 face from you, that he will not h'.
65: 12 when I spake, ye did not h'; but
24 while they are yet speaking, I will h'.
66: 4 when I spake, they did not h': but
5 H' the word of the Lord, ye that
Jer 2: 4 H' ye the word of the Lord, O house
4: 21 and h' the sound of the trumpet?
5: 21 H' now this, O foolish people, and
21 which have ears, and h' not:
6: 10 and give warning, that they may h'?
18 Therefore h', ye nations, and know,
19 H', O earth: behold, I will bring
7: 2 H' the word of the Lord, all ye of
16 to me: for I will not h' thee.
9: 10 can men h' the voice of the cattle;
20 h' the word of the Lord, O ye women,
10: 1 H' ye the word which the Lord
11: 2, 6 H' ye the words of this covenant,
10 which refused to h' my words;
14 for I will not h' them in the time
13: 10 people, which refuse to h' my words,
11 for a glory: but they would not h'.
15 H' ye, and give ear; be not proud:
17 But if ye will not h' it, my soul shall
14: 12 they fast, I will not h' their cry;
17: 20 H' ye the word of the Lord, ye kings
23 neck stiff, that they might not h',
18: 2 I will cause thee to h' my words.
19: 3 H' ye the word of the Lord, O kings
15 that they might not h' my words.
20: 16 let him h' the cry in the morning,
21: 11 say, H' ye the word of the Lord;
22: 2 H' the word of the Lord, O king of
5 But if ye will not h' these words,
21 but thou saidst, I will not h'.
29 O earth, earth, earth, h' the word
23: 22 caused my people to h' my words,
25: 4 nor inclined your ear to h'.
Jer 28: 7 h' thou now this word that I speak
15 H' now, Hananiah; the Lord hath
29: 19 but ye would not h', saith the Lord.
20 H' ye therefore the word of the
31: 10 H' the word of the Lord, O ye
33: 9 which shall h' all the good that I do
34: 4 Yet h' the word of the Lord, O
36: 3 Judah will h' all the evil which I
25 the roll: but he would not h' them.
37: 20 h' now, I pray thee, O my lord the
38: 25 if the princes h' that I have talked
42: 14 nor h' the sound of the trumpet,
15 therefore h' the word of the Lord,
44: 24 H' the word of the Lord, all Judah
26 h' ye the word of the Lord, all
49: 20 h' the counsel of the Lord, that the
50: 45 h' ye the counsel of the Lord, that
La 1: 18 h', I pray you, all people, and
Eze 2: 5, 7 whether they will h', or whether
8 h' what I say unto thee; Be not
3: 10 thine heart, and h' with thine ears.
11 whether they will h', or whether
17 therefore h' the word at my mouth,
27 He that heareth, let him h'; and he
6: 3 h' the word of the Lord God: Thus
8: 18 a loud voice, yet will I not h' them.
12: 2 they have ears to h', and h' not:
13: 2 hearts, H' ye the word of the Lord;
19 lying to my people that h' your lies?
16: 35 O harlot, h' the word of the Lord:
18: 25 H' now, O house of Israel; Is not
20: 47 H' the word of the Lord; Thus
24: 26 to cause thee to h' it with thine
25: 3 H' the word of the Lord God;
33: 7 thou shalt h' the word at my mouth,
30 h' what is the word that cometh
31 and they h' thy words, but they will
32 for they h' thy words, but they do
34: 7, 9 ye shepherds, h' the word of the
36: 1 Ye mountains of Israel, h' the word
4 h' the word of the Lord God; Thus
15 Neither will I cause men to h' in
37: 4 O ye dry bones, h' the word of the
40: 4 h' with thine ears, and set thine
44: 5 h' with thine ears all that I say unto
Da 3: 5 time ye h' the sound of the cornet,
10 shall h' the sound of the cornet,
15 time ye h' the sound of the cornet,
5: 23 which see not, nor h', nor know;
9: 17 h' the prayer of thy servant, and
18 O my God, incline thine ear, and h';
19 O Lord, h'; O Lord, forgive; O Lord,
Ho 2: 21 to pass in that day, I will h', saith
21 the Lord, I will h' the heavens,
21 and they shall h' the earth;
22 And the earth shall h' the corn,
22 the oil; and they shall h' Jezreel.
4: 1 H' the word of the Lord, ye
5: 1 H' ye this, O priests; and hearken,
Joe 1: 2 H' this, ye old men, and give ear,
Am 3: 1 H' this word that the Lord hath
13 H' ye, and testify in the house of
4: 1 H' this word, ye kine of Bashan,
5: 1 H' ye this word which I take up
23 I will not h' the melody of thy viols,
7: 16 h' thou the word of the Lord: Thou
8: 4 H' this, O ye that swallow up the
Mic 1: 2 H', all ye people; hearken, O earth,
3: 1 H', I pray you, O heads of Jacob,
4 the Lord, but he will not h' them:
9 H' this, I pray you, ye heads of
6: 1 H' ye now what the Lord saith;
1 and let the hills h' thy voice.
2 H' ye, O mountains, the Lord's
9 h' ye the rod, and who hath
7: 7 my salvation: my God will h' me.
Na 3: 19 all that h' the bruit of thee shall
Hab 1: 2 shall I cry, and thou wilt not h'!
Zec 1: 4 but they did not h', nor hearken
3: 8 H' now, O Joshua the high priest,
7: 7 Should ye not h' the words which
11 their ears, that they should not h'.
12 lest they should h' the law, and the
13 as he cried, and they would not h';
13 so they cried, and I would not h',
8: 9 be strong, ye that h' in these days
10: 6 Lord their God, and will h' them.
13: 9 call on my name, and I will h' them:
Mal 2: 2 If ye will not h', and if ye will not
M't 10: 14 not receive you, nor h' your words,
27 what ye h' in the ear, that preach
11: 4 those things which ye do h' and see:
5 lepers are cleansed, and the deaf h',
15 He that hath ears to h', let him h'.
12: 19 any man h' his voice in the streets.
42 to h' the wisdom of Solomon; and,
13: 9 Who hath ears to h', let him
9 Who hath ears...let him h'.
13 see not; and hearing they h' not,
14 By hearing ye shall h', and shall not
15 their eyes, and h' with their ears,
16 they see: and your ears, for they h'.
17 and to h' those things which ye h',
18 H' ye therefore the parable of the
43 Who hath ears to h', let him
43 Who hath ears...let him h'.
15: 10 said unto them, H', and understand:
17: 5 whom I am well pleased; h' ye him.
18: 15 if he shall h' thee, thou hast gained
16 if he will not h' thee, then take with
17 And if he shall neglect to h' them,
17 but if he neglect to h' the church,
21: 33 H' another parable: There was a
24: 6 ye shall h' of wars and rumours of
M'r 4: 9 He that hath ears to h', let him h'.
12 they may h', and not understand;
M'r 4: 18 among thorns; such as h' the word,
20 such as h' the word, and receive it,
23 any man have ears to h', let him h'.
24 Take heed what ye h': with what
24 you that h' shall more be given.
33 unto them, as they were able to h' it.
6: 11 shall not receive you, nor h' you,
7: 16 any man have ears to h', let him h'.
37 he maketh both the deaf to h', and
8: 18 see ye not? having ears, h' ye not?
9: 7 This is my beloved Son: h' him.
12: 29 H', O Israel; the Lord our God is one
13: 7 ye shall h' of wars and rumours of
Lu 5: 1 upon him to h' the word of God,
15 multitudes came together to h', and
6: 17 came to h' him, and to be healed of
27 I say unto you which h', Love your
7: 22 lepers are cleansed, the deaf h', the
8: 8 He that hath ears to h', let him h'.
12 by the way side are they that h';
13 they h', receive the word with
18 Take heed therefore how ye h': for
21 which h' the word of God, and do it.
9: 9 is this, of whom I h' such things?
35 This is my beloved Son: h' him.
10: 24 to h' those things which ye h', and
11: 28 blessed are they that h' the word of
31 to h' the wisdom of Solomon; and,
14: 35 He that hath ears to h', let him h'.
15: 1 publicans and sinners for to h' him.
16: 2 him, How is it that I h' this of thee?
29 and the prophets; let them h' them.
31 they h' not Moses and the prophets,
18: 6 said, H' what the unjust judge saith.
19: 48 people were very attentive to h' him.
21: 9 ye shall h' of wars and commotions,
38 to him in the temple, for to h' him.
Joh 5: 25 the dead shall h' the voice of God:
25 God: and they that h' shall live.
28 are in the graves shall h' his voice,
30 as I h', I judge: and my judgment is
6: 60 This is an hard saying; who can h' it?
7: 51 law judge any man, before it h' him,
8: 43 even because ye cannot h' my word.
47 ye therefore h' them not, because ye
9: 27 told you already, and ye did not h':
27 wherefore would ye h' it again?
10: 3 and the sheep h' his voice: and he
8 but the sheep did not h' them.
16 and they shall h' my voice; and they
20 a devil, and is mad; why h' ye him?
27 My sheep h' my voice, and I know
12: 47 if any man h' my words, and believe
14: 24 the word which ye h' is not mine,
16: 13 whatsoever he shall h', that shall he
Ac 2: 8 h' we every man in our own tongue,
11 we do h' them speak in our tongues,
22 Ye men of Israel, h' these words;
33 forth this, which ye now see and h'.
3: 22 shall ye h' in all things whatsoever
23 which will not h' that prophet,
7: 37 like unto me; him shall ye h'.
10: 22 his house, and to h' words of thee.
33 to h' all things that are commanded
13: 7 and desired to h' the word of God.
44 city together, to h' the word of God.
15: 7 should h' the word of the gospel,
17: 21 either to tell, or to h' some new thing.
32 We will h' thee again of this matter.
19: 26 see and h', that not alone at Ephesus,
21: 22 for they will h' that thou art come.
22: 1 h' ye my defence which I make
14 shouldest h' the voice of his mouth.
23: 35 I will h' thee, said he, when thine
24: 4 wouldest h' us of thy clemency a
25: 22 I would also h' the man myself.
22 morrow, said he, thou shalt h' him.
26: 3 I beseech thee to h' me patiently.
29 thou, but also all that h' me this day,
28: 22 to h' of thee what thou thinkest:
26 Hearing ye shall h', and shall not
27 their eyes, and h' with their ears,
28 the Gentiles, and that they will h' it.
Ro 10: 14 shall they h' without a preacher?
11: 8 see, and ears that they should not h';
1Co 11: 18 I h' that there be divisions among
14: 21 yet for all that will they not h' me,
Ga 4: 21 under the law, do ye not h' the law?
Ph'p 1: 27 be absent, I may h' of your affairs,
30 saw in me, and now h' to be in me.
2Th 3: 11 h' that there are some which walk
1Ti 4: 16 save thyself, and them that h' thee.
2Ti 4: 17 and that all the Gentiles might h':
Heb 3: 7, 15 To day if ye will h' his voice,
4: 7 said, To day if ye will h' his voice,
Jas 1: 19 let every man be swift to h', slow to
1Jo 5: 15 that he h' us, whatsoever we ask,
3Jo 4 no greater joy than to h' that my
Re 1: 3 that h' the words of this prophecy,
2: 7, 11, 17, 29 that hath an ear, let him h'
3: 6, 13 He that hath an ear, let him h'
20 if any man h' my voice, and open
22 He that hath an ear, let him h'
9: 20 neither can see, nor h', nor walk:
13: 9 If any man have an ear, let him h'.

heard See also HEARDEST.

Ge 3: 8 And they h' the voice of the Lord
10 I h' thy voice in the garden, and I
14: 14 Abraham h' that his brother was
16: 11 the Lord hath h' thy affliction.
17: 20 And as for Ishmael, I have h' thee:
18: 10 Sarah h' it in the tent door, which
21: 17 And God h' the voice of the lad;
17 God hath h' the voice of the lad
26 thou tell me, neither yet h' I of it,
24: 30 when he h' the words of Rebekah

Ge 24:52 Abraham's servant h' their words,
27: 5 Rebekah h' when Isaac spake to
6 I h' thy father speak unto Esau thy
34 And when Esau h' the words of his
29:13 when Laban h' the tidings of Jacob
33 the Lord hath h' that I was hated,
30: 6 and hath also h' my voice, and hath
31: 1 he h' the words of Laban's sons,
34: 5 And Jacob h' that he had defiled
7 came out of the field when they h' it:
35:22 father's concubine: and Israel h' it.
37:17 I h' them say, Let us go to Dothan.
21 And Reuben h' it, and he delivered
39:15 when he h' that I lifted up my voice
19 his master h' the words of his wife,
41:15 have h' say of thee, that thou canst
42: 2 have h' that there is corn in Egypt:
43:25 they h' that they should eat bread
45: 2 and the house of Pharaoh h'.
16 fame thereof was h' in Pharaoh's
Ex 2:15 Now when Pharaoh h' this thing, he
24 And God h' their groaning, and
3: 7 have h' their cry by reason of their
4:31 they h' that the Lord had visited
6: 5 I have also h' the groaning of the
16: 9 for he hath h' your murmurings.
12 I have h' the murmurings of the
18: 1 Midian, Moses' father in law, h' of all
23:13 neither let it be h' out of thy mouth.
28:35 be h' when he goeth into the holy
32:17 Joshua h' the noise of the people
33: 4 the people h' these evil tidings,
Le 10:20 when Moses h' that, he was content.
24:14 let all that h' him lay their hands
Nu 7:89 then he h' the voice of one speaking
11: 1 and the Lord h' it; and his anger
10 Then Moses h' the people weep
12: 2 also by us? And the Lord h' it.
14:14 have h' that thou Lord art seen face
15 the nations which have h' the fame
27 I have h' the murmurings of the
16: 4 Moses h' it, he fell upon his face:
20:16 he h' our voice, and sent an angel,
21: 1 h' tell that Israel came by the way
22:36 Balak h' that Balaam was come,
24: 4 which h' the words of God, which
16 which h' the words of God, and
30: 7 husband h' it, and held his peace
7 at her in the day that he h' it:
8 the day that he h' it; then he shall
11 husband h' it, and held his peace
12 them void on the day he h' them;
14 at her in the day that he h' them.
15 void after that he hath h' them;
33:40 h' of the coming of the children of
De 1:34 the Lord h' the voice of your words,
4:12 ye h' the voice of the words, but saw
12 no similitude; only ye h' a voice.
32 thing is, or hath been h' like it?
33 of the fire, as thou hast h', and live?
5:23 ye h' the voice out of the midst
24 have h' his voice out of the midst
26 hath h' the voice of the living God
28 the Lord h' the voice of your words,
28 I have h' the voice of the words of
9: 2 and of whom thou hast h' say,
17: 4 be told thee, and thou hast h' of it,
26: 7 the Lord h' our voice, and looked
Jos 2:10 we have h' how the Lord dried up
11 as soon as we had h' these things,
5: 1 h' that the Lord had dried up
6:20 people h' the sound of the trumpet,
9: 1 Hivite, and the Jebusite, h' thereof;
3 when the inhabitants of Gibeon h'
9 for we have h' the fame of him,
16 h' that they were their neighbours,
10: 1 had h' how Joshua had taken Ai,
11: 1 when Jabin king of Hazor had h'
22:11 And the children of Israel h' say,
12 when the children of Israel h' of it,
30 h' the words that the children of
24:27 it hath h' all the words of the Lord
J'g 7:15 Gideon h' the telling of the dream,
9:30 ruler of the city h' the words of Gaal
46 the men of the tower of Shechem h'
18:25 Let not thy voice be h' among us,
20: 3 Now the children of Benjamin h'
Ru 1: 6 she had h' in the country of Moab
1Sa 1:13 lips moved, but her voice was not h':
2:22 and h' all that his sons did unto all
4: 6 Philistines h' the noise of the shout,
14 when Eli h' the noise of the crying,
19 h' the tidings that the ark of God
7: 7 when the Philistines h' that the
7 when the children of Israel h' it,
9 for Israel; and the Lord h' him.
8:21 And Samuel h' all the words of the
11: 6 upon Saul when he h' those tidings,
13: 3 in Geba, and the Philistines h' of it.
4 Israel h' say that Saul had smitten
14:22 they h' that the Philistines fled,
27 Jonathan h' not when his father
17:11 Saul and all Israel h' those words
23 the same words: and David h' them.
28 And Eliab his eldest brother h'
31 And when the words were h'
22: 1 all his father's house h' it, they
6 Saul h' that David was discovered,
23:10 hath certainly h' that Saul seeketh
11 come down, as thy servant hath h'?
25 And when Saul h' that, he pursued
25: 4 And David h' in the wilderness
7 I have h' that thou hast shearers:
39 David h' that Nabal was dead,
31:11 inhabitants of Jabesh-gilead h' of
2Sa 3:28 afterward when David h' it, he

2Sa 4: 1 Saul's son h' that Abner was dead
5:17 Philistines h' that they had anointed
17 and David h' of it, and went down
7:22 to all that we have h' with our ears.
8: 9 Toi king of Hamath h' that David
10: 7 when David h' of it, he sent Joab,
11:26 the wife of Uriah h' that Uriah
13:21 But when king David h' of all these
18: 5 the people h' when the king gave
19: 2 people h' say that day how the king
1Ki 1:11 Hast thou not h' that Adonijah
41 h' it as they had made an end of
41 Joab h' the sound of the trumpet,
45 This is the noise that ye have h'.
2:42 The word that I have h' is good.
3:28 And all Israel h' of the judgment
4:34 earth, which had h' of his wisdom.
5: 1 he had h' that they had anointed
7 Hiram h' the words of Solomon,
6: 7 nor any tool of iron h' in the house,
9: 3 I have h' thy prayer and thy
10: 1 the queen of Sheba h' of the fame
6 report that I h' in mine own land
7 exceedeth the fame which I h'.
11:21 when Hadad h' in Egypt that David
12: 2 Jeroboam the son of Nebat,...h' of it
20 when all Israel h' that Jeroboam
13: 4 when king Jeroboam h' the saying
26 him back from the way h' thereof,
14: 6 Ahijah h' the sound of her feet,
15:21 when Baasha h' thereof, that he
16:16 people that were encamped h' say,
17:22 the Lord h' the voice of Elijah;
19:13 when Elijah h' it, that he wrapped
20:12 when Ben-hadad h' this message,
31 we have h' that the kings of the
21:15 Jezebel h' that Naboth was stoned,
16 when Ahab h' that Naboth was dead,
27 to pass, when Ahab h' those words,
2Ki 3:21 Moabites h' that the kings were
5: 8 when Elisha the man of God had h'
6:30 the king h' the words of the woman,
9:30 come to Jezreel, Jezebel h' of it;
11:13 Athaliah h' the noise of the guard
19: 1 to pass, when king Hezekiah h' it,
4 which the Lord thy God hath h':
6 of the words which thou hast h',
8 for he had h' that he was departed
9 And when he h' say of Tirhakah
11 hast h' what the kings of Assyria
20 king of Assyria I have h'.
25 Hast thou not h' long ago how I
20: 5 h' thy prayer, I have seen thy tears,
12 had h' that Hezekiah had been sick.
22:11 king had h' the words of the book
18 the words which thou hast h';
19 I also have h' thee, saith the Lord.
25:23 h' that the king of Babylon had
1Ch 10:11 when all Jabesh-gilead h' all that
14: 8 h' that David was anointed king
8 David h' of it, and went out against
17:20 to all that we have h' with our ears.
18: 9 Tou king of Hamath h' how David
19: 8 when David h' of it, he sent Joab,
2Ch 5:13 make one sound to be h' in praising
7:12 have h' thy prayer, and have chosen
9: 1 the queen of Sheba h' of the fame
5 report which I h' in mine own land
6 thou exceedest the fame that I h'.
10: 2 Jeroboam the son of Nebat,...h' it,
15: 8 And when Asa h' these words, and
16: 5 when Baasha h' it, that he left off
20:29 they had h' that the Lord fought
23:12 Athaliah h' the noise of the people
30:27 and their voice was h', and their
33:13 and h' his supplication, and brought
34:19 king had h' the words of the law,
26 the words which thou hast h';
27 I have even h' thee also, saith the
Ezr 3:13 shout, and the noise was h' afar off.
4: 1 of Judah and Benjamin h' that the
9: 3 And when I h' this thing, I rent my
Ne 1: 4 when I h' these words, that I sat
2:10 Ammonite, h' of it, it grieved them
19 Arabian, h' it, they laughed us to
4: 1 when Sanballat h' that we builded
7 h' that the walls of Jerusalem were
15 our enemies h' that it was known
5: 6 I was very angry when I h' their cry
6: 1 h' that I had builded the wall,
16 when all our enemies h' thereof,
8: 9 when they h' the words of the law.
12:43 joy of Jerusalem was h' even afar off.
13: 3 when they had h' the law, that they
Es 1:18 have h' of the deed of the queen.
2: 8 commandment and...decree was h',
Job 2:11 when Job's three friends h' of all
4:16 there was silence, and I h' a voice,
13: 1 mine ear hath h' and understood it.
15: 8 Hast thou h' the secret of God?
16: 2 I have h' many such things:
19: 7 I cry out of wrong, but I am not h':
20: 3 have h' the check of my reproach,
26:14 how little a portion is h' of him?
28:22 We have h' the fame thereof with
29:11 When the ear h' me, then it blessed
33: 8 and I have h' the voice of thy words,
37: 4 not stay them when his voice is h'.
42: 5 I have h' of thee by the hearing of
Ps 3: 4 and he h' me out of his holy hill.
6: 8 hath h' the voice of my weeping.
9 The Lord hath h' my supplication;
10:17 hast h' the desire of the humble:
18: 6 he h' my voice out of his temple,
19: 3 language, where their voice is not h'.
22:21 thou hast h' me from the horns of

Ps 22:24 when he cried unto him, he h'.
28: 6 h' the voice of my supplications.
31:13 For I have h' the slander of many:
34: 4 I sought the Lord, and he h' me,
6 poor man cried, and the Lord h'
38:13 But I, as a deaf man, h' not;
40: 1 he inclined unto me, and h' my cry
44: 1 We have h' with our ears, O God,
48: 8 As we have h', so have we seen in
61: 5 For thou, O God, hast h' my vows:
62:11 twice have I h' this; that power
66: 8 make the voice of his praise to be h':
19 But verily God hath h' me; he hath
76: 8 didst cause judgment to be h' from
78: 3 Which we have h' and known, and
21 the Lord h' this, and was wroth:
59 When God h' this, he was wroth,
81: 5 h' a language that I understood not.
97: 8 Zion h', and was glad; and the
106:44 their affliction, when he h' their cry:
116: 1 because he hath h' my voice and
118:21 h' me, and...become my salvation.
120: 1 cried unto the Lord, and he h' me.
132: 6 Lo, we h' of it at Ephratah:
Pr 21:13 cry himself, but shall not be h'.
Ec 9:16 despised, and his words are not h'.
17 words of wise men are h' in quiet
Ca 2:12 voice of the turtle is h' in our land;
Isa 6: 8 Also I h' the voice of the Lord,
10:30 cause it to be h' unto Laish,
15: 4 voice shall be h' even unto Jahaz:
16: 6 We have h' of the pride of Moab;
21:10 that which I have h' of the Lord of
24:16 part of the earth have we h' songs,
28:22 for I have h' from the Lord of hosts
30:30 cause his glorious voice to be h',
37: 1 to pass, when king Hezekiah h' it,
4 which the Lord thy God hath h':
6 afraid of the words that thou hast h',
8 he had h' that he was departed
9 And he h' say concerning Tirhakah
9 when he h' it, he sent messengers
11 hast h' what the kings of Assyria
26 Hast thou not h' long ago, how I
38: 5 I have h' thy prayer, I have seen
39: 1 for he had h' that he had been sick,
40:21 have ye not known? have ye not h'?
28 hast thou not h', that the everlasting
42: 2 cause his voice to be h' in the street.
48: 6 Thou hast h', see all this; and will
49: 8 In an acceptable time have I h'
52:15 had not h' shall they consider.
58: 4 to make your voice to be h' on high.
60:18 Violence shall no more be h' in thy
64: 4 men have not h', nor perceived by
65:19 voice of weeping shall be no more h'
66: 8 Who hath h' such a thing? who
19 isles...that have not h' my fame,
Jer 3:21 voice was h' upon the high places,
4:19 thou hast h', O my soul, the sound
31 For I have h' a voice as of a woman
6: 7 violence and spoil is h' in her;
24 We have h' the fame thereof: our
7:13 early and speaking, but ye h' not;
8: 6 I hearkened and h', but they spake
16 The snorting of his horses was h'
9:19 a voice of wailing is h' out of Zion,
18:13 heathen, who hath h' such things;
22 Let a cry be h' from their houses,
20: 1 h' that Jeremiah prophesied these
10 For I h' the defaming of many,
23:18 hath perceived and h' his word?
18 hath marke his word, and h' it?
25 I have h' what the prophets said,
25: 8 Because ye have not h' my words,
36 principal of the flock, shall be h':
26: 7 the prophets and all the people h'
10 When the princes of Judah h' these
11 city, as ye have h' with your ears.
12 all the words that ye have h'.
21 and all the princes, h' his words,
21 but when Urijah h' it, he was afraid,
30: 5 We have h' a voice of trembling,
31:15 voice was h' in Ramah, lamentation,
18 have surely h' Ephraim bemoaning
33:10 Again there shall be h' in this place,
34:10 h' that every one should let his
35:17 unto them, but they have not h';
36:11 had h' out of the book all the words
13 them all the words that he had h',
16 pass, when they had h' all the words,
24 his servants that h' all these words.
37: 5 that besieged Jerusalem h' tidings
38: 1 h' the words that Jeremiah had
7 h' that they had put Jeremiah in
40: 7 h' that the king of Babylon had
11 h' that the king of Babylon had left
41:11 h' of all the evil that Ishmael
42: 4 said unto them, I have h' you;
46:12 The nations have h' of thy shame,
48: 4 little ones have caused a cry to be h'.
5 enemies have h' a cry of destruction.
29 We have h' the pride of Moab,
49: 2 will cause an alarm of war to be h'
14 I have h' a rumour from the Lord,
21 noise thereof was h' in the Red sea.
23 for they have h' evil tidings;
50:43 king of Babylon hath h' the report
46 and the cry is h' among the nations.
51:46 rumour that shall be h' in the land;
51 because we have h' reproach:
La 1:21 They have h' that I sigh: there is
21 mine enemies have h' of my trouble;
3:56 Thou hast h' my voice: hide not
61 Thou hast h' their reproach, O Lord,
Eze 1:24 went, I h' the noise of their wings,

Eze 1:28 and I *h'* a voice of one that spake.
2: 2 that I *h'* him that spake unto me.
3:12 I *h'* behind me a voice of a great
13 I *h'* also the voice of the wings of
10: 5 the cherubims' wings was *h'* even
19: 4 The nations also *h'* of him; he was
9 no more be *h'* upon the mountains
26:13 of thy harps shall be no more *h'*.
27:30 And shall cause their voice to be *h'*
33: 5 He *h'* the sound of the trumpet,
35:12 I have *h'* all thy blasphemies which
13 words against me: I have *h'* them.
43: 6 And I *h'* him speaking unto me out
Da 3: 7 people *h'* the sound of the cornet,
5:14 have even *h'* of thee, that the spirit
16 I have *h'* of thee, that thou canst
6:14 the king, when he *h'* these words,
8:13 Then I *h'* one saint speaking, and
16 And I *h'* a man's voice between the
10: 9 Yet *h'* I the voice of his words:
9 and when I *h'* the voice of his words,
12 thy words were *h'*, and I am come
12: 7 And I *h'* the man clothed in linen,
8 And I *h'*, but I understood not:
Ho 7:12 them, as their congregation hath *h'*.
14: 8 I have *h'* him, and observed him:
Ob 1 We have *h'* a rumour from the
Jon 2: 2 unto the Lord, and he *h'* me;
Mic 5:15 heathen, such as they have not *h'*.
Na 2:13 thy messengers shall no more be *h'*.
Hab 3: 2 O Lord, I have *h'* thy speech, and
16 When I *h'*, my belly trembled; my
Zep 2: 8 I have *h'* the reproach of Moab,
Zec 8:23 for we have *h'* that God is with you
Mal 3:16 and the Lord hearkened, and *h'* it,
M't 2: 3 When Herod the king had *h'* these
9 When they had *h'* the king, they
18 In Rama was there a voice *h'*,
2:22 when he *h'* that Archelaus did reign
4:12 Jesus had *h'* that John was cast into
5:21, 27 Ye have *h'* that it was said by
33 ye have *h'* that it hath been said by
38, 43 Ye have *h'* that it hath been said.
6: 7 shall be *h'* for their much speaking.
8:10 When Jesus *h'* it, he marvelled, and
9:12 But when Jesus *h'* that, he said unto
11: 2 when John had *h'* in the prison the
12:24 when the Pharisees *h'* it, they said,
13:17 which ye hear, and have not *h'* them.
14: 1 Herod the tetrarch *h'* of the fame of
13 When Jesus *h'* of it, he departed
13 people had *h'* thereof, they followed
15:12 offended, after they *h'* this saying?
17: 6 when the disciples *h'* it, they fell on
19:22 when the young man *h'* that saying,
25 When his disciples *h'* it, they were
20:24 when the ten *h'* it, they were moved
30 when they *h'* that Jesus passed by,
21:45 chief priests and Pharisees had *h'*
22: 7 the king *h'* thereof, he was wroth:
22 had *h'* these words, they marvelled,
33 when the multitude *h'* this, they were
34 had *h'* that he had put the Sadducees
26:65 now ye have *h'* his blasphemy.
27:47 they *h'* that, said, This man calleth
M'r 2:17 When Jesus *h'* it, he saith unto them,
3: 8 when they had *h'* what great things
21 when his friends *h'* of it, they went
4:15 when they have *h'*, Satan cometh
16 who, when they have *h'* the word,
5:27 When she had *h'* of Jesus, came
36 As soon as Jesus *h'* the word that
6:14 king Herod *h'* of him; for his name
16 Herod *h'* thereof, he said, It is John,
20 when he *h'* him, he did many things,
20 did many things, and *h'* him gladly.
29 when his disciples *h'* of it, they came
55 that were sick, where they *h'* he was.
7:25 had an unclean spirit, *h'* of him,
10:41 when the ten *h'* it, they began to be
47 when he *h'* that it was Jesus of
11:14 for ever. And his disciples *h'* it.
18 the scribes and chief priests *h'* it,
12:28 having *h'* them reasoning together,
37 the common people *h'* him gladly.
14:11 And when they *h'* it, they were glad,
58 We *h'* him say, I will destroy this
64 Ye have *h'* the blasphemy: what
15:35 *h'* it, said, Behold, he calleth Elias.
16:11 when they had *h'* that he was alive,
Lu 1:13 for thy prayer is *h'*; and thy wife
41 when Elisabeth *h'* the salutation of
58 cousins *h'* how the Lord had shewed
66 *h'* them laid them up in their hearts,
2:18 all they that *h'* it, wondered at those
20 things that they had *h'* and seen,
47 all that *h'* him were astonished at his
4:23 we have *h'* done in Capernaum, do
28 when they *h'* these things, were filled
7: 3 when he *h'* of Jesus, he sent unto
9 Jesus *h'* these things, he marvelled
22 what things ye have seen and *h'*;
29 all the people that *h'* him, and the
8:14 which, when they have *h'*, go forth,
15 having *h'* the word, keep it, and bring
50 when Jesus *h'* it, he answered him,
9: 7 Herod the tetrarch *h'* of all that was
10:24 which ye hear, and have not *h'* them.
39 sat at Jesus' feet, and *h'* his word.
12: 3 in darkness shall be *h'* in the light;
14:15 sat at meat with him *h'* these things,
15:25 house, he *h'* musick and dancing.
16:14 were covetous, *h'* all these things:
18:22 when Jesus *h'* these things, he said
23 he *h'* this, he was very sorrowful:
26 *h'* it said, Who then can be saved?

Lu 19:11 as they *h'* these things, he added
20:16 they *h'* it, they said, God forbid.
22:71 ourselves have *h'* of his own mouth.
23: 6 When Pilate *h'* of Galilee, he asked
8 he had *h'* many things of him;
Joh 1:37 the two disciples *h'* him speak, and
40 One of the two which *h'* John speak,
3:32 hath seen and *h'*, that he testifieth;
4: 1 Pharisees had *h'* that Jesus made
42 for we have *h'* him ourselves, and
47 When he *h'* that Jesus was come out
5:37 Ye have neither *h'* his voice at any
6:45 Every man therefore that hath *h'*,
60 disciples, when they had *h'* this, said,
7:32 The Pharisees *h'* that the people
40 when they *h'* this saying, said, Of a
8: 6 the ground, as though he *h'* them not.
9 they which *h'* it, being convicted by
26 those things which I have *h'* of him.
40 the truth, which I have *h'* of God:
9:32 world began was it not *h'* that any
35 Jesus *h'* that they had cast him out;
40 Pharisees which were with him *h'*
11: 4 Jesus *h'* that, he said, This sickness
6 had *h'* therefore that he was sick,
20 soon as she *h'* that Jesus was coming,
29 As soon as she *h'* that, she arose
41 I thank thee that thou hast *h'* me.
12:12 when they *h'* that Jesus was coming
18 *h'* that he had done this miracle.
29 and *h'* it, said that it thundered:
34 have *h'* out of the law that Christ
14:28 Ye have *h'* how I said unto you, I go
15:15 things that I have *h'* of my Father
18:21 ask them which *h'* me, what I have
19: 8 When Pilate...*h'* that saying, he was
13 Pilate...*h'* that saying, he brought
21: 7 Simon Peter *h'* that it was the Lord,
Ac 1: 4 which, saith he, ye have *h'* of me.
2: 6 every man *h'* them speak in his own
37 when they *h'* this, they were pricked
4: 4 of them which *h'* the word believed;
20 things which we have seen and *h'*.
24 they *h'* that, they lifted up their voice
5: 5 fear came on all them that *h'* these
11 upon as many as *h'* these things.
21 when they *h'* that, they entered into
24 priests *h'* these things, they doubted
33 When they *h'* that, they were cut to
6:11 We have *h'* him speak blasphemous
14 have *h'* him say, that this Jesus
7:12 when Jacob *h'* that there was corn in
34 have *h'* their groaning, and am come
54 they *h'* these things, they were cut
8:14 at Jerusalem *h'* that Samaria had
30 and *h'* him read the prophet Esaias,
9: 4 he fell to the earth, and *h'* a voice
13 I have *h'* by many of this man, how
21 all that *h'* him were amazed, and
38 the disciples had *h'* that Peter was
10:31 said, Cornelius, thy prayer is *h'*,
44 fell on all them which *h'* the word.
46 they *h'* them speak with tongues,
11: 1 in Judæa *h'* that the Gentiles had
7 I *h'* a voice saying unto me, Arise,
18 When they *h'* these things, they held
13:48 the Gentiles *h'* this, they were glad
14: 9 The same *h'* Paul speak: who
14 Barnabas and Paul, *h'* of, they rent
15:24 Forasmuch as we have *h'*, that
16:14 which worshipped God, *h'* us: whose
25 God: and the prisoners *h'* them.
38 when they *h'* that they were Romans.
17: 8 of the city, when they *h'* these things.
32 when they *h'* of the resurrection of
18:26 when Aquila and Priscilla had *h'*,
19: 2 We have not so much as *h'* whether
5 they *h'* this, they were baptized
10 dwelt in Asia *h'* the word of the Lord
28 *h'* these sayings, they were full of
21:12 when we *h'* these things, both we,
20 when they *h'* it, they glorified the
22: 2 they *h'* that he spake in the Hebrew
7 *h'* a voice saying unto me, Saul, Saul,
9 *h'* not the voice of him that spake to
15 men of what thou hast seen and *h'*.
26 When the centurion *h'* that, he went
23:16 Paul's sister's son *h'* of their lying
24:22 when Felix *h'* these things, having
24 sent for Paul, and *h'* him concerning
26:14 I *h'* a voice speaking unto me, and
28:15 brethren *h'* of us, they came to meet
Ro 10:14 in him of whom they have not *h'*?
18 I say, Have they not *h'*? Yes verily,
15:21 that have not *h'* shall understand.
1Co 2: 9 Eye hath not seen, nor ear *h'*,
2Co 6: 2 I have *h'* thee in a time accepted,
12: 4 into paradise, and *h'* unspeakable
Ga 1:13 ye have *h'* of my conversation in
23 *h'* only, That he which persecuted
Eph 1:13 after that ye *h'* the word of truth,
15 after I *h'* of your faith in the Lord
3: 2 If ye have *h'* of the dispensation of
4:21 If so be that ye have *h'* him, and
Ph'p 2:26 that ye had *h'* that he had been sick
4: 9 both learned, and received, and *h'*,
Col 1: 4 Since we *h'* of your faith in Christ
5 whereof ye *h'* before in the word of
6 since the day ye *h'* of it, and knew
9 since the day we *h'* it, do not cease
23 the gospel, which ye have *h'*, and
1Th 2:13 the word of God which ye *h'* of us,
2Ti 1:13 words, which thou hast *h'* of me,
2: 2 the things that thou hast *h'* of me
Heb 2: 1 heed to the things which we have *h'*,
3 confirmed unto us by them that *h'*

Heb 3:16 when they had *h'*, did provoke:
4: 2 mixed with faith in them that *h'* it.
5: 7 and was *h'* in that he feared;
12:19 which voice they that *h'* intreated
Jas 5:11 Ye have *h'* of the patience of Job,
2Pe 1:18 voice which came from heaven we *h'*,
1Jo 1: 1 which we have *h'*, which we have seen
3 we have seen and *h'* declare we
5 message which we have *h'* of him,
2: 7 the word which ye *h'* heard from
18 have *h'* that antichrist shall come,
24 which ye have *h'* from the beginning.
24 which ye have *h'* from the beginning
3:11 that ye *h'* from the beginning,
4: 3 ye have *h'* that it should come;
2Jo 6 as ye have *h'* from the beginning,
Re 1:10 *h'* behind me a great voice, as of a
3: 3 how hast thou received and *h'*, and
4: 1 first voice which I *h'* was as it were
5:11 I *h'* the voice of many angels round
13 and all that are in them, *h'* I saying,
6: 1 I *h'*, as it were, the noise of thunder,
3 I *h'* the second beast say, Come
5 I *h'* the third beast say, Come and
6 I *h'* a voice in the midst of the four
7 I *h'* the voice of the fourth beast say,
7: 4 I *h'* the number of them which were
8:13 I beheld, and *h'* an angel flying
9:13 I *h'* a voice from the four horns of
16 and I *h'* the number of them.
10: 4 I *h'* a voice from heaven saying unto
8 the voice which I *h'* from heaven
11:12 they *h'* a great voice from heaven
12:10 I *h'* a loud voice saying in heaven,
14: 2 I *h'* a voice from heaven, as the voice
2 I *h'* the voice of harpers harping
13 I *h'* a voice from heaven saying unto
16: 1 I *h'* a great voice out of the temple
5 I *h'* the angel of the waters say,
7 I *h'* another out of the altar say,
18: 4 I *h'* another voice from heaven,
22 trumpeters, shall be *h'* no more at all
22 millstone shall be *h'* no more at all
23 the bride shall be *h'* no more at all
19: 1 I *h'* a great voice of much people
6 I *h'*, as it were, the voice of a great
21: 3 I *h'* a great voice out of heaven
22: 8 I John saw these things, and *h'*
8 them. And when I had *h'* and seen,

heardest
De 4:36 thou *h'* his words out of the midst
Jos 14:12 thou *h'* in that day how the Anakims
2Ki 22:19 *h'* what I spake against this place,
2Ch 34:27 thou *h'* his words against this place,
Ne 9: 9 and *h'* their cry by the Red sea;
27, 28 thee, thou *h'* them from heaven;
Ps 31:22 thou *h'* the voice of my supplications
119:26 declared my ways, and thou *h'* me:
Isa 48: 7 the day when thou *h'* them not;
8 Yea, thou *h'* not; yea, thou knewest
Jon 2: 2 hell cried I, and thou *h'* my voice.

hearer See also HEARERS.
Jas 1:23 if any be a *h'* of the word, and not
25 he being not a forgetful *h'*, but

hearers
Ro 2:13 For not the *h'* of the law are just
Eph 4:29 may minister grace unto the *h'*.
2Ti 2:14 but to the subverting of the *h'*.
Jas 1:22 doers of the word, and not *h'* only,

hearest
Ru 2: 8 Boaz unto Ruth, *H'* thou not, my
1Sa 24: 9 Wherefore *h'* thou men's words,
2Sa 5:24 when thou *h'* the sound of a going
1Ki 8:30 and when thou *h'*, forgive.
2Ch 6:21 and when thou *h'*, forgive.
Ps 22: 2 in the daytime, but thou *h'* not;
65: 2 O thou that *h'* prayer, unto thee
M't 21:16 unto him, *H'* thou what these say?
27:13 *H'* thou not how many things they
Joh 3: 8 and thou *h'* the sound thereof, but
11:42 I knew that thou *h'* me always:

heareth
Ex 16: 7 for that he *h'* your murmurings
8 that the Lord *h'* your murmurings
Nu 30: 5 disallow her in the day that he *h'*;
De 29:19 when he *h'* the words of this curse,
1Sa 3: 9 Speak, Lord; for thy servant *h'*.
10 answered, Speak; for thy servant *h'*.
11 of every one that *h'* it shall tingle.
2Sa 17: 9 first, that whosoever *h'* it will say,
2Ki 21:12 that whosoever *h'* of it, both his ears
Job 34:28 and he *h'* the cry of the afflicted.
Ps 34:17 and the Lord *h'* and delivereth
38:14 I was as a man that *h'* not,
69:33 for the Lord *h'* the poor, and
Pr 8:34 Blessed is the man that *h'* me,
13: 1 wise son *h'* his father's instruction:
1 but a scorner *h'* not rebuke.
8 riches: but the poor *h'* not rebuke.
15:29 he *h'* the prayer of the righteous.
31 The ear that *h'* the reproof of life
32 *h'* reproof getteth understanding.
18:13 answereth a matter before he *h'* it,
21:28 man that *h'* speaketh constantly.
25:10 Lest he that *h'* it put thee to shame,
29:24 he *h'* cursing, and bewrayeth it not.
Isa 41:26 there is none that *h'* your words.
42:20 opening the ears, but he *h'* not.
Jer 19: 3 whosoever *h'*, his ears shall tingle.
Eze 3:27 He that *h'*, let him hear: and he
33: 4 Then whosoever *h'* the sound of the
M't 7:24 whosoever *h'* these sayings of mine,
26 every one that *h'* these sayings of
13:19 any one *h'* the word of the kingdom,
20 the same is he that *h'* the word,

M't 13:22 the thorns is he that h' the word;
23 good ground is he that h' the word,
Lu 6:47 cometh to me, and h' my sayings,
49 he that h', and doeth not, is like
10:16 He that h' you h' me; and he that
Joh 3:29 bridegroom, which standeth and h'
5:24 He that h' my word, and believeth
8:47 He that is of God h' God's words:
9:31 we know that God h' not sinners:
31 of God, and doeth his will, him he h'.
18:37 one that is of the truth h' my voice.
2Co 12: 6 seeth me to be, or that he h' of me.
1Jo 4: 5 of the world, and the world h' them.
6 he that knoweth God h' us; he that
6 he that is not of God h' not us.
5:14 thing according to his will, he h' us:
Re 22:17 And let him that h' say, Come.
18 that h' the words of the prophecy of

hearing^
De 31:11 this law before all Israel in their h'.
2Sa 18:12 for in our h' the king charged thee
2Ki 4:31 there was neither voice, nor h'.
Job 33: 8 Surely thou hast spoken in mine h',
42: 5 heard of thee by the h' of the ear:
Pr 20:12 The h' ear, and the seeing eye,
28: 9 turneth away his ear from h' the law,
Ec 1: 8 seeing, nor the ear filled with h'.
Isa 11: 3 reprove after the h' of his ears:
21: 3 I was bowed down at the h' of it;
33:15 stoppeth his ears from h' of blood,
Eze 9: 5 to the others he said in mine h',
10:13 it was cried unto them in my h',
Am 8:11 but of h' the words of the Lord:
M't 13:13 seeing see not; and h' they hear not,
14 By h' ye shall hear, and shall not
15 and their ears are dull of h',
M'r 6: 2 and many h' him were astonished,
Lu 2:46 both h' them, and asking them
8:10 and h' they might not understand.
18:36 h' the multitude pass by, he asked
Ac 5: 5 Ananias h' these words fell down,
8: 6 Philip spake, h' and seeing the
9: 7 h' a voice, but seeing no man.
18: 8 many of the Corinthians h' believed,
25:21 reserved unto the h' of Augustus,
23 and was entered into the place of h',
28:26 H' ye shall hear, and shall not
27 and their ears are dull of h',
Ro 10:17 So then faith cometh by h',
17 and h' by the word of God.
1Co 12:17 body were an eye, where were the h'?
17 whole were h', where...the smelling?
Ga 3: 2, 5 of the law, or by the h' of faith?
Ph'm 5 H' of thy love and faith, which thou
Heb 5:11 to be uttered, seeing ye are dull of h'.
2Pe 2: 8 them, in seeing and h', vexed his

hearken See also HEARKENED; HEARKENETH; HEARKENING.
Ge 4:23 wives of Lamech, h' unto...speech:
21:12 said unto thee, h' unto her voice;
23:15 My lord, h' unto me: the land is
34:17 not h' unto us, to be circumcised;
49: 2 and h' unto Israel your father.
Ex 3:18 And they shall h' to thy voice:
4: 1 they will not believe me, nor h' unto
8 neither h' to the voice of the first
9 two signs, neither h' unto thy voice,
6:30 and how shall Pharaoh h' unto me?
7: 4 But Pharaoh shall not h' unto you,
22 neither did he h' unto them; as
11: 9 Pharaoh shall not h' unto you;
15:26 If thou wilt diligently h' to the voice
18:19 H' now unto my voice, I will give
Le 26:14 But if ye will not h' unto me,
18 ye will not yet for all this h' unto
21 will not h' unto me; I will bring
27 if ye will not for all this h' unto me,
Nu 23:18 h' unto me, thou son of Zippor:
De 1:45 Lord would not h' to your voice,
4: 1 Now therefore h', O Israel, unto the
7:12 if ye h' to these judgments, and
11:13 if ye shall h' diligently unto my
13: 3 Thou shalt not h' unto the words
8 consent unto him, nor h' unto him;
18 shalt h' to the voice of the Lord
15: 5 if thou carefully h' unto the voice
17:12 h' unto the priest that standeth
18:15 like unto me; unto him ye shall h';
19 whosoever will not h' unto my words
21:18 chastened him, will not h' unto
23: 5 thy God would not h' unto Balaam;
26:17 judgments, and to h' unto his voice:
27: 9 Take heed, and h', O Israel; this day
28: 1 shalt h' diligently unto the voice of
2 if thou shalt h' unto the voice of the
13 thou h' unto the commandments
15 if thou wilt not h' unto the voice of
30:10 If thou shalt h' unto the voice of
Jos 1:17 in all things, so will we h' unto thee:
18 will not h' unto thy words in all that
24:10 But I would not h' unto Balaam;
J'g 2:17 would not h' unto their judges,
3: 4 would h' unto the commandments
9: 7 H' unto me, ye men of Shechem,
7 Shechem, that God may h' unto you.
11:17 king of Edom would not h' thereto.
19:25 But the men would not h' to him:
20:13 Benjamin would not h' to the voice
1Sa 8: 7 H' unto the voice of the people in all
9 Now therefore h' unto their voice:
22 H' unto their voice, and make them
15: 1 therefore h' thou unto the voice of
22 better...to h' than the fat of rams.
28:22 h' thou also unto the voice of thine
30:24 For who will h' unto you in this

2Sa 12:18 he would not h' unto our voice:
13:14 he would not h' unto her voice:
16 But he would not h' unto her.
1Ki 8:28 to h' unto the cry and to the prayer,
29 that thou mayest h' unto the prayer,
30 And h' thou to the supplication of
52 to h' unto them in all that they call
11:38 thou wilt h' unto all that I command
20: 8 H' not unto him, nor consent.
22:28 H', O people, every one of you.
2Ki 10: 6 if ye will h' unto my voice, take ye
17:40 Howbeit they did not h', but they
18:31 H' not to Hezekiah: for thus saith
32 and h' not unto Hezekiah, when he
2Ch 6:19 to h' unto the cry and the prayer
20 to h' unto the prayer which thy
21 H' therefore unto the supplications
10:16 the king would not h' unto them,
18:27 And he said, H', all ye people.
20:15 H' ye, all Judah, and ye
33:10 his people: but they would not h'.
Ne 13:27 Shall we then h' unto you to do all
Job 13: 6 and h' to the pleadings of my lips.
32:10 H' to me; I also will shew mine
33: 1 speeches, and h' to all my words.
31 Mark well, O Job, h' unto me:
33 If not, h' unto me: hold thy peace,
34:10 Therefore h' unto me, ye men of
16 this; h' to the voice of my words.
34 and let a wise man h' unto me.
37:14 H' unto this, O Job: stand still,
Ps 5: 2 H' unto the voice of my cry,
34:11 Come, ye children, h' unto me: I
45:10 H', O daughter, and consider, and
58: 5 not h' to the voice of charmers,
81: 8 O Israel, if thou wilt h' unto me;
11 But my people would not h' to my
Pr 7:24 H' unto me now therefore, O ye
8:32 Now therefore h' unto me, O ye
23:22 H' unto thy father that begat thee,
29:12 If a ruler h' to lies, all his servants
Ca 8:13 the companions h' to thy voice:
Isa 28:23 my voice; h', and hear my speech.
32: 3 the ears of them that hear shall h'.
34: 1 h', ye people: let the earth hear,
36:16 H' not to Hezekiah: for thus saith
42:23 who will h' and hear for the time
46: 3 H' unto me, O house of Jacob,
12 H' unto me, ye stouthearted, that
48:12 H' unto me, O Jacob and Israel,
49: 1 and h', ye people, from far; The
51: 1 H' to me, ye that follow after
4 H' unto me, my people; and give
7 H' unto me, ye that know
55: 2 h' diligently unto me, and eat ye
Jer 6:10 uncircumcised, and they cannot h':
17 H' to the sound of the trumpet. But
17 But they said, We will not h'.
7:27 but they will not h' to thee: thou
11:11 cry unto me, I will not h' unto them.
16:12 heart, that they may not h' unto me:
17:24 to pass, if ye diligently h' unto me,
27 h' unto me to hallow the sabbath
18:19 h' to the voice of them that contend
23:16 H' not unto the words of the
26: 3 If so be they will h', and turn every
4 If ye will not h' to me, to walk in
5 To h' to the words of my servants
27: 9 h' not ye to your prophets, nor to
14 h' not unto the words of the
16 H' not to the words of your
17 H' not unto them; serve the king of
29: 8 neither h' to your dreams which ye
12 pray unto me, and I will h' unto you.
35:13 Will ye not receive instruction to h'
37: 2 did h' unto the words of the Lord,
38:15 counsel, wilt thou not h' unto me?
44:16 of the Lord, we will not h' unto thee.
Eze 3: 7 the house of Israel will not h' unto
7 thee; for they will not h' unto me:
20: 8 me, and would not h' unto me: they
39 also, if ye will not h' unto me:
Da 9:19 O Lord, h' and do; defer not,
Ho 5: 1 h', ye house of Israel; and give ye
9:17 because they did not h' unto him:
Mic 1: 2 h', O earth, and all that therein is:
Zec 1: 4 did not hear, nor h' unto me,
7:11 they refused to h', and pulled away
M'r 4: 3 H'; Behold, there went out a sower
7:14 H' unto me every one of you,
Ac 2:14 unto you, and h' to my words:
4:19 right in the sight of God to h' unto
7: 2 Men, brethren, and fathers, h'; The
12:13 damsel came to h', named Rhoda,
15:13 Men and brethren, h' unto me:
Jas 2: 5 H', my beloved brethren, Hath not

hearkened^ See also HEARKENEDST.
Ge 3:17 hast h' unto the voice of thy wife,
16: 2 And Abram h' to the voice of Sarai.
23:16 And Abraham h' unto Ephron; and
30:17 And God h' unto Leah, and she
22 and God h' to her, and opened her
34:24 and unto Shechem his son h' all
39:10 that he h' not unto her, to lie by her.
Ex 6: 9 they h' not unto Moses for anguish
12 Israel have not h' unto me; how
7:13 Pharaoh's heart, that he h' not
8:15 hardened his heart, and h' not
19 heart was hardened, and he h' not
9:12 heart of Pharaoh, and he h' not
16:20 they h' not unto Moses; but some
18:24 So Moses h' to the voice of his father
Nu 14:22 and have not h' to my voice;
21: 3 the Lord h' to the voice of Israel,
De 9:19 Lord h' unto me at that time also.
23 believed him not, nor h' to his voice.

De 10:10 Lord h' unto me at that time also,
18:14 h' unto observers of times, and unto
26:14 I have h' to the voice of the Lord
34: 9 the children of Israel h' unto him,
Jos 1:17 as we h' unto Moses in all things,
10:14 the Lord h' unto the voice of a man:
J'g 2:20 and have not h' unto my voice;
11:28 Ammon h' not unto the words of
13: 9 And God h' to the voice of Manoah;
1Sa 2:25 h' not unto the voice of their father,
12: 1 I have h' unto your voice in all that
19: 6 Saul h' unto the voice of Jonathan:
25:35 I have h' to thy voice, and have
28:21 and have h' unto thy words which
23 him; and he h' unto their voice.
1Ki 12:15 the king h' not unto the people;
16 Israel saw that the king h' not
24 They h' therefore to the word of the
15:20 So Ben-hadad h' unto king Asa,
2Ki 13: 4 and the Lord h' unto him: for he saw
16: 9 And the king of Assyria h' unto him:
20:13 And Hezekiah h' unto them, and
21: 9 But they h' not: and Manasseh
22:13 because our fathers have not h' unto
2Ch 10:15 So the king h' not unto the people:
16: 4 And Ben-hadad h' unto king Asa,
24:17 Then the king h' unto them.
25:16 and hast not h' unto my counsel.
30:20 Lord h' to Hezekiah, and healed
35:22 and h' not unto the words of Necho
Ne 9:16 and h' not to thy commandments,
29 h' not unto thy commandments, but
34 nor h' unto thy commandments
Es 3: 4 unto him, he h' not unto them, that
Job 9:16 that he had h' unto my voice.
Ps 81:13 Oh that my people had h' unto me,
106:25 h' not unto the voice of the Lord.
Isa 21: 7 he h' diligently with much heed:
48:18 hadst h' to my commandments!
Jer 6:19 they have not h' unto my words,
7:24 But they h' not, nor inclined their
26 Yet they h' not unto me, nor inclined
8: 6 I h' and heard, but they spake not
25: 3 and speaking; but ye have not h'.
4 but ye have not h', nor inclined
7 Yet ye have not h' unto me, saith
26: 5 sending them, but ye have not h';
29:19 they have not h' to my words, saith
32:33 have not h' to receive instruction.
34:14 but your fathers h' not unto me,
17 have not h' unto me, in proclaiming
35:14 speaking; but ye h' not unto me.
15 inclined your ear, nor h' unto me.
16 but this people hath not h' unto me:
36:31 against them; but they h' not.
37:14 But he h' not to him: so Irijah took
44: 5 But they h' not, nor inclined their
Eze 3: 6 them, they would have h' unto thee.
Da 9: 6 have we h' unto thy servants the
Mal 3:16 and the Lord h', and heard it, and
Ac 27:21 Sirs, ye should have h' unto me,

hearkenedst
De 28:45 because thou h' not unto the voice

hearkeneth
Pr 1:33 But whoso h' unto me shall dwell
12:15 but he that h' unto counsel is wise.

hearkening
Ps 103:20 h' unto the voice of his word.

heart See also HEARTED; HEART'S; HEARTS.
Ge 6: 5 thoughts of his h' was only evil
6 earth, and it grieved him at his h'.
8:21 Lord said in his h', I will not again
21 the imagination of man's h' is evil
17:17 said in his h', Shall a child be born
20: 5 integrity of my h' and innocency
6 didst this in the integrity of thy h':
24:45 I had done speaking in mine h',
27:41 Esau said in his h', The days of
42:28 their h' failed them, and they were
45:26 Jacob's h' fainted, for he believed
Ex 4:14 seeth thee, he will be glad in his h'.
21 I will harden his h', that he shall
7: 3 harden Pharaoh's h', and multiply
13 hardened Pharaoh's h', that he
14 Pharaoh's h' is hardened, he
22 Pharaoh's h' was hardened, neither
23 neither did he set his h' to this also.
8:15 was respite, he hardened his h',
19 and Pharaoh's h' was hardened,
32 Pharaoh hardened his h' at this
9: 7 the h' of Pharaoh was hardened,
12 Lord hardened the h' of Pharaoh,
14 send all my plagues upon thine h',
34 and hardened his h', he and his
35 the h' of Pharaoh was hardened,
10: 1 for I have hardened his h', and
1 and the h' of his servants, that I
20 hardened Pharaoh's h', so that he
27 Lord hardened Pharaoh's h', and he
11:10 hardened Pharaoh's h', so that he
14: 4 will harden Pharaoh's h', that he
5 h' of Pharaoh and of his servants
8 Lord hardened the h' of Pharaoh
15: 8 were congealed in the h' of the sea.
23: 9 for ye know the h' of a stranger,
25: 2 giveth it willingly with his h' ye
28:29 breastplate of judgment upon his h',
30 and they shall be upon Aaron's h',
30 Israel upon his h' before the Lord
35: 5 whosoever is of a willing h', let him
21 every one whose h' stirred him up,
26 the women whose h' stirred them up
29 whose h' made them willing to bring
34 hath put in his h' that he may teach,
35 hath he filled with wisdom of h',

Ex 36: 2 whose *h'* the Lord had put wisdom,
2 every one whose *h'* stirred him up
Le 19:17 not hate thy brother in thine *h'*:
26:16 the eyes, and cause sorrow of *h'*:
Nu 15:39 that ye seek not after your own *h'*
32: 7 discourage ye the *h'* of the children
9 discouraged the *h'* of the children
De 1:28 brethren have discouraged our *h'*,
2:30 spirit, and made his *h'* obstinate,
4: 9 lest they depart from thy *h'* all the
29 if thou seek him with all thy *h'* and
39 consider it in thine *h'*, that the Lord
5:29 that there were such an *h'* in them,
6: 5 the Lord thy God with all thine *h'*,
6 thee this day, shall be in thine *h'*:
7:17 say in thine *h'*, These nations are
8: 2 to know what was in thine *h'*:
5 Thou shalt also consider in thine *h'*,
14 thine *h'* be lifted up, and thou forget
17 And thou say in thine *h'*, My power
9: 4 Speak not thou in thine *h'*, after
5 or for the uprightness of thine *h'*,
10:12 the Lord thy God with all thy *h'* and
16 the foreskin of your *h'*, and be no
11:13 serve him with all your *h'* and with
16 that your *h'* be not deceived, and ye
18 lay up these my words in your *h'*
13: 3 the Lord your God with all your *h'*
15: 7 thou shalt not harden thine *h'*, nor
9 be not a thought in thy wicked *h'*,
10 thine *h'* shall not be grieved when
17:17 that his *h'* turn not away: neither
20 That his *h'* be not lifted up above
18:21 if thou say in thine *h'*, How shall we
19: 6 the slayer, while his *h'* is hot, and
20: 8 brethren's *h'* faint as well as his *h'*.
24:15 he is poor, ... setteth his *h'* upon it:
26:16 keep and do them with all thine *h'*,
28:28 blindness, and astonishment of *h'*:
47 joyfulness, and with gladness of *h'*,
65 a trembling *h'*, and failing of eyes,
67 for the fear of thine *h'* wherewith
29: 4 not given you an *h'* to perceive,
18 whose *h'* turneth away this day
19 he bless himself in his *h'*, saying, I
19 walk in the imagination of mine *h'*,
30: 2 all thine *h'*, and with all thy soul;
6 thy God will circumcise thine *h'*,
6 and the *h'* of thy seed, to love the
6 Lord thy God with all thine *h'*, and
10 the Lord thy God with all thine *h'*,
14 thy mouth, and in thy *h'*, that thou
17 if thine *h'* turn away, so that thou
Jos 5: 1 their *h'* melted, neither was there
14: 7 word again as it was in mine *h'*.
8 made the *h'* of the people melt:
22: 5 to serve him with all your *h'* and
24:23 incline your *h'* unto the Lord God
J'g 5: 9 My *h'* is toward the governors of
15 there were great thoughts of *h'*.
16 there were great searchings of *h'*.
16:15 thee, when thine *h'* is not with me?
17 That he told her all his *h'*, and said
18 saw that he had told her all his *h'*,
18 for he hath shewed me all his *h'*.
18:20 the priest's *h'* was glad, and he took
19: 5 Comfort thine *h'* with a morsel of
6 all night, and let thine *h'* be merry.
8 said, Comfort thine *h'*, I pray thee.
9 here, that thine *h'* may be merry;
Ru 3: 7 his *h'* was merry, he went to lie
1Sa 1: 8 not? and why is thy *h'* grieved?
13 Now Hannah, she spake in her *h'*;
2: 1 My *h'* rejoiceth in the Lord, mine
33 thine eyes, and to grieve thine *h'*:
35 is in mine *h'* and in my mind:
4:13 his *h'* trembled for the ark of God.
9:19 will tell thee all that is in thine *h'*.
10: 9 Samuel, God gave him another *h'*:
12:20 serve the Lord with all your *h'*;
24 serve him in truth with all your *h'*:
13:14 sought him a man after his own *h'*,
14: 7 Do all that is in thine *h'*: turn thee;
7 I am with thee according to thy *h'*.
16: 7 but the Lord looketh on the *h'*.
17:28 the naughtiness of thine *h'*; for thou
32 Let no man's *h'* fail because of
21:12 David laid up these words in his *h'*,
24: 5 David's *h'* smote him, because he
25:31 nor offence of *h'* unto my lord,
36 and Nabal's *h'* was merry within
37 that his *h'* died within him, and he
27: 1 David said in his *h'*, I shall now
28: 5 afraid, and his *h'* greatly trembled.
2Sa 3:21 over all that thine *h'* desireth.
6:16 and she despised him in her *h'*.
7: 3 king, Go, do all that is in thine *h'*;
21 to thine own *h'*, hast thou done
27 thy servant found in his *h'* to pray
13:28 when Amnon's *h'* is merry with wine,
33 the king take the thing to his *h'*,
14: 1 the king's *h'* was toward Absalom.
17:10 whose *h'* is as the *h'* of a lion,
18:14 them through the *h'* of Absalom,
19:14 the *h'* of all the men of Judah,
14 of Judah, even as the *h'* of one man;
19 the king should take it to his *h'*.
24:10 David's *h'* smote him after that he
1Ki 2: 4 all their *h'* and with all their soul,
44 wickedness which thine *h'* is privy to,
3: 6 and in uprightness of *h'* with thee;
9 an understanding *h'* to judge thy
12 wise and an understanding *h'*;
4:29 largeness of *h'*, even as the sand
8:17 the *h'* of David my father to build
18 it was in thine *h'* to build an house

1Ki 8:18 didst well that it was in thine *h'*.
23 walk before thee with all their *h'*:
38 every man the plague of his own *h'*,
39 to his ways, whose *h'* thou knowest;
48 return unto thee with all their *h'*,
61 Let your *h'* therefore be perfect
66 and glad of *h'* for all the goodness
9: 3 mine eyes and mine *h'* shall be there
4 integrity of *h'*, and in uprightness,
10: 2 with him of all that was in her *h'*.
24 wisdom...God had put in his *h'*.
11: 2 they will turn away your *h'* after
3 and his wives turned away his *h'*.
4 wives turned away his *h'* after
4 and his *h'* was not perfect with
4 was the *h'* of David his father.
9 his *h'* was turned from the Lord
12:26 And Jeroboam said in his *h'*,
27 the *h'* of this people turn again
33 which he had devised of his own *h'*;
14: 8 followed me with all his *h'*, to do
15: 3 his *h'* was not perfect with the Lord
3 God, as the *h'* of David his father.
14 Asa's *h'* was perfect with the Lord
18:37 hast turned their *h'* back again.
21: 7 eat bread, and let thine *h'* be merry:
2Ki 5:26 Went not mine *h'* with thee, when
6:11 the *h'* of the king of Syria was sore
9:24 and the arrow went out at his *h'*,
10:15 *h'* right, as my *h'* is with thy *h'*?
30 according to all that was in mine *h'*,
31 Lord God of Israel with all his *h'*:
12: 4 cometh into any man's *h'* to bring
14:10 and thine *h'* hath lifted thee up:
20: 3 in truth and with a perfect *h'*,
22:19 thine *h'* was tender, and thou hast
23: 3 with all their *h'* and all their soul,
25 turned to the Lord with all his *h'*,
1Ch 12:17 mine *h'* shall be knit unto you:
33 rank: they were not of double *h'*.
38 came with a perfect *h'* to Hebron,
38 were of one *h'* to make David king.
15:29 and she despised him in her *h'*.
16:10 the *h'* of them rejoice that seek the
17: 2 David, Do all that is in thine *h'*;
19 according to thine own *h'*, hast thou
25 found in his *h'* to pray before thee.
22:19 set your *h'* and your soul to seek
28: 2 I had in mine *h'* to build an house
9 serve him with a perfect *h'* and
29: 9 with perfect *h'* they offered willingly
17 triest the *h'*, and hast pleasure in
17 the uprightness of mine *h'* I have
18 the thoughts of the *h'* of thy people,
18 and prepare their *h'* unto thee:
19 give...Solomon my son a perfect *h'*,
2Ch 1:11 Because this was in thine *h'*, and
6: 7 was in the *h'* of David my father
8 as it was in thine *h'* to build an
8 didst well in that it was in thine *h'*:
30 his ways, whose *h'* thou knowest;
38 they return to thee with all their *h'*
7:10 and merry in *h'* for the goodness
11 came into Solomon's *h'* to make in
16 mine eyes and mine *h'* shall be there
9: 1 with him of all that was in her *h'*.
23 wisdom, that God had put in his *h'*.
12:14 prepared not his *h'* to seek the Lord.
15:12 all their *h'* and with all their soul;
15 for they had sworn with all their *h'*,
17 *h'* of Asa was perfect all his days.
16: 9 whose *h'* is perfect toward him.
17: 6 his *h'* was lifted up in the ways
19: 3 hast prepared thine *h'* to seek God.
9 faithfully, and with a perfect *h'*.
22: 9 who sought the Lord with all his *h'*.
25: 2 the Lord, but not with a perfect *h'*.
19 thine *h'* lifteth thee up to boast:
26:16 *h'* was lifted up to his destruction:
29:10 it is in mine *h'* to make a covenant
31 as many as were of a free *h'* burnt
34 Levites were more upright in *h'*
30:12 one *h'* to do the commandment of
19 That prepareth his *h'* to seek God,
31:21 did it with all his *h'*, and prospered
32:25 for his *h'* was lifted up: therefore
26 himself for the pride of his *h'*,
31 might know all that was in his *h'*.
34:27 Because thine *h'* was tender, and
31 and his statutes, with all his *h'*,
36:13 hardened his *h'* from turning unto
Ezr 6:22 turned the *h'* of the king of Assyria
7:10 Ezra had prepared his *h'* to seek
27 a thing as this in the king's *h'*,
Ne 2: 2 nothing else but sorrow of *h'*.
12 had put in my *h'* to do at Jerusalem:
6: 8 feignest them out of thine own *h'*.
7: 5 my God put into mine *h'* to gather
9: 8 foundest his *h'* faithful before thee,
Es 1:10 the *h'* of the king was merry with
5: 9 that day joyful and with a glad *h'*:
6: 6 Haman thought in his *h'*, For whom
7: 5 durst presume in his *h'* to do so?
Job 7:17 shouldest set thine *h'* upon him?
8:10 and utter words out of their *h'*?
9: 4 He is wise in *h'*, and mighty in
10:13 things hast thou hid in thine *h'*:
11:13 thou prepare thine *h'*, and stretch
12:24 the *h'* of the chief of the people
15:12 Why doth thine *h'* carry thee away?
17: 4 hid their *h'* from understanding:
11 off, even the thoughts of my *h'*.
22:22 and lay up his words in thine *h'*.
23:16 God maketh my *h'* soft, and the
27: 6 my *h'* shall not reproach me so
29:13 and I caused the widow's *h'* to sing

Job 31: 7 mine *h'* walked after mine eyes,
9 If mine *h'* have been deceived by a
27 my *h'* hath been secretly enticed,
33: 3 be of the uprightness of my *h'*:
34:14 If he set his *h'* upon man,
36:13 hypocrites in *h'* heap up wrath:
37: 1 At this also my *h'* trembleth, and is
24 not any that are wise of *h'*.
38:36 given understanding to the *h'*?
41:24 His *h'* is as firm as a stone;
Ps 4: 4 commune with your own *h'* upon
7 Thou hast put gladness in my *h'*,
7:10 God, which saveth the upright in *h'*.
9: 1 thee, O Lord, with my whole *h'*;
10: 6 said in his *h'*, I shall not be moved:
11 said in his *h'*, God hath forgotten:
13 said in his *h'*, Thou wilt not require
17 thou wilt prepare their *h'*, thou wilt
11: 2 privily shoot at the upright in *h'*.
12: 2 and with a double *h'* do they speak.
13: 2 soul, having sorrow in my *h'* daily?
5 *h'* shall rejoice in thy salvation.
14: 1 The fool hath said in his *h'*, There
15: 2 and speaketh the truth in his *h'*.
16: 9 Therefore my *h'* is glad, and my
17: 3 Thou hast proved mine *h'*; thou
19: 8 Lord are right, rejoicing the *h'*:
14 mouth, and the meditation of my *h'*.
20: 4 thee according to thine own *h'*,
22:14 my *h'* is like wax; it is melted in
26 him: your *h'* shall live for ever.
24: 4 hath clean hands, and a pure *h'*;
25:17 The troubles of my *h'* are enlarged:
26: 2 prove me; try my reins and my *h'*.
27: 3 against me, my *h'* shall not fear:
8 my *h'* said unto thee, Thy face,
14 and he shall strengthen thine *h'*:
28: 7 *h'* trusted in him, and I am helped:
7 therefore my *h'* greatly rejoiceth;
31:24 he shall strengthen your *h'*, all ye
32:11 joy, all ye that are upright in *h'*.
33:11 of his *h'* to all generations.
21 our *h'* shall rejoice in him, because
34:18 unto them that are of a broken *h'*;
36: 1 saith within my *h'*, that there is no
10 righteousness to the upright in *h'*.
37: 4 give thee the desires of thine *h'*.
15 sword shall enter into their own *h'*,
31 The law of his God is in his *h'*;
38: 8 reason of the disquietness of my *h'*.
10 My *h'* panteth, my strength faileth
39: 3 My *h'* was hot within me, while I
40: 8 God: yea, thy law is within my *h'*.
10 thy righteousness within my *h'*;
12 head: therefore my *h'* faileth me.
41: 6 his *h'* gathereth iniquity to itself;
44:18 Our *h'* is not turned back, neither
21 he knoweth the secrets of the *h'*.
45: 1 My *h'* is inditing a good matter:
5 in the *h'* of the king's enemies;
49: 3 the meditation of my *h'* shall be of
51:10 Create in me a clean *h'*, O God;
17 a broken and a contrite *h'*, O God,
53: 1 The fool hath said in his *h'*, There
55: 4 My *h'* is sore pained within me:
21 than butter, but war was in his *h'*:
57: 7 My *h'* is fixed, O God, my *h'* is fixed:
58: 2 in *h'* ye work wickedness; ye weigh
61: 2 thee, when my *h'* is overwhelmed:
62: 8 pour out your *h'* before him:
10 increase, set not your *h'* upon them.
64: 6 one of them, and the *h'*, is deep.
10 and all the upright in *h'* shall glory.
66:18 I regard iniquity in my *h'*, the Lord
69:20 Reproach hath broken my *h'*; and
32 your *h'* shall live that seek God.
73: 1 even to such as are of a clean *h'*.
7 they have more than *h'* could wish.
13 I have cleansed my *h'* in vain,
21 Thus my *h'* was grieved, and I was
26 My flesh and my *h'* faileth: but God
26 but God is the strength of my *h'*,
77: 6 I commune with mine own *h'*: and
78: 8 that set not their *h'* aright, and
18 they tempted God in their *h'* by
37 their *h'* was not right with him,
72 to the integrity of his *h'*; and
84: 2 my *h'* and my flesh crieth out for
5 in whose *h'* are the ways of them.
86:11 truth: unite my *h'* to fear thy name.
12 O Lord my God, with all my *h'*:
94:15 all the upright in *h'* shall follow it.
95: 8 Harden not your *h'*, as in the
10 It is a people that do err in their *h'*,
97:11 and gladness for the upright in *h'*.
101: 2 within my house with a perfect *h'*.
4 A froward *h'* shall depart from me:
5 hath an high look and a proud *h'*
102: 4 My *h'* is smitten, and withered like
104:15 that maketh glad the *h'* of man,
15 which strengtheneth man's *h'*.
105: 3 let the *h'* of them rejoice that seek
25 turned their *h'* to hate his people,
107:12 brought down their *h'* with labour;
108: 1 O God, my *h'* is fixed; I will sing
109:16 might even slay the broken in *h'*.
22 and my *h'* is wounded within me.
111: 1 praise the Lord with my whole *h'*,
112: 7 his *h'* is fixed, trusting in the Lord.
8 His *h'* is established, he shall not
119: 2 that seek him with the whole *h'*.
7 praise thee with uprightness of *h'*,
10 With my whole *h'* have I sought
11 Thy word have I hid in mine *h'*,
32 when thou shalt enlarge my *h'*.
34 I shall observe it with my whole *h'*.

Ps 119: 36 Incline my h' unto thy testimonies,
58 thy favour with my whole h': but
69 keep thy precepts with my whole h'.
70 Their h' is as fat as grease; but I
80 Let my h' be sound in thy statutes;
111 for they are the rejoicing of my h'.
112 I have inclined mine h' to perform
145 I cried with my whole h'; hear me,
161 my h' standeth in awe of thy word.
131: 1 my h' is not haughty, nor mine eyes
138: 1 will praise thee with my whole h':
139: 23 Search me...and know my h':
140: 2 imagine mischiefs in their h';
141: 4 Incline not my h' to any evil thing,
143: 4 me; my h' within me is desolate.
147: 3 He healeth the broken in h', and
Pr 2: 2 apply thine h' to understanding;
10 wisdom entereth into thine h', and
3: 1 thine h' keep my commandments:
3 them upon the table of thine h':
5 Trust in the Lord with all thine h';
4: 4 Let thine h' retain my words: keep
21 keep them in the midst of thine h'.
23 Keep thy h' with all diligence; for
5: 12 and my h' despised reproof;
6: 14 Frowardness is in his h', he deviseth
18 An h' that deviseth wicked
21 Bind them continually upon thine h',
25 not after her beauty in thine h';
7: 3 them upon the table of thine h'.
10 attire of an harlot, and subtil of h'.
25 Let not thine h' decline to her ways,
8: 5 fools, be ye of an understanding h'.
10: 8 The wise in h' will receive
20 the h' of the wicked is little worth.
11: 20 They that are of a froward h' are
29 shall be servant to the wise of h'.
12: 8 of a perverse h' shall be despised.
20 Deceit is in the h' of them that
23 but the h' of fools proclaimeth
25 Heaviness in the h' of man maketh
13: 12 Hope deferred maketh the h' sick:
14: 10 The h' knoweth his own bitterness;
13 in laughter the h' is sorrowful;
14 The backslider in h' shall be filled
30 A sound h' is the life of the flesh:
33 Wisdom resteth in the h' of him
15: 7 the h' of the foolish doeth not so.
13 A merry h' maketh a cheerful
13 but by sorrow of the h' the spirit
14 h' of him that hath understanding
15 is of a merry h' hath a continual
28 The h' of the righteous studieth to
30 The light of the eyes rejoiceth the h':
16: 1 The preparations of the h' in man,
5 Every one that is proud in h' is an
9 A man's h' deviseth his way; but
21 wise in h' shall be called prudent:
23 h' of the wise teacheth his mouth,
17: 16 wisdom, seeing he hath no h' to it?
20 He that hath a froward h' findeth
22 A merry h' doeth good like a
18: 2 but that his h' may discover itself.
12 the h' of man is haughty, and
15 The h' of the prudent getteth
19: 3 his h' fretteth against the Lord.
21 are many devices in a man's h';
20: 5 Counsel in the h' of man is like
9 I have made my h' clean, I am pure
21: 1 The king's h' is in the hand of the
4 An high look, and a proud h',
22: 11 He that loveth pureness of h',
15 Foolishness is bound in the h' of a
17 apply thine h' unto my knowledge.
23: 7 as he thinketh in his h', so is he:
7 but his h' is not with thee.
12 Apply thine h' unto instruction,
15 thine h' be wise, my h' shall rejoice,
17 Let not thine h' envy sinners:
19 wise, and guide thine h' in the way.
26 My son, give me thine h', and
33 and thine h' shall utter perverse
24: 2 For their h' studieth destruction,
12 he that pondereth the h' consider
17 let not thine h' be glad when he
25: 3 the h' of kings is unsearchable.
20 he that singeth songs to an heavy h'.
26: 23 Burning lips and a wicked h' are
25 are seven abominations in his h'.
27: 9 Ointment...perfume rejoice the h':
11 son, be wise, and make my h' glad,
19 to face, so the h' of man to man.
28: 14 he that hardeneth his h' shall fall
25 He that is of a proud h' stirreth up
26 trusteth in his own h' is a fool:
31: 11 The h' of her husband doth safely
Ec 1: 13 I gave my h' to seek and search out
16 I communed with mine own h',
16 yea, my h' had great experience of
17 And I gave my h' to know wisdom,
2: 1 I said in mine h', Go to now, I will
3 I sought in mine h' to give myself
3 acquainting mine h' with wisdom;
10 I withheld not my h' from any joy;
10 for my h' rejoiced in all my labour:
15 said I in my h', As it happeneth
15 Then I said in my h', that this also
20 to cause my h' to despair of all the
22 labour, and of the vexation of his h',
23 his h' taketh not rest in the night.
3: 11 he hath set the world in their h',
17 I said in mine h', God shall judge
18 in mine h' concerning the estate of
5: 2 and let not thine h' be hasty to utter
20 answereth him in the joy of his h'.
7: 2 and the living will lay it to his h'.

Ec 7: 3 countenance the h' is made better.
4 The h' of the wise is in the house of
4 h' of fools is in the house of mirth.
7 mad; and a gift destroyeth the h'.
22 oftentimes...thine own h' knoweth
25 I applied mine h' to know, and to
26 woman, whose h' is snares and nets,
8: 5 wise man's h' discerneth both time
9 and applied my h' unto every work
11 the h' of the sons of men is fully set
16 I applied mine h' to know wisdom,
9: 1 For all this I considered in my h'
3 the h' of the sons of men is full of
3 and madness is in their h' while
7 drink thy wine with a merry h';
10: 2 wise man's h' is at his right hand;
2 hand; but a fool's h' at his left.
11: 9 let thy h' cheer thee in the days of
9 and walk in the ways of thine h',
10 remove sorrow from thy h', and put
Ca 3: 11 in the day of the gladness of his h'.
4: 9 Thou hast ravished my h', my
9 thou hast ravished my h' with one
5: 2 I sleep, but my h' waketh: it is
8: 6 Set me as a seal upon thine h',
Isa 1: 5 head is sick, and the whole h' faint.
6: 10 Make the h' of this people fat,
10 and understand with their h', and
7: 2 And his h' was moved, and the h' of
9: 9 say in the pride and stoutness of h',
10: 7 neither doth his h' think so;
7 but it is in his h' to destroy and
12 the stout h' of the king of Assyria,
13: 7 faint, and every man's h' shall melt:
14: 13 hast said in thine h', I will ascend
15: 5 My h' shall cry out for Moab;
19: 1 and the h' of Egypt shall melt in
21: 4 h' panted, fearfulness affrighted
29: 13 have removed their h' far from me,
30: 29 gladness of h', as when one goeth
32: 4 The h' also of the rash shall
6 and his h' shall work iniquity, to
33: 18 Thine h' shall meditate terror.
35: 4 Say to them that are of a fearful h',
38: 3 in truth and with a perfect h',
42: 25 burned him, yet he laid it not to h'.
44: 19 none considereth in his h', neither
20 deceived h' hath turned him aside,
47: 7 didst not lay these things to thy h',
8 that sayest in thine h', I am, and
10 thou hast said in thine h', I am
49: 21 Then shalt thou say in thine h',
51: 7 the people in whose h' is my law;
57: 1 and no man layeth it to h':
11 remembered...nor laid it to thy h'?
15 revive the h' of the contrite ones.
17 on frowardly in the way of his h'.
59: 13 from the h' words of falsehood.
60: 5 and thine h' shall fear, and be
63: 4 the day of vengeance is in mine h',
17 and hardened our h' from thy fear?
65: 14 my servants shall sing for joy of h',
14 but ye shall cry for sorrow of h',
66: 14 ye see this, your h' shall rejoice,
Jer 3: 10 turned unto me with her whole h',
15 you pastors according to mine h',
17 the imagination of their evil h'.
4: 4 take away the foreskins of your h',
9 that the h' of the king shall perish,
9 perish, and the h' of the princes;
14 wash thine h' from wickedness,
18 because it reacheth unto thine h'.
19 I am pained at my very h';
19 my h' maketh a noise in me;
5: 23 hath a revolting and a rebellious h';
24 Neither say they in their h', Let
7: 24 in the imagination of their evil h',
31 not, neither came it into my h'.
8: 18 against sorrow, my h' is faint in me.
9: 8 but in h' he layeth his wait.
14 the imagination of their own h',
26 Israel are uncircumcised in the h'.
11: 8 in the imagination of their evil h':
20 that triest the reins and the h',
12: 3 and tried mine h' toward thee:
11 because no man layeth it to h'.
13: 10 walk in the imagination of their h',
22 if thou say in thine h', Wherefore
14: 14 nought, and the deceit of their h'.
15: 16 me the joy and rejoicing of mine h':
16: 12 after the imagination of his evil h',
17: 1 graven upon the table of their h',
5 whose h' departeth from the Lord.
9 The h' is deceitful above all things,
10 I the Lord search the h', I try the
18: 12 do the imagination of his evil h'.
20: 9 word was in mine h' as a burning
12 seest the reins and the h', let me see
22: 17 thine eyes and thine h' are not but
23: 9 Mine h' within me is broken
16 they speak a vision of their own h',
17 after the imagination of his own h',
20 performed the thoughts of his h':
26 the h' of the prophets that prophesy
26 of the deceit of their own h';
24: 7 I will give them an h' to know me,
7 return unto me with their whole h'.
29: 13 shall search for me with all your h'.
30: 21 engaged his h' to approach unto
24 performed the intents of his h':
31: 21 set thine h' toward the highway.
32: 39 will give them one h', and one way,
41 with my whole h' and with my whole
48: 29 pride, and the haughtiness of his h'.
31 mine h' shall mourn for the men
36 mine h' shall sound for Moab like

Jer 48: 36 and mine h' shall sound like pipes
41 as the h' of a woman in her pangs.
49: 16 the pride of thine h', O thou that
22 the h' of the mighty men of Edom
22 as the h' of a woman in her pangs.
51: 46 And lest your h' faint, and ye fear
La 1: 20 mine h' is turned within me; for I
22 my sighs are many, and my h' is
2: 18 Their h' cried unto the Lord, O wall
19 pour out thine h' like water before
3: 41 Let us lift up our h' with our hands
51 eye affecteth mine h' because of
65 Give them sorrow of h', thy curse
5: 15 The joy of our h' is ceased; our
17 For this our h' is faint; for these
Eze 3: 10 receive in thine h', and hear with
6: 9 am broken with their whorish h',
11: 19 I will give them one h', and I will
19 I will take the stony h' out of their
19 and will give them an h' of flesh:
21 whose h' walketh after the h' of their
13: 17 which prophesy out of their own h';
22 have made the h' of the righteous
14: 3 have set up their idols in their h',
4 that setteth up his idols in his h',
5 the house of Israel in their own h',
7 and setteth up his idols in his h',
16: 30 weak is thine h', saith the Lord
18: 31 and make you a new h' and a new
20: 16 for their h' went after their idols.
21: 7 every h' shall melt, and all hands
15 that their h' may faint, and their
22: 14 Can thine h' endure, or can thine
25: 6 rejoiced in h' with all thy despite
15 vengeance with a despiteful h',
27: 31 weep for thee with bitterness of h'
28: 2 thine h' is lifted up, and thou hast
2 thou set thine h' as the h' of God:
5 thine h' is lifted up because of thy
6 set thine h' as the...of God;
6 set thine h' [3824] as the h' of God;
17 Thine h' was lifted up because of
31: 10 his h' is lifted up in his height;
33: 31 h' goeth after their covetousness.
36: 5 with the joy of all their h',
26 A new h' also will I give you, and
26 I will take away the stony h' out of
26 and I will give you an h' of flesh.
40: 4 set thine h' upon all that I shall
44: 7 strangers, uncircumcised in h', and
9 No stranger, uncircumcised in h',
Da 1: 8 Daniel purposed in his h' that he
2: 30 know the thoughts of thy h'.
4: 16 Let his h' be changed from man's,
16 let a beast's h' be given unto him;
5: 20 But when his h' was lifted up,
21 and his h' was made like the beasts,
22 hast not humbled thine h', though
6: 14 set his h' on Daniel to deliver him:
7: 4 and a man's h' was given to it.
28 but I kept the matter in my h'.
8: 25 he shall magnify himself in his h',
10: 12 didst set thine h' to understand,
11: 12 multitude, his h' shall be lifted up;
28 and his h' shall be against the holy
Ho 4: 8 they set their h' on their iniquity.
11 and new wine take away the h'.
7: 6 made ready their h' like an oven,
11 is like a silly dove without h':
14 have not cried unto me with their h',
10: 2 Their h' is divided; now shall they
11: 8 mine h' is turned within me, my
13: 6 were filled, and their h' was exalted;
8 and will rend the caul of their h',
Joe 2: 12 turn ye even to me with all your h',
13 And rend your h', and not your
Ob 3 The pride of thine h' hath deceived
3 that saith in his h', Who shall
Na 2: 10 and the h' melteth, and the knees
Zep 1: 12 that say in their h', The Lord will
2: 15 that said in her h', I am, and there
3: 14 be glad and rejoice with all the h',
Zec 7: 10 evil against his brother in your h'.
10: 7 h' shall rejoice as through wine:
7 their h' shall rejoice in the Lord.
12: 5 of Judah shall say in their h',
Mal 2: 2 if ye will not lay it to h', to give glory
2 because ye do not lay it to h'.
4: 6 he shall turn the h' of the fathers to
6 and the h' of the children to their
M't 5: 8 Blessed are the pure in h': for they
28 adultery with her already in his h'.
6: 21 treasure is, there will your h' be
11: 29 for I am meek and lowly in h':
12: 34 the abundance of the h' the mouth
35 out of the good treasure of the h'
40 three nights in the h' of the earth.
13: 15 this people's h' is waxed gross, and
15 should understand with their h',
19 away that which was sown in his h'.
15: 8 lips; but their h' is far from me.
18 the mouth come forth from the h';
19 out of the h' proceed evil thoughts,
22: 37 the Lord thy God with all thy h',
24: 48 that evil servant shall say in his h',
M'r 6: 52 loaves: for their h' was hardened.
7: 6 lips, but their h' is far from me.
19 Because it entereth not into his h',
21 out of the h' of men, proceed evil
8: 17 have ye your h' yet hardened?
10: 5 the hardness of your h' he wrote
11: 23 and shall not doubt in his h', but
12: 30 the Lord thy God with all thy h',
33 And to love him with all the h',
16: 14 their unbelief and hardness of h',
Lu 2: 19 and pondered them in her h'.

Lu 2:51 kept all these sayings in her h'.
6:45 out of the good treasure of his h'
45 out of the evil treasure of his h'
45 abundance of the h' his mouth
8:15 which in an honest and good h',
9:47 perceiving the thought of their h',
10:27 the Lord thy God with all thy h',
12:34 treasure is, there will your h' be
45 But and if that servant say in his h',
24:25 and slow of h' to believe all that the
32 Did not our h' burn within us, while
Joh 12:40 their eyes, and hardened their h';
40 eyes, nor understand with their h',
13:2 having now put into the h' of Judas
14:1 Let not your h' be troubled: ye
27 Let not your h' be troubled, neither
16:6 unto you, sorrow hath filled your h'.
22 and your h' shall rejoice, and your
Ac 2:26 Therefore did my h' rejoice, and my
37 they were pricked in their h', and
46 with gladness and singleness of h',
4:32 were of one h', and of one soul:
5:3 why hath Satan filled thine h' to lie
4 conceived this thing in thine h'?
33 heard that, they were cut to the h',
7:23 into his h' to visit his brethren
51 and uncircumcised in h' and ears,
54 they were cut to the h', and they
8:21 thy h' is not right in the sight of
22 the thought of thine h' may be
37 If thou believest with all thine h',
11:23 with purpose of h' they would cleave
13:22 Jesse, a man after mine own h',
16:14 whose h' the Lord opened, that she
21:13 ye to weep and to break mine h'?
28:27 For the h' of this people is waxed
27 understand with their h', and should
Ro 1:21 and their foolish h' was darkened.
2:5 after thy hardness and impenitent h'
29 and circumcision is that of the h',
6:17 have obeyed from the h' that form
9:2 and continual sorrow in my h'.
10:6 Say not in thine h', Who shall ascend
8 even in thy mouth, and in thy h':
9 shalt believe in thine h' that God
10 For with the h' man believeth unto
1Co 2:9 have entered into the h' of man,
7:37 he that standeth stedfast in his h',
37 and hath so decreed in his h' that
14:25 the secrets of his h' made manifest;
2Co 2:4 and anguish of h' I wrote unto you
3:3 stone, but in fleshy tables of the h'.
15 is read, the vail is upon their h'.
5:12 glory in appearance, and not in h'.
6:11 open unto you, our h' is enlarged.
8:16 care into the h' of Titus for you.
9:7 as he purposeth in his h', so let him
Eph 4:18 because of the blindness of their h':
5:19 making melody in your h' to the
6:5 in singleness of your h', as unto
6 doing the will of God from the h';
Ph'p 1:7 all, because I have you in my h';
Col 3:22 but in singleness of h', fearing God:
1Th 2:17 short time in presence, not in h',
1Ti 1:5 is charity out of a pure h', and of a
2Ti 2:22 call on the Lord out of a pure h'.
Heb 3:10 They do alway err in their h';
12 be in any of you an evil h' of
4:12 of thoughts and intents of the h'.
10:22 Let us draw near with a true h' in
13:9 thing that the h' be established
Jas 1:26 his tongue, but deceiveth his own h',
1Pe 1:22 ye love one another with a pure h'
3:4 let it be the hidden man of the h',
2Pe 2:14 an h' they have exercised with
1Jo 3:20 For if our h' condemn us, God is
20 God is greater than our h', and
21 if our h' condemn us not, then have
Re 18:7 for she saith in her h', I sit a queen,

hearted See also BROKENHEARTED; FAINTHEARTED; HARDHEARTED; MERRYHEARTED; STIFFHEARTED; STOUTHEARTED; TENDERHEARTED.
Ex 28:3 speak unto all that are wise h',
31:6 in the hearts of all that are wise h'
35:10 And every wise h' among you shall
22 as many as were willing h', and
25 And all the women that were wise h'
36:1 and every wise h' man, in whom
2 and every wise h' man, in whose
8 And every wise h' man among them

hearth
Ge 18:6 knead it and make cakes upon the h'.
Ps 102:3 my bones are burned as an h'.
Isa 30:14 a sherd to take fire from the h', or
Jer 36:22 fire on the h' burning before him.
23 it into the fire that was on the h',
23 in the fire that was on the h'.
Zec 12:6 like an h' of fire among the wood,

heartily
Col 3:23 whatsoever ye do, do it h', as to

heart's
Ps 10:3 wicked boasteth of his h' desire,
21:2 Thou hast given him his h' desire,
Ro 10:1 my h' desire and prayer to God

hearts
Ge 18:5 of bread, and comfort ye your h';
Ex 14:17 will harden the h' of the Egyptians,
31:6 the h' of all that are wise hearted
Le 26:36 will send a faintness into their h'
41 uncircumcised h' be humbled,
De 20:3 let not your h' faint, fear not, and
32:46 Set your h' unto all the words
Jos 2:11 our h' did melt, neither did there
7:5 the h' of the people melted, and
11:20 was of the Lord to harden their h',
Jos 23:14 ye know in all your h' and in all
J'g 9:3 h' inclined to follow Abimelech;
16:25 to pass, when their h' were merry,
19:22 they were making their h' merry,
1Sa 6:6 then do ye harden your h', as the
6 and Pharaoh hardened their h?
7:3 unto the Lord with all your h',
3 and prepare your h' unto the Lord,
10:26 men, whose h' God had touched.
2Sa 15:6 Absalom stole the h' of the men of
13 The h' of the men of Israel are
1Ki 8:39 thou only, knowest the h' of all
58 he may incline our h' unto him,
1Ch 28:9 for the Lord searcheth all h', and
2Ch 6:14 walk before thee with all their h':
30 for thou only knowest the h' of the
11:16 such as set their h' to seek the Lord
20:33 the people had not prepared their h'
Job 1:5 sinned, and cursed God in their h'.
Ps 7:9 the righteous God trieth the h' and
28:3 but mischief is in their h'.
33:15 He fashioneth their h' alike; he
35:25 Let them not say in their h', Ah, so
74:8 said in their h', Let us destroy
90:12 may apply our h' unto wisdom.
125:4 them that are upright in their h'.
Pr 15:11 then the h' of the children of men?
17:3 for gold: but the Lord trieth the h'.
21:2 eyes: but the Lord pondereth the h'.
31:6 unto those that be of heavy h'.
Isa 44:18 see; and their h', that they cannot
Jer 31:33 and write it in their h'; and will
32:40 but I will put my fear in their h',
42:20 ye dissembled in your h', when ye
48:41 the mighty men's h' in Moab at
Eze 13:2 that prophesy out of their own h',
32:9 will also vex the h' of many people,
Da 11:27 both these kings' h' shall be to do
Ho 7:2 they consider not in their h' that I
Zec 7:12 they made their h' as an adamant
8:17 none of you imagine evil in your h'
M't 9:4 Wherefore think ye evil in your h'?
18:35 from your h' forgive not every one
19:8 because of the hardness of your h'
M'r 2:6 there, and reasoning in their h',
8 reason ye these things in your h'?
3:5 grieved for the hardness of their h',
4:15 word that was sown in their h'.
Lu 1:17 to turn the h' of the fathers to the
51 in the imagination of their h'.
66 laid them up in their h', saying,
2:35 the thoughts of many h' may be
3:15 all men mused in their h' of John,
5:22 them, What reason ye in your h'?
8:12 away the word out of their h',
16:15 but God knoweth your h': for that
21:14 Settle it therefore in your h', not to
26 Men's h' failing them for fear, and
34 any time your h' be overcharged
24:38 why do thoughts arise in your h'?
Ac 1:24 which knowest the h' of all men,
7:39 in their h' turned back again into
14:17 filling our h' with food and gladness,
15:8 And God, which knoweth the h',
9 them, purifying their h' by faith.
Ro 1:24 through the lusts of their own h',
2:15 work of the law written in their h',
5:5 love of God is shed abroad in our h'
8:27 he that searcheth the h' knoweth
16:18 deceive the h' of the simple.
1Co 4:5 manifest the counsels of the h':
2Co 1:22 the earnest of the Spirit in our h'.
3:2 written in our h', known and read
4:6 hath shined in our h', to give the
7:3 that ye are in our h' to die and live
Ga 4:6 the Spirit of his Son into your h',
Eph 3:17 That Christ may dwell in your h' by
6:22 and that he might comfort your h'.
Ph'p 4:7 shall keep your h' and minds
Col 2:2 That their h' might be comforted,
3:15 let the peace of God rule in your h',
16 singing with grace in your h' to the
4:8 your estate, and comfort your h';
1Th 2:4 men, but God, which trieth our h'.
3:13 he may stablish your h' unblamable
2Th 2:17 Comfort your h', and stablish you
3:5 And the Lord direct your h' into the
Heb 3:8 Harden not your h', as in the
15 voice, harden not your h', as in the
4:7 hear his voice, harden not your h'.
8:10 mind, and write them in their h':
10:16 I will put my laws into their h',
22 having our h' sprinkled from an evil
Jas 3:14 envying and strife in your h',
4:8 purify your h', ye double minded.
5:5 ye have nourished your h', as in a
8 ye also patient; stablish your h':
1Pe 3:15 sanctify the Lord God in your h':
2Pe 1:19 and the day star arise in your h':
1Jo 3:19 and shall assure our h' before him.
Re 2:23 which searcheth the reins and h':
17:17 God hath put in their h' to fulfil

hearts'
Ps 81:12 them up unto their own h' lust:

hearty
Pr 27:9 of a man's friend by h' counsel.

he-asses See ASSES.

heat See also HEATED.
Ge 8:22 and cold and h', and summer and
18:1 in the tent door in the h' of the day;
De 29:24 meaneth the h' of this great anger?
32:24 devoured with burning h', and
1Sa 11:11 Ammonites until the h' of the day:
2Sa 4:5 came about the h' of the day to her
1Ki 1:1 him with clothes, but he gat no h'.
2 that my lord the king may get h'.
Job 24:19 Drought and h' consume the snow
30:30 and my bones are burned with h'.
Ps 19:6 nothing hid from the h' thereof.
Ec 4:11 lie together, then they have h':
Isa 4:6 shadow in the daytime from the h',
18:4 like a clear h' upon herbs, and like
4 a cloud of dew in the h' of harvest.
25:4 the storm, a shadow from the h',
5 strangers, as the h' in a dry place;
5 the h' with the shadow of a cloud:
49:10 neither shall the h' nor sun smite
Jer 17:8 and shall not see when h' cometh,
36:30 be cast out in the day to the h',
51:39 their h' I will make their feasts,
Eze 3:14 bitterness, in the h' of my spirit;
Da 3:19 that they should h' the furnace
M't 20:12 borne the burden and h' of the
Lu 12:55 ye say, There will be h'; and it
Ac 28:3 there came a viper out of the h',
Jas 1:11 no sooner risen with a burning h',
2Pe 3:10 elements shall melt with fervent h',
12 elements shall melt with fervent h'?
Re 7:16 the sun light on them, nor any h'.
16:9 men were scorched with great h',

heated
Da 3:19 more than it was wont to be h'.
Ho 7:4 as an oven h' by the baker,

heath
Jer 17:6 shall be like the h' in the desert,
48:6 be like the h' in the wilderness.

heathen
Le 25:44 the h' that are round about you;
26:33 I will scatter you among the h',
38 And ye shall perish among the h',
45 land of Egypt in the sight of the h',
De 4:27 left few in number among the h',
2Sa 22:44 hast kept me to be head of the h':
50 unto thee, O Lord, among the h',
2Ki 16:3 to the abominations of the h',
17:8 walked in the statutes of the h',
11 did the h' whom the Lord carried
15 went after the h' that were round
21:2 after the abominations of the h',
1Ch 16:24 Declare his glory among the h';
35 deliver us from the h', that we may
2Ch 20:6 over all the kingdoms of the h'?
28:3 after the abominations of the h'
33:2 unto the abominations of the h',
9 to do worse than the h', whom the
36:14 all the abominations of the h';
Ezr 6:21 the filthiness of the h' of the land,
Ne 5:8 Jews, which were sold unto the h';
9 because of the reproach of the h'
17 came unto us from among the h'
6:6 It is reported among the h', and
16 all the h' that were about us saw
Ps 2:1 Why do the h' rage, and the people
8 I shall give thee the h' for thine
9:5 Thou hast rebuked the h', thou
15 The h' are sunk down in the pit
19 let the h' be judged in thy sight.
10:16 the h' are perished out of his land.
18:43 hast made me the head of the h':
49 unto thee, O Lord, among the h',
33:10 the counsel of the h' to nought:
44:2 thou didst drive out the h' with
11 hast scattered us among the h'.
14 us a byword among the h', a
46:6 The h' raged, the kingdoms were
10 I will be exalted among the h',
47:8 God reigneth over the h': God
59:5 of Israel, awake to visit all the h':
8 shalt have all the h' in derision.
78:55 cast out the h' also before them,
79:1 h' are come into thine inheritance;
6 Pour out thy wrath upon the h' that
10 Wherefore should the h' say, Where
10 let him be known among the h' in
80:8 hast cast out the h', and planted
94:10 He that chastiseth the h', shall not
96:3 Declare his glory among the h',
10 Say among the h' that the Lord
98:2 shewed in the sight of the h'.
102:15 So the h' shall fear the name of
105:44 And gave them the lands of the h':
106:35 But were mingled among the h',
41 gave them into the hand of the h';
47 and gather us from among the h',
110:6 He shall judge among the h', he
111:6 give them the heritage of the h'.
115:2 Wherefore should the h' say,
126:2 then said they among the h', The
135:15 The idols of the h' are silver and
149:7 To execute vengeance upon the h',
Isa 16:8 lords of the h' have broken down
Jer 9:16 scatter them also among the h',
10:2 Learn not the way of the h', and
2 for the h' are dismayed at them.
25 Pour out thy fury upon the h' that
18:13 Ask ye now among the h', who
49:14 an ambassador is sent unto the h',
15 make thee small among the h',
La 1:3 she dwelleth among the h', she
10 she hath seen that the h' entered
4:15 they said among the h', They shall
20 shadow we shall live among the h'.
Eze 7:24 I will bring the worst of the h',
11:12 after the manners of the h' that
16 cast them far off among the h', and
12:16 their abominations among the h'
16:14 renown went forth among the h'
20:9 be polluted before the h', among
14 be polluted before the h', in

Eze 20:22 be polluted in the sight of the h'.
23 would scatter them among the h',
32 say, We will be as the h', as the
41 be sanctified in you before the h'.
22: 4 made thee a reproach unto the h',
15 will scatter thee among the h',
16 in thyself in the sight of the h',
23: 30 hast gone a whoring after the h',
25: 7 deliver thee for a spoil to the h';
8 of Judah is like unto all the h';
28: 25 sanctified...in the sight of the h',
30: 3 it shall be the time of the h'.
31: 11 hand of the mighty one of the h';
17 shadow in the midst of the h'.
34: 28 shall no more be a prey to the h',
29 neither bear the shame of the h'
36: 3 unto the residue of the h', and ye
4 to the residue of the h' that are
5 against the residue of the h', and
6 ye have born the shame of the h':
7 Surely the h' that are about you,
15 the shame of the h' any more,
19 I scattered them among the h',
20 And when they entered unto the h',
21 Israel had profaned among the h',
22 ye have profaned among the h',
23 which was profaned among the h',
23 h' shall know that I am the Lord,
24 will take you from among the h',
30 reproach of famine among the h'.
36 Then the h' that are left round
37: 21 Israel from among the h', whither
28 h' shall know that I the Lord do
38: 16 that the h' may know me, when
39: 7 h' shall know that I am the Lord,
21 I will set my glory among the h'
21 all the h' shall see my judgment
23 the h' shall know that the house
28 led into captivity among the h':
Joe 2: 17 that the h' should rule over them:
19 you a reproach among the h':
3: 11 and come, all ye h', and gather
12 Let the h' be wakened, and come
12 to judge all the h' round about.
Am 9: 12 of all the h', which are called by
Ob 1 ambassador is sent among the h',
2 made thee small among the h':
15 the Lord is near upon all the h':
16 shall all the h' drink continually,
Mic 5: 15 in anger and fury upon the h',
Hab 1: 5 Behold ye among the h', and
3: 12 thou didst thresh the h' in anger.
Zep 2: 11 even all the isles of the h'.
Hag 2: 22 of the kingdoms of the h'; and I
Zec 1: 15 sore displeased with the h' that
8: 13 as ye were a curse among the h',
9: 10 he shall speak peace unto the h':
14: 14 the wealth of all the h' round
18 smite the h' that come not up
Mal 1: 11 name shall be great among the h',
14 name is dreadful among the h'.
M't 6: 7 not vain repetitions, as the h' do:
18: 17 let him be unto thee as an h' man
Ac 4: 25 Why did the h' rage, and the
2Co 11: 26 in perils by the h', in perils in the
Ga 1: 16 I might preach him among the h';
2: 9 that we should go unto the h', and
3: 8 that God would justify the h'

heave See also HEAVED.
Ex 29: 27 the shoulder of the h' offering,
28 for it is an h' offering: and it shall
28 be an h' offering from the children
28 their h' offering unto the Lord.
Le 7: 14 an h' offering unto the Lord, and it
32 an h' offering of the sacrifices of
34 and the h' shoulder have I taken of
10: 14 the wave breast and h' shoulder
15 The h' shoulder and the wave
Nu 6: 20 the wave breast and h' shoulder:
15: 19 shall offer up an h' offering unto the
20 of your dough for an h' offering:
20 h' offering of the threshingfloor,
20 threshingfloor, so shall ye h' it.
21 the Lord an h' offering in your
18: 8 the charge of mine h' offerings of
11 the h' offering of their gift, with all
19 the h' offerings of the holy things,
24 which they offer as an h' offering
26 ye shall offer up an h' offering of
27 your h' offering shall be reckoned
28 offer an h' offering unto the Lord
28 the Lord's h' offering to Aaron the
29 offer every h' offering of the Lord,
31: 29 for an h' offering of the Lord.
41 which was the Lord's h' offering,
De 12: 6 h' offerings of your hand, and your
11 and the h' offering of your hand,
17 or h' offering of thine hand:

heaved
Ex 29: 27 is waved, and which is h' up, of
Nu 18: 30 When ye have h' the best thereof
32 when ye have h' from it the best of

heaven See also HEAVEN'S; HEAVENS.
Ge 1: 1 the beginning God created the h'
8 And God called the firmament H'.
9 waters under the h' be gathered
14, 15 lights in the firmament of the h'
17 set them in the firmament of the h'
20 earth in the open firmament of h'.
6: 17 the breath of life, from under h';
7: 11 and the windows of h' were opened.
19 hills, that were under the whole h',
23 things, and the fowl of the h'; and
8: 2 the windows of h' were stopped, and
2 the rain from h' was restrained;
Ge 11: 4 whose top may reach unto h'; and
14: 19 high God, possessor of h' and earth:
22 God, the possessor of h' and earth,
15: 5 Look now toward h', and tell the
19: 24 and fire from the Lord out of h';
21: 17 of God called to Hagar out of h',
22: 11 the Lord called unto him out of h',
15 Lord called unto Abraham out of h'
17 thy seed as the stars of the h',
24: 3 the Lord, the God of h', and the God
7 The Lord God of h', which took me
26: 4 seed to multiply as the stars of h',
27: 28 God give thee of the dew of h', and
39 and of the dew of h' from above;
28: 12 and the top of it reached to h': and
17 of God, and this is the gate of h'.
49: 25 bless thee with blessings of h' above,
Ex 9: 8 sprinkle it toward the h' in the sight
10 Moses sprinkled it up toward h';
22 Stretch forth thine hand toward h',
23 stretched forth his rod toward h':
10: 21 Stretch out thine hand toward h',
22 stretched forth his hand toward h':
16: 4 I will rain bread from h' for you;
17: 14 of Amalek from under h'.
20: 4 likeness of any thing that is in h'
11 days the Lord made h' and earth,
22 that I have talked with you from h'.
24: 10 were the body of h' in his clearness.
31: 17 days the Lord made h' and earth,
32: 13 multiply your seed as the stars of h',
Le 26: 19 and I will make your h' as iron, and
De 1: 10 as the stars of h' for multitude.
28 cities are great and walled up to h';
2: 25 nations that are under the whole h',
3: 24 what God is there in h' or in earth,
4: 11 with fire unto the midst of h', with
19 lest thou lift up thine eyes unto h',
19 and the stars, even all the host of h',
19 unto all nations under the whole h'.
26 I call h' and earth to witness against
32 the one side of h' unto the other,
36 Out of h' he made thee to hear his
39 he is God in h' above, and upon the
5: 8 likeness of any thing that is in h'
7: 24 destroy their name from under h':
9: 1 cities great and fenced up to h',
14 blot out their name from under h':
10: 14 the h' and the h' of heavens is the
22 thee as the stars of h' for multitude.
11: 11 and drinketh water of the rain of h':
17 and he shut up the h', that there be
21 as the days of h' upon the earth.
17: 3 or moon, or any of the host of h',
25: 19 of Amalek from under h'; thou
26: 15 from thy holy habitation, from h',
28: 12 the h' to give the rain unto thy land
23 thy h' that is over thy head shall be
24 h' shall it come down upon thee,
62 as the stars of h' for multitude;
29: 20 blot out his name from under h'.
30: 4 out unto the uttermost parts of h',
12 It is not in h', that thou shouldest
12 say, Who shall go up for us to h',
19 I call h' and earth to record this day
31: 28 call h' and earth to record against
32: 40 For I lift up my hand to h', and say,
33: 13 precious things of h', for the dew,
26 who rideth upon the h' in thy help,
Jos 2: 11 he is God in h' above, and in earth
8: 20 smoke of the city ascended up to h',
10: 11 Lord cast down great stones from h'
13 the sun stood still in the midst of h',
J'g 5: 20 They fought from h'; the stars in
13: 20 the flame went up toward h' from
20: 40 flame of the city ascended up to h'.
1Sa 2: 10 of h' shall he thunder upon them:
5: 12 the cry of the city went up to h'.
2Sa 18: 9 taken up between the h' and the
21: 10 water dropped upon them out of h',
22: 8 foundations of h' moved and shook,
14 The Lord thundered from h', and
1Ki 8: 22 spread forth his hands toward h':
23 is no God like thee, in h' above, or
27 h' and h' of heavens cannot contain
30 hear thou in h' thy dwelling place:
32 hear thou in h', and do, and judge
34 Then hear thou in h', and forgive
35 When h' is shut up, and there is no
36 Then hear thou in h', and forgive
39, 43 hear thou in h' thy dwelling place,
45 hear thou in h' their prayer and
49 in h' thy dwelling place, and
54 with his hands spread up to h'.
18: 45 that the h' was black with clouds
22: 19 all the host of h' standing by him
2Ki 1: 10 then let fire come down from h',
10 And there came down fire from h',
12 of God, let fire come down from h',
12 the fire of God came down from h',
14 came fire down from h', and burnt
2: 1 Lord would take up Elijah into h'
11 went up by a whirlwind into h'.
7: 2 Lord would make windows in h',
19 Lord should make windows in h',
14: 27 the name of Israel from under h':
17: 16 and worshipped all the host of h',
19: 15 thou hast made h' and earth.
21: 3 all the host of h', and served them.
5 he built altars for all the host of h'
23: 4 the grove, and for all the host of h':
5 planets, and to all the host of h'.
1Ch 21: 16 stand between the earth and the h',
26 he answered him from h' by fire
29: 11 all that is in the h' and in the earth
2Ch 2: 6 h' and h' of heavens cannot contain
2Ch 2: 12 of Israel, that made h' and earth,
6: 13 spread forth his hands toward h',
14 no God like thee in the h', nor in the
18 h' and the h' of heavens cannot
21 thy dwelling place, even from h';
23 Then hear thou from h', and do, and
26 the h' is shut up, and there is no
27 hear thou from h', and forgive the
30 hear thou from h' thy dwelling
7: 1 the fire came down from h', and
13 If I shut up h' that there be no rain,
14 then will I hear from h', and will
18: 18 the host of h' standing on his right
20: 6 our fathers, art not thou God in h'?
28: 9 in a rage that reacheth up unto h'.
30: 27 holy dwelling place, even unto h'.
32: 20 son of Amoz, prayed and cried to h'.
33: 3 and worshipped all the host of h',
5 he built altars for all the host of h'
36: 23 hath the Lord God of h' given me;
Ezr 1: 2 The Lord God of h' hath given me
5: 11 We are the servants of the God of h'
12 fathers had provoked the God of h'
6: 9 the burnt offerings of the God of h',
10 sweet savours unto the God of h',
7: 12, 21 scribe of the law of the God of h',
23 is commanded by the God of h', let
23 done for the house of the God of h':
Ne 1: 4 and prayed before the God of h',
5 O Lord God of h', the great and
9 unto the uttermost part of the h',
2: 4 So I prayed to the God of h'.
20 The God of h', he will prosper us;
9: 6 thou hast made h', the h' of heavens,
6 and the host of h' worshippeth thee.
13 and spakest with them from h',
15 gavest them bread from h' for their
23 multipliedst thou as the stars of h',
27, 28 thou heardest them from h'; and
Job 1: 16 The fire of God is fallen from h',
2: 12 dust upon their heads toward h'.
11: 8 It is as high as h'; what canst thou
16: 19 behold, my witness is in h', and my
20: 27 The h' shall reveal his iniquity;
22: 12 Is not God in the height of h'?
14 and he walketh in the circuit of h'.
26: 11 The pillars of h' tremble and are
28: 24 earth, and seeth under the whole h';
35: 11 maketh us wiser than the fowls of h'?
37: 3 He directeth it under the whole h',
38: 29 and the hoary frost of h', who hath
33 Knowest thou the ordinances of h'?
37 or who can stay the bottles of h',
41: 11 is under the whole h' is mine.
Ps 11: 4 temple, the Lord's throne is in h':
14: 2 The Lord looked down from h' upon
19: 6 forth is from the end of the h', and
20: 6 he will hear him from his holy h'
33: 13 Lord looketh from h'; he beholdeth
53: 2 God looked down from h' upon the
57: 3 He shall send from h', and save me
69: 34 Let the h' and earth praise him,
73: 25 Whom have I in h' but thee? and
76: 8 judgment to be heard from h';
77: 18 of thy thunder was in the h'; the
78: 23 above, and opened the doors of h',
24 had given them of the corn of h'.
26 an east wind to blow in the h':
79: 2 be meat unto the fowls of the h',
80: 14 look down from h', and behold, and
85: 11 righteousness shall look...from h'.
89: 6 who in the h' can be compared
29 and his throne as the days of h'.
37 and as a faithful witness in h'.
102: 19 from h' did the Lord behold the
103: 11 as the h' is high above the earth,
104: 12 shall the fowls of the h' have their
105: 40 them with the bread of h'.
107: 26 They mount up to the h', they go
113: 6 the things that are in h', and in the
115: 15 the Lord which made h' and earth.
16 The h', even the heavens, are the
119: 89 O Lord, thy word is settled in h'.
121: 2 the Lord, which made h' and earth.
124: 8 the Lord, who made h' and earth.
134: 3 The Lord that made h' and earth
135: 6 the Lord pleased, that did he in h',
136: 26 O give thanks unto the God of h':
139: 8 If I ascend up into h', thou art there:
146: 6 Which made h', and earth, the sea,
147: 8 Who covereth the h' with clouds,
148: 13 his glory is above the earth and h'.
Pr 23: 5 they fly away as an eagle toward h'.
25: 3 The h' for height, and the earth for
30: 4 Who hath ascended up into h', or
Ec 1: 13 all things that are done under h':
2: 3 should do under the h' all the days
3: 1 time to every purpose under the h';
5: 2 God is in h', and thou upon earth:
Isa 13: 5 a far country, from the end of h',
10 the stars of h' and the constellations
14: 12 How art thou fallen from h', O
13 I will ascend into h', I will exalt
34: 4 all the host of h' shall be dissolved,
5 for my sword shall be bathed in h':
37: 16 earth: thou hast made h' and earth.
40: 12 and meted out h' with the span,
55: 10 cometh down, and the snow from h',
63: 15 Look down from h', and behold
66: 1 The h' is my throne, and the earth
Jer 7: 18 to make cakes to the queen of h',
33 shall be meat for the fowls of the h'.
8: 2 the moon, and all the host of h',
7 Yea, the stork in the h' knoweth her
10: 2 be not dismayed at the signs of h';
15: 3 the fowls of the h', and the beasts

Jer 16: 4 shall be meat for the fowls of h'.
19: 7 to be meat for the fowls of the h',
13 incense unto all the host of h', and
23: 24 Do not I fill h' and earth? saith
31: 37 If h' above can be measured, and
32: 17 thou hast made the h' and the earth
33: 22 the host of h' cannot be numbered,
25 the ordinances of h' and earth;
34: 20 be for meat unto the fowls of the h',
44: 17 burn incense unto the queen of h',
18 to burn incense to the queen of h',
19 burned incense to the queen of h',
25 to burn incense to the queen of h',
49: 36 winds from the four quarters of h',
51: 9 for her judgment reacheth unto h',
15 hath stretched out the h' by his
48 the h' and the earth, and all that is
53 Babylon should mount up to h',
La 2: 1 cast down from h' unto the earth
3: 50 Lord look down, and behold from h'.
4: 19 swifter than the eagles of the h':
Eze 8: 3 up between the earth and the h',
29: 5 of the field and to the fowls of the h'.
31: 6 All the fowls of h' made their nests
13 shall all the fowls of the h' remain,
32: 4 all the fowls of the h' to remain
7 I will cover the h', and make the
8 All the bright lights of h' will I
38: 20 the fowls of the h', and the beasts
Da 2: 18 desire mercies of the God of h'
19 Then Daniel blessed the God of h'.
28 there is a God in h' that revealeth
37 for the God of h' hath given thee a
38 the fowls of the h' hath he given
44 shall the God of h' set up a kingdom,
4: 11 height thereof reached unto h', and
12 and the fowls of the h' dwelt in the
13 and an holy one came down from h';
15 let it be wet with the dew of h', and
20 whose height reached unto the h',
21 branches the fowls of the h' had
22 is grown, and reacheth unto h', and
23 an holy one coming down from h',
23 and let it be wet with the dew of h',
25 shall wet thee with the dew of h',
31 there fell a voice from h', saying,
33 his body was wet with the dew of h',
34 lifted up mine eyes unto h', and
35 to his will in the army of h', and
37 and extol and honour the King of h',
5: 21 his body was wet with the dew of h';
23 up thyself against the Lord of h';
6: 27 he worketh signs and wonders in h'
7: 2 the four winds of the h' strove
13 of man came with the clouds of h',
27 of the kingdom under the whole h',
8: 8 ones toward the four winds of h'.
10 waxed great, even to the host of h';
9: 12 under the whole h' hath not been
11: 4 divided toward the four winds of h';
12: 7 right hand and his left hand unto h',
Ho 2: 18 and with the fowls of h', and with
4: 3 the field, and with the fowls of h';
7: 12 them down as the fowls of the h';
Am 9: 2 though they climb up to h', thence
6 that buildeth his stories in the h',
Jon 1: 9 the Lord, the God of h', which hath
Na 3: 16 thy merchants above the stars of h':
Zep 1: 3 I will consume the fowls of the h',
5 them that worship the host of h'
Hag 1: 10 the h' over you is stayed from dew,
Zec 2: 6 abroad as the four winds of the h',
5: 9 ephah between the earth and the h'.
Mal 3: 10 will not open you the windows of h',
M't 3: 2 for the kingdom of h' is at hand.
17 And lo a voice from h', saying,
4: 17 for the kingdom of h' is at hand.
5: 3, 10 for theirs is the kingdom of h'.
12 for great is your reward in h': for so
16 glorify your Father which is in h'.
18 Till h' and earth pass, one jot or one
19 called the least in the kingdom of h':
19 be called great in the kingdom of h'.
20 case enter into the kingdom of h'.
34 Swear not at all; neither by h'; for
5: 45 of your Father which is in h':
48 your Father which is in h' is perfect.
6: 1 reward of your Father which is in h'.
9 pray ye: Our Father which art in h',
10 will be done in earth, as it is in h'.
20 up for yourselves treasures in h',
7: 11 your Father which is in h' give good
21 shall enter into the kingdom of h';
21 the will of my Father which is in h'.
8: 11 and Jacob, in the kingdom of h'.
10: 7 saying, The kingdom of h' is at hand.
32 also before my Father which is in h'.
33 deny before my Father which is in h'
11: 11 he that is least in the kingdom of h'
12 the kingdom of h' suffereth violence,
23 which art exalted unto h', shalt be
25 O Father, Lord of h' and earth,
12: 50 will of my Father which is in h', the
13: 11 the mysteries of the kingdom of h',
24 kingdom of h' is likened unto a man
31 The kingdom of h' is like to a grain
33 kingdom of h' is like unto leaven,
44, 45 Again, the kingdom of h' is like
47 the kingdom of h' is like unto a net,
52 instructed unto the kingdom of h' is
14: 19 and looking up to h', he blessed, and
16: 1 he would shew them a sign from h'.
17 thee, but my Father which is in h'.
19 thee the keys of the kingdom of h':
19 bind on earth shall be bound in h':
19 loose on earth shall be loosed in h'.

M't 18: 1 the greatest in the kingdom of h'?
3 not enter into the kingdom of h'.
4 is greatest in the kingdom of h'.
10 in h' their angels do always behold
10 the face of my Father which is in h'.
14 of your Father which is in h', that
18 bind on earth shall be bound in h':
18 loose on earth shall be loosed in h'.
19 them of my Father which is in h'.
23 the kingdom of h' is likened unto a
19: 14 me: for of such is the kingdom of h'.
21 and thou shalt have treasure in h':
23 hardly enter into the kingdom of h'.
20: 1 the kingdom of h' is like unto a man
21: 25 whence was it? from h', or of men?
25 If we shall say, From h'; he will say
22: 2 The kingdom of h' is like unto a
30 but are as the angels of God in h'.
23: 9 one is your Father, which is in h'.
13 shut up the kingdom of h' against
22 that shall swear by h', sweareth by
24: 29 the stars shall fall from h', and the
30 the sign of the Son of man in h':
30 Son of man coming in the clouds of h'
31 from one end of h' to the other.
35 H' and earth shall pass away, but
36 not the angels of h', but my Father
25: 1 the kingdom of h' be likened unto
14 For the kingdom of h' is as a man
26: 64 and coming in the clouds of h'.
28: 2 of the Lord descended from h', and
18 is given unto me in h' and in earth.
M'r 1: 11 there came a voice from h', saying,
6: 41 he looked up to h', and blessed, and
7: 34 And looking up to h', he sighed, and
8: 11 him, seeking of him a sign from h',
10: 21 and thou shalt have treasure in h':
11: 25 your Father also which is in h' may
26 your Father which is in h' forgive
30 John, was it from h', or of men?
31 If we shall say, From h'; he will say,
12: 25 are as the angels which are in h'.
13: 25 the stars of h' shall fall, and the
25 the powers that are in h' shall be
27 earth to the uttermost part of h'.
31 H' and earth shall pass away: but
32 no, not the angels which are in h',
14: 62 and coming in the clouds of h'.
16: 19 he was received up into h', and sat
Lu 2: 15 were gone away from them into h',
3: 21 and praying, the h' was opened, And
22 and a voice came from h', which
4: 25 when the h' was shut up three years
6: 23 your reward is great in h': for in
9: 16 and looking up to h', he blessed
54 command fire to come down from h',
10: 15 which art exalted to h', shalt be
18 Satan as lightning fall from h'.
20 your names are written in h'.
21 O Father, Lord of h' and earth, that
11: 2 say, Our Father which art in h',
2 will be done as in h', so in earth.
16 him, sought of him a sign from h'.
15: 7 joy shall be in h' over one sinner
18 I have sinned against h', and before
21 Father, I have sinned against h',
16: 17 it is easier for h' and earth to pass,
17: 24 out of the one part under h', shineth
24 unto the other part under h';
29 rained fire and brimstone from h',
18: 13 lift up so much as his eyes unto h',
22 and thou shalt have treasure in h':
19: 38 peace in h', and glory in the highest
20: 4 baptism of John, was it from h', or
5 If we shall say, From h'; he will
21: 11 great signs shall there be from h'.
26 the powers of h' shall be shaken.
33 H' and earth shall pass away: but
22: 43 appeared an angel unto him from h',
24: 51 from them, and carried up into h'.
Jo 1: 32 descending from h' like a dove, and
51 Hereafter ye shall see h' open, and
3: 13 And no man hath ascended up to h',
13 but he that came down from h', even
13 even the Son of man which is in h'.
27 except it be given him from h'.
31 he that cometh from h' is above all.
6: 31 He gave them bread from h' to eat.
32 gave you not that bread from h';
32 giveth you the true bread from h'.
33 is he which cometh down from h',
38 I came down from h', not to do mine
41 the bread which came down from h'.
42 that he saith, I came down from h'?
50 bread which cometh down from h',
51, 58 bread which came down from h':
12: 28 Then came there a voice from h',
17: 1 and lifted up his eyes to h', and said,
Ac 1: 10 looked stedfastly toward h' as he
11 why stand ye gazing up into h'?
11 which is taken up from you into h',
11 as ye have seen him go into h'.
2: 2 there came a sound from h' as of a
5 men, out of every nation under h'.
19 I will shew wonders in h' above, and
3: 21 Whom the h' must receive until the
4: 12 none other name under h' given
24 which hast made h', and earth, and
7: 42 them up to worship the host of h';
49 H' is my throne, and earth is my
55 looked up stedfastly into h', and saw
9: 3 round about him a light from h':
10: 11 And saw h' opened, and a certain
16 vessel was received up again into h'.
11: 5 let down from h' by four corners;
9 voice answered me again from h',

Ac 14: 10 and all were drawn up again into h'.
15 which made h', and earth, and the
17 gave us rain from h', and fruitful
17: 24 that he is Lord of h' and earth,
22: 6 there shone from h' a great light
26: 13 I saw in the way a light from h',
Ro 1: 18 wrath of God is revealed from h'
10: 6 heart, Who shall ascend into h'?
1Co 8: 5 gods, whether in h' or in earth, as
15: 47 the second man is the Lord from h'.
2Co 5: 2 with our house which is from h':
12: 2 an one caught up to the third h'.
Ga 1: 8 we, or an angel from h', preach any
Eph 1: 10 both which are in h', and which
3: 15 family in h' and earth is named,
6: 9 your Master also is in h'; neither
Ph'p 2: 10 of things in h', and things in earth
3: 20 For our conversation is in h'; from
Col 1: 5 hope which is laid up for you in h',
16 that are in h', and that are in earth,
20 be things in earth, or things in h'.
23 every creature which is under h';
4: 1 knowing ye also have a Master in h'.
1Th 1: 10 And to wait for his Son from h',
4: 16 shall descend from h' with a shout,
2Th 1: 7 Jesus shall be revealed from h'
Heb 9: 24 but into h' itself, now to appear in
10: 34 that ye have in h' a better and an
12: 23 firstborn, which are written in h',
25 from him that speaketh from h':
26 shake not the earth only, but also h'.
Jas 5: 12 swear not neither by h', neither
18 and the h' gave rain, and the earth
1Pet 1: 4 not away, reserved in h' for you,
12 the Holy Ghost sent down from h';
3: 22 Who is gone into h', and is on the
2Pe 1: 18 this voice which came from h' we
1Jo 5: 7 are three that bear record in h', the
Re 3: 12 cometh down out of h' from my God:
4: 1 behold, a door was opened in h':
2 a throne was set in h', and one sat
5: 3 And no man in h', nor in earth,
13 every creature which is in h', and
6: 13 the stars of h' fell unto the earth,
14 And the h' departed as a scroll when
8: 1 was silence in h' about the space of
10 and there fell a great star from h',
13 flying through the midst of h',
9: 1 I saw a star fall from h' unto the
10: 1 angel come down from h', clothed
4 I heard a voice from h' saying unto
5 the earth lifted up his hand to h',
6 who created h', and the things that
8 voice which I heard from h' spake
11: 6 These have power to shut h', that it
12 heard a great voice from h' saying
12 they ascended up to h' in a cloud;
13 and gave glory to the God of h'.
15 were great voices in h', saying, The
19 the temple of God was opened in h',
12: 1 appeared a great wonder in h';
3 appeared another wonder in h';
4 third part of the stars of h', and did
7 And there was war in h': Michael
8 was their place found any more in h'.
10 heard a loud voice saying in h', Now
13: 6 and them that dwell in h'.
13 fire come down from h' on the earth
14: 2 I heard a voice from h', as the voice
6 another angel fly in the midst of h',
7 that made h', and earth, and the
13 I heard a voice from h' saying unto
17 out of the temple which is in h', he
15: 1 I saw another sign in h', great and
5 the tabernacle of the testimony in h'
16: 11 blasphemed the God of h' because
17 great voice out of the temple of h',
21 fell upon men a great hail out of h',
18: 1 another angel come down from h',
4 and I heard another voice from h',
5 For her sins have reached unto h',
20 Rejoice over her, thou h', and ye
19: 1 a great voice of much people in h',
11 And I saw h' opened, and behold a
14 armies which were in h' followed
17 the fowls that fly in the midst of h',
20: 1 angel come down from h', having
9 fire came down from God out of h',
11 face the earth and the h' fled away;
21: 1 I saw a new h' and a new earth:
1 for the first h' and the first earth
2 coming down from God out of h',
3 heard a great voice out of h' saying,
10 holy Jerusalem, descending out of h'

heavenly

M't 6: 14 your h' Father will also forgive
26 yet your h' Father feedeth them.
32 h' Father knoweth that ye have need
15: 13 my h' Father hath not planted,
18: 35 shall my h' Father do also unto
Lu 2: 13 a multitude of the h' host praising
11: 13 your h' Father give the Holy
Joh 3: 12 believe, if I tell you of h' things?
Ac 26: 19 disobedient unto the h' vision:
1Co 15: 48 and as is the h', such are they also
48 such are they also that are h'.
49 shall also bear the image of the h'.
Eph 1: 3 spiritual blessings in h' places in
20 own right hand in the h' places,
2: 6 together in h' places in Christ Jesus:
3: 10 powers in h' places might be known
2Ti 4: 18 preserve me unto his h' kingdom:
Heb 3: 1 brethren, partakers of the h' calling,
6: 4 tasted of the h' gift, and were made
8: 5 example and shadow of h' things,
9: 23 but the h' things themselves with

Heb 11:16 a better country, that is, an h':
12:22 of the living God, the h' Jerusalem,

heaven's
M't 19:12 eunuchs for the kingdom of h' sake.

heavens
Ge 2: 1 the h' and the earth were finished,
4 the generations of the h' and of
4 God made the earth and the h',
De 10:14 and the heaven of h' is the Lord's
32: 1 Give ear, O ye h', and I will speak;
33:28 also his h' shall drop down dew.
J'g 5: 4 and the h' dropped, the clouds also
2Sa 22:10 He bowed the h' also, and came
1Ki 8:27 heaven of h' cannot contain thee;
1Ch 16:26 are idols: but the Lord made the h'.
31 Let the h' be glad, and let the earth
27:23 Israel like to the stars of the h'.
2Ch 2: 6 heaven of h' cannot contain him?
6:18 heaven of h' cannot contain thee;
25 Then hear thou from the h', and
33 Then hear thou from the h', even
35 hear thou from the h' their prayer
39 Then hear thou from the h', even
Ezr 9: 6 our trespass is grown up unto the h'.
Ne 9: 6 hast made heaven, the heaven of h',
Job 9: 8 Which alone spreadeth out the h',
14:12 till the h' be no more, they shall not
15:15 yea, the h' are not clean in his sight.
20: 6 his excellency mount up to the h',
26:13 his spirit he hath garnished the h';
35: 5 Look unto the h', and see; and
Ps 2: 4 He that sitteth in the h' shall laugh:
8: 1 who hast set thy glory above the h'.
3 When I consider thy h', the work of
18: 9 He bowed the h' also, and came
13 The Lord also thundered in the h',
19: 1 The h' declare the glory of God;
33: 6 word of the Lord were the h' made;
36: 5 Thy mercy, O Lord, is in the h';
50: 4 He shall call to the h' from above,
6 h' shall declare his righteousness:
57: 5 Be thou exalted, O God, above the h';
10 For thy mercy is great unto the h',
11 Be thou exalted, O God, above the h':
68: 4 extol him that rideth upon the h'
8 h' also dropped at the presence
33 To him that rideth upon the h' of h',
73: 9 They set their mouth against the h',
89: 2 shalt thou establish in the very h'.
5 And the h' shall praise thy wonders,
11 The h' are thine, the earth also is
96: 5 are idols: but the Lord made the h'.
11 Let the h' rejoice, and let the earth
97: 6 The h' declare his righteousness,
102:25 and the h' are the work of thy hands.
103:19 hath prepared his throne in the h';
104: 2 stretchest out the h' like a curtain:
108: 4 For thy mercy is great above the h':
5 Be thou exalted, O God, above the h':
113: 4 nations, and his glory above the h'.
115: 3 our God is in the h': he hath done
16 heaven, even the h', are the Lord's:
123: 1 eyes, O thou that dwellest in the h'.
136: 5 To him that by wisdom made the h':
144: 5 Bow thy h', O Lord, and come down:
148: 1 Praise ye the Lord from the h':
4 Praise him, ye h' of h', and ye waters
4 and ye waters that be above the h'.
Pr 3:19 hath he established the h'.
8:27 he prepared the h', I was there:
Isa 1: 2 Hear, O h', and give ear, O earth:
5:30 light is darkened in the h' thereof.
13:13 Therefore I will shake the h', and
34: 4 the h' shall be rolled together as a
40:22 stretcheth out the h' as a curtain,
42: 5 he that created the h', and stretched
44:23 Sing, O ye h'; for the Lord hath
24 that stretcheth forth the h' alone;
45: 8 Drop down, ye h', from above, and
12 have stretched out the h', and all
18 saith the Lord that created the h';
48:13 my right hand hath spanned the h':
49:13 Sing, O h'; and be joyful, O earth;
50: 3 I clothe the h' with blackness, and
51: 6 Lift up your eyes to the h', and look
6 the h' shall vanish away like smoke,
13 hath stretched forth the h', and laid
16 that I may plant the h', and lay the
55: 9 as the h' are higher than the earth,
64: 1 Oh that thou wouldest rend the h',
65:17 I create new h' and a new earth:
66:22 as the new h' and the new earth,
Jer 2:12 Be astonished, O ye h', at this, and
4:23 and the h', and they had no light.
25 and all the birds of the h' were fled.
28 mourn, and the h' above be black:
9:10 the fowl of the h' and the beast are
10:11 gods that have not made the h'
11 the earth, and from under these h'.
12 hath stretched out the h' by his
13 is a multitude of waters in the h',
14:22 rain? or can the h' give showers?
51:16 is a multitude of waters in the h';
La 3:41 with our hands unto God in the h'.
66 in anger from under the h' of the
Eze 1: 1 that the h' were opened, and I saw
Da 4:26 have known that the h' do rule.
Ho 2:21 I will hear the h', and they shall
Joe 2:10 the h' shall tremble: the sun and
30 I will shew wonders in the h' and in
3:16 the h' and the earth shall shake:
Hab 3: 3 His glory covered the h', and the
Hag 2: 6 I will shake the h', and the earth,
21 I will shake the h' and the earth;
Zec 6: 5 These the four spirits of the h',
8:12 and the h' shall give their dew:
12: 1 stretcheth forth the h', and layeth
M't 3:16 lo, the h' were opened unto him,
24:29 powers of the h' shall be shaken:
M'r 1:10 he saw the h' opened, and the Spirit
Lu 12:33 a treasure in the h' that faileth not,
Ac 2:34 David is not ascended into the h':
7:56 Behold, I see the h' opened, and the
2Co 5: 1 made with hands, eternal in the h'.
Eph 4:10 that ascended up far above all h',
Heb 1:10 and the h' are the works of thine
4:14 priest, that is passed into the h',
7:26 and made higher than the h';
8: 1 the throne of the Majesty in the h';
9:23 patterns of things in the h' should
2Pe 3: 5 the word of God the h' were of old,
7 But the h' and the earth, which are
10 the h' shall pass away with a great
12 h' being on fire shall be dissolved,
13 look for new h' and a new earth,
Re 12:12 Therefore rejoice, ye h', and ye that

heave-offering See HEAVE and OFFERING.

heave-shoulder See HEAVE and SHOULDER.

heavier
Job 6: 3 now it would be h' than the sand
23: 2 my stroke is h' than my groaning.
Pr 27: 3 a fool's wrath is h' than them both.

heavily
Ex 14:25 wheels, that they drave them h':
Ps 35:14 I bowed down h', as one that
Isa 47: 6 hast thou very h' laid thy yoke.

heaviness
Ezr 9: 5 sacrifice I arose up from my h';
Job 9:27 I will leave off my h', and comfort
Ps 69:20 and I am full of h': and I looked
119:28 My soul melteth for h': strengthen
Pr 10: 1 foolish son is the h' of his mother.
12:25 H' in the heart of man maketh it
14:13 but the end of that mirth is h'.
Isa 29: 2 and there shall be h' and sorrow:
61: 3 of praise for the spirit of h';
Ro 9: 2 great h' and continual sorrow
2Co 2: 1 would not come again to you in h'
Ph'p 2:26 and was full of h', because that
Jas 4: 9 to mourning, and your joy to h'.
1Pe 1: 6 ye are in h' through manifold

heavy See also HEAVIER.
Ex 17:12 Moses' hands were h'; and they
18:18 for this thing is too h' for thee;
Nu 11:14 alone, because it is too h' for me.
1Sa 4:18 for he was an old man, and h'.
5: 6 But the hand of the Lord was h'
11 the hand of God was very h' there.
2Sa 14:26 because the hair was h' on him,
1Ki 12: 4 his h' yoke which he put upon us,
10 Thy father made our yoke h', but
11 father did lade you with a h' yoke,
14 My father made your yoke h', and
14: 6 I am sent to thee with h' tidings.
20:43 went to his house h' and displeased,
21: 4 Ahab came into his house h' and
2Ch 10: 4 his h' yoke that he put upon us,
10 Thy father made our yoke h', but
11 my father put a h' yoke upon you,
14 My father made your yoke h', but
Ne 5:18 bondage was h' upon this people.
Job 33: 7 neither shall my hand be h' upon
Ps 32: 4 night thy hand was h' upon me:
38: 4 over mine head: as an h' burden
4 burden they are too h' for me.
Pr 25:20 that singeth songs to an h' heart.
27: 3 stone is h', and the sand weighty;
31: 6 unto those that be of h' hearts.
Isa 6:10 make their ears h', and shut their
24:20 transgression thereof shall be h'
30:27 and the burden thereof is h':
46: 1 your carriages were h' loaden;
58: 6 to undo the h' burdens, and to let
59: 1 neither his ear h', that it cannot
La 3: 7 get out: he hath made my chain h'.
M't 11:28 all ye that labour and are h' laden,
23: 4 For they bind h' burdens and
26:37 began to be sorrowful and very h'.
43 asleep again: for their eyes were h'.
M'r 14:33 be sore amazed, and to be very h';
40 asleep again, for their eyes were h',
Lu 9:32 were with him were h' with sleep:

Heber (*he'-bur*) See also EBER; HEBER'S; HEBERITES.
Ge 46:17 and the sons of Beriah; H', and
Nu 26:45 the sons of Beriah: of H', the
J'g 4:11 Now H' the Kenite, which was of
17 the tent of Jael the wife of H' the
17 and the house of H' of Kenite.
5:24 Jael the wife of H' the Kenite be,
1Ch 4:18 and H' the father of Socho, and
5:13 Jachan, and Zia and H', seven.
7:31 And the sons of Beriah; H',
32 And H' begat Japhlet, and Shomer,
8:17 Meshullam, and Hezeki, and H',
22 And Ishpan, and H', and Eliel,
Lu 3:35 Phalec, which was the son of H',

Heberites (*he'-bur-ites*)
Nu 26:45 of Heber, the family of the H': of

Heber's (*he'-burs*)
J'g 4:21 Then Jael H' wife took a nail of

Hebrew (*he'-broo*) See also HEBREWESS; HEBREWS.
Ge 14:13 escaped, and told Abram the H';
39:14 he hath brought in a H' unto us
17 The H' servant, which thou hast
41:12 with us a young man, an H',
Ex 1:15 Egypt spake to the H' midwives,
1:16 of a midwife to the H' women,
19 Because the H' women are not as
2: 7 to thee a nurse of the H' women,
11 spied an Egyptian smiting a H',
21: 2 If thou buy an H' servant, six years
De 15:12 an H' man, or an H' woman,
Jer 34: 9 being an H' or an Hebrewess, go
14 every man his brother an H', which
Jon 1: 9 And he said unto them, I am a H';
Lu 23:38 of Greek, and Latin, and H',
Joh 5: 2 called in the H' tongue Bethesda,
19:13 Pavement, but in the H', Gabbatha.
17 which is called in the H' Golgotha:
20 written in H', and Greek, and Latin.
Ac 21:40 spake unto them in the H' tongue,
22: 2 that he spake in the H' tongue to
26:14 saying in the H' tongue, Saul, Saul,
Ph'p 3: 5 of Benjamin, an H' of the Hebrews;
Re 9:11 name in the H' tongue is Abaddon,
16:16 in the H' tongue Armageddon.

Hebrewess (*he'-broo-ess*)
Jer 34: 9 being an Hebrew or an H', go free;

Hebrews[A] (*he'-brooz*) See also HEBREWS'.
Ge 40:15 away out of the land of the H':
43:32 might not eat bread with the H';
Ex 2:13 two men of the H' strove together:
3:18 God of the H' hath met with us:
5: 3 God of the H' hath met with us:
7:16 The Lord God of the H' hath sent
9: 1, 13 saith the Lord God of the H',
10: 3 Thus saith the Lord God of the H',
1Sa 4: 6 great shout in the camp of the H'?
9 that ye be not servants unto the H'
13: 3 all the land, saying, Let the H' hear.
7 some of the H' went over Jordan
19 the H' make them swords or spears:
14:11 the H' come forth out of the holes
21 H' that were with the Philistines
29: 3 What do these H' here? And
Ac 6: 1 of the Grecians against the H',
2Co 11:22 Are they H'? so am I. Are they
Ph'p 3: 5 of Benjamin, an Hebrew of the H';
Heb *subscr.* Written to the H' from Italy

Hebrews' (*he'-brooz*)
Ex 2: 6 This is one of the H' children.

Hebron (*he'-brun*) See also HEBRONITES.
Ge 13:18 plain of Mamre, which is in H',
23: 2 same is H' in the land of Canaan:
19 same is H' in the land of Canaan.
35:27 unto the city of Arbah, which is H',
37:14 So he sent him out of the vale of H',
Ex 6:18 Amram, and Izhar, and H', and
Nu 3:19 Amram, and Izehar, H', and Uzziel.
13:22 by the south, and came unto H';
22 Now H' was built seven years before
Jos 10: 3 sent unto Hoham king of H', and
5 king of Jerusalem, the king of H',
23 king of Jerusalem the king of H',
36 and all Israel with him, unto H';
39 as he had done to H', so he did to
11:21 from the mountains, from H', from
12:10 Jerusalem, one; the king of H', one;
14:13 Jephunneh H' for an inheritance.
14 H' therefore became the
15 name of H' before was Kirjath-arba;
15:13 father of Anak, which city is H'.
54 and Kirjath-arba, which is H', and
19:28 And H', and Rehob, and Hammon,
20: 7 and Kirjath-arba, which is H',
21:11 H', in the hill country of Judah,
13 H' with her suburbs, to be a city
J'g 1:10 the Canaanites that dwelt in H',
10 now the name of H' before was
20 And they gave H' unto Caleb, as
16: 3 the top of an hill that is before H'.
1Sa 30:31 to them which were in H', and to
2Sa 2: 1 I go up? And he said, Unto H'.
3 and they dwelt in the cities of H'.
11 David was king in H' over the house
32 they came to H' at break of day.
3: 2 unto David were sons born in H':
5 These were born to David in H'.
19 to speak in the ears of David in H'
20 So Abner came to David to H', and
22 Abner was not with David in H';
27 when Abner was returned to H',
32 And they buried Abner in H': and
4: 1 heard that Abner was dead in H',
8 of Ish-bosheth unto David to H',
12 hanged them up over the pool in H'.
12 it in the sepulchre of Abner in H'.
5: 1 tribes of Israel to David unto H',
3 of Israel came to the king to H';
3 made a league with them in H'
5 In H' he reigned over Judah seven
13 after he was come from H': and
15: 7 I have vowed unto the Lord, in H'.
9 peace. So he arose, and went to H'.
10 shall say, Absalom reigneth in H'.
1Ki 2:11 seven years reigned he in H', and
1Ch 2:42 sons of Mareshah the father of H'.
43 And the sons of H'; Korah, and
3: 1 which were born unto him in H';
4 These six were born unto him in H';
6: 2 Kohath; Amram, Izhar, and H', and
18 were, Amram, and Izhar, and H',
55 gave them H' in the land of Judah,
57 namely, H', the city of refuge,
11: 1 themselves to David unto H',
3 elders of Israel to the king to H';
3 made a covenant with them in H'
12:23 came to David to H', to turn the
38 came with a perfect heart to H', to
15: 9 Of the sons of H'; Eliel the chief,

1Ch 23:12 Amram, Izhar, H', and Uzziel, four.
19 Of the sons of H'; Jeriah the first,
24:23 And the sons of H'; Jeriah the
29:27 seven years reigned he in H', and
2Ch 11:10 Zorah, and Aijalon, and H', which

Hebronites (*he'-brun-ites*)
Nu 3:27 and the family of the H', and the
26:58 the family of the H', the family of
1Ch 26:23 and the Izharites, the H', and the
30 And of the H', Hashabiah and his
31 Among the H' was Jerijah the chief,
31 even among the H', according to

hedge See also HEDGED; HEDGES.
Job 1:10 not thou made an h' about him,
Pr 15:19 slothful man is as an h' of thorns:
Ec 10: 8 whoso breaketh an h', a serpent
Isa 5: 5 I will take away the h' thereof,
Eze 13: 5 the h' for the house of Israel
22:30 them, that should make up the h',
Ho 2: 6 I will h' up thy way with thorns,
Mic 7: 4 upright is sharper than a thorn h':
M'r 12: 1 and set an h' about it, and digged

hedged
Job 3:23 is hid, and whom God hath h' in?
La 3: 7 He hath h' me about, that I cannot
M't 21:33 a vineyard, and h' it round

hedges
1Ch 4:23 that dwelt among plants and h':
Ps 80:12 thou then broken down her h',
89:40 Thou hast broken down all his h';
Jer 49: 3 and run to and fro by the h'; for
Na 3:17 which camp in the h' in the cold
Lu 14:23 Go out into the highways and h',

heed
Ge 31:24 Take h' that thou speak not to
29 Take thou h' that thou speak not
Ex 10:28 Get thee from me, take h' to thyself,
19:12 Take h' to yourselves, that ye go not
34:12 Take h' to thyself, lest thou make
Nu 23:12 Must I not take h' to speak that
De 2: 4 take ye good h' unto yourselves
4: 9 Only take h' to thyself, and keep thy
15 Take ye therefore good h' unto
23 Take h' unto yourselves, lest ye
11:16 Take h' to yourselves, that your
12:13 Take h' to thyself that thou offer not
19 Take h' to thyself that thou forsake
30 Take h' to thyself that thou be not
24: 8 Take h' in the plague of leprosy,
27: 9 Take h', and hearken, O Israel;
Jos 22: 5 But take diligent h' to do the
23:11 Take good h' therefore unto your
1Sa 19: 2 take h' to thyself until the morning,
2Sa 20:10 Amasa took no h' to the sword that
1Ki 2: 4 If thy children take h' to their way,
8:25 thy children take h' to their way,
2Ki 10:31 Jehu took no h' to walk in the law
1Ch 22:13 prosper if thou takest h' to fulfil
28:10 Take h' now; for the Lord hath
2Ch 6:16 thy children take h' to their way
19: 6 Take h' what ye do: for ye judge
7 take h' and do it: for there is no
33: 8 so that they will take h' to do all
Ezr 4:22 Take h' now that ye fail not to do
Job 36:21 Take h', regard not iniquity: for
Ps 39: 1 I said, I will take h' to my ways,
119: 9 by taking h' thereto according to
Pr 17: 4 wicked doer giveth h' to false lips;
Ec 7:21 Also take no h' unto all words
12: 9 he gave good h', and sought out,
Isa 7: 4 Take h', and be quiet; fear him,
21: 7 hearkened diligently with much h':
Jer 9: 4 Take ye h' every one of his
17:21 Take h' to yourselves, and bear no
18:18 us not give h' to any of his words.
19 Give h' to me, O Lord, and hearken
Ho 4:10 have left off to take h' to the Lord.
Mal 2:15 Therefore take h' to your spirit, and
16 therefore take h' to your spirit, that
M't 6: 1 Take h' that ye do not your alms
16: 6 Take h' and beware of the leaven
18:10 Take h' that ye despise not one of
24: 4 Take h' that no man deceive you.
M'r 4:24 Take h' what ye hear: with what
8:15 Take h', beware of the leaven of
13: 5 Take h' lest any man deceive you:
9 take h' to yourselves: for they shall
23 take ye h': behold, I have foretold
33 Take ye h', watch and pray: for ye
Lu 8:18 Take h' therefore how ye hear: for
11:35 Take h' therefore that the light
12:15 Take h', ... beware of covetousness:
17: 3 Take h' to yourselves: If thy
21: 8 Take h' that ye be not deceived:
34 take h' to yourselves, lest at any
Ac 3: 5 he gave h' unto them, expecting to
5:35 take h' to yourselves what ye
8: 6 accord gave h' unto those things
10 To whom they all gave h', from the
20:28 Take h' therefore unto yourselves,
22:26 Take h' what thou doest: for this
Ro 11:21 take h' lest he also spare not thee.
1Co 3:10 every man take h' how he buildeth
8: 9 But take h' lest by any means this
10:12 thinketh he standeth take h' lest he
Ga 5:15 take h' that ye be not consumed one
Col 4:17 Take h' to the ministry which thou
1Ti 1: 4 give h' to fables and endless
4: 1 giving h' to seducing spirits, and
16 Take h' unto thyself, and unto the
Tit 1:14 Not giving h' to Jewish fables, and
Heb 2: 1 the more earnest h' to the things
3:12 Take h' brethren, lest there be in
2Pe 1:19 ye do well that ye take h', as unto

heel See also HEELS.
Ge 3:15 head, and thou shalt bruise his h'.
25:26 his hand took hold on Esau's h';
Job 18: 9 The gin shall take him by the h'.
Ps 41: 9 hath lifted up his h' against me.
Ho 12: 3 He took his brother by the h' in the
Joh 13:18 hath lifted up his h' against me.

heels
Ge 49:17 adder ... that biteth the horse h',
Job 13:27 thou settest a print upon the h' of
Ps 49: 5 iniquity of my h' shall compass
Jer 13:22 discovered, and thy h' made bare.

Hegai (*he'-gahee*) See also HEGE.
Es 2: 8 the palace, to the custody of H',
8 custody of H', keeper of the women.
15 H' the king's chamberlain, the

Hege (*he'-ghe*) See also HEGAI.
Es 2: 3 unto the custody of H' the king's

heifer See also HEIFER'S.
Ge 15: 9 Take me an h' of three years old,
Nu 19: 2 bring thee a red h' without spot,
5 one shall burn the h' in his sight;
6 the midst of the burning of the h'.
9 shall gather up the ashes of the h',
10 gathereth the ashes of the h' shall
17 ashes of the burnt h' of purification
De 21: 3 elders of that city shall take an h',
4 down the h' unto a rough valley,
6 shall wash their hands over the h'
J'g 14:18 If ye had not plowed with my h', ye
1Sa 16: 2 Take an h' with thee, and say, I am
Isa 15: 5 unto Zoar, an h' of three years old:
Jer 46:20 Egypt is like a very fair h', but
48:34 voice, ... as an h' of three years old:
50:11 ye are grown fat as the h' at grass,
Ho 4:16 slideth back as a backsliding h':
10:11 Ephraim is as an h' that is taught,
Heb 9:13 the ashes of an h' sprinkling the

heifer's
De 21: 4 shall strike off the h' neck there

height See also HEIGHTS.
Ge 6:15 and the h' of it thirty cubits.
Ex 25:10, 23 a cubit and a half the h' thereof.
27: 1 the h' thereof shall be three cubits.
18 and the h' five cubits of fine twined
30: 2 two cubits shall be the h' thereof:
37: 1 and a cubit and a half the h' of it:
10 a cubit and a half the h' thereof:
25 and two cubits was the h' of it; the
38: 1 and three cubits the h' thereof.
18 the h' in the breadth was five cubits
1Sa 16: 7 or on the h' of his stature;
17: 4 whose h' was six cubits and a span.
1Ki 6: 2 and the h' thereof thirty cubits.
20 and twenty cubits in the h' thereof:
26 The h' of the one cherub was ten
7: 2 the h' thereof thirty cubits, upon
16 the h' of the one chapiter was five
16 the h' of the other chapiter was five
23 all about, his h' was five cubits: and
27 thereof, and three cubits the h' of it.
32 the h' of a wheel was a cubit and
2Ki 19:23 come up to the h' of the mountains,
25:17 h' of the one pillar was eighteen
17 the h' of the chapiter three cubits:
2Ch 3: 4 the h' was an hundred and twenty:
4: 1 and ten cubits the h' thereof.
2 and five cubits the h' thereof; and a
33:14 and raised it up a very great h',
Ezr 6: 3 the h' thereof threescore cubits,
Job 22:12 Is not God in the h' of heaven? and
12 behold the h' of the stars, how high
Ps 102:19 down from the h' of his sanctuary;
Pr 25: 3 The heaven for h', and the earth
Isa 7:11 in the depth; or in the h' above.
37:24 come up to the h' of the mountains,
24 will enter into the h' of his border,
Jer 31:12 come and sing in the h' of Zion, and
49:16 rock, that holdest the h' of the hill;
51:53 should fortify the h' of her strength,
52:21 the h' of one pillar was eighteen
22 and the h' of one chapiter was five
Eze 17:23 In the mountain of the h' of Israel
19:11 and she appeared in her h' with the
20:40 in the mountain of the h' of Israel,
31: 5 his h' was exalted above all the
10 thou hast lifted up thyself in h',
10 and his heart is lifted up in his h';
14 exalt themselves for their h',
14 their trees stand up in their h',
32: 5 and fill the valleys with thy h'.
40: 5 one reed; and the h', one reed.
41: 8 I saw also the h' of the house
Da 3: 1 whose h' was threescore cubits,
4:10 earth, and the h' thereof was great.
11 the h' thereof reached unto heaven,
20 whose h' reached unto the heaven,
Am 2: 9 Amorite before them, whose h' was
9 was like the h' of the cedars, and
Ro 8:39 Nor h', nor depth, nor any other
Eph 3:18 and length, and depth, and h';
Re 21:16 breadth and the h' of it are equal.

heights
Ps 148: 1 the heavens: praise him in the h'.
Isa 14:14 ascend above the h' of the clouds:

heinous
Job 31:11 For this is an h' crime; yea, it is an

heir See also HEIRS.
Ge 15: 3 one born in my house is mine h'.
4 This shall not be thine h'; but he
4 thine own bowels shall be thine h'.
21:10 of this bondwoman shall not be h'
2Sa 14: 7 and we will destroy the h' also:
Pr 30:23 handmaid that is h' to her mistress
Jer 49: 1 Hath Israel no sons? hath he no h'?
2 then shall Israel be h' unto them
Mic 1:15 Yet will I bring an h' unto thee,
M't 21:38 This is the h'; come, let us kill him,
M'r 12: 7 This is the h'; come, let us kill him,
Lu 20:14 This is the h'; come, let us kill him,
Ro 4:13 he should be the h' of the world,
Ga 4: 1 That the h', as long as he is a child,
7 then an h' of God through Christ.
30 shall not be h' with the son of the
Heb 1: 2 whom...appointed h' of all things,
11: 7 and became h' of the righteousness

heirs See also FELLOWHEIRS; JOINT-HEIRS.
Jer 49: 2 unto them that were his h', saith
Ro 4:14 if they which are of the law be h',
8:17 And if children, then h'; h' of God,
Ga 3:29 and h' according to the promise.
Tit 3: 7 by his grace, we should be made h'
Heb 1:14 them who shall be h' of salvation?
6:17 to shew unto the h' of promise
11: 9 h' with him of the same promise:
Jas 2: 5 rich in faith, and h' of the kingdom
1Pe 3: 7 h' together of the grace of life;

Helah (*he'-lah*)
1Ch 4: 5 had two wives, H', and Naarah.
7 the sons of H' were, Zereth, and

Helam (*he'-lam*)
2Sa 10:16 the river: and they came to H': and
17 passed over Jordan, and came to H'.

Helbah (*hel'-bah*)
J'g 1:31 nor of H', nor of Aphik, nor of

Helbon (*hel'-bon*)
Eze 27:18 in the wine of H', and white wool.

held See also BEHELD; HOLDEN; UPHELD; WITHHELD.
Ge 24:21 wondering at her h' his peace, to
34: 5 and Jacob h' his peace until they
48:17 and he h' up his father's hand, to
Ex 17:11 when Moses h' up his hand, that
36:12 the loops h' one curtain to another.
Le 10: 3 glorified. And Aaron h' his peace.
Nu 30: 7 and h' his peace at her in the day
11 heard it, and h' his peace at her,
14 he h' his peace at her in the day he
J'g 7:20 h' the lamps in their left hands,
16:26 unto the lad that h' him by the hand,
Ru 3:15 And when she h' it, he measured
1Sa 10:27 no presents. But he h' his peace.
25:36 behold, he h' a feast in his house,
2Sa 18:16 Israel: for Joab h' back the people.
1Ki 8:65 at that time Solomon h' a feast,
2Ki 18:36 But the people h' their peace, and
2Ch 4: 5 received and h' three thousand
Ne 4:16 half of them h' both the spears,
17 with the other hand h' a weapon.
21 half of them h' the spears from
5: 8 Then h' they their peace, and
Es 5: 2 king h' out to Esther the golden
7: 4 I had h' my tongue, although
8: 4 the king h' out the golden sceptre
Job 23:11 My foot hath h' his steps, his
29:10 The nobles h' their peace, and
Ps 32: 9 whose mouth must be h' in with
39: 2 I h' my peace, even from good;
94:18 thy mercy, O Lord, h' me up.
Ca 3: 4 I h' him, and would not let him go,
7: 5 the king is h' in the galleries.
Isa 36:21 they h' their peace, and answered
57:11 have not I h' my peace even of old,
Jer 50:33 took them captives h' them fast;
Da 12: 7 when he h' up his right hand and
M't 12:14 and h' a council against him, how
26:63 But Jesus h' his peace. And the
28: 9 they came and h' him by the feet,
M'k 3: 4 or to kill? But they h' their peace.
9:34 But they h' their peace: for by the
14:61 But he h' his peace, and answered
15: 1 the chief priests h' a consultation
Lu 14: 4 And they h' their peace. And he
20:26 at his answer, and h' their peace.
22:63 the men that h' Jesus mocked him,
Ac 3:11 man which was healed h' Peter
11:18 they h' their peace, and glorified
14: 4 and part h' with the Jews, and part
15:13 and after they had h' their peace,
Ro 7: 6 being dead wherein we were h';
Re 6: 9 for the testimony which they h':

Heldai (*hel'-dahee*) See also HELED; HELEM.
1Ch 27:15 H' the Netophathite, of Othniel:
Zec 6:10 of them of the captivity, even of H',

heldest See WITHHELDEST.

Heleb (*he'-leb*) See also HELED.
2Sa 23:29 H' the son of Baanah, a

Heled (*he'-led*) See also HELEB; HELDAI.
1Ch 11:30 H' the son of Baanah the

Helek (*he'-lek*) See also HELEKITES.
Nu 26:30 of H', the family of the Helekites:
Jos 17: 2 and for the children of H', and for

Helekites (*he'-lek-ites*)
Nu 26:30 of Helek, the family of the H':

Helem (*he'-lem*) See also HELDAI.
1Ch 7:35 And the sons of his brother H';
Zec 6:14 And the crowns shall be to H',

Heleph (*he'-lef*)
Jos 19:33 And their coast was from H',

Helez (*he'-lez*)
2Sa 23:26 H' the Paltite, Ira the son of
1Ch 2:39 Azariah begat H', and H' begat
11:27 the Harorite, H' the Pelonite,
27:10 seventh month was H' the Pelonite,

Heli (*he'-li*) See also ELI.
Lu 3:23 Joseph, which was the son of *H'*.
Helkai (*hel'-kahee*)
Ne 12:15 Of Harim, Adna; of Meraioth, *H'*;
Helkath (*hel'-kath*) See also HELKATH-HAZZURIM; HUKOK.
Jos 19:25 their border was *H'*, and Hali, and
21:31 *H'* with her suburbs, and Rehob
Helkath-hazzurim (*hel"-kath-haz'-zu-rim*)
2Sa 2:16 that place was called *H'*, which is
hell
De 32:22 shall burn unto the lowest *h'*,
2Sa 22: 6 The sorrows of *h'* compassed me
Job 11: 8 deeper than *h'*; what canst thou
26: 6 *H'* is naked before him, and
Ps 9:17 The wicked shall be turned into *h'*,
16:10 thou wilt not leave my soul in *h'*;
18: 5 The sorrows of *h'* compassed me
55:15 let them go down quick into *h'*:
86:13 my soul from the lowest *h'*.
116: 3 the pains of *h'* gat hold upon me:
139: 8 if I make my bed in *h'*, behold,
Pr 5: 5 death; her steps take hold on *h'*.
7:27 Her house is the way to *h'*, going
9:18 her guests are in the depths of *h'*.
15:11 *H'* and destruction are before the
24 he may depart from *h'* beneath.
23:14 and shalt deliver his soul from *h'*.
27:20 *H'* and destruction are never full;
Isa 5:14 Therefore *h'* hath enlarged herself,
14: 9 *H'* from beneath is moved for thee
15 thou shalt be brought down to *h'*,
28:15 and with *h'* are we at agreement;
18 agreement with *h'* shall not stand;
57: 9 didst debase thyself even unto *h'*.
Eze 31:16 I cast him down to *h'* with them
17 They also went down into *h'* with
32:21 speak to him out of the midst of *h'*
27 gone down to *h'* with their weapons
Am 9: 2 Though they dig into *h'*, thence
Jon 2: 2 out of the belly of *h'* cried I, and
Hab 2: 5 who enlargeth his desire as *h'*, and
M't 5:22 fool, shall be in danger of *h'* fire.
29, 30 body should be cast into *h'*.
10:28 to destroy both soul and body in *h'*.
11:23 shalt be brought down to *h'*: for if
16:18 and the gates of *h'* shall not prevail
18: 9 two eyes to be cast into *h'* fire.
23:15 more the child of *h'* than yourselves.
33 can ye escape the damnation of *h'*?
M'r 9:43 than having two hands to go into *h'*,
45 having two feet to be cast into *h'*,
47 having two eyes to be cast into *h'* fire
Lu 10:15 heaven, shalt be thrust down to *h'*.
12: 5 killed hath power to cast into *h'*;
16:23 in *h'* he lift up his eyes, being in
Ac 2:27 thou wilt not leave my soul in *h'*,
31 that his soul was not left in *h'*,
Jas 3: 6 nature; and it is set on fire of *h'*.
2Pe 2: 4 sinned, but cast them down to *h'*,
Re 1:18 have the keys of *h'* and of death.
6: 8 Death, and *H'* followed with him.
20:13 death and *h'* delivered up the dead
14 death and *h'* were cast into the lake
hell-fire See HELL and FIRE.
helm
Jas 3: 4 turned about with a very small *h'*,
helmet See also HELMETS.
1Sa 17: 5 had an *h'* of brass upon his head,
38 put an *h'* of brass upon his head;
Isa 59:17 an *h'* of salvation upon his head;
Eze 23:24 buckler and shield and *h'* round
27:10 hanged the shield and *h'* in thee;
38: 5 all of them with shield and *h'*:
Eph 6:17 And take the *h'* of salvation, and
1Th 5: 8 and for an *h'*, the hope of salvation.
helmets
2Ch 26:14 spears, and *h'*, and habergeons,
Jer 46: 4 stand forth with your *h'*; furbish
Helon (*he'-lon*)
Nu 1: 9 Of Zebulun; Eliab the son of *H'*.
2: 7 Eliab the son of *H'* shall be captain
7:24 Eliab the son of *H'*, prince of the
29 the offering of Eliab the son of *H'*.
10:16 of Zebulun was Eliab the son of *H'*.
help See also HELPED; HELPETH; HELPING; HELPS; HOLPEN.
Ge 2:18 will make him an *h'* meet for him.
20 was not found an *h'* meet for him.
49:25 of thy father, who shall *h'* thee;
Ex 18: 4 of my father, said he, was mine *h'*,
23: 5 and wouldest forbear to *h'* him,
5 thou shalt surely *h'* with him.
De 22: 4 shalt surely *h'* him to lift them up
32:38 let them rise up and *h'* you, and
33: 7 an *h'* to him from his enemies.
26 rideth upon the heaven in thy *h'*,
29 Lord, the shield of thy *h'*, and who is
Jos 1:14 men of valour, and *h'* them;
10: 4 Come up unto me, and *h'* me, that
6 us quickly, and save us, and *h'* us:
33 of Gezer came up to *h'* Lachish;
J'g 5:23 came not to the *h'* of the Lord,
23 *h'* of the Lord against the mighty.
1Sa 11: 9 the sun be hot, ye shall have *h'*.
2Sa 10:11 for me, then thou shalt *h'* me:
11 thee, then I will come and *h'* thee.
19 Syrians feared to *h'* the children of
14: 4 did obeisance, and said, *H'*, O king.
2Ki 6:26 him, saying, *H'*, my lord, O king.
27 not *h'* thee, whence shall I *h'* thee?
1Ch 12:17 come peaceably unto me to *h'* me,
22 day there came to David to *h'* him,
1Ch 18: 5 Syrians of Damascus came to *h'*
19:12 for me, then thou shalt *h'* me: but
12 strong for thee, then I will *h'* thee.
19 Syrians *h'* the children of Ammon
22:17 princes of Israel to *h'* Solomon
2Ch 14:11 Lord, it is nothing with thee to *h'*,
11 no power: *h'* us, O Lord our God;
19: 2 Shouldest thou *h'* the ungodly,
20: 4 together, to ask *h'* of the Lord: even
9 then thou wilt hear and *h'*.
25: 8 God hath power to *h'*, and to cast
26:13 to *h'* the king against the enemy.
28:16 unto the kings of Assyria to *h'* him.
23 the gods of the kings of Syria to *h'*
23 I sacrifice to them, that they may *h'*
29:34 brethren the Levites did *h'* them,
32: 3 the city: and they did *h'* him.
8 with us is the Lord our God to *h'* us,
Ezr 1: 4 of his place *h'* him with silver,
8:22 of soldiers and horsemen to *h'* us
Job 6:13 Is not my *h'* in me? and is wisdom
8:20 neither will he *h'* the evil doers:
29:12 and him that had none to *h'* him.
31:21 when I saw my *h'* in the gate:
Ps 3: 2 soul, There is no *h'* for him in God.
12: 1 *H'*, Lord; for the godly man
20: 2 Send thee *h'* from the sanctuary,
22:11 trouble is near; there is none to *h'*.
19 O my strength, haste thee to *h'* me.
27: 9 thou hast been my *h'*; leave me not,
33:20 Lord: he is our *h'* and our shield.
35: 2 buckler, and stand up for mine *h'*.
37:40 And the Lord shalt *h'* them, and
38:22 Make haste to *h'* me, O Lord my
40:13 me: O Lord, make haste to *h'* me.
17 thou art my *h'* and my deliverer;
42: 5 for the *h'* of his countenance.
44:26 Arise for our *h'*, and redeem us
46: 1 a very present *h'* in trouble.
5 God shall *h'* her, and that right
59: 4 fault: awake to *h'* me, and behold.
60:11 Give us *h'* from trouble: for vain
11 trouble: for vain is the *h'* of man.
63: 7 Because thou hast been my *h'*,
70: 1 me; make haste to *h'* me, O Lord.
5 thou art my *h'* and my deliverer;
71:12 O my God, make haste for my *h'*,
79: 9 *H'* us, O God of our salvation, for
89:19 I have laid *h'* upon one that is
94:17 Unless the Lord had been my *h'*,
107:12 fell down, and there was none to *h'*
108:12 Give us *h'* from trouble: for vain
12 trouble: for vain is the *h'* of man.
109:26 *H'* me, O Lord my God: O save me
115: 9, 10, 11 is their *h'* and their shield.
118: 7 my part with them that *h'* me:
119:86 persecute me wrongfully; *h'* thou
173 Let thine hand *h'* me; for I have
175 thee; and let thy judgments *h'* me.
121: 1 hills, from which cometh my *h'*.
2 My *h'* cometh from the Lord, which
124: 8 Our *h'* is in the name of the Lord,
146: 3 son of man, in whom there is no *h'*.
5 hath the God of Jacob for his *h'*,
Ec 4:10 he hath not another to *h'* him up.
Isa 10: 3 to whom will ye flee for *h'*? and
20: 6 whither we flee for *h'* to be delivered
30: 5 be an *h'* nor profit, but a shame,
7 For the Egyptians shall *h'* in vain,
31: 1 them that go down to Egypt for *h'*;
2 the *h'* of them that work iniquity.
41:10 I will *h'* thee; yea, I will uphold
13 unto thee, Fear not; I will *h'* thee.
14 I will *h'* thee, saith the Lord, and
44: 2 from the womb, which will *h'* thee;
50: 7 the Lord God will *h'* me; therefore
9 Behold, the Lord God will *h'* me;
63: 5 I looked, and there was none to *h'*;
Jer 37: 7 which is come forth to *h'* you,
La 1: 7 the enemy, and none did *h'* her:
4:17 eyes as yet failed for our vain *h'*:
Eze 12:14 all that are about him to *h'* him,
32:21 midst of hell with them that *h'* him:
Da 10:13 of the chief princes, came to *h'* me;
11:34 they shall be holpen with a little *h'*:
45 to his end, and none shall *h'* him.
Ho 13: 9 thyself; but in me is thine *h'*.
M't 15:25 worshipped him, saying, Lord, *h'* me.
M'r 9:22 have compassion on us, and *h'* us.
24 I believe; *h'* thou mine unbelief.
Lu 5: 7 that they should come and *h'* them.
10:40 bid her therefore that she *h'* me.
Ac 16: 9 over into Macedonia, and *h'* us.
21:28 Crying out, Men of Israel, *h'*: This
26:22 Having therefore obtained *h'* of
Ph'p 4: 3 *h'* those women which laboured
Heb 4:16 find grace to *h'* in time of need.
helped See also HOLPEN.
Ex 2:17 Moses stood up and *h'* them, and
1Sa 7:12 Hitherto hath the Lord *h'* us.
1Ki 1: 7 and they following Adonijah *h'* him.
20:16 the thirty and two kings that *h'* him.
1Ch 5:20 And they were *h'* against them, and
12:19 Saul to battle: but they *h'* them not:
21 And they *h'* David against the band
15:26 when God *h'* the Levites that bare
2Ch 18:31 cried out, and the Lord *h'* him; and
20:23 every one *h'* to destroy another.
26: 7 God *h'* him against the Philistines,
15 marvellously *h'*, till he was strong.
28:21 king of Assyria: but he *h'* him not.
Ezr 10:15 and Shabbethai the Levite *h'* them.
Es 9: 3 officers of the king, *h'* the Jews;
Job 26: 2 thou *h'* him that is without power?
Ps 28: 7 heart trusted in him, and I am *h'*:
116: 6 I was brought low, and he *h'* me.
Ps 118:13 I might fall: but the Lord *h'* me.
Isa 41: 6 They *h'* every one his neighbour;
49: 8 in a day of salvation have I *h'* thee:
Zec 1:15 and they *h'* forward the affliction.
Ac 18:27 *h'* them much which had believed
Re 12:16 the earth *h'* the woman, and the
helper See also HELPERS.
2Ki 14:26 nor any left, nor any *h'* for Israel.
Job 30:13 my calamity, they have no *h'*.
Ps 10:14 thou art the *h'* of the fatherless.
30:10 upon me: Lord, be thou my *h'*.
54: 4 Behold, God is mine *h'*: the Lord is
72:12 poor also, and him that hath no *h'*.
Jer 47: 4 and Zidon every *h'* that remaineth:
Ro 16: 9 Salute Urbane, our *h'* in Christ,
Heb 13: 6 Lord is my *h'*, and I will not fear
helpers See also FELLOWHELPERS.
1Ch 12: 1 the mighty men, *h'* of the war.
18 unto thee, and peace be to thine *h'*,
Job 9:13 the proud *h'* do stoop under him.
Eze 30: 8 when all her *h'* shall be destroyed.
Na 3: 9 Put and Lubim were thy *h'*.
Ro 16: 3 and Aquila my *h'* in Christ Jesus:
2Co 1:24 your faith, but are *h'* of your joy:
helpeth
1Ch 12:18 thine helpers; for thy God *h'* thee.
Isa 31: 3 both he that *h'* shall fall, and he
Ro 8:26 the Spirit also *h'* our infirmities:
1Co 16:16 and to every one that *h'* with us,
helping
Ezr 5: 2 were the prophets of God *h'* them.
Ps 22: 1 why art thou so far from *h'* me,
2Co 1:11 Ye also *h'* together by prayer for us,
helps
Ac 27:17 they used *h'*, undergirding the ship
1Co 12:28 gifts of healings, *h'*, governments,
helve
De 19: 5 and the head slippeth from the *h'*,
hem See also HEMS.
Ex 28:33 upon the *h'* of it thou shall make
33 scarlet, round about the *h'* thereof:
34 upon the *h'* of the robe round
39:25 upon the *h'* of the robe, round
26 round about the *h'* of the robe to
M't 9:20 touched the *h'* of his garment:
14:36 only touch the *h'* of his garment:
Hemam (*he'-mam*) See also HOMAM.
Ge 36:22 of Lotan were Hori and *H'*;
Heman (*he'-man*)
1Ki 4:31 than Ethan the Ezrahite, and *H'*,
1Ch 2: 6 of Zerah; Zimri, and Ethan, and *H'*,
6:33 *H'* a singer, the son of Joel, the son
15:17 So the Levites appointed *H'* the son
19 the singers, *H'*, Asaph, and Ethan,
16:41 And with them *H'* and Jeduthun,
42 *H'* and Jeduthun with trumpets
25: 1 of the sons of Asaph, and of *H'*, and
4 Of *H'*: the son of *H'*; Bukkiah,
5 *H'* the king's seer in the words of
5 And God gave to *H'* fourteen sons
6 order to Asaph, Jeduthun, and *H'*.
2Ch 5:12 of Asaph, of *H'*, of Jeduthun, with
29:14 the sons of *H'*; Jehiel, and Shimei:
35:15 and Asaph, and *H'*, and Jeduthun
Ps 88: *title* Maschil of *H'* the Ezrahite.
Hemath (*he'-math*) See also HAMATH.
1Ch 2:55 the Kenites that came of *H'*, the
13: 5 even unto the entering of *H'*,
Am 6:14 the entering in of *H'* unto the
Hemdan (*hem'-dan*) See also AMRAM.
Ge 36:26 *H'*, and Eshban, and Ithran, and
hemlock
Ho 10: 4 as *h'* in the furrows of the field.
Am 6:12 the fruit of righteousness into *h'*:
hems
Ex 39:24 they made upon the *h'* of the robe
hen
M't 23:37 even as a *h'* gathereth her chickens
Lu 13:34 as a *h'* doth gather her brood under
Hen (*hen*)
Zec 6:14 and to *H'* the son of Zephaniah,
Hena (*he'-nah*)
2Ki 18:34 gods of Sepharvaim, *H'*, and Ivah?
19:13 city of Sepharvaim, of *H'*, and Ivah?
Isa 37:13 city of Sepharvaim, *H'*, and Ivah?
Henadad (*hen'-a-dad*)
Ezr 3: 9 the sons of *H'*, with their sons and
Ne 3:18 Bavai the son of *H'*, the ruler of the
24 him repaired Binnui the son of *H'*
10: 9 Binnui of the sons of *H'*, Kadmiel;
hence See also HENCEFORTH; HENCEFORWARD.
Ge 37:17 They are departed *h'*; for I heard
42:15 ye shall not go forth *h'*, except your
50:25 ye shall carry up my bones from *h'*.
Ex 11: 1 afterwards he will let you go *h'*:
1 surely thrust you out *h'* altogether.
13:19 carry up my bones away *h'* with you.
33: 1 and go up *h'*, thou and the people
15 go not with me, carry us not up *h'*.
De 9:12 Arise, get thee down quickly from *h'*,
Jos 4: 3 you *h'* out of the midst of Jordan,
J'g 6:18 Depart not *h'*, I pray thee, until I
Ru 2: 8 neither go from *h'*, but abide here
1Ki 17: 3 Get thee *h'*, and turn thee eastward,
Ps 39:13 strength, before I go *h'*, and be no more.
Isa 30:22 thou shalt say unto it, Get thee *h'*.
Jer 38:10 Take from *h'* thirty men with thee,
Zec 6: 7 Get you *h'*, walk to and fro through
M't 4:10 Get thee *h'*, Satan: for it is written,
17:20 Remove *h'* to yonder place; and it

Lu 4: 9 of God, cast thyself down from h':
13:31 Get thee out, and depart h': for
16:26 would pass from h' to you cannot;
Joh 2:16 Take these things h'; make not my
7: 3 Depart h', and go into Judæa, that
14:31 even so I do. Arise, let us go h'.
18:36 but now is my kingdom not from h'.
20:15 Sir, if thou have borne him h', tell me
Ac 1: 5 Holy Ghost not many days h'.
22:21 send thee far h' unto the Gentiles.
Jas 4: 1 come they not h', even of your lusts

henceforth
Ge 4:12 it shall not h' yield unto thee her
Nu 18:22 Israel h' come nigh the tabernacle
De 17:16 Ye shall h' return no more that
19:20 shall h' commit no more any such
J'g 2:21 will not h' drive out any from before
2Ki 5:17 for thy servant will h' offer neither
2Ch 16: 9 from h' thou shalt have wars.
Ps 125: 2 his people from h' even for ever.
131: 3 in the Lord from h' and for ever.
Isa 9: 7 with justice from h' even for ever.
52: 1 for h' there shall no more come into
59:21 saith the Lord, from h' and for ever.
Eze 36:12 shalt no more h' bereave them of
M't 23:39 Ye shall not see me h', till ye
26:29 I will not drink h' of this fruit of
Lu 1:48 from h' all generations shall call me
5:10 not; from h' thou shalt catch men.
12:52 h' there shall be five in one house
Joh 14: 7 from h' ye know him, and have seen
15:15 H' I call you not servants; for the
Ac 4:17 speak h' to no man in this name.
18: 6 from h' I will go unto the Gentiles.
Ro 6: 6 that h' we should not serve sin.
2Co 5:15 should not h' live unto themselves,
16 h' know we no man after
16 yet now h' know we him no more.
Ga 6:17 From h' let no man trouble me:
Eph 4:14 That we h' be no more children,
17 ye h' walk not as other Gentiles
2Ti 4: 8 H' there is laid up for me a crown
Heb10:13 From h' expecting till his enemies
Re 14:13 dead which die in the Lord from h':

henceforward
Nu 15:23 and h' among your generations;
M't 21:19 no fruit grow on thee h' for ever.

Henoch (*he'-nok*) See also ENOCH.
1Ch 1: 3 H', Methuselah, Lamech, Noah
33 Epher, and H', and Abido, and

Hepher (*he'-fer*) See also GATH-HEPHER; HEPHERITES.
Nu 26:32 of H', the family of the Hepherites.
33 Zelophehad the son of H' had no
27: 1 the son of H', the son of Gilead,
Jos 12:17 Tappuah, one; the king of H', one;
17: 2 for the children of H', and for the
3 But Zelophehad, the son of H', the
1Ki 4:10 Sochoh, and all the land of H':
1Ch 4: 6 Naarah bare him Ahuzam, and H',
11:36 H' the Mecherathite, Ahijah the

Hepherites (*he'-fer-ites*)
Nu 26:32 of Hepher, the family of the H'.

Hephzi-bah (*hef'-zi-bah*)
2Ki 21: 1 And his mother's name was H'.
Isa 62: 4 but thou shalt be called H', and

herald
Da 3: 4 Then an h' cried aloud, To you it is

herb See also HERBS.
Ge 1:11 the h' yielding seed, and the fruit
12 h' yielding seed after his kind, and
29 I have given you every h' bearing
30 have given every green h' for meat:
2: 5 every h' of the field before it grew:
3:18 and thou shalt eat the h' of the field;
9: 3 even as the green h' have I given
Ex 9:22 every h' of the field, throughout
25 the hail smote every h' of the field,
10:12 and eat every h' of the land, even all
15 and they did eat every h' of the land,
De 32: 2 the small rain upon the tender h',
2Ki 19:26 and as the green h', as the grass on
Job 8:12 it withereth before any other h'.
38:27 the bud of the tender h' to spring
Ps 37: 2 grass, and wither as the green h'.
104:14 and h' for the service of man: that
Isa 37:27 of the field, and as the green h', as
66:14 your bones shall flourish like an h':

herbs
Ex 10:15 the trees, or in the h' of the field,
12: 8 and with bitter h' they shall eat it.
Nu 9:11 with unleavened bread and bitter h'.
De 11:10 it with thy foot, as a garden of h':
1Ki 21: 2 I may have it for a garden of h',
2Ki 4:39 went out into the field to gather h',
Ps 105:35 did eat up all the h' in their land,
Pr 15:17 Better is a dinner of h' where love
27:25 h' of the mountains are gathered.
Isa 18: 4 like a clear heat upon h', and like
26:19 thy dew is as the dew of h', and the
42:15 and hills, and dry up all their h';
Jer 12: 4 and the h' of every field wither, for
M't 13:32 grown, it is the greatest among h',
M'r 4:32 up, and becometh greater than all h',
Lu 11:42 mint and rue and all manner of h',
Ro 14: 2 another, who is weak, eateth h'.
Heb 6: 7 and bringeth forth h' meet for them

herd See also HERDMAN; HERDS; SHEPHERD.
Ge 18: 7 And Abraham ran unto the h',
Le 1: 2 even of the h', and of the flock.
3 offering be a burnt sacrifice of the h',
Le 3: 1 peace offering, if he offer it of the h';
27:32 concerning the tithe of the h', or of
Nu 15: 3 the Lord, of the h', or of the flock:
De 12:21 shalt kill of thy h' and of thy flock,
15:19 that come of thy h' and of thy flock
16: 2 of the flock and the h', in the place
1Sa 11: 5 came after the h' out of the field
2Sa 12: 4 of his own flock and of his own h',
Jer 31:12 the young of the flock and of the h':
Jon 3: 7 man nor beast, h' nor flock, taste
Hab 3:17 and there shall be no h' in the stalls:
M't 8:30 them an h' of many swine feeding.
31 us to go away into the h' of swine.
32 they went into the h' of swine: and,
32 the whole h' of swine ran violently
M'r 5:11 mountains a great h' of swine feeding.
13 the h' ran violently down a steep place
Lu 8:32 an h' of many swine feeding on the
33 the h' ran violently down a steep place

herdman See also HERDMEN.
Am 7:14 but I was an h', and a gatherer of

herdmen
Ge 13: 7 between the h' of Abram's cattle
7 cattle and the h' of Lot's cattle:
8 between my h' and thy h'; for we be
26:20 And the h' of Gerar did strive with
20 of Gerar did strive with Isaac's h',
1Sa 21: 7 the chiefest of the h' that belonged to
Am 1: 1 who was among the h' of Tekoa,

herds See also SHEPHERDS.
Ge 13: 5 with Abram, had flocks, and h', and
24:35 hath given him flocks, and h', and
26:14 and possession of h', and great store
32: 7 the flocks, and h', and the camels,
33:13 and the flocks and h' with young are
45:10 and thy h', and all that thou hast:
46:32 and their h', and all that they have.
47: 1 and their h', and all that they have,
17 for the cattle of the h', and for the
18 my lord also hath our h' of cattle;
50: 8 their flocks, and their h', they left
Ex 10: 9 flocks and with our h' will we go;
24 your flocks and your h' be stayed:
12:32 take your flocks and your h', as ye
38 flocks, and h', even very much cattle
34: 3 flocks nor h' feed before that mount.
Nu 11:22 Shall the flocks and the h' be slain
De 8:13 when thy h' and thy flocks multiply,
12: 6 firstlings of your h' and of your
17 firstlings of thy h' or of thy flock,
14:23 the firstlings of thy h' and of thy
1Sa 30:20 David took all the flocks and the h',
2Sa 12: 2 had exceeding many flocks and h':
1Ch 27:29 And over the h' that fed in Sharon
29 over the h' that were in the valleys
2Ch 32:29 and possessions of flocks and h' in
Ne 10:36 firstlings of our h' and of our flocks,
Pr 27:23 thy flocks, and look well to thy h'.
Isa 65:10 a place for the h' to lie down in,
Jer 3:24 their flocks and their h', their sons
5:17 shall eat up thy flocks and thine h':
Hos 5: 6 and with their h' to seek the Lord;
Joe 1:18 the h' of cattle are perplexed,

here See also HEREAFTER; HEREBY; HEREIN; HEREOF; HERETOFORE; HEREUNTO; HEREWITH.
Ge 16:13 Have I also h' looked after him that
19:12 unto Lot, Hast thou h' any besides?
15 thy two daughters, which are h';
21:23 swear unto me h' by God that thou
22: 1 Abraham: and he said, Behold, h' I am.
5 Abide ye h' with the ass; and I and
7 and he said, H' am I, my son.
11 Abraham: and he said, H' am I.
24:13 Behold, I stand h' by the well of water;
27: 1 and he said unto him, Behold, h' am I.
18 H' am I; who art thou, my son?
31:11 saying, Jacob: And I said, H' am I.
37 set it h' before my brethren and thy
37:13 And he said to him, H' am I.
40:15 and h' also have I done nothing
42:33 leave one of your brethren h' with me,
46: 2 Jacob, Jacob. And he said, H' am I.
47:23 h' is seed for you, and ye shall sow the
Ex 3: 4 Moses. And he said, H' am I.
24:14 Tarry ye h' for us, until we come
33:16 wherein shall it be known h' that I
Nu 14:40 Lo we be h', and will go up unto the
22: 8 said unto them, Lodge h' this night.
19 pray you, tarry ye also h' this night,
23: 1 unto Balak, Build me h' seven altars,
1 and prepare me h' seven oxen and
15 Stand h' by thy burnt-offering,
29 Balak, Build me h' seven altars,
29 and prepare me h' seven bullocks
32: 6 go to war, and shall ye sit h'?
16 will build sheepfolds h' for our cattle,
De 5: 3 who are all of us h' alive this day.
31 But as for thee, stand thou h' by me,
12: 8 the things that we do h' this day,
29:15 him that standeth h' with us this day
15 him that is not h' with us this day:
Jos 18: 6 cast lots for you h' before the Lord
8 that I may h' cast lots for you before
21: 9 cities which are h' mentioned by name,
J'g 4:20 thee, and say, Is there any man h'?
18: 3 this place? and what hast thou h'?
19: 9 lodge h', that thine heart may be
24 Behold, h' is my daughter a maiden,
20: 7 give h' your advice and counsel.
Ru 2: 8 but abide h' fast by my maidens:
4: 1 turn aside, sit down h'. And he
2 Sit ye down h'. And they sat down.
1Sa 1:26 the woman that stood by thee h',
3: 4 Samuel: and he answered, H' am I.
5 he said, H' am I; for thou calledst
1Sa 3: 6, 8 H' am I; for thou didst call me.
16 my son. And he answered, H' am I.
9: 8 I have h' at hand the fourth part of
11 and said unto them, Is the seer h'?
12: 3 behold, h' I am: witness against me
14:34 sheep, and slay them h', and eat;
16:11 Jesse, Are h' all thy children?
21: 8 not h' under thine hand spear or
9 behold, it is h' wrapped in a cloth
9 for there is no other save that h'.
22:12 he answered, H' I am, my lord.
23: 3 Behold, we be afraid h' in Judah:
29: 3 What do these Hebrews h'? And
2Sa 1: 7 And I answered, H' am I.
11:12 Tarry h' to day also, and to-morrow
15:26 behold, h' am I, let him do to me as
18:30 Turn aside, and stand h'. And he
20: 4 three days, and be thou h' present.
24:22 behold, h' be oxen for burnt sacrifice,
1Ki 2:30 And he said, Nay; but I will die h'.
18: 8, 11 tell thy lord, Behold, Elijah is h'.
14 tell thy lord, Behold, Elijah is h'.
19: 9, 13 What doest thou h', Elijah?
20:40 thy servant was busy h' and there,
22: 7 Is there not h' a prophet of the
2Ki 2: 2 Tarry h', I pray thee; for the Lord
4 tarry h', I pray thee; for the Lord
6 Tarry, I pray thee, h'; for the Lord
3:11 Is there not h' a prophet of the Lord,
11 H' is Elisha, the son of Shaphat,
7: 3 Why sit we h', until we die?
4 and if we sit still h', we die also.
10:23 be h' with you none of the servants
1Ch 29:17 joy thy people, which are present h',
Job 38:11 h' shall thy proud waves be stayed?
35 and say unto thee, H' we are?
Ps 132:14 h' will I dwell; for I have desired it.
Isa 6: 8 Then said I, H' am I; send me.
21: 9 behold, h' cometh a chariot of men,
22:16 What hast thou h'? and whom
16 and whom hast thou h', that thou
16 hast hewed thee out a sepulchre h',
28:10 line; h' a little, and there a little:
13 line; h' a little, and there a little;
52: 5 what have I h', saith the Lord, that
58: 9 shalt cry, and he shall say, H' I am.
Eze 8: 6 house of Israel committeth h',
9 wicked abominations that they do h'.
17 abominations which they commit h'?
Ho 7: 9 gray hairs are h' and there upon
M't 12:41 behold, a greater than Jonas is h'.
42 behold, a greater than Solomon is h'.
14: 8 Give me h' John Baptist's head in a
17 We have h' but five loaves, and two
16:28 standing h', which shall not taste
17: 4 Lord, it is good for us to be h':
4 let us make h' three tabernacles;
20: 6 Why stand ye h' all the day idle?
24: 2 shall not be left h' one stone upon
23 unto you, Lo, h' is Christ, or there;
26:36 Sit ye h', while I go and pray yonder.
38 tarry ye h', and watch with me.
28: 6 He is not h': for he is risen, as
M'r 6: 3 and are not his sisters h' with us?
8: 4 with bread h' in the wilderness?
9: 1 there be some of them that stand h',
5 Master, it is good for us to be h':
13: 1 of stones and what buildings are h'!
21 Lo, h' is Christ; or, lo, he is there;
14:32 Sit ye h', while I shall pray.
34 unto death: tarry ye h', and watch.
16: 6 he is risen; he is not h': behold the
Lu 4:23 Capernaum, do...h' in thy country.
9:12 for we are h' in a desert place.
27 standing h', which shall not taste
33 Master, it is good for us to be h':
11:31 behold, a greater than Solomon is h'.
32 behold, a greater than Jonas is h'.
17:21 shall they say, Lo h'! or, lo there!
23 And they shall say to you, See h'; or
19:20 Lord, behold, h' is thy pound, which I
22:38 Lord, behold, h' are two swords.
24: 6 He is not h', but is risen: remember
41 unto them, Have ye h' any meat?
Joh 6: 9 There is a lad h', which hath five
11:21, 32 if thou hadst been h', my brother
Ac 4:10 doth this man stand h' before you
9:10 And he said, Behold, I am h', Lord.
14 And h' he hath authority from the
10:33 Now therefore are we all h' present
16:28 thyself no harm: for we are all h'.
24:19 ought to have been h' before thee,
20 Or else let these same h' say, if they
25:24 men which are h' present with us,
24 me, both at Jerusalem, and also h',
Col 4: 9 you all things which are done h'.
Heb 7: 8 And h' men that die receive tithes;
13:14 For h' have we no continuing city,
Jas 2: 3 unto him, Sit thou h' in a good place:
3 there, or sit h' under my footstool:
1Pe 1:17 the time of your sojourning h' in fear.
Re 13:10 H' is the patience and the faith of
18 H' is wisdom. Let him that hath
14:12 H' is the patience of the saints:
12 h' are they that keep the
17: 9 h' is the mind which hath wisdom.

hereafter
Isa 41:23 Shew the things that are to come h',
Eze 20:39 and h' also, if ye will not hearken
Da 2:29 what should come to pass h':
45 what shall come to pass h':
M't 26:64 H' shall ye see the Son of man
M'r 11:14 man eat fruit of thee h' for ever.
Lu 22:69 H' shall the Son of man sit on
Joh 1:51 H' ye shall see heaven open,
13: 7 now; but thou shalt know h'.

Joh 14:30 H' I will not talk much with you:
1Ti 1:16 should h' believe on him to life
Re 1:19 the things which shall be h';
4: 1 thee things which must be h'.
9:12 there come two woes more h'.
hereby
Ge 42:15 H' ye shall be proved: By the life
33 H' shall I know that ye are true men;
Nu 16:28 And Moses said, H' ye shall know
Jos 3:10 And Joshua said, H' ye shall know
1Co 4: 4 yet am I not h' justified: but
1Jo 2: 3 And h' we do know that we do
5 h' know we that we are in him.
3:16 H' perceive we the love of God,
19 And h' we know that we are of
24 h' we know that he abideth in
4: 2 H' know ye the Spirit of God:
6 H' know we the spirit of truth,
13 H' know we that we dwell in
herein
Ge 34:22 Only h' will the men consent unto
2Ch 16: 9 H' thou hast done foolishly:
Joh 4:37 And h' is that saying true, One
9:30 Why h' is a marvellous thing,
15: 8 H' is my Father glorified, that
Ac 24:16 And h' do I exercise myself, to
2Co 8:10 And h' I give my advice: for
1Jo 4:10 H' is love, not that we loved God,
17 H' is our love made perfect,
hereof
M't 9:26 the fame h' went abroad into all
Heb 5: 3 And by reason h' he ought, as for
Heres (*he'-res*) See also KIR-HERES; TIMMATH-HERES.
J'g 1:35 Amorites would dwell in mount H'
Heresh (*he'-resh*)
1Ch 9:15 Bakbakkar, H', and Galal, and
heresies
1Co 11:19 there must be also h' among you,
Ga 5:20 wrath, strife, seditions, h', envyings,
2Pe 2: 1 shall bring in damnable h', even
heresy See also HERESIES.
Ac 24:14 after the way which they call h', so
heretick
Tit 3:10 A man that is an h' after the first
heretofore
Ex 4:10 eloquent, neither h', nor since
5: 7 straw to make brick, as h':
8 the bricks,...they did make h',
14 yesterday and to day, as h'?
Jos 3: 4 ye have not passed this way h'.
Ru 2:11 people...thou knewest not h'.
1Sa 4: 7 hath not been such a thing h'.
2Co 13: 2 write to them which h' have sinned,
hereunto
Ec 2:25 who else can hasten h', more than I?
1Pe 2:21 For even h' were ye called:
herewith
Eze 16:29 and yet thou wast not satisfied h'.
Mal 3:10 prove me now h', saith the Lord of
heritage See also HERITAGES.
Ex 6: 8 and I will give it you for an h':
Job 20:29 the h' appointed unto him by God.
27:13 and the h' of oppressors, which they
Ps 16: 6 places; yea, I have a goodly h'.
61: 5 the h' of those that fear thy name.
94: 5 people, O Lord, and afflict thine h'.
111: 6 may give them the h' of the heathen.
119:111 testimonies have I taken as an h'
127: 3 Lo, children are an h' of the Lord:
135:12 And gave their land for an h',
12 an h' unto Israel his people.
136:21 And gave their land for an h': for his
22 Even an h' unto Israel his servant:
Isa 54:17 the h' of the servants of the Lord,
58:14 thee with the h' of Jacob thy father:
Jer 2: 7 and made mine h' an abomination.
3:19 a goodly h' of the hosts of nations?
12: 7 I have left mine h'; I have given the
8 Mine h' is unto me as a lion in the
9 Mine h' is unto me as a speckled
15 every man to his h', and every man
17: 4 discontinue from thine h' that I gave
50:11 O ye destroyers of mine h', because
Joe 2:17 give not thine h' to reproach, that
3: 2 for my people and for my h' Israel,
Mic 2: 2 his house, even a man and his h'.
7:14 the flock of thine h', which dwell
18 the remnant of his h'? he retaineth
Mal 1: 3 laid his mountains and his h' waste
1Pe 5: 3 as being lords over God's h', but
heritages
Isa 49: 8 to cause to inherit the desolate h';
Hermas (*her'-mas*)
Ro 16:14 Phlegon, H', Patrobas, Hermes,
Hermes (*her'-mees*)
Ro 16:14 H', and the brethren which are
Hermogenes (*her-moj'-e-nees*)
2Ti 1:15 of whom are Phygellus and H'.
Hermon (*her'-mon*) See also BAAL-HERMON; HERMONITES.
De 3: 8 the river of Arnon unto mount H';
9 which H' the Sidonians call Sirion;
4:48 even unto mount Sion, which is H',
Jos 11: 3 under H' in the land of Mizpeh.
17 valley of Lebanon under mount H':
12: 1 unto mount H', and all the plain on
5 And reigned in mount H', and in
13: 5 from Baal-gad under mount H' unto
11 and all mount H', and all Bashan
1Ch 5:23 and Senir, and unto mount H'.
Ps 89:12 Tabor and H' shall rejoice in thy
133: 3 As the dew of H', and as the dew
Ca 4: 8 from the top of Shenir and H',
Hermonites (*her'-mon-ites*) See also HERMON.
Ps 42: 6 land of Jordan, and of the H',
Herod (*her'-od*) See also HERODIANS; HEROD'S.
M't 2: 1 in the days of H' the king, behold,
3 When H' the king had heard these
7 Then H', when he had privily
12 that they should not return to H',
13 for H' will seek the young child to
15 was there until the death of H':
16 Then H', when he saw that he was
19 But when H' was dead, behold, an
22 in the room of his father H', he
14: 1 At that time H' the tetrarch heard
3 For H' had laid hold on John, and
6 danced before them, and pleased H'.
M'r 6:14 king H' heard of him; for his name
16 But when H' heard thereof, he said,
17 H' himself had sent forth and laid
18 For John had said unto H', It is not
20 For H' feared John, knowing that
21 H' on his birthday made a supper
22 came in, and danced, and pleased H'
8:15 Pharisees, and of the leaven of H'.
Lu 1: 5 There was in the days of H', the
3: 1 and H' being tetrarch of Galilee,
19 H' the tetrarch, being reproved
19 for all the evils which H' had done,
9: 7 H' the tetrarch heard of all that was
9 And H' said, John have I beheaded:
13:31 depart hence: for H' will kill thee.
23: 7 he sent him to H', who himself also
8 And when H' saw Jesus, he was
11 And H' with his men of war set him
12 Pilate and H' were made friends
15 nor yet H': for I sent you to him;
Ac 4:27 whom thou hast anointed, both H'
12: 1 Now about that time H' the king
6 H' would have brought him forth,
11 delivered me out of the hand of H',
19 And when H' had sought for him,
20 H' was highly displeased with them
21 And upon a set day H', arrayed in
13: 1 brought up with H' the tetrarch,
Herodians (*he-ro'-de-uns*)
M't 22:16 their disciples with the H', saying,
M'r 3: 6 took counsel with the H' against
12:13 of the Pharisees and of the H', to
Herodias (*he-ro'-de-as*) See also HERODIAS'.
M't 14: 6 the daughter of H' danced before
M'r 6:19 Therefore H' had a quarrel against
22 when the daughter of the said H'
Lu 3:19 being reproved by him for H' his
Herodias' (*he-ro'-de-as*)
M't 14: 3 and put him in prison for H' sake,
M'r 6:17 bound him in prison for H' sake,
Herodion (*he-ro'-de-on*)
Ro 16:11 Salute H' my kinsman. Greet
Herod's (*her'-ods*)
M't 14: 6 when H' birthday was kept, the
Lu 8: 3 the wife of Chuza H' steward, and
23: 7 he belonged unto H' jurisdiction,
Ac 23:35 him to be kept in H' judgment hall.
heron
Le 11:19 stork, the h' after her kind, and the
De 14:18 and the h' after her kind, and the
hers See also HERSELF.
De 21:15 if the firstborn be h' that was hated:
1Sa 25:42 with five damsels of h' that went after
2Ki 8: 6 Restore all that was h', and all the
Job 39:16 ones, as though they were not h': her
herself
Ge 18:12 Therefore Sarah laughed within h',
20: 5 even she h', said, He is my brother:
24:65 she took a vail, and covered h'.
38:14 covered...with a vail, and wrapped h',
Ex 2: 5 came down to wash h' at the river;
Le 15:28 she shall number to h' seven days,
21: 9 if she profane h' by playing the whore,
Nu 22:25 she thrust h' unto the wall: and
30: 3 and bind h' by a bond, being in her
J'g 5:29 her, yea, she returned answer to h',
Ru 2:10 her face, and bowed h' to the ground,
1Sa 4:19 husband were dead, she bowed h' and
25:23 on her face, and bowed h' to the ground,
41 she arose, and bowed h' on her face
2Sa 11: 2 the roof he saw a woman washing h';
1Ki 14: 5 she shall feign h' to be another woman.
2Ki 4:37 and bowed h' to the ground, and took
Job 39:18 What time she lifteth up h' on high,
Ps 84: 3 and the swallow a nest for h', where
Pr 31:22 She maketh h' coverings of tapestry;
Isa 5:14 Therefore hell hath enlarged h',
34:14 there, and find for h' a place of rest.
61:10 as a bride adorneth h' with her jewels.
Jer 3:11 backsliding Israel hath justified h'
4:31 Zion, that bewaileth h', that spreadeth
49:24 and turneth h' to flee, and fear hath
Eze 22: 3 maketh idols against h' to defile
3 maketh idols against..., to defile h'.
23: 7 with all their idols she defiled h'.
24:12 She hath wearied h' with lies, and her
Ho 2:13 she decked h' with her earrings and
Zec 9: 3 And Tyrus did build h' a strong hold,
M't 9:21 For she said within h', If I may but
M'r 4:28 the earth bringeth forth fruit of h';
Lu 1:24 and hid h' five months, saying,
13:11 together, and could in no wise lift up h'.
Joh 20:14 she turned h' back, and saw Jesus
16 She turned h', and saith unto him,
Heb 11:11 Through faith also Sara h' received
Re 2:20 woman Jezebel, which calleth h' a
18: 7 How much she hath glorified h', and
19: 7 and his wife hath made h' ready.
Hesed (*he'-sed*) See also JUSHAB-HESED.
1Ki 4:10 The son of H', in Aruboth; to him
Heshbon (*hesh'-bon*)
Nu 21:25 in H', and in all the villages thereof.
26 For H' was the city of Sihon the king
27 Come into H', let the city of Sihon
28 For there is a fire gone out of H',
30 H' is perished even unto Dibon, and
34 of the Amorites, which dwelt at H'.
32: 3 Nimrah, and H', and Elealeh, and
37 the children of Reuben built H',
De 1: 4 of the Amorites, which dwelt in H',
2:24 hand Sihon the Amorite, king of H',
26 unto Sihon king of H' with words
30 Sihon king of H' would not let us
3: 2 of the Amorites, which dwelt at H'.
6 as we did unto Sihon king of H',
4:46 of the Amorites, who dwelt at H',
29: 7 unto this place, Sihon the king of H',
Jos 9:10 beyond Jordan, to Sihon king of H',
12: 2 of the Amorites, who dwelt in H',
5 the border of Sihon king of H'.
13:10 the Amorites, which reigned in H',
17 H', and all her cities that are in the
21 the Amorites, which reigned in H',
26 And from H' unto Ramath-mizpeh,
27 the kingdom of Sihon king of H',
21:39 H' with her suburbs, Jazer with her
J'g 11:19 of the Amorites, the king of H';
26 While Israel dwelt in H' and her
1Ch 6:81 H' with her suburbs, and Jazer with
Ne 9:22 and the land of the king of H', and
Ca 7: 4 thine eyes like the fishpools in H',
Isa 15: 4 And H' shall cry, and Elealeh: their
16: 8 fields of H' languish, and the vine
9 will water thee with my tears, O H',
Jer 48: 2 in H' they have devised evil against
34 the cry of H', even unto Elealeh,
45 fled stood under the shadow of H'
45 but a fire shall come forth out of H',
49: 3 Howl, O H', for Ai is spoiled: cry,
Heshmon (*hesh'-mon*) See also AZMON.
Jos 15:27 And Hazar-gaddah, and H', and
Heth (*heth*)
Ge 10:15 begat Sidon his firstborn, and H',
23: 3 spake unto the sons of H', saying,
5 And the children of H' answered
7 the land, even to the children of H'.
10 dwelt among the children of H':
10 the audience of the children of H',
16 in the audience of the sons of H',
18 the presence of the children of H',
20 of a buryingplace by the sons of H'.
25:10 purchased of the sons of H':
27:46 because of the daughters of H':
46 take a wife of the daughters of H',
49:32 therein was from the children of H'.
1Ch 1:13 begat Zidon his firstborn, and H',
Hethlon (*heth'-lon*)
Eze 47:15 way of H', as men go to Zedad;
48: 1 end to the coast of the way of H',
hew See also HEWED; HEWETH; HEWN.
Ex 34: 1 H' thee two tables of stone like
De 10: 1 H' thee two tables of stone like
12: 3 shall h' down the graven images of
19: 5 with his neighbour to h' wood, and
1Ki 5: 6 that they h' me cedar trees out of
6 to h' timber like unto the Sidonians.
18 and Hiram's builders did h' them,
1Ch 22: 2 set masons to h' wrought stones
2Ch 2: 2 thousand to h' in the mountain,
Jer 6: 6 H' ye down trees, and cast them
Da 4:14 H' down the tree, and cut off his
23 H' the tree down, and destroy it;
hewed See also HEWN.
Ex 34: 4 And he h' two tables of stone like
De 10: 3 and h' two tables of stone like unto
1Sa 11: 7 of oxen, and h' them in pieces,
15:33 And Samuel h' Agag in pieces
1Ki 5:17 costly stones, and h' stones, to lay
6:36 with three rows of h' stone, and a
7: 9 to the measures of h' stones, sawed
11 after the measures of h' stones,
12 with three rows of h' stones, and a
2Ki 12:12 and to buy timber and h' stone to
Isa 22:16 thou hast h' thee out a sepulchre
Jer 2:13 and h' them out cisterns, broken
Ho 6: 5 have I h' them by the prophets;
hewer See also HEWERS.
De 29:11 the h' of thy wood unto the drawer
hewers
Jos 9:21 let them be h' of wood and drawers
23 bondmen, and h' of wood and
27 make them that day h' of wood and
1Ki 5:15 thousand h' in the mountains;
2Ki 12:12 masons, and h' of stone, and to buy
1Ch 22:15 h' and workers of stone and timber,
2Ch 2:10 thy servants, the h' that cut timber,
18 thousand to be h' in the mountain
Jer 46:22 her with axes, as h' of wood.
heweth
Isa 10:15 axe boast itself against him that h'
22:16 as he that h' him out a sepulchre
44:14 He h' him down cedars, and taketh
hewn See also HEWED.
Ex 20:25 thou shalt not build it of h' stone:
2Ki 22: 6 timber and h' stone to repair the
2Ch 34:11 to buy h' stone, and timber for
Pr 9: 1 she hath h' out her seven pillars:
Isa 9:10 but we will build with h' stones:

Isa 10:33 ones of stature shall be *h'* down,
33: 9 Lebanon is ashamed and *h'* down:
51: 1 unto the rock whence ye are *h'*,
La 3: 9 inclosed my ways with *h'* stone,
Eze 40:42 four tables were of *h'* stone for the
Am 5:11 ye have built houses of *h'* stone,
M't 3:10 is *h'* down, and cast into the fire.
7:19 is *h'* down, and cast into the fire.
27:60 which he had *h'* out in the rock;
M'r 15:46 in a sepulchre which was *h'* out of a
Lu 3: 9 is *h'* down, and cast into the fire.
23:53 a sepulchre that was *h'* in stone,

Hezeki (*hez'-e-ki*)
1Ch 8:17 and Meshullam, and *H'*, and

Hezekiah (*hez-e-ki'-ah*) See also EZEKIAS; HIZKIAH.
2Ki 16:20 *H'* his son reigned in his stead.
18: 1 that *H'* the son of Ahaz king of
9 pass in the fourth year of king *H'*,
10 even in the sixth year of *H'*, that
13 fourteenth year of king *H'* did
14 And *H'* king of Judah sent to the
14 king of Assyria appointed unto *H'*
15 And *H'* gave him all the silver that
16 At that time did *H'* cut off the gold
16 pillars which *H'* king of Judah had
17 from Lachish to king *H'* with a
19 Speak ye now to *H'*, Thus saith
22 whose altars *H'* hath taken away,
29 saith the king, Let not *H'* deceive
30 Neither let *H'* make you trust in the
31 Hearken not to *H'*: for thus saith
32 and hearken not unto *H'*, when he
37 to *H'* with their clothes rent, and
19: 1 when king *H'* heard it, that he rent
3 Thus saith *H'*, This day is a day of
5 servants of king *H'* came to Isaiah.
9 he sent messengers again unto *H'*,
10 Thus shall ye speak to *H'* king of
14 And *H'* received the letter of the
14 and *H'* went up into the house of
15 And *H'* prayed before the Lord,
20 Isaiah the son of Amoz sent to *H'*,
20: 1 those days was *H'* sick unto death.
3 in thy sight. And *H'* wept sore.
5 Turn again, and tell *H'* the captain
8 And *H'* said unto Isaiah, What
10 *H'* answered, It is a light thing for
12 sent letters and a present unto *H'*:
12 he had heard that *H'* had been sick.
13 And *H'* hearkened unto them, and
13 dominion, that *H'* shewed them not.
14 Isaiah the prophet unto king *H'*,
14 And *H'* said, They are come from
15 And *H'* answered, All the things
16 Isaiah said unto *H'*, Hear the word
19 Then said *H'* unto Isaiah, Good is
20 And the rest of the acts of *H'*, and
21 And *H'* slept with his fathers: and
21: 3 high places which *H'* his father had
1Ch 3:13 Ahaz his son, *H'* his son, Manasseh
23 of Neariah: Elioenai, and *H'*, and
4:41 came in the days of *H'* king of
2Ch 28:27 *H'* his son reigned in his stead.
29: 1 *H'* began to reign when he was five
18 Then they went into *H'* the king,
20 Then *H'* the king rose early, and
27 And *H'* commanded to offer the
30 *H'* the king and the princes
31 Then *H'* answered and said, Now
36 And *H'* rejoiced, and all the people,
30: 1 And *H'* sent to all Israel and Judah,
18 But *H'* prayed for them, saying, The
20 Lord hearkened to *H'*, and healed
22 *H'* spake comfortably unto all the
24 For *H'* king of Judah did give to
31: 2 *H'* appointed the courses of the
8 when *H'* and the princes came and
9 *H'* questioned with the priests
11 Then *H'* commanded to prepare
13 the commandment of *H'* the king,
20 thus did *H'* throughout all Judah,
32: 2 when *H'* saw that Sennacherib was
8 themselves upon the words of *H'*
9 unto *H'* king of Judah, and unto all
11 Doth not *H'* persuade you to give
12 Hath not the same *H'* taken away
15 therefore let not *H'* deceive you,
16 God, and against his servant *H'*.
17 so shall not the God of *H'* deliver
20 And for this cause *H'* the king,
22 Lord saved *H'* and the inhabitants
23 and presents to *H'* king of Judah:
24 those days *H'* was sick to the death,
25 *H'* rendered not again according
26 *H'* humbled himself for the pride
26 not upon them in the days of *H'*.
27 *H'* had exceeding much riches and
30 same *H'* also stopped the upper
30 And *H'* prospered in all his works.
32 the rest of the acts of *H'*, and his
33 *H'* slept with his fathers, and they
33: 3 high places which *H'* his father had
Ezr 2:16 The children of Ater of *H'*, ninety
Ne 7:21 The children of Ater of *H'*, ninety
Pr 25: 1 men of *H'* king of Judah copied out.
Isa 1: 1 Ahaz, and *H'*, kings of Judah.
36: 1 in the fourteenth year of king *H'*,
2 unto king *H'* with a great army.
4 Say ye now to *H'*, Thus saith the
7 whose altars *H'* hath taken away,
14 saith the king, Let not *H'* deceive
15 Neither let *H'* make you trust in the
16 Hearken not to *H'*: for thus saith
18 Beware lest *H'* persuade you,

Isa 36:22 to *H'* with their clothes rent, and
37: 1 when king *H'* heard it, that he rent
3 Thus saith *H'*, This day is a day of
5 servants of king *H'* came to Isaiah.
9 he sent messengers to *H'*, saying,
10 Thus shall ye speak to *H'* king of
14 And *H'* received the letter from the
14 and *H'* went up unto the house of
15 *H'* prayed unto the Lord, saying,
21 Isaiah the son of Amoz sent unto *H'*,
38: 1 those days was *H'* sick unto death.
2 Then *H'* turned his face toward the
3 in thy sight. And *H'* wept sore.
5 Go, and say to *H'*, Thus saith the
9 The writing of *H'* king of Judah,
22 *H'* also had said, What is the sign
39: 1 sent letters and a present to *H'*:
2 *H'* was glad of them, and shewed
2 dominion, that *H'* shewed them not
3 Isaiah the prophet unto king *H'*,
3 And *H'* said, They are come from
4 And *H'* answered, All that is in mine
5 Then said Isaiah to *H'*, Hear the
8 Then said *H'* to Isaiah, Good is the
Jer 15: 4 because of Manasseh the son of *H'*
26:18 prophesied in the days of *H'* king
19 Did *H'* king of Judah and all Judah
Ho 1: 1 Uzziah, Jotham, Ahaz, and *H'*, kings
Mic 1: 1 the days of Jotham, Ahaz, and *H'*,

Hezion (*he'-zi-on*)
1Ki 15:18 the son of *H'*, king of Syria, that

Hezir (*he'-zur*)
1Ch 24:15 seventeenth to *H'*, the eighteenth
Ne 10:20 Magpiash, Meshullam, *H'*,

Hezrai (*hez'-rahee*) See also HEZRO.
2Sa 23:35 *H'* the Carmelite, Paarai the

Hezro (*hez'-ro*) See also HEZRAI.
1Ch 11:37 *H'* the Carmelite, Naarai the son

Hezron (*hez'-ron*) See also HAZOR; HEZRONITES; HEZRON'S.
Ge 46: 9 Hanoch, and Phallu, and *H'*, and
12 sons of Pharez were *H'* and Hamul.
Ex 6:14 Hanoch, and Pallu, *H'*, and Carmi:
Nu 26: 6 Of *H'*, the family of the Hezronites:
21 of *H'*, the family of the Hezronites:
Jos 15: 3 and passed along to *H'*, and went
25 Kerioth, and *H'*, which is Hazor,
Ru 4:18 of Pharez: Pharez begat *H'*,
19 And *H'* begat Ram, and Ram begat
1Ch 2: 5 The sons of Pharez; *H'*, and Hamul.
9 The sons also of *H'*, that were born
18 Caleb the son of *H'* begat children
21 *H'* went in to the daughter of Machir
24 And after that *H'* was dead in
25 Jerahmeel the firstborn of *H'* were,
4: 1 The sons of Judah; Pharez, *H'*, and
5: 3 were, Hanoch, and Pallu, *H'*, and

Hezronites (*hez'-ron-ites*)
Nu 26: 6 Of Hezron, the family of the *H'*:
21 of Hezron, the family of the *H'*:

Hezron's (*hez'-ronz*)
1Ch 2:24 Abiah *H'* wife bare him Ashur

hid See also HIDDEN.
Ge 3: 8 Adam and his wife *h'* themselves
10 I was naked; and I *h'* myself.
4:14 and from thy face shall I be *h'*;
35: 4 and Jacob *h'* them under the oak
Ex 2: 2 child, she *h'* him three months.
12 Egyptian, and *h'* him in the sand.
3: 6 And Moses *h'* his face; for he was
Le 4:13 and the thing be *h'* from the eyes
5: 3 defiled withal, and it be *h'* from him;
4 with an oath, and it be *h'* from him;
Nu 5:13 be *h'* from the eyes of her husband,
De 33:19 and of treasures *h'* in the sand.
Jos 2: 4 took the two men, and *h'* them,
6 *h'* them with the stalks of flax,
6:17 because she *h'* the messengers
25 because she *h'* the messengers,
7:21 are *h'* in the earth in the midst
22 behold, it was *h'* in his tent, and the
10:16 five kings fled, and *h'* themselves
17 five kings are found *h'* in a cave
27 cave wherein they had been *h'*,
J'g 9: 5 Jerubbaal was left; for he *h'* himself.
1Sa 3:18 whit, and *h'* nothing from him.
10:22 hath *h'* himself among the stuff.
14:11 holes where they had *h'* themselves.
22 which had *h'* themselves in mount
20:24 So David *h'* himself in the field:
2Sa 17: 9 he is *h'* now in some pit, or in some
18:13 there is no matter *h'* from the king,
1Ki 10: 3 was not any thing *h'* from the king,
18: 4 and *h'* them by fifty in a cave, and
13 how I *h'* an hundred men of the
2Ki 4:27 and the Lord hath *h'* it from me,
6:29 eat him: and she hath *h'* her son.
7: 8 and raiment, and went and *h'* it;
8 thence also, and went and *h'* it.
11: 2 and they *h'* him, even him and his
3 he was with her *h'* in the house of
1Ch 21:20 four sons with him *h'* themselves.
2Ch 9: 2 nothing *h'* from Solomon which
22: 9 for he was *h'* in Samaria, and
11 of Ahaziah, *h'* him from Athaliah,
12 *h'* in the house of God six years:
Job 3:10 nor *h'* sorrow from mine eyes.
21 for it more than for *h'* treasures;
23 given to a man whose way is *h'*,
5:21 Thou shalt be *h'* from the scourge
6:16 ice, and wherein the snow is *h'*:
10:13 things hast thou *h'* in thine heart:
15:18 their fathers, and have not *h'* it:
17: 4 For thou hast *h'* their heart from

Job 20:26 darkness shall be *h'* in his secret
28:11 thing that is *h'* bringeth he forth
21 Seeing it is *h'* from the eyes of all
29: 8 men saw me, and *h'* themselves:
38:30 The waters are *h'* as with a stone,
Ps 9:15 net which they *h'* is their own foot
17:14 thou fillest with thy *h'* treasure:
19: 6 there is nothing *h'* from the heat
22:24 neither hath he *h'* his face from him;
32: 5 and mine iniquity have I not *h'*.
35: 7 have they *h'* for me their net in a
8 net that he hath *h'* catch himself:
38: 9 my groaning is not *h'* from thee.
40:10 I have not *h'* thy righteousness
55:12 then I would have *h'* myself from
69: 5 and my sins are not *h'* from thee.
119:11 Thy word have I *h'* in mine heart,
139:15 My substance was not *h'* from
140: 5 The proud have *h'* a snare for me,
Pr 2: 4 for her as for *h'* treasures;
Isa 28:15 falsehood have we *h'* ourselves:
29:14 of their prudent men shall be *h'*.
40:27 My way is *h'* from the Lord, and my
42:22 and they are *h'* in prison houses:
49: 2 shadow of his hand hath he *h'* me.
2 in his quiver hath he *h'* me;
50: 6 I *h'* not my face from shame and
53: 3 and we *h'* as it were our faces from
54: 8 In a little wrath I *h'* my face from
57:17 I *h'* me, and was wroth, and he went
59: 2 your sins have *h'* his face from you,
64: 7 for thou hast *h'* thy face from us,
65:16 because they are *h'* from mine eyes.
Jer 13: 5 So I went, and *h'* it by Euphrates,
7 from the place where I had *h'* it:
16:17 they are not *h'* from my face,
17 is their iniquity *h'* from mine eyes.
18:22 take me, and *h'* snares for my feet.
33: 5 I have *h'* my face from this city.
36:26 the prophet: but the Lord *h'* them.
43:10 upon these stones that I have *h'*;
Eze 22:26 *h'* their eyes from my sabbaths,
39:23 therefore *h'* I my face from them,
24 them, and *h'* my face from them.
Ho 5: 3 and Israel is not *h'* from me:
13:12 is bound up; his sin is *h'*.
14 repentance shall be *h'* from mine
Am 9: 3 be *h'* from my sight in the bottom
Na 3:11 thou shalt be *h'*, thou also shalt
Zep 2: 3 it may be ye shall be *h'* in the day
M't 5:14 that is set on an hill cannot be *h'*.
10:26 and *h'*, that shall not be known.
11:25 because thou hast *h'* these things
13:33 and *h'* in three measures of meal,
44 is like unto treasure *h'* in a field;
25:18 the earth, and *h'* his lord's money.
25 went and *h'* thy talent in the earth:
M'r 4:22 For there is nothing *h'*, which shall
7:24 know it: but he could not be *h'*.
Lu 1:24 and *h'* herself five months, saying,
8:17 neither any thing *h'*, that shall not
47 saw that she was not *h'*, she came
9:45 and it was *h'* from them, that they
10:21 that thou hast *h'* these things from
12: 2 neither *h'*, that shall not be known.
13:21 and *h'* in three measures of meal,
18:34 and this saying was *h'* from them,
19:42 now they are *h'* from thine eyes.
Joh 8:59 but Jesus *h'* himself, and went out
2Co 4: 3 if our gospel be *h'*, it is *h'* to them
Eph 3: 9 hath been *h'* in God, who created
Col 1:26 which hath been *h'* from ages and
2: 3 In whom are *h'* all the treasures
3: 3 your life is *h'* with Christ in God.
1Ti 5:25 that are otherwise cannot be *h'*.
Heb 11:23 was *h'* three months of his parents,
Re 6:15 *h'* themselves in the dens and in

Hiddai (*hid'-dahee*) See also HURAI.
2Sa 23:30 *H'* of the brooks of Gaash,

Hiddekel (*hid'-de-kel*)
Ge 2:14 the name of the third river is *H'*:
Da 10: 4 side of the great river, which is *H'*.

hidden See also HID.
Le 5: 2 and if it be *h'* from him; he also
De 30:11 it is not *h'* from thee, neither is
Job 3:16 Or as an *h'* untimely birth I had
15:20 of years is *h'* to the oppressor.
24: 1 times are not *h'* from the Almighty,
Ps 51: 6 in the *h'* part thou shalt make me
83: 3 and consulted against thy *h'* ones.
Pr 28:12 when the wicked rise, a man is *h'*.
Isa 45: 3 and *h'* riches of secret places, that
48: 6 from this time, even *h'* things, and
Ob 6 how are his *h'* things sought up!
Ac 26:26 none of these things are *h'* from
1Co 2: 7 the *h'* wisdom, which God ordained
4: 5 bring to the light the *h'* things of
2Co 4: 2 the *h'* things of dishonesty, not
1Pe 3: 4 But let it be the *h'* man of the heart,
Re 2:17 will I give to eat of the *h'* manna,

hide See also HID; HIDDEN; HIDEST; HIDETH; HIDING.
Ge 18:17 Shall I *h'* from Abraham that thing
47:18 We will not *h'* it from my lord, how
Ex 2: 3 when she could not longer *h'* him.
Le 8:17 the bullock, and his *h'*, his flesh,
9:11 flesh and the *h'* he burnt with fire
20: 4 ways *h'* their eyes from the man,
De 7:20 left, and *h'* themselves from thee,
22: 1 astray, and *h'* myself from them:
3 likewise thou mayest not *h'* thyself.
4 the way, and *h'* thyself from them:
31:17 and I will *h'* my face from them,
18 I will surely *h'* my face in that day
32:20 said, I will *h'* my face from them,

Jos 2:16 h· yourselves there three days,
7:19 thou hast done; h· it not from me.
J'g 6:11 to h· it from the Midianites.
1Sa 3:17 I pray thee h· it not from me: God
17 if thou h· any thing from me of all
13: 6 people did h· themselves in caves,
19: 2 in a secret place, and h· thyself:
20: 2 why should my father h· this thing
5 that I may h· myself in the field
19 the place where thou didst h· thyself
23:19 Doth not David h· himself with us
26: 1 Doth not David h· himself in the
2Sa 14:18 H· not from me, I pray thee, the
1Ki 17: 3 h· thyself by the brook Cherith,
22:25 an inner chamber to h· thyself.
2Ki 7:12 out of the camp to h· themselves
2Ch 18:24 an inner chamber to h· thyself.
Job 13:20 then will I not h· myself from thee.
14:13 thou wouldest h· me in the grave,
20:12 though he h· it under his tongue;
24: 4 poor of the earth h· themselves
33:17 purpose, and h· pride from man.
34:22 of iniquity may h· themselves.
40:13 H· them in the dust together;
Ps 13: 1 how long wilt thou h· thy face
17: 8 h· me under the shadow of thy
27: 5 the time of trouble he shall h· me
5 of his tabernacle shall he h· me;
9 H· not thy face far from me; put
30: 7 thou didst h· thy face, and I was
31:20 Thou shalt h· them in the secret
51: 9 H· thy face from my sins, and blot
54 *title* Doth not David h· himself with
55: 1 O God, and h· not thyself from my
56: 6 they h· themselves, they mark my
64: 2 H· me from the secret counsel of
69:17 h· not thy face from thy servant;
78: 4 not h· them from their children,
89:46 Lord? wilt thou h· thyself for ever?
102: 2 H· not thy face from me in the day
119:19 h· not thy commandments from me.
143: 7 h· not thy face from me, lest I be
9 enemies: I flee unto thee to h· me.
Pr 2: 1 h· my commandments with thee;
28:28 wicked rise, men h· themselves;
Isa 1:15 I will h· mine eyes from you: yea,
2:10 and h· thee in the dust, for fear of
3: 9 their sin as Sodom, they h· it not.
16: 3 h· the outcasts; bewray not him
26:20 h· thyself as it were for a little
29:15 that seek deep to h· their counsel
58: 7 thou h· not thyself from thine own
Jer 13: 4 Euphrates, and h· it there in a hole
6 which I commanded thee to h· there.
23:24 Can any h· himself in secret places
36:19 Go, h· thee, thou and Jeremiah; and
38:14 thee a thing; h· nothing from me.
25 h· it not from us, and we will not
43: 9 and h· them in the clay in the
49:10 he shall not be able to h· himself:
La 3:56 h· not thine ear at my breathing,
Eze 28: 3 no secret that they can h· from
31: 8 the garden of God could not h· him:
39:29 Neither will I h· my face any more
Da 10: 7 so that they fled to h· themselves.
Am 9: 3 they h· themselves in the top
Mic 3: 4 he will even h· his face from them
Joh 12:36 and did h· himself from them.
Jas 5:20 and shall h· a multitude of sins.
Re 6:16 h· us from the face of him that

hidest
Job 13:24 Wherefore h· thou thy face, and
Ps 10: 1 why h· thou thyself in times of
44:24 Wherefore h· thou thy face, and
88:14 why h· thou thy face from me?
104:29 Thou h· thy face, they are troubled:
Isa 45:15 thou art a God that h· thyself, O

hideth
1Sa 23:23 places where he h· himself, and
Job 23: 9 he h· himself on the right hand,
34:29 and when he h· his face, who then
42: 3 Who is he that h· counsel without
Ps 10:11 he h· his face; he will never see it.
139:12 the darkness h· not from thee;
Pr 10:18 He that h· hatred with lying lips,
19:24 man h· his hand in his bosom,
22: 3 foreseeth the evil, and h· himself:
26:15 slothful h· his hand in his bosom;
27:12 foreseeth the evil, and h· himself;
16 Whosoever h· her h· the wind, and
28:27 that h· his eyes shall have many a
Isa 8:17 that h· his face from the house of
M't 13:44 when a man hath found, he h·,

hiding
Job 31:33 by h· mine iniquity in my bosom:
Ps 32: 7 Thou art my h· place; thou shalt
119:114 art my h· place and my shield:
Isa 28:17 waters shall overflow the h· place.
32: 2 be as an h· place from the wind,
Hab 3: 4 and there was the h· of his power.

hiding-place See HIDING and PLACE.

Hiel (*hi'-el*)
1Ki 16:34 H· the Beth-elite build Jericho:

Hierapolis (*hi-e-rap'-o-lis*)
Col 4:13 are in Laodicea, and them in H·.

Higgaion (*hig-gah'-yon*)
Ps 9:16 work of his own hands. H·. Selah.

high See also HIGHER; HIGHEST; HIGHMINDED; HIGHWAY.
Ge 7:19 all the h· hills, that were under the
14:18 was the priest of the most h· God.
19 be Abram of the most h· God,
20 And blessed be the most h· God,
14:22 unto the Lord, the most h· God,
29: 7 Lo, it is yet h· day, neither is it
Ex 14: 8 of Israel went out with an h· hand.
25:20 stretch forth their wings on h·,
37: 9 spread out their wings on h·, and
39:31 to fasten it on h· upon the mitre;
Le 21:10 And he that is the h· priest among
26:22 and your h· ways shall be desolate.
30 I will destroy your h· places, and
Nu 11:31 it were two cubits h· upon the face of
20:17 we will go by the king's h· way,
19 We will go by the h· way: and if I
21:22 we will go along by the king's h· way,
28 the lords of the h· places of Arnon.
22:41 him up into the h· places of Baal,
23: 3 thee. And he went to an h· place.
24:16 the knowledge of the most H·,
33: 3 of Israel went out with an h· hand
52 pluck down all their h· places:
35:25 in it unto the death of the h· priest,
28 until the death of the h· priest: but
28 after the death of the h· priest the
De 2:27 I will go along by the h· way, I will
3: 5 cities were fenced with h· walls,
12: 2 upon the h· mountains, and upon
26:19 to make thee h· above all nations
28: 1 thy God will set thee on h· above all
43 shall get up above thee very h·;
52 thy h· and fenced walls come down,
32: 8 When the most H· divided to the
13 He made him ride on the h· places
27 Our hand is h·, and the Lord hath
33:29 shalt tread upon their h· places.
Jos 20: 6 and until the death of the h· priest
J'g 5:18 death in the h· places of the field.
1Sa 9:12 of the people to day in the h· place:
13 before he go up to the h· place to eat;
14 them, for to go up to the h· place.
19 go up before me unto the h· place;
25 from the h· place into the city,
10: 5 coming down from the h· place with
13 prophesying, he came to the h· place
13: 6 in rocks, and in h· places, and in
2Sa 1:19 Israel is slain upon thy h· places:
25 thou wast slain in thine h· places.
22: 3 my h· tower, and my refuge, my
14 and the most H· uttered his voice.
34 and setteth me upon my h· places.
49 hast lifted me up on h· above them
23: 1 the man who was raised up on h·,
1Ki 3: 2 the people sacrificed in h· places,
3 and burnt incense in h· places.
4 for that was the great h· place:
6:10 all the house, five cubits h·: and
23 of olive tree, each ten cubits h·.
7:15 brass, of eighteen cubits h· apiece:
35 a round compass of half a cubit h·:
9: 8 this house, which is h·, every one
11: 7 Solomon build an h· place for
12:31 he made an house of h· places, and
32 the priests of the h· places which
13: 2 he offer the priests of the h· places
32 all the houses of the h· places which
33 the people priests of the h· places:
33 one of the priests of the h· places.
14:23 For they also built them h· places,
23 on every h· hill, and under every
15:14 the h· places were not removed:
21: 9 set Naboth on h· among the people:
12 set Naboth on h· among the people.
22:43 the h· places were not taken away;
43 burnt incense yet in the h· places.
2Ki 12: 3 the h· places were not taken away:
3 and burnt incense in the h· places.
10 scribe and the h· priest came up,
14: 4 Howbeit the h· places were not
4 and burnt incense on the h· places.
15: 4 the h· places were not removed: the
4 burnt incense still on the h· places.
35 the h· places were not removed: the
35 burned incense still in the h· places.
16: 4 burnt incense in the h· places, and
17: 9 they built them h· places in all their
10 groves in every h· hill, and under
11 burnt incense in all the h· places,
29 them in the houses of the h· places
32 of them priests of the h· places,
32 them in the houses of the h· places.
18: 4 He removed the h· places, and brake
22 whose h· places and whose altars
19:22 and lifted up thine eyes on h·?
21: 3 For he built up again the h· places
22: 4 Go up to Hilkiah the h· priest, that
8 And Hilkiah the h· priest said unto
23: 4 commanded Hilkiah the h· priest,
5 to burn incense in the h· places in
8 and defiled the h· places where the
8 down the h· places of the gates
9 the priests of the h· places came not
13 And the h· places that were before
15 and the h· place which Jeroboam
15 both that altar and the h· place he
15 brake down, and burned the h· place,
19 all the houses also of the h· places
20 slew all the priests of the h· places
1Ch 14: 2 his kingdom was lifted up on h·,
16:39 in the h· place that was at Gibeon,
17:17 to the estate of a man of h· degree,
21:29 season in the h· place at Gibeon.
2Ch 1: 3 to the h· place that was at Gibeon;
13 to the h· place that was at Gibeon
3:15 pillars of thirty and five cubits h·,
6:13 and three cubits h·, and had set it
7:21 this house, which is h·, shall be
11:15 priests for the h· places, and for
14: 3 and the h· places, and brake down
2Ch 14: 5 the h· places and the images: and
15:17 the h· places were not taken away
17: 6 took away the h· places and groves
20:19 of Israel with a loud voice on h·.
33 the h· places were not taken away:
21:11 made h· places in the mountains
23:20 through the h· gate into the king's
24:11 and the h· priest's officer came
27: 3 He built the h· gate of the house
28: 4 and burnt incense in the h· places,
25 he made h· places to burn incense
31: 1 threw down the h· places and the
32:12 taken away his h· places and his
33: 3 he built again the h· places which
17 did sacrifice still in the h· places,
19 places wherein he built h· places,
34: 3 Jerusalem from the h· places, and
4 the images, that were on h· above
9 they came to Hilkiah the h· priest,
Ne 3: 1 Eliashib the h· priest rose up with
20 the house of Eliashib the h· priest.
25 lieth out from the king's h· house,
13:28 the son of Eliashib the h· priest,
Es 5:14 gallows be made of fifty cubits h·,
7: 9 the gallows fifty cubits h·, which
Job 5:11 To set up on h· those that be low;
11: 8 It is as h· as heaven; what canst
16:19 in heaven, and my record is on h·.
21:22 seeing he judgeth those that are h·.
22:12 height of the stars, how h· they are!
25: 2 he maketh peace in his h· places.
31: 2 of the Almighty from on h·?
38:15 and the h· arm shall be broken.
39:18 time she lifteth up herself on h·,
27 command, and make her nest on h·?
41:34 He beholdeth all h· things: he is
Ps 7: 7 sakes therefore return thou on h·.
17 to the name of the Lord most h·.
9: 2 praise to thy name, O thou most H·.
18: 2 of my salvation, and my h· tower.
27 but wilt bring down h· looks.
33 and setteth me upon my h· places.
21: 7 through the mercy of the most H·
46: 4 of the tabernacles of the most H·.
47: 2 the Lord most h· is terrible; he is
49: 2 Both low and h·, rich and poor,
50:14 pay thy vows unto the most H·:
56: 2 fight against me, O thou most H·.
57: 2 I will cry unto God most h·; unto
62: 9 and men of h· degree are a lie:
68:15 an h· hill as the hill of Bashan.
16 Why leap ye, ye h· hills? this is the
18 Thou hast ascended on h·, thou
69:29 salvation, O God, set me up on h·.
71:19 also, O God, is very h·, who hast
73:11 is there knowledge in the most H·?
75: 5 Lift not up your horn on h·: speak
77:10 of the right hand of the most H·.
78:17 by provoking the most H· in the
35 and the h· God their redeemer.
56 and provoked the most h· God, and
58 to anger with their h· places, and
69 built his sanctuary like h· palaces,
82: 6 of you are children of the most H·.
83:18 art the most h· over all the earth.
89:13 thy hand, and h· is thy right hand.
91: 1 in the secret place of the most H·
9 even the most H·, thy habitation;
14 I will set him on h·, because he
92: 1 praises unto thy name, O most H·:
8 Lord, art most h· for evermore.
93: 4 The Lord on h· is mightier than the
97: 9 Lord, art h· above all the earth:
99: 2 and he is h· above all the people.
101: 5 hath an h· look and a proud heart
103:11 the heaven is h· above the earth,
104:18 The h· hills are a refuge for the
107:11 the counsel of the most H·:
41 Yet setteth he the poor on h· from
113: 4 The Lord is h· above all nations,
5 our God, who dwelleth on h·,
131: 1 matters, or in things too h· for me.
138: 6 Though the Lord be h·, yet hath
139: 6 it is h·, I cannot attain unto it.
144: 2 my h· tower, and my deliverer;
149: 6 the h· praises of God be in their
150: 5 him upon the h· sounding cymbals.
Pr 8: 2 standeth in the top of the h· places,
9:14 a seat in the h· places of the city.
18:11 as an h· wall in his own conceit.
21: 4 An h· look, and a proud heart, and
24: 7 Wisdom is too h· for a fool: he
Ec 12: 5 shall be afraid of that which is h·,
Isa 2:13 the cedars of Lebanon, that are h·
14 upon all the h· mountains, and upon
15 upon every h· tower, and upon
6: 1 upon a throne, h· and lifted up,
10:12 and the glory of his h· looks.
33 the h· ones of stature shall be hewn
13: 2 a banner upon the h· mountain,
14:14 clouds; I will be like the most H·.
15: 2 gone up to...the h· places, to weep:
16:12 that Moab is weary on the h· place,
22:16 heweth him out a sepulchre on h·,
24:18 the windows from on h· are open,
21 the host of the h· ones that are on h·,
25:12 fortress of the h· fort of thy walls
26: 5 down them that dwell on h·; the
30:13 swelling out in a h· wall, whose
25 upon every h· mountain, and upon
25 and upon every h· hill, rivers and
32:15 be poured upon us from on h·,
33: 5 is exalted; for he dwelleth on h·:
16 He shall dwell on h·: his place of
36: 7 whose h· places and whose altars
37:23 and lifted up thine eyes on h·? even

Isa 40: 9 get thee up into the h· mountain;
26 Lift up your eyes on h·, and behold
41:18 I will open rivers in h· places, and
49: 9 pastures shall be in all h· places.
52:13 and extolled, and be very h·.
57: 7 Upon a lofty and h· mountain hast
15 the h· and lofty One that inhabiteth
15 I dwell in the h· and holy place,
58: 4 make your voice to be heard on h·.
14 ride upon the h· places of the earth,
Jer 2:20 when upon every h· hill and under
3: 2 up thine eyes unto the h· places,
6 upon every h· mountain and under
21 was heard upon the h· places,
4:11 A dry wind of the h· places in the
7:29 take up a lamentation on h· places;
31 have built the h· places of Tophet,
12:12 are come upon all h· places
14: 6 asses did stand in the h· places,
17: 2 by the green trees upon the h· hills.
3 thy h· places for sin, throughout
12 A glorious h· throne from the
19: 5 built also the h· places of Baal,
20: 2 were in the h· gate of Benjamin,
25:30 The Lord shall roar from on h·,
26:18 house as the h· places of a forest.
31:21 up waymarks, make thee h· heaps:
32:35 they built the h· places of Baal,
48:35 him that offereth in the h· places,
49:16 make thy nest as h· as the eagle,
51:58 her h· gates shall be burned with
La 3:35 before the face of the most H·.
38 Out of the mouth of the most H·
Eze 1:18 were so h· that they were dreadful;
6: 3 and I will destroy your h· places.
6 and the h· places shall be desolate;
13 upon every h· hill, in all the tops
16:16 deckedst thy h· places with divers
24 thee an h· place in every street.
25 built thy h· place at every head of
31 and makest thine h· place in every
39 shall break down thy h· places:
17:22 highest branch of the h· cedar,
22 will plant it upon an h· mountain
24 Lord have brought down the h· tree,
20:28 then they saw every h· hill, and all
29 What is the h· place whereunto ye
21:26 is low, and abase him that is h·.
31: 3 and of an h· stature; and his top
4 the deep set him up on h· with her
34: 6 mountains, and upon every h· hill:
14 the h· mountains of Israel shall
36: 2 even the ancient h· places are ours
40: 2 set me upon a very h· mountain,
42 and one cubit h·: whereupon also
41:22 altar of wood was three cubits h·,
43: 7 of their kings in their h· places.
Da 3:26 ye servants of the most h· God,
4: 2 and wonders that the h· God hath
17 the most H· ruleth in the kingdom
24 this is the decree of the most H·,
25, 32 most H· ruleth in the kingdom
34 and I blessed the most H·, and I
5:18 most h· God gave Nebuchadnezzar
21 most h· God ruled in the kingdom
7:18 But the saints of the most H· shall
22 given to the saints of the most H·;
25 great words against the most H·,
25 wear out the saints of the most H·,
27 people of the saints of the most H·,
8: 3 and the two horns were h·; but one
Ho 7:16 return, but not to the most H·:
10: 8 The h· places also of Aven, the sin
11: 7 they called them to the most H·,
Am 4:13 treadeth upon the h· places of the
7: 9 h· places of Isaac shall be desolate,
Ob 3 whose habitation is h·; that saith
Mic 1: 3 and tread upon the h· places of the
5 what are the h· places of Judah?
3:12 house as the h· places of the forest.
6: 6 and bow myself before the h· God?
Hab 2: 9 that he may set his nest on h·, that
3:10 voice, and lifted up his hands on h·.
19 me to walk upon mine h· places.
Zep 1:16 cities, and against the h· towers.
Hag 1: 1, 12, 14, of Josedech, the h· priest,
2: 2 the son of Josedech, the h· priest,
4 the son of Josedech, the h· priest;
Zec 3: 1 he shewed me Joshua the h· priest
8 Hear now, O Joshua the h· priest,
6:11 the son of Josedech, the h· priest;
M't 4: 8 up into an exceeding h· mountain,
17: 1 them up into an h· mountain apart,
26: 3 the palace of the h· priest, who was
51 struck a servant of the h· priest's,
57 him away to Caiaphas the h· priest,
58 afar off unto the h· priest's palace,
62 And the h· priest arose, and said unto
63 And the h· priest answered and said
65 Then the h· priest rent his clothes,
M'r 2:26 days of Abiathar the h· priest, and
5: 7 Jesus, thou Son of the most h· God?
6:21 supper to his lords, h· captains, and
9: 2 them up into an h· mountain apart
14:47 and smote a servant of the h· priest,
53 led Jesus away to the h· priest: and
54 into the palace of the h· priest: and
60 the h· priest stood up in the midst,
61 Again the h· priest asked him, and
63 Then the h· priest rent his clothes,
66 one of the maids of the h· priest:
Lu 1:78 dayspring from on h· hath visited
3: 2 and Caiaphas being the h· priests,
4: 5 taking him up into an h· mountain,
8:28 Jesus, thou Son of God most h·?
22:50 smote the servant of the h· priest,
Lu 22:54 him into the h· priest's house. And
24:49 be endued with power from on h·.
Joh 11:49 being the h· priest that same year,
51 but being h· priest that year, he
18:10 and smote the h· priest's servant, and
13 which was the h· priest that same
15 was known unto the h· priest, and
15 Jesus into the palace of the h· priest.
16 which was known unto the h· priest,
19 The h· priest then asked Jesus of his
22 Answerest thou the h· priest so?
24 bound unto Caiaphas the h· priest.
26 of the servants of the h· priest,
19:31 that sabbath day was an h· day,
Ac 4: 6 Annas the h· priest, and Caiaphas,
6 were of the kindred of the h· priest,
5:17 the h· priest rose up, and all they
21 But the h· priest came, and they that
24 the h· priest and the captain of the
27 and the h· priest asked them,
7: 1 said the h· priest, Are these things
48 most H· dwelleth not in temples
9: 1 And Saul...went unto the h· priest,
13:17 with an h· arm brought he them
16:17 are the servants of the most h· God,
22: 5 the h· priest doth bear me witness,
23: 2 the h· priest Ananias commanded
4 said, Revilest thou God's h· priest?
5 wist not...that he was the h· priest:
24: 1 Ananias the h· priest descended with
25: 2 Then the h· priest and the chief of
Ro 12:16 Mind not h· things, but condescend
13:11 it is h· time to awake out of sleep:
2Co 10: 5 and every h· thing that exalteth
Eph 4: 8 When he ascended up on h·, he led
6:12 spiritual wickedness in h· places.
Ph'p 3:14 the prize of the h· calling of God in
Heb 1: 3 the right hand of the Majesty on h·;
2:17 a merciful and faithful h· priest in
3: 1 consider the Apostle and H· Priest of
4:14 that we have a great h· priest, that is
15 we have not an h· priest which cannot
5: 1 For every h· priest taken from among
5 not himself to be made an h· priest;
10 of God an h· priest after the order of
6:20 an h· priest for ever after the order
7: 1 of Salem, priest of the most h· God,
26 For such an h· priest became
27 not daily, as those h· priests, to offer
28 the law maketh men h· priests which
8: 1 We have such an h· priest, who is set
3 every h· priest is ordained to offer
9: 7 went the h· priest alone once every
11 an h· priest of good things to come,
25 as the h· priest entereth into the holy
10:21 having an h· priest over the house
13:11 sanctuary by the h· priest for sin,
Re 21:10 spirit to a great and h· mountain,
12 And had a wall great and h·, and had

higher
Nu 24: 7 and his king shall be h· than Agag,
1Sa 9: 2 he was h· than any of the people.
10:23 he was h· than any of the people
2Ki 15:35 He built the h· gate of the house
Ne 4:13 the wall, and on the h· places, I
Job 35: 5 the clouds which are h· than thou.
Ps 61: 2 me to the rock that is h· than I.
89:27 h· than the kings of the earth.
Ec 5: 8 for he that is h· than the highest
8 and there be h· than they.
Isa 55: 9 the heavens are h· than the earth,
9 so are my ways h· than your ways,
Jer 36:10 in the h· court, at the entry of the
Eze 9: 2 came from the way of the h· gate,
42: 5 the galleries were h· than these,
43:13 shall be the h· place of the altar.
Da 8: 3 but one was h· than the other, and
3 the other, and the h· came up last.
Lu 14:10 may say unto thee, Friend, go up h·:
Ro 13: 1 soul be subject unto the h· powers.
Heb 7:26 and made h· than the heavens;

highest
Ps 18:13 and the H· gave his voice;
87: 5 the h· himself shall establish her.
Pr 8:26 h· part of the dust of the world.
9: 3 upon the h· places of the city,
Ec 5: 8 for he that is higher than the h·
Eze 17: 3 took the h· branch of the cedar:
22 of the h· branch of the high cedar,
41: 7 from the lowest chamber to the h·
M't 21: 9 of the Lord; Hosanna in the h·.
M'r 11:10 of the Lord: Hosanna in the h·.
Lu 1:32 shall be called the Son of the H·:
35 power of the H· shall overshadow
76 be called the prophet of the H·:
2:14 Glory to God in the h·, and on earth
6:35 ye shall be the children of the H·:
14: 8 sit not down in the h· room; lest
19:38 peace in heaven, and glory in the h·.
20:46 the h· seats in the synagogues,

highly
Lu 1:28 said, Hail, thou that art h· favoured,
16:15 which is h· esteemed among men
Ac 12:20 Herod was h· displeased with them
Ro 12: 3 not to think of himself more h· than
Ph'p 2: 9 God also hath h· exalted him, and
1Th 5:13 to esteem them very h· in love

highminded
Ro 11:20 by faith. Be not h·, but fear:
1Ti 6:17 they be not h·, nor trust in uncertain
2Ti 3: 4 heady, h·, lovers of pleasures more

highness
Job 31:23 by reason of his h· I could not
Isa 13: 3 even them that rejoice in my h·.

high-place See HIGH and PLACE.

high-priest See HIGH and PRIEST.

highway See also HIGH; HIGHWAYS.
J'g 21:19 on the east side of the h· that goeth
1Sa 6:12 went along the h·, lowing as they
2Sa 20:12 in blood in the midst of the h·. And
12 he removed Amasa out of the h· into
13 When he was removed out of the h·,
2Ki 18:17 which is in the h· of the fuller's field.
Pr 16:17 The h· of the upright is to depart
Isa 7: 3 pool in the h· of the fuller's field;
11:16 there shall be an h· for the remnant
19:23 day shall there be a h· out of Egypt
35: 8 And an h· shall be there, and a way,
36: 2 pool in the h· of the fuller's field.
40: 3 in the desert a h· for our God.
62:10 cast up, cast up the h·; gather out
Jer 31:21 set thine heart toward the h·, even
M'r 10:46 Timæus, sat by the h· side begging.

highways
J'g 5: 6 the h· were unoccupied, and the
20:31 in the h·, of which one goeth up
32 draw them from the city unto the h·.
45 they gleaned of them in the h· five
Isa 33: 8 The h· lie waste, the wayfaring man
49:11 a way, and my h· shall be exalted.
Am 5:16 they shall say in all the h·, Alas!
M't 22: 9 Go ye therefore into the h·,
10 servants went out into the h·, and
Lu 14:23 Go out into the h· and hedges, and

Hilen (*hi'-len*) See also HOLON.
1Ch 6:58 And H· with her suburbs, Debir

Hilkiah (*hil-ki'-ah*) See also HELKAI; HILKIAH'S.
2Ki 18:18 out to them Eliakim the son of H·,
26 Then said Eliakim the son of H·,
37 Then came Eliakim the son of H·,
22: 4 Go up to H· the high priest, that he
8 And H· the high priest said unto
8 And H· gave the book to Shaphan,
10 H· the priest hath delivered me a
12 the king commanded H· the priest,
14 So H· the priest, and Ahikam, and
23: 4 the king commanded H· the high
24 the book that H· the priest found in
1Ch 6:13 Shallum begat H·, and H· begat
45 the son of Amaziah, the son of H·,
9:11 Azariah the son of H·, the son of
26:11 H· the second, Tebaliah the third,
2Ch 34: 9 they came to H· the high priest,
14 H· the priest found a book of the
15 H· answered and said to Shaphan
15 H· delivered the book to Shaphan.
18 H· the priest hath given me a book.
20 And the king commanded H·, and
22 H·,...went to Huldah the prophetess,
35: 8 H· and Zechariah and Jehiel, rulers
Ezr 7: 1 the son of Azariah, the son of H·,
Ne 8: 4 and Urijah, and H·, and Maaseiah,
11:11 Seraiah the son of H·, the son of
12: 7 Sallu, Amok, H·, Jedaiah. These
21 Of H·, Hashabiah; of Jedaiah,
Isa 22:20 my servant Eliakim the son of H·:
36:22 Then came Eliakim, the son of H·,
Jer 1: 1 words of Jeremiah the son of H·,
29: 3 and Gemariah the son of H·, whom

Hilkiah's (*hil-ki'ahs*)
Isa 36: 3 H· son, which was over the house,

hill See also DUNGHILL; HILL'S; HILLS.
Ex 17: 9 I will stand on the top of the h· with
10 and Hur went up to the top of the h·.
24: 4 builded an altar under the h·, and
Nu 14:44 presumed to go up unto the h· top:
45 which dwelt in that h·, and smote
De 1:41 ye were ready to go up into the h·.
43 went presumptuously up into the h·.
Jos 5: 3 of Israel at the h· of the foreskins.
13: 6 the inhabitants of the h· country
15: 9 drawn from the top of the h· unto
17:16 The h· is not enough for us: and
18:13 near the h· that lieth on the south
14 the h· that lieth before Beth-horon
21:11 Hebron, in the h· country of Judah,
24:30 on the north side of the h· of Gaash.
33 buried him in a h· that pertained
J'g 2: 9 on the north side of the h· Gaash.
7: 1 by the h· of Moreh, in the valley.
16: 3 carried them up to the top of an h·
1Sa 7: 1 the house of Abinadab in the h·,
9:11 they went up to the h· to the city,
10: 5 thou shalt come to the h· of God,
10 they came thither to the h·, behold,
23:19 in the h· of Hachilah, which is on
25:20 came down by the covert of the h·,
26: 1 not David hide himself in the h· of
3 Saul pitched in the h· of Hachilah,
13 stood on the top of an h· afar off;
2Sa 2:24 they were come to the h· of Ammah,
25 troop, and stood on the top of an h·.
13:34 the way of the h· side behind him.
16: 1 was a little past the top of the h·,
21: 9 they hanged them in the h· before
1Ki 11: 7 in the h· that is before Jerusalem,
14:23 groves, on every high h·, and under
16:24 bought the h· Samaria of Shemer
24 and built on the h·, and called the
24 of Shemer, owner of the h·, Samaria.
2Ki 1: 9 behold, he sat on the top of an h·.
4:27 she came to the man of God to the h·,
17:10 groves in every high h·, and under
Ps 2: 6 my king upon my holy h· of Zion.
3: 4 and he heard me out of his holy h·.
15: 1 who shall dwell in thy holy h·?
24: 3 Who shall ascend into the h· of the

Ps 42: 6 the Hermonites, from the h' Mizar.
43: 3 let them bring me unto thy holy h',
68: 15 h' of God is as the h' of Bashan;
15 an high h' as the h' of Bashan.
16 this is the h' which God desireth to
99: 9 our God, and worship at his holy h';
Ca 4: 6 and to the h' of frankincense.
Isa 5: 1 a vineyard in a very fruitful h':
10: 32 of Zion, the h' of Jerusalem.
30: 17 mountain, and as an ensign on an h'.
25 and upon every high h', rivers and
31: 4 mount Zion, and for the h' thereof.
40: 4 mountain and h' shall be made low:
Jer 2: 20 when upon every high h' and under
16: 16 from every h', and out of the holes
31: 39 over against it upon the h' Gareb,
49: 16 that holdest the height of the h':
50: 6 they have gone from mountain to h',
Eze 6: 13 altars, upon every high h', in all the
20: 28 they saw every high h', and all the
34: 6 mountains, and upon every high h':
26 round about my h' a blessing;
M't 5: 14 A city that is set on an h' cannot
Lu 1: 39 went into the h' country with haste,
65 throughout all the h' country of
3: 5 mountain and h' shall be brought
4: 29 led him unto the brow of the h',
9: 37 they were come down from the h',
Ac 17: 22 Paul stood in the midst of Mars' h',

hill-country See HILL and COUNTRY.

Hillel (*hil'-lel*)
J'g 12: 13 And after him Abdon the son of H',
15 the son of H' the Pirathonite died,

hill's
2Sa 16: 13 Shimei went along on the h' side

hills
Ge 7: 19 all the high h', that were under
49: 26 utmost bound of the everlasting h':
Nu 23: 9 him, and from the h' I behold him:
De 1: 7 in the h', and in the vale, and in
8: 7 that spring out of valleys and h';
9 out of whose h' thou mayest dig
11: 11 it, is a land of h' and valleys, and
12: 2 upon the h', and under every green
33: 15 the precious things of the lasting h',
Jos 9: 1 on this side Jordan, in the h', and
10: 40 smote all the country of the h', and
11: 16 the h', and all the south country,
1Ki 20: 23 Their gods are gods of the h';
28 The Lord is God of the h', but he is
22: 17 saw all Israel scattered upon the h',
2Ki 16: 4 on the h', and under every green
2Ch 28: 4 on the h', and under every green
Job 15: 7 wast thou made before the h'?
Ps 18: 7 foundations also of the h' moved
50: 10 and the cattle upon a thousand h'.
65: 12 and the little h' rejoice on every
68: 16 Why leap ye, ye high h'? this is
72: 3 and the little h', by righteousness.
80: 10 The h' were covered with the
95: 4 the strength of the h' is his also.
97: 5 h' melted like wax at the presence
98: 8 hands: let the h' be joyful together
104: 10 valleys, which run among the h'.
13 watereth the h' from his chambers:
18 The high h' are a refuge for the
32 he toucheth the h', and they smoke.
114: 4 rams, and the little h' like lambs.
6 rams; and ye little h', like lambs?
121: 1 I will lift up mine eyes unto the h',
148: 9 Mountains, and all h'; fruitful
Pr 8: 25 before the h' was I brought forth:
Ca 2: 8 mountains, skipping upon the h'.
Isa 2: 2 shall be exalted above the h'; and
14 upon all the h' that are lifted up,
5: 25 the h' did tremble, and their
7: 25 all h' that shall be digged with the
40: 12 in scales, and the h' in a balance?
41: 15 and shalt make the h' as chaff.
42: 15 make waste mountains and h', and
54: 10 depart, and the h' be removed; but
55: 12 the mountains and the h' shall break
65: 7 and blasphemed me upon the h':
Jer 3: 23 salvation is hoped for from the h',
4: 24 and all the h' moved lightly
13: 27 abominations on the h' in the fields.
17: 2 by the green trees upon the high h'.
Eze 6: 3 and to the h', to the rivers, and to
35: 8 in thy h', and in thy valleys, and in
36: 4, 6 and to the h', to the rivers, and to
Ho 4: 13 and burn incense upon the h', under
10: 8 Cover us; and to the h', Fall on us.
Joe 3: 18 and the h' shall flow with milk, and
Am 9: 13 sweet wine, and all the h' shall melt.
Mic 4: 1 it shall be exalted above the h'; and
6: 1 and let the h' hear thy voice.
Na 1: 5 the h' melt, and the earth is burned
Hab 3: 6 the perpetual h' did bow: his ways
Zep 1: 10 and a great crashing from the h'.
Lu 23: 30 Fall on us; and to the h', Cover us.

hill-top See HILL and TOP.

himself^
Ge 14: 15 And he divided h' against them, he
18: 2 door, and bowed h' toward the ground,
19: 1 and he bowed h' with his face toward
22: 8 My son, God will provide h' a lamb for
23: 7 And Abraham stood up, and bowed h'
12 And Abraham bowed down h' before
24: 52 worshipped the Lord, bowing h' to the
27: 42 doth comfort h', purposing to kill
30: 36 three days' journey betwixt h' and
32: 21 h' lodged that night in...company.
33: 3 bowed h' to the ground seven times,
Ge 41: 14 shaved h', and changed his raiment,
42: 7 but made h' strange unto them,
24 And he turned h' about from them,
43: 31 refrained h', and said, Set on bread.
32 And they set on for him by h', and for
45: 1 Then Joseph could not refrain h' before
1 while Joseph made h' known unto his
46: 29 to Goshen, and presented h' unto him;
47: 31 Israel bowed h' upon the bed's head.
48: 2 and Israel strengthened h', and sat
12 and he bowed h' with his face to the
Ex 10: 6 and he turned h', and went out from
21: 3 If he came in by h', he shall go out
3 he shall go out by h': if he were
4 master's, and he shall go out by h'.
8 master, who hath betrothed her to h',
Le 7: 8 the priest shall have to h' the skin of
9: 8 of the sin offering, which was for h'.
14: 8 wash h' in water, that he may be clean:
15: 5, 6, 7, 8, 10, 11, 22, 27 bathe h' in water,
16: 6 of the sin offering, which is for h',
6 and make an atonement for h', and for
11 of the sin offering, which is for h',
11 and shall make an atonement for h',
11 of the sin offering which is for h':
17 and have made an atonement for h',
24 an atonement for h', and for the people,
17: 15 and bathe h' in water, and be unclean
21: 4 he shall not defile h', being a chief
4 man among his people, to profane h'.
11 nor defile h' for his father, or for his
22: 8 he shall not eat to defile h' therewith:
25: 26 it, and h' be able to redeem it;
47 wax poor, and sell h' unto the stranger
49 or if he be able, he may redeem h'.
27: 8 then he will present h' before the
Nu 6: 3 He shall separate h' from wine and
5 in the which he separateth h' unto the
6 All the days that he separateth h' unto
7 He shall not make h' unclean for his
16: 9 bring you near to h' to do the service
19: 12 shall purify h' with it on the third
12 but if he purify not h' the third day,
13 purifieth not h', defileth the tabernacle
19 on the seventh day he shall purify h',
19 wash his clothes, and bathe h' in water,
20 and shall not purify h', that soul shall
23: 24 lion, and lift up h' as a young lion:
25: 3 And Israel joined h' unto Baal-peor:
31: 53 war had taken spoil, every man for h'.
35: 19 revenger of blood h' shall slay the
36: 7 Israel shall keep h' to the inheritance
9 shall keep h' to his own inheritance.
De 7: 6 thee to be a special people unto h',
14: 2 thee to be a peculiar people unto h',
17: 16 But he shall not multiply horses to h',
17 Neither shall he multiply wifes to h',
17 shall he greatly multiply to h' silver
23: 11 cometh on, he shall wash h' with water:
28: 9 establish thee a holy people unto h',
29: 13 thee to day for a people unto h', and
19 that he bless h' in his heart, saying, I
32: 36 and repent h' for his servants, when he
33: 21 And he provided the first part for h',
Jos 22: 23 thereon, let the Lord h' require it;
J'g 3: 19 he h' turned again from the quarries
20 parlour, which he had for h' alone.
4: 11 in law of Moses, had severed h' from
6: 31 if he be a god, let him plead for h',
7: 5 a dog lappeth, him shalt thou set by h';
9: 5 son of Jerubbaal was left; for he hid h'.
16: 30 And he bowed h' with all his might;
Ru 3: 8 the man was afraid, and turned h':
1Sa 2: 14 brought up the priest took for h'.
3: 21 Lord revealed h' to Samuel in Shiloh
8: 11 your sons, and appoint them for h',
10: 19 your God, who h' saved you out of
22 he hath hid h' among the stuff.
14: 47 whithersoever he turned h', he vexed
17: 16 evening, and presented h' forty days.
18: 4 And Jonathan stripped h' of the robe
5 Saul sent him, and behaved h' wisely:
14 And David behaved h' wisely in all his
15 Saul saw that he behaved h' very wisely,
30 that David behaved h' more wisely than
20: 24 So David hid h' in the field: and when
41 the ground, and bowed h' three times:
21: 13 and feigned h' mad in their hands, and
23: 19 Doth not David hide h' with us in the
23 the lurking places where he hideth h',
24: 8 with his face to the earth, and bowed h'.
25: 31 or that my lord hath avenged h': but
26: 1 Doth not David hide h' in the hill of
28: 8 And Saul disguised h', and put on other
14 his face to the ground, and bowed h'.
29: 4 he reconcile h' unto his master?
30: 6 but David encouraged h' in the Lord
31 David h' and his men were wont to
2Sa 3: 6 Abner made h' strong for the house
31 And king David h' followed the bier.
6: 20 who uncovered h' to day in the eyes of
20 fellows shamelessly uncovereth h'!
7: 23 God went to redeem for a people to h',
9: 8 And he bowed h', and said, What is thy
12: 18 how will he then vex h', if we tell him
20 anointed h', and changed his apparel,
13: 6 Amnon lay down, and made h' sick:
14: 22 and bowed h', and thanked the king:
33 bowed h' on his face to the ground
15: 23 the king also h' passed over the brook
17: 23 hanged h', and died, and was buried
18: 21 And Cushi bowed h' unto Joab, and ran.
24: 20 bowed h' before the king on his face
1Ki 1: 5 the son of Haggith exalted h', saying, I
23 he bowed h' before the king with his
47 And the king bowed h' upon the bed.
1Ki 1: 52 said, If he will shew h' a worthy man,
53 and bowed h' to king Solomon: and
2: 19 and bowed h' unto her, and sat down
11: 29 he had clad h' with a new garment;
15: 15 and the things which h' had dedicated,
16: 9 drinking h' drunk in the house of Azra
17: 21 And he stretched h' upon the child
18: 2 And Elijah went to shew h' unto Ahab.
6 Ahab went one way by h', and Obadiah
6 and Obadiah went another way by h'.
42 And he cast h' down upon the earth,
19: 4 But he h' went a day's journey into
4 requested for h' that he might die;
20: 11 that girdeth on his harness boast h' as
16 Ben-hadad was drinking h' drunk in
38 disguised h' with ashes upon his face.
21: 25 which did sell h' to work wickedness
29 how Ahab humbleth h' before me?
29 he humbleth h' before me, I will not
22: 30 king of Israel disguised h', and went
2Ki 4: 34 and he stretched h' upon the child;
35 and stretched h' upon him: and the
5: 14 and dipped h' seven times in Jordan,
6: 10 and saved h' there, not once nor twice.
19: 1 covered h' with sackcloth, and went
23: 16 And as Josiah turned h', he spied the
1Ch 12: 1 he yet kept h' close because of Saul
13: 13 brought not the ark home to h' to
21: 21 and bowed h' to David with his face to
2Ch 12: 1 and had strengthened h', he forsook
12 And when he humbled h', the wrath of
13 So king Rehoboam strengthened h' in
13: 9 cometh to consecrate h' with a
12 God h' is with us for our captain, and
15: 18 and that he h' had dedicated, silver,
16: 9 to shew h' strong in the behalf of them
14 sepulchres, which he had made for h'
17: 1 and strengthened h' against Israel
16 Zichri, who willingly offered h' unto
18: 29 So the king of Israel disguised h'; and
34 of Israel stayed h' up in his chariot
20: 3 and set h' to seek the Lord, and
35 Jehoshaphat king of Judah join h' with
36 he joined h' with him to make ships
21: 4 he strengthened h', and slew all his
23: 1 Jehoiada strengthened h', and took
25: 11 And Amaziah strengthened h', and
14 and bowed down h' before them, and
26: 8 for he strengthened h' exceedingly.
20 yea, h' hasted also to go out,
32: 1 cities, and thought to win them for h'.
5 Also he strengthened h', and built up
9 he h' laid siege against Lachish,
26 Hezekiah humbled h' for the pride of
27 he made h' treasuries for silver, and
33: 12 and humbled h' greatly before the God
23 And humbled not h' before the Lord,
23 Manasseh his father had humbled h';
35: 22 but disguised h', that he might fight
36: 12 and humbled not h' before Jeremiah
Ezr 10: 1 weeping and casting h' down before
8 forfeited, and h' separated from
Es 5: 10 Nevertheless Haman refrained h': and
Job 1: 12 only upon h' put not forth thine hand.
2: 1 among them to present h' before the
8 a potsherd to scrape h' withal; and he
4: 2 who can withhold h' from speaking?
9: 4 who hath hardened h' against him,
15: 25 strengthened h' against the Almighty.
17: 8 shall stir up h' against the hypocrite.
18: 4 He teareth h' in his anger: shall
22: 2 that is wise may be profitable unto h'?
23: 9 he hideth h' on the right hand, that I
27: 10 Will he delight h' in the Almighty?
32: 2 he justified h' rather than God.
34: 9 that he should delight h' with God.
14 gather unto h' his spirit and his breath;
41: 25 When he raiseth up h', the mighty are
Ps 4: 3 hath set apart him that is godly for h':
10: 10 He croucheth, and humbleth h', that
14 the poor committeth h' unto thee; thou
35: 8 let his net that he hath hid catch h':
36: 2 For he flattereth h' in his own eyes,
4 he setteth h' in a way that is not good;
37: 35 and spreading h' like a green bay tree.
50: 6 righteousness: for God is judge h'.
52: 7 and strengthened h' in his wickedness.
54: *title* Doth not David hide h' with us?
55: 12 me that did magnify h' against me:
68: 30 one submit h' with pieces of silver:
87: 5 the Highest h' shall establish her.
93: 1 strength, wherewith he hath girded h':
109: 18 As he clothed h' with cursing like as
113: 6 Who humbleth h' to behold the things
132: 18 But upon h' shall his crown flourish.
135: 4 the Lord hath chosen Jacob unto h',
14 will repent h' concerning his servants.
Pr 5: 22 own iniquities shall take the wicked h',
9: 7 a scorner getteth to h' shame: and he
10: 7 a wicked man getteth h' a blot.
11: 25 watereth shall be watered also h'.
12: 9 better than he that honoureth h', and
13: 7 that maketh h' rich, yet hath nothing:
7 maketh h' poor, yet hath great riches.
14: 14 a good man shall be satisfied from h'.
16: 4 Lord hath made all things for h':
26 He that laboureth laboureth for h';
18: 1 a man, having separated h', seeketh
24 hath friends must shew h' friendly:
21: 13 shall cry h', but shall not be heard.
22: 3 man foreseeth the evil, and hideth h';
25: 9 Debate thy cause with thy neighbour h';
14 Whoso boasteth h' of a false gift is
27: 12 man foreseeth the evil, and hideth h';
28: 10 he shall fall h' into his own pit:
29: 15 child left to h' bringeth his mother to

Ec 5: 9 the king *h'* is served by the field.
10: 12 but the lips of a fool will swallow up *h'*.
Ca 2: 9 shewing *h'* through the lattice.
3: 9 King Solomon made *h'* a chariot of the
5: 6 but my beloved had withdrawn *h'*, and
Isa 2: 9 and the great man humbleth *h'*:
20 they made each one for *h'* to worship.
3: 5 the child shall behave *h'* proudly
7: 14 the Lord *h'* shall give you a sign;
8: 13 Sanctify the Lord of hosts *h'*; and let
19: 17 mention thereof shall be afraid in *h'*,
22: 16 graveth a habitation for *h'* in a rock?
28: 20 than that a man can stretch *h'* on it:
20 narrower than that he can wrap *h'* in
31: 4 nor abase *h'* for the noise of them:
37: 1 clothes, and covered *h'* with sackcloth,
38: 15 both spoken...and *h'* hath done it:
44: 5 and another shall call *h'* by the name
5 and surname *h'* by the name of Israel.
14 oak, which he strengtheneth for *h'*
15 for he will take thereof, and warm *h'*;
16 yea, he warmeth *h'*, and saith, Aha,
23 Jacob, and glorified *h'* in Israel.
45: 18 God *h'* that formed the earth and
56: 3 that hath joined *h'* to the Lord, speak,
59: 15 departeth from evil maketh *h'* a prey:
61: 10 as a bridegroom decketh *h'* with
63: 12 them, to make *h'* an everlasting name?
64: 7 that stirreth up *h'* to take hold of thee:
65: 16 That he who blesseth *h'* in the earth
16 shall bless *h'* in the God of truth; and
Jer 10: 23 know that the way of man is not in *h'*:
16: 20 Shall a man make gods unto *h'*, and
23: 24 Can any hide *h'* in secret places that I
29: 26 that is mad, and maketh *h'* a prophet,
27 which maketh *h'* a prophet to you?
31: 18 heard Ephraim bemoaning *h'* thus;
34: 9 none should serve *h'* of them, to wit, of
37: 12 to separate *h'* thence in the midst of
43: 12 shall array *h'* with the land of Egypt,
48: 26 for he magnified *h'* against the Lord:
42 because he hath magnified *h'* against
49: 10 he shall not be able to hide *h'*: his seed
51: 3 and against him that lifteth *h'* up in his
14 The Lord of hosts hath sworn by *h'*,
La 1: 9 for the enemy hath magnified *h'*.
Eze 7: 13 neither shall any strengthen *h'* in the
14: 7 Israel, which separateth *h'* from me,
24: 2 the king of Babylon set *h'* against
25: 12 offended, and revenged *h'* upon them;
45: 22 prepare for *h'* and for all the people
Da 1: 8 not defile *h'* with the portion of the
8 eunuchs that he might not defile *h'*.
6: 14 was sore displeased with *h'*, and set
8: 11 he magnified *h'* even to the prince
25 and he shall magnify *h'* in his heart,
9: 26 Messiah be cut off, but not for *h'*:
11: 36 to his will; and he shall exalt *h'*, and
36 and magnify *h'* above every god, and
37 for he shall magnify *h'* above all.
Ho 5: 6 he hath withdrawn *h'* from them.
7: 8 hath mixed *h'* among the people;
8: 9 up to Assyria, a wild ass alone by *h'*:
10: 1 vine, he bringeth forth fruit unto *h'*:
13: 1 he exalted *h'* in Israel; but when
Am 2: 14 neither shall the mighty deliver *h'*:
15 is swift of foot shall not deliver *h'*:
15 he that rideth the horse deliver *h'*.
6: 8 The Lord God hath sworn by *h'*,
Jon 4: 8 he fainted, and wished in *h'* to die,
Hab 2: 6 him that ladeth *h'* with thick clay!
M't 6: 4 secret *h'* shall reward thee openly.
8: 17 *H'* took our infirmities, and bare our
12: 15 knew it, he withdrew *h'* from thence:
26 out Satan, he is divided against *h'*;
45 taketh with *h'* seven other spirits
45 other spirits more wicked than *h'*,
13: 21 Yet hath he not root in *h'*, but
16: 24 will come after me, let him deny *h'*,
18: 4 shall humble *h'* as this little child,
23: 12 shall exalt *h'* shall be abased; and
12 shall humble *h'* shall be exalted.
27: 3 repented *h'*, and brought again the
5 departed, and went and hanged *h'*.
42 He saved others; *h'* he cannot save.
57 who also *h'* was Jesus' disciple:
M'r 3: 7 Jesus withdrew *h'* with his disciples
21 on him: for they said, He is beside *h'*.
26 If Satan rise up against *h'*, and be
5: 5 crying, and cutting *h'* with stones.
30 knowing in *h'* that virtue had gone
6: 17 For Herod *h'* had sent forth and laid
8: 34 let him deny *h'*, and take up his
12: 33 and to love his neighbour as *h'*, is
36 David *h'* said by the Holy Ghost,
37 David therefore *h'* calleth him Lord:
14: 54 the servants, and warmed *h'* at the fire.
67 saw Peter warming *h'*, she looked upon
15: 31 He saved others; *h'* he cannot save.
Lu 3: 23 Jesus *h'* began to be about thirty
5: 16 And he withdrew *h'* into the wilderness,
6: 3 David did, when *h'* was an hungred,
7: 39 he spake within *h'*, saying, This
9: 23 let him deny *h'*, and take up his
25 world, and lose *h'*, or be cast away?
10: 1 place, whither he *h'* would come.
29 he, willing to justify *h'*, said unto
11: 18 If Satan also be divided against *h'*,
26 other spirits more wicked than *h'*;
12: 17 And he thought within *h'*, saying,
21 layeth up treasure for *h'*, and is not
37 he shall gird *h'*, and make them to sit
47 will, and prepared not *h'*, neither did
14: 11 whosoever exalteth *h'* shall be
11 and he that humbleth *h'* shall be
15: 15 And he went and joined *h'* to a citizen

Lu 15: 17 And when he came to *h'*, he said,
16: 3 the steward said within *h'*, What
18: 4 he said within *h'*, Though I fear not
11 stood, and prayed thus with *h'*, God,
14 that exalteth *h'* shall be abased;
14 that humbleth *h'* shall be exalted.
19: 12 to receive for *h'* a kingdom, and to
20: 42 And David *h'* saith in the book of
23: 2 saying that he *h'* is Christ a King.
7 who *h'* also was at Jerusalem at
35 let him save *h'*, if he be Christ, the
51 who also *h'* waited for the kingdom
24: 12 wondering in *h'* at that which was
15 Jesus *h'* drew near, and went with
27 the things concerning *h'*.
36 Jesus *h'* stood in the midst of them,
Joh 2: 24 Jesus did not commit *h'* unto them,
4: 2 Though Jesus *h'* baptized not, but
12 drank thereof *h'*, and his children,
44 For Jesus *h'* testified, that a prophet
53 and *h'* believed, and his whole house.
5: 13 for Jesus had conveyed *h'* away, a
18 Father, making *h'* equal with God.
19 Son can do nothing of *h'*, but what
20 sheweth him all things that *h'* doeth:
26 For as the Father hath life in *h'*;
26 given to the Son to have life in *h'*;
37 And the Father *h'*, which hath sent
6: 6 for he *h'* knew what he would do.
15 again into a mountain *h'* alone.
61 Jesus knew in *h'* that his disciples
7: 4 he *h'* seeketh to be known openly.
18 He that speaketh of *h'* seeketh his
8: 7 he lifted up *h'*, and said unto them,
10 When Jesus had lifted up *h'*, and saw
22 Will he kill *h'*? because he saith,
59 Jesus hid *h'*, and went out of the temple,
9: 21 age; ask him; he shall speak for *h'*.
11: 33 groaning in *h'* cometh to the grave.
51 this spake he not of *h'*: but being
12: 36 departed, and did hide *h'* from them.
13: 4 and took a towel, and girded *h'*.
32 God shall also glorify him in *h'*, and
16: 13 for he shall not speak of *h'*; but
27 the Father *h'* loveth you, because
18: 18 Peter stood with them, and warmed *h'*.
25 And Simon Peter stood and warmed *h'*.
19: 7 because he made *h'* the Son of God.
12 whosoever maketh *h'* a king
21: 1 things Jesus shewed *h'* again to the
1 and on this wise shewed he *h'*.
7 naked, and did cast *h'* into the sea.
14 that Jesus shewed *h'* to his disciples,
Ac 1: 3 To whom also he shewed *h'* alive
2: 34 he saith *h'*, The Lord said unto my
5: 13 rest durst no man join *h'* to them:
36 boasting *h'* to be somebody; to
7: 26 next day he shewed *h'* unto them as
8: 9 out that he *h'* was some great one:
13 Then Simon *h'* believed also: and
34 this? of *h'*, or of some other man?
9: 26 he assayed to join *h'* to the disciples:
10: 17 while Peter doubted in *h'* what this
12: 11 when Peter was come to *h'*, he said,
14: 17 he left not *h'* without witness, in that
16: 27 and would have killed *h'*, supposing
18: 19 he *h'* entered into the synagogue,
19: 22 but he *h'* stayed in Asia for a season.
31 not adventure *h'* into the theatre.
20: 13 he appointed, minding *h'* to go afoot.
21: 26 the next day purifying *h'* with them
25: 4 he *h'* would depart shortly thither.
8 he answered for *h'*, Neither against
16 to answer for *h'* concerning the crime
25 he *h'* hath appealed to Augustus,
26: 1 forth the hand, and answered for *h'*:
24 And as he thus spake for *h'*, Festus,
27: 3 to go unto his friends to refresh *h'*.
28: 16 suffered to dwell by *h'* with a soldier
Ro 12: 3 not to think of *h'* more highly than he
14: 7 liveth to *h'*, and no man dieth to *h'*.
12 shall give an account of *h'* to God.
22 Happy is he that condemneth not *h'*
15: 3 For even Christ pleased not *h'*; but,
1Co 2: 15 things, yet he *h'* is judged of no man.
3: 15 he *h'* shall be saved; yet so as by fire.
18 Let no man deceive *h'*. If any man
7: 36 that he behaveth *h'* uncomely toward
11: 28 But let a man examine *h'*, and so
29 eateth and drinketh damnation to *h'*,
14: 4 in an unknown tongue edifieth *h'*;
8 who shall prepare *h'* to the battle?
28 and let him speak to *h'*, and to God.
37 If any man think *h'* to be a prophet,
15: 28 then shall the Son also *h'* be subject
2Co 5: 18 who hath reconciled us to *h'* by
19 reconciling the world unto *h'*, not
10: 7 man trust to *h'* that he is Christ's,
7 let him of *h'* think this again, that,
18 For not he that commendeth *h'* is
11: 14 Satan *h'* is transformed into an angel
20 if a man exalt *h'*, if a man smite you
Ga 1: 4 Who gave *h'* for our sins, that he
2: 12 withdrew and separated *h'*, fearing
20 who loved me, and gave *h'* for me.
6: 3 if a man think *h'* to be something,
3 when he is nothing, he deceiveth *h'*.
4 shall he have rejoicing in *h'* alone,
Eph 1: 5 of children by Jesus Christ to *h'*,
9 which he hath purposed in *h'*:
2: 15 make in *h'* of twain one new man,
20 Jesus Christ *h'* being the chief corner
5: 2 loved us, and hath given *h'* for us
25 loved the church, and gave *h'* for it;
27 present it to *h'* a glorious church,
28 He that loveth his wife loveth *h'*.

Eph 5: 33 so love his wife even as *h'*; and the
Ph'p 2: 7 But made *h'* of no reputation, and
8 in fashion as a man, he humbled *h'*,
3: 21 even to subdue all things unto *h'*.
Col 1: 20 him to reconcile all things unto *h'*;
1Th 3: 11 Now God *h'* and our Father, and
4: 16 Lord *h'* shall descend from heaven
2Th 2: 4 opposeth and exalteth *h'* above all
4 of God, shewing *h'* that he is God.
16 Now our Lord Jesus Christ *h'*, and
3: 16 Now the Lord of peace *h'* give you
1Ti 2: 6 Who gave *h'* a ransom for all, to be
2Ti 2: 4 No man that warreth entangleth *h'*
13 abideth faithful: he cannot deny *h'*.
21 If a man therefore purge *h'* from
Tit 2: 14 Who gave *h'* for us, that he might
14 and purify unto *h'* a peculiar people,
3: 11 sinneth, being condemned of *h'*.
Heb 1: 3 when he had by *h'* purged our sins,
2: 14 *h'* likewise took part of the same:
18 For in that he *h'* hath suffered being
5: 2 for that he *h'* is also compassed with
3 so also for *h'*, to offer for sins.
4 no man taketh this honour unto *h'*,
5 So also Christ glorified not *h'* to be
6: 13 swear by no greater, he sware by *h'*.
7: 27 he did once, when he offered up *h'*.
9: 7 blood, which he offered for *h'*, and
14 eternal Spirit offered *h'* without spot
25 Nor yet that he should offer *h'* often,
26 put away sin by the sacrifice of *h'*.
12: 3 contradiction of sinners against *h'*,
Jas 1: 24 For he beholdeth *h'*, and goeth his
27 and to keep *h'* unspotted from the
1Pe 2: 23 but committed *h'* to him that judgeth
1Jo 2: 6 ought *h'* also so to walk, even as he
3: 3 hath this hope in him purifieth *h'*,
5: 10 Son of God hath the witness in *h'*:
18 that is begotten of God keepeth *h'*,
3Jo 10 doth he *h'* receive the brethren,
Re 19: 12 written, that no man knew, but he *h'*.
21: 3 God *h'* shall be with them, and be

hin
Ex 29: 40 fourth part of an *h'* of beaten oil;
40 the fourth part of an *h'* of wine for
30: 24 the sanctuary, and of oil olive an *h'*:
Le 19: 36 ephah, and a just *h'*, shall ye have:
23: 13 be of wine, the fourth part of an *h'*.
Nu 15: 4 with the fourth part of an *h'* of oil.
5 the fourth part of an *h'* of wine for
6 with the third part of an *h'* of oil.
7 offer the third part of an *h'* of wine,
9 flour mingled with half an *h'* of oil.
10 half an *h'* of wine, for an offering
28: 5 fourth part of an *h'* of beaten oil.
7 part of an *h'* for the one lamb:
14 be half an *h'* of wine unto a bullock,
14 the third part of an *h'* unto a ram,
14 a fourth part of an *h'* unto a lamb:
Eze 4: 11 by measure; the sixth part of an *h'*:
45: 24 for a ram, an *h'* of oil for an ephah.
46: 5 to give, and an *h'* of oil to an ephah.
7 unto, and an *h'* of oil to an ephah
11 to give, and an *h'* of oil to an ephah.
14 and the third part of an *h'* of oil, to

hind See also BEHIND; HINDER; HINDMOST; HINDS.
Ge 49: 21 Naphtali is a *h'* let loose: he giveth
Pr 5: 19 Let her be as the loving *h'* and
Jer 14: 5 the *h'* also calved in the field, and

hinder See also HINDERED; HINDERETH; HINDERMOST.
Ge 24: 56 And he said unto them, *H'* me not,
Nu 22: 16 thee, *h'* thee from coming unto me:
2Sa 2: 23 the *h'* end of the spear smote him
1Ki 7: 25 and all their *h'* parts were inward.
2Ch 4: 4 and all their *h'* parts were inward.
Ne 4: 8 against Jerusalem, and to *h'*
Job 9: 12 he taketh away, who can *h'* him?
11: 10 together, then who can *h'* him?
Ps 78: 66 smote his enemies in the *h'* parts:
Joe 2: 20 his *h'* part toward the utmost sea,
Zec 14: 8 and half of them toward the *h'* sea:
M'r 4: 38 he was in the *h'* part of the ship,
Ac 8: 36 what doth *h'* me to be baptized?
27: 41 but the *h'* part was broken with
1Co 9: 12 we should *h'* the gospel
Ga 5: 7 did *h'* you that ye should not obey

hindered
Ezr 6: 8 unto these men, that they be not *h'*.
Lu 11: 52 them that were entering in ye *h'*.
Ro 15: 22 been much *h'* from coming to you.
1Th 2: 18 once and again; but Satan *h'* us.
1Pe 3: 7 of life; that your prayers be not *h'*.

hindereth
Isa 14: 6 anger, is persecuted, and none *h'*.

hindermost See also HINDMOST.
Ge 33: 2 after, and Rachel and Joseph *h'*.
Jer 50: 12 the *h'* of the nations shall be a

hindmost See also HINDERMOST.
Nu 2: 31 They shall go *h'* with their standards.
De 25: 18 and smote the *h'* of thee, even all
Jos 10: 19 enemies, and smite the *h'* of them;

hinds See also HINDS'.
Job 39: 1 thou mark when the *h'* do calve?
Ps 29: 9 of the Lord maketh the *h'* to calve,
Ca 2: 7 the *h'* of the field, that ye stir not up,
3: 5 the *h'* of the field that ye stir not up,

hinds'
2Sa 22: 34 He maketh my feet like *h'* feet:
Ps 18: 33 He maketh my feet like *h'* feet, and
Hab 3: 19 and he will make my feet like *h'* feet,

hinges
1Ki 7:50 and the *h'* of gold, both for the
Pr 26:14 As the door turneth upon its *h'*, so

Hinnom (*hin'-nom*)
Jos 15: 8 up by the valley of the son of *H'*
8 before the valley of *H'* westward,
18:16 before the valley of the son of *H'*,
16 and descended to the valley of *H'*,
2Ki 23:10 in the valley of the children of *H'*,
2Ch 28: 3 incense in the valley of the son of *H'*,
33: 6 the fire in the valley of the son of *H'*:
Ne 11:30 Beer-sheba unto the valley of *H'*.
Jer 7:31 is in the valley of the son of *H'*,
32 nor the valley of the son of *H'*, but
19: 2 forth unto the valley of the son of *H'*,
6 nor The valley of the son of *H'*, but
32:35 are in the valley of the son of *H'*,

hip
J'g 15: 8 he smote them *h'* and thigh with a

Hirah (*hi'-rah*)
Ge 38: 1 Adullamite, whose name was *H'*.
12 he and his friend *H'* the Adullamite.

Hiram (*hi'-ram*) See also HIRAM'S; HURAM.
2Sa 5:11 *H'* king of Tyre sent messengers
1Ki 5: 1 *H'* king of Tyre sent his servants
1 for *H'* was ever a lover of David.
2 And Solomon sent to *H'*, saying,
7 *H'* heard the words of Solomon,
8 And *H'* sent to Solomon, saying,
10 *H'* gave Solomon cedar trees and
11 Solomon gave *H'* twenty thousand
11 gave Solomon to *H'* year by year.
12 was peace between *H'* and Solomon;
7:13 sent and fetched *H'* out of Tyre.
40 *H'* made the lavers, and the shovels,
40 *H'* made an end of...all the work
45 which *H'* made to king Solomon
9:11 *H'* the king of Tyre had furnished
11 king Solomon gave *H'* twenty cities
12 *H'* came out from Tyre to see the
14 And *H'* sent to the king sixscore
27 *H'* sent in the navy his servants,
10:11 navy also of *H'*, that brought gold
22 of Tharshish with the navy of *H'*:
1Ch 14: 1 *H'* king of Tyre sent messengers to

Hiram's (*hi'-rams*)
1Ki 5:18 Solomon's builders and *H'* builders

hire See also HIRED; HIRES; HIREST.
Ge 30:18 God hath given me my *h'*, because
32 Goats: and of such shall be my *h'*.
33 shall come for my *h'* before thy face:
31: 8 The ringstraked shall be thy *h'*;
Ex 22:15 an hired thing, it came for his *h'*.
De 23:18 shalt not bring the *h'* of a whore,
24:15 At his day thou shalt give him his *h'*.
1Ki 5: 6 thee will I give *h'* for thy servants
1Ch 19: 6 to *h'* them chariots and horsemen
Isa 23:17 Tyre, and she shall turn to her *h'*,
18 her *h'* shall be holiness to the Lord:
46: 6 the balance, and *h'* a goldsmith;
Eze 16:31 an harlot, in that thou scornest *h'*;
41 thou also shalt give no *h'* any more.
Mic 1: 7 she gathered it of the *h'* of an harlot,
7 shall return to the *h'* of an harlot.
3:11 the priests thereof teach for *h'*, and
Zec 8:10 no *h'* for man, nor any *h'* for beast;
M't 20: 1 to *h'* labourers into his vineyard.
8 give them their *h'*, beginning from
Lu 10: 7 for the labourer is worthy of his *h'*.
Jas 5: 4 *h'* of the labourers who have reaped

hired
Ge 30:16 surely I have *h'* thee with my son's
Ex 12:45 an *h'* servant shall not eat thereof.
22:15 be an *h'* thing, it came for his hire.
Le 19:13 the wages of him that is *h'* shall not
22:10 *h'* servant, shall not eat of the holy
25: 6 thy *h'* servant and for thy stranger
40 as an *h'* servant, and as a sojourner,
50 to the time of an *h'* servant shall it
53 as a yearly *h'* servant shall he be
De 15:18 worth a double *h'* servant to thee,
23: 4 *h'* against thee Balaam the son of
24:14 oppress an *h'* servant that is poor
J'g 9: 4 wherewith Abimelech *h'* vain and
18: 4 Micah with me, and hath *h'* me, and
1Sa 2: 5 full have *h'* out themselves for bread;
2Sa 10: 6 Ammon sent and *h'* the Syrians of
2Ki 7: 6 Israel hath *h'* against us the kings
1Ch 19: 7 So they *h'* thirty and two thousand
2Ch 24:12 *h'* masons and carpenters to repair
25: 6 He *h'* also an hundred thousand
Ezr 4: 5 And *h'* counsellers against them, to
Ne 6:12 for Tobiah and Sanballat had *h'* him.
13 Therefore was he *h'*, that I should
13: 2 but *h'* Balaam against them, that he
Isa 7:20 Lord shave with a rasor that is *h'*,
Jer 46:21 her *h'* men are in the midst of her
Ho 8: 9 himself: Ephraim hath *h'* lovers.
10 they have *h'* among the nations,
M't 20: 7 him, Because no man hath *h'* us.
9 were *h'* about the eleventh hour,
M'r 1:20 the ship with the *h'* servants, and
Lu 15:17 many *h'* servants of my father's
19 make me as one of thy *h'* servants.
Ac 28:30 whole years in his own *h'* house,

hireling
Job 7: 1 days also like the days of an *h'*?
2 and as an *h'* looketh for the reward
14: 6 shall accomplish, as an *h'*, his day.
Isa 16:14 three years, as the years of an *h'*,
21:16 year, according to the years of an *h'*,
Mal 3: 5 that oppress the *h'* in his wages,
Joh 10:12 is an *h'*, and not the shepherd,
13 The *h'* fleeth, because he is an
13 because he is an *h'*, and careth not

hires
Mic 1: 7 all the *h'* thereof shall be burned

hirest
Eze 16:33 gifts to all thy lovers, and *h'* them,

hiss See also HISSING.
1Ki 9: 8 shall be astonished, and shall *h'*;
Job 27:23 and shall *h'* him out of his place.
Isa 5:26 will *h'* unto them from the end of
7:18 the Lord shall *h'* for the fly that is
Jer 19: 8 shall be astonished and *h'* because
49:17 shall *h'* at all the plagues thereof.
50:13 astonished and *h'* at all her plagues.
La 2:15 they *h'* and wag their head at the
16 they *h'* and gnash the teeth: they
Eze 27:36 merchants among the people shall *h'*
Zep 2:15 one that passeth by her shall *h'*,
Zec 10: 8 I will *h'* for them, and gather them;

hissing
2Ch 29: 8 to astonishment, and to *h'*, as ye
Jer 18:16 land desolate, and a perpetual *h'*;
19: 8 make this city desolate, and an *h'*;
25: 9 an astonishment, and an *h'*, and
18 astonishment, an *h'*, and a curse;
29:18 an astonishment, and an *h'*, and a
51:37 an astonishment, and an *h'*, without
Mic 6:16 and the inhabitants thereof an *h'*:

hit
1Sa 31: 3 Saul, and the archers *h'* him:
1Ch 10: 3 Saul, and the archers *h'* him,

hither^ See also HITHERTO.
Ge 15:16 they shall come *h'* again: for the
42:15 your youngest brother come *h'*.
45: 5 with yourselves, that ye sold me *h'*:
8 not you that sent me *h'*, but God:
13 haste and bring down my father *h'*.
Ex 3: 5 Draw not nigh *h'*: put off thy shoes
Jos 2: 2 there came men in *h'* to night
3: 9 Come *h'*, and hear the words of
18: 6 and bring the description *h'* to me,
J'g 16: 2 Gazites, saying, Samson is come *h'*.
18: 3 Who brought thee *h'*? and what
19:12 We will not turn aside *h'* into the
Ru 2:14 At mealtime come thou *h'*, and eat
1Sa 13: 9 Bring *h'* a burnt offering to me,
14:18 Bring *h'* the ark of God. For the ark
34 Bring me *h'* every man his ox, and
36 Let us draw near *h'* unto God.
38 Draw ye near *h'*, all the chief of the
15:32 Bring ye *h'* to me Agag the king of
16:11 we will not sit down till he come *h'*.
17:28 he said, Why camest thou down *h'*?
23: 9 the priest, Bring *h'* the ephod.
30: 7 I pray thee, bring me *h'* the ephod.
2Sa 1:10 Have brought them *h'* unto my
5: 6 the lame, thou shalt not come in *h'*:
6 thinking, David cannot come in *h'*.
14:32 Come *h'*, that I may send thee unto
20:16 Come near *h'*, that I may speak
1Ki 22: 9 Hasten *h'* Micaiah the son of Imlah.
2Ki 2: 8 they were divided *h'* and thither,
14 waters, they parted *h'* and thither:
8: 7 The man of God is come *h'*.
1Ch 11: 5 to David, Thou shalt not come *h'*.
2Ch 28:13 Ye shall not bring in the captives *h'*:
Ezr 4: 2 of Assur, which brought us up *h'*
Ps 73:10 Therefore his people return *h'*:
81: 2 Take a psalm, and bring *h'* the timbrel
Pr 9: 4, 16 is simple, let him turn in *h'*:
Isa 57: 3 draw near *h'*, ye sons of the sorceress,
Eze 40: 4 them unto thee art thou brought *h'*:
Da 3:26 high God, come forth, and come *h'*.
M't 8:29 art thou come *h'* to torment us
14:18 He said, Bring them *h'* to me.
17:17 I suffer you? bring him *h'* to me.
22:12 thou in *h'* not having a wedding
M'r 11: 3 and straightway he will send him *h'*.
Lu 9:41 and suffer you? Bring thy son *h'*.
14:21 bring in *h'* the poor, and...maimed.
15:23 And bring *h'* the fatted calf, and kill
19:27 bring *h'*, and slay them before me.
30 man sat: loose him, and bring him *h'*.
Joh 4:15 thirst not, neither come *h'* to draw
16 Go, call thy husband, and come *h'*.
6:25 him, Rabbi, when camest thou *h'*?
20:27 Reach *h'* thy finger, and behold my
27 and reach *h'* thy hand, and thrust
Ac 9:21 and came *h'* for that intent, that he
10:32 and call *h'* Simon, whose surname
17: 6 upside down are come *h'* also;
19:37 For ye have brought *h'* these men,
25:17 when they were come *h'*, without
Re 4: 1 Come up *h'*, and I will shew thee
11:12 saying unto them, Come up *h'*. And
17: 1 Come *h'*; I will shew unto thee the
21: 9 Come *h'*, I will shew thee the bride,

hitherto
Ex 7:16 *h'* thou wouldest not hear.
Jos 17:14 as the Lord hath blessed me *h'*?
J'g 16:13 *H'* thou hast mocked me, and
1Sa 1:16 and grief have I spoken *h'*.
7:12 *H'* hath the Lord helped us.
2Sa 7:18 that thou hast brought me *h'*?
15:34 have been thy father's servant *h'*,
1Ch 9:18 Who *h'* waited in...king's gate
12:29 *h'* the greatest part of them had
17:16 that thou hast brought me *h'*?
Job 38:11 *H'* shalt thou come, but no
Ps 71:17 *h'* have I declared thy wondrous
Isa 18: 2, 7 terrible from their beginning *h'*;
Da 7:28 *H'* is the end of the matter.
Joh 5:17 My father worketh *h'*, and I
16:24 *H'* have ye asked nothing in my
Ro 1:13 to come unto you, but was let *h'*,
1Co 3: 2 for *h'* ye were not able to bear it,

Hittite (*hit'-tite*) See also HITTITES.
Ge 23:10 and Ephron the *H'* answered
25: 9 of Ephron the son of Zohar the *H'*,
26:34 Judith the daughter of Beeri the *H'*,
34 the daughter of Elon the *H'*:
36: 2 Adah the daughter of Elon the *H'*,
49:29 is in the field of Ephron the *H'*,
30 with the field of Ephron the *H'* for
50:13 a buryingplace of Ephron the *H'*,
Ex 23:28 and the *H'*, from before thee.
33: 2 Canaanite, the Amorite, and the *H'*,
34:11 and the Canaanite, and the *H'*, and
Jos 9: 1 sea over against Lebanon, the *H'*,
11: 3 and to the Amorite, and the *H'*, and
1Sa 26: 6 David and said to Ahimelech the *H'*,
2Sa 11: 3 of Eliam, the wife of Uriah the *H'*?
6 Joab, saying, Send me Uriah the *H'*.
17 and Uriah the *H'* died also.
21, 24 servant Uriah the *H'* is dead also.
12: 9 killed Uriah the *H'* with the sword,
10 wife of Uriah the *H'* to be thy wife.
23:39 Uriah the *H'*: thirty and seven in all.
1Ki 15: 5 only in the matter of Uriah the *H'*.
1Ch 11:41 Uriah the *H'*, Zabad the son of
Eze 16: 3 an Amorite, and thy mother an *H'*.
45 your mother was an *H'*, and your

Hittites (*hit'-tites*)
Ge 15:20 And the *H'*, and the Perizzites,
Ex 3: 8 place of the Canaanites, and the *H'*,
17 land of the Canaanites, and the *H'*,
13: 5 land of the Canaanites, and the *H'*,
23:23 in unto the Amorites and the *H'*,
Nu 13:29 and the *H'*, and the Jebusites, and
De 7: 1 many nations before thee, the *H'*,
20:17 destroy them; namely, the *H'*, and
Jos 1: 4 all the land of the *H'*, and unto the
3:10 you the Canaanites, and the *H'*,
12: 8 and in the south country; the *H'*,
24:11 and the Canaanites, and the *H'*,
J'g 1:26 man went into the land of the *H'*,
3: 5 dwelt among the Canaanites, *H'*,
1Ki 9:20 that were left of the Amorites, *H'*,
10:29 and so for all the kings of the *H'*,
11: 1 Edomites, Zidonians, and *H'*;
2Ki 7: 6 hired against us the kings of the *H'*,
2Ch 1:17 horses for all the kings of the *H'*,
8: 7 the people that were left of the *H'*,
Ezr 9: 1 even of the Canaanites, the *H'*, the
Ne 9: 8 the land of the Canaanites, the *H'*,

Hivite (*hi'-vite*) See also HIVITES.
Ge 10:17 And the *H'*, and the Arkite, and
34: 2 Shechem the son of Hamor the *H'*,
36: 2 Anah the daughter of Zibeon the *H'*;
Ex 23:28 which shall drive out the *H'*, the
33: 2 Hittite, and the Perizzite, the *H'*,
34:11 and the Perizzite, and the *H'*, and
Jos 9: 1 Perizzite, the *H'*, and the Jebusite,
11: 3 and to the *H'* under Hermon in the
1Ch 1:15 And the *H'*, and the Arkite, and

Hivites (*hi'-vites*)
Ex 3: 8 and the *H'*, and the Jebusites.
17 and the *H'*, and the Jebusites,
13: 5 and the *H'*, and the Jebusites,
23:23 and the Canaanites, the *H'*, and the
De 7: 1 and the *H'*, and the Jebusites,
20:17 the *H'*, and the Jebusites; as the
Jos 3:10 *H'*, and the Perizzites, and the
9: 7 the men of Israel said unto the *H'*,
11:19 Israel, save the *H'* the inhabitants
12: 8 the Perizzites, the *H'*, and the
24:11 and the Girgashites, the *H'*, and
J'g 3: 3 *H'* that dwelt in mount Lebanon;
5 Amorites, and Perizzites, and *H'*,
2Sa 24: 7 and to all the cities of the *H'*, and
1Ki 9:20 *H'*, and Jebusites, which were not
2Ch 8: 7 the *H'*, and the Jebusites, which

Hizkiah (*hiz-ki'-ah*) See also HEZEKIAH; HIZKIJAH.
Zep 1: 1 the son of *H'*, in the days of Josiah

Hizkijah (*hiz-ki'-jah*) See also HIZKIAH.
Ne 10:17 Ater, *H'*, Azzur, Hodijah, Bani,

ho^
Isa 55: 1 *H'*, every one that thirsteth, come
Zec 2: 6 *H'*, *h'*, come forth, and flee from the

hoar See also HOARFROST; HOARY.
Ex 16:14 small as the *h'* frost on the ground.
1Ki 2: 6 let not his *h'* head go down to the
9 his *h'* head bring thou down to the
Isa 46: 4 even to *h'* hairs will I carry you:

hoarfrost See also HOAR; HOARY; and FROST.
Ps 147:16 he scattereth the *h'* like ashes.

hoary
Le 19:32 shalt rise up before the *h'* head,
Job 38:29 and the *h'* frost of heaven, who hath
41:32 one would think the deep to be *h'*.
Pr 16:31 The *h'* head is a crown of glory, if

Hobab (*ho'-bab*) See also JETHRO.
Nu 10:29 And Moses said unto *H'*, the son of
J'g 4:11 the children of *H'* the father in law

Hobah (*ho'-bah*)
Ge 14:15 and pursued them unto *H'*, which

Hod (*hod*)
1Ch 7:37 Bezer, and *H'*, and Shamma, and

Hodaiah (*ho-da-i'-ah*) See also HODAVIAH.
1Ch 3:24 the sons of Elioenai were, *H'*, and

Hodaviah (*ho-da-vi'ah*) See also HODAIAH; HO-DEVAH.
1Ch 5:24 and Jeremiah, and *H'*, and Jahdiel,
9: 7 the son of *H'*, the son of Hasenuah,
Ezr 2:40 children of *H'*, seventy and four.
Hodesh (*ho'-desh*)
1Ch 8: 9 begat of *H'* his wife, Jobab, and
Hodevah (*ho-de'-vah*) See also HODAVIAH.
Ne 7:43 children of *H'*, seventy and four.
Hodiah (*ho-di'-ah*) See also HODIJAH.
1Ch 4:19 the sons of his wife *H'* the sister
Hodijah (*ho-di'-jah*) See also HODIAH.
Ne 8: 7 Shabbethai, *H'*, Maaseiah, Kelita,
9: 5 Sherebiah, *H'*, Shebaniah, and
10:10 Shebaniah, *H'*, Kelita, Pelaiah,
13 *H'*, Bani, Beninu.
18 *H'*, Hashum, Bezai,
Hodshi See TAHTIM-HODSHI.
Hoglah (*hog'-lah*) See also BETH-HOGLAH.
Nu 26:33 were Mahlah, and Noah, *H'*,
27: 1 daughters; Mahlah, Noah, and *H'*,
36:11 and *H'*, and Milcah, and Noah, the
Jos 17: 3 daughters, Mahlah, and Noah, *H'*,
Hoham (*ho'-ham*)
Jos 10: 3 sent unto *H'* king of Hebron, and
hoised
Ac 27:40 and *h'* up the mainsail to the wind,
hoist See HOISED.
hold See also BEHOLD; HELD; HOLDEN; HOLDEST; HOLDETH; HOLDING; HOLDS; HOUSEHOLD; UPHOLD; WITHHOLD.
Ge 19:16 the men laid *h'* upon his hand,
21:18 up the lad, and *h'* him in thine hand;
25:26 his hand took *h'* on Esau's heel;
Ex 5: 1 that they may *h'* a feast unto me
9: 2 let them go, and wilt *h'* them still,
10: 9 we must *h'* a feast unto the Lord.
14:14 for you, and ye shall *h'* your peace.
15:14 sorrow shall take *h'* on the
15 trembling shall take *h'* upon them;
20: 7 the Lord will not *h'* him guiltless
26: 5 loops may take *h'* one of another.
Nu 30: 4 and her father shall *h'* his peace
14 *h'* his peace at her from day to day;
De 5:11 the Lord will not *h'* him guiltless
21:19 father and his mother lay *h'* on him,
22:28 and lay *h'* on her, and lie with her,
32:41 and mine hand take *h'* on judgment;
J'g 9:46 entered into an *h'* of the house
49 Abimelech, and put them to the *h'*,
49 and set the *h'* on fire upon them;
16:29 Samson took *h'* of the two middle
18:19 they said unto him, *H'* thy peace,
19:29 knife, and laid *h'* on his concubine,
Ru 3:15 that thou hast upon thee, and *h'* it.
1Sa 15:27 laid *h'* upon the skirt of his mantle,
22: 4 the while that David was in the *h'*.
5 said unto David, Abide not in the *h'*
24:22 his men gat them up unto the *h'*.
2Sa 1:11 then David took *h'* on his clothes,
2:21 lay thee *h'* on one of the young men,
22 I *h'* up my face to Joab my brother?
4:10 I took *h'* of him, and slew him in
5: 7 David took the strong *h'* of Zion:
17 heard of it; and went down to the *h'*.
6: 6 to the ark of God, and took *h'* of it;
13:11 he took *h'* of her, and said unto her,
20 but *h'* now thy peace, my sister:
18: 9 and his head caught *h'* of the oak,
23:14 David was then in an *h'*, and the
24: 7 And came to the strong *h'* of Tyre,
1Ki 1:50 caught *h'* on the horns of the altar.
51 caught *h'* on the horns of the altar,
2: 9 *h'* him not guiltless: for thou art
28 caught *h'* on the horns of the altar.
9: 9 and have taken *h'* upon other gods,
13: 4 the altar, saying, Lay *h'* on him.
2Ki 2: 3, 5 Yea, I know it; *h'* ye your peace.
12 and he took *h'* of his own clothes,
6:32 door, and *h'* him fast at the door:
7: 9 good tidings, and we *h'* our peace:
1Ch 11:16 David was then in the *h'*, and the
12: 8 David into the *h'* to the wilderness
16 and Judah to the *h'* unto David.
13: 9 put forth his hand to *h'* the ark;
2Ch 7:22 Egypt, and laid *h'* on other gods,
Ne 8:11 saying, *H'* your peace, for the day
Es 4:11 the king shall *h'* out the golden
Job 6:24 Teach me, and I will *h'* my tongue:
8:15 he shall *h'* it fast, but it shall not
9:28 that thou wilt not *h'* me innocent.
11: 3 thy lies make men *h'* their peace?
13: 5 ye would altogether *h'* your peace!
13 *H'* your peace, let me alone, that
19 for now, if I *h'* my tongue, I shall
17: 9 righteous shall also *h'* on his way,
21: 6 am afraid, and trembling taketh *h'*
27: 6 My righteousness I *h'* fast, and
20 Terrors take *h'* on him as waters,
30:16 days of affliction have taken *h'* upon
33:31 *h'* thy peace, and I will speak.
33 *h'* thy peace, and I shall teach thee
36:17 judgment and justice take *h'* on
38:13 take *h'* of the ends of the earth,
41:26 him that layeth at him cannot *h'*:
Ps 17: 5 *H'* up my goings in thy paths,
35: 2 Take *h'* of shield and buckler, and
39:12 *h'* not thy peace at my tears: for I
40:12 iniquities have taken *h'* upon me,
48: 6 Fear took *h'* upon them there, and
69:24 wrathful anger take *h'* of them.
83: 1 *h'* not thy peace, and be not still,
Ps 109: 1 *H'* not thy peace, O God of my
116: 3 the pains of hell gat *h'* upon me:
119:53 Horror hath taken *h'* upon me
117 *H'* thou me up, and I shall be safe:
143 and anguish have taken *h'* on me:
139:10 me, and thy right hand shall *h'* me.
Pr 2:19 neither take they *h'* of the paths
3:18 life to them that lay *h'* upon her:
4:13 Take fast *h'* of instruction; let her
5: 5 to death; her steps take *h'* on hell.
30:28 spider taketh *h'* with her hands,
31:19 and her hands *h'* the distaff.
Ec 2: 3 and to lay *h'* on folly, till I might
7:18 that thou shouldest take *h'* of this;
Ca 3: 8 They all *h'* swords, being expert
7: 8 I will take *h'* of the boughs thereof:
Isa 3: 6 a man shall take *h'* of his brother
4: 1 seven women shall take *h'* of one
5:29 shall roar, and lay *h'* of the prey,
13: 8 and sorrows shall take *h'* of them;
21: 3 pangs have taken *h'* upon me, as
27: 5 Or let him take *h'* of my strength,
31: 9 pass over to his strong *h'* for fear,
41:13 Lord thy God will *h'* thy right hand,
42: 6 and will *h'* thine hand, and will keep
56: 2 the son of man that layeth *h'* on it;
4 me, and take *h'* of my covenant;
6 it, and taketh *h'* of my covenant;
62: 1 Zion's sake will I not *h'* my peace,
6 never *h'* their peace day nor night:
64: 7 stirreth up himself to take *h'* of
12 wilt thou *h'* thy peace, and afflict
Jer 2:13 cisterns, that can *h'* no water.
4:19 I cannot *h'* my peace, because thou
6:23 They shall lay *h'* on bow and spear;
24 anguish hath taken *h'* of us, and
8: 5 *h'* fast deceit, they refuse to return.
21 astonishment hath taken *h'* on me.
50:42 They shall *h'* the bow and the lance:
43 feeble: anguish took *h'* of him,
Eze 29: 7 they took *h'* of thee by thy hand,
30:21 to make it strong to *h'* the sword.
41: 6 round about that they might have *h'*,
6 had not *h'* in the wall of the house.
Am 6:10 Then shall he say, *H'* thy tongue:
Mic 4: 8 strong *h'* of the daughter of Zion,
6:14 take *h'*, but shalt not deliver;
Na 1: 7 a strong *h'* in the day of trouble;
Hab 1:10 they shall deride every strong *h'*;
Zep 1: 7 *H'* thy peace at the presence of
Zec 1: 6 they not take *h'* of your fathers?
8:23 ten men shall take *h'* out of all
23 even shall take *h'* of the skirt of
9: 3 Tyrus did build herself a strong *h'*,
12 Turn you to the strong *h'*, ye
11: 5 and *h'* themselves not guilty; and
14:13 shall lay *h'* every one on the hand
M't 6:24 or else he will *h'* to the one, and
12:11 he not lay *h'* on it, and lift it out?
14: 3 For Herod had laid *h'* on John, and
20:31 because they should *h'* their peace:
21:26 for all *h'* John as a prophet.
26:48 kiss, that same is he: *h'* him fast.
55 temple, and ye laid no *h'* on me.
57 they that had laid *h'* on Jesus led
M'r 1:25 *H'* thy peace, and come out of him.
3:21 they went out to lay *h'* on him:
6:17 and laid *h'* upon John, and bound
7: 4 which they have received to *h'*, as
8 ye *h'* the tradition of men, as the
10:48 that he should *h'* his peace: but
12:12 and they sought to lay *h'* on him,
14:51 and the young men laid *h'* on him:
Lu 4:35 *H'* thy peace, and come out of him.
16:13 or else he will *h'* to the one, and
18:39 him, that he should *h'* his peace:
19:40 if these should *h'* their peace, the
20:20 that they might take *h'* of his words,
26 they could not take *h'* of his words
23:26 they laid *h'* upon one Simon, a
Ac 4: 3 put them in *h'* unto the next day:
12:17 with the hand to *h'* their peace,
18: 9 but speak, and *h'* not thy peace:
Ro 1:18 *h'* the truth in unrighteousness;
1Co 14:30 sitteth by, let the first *h'* his peace.
Ph'p 2:29 gladness; and *h'* such in reputation.
1Th 5:21 things; *h'* fast that which is good.
2Th 2:15 stand fast, and *h'* the traditions
1Ti 6:12 of faith, lay *h'* on eternal life,
19 that they may lay *h'* on eternal life.
2Ti 1:13 *H'* fast the form of sound words,
Heb 3: 6 if we *h'* fast the confidence and the
14 Christ, if we *h'* the beginning of our
4:14 of God, let us *h'* fast our profession.
6:18 lay *h'* upon the hope set before us:
10:23 Let us *h'* fast the profession of our
Re 2:14 that *h'* the doctrine of Balaam,
15 *h'* the doctrine of the Nicolaitanes,
25 ye have already *h'* fast till I come.
3: 3 and heard, and *h'* fast, and repent.
11 *h'* that fast which thou hast, that
18: 2 and the *h'* of every foul spirit, and
20: 2 And he laid *h'* on the dragon, that
holden See also HELD; UPHOLDEN; WITHHOLDEN.
2Ki 23:22 there was not *h'* such a passover
23 this passover was *h'* to the Lord
Job 36: 8 and be *h'* in cords of affliction;
Ps 18:35 and thy right hand hath *h'* me up,
71: 6 By thee have I been *h'* up from the
73:23 thou hast *h'* me by my right hand.
Pr 5:22 be *h'* with the cords of his sins.
Isa 42:14 I have long time *h'* my peace; I
45: 1 Cyrus, whose right hand I have *h'*,
Lu 24:16 But their eyes were *h'* that they
Ac 2:24 possible that he should be *h'* of it.
Ro 14: 4 Yea, he shall be *h'* up: for God is
holder See HOUSEHOLDER.
holdest See also BEHOLDEST; UPHOLDEST.
Es 4:14 if thou altogether *h'* thy peace at
Job 13:24 face, and *h'* me for thine enemy?
Ps 77: 4 Thou *h'* mine eyes waking: I am so
Jer 49:16 rock, that *h'* the height of the hill:
Hab 1:13 *h'* thy tongue when the wicked
Re 2:13 and thou *h'* fast my name, and
holdeth See also BEHOLDETH; UPHOLDETH; WITHHOLDETH.
Job 2: 3 and still he *h'* fast his integrity,
26: 9 He *h'* back the face of his throne,
Ps 66: 9 Which *h'* our soul in life, and
Pr 11:12 man of understanding *h'* his peace.
17:28 a fool, when he *h'* his peace,
Da 10:21 none that *h'* with me in these
Am 1: 5 that *h'* the sceptre from the house
8 that *h'* the sceptre from Ashkelon,
Re 2: 1 saith he that *h'* the seven stars in
holding See also BEHOLDING; UPHOLDING.
Isa 33:15 his hands from *h'* of bribes,
Jer 6:11 I am weary with *h'* in: I will pour
M'r 7: 3 not, *h'* the tradition of the elders.
Ph'p 2:16 *H'* forth the word of life; that I
Col 2:19 And not *h'* the Head, from which
1Ti 1:19 *H'* faith, and a good conscience;
3: 9 *H'* the mystery of the faith in a
Tit 1: 9 *H'* fast the faithful word as he
Re 7: 1 *h'* the four winds of the earth,
holds^ See also HOUSEHOLDS.
Nu 13:19 whether in tents, or in strong *h'*;
J'g 6: 2 mountains...caves, and strong *h'*.
1Sa 23:14 abode in the wilderness in strong *h'*,
19 hide himself with us in strong *h'*
29 and dwelt in strong *h'* at En-gedi.
2Ki 8:12 their strong *h'* wilt thou set on fire,
2Ch 11:11 he fortified the strong *h'*, and put
Ps 89:40 hast brought his strong *h'* to ruin.
Isa 23:11 to destroy the strong *h'* thereof.
Jer 48:18 and he shall destroy thy strong *h'*.
41 and the strong *h'* are surprised,
51:30 they have remained in their *h'*:
La 2: 2 strong *h'* of the daughter of Judah;
5 he hath destroyed his strong *h'*,
Eze 19: 9 they brought him into *h'*, that his
Da 11:24 his devices against the strong *h'*,
39 shall he do in the most strong *h'*
Mic 5:11 and throw down all thy strong *h'*:
Na 3:12 All thy strong *h'* shall be like fig
14 fortify thy strong *h'*: go into clay,
hole See also HOLE'S; HOLES.
Ex 28:32 there shall be an *h'* in the top of it,
32 woven work round about the *h'* of it,
32 as it were the *h'* of an habergeon,
39:23 And there was an *h'* in the midst of
23 the robe, as the *h'* of an habergeon,
23 with a band round about the *h'*,
2Ki 12: 9 a chest, bored a *h'* in the lid of it,
Ca 5: 4 put in his hand by the *h'* of the door,
Isa 11: 8 shall play on the *h'* of the asp,
51: 1 *h'* of the pit whence ye are digged.
Jer 13: 4 and hid it there in a *h'* of the rock.
Eze 8: 7 I looked, behold a *h'* in the wall.
hole's
Jer 48:28 nest in the sides of the *h'* mouth.
holes See also ARMHOLES.
1Sa 14:11 Hebrews come forth out of the *h'*
Isa 2:19 shall go into the *h'* of the rocks,
7:19 valleys, and in the *h'* of the rocks,
42:22 all of them snared in *h'*, and they
Jer 16:16 hill, and out of the *h'* of the rocks.
Mic 7:17 they shall move out of their *h'*
Na 2:12 filled his *h'* with prey, and his dens
Hag 1: 6 wages to put it into a bag with *h'*.
Zec 14:12 shall consume away in their *h'*,
M't 8:20 The foxes have *h'*, and the birds
Lu 9:58 Foxes have *h'*, and the birds of the
holiday See HOLYDAY.
holier
Isa 65: 5 near to me; for I am *h'* than thou.
holiest
Heb 9: 3 which is called the *H'* of all;
8 the way into the *h'* of all was not
10:19 into the *h'* by the blood of Jesus,
holily
1Th 2:10 how *h'* and justly and unblameably
holiness
Ex 15:11 who is like thee, glorious in *h'*,
28:36 of a signet, *H'* to the Lord.
39:30 of a signet, *H'* to the Lord.
1Ch 16:29 worship the Lord in the beauy of *h'*.
2Ch 20:21 that should praise the beauty of *h'*,
31:18 they sanctified themselves in *h'*:
Ps 29: 2 worship the Lord in the beauty of *h'*.
30: 4 at the remembrance of his *h'*.
47: 8 sitteth upon the throne of his *h'*.
48: 1 our God, in the mountain of his *h'*.
60: 6 God hath spoken in his *h'*; I will
89:35 Once have I sworn by my *h'* that I
93: 5 *h'* becometh thine house, O Lord,
96: 9 worship the Lord in the beauty of *h'*:
97:12 thanks at the remembrance of his *h'*.
108: 7 God hath spoken in his *h'*; I will
110: 3 in the beauties of *h'* from the
Isa 23:18 and her hire shall be *h'* to the Lord:
35: 8 and it shall be called The way of *h'*;
62: 9 shall drink it in the courts of my *h'*.
63:15 behold from the habitation of thy *h'*
18 people of thy *h'* have possessed it
Jer 2: 3 Israel was *h'* unto the Lord, and the
23: 9 and because of the words of his *h'*.
31:23 of justice, and mountain of *h'*.

Am 4: 2 The Lord God hath sworn by his *h'*
Ob 17 deliverance, and there shall be *h'*;
Zec 14: 20 of the horses, *H'* unto the Lord;
21 shall be *h'* unto the Lord of hosts:
Mal 2: 11 Judah hath profaned the *h'* of the
Lu 1: 75 In *h'* and righteousness before him.
Ac 3: 12 though by our own power or *h'* we
Ro 1: 4 power, according to the spirit of *h'*,
6: 19 servants to righteousness unto *h'*.
22 have your fruit unto *h'*, and the end
2Co 7: 1 perfecting *h'* in the fear of God.
Eph 4: 24 in righteousness and true *h'*.
1Th 3: 13 hearts unblameable in *h'* before God,
4: 7 us unto uncleanness, but unto *h'*.
1Ti 2: 15 faith ... charity and *h'* with sobriety.
Tit 2: 3 be in behaviour as becometh *h'*,
Heb 12: 10 that we might be partakers of his *h'*.
14 Follow peace with all men, and *h'*,

hollow
Ge 32: 25 him, he touched the *h'* of his thigh;
25 and the *h'* of Jacob's thigh was out
32 the *h'* of the thigh, unto this day:
32 because he touched the *h'* of Jacob's
Ex 27: 8 *H'* with boards shalt thou make it:
38: 7 he made the altar *h'* with boards.
Le 14: 37 walls of the house with *h'* strakes,
J'g 15: 19 God clave an *h'* place that was
Isa 40: 12 the waters in the *h'* of his hand,
Jer 52: 21 thereof was four fingers: it was *h'*.

Holon (*ho'-lon*) See also HILEN.
Jos 15: 51 And Goshen, and *H'*, and Giloh;
21: 15 And *H'* with her suburbs, and Debir
Jer 48: 21 upon *H'*, and upon Jahazah, and

holpen See also HELPED.
Ps 83: 8 they have *h'* the children of Lot.
86: 17 because thou, Lord, has *h'* me,
Isa 31: 3 he that is *h'* shall fall down, and
Da 11: 34 they shall be *h'* with a little help:
Lu 1: 54 He hath *h'* his servant Israel, in

holy See also HOLIER; HOLIEST; HOLYDAY; UNHOLY.
Ex 3: 5 whereon thou standest is *h'* ground.
12: 16 there shall be an *h'* convocation,
16 shall be an *h'* convocation to you;
15: 13 thy strength unto thy *h'* habitation.
16: 23 of the *h'* sabbath unto the Lord:
19: 6 of priests, and an *h'* nation.
20: 8 the sabbath day, to keep it *h'*.
22: 31 And ye shall be *h'* men unto me:
26: 33 between the *h'* place and the most *h'*.
34 of the testimony in the most *h'* place.
28: 2 shalt make *h'* garments for Aaron
4 shall make *h'* garments for Aaron
29 when he goeth in unto the *h'* place,
35 when he goeth in unto the *h'* place
38 bear the iniquity of the *h'* things,
38 shall hallow in all their *h'* gifts;
43 the altar to minister in the *h'* place;
29: 6 and put the *h'* crown upon the mitre.
29 the *h'* garments of Aaron shall be
30 cometh...to minister in the *h'* place.
31 seethe his flesh in the *h'* place.
33 eat thereof, because they are *h'*.
34 shall not be eaten, because it is *h'*.
37 it; and it shall be an altar most *h'*:
37 toucheth the altar shall be *h'*.
30: 10 it is most *h'* unto the Lord.
25 shalt make it an oil of *h'* ointment,
25 it shall be an *h'* anointing oil.
29 them, that they may be most *h'*:
29 whatsoever toucheth them...be *h'*.
31 This shall be an *h'* anointing oil
32 it is *h'*, and it shall be *h'* unto you.
35 tempered together, pure and *h'*:
36 thee: it shall be unto you most *h'*.
37 shall be unto thee *h'* for the Lord.
31: 10 the *h'* garments for Aaron the priest,
11 and sweet incense for the *h'* place:
14 sabbath therefore; for it is *h'* unto
15 sabbath to rest, *h'* to the Lord:
35: 2 day there shall be to you an *h'* day,
19 service, to do service in the *h'* place,
19 the *h'* garments for Aaron the priest,
21 service, and for the *h'* garments.
37: 29 And he made the *h'* anointing oil,
38: 24 work in all the work of the *h'* place,
39: 1 to do service in the *h'* place, and
1 made the *h'* garments for Aaron;
30 plate of the *h'* crown of pure gold,
41 to do service in the *h'* place, and
41 the *h'* garments for Aaron the priest,
40: 9 vessels thereof: and it shall be *h'*.
10 altar: and it shall be an altar most *h'*.
13 put upon Aaron the *h'* garments,
Le 2: 3, 10 is a thing most *h'* of the offerings
5: 15 in the *h'* things of the Lord; then
16 that he hath done in the *h'* thing,
6: 16 shall it be eaten in the *h'* place;
17 it is most *h'*, as is the sin offering,
18 one that toucheth them shall be *h'*.
25 before the Lord: it is most *h'*.
26 in the *h'* place shall it be eaten, in
27 touch the flesh thereof shall be *h'*:
27 it was sprinkled in the *h'* place.
29 shall eat thereof: it is most *h'*.
30 to reconcile withal in the *h'* place,
7: 1 trespass offering: it is most *h'*.
6 it shall be eaten in the *h'* place:
6 eaten in the...place: it is most *h'*.
8: 9 put the golden plate, the *h'* crown;
10: 10 difference between *h'* and unholy,
12 beside the altar: for it is most *h'*:
13 And ye shall eat it in the *h'* place,
17 have ye not eaten...in the *h'* place,
Le 10: 17 seeing it is most *h'*, and God hath
18 not brought in within the *h'* place:
18 indeed have eaten it in the *h'* place,
11: 44 and ye shall be *h'*; for I am *h'*:
45 ye shall therefore be *h'*, for I am *h'*.
14: 13 the burnt offering, in the *h'* place:
13 the trespass offering: it is most *h'*:
16: 2 not at all times into the *h'* place
3 shall Aaron come into the *h'* place:
4 He shall put on the *h'* linen coat,
4 these are *h'* garments; be attired:
16 make an atonement for the *h'* place,
17 make an atonement in the *h'* place,
20 an end of reconciling the *h'* place,
23 when he went into the *h'* place,
24 his flesh with water in the *h'* place,
27 to make atonement in the *h'* place,
32 linen clothes, even the *h'* garments:
33 an atonement for the *h'* sanctuary,
19: 2 and say unto them, Ye shall be *h'*:
2 for I the Lord your God am *h'*.
24 fruit thereof shall be *h'* to praise
20: 3 and to profane my *h'* name.
7 be ye *h'*: for I am the Lord your
26 be *h'* unto me: for I the Lord am *h'*,
21: 6 They shall be *h'* unto their God, and
6 do offer: therefore they shall be *h'*.
7 husband: for he is *h'* unto his God.
8 thy God: he shall be *h'* unto thee:
8 the Lord which sanctify you, am *h'*.
22 both of the most *h'*, and of the *h'*.
22: 2 themselves from the *h'* things of
2 that they profane not my *h'* name
3 that goeth unto the *h'* things, which
4 he shall not eat of the *h'* things,
6 and shall not eat of the *h'* things,
7 shall afterward eat of the *h'* things;
10 shall no stranger eat of the *h'* thing:
10 servant, shall not eat of the *h'* thing.
12 eat of an offering of the *h'* things.
14 man eat of the *h'* thing unwittingly,
14 it unto the priest with the *h'* thing.
15 they shall not profane the *h'* things
16 when they eat their *h'* things: for
32 Neither shall ye profane my *h'* name;
23: 2 which ye shall proclaim to be *h'*
3 sabbath of rest, an *h'* convocation;
4 even *h'* convocations, which ye
7 day ye shall have an *h'* convocation:
8 seventh day is an *h'* convocation:
20 shall be *h'* to the Lord for the priest.
21 may be an *h'* convocation unto you:
24 of trumpets, an *h'* convocation.
27 shall be an *h'* convocation unto you;
35 first day shall be an *h'* convocation:
36 eighth day shall be an *h'* convocation
37 shall proclaim to be *h'* convocations,
24: 9 and they shall eat it in the *h'* place:
9 is most *h'* unto him of the offerings
25: 12 it shall be *h'* unto you: ye shall eat
27: 9 of such unto the Lord shall be *h'*.
10 and the exchange thereof shall be *h'*.
14 man shall sanctify his house to be *h'*
21 shall be *h'* unto the Lord, as a field
23 that day, as a *h'* thing unto the Lord.
28 every devoted thing is most *h'* unto
30 is the Lord's: it is *h'* unto the Lord.
32 the tenth shall be *h'* unto the Lord.
33 it the change thereof shall be *h'*;
Nu 4: 4 about the most *h'* things:
15 they shall not touch any *h'* thing,
19 approach unto the most *h'* things:
20 see when the *h'* things are covered,
5: 9 every offering of the *h'* things of the
17 the priest shall take *h'* water in an
6: 5 he shall be *h'*, and shall let the locks
8 separation he is *h'* unto the Lord.
20 this is *h'* for the priest, with the
15: 40 and be *h'* unto your God.
16: 3 seeing all the congregation are *h'*,
5 will shew who are his, and who is *h'*;
7 Lord doth choose, he shall be *h'*:
18: 9 shall be thine of the most *h'* things,
9 be most *h'* for thee and for thy sons.
10 In the most *h'* place shalt thou eat
10 shall eat it: it shall be *h'* unto thee.
17 they are *h'*: thou shalt sprinkle
19 the heave offerings of the *h'* things,
32 neither shall ye pollute the *h'* things
28: 7 in the *h'* place shalt thou cause the
18 first day shall be an *h'* convocation;
25, 26 ye shall have an *h'* convocation;
29: 1 ye shall have an *h'* convocation;
7 seventh month an *h'* convocation;
12 ye shall have an *h'* convocation; ye
31: 6 to the war, with the *h'* instruments,
35: 25 which was anointed with the *h'* oil.
De 7: 6 thou art an *h'* people unto the Lord
12: 26 Only thy *h'* things which thou hast,
14: 2 for thou art an *h'* people unto the
21 For thou art an *h'* people unto the
23: 14 therefore shall thy camp be *h'*: that
26: 15 Look down from thy *h'* habitation,
19 thou mayest be an *h'* people unto
28: 9 shall establish thee an *h'* people
33: 8 Urim be with thy *h'* one, whom
Jos 5: 15 place whereon thou standest is *h'*.
24: 19 serve the Lord: for he is an *h'* God;
1Sa 2: 2 There is none *h'* as the Lord: for
6: 20 to stand before this *h'* Lord God?
21: 5 vessels of the young men are *h'*,
1Ki 6: 16 oracle, even for the most *h'* place.
7: 50 the inner house, the most *h'* place,
8: 4 all the *h'* vessels that were in the
6 of the house, to the most *h'* place,
8 out in the *h'* place before the oracle,
1Ki 8: 10 priests were come out of the *h'* place,
2Ki 4: 9 I perceive that this is an *h'* man
19: 22 even against the *H'* One of Israel.
1Ch 6: 49 all the work of the place most *h'*,
16: 10 Glory ye in his *h'* name: let the
35 we may give thanks to thy *h'* name,
22: 19 the *h'* vessels of God, into the house
23: 13 should sanctify the most *h'* things,
28 in the purifying of all *h'* things,
32 and the charge of the *h'* place,
29: 3 I have prepared for the *h'* house,
16 build thee an house for thine *h'* name
2Ch 3: 8 and he made the most *h'* house, the
10 in the most *h'* house he made two
4: 22 doors thereof for the most *h'* place,
5: 5 all the *h'* vessels that were in the
7 into the most *h'* place, even under
11 were come out of the *h'* place:
8: 11 of Israel, because the places are *h'*,
23: 6 they shall go in, for they are *h'*: but
29: 5 the filthiness out of the *h'* place.
7 burnt offerings in the *h'* place unto
30: 27 came up to his *h'* dwelling place,
31: 6 the tithe of *h'* things which were
14 of the Lord, and the most *h'* things.
35: 3 which were *h'* unto the Lord,
3 Put the *h'* ark in the house which
5 stand in the *h'* place according to
13 but the other *h'* offerings sod they
Ezr 2: 63 should not eat of the most *h'* things,
8: 28 unto them, Ye are *h'* unto the Lord;
28 Lord; the vessels are *h'* also; and
9: 2 *h'* seed have mingled themselves
8 to give us a nail in his *h'* place,
Ne 7: 65 should not eat of the most *h'* things,
8: 9 This day is *h'* unto the Lord your
10 for this day is *h'* unto our Lord:
11 Hold your peace, for the day is *h'*;
9: 14 known unto them thy *h'* sabbath,
10: 31 on the sabbath, or on the *h'* day:
33 the set feasts, and for the *h'* things,
11: 1 to dwell in Jerusalem the *h'* city,
18 All the Levites in the *h'* city
12: 47 and they sanctified *h'* things unto
Job 6: 10 concealed the words of the *H'* One.
Ps 2: 6 my king upon my *h'* hill of Zion.
3: 4 and he heard me out of his *h'* hill.
5: 7 will I worship toward thy *h'* temple.
11: 4 The Lord is in his *h'* temple, the
15: 1 who shall dwell in thy *h'* hill?
16: 10 thou suffer thine *H'* One to see
20: 6 will hear him from his *h'* heaven
22: 3 thou art *h'*, O thou that inhabitest
24: 3 or who shall stand in his *h'* place?
28: 2 up my hands toward thy *h'* oracle.
33: 21 we have trusted in his *h'* name.
43: 3 let them bring me unto thy *h'* hill,
46: 4 the *h'* place of the tabernacles of
51: 11 take not thy *h'* spirit from me.
65: 4 thy house, even of thy *h'* temple.
68: 5 widows, is God in his *h'* habitation.
17 them, as in Sinai, in the *h'* place.
35 art terrible out of thy *h'* places:
71: 22 the harp, O thou *H'* One of Israel.
78: 41 and limited the *H'* One of Israel.
79: 1 thy *h'* temple have they defiled;
86: 2 Preserve my soul; for I am *h'*: O
87: 1 foundation is in the *h'* mountains.
89: 18 the *H'* One of Israel is our king.
19 spakest in vision to thy *h'* one,
20 with my *h'* oil have I anointed him:
98: 1 his right hand, and his *h'* arm,
99: 3 and terrible name; for it is *h'*.
5 at his footstool; for he is *h'*.
9 our God, and worship at his *h'* hill;
9 hill; for the Lord our God is *h'*.
103: 1 is within me, bless his *h'* name.
105: 3 Glory ye in his *h'* name: let the
42 For he remembered his *h'* promise,
106: 47 to give thanks unto thy *h'* name,
111: 9 ever: *h'* and reverend is his name.
138: 2 will worship toward thy *h'* temple,
145: 17 his ways, and *h'* in all his works.
21 bless his *h'* name for ever and ever.
Pr 9: 10 and the knowledge of the *h'* is
20: 25 who devoureth that which is *h'*,
30: 3 nor have the knowledge of the *h'*.
Ec 8: 10 and gone from the place of the *h'*,
Isa 1: 4 have provoked the *H'* One of Israel
4: 3 in Jerusalem, shall be called *h'*,
5: 16 God that is *h'* shall be sanctified
19 counsel of the *H'* One of Israel draw
24 despised the word of the *H'* One
6: 3 said, *H'*, *h'*, *h'*, is the Lord of hosts:
13 the *h'* seed shall be the substance
10: 17 fire, and his *H'* One for a flame:
20 stay upon the Lord, the *H'* One of
11: 9 nor destroy in all my *h'* mountain:
12: 6 great is the *H'* One of Israel in the
17: 7 shall have respect to the *H'* One
27: 13 worship the Lord in the *h'* mount
29: 19 rejoice in the *H'* One of Israel.
23 sanctify the *H'* One of Jacob, and
30: 11 cause the *H'* One of Israel to cease
12 thus saith the *H'* One of Israel,
15 the Lord God, the *H'* One of Israel;
29 night when a *h'* solemnity is kept;
31: 1 look not unto the *H'* One of Israel,
37: 23 even against the *H'* One of Israel.
40: 25 shall I be equal? saith the *H'* One.
41: 14 thy redeemer, the *H'* One of Israel.
16 shalt glory in the *H'* One of Israel.
20 the *H'* One of Israel hath created it.
43: 3 Lord thy God, the *H'* One of Israel,
14 your redeemer, the *H'* One of Israel;
15 I am the Lord, your *H'* One, the

Isa 45:11 saith the Lord, the *H'* One of Israel,
47: 4 is his name, the *H'* One of Israel.
48: 2 they call themselves of the *h'* city,
17 Redeemer, the *H'* One of Israel;
49: 7 Redeemer of Israel, and his *H'* One,
7 the *H'* One of Israel, and he shall
52: 1 garments, O Jerusalem, the *h'* city:
10 The Lord hath made bare his *h'* arm
54: 5 Redeemer the *H'* One of Israel;
55: 5 God, and for the *H'* One of Israel;
56: 7 will I bring to my *H'* mountain,
57:13 and shall inherit my *h'* mountain;
15 eternity, whose name is *H'*; I dwell
15 I dwell in the high and *h'* place,
58:13 doing thy pleasure on my *h'* day;
13 the *h'* of the Lord, honourable;
60: 9 God, and to the *H'* One of Israel,
14 The Zion of the *H'* One of Israel.
62:12 they shall call them, The *h'* people,
63:10 rebelled, and vexed his *h'* Spirit:
11 he that put his *h'* Spirit within him?
64:10 Thy *h'* cities are a wilderness, Zion
11 Our *h'* and our beautiful house,
65:11 Lord, that forget my *h'* mountain,
25 nor destroy in all my *h'* mountain,
66:20 to my *h'* mountain Jerusalem, saith
Jer 11:15 the *h'* flesh is passed from thee?
25:30 his voice from his *h'* habitation;
31:40 shall be *h'* unto the Lord; it shall
50:29 Lord, against the *H'* One of Israel.
51: 5 sin against the *H'* One of Israel.
Eze 7:24 and their *h'* places shall be defiled.
20:39 but pollute ye my *h'* name no more
40 mine *h'* mountain, in the mountain
40 oblations, with all your *h'* things.
21: 2 drop thy word toward the *h'* place,
22: 8 Thou hast despised mine *h'* things,
26 and have profaned mine *h'* things,
26 between the *h'* and profane,
28:14 thou wast upon the *h'* mountain
36:20 they profaned my *h'* name, when
21 I had pity for mine *h'* name, which
22 but for mine *h'* name's sake, which
38 As the *h'* flock, as the flock of
39: 7 So will I make my *h'* name known
7 will not let them pollute my *h'* name
7 I am the Lord, the *H'* One in Israel.
25 will be jealous for my *h'* name;
41: 4 unto me, This is the most *h'* place.
42:13 separate place, they be *h'* chambers,
13 shall eat the most *h'* things:
13 shall they lay the most *h'* things,
13 trespass offering...the place is *h'*.
14 shall they not go out of the *h'* place
14 they minister; for they are *h'*;
43: 7 and my *h'* name, shall the house of
8 they have even defiled my *h'* name
12 round about shall be most *h'*.
44: 8 kept the charge of mine *h'* things:
13 to come near to any of my *h'* things,
13 in the most *h'* place: but they shall
19 lay them in the *h'* chambers, and
23 between the *h'* and profane.
45: 1 the Lord, an *h'* portion of the land:
1 This shall be *h'* in all the borders
3 sanctuary and the most *h'* place.
4 The *h'* portion of the land shall be
4 and an *h'* place for the sanctuary.
6 the oblation of the *h'* portion:
7 of the oblation of the *h'* portion,
7 before the oblation of the *h'* portion,
46:19 into the *h'* chambers of the priests,
48:10 the priests, shall be this *h'* oblation;
12 shall be unto them a thing most *h'*
14 the land: for it is *h'* unto the Lord.
18 the oblation of the *h'* portion shall
18 the oblation of the *h'* portion;
20 ye shall offer the *h'* oblation
21 and on the other of the *h'* oblation,
21 and it shall be the *h'* oblation;
Da 4: 8 in whom is the spirit of the *h'* gods:
9 the spirit of the *h'* gods is in thee,
13 a watcher and an *h'* one came down
17 demand by the word of the *h'* ones:
18 the spirit of the *h'* gods is in thee.
23 a watcher and an *h'* one coming
5:11 whom is the spirit of the *h'* gods;
8:24 destroy the mighty...*h'* people.
9:16 city Jerusalem, thy *h'* mountain:
20 God for the *h'* mountain of my God;
24 thy people and upon thy *h'* city,
24 prophecy, and to anoint the most *H'*.
11:28 shall be against the *h'* covenant;
30 indignation against the *h'* covenant:
30 them that forsake the *h'* covenant.
45 seas in the glorious *h'* mountain;
12: 7 scatter the power of the *h'* people,
Ho 11: 9 the *H'* One in the midst of thee:
Joe 2: 1 sound an alarm in my *h'* mountain:
3:17 dwelling in Zion, my *h'* mountain:
17 then shall Jerusalem be *h'*, and
Am 2: 7 same maid, to profane my *h'* name:
Ob 16 have drunk upon my *h'* mountain,
Jon 2: 4 look again toward thy *h'* temple.
7 unto thee, into thine *h'* temple.
Mic 1: 2 you, the Lord from his *h'* temple.
Hab 1:12 O Lord my God, mine *H'* One?
2:20 but the Lord is in his *h'* temple:
3: 3 and the *H'* One from mount Paran.
Zep 3:11 because of my *h'* mountain.
Hag 2:12 If one bear *h'* flesh in the skirt of
12 oil, or any meat, shall it be *h'*?
Zec 2:12 Judah his portion in the *h'* land,
13 raised up out of his *h'* habitation.
8: 3 the Lord of hosts the *h'* mountain.
M't 1:18 found with child of the *H'* Ghost.

M't 1:20 in her is of the *H'* Ghost.
3:11 baptize you with the *H'* Ghost,
4: 5 devil taketh him up into the *h'* city,
7: 6 not that which is *h'* unto the dogs,
12:31 the blasphemy against the *H'* Ghost
32 speaketh against the *H'* Ghost,
24:15 of desolation,...stand in the *h'* place,
25:31 glory, and all the *h'* angels with him,
27:53 went into the *h'* city, and appeared
28:19 of the Son, and of the *H'* Ghost:
M'r 1: 8 baptize you with the *H'* Ghost.
24 who thou art, the *H'* One of God.
3:29 blaspheme against the *H'* Ghost
6:20 that he was a just man and an *h'*,
8:38 of his Father with the *h'* angels.
12:36 himself said by the *H'* Ghost,
13:11 not ye that speak, but the *H'* Ghost.
Lu 1:15 shall be filled with the *H'* Ghost,
35 The *H'* Ghost shall come upon
35 that *h'* thing which shall be born
41 was filled with the *H'* Ghost:
49 great things; and *h'* is his name.
67 was filled with the *H'* Ghost,
70 the mouth of his *h'* prophets, which
72 and to remember his *h'* covenant;
2:23 womb shall be called *h'* to the Lord;
25 and the *H'* Ghost was upon him.
26 unto him by the *H'* Ghost, that
3:16 baptize you with the *H'* Ghost
22 the *H'* Ghost descended in a bodily
4: 1 Jesus being full of the *H'* Ghost
34 who thou art; the *H'* One of God.
9:26 in his Father's, and of the *h'* angels.
11:13 give the *H'* Spirit to them that ask
12:10 against the *H'* Ghost it shall
12 For the *H'* Ghost shall teach you
Joh 1:33 which baptizeth with the *H'* Ghost.
7:39 for the *H'* Ghost was not yet given;
14:26 Comforter, which is the *H'* Ghost,
17:11 *H'* Father, keep through thine own
20:22 them, Receive ye the *H'* Ghost:
Ac 1: 2 he through the *H'* Ghost had given
5 be baptized with the *H'* Ghost not
8 that the *H'* Ghost is come upon
16 the *H'* Ghost by the mouth of David
2: 4 were all filled with the *H'* Ghost,
27 thine *H'* One to see corruption.
33 the promise of the *H'* Ghost, he
38 receive the gift of the *H'* Ghost.
3:14 ye denied the *H'* One and the Just,
21 by the mouth of all his *h'* prophets
4: 8 Peter, filled with the *H'* Ghost, said
27 of a truth against thy *h'* child Jesus,
30 by the name of thy *h'* child Jesus.
31 were all filled with the *H'* Ghost,
5: 3 heart to lie to the *H'* Ghost, and
32 so is also the *H'* Ghost, whom
6: 3 full of the *H'* Ghost and wisdom,
5 full of faith and of the *H'* Ghost,
13 words against this *h'* place, and the
7:33 where thou standest is *h'* ground.
51 do always resist the *H'* Ghost:
55 he, being full of the *H'* Ghost,
8:15 they might receive the *H'* Ghost:
17 and they received the *H'* Ghost.
18 hands the *H'* Ghost was given, he
19 he may receive the *H'* Ghost.
9:17 and be filled with the *H'* Ghost.
31 in the comfort of the *H'* Ghost,
10:22 was warned from God by an *h'* angel
38 with the *H'* Ghost and with power:
44 the *H'* Ghost fell on all them
45 out the gift of the *H'* Ghost
47 have received the *H'* Ghost as well
11:15 the *H'* Ghost fell on them, as on
16 shall be baptized with the *H'* Ghost.
24 full of the *H'* Ghost and of faith:
13: 2 the *H'* Ghost said, Separate me
4 being sent forth by the *H'* Ghost,
9 filled with the *H'* Ghost, set his
35 thine *H'* One to see corruption.
52 with joy, and with the *H'* Ghost.
15: 8 giving them the *H'* Ghost, even
28 it seemed good to the *H'* Ghost,
16: 6 were forbidden of the *H'* Ghost
19: 2 Have ye received the *H'* Ghost
2 whether there be any *H'* Ghost.
6 the *H'* Ghost came on them;
20:23 Save that the *H'* Ghost witnesseth
28 *H'* Ghost hath made you overseers,
21:11 said, Thus saith the *H'* Ghost, So
28 and hath polluted this *h'* place.
28:25 Well spake the *H'* Ghost by Esaias
Ro 1: 2 by his prophets in the *h'* scriptures,
5: 5 in our hearts by the *H.* Ghost
7:12 law is *h'*, and the commandment *h'*,
9: 1 me witness in the *H'* Ghost,
11:16 For if the firstfruit be *h'*, the lump is
16 the lump is also *h'*: and if the lump
16 if the root be *h'*, so are the branches.
12: 1 a living sacrifice, *h'*, acceptable unto
14:17 peace, and joy in the *H'* Ghost.
15:13 through the power of the *H'* Ghost.
16 being sanctified by the *H'* Ghost.
16:16 Salute one another with an *h'* kiss.
1Co 2:13 which the *H'* Ghost teacheth;
3:17 for the temple of God is *h'*, which
6:19 is the temple of the *H'* Ghost
7:14 children unclean; but now are they *h'*.
34 may be *h'* both in body and in spirit:
9:13 which minister about *h'* things
12: 3 is the Lord, but by the *H'* Ghost.
16:20 Greet ye one another with an *h'* kiss
2Co 6: 6 by kindness, by the *H'* Ghost, by
13:12 Greet one another with an *h'* kiss.
14 communion of the *H'* Ghost, be

Eph 1: 4 we should be *h'* and without blame
13 sealed with that *h'* Spirit of promise,
2:21 groweth unto an *h'* temple in the
3: 5 unto his *h'* apostles and prophets
4:30 And grieve not the *h'* Spirit of God,
5:27 it should be *h'* and without blemish.
Col 1:22 to present you *h'* and unblameable
3:12 as the elect of God, *h'* and beloved,
1Th 1: 5 in power, and in the *H'* Ghost,
6 affliction with joy of the *H'* Ghost:
4: 8 hath also given unto us his *h'* Spirit.
5:26 Greet all the brethren with an *h'* kiss.
27 be read unto all the *h'* brethren.
1Ti 2: 8 lifting up *h'* hands, without wrath
2Ti 1: 9 us, and called us with an *h'* calling,
14 by the *H'* Ghost which dwelleth
3:15 thou hast known the *h'* scriptures,
Tit 1: 8 sober, just, *h'*, temperate; Holding
3: 5 and renewing of the *H'* Ghost;
Heb 2: 4 miracles and gifts of the *H'* Ghost,
3: 1 Wherefore, *h'* brethren, partakers of
7 as the *H'* Ghost saith, To day if
6: 4 made partakers of the *H'* Ghost,
7:26 who is *h'*, harmless, undefiled,
9: 8 The *H'* Ghost this signifying,
12 he entered in once into the *h'* place,
24 into the *h'* places made with hands,
25 entereth into the *h'* place every year
10:15 the *H'* Ghost also is a witness to
1Pe 1:12 you with the *H'* Ghost sent down
15 hath called you is *h'*, so be ye *h'* in all
16 it is written, Be ye *h'*; for I am *h'*.
2: 5 spiritual house, an *h'* priesthood, to
9 a royal priesthood, an *h'* nation, a
3: 5 in the old time the *h'* women also,
2Pe 1:18 we were with him in the *h'* mount.
21 *h'* men of God spake as they were
21 were moved by the *H'* Ghost.
2:21 from the *h'* commandment delivered
3: 2 spoken before by the *h'* prophets,
11 in all *h'* conversation and godliness,
1Jo 2:20 ye have an unction from the *H'* One,
5: 7 the Word, and the *H'* Ghost:
Jude 20 yourselves in your most *h'* faith,
20 faith, praying in the *H'* Ghost,
Re 3: 7 saith he that is *h'*, he that is true,
4: 8 night, saying, *H'*, *h'*, *h'*, Lord God
6:10 How long, O Lord, *h'* and true, dost
11: 2 the *h'* city shall they tread under foot
14:10 the presence of the *h'* angels, and in
15: 4 for thou only art *h'*: for all nations
18:20 and ye *h'* apostles and prophets;
20: 6 Blessed and *h'* is he that hath part
21: 2 John saw the *h'* city, new Jerusalem,
10 me that great city, the *h'* Jerusalem,
22: 6 God of the *h'* prophets sent his angel
11 and that is *h'*, let him be...still.
11 and he that is..., let him be *h'* still.
19 book of life, and out of the *h'* city,

holyday See also HOLY and DAY.
Ps 42: 4 with a multitude that kept *h'*.
Col 2:16 in respect of an *h'*, or of the new

Holy-Ghost See HOLY and GHOST.

Holy-One See HOLY and ONE.

Holy-place See HOLY and PLACE.

Holy-Spirit See HOLY and SPIRIT.

Homam (*ho'-mam*) See also HEMAM.
1Ch 1:39 the sons of Lotan; Hori and *H'*:

home See also HOMEBORN.
Ge 39:16 by her, until his lord came *h'*.
43:16 Bring these men *h'*, and slay, and
26 And when Joseph came *h'*, they
Ex 9:19 the field, and shall not be brought *h'*,
Le 18: 9 she be born at *h'*, or born abroad,
De 21:12 shalt bring her *h'* to thine house;
24: 5 but he shall be free at *h'* one year,
Jos 2:18 father's household, *h'* unto thee.
J'g 11: 9 If ye bring me *h'* again to fight
19: 9 your way, that thou mayest go *h'*.
Ru 1:21 hath brought me *h'* again empty:
1Sa 2:20 And they went unto their own *h'*.
6: 7 bring their calves *h'* from them:
10 cart, and shut up their calves at *h'*:
10:26 And Saul also went *h'* to Gibeah;
18: 2 go no more *h'* to his father's house.
24:22 And Saul went *h'*; but David and
2Sa 13: 7 David sent *h'* to Tamar, saying,
14:13 not fetch *h'* again his banished.
17:23 and gat him *h'* to his house, to his
1Ki 5:14 in Lebanon, and two months at *h'*:
13: 7 Come *h'* with me, and refresh thyself,
15 Come *h'* with me, and eat bread.
2Ki 14:10 glory of this, and tarry at *h'*: for
1Ch 13:12 shall I bring the ark of God *h'* to me?
13 So David brought not the ark *h'* to
2Ch 25:10 out of Ephraim, to go *h'* again:
10 and they returned *h'* in great anger.
19 abide now at *h'*; why shouldest
Es 5:10 and when he came *h'*, he sent and
Job 39:12 him, that he will bring *h'* thy seed,
Ps 68:12 that tarried at *h'* divided the spoil.
Pr 7:19 For the goodman is not at *h'*, he is
20 will come *h'* at the day appointed.
Ec 12: 5 man goeth to his long *h'*, and the
Jer 39:14 that he should carry him *h'*: so he
La 1:20 bereaveth, at *h'* there is as death.
Hab 2: 5 proud man, neither keepeth at *h'*,
Hag 1: 9 when ye brought it *h'*, I did blow
M't 8: 6 my servant lieth at *h'* sick of the
M'r 5:19 Go *h'* to thy friends, and tell them
Lu 9:61 bid them farewell, which are at *h'* at
15: 6 And when he cometh *h'*, he calleth
Joh 19:27 that disciple took her unto his own *h'*.
20:10 went away again unto their own *h'*.

Ac 21: 6 ship; and they returned *h'* again.
1Co 11: 34 any man hunger, let him eat at *h'*;
14: 35 let them ask their husbands at *h'*:
2Co 5: 6 whilst we are at *h'* in the body, we
1Ti 5: 4 learn first to shew piety at *h'*, and
Tit 2: 5 be discreet, chaste, keepers at *h'*,

homeborn
Ex 12: 49 One law shall be to him that is *h'*,
Jer 2: 14 Israel a servant? is he a *h'* slave?

homer (*ho'-mer*) See also HOMERS.
Le 27: 16 an *h'* of barley seed shall be valued
Isa 5: 10 seed of an *h'* shall yield an ephah.
Eze 45: 11 may contain the tenth part of an *h'*,
11 the ephah the tenth part of an *h'*:
11 measure thereof shall be after the *h'*.
13 part of an ephah of an *h'* of wheat,
13 part of an ephah of an *h'* of barley:
14 the cor, which is an *h'* of ten baths;
14 ten baths; for ten baths are an *h'*:
Ho 3: 2 of silver, and for an *h'* of barley,
2 of barley, and an half *h'* of barley:

homers (*ho'-mers*)
Nu 11: 32 gathered least gathered ten *h'*:

honest See also DISHONEST.
Lu 8: 15 they, which in an *h'* and good heart,
Ac 6: 3 you seven men of *h'* report, full of the
Ro 12: 17 things *h'* in the sight of all men.
2Co 8: 21 Providing for *h'* things, not only in
13: 7 but ye should do that which is *h'*,
Ph'p 4: 8 are true, whatsoever things are *h'*,
1Pe 2: 12 your conversation *h'* among the

honestly
Ro 13: 13 Let us walk *h'*, as in the day; not
1Th 4: 12 That ye may walk *h'* toward them
Heb13: 18 in all things willing to live *h'*.

honesty See also DISHONESTY.
1Ti 2: 2 quiet...life in all godliness and *h'*.

honey See also HONEYCOMB.
Ge 43: 11 a little balm, and a little *h'*, spices,
Ex 3: 8 a land flowing with milk and *h'*;
17 a land flowing with milk and *h'*.
13: 5 a land flowing with milk and *h'*,
16: 31 of it was like wafers made with *h'*.
33: 3 a land flowing with milk and *h'*:
Le 2: 11 burn no leaven, nor any *h'*, in any
20: 24 land that floweth with milk and *h'*:
Nu 13: 27 surely it floweth with milk and *h'*;
14: 8 land which floweth with milk and *h'*.
16: 13, 14 that floweth with milk and *h'*,
De 6: 3 land that floweth with milk and *h'*.
8: 8 a land of oil olive, and *h'*;
11: 9 land that floweth with milk and *h'*.
26: 9, 15 that floweth with milk and *h'*.
27: 3 land that floweth with milk and *h'*;
31: 20 that floweth with milk and *h'*; and
32: 13 made him to suck *h'* out of the rock,
Jos 5: 6 land that floweth with milk and *h'*.
J'g 14: 8 was a swarm of bees and *h'* in the
9 had taken the *h'* out of the carcase
18 What is sweeter than *h'*? and what
1Sa 14: 25 and there was *h'* upon the ground.
26 the *h'* dropped; but no man put his
29 because I tasted a little of this *h'*.
43 I did but taste a little *h'* with the
2Sa 17: 29 And *h'*, and butter, and sheep, and
1Ki 14: 3 and cracknels, and a cruse of *h'*,
2Ki 18: 32 a land of oil olive and of *h'*, that ye
2Ch 31: 5 wine, and oil, and *h'*, and of all the
Job 20: 17 floods, the brooks of *h'* and butter.
Ps 19: 10 gold: sweeter also than *h'* and the
81: 16 and with *h'* out of the rock should I
119: 103 yea, sweeter than *h'* to my mouth!
Pr 24: 13 son, eat thou *h'*, because it is good;
25: 16 Hast thou found *h'*? eat so much as
27 It is not good to eat much *h'*: so for
Ca 4: 11 *h'* and milk are under thy tongue;
5: 1 eaten my honeycomb with my *h'*;
Isa 7: 15 Butter and *h'* shall he eat, that he
22 for butter and *h'* shall every one eat
Jer 11: 5 a land flowing with milk and *h'*, as
32: 22 a land flowing with milk and *h'*;
41: 8 and of barley, and of oil, and of *h'*.
Eze 3: 3 in my mouth as *h'* for sweetness.
16: 13 didst eat fine flour, and *h'*, and oil:
19 gave thee, fine flour, and oil, and *h'*,
20: 6, 15 flowing with milk and *h'*, which
27: 17 Pannag, and *h'*, and oil, and balm.
M't 3: 4 his meat was locusts and wild *h'*.
M'r 1: 6 and he did eat locusts and wild *h'*;
Re 10: 9 it shall be in thy mouth sweet as *h'*.
10 it was in my mouth sweet as *h'*:

honeycomb
1Sa 14: 27 and dipped it in an *h'*, and put
Ps 19: 10 also than honey and the *h'*.
Pr 5: 3 a strange woman drop as an *h'*.
16: 24 Pleasant words are as an *h'*,
24: 13 the *h'*, which is sweet to thy taste:
27: 7 The full soul loatheth an *h'*; but to
Ca 4: 11 lips, O my spouse, drop as the *h'*:
5: 1 have eaten my *h'* with my honey;
Lu 24: 42 a broiled fish, and of an *h'*.

honour See also DISHONOUR; HONOURABLE; HONOURED; HONOUREST; HONOURETH; HONOURS.
Ge 49: 6 mine *h'*, be not thou united: for
Ex 14: 17 and I will get me *h'* upon Pharaoh,
18 I have gotten me *h'* upon Pharaoh,
20: 12 *H'* thy father and thy mother: that
Le 19: 15 nor *h'* the person of the mighty:
32 and *h'* the face of the old man, and
Nu 22: 17 promote thee unto very great *h'*,
37 able indeed to promote thee to *h'*?
24: 11 to promote thee unto great *h'*; but,
Nu 24: 11 Lord hath kept thee back from *h'*.
27: 20 put some of thine *h'* upon him,
De 5: 16 *H'* thy father and thy mother, as
26: 19 in praise, and in name, and in *h'*;
J'g 4: 9 thou takest shall not be for thine *h'*;
9: 9 by me they *h'* God and man, and
13: 17 come to pass we may do thee *h'*?
1Sa 2: 30 them that *h'* me I will *h'*, and they
15: 30 sinned: yet *h'* me now, I pray thee,
2Sa 6: 22 of, of them shall I be had in *h'*.
10: 3 thou that David doth *h'* thy father,
1Ki 3: 13 hast not asked, both riches, and *h'*:
1Ch 16: 27 Glory and *h'* are in his presence;
17: 18 to thee, for the *h'* of thy servant?
19: 3 thou that David doth *h'* thy father,
29: 12 Both riches and *h'* come of thee,
28 old age, full of days, riches, and *h'*:
2Ch 1: 11 hast not asked riches, wealth, or *h'*,
12 give thee riches, and wealth, and *h'*,
17: 5 he had riches and *h'* in abundance.
18: 1 had riches and *h'* in abundance, and
26: 18 neither shall it be for thine *h'* from
32: 27 exceeding much riches and *h'*: and
33 inhabitants of Jerusalem did him *h'*
Es 1: 4 and the *h'* of his excellent majesty
20 shall give to their husbands *h'*, both
6: 3 What *h'* and dignity hath been done
6 whom the king delighteth to *h'*?
6 would the king delight to do *h'* more
7, 9 whom the king delighteth to *h'*,
9, 11 whom the king delighteth to *h'*.
8: 16 light, and gladness, and joy, and *h'*.
Job 14: 21 sons come to *h'*, and he knoweth
Ps 7: 5 earth, and lay mine *h'* in the dust.
8: 5 crowned him with glory and *h'*.
21: 5 *h'* and majesty hast thou laid upon
26: 8 the place where thine *h'* dwelleth.
49: 12 man being in *h'* abideth not: he is
20 that is in *h'*, and understandeth not,
66: 2 Sing forth the *h'* of his name:
71: 8 praise and with thy *h'* all the day.
91: 15 I will deliver him, and *h'* him.
96: 6 *H'* and majesty are before him:
104: 1 art clothed with *h'* and majesty.
112: 9 his horn shall be exalted with *h'*.
145: 5 the glorious *h'* of thy majesty, and
149: 9 written: this *h'* have all his saints.
Pr 3: 9 *H'* the Lord with thy substance,
16 and in her left hand riches and *h'*.
4: 8 she shall bring thee to *h'*, when
5: 9 Lest thou give thine *h'* unto others,
8: 18 Riches and *h'* are with me; yea,
11: 16 A gracious woman retaineth *h'*:
14: 28 multitude of people is the king's *h'*:
15: 33 wisdom; and before *h'* is humility.
18: 12 haughty, and before *h'* is humility.
20: 3 It is an *h'* for a man to cease from
21: 21 findeth life, righteousness, and *h'*.
22: 4 the Lord are riches, and *h'*, and life.
25: 2 but the *h'* of kings is to search out
26: 1 harvest, so *h'* is not seemly for a fool.
8 so is he that giveth *h'* to a fool.
29: 23 *h'* shall uphold the humble in spirit.
31: 25 Strength and *h'* are her clothing;
Ec 6: 2 riches, wealth, and *h'*, so that he
10: 1 is in reputation for wisdom and *h'*.
Isa 29: 13 with their lips do *h'* me, but have
43: 20 The beast of the field shall *h'* me,
58: 13 and shalt *h'* him, not doing thine
Jer 33: 9 a praise and an *h'* before all the
Da 2: 6 me gifts and rewards and great *h'*:
4: 30 of my power, and for the *h'* of my
36 mine *h'* and brightness returned
37 extol and *h'* the King of heaven, all
5: 18 and majesty, and glory, and *h'*:
11: 21 not give the *h'* of the kingdom:
38 shall he *h'* the God of forces: and
38 his fathers knew not shall he *h'*
Mal 1: 6 I be a father, where is mine *h'*?
M't 13: 57 A prophet is not without *h'*, save in
15: 4 *H'* thy father and mother: and he
6 *h'* not his father or his mother, he
19: 19 *H'* thy father and thy mother: and,
M'r 6: 4 A prophet is not without *h'*, but in
7: 10 *H'* thy father and thy mother;
10: 19 not; *H'* thy father and mother.
Lu 18: 20 *h'* thy father and thy mother.
Joh 4: 44 hath no *h'* in his own country.
5: 23 that all men should *h'* the Son,
23 the Son, even as they *h'* the Father.
41 I receive not *h'* from men.
44 which receive *h'* one of another,
44 the *h'* that cometh from God only?
8: 49 but I *h'* my Father, and ye do
54 Jesus answered, If I *h'* myself,
54 If I...myself, my *h'* is nothing:
12: 26 serve me, him will my Father *h'*.
Ro 2: 7 for glory and *h'* and immortality,
10 But glory, *h'*, and peace, to every
9: 21 to make one vessel unto *h'*, and
12: 10 love; in *h'* preferring one another;
13: 7 fear to whom fear; *h'* to whom *h'*.
1Co 12: 23 these we bestow more abundant *h'*;
24 given more abundant *h'* to that
2Co 6: 8 *h'* and dishonour, by evil report
Eph 6: 2 *H'* thy father and mother; which
Col 2: 23 not in any *h'* to the satisfying of
1Th 4: 4 his vessel in sanctification and *h'*;
1Ti 1: 17 be *h'* and glory for ever and ever.
5: 3 *H'* widows that are widows indeed.
17 be counted worthy of double *h'*,
6: 1 their own masters worthy of all *h'*,
16 whom be *h'* and power everlasting:
2Ti 2: 20 some to *h'*, and some to dishonour.
21 be a vessel unto *h'*, sanctified, and
Heb 2: 7 crownedst him with glory and *h'*,
Heb 2: 9 death, crowned with glory and *h'*;
3: 3 builded the house hath more *h'*
5: 4 no man taketh this *h'* unto himself,
1Pe 1: 7 might be found unto praise and *h'*
2: 17 *H'* all men. Love the brotherhood.
17 Fear God. *H'* the king.
3: 7 giving *h'* unto the wife, as unto
2Pe 1: 17 from God the Father *h'* and glory,
Re 4: 9 beasts give glory and *h'* and thanks
11 to receive glory and *h'* and power:
5: 12 and *h'*, and glory, and blessing.
13 Blessing, and *h'*, and glory, and
7: 12 *h'*, and power, and might, be unto
19: 1 Salvation, and glory, and *h'*, and
7 and rejoice, and give *h'* to him:
21: 24 do bring their glory and *h'* into it.
26 bring the glory and *h'* of the nations

honourable
Ge 34: 19 was more *h'* than all the house of
Nu 22: 15 more, and more *h'* than they.
1Sa 9: 6 man of God, and he is an *h'* man;
22: 14 bidding, and is *h'* in thine house?
2Sa 23: 19 Was he not most *h'* of three?
23 He was more *h'* than the thirty,
2Ki 5: 1 man with his master, and *h'*,
1Ch 4: 9 was more *h'* than his brethren:
11: 21 three, he was more *h'* than the two;
25 he was *h'* among the thirty, but
Job 22: 8 and the *h'* man dwelt in it.
Ps 45: 9 were among thy *h'* women: upon
111: 3 His work is *h'* and glorious: and
Isa 3: 3 of fifty, and the *h'* man, and
5 ancient, and...base against the *h'*.
5: 13 and their *h'* men are famished, and
9: 15 ancient and *h'*, he is the head;
23: 8 traffickers are the *h'* of the earth?
9 contempt all the *h'* of the earth.
42: 21 magnify the law, and make it *h'*.
43: 4 thou hast been *h'*, and I have loved
58: 13 delight, the holy of the Lord, *h'*; and
Na 3: 10 and they cast lots for her *h'* men,
M'r 15: 43 of Arimathæa, an *h'* counsellor,
Lu 14: 8 more *h'* man than thou be bidden
Ac 13: 50 up the devout and *h'* women,
17: 12 of *h'* women which were Greeks,
1Co 4: 10 ye are *h'*, but we are despised.
12: 23 body, which we think to be less *h'*,
Heb13: 4 Marriage is *h'* in all, and the bed

honoured
Ex 14: 4 and I will be *h'* upon Pharaoh,
Pr 13: 18 that regardeth reproof shall be *h'*.
27: 18 waiteth on his master shall be *h'*.
Isa 43: 23 hast thou *h'* me with thy sacrifices.
La 1: 8 all that *h'* her despise her, because
5: 12 the faces of elders were not *h'*.
Da 4: 34 and *h'* him that liveth for ever,
Ac 28: 10 also *h'* us with many honours;
1Co 12: 26 one member be *h'*, all the members

honourest See also DISHONOUREST.
1Sa 2: 29 and *h'* thy sons above me, to make

honoureth See also DISHONOURETH.
Ps 15: 4 but he *h'* them that fear the Lord.
Pr 12: 9 better than he that *h'* himself, and
14: 31 that *h'* him hath mercy on the poor.
Mal 1: 6 A son *h'* his father, and a servant
M't 15: 8 mouth, and *h'* me with their lips;
M'r 7: 6 This people *h'* me with their lips,
Joh 5: 23 that *h'* not the Son *h'* not the Father
8: 54 it is my Father that *h'* me; of

honours
Ac 28: 10 also honoured us with many *h'*;

hoods
Isa 3: 23 linen, and the *h'*, and the vails.

hoof See also HOOFS.
Ex 10: 26 shall not an *h'* be left behind;
Le 11: 3 Whatsoever parteth the *h'*, and is
4 cud, or of them that divide the *h'*:
4, 5, 6 cud, but divideth not the *h'*:
7 the swine, though he divide the *h'*
26 every beast which divideth the *h'*,
De 14: 6 And every beast that parteth the *h'*,
7 of them that divide the cloven *h'*;
7 chew the cud, but divide not the *h'*;
8 swine, because it divideth the *h'*,

hoofs See also HORSEHOOFS.
Ps 69: 31 or bullock that hath horns and *h'*.
Isa 5: 28 horses' *h'* shall be counted like
Jer 47: 3 the noise of the stamping of the *h'*
Eze 26: 11 the *h'* of his horses shall he tread
32: 13 nor the *h'* of beasts trouble them.
Mic 4: 13 iron, and I will make thy *h'* brass:

hook See also HOOKS.
2Ki 19: 28 I will put my *h'* in thy nose,
Job 41: 1 draw out leviathan with an *h'*?
2 thou put an *h'* into his nose?
Isa 37: 29 will I put my *h'* in thy nose,
M't 17: 27 go thou to the sea, and cast an *h'*,

hooks See also FISHHOOKS; PRUNINGHOOKS.
Ex 26: 32 their *h'* shall be of gold, upon the
37 gold, and their *h'* shall be of gold:
27: 10, 11 *h'* of the pillars and their fillets
17 their *h'* shall be of silver, and their
36: 36 with gold: their *h'* were of gold;
38 the five pillars of it with their *h'*:
38: 10, 11, 12, 17, the *h'* of the pillars and
19 their *h'* of silver, and the overlaying
28 shekels he made *h'* for the pillars,
Isa 18: 5 cut off the sprigs with pruning *h'*,
Eze 29: 4 But I will put *h'* in thy jaws, and
38: 4 thee back, and put *h'* into thy jaws,
40: 43 And within were *h'*, an hand broad,
Am 4: 2 that he will take you away with *h'*,

hope See also HOPED; HOPE'S; HOPETH; HOPING.
Ru 1:12 If I should say, I have *h*·, if I
Ezr 10: 2 yet now there is *h*· in Israel
Job 4: 6 thy fear, thy confidence, thy *h*·,
5:16 So the poor hath *h*·, and iniquity
6:11 is my strength, that I should *h*·?
7: 6 shuttle, and are spent without *h*·.
8:13 and the hypocrite's *h*· shall perish:
14 Whose *h*· shall be cut off; and
11:18 be secure, because there is *h*·:
20 their *h*· shall be as the giving up
14: 7 there is *h*· of a tree, if it be cut down,
19 and thou destroyest the *h*· of man.
17:15 And where is now my *h*·? as for
15 as for my *h*·, who shall see it?
19:10 mine *h*· hath he removed like a tree.
27: 8 For what is the *h*· of the hypocrite,
31:24 If I have made gold my *h*·, or have
41: 9 Behold, the *h*· of him is in vain:
Ps 16: 9 my flesh also shall rest in *h*·.
22: 9 didst make me *h*· when I was upon
31:24 heart, all ye that *h*· in the Lord.
33:18 upon them that *h*· in his mercy;
22 upon us, according as we *h*· in thee.
38:15 in thee, O Lord, do I *h*·: thou wilt
39: 7 what wait I for? my *h*· is in thee.
42: 5 disquieted in me? *h*· thou in God:
11 within me? *h*· thou in God:
43: 5 disquieted within me? *h*· in God:
71: 5 For thou art my *h*·, O Lord God:
14 But I will *h*· continually, and will
78: 7 they might set their *h*· in God,
119:49 which thou hast caused me to *h*·.
81 salvation: but I *h*· in thy word.
114 and my shield: I *h*· in thy word.
116 let me not be ashamed of my *h*·.
130: 5 doth wait, and in his word do I *h*·.
7 Let Israel *h*· in the Lord: for with
131: 3 Let Israel *h*· in the Lord from
146: 5 whose *h*· is in the Lord his God:
147:11 him, in those that *h*· in his mercy.
Pr 10:28 The *h*· of the righteous shall be
11: 7 and the *h*· of unjust men perisheth.
13:12 *H*· deferred maketh the heart sick:
14:32 the righteous hath *h*· in his death.
19:18 Chasten thy son while there is *h*·,
26:12 is more *h*· of a fool than of him.
29:20 is more *h*· of a fool than of him.
Ec 9: 4 joined to all the living there is *h*·:
Isa 38:18 into the pit cannot *h*· for thy truth.
57:10 saidst thou not, There is no *h*·:
Jer 2:25 but thou saidst, There is no *h*·:
14: 8 O the *h*· of Israel, the saviour
17: 7 Lord, and whose *h*· the Lord is.
13 O Lord, the *h*· of Israel, all that
17 thou art my *h*· in the day of evil.
18:12 And they said, There is no *h*·:
31:17 And there is *h*· in thine end, saith
50: 7 the Lord, the *h*· of their fathers.
La 3:18 strength and my *h*· is perished
21 to my mind, therefore have I *h*·.
24 soul; therefore will I *h*· in him.
26 good that a man should both *h*·
29 the dust; if so be there may be *h*·.
Eze 13: 6 and they have made others to *h*·
19: 5 had waited, and her *h*· was lost,
37:11 bones are dried, and our *h*· is lost:
Ho 2:15 the valley of Achor for a door of *h*·:
Joe 3:16 Lord will be the *h*· of his people,
Zec 9:12 the strong hold, ye prisoners of *h*·:
Lu 6:34 to them of whom ye *h*· to receive,
Ac 2:26 also my flesh shall rest in *h*·:
16:19 that the *h*· of their gains was gone,
23: 6 the *h*· and resurrection of the dead
24:15 And have *h*· toward God, which
26: 6 am judged for the *h*· of the promise
7 God day and night, *h*· to come.
27:20 all *h*· that we should be saved was
28:20 that for the *h*· of Israel I am bound
Ro 4:18 Who against *h*· believed in *h*·, that
5: 2 and rejoice in *h*· of the glory of God.
4 experience; and experience, *h*·:
5 And *h*· maketh not ashamed:
8:20 who hath subjected the same in *h*·,
24 for we are saved by *h*·:
24 but *h*· that is seen is not *h*·:
24 man seeth, why doth he yet *h*· for?
25 But if we *h*· for that we see not,
12:12 Rejoicing in *h*·; patient in
15: 4 of the scriptures might have *h*·.
13 the God of *h*· fill you with all joy and
13 that ye may abound in *h*·, through
1Co 9:10 he that ploweth should plow in *h*·:
10 and that he that thresheth in *h*·
10 should be partaker of his *h*·.
13:13 And now abideth faith, *h*·, charity,
15:19 If in this life only we have *h*· in
2Co 1: 7 And our *h*· of you is stedfast,
3:12 Seeing then that we have such *h*·,
10:15 but having *h*·, when your faith is
Ga 5: 5 wait for the *h*· of righteousness by
Eph 1:18 know what is the *h*· of his calling,
2:12 having no *h*·, and without God in
4: 4 are called in one *h*· of your calling;
Ph'p 1:20 my earnest expectation and my *h*·,
2:23 Him therefore I *h*· to send
Col 1: 5 the *h*· which is laid up for you in
23 away from the *h*· of the gospel,
27 Christ in you, the *h*· of glory:
1Th 1: 3 patience of *h*· in our Lord Jesus
2:19 For what is our *h*·, or joy, or crown
4:13 even as others which have no *h*·.
5: 8 for an helmet, the *h*· of salvation.
2Th 2:16 and good *h*· through grace,
1Ti 1: 1 Lord Jesus Christ, which is our *h*·;
Tit 1: 2 In *h*· of eternal life, which God,
Tit 2:13 Looking for that blessed *h*·, and
3: 7 according to the *h*· of eternal life.
Heb 3: 6 confidence and rejoicing of the *h*·
6:11 full assurance of *h*· unto the end:
18 lay hold upon the *h*· set before us:
19 which *h*· we have as an anchor of
7:19 the bringing in of a better *h*· did;
1Pe 1: 3 begotten us again unto a lively *h*·
13 and *h*· to the end for the grace that
21 your faith and *h*· might be in God.
3:15 a reason of the *h*· that is in you
1Jo 3: 3 every man that hath this *h*· in him

hoped
Es 9: 1 the enemies of the Jews *h*· to have
Job 6:20 confounded because they had *h*·;
Ps 119:43 for I have *h*· in thy judgments.
74 because I have *h*· in thy word.
147 and cried: I *h*· in thy word.
166 Lord, I have *h*· for thy salvation,
Jer 3:23 Truly in vain is salvation *h*· for from
Lu 23: 8 he *h*· to have seen some miracle
Ac 24:26 He *h*· also that the money should
2Co 8: 5 And this they did, not as we *h*·, but
Heb11: 1 is the substance of things *h*· for,

hope's
Ac 26: 7 For which *h*· sake, king Agrippa, I

hopeth
1Co 13: 7 believeth all things, *h*· all things,

Hophni (*hof'-ni*)
1Sa 1: 3 two sons of Eli, *H*· and Phinehas,
2:34 thy two sons, on *H*· and Phinehas;
4: 4 *H*· and Phinehas, were there with
11 two sons of Eli, *H*· and Phinehas,
17 *H*· and Phinehas are dead, and

Hophra See PHARAOH-HOPHRA.

hoping
Lu 6:35 and lend, *h*· for nothing again;
1Ti 3:14 thee, *h*· to come unto thee shortly:

hopper See GRASSHOPPER.

Hor (*hor*) See also HOR-HAGIDGAD.
Nu 20:22 Kadesh, and came unto mount *H*·.
23 unto Moses and Aaron in mount *H*·,
25 and bring them up unto mount *H*·:
27 and they went up into mount *H*·
21: 4 And they journeyed from mount *H*·
33:37 Kadesh, and pitched in mount *H*·,
38 the priest went up into mount *H*·
39 years old when he died in mount *H*·.
41 And they departed from mount *H*·,
34: 7 ye shall point out for you mount *H*·:
8 From mount *H*· ye shall point out
De 32:50 thy brother died in mount *H*·, and

Horam (*ho'-ram*)
Jos 10:33 Then *H*· king of Gezer came up

Horeb (*ho'-reb*) See also SINAI.
Ex 3: 1 the mountain of God, even to *H*·.
17: 6 thee there upon the rock in *H*·;
33: 6 their ornaments by the mount *H*·.
De 1: 2 are eleven days' journey from *H*·
6 Lord our God spake unto us in *H*·,
19 And when we departed from *H*·, we
4:10 before the Lord thy God in *H*·,
15 Lord spake unto you in *H*· out of
5: 2 God made a covenant with us in *H*·.
9: 8 Also in *H*· ye provoked the Lord to
18:16 desiredst of the Lord thy God in *H*·
29: 1 which he made with them in *H*·.
1Ki 8: 9 stone, which Moses put there at *H*·,
19: 8 nights unto *H*· the mount of God.
2Ch 5:10 which Moses put therein at *H*·,
Ps 106:19 made a calf in *H*·, and worshipped
Mal 4: 4 which I commanded unto him in *H*·

Horem (*ho'-rem*)
Jos 19:38 And Iron, and Migdal-el, *H*·, and

Hor-hagidgad (*hor-hag-id'-gad*) See also GUDGODAH.
Nu 33:32 Bene-jaakan, and encamped at *H*·.
33 they went from *H*·, and pitched

Hori (*ho'-ri*) See also HORITE.
Ge 36:22 of Lotan were *H*· and Hemam;
30 are the dukes that came of *H*·,
Nu 13: 5 of Simeon, Shaphat, the son of *H*·.
1Ch 1:39 the sons of Lotan; *H*·, and Homam:

Horims (*ho'-rims*) See also HORITES.
De 2:12 The *H*· also dwelt in Seir
22 when he destroyed the *H*· from

Horite (*ho'-rite*) See also HORI; HORITES.
Ge 36:20 These are the sons of Seir the *H*·,

Horites (*ho'-rites*) See also HORIMS.
Ge 14: 6 And the *H*· in their mount Seir,
36:21 these are the dukes of the *H*·, the
29 are the dukes that came of the *H*·;

Hormah (*hor'-mah*) See also ZEPHATH.
Nu 14:45 discomfited them, even unto *H*·.
21: 3 he called the name of the place *H*·.
De 1:44 destroyed you in Seir, even unto *H*·.
Jos 12:14 The king of *H*·, one; the king of
15:30 And Eltolad, and Chesil, and *H*·,
19: 4 And Eltolad, and Bethul, and *H*·,
J'g 1:17 the name of the city was called *H*·.
1Sa 30:30 And to them which were in *H*·,
1Ch 4:30 And at Bethuel, and at *H*·, and at

horn See also HORNS; INKHORN.
Ex 21:29 ox were wont to push with his *h*·
Jos 6: 5 a long blast with the ram's *h*·,
1Sa 2: 1 mine *h*· is exalted in the Lord: my
10 and exalt the *h*· of his anointed.
16: 1 fill thine *h*· with oil, and go, I will
13 Then Samuel took the *h*· of oil, and
2Sa 22: 3 shield, and the *h*· of my salvation,
1Ki 1:39 Zadok the priest took an *h*· of oil
1Ch 25: 5 the words of God, to lift up the *h*·.
Job 16:15 skin, and defiled my *h*· in the dust.
Ps 18: 2 buckler, and the *h*· of my salvation,
75: 4 to the wicked, Lift not up the *h*·:
5 Lift not up your *h*· on high: speak
89:17 thy favour our *h*· shall be exalted.
24 in my name shall his *h*· be exalted.
92:10 But my *h*· shalt thou exalt like
10 thou exalt like the *h*· of an unicorn:
112: 9 his *h*· shalt be exalted with honour.
132:17 will I make the *h*· of David to bud:
148:14 also exalteth the *h*· of his people,
Jer 48:25 The *h*· of Moab is cut off, and his
La 2: 3 his fierce anger all the *h*· of Israel:
17 set up the *h*· of thine adversaries.
Eze 29:21 the *h*· of the house of Israel to bud
Da 7: 8 up among them another little *h*·,
8 in this *h*· were eyes like the eyes of
11 great words which the *h*· spake:
20 even of that *h*· that had eyes, and
21 same *h*· made war with the saints,
8: 5 the goat had a notable *h*· between
8 strong, the great *h*· was broken;
9 one of them came forth a little *h*·,
21 great *h*· that is between his eyes
Mic 4:13 I will make thine *h*· iron, and I will
Zec 1:21 the Gentiles, which lifted up their *h*·
Lu 1:69 hath raised up an *h*· of salvation

hornet See also HORNETS.
De 7:20 God will send the *h*· among them,
Jos 24:12 I sent the *h*· before you, which drave

hornets
Ex 23:28 And I will send *h*· before thee,

horns ^
Ge 22:13 ram caught in a thicket by his *h*·:
Ex 27: 2 And thou shalt make the *h*· of it
2 his *h*· shall be of the same: and
29:12 and put it upon the *h*· of the altar
30: 2 the *h*· thereof shall be of the same.
3 round about, and the *h*· thereof:
10 an atonement upon the *h*· of it once
37:25 the *h*· thereof were of the same.
26 round about, and the *h*· of it: also
38: 2 he made the *h*· thereof on the four
2 it; the *h*· thereof were of the same:
Le 4: 7 blood upon the *h*· of the altar of
18 blood upon the *h*· of the altar which
25, 30, 34 upon the *h*· of the altar of
8:15 and put it upon the *h*· of the altar
9: 9 and put it upon the *h*· of the altar,
16:18 and put it upon the *h*· of the altar
De 33:17 his *h*· are like the *h*· of unicorns:
Jos 6: 4 ark seven trumpets of rams' *h*·:
6 bear seven trumpets of rams' *h*·
13 seven trumpets of rams' *h*· before
1Ki 1:50 caught hold on the *h*· of the altar.
51 caught hold on the *h*· of the altar,
2:28 caught hold on the *h*· of the altar.
22:11 And Zedekiah...made him *h*· of iron:
2Ch 18:10 And Zedekiah...made him *h*· of iron,
Ps 22:21 me from the *h*· of the unicorns.
69:31 or bullock that hath *h*· and hoofs.
75:10 the *h*· of the wicked also will I cut
10 *h*· of the righteous shall be exalted.
118:27 even unto the *h*· of the altar.
Jer 17: 1 and upon the *h*· of your altars;
Eze 27:15 for a present *h*· of ivory and ebony.
34:21 pushed all the diseased with your *h*·
43:15 altar and upward shall be four *h*·.
20 thereof, and on the four *h*· of it,
Da 7: 7 were before it; and it had ten *h*·.
8 I considered the *h*·, and behold,
8 three of the first *h*· plucked up by
20 the ten *h*· that were in his head,
24 And the ten *h*· out of this kingdom
8: 3 the river a ram which had two *h*·:
3 and the two *h*· were high; but one
6 came to the ram that had two *h*·,
7 smote the ram, and brake his two *h*·:
20 sawest having two *h*· are the kings
Am 3:14 the *h*· of the altar shall be cut off,
6:13 Have we not taken to us *h*· by our
Hab 3: 4 he had *h*· coming out of his hand:
Zec 1:18 eyes, and saw, and behold four *h*·.
19, 21 *h*· which have scattered Judah,
21 to cast out the *h*· of the Gentiles,
Re 5: 6 having seven *h*· and seven eyes,
9:13 from the four *h*· of the golden altar
12: 3 having seven heads and ten *h*·,
13: 1 sea, having seven heads and ten *h*·,
1 and upon his *h*· ten crowns, and
11 he had two *h*· like a lamb, and he
17: 3 having seven heads and ten *h*·,
7 hath the seven heads and ten *h*·.
12 the ten *h*· which thou sawest are
16 the ten *h*· which thou sawest upon

Horon See BETH-HORON; HORONITE.

Horonaim (*hor-o-na'-im*) See also HOLON.
Isa 15: 5 in the way of *H*· they shall raise
Jer 48: 3 A voice of crying shall be from *H*·,
5 for in the going down of *H*· the
34 voice, from Zoar even unto *H*·,

Horonite (*ho'-ron-ite*)
Ne 2:10 When Sanballat the *H*·, and
19 But when Sanballat the *H*·, and
13:28 was son in law to Sanballat the *H*·:

horrible
Ps 11: 6 brimstone, and an *h*· tempest:
40: 2 brought me up also out of an *h*· pit,
Jer 5:30 A wonderful and *h*· thing is
18:13 Israel hath done a very *h*· thing.
23:14 prophets of Jerusalem an *h*· thing:
Ho 6:10 I have seen an *h*· thing in the house

horribly
Jer 2:12 heavens, at this, and be *h'* afraid,
Eze 32:10 their kings shall be *h'* afraid for

horror
Ge 15:12 an *h'* of great darkness fell upon
Ps 55: 5 and *h'* hath overwhelmed me.
119:53 *H'* hath taken hold upon me
Eze 7:18 *h'* shall cover them; and shame

horse See also HORSEBACK; HORSEHOOFS; HORSELEACH; HORSEMAN; HORSES.
Ge 49:17 the path, that biteth the *h'* heels,
Ex 15: 1 the *h'* and his rider hath he thrown
19 For the *h'* of Pharaoh went in with
21 the *h'* and his rider hath he thrown
1Ki 10:29 and an *h'* for an hundred and fifty:
20:20 king of Syria escaped on an *h'* with
25 *h'* for *h'*, and chariot for chariot:
2Ch 1:17 and an *h'* for an hundred and fifty:
23:15 come to the entering of the *h'* gate
Ne 3:28 From above the *h'* gate repaired
Es 6: 8 the *h'* that the king rideth upon,
9 this apparel and *h'* be delivered
10 and take the apparel and the *h'*,
11 took Haman the apparel and the *h'*,
Job 39:18 she scorneth the *h'* and his rider.
19 Hast thou given the *h'* strength?
Ps 32: 9 Be ye not as the *h'*, or as the mule,
33:17 An *h'* is a vain thing for safety:
76: 6 both the chariot and *h'* are cast
147:10 not in the strength of the *h'*:
Pr 21:31 The *h'* is prepared against the day
26: 3 A whip for the *h'*, a bridle for the
Isa 43:17 bringeth forth the chariot and *h'*,
63:13 the deep, as an *h'* in the wilderness,
Jer 8: 6 as the *h'* rusheth into the battle.
31:40 unto the corner of the *h'* gate toward
51:21 break in pieces the *h'* and his rider;
Am 2:15 he that rideth the *h'* deliver himself.
Zec 1: 8 behold a man riding upon a red *h'*,
9:10 and the *h'* from Jerusalem,
10: 3 them as his goodly *h'* in the battle.
12: 4 smite every *h'* with astonishment,
4 smite every *h'* of the people with
14:15 And so shall be the plague of the *h'*,
Re 6: 2 I saw, and behold a white *h'*: and
4 went out another *h'* that was red:
5 I beheld, and lo a black *h'*; and he
8 And I looked, and behold a pale *h'*:
14:20 winepress, even unto the *h'* bridles,
19:11 opened, and behold a white *h'*;
19 war against him that sat on the *h'*,
21 sword of him that sat upon the *h'*,

horseback
2Ki 9:18 there went one on *h'* to meet
19 Then he sent out a second on *h'*,
Es 6: 9 on *h'* through the street of the
11 on *h'* through the street of the city,
8:10 and sent letters by posts on *h'*,

horse-gate See HORSE and GATE.

horse-heels See HORSE and HEELS.

horsehoofs
J'g 5:22 Then were the *h'* broken by

horseleach
Pr 30:15 the *h'* hath two daughters,

horseman See also HORSEMEN.
2Ki 9:17 Joram said, Take an *h'*, and send
Na 3: 3 The *h'* lifteth up both the bright

horsemen
Ge 50: 9 up with him both chariots and *h'*:
Ex 14: 9 chariots of Pharaoh, and his *h'*,
17, 18 his chariots, and upon his *h'*.
23 horses, his chariots, and his *h'*.
26 their chariots, and upon their *h'*.
28 covered the chariots, and the *h'*,
15:19 in with his chariots and with his *h'*
Jos 24: 6 with chariots and *h'* unto the Red
1Sa 8:11 for his chariots, and to be his *h'*;
13: 5 chariots, and six thousand *h'*,
2Sa 1: 6 *h'* followed hard after him.
8: 4 chariots, and seven hundred *h'*,
10:18 the Syrians, and forty thousand *h'*,
1Ki 1: 5 he prepared him chariots and *h'*,
4:26 chariots, and twelve thousand *h'*.
9:19 for his chariots, and cities for his *h'*,
22 rulers of his chariots, and his *h'*.
10:26 gathered together chariots and *h'*:
26 chariots, and twelve thousand *h'*,
20:20 escaped on an horse with the *h'*.
2Ki 2:12 chariot of Israel, and the *h'* thereof.
13: 7 he leave of the people...but fifty *h'*,
14 chariot of Israel, and the *h'* thereof.
18:24 on Egypt for chariots and for *h'*?
1Ch 18: 4 chariots, and seven thousand *h'*,
19: 6 silver to hire them chariots and *h'*
2Ch 1:14 Solomon gathered chariots and *h'*:
14 chariots, and twelve thousand *h'*,
8: 6 cities, and the cities of the *h'*, and
9 and captains of his chariots and *h'*.
9:25 chariots, and twelve thousand *h'*;
12: 3 and threescore thousand *h'*:
16: 8 with very many chariots and *h'*?
Ezr 8:22 a band of soldiers and *h'* to help us
Ne 2: 9 had sent captains of the army and *h'*
Isa 21: 7 he saw a chariot with a couple of *h'*,
9 chariot of men, with a couple of *h'*,
22: 6 quiver with chariots of men and *h'*,
7 the *h'* shall set themselves in array
28:28 his cart, nor bruise it with his *h'*.
31: 1 in *h'*, because they are very strong;
36: 9 on Egypt for chariots and for *h'*?
Jer 4:29 for the noise of the *h'* and bowmen;
46: 4 get up, ye *h'*, and stand forth with
Eze 23: 6 young men, *h'* riding upon horses.
Eze 23:12 *h'* riding upon horses, all of them
26: 7 with chariots, and with *h'*, and
10 shall shake at the noise of the *h'*,
27:14 in thy fairs with horses and *h'* and
38: 4 and all thine army, horses and *h'*,
Da 11:40 with chariots, and with *h'*, and with
Ho 1: 7 nor by battle, by horses, nor by *h'*.
Joe 2: 4 and as *h'*, so shall they run.
Hab 1: 8 their *h'* shall spread themselves,
8 and their *h'* shall come from far;
Ac 23:23 and *h'* threescore and ten, and
32 they left the *h'* to go with him,
Re 9:16 the number of the army of the *h'*

horses^ See also HORSES'.
Ge 47:17 them bread in exchange for *h'*,
Ex 9: 3 field, upon the *h'*, upon the asses,
14: 9 all the *h'* and chariots of Pharaoh,
23 even all Pharaoh's *h'*, his chariots,
De 11: 4 unto their *h'*, and to their chariots;
17:16 he shall not multiply *h'* to himself,
16 the end that he should multiply *h'*:
20: 1 and seest *h'*, and chariots, and a
Jos 11: 4 with *h'* and chariots very many.
6 thou shalt hough their *h'*, and burn
9 he houghed their *h'*, and burnt
2Sa 15: 1 prepared him chariots and *h'*,
1Ki 4:26 had forty thousand stalls of *h'* for
28 Barley also and straw for the *h'* and
10:25 armour, and spices, *h'*, and mules.
28 had *h'* brought out of Egypt,
18: 5 grass to save the *h'* and mules alive,
20: 1 with him, and *h'*, and chariots:
21 and smote the *h'* and chariots, and
22: 4 people as thy people, my *h'* as thy *h'*.
2Ki 2:11 a chariot of fire, and *h'* of fire, and
3: 7 as thy people, and my *h'* as thy *h'*.
5: 9 Naaman came with his *h'* and with
6:14 sent he thither *h'*, and chariots,
15 the city both with *h'* and chariots.
17 was full of *h'* and chariots of fire
7: 6 noise of chariots, and a noise of *h'*,
7 left their tents, and their *h'*, and
10 but *h'* tied, and asses tied, and the
13 five of the *h'* that remain, which
14 They took therefore two chariot *h'*:
9:33 sprinkled on the wall, and on the *h'*:
10: 2 there are with you chariots and *h'*,
11:16 way by the which the *h'* came into
14:20 And they brought him on *h'*: and
18:23 I will deliver thee two thousand *h'*,
23:11 he took away the *h'* that the kings
1Ch 18: 4 also houghed all the chariot *h'*, but
2Ch 1:16 had *h'* brought out of Egypt,
17 so brought they out *h'* for all the
9:24 harness, and spices, *h'*, and mules,
25 had four thousand stalls for *h'* and
28 unto Solomon *h'* out of Egypt,
25:28 And they brought him upon *h'*, and
Ezr 2:66 Their *h'* were seven hundred thirty
Ne 7:68 Their *h'*, seven hundred thirty and
Ps 20: 7 trust in chariots, and some in *h'*:
Ec 10: 7 I have seen servants upon *h'*, and
Ca 1: 9 to a company of *h'* in Pharaoh's
Isa 2: 7 their land is also full of *h'*, neither
30:16 said, No; for we will flee upon *h'*;
31: 1 stay on *h'*, and trust in chariots,
3 and their *h'* flesh, and not spirit.
36: 8 I will give thee two thousand *h'*,
66:20 the Lord out of all nations upon *h'*,
Jer 4:13 his *h'* are swifter than eagles.
5: 8 They were as fed *h'* in the morning:
6:23 they ride upon *h'*, set in array as
8:16 The snorting of his *h'* was heard
12: 5 how canst thou contend with *h'*?
17:25 riding in chariots and on *h'*, they,
22: 4 riding in chariots and on *h'*, he,
46: 4 Harness the *h'*; and get up, ye
9 Come up, ye *h'*; and rage, ye
47: 3 stamping of...hoofs of his strong *h'*,
50:37 A sword is upon their *h'*, and upon
42 they shall ride upon *h'*, every one
51:27 cause the *h'* to come up as the rough
Eze 17:15 that they might give him *h'* and
23: 6 men, horsemen riding upon *h'*.
12 horsemen riding upon *h'*, all of
20 whose issue is like the issue of *h'*.
23 renowned, all of them riding upon *h'*.
26: 7 with *h'*, and with chariots, and with
10 By reason of the abundance of his *h'*
11 the hoofs of his *h'* shall he tread
27:14 with *h'* and horsemen and mules.
38: 4 all thine army, *h'* and horsemen,
15 all of them riding upon *h'*, a great
39:20 at my table with *h'* and chariots,
Ho 1: 7 by battle, by *h'*, nor by horsemen.
14: 3 save us; we will not ride upon *h'*:
Joe 2: 4 of them is as the appearance of *h'*;
Am 4:10 and have taken away your *h'*;
6:12 Shall *h'* run upon the rock? will one
Mic 5:10 that I will cut off thy *h'* out of the
Na 3: 2 of the wheels and of the pransing *h'*,
Hab 1: 8 Their *h'* are also swifter than the
3: 8 that thou didst ride upon thine *h'*
15 walk through the sea with thine *h'*,
Hag 2:22 the *h'* and their riders shall come
Zec 1: 8 and behind him were there red *h'*,
6: 2 In the first chariot were red *h'*;
2 and in the second chariot black *h'*;
3 And in the third chariot white *h'*;
3 fourth chariot grisled and bay *h'*.
6 The black *h'* which are therein go
10: 5 riders on *h'* shall be confounded.
14:20 there be upon the bells of the *h'*,
Re 9: 7 of the locusts were like unto *h'*
9 the chariots of many *h'* running to
17 And thus I saw the *h'* in the vision,
Re 9:17 heads of the *h'* were as the heads
18:13 and *h'*, and chariots, and slaves,
19:14 heaven followed him upon white *h'*,
18 of mighty men, and the flesh of *h'*,

horses'
Isa 5:28 their *h'* hoofs shall be counted
Jas 3: 3 we put bits in the *h'* mouths, that

Hosah (*ho'-sah*)
Jos 19:29 and the coast turneth to *H'*;
1Ch 16:38 of Jeduthun and *H'* to be porters:
26:10 Also *H'*, of the children of Merari,
11 and brethren of *H'* were thirteen.
16 To Shuppim and *H'* the lot came

hosanna (*ho-zan'-nah*)
M't 21: 9 *H'* to the son of David: Blessed
9 name of the Lord; *H'* in the highest.
15 and saying, *H'* to the son of David;
M'r 11: 9 *H'*; Blessed is he that cometh in
10 name of the Lord; *H'* in the highest.
Joh 12:13 *H'*: Blessed is the King of Israel

Hosea^ (*ho-se'-ah*) See also HOSHEA; OSEE; OSHEA.
Ho 1: 1 of the Lord that came unto *H'*,
2 of the word of the Lord by *H'*.
2 Lord said to *H'*, Go, take unto thee

hosen
Da 3:21 were bound in their coats, their *h'*,

Hoshaiah (*ho-sha-i'-ah*)
Ne 12:32 And after them went *H'*, and half
Jer 42: 1 and Jezaniah the son of *H'*,
43: 2 Then spake Azariah the son of *H'*,

Hoshama (*ho-sha'-mah*)
1Ch 3:18 Jecamiah, *H'*, and Nedabiah.

Hoshea (*ho-she'-ah*) See also HOSEA.
De 32:44 people, he, and *H'* the son of Nun.
2Ki 15:30 And *H'* the son of Elah made a
17: 1 began *H'* the son of Elah to reign
3 and *H'* became his servant, and
4 of Assyria found conspiracy in *H'*:
6 In the ninth year of *H'* the king of
18: 1 in the third year of *H'* son of Elah
9 which was the seventh year of *H'*
10 that is the ninth year of *H'* king of
1Ch 27:20 of Ephraim, *H'* the son of Azaziah:
Ne 10:23 *H'*, Hananiah, Hashub,

hospitality
Ro 12:13 necessity of saints; given to *h'*.
1Ti 3: 2 given to *h'*, apt to teach;
Tit 1: 8 But a lover of *h'*, a lover of good
1Pe 4: 9 Use *h'* one to another without

host^ See also HOSTS.
Ge 2: 1 finished, and all the *h'* of them.
21:22 chief captain of his *h'* spake unto
32 Phichol the chief captain of his *h'*,
32: 2 them, he said, This is God's *h'*:
Ex 14: 4 upon Pharaoh, and upon all his *h'*;
17 upon Pharaoh, and upon all his *h'*,
24 unto the *h'* of the Egyptians,
24 troubled the *h'* of the Egyptians,
28 all the *h'* of Pharaoh that came
15: 4 Pharaoh's chariots and his *h'* hath
16:13 the dew lay round about the *h'*.
Nu 2: 4, 6, 8, 11, 13, 15, 19, 21, 23, 26, 28,
30 And his *h'*, and those that were
4: 3 all that enter into the *h'*, to do the
10:14 and over his *h'* was Nahshon the son
15, 16 over the *h'* of the tribe of the
18 and over his *h'* was Elizur the son
19, 20 over the *h'* of the tribe of the
22 and over his *h'* was Elishama the
23, 24 over the *h'* of the tribe of the
25 and over his *h'* was Ahiezer the
26, 27 over the *h'* of the tribe of the
31:14 wroth with the officers of the *h'*,
48 were over thousands of the *h'*,
De 2:14 wasted out from among the *h'*,
15 destroy them from among the *h'*,
4:19 stars, even all the *h'* of heaven,
17: 3 moon, or any of the *h'* of heaven,
23: 9 When the *h'* goeth forth against
Jos 1:11 Pass through the *h'*, and command
3: 2 the officers went through the *h'*;
5:14 captain of the *h'* of the Lord am
15 captain of the Lord's *h'* said unto
8:13 all the *h'* that was on the north of
18: 9 came again to Joshua to the *h'* at
J'g 4: 2 captain of whose *h'* was Sisera,
15 all his chariots, and all his *h'*,
16 after the chariots, and after the *h'*,
16 all the *h'* of Sisera fell upon the
7: 1 so that the *h'* of the Midianites
8 and the *h'* of Midian was beneath
9 Arise, get thee down unto the *h'*;
10 thy servant down to the *h'*:
11 strengthened to go...unto the *h'*:
11 armed men that were in the *h'*.
13 bread tumbled into the *h'* of
14 delivered Midian, and all the *h'*.
15 and returned into the *h'* of Israel,
15 into your hand the *h'* of Midian.
21 the *h'* ran, and cried, and fled.
22 even throughout all the *h'*: and the
22 and the *h'* fled to Beth-shittah in
8:11 smote the *h'*: for the *h'* was secure.
12 Zalmunna, discomfited all the *h'*.
1Sa 11:11 came into the midst of the *h'*
12: 9 captain of the *h'* of Hazor, and
14:15 there was trembling in the *h'*, in
19 the noise that was in the *h'* of the
48 And he gathered an *h'*, and smote
50 the captain of his *h'* was Abner,
17:20 as the *h'* was going forth to the
46 the carcases of the *h'* of the

1Sa 17: 55 unto Abner, the captain of the h'.
26: 5 son of Ner, the captain of his h':
28: 5 Saul saw the h' of the Philistines,
19 also shall deliver the h' of Israel
29: 6 thy coming in with me in the h' is
2Sa 2: 8 Son of Ner, captain of Saul's h',
3:23 Joab and all the h' that was with
5:24 to smite the h' of the Philistines.
8: 9 David had smitten all the h' of
16 son of Zeruiah was over the h';
10: 7 and all the h' of the mighty men.
16 Shobach the captain of the h' of
18 Shobach the captain of their h',
17:25 Amasa captain of the h' instead of
19:13 be not captain of the h' before me
20:23 Joab was over all the h' of Israel:
23:16 through the h' of the Philistines,
24: 2 said to Joab the captain of the h',
4 and against the captains of the h'.
4 and the captain of the h' went
1Ki 1:19 Joab the captain of the h':
25 and the captains of the h', and
2:32 of Ner, captain of the h' of Israel,
32 Jether, captain of the h' of Judah.
35 Jehoiada in his room over the h':
4: 4 son of Jehoiada was over the h':
11:15 and Joab the captain of the h' was
21 Joab the captain of the h' was
16:16 made Omri, the captain of the h',
20: 1 Syria gathered all his h' together:
22:34 hand, and carry me out of the h';
36 a proclamation throughout the h'
2Ki 3: 9 there was no water for the h', and
4:13 king, or to the captain of the h'?
5: 1 Naaman, captain of the h' of the
6:14 and chariots, and a great h':
15 an h' compassed the city both with
24 king of Syria gathered all his h',
7: 4 let us fall unto the h' of the
6 had made the h' of the Syrians
6 even the noise of a great h':
14 sent after the h' of the Syrians,
9: 5 the captains of the h' were sitting;
11:15 the hundreds, the officers of the h',
17:16 worshipped all the h' of heaven,
18:17 Hezekiah with a great h' against
21: 3 worshipped all the h' of heaven,
5 built altars for all the h' of heaven
23: 4 grove, and for all the h' of heaven:
5 planets, and to all the h' of heaven.
25: 1 Babylon came, he, and all his h',
19 the principal scribe of the h',
1Ch 9:19 being over the h' of the Lord,
11:15 the h' of the Philistines encamped
18 brake through the h' of the
12:14 sons of Gad, captains of the h':
21 valour, and were captains in the h'.
22 was a great h', like the h' of God.
14:15 to smite the h' of the Philistines.
16 they smote the h' of the Philistines
18: 9 smitten all the h' of Hadarezer
15 the son of Zeruiah was over the h';
19: 8 and all the h' of the mighty men,
16 Shophach the captain of the h' of
18 Shophach the captain of the h'.
25: 1 David and the captains of the h'
26:26 captains of the h', had dedicated,
27: 3 of all the captains of the h' for the
5 The third captain of the h' for the
2Ch 14: 9 an h' of a thousand thousand,
13 before the Lord, and before his h';
16: 7 the h' of the king of Syria escaped
8 and the Lubims a huge h',
18:18 all the h' of heaven standing on
33 thou mayest carry me out of the h':
23:14 hundreds that were set over the h',
24:23 the h' of Syria came up against
24 the Lord delivered a very great h'
26:11 Uzziah had an h' of fighting men,
14 for them throughout all the h'
28: 9 before the h' that came to Samaria,
33: 3 worshipped all the h' of heaven,
5 built altars for all the h' of heaven
11 the captains of the h' of the king of
Ne 9: 6 heaven of heavens, with all their h',
6 the h' of heaven worshippeth thee.
Ps 27: 3 Though an h' should encamp
33: 6 and all the h' of them by the
16 saved by the multitude of an h':
136:15 overthrew Pharaoh and his h' in
Isa 13: 4 mustereth the h' of the battle.
24:21 shall punish the h' of the high ones
34: 4 all the h' of heaven shall be
4 all their h' shall fall down, as the
40:26 bringeth out their h' by number:
45:12 and all their h' have I commanded.
Jer 8: 2 the moon, and all the h' of heaven,
19:13 incense unto all the h' of heaven,
33:22 h' of heaven cannot be numbered,
51: 3 men; destroy ye utterly all her h'.
52:25 the principal scribe of the h', who
Eze 1:24 of speech, as the noise of an h':
Da 8:10 great, even to the h' of heaven;
10 some of the h' and of the stars
11 himself even to the prince of the h',
12 And an h' was given him against
13 give both the sanctuary and the h'
Ob 20 captivity of this h' of the children
Zep 1: 5 that worship the h' of heaven
Lu 2:13 a multitude of the heavenly h'
10:35 pence, and gave them to the h',
Ac 7:42 up to worship the h' of heaven;
Ro 16:23 Gaius mine h', and of the whole

hostages
2Ki 14:14 house, and h', and returned
2Ch 25:24 house, the h' also, and returned

hosts
Ex 12:41 the h' of the Lord went out from
Nu 1:52 standard, throughout their h'.
2:32 of the camps throughout their h'
10:25 all the camps throughout their h':
Jos 10: 5 and went up, they and all their h',
11: 4 went out, they and all their h' with
J'g 8:10 in Karkor, and their h' with them,
10 that were left of all the h' of the
1Sa 1: 3 unto the Lord of h' in Shiloh.
11 O Lord of h', if thou wilt indeed
4: 4 of the covenant of the Lord of h',
15: 2 Thus saith the Lord of h', I
17:45 thee in the name of the Lord of h',
2Sa 5:10 the Lord God of h' was with him.
6: 2 called by the name of the Lord of h'
18 in the name of the Lord of h'.
7: 8 Thus saith the Lord of h', I took
26 The Lord of h' is the God over
27 For thou, O Lord of h', God of
1Ki 2: 5 did to the two captains of the h' of
15:20 sent the captains of the h' which
18:15 As the Lord of h' liveth, before
19:10, 14 jealous for the Lord God of h':
2Ki 3:14 As the Lord of h' liveth, before
19:31 zeal of the Lord of h' shall do this.
1Ch 11: 9 and greater: for the Lord of h'
17: 7 Thus saith the Lord of h', I took
24 The Lord of h' is the God of Israel,
Ps 24:10 Lord of h', he is the King of glory.
46: 7, 11 The Lord of h' is with us; the
48: 8 seen in the city of the Lord of h',
59: 5 O Lord God of h', the God of Israel,
69: 6 that wait on thee, O Lord God of h',
80: 4 O Lord God of h', how long wilt
7 Turn us again, O God of h', and
14 we beseech thee, O God of h':
19 Turn us again, O Lord God of h',
84: 1 are thy tabernacles, O Lord of h'!
3 O Lord of h', my King, and my God.
8 O Lord God of h', hear my prayer:
12 O Lord of h', blessed is the man
89: 8 O Lord God of h', who is a strong
103:21 Bless ye the Lord, all ye his h'; ye
108:11 thou, O God, go forth with our h'?
148: 2 angels: praise ye him, all his h'.
Isa 1: 9 Except the Lord of h' had left unto
24 saith the Lord, the Lord of h',
2:12 For the day of the Lord of h' shall
3: 1 the Lord, the Lord of h', doth take
15 the poor? saith the Lord God of h'.
5: 7 For the vineyard of the Lord of h'
9 In mine ears said the Lord of h',
16 But the Lord of h' shall be exalted
24 cast away the law of the Lord of h',
6: 3 Holy, holy, holy, is the Lord of h':
5 have seen the King, the Lord of h'.
8:13 Sanctify the Lord of h' himself;
18 in Israel from the Lord of h', which
9: 7 The zeal of the Lord of h' will
13 neither do they seek the Lord of h'.
19 Through the wrath of the Lord of h'
10:16 shall the Lord, the Lord of h',
23 For the Lord God of h' shall make
24 thus saith the Lord God of h', O my
26 And the Lord of h' shall stir up a
33 Behold, the Lord, the Lord of h',
13: 4 the Lord of h' mustereth the h' of
13 in the wrath of the Lord of h', and
14:22 against them, saith the Lord of h',
23 of destruction, saith the Lord of h'.
24 The Lord of h' hath sworn, saying,
27 For the Lord of h' hath purposed,
17: 3 of Israel, saith the Lord of h'.
18: 7 be brought unto the Lord of h'
7 place of the name of the Lord of h',
19: 4 saith the Lord, the Lord of h'.
12 what the Lord of h' hath purposed
16 of the hand of the Lord of h', which
17 of the counsel of the Lord of h',
18 and swear to the Lord of h'; one
20 for a witness unto the Lord of h'
25 Whom the Lord of h' shall bless,
21:10 I have heard of the Lord of h', the
22: 5 perplexity by the Lord God of h'
12 that day did the Lord God of h' call
14 in mine ears by the Lord of h',
14 till ye die, saith the Lord God of h'.
15 Thus saith the Lord God of h', Go,
25 In that day, saith the Lord of h',
23: 9 The Lord of h' hath purposed it, to
24:23 Lord of h' shall reign in mount Zion,
25: 6 this mountain shall the Lord of h'
28: 5 Lord of h' be for a crown of glory,
22 have heard from the Lord God of h'
29 cometh forth from the Lord of h',
29: 6 be visited of the Lord of h' with
31: 4 the Lord of h' come down to fight
5 the Lord of h' defend Jerusalem;
37:16 O Lord of h', God of Israel, that
32 zeal of the Lord of h' shall do this.
39: 5 Hear the word of the Lord of h':
44: 6 and his redeemer the Lord of h';
45:13 nor reward, saith the Lord of h'.
47: 4 the Lord of h' is his name, the
48: 2 Israel; the Lord of h' is his name.
51:15 roared: The Lord of h' is his name.
54: 5 husband; the Lord of h' is his name;
Jer 2:19 in thee, saith the Lord God of h'.
3:19 goodly heritage of the h' of nations?
5:14 thus saith the Lord God of h',
6: 6 For thus hath the Lord of h' said
9 Thus saith the Lord of h', They
7: 3 the Lord of h', the God of Israel,
21 the Lord of h', the God of Israel;
8: 3 driven them, saith the Lord of h'.
Jer 9: 7 Therefore saith the Lord of h',
15 the Lord of h', the God of Israel;
17 Thus saith the Lord of h', Consider
10:16 The Lord of h' is his name.
11:17 For the Lord of h', that planted
20 Lord of h', that judgest righteously,
22 Therefore thus saith the Lord of h',
15:16 by thy name, O Lord God of h'.
16: 9 the Lord of h', the God of Israel;
19: 3 the Lord of h', the God of Israel;
11 Thus saith the Lord of h'; Even so
15 the Lord of h', the God of Israel;
20:12 Lord of h', that triest the righteous,
23:15 Therefore thus saith the Lord of h'
16 Thus saith the Lord of h', Hearken
36 living God, of the Lord of h' our God.
25: 8 Therefore thus saith the Lord of h';
27 the Lord of h', the God of Israel;
28 Thus saith the Lord of h'; Ye shall
29 of the earth, saith the Lord of h'.
32 Thus saith the Lord of h', Behold,
26:18 Thus saith the Lord of h'; Zion
27: 4 the Lord of h', the God of Israel;
18 make intercession to the Lord of h',
19 For thus saith the Lord of h'
21 the Lord of h', the God of Israel,
28: 2 the Lord of h', the God of Israel,
14 the Lord of h', the God of Israel;
29: 4 the Lord of h', the God of Israel,
8 the Lord of h', the God of Israel;
17 Thus saith the Lord of h'; Behold,
21, 25 the Lord of h', the God of Israel,
30: 8 saith the Lord of h', that I will break
31:23 the Lord of h', the God of Israel;
35 The Lord of h' is his name:
32:14, 15 the Lord of h', the God of Israel;
18 the Mighty God, the Lord of h', is
33:11 Praise the Lord of h': for the Lord
12 Thus saith the Lord of h'; Again
35:13, 17, 18, 19, the Lord of h', the God of
38:17 the God of h', the God of Israel;
39:16 the Lord of h', the God of Israel;
42:15, 18 the Lord of h', the God of Israel;
43:10 the Lord of h', the God of Israel;
44: 2 the Lord of h', the God of Israel;
7 thus saith the Lord, the God of h',
11 the Lord of h', the God of Israel;
25 the Lord of h', the God of Israel,
46:10 is the day of the Lord God of h',
10 the Lord God of h' hath a sacrifice
18 King, whose name is the Lord of h',
25 The Lord of h', the God of Israel,
48: 1 the Lord of h', the God of Israel:
15 King, whose name is the Lord of h'.
49: 5 upon thee, saith the Lord God of h',
7 Edom, thus saith the Lord of h';
26 off in that day, saith the Lord of h'.
35 Thus saith the Lord of h'; Behold,
50:18 the Lord of h', the God of Israel;
25 the work of the Lord God of h' in
31 proud, saith the Lord God of h':
33 Thus saith the Lord of h'; The
34 strong; the Lord of h' is his name:
51: 5 Judah of his God, of the Lord of h';
14 The Lord of h' hath sworn by
19 the Lord of h' is his name.
33 the Lord of h', the God of Israel;
57 King, whose name is the Lord of h'.
58 Thus saith the Lord of h'; The
Ho 12: 5 Even the Lord God of h'; the Lord
Am 3:13 saith the Lord God, the God of h',
4:13 Lord, the God of h', is his name.
5:14 the Lord, the God of h', shall be
15 Lord God of h' will be gracious
16 Therefore the Lord, the God of h',
27 Lord, whose name is The God of h'.
6: 8 saith the Lord the God of h', I
14 Israel, saith the Lord the God of h';
9: 5 Lord God of h' is he that toucheth
Mic 4: 4 of the Lord of h' hath spoken it.
Na 2:13 against thee, saith the Lord of h',
3: 5 against thee, saith the Lord of h';
Hab 2:13 not of the Lord of h' that the people
Zep 2: 9 the Lord of h', the God of Israel,
10 against the people of the Lord of h'.
Hag 1: 2 Thus speaketh the Lord of h',
5 therefore thus saith the Lord of h';
7 saith the Lord of h'; Consider your
9 Why? saith the Lord of h'. Because
14 work in the house of the Lord of h',
2: 4 I am with you, saith the Lord of h':
6 For thus saith the Lord of h'; Yet
7 with glory, saith the Lord of h'.
8 gold is mine, saith the Lord of h'.
9 of the former, saith the Lord of h':
9 I give peace, saith the Lord of h'.
11 Thus saith the Lord of h'; Ask now
23 In that day, saith the Lord of h',
23 chosen thee, saith the Lord of h'.
Zec 1: 3 them, Thus saith the Lord of h';
3 ye unto me, saith the Lord of h',
3 turn unto you, saith the Lord of h'.
4 Thus saith the Lord of h'; Turn ye
6 Like as the Lord of h' thought to do
12 O Lord of h', how long wilt thou not
14 Thus saith the Lord of h'; I am
16 be built in it, saith the Lord of h',
17 Thus saith the Lord of h'; My cities
2: 8 For thus saith the Lord of h';
9 that the Lord of h' hath sent me.
11 that the Lord of h' hath sent me unto
3: 7 Thus saith the Lord of h'; If thou
9 thereof, saith the Lord of h'.
10 In that day, saith the Lord of h',
4: 6 by my spirit, saith the Lord of h'.
9 that the Lord of h' hath sent me unto

Zec 5: 4 bring it forth, saith the Lord of h'.
6:12 Thus speaketh the Lord of h',
15 that the Lord of h' hath sent me unto
7: 3 were in the house of the Lord of h',
4 came the word of the Lord of h'
9 Thus speaketh the Lord of h',
12 which the Lord of h' hath sent in
12 a great wrath from the Lord of h'.
13 would not hear, saith the Lord of h':
8: 1 the word of the Lord of h' came to
2 Thus saith the Lord of h'; I was
3 the mountain of the Lord of h' the
4 Thus saith the Lord of h'; There
6 Thus saith the Lord of h'; If it be
6 in mine eyes? saith the Lord of h'.
7 Thus saith the Lord of h'; Behold,
9 Thus saith the Lord of h'; Let your
9 the house of the Lord of h' was laid,
11 former days, saith the Lord of h'.
14 For thus saith the Lord of h'; As I
14 saith the Lord of h', and I repented
18 the word of the Lord of h' came
19 Thus saith the Lord of h'; The fast
20 Thus saith the Lord of h'; It shall
21 and to seek the Lord of h': I will
22 shall come to seek the Lord of h' in
23 Thus saith the Lord of h'; In those
9:15 The Lord of h' shall defend them;
10: 3 the Lord of h' hath visited his flock
12: 5 strength in the Lord of h' their God.
13: 2 in that day, saith the Lord of h',
7 is my fellow, saith the Lord of h':
14:16, 17 worship the King, the Lord of h',
21 be holiness unto the Lord of h':
21 in the house of the Lord of h'.
Mal 1: 4 thus saith the Lord of h', They
6 saith the Lord of h' unto you, O
8 thy person? saith the Lord of h'.
9 your persons? saith the Lord of h'.
10 pleasure in you, saith...Lord of h',
11 the heathen, saith the Lord of h'.
13 snuffed at it, saith the Lord of h';
14 a great King, saith the Lord of h',
2: 2 unto my name, saith the Lord of h',
4 be with Levi, saith the Lord of h'.
7 is the messenger of the Lord of h'.
8 of Levi, saith the Lord of h'.
12 an offering unto the Lord of h'.
16 his garment, saith the Lord of h':
3: 1 he shall come, saith the Lord of h'.
5 fear not me, saith the Lord of h'.
7 unto you, saith the Lord of h'.
10 now herewith, saith the Lord of h',
11 in the field, saith the Lord of h'.
12 delightsome land, saith...Lord of h'.
14 mournfully before the Lord of h'?
17 shall be mine, saith the Lord of h',
4: 1 burn them up, saith the Lord of h',
3 I shall do this, saith the Lord of h'.

hot See also HOTTEST.
Ex 16:21 when the sun waxed h', it melted.
22:24 And my wrath shall wax h', and I
32:10 that my wrath may wax h' against
11 why doth thy wrath wax h' against
19 and Moses' anger waxed h', and he
22 not the anger of my lord wax h':
Le 13:24 skin whereof there is a h' burning,
De 9:19 of the anger and h' displeasure,
19: 6 the slayer, while his heart is h',
Jos 9:12 This our bread we took h' for our
J'g 2:14, 20 the anger of the Lord was h'
3: 8 anger of the Lord was h' against
6:39 Let not thine anger be h' against
10: 7 anger of the Lord was h' against
1Sa 11: 9 by that time the sun be h', ye shall
21: 6 to put h' bread in the day when it
Ne 7: 3 be opened until the sun be h';
Job 6:17 when it is h', they are consumed
Ps 6: 1 chasten me in thy h' displeasure.
38: 1 chasten me in thy h' displeasure.
39: 3 My heart was h' within me, while
78:48 their flocks to h' thunderbolts.
Pr 6:28 Can one go upon h' coals, and his feet
Eze 24:11 that the brass of it may be h', and
Da 3:22 and the furnace exceeding h', the
Ho 7: 7 They are all h' as an oven, and
1Ti 4: 2 conscience seared with a h' iron;
Re 3:15 that thou art neither cold nor h':
15 I would thou wert cold or h'.
16 lukewarm, and neither cold nor h',

Hotham (*ho'-tham*) See also HOTHAN.
1Ch 7:32 Japhlet, and Shomer, and H',
Hothan (*ho'-than*) See also HOTHAM.
1Ch 11:44 Shama and Jehiel the sons of H'
Hothir (*ho'-thur*)
1Ch 25: 4 Mallothi, H', and Mahazioth:
28 The one and twentieth to H', he,
hotly
Ge 31:36 thou hast so h' pursued after me?
hottest
2Sa 11:15 in the forefront of the h' battle,
hough See also HOUGHED.
Jos 11: 6 shalt h' their horses, and burn
houghed
Jos 11: 9 he h' their horses, and burnt their
2Sa 8: 4 David h' all the chariot horses, but
1Ch 18: 4 David also h' all the chariot horses,
hound See GREYHOUND.
hour See also HOURS.
Da 3: 6 the same h' be cast into the midst
15 be cast the same h' into the midst
4:19 was astonied for one h', and his
33 The same h' was the thing fulfilled
Da 5: 5 In the same h' came forth fingers
M't 8:13 was healed in the selfsame h'.
9:22 was made whole from that h'.
10:19 that same h' what ye shall speak.
15:28 was made whole from that very h'.
17:18 child was cured from that very h'.
20: 3 he went out about the third h', and
5 out about the sixth and ninth h',
6 about the eleventh h' he went out,
9 were hired about the eleventh h',
12 These last have wrought but one h',
24:36 of that day and h' knoweth no man,
42 not what h' your Lord doth come.
44 such an h' as ye think not the Son
50 and in an h' that he is not aware of,
25:13 ye know neither the day nor the h'
26:40 could ye not watch with me one h'?
45 the h' is at hand, and the Son of
55 In that same h' said Jesus to the
27:45 the sixth h' there was darkness
45 over all the land unto the ninth h'.
46 about the ninth h' Jesus cried with
M'r 13:11 given you in that h', that speak ye:
32 day and that h' knoweth no man,
14:35 possible, the h' might pass from
37 couldest not thou watch one h'?
41 it is enough, the h' is come; behold,
15:25 was the third h', and they crucified
33 And when the sixth h' was come,
33 the whole land until the ninth h'.
34 the ninth h' Jesus cried with a loud
Lu 7:21 And in that same h' he cured many
10:21 In that h' Jesus rejoiced in spirit,
12:12 in the same h' what ye ought to say.
39 known what h' the thief would
40 cometh at an h' when ye think not.
46 at an h' when he is not aware, and
20:19 the same h' sought to lay hands
22:14 when the h' was come, he sat down,
53 but this is your h', and the power of
59 And about the space of one h' after
23:44 it was about the sixth h', and there
44 over all the earth until the ninth h'.
24:33 rose up the same h', and returned
Joh 1:39 day: for it was about the tenth h'.
2: 4 with thee? mine h' is not yet come.
4: 6 well: and it was about the sixth h'.
21 Woman, believe me, the h' cometh,
23 the h' cometh, and now is, when the
52 enquired he of them the h' when he
52 Yesterday at the seventh h' the
53 knew that it was at the same h',
5:25 The h' is coming, and now is, when
28 the h' is coming, in the which all
7:30 because his h' was not yet come.
8:20 on him; for his h' was not yet come.
12:23 The h' is come, that the Son of man
27 I say? Father, save me from this h':
27 for this cause came I unto this h'.
13: 1 when Jesus knew that his h' was
16:21 sorrow, because her h' is come:
32 the h' cometh, yea, is now come,
17: 1 and said, Father, the h' is come;
19:14 the passover, and about the sixth h':
27 from that h' that disciple took her
Ac 2:15 seeing it is but the third h' of the
3: 1 into the temple at the h' of prayer,
1 of prayer, being the ninth h'.
10: 3 the ninth h' of the day an angel
9 housetop to pray about the sixth h':
30 days ago I was fasting until this h';
30 the ninth h' I prayed in my house,
16:18 her. And he came out the same h'.
33 took them the same h' of the night,
22:13 And the same h' I looked up upon
23:23 hundred, at the third h' of the night;
1Co 4:11 this present h' we both hunger,
8: 7 of the idol unto this h' eat it as a
15:30 stand we in jeopardy every h'?
Ga 2: 5 by subjection, no, not for an h';
Re 3: 3 shalt not know what h' I will come
10 keep thee from the h' of temptation,
8: 1 about the space of half an h'.
9:15 prepared for an h', and a day, and
11:13 same h' was there a great
14: 7 for the h' of his judgment is come:
17:12 power as kings one h' with the
18:10 for in one h' is thy judgment come.
17 in one h' so great riches is come
19 for in one h' is she made desolate.
hours
Joh 11: 9 Are there not twelve h' in the
Ac 5: 7 about the space of three h' after,
19:34 about the space of two h' cried out,
house See also HOUSEHOLD; HOUSES; HOUSETOP; STOREHOUSES; WINTERHOUSE.
Ge 7: 1 thou and all thy h' into the ark;
12: 1 kindred, and from thy father's h',
15 woman was taken into Pharaoh's h'.
17 plagued Pharaoh and his h' with
14:14 trained servants, born in his own h',
15: 2 the steward of my h' is this Eliezer
3 one born in my h' is mine heir.
17:12 he that is born in the h', or bought
13 He that is born in thy h', and he
23 son, and all that were born in his h',
23 among the men of Abraham's h';
27 all the men of his h', born in the h',
19: 2 I pray you, into your servant's h',
3 unto him, and entered into his h';
4 of Sodom, compassed the h' round,
10 pulled Lot into the h' to them,
11 at the door of the h' with blindness,
20:13 me to wander from my father's h',
18 the wombs of the h' of Abimelech,
24: 2 unto his eldest servant of his h',
Ge 24: 7 which took me from my father's h',
23 is there room in thy father's h' for
27 to the h' of my master's brethren.
28 told them of her mother's h' these
31 for I have prepared the h', and room
32 the man came into the h': and he
38 go unto my father's h', and to my
40 my kindred, and of my father's h':
27:15 which were with her in the h',
28: 2 to the h' of Bethuel thy mother's
17 none other but the h' of God, and
21 again to my father's h' in peace;
22 set for a pillar, shall be God's h':
29:13 him, and brought him to his h'.
30:30 I provide for mine own h' also?
31:14 inheritance for us in our father's h'?
30 sore longedst after thy father's h',
41 have I been twenty years in thy h';
33:17 built him an h', and made booths
34:19 than all the h' of his father.
26 took Dinah out of Shechem's h',
29 spoiled even all that was in the h'.
30 I shall be destroyed, I and my h'.
36: 6 and all the persons of his h',
38:11 Remain a widow at thy father's h',
11 went and dwelt in her father's h'.
39: 2 he was in the h' of his master the
4 he made him overseer over his h',
5 he had made him overseer in his h',
5 Lord blessed the Egyptian's h'
5 was upon all that he had in the h',
8 not what is with me in the h',
9 is none greater in this h' than I;
11 that Joseph went into the h' to do
11 was none of the men of the h' there
14 she called unto the men of her h',
40: 3 in ward in the h' of the captain of
7 with him in the ward of his lord's h',
14 and bring me out of this h':
41:10 in the captain of the guard's h',
40 Thou shalt be over my h', and
51 all my toil, and all my father's h'.
42:19 be bound in the h' of your prison:
43:16 he said to the ruler of his h',
17 brought the men into Joseph's h'.
18 they were brought into Joseph's h';
19 near to the steward of Joseph's h',
19 with him at the door of the h',
24 brought the men into Joseph's h',
26 which was in their hand into the h',
44: 1 commanded the steward of his h',
8 should we steal out of thy lord's h'
14 his brethren came to Joseph's h';
45: 2 and the h' of Pharaoh heard.
8 to Pharaoh, and lord of all his h',
16 thereof was heard in Pharaoh's h',
46:27 all the souls of the h' of Jacob,
31 brethren, and unto his father's h',
31 My brethren, and my father's h',
47:14 the money into Pharaoh's h'.
50: 4 spake unto the h' of Pharaoh,
7 the elders of his h', and all the
8 and all the h' of Joseph, and his
8 and his father's h': only their little
22 in Egypt, he, and his father's h':
Ex 2: 1 there went a man of the h' of Levi,
3:22 of her that sojourneth in her h',
7:23 Pharaoh turned and went into his h',
8: 3 shall go up and come into thine h',
3 and into the h' of thy servants, and
24 of flies into the h' of Pharaoh,
12: 3 according to the h' of their fathers,
3 of their fathers, a lamb for an h':
4 and his neighbour next unto his h'
22 go out at the door of his h' until
30 there was not a h' where there was
46 In one h' shall it be eaten; thou
46 of the flesh abroad out of the h';
13: 3 Egypt, out of the h' of bondage;
14 Egypt, from the h' of bondage:
16:31 the h' of Israel called the name
19: 3 shalt thou say to the h' of Jacob,
20: 2 Egypt out of the h' of bondage.
17 shalt not covet thy neighbour's h',
22: 7 and it be stolen out of the man's h';
8 then the master of the h' shall be
23:19 bring into the h' of the Lord thy
34:26 bring unto the h' of the Lord thy
40:38 in the sight of all the h' of Israel,
Le 10: 6 the whole h' of Israel, bewail the
14:34 the plague of leprosy in a h' of the
35 And he that owneth the h' shall
35 is as it were a plague in the h':
36 that they empty the h', before the
36 all that is in the h' be not made
36 priest shall go in to see the h':
37 in the walls of the h' with hollow
38 out of the h' to the door of the h',
38 and shut up the h' seven days:
39 be spread in the walls of the h';
41 shall cause the h' to be scraped
42 mortar, and shall plaister the h'.
43 again, and break out in the h',
43 and after he hath scraped the h',
44 if the plague be spread in the h',
44 it is a fretting leprosy in the h':
45 he shall break down the h', the
45 thereof, and all the mortar of the h';
46 he that goeth into the h' all the
47 he that lieth in the h' shall wash
47 he that eateth in the h' shall wash
48 plague hath not spread in the h',
48 after the h' was plaistered: then the
48 priest shall pronounce the h' clean,
49 take to cleanse the h' two birds,
51 water, sprinkle the h' seven times:

Le 14:52 cleanse the h' with the blood of the
53 make an atonement for the h': and
55 leprosy of a garment, and of a h',
16: 6 atonement for himself, and for his h'.
11 atonement for himself, and for his h',
17: 3 be of the h' of Israel, that killeth
8 the h' of Israel, or of the strangers
10 man there be of the h' of Israel,
22:11 of it, and he that is born in his h':
13 is returned unto her father's h', as
18 he be of the h' of Israel, or of the
25:29 if a man sell a dwelling h' in a
30 then the h' that is in the walled city
33 then the h' that was sold, and the
27:14 man shall sanctify his h' to be holy
15 that sanctified it will redeem his h',
Nu 1: 2 families, by the h' of their fathers,
4 every one head of the h' of his
18, 20, 22, 24, 26, 28, 30, 32, 34, 36, 38,
40, 42, by the h' of their fathers,
44 one was for the h' of his fathers.
45 Israel, by the h' of their fathers,
2: 2 the ensign of their father's h':
32 Israel by the h' of their fathers:
34 according to the h' of their fathers.
3:15 after the h' of their fathers, by
20 according to the h' of their fathers.
24 the chief of the h' of the father of
30 the h' of the father of the families
35 the chief of the h' of the father of
4: 2 families, by the h' of their fathers,
29 families, by the h' of their fathers;
34 and after the h' of their fathers,
38 and by the h' of their fathers,
40, 42 families, by the h' of...fathers,
46 and after the h' of their fathers,
7: 2 heads of the h' of their fathers,
12: 7 so, who is faithful in all mine h'.
17: 2 according to the h' of their fathers,
2 according to the h' of their fathers
3 head of the h' of their fathers.
8 the rod of Aaron for the h' of Levi
18: 1 and thy sons, and thy father's h'
11 every one that is clean in thy h'
13 every one that is clean in thine h'
20:29 thirty days, even all the h' of Israel.
22:18 give me his h' full of silver and gold,
24:13 give me his h' full of silver and gold,
25:14 a prince of a chief h' among the
15 people, and of a chief h' in Midian.
26: 2 throughout their fathers' h', all
30: 3 in her father's h' in her youth;
10 if she vowed in her husband's h',
16 yet in her youth in her father's h'.
34:14 according to the h' of their fathers,
14 according to the h' of their fathers,
De 5: 6 of Egypt, from the h' of bondage.
21 thou covet thy neighbour's h', his
6: 7 when thou sittest in thine h', and
9 write them upon the posts of thy h',
12 of Egypt, from the h' of bondage.
7: 8 you out of the h' of bondmen,
26 bring an abomination into thine h',
8:14 of Egypt, from the h' of bondage;
11:19 them when thou sittest in thine h',
20 upon the door posts of thine h',
13: 5 you out of the h' of bondage,
10 of Egypt, from the h' of bondage.
15:16 because he loveth thee and thine h',
20: 5 is there that hath built a new h',
5 let him go and return to his h', lest
6 him also go and return unto his h',
7, 8 let him go and return unto his h',
21:12 shalt bring her home to thine h';
13 shall remain in thine h', and bewail
22: 2 shalt bring it unto thine own h',
8 When thou buildest a new h', then
8 thou bring not blood upon thine h',
21 damsel to the door of her father's h',
21 to play the whore in her father's h':
23:18 into the h' of the Lord thy God
24: 1 hand, and send her out of his h'.
2 when she is departed out of his h',
3 hand, and sendeth her out of his h';
10 not go into his h' to fetch his pledge.
25: 9 will not build up his brother's h'.
10 The h' of him that hath his shoe
14 Thou shalt not have in thine h'
26:11 given unto thee, and unto thine h',
13 the hallowed things out of mine h',
28:30 thou shalt build an h', and thou
Jos 2: 1 went, and came into an harlot's h',
3 which are entered into thine h':
6 brought them up to the roof of the h',
12 shew kindness unto my father's h',
15 for her h' was upon the town wall,
19 shall go out of the doors of thy h'
19 shall be with thee in the h',
6:17 and all that are with her in the h',
22 Go into the harlot's h', and bring
24 the treasury of the h' of the Lord.
9:23 of water for the h' of my God.
17:17 Joshua spake unto the h' of Joseph,
18: 5 and the h' of Joseph shall abide in
20: 6 his own city, and unto his own h',
21:45 had spoken unto the h' of Israel;
22:14 of each chief h' a prince throughout
14 an head of the h' of their fathers
24:15 as for me and my h', we will serve
17 of Egypt, from the h' of bondage,
J'g 1:22 the h' of Joseph, they also went up
23 And the h' of Joseph sent to descry
35 hand of the h' of Joseph prevailed,
4:17 and the h' of Heber the Kenite.
6: 8 you forth out of the h' of bondage;
15 I am the least in my father's h'.

J'g 8:27 a snare unto Gideon, and to his h'.
29 Joash went and dwelt in his own h'.
35 kindness to the h' of Jerubbaal,
9: 1 of the h' of his mother's father,
4 silver out of the h' of Baal-berith,
5 And he went unto his father's h'
6 all the h' of Millo, and went, and
16 well with Jerubbaal and his h',
18 are risen up against my father's h'
19 with Jerubbaal and with his h' this
20 of Shechem, and the h' of Millo;
20 Shechem, and from the h' of Millo,
27 and went into the h' of their god,
46 an hold of the h' of the god Berith.
10: 9 and against the h' of Ephraim;
11: 2 shalt not inherit in our father's h';
7 and expel me out of my father's h'?
31 cometh forth of the doors of my h'
34 came to Mizpeh unto his h', and,
12: 1 we will burn thine h' upon thee
14:15 we burn thee and thy father's h'
19 and he went up to his father's h'.
16:21 and he did grind in the prison h'.
25 for Samson out of the prison h';
26 pillars whereupon the h' standeth,
27 Now the h' was full of men and
29 pillars upon which the h' stood,
30 and the h' fell upon the lords, and
31 and all the h' of his father came
17: 4 and they were in the h' of Micah.
5 the man Micah had an h' of gods,
8 to the h' of Micah, as he journeyed.
12 priest, and was in the h' of Micah.
18: 2 to the h' of Micah, they lodged
3 When they were by the h' of Micah,
13 and came unto the h' of Micah.
15 came to the h' of the young man
15 Levite, even unto the h' of Micah,
18 these went into Micah's h', and
19 be a priest unto the h' of one man,
22 good way from the h' of Micah,
22 in the houses near to Micah's h'
26 turned and went back unto his h'.
31 that the h' of God was in Shiloh.
19: 2 away from him unto her father's h'
3 brought him into her father's h':
15 took them into his h' to lodging.
18 am now going to the h' of the Lord;
18 is no man that receiveth me to h'.
21 So he brought him into his h', and
22 of Belial, beset the h' round about,
22 spake to the master of the h', the
22 the man that came into thine h',
23 man, the master of the h', went out
23 that this man is come into mine h',
26 fell down at the door of the man's h'
27 opened the doors of the h', and
27 fallen down at the door of the h',
29 when he was come into his h', he
20: 5 beset the h' round about upon me
8 will we any of us turn into his h'.
18 and went up to the h' of God,
26 came unto the h' of God, and wept,
31 one goeth up to the h' of God,
21: 2 the people came to the h' of God,
Ru 1: 8 Go, return each to her mother's h':
9 each of you in the h' of her husband.
2: 7 that she tarried a little in the h'.
4:11 is come into thine h' like Rachel
11 which two did build the h' of Israel:
12 let thy h' be like the h' of Pharez,
1Sa 1: 7 she went up to the h' of the Lord,
19 and came to their h' to Ramah:
21 the man Elkanah, and all his h',
24 unto the h' of the Lord in Shiloh:
2:11 Elkanah went to Ramah to his h'.
27 appear unto the h' of thy father,
27 were in Egypt in Pharaoh's h'?
28 I give unto the h' of thy father all
30 that thy h', and the h' of thy father,
31 and the arm of thy father's h',
31 shall not be an old man in thine h'.
32 an old man in thine h' for ever.
33 the increase of thine h' shall die in
35 I will build him a sure h'; and he
36 every one that is left in thine h'
3:12 I have spoken concerning his h':
13 that I will judge his h' for ever for
14 I have sworn unto the h' of Eli,
14 iniquity of Eli's h' shall not be
15 the doors of the h' of the Lord.
5: 2 brought it into the h' of Dagon,
5 nor any that come into Dagon's h',
7: 1 brought it into the h' of Abinadab
2 all the h' of Israel lamented after
3 spake unto all the h' of Israel,
17 for there was his h'; and there he
9:18 I pray thee, where the seer's h' is.
20 on thee, and on all thy father's h'?
25 with Saul upon the top of the h'.
26 called Saul to the top of the h',
10:25 people away, every man to his h'.
15:34 Saul went up to his h' to Gibeah
17:25 make his father's h' free in Israel.
18: 2 go no more home to his father's h'.
10 prophesied in the midst of the h':
19: 9 he sat in his h' with his javelin in
11 sent messengers unto David's h',
20:15 thy kindness from my h' for ever:
16 a covenant with the h' of David,
21:15 shall this fellow come into my h'?
22: 1 and all his father's h' heard it,
11 son of Ahitub, and all his father's h',
14 and is honourable in thine h'?
15 nor to all the h' of my father:
16 thou, and all thy father's h'.

1Sa 22:22 of all the persons of thy father's h'.
23:18 wood, and Jonathan went to his h'.
24:21 my name out of my father's h'.
25: 1 and buried him in his h' at Ramah.
3 and he was of the h' of Caleb.
6 to thee, and peace be to thine h',
28 certainly make my lord a sure h';
35 unto her, Go up in peace to thine h';
36 he held a feast in his h', like the
28:24 the woman had a fat calf in the h';
31: 9 to publish it in the h' of their idols,
10 his armour in the h' of Ashtaroth:
2Sa 1:12 the Lord, and for the h' of Israel;
2: 4 David king over the h' of Judah.
7 the h' of Judah have anointed me
10 But the h' of Judah followed David.
11 king in Hebron over the h' of Judah
3: 1 the h' of Saul and the h' of David:
1 the h' of Saul waxed weaker and
6 the h' of Saul and the h' of David,
6 himself strong for the h' of Saul.
8 day unto the h' of Saul thy father,
10 the kingdom from the h' of Saul,
19 good to the whole h' of Benjamin.
29 of Joab, and on all his father's h';
29 there not fail from the h' of Joab
4: 5 of the day to the h' of Ish-bosheth,
6 thither into the midst of the h',
7 For when they came into the h', he
11 a righteous person in his own h'
5: 8 the lame shall not come into the h'.
5:11 masons: and they built David an h'.
6: 3, 4 it out of the h' of Abinadab
5 and all the h' of Israel played
10 aside into the h' of Obed-edom
11 continued in the h' of Obed-edom
12 hath blessed the h' of Obed-edom,
12 ark of God from the h' of Obed-edom
15 David and all the h' of Israel
19 people departed every one to his h'.
21 thy father, and before all his h',
7: 1 to pass, when the king sat in his h',
2 I dwell in an h' of cedar, but the ark
5 Shalt thou build me an h' for me
6 I have not dwelt in any h' since
7 Why build ye not me an h' of cedar?
11 thee that he will make thee an h'.
13 He shall build an h' for my name,
16 And thine h' and thy kingdom shall
18 and what is my h', that thou hast
19 hast spoken also of thy servant's h'
25 thy servant, and concerning his h',
26 and let the h' of thy servant David
27 saying, I will build thee an h':
29 thee to bless the h' of thy servant,
29 let the h' of thy servant be blessed
9: 1 any that is left of the h' of Saul,
2 there was of the h' of Saul a servant
3 there not yet any of the h' of Saul,
4 Behold, he is in the h' of Machir,
5 fetched him out of the h' of Machir,
9 pertained to Saul and to all his h'.
12 in the h' of Ziba were servants
11: 2 upon the roof of the king's h':
4 and she returned unto her h'.
8 Go down to thy h', and wash thy
8 Uriah departed out of the king's h',
9 slept at the door of the king's h'
9 lord, and went not down to his h'.
10 Uriah went not down unto his h',
10 thou not go down unto thine h'?
11 shall I then go into mine h', to eat
13 lord, but went not down to his h'.
27 David sent and fetched her to his h',
12: 8 I gave thee thy master's h', and
8 and gave thee the h' of Israel and
10 shall never depart from thine h';
11 against thee out of thine own h',
15 And Nathan departed unto his h'.
17 And the elders of his h' arose,
20 came into the h' of the Lord, and
20 then he came to his own h'; and
13: 7 Go now to thy brother Amnon's h',
8 went to her brother Amnon's h';
20 in her brother Absalom's h'.
14: 8 Go to thine h', and I will give
9 be on me, and on my father's h':
24 Let him turn to his own h', and
24 So Absalom returned to his own h',
31 and came to Absalom unto his h',
15:16 were concubines, to keep the h'.
35 thou shalt hear out of the king's h',
16: 3 To day shall the h' of Israel restore
5 man of the family of the h' of Saul,
8 thee all the blood of the h' of Saul,
21 which he hath left to keep the h';
22 a tent upon the top of the h';
17:18 quickly, and came to a man's h' in
20 came to the woman to the h',
23 arose, and gat him home to his h',
19: 5 Joab came into the h' to the king,
11 to bring the king back to his h'?
11 is come to the king, even to his h'.
17 Ziba the servant of the h' of Saul,
20 of all the h' of Joseph to go down
28 my father's h' were but dead men
30 again in peace unto his own h'.
20: 3 David came to his h' at Jerusalem;
3 whom he had left to keep the h',
21: 1 It is for Saul, and for his bloody h',
4 silver nor gold of Saul, nor of his h';
23: 5 Although my h' be not so with God;
24:17 me, and against my father's h'.
1Ki 1:53 said unto him, Go to thine h'.
2:24 and who hath made me an h', as
27 he spake concerning the h' of Eli

1Ki 2:31 me, and from the h' of my father.
33 upon his h', and upon his throne,
34 he was buried in his own h' in the
36 Build thee an h' in Jerusalem,
3: 1 made an end of building his own h',
1 the h' of the Lord, and the wall of
2 because there was no h' built unto
17 I and this woman dwell in one h';
17 delivered of a child...in the h'.
18 us in the h', save we two in the h'.
5: 3 my father could not build an h'
5 I purpose to build an h' unto the
5 he shall build an h' unto my name.
17 to lay the foundation of the h'.
18 timber and stones to build the h'.
6: 1 he began to build the h' of the Lord.
2 the h' which king Solomon built
3 porch before the temple of the h',
3 according to the breadth of the h';
3 the breadth thereof before the h'.
4 for the h' he made windows of
5 And against the wall of the h' he
5 against the walls of the h' round
6 wall of the h' he made narrowed
6 not be fastened in the wall of the h'.
7 And the h', when it was in building,
7 nor any tool of iron heard in the h',
8 was in the right side of the h':
9 So he built the h', and finished it;
9 covered the h' with beams and
10 he built chambers against all the h',
10 rested on the h' with timber of cedar.
12 this h' which thou art in building,
14 built the h', and finished it.
15 he built the walls of the h' within
15 floor of the h', and the walls of the
15 covered the floor of the h' with
16 twenty cubits on the sides of the h',
17 And the h', that is, the temple
18 And the cedar of the h' within
19 the oracle he prepared in the h'
21 overlaid the h' within with pure
22 the whole h' he overlaid with gold,
22 until he had finished all the h':
27 the cherubims within the inner h':
27 one another in the midst of the h'.
29 And he carved all the walls of the h'
30 the floor of the h' he overlaid with
37 the foundation of the h' of the Lord
38 was the h' finished throughout
7: 1 Solomon was building his own h'
1 years, and he finished all his h'.
2 He built also the h' of the forest
8 And his h' where he dwelt had
8 also an h' for Pharaoh's daughter,
12 inner court of the h' of the Lord,
12 and for the porch of the h'.
39 bases on the right side of the h',
39 and five on the left side of the h':
39 set the sea on the right side of the h'
40 king Solomon for the h' of the Lord:
45 vessels...for the h' of the Lord,
48 pertained unto the h' of the Lord:
50 of the inner h', the most holy place,
50 and for the doors of the h', to wit,
51 all the work...for the h' of the Lord.
51 the treasures of the h' of the Lord.
8: 6 into the oracle of the h', to the
10 the cloud filled the h' of the Lord,
11 glory of the Lord had filled the h'
13 surely built thee an h' to dwell in,
16 all the tribes of Israel to build an h',
17 David my father to build an h' for
18 heart to build an h' unto my name,
19 thou shalt not build the h'; but thy
19 of thy loins, he shall build the h'
20 built an h' for the name of the Lord
27 how much less this h' that I have
29 eyes may be open toward this h'
31 come before thine altar in this h':
33 supplication unto thee in this h':
38 forth his hands toward this h':
42 shall come and pray toward this h';
43 that this h', which I have builded,
44 toward the h' that I have built
48 and the h' which I have built for
63 Israel, dedicated the h' of the Lord.
64 that was before the h' of the Lord:
9: 1 had finished the building of the h'
1 king's h', and all Solomon's desire
3 I have hallowed this h', which thou
7 and this h', which I have hallowed
8 And at this h', which is high, every
8 thou unto this land, and to this h'?
10 the h' of the Lord, and the king's h',
15 the h' of the Lord, and his own h',
24 unto her h' which Solomon had
25 the Lord. So he finished the h'.
10: 4 wisdom, and the h' that he had built,
5 he went up unto the h' of the Lord;
12 trees pillars for the h' of the Lord,
12 and for the king's h', harps also
17 in the h' of the forest of Lebanon.
21 of the h' of the forest of Lebanon
11:18 which gave him an h', and appointed
20 Tahpenes weaned in Pharaoh's h':
28 all the charge of the h' of Joseph.
38 with thee, and build thee a sure h',
12:16 now see to thine own h', David.
19 rebelled against the h' of David
20 none that followed the h' of David,
21 he assembled all the h' of Judah,
21 to fight against the h' of Israel,
23 all the h' of Judah and Benjamin,
24 return every man to his h'; for this
26 kingdom return to the h' of David:

1Ki 12:27 sacrifice in the h' of the Lord at
31 he made an h' of high places, and
13: 2 shall be born unto the h' of David,
8 If thou wilt give me half thine h',
18 him back with thee into thine h',
19 eat bread in his h', and drank water,
34 became sin unto the h' of Jeroboam,
14: 4 and came to the h' of Ahijah.
8 kingdom away from the h' of David,
10 bring evil upon the h' of Jeroboam,
10 remnant of the h' of Jeroboam,
12 get thee to thine own h': and
13 God of Israel in the h' of Jeroboam.
14 cut off the h' of Jeroboam that day:
26 the treasures of the h' of the Lord,
26 and the treasures of the king's h';
27 which kept the door of the king's h'.
28 king went into the h' of the Lord,
15:15 into the h' of the Lord, silver, and
18 the treasures of the h' of the Lord,
18 and the treasures of the king's h',
27 son of Ahijah, of the h' of Issachar,
29 he smote all the h' of Jeroboam;
16: 3 and the posterity of his h'; and will
3 make thy h' like the h' of Jeroboam
7 against Baasha, and against his h',
7 in being like the h' of Jeroboam;
9 drinking himself drunk in the h' of
9 of Arza steward of his h' in Tirzah.
11 that he slew all the h' of Baasha:
12 Zimri destroy all the h' of Baasha,
18 went into the palace of the king's h',
18 burnt the king's h' over him with
32 an altar to Baal in the h' of Baal,
17:15 he and her h', did eat many days.
17 the mistress of the h', fell sick;
23 down out of the chamber into the h',
18: 3 which was the governor of his h'.
18 but thou, and thy father's h', in that
20: 6 they shall search thine h', and the
31 the h' of Israel are merciful kings:
43 king of Israel went to his h' heavy
21: 2 because it is near unto my h':
4 And Ahab came into his h' heavy
22 make thine h' like the h' of Jeroboam
22 and like the h' of Baasha the son of
29 will I bring the evil upon his h'.
22:17 return every man to his h' in peace.
39 and the ivory h' which he made,
2Ki 4: 2 tell me, what hast thou in the h'?
2 hath not any thing in the h', save
32 Elisha was come into the h', behold,
35 and walked in the h' to and fro;
5: 9 stood at the door of the h' of Elisha
18 into the h' of Rimmon to worship
18 I bow myself in the h' of Rimmon:
18 down myself in the h' of Rimmon,
24 hand, and bestowed them in the h':
6:32 But Elisha sat in his h', and the
7:11 they told it to the king's h' within.
8: 3 to cry unto the king for her h' and
5 cried to the king for her h' and for
18 of Israel, as did the h' of Ahab:
27 walked in the way of the h' of Ahab,
27 of the Lord, as did the h' of Ahab:
27 was the son in law of the h' of Ahab.
9: 6 And he arose, and went into the h';
7 smite the h' of Ahab thy master,
8 the whole h' of Ahab shall perish:
9 h' of Ahab like the h' of Jeroboam
9 and like the h' of Baasha the son
27 he fled by the way of the garden h'.
10: 3 and fight for your master's h'.
5 And he that was over the h', and
10 spake concerning the h' of Ahab:
11 all that remained of the h' of Ahab
12 was at the shearing h' in the way,
14 them at the pit of the shearing h',
21 And they came into the h' of Baal;
21 and the h' of Baal was full from
23 And Jehu went...into the h' of Baal,
25 went to the city of the h' of Baal.
26 images out of the h' of Baal, and
27 and brake down the h' of Baal,
27 and made it a draught h' unto this day.
30 eyes, hast done unto the h' of Ahab
11: 3 hid in the h' of the Lord six years.
4 them to him into the h' of the Lord,
4 oath of them in the h' of the Lord,
5 of the watch of the king's h';
6 so shall ye keep the watch of the h',
7 keep the watch of the h' of the Lord
15 not be slain in the h' of the Lord.
16 the horses came into the king's h':
18 went into the h' of Baal, and brake
18 officers over the h' of the Lord.
19 the king from the h' of the Lord,
19 gate of the guard to the king's h'.
20 with the sword beside the king's h'.
12: 4 is brought into the h' of the Lord,
4 to bring into the h' of the Lord,
5 them repair the breaches of the h',
6 not repaired the breaches of the h'.
7 repair ye not the breaches of the h'?
7 deliver it for the breaches of the h'.
8 to repair the breaches of the h'.
9 one cometh into the h' of the Lord:
9 was brought into the h' of the Lord
10 was found in the h' of the Lord.
11 the oversight of the h' of the Lord:
11 wrought upon the h' of the Lord,
12 the breaches of the h' of the Lord,
12 was laid out for the h' to repair it.
13 the h' of the Lord bowls of silver,
13 was brought into the h' of the Lord:
14 repaired therewith the h' of the

2Ki 12:16 not brought into the h' of the Lord:
18 the treasures of the h' of the Lord,
18 and in the king's h', and sent it
20 and slew Joash in the h' of Millo,
13: 6 from the sins of the h' of Jeroboam,
14:14 were found in the h' of the Lord;
14 in the treasures of the king's h',
15: 5 his death, and dwelt in a several h'.
5 the king's son was over the h',
25 in the palace of the king's h', with
35 higher gate of the h' of the Lord,
16: 8 gold that was found in the h' of
8 in the treasures of the king's h',
14 Lord, from the forefront of the h',
14 the altar and the h' of the Lord,
18 sabbath that they had built in the h',
18 turned he from the h' of the Lord
17:21 rent Israel from the h' of David;
18:15 silver that was found in the h' of
15 in the treasures of the king's h'.
19: 1 and went into the h' of the Lord.
14 went up into the h' of the Lord,
26 as the grass on the h' tops, and as corn
30 that is escaped of the h' of Judah
37 worshipping in the h' of Nisroch
20: 1 Set thine h' in order; for thou shalt
5 shalt go up unto the h' of the Lord.
8 I shall go up into the h' of the Lord
13 and all the h' of his precious things,
13 and all the h' of his armour, and all
13 there was nothing in his h', nor in
15 What have they seen in thine h'?
15 that are in mine h' have they seen:
17 that all that is in thine h', and that
21: 4 he built altars in the h' of the Lord,
5 the two courts of the h' of the Lord.
7 grove that he had made in the h',
7 In this h', and in Jerusalem, which
13 and the plummet of the h' of Ahab:
18 buried in the garden of his own h',
23 and slew the king in his own h'.
22: 3 the scribe, to the h' of the Lord,
4 is brought into the h' of the Lord,
5 the oversight of the h' of the Lord:
5 work which is in the h' of the Lord,
5 to repair the breaches of the h',
6 and hewn stone to repair the h'.
8 found the book of the law in the h'
9 the money that was found in the h',
9 the oversight of the h' of the Lord.
23: 2 king went up into the h' of the Lord,
2 was found in the h' of the Lord.
6 the grove from the h' of the Lord,
7 that were by the h' of the Lord,
11 entering in of the h' of the Lord,
12 the two courts of the h' of the Lord,
24 priest found in the h' of the Lord.
27 and the h' of which I said, My name
24:13 the treasures of the h' of the Lord,
13 and the treasures of the king's h',
25: 9 the h' of the Lord, and the king's h',
9 great man's h' burnt he with fire.
13 brass that were in the h' of the
13 sea that was in the h' of the Lord,
16 had made for the h' of the Lord;
1Ch 2:54 Ataroth, the h' of Joab, and half
55 the father of the h' of Rechab.
4:21 the families of the h' of them that
21 fine linen, of the h' of Ashbea,
38 the h' of their fathers increased
5:13 brethren of the h' of their fathers
15 Guni, chief of the h' of their
24 heads of the h' of their fathers,
24 heads of the h' of their fathers.
6:31 service of song in the h' of the Lord,
32 Solomon had built the h' of the
48 of the tabernacle of the h' of God.
7: 2 heads of their father's h', to wit,
4 generations, after the h' of their
7, 9 heads of the h' of their fathers,
23 because it went evil with his h'.
40 heads of their fathers' h', choice
9: 9 fathers in the h' of their fathers.
11 Ahitub, the ruler of the h' of God;
13 heads of the h' of their fathers,
13 work of the service of the h' of God.
19 his brethren, of the h' of his father,
23 of the gates of the h' of the Lord,
23 namely, the h' of the tabernacle, by
26 and treasuries of the h' of God.
27 lodged round about the h' of God.
10: 6 sons, and all his h' died together.
10 his armour in the h' of their gods,
12:28 of his father's h' twenty and two
29 had kept the ward of the h' of Saul.
30 famous throughout the h' of their
13: 7 new cart out of the h' of Abinadab:
13 it aside into the h' of Obed-edom
14 Obed-edom in his h' three months.
14 Lord blessed the h' of Obed-edom,
14: 1 and carpenters, to build him an h'.
15:25 out of the h' of Obed-edom with joy.
16:43 departed every man to his h':
43 and David returned to bless his h'.
17: 1 came to pass, as David sat in his h',
1 Lo, I dwell in an h' of cedars, but
4 Thou shalt not build me an h' to
5 For I have not dwelt in an h' since
6 ye not built me an h' of cedars?
10 that the Lord will build thee an h'.
12 He shall build me an h', and I will
14 But I will settle him in mine h' and
16 I, O Lord God, and what is mine h',
17 spoken of thy servant's h' for a
23 thy servant and concerning his h'
24 and let the h' of David thy servant

1Ch 17: 25 that thou wilt build him an *h'*:
27 thee to bless the *h'* of thy servant,
21: 17 be on me, and on my father's *h'*;
22: 1 said, This is the *h'* of the Lord God,
2 stones to build the *h'* of God.
5 the *h'* that is to be builded for the
6 him to build an *h'* for the Lord God
7 it was in my mind to build an *h'*
8 shalt not build an *h'* unto my name,
10 He shall build an *h'* for my name;
11 build the *h'* of the Lord thy God,
14 I have prepared for the *h'* of the
19 into the *h'* that is to be built to the
23: 4 to set forward the work of the *h'* of
11 according to their father's *h'*.
24 Levi after the *h'* of their fathers;
24 for the service of the *h'* of the Lord,
28 for the service of the *h'* of the Lord,
28 work of the service of the *h'* of God;
32 in the service of the *h'* of the Lord.
24: 4 chief men of the *h'* of their fathers,
4 acording to the *h'* of their fathers.
5 and governors of the *h'* of God,
19 to come into the *h'* of the Lord,
30 after the *h'* of their fathers.
25: 6 for song in the *h'* of the Lord,
6 for the service of the *h'* of God,
26: 6 ruled throughout the *h'* of their
12 to minister in the *h'* of the Lord.
13 according to the *h'* of their
15 and to his sons the *h'* of Asuppim.
20 over the treasures of the *h'* of God,
22 the treasures of the *h'* of the Lord.
27 to maintain the *h'* of the Lord.
28: 2 to build an *h'* of rest for the ark
3 shalt not build an *h'* for my name,
4 chose me before all the *h'* of my
4 the *h'* of Judah, the *h'* of my father;
6 thy son, he shall build my *h'* and
10 to build an *h'* for the sanctuary:
12 of the courts of the *h'* of the Lord,
12 of the treasuries of the *h'* of God,
13 of the service of the *h'* of the Lord,
13 of service in the *h'* of the Lord.
20 for the service of the *h'* of the Lord.
21 for all the service of the *h'* of God:
29: 2 for the *h'* of my God the gold for
3 my affection to the *h'* of my God,
3 which I have given to the *h'* of God,
3 all I have prepared for the holy *h'*,
7 gave for the service of the *h'* of God
8 to the treasure of the *h'* of the Lord,
16 have prepared to build thee an *h'*
2Ch 2: 1 Solomon determined to build an *h'*
1 Lord, and an *h'* for his kingdom.
3 to build him an *h'* to dwell therein,
4 build an *h'* to the name of the Lord
5 And the *h'* which I build is great:
6 But who is able to build him an *h'*,
6 then, that I should build him an *h'*,
9 the *h'* which I am about to build
12 that might build an *h'* for the Lord,
12 Lord, and an *h'* for his kingdom.
3: 1 began to build the *h'* of the Lord
3 for the building of the *h'* of God.
4 porch that was in front of the *h'*,
4 according to the breadth of the *h'*,
5 And the greater *h'* he cieled with
6 he garnished the *h'* with precious
7 He overlaid also the *h'*, the beams,
8 he made the most holy *h'*, the length
8 according to the breadth of the *h'*,
10 in the most holy *h'* he made two
11, 12 reaching to the wall of the *h'*;
15 he made before the *h'* two pillars
4: 11 king Solomon for the *h'* of God;
16 Solomon for the *h'* of the Lord of
19 all the vessels that were for the *h'*
22 the entry of the *h'*, the inner doors
22 the doors of the *h'* of the temple,
5: 1 Solomon made for the *h'* of the
1 among the treasures of the *h'* of
7 to the oracle of the *h'*, into the most
13 *h'* was filled with a cloud, even the *h'*
14 glory of the Lord had filled the *h'* of
6: 2 I have built an *h'* of habitation for
5 the tribes of Israel to build an *h'* in,
7 David my father to build an *h'* for
8 heart to build an *h'* for my name,
9 thou shalt not build the *h'*; but thy
9 he shall build the *h'* for my name.
10 have built the *h'* for the name of
18 how much less this *h'* which I have
20 eyes may be open upon this *h'* day
22 come before thine altar in this *h'*;
24 supplication before thee in this *h'*;
29 spread forth his hands in this *h'*;
32 if they come and pray in this *h'*;
33 may know that this *h'* which I have
34 and the *h'* which I have built for
38 toward the *h'* which I have built for
7: 1 the glory of the Lord filled the *h'*.
2 priests could not enter into the *h'*
2 of the Lord had filled the Lord's *h'*.
3 the glory of the Lord upon the *h'*,
5 the people dedicated the *h'* of God.
7 that was before the *h'* of the Lord:
11 the *h'* of the Lord, and the king's *h'*:
11 the *h'* of the Lord, and in his own *h'*,
12 place to myself for an *h'* of sacrifice.
16 have I chosen and sanctified this *h'*,
20 and this *h'*, which I have sanctified
21 And this *h'*, which is high, shall be
21 unto this land, and unto this *h'*?
8: 1 the *h'* of the Lord, and his own *h'*,
11 unto the *h'* that he had built for her:

2Ch 8: 11 My wife shall not dwell in the *h'* of
16 the foundation of the *h'* of the Lord,
16 So the *h'* of the Lord was perfected.
9: 3 Solomon, and the *h'* that he had
4 he went up into the *h'* of the Lord;
11 trees terraces to the *h'* of the Lord
16 in the *h'* of the forest of Lebanon.
20 of the *h'* of the forest of Lebanon
10: 16 and now, David, see to thine own *h'*.
19 rebelled against the *h'* of David
11: 1 he gathered of the *h'* of Judah and
4 return every man to his *h'*: for
12: 9 the treasures of the *h'* of the Lord,
9 and the treasures of the king's *h'*;
10 kept the entrance of the king's *h'*.
11 king entered into the *h'* of the Lord,
15: 18 he brought into the *h'* of God the
16: 2 *h'* of the Lord, and of the king's *h'*,
10 seer, and put him in a prison *h'*;
17: 14 according to the *h'* of their fathers:
18: 16 every man to his *h'* in peace.
19: 1 Judah returned to his *h'* in peace
11 the ruler of the *h'* of Judah,
20: 5 in the *h'* of the Lord, before the new
9 we stand before this *h'*, and in thy
9 for thy name is in this *h'*, and cry
28 trumpets unto the *h'* of the Lord.
21: 6 of Israel, like as did the *h'* of Ahab:
7 would not destroy the *h'* of David,
13 to the whoredoms of the *h'* of Ahab,
13 slain thy brethren of thy father's *h'*,
17 that was found in the king's *h'*,
22: 3 also in the ways of the *h'* of Ahab:
4 of the Lord like the *h'* of Ahab:
7 anointed to cut off the *h'* of Ahab.
8 judgment upon the *h'* of Ahab,
9 So the *h'* of Ahaziah had no power
10 all the seed royal of the *h'* of Judah.
12 them hid in the *h'* of God six years:
23: 3 with the king in the *h'* of God.
5 third part shall be at the king's *h'*;
5 in the courts of the *h'* of the Lord.
6 none come into the *h'* of the Lord,
7 cometh into the *h'*, he shall be put
9 David's, which were in the *h'* of God.
12 the people into the *h'* of the Lord:
14 Slay her not in the *h'* of the Lord.
15 of the horse gate by the king's *h'*,
17 went to the *h'* of Baal, and brake it
18 the offices of the *h'* of the Lord
18 distributed in the *h'* of the Lord,
19 at the gates of the *h'* of the Lord,
20 the king from the *h'* of the Lord:
20 the high gate into the king's *h'*,
24: 4 minded to repair the *h'* of the Lord.
5 repair the *h'* of your God from year
7 had broken up the *h'* of God; and
7 dedicated things of the *h'* of the
8 at the gate of the *h'* of the Lord.
12 of the service of the *h'* of the Lord,
12 to repair the *h'* of the Lord,
12 brass to mend the *h'* of the Lord.
13 they set the *h'* of God in his state,
14 made vessels for the *h'* of the Lord,
14 burnt offerings in the *h'* of the Lord
16 both toward God, and toward his *h'*.
18 And they left the *h'* of the Lord God
21 in the court of the *h'* of the Lord.
27 and the repairing of the *h'* of God,
25: 24 that were found in the *h'* of God
24 and the treasures of the king's *h'*,
26: 19 before the priests in the *h'* of the
21 dwelt in a several *h'*, being a leper;
21 was cut off from the *h'* of the Lord:
21 his son was over the king's *h'*,
27: 3 the high gate of the *h'* of the Lord,
28: 7 Azrikam the governor of the *h'*, and
21 a portion out of the *h'* of the Lord,
21 and out of the *h'* of the king, and of
24 together the vessels of the *h'* of God,
24 pieces the vessels of the *h'* of God,
24 up the doors of the *h'* of the Lord,
29: 3 the doors of the *h'* of the Lord,
5 sanctify the *h'* of the Lord God of
15 Lord, to cleanse the *h'* of the Lord.
16 the inner part of the *h'* of the Lord,
16 into the court of the *h'* of the Lord.
17 so they sanctified the *h'* of the Lord
18 We have cleansed all the *h'* of the
20 and went up to the *h'* of the Lord.
25 set the Levites in the *h'* of the Lord
31 offerings into the *h'* of the Lord.
35 the service of the *h'* of the Lord was
30: 1 should come to the *h'* of the Lord
15 offerings into the *h'* of the Lord.
31: 10 the chief priest of the *h'* of Zadok
10 the offerings into the *h'* of the Lord,
11 chambers in the *h'* of the Lord;
13 Azariah the ruler of the *h'* of God.
16 that entereth into the *h'* of the Lord,
17 priests by the *h'* of their fathers,
21 began in the service of the *h'* of God,
32: 21 he was come into the *h'* of his god,
33: 4 he built altars in the *h'* of the Lord,
5 the two courts of the *h'* of the Lord.
7 idol...he had made, in the *h'* of God,
7 In this *h'*, and in Jerusalem, which
15 the idol out of the *h'* of the Lord,
15 in the mount of the *h'* of the Lord,
20 and they buried him in his own *h'*:
24 him, and slew him in his own *h'*.
34: 8 he had purged the land, and the *h'*,
8 to repair the *h'* of the Lord his God.
9 that was brought into the *h'* of God,
10 the oversight of the *h'* of the Lord,
10 workmen that wrought in the *h'* of

2Ch 34: 10 Lord, to repair and amend the *h'*:
14 was brought into the *h'* of the Lord,
15 book of the law in the *h'* of the Lord.
17 money that was found in the *h'* of
30 king went up into the *h'* of the Lord,
30 that was found in the *h'* of the Lord.
35: 2 to the service of the *h'* of the Lord,
3 Put the holy ark in the *h'* which
8 and Jehiel, rulers of the *h'* of God,
21 against the *h'* wherewith I have war:
36: 7 of the vessels of the *h'* of the Lord
10 goodly vessels of the *h'* of the Lord,
14 polluted the *h'* of the Lord which
17 sword in the *h'* of their sanctuary,
18 all the vessels of the *h'* of God,
18 the treasures of the *h'* of the Lord,
19 And they burnt the *h'* of God, and
23 charged me to build him an *h'* in
Ezr 1: 2 charged me to build him an *h'* at
3 and build the *h'* of the Lord God of
4 freewill offering for the *h'* of God
5 to go up to build the *h'* of the Lord
7 the vessels of the *h'* of the Lord,
7 had put them in the *h'* of his gods;
2: 36 of the *h'* of Jeshua, nine hundred
59 could not shew their father's *h'*,
68 when they came to the *h'* of the Lord
68 offered freely for the *h'* of God
3: 8 of their coming unto the *h'* of God
8 the work of the *h'* of the Lord.
9 the workmen in the *h'* of God:
11 foundation of the *h'* of the Lord was
12 men, that had seen the first *h'*,
12 the foundation of this *h'* was laid
4: 3 nothing to do with us to build an *h'*
24 ceased the work of the *h'* of God
5: 2 and began to build the *h'* of God
3 commanded you to build this *h'*,
8 to the *h'* of the great God, which is
9 commanded you to build this *h'*,
11 and build the *h'* that was builded
12 who destroyed this *h'*, and carried
13 a decree to build this *h'* of God.
14 of gold and silver of the *h'* of God,
15 let the *h'* of God be builded in his
16 laid the foundation of the *h'* of God
17 made in the king's treasure *h'*,
17 to build this *h'* of God at Jerusalem,
6: 1 was made in the *h'* of the rolls,
3 a decree concerning the *h'* of God
3 Let the *h'* be builded, the place
4 be given out of the king's *h'*:
5 and silver vessels of the *h'* of God,
5 and place them in the *h'* of God.
7 Let the work of this *h'* of God alone;
7 elders of the Jews build this *h'* of
8 for the building of this *h'* of God:
11 timber be pulled down from his *h'*,
11 and let his *h'* be made a dunghill
12 alter and to destroy this *h'* of God
15 And this *h'* was finished on the
16 kept the dedication of this *h'* of God
17 at the dedication of this *h'* of God
22 hands in the work of the *h'* of God,
7: 16 willingly for the *h'* of their God
17 upon the altar of the *h'* of your God
19 for the service of the *h'* of thy God,
20 be needful for the *h'* of thy God,
20 it out of the king's treasure *h'*.
23 done for the *h'* of the God of heaven:
24 or ministers of this *h'* of God,
27 to beautify the *h'* of the Lord
8: 17 us ministers for the *h'* of our God.
25 the offering of the *h'* of our God,
29 the chambers of the *h'* of the Lord.
30 to Jerusalem unto the *h'* of our God.
33 vessels weighed in the *h'* of our God
36 the people, and the *h'* of God.
9: 9 reviving, to set up the *h'* of our God,
10: 1 himself down before the *h'* of God,
6 rose up from before the *h'* of God,
9 sat in the street of the *h'* of God,
16 after the *h'* of their fathers, and all
Ne 1: 6 I and my father's *h'* have sinned.
2: 8 palace which appertained to the *h'*,
8 and for the *h'* that I shall enter into.
3: 10 Harumaph, even over against his *h'*.
16 and unto the *h'* of the mighty.
20 unto the door of the *h'* of Eliashib
21 from the door of the *h'* of Eliashib
21 even to the end of the *h'* of Eliashib.
23 and Hashub over against their *h'*.
23 the son of Ananiah by his *h'*.
24 from the *h'* of Azariah unto the
25 lieth out from the king's high *h'*,
28 every one over against his *h'*.
29 son of Immer over against his *h'*.
4: 16 were behind all the *h'* of Judah.
5: 13 shake out every man from his *h'*,
6: 10 I came unto the *h'* of Shemaiah
10 us meet together in the *h'* of God,
7: 3 every one to be over against his *h'*.
39 of the *h'* of Jeshua, nine hundred
61 could not shew their father's *h'*,
8: 16 every one upon the roof of his *h'*,
16 and in the courts of the *h'* of God,
10: 32 for the service of the *h'* of our God;
33 for all the work of the *h'* of our God.
34 to bring it into the *h'* of our God,
35 by year, unto the *h'* of the Lord:
36 flocks, to bring to the *h'* of our God,
36 that minister in the *h'* of our God:
37 the chambers of the *h'* of our God;
38 of the tithes unto the *h'* of our God,
38 the chambers, into the treasure *h'*.
39 will not forsake the *h'* of our God.

Ne 11:11 was the ruler of the *h'* of God.
12 brethren that did the work of the *h'*
16 outward business of the *h'* of God.
22 over the business of the *h'* of God.
12:29 Also from the *h'* of Gilgal, and out
37 above the *h'* of David, even unto
40 that gave thanks in the *h'* of God,
13: 4 the chamber of the *h'* of our God,
7 in the courts of the *h'* of God.
9 again the vessels of the *h'* of God,
11 Why is the *h'* of God forsaken?
14 I have done for the *h'* of my God,
Es 1: 8 appointed to all the officers of his *h'*,
9 feast for the women in the royal *h'*
22 man should bear rule in his own *h'*,
2: 3 the palace, to the *h'* of the women,
8 was brought also unto the king's *h'*,
9 be given her, out of the king's *h'*:
9 best place of the *h'* of the women.
11 before the court of the women's *h'*,
13 her out of the *h'* of the women
13 of the women unto the king's *h'*.
14 into the second *h'* of the women,
16 king Ahasuerus into his *h'* royal
4:13 thou shalt escape in the king's *h'*,
14 thy father's *h'* shall be destroyed:
5: 1 in the inner court of the king's *h'*,
1 over against the king's *h'*:
1 upon his royal throne in the royal *h'*,
1 over against the gate of the *h'*.
6: 4 the outward court of the king's *h'*,
12 Haman hasted to his *h'* mourning,
7: 8 the queen also before me in the *h'*?
9 king, standeth in the *h'* of Haman.
8: 1 give the *h'* of Haman the Jews'
2 set Mordecai over the *h'* of Haman.
7 have given Esther the *h'* of Haman,
9: 4 Mordecai was great in the king's *h'*,
Job 1:10 hedge about him, and about his *h'*,
13, 18 wine in their eldest brother's *h'*:
19 smote the four corners of the *h'*,
7:10 He shall return no more to his *h'*,
8:15 He shall lean upon his *h'*, but it
17:13 If I wait, the grave is mine *h'*:
19:15 They that dwell in mine *h'*, and my
20:19 violently taken away an *h'* which
28 The increase of his *h'* shall depart,
21:21 pleasure hath he in his *h'* after him,
28 say, Where is the *h'* of the prince?
27:18 He buildeth his *h'* as a moth, and as
30:23 to the *h'* appointed for all living.
38:20 know the paths to the *h'* thereof?
39: 6 *h'* I have made the wilderness,
42:11 did eat bread with him in his *h'*:
Ps 5: 7 as for me, I will come into thy *h'* in
23: 6 dwell in the *h'* of the Lord for ever.
26: 8 have loved the habitation of thy *h'*,
27: 4 I may dwell in the *h'* of the Lord all
30 *title* at the dedication of the *h'* of David.
31: 2 for an *h'* of defence to save me.
36: 8 satisfied with the fatness of thy *h'*;
42: 4 I went with them to the *h'* of God,
45:10 own people, and thy father's *h'*;
49:16 the glory of his *h'* is increased;
50: 9 I will take no bullock out of thy *h'*,
52 *title* come to the *h'* of Abimelech.
8 a green olive tree in the *h'* of God:
55:14 and walked unto the *h'* of God in
59 *title* they watched the *h'* to kill him.
65: 4 satisfied with the goodness of thy *h'*,
66:13 I will go into thy *h'* with burnt
69: 9 the zeal of thine *h'* hath eaten me
84: 3 the sparrow hath found an *h'*, and
4 are they that dwell in thy *h'*: they
10 a doorkeeper in the *h'* of my God,
92:13 be planted in the *h'* of the Lord
93: 5 holiness becometh thine *h'*, O Lord,
98: 3 his truth toward the *h'* of Israel:
101: 2 walk within my *h'* with a perfect
7 deceit shall not dwell within my *h'*:
102: 7 a sparrow alone upon the *h'* top.
104:17 the stork, the fir trees are her *h'*.
105:21 He made him lord of his *h'*, and
112: 3 Wealth and riches shall be in his *h'*:
113: 9 the barren woman to keep *h'*, and
114: 1 the *h'* of Jacob from a people of
115:10 O *h'* of Aaron, trust in the Lord:
12 he will bless the *h'* of Israel;
12 he will bless the *h'* of Aaron.
116:19 In the courts of the Lord's *h'*, in
118: 3 Let the *h'* of Aaron now say, that
26 blessed you out of the *h'* of the
119:54 songs in the *h'* of my pilgrimage.
122: 1 Let us go into the *h'* of the Lord.
5 the thrones of the *h'* of David.
9 Because of the *h'* of the Lord our
127: 1 Except the Lord build the *h'*, they
128: 3 vine by the sides of thine *h'*:
132: 3 come into the tabernacle of my *h'*,
134: 1 night stand in the *h'* of the Lord.
135: 2 Ye that stand in the *h'* of the Lord,
2 in the courts of the *h'* of our God,
19 Bless the Lord, O *h'* of Israel:
19 bless the Lord, O *h'* of Aaron:
20 Bless the Lord, O *h'* of Levi: ye
Pr 2:18 For her *h'* inclineth unto death,
3:33 the Lord is in the *h'* of the wicked:
5: 8 come not nigh the door of her *h'*:
10 labours be in the *h'* of a stranger;
6:31 give all the substance of his *h'*.
7: 6 For at the window of my *h'* I looked
8 he went the way to her *h'*, and
11 her feet abide not in her *h'*:
27 Her *h'* is the way to hell, going
9: 1 Wisdom hath builded her *h'*, she
14 she sitteth at the door of her *h'*,

Pr 11:29 He that troubleth his own *h'* shall
12: 7 the *h'* of the righteous shall stand.
14: 1 wise woman buildeth her *h'*: but
11 The *h'* of the wicked shall be
15: 6 In the *h'* of the righteous is much
25 will destroy the *h'* of the proud:
27 greedy of gain troubleth his own *h'*;
17: 1 than an *h'* full of sacrifices with
13 evil shall not depart from his *h'*.
19:14 *H'* and riches are the inheritance
21: 9 a brawling woman in a wide *h'*.
12 considereth the *h'* of the wicked:
24: 3 Through wisdom is an *h'* builded;
27 and afterwards build thine *h'*.
25:17 thy foot from thy neighbour's *h'*;
24 brawling woman and in a wide *h'*.
27:10 neither go into thy brother's *h'* in
Ec 2: 7 and had servants born in my *h'*;
5: 1 when thou goest to the *h'* of God,
7: 2 better to go to the *h'* of mourning,
2 than to go to the *h'* of feasting:
4 the wise is in the *h'* of mourning;
4 heart of fools is in the *h'* of mirth.
10:18 of the hands the *h'* droppeth
12: 3 the keepers of the *h'* shall tremble,
Ca 1:17 The beams of our *h'* are cedar, and
2: 4 brought me to the banqueting *h'*,
3: 4 brought him into my mother's *h'*,
8: 2 bring thee into my mother's *h'*,
7 all the substance of his *h'* for love,
Isa 2: 2 the mountain of the Lord's *h'* shall
3 Lord, to the *h'* of the God of Jacob;
5 O *h'* of Jacob, come ye, and let us
6 forsaken thy people the *h'* of Jacob,
3: 6 his brother of the *h'* of his father,
7 for in my *h'* is neither bread nor
5: 7 Lord of hosts is the *h'* of Israel,
8 Woe unto them that join *h'* to *h'*,
6: 4 and the *h'* was filled with smoke.
7: 2 it was told the *h'* of David, saying,
13 said, Hear ye now, O *h'* of David;
17 and upon thy father's *h'*, days that
8:17 hideth his face from the *h'* of Jacob,
10:20 as are escaped of the *h'* of Jacob,
14: 1 they shall cleave to the *h'* of Jacob.
2 the *h'* of Israel shall possess them
17 opened not the *h'* of his prisoners?
18 in glory, every one in his own *h'*.
22: 8 the armour of the *h'* of the forest.
15 Shebna, which is over the *h'*, and
18 shall be the shame of thy Lord's *h'*.
21 Jerusalem, and to the *h'* of Judah.
22 the key of the *h'* of David will I lay
23 a glorious throne to his father's *h'*.
24 him all the glory of his father's *h'*,
23: 1 is laid waste, so that there is no *h'*,
24:10 every *h'* is shut up, that no man
29:22 concerning the *h'* of Jacob, Jacob
31: 2 arise against the *h'* of the evildoers,
36: 3 son, which was over the *h'*, and
37: 1 and went into the *h'* of the Lord.
14 went up unto the *h'* of the Lord,
31 escaped of the *h'* of Judah shall
38 worshipping in the *h'* of Nisroch
38: 1 Set thine *h'* in order: for thou shalt
20 days of our life in the *h'* of the Lord.
22 I shall go up to the *h'* of the Lord?
39: 2 them the *h'* of his precious things,
2 and all the *h'* of his armour, and all
2 there was nothing in his *h'*, nor in
4 What have they seen in thy *h'*? And
4 All that is in mine *h'* have they
6 all that is in thine *h'*, and that
42: 7 in darkness out of the prison *h'*.
44:13 man; that it may remain in the *h'*.
46: 3 Hearken unto me, O *h'* of Jacob,
3 all the remnant of the *h'* of Israel,
48: 1 Hear ye this, O *h'* of Jacob, which
56: 5 will I give in mine *h'* and within
7 them joyful in my *h'* of prayer:
7 mine *h'* shall be called an *h'* of
58: 1 and the *h'* of Jacob their sins.
7 the poor that are cast out to thy *h'*?
60: 7 I will glorify the *h'* of my glory.
63: 7 goodness toward the *h'* of Israel,
64:11 Our holy and our beautiful *h'*,
66: 1 where is the *h'* that ye build unto
20 clean vessel into the *h'* of the Lord.
Jer 2: 4 word of the Lord, O *h'* of Jacob,
4 all the families of the *h'* of Israel:
26 so is the *h'* of Israel ashamed; they,
3:18 In those days the *h'* of Judah shall
18 walk with the *h'* of Israel, and they
20 with me, O *h'* of Israel,
5:11 the *h'* of Israel and the *h'* of Judah
15 upon you from far, O *h'* of Israel,
20 Declare this in the *h'* of Jacob,
7: 2 Stand in the gate of the Lord's *h'*,
10 come and stand before me in this *h'*,
11 Is this *h'*, which is called by my
14 will I do unto this *h'*, which is
30 the *h'* which is called by my name,
9:26 *h'* of Israel are uncircumcised in
10: 1 speaketh unto you, O *h'* of Israel:
11:10 the *h'* of Israel and the *h'* of Judah
15 hath my beloved to do in mine *h'*,
17 *h'* of Israel and of the *h'* of Judah,
12: 6 brethren, and the *h'* of thy father,
7 I have forsaken mine *h'*, I have left
14 pluck out the *h'* of Judah from
13:11 to cleave unto me the whole *h'* of
11 whole *h'* of Judah, saith the Lord;
16: 5 Enter not into the *h'* of mourning,
8 not also go into the *h'* of feasting,
17:26 of praise, unto the *h'* of the Lord.
18: 2 go down to the potter's *h'*, and

Jer 18: 3 Then I went down to the potter's *h'*,
6 O *h'* of Israel, cannot I do with you
6 are ye in mine hand, O *h'* of Israel.
19:14 stood in the court of the Lord's *h'*;
20: 1 chief governor in the *h'* of the Lord,
2 which was by the *h'* of the Lord.
6 all that dwell in thine *h'* shall go
21:11 And touching the *h'* of the king of
12 O *h'* of David, thus saith the Lord;
22: 1 down to the *h'* of the king of Judah,
4 enter in by the gates of this *h'*
5 Lord, that this *h'* shall become a
6 Lord unto the king's *h'* of Judah;
13 buildeth his *h'* by unrighteousness,
14 I will build me a wide *h'* and large
23: 8 led the seed of the *h'* of Israel out
11 in my *h'* have I found their
34 will even punish the man and his *h'*.
26: 2 Stand in the court of the Lord's *h'*,
2 come to worship in the Lord's *h'*,
6 Then will I make this *h'* like Shiloh,
7 these words in the *h'* of the Lord.
9 saying, This *h'* shall be like Shiloh,
9 Jeremiah in the *h'* of the Lord.
10 from the king's *h'* unto the *h'* of the
10 entry of the new gate of the Lord's *h'*.
12 to prophesy against this *h'* and
18 *h'* as the high places of a forest.
27:16 the vessels of the Lord's *h'* shall
18 which are left in the *h'* of the Lord,
18 and in the *h'* of the king of Judah,
21 that remain in the *h'* of the Lord,
21 and in the *h'* of the king of Judah
28: 1 spake unto me in the *h'* of the Lord,
3 place all the vessels of the Lord's *h'*,
5 that stood in the *h'* of the Lord,
6 again the vessels of the Lord's *h'*,
29:26 officers in the *h'* of the Lord, for
31:27 that I will sow the *h'* of Israel
27 and the *h'* of Judah with the seed
31 new covenant with the *h'* of Israel,
31 and with the *h'* of Judah:
33 I will make with the *h'* of Israel;
32: 2 which was in the king of Judah's *h'*.
34 set their abominations in the *h'*,
33:11 of praise into the *h'* of the Lord.
14 the *h'* of Israel...to the *h'* of Judah.
17 upon the throne of the *h'* of Israel;
34:13 out of the *h'* of bondmen, saying,
15 before me in the *h'* which is called
35: 2 Go unto the *h'* of the Rechabites,
2 bring them into the *h'* of the Lord,
3 and the whole *h'* of the Rechabites;
4 brought them into the *h'* of the Lord,
5 the sons of the *h'* of the Rechabites
7 shall ye build *h'*, nor sow seed, nor
18 said unto the *h'* of the Rechabites,
36: 3 that the *h'* of Judah will hear all the
5 cannot go into the *h'* of the Lord:
6 in the Lord's *h'* upon the fasting
8 words of the Lord in the Lord's *h'*.
10 of Jeremiah in the *h'* of the Lord,
10 the new gate of the Lord's *h'*, in
12 he went down into the king's *h'*,
37:15 in prison in the *h'* of Jonathan the
17 king asked him secretly in his *h'*,
20 not to return to the *h'* of Jonathan
38: 7 eunuchs which was in the king's *h'*,
8 went forth out of the king's *h'*, and
11 went into the *h'* of the king under
14 the third entry that is in the *h'* of
17 and thou shalt live, and thine *h'*:
22 are left in the king of Judah's *h'*
26 to return to Jonathan's *h'*, to die
39: 8 Chaldeans burned the king's *h'*,
41: 5 bring them to the *h'* of the Lord.
43: 9 at the entry of Pharaoh's *h'* in
48:13 as the *h'* of Israel was ashamed of
51:51 the sanctuaries of the Lord's *h'*.
52:13 the *h'* of the Lord, and the king's *h'*;
17 brass that were in the *h'* of the Lord,
17 sea that was in the *h'* of the Lord,
20 had made in the *h'* of the Lord:
La 2: 7 made a noise in the *h'* of the Lord,
Eze 2: 5 for they are a rebellious *h'*, yet
6 looks, though they be a rebellious *h'*.
8 rebellious like that rebellious *h'*:
3: 1 and go speak unto the *h'* of Israel.
4 go, get thee unto the *h'* of Israel,
5 language, but to the *h'* of Israel;
7 the *h'* of Israel will not hearken
7 all the *h'* of Israel are impudent
9 though they be a rebellious *h'*.
17 a watchman unto the *h'* of Israel:
24 me, Go, shut thyself within thine *h'*.
26 reprover: for they are a rebellious *h'*.
27 forbear: for they are a rebellious *h'*.
4: 3 shall be a sign to the *h'* of Israel.
4 iniquity of the *h'* of Israel upon it:
5 bear the iniquity of the *h'* of Israel.
6 the iniquity of the *h'* of Judah forty
5: 4 come forth into all the *h'* of Israel.
6:11 abominations of the *h'* of Israel!
8: 1 I sat in mine *h'*, and the elders of
6 that the *h'* of Israel committeth
10 and all the idols of the *h'* of Israel,
11 of the ancients of the *h'* of Israel,
12 the ancients of the *h'* of Israel do
14 door of the gate of the Lord's *h'*
16 the inner court of the Lord's *h'*,
17 Is it a light thing to the *h'* of Judah
9: 3 he was, to the threshold of the *h'*.
6 men which were before the *h'*.
7 Defile the *h'*, and fill the courts
9 The iniquity of the *h'* of Israel and
10: 3 stood on the right side of the *h'*,

Eze 10: 4 stood over the threshold of the h';
4 the h' was filled with the cloud,
18 from off the threshold of the h',
19 of the east gate of the Lord's h';
11: 1 unto the east gate of the Lord's h',
5 Thus have ye said, O h' of Israel:
15 and all the h' of Israel wholly, are
12: 2 in the midst of a rebellious h',
2 not: for they are a rebellious h'.
3 though they be a rebellious h'.
6 thee for a sign unto the h' of Israel.
9 the h' of Israel, the rebellious h',
10 all the h' of Israel that are among
24 divination within the h' of Israel.
25 O rebellious h', will I say the word,
27 they of the h' of Israel say, The
13: 5 hedge for the h' of Israel to stand
9 in the writing of the h' of Israel,
14: 4 Every man of the h' of Israel that
5 I may take the h' of Israel in their
6 say unto the h' of Israel, Thus saith
7 every one of the h' of Israel, or of
11 That the h' of Israel may go no
17: 2 a parable unto the h' of Israel;
12 Say now to the rebellious h', Know
18: 6, 15 to the idols of the h' of Israel,
25 Hear now, O h' of Israel; Is not my
29 Yet saith the h' of Israel, The way
29 O h' of Israel, are not my ways
30 I will judge you, O h' of Israel,
31 for why will ye die, O h' of Israel?
20: 5 unto the seed of the h' of Jacob,
13 But the h' of Israel rebelled against
27 speak unto the h' of Israel, and say
30 Wherefore say unto the h' of Israel,
31 enquired of by you, O h' of Israel?
39 As for you, O h' of Israel, thus
40 there shall all the h' of Israel, all of
44 corrupt doings, O ye h' of Israel,
22: 18 the h' of Israel is to me become
23: 39 they done in the midst of mine h'.
24: 3 a parable unto the rebellious h',
21 Speak unto the h' of Israel, Thus
25: 3 against the h' of Judah, when they
8 the h' of Judah is like unto all the
12 against the h' of Judah by taking
27: 14 They of the h' of Togarmah traded
28: 24 pricking brier unto the h' of Israel,
25 shall have gathered the h' of Israel
29: 6 a staff of reed to the h' of Israel.
16 the confidence of the h' of Israel,
21 the horn of the h' of Israel to bud
33: 7 watchman unto the h' of Israel;
10 man, speak unto the h' of Israel;
11 for why will ye die, O h' of Israel?
20 O ye h' of Israel, I will judge you
34: 30 the h' of Israel, are my people,
35: 15 the inheritance of the h' of Israel,
36: 10 all the h' of Israel, even all of it:
17 when the h' of Israel dwelt in their
21 the h' of Israel had profaned among
22 say unto the h' of Israel, Thus saith
22 this for your sakes, O h' of Israel,
32 for your own ways, O h' of Israel.
37 be enquired of by the h' of Israel,
37: 11 bones are the whole h' of Israel:
16 all the h' of Israel his companions:
38: 6 the h' of Togarmah of the north
39: 12 shall the h' of Israel be burying of
22 So the h' of Israel shall know that
23 the h' of Israel went into captivity
25 mercy upon the whole h' of Israel,
29 out my spirit upon the h' of Israel,
40: 4 that thou seest to the h' of Israel.
5 wall on the outside of the h' round
45 the keepers of the charge of the h'.
47 the altar that was before the h'.
48 brought me to the porch of the h',
41: 5 he measured the wall of the h', six
5 round about the h' on every side.
6 into the wall which was of the h'
6 had not hold in the wall of the h'.
7 the winding about of the h' went
7 still upward round about the h':
7 breadth of the h' was still upward,
8 I saw also the height of the h' round
10 round about the h' on every side.
13 So he measured the h', an hundred
14 the breadth of the face of the h',
17 the door, even unto the inner h',
19 through all the h' round about.
26 the side chambers of the h', and
42: 15 an end of measuring the inner h',
43: 4 glory of the Lord came into the h'
5 the glory of the Lord filled the h'.
6 speaking unto me out of the h';
7 shall the h' of Israel no more defile
10 shew the h' to the h' of Israel, that
11 shew them the form of the h', and
12 This is the law of the h'; upon the
12 Behold, this is the law of the h'.
21 it in the appointed place of the h',
44: 4 way of the north gate before the h':
4 the Lord filled the h' of the Lord:
5 ordinances of the h' of the Lord,
5 mark well the entering in of the h',
6 rebellious, even to the h' of Israel,
6 the Lord God; O ye h' of Israel,
7 sanctuary, to pollute it, even my h',
11 having charge at the gates of the h',
11 and ministering to the h':
12 the h' of Israel to fall into iniquity;
14 keepers of the charge of the h',
22 of the seed of the h' of Israel,
30 the blessing to rest in thine h'.
45: 5 the Levites, the ministers of the h',
Eze 45: 6 shall be for the whole h' of Israel.
8 shall they give to the h' of Israel
17 all solemnities of the h' of Israel:
17 reconciliation for the h' of Israel.
19 upon the posts of the h', and upon
20 so shall ye reconcile the h'.
46: 24 the ministers of the h' shall boil the
47: 1 me again unto the door of the h';
1 the threshold of the h' eastward:
1 forefront of the h' stood toward the
1 under from the right side of the h',
48: 21 the sanctuary of the h' shall be in
Da 1: 2 part of the vessels of the h' of God:
2 land of Shinar to the h' of his god;
2 into the treasure h' of his god.
2: 17 Daniel went to his h', and made
4: 4 was at rest in mine h',
30 built for the h' of the kingdom
5: 3 out of the temple of the h' of God
10 his lords came into the banquet h':
23 brought the vessels of his h' before
6: 10 was signed, he went into his h';
Ho 1: 4 of Jezreel upon the h' of Jehu,
4 the kingdom of the h' of Israel.
6 have mercy upon the h' of Israel;
7 have mercy upon the h' of Judah,
5: 1 and hearken, ye h' of Israel;
1 and give ye ear, O h' of the king;
12 to the h' of Judah as rottenness.
14 as a young lion to the h' of Judah:
6: 10 horrible thing in the h' of Israel:
8: 1 an eagle against the h' of the Lord,
9: 4 not come into the h' of the Lord.
8 and hatred in the h' of his God.
15 I will drive them out of mine h',
11: 12 and the h' of Israel with deceit:
Joe 1: 9 is cut off from the h' of the Lord;
13 withholden from the h' of your God.
14 into the h' of the Lord your God,
16 gladness from the h' of our God?
3: 18 come forth of the h' of the Lord,
Am 1: 4 will send a fire into the h' of Hazael,
5 the sceptre from the h' of Eden:
2: 8 condemned in the h' of their god.
3: 13 ye, and testify in the h' of Jacob,
15 the winter h' with the summer h';
5: 1 even a lamentation, O h' of Israel.
3 shall leave ten, to the h' of Israel.
4 saith the Lord unto the h' of Israel,
6 out like fire in the h' of Joseph,
19 or went into the h', and leaned his
25 forty years, O h' of Israel?
6: 1 to whom the h' of Israel came!
9 remain ten men in one h', that they
10 to bring out the bones out of the h',
10 him that is by the sides of the h',
11 smite the great h' with breaches,
11 and the little h' with clefts.
14 against you a nation, O h' of Israel,
7: 9 will rise against the h' of Jeroboam
10 thee in the midst of the h' of Israel:
16 not thy word against the h' of Isaac.
9: 8 not utterly destroy the h' of Jacob,
9 I will sift the h' of Israel among all
Ob 17 and the h' of Jacob shall possess
18 And the h' of Jacob shall be a fire,
18 and the h' of Joseph a flame,
18 and the h' of Esau for stubble,
18 be any remaining of the h' of Esau;
Mic 1: 5 and for the sins of the h' of Israel,
10 in the h' of Aphrah roll thyself in
2: 2 so they oppress a man and his h',
7 thou that art named the h' of Jacob,
3: 1 and ye princes of the h' of Israel;
9 and you, ye heads of the h' of Jacob,
9 and princes of the h' of Israel, that
12 mountain of the h' as the high
4: 1 the mountain of the h' of the Lord
2 and to the h' of the God of Jacob;
6: 4 thee out of the h' of servants;
10 wickedness in the h' of the wicked,
16 all the works of the h' of Ahab, and
7: 6 enemies are the men of his own h'.
Na 1: 14 out of the h' of thy gods will I cut
Hab 2: 9 an evil covetousness to his h',
10 hast consulted shame to thy h' by
3: 13 head out of the h' of the wicked, by
Zep 2: 7 for the remnant of the h' of Judah;
Hag 1: 2 that the Lord's h' should be built.
4 cieled houses, and this h' lie waste?
8 and bring wood, and build the h';
9 Because of mine h' that is waste,
9 ye run every man unto his own h'.
14 work in the h' of the Lord of hosts,
2: 3 among you that saw this h' in her
7 and I will fill this h' with glory,
9 The glory of this latter h' shall be
Zec 1: 16 my h' shall be built in it, saith the
3: 7 thou shalt also judge my h', and
4: 9 have laid the foundation of this h';
5: 4 shall enter into the h' of the thief,
4 the h' of him that sweareth falsely
4 shall remain in the midst of his h',
11 build it an h' in the land of Shinar:
6: 10 go into the h' of Josiah the son of
7: 2 they had sent unto the h' of God
3 priests which were in the h' of the
8: 9 the foundation of the h' of the Lord
13 O h' of Judah, and h' of Israel;
15 Jerusalem and to the h' of Judah:
19 to the h' of Judah joy and gladness,
9: 8 And I will encamp about mine h'
10: 3 visited his flock the h' of Judah,
6 I will strengthen the h' of Judah,
6 and I will save the h' of Joseph,
11: 13 to the potter in the h' of the Lord.
Zec 12: 4 mine eyes upon the h' of Judah,
7 that the glory of the h' of David
8 and the h' of David shall be as God,
10 I will pour upon the h' of David,
12 the family of the h' of David apart,
12 family of the h' of Nathan apart,
13 The family of the h' of Levi apart,
13: 1 fountain opened to the h' of David
6 wounded in the h' of my friends.
14: 20 the pots in the Lord's h' shall be
21 in the h' of the Lord of hosts.
Mal 3: 10 there may be meat in mine h', and
M't 2: 11 when they were come into the h',
5: 15 light unto all that are in the h'.
7: 24 which built his h' upon a rock:
25 winds blew, and beat upon that h';
26 which built his h' upon the sand:
27 winds blew, and beat upon that h';
8: 14 Jesus was come into Peter's h', he
9: 6 up thy bed, and go unto thine h'.
7 he arose, and departed to his h'.
10 as Jesus sat at meat in the h',
23 when Jesus came into the ruler's h',
28 And when he was come into the h',
10: 6 the lost sheep of the h' of Israel.
12 when ye come into an h', salute it.
13 And if the h' be worthy, let your
14 when ye depart out of that h' or
25 call the master of the h' Beelzebub,
12: 4 How he entered into the h' of God,
25 city or h' divided against itself
29 one enter into a strong man's h',
29 man? and then he will spoil his h'.
44 return into my h' from whence I
13: 1 same day went Jesus out of the h',
36 away, and went into the h':
57 his own country, and in his own h'.
15: 24 the lost sheep of the h' of Israel.
17: 25 And when he was come into the h',
20: 11 against the goodman of the h',
21: 13 My h' shall be called the h' of
23: 38 your h' is left unto you desolate.
24: 17 to take any thing out of his h':
43 goodman of the h' had known in
43 suffered his h' to be broken up.
26: 6 in the h' of Simon the leper,
18 I will keep the passover at thy h'
M'r 1: 29 entered into the h' of Simon and
2: 1 was noised that he was in the h'.
11 bed, and go thy way into thine h'.
15 that, as Jesus sat at meat in his h',
26 How he went into the h' of God in
3: 19 him: and they went into an h'.
25 And if a h' be divided against itself,
25 itself, that h' cannot stand.
27 can enter into a strong man's h',
27 man; and then he will spoil his h'.
5: 35 from the ruler of the synagogue's h'
38 cometh to the h' of the ruler of the
6: 4 his own kin, and in his own h'.
10 ye enter into a h', there abide till ye
7: 17 when he was entered into the h'
24 and Sidon, and entered into an h',
30 when she was come to her h', she
8: 26 And he sent him away to his h',
9: 28 when he was come into the h', his
33 and being in the h' he asked them,
10: 10 And in the h' his disciples asked
29 There is no man that hath left h', or
11: 17 not written, My h' shall be called
17 of all nations the h' of prayer?
13: 15 housetop not go down into the h',
15 to take any thing out of his h':
34 taking a far journey, who left his h',
35 when the master of the h' cometh,
14: 3 Bethany in the h' of Simon the leper,
14 say ye to the goodman of the h',
Lu 1: 23 he departed to his own h'.
27 was Joseph, of the h' of David;
33 reign over the h' of Jacob for ever;
40 entered into the h' of Zacharias,
56 months, and returned to her own h'.
69 us in the h' of his servant David;
2: 4 was of the h' and lineage of David:
4: 38 and entered into Simon's h'.
5: 24 up thy couch, and go into thine h';
25 he lay, and departed to his own h',
29 him a great feast in his own h':
6: 4 How he went into the h' of God,
48 He is like a man which built an h',
48 beat vehemently upon that h',
49 built an h' upon the earth; against
49 and the ruin of that h' was great.
7: 6 he was now not far from the h',
10 that were sent, returning to the h',
36 he went into the Pharisee's h', and
37 sat at meat in the Pharisee's h',
44 I entered into thine h', thou gavest
8: 27 neither abode in any h', but in the
39 Return to thine own h', and shew
41 him that he would come into his h':
49 from the ruler of the synagogue's h',
51 And when he came into the h', he
9: 4 whatsoever h' ye enter into, there
61 which are at home at my h'.
10: 5 into whatsoever h' ye enter, first
5 first say, Peace be to this h'.
7 in the same h' remain, eating and
7 of his hire. Go not from h' to h'.
38 Martha received him into her h'.
11: 17 and a h' divided against a h' falleth.
24 I will return unto my h' whence I
12: 39 the goodman of the h' had known
39 have suffered his h' to be broken
52 there shall be five in one h' divided,
13: 25 the master of the h' is risen up,

Lu 13:35 your h' is left unto you desolate:
14: 1 the h' of one of the chief Pharisees
21 the master of the h' being angry
23 to come in, that my h' may be filled.
15: 8 sweep the h', and seek diligently
25 he came and drew nigh to the h',
16:27 send him to my father's h':
17:31 housetop, and his stuff in the h',
18:14 man went down to his h' justified
29 no man that hath left h', or parents,
19: 5 for to day I must abide at thy h'.
9 This day is salvation come to this h',
46 written, My h' is the h' of prayer:
22:10 follow him into the h' where he
11 say unto the goodman of the h',
54 him into the high priest's h'.
Joh 2:16 Father's h' an h' of merchandise.
17 zeal of thine h' hath eaten me up.
4:53 himself believed, and his whole h'.
7:53 every man went unto his own h'.
8:35 abideth not in the h' for ever:
11:20 him: but Mary sat still in the h'.
31 which were with her in the h',
12: 3 the h' was filled with the odour of
14: 2 my Father's h' are many mansions:
Ac 2: 2 all the h' where they were sitting.
36 let all the h' of Israel know
46 breaking bread from h' to h',
5:42 in the temple, and in every h',
7:10 governor over Egypt and all his h'.
20 up in his father's h' three months:
42 O ye h' of Israel, have ye offered to
47 But Solomon built him an h'.
49 what h' will ye build me? saith
8: 3 entering into every h', and
9:11 enquire in the h' of Judas for one
17 his way, and entered into the h';
10: 2 one that feared God with all his h',
6 tanner, whose h' is by the sea side:
17 had made enquiry for Simon's h',
22 angel to send for thee into his h',
30 ninth hour I prayed in my h', and,
32 he is lodged in the h' of one Simon
11:11 three men already come unto the h'
12 and we entered into the man's h':
13 how he had seen an angel in his h',
14 thou and all thy h' shall be saved.
12:12 came to the h' of Mary the mother
16:15 Lord, come into my h', and abide
31 and thou shalt be saved, and thy h'.
32 Lord, and to all that were in his h'.
34 he had brought them into his h',
34 believing in God with all his h'.
40 and entered into the h' of Lydia:
17: 5 and assaulted the h' of Jason,
18: 7 a certain man's h', named Justus,
7 h' joined hard to the synagogue.
8 believed on the Lord with all his h';
19:16 they fled out of that h' naked and
20:20 you publickly, and from h' to h',
21: 8 we entered into the h' of Philip the
28:30 whole years in his own hired h',
Ro 16: 5 greet the church that is in their h'.
1Co 1:11 them which are of the h' of Chloe,
16:15 ye know the h' of Stephanas, that
19 with the church that is in their h'.
2Co 5: 1 we know that if our earthly h' of
1 an h' not made with hands, eternal
2 with our h' which is from heaven:
Col 4:15 and the church which is in his h'.
1Ti 3: 4 One that ruleth well his own h',
5 know not how to rule his own h',
15 to behave thyself in the h' of God,
5: 8 specially for those of his own h',
13 wandering about from h' to h';
14 bear children, guide the h', give
2Ti 1:16 mercy unto the h' of Onesiphorus;
2:20 But in a great h' there are not only
Ph'm 2 and to the church in thy h':
Heb 3: 2 also Moses was faithful in all his h'.
3 as he who hath builded the h'
3 hath more honour than the h'.
4 every h' is builded by some man;
5 verily was faithful in all his h',
6 But Christ as a son over his own h';
6 whose h' are we, if we hold fast the
8: 8 h' of Israel and with the h' of Judah:
10 I will make with the h' of Israel
10:21 an high priest over the h' of God;
11: 7 an ark to the saving of his h';
1Pe 2: 5 stones, are built up a spiritual h',
4:17 must begin at the h' of God:
2Jo 10 receive him not into your h',

house-full See HOUSE and FULL.

household See also HOUSEHOLDS.
Ge 18:19 his children and his h' after him,
31:37 hast thou found of all thy h' stuff?
35: 2 Jacob said unto his h', and to all
45:11 lest thou, and thy h', and all that
47:12 and all his father's h', with bread,
Ex 1: 1 man and his h' came with Jacob.
12: 4 if the h' be too little for the lamb,
Le 16:17 for himself, and for his h', and for
De 6:22 upon Pharaoh, and upon all his h',
14:26 thou shalt rejoice, thou, and thine h',
15:20 Lord shall choose, thou and thy h'.
Jos 2:18 all thy father's h', home unto thee.
6:25 harlot alive, and her father's h',
7:14 the h' which the Lord shall take
18 And he brought his h' man by man;
J'g 6:27 because he feared his father's h',
18:25 lose thy life, with the lives of thy h'.
1Sa 25:17 our master, and against all his h':
27: 3 and his men, every man with his h',
2Sa 2: 3 bring up, every man with his h':
6:11 blessed Obed-edom, and all his h'.
20 Then David returned to bless his h'.
15:16 went forth, and all his h' after him.
16: 2 asses be for the king's h' to ride on;
17:23 put his h' in order, and hanged
19:18 ferry boat to carry over the king's h',
41 have brought the king, and his h',
1Ki 4: 6 Ahishar was over the h': and
7 victuals for the king and his h':
5: 9 my desire, in giving food for my h'.
11 measures of wheat for food to his h',
11:20 and Genubath was in Pharaoh's h'
2Ki 7: 9 we may go and tell the king's h'.
8: 1 go thou and thine h', and sojourn
2 she went with her h', and sojourned
18:18, 37 Hilkiah, which was over the h',
19: 2 sent Eliakim, which was over the h',
1Ch 24: 6 one principal h' being taken for
Ne 13: 8 I cast forth all the h' stuff of Tobiah
Job 1: 3 she asses, and a very great h';
Pr 27:27 for the food of thy h', and for the
31:15 giveth meat to her h', and a portion
21 not afraid of the snow for her h':
21 for all her h' are clothed with scarlet.
27 looketh well to the ways of her h',
Isa 36:22 son of Hilkiah, that was over the h',
37: 2 sent Eliakim, who was over the h',
M't 10:25 more shall they call them of his h'?
36 man's foes shall be they of his own h'.
24:45 his lord hath made ruler over his h',
Lu 12:42 his lord shall make ruler over his h',
Ac 10: 7 he called two of his h' servants,
16:15 when she was baptized, and her h',
Ro 16:10 them which are of Aristobulus' h'.
11 them that be of the h' of Narcissus,
1Co 1:16 baptized also the h' of Stephanas:
Ga 6:10 unto them who are of the h' of faith.
Eph 2:19 with the saints, and of the h' of God;
Ph'p 4:22 chiefly they that are of Cæsar's h'.
2Ti 4:19 and the h' of Onesiphorus.

householder
M't 13:27 servants of the h' came and said
52 is like unto a man that is an h',
20: 1 is like unto a man that is an h',
21:33 was a certain h', which planted a

households
Ge 42:33 food for the famine of your h',
45:18 take your father and your h', and
47:24 your food, and for them of your h',
Nu 18:31 eat it in every place, ye and your h':
De 11: 6 swallowed them up, and their h',
12: 7 put your hand unto, ye and your h',
Jos 7:14 Lord shall take shall come by h';

houses^ See also STOREHOUSES.
Ge 42:19 corn for the famine of your h':
Ex 1:21 feared God, that he made them h'.
6:14 be the heads of their fathers' h':
8: 9 the frogs from thee and thy h',
11 depart from thee, and from thy h',
13 the frogs died out of the h', out of
21 upon thy people, and into thy h':
21 h' of the Egyptians shall be full of
24 into his servants' h', and into all the
9:20 and his cattle flee into the h':
10: 6 And they shall fill thy h', and the
6 and the h' of all thy servants, and
6 and the h' of all the Egyptians;
12: 7 on the upper door post of the h',
13 for a token upon the h' where ye are:
15 put away leaven out of your h':
19 be no leaven found in your h': for
23 destroyer to come in unto your h' to
27 over the h' of the children of Israel
27 the Egyptians, and delivered our h'.
Le 25:31 But the h' of the villages which no
32 and the h' of the cities of their
33 the h' of the cities of the Levites
Nu 4:22 throughout the h' of their fathers,
16:32 swallowed them up, and their h',
17: 6 according to their fathers' h', even
32:18 We will not return unto our h', until
De 6:11 and h' full of all good things, which
8:12 and hast built goodly h', and dwelt
19: 1 in their cities, and in their h';
Jos 9:12 hot for our provision out of our h'
J'g 18:14 that there is in these h' an ephod,
22 that were in the h' near to Micah's
1Ki 9:10 Solomon had built the two h', the
13:32 against all the h' of the high places
20: 6 house, and the h' of thy servants;
2Ki 17:29 for them in the h' of the high places
32 for them in the h' of the high places.
23: 7 brake down the h' of the sodomites,
19 all the h' also of the high places
25: 9 and all the h' of Jerusalem, and
1Ch 15: 1 David made him h' in the city of
29: 4 to overlay the walls of the h' withal:
2Ch 25: 5 according to the h' of their fathers,
34:11 floor the h' which the kings of Judah
35: 4 yourselves by the h' of your fathers,
Ne 4:14 daughters, your wives, and your h'.
5: 3 our lands, vineyards, and h', that
11 their oliveyards, and their h', also
9:25 and possessed h' full of all goods,
10:34 our God, after the h' of our fathers,
Job 1: 4 sons went and feasted in their h',
3:15 gold, who filled their h' with silver:
4:19 less in them that dwell in h' of clay,
15:28 and in h' which no man inhabiteth,
21: 9 Their h' are safe from fear, neither
22:18 he filled their h' with good things:
24:16 In the dark they dig through h',
Ps 49:11 that their h' shall continue for ever,
83:12 us take to ourselves the h' of God
Pr 1:13 we shall fill our h' with spoil:
Ec 2: 4 I builded me h'; I planted me
Isa 3:14 the spoil of the poor is in your h'.
5: 9 a truth many h' shall be desolate,
6:11 and the h' without man, and the
8:14 of offence to both the h' of Israel,
13:16 their h' shall be spoiled, and their
21 and their h' shall be full of doleful
22 shall cry in their desolate h',
15: 3 on the tops of their h', and in their
22:10 numbered the h' of Jerusalem,
10 h' have ye broken down to fortify
32:13 upon all the h' of joy in the joyous
42:22 and they are hid in the prison h':
65:21 And they shall build h', and inhabit
Jer 5: 7 by troops in the harlots' h'.
27 birds, so are their h' full of deceit:
6:12 their h' shall be turned unto others,
17:22 carry forth a burden out of your h'
18:22 Let a cry be heard from their h',
19:13 And the h' of Jerusalem, and the h'
13 because of all the h' upon whose
29: 5 Build ye h', and dwell in them; and
28 build ye h', and dwell in them; and
32:15 H' and fields and vineyards shall be
29 on this city, and burn it with the h',
33: 4 concerning the h' of this city, and
4 the h' of the kings of Judah, which
35: 9 Nor to build h' for us to dwell in:
39: 8 and the h' of the people, with fire,
43:12 fire in the h' of the gods of Egypt;
13 the h' of the gods of the Egyptians
52:13 and all the h' of Jerusalem, and all
13 the h' of the great men, burned he
La 5: 2 turned to strangers, our h' to aliens.
Eze 7:24 then, and they shall possess their h':
11: 3 say, It is not near; let us build h':
16:41 they shall burn thine h' with fire,
23:47 and burn up their h' with fire.
26:12 walls and destroy thy pleasant h':
28:26 therein, and shall build h', and plant
33:30 the walls and in the doors of the h',
45: 4 It shall be a place for their h', and
Da 2: 5 your h' shall be made a dunghill.
3:29 their h' shall be made a dunghill:
Ho 11:11 I will place them in their h', saith
Joe 2: 9 they shall climb up upon the h';
Am 3:15 and the h' of ivory shall perish, and
15 and the great h' shall have an end,
5:11 ye have built h' of hewn stone, but
Mic 1:14 the h' of Achzib shall be a lie to the
2: 2 and h', and take them away: so they
9 cast out from their pleasant h';
Zep 1: 9 fill their master's h' with violence
13 a booty, and their h' a desolation:
13 they shall also build h', but not
2: 7 in the h' of Ashkelon shall they lie
Hag 1: 4 to dwell in your cieled h', and this
Zec 14: 2 city shall be taken, and the h' rifled,
M't 11: 8 wear soft clothing are in kings' h'.
19:29 that hath forsaken h', or brethren,
23:14 ye devour widows' h', and for a
M'r 8: 3 away, fasting to their own h', they
10:30 h', and brethren, and sisters, and
12:40 Which devour widows' h', and for a
Lu 16: 4 they may receive me into their h'.
20:47 Which devour widows' h', and for
Ac 4:34 possessors of lands or h' sold them,
1Co 11:22 ye not h' to eat and to drink in?
1Ti 3:12 their children and their own h' well.
2Ti 3: 6 sort are they which creep into h',
Tit 1:11 who subvert whole h', teaching

housetop See also HOUSE and TOP; HOUSETOPS.
Pr 21: 9 better to dwell in a corner of the h',
25:24 better to dwell in the corner of the h',
M't 24:17 Let him which is on the h' not
M'r 13:15 let him that is on the h' not go down
Lu 5:19 they went upon the h', and let him
17:31 he which shall be upon the h', and
Ac 10: 9 Peter went up upon the h' to pray

housetops
Ps 129: 6 them be as the grass upon the h',
Isa 22: 1 thou art wholly gone up to the h'?
37:27 as the grass on the h', and as corn
Jer 48:38 upon all the h' of Moab, and in the
Zep 1: 5 the host of heaven upon the h';
M't 10:27 the ear, that preach ye upon the h'.
Lu 12: 3 shall be proclaimed upon the h'.

houshold See HOUSEHOLD.

how^ See also HOWBEIT; HOWSOEVER.
Ge 26: 9 h' saidst thou, She is my sister?
27:20 H' is it that thou hast found it so
28:17 H' dreadful is this place! this is
30:29 knowest h' I have served thee,
29 and h' thy cattle was with me.
38:29 said, H' hast thou broken forth?
39: 9 his wife: h' then can I do this great
44: 8 h' then should we steal out of thy
16 or h' shall we clear ourselves?
34 h' shall I go up to my father, and
47: 8 said unto Jacob, H' old art thou?
18 h' that our money is spent;
Ex 2:18 H' is it that ye are come so soon
6:30 h' shall Pharaoh hearken unto me?
9:29 h' that the earth is the Lord's.
10: 2 may know h' that I am the Lord.
3 H' long wilt thou refuse to humble
16:28 H' long refuse ye to keep my
18: 8 way, and h' the Lord delivered them.
19: 4 h' I bare you on eagles' wings, and
36: 1 know h' to work all manner of work
Nu 10:31 h' we are to encamp in the wilderness,
14:11 H' long will this people provoke
11 h' long will it be ere they believe
27 H' long shall I bear with this evil

Nu 20:15 H' our fathers went down into Egypt,
23: 8 H' shall I curse, whom God hath
8 h' shall I defy, whom the Lord hath
24: 5 H' goodly are thy tents, O Jacob,
De 1:12 H' can I myself alone bear your
31 h' that the Lord thy God bare thee,
7:17 than I; h' can I dispossess them?
9: 7 h' thou provokedst the Lord
11: 4 h' he made the water of the Red
4 and h' the Lord hath destroyed them
6 h' the earth opened her mouth, and,
12:30 H' did these nations serve their
18:21 H' shall we know the word which
25:18 H' he met thee by the way, and
29:16 h' we have dwelt in the land of
16 and h' we came through the
31:27 and h' much more after my death?
32:30 H' should one chase a thousand,
Jos 2:10 h' the Lord dried up the water of
9: 7 h' shall we make a league with you?
24 h' that the Lord...commanded his
10: 1 h' Joshua had taken Ai, and had
1 h' the inhabitants of Gibeon had
14:12 that day h' the Anakims were there,
18: 3 H' long are ye slack to go to
J'g 13:12 H' shall we order the child, and
12 and h' shall we do unto him?
16:15 H' canst thou say, I love thee,
18: 7 h' they dwelt careless, after the
20: 3 Tell us, h' was this wickedness?
21: 7, 16 H' shall we do for wives for
Ru 1: 6 h' that the Lord had visited his
2:11 h' thou hast left thy father and thy
3:18 thou know h' the matter will fall
1Sa 1:14 H' long wilt thou be drunken? put
2:22 h' they lay with the women that
10:27 said, H' shall this man save us?
12:24 h' great things he hath done for
14:29 h' mine eyes have been enlightened
30 H' much more, if haply the
15: 2 h' he laid wait for him in the way,
16: 1 H' long wilt thou mourn for Saul,
2 H' can I go? if Saul hear it, he will
17:18 and look h' thy brethren fare, and
23: 3 h' much more then if we come to
24:10 h' that the Lord had delivered thee
18 h' that thou hast dealt well with
28: 9 h' he hath cut off those that have
2Sa 1: 4 unto him, H' went the matter?
5 H' knowest thou that Saul and
14 H' wast thou not afraid to stretch
19 places: h' are the mighty fallen!
25 H' are the mighty fallen in the
27 H' are the mighty fallen, and the
2:22 h' then should I hold up my face to
26 h' long shall it be then, ere thou
4:11 H' much more, when wicked men
6:20 H' glorious was the king of Israel
11: 7 demanded of him h' Joab did, and
7 and h' the people did, and h' the war
12:18 h' will he then vex himself, if we
16:11 h' much more now may this
18:19 h' that the Lord hath avenged him
19: 2 h' the king was grieved for his son.
34 H' long have I to live, that I should
24: 3 people, h' many soever they be, an
1Ki 3: 7 I know not h' to go out or come in.
5: 3 h' that David my father could not
8:27 h' much less this house that I
12: 6 H' do ye advise that I may answer
14:19 h' he warred, and h' he reigned,
18:13 h' I hid an hundred men of the Lord's
21 H' long halt ye between two
19: 1 h' he had slain all the prophets
20: 7 see h' this man seeketh mischief:
21:29 thou h' Ahab humbleth himself
22:16 H' many times shall I adjure
45 of Jehoshaphat,...and h' he warred,
2Ki 5: 7 h' he seeketh a quarrel against me.
13 h' much rather then, when he
6:15 Alas, my master! h' shall we do?
32 h' this son of a murderer hath sent
8: 5 h' he had restored a dead body to
9:25 h' that, when I and thou rode together
10: 4 before him: h' then shall we stand?
14:15 h' he fought with Amaziah king of
28 h' he warred, and h' he recovered
17:28 them h' they should fear the Lord.
18:24 H' then wilt thou turn away the face
19:25 not heard long ago h' I have done it,
20: 3 h' I have walked before thee in
20 and h' he made a pool, and a conduit,
1Ch 13:12 H' shall I bring the ark of God
18: 9 h' David had smitten all the host
2Ch 6:18 h' much less this house which I
7: 3 saw h' the fire came down, and the
18:15 H' many times shall I adjure
20:11 Behold, I say, h' they reward us,
32:15 h' much less shall your God
33:19 also, and h' God was intreated of him,
Ezr 7:22 and salt without prescribing h' much.
Ne 2: 6 For h' long shall thy journey be?
17 h' Jerusalem lieth waste, and the
Es 2:11 to know h' Esther did, and what should
5:11 h' he had advanced him above the
8: 6 h' can I endure to see the evil that
6 h' can I endure to see the destruction
Job 4:19 H' much less in them that dwell in
6:25 H' forcible are right words! but
7:19 H' long wilt thou not depart
8: 2 H' long wilt thou speak these
2 h' long shall the words of thy mouth
9: 2 h' should man be just with God?
14 H' much less shall I answer him,
13:23 H' many are mine iniquities and
15:16 H' much more abominable
Job 18: 2 H' long will it be ere ye make
19: 2 H' long will ye vex my soul, and
21:17 H' oft is the candle of the wicked
17 and h' oft cometh their destruction
34 H' then comfort ye me in vain,
22:12 the height of the stars, h' high
13 thou sayest, H' doth God know?
25: 4 H' then can man be justified with
4 or h' can he be clean that is born of
6 H' much less man, that is a
26: 2 H' hast thou helped him that is
2 h' savest thou the arm that hath no
3 H' hast thou counselled him that
3 h' hast thou plentifully declared the
14 h' little a portion is heard of him?
34:19 H' much less to him that accepted
37:17 H' thy garments are warm, when he
Ps 3: 1 h' are they increased that trouble
4: 2 h' long will ye turn my glory
2 h' long will ye love vanity, and seek
6: 3 vexed: but thou, O Lord, h' long?
8: 1, 9 h' excellent is thy name in all the
11: 1 h' say ye to my soul, Flee as a bird
13: 1 H' long wilt thou forget me, O
1 h' long wilt thou hide thy face from
2 H' long shall I take counsel in my
2 h' long shall mine enemy be exalted
21: 1 h' greatly shall he rejoice!
31:19 Oh h' great is thy goodness, which
35:17 Lord, h' long wilt thou look on?
36: 7 H' excellent is thy lovingkindness,
39: 4 it is: that I may know h' frail I am.
44: 2 H' thou didst drive out the heathen
2 h' thou didst afflict the people, and
62: 3 H' long will ye imagine mischief
66: 3 H' terrible art thou in thy works!
73:11 H' doth God know? and is there
19 H' are they brought into desolation,
74: 9 us any that knoweth h' long.
10 God, h' long shall the adversary
22 h' the foolish man reproacheth thee
78:40 H' oft did they provoke him in the
43 H' he had wrought his signs in
79: 5 H' long, Lord? wilt thou be angry
80: 4 hosts, h' long wilt thou be angry
82: 2 H' long will ye judge unjustly, and
84: 1 H' amiable are thy tabernacles, O
89:46 H' long, Lord? wilt thou hide
47 Remember h' short my time is:
50 h' I do bear in my bosom the reproach
90:13 Return, O Lord, h' long? and let it
92: 5 O Lord, h' great are thy works!
94: 3 h' long shall the wicked, h' long
4 H' long shall they utter and speak hard
104:24 h' manifold are thy works! in
119:84 H' many are the days of thy
97 O h' love I thy law! it is my
103 H' sweet are thy words unto my
159 Consider h' I love thy precepts:
132: 2 H' he sware unto the Lord, and
133: 1 h' good and h' pleasant it is for
137: 4 H' shall we sing the Lord's song in
139:17 H' precious also are thy thoughts
17 O God! h' great is the sum of them!
Pr 1:22 H' long, ye simple ones, will ye
5:12 H' have I hated instruction, and
6: 9 H' long wilt thou sleep, O
15:11 h' much more then the hearts
23 spoken in due season, h' good is it!
16:16 H' much better is it to get wisdom
19: 7 h' much more do his friends
20:24 h' can a man then understand his
21:27 h' much more, when he
30:13 O h' lofty are their eyes!
Ec 2:16 And h' dieth the wise man? as the
4:11 but h' can one be warm alone?
10:15 he knoweth not h' to go to the city.
11: 5 h' the bones do grow in the womb of
Ca 4:10 H' fair is thy love, my sister, my
10 h' much better is thy love than
5: 3 off my coat; h' shall I put it on?
3 my feet; h' shall I defile them?
7: 1 H' beautiful are thy feet with
6 H' fair and h' pleasant art thou,
Isa 1:21 H' is the faithful city become an
6:11 Then said I, Lord, h' long? And
14: 4 H' hath the oppressor ceased! the
12 H' art thou fallen from heaven, O
19:11 h' say ye unto Pharaoh, I am the son
20: 6 Assyria: and h' shall we escape?
36: 9 H' then wilt thou turn away the face
37:26 heard long ago, h' I have done it;
38: 3 h' I have walked before thee in
48:11 h' should my name be polluted?
50: 4 know h' to speak a word in season
52: 7 H' beautiful upon the mountains
Jer 2:21 h' then art thou turned into the
23 H' canst thou say, I am not polluted,
3:19 H' shall I put thee among the
4:14 H' long shall thy vain thoughts
21 H' long shall I see the standard,
5: 7 H' shall I pardon thee for this?
8: 8 H' do ye say, We are wise, and the
9: 7 h' shall I do for the daughter of my
19 H' are we spoiled! we are greatly
12: 4 H' long shall the land mourn, and
5 h' canst thou contend with horses?
5 h' wilt thou do in the swelling of
15: 5 shall go aside to ask h' thou doest?
22:23 h' gracious shalt thou be when
23:26 H' long shall this be in the heart
31:22 H' long wilt thou go about, O thou
36:17 H' didst thou write all these words
46:13 h' Nebuchadrezzar king of Babylon
47: 6 h' long will it be ere thou be quiet?
7 H' can it be quiet, seeing the Lord
Jer 48:14 H' say ye, We are mighty and strong
17 H' is the strong staff broken, and
39 howl, saying, H' is it broken down!
39 h' hath Moab turned the back
49:25 H' is the city of praise not left, the
50:23 H' is the hammer of the whole earth
23 h' is Babylon become a desolation
51:41 H' is Sheshach taken! and
41 h' is the praise of the whole earth
41 h' is Babylon...an astonishment
La 1: 1 H' doth the city sit solitary, that
1 h' is she become as a widow! she that
1 provinces, h' is she become tributary!
2: 1 H' hath the Lord covered the
4: 1 H' is the gold become dim!
1 h' is the fine gold changed!
Eze 14:21 H' much more when I send
15: 5 h' much less shall it be meet
16:30 H' weak is thine heart, saith the
26:17 H' art thou destroyed, that wast
33:10 in them, h' should we then live?
Da 4: 3 H' great are his signs! and
3 and how mighty are his wonders!
8:13 H' long shall be the vision
10:17 For h' can the servant of this my
12: 6 H' long shall it be to the end of
Ho 8: 5 h' long will it be ere they attain to
11: 8 H' shall I give thee up, Ephraim?
8 h' shall I deliver thee, Israel?
8 h' shall I make thee as Adinah?
8 h' shall I set thee as Zeboim? mine
Joe 1:18 H' do the beasts groan! the
Ob 5 h' art thou cut off! would they not
6 H' are the things of Esau searched
6 h' are his hidden things sought up!
Mic 2: 4 h' hath he removed it from me!
Hab 1: 2 O Lord, h' long shall I cry, and
2: 6 that which is not his! h' long?
Zep 2:15 h' is she become a desolation, a
Hag 2: 3 and h' do ye see it now? is it not
Zec 1:12 h' long wilt thou not have mercy
9:17 For h' great is his goodness, and
17 and h' great is his beauty!
M't 6:23 h' great is that darkness!
28 lilies of the field, h' they grow;
7: 4 Or h' wilt thou say to thy brother,
11 h' to give good gifts unto your
11 h' much more shall your Father
10:19 thought h' or what ye shall speak:
25 h' much more shall they call them
12: 4 H' he entered into the house of
5 h' that on the sabbath days the
12 H' much then is a man better
14 him, h' they might destroy him.
26 h' shall then his kingdom stand?
29 h' can one enter into a strong man's
34 h' can ye, being evil, speak good
15:34 them, H' many loaves have ye?
16: 9, 10 and h' many baskets ye took up?
11 H' is it that ye do not understand
12 H' that he bade them not beware
21 h' that he must go unto Jerusalem,
17:17 h' long shall I be with you?
17 h' long shall I suffer you? bring
18:12 H' think ye? if a man have an
21 Lord, h' oft shall my brother sin
21:20 H' soon is the fig tree withered
22:12 h' camest thou in hither not having
15 h' they might entangle him in his
43 H' then doth David in spirit call
45 then call him Lord, h' is he his son?
23:33 h' can ye escape the damnation
37 h' often would I have gathered thy
26:54 h' then shall the scriptures be
27:13 not h' many things they witness
M'r 2:16 H' is it that he eateth and
26 H' he went into the house of God
3: 6 him, h' they might destroy him.
23 H' can Satan cast out Satan?
4:13 h' then will ye know all parables?
27 and grow up, he knoweth not h'.
40 h' is it that ye have no faith?
5:16 h' it befell to him that was possessed
19 h' great things the Lord hath done
20 h' great things Jesus had done for
6:38 H' many loaves have ye? go and
8: 5 H' many loaves have ye? And they
19, 20 h' many baskets full of fragments
21 H' is it that ye do not understand?
9:12 h' it is written of the Son of man,
19 h' long shall I be with you?
19 h' long shall I suffer you? bring
21 H' long is it ago since this came
10:23 H' hardly shall they that have
24 h' hard is it for them that trust in
11:18 sought h' they might destroy him:
12:26 h' in the bush God spake unto
35 H' say the scribes that Christ is
41 h' the people cast money into the
14: 1 h' they might take him by craft,
11 h' he might conveniently betray
15: 4 h' many things they witness
Lu 1:34 H' shall this be, seeing I know not
58 h' the Lord had shewed great
62 h' he would have him called.
2:49 them, H' is it that ye sought me?
6: 4 H' he went into the house of God,
42 h' canst thou say to thy brother,
7:22 h' that the blind see, the lame
8:18 Take heed therefore h' ye hear:
39 h' great things God hath done
39 h' great things Jesus had done
47 h' she was healed immediately,
9:41 h' long shall I be with you,
10:26 written in the law? h' readest thou?
11:13 h' to give good gifts unto your

Lu 11:13 h' much more shall your heavenly
18 h' shall his kingdom stand?
12:11 h' or what thing ye shall answer,
24 h' much more are ye better than
27 Consider the lilies h' they grow:
28 h' much more will he clothe you,
50 and h' am I straitened till it be
56 h' is it that ye do not discern this
13:34 h' often would I have gathered
14: 7 h' they chose out the chief rooms;
15:17 H' many hired servants of my
16: 2 H' is it that I hear this of thee?
5 H' much owest thou unto my lord?
7 another, And h' much owest thou?
18:24 H' hardly shall they that have
19:15 h' much every man had gained by
20:41 H' say they that Christ is David's
44 him Lord, h' is he then his son?
21: 5 h' it was adorned with goodly
22: 2 scribes sought h' they might kill
4 h' he might betray him unto them.
61 h' he had said unto him, Before
23:55 sepulchre, and h' his body was laid.
24: 6 h' he spake unto you when he was
20 h' the chief priests and our rulers
35 and h' he was known of them in
Joh 3: 4 H' can a man be born when he is
9 unto him, H' can these things be?
12 h' shall ye believe, if I tell you of
4: 1 h' the Pharisees had heard that
9 H' is it that thou, being a Jew,
5:44 H' can ye believe, which receive
47 h' shall ye believe my words?
6:42 h' is it then that he saith, I came
52 H' can this man give us of his flesh
7:15 H' knoweth this man letters,
8:33 h' sayest thou, Ye shall be made
9:10 him, H' were thine eyes opened?
15 him h' he had received his sight.
16 H' can a man that is a sinner do
19 blind? h' then doth he now see?
26 to thee? h' opened he thine eyes?
10:24 H' long dost thou make us to
11:36 the Jews, Behold h' he loved him!
12:19 Perceive ye h' ye prevail nothing?
*34 h' sayest thou, The Son of man
14: 5 goest; and h' can we know the way?
9 h' sayest thou then, Shew us the
22 h' is it that thou wilt manifest
28 h' I said unto you, I go away, and
Ac 2: 8 h' hear we every man in our own
4:21 nothing h' they might punish them,
5: 9 H' is it that ye have agreed
7:25 h' that God by his hand would
8:31 H' can I, except some man should
9:13 h' much evil he hath done to thy
16 him h' great things he must suffer
27 h' he had seen the Lord in the way,
27 and h' he had preached boldly at
10:28 h' that it is an unlawful thing for
38 H' God anointed Jesus of Nazareth
11:13 h' he had seen an angel in his
16 h' that he said, John indeed
12:14 h' Peter stood before the gate.
17 h' the Lord had brought him out
13:32 h' that the promise which was
14:27 h' he had opened the door of faith
15: 7 h' that a good while ago God made
14 h' God at the first did visit the
36 of the Lord, and see h' they do.
20:20 And h' I kept back nothing that
35 h' that so labouring ye ought to
35 h' he said, It is more blessed to
21:20 h' many thousands of Jews there
23:30 h' that the Jews laid wait for the
Ro 3: 6 h' then shall God judge the world?
4:10 H' was it then reckoned? when
6: 2 H' shall we, that are dead to sin,
7: 1 h' that the law hath dominion over
18 h' to perform that which is good
8:32 h' shall he not with him also freely
10:14 H' then shall they call on him in
14 h' shall they believe in him of whom
14 h' shall they hear without a
15 h' shall they preach, except they
15 H' beautiful are the feet of them
11: 2 h' he maketh intercession to God
12 h' much more their fulness?
24 h' much more shall these, which
33 h' unsearchable are his judgments,
1Co 1:26 h' that not many wise men after
3:10 heed h' he buildeth thereupon.
6: 3 h' much more things that pertain
7:16 or h' knowest thou, O man,
32 Lord, h' he may please the Lord:
33 world, h' he may please his wife.
34 h' she may please her husband.
10: 1 h' that all our fathers were under
14: 7 h' shall it be known what is piped
9 h' shall it be known what is spoken?
16 h' shall he that occupieth the room
26 H' is it then, brethren? when ye
15: 3 h' that Christ died for our sins
12 h' say some among you that there
35 H' are the dead raised up? and
2Co 3: 8 H' shall not the ministration of the
7:15 h' with fear and trembling ye
8: 2 H' that in a great trial of affliction
12: 4 H' that he was caught up into
13: 5 h' that Jesus Christ is in you,
Ga 1:13 h' that beyond measure I persecuted
4: 9 h' turn ye again to the weak and
13 h' through infirmity of the flesh
6:11 Ye see h' large a letter I have
Eph 3: 3 H' that by revelation he made
6:21 may know my affairs, and h' I do,
Ph'p 1: 8 h' greatly I long after you all in
2:23 as I shall see h' it will go with me.
4:12 h' to be abased, and I know how to
Col 4: 6 h' ye ought to answer every man.
1Th 1: 9 h' ye turned to God from idols to
2:10 God also, h' holily and justly and
11 h' we exhorted and comforted and
4: 1 h' ye ought to walk and to please
4 know h' to possess his vessel in
2Th 3: 7 know h' ye ought to follow us:
1Ti 3: 5 know not h' to rule his own house,
5 h' shall he take care of the church
15 h' thou oughtest to behave thyself
2Ti 1:18 h' many things he ministered unto
Ph'm 16 me, but h' much more unto thee,
19 h' thou owest unto me even thine
Heb 2: 3 H' shall we escape, if we neglect
7: 4 consider h' great this man was,
8: 6 by h' much also he is the mediator
9:14 H' much more shall the blood of
10:29 Of h' much sorer punishment,
12:17 For ye know h' that afterward,
Jas 2:22 h' faith wrought with his works,
24 h' that by works a man is justified,
3: 5 h' great a matter a little fire
2Pe 2: 9 knoweth h' to deliver the godly out
1Jo 3:17 h' dwelleth the love of God in him?
4:20 h' can he love God whom he hath
Jude 5 h' that the Lord, having saved the
18 H' that they told you there should
Re 2: 2 h' thou canst not bear them which
3: 3 h' thou hast received and heard,
6:10 H' long, O Lord, holy and
18: 7 H' much she hath glorified herself,

howbeit
J'g 4:17 H' Sisera fled away on his feet to the
11:28 H' the king of the children of Ammon
16:22 H' the hair of his head began to grow
18:29 h' the name of the city was Laish
21:18 H' we may not give them wives of our
Ru 3:12 h' there is a kinsman nearer than I.
1Sa 8: 9 h' yet protest solemnly unto them
2Sa 2:23 H' he refused to turn aside: wherefore
12:14 H', because by this deed thou hast
13:14 H' he would not hearken unto her
25 h' he would not go, but blessed him.
23:19 h' he attained not unto the first three.
1Ki 2:15 h' the kingdom is turned about, and is
10: 7 H' I believed not the words, until I
11:13 H' I will not rend away all the
22 Nothing: h' let me go in any wise.
34 H' I will not take the whole kingdom
2Ki 3:25 h' the slingers went about it, and
8:10 h' the Lord hath shewed me that he
10:29 H' from the sins of Jeroboam the
12:13 H' there were not made for the
14: 4 H' the high places were not taken
15:35 H' the high places were not removed:
17:29 H' every nation made gods of their
40 H' they did not hearken, but they did
22: 7 H' there was no reckoning made
1Ch 11:21 h' he attained not to the first three.
28: 4 H' the Lord God of Israel chose me
2Ch 9: 6 H' I believed not their words, until I
18:34 h' the king of Israel stayed himself up
20:33 H' the high places were not taken
21: 7 H' the Lord would not destroy the
20 H' they buried him in the city of
24: 5 H' the Levites hastened it not.
27: 2 h' he entered not into the temple of
32:31 H' in the business of the
Ne 9:33 H' thou art just in all that is brought
13: 2 h' our God turned the curse into a
Job 30:24 H' he will not stretch out his hand
Isa 10: 7 H' he meaneth not so, neither doth his
Jer 44: 4 H' I sent unto you all my servants the
M't 17:21 H' this kind goeth not out but by
M'r 5:19 H' Jesus suffered him not, but saith
7: 7 H' in vain do they worship me,
Joh 6:23 H' there came other boats from
7:13 H' no man spake openly of him
27 H' we know this man whence he is:
11:13 H' Jesus spake of his death: but they
16:13 H' when he, the Spirit of truth, is
Ac 4: 4 H' many of them which heard the
7:48 H' the most High dwelleth not in
14:20 H', as the disciples stood round
17:34 H' certain men clave unto him, and
27:26 H' we must be cast upon a certain
28: 6 H' they looked when he should have
1Co 2: 6 H' we speak wisdom among them
8: 7 H' there is not in every man that
14: 2 h' in the spirit he speaketh mysteries.
20 h' in malice be ye children, but in
15:46 H' that was not first which is
2Co 11:21 H' whereinsoever any is bold,
Ga 4: 8 H' then, when ye know not God,
1Ti 1:16 H' for this cause I obtained mercy,
Heb 3:16 h' not all that came out of Egypt

howl See also HOWLED; HOWLING.
Isa 13: 6 H' ye; for the day of the Lord
14:31 H', O gate; cry, O city; thou,
15: 2 Moab shall h' over Nebo, and
3 every one shall h', weeping
16: 7 h' for Moab, every one shall h':
23: 1 H', ye ships of Tarshish; for it
6 h', ye inhabitants of the isle.
14 H', ye ships of Tarshish, for your
52: 5 rule over them make them to h',
65:14 and shall h' for vexation of spirit.
Jer 4: 8 you with sackcloth, lament and h':
25:34 H', ye shepherds, and cry; and
47: 2 the inhabitants of the land shall h'.
48:20 h' and cry; tell ye it in Arnon,
31 Therefore will I h' for Moab, and
Jer 48:39 They shall h', saying, How is it
49: 3 H', O Heshbon, for Ai is spoiled:
51: 8 fallen and destroyed: h' for her:
Eze 21:12 Cry and h', son of man: for it
30: 2 Thus saith the Lord God; H' ye,
Joe 1: 5 and h', all ye drinkers of wine,
11 h', O ye vinedressers, for the
13 h', ye ministers of the altar; come
Mic 1: 8 I will wail and h', I will go stripped
Zep 1:11 H', ye inhabitants of Maktesh,
Zec 11: 2 H', fir tree; for the cedar is fallen;
2 h', O ye oaks of Bashan; for the
Jas 5: 1 weep and h' for your miseries that

howled
Ho 7:14 when they h' upon their beds:

howling See also HOWLINGS.
De 32:10 and in the waste h' wilderness; he
Isa 15: 8 Moab: the h' thereof unto Eglaim,
8 and the h' thereof unto Beer-elim.
Jer 25:36 an h' of the principal of the flock,
Zep 1:10 and an h' from the second, and
Zec 11: 3 voice of the h' of the shepherds;

howlings
Am 8: 3 songs of the temple shall be h'

howsoever
J'g 19:20 h' let all thy wants lie upon me;
2Sa 18:22 h', let me, I pray thee, also
23 But h', said he, let me run.
Zep 3: 7 be cut off, h' I punished them:

Hozeh See COL-HOZEH.

huge
2Ch 16: 8 and the Lubims a h' host, with

Hukkok (*huk'-kok*) See also HELKATH; HUKOK.
Jos 19:34 and goeth out from thence to H',

Hukok (*hu'-kok*) See also HUKKOK.
1Ch 6:75 And H' with her suburbs, and

Hul (*hul*)
Ge 10:23 Uz, and H', and Gether, and Mash.
1Ch 1:17 and Aram, Uz, and H', and Gether,

Huldah (*hul'-dah*)
2Ki 22:14 went unto H' the prophetess, the
2Ch 34:22 went to H' the prophetess, the

humble See also HUMBLED; HUMBLETH.
Ex 10: 3 long wilt thou refuse to h' thyself
De 8: 2 to h' thee, and to prove thee,
16 that he might h' thee, and that he
J'g 19:24 and h' ye them, and do with them
2Ch 7:14 If my people,...shall h' themselves,
34:27 thou didst h' thyself before God,
Job 22:29 and he shall save the h'
Ps 9:12 he forgetteth not the cry of the h'.
10:12 up thine hand: forget not the h'.
17 hast heard the desire of the h':
34: 2 the h' shall hear thereof, and be
69:32 The h' shall see this, and be glad
Pr 6: 3 go, h' thyself, and make sure thy
16:19 Better it is to be of an h' spirit
29:23 but honour shall uphold the h' in
Isa 57:15 that is of a contrite and h' spirit,
15 to revive the spirit of the h', and
Jer 13:18 the queen, H' yourselves, sit down:
M't 18: 4 Whosoever therefore shall h'
23:12 and he that shall h' himself shall
2Co 12:21 my God will h' me among you,
Jas 4: 6 but giveth grace unto the h'.
10 H' yourselves in the sight of the
1Pe 5: 5 proud, and giveth grace to the h'.
6 H' yourselves therefore under

humbled See also HUMBLEDST.
Le 26:41 their uncircumcised hearts be h',
De 8: 3 And he h' thee, and suffered thee
21:14 her, because thou hast h' her.
22:24 he hath h' his neighbour's wife:
29 because he hath h' her, he may not
2Ki 22:19 and thou hast h' thyself before
2Ch 12: 6 Israel and the king h' themselves;
7 Lord saw that they h' themselves,
7 saying, They have h' themselves;
12 And when he h' himself, the wrath
30:11 and of Zebulun h' themselves, and
32:26 Hezekiah h' himself for the pride
33:12 and h' himself greatly before the
19 graven images, before he was h':
23 And h' not himself before the Lord,
23 Manasseh his father had h' himself;
36:12 h' not himself before Jeremiah
Ps 35:13 I h' my soul with fasting; and
Isa 2:11 The lofty looks of man shall be h',
5:15 and the mighty man shall be h',
15 the eyes of the lofty shall be h':
10:33 down, and the haughty shall be h'.
Jer 44:10 They are not h' even unto this
La 3:20 remembrance, and is h' in me.
Eze 22:10 thee have they h' her that was set
11 another in thee hath h' his sister,
Da 5:22 Belshazzar, hast not h' thine heart,
Ph'p 2: 8 he h' himself, and became obedient

humbledst
2Ch 34:27 and h' thyself before me, and

humbleness
Col 3:12 kindness, h' of mind, meekness,

humbleth
1Ki 21:29 how Ahab h' himself before me?
29 because he h' himself before me,
Ps 10:10 He croucheth, and h' himself,
113: 6 Who h' himself to behold the
Isa 2: 9 and the great man h' himself:
Lu 14:11 that h' himself shall be exalted.
18:14 that h' himself shall be exalted.

humbly
2Sa 16: 4 I *h*· beseech thee that I may find
Mic 6: 8 love mercy, and to walk *h*· with
humiliation
Ac 8:33 In his *h*· his judgment was taken
humility
Pr 15:33 wisdom; and before honour is *h*·.
18:12 haughty, and before honour is *h*·.
22: 4 By *h*· and the fear of the Lord are
Ac 20:19 Serving the Lord with all *h*· of
Col 2:18 your reward in a voluntary *h*· and
23 and *h*·, and neglecting of the body;
1Pe 5: 5 another and be clothed with *h*·:
Humtah (*hum'-tah*)
Jos 15:54 And *H*·, and Kirjath-arba, which
hundred See also HUNDREDFOLD; HUNDREDS.
Ge 5: 3 Adam lived an *h*· and thirty years,
4 begotten Seth were eight *h*· years:
5 lived were nine *h*· and thirty years:
6 And Seth lived an *h*· and five years,
7 Enos eight *h*· and seven years,
8 were nine *h*· and twelve years:
10 Cainan eight *h*· and fifteen years,
11 Enos were nine *h*· and five years:
13 Mahalaleel eight *h*· and forty years,
14 Cainan were nine *h*· and ten years:
16 Jared eight *h*· and thirty years,
17 were eight *h*· ninety and five years:
18 Jared lived an *h*· sixty and two
19 he begat Enoch eight *h*· years,
20 were nine *h*· sixty and two years:
22 he begat Methuselah three *h*· years,
23 were three *h*· sixty and five years:
25 Methuselah lived an *h*· eighty and
26 seven *h*· eighty and two years,
27 were nine *h*· sixty and nine years:
28 Lamech lived an *h*· eighty and two
30 Noah five *h*· ninety and five years,
31 seven *h*· seventy and seven years:
32 And Noah was five *h*· years old:
6: 3 his days shall be an *h*· and twenty
15 of the ark shall be three *h*· cubits,
7: 6 And Noah was six *h*· years old
24 upon the earth an *h*· and fifty days
8: 3 after the end of the *h*· and fifty days
9:28 flood three *h*· and fifty years.
29 of Noah nine *h*· and fifty years:
11:10 Shem was an *h*· years old, and
11 he begat Arphaxad five *h*· years,
13 begat Salah four *h*· and three years,
15 begat Eber four *h*· and three years,
17 begat Peleg four *h*· and thirty years
19 begat Reu two *h*· and nine years,
21 begat Serug two *h*· and seven years.
23 after he begat Nahor two *h*· years,
25 Terah an *h*· and nineteen years,
32 Terah were two *h*· and five years:
14:14 own house, three *h*· and eighteen,
15:13 shall afflict them four *h*· years;
17:17 unto him that is an *h*· years old?
21: 5 Abraham was an *h*· years old,
23: 1 an *h*· and seven and twenty years
15 land is worth four *h*· shekels of
16 four *h*· shekels of silver, current
25: 7 an *h*· threescore and fifteen years.
17 an *h*· and thirty and seven years:
32: 6 thee, and four *h*· men with him.
14 Two *h*· she goats and twenty he
14 two *h*· ewes, and twenty rams,
33: 1 Esau came, and with him four *h*·
19 father, for an *h*· pieces of money.
35:28 Isaac were an *h*· and fourscore
45:22 gave three *h*· pieces of silver,
47: 9 of my pilgrimage are an *h*· and
28 was an *h*· forty and seven years.
50:22 Joseph lived an *h*· and ten years.
26 being an *h*· and ten years old:
Ex 6:16 were an *h*· thirty and seven years.
18 were an *h*· thirty and three years.
20 Amram were an *h*· and thirty and
12:37 about six *h*· thousand on foot that
40 was four *h*· and thirty years.
41 end of the four *h*· and thirty years,
14: 7 And he took six *h*· chosen chariots,
27: 9 fine twined linen of an *h*· cubits
11 be hangings of an *h*· cubits long,
18 the court shall be an *h*· cubits,
30:23 of pure myrrh five *h*· shekels, and
23 two *h*· and fifty shekels, and of
23 calamus two *h*· and fifty shekels,
24 And of cassia five *h*· shekels,
38: 9 fine twined linen, an *h*· cubits:
11 the hangings were an *h*· cubits,
24 seven *h*· and thirty shekels, after
25 congregation was an *h*· talents,
25 seven *h*· and threescore and fifteen
26 old and upward, for six *h*· thousand
26 thousand and five *h*· and fifty men
27 of the *h*· talents of silver were cast
27 an *h*· sockets of the *h*· talents,
28 seven *h*· seventy and five shekels
29 two thousand and four *h*· shekels.
Le 26: 8 five of you shall chase an *h*·, and an
8 *h*· of you shall put ten thousand to
Nu 1:21 forty and six thousand and five *h*·.
23 fifty and nine thousand and three *h*·.
25 and five thousand six *h*· and fifty.
27 and fourteen thousand and six *h*·.
29 fifty and four thousand and four *h*·.
31 and seven thousand and four *h*·.
33 were forty thousand and five *h*·.
35 thirty and two thousand and two *h*·
37 and five thousand and four *h*·.
39 and two thousand and seven *h*·.
Nu 1:41 forty and one thousand and five *h*·.
43 fifty and three thousand and four *h*·.
46 numbered were six *h*· thousand and
46 three thousand and five *h*· and fifty.
2: 4 and fourteen thousand and six *h*·.
6 fifty and four thousand and four *h*·.
8 and seven thousand and four *h*·.
9 an *h*· thousand and fourscore
9 and four *h*·, throughout their armies.
11 forty and six thousand and five *h*·.
13 fifty and nine thousand and three *h*·.
15 forty and five thousand and six *h*·
16 of Reuben were an *h*· thousand
16 one thousand and four *h*· and fifty,
19 were forty thousand and five *h*·.
21 thirty and two thousand and two *h*·.
23 thirty and five thousand and four *h*·.
24 of Ephraim were an *h*· thousand
24 and eight thousand and an *h*·.
26 and two thousand and seven *h*·.
28 forty and one thousand and five *h*·.
30 fifty and three thousand and four *h*·.
31 camp of Dan were an *h*· thousand
31 fifty and seven thousand and six *h*·.
32 their hosts were six *h*· thousand
32 three thousand and five *h*· and fifty.
3:22 were seven thousand and five *h*·.
28 eight thousand and six *h*·, keeping
34 were six thousand and two *h*·.
43 two thousand two *h*· and threescore
46 two *h*· and threescore and thirteen
50 a thousand three *h*· and threescore
4:36 two thousand seven *h*· and fifty.
40 two thousand and six *h*· and thirty.
44 were three thousand and two *h*·.
48 thousand and five *h*· and fourscore.
7:13, 19, 25, 31, 37, 43, 49, 55, 61, 67, 73,
79, 85 an *h*· and thirty shekels,
85 two thousand and four *h*· shekels,
86 spoons was an *h*· and twenty shekels.
11:21 I am, are six *h*· thousand footmen;
16: 2 two *h*· and fifty princes of the
17 his censer, two *h*· and fifty censers;
35 consumed the two *h*· and fifty men
49 were fourteen thousand and seven *h*·.
26: 7 thousand and seven *h*· and thirty.
10 fire devoured two *h*· and fifty men:
14 twenty and two thousand and two *h*·.
18 of them, forty thousand and five *h*·.
22 and sixteen thousand and five *h*·.
25 and four thousand and three *h*·.
27 threescore thousand and five *h*·.
34 fifty and two thousand and seven *h*·.
37 thirty and two thousand and five *h*·.
41 forty and five thousand and six *h*·.
43 and four thousand and four *h*·.
47 fifty and three thousand and four *h*·.
50 forty and five thousand and four *h*·.
51 children of Israel, six *h*· thousand
51 and a thousand seven *h*· and thirty.
31:28 one soul of five *h*·, both of the
32 six *h*· thousand and seventy
36 number three *h*· thousand and seven
36 thirty thousand and five *h*· sheep:
37 six *h*· and threescore and fifteen.
39 were thirty thousand and five *h*·;
43 three *h*· thousand and thirty
43 seven thousand and five *h*· sheep,
45 thirty thousand asses and five *h*·,
52 thousand seven *h*· and fifty shekels.
33:39 Aaron was an *h*· and twenty and
De 22:19 amerce him in an *h*· shekels of
31: 2 I am an *h*· and twenty years
34: 7 Moses was an *h*· and twenty years
Jos 7:21 and two *h*· shekels of silver,
24:29 died, being an *h*· and ten years old.
32 Shechem for an *h*· pieces of silver:
J'g 2: 8 died, being an *h*· and ten years old.
3:31 slew of the Philistines six *h*· men
4: 3 for he had nine *h*· chariots of iron;
13 nine *h*· chariots of iron, and all the
7: 6 to their mouth, were three *h*· men:
7 By the three *h*· men that lapped will
8 and retained those three *h*· men:
16 he divided the three *h*· men into
19 Gideon, and the *h*· men that were
22 And the three *h*· blew the trumpets,
8: 4 three *h*· men that were with him,
10 an *h*· and twenty thousand men that
26 a thousand and seven *h*· shekels of
11:26 coasts of Arnon, three *h*· years?
15: 4 went and caught three *h*· foxes,
16: 5 one of us eleven *h*· pieces of silver
17: 2 The eleven *h*· shekels of silver that
3 restored the eleven *h*· shekels of
4 his mother took two *h*· shekels of
18:11 six *h*· men appointed with weapons
16 six *h*· men appointed with their
17 six *h*· men that were appointed with
20: 2 four *h*· thousand footmen that drew
10 And we will take ten men of an *h*·
10 of Israel, and an *h*· of a thousand,
15 numbered seven *h*· chosen men.
16 there were seven *h*· chosen men
17 four *h*· thousand men that drew
35 and five thousand and an *h*· men:
47 But six *h*· men turned and fled to
21:12 four *h*· young virgins, that had
1Sa 11: 8 of Israel were three *h*· thousand,
13:15 present with him, about six *h*· men.
14: 2 with him were about six *h*· men;
15: 4 Telaim, two *h*· thousand footmen,
17: 7 weighed six *h*· shekels of iron:
18:25 an *h*· foreskins of the Philistines,
27 slew of the Philistines two *h*· men;
22: 2 were with him about four *h*· men.
1Sa 23:13 his men, which were about six *h*·,
25:13 up after David about four *h*· men;
13 and two *h*· abode by the stuff.
18 made haste, and took two *h*· loaves,
18 corn, and an *h*· clusters of raisins,
18 and two *h*· cakes of figs, and laid
27: 2 he passed over with the six *h*· men
30: 9 David went, he and the six *h*· men
10 David pursued, he and four *h*· men:
10 for two *h*· abode behind, which were
17 four *h*· young men, which rode upon
21 And David came to the two *h*· men,
2Sa 2:31 three *h*· and threescore men died.
3:14 I espoused to me for an *h*· foreskins
8: 4 chariots, and seven *h*· horsemen,
4 reserved of them for an *h*· chariots.
10:18 slew the men of seven *h*· chariots
14:26 hair of his head at two *h*· shekels
15:11 with Absalom went two *h*· men out
18 six *h*· men which came after him
16: 1 upon them two *h*· loaves of bread,
1 and an *h*· bunches of raisins,
1 and an *h*· of summer fruits, and a
21:16 weighed three *h*· shekels of brass
23: 8 lift up his spear against eight *h*·,
18 lifted up his spear against three *h*·,
24: 9 Israel eight *h*· thousand valiant men
9 of Judah were five *h*· thousand men.
1Ki 4:23 and an *h*· sheep, beside harts, and
5:16 three thousand and three *h*·, which
6: 1 in the four *h*· and eightieth year
7: 2 the length thereof was an *h*· cubits,
20 the pomegranates were two *h*· in
42 And four *h*· pomegranates for the
8:63 an *h*· and twenty thousand sheep.
9:23 five *h*· and fifty, which bare rule
28 gold, four *h*· and twenty talents,
10:10 an *h*· and twenty talents of gold,
14 six *h*· threescore and six talents of
16 six *h*· shekels of gold went to one
16 made two *h*· targets of beaten gold:
17 he made three *h*· shields of beaten
26 had a thousand and four *h*· chariots,
29 of Egypt for six *h*· shekels of silver,
29 and an horse for an *h*· and fifty: and
11: 3 he had seven *h*· wives, princesses,
3 and three *h*· concubines: and his
12:21 an *h*· and fourscore thousand chosen
18: 4 Obadiah took an *h*· prophets, and
13 how I hid an *h*· men of the Lord's
19 prophets of Baal four *h*· and fifty,
19 the prophets of the groves four *h*·,
22 prophets are four *h*· and fifty men.
20:15 and they were two *h*· and thirty two:
29 an *h*· thousand footmen in one day.
22: 6 the prophets together, about four *h*·
2Ki 3: 4 of Israel an *h*· thousand lambs, and
4 an *h*· thousand rams, with the wool.
26 he took with him seven *h*· men that
4:43 should I set this before an *h*· men?
14:13 unto the corner gate, four *h*· cubits.
18:14 of Judah three *h*· talents of silver
19:35 an *h*· fourscore and five thousand:
23:33 a tribute of an *h*· talents of silver,
1Ch 4:42 of the sons of Simeon, five *h*· men,
5:18 thousand seven *h*· and threescore,
21 of sheep two *h*· and fifty thousand,
21 and of men an *h*· thousand.
7: 2 two and twenty thousand and six *h*·.
9 was twenty thousand and two *h*·.
11 thousand and two *h*· soldiers, fit to
8:40 sons, and sons' sons, an *h*· and fifty.
9: 6 their brethren, six *h*· and ninety.
9 generations, nine *h*· and fifty and six.
13 and seven *h*· and threescore;
22 in the gates were two *h*· and twelve.
11:11 up his spear against three *h*· slain
20 lifting up his spear against three *h*·,
12:14 one of the least was over an *h*·, and
24 six thousand and eight *h*·, ready
25 the war, seven thousand and one *h*·.
26 of Levi four thousand and six *h*·.
27 were three thousand and seven *h*·;
30 twenty thousand and eight *h*·,
32 the heads of them were two *h*·; and
35 and eight thousand and six *h*·.
37 battle, an *h*· and twenty thousand.
15: 5 and his brethren an *h*· and twenty:
6 and his brethren two *h*· and twenty:
7 his brethren an *h*· and thirty: and
8 the chief, and his brethren two *h*·:
10 his brethren an *h*· and twelve, and
18: 4 but reserved of them an *h*· chariots.
21: 3 Lord make his people an *h*· times
5 an *h*· thousand men that drew
5 Judah was four *h*· threescore and
25 for the place six *h*· shekels of gold
22:14 Lord an *h*· thousand talents of gold,
25: 7 was two *h*· fourscore and eight.
26:30 of valour, a thousand and seven *h*·,
32 thousand and seven *h*· chief fathers,
29: 7 and one *h*· thousand talents of iron.
2Ch 1:14 had a thousand and four *h*· chariots,
17 a chariot for six *h*· shekels of silver,
17 and an horse for an *h*· and fifty:
2: 2 three thousand and six *h*· to oversee
17 were found an *h*· and fifty thousand
17 and three thousand and six *h*·.
18 thousand and six *h*· overseers to set
3: 4 the height was an *h*· and twenty:
8 gold, amounting to six *h*· talents.
16 and made an *h*· pomegranates, and
4: 8 And he made an *h*· basons of gold.
13 four *h*· pomegranates on the two
5:12 an *h*· and twenty priests sounding
7: 5 an *h*· and twenty thousand sheep:

2Ch 8:10 officers, even two h' and fifty, that
18 four h' and fifty talents of gold,
9: 9 an h' and twenty talents of gold,
13 six h' and threescore and six talents
15 Solomon made two h' targets of
15 six h' shekels of beaten gold went
16 three h' shields made he of beaten
16 three h' shekels of gold went to one
11: 1 an h' and fourscore thousand
12: 3 With twelve h' chariots, and
13: 3 even four h' thousand chosen men:
3 with eight h' thousand chosen men,
17 Israel five h' thousand chosen men.
14: 8 out of Judah three h' thousand;
8 two h' and fourscore thousand:
9 thousand, and three h' chariots;
15:11 brought, seven h' oxen and seven
17:11 seven thousand and seven h' rams,
11 thousand and seven h' he goats.
14 men of valour three h' thousand.
15 him two h' and fourscore thousand.
16 him two h' thousand mighty men
17 bow and shield two h' thousand.
18 an h' and fourscore thousand ready
18: 5 together of prophets four h' men,
24:15 an h' and thirty years old was he
25: 5 three h' thousand choice men, able
6 hired...an h' thousand mighty men
6 of Israel for an h' talents of silver.
9 the h' talents which I have given to
23 to the corner gate, four h' cubits.
26:12 valour were two thousand and six h'.
13 army, three h' thousand and seven
13 thousand and five h', that made war
27: 5 same year an h' talents of silver,
28: 6 an h' and twenty thousand in one
8 of their brethren two h' thousand,
29:32 an h' rams, and two h' lambs:
33 consecrated things were six h' oxen
35: 8 thousand and six h' small cattle,
8 small cattle, and three h' oxen.
9 small cattle, and five h' oxen.
36: 3 condemned the land in an h' talents
Ezr 1:10 of a second sort four h' and ten,
11 were five thousand and four h'.
2: 3 thousand an h' seventy and two.
4 Shephatiah, three h' seventy and
5 of Arah, seven h' seventy and five.
6 two thousand eight h' and twelve.
7 a thousand two h' fifty and four.
8 of Zattu, nine h' forty and five.
9 of Zaccai, seven h' and threescore.
10 children of Bani, six h' forty and two.
11 of Bebai, six h' twenty and three.
12 a thousand two h' twenty and two.
13 of Adonikam, six h' sixty and six.
15 of Adin, four h' fifty and four.
17 of Bezai, three h' twenty and three.
18 children of Jorah, an h' and twelve.
19 of Hashum, two h' twenty and three.
21 Beth-lehem, an h' twenty and three.
23 of Anathoth, an h' twenty and eight.
25 Beeroth, seven h' and forty and three.
26 and Gaba, six h' twenty and one.
27 of Michmas, an h' twenty and two.
28 and Ai, two h' twenty and three.
30 of Magbish, an h' fifty and six.
31 a thousand two h' fifty and four.
32 of Harim, three h' and twenty.
33 and Ono, seven h' twenty and five.
34 of Jericho, three h' forty and five.
35 three thousand and six h' and thirty.
36 of Jeshua, nine h' seventy and three.
38 a thousand two h' forty and seven.
41 of Asaph, an h' twenty and eight.
42 Shobai, in all an h' thirty and nine.
58 were three h' ninety and two.
60 of Nekoda, six h' fifty and two.
64 thousand three h' and threescore,
65 thousand three h' thirty and seven:
65 two h' singing men and singing
66 horses were seven h' thirty and six;
66 their mules, two h' forty and five;
67 their camels, four h' thirty and five;
67 six thousand seven h' and twenty.
69 silver, and one h' priests' garments.
6:17 an h' bullocks, two h' rams, four h'
7:22 Unto an h' talents of silver,
22 and to an h' measures of wheat,
22 and to an h' baths of wine,
22 and to an h' baths of oil, and salt
8: 3 of the males an h' and fifty.
4 and with him two h' males.
5 and with him three h' males.
9 with him two h' and eighteen males.
10 him an h' and threescore males.
12 and with him an h' and ten males.
20 two h' and twenty Nethinims: all of
26 six h' and fifty talents of silver,
26 and silver vessels an h' talents,
26 and of gold an h' talents;
Ne 5:17 my table an h' and fifty of the Jews
7: 8 thousand an h' seventy and two.
9 three h' seventy and two.
10 of Arah, six h' fifty and two.
11 thousand and eight h' and eighteen.
12 a thousand two h' fifty and four.
13 of Zattu, eight h' forty and five.
14 of Zaccai, seven h' and threescore.
15 of Binnui, six h' forty and eight.
16 of Bebai, six h' twenty and eight.
17 thousand three h' twenty and two.
18 six h' threescore and seven.
20 children of Adin, six h' fifty and five.
22 Hashum, three h' twenty and eight.
23 of Bezai, three h' twenty and four.
Ne 7: 24 children of Hariph, an h' and twelve.
26 an h' fourscore and eight.
27 Anathoth, an h' twenty and eight.
29 Beeroth, seven h' forty and three.
30 and Gaba, six h' twenty and one.
31 Michmas, an h' and twenty and two.
32 and Ai, an h' twenty and three.
34 a thousand two h' fifty and four.
35 of Harim, three h' and twenty.
36 of Jericho, three h' forty and five.
37 and Ono, seven h' twenty and one.
38 three thousand nine h' and thirty.
39 Jeshua, nine h' seventy and three.
41 a thousand two h' forty and seven.
44 of Asaph, an h' forty and eight.
45 of Shobai, an h' thirty and eight.
60 were three h' ninety and two.
62 of Nekoda, six h' forty and two.
66 thousand three h' and threescore,
67 thousand three h' thirty and seven:
67 two h' forty and five singing men
68 horses, seven h' thirty and six:
68 their mules, two h' forty and five:
69 their camels, four h' thirty and five:
69 thousand seven h' and twenty asses.
70 five h' and thirty priests' garments.
71 thousand and two h' pound of silver.
11: 6 four h' threescore and eight valiant
8 Sallai, nine h' twenty and eight.
12 were eight h' twenty and two:
13 of the fathers, two h' forty and two:
14 of valour, an h' twenty and eight:
18 city were two h' fourscore and two:
19 gates, were an h' seventy and two.
Es 1: 1 h' and seven and twenty provinces:
4 days, even an h' and fourscore days
8: 9 an h' twenty and seven provinces,
9: 6 Jews slew and destroyed five h' men.
12 have slain and destroyed five h' men
15 and slew three h' men at Shushan;
30 the h' twenty and seven provinces
Job 1: 3 five h' yoke of oxen, and five h' she
42:16 this lived Job an h' and forty years,
Pr 17:10 man than an h' stripes into a fool.
Ec 6: 3 If a man beget an h' children, and
8:12 Though a sinner do evil an h' times,
Ca 8:12 that keep the fruit thereof two h'.
Isa 37:36 a h' and fourscore and five thousand:
65:20 the child shall die an h' years old;
20 sinner being an h' years old shall
Jer 52:23 upon the network were an h' round
29 eight h' thirty and two persons:
30 seven h' forty and five persons:
30 were four thousand and six h'.
Eze 4: 5 the days, three h' and ninety days:
9 three h' and ninety days shalt thou
40:19 h' cubits eastward and northward.
23 from gate to gate an h' cubits.
27 gate toward the south an h' cubits.
47 an h' cubits long, and an h' cubits
41:13 the house, an h' cubits long;
13 the walls thereof, an h' cubits long;
14 place toward the east, an h' cubits.
15 and on the other side, an h' cubits,
42: 2 length of an h' cubits was the north
8 before the temple were an h' cubits.
16 measuring reed, five h' reeds,
17 the north side, five h' reeds,
18 the south side, five h' reeds,
19 and measured five h' reeds with the
20 five h' reeds long, and five h' broad.
45: 2 for the sanctuary five h' in length,
2 with five h' in breadth, square round
15 lamb out of the flock, out of two h',
48:16 north side four thousand and five h',
16 south side four thousand and five h',
16 east side four thousand and five h',
16 west side four thousand and five h'.
17 toward the north two h' and fifty,
17 toward the south two h' and fifty,
17 toward the east two h' and fifty,
17 toward the west two h' and fifty.
30 four thousand and five h' measures.
32 east side four thousand and five h':
33 four thousand and five h' measures:
34 west side four thousand and five h',
Da 6: 1 kingdom an h' and twenty princes,
8:14 two thousand and three h' days;
12:11 a thousand two h' and ninety days.
12 three h' and five and thirty days.
Am 5: 3 out by a thousand shall leave an h',
3 went forth by an h' shall leave ten,
M't 18:12 if a man have an h' sheep, and one
28 which owed him an h' pence:
M'r 4: 8 and some sixty, and some an h'.
20 some sixty, and some an h'.
6:37 buy two h' pennyworth of bread,
14: 5 sold for more than three h' pence,
Lu 7:41 the one owed five h' pence, and
15: 4 man of you, having an h' sheep,
16: 6 And he said, An h' measures of oil.
7 he said, An h' measures of wheat.
Joh 6: 7 Two h' pennyworth of bread is not
12: 5 ointment sold for three h' pence,
19:39 aloes, about an h' pound weight.
21: 8 land, but as it were two h' cubits,
11 great fishes, an h' and fifty and
Ac 1:15 were about an h' and twenty,
5:36 a number of men, about four h',
7: 6 and entreat them evil four h' years.
13:20 the space of four h' and fifty years,
23:23 Make ready two h' soldiers to go
23 and spearmen two h', at the third
27:37 two h' threescore and sixteen souls.
Ro 4:19 when he was about an h' years old,
1Co 15: 6 of above five h' brethren at once;
Ga 3:17 was four h' and thirty years after,
Re 7: 4 an h' and forty and four thousand
9:16 were two h' thousand thousand:
11: 3 a thousand two h' and threescore
12: 6 a thousand two h' and threescore
13:18 number is Six h' threescore and six.
14: 1 him an h' forty and four thousand,
3 the h' and forty and four thousand,
20 of a thousand and six h' furlongs.
21:17 an h' and forty and four cubits,

hundredfold
Ge 26:12 in the same year an h':
2Sa 24: 3 many soever they be, an h',
M't 13: 8 some an h', some sixtyfold, some
23 bringeth forth, some an h', some
19:29 shall receive an h', and shall
M'r 10:30 he shall receive an h' now in this
Lu 8: 8 sprang up, and bare fruit an h'.

hundreds
Ex 18:21,25 rulers of h', rulers of fifties,
Nu 31:14 thousands, and captains over h',
48 and captains of h', came near unto
52 thousands, and of the captains of h',
54 the captains of thousands and of h',
De 1:15 captains over h', and captains over
1Sa 22: 7 of thousands, and captains of h';
29: 2 of the Philistines passed on by h',
2Sa 18: 1 thousands and captains of h' over
4 all the people came out by h' and
2Ki 11: 4 sent and fetched the rulers over h',
9 captains over the h' did according
10 the captains over h' did the priest
15 commanded the captains of the h',
19 he took the rulers over h', and the
1Ch 13: 1 the captains of thousands and h',
26:26 the captains over thousands and h',
27: 1 and captains of thousands and h',
28: 1 captains over the h', and the
29: 6 the captains of thousands and of h',
2Ch 1: 2 the captains of thousands and of h',
23: 1 himself, and the captains of h',
9 to the captains of h' spears, and
14 the captains of h' that were set
20 And he took the captains of h', and
25: 5 captains over h', according to the
M'r 6:40 in ranks, by h', and by fifties.

hundredth
Ge 7:11 In the six h' year of Noah's life, in
8:13 in the six h' and first year, in the
Ne 5:11 also the h' part of the money, and

hundred-thousand See HUNDRED and THOUSAND.

hung See HANGED.

hunger See also HUNGERBITTEN; HUNGERED.
Ex 16: 3 to kill the whole assembly with h'.
De 8: 3 thee, and suffered thee to h',
28:48 in h', and in thirst, and in
32:24 They shall be burnt with h', and
Ne 9:15 bread from heaven for their h',
Ps 34:10 young lions do lack, and suffer h':
Pr 19:15 sleep; an idle soul shall suffer h'.
Isa 49:10 They shall not h' nor thirst;
Jer 38: 9 he is like to die for h' in the place
42:14 trumpet, nor have h' of bread;
La 2:19 young children, that faint for h'
4: 9 than they that be slain with h':
Eze 34:29 shall be no more consumed with h'
M't 5: 6 Blessed are they which do h' and
Lu 6:21 Blessed are ye that h' now: for ye
25 you that are full! for ye shall h'.
15:17 and to spare, and I perish with h'!
Joh 6:35 that cometh to me shall never h';
Ro 12:20 Therefore if thine enemy h', feed
1Co 4:11 we both h', and thirst, and are
11:34 And if any man h', let him eat at
2Co 11:27 often, in h' and thirst, in fastings
Re 6: 8 to kill with sword, and with h',
7:16 They shall h' no more, neither

hungerbitten
Job 18:12 His strength shall be h', and

hungered See also HUNGRED; HUNGRY.
M't 21:18 as he returned into the city, he h'.
Lu 4: 2 they were ended, he afterward h'.

hungred See also HUNGERED.
M't 4: 2 nights, he was afterward an h'.
12: 1 his disciples were an h', and began
3 what David did, when he was an h',
25:35 I was an h', and ye gave me meat:
37 when saw we thee an h', and fed
42 For I was an h', and ye gave me no
44 Lord, when saw we thee an h', or
M'r 2:25 when he had need, and was an h',
Lu 6: 3 David did, when himself was an h',

hungry See also HUNGERED.
1Sa 2: 5 and they that were h' ceased:
2Sa 17:29 The people is h', and weary, and
2Ki 7:12 They know that we be h'; therefore
Job 5: 5 Whose harvest the h' eateth up,
22: 7 hast withholden bread from the h'.
24:10 take away the sheaf from the h';
Ps 50:12 If I were h', I would not tell thee:
107: 5 H' and thirsty, their soul fainted
9 filleth the h' soul with goodness.
36 there he maketh the h' to dwell,
146: 7 which giveth food to the h'.
Pr 6:30 to satisfy his soul when he is h';
25:21 If thine enemy be h', give him bread
27: 7 to the h' soul every bitter thing is
Isa 8:21 through it, hardly bestead and h':
21 that when they shall be h', they
9:20 snatch on the right hand, and be h';
29: 8 be as when an h' man dreameth.

Isa 32: 6 to make empty the soul of the h·.
44:12 he is h·, and his strength faileth:
58: 7 Is it not to deal thy bread to the h·,
10 if thou draw out thy soul to the h·,
65:13 servants shall eat, but ye shall be h·:
Eze 18: 7, 16 hath given his bread to the h·,
M'r 11:12 come from Bethany, he was h·:
Lu 1:53 He hath filled the h· with good
Ac 10:10 And he became very h·, and would
1Co 11:21 one is h·, and another is drunken.
Ph'p 4:12 both to be full and to be h·, both

hunt See also HUNTED; HUNTEST; HUNTETH; HUNTING.
Ge 27: 5 went to the field to h· for venison,
1Sa 26:20 h· a partridge in the mountains.
Job 38:39 Wilt thou h· the prey for the lion?
Ps 140:11 evil shall h· the violent man to
Pr 6:26 adulteress will h· for the precious
Jer 16:16 shall h· them from every mountain,
La 4:18 They h· our steps, that we cannot
Eze 13:18 head of every stature to h· souls!
18 Will ye h· the souls of my people,
20 wherewith ye there h· the souls to
20 even the souls that ye h· to make
Mic 7: 2 they h· every man his brother with

hunted
Eze 13:21 be no more in your hand to be h·;

hunter See also HUNTERS.
Ge 10: 9 was a mighty h· before the Lord:
9 Even as Nimrod the mighty h·
25:27 Esau was a cunning h·, a man of
Pr 6: 5 as a roe from the hand of the h·,

hunters
Jer 16:16 and after will I send for many h·,

huntest
1Sa 24:11 thee; yet thou h· my soul to take it.
Job 10:16 Thou h· me as a fierce lion: and

hunteth
Le 17:13 which h· and catcheth any beast

hunting
Ge 27:30 his brother came in from his h·.
Pr 12:27 roasteth not that...he took in h·:

Hupham (hu'-fam) See also HUPPIM; HUPHAMITES.
Nu 26:39 H·, the family of the Huphamites.

Huphamites (hu'-fam-ites)
Nu 26:39 of Hupham, the family of the H·.

Huppah (hup'-pah)
1Ch 24:13 thirteenth to H·, the fourteenth

Huppim (hup'-pim) See also HUPHAM.
Ge 46:21 Rosh, Muppim, and H·, and Ard.
1Ch 7:12 Shuppim also, and H·, the children
15 Machir took to wife the sister of H·

Hur (hur)
Ex 17:10 Moses, Aaron, and H· went up to
12 Aaron and H· stayed up his hands,
24:14 behold, Aaron and H· are with you:
31: 2 the son of Uri, the son of H·, of the
35:30 the son of Uri, the son of H·, of the
38:22 the son of Uri, the son of H·, of the
Nu 31: 8 Zur, and H·, and Reba, five kings
Jos 13:21 Zur, and H·, and Reba, which were
1Ki 4: 8 The son of H·, in mount Ephraim:
1Ch 2:19 him Ephrath, which bare him H·.
20 And H· begat Uri, and Uri begat
50 were the sons of Caleb the son of H·,
4: 1 and Carmi, and H·, and Shobal.
4 are sons of H·, the firstborn of
2Ch 1: 5 the son of Uri, the son of H·, had
Ne 3: 9 repaired Rephaiah the son of H·.

Hurai (hu'-rahee) See also HIDDAI.
1Ch 11:32 H· of the brooks of Gaash, Abiel

Huram (hu'-ram) See also HIRAM.
1Ch 8: 5 Gera, and Shephuphan, and H·.
2Ch 2: 3 Solomon sent to H· the king of Tyre,
11 H· the king of Tyre answered
12 H· said moreover, Blessed be the
13 understanding, of H· my father's,
4:11 And H· made the pots, and the
11 And H· finished the work that he
16 did H· his father make to king
8: 2 cities which H· had restored to
18 And H· sent him by the hands of
9:10 And the servants also of H·, and
21 to Tarshish with the servants of H·:

Huri (hu'-ri)
1Ch 5:14 Abihail the son of H·, the son of

hurl See also HURLETH; HURLING.
Nu 35:20 or h· at him by laying of wait,

hurleth
Job 27:21 as a storm h· him out of his place.

hurling
1Ch 12: 2 in h· stones and shooting arrows out

hurt See also HURTFUL; HURTING.
Ge 4:23 and a young man to my h·.
26:29 That thou wilt do us no h·, as we
31: 7 but God suffered him not to h· me.
29 the power of my hand to do you h·:
Ex 21:22 strive, and h· a woman with child,
35 if one man's ox h· another's, that he
22:10 and it die, or be h·, or driven away,
14 ought of his neighbour, and it be h·,
Nu 16:15 neither have I h· one of them.
Jos 24:20 then he will turn and do you h·,
1Sa 20:21 there is peace to thee, and no h·;
24: 9 Behold, David seeketh thy h·?
25: 7 which were with us, we h· them not,
15 good unto us, and we were not h·,
2Sa 18:32 rise against thee to do thee h·,

2Ki 14:10 shouldest thou meddle to thy h·,
2Ch 25:19 shouldest thou meddle to thine h·,
Ezr 4:22 grow to the h· of the kings?
Es 9: 2 hand on such as sought their h·:
Job 35: 8 Thy wickedness may h· a man as thou
Ps 15: 4 He that sweareth to his own h·,
35: 4 to confusion that devise my h·.
26 together that rejoice at mine h·:
38:12 that seek my h· speak mischievous
41: 7 against me do they devise my h·.
70: 2 put to confusion, that desire my h·.
71:13 and dishonour that seek my h·.
24 unto shame, that seek my h·.
105:18 Whose feet they h· with fetters:
Ec 5:13 for the owners thereof to their h·.
8: 9 ruleth over another to his own h·.
10: 9 Whoso removeth stones shall be h·
Isa 11: 9 They shall not h· nor destroy in all
27: 3 lest any h· it, I will keep it night
65:25 They shall not h· nor destroy in all
Jer 6:14 healed also the h· of the daughter
7: 6 walk after other gods to your h·:
8:11 healed the h· of the daughter of
21 the h· of the daughter of my people
21 the daughter of my people am I h·;
10:19 Woe is me for my h·! my wound is
24: 9 kingdoms of the earth for their h·,
25: 6 hands; and I will do you no h·.
7 works of your hands to your own h·.
38: 4 the welfare of this people, but the h·.
Da 3:25 of the fire, and they have no h·;
6:22 mouths, that they have not h· me:
22 thee, O king, have I done no h·.
23 no manner of h· was found upon
M'r 16:18 deadly thing, it shall not h· them;
Lu 4:35 he came out of him, and h· him not.
10:19 nothing shall by any means h· you.
Ac 18:10 no man shall set on thee to h· thee:
27:10 will be with h· and much damage,
Re 2:11 shall not be h· of the second death.
6: 6 see thou h· not the oil and the wine.
7: 2 it was given to h· the earth and the
3 H· not the earth, neither the sea,
9: 4 should not h· the grass of the earth,
10 power was to h· men five months.
19 had heads, and with them they do h·.
11: 5 any man will h· them, fire proceedeth
5 if any man will h· them, he must in

hurtful
Ezr 4:15 rebellious city, and h· unto kings
Ps 144:10 his servant from the h· sword.
1Ti 6: 9 and into many foolish and h· lusts,

hurting
1Sa 25:34 hath kept me back from h· thee,

husband See also HUSBANDMAN; HUSBAND'S; HUSBANDS.
Ge 3: 6 and gave also unto her h· with her;
16 and thy desire shall be to thy h·,
16: 3 gave her to her h· Abram to be his
29:32 now therefore my h· will love me.
34 time will my h· be joined unto me,
30:15 matter that thou hast taken my h·?
18 I have given my maiden to my h·:
20 now will my h· dwell with me,
Ex 4:25 Surely a bloody h· art thou to me.
26 A bloody h· thou art, because of
21:22 as the woman's h· will lay upon
Le 19:20 is a bondmaid, betrothed to an h·,
21: 3 nigh unto him, which hath had no h·;
7 take a woman put away from her h·:
Nu 5:13 and it be hid from the eyes of her h·,
19 with another instead of thy h·;
20 aside to another, instead of thy h·,
20 have lain with thee beside thine h·:
27 have done trespass against her h·,
29 aside to another instead of her h·,
30: 6 had at all an h·, when she vowed,
7 her h· heard it, and held his peace
8 if her h· disallowed her on the day
11 her h· heard it, and held his peace
12 if her h· hath utterly made them void
12 her h· hath made them void;
13 afflict the soul, her h· may establish
13 it, or her h· may make it void.
14 if her h· altogether hold his peace
De 21:13 and be her h·, and she shall be thy
22:22 with a woman married to an h·, then
23 a virgin be betrothed unto an h·,
24: 3 if the latter h· hate her, and write
3 or if the latter h· die, which took her
4 former h·, which sent her away,
25:11 to deliver her h· out of the hand of
28:56 be evil toward the h· of her bosom,
J'g 13: 6 the woman came and told her h·,
9 but Manoah her h· was not with her.
10 haste, and ran, and shewed her h·,
14:15 Entice thy h·, that he may declare
19: 3 And her h· arose, and went after her,
20: 4 And the Levite, the h· of the woman
Ru 1: 3 Elimelech Naomi's h· died; and she
5 was left of her two sons and her h·.
9 each of you in the house of her h·.
12 way; for I am too old to have a h·.
12 I should have an h· also to night,
2:11 in law since the death of thine h·:
1Sa 1: 8 Then said Elkanah her h· to her,
22 for she said unto her h·, I will not
23 And Elkanah her h· said unto her,
2:19 she came up with her h· to offer
4:19 father in law and her h· were dead,
21 of her father in law and her h·.
25:19 But she told not her h· Nabal.
2Sa 3:15 and took her from her h·, even from
16 her h· went with her along weeping
11:26 heard that Uriah her h· was dead,

2Sa 11:26 was dead, she mourned for her h·.
14: 5 widow woman, and mine h· is dead.
7 shall not leave to my h· neither name
2Ki 4: 1 Thy servant my h· is dead; and thou
9 she said unto her h·, Behold now, I
14 she hath no child, and her h· is old.
22 And she called unto her h·, and said,
26 Is it well with thy h·? is it well with
Pr 12: 4 woman is a crown to her h·:
31:11 The heart of her h· doth safely trust
23 Her h· is known in the gates,
28 her h· also, and he praiseth her.
Isa 54: 5 For thy Maker is thine h·; the Lord
Jer 3:20 treacherously departeth from her h·,
6:11 the h· with the wife shall be taken,
31:32 an h· unto them, saith the Lord:
Eze 16:32 taketh strangers instead of her h·!
45 that lotheth her h· and her children;
44:25 or for sister that hath had no h·,
Ho 2: 2 is not my wife, neither am I her h·:
7 I will go and return to my first h·;
Joe 1: 8 sackcloth for the h· of her youth.
M't 1:16 begat Joseph the h· of Mary, of
19 Then Joseph her h·, being a just man,
M'r 10:12 a woman shall put away her h·, and
Lu 2:36 had lived with an h· seven years
16:18 her that is put away from her h·
Joh 4:16 Go, call thy h·, and come hither.
17 answered and said, I have no h·.
17 Thou hast well said, I have no h·:
18 whom thou now hast is not thy h·:
Ac 5: 9 which have buried thy h· are at the
10 her forth, buried her by her h·.
Ro 7: 2 woman which hath an h· is bound
2 by the law to her h· so long as he
2 if the h· be dead, she is loosed from
2 she is loosed from the law of her h·.
3 while her h· liveth, she be married
3 if her h· be dead, she is free from
1Co 7: 2 let every woman have her own h·.
3 Let the h· render unto the wife due
3 likewise also the wife unto the h·.
4 power of her own body, but the h·:
4 likewise also the h· hath not power
10 Let not the wife depart from her h·:
11 or be reconciled to her h·: and let
11 and let not the h· put away his wife.
13 which hath an h· that believeth not,
14 the unbelieving h· is sanctified by
14 wife is sanctified by the h·:
16 whether thou shalt save thy h·? or
34 world, how she may please her h·.
39 by the law as long as her h· liveth;
39 if her h· be dead, she is at liberty
2Co 11: 2 for I have espoused you to one h·,
Ga 4:27 children than she which hath an h·.
Eph 5:23 For the h· is the head of the wife,
33 wife see that she reverence her h·.
1Ti 3: 2 the h· of one wife, vigilant, sober,
Tit 1: 6 the h· of one wife, having faithful
Re 21: 2 as a bride adorned for her h·.

husbandman See also HUSBANDMEN.
Ge 9:20 Noah began to be an h·, and he
Jer 51:23 I break in pieces the h· and his yoke
Am 5:16 they shall call the h· to mourning,
Zec 13: 5 I...no prophet, I am an h·;
Joh 15: 1 true vine, and my Father is the h·.
2Ti 2: 6 The h· that laboureth must be first
Jas 5: 7 the h· waiteth for the precious fruit

husbandmen
2Ki 25:12 the land to be vine dressers and h·.
2Ch 26:10 h· also, and vine dressers in the
Jer 31:24 h·, and they that go with flocks.
52:16 land for vinedressers and for h·.
Joe 1:11 Be ye ashamed, O ye h·; howl, O
M't 21:33 let it out to h·, and went into a far
34 he sent his servants to the h·, that
35 the h· took his servants, and beat
38 when the h· saw the son, they said
40 what will he do unto those h·?
41 let out his vineyard unto other h·,
M'r 12: 1 let it out to h·, and went into a far
2 he sent to the h· a servant, that he
2 receive from the h· of the fruit of
7 those h· said among themselves,
9 will come and destroy the h·, and
Lu 20: 9 a vineyard and let it forth to h·,
10 sent a servant to the h·, that they
10 the h· beat him, and sent him away
14 when the h· saw him, they reasoned
16 shall come and destroy these h·,

husbandry
2Ch 26:10 and in Carmel: for he loved h·.
1Co 3: 9 with God: ye are God's h·, ye are

husband's
Nu 30:10 vowed in her h· house, or bound
De 25: 5 her h· brother shall go in unto her,
5 perform the duty of an h· brother
7 My h· brother refuseth to raise up
7 perform the duty of my h· brother.
Ru 2: 1 kinsman of her h·, a mighty man

husbands
Ru 1:11 womb, that they may be your h·?
13 ye stay for them from having h·?
Es 1:17 they shall despise their h· in their
20 wives shall give to their h· honour,
Jer 29: 6 and give your daughters to h·, that
Eze 16:45 lothed their h· and their children:
Joh 4:18 For thou hast had five h·; and he
1Co 14:35 let them ask their h· at home: for it
Eph 5:22 submit yourselves unto your own h·,
24 be to their own h· in every thing.
25 H·, love your wives, even as Christ
Col 3:18 submit yourselves unto your own h·,

Col 3:19 H', love your wives, and be not bitter
1Ti 3:12 deacons be the h' of one wife, ruling
Tit 2: 4 love their h', to love their children,
5 obedient to their own h', that the
1Pe 3: 1 wives, in subjection to your own h';
5 in subjection unto their own h':
7 Likewise, ye h', dwell with them

Hushah (*hu'-shah*) See also HUSHATHITE; SHUAH.
1Ch 4: 4 Gedor, and Ezer the father of H'.

Hushai (*hu'-shahee*)
2Sa 15:32 H' the Archite came to meet him
37 So H' David's friend came into the
16:16 when H' the Archite, David's friend,
16 that H' said unto Absalom, God
17 Absalom said to H', Is this thy
18 H' said unto Absalom, Nay; but
17: 5 Call now H' the Archite also, and
6 when H' was come to Absalom,
7 And H' said unto Absalom, The
8 For, said H', thou knowest thy
14 The counsel of H' the Archite is
15 Then said H' unto Zadok and to
1Ki 4:16 Baanah the son of H' was in Asher
1Ch 27:33 and H' the Archite was the king's

Husham (*hu'-sham*)
Ge 36:34 and H' of the land of Temani
35 And H' died, and Hadad the son of
1Ch 1:45 H' of the land of the Temanites
46 when H' was dead, Hadad the son

Hushathite (*hu'-shath-ite*)
2Sa 21:18 then Sibbechai the H' slew Saph,
23:27 the Anethothite, Mebunnai the H',
1Ch 11:29 Sibbecai the H', Ilai the Ahohite,
20: 4 time Sibbechai the H' slew Sippai,
27:11 eighth month was Sibbecai the H',

Hushim (*hu'-shim*) See also SHUHAM.
Ge 46:23 And the sons of Dan; H'.
1Ch 7:12 the children of Ir, and H', the sons
8: 8 H' and Baara were his wives.
11 And of H' he begat Abitub, and

husk See also HUSKS.
Nu 6: 4 from the kernels even to the h'.
2Ki 4:42 ears of corn in the h' thereof.

husks
Lu 15:16 filled his belly with the h' that

Huz (*huz*)
Ge 22:21 H' his firstborn, and Buz his

Huzoth See KIRJATH-HUZOTH.

Huzzab (*huz'-zab*)
Na 2: 7 And H' shall be led away captive,

hyacinth See JACINTH.

Hymenæus (*hy-men-e'-us*)
1Ti 1:20 Of whom is H' and Alexander;
2Ti 2:17 Of whom is H' and Philetus;

hymn See also HYMNS.
M't 26:30 they had sung an h', they went out
M'r 14:26 they had sung an h', they went out

hymns
Eph 5:19 in psalms and h' and spiritual
Col 3:16 in psalms and h' and spiritual

hypocrisies
1Pe 2: 1 and all guile, and h', and envies,

hypocrisy See also HYPOCRISIES.
Isa 32: 6 work iniquity, to practise h', and
M't 23:28 within ye are full of h' and
M'r 12:15 knowing their h', said unto them,
Lu 12: 1 leaven of the Pharisees, which is h'.
1Ti 4: 2 Speaking lies in h'; having their
Jas 3:17 without partiality, and without h'.

hypocrite See also HYPOCRITE'S; HYPOCRITES.
Job 13:16 for an h' shall not come before
17: 8 stir up himself against the h'.
20: 5 the joy of the h' but for a moment?
27: 8 For what is the hope of the h',
34:30 That the h' reign not, lest
Pr 11: 9 An h' with his mouth destroyeth
Isa 9:17 for every one is a h' and an
M't 7: 5 Thou h', first cast out the beam
Lu 6:42 Thou h', cast out first the beam
13:15 Thou h', doth not each one of you

hypocrite's
Job 8:13 and the h' hope shall perish:

hypocrites
Job 15:34 the congregation of h' shall be
36:13 But the h' in heart heap up wrath:
Isa 33:14 hath surprised the h'.
M't 6: 2 as the h' do in the synagogues
5 thou shalt not be as the h' are: for
16 when ye fast, be not, as the h', of
15: 7 Ye h', well did Esaias prophesy of
16: 3 O ye h', ye can discern the face
22:18 and said, Why tempt ye me, ye h'?
23:13 scribes and Pharisees, h'! for ye
14 scribes and Pharisees, h'! for ye
15, 23, 25, 27 scribes and Pharisees, h'!
29 scribes and Pharisees, h'! because
24:51 appoint him his portion with the h':
M'r 7: 6 Esaias prophesied of you h', as it is
Lu 11:44 scribes and Pharisees, h'! for ye
12:56 Ye h', ye can discern the face of the

hypocritical
Ps 35:16 With h' mockers in feasts, they
Isa 10: 6 will send him against an h' nation,

hyssop
Ex 12:22 ye shall take a bunch of h', and dip
Le 14: 4 cedar wood, and scarlet, and h':
6 wood, and the scarlet, and the h',
49 cedar wood, and scarlet, and h':
51 the cedar wood, and the h', and the
52 cedar wood, and with the h', and
Nu 19: 6 cedar wood, and h', and scarlet,
18 a clean person shall take h', and
1Ki 4:33 the h' that springeth out of the
Ps 51: 7 Purge me with h', and I shall be
Joh 19:29 with vinegar, and put it upon h',
Heb 9:19 water, and scarlet wool, and h', and

I.

I-Am See AM.

Ibhar (*ib'-har*)
2Sa 5:15 I' also, and Elishua, and Nepheg,
1Ch 3: 6 I' also, and Elishama, and
14: 5 And I', and Elishua, and Elpalet,

Ibleam (*ib'-le-am*)
Jos 17:11 and I' and her towns, and the
J'g 1:27 nor the inhabitants of I' and her
2Ki 9:27 going up to Gur, which is by I'.

Ibneiah (*ib-ne-i'-ah*)
1Ch 9: 8 And I' the son of Jeroham, and

Ibnijah (*ib-ni'-jah*)
1Ch 9: 8 the son of Reuel, the son of I';

Ibri (*ib'-ri*)
1Ch 24:27 and Shoham, and Zaccur, and I'.

Ibzan (*ib'-zan*)
J'g 12: 8 And after him I' of Bethlehem
10 Then died I', and was buried at

ice
Job 6:16 are blackish by reason of the i',
38:29 Out of whose womb came the i'?
Ps 147:17 He casteth forth his i' like morsels:

I-chabod (*ik'-a-bod*) See also I-CHABOD'S.
1Sa 4:21 she named the child I', saying,

I-chabod's (*ik'-a-bods*)
1Sa 14: 3 the son of Ahitub, I' brother,

Iconium (*i-co'-ne-um*)
Ac 13:51 against them, and came unto I'.
14: 1 And it came to pass in I', that they
19 certain Jews from Antioch and I',
21 to Lystra, and to I', and Antioch,
16: 2 brethren that were at Lystra and I'.
2Ti 3:11 unto me at Antioch, at I', at Lystra;

Idalah (*id'-a-lah*)
Jos 19:15 and Shimron, and I', and

Idbash (*id'-bash*)
1Ch 4: 3 Jezreel, and Ishma, and I': and

Iddo (*id'-do*)
1Ki 4:14 Ahinadab the son of I' had
1Ch 6:21 Joah his son, I' his son, Zerah his
27:21 I' the son of Zechariah: of
2Ch 9:29 and in the visions of I' the seer
12:15 and of I' the seer concerning
13:22 written in the story of the prophet I'.
Ezr 5: 1 and Zechariah the son of I',
6:14 and Zechariah the son of I'.
8:17 with commandment unto I' the
17 what they should say unto I', and
Ne 12: 4 I', Ginnetho, Abijah,
16 Of I', Zechariah; of Ginnethon,
Zec 1: 1 the son of Berechiah, the son of I'
7 the son of I' the prophet, saying,

idle
Ex 5: 8 for they be i'; therefore they cry,
17 But he said, Ye are i', ye are i':
Pr 19:15 and an i' soul shall suffer hunger.
M't 12:36 That every i' word that men shall
20: 3 and saw others standing i' in the
6 found others standing i', and saith
6 Why stand ye here all the day i'?
Lu 24:11 words seemed to them as i' tales,
1Ti 5:13 And withal they learn to be i',
13 not only i', but tattlers also and

idleness
Pr 31:27 and eateth not the bread of i'.
Ec 10:18 and through i' of the hands the
Eze 16:49 and abundance of i' was in her

idol See also IDOL'S; IDOLS.
1Ki 15:13 she had made an i' in a grove;
13 Asa destroyed her i', and burnt it
2Ch 15:16 because she had made an i' in a
16 grove: and Asa cut down her i',
33: 7 image, the i' which he had made,
15 the i' out of the house of the Lord,
Isa 48: 5 Mine i' hath done them, and my
66: 3 incense, as if he blessed an i'.
Jer 22:28 man Coniah a despised broken i'?
Zec 11:17 Woe to the i' shepherd that leaveth
Ac 7:41 and offered a sacrifice unto the i',
1Co 8: 4 we know that an i' is nothing in
7 with conscience of the i' unto this
7 eat it as a thing offered unto an i';
10:19 say I then? that the i' is any thing,

idolater See also IDOLATERS.
1Co 5:11 a fornicator, or covetous, or an i',
Eph 5: 5 nor covetous man, who is an i'.

idolaters
1Co 5:10 or extortioners, or with i';
6: 9 neither fornicators, nor i', nor
10: 7 Neither be i', as were some of
Re 21: 8 i', and all liars, shall have their
22:15 and murderers, and i', and

idolatries
1Pe 4: 3 banquetings, and abominable i':

idolatrous
2Ki 23: 5 he put down the i' priests, whom

idolatry See also IDOLATRIES.
1Sa 15:23 stubbornness is as iniquity and i'.
Ac 17:16 he saw the city wholly given to i'.
1Co 10:14 my dearly beloved, flee from i'.
Ga 5:20 I', witchcraft, hatred, variance,
Col 3: 5 and covetousness, which is i':

idol's
1Co 8:10 sit at meat in the i' temple, shall

idols
Le 19: 4 Turn ye not unto i', nor make
26: 1 Ye shall make you no i' nor graven
30 upon the carcases of your i',
De 29:17 and their i', wood and stone, silver
1Sa 31: 9 publish it in the house of their i',
1Ki 15:12 and removed all the i' that his
21:26 did very abominably in following i',
2Ki 17:12 For they served i', whereof the
21:11 made Judah also to sin with his i':
21 served the i' that his father served,
23:24 and the images, and the i', and all
1Ch 10: 9 to carry tidings unto their i', and
16:26 all the gods of the people are i':
2Ch 15: 8 put away the abominable i' out
24:18 and served groves and i': and
34: 7 cut down all the i' throughout all
Ps 96: 5 the gods of the nations are i': but
97: 7 that boast themselves of i': worship
106:36 And they served their i': which
106:38 sacrificed unto the i' of Canaan:
115: 4 Their i' are silver and gold, the
135:15 The i' of the heathen are silver and
Isa 2: 8 Their land also is full of i'; they
18 and the i' he shall utterly abolish.
20 day a man shall cast his i' of silver,
20 and his i' of gold, which they made
10:10 hath found the kingdoms of the i',
11 have done unto Samaria and her i',
11 so do to Jerusalem and her i'?
19: 1 the i' of Egypt shall be moved at
3 and they shall seek to the i', and to
31: 7 man shall cast away his i' of silver,
7 and his i' of gold, which your own
45:16 together that are makers of i'.
46: 1 their i' were upon the beasts, and
57: 5 Enflaming yourselves with i' under
Jer 50: 2 her i' are confounded, her images
38 and they are mad upon their i'.
Eze 6: 4 your slain men before your i'.
5 children of Israel before their i';
6 your i' may be broken and cease,
9 which go a whoring after their i':
13 shall be among their i' round about
13 offer sweet savour to all their i'.
8:10 and all the i' of the house of Israel,
14: 3 man, these men have set up their i'
4 that setteth up his i' in his heart,
4 according to the multitude of his i';
5 estranged from me through their i'.
6 turn yourselves from your i'; and
7 setteth up his i' in his heart, and
16:36 with all the i' of thy abominations,
18: 6 eyes to the i' of the house of Israel,
12 hath lifted up his eyes to the i',
15 eyes to the i' of the house of Israel,
20: 7 not yourselves with the i' of Egypt:
8 did they forsake the i' of Egypt:
16 for their heart went after their i'.
18 nor defile yourselves with their i':
24 eyes were after their fathers' i'.
31 pollute yourselves with all your i',
39 Go ye, serve ye every one his i', and
39 with your gifts, and with your i'.
22: 3 maketh i' against herself to defile
4 defiled thyself in thine i' which
23: 7 with all their i' she defiled herself.
30 thou art polluted with their i'.
37 with their i' have they committed
39 had slain their children to their i',
49 you, and ye bear the sins of your i':
30:13 I will also destroy the i', and I will
33:25 lift up your eyes toward your i',
36:18 shed upon the land, and for their i'
25 from all your i', will I cleanse you.
37:23 themselves any more with their i',
44:10 astray away from me after their i';
12 unto them before their i', and
Ho 4:17 Ephraim is joined to i': let him
8: 4 their gold have they made them i',
13: 2 and i' according to their own
14: 8 have I to do any more with i'? I
Mic 1: 7 all the i' thereof will I lay desolate:
Hab 2:18 trusteth therein, to make dumb i'?
Zec 10: 2 For the i' have spoken vanity,
13: 2 cut off the names of the i' out of
Ac 15:20 they abstain from pollutions of i',

Ac 15:29 abstain from meats offered to i·,
21:25 from things offered to i·, and from
Ro 2:22 thou that abhorrest i·, dost thou
1Co 8: 1 as touching things offered to i·, we
4 that are offered in sacrifice unto i·,
10 those things which are offered to i·;
10:19 which is offered in sacrifice to i· is
28 offered in sacrifice unto i·, eat not
12: 2 carried away unto these dumb i·,
2Co 6:16 hath the temple of God with i·?
1Th 1: 9 ye turned to God from i· to serve
1Jo 5:21 children, keep yourselves from i·.
Re 2:14 eat things sacrificed unto i·, and
20 and to eat things sacrificed unto i·.
9:20 i· of gold, and silver, and brass,

Idumæa (*i-doo-me'-ah*) See also IDUMEA.
M'r 3: 8 from Jerusalem, and from I·, and

Idumea (*i-doo-me'-ah*) See also EDOM; IDUMÆA.
Isa 34: 5 it shall come down upon I·, and
6 great slaughter in the land of I·.
Eze 35:15 O Mount Seir, and all I·, even all
36: 5 of the heathen, and against all I·,

if
Ge 4: 7 I· thou doest well, shalt thou not
7 i· thou doest not well, sin lieth at
24 I· Cain should be avenged
8: 8 to see i· the waters were abated from
13: 9 i· thou wilt take the left hand, then
9 or i· thou depart to the right hand,
16 so that i· a man can number the
15: 5 i· thou be able to number them:
18: 3 My Lord, i· now I have found favour
21 unto me; and i· not, I will know.
26 I· I find in Sodom fifty righteous
28 I· I find there forty and five, I will
30 I will not do it, i· I find thirty there.
20: 7 and i· thou restore her not, know
24:41 and i· they give not thee one, thou
42 i· now thou do prosper my way
49 i· ye will deal kindly and truly with
49 and i· not, tell me; that I may turn
25:22 I· it be so, why am I thus! And she
27:46 i· Jacob take a wife of the daughters
28:20 I· God will be with me, and will
30:27 i· I have found favour in thine eyes,
31 i· thou wilt do this thing for me, I
31: 8 I· he said thus, The speckled shall
8 and i· he said thus, The ringstraked
50 I· thou shalt afflict my daughters,
50 or i· thou shalt take other wives
32: 8 I· Esau come to the one company,
33:10 i· now I have found grace in thy
13 and i· men shall overdrive them one
34:15 I· ye will be as we be, that every
17 But i· ye will not hearken unto us,
22 i· every male among us be
37:26 What profit is it i· we slay our
42:19 I· ye be true men, let one of your
38 i· mischief befall him by the way in
43: 4 I· thou wilt send our brother with
5 But i· thou wilt not send him, we
9 i· I bring him not unto thee, and set
11 I· it must be so now, do this; take
14 I· I be bereaved of my children, I
44:22 for i· he should leave his father, his
26 i· our youngest brother be with us,
29 And i· ye take this also from me,
32 I· I bring him not unto thee, then
47: 6 and i· thou knowest any man of
16 you for your cattle, i· money fail.
29 I· now I have found grace in thy
50: 4 I· now I have found grace in your
Ex 4: 8 i· they will not believe thee, neither
9 i· they will not believe also these
23 and i· thou refuse to let him go,
8: 2 and i· thou refuse to let them go,
21 Else, i· thou wilt not let my people
9: 2 For i· thou refuse to let them go,
10: 4 Else, i· thou refuse to let my people
12: 4 And i· the household be too little for
13:13 i· thou wilt not redeem it, then thou
15:26 I· thou wilt diligently hearken to
18:23 I· thou shalt do this thing, and God
19: 5 i· ye will obey my voice indeed, and
20:25 And i· thou wilt make me an altar
25 for i· thou lift up thy tool upon it,
21: 2 I· thou buy an Hebrew servant,
3 I· he came in by himself, he shall
3 i· he were married, then his wife
4 I· his master have given him a wife,
5 i· the servant shall plainly say, I
7 i· a man sell his daughter to be a
8 I· she please not her master, who
9 And i· he have betrothed her unto
10 I· he take him another wife; her
11 i· he do not these three unto her,
13 i· a man lie not in wait, but God
14 i· a man come presumptuously
16 i· he be found in his hand, he shall
18 i· men strive together, and one
19 I· he rise again, and walk abroad
20 i· a man smite his servant, or his
21 i· he continue a day or two, he
22 I· men strive, and hurt a woman
23 i· any mischief follow, then thou
26 i· any man smite the eye of his
27 i· he smite out his manservant's
28 I· an ox gore a man or a woman,
29 I· the ox were wont to push with
30 I· there be laid on him a sum of
32 I· the ox shall push a manservant
33 i· a man shall open a pit, or i· a man
35 i· one man's ox hurt another's,
22: 1 I· a man shall steal an ox, or a
2 I· a thief be found breaking up,
Ex 22: 3 I· the sun be risen upon him, there
3 i· he have nothing, then he shall be
4 I· the theft be certainly found in
5 I· a man shall cause a field or
6 I· fire break out, and catch in
7 I· a man shall deliver unto his
7 i· the thief be found, let him pay
8 I· the thief be not found, then the
10 I· a man deliver unto his
12 i· it be not stolen from him, he
13 I· it be torn in pieces, then let him
14 And i· a man borrow ought of his
15 i· the owner thereof be with it, he
15 i· it be an hired thing, it came for
16 i· a man entice a maid that is not
17 I· her father utterly refuse to give
23 I· thou afflict them in any wise,
25 I· thou lend money to any of my
26 I· thou at all take thy neighbour's
23: 4 I· thou meet thine enemy's ox or
5 I· thou see the ass of him that
22 i· thou shalt indeed obey his voice,
33 i· thou serve their gods, it will surely
24:14 i· any man have any matters to do,
29:34 And i· ought of the flesh of the
32:32 now, i· thou wilt forgive their sin;
32 and i· not, blot me, I pray thee, out
33:13 i· I have found grace in thy sight,
15 I· thy presence go not with me,
34: 9 I· now I have found grace in thy
20 and i· thou redeem him not, then
40:37 But i· the cloud were not taken up
Le 1: 2 I· any man of you bring an
3 I· his offering be a burnt sacrifice
10 And i· his offering be of the flocks,
14 And i· the burnt sacrifice for his
2: 4 And i· thou bring an oblation of
5, 7 And i· thy oblation be a meat
14 And i· thou offer a meat offering of
3: 1 And i· his oblation be a sacrifice of
1 i· he offer it of the herd; whether it
6 And i· his offering for a sacrifice of
7 I· he offer a lamb for his offering,
12 And i· his offering be a goat, then
4: 2 I· a soul shall sin through
3 I· the priest that is anointed do
13 And i· the whole congregation of
23 Or i· his sin, wherein he hath
27 And i· any one of the common
28 Or i· his sin, which he hath sinned,
32 And i· he bring a lamb for a sin
5: 1 And i· a soul sin, and hear the
1 i· he do not utter it, then he shall
2 Or i· a soul touch any unclean
3 Or i· he touch the uncleanness of
4 Or i· a soul swear, pronouncing
7 And i· he be not able to bring a
11 But i· he be not able to bring two
15 I· a soul commit a trespass, and
17 And i· a soul sin, and commit any
6: 2 I· a soul sin, and commit a
28 and i· it be sodden in a brasen pot,
7:12 I· he offer it for a thanksgiving,
16 But i· the sacrifice of his offering
18 And i· any of the flesh of the
10:19 and i· I had eaten the sin offering
11:37 And i· any part of their carcase
38 But i· any water be put upon the
39 And i· any beast, of which ye may
12: 2 I· a woman have conceived seed,
5 But i· she bear a maid child, then
8 And i· she be not able to bring a
13: 4 I· the bright spot be white in the
5 behold, i· the plague in his sight be at
6 behold, i· the plague be somewhat
7 But i· the scab spread much abroad
8 And i· the priest see that, behold, the
10 behold, i· the rising be white in the
12 And i· a leprosy break out abroad
13 i· the leprosy have covered all his
16 Or i· the raw flesh turn again,
17 i· the plague be turned into white;
20 And i·, when the priest seeth it,
21 But i· the priest look on it, and,
21 and i· it be not lower than the skin,
22 And i· it spread much abroad in
23 But i· the bright spot stay in his
24 Or i· there be any flesh, in the
25 behold, i· the hair in the bright spot
26 But i· the priest look on it, and,
27 and i· it be spread much abroad in
28 And i· the bright spot stay in his
29 I· a man or woman have a
30 behold, i· it be in sight deeper than
31 And i· the priest look on the
32 i· the scall spread not, and there be in
34 i· the scall be not spread in the skin.
35 But i· the scall spread much in
36 i· the scall be spread in the skin, the
37 But i· the scall be in his sight at a
38 I· a man also or a woman have
39 behold, i· the bright spots in the skin,
42 And i· there be in the bald head,
43 i· the rising of the sore be white
49 And i· the plague be greenish or
51 i· the plague be spread in the
53 And i· the priest shall look, and,
55 i· the plague have not changed his
56 And i· the priest look, and, behold,
57 And i· it appear still in the
14: 3 i· the plague of leprosy be healed in
21 And i· he be poor, and cannot get
37 i· the plague be in the walls of the
39 i· the plague be spread in the walls of
43 And i· the plague come again, and
44 i· the plague be spread in the house, it
Le 14:48 And i· the priest shall come in, and
15: 8 And i· he that hath the issue spit
16 And i· any man's seed of copulation
19 And i· a woman have an issue, and
23 And i· it be on her bed, or on
24 And i· any man lie with her at all,
25 And i· a woman have an issue of
25 or i· it run beyond the time of her
28 But i· she be cleansed of her issue,
17:16 But i· he wash them not, nor bathe
18: 5 which i· a man do, he shall live in
19: 5 And i· ye offer a sacrifice of peace
6 and i· ought remain until the third
7 And i· it be eaten at all on the third
33 And i· a stranger sojourn with
20: 4 And i· the people of the land do
12 And i· a man lie with his daughter
13 I· a man also lie with mankind, as
14 And i· a man take a wife and her
15 And i· a man lie with a beast, he
16 And i· a woman approach unto any
17 And i· a man shall take his sister,
18 And i· a man shall lie with a woman
20 And i· a man shall lie with his
21 And i· a man shall take his brother's
21: 9 i· she profane herself by playing
22: 9 i· they profane it: I the Lord do
11 But i· the priest buy any soul with
12 I· the priest's daughter also be
13 But i· the priest's daughter be a
14 And i· a man eat of the holy thing
24:19 And i· a man cause a blemish in
25:14 And i· thou sell ought unto thy
20 And i· ye shall say, What shall we
25 I· thy brother be waxen poor, and
25 and i· any of his kin come to redeem
26 And i· the man have none to
28 But i· he be not able to restore it
29 And i· a man sell a dwelling house
30 And i· it be not redeemed within
33 And i· a man purchase of the
35 And i· thy brother be waxen poor,
39 And i· thy brother that dwelleth by
47 And i· a sojourner or stranger wax
49 or i· he be able, he may redeem
51 I· there be yet many years behind,
52 And i· there remain but few years
54 And i· he be not redeemed in these
26: 3 I· ye walk in my statutes, and keep
14 But i· ye will not hearken unto me,
15 And i· ye shall despise my statutes,
18 And i· ye will not yet for all this
21 And i· ye walk contrary unto me,
23 And i· ye will not be reformed by
27 And i· ye will not for all this
40 I· they shall confess their iniquity,
41 i· then their uncircumcised hearts
27: 4 And i· it be a female, then thy
5 i· it be from five years old even unto
6 i· it be from a month old even unto
7 i· it be from sixty years old and
7 i· it be a male, then thy estimation
8 i· he be poorer than thy estimation
9 i· it be a beast, whereof men bring
10 i· he shall at all change beast for
11 And i· it be any unclean beast, of
13 But i· he will at all redeem it, then
15 And i· he that sanctified it will
16 And i· a man shall sanctify unto
17 I· he sanctify his field from the
18 But i· he sanctify his field after
19 And i· he that sanctified the field
20 And i· he will not redeem the field,
20 i· he have sold the field to another
22 And i· a man sanctify unto the
27 And i· it be of an unclean beast,
27 or i· it be not redeemed, then it
31 And i· a man will at all redeem
33 and i· he change it all, then both it
Nu 5: 8 But i· the man have no kinsman
12 I· any man's wife go aside, and
14 or i· the spirit of jealousy come upon
19 I· no man have lain with thee,
19 and i· thou hast not gone aside to
20 But i· thou hast gone aside to
20 and i· thou be defiled, and some
27 i· she be defiled, and have done
28 And i· the woman be not defiled,
6: 9 And i· any man die very suddenly
9:10 I· any man of you or your posterity
14 And i· a stranger shall sojourn
10: 4 And i· they blow but with one
9 And i· ye go to war in your land
32 i· thou go with us, yea, it shall be,
11:15 And i· thou deal thus with me,
15 i· I have found favour in thy sight;
12: 6 I· there be a prophet among you,
14 I· her father had but spit in her face,
14: 8 I· the Lord delight in us, then
15 Now i· thou shalt kill all this people as
15:14 And i· a stranger sojourn with
22 And i· ye have erred, and not
24 i· ought be committed by ignorance
27 i· any soul sin through ignorance,
16:29 I· these men die the common death
29 or i· they be visited after the visitation
30 But i· the Lord make a new thing
20:19 and i· I and my cattle drink of thy
21: 2 I· thou wilt indeed deliver this
9 that i· a serpent had bitten any man
22:18 I· Balak would give me his house
20 I· the men come to call thee, rise
34 i· it displease thee, I will get me
24:13 I· Balak would give me his house
27: 8 I· a man die, and have no son,
9 And i· he have no daughter, then

Nu 27:10 And i' he have no brethren, then
11 And i' his father have no brethren,
30: 2 I' a man vow a vow unto the
3 I' a woman also vow a vow unto the
5 But i' her father disallow her in
6 And i' she had at all an husband,
8 But i' her husband disallowed her
10 And i' she vowed in her husband's
12 But i' her husband hath utterly
14 But i' her husband altogether hold
15 i' he shall any ways make them void
32: 5 i' we have found grace in thy sight,
15 For i' ye turn away from after
20 I' ye will do this thing, i' ye will go
23 But i' ye will not do so, behold, ye
29 I' the children of Gad and the
30 But i' they will not pass over with
33:55 But i' ye will not drive out the
35:16 i' he smite him with an instrument
17 And i' he smite him with throwing
18 Or i' he smite him with an hand
20 But i' he thrust him of hatred, or
22 But i' he thrust him suddenly
26 But i' the slayer shall at any time
36: 3 And i' they be married to any of the
De 4:29 But i' from thence thou shalt seek the
29 i' thou seek him with all thy heart
30 i' thou turn to the Lord thy God, and
5:25 i' we hear the voice of the Lord
6:25 i' we observe to do all these
7:12 i' ye hearken to these judgments,
17 I' thou shalt say in thine heart,
8:19 i' thou do at all forget the Lord
11:13 i' ye shall hearken diligently unto
22 For i' ye shall diligently keep all
27 i' ye obey the commandments of
28 i' ye will not obey the
12:21 I' the place which the Lord thy
13: 1 I' there arise among you a prophet,
6 I' thy brother, the son of thy
12 I' thou shalt hear say in one of thy
14 i' it be truth, and the thing certain,
14:24 i' the way be too long for thee,
24 or i' the place be too far from thee
15: 5 Only i' thou carefully hearken
7 I' there be among you a poor man
12 And i' thy brother, an Hebrew man,
16 i' he say unto thee, I will not go
21 And i' there be any blemish therein,
21 as i' it be lame, or blind, or have any
17: 2 I' there be found among you,
8 I' there arise a matter too hard for
18: 6 And i' a Levite come from any of
21 And i' thou say in thine heart,
22 i' the thing follow not, nor come to
19: 8 And i' the Lord thy God enlarge
9 I' thou shalt keep all these
11 But i' any man hate his neighbour,
16 I' a false witness rise up against
18 and, behold, i' the witness be a false
20:11 i' it make thee answer of peace, and
12 And i' it will make no peace with
21: 1 I' one be found slain in the land
14 i' thou have no delight in her, then
15 I' a man have two wives, one
15 and i' the firstborn son be hers that
18 I' a man have a stubborn and
22 And i' a man have committed a sin
22: 2 And i' thy brother be not nigh
2 or i' thou know him not, then thou
6 I' a bird's nest chance to be
8 house, i' any man fall from thence.
13 I' any man take a wife, and go in
20 But i' this thing be true, and the
22 I' a man be found lying with a
23 I' a damsel that is a virgin be
25 But i' a man find a betrothed
28 I' a man find a damsel that is a
23:10 I' there be among you any man,
22 But i' thou shalt forbear to vow, it
24: 3 And i' the latter husband hate her,
3 or i' the latter husband die,
7 I' a man be found stealing any of
12 And i' the man be poor, thou shalt
25: 1 I' there be a controversy between
2 i' the wicked man be worthy to be
3 lest, i' he should exceed, and beat
5 I' brethren dwell together, and
7 And i' the man like not to take
8 and i' he stand to it, and say, I like
28: 1 i' thou shalt hearken diligently
2 i' thou shalt hearken unto the
9 i' thou shalt keep...commandments
13 i' that thou hearken unto the
15 i' thou wilt not hearken unto the
58 I' thou wilt not observe to do all
30: 4 I' any of thine be driven out unto
10 I' thou shalt hearken unto the
10 and i' thou turn unto the Lord thy
32:41 I' I whet my glittering sword, and
Jos 2:14 i' ye utter not this our business.
19 our head, i' any hand be upon him.
20 And i' thou utter this our business,
8:15 as i' they were beaten before them,
9: 4 as i' they had been ambassadors, and
14:12 i' so be the Lord will be with me,
17:15 I' thou be a great people, then
15 i' mount Ephraim be too narrow
20: 5 And i' the avenger of blood pursue
22:19 i' the land of your possession be
22 i' it be in rebellion, or i' in
23 or i' to offer thereon burnt offering
23 or i' to offer peace offerings thereon,
24 And i' we have not rather done it for
24:15 And i' it seem evil unto you to serve
20 I' ye forsake the Lord, and serve

J'g 4: 8 I' thou wilt go with me, then I
8 but i' thou wilt not go with me,
6:13 i' the Lord be with us, why then is all
17 I' now I have found grace in thy
31 i' he be a god, let him plead for
36 I' thou wilt save Israel by mine
37 and i' the dew be on the fleece
7:10 But i' thou fear to go down, go thou
8:19 i' ye had saved them alive, I would
9:15 I' in truth ye anoint me king over
15 and i' not, let fire come out of the
16 i' ye have done truly and sincerely,
16 and i' ye have dealt well with
19 I' ye then have dealt truly and
20 But i' not, let fire come out from
36 of the mountains as i' they were men.
11: 9 I' ye bring me home again to fight
10 i' we do not so according to thy
30 I' thou shalt without fail deliver
36 i' thou hast opened thy mouth unto
12: 5 thou an Ephraimite? I' he said, Nay;
13:16 i' thou wilt offer a burnt offering,
23 I' the Lord were pleased to kill
14:12 i' ye can certainly declare it me
13 i' ye cannot declare it me, then
18 I' ye had not ploughed with my
16: 7 I' they bind me with seven green
11 I' they bind me fast with new ropes
13 I' thou weavest the seven locks of
17 i' I be shaven, then my strength will
21:21 i' the daughters of Shiloh come out
Ru 1:12 I' I should say, I have hope, i' I
17 also, i' ought but death part thee
3:13 that i' he will perform unto thee
13 but i' he will not do the part of a
4: 4 I' thou wilt redeem it, redeem it:
4 but i' thou wilt not redeem it, then
1Sa 1:11 i' thou wilt indeed look on the
2:16 And i' any man said unto him, Let
16 me now: and i' not, I will take it
25 I' one man sin against another, the
25 but i' a man sin against the Lord,
3: 9 i' he call thee, that thou shalt say,
17 also, i' thou hide anything from me
6: 3 I' ye send away the ark of the God
9 i' it goeth up by the way of his own
9 but i' not, then we shall know that
7: 3 I' ye do return unto the Lord with
9: 7 behold, i' we go, what shall we
10:22 i' the man should yet come thither.
11: 3 i' there be no man to save us, we
12:14 I' ye will fear the Lord, and serve
15 But i' ye will not obey the voice of
25 But i' ye shall still do wickedly, ye
14: 9 I' they say thus unto us, Tarry
10 But i' they say thus, Come up unto
30 i' haply the people had eaten freely
16: 2 i' Saul hear it, he will kill me. And the
17: 9 I' he be able to fight with me, and
9 but i' I prevail against him, and kill
19:11 saying, I' thou save not thy life
20: 6 I' thy father at all miss me, then
7 I' he say thus, It is well; thy
7 but i' he be very wroth, then be sure
8 i' there be in me iniquity, slay me
9 for i' I knew certainly that evil
10 or what i' thy father answer thee
12 behold, i' there be good toward
13 but i' it please my father to do
21 I' I expressly say unto the lad,
22 But i' I say thus unto the young
29 i' I have found favour in thine eyes,
21: 4 i' the young men have kept
9 i' thou wilt take that, take it; for
23: 3 i' we come to Keilah against the
23 i' he be in the land, that I will
24:19 For i' a man find his enemy, will
25:22 i' I leave of all that pertain to him
26:19 I' the Lord have stirred thee up
19 but i' they be the children of men,
27: 5 I' I have now found grace in thine
2Sa 3:35 i' I taste bread, or ought else, 3588.
7:14 I' he commit iniquity, I will chasten
10:11 I' the Syrians be too strong for
11 i' the children of Ammon be too
11:20 And i' so be that the king's wrath
12: 8 and i' that had been too little, I
18 i' we tell him that the child is dead?
13:26 I' not, I pray thee, let my brother
14:32 and i' there be any iniquity in me,
15: 8 I' the Lord shall bring me again
26 But i' he thus say, I have no delight
33 I' thou passest on with me, then
34 But i' thou return to the city, and
16:23 was as i' a man had enquired at
17: 3 whom thou seekest is as i' all returned:
6 after his saying? i' not; speak thou.
13 Moreover, i' he be gotten into a city,
18: 3 for i' we flee away, they will not
3 neither i' half of us, will they care
25 I' he be alone, there is tidings in
19: 6 that i' Absalom had lived, and all
7 i' thou go not forth, there will not
13 i' thou be not captain of the host
1Ki 1:52 I' he will shew himself a worthy
52 i' wickedness shall be found in him,
2: 4 I' thy children take heed to their
23 i' Adonijah have not spoken this
3:14 And i' thou wilt walk in my ways,
6:12 i' thou wilt walk in my statutes,
8:31 I' any man trespass against his
35 i' they pray toward this place, and
37 I' there be in the land famine,
37 i' there be pestilence, blasting,
37 or i' there be caterpiller; i' their
44 I' thy people go out to battle

1Ki 8:46 I' they sin against thee, (for there
9: 4 And i' thou wilt walk before me, as
6 But i' ye shall at all turn from
11:38 i' thou wilt hearken unto all that I
12: 7 I' thou wilt be a servant unto this
27 I' this people go up to do sacrifice
13: 8 I' thou wilt give me half thine
16:31 as i' it had been a light thing for him to
18:21 i' the Lord be God, follow him: but
21 but i' Baal, then follow him. And
19: 2 i' I make not thy life as the life of
20:39 i' by any means he be missing,
21: 2 or, i' it seem good to thee, I will
6 or else, i' it please thee, I will give
22:28 I' thou return at all in peace, the
2Ki 1:10 I' I be a man of God, then let fire
12 I' I be a man of God, let fire come
2:10 i' thou see me when I am taken
10 unto thee; but i' not, it shall not be
4:29 i' thou meet any man, salute him
29 and i' any salute thee, answer him
5:13 i' the prophet had bid thee do some
6:27 I' the Lord do not help thee, whence
31 i' the head of Elisha the son of
7: 2 i' the Lord would make windows
4 I' we say, We will enter into the
4 and i' we sit still here, we die also.
4 i' they save us alive, we shall live;
4 and i' they kill us, we shall but die:
9 i' we tarry till the morning light,
19 i' the Lord shall make windows in
9:15 I' it be your minds, then let none
10: 6 time to them, saying, I' ye be mine,
6 and i' ye will hearken unto my voice,
15 I' it be, give me thine hand. And he
24 I' any of the men whom I have
18:21 on which i' a man lean, it will go
22 But i' ye say unto me, We trust in
23 i' thou be able on thy part to set
20:19 i' peace and truth be in my days?
21: 8 only i' they will observe to do
1Ch 12:17 I' ye be come peaceably unto me to
17 but i' ye be come to betray me to
13: 2 I' it seem good unto you, and that
19:12 he said, I' the Syrians be too strong
12 but i' the children of Ammon be too
22:13 i' thou takest heed to fulfill the
28: 7 i' he be constant to do my
9 i' thou seek him, he will be found
9 but i' thou forsake him, he will cast
2Ch 6:22 I' a man sin against his neighbour,
24 And i' thy people Israel be put to
28 I' there be a dearth in the land,
28 I' there be pestilence, i' there be
28 i' their enemies besiege them in
32 i' they come and pray in this house;
34 I' thy people go out to war against
36 I' they sin against thee, (for there
37 Yet i' they bethink themselves in the
38 I' they return to thee with all their
7:13 I' I shut up heaven that there be
13 or i' I command the locust to
13 or i' I send pestilence among my
14 I' my people, which are called by my
17 i' thou wilt walk before me, as
19 But i' ye turn away, and forsake my
10: 7 I' thou be kind to this people, and
15: 2 and i' ye seek him, he will be found
2 but i' ye forsake him, he will forsake
18:27 I' thou certainly return in peace,
20: 9 I', when evil cometh upon us, as the
25: 8 But i' thou wilt go, do it, be strong
30: 9 For i' ye turn again unto the Lord,
9 from you, i' ye return unto him.
Ezr 4:13 i' this city be builded, and the
16 i' this city be builded again, and
5:17 i' it seem good to the king, let there
Ne 1: 8 I' ye transgress, I will scatter you
9 But i' ye turn unto me, and keep my
2: 5 I' it please the king, and if thy
7 I' it please the king, let letters be
4: 3 i' a fox go up, he shall even break
9:29 (which i' a man do, he shall live in
10:31 And i' the people of the land bring
13:21 i' ye do so again, I will lay hands
Es 1:19 I' it please the king, let there go a
3: 9 I' it please the king, let it be
4:14 For i' thou altogether holdest thy
16 the law: and i' I perish, I perish.
5: 4 I' it seem good unto the king, let
8 I' I have found favour in the sight
8 and i' it please the king to grant my
6:13 I' Mordecai be of the seed of the
7: 3 and said, I' I have found favour in
3 and i' it please the king, let my life
4 But i' we had been sold for
8: 5 I' it please the king, and i' I have
9:13 I' it please the king, let it be
Job 4: 2 I' we assay to commune with thee,
5: 1 i' there be any that will answer thee;
6:28 for it is evident unto you i' I lie.
8: 4 I' thy children have sinned against
5 I' thou wouldest seek unto God
6 I' thou wert pure and upright;
18 I' he destroy him from his place,
9: 3 I' he will contend with him, he
13 I' God will not withdraw his anger,
16 I' I had called, and he had
19 I' I speak of strength, lo, he is
19 and i' of judgment, who shall set
20 I' I justify myself, mine own mouth
20 i' I say, I am perfect, it shall also
23 I' the scourge slay suddenly, he
24 thereof; i' not, where, and who is he?
27 I' I say, I will forget my complaint,
29 I' I be wicked, why then labour I in

Job 9:30 I' I wash myself with snow water,
10:14 I' I sin, then thou markest me, and
15 I' I be wicked, woe unto me;
15 and i' I be righteous, yet will I not
11:10 I' he cut off, and shut up, or gather
13 I' thou prepare thine heart, and
14 I' iniquity be in thine hand, put it
13:10 i' ye do secretly accept persons.
19 now, i' I hold my tongue, I shall
14:14 I' a man die, shall he live again?
16: 4 i' your soul were in my soul's
17:13 I' I wait, the grave is mine house:
19: 5 I' indeed ye will magnify yourselves
21: 4 and i' it were so, why should not my
22:23 I' thou return to the Almighty,
24:17 i' one know them, they are in the
25 And i' it be not so now, who will
27:14 I' his children be multiplied, it is
29:24 I' I laughed on them, they believed
31: 5 I' I have walked with vanity,
5 or i' my foot hath hasted to deceit;
7 I' my step hath turned out of the
7 and i' any blot hath cleaved to mine
9 I' mine heart have been deceived
9 or i' I have laid wait at my neighbour's
13 I' I did despise the cause of my
16 I' have withheld the poor from their
19 I' I have seen any perish for want
20 I' his loins have not blessed me,
20 and i' he were not warmed with the
21 I' I have lifted up my hand against
24 I' I have made gold my hope, or
25 I' I rejoiced because my wealth was
26 I' I beheld the sun when it shined,
29 I' I rejoiced at the destruction of
31 I' the men of my tabernacle said
33 I' I covered my transgressions as
38 I' my land cry against me, or that
39 I' I have eaten the fruits thereof
33: 5 I' thou canst answer me, set thy
23 I' there be a messenger with him,
27 and i' any say, I have sinned, and
32 I' thou hast anything to say,
33 I' not, hearken unto me: hold thy
34:14 I' he set his heart upon man,
14 i' he gather unto himself his spirit
16 I' now thou hast understanding,
32 i' I have done iniquity, I will do no
35: 3 I have, i' I be cleansed from my sin?
6 I' thou sinnest, what doest thou
6 or i' thy transgressions be multiplied,
7 I' thou be righteous, what givest
36: 8 And i' they be bound in fetters, and
11 I' they obey and serve him, they
12 But i' they obey not, they shall
37:20 i' a man speak, surely he shall be
38: 5 measures thereof, i' thou knowest?
8 as i' it had issued out of the womb?
18 the earth? declare i' thou knowest
Ps 7: 3 O Lord my God, i' I have done this;
3 i' there be iniquity in my hands;
4 I' I have rewarded evil unto him
12 I' he turn not, he will whet his
11: 3 I' the foundations be destroyed,
14: 2 to see i' there were any that did
28: 1 i' thou be silent to me, I become like
40: 5 i' I would declare and speak of them,
41: 6 And i' he come to see me, he
44:20 I' we have forgotten the name of
50:12 I' I were hungry, I would not tell
59:15 and grudge i' they be not satisfied.
66:18 I' I regard iniquity in my heart, the
73:15 I' I say, I will speak thus; behold,
81: 8 Israel, i' thou wilt hearken unto me;
89:30 I' his children forsake my law, and
31 I' they break my statutes, and keep
90:10 and i' by reason of strength they be
95: 7 To day i' ye will hear his voice,
124: 1, 2 I' it had not been the Lord who
130: 3 I' thou, Lord, shouldest mark
132:12 I' thy children will keep my
137: 5 I' I forget thee, O Jerusalem, let my
6 I' I do not remember thee, let my
6 i' I prefer not Jerusalem above my
139: 8 I' I ascend up into heaven, thou art
8 i' I make my bed in hell, behold,
9 I' I take the wings of the morning,
11 I' I say, Surely the darkness shall
18 I' I should count them, they are more
24 And see i' there be any wicked way
Pr 1:10 i' sinners entice thee, consent...not.
11 I' they say, Come with us, let us lay
2: 1 i' thou wilt receive my words, and
3 Yea, i' thou criest after knowledge,
4 I' thou seekest her as silver, and
3:30 without cause, i' he have done thee
6: 1 i' thou be surety for thy friend,
1 i' thou hast stricken thy hand with
31 But i' he be found, he shall restore
9:12 I' thou be wise, thou shalt be wise
12 but i' thou scornest, thou alone shall
16:31 i' it be found in...way of righteousness.
19:19 for i' thou deliver him, yet thou
22:18 pleasant thing i' thou keep them
27 I' thou hast nothing to pay, why
23: 2 i' thou be a man given to appetite.
15 i' thine heart be wise, my heart shalt
24:10 I' thou faint in the day of adversity,
11 I' thou forbear to deliver them that
12 I' thou sayest, Behold, we knew it
25:21 I' thine enemy be hungry, give
21 and i' he be thirsty, give him water
30:32 I' thou hast done foolishly in lifting
32 or i' thou hast thought evil, lay thine
Ec 4:10 For i' they fall, the one will lift up
5: 8 I' thou seest the oppression of the

Ec 6: 3 I' a man beget an hundred children,
10:10 I' the iron be blunt, and he do not
11: 3 I' the clouds be full of rain, they
Ca 1: 8 I' thou know not, O thou fairest
8: 7 i' a man would give all the substance
9 I' she be a wall, we will build upon
Isa 1:19 I' ye be willing and obedient, ye
20 But i' ye refuse and rebel, ye shall
5:30 and i' one look unto the land, behold
7: 9 I' ye will not believe, surely ye
8:20 i' they speak not according to this
10:15 as i' the rod should shake itself
15 or as i' the staff should lift up itself
15 itself, as i' it were no wood.
21:12 i' ye will enquire, enquire ye:
36: 6 whereon i' a man lean, it will go
8 i' thou be able on thy part to set
47:12 i' so be thou shalt be able to profit,
12 i' so be thou mayest prevail.
58: 9 I' thou take away from the midst
10 And i' thou draw out thy soul to the
13 I' thou turn away thy foot from
59:10 and we grope as i' we had no eyes:
66: 3 killeth an ox is as i' he slew a man;
3 lamb, as i' he cut off a dog's neck;
3 as i' he offered swine's blood; he
3 incense, as i' he blessed an idol.
Jer 4: 1 I' thou wilt return, O Israel, saith
5: 1 places thereof, i' ye can find a man,
1 i' there be any that executeth
7: 5 For i' ye throughly amend your
5 i' ye throughly execute judgment
6 I' ye oppress not the stranger, the
12: 5 I' thou hast run with thy footmen,
5 i' in the land of peace, wherein thou
16 i' they will diligently learn the
17 But i' they will not obey, I will
13:17 But i' ye will not hear it, my soul
22 And i' thou say in thine heart,
14:18 I' I go forth into the field, then
18 and i' I enter into the city, then
15: 2 i' they say unto thee, Whither
19 I' thou return, then will I bring
19 and i' thou take forth the precious
17:24 i' ye diligently hearken unto me,
27 But i' ye will not hearken unto me
18: 8 I' that nation, against whom I have
10 I' it do evil in my sight, that it obey
21: 2 i' so be that the Lord will deal
22: 4 For i' ye do this thing indeed, then
5 But i' ye will not hear these words,
26: 3 I' so be they will hearken, and
4 I' ye will not hearken to me,
15 that i' ye put me to death, ye shall
27:18 But i' they be prophets, and i' the
31:36 I' those ordinances depart from
37 I' heaven above can be measured,
33:20 I' ye can break my covenant of the
25 I' my covenant be not with day
25 and i' I have not appointed the
38:15 I' I declare it unto thee, wilt thou
15 i' I give thee counsel, wilt thou not
17 I' thou wilt assuredly go forth unto
18 But i' thou wilt not go forth to
25 But i' the princes hear that I
40: 4 I' it seem good unto thee to come
4 but i' it seem ill unto thee to come
42:10 I' ye will still abide in this land,
13 But i' ye say, We will not dwell in
15 I' ye wholly set your faces to enter
49: 9 I' grapegatherers come to thee,
9 i' thieves by night, they will destroy
51: 8 pain, i' so be she may be healed.
La 1:12 and see i' there be any sorrow like
2: 6 tabernacle, as i' it were of a garden:
3:29 dust; i' so be there may be hope.
Eze 3:19 Yet i' thou warn the wicked, and
21 Nevertheless i' thou warn the
10:10 as i' a wheel had been in the
14: 9 And i' the prophet be deceived
15 I' I cause noisome beasts to pass
17 Or i' I bring a sword upon that land,
19 Or i' I send a pestilence into that
16:47 but, as i' that were a very little thing,
18: 5 But i' a man be just, and do that
10 I' he beget a son that is a robber,
14 Now, lo, i' he beget a son, that
20:11, 13, 21 which i' a man do, he shall
39 i' ye will not hearken unto me:
21:13 and what i' the sword contemn
33: 2 i' the people of the land take a man
3 I' when he seeth the sword come
4 i' the sword come, and take him
6 But i' the watchman see the
6 i' the sword come, and take any
8 i' thou dost not speak to warn the
9 i' thou warn the wicked of his
9 i' he do not turn from his way,
10 I' our transgressions and our
13 i' he trust to his own righteousness,
14 i' he turn from his sin, and do that
15 I' the wicked restore the pledge,
19 But i' the wicked turn from his
43:11 And i' they be ashamed of all that
46:16 I' the prince give a gift unto any
17 But i' he give a gift of his
Da 2: 5 i' ye will not make known unto
6 But i' ye shew the dream, and the
9 But i' ye will not make known
3:15 Now i' ye be ready that at what
15 but i' ye worship not, ye shall be
17 I' it be so, our God whom we serve
4:27 i' it may be the lengthening of thy
5:16 now i' thou canst read the writing,
Ho 6: 3 i' we follow on to know the Lord:
8: 7 i' so be it yield, the strangers shall

Joe 2:14 Who knoweth i' he will return and
3: 4 and i' ye recompense me, swiftly
Am 3: 4 out of his den, i' he have taken
5:19 As i' a man did flee from a lion,
6: 9 i' there remain ten men in one
Ob 5 I' thieves came to thee,
5 i' robbers by night, how art thou
5 i' the grapegatherers came to thee,
Jon 1: 6 i' so be that God will think upon
3: 9 Who can tell i' God will turn and
Mic 2:11 I' a man walking in the spirit
5: 8 who, i' he go through, both
Na 3:12 i' they be shaken, they shall even
Hag 2:12 I' one bear holy flesh in the skirt
13 I' one that is unclean by a dead
Zec 3: 7 I' thou wilt walk in my ways, and
7 and i' thou wilt keep my charge,
8: 6 I' it be marvellous in the eyes of
11:12 I' ye think good, give me my price;
12 and i' not forbear. So they weighed
Mal 1: 6 i' then I be a father, where is mine
6 and i' I be a master, where is my
8 And i' ye offer the blind for
8 and i' ye offer the lame and sick,
2: 2 I' ye will not hear, and i' ye will
3:10 i' I will not open you the windows of
M't 4: 3 I' thou be the Son of God, command
6 I' thou be the Son of God, cast
9 i' thou wilt fall down and worship
5:13 but i' the salt have lost his savour,
23 Therefore i' thou bring thy gift to the
29 And i' thy right eye offend thee,
30 And i' thy right hand offend thee, cut
46 For i' ye love them which love you,
47 And i' ye salute your brethren only,
6:14 For i' ye forgive men their
15 But i' ye forgive not men their
22 i' therefore thine eye be single,
23 But i' thine eye be evil, thy whole
23 I' therefore the light that is in
30 Wherefore, i' God so clothed the
7: 9 i' his son ask bread, will he give
10 Or i' he ask a fish, will he give him
11 I' ye then, being evil, know how to
8: 2 i' thou wilt, thou canst make me
31 I' thou cast us out, suffer us to
9:21 I' I may but touch his garment,
10:13 And i' the house be worthy, let
13 but i' it be not worthy, let your
25 I' they have called the master of
11:14 And i' ye will receive it, this is
21 for i' the mighty works, which
23 for i' the mighty works, which
12: 7 But i' ye had known what this
11 and i' it fall into a pit on the
26 And i' Satan cast out Satan, he
27 And i' I by Beelzebub cast out
28 But i' I cast out devils by the Spirit
14:28 Lord, i' it be thou, bid me come
15:14 And i' the blind lead the blind,
16:24 I' any man will come after me, let
17: 4 i' thou wilt, let us make here three
20 I' ye have faith as a grain of
18: 8 Wherefore i' thy hand or thy foot
9 And i' thine eye offend thee, pluck
12 i' a man have an hundred sheep,
13 And i' so be that he find it, verily
15 Moreover i' thy brother shall
15 i' he shall hear thee, thou hast
16 But i' he will not hear thee, then
17 And i' he shall neglect to hear them,
17 but i' he neglect to hear the church,
19 That i' two of you shall agree on
35 i' ye from your hearts forgive not
19:10 I' the case of the man be so with
17 but i' thou wilt enter into life, keep
21 I' thou wilt be perfect, go and sell
21: 3 And i' any man say ought unto
21 I' ye have faith, and doubt not, ye
21 but also i' ye shall say unto this
24 which i' ye tell me, I in like wise
25 I' we shall say, From heaven; he
26 But i' we shall say, Of men; we
22:24 Moses said, I' a man die, having
45 I' David then call him Lord, how
23:30 I' we had been in the days of our
24:23 Then i' any man shall say unto
24 i' it were possible, they shall
26 Wherefore i' they shall say unto
43 that i' the goodman of the house
48 But and i' that evil servant shall
26:24 good for that man i' he had not
39 i' it be possible, let this cup pass
42 i' this cup may not pass away from
27:40 I' thou be the Son of God, come
42 I' he be the King of Israel, let
43 i' he will have him: for he said, I
28:14 And i' this come to the governor's
M'r 1:40 I' thou wilt, thou canst make me
3:24 i' a kingdom be divided against
25 And i' a house be divided against
26 i' Satan rise up against himself,
4:23 I' any man have ears to hear, let him
26 as i' a man should cast seed into
5:28 I' I may touch but his clothes, I
6:56 touch i' it were but the border of
7:11 I' a man shall say to his father or
8: 3 And i' I send them away fasting to
36 i' he shall gain the whole world,
9:23 I' thou canst believe, all things
35 I' any man desire to be first, the
43 i' thy hand offend thee, cut it off:
45 And i' thy foot offend thee, cut it off:
47 i' thine eye offend thee, pluck it out:
50 i' the salt have lost his saltness,
10:12 And i' a woman shall put away her

M'r 11: 3 i' any man say unto you, Why do
13 i' haply he might find any thing
25 forgive, i' ye have ought against
26 But i' ye do not forgive, neither
31 I' we shall say, From heaven; he
32 I' we shall say, Of men; they feared
12:19 I' a man's brother die, and leave
13:21 then i' any man shall say to you,
22 to seduce, i' it were possible, even
14:21 that man i' he had never been born.
31 I' I should die with thee, I will not
35 and prayed that, i' it were possible,
15:44 marvelled i' he were already dead:
16:18 and i' they drink any deadly thing,
Lu 4: 3 I' thou be the Son of God,
7 I' thou therefore wilt worship me,
9 I' thou be the Son of God, cast
5:12 i' thou wilt, thou canst make me
36 i' otherwise, then both the new
6:32 For i' ye love them which love you,
33 And i' ye do good to them which
34 i' ye lend to them of whom ye hope
7:39 This man, i' he were a prophet,
9:23 I' any man will come after me, let
25 i' he gain the whole world, and lose
10: 6 And i' the son of peace be there,
6 i' not, it shall turn to you again.
13 i' the mighty works had been done
11:11 I' a son shall ask bread of any of you
11 i' he ask a fish, will he for a fish give
12 i' he shall ask an egg, will he offer
13 I' ye then, being evil, know how to
18 I' Satan also be divided against
19 i' I by Beelzebub cast out devils, by
20 But i' I with the finger of God cast
36 I' thy whole body therefore be full
12:26 I' ye then be not able to do that
28 I' then God so clothe the grass,
38 And i' he shall come in the second
39 that i' the goodman of the house
45 But and i' that servant say in his
49 will I, i' it be already kindled?
13: 9 And i' it bear fruit, well: and
9 and i' not, then after that thou
14:34 but i' the salt have lost his savour,
15: 4 i' he lose one of them, doth not leave
8 i' she lose one piece, doth not light
16:11 I' therefore ye have not been
12 And i' ye have not been faithful in
30 but i' one went unto them from the
31 I' they hear not Moses and the
17: 3 I' thy brother trespass against
3 and i' he repent, forgive him.
4 i' he trespass against thee seven
6 I' ye had faith as a grain of
19: 8 and i' I have taken any thing from
31 And i' any man ask you, Why do
40 i' these should hold their peace, the
42 I' thou hadst known, even thou,
20: 5 I' we shall say, From heaven; he
6 But and i' we say, Of men; all the
28 I' any man's brother die, having a
22:42 i' thou be willing, remove this cup
67 I' I tell you, ye will not believe:
68 And i' I also ask you, ye will not
23:31 i' they do these things in a green
35 himself, i' he be Christ, the chosen
37 I' thou be the king of the Jews, save
39 I' thou be Christ, save thyself and
Joh 1:25 i' thou be not that Christ, nor Elias,
3:12 I' I have told you earthly things,
12 i' I tell you of heavenly things?
4:10 I' thou knewest the gift of God,
5:31 I' I bear witness of myself, my
43 i' another shall come in his own
47 But i' ye believe not his writings,
6:51 i' any man eat of this bread, he
62 What and i' ye shall see the Son
7: 4 I' thou do these things, shew
17 I' any man will do his will, he
23 I' a man on the sabbath day
37 I' any man thirst, let him come
8:16 And yet i' I judge, my judgment is
19 i' ye had known me, ye should
24 for i' ye believe not that I am he,
31 I' ye continue in my word, then
36 I' the Son therefore shall make you
39 I' ye were Abraham's children,
42 I' God were your Father, ye would
46 i' I say the truth, why do ye not
51, 52 I' a man keep my saying, he
54 I' I honour myself, my honour is
55 and i' I should say, I know him not
9:22 that i' any man did confess that he
31 but i' any man be a worshipper of
33 I' this man were not of God, he
41 I' ye were blind, ye should have
10: 9 by me i' any man enter in, he shall
24 I' thou be the Christ, tell us
35 I' he called them gods, unto whom
37 I' I do not the works of my Father,
38 But i' I do, though ye believe not
11: 9 I' any man walk in the day, he
10 But i' a man walk in the night, he
12 Lord, i' he sleep, he shall do well.
21, 32 i' thou hadst been here, my brother
40 i' thou wouldest believe, thou
48 I' we let him thus alone, all men
57 i' any man knew where he were, he
12:24 but i' it die, it bringeth forth much
26 I' any man serve me, let him follow
26 i' any man serve me, him will my
32 I, i' I be lifted up from the earth,
47 And i' any man hear my words, and
13: 8 I' I wash thee not, thou hast no part
14 I' I then, your Lord and Master,
Joh 13:17 I' ye know these things,
17 happy are ye i' ye do them.
32 I' God be glorified in him, God
35 disciples, i' ye have love one to
14: 2 i' it were not so, I would have told
3 And i' I go and prepare a place
7 I' ye had known me, ye should
14 I' ye shall ask any thing in my
15 I' ye love me, keep my
23 I' a man love me, he will keep my
28 I' ye loved me, ye would rejoice,
15: 6 I' a man abide not in me, he is cast
7 I' ye abide in me, and my words
10 I' ye keep my commandments, ye
14 my friends, i' ye do whatsoever I
18 I' the world hate you, ye know
19 I' ye were of the world, the world
20 I' they have persecuted me, they
20 i' they have kept my saying, they
22 I' I had not come and spoken unto
24 I' I had not done among them the
16: 7 for i' I go not away, the Comforter
7 i' I depart, I will send him unto
18: 8 i' therefore ye seek me, let these go
23 I' I have spoken evil, bear witness
23 but i' well, why smitest thou me?
30 I' he were not a malefactor, we
36 i' my kingdom were of this world,
19:12 I' thou let this man go, thou art
20:15 i' thou have borne him hence, tell
21:22 I' I will that he tarry till I come,
23 but, I' I will that he tarry till I
25 i' they should be written every one,
Ac 4: 9 I' we this day be examined of the
5:38 for i' this counsel or this work be
39 But i' it be of God, ye cannot
8:22 i' perhaps the thought of thine
37 I' thou believest with all thine
9: 2 that i' he found any of this way,
13:15 i' ye have any word of exhortation
15:29 from which i' ye keep yourselves, ye
16:15 I' ye have judged me to be faithful
17:27 i' haply they might feel after him,
18:14 I' it were a matter of wrong or
15 But i' it be a question of words and
21 will return again unto you, i' God will.
19:38 Wherefore i' Demetrius, and the
39 i' ye enquire any thing concerning
20:16 i' it were possible for him, to be at
23: 9 i' a spirit or an angel hath spoken
24:19 i' they had ought against me.
20 i' they have found any evil doing
25: 5 i' there be any wickedness in him.
11 For i' I be an offender, or have
11 but i' there be none of these things
26: 5 i' they would testify, that after
32 i' he had not appealed unto Cæsar.
27:12 i' by any means they might attain
39 i' it were possible, to thrust in
Ro 1:10 i' by any means now at length I
2:25 profiteth, i' thou keep the law:
25 but i' thou be a breaker of the law,
26 Therefore i' the uncircumcision
27 i' it fulfil the law, judge thee, who
3: 3 For what i' some do not believe?
5 i' our unrighteousness commend
7 For i' the truth of God hath more
4: 2 For i' Abraham were justified by
14 For i' they which are of the law be
24 i' we believe on him that raised up
5:10 For i', when we were enemies, we
15 For i' through the offence of one
17 For i' by one man's offence death
6: 5 i' we have been planted together
8 Now i' we be dead with Christ, we
7: 2 but i' the husband be dead, she
3 So then i', while her husband liveth,
3 but i' her husband be dead, she is
16 I' then I do that which I would
20 Now i' I do that I would not, it is
8: 9 i' so be that the Spirit of God
9 Now i' any man have not the Spirit
10 And i' Christ be in you, the body
11 But i' the Spirit of him that raised
13 For i' ye live after the flesh, ye
13 but i' ye through the Spirit do
17 And i' children, then heirs; heirs
17 i' so be that we suffer with him,
25 But i' we hope for that we see not,
31 I' God be for us, who can be
9:22 What i' God, willing to shew his
10: 9 That i' thou shalt confess with
11: 6 And i' by grace, then is it no more
6 But i' it be of works, then is it no
12 Now i' the fall of them be the riches
14 I' by any means I may provoke
15 For i' the casting away of them be
16 For i' the firstfruit be holy, the
16 and i' the root be holy, so are the
17 And i' some of the branches be
18 But i' thou boast, thou bearest
21 For i' God spared not the natural
22 i' thou continue in his goodness:
23 i' they abide not still in unbelief,
24 For i' thou wert cut out of the
12:18 I' it be possible, as much as lieth
20 Therefore i' thine enemy hunger,
20 i' he thirst, give him drink: for in
13: 4 But i' thou do that which is evil,
9 and i' there be any other
14:15 But i' thy brother be grieved with
23 is damned i' he eat, because he
15:24 i' first I be somewhat filled with
27 For i' the Gentiles have been made
1Co 3:12 Now i' any man build upon this
14 I' any man's work abide which
1Co 3:15 I' any man's work shall be burned,
17 I' any man defile the temple of
18 I' any man among you seemeth to
4: 7 now i' thou didst receive it, why
7 glory, as i' thou hadst not received it?
19 to you shortly, i' the Lord will,
5:11 i' any man that is called a brother
6: 2 and i' the world shall be judged
4 I' then ye have judgments of
7: 8 It is good for them i' they abide
9 But i' they cannot contain, let
11 But and i' she depart, let her
12 i' any brother hath a wife that
13 and i' he be pleased to dwell with her,
15 But i' the unbelieving depart, let
21 but i' thou mayest be made free,
28 But and i' thou marry, thou hast
28 and i' a virgin marry, she hath not
36 But i' any man think that he
36 i' she pass the flower of her age,
39 but i' her husband be dead, she is
40 But she is happier i' she so abide,
8: 2 And i' any man think that he
3 But i' any man love God, the same
8 for neither, i' we eat, are we the
8 neither, i' we eat not, are we the
10 For i' any man see thee which hast
13 i' meat make my brother to offend,
9: 2 I' I be not an apostle unto others,
11 I' we have sown unto you spiritual
11 i' we shall reap your carnal things?
12 I' others be partakers of this
16 unto me, i' I preach not the gospel!
17 For i' I do this thing willingly, I
17 i' against my will, a dispensation
10:27 I' any of them that believe not
28 But i' any man say unto you, This
30 For i' I by grace be a partaker,
11: 5 is even all one as i' she were shaven.
6 For i' the woman be not covered,
6 but i' it be a shame for a woman
14 i' a man have long hair, it is a
15 But i' a woman have long hair, it is
16 But i' any man seem to be
31 For i' we would judge ourselves,
34 i' any man hunger, let him eat at
12:15 I' the foot shall say, Because I
16 And i' the ear shall say, Because I
17 I' the whole body were an eye,
17 I' the whole were hearing, where
19 And i' they were all one member,
14: 6 i' I come unto you speaking with
8 i' the trumpet give an uncertain
11 Therefore i' I know not the meaning
14 For i' I pray in an unknown tongue,
23 I' therefore the whole church be
24 But i' all prophesy, and there come
27 I' any man speak in an unknown
28 But i' there be no interpreter,
30 I' any thing be revealed to another
35 And i' they will learn any thing,
37 I' any man think himself to be a
38 But i' any man be ignorant,
15: 2 saved, i' ye keep in memory what I
12 Now i' Christ be preached that he
13 But i' there be no resurrection of
14 And i' Christ be not risen, then is
15 i' so be that the dead rise not.
16 For i' the dead rise not, then is
17 And i' Christ be not raised, your
19 I' in this life only we have hope in
29 the dead, i' the dead rise not at all?
32 I' after the manner of men I have
32 what advantageth it me, i' the dead
16: 4 And i' it be meet that I go also,
7 while with you, i' the Lord permit.
10 Now i' Timotheus come, see that
22 I' any man love not the Lord Jesus
2Co 2: 2 For i' I make you sorry, who is he
5 But i' any have caused grief,
10 for i' I forgave any thing, to whom
3: 7 But i' the ministration of death,
9 For i' the ministration of
11 For i' that which is done away was
4: 3 But i' our gospel be hid, it is hid
5: 1 For we know that i' our earthly
3 I' so be that being clothed we
14 that i' one died for all, then were
17 Therefore i' any man be in Christ,
7:14 For i' I have boasted any thing to
8:12 For i' there be first a willing mind,
9: 4 Lest haply i' they of Macedonia
10: 2 as i' we walked according to the flesh.
7 I' any man trust to himself that
9 as i' I would terrify you by letters.
11: 4 For i' he that cometh preacheth
4 or i' ye receive another spirit, which
15 i' his ministers also be transformed
16 i' otherwise, yet as a fool receive
20 i' a man bring you into bondage,
20 i' a man devour you, i' a man take
20 i' a man exalt himself, i' a man
30 I' I must needs glory, I will glory
13: 2 as i' I were present, the second
2 that, i' I come again, I will not spare:
Ga 1: 9 I' any man preach any other gospel
10 for i' I yet pleased men, I should
2:14 I' thou, being a Jew, livest after
17 But i', while we seek to be justified
18 For i' I build again the things which
21 i' righteousness come by the law,
3: 4 in vain? i' it be yet in vain.
15 yet i' it be confirmed, no man
18 For i' the inheritance be of the law
21 for i' there had been a law given
29 And i' ye be Christ's, then are ye

Ga 4: 7 and *i·* a son, then an heir of God
15 that, *i·* it had been possible, ye
5: 2 that *i·* ye be circumcised, Christ
11 *i·* I yet preach circumcision, why
15 But *i·* ye bite and devour one
18 But *i·* ye be led of the Spirit, ye are
25 *I·* we live in the Spirit, let us also
6: 1 *i·* a man be overtaken in a fault,
3 For *i·* a man think himself to be
9 season we shall reap, *i·* we faint not.
Eph 3: 2 *I·* ye have heard of the
4: 21 *I·* so be that ye have heard him,
Ph'p 1: 22 But *i·* I live in the flesh, this is
2: 1 *I·* there be...any consolation in
1 *i·* any comfort of love,
1 *i·* any fellowship of the Spirit,
1 *i·* any bowels and mercies,
17 Yea, and *i·* I be offered upon the
3: 4 *I·* any other man thinketh that he
11 *I·* by any means I might attain
12 *i·* that I may apprehend that for
15 *i·* in any thing ye be otherwise
4: 8 good report; *i·* there be any virtue,
8 and *i·* there be any praise, think on
Col 1: 23 *I·* ye continue in the faith
2: 20 Wherefore *i·* ye be dead with
3: 1 *I·* ye then be risen with Christ,
13 *i·* any man have a quarrel against
4: 10 *i·* he come unto you, receive him;
1Th 3: 8 For now we live, *i·* ye stand fast in
4: 14 For *i·* we believe that Jesus died
2Th 3: 10 that *i·* any would not work, neither
14 And *i·* any man obey not our word
1Ti 1: 8 is good, *i·* a man use it lawfully;
10 and *i·* there be any other thing
2: 15 *i·* they continue in faith and
3: 1 *I·* a man desire the office of a
5 For *i·* a man know not how to
15 But *i·* I tarry long, that thou mayest
4: 4 *i·* it be received with thanksgiving:
6 *I·* thou put the brethren in
5: 4 *i·* any widow have children or
8 But *i·* any provide not for his own,
10 *i·* she have brought up children
10 *i·* she have lodged strangers,
10 *i·* she have washed the saints' feet,
10 *i·* she have relieved the afflicted,
10 *i·* she have diligently followed every
16 *I·* any man or woman that
6: 3 *I·* any man teach otherwise, and
2Ti 2: 5 *i·* a man also strive for masteries,
11 For *i·* we be dead with him, we
12 *I·* we suffer, we shall also reign
12 *i·* we deny him, he also will deny
13 *I·* we believe not, yet he abideth
21 *I·* a man therefore purge himself
25 *i·* God peradventure will give them
Tit 1: 6 *I·* any be blameless, the husband of
Ph'm 17 *I·* thou count me therefore a
18 *I·* he hath wronged thee, or oweth
Heb 2: 2 For *i·* the word spoken by angels
3 *i·* we neglect so great salvation;
3: 6 *i·* we hold fast the confidence and
7 To day *i·* ye will hear his voice,
14 *i·* we hold the beginning of our
15 To day *i·* ye will hear his voice,
4: 3 *i·* they shall enter into my rest:
5 *I·* they shall enter into my rest.
7 To day *i·* ye will hear his voice,
8 For *i·* Jesus had given them rest,
6: 3 And this will we do, *i·* God permit.
6 *I·* they shall fall away, to renew
7: 11 *I·* therefore perfection were by
8: 4 For *i·* he were on earth, he should
7 For *i·* that first covenant had been
9: 13 For *i·* the blood of bulls and of
10: 26 For *i·* we sin wilfully after that we
38 but *i·* any man draw back, my soul
11: 15 *i·* they had been mindful of that
12: 7 *I·* ye endure chastening, God
8 But *i·* ye be without chastisement,
20 And *i·* so much as a beast touch the
25 for *i·* they escaped not who refused
25 *i·* we turn away from him that
13: 23 *i·* he come shortly, I will see you.
Jas 1: 5 *I·* any of you lack wisdom, let him
23 For *i·* any be a hearer of the word,
26 *I·* any man among you seem to be
2: 2 *i·* there come unto your assembly
8 *I·* ye fulfil the royal law according
9 But *i·* ye have respect to persons,
11 Now *i·* thou commit no adultery,
11 yet *i·* thou kill, thou art become a
15 *I·* a brother or sister be naked,
17 *i·* it hath not works, is dead,
3: 2 *I·* any man offend not in word,
14 But *i·* ye have bitter envying and
4: 11 but *i·* thou judge the law, thou art
15 *I·* the Lord will, we shall live, and
5: 15 and *i·* he have committed sins, they
19 Brethren, *i·* any of you do err from
1Pe 1: 6 *i·* need be, ye are in heaviness
17 And *i·* ye call on the Father, who
2: 3 *I·* so be ye have tasted that the
19 *i·* a man for conscience toward God
20 *i·*, when ye be buffeted for your
20 *i·*, when ye do well, and suffer for
3: 1 that, *i·* any obey not the word, they
13 *i·* ye be followers of that which is
14 and *i·* ye suffer for righteousness' sake,
17 *i·* the will of God be so, that ye
4: 11 *I·* any man speak, let him speak
11 *i·* any man minister, let him do it
14 *I·* ye be reproached for the name
16 Yet *i·* any man suffer as a Christian,
17 and *i·* it first begin at us, what
1Pe 4: 18 And *i·* the righteous scarcely be
2Pe 1: 8 For *i·* these things be in you, and
10 for *i·* ye do these things, ye shall never
2: 4 For *i·* God spared not the angels
20 For *i·* after they have escaped the
1Jo 1: 6 *I·* we say that we have fellowship
7 But *i·* we walk in the light, as he is
8 *I·* we say that we have no sin, we
9 *I·* we confess our sins, he is
10 *I·* we say that we have not sinned,
2: 1 And *i·* any man sin, we have an
3 *i·* we keep his commandments.
15 *I·* any man love the world, the love
19 for *i·* they had been of us, they
24 *I·* that which ye have heard from
29 *I·* ye know that he is righteous, ye
3: 13 my brethren, *i·* the world hate you
20 For *i·* our heart condemn us, God
21 *i·* our heart condemn us not,
4: 11 Beloved, *i·* God so loved us, we
12 *I·* we love one another, God
20 *I·* a man say, I love God, and
5: 9 *I·* we receive the witness of men,
14 *i·* we ask any thing according to
15 And *i·* we know that he hear us,
16 *I·* any man see his brother sin a
2Jo 10 *I·* there come any unto you, and
3Jo 6 whom *i·* thou bring forward on their
10 *i·* I come, I will remember his
Re 1: 15 brass, as *i·* they burned in a furnace;
3: 3 *I·* therefore thou shalt not
20 *i·* any man hear my voice, and open
11: 5 And *i·* any man will hurt them,
5 and *i·* any man will hurt them, he
13: 9 *I·* any man have an ear, let him
14: 9 *I·* any man worship the beast and
22: 18 *I·* any man shall add unto these
19 And *i·* any man shall take away

Igal (*i'-gal*) See also IGEAL.
Nu 13: 7 Issachar, *I·* the son of Joseph.
2Sa 23: 36 *I·* the son of Nathan of Zobah,

Igdaliah (*ig-da-li'-ah*)
Jer 35: 4 of *I·*, a man of God, which was

Igeal (*ig'-e-al*) See also IGAL.
1Ch 3: 22 Hattush, and *I·*, and Bariah, and

ignominy
Pr 18: 3 contempt, and with *i·* reproach.

ignorance
Le 4: 2 If a soul shall sin through *i·*
13 of Israel sin through *i·*,
22 done somewhat through *i·*
27 common people sin through *i·*,
5: 15 a trespass, and sin through *i·*,
18 his *i·* wherein he erred and wist it
Nu 15: 24 if ought be committed by *i·*
25 shall be forgiven them; for it is *i·*:
25 before the Lord, for their *i·*:
26 seeing all the people were in *i·*.
27 if any soul sin through *i·*, then he
28 he sinneth by *i·* before the Lord,
29 for him that sinneth through *i·*,
Ac 3: 17 brethen, I wot that through *i·* ye did
17: 30 the times of this *i·* God winked at;
Eph 4: 18 God through the *i·* that is in them,
1Pe 1: 14 to the former lusts in your *i·*:
2: 15 to silence the *i·* of foolish men:

ignorant
Ps 73: 22 So foolish was I, and *i·*: I was
Isa 56: 10 they are all *i·*, they are all
63: 16 though Abraham be *i·* of us,
Ac 4: 13 they were unlearned and *i·* men,
Ro 1: 13 Now I would not have you *i·*,
10: 3 For they being *i·* of God's
11: 25 that ye should be *i·* of this mystery,
1Co 10: 1 I would not that ye should be *i·*,
12: 1 brethren, I would not have you *i·*.
14: 38 if any man be *i·*, let him be *i·*.
2Co 1: 8 would not, brethren, have you *i·* of
2: 11 of us: for we are not *i·* of his devices.
1Th 4: 13 But I would not have you to be *i·*,
Heb 5: 2 Who can have compassion on the *i·*,
2Pe 3: 5 For this they willingly are *i·* of
8 beloved, be not *i·* of this one thing,

ignorantly
Nu 15: 28 for the soul that sinneth *i·*, when
De 19: 4 Whoso killeth...neighbour *i·*,
Ac 17: 23 Whom therefore ye *i·* worship, him
1Ti 1: 13 mercy, because I did it *i·* in unbelief.

Iim (*i'-im*) See also IJE-ABARIM.
Nu 33: 45 And they departed from *I·*, and
Jos 15: 29 Baalah, and *I·*, and Azem,

Ije-abarim (*i''-je-ab'-a-rim*) See also IIM.
Nu 21: 11 and pitched at *I·*, in the
33: 44 and pitched in *I·*, in the border

Ijon (*i'-jon*)
1Ki 15: 20 and smote *I·*, and Dan, and
2Ki 15: 29 took *I·*, and Abel-beth-maachah,
2Ch 16: 4 and they smote *I·*, and Dan, and

Ikkesh (*ik'-kesh*)
2Sa 23: 26 Ira the son of *I·* the Tekoite,
1Ch 11: 28 Ira the son of *I·* the Tekoite,
27: 9 sixth month was Ira the son of *I·*

Ilai (*i'-lahee*) See also ZALMON.
1Ch 11: 29 the Hushathite, *I·* the Ahohite,

ill
Ge 41: 3 them out of the river, *i·* favoured
4 the *i·* favoured and leanfleshed kine
19 up after them, poor and very *i·*
20 the lean and the *i·* favoured kine
Ge 41: 21 they were still *i·* favoured, as at
27 the seven thin and *i·* favoured kine
43: 6 dealt so *i·* with me, as to tell
De 15: 21 blind, or have any *i·* blemish,
Job 20: 26 it shall go *i·* with him that is left
Ps 106: 32 so that it went *i·* with Moses for
Isa 3: 11 it shall be *i·* with him: for the
Jer 40: 4 if it seem *i·* unto thee to come
Joel 2: 20 and his *i·* savour shall come up,
Mic 3: 4 they have behaved themselves *i·*
Ro 13: 10 Love worketh no *i·* to his

ill-favoured See ILL and FAVOURED.

illuminated
Heb10: 32 in which, after ye were *i·*, ye

Illyricum (*il-lir'-ic-um*)
Ro 15: 19 and round about unto *I·*, I have

image See also IMAGE'S; IMAGES.
Ge 1: 26 said, Let us make man in our *i·*,
27 God created man in his own *i·*,
27 in the *i·* of God created he him;
5: 3 in his own likeness, after his *i·*;
9: 6 for in the *i·* of God made he man.
Ex 20: 4 not make unto thee any graven *i·*,
Le 26: 1 make you no idols nor graven *i·*,
1 neither rear you up a standing *i·*,
1 neither shall ye set up any *i·* of
De 4: 16 and make you a graven *i·*, the
23 and make you a graven *i·*, or the
25 and make a graven *i·*, or the
5: 8 shalt not make thee any graven *i·*,
9: 12 they have made them a molten *i·*.
16: 22 shalt thou set thee up any *i·*;
27: 15 maketh any graven or molten *i·*,
J'g 17: 3 for my son, to make a graven *i·*
3 and a molten *i·*: now therefore I
4 thereof a graven *i·*, and a molten *i·*:
18: 14 and a graven *i·* and a molten *i·*?
17 and took the graven *i·*, and the
17 teraphim, and the molten *i·*: and the
18 and fetched the carved *i·*, the ephod,
18 the teraphim, and the molten *i·*,
20 the teraphim, and the graven *i·*,
30 children of Dan set up the graven *i·*:
31 them up Micah's graven *i·*, which
1Sa 19: 13 Michal took an *i·*, and laid it in
16 behold, there was an *i·* in the bed,
2Ki 3: 2 he put away the *i·* of Baal that
10: 27 they brake down the *i·* of Baal, and
21: 7 he set a graven *i·* of the grove that he
2Ch 3: 10 he made two cherubims of *i·* work,
33: 7 And he set a carved *i·*, the idol
Job 4: 16 an *i·* was before mine eyes, there
Ps 73: 20 thou shalt despise their *i·*.
106: 19 Horeb, and worshipped the molten *i·*.
Isa 40: 19 The workman melteth a graven *i·*,
20 workman to prepare a graven *i·*,
44: 9 They that make a graven *i·* are all
10 formed a god, or molten a graven *i·*
15 he maketh it a graven *i·*, and falleth
17 he maketh a god, even his graven *i·*:
45: 20 set up the wood of their graven *i·*,
48: 5 hath done them, and my graven *i·*,
5 and my molten *i·*, hath commanded
Jer 10: 14 is confounded by the graven *i·*:
14 for his molten *i·* is falsehood, and
51: 17 is confounded by the graven *i·*:
17 for his molten *i·* is falsehood, and
Eze 8: 3 was the seat of the *i·* of jealousy,
5 altar this *i·* of jealousy in the entry.
Da 2: 31 king, sawest, and behold a great *i·*.
31 This great *i·*, whose brightness was
34 which smote the *i·* upon his feet,
35 and the stone that smote the *i·*
3: 1 the king made an *i·* of gold, whose
2 to the dedication of the *i·* which
3 unto the dedication of the *i·* that
3 set up; and they stood before the *i·*
5 fall down and worship the golden *i·*
7 down and worshipped the golden *i·*
10 fall down and worship the golden *i·*:
12 nor worship the golden *i·* which
14 nor worship the golden *i·* which I
15 fall down and worship the *i·* which
18 nor worship the golden *i·* which
Ho 3: 4 and without an *i·*, and without an
Na 1: 14 cut off the graven *i·* and the molten *i·*:
Hab 2: 18 What profiteth the graven *i·* that
18 the molten *i·*, and a teacher of lies,
M't 22: 20 Whose is this *i·* and superscription?
M'r 12: 16 Whose is this *i·* and superscription?
Lu 20: 24 Whose *i·* and superscription hath
Ac 19: 35 *i·* which fell down from Jupiter?
Ro 1: 23 into an *i·* made like to corruptible
8: 29 conformed to the *i·* of his Son, that
11: 4 not bowed the knee to the *i·* of Baal.
1Co 11: 7 as he is the *i·* and glory of God:
15: 49 as we have borne the *i·* of the earthy,
49 also bear the *i·* of the heavenly.
2Co 3: 18 changed into the same *i·* from glory
4: 4 gospel of Christ, who is the *i·* of God,
Col 1: 15 Who is the *i·* of the invisible God,
3: 10 after the *i·* of him that created him:
Heb 1: 3 and the express *i·* of his person,
10: 1 not the very image of the things,
Re 13: 14 they should make an *i·* to the beast,
15 to give life unto the *i·* of the beast,
15 *i·* of the beast should both speak,
15 not worship the *i·* of the beast
14: 9 man worship the beast and his *i·*,
11 who worship the beast and his *i·*,
15: 2 victory over the beast, and over his *i·*,
16: 2 upon them which worshipped his *i·*.
19: 20 and them that worshipped his *i·*.
20: 4 worshipped the beast, neither his *i·*,

imagery
Eze 8:12 man in the chambers of his *i*?
image's
Da 2:32 This *i* head was of fine gold,
images
Ge 31:19 Rachel had stolen the *i* that were
34 Rachel had taken the *i*, and put
35 he searched, but found not the *i*.
Ex 23:24 and quite break down their *i*.
34:13 break their *i*, and cut down their
Le 26:30 cut down your *i*, and cast your
Nu 33:52 destroy all their molten *i*, and
De 7: 5 and break down their *i*, and cut
5 and burn their graven *i* with fire.
25 The graven *i* of their gods shall ye
12: 3 ye shall hew down the graven *i* of
1Sa 6: 5 ye shall make *i* of your emerods,
5 and *i* of your mice that mar the
11 of gold and the *i* of their emerods,
2Sa 5:21 And there they left their *i*, and
1Ki 14: 9 made thee other gods, and molten *i*,
23 built them high places, and *i*,
2Ki 10:26 forth the *i* out of the house of Baal,
11:18 and his *i* brake they in pieces
17:10 they set them up *i* and groves
16 made them molten *i*, even two calves,
41 and served their graven *i*, both
18: 4 brake the *i*, and cut down the
23:14 And he brake in pieces the *i*,
24 wizards, and the *i*, and the idols,
2Ch 14: 3 and brake down the *i*, and cut
5 away...the high places and the *i*:
23:17 his altars and his *i* in pieces,
28: 2 and made also molten *i* for Baalim.
31: 1 Judah, and brake the *i* in pieces,
33:19 and set up groves and graven *i*,
22 sacrificed unto all the carved *i*
34: 3 and the groves, and the carved *i*,
3 the groves,...and the molten *i*,
4 and the *i*, that were on high above
4 and the groves, and the carved *i*,
4 the groves,...and the molten *i*,
7 beaten the graven *i* into powder,
Ps 78:58 him to jealousy with their graven *i*.
97: 7 be all they that serve graven *i*,
Isa 10:10 and whose graven *i* did excel
17: 8 made, either the groves, or the *i*.
21: 9 and all the graven *i* of her gods
27: 9 the groves and *i* shall not stand
30:22 covering of thy graven *i* of silver,
22 ornament of thy molten *i* of gold:
41:29 their molten *i* are wind and confusion.
42: 8 neither my praise to graven *i*.
17 ashamed, that trust in graven *i*,
17 that say to the molten *i*, Ye are our
Jer 8:19 me to anger with their graven *i*,
43:13 He shall break also the *i* of
50: 2 confounded, her *i* are broken in
38 for it is the land of graven *i*, and
51:47 upon the graven *i* of Babylon:
52 do judgment upon her graven *i*:
Eze 6: 4 your *i* shall be broken: and I will
6 and your *i* may be cut down, and
7:20 made the *i* of their abominations
16:17 and madest to thyself *i* of men, and
21:21 he consulted with *i*, he looked in
23:14 the *i* of the Chaldeans pourtrayed
30:13 cause their *i* to cease out of Noph;
Ho 10: 1 his land they have made goodly *i*.
2 their altars, he shall spoil their *i*.
11: 2 and burned incense to graven *i*.
13: 2 and have made them molten *i* of their
Am 5:26 Moloch and Chiun your *i*, the
Mic 1: 7 all the graven *i* thereof shall be
5:13 Thy graven *i* also will I cut off,
13 and thy standing *i* out of the midst
image-work See IMAGE and WORK.
imagination See also IMAGINATIONS.
Ge 6: 5 every *i* of the thoughts of his
8:21 the *i* of man's heart is evil from
De 29:19 I walk in the *i* of mine heart,
31:21 for I know their *i* which they go
1Ch 29:18 keep this for ever in the *i* of the
Jer 3:17 after the *i* of their evil heart.
7:24 and in the *i* of their evil heart,
9:14 the *i* of their own heart, and after
11: 8 one in the *i* of their evil heart:
13:10 walk in the *i* of their heart, and
16:12 one after the *i* of his evil heart,
18:12 every one do the *i* of his evil heart.
23:17 after the *i* of his own heart,
Lu 1:51 proud in the *i* of their hearts.
imaginations
1Ch 28: 9 all the *i* of the thoughts: if thou
Pr 6:18 An heart that deviseth wicked *i*,
La 3:60 and all their *i* against me.
61 Lord, and all their *i* against me;
Ro 1:21 became vain in their *i*, and their
2Co 10: 5 Casting down *i*, and every high
imagine See also IMAGINED; IMAGINETH.
Job 6:26 Do ye *i* to reprove words, and
21:27 the devices which ye wrongfully *i*
Ps 2: 1 and the people *i* a vain thing?
38:12 and *i* deceits all the day long.
62: 3 will ye *i* mischief against a man?
140: 2 Which *i* mischiefs in their heart;
Pr 12:20 in the heart of them that *i* evil:
Ho 7:15 yet do they *i* mischief against
Na 1: 9 What do ye *i* against the Lord?
Zec 7:10 you *i* evil against his brother
8:17 none of you *i* evil in your hearts
Ac 4:25 rage, and the people *i* vain things?
imagined
Ge 11: 6 them, which they have *i* to do.
Ps 10: 2 in the devices that they have *i*.
21:11 they *i* a mischievous device,
imagineth
Na 1:11 that *i* evil against the Lord,
Imla (*im'-lah*) See also IMLAH.
2Ch 18: 7 the same is Micaiah the son of *I*.
8 quickly Micaiah the son of *I*.
Imlah (*im'-lah*) See also IMLA.
1Ki 22: 8 one man, Micaiah the son of *I*.
9 hither Micaiah the son of *I*.
Immanuel (*im-man'-u-el*) See also EMMANUEL.
Is 7:14 a son, and shall call his name *I*.
8: 8 fill the breadth of the land, O *I*.
immediately
M't 4:22 And they *i* left the ship, and
8: 3 And *i* his leprosy was cleansed.
14:31 And *i* Jesus stretched forth his
20:34 *i* their eyes received sight, and
24:29 *i* after the tribulation of those
26:74 the man. And *i* the cock crew.
M'r 1:12 *i* the spirit driveth him into the
28 *i* his fame spread abroad
31 *i* the fever left her, and she
42 *i* the leprosy departed from him,
2: 8 *i* when Jesus perceived in his
12 And *i* he arose, took up the bed,
4: 5 and *i* it sprang up, because it
15 Satan cometh *i*, and taketh away
16 word, *i* receive it with gladness;
17 word's sake, *i* they are offended.
29 *i* he putteth in the sickle,
5: 2 *i* there met him out of the tombs
30 Jesus, *i* knowing in himself that
6:27 *i* the king sent an executioner,
50 *i* he talked with them, and saith
10:52 And *i* he received his sight, and
14:43 And *i*, while he yet spake,
Lu 1:64 And his mouth was opened *i*, and
4:39 *i* she arose and ministered unto
5:13 *i* the leprosy departed from him.
25 And *i* he rose up before them,
6:49 beat vehemently, and *i* it fell;
8:44 and *i* her issue of blood stanched.
47 him, and how she was healed *i*.
12:36 they may open unto him *i*.
13:13 and *i* she was made straight,
18:43 And *i* he received his sight, and
19:11 kingdom of God should *i* appear.
40 peace, the stones would *i* cry out.
22:60 And *i*, while he yet spake, the
Joh 5: 9 *i* the man was made whole, and
6:21 *i* the ship was at the land
13:30 received the sop went *i* out:
18:27 again: and *i* the cock crew.
21: 3 forth, and entered into a ship *i*;
Ac 3: 7 and *i* his feet and ancle bones
9:18 *i* there fell from his eyes as it
34 make thy bed. And he arose *i*.
10:33 *I* therefore I sent to thee; and
11:11 *i* there were three men already
12:23 And *i* the angel of the Lord smote
13:11 And *i* there fell on him a mist and
16:10 *i* we endeavoured to go into
26 and *i* all the doors were opened,
17:10 the brethren *i* sent away Paul
14 *i* the brethren sent away Paul
21:32 Who *i* took soldiers and
Ga 1:16 *i* I conferred not with flesh and
Re 4: 2 And *i* I was in the spirit: and
Immer (*im'-mur*)
1Ch 9:12 son of Meshillemith, the son of *I*;
24:14 to Bilgah, the sixteenth to *I*,
Ezr 2:37 The children of *I*, a thousand fifty
59 Tel-harsa, Cherub, Addan, and *I*:
10:20 of the sons of *I*; Hanani, and
Ne 3:29 them repaired Zadok the son of *I*
7:40 The children of *I*, a thousand fifty
61 Tel-haresha, Cherub, Addon, and *I*:
11:13 son of Meshillemoth, the son of *I*,
Jer 20: 1 Now Pashur the son of *I* the priest,
immortal
1Ti 1:17 Now unto the King eternal, *i*,
immortality
Ro 2: 7 glory and honour and *i*, eternal
1Co 15:53 and this mortal must put on *i*.
54 this mortal shall have put on *i*,
1Ti 6:16 Who only hath *i*, dwelling in the
2Ti 1:10 hath brought life and *i* to light
immovable See UNMOVEABLE.
immutability
Heb 6:17 the *i* of his counsel, confirmed it
immutable
Heb 6:18 That by two *i* things, in which it
Imna (*im'-nah*) See also IMNAH; JIMNA.
1Ch 7:35 Zophah, and *I*, and Shelesh, and
Imnah (*im'-nah*) See also IMNA; JIMNAH.
1Ch 7:30 sons of Asher; *I*, and Ishuah,
2Ch 31:14 And Kore the son of *I* the Levite,
impart See also IMPARTED.
Lu 3:11 let him *i* to him that hath none;
Ro 1:11 *i* unto you some spiritual gift,
imparted
Job 39:17 hath he *i* to her understanding.
1Th 2: 8 were willing to have *i* unto you,
impediment
M'r 7:32 deaf, and had an *i* in his speech;
impenitent
Ro 2: 5 But, after thy hardness and *i* heart
imperfect See UNPERFECT.
imperious
Eze 16:30 the work of an *i* whorish woman;
implacable
Ro 1:31 without natural affection, *i*,
implead
Ac 19:38 deputies: let them *i* one another.
importunity
Lu 11: 8 yet because of his *i* he will rise
impose See also IMPOSED.
Ezr 7:24 it shall not be lawful to *i* toll,
imposed
Heb 9:10 *i* on them until the time of
impossible
M't 17:20 and nothing shall be *i* unto you.
19:26 With men this is *i*; but with God
M'r 10:27 With men it is *i*, but not with God:
Lu 1:37 with God nothing shall be *i*.
17: 1 is *i* but that offences will come:
18:27 things which are *i* with men are
Heb 6: 4 For it is *i* for those who were once
18 in which it was *i* for God to lie,
11: 6 without faith it is *i* to please him:
impotent
Joh 5: 3 lay a great multitude of *i* folk,
7 The *i* man answered him, Sir, I
Ac 4: 9 the good deed done to the *i* man,
14: 8 certain man at Lystra, *i* in his feet,
impoverish See also IMPOVERISHED.
Jer 5:17 they shall *i* thy fenced cities,
impoverished
J'g 6: 6 And Israel was greatly *i* because
Isa 40:20 is so *i* that he hath no oblation
Mal 1: 4 Whereas, Edom saith, We are *i*,
imprisoned
Ac 22:19 know that I *i* and beat in every
imprisonment See also IMPRISONMENTS.
Ezr 7:26 or to confiscation of goods, or to *i*.
Heb 11:36 yea, moreover of bonds and *i*:
imprisonments
2Co 6: 5 In stripes, in *i*, in tumults, in
impudent
Pr 7:13 kissed him, and with an *i* face
Eze 2: 4 *i* children and stiff hearted.
3: 7 all the house of Israel are *i*
impute See also IMPUTED; IMPUTETH; IMPUTING.
1Sa 22:15 king *i* any thing unto his servant,
2Sa 19:19 Let not my lord *i* iniquity unto
Ro 4: 8 to whom the Lord will not *i* sin.
imputed
Le 7:18 it be *i* unto him that offereth it:
17: 4 blood shall be *i* unto that man; he
Ro 4:11 might be *i* unto them also:
22 therefore it was *i* to him for
23 sake alone, that it was *i* to him;
24 to whom it shall be *i*, if we believe
5:13 sin is not *i* when there is no law.
Jas 2:23 and it was *i* unto him for
imputeth
Ps 32: 2 whom the Lord *i* not iniquity,
Ro 4: 6 unto whom God *i* righteousness
imputing
Hab 1:11 offend, *i* this his power unto his God.
2Co 5:19 not *i* their trespasses unto them;
Imrah (*im'-rah*)
1Ch 7:36 and Shual, and Beri, and *I*,
Imri (*im'-ri*)
1Ch 9: 4 the son of *I*, the son of Bani,
Ne 3: 2 them builded Zaccur the son of *I*.

inasmuch
De 19: 6 of death, *i* as he hated him not
Ru 3:10 *i* as thou followedst not young
M't 25:40 *I* as ye have done it unto one
45 *I* as ye did it not to one of the
Ro 11:13 *i* as I am the apostle of the
Ph'p 1: 7 *i* as both in my bonds, and in
Heb 3: 3 *i* as he who hath builded the
7:20 And *i* as not without an oath
1Pe 4:13 *i* as ye are partakers of Christ's
incense See also FRANKINCENSE; INCENSED.
Ex 25: 6 for anointing oil, and for sweet *i*,
30: 1 make an altar to burn *i* upon:
7 shall burn thereon sweet *i* every
7 the lamps, he shall burn *i* upon it.
8 at even, he shall burn *i* upon it,
8 a perpetual *i* before the Lord
9 Ye shall offer no strange *i* thereon,
27 and his vessels, and the altar of *i*,
31: 8 all his furniture, and the altar of *i*,
11 and sweet *i* for the holy place:
35: 8 anointing oil, and for the sweet *i*,
15 And the *i* altar, and his staves,
15 the anointing oil, and the sweet *i*,
28 anointing oil, and for the sweet *i*.
37:25 made the *i* altar of shittim wood:
29 and the pure *i* of sweet spices,
39:38 the anointing oil, and the sweet *i*,
40: 5 altar of gold for the *i* before the ark
27 And he burnt sweet *i* thereon; as
Le 4: 7 the horns of the altar of sweet *i*

Le 10: 1 put fire therein, and put *i* thereon,
16:12 and his hands full of sweet *i* beaten
13 he shall put the *i* upon the fire
13 of the *i* may cover the mercy seat
Nu 4:16 light, and the sweet *i*, and the daily
7:14 of ten shekels of gold, full of *i*:
20 of gold of ten shekels, full of *i*:
26, 32, 38, 44, 50, 56, 62, 68, 74, 80 One golden spoon of ten shekels, full of *i*:
86 golden spoons were twelve, full of *i*,
16: 7 put *i* in them before the Lord to
17 man his censer, and put *i* in them,
18 fire in them, and laid *i* thereon,
35 hundred and fifty men that offered *i*.
40 near to offer *i* before the Lord;
46 from off the altar, and put on *i*,
47 put on *i*, and made an atonement
De 33:10 they shall put *i* before thee, and
1Sa 2:28 to burn *i*, to wear an ephod before
1Ki 3: 3 he sacrificed and burnt *i* in high
9:25 and he burnt *i* upon the altar that
11: 8 wives, which burnt *i* and sacrificed
12:33 offered upon the altar, and burnt *i*.
13: 1 stood by the altar to burn *i*.
2 high places that burn *i* upon thee,
22:43 the people offered and burnt *i* yet
2Ki 12: 3 people still sacrificed and burnt *i*
14: 4 people did sacrifice and burnt *i* on
15: 4 people sacrificed and burnt *i* still
35 and burned *i* still in the high
16: 4 and burnt *i* in the high places,
17:11 they burnt *i* in all the high places,
18: 4 children of Israel did burn *i* to it:
22:17 and have burned *i* unto other gods,
23: 5 had ordained to burn *i* in the high
5 them also that burned *i* unto Baal,
8 where the priests had burned *i*,
1Ch 6:49 offering, and on the altar of *i*,
23:13 for ever, to burn *i* before the Lord,
28:18 for the altar of *i* refined gold by
2Ch 2: 4 and to burn before him sweet *i*,
13:11 burnt sacrifices and sweet *i*:
25:14 before them, and burned *i* to them.
26:16 to burn *i* upon the altar of
16 to burn...upon the altar of *i*.
18 Uzziah, to burn *i* unto the Lord,
18 that are consecrated to burn *i*:
19 had a censer in his hand to burn *i*:
19 the Lord, from beside the *i* altar.
28: 3 he burnt *i* in the valley of the son
4 also and burnt *i* in the high places,
25 places to burn *i* unto other gods,
29: 7 not burned *i* nor offered burnt
11 minister unto him, and burn *i*.
30:14 all the altars for *i* took they away,
32:12 one altar, and burn *i* upon it?
34:25 and have burned *i* unto other gods,
Ps 66:15 of fatlings, with the *i* of rams;
141: 2 prayer be set forth before thee as *i*
Isa 1:13 *i* is an abomination unto me;
43:23 offering, nor wearied thee with *i*.
60: 6 they shall bring gold and *i*; and
65: 3 burneth *i* upon altars of brick;
7 burned *i* upon the mountains,
66: 3 he that burneth *i*, as if he blessed
Jer 1:16 have burned *i* unto other gods,
6:20 cometh there to me *i* from Sheba,
7: 9 and burn *i* unto Baal, and walk
11:12 the gods unto whom they offer *i*:
13 even altars to burn *i* unto Baal.
17 me to anger in offering *i* unto Baal.
17:26 and meat offerings, and *i*, and
18:15 they have burned *i* to vanity, and
19: 4 have burned *i* in it unto other gods,
13 *i* unto all the host of heaven,
32:29 roofs they have offered *i* unto Baal,
41: 5 with offerings and *i* in their hand,
44: 3 in that they went to burn *i*, and
5 to burn no *i* unto other gods.
8 burning *i* unto other gods in the
15 wives had burned *i* unto other gods,
17 to burn *i* unto the queen of
18 to burn *i* to the queen of heaven,
19 burned *i* to the queen of heaven,
21 The *i* that ye burned in the cities
23 Because ye have burned *i*, and
25 to burn *i* to the queen of heaven,
48:35 and him that burneth *i* to his gods.
Eze 8:11 and a thick cloud of *i* went up.
16:18 set mine oil and mine *i* before
23:41 thou hast set mine *i* and mine oil.
Ho 2:13 wherein she burned *i* to them,
4:13 burn *i* upon the hills, under oaks
11: 2 and burned *i* to graven images.
Hab 1:16 and burn *i* unto their drag;
Mal 1:11 in every place *i* shall be offered
Lu 1: 9 his lot was to burn *i* when he went
10 praying without at the time of *i*.
11 on the right side of the altar of *i*.
Re 8: 3 there was given unto him much *i*,
4 the smoke of the *i*, which came

incensed
Isa 41:11 all they that were *i* against thee
45:24 and all that are *i* against him shall

incline See also INCLINED; INCLINETH.
Jos 24:23 and *i* your heart unto the Lord
1Ki 8:58 That he may *i* our hearts unto him,
Ps 17: 6 *i* thine ear unto me, and hear my
45:10 and consider, and *i* thine ear;
49: 4 I will *i* mine ear to a parable:
71: 2 escape: *i* thine ear unto me, and
78: 1 *i* your ears to the words of my
88: 2 thee: *i* thine ear unto my cry;
102: 2 *i* thine ear unto me: in the day
119:36 *I* my heart unto thy testimonies,
Ps 141: 4 *I* not my heart to any evil thing,
Pr 2: 2 thou *i* thine ear unto wisdom,
4:20 *i* thine ear unto my sayings.
Isa 37:17 *I* thine ear, O Lord, and hear;
55: 3 *I* your ear, and come unto me:
Da 9:18 O my God, *i* thine ear, and hear;

inclined
J'g 9: 3 and their hearts *i* to follow
Ps 40: 1 and he *i* unto me, and heard my
116: 2 Because he hath *i* his ear unto me,
119:112 I have *i* mine heart to perform
Pr 5:13 nor *i* mine ear to them that
Jer 7:24 hearkened not, nor *i* their ear,
26 not unto me, nor *i* their ear,
11: 8 they obeyed not, nor *i* their ear,
17:23 obeyed not, neither *i* their ear,
25: 4 hearkened, nor *i* your ear to hear.
34:14 not unto me, neither *i* their ear.
35:15 ye have not *i* your ear, nor
44: 5 nor *i* their ear to turn from their

inclineth
Pr 2:18 her house *i* unto death, and her

inclose See also INCLOSED; INCLOSINGS.
Ca 8: 9 we will *i* her with boards of cedar.

inclosed
Ex 39: 6 onyx stones *i* in ouches of gold,
13 they were *i* in ouches of gold in
J'g 20:43 Thus they *i* the Benjamites
Ps 17:10 They are *i* in their own fat: with
22:16 assembly of the wicked have *i* me:
Ca 4:12 A garden *i* is my sister, my
La 3: 9 He hath *i* my ways with hewn
Lu 5: 6 they *i* a great multitude of fishes:

inclosings
Ex 28:20 shall be set in gold in their *i*.
39:13 in ouches of gold in their *i*.

incontinency
1Co 7: 5 Satan tempt you not for your *i*.

incontinent
2Ti 3: 3 false accusers, *i*, fierce, despisers

incorruptible See also UNCORRUPTIBLE.
1Co 9:25 corruptible crown; but we an *i*.
15:52 and the dead shall be raised *i*,
1Pe 1: 4 To an inheritance *i*, and undefiled,
23 corruptible seed, but of *i*,

incorruption
1Co 15:42 in corruption; it is raised in *i*:
50 neither doth corruption inherit *i*.
53 must put on *i*, and this mortal
54 corruptible shall have put on *i*,

increase See also INCREASED; INCREASEST; INCREASETH; INCREASING.
Ge 47:24 to pass in the *i*, that ye shall give
Le 19:25 may yield unto you the *i* thereof:
25: 7 shall all the *i* thereof be meat.
12 ye shall eat the *i* thereof out of
16 thou shalt *i* the price thereof, and
20 shall not sow, nor gather in our *i*:
36 Take thou no usury of him, or *i*:
37 nor lend him thy victuals for *i*.
26: 4 the land shall yield her *i*, and the
20 your land shall not yield her *i*,
Nu 18:30 as the *i* of the threshingfloor,
30 and as the *i* of the winepress.
32:14 an *i* of sinful men, to augment
De 6: 3 that ye may *i* mightily, as the
7:13 the *i* of thy kine, and the flocks
22 once, lest the beasts of the field *i*
14:22 truly tithe all the *i* of thy seed,
28 bring forth all the tithe of thine *i*
16:15 God shall bless thee in all thine *i*,
26:12 tithing all the tithes of thine *i* the
28: 4 thy cattle, the *i* of thy kine,
18 the *i* of thy kine, and the flocks of
51 or the *i* of thy kine, or flocks of thy
32:13 he might eat the *i* of the fields;
22 consume the earth with her *i*,
J'g 6: 4 and destroyed the *i* of the earth,
9:29 *I* thine army, and come out.
1Sa 2:33 all the *i* of thine house shall die
1Ch 27:23 Lord had said he would *i* Israel
27 over the *i* of the vineyards for the
2Ch 31: 5 and of all the *i* of the field;
32:28 Storehouses also for the *i* of corn,
Ezr 10:10 wives, to *i* the trespass of Israel.
Ne 9:37 yieldeth much *i* unto the kings
Job 8: 7 thy latter end should greatly *i*.
20:28 The *i* of his house shall depart,
31:12 and would root out all mine *i*.
Ps 44:12 not *i* thy wealth by their price.
62:10 if riches *i*, set not your heart upon
67: 6 Then shall the earth yield her *i*;
71:21 Thou shalt *i* my greatness, and
73:12 in the world; they *i* in riches.
78:46 also their *i* unto the caterpiller,
85:12 and our land shall yield her *i*.
107:37 which may yield fruits of *i*.
115:14 The Lord shall *i* you more and
Pr 1: 5 man will hear, and will *i* learning;
3: 9 with the firstfruits of all thine *i*:
9: 9 man, and he will *i* in learning.
13:11 that gathereth by labour shall *i*.
14: 4 much *i* is by the strength of the ox.
18:20 the *i* of his lips shall he be filled
22:16 oppresseth the poor to *i* his riches,
28:28 when they perish, the righteous *i*.
Ec 5:10 he that loveth abundance with *i*:
11 When goods *i*, they are increased
6:11 there be many things that *i* vanity,
Isa 9: 7 Of the *i* of his government and
29:19 The meek also shall *i* their joy
30:23 and bread of the *i* of the earth,
Isa 57: 9 and didst *i* thy perfumes, and
Jer 2: 3 and the firstfruits of his *i*: all that
23: 3 and they shall be fruitful and *i*.
Eze 5:16 I will *i* the famine upon you, and
18: 8 usury, neither hath taken any *i*,
13 upon usury, and hath taken *i*:
17 that hath not received usury nor *i*,
22:12 thou hast taken usury and *i*, and
34:27 and the earth shall yield her *i*,
36:11 and they shall *i* and bring fruit:
29 I will call for the corn, and will *i* it,
30 of the tree, and the *i* of the field,
37 I will *i* them with men like a flock.
48:18 and the *i* thereof shall be for food
Da 11:39 acknowledge and *i* with glory:
Ho 4:10 whoredom, and shall not *i*:
Zec 8:12 and the ground shall give her *i*,
10: 8 shall *i* as they have increased.
Lu 17: 5 said unto the Lord, *I* our faith.
Joh 3:30 He must *i*, but I must decrease.
1Co 3: 6 Apollos watered; but God gave the *i*.
7 watereth; but God that giveth the *i*.
2Co 9:10 *i* the fruits of your righteousnesss;
Eph 4:16 *i* of the body unto the edifying
Col 2:19 increaseth with the *i* of God.
1Th 3:12 the Lord make you to *i* and abound
4:10 that ye *i* more and more;
2Ti 2:16 they will *i* unto more ungodliness.

increased
Ge 7:17 and the waters *i*, and bare up the
18 and were *i* greatly upon the earth:
30:30 and it is now *i* unto a multitude;
43 And the man *i* exceedingly, and
Ex 1: 7 were fruitful, and *i* abundantly,
23:30 thou be *i*, and inherit the land.
1Sa 14:19 of the Philistines went on and *i*:
2Sa 15:12 for the people *i* continually with
1Ki 22:35 And the battle *i* that day: and
1Ch 4:38 house of their fathers *i* greatly.
5:23 they *i* from Bashan unto
2Ch 18:34 And the battle *i* that day: howbeit
Ezr 9: 6 for our iniquities are *i* over our
Job 1:10 and his substance is *i* in the land.
Ps 3: 1 Lord, how are they *i* that trouble
4: 7 that their corn and their wine *i*.
49:16 when the glory of his house is *i*;
105:24 And he *i* his people greatly; and
Pr 9:11 and the years of thy life shall be *i*.
Ec 2: 9 So I was great, and *i* more than
5:11 increase, they are *i* that eat them:
Isa 9: 3 the nation, and not *i* the joy:
26:15 Thou hast *i* the nation, O Lord,
15 thou hast *i* the nation: thou art
51: 2 and blessed him, and *i* him.
Jer 3:16 ye be multiplied and *i* in the land,
5: 6 and their backslidings are *i*.
15: 8 Their widows are *i* to me above
29: 6 that ye may be *i* there, and not
30:14 iniquity; because thy sins were *i*.
15 because thy sins were *i*, I have
La 2: 5 hath *i* in the daughter of Judah
Eze 16: 7 and thou hast *i* and waxen great,
26 and hast *i* thy whoredoms, to
23:14 And that she *i* her whoredoms:
28: 5 thy traffick hast thou *i* thy riches.
41: 7 so *i* from the lowest chamber
Da 12: 4 and fro, and knowledge shall be *i*.
Ho 4: 7 As they were *i*, so they sinned
10: 1 of his fruit he hath *i* the altars;
Am 4: 9 fig trees and your olive trees *i*,
Zec 10: 8 they shall increase as they have *i*.
M'r 4: 8 yield fruit that sprang up and *i*,
Lu 2:52 Jesus *i* in wisdom and stature,
Ac 6: 7 And the word of God *i*; and the
9:22 Saul *i* the more in strength, and
16: 5 the faith, and *i* in number daily.
2Co 10:15 having hope, when your faith is *i*,
Re 3:17 I am rich, and *i* with goods, and

increasest
Job 10:17 and *i* thine indignation upon me;

increaseth
Job 10:16 For it *i*. Thou huntest me as a
12:23 He *i* the nations, and destroyeth
Ps 74:23 rise up against thee *i* continually.
Pr 11:24 is that scattereth, and yet *i*;
16:21 sweetness of the lips *i* learning.
23:28 *i* the transgressors among men.
24: 5 yea, a man of knowledge *i* strength.
28: 8 that by usury and unjust gain *i*
29:16 are multiplied, transgression *i*:
Ec 1:18 he that *i* knowledge, *i* sorrow.
Isa 40:29 that have no might he *i* strength.
Ho 12: 1 he daily *i* lies and desolation;
Hab 2: 6 to him that *i* that which is not his
Col 2:19 together, *i* with the increase of God.

increasing
Col 1:10 and *i* in the knowledge of God;

incredible
Ac 26: 8 it be thought a thing *i* with you,

incurable
2Ch 21:18 his bowels with an *i* disease.
Job 34: 6 wound is *i* without transgression.
Jer 15:18 my wound *i*, which refuseth to be
30:12 Thy bruise is *i*, and thy wound is
15 thy sorrow is *i* for the multitude
Mic 1: 9 For her wound is *i*; for it is come

indebted
Lu 11: 4 forgive every one that is *i* to us.

indeed
Ge 17:19 thy wife shall bear thee a son *i*;
20:12 And yet *i* she is my sister; she is
37: 8 to him, Shalt thou *i* reign over us?
8 or shalt thou *i* have dominion over us?

Ge 37:10 thy brethren i' come to bow down
40:15 For i' I was stolen away out of the
43:20 And said, O sir, we came i' down at
44: 5 drinketh, and whereby i' he divineth?
Ex 19: 5 if ye will obey my voice i', and keep
23:22 But if thou shalt i' obey his voice, and
Le 10:18 ye should i' have eaten it in the holy
Nu 12: 2 Hath the Lord i' spoken only by
21: 2 If thou wilt i' deliver this people
22:37 am I not able i' to promote thee to
De 2:15 For i' the hand of the Lord was
21:16 of the hated, which is i' the firstborn:
Jos 7:20 I' I have sinned against the Lord
1Sa 1:11 if thou wilt i' look on the affliction of
2:30 I said i' that thy house, and the house
2Sa 14: 5 I am i' a widow woman, and mine
15: 8 shall bring me again i' to Jerusalem,
1Ki 8:27 But will God i' dwell on the earth?
2Ki 14:10 Thou hast i' smitten Edom, and thine
1Ch 4:10 Oh that thou wouldest bless me i', and
21:17 I it is that have sinned and done evil i';
Job 19: 4 And be it i' that I have erred,
5 If i' ye will magnify yourselves
Ps 58: 1 Do ye i' speak righteousness, O
Isa 6: 9 people, Hear ye i', but understand not;
9 and see ye i', but perceive not.
Jer 22: 4 For if ye do this thing i', then shall
M't 3:11 I i' baptize you with water unto
13:32 Which i' is the least of all seeds:
20:23 them, Ye shall drink i' of my cup,
23:27 which i' appear beautiful outward,
26:41 the spirit i' is willing, but the flesh
M'r 1: 8 I i' have baptized you with water:
9:13 That Elias is i' come, and they
10:39 Ye shall i' drink of the cup that
11:32 John, that he was a prophet i'.
14:21 The Son of man i' goeth, as it is
Lu 3:16 I i' baptize you with water; but
11:48 for they i' killed them, and ye build
23:41 And we i' justly; for we receive the
24:34 Saying, The Lord is risen i', and
Joh 1:47 Behold an Israelite i', in whom is
4:42 this is i' the Christ, the Saviour of
6:55 For my flesh is meat i',
55 and my blood is drink i'.
7:26 know i' that this is the very Christ?
8:31 word, then are ye my disciples i';
36 make you free, ye shall be free i'.
Ac 4:16 for that i' a noble miracle hath
11:16 John i' baptized with water; but ye
22: 9 that were with me saw i' the light,
Ro 6:11 to be dead i' unto sin, but alive
8: 7 the law of God, neither i' can be.
14:20 All things i' are pure; but it is evil
1Co 11: 7 For a man i' ought not to cover his
2Co 8:17 For i' he accepted the exhortation;
11: 1 in my folly: and i' bear with me.
Ph'p 1:15 Some i' preach Christ even of envy
2:27 For i' he was sick nigh unto death:
3: 1 to me i' is not grievous, but for you
Col 2:23 Which things have i' a shew of
1Th 4:10 And i' ye do it toward all the
1Ti 5: 3 Honour widows that are widows i'.
5 Now she that is a widow i', and
16 relieve them that are widows i'.
1Pe 2: 4 disallowed i' of men, but chosen of

India (*in'-de-ah*)
Es 1: 1 from I' even unto Ethiopia,
8: 9 which are from I' unto Ethiopia,

indignation
De 29:28 and in wrath, and in great i', and
2Ki 3:27 there was great i' against Israel:
Ne 4: 1 was wroth, and took great i', and
Es 5: 9 he was full of i' against Mordecai.
Job 10:17 and increasest thine i' upon me;
Ps 69:24 Pour out thine i' upon them, and
78:49 anger, wrath, and i', and trouble,
102:10 Because of thine i' and thy wrath:
Isa 10: 5 the staff in their hand is mine i'.
25 the i' shall cease, and mine anger
13: 5 the weapons of his i', to destroy the
26:20 moment, until the i' be overpast.
30:27 his lips are full of i', and his tongue
30 with the i' of his anger, and with
34: 2 i' of the Lord is upon all nations,
66:14 and his i' toward his enemies.
Jer 10:10 shall not be able to abide his i'.
15:17 hand: for thou hast filled me with i'.
50:25 brought forth the weapons of his i':
La 2: 6 hath despised in the i' of his anger
Eze 21:31 I will pour out mine i' upon thee,
22:24 nor rained upon in the day of i'.
31 I poured out mine i' upon them;
Da 8:19 shall be in the last end of the i':
11:30 have i' against the holy covenant:
36 prosper till the i' be accomplished:
Mic 7: 9 I will bear the i' of the Lord,
Na 1: 6 Who can stand before his i'? and
Hab 3:12 didst march through the land in i',
Zep 3: 8 to pour upon them mine i', even all
Zec 1:12 hast had i' these threescore and
Mal 1: 4 whom the Lord hath i' for ever.
M't 20:24 were moved with i' against the two
26: 8 they had i', saying, To what purpose
M'r 14: 4 some that had i' within themselves,
Lu 13:14 of the synagogue answered with i',
Ac 5:17 Sadducees, and were filled with i',
Ro 2: 8 unrighteousness, i', and wrath,
2Co 7:11 yea, what i', yea, what fear, yea,
Heb 10:27 of judgment and fiery i', which
Re 14:10 mixture into the cup of his i';

inditing
Ps 45: 1 My heart is i' a good matter: I

industrious
1Ki 11:28 young man that he was i', he

inexcusable
Ro 2: 1 Therefore thou art i', O man,

infallible
Ac 1: 3 by many i' proofs, being seen of them

infamous
Eze 22: 5 shall mock thee, which art i'

infamy
Pr 25:10 shame, and thine i' turn not away.
Eze 36: 3 talkers, and are an i' of the people:

infant See also INFANTS.
1Sa 15: 3 slay both man and woman, i' and
Isa 65:20 be no more thence an i' of days,

infants
Job 3:16 been; as i' which never saw light.
Ho 13:16 their i' shall be dashed in pieces,
Lu 18:15 they brought unto him also i',

inferior
Job 12: 3 I am not i' to you: yea, who
13: 2 I know also: I am not i' unto you.
Da 2:39 arise another kingdom i' to thee,
2Co 12:13 you were i' to other churches,

infidel
2Co 6:15 hath he that believeth with an i'?
1Ti 5: 8 the faith, and is worse than an i'.

infinite
Job 22: 5 great? and thine iniquities i'?
Ps 147: 5 power: his understanding is i'.
Na 3: 9 her strength, and it was i';

infirmities
M't 8:17 Himself took our i', and bare our
Lu 5:15 and to be healed by him of their i'.
7:21 cured many of their i' and plagues,
8: 2 been healed of evil spirits and i',
Ro 8:26 the Spirit also helpeth our i': for
15: 1 to bear the i' of the weak, and not
2Co 11:30 of the things which concern my i'.
12: 5 I will not glory, but in mine i'.
9 will I rather glory in my i', that the
10 Therefore I take pleasure in i', in
1Ti 5:23 stomach's sake and thine often i'.
Heb 4:15 touched with the feeling of our i';

infirmity See also INFIRMITIES.
Le 12: 2 days of the separation for her i'
Ps 77:10 And I said, This is my i': but I
Pr 18:14 spirit of a man will sustain his i';
Lu 13:11 a woman which had a spirit of i'
12 thou art loosed from thine i'.
Joh 5: 5 had an i' thirty and eight years.
Ro 6:19 men because of the i' of your flesh:
Ga 4:13 Ye know how through i' of the flesh
Heb 5: 2 himself also is compassed with i'.
7:28 men high priests which have i';

inflame See also ENFLAME.
Isa 5:11 until night, till wine i' them!

inflammation
Le 13:28 clean: for it is an i' of the burning.
De 28:22 and with a fever, and with an i',

inflicted
2Co 2: 6 this punishment, which was i' of many.

influences
Job 38:31 Canst thou bind the sweet i' of Pleiades,

infolding
Eze 1: 4 a fire i' itself, and a brightness

inform See also INFORMED.
De 17:10 according to all that they i' thee:

informed
Da 9:22 And he i' me, and talked with me,
Ac 21:21 are i' of thee, that thou teachest
24 they were i' concerning thee,
24: 1 who i' the governor against Paul.
25: 2 of the Jews i' him against Paul, and
15 and the elders of the Jews i' me,

ingathering
Ex 23:16 and the feast of i', which is in the
34:22 the feast of i' at the year's end.

inhabit See also INHABITED; INHABITEST; INHABITETH; INHABITING.
Nu 35:34 the land which ye shall i', wherein
Pr 10:30 the wicked shall not i' the earth.
Isa 42:11 the villages that Kedar doth i':
65:21 shall build houses, and i' them;
22 shall not build and another i'; they
Jer 17: 6 but shall i' the parched places in
48:18 Thou daughter that dost i' Dibon,
Eze 33:24 they that i' those wastes of the land
Am 9:14 build the waste cities, and i' them;
Zep 1:13 also build houses, but not i' them;

inhabitant See also INHABITANTS.
Job 28: 4 flood breaketh out from the i';
Isa 5: 9 even great and fair, without i'.
6:11 Until the cities be wasted without i',
9: 9 and the i' of Samaria that say in
12: 6 Cry out and shout, thou i' of Zion:
20: 6 And the i' of this isle shall say in
24:17 are upon thee, O i' of the earth.
33:24 And the i' shall not say, I am sick:
Jer 2:15 his cities are burned without i'.
4: 7 shall be laid waste, without an i'.
9:11 of Judah desolate, without an i'.
10:17 out of the land, O i' of the fortress.
21:13 I am against thee, O i' of the valley,
22:23 O i' of Lebanon, that makest thy
26: 9 city shall be desolate without an i'?
33:10 without man, and without i', and
34:22 of Judah a desolation without an i'.
44:22 and a curse, without an i', as at
46:19 waste and desolate without an i'.
48:19 O i' of Aroer, stand by the way, and
43 thee, O i' of Moab, saith the Lord.
51:29 Babylon a desolation without an i'.
Jer 51:35 Babylon, shall the i' of Zion say;
37 and an hissing, without an i'.
Am 1: 5 cut off the i' from the plain of Aven,
8 I will cut off the i' from Ashdod,
Mic 1:11 Pass ye away, thou i' of Saphir,
11 the i' of Zaanan came not forth in
12 the i' of Maroth waited carefully for
13 O thou i' of Lachish, bind the
15 heir unto thee, O i' of Mareshah:
Zep 2: 5 thee, that there shall be no i'.
3: 6 is no man, that there is none i'.

inhabitants See also INHABITERS.
Ge 19:25 and all the i' of the cities, and all
34:30 to stink among the i' of the land,
50:11 the i' of the land, the Canaanites,
Ex 15:14 take hold on the i' of Palestina.
15 all the i' of Canaan shall melt away.
23:31 I will deliver the i' of the land into
34:12 with the i' of the land whither thou
15 a covenant with the i' of the land,
Le 18:25 the land itself vomiteth out her i'.
25:10 all the land unto all the i' thereof:
Nu 13:32 land that eateth up the i' thereof;
14:14 they will tell it to the i' of this land:
32:17 cities because of the i' of the land.
33:52 ye shall drive out the i' of the land
53 ye shall dispossess the i' of the land,
55 will not drive out the i' of the land
De 13:13 have withdrawn the i' of their city,
15 shalt surely smite the i' of that city
Jos 2: 9 all the i' of the land faint because
24 all the i' of the country do faint
7: 9 all the i' of the land shall hear of it,
8:24 of slaying all the i' of Ai in the field,
26 had utterly destroyed all the i' of Ai.
9: 3 And when the i' of Gibeon heard
11 all the i' of our country spake to us,
24 to destroy all the i' of the land from
10: 1 the i' of Gibeon had made peace
11:19 save the Hivites the i' of Gibeon:
13: 6 All the i' of the hill country from
15:15 he went up thence to the i' of Debir:
63 the Jebusites the i' of Jerusalem,
17: 7 hand unto the i' of En-tappuah.
11 and the i' of Dor and her towns,
11 and the i' of En-dor and her towns,
11 the i' of Taanach and her towns,
11 the i' of Megiddo and her towns,
12 not drive out the i' of those cities;
J'g 1:11 he went against the i' of Debir:
19 he drave out the i' of the mountain;
19 not drive out the i' of the valley,
27 the i' of Beth-shean and her towns,
27 nor the i' of Dor and her towns,
27 nor the i' of Ibleam and her towns,
27 the i' of Megiddo and her towns:
30 Zebulun drive out the i' of Kitron,
30 nor the i' of Nahalol; but the
31 did Asher drive out the i' of Accho,
31 nor the i' of Zidon, nor of Ahlab,
32 the Canaanites, the i' of the land:
33 drive out the i' of Beth-shemesh,
33 nor the i' of Beth-anath;
33 the Canaanites, the i' of the land:
33 nevertheless the i' of Beth-shemesh
2: 2 no league with the i' of this land;
5: 7 The i' of the villages ceased, they
11 toward the i' of his villages in Israel:
23 curse ye bitterly the i' thereof;
10:18 be head over all the i' of Gilead.
11: 8 our head over all the i' of Gilead.
21 the Amorites, the i' of that country.
20:15 i' of Gibeah, which were numbered
21: 9 none of the i' of Jabesh-gilead there.
10 Go and smite the i' of Jabesh-gilead
12 found among the i' of Jabesh-gilead
Ru 4: 4 Buy it before the i', and before the
1Sa 6:21 to the i' of Kirjath-jearim, saying,
23: 5 So David saved the i' of Keilah.
27: 8 nations were of old the i' of the land,
31: 11 when the i' of Jabesh-gilead heard
2Sa 5: 6 the Jebusites, the i' of the land:
1Ki 17: 1 who was of the i' of Gilead,
21:11 nobles who were the i' in his city,
2Ki 19:26 their i' were of small power,
22:16 this place, and upon the i' thereof,
19 place, and against the i' thereof,
23: 2 and all the i' of Jerusalem with him,
1Ch 8: 6 of the fathers of the i' of Geba, and
13 of the fathers of the i' of Aijalon,
13 who drove away the i' of Gath:
9: 2 Now the first i' that dwelt in their
11: 4 Jebusites were, the i' of the land.
5 And the i' of Jebus said to David,
22:18 the i' of the land into mine hand;
2Ch 15: 5 were upon all the i' of the countries.
20: 7 the i' of this land before thy people
15 all Judah, and ye i' of Jerusalem,
18 and the i' of Jerusalem fell before
20 O Judah, and ye i' of Jerusalem;
23 up against the i' of mount Seir,
23 had made an end of the i' of Seir,
21:11 caused the i' of Jerusalem to commit
13 the i' of Jerusalem to go a whoring,
22: 1 i' of Jerusalem made Ahaziah king
32:22 the i' of Jerusalem from the hand of
26 both he and the i' of Jerusalem, so
33 the i' of Jerusalem did him honour
33: 9 Judah and the i' of Jerusalem to err,
34:24 this place, and upon the i' thereof,
27 place, and against the i' thereof,
28 place, and upon the i' of the same.
30 of Judah, and the i' of Jerusalem,
32 the i' of Jerusalem did according to
35:18 present, and the i' of Jerusalem.
Ezr 4: 6 the i' of Judah and Jerusalem.

Ne 3:13 and the i' of Zanoah; they built it,
7: 3 watches of the i' of Jerusalem,
9:24 the i' of the land, the Canaanites,
Job 26: 5 the waters, and the i' thereof.
Ps 33: 8 all the i' of the world stand in awe
14 looketh upon all the i' of the earth.
49: 1 give ear, all ye i' of the world:
75: 3 and all the i' thereof are dissolved:
83: 7 the Philistines with the i' of Tyre;
Isa 5: 3 O i' of Jerusalem, and men of Judah,
8:14 for a snare to the i' of Jerusalem.
10:13 have put down the i' like a valiant
31 the i' of Gebim gather themselves
18: 3 All ye i' of the world, and dwellers
21:14 The i' of the land of Tema brought
22:21 be a father to the i' of Jerusalem,
23: 2 Be still, ye i' of the isle; thou whom
6 to Tarshish; howl, ye i' of the isle.
24: 1 scattereth abroad the i' thereof.
5 also is defiled under the i' thereof;
6 the i' of the earth are burned, and
26: 9 the i' of the world will learn
18 have the i' of the world fallen.
21 to punish the i' of the earth for
37:27 their i' were of small power,
38:11 no more with the i' of the world.
40:22 the i' thereof are as grasshoppers;
42:10 therein; the isles, and the i' thereof.
11 let the i' of the rock sing, let them
49:19 be too narrow by reason of the i',
Jer 1:14 forth upon all the i' of the land.
4: 4 men of Judah and i' of Jerusalem:
6:12 out my hand upon the i' of the land,
8: 1 the bones of the i' of Jerusalem,
10:18 I will sling out the i' of the land
11: 2 Judah, and to the i' of Jerusalem;
9 and among the i' of Jerusalem.
12 of Judah and i' of Jerusalem go,
13:13 I will fill all the i' of this land even
13 prophets, and all the i' of Jerusalem,
17:20 Judah, and all the i' of Jerusalem,
25 of Judah, and the i' of Jerusalem:
18:11 Judah, and to the i' of Jerusalem,
19: 3 of Judah, and i' of Jerusalem;
12 this place,...and to the i' thereof,
21: 6 I will smite the i' of this city, both
23:14 and the i' thereof as Gomorrah.
25: 2 Judah, and to all the i' of Jerusalem,
9 against the i' thereof, and against
29 sword upon all the i' of the earth,
30 grapes, against all the i' of the earth.
26:15 this city, and upon the i' thereof:
32:32 of Judah, and the i' of Jerusalem.
35:13 of Judah and the i' of Jerusalem,
17 all the i' of Jerusalem all the evil
36:31 upon the i' of Jerusalem, and upon
42:18 forth upon the i' of Jerusalem;
46: 8 I will destroy the city and the i'
47: 2 and all the i' of the land shall howl.
49: 8 back, dwell deep, O i' of Dedan;
20 purposed against the i' of Teman:
30 far off, dwell deep, O ye i' of Hazor,
50:21 it, and against the i' of Pekod:
34 and disquiet the i' of Babylon.
35 upon the i' of Babylon, and upon
51:12 he spake against the i' of Babylon.
24 to all the i' of Chaldea all their evil
35 my blood upon the i' of Chaldea,
La 4:12 the earth and all the i' of the world,
Eze 11:15 whom the i' of Jerusalem have said,
12:19 Lord God of the i' of Jerusalem,
15: 6 so will I give the i' of Jerusalem.
26:17 she and her i', which cause their
27: 8 The i' of Zidon and Arvad were thy
35 the i' of the isles shall be astonished
29: 6 all the i' of Egypt shall know that I
Da 4:35 all the i' of the earth are reputed
35 and among the i' of the earth: and
9: 7 Judah, and to the i' of Jerusalem,
Ho 4: 1 controversy with the i' of the land,
10: 5 The i' of Samaria shall fear
Joe 1: 2 and give ear, all ye i' of the land.
14 the i' of the land into the house of
2: 1 let all the i' of the land tremble:
Mic 6:12 and the i' thereof have spoken lies,
16 and the i' thereof an hissing:
Zep 1: 4 and upon all the i' of Jerusalem;
11 Howl, ye i' of Maktesh, for all the
2: 5 Woe unto the i' of the sea coast,
Zec 8:20 people, and the i' of many cities:
21 the i' of one city shall go to another,
11: 6 I will no more pity the i' of the land,
12: 5 The i' of Jerusalem shall be my
7 the i' of Jerusalem do not magnify
8 the Lord defend the i' of Jerusalem;
10 David, and upon the i' of Jerusalem,
13: 1 of David and to the i' of Jerusalem
Re 17: 2 the i' of the earth have been made

inhabited
Ge 36:20 of Seir the Horite, who i' the land;
Ex 16:35 years, until they came to a land i';
Le 16:22 their iniquities unto a land not i':
J'g 1:17 the Canaanites that i' Zephath,
21 out the Jebusites that i' Jerusalem;
1Ch 5: 9 eastward he i' unto the entering in
Isa 13:20 It shall never be i', neither shall it
44:26 saith to Jerusalem, Thou shalt be i';
45:18 it not in vain, he formed it to be i':
54: 3 make the desolate cities to be i'.
Jer 6: 8 make thee desolate, a land not i'.
17: 6 wilderness, in a salt land and not i'.
22: 6 and cities which are not i'.
46:26 and afterward it shall be i', as in
50:13 it shall not be i', but it shall be
39 it shall be no more i' for ever;
Eze 12:20 cities that are i' shall be laid waste,
26:17 that wast i' of seafaring men,
19 city, like the cities that are not i';
20 down to the pit, that thou be not i';
29:11 it, neither shall it be i' forty years.
34:13 in all the i' places of the country.
36:10 and the cities shall be i', and the
35 cities are become fenced, and are i'.
38:12 the desolate places that are now i',
Zec 2: 4 Jerusalem shall be i' as towns
7: 7 when Jerusalem was i' and in
7 men i' the south and the plain?
9: 5 Gaza, and Ashkelon shall not be i'.
12: 6 and Jerusalem shall be i' again in
14:10 be lifted up, and i' in her place,
11 but Jerusalem shall be safely i'.

inhabiters See also INHABITANTS.
Re 8:13 woe, woe, to the i' of the earth
12:12 Woe to the i' of the earth and of

inhabitest
Ps 22: 3 O thou that i' the praises of Israel.

inhabiteth
Job 15:28 and in houses which no man i',
Isa 57:15 high and lofty One that i' eternity,

inhabiting
Ps 74:14 to the people i' the wilderness.

inherit See also DISINHERIT; INHERITED; INHERITETH.
Ge 15: 7 to give thee this land to i' it.
8 shall I know that I shall i' it?
28: 4 that thou mayest i' the land
Ex 23:30 thou be increased, and i' the land.
32:13 seed, and they shall i' it for ever.
Le 20:24 Ye shall i' their land, and I will
25:46 you, to i' them for a possession;
Nu 18:24 I have given to the Levites to i':
26:55 tribes of their fathers they shall i'.
32:19 we will not i' with them on yonder
33:54 the tribes of your fathers ye shall i'.
34:13 is the land which ye shall i' by lot,
De 1:38 for he shall cause Israel to i' it.
2:31 that thou mayest i' his land.
3:28 he shall cause them to i' the land
12:10 the Lord your God giveth you to i',
16:20 thou mayest live, and i' the land
19: 3 the Lord thy God giveth thee to i',
14 which thou shalt i' in the land that
21:16 his sons to i' that which he hath,
31: 7 and thou shalt cause them to i' it.
Jos 17:14 but one lot and one portion to i',
J'g 11: 2 shalt not i' in our father's house,
1Sa 2: 8 to make them i' the throne of glory:
2Ch 20:11 which thou hast given us to i'.
Ps 25:13 and his seed shall i' the earth.
37: 9 the Lord, they shall i' the earth.
11 But the meek shall i' the earth;
22 blessed of him shall i' the earth;
29 The righteous shall i' the land,
34 he shall exalt thee to i' the land:
69:36 seed also of his servants shall i' it:
82: 8 earth: for thou shalt i' all nations.
Pr 3:35 The wise shall i' glory: but shame
8:21 those that love me to i' substance;
11:29 his own house shall i' the wind:
14:18 The simple i' folly: but the prudent
Isa 49: 8 to cause to i' the desolate heritages;
54: 3 and thy seed shall i' the Gentiles,
57:13 and shall i' my holy mountain;
60:21 they shall i' the land for ever, the
65: 9 and mine elect shall i' it, and my
Jer 8:10 fields to them that shall i' them:
12:14 caused my people Israel to i';
49: 1 why then doth their king i' Gad,
Eze 47:13 whereby ye shall i' the land
14 shall i' it, one as well as another:
Zec 2:12 And the Lord shall i' Judah his
M't 5: 5 meek: for they shall i' the earth.
19:29 and shall i' everlasting life.
25:34 i' the kingdom prepared for you
M'r 10:17 shall I do that I may i' eternal life?
Lu 10:25 what shall I do to i' eternal life?
18:18 what shall I do to i' eternal life?
1Co 6: 9 shall not i' the kingdom of God?
10 shall i' the kingdom of God.
15:50 and blood cannot i' the kingdom
50 doth corruption i' incorruption.
Ga 5:21 shall not i' the kingdom of God.
Heb 6:12 faith and patience i' the promises.
1Pe 3: 9 called, that ye should i' a blessing.
Rev 21: 7 that overcometh shall i' all things;

inheritance See also INHERITANCES.
Ge 31:14 yet any portion or i' for us in our
48: 6 name of their brethren in their i'.
Ex 15:17 in the mountain of thine i', in the
34: 9 our sin, and take us for thine i'.
Le 25:46 them as an i' for your children
Nu 16:14 given us i' of fields and vineyards:
18:20 Thou shalt have no i' in their land,
20 I am thy part and thine i' among
21 Levi all the tenth in Israel for an i',
23 children of Israel they have no i'.
24 of Israel they shall have no i'.
26 given you from them for your i',
26:53 the land shall be divided for an i'
54 many thou shalt give the more i',
54 and to few thou shalt give the less i':
54 to every one shall his i' be given
62 because there was no i' given
27: 7 an i' among their father's brethren;
7 i' of their father to pass unto them.
8 his i' to pass unto his daughter.
9 shall give his i' unto his brethren.
10 his i' unto his father's brethren.
11 shall give his i' unto his kinsman
32:18 have inherited every man his i'.
Nu 32:19 our i' is fallen to us on this side
32 the possession of our i' on this side
33:54 divide the land by lot for an i'
54 the more ye shall give the more i',
54 to the fewer ye shall give the less i':
54 every man's i' shall be in the place
34: 2 that shall fall unto you for an i',
14 fathers, have received their i';
14 of Manasseh have received their i':
15 have received their i' on this side
18 every tribe, to divide the land by i'.
29 Lord commanded to divide the i'
35: 2 the i' of their possession cities to
8 to his i' which he inheriteth.
36: 2 to give the land for an i' by lot to
2 the i' of Zelophehad our brother
3 their i' be taken from the i' of our
3 shall be put to the i' of the tribe
3 it be taken from the lot of our i'.
4 their i' be put unto the i' of the
4 their i' be taken away from the i'
7 not the i' of the children of Israel
7 to the i' of the tribe of his fathers.
8 daughter, that possesseth an i' in
8 enjoy every man the i' of his fathers.
9 Neither shall the i' remove from
9 shall keep himself to his own i'.
12 and their i' remained in the tribe
De 4:20 to be unto him a people of i', as ye
21 Lord thy God giveth thee for an i':
38 to give thee their land for an i', as it
9:26 destroy not thy people and thine i',
29 they are thy people and thine i',
10: 9 no part nor i' with his brethren;
9 the Lord is his i', according as the
12: 9 as yet come to the rest and to the i',
12 as he hath no part nor i' with you.
14:27 for he hath no part nor i' with thee.
29 he hath no part nor i' with thee,
15: 4 Lord thy God giveth thee for an i'
18: 1 have no part nor i' with Israel:
1 the Lord made by fire, and his i'.
2 Therefore shall they have no i'
2 the Lord is their i', as he hath said
19:10 Lord thy God giveth thee for an i',
14 they of old time have set in thine i',
20:16 thy God doth give thee for an i',
21:23 Lord thy God giveth thee for an i'.
24: 4 Lord thy God giveth thee for an i'.
25:19 giveth thee for an i' to possess it,
26: 1 Lord thy God giveth thee for an i',
29: 8 it for an i' unto the Reubenites,
32: 8 divided to the nations their i',
9 people; Jacob is the lot of his i'.
33: 4 the i' of the congregation of Jacob.
Jos 1: 6 shalt thou divide for an i' the land,
11:23 and Joshua gave it for an i' unto
13: 6 by lot unto the Israelites for an i',
7 land for an i' unto the nine tribes,
8 the Gadites have received their i',
14 the tribe of Levi he gave none i';
14 of Israel made by fire are their i',
15 the children of Reuben i' according
23 the i' of the children of Reuben
24 Moses gave i' unto the tribe of Gad
28 is the i' of the children of Gad
29 And Moses gave the i' unto the half
32 which Moses did distribute for i'
33 of Levi Moses gave not any i':
33 the Lord God of Israel was their i',
14: 1 Israel, distributed for i' to them.
2 By lot was their i', as the Lord
3 Moses had given the i' of two tribes
3 unto the Levites he gave none i'
9 feet have trodden shall be thine i',
13 son of Jephunneh Hebron for an i'.
14 Hebron therefore became the i' of
15:20 i' of the tribe of...children of Judah
16: 4 and Ephraim, took their i'.
5 the border of their i' on the east
8 the i' of the tribe of the children of
9 the i' of the children of Manasseh,
17: 4 to give us an i' among our brethren.
4 them an i' among the brethren of
6 daughters of Manasseh had an i'
18: 2 which had not yet received their i'.
4 it according to the i' of them;
7 priesthood of the Lord is their i':
7 received their i' beyond Jordan
20 the i' of the children of Benjamin,
28 the i' of the children of Benjamin
19: 1 i' was within the i' of the children
2 and they had in their i' Beer-sheba,
8 This is the i' of the tribe of the
9 the i' of the children of Simeon:
9 the children of Simeon had their i'
9 had their...within the i' of them.
10 border of their i' was unto Sarid:
16 is the i' of the children of Zebulun
23, 31, 39 This is the i' of the tribe of
41 And the coast of their i' was Zorah,
48 This is the i' of the tribe of the
49 an end of dividing the land for i'
49 of Israel gave an i' to Joshua the
51 divided for an i' by lot in Shiloh
21: 3 unto the Levites out of their i',
23: 4 to be an i' for your tribes, from
24:28 depart, every man unto his i'.
30 buried him in the border of his i'
32 the i' of the children of Joseph.
J'g 2: 6 every man unto his i' to possess
9 buried him in the border of his i'
18: 1 the Danites sought them an i' to
1 all their i' had not fallen unto them
20: 6 all the country of the i' of Israel:
21:17 There must be an i' for them that

J'g 21:23 went and returned unto their i'.
24 from thence every man unto his i'.
Ru 4: 5 up the name of the dead upon his i'.
6 for myself, lest I mar mine own i':
10 up the name of the dead upon his i'.
1Sa 10: 1 thee to be captain over his i'?
26:19 from abiding in the i' of the Lord,
2Sa 14:16 my son together out of the i' of God.
20: 1 have we i' in the son of Jesse:
19 thou swallow up the i' of the Lord?
21: 3 ye may bless the i' of the Lord?
1Ki 8:36 hast given to thy people for an i'.
51 For they be thy people, and thine i',
53 people of the earth to be thine i'.
12:16 have we i' in the son of Jesse:
21: 3 I should give the i' of my fathers
4 not give thee the i' of my fathers.
2Ki 21:14 will forsake the remnant of mine i',
1Ch 16:18 land of Canaan, the lot of your i';
28: 8 leave it for an i' for your children
2Ch 6:27 given unto thy people for an i'.
10:16 we have none i' in the son of Jesse:
Ezr 9:12 leave it for an i' to your children
Ne 11:20 cities of Judah, every one in his i'.
Job 31: 2 i' of the Almighty from on high?
42:15 gave them i' among their brethren.
Ps 2: 8 give thee the heathen for thine i',
16: 5 The Lord is the portion of mine i'
28: 9 Save thy people, and bless thine i':
33:12 whom he hath chosen for his own i'.
37:18 and their i' shall be for ever.
47: 4 He shall choose our i' for us,
68: 9 whereby thou didst confirm thine i',
74: 2 the rod of thine i', which thou hast
78:55 and divided them an i' by line, and
62 and was wroth with his i'.
71 Jacob his people, and Israel his i'.
79: 1 the heathen are come into thine i';
94:14 people, neither will he forsake his i'.
105:11 land of Canaan, the lot of your i':
106: 5 that I may glory with thine i'.
40 that he abhorred his own i'.
Pr 13:22 A good man leaveth an i' to his
17: 2 part of the i' among the brethren
19:14 and riches are the i' of fathers:
20:21 An i' may be gotten hastily at the
Ec 7:11 Wisdom is good with an i': and by
Isa 19:25 of my hands, and Israel mine i'.
47: 6 I have polluted mine i', and given
63:17 servants' sake, the tribes of thine i'.
Jer 3:18 given for an i' unto your fathers.
10:16 and Israel is the rod of his i': The
12:14 evil neighbours, that touch the i'
16:18 filled mine i' with the carcases of
32: 8 for the right of i' is thine, and the
51:19 and Israel is the rod of his i': The
La 5: 2 Our i' is turned to strangers, our
Eze 22:16 And thou shalt take thine i' in
33:24 many; the land is given us for i'.
35:15 at the i' of the house of Israel,
36:12 and thou shalt be their i', and thou
44:28 be unto them for an i': I am their i':
45: 1 shall divide by lot the land for i',
46:16 the i' thereof shall be his sons';
16 it shall be their possession by i'.
17 gift of his i' to one of his servants,
17 his i' shall be his sons' for them.
18 shall not take of the people's i' by
18 shall give his sons i' out of his own
47:14 this land shall fall unto you for i'.
22 divide it by lot for an i' unto you,
22 they shall have i' with you among
23 there shall ye give him his i', saith
48:29 lot unto the tribes of Israel for i',
M't 21:38 kill him, and let us seize on his i'.
M'r 12: 7 kill him, and the i' shall be ours.
Lu 12:13 that he divide the i' with me.
20:14 kill him, that the i' may be ours.
Ac 7: 5 And he gave him none i' in it,
20:32 to give you an i' among all them
26:18 i' among them which are sanctified
Ga 3:18 if the i' be of the law, it is no more
Eph 1:11 In whom...we...obtained an i',
14 is the earnest of our i' until the
18 of the glory of his i' in the saints.
5: 5 hath any i' in the kingdom of Christ
Col 1:12 be partakers of the i' of the saints
3:24 shall receive the reward of the i':
Heb 1: 4 as he hath by i' obtained a more
9:15 receive the promise of eternal i'.
11: 8 he should after receive for an i',
1Pe 1: 4 an i' incorruptible, and undefiled,

inheritances
Jos 19:51 These are the i', which Eleazer

inherited
Nu 32:18 have i' every man his inheritance.
Jos 14: 1 of Israel i' in the land of Canaan,
Ps 105:44 they i' the labour of the people;
Jer 16:19 Surely our fathers have i' lies,
Eze 33:24 and he i' the land: but we are
Heb 12:17 he would have i' the blessing,

inheriteth
Nu 35: 8 to his inheritance which he i'.

inheritor
Isa 65: 9 of Judah an i' of my mountains:

iniquities
Le 16:21 all the i' of the children of Israel,
22 goat shall bear upon him all their i'
26:39 i' of their fathers shall they pine
Nu 14:34 day for a year, shall ye bear your i',
Ezr 9: 6 our i' are increased over our head,
7 for our i' have we, our kings, and
13 punished us less than our i' deserve,
Ne 9: 2 sins, and the i' of their fathers.
Job 13:23 How many are mine i' and sins?
26 me to possess the i' of my youth.
22: 5 great? and thine i' infinite?
Ps 38: 4 mine i' are gone over mine head: as
40:12 mine i' have taken hold upon me,
51: 9 my sins, and blot out all mine i'.
64: 6 They search out i'; they
65: 3 I' prevail against me: as for
79: 8 remember not against us former i':
90: 8 Thou hast set our i' before thee,
103: 3 Who forgiveth all thine i'; who
10 rewarded us according to our i'.
107:17 and because of their i', are afflicted.
130: 3 If thou, Lord, shouldest mark i', O
8 shall redeem Israel from all his i'.
Pr 5:22 His own i' shall take the wicked
Isa 43:24 thou hast wearied me with thine i'.
50: 1 for your i' have ye sold yourselves,
53: 5 he was bruised for our i':
11 many; for he shall bear their i'.
59: 2 But your i' have separated between
12 and as for our i', we know them;
64: 6 our i', like the wind, have taken
7 consumed us, because of our i'.
65: 7 Your i', and the i' of your fathers
Jer 5:25 Your i' have turned away these
11:10 back to the i' of their forefathers,
14: 7 though our i' testify against us,
33: 8 and I will pardon all their i'.
La 4:13 the i' of her priests, that have shed
5: 7 not; and we have borne their i'.
Eze 24:23 but ye shall pine away for your i',
28:18 by the multitude of thine i', by the
32:27 their i' shall be upon their bones,
36:31 in your own sight for your i' and
33 have cleansed you from all your i'
43:10 they may be ashamed of their i':
Da 4:27 and thine i' by shewing mercy to
9:13 that we might turn from our i',
16 sins, and for the i' of our fathers,
Am 3: 2 I will punish you for all your i'.
Mic 7:19 he will subdue our i'; and thou
Ac 3:26 away every one of you from his i'.
Ro 4: 7 are they whose i' are forgiven,
Heb 8:12 their i' will I remember no more.
10:17 sins and i' will I remember no more.
Re 18: 5 and God hath remembered her i'.

iniquity See also INIQUITIES.
Ge 15:16 i' of the Amorites is not yet full.
19:15 be consumed in the i' of the city.
44:16 found out the i' of thy servants:
Ex 20: 5 visiting the i' of the fathers upon
28:38 may bear the i' of the holy things,
43 that they bear not i', and die:
34: 7 forgiving i' and transgression and
7 visiting the i' of the fathers upon
9 and pardon our i' and our sin, and
Le 5: 1 utter it, then he shall bear his i'.
17 is he guilty, and shall bear his i'.
7:18 that eateth of it shall bear his i'.
10:17 to bear the i' of the congregation,
17:16 his flesh; then he shall bear his i'.
18:25 I do visit the i' thereof upon it,
19: 8 one that eateth it shall bear his i',
20:17 nakedness; he shall bear his i'.
19 near kin: they shall bear their i'.
22:16 them to bear the i' of trespass,
26:39 of you shall pine away in their i' in
40 confess their i', and the i' of their
41, 43 of the punishment of their i':
Nu 5:15 bringing i' to remembrance.
31 shall the man be guiltless from i',
31 and this woman shall bear her i'.
14:18 forgiving i' and transgression,
18 visiting the i' of the fathers upon
19 I beseech thee, the i' of this people
15:31 cut off; his i' shall be upon him.
18: 1 shall bear the i' of the sanctuary:
1 shall bear the i' of your priesthood.
23 and they shall bear their i': it shall
23:21 He hath not beheld i' in Jacob,
30:15 them; then he shall bear her i'.
De 5: 9 visiting the i' of the fathers upon
19:15 not rise up against a man for any i',
32: 4 a God of truth and without i',
Jos 22:17 Is the i' of Peor too little for us,
20 man perished not alone in his i'.
1Sa 3:13 ever for the i' which he knoweth;
14 i' of Eli's house shall not be purged
15:23 stubbornness is as i' and idolatry.
20: 1 have I done? what is mine i'?
8 if there be in me i', slay me
25:24 me, my lord, upon me let this i' be:
2Sa 7:14 If he commit i', I will chasten him
14: 9 the i' be on me, and on my father's
32 if there be any i' in me, let him kill
19:19 Let not my lord impute i' unto me,
22:24 and have kept myself from mine i'.
24:10 take away the i' of thy servant;
1Ch 21: 8 do away the i' of thy servant; for
2Ch 19: 7 is no i' with the Lord our God,
Ne 4: 5 And cover not their i', and let not
Job 4: 8 that plow i', and sow wickedness,
5:16 hope, and i' stoppeth her mouth.
6:29 Return, I pray you, let it not be i';
30 Is there i' in my tongue? cannot
7:21 and take away mine i'?
10: 6 That thou enquirest after thine i',
14 wilt not acquit me from mine i'.
11: 6 thee less than thine i' deserveth.
14 If i' be in thine hand, put it far
14:17 a bag, and thou sewest up mine i'.
15: 5 thy mouth uttereth thine i', and
16 man, which drinketh i' like water?
20:27 The heaven shall reveal his i'; and
21:19 God layeth up his i' for his children:
Job 22:23 away i' far from thy tabernacles.
31: 3 punishment to the workers of i'?
11 an i' to be punished by the judges.
28 an i' to be punished by the judge:
33 by hiding mine i' in my bosom:
33: 9 innocent; neither is there i' in me.
34: 8 in company with the workers of i',
10 that he should commit i'.
22 where the workers of i' may hide
32 if I have done i', I will do no more.
36:10 that they return from i'.
21 Take heed, regard not i': for this
23 can say, Thou hast wrought i'?
Ps 5: 5 sight: thou hatest all workers of i'.
6: 8 Depart from me, all ye workers of i';
7: 3 this; if there be i' in my hands;
14 Behold, he travaileth with i', and
14: 4 all the workers of i' no knowledge?
18:23 and I kept myself from mine i'.
25:11 O Lord, pardon mine i'; for it is
28: 3 with the workers of i', which speak
31:10 strength faileth because of mine i',
32: 2 whom the Lord imputeth not i',
5 thee, and mine i' have I not hid.
5 and thou forgavest the i' of my sin.
36: 2 until his i' be found to be hateful.
3 The words of his mouth are i' and
12 There are the workers of i' fallen:
37: 1 envious against the workers of i'.
38:18 For I will declare mine i'; I will
39:11 with rebukes dost correct man for i',
41: 6 his heart gathereth i' to itself;
49: 5 the i' of my heels shall compass
51: 2 Wash me thoroughly from mine i',
5 I was shapen in i'; and in sin
53: 1 and have done abominable i':
4 the workers of i' no knowledge?
55: 3 for they cast i' upon me, and in
56: 7 Shall they escape by i'? in thine
59: 2 Deliver me from the workers of i',
64: 2 insurrection of the workers of i':
66:18 If I regard i' in my heart, the Lord
69:27 Add i' unto their i': and let them
78:38 full of compassion, forgave their i',
85: 2 hast forgiven the i' of thy people,
89:32 the rod, and their i' with stripes.
92: 7 all the workers of i' do flourish;
9 the workers of i' shall be scattered.
94: 4 the workers of i' boast themselves.
16 up for me against the workers of i'?
20 the throne of i' have fellowship
23 shall bring upon them their own i',
106: 6 we have committed i', we have
43 and were brought low for their i'.
107:42 and all i' shall stop her mouth.
109:14 i' of his fathers be remembered
119: 3 They also do no i': they walk in
133 let not any i' have dominion over
125: 3 put forth their hands unto i'.
5 them forth with the workers of i'.
141: 4 wicked works with men that work i':
9 and the gins of the workers of i'.
Pr 10:29 shall be to the workers of i'.
16: 6 By mercy and truth i' is purged:
19:28 mouth of the wicked devoureth i'.
21:15 shall be to the workers of i'.
22: 8 that soweth i' shall reap vanity:
Ec 3:16 righteousness, that i' was there.
Isa 1: 4 nation, a people laden with i',
13 it is i', even the solemn meeting.
5:18 unto them that draw i' with cords
6: 7 thine i' is taken away, and thy sin
13:11 evil, and the wicked for their i'; and
14:21 children for the i' of their fathers;
22:14 Surely this i' shall not be purged
26:21 inhabitants of the earth for their i':
27: 9 shall the i' of Jacob be purged;
29:20 all that watch for i' are cut off:
30:13 this i' shall be to you as a breach
31: 2 the help of them that work i'.
32: 6 his heart will work i', to practise
33:24 therein shall be forgiven their i'.
40: 2 her i' is pardoned: for she hath
53: 6 hath laid on him the i' of us all.
57:17 For the i' of his covetousness was I
59: 3 with blood, and your fingers with i';
4 conceive mischief, and bring forth i'.
6 their works are works of i', and the
7 their thoughts are thoughts of i';
64: 9 neither remember i' for ever:
Jer 2: 5 What i' have your fathers found
22 yet thine i' is marked before me,
3:13 Only acknowledge thine i', that
9: 5 weary themselves to commit i'.
13:22 For the greatness of thine i' are
14:10 he will now remember their i',
20 wickedness, and the i' of our fathers:
16:10 or what is our i'? or what is our sin
17 neither is their i' hid from mine
18 I will recompense their i' and their
18:23 forgive not their i', neither blot out
25:12 nation, saith the Lord, for their i',
30:14 for the multitude of thine i';
15 for the multitude of thine i':
31:30 every one shall die for his own i':
34 for I will forgive their i', and I will
32:18 recompensest the i' of the fathers
33: 8 I will cleanse them from all their i',
36: 3 I may forgive their i' and their sin.
31 seed and his servants for their i';
50:20 the i' of Israel shall be sought for,
51: 6 be not cut off in her i'; for this
La 2:14 they have not discovered thine i',
4: 6 punishment of the i' of the daughter
22 The punishment of thine i' is
22 he will visit thine i', O daughter of

Eze 3:18 same wicked man shall die in his i';
19 wicked way, he shall die in his i';
20 his righteousness, and commit i',
4: 4 lay the i' of the house of Israel
4 lie upon it thou shalt bear their i'.
5 laid upon thee the years of their i',
5 shalt thou bear the i' of the house
6 thou shalt bear the i' of the house
17 and consume away for their i'.
7:13 himself in the i' of his life.
16 mourning, every one for his i'.
19 it is the stumblingblock of their i'.
9: 9 i' of the house of Israel and Judah
14: 3 the stumblingblock of their i'
4, 7 the stumblingblock of his i'
10 bear the punishment of their i':
16:49 this was the i' of thy sister Sodom,
18: 8 hath withdrawn his hand from i',
17 not die for the i' of his father, he
18 lo, even he shall die in his i'.
19 not the son bear the i' of the father?
20 shall not bear the i' of the father,
20 the father bear the i' of the son:
24 and committeth i', and doeth
26 committeth i', and dieth in them;
26 his i' that he hath done shall he die.
30 so i' shall not be your ruin.
21:23 he will call to remembrance the i',
24 made your i' to be remembered,
25 is come, when i' shall have an end,
29 when their i' shall have an end.
28:15 created, till i' was found in thee.
18 by the i' of thy traffick;
29:16 bringeth their i' to remembrance,
33: 6 them, he is taken away in his i';
8 that wicked man shall die in his i';
9 from his way, he shall die in his i';
13 own righteousness, and commit i',
13 for his i' that he hath committed,
15 of life, without committing i';
18 righteousness, and committeth i',
35: 5 the time that their i' had an end:
39:23 went into captivity for their i':
44:10 idols; they shall even bear their i'.
12 the house of Israel to fall into i';
12 God, and they shall bear their i'.
Da 9: 5 sinned, and have committed i',
24 and to make reconciliation for i',
Ho 4: 8 and they set their heart on their i'.
5: 5 Israel and Ephraim fall in their i';
6: 8 Gilead is a city of them that work i',
7: 1 the i' of Ephraim was discovered,
8:13 now will he remember their i',
9: 7 for the multitude of thine i', and
9 he will remember their i', he will
10: 9 battle...against the children of i'
13 wickedness, ye have reaped i'; ye
12: 8 find none i' in me that were sin.
11 Is there i' in Gilead? surely they
13:12 The i' of Ephraim is bound up;
14: 1 for thou hast fallen by thine i'.
2 Take away all i', and receive us
Mic 2: 1 Woe to them that devise i', and
3:10 with blood, and Jerusalem with i'.
7:18 like unto thee, that pardoneth i',
Hab 1: 3 Why dost thou shew me i', and
13 evil, and canst not look on i':
2:12 blood, and stablisheth a city by i'!
Zep 3: 5 the midst thereof; he will not do i':
13 remnant of Israel shall not do i',
Zec 3: 4 I have caused thine i' to pass
9 will remove the i' of that land in one
Mal 2: 6 and i' was not found in his lips:
6 and did turn many away from i'.
M't 7:23 depart from me, ye that work i'.
13:41 that offend, and them which do i';
23:28 within ye are full of hypocrisy and i'.
24:12 because i' shall abound, the love of
Lu 13:27 depart from me, all ye workers of i'.
Ac 1:18 a field with the reward of i';
8:23 of bitterness, and in the bond of i'.
Ro 6:19 to uncleanness and to i' unto i';
1Co 13: 6 Rejoiceth not in i', but rejoiceth in
2Th 2: 7 mystery of i' doth already work:
2Ti 2:19 the name of Christ depart from i'.
Tit 2:14 might redeem us from all i', and
Heb 1: 9 loved righteousness, and hated i';
Jas 3: 6 And the tongue is a fire, a world of i':
2Pe 2:16 But was rebuked for his i': the

injoin See ENJOIN.

injured
Ga 4:12 as ye are: ye have not i' me at all.

injurious
1Ti 1:13 and a persecutor, and i': but I

injustice
Job 16:17 Not for any i' in mine hands: also

ink See also INKHORN.
Jer 36:18 and I wrote them with i' in the
2Co 3: 3 written not with i', but with the
2Jo 12 would not write with paper and i':
3Jo 13 I will not with i' and pen write unto

inkhorn
Eze 9: 2 with a writer's i' by his side:
3 had the writer's i' by his side;
11 linen, which had the i' by his side,

inn
Ge 42:27 to give his ass provender in the i',
43:21 when we came to the i', that we
Ex 4:24 came to pass by the way in the i',
Lu 2: 7 was no room for them in the i'.
10:34 and brought him to an i', and took

inner See also INNERMOST.
1Ki 6:27 the cherubims within the i' house:
6:36 he built the i' court with three rows
7:12 for the i' court of the house of the
50 the doors of the i' house, the most
20:30 into the city, into an i' chamber.
22:25 shalt go into an i' chamber to hide
2Ki 9: 2 and carry him to an i' chamber;
1Ch 28:11 and of the i' parlours thereof, and
2Ch 4:22 the i' doors thereof for the most
18:24 shalt go into an i' chamber to hide
29:16 went into the i' part of the house
Es 4:11 unto the king into the i' court,
5: 1 stood in the i' court of the king's
Eze 8: 3 the door of the i' gate that looketh
16 he brought me into the i' court
10: 3 and the cloud filled the i' court.
40:15 the porch of the i' gate were fifty
19 unto the forefront of the i' court
23 the gate of the i' court was over
27 a gate in the i' court toward the
28 he brought me to the i' court by
32 he brought me into the i' court
44 the i' gate were the chambers
44 of the singers in the i' court, which
41:15 with the i' temple, and the porches
17 the door, even unto the i' house,
42: 3 cubits which were for the i' court,
15 an end of measuring the i' house,
43: 5 and brought me into the i' court;
44:17 enter in at the gates of the i' court,
17 minister in the gates of the i' court,
21 when they enter into the i' court.
27 into the sanctuary, unto the i' court,
45:19 the posts of the gate of the i' court.
46: 1 The gate of the i' court that looketh
Ac 16:24 thrust them into the i' prison, and
Eph 3:16 might by his Spirit in the i' man;

innermost
Pr 18: 8 down into the i' parts of the belly.
26:22 down into the i' parts of the belly.

innocency
Ge 20: 5 and i' of my hands have I done
Ps 26: 6 I will wash mine hands in i': so will
73:13 in vain, and washed my hands in i'.
Da 6:22 as before him i' was found in me;
Ho 8: 5 long will it be ere they attain to i'?

innocent See also INNOCENTS.
Ex 23: 7 the i' and righteous slay thou not:
De 19:10 That i' blood be not shed in thy
13 the guilt of i' blood from Israel,
21: 8 and lay not i' blood unto thy people
9 put away the guilt of i' blood from
27:25 taketh reward to slay an i' person.
1Sa 19: 5 then wilt thou sin against i' blood,
1Ki 2:31 mayest take away the i' blood,
2Ki 21:16 Manasseh shed i' blood very much,
24: 4 also for the i' blood that he shed:
4 he filled Jerusalem with i' blood;
Job 4: 7 thee, who ever perished, being i'?
9:23 he will laugh at the trial of the i'.
28 know that thou wilt not hold me i'.
17: 8 the i' shall stir up himself against
22:19 and the i' laugh them to scorn.
30 He shall deliver the island of the i':
27:17 on, and the i' shall divide the silver.
33: 9 without transgression, I am i';
Ps 10: 8 places doth he murder the i':
15: 5 nor taketh reward against the i'.
19:13 i' from the great transgression.
94:21 and condemn the i' blood.
106:38 And shed i' blood, even the blood
Pr 1:11 let us lurk privily for the i' without
6:17 and hands that shed i' blood,
29 toucheth her shall not be i'.
28:20 haste to be rich shall not be i'.
Isa 59: 7 they make haste to shed i' blood:
Jer 2:35 Yet thou sayest, Because I am i',
7: 6 and shed not i' blood in this place,
22: 3 neither shed i' blood in this place.
17 and for to shed i' blood, and for
26:15 ye shall surely bring i' blood upon
Joe 3:19 they have shed i' blood in their land.
Jon 1:14 and lay not upon us i' blood: for
M't 27: 4 in that I have betrayed the i' blood.
24 I am i' of the blood of this just

innocents
Jer 2:34 blood of the souls of the poor i':
19: 4 filled this place with the blood of i';

innumerable
Job 21:33 as there are i' before him.
Ps 40:12 For i' evils have compassed me
104:25 wherein are things creeping i',
Jer 46:23 the grasshoppers, and are i'.
Lu 12: 1 an i' multitude of people;
Heb 11:12 sand which is by the sea shore i'.
12:22 and to an i' company of angels,

inordinate
Eze 23:11 was more corrupt in her i' love
Col 3: 5 uncleanness, i' affection, evil

inquire See ENQUIRE.

inquisition
De 19:18 the judges shall make diligent i':
Es 2:23 when i' was made of the matter,
Ps 9:12 When he maketh i' for blood, he

insatiable See UNSATIABLE.

inscription
Ac 17:23 altar with this i', To The Unknown

inside
1Ki 6:15 covered them on the i' with wood,

insomuch See also FORASMUCH; INASMUCH.
Mal 2:13 i' that he regardeth not the offering
M't 8:24 i' that the ship was covered with
12:22 i' that the blind and dumb both
13:54 i' that they were astonished, and
15:31 I' that the multitude wondered,
24:24 i' that, if it were possible, they shall
27:14 i' that the governor marvelled
M'r 1:27 i' that they questioned among
45 i' that Jesus could no more openly
2: 2 i' that there was no room to receive
12 i' that they were all amazed, and
3:10 i' that they pressed upon him for to
9:26 dead: i' that many said, He is dead.
Lu 12: 1 i' that they trode one upon another,
Ac 1:19 i' as that field is called in their
5:15 I' that they brought forth the sick
2Co 1: 8 i' that we despaired even of life:
8: 6 I' that we desired Titus, that as
Ga 2:13 i' that Barnabas also was carried

inspiration
Job 32: 8 the i' of the Almighty giveth them
2Ti 3:16 scripture is given by i' of God,

instant
Isa 29: 5 yea, it shall be at an i' suddenly.
30:13 breaking cometh suddenly at an i'.
Jer 18: 7 At what i' I shall speak concerning
9 at what i' I shall speak concerning
Lu 2:38 she coming in that i' gave thanks
23:23 And they were i' with loud voices,
Ro 12:12 continuing i' in prayer;
2Ti 4: 2 be i' in season, out of season;

instantly
Lu 7: 4 they besought him i', saying,
Ac 26: 7 i' serving God day and night,

instead
Ge 2:21 and closed up the flesh i' thereof;
4:25 me another seed instead of Abel,
44:33 let thy servant abide i' of the lad a
Ex 4:16 even he shall be to thee i' of a mouth,
16 and thou shalt be to him i' of God.
5:12 of Egypt to gather stubble i' of straw.
Nu 3:12 of Israel i' of all the firstborn
41 i' of all the firstborn among the
41 i' of all the firstlings among the
45 the Levites i' of all the firstborn
45 of the Levites i' of their cattle;
5:19 with another i' of thy husband,
20 aside to another i' of thy husband,
29 aside to another i' of her husband,
8:16 i' of such as open every womb,
16 even i' of the firstborn of all the
10:31 thou mayest be to us i' of eyes.
J'g 15: 2 she? take her, I pray thee, i' of her.
2Sa 17:25 captain of the host i' of Joab:
1Ki 3: 7 made thy servant king i' of David
2Ki 14:21 him king i' of his father Amaziah.
17:24 of Samaria i' of the children of
1Ch 29:23 as king i' of David his father, and
2Ch 12:10 I' of which king Rehoboam made
Es 2: 4 the king be queen i' of Vashti.
17 and made her queen i' of Vashti.
Job 31:40 i' of wheat, and cockle i' of barley.
Ps 45:16 I' of thy fathers shall be thy
Isa 3:24 i' of sweet smell there shall be
24 stink; and i' of a girdle a rent;
24 and i' of well set hair baldness;
24 and i' of a stomacher a girding of
24 sackcloth; and burning i' of beauty.
55:13 I' of the thorn shall come up the fir
13 i' of the brier shall come up the
Jer 22:11 which reigned i' of Josiah his father,
37: 1 son of Josiah reigned i' of Coniah
Eze 16:32 taketh strangers i' of her husband!

instruct See also INSTRUCTED; INSTRUCTING.
De 4:36 his voice, that he might i' thee:
Ne 9:20 also thy good spirit to i' them,
Job 40: 2 with the Almighty i' him?
Ps 16: 7 my reins also i' me in the night
32: 8 I will i' thee and teach thee in the
Ca 8: 2 mother's house, who would i' me:
Isa 28:26 his God doth i' him to discretion,
Da 11:33 among the people shall i' many:
1Co 2:16 of the Lord, that he may i' him?

instructed
De 32:10 he i' him, he kept him as the
2Ki 12: 2 Jehoiada the priest i' him.
1Ch 15:22 he i' about the song, because he
25: 7 brethren that were i' in the songs
2Ch 3: 3 Solomon was i' for the building
Job 4: 3 Behold, thou hast i' many, and
Ps 2:10 be i', ye judges of the earth.
Pr 5:13 mine ear to them that i' me!
21:11 when the wise is i', he receiveth
Isa 8:11 and i' me that I should not walk
40:14 and who i' him, and taught him
Jer 6: 8 Be thou i', O Jerusalem, lest my
31:19 and after that I was i', I smote
M't 13:52 is i' unto the kingdom of heaven
14: 8 being before i' of her mother,
Lu 1: 4 things, wherein thou hast been i'.
Ac 18:25 man was i' in the way of the Lord;
Ro 2:18 excellent, being i' out of the law;
Ph'p 4:12 all things I am i' both to be full

instructer See also INSTRUCTERS; INSTRUCTOR.
Ge 4:22 an i' of every artificer in brass

instructers [in some eds. INSTRUCTORS]
1Co 4:15 ye have ten thousand i' in Christ,

instructing
2Ti 2:25 In meekness i' those that oppose

instruction
Job 33:16 ears of men, and sealeth their i',
Ps 50:17 Seeing thou hatest i', and castest
Pr 1: 2 To know wisdom and i'; to
3 To receive the i' of wisdom,
7 but fools despise wisdom and i'.

Pr 1: 8 My son, hear the i· of thy father,
4: 1 Hear, ye children, the i· of a father,
13 Take fast hold of i·; let her not go:
5: 12 How have I hated i·, and my heart
23 He shall die without i·; and in the
6: 23 reproofs of i· are the way of life:
8: 10 Receive my i·, and not silver; and
33 Hear i·, and be wise, and refuse it
9: 9 Give i· to a wise man, and he will be
10: 17 in the way of life that keepeth i·:
12: 1 Whoso loveth i· loveth knowledge:
13: 1 A wise son heareth his father's i·:
18 shall be to him that refuseth i·:
15: 5 A fool despiseth his father's i·:
32 refuseth i· despiseth his own soul:
33 fear of the Lord is the i· of wisdom;
16: 22 hath it: but the i· of fools is folly.
19: 20 Hear counsel, and receive i·, that
27 to hear the i· that causeth to err
23: 12 Apply thine heart unto i·, and
23 wisdom, and i·, and understanding.
24: 32 I looked upon it, and received i·.
Jer 17: 23 they might not hear, nor receive i·.
32: 33 have not hearkened to receive i·.
35: 13 Will ye not receive i· to hearken to
Eze 5: 15 an i· and an astonishment unto
Zep 3: 7 wilt fear me, thou wilt receive i·;
2Ti 3: 16 correction, for i· in righteousness:

instructor See also INSTRUCTER.
Ro 2: 20 An i· of the foolish, a teacher of

instrument See also INSTRUMENTS.
Nu 35: 16 if he smite him with an i· of iron,
Ps 33: 2 the psaltery and an i· of ten strings.
92: 3 Upon an i· of ten strings, and upon
144: 9 upon a psaltery and an i· of ten strings
Isa 28: 27 are not threshed with a threshing i·,
41: 15 make thee a new sharp threshing i·
54: 16 bringeth forth an i· for his work;
Eze 33: 32 voice, and can play well on an i·:

instruments
Ge 49: 5 i· of cruelty are in their
Ex 25: 9 the pattern of all the i· thereof,
Nu 3: 8 keep all the i· of the tabernacle
4: 12 shall take all the i· of ministry,
26 cords, and all the i· of their service,
32 with all their i·, and with all their
32 ye shall reckon the i· of the charge
7: 1 sanctified it, and all the i· thereof,
31: 6 with the holy i·, and the trumpets
1Sa 8: 12 his i· of war, and i· of his chariots.
18: 6 with joy, and with i· of musick.
2Sa 6: 5 on all manner of i· made of fir wood,
24: 22 burnt sacrifice, and threshing i·
22 and other i· of the oxen for wood.
1Ki 19: 21 their flesh with the i· of the oxen,
1Ch 9: 29 and all the i· of the sanctuary,
12: 33 with all i· of war, fifty thousand,
37 with all manner of i· of war for the
15: 16 to be the singers with i· of musick,
16: 42 sound, and with musical i· of God.
21: 23 and the threshing i· for wood, and the
23: 5 Lord with the i· which I made,
28: 14 for all i· of all manner of service;
14 silver also for all i· of silver by
14 for all i· of every kind of service:
2Ch 4: 16 and all their i·, did Huram his
5: 1 and all the i·, put he among the
13 and cymbals and i· of musick, and
7: 6 also with i· of musick of the Lord,
23: 13 the singers with i· of musick, and
29: 26 Levites stood with the i· of David,
27 with the i· ordained by David king
30: 21 singing with loud i· unto the Lord.
34: 12 all that could skill of i· of musick.
Ne 12: 36 with the musical i· of David the
Ps 7: 13 prepared for him the i· of death;
68: 25 the players on i· followed after;
87: 7 as the players on i· shall be there:
150: 4 him with stringed i· and organs.
Ec 2: 8 as musical i·, and that of all sorts.
Isa 32: 7 The i· also of the churl are evil:
38: 20 sing my songs to the stringed i·
Eze 40: 42 i· wherewith they slew the burnt
Da 6: 18 neither were i· of musick brought
Am 1: 3 Gilead with threshing i· of iron:
6: 5 invent to themselves i· of musick,
Hab 3: 19 chief singer on my stringed i·.
Zec 11: 15 yet the i· of a foolish shepherd.
Ro 6: 13 as i· of unrighteousness unto sin:
13 as i· of righteousness unto God.

insurrection
Ezr 4: 19 time hath made i· against kings,
Ps 64: 2 the i· of the workers of iniquity:
M'r 15: 7 bound with them that had made i·
7 had committed murder in the i·.
Ac 18: 12 the Jews made i· with one accord

intangle See ENTANGLE.

integrity
Ge 20: 5 the i· of my heart and innocency
6 didst this in the i· of thy heart;
1Ki 9: 4 thy father walked, in i· of heart,
Job 2: 3 and still he holdeth fast his i·,
9 him, Dost thou still retain thine i·?
27: 5 till I die I will not remove mine i·
31: 6 that God may know mine i·.
Ps 7: 8 according to mine i· that is in me.
25: 21 Let i· and uprightness preserve
26: 1 Lord; for I have walked in mine i·:
11 as for me, I will walk in mine i·:
41: 12 me, thou upholdest me in mine i·,
78: 72 according to the i· of his heart;
Pr 11: 3 The i· of the upright shall guide
19: 1 is the poor that walketh in his i·,
20: 7 The just man walketh in his i·: his

intelligence
Da 11: 30 and have i· with them that forsake

intend See also INTENDED; INTENDEST; INTENDING.
Jos 22: 33 and did not i· to go up against
2Ch 28: 13 ye i· to add more to our sins and to
Ac 5: 28 and i· to bring this man's blood
35 what ye i· to do as touching these

intended
Ps 21: 11 For they i· evil against thee: they

intendest
Ex 2: 14 i· thou to kill me, as thou killedst

intending
Lu 14: 28 which of you, i· to build a tower,
Ac 12: 4 i· after Easter to bring him forth
20: 13 Assos, there i· to take in Paul:

intent See also INTENTS.
2Sa 17: 14 i· that the Lord might bring evil
2Ki 10: 19 to the i· that he might destroy the
2Ch 16: 1 to the i· that he might let none go out
Eze 40: 4 the i· that I might shew them unto
Da 4: 17 to the i· that the living may know
Joh 11: 15 not there, to the i· ye may believe;
13: 28 for what i· he spake this unto
Ac 9: 21 and came hither for that i·,
10: 29 for what i· ye have sent for me?
1Co 10: 6 to the i· we should not lust after
Eph 3: 10 To the i· that now unto the

intents
Jer 30: 24 have performed the i· of his heart:
Heb 4: 12 of the thoughts and i· of the heart.

intercession See also INTERCESSIONS.
Isa 53: 12 and made i· for the transgressors.
Jer 7: 16 for them, neither make i· to me:
27: 18 let them now make i· to the Lord
36: 25 Gemariah had made i· to the king
Ro 8: 26 the Spirit itself maketh i· for us
27 maketh i· for the saints according
34 of God, who also maketh i· for us.
11: 2 he maketh i· to God against Israel,
Heb 7: 25 he ever liveth to make i· for them.

intercessions
1Ti 2: 1 prayers, i·, and giving of thanks,

intercessor
Isa 59: 16 wondered that there was no i·:

intermeddle See also INTERMEDDLETH.
Pr 14: 10 a stranger doth not i· with his joy.

intermeddleth
Pr 18: 1 seeketh and i· with all wisdom.

intermission
La 3: 49 and ceaseth not, without any i·,

interpret See also INTERPRETED; INTERPRETING.
Ge 41: 8 there was none that could i· them
12 according to his dream he did i·.
15 and there is none that can i· it:
15 canst understand a dream to i· it.
1Co 12: 30 all speak with tongues? do all i·?
14: 5 speaketh with tongues, except he i·,
13 tongue pray that he may i·.
27 and that by course; and let one i·.

interpretation See also INTERPRETATIONS.
Ge 40: 5 according to the i· of his dream,
12 This is the i· of it: The three
16 baker saw that the i· was good,
18 This is the i· thereof: The three
41: 11 according to the i· of his dream.
J'g 7: 15 of the dream, and the i· therof,
Pr 1: 6 understand a proverb, and the i·;
Ec 8: 1 who knoweth the i· of a thing?
Da 2: 4 the dream, and we will shew the i·.
5 me the dream, with the i· thereof,
6 shew the dream and the i· thereof,
6 me the dream, and the i· thereof.
7 dream, and we will shew the i· of it.
9 that ye can shew me the i· thereof.
16 that he would shew the king the i·.
24 I will shew unto the king the i·.
25 make known unto the king the i·.
26 I have seen, and the i· thereof?
30 make known the i· to the king,
36 and we will tell the i· thereof before
45 is certain, and the i· thereof sure.
4: 6 known unto me the i· of the dream.
7 make known unto me the i· thereof.
9 that I have seen, and the i· thereof.
18 declare the i· thereof, forasmuch
18 able to make known unto me the i·:
19 dream, or the i· thereof, trouble
19 and the i· thereof to thine enemies.
24 This is the i·, O king, and this is
5: 7 writing, and shew me the i· thereof,
8 known to the king the i· thereof.
12 be called, and he will shew the i·.
15 make known unto me the i· thereof:
15 could not shew the i· of the thing:
16 known to me the i· thereof, thou
17 and make known to him the i·.
26 This is the i· of the thing: Mene;
7: 16 made me know the i· of the things.
Joh 1: 42 Cephas, which is by i·, A stone.
9: 7 pool of Siloam, which is by i·, Sent.
Ac 9: 36 which by i· is called Dorcas: this
13: 8 sorcerer (for so is his name by i·)
1Co 12: 10 to another the i· of tongues:
14: 26 tongue, hath a revelation, hath an i·.
Heb 7: 2 being by i· King of righteousness,
2Pe 1: 20 the scripture is of any private i·.

interpretations
Ge 40: 8 Do not i· belong to God? tell me
Da 5: 16 that thou canst make i·, and

interpreted
Ge 40: 22 baker: as Joseph had i· to them.
41: 12 him, and he i· to us our dreams;
13 to pass, as he i· to us, so it was;
Ezr 4: 7 and i· in the Syrian tongue.
M't 1: 23 which being i· is, God with us.
M'r 5: 41 cumi; which is, being i·, Damsel,
15: 22 is, being i·, The place of a skull.
34 which is, being i·, My God, my God,
Joh 1: 38 which is to say, being i·, Master,
41 which is, being i·, the Christ.
Ac 4: 36 being i·, The son of consolation,

interpreter
Ge 40: 8 a dream, and there is no i· of it.
42: 23 for he spake unto them by an i·.
Job 33: 23 an i·, one among a thousand, to
1Co 14: 28 if there be no i·, let him keep

interpreting
Da 5: 12 understanding, i· of dreams, and

into^ See also THEREINTO.
Ge 2: 7 breathed i· his nostrils the breath of
10 parted, and became i· four heads.
15 and put him i· the garden of Eden
6: 18 and thou shalt come i· the ark,
19 sort shalt thou bring i· the ark,
7: 1 thou and all thy house i· the ark;
7 his sons' wives with him, i· the ark,
9 two and two unto Noah i· the ark,
13 of his sons with them, i· the ark,
15 went in unto Noah i· the ark, two
8: 9 she returned unto him i· the ark;
9 pulled her in unto him i· the ark.
9: 2 sea; i· your hands are they delivered.
11: 31 Chaldees, to go i· the land of Canaan;
12: 5 went forth to go i· the land of Canaan;
5 and i· the land of Canaan they came.
10 Abram went down i· Egypt to sojourn
11 he was come near to enter i· Egypt,
14 that, when Abram was come i· Egypt,
15 woman was taken i· Pharaoh's house.
13: 1 he had, and Lot with him, i· the south.
14: 20 delivered thine enemies i· thy hand.
16: 5 I have given my maid i· thy bosom;
18: 6 And Abraham hastened i· the tent
19: 2 I pray you, i· your servant's house,
3 unto him, and entered i· his house;
10 and pulled Lot i· the house to them,
23 the earth when Lot entered i· Zoar.
21: 32 i· the land of the Philistines.
22: 2 and get thee i· the land of Moriah;
24: 20 emptied her pitcher i· the trough,
32 And the man came i· the house: and
67 Isaac brought her i· his mother
26: 2 Go not down i· Egypt; dwell in the
27: 17 prepared, i· the hand of her son Jacob.
28: 15 will bring thee again i· this land;
29: 1 came i· the land of the people of the
30: 35 gave them i· the hand of his sons.
31: 33 went i· Jacob's tent, and i· Leah's tent,
33 and i· the two maidservants' tents;
33 tent, and entered i· Rachel's tent.
32: 17 herds, and the camels, i· two bands;
6 delivered them i· the hand of his
36: 6 went i· the country from the face
37: 20 us slay him, and cast him i· some pit,
22 cast him i· this pit that is in the
24 they took him, and cast him i· a pit:
28 and they brought Joseph i· Egypt.
35 I will go down i· the grave unto my
36 Midianites sold him i· Egypt unto
39: 4 and all that he had he put i· his hand.
11 that Joseph went i· the house to do
20 took him, and put him i· the prison,
40: 3 i· the prison, the place where Joseph
11 and pressed them i· Pharaoh's cup,
11 I gave the cup i· Pharaoh's hand.
13 deliver Pharaoh's cup i· his hand,
15 they should put me i· the dungeon.
21 gave the cup i· Pharaoh's hand:
41: 57 And all countries came i· Egypt to
42: 17 all together i· ward three days.
25 every man's money i· his sack,
37 deliver him i· my hand, and I will
43: 17 brought the men i· Joseph's house.
18 they were brought i· Joseph's
24 brought the men i· Joseph's house,
26 which was in their hand i· the house,
30 he entered i· his chamber, and wept
45: 4 your brother, whom ye sold i· Egypt.
25 and came i· the land of Canaan unto
46: 3 fear not to go down i· Egypt; for I will
4 I will go down with thee i· Egypt; for
6 and came i· Egypt, Jacob, and all his
7 seed brought he with him i· Egypt.
8 of Israel, which came i· Egypt,
27 house of Jacob, which came i· Egypt,
28 they came i· the land of Goshen.
47: 14 brought the money i· Pharaoh's house.
48: 5 I came unto thee i· Egypt, are mine;
16 let them grow i· a multitude in the
49: 6 my soul, come not thou i· their secret;
33 he gathered up his feet i· the bed,
50: 13 his sons carried him i· the land of
14 And Joseph returned i· Egypt, he, and
Ex 1: 1 of Israel, which came i· Egypt;
22 son that is born ye shall cast i· the
3: 18 three days' journey i· the wilderness,
4: 6 him, Put now thine hand i· thy bosom.
6 he put his hand i· his bosom: and
7 Put thine hand i· thy bosom again.
7 put his hand i· his bosom again;
19 Moses in Midian, Go, return i· Egypt:
21 When thou goest to return i· Egypt,
27 Go i· the wilderness to meet Moses.

Ex 5: 3 thee, three days' journey i' the desert.
7:23 turned and went i' his house,
8: 3 shall go up and come i' thine house,
3 and i' thy bedchamber, and upon thy
3 and i' the house of thy servants, and
3 upon thy people and i' thine ovens,
3 and i' thy kneading troughs:
21 upon thy people, and i' thy houses:
24 grievous swarm of flies i' the house of
24 i' his servants' houses, and i' all the
27 three days' journey i' the wilderness,
9:20 and his cattle flee i' the houses:
10: 4 will I bring the locusts i' thy coast:
19 locusts, and cast them i' the Red sea;
11: 4 midnight will I go out i' the midst
13: 5, 11 thee i' the land of the Canaanites,
14:22 of Israel went i' the midst of the sea
28 that came i' the sea after them;
15: 1 his rider hath he thrown i' the sea.
4 and his host hath he cast i' the sea:
5 they sank i' the bottom as a stone.
19 and with his horsemen i' the sea,
21 his rider hath he thrown i' the sea.
22 went out i' the wilderness of Shur;
25 when he had cast i' the waters,
16: 3 brought us forth i' this wilderness,
18: 5 his wife unto Moses i' the wilderness,
7 welfare; and they came i' the tent.
27 he went his way i' his own land.
19: 1 came they i' the wilderness of Sinai.
12 that ye go not up i' the mount, or
21:13 but God deliver him i' his hand;
23:19 shalt bring i' the house of the Lord thy
20 bring thee i' the place which I have
31 inhabitants of the land i' your hand;
24:12 Come up to me i' the mount, and be
13 Moses went up i' the mount of God.
15 Moses went up i' the mount, and a
18 Moses went i' the midst of the cloud,
18 and gat him i' the mount: and
25:14 thou shalt put the staves i' the rings
16 shalt put i' the ark the testimony
26:11 put the taches i' the loops, and couple
27: 7 the staves shall be put i' the rings, and
29: 3 thou shalt put them i' one basket,
30 i' the tabernacle of...congregation
30:20 i' the tabernacle of the congregation,
32:24 then I cast it i' the fire, and there
33: 5 I will come up i' the midst of thee
8 until he was gone i' the tabernacle.
9 as Moses entered i' the tabernacle,
11 And he turned again i' the camp:
37: 5 And he put the staves i' the rings by
38: 7 And he put the staves i' the rings on
39: 3 did beat the gold i' thin plates,
3 and cut it i' wires, to work it in the
40:20 and put the testimony i' the ark,
21 brought the ark i' the tabernacle,
32 went i' the tent of the congregation,
35 was not able to enter i' the tent
Le 1: 6 burnt offering, and cut it i' his pieces.
12 And he shall cut it i' his pieces, with
6:30 blood is brought i' the tabernacle
8:20 he cut the ram i' pieces; and Moses
9:23 and Aaron went i' the tabernacle
10: 9 with ye, when ye go i' the tabernacle
11:32 it must be put i' water, and it shall
12: 4 thing, nor come i' the sanctuary,
13:17 if the plague be turned i' white;
14: 7 living bird loose i' the open field.
8 that he shall come i' the camp,
15 pour it i' the palm of his own left
26 oil i' the palm of his own left hand:
34 ye be come i' the land of Canaan,
36 the priest go i' it to see the plague,
40 shall cast them i' an unclean place
41 without the city i' an unclean place:
45 out of the city i' an unclean place.
46 he that goeth i' the house all the
53 bird out of the city i' the open fields,
16: 2 not at all times i' the holy place
3 shall Aaron come i' the holy place:
10 go for a scapegoat i' the wilderness.
21 hand of a fit man i' the wilderness:
23 Aaron shall come i' the tabernacle
23 on when he went i' the holy place,
26 and afterward come i' the camp.
28 afterward he shall come i' the camp.
19:23 when ye shall come i' the land, and
23:10 ye be come i' the land which I give
25: 2 ye come i' the land which I give you,
26:25 be delivered i' the hand of the enemy.
32 will bring the land i' desolation:
36 send a faintness i' their hearts in the
41 them i' the land of their enemies;
Nu 4:30, 35, 39, 43 that entereth i' the service,
5:17 shall take, and put it i' the water:
27 causeth the curse shall enter i' her,
7:89 Moses was gone i' the tabernacle
11:30 Moses gat him i' the camp, he and
13:17 and go up i' the mountain:
14: 3 it not better for us to return i' Egypt?
4 captain, and let us return i' Egypt.
8 he will bring us i' this land, and
16 able to bring this people i' the land
24 him will I bring i' the land whereinto
25 get you i' the wilderness by the way
30 ye shall not come i' the land,
40 them up i' the top of the mountain,
15: 2 come i' the land of your habitations,
18 ye come i' the land whither I bring
16:14 i' a land that floweth with milk and
30 they go down quick i' the pit; then ye
33 went down alive i' the pit, and the
47 ran i' the midst of the congregation;
17: 8 went i' the tabernacle of witness;

Nu 19: 6 i' the midst of the burning of the
7 he shall come i' the camp, and the
14 all that come i' the tent, and all that
20: 1 congregation, i' the desert of Zin in the
4 of the Lord i' this wilderness,
12 i' the land which I have given them.
15 How our fathers went down i' Egypt,
24 he shall not enter i' the land which
27 they went up i' mount Hor in the
21: 2 indeed deliver this people i' my hand,
22 turn i' the fields, or i' the vineyards;
23 out against Israel i' the wilderness:
27 Come i' Heshbon, let the city of Sihon
29 i' captivity unto Sihon king of the
34 I have delivered him i' thy hand, and
22:13 Get you i' your land: for the Lord
23 out of the way, and went i' the field:
23 smote the ass, to turn her i' the way.
41 brought him up i' the high places of
23:14 he brought him i' the field of Zophim,
24: 4, 16 falling i' a trance, but having his
25: 8 after the man of Israel i' the tent,
27:12 Get thee up i' this mount Abarim,
31:24 afterward ye shall come i' the camp.
27 And divide the prey i' two parts;
54 brought it i' the tabernacle of the
32: 7 from going over i' the land which
9 they should not go i' the land which
32 before the Lord i' the land of Canaan,
33: 8 midst of the sea i' the wilderness,
38 the priest went up i' mount Hor
51 over Jordan i' the land of Canaan;
34: 2 ye come i' the land of Canaan;
35:10 over Jordan i' the land of Canaan;
28 slayer shall return i' the land of his
36:12 married i' the families of the sons of
De 1:22 and i' what cities we shall come.
24 turned and went up i' the mountain,
27 deliver us i' the hand of the Amorites,
31 went, until ye came i' this place.
40 take your journey i' the wilderness
41 war, ye were ready to go up i' the hill.
43 went presumptuously up i' the hill.
2: 1 took our journey i' the wilderness by
24 behold, I have given i' thine hand Sihon
29 i' the land which the Lord our God
30 that he might deliver him i' thy hand,
3: 2 his people, and his land, i' thy hand;
3 God delivered i' our hands Og also,
27 Get thee up i' the top of Pisgah, and
5: 5 and went not up i' the mount: saying,
30 to them, Get you i' your tents again.
6:10 i' the land which he sware unto thy
7: 1 thy God shall bring thee i' the land
24 shall deliver their kings i' thine hand,
26 an abomination i' thine house,
8: 7 God bringeth thee i' a good land,
9: 9 i' the mount to receive the tables of
21 I cast the dust thereof i' the brook
28 not able to bring them i' the land
10: 1 and come up unto me i' the mount,
3 and went up i' the mount, having the
22 Thy fathers went down i' Egypt with
11: 5 until ye came i' this place;
13:16 spoil of it i' the midst of the street
14: 6 and cleaveth the cleft i' two claws,
25 turn it i' money, and bind up the
17: 8 get thee up i' the place which the
18: 9 thou art come i' the land which
19: 3 i' three parts, that every slayer may
5 i' the wood with his neighbour to
11 die, and fleeth i' one of these cities:
12 deliver him i' the hand of the avenger
20:13 thy God hath delivered it i' thine hands,
21:10 God hath delivered them i' thine hands,
23: 1 off, shall not enter i' the congregation
2 shall not enter i' the congregation of
2 shall he not enter i' the congregation
3 shall not enter i' the congregation of
3 they not enter i' the congregation of
5 turned the curse i' a blessing unto
8 shall enter i' the congregation of the
11 he shall come i' the camp again.
18 i' the house of the Lord thy God for
24 When thou comest i' thy neighbour's
25 When thou comest i' the standing corn
24:10 not go i' his house to fetch his
26: 5 he went down i' Egypt, and sojourned
9 and he hath brought us i' this land,
28:25 shalt be removed i' all the kingdoms?
38 shalt carry much seed out i' the field,
41 them; for they shall go i' captivity.
68 Lord shall bring thee i' Egypt again
29:12 enter i' covenant with the Lord thy
12 i' his oath, which the Lord thy God
28 and cast them i' another land,
30: 5 thy God will bring thee i' the land
31:20 shall have brought them i' the land
21 them i' the land which I sware.
23 the children of Israel i' the land
32:26 I said, I would scatter them i' corners,
49 Get thee up i' this mountain
Jos 2: 1 and came i' an harlot's house, named
3 thee, which are entered i' thine house:
18 when we come i' the land, thou shalt
19 of the doors of thy house i' the street,
24 Lord hath delivered i' our hands all
3:11 passeth over before you i' Jordan.
4: 5 your God i' the midst of Jordan,
6: 2 I have given i' thine hand Jericho,
11 and they came i' the camp, and
14 city once, and returned i' the camp.
19 shall come i' the treasury of the Lord.
20 so that the people went up i' the city,
22 Go i' the harlot's house, and bring out
24 put i' the treasury of the house of the

Jos 7: 7 deliver us i' the hand of the Amorites,
8: 1 given i' thy hand the king of Ai, and
7 your God will deliver it i' your hand.
13 Joshua went that night i' the midst of
18 Ai; for I will give it i' thine hand.
19 and they entered i' the city, and took
10: 8 for I have delivered them i' thine hand;
19 suffer them not to enter i' their
19 God hath delivered them i' your hand.
20 of them entered i' fenced cities.
27 and cast them i' the cave wherein
30 king thereof, i' the hand of Israel;
32 delivered Lachish i' the hand of Israel,
11: 8 delivered them i' the hand of Israel,
13: 5 Hermon unto the entering i' Hamath.
18: 5 shall divide it i' seven parts: Judah
6 describe the land i' seven parts,
9 described it by cities i' seven parts
20: 4 take him i' the city unto them, and
5 not deliver the slayer up i' his hand;
21:44 delivered all their enemies i' their
22:13 of Manasseh, i' the land of Gilead,
24: 4 and his children went down i' Egypt.
8 And I brought you i' the land of the
8 and I gave them i' your hand, that ye
11 and I delivered them i' your hand.
J'g 1: 2 I have delivered the land i' his hand.
3 Come up with me i' my lot, that we
3 I likewise will go with thee i' thy lot.
4 and the Perizzites i' their hand:
16 of Judah i' the wilderness of Judah,
24 we pray thee, the entrance i' the city,
25 he shewed them the entrance i' the
26 man went i' the land of the Hittites,
34 the children of Dan i' the mountain:
2:14 he delivered them i' the hands of
14 he sold them i' the hands of their
23 he them i' the hand of Joshua.
3: 8 and he sold them i' the hand of
10 king of Mesopotamia i' his hand; and
21 right thigh, and thrust it i' his belly:
28 your enemies the Moabites i' your
4: 2 sold them i' the hand of Jabin king of
7 and I will deliver him i' thine hand.
9 sell Sisera i' the hand of a woman.
14 hath delivered Sisera i' thine hand:
18 had turned in unto her i' the tent, she
21 and smote the nail i' his temples,
21 fastened it i' the ground: for he was
22 And when he came i' her tent, behold,
5:15 he was sent on foot i' the valley.
6: 1 delivered them i' the hand of Midian
5 they entered i' the land to destroy it.
13 delivered us i' the hands of the
7: 2 to give the Midianites i' their hands,
7 deliver the Midianites i' thine hand:
9 for I have delivered it i' thine hand.
13 of barley bread tumbled i' the host
14 for i' his hand hath God delivered
15 returned i' the host of Israel, and
15 delivered i' your hand the host of
16 three hundred men i' three companies,
8: 3 delivered i' your hands the princes
7 Zebah and Zalmunna i' mine hand,
9:27 And they went out i' the fields, and
27 and went i' the house of their God,
42 that the people went out i' the field;
43 and divided them i' three companies,
46 entered i' an hold of the house of
10: 7 them i' the hands of the Philistines,
7 i' the hands of the children of Ammon.
11:19 thee, through my land i' my place.
21 and all his people i' the hand of Israel,
30 the children of Ammon i' mine hands,
32 the Lord delivered them i' his hands.
12: 3 the Lord delivered them i' my hand:
13: 1 them i' the hand of the Philistines
15: 1 I will go in to my wife i' the chamber.
5 them go i' the standing corn of the
12 thee i' the hand of the Philistines.
13 fast, and deliver thee i' their hand:
18 deliverance i' the hand of thy servant:
18 fall i' the hand of the uncircumcised?
16:23 Samson our enemy i' our hand.
24 hath delivered i' our hands our enemy,
18:10 for God hath given it i' your hands;
18 these went i' Micah's house, and
19: 3 she brought him i' her father's house:
11 turn in i' this city of the Jebusites,
12 aside hither i' the city of a stranger,
15 took them i' his house to lodging.
21 So he brought him i' his house, and
22 the man that came i' thine house,
23 that this man is come i' mine house,
29 when he was come i' his house, he
29 with her bones, i' twelve pieces,
29 and sent her i' all the coasts of Israel.
20: 4 i' Gibeah that belongeth to Benjamin,
8 will we any of us turn i' his house.
28 I will deliver them i' thine hand.
Ru 1: 2 And they came i' the country of Moab,
2:18 she took it up, and went i' the city:
3:14 known that a woman came i' the floor.
15 it on her: and she went i' the city.
4:11 woman that is come i' thine house
1Sa 2:14 And he struck it i' the pan, or kettle, or
36 thee, i' one of the priests' offices,
4: 3 the people were come i' the camp,
5 ark...of the Lord came i' the camp,
6 of the Lord was come i' the camp.
7 they said, God is come i' the camp.
10 and they fled every man i' his tent:
13 when the man came i' the city, and
5: 2 they brought it i' the house of Dagon,
5 nor any that come i' Dagon's house,
6:14 the cart came i' the field of Joshua,

1Sa 6:19 they had looked *i'* the ark of the Lord,
7: 1 brought it *i'* the house of Abinadab
13 came no more *i'* the coast of Israel:
9:13 As soon as ye be come *i'* the city, ye
14 And they went up *i'* the city:
14 when they were come *i'* the city,
22 and brought them *i'* the parlour, and
25 down from the high place *i'* the city,
10: 6 and shalt be turned *i'* another man.
11:11 they came *i'* the midst of the host in
12: 8 When Jacob was come *i'* Egypt, and
9 he sold them *i'* the hand of Sisera,
9 and *i'* the hand of the Philistines,
9 and *i'* the hand of the king of Moab,
14:10 Lord hath delivered them *i'* our hand:
12 delivered them *i'* the hand of Israel.
21 went up with them *i'* the camp from
26 the people were come *i'* the wood,
37 deliver them *i'* the hand of Israel?
17:22 and ran *i'* the army, and came and
46 the Lord deliver thee *i'* mine hand;
47 and he will give you *i'* our hands.
49 that the stone sunk *i'* his forehead;
19:10 and he smote the javelin *i'* the wall:
20: 8 hast brought thy servant *i'* a covenant
11 Come, and let us go out *i'* the field.
35 that Jonathan went out *i'* the field at
42 and Jonathan went *i'* the city.
21:15 shall this fellow come *i'* my house?
22: 5 and get thee *i'* the land of Judah.
5 and came *i'* the forest of Hareth.
23: 4 deliver the Philistines *i'* thine hand.
7 God hath delivered him *i'* mine hand;
7 by entering *i'* a town that hath gates
11 of Keilah deliver me up *i'* his hand?
12 me and my men *i'* the hand of Saul?
14 but God delivered him not *i'* his hand.
16 and went to David *i'* the wood, and
20 be to deliver him *i'* the king's hand.
25 he came down *i'* a rock, and abode in
24: 4 deliver thine enemy *i'* thine hand,
10 thee to day *i'* mine hand in the cave:
18 Lord had delivered me *i'* thine hand,
26: 3 Saul came after him *i'* the wilderness.
8 thine enemy *i'* thine hand this day:
10 or he shall descend *i'* battle, and
23 Lord delivered thee *i'* my hand to day,
27: 1 *i'* the land of the Philistines;
28:19 with thee *i'* the hand of the Philistines:
19 of Israel *i'* the hand of the Philistines.
29:11 return *i'* the land of the Philistines.
30:15 deliver me *i'* the hands of my master,
23 that came against us *i'* our hand.
31: 9 and sent *i'* the land of the Philistines
2Sa 2: 1 I go up *i'* any of the cities of Judah?
3: 8 delivered thee *i'* the hand of David,
34 not bound, nor thy feet put *i'* fetters:
4: 6 thither *i'* the midst of the house,
7 For when they came *i'* the house, he
5: 8 lame shall not come *i'* the house.
19 wilt thou deliver them *i'* mine hand?
19 deliver the Philistines *i'* thine hand.
6:10 Lord unto him *i'* the city of David:
10 it aside *i'* the house of Obed-edom
12 the house of Obed-edom *i'* the city of
16 of the Lord came *i'* the city of David,
10: 2 servants came *i'* the land of the
10 he delivered *i'* the hand of Abishai
14 before Abishai, and entered *i'* the city.
11:11 I then go *i'* mine house, to eat and to
23 us, and came out unto us *i'* the field,
12: 8 and thy master's wives *i'* thy bosom,
20 came *i'* the house of the Lord, and
13:10 Bring the meat *i'* the chamber, that I
10 brought them *i'* the chamber to Amnon
15:25 Carry back the ark of God *i'* the city:
27 return *i'* the city in peace, and your
31 the counsel of Ahithophel *i'* foolishness.
37 Hushai David's friend came *i'* the city,
37 and Absalom came *i'* Jerusalem.
16: 8 the kingdom *i'* the hand of Absalom
17:13 if he be gotten *i'* a city, then shall
13 and we will draw it *i'* the river,
17 might not be seen to come *i'* the city:
18: 6 went out *i'* the field against Israel:
17 cast him *i'* a great pit in the wood,
19: 2 that day was turned *i'* mourning
3 them by stealth that day *i'* the city,
5 Joab came *i'* the house to the king,
20:12 Amasa out of the highway *i'* the field,
21: 9 them *i'* the hands of the Gibeonites,
22: 7 temple, and my cry did enter *i'* his ears.
20 brought me forth also *i'* a large place:
23:11 were gathered together *i'* a troop,
24:14 let us fall now *i'* the hand of the Lord;
14 and let me not fall *i'* the hand of man.
1Ki 1:15 went in unto the king *i'* the chamber:
28 she came *i'* the king's presence, and,
3: 1 brought her *i'* the city of David,
6: 8 with winding stairs *i'* the middle
8 and out of the middle *i'* the third.
8: 6 *i'* the oracle of the house, to the
11:17 servants with him, to go *i'* Egypt;
40 and fled *i'* Egypt, unto Shishak king of
13:18 him back with thee *i'* thine house,
14:12 and when thy feet enter *i'* the city, the
28 the king went *i'* the house of the Lord,
28 them back *i'* the guard chamber.
15:15 dedicated, *i'* the house of the Lord,
18 them *i'* the hand of his servants:
16:18 *i'* the palace of the king's house,
21 the people of Israel divided *i'* two parts:
17:19 and carried him up *i'* a loft, where
21 this child's soul come *i'* him again,
22 soul of the child came *i'* him again,
23 down out of the chamber *i'* the house,
1Ki 18: 5 Go *i'* the land, unto all fountains of
9 deliver thy servant *i'* the hand of Ahab,
19: 4 went a day's journey *i'* the wilderness,
20: 2 to Ahab king of Israel *i'* the city, and
13 I will deliver it *i'* thine hand this day;
28 all this great multitude *i'* thine hand,
30 the rest fled to Aphek, *i'* the city;
30 Ben-hadad fled and came *i'* the city,
30 fled, and came...*i'* an inner chamber.
33 him to come up *i'* the chariot.
39 went out *i'* the midst of the battle;
21: 4 Ahab came *i'* his house heavy and
22: 6 shall deliver it *i'* the hand of the king.
12 Lord shall deliver it *i'* the king's hand.
15 shall deliver it *i'* the hand of the king.
25 shalt go *i'* an inner chamber to hide
30 thyself, and enter *i'* the battle;
30 himself, and went *i'* the battle.
35 wound *i'* the midst of the chariot.
2Ki 2: 1 up Elijah *i'* heaven by a whirlwind,
11 went up by a whirlwind *i'* heaven.
16 upon some mountain, or *i'* some valley.
3:10 to deliver them *i'* the hand of Moab!
13 to deliver them *i'* the hand of Moab,
18 deliver the Moabites also *i'* your hand.
4: 4 shalt pour out *i'* all those vessels,
11 and he turned *i'* the chamber, and
32 when Elisha was come *i'* the house,
39 went out *i'* the field to gather herbs,
39 shred them *i'* the pot of pottage:
41 bring meal. And he cast it *i'* the pot:
5:18 master goeth *i'* the house of Rimmon
6: 5 the axe head fell *i'* the water: and
20 when they were come *i'* Samaria, that
23 came no more *i'* the land of Israel.
7: 4 If we say, We will enter *i'* the city,
8 they went *i'* one tent, and did eat
8 and entered *i'* another tent, and
12 catch them alive, and get *i'* the city.
8:21 and the people fled *i'* their tents.
9: 6 And he arose, and went *i'* the house;
26 and cast him *i'* the plat of ground,
10:15 took him up to him *i'* the chariot.
21 And they came *i'* the house of Baal;
23 son of Rechab, *i'* the house of Baal,
24 I have brought *i'* your hands
11: 4 them to him *i'* the house of the Lord,
13 the people *i'* the temple of the Lord.
16 the horses came *i'* the king's house:
18 of the land went *i'* the house of Baal,
12: 4 is brought *i'* the house of the Lord,
4 that cometh *i'* any man's heart
4 to bring *i'* the house of the Lord,
9 one cometh *i'* the house of the Lord:
9 brought *i'* the house of the Lord.
11 *i'* the hands of them that did the
13 brought *i'* the house of the Lord:
15 *i'* whose hand they delivered the
16 brought *i'* the house of the Lord:
13: 3 delivered them *i'* the hand of Hazael
3 and *i'* the hand of Ben-hadad the son
21 the man *i'* the sepulchre of Elisha:
17: 6 and carried Israel away *i'* Assyria,
20 them *i'* the hand of spoilers,
18:21 if a man lean, it will go *i'* his hand,
30 be delivered *i'* the hand of the king
19: 1 and went *i'* the house of the Lord.
10 be delivered *i'* the hand of the king
14 went up *i'* the house of the Lord,
18 And have cast their gods *i'* the fire:
23 enter *i'* the lodgings of his borders,
23 and *i'* the forest of his Carmel.
25 waste fenced cities *i'* ruinous heaps.
28 the tumult is come up *i'* mine ears,
32 He shall not come *i'* this city, nor
33 and shall not come *i'* this city,
37 they escaped *i'* the land of Armenia.
20: 4 was gone out *i'* the middle court,
8 I shall go up *i'* the house of the Lord
20 conduit, and brought water *i'* the city,
21:14 them *i'* the hand of their enemies;
22: 4 brought *i'* the house of the Lord,
5 deliver it *i'* the hand of the doers
7 that was delivered *i'* their hand,
9 delivered it *i'* the hand of them that
20 be gathered *i'* thy grave in peace;
23: 2 went up *i'* the house of the Lord,
12 dust of them *i'* the brook Kidron.
24:15 carried he *i'* captivity from Jerusalem
1Ch 5:20 Hagarites were delivered *i'* their hand,
6:15 And Jehozadak went *i'* captivity,
10: 9 and sent *i'* the land of the Philistines
11:15 to David, *i'* the cave of Adullam;
12: 8 David *i'* the hold to the wilderness
13:13 it aside *i'* the house of Obed-edom
14:10 wilt thou deliver them *i'* mine hand?
10 for I will deliver them *i'* thine hand.
17 fame of David went out *i'* all lands;
16: 7 *i'* the hand of Asaph and his brethren.
19: 2 *i'* the land of the children of Ammon
15 his brother, and entered *i'* the city.
21:13 let me fall now *i'* the hand of the Lord;
13 but let me not fall *i'* the hand of man.
27 up his sword again *i'* the sheath
22:18 inhabitants of the land *i'* mine hand;
19 *i'* the house that is to be built to the
23: 6 David divided them *i'* courses among
24:19 service to come *i'* the house of the Lord,
2Ch 5: 7 the house, *i'* the most holy place,
6:41 arise, O Lord God, *i'* thy resting place,
7: 2 not enter *i'* the house of the Lord,
10 he sent the people away *i'* their tents,
11 all that came *i'* Solomon's heart
9: 4 he went up *i'* the house of the Lord;
12:11 king entered *i'* the house of the Lord,
11 them again *i'* the guard chamber.
2Ch 13:16 and God delivered them *i'* their hand.
15:12 And they entered *i'* a covenant to seek
18 And he brought *i'* the house of God
16: 8 Lord, he delivered them *i'* thine hand.
18: 5 for God will deliver it *i'* the king's hand.
11 shall deliver it *i'* the hand of the king.
14 they shall be delivered *i'* your hand.
24 shalt go *i'* an inner chamber to hide
20:20 went forth *i'* the wilderness of Tekoa:
21:17 And they came up *i'* Judah,
17 and brake *i'* it, and carried away
23: 1 the son of Zichri, *i'* covenant with him.
6 none come *i'* the house of the Lord,
7 whosoever else cometh *i'* the house,
12 to the people *i'* the house of the Lord:
20 the high gate *i'* the king's house,
24:10 and cast *i'* the chest, until they had
24 a very great host *i'* their hand, because
25:20 them *i'* the hand of their enemies,
26:16 and went *i'* the temple of the Lord
27: 2 not *i'* the temple of the Lord. And
28: 5 him *i'* the hand of the king of Syria;
5 *i'* the hand of the king of Israel.
9 he hath delivered them *i'* your hand,
27 they brought him not *i'* the sepulchres
29: 4 them together *i'* the east street,
16 *i'* the inner part of the house of the
16 *i'* the court of the house of the Lord.
16 it out abroad *i'* the brook Kidron.
31 offerings *i'* the house of the Lord.
30: 8 enter *i'* his sanctuary, which he hath
9 that they shall come again *i'* this land:
14 and cast them *i'* the brook Kidron.
15 offerings *i'* the house of the Lord.
31: 1 to his possession, *i'* their own cities.
10 the offerings *i'* the house of the Lord,
16 that entereth *i'* the house of the Lord,
32: 1 and entered *i'* Judah, and encamped
21 he was come *i'* the house of his god,
33:13 again to Jerusalem *i'* his kingdom.
34: 7 beaten the graven images *i'* powder,
9 was brought *i'* the house of God,
14 brought *i'* the house of the Lord,
17 it *i'* the hand of the overseers,
30 king went up *i'* the house of the Lord,
36:17 for age: he gave them all *i'* his hand.
Ezr 5: 8 we went *i'* the province of Judea, to
12 them *i'* the hand of Nebuchadnezzar
12 carried the people away *i'* Babylon.
14 brought them *i'* the temple of Babylon,
15 carry them *i'* the temple that is in
7: 7 delivered *i'* the hand of the kings of
10: 6 went *i'* the chamber of Johanan
Ne 2: 7 convey me over till I come *i'* Judah;
8 for the house that I shall enter *i'*.
5: 5 we bring *i'* bondage our sons and
6:11 go *i'* the temple to save his life?
7: 5 my God put *i'* mine heart to gather
8: 1 as one man *i'* the street that was
9:11 persecutors thou threwest *i'* the deeps,
11 as a stone *i'* the mighty waters.
22 and didst divide them *i'* corners: so
23 and broughtest them *i'* the land,
24 and gavest them *i'* their hands, with
27 them *i'* the hands of their enemies,
30 *i'* the hand of the people of the lands.
10:29 their nobles, and entered *i'* a curse,
29 and *i'* an oath, to walk in God's law,
34 to bring it *i'* the house of our God,
38 the chambers, *i'* the treasure-house.
12:44 to gather *i'* them out of the fields of
13: 1 not come *i'* the congregation of God
2 our God turned the curse *i'* a blessing.
15 *i'* Jerusalem on the sabbath day:
Es 1:22 letters *i'* all the king's provinces,
22 *i'* every province according to the
2:14 she returned *i'* the second house
16 Ahasuerus *i'* his house royal in the
3: 9 to bring it *i'* the king's treasuries.
13 by posts *i'* all the king's provinces,
4: 1 out *i'* the midst of the city, and
2 none might enter *i'* the king's gate
11 unto the king *i'* the inner court,
6: 4 Haman was come *i'* the outward court
7: 7 wrath went *i'* the palace garden:
8 the palace garden *i'* the place of the
9:22 and from mourning *i'* a good day:
Job 3: 6 come *i'* the number of the months.
9:24 is given *i'* the hand of the wicked:
10: 9 wilt thou bring me *i'* dust again?
12: 6 *i'* whose hand God bringeth
14: 3 bringest me *i'* judgment with thee?
16:11 over *i'* the hands of the wicked.
17:12 They change the night *i'* day: the
18: 8 For he is cast *i'* a net by his own feet,
18 be driven from light *i'* darkness,
22: 4 will he enter with thee *i'* judgment?
30: 3 fleeing *i'* the wilderness in former
19 He hath cast me *i'* the mire, and I am
31 and my organ *i'* the voice of them that
33:28 deliver his soul from going *i'* the pit,
36:16 thee out of the strait *i'* a broad place,
37: 8 Then the beasts go *i'* dens, and
38:16 Hast thou entered *i'* the springs of
22 Hast thou entered *i'* the treasures
38 When the dust groweth *i'* hardness,
39:12 thy seed, and gather it *i'* thy barn?
40:23 can draw up Jordan *i'* his mouth.
41: 2 Canst thou put a hook *i'* his nose?
22 sorrow is turned *i'* joy before him.
28 are turned with him *i'* stubble.
Ps 4: 2 long will ye turn my glory *i'* shame?
5: 7 I will come *i'* thy house in the
7:15 and is fallen *i'* the ditch which he
9:17 The wicked shall be turned *i'* hell,
10: 9 poor, when he draweth him *i'* his net.

Ps 16: 4 take up their names *i'* my lips.
18: 6 cry came before him, even *i'* his ears.
19 brought me forth also *i'* a large place;
22: 15 hast brought me *i'* the dust of death.
24: 3 shall ascend *i'* the hill of the Lord?
28: 1 like them that go down *i'* the pit.
30: 11 for me my mourning *i'* dancing:
31: 5 *I'* thine hand I commit my spirit:
8 not shut me up *i'* the hand of the
32: 4 is turned *i'* the drought of summer.
35: 8 *i'* that very destruction let him fall.
13 my prayer returned *i'* mine own
37: 15 sword shall enter *i'* their own heart,
20 *i'* smoke shall they consume away.
45: 2 grace is poured *i'* thy lips: therefore
15 they shall enter *i'* the King's palace.
46: 2 be carried *i'* the midst of the sea;
55: 15 and let them go down quick *i'* hell:
23 them down *i'* the pit of destruction:
56: 8 put thou my tears *i'* thy bottle: are
57: 6 *i'* the midst whereof they are fallen
60: 9 Who will bring me *i'* the strong city?
9 who will lead me *i'* Edom?
63: 9 shall go *i'* the lower parts of the earth.
66: 6 He turned the sea *i'* dry land: they
11 Thou broughtest us *i'* the net; thou
12 broughtest us out *i'* a wealthy place.
13 go *i'* thy house with burnt offerings:
69: 2 I am come *i'* deep waters, where the
27 them not come *i'* thy righteousness.
73: 17 I went *i'* the sanctuary of God;
18 castedst them down *i'* destruction.
19 How are they brought *i'* desolation.
74: 7 They have cast fire *i'* thy sanctuary,
76: 6 and horse are cast *i'* a dead sleep.
78: 44 And had turned their rivers *i'* blood;
61 And delivered his strength *i'* captivity,
61 his glory *i'* the enemy's hand.
79: 1 heathen are come *i'* thine inheritance:
12 neighbours sevenfold *i'* their bosom
88: 4 with them that go down *i'* the pit:
18 and mine acquaintance *i'* darkness.
95: 11 they should not enter *i'* my rest.
96: 8 an offering, and come *i'* his courts.
100: 4 Enter *i'* his gates with thanksgiving,
4 and *i'* his courts with praise: be
104: 10 He sendeth the springs *i'* the valleys,
105: 23 Israel also came *i'* Egypt; and Jacob
29 He turned their waters *i'* blood, and
106: 15 but sent leanness *i'* their soul,
20 changed their glory *i'* the similitude
41 And he gave them *i'* the hand of the
42 they were brought *i'* subjection
107: 33 He turneth rivers *i'* a wilderness, and
33 the watersprings *i'* dry ground;
34 A fruitful land *i'* barrenness, for the
35 the wilderness *i'* a standing water,
35 and dry ground *i'* watersprings.
108: 10 Who will bring me *i'* the strong city?
10 who will lead me *i'* Edom?
109: 18 let it come *i'* his bowels like water,
18 and like oil *i'* his bones.
114: 8 turned the rock *i'* a standing water,
8 the flint *i'* a fountain of waters.
115: 17 neither any that go down *i'* silence.
118: 19 I will go *i'* them, and I will praise the
20 *i'* which the righteous shall enter.
122: 1 Let us go *i'* the house of the Lord.
132: 3 I will not come *i'* the tabernacle of
3 of my house, nor go up *i'* my bed;
7 We will go *i'* his tabernacles: we will
8 Arise, O Lord, *i'* thy rest; thou, and
135: 9 and wonders *i'* the midst of thee,
136: 13 which divided the Red sea *i'* parts:
139: 8 If I ascend up *i'* heaven, thou art
140: 10 them: let them be cast *i'* the fire;
10 *i'* deep pits, that they rise not up
141: 10 Let the wicked fall *i'* their own nets,
143: 2 not *i'* judgment with thy servant:
7 unto them that go down *i'* the pit.
10 lead me *i'* the land of uprightness.
Pr 1: 12 as those that go down *i'* the pit:
2: 10 wisdom entereth *i'* thine heart,
4: 14 Enter not *i'* the path of the wicked,
6: 3 art come *i'* the hand of thy friend;
13: 17 wicked messenger falleth *i'* mischief:
16: 29 him *i'* the way that is not good.
33 The lot is cast *i'* the lap; but the
17: 10 reproof entereth more *i'* a wise man
10 than an hundred stripes *i'* a fool.
20 a perverse tongue falleth *i'* mischief.
18: 6 A fool's lips enter *i'* contention, and
8 *i'* the innermost parts of the belly.
10 righteous runneth *i'* it, and is safe.
19: 15 Slothfulness casteth *i'* a deep sleep;
23: 10 enter not *i'* the fields of the fatherless:
24: 16 but the wicked shall fall *i'* mischief.
26: 9 goeth up *i'* the hand of a drunkard,
22 *i'* the innermost parts of the belly.
27: 10 neither go *i'* thy brother's house in
28: 10 he shall fall himself *i'* his own pit:
14 his heart shall fall *i'* mischief.
29: 8 men bring a city *i'* a snare:
30: 4 Who hath ascended up *i'* heaven,
Ec 1: 7 All the rivers run *i'* the sea; yet
10: 8 He that diggeth a pit shall fall *i'* it;
11: 9 God will bring thee *i'* judgment.
12: 14 shall bring every work *i'* judgment,
Ca 1: 4 hath brought me *i'* his chambers:
3: 4 brought him *i'* my mother's house,
4 *i'* the chamber of her that conceived
4: 16 Let my beloved come *i'* his garden,
5: 1 I am come *i'* my garden, my sister, my
6: 2 beloved is gone down *i'* his garden,
11 I went down *i'* the garden of nuts
7: 11 beloved, let us go forth *i'* the field;

Ca 8: 2 bring thee *i'* my mother's house,
Isa 2: 4 beat their swords *i'* plowshares,
4 and their spears *i'* pruninghooks:
10 Enter *i'* the rock, and hide thee in the
19 they shall go *i'* the holes of the rocks,
19 and *i'* the caves of the earth, for fear
21 To go *i'* the clefts of the rocks,
21 and *i'* the tops of the ragged rocks,
3: 14 The Lord will enter *i'* judgment with
5: 13 my people are gone *i'* captivity,
14 he that rejoiceth, shall descend *i'* it.
9: 8 The Lord sent a word *i'* Jacob, and it
10 but we will change them *i'* cedars.
13: 2 they may go *i'* the gates of the nobles.
14 and flee every one *i'* his own land.
14: 7 quiet: they break forth *i'* singing.
13 I will ascend *i'* heaven, I will exalt my
19: 1 swift cloud, and shall come *i'* Egypt:
4 I give over *i'* the hand of a cruel lord;
8 they that cast angle *i'* the brooks
23 the Assyrian shall come *i'* Egypt,
23 and the Egyptian *i'* to Assyria, and the
21: 4 of my pleasure hath he turned *i'* fear
22: 18 thee like a ball *i'* a large country:
21 commit thy government *i'* his hand:
23: 9 *i'* contempt all the honourable
24: 18 noise of the fear shall fall *i'* the pit;
26: 20 my people, enter thou *i'* thy chambers,
29: 17 shall be turned *i'* a fruitful field,
30: 2 That walk to go down *i'* Egypt, and
6 *i'* the land of trouble and anguish,
20 be removed *i'* a corner any more,
29 to come *i'* the mountain of the Lord,
34: 9 thereof shall be turned *i'* pitch,
9 and the dust thereof *i'* brimstone,
36: 6 it will go *i'* his hand, and pierce it:
15 be delivered *i'* the hand of the king
37: 1 and went *i'* the house of the Lord.
10 not be given *i'* the hand of the king
19 And have cast their gods *i'* the fire:
24 I will enter *i'* the height of his border,
26 waste defenced cities *i'* ruinous heaps.
29 thy tumult, is come up *i'* mine ears,
33 He shall not come *i'* this city,
34 shall not come *i'* this city, saith the
38 they escaped *i'* the land of Armenia:
38: 18 go down *i'* the pit cannot hope for thy
40: 9 get thee up *i'* the high mountain;
44: 23 break forth *i'* singing, ye mountains,
46: 2 but themselves are gone *i'* captivity.
47: 5 thou silent, and get thee *i'* darkness,
6 and given them *i'* thine hand:
49: 13 break forth *i'* singing, O mountains:
51: 23 put it *i'* the hand of them that afflict
52: 1 there shall no more come *i'* thee the
4 people went down aforetime *i'* Egypt
9 Break forth *i'* joy, sing together,
54: 1 break forth *i'* singing, and cry aloud,
55: 12 shall break forth before you *i'* singing,
57: 2 He shall enter *i'* peace: they shall
59: 5 is crushed breaketh out *i'* a viper.
63: 14 As a beast goeth down *i'* the valley,
65: 6 even recompense *i'* their bosom,
7 their former work *i'* their bosom.
17 be remembered, nor come *i'* mind.
66: 20 offering in a clean vessel *i'* the house
Jer 2: 7 brought you *i'* a plentiful country,
21 art thou turned *i'* the degenerate plant
4: 5 and let us go *i'* the defenced cities.
29 they shall go *i'* thickets, and climb
6: 9 as a grapegatherer *i'* the baskets.
25 Go not forth *i'* the field, nor walk by
7: 31 not, neither came it *i'* my heart.
8: 6 as the horse rusheth *i'* the battle.
14 let us enter *i'* the defenced cities,
9: 21 For death is come up *i'* our windows,
21 and is entered *i'* our palaces, to cut off
10: 9 Silver spread *i'* plates is brought
12: 7 of my soul *i'* the hand of her enemies.
13: 16 he turn it *i'* the shadow of death,
14: 18 If I go forth *i'* the field, then behold
18 and if I enter *i'* the city, then behold
18 about *i'* a land that they know not.
15: 4 removed *i'* all kingdoms of the earth,
14 *i'* a land which thou knowest not:
16: 5 Enter not *i'* the house of mourning,
8 not also go *i'* the house of feasting,
13 land *i'* a land that ye know not,
15 *i'* their land that I gave unto their
17: 25 there enter *i'* the gates of this city
19: 5 neither came it *i'* my mind:
20: 4 all Judah *i'* the hand of the king
4 shall carry them captive *i'* Babylon,
5 I give *i'* the hand of their enemies,
6 in thine house, shall go *i'* captivity:
21: 4 them *i'* the midst of this city.
7 *i'* the hand of Nebuchadrezzar king
7 and *i'* the hand of their enemies,
7 and *i'* the hand of those that seek
10 *i'* the hand of the king of Babylon,
13 or who shall enter *i'* our habitations?
22: 7 cedars, and cast them *i'* the fire.
22 and thy lovers shall go *i'* captivity:
25 *i'* the hand of them that seek thy life,
25 and *i'* the hand of them whose face
25 even *i'* the hand of Nebuchadrezzar
25 and *i'* the hand of the Chaldeans.
26 *i'* another country, where ye were
28 cast *i'* a land which they know not?
23: 15 profaneness gone forth *i'* all the land.
24: 5 this place *i'* the land of the Chaldeans,
9 to be removed *i'* all the kingdoms of
26: 21 was afraid, and fled, and went *i'* Egypt;
22 the king sent men *i'* Egypt, namely,
22 and certain men with him *i'* Egypt.
23 *i'* the graves of the common people.

Jer 26: 24 not give him *i'* the hand of the people
27: 6 lands *i'* the hand of Nebuchadnezzar
28: 3 again *i'* this place all the vessels of
4 of Judah, that went *i'* Babylon, saith
6 captive, from Babylon *i'* this place.
29: 14 bring you again *i'* the place whence
16 are not gone forth with you *i'* captivity;
21 them *i'* the hand of Nebuchadrezzar
30: 6 and all faces are turned *i'* paleness?
16 every one of them, shall go *i'* captivity;
31: 13 for I will turn their mourning *i'* joy,
32: 3 give this city *i'* the hand of the king of
4 be delivered *i'* the hand of the king of
18 of the fathers *i'* the bosom of their
24 is given *i'* the hand of the Chaldeans,
25 is given *i'* the hand of the Chaldeans.
28 this city *i'* the hand of the Chaldeans,
28 and *i'* the hand of Nebuchadrezzar
35 neither came it *i'* my mind, that
36 be delivered *i'* the hand of the king of
43 it is given *i'* the hand of the Chaldeans.
33: 11 of praise *i'* the house of the Lord.
34: 2 give this city *i'* the hand of the king
3 be taken, and delivered *i'* his hand;
10 which had entered *i'* the covenant,
11 and brought them *i'* subjection for
16 and brought them *i'* subjection, to be
17 to be removed *i'* all the kingdoms of
20 give them *i'* the hand of their enemies,
20 and *i'* the hand of them that seek their
21 I give *i'* the hand of their enemies,
21 and *i'* the hand of them that seek their
21 and *i'* the hand of the king of Babylon's
35: 2 bring them *i'* the house of the Lord,
2 *i'* one of the chambers, and give
4 brought them *i'* the house of the Lord,
4 *i'* the chamber of the sons of Hanan,
11 king of Babylon came up *i'* the land,
36: 5 I cannot go *i'* the house of the Lord:
12 Then he went down *i'* the king's house,
12 *i'* the scribe's chamber: and, lo,
20 they went in to the king *i'* the court,
23 *i'* the fire that was on the hearth,
37: 4 for they had not put him *i'* prison.
7 return to Egypt *i'* their own land.
12 to go *i'* the land of Benjamin,
16 was entered *i'* the dungeon, and
16 and *i'* the cabins, and Jeremiah
17 be delivered *i'* the hand of the king
21 Jeremiah *i'* the court of the prison,
38: 3 be given *i'* the hand of the king surely
6 him *i'* the dungeon of Malchiah
9 whom they have cast *i'* the dungeon;
11 and went *i'* the house of the king
11 down by cords *i'* the dungeon
14 prophet unto him *i'* the third entry
16 I give thee *i'* the hand of these men
18 be given *i'* the hand of the Chaldeans,
19 lest they deliver me *i'* their hand, and
39: 9 carried away captive *i'* Babylon the
17 given *i'* the hand of the men of whom
40: 4 good...to come with me *i'* Babylon,
4 ill...to come with me *i'* Babylon,
41: 7 they came *i'* the midst of the city,
7 and cast them *i'* the midst of the pit,
17 Beth-lehem, to go to enter *i'* Egypt,
42: 14 we will go *i'* the land of Egypt, where
15 set your faces to enter *i'* Egypt,
17 to go *i'* Egypt to sojourn there;
18 when ye shall enter *i'* Egypt:
19 Go ye not *i'* Egypt: know certainly
43: 2 to say, Go not *i'* Egypt to sojourn there:
3 carry us away captives *i'* Babylon.
7 So they came *i'* the land of Egypt: for
44: 12 faces to go *i'* the land of Egypt
14 gone *i'* the land of Egypt to sojourn
14 should return *i'* the land of Judah,
21 them, and came it not *i'* his mind?
28 the land of Egypt *i'* the land of Judah,
28 gone *i'* the land of Egypt to sojourn
30 of Egypt *i'* the hand of his enemies,
30 *i'* the hand of them that seek his life;
30 Judah *i'* the hand of Nebuchadrezzar
46: 11 Go up *i'* Gilead, and take balm, O
19 furnish thyself to go *i'* captivity: for
24 *i'* the hand of the people of the north.
26 them *i'* the hand of those that seek
26 and *i'* the hand of Nebuchadrezzar
26 and *i'* the hand of his servants: and
47: 6 put up thyself *i'* thy scabbard,
48: 7 Chemosh shall go forth *i'* captivity
11 neither hath he gone *i'* captivity:
44 from the fear shall fall *i'* the pit;
49: 3 for their king shall go *i'* captivity, and
32 I will scatter *i'* all winds them that
51: 9 us go every one *i'* his own country:
50 let Jerusalem come *i'* your mind.
51 come *i'* the sanctuaries of the Lord's
59 Zedekiah the king of Judah *i'* Babylon
63 cast it *i'* the midst of Euphrates:
52: 12 the king of Babylon, *i'* Jerusalem,
La 1: 3 Judah is gone *i'* captivity because
5 her children are gone *i'* captivity
7 people fell *i'* the hand of the enemy,
10 the heathen entered *i'* her sanctuary,
10 should not enter *i'* thy congregation.
13 above hath he sent fire *i'* my bones,
14 Lord hath delivered me *i'* their hands,
18 my young men are gone *i'* captivity.
2: 7 given up *i'* the hand of the enemy the
9 Her gates are sunk *i'* the ground; he
12 poured out *i'* their mothers' bosom.
3: 2 and brought me *i'* darkness, but not
13 of his quiver to enter *i'* my reins.
4: 12 entered *i'* the gates of Jerusalem.
22 more carry thee away *i'* captivity:

La 5:15 our dance is turned *i'* mourning.
Eze 2: 2 the spirit entered *i'* me when he spake
3:22 Arise, go forth *i'* the plain, and I
23 I arose, and went forth *i'* the plain:
24 the spirit entered *i'* me, and set me
4:14 there abominable flesh *i'* my mouth.
5: 4 cast them *i'* the midst of the fire,
4 come forth *i'* all the house of Israel.
6 changed my judgments *i'* wickedness
10 of thee will I scatter *i'* all the winds.
12 scatter a third part *i'* all the winds,
7:11 is risen up *i'* a rod of wickedness:
21 will give it *i'* the hands of the strangers
22 for the robbers shall enter *i'* it, and
8:16 he brought me *i'* the inner court
10: 7 and put it *i'* the hands of him that
11: 5 the things that come *i'* your mind,
9 deliver you *i'* the hands of strangers,
24 vision by the Spirit of God *i'* Chaldea,
12: 4 as they that go forth *i'* captivity.
13: 5 Ye have not gone up *i'* the gaps,
9 shall they enter *i'* the land of Israel:
14:19 Or if I send a pestilence *i'* that land,
15: 4 Behold, it is cast *i'* the fire for fuel;
16: 8 and entered *i'* a covenant with thee,
13 and thou didst prosper *i'* a kingdom.
39 And I will also give thee *i'* their hand,
17: 4 and carried it *i'* a land of traffick; he
15 in sending his ambassadors *i'* Egypt,
19: 9 they brought him *i'* holds, that his
20: 6 *i'* a land that I had espied for them,
10 and brought them *i'* the wilderness.
15 not bring them *i'* the land which I
28 when I had brought them *i'* the land,
32 that which cometh *i'* your mind
35 I will bring you *i'* the wilderness
37 bring you *i'* the bond of the covenant:
38 shall not enter *i'* the land of Israel:
42 shall bring you *i'* the land of Israel,
42 *i'* the country for the which I lifted
21:11 to give it *i'* the hand of the slayer.
14 which entereth *i'* their privy chambers.
30 I cause it to return *i'* his sheath?
31 thee *i'* the hand of brutish men,
22:19 you *i'* the midst of Jerusalem.
20 *i'* the midst of the furnace, to blow
23: 9 delivered her *i'* the hand of her lovers,
9 *i'* the hand of the Assyrians, upon
16 messengers unto them *i'* Chaldea.
17 came to her *i'* the bed of love,
28 deliver thee *i'* the hand of them whom
28 *i'* the hand of them from whom thy
31 will I give her cup *i'* thine hand.
39 the same day *i'* my sanctuary
24: 3 set it on, and also pour water *i'* it:
4 Gather the pieces thereof *i'* it, even
25: 3 Judah, when they went *i'* captivity;
26:10 when he shall enter *i'* thy gates,
10 as men enter *i'* a city wherein is
20 with them that descend *i'* the pit,
27:26 have brought thee *i'* great waters:
27 shall fall *i'* the midst of the seas in
28: 4 gold and silver *i'* thy treasures:
23 For I will send *i'* her pestilence, and
23 and blood *i'* her streets; and the
29: 5 leave thee thrown *i'* the wilderness,
14 them to return *i'* the land of Pathros,
14 *i'* the land of their habitation.
30:12 the land *i'* the hand of the wicked:
17 and these cities shall go *i'* captivity.
18 her daughters shall go *i'* captivity.
25 put my sword *i'* the hand of the king
31:11 him *i'* the hand of the mighty one
16 hell with them that descend *i'* the pit:
17 They also went down *i'* hell with him
32: 9 *i'* the countries which thou hast
18 with them that go down *i'* the pit.
24 down uncircumcised *i'* the nether
36: 5 my land *i'* their possession with the
24 will bring you *i'* your own land.
37: 5 I will cause breath to enter *i'* you,
10 and the breath came *i'* them, and they
12 and bring you *i'* the land of Israel.
17 join them one to another *i'* one stick;
21 and bring them *i'* their own land:
22 be divided *i'* two kingdoms any more
38: 4 and put hooks *i'* thy jaws, and I will
8 thou shalt come *i'* the land that is
10 shall things come *i'* thy mind,
39:23 went *i'* captivity for their iniquity:
23 them *i'* the hand of their enemies:
28 them to be led *i'* captivity among
40: 2 brought he me *i'* the land of Israel,
17 brought he me *i'* the outward court,
32 he brought me *i'* the inner court
41: 6 they entered *i'* the wall which was of
42: 1 brought me forth *i'* the utter court,
1 and he brought me *i'* the chamber
9 as one goeth *i'* them from the utter
12 the east, as one entereth *i'* them.
14 of the holy place *i'* the utter court,
43: 4 Lord came *i'* the house by the way
5 brought me *i'* the inner court; and,
44: 7 brought *i'* my sanctuary strangers
9 shall enter *i'* my sanctuary, of any
12 the house of Israel to fall *i'* iniquity;
16 They shall enter *i'* my sanctuary,
19 they go forth *i'* the utter court, even
19 even *i'* the utter court to the people,
21 when they enter *i'* the inner court.
27 day that he goeth *i'* the sanctuary,
46:19 *i'* the holy chambers of the priests,
20 they bear them not out *i'* the utter
21 brought me forth *i'* the utter court,
47: 8 country, and go down *i'* the desert,
8 the desert, and go down *i'* the sea:
Eze 47: 8 which being brought forth *i'* the sea,
Da 1: 2 Jehoiakim king of Judah *i'* his hand,
2 *i'* the land of Shinar to the house of
2 brought the vessels *i'* the treasure
9 brought Daniel *i'* favour and tender
2:29 came *i'* thy mind upon thy bed,
38 heaven hath he given *i'* thine hand,
3: 6, 11, 15 *i'* the midst of a burning fiery
20 cast them *i'* the burning fiery furnace.
21 cast *i'* the midst of the burning fiery
23 bound *i'* the midst of the burning fiery
24 men bound *i'* the midst of the fire?
5:10 his lords came *i'* the banquet house:
6: 7 he shall be cast *i'* the den of lions.
10 was signed, he went *i'* his house; and his
12 king, shall be cast *i'* the den of lions?
16 and cast him *i'* the den of lions.
24 they cast them *i'* the den of lions,
7:25 they shall be given *i'* his hand until
10: 8 was turned in me *i'* corruption, and
11: 7 shall enter *i'* the fortress of the king
8 also carry captives *i'* Egypt their gods,
9 the south shall come *i'* his kingdom,
9 and shall return *i'* his own land.
11 multitude shall be given *i'* his hand.
28 he return *i'* his land with great riches;
40 and he shall enter *i'* the countries,
41 He shall enter also *i'* the glorious land,
Ho 2:14 her, and bring her *i'* the wilderness,
4: 7 will I change their glory *i'* shame.
9: 4 not come *i'* the house of the Lord.
11: 5 not return *i'* the land of Egypt,
9 thee: and I will not enter *i'* the city.
12: 1 Assyrians, and oil is carried *i'* Egypt.
12 And Jacob fled *i'* the country of Syria,
Joe 1:14 land *i'* the house of the Lord your God,
2:20 will drive him *i'* a land barren and
31 The sun shall be turned *i'* darkness,
31 and the moon *i'* blood, before the
3: 2 bring them down *i'* the valley of
5 and have carried *i'* your temples my
8 daughters *i'* the hand of the children
10 Beat your plowshares *i'* swords,
10 and your pruninghooks *i'* spears;
Am 1: 4 send a fire *i'* the house of Hazael,
5 Syria shall go *i'* captivity unto Kir,
15 their king shall go *i'* captivity, he and
2: 1 the bones of the king of Edom *i'* lime:
4: 3 ye shall cast them *i'* the palace, saith
5: 5 seek not Beth-el, nor enter *i'* Gilgal,
5 Gilgal shall surely go *i'* captivity,
8 the shadow of death *i'* the morning,
19 or went *i'* the house, and leaned his
27 will I cause you to go *i'* captivity
6:12 ye have turned judgment *i'* gall, and
12 the fruit of righteousness *i'* hemlock:
7:12 flee thee away *i'* the land of Judah.
17 Israel shall surely go *i'* captivity
8:10 I will turn your feasts *i'* mourning,
10 all your songs *i'* lamentation; and I
9: 2 Though they dig *i'* hell, thence shall
4 though they go *i'* captivity before
Ob 11 and foreigners entered *i'* his gates,
13 shouldest not have entered *i'* the gate
Jon 1: 3 and went down *i'* it, to go with them
4 sent out a great wind *i'* the sea,
5 that were in the ship *i'* the sea, to
5 gone down *i'* the sides of the ship;
12 me up, and cast me forth *i'* the sea;
15 Jonah, and cast him forth *i'* the sea:
2: 3 For thou hadst cast me *i'* the deep,
7 in unto thee, *i'* thine holy temple.
3: 4 to enter *i'* the city a day's journey,
Mic 1: 6 down the stones thereof *i'* the valley,
16 for they are gone *i'* captivity from
3: 5 that putteth not *i'* their mouths,
4: 3 shall beat their swords *i'* plowshares,
3 and their spears *i'* pruninghooks:
12 gather them as the sheaves *i'* the floor.
5: 5 the Assyrian shall come *i'* our land:
6 when he cometh *i'* our land, and when
7:19 all their sins *i'* the depths of the sea.
Na 3:10 carried away, she went *i'* captivity:
12 fall *i'* the mouth of the eater.
14 go *i'* clay, and tread the morter, make
Hab 3:16 rottenness entered *i'* my bones, and I
Hag 1: 6 wages to put it *i'* a bag with holes.
Zec 5: 4 shall enter *i'* the house of the thief,
4 *i'* the house of him that sweareth
8 he cast it *i'* the midst of the ephah;
6: 6 go forth *i'* the north country;
10 and go *i'* the house of Josiah the son
10:10 bring them *i'* the land of Gilead
11: 6 men every one *i'* his neighbour's hand,
6 and *i'* the hand of his king: and they
14: 2 of the city shall go forth *i'* captivity,
Mal 3:10 all the tithes *i'* the storehouse,
M't 1:17 until the carrying away *i'* Babylon
17 from the carrying away *i'* Babylon
2:11 when they were come *i'* the house,
12 departed *i'* their own country
13 and his mother, and flee *i'* Egypt,
14 by night, and departed *i'* Egypt:
20 mother, and go *i'* the land of Israel:
21 and came *i'* the land of Israel.
22 turned aside *i'* the parts of Galilee:
3:10 is hewn down, and cast *i'* the fire.
12 gather his wheat *i'* the garner;
4: 1 *i'* the wilderness to be tempted of
5 devil taketh him up *i'* the holy city,
8 up *i'* an exceeding high mountain,
12 that John was cast *i'* prison,
12 prison, he departed *i'* Galilee;
18 casting a net *i'* the sea: for they
5: 1 he went up *i'* a mountain: and
20 in no case enter *i'* the kingdom
M't 5:25 officer, and thou be cast *i'* prison.
29, 30 whole body should be cast *i'* hell.
6: 6 thou prayest, enter *i'* thy closet,
13 lead us not *i'* temptation, but
26 do they reap, nor gather *i'* barns;
30 and to morrow is cast *i'* the oven,
7:19 is hewn down, and cast *i'* the fire.
21 enter *i'* the kingdom of heaven;
8: 5 Jesus was entered *i'* Capernaum,
12 shall be cast out *i'* outer darkness:
14 Jesus was come *i'* Peter's house,
23 And when he was entered *i'* a ship,
28 *i'* the country of the Gergesenes,
31 us to go away *i'* the herd of swine.
32 out, they went *i'* the herd of swine:
32 down a steep place *i'* the sea,
33 fled, and went their ways *i'* the city,
9: 1 And he entered *i'* a ship, and passed
1 over, and came *i'* his own city.
17 do men put new wine *i'* old bottles:
17 they put new wine *i'* new bottles,
23 Jesus came *i'* the ruler's house, and
26 hereof went abroad *i'* all that land.
28 when he was come *i'* the house, the
38 send forth labourers *i'* his harvest
10: 5 Go not *i'* the way of the Gentiles,
5 *i'* any city of the Samaritans enter
11 And *i'* whatsoever city or town ye
12 when ye come *i'* an house, salute it.
23 you in this city, flee ye *i'* another:
11: 7 went ye out *i'* the wilderness to see?
12: 4 How he entered *i'* the house of God,
9 thence, he went *i'* their synagogue:
11 if it fall *i'* a pit on the sabbath day,
29 one enter *i'* a strong man's house,
44 I will return *i'* my house from
13: 2 so that he went *i'* a ship, and sat;
8 But other fell *i'* good ground, and
20 received the seed *i'* stony places,
23 received seed *i'* the good ground is
30 but gather the wheat *i'* my barn.
36 away, and went *i'* the house:
42 shall cast them *i'* a furnace of fire:
47 unto a net, that was cast *i'* the sea,
48 and gathered the good *i'* vessels,
50 cast them *i'* the furnace of fire:
54 he was come *i'* his own country, he
14:13 thence by ship *i'* a desert place
15 that they may go *i'* the villages,
22 his disciples to get *i'* a ship, and to
23 up *i'* a mountain apart to pray: and
32 when they were come *i'* the ship,
34 came *i'* the land of Gennesaret.
35 they sent out *i'* all that country
15:11 Not that which goeth *i'* the mouth
14 blind, both shall fall *i'* the ditch.
17 in at the mouth goeth *i'* the belly,
17 and is cast out *i'* the draught?
21 *i'* the coasts of Tyre and Sidon.
29 and went up *i'* a mountain, and sat
39 and came *i'* the coasts of Magdala.
16:13 When Jesus came *i'* the coasts of
17: 1 them up *i'* an high mountain apart,
15 for ofttimes he falleth *i'* the fire,
15 and oft *i'* the water.
22 be betrayed *i'* the hands of men:
25 when he was come *i'* the house,
18: 3 shall not enter *i'* the kingdom of
8 thee to enter *i'* life halt or maimed,
8 two feet to be cast *i'* everlasting fire.
9 thee to enter *i'* life with one eye,
9 two eyes to be cast *i'* hell fire.
12 and goeth *i'* the mountains, and
30 but went and cast him *i'* prison,
19: 1 and came *i'* the coasts of Judæa
17 if thou wilt enter *i'* life, keep the
23 enter *i'* the kingdom of heaven.
24 man to enter *i'* the kingdom of God.
20: 1 to hire labourers *i'* his vineyard.
2 a day, he sent them *i'* his vineyard.
4 Go ye also *i'* the vineyard, and
7 them, Go ye also *i'* the vineyard; and
21: 2 Go *i'* the village over against you,
10 when he was come *i'* Jerusalem,
12 Jesus went *i'* the temple of God,
17 went out of the city *i'* Bethany;
18 as he returned *i'* the city, he
21 removed, and be thou cast *i'* the sea;
23 when he was come *i'* the temple,
31 harlots go *i'* the kingdom of God
33 to husbandmen, and went *i'* a far
22: 9 Go ye therefore *i'* the highways,
10 servants went out *i'* the highways,
13 cast him *i'* outer darkness; there
24:16 be in Judæa flee *i'* the mountains:
38 day that Noe entered *i'* the ark.
25:14 as a man travelling *i'* a far country,
21, 23 enter thou *i'* the joy of thy lord.
30 ye the unprofitable servant *i'* outer
41 me, ye cursed, *i'* everlasting fire,
46 go away *i'* everlasting punishment:
46 but the righteous *i'* life eternal.
26:18 Go *i'* the city to such a man, and
30 they went out *i'* the mount of Olives.
32 again, I will go before you *i'* Galilee.
41 that ye enter not *i'* temptation:
45 is betrayed *i'* the hands of sinners.
52 Put up again thy sword *i'* his place:
71 when he was gone out *i'* the porch,
27: 6 for to put them *i'* the treasury,
27 took Jesus *i'* the common hall,
53 and went *i'* the holy city, and
28: 7 he goeth before you *i'* Galilee;
10 my brethren that they go *i'* Galilee,
11 some of the watch came *i'* the city,
16 disciples went away *i'* Galilee.

M't 28: 16 i' a mountain where Jesus had
M'r 1: 12 spirit driveth him i' the wilderness.
14 Jesus came i' Galilee, preaching
16 brother casting a net i' the sea:
21 And they went i' Capernaum; and
21 day he entered i' the synagogue,
29 they entered i' the house of Simon
35 and departed i' a solitary place,
38 Let us go i' the next towns, that I
45 no more openly enter i' the city,
2: 1 again he entered i' Capernaum after
11 and go thy way i' thine house.
22 putteth new wine i' old bottles:
22 wine must be put i' new bottles.
26 he went i' the house of God in the
3: 1 he entered again i' the synagogue;
13 he goeth up i' a mountain, and
19 him: and they went i' an house.
27 can enter i' a strong man's house,
4: 1 that he entered i' a ship, and sat
26 should cast seed i' the ground;
37 the waves beat i' the ship, so that
5: 1 i' the country of the Gadarenes.
12 him, saying, Send us i' the swine,
12 that we may enter i' them.
13 went out, and entered i' the swine:
13 down a steep place i' the sea.
18 And when he was come i' the ship,
6: 1 and came i' his own country; and
10 place soever ye enter i' an house,
31 yourselves apart i' a desert place,
32 i' a desert place by ship privately.
36 may go i' the country round about,
36 and i' the villages, and buy
45 his disciples to get i' the ship, and
46 he departed i' a mountain to pray.
51 went up unto them i' the ship; and
53 came i' the land of Gennesaret,
56 he entered, i' villages, or cities, or
7: 15 that entering i' him can defile him:
17 And when he was entered i' the
18 from without entereth i' the man,
19 not i' his heart, but i' the belly
19 and goeth out i' the draught,
24 i' the borders of Tyre and Sidon,
24 and entered i' a house, and would
33 and put his fingers i' his ears, and
8: 10 entered i' a ship with his disciples,
10 came i' the parts of Dalmanutha.
13 and entering i' the ship again
26 Neither go i' the town, nor tell it to
27 i' the towns of Cæsarea Philippi:
9: 2 up i' a high mountain apart by
22 ofttimes it hath cast him i' the fire,
22 and i' the waters, to destroy him:
25 of him, and enter no more i' him.
28 when he was come i' the house, his
31 is delivered i' the hands of men,
42 neck, and he were cast i' the sea.
43 for thee to enter i' life maimed,
43 than having two hands to go i' hell,
43 i' the fire that never shall be
45 better for thee to enter halt i' life,
45 having two feet to be cast i' hell,
45 i' the fire that never shall be
47 to enter i' the kingdom of God
47 having two eyes to be cast i' hell
10: 1 i' the coast of Judæa by the farther
17 when he was gone forth i' the way,
23 have riches enter i' the kingdom of
24 to enter i' the kingdom of God!
25 man to enter i' the kingdom of God.
11: 2 way i' the village over against you:
2 as soon as ye be entered i' it, ye
11 And Jesus entered i' Jerusalem,
11 and i' the temple: and when he
15 and Jesus went i' the temple, and
23 be thou cast i' the sea; and shall
12: 1 husbandmen, and went i' a far country.
41 people cast money i' the treasury:
43 which have cast i' the treasury:
13: 15 housetop not go down i' the house,
14: 13 Go ye i' the city, and there shall
16 came i' the city, and found as he
26 they went out i' the mount of Olives.
28 risen, I will go before you i' Galilee.
38 pray, lest ye enter i' temptation.
41 is betrayed i' the hands of sinners.
54 i' the palace of the high priest:
68 he went out i' the porch; and the
15: 16 soldiers led him away i' the hall,
16: 5 And entering i' the sepulchre, they
7 that he goeth before you i' Galilee:
12 walked, and went i' the country.
15 Go ye i' all the world, and preach
19 he was received up i' heaven, and
Lu 1: 9 he went i' the temple of the Lord.
39 went i' the hill country with haste,
39 with haste, i' a city of Juda;
40 entered i' the house of Zacharias,
79 guide our feet i' the way of peace.
2: 3 be taxed, every one i' his own city.
4 i' Judæa, unto the city of David
15 gone away from them i' heaven,
27 he came by the Spirit i' the temple:
39 they returned i' Galilee, to their
3: 3 he came i' all the country about
9 is hewn down, and cast i' the fire.
17 will gather the wheat i' his garner;
4: 1 led by the Spirit i' the wilderness,
5 taking him up i' a high mountain,
14 the power of the Spirit i' Galilee:
16 i' the synagogue on the sabbath
37 out i' every place of the country
38 and entered i' Simon's house. And
42 departed and went i' a desert place:

Lu 5: 3 And he entered i' one of the ships,
4 Launch out i' the deep, and let
16 withdrew himself i' the wilderness,
19 couch i' the midst before Jesus.
24 up thy couch, and go i' thine house.
37 putteth new wine i' old bottles;
38 wine must be put i' new bottles;
6: 4 How he went i' the house of God,
6 he entered i' the synagogue and
12 he went out i' a mountain to pray,
38 over, shall men give i' your bosom.
39 shall they not both fall i' the ditch?
7: 1 people, he entered i' Capernaum.
11 that he went i' a city called Nain;
24 ye out i' the wilderness for to see?
36 he went i' the Pharisee's house,
44 I entered i' thine house, thou
8: 22 went i' a ship with his disciples:
29 driven of the devil i' the wilderness.
30 many devils were entered i' him.
31 command them to go out i' the deep.
32 would suffer them to enter i' them.
33 the man, and entered i' the swine:
33 down a steep place i' the lake,
37 and he went up i' the ship, and
41 that he would come i' his house:
51 And when he came i' the house, he
9: 4 whatsoever house ye enter i', there
10 aside privately i' a desert place
12 may go i' the towns and country
28 and went up i' a mountain to pray.
34 feared as they entered i' the cloud.
44 sayings sink down i' your ears:
44 be delivered i' the hands of men.
52 i' a village of the Samaritans,
10: 1 two before his face i' every city
2 send forth labourers i' his harvest.
5 And i' whatsoever house ye enter,
8 And i' whatsoever city ye enter,
10 But i' whatsoever city ye enter,
10 ways out i' the streets of the same,
38 that he entered i' a certain village:
38 Martha received him i' her house.
11: 4 And lead us not i' temptation; but
12: 5 killed hath power to cast i' hell;
28 and to morrow is cast i' the oven;
58 and the officer cast thee i' prison.
13: 19 a man took, and cast i' his garden;
14: 1 i' the house of one of the chief
5 have an ass or an ox fallen i' a pit,
21 out quickly i' the streets and lanes
23 Go out i' the highways and hedges,
15: 13 took his journey i' a far country,
15 sent him i' his fields to feed swine.
16: 4 they may receive me i' their houses.
9 you i' everlasting habitations.
16 and every man presseth i' it.
22 by the angels i' Abraham's bosom:
28 also come i' this place of torment.
17: 2 his neck, and he cast i' the sea,
12 as he entered i' a certain village,
27 the day that Noe entered i' the ark,
18: 10 men went up i' the temple to pray;
24 riches enter i' the kingdom of God!
25 man to enter i' the kingdom of God.
19: 4 up i' a sycomore tree to see him:
12 nobleman went i' a far country
23 not thou my money i' the bank,
30 ye i' the village over against you;
45 And he went i' the temple, and
20: 9 went i' a far country for a long time.
21: 1 casting their gifts i' the treasury.
12 up to the synagogues, and i' prisons,
24 be led away captive i' all nations:
22: 3 Satan i' Judas surnamed Iscariot,
10 when ye are entered i' the city,
10 him i' the house where he entereth
33 thee, both i' prison, and to death.
40 that ye enter not i' temptation.
46 pray, lest ye enter i' temptation.
54 him i' the high priest's house.
66 and led him i' their council, saying,
23: 19 and for murder, was cast i' prison.
25 and murder, was cast i' prison,
42 when thou comest i' thy kingdom.
46 i' thy hands I commend my spirit:
24: 7 delivered i' the hands of sinful men,
26 things, and to enter i' his glory?
51 them, and carried up i' heaven.
Joh 1: 9 every man that cometh i' the world.
43 Jesus would go forth i' Galilee,
3: 4 second time i' his mother's womb,
5 cannot enter i' the kingdom of God.
17 not his Son i' the world to condemn
19 that light is come i' the world, and
22 his disciples i' the land of Judæa;
24 For John was not yet cast i' prison.
35 hath given all things i' his hand.
4: 3 and departed again i' Galilee.
14 springing up i' everlasting life.
28 went her way i' the city, and saith
38 and ye are entered i' their labours.
43 thence, and went i' Galilee.
45 Then when he was come i' Galilee,
46 Jesus came again i' Cana of Galilee,
47 was come out of Judæa i' Galilee,
54 was come out of Judæa i' Galilee.
5: 4 down at a certain season i' the pool,
7 is troubled, to put me i' the pool:
24 shall not come i' condemnation;
6: 3 And Jesus went up i' a mountain,
14 that should come i' the world.
15 again i' a mountain himself alone.
17 And entered i' a ship, and went
21 willingly received him i' the ship:
22 not with his disciples i' the boat,

Joh 7: 3 and go i' Judæa, that thy disciples
14 feast Jesus went up i' the temple,
8: 2 he came again i' the temple,
9: 39 judgment I am come i' this world,
10: 1 not by the door i' the sheepfold,
36 sanctified, and sent i' the world,
40 Jordan i' the place where John
11: 7 disciples, Let us go i' Judæa again.
27 which should come i' the world.
30 Jesus was not yet come i' the town,
54 wilderness, i' a city called Ephraim,
12: 24 a corn of wheat fall i' the ground
46 I am come a light i' the world, that
13: 2 having now put i' the heart of Judas
3 had given all things i' his hands,
5 that he poureth water i' a bason,
27 after the sop Satan entered i' him.
15: 6 them, and cast them i' the fire,
16: 13 come, he will guide you i' all truth:
20 your sorrow shall be turned i' joy.
21 joy that a man is born i' the world.
28 Father, and am come i' the world:
17: 18 As thou hast sent me i' the world,
18 have I also sent them i' the world.
18: 1 a garden, i' the which he entered,
11 Put up thy sword i' the sheath:
15 i' the palace of the high priest.
28 went not i' the judgment hall, lest
33 entered i' the judgment hall again,
37 for this cause came I i' the world,
19: 9 went again i' the judgment hall,
17 cross went forth i' a place called
20: 6 and went i' the sepulchre, and seeth
11 down, and looked i' the sepulchre,
25 my finger i' the print of the nails,
25 and thrust my hand i' his side, I will
27 thy hand, and thrust it i' my side:
21: 3 and entered i' a ship immediately;
7 and did cast himself i' the sea.
Ac 1: 11 why stand ye gazing up i' heaven?
11 is taken up from you i' heaven,
11 as ye have seen him go i' heaven.
13 they went up i' an upper room,
2: 20 The sun shall be turned i' darkness,
20 and the moon i' blood, before that
34 is not ascended i' the heavens:
3: 1 i' the temple at the hour of prayer,
2 of them that entered i' the temple;
3 and John about to go i' the temple,
8 entered with them i' the temple,
5: 15 brought forth the sick i' the streets,
21 i' the temple early in the morning,
7: 3 i' the land which I shall shew thee.
4 removed him i' this land, wherein
6 they should bring them i' bondage,
9 with envy, sold Joseph i' Egypt:
15 Jacob went down i' Egypt, and died,
16 were carried over i' Sychem, and
23 i' his heart to visit his brethren
34 come, I will send thee i' Egypt.
39 hearts turned back again i' Egypt,
45 i' the possession of the Gentiles,
55 looked up stedfastly i' heaven,
8: 3 entering i' every house, and haling
38 they went down both i' the water,
9: 6 Arise, and go i' the city, and it shall
8 and brought him i' Damascus.
11 i' the street...called Straight.
17 his way, and entered i' the house;
39 brought him i' the upper chamber:
10: 10 they made ready, he fell i' a trance,
16 was received up again i' heaven.
22 angel to send for thee i' his house,
24 after they entered i' Cæsarea.
11: 8 at any time entered i' my mouth.
10 all were drawn up again i' heaven.
12 and we entered i' the man's house:
12: 17 departed, and went i' another place:
13: 14 i' the synagogue on the sabbath
14: 1 i' the synagogue of the Jews,
20 he rose up, and came i' the city:
22 enter i' the kingdom of God.
25 Perga, they went down i' Attalia:
16: 7 they assayed to go i' Bithynia:
9 Come over i' Macedonia, and help
10 endeavoured to go i' Macedonia,
15 Lord, come i' my house, and abide
19 i' the marketplace unto the rulers,
23 they cast them i' prison, charging
24 thrust them i' the inner prison,
34 he had brought them i' his house,
37 Romans, and have cast us i' prison;
40 and entered i' the house of Lydia:
17: 10 went i' the synagogue of the Jews.
18: 7 entered i' a certain man's house,
18 sailed thence i' Syria, and with him
19 he himself entered i' the synagogue,
27 he was disposed to pass i' Achaia,
19: 8 he went i' the synagogue, and spake
22 he sent i' Macedonia two of them
29 with one accord i' the theatre.
31 adventure himself i' the theatre.
20: 1 departed for to go i' Macedonia.
2 exhortation, he came i' Greece,
3 as he was about to sail i' Syria,
4 accompanied him i' Asia Sopater
9 Eutychus, being fallen i' a deep sleep:
18 the first day that I came i' Asia,
21: 3 sailed i' Syria, and landed at Tyre:
8 entered i' the house of Philip the
11 him i' the hands of the Gentiles.
26 with them entered i' the temple,
28 brought Greeks also i' the temple,
29 that Paul had brought i' the temple.
34 him to be carried i' the castle.
37 as Paul was to be led i' the castle.

Ac 21:38 and leddest out *i'* the wilderness
22: 4 *i'* prisons both men and women.
10 Arise, and go *i'* Damascus; and
11 were with me, I came *i'* Damascus.
23 clothes, and threw dust *i'* the air,
24 him to be brought *i'* the castle,
23:10 them, and to bring him *i'* the castle.
16 he went and entered *i'* the castle,
20 down Paul to morrow *i'* the council,
28 brought him forth *i'* their council:
24:27 Porcius Festus came *i'* Felix' room:
25: 1 when Festus was come *i'* the province,
23 was entered *i'* the place of hearing,
27: 1 determined...we should sail *i'* Italy,
2 entering *i'* a ship of Adramyttium,
6 ship of Alexandria sailing *i'* Italy;
15 and could not bear up *i'* the wind,
17 they should fall *i'* the quicksands,
30 had let down the boat *i'* the sea,
38 and cast out the wheat *i'* the sea.
39 *i'* the which they were minded,
41 *i'* a place where two seas met,
43 should cast themselves first *i'* the sea,
28: 5 he shook off the beast *i'* the fire,
17 *i'* the hands of the Romans:
23 came many to him *i'* his lodging;
Ro 1:23 *i'* an image made like to corruptible
25 changed the truth of God *i'* a lie,
26 *i'* that which is against nature:
5: 2 faith *i'* this grace wherein we stand,
12 one man sin entered *i'* the world,
6: 3 us as were baptized *i'* Jesus Christ
3 were baptized *i'* his death?
4 with him by baptism *i'* death:
7:23 me *i'* captivity to the law of sin
8:21 *i'* the glorious liberty of the
10: 6 Who shall ascend *i'* heaven? that is,
7 Or, Who shall descend *i'* the deep?
18 their sound went *i'* all the earth,
11:24 to nature *i'* a good olive tree:
24 be graffed *i'* their own olive tree?
15:24 I take my journey *i'* Spain, I will
28 fruit, I will come by you *i'* Spain.
1Co 2: 9 have entered *i'* the heart of man,
4:17 bring you *i'* remembrance of my ways
9:27 my body, and bring it *i'* subjection:
11:20 together therefore *i'* one place,
12:13 are we all baptized *i'* one body,
13 been all made to drink *i'* one Spirit.
14: 9 spoken? for ye shall speak *i'* the air.
23 be come together *i'* one place,
2Co 1:16 And to pass by you *i'* Macedonia,
2:13 I went from thence *i'* Macedonia.
3:18 *i'* the same image from glory to glory,
7: 5 when we were come *i'* Macedonia,
8:16 earnest care *i'* the heart of Titus
10: 5 bringing *i'* captivity every thought to
11:13 themselves *i'* the apostles of Christ.
14 is transformed *i'* an angel of light.
20 if a man bring you *i'* bondage,
12: 4 that he was caught up *i'* paradise,
Ga 1: 6 called you *i'* the grace of Christ
17 but I went *i'* Arabia, and returned
21 *i'* the regions of Syria and Cilicia;
2: 4 they might bring us *i'* bondage:
3:27 baptized *i'* Christ have put on
4: 6 the Spirit of his Son *i'* your hearts,
Eph 4: 9 *i'* the lower parts of the earth?
15 may grow up *i'* him in all things,
Col 1:13 translated us *i'* the kingdom of his
2:18 intruding *i'* those things which
2Th 3: 5 direct your hearts *i'* the love of God,
5 and *i'* the patient waiting for Christ.
1Ti 1: 3 when I went *i'* Macedonia, that
12 faithful, putting me *i'* the ministry;
15 came *i'* the world to save sinners;
3: 6 *i'* the condemnation of the devil.
7 he fall *i'* reproach and the snare of
16 in the world, received up *i'* glory.
5: 9 not a widow be taken *i'* the number
6: 7 we brought nothing *i'* this world,
9 rich fall *i'* temptation and a snare,
9 *i'* many foolish and hurtful lusts,
2Ti 3: 6 are they which creep *i'* houses,
Heb 1: 6 in the firstbegotten *i'* the world, he
3:11 They shall not enter *i'* my rest.
18 they should not enter *i'* his rest,
4: 1 being left us of entering *i'* his rest,
3 which have believed do enter *i'* rest,
3 wrath, if they shall enter *i'* my rest:
5 again, If they shall enter *i'* my rest.
10 For he that is entered *i'* his rest, he
11 labour therefore to enter *i'* that rest,
14 priest, that is passed *i'* the heavens
6:19 entereth *i'* that within the veil;
8:10 I will put my laws *i'* their mind,
9: 6 went always *i'* the first tabernacle,
7 *i'* the second went the high priest
8 the way *i'* the holiest of all was not yet
12 he entered in once *i'* the holy place,
24 is not entered *i'* the holy places
24 but *i'* heaven itself, now to appear
25 entereth *i'* the holy place every
10: 5 when he cometh *i'* the world, he
16 I will put my laws *i'* their hearts,
19 *i'* the holiest by the blood of Jesus,
31 fall *i'* the hands of the living God.
11: 8 *i'* a place which he should after
13:11 blood is brought *i'* the sanctuary by
Jas 1: 2 joy when ye fall *i'* divers temptations;
25 looketh *i'* the perfect law of liberty,
4:13 to morrow we will go *i'* such a city,
5: 4 *i'* the ears of the Lord of sabaoth.
12 lest ye fall *i'* condemnation.
1Pe 1:12 things the angels desire to look *i'*.
2: 9 darkness *i'* his marvellous light:
1Pe 3:22 Who is gone *i'* heaven, and is on
2Pe 1:11 *i'* the everlasting kingdom of our
2: 4 delivered them *i'* chains of darkness,
6 of Sodom and Gomorrha *i'* ashes
1Jo 4: 1 prophets are gone out *i'* the world.
9 his only begotten Son *i'* the world,
2Jo 7 deceivers are entered *i'* the world,
10 receive him not *i'* your house,
Jude 4 grace of our God *i'* lasciviousness,
Re 2:10 shall cast some of you *i'* prison,
22 Behold, I will cast her *i'* a bed,
22 with her *i'* great tribulation,
5: 6 of God sent forth *i'* all the earth.
8: 5 the altar, and cast it *i'* the earth:
8 with fire was cast *i'* the sea:
11:11 of life from God entered *i'* them,
12: 6 the woman fled *i'* the wilderness,
9 he was cast out *i'* the earth, and
14 she might fly *i'* the wilderness,
14 *i'* her place, where she is nourished
13:10 He that leadeth *i'* captivity shall
10 captivity shall go *i'* captivity:
14:10 *i'* the cup of his indignation;
19 thrust in his sickle *i'* the earth,
19 *i'* the great winepress of the wrath
15: 8 man was able to enter *i'* the temple,
16:16 gathered them together *i'* a place
17 angel poured out his vial *i'* the air;
19 great city was divided *i'* three parts,
17: 3 away in the spirit *i'* the wilderness:
8 bottomless pit, and go *i'* perdition:
11 of the seven, and goeth *i'* perdition.
18:21 millstone, and cast it *i'* the sea,
19:20 alive *i'* a lake of fire burning with
20: 3 And cast him *i'* the bottomless pit,
10 was cast *i'* the lake of fire and
14 and hell were cast *i'* the lake of fire.
15 of life was cast *i'* the lake of fire.
21:24 bring their glory and honour *i'* it.
26 and honour of the nations *i'* it.
27 enter *i'* it any thing that defileth,
22:14 in through the gates *i'* the city.

intreat See also ENTREAT; INTREATED.
Ge 23: 8 *i'* for me to Ephron the son of
Ex 8: 8 *I'* the Lord, that he may take
9 when shall I *i'* for thee, and for thy
28 not go very far away: *i'* for me.
29 *i'* the Lord that the swarms of flies
9:28 *I'* the Lord (for it is enough) that
10:17 once, and *i'* the Lord your God,
Ru 1:16 Ruth said, *I'* me not to leave thee,
1Sa 2:25 the Lord, who shall *i'* for him?
1Ki 13: 6 *I'* now the face of the Lord thy
Ps 45:12 the people shall *i'* thy favour.
Pr 19: 6 will *i'* the favour of the prince:
1Co 4:13 Being defamed, we *i'*: we are
Ph'p 4: 3 I *i'* thee also, true yokefellow,
1Ti 5: 1 an elder, but *i'* him as a father;

intreated See also ENTREATED.
Ge 25:21 Isaac *i'* the Lord for his wife,
21 and the Lord was *i'* of him, and
Ex 8:30 out from Pharaoh, and *i'* the Lord.
10:18 out from Pharaoh, and *i'* the Lord.
J'g 13: 8 Then Manoah *i'* the Lord, and said,
2Sa 21:14 after that God was *i'* for the land.
24:25 So the Lord was *i'* for the land, and
1Ch 5:20 in the battle, and he was *i'* of them;
2Ch 33:13 and he was *i'* of him, and heard
19 also, and how God was *i'* of him,
Ezr 8:23 God for this: and he was *i'* of us.
Job 19:16 answer; I *i'* him with my mouth.
17 I *i'* for the children's sake of
Ps 119:58 I *i'* thy favour with my whole
Isa 19:22 Lord, and he shall be *i'* of them,
Lu 15:28 came his father out, and *i'* him.
Heb 12:19 *i'* that the word should not be
Jas 3:17 and easy to be *i'*, full of mercy and

intreateth See ENTREATETH.

intreaties
Pr 18:23 The poor useth *i'*; but the rich

intreaty See also INTREATIES.
2Co 8: 4 Praying us with much *i'* that we

intruding
Col 2:18 *i'* into those things which he hath

invade See also INVADED.
2Ch 20:10 thou wouldest not let Israel *i'*,
Hab 3:16 he will *i'* them with his troops.

invaded
1Sa 23:27 for the Philistines have *i'* the land.
27: 8 went up, and *i'* the Geshurites,
30: 1 the Amalekites had *i'* the south,
2Ki 13:20 bands of the Moabites *i'* the land
2Ch 28:18 Philistines also had *i'* the cities

invasion
1Sa 30:14 We made an *i'* upon the south of

invent See also INVENTED.
Am 6: 5 *i'* to themselves instruments of

invented
2Ch 26:15 engines, *i'* by cunning men,

inventions
Ps 99: 8 thou tookest vengeance of their *i'*.
106:29 provoked him to anger with their *i'*:
39 went a whoring with their own *i'*.
Pr 8:12 and find out knowledge of witty *i'*.
Ec 7:29 but they have sought out many *i'*.

inventors
Ro 1:30 *i'* of evil things, disobedient to

invisible
Ro 1:20 For the *i'* things of him from the
Col 1:15 Who is the image of the *i'* God,
16 and that are in earth, visible and *i'*,
1Ti 1:17 unto the King eternal, immortal, *i'*,
Heb 11:27 endured, as seeing him who is *i'*.

invited
1Sa 9:24 since I said, I have *i'* the people.
2Sa 13:23 and Absalom *i'* all the king's sons.
Es 5:12 am I *i'* unto her also with the king.

inward See also INWARDS.
Ex 28:26 is in the side of the ephod *i'*.
39:19 was on the side of the ephod *i'*.
Le 13:55 it is fret *i'*, whether it be bare
2Sa 5: 9 round about from Millo and *i'*.
1Ki 7:25 and all their hinder parts were *i'*.
2Ch 3:13 their feet, and their faces were *i'*.
4: 4 and all their hinder parts were *i'*.
Job 19:19 All my *i'* friends abhorred me:
38:36 hath put wisdom in the *i'* parts?
Ps 5: 9 their *i'* part is very wickedness;
49:11 Their *i'* thought is, that their
51: 6 thou desirest truth in the *i'* parts:
64: 6 *i'* thought of every one of them,
Pr 20:27 all the *i'* parts of the belly.
30 do stripes the *i'* parts of the belly.
Isa 16:11 and mine *i'* parts for Kir-haresh.
Jer 31:33 I will put my law in their *i'* parts,
Eze 40: 9 and the porch of the gate was *i'*.
16 and windows were round about *i'*:
41: 3 Then went he *i'*, and measured the
42: 4 a walk of ten cubits breadth *i'*,
Lu 11:39 your *i'* part is full of ravening and
Ro 7:22 the law of God after the *i'* man:
2Co 4:16 the *i'* man is renewed day by day.
7:15 his *i'* affection is more abundant

inwardly
Ps 62: 4 their mouth, but they curse *i'*.
M't 7:15 but *i'* they are ravening wolves.
Ro 2:29 he is a Jew, which is one *i'*;

inwards
Ex 29:13 all the fat that covereth the *i'*,
17 in pieces, and wash the *i'* of him,
22 and the fat that covereth the *i'*, and
Le 1: 9 his *i'* and his legs shall he wash in
13 he shall wash the *i'* and the legs
3: 3 the fat that covereth the *i'*,
3 and all the fat that is upon the *i'*,
9 and the fat that covereth the *i'*,
9 and all the fat that is upon the *i'*,
14 the fat that covereth the *i'*,
14 and all the fat that is upon the *i'*,
4: 8 the fat that covereth the *i'*,
8 and all the fat that is upon the *i'*,
11 and with his legs, and his *i'*, and his
7: 3 and the fat that covereth the *i'*,
8:16 took all the fat that was upon the *i'*,
21 And he washed the *i'* and the legs
25 and all the fat that was upon the *i'*,
9:14 he did wash the *i'* and the legs,
19 and that which covereth the *i'*, and

Iphedeiah (*if-e-di'-ah*)
1Ch 8:25 And *I'*, and Penuel, the sons of

Ir (*ur*) See also IR-NAHASH; IR-SHEMESH.
1Ch 7:12 and Huppim, the children of *I'*.

Ira (*i'-rah*)
2Sa 20:26 *I'* also the Jairite was a chief
23:26 *I'* the son of Ikkesh the Tekoite,
38 *I'* an Ithrite, Gareb an Ithrite,
1Ch 11:28 *I'* the son of Ikkesh the Tekoite,
40 *I'* the Ithrite, Gareb the Ithrite,
27: 9 *I'* the son of Ikkesh the Tekoite:

Irad (*i'-rad*)
Ge 4:18 And unto Enoch was born *I'*:
18 *I'* begat Mehujael: and Mehujael

Iram (*i'-ram*)
Ge 36:43 Duke Magdiel, duke *I'*: these be
1Ch 1:54 Duke Magdiel, duke *I'*. These are

Iri (*i'-ri*)
1Ch 7: 7 and *I'*, five; heads of the house

Irijah (*i-ri'-jah*)
Jer 37:13 whose name was *I'*, the son of
14 *I'* took Jeremiah, and brought him

Ir-nahash (*ur-na'-hash*)
1Ch 4:12 and Tehinnah, the father of *I'*.

iron See also IRONS.
Ge 4:22 of every artificer in brass and *i'*:
Le 26:19 I will make your heaven as *i'*, and
Nu 31:22 the silver, the brass, the *i'*, the tin,
35:16 smite him with an instrument of *i'*,
De 3:11 his bedstead was a bedstead of *i'*;
4:20 you forth out of the *i'* furnace, even
8: 9 a land whose stones are *i'*, and out
27: 5 thou shalt not lift up any *i'* tool
28:23 earth that is under thee shall be *i'*.
48 shall put a yoke of *i'* upon thy neck,
33:25 Thy shoes shall be *i'* and brass;
Jos 6:19 gold, and vessels of brass and *i'*,
24 and the vessels of brass and of *i'*,
8:31 which no man hath lift up any *i'*:
17:16 of the valley have chariots of *i'*,
18 though they have *i'* chariots, and
22: 8 gold, and with brass, and with *i'*,
J'g 1:19 because they had chariots of *i'*.
4: 3 he had nine hundred chariots of *i'*;
13 even nine hundred chariots of *i'*,
1Sa 17: 7 weighed six hundred shekels of *i'*:
2Sa 12:31 saws, and under harrows of *i'*,
31 and under axes of *i'*, and made
23: 7 be fenced with *i'* and the staff of a
1Ki 6: 7 any tool of *i'* heard in the house,
8:51 from the midst of the furnace of *i'*.
22:11 Chenaanah made him horns of *i'*:
2Ki 6: 6 it in thither; and the *i'* did swim.
1Ch 20: 3 with harrows of *i'*, and with axes.

1Ch 22: 3 David prepared i' in abundance
14 and of brass and i' without weight;
16 the brass, and the i', there is no
29: 2 of brass, the i' for things of i',
7 one hundred thousand talents of i'.
2Ch 2: 7 in brass, and in i', and in purple,
14 in silver, in brass, in i', in stone,
18: 10 had made him horns of i',
24: 12 also such as wrought i' and brass
Job 19: 24 they were graven with an i' pen
20: 24 He shall flee from the i' weapon,
28: 2 I' is taken out of the earth, and
40: 18 brass; his bones are like bars of i'.
41: 27 He esteemeth i' as straw, and brass
Ps 2: 9 shalt break them with a rod of i';
105: 18 hurt with fetters: he was laid in i':
107: 10 being bound in affliction and i';
16 and cut the bars of i' in sunder.
149: 8 and their nobles with fetters of i';
Pr 27: 17 I' sharpeneth i'; so a man
Ec 10: 10 If the i' be blunt, and he do not
Isa 10: 34 the thickets of the forest with i',
45: 2 and cut in sunder the bars of i':
48: 4 thy neck is as an i' sinew, and thy
60: 17 gold, and for i' I will bring silver,
17 for wood brass, and for stones i':
Jer 1: 18 and an i' pillar, and brasen walls
6: 28 they are brass and i'; they are all
11: 4 land of Egypt, from the i' furnace,
15: 12 Shall i' break the northern i' and
17: 1 of Judah is written with a pen of i',
28: 13 shalt make for them yokes of i'.
14 have put a yoke of i' upon the neck
Eze 4: 3 take thou unto thee an i' pan,
3 and set it for a wall of i' between
22: 18 are brass, and tin, and i', and lead,
20 silver, and brass, and i', and lead,
27: 12 with silver, i', tin, and lead, they
19 bright i', cassia, and calamus, were
Da 2: 33 His legs of i', his feet part of i' and
34 image upon his feet that were of i'
35 Then was the i', the clay, the brass,
40 kingdom shall be strong as i':
40 i' breaketh in pieces and subdueth
40 and as i' that breaketh all these,
41 part of potters' clay, and part of i',
41 be in it of the strength of the i',
41 sawest the i' mixed with miry clay.
42 the toes of the feet were part of i',
43 sawest i' mixed with miry clay,
43 even as i' is not mixed with clay.
45 it brake in pieces the i', the brass,
4: 15, 23 even with a band of i' and brass,
5: 4 of gold, and of silver, of brass, of i',
23 gods of silver, and gold, of brass, i',
7: 7 it had great i' teeth: it devoured
19 whose teeth were of i', and his nails
Am 1: 3 with threshing instruments of i':
Mic 4: 13 for I will make thine horn i', and I
Ac 12: 10 they came unto the i' gate that
1Ti 4: 2 conscience seared with a hot i';
Re 2: 27 he shall rule them with a rod of i';
9: 9 as it were breastplates of i';
12: 5 to rule all nations with a rod of i':
18: 12 and of brass, and i', and marble,
19: 15 he shall rule them with a rod of i':

Iron (*i'-ron*)
Jos 19: 38 And I', and Migdal-el, Horem,

irons
Job 41: 7 thou fill his skin with barbed i'?

Irpeel (*ur'-pe-el*)
Jos 18: 27 Rekem, and I', and Taralah,

Ir-shemesh (*ur-she'-mesh*)
Jos 19: 41 was Zorah, and Eshtaol, and I',

Iru (*i'-ru*)
1Ch 4: 15 Caleb the son of Jephunneh; I',

Isaac (*i'-za-ak*) See also Isaac's.
Ge 17: 19 and thou shalt call his name I':
21 covenant will I establish with I',
21: 3 him, whom Sarah bare to him, I'.
4 Abraham circumcised his son I'
5 when his son I' was born unto him.
8 the same day that I' was weaned.
10 be heir with my son, even with I'.
12 for in I' shall thy seed be called.
22: 2 Take now thy son, thine only son I'
3 men with him, and I' his son,
6 offering, and laid it upon I' his son;
7 and I' spake unto Abraham his
9 and bound I' his son, and laid him
24: 4 and take a wife unto my son I'.
14 hast appointed for thy servant I';
62 I' came from the way of the well
63 I' went out to meditate in the field
64 saw I', she lighted off the camel.
66 told I' all things that he had done.
67 I' brought her into his mother
67 I' was comforted after his mother's
25: 5 gave all that he had unto I'.
6 sent them away from I' his son,
9 his sons I' and Ishmael buried him
11 that God blessed his son I';
11 and I' dwelt by the well Lahai-roi.
19 these are the generations of I',
19 Abraham's son: Abraham begat I':
20 I' was forty years old when he took
21 I' entreated the Lord for his wife,
26 I' was threescore years old when
28 I' loved Esau, because he did eat
26: 1 I' went unto Abimelech king of
6 And I' dwelt in Gerar:
8 I' was sporting with Rebekah his
9 Abimelech called I', and said,
Ge 26: 9 I' said unto him, Because I said,
12 I' sowed in that land, and received
16 Abimelech said unto I', Go from
17 I' departed thence, and pitched
18 I' digged again the wells of water,
27 I' said unto them, Wherefore come
31 I' sent them away, and they
35 which were a grief of mind unto I'
27: 1 when I' was old, and his eyes were
5 when I' spake to Esau his son.
20 I' said unto his son, How is it that
21 I' said unto Jacob, Come near, I
22 Jacob went near unto I' his father;
26 his father I' said unto him, Come
30 I' had made an end of blessing
30 gone out from the presence of I'
32 I' his father said unto him, Who
33 I' trembled very exceedingly, and
37 I' answered and said unto Esau,
39 I' his father answered and said
46 Rebekah said to I', I am weary of
28: 1 I' called Jacob, and blessed him,
5 I' sent away Jacob: and he went
6 saw that I' had blessed Jacob,
8 daughters of Canaan pleased not I'
13 thy father, and the God of I':
31: 18 for to go to I' his father in the land
42 Abraham, and the fear of I', had
53 sware by the fear of his father I'.
32: 9 and God of my father I', the Lord
35: 12 land which I gave Abraham and I',
27 Jacob came unto I' his father unto
27 where Abraham and I' sojourned.
28 I' were a hundred and fourscore
29 And I' gave up the ghost, and died,
46: 1 unto the God of his father I'.
48: 15 fathers Abraham and I' did walk,
16 of my fathers Abraham and I';
49: 31 buried I' and Rebekah his wife;
50: 24 to Abraham, to I', and to Jacob.
Ex 2: 24 Abraham, with I', and with Jacob.
3: 6 Abraham, the God of I', and the
15 the God of I', and the God of Jacob,
16 God of Abraham, of I', and of
4: 5 the God of I', and the God of Jacob,
6: 3 I appeared unto Abraham, unto I',
8 give it to Abraham, to I', and to
32: 13 Remember Abraham, I', and Israel,
33: 1 swear unto Abraham, to I', and to
Le 26: 42 and also my covenant with I',
Nu 32: 11 swear unto Abraham, unto I', and
De 1: 8 your fathers, Abraham, I', and
6: 10 to Abraham, to I', and to Jacob,
9: 5 fathers, Abraham, I', and Jacob.
27 servants, Abraham, I', and Jacob;
29: 13 to Abraham, to I', and to Jacob.
30: 20 to Abraham, to I', and to Jacob,
34: 4 I sware unto Abraham, unto I',
Jos 24: 3 multiplied his seed, and gave him I'.
4 I gave unto I' Jacob and Esau:
1Ki 18: 36 God of Abraham, I', and of Israel,
2Ki 13: 23 his covenant with Abraham, I', and
1Ch 1: 28 sons of Abraham; I', and Ishmael.
34 And Abraham begat I'.
34 The sons of I'; Esau and Israel.
16: 16 Abraham, and of his oath unto I';
29: 18 God of Abraham, I', and of Israel,
2Ch 30: 6 God of Abraham, I', and Israel,
Ps 105: 9 Abraham, and his oath unto I';
Jer 33: 26 seed of Abraham, I', and Jacob:
Am 7: 9 high places of I' shall be desolate,
16 thy word against the house of I'.
M't 1: 2 begat I'; and I' begat Jacob;
8: 11 sit down with Abraham, and I',
22: 32 God of I', and the God of Jacob?
M'r 12: 26 God of Abraham, and the God of I',
Lu 3: 34 which was the son of I', which was
13: 28 see Abraham, and I', and Jacob,
20: 37 and the God of I', and the God of
Ac 3: 13 The God of Abraham, and of I',
7: 8 Abraham begat I', and circumcised
8 and I' begat Jacob; and Jacob
32 God of Abraham, and the God of I',
Ro 9: 7 but, In I' shall thy seed be called.
10 by one, even by our father I';
Ga 4: 28 Now we, brethren, as I' was, are
Heb 11: 9 dwelling in tabernacles with I' and
17 when he was tried, offered up I':
18 That in I' shall thy seed be called:
20 By faith I' blessed Jacob and Esau
Jas 2: 21 offered I' his son upon the altar?

Isaac's (*i'-za-aks*)
Ge 26: 19 I' servants digged in the valley,
20 Gerar did strive with I' herdmen,
25 and there I' servants digged a well.
32 I' servants came, and told him

Isaiah^ (*i-za'-yah*) See also Esaias.
2Ki 19: 2 to I' the prophet the son of Amoz.
5 of king Hezekiah came to I'.
6 And I' said unto them, Thus shall
20 Then I' the son of Amoz sent to
20: 1 I' the son of Amoz came to him,
4 I' was gone out into the middle
7 And I' said, Take a lump of figs.
8 Hezekiah said unto I', What shall
9 I' said, This sign shalt thou have of
11 I' the prophet cried unto the Lord:
14 I' the prophet unto king Hezekiah,
16 I' said unto Hezekiah, Hear the
19 said Hezekiah unto I', Good is the
2Ch 26: 22 did I' the prophet, the son of Amoz,
32: 20 I' the son of Amoz, prayed and
32 in the vision of I' the prophet,
Isa 1: 1 The vision of I' the son of Amoz,
2: 1 word that I' the son of Amoz saw
Isa 7: 3 Then said the Lord unto I', Go
13: 1 which I' the son of Amoz did see.
20: 2 the same time spake the Lord by I'
3 my servant I' hath walked naked
37: 2 unto I' the prophet the son of Amoz.
5 of king Hezekiah came to I'.
6 I' said unto them, Thus shall ye say
21 Then I' the son of Amoz sent unto
38: 1 I' the prophet the son of Amoz
4 came the word of the Lord to I',
21 I' had said, Let them take a lump
39: 3 I' the prophet unto king Hezekiah,
5 Then said I' to Hezekiah, Hear the
8 Then said Hezekiah to I', Good is

Iscah (*is'-cah*) See also Sarah.
Ge 11: 29 of Milcah, and the father of I'.

Iscariot (*is-car'-e-ot*) See also Judas.
M't 10: 4 Judas I', who also betrayed him.
26: 14 one of the twelve, called Judas I',
M'r 3: 19 Judas I', which also betrayed him:
14: 10 And Judas I', one of the twelve,
Lu 6: 16 Judas I', which also was the traitor.
22: 3 Satan into Judas surnamed I',
Joh 6: 71 spake of Judas I' the son of Simon:
12: 4 one of his disciples, Judas I',
13: 3 now put it into the heart of Judas I',
26 the sop, he gave it to Judas I', the
14: 22 Judas saith unto him, not I', Lord,

Ish See Ish-bosheth; Ish-tob.

Ishbah (*ish'-bah*)
1Ch 4: 17 and I' the father of Eshtemoa.

Ishbak (*ish'-bak*)
Ge 25: 2 and Midian, and I', and Shuah.
1Ch 1: 32 and Midian, and I', and Shuah.

Ishbi-benob (*ish''-bi-be'-nob*)
2Sa 21: 16 And I', which was of the sons of

Ish-bosheth (*ish-bo'-sheth*) See also Esh-baal.
2Sa 2: 8 took I' the son of Saul, and
10 I' Saul's son was forty years old
12 the servants of I' the son of Saul,
15 pertained to I' the son of Saul,
3: 7 I' said to Abner, Wherefore hast
8 very wroth for the words of I',
14 David sent messengers to I' Saul's
15 I' sent, and took her from her
4: 5 heat of the day to the house of I',
8 brought the head of I' unto David
8 Behold the head of I' the son of
12 they took the head of I', and buried

Ishi (*i'-shi*)
1Ch 2: 31 of Appaim; I'. And the sons of I';
4: 20 the sons of I' were, Zoheth, and
42 and Uzziel, the sons of I'.
5: 24 of their fathers, even Epher, and I',
Ho 2: 16 Lord, that thou shalt call me I';

Ishiah (*i-shi'-ah*) See also Ishijah; Isshiah.
1Ch 7: 3 and Obadiah, and Joel, I', five:

Ishijah (*i-shi'-jah*) See also Ishiah; Jesiah.
Ezr 10: 31 the sons of Harim; Eliezer, I',

Ishma (*ish'-mah*)
1Ch 4: 3 Jezreel, and I', and Idbash: and

Ishmael (*ish'-ma-el*) See also Ishmaelite; Ishmael's.
Ge 16: 11 a son, and shalt call his name I';
15 son's name, which Hagar bare, I'.
16 old, when Hagar bare I' to Abram.
17: 18 O that I' might live before thee!
20 And as for I', I have heard thee:
23 And Abraham took I' his son, and
25 I' his son was thirteen years old,
26 circumcised, and I' his son.
25: 9 his sons Isaac and I' buried him
12 these are the generations of I',
13 are the names of the sons of I',
13 the firstborn of I', Nebajoth; and
16 These are the sons of I', and these
17 these are the years of the life of I',
28: 9 Then went Esau unto I', and took
9 Mahalath the daughter of I',
2Ki 25: 23, 25 even I' the son of Nethaniah,
1Ch 1: 28 sons of Abraham; Isaac, and I'.
29 The firstborn of I', Nebaioth; then
31 Kedemah. These are the sons of I'.
8: 38 I', and Sheariah, and Obadiah, and
9: 44 I', and Sheariah, and Obadiah, and
2Ch 19: 11 Zebadiah the son of I', the ruler
23: 1 I' the son of Jehohanan, and
Ezr 10: 22 Pashur; Elioenai, Maaseiah, I',
Jer 40: 8 even I' the son of Nethaniah, and
14 hath sent I' the son of Nethaniah
15 I will slay I' the son of Nethaniah,
16 for thou speakest falsely of I'.
41: 1 month, that I' the son of Nethaniah
2 Then arose I' the son of Nethaniah,
3 I' also slew all the Jews that were
6 And I' the son of Nethaniah went
7 I' the son of Nethaniah slew them,
8 among them that said unto I',
9 I' had cast all the dead bodies
9 I' the son of Nethaniah filled it with
10 I' carried away captive all the
10 I' the son of Nethaniah carried
11 I' the son of Nethaniah had done,
12 fight with I' the son of Nethaniah,
13 which were with I' saw Johanan
14 people that I' had carried away
15 But I' the son of Nethaniah escaped
16 he had recovered from I' the son of
18 I' the son of Nethaniah had slain

Ishmaelite (*ish'-ma-el-ite*) See also Ishmaelites; Ishmeelite.
1Ch 27: 30 the camels also was Obil the I':

Ishmaelites (*ish'-ma-el-ites*) See also ISHMEELITES.
J'g 8:24 earrings, because they were *I'*.
Ps 83: 6 tabernacles of Edom, and the *I'*;
Ishmael's (*ish'-ma-els*)
Ge 36: 3 AndBashemath *I'* daughter, sister
Ishmaiah (*ish-ma-i'-ah*) See also ISMAIAH.
1Ch 27:19 Zebulun, *I'* the son of Obadiah:
Ishmeelite (*ish'-me-el-ite*) See also ISHMAELITE; ISHMEELITES.
1Ch 2:17 of Amasa was Jether the *I'*.
Ishmeelites (*ish'-me-el-ites*) See also ISHMAELITES.
Ge 37:25 *I'* came from Gilead, with their
27 Come, and let us sell him to the *I'*.
28 sold Joseph to the *I'* for twenty
39: 1 bought him of the hands of the *I'*.
Ishmerai (*ish'-me-rahee*)
1Ch 8:18 *I'* also, and Jezliah, and Jobab,
Ishod (*i'-shod*)
1Ch 7:18 his sister Hammoleketh bare *I'*,
Ishpan (*ish'-pan*)
1Ch 8:22 And *I'*, and Heber, and Eliel,
Ish-tob (*ish'-tob*)
2Sa 10: 6 and of *I'* twelve thousand men.
8 of Zoba, and of Rehob, and *I'*.
Ishuah (*ish'-u-ah*) See also ISUAH.
Ge 46:17 and *I'*, and Isui, and Beriah,
Ishuai (*ish'-u-ahee*) See also ISHUI.
1Ch 7:30 and Isuah, and *I'*, and Beriah,
Ishui (*ish'-u-i*) See also ISHUAI; JESUI.
1Sa 14:49 Saul were Jonathan, and *I'*, and
island See also ISLANDS; ISLE.
Job 22:30 shall deliver the *i'* of the innocent,
Isa 34:14 meet with the wild beasts of the *i'*,
Ac 27:16 a certain *i'* which is called Clauda,
26 we must be cast upon a certain *i'*.
28: 1 knew that the *i'* was called Melita.
7 the chief man of the *i'*, whose name
9 which had diseases in the *i'*, came,
Re 6:14 every mountain and *i'* were moved
16:20 And every *i'* fled away, and the
islands See also ISLES.
Isa 11:11 Hamath, and from the *i'* of the sea.
13:22 the wild beasts of the *i'* shall cry in
41: 1 Keep silence before me, O *i'*; and
42:12 and declare his praise in the *i'*.
15 I will make the rivers *i'*, and I will
59:18 to the *i'* he will repay recompence.
Jer 50:39 beasts of the *i'* shall dwell there,
isle See also ISLAND; ISLES.
Isa 20: 6 inhabitants of this *i'* shall say in
23: 2 Be still, ye inhabitants of the *i'*;
6 howl, ye inhabitants of the *i'*.
Ac 13: 6 gone through the *i'* unto Paphos,
28:11 which had wintered in the *i'*, whose
Re 1: 9 was in the *i'* that is called Patmos,
isles See also ISLANDS.
Ge 10: 5 were the *i'* of the Gentiles divided
Es 10: 1 the land, and upon the *i'* of the sea.
Ps 72:10 and of the *i'* shall bring presents:
97: 1 the multitude of *i'* be glad thereof.
Isa 24:15 God of Israel in the *i'* of the sea.
40:15 taketh up the *i'* as a very little thing.
41: 5 The *i'* saw it, and feared; the ends
42: 4 and the *i'* shall wait for his law.
10 the *i'*, and the inhabitants thereof.
49: 1 Listen, O *i'*, unto me; and hearken,
51: 5 the *i'* shall wait upon me, and on
60: 9 Surely the *i'* shall wait for me, and
66:19 to Tubal, and Javan, to the *i'* afar off,
Jer 2:10 pass over the *i'* of Chittim, and see;
25:22 the *i'* which are beyond the sea,
31:10 declare it in the *i'* afar off, and say,
Eze 26:15 the *i'* shake at the sound of thy fall,
18 the *i'* tremble in the day of thy fall;
18 the *i'* that are in the sea shall be
27: 3 merchant of the people for many *i'*,
6 brought out of the *i'* of Chittim.
7 and purple from the *i'* of Elishah
15 many *i'* were the merchandise of
35 All the inhabitants of the *i'* shall be
39: 6 them that dwell carelessly in the *i'*:
Da 11:18 shall he turn his face unto the *i'*,
Zep 2:11 place, even all the *i'* of the heathen.
Ismachiah (*is-ma-ki'-ah*)
2Ch 31:13 and Jozabad, and Eliel, and *I'*,
Ismaiah (*is-ma-i'-ah*) See also ISHMAIAH.
1Ch 12: 4 And *I'* the Gibeonite, a mighty
Ispah (*is'-pah*)
1Ch 8:16 And Michael, and *I'*, and Joha,
Israel^ (*iz'-ra-el*) See also EL-ELOHE-ISRAEL; ISRAELITE; ISRAEL'S; JACOB; JESHURUN.
Ge 32:28 be called no more Jacob, but *I'*:
32 children of *I'* eat not of the sinew
34: 7 because he had wrought folly in *I'*
35:10 Jacob, but *I'* shall be thy name;
10 and he called his name *I'*.
21 *I'* journeyed, and spread his tent
22 when *I'* dwelt in that land, that
22 father's concubine: and *I'* heard it.
36:31 any king over the children of *I'*.
37: 3 *I'* loved Joseph more than all his
13 *I'* said unto Joseph, Do not thy
42: 5 the sons of *I'* came to buy corn
43: 6 *I'* said, Wherefore dealt ye so ill
8 Judah said unto *I'* his father,
11 *I'* said unto them, If it must be so
Ge 45:21 And the children of *I'* did so: and
28 *I'* said, It is enough; Joseph my
46: 1 *I'* took his journey with all that he
2 God spake unto *I'* in the visions of
5 the sons of *I'* carried Jacob their
8 are the names of the children of *I'*,
29 went up to meet *I'* his father, to
30 *I'* said unto Joseph, Now let me die
47:27 And *I'* dwelt in the land of Egypt,
29 time drew nigh that *I'* must die:
31 *I'* bowed himself upon the bed's
48: 2 *I'* strengthened himself, and sat
8 *I'* beheld Joseph's sons, and said,
10 the eyes of *I'* were dim for age,
11 *I'* said unto Joseph, I had not
14 And *I'* stretched out his right hand,
20 In thee shall *I'* bless, saying, God
21 *I'* said unto Joseph, Behold, I die:
49: 2 and hearken unto *I'* your father.
7 in Jacob, and scatter them in *I'*.
16 people, as one of the tribes of *I'*.
24 is the shepherd, the stone of *I'*:
28 these are the twelve tribes of *I'*:
50: 2 and the physicians embalmed *I'*.
25 took an oath of the children of *I'*,
Ex 1: 1 are the names of the children of *I'*,
7 the children of *I'* were fruitful, and
9 the children of *I'* are more and
12 because of the children of *I'*.
13 children of *I'* to serve with rigour:
2:23 of *I'* sighed by reason of bondage,
25 God looked upon the children of *I'*,
3: 9 the cry of the children of *I'* is come
10 forth my people the children of *I'*
11 bring forth the children of *I'* out of
13 when I come unto the children of *I'*,
14, 15 thou say unto the children of *I'*,
16 gather the elders of *I'* together,
18 come, thou and the elders of *I'*,
4:22 Thus saith the Lord, *I'* is my son,
29 all the elders of the children of *I'*:
31 Lord had visited the children of *I'*,
5: 1 Thus saith the Lord God of *I'*, Let
2 should obey his voice to let *I'* go?
2 the Lord, neither will I let *I'* go.
14 the officers of the children of *I'*,
15 officers of the children of *I'* came
19 officers of the children of *I'* did see
6: 5 the groaning of the children of *I'*,
6 say unto the children of *I'*, I am
9 spake so unto the children of *I'*:
11 children of *I'* go out of his land.
12 of *I'* have not hearkened unto me;
13 a charge unto the children of *I'*,
13 the children of *I'* out of the land of
14 sons of Reuben the firstborn of *I'*;
26 Bring out the children of *I'* from
27 to bring out the children of *I'* from
7: 2 that he send the children of *I'* out
4 and my people the children of *I'*,
5 and bring out the children of *I'*.
9: 4 shall sever between the cattle of *I'*
4 die of all that is the children's of *I'*.
6 cattle of the children of *I'* died not
26 where the children of *I'* were, was
35 would he let the children of *I'* go;
10:20 would not let the children of *I'* go.
23 of *I'* had light in their dwellings.
11: 7 children of *I'* shall not a dog move
7 between the Egyptians and *I'*.
10 the children of *I'* go out of his land.
12: 3 ye unto all the congregation of *I'*,
6 assembly of the congregation of *I'*
15 that soul shall be cut off from *I'*.
19 cut off from the congregation of *I'*,
21 Moses called for all the elders of *I'*,
27 the houses of the children of *I'* in
28 And the children of *I'* went away,
31 both ye and the children of *I'*;
35 of *I'* did according to the word of
37 And the children of *I'* journeyed
40 the sojourning of the children of *I'*,
42 children of *I'* in their generations.
47 the congregation of *I'* shall keep it.
50 Thus did all the children of *I'*; as
51 bring the children of *I'* out of the
13: 2 womb among the children of *I'*,
18 children of *I'* went up harnessed
19 straitly sworn the children of *I'*,
14: 2 Speak unto the children of *I'*, that
3 will say of the children of *I'*, They
5 we have let *I'* go from serving us?
8 he pursued after the children of *I'*:
8 of *I'* went out with an high hand.
10 children of *I'* lifted up their eyes
10 of *I'* cried out unto the Lord.
15 Speak unto the children of *I'*, that
16 of *I'* shall go on dry ground
19 which went before the camp of *I'*,
20 the Egyptians and the camp of *I'*;
22 of *I'* went into the midst of the sea
25 Let us flee from the face of *I'*; for
29 children of *I'* walked upon dry land
30 the Lord saved *I'* that day out of
30 *I'* saw the Egyptians dead upon
31 *I'* saw that great work which the
15: 1 sang Moses and the children of *I'*
19 the children of *I'* went on dry land
22 Moses brought *I'* from the Red sea,
16: 1 congregation of the children of *I'*
2 children of *I'* murmured against
3 the children of *I'* said unto them,
6 said unto all the children of *I'*,
9 all the congregation of the...of *I'*,
10 whole congregation of the...of *I'*,
12 murmurings of the children of *I'*:
Ex 16:15 when the children of *I'* saw it, they
17 And the children of *I'* did so, and
31 *I'* called the name thereof Manna:
35 children of *I'* did eat manna forty
17: 1 *I'* journeyed from the wilderness
5 take with thee of the elders of *I'*;
6 so in the sight of the elders of *I'*.
7 the chiding of the children of *I'*,
8 and fought with *I'* in Rephidim.
11 held up his hand, that *I'* prevailed:
18: 1 for Moses, and for *I'* his people,
1 Lord had brought *I'* out of Egypt;
9 which the Lord had done to *I'*,
12 Aaron came, and all the elders of *I'*,
25 Moses chose able men out of all *I'*,
19: 1 children of *I'* were gone forth out
2 there *I'* camped before the mount.
3 Jacob, and tell the children of *I'*;
6 shalt speak unto the children of *I'*.
20:22 shalt say unto the children of *I'*,
24: 1 and seventy of the elders of *I'*;
4 according to the twelve tribes of *I'*.
5 young men of the children of *I'*,
9 and seventy of the elders of *I'*:
10 And they saw the God of *I'*: and
11 the nobles of the children of *I'* he
17 in the eyes of the children of *I'*.
25: 2 Speak unto the children of *I'*, that
22 unto the children of *I'*.
27:20 shalt command the children of *I'*,
21 on the behalf of the children of *I'*.
28: 1 from among the children of *I'*, that
9, 11 the names of the children of *I'*:
12 memorial unto the children of *I'*:
21 the names of the children of *I'*,
29 bear the names of the children of *I'*
30 the judgment of the children of *I'*
38 *I'* shall hallow in all their holy
29:28 for ever from the children of *I'*:
28 offering from the children of *I'*
43 will meet with the children of *I'*,
45 will dwell among the children of *I'*,
30:12 takest the sum of the children of *I'*
16 money of the children of *I'*,
16 memorial unto the children of *I'*
31 shalt speak unto the children of *I'*,
31:13 thou also unto the children of *I'*,
16 of *I'* shall keep the sabbath,
17 between me and the children of *I'*
32: 4, 8 These be thy gods, O *I'*, which
13 Remember Abraham, Isaac, and *I'*,
20 made the children of *I'* drink of it.
27 Thus saith the Lord God of *I'*, Put
33: 5 Say unto the children of *I'*, Ye are
6 of *I'* stripped themselves of their
34:23 before the Lord God, the God of *I'*.
27 covenant with thee and with *I'*.
30 all the children of *I'* saw Moses,
32 all the children of *I'* came nigh:
34 and spake unto the children of *I'*
35 children of *I'* saw the face of Moses,
35: 1 congregation of the children of *I'*
4 congregation of the children of *I'*,
20 children of *I'* departed from
29 of *I'* brought a willing offering unto
30 Moses said unto the children of *I'*,
36: 3 of *I'* had brought for the service
39: 6 the names of the children of *I'*,
7 a memorial to the children of *I'*;
14 to the names of the children of *I'*,
32 children of *I'* did according to all
42 children of *I'* made all the work.
40:36 of *I'* went onward in all their
38 in the sight of all the house of *I'*,
Le 1: 2 Speak unto the children of *I'*, and
4: 2 Speak unto the children of *I'*,
13 congregation of *I'* sin through
7:23, 29 Speak unto the children of *I'*,
34 have I taken of the children of *I'*
34 ever from among the children of *I'*.
36 be given them of the children of *I'*.
38 the children of *I'* to offer their
9: 1 and his sons, and the elders of *I'*;
3 the children of *I'* thou shalt speak,
10: 6 brethren, the whole house of *I'*,
11 that ye may teach the children of *I'*
14 peace offerings of the children of *I'*.
11: 2 Speak unto the children of *I'*,
12: 2 Speak unto the children of *I'*,
15: 2 Speak unto the children of *I'*, and
31 shall ye separate the children of *I'*
16: 5 of *I'* two kids of the goats for a sin
16 uncleanness of the children of *I'*,
17 and for all the congregation of *I'*.
19 uncleanness of the children of *I'*.
21 the iniquities of the children of *I'*,
34 the children of *I'* for all their sins
17: 2 unto all the children of *I'*, and say
3 soever there be of the house of *I'*,
5 of *I'* may bring their sacrifices,
8, 10 man there be of the house of *I'*
12 I said unto the children of *I'*, No
13 man there be of the children of *I'*,
14 I said unto the children of *I'*, Ye
18: 2 Speak unto the children of *I'*, and
19: 2 congregation of the children of *I'*,
20: 2 shalt say to the children of *I'*,
2 he be of the children of *I'*, or of the
2 strangers that sojourn in *I'*, that
21:24 and unto all the children of *I'*.
22: 2 holy things of the children of *I'*,
3 children of *I'* hallow unto the Lord,
15 holy things of the children of *I'*,
18 and unto all the children of *I'*,
18 Whatsoever he be of the house of *I'*,
18 the strangers in *I'*, that will offer

Le 22: 32 hallowed among the children of I':
23: 2, 10 Speak unto the children of I', and
24, 34 Speak unto the children of I',
43 children of I' to dwell in booths,
44 unto the children of I' the feasts of
24: 2 Command the children of I', that
8 being taken from the children of I'
10 went out among the children of I':
10 of I' strove together in the camp;
15 speak unto the children of I',
23 Moses spake to the children of I',
23 of I' did as the Lord commanded
25: 2 Speak unto the children of I', and
33 possession among the children of I'.
46 your brethren the children of I',
55 me the children of I' are servants;
26: 46 between him and the children of I'
27: 2 Speak unto the children of I', and
34 Moses for the children of I' in
Nu 1: 2 congregation of the children of I',
3 are able to go forth to war in I':
16 fathers, heads of thousands in I'.
44 the princes of I', being twelve men:
45 numbered of the children of I',
45 were able to go forth to war in I';
49 of them among the children of I':
52 children of I' shall pitch their tents,
53 congregation of the children of I':
54 children of I' did according to all
2: 2 children of I' shall pitch by his own
32 were numbered of the children of I'
33 numbered among the children of I';
34 children of I' did according to all
3: 8 the charge of the children of I', to
9 unto him out of the children of I'.
12 from among the children of I'
12 matrix among the children of I':
13 unto me all the firstborn in I',
38 for the charge of the children of I';
40 of the males of the children of I'
41 firstborn among the children of I';
41 the cattle of the children of I'.
42 firstborn among the children of I'.
45 firstborn among the children of I',
46 the firstborn of the children of I',
50 the firstborn of the children of I'
4: 46 Aaron and the chief of I' numbered,
5: 2 Command the children of I', that
4 the children of I' did so, and put
4 unto Moses, so did the children of I'.
6 Speak unto the children of I', When
9 holy things of the children of I',
12 Speak unto the children of I', and
6: 2 Speak unto the children of I', and
23 ye shall bless the children of I',
27 my name upon the children of I';
7: 2 That the princes of I', heads of the
84 was anointed, by the princes of I':
8: 6 from among the children of I',
9 whole assembly of the children of I'
10 children of I' shall put their hands
11 for an offering of the children of I',
14 from among the children of I':
16 me from among the children of I';
16 firstborn of all the children of I',
17 firstborn of the children of I' are
18 the firstborn of the children of I'.
19 sons from among the children of I',
19 do the service of the children of I'
19 atonement for the children of I':
19 no plague among the children of I',
19 the children of I' come nigh unto
20 congregation of the children of I',
20 so did the children of I' unto them.
9: 2 children of I' also keep the passover
4 Moses spake unto the children of I',
5 Moses, so did the children of I'.
7 season among the children of I'?
10 Speak unto the children of I',
17 that the children of I' journeyed:
17 children of I' pitched their tents.
18 Lord the children of I' journeyed,
19 of I' kept the charge of the Lord,
22 children of I' abode in their tents,
10: 4 are heads of the thousands of I',
12 children of I' took their journeys
28 journeyings of the children of I'
29 hath spoken good concerning I'.
36 unto the many thousands of I'.
11: 4 the children of I' also wept again,
16 me seventy men of the elders of I',
30 the camp, he and the elders of I'.
13: 2 which I give unto the children of I':
3 were heads of the children of I'.
24 which the children of I' cut down
26 congregation of the children of I',
32 had searched unto the children of I',
14: 2 of I' murmured against Moses and
5 congregation of the children of I'.
7 the company of the children of I',
10 before all the children of I'.
27 murmurings of the children of I',
39 sayings unto all the children of I':
15: 2, 18 Speak unto the children of I',
25, 26 congregation of the children of I',
29 is born among the children of I',
32 of I' were in the wilderness,
38 Speak unto the children of I', and
16: 2 with certain of the children of I',
9 the God of I' hath separated you
9 you from the congregation of I', to
25 and the elders of I' followed him.
34 all I' that were round about them
38 be a sign unto the children of I'.
40 memorial unto the children of I',
41 children of I' murmured against

Nu 17: 2 Speak unto the children of I', and
5 murmurings of the children of I',
6 Moses spake unto the children of I',
9 Lord unto all the children of I':
12 the children of I' spake unto Moses,
18: 5 any more upon the children of I'.
6 from among the children of I':
8 hallowed things of the children of I';
11 wave offerings of the children of I':
14 Every thing devoted in I' shall be
19 which the children of I' offer unto
20 inheritance among the children of I'
21 the tenth in I' for an inheritance,
22 children of I' henceforth come nigh
23 of I' they have no inheritance.
24 But the tithes of the children of I',
24 of I' they shall have no inheritance.
26 take of the children of I' the tithes
28 ye receive of the children of I';
32 the holy things of the children of I',
19: 2 Speak unto the children of I', that
9 congregation of the children of I'
10 it shall be unto the children of I',
13 that soul shall be cut off from I':
20: 1 Then came the children of I', even
12 me in the eyes of the children of I',
13 children of I' strove with the Lord,
14 Thus saith thy brother I', Thou
19 the children of I' said unto him,
21 Edom refused to give I' passage
21 wherefore I' turned away from him.
22 the children of I', even the whole
24 I have given unto the children of I',
29 thirty days, even all the house of I'.
21: 1 I' came by the way of the spies;
1 he fought against I', and took some
2 And I' vowed a vow unto the Lord,
3 Lord hearkened to the voice of I',
6 people; and much people of I' died.
10 the children of I' set forward, and
17 I' sang this song, Spring up, O
21 I' sent messengers unto Sihon
23 suffer I' to pass through his border:
23 out against I' into the wilderness:
23 to Jahaz, and fought against I'.
24 I' smote him with the edge of the
25 And I' took all these cities:
25 and I' dwelt in all the cities of the
31 I' dwelt in the land of the Amorites.
22: 1 the children of I' set forward, and
2 that I' had done to the Amorites.
3 because of the children of I'.
23: 7 curse me Jacob, and come, defy I'.
10 number of the fourth part of I'?
21 hath he seen perverseness in I':
23 is there any divination against I':
23 it shall be said of Jacob and of I',
24: 1 that it pleased the Lord to bless I',
2 and he saw I' abiding in his tents
5 O Jacob, and thy tabernacles, O I'!
17 a Sceptre shall rise out of I', and
18 enemies; and I' shall do valiantly.
25: 1 And I' abode in Shittim, and the
3 I' joined himself unto Baal-peor:
3 of the Lord was kindled against I'.
4 Lord may be turned away from I',
5 Moses said unto the judges of I',
6 behold, one of the children of I'
6 congregation of the children of I',
8 after the man of I' into the tent,
8 the man of I', and the woman
8 was stayed from the children of I'.
11 wrath away from the children of I',
11 the children of I' in my jealousy.
13 an atonement for the children of I'.
26: 2 congregation of the children of I',
2 all that are able to go to war in I'.
4 Moses and the children of I',
5 Reuben, the eldest son of I': the
51 the numbered of the children of I',
62 numbered among the children of I',
62 them among the children of I'.
63 the children of I' in the plains of
64 the children of I' in the wilderness
27: 8 shalt speak unto the children of I',
11 children of I' a statute of judgment,
12 I have given unto the children of I'.
20 the children of I' may be obedient.
21 and all the children of I' with him,
28: 2 Command the children of I', and
29: 40 of I' according to all that the Lord
30: 1 tribes concerning the children of I',
31: 2 children of I' of the Midianites:
4 throughout all the tribes of I', shall
5 delivered out of the thousands of I',
9 children of I' took all the women
12 congregation of the children of I',
16 these caused the children of I',
54 the children of I' before the Lord.
32: 4 smote before the congregation of I',
7 ye the heart of the children of I'
9 the heart of the children of I',
13 Lord's anger was kindled against I',
14 fierce anger of the Lord toward I'.
17 armed before the children of I',
18 of I' have inherited every man his
22 before the Lord, and before I';
28 of the tribes of the children of I':
33: 1 the journeys of the children of I',
3 after the passover the children of I'
5 of I' removed from Rameses,
38 of I' were come out of the land of
40 of the coming of the children of I'.
51 Speak unto the children of I', and
34: 2 Command the children of I', and,
13 commanded the children of I',

Nu 34: 29 children of I' in the land of Canaan.
35: 2 Command the children of I', that
8 the possession of the children of I':
10 Speak unto the children of I', and
15 both for the children of I', and for
34 dwell among the children of I'.
36: 1 chief fathers of the children of I':
2 by lot to the children of I':
3 other tribes of the children of I',
4 jubile of the children of I' shall be,
5 Moses commanded the children of I'
7 of I' remove from tribe to tribe:
7 Every one of the children of I' shall
8 in any tribe of the children of I',
8 of I' may enjoy every man the
9 of I' shall keep himself to his own
13 children of I' in the plains of Moab
De 1: 1 words which Moses spake unto all I'
3 Moses spake unto the children of I',
38 for he shall cause I' to inherit it.
2: 12 as I' did unto the land of his
3: 18 your brethren the children of I',
4: 1 Now therefore hearken, O I', unto
44 Moses set before the children of I':
45 Moses spake unto the children of I',
46 Moses and the children of I' smote,
5: 1 Moses called all I', and said unto
1 Hear, O I', the statutes and
6: 3 Hear therefore, O I', and observe
4 Hear, O I': The Lord our God is
9: 1 Hear, O I': Thou art to pass over
10: 6 the children of I' took their journey
12 I', what doth the Lord thy God
11: 6 possession, in the midst of all I':
13: 11 And all I' shall hear, and fear, and
17: 4 such abomination is wrought in I':
12 shalt put away the evil from I'.
20 and his children, in the midst of I'.
18: 1 no part nor inheritance with I':
6 from any of thy gates out of all I',
19: 13 guilt of innocent blood from I',
20: 3 Hear, O I', ye approach this day
21: 8 merciful, O Lord, unto thy people I',
21 you; and all I' shall hear, and fear.
22: 19 an evil name upon a virgin of I':
21 she hath wrought folly in I', to play
22 shalt thou put away evil from I'.
23: 17 be no whore of the daughters of I',
17 nor a sodomite of the sons of I'.
24: 7 his brethren of the children of I',
25: 6 that his name be not put out of I'.
7 up unto his brother a name in I',
10 his name shall be called in I', The
26: 15 and bless thy people I', and the
27: 1 elders of I' commanded the people,
9 the Levites spake unto all I',
9 Take heed, and hearken, O I'; this
14 and say unto all the men of I' with
29: 1 children of I' in the land of Moab,
2 And Moses called unto all I', and
10 officers, with all the men of I',
21 unto evil out of all the tribes of I',
31: 1 and spake these words unto all I'.
7 said unto him in the sight of all I',
9 Lord, and unto all the elders of I'.
11 I' is come to appear before the Lord
11 law before all I' in their hearing.
19 and teach it the children of I': put
19 for me against the children of I'.
22 and taught it the children of I'.
23 bring the children of I' into the land
30 ears of all the congregation of I'
32: 8 to the number of children of I'.
45 speaking all these words to all I':
49 the children of I' for a possession:
51 against me among the children of I'
51 in the midst of the children of I'.
52 which I give the children of I'.
33: 1 of God blessed the children of I'
5 of the people and the tribes of I'
10 thy judgments, and I' thy law.
21 Lord, and his judgments with I'.
28 I' then shall dwell in safety alone:
29 Happy art thou, O I': who is like
34: 8 of I' wept for Moses in the plains
9 children of I' hearkened unto him,
10 prophet since in I' like unto Moses,
12 Moses shewed in the sight of all I'.
Jos 1: 2 them, even to the children of I'.
2: 2 of I' to search out the country.
3: 1 Jordan, he and all the children of I',
7 magnify thee in the sight of all I',
9 Joshua said unto the children of I',
12 twelve men out of the tribes of I',
4: 4 had prepared of the children of I',
5 of the tribes of the children of I':
7 a memorial unto the children of I'
8 of I' did so as Joshua commanded,
8 of the tribes of the children of I',
12 armed before the children of I',
14 Joshua in the sight of all I';
21 he spake unto the children of I',
22 I' came over this Jordan on dry
5: 1 from before the children of I',
1 more, because of the children of I'.
2 circumcise again the children of I'
3 and circumcised the children of I'
6 children of I' walked forty years
10 children of I' encamped in Gilgal,
12 children of I' manna any more;
6: 1 up because of the children of I':
18 and make the camp of I' a curse,
23 left them without the camp of I',
25 and she dwelleth in I' even unto
7: 1 children of I' committed a trespass
1 kindled against the children of I'.

Jos 7: 6 he and the elders of I·, and put
8 I say, when I· turneth their backs
11 I· hath sinned, and they have also
12 the children of I· could not stand
13 for thus saith the Lord God of I·,
13 thing in the midst of thee, O I·:
15 because he hath wrought folly in I·.
16 and brought I· by their tribes;
19 thee, glory to the Lord God of I·,
20 sinned against the Lord God of I·,
23 and unto all the children of I·,
24 And Joshua, and all I· with him,
25 And all I· stoned him with stones,
8: 10 and went up, he and the elders of I·,
14 city went out against I· to battle,
15 all I· made as if they were beaten
17 Beth-el, that went not out after I·:
17 the city open, and pursued after I·.
21 I· saw that the ambush had taken
22 so they were in the midst of I·,
24 when I· had made an end of slaying
27 and the spoil of that city I· took
30 an altar unto the Lord God of I·
31 Lord commanded the children of I·,
32 the presence of the children of I·.
33 all I·, and their elders, and officers,
33 they should bless the people of I·.
35 before all the congregation of I·,
9: 2 to fight with Joshua, and with I·,
6 said unto him, and to the men of I·,
7 the men of I· said unto the Hivites,
17 And the children of I· journeyed,
18 the children of I· smote them not,
18 unto them by the Lord God of I·.
19 unto them by the Lord God of I·:
26 out of the hand of the children of I·,
10: 1 of Gibeon had made peace with I·,
4 Joshua and with the children of I·.
10 Lord discomfited them before I·,
11 came to pass, as they fled before I·,
11 children of I· slew with the sword.
12 Amorites before the children of I·,
12 he said in the sight of I·, Sun, stand
14 a man: for the Lord fought for I·.
15 returned, and all I· with him,
20 of I· had made an end of slaying
21 against any of the children of I·.
24 Joshua called for all the men of I·,
29 Makkedah, and all I· with him,
30 king thereof, into the hand of I·;
31 from Libnah, and all I· with him,
32 Lachish into the hand of I·,
34 unto Eglon, and all I· with him;
36 up from Eglon, and all I· with him,
38 returned, and all I· with him, to
40 as the Lord God of I· commanded.
42 the Lord God of I· fought for I·.
43 returned, and all I· with him, unto
11: 5 waters of Merom, to fight against I·.
6 deliver them up all slain before I·:
8 delivered them into the hand of I·,
13 I· burned none of them, save Hazor
14 the children of I· took for a prey
16 mountain of I·, and the valley
19 made peace with the children of I·,
20 should come against I· in battle,
21 and from all the mountains of I·:
22 in the land of the children of I·:
23 gave it for an inheritance unto I·
12: 1 which the children of I· smote, and
6 Lord and the children of I· smite:
7 of I· smote on this side Jordan on
7 unto the tribes of I· for a possession
13: 6 out from before the children of I·:
13 of I· expelled not the Geshurites,
14 of the Lord God of I· made by fire
22 the children of I· slay with sword
33 God of I· was their inheritance,
14: 1 which the children of I· inherited
1 of the tribes of the children of I·,
5 Moses, so the children of I· did,
10 of I· wandered in the wilderness:
14 wholly followed the Lord God of I·.
17: 13 children of I· were waxen strong,
18: 1 of I· assembled together at Shiloh,
2 the children of I· seven tribes,
3 Joshua said unto the children of I·,
10 the land unto the children of I·
19: 49 of I· gave an inheritance to Joshua
51 of the tribes of the children of I·,
20: 2 Speak to the children of I·, saying,
9 appointed for all the children of I·,
21: 1 of the tribes of the children of I·;
3 children of I· gave unto the Levites
8 of I· gave by lot unto the Levites
41 the possession of the children of I·
43 the Lord gave unto I· all the land
45 had spoken unto the house of I·;
22: 9 departed from the children of I·
11 children of I· heard say, Behold,
11 at the passage of the children of I·.
12 when the children of I· heard of it,
12 of I· gathered themselves together
13 I· sent unto the children of Reuben,
14 throughout all the tribes of I·;
14 fathers among the thousands of I·.
16 committed against the God of I·,
18 with the whole congregation of I·.
20 fell on all the congregation of I·?
21 the heads of the thousands of I·,
22 he knoweth, and I· he shall know;
24 ye to do with the Lord God of I·?
30 and heads of the thousands of I·
31 ye have delivered the children of I·
32 land of Canaan, to the children of I·,
33 thing pleased the children of I·;

Jos 22: 33 and the children of I· blessed God,
23: 1 that the Lord had given rest unto I·
2 And Joshua called for all I·, and
24: 1 all the tribes of I· to Shechem,
1 and called for the elders of I·, and
2 Thus saith the Lord God of I·,
9 Moab, arose and warred against I·,
23 your heart unto the Lord God of I·.
31 I· served the Lord all the days of
31 the Lord, that he had done for I·.
32 of I· brought up out of Egypt,
J'g 1: 1 the children of I· asked the Lord,
28 came to pass, when I· was strong,
2: 4 words unto all the children of I·,
6 children of I· went every man unto
7 of the Lord, that he did for I·.
10 works which he had done for I·.
11 I· did evil in the sight of the Lord,
14 of the Lord was hot against I·,
20 of the Lord was hot against I·;
22 That through them I may prove I·,
3: 1 the Lord left, to prove I· by them,
1 as many of I· as had not known
2 of the children of I· might know, to
4 And they were to prove I· by them,
5 of I· dwelt among the Canaanites,
7 I· did evil in the sight of the Lord,
8 of the Lord was hot against I·,
8 the children of I· served...eight
9 children of I· cried unto the Lord,
9 up a deliverer to the children of I·,
10 came upon him, and he judged I·,
12 I· did evil again in the sight of the
12 Eglon the king of Moab against I·,
13 Amalek, and went and smote I·,
14 children of I· served Eglon the king
15 children of I· cried unto the Lord,
15 of I· sent a present unto Eglon the
27 children of I· went down with him
30 that day under the hand of I·.
31 ox goad: and he also delivered I·.
4: 1 I· again did evil in the sight of the
3 children of I· cried unto the Lord:
3 oppressed the children of I·.
4 she judged I· at that time.
5 of I· came up to her for judgment.
6 not the Lord God of I· commanded,
23 of Canaan before the children of I·.
24 hand of the children of I· prospered,
5: 2 ye the Lord for the avenging of I·,
3 sing praise to the Lord God of I·.
5 from before the Lord God of I·.
7 villages ceased, they ceased in I·,
7 arose, that I arose a mother in I·.
8 seen among forty thousand in I·?
9 heart is toward the governors of I·,
11 the inhabitants of his villages in I·:
6: 1 I· did evil in the sight of the Lord;
2 of Midian prevailed against I·:
2 children of I· made them the dens
3 I· had sown, that the Midianites
4 left no sustenance for I·, neither
6 And I· was greatly impoverished
6 children of I· cried unto the Lord.
7 children of I· cried unto the Lord
8 a prophet unto the children of I·,
8 Thus saith the Lord God of I·, I
14 shalt save I· from the hand of the
15 Lord, wherewith shall I save I·?
36 said unto God, If thou wilt save I·
37 shall I know that thou wilt save I·
7: 2 I· vaunt themselves against me,
8 rest of I· every man unto his tent,
14 the son of Joash, a man of I·:
15 and returned into the host of I·,
23 I· gathered themselves together
8: 22 the men of I· said unto Gideon,
27 I· went thither a whoring after it:
28 subdued before the children of I·,
33 the children of I· turned again,
34 of I· remembered not the Lord
35 which he had shewed unto I·.
9: 22 had reigned three years over I·,
55 of I· saw that Abimelech was dead,
10: 1 there arose to defend I· Tola the
2 And he judged I· twenty and three
3 Jair, a Gileadite, and judged I·
6 I· did evil again in the sight of the
7 of the Lord was hot against I·,
8 and oppressed the children of I·:
8 of I· that were on the other side
9 so that I· was sore distressed.
10 children of I· cried unto the Lord,
11 Lord said unto the children of I·,
15 children of I· said unto the Lord,
16 was grieved for the misery of I·.
17 I· assembled themselves together,
11: 4 of Ammon made war against I·.
5 of Ammon made war against I·,
13 Because I· took away my land,
15 I· took not away the land of Moab,
16 But when I· came up from Egypt,
17 I· sent messengers unto the king
17 consent: and I· abode in Kadesh.
19 I· sent messengers unto Sihon
19 I· said unto him, Let us pass, we
20 But Sihon trusted not I· to pass
20 in Jahaz, and fought against I·.
21 Lord God of I· delivered Sihon and
21 all his people into the hand of I·,
21 so I· possessed all the land of the
23 God of I· hath dispossessed the
23 from before his people I·, and
25 did he ever strive against I·, or did
26 While I· dwelt in Heshbon and her
27 between the children of I· and the

J'g 11: 33 subdued before the children of I·.
39 no man. And it was a custom in I·,
40 the daughters of I· went yearly to
12: 7 And Jephthah judged I· six years.
8 him Ibzan of Beth-lehem judged I·.
9 And he judged I· seven years.
11 him Elon, a Zebulonite, judged I·;
11 and he judged I· ten years.
13 of Hillel, a Pirathonite, judged I·.
14 colts: and he judged I· eight years.
13: 1 I· did evil again in the sight of the
5 I· out of the hand of the Philistines.
14: 4 Philistines had dominion over I·.
15: 20 he judged I· in the days of the
16: 31 And he judged I· twenty years.
17: 6 those days there was no king in I·,
18: 1 those days there was no king in I·:
1 unto them among the tribes of I·.
19 unto a tribe and a family in I·?
29 their father, who was born unto I·:
19: 1 days, when there was no king in I·,
12 that is not of the children of I·;
29 and sent her into all the coasts of I·.
30 I· came up out of the land of Egypt
20: 1 Then all the children of I· went out,
2 even of all the tribes of I·, presented
3 heard that the children of I· were
3 Then said the children of I·, Tell
6 country of the inheritance of I·:
6 committed lewdness and folly in I·.
7 Behold, ye are all children of I·;
10 throughout all the tribes of I·,
10 folly that they have wrought in I·.
11 all the men of I· were gathered
12 tribes of I· sent men through all
13 death, and put away evil from I·.
13 of their brethren the children of I·:
14 to battle against the children of I·.
17 men of I·, beside Benjamin, were
18 And the children of I· arose, and
19 children of I· rose up in the morning,
20 the men of I· went out to battle
20 I· put themselves in array to fight
22 men of I· encouraged themselves,
23 children of I· went up and wept
24 children of I· came near against
25 I· again eighteen thousand men;
26 Then all the children of I·, and all
27 children of I· enquired of the Lord,
29 I· set liers in wait round about
30 I· went up against the children of
31 in the field, about thirty men of I·.
32 the children of I· said, Let us flee,
33 men of I· rose up out of their place,
33 liers in wait of I· came forth out of
34 thousand chosen men out of all I·,
35 Lord smote Benjamin before I·:
35 of I· destroyed of the Benjamites
36 of I· gave place to the Benjamites,
38 sign between the men of I· and the
39 the men of I· retired in the battle,
39 the men of I· about thirty persons:
41 when the men of I· turned again,
42 their backs before the men of I·
48 I· turned again upon the children
21: 1 men of I· had sworn in Mizpeh,
3 And said, O Lord God of I·, why is
3 why is this come to pass in I·, that
3 be to day one tribe lacking in I·?
5 And the children of I· said, Who is
5 all the tribes of I· that came not up
6 of I· repented them for Benjamin
6 one tribe cut off from I· this day.
8 of I· that came not up to Mizpeh to
15 made a breach in the tribes of I·.
17 a tribe be not destroyed out of I·.
18 for the children of I· had sworn,
24 the children of I· departed thence
25 those days there was no king in I·:
Ru 2: 12 be given thee of the Lord God of I·,
4: 7 the manner in former time in I·
7 and this was a testimony in I·.
11 which two did build the house of I·:
14 that his name may be famous in I·.
1Sa 1: 17 God of I· grant thee thy petition
2: 22 all that his sons did unto all I·;
28 choose him out of all the tribes of I·
28 made by fire of the children of I·?
29 all the offerings of I· my people?
30 Wherefore the Lord God of I· saith,
32 the wealth which God shall give I·:
3: 11 Behold, I will do a thing in I·, at
20 all I· from Dan even to Beer-sheba
4: 1 the word of Samuel came to all I·.
1 I· went out against the Philistines
2 put themselves in array against I·:
2 I· was smitten before the
3 I· said, Wherefore hath the Lord
5 all I· shouted with a great shout,
10 fought, and I· was smitten, and they
10 fell of I· thirty thousand footmen.
17 I· is fled before the Philistines,
18 And he had judged I· forty years.
21, 22 The glory is departed from I·:
5: 7 ark of the God of I· shall not abide
8 do with the ark of the God of I·?
8 the ark of the God of I· be carried
8 they carried the ark of the God of I·
10 about the ark of the God of I· to us,
11 Send away the ark of the God of I·,
6: 3 send away the ark of the God of I·,
5 shall give glory unto the God of I·:
7: 2 house of I· lamented after the Lord.
3 spake unto all the house of I·,
4 of I· did put away Baalim and
5 Gather all I· to Mizpeh, and I will

1Sa 7: 6 judged the children of I· in Mizpeh.
7 of I· were gathered together to
7 the Philistines went up against I·.
7 when the children of I· heard it,
8 the children of I· said to Samuel,
9 Samuel cried unto the Lord for I·;
10 drew near to battle against I·:
10 and they were smitten before I·.
11 the men of I· went out of Mizpeh,
13 came no more into the coast of I·:
14 taken from I· were restored to I·,
14 I· deliver out of the hands of the
14 peace between I· and the Amorites.
15 judged I· all the days of his life.
16 and judged I· in all those places.
17 and there he judged I·; and there
8: 1 he made his sons judges over I·.
4 elders of I· gathered themselves
22 Samuel said unto the men of I·,
9: 2 of I· a goodlier person than he:
9 Beforetime in I·, when a man went
16 to be captain over my people I·,
20 on whom is all the desire of I·? Is
21 the smallest of the tribes of I·?
10: 18 And said unto the children of I·,
18 Thus saith the Lord God of I·,
18 I brought up I· out of Egypt, and
20 all the tribes of I· to come near,
11: 2 lay it for a reproach upon all I·.
3 messengers unto all the coasts of I·:
7 them throughout all the coasts of I·
8 of I· were three hundred thousand,
13 Lord hath wrought salvation in I·.
15 all the men of I· rejoiced greatly.
12: 1 And Samuel said unto all I·,
13: 1 he had reigned two years over I·,
2 chose...three thousand men of I·;
4 I· heard say that Saul had smitten
4 that I· also was had in abomination
5 themselves together to fight with I·,
6 of I· saw that they were in a strait,
13 thy kingdom upon I· for ever.
19 found throughout all the land of I·:
14: 12 delivered them into the hand of I·.
18 at that time with the children of I·.
22 men of I· which had hid themselves
23 So the Lord saved I· that day: and
24 men of I· were distressed that day:
37 deliver them into the hand of I·?
39 as the Lord liveth, which saveth I·,
40 Then said he unto all I·, Be ye on
41 Saul said unto the Lord God of I·,
45 wrought this great salvation in I·?
47 So Saul took the kingdom over I·,
48 and delivered I· out of the hands of
15: 1 to be king over his people, over I·:
2 that which Amalek did to I·, how
6 kindness to all the children of I·,
17 not made the head of the tribes of I·,
17 the Lord anointed thee king over I·?
26 thee from being king over I·.
28 rent the kingdom of I· from thee
29 Strength of I· will not lie nor repent:
30 elders of my people, and before I·,
35 that he had made Saul king over I·.
16: 1 rejected him from reigning over I·?
17: 2 men of I· were gathered together,
3 I· stood on a mountain on the other
8 and cried unto the armies of I·,
10 I defy the armies of I· this day;
11 Saul and all I· heard those words
19 and they, and all the men of I·,
21 I· and the Philistines had put the
24 all the men of I·, when they saw
25 men of I· said, Have ye seen this
25 surely to defy I· is he come up:
25 make his father's house free in I·.
26 taketh away the reproach from I·?
45 hosts, the God of the armies of I·,
46 may know that there is a God in I·.
52 the men of I· and of Judah arose,
53 of I· returned from chasing after
18: 6 women came out of all cities of I·,
16 But all I· and Judah loved David,
18 my life, or my father's family in I·,
19: 5 wrought a great salvation for all I·:
20: 12 said unto David, O Lord God of I·,
23: 10 Then said David, O Lord God of I·,
11 O Lord God of I·, I beseech thee,
17 and thou shalt be king over I·, and
24: 2 thousand chosen men out of all I·,
14 whom is the king of I· come out?
20 kingdom of I· shall be established
25: 30 have appointed thee ruler over I·;
32 Blessed be the Lord God of I·,
34 deed, as the Lord God of I· liveth,
26: 2 three thousand chosen men of I·
15 man? and who is like to thee in I·?
20 king of I· is come out to seek a flea,
27: 1 me any more in any coast of I·:
12 his people I· utterly to abhor him;
28: 1 for warfare, to fight with I·.
3 dead, and all I· had lamented him,
4 Saul gathered all I· together, and
19 the Lord will also deliver I· with
19 Lord also shall deliver the host of I·
29: 3 the servant of Saul the king of I·,
30: 25 a statute and an ordinance for I·
31: 1 the Philistines fought against I·:
1 I· fled from before the Philistines,
7 of I· that were on the other side
7 Jordan, saw that the men of I· fled,
2Sa 1: 3 Out of the camp of I· am I escaped.
12 the Lord, and for the house of I·;
19 beauty of I· is slain upon thy high
24 Ye daughters of I·, weep over Saul,

2Sa 2: 9 and over Benjamin, and over all I·.
10 old when he began to reign over I·,
17 Abner was beaten, and the men of I·,
28 still, and pursued after I· no more,
3: 10 set up the throne of David over I·
12 to bring about all I· unto thee.
17 communication with the elders of I·,
18 I will save my people I· out of the
19 Hebron all that seemed good to I·,
21 gather all I· unto my lord the king,
37 all the people and all I· understood
38 a great man fallen this day in I·?
5: 1 came all the tribes of I· to David
2 leddest out and broughtest in I·:
2 thee, Thou shalt feed my people I·,
2 and thou shalt be a captain over I·.
3 elders of I· came to the king to
3 they anointed David king over I·.
5 thirty and three years over all I·
12 had established him king over I·,
17 had anointed David king over I·,
6: 1 together all the chosen men of I·,
5 house of I· played before the Lord
15 the house of I· brought up the ark
19 among the whole multitude of I·,
20 glorious was the king of I· to day,
21 over the people of the Lord, over I·:
7: 6 up the children of I· out of Egypt,
7 walked with all the children of I·
7 a word with any of the tribes of I·,
7 I commanded to feed my people I·,
8 to be ruler over my people, over I·:
10 appoint a place for my people I·,
11 judges to be over my people I·,
23 is like thy people, even like I·,
24 confirmed to thyself thy people I·
26 Lord of hosts is the God over I·:
27 For thou, O Lord of hosts, God of I·,
8: 15 And David reigned over all I·; and
10: 9 he chose of all the choice men of I·,
15 that they were smitten before I·,
17 he gathered all I· together, and
18 And the Syrians fled before I·; and
19 that they were smitten before I·,
19 they made peace with I·, and served
11: 1 his servants with him, and all I·;
11 The ark, and I·, and Judah, abide
12: 7 Thus saith the Lord God of I·,
7 I anointed thee king over I·, and
8 thee the house of I· and of Judah;
12 I will do this thing before all I·,
13: 12 such thing ought to be done in I·:
13 shalt be as one of the fools in I·.
14: 25 in all I· there was none to be so
15: 2 servant is of one of the tribes of I·.
6 this manner did Absalom to all I·
6 stole the hearts of the men of I·.
10 spies throughout all the tribes of I·,
13 hearts of the men of I· are after
16: 3 house of I· restore me the kingdom
15 and all the people the men of I·,
18 this people, and all the men of I·,
21 I· shall hear that thou art abhorred
22 concubines in the sight of all I·.
17: 4 well, and all the elders of I·.
10 all I· knoweth that thy father is a
11 that all I· be generally gathered
13 shall all I· bring ropes to that city,
14 Absalom and all the men of I· said,
15 Absalom and the elders of I·;
24 he and all the men of I· with him.
26 I· and Absalom pitched in the land
18: 6 went out into the field against I·:
7 the people of I· were slain before
16 returned from pursuing after I·:
17 all I· fled every one to his tent.
19: 8 I· had fled every man to his tent.
9 strife throughout all the tribes of I·,
11 speech of all I· is come to the king,
22 man be put to death this day in I·?
22 that I am this day king over I·?
40 king, and also half the people of I·.
41 all the men of I· came to the king,
42 of Judah answered the men of I·,
43 the men of I· answered the men of
43 than the words of the men of I·.
20: 1 Jesse: every man to his tents, O I·.
2 man of I· went up from after David,
14 he went through all the tribes of I·
19 are peaceable and faithful in I·:
19 destroy a city and a mother in I·:
23 Joab was over all the host of I·:
21: 2 were not of the children of I·, but
2 and the children of I· had sworn
2 zeal to the children of I· and Judah.
4 for us shalt thou kill any man in I·.
5 remaining in any of the coasts of I·,
15 had yet war again with I·;
17 that thou quench not the light of I·.
21 when he defied I·, Jonathan the
23: 1 Jacob, and the sweet psalmist of I·,
3 God of I· said, the Rock of I· spake
9 and the men of I· were gone away:
24: 1 of the Lord was kindled against I·,
1 to say, Go, number I· and Judah.
2 Go now through all the tribes of I·,
4 king, to number the people of I·.
9 were in I· eight hundred thousand
15 the Lord sent a pestilence upon I·
25 the plague was stayed from I·.
1Ki 1: 3 throughout all the coast of I·,
20 the eyes of all I· are upon thee,
30 unto thee by the Lord God of I·,
34 anoint him there king over I·:
35 appointed him to be ruler over I·
48 Blessed be the Lord God of I·,

1Ki 2: 4 (said he) a man on the throne of I·.
5 the two captains of the hosts of I·,
11 David reigned over I· were forty
15 that all I· set their faces on me,
32 son of Ner, captain of the host of I·,
3: 28 I· heard of the judgment which the
4: 1 king Solomon was king over all I·.
7 had twelve officers over all I·,
20 Judah and I· were many, as the
25 Judah and I· dwelt safely, every
5: 13 Solomon raised a levy out of all I·;
6: 1 of I· were come out of the land of
1 year of Solomon's reign over I·,
13 will dwell among the children of I·,
13 and will not forsake my people I·.
8: 1 Solomon assembled the elders of I·,
1 the fathers of the children of I·,
2 men of I· assembled themselves
3 all the elders of I· came, and all the
5 and all the congregation of I·, that
9 a covenant with the children of I·,
14 blessed all the congregation of I·:
14 all the congregation of I· stood;
15 Blessed be the Lord God of I·,
16 forth my people I· out of Egypt,
16 no city out of all the tribes of I·
16 chose David to be over my people I·.
17 for the name of the Lord God of I·.
20 father, and sit on the throne of I·,
20 for the name of the Lord God of I·.
22 of all the congregation of I·,
23 Lord God of I·, there is no God like
25 Lord God of I·, Keep with thy
25 my sight to sit on the throne of I·;
26 O God of I·, let thy word, I pray
30 of thy people I·, when they shall
33 people I· be smitten down before
34 forgive the sin of thy people I·,
36 thy servants, and of thy people I·,
38 any man, or by all thy people I·,
41 stranger, that is not of thy people I·,
43 to fear thee, as do thy people I·;
52 the supplication of thy people I·,
55 congregation of I· with a loud voice,
56 hath given rest unto his people I·,
59 cause of his people I· at all times,
62 And the king, and all I· with him,
63 I· dedicated the house of the Lord.
65 held a feast, and all I· with him,
66 his servant, and for I· his people.
9: 5 the throne of thy kingdom upon I·
5 thee a man upon the throne of I·.
7 I cut off I· out of the land which I
7 I· shall be a proverb and a byword
20 which were not of the children of I·,
21 of I· also were not able utterly to
22 I· did Solomon make no bondmen:
10: 9 thee, to set thee on the throne of I·:
9 the Lord loved I· forever, therefore
11: 2 Lord said unto the children of I·,
9 turned from the Lord God of I·,
16 did Joab remain there with all I·,
25 And he was an adversary to I· all
25 and he abhorred I·, and reigned
31 thus saith the Lord, the God of I·,
32 chosen out of all the tribes of I·:
37 desireth, and shall be king over I·.
38 David, and will give I· unto thee.
42 reigned in Jerusalem over all I·
12: 1 I· were come to Shechem to make
3 and all the congregation of I· came,
16 I· saw that the king hearkened not
16 to your tents, O I·: now see to
16 So I· departed unto their tents.
17 children of I· which dwelt in the
18 all I· stoned him with stones, that
19 So I· rebelled against the house of
20 I· heard that Jeroboam was come
20 and made him king over all I·:
21 to fight against the house of I·,
24 your brethren the children of I·:
28 thy gods, O I·, which brought thee
33 a feast unto the children of I·:
14: 7 thus saith the Lord God of I·,
7 made thee prince over my people I·,
10 him that is shut up and left in I·,
13 I· shall mourn for him, and bury
13 God of I· in the house of Jeroboam.
14 shall raise him up a king over I·,
15 the Lord shall smite I·, as a reed
15 he shall root up I· out of this good
16 give I· up because of the sin of
16 did sin, and who made I· to sin.
18 him; and all I· mourned for him,
19 of the chronicles of the kings of I·.
21 did choose out of all the tribes of I·,
24 cast out before the children of I·.
15: 9 year of Jeroboam king of I· reigned
16 between Asa and Baasha king of I·
17 king of I· went up against Judah,
19 thy league with Baasha king of I·,
20 which he had against the cities of I·,
25 Jeroboam began to reign over I·
25 and reigned over I· two years.
26 sin wherewith he made I· to sin.
27 and all I· laid siege to Gibbethon.
30 and which he made I· sin, by his
30 provoked the Lord God of I· to
31 the chronicles of the kings of I·?
32 Baasha king of I· all their days.
33 to reign over all I· in Tirzah,
34 sin wherewith he made I· to sin.
16: 2 made thee prince over my people I·;
2 hast made my people I· to sin, to
5 of the chronicles of the kings of I·?
8 Baasha to reign over I· in Tirzah,

1Ki 16:13 by which they made I' to sin, in
13 Lord God of I' to anger with their
14 of the chronicles of the kings of I'?
16 wherefore all I' made Omri, the
16 king over I' that day in the camp.
17 from Gibbethon, and all I' with him,
19 which he did, to make I' to sin.
20 of the chronicles of the kings of I'?
21 people of I' divided into two parts:
23 began Omri to reign over I', twelve
26 his sin wherewith he made I' to sin,
26 Lord God of I' to anger with their
27 of the chronicles of the kings of I'?
29 the son of Omri to reign over I':
29 Omri reigned over I' in Samaria
33 provoke the Lord God of I' to anger
33 kings of I' that were before him.
17: 1 As the Lord God of I' liveth, before
14 thus saith the Lord God of I', The
18:17 him, Art thou he that troubleth I'?
18 answered, I have not troubled I';
19 to me all I' unto mount Carmel,
20 sent unto all the children of I',
31 came, saying, I' shall be thy name:
36 God of Abraham, Isaac, and of I',
36 this day that thou art God in I',
19:10, 14 of I' have forsaken thy covenant,
16 thou anoint to be king over I':
18 have left me seven thousand in I',
20: 2 messengers to Ahab king of I'
4 the king of I' answered and said,
7 the king of I' called all the elders
11 the king of I' answered and said,
13 a prophet unto Ahab, king of I',
15 even all the children of I', being
20 Syrians fled; and I' pursued them:
21 the king of I' went out, and smote
22 the prophet came to the king of I',
26 up to Aphek, to fight against I'.
27 the children of I' were numbered,
27 of I' pitched before them like two
28 spake unto the king of I', and
29 children of I' slew of the Syrians
31 that the kings of the house of I'
31 heads, and go out to the king of I':
32 came to the king of I', and said,
40 the king of I' said unto him, So
41 king of I' discerned him that he
43 king of I' went to his house heavy
21: 7 thou now govern the kingdom of I'?
18 go down to meet Ahab king of I',
21 him that is shut up and left in I',
22 me to anger, and made I' to sin.
26 cast out before the children of I'.
22: 1 without war between Syria and I'.
2 Judah came down to the king of I'.
3 king of I' said unto his servants,
4 Jehoshaphat said to the king of I',
5 said unto the king of I', Enquire,
6 king of I' gathered the prophets
8 king of I' said unto Jehoshaphat,
9 king of I' called an officer, and
10 king of I' and Jehoshaphat the
17 saw all I' scattered upon the hills,
18 king of I' said unto Jehoshaphat,
26 the king of I' said, Take Micaiah,
29 king of I' and Jehoshaphat the
30 king of I' said unto Jehoshaphat,
30 the king of I' disguised himself,
31 great, save only with the king of I'.
32 they said, Surely it is the king of I'.
33 that it was not the king of I',
34 smote the king of I' between the
39 of the chronicles of the kings of I'?
41 the fourth year of Ahab king of I'.
44 made peace with the king of I'.
51 son of Ahab began to reign over I'
51 and reigned two years over I'.
52 son of Nebat, who made I' to sin:
53 to anger the Lord God of I',
2Ki 1: 1 Moab rebelled against I' after the
3, 6 because there is not a God in I',
16 not because there is no God in I' to
18 of the chronicles of the kings of I'?
2:12 the chariot of I', and the horsemen
3: 1 son of Ahab began to reign over I'
3 son of Nebat, which made I' to sin;
4 of I' an hundred thousand lambs,
5 Moab rebelled against the king of I'.
6 the same time, and numbered all I'.
9 So the king of I' went, and the king
10 king of I' said, Alas! that the Lord
12 king of I' and Jehoshaphat and the
13 And Elisha said unto the king of I',
13 the king of I' said unto him, Nay:
24 when they came to the camp of I',
27 was great indignation against I':
5: 2 out of the land of I' a little maid;
4 the maid that is of the land of I'.
5 send a letter unto the king of I'.
6 the letter unto the king of I',
7 the king of I' had read the letter,
8 the king of I' had rent his clothes,
8 know that there is a prophet in I'.
12 better than all the waters of I'?
15 no God in all the earth, but in I':
6: 8 king of Syria warred against I',
9 man of God sent unto the king of I',
10 king of I' sent to the place which
11 which of us is for the king of I'?
12 Elisha, the prophet that is in I',
12 telleth the king of I' the words that
21 king of I' said unto Elisha, when
23 came no more into the land of I'.
26 king of I' was passing by upon the
7: 6 king of I' hath hired against us

2Ki 7:13 they are as all the multitude of I'
8:12 thou wilt do unto the children of I':
16 fifth year of Joram the...king of I',
18 walked in the way of the kings of I'
25 twelfth year of Joram...king of I'
26 the daughter of Omri king of I'.
9: 3 I have anointed thee king over I'.
6 Thus saith the Lord God of I',
6 the people of the Lord, even over I'.
8 him that is shut up and left in I':
12 I have anointed thee king over I'.
14 he and all I', because of Hazael
21 Joram king of I' and Ahaziah king
10:21 And Jehu sent through all I': and
28 Thus Jehu destroyed Baal out of I'.
29 son of Nebat, who made I' to sin,
30 shall sit on the throne of I'.
31 walk in the law of the Lord God of I'
31 of Jeroboam, which made I' to sin.
32 the Lord began to cut I' short:
32 smote them in all the coasts of I';
34 of the chronicles of the kings of I'?
36 Jehu reigned over I' in Samaria
13: 1 son of Jehu began to reign over I'
2 son of Nebat, which made I' to sin;
3 of the Lord was kindled against I',
4 for he saw the oppression of I',
5 And the Lord gave I' a saviour, so
5 children of I' dwelt in their tents,
6 of Jeroboam, who made I' sin,
8 of the chronicles of the kings of I'?
10 to reign over I' in Samaria, and
11 the son of Nebat, who made I' sin:
12 of the chronicles of the kings of I'?
13 in Samaria with the kings of I'.
14 the king of I' came down unto him,
14 the chariot of I', and the horsemen
16 And he said to the king of I', Put
18 he said unto the king of I', Smite
22 Hazael king of Syria oppressed I'
25 him, and recovered the cities of I'.
14: 1 second year of Joash...king of I'
8 messengers to Joash,...king of I',
9 the king of I' sent to Amaziah
11 Jehoash king of I' went up;
12 was put to the worse before I';
13 Jehoash king of I' took Amaziah
15 of the chronicles of the kings of I'?
16 in Samaria with the kings of I';
17 Jehoahaz king of I' fifteen years.
23 of Joash king of I' began to reign
24 son of Nebat, who made I' to sin.
25 He restored the coast of I' from
25 to the word of the Lord God of I',
26 For the Lord saw the affliction of I',
26 nor any left, nor any helper for I'.
27 he would blot out the name of I'
28 which belonged to Judah, for I',
28 of the chronicles of the kings of I'?
29 fathers, even with the kings of I';
15: 1 year of Jeroboam king of I' began
8 the son of Jeroboam reigned over I'
9 son of Nebat, who made I' to sin.
11 of the chronicles of the kings of I'.
12 Thy sons shall sit on the throne of I
15 of the chronicles of the kings of I'.
17 the son of Gadi to reign over I',
18 son of Nebat, who made I' to sin.
20 Menahem exacted the money of I',
21 of the chronicles of the kings of I'?
23 of Menahem began to reign over I'
24 son of Nebat, who made I' to sin.
26 of the chronicles of the kings of I'.
27 of Remaliah began to reign over I'
28 son of Nebat, who made I' to sin.
29 In the days of Pekah king of I'
31 of the chronicles of the kings of I'.
32 Pekah the son of Remaliah king of I'
16: 3 walked in the way of the kings of I',
3 out from before the children of I'.
5 Pekah son of Remaliah king of I'
7 out of the hand of the king of I',
17: 1 of Elah to reign in Samaria over I'
2 kings of I' that were before him.
6 and carried I' away into Assyria,
7 of I' had sinned against the Lord
8 out from before the children of I',
8 and of the kings of I', which they
9 children of I' did secretly those
13 Yet the Lord testified against I',
18 the Lord was very angry with I',
19 walked in the statutes of I' which
20 the Lord rejected all the seed of I',
21 he rent I' from the house of David;
21 Jeroboam drave I' from following
22 I' walked in all the sins of Jeroboam
23 Lord removed I' out of his sight,
23 was I' carried away out of their own
24 instead of the children of I':
34 of Jacob, whom he named I';
18: 1 of Hoshea son of Elah king of I',
4 of I' did burn incense to it:
5 He trusted in the Lord God of I';
9 of Hoshea son of Elah king of I',
10 ninth year of Hoshea king of I',
11 king of Assyria did carry away I'
19:15 O Lord God of I', which dwellest
20 Thus saith the Lord God of I',
22 even against the Holy One of I'.
21: 2 cast out before the children of I'.
3 a grove, as did Ahab king of I';
7 have chosen out of all tribes of I',
8 make the feet of I' move any more
9 destroyed before the children of I'.
12 thus saith the Lord God of I',
22:15, 18 Thus saith the Lord God of I',

2Ki 23:13 Solomon the king of I' had builded
15 son of Nebat, who made I' to sin,
19 kings of I' had made to provoke the
22 days of the judges that judged I',
22 nor in all the days of the kings of I',
27 of my sight, as I have removed I',
24:13 gold which Solomon king of I' had
1Ch 1:34 The sons of Isaac; Esau and I'.
43 reigned over the children of I';
2: 1 These are the sons of I'; Reuben,
7 Achar, the troubler of I', who
4:10 Jabez called on the God of I',
5: 1 sons of Reuben the firstborn of I',
1 the sons of Joseph the son of I':
3 of Reuben the firstborn of I' were,
17 the days of Jeroboam king of I'.
26 the God of I' stirred up the spirit
6:38 the son of Levi, the son of I'.
49 and to make an atonement for I',
64 I' gave to the Levites these cities
7:29 the children of Joseph the son of I'.
9: 1 I' were reckoned by genealogies;
1 book of the kings of I' and Judah,
10: 1 the Philistines fought against I';
1 men of I' fled from before the
7 men of I' that were in the valley
11: 1 all I' gathered themselves to David
2 leddest out and broughtest in I':
2 Thou shalt feed my people I', and
2 shalt be ruler over my people I'.
3 came all the elders of I' to the king
3 they anointed David king over I',
4 David and all I' went to Jerusalem,
10 and with all I', to make him king,
10 the word of the Lord concerning I'.
12:32 to know what I' ought to do;
38 to make David king over all I':
38 all the rest of I' were of one heart
40 for there was joy in I'.
13: 2 unto all the congregation of I',
2 that are left in all the land of I',
5 So David gathered all I' together,
6 And David went up, and all I', to
8 David and all I' played before God
14: 2 had confirmed him king over I',
2 on high, because of his people I'.
8 David was anointed king over all I',
15: 3 David gathered all I' together to
12 up the ark of the Lord God of I'
14 up the ark of the Lord God of I'.
25 the elders of I', and the captains
28 Thus all I' brought up the ark of
16: 3 And he dealt to every one of I',
4 thank and praise the Lord God of I':
13 O ye seed of I' his servant, ye
17 to I' for an everlasting covenant,
36 Blessed be the Lord God of I' for
40 the Lord, which he commanded I';
17: 5 since the day that I brought up I'
6 I have walked with all I', spake I
6 a word to any of the judges of I',
7 be ruler over my people I':
9 will ordain a place for my people I',
10 judges to be over my people I'.
21 in the earth is like thy people I',
22 thy people I' didst thou make thine
24 is the God of I', even a God to I':
18:14 So David reigned over all I', and
19:10 he chose out of all the choice of I',
16 were put to the worse before I',
17 he gathered all I', and passed over
18 But the Syrians fled before I': and
19 were put to the worse before I',
20: 7 But when he defied I', Jonathan
21: 1 And Satan stood up against I',
1 and provoked David to number I'.
2 number I' from Beer-sheba even to
3 will he be a cause of trespass to I'?
4 and went throughout all I', and
5 And all they of I' were a thousand
7 this thing; therefore he smote I'.
12 throughout all the coasts of I'.
14 the Lord sent pestilence upon I':
14 fell of I' seventy thousand men.
16 Then David and the elders of I',
22: 1 altar of the burnt offering for I'.
2 the strangers...in the land of I';
6 an house for the Lord God of I'.
9 give peace and quietness unto I'
10 the throne of his kingdom over I'
12 give thee charge concerning I',
13 charged Moses with concerning I':
17 commanded all the princes of I' to
23: 1 made Solomon his son king over I'.
2 together all the princes of I',
25 Lord God of I' hath given rest unto
24:19 Lord God of I' had commanded
26:29 for the outward business over I',
30 were officers among them of I' on
27: 1 children of I' after their number,
16 Furthermore over the tribes of I':
22 were the princes of the tribes of I'.
23 would increase I' like to the stars
24 there fell wrath for it against I';
28: 1 assembled all the princes of I',
4 Lord God of I' chose me before all
4 of my father to be king over I'
4 me to make me king over all I':
5 of the kingdom of the Lord over I'.
8 sight of all I' the congregation of
29: 6 and princes of the tribes of I',
10 thou, Lord God of I' our father,
18 God of Abraham, Isaac, and of I',
21 sacrifices in abundance for all I':
23 prospered; and all I' obeyed him.
25 exceedingly in the sight of all I',

1Ch 29: 25 been on any king before him in I'.
26 the son of Jesse reigned over all I'.
27 the time that he reigned over I' was
30 that went over him, and over I',
2Ch 1: 2 Then Solomon spake unto all I',
2 and to every governor in all I',
13 congregation, and reigned over I'.
2: 4 This is an ordinance for ever to I'.
12 Blessed be the Lord God of I', that
17 all the strangers...in the land of I',
5: 2 Solomon assembled the elders of I'
2 of the fathers of the children of I',
3 men of I' assembled themselves
4 And all the elders of I' came; and
6 all the congregation of I' that were
10 a covenant with the children of I',
6: 3 the whole congregation of I':
3 all the congregation of I' stood.
4 Blessed be the Lord God of I',
5 no city among all the tribes of I'
5 man to be a ruler over my people I':
6 David to be over my people I'.
7 for the name of the Lord God of I'.
10 and am set on the throne of I', as
10 for the name of the Lord God of I'.
11 he made with the children of I'.
12 of all the congregation of I',
13 before all the congregation of I',
14 God of I', there is no God like thee
16 God of I', keep with thy servant
16 sight to sit upon the throne of I';
17 O Lord God of I', let thy word be
21 of thy servant, and of thy people I',
24 thy people I' be put to the worse
25 and forgive the sin of my people I',
27 thy servants, and of thy people I',
29 of any man, or of all thy people I',
32 which is not of thy people I',
33 fear thee, as doth thy people I',
7: 3 of I' saw how the fire came down,
6 before them, and all I' stood.
8 seven days, and all I' with him,
10 to Solomon, and to I' his people.
18 not fail thee a man to be ruler in I'.
8: 2 the children of I' to dwell there.
7 the Jebusites, which were not of I',
8 whom the children of I' consumed
9 children of I' did Solomon make no
11 in the house of David king of I',
9: 8 because thy God loved I', to
30 in Jerusalem over all I' forty years.
10: 1 for to Shechem were all I' come to
3 all I' came and spake to Rehoboam,
16 all I' saw that the king would not
16 every man to your tents, O I': and
16 So all I' went to their tents.
17 I' that dwelt in the cities of Judah
18 of I' stoned him with stones, that
19 I' rebelled against the house of
11: 1 were warriors, to fight against I',
3 to all I' in Judah and Benjamin,
13 and the Levites that were in all I'
16 after them out of all the tribes of I'
16 hearts to seek the Lord God of I'
12: 1 law of the Lord, and all I' with him.
6 princes of I' and the king humbled
13 chosen out of all the tribes of I',
13: 4 me, thou Jeroboam, and all I';
5 know that the Lord God of I' gave
5 gave the kingdom over I' to David
12 children of I', fight ye not against
15 God smote Jeroboam and all I'
16 children of I' fled before Judah:
17 slain of I' five hundred thousand
18 children of I' were brought under
15: 3 I' hath been without the true God,
4 did turn unto the Lord God of I',
9 fell to him out of I' in abundance,
13 would not seek the Lord God of I'
17 were not taken away out of I':
16: 1 king of I' came up against Judah,
3 thy league with Baasha king of I',
4 his armies against the cities of I':
11 book of the kings of Judah and I'.
17: 1 strengthened himself against I'.
4 and not after the doings of I'.
18: 3 king of I' said unto Jehoshaphat
4 Jehoshaphat said unto the king of I',
5 of I' gathered together of prophets
7 king of I' said unto Jehoshaphat,
8 of I' called for one of his officers,
9 the king of I' and Jehoshaphat king
16 I' scattered upon the mountains,
17 the king of I' said to Jehoshaphat,
19 Who shall entice Ahab king of I',
25 Then the king of I' said, Take ye
28 So the king of I' and Jehoshaphat
29 king of I' said unto Jehoshaphat, I
29 So the king of I' disguised himself;
30 great, save only with the king of I'.
31 that they said, It is the king of I'.
32 that it was not the king of I', they
33 smote the king of I' between the
34 I' stayed himself up in his chariot
19: 8 and of the chief of the fathers of I',
20: 7 of this land before thy people I',
10 thou wouldest not let I' invade,
19 up to praise the Lord God of I'
29 fought against the enemies of I'.
34 in the book of the kings of I'.
35 himself with Ahaziah king of I',
21: 2 the sons of Jehoshaphat king of I'.
4 and divers also of the princes of I'.
6, 13 in the way of the kings of I',
22: 5 Ahab king of I' to war against
23: 2 and the chief of the fathers of I'.

2Ch 24: 5 gather of all I' money to repair the
6 and of the congregation of I', for
9 the servant of God laid upon I'
16 he had done good in I', both toward
25: 6 mighty men of valour out of I'
7 let not the army of I' go with thee;
7 for the Lord is not with I', to wit,
9 which I have given to the army of I'?
17 the son of Jehu, king of I', saying,
18 king of I' sent to Amaziah king of
21 So Joash the king of I' went up;
22 was put to the worse before I',
23 king of I' took Amaziah king of
25 of Joash son of Jehoahaz king of I'
26 book of the kings of Judah and I'?
27: 7 book of the kings of I' and Judah.
28: 2 walked in the ways of the kings of I',
3 cast out before the children of I'.
5 into the hand of the king of I',
8 of I' carried away captive of their
13 and there is fierce wrath against I'.
19 low because of Ahaz king of I';
23 were the ruin of him, and of all I'.
26 book of the kings of Judah and I'.
27 the sepulchres of the kings of I':
29: 7 the holy place unto the God of I'.
10 covenant with the Lord God of I',
24 to make an atonement for all I':
24 offering should be made for all I'.
27 ordained by David king of I'.
30: 1 Hezekiah sent to all I' and Judah,
1 passover unto the Lord God of I'.
5 proclamation throughout all I',
5 passover unto the Lord God of I'
6 and his princes throughout all I'
6 Ye children of I', turn again unto
6 God of Abraham, Isaac, and I',
21 I' that were present at Jerusalem
25 congregation that came out of I',
25 that came out of the land of I',
26 Solomon the son of David king of I'
31: 1 all I' that were present went out to
1 Then all the children of I' returned,
5 of I' brought in abundance the first
6 the children of I' and Judah,
8 blessed the Lord, and his people I'.
32: 17 letters to rail on the Lord God of I',
32 book of the kings of Judah and I'.
33: 2 cast out before the children of I'.
7 chosen before all the tribes of I',
8 I any more remove the foot of I'
9 destroyed before the children of I'.
16 Judah to serve the Lord God of I'.
18 in the name of the Lord God of I',
18 in the book of the kings of I'.
34: 7 idols throughout all the land of I',
9 and of all the remnant of I',
21 them that are left in I' and in Judah,
23 Thus saith the Lord God of I', Tell
26 of I' concerning the words which
33 that pertained to the children of I',
33 all that were present in I' to serve,
35: 3 unto the Levites that taught all I',
3 son of David king of I' did build;
3 Lord your God, and his people I',
4 to the writing of David king of I',
17 of I' that were present kept the
18 no passover like to that kept in I'
18 kings of I' keep such a passover as
18 all Judah and I' that were present,
25 and made them an ordinance in I':
27 in the book of the kings of I'
36: 8 in the book of the kings of I'
13 turning unto the Lord God of I'.
Ezr 1: 3 the house of the Lord God of I',
2: 2 of the men of the people of I':
59 their seed, whether they were of I':
70 their cities, and all I' in their cities.
3: 1 the children of I' were in the cities,
2 builded the altar of the God of I',
10 the ordinance of David king of I'.
11 mercy endureth for ever toward I'.
4: 1 temple unto the Lord God of I';
3 rest of the chief of the fathers of I',
3 will build unto the Lord God of I',
5: 1 in the name of the God of I', even
11 which a great king of I' builded
6: 14 the commandment of the God of I',
16 the children of I', the priests, and
17 and for a sin offering for all I',
17 to the number of the tribes of I'.
21 I', which were come again out of
21 land, to seek the Lord God of I',
22 of the house of God, the God of I'.
7: 6 which the Lord God of I' had given:
7 went up some of the children of I',
10 teach in I' statutes and judgments.
11 the Lord, and of his statutes to I'.
13 that all they of the people of I',
15 freely offered unto the God of I',
28 out of I' chief men to go up with
8: 18 Mahli, the son of Levi, the son of I';
25 his lords, and all I' there present,
29 and chief of the fathers of I',
35 burnt offerings unto the God of I',
35 twelve bullocks for all I', ninety
9: 1 The people of I', and the priests,
4 at the words of the God of I',
15 Lord God of I', thou art righteous;
10: 1 assembled unto him out of I' a
2 is hope in I' concerning this thing.
5 all I', to swear that they should do
10 wives, to increase the trespass of I'.
25 Moreover of I': of the sons of
Ne 1: 6 for the children of I' thy servants,
6 confess the sins of the children of I',

Ne 2: 10 the welfare of the children of I'.
7: 7 say, of the men of the people of I'
61 their seed, whether they were of I'.
73 and all I', dwelt in their cities;
73 children of I' were in their cities.
8: 1 the Lord had commanded to I'.
14 children of I' should dwell in booths
17 had not the children of I' done so.
9: 1 of I' were assembled with fasting,
2 I' separated themselves from all
10: 33 to make an atonement for I',
39 the children of I' and the children
11: 3 to wit, I', the priests, and the
20 And the residue of I', of the priests,
12: 47 all I' in the days of Zerubbabel,
13: 2 of I' with bread and with water,
3 separated from I' all the mixed
18 wrath upon I' by profaning the
26 king of I' sin by these things?
26 and God made him king over all I':
Ps 14: 7 salvation of I' were come out of
7 shall rejoice, and I' shall be glad.
22: 3 that inhabitest the praises of I'.
23 and fear him, all ye the seed of I'.
25: 22 Redeem I', O God, out of all his
41: 13 Blessed be the Lord God of I' from
50: 7 O I', and I will testify against thee:
53: 6 salvation of I' were come out of
6 shall rejoice, and I' shall be glad.
59: 5 Lord God of hosts, the God of I',
68: 8 the presence of God, the God of I'.
26 the Lord, from the fountain of I'.
34 his excellency is over I', and his
35 God of I' is he that giveth strength
69: 6 confounded for my sake, O God of I'.
71: 22 the harp, O thou Holy One of I'.
72: 18 be the Lord God, the God of I',
73: 1 God is good to I', even to such as
76: 1 God known: his name is great in I'.
78: 5 Jacob, and appointed a law in I',
21 and anger also came up against I';
31 smote down the chosen men of I'.
41 and limited the Holy One of I'.
55 tribes of I' to dwell in their tents.
59 wroth, and greatly abhorred I':
71 his people, and I' his inheritance.
80: 1 Give ear, O Shepherd of I', thou
81: 4 For this was a statute for I', and
8 O I', if thou wilt hearken unto me;
11 voice; and I' would none of me.
13 me, and I' had walked in my ways!
83: 4 name of I' may be no more in
89: 18 and the Holy One of I' is our king.
98: 3 his truth toward the house of I':
103: 7 his acts unto the children of I'.
105: 10 to I' for an everlasting covenant:
23 I' also came into Egypt; and Jacob
106: 48 Blessed be the Lord God of I' from
114: 1 When I' went out of Egypt, the
2 his sanctuary, and I' his dominion.
115: 9 O I', trust thou in the Lord: he is
12 he will bless the house of I'; he
118: 2 I' now say, that his mercy endureth
121: 4 keepeth I' shall neither slumber
122: 4 unto the testimony of I', to give
124: 1 was on our side, now may I' say;
125: 5 but peace shall be upon I'.
128: 6 children, and peace upon I'.
129: 1 from my youth, may I' now say:
130: 7 Let I' hope in the Lord: for with
8 And he shall redeem I' from all
131: 3 Let I' hope in the Lord from
135: 4 and I' for his peculiar treasure.
12 an heritage unto I' his people.
19 Bless the Lord, O house of I':
136: 11 brought out I' from among them:
14 made I' to pass through the midst
22 an heritage unto I' his servant:
147: 2 together the outcasts of I'.
19 statutes and his judgments unto I'.
148: 14 the children of I', a people near
149: 2 Let I' rejoice in him that made
Pr 1: 1 the son of David, king of I':
Ec 1: 12 was king over I' in Jerusalem.
Ca 3: 7 are about it, of the valiant of I'.
Isa 1: 3 I' doth not know, my people doth
4 provoked the Holy One of I' unto
24 Lord of hosts, the Mighty One of I'.
4: 2 for them that are escaped of I'.
5: 7 Lord of hosts is the house of I',
19 of the Holy One of I' draw nigh
24 the word of the Holy One of I'.
7: 1 the son of Remaliah, king of I',
8: 14 of offence to both the houses of I',
18 for signs and for wonders in I'
9: 8 Jacob, and it hath lighted upon I'.
12 shall devour I' with open mouth.
14 Lord will cut off from I' head and
10: 17 the light of I' shall be for a fire,
20 that the remnant of I', and such as
20 upon the Lord, the Holy One of I',
22 people I' be as the sand of the sea,
11: 12 shall assemble the outcasts of I',
16 like as it was to I' in the day that
12: 6 great is the Holy One of I' in the
14: 1 will yet choose I', and set them in
2 the house of I' shall possess them
17: 3 be as the glory of the children of I',
6 thereof, saith the Lord God of I'.
7 have respect to the Holy One of I'.
9 left because of the children of I':
19: 24 In that day shall I' be the third
25 my hands, and I' mine inheritance.
21: 10 of the Lord of hosts, the God of I',
17 the Lord God of I' hath spoken it,
24: 15 of the Lord God of I' in the isles of

Isa 27: 6 *I'* shall blossom and bud, and fill
12 one by one, O ye children of *I'*.
29: 19 shall rejoice in the Holy One of *I'*.
23 and shall fear the God of *I'*.
30: 11 cause the Holy One of *I'* to cease
12 thus saith the Holy One of *I'*,
15 the Lord God, the Holy One of *I'*;
29 the Lord, to the mighty One of *I'*.
31: 1 look not unto the Holy One of *I'*,
6 children of *I'* have deeply revolted.
37: 16 O Lord of hosts, God of *I'*, that
21 Thus saith the Lord God of *I'*,
23 even against the Holy One of *I'*.
40: 27 thou, O Jacob, and speakest, O *I'*,
41: 8 But thou, *I'*, art my servant, Jacob
14 thou worm Jacob, and ye men of *I'*;
14 thy redeemer, the Holy One of *I'*.
16 shalt glory in the Holy One of *I'*.
17 the God of *I'* will not forsake them.
20 the Holy One of *I'* hath created it.
42: 24 for a spoil, and *I'* to the robbers?
43: 1 and he that formed thee, O *I'*, Fear
3 Lord thy God, the Holy One of *I'*,
14 redeemer, the Holy One of *I'*;
15 One, the Creator of *I'*, your King.
22 thou hast been weary of me, O *I'*.
28 the curse, and *I'* to reproaches.
44: 1 and *I'*, whom I have chosen:
5 surname himself by the name of *I'*.
6 Thus saith the Lord the King of *I'*,
21 Remember these, O Jacob and *I'*;
21 O *I'*, thou shalt not be forgotten of
23 Jacob, and glorified himself in *I'*.
45: 3 thee by thy name, am the God of *I'*.
4 servant's sake, and *I'* mine elect,
11 saith the Lord, the Holy One of *I'*,
15 God that hidest thyself, O God of *I'*,
17 But *I'* shall be saved in the Lord
25 shall all the seed of *I'* be justified,
46: 3 all the remnant of the house of *I'*,
13 salvation in Zion for *I'* my glory.
47: 4 is his name, the Holy One of *I'*.
48: 1 which are called by the name of *I'*,
1 and make mention of the God of *I'*,
2 stay themselves upon the God of *I'*;
12 Hearken unto me, O Jacob and *I'*,
17 thy Redeemer, the Holy One of *I'*;
49: 3 Thou art my servant, O *I'*, in whom
5 Though *I'* be not gathered, yet
6 and to restore the preserved of *I'*:
7 Redeemer of *I'*, and his Holy One,
7 is faithful, and the Holy One of *I'*,
52: 12 the God of *I'* will be your rereward.
54: 5 thy Redeemer the Holy One of *I'*;
55: 5 thy God, and for the Holy One of *I'*;
56: 8 which gathereth the outcasts of *I'*
60: 9 thy God, and to the Holy One of *I'*,
14 The Zion of the Holy One of *I'*.
63: 7 goodness toward the house of *I'*,
16 of us, and *I'* acknowledge us not:
66: 20 of *I'* bring an offering in a clean
Jer 2: 3 *I'* was holiness unto the Lord, and
4 all the families of the house of *I'*:
14 Is *I'* a servant? is he a homeborn
26 so is the house of *I'* ashamed;
31 Have I been a wilderness unto *I'*?
3: 6 which backsliding *I'* hath done?
8 backsliding *I'* committed adultery
11 The backsliding *I'* hath justified
12 Return, thou backsliding *I'*, saith
18 shall walk with the house of *I'*,
20 dealt treacherously...O house of *I'*,
21 supplications of the children of *I'*:
23 Lord our God is the salvation of *I'*.
4: 1 wilt return, O *I'*, saith the Lord,
5: 11 house of *I'* and the house of Judah
15 upon you from far, O house of *I'*,
6: 9 glean the remnant of *I'* as a vine:
7: 3 the Lord of hosts, the God of *I'*,
12 the wickedness of my people *I'*.
21 the Lord of hosts, the God of *I'*;
9: 15 the Lord of hosts, the God of *I'*;
26 the house of *I'* are uncircumcised
10: 1 speaketh unto you, O house of *I'*:
16 and *I'* is the rod of his inheritance:
11: 3 Thus saith the Lord God of *I'*;
10 house of *I'* and the house of Judah
17 for the evil of the house of *I'* and of
12: 14 caused my people *I'* to inherit;
13: 11 cleave unto me...whole house of *I'*
12 Thus saith the Lord God of *I'*,
14: 8 the hope of *I'*, the saviour thereof
16: 9 the Lord of hosts, the God of *I'*;
14 of *I'* out of the land of Egypt;
15 of *I'* from the land of the north,
17: 13 O Lord, the hope of *I'*, all that
18: 6 O house of *I'*, cannot I do with you
6 are ye in mine hand, O house of *I'*.
13 virgin of *I'* hath done a...horrible
19: 3, 15 the Lord of hosts, the God of *I'*;
21: 4 Thus saith the Lord God of *I'*;
23: 2 Lord God of *I'* against the pastors
6 be saved, and *I'* shall dwell safely:
7 of *I'* out of the land of Egypt;
8 which led the seed of the house of *I'*
13 and caused my people *I'* to err.
24: 5 Thus saith the Lord, the God of *I'*;
25: 15 saith the Lord God of *I'* unto me;
27 the Lord of hosts, the God of *I'*;
27: 4 the Lord of hosts, the God of *I'*;
21 the Lord of hosts, the God of *I'*,
28: 2 the Lord of hosts, the God of *I'*,
14 the Lord of hosts, the God of *I'*;
29: 4 the Lord of hosts, the God of *I'*,
8 the Lord of hosts, the God of *I'*;
21 the Lord of hosts, the God of *I'*,

Jer 29: 23 they have committed villainy in *I'*,
25 the Lord of hosts, the God of *I'*,
30: 2 Thus speaketh the Lord God of *I'*,
3 again the captivity of my people *I'*
4 that the Lord spake concerning *I'*
10 neither be dismayed, O *I'*: for, lo,
31: 1 be the God of all the families of *I'*,
2 even *I'*, when I went to cause him
4 thou shalt be built, O virgin of *I'*:
7 save thy people, the remnant of *I'*.
9 for I am a father to *I'*, and Ephraim
10 He that scattered *I'* will gather
21 O virgin of *I'*, turn again to these
23 the Lord of hosts, the God of *I'*;
27 I will sow the house of *I'* and the
31 new covenant with the house of *I'*,
33 I will make with the house of *I'*;
36 the seed of *I'* also shall cease from
37 I will also cast off all the seed of *I'*
32: 14, 15 the Lord of hosts, the God of *I'*;
20 and in *I'*, and among other men;
21 people *I'* out of the land of Egypt
30 the children of *I'* and the children
30 children of *I'* have only provoked
32 of all the evil of the children of *I'*
36 thus saith the Lord, the God of *I'*,
33: 4 thus saith the Lord, the God of *I'*,
7 and the captivity of *I'* to return,
14 have promised unto the house of *I'*
17 upon the throne of the house of *I'*;
34: 2, 13 saith the Lord, the God of *I'*;
35: 13 the Lord of hosts, the God of *I'*;
17 Lord God of hosts, the God of *I'*;
18, 19 the Lord of hosts, the God of *I'*;
36: 2 I have spoken unto thee against *I'*,
37: 7 Thus saith the Lord, the God of *I'*;
38: 17 the God of hosts, the God of *I'*;
39: 16 the Lord of hosts, the God of *I'*;
41: 9 made for fear of Baasha king of *I'*:
42: 9 Thus saith the Lord, the God of *I'*,
15, 18 the Lord of hosts, the God of *I'*;
43: 10 the Lord of hosts, the God of *I'*;
44: 2 the Lord of hosts, the God of *I'*;
7 the God of hosts, the God of *I'*;
11 the Lord of hosts, the God of *I'*;
25 the Lord of hosts, the God of *I'*,
45: 2 Thus saith the Lord, the God of *I'*,
46: 25 The Lord of hosts, the God of *I'*,
27 Jacob, and be not dismayed, O *I'*:
48: 1 the Lord of hosts, the God of *I'*;
13 house of *I'* was ashamed of Beth-el
27 For was not *I'* a derision to thee?
49: 1 Hath *I'* no sons? hath he no heir?
2 shall *I'* be heir unto them that were
50: 4 the children of *I'* shall come,
17 *I'* is a scattered sheep; the lions
18 the Lord of hosts, the God of *I'*;
19 will bring *I'* again to his habitation,
20 iniquity of *I'* shall be sought for,
29 Lord, against the Holy One of *I'*.
33 of *I'* and...Judah were oppressed
51: 5 For *I'* hath not been forsaken, nor
5 with sin against the Holy One of *I'*.
33 the Lord of hosts, the God of *I'*;
49 hath caused the slain of *I'* to fall,
La 2: 1 unto the earth the beauty of *I'*,
3 his fierce anger all the horn of *I'*:
5 enemy: he hath swallowed up *I'*,
Eze 2: 3 I send thee to the children of *I'*,
3: 1 and go speak unto the house of *I'*.
4 go, get thee unto the house of *I'*,
5 language, but to the house of *I'*;
7 of *I'* will not hearken unto thee;
7 *I'* are impudent and hardhearted.
17 a watchman unto the house of *I'*:
4: 3 shall be a sign to the house of *I'*.
4 iniquity of the house of *I'* upon it:
5 bear the iniquity of the house of *I'*.
13 children of *I'* eat their defiled bread
5: 4 come forth into all the house of *I'*.
6: 2 face toward the mountains of *I'*,
3 Ye mountains of *I'*, hear the word
5 dead carcases of the children of *I'*
11 abominations of the house of *I'*!
7: 2 the Lord God unto the land of *I'*;
8: 4 glory of the God of *I'* was there,
6 that the house of *I'* committeth
10 and all the idols of the house of *I'*,
11 of the ancients of the house of *I'*,
12 the ancients of the house of *I'* do in
9: 3 glory of the Lord of *I'* was gone up
8 thou destroy all the residue of *I'*
9 The iniquity of the house of *I'* and
10: 19 glory of the God of *I'* was over them
20 that I saw under the God of *I'*
11: 5 Thus have ye said, O house of *I'*:
10 I will judge you in the border of *I'*;
11 I will judge you in the border of *I'*:
13 a full end of the remnant of *I'*?
15 and all the house of *I'* wholly,
17 and I will give you the land of *I'*.
22 glory of the God of *I'* was over them
12: 6 thee for a sign unto the house of *I'*.
9 of man, hath not the house of *I'*,
10 house of *I'* that are among them.
19 of Jerusalem, and of the land of *I'*;
22 proverb...ye have in the land of *I'*,
23 no more use it as a proverb in *I'*;
24 divination within the house of *I'*.
27 behold, they of the house of *I'* say,
13: 2 prophesy against the prophets of *I'*
4 O *I'*, thy prophets are like the foxes
5 up the hedge for the house of *I'*
9 in the writing of the house of *I'*,
9 shall they enter into the land of *I'*;
16 the prophets of *I'* which prophesy

Eze 14: 1 certain of the elders of *I'* unto me,
4 Every man of the house of *I'* that
5 the house of *I'* in their own heart,
6 Therefore say unto the house of *I'*,
7 For every one of the house of *I'*,
7 the stranger that sojourneth in *I'*,
9 him from the midst of my people *I'*.
11 house of *I'* may go no more astray
17: 2 a parable unto the house of *I'*;
23 In the mountain of the height of *I'*
18: 2 proverb concerning the land of *I'*,
3 any more to use this proverb in *I'*
6, 15 to the idols of the house of *I'*,
25 Hear now, O house of *I'*; Is not my
29 Yet saith the house of *I'*, The way
29 O house of *I'*, are not my ways
30 I will judge you, O house of *I'*,
31 for why will ye die, O house of *I'*?
19: 1 a lamentation for the princes of *I'*,
9 be heard upon the mountains of *I'*.
20: 1 of the elders of *I'* came to enquire
3 of man, speak unto the elders of *I'*,
5 In the day when I chose *I'*, and
13 the house of *I'* rebelled against me
27 of man, speak unto the house of *I'*,
30 Wherefore say unto the house of *I'*,
31 enquired of by you, O house of *I'*?
38 shall not enter into the land of *I'*:
39 As for you, O house of *I'*, thus saith
40 in the mountain of the height of *I'*,
40 there shall all the house of *I'*, all
42 shall bring you into the land of *I'*,
44 corrupt doings, O ye house of *I'*,
21: 2 prophesy against the land of *I'*,
3 say to the land of *I'*, Thus saith
12 shall be upon all the princes of *I'*:
25 thou, profane wicked prince of *I'*,
22: 6 Behold, the princes of *I'*, every one
18 house of *I'* is to me become dross:
24: 21 Speak unto the house of *I'*, Thus
25: 3 against the land of *I'*, when it was
6 thy despite against the land of *I'*;
14 Edom by the hand of my people *I'*:
27: 17 land of *I'*, they were thy merchants:
28: 24 pricking brier unto the house of *I'*,
25 shall have gathered the house of *I'*
29: 6 a staff of reed to the house of *I'*.
16 the confidence of the house of *I'*,
21 horn of the house of *I'* to bud forth,
33: 7 a watchman unto the house of *I'*;
10 of man, speak unto the house of *I'*;
11 for why will ye die, O house of *I'*?
20 O ye house of *I'*, I will judge you
24 those wastes of the land of *I'*
28 mountains of *I'* shall be desolate,
34: 2 against the shepherds of *I'*,
2 Woe be to the shepherds of *I'* that
13 feed them upon the mountains of *I'*
14 upon the high mountains of *I'* shall
14 they feed upon the mountains of *I'*.
30 even the house of *I'*, are my people,
35: 5 shed blood of the children of *I'* by
12 spoken against the mountains of *I'*,
15 the inheritance of the house of *I'*,
36: 1 prophesy unto the mountains of *I'*,
1 Ye mountains of *I'*, hear the word
4 ye mountains of *I'*, hear the word
6 therefore concerning the land of *I'*,
8 But ye, O ye mountains of *I'*, ye
8 yield your fruit to my people of *I'*;
10 all the house of *I'*, even all of it;
12 walk upon you, even my people *I'*;
17 house of *I'* dwelt in their own land,
21 which the house of *I'* had profaned
22 Therefore say unto the house of *I'*,
22 this for your sakes, O house of *I'*,
32 for your own ways, O house of *I'*.
37 be enquired of by the house of *I'*,
37: 11 bones are the whole house of *I'*:
12 and bring you into the land of *I'*.
16 the children of *I'* his companions:
16 all the house of *I'* his companions:
19 the tribes of *I'* his fellows, and will
21 I will take the children of *I'* from
22 the land upon the mountains of *I'*;
28 know that I the Lord do sanctify *I'*,
38: 8 people, against the mountains of *I'*,
14 my people of *I'* dwelleth safely,
16 come up against my people of *I'*,
17 by my servants the prophets of *I'*,
18 shall come against the land of *I'*,
19 a great shaking in the land of *I'*;
39: 2 thee upon the mountains of *I'*:
4 shalt fall upon the mountains of *I'*,
7 known in the midst of my people *I'*;
7 I am the Lord, the Holy One in *I'*.
9 they that dwell in the cities of *I'*
11 Gog a place there of graves in *I'*,
12 the house of *I'* be burying of them,
17 sacrifice upon the mountains of *I'*,
22 house of *I'* shall know that I am
23 house of *I'* went into captivity for
25 mercy upon the whole house of *I'*,
29 out my spirit upon the house of *I'*,
40: 2 brought he me into the land of *I'*,
4 that thou seest to the house of *I'*.
43: 2 glory of the God of *I'* came from
7 in the midst of the children of *I'*
7 shall the house of *I'* no more defile,
10 shew the house to the house of *I'*,
44: 2 Lord, the God of *I'*, hath entered in
6 rebellious, even to the house of *I'*,
6 O ye house of *I'*, let it suffice you
9 that is among the children of *I'*.
10 far from me, when *I'* went astray,
12 the house of *I'* to fall into iniquity;

Eze 44:15 children of I' went astray from me,
22 take maidens...of the house of I',
28 shall give them no possession in I':
29 dedicated thing in I' shall be theirs.
45: 6 shall be for the whole house of I'.
8 land shall be his possession in I':
8 shall they give to the house of I'
9 Let it suffice you, O princes of I':
15 out of the fat pastures of I';
16 this oblation for the prince in I'.
17 all solemnities of the house of I':
17 reconciliation for the house of I'.
47:13 according to the twelve tribes of I':
18 and from the land of I' by Jordan,
21 you according to the tribes of I'.
22 country among the children of I';
22 with you among the tribes of I'.
48:11 when the children of I' went astray,
19 serve it out of all the tribes of I'.
29 unto the tribes of I' for inheritance,
31 after the names of the tribes of I':
Da 1: 3 bring certain of the children of I',
9: 7 of Jerusalem, and unto all I',
11 all I' have transgressed thy law,
20 my sin and the sin of my people I',
Ho 1: 1 the son of Joash, king of I'.
4 the kingdom of the house of I'.
5 break the bow of I' in the valley
6 have mercy upon the house of I';
10 I' shall be as the sand of the sea,
11 children of I' be gathered together,
3: 1 Lord toward the children of I',
4 I' shall abide many days without a
5 shall the children of I' return, and
4: 1 word of the Lord, ye children of I':
15 Though thou, I', play the harlot, yet
16 I' slideth back as a backsliding
5: 1 and hearken, ye house of I';
3 Ephraim, and I' is not hid from me:
3 whoredom, and I' is defiled.
5 pride of I' doth testify to his face:
5 shall I' and Ephraim fall in their
9 tribes of I' have I made known that
6:10 horrible thing in the house of I':
10 whoredom of Ephraim, I' is defiled.
7: 1 When I would have healed I', then
10 the pride of I' testifieth to his face:
8: 2 I' shall cry unto me, My God, we
3 I' hath cast off the thing that is
6 from I' was it also: the workman
8 I' is swallowed up: now shall they
14 I' hath forgotten his Maker, and
9: 1 Rejoice not, O I', for joy, as other
7 are come; I' shall know it:
10 I' like grapes in the wilderness;
10: 1 I' is an empty vine, he bringeth
6 I' shall be ashamed of his own
8 the sin of I', shall be destroyed:
9 I', thou hast sinned from the days
15 shall the king of I' utterly be cut off.
11: 1 When I' was a child, then I loved
8 how shall I deliver thee, I'? how
12 and the house of I' with deceit:
12:12 I' served for a wife, and for a wife
13 the Lord brought I' out of Egypt,
13: 1 trembling, he exalted himself in I';
9 O I', thou hast destroyed thyself;
14: 1 O I', return unto the Lord thy God;
5 I will be as the dew unto I': he
Joe 2:27 know that I am in the midst of I',
3: 2 my people and for my heritage I',
16 the strength of the children of I'.
Am 1: 1 concerning I' in the days of Uzziah
1 the son of Joash king of I',
2: 6 For three transgressions of I', and
11 not even thus, O ye children of I'?
3: 1 spoken against you, O children of I',
12 shall the children of I' be taken out
14 I shall visit the transgressions of I'
4: 5 this liketh you, O ye children of I',
12 thus will I do unto thee, O I':
12 prepare to meet thy God, O I'.
5: 1 even a lamentation, O house of I'.
2 The virgin of I' is fallen; she shall
3 shall leave ten, to the house of I'.
4 saith the Lord unto the house of I',
25 wilderness forty years, O house of I'?
6: 1 to whom the house of I' came!
14 against you a nation, O house of I',
7: 8 in the midst of my people I':
9 sanctuaries of I' shall be laid waste;
10 Beth-el sent to Jeroboam king of I',
10 thee in the midst of the house of I':
11 I' shall surely be led away captive
15 Go, prophesy unto my people I'.
16 sayest, Prophesy not against I',
17 and I' shall surely go into captivity
8: 2 end is come upon my people of I';
9: 7 unto me, O children of I'?
7 not I brought up I' out of the land
9 will sift the house of I' among all
14 the captivity of my people of I',
Ob 20 of this host of the children of I'
Mic 1: 5 and for the sins of the house of I'.
13 transgressions of I' were found in
14 shall be a lie to the kings of I'.
15 come unto Adullam the glory of I'.
2:12 surely gather the remnant of I';
3: 1 and ye princes of the house of I';
8 his transgression, and to I' his sin.
9 and princes of the house of I',
5: 1 smite the judge of I' with a rod
2 unto me that is to be ruler in I';
3 shall return unto the children of I'
6: 2 people, and he will plead with I'.
Na 2: 2 of Jacob, as the excellency of I':

Zep 2: 9 the Lord of hosts, the God of I',
3:13 remnant of I' shall not do iniquity,
14 O daughter of Zion; shout, O I'; be
15 the king of I', even the Lord, is in
Zec 1:19 scattered Judah, I', and Jerusalem.
8:13 O house of Judah, and house of I';
9: 1 of man, as of all the tribes of I',
11:14 brotherhood between Judah and I'.
12: 1 of the word of the Lord for I',
Mal 1: 1 word of the Lord to I' by Malachi.
5 be magnified from the border of I'.
2:11 an abomination is committed in I'
16 the Lord, the God of I', saith that
4: 4 unto him in Horeb for all I',
M't 2: 6 that shall rule my people I'.
20 mother, and go into the land of I':
21 and came into the land of I'.
8:10 found so great faith, no, not in I'.
9:33 saying, It was never so seen in I'.
10: 6 to the lost sheep of the house of I'.
23 not have gone over the cities of I',
15:24 unto the lost sheep of the house of I'
31 and they glorified the God of I'.
19:28 judging the twelve tribes of I'.
27: 9 they of the children of I' did value;
42 If he be the King of I', let him now
M'r 12:29 the commandments is, Hear, O I';
15:32 Let Christ the King of I' descend
Lu 1:16 of the children of I' shall he turn
54 He hath holpen his servant I',
68 Blessed be the Lord God of I'; for
80 till the day of his shewing unto I'.
2:25 waiting for the consolation of I':
32 and the glory of thy people I'.
34 fall and rising again of many in I';
4:25 many widows were in I' in the days
27 many lepers were in I' in the time of
7: 9 found so great faith, no, not in I'.
22:30 judging the twelve tribes of I'.
24:21 he which should have redeemed I':
Joh 1:31 he should be made manifest to I',
49 Son of God; thou art the King of I'.
3:10 Art thou a master of I', and
12:13 King of I' that cometh in the name
Ac 1: 6 restore again the kingdom to I'?
2:22 Ye men of I', hear these words;
36 all the house of I' know assuredly,
3:12 Ye men of I', why marvel ye at this?
4: 8 of the people, and elders of I',
10 you all, and to all the people of I',
27 the Gentiles, and the people of I',
5:21 all the senate of the children of I',
31 for to give repentance to I', and
35 Ye men of I', take heed to
7:23 his brethren the children of I'.
37 which said unto the children of I',
42 O ye house of I', have ye offered to
9:15 and kings, and the children of I':
10:36 God sent unto the children of I',
13:16 Men of I', and ye that fear God,
17 The God of this people of I' chose
23 promise raised unto I' a Saviour,
24 repentance to all the people of I'.
21:28 Crying out, Men of I', help: This
28:20 that for the hope of I' I am bound
Ro 9: 6 they are not all I', which are of I':
27 Esaias also crieth concerning I',
27 children of I' be as the sand of the
31 But I', which followed after the law
10: 1 desire and prayer to God for I' is,
19 But I say, Did not I' know?
21 But to I' he saith, All day long I
11: 2 intercession to God against I',
7 I' hath not obtained that which he
25 blindness in part is happened to I',
26 And so all I' shall be saved: as it is
1Co 10:18 Behold I' after the flesh: are not
2Co 3: 7 of I' could not stedfastly behold
13 of I' could not stedfastly look to
Ga 6:16 and mercy, and upon the I' of God.
Eph 2:12 aliens from the commonwealth of I'
Ph'p 3: 5 of the stock of I', of the tribe of
Heb 8: 8 a new covenant with the house of I'
10 that I will make with the house of I'
11:22 the departing of the children of I';
Re 2:14 cast a stumblingblock before...of I',
7: 4 of all the tribes of the children of I'.
21:12 twelve tribes of the children of I':

Israelite (*iz'-ra-el-ite*) See also ISRAELITES; ISRAELITISH.
Nu 25:14 name of the I' that was slain,
2Sa 17:25 son, whose name was Ithra an I',
Joh 1:47 Behold an I' indeed, in whom is
Ro 11: 1 For I also am an I', of the seed of

Israelites (*iz'-ra-el-ites*)
Ex 9: 7 not one of the cattle of the I' dead.
Le 23:42 are I' born shall dwell in booths:
Jos 3:17 the I' passed over on dry ground,
8:24 all the I' returned unto Ai, and
13: 6 lot unto the I' for an inheritance,
13 dwell among the I' until this day.
J'g 20:21 to the ground of the I' that day
1Sa 2:14 in Shiloh unto all the I' that came
13:20 the I' went down to the Philistines,
14:21 be with the I' that were with Saul
25: 1 all the I' were gathered together,
29: 1 I' pitched by a fountain which is
2Sa 4: 1 feeble, and all the I' were troubled.
2Ki 3:24 I' rose up and smote the Moabites,
7:13 even as all the multitude of the I'
1Ch 9: 2 the I', the priests, Levites, and
Ro 9: 4 Who are I'; to whom pertaineth
2Co 11:22 Are they I'? so am I. Are they

Israelitish (*iz'-ra-el-i-tish*)
Le 24:10 the son of an I' woman, whose
10 this son of the I' woman and a man
11 the I' woman's son blasphemed

Israel's (*iz'-ra-els*)
Ge 48:13 his right hand toward I' left hand,
13 his left hand toward I' right hand,
Ex 18: 8 and to the Egyptians for I' sake,
Nu 1:20 children of Reuben, I' eldest son,
31:30 the children of I' half, thou shalt
42 the children of I' half, which Moses
47 Even of the children of I' half,
De 21: 8 blood unto thy people of I' charge.
2Sa 5:12 his kingdom for his people I' sake.
2Ki 3:11 And one of the king of I' servants

Issachar (*is'-sa-kar*)
Ge 30:18 and she called his name I'.
35:23 and Judah, and I', and Zebulun:
46:13 the sons of I'; Tola, and Phuvah,
49:14 I' is a strong ass couching down
Ex 1: 3 I', Zebulun, and Benjamin,
Nu 1: 8 Of I'; Nethaneel the son of Zuar.
28 children of I', by their generations,
29 of the tribe of I', were fifty and four
2: 5 unto him shall be the tribe of I':
5 shall be captain of the children of I'.
7:18 the son of Zuar, prince of I',
10:15 host of the tribe of the children of I'
13: 7 tribe of I', Igal the son of Joseph.
26:23 the sons of I' after their families:
25 These are the families of I'
34:26 of the tribe of the children of I',
De 27:12 Judah, and I', and Joseph, and
33:18 thy going out; and, I', in thy tents.
Jos 17:10 on the north, and in I' on the east.
11 Manasseh had in I' and in Asher
19:17 came out to I', for the children of I'
23 of the tribe of the children of I'
21: 6 out of the families of the tribe of I',
28 out of the tribe of I', Kishon with
J'g 5:15 of I' were with Deborah; even I',
10: 1 Puah, the son of Dodo, a man of I';
1Ki 4:17 the son of Paruah, in I':
15:27 son of Ahijah, of the house of I',
1Ch 2: 1 Simeon, Levi, and Judah, I', and
6:62 their families out of the tribe of I',
72 And out of the tribe of I'; Kedesh
7: 1 sons of I' were, Tola, and Puah,
5 the families of I' were valiant men
12:32 the children of I', which were men
40 that were nigh them, even unto I'
26: 5 Ammiel the sixth, I' the seventh,
27:18 of I', Omri the son of Michael:
2Ch 30:18 many of Ephraim, and Manasseh, I',
Eze 48:25 unto the west side, I' a portion.
26 And by the border of I', from the
33 one gate of I', one gate of Zebulun.
Re 7: 7 Of the tribe of I' were sealed

Isshiah (*is-shi'-ah*) See also ISAIAH; JESIAH.
1Ch 24:21 sons of Rehabiah, the first was I'.
25 The brother of Michah was I':

issue See also ISSUED; ISSUES.
Ge 48: 6 And thy i', which thou begettest
Le 12: 7 cleansed from the i' of her blood.
15: 2 When any man hath a running i'
2 because of his i' he is unclean.
3 shall be his uncleanness in his i':
3 whether his flesh run with his i', or
3 his flesh be stopped from his i',
4 whereon he lieth that hath the i',
6 whereon he sat that hath the i'
7 the flesh of him that hath the i'
8 if he that hath the i' spit upon him
9 he rideth upon that hath the i' shall
11, 12 he toucheth that hath the i',
13 And when he that hath an i'
13 is cleansed of his i',
15 for him before the Lord for his i'.
19 And if a woman have an i',
19 and her i' in her flesh be blood,
25 if a woman have an i' of her blood
25 days of the i' of her uncleanness
26 she lieth all the days of her i'
28 But if she be cleansed of her i',
30 atonement before the Lord for the i'
32 is the law of him that hath an i',
33 of him that hath an i', of the man,
22: 4 is a leper, or hath a running i';
Nu 5: 2 leper, and every one that hath an i',
2Sa 3:29 house of Joab one that hath an i',
2Ki 20:18 of thy sons that shall i' from thee,
Isa 22:24 house, the offspring and the i', all
39: 7 thy sons that shall i' from thee,
Eze 23:20 and whose i' is like the i' of horses.
47: 8 waters i' out toward the east
M't 9:20 with an i' of blood twelve years,
22:25 having no i', left his wife unto his
M'r 5:25 had an i' of blood twelve years,
Lu 8:43 having an i' of blood twelve years,
44 and immediately her i' of blood

issued
Jos 8:22 the other i' out of the city against
Job 38: 8 as if it had i' out of the womb?
Eze 47: 1 waters i' out from under the
12 waters they i' out of the sanctuary:
Da 7:10 A fiery stream i' and came forth
Re 9:17 out of their mouths i' fire and
18 which i' out of their mouths.

issues
Ps 68:20 the Lord belong the i' from death.
Pr 4:23 for out of it are the i' of life.

Isuah (*is'-u-ah*) See also ISHUAH.
1Ch 7:30 Imnah, and I', and Ishuai, and

Isui (*is'-u-i*) See also ISHUI.
Ge 46:17 Jimnah, and Ishuah, and I', and

Italian (*it-al'-yan*)
Ac 10: 1 of the band called the *I'* band,

Italy (*it'-a-lee*)
Ac 18: 2 in Pontus, lately come from *I'*,
27: 1 that we should sail into *I'*,
6 ship of Alexandria sailing into *I'*;
Heb13: 24 the saints. They of *I'* salute you.
subsc. Written to the Hebrews from *I'*

itch See also ITCHING.
De 28: 27 and with the scab, and with the *i'*,

itching
2Ti 4: 3 teachers, having *i'* ears;

Ithai (*ith'-a-i*) See also ITTAI.
1Ch 11: 31 *I'* the son of Ribai of Gibeah, that

Ithamar (*ith'-a-mar*)
Ex 6: 23 Nadab and Abihu, Eleazar, and *I'*.
28: 1 Abihu, Eleazar and *I'*, Aaron's sons.
38: 21 by the hand of *I'*, son to Aaron the
Le 10: 6 unto Eleazar and unto *I'*, his sons,
12 Aaron, unto Eleazar and unto *I'*,
16 he was angry with Eleazar and *I'*,
Nu 3: 2 firstborn, and Abihu, Eleazar, and *I'*.
4 *I'* ministered in the priest's office
4: 28 shall be under the hand of *I'* the
33 under the hand of *I'* the son of
7: 8 under the hand of *I'* the son of
26: 60 Nadab, and Abihu, Eleazar, and *I'*.
1Ch 6: 3 Nadab, and Abihu, Eleazar, and *I'*.
24: 1 Nadab, and Abihu, Eleazar, and *I'*.
2 Eleazar and *I'* executed the priest's
3 and Ahimelech of the sons of *I'*,
4 of Eleazar than of the sons of *I'*;
4 and eight among the sons of *I'*
5 of Eleazar, and of the sons of *I'*.
6 for Eleazar, and one taken for *I'*.
Ezr 8: 2 Gershom: of the sons of *I'*: Daniel:

Ithiel (*ith'-e-el*)
Ne 11: 7 son of Maaseiah, the son of *I'*, the
Pr 30: 1 man spake unto *I'*, even unto *I'* and

Ithmah (*ith'-mah*)
1Ch 11: 46 of Elnaam, and *I'* the Moabite,

Ithnan (*ith'-nan*)
Jos 15: 23 And Kedesh, and Hazor, and *I'*,

Ithra (*ith'-rah*) See also JETHER.
2Sa 17: 25 whose name was *I'* an Israelite,

Ithran (*ith'-ran*)
Ge 36: 26 Hemdan, and Eshban, and *I'*,
1Ch 1: 41 Amram, and Eshban, and *I'*,
7: 37 and Shilshah, and *I'*, and Beera.

Ithream (*ith'-re-am*)
2Sa 3: 5 sixth, *I'*, by Eglah David's wife.
1Ch 3: 3 the sixth, *I'* by Eglah his wife.

Ithrite (*ith'-rite*) See also ITHRITES.
2Sa 23: 38 Ira an *I'*, Gareb an *I'*,
1Ch 11: 40 Ira the *I'*, Gareb the *I'*,

Ithrites (*ith'-rites*)
1Ch 2: 53 families of Kirjath-jearim; the *I'*,

its
Le 25: 5 That which groweth of *i'* own accord

itself
Ge 1: 11 whose seed is in *i'*, upon the earth:
12 yielding fruit, whose seed was in *i'*,
Le 7: 24 fat of the beast that dieth of *i'*, and
17: 15 soul that eateth that which dieth of *i'*
18: 25 land *i'* vomiteth out her inhabitants.
22: 8 That which dieth of *i'*, or is torn
25: 11 neither reap that which groweth of *i'*
De 14: 21 not eat of any thing that died of *i'*:
1Ki 7: 34 undersetters were of the very base *i'*.
Job 10: 22 A land of darkness, as darkness *i'*;
Ps 41: 6 his heart gathereth iniquity to *i'*;
68: 8 Sinai *i'* was moved at...presence
Pr 18: 2 but that his heart may discover *i'*.
23: 31 in the cup, when it moveth *i'* aright.
27: 16 of his right hand, which bewrayeth *i'*.
25 and the tender grass sheweth *i'*,
Isa 10: 15 Shall the axe boast *i'* against him that
15 shall the saw magnify *i'* against him
15 rod should shake *i'* against them that
15 as if the staff should lift up *i'*, as if it
37: 30 eat this year such as groweth of *i'*; and
55: 2 and let your soul delight *i'* in fatness.
60: 20 neither shall thy moon withdraw *i'*:
Jer 31: 24 there shall dwell in Judah *i'*, and in
Eze 1: 4 a great cloud, and a fire infolding *i'*,
4: 14 not eaten of that which dieth of *i'*,
17: 14 be base, that it might not lift *i'* up,
29: 15 neither shall it exalt *i'* any more above
44: 31 eat of any thing that is dead of *i'*,
Da 7: 5 a bear, and it raised up *i'* on one side.
Mt 6: 34 take thought for the things of *i'*.
12: 25 Every kingdom divided against *i'*
25 city or house divided against *i'*
M'r 3: 24 if a kingdom be divided against *i'*,
25 if a house be divided against *i'*,
Lu 11: 17 Every kingdom divided against *i'* is
Jo 15: 4 the branch cannot bear fruit of *i'*,
20: 7 wrapped together in a place by *i'*.
21: 25 even the world *i'* could not contain
Ro 8: 16 Spirit *i'* beareth witness with our
21 creature *i'* also shall be delivered
26 the Spirit *i'* maketh intercession for
14: 14 there is nothing unclean of *i'*: but
1Co 11: 14 Doth not even nature *i'* teach you,
13: 4 charity vaunteth not *i'*, is not puffed
5 Doth not behave *i'* unseemly,
2Co 10: 5 every high thing that exalteth *i'*
Eph 4: 16 of the body unto the edifying of *i'*
Heb 9: 24 into heaven *i'*, now to appear in the
3Jo 12 of all men, and of the truth *i'*:

Ittah-kazin (*it''-tah-ka'-zin*)
Jos 19: 13 the east to Gittah-hepher, to *I'*,

Ittai (*it'-ta-i*) See also ITHAI.
2Sa 15: 19 said the king to *I'* the Gittite,
21 *I'* answered the king, and said,
22 David said to *I'*, Go and pass over.
22 And *I'* the Gittite passed over,
18: 2 a third part...under the hand of *I'*
5 commanded Joab and Abishai and *I'*,
12 charged thee and Abishai and *I'*,
23: 29 *I'* the son of Ribai out of Gibeah

Ituræa (*i-tu-re'-ah*)
Lu 3: 1 his brother Philip tetrarch of *I'*

Ivah (*i'-vah*) See also AHAVA; AVA.
2Ki 18: 34 of Sepharvaim, Hena, and *I'*?
19: 13 of Sepharvaim, of Hena, and *I'*?
Isa 37: 13 city of Sepharvaim, Hena, and *I'*?

ivory
1Ki 10: 18 the king made a great throne of *i'*,
22 silver, *i'*, and apes, and peacocks.
22: 39 and the *i'* house which he made,
2Ch 9: 17 the king made a great throne of *i'*,
21 silver, *i'*, and apes, and peacocks.
Ps 45: 8 and cassia, out of the *i'* palaces,
Ca 5: 14 his belly is as bright *i'* overlaid
7: 4 Thy neck is as a tower of *i'*; thine
Eze 27: 6 have made thy benches of *i'*,
15 for a present horns of *i'* and ebony.
Am 3: 15 houses of *i'* shall perish, and the
6: 4 That lie upon beds of *i'*, and stretch
Re 18: 12 wood, and all manner vessels of *i'*,

Izehar (*iz'-e-har*) See also IZEHARITES; IZHAR.
Nu 3: 19 families; Amram, and *I'*, Hebron,

Izeharites (*iz'-e-har-ites*) See also IZHARITE.
Nu 3: 27 and the family of the *I'*, and the

Izhar (*iz'-har*) See also IZEHAR; IZHARITES.
Ex 6: 18 sons of Kohath; Amram, and *I'*,
21 the sons of *I'*; Korah, and Nepheg,
Nu 16: 1 the son of *I'*, the son of Kohath,
1Ch 6: 2 the sons of Kohath; Amram, *I'*,
18 of Kohath were, Amram, and *I'*,
38 The son of *I'*, the son of Kohath,
23: 12 of Kohath; Amram, *I'*, Hebron,
18 sons of *I'*; Shelomith the chief:

Izharites (*iz'-har-ites*) See also IZEHARITES.
1Ch 24: 22 Of the *I'*; Shelomoth: of the sons
26: 23 Of the Amramites, and the *I'*,
29 Of the *I'*, Chenaniah and his sons

Izrahiah (*iz-ra-hi'-ah*) See also JEZRAHIAH.
1Ch 7: 3 And the sons of Uzzi; *I'*: and the
3 sons of *I'*; Michael, and Obadiah,

Izrahite (*iz'-ra-hite*) See also EZRAHITE.
1Ch 27: 8 fifth month was Shamhuth the *I'*:

Izri (*iz'-ri*) See also ZERI.
1Ch 25: 11 fourth to *I'*, he, his sons, and his

J.

Jaakan (*ja'-a-kan*) See also AKAN; BENE-JAAKAN.
De 10: 6 Beeroth of the children of *J'* to

Jaakobah (*ja-ak'-o-bah*)
1Ch 4: 36 Elioenai, and *J'*, and Jeshohaiah,

Jaala (*ja'-a-lah*) See also JAALAH.
Ne 7: 58 The children of *J'*, the children

Jaalah (*ja'-a-lah*) See also JAALA.
Ezr 2: 56 The children of *J'*, the children of

Jaalam (*ja'-a-lam*)
Ge 36: 5 Aholibamah bare Jeush, and *J'*,
14 to Esau Jeush and *J'*, and Korah
18 duke Jeush, duke *J'*, duke Korah:
1Ch 1: 35 and Jeush, and *J'*, and Korah.

Jaan See DAN-JAAN.

Jaanai (*ja'-a-nahee*)
1Ch 5: 12 and *J'*, and Shaphat in Bashan.

Jaare-oregim (*ja''-a-re-or'-eg-im*) See also JAIR.
2Sa 21: 19 where Elhanan the son of *J'*,

Jaasau (*ja-a'-saw*)
Ezr 10: 37 Mattaniah, Mattenai, and *J'*,

Jaasiel (*ja-a'-se-el*)
1Ch 27: 21 of Benjamin, *J'* the son of Abner:

Jaazaniah (*ja-az-a-ni'-ah*) See also JEZANIAH.
2Ki 25: 23 and *J'* the son of a Maachathite,
Jer 35: 3 Then I took *J'* the son of Jeremiah,
Eze 8: 11 them stood *J'* the son of Shaphan,
11: 1 whom I saw *J'* the son of Azur,

Jaazer (*ja-a'-zer*) See also JAZER.
Nu 21: 32 And Moses sent to spy out *J'*,
32: 35 And Atroth, Shophan, and *J'*,

Jaaziah (*ja-a-zi'-ah*)
1Ch 24: 26 and Mushi: the sons of *J'*; Beno
27 The sons of Merari by *J'*; Beno, and

Jaaziel (*ja-a'-ze-el*) See also AZIEL.
1Ch 15: 18 degree, Zechariah, Ben, and *J'*,

Jabal (*ja'-bal*)
Ge 4: 20 Adah bare *J'*: he was the father

Jabbok (*jab'-bok*)
Ge 32: 22 and passed over the ford *J'*.
Nu 21: 24 his land from Arnon unto *J'*,
De 2: 37 nor unto any place of the river *J'*,
3: 16 the border even unto the river *J'*,
Jos 12: 2 half Gilead, even unto the river *J'*,
J'g 11: 13 from Arnon even unto *J'*, and unto
22 Amorites, from Arnon even unto *J'*,

Jabesh (*ja'-besh*) See also JABESH-GILEAD.
1Sa 11: 1 the men of *J'* said unto Nahash,
3 And the elders of *J'* said unto him,
5 him the tidings of the men of *J'*,
9 and shewed it to the men of *J'*;
10 the men of *J'* said, To morrow we
31: 12 and came to *J'*, and burnt them
13 and buried them under a tree at *J'*,
2Ki 15: 10 the son of *J'* conspired against him,
13 the son of *J'* began to reign
14 and smote Shallum the son of *J'*
1Ch 10: 12 and brought them to *J'*, and buried
12 their bones under the oak in *J'*,

Jabesh-gilead (*ja''-besh-ghil'-e-ad*)
J'g 21: 8 none to the camp from *J'* to
9 none of the inhabitants of *J'*
10 and smite the inhabitants of *J'*
12 among the inhabitants of *J'*
14 saved alive of the women of *J'*:
1Sa 11: 1 up, and encamped against *J'*:
9 shall ye say unto the men of *J'*,
31: 11 inhabitants of *J'* heard of that
2Sa 2: 4 men of *J'* were they that buried
5 messengers unto the men of *J'*,
21: 12 his son from the men of *J'*,
1Ch 10: 11 *J'* heard all that the Philistines

Jabez (*ja'-bez*)
1Ch 2: 55 of the scribes which dwelt at *J'*;
4: 9 *J'* was more honourable than his
9 and his mother called his name *J'*,
10 And *J'* called on the God of Israel,

Jabin (*ja'-bin*) See also JABIN'S.
Jos 11: 1 when *J'* king of Hazor had heard
J'g 4: 2 into the hand of *J'* king of Canaan,
17 was peace between *J'* the king of
23 God subdued on that day *J'* the
24 prevailed against *J'* the king of
24 until they had destroyed *J'* king of
Ps 83: 9 as to *J'* at the brook of Kison:

Jabin's (*ja'-bins*)
J'g 4: 7 Sisera, the captain of *J'* army,

Jabneel (*jab'-ne-el*) See also JABNEH.
Jos 15: 11 mount Baalah, and went unto *J'*;
19: 33 Adami, Nekeb, and *J'*, unto Lakum;

Jabneh (*jab'-neh*) See also JABNEEL.
2Ch 26: 6 wall of Gath, and the wall of *J'*,

Jachan (*ja'-kan*) See also AKAN.
1Ch 5: 13 Jorai, and *J'*, and Zia, and Heber.

Jachin (*ja'-kin*) See also JACHINITES; JARIB.
Ge 46: 10 Jamin, and Ohad, and *J'*, and
Ex 6: 15 Jamin, and Ohad, and *J'*, and
Nu 26: 12 of *J'*, the family of the Jachinites:
1Ki 7: 21 and called the name thereof *J'*:
1Ch 9: 10 Jedaiah, and Jehoiarib, and *J'*,
24: 17 The one and twentieth to *J'*, the
2Ch 3: 17 name of that on the right hand *J'*,
Ne 11: 10 Jedaiah the son of Joiarib, *J'*.

Jachinites (*ja'-kin-ites*)
Nu 26: 12 of Jachin, the family of the *J'*:

jacinth
Re 9: 17 breastplates of fire, and of *j'*,
21: 20 the eleventh, a *j'*; the twelfth, an

Jacob (*ja'-cub*) See also ISRAEL; JACOB'S; JAMES.
Ge 25: 26 heel; and his name was called *J'*:
27 *J'* was a plain man, dwelling in
28 venison: but Rebekah loved *J'*.
29 And *J'* sod pottage: and Esau came
30 Esau said to *J'*, Feed me, I pray
31 and *J'* said, Sell me this day thy
33 And *J'* said, Swear to me this day;
33 and he sold his birthright unto *J'*.
34 *J'* gave Esau bread and pottage of
27: 6 Rebekah spake unto *J'* her son,
11 *J'* said to Rebekah his mother,
15 put them upon *J'* her younger son:
17 into the hand of her son *J'*.
19 *J'* said unto his father, I am Esau
21 Isaac said unto *J'*, Come near, I
22 *J'* went near unto Isaac his father;
30 had made an end of blessing *J'*,
30 *J'* was yet scarce gone out from
36 said, Is not he rightly named *J'*?
41 Esau hated *J'* because of the
41 then will I slay my brother *J'*.
42 sent and called *J'* her younger son,
46 if *J'* take a wife of the daughters of
28: 1 Isaac called *J'*, and blessed him,
5 Isaac sent away *J'*: and he went
6 Esau saw that Isaac had blessed *J'*,
7 *J'* obeyed his father and his mother,
10 *J'* went out from Beer-sheba, and
16 *J'* awaked out of his sleep, and he
18 *J'* rose up early in the morning,
20 *J'* vowed a vow, saying, If God will
29: 1 Then *J'* went on his journey, and
4 *J'* said unto them, My brethren,
10 when *J'* saw Rachel the daughter
10 *J'* went near, and rolled the stone

Ge 29:11 and J' kissed Rachel, and lifted up
12 J' told Rachel that he was her
13 when Laban heard the tidings of J'
15 Laban said unto J', Because thou
18 J' loved Rachel; and said, I will
20 J' served seven years for Rachel;
21 J' said unto Laban, Give me my
28 J' did so, and fulfilled her week:
30: 1 saw that she bare J' no children,
1 and said unto J', Give me children,
4 to wife: and J' went in unto her.
5 Bilhah conceived, and bare J' a son.
7 again, and bare J' a second son.
9 her maid, and gave her J' to wife.
10 Zilpah Leah's maid bare J' a son.
12 Leah's maid bare J' a second son.
16 And J' came out of the field in the
17 conceived, and bare J' the fifth son.
19 again, and bare J' the sixth son.
25 J' said unto Laban, Send me away,
31 J' said, Thou shalt not give me any
36 journey betwixt himself and J':
36 J' fed the rest of Laban's flocks.
37 J' took him rods of green poplar,
40 J' did separate the lambs, and set
41 that J' laid the rods before the eyes
31: 1 J' hath taken away all that was our
2 J' beheld the countenance of
3 the Lord said unto J', Return unto
4 J' sent and called Rachel and Leah
11 unto me in a dream, saying, J':
17 J' rose up, and set his sons and his
20 J' stole away unawares to Laban
22 on the third day that J' was fled.
24 speak not to J' either good or bad.
25 Then Laban overtook J'.
25 Now J' had pitched his tent in the
26 Laban said to J', What hast thou
29 speak not to J' either good or bad.
31 J' answered and said to Laban,
32 J' knew not that Rachel had stolen
36 And J' was wroth, and chode with
36 and J' answered and said to Laban,
43 Laban answered and said unto J',
45 J' took a stone, and set it up for a
46 J' said unto his brethren, Gather
47 but J' called it Galeed.
51 Laban said to J', Behold this heap,
53 J' sware by the fear of his father
54 J' offered sacrifice upon the mount,
32: 1 J' went on his way, and the angels
2 when J' saw them, he said, This is
3 J' sent messengers before him to
4 Esau; Thy servant J' saith thus,
6 the messengers returned to J',
7 Then J' was greatly afraid and
9 And J' said, O God of my father
20 Behold, thy servant J' is behind us.
24 And J' was left alone; and there
27 What is thy name? And he said, J'.
28 name shall be called no more J',
29 J' asked him, and said, Tell me,
30 And J' called the name of the place
33: 1 J' lifted up his eyes, and looked,
10 And J' said, Nay, I pray thee, if
17 J' journeyed to Succoth, and built
18 And J' came to Shalem, a city of
34: 1 of Leah, which she bare unto J',
3 unto Dinah the daughter of J',
5 J' heard that he had defiled Dinah
5 J' held his peace until they were
6 out unto J' to commune with him.
7 the sons of J' came out of the field
13 the sons of J' answered Shechem
25 two of the sons of J', Simeon and
27 The sons of J' came upon the slain,
30 J' said to Simeon and Levi, Ye have
35: 1 God said unto J', Arise, go up to
2 J' said unto his household, and to
4 gave unto J' all the strange gods
4 J' hid them under the oak which
5 did not pursue after the sons of J'.
6 J' came to Luz, which is in the land
9 God appeared unto J' again, when
10 said unto him, Thy name is J':
10 shall not be called any more J',
14 J' set up a pillar in the place where
15 And J' called the name of the place
20 And J' set a pillar upon her grave:
22 Now the sons of J' were twelve:
26 these are the sons of J', which were
27 J' came unto Isaac his father unto
27 his sons Esau and J' buried him.
36: 6 from the face of his brother J'.
37: 1 J' dwelt in the land wherein his
2 These are the generations of J'.
34 And J' rent his clothes, and put
42: 1 when J' saw that there was corn in
1 J' said unto his sons, Why do ye
4 J' sent not with his brethren;
29 they came unto J' their father unto
36 And J' their father said unto them,
45:25 into the land of Canaan unto J'
27 the spirit of J' their father revived:
46: 2 of the night, and said, J', J'.
5 And J' rose up from Beer-sheba:
5 the sons of Israel carried J' their
6 came into Egypt, J', and all his
8 came into Egypt, J' and his sons:
15 of Leah, which she bare unto J' in
18 and these she bare unto J', even
22 of Rachel, which were born to J':
25 and she bare these unto J': all the
26 souls that came with J' into Egypt,
27 all the souls of the house of J',
47: 7 Joseph brought in J' his father,

Ge 47: 7 Pharaoh: and J' blessed Pharaoh.
8 Pharaoh said unto J', How old art
9 J' said unto Pharaoh, The days of
10 J' blessed Pharaoh, and went out
28 And J' lived in the land of Egypt
28 whole age of J' was an hundred
48: 2 one told J', and said, Behold, thy
3 J' said unto Joseph, God Almighty
49: 1 J' called unto his sons, and said,
2 together, and hear, ye sons of J';
7 I will divide them in J', and scatter
24 the hands of the mighty God of J';
33 J' had made an end of commanding
50:24 to Abraham, to Isaac, and to J'.
Ex 1: 1 and his household came with J'.
5 that came out of the loins of J'.
2:24 Abraham, with Isaac, and with J'.
3: 6, 15 God of Isaac, and the God of J'.
16 of Abraham, of Isaac, and of J',
4: 5 the God of Isaac, and the God of J',
6: 3 Abraham, unto Isaac, and unto J',
8 to Abraham, to Isaac, and to J';
19: 3 shalt thou say to the house of J',
33: 1 to Abraham, to Isaac, and to J',
Le 26:42 I remember my covenant with J',
Nu 23: 7 Come, curse me J', and come, defy
10 Who can count the dust of J', and
21 He hath not beheld iniquity in J',
23 there is no enchantment against J',
23 this time it shall be said of J' and
24: 5 How goodly are thy tents, O J',
17 there shall come a Star out of J',
19 Out of J' shall come he that shall
32:11 Abraham, unto Isaac, and unto J';
De 1: 8 fathers, Abraham, Isaac, and J',
6:10 to Abraham, to Isaac, and to J',
9: 5 fathers, Abraham, Isaac, and J'.
27 servants, Abraham, Isaac, and J';
29:13 to Abraham, to Isaac, and to J'.
30:20 to Abraham, to Isaac, and to J'.
32: 9 J' is the lot of his inheritance.
33: 4 inheritance of...congregation of J'.
10 They shall teach J' thy judgments,
28 fountain of J' shall be upon a land
34: 4 Abraham, unto Isaac, and unto J',
Jos 24: 4 And I gave unto Isaac J' and Esau:
4 but J' and his children went down
32 parcel of ground which J' bought
1Sa 12: 8 When J' was come into Egypt, and
2Sa 23: 1 the anointed of the God of J', and
1Ki 18:31 of the tribes of the sons of J',
2Ki 13:23 with Abraham, Isaac, and J', and
17:34 Lord commanded the children of J',
1Ch 16:13 ye children of J', his chosen ones.
17 confirmed the same to J' for a law,
Ps 14: 7 J' shall rejoice, and Israel shall be
20: 1 name of the God of J' defend thee;
22:23 all ye the seed of J', glorify him;
24: 6 seek him, that seek thy face, O J'.
44: 4 God: command deliverances for J'.
46: 7, 11 the God of J' is our refuge.
47: 4 the excellency of J' whom he loved.
53: 6 J' shall rejoice, and Israel shall be
59:13 let them know that God ruleth in J'
75: 9 I will sing praises to the God of J'.
76: 6 At thy rebuke, O God of J', both
77:15 people, the sons of J' and Joseph.
78: 5 he established a testimony in J',
21 so a fire was kindled against J',
71 brought him to feed J' his people,
79: 7 For they have devoured J', and
81: 1 a joyful noise unto the God of J'.
4 Israel, and a law of the God of J'.
84: 8 my prayer: give ear, O God of J'.
85: 1 brought back the captivity of J'.
87: 2 more than all the dwellings of J'.
94: 7 neither shall the God of J' regard it.
99: 4 judgment and righteousness in J'.
105: 6 ye children of J' his chosen.
10 confirmed the same unto J' for a
23 J' sojourned in the land of Ham.
114: 1 house of J' from a people of strange
7 at the presence of the God of J';
132: 2 vowed unto the mighty God of J';
5 habitation for the mighty God of J'.
135: 4 Lord hath chosen J' unto himself,
146: 5 that hath the God of J' for his help,
147:19 He sheweth his word unto J', his
Isa 2: 3 Lord, to the house of the God of J';
5 O house of J', come ye, and let us
6 forsaken thy people the house of J',
8:17 his face from the house of J',
9: 8 The Lord sent a word into J', and
10:20 as are escaped of the house of J',
21 return, even the remnant of J',
14: 1 For the Lord will have mercy on J',
1 they shall cleave to the house of J'.
17: 4 the glory of J' shall be made thin,
27: 6 them that come of J' to take root:
9 shall the iniquity of J' be purged;
29:22 concerning the house of J',
22 J' shall not now be ashamed,
23 and sanctify the Holy One of J',
40:27 Why sayest thou, O J', and
41: 8 J' whom I have chosen, the seed
14 Fear not, thou worm J', and ye
21 strong reasons, saith the King of J'.
42:24 Who gave J' for a spoil, and Israel
43: 1 the Lord that created thee, O J',
22 thou hast not called upon me, O J';
28 and have given J' to the curse, and
44: 1 Yet now hear, O J' my servant;
2 Fear not, O J', my servant; and
5 shall call himself by the name of J';
21 Remember these, O J' and Israel;
23 for the Lord hath redeemed J',

Isa 45: 4 For J' my servant's sake, and
19 I said not unto the seed of J', Seek
46: 3 Hearken unto me, O house of J',
48: 1 Hear ye this, O house of J', which
12 Hearken unto me, O J' and Israel,
20 Lord hath redeemed his servant J'.
49: 5 servant, to bring J' again to him,
6 servant to raise up the tribes of J',
26 thy Redeemer, the mighty One of J'.
58: 1 and the house of J' their sins.
14 feed thee with the heritage of J'
59:20 that turn from transgression in J',
60:16 thy Redeemer, the mighty One of J'.
65: 9 I will bring forth a seed out of J',
Jer 2: 4 word of the Lord, O house of J',
5:20 Declare this in the house of J', and
10:16 The portion of J' is not like them:
25 for they have eaten up J', and
30:10 fear thou not, O my servant J',
10 and J' shall return, and shall be in
31: 7 Sing with gladness for J', and
11 For the Lord hath redeemed J',
33:26 Then will I cast away the seed of J',
26 the seed of Abraham, Isaac, and J':
46:27 fear not thou, O my servant J',
27 J' shall return, and be in rest and
28 Fear thou not, O J' my servant,
51:19 The portion of J' is not like them;
La 1:17 hath commanded concerning J',
2: 2 swallowed...the habitations of J',
3 burned against J' like a flaming
Eze 20: 5 unto the seed of the house of J',
28:25 that I have given to my servant J'
37:25 the land that I have given unto J'
39:25 I bring again the captivity of J',
Ho 10:11 plow, and J' shall break his clods.
12: 2 punish J' according to his ways;
12 J' fled into the country of Syria,
Am 3:13 ye, and testify in the house of J',
6: 8 I abhor the excellency of J', and
7: 2, 5 thee: by whom shall J' arise?
8: 7 hath sworn by the excellency of J',
9: 8 not utterly destroy the house of J',
Ob 10 thy violence against thy brother J'
17 J' shall possess their possessions.
18 And the house of J' shall be a fire,
Mic 1: 5 the transgression of J' is all this,
5 What is the transgression of J'?
2: 7 that art named the house of J',
12 surely assemble, O J', all of thee;
3: 1 Hear, I pray you, O heads of J',
8 declare unto J' his transgression,
9 you, ye heads of the house of J',
4: 2 and to the house of the God of J';
5: 7 remnant of J' shall be in the midst
8 remnant of J' shall be among the
7:20 Thou wilt perform the truth to J',
Na 2: 2 turned away the excellency of J',
Mal 1: 2 saith the Lord: yet I loved J',
2:12 out of the tabernacles of J',
3: 6 ye sons of J' are not consumed.
M't 1: 2 begat J'; and J' begat Judas
15 Matthan; and Matthan begat J';
16 And J' begat Joseph the husband
8:11 with Abraham, and Isaac, and J',
22:32 the God of Isaac, and the God of J'?
M'r 12:26 the God of Isaac, and the God of J'?
Lu 1:33 he shall reign over the house of J'
3:34 Which was the son of J', which was
13:28 see Abraham, and Isaac, and J',
20:37 the God of Isaac, and the God of J'.
Joh 4: 5 that J' gave to his son Joseph.
12 Art thou greater than our father J',
Ac 3:13 of Abraham, and of Isaac, and of J',
7: 8 begat J'; and J' begat the twelve
12 when J' heard that there was corn
14 and called his father J' to him,
15 J' went down into Egypt, and died,
32 the God of Isaac, and the God of J'.
46 find a tabernacle for the God of J'.
Ro 9:13 J' have I loved, but Esau have I
11:26 turn away ungodliness from J':
Heb 11: 9 in tabernacles with Isaac and J',
20 By faith, Isaac blessed J' and Esau
21 By faith J', when he was a dying,

Jacob's (*ja'-cubs*)
Ge 27:22 voice is J' voice, but the hands
28: 5 Rebekah, J' and Esau's mother.
30: 2 And J' anger was kindled against
42 were Laban's, and the stronger J'.
31:33 And Laban went into J' tent, and
32:18 shalt say, They be thy servant J';
25 hollow of J' thigh was out of joint,
32 he touched the hollow of J' thigh
34: 7 in Israel in lying with J' daughter;
19 he had delight in J' daughter:
35:23 Reuben, J' firstborn, and Simeon,
45:26 J' heart fainted, for he believed
46: 8 and his sons: Reuben, J' firstborn.
19 sons of Rachel J' wife; Joseph, and
26 of his loins, besides J' son's wives,
Jer 30: 7 it is even the time of J' trouble;
18 again the captivity of J' tents,
Mal 1: 2 Was not Esau J' brother? saith
Joh 4: 6 Now J' well was there. Jesus

Jada (*ja'-dah*)
1Ch 2:28 of Onam were, Shammai, and J'.
32 And the sons of J' the brother of

Jadau (*ja'-daw*)
Ezr 10:43 Zabad, Zebina, J', and Joel,

Jaddua (*jad'-du-ah*)
Ne 10:21 Meshezabeel, Zadok, J',
12:11 Jonathan, and Jonathan begat J'.
22 Joiada, and Johanan, and J',

Jadon (*ja'-don*)
Ne 3: 7 and J' the Meronothite, the men

Jael (*ja'-el*)
J'g 4:17 away on his feet to the tent of J'
18 And J' went out to meet Sisera, and
21 J' Heber's wife took a nail of the
22 J' came out to meet him, and said
5: 6 in the days of J', the highways were
24 Blessed above women shall J' the

Jagur (*ja'-gur*)
Jos 15:21 were Kabzeel, and Eder, and J',

Jah (*jah*) See also JEHOVAH.
Ps 68: 4 upon the heavens by his name J',

Jahath (*ja'-hath*)
1Ch 4: 2 Reaiah the son of Shobal begat J';
2 and J' begat Ahumai, and Lahad.
6:20 Libni his son, J' his son, Zimmah
43 The son of J', the son of Gershom,
23:10 sons of Shimei were, J', Zina, and
11 And J' was the chief, and Zizah the
24:22 of the sons of Shelomoth; J'.
2Ch 34:12 the overseers of them were J' and

Jahaz (*ja'-haz*) See also JAHAZA; JAHAZAH; JAHZAH.
Nu 21:23 he came to J', and fought against
De 2:32 he and all his people, to fight at J'.
J'g 11:20 pitched in J', and fought against
Isa 15: 4 voice shall be heard even unto J':
Jer 48:34 even unto J', have they uttered

Jahaza (*ja-ha'-zah*) See also JAHAZ.
Jos 13:18 J', and Kedemoth, and Mephaath,

Jahazah (*ja-ha'-zah*) See also JAHAZ.
Jos 21:36 suburbs, and J' with...suburbs,
Jer 48:21 and upon J', and upon Mephaath,

Jahaziah (*ja-ha-zi'-ah*)
Ezr 10:15 and J' the son of Tikvah were

Jahaziel (*ja-ha'-ze-el*)
1Ch 12: 4 Jeremiah, and J', and Johanan,
16: 6 Benaiah also and J' the priests
23:19 J' the third, and Jekameam the
24:23 J' the third, Jekameam the fourth.
2Ch 20:14 Then upon J' the son of Zechariah,
Ezr 8: 5 the son of J', and with him three

Jahdai (*jah'-dahee*)
1Ch 2:47 sons of J'; Regem, and Jotham,

Jahdiel (*jah'-de-el*)
1Ch 5:24 and J', mighty men of valour,

Jahdo (*jah'-do*)
1Ch 5:14 the son of J', the son of Buz;

Jahleel (*jah'-le-el*) See also JAHLEELITES.
Ge 46:14 Zebulun; Sered, and Elon, and J'.
Nu 26:26 of J', the family of the Jahleelites.

Jahleelites (*jah'-le-el-ites*)
Nu 26:26 of Jahleel, the family of the J'.

Jahmai (*jah'-mahee*)
1Ch 7: 2 and Jeriel, and J', and Jibsam,

Jahzah (*jah'-zah*) See also JAHAZ.
1Ch 6:78 suburbs, and J' with her suburbs,

Jahzeel (*jah'-ze-el*) See also JAHZEELITES; JAHZIEL.
Ge 46:24 sons of Naphtali; J', and Guni,
Nu 26:48 J', the family of the Jahzeelites:

Jahzeelites (*jah'-ze-el-ites*)
Nu 26:48 of Jahzeel, the family of the J': of

Jahzerah (*jah'-ze-rah*) See also AHAZAI.
1Ch 9:12 Adiel, the son of J', the son of

Jahziel (*jah'-ze-el*) See also JAHZEEL.
1Ch 7:13 sons of Naphtali; J', and Guni,

jailor
Ac 16:23 charging the j' to keep them

Jair^ (*ja'-ur*) See also HAVOTH-JAIR; JAARE-OREGIM; JAIRITE.
Nu 32:41 J' the son of Manasseh went and
Jos 13:30 towns of J', which are in Bashan,
J'g 10: 3 And after him arose J', a Gileadite,
5 J' died, and was buried in Camon.
1Ki 4:13 to him pertained the towns of J'
1Ch 2:22 Segub begat J', who had three and
23 and Aram, with the towns of J',
20: 5 Elhanan the son of J' slew Lahmi
Es 2: 5 name was Mordecai, the son of J',

Jairite (*ja'-ur-ite*)
2Sa 20:26 Ira also the J' was a chief ruler

Jairus (*ja-i'-rus*)
M'r 5:22 of the synagogue, J' by name;
Lu 8:41 there came a man named J', and

Jakan (*ja'-kan*) See also AKAN; JAAKAN.
1Ch 1:42 Ezer; Bilhan, and Zavan, and J'.

Jakeh (*ja'-keh*)
Pr 30: 1 The words of Agur the son of J',

Jakim (*ja'-kim*)
1Ch 8:19 And J', and Zichri, and Zabdi,
24:12 to Eliashib, the twelfth to J',

Jalon (*ja'-lon*)
1Ch 4:17 and Mered, and Epher, and J':

Jambres (*jam'-brees*)
2Ti 3: 8 Jannes and J' withstood Moses.

James^ (*james*) See also JACOB.
M't 4:21 J' the son of Zebedee, and John
10: 2 J' the son of Zebedee, and John
3 J' the son of Alphæus, and
13:55 brethren, J', and Joses, and Simon,
17: 1 Jesus taketh Peter, J', and John his
27:56 Mary the mother of J' and Joses,
M'r 1:19 J' the son of Zebedee, and John
29 and Andrew, with J' and John.
3:17 J'...and John the brother of J';
18 and J' the son of Alphæus, and
5:37 and J', and John the brother of J'.
6: 3 the brother of J', and Joses, and of
9: 2 with him Peter, and J', and John,
10:35 J' and John, the sons of Zebedee,
41 much displeased with J' and John
13: 3 Peter and J' and John and Andrew
14:33 with him Peter and J' and John,
15:40 Mary the mother of J' the less and
16: 1 Mary the mother of J', and Salome,
Lu 5:10 J', and John, the sons of Zebedee,
6:14 Andrew his brother, J' and John,
15 Thomas, J' the son of Alphæus,
16 And Judas the brother of J', and
8:51 go in, save Peter, and J', and John,
9:28 he took Peter and John and J', and
54 his disciples J' and John saw this,
24:10 and Mary the mother of J', and
Ac 1:13 abode...Peter, and J', and John,
13 Matthew, J' the son of Alphæus,
13 and Judas the brother of J'.
12: 2 he killed J' the brother of John
17 Go shew these things unto J', and
15:13 J' answered, saying, Men and
21:18 Paul went in with us unto J';
1Co 15: 7 After that, he was seen of J'; then
Ga 1:19 I none, save J' the Lord's brother.
2: 9 J', Cephas, and John, who seemed
12 before that certain came from J',
Jas 1: 1 J', a servant of God and of the
Jude 1 of Jesus Christ, and brother of J',

Jamin (*ja'-min*) See also JAMINITES.
Ge 46:10 Jemuel, and J', and Ohad, and
Ex 6:15 Jemuel, and J', and Ohad, and
Nu 26:12 of J', the family of the Jaminites:
1Ch 2:27 of Jerahmeel were, Maaz, and J',
4:24 of Simeon were, Nemuel, and J',
Ne 8: 7 Sherebiah, J', Akkub, Shabbethai,

Jaminites (*ja'-min-ites*)
Nu 26:12 of Jamin, the family of the J':

Jamlech (*jam'-lek*)
1Ch 4:34 Meshobab, and J', and Joshah

jangling
1Ti 1: 6 turned aside unto vain j'; have

Janna (*jan'-nah*)
Lu 3:24 Melchi, which was the son of J',

Jannes (*jan'-nees*)
2Ti 3: 8 J' and Jambres withstood Moses,

Janoah (*ja-no'-ah*) See also JANOHAH.
2Ki 15:29 J', and Kedesh, and Hazor, and

Janohah (*ja-no'-hah*) See also JANOAH.
Jos 16: 6 and passed by it on the east to J';
7 it went down from J' to Ataroth,

Janum (*ja'-num*)
Jos 15:53 And J', and Beth-tappuah, and

Japheth (*ja'-feth*)
Ge 5:32 Noah begat Shem, Ham, and J'.
6:10 three sons, Shem, Ham, and J'.
7:13 Noah, and Shem, and Ham, and J',
9:18 ark, were Shem, and Ham, and J':
23 And Shem and J' took a garment,
27 shall enlarge J', and he shall dwell
10: 1 sons of Noah, Shem, Ham, and J':
2 The sons of J'; Gomer, and Magog,
21 of Eber, brother of J' the elder,
1Ch 1: 4 Noah, Shem, Ham, and J'.
5 The sons of J'; Gomer, and Magog,

Japhia (*ja-fi'-ah*)
Jos 10: 3 and unto J' king of Lachish, and
19:12 out to Daberath, and goeth up to J',
2Sa 5:15 and Elishua, and Nepheg, and J',
1Ch 3: 7 And Nogah, and Nepheg, and J',
14: 6 And Nogah, and Nepheg, and J',

Japhlet (*jaf'-let*) See also JAPHLETI.
1Ch 7:32 Heber begat J', and Shomer, and
33 And the sons of J'; Pasach, and
33 These are the children of J'.

Japhleti (*jaf'-let-i*) See also JAPHLET.
Jos 16: 3 down westward to the coast of J',

Japho (*ja'-fo*) See also JOPPA.
Jos 19:46 Rakkon, with the border before J'.

Jarah (*ja'-rah*) See also JEHOADAH.
1Ch 9:42 And Ahaz begat J'; and J' begat

Jareb (*ja'-reb*)
Ho 5:13 the Assyrian, and sent to king J':
10: 6 Assyria for a present to king J':

Jared (*ja'-red*) See also JERED.
Ge 5:15 sixty and five years, and begat J':
16 Mahalaleel lived after he begat J'
18 J' lived an hundred sixty and two
19 And J' lived after he begat Enoch
20 the days of J' were nine hundred
Lu 3:37 Enoch, which was the son of J',

Jaresiah (*ja-re-si'-ah*)
1Ch 8:27 J', and Eliah, and Zichri, the sons

Jarha (*jar'-hah*)
1Ch 2:34 an Egyptian, whose name was J'.
35 Sheshan gave his daughter to J'

Jarib (*ja'-rib*) See also JACHIN.
1Ch 4:24 and Jamin, J', Zerah, and Shaul:
Ezr 8:16 for Elnathan, and for J', and for
10:18 and Eliezer, and J', and Gedaliah.

Jarkon See ME-JARKON.

Jarmuth (*jar'-muth*) See also REMETH.
Jos 10: 3 unto Piram king of J', and unto
5, 23 king of J', the king of Lachish,
12:11 The king of J', one; the king of
15:35 J', and Adullam, Socoh, and Azekah,
21:29 J' with her suburbs, En-gannim
Ne 11:29 and at Zareah, and at J',

Jaroah (*ja-ro'-ah*)
1Ch 5:14 the son of Huri, the son of J',

Jashen (*ja'-shen*) See also HASHEM.
2Sa 23:32 the Shaalbonite, of the sons of J',

Jasher (*ja'-shur*)
Jos 10:13 not this written in the book of J'?
2Sa 1:18 it is written in the book of J'.

Jashobeam (*jash-o'-be-am*)
1Ch 11:11 J', an Hachmonite, the chief of the
12: 6 and Joezer, and J', the Korhites,
27: 2 month was J' the son of Zabdiel:

Jashub (*ja'-shub*) See also JASHUBI-LEHEM; JOB; JASHUBITES; SHEAR-JASHUB.
Nu 26:24 J', the family of the Jashubites:
1Ch 7: 1 Puah, J', and Shimrom, four.
Ezr 10:29 and Adaiah, J', and Sheal, and

Jashubi-lehem (*jash"-u-bi-le'-hem*)
1Ch 4:22 had the dominion in Moab, and J'.

Jashubites (*jash'-u-bites*)
Nu 26:24 Of Jashub, the family of the J':

Jasiel (*ja'-se-el*)
1Ch 11:47 and Obed, and J' the Mesobaite.

Jason (*ja'-sun*)
Ac 17: 5 and assaulted the house of J', and
6 they drew J' and certain brethren
7 Whom J' hath received: and these
9 when they had taken security of J',
Ro 16:21 Lucius, and J', and Sosipater, my

jasper
Ex 28:20 a beryl, and an onyx, and a j':
39:13 row, a beryl, an onyx, and a j':
Eze 28:13 the onyx, and the j', the sapphire,
Re 4: 3 to look upon like a j' and a sardine
21:11 even like a j' stone, clear as crystal;
18 building of the wall of it was of j':
19 The first foundation was j'; the

Jathniel (*jath'-ne-el*)
1Ch 26: 2 Zebadiah the third, J' the fourth,

Jattir (*jat'-tur*)
Jos 15:48 in the mountains, Shamir, and J',
21:14 J' with her suburbs, and Eshtemoa
1Sa 30:27 and to them which were in J',
1Ch 6:57 Libnah with her suburbs, and J',

Javan (*ja'-van*)
Ge 10: 2 and J', and Tubal, and Meshech,
4 And the sons of J'; Elishah, and
1Ch 1: 5 and J', and Tubal, and Meshech,
7 And the sons of J'; Elishah, and
Isa 66:19 that draw the bow, to Tubal, and J',
Eze 27:13 J', Tubal, and Meshech, they were
19 Dan also and J' going to and fro

javelin
Nu 25: 7 and took a j' in his hand;
1Sa 18:10 and there was a j' in Saul's hand.
11 And Saul cast the j'; for he said, I
19: 9 in his house with his j' in his hand:
10 David even to the wall with the j';
10 and he smote the j' into the wall:
20:33 Saul cast a j' at him to smite him:

jaw See also JAWBONE; JAWS.
J'g 15:16 with the j' of an ass have I slain a
19 clave an hollow place that in the j',
Job 41: 2 or bore his j' through with a thorn?
Pr 30:14 their j' teeth as knives, to devour

jawbone
J'g 15:15 he found a new j' of an ass, and
16 With the j' of an ass, heaps upon
17 he cast away the j' out of his hand,

jaws
Job 29:17 I brake the j' of the wicked, and
Ps 22:15 and my tongue cleaveth to my j';
Isa 30:28 be a bridle in the j' of the people,
Eze 29: 4 I will put hooks in thy j', and I will
38: 4 thee back, and put hooks into thy j',
Ho 11: 4 that take off the yoke on their j',

jaw-teeth See JAW and TEETH.

Jazer (*ja'-zur*) See also JAAZER.
Nu 32: 1 and when they saw the land of J',
3 Ataroth, and Dibon, and J', and
Jos 13:25 their coast was J', and all the cities
21:39 her suburbs, J' with her suburbs;
2Sa 24: 5 of the river of Gad, and toward J':
1Ch 6:81 suburbs, and J' with her suburbs.
26:31 them men of valour at J' of Gilead.
Isa 16: 8 they are come even unto J', they
9 I will bewail with the weeping of J'
Jer 48:32 weep for thee with the weeping of J':
32 they reach even to the sea of J':

Jaziz (*ja'-ziz*)
1Ch 27:31 over the flocks was J' the Hagerite

jealous
Ex 20: 5 Lord thy God am a j' God, visiting
34:14 Lord, whose name is J', is a j' God:
Nu 5:14 and he be j' of his wife, and she be
14 he be j' of his wife, and she be not
30 and he be j' over his wife, and shall
De 4:24 is a consuming fire, even a j' God.
5: 9 for I the Lord thy God am a j' God.
6:15 Lord thy God is a j' God among you)
Jos 24:19 he is an holy God; he is a j' God;
1Ki 19:10,14 I have been very j' for the Lord
Eze 39:25 and will be j' for my holy name;
Joe 2:18 Then will the Lord be j' for his land,
Na 1: 2 God is j', and the Lord revengeth;
Zec 1:14 I am j' for Jerusalem and for Zion

Zec 8: 2 I was *j* for Zion with great jealousy,
2 and I was *j* for her with great fury.
2Co 11: 2 am *j* over you with godly jealousy:

jealousies
Nu 5: 29 This is the law of *j*, when a wife

jealousy See also JEALOUSIES.
Nu 5: 14 And the spirit of *j* come upon him,
14 or if the spirit of *j* come upon him,
15 for it is an offering of *j*, an offering
18 her hands, which is the *j* offering:
25 the priest shall take the *j* offering
30 the spirit of *j* cometh upon him,
25: 11 not the children of Israel in my *j*.
De 29: 20 his *j* shall smoke against that man,
32: 16 provoked him to *j* with strange
21 They have moved me to *j* with that
21 I will move them to *j* with those
1Ki 14: 22 provoked him to *j* with their sins
Ps 78: 58 moved him to *j* with their graven
79: 5 for ever? shall thy *j* burn like fire?
Pr 6: 34 For *j* is the rage of a man:
Ca 8: 6 as death; *j* is cruel as the grave:
Isa 42: 13 he shall stir up *j* like a man of war:
Eze 8: 3 was the seat of the image of *j*,
3 which provoketh to *j*.
5 altar this image of *j* in the entry.
16: 38 I will give thee blood in fury and *j*.
42 and my *j* shall depart from thee,
23: 25 And I will set my *j* against thee,
36: 5 in the fire of my *j* have I spoken
6 have spoken in my *j* and in my fury,
38: 19 in my *j* and in the fire of my wrath
Zep 1: 18 be devoured by the fire of his *j*:
3: 8 be devoured with the fire of my *j*.
Zec 1: 14 jealous...for Zion with a great *j*.
8: 2 I was jealous for Zion with great *j*,
Ro 10: 19 I will provoke you to *j* by them
11: 11 Gentiles, for to provoke them to *j*.
1Co 10: 22 Do we provoke the Lord to *j*? are we
2Co 11: 2 am jealous over you with godly *j*:

Jearim *(je'-a-rim)* See also KIRJATH-JEARIM.
Jos 15: 10 passed along unto the side of mount *J*.

Jeaterai *(je-at'-e-rahee)*
1Ch 6: 21 his son, Zerah his son, *J* his son.

Jeberechiah *(je-ber''-e-ki'-ah)*
Isa 8: 2 priest, and Zechariah the son of *J*.

Jebus *(je'-bus)* See also JEBUSI; JEBUSITE; JERUSALEM.
J'g 19: 10 departed...came over against *J*.
11 And when they were by *J*, the day
1Ch 11: 4 went to Jerusalem, which is *J*;
5 the inhabitants of *J* said to David,

Jebusi *(jeb'-u-si)* See also JEBUSITE.
Jos 18: 16 to the side of *J* on the south,
28 Eleph, and *J*, which is Jerusalem,

Jebusite *(jeb'-u-site)* See also JEBUSITES.
Ge 10: 16 the *J*, and the Amorite, and the
Ex 33: 2 the Perizzite, the Hivite, and the *J*:
34: 11 Perizzite, and the Hivite, and the *J*.
Jos 9: 1 Hivite, and the *J*, heard thereof;
11: 3 and the *J* in the mountains,
15: 8 unto the south side of the *J*;
2Sa 24: 16 threshingplace of Araunah the *J*.
18 threshingfloor of Araunah the *J*.
1Ch 1: 14 The *J* also, and the Amorite, and
21: 15, 18 threshingfloor of Ornan the *J*.
28 the threshingfloor of Ornan the *J*,
2Ch 3: 1 the threshingfloor of Ornan the *J*.
Zec 9: 7 in Judah, and Ekron as a *J*.

Jebusites *(jeb'-u-sites)*
Ge 15: 21 and the Girgashites, and the *J*.
Ex 3: 8 and the Hivites, and the *J*.
17 and the Hivites, and the *J*, unto a
13: 5 and the Hivites, and the *J*, which
23: 23 Canaanites, the Hivites, and the *J*:
Nu 13: 29 the *J*, and the Amorites, dwell in
De 7: 1 and the Hivites, and the *J*, seven
20: 17 Perizzites, the Hivites, and the *J*;
Jos 3: 10 and the Amorites, and the *J*.
12: 8 Perizzites, the Hivites, and the *J*:
15: 63 *J* the inhabitants of Jerusalem,
63 *J* dwell with the children of Judah
24: 11 Girgashites, the Hivites, and the *J*;
J'g 1: 21 out the *J* that inhabited Jerusalem;
21 the *J* dwell with the children of
3: 5 and Perizzites, and Hivites, and *J*:
19: 11 let us turn in into this city of the *J*,
2Sa 5: 6 men went to Jerusalem unto the *J*,
8 and smiteth the *J*, and the lame
1Ki 9: 20 Hittites, Perizzites, Hivites, and *J*,
1Ch 11: 4 where the *J* were, the inhabitants
6 Whosoever smiteth the *J* first shall
2Ch 8: 7 and the Hivites, and the *J*, which
Ezr 9: 1 the Hittites, the Perizzites, the *J*,
Ne 9: 8 and the *J*, and the Girgashites,

Jecamiah *(jek-a-mi'-ah)* See also JEKAMIAH.
1Ch 3: 18 and Shenazar, *J*, Hoshama, and

Jecholiah *(jek-o-li'-ah)* See also JECOLIAH.
2Ki 15: 2 And his mother's name was *J* of

Jechonias *(jek-o-ni'-as)* See also JECONIAH.
M't 1: 11 Josias begat *J* and his brethren,
12 to Babylon, *J* begat Salathiel;

Jecoliah *(jek-o-li'-ah)* See also JECHOLIAH.
2Ch 26: 3 His mother's name also was *J* of

Jeconiah *(jek-o-ni'-ah)* See also CONIAH; JECHONIAS; JEHOIACHIN.
1Ch 3: 16 *J* his son, Zedekiah his son.
17 the sons of *J*; Assir, Salathiel his
Es 2: 6 which had been carried away with *J*
Jer 24: 1 had carried away captive *J* the son
27: 20 when he carried away captive *J*
Jer 28: 4 I will bring again to this place *J*
29: 2 (After that *J* the king, and the

Jedaiah *(jed-a-i'-ah)*
1Ch 4: 37 the son of Allon, the son of *J*, the
9: 10 of the priests; *J*, and Jehoiarib,
24: 7 forth to Jehoiarib, the second to *J*,
Ezr 2: 36 the children of *J*, of the house of
Ne 3: 10 repaired *J* the son of Harumaph,
7: 39 the children of *J*, of the house of
11: 10 Of the priests: *J* the son of Joiarib,
12: 6 Shemaiah, and Joiarib, *J*,
7 Sallu, Amok, Hilkiah, *J*.
19 of Joiarib, Mattenai; of *J*, Uzzi;
21 Hashabiah; of *J*, Nethaneel.
Zec 6: 10 of Heldai, of Tobijah, and of *J*,
14 Helem, and to Tobijah, and to *J*,

Jediael *(jed-e-a'-el)*
1Ch 7: 6 Bela, and Becher, and *J*, three.
10 The sons also of *J*; Bilhan: and
11 All these the sons of *J*, by the
11: 45 *J* the son of Shimri, and Joha his
12: 20 and Jozabad, and *J*, and Michael,
26: 2 the firstborn, *J* the second,

Jedidah *(je-di'-dah)*
2Ki 22: 1 his mother's name was *J*, the

Jedidiah *(jed-id-i'-ah)* See also SOLOMON.
2Sa 12: 25 called his name *J*, because of the

Jeduthun *(jed'-u-thun)*
1Ch 9: 16 son of Galal, the son of *J*, and
16: 38 Obed-edom also the son of *J* and
41 And with them Heman and *J*, and
42 And with them Heman and *J* with
42 And the sons of *J* were porters.
25: 1 of Asaph, and of Heman, and of *J*,
3 Of *J*: the sons of *J*; Gedaliah, and
3 under the hands of their father *J*,
6 order to Asaph, *J*, and Heman.
2Ch 5: 12 of them of Asaph, of Heman, of *J*,
29: 14 and of the sons of *J*; Shemaiah,
35: 15 and Heman, and *J* the king's seer;
Ne 11: 17 the son of Galal, the son *J*.
Ps 39: *title* To the chief Musician, even to *J*,
62: *title* To the chief Musician, to *J*,
77: *title* To the chief Musician, to *J*.

Jeezer *(je-e'-zur)*. See also ABIEZER; JEEZERITES.
Nu 26: 30 of *J*, the family of the Jeezerites:

Jeezerites *(je-e'-zur-ites)*
Nu 26: 30 of Jeezer, the family of the *J*:

Jegar-sahadutha *(je''-gar-sa-ha-du'-thah)* See also GALEED.
Ge 31: 47 And Laban called it *J*: but Jacob

Jehaleleel *(je-hal-e'-le-el)* See also JEHALELEL.
1Ch 4: 16 the sons of *J*: Ziph, and Ziphah,

Jehalelel *(je-hal'-e-lel)* See also JEHALELEEL.
2Ch 29: 12 and Azariah the son of *J*:

Jehdeiah *(jeh-di'-ah)*
1Ch 24: 20 of the sons of Shubael; *J*.
27: 30 the asses was *J* the Meronothite:

Jehezekel *(je-hez'-e-kel)* See also EZEKIEL.
1Ch 24: 16 to Pethahiah, the twentieth to *J*,

Jehiah *(je-hi'-ah)* See also JEHIEL.
1Ch 15: 24 *J* were doorkeepers for the ark.

Jehiel *(je-hi'-el)* See also JEHIAH; JEIEL; JEHIELI.
1Ch 9: 35 dwelt the father of Gibeon, *J*,
11: 44 Shama and *J* the sons of Hothan
15: 18, 20 Shemiramoth, and *J*, and Unni,
16: 5 and Shemiramoth, and *J*, and
23: 8 the chief was *J*, and Zetham, and
27: 32 *J* the son of Hachmoni was with the
29: 8 by the hand of *J* the Gershonite.
2Ch 21: 2 Azariah, and *J*, and Zechariah,
29: 14 sons of Heman; *J*, and Shimei:
31: 13 And *J*, and Azaziah, and Nahath,
35: 8 and Zechariah and *J*, rulers of the
Ezr 8: 9 Obadiah the son of *J*, and with him
10: 2 Shechaniah the son of *J*, one of the
21 and Elijah, and Shemaiah, and *J*,
26 Zechariah, and *J*, and Abdi, and

Jehieli *(je-hi'-el-i)* See also JEHIEL.
1Ch 26: 21 Laadan the Gershonite, were *J*.
22 The sons of *J*; Zetham, and Joel

Jehizkiah *(je-hiz-ki'-ah)* See also HEZEKIAH.
2Ch 28: 12 *J* the son of Shallum, and Amasa

Jehoadah *(je-ho'-a-dah)* See also JARAH.
1Ch 8: 36 Ahaz begat *J*; and *J* begat

Jehoaddan *(je-ho-ad'-dan)*
2Ki 14: 2 And his mother's name was *J* of
2Ch 25: 1 And his mother's name was *J* of

Jehoahaz *(je-ho'-a-haz)* See also AHAZIAH; JOAHAZ; SHALLUM.
2Ki 10: 35 *J* his son reigned in his stead.
13: 1 *J* the son of Jehu began to reign
4 *J* besought the Lord, and the Lord
7 leave of the people to *J* but fifty
8 the rest of the acts of *J*, and all
9 *J* slept with his fathers; and they
10 began Jehoash the son of *J* to reign
22 oppressed Israel all the days of *J*.
25 Jehoash the son of *J* took again
25 he had taken out of the hand of *J*
14: 1 the second year of Joash son of *J*
8 Jehoash, the son of *J* son of Jehu,
17 after the death of Jehoash son of *J*
23: 30 the land took *J* the son of Josiah,
31 *J* was twenty and three years old
34 to Jehoiakim, and took *J* away:
2Ch 21: 17 save *J*, the youngest of his sons.
25: 17 and sent to Joash, the son of *J*,
2Ch 25: 23 the son of Joash, the son of *J*, at
25 after the death of Joash son of *J*
36: 1 the land took *J* the son of Josiah,
2 *J* was twenty and three years old
4 Necho took *J* his brother, and

Jehoash *(je-ho'-ash)* See also JOASH.
2Ki 11: 21 Seven years old was *J* when he
12: 1 year of Jehu *J* began to reign;
2 *J* did that which was right in the
4 *J* said to the priests, All the money
6 three and twentieth year of king *J*
7 Then king *J* called for Jehoiada the
18 And *J* king of Judah took all the
13: 10 began *J* the son of Jehoahaz to
25 *J* the son of Jehoahaz took again
14: 8 Amaziah sent messengers to *J*,
9 *J* the king of Israel sent to Amaziah
11 Therefore *J* king of Israel went up;
13 And *J* king of Israel took Amaziah
13 the son of *J* the son of Ahaziah,
15 rest of the acts of *J* which he did,
16 *J* slept with his fathers, and was
17 the death of *J* son of Jehoahaz

Jehohanan *(je-ho'-ha-nan)* See also JOHANAN; JOHN.
1Ch 26: 3 *J* the sixth, Elioenai the seventh.
2Ch 17: 15 And next to him was *J* the captain
23: 1 Jeroham, and Ishmael the son of *J*,
Ezr 10: 28 Of the sons also of Bebai; *J*,
Ne 12: 13 Ezra, Meshullam; of Amariah, *J*;
42 Uzzi, and *J*, and Malchijah, and

Jehoiachin *(je-hoy'-a-kin)* See also CONIAH; JECONIAH; JECONIAS; JEHOIACHIN'S.
2Ki 24: 6 *J* his son reigned in his stead.
8 *J* was eighteen years old when he
12 *J* the king of Judah went out to
15 he carried away *J* to Babylon, and
25: 27 thirtieth year of the captivity of *J*
27 lift up the head of *J* king of Judah
2Ch 36: 8 *J* his son reigned in his stead.
9 *J* was eight years old when he
Jer 52: 31 thirtieth year of the captivity of *J*
31 lifted up the head of *J* king of

Jehoiachin's *(je-hoy'-a-kins)*
Eze 1: 2 fifth year of king *J* captivity,

Jehoiada *(je-hoy'-a-dah)* See also BERECHIAS; JOIADA.
2Sa 8: 18 Benaiah the son of *J* was over
20: 23 Benaiah the son of *J* was over the
23: 20 Benaiah the son of *J*, the son of a
22 things did Benaiah the son of *J*,
1Ki 1: 8 and Benaiah the son of *J*, and
26 and Benaiah the son of *J*, and thy
32 prophet, and Benaiah the son of *J*.
36 Benaiah the son of *J* answered
38, 44 and Benaiah the son of *J*, and
2: 25 the hand of Benaiah the son of *J*;
29 Solomon sent Benaiah the son of *J*,
34 So Benaiah the son of *J* went up,
35 Benaiah the son of *J* in his room
46 commanded Benaiah the son of *J*;
4: 4 Benaiah the son of *J* was over the
2Ki 11: 4 *J* sent and fetched the rulers over
9 that *J* the priest commanded:
9 sabbath, and came to *J* the priest.
15 But *J*...commanded the captains
17 *J* made a covenant between the
12: 2 *J* the priest instructed him.
7 Jehoash called for *J* the priest,
9 *J* the priest took a chest, and bored
1Ch 11: 22 Benaiah the son of *J*, the son of
24 things did Benaiah the son of *J*,
12: 27 *J* was the leader of the Aaronites,
18: 17 And Benaiah the son of *J* was over
27: 5 month was Benaiah the son of *J*,
34 was *J* the son of Benaiah, and
2Ch 22: 11 But Jehoshabeath,...the wife of *J*
23: 1 year *J* strengthened himself,
8 that *J* the priest had commanded,
8 for *J*...dismissed not the courses.
9 *J*...delivered to the captains
11 *J* and his sons anointed him, and
14 Then *J*...brought out the captains
16 *J* made a covenant between him,
18 *J* appointed the offices of the house
24: 2 sight of the Lord all the days of *J*
3 *J* took for him two wives; and he
6 the king called for *J* the chief, and
12 *J* gave it to such as did the work
14 the money before the king and *J*,
14 Lord continually all the days of *J*.
15 *J* waxed old, and was full of days
17 the death of *J* came the princes
20 came upon Zechariah the son of *J*
22 kindness which *J* his father had
25 him for the blood of the sons of *J*
Ne 3: 6 gate repaired *J* the son of Paseah,
Jer 29: 26 made thee priest in the stead of *J*

Jehoiakim *(je-hoy'-a-kim)* See also ELIAKIM; JOIAKIM.
2Ki 23: 34 father, and turned his name to *J*,
35 *J* gave the silver and the gold to
36 *J* was twenty and five years old
24: 1 *J* became his servant three years:
5 Now the rest of the acts of *J*,
6 So *J* slept with his fathers:
19 according to all that *J* had done.
1Ch 3: 15 firstborn Johanan, the second *J*,
16 the sons of *J*: Jeconiah his son,
2Ch 36: 4 and turned his name to *J*.
5 *J* was twenty and five years old
8 Now the rest of the acts of *J*,
Jer 1: 3 It came also in the days of *J*
22: 18 thus saith the Lord concerning *J*

Jer 22: 24 Coniah the son of J· king of Judah
24: 1 away captive Jeconiah the son of J·
25: 1 fourth year of J· the son of Josiah
26: 1 In the beginning of the reign of J·
21 J· the king, with all his mighty
22 J· the king sent men into Egypt,
23 and brought him unto J· the king;
27: 1 In the beginning of the reign of J·
20 away captive Jeconiah the son of J·
28: 4 to this place Jeconiah the son of J·
35: 1 in the days of J· the son of Josiah
36: 1 came to pass in the fourth year of J·
9 came to pass in the fifth year of J·
28 J· the king of Judah hath burned.
29 thou shalt say to J· king of Judah,
30 saith the Lord of J· king of Judah;
32 which J·...had burned in the fire:
37: 1 instead of Coniah the son of J·,
45: 1 fourth year of J· the son of Josiah
46: 2 smote in the fourth year of J·
52: 2 according to all that J· had done.
Da 1: 1 In the third year of the reign of J·
2 the Lord gave J· king of Judah into

Jehoiarib (*je-hoy'-a-rib*) See also JOIARIB.
1Ch 9: 10 Jedaiah, and J·, and Jachin,
24: 7 Now the first lot came forth to J·,

Jehonadab (*je-hon'-a-dab*) See also JONADAB.
2Ki 10: 15 he lighted on J· the son of Rechab
15 thy heart? And J· answered, It is.
23 went, and J· the son of Rechab,

Jehonathan (*je-hon'-a-than*) See also JONATHAN.
1Ch 27: 25 castles, was J· the son of Uzziah:
2Ch 17: 8 and Shemiramoth, and J·, and
Ne 12: 18 Shammua: of Shemaiah, J·;

Jehoram (*je-ho'-ram*) See also HADORAM; JORAM.
1Ki 22: 50 J· his son reigned in his stead.
2Ki 1: 17 And J· reigned in his stead
17 in the second year of J· the son of
3: 1 J· the son of Ahab began to reign
6 And king J· went out of Samaria
8: 16 J· the son of Jehoshaphat king of
25 Ahaziah the son of J· king of Judah
29 son of J· king of Judah went down
9: 24 and smote J· between his arms,
12: 18 J·, and Ahaziah, his fathers, kings
2Ch 17: 8 with them Elishama and J·, priests.
21: 1 And J· his son reigned in his stead.
3 but the kingdom gave he to J·;
4 J· was risen up to the kingdom of
5 J· was thirty and two years old
9 Then J· went forth with his princes,
16 Lord stirred up against J· the spirit
22: 1 Ahaziah the son of J· king of Judah
5 J· the son of Ahab king of Israel
6 Azariah the son of J· king of Judah
6 went down to see J· the son of Ahab
7 he went out with J· against Jehu
11 the daughter of king J·, the wife of

Jehoshabeath (*je-ho-shab'-e-ath*) See also JEHOSHEBA.
2Ch 22: 11 But J·, the daughter of the king,
11 J·, the daughter of king Jehoram,

Jehoshaphat (*je-hosh'-a-fat*) See also JOSAPHAT; JOSHAPHAT.
2Sa 8: 16 J· the son of Ahilud was recorder;
20: 24 J· the son of Ahilud was recorder:
1Ki 4: 3 J· the son of Ahilud, the recorder.
17 J· the son of Paruah, in Issachar:
15: 24 and J· his son reigned in his stead.
22: 2 J· the king of Judah came down
4 he said unto J·, Wilt thou go with
4 J· said to the king of Israel, I am
5 And J· said unto the king of Israel,
7 J· said, Is there not here a prophet
8 said unto J·, There is yet one man,
8 And J· said, Let not the king say so.
10 and J· the king of Judah sat each
18 king of Israel said unto J·, Did I
29 and J· the king of Judah went up
30 king of Israel said unto J·, I will
32 captains of the chariots saw J·, that
32 fight against him: and J· cried out.
41 J· the son of Asa began to reign
42 J· was thirty and five years old
44 J· made peace with the king of
45 the rest of the acts of J·, and his
48 J· made ships of Tharshish to go
49 Ahaziah the son of Ahab unto J·,
49 in the ships. But J· would not.
50 J· slept with his fathers, and was
51 the seventeenth year of J· king of
2Ki 1: 17 year of Jehoram the son of J· king
3: 1 the eighteenth year of J· king of
7 and sent to J· the king of Judah,
11 J· said, Is there not here a prophet
12 J· said, The word of the Lord is
12 J· and the king of Edom went down
14 not that I regard the presence of J·
8: 16 Israel, J· being then king of Judah,
16 Jehoram the son of J· king of Judah
9: 2 look out there Jehu the son of J·
14 Jehu the son of J·...conspired
12: 18 took all the hallowed things that J·,
1Ch 3: 10 his son, Asa his son, J· his son,
15: 24 Shebaniah, and J·, and Nethaneel,
18: 15 and J· the son of Alihud, recorder.
2Ch 17: 1 And J· his son reigned in his stead,
3 the Lord was with J·, because he
5 all Judah brought to J· presents;
10 that they made no war against J·.
11 the Philistines brought J· presents,
12 And J· waxed great exceedingly;
18: 1 Now J· had riches and honour in

2Ch 18: 3 Ahab king of Israel said unto J·
4 And J· said unto the king of Israel,
6 J· said, Is there not here a prophet
7 And the king of Israel said unto J·,
7 And J· said, Let not the king say so.
9 and J· king of Judah sat either
17 And the king of Israel said to J·,
28 and J· the king of Judah went up
29 And the king of Israel said unto J·,
31 the captains of the chariot saw J·,
31 J· cried out, and the Lord helped
19: 1 J· the king of Judah returned to
2 to meet him, and said to king J·,
4 And J· dwelt at Jerusalem: and he
8 Jerusalem did J· set of the Levites,
20: 1 came against J· to battle.
2 Then there came some that told J·,
3 J· feared, and set himself to seek
5 J· stood in the congregation of
15 of Jerusalem, and thou king J·,
18 J· bowed his head with his face to
20 J· stood and said, Hear me, O Judah,
25 J· and his people came to take away
27 J· in the forefront of them, to go
30 So the realm of J· was quiet: for
31 And J· reigned over Judah: he was
34 Now the rest of the acts of J·, first
35 did J· king of Judah join himself
37 of Mareshah prophesied against J·,
21: 1 J· slept with his fathers, and was
2 And he had brethren the sons of J·,
2 all these were the sons of J· king
12 hast not walked in the ways of J·
22: 9 said they, he is the son of J·, who
Joe 3: 2 them down into the valley of J·,
12 and come up to the valley of J·:

Jehosheba (*je-hosh'-e-bah*) See also JEHOSHABEATH.
2Ki 11: 2 J·, the daughter of king Joram,

Jehoshua (*je-hosh'-u-ah*) See also JEHOSHUAH; JOSHUA.
Nu 13: 16 called Oshea the son of Nun J·.

Jehoshuah (*je-hosh'-u-ah*) See also JEHOSHUA.
1Ch 7: 27 Non his son, J· his son.

Jehovah (*je-ho'-vah*) See also GOD; JAH; JEHOVAH-JIREH; JEHOVAH-NISSI; JEHOVAH-SHALOM; LORD.
Ex 6: 3 name J· was I not known to them.
Ps 83: 18 thou, whose name alone is J·, art
Isa 12: 2 J· is my strength and my song;
26: 4 the Lord J· is everlasting strength.

Jehovah-jireh (*je-ho"-vah-ji'-reh*)
Ge 22: 14 called the name of that place J·:

Jehovah-nissi (*je-ho"-vah-nis'-si*)
Ex 17: 15 altar, and called the name of it J·:

Jehovah-shalom (*je-ho"-vah-sha'-lom*)
J'g 6: 24 unto the Lord, and called it J·:

Jehozabad (*je-hoz'-a-bad*) See also JOZABAD.
2Ki 12: 21 J· the son of Shomer, his servants,
1Ch 26: 4 J· the second, Joah the third,
2Ch 17: 18 next him was J·, and with him an
24: 26 J· the son of Shimrith a Moabitess.

Jehozadak (*je-hoz'-a-dak*) See also JOZADAK.
1Ch 6: 14 Seraiah, and Seraiah begat J·,
15 J· went into captivity, when the

Jehu (*je-hu*)
1Ki 16: 1 word of the Lord came to J· the
7 also by the hand of the prophet J·
12 he spake against Baasha by J· the
19: 16 J·...shalt thou anoint to be king
17 the sword of Hazael shall J· slay:
17 that escapeth from the sword of J·
2Ki 9: 2 there J· the son of Jehoshaphat
5 And J· said, Unto which of all us?
11 J· came forth to the servants of his
13 with trumpets, saying, J· is king.
14 J· the son of Jehoshaphat the son
15 And J· said, If it be your minds,
16 So J· rode in a chariot, and went to
17 spied the company of J· as he came,
18 J· said, What hast thou to do with
19 J· answered, What hast thou to do
20 the driving is like the driving of J·
21 they went out against J·, and met
22 it came to pass, when Joram saw J·,
22 that he said, Is it peace, J·?
24 And J· drew a bow with his full
25 Then said J· to Bidkar his captain,
27 J· followed after him, and said,
30 And when J· was come to Jezreel,
31 as J· entered in at the gate, she
10: 1 And J· wrote letters, and sent to
5 up of the children, sent to J·, saying,
11 J· slew all that remained of the
13 J· met with the brethren of Ahaziah
18 J· gathered all the people together,
18 little; but J· shall serve him much.
19 J· did it in subtilty, to the intent
20 And J· said, Proclaim a solemn
21 And J· sent through all Israel:
23 J· went, and Jehonadab the son of
24 J· appointed fourscore men without,
25 And J· said to the guard and to the
28 J· destroyed Baal out of Israel.
29 J· departed not from after them,
30 the Lord said unto J·, Because thou
31 J· took no heed to walk in the law
34 the rest of the acts of J·, and all
35 And J· slept with his fathers: and
36 time that J· reigned over Israel
12: 1 seventh year of J· Jehoash began
13: 1 Jehoahaz the son of J· began to

2Ki 14: 8 the son of Jehoahaz son of J·,
15: 12 of the Lord which he spake unto J·,
1Ch 2: 38 And Obed begat J·, and J· begat
4: 35 Joel, and J· the son of Josibiah,
12: 3 Berachah, and J· the Antothite,
2Ch 19: 2 J· the son of Hanani the seer went
20: 34 they are written in the book of J·
22: 7 went out with Jehoram against J·
8 J· was executing judgment upon
9 in Samaria,) and brought him to J·:
25: 17 the son of Jehoahaz, the son of J·,
Ho 1: 4 of Jezreel upon the house of J·,

Jehubbah (*je-hub'-bah*)
1Ch 7: 34 of Shamer; Ahi, and Rohgah, J·,

Jehucal (*je-hu'-kal*) See also JUCAL.
Jer 37: 3 king sent J· the son of Shelemiah

Jehud (*je'-hud*)
Jos 19: 45 And J·, and Bene-berak, and

Jehudi (*je-hu'-di*)
Jer 36: 14 Therefore all the princes sent J·
21 So the king sent J· to fetch the roll:
21 J· read it in the ears of the king,
23 J· had read three or four leaves, he

Jehudijah (*je-hu-di'-jah*) See also HODIAH.
1Ch 4: 18 And his wife J· bare Jered the

Jehush (*je'-hush*) See also JEUSH.
1Ch 8: 39 J· the second, and Eliphelet the

Jeiel (*je-i'-el*) See also JEHIEL; JEUEL.
1Ch 5: 7 were the chief, J·, and Zecariah,
15: 18 Obed-edom, and J·, the porters.
21 Obed-edom, and J·, and Azaziah,
16: 5 and next to him Zechariah, J·, and
5 J· with psalteries and with harps;
2Ch 20: 14 of Benaiah, the son of J·, the son of
26: 11 account by the hand of J· the scribe
29: 13 sons of Elizaphan; Shimri, and J·:
35: 9 Hashabiah and J· and Jozabad,
Ezr 8: 13 names are these, Eliphelet, J·, and
10: 43 the sons of Nebo; J·, Mattithiah,

Jekabzeel (*je-kab'-ze-el*) See also KABZEEL.
Ne 11: 25 at J·, and in the villages thereof,

Jekameam (*je-kam'-e-am*)
1Ch 23: 19 the third, and J· the fourth.
24: 23 Jahaziel the third, J· the fourth.

Jekamiah (*jek-a-mi'-ah*) See also JECAMIAH.
1Ch 2: 41 Shallum begat J·, and J· begat

Jekuthiel (*je-ku'-the-el*)
1Ch 4: 18 and J· the father of Zanoah.

Jemima (*je-mi'-mah*)
Job 42: 14 he called the name of the first, J·;

Jemuel (*je-mu'-el*) See also NEMUEL.
Ge 46: 10 sons of Simeon; J·, and Jamin,
Ex 6: 15 the sons of Simeon; J·, and Jamin,

jeoparded
J'g 5: 18 a people that j· their lives unto the

jeopardy
2Sa 23: 17 the men that went in j· of their lives?
1Ch 11: 19 that have put their lives in j·?
19 for with the j· of their lives they brought
12: 19 master Saul to the j· of our heads.
Lu 8: 23 filled with water, and were in j·.
1Co 15: 30 And why stand we in j· every hour?

Jephthae (*jef'-thah-e*) See also JEPHTHAH.
Heb 11: 32 Barak, and of Samson, and of J·;

Jephthah (*jef'-thah*) See also JEPHTHAE; JIPHTHAH-EL.
J'g 11: 1 Now J· the Gileadite was a mighty
1 of an harlot: and Gilead begat J·.
2 they thrust out J·, and said unto
3 Then J· fled from his brethren,
3 there were gathered vain men to J·,
5 the elders of Gilead went to fetch J·
6 they said unto J·, Come, and be our
7 J· said unto the elders of Gilead,
8 the elders of Gilead said unto J·,
9 J· said unto the elders of Gilead,
10 the elders of Gilead said unto J·,
11 J· went with the elders of Gilead,
11 J· uttered all his words before the
12 J· sent messengers unto the king
13 answered...the messengers of J·,
14 J· sent messengers again unto the
15 Thus saith J·, Israel took not away
28 hearkened not unto the words of J·
29 Spirit of the Lord came upon J·,
30 J· vowed a vow unto the Lord, and
32 J· passed over unto the children of
34 J· came to Mizpeh unto his house,
40 yearly to lament the daughter of J·
12: 1 went northward, and said unto J·,
2 J· said unto them, I and my people
4 J· gathered together all the men of
7 And J· judged Israel six years.
7 Then died J· the Gileadite, and was
1Sa 12: 11 sent Jerubbaal, and Bedan, and J·,

Jephunneh (*je-fun'-neh*)
Nu 13: 6 tribe of Judah, Caleb the son of J·.
14: 6 son of Nun, and Caleb the son of J·,
30 therein, save Caleb the son of J·,
38 son of Nun, and Caleb the son of J·,
26: 65 of them, save Caleb the son of J·,
32: 12 Save Caleb the son of J· the
34: 19 tribe of Judah, Caleb the son of J·.
De 1: 36 Save Caleb the son of J·; he shall
Jos 14: 6 Caleb the son of J· the Kenezite said
13 and gave unto Caleb the son of J·
14 inheritance of Caleb the son of J·
15: 13 unto Caleb the son of J· he gave a

Jos 21:12 gave they to Caleb the son of J·
1Ch 4:15 the sons of Caleb the son of J·; Iru,
6:56 they gave to Caleb the son of J·.
7:38 the sons of Jether; J·, and Pispah.

Jerah (*je'-rah*)
Ge 10:26 and Hazarmaveth, and J·,
1Ch 1:20 and Hazarmaveth, and J·,

Jerahmeel (*je-rah'-me-el*) See also JERAHMEELITES.
1Ch 2: 9 J·, and Ram, and Chelubai.
25 sons of J· the firstborn of Hezron
26 J· had also another wife, whose
27 the sons of Ram the firstborn of J·
33 These were the sons of J·.
42 sons of Caleb the brother of J· were,
24:29 Kish: the son of Kish was J·.
Jer 36:26 J· the son of Hammelech,

Jerahmeelites (*je-rah'-me-el-ites*)
1Sa 27:10 and against the south of the J·,
30:29 which were in the cities of the J·.

Jered (*je'-red*) See also JARED.
1Ch 1: 2 Kenan, Mahalaleel, J·,
4:18 wife Jehudijah bare J· the father of

Jeremai (*jer'-e-mahee*)
Ezr 10:33 Zabad, Eliphelet, J·, Manasseh,

Jeremiah (*jer-e-mi'-ah*) See also JEREMIAH'S; JEREMIAS; JEREMY.
2Ki 23:31 the daughter of J· of Libnah.
24:18 the daughter of J· of Libnah.
1Ch 5:24 and Azriel, and J·, and Hodaviah,
12: 4 and J·, and Jahaziel, and Johanan,
10 the fourth, J· the fifth,
13 J· the tenth, Machbanai the
2Ch 35:25 And J· lamented for Josiah:
36:12 and humbled not himself before J·
21 word of the Lord by the mouth of J·,
22 the Lord spoken by the mouth of J·
Ezr 1: 1 word of the Lord by the mouth of J·
Ne 10: 2 Seraiah, Azariah, J·,
12: 1 and Jeshua: Seraiah, J·, Ezra,
12 Seraiah, Meraiah; of J·, Hananiah;
34 Benjamin, and Shemaiah, and J·,
Jer 1: 1 The words of J· the son of Hilkiah,
11 me, saying, J·, what seest thou?
7: 1 word that came to J· from the Lord,
11: 1 word that came to J· from the Lord,
14: 1 came to J· concerning the dearth.
18: 1 word which came to J· from the
18 let us devise devices against J·;
19:14 Then came J· from Tophet,
20: 1 heard that J· prophesied these
2 Then Pashur smote J· the prophet,
3 brought forth J· out of the stocks.
3 Then said J· unto him, The Lord
21: 1 which came unto J· from the Lord,
3 Then said J· unto them, Thus shall
24: 3 Lord unto me, What seest thou, J·?
25: 1 word that came to J· concerning
2 The which J· the prophet spake
13 J· hath prophesied against all the
26: 7 the people heard J· speaking these
8 J· had made an end of speaking all
9 people were gathered against J· in
12 spake J· unto all the princes and
20 according to all the words of J·;
24 the son of Shaphan was with J·,
27: 1 this word unto J· from the Lord,
28: 5 J· said unto the prophet Hananiah
6 prophet J· said, Amen: the Lord do
11 And the prophet J· went his way.
12 word of the Lord came unto J· the
12 from off the neck of the prophet J·,
15 said the prophet J· unto Hananiah
29: 1 are the words of the letter that J·
27 why hast thou not reproved J· of
29 read this letter in the ears of J·
30 came the word of the Lord unto J·,
30: 1 word that came to J· from the Lord,
32: 1 The word that came to J· from the
2 J· the prophet was shut up in the
6 J· said, The word of the Lord came
26 came the word of the Lord unto J·,
33: 1 Lord came unto J· the second time,
19 the word of the Lord came unto J·,
23 the word of the Lord came to J·,
34: 1 which came unto J· from the Lord,
6 Then J· the prophet spake all these
8 that came unto J· from the Lord,
12 the word of the Lord came to J·
35: 1 which came unto J· from the Lord,
3 I took Jaazaniah the son of J·,
12 came the word of the Lord unto J·,
18 And J· said unto...the Rechabites,
36: 1 word came unto J· from the Lord,
4 J· called Baruch the son of Neriah:
4 Baruch wrote from the mouth of J·
5 J· commanded Baruch, saying, I
8 J· the prophet commanded him,
10 Baruch in the book the words of J·
19 Baruch, Go, hide thee, thou and J·;
26 the scribe and J· the prophet:
27 the word of the Lord came to J·,
27 Baruch wrote at the mouth of J·,
32 Then took J· another roll, and gave
32 wrote therein from the mouth of J·
37: 2 which he spake by the prophet J·.
3 the priest to the prophet J·, saying,
4 J· came in and went out among
6 of the Lord unto the prophet J·,
12 Then J· went forth out of Jerusalem
13 and he took J· the prophet, saying,
14 Then said J·, It is false; I fall not
14 so Irijah took J·, and brought him
15 the princes were wroth with J·,
Jer 37:16 J· was entered into the dungeon,
16 J· had remained there many days;
17 And J· said, There is: for, said he,
18 J· said unto king Zedekiah, What
21 should commit J· into the court of
21 J· remained in the court of the
38: 1 heard the words that J· had spoken
6 took they J·, and cast him into the
6 and they let down J· with cords.
6 but mire: so J· sunk in the mire.
7 they had put J· in the dungeon;
9 evil in all that they have done to J·
10 J· the prophet out of the dungeon,
11 by cords into the dungeon to J·.
12 the Ethiopian said unto J·, Put now
12 under the cords. And J· did so.
13 So they drew up J· with cords, and
13 J· remained in the court of the
14 and took J· the prophet unto him
14 the king said unto J·, I will ask
15 J· said unto Zedekiah, If I declare
16 the king sware secretly unto J·,
17 said J· unto Zedekiah, Thus saith
19 Zedekiah the king said unto J·, I
20 J· said, They shall not deliver thee.
24 Then said Zedekiah unto J·, Let no
27 Then came all the princes unto J·,
28 J· abode in the court of the prison
39:11 Babylon gave charge concerning J·
14 sent, and took J· out of the court
15 the word of the Lord came unto J·,
40: 1 that came to J· from the Lord,
2 the captain of the guard took J·,
6 Then went J· unto Gedaliah the
42: 2 And said unto J· the prophet, Let,
4 J· the prophet said unto them, I
5 they said to J·, The Lord be a true
7 the word of the Lord came unto J·.
43: 1 J· had made an end of speaking
2 and all proud men, saying unto J·,
6 J· the prophet and Baruch the son
8 came the word of the Lord unto J·
44: 1 word that came to J· concerning
15 in Pathros, answered J·, saying,
20 Then J· said unto all the people, to
24 J· said unto all the people, and to
45: 1 word that J· the prophet spake unto
1 words in a book at the mouth of J·,
46: 1 word of the Lord which came to J·
13 The word that the Lord spake to J·
47: 1 word of the Lord that came to J·
49:34 word of the Lord that came to J·
50: 1 the land of the Chaldeans by J·
51:59 which J· the prophet commanded
60 J· wrote in a book all the evil that
61 J· said to Seraiah, When thou comest
64 Thus far are the words of J·.
52: 1 the daughter of J· of Libnah.
Da 9: 2 the word of the Lord came to J· the

Jeremiah's (*jer-e-mi'-ahz*)
Jer 28:10 yoke from off the prophet J· neck,

Jeremias (*jer-e-mi'-as*) See also JEREMIAH.
M't 16:14 others, J·, or one of the prophets.

Jeremoth (*jer'-e-moth*) See also JERIMOTH.
1Ch 8:14 And Ahio, Shashak, and J·,
23:23 Mahli, and Eder, and J·, three.
25:22 The fifteenth to J·, he, his sons, and
Ezr 10:26 and Jehiel, and Abdi, and J·, and
27 Mattaniah, and J·, and Zabad, and

Jeremy (*jer'-e-mee*) See also JEREMIAH.
M't 2:17 that which was spoken by J· the
27: 9 that which was spoken by J· the

Jeriah (*je-ri'-ah*) See also JERIJAH.
1Ch 23:19 Of the sons of Hebron; J· the first,
24:23 J· the first, Amariah the second,

Jeribai (*jer'-ib-ahee*)
1Ch 11:46 Eliel the Mahavite, and J·, and

Jericho (*jer'-ik-o*)
Nu 22: 1 of Moab on this Jordan by J·.
26: 3 plains of Moab by Jordan near J·,
63 plains of Moab by Jordan near J·.
31:12 Moab, which are by Jordan near J·.
33:48 plains of Moab by Jordan near J·.
50 plains of Moab by Jordan near J·,
34:15 this side Jordan near J· eastward,
35: 1 plains of Moab by Jordan near J·,
36:13 plains of Moab by Jordan near J·.
De 32:49 of Moab, that is over against J·;
34: 1 of Pisgah, that is over against J·.
3 and the plain of the valley of J·, the
Jos 2: 1 saying, Go view the land, even J·.
2 it was told the king of J·, saying,
3 And the king of J· sent unto Rahab,
3:16 people passed over right against J·.
4:13 Lord unto battle, to the plains of J·.
19 in Gilgal, in the east border of J·.
5:10 month at even in the plains of J·.
13 to pass, when Joshua was by J·,
6: 1 J· was straitly shut up because of
2 I have given into thine hand J·,
25 which Joshua sent to spy out J·.
26 riseth up and buildeth this city J·:
7: 2 And Joshua sent men from J· to Ai,
8: 2 as thou didst unto J· and her king:
9: 3 what Joshua had done unto J·
10: 1 as he had done to J· and her king,
28 as he did unto the king of J·.
30 thereof as he did unto the king of J·.
12: 9 The king of J·, one; the king of Ai,
13:32 Moab, on the other side Jordan, by J·,
16: 1 of Joseph fell from Jordan by J·,
1 unto the water of J· on the east,
1 wilderness that goeth up from J·
7 and to Naarath, and came to J·,
Jos 18:12 border went up to the side of J· on
21 according to their families were J·,
20: 8 And on the other side Jordan by J·
24:11 over Jordan, and came unto J·:
11 the men of J· fought against you,
2Sa 10: 5 Tarry at J· until your beards be
1Ki 16:34 did Hiel the Beth-elite build J·:
2Ki 2: 4 for the Lord hath sent me to J·.
4 not leave thee. So they came to J·.
5 sons of the prophets that were at J·
15 prophets which were to view at J·
18 again to him, (for he tarried at J·,)
25: 5 overtook him in the plains of J·:
1Ch 6:78 And on the other side Jordan by J·,
19: 5 Tarry at J· until your beards be
2Ch 28:15 upon asses, and brought them to J·,
Ezr 2:34 The children of J·, three hundred
Ne 3: 2 unto him builded the men of J·.
7:36 The children of J·, three hundred
Jer 39: 5 Zedekiah in the plains of J·:
52: 8 Zedekiah in the plains of J·;
M't 20:29 And as they departed from J·, a
M'r 10:46 came to J·: and as he went out of J·
Lu 10:30 went down from Jerusalem to J·,
18:35 that as he was come nigh unto J·,
19: 1 entered and passed through J·.
Heb11:30 By faith the walls of J· fell down,

Jeriel (*je-ri'-el*)
1Ch 7: 2 Uzzi, and Rephaiah, and J·, and

Jerijah (*je-ri'-jah*) See also JERIAH.
1Ch 26:31 the Hebronites was J· the chief,

Jerimoth (*jer'-im-oth*) See also JEREMOTH.
1Ch 7: 7 Uzzi, and Uzziel, and J·, and Iri,
8 and Elioenai, and Omri, and J·,
12: 5 Eluzai, and J·, and Bealiah, and
24:30 of Mushi; Mahli, and Eder, and J·,
25: 4 Mattaniah, Uzziel, Shebuel, and J·,
27:19 of Naphtali, J· the son of Azriel:
2Ch 11:18 him Mahalath the daughter of J·
31:13 and Nahath, and Asahel, and J·,

Jerioth (*je'-re-oth*)
1Ch 2:18 of Azubah his wife, and of J·:

Jeroboam (*jer-o-bo'-am*) See also JEROBOAM'S.
1Ki 11:26 J· the son of Nebat, an Ephrathite
28 J· was a mighty man of valour:
29 when J· went out of Jerusalem,
31 And he said to J·, Take thee ten
40 Solomon sought therefore to kill J·.
40 And J· arose, and fled into Egypt,
12: 2 to pass, when J· the son of Nebat,
2 Solomon, and J· dwelt in Egypt;)
3 And J· and all the congregation of
12 So J· and all the people came to
15 by Ahijah the Shilonite unto J·
20 all Israel heard that J· was come
25 Then J· built Shechem in mount
26 J· said in his heart, Now shall the
32 J· ordained a feast in the eighth
13: 1 and J· stood by the altar to burn
4 J· heard the saying of the man of
33 J· returned not from his evil way,
34 became sin unto the house of J·,
14: 1 time Abijah the son of J· fell sick.
2 J· said to his wife, Arise, I pray
2 be not known to be the wife of J·;
5 Behold, the wife of J· cometh to ask
6 he said, Come in, thou wife of J·;
7 Go, tell J·, Thus saith the Lord God
10 will bring evil upon the house of J·,
10 will cut off from J· him that pisseth
10 the remnant of the house of J·,
11 Him that dieth of J· in the city
13 only of J· shall come to the grave,
13 God of Israel in the house of J·.
14 cut off the house of J· that day:
16 Israel up because of the sins of J·,
19 the rest of the acts of J·, how he
20 J· reigned were two and twenty
30 was war between Rehoboam and J·
15: 1 in the eighteenth year of king J·
6 was war between Rehoboam and J·
7 was war between Abijam and J·.
9 twentieth year of J· king of Israel
25 Nadab the son of J· began to reign
29 that he smote all the house of J·;
29 he left not to J· any that breathed,
30 of the sins of J· which he sinned,
34 walked in the way of J·, and in his
16: 2 thou hast walked in the way of J·,
3 make thy house like the house of J·
7 in being like the house of J·;
19 in walking in the way of J·, and in
26 For he walked in all the way of J·
31 for him to walk in the sins of J·
21:22 thine house like the house of J·
22:52 of his mother, and in the way of J·
2Ki 3: 3 he cleaved unto the sins of J· the
9: 9 house of Ahab like the house of J·
10:29 from the sins of J· the son of Nebat,
31 he departed not from the sins of J·,
13: 2 and followed the sins of J· the son
6 not from the sins of the house of J·,
11 departed not from all the sins of J·
13 and J· sat upon his throne:
14:16 and J· his son reigned in his stead.
23 J· the son of Joash king of Israel
24 departed not from all the sins of J·
27 he saved them by the hand of J·
28 the rest of the acts of J·, and all
29 J· slept with his fathers, even with
15: 1 twenty and seventh year of J· king
8 did Zachariah the son of J· reign
9 he departed not from the sins of J·
18 not all his days from the sins of J·

2Ki 15: 24, 28 departed not from the sins of *J'*
17: 21 they made *J'* the son of Nebat king:
21 *J'* drave Israel from following the
22 of Israel walked in all the sins of *J'*
23: 15 the high place which *J'* the son of
1Ch 5: 17 and in the days of *J'* king of Israel.
2Ch 9: 29 visions of Iddo the seer against *J'*
10: 2 came to pass, when *J'*...heard it,
2 it, that *J'* returned out of Egypt.
3 *J'* and all Israel came and spake to
12 So *J'* and all the people came to
15 hand of Ahijah the Shilonite to *J'*
11: 4 returned from going against *J'*.
14 *J'* and his sons had cast them off
12: 15 wars between Rehoboam and *J'*
13: 1 in the eighteenth year of king *J'*
2 was war between Abijah and *J'*.
3 *J'* also set the battle in array
4 Hear me, thou *J'*, and all Israel;
6 *J'* the son of Nebat, the servant of
8 calves, which *J'* made you for gods.
13 *J'* caused an ambushment to come
15 God smote *J'* and all Israel before
19 Abijah pursued after *J'*, and took
20 Neither did *J'* recover strength
Ho 1: 1 in the days of *J'* the son of Joash,
Am 1: 1 in the days of *J'* the son of Joash
7: 9 I will rise against the house of *J'*
10 the priest of Beth-el sent to *J'* king
11 saith, *J'* shall die by the sword,

Jeroboam's (*jer-o-bo'-ams*)
1Ki 14: 4 And *J'* wife did so, and arose, and
17 *J'* wife arose, and departed, and

Jeroham (*je-ro'-ham*)
1Sa 1: 1 name was Elkanah, the son of *J'*.
1Ch 6: 27 son, *J'* his son, Elkanah his son.
34 The son of Elkanah, the son of *J'*,
8: 27 Eliah, and Zichri, the sons of *J'*.
9: 8 Ibneiah the son of *J'*, and Elah the
12 And Adaiah the son of *J'*, the son of
12: 7 Zebadiah, the sons of *J'* of Gedor.
27: 22 Of Dan, Azareel the son of *J'*.
2Ch 23: 1 Azariah the son of *J'*, and Ishmael
Ne 11: 12 and Adaiah the son of *J'*, the son of

Jerubbaal (*je-rub'-ba-al*) See also GIDEON; JERUBBESHETH.
J'g 6: 32 on that day he called him *J'*,
7: 1 *J'*, who is Gideon, and all the people
8: 29 *J'* the son of Joash went and dwelt
35 they kindness to the house of *J'*,
9: 1 Abimelech the son of *J'* went to
2 that all the sons of *J'*,...reign over
5 slew his brethren the sons of *J'*,
5 the youngest son of *J'* was left;
16 and if ye have dealt well with *J'*
19 dealt truly and sincerely with *J'*
24 and ten sons of *J'* might come,
28 serve him? is not he the son of *J'*?
57 the curse of Jotham the son of *J'*.
1Sa 12: 11 And the Lord sent *J'*, and Bedan,

Jerubbesheth (*je-rub'-be-sheth*) See also JERUBBAAL.
2Sa 11: 21 smote Abimelech the son of *J'*?

Jeruel (*je-ru'-el*)
2Ch 20: 16 brook, before the wilderness of *J'*.

Jerusalem (*je-ru'-sa-lem*) See also JERUSALEM'S; SALEM.
Jos 10: 1 king of *J'* had heard how Joshua
3 king of *J'* sent unto Hoham king of
5, 23 king of *J'*, the king of Hebron,
12: 10 The king of *J'*, one; the king of
15: 8 side of the Jebusite; the same is *J'*:
63 the Jebusites the inhabitants of *J'*,
63 with the children of Judah at *J'*
18: 28 Eleph, and Jebusi, which is *J'*,
J'g 1: 7 they brought him to *J'*, and there
8 of Judah had fought against *J'*,
21 out the Jebusites that inhabited *J'*;
21 of Benjamin in *J'* unto this day.
19: 10 over against Jebus, which is *J'*;
1Sa 17: 54 the Philistine, and brought it to *J'*;
2Sa 5: 5 in *J'* he reigned thirty and three
6 the king and his men went to *J'*
13 concubines and wives out of *J'*,
14 those that were born unto him in *J'*;
8: 7 Hadadezer, and brought them to *J'*.
9: 13 So Mephibosheth dwelt in *J'*: for
10: 14 children of Ammon, and came to *J'*.
11: 1 But David tarried still at *J'*.
12 So Uriah abode in *J'* that day, and
12: 31 and all the people returned unto *J'*.
14: 23 Geshur, and brought Absalom to *J'*.
28 Absalom dwelt two full years in *J'*,
15: 8 shall bring me again indeed to *J'*,
11 went two hundred men out of *J'*,
14 servants that were with him at *J'*,
29 carried the ark of God again to *J'*:
37 the city, and Absalom came into *J'*.
16: 3 the king, Behold, he abideth at *J'*:
15 people the men of Israel, came to *J'*,
17: 20 not find them, they returned to *J'*.
19: 19 that my lord the king went out of *J'*,
25 he was come to *J'* to meet the king,
33 and I will feed thee with me in *J'*,
34 should go up with the king unto *J'*?
20: 2 their king, from Jordan even to *J'*.
3 And David came to his house at *J'*;
7 and they went out of *J'*, to pursue
22 Joab returned to *J'* unto the king.
24: 8 they came to *J'* at the end of nine
16 out his hand upon *J'* to destroy it,
1Ki 2: 11 and three years reigned he in *J'*.
36 unto him, Build thee an house in *J'*,
38 And Shimei dwelt in *J'* many days.
1Ki 2: 41 Shimei had gone from *J'* to Gath,
3: 1 and the wall of *J'* round about.
15 he came to *J'*, and stood before the
8: 1 of Israel, unto king Solomon in *J'*,
9: 15 and the wall of *J'*, and Hazor, and
19 Solomon desired to build in *J'*,
10: 2 she came to *J'* with a very great
26 chariots, and with the king at *J'*.
27 made silver to be in *J'* as stones,
11: 7 in the hill that is before *J'*, and for
29 when Jeroboam went out of *J'*,
36 have a light alway before me in *J'*,
42 the time that Solomon reigned in *J'*
12: 18 him up to his chariot, to flee to *J'*.
21 when Rehoboam was come to *J'*,
27 in the house of the Lord at *J'*,
28 is too much for you to go up to *J'*:
14: 21 he reigned seventeen years in *J'*,
25 king of Egypt came up against *J'*:
15: 2 Three years reigned he in *J'*.
4 Lord his God give him a lamp in *J'*,
4 son after him, and to establish *J'*:
10 forty and one years reigned he in *J'*.
22: 42 reigned twenty and five years in *J'*.
2Ki 8: 17 and he reigned eight years in *J'*.
26 and he reigned one year in *J'*.
9: 28 carried him in a chariot to *J'*,
12: 1 and forty years reigned he in *J'*.
17 Hazael set his face to go up to *J'*.
18 of Syria: and he went away from *J'*.
14: 2 reigned twenty and nine years in *J'*.
2 name was Jehoaddan of *J'*.
13 at Beth-shemesh, and came to *J'*,
13 and brake down the wall of *J'* from
19 a conspiracy against him in *J'*:
20 he was buried at *J'* with his fathers
15: 2 reigned two and fifty years in *J'*.
2 name was Jecholiah of *J'*.
33 and he reigned sixteen years in *J'*.
16: 2 and reigned sixteen years in *J'*,
5 king of Israel came up to *J'* to war:
18: 2 reigned twenty and nine years in *J'*.
17 with a great host against *J'*:
17 And they went up and came to *J'*,
22 and hath said to Judah and *J'*,
22 worship before this altar in *J'*?
35 should deliver *J'* out of mine hand?
19: 10 *J'* shall not be delivered into the
21 daughter of *J'* hath shaken her head
31 out of *J'* shall go forth a remnant,
21: 1 reigned fifty and five years in *J'*.
4 Lord said, In *J'* will I put my name.
7 and in *J'*, which I have chosen
12 I am bringing such evil upon *J'* and
13 stretch over *J'* the line of Samaria,
13 wipe *J'* as a man wipeth a dish,
16 filled *J'* from one end to another;
19 and he reigned two years in *J'*.
22: 1 reigned thirty and one years in *J'*.
14 (now she dwelt in *J'* in the college;)
23: 1 all the elders of Judah and of *J'*.
2 all the inhabitants of *J'* with him,
4 he burned them without *J'* in the
5 and in the places round about *J'*;
6 without *J'*, unto the brook Kidron,
9 not up to the altar of the Lord in *J'*,
13 the high places that were before *J'*,
20 upon them, and returned to *J'*.
23 was holden to the Lord in *J'*.
24 spied in the land of Judah and in *J'*,
27 off this city *J'* which I have chosen,
30 brought him to *J'*, and buried him
31 and he reigned three months in *J'*.
33 that he might not reign in *J'*;
36 and he reigned eleven years in *J'*.
24: 4 for he filled *J'* with innocent blood;
8 and he reigned in *J'* three months.
8 the daughter of Elnathan of *J'*.
10 king of Babylon came up against *J'*,
14 he carried away all *J'*, and all the
15 carried he into captivity from *J'* to
18 and he reigned eleven years in *J'*.
20 it came to pass in *J'* and Judah,
25: 1 he, and all his host, against *J'*,
8 of the king of Babylon, unto *J'*:
9 house, and all the houses of *J'*,
10 down the walls of *J'* round about.
1Ch 3: 4 in *J'* he reigned thirty and three
5 these were born unto him in *J'*;
6: 10 temple that Solomon built in *J'*:)
15 Lord carried away Judah and *J'*
32 built the house of the Lord in *J'*:
8: 28 chief men. These dwelt in *J'*.
32 dwelt with their brethren in *J'*,
9: 3 in *J'* dwelt of the children of Judah,
34 their generations; these dwelt at *J'*.
38 dwelt with their brethren at *J'*,
11: 4 David and all Israel went to *J'*,
14: 3 And David took more wives at *J'*:
4 of his children which he had in *J'*;
15: 3 gathered all Israel together to *J'*,
18: 7 Hadarezer, and brought them to *J'*.
19: 15 into the city. Then Joab came to *J'*.
20: 1 But David tarried at *J'*. And Joab
3 and all the people returned to *J'*.
21: 4 throughout all Israel, and came to *J'*.
15 And God sent an angel unto *J'* to
16 in his hand stretched out over *J'*.
23: 25 that they may dwell in *J'* for ever:
28: 1 with all the valiant men, unto *J'*.
29: 27 and three years reigned he in *J'*.
2Ch 1: 4 he had pitched a tent for it at *J'*.
13 high place that was at Gibeon to *J'*,
14 cities, and with the king at *J'*.
15 silver and gold at *J'* as plenteous
2: 7 are with me in Judah and in *J'*,
2Ch 2: 16 and thou shalt carry it up to *J'*.
3: 1 to build the house of the Lord at *J'*
5: 2 unto *J'*, to bring up the ark of
6: 6 But I have chosen *J'*, that my name
8: 6 that Solomon desired to build in *J'*,
9: 1 Solomon with hard questions at *J'*,
25 cities, and with the king at *J'*.
27 king made silver in *J'* as stones,
30 And Solomon reigned in *J'* over all
10: 18 him up to his chariot, to flee to *J'*.
11: 1 when Rehoboam was come to *J'*,
5 Rehoboam dwelt in *J'*, and built
14 and came to Judah and *J'*:
16 the Lord God of Israel came to *J'*,
12: 2 king of Egypt came up against *J'*,
4 pertained to Judah, and came to *J'*.
5 that were gathered together to *J'*
7 shall not be poured out upon *J'*
9 king of Egypt came up against *J'*,
13 strengthened himself in *J'*, and
13 he reigned seventeen years in *J'*,
13: 2 He reigned three years in *J'*. His
14: 15 in abundance, and returned to *J'*.
15: 10 gathered themselves together at *J'*
17: 13 mighty men of valour, were in *J'*.
19: 1 returned to his house in peace to *J'*.
4 Jehoshaphat dwelt at *J'*: and he
8 in *J'* did Jehoshaphat set of the
8 when they returned to *J'*.
20: 5 the congregation of Judah and *J'*,
15 all Judah, and ye inhabitants of *J'*,
17 the Lord with you, O Judah and *J'*:
18 the inhabitants of *J'* fell before the
20 O Judah, and ye inhabitants of *J'*;
27 every man of Judah and *J'*,
27 of them, to go again to *J'* with joy;
28 they came to *J'* with psalteries and
31 reigned twenty and five years in *J'*.
21: 5 and he reigned eight years in *J'*.
11 the inhabitants of *J'* to commit
13 inhabitants of *J'* to go a whoring,
20 he reigned in *J'* eight years, and
22: 1 inhabitants of *J'* made Ahaziah his
2 reign, and he reigned one year in *J'*.
23: 2 of Israel, and they came to *J'*.
24: 1 and he reigned forty years in *J'*.
6 Judah and out of *J'* the collection,
9 proclamation through Judah and *J'*,
18 wrath came upon Judah and *J'* for
23 and they came to Judah and *J'*, and
25: 1 reigned twenty and nine years in *J'*.
1 mother's name...Jehoaddan of *J'*.
23 and brought him to *J'*, and brake
23 brake down the wall of *J'* from the
27 a conspiracy against him in *J'*;
26: 3 he reigned fifty and two years in *J'*.
3 name also was Jecoliah of *J'*.
9 Moreover Uzziah built towers in *J'*
15 he made in *J'* engines, invented
27: 1 and he reigned sixteen years in *J'*.
8 and reigned sixteen years in *J'*.
28: 1 and he reigned sixteen years in *J'*:
10 under the children of Judah and *J'*
24 him altars in every corner of *J'*.
27 buried him in the city, even in *J'*:
29: 1 reigned nine and twenty years in *J'*.
8 of the Lord was upon Judah and *J'*,
30: 1 come to the house of the Lord at *J'*,
2 and all the congregation in *J'*,
3 gathered themselves together to *J'*.
5 unto the Lord God of Israel at *J'*:
11 themselves, and came to *J'*.
13 there assembled at *J'* much people
14 took away the altars that were in *J'*,
21 of Israel that were present at *J'*
26 So there was great joy in *J'*: for
26 Israel there was not the like in *J'*.
31: 4 the people that dwelt in *J'* to give
32: 2 he was purposed to fight against *J'*,
9 of Assyria send his servants to *J'*,
9 and unto all Judah that were at *J'*,
10 that ye abide in the siege in *J'*?
12 and commanded Judah and *J'*,
18 people of *J'* that were on the wall,
19 they spake against the God of *J'*,
22 Hezekiah and the inhabitants of *J'*
23 brought gifts unto the Lord to *J'*:
25 upon him, and upon Judah and *J'*.
26 both he and the inhabitants of *J'*,
33 inhabitants of *J'* did him honour at
33: 1 he reigned fifty and five years in *J'*:
4 In *J'* shall my name be for ever.
7 and in *J'*, which I have chosen
9 and the inhabitants of *J'* to err,
13 him again to *J'* into his kingdom.
15 in *J'*, and cast them out of the city.
21 reign, and reigned two years in *J'*.
34: 1 reigned in *J'* one and thirty years.
3 he began to purge Judah and *J'*
5 altars, and cleansed Judah and *J'*.
7 land of Israel, he returned to *J'*.
9 Benjamin; and they returned to *J'*.
22 (now she dwelt in *J'* in the college:)
29 all the elders of Judah and *J'*.
30 of Judah, and the inhabitants of *J'*,
32 he caused all that were present in *J'*
32 the inhabitants of *J'* did according
35: 1 kept a passover unto the Lord in *J'*:
18 present, and the inhabitants of *J'*.
24 they brought him to *J'*, and he died,
24 Judah and *J'* mourned for Josiah.
36: 1 him king in his father's stead in *J'*.
2 and he reigned three months in *J'*.
3 king of Egypt put him down at *J'*,
4 his brother king over Judah and *J'*,
5 and he reigned eleven years in *J'*:

2Ch 36: 9 three months and ten days in J':
10 his brother king over Judah and J'.
11 and reigned eleven years in J'.
14 Lord which he had hallowed in J'.
19 and brake down the wall of J'.
23 me to build him an house in J'.
Ezr 1: 2 me to build him an house at J'.
3 with him, and let him go up to J'.
3 (he is the God,) which is in J'.
4 for the house of God that is in J'.
5 house of the Lord which is in J'.
7 had brought forth out of J'.
11 brought up from Babylon unto J'.
2: 1 and came again unto J' and Judah,
68 house of the Lord which is at J',
3: 1 together as one man to J'.
8 coming unto the house of God at J',
8 come out of the captivity unto J';
4: 6 the inhabitants of Judah and J'.
8 the scribe wrote a letter against J'
12 from thee to us are come unto J',
20 have been mighty kings also over J',
23 up in haste to J' unto the Jews,
24 of the house of God which is at J'.
5: 1 the Jews that were in Judah and J'
2 the house of God which is at J':
14 out of the temple that was in J',
15 them into the temple that is in J',
16 of the house of God which is in J':
17 to build this house of God at J',
6: 3 concerning the house of God at J',
5 out of the temple which is at J',
5 again unto the temple which is at J',
9 of the priests which are at J',
12 this house of God which is at J'.
18 the service of God, which is at J';
7: 7 and the Nethinims, unto J',
8 he came to J' in the fifth month,
9 of the fifth month came he to J',
13 their own freewill to go up to J',
14 enquire concerning Judah and J',
15 of Israel, whose habitation is in J',
16 house of their God which is in J':
17 house of your God which is in J'.
19 deliver thou before the God of J'.
27 house of the Lord which is in J':
8: 29 at J', in the chambers of the house
30 to bring them to J' unto the house
31 of the first month, to go unto J':
32 And we came to J', and abode there
9: 9 give us a wall in Judah and in J'.
10: 7 made proclamation throughout...J'
7 gather themselves together unto J';
9 together unto J' within three days.
Ne 1: 2 of the captivity, and concerning J'.
3 the wall of J' also is broken down,
2: 11 So I came to J', and was there three
12 God had put in my heart to do at J':
13 viewed the walls of J', which were
17 how J' lieth waste, and the gates
17 let us build up the wall of J', that
20 nor right, nor memorial, in J'.
3: 8 fortified J' unto the broad wall.
9 Hur, the ruler of the half part of J'.
12 the ruler of the half part of J',
4: 7 that the walls of J' were made up,
8 to come and to fight against J',
22 with his servant lodge within J',
6: 7 prophets to preach of thee at J',
7: 2 ruler of the palace, charge over J':
3 Let not the gates of J' be opened
3 watches of the inhabitants of J',
6 and came again to J' and to Judah,
8: 15 proclaim in...their cities, and in J',
11: 1 the rulers of the people dwelt at J':
1 of ten to dwell in J' the holy city,
2 offered themselves to dwell at J'.
3 of the province that dwelt in J':
4 at J' dwelt certain of the children
6 the sons of Perez that dwelt at J'
22 overseer also of the Levites at J'
12: 27 at the dedication of the wall of J'
27 to bring them to J', to keep the
28 the plain country round about J',
29 them villages round about J'.
43 the joy of J' was heard even afar off.
13: 6 But in all this time was not I at J':
7 I came to J', and understood of the
15 they brought into J' on the sabbath
16 the children of Judah, and in J'.
19 the gates of J' began to be dark
20 all kind of ware lodged without J'
Es 2: 6 Who had been carried away from J'
Ps 51: 18 Zion: build thou the walls of J'.
68: 29 of thy temple at J' shall kings bring
79: 1 defiled; they have laid J' on heaps.
3 shed like water round about J';
102: 21 Lord in Zion, and his praise in J';
116: 19 house, in the midst of thee, O J'.
122: 2 shall stand within thy gates, O J'.
3 J' is builded as a city that is
6 Pray for the peace of J': they shall
125: 2 the mountains are round about J',
128: 5 thou shalt see the good of J' all the
135: 21 out of Zion, which dwelleth at J'.
137: 5 If I forget thee, O J', let my right
6 if I prefer not J' above my chief joy.
7 children of Edom in the day of J';
147: 2 The Lord doth build up J': he
12 Praise the Lord, O J'; praise thy
Ec 1: 1 the son of David, king in J'.
12 Preacher was king over Israel in J'.
16 they that have been before me in J':
2: 7 above all that were in J' before me:
9 than all that were before me in J':
Ca 1: 5 but comely, O ye daughters of J',

Ca 2: 7 I charge you, O ye daughters of J',
3: 5 I charge you, O ye daughters of J',
10 with love, for the daughters of J'.
5: 8 I charge you, O daughters of J',
16 this is my friend, O daughters of J'.
6: 4 O my love, as Tirzah, comely as J',
8: 4 I charge you, O daughters of J',
Isa 1: 1 he saw concerning Judah and J'
2: 1 Amoz saw concerning Judah and J'.
3 and the word of the Lord from J'.
3: 1 take away from J' and from Judah
8 J' is ruined, and Judah is fallen:
4: 3 and he that remaineth in J', shall be
3 is written among the living in J':
4 shall have purged the blood of J'
5: 3 now, O inhabitants of J', and men of
7: 1 went up toward J' to war against
8: 14 for a snare to the inhabitants of J'.
10: 10 graven images did excel them of J'
11 her idols, so do to J' and her idols?
12 work upon mount Zion and on J',
32 the daughter of Zion, the hill of J'.
22: 10 ye have numbered the houses of J',
21 be a father to the inhabitants of J',
24: 23 shall reign in mount Zion, and in J',
27: 13 the Lord in the holy mount at J'.
28: 14 that rule this people which is in J'.
30: 19 the people shall dwell in Zion at J':
31: 5 so will the Lord of hosts defend J';
9 fire is in Zion, and his furnace in J'.
33: 20 eyes shall see J' a quiet habitation,
36: 2 sent Rabshakeh from Lachish to J'
7 away, and said to Judah and to J',
20 Lord should deliver J' out of my
37: 10 J' shall not be given into the hand
22 the daughter of J' hath shaken her
32 out of J' shall go forth a remnant,
40: 2 Speak ye comfortably to J', and cry
9 O J', that bringest good tidings,
41: 27 give to J' one that bringeth good
44: 26 saith to J', Thou shalt be inhabited;
28 saying to J', Thou shalt be built;
51: 17 Awake, awake, stand up, O J',
52: 1 put on thy beautiful garments, O J',
2 arise, and sit down, O J': loose
9 sing together, ye waste places of J':
9 his people, he hath redeemed J'.
62: 6 set watchmen upon thy walls, O J',
7 till he make J' a praise in the earth.
64: 10 Zion is a wilderness, J' a desolation.
65: 18 I create J' a rejoicing, and her
19 I will rejoice in J', and joy in my
66: 10 Rejoice ye with J', and be glad with
13 and ye shall be comforted in J'.
20 beasts, to my holy mountain J',
Jer 1: 3 unto the carrying away of J' captive
15 at the entering of the gates of J',
2: 2 Go and cry in the ears of J', saying,
3: 17 shall call J' the throne of the Lord;
17 it, to the name of the Lord, to J':
4: 3 Lord to the men of Judah and J',
4 men of Judah and inhabitants of J':
5 ye in Judah, and publish in J';
10 greatly deceived this people and J',
11 it be said to this people and to J',
14 O J', wash thine heart from
16 publish against J', that watchers
5: 1 to and fro through the streets of J',
6: 1 to flee out of the midst of J',
6 trees, and cast a mount against J':
8 Be thou instructed, O J', lest my
7: 17 of Judah and in the streets of J'?
29 Cut off thine hair, O J', and cast it
34 Judah, and from the streets of J',
8: 1 the bones of the inhabitants of J',
5 is this people of J' slidden back
9: 11 I will make J' heaps, and a den of
11: 2 Judah, and to the inhabitants of J';
6 of Judah, and in the streets of J',
9 and among the inhabitants of J'.
12 of Judah and inhabitants of J' go,
13 to the number of streets of J'
13: 9 of Judah, and the great pride of J'.
13 all the inhabitants of J', and
27 Woe unto thee, O J'! wilt thou not
14: 2 and the cry of J' is gone up.
16 shall be cast out in the streets of J'
15: 4 Judah, for that which he did in J'.
5 shall have pity upon thee, O J'?
17: 19 go out, and in all the gates of J';
20 all the inhabitants of J', that enter
21 nor bring it in by the gates of J';
25 Judah, and the inhabitants of J':
26 Judah, and from the places about J',
27 even entering in at the gates of J'
27 it shall devour the palaces of J',
18: 11 Judah, and to the inhabitants of J',
19: 3 of Judah, and inhabitants of J';
7 void the counsel of Judah and J'
13 the houses of J', and the houses of
22: 19 cast forth beyond the gates of J'.
23: 14 have seen also in the prophets of J'
15 the prophets of J' is profaneness
24: 1 the carpenters and smiths, from J',
8 his princes, and the residue of J',
25: 2 to all the inhabitants of J', saying,
18 To wit, J', and the cities of Judah,
26: 18 a field, and J' shall become heaps,
27: 3 of the messengers which come to J'
18 of the king of Judah, and at J', go
20 king of Judah from J' to Babylon,
20 and all the nobles of Judah and J';
21 of the king of Judah and of J';
29: 1 Jeremiah the prophet sent from J'
1 away captive from J' to Babylon;
2 the princes of Judah and J', and

Jer 29: 2 the smiths, were departed from J';)
4 caused to be carried away from J'
20 I have sent from J' to Babylon:
25 unto all the people that are at J',
32: 2 king of Babylon's army besieged J':
32 of Judah, and the inhabitants of J'.
44 and in the places about J', and in
33: 10 the streets of J', that are desolate,
13 and in the places about J', and in
16 be saved, and J' shall dwell safely:
34: 1 all the people, fought against J',
6 unto Zedekiah king of Judah in J',
7 Babylon's army fought against J',
8 with all the people which were at J',
19 of Judah, and the princes of J',
35: 11 Come, and let us go to J' for fear
11 of the Syrians: so we dwell at J'.
13 of Judah and the inhabitants of J',
17 upon all the inhabitants of J' all
36: 9 the Lord to all the people in J',
9 from the cities of Judah unto J'.
31 and upon the inhabitants of J',
37: 5 Chaldeans that besieged J' heard
5 of them, they departed from J'.
11 was broken up from J' for fear of
12 Jeremiah went forth out of J' to go
38: 28 until the day that J' was taken:
28 he was there when J' was taken.
39: 1 Babylon and all his army against J',
8 and brake down the walls of J'.
40: 1 away captive of J' and Judah,
42: 18 forth upon the inhabitants of J';
44: 2 evil that I have brought upon J',
6 of Judah and in the streets of J';
9 of Judah, and in the streets of J'?
13 as I have punished J', by the sword,
17 of Judah, and in the streets of J':
21 of Judah, and in the streets of J',
51: 35 inhabitants of Chaldea, shall J' say.
50 and let J' come into your mind.
52: 1 and he reigned eleven years in J'.
3 it came to pass in J' and Judah,
4 he and all his army, against J',
12 served the king of Babylon, into J',
13 and all the houses of J', and all the
14 brake down all the walls of J' round
29 he carried away captive from J'
La 1: 7 J' remembered in the days of her
8 J' hath grievously sinned;
17 J' is as a menstruous woman
2: 10 virgins of J' hang down their heads
13 I liken to thee, O daughter of J'?
15 their head at the daughter of J',
4: 12 have entered into the gates of J'.
Eze 4: 1 pourtray upon it the city, even J':
7 set thy face toward the siege of J',
16 I will break the staff of bread in J':
5: 5 saith the Lord God; This is J':
8: 3 me in the visions of God to J',
9: 4 of the city, through the midst of J',
8 pouring out of thy fury upon J'?
11: 15 the inhabitants of J' have said,
12: 10 burden concerneth the prince in J',
19 Lord God of the inhabitants of J',
13: 16 which prophesy concerning J',
14: 21 my four sore judgments upon J',
22 evil that I have brought upon J',
15: 6 so will I give the inhabitants of J'.
16: 2 cause J' to know her abominations,
3 Thus saith the Lord God unto J';
17: 12 the king of Babylon is come to J',
21: 2 Son of man, set thy face toward J',
20 and to Judah in J' the defenced.
22 right hand was the divination for J',
22: 19 will gather you into the midst of J'.
23: 4 Samaria is Aholah, and J' Aholibah.
24: 2 of Babylon set himself against J'
26: 2 that Tyrus hath said against J',
33: 21 one that had escaped out of J' came
36: 38 the flock of J' in her solemn feasts;
Da 1: 1 came Nebuchadnezzar...unto J',
5: 2 out of the temple which was in J';
3 the house of God which was at J';
6: 10 open in his chamber toward J',
9: 2 years in the desolations of J'.
7 Judah, and to the inhabitants of J',
12 done as hath been done upon J'.
16 be turned away from thy city J',
16 J' and thy people are become a
25 to restore and to build J' unto the
Joe 2: 32 Zion and in J' shall be deliverance,
3: 1 again the captivity of Judah and J',
6 the children of J' have ye sold unto
16 of Zion, and utter his voice from J';
17 mountain: then shall J' be holy,
20 J' from generation to generation.
Am 1: 2 Zion, and utter his voice from J';
2: 5 it shall devour the palaces of J'.
Ob 11 his gates, and cast lots upon J',
20 Zarephath; and the captivity of J',
Mic 1: 1 he saw concerning Samaria and J'.
5 places of Judah? are they not J'?
9 the gate of my people, even to J'.
12 from the Lord unto the gate of J'.
3: 10 with blood, and J' with iniquity.
12 a field, and J' shall become heaps,
4: 2 and the word of the Lord from J'.
8 shall come to the daughter of J'.
Zep 1: 4 and upon all the inhabitants of J';
12 that I will search J' with candles,
3: 14 with all the heart, O daughter of J'.
16 In that day it shall be said to J',
Zec 1: 12 long wilt thou not have mercy on J
14 I am jealous for J' and for Zion
16 I am returned to J' with mercies:
16 shall be stretched forth upon J'.

Zec 1:17 Zion, and shall yet choose J'.
19 scattered Judah, Israel, and J'.
2: 2 he said unto me, To measure J'.
4 J' shall be inhabited as towns
12 land, and shall choose J' again.
3: 2 Lord that hath chosen J' rebuke
7: 7 J' was inhabited and in prosperity,
8: 3 and will dwell in the midst of J':
3 J' shall be called a city of truth;
4 women dwell in the streets of J',
8 they shall dwell in the midst of J':
15 to do well unto J' and to the house
22 come to seek the Lord of hosts in J',
9: 9 shout, O daughter of J': behold,
10 Ephraim, and the horse from J',
12: 2 I will make J' a cup of trembling
2 both against Judah and against J'.
3 make J' a burdensome stone for all
5 The inhabitants of J' shall be my
6 and J' shall be inhabited again
6 in her own place, even in J'.
7 the glory of the inhabitants of J'
8 Lord defend the inhabitants of J';
9 the nations that come against J'.
10 and upon the inhabitants of J', the
11 there be a great mourning in J',
13: 1 and to the inhabitants of J' for sin
14: 2 I will gather all nations against J'
4 which is before J' on the east,
8 living waters shall go out from J';
10 from Geba to Rimmon south of J':
11 but J' shall be safely inhabited.
12 people that have fought against J';
14 And Judah also shall fight at J';
16 the nations which came against J'
17 earth unto J' to worship the King,
21 every pot in J' and in Judah shall
Mal 2:11 is committed in Israel and in J';
3: 4 offering of Judah and J' be pleasant
M't 2: 1 wise men from the east to J',
3 was troubled, and all J' with him.
3: 5 went out to him J', and all Judæa,
4:25 from J', and from Judæa, and from
5:35 neither by J'; for it is the city of
15: 1 and Pharisees, which were of J',
16:21 how that he must go unto J', and
20:17 And Jesus going up to J' took the
18 Behold, we go up to J'; and the
21: 1 And when they drew nigh unto J',
10 when he was come into J', all the
23:37 O J', J', thou that killest the
M'r 1: 5 the land of Judæa, and they of J',
3: 8 And from J', and from Idumæa, and
22 scribes which came down from J'
7: 1 of the scribes, which came from J'.
10:32 were in the way going up to J';
33 Saying, Behold, we go up to J';
11: 1 when they came nigh to J', unto
11 Jesus entered into J', and into the
15 they come to J': and Jesus went
27 And they come again to J': and as
15:41 which came up with him unto J'.
Lu 2:22 they brought him to J', to present
25 there was a man in J', whose
38 that looked for redemption in J'.
41 his parents went to J' every year
42 went up to J' after the custom
43 child Jesus tarried behind in J';
45 not, they turned back again to J',
4: 9 he brought him to J', and set him
5:17 town of Galilee, and Judæa, and J':
6:17 of people out of all Judæa and J',
9:31 which he should accomplish at J'.
51 stedfastly set his face to go to J',
53 was as though he would go to J'.
10:30 man went down from J' to Jericho,
13: 4 above all men that dwelt in J'?
22 teaching, and journeying toward J'.
33 be that a prophet perish out of J'.
34 O J', J', which killest the prophets,
17:11 it came to pass, as he went to J',
18:31 unto them, Behold, we go up to J',
19:11 parable, because he was nigh to J',
28 he went before, ascending up to J'.
21:20 see J' compassed with armies,
24 and J' shall be trodden down of the
23: 7 himself also was at J' at that
28 Daughters of J', weep not for me,
24:13 from J' about threescore furlongs.
18 him, Art thou only a stranger in J',
33 the same hour, and returned to J',
47 among all nations, beginning at J'.
49 tarry ye in the city of J', until ye
52 and returned to J' with great joy:
Joh 1:19 sent priests and Levites from J'
2:13 at hand, and Jesus went up to J',
23 when he was in J' at the passover,
4:20 in J' is the place where men ought
21 in this mountain, nor yet at J',
45 things that he did at J' at the feast:
5: 1 the Jews; and Jesus went up to J'.
2 is at J' by the sheep market a pool,
7:25 Then said some of them of J', Is
10:22 was at J' the feast of the dedication,
11:18 Now Bethany was nigh unto J',
55 went out of the country up to J'
12:12 heard that Jesus was coming to J',
Ac 1: 4 they should not depart from J',
8 be witnesses unto me both in J',
12 Then returned they unto J' from
12 is from J' a sabbath day's journey.
19 known unto all the dwellers at J';
2: 5 there were dwelling at J' Jews,
14 Judæa, and all ye that dwell at J',
4: 6 were gathered together at J'.
16 to all them that dwell in J';

Ac 5:16 of the cities round about unto J',
28 ye have filled J' with your doctrine,
6: 7 disciples multiplied in J' greatly;
8: 1 the church which was at J';
14 the apostles which were at J' heard
25 returned to J', and preached the
26 that goeth down from J' unto Gaza,
27 and had come to J' for to worship,
9: 2 might bring them bound unto J'.
13 evil he hath done to thy saints at J'
21 which called on this name in J',
26 And when Saul was come to J',
28 them coming in and going out at J'.
10:39 in the land of the Jews, and in J';
11: 2 when Peter was come up to J',
22 ears of the church which was in J':
27 prophets from J' unto Antioch.
12:25 and Saul returned from J',
13:13 John departing...returned to J'.
27 For they that dwell at J', and their
31 up with him from Galilee to J',
15: 2 go up to J' unto the apostles and
4 And when they were come to J',
16: 4 and elders which were at J'.
18:21 keep this feast that cometh in J':
19:21 Macedonia and Achaia, to go to J',
20:16 to be at J' the day of Pentecost.
22 I go bound in the spirit unto J',
21: 4 that he should not go up to J'.
11 So shall the Jews at J' bind the man
12 besought him not to go up to J'.
13 to die at J' for the name of the Lord
15 up our carriages, and went up to J'.
17 And when we were come to J',
31 band, that all J' was in an uproar.
22: 5 which were there bound unto J',
17 that, when I was come again to J',
18 and get thee quickly out of J':
23:11 as thou hast testified of me in J',
24:11 since I went up to J' for to worship.
25: 1 he ascended from Cæsarea to J'.
3 that he would send for him to J',
7 Jews which came down from J'
9 Wilt thou go up to J', and there be
15 About whom, when I was at J', the
20 him whether he would go to J',
24 dealt with me, both at J', and also
26: 4 first among mine own nation at J',
10 Which thing I also did in J':
20 unto them of Damascus, and at J',
28:17 yet was I delivered prisoner from J'
Ro 15:19 so that from J', and round about
25 But now I go unto J' to minister
26 for the poor saints which are at J'.
31 that my service which I have for J'
1Co 16: 3 to bring your liberality unto J'.
Ga 1:17 Neither went I up to J' to them
18 I went up to J' to see Peter,
2: 1 I went up again to J' with Barnabas,
4:25 and answereth to J' which now is,
26 But J' which is above is free, which
Heb12:22 of the living God, the heavenly J',
Re 3:12 the city of my God, which is new J',
21: 2 saw the holy city, new J', coming
10 great city, the holy J', descending

Jerusalem's (*je-ru'-sa-lems*)
1Ki 11:13 for J' sake which I have chosen.
32 David's sake, and for J' sake, the
Isa 62: 1 and for J' sake I will not rest, until

Jerusha (*je-ru'-shah*) See also JERUSHAH.
2Ki 15:33 And his mother's name was J', the

Jerushah (*je-ru'-shah*) See also JERUSHA.
2Ch 27: 1 His mother's name also was J',

Jesaiah (*jes-a-i'-ah*) See also ISAIAH; JESHAIAH.
1Ch 3:21 of Hananiah; Pelatiah, and J':
Ne 11: 7 the son of Ithiel, the son of J'.

Jeshaiah (*jesh-a-i'-ah*) See also JESAIAH.
1Ch 25: 3 and Zeri, and J', Hashabiah, and
15 The eighth to J', he, his sons, and
26:25 Rehabiah his son, and J' his son,
Ezr 8: 7 of Elam; J' the son of Athaliah,
19 with him J' of the sons of Merari.

Jeshanah (*je-sha'-nah*)
2Ch 13:19 and J' with the towns thereof, and

Jesharelah (*je-shar'-e-lah*) See also ASARELAH.
1Ch 25:14 The seventh to J', he, his sons,

Jeshebeab (*je-sheb'-e-ab*)
1Ch 24:13 to Huppah, the fourteenth to J',

Jesher (*je'-shur*)
1Ch 2:18 sons are these; J', and Shobab,

Jeshimon (*jesh'-im-on*)
Nu 21:20 Pisgah, which looketh toward J'.
23:28 of Peor, that looketh toward J'.
1Sa 23:19 which is on the south of J'?
24 in the plain on the south of J'.
26: 1 of Hachilah, which is before J'?
3 hill of Hachilah, which is before J',

Jeshimoth See BETH-JESHIMOTH.

Jeshishai (*jesh'-i-shahee*)
1Ch 5:14 the son of J', the son of Jahdo,

Jeshohaiah (*je-sho-ha-i'-ah*)
1Ch 4:36 Elioenai, and Jaakobah, and J',

Jeshua (*jesh'-u-ah*) See also JESHUAH; JOSHUA.
2Ch 31:15 were Eden, and Miniamin, and J',
Ezr 2: 2 J', Nehemiah, Seraiah, Reelaiah,
6 of the children of J' and Joab, two
36 of Jedaiah, of the house of J', nine
40 the children of J' and Kadmiel, of
3: 2 stood up J' the son of Jozadak,
8 and J' the son of Jozadak, and the

Ezr 3: 9 Then stood J' with his sons and his
4: 3 But Zerubbabel, and J', and the rest
5: 2 and J' the son of Jozadak,
8:33 them was Jozabad the son of J',
10:18 the sons of J' the son of Jozadak,
Ne 3:19 to him repaired Ezer the son of J',
7: 7 with Zerubbabel, J', Nehemiah,
11 of the children of J' and Joab,
39 of Jedaiah, of the house of J',
43 the children of J', of Kadmiel, and
8: 7 Also J', and Bani, and Sherebiah,
17 since the days of J' the son of Nun
9: 4 stairs, of the Levites, J', and Bani,
5 Then the Levites, J', and Kadmiel,
10: 9 both J' the son of Azaniah, Binnui
11:26 And at J', and at Moladah, and at
12: 1 the son of Shealtiel, and J':
7 of their brethren in the days of J'.
8 the Levites: J', Binnui, Kadmiel,
10 And J' begat Joiakim, Joiakim also
24 and J' the son of Kadmiel,
26 the days of Joiakim the son of J',

Jeshuah (*jesh'-u-ah*) See also JESHUA.
1Ch 24:11 The ninth to J', the tenth to

Jeshurun (*jesh'-u-run*) See also ISRAEL; JESURUN.
De 32:15 But J' waxed fat, and kicked:
33: 5 he was king in J', when the heads
26 is none like unto the God of J',

Jesiah (*je-si'-ah*) See also ISHIAH.
1Ch 12: 6 Elkanah, and J', and Azareel,
23:20 Micah the first, and J' the second

Jesimiel (*je-sim'-e-el*)
1Ch 4:36 and Adiel, and J', and Benaiah,

Jesimoth See BETH-JESIMOTH.

Jesse (*jes'-se*)
Ru 4:17 he is the father of J', the father
22 Obed begat J', and J' begat David.
1Sa 16: 1 send thee to J' the Beth-lehemite:
3 call J' to the sacrifice, and I will
5 And he sanctified J' and his sons,
8 J' called Abinadab, and made him
9 Then J' made Shammah to pass
10 J' made seven of his sons to pass
10 Samuel said unto J', The Lord hath
11 Samuel said unto J', Are here all
11 And Samuel said unto J', Send and
18 Behold, I have seen a son of J'
19 Saul sent messengers unto J', and
20 J' took an ass laden with bread,
22 Saul sent to J', saying, Let David, I
17:12 whose name was J'; and he had
13 three eldest sons of J' went and
17 J' said unto David his son, Take
20 and went, as J' had commanded
58 I am the son of thy servant J' the
20:27 cometh not the son of J' to meat,
30 chosen the son of J' to thine own
31 as long as the son of J' liveth upon
22: 7 the son of J' give every one of you
8 made a league with the son of J',
9 I saw the son of J' coming to Nob,
13 against me, thou and the son of J',
25:10 David? and who is the son of J'?
2Sa 20: 1 we inheritance in the son of J':
23: 1 David the son of J' said, and the
1Ki 12:16 we inheritance in the son of J':
1Ch 2:12 begat Obed, and Obed begat J',
13 And J' begat his firstborn Eliab,
10:14 kingdom unto David the son of J'.
12:18 and on thy side, thou son of J':
29:26 David the son of J' reigned over all
2Ch 10:16 none inheritance in the son of J':
11:18 daughter of Eliab the son of J';
Ps 72:20 The prayers of David the son of J'
Isa 11: 1 forth a rod out of the stem of J',
10 that day there shall be a root of J',
M't 1: 5 Obed of Ruth; and Obed begat J';
6 And J' begat David the king; and
Lu 3:32 Which was the son of J', which was
Ac 13:22 I have found David the son of J',
Ro 15:12 saith, There shall be a root of J',

jesting
Eph 5: 4 nor foolish talking, nor j', which

Jesui (*jes'-u-i*) See also ISHUI; JESUITES.
Nu 26:44 of J', the family of the Jesuites:

Jesuites (*jes'-u-ites*)
Nu 26:44 of Jesui, the family of the J': of

Jesurun (*jes'-u-run*) See also JESHURUN.
Isa 44: 2 thou, J', whom I have chosen.

Jesus (*je'-zus*) See also BAR-JESUS; CHRIST; JESUS'; JOSHUA; JUSTUS.
M't 1: 1 book of the generation of J' Christ,
16 of whom was born J', who is called
18 birth of J' Christ was on this wise:
21 son, and thou shalt call his name J':
25 son: and he called his name J'.
2: 1 when J' was born in Bethlehem of
3:13 cometh J' from Galilee to Jordan
15 J' answering said unto him, Suffer
16 J', when he was baptized, went up
4: 1 was J' led up of the spirit into the
7 J' said unto him, It is written
10 saith J' unto him, Get thee hence,
12 J' had heard that John was cast
17 From that time J' began to preach,
18 J', walking by the sea of Galilee,
23 J' went about all Galilee, teaching
7:28 when J' had ended these sayings,
8: 3 J' put forth his hand, and touched
4 J' saith unto him, See thou tell no
5 J' was entered into Capernaum,

M't 8: 7 J' saith unto him, I will come and
10 When J' heard it, he marvelled,
13 J' said unto the centurion, Go thy
14 J' was come into Peter's house,
18 Now when J' saw great multitudes
20 J' saith unto him, The foxes have
22 But J' said unto him, Follow me;
29 do with thee, J', thou son of God?
34 the whole city came out to meet J':
9: 2 J' seeing their faith said unto the
4 And J' knowing their thoughts said,
9 And as J' passed forth from thence,
10 pass, as J' sat at meat in the house,
12 when J' heard that, he said unto
15 J' said unto them, Can the children
19 J' arose, and followed him, and so
22 J' turned him about, and when he
23 when J' came into the ruler's house,
27 when J' departed thence, two blind
28 J' saith unto them, Believe ye that
30 and Jesus straitly charged them,
35 And J' went about all the cities and
10: 5 These twelve J' sent forth, and
11: 1 J'...made an end of commanding
4 J' answered and said unto them,
7 J' began to say unto the multitudes
25 J' answered and said, I thank thee,
12: 1 J' went on the sabbath day through
15 But when J' knew it, he withdrew
25 J' knew their thoughts, and said
13: 1 same day went J' out of the house,
34 things spake J' unto the multitudes
36 Then J' sent the multitude away,
51 J' saith...,Have ye understood all
53 when J' had finished these parables,
57 But J' said unto them, A prophet is
14: 1 tetrarch heard of the fame of J',
12 and buried it, and went and told J'.
13 When J' heard of it, he departed
14 J' went forth, and saw a great
16 J' said unto them, They need not
22 J' constrained his disciples to get
25 fourth watch of the night J' went
27 straightway J' spake unto them,
29 he walked on the water, to go to J'.
31 immediately J' stretched forth his
15: 1 came to J' scribes and Pharisees,
16 J' said, Are ye also yet without
21 J' went thence, and departed into
28 J' answered and said unto her, O
29 J' departed from thence, and came
32 J' called his disciples unto him,
34 And J' saith unto them, How many
16: 6 Then J' said unto them, Take heed
8 Which when J' perceived, he said
13 When J' came into the coasts of
17 J' answered and said unto him,
20 should tell no man that he was J'
21 that time forth began J' to shew
24 said J' unto his disciples, If any
17: 1 And after six days J' taketh Peter,
4 and said unto J', Lord, it is good
7 J' came and touched them, and
8 they saw no man, save J' only.
9 the mountain, J' charged them,
11 J' answered and said unto them,
17 J' answered and said, O faithless
18 and J' rebuked the devil; and he
19 Then came the disciples to J' apart,
20 J' said unto them, Because of your
22 abode in Galilee, J' said unto them,
25 into the house, J' prevented him,
26 J' saith unto him, Then are the
18: 1 time came the disciples unto J',
2 J' called a little child unto him,
22 J' saith unto him, I say not unto
19: 1 when J' had finished these sayings,
14 J' said, Suffer little children, and
18 J' said, Thou shalt do no murder,
21 J' said unto him, If thou wilt be
23 said J' unto his disciples, Verily I
26 J' beheld them, and said unto them,
28 J' said unto them, Verily I say unto
20: 17 J' going up to Jerusalem took the
22 J' answered and said, Ye know not
25 J' called them unto him, and said,
30 when they heard that J' passed by,
32 J' stood still, and called them, and
34 J' had compassion on them, and
21: 1 Olives, then sent J' two disciples,
6 and did as J' commanded them,
11 This is J' the prophet of Nazareth
12 J' went into the temple of God, and
16 J' said unto them, Yea; have ye
21 J' answered and said unto them,
24 J' answered and said unto them, I
27 they answered J', and said, We
31 J' saith unto them, Verily I say
42 J' saith unto them, Did ye never
22: 1 J' answered and spake unto them
18 But J' perceived their wickedness,
29 J' answered and said unto them,
37 J' said unto him, thou shalt love
41 gathered together, J' asked them,
23: 1 Then spake J' to the multitude,
24: 1 J' went out, and departed from the
2 J' said unto them, See ye not all
4 J' answered and said unto them,
26: 1 when J' had finished all these
4 that they might take J' by subtilty,
6 J' was in Bethany, in the house of
10 When J' understood it, he said
17 bread the disciples came to J',
19 disciples did as J' had appointed
26 J' took bread, and blessed it,
31 saith J' unto them, All ye shall be

M't 26: 34 J' said unto him, Verily I say unto
36 cometh J' with them unto a place
49 forthwith he came to J', and said,
50 J' said unto him, Friend, wherefore
50 came they, and laid hands on J',
51 which were with J' stretched out
52 said J' unto him, Put up again thy
55 In that same hour said J' to the
57 they that had laid hold on J' led
59 sought false witness against J',
63 J' held his peace. And the high
64 J' saith unto him, Thou hast said:
69 Thou also wast with J' of Galilee.
71 was also with J' of Nazareth.
75 Peter remembered the word of J',
27: 1 took counsel against J' to put him
11 And J' stood before the governor:
11 J' said unto him, Thou sayest.
17 or J' which is called Christ?
20 ask Barabbas, and destroy J'.
22 then with J' which is called Christ?
26 he had scourged J', he delivered
27 soldiers of the governor took J'
37 This Is J' The King Of The Jews.
46 ninth hour J' cried with a loud
50 J', when he had cried again with a
54 watching J', saw the earthquake,
55 which followed J' from Galilee,
58 Pilate, and begged the body of J'.
28: 5 I know that ye seek J', which was
9 J' met them, saying, All hail. And
10 said J' unto them, Be not afraid:
16 into a mountain where J' had
18 J' came and spake unto them,
M'r 1: 1 beginning of the gospel of J' Christ,
9 J' came from Nazareth of Galilee,
14 J' came into Galilee, preaching the
17 J' said unto them, Come ye after
24 do with thee, thou J' of Nazareth?
25 J' rebuked him, saying, Hold thy
41 J', moved with compassion, put
45 insomuch that J' could no more
2: 5 When J' saw their faith, he said
8 when J' perceived in his spirit
15 that, as J' sat at meat in his house,
15 sat also together with J' and his
17 When J' heard it, he saith unto
19 J' said unto them, Can the children
3: 7 J' withdrew himself with his
5: 6 when he saw J' afar off, he ran and
7 What have I to do with thee, J',
13 And forthwith J' gave them leave.
15 they come to J', and see him that
19 Howbeit J' suffered him not, but
20 great things J' had done for him:
21 when J' was passed over again by
24 J' went with him; and much
27 When she had heard of J', came in
30 J', immediately knowing in
36 As soon as J' heard the word that
6: 4 J' said unto them, A prophet is not
30 themselves together unto J',
34 J', when he came out, saw much
7: 27 J' said unto her, Let the children
8: 1 J' called his disciples unto him,
17 And when J' knew it, he saith unto
27 And J' went out, and his disciples,
9: 2 six days J' taketh with him Peter,
4 and they were talking with J'.
5 Peter answered and said to J',
8 more, save J' only with themselves.
23 J' said unto him, If thou canst
25 When J' saw that the people came
27 J' took him by the hand, and lifted
39 J' said, Forbid him not: for there
10: 5 J' answered and said unto them,
14 when J' saw it, he was much
18 J' said unto him, Why callest thou
21 Then J' beholding him loved him,
23 J' looked round about, and saith
24 J' answereth again, and saith unto
27 J' looking upon them saith, With
29 J' answered and said, Verily I say
32 J' went before them: and they were
38 J' said unto them, Ye know not
39 J' said unto them, Ye shall indeed
42 J' called them to him, and saith
47 he heard that it was J' of Nazareth,
47 out, and say, J', thou son of David,
49 J' stood still, and commanded him
50 his garment, rose, and came to J'.
51 J' answered and said unto him,
52 And J' said unto him, Go thy way;
52 sight, and followed J' in the way.
11: 6 them even as J' had commanded:
7 they brought the colt to J', and
11 J' entered into Jerusalem, and into
14 J' answered and said unto it, No
15 J' went into the temple, and began
22 J' answering saith unto them,
29 J' answered and said unto them,
33 they answered and said unto J',
33 J' answering saith unto them,
12: 17 J' answering said unto them,
24 J' answering said unto them, Do
29 J' answered him, The first of all
34 when J' saw that he answered
35 J' answered and said, while he
41 J' sat over against the treasury,
13: 2 J' answering said unto him, Seest
5 J' answering them began to say,
14: 6 J' said, Let her alone; why trouble
18 eat, J' said, Verily I say unto you,
22 J' took bread, and blessed, and
27 And J' saith unto them, All ye shall
30 And J' saith unto him, Verily I say

M'r 14: 48 J' answered and said unto them,
53 they led J' away to the high priest:
55 sought for witness against J' to put
60 and asked J', saying, Answerest
62 And J' said, I am: and ye shall see
67 thou also wast with J' of Nazareth.
72 called to mind the word that J' said
15: 1 bound J', and carried him away,
5 J' yet answered nothing; so that
15 delivered J', when he had scourged
34 ninth hour J' cried with a loud
37 and J' cried with a loud voice, and
43 Pilate, and craved the body of J'.
16: 6 Ye seek J' of Nazareth, which was
9 Now when J' was risen early the
Lu 1: 31 son, and shalt call his name J'.
2: 21 his name was called J', which was
27 the parents brought in the child J',
43 the child J' tarried behind in
52 And J' increased in wisdom and
3: 21 pass, that J' also being baptized,
23 J' himself began to be about thirty
4: 1 And J' being full of the Holy Ghost
4 And J' answered him, saying, It is
8 J' answered and said unto him,
12 J' answering said unto him, It is
14 J' returned in the power of the
34 J' of Nazareth? art thou come to
35 And J' rebuked him, saying, Hold
5: 10 And J' said unto Simon, Fear not:
12 who seeing J' fell on his face,
19 his couch into the midst before J'.
22 But when J' perceived their
31 And J' answering said unto them,
6: 3 J' answering them said, Have ye
9 Then said J' unto them, I will ask
11 another what they might do to J'.
7: 3 And when he heard of J', he sent
4 when they came to J', they
6 Then J' went with them. And
9 When J' heard these things, he
19 two of his disciples sent them to J',
22 Then J' answering said unto them,
37 when she knew that J' sat at meat
40 And J' answering said unto him,
8: 28 When he saw J', he cried out, and
28 What have I to do with thee, J',
30 J' asked him, saying, What is thy
35 and came to J', and found the man,
35 sitting at the feet of J', clothed,
38 be with him: but J' sent him away,
39 great things J' had done unto him.
40 pass, that, when J' was returned,
45 J' said, Who touched me? When all
46 J' said, Somebody hath touched
50 But when J' heard it, he answered
9: 33 Peter said unto J', Master, it is
36 voice was past, J' was found alone.
41 And J' answering said, O faithless
42 And J' rebuked the unclean spirit,
43 every one at all things which J' did,
47 And J', perceiving the thought of
50 And J' said unto him, Forbid him
58 And J' said unto him, Foxes have
60 J' said unto him, Let the dead bury
62 And J' said unto him, No man,
10: 21 In that hour J' rejoiced in spirit,
29 said unto J', And who is my
30 And J' answering said, A certain
37 Then said J' unto him, Go, and do
41 And J' answered and said unto
13: 2 And J' answering said unto them,
12 And when J' saw her, he called her
14 J' had healed on the sabbath day,
14: 3 And J' answering spake unto the
17: 13 J', Master, have mercy on us.
17 J' answering said, Were there not
18: 16 J' called them unto him, and said,
19 J' said unto him, Why callest thou
22 Now when J' heard these things, he
24 when J' saw that he was very
37 him, that J' of Nazareth passeth by.
38 saying, J', thou son of David, have
40 J' stood, and commanded him to be
42 J' said unto him, Receive thy sight:
19: 1 J' entered and passed through
3 he sought to see J' who he was;
5 And when J' came to the place, he
9 And J' said unto him, This day is
35 they brought him to J': and they
35 the colt, and they set J' thereon.
20: 8 J' said unto them, Neither tell I
34 And J' answering said unto them,
22: 47 and drew near unto J' to kiss him.
48 J' said unto him, Judas, betrayest
51 J' answered and said, Suffer ye
52 Then J' said unto the chief priests,
63 the men that held J' mocked him,
23: 8 And when Herod saw J', he was
20 willing to release J', spake again
25 but he delivered J' to their will.
26 cross, that he might bear it after J'.
28 But J' turning unto them said,
34 Then said J', Father, forgive them;
42 he said unto J', Lord, remember
43 J' said unto him, Verily I say unto
46 when J' had cried with a loud
52 Pilate, and begged the body of J'.
24: 3 found not the body of the Lord J'.
15 J' himself drew near, and went
19 Concerning J' of Nazareth, which
36 J' himself stood in the midst of
Joh 1: 17 grace and truth came by J' Christ.
29 John seeth J' coming unto him,
36 looking upon J' as he walked, he
37 him speak, and they followed J'.

Joh 1:38 J· turned, and saw them following,
42 And he brought him to J·.
42 when J· beheld him, he said, Thou
43 The day following J· would go
45 prophets, did write, J· of Nazareth,
47 J· saw Nathanael coming to him,
48, 50 J· answered and said unto him,
2: 1 and the mother of J· was there:
2 J· was called, and his disciples, to
3 the mother of J· saith unto him,
4 J· saith unto her, Woman, what
7 J· saith unto them, Fill the
11 This beginning of miracles did J·
13 hand, and J· went up to Jerusalem.
19 J· answered and said unto them,
22 and the word which J· had said.
24 J· did not commit himself unto
3: 2 The same came to J· by night, and
3 J· answered and said unto him,
5 J· answered, Verily, verily, I say
10 J· answered and said unto him,
22 After these things came J· and his
4: 1 that J· made and baptized more
2 Though J· himself baptized not,
6 J· therefore, being wearied with
7 J· saith unto her, Give me to drink.
10, 13 J· answered and said unto her,
16 J· saith unto her, Go, call thy
17 J· said unto her, Thou hast well
21 J· saith unto her, Woman, believe
26 J· saith unto her, I that speak unto
34 J· saith unto them, My meat is to
44 J· himself testified, that a prophet
46 J· came again into Cana of Galilee,
47 he heard that J· was come out of
48 Then said J· unto him, Except ye
50 J· saith unto him, Go thy way;
50 man believed the word that J· had
53 J· said unto him, Thy son liveth:
54 the second miracle that J· did,
5: 1 and J· went up to Jerusalem.
6 When J· saw him lie, and knew
8 J· saith unto him, Rise, take up
13 for J· had conveyed himself away,
14 Afterward J· findeth him in the
15 told the Jews that it was J·, which
16 therefore did the Jews persecute J·,
17 J· answered them, My Father
19 Then answered J· and said unto
6: 1 J· went over the sea of Galilee,
3 J· went up into a mountain, and
5 When J· then lifted up his eyes,
10 J· said, Make the men sit down.
11 J· took the loaves; and when he
14 had seen the miracle that J· did,
15 When J· therefore perceived that
17 dark, and J· was not come to them.
19 they see J· walking on the sea, and
22 that J· went not with his disciples
24 therefore saw that J· was not there,
24 came to Capernaum, seeking for J·.
26 J· answered them and said, Verily,
29 J· answered and said unto them,
32 Then J· said unto them, Verily,
35 J· said unto them, I am the bread
42 Is not this J·, the son of Joseph,
43 J· therefore answered and said
53 Then J· said unto them, Verily,
61 When J· knew in himself that his
64 J· knew from the beginning who
67 Then said J· unto the twelve, Will
70 J· answered them, Have not I
7: 1 these things J· walked in Galilee:
6 Then J· said unto them, My time
14 feast J· went up into the temple,
16 J· answered them, and said, My
21 J· answered and said unto them,
28 Then cried J· in the temple as he
33 Then said J· unto them, Yet a little
37 J· stood and cried, saying, If any
39 that J· was not yet glorified.
50 (he that came to J· by night, being
8: 1 J· went unto the mount of Olives.
6 But J· stooped down, and with his
9 J· was left alone, and the woman
10 When J· had lifted up himself, and
11 And J· said unto her, Neither do I
12 Then spake J· again unto them,
14 J· answered and said unto them,
19 J· answered, Ye neither know me
20 These words spake J· in the
21 Then said J· again unto them, I go
25 J· saith unto them, Even the same
28 Then said J· unto them, When ye
31 Then said J· to those Jews which
34 J· answered them, Verily, verily, I
39 J· saith unto them, If ye were
42 J· said unto them, If God were
49 J· answered, I have not a devil;
54 J· answered, If I honour myself,
58 J· said unto them, Verily, verily, I
59 J· hid himself, and went out of the
9: 1 And as J· passed by, he saw a man
3 J· answered, Neither hath this
11 A man that is called J· made clay,
14 sabbath day when J· made the clay,
35 J· heard that they had cast him
37 J· said unto him, Thou hast both
39 J· said, For judgment I am come
41 J· said unto them, If ye were blind,
10: 6 This parable spake J· unto them:
7 Then said J· unto them again,
23 J· walked in the temple in
25 J· answered them, I told you, and
32 J· answered them, Many good
34 J· answered them, Is it not written

Joh 11: 4 When J· heard that, he said, This
5 J· loved Martha, and her sister,
9 J· answered, Are there not twelve
13 Howbeit J· spake of his death: but
14 Then said J· unto them plainly,
17 when J· came, he found that he had
20 as soon as she heard that J· was
21 Then said Martha unto J·, Lord,
23 J· saith unto her, Thy brother
25 J· saith...,I am the resurrection,
30 Now J· was not yet come into the
32 when Mary was come where J· was,
33 When J· therefore saw her weeping,
35 J· wept.
38 J· therefore again groaning in
39 J· said, Take ye away the stone.
40 J· saith unto her, Said I not unto
41 And J· lifted up his eyes, and said,
44 J· saith unto them, Loose him, and
45 had seen the things which J· did,
46 told them what things J· had done.
51 that J· should die for that nation;
54 J· therefore walked no more openly
56 Then sought they for J·, and spake
12: 1 J· six days before the passover
3 and anointed the feet of J·, and
7 Then said J·, Let her alone:
11 Jews went away, and believed on J·
12 they heard that J· was coming to
14 And J·, when he had found a young
16 but when J· was glorified, then
21 him, saying, Sir, we would see J·.
22 again Andrew and Philip tell J·.
23 And J· answered them, saying,
30 J· answered and said, This voice
35 Then J· said unto them, Yet a little
36 things spake J·, and departed, and
44 J· cried and said, He that believeth
13: 1 J· knew that his hour was come
3 J· knowing that the Father had
7 J· answered and said unto him,
8 J· answered him, If I wash thee
10 J· saith to him, He that is washed
21 When J· had thus said, he was
23 one of his disciples, whom J· loved.
26 J· answered, He it is, to whom I
27 Then said J· unto him, That thou
29 J· had said unto him, Buy those
31 J· said, Now is the Son of man
36 J· answered him, Whither I go,
38 J· answered him, Wilt thou lay
14: 6 J· saith unto him, I am the way,
9 J· saith unto him, Have I been so
23 J· answered and said unto him, If
16:19 J· knew that they were desirous
31 J· answered...,Do ye now believe?
17: 1 These words spake J·, and lifted up
3 J· Christ, whom thou hast sent.
18: 1 When J· had spoken these words,
2 for J· ofttimes resorted thither
4 J· therefore, knowing all things
5 They answered him, J· of Nazareth.
5 J· saith unto them, I am he.
7 And they said, J· of Nazareth.
8 J· answered, I have told you that
11 Then said J· unto Peter, Put up thy
12 and officers of the Jews took J·,
15 Simon Peter followed J·, and so
15 went in with J· into the palace of
19 The high priest then asked J· of
20 J· answered him, I spake openly to
22 struck J· with the palm of his hand,
23 J· answered him, If I have spoken
28 Then led they J· from Caiaphas
32 the saying of J· might be fulfilled,
33 and called J·, and said unto him,
34 J· answered him, Sayest thou this
36 J· answered, My kingdom is not of
37 J· answered, Thou sayest that I
19: 1 Then Pilate therefore took J·, and
5 came J· forth, wearing the crown
9 saith unto J·, Whence art thou?
9 But J· gave him no answer.
11 J· answered, Thou couldest have
13 he brought J· forth, and sat down
16 they took J·, and led him away.
18 side one, and J· in the midst.
19 J· of Nazareth the King of the
20 the place where J· was crucified
23 when they had crucified J·, took
25 stood by the cross of J· his mother,
26 When J· therefore saw his mother,
28 J· knowing that all things were
30 When J· therefore had received
33 when they came to J·, and saw that
38 Arimathæa, being a disciple of J·,
38 he might take away the body of J·:
38 therefore, and took the body of J·.
39 at the first came to J· by night,
40 Then took they the body of J·,
42 There laid they J· therefore
20: 2 the other disciple, whom J· loved,
12 where the body of J· had lain.
14 herself back, and saw J· standing,
14 and knew not that it was J·.
15 J· saith unto her, Woman, why
16 J· saith unto her, Mary. She
17 J· saith unto her, Touch me not;
19 came J· and stood in the midst,
21 Then said J· to them again, Peace
24 was not with them when J· came.
26 then came J·, the doors being shut,
29 J· saith unto him, Thomas, because
30 many other signs truly did J· in
31 might believe that J· is the Christ,
21: 1 J· shewed himself again to his

Joh 21: 4 now come, J· stood on the shore,
4 disciples knew not that it was J·.
5 J· saith unto them, Children, have
7 that disciple whom J· loved saith
10 J· saith unto them, Bring of the fish
12 J· saith unto them, Come and dine.
13 J· then cometh, and taketh bread,
14 third time that J· shewed himself
15 J· saith to Simon Peter, Simon,
17 J· saith unto him, Feed my sheep.
20 disciple whom J· loved following;
21 Peter seeing him saith to J·, Lord,
22 J· saith unto him, If I will that he
23 yet J· said not unto him, He shall
25 many other things which J· did,
Ac 1: 1 that J· began both to do and teach,
11 this same J·, which is taken up
14 Mary the mother of J·, and with
16 was guide to them that took J·.
21 Lord J· went in and out among us,
2:22 J· of Nazareth, a man approved of
32 This J· hath God raised up,
36 God hath made that same J·, whom
38 one of you in the name of J· Christ
3: 6 In the name of J· Christ of
13 fathers, hath glorified his Son J·;
20 he shall send J· Christ, which
26 God, having raised up his Son J·,
4: 2 preached through J· the
10 the name of J· Christ of Nazareth,
13 them, that they had been with J·.
18 at all nor teach in the name of J·.
27 a truth against thy holy child J·,
30 by the name of thy holy child J·.
33 of the resurrection of the Lord J·:
5:30 God of our fathers raised up J·,
40 should not speak in the name of J·
42 not to teach and preach J· Christ.
6:14 J· of Nazareth shall destroy this
7:45 with J· into the possession of the
55 J· standing on the right hand of
59 saying, Lord J·, receive my spirit.
8:12 of God, and the name of J· Christ,
16 baptized in the name of the Lord J·.)
35 and preached unto him J·.
37 that J· Christ is the Son of God.
9: 5 I am J· whom thou persecutest:
17 even J·, that appeared unto thee in
27 at Damascus in the name of J·.
29 boldly in the name of the Lord J·,
34 J· Christ maketh thee whole:
10:36 preaching peace by J· Christ: (he is
38 How God anointed J· of Nazareth
11:17 who believed on the Lord J· Christ;
20 Grecians, preaching the Lord J·.
13:23 raised unto Israel a Saviour, J·:
33 in that he hath raised up J· again;
15:11 the grace of the Lord J· Christ we
26 for the name of our Lord J· Christ.
16:18 in the name of J· Christ to come out
31 Believe on the Lord J· Christ, and
17: 3 this J·, whom I preach unto you,
7 that there is another king, one J·.
18 because he preached unto them J·,
18: 5 to the Jews that J· was Christ.
28 by the scriptures that J· was Christ.
19: 4 come after him, that is, on Christ J·.
5 baptized in the name of the Lord J·.
10 Asia heard the word of the Lord J·,
13 evil spirits the name of the Lord J·,
13 We adjure you by J· whom Paul
15 said, J· I know, and Paul I know;
17 name of the Lord J· was magnified.
20:21 and faith toward our Lord J· Christ.
24 which I have received of the Lord J·,
35 remember the words of the Lord J·,
21:13 to die...for the name of the Lord J·.
22: 8 said unto me, I am J· of Nazareth,
25:19 and of one J·, which was dead,
26: 9 things contrary to the name of J· of
15 I am J· whom thou persecutest.
28:23 persuading them concerning J·,
31 which concern the Lord J· Christ,
Ro 1: 1 Paul, a servant of J· Christ, called
3 concerning his Son J· Christ our
6 are ye also the called of J· Christ:
7 our Father, and the Lord J· Christ.
8 I thank my God through J· Christ
2:16 the secrets of men by J· Christ.
3:22 of God which is by faith of J· Christ
24 the redemption that is in Christ J·:
26 of him which believeth in J·.
4:24 believe on him that raised up J·
5: 1 God through our Lord J· Christ:
11 in God through our Lord J· Christ,
15 which is by one man, J· Christ,
17 shall reign in life by one, J· Christ.)
21 unto eternal life by J· Christ our
6: 3 us as were baptized into J· Christ
11 unto God through J· Christ our
23 God is eternal life through J· Christ
7:25 I thank God through J· Christ our
8: 1 to them which are in Christ J·,
2 law of the Spirit of life in Christ J·
11 if the Spirit of him that raised up J·
39 God, which is in Christ J· our Lord.
10: 9 confess with thy mouth the Lord J·,
13:14 But put ye on the Lord J· Christ,
14:14 and am persuaded by the Lord J·,
15: 5 another according to Christ J·:
6 the Father of our Lord J· Christ.
8 I say that J· Christ was a minister
16 should be the minister of J· Christ
17 I may glory through J· Christ in
30 for the Lord J· Christ's sake,
16: 3 Aquilla my helpers in Christ J·:

Ro 16:18 such serve not our Lord J· Christ,
20 grace of our Lord J· Christ be with
24 grace of our Lord J· Christ be with
25 and the preaching of J· Christ,
27 be glory through J· Christ for ever.
1Co 1: 1 called to be an apostle of J· Christ
2 them that are sanctified in Christ J·,
2 call upon the name of J· Christ our
3 Father, and from the Lord J· Christ.
4 which is given you by J· Christ;
7 the coming of our Lord J· Christ:
8 in the day of our Lord J· Christ.
9 of his Son J· Christ our Lord.
10 by the name of our Lord J· Christ,
30 But of him are ye in Christ J·,
2: 2 save J· Christ, and him crucified.
3:11 than that is laid, which is J· Christ.
4:15 for in Christ J· I have begotten you
5: 4 In the name of our Lord J· Christ,
4 the power of our Lord J· Christ,
5 be saved in the day of the Lord J·.
6:11 justified in the name of the Lord J·,
8: 6 and one Lord J· Christ, by whom are
9: 1 have I not seen J· Christ our Lord?
11:23 the Lord J· the same night in which
12: 3 Spirit of God calleth J· accursed:
3 no man can say that J· is the Lord,
15:31 rejoicing which I have in Christ J·
57 victory through our Lord J· Christ.
16:22 man love not the Lord J· Christ,
23 The grace of our Lord J· Christ be
24 My love be with you all in Christ J·.
2Co 1: 1 Paul, an apostle of J· Christ by the
2 Father, and from the Lord J· Christ.
3 the Father of our Lord J· Christ,
14 are ours in the day of the Lord J·.
19 For the Son of God, J· Christ, who
4: 5 ourselves, but Christ J· the Lord;
6 glory of God in the face of J· Christ.
10 the body the dying of the Lord J·,
10, 11 the life also of J· might be made
14 that he which raised up the Lord J·
14 shall raise up us also by J·, and
5:18 hath reconciled us...by J· Christ,
8: 9 the grace of our Lord J· Christ,
11: 4 that cometh preacheth another J·,
31 and Father of our Lord J· Christ,
13: 5 how that J· Christ is in you, except
14 The grace of the Lord J· Christ,
Ga 1: 1 neither by man, but by J· Christ,
3 Father, and from our Lord J· Christ,
12 but by the revelation of J· Christ.
2: 4 liberty which we have in Christ J·,
16 law, but by the faith of J· Christ,
16 even we have believed in J· Christ,
3: 1 J· Christ hath been evidently set
14 on the Gentiles through J· Christ;
22 that the promise by faith of J· Christ
26 of God by faith in Christ J·.
28 for ye are all one in Christ J·.
4:14 an angel of God, even as Christ J·.
5: 6 in J· Christ neither circumcision
6:14 in the cross of our Lord J· Christ,
15 in Christ J· neither circumcision
17 my body the marks of the Lord J·.
18 grace of our Lord J· Christ be with
Eph 1: 1 Paul, an apostle of J· Christ by the
1 and to the faithful in Christ J·:
2 Father, and from the Lord J· Christ.
3 and Father of our Lord J· Christ,
5 adoption of children by J· Christ
15 I heard of your faith in the Lord J·,
17 That the God of our Lord J· Christ,
2: 6 in heavenly places in Christ J·:
7 toward us through Christ J·.
10 created in Christ J· unto good works,
13 in Christ J· ye who sometimes were
20 J· Christ himself being the chief
3: 1 the prisoner of J· Christ for you
9 who created all things by J· Christ:
11 he purposed in Christ J· our Lord:
14 the Father of our Lord J· Christ,
21 be glory in the church by Christ J·
4:21 taught by him, as the truth is in J·:
5:20 in the name of our Lord J· Christ;
6:23 the Father and the Lord J· Christ.
24 love our Lord J· Christ in sincerity.
Ph'p 1: 1 the servants of J· Christ,
1 to all the saints in Christ J· which
2 Father, and from the Lord J· Christ.
6 perform it until the day of J· Christ:
8 you all in the bowels of J· Christ.
11 which are by J· Christ, unto the
19 the supply of the Spirit of J· Christ,
26 may be more abundant in J· Christ
2: 5 in you, which was also in Christ J·:
10 That at the name of J· every knee
11 confess that J· Christ is Lord,
19 But I trust in the Lord J· to send
21 not the things which are J· Christ's.
3: 3 the spirit, and rejoice in Christ J·,
8 knowledge of Christ J· my Lord:
12 also I am apprehended of Christ J·.
14 the high calling of God in Christ J·.
20 for the Saviour, the Lord J· Christ:
4: 7 hearts and minds through Christ J·.
19 to his riches in glory by Christ J·.
21 Salute every saint in Christ J·. The
23 grace of our Lord J· Christ be with
Col 1: 1 Paul, an apostle of J· Christ by the
2 our Father and the Lord J· Christ.
3 the Father of our Lord J· Christ,
4 we heard of your faith in Christ J·,
28 every man perfect in Christ J·:
2: 6 received Christ J· the Lord, so walk
3:17 do all in the name of the Lord J·
Col 4:11 And J·, which is called Justus, who
1Th 1: 1 Father and in the Lord J· Christ:
1 Father, and the Lord J· Christ.
3 of hope in our Lord J· Christ,
10 he raised from the dead, even J·,
2:14 which in Judæa are in Christ J·:
15 Who both killed the Lord J·, and
19 the presence of our Lord J· Christ
3:11 Father, and our Lord J· Christ,
13 at the coming of our Lord J· Christ
4: 1 and exhort you by the Lord J·, that
2 we gave you by the Lord J·.
14 if we believe that J· died and rose
14 which sleep in J· will God bring
5: 9 salvation by our Lord J· Christ,
18 this is the will of God in Christ J·
23 the coming of our Lord J· Christ.
28 grace of our Lord J· Christ be with
2Th 1: 1 our Father and the Lord J· Christ:
2 our Father and the Lord J· Christ.
7 the Lord J· shall be revealed from
8 not the gospel of our Lord J· Christ:
12 name of our Lord J· Christ may be
12 of our God and the Lord J· Christ.
2: 1 the coming of our Lord J· Christ,
14 of the glory of our Lord J· Christ.
16 Now our Lord J· Christ himself,
3: 6 in the name of our Lord J· Christ,
12 and exhort by our Lord J· Christ,
18 grace of our Lord J· Christ be with
1Ti 1: 1 Paul, an apostle of J· Christ by the
1 our Saviour, and Lord J· Christ,
2 our Father and J· Christ our Lord.
12 And I thank Christ J· our Lord,
14 faith and love which is in Christ J·.
15 Christ J· came into the world to save
16 in me first J· Christ might shew
2: 5 God and men, the man Christ J·;
3:13 in the faith which is in Christ J·.
4: 6 shalt be a good minister of J· Christ,
5:21 before God, and the Lord J· Christ,
6: 3 the words of our Lord J· Christ,
13 all things, and before Christ J·,
14 appearing of our Lord J· Christ:
2Ti 1: 1 Paul, an apostle of J· Christ by the
1 promise of life which is in Christ J·,
2 the Father and Christ J· our Lord.
9 was given us in Christ J· before the
10 appearing of our Saviour J· Christ,
13 faith and love which is in Christ J·.
2: 1 in the grace that is in Christ J·.
3 as a good soldier of J· Christ.
8 that J· Christ of the seed of David
10 the salvation which is in Christ J·
3:12 all that will live godly in Christ J·
15 through faith which is in Christ J·.
4: 1 before God, and the Lord J· Christ,
22 Lord J· Christ be with thy spirit.
Tit 1: 1 of God, and an apostle of J· Christ,
4 and the Lord J· Christ our Saviour.
2:13 God and our Saviour J· Christ;
3: 6 through J· Christ our Saviour;
Ph'm 1 Paul, a prisoner of J· Christ, and
3 our Father and the Lord J· Christ.
5 which thou hast toward the Lord J·,
6 thing which is in you in Christ J·.
9 now also a prisoner of J· Christ.
23 my fellowprisoner in Christ J·;
25 grace of our Lord J· Christ be with
Heb 2: 9 see J·, who was made a little lower
3: 1 Priest of our profession, Christ J·;
4: 8 For if J· had given them rest, then
14 the heavens, J· the Son of God,
6:20 even J·, made an high priest for ever
7:22 was J· made a surety of a better
10:10 of the body of J· Christ once for all.
19 into the holiest by the blood of J·
12: 2 Looking unto J· the author and
24 And to J· the mediator of the new
13: 8 J· Christ the same yesterday, and
12 Wherefore J· also, that he might
20 again from the dead our Lord J·,
21 in his sight, through J· Christ;
Jas 1: 1 of God and of the Lord J· Christ,
2: 1 not the faith of our Lord J· Christ,
1Pe 1: 1 Peter, an apostle of J· Christ, to the
2 sprinkling of the blood of J· Christ:
3 and Father of our Lord J· Christ,
3 hope by the resurrection of J· Christ
7 glory at the appearing of J· Christ:
13 you at the revelation of J· Christ;
2: 5 acceptable to God by J· Christ.
3:21 by the resurrection of J· Christ:
4:11 may be glorified through J· Christ,
5:10 unto his eternal glory by Christ J·,
14 be with you all that are in Christ J·.
2Pe 1: 1 servant and an apostle of J· Christ,
1 of God and our Saviour J· Christ:
2 the knowledge...of J· our Lord,
8 knowledge of our Lord J· Christ.
11 of our Lord and Saviour J· Christ.
14 our Lord J· Christ hath shewed me.
16 and coming of our Lord J· Christ,
2:20 of the Lord and Saviour J· Christ,
3:18 of our Lord and Saviour J· Christ.
1Jo 1: 3 Father, and with his Son J· Christ.
7 blood of J· Christ his Son cleanseth
2: 1 the Father, J· Christ the righteous:
22 that denieth that J· is the Christ?
3:23 on the name of his Son J· Christ,
4: 2, 3 that J· Christ is come in the flesh
15 shall confess that J· is the Son of
5: 1 believeth that J· is the Christ is
5 believeth that J· is the Son of God?
6 by water and blood, even J· Christ;
20 is true, even in his Son J· Christ.
2Jo 3 from the Lord J· Christ, the Son of
7 that J· Christ is come in the flesh.
Jude 1 Jude, the servant of J· Christ, and
1 preserved in J· Christ, and called:
4 Lord God, and our Lord J· Christ.
17 the apostles of our Lord J· Christ;
21 for the mercy of our Lord J· Christ
Re 1: 1 The Revelation of J· Christ, which
2 and of the testimony of J· Christ,
5 from J· Christ, who is the faithful
9 kingdom and patience of J· Christ,
9 and for the testimony of J· Christ.
12:17 and have the testimony of J· Christ.
14:12 of God, and the faith of J·.
17: 6 with the blood of the martyrs of J·:
19:10 that have the testimony of J·:
10 the testimony of J· is the spirit of
20: 4 were beheaded for the witness of J·,
22:16 I J· have sent mine angel to testify
20 Amen. Even so, come, Lord J·.
21 grace of our Lord J· Christ be with

Jesus' (je'-zus)
M't 15:30 and cast them down at J· feet;
27:57 who also himself was J· disciple:
Lu 5: 8 saw it, he fell down at J· knees,
8:41 fell down at J· feet, and besought
10:39 Mary, which also sat at J· feet,
Joh 12: 9 they came not for J· sake only, but
13:23 Now there was leaning on J· bosom
25 He then lying on J· breast saith
2Co 4: 5 ourselves your servants for J· sake.
11 delivered unto death for J· sake,

Jesus Christ See JESUS and CHRIST.

Jether (je'-thur) See also HOBAB; ITHRA; ITHRITES; JETHRO; RAGUEL.
J'g 8:20 he said unto J· his firstborn, Up,
1Ki 2: 5 Ner, and unto Amasa the son of J·,
32 and Amasa the son of J·, captain of
1Ch 2:17 and the father of Amasa was J· the
32 of Shammai; J·, and Jonathan:
32 and J· died without children.
4:17 sons of Ezra were, J·, and Mered,
7:38 sons of J·; Jephunneh, and Pispah,

Jetheth (je'-theth)
Ge 36:40 Timnah, duke Alvah, duke J·,
1Ch 1:51 Timnah, duke Aliah, duke J·,

Jethlah (jeth'-lah)
Jos 19:42 Shaalabbin, and Ajalon, and J·,

Jethro (je'-thro) See also JETHER.
Ex 3: 1 Now Moses kept the flock of J· his
4:18 Moses went and returned to J· his
18 And J· said to Moses, Go in peace.
18: 1 When J·, the priest of Midian,
2 Then J·, Moses' father in law, took
5 J·, Moses' father in law, came with
6 father in law J· am come unto thee,
9 J· rejoiced for all the goodness
10 J· said, Blessed be the Lord, who
12 J·, Moses' father in law, took a

Jetur (je'-tur)
Ge 25:15 Hadar, and Tema, J·, Naphish,
1Ch 1:31 J·, Naphish, and Kedemah. These
5:19 Hagarites, with J·, and Nephish,

Jeuel (je-u'-el) See also JEIEL.
1Ch 9: 6 the sons of Zerah; J·, and their

Jeush (je'-ush) See also JEHUSH.
Ge 36: 5 Aholibamah bare J·, and Jaalam,
14 she bare to Esau J·, and Jaalam,
18 duke J·, duke Jaalam, duke Korah:
1Ch 1:35 Reuel, and J·, and Jaalam, and
7:10 J·, and Benjamin, and Ehud, and
23:10 Jahath, Zina, and J·, and Beriah.
11 J· and Beriah had not many sons;
2Ch 11:19 J·, and Shamariah, and Zaham.

Jeuz (je'-uz)
1Ch 8:10 And J·, and Shachia, and Mirma.

Jew (jew) See also JEWESS; JEWISH; JEWS.
Es 2: 5 the palace there was a certain J·,
3: 4 he had told them that he was a J·.
5:13 Mordecai the J· sitting at the king's
6:10 do even so to Mordecai the J·, that
8: 7 the queen and to Mordecai the J·,
9:29 of Abihail, and Mordecai the J·,
31 Mordecai the J· and Esther the
10: 3 Mordecai the J· was next unto king
Jer 34: 9 them, to wit, of a J· his brother.
Zec 8:23 hold of the skirt of him that is a J·,
Joh 4: 9 being a J·, askest drink of me,
18:35 Pilate answered, Am I a J·? Thine
Ac 10:28 man that is a J· to keep company,
13: 6 a J·, whose name was Bar-jesus:
18: 2 found a certain J· named Aquila,
24 certain J· named Apollos, born at
19:14 Sceva, a J·, and chief of the priests,
34 when they knew that he was a J·,
21:39 a man which am a J· of Tarsus,
22: 3 man which am a J· born in Tarsus,
Ro 1:16 the J· first, and also to the Greek.
2: 9 the J· first, and also of the Gentile;
10 the J· first, and also to the Gentile:
17 Behold, thou art called a J·, and
28 is not a J·, which is one outwardly;
29 he is a J·, which is one inwardly;
3: 1 What advantage then hath the J·?
10:12 between the J· and the Greek:
1Co 9:20 And to the Jews I became as a J·,
Ga 2:14 If thou, being a J·, livest after the
3:28 There is neither J· nor Greek,
Col 3:11 Where there is neither Greek nor J·,

jewel See also JEWELS.
Pr 11:22 As a j· of gold in a swine's snout,

Pr 20:15 lips of knowledge are a precious *j*·.
Eze 16:12 I put a *j*· on thy forehead, and

Jewels
Ge 24:53 servant brought forth *j*· of silver,
53 and *j*· of gold, and raiment, and
Ex 3:22 sojourneth in her house, *j*· of silver,
22 and *j*· of gold, and raiment: and ye
11: 2 neighbour, *j*· of silver, and *j*· of gold.
12:35 of the Egyptians *j*· of silver,
35 and *j*· of gold, and raiment:
35:22 rings, and tablets, all *j*· of gold:
Nu 31:50 of *j*· of gold, chains, and bracelets,
51 gold of them, even all wrought *j*·.
1Sa 6: 8 put the *j*· of gold, which ye return
15 with it, wherein the *j*· of gold were.
2Ch 20:25 precious *j*·, which they stripped off
32:27 and for all manner of pleasant *j*·;
Job 28:17 it shall not be for *j*· of fine gold.
Ca 1:10 cheeks are comely with rows of *j*·,
7: 1 joints of thy thighs are like *j*·, the
Isa 3:21 The rings, and nose *j*·,
61:10 bride adorneth herself with her *j*·.
Eze 16:17 Thou hast also taken thy fair *j*· of
39 shall take thy fair *j*·, and leave thee
23:26 clothes, and take away thy fair *j*·.
Ho 2:13 with her earrings and her *j*·,
Mal 3:17 that day when I make up my *j*·;

Jewess (*jew'-ess*)
Ac 16: 1 certain woman, which was a *J*·,
24:24 his wife Drusilla, which was a *J*·.

Jewish (*jew'-ish*)
Tit 1:14 Not giving heed to *J*· fables, and

Jewry (*jew'-ree*) See also JUDÆA.
Da 5:13 king my father brought out of *J*·?
Lu 23: 5 people, teaching throughout all *J*·,
Joh 7: 1 he would not walk in *J*·, because

Jews (*jews*) See also JEWS'.
2Ki 16: 6 Syria, and drave the *J*· from Elath:
25:25 the *J*· and the Chaldees that were
Ezr 4:12 the *J*· which came up from thee to
23 in haste to Jerusalem unto the *J*·,
5: 1 son of Iddo, prophesied unto the *J*·
5 God was upon the elders of the *J*·,
6: 7 alone; let the governors of the *J*·
7 and the elders of the *J*· built this
8 shall do to the elders of these *J*·
14 the elders of the *J*· builded, and
Ne 1: 2 concerning the *J*· that had escaped,
2:16 neither had I as yet told it to the *J*·,
4: 1 indignation, and mocked the *J*·,
2 and said, What do these feeble *J*·?
12 the *J*· which dwelt by them came,
5: 1 wives against their brethren the *J*·.
8 have redeemed our brethren the *J*·,
17 were at my table... *J*· and rulers,
6: 6 that thou and the *J*· think to rebel:
13:23 In those days also saw I *J*· that
Es 3: 6 Haman sought to destroy all the *J*·
13 kill, and to cause to perish, all *J*·,
4: 3 was great mourning among the *J*·,
7 to the king's treasuries for the *J*·,
13 king's house, more than all the *J*·.
14 and deliverance arise to the *J*·
16 gather together all the *J*· that are
6:13 Mordecai be of the seed of the *J*·,
8: 3 that he had devised against the *J*·.
5 which he wrote to destroy the *J*·
7 he laid his hand upon the *J*·.
8 Write ye also for the *J*·, as it liketh
9 Mordecai commanded unto the *J*·,
9 the *J*· according to their writing,
11 Wherein the king granted the *J*·
13 *J*· should be ready against that day
16 The *J*· had light, and gladness, and
17 the *J*· had joy and gladness, a feast
17 the people of the land became *J*·;
17 the fear of the *J*· fell upon them.
9: 1 *J*· hoped to have power over them,
1 the *J*· had rule over them that
2 *J*· gathered themselves together
3 officers of the king, helped the *J*·;
5 the *J*· smote all their enemies with
6 Shushan the palace the *J*· slew and
10 the enemy of the *J*·, slew they;
12 The *J*· have slain and destroyed
13 king, let it be granted to the *J*·
15 For the *J*· that were in Shushan
16 *J*· that were in the king's provinces
18 *J*· that were in Shushan assembled
19 Therefore the *J*· of the villages,
20 sent letters unto all the *J*· that
22 the *J*· rested from their enemies,
23 the *J*· undertook to do as they had
24 Agagite, the enemy of all the *J*·,
24 devised against the *J*· to destroy
25 which he devised against the *J*·,
27 *J*· ordained, and took upon them,
28 should not fail from among the *J*·,
30 he sent the letters unto all the *J*·,
10: 3 Ahasuerus, great among the *J*·,
Jer 32:12 *J*· that sat in the court of the prison.
38:19 afraid of the *J*· that are fallen to
40:11 when all the *J*· that were in Moab,
12 all the *J*· returned out of all places
15 all the *J*· which are gathered unto
41: 3 Ishmael also slew all the *J*· that
44: 1 concerning all the *J*· which dwell
52:28 the seventh year three thousand *J*·
30 carried away captive of the *J*·
Da 3: 8 came near, and accused the *J*·.
12 certain *J*· whom thou hast set
M't 2: 2 is he that is born King of the *J*·?
27:11 saying, Art thou the King of the *J*·?
29 him, saying, Hail, King of the *J*·!
M't 27:37 This Is Jesus The King Of The *J*·.
28:15 is commonly reported among the *J*·
M'r 7: 3 For the Pharisees, and all the *J*·,
15: 2 him, Art thou the King of the *J*·?
9 release unto you the King of the *J*·?
12 whom ye call the King of the *J*·?
18 to salute him, Hail, King of the *J*·!
26 written over, The King Of The *J*·.
Lu 7: 3 sent unto him the elders of the *J*·,
23: 3 saying, Art thou the King of the *J*·?
37 If thou be the king of the *J*·, save
38 This Is The King Of The *J*·.
51 was of Arimathæa, a city of the *J*·:
Joh 1:19 when the *J*· sent priests and Levites
2: 6 manner of the purifying of the *J*·,
18 Then answered the *J*· and said unto
20 Then said the *J*·, Forty and six
3: 1 named Nicodemus, a ruler of the *J*·:
25 of John's disciples and the *J*·
4: 9 the *J*· have no dealings with the
22 worship: for salvation is of the *J*·.
5: 1 this there was a feast of the *J*·;
10 *J*· therefore said unto him that was
15 and told the *J*· that it was Jesus,
16 therefore did the *J*· persecute Jesus,
18 the *J*· sought the more to kill him,
6: 4 passover, a feast of the *J*·, was nigh.
41 The *J*· then murmured at him,
52 The *J*· therefore strove among
7: 1 because the *J*· sought to kill him.
11 Then the *J*· sought him at the feast,
13 openly of him for fear of the *J*·.
15 And the *J*· marvelled, saying, How
35 said the *J*· among themselves,
8:22 said the *J*·, Will he kill himself?
31 Jesus to those *J*· which believed
48 Then answered the *J*·, and said
52 Then said the *J*· unto him, Now we
57 Then said the *J*· unto him, Thou
9:18 the *J*· did not believe concerning
22 parents, because they feared the *J*·:
22 for the *J*· had agreed already, that
10:19 was a division...again among the *J*·
24 Then came the *J*· round about him,
31 Then the *J*· took up stones again
33 The *J*· answered him, saying, For
11: 8 the *J*· of late sought to stone thee;
19 many of the *J*· came to Martha
31 The *J*· then which were with her
33 weeping, and the *J*· also weeping
36 Then said the *J*·, Behold how he
45 many of the *J*· which came to Mary,
54 no more openly among the *J*·;
12: 9 people of the *J*· therefore knew
11 of him many of the *J*· went away,
13:33 as I said unto the *J*·, Whither I go,
18:12 and officers of the *J*· took Jesus,
14 he, which gave counsel to the *J*·,
20 whither the *J*· always resort;
31 The *J*· therefore said unto him, It
33 him, Art thou the King of the *J*·?
36 I should not be delivered to the *J*·:
38 he went out again unto the *J*·, and
39 release unto you the King of the *J*·?
19: 3 And said, Hail, King of the *J*·! and
7 *J*· answered him, We have a law,
12 but the *J*· cried out, saying, If thou
14 he saith unto the *J*·, Behold your
19 Of Nazareth The King Of The *J*·.
20 This title then read many of the *J*·:
21 Then said the chief priests of the *J*·
21 Write not, The King of the *J*·; but
21 that he said, I am King of the *J*·.
31 The *J*· therefore,...besought Pilate
38 but secretly for fear of the *J*·,
40 as the manner of the *J*· is to bury.
20:19 were assembled for fear of the *J*·,
Ac 2: 5 were dwelling at Jerusalem *J*·,
10 of Rome, *J*· and proselytes,
9:22 the *J*· which dwelt at Damascus,
23 the *J*· took counsel to kill him:
10:22 among all the nation of the *J*·,
39 he did both in the land of the *J*·,
11:19 word to none but unto the *J*· only.
12: 3 because he saw it pleased the *J*·,
11 expectation of the people of the *J*·.
13: 5 of God in the synagogues of the *J*·:
42 *J*· were gone out of the synagogue,
43 many of the *J*· and religious
45 when the *J*· saw the multitudes,
50 the *J*· stirred up the devout and
14: 1 into the synagogue of the *J*·,
1 great multitude both of the *J*· and
2 the unbelieving *J*· stirred up the
4 and part held with the *J*·, and part
5 and also of the *J*· with their rulers,
13 thither certain *J*· from Antioch
16: 3 circumcised him because of the *J*·
20 being *J*·, do exceedingly trouble
17: 1 where was a synagogue of the *J*·:
5 But the *J*· which believed not,
10 went into the synagogue of the *J*·.
13 But when the *J*· of Thessalonica
17 he in the synagogue of the *J*·,
18: 2 all *J*· to depart from Rome:)
4 persuaded the *J*· and the Greeks.
5 testified to the *J*· that Jesus was
12 the *J*· made insurrection with one
14 Gallio said unto the *J*·, If it were
14 O ye *J*·, reason would that I should
19 and reasoned with the *J*·.
28 For he mightily convinced the *J*·,
19:10 Lord Jesus, both *J*· and Greeks.
13 Then certain of the vagabond *J*·,
17 And this was known to all the *J*·
33 the *J*· putting him forward.
Ac 20: 3 And when the *J*· laid wait for him,
19 me by the lying in wait of the *J*·:
21 Testifying both to the *J*·, and also
21:11 So shall the *J*· at Jerusalem bind
20 how many thousands of *J*· there are
21 thou teachest all the *J*· which are
27 the *J*· which were of Asia, when
22:12 a good report of all the *J*· which
30 wherefore he was accused of the *J*·,
23:12 certain of the *J*· banded together,
20 The *J*· have agreed to desire thee
27 This man was taken of the *J*·,
30 that the *J*· laid wait for the man,
24: 5 mover of sedition among all the *J*·
9 the *J*· also assented, saying that
18 certain *J*· from Asia found me
27 willing to shew the *J*· a pleasure,
25: 2 the chief of the *J*· informed him
7 the *J*· which came down from
8 Neither against the law of the *J*·,
9 willing to do the *J*· a pleasure,
10 to the *J*· have I done no wrong, as
15 the elders of the *J*· informed me,
24 the multitude of the *J*· have dealt
26: 2 whereof I am accused of the *J*·:
3 questions which are among the *J*·:
4 at Jerusalem, know all the *J*·;
7 Agrippa, I am accused of the *J*·.
21 the *J*· caught me in the temple,
28:17 days Paul called the chief of the *J*·
19 But when the *J*· spake against it,
29 said these words, the *J*· departed,
Ro 3: 9 before proved both *J*· and Gentiles,
29 Is he the God of the *J*· only?
9:24 called, not of the *J*· only, but also
1Co 1:22 For the *J*· require a sign, and the
23 unto the *J*· a stumblingblock, and
24 are called, both *J*· and Greeks,
9:20 And unto the *J*· I became as a Jew,
20 that I might gain the *J*·; to them
10:32 none offence, neither to the *J*·, nor
12:13 whether we be *J*· or Gentiles,
2Co 11:24 Of the *J*· five times received I forty
Ga 2:13 the other *J*· dissembled likewise
14 of Gentiles, and not as do the *J*·,
14 the Gentiles to live as do the *J*·?
15 We who are *J*· by nature, and not
1Th 2:14 even as they have of the *J*·:
Re 2: 9 which say they are *J*·, and are not,
3: 9 which say they are *J*·, and are not,

Jews' (*jews*)
2Ki 18:26 talk not with us in the *J*· language
28 a loud voice in the *J*· language,
2Ch 32:18 with a loud voice in the *J*· speech
Ne 13:24 not speak in the *J*· language, but
Es 3:10 the Agagite, the *J*· enemy.
8: 1 the house of Haman the *J*· enemy
Isa 36:11 speak not to us in the *J*· language,
13 a loud voice in the *J*· language,
Joh 2:13 the *J*· passover was at hand, and
7: 2 the *J*· feast of tabernacles was at
11:55 the *J*· passover was nigh at hand:
19:42 because of the *J*· preparation day;
Ga 1:13 in time past in the *J*· religion,
14 profited in the *J*· religion above

Jezaniah (*jez-a-ni'-ah*) See also JAAZANIAH.
Jer 40: 8 and *J*· the son of a Maachathite,
42: 1 Kareah, and *J*· the son of Hoshaiah,

Jezebel (*jez'-e-bel*) See also JEZEBEL'S.
1Ki 16:31 he took to wife *J*· the daughter of
18: 4 when *J*· cut off the prophets of the
13 what I did when *J*· slew the prophets
19: 1 And Ahab told *J*· all that Elijah had
2 *J*· sent a messenger unto Elijah,
21: 5 *J*· his wife came to him, and said
7 *J*· his wife said unto him, Dost thou
11 did as *J*· had sent unto them, and
14 sent to *J*·, saying, Naboth is stoned,
15 *J*· heard that Naboth was stoned,
15 that *J*· said to Ahab, Arise, take
23 And of *J*· also spake the Lord,
23 The dogs shall eat *J*· by the wall of
25 Lord, whom *J*· his wife stirred up.
2Ki 9: 7 of the Lord, at the hand of *J*·.
10 the dogs shall eat *J*· in the portion
22 as the whoredoms of thy mother *J*·
30 was come to Jezreel, *J*· heard of it;
36 Jezreel shall dogs eat the flesh of *J*·:
37 the carcase of *J*· shall be as dung
37 so that they shall not say, This is *J*·.
Re 2:20 thou sufferest that woman *J*·,

Jezebel's (*jez'-e-bels*)
1Ki 18:19 four hundred which eat at *J*· table.

Jezer (*je'-zur*) See also JEZERITES.
Ge 46:24 and Guni, and *J*·, and Shillem.
Nu 26:49 Of *J*·, the family of the Jezerites:
1Ch 7:13 and Guni, and *J*·, and Shallum,

Jezerites (*je'-zur-ites*)
Nu 26:49 of Jezer, the family of the *J*·:

Jeziah (*je-zi'-ah*)
Ezr 10:25 Ramiah, and *J*·, and Malchiah,

Jeziel (*je'-ze-el*)
1Ch 12: 3 and *J*·, and Pelet, the sons of

Jezliah (*jez-li'-ah*)
1Ch 8:18 *J*·, and Jobab, the sons of Elpaal;

Jezoar (*je-zo'-ar*) See also ZOAR.
1Ch 4: 7 of Helah were, Zereth, and *J*·,

Jezrahiah (*jez-ra-hi'-ah*) See also IZRAHIAH.
Ne 12:42 sang loud, with *J*· their overseer.

Jezreel (*jez'-re-el*) See also JEZREELITE.
Jos 15:56 *J*·, and Jokdeam, and Zanoah,
17:16 they who are of the valley of *J*·.

Jos 19:18 And their border was toward J'.
J'g 6:33 and pitched in the valley of J'.
1Sa 25:43 David also took Ahinoam of J';
29: 1 pitched by a fountain which is in J'.
11 And the Philistines went up to J'.
2Sa 2: 9 and over J', and over Ephraim, and
4: 4 of Saul and Jonathan out of J',
1Ki 4:12 which is by Zartanah beneath J',
18:45 And Ahab rode, and went to J'.
46 before Ahab to the entrance of J'.
21: 1 had a vineyard, which was in J',
23 shall eat Jezebel by the wall of J'.
2Ki 8:29 Joram went back to be healed in J'
29 to see Joram the son of Ahab in J',
9:10 eat Jezebel in the portion of J',
15 was returned to be healed in J'
15 out of the city to go to tell it in J'.
16 rode in a chariot, and went to J';
17 a watchman on the tower of J',
30 And when Jehu was come to J',
36 In the portion of J' shall dogs eat
37 of the field in the portion of J';
10: 1 to Samaria, unto the rulers of J',
6 and come to me to J' by to morrow
7 baskets, and sent him them to J'.
11 remained of the house of Ahab in J',
1Ch 4: 3 Etam; J', and Ishma, and Idbash:
2Ch 22: 6 he returned to be healed in J'
6 Jehoram the son of Ahab at J',
Ho 1: 4 said unto him, Call his name J';
4 I will avenge the blood of J' upon
5 bow of Israel in the valley of J'.
11 for great shall be the day of J'.
2:22 the oil; and they shall hear J'.

Jezreelite (*jez'-re-el-ite*) See also JEZREELITESS.
1Ki 21: 1 that Naboth the J' had a vineyard,
4 Naboth the J' had spoken to him:
6 Because I spake unto Naboth the J',
7 thee the vineyard of Naboth the J'.
15 of the vineyard of Naboth the J',
16 to the vineyard of Naboth the J',
2Ki 9:21 him in the portion of Naboth the J'.
25 of the field of Naboth the J':

Jezreelitess (*jez'-re-el-i-tess*)
1Sa 27: 3 his two wives, Ahinoam the J',
30: 5 taken captives, Ahinoam the J',
2Sa 2: 2 two wives also, Ahinoam the J',
3: 2 was Amnon, of Ahinoam the J';
1Ch 3: 1 Amnon, of Ahinoam the J';

Jibsam (*jib'-sam*)
1Ch 7: 2 and Jahmai, and J', and Shemuel,

Jidlaph (*jid'-laf*)
Ge 22:22 and Pildash, and J', and Bethuel.

Jimna (*jim'-nah*) See also IMNA; JIMNAH; JIMNITES.
Nu 26:44 of J', the family of the Jimnites:

Jimnah (*jim'-nah*) See also JIMNA.
Ge 46:17 sons of Asher; J', and Ishuah,

Jimnites (*jim'-nites*)
Nu 26:44 of Jimna, the family of the J':

Jiphtah (*jif'-tah*) See also JEPHTHAH; JIPHTHAH-EL.
Jos 15:43 And J', and Ashnah, and Nezib,

Jiphthah-el (*jif'-thah-el*)
Jos 19:14 thereof are in the valley of J':
27 to the valley of J' toward the north

Joab (*jo'-ab*) See also ATAROTH; HOUSE; JOAB'S.
1Sa 26: 6 the son of Zeruiah, brother to J',
2Sa 2:13 J' the son of Zeruiah, and the
14 Abner said to J', Let the young
14 And J' said, Let them arise.
18 three sons of Zeruiah there, J', and
22 should I hold up my face to J'
24 J' also and Abishai pursued after
26 Abner called to J', and said, Shall
27 J' said, As God liveth, unless thou
28 So J' blew a trumpet, and all the
30 J' returned from following Abner:
32 J' and his men went all night, and
3:22 servants of David and J' came
23 When J' and all the host that was
23 they told J', saying, Abner the son
24 Then J' came to the king, and
26 when J' was come out from David,
27 J' took him aside in the gate to
29 Let it rest on the head of J', and on
29 not fail from the house of J' one
30 So J' and Abishai his brother slew
31 David said to J', and to all the
8:16 J' the son of Zeruiah was over the
10: 7 when David heard of it, he sent J',
9 When J' saw that the front of the
13 J' drew nigh, and the people that
14 So J' returned from the children
11: 1 that David sent J', and his servants
6 David sent to J', saying, Send me
6 And J' sent Uriah to David.
7 David demanded of him how J' did,
11 and my lord J', and the servants
14 David wrote a letter to J', and sent
16 to pass, when J' observed the city,
17 city went out, and fought with J':
18 J' sent and told David all the
22 David all that J' had sent him for.
25 Thus shalt thou say unto J', Let
12:26 J' fought against Rabbah of the
27 J' sent messengers to David, and
14: 1 J' the son of Zeruiah perceived
2 J' sent to Tekoah, and fetched
3 So J' put the words in her mouth.
19 Is not the hand of J' with thee in
2Sa 14:19 for thy servant J', he bade me,
20 hath thy servant J' done this thing:
21 the king said unto J', Behold now,
22 J' fell to the ground on his face,
22 J' said, To day thy servant knoweth
23 J' arose and went to Geshur, and
29 Absalom sent for J', to have sent
31 J' arose, and came to Absalom
32 Absalom answered J', Behold, I
33 J' came to the king, and told him:
17:25 captain of the host instead of J':
18: 2 of the people under the hand of J',
5 the king commanded J' and
10 a certain man saw it, and told J',
11 J' said unto the man that told him,
12 the man said unto J', Though I
14 Then said J', I may not tarry thus
16 J' blew the trumpet, and the people
16 for J' held back the people.
20 J' said unto him, Thou shalt not
21 Then said J' to Cushi, Go tell the
21 Cushi bowed himself unto J', and
22 the son of Zadok yet again to J',
22 J' said, Wherefore wilt thou run,
29 When J' sent the king's servant,
19: 1 it was told J', Behold, the king
5 J' came into the house to the king,
13 me continually in the room of J'.
20: 9 J' said to Amasa, Art thou in
9 J' took Amasa by the beard with
10 So J' and Abishai his brother
11 and said, He that favoureth J',
11 is for David, let him go after J'.
13 all the people went on after J', to
15 people that were with J' battered
16 say, I pray you, unto J', Come near
17 her, the woman said, Art thou J'?
20 J' answered and said, Far be it,
21 the woman said unto J', Behold,
22 son of Bichri, and cast it out to J'.
22 J' returned to Jerusalem unto the
23 J' was over all the host of Israel:
23:18 Abishai, the brother of J', the son
24 brother of J' was one of the thirty;
37 armourbearer to J' the son of
24: 2 the king said to J' the captain of
3 J' said unto the king, Now the
4 king's word prevailed against J',
4 J' and the captains of the host
9 J' gave up the sum of the number
1Ki 1: 7 he conferred with J' the son of
19 and J' the captain of the host:
41 J' heard the sound of the trumpet,
2: 5 J' the son of Zeruiah did to me,
22 and for J' the son of Zeruiah.
28 Then tidings came to J':
28 for J' had turned after Adonijah,
28 J' fled unto the tabernacle of the
29 that J' was fled unto the tabernacle
30 Thus said J', and thus he answered
31 the innocent blood, which J' shed,
33 therefore return upon the head of J',
11:15 J' the captain of the host was gone
16 For six months did J' remain there
21 J' the captain of the host was dead,
1Ch 2:16 sons of Zeruiah; Abishai and J',
54 Ataroth, the house of J', and half
4:14 Seraiah begat J', the father of
11: 6 So J' the son of Zeruiah went first
8 J' repaired the rest of the city.
20 the brother of J', he was chief of
26 were, Asahel the brother of J',
39 the armourbearer of J' the son of
18:15 J' the son of Zeruiah was over the
19: 8 when David heard of it, he sent J',
10 when J' saw that the battle was
14 So J' and the people that were
15 city. Then J' came to Jerusalem.
20: 1 J' led forth the power of the army,
1 J' smote Rabbah, and destroyed it.
21: 2 David said to J' and to the rulers
3 And J' answered, The Lord make
4 king's word prevailed against J'.
4 Wherefore J' departed, and went
5 J' gave the sum of the number of
6 king's word was abominable to J'.
26:28 and J' the son of Zeruiah, had
27: 7 month was Asahel the brother of J',
24 J' the son of Zeruiah began to
34 general of the king's army was J'.
Ezr 2: 6 of the children of Jeshua and J',
8: 9 Of the sons of J'; Obadiah the son
Ne 7:11 of the children of Jeshua and J',
Ps 60: *title* when J' returned, and smote of

Joab's (*jo'-abs*)
2Sa 14:30 J' field is near mine, and he hath
17:25 Nahash, sister to Zeruiah J' mother,
18: 2 the son of Zeruiah, J' brother,
15 young men that bare J' armour
20: 7 there went out after him J' men,
8 J' garment that he had put on was
10 to the sword that was in J' hand:
11 one of J' men stood by him, and

Joah (*jo'-ah*) See also ETHAN.
2Ki 18:18 J' the son of Asaph the recorder.
26 Shebna, and J', unto Rab-shakeh,
37 J' the son of Asaph the recorder,
1Ch 6:21 J' his son, Iddo his son, Zerah his
26: 4 J' the third, and Sacar the fourth,
2Ch 29:12 Gershonites; J' the son of Zimmah,
12 and Eden the son of J':
34: 8 J' the son of Joahaz the recorder,
Isa 36: 3 and J', Asaph's son, the recorder.
11 Shebna and J' unto Rabshakeh,
22 J', the son of Asaph, the recorder,

Joahaz (*jo'-a-haz*) See also JEHOAHAZ.
2Ch 34: 8 Joah the son of J' the recorder,

Joanna (*jo-an'-nah*)
Lu 3:27 Which was the son of J', which
8: 3 And J' the wife of Chuza Herod's
24:10 It was Mary Magdalene, and J',

Joash (*jo'-ash*) See also JEHOASH.
J'g 6:11 pertained unto J' the Abi-ezrite:
29 the son of J' hath done this thing.
30 men of the city said unto J', Bring
31 J' said unto all that stood against
7:14 the sword of Gideon the son of J',
8:13 the son of J' returned from battle
29 the son of J' went and dwelt in his
32 Gideon the son of J' died in a good
32 in the sepulchre of J' his father,
1Ki 22:26 the city, and to J' the king's son;
2Ki 11: 2 took J' the son of Ahaziah, and
12:19 the rest of the acts of J', and all
20 slew J' in the house of Millo, which
13: 1 the three and twentieth year of J'
9 and J' his son reigned in his stead.
10 the thirty and seventh year of J'
12 the rest of the acts of J', and all
13 And J' slept with his fathers; and
13 J' was buried in Samaria with the
14 J' the king of Israel came down
25 Three times did J' beat him, and
14: 1 second year of J' son of Jehoahaz
1 the son of J' king of Judah.
3 to all things as J' his father did.
17 the son of J' king of Judah
23 year of Amaziah the son of J'
23 Jeroboam the son of J' king of
27 the hand of Jeroboam the son of J'.
1Ch 3:11 son, Ahaziah his son, J' his son,
4:22 J', and Saraph, who had the
7: 8 Zemira, and J', and Eliezer, and
12: 3 The chief was Ahiezer, then J',
27:28 and over the cellars of oil was J':
2Ch 18:25 the city, and to J' the king's son;
22:11 took J' the son of Ahaziah, and
24: 1 J' was seven years old when he
2 J' did that which was right in the
4 J' was minded to repair the house
22 Thus J' the king remembered not
24 they executed judgment against J'.
25:17 Judah took advice, and sent to J',
18 J' king of Israel sent to Amaziah
21 so J' the king of Israel went up;
23 J' the king of Israel took Amaziah
23 king of Judah, the son of J', the
25 Amaziah the son of J' king of Judah
25 death of J' son of Jehoahaz king of
Ho 1: 1 days of Jeroboam the son of J',
Am 1: 1 days of Jeroboam the son of J'

Joatham (*jo'-a-tham*) See also JOTHAM.
M't 1: 9 And Ozias begat J'; and J' begat

Job^ (*jobe*) See also JASHUB; JOB'S.
Ge 46:13 Tola, and Phuvah, and J', and
Job 1: 1 land of Uz, whose name was J';
5 that J' sent and sanctified them,
5 J' said, It may be that my sons have
5 hearts. Thus did J' continually.
8 Hast thou considered my servant J',
9 said, Doth J' fear God for nought?
14 there came a messenger unto J',
20 Then J' arose, and rent his mantle,
22 In all this J' sinned not, nor charged
2: 3 Hast thou considered my servant J',
7 smote J' with sore boils from the
10 In all this did not J' sin with his
3: 1 After this opened J' his mouth, and
2 And J' spake, and said,
6: 1 But J' answered, and said,
9: 1 Then J' answered and said,
12: 1 And J' answered and said,
16: 1 Then J' answered and said,
19: 1 Then J' answered and said,
21: 1 But J' answered and said,
23: 1 Then J' answered and said,
26: 1 But J' answered and said,
27: 1 Moreover J' continued his parable,
29: 1 Moreover J' continued his parable,
31:40 barley. The words of J' are ended.
32: 1 three men ceased to answer J',
2 against J' was his wrath kindled,
3 and yet had condemned J'.
4 Elihu had waited till J' had spoken,
12 was none of you that convinced J',
33: 1 J', I pray thee, hear my speeches,
31 Mark well, O J', hearken unto me:
34: 5 For J' hath said, I am righteous:
7 What man is like J', who drinketh
35 J' hath spoken without knowledge,
36 My desire is that J' may be tried
35:16 doth J' open his mouth in vain;
37:14 Hearken unto this, O J': stand still,
38: 1 the Lord answered J' out of the
40: 1 the Lord answered J', and said,
3 J' answered the Lord, and said,
6 answered the Lord unto J' out of
42: 1 J' answered the Lord, and said,
7 had spoken these words unto J',
7 that is right, as my servant J' hath.
8 go to my servant J', and offer up
8 my servant J' shall pray for you:
8 which is right, like my servant J',
9 them: the Lord also accepted J'.
10 the Lord turned the captivity of J',
10 gave J' twice as much as he had
12 Lord blessed the latter end of J'
15 found so fair as the daughter of J':
16 lived J' a hundred and forty years,

Job 42:17 So J· died, being old and full of
Eze 14:14 three men, Noah, Daniel, and J·,
20 Noah, Daniel, and J·, were in it, as
Jas 5:11 have heard of the patience of J·.
Jobab (*jo'-bab*)
Ge 10:29 And Ophir, and Havilah, and J·:
36:33 and J· the son of Zerah of Bozrah
34 And J· died, and Husham of the
Jos 11: 1 he sent to J· king of Madon, and
1Ch 1:23 And Ophir, and Havilah, and J·.
44 J· the son of Zerah of Bozrah
45 And when J· was dead, Husham
8: 9 he begat of Hodesh his wife, J·,
18 Ishmerai also, and Jezliah, and J·.
Job's (*jobes*)
Job 2:11 when J· three friends heard of all
Jochebed (*jok'-e-bed*)
Ex 6:20 Amram took him J· his father's
Nu 26:59 the name of Amram's wife was J·.
Joed (*jo'-ed*)
Ne 11: 7 the son of J·, the son of Pedaiah,
Joel (*jo'-el*)
1Sa 8: 2 the name of his firstborn was J·;
1Ch 4:35 J·, and Jehu the son of Josibiah,
5: 4 The sons of J·; Shemaiah his son,
8 the son of J·, who dwelt in Aroer,
12 J· the chief, and Shapham the next,
6:33 Heman a singer, the son of J·, the
36 Elkanah, the son of J·, the son of
7: 3 and Obadiah, and J·, Ishiah, five:
11:38 J· the brother of Nathan, Mibhar
15: 7 the sons of Gershom; J· the chief,
11 Levites, for Uriel, Asaiah, and J·,
17 appointed Heman the son of J·;
23: 8 Jehiel, and Zatham, and J·, three.
26:22 Zetham, and J· his brother, which
27:20 Manasseh, J· the son of Pedaiah:
2Ch 29:12 Amasai, and J· the son of Azariah,
Ezr 10:43 Zabad, Zebina, Jadau, and J·,
Ne 11: 9 And J· the son of Zichri was their
Joe 1: 1 word of the Lord that came to J·
Ac 2:16 was spoken by the prophet J·;
Joelah (*jo-e'-lah*)
1Ch 12: 7 J·, and Zebadiah, the sons of
Joezer (*jo-e'-zer*)
1Ch 12: 6 and Jesiah, and Azareel, and J·,
Jogbehah (*jog'-be-hah*)
Nu 32:35 Shophan, and Jaazer, and J·,
J'g 8:11 tents on the east of Nobah and J·,
Jogli (*jog'-li*)
Nu 34:22 of Dan, Bukki the son of J·.
Joha (*jo'-hah*)
1Ch 8:16 And Michael, and Ispah, and J·,
11:45 son of Shimri, and J· his brother,
Johanan (*jo-ha'-nan*) See also JEHOHANAN; JOHN.
2Ki 25:23 and J· the son of Careah,
1Ch 3:15 sons of Josiah were, the firstborn J·,
24 and J·, and Dalaiah, and Anani,
6: 9 Azariah, and Azariah begat J·,
10 J· begat Azariah, (he it is that
12: 4 Jahaziel, and J·, and Josabad the
12 J· the eighth, Elzabad the ninth,
2Ch 28:12 Ephraim, Azariah the son of J·,
Ezr 8:12 J· the son of Hakkatan, and with
10: 6 and went into the chamber of J·,
Ne 6:18 his son J· had taken the daughter
12:22 J·, and Jaddua, were recorded
23 even until the days of J· the son of
Jer 40: 8 and J· and Jonathan the sons of
13 Moreover J· the son of Kareah, and
15 Then J· the son of Kareah spake to
16 the son of Ahikam said unto J· the
41:11 But when J· the son of Kareah,
13 which were with Ishmael saw J·
14 and went unto J· the son of Kareah.
15 escaped from J· with eight men,
16 Then took J· the son of Kareah,
42: 1 the captains of the forces, and J·
8 Then called he J· the son of Kareah,
43: 2 J· the son of Kareah, and all the
4 So J· the son of Kareah, and all
5 But J· the son of Kareah, and all
John (*jon*) See also BAPTIST; JEHOHANAN; JOHN'S; MARK.
M't 3: 1 In these days came J· the Baptist,
4 same J· had his raiment of camel's
13 from Galilee to Jordan unto J·,
14 J· forbade him, saying, I have need
4:12 heard that J· was cast into prison,
21 son of Zebedee, and J· his brother,
9:14 came to him the disciples of J·,
10: 2 son of Zebedee, and J· his brother;
11: 2 when J· had heard in the prison
4 Go and shew J· again those things
7 unto the multitudes concerning J·,
11 risen a greater than J· the Baptist:
12 from the days of J· the Baptist
13 and the law prophesied until J·.
18 J· came neither eating nor drinking,
14: 2 his servants, This is J· the Baptist;
3 For Herod had laid hold on J·,
4 J· said unto him, It is not lawful
8 J· the Baptist's head in a charger.
10 sent, and beheaded J· in the prison.
16:14 say that thou art J· the Baptist;
17: 1 Peter, James, and J· his brother,
13 spake unto them of J· the Baptist.
21:25 The baptism of J·, whence was it?
26 people; for all hold J· as a prophet.
32 J· came unto you in the way of
M'r 1: 4 J· did baptize in the wilderness,
6 J· was clothed with camel's hair,
M'r 1: 9 and was baptized of J· in Jordan.
14 Now after that J· was put in prison,
19 son of Zebedee, and J· his brother,
29 and Andrew, with James and J·.
2:18 the disciples of J· and of the
18 Why do the disciples of J· and of
3:17 and J· the brother of James;
5:37 James, and J· the brother of James.
6:14 J· the Baptist was risen from the
16 he said, It is J·, whom I beheaded:
17 laid hold upon J·, and bound him
18 J· had said unto Herod, It is not
20 Herod feared J·, knowing that he
24 said, The head of J· the Baptist.
25 charger the head of J· the Baptist.
8:28 they answered, J· the Baptist:
9: 2 with him Peter and James, and J·,
38 J· answered him, saying, Master,
10:35 James and J·, the sons of Zebedee,
41 much displeased with James and J·.
11:30 baptism of J·, was it from heaven,
32 all men counted J·, that he was a
13: 3 Peter, and James, and J·, and
14:33 with him Peter and James and J·,
Lu 1:13 and thou shalt call his name J·.
60 Not so; but he shall be called J·.
63 and wrote, saying, His name is J·.
3: 2 the word of God came unto J· the
15 all men mused in their hearts of J·,
16 J· answered, saying unto them all,
20 all, that he shut up J· in prison.
5:10 James, and J·, the sons of Zebedee,
33 Why do the disciples of J· fast often,
6:14 and J·, Philip and Bartholomew,
7:18 disciples of J· shewed him of all
19 J· calling unto him two of his
20 J· the Baptist hath sent us...thee,
22 tell J· what things ye have seen
24 messengers of J· were departed,
24 unto the people concerning J·,
28 greater prophet than J· the Baptist:
29 baptized with the baptism of J·.
33 J· the Baptist came neither eating
8:51 save Peter, and James, and J·,
9: 7 that J· was risen from the dead;
9 Herod said, J· have I beheaded:
19 answering said, J· the Baptist;
28 he took Peter and J· and James,
49 And J· answered and said, Master,
54 his disciples James and J· saw this,
11: 1 as J· also taught his disciples.
16:16 law and the prophets were until J·:
20: 4 baptism of J·, was it from heaven,
6 be persuaded that J· was a prophet.
22: 8 he sent Peter and J·, saying, Go and
Joh 1: 6 sent from God, whose name was J·.
15 J· bare witness of him, and cried,
19 And this is the record of J·, when
26 J· answered them, saying, I baptize
28 Jordan, where J· was baptizing.
29 The next day J· seeth Jesus coming
32 And J· bare record, saying, I saw
35 J· stood, and two of his disciples;
40 of the two which heard J· speak,
3:23 And J· also was baptizing in Ænon
24 For J· was not yet cast into prison.
26 And they came unto J·, and said
27 J· answered and said, A man can
4: 1 baptized more disciples than J·,
5:33 sent unto J·, and he bare witness
36 have greater witness than that of J·:
10:40 the place where J· at first baptized;
41 him, and said, J· did no miracle:
41 that J· spake of this man were true.
Ac 1: 5 For J· truly baptized with water;
13 abode both Peter, and James, and J·,
22 Beginning from the baptism of J·,
3: 1 Peter and J· went up together into
3 seeing Peter and J· about to go into
4 fastening his eyes upon him with J·,
11 which was healed held Peter and J·,
4: 6 Caiaphas, and J·, and Alexander,
13 saw the boldness of Peter and J·,
19 But Peter and J· answered and said
8:14 they sent unto them Peter and J·:
10:37 the baptism which J· preached;
11:16 J· indeed baptized with water;
12: 2 killed James the brother of J· with
12 of J·, whose surname was Mark;
25 them J·, whose surname was Mark.
13: 5 they had also J· to their minister.
13 J· departing from them returned
24 When J· had first preached before
25 And as J· fulfilled his course, he
15:37 them J·, whose surname was Mark.
18:25 knowing only the baptism of J·.
19: 4 J· verily baptized with the baptism
Gal 2: 9 Cephas, and J·, who seemed to be
Re 1: 1 it by his angel unto his servant J·:
4 J· to the seven churches which are
9 I J·, who also am your brother,
21: 2 And I J· saw the holy city, new
22: 8 And I J· saw these things, and
John's (*jonz*)
Joh 3:25 between some of J· disciples and
Ac 19: 3 And they said, Unto J· baptism.
Joiada (*joy'-a-dah*) See also JEHOIADA.
Ne 12:10 Eliashib, and Eliashib begat J·,
11 J· begat Jonathan, and Jonathan
22 Levites in the days of Eliashib, J·,
13:28 one of the sons of J·, the son of
Joiakim (*joy'-a-kim*) See also JEHOIAKIM.
Ne 12:10 Jeshua begat J·, J· also begat
12 in the days of J· were priests, the
26 in the days of J· the son of Jeshua,
Joiarib (*joy'-a-rib*) See also JEHOIARIB.
Ezr 8:16 for J·, and for Elnathan, men of
Ne 11: 5 the son of Adaiah, the son of J·,
10 the priests: Jedaiah the son of J·,
12: 6 Shemaiah, and J·, Jedaiah,
19 of J·, Mattenai; of Jedaiah, Uzzi;
join See also JOINED; JOINING.
Ex 1:10 they j· also unto our enemies, and
2Ch 20:35 king of Judah j· himself with
Ezr 9:14 and j· in affinity with the people of
Pr 11:21 Though hand j· in hand, the wicked
16: 5 though hand j· in hand, he shall not be
Isa 5: 8 unto them that j· house to house,
9:11 him, and j· his enemies together;
56: 6 that j· themselves to the Lord, to
Jer 50: 5 let us j· ourselves to the Lord in a
Eze 37:17 j· them one to another into one
Da 11: 6 they shall j· themselves together;
Ac 5:13 durst no man j· himself to them:
8:29 near, and j· thyself to this chariot.
9:26 assayed to j· himself to the disciples:
joined See also ENJOINED.
Ge 14: 3 these were j· together in the vale
14: 8 they j· battle with them in the vale
29:34 will my husband be j· unto me,
Ex 28: 7 shoulderpieces thereof j· at the two
7 and so it shall be j· together.
Nu 18: 2 that they may be j· unto thee, and
4 they shall be j· unto thee, and keep
25: 3 Israel j· himself unto Baal-peor:
5 men that were j· unto Baal-peor.
1Sa 4: 2 they j· battle, Israel was smitten
1Ki 7:32 of the wheels were j· to the base:
20:29 the seventh day the battle was j·:
2Ch 18: 1 and j· affinity with Ahab.
20:36 j· himself with him to make ships
37 thou hast j· thyself with Ahaziah,
Ezr 4:12 thereof, and j· the foundations.
Ne 4: 6 all the wall was j· together unto
Es 9:27 such as j· themselves unto them,
Job 3: 6 not be j· unto the days of the year,
41:17 They are j· one to another, they
23 flakes of his flesh are j· together:
Ps 83: 8 Assur also is j· with them: they
106:28 j· themselves also unto Baal-peor,
Ec 9: 4 to him that is j· to all the living
Isa 13:15 every one that is j· unto them
14: 1 strangers shall be j· with them,
20 shalt not be j· with them in burial,
56: 3 that hath j· himself to the Lord,
Eze 1: 9 wings were j· one to another;
11 two wings of every one were j· one
46:22 there were courts j· of forty cubits
Ho 4:17 Ephraim is j· to idols: let him
Zec 2:11 nations shall be j· to the Lord
M't 19: 6 therefore God hath j· together,
M'r 10: 9 therefore God hath j· together,
Lu 15:15 and j· himself to a citizen of that
Ac 5:36 about four hundred, j· themselves:
18: 7 house j· hard to the synagogue.
1Co 1:10 that ye be perfectly j· together
6:16 not that he which is j· to an harlot
17 he that is j· unto the Lord is one
Eph 4:16 the whole body fitly j· together
5:31 shall be j· unto his wife, and they
joining See also JOININGS.
2Ch 3:12 j· to the wing of the other cherub.
joinings
1Ch 22: 3 doors of the gates, and for the j·;
joint See also JOINT-HEIRS; JOINTS.
Ge 32:25 of Jacob's thigh was out of j·,
Ps 22:14 and all my bones are out of j·:
Pr 25:19 broken tooth, and a foot out of j·.
Eph 4:16 by that which every j· supplieth,
joint-heirs
Ro 8:17 heirs of God, and j· with Christ;
joints
1Ki 22:34 between the j· of the harness:
2Ch 18:33 between the j· of the harness:
Ca 7: 1 the j· of thy thighs are like jewels,
Da 5: 6 that the j· of his loins were loosed,
Col 2:19 all the body by j· and bands having
Heb 4:12 spirit, and of the j· and marrow,
Jokdeam (*jok'-de-am*)
Jos 15:56 And Jezreel, and J·, and Zanoah,
Jokim (*jo'-kim*)
1Ch 4:22 J·, and the men of Chozeba, and
Jokmeam (*jok'-me-am*) See also JOKNEAM.
1Ch 6:68 and J· with her suburbs, and
Jokneam (*jok'-ne-am*) See also JOKMEAM; KIBZAIM.
Jos 12:22 the king of J· of Carmel, one;
19:11 to the river that is before J·;
21:34 J· with her suburbs, and Kartah
1Ki 4:12 unto the place that is beyond J·:
Jokshan (*jok'-shan*)
Ge 25: 2 she bare him Zimran, and J·, and
3 And J· begat Sheba, and Dedan.
1Ch 1:32 she bare Zimran, and J·, and
32 the sons of J·; Sheba, and Dedan.
Joktan (*jok'-tan*)
Ge 10:25 and his brother's name was J·.
26 J· begat Almodad, and Sheleph,
29 Jobab: all these were the sons of J·
1Ch 1:19 and his brother's name was J·.
20 J· begat Almodad, and Sheleph,
23 Jobab. All these were the sons of J·.

Joktheel (*jok'-the-el*) See also SELAH.
Jos 15: 38 and Dilean, and Mizpeh, and J·,
2Ki 14: 7 and called the name of it J· unto

Jona (*jo'-nah*) See also BAR-JONA; JONAH; JONAS.
Joh 1: 42 Thou art Simon the son of J·:

Jonadab (*jon'-a-dab*) See also JEHONADAB.
2Sa 13: 3 had a friend, whose name was J·,
3 and J· was a very subtle man.
5 J· said unto him, Lay thee down
32 and J·, the son of Shimeah David's
35 And J· said unto the king, Behold,
Jer 35: 6 for J· the son of Rechab our father
8 have we obeyed the voice of J·
10 that J· our father commanded us.
14 the words of J· the son of Rechab
16 the sons of J· the son of Rechab
18 obeyed the commandment of J·
19 J· the son of Rechab shall not

Jonah^ (*jo'-nah*) See also JONA; JONAS.
2Ki 14: 25 by the hand of his servant J·,
Jon 1: 1 the word of the Lord came unto J·
3 J· rose up to flee unto Tarshish
5 J· was gone down into the sides of
7 cast lots, and the lot fell upon J·.
15 took up J·, and cast him forth into
17 a great fish to swallow up J·.
17 J· was in the belly of the fish three
2: 1 J· prayed unto the Lord his God
10 it vomited out J· upon the dry land.
3: 1 word of the Lord came unto J· the
3 So J· arose, and went unto Nineveh,
4 J· began to enter into the city a
4: 1 But it displeased J· exceedingly,
5 J· went out of the city, and sat on
6 and made it to come up over J·,
6 J· was exceeding glad of the gourd.
8 the sun beat upon the head of J·,
9 God said unto J·, Doest thou well

Jonan (*jo'-nan*)
Lu 3: 30 Joseph, which was the son of J·,

Jonas (*jo'-nas*) See also JONA; JONAH.
M't 12: 39 it, but the sign of the prophet J·:
40 For as J· was three days and three
41 repented at the preaching of J·;
41 behold, a greater than J· is here
16: 4 it, but the sign of the prophet J·.
Lu 11: 29 it, but the sign of J· the prophet.
30 J· was a sign unto the Ninevites,
32 repented at the preaching of J·;
32 behold, a greater than J· is here.
Joh 21: 15, 16, 17 Simon, son of J·, lovest thou

Jonathan (*jon'-a-than*) See also JEHONATHAN; JONATHAN'S.
J'g 18: 30 J·, the son of Gershom, the son of
1Sa 13: 2 a thousand were with J· in Gibeah
3 J· smote the garrison of the
16 Saul, and J· his son, and the people
22 people that were with Saul and J·:
22 with J· his son was there found.
14: 1 J· the son of Saul said unto the
3 people knew not that J· was gone.
4 which J· sought to go over unto
6 J· said to the young man that
8 said J·, Behold, we will pass over
12 J· and his armourbearer,
12 J· said unto his armourbearer,
13 J· climbed up upon his hands and
13 and they fell before J·; and his
14 which J· and his armourbearer
17 behold, J· and his armourbearer
21 that were with Saul and J·.
27 But J· heard not when his father
29 said J·, My father hath troubled
39 it be in J· my son, he shall surely
40 I and J· my son will be on the
41 Saul and J· were taken: but the
42 lots between me and J· my son.
42 And J· was taken.
43 Then Saul said to J·, Tell me what
43 And J· told him, and said, I did but
44 also: for thou shalt surely die, J·.
45 people said unto Saul, Shall J· die,
45 So the people rescued J·, that he
49 the sons of Saul were J·, and Ishui,
18: 1 soul of J· was knit with the soul of
1 and J· loved him as his own soul.
3 J· and David made a covenant,
4 J· stripped himself of the robe that
19: 1 Saul spake to J· his son, and to all
2 J· Saul's son delighted much in
2 J· told David, saying, Saul my
4 J· spake good of David unto Saul
6 hearkened unto the voice of J·:
7 J· called David, and J· shewed him
7 J· brought David to Saul, and he
20: 1 said before J·, What have I done?
3 Let not J· know this, lest he be
4 Then said J· unto David,
5 And David said to J·, Behold
9 And J· said, Far be it from thee:
10 Then said David to J·, Who shall
11 J· said unto David, Come, and let
12 J· said unto David, O Lord God of
13 Lord do so and much more to J·:
16 J· made a covenant with the house
17 J· caused David to swear again,
18 J· said to David, To-morrow is the
25 J· arose, and Abner sat by Saul's
27 Saul said unto J· his son, Wherefore
28 J· answered Saul, David earnestly
30 Saul's anger was kindled against J·,
32 J· answered Saul his father, and
33 J· knew that it was determined
34 So J· arose from the table in fierce
1Sa 20: 35 J· went out into the field at the time
37 of the arrow which J· had shot,
37 J· cried after the lad, and said, Is
38 J· cried after the lad, Make speed,
39 only J· and David knew the matter.
40 J· gave his artillery unto his lad,
42 And J· said to David, Go in peace,
42 departed: and J· went into the city.
23: 16 J· Saul's son arose, and went to
18 the wood, and J· went to his house.
31: 2 Philistines slew J·, and Abinadab,
2Sa 1: 4 Saul and J· his son are dead also.
5 that Saul and J· his son be dead?
12 even, for Saul, and for J· his son,
17 lamentation over Saul and over J·
22 the bow of J· turned not back, and
23 Saul and J· were lovely and
25 O J·, thou wast slain in thine high
26 distressed for thee, my brother J·:
4: 4 J·, Saul's son, had a son that was
4 the tidings came of Saul and J·
9: 3 J· hath yet a son, which is lame
6 when Mephibosheth, the son of J·,
7 kindness for J· thy father's sake,
15: 27 thy son, and J· the son of Abiathar.
36 Zadok's son, and J· Abiathar's son;
17: 17 Now J· and Ahimaaz stayed by
20 said, Where is Ahimaaz and J·?
21: 7 spared Mephibosheth, the son of J·
7 between David and J· the son of
12 bones of Saul and the bones of J·
13 Saul and the bones of J· his son;
14 the bones of Saul and J· his son
21 J· the son of Shimeah the brother
23: 32 of the sons of Jashen, J·,
1Ki 1: 42 J· the son of Abiathar the priest
43 J· answered and said to Adonijah,
1Ch 2: 32 of Shammai; Jether, and J·:
33 And the sons of J·; Peleth, and
8: 33 Saul begat J·, and Malchi-shua,
34 And the son of J· was Merib-baal;
9: 39 Saul begat J·, and Malchi-shua,
40 And the son of J· was Merib-baal:
10: 2 and the Philistines slew J·, and
11: 34 J· the son of Shage the Hararite,
20: 7 J· the son of Shimea David's
27: 32 J· David's uncle was a counseller,
Ezr 8: 6 Ebed the son of J·, and with him
10: 15 Only J· the son of Asahel and
Ne 12: 11 And Joiada begat J·, and J· begat
14 Of Melicu, J·; of Shebaniah,
35 Zechariah the son of J·, the son of
Jer 37: 15 prison in the house of J· the scribe:
20 return to the house of J· the scribe,
40: 8 Johanan and J· the sons of Kareah,

Jonathan's (*jon'-a-thans*)
1Sa 20: 38 J· lad gathered up the arrows,
2Sa 9: 1 shew him kindness for J· sake?
Jer 38: 26 to return to J· house, to die there.

Jonath-elem-rechokim (*jo'''-nath-e''-lem-re-ko'-kim*)
Ps 56: *title* the chief Musician upon J·,

Joppa (*jop'-pah*) See also JAPHO.
2Ch 2: 16 it to thee in floats by sea to J·,
Ezr 3: 7 trees from Lebanon to the sea of J·
Jon 1: 3 of the Lord, and went down to J·;
Ac 9: 36 there was at J· a certain disciple
38 as Lydda was nigh to J·, and the
42 it was known throughout all J·;
43 he tarried many days in J· with one
10: 5 now send men to J·, and call for one
8 unto them, he sent them to J·.
23 and certain brethren from J·
32 Send therefore to J·, and call
11: 5 I was in the city of J· praying: and
13 Send men to J·, and call for Simon,

Jorah (*jo'-rah*) See also HARIPH.
Ezr 2: 18 The children of J·, an hundred and

Jorai (*jo'-rahee*)
1Ch 5: 13 Sheba, and J·, and Jachan, and

Joram (*jo'-ram*) See also JEHORAM.
2Sa 8: 10 Toi sent J· his son unto king David,
10 J· brought with him vessels of silver,
2Ki 8: 16 the fifth year of J· the son of Ahab
21 So J· went over to Zair, and all the
23 And the rest of the acts of J·, and all
24 J· slept with his fathers, and was
25 twelfth year of J· the son of Ahab
28 he went with J· the son of Ahab to
28 and the Syrians wounded J·.
29 And king J· went back to be healed
29 went down to see J· the son of Ahab
9: 14 son of Nimshi conspired against J·.
14 (Now J· had kept Ramoth-gilead, he
15 king J· was returned to be healed
16 went to Jezreel; for J· lay there.
16 of Judah was come down to see J·.
17 And J· said, Take an horseman,
21 And J· said, Make ready. And his
21 J· king of Israel and Ahaziah king
22 it came to pass, when J· saw Jehu,
23 And J· turned his hands, and fled,
29 eleventh year of J· the son of Ahab
11: 2 Jehosheba, the daughter of king J·,
1Ch 3: 11 J· his son, Ahaziah his son, Joash
26: 25 J· his son, and Zichri his son, and
2Ch 22: 5 and the Syrians smote J·.
7 was of God by coming to J·:
M't 1: 8 Josaphat begat J·; and J· begat

Jordan (*jor'-dan*)
Ge 13: 10 and beheld all the plain of J·,
11 Lot chose him all the plain of J·;
32: 10 with my staff I passed over this J·;
Ge 50: 10 of Atad, which is beyond J·, and
11 Abel-mizraim, which is beyond J·.
Nu 13: 29 of the sea, and by the coast of J·.
22: 1 in the plains of Moab on this side J·
26: 3 them in the plains of Moab by J·
63 Israel in the plains of Moab by J·
31: 12 the plains of Moab, which are by J·.
32: 5 possession, and bring us not over J·.
19 inherit with them on yonder side J·,
19 fallen to us on this side J· eastward.
21 And will go all of you armed over J·
29 Reuben will pass with you over J·,
32 on this side J· may be ours.
33: 48 pitched in the plains of Moab by J.
49 pitched by J·, from Beth-jesimoth
50 Moses in the plains of Moab by J·
51 over J· into the land of Canaan;
34: 12 the border shall go down to J·, and
15 their inheritance this side J· near
35: 1 Moses in the plains of Moab by J·
10 ye be come over J· into the land of
14 give three cities on this side J·,
36: 13 Israel in the plains of Moab by J·.
De 1: 1 on this side J· in the wilderness,
5 On this side J·, in the land of Moab,
2: 29 until I shall pass over J· into the
3: 8 the land that was on this side J·,
17 plain also, and J·, and the coast,
20 God hath given them beyond J·:
25 see the good land that is beyond J·,
27 for thou shalt not go over this J·.
4: 21 sware that I should not go over J·,
22 in this land, I must not go over J·:
26 whereunto ye go over J· to possess
41 severed three cities on this side J·
46 On this side J·, in the valley over
47 this side J· toward the sunrising;
49 And all the plain on this side J·
9: 1 Thou art to pass over J· this day,
11: 30 Are they not on the other side J·,
31 For ye shall pass over J· to go in to
12: 10 But when ye go over J·, and dwell
27: 2 when ye shall pass over J· unto the
4 shall be when ye be gone over J·,
12 people, when ye are come over J·;
30: 18 passest over J· to go to possess it.
31: 2 Thou shalt not go over this J·.
13 in the land whither ye go over J·
32: 47 whither ye go over J· to possess it.
Jos 1: 2 go over this J·, thou, and all this
11 days ye shall pass over this J·,
14 Moses gave you on this side J·;
15 this side J· toward the sunrising.
2: 7 them the way to J· unto the fords:
10 were on the other side J·, Sihon
3: 1 from Shittim, and came to J·,
8 to the brink of the water of J·,
8 ye shall stand still in J·.
11 passeth over before you into J·.
13 earth, shall rest in the waters of J·,
13 the waters of J· shall be cut off
14 from their tents, to pass over J·,
15 bare the ark were come unto J·,
15 J· overfloweth all his banks all the
17 on dry ground in the midst of J·,
17 people were passed clean over J·.
4: 1 people were clean passed over J·,
3 you hence out of the midst of J·,
5 Lord your God into the midst of J·,
7 the waters of J· were cut off before
7 the Lord; when it passed over J·,
7 the waters of J· were cut off: and
8 twelve stones out of the midst of J·,
9 up twelve stones in the midst of J·,
10 the ark stood in the midst of J·,
16 that they come up out of J·.
17 saying, Come ye up out of J·.
18 come up out of the midst of J·,
18 waters of J· returned unto their
19 came up out of J· on the tenth day
20 stones, which they took out of J·,
22 Israel came over this J· on dry
23 God dried up the waters of J· from
5: 1 were on the side of J· westward,
1 Lord had dried up the waters of J·
7: 7 at all brought this people over J·,
7 and dwelt on the other side J·!
9: 1 kings which were on this side J·,
10 the Amorites, that were beyond J·,
12: 1 their land on the other side J·
7 smote on this side J· on the west,
13: 8 gave them, beyond J· eastward,
23 And the border...of Reuben was J·,
27 of Heshbon, J· and his border,
27 on the other side J· eastward.
32 plains of Moab, on the other side J·,
14: 3 an half tribe on the other side J·:
15: 5 salt sea, even unto the end of J·.
5 the sea at the uttermost part of J·:
16: 1 of Joseph fell from J· by Jericho,
7 to Jericho, and went out at J·.
17: 5 which were on the other side J·;
18: 7 received their inheritance beyond J·
12 on the north side was from J·;
19 the salt sea at the south end of J·:
20 J· was the border of it on the east
19: 22 outgoings of their border were at J·:
33 the outgoings thereof were at J·:
34 to Judah upon J· toward the
20: 8 other side J· by Jericho eastward,
22: 4 Lord gave you on the other side J·.
7 brethren on this side J· westward.
10 they came unto the borders of J·,
10 Manasseh built there an altar by J·,
11 in the borders of J·, at the passage
25 the Lord hath made J· a border

Jos 23: 4 inheritance for your tribes, from J'.
24: 8 which dwelt on the other side J';
11 ye went over J', and came unto
J'g 3: 28 took the fords of J' toward Moab,
5: 17 Gilead abode beyond J': and why
7: 24, 24 waters unto Beth-barah and J'.
25 Zeeb to Gideon on the other side J'.
8: 4 Gideon came to J', and passed over,
10: 8 that were on the other side J' in
9 children of Ammon passed over J'
11: 13 even unto Jabbok, and unto J':
22 from the wilderness even unto J'.
12: 5 Gileadites took the passages of J'
6 slew him at the passages of J':
1Sa 13: 7 some of the Hebrews went over J'
31: 7 they that were on the other side J',
2Sa 2: 29 passed over J', and went through
10: 17 Israel together, and passed over J',
17: 22 with him, and they passed over J':
22 of them that was not gone over J'.
24 Absalom passed over J', he and all
19: 15 the king returned, and came to J'.
15 king, to conduct the king over J'.
17 they went over J' before the king.
18 the king, as he was come over J';
31 from Rogelim, and went over J'
31 the king, to conduct him over J'.
36 servant will go a little way over J'
39 And all the people went over J'.
41 David's men with him, over J'?
20: 2 king, from J' even to Jerusalem.
24: 5 they passed over J', and pitched
1Ki 2: 8 he came down to meet me at J'.
7: 46 In the plain of J' did the king cast
17: 3, 5 brook Cherith, that is before J'.
2Ki 2: 6 for the Lord hath sent me to J'.
7 afar off: and they two stood by J'.
13 back, and stood by the bank of J';
5: 10 Go and wash in J' seven times,
14 dipped himself seven times in J',
6: 2 Let us go, we pray thee, unto J',
4 when they came to J', they cut
7: 15 they went after them unto J': and,
10: 33 From J' eastward, all...Gilead,
1Ch 6: 78 on the other side J' by Jericho,
78 on the east side of J', were given
12: 15 they that went over J' in the first
37 on the other side of J', of the
19: 17 all Israel, and passed over J',
26: 30 among them of Israel on this side J'
2Ch 4: 17 In the plain of J' did the king cast
Job 40: 23 he can draw up J' into his mouth.
Ps 42: 6 remember thee from the land of J',
114: 3 and fled: J' was driven back.
5 thou J', that thou wast driven back?
Isa 9: 1 by the way of the sea, beyond J',
Jer 12: 5 wilt thou do in the swelling of J'?
49: 19 like a lion from the swelling of J'
50: 44 like a lion from the swelling of J'
Eze 47: 18 and from the land of Israel by J',
Zec 11: 3 lions; for the pride of J' is spoiled.
M't 3: 5 and all the region round about J',
6 baptized of him in J', confessing
13 cometh Jesus from Galilee to J'
4: 15 by the way of the sea, beyond J',
25 from Judæa, and from beyond J'.
19: 1 into the coasts of Judæa beyond J';
M'r 1: 5 baptized of him in the river of J',
9 and was baptized of John in J',
3: 8 Idumæa, and from beyond J';
10: 1 of Judæa by the farther side of J':
Lu 3: 3 came into all the country about J',
4: 1 the Holy Ghost returned from J',
Joh 1: 28 were done in Bethabara beyond J',
3: 26 he that was with thee beyond J',
10: 40 went away again beyond J' into

Jorim (*jo'-rim*)
Lu 3: 29 Eliezer, which was the son of J',

Jorkoam (*jor'-ko-am*)
1Ch 2: 44 begat Raham, the father of J':

Josabad (*jos'-a-bad*) See also JOZABAD.
1Ch 12: 4 Johanan, and J' the Gederathite,

Josaphat (*jos'-a-fat*) See also JEHOSHAPHAT.
M't 1: 8 Asa begat J'; and J' begat Joram;

Jose (*jo'-ze*) See also JOSES.
Lu 3: 29 Which was the son of J', which

Josedech (*jos'-e-dek*) See also JOZADAK.
Hag 1: 1 to Joshua the son of J', the high
12 and Joshua the son of J', the high
14 spirit of Joshua the son of J', the
2: 2 to Joshua the son of J', the high
4 Joshua, son of J', the high priest;
Zec 6: 11 the head of Joshua the son of J',

Joseph (*jo'-zef*) See also BARSABAS; JOSEPH'S.
Ge 30: 24 And she called his name J'; and
25 to pass, when Rachel had borne J',
33: 2 and Rachel and J' hindermost.
7 and after came J' near and Rachel,
35: 24 sons of Rachel; J', and Benjamin:
37: 2 J', being seventeen years old, was
2 J' brought unto his father...report.
3 Israel loved J' more than all his
5 J' dreamed a dream, and he told
13 Israel said unto J', Do not thy
17 J' went after his brethren, and
23 when J' was come unto his brethren,
23 that they stript J' out of his coat,
28 drew and lifted up J' out of the pit,
28 and sold J' to the Ishmeelites for
28 and they brought J' into Egypt.
29 behold, J' was not in the pit; and
33 J' is without doubt rent in pieces.
39: 1 J' was brought down to Egypt;
2 And the Lord was with J', and he
Ge 39: 4 J' found grace in his sight, and
6 J' was a goodly person, and well
7 master's wife cast her eyes upon J';
10 as she spake to J' day by day,
11 that J' went into the house to do
21 But the Lord was with J', and
40: 3 the place where J' was bound.
4 of the guard charged J' with them,
6 And J' came in unto them in the
8 And J' said unto them, Do not
9 chief butler told his dream to J',
12 And J' said unto him, This is the
16 he said unto J', I also was in my
18 J' answered and said, This is the
22 as J' had interpreted to them.
23 not the chief butler remember J',
41: 14 Pharaoh sent and called J', and
15 And Pharaoh said unto J', I have
16 J' answered Pharaoh, saying, It is
17 Pharaoh said unto J', In my dream,
25 J' said unto Pharaoh, The dream
39 Pharaoh said unto J', Forasmuch
41 Pharaoh said unto J', See, I have
44 Pharaoh said unto J', I am
45 And J' went out over all the land of
46 J' was thirty years old when he
46 J' went out from the presence of
49 J' gathered corn as the sand of the
50 unto J' were born two sons before
51 J' called the name of the firstborn
54 to come, according as J' had said:
55 unto all the Egyptians, Go unto J';
56 J' opened all the storehouses, and
57 came into Egypt to J' for to buy
42: 6 J' was the governor over the land,
7 J' saw his brethren, and he knew
8 J' knew his brethren, but they knew
9 J' remembered the dreams which
14 J' said unto them, That is it that I
18 J' said unto them the third day,
23 knew not that J' understood them;
25 J' commanded to fill their sacks
36 J' is not, and Simeon is not, and ye
43: 15 down to Egypt, and stood before J'.
16 when J' saw Benjamin with them,
17 And the man did as J' bade; and
25 present against J' came at noon:
26 when J' came home, they brought
30 J' made haste; for his bowels did
44: 2 to the word that J' had spoken.
4 J' said unto his steward, Up, follow
15 J' said unto them, What deed is
45: 1 Then J' could not refrain himself
1 while J' made himself known unto
3 J' said unto his brethren, I am J';
4 J' said unto his brethren, Come
4 I am J' your brother, whom ye sold
9 Thus saith thy son J', God hath
17 Pharaoh said unto J', Say unto thy
21 J' gave them wagons, according to
26 told him, saying, J' is yet alive,
27 they told him all the words of J',
27 saw the wagons which J' had sent
28 It is enough; J' my son is yet alive:
46: 4 J' shall put his hand upon thine
19 sons of Rachel Jacob's wife; J', and
20 unto J' in the land of Egypt were
27 sons of J', which were born him in
28 he sent Judah before him unto J',
29 J' made ready his chariot, and went
30 Israel said unto J', Now let me die,
31 J' said unto his brethren, and unto
47: 1 Then J' came and told Pharaoh, and
5 And Pharaoh spake unto J', saying,
7 And J' brought in Jacob his father,
11 And J' placed his father and his
12 J' nourished his father, and his
14 J' gathered up all the money that
14 J' brought the money into Pharaoh's
15 the Egyptians came unto J', and
16 J' said, Give your cattle; and I will
17 they brought their cattle unto J':
17 J' gave them bread in exchange for
20 J' bought all the land of Egypt for
23 J' said unto the people, Behold, I
26 J' made it a law over the land of
29 and he called his son J', and said
48: 1 told J', Behold, thy father is sick:
2 thy son J' cometh unto thee:
3 Jacob said unto J', God Almighty
9 J' said unto his father, They are
11 And Israel said unto J', I had not
12 J' brought them out from between
13 J' took them both, Ephraim in his
15 he blessed J', and said, God, before
17 when J' saw that his father laid his
18 J' said unto his father, Not so, my
21 Israel said unto J', Behold, I die:
49: 22 J' is a fruitful bough, even a fruitful
26 shall be on the head of J', and on
50: 1 J' fell upon his father's face, and
2 J' commanded...the physicians to
4 J' spake unto the house of Pharaoh,
7 J' went up to bury his father: and
8 And all the house of J', and his
14 J' returned into Egypt, he, and his
15 said, J' will peradventure hate us,
16 And they sent a messenger unto J',
17 So shall ye say unto J', Forgive, I
17 J' wept when they spake unto him.
19 J' said unto them, Fear not: for am
22 And J' dwelt in Egypt, he, and his
22 J' lived an hundred and ten years.
23 J' saw Ephraim's children of the
24 J' said unto his brethren, I die:
25 J' took an oath of the children of
Ge 50: 26 J' died, being an hundred and ten
Ex 1: 5 souls: for J' was in Egypt already.
6 J' died, and all his brethren, and
8 king over Egypt, which knew not J'
13: 19 Moses took the bones of J' with
Nu 1: 10 Of the children of J': of Ephraim;
32 Of the children of J', namely, of
13: 7 tribe of Issachar, Igal the son of J'.
11 Of the tribe of J', namely, of the
26: 28 The sons of J' after their families
37 the sons of J' after their families.
27: 1 families of Manasseh the son of J':
32: 33 tribe of Manasseh the son of J',
34: 23 prince of the children of J', for the
36: 1 of the families of the sons of J',
5 The tribe of the sons of J' hath said
12 the sons of Manasseh the son of J',
De 27: 12 Issachar, and J', and Benjamin:
33: 13 And of J' he said, Blessed of the
16 blessing come upon the head of J',
Jos 14: 4 the children of J' were two tribes,
16: 1 the children of J' fell from Jordan
4 So the children of J', Manasseh and
17: 1 for he was the firstborn of J';
2 children of Manasseh the son of J'
14 children of J' spake unto Joshua,
16 And the children of J' said, The hill
17 Joshua spake unto the house of J',
18: 5 the house of J' shall abide in their
11 of Judah and the children of J'.
24: 32 And the bones of J', which the
32 the inheritance of the children of J'.
J'g 1: 22 the house of J', they also went up
23 house of J' sent to descry Beth-el.
35 hand of the house of J' prevailed,
2Sa 19: 20 first this day of all the house of J'
1Ki 11: 28 all the charge of the house of J'.
1Ch 2: 2 Dan, J', and Benjamin, Naphtali,
5: 1 was given unto the sons of J'
7: 29 In these dwelt the children of J'
25: 2 the sons of Asaph; Zaccur, and J',
9 first lot came forth for Asaph to J':
Ezr 10: 42 Shallum, Amariah, and J'.
Ne 12: 14 Melicu, Jonathan; of Shebaniah, J';
Ps 77: 15 thy people, the sons of Jacob and J'.
78: 67 he refused the tabernacle of J',
80: 1 thou that leadest J' like a flock;
81: 5 he ordained in J' for a testimony,
105: 17 sent a man before them, even J',
Eze 37: 16 For J', the stick of Ephraim, and
19 I will take the stick of J', which is
47: 13 Israel: J' shall have two portions.
48: 32 and one gate of J', one gate of
Am 5: 6 out like fire in the house of J', and
15 be gracious unto the remnant of J'.
6: 6 not grieved for the affliction of J'.
Ob 18 a fire, and the house of J' a flame,
Zec 10: 6 and I will save the house of J', and
M't 1: 16 begat J' the husband of Mary,
18 mother Mary was espoused to J',
19 Then J' her husband, being a just
20 J', thou son of David, fear not to
24 J' being raised from sleep did as
2: 13 Lord appeareth to J' in a dream,
19 Lord appeareth in a dream to J'
27: 57 rich man of Arimathæa, named J',
59 And when J' had taken the body, he
M'r 15: 43 J' of Arimathæa, an honourable
45 centurion, he gave the body to J'.
Lu 1: 27 to a man whose name was J',
2: 4 And J' also went up from Galilee,
16 found Mary, and J', and the babe
33 J' and his mother marvelled at
43 J' and his mother knew not of it.
3: 23 (as was supposed) the son of J',
24 of Janna, which was the son of J',
26 of Semei, which was the son of J',
30 of Juda, which was the son of J',
23: 50 was a man named J', a counsellor;
Joh 1: 45 Jesus of Nazareth, the son of J'.
4: 5 that Jacob gave to his son J'.
6: 42 Is not this Jesus, the son of J',
19: 38 after this J' of Arimathæa, being a
Ac 1: 23 J' called Barsabas, who was
7: 9 with envy, sold J' into Egypt:
13 J' was made known to his brethren;
14 Then sent J', and called his father
18 king arose, which knew not J'.
Heb 11: 21 dying, blessed both the sons of J';
22 By faith J', when he died, made
Re 7: 8 Of the tribe of J' were sealed

Joseph's (*jo'-zefs*)
Ge 37: 31 they took J' coat, and killed a kid
39: 5 the Egyptian's house for J' sake;
6 he left all that he had in J' hand;
20 J' master took him, and put him
22 prison committed to J' hand all the
41: 42 his hand, and put it upon J' hand,
45 called J' name Zaphnath-paaneah;
42: 3 J' ten brethren went down to buy
4 Benjamin, J' brother, Jacob sent
6 J' brethren came, and bowed down
43: 17 man brought the men into J' house.
18 they were brought into J' house;
19 near to the steward of J' house,
24 man brought the men into J' house,
44: 14 and his brethren came to J' house;
45: 16 house, saying, J' brethren are come:
48: 8 Israel beheld J' sons, and said, Who
50: 15 J' brethren saw that their father
23 were brought up upon J' knees.
1Ch 5: 2 ruler; but the birthright was J':)
Lu 4: 22 And they said, Is not this J' son?
Ac 7: 13 J' kindred was made known unto

Joses (*jo'-zez*) See also JOSE.
M't 13:55 James, and J', and Simon, and
27:56 Mary the mother of James and J',
M'r 6: 3 the brother of James, and J', and
15:40 mother of James the less and of J',
47 Mary the mother of J' beheld where
Ac 4:36 J', who...was surnamed Barnabas,
Joshah (*jo'-shah*)
1Ch 4:34 and J' the son of Amaziah,
Joshaphat (*josh'-a-fat*) See also JEHOSHAPHAT; JOSAPHAT.
1Ch 11:43 Maachah, and J' the Mithnite,
Joshaviah (*josh-a-vi'-ah*)
1Ch 11:46 Jeribai, and J', the sons of Elnaam,
Joshbekashah (*josh-bek'-a-shah*)
1Ch 25: 4 J', Mallothi, Hothir, and
24 The seventeenth to J', he, his sons,
Joshua^ (*josh'-u-ah*) See also HOSEA; HOSHEA; JEHOSHUAH; JESHUA; JESHUAH; JESUS; OSEA; OSHEA.
Ex 17: 9 Moses said unto J', Choose us out
10 So J' did as Moses had said to him,
13 And J' discomfited Amalek and his
14 and rehearse it in the ears of J':
24:13 Moses rose up, and his minister J':
32:17 And when J' heard the noise of the
33:11 but his servant J', the son of Nun,
Nu 11:28 J' the son of Nun, the servant of
14: 6 J' the son of Nun, and Caleb the
30 Jephunneh, and J' the son of Nun.
38 But J' the son of Nun, and Caleb
26:65 Jephunneh, and J' the son of Nun.
27:18 Take thee J' the son of Nun, a man
22 and he took J', and set him before
32:12 the Kenezite, and J' the son of Nun:
28 J' the son of Nun, and the chief
34:17 the priest, and J' the son of Nun.
De 1:38 J' the son of Nun, which standeth
3:21 And I commanded J' at that time,
28 But charge J', and encourage him,
31: 3 and J', he shall go over before thee,
7 Moses called unto J', and said unto
14 call J', and present yourselves in
14 Moses and J' went, and presented
23 he gave J' the son of Nun a charge,
34: 9 J' the son of Nun was full of the
Jos 1: 1 Lord spake unto J' the son of Nun,
10 Then J' commanded the officers of
12 half the tribe of Manasseh, spake J',
16 they answered J', saying, All that
2: 1 And J' the son of Nun sent out of
23 came to J' the son of Nun, and told
24 said unto J', Truly the Lord hath
3: 1 J' rose early in the morning; and
5 J' said unto the people, Sanctify
6 J' spake unto the priests, saying,
7 the Lord said unto J', This day will
9 J' said unto the children of Israel,
10 J' said, Hereby ye shall know that
4: 1 that the Lord spake unto J', saying,
4 Then J' called the twelve men,
5 J' said unto them, Pass over before
8 of Israel did so as J' commanded,
8 Jordan, as the Lord spake unto J',
9 J' set up twelve stones in the midst
10 Lord commanded J' to speak unto
10 to all that Moses commanded J':
14 On that day the Lord magnified J'
15 And the Lord spake unto J', saying,
17 J' therefore commanded the priests,
20 out of Jordan, did J' pitch in Gilgal.
5: 2 At that time the Lord said unto J',
3 And J' made him sharp knives, and
4 the cause why J' did circumcise:
7 their stead, them J' circumcised:
9 Lord said unto J', This day have I
13 to pass, when J' was by Jericho,
13 J' went unto him, and said unto
14 J' fell on his face to the earth, and
15 the Lord's host said unto J', Loose
15 standest is holy. And J' did so.
6: 2 Lord said unto J', See, I have given
6 J' the son of Nun called the priests,
8 when J' had spoken unto the people,
10 J' had commanded the people,
12 J' rose early in the morning, and
16 J' said unto the people, Shout; for
22 J' had said unto the two men that
25 J' saved Rahab the harlot alive,
25 which J' sent to spy out Jericho.
26 And J' adjured them at that time,
27 So the Lord was with J'; and his
7: 2 J' sent men from Jericho to Ai,
3 they returned to J', and said unto
6 J' rent his clothes, and fell to the
7 J' said, Alas, O Lord God, wherefore
10 the Lord said unto J', Get thee up;
16 So J' rose up early in the morning,
19 J' said unto Achan, My son, give, I
20 Achan answered J', and said, indeed
22 So J' sent messengers, and they
23 brought them unto J', and unto all
24 J', and all Israel with him, took
25 J' said, Why hast thou troubled us?
8: 1 Lord said unto J', Fear not, neither
3 J' arose, and all the people of war,
3 J' chose out thirty thousand...men
9 J' therefore sent them forth; and
9 J' lodged that night among the
10 J' rose up early in the morning,
13 J' went that night into the midst of
15 J' and all Israel made as if they
16 they pursued after J', and were
18 Lord said unto J', Stretch out the
18 J' stretched out the spear that he
Jos 8:21 when J' and all Israel saw that
23 took alive, and brought him to J'.
26 for J' drew not his hand back,
27 the Lord which he commanded J'.
28 J' burnt Ai, and made it an heap for
29 J' commanded that they should
30 J' built an altar unto the Lord
35 which J' read not before all the
9: 2 to fight with J' and with Israel,
3 Gibeon heard what J' had done
6 went to J' unto the camp at Gilgal,
8 And they said unto J', We are thy
8 And J' said unto them, Who are ye?
15 J' made peace with them, and
22 J' called for them, and he spake
24 they answered J', and said, Because
27 J' made them that day hewers of
10: 1 had heard how J' had taken Ai,
4 it hath made peace with J' and
6 men of Gibeon sent unto J' to the
7 So J' ascended from Gilgal, he, and
8 Lord said unto J', Fear them not:
9 J' therefore came unto them
12 Then spake J' to the Lord in the
15 J' returned, and all Israel with him,
17 it was told J', saying, the five kings
18 J' said, Roll great stones upon the
20 when J' and the children of Israel
21 people returned to the camp to J'
22 said J', Open the mouth of the cave,
24 brought out those kings unto J',
24 J' called for all the men of Israel,
25 J' said unto them, Fear not, nor be
26 afterward J' smote them, and slew
27 that J' commanded, and they took
28 that day J' took Makkedah, and
29 J' passed from Makkedah, and all
31 J' passed from Libnah, and all
33 J' smote him and his people, until
34 from Lachish J' passed unto Eglon,
36 J' went up from Eglon, and all
38 J' returned, and all Israel with him,
40 So J' smote all the country of the
41 J' smote them from Kadesh-barnea
42 their land did J' take at one time,
43 J' returned, and all Israel with him,
11: 6 Lord said unto J', Be not afraid
7 J' came, and all the people of war
9 J' did unto them as the Lord bade
10 J' at that time turned back, and
12 all the kings of them, did J' take,
13 save Hazor only; that did J' burn.
15 Moses command J', and so did J';
16 So J' took all that land, the hills,
18 J' made war a long time with all
21 at that time came J', and cut off
21 J' destroyed them utterly with
23 So J' took the whole land, according
23 J' gave it for an inheritance unto
12: 7 the kings of the country which J'
7 J' gave unto the tribes of Israel
13: 1 J' was old and stricken in years;
14: 1 the priest, and J' the son of Nun,
6 children of Judah came unto J'
13 J' blessed him, and gave unto Caleb
15:13 commandment of the Lord to J',
17: 4 priest, and before J' the son of Nun,
14 children of Joseph spake unto J',
15 J' answered them, If thou be a
17 J' spake unto the house of Joseph,
18: 3 J' said unto the children of Israel,
8 J' charged them that went to
9 again to J' to the host at Shiloh.
10 J' cast lots for them in Shiloh
10 there J' divided the land unto the
19:49 of Israel gave an inheritance to J'
51 J' the son of Nun, and the heads of
20: 1 The Lord also spake unto J', saying,
21: 1 unto J' the son of Nun, and unto
22: 1 Then J' called the Reubenites, and
6 So J' blessed them, and sent them
7 unto the other half thereof gave J'
7 when J' sent them away also unto
23: 1 J' waxed old and stricken in age.
2 J' called for all Israel, and for their
24: 1 J' gathered all the tribes of Israel
2 J' said unto all the people, Thus
19 J' said unto the people, Ye cannot
21 And the people said unto J', Nay;
22 J' said unto the people, Ye are
24 the people said unto J', The Lord
25 J' made a covenant with the people
26 J' wrote these words in the book of
27 J' said unto all the people, Behold,
28 So J' let the people depart, every
29 J' the son of Nun, the servant of
31 served the Lord all the days of J',
31 days of the elders that overlived J',
J'g 1: 1 after the death of J' it came to pass,
2: 6 when J' had let the people go, the
7 served the Lord all the days of J',
7 days of the elders that outlived J',
8 J' the son of Nun, the servant of
21 nations which J' left when he died:
23 he them into the hand of J'.
1Sa 6:14 the cart came into the field of J',
18 unto this day in the field of J', the
1Ki 16:34 he spake by J' the son of Nun.
2Ki 23: 8 in the entering in of the gate of J'
Hag 1: 1 and to J' the son of Josedech, the
12 J' the son of Josedech, the high
14 the spirit of J' the son of Josedech,
2: 2 and to J' the son of Josedech, the
4 be strong, O J', son of Josedech,
Zec 3: 1 he shewed me J' the high priest
3 Now J' was clothed with filthy
Zec 3: 6 angel of the Lord protested unto J',
8 Hear now, O J' the high priest,
9 stone that I have laid before J';
6:11 and set them upon the head of J'
Josiah (*jo-si'-ah*) See also JOSIAS.
1Ki 13: 2 the house of David, J' by name;
2Ki 21:24 of the land made J' his son king
26 and J' his son reigned in his stead.
22: 1 J' was eight years old when he
3 in the eighteenth year of king J',
23:16 as J' turned himself, he spied the
19 J' took away, and did to them
23 in the eighteenth year of king J',
24 J' put away, that he might perform
28 the rest of the acts of J', and all
29 king J' went against him; and he
30 land took Jehoahaz the son of J',
34 the son of J' king in the room of J'
1Ch 3:14 Amon his son, J' his son.
15 the sons of J' were, the firstborn
2Ch 33:25 of the land made J' his son king
34: 1 J' was eight years old when he
33 J' took away all the abominations
35: 1 J' kept a passover unto the Lord in
7 J' gave to the people, of the flock,
16 to the commandment of king J'.
18 keep such a passover as J' kept,
19 reign of J' was this passover kept.
20 when J' had prepared the temple,
20 and J' went out against him.
22 J' would not turn his face from him,
23 the archers shot at king J'; and
24 and Jerusalem mourned for J'.
25 Jeremiah lamented for J': and all
25 spake of J' in their lamentations
26 the rest of the acts of J', and his
36: 1 land took Jehoahaz the son of J',
Jer 1: 2 days of J' the son of Amon king of
3 days of Jehoiakim the son of J' king
3 year of Zedekiah the son of J' king
3: 6 said also unto me in the days of J'
22:11 Lord touching Shallum the son of J'
11 reigned instead of J' his father,
18 concerning Jehoiakim the son of J'
25: 1 year of Jehoiakim the son of J' king
3 year of J' the son of Amon king of
26: 1 the reign of Jehoiakim the son of J'
27: 1 the reign of Jehoiakim the son of J'
35: 1 the days of Jehoiakim the son of J'
36: 1 year of Jehoiakim the son of J'
2 from the days of J', even unto this
9 year of Jehoiakim the son of J' king
37: 1 Zedekiah the son of J' reigned
45: 1 year of Jehoiakim the son of J' king
46: 2 year of Jehoiakim the son of J' king
Zep 1: 1 days of J' the son of Amon, king of
Zec 6:10 house of J' the son of Zephaniah;
Josias (*jo-si'-as*) See also JOSIAH.
M't 1:10 begat Amon; and Amon begat J';
11 And J' begat Jechonias and his
Josibiah (*jos-ib-i'-ah*)
1Ch 4:35 And Joel, and Jehu the son of J',
Josiphiah (*jos-if-i'-ah*)
Ezr 8:10 sons of Shelomith; the son of J',
jostle See JUSTLE.
jot
M't 5:18 one j' or one tittle shall in no wise
Jotbah (*jot'-bah*)
2Ki 21:19 the daughter of Haruz of J'.
Jotbath (*jot'-bath*) See also JOTBATHAH.
De 10: 7 from Gudgodah to J', a land of
Jotbathah (*jot'-ba-thah*) See also JOTBATH.
Nu 33:33 Hor-hagidgad, and pitched in J'.
34 removed from J', and encamped
Jotham (*jo'-tham*) See also JOATHAM.
J'g 9: 5 J' the youngest son of Jerubbaal
7 And when they told it to J', he went
21 J' ran away, and fled, and went to
57 upon them came the curse of J'
2Ki 15: 5 And J' the king's son was over the
7 and J' his son reigned in his stead.
30 year of J' the son of Uzziah.
32 J' the son of Uzziah king of Judah
36 the rest of the acts of J', and all
38 J' slept with his fathers, and was
16: 1 Ahaz the son of J' king of Judah
1Ch 2:47 the sons of Jahdai; Regem, and J',
3:12 his son, Azariah his son, J' his son,
5:17 by genealogies in the days of J'
2Ch 26:21 and J' his son was over the king's
23 and J' his son reigned in his stead.
27: 1 J' was twenty and five years old
6 So J' became mighty, because he
7 the rest of the acts of J', and all
9 J' slept with his fathers, and they
Isa 1: 1 in the days of Uzziah, J', Ahaz, and
7: 1 in the days of Ahaz the son of J',
Ho 1: 1 in the days of Uzziah, J', Ahaz, and
Mic 1: 1 the days of J', Ahaz, and Hezekiah,
journey See also JOURNEYED; JOURNEYING; JOURNEYS.
Ge 24:21 had made his j' prosperous or not.
29: 1 Jacob went on his j', and
30:36 set three days' j' betwixt himself
31:23 pursued after him seven days' j';
33:12 Let us take our j', and let us go,
46: 1 Israel took his j' with all that he
Ex 3:18 three days' j' into the wilderness,
5: 3 thee, three days' j' into the desert,
8:27 three days' j' into the wilderness,
13:20 they took their j' from Succoth,
16: 1 And they took their j' from Elim,

Nu 9:10 or be in a j' afar off, yet he shall
13 man that is clean, and is not in a j'.
10: 6 the south side shall take their j':
13 they first took their j' according to
33 mount of the Lord three days' j':
33 before them in the three days' j',
11: 31 as it were a day's j' on this side,
31 it were a day's j' on the other side,
33: 8 went three days' j' in the wilderness
12 took their j' out of the wilderness
De 1: 2 eleven days' j' from Horeb by the way
7 Turn you, and take your j', and
40 take your j' into the wilderness by
2: 1 took our j' into the wilderness by
24 take your j', and pass over the river
10: 6 of Israel took their j' from Beeroth
11 Arise, take thy j' before the people,
Jos 9: 11 Take victuals with you for the j',
13 old by reason of the very long j'.
J'g 4: 9 the j' that thou takest shall not be
1Sa 15: 18 the Lord sent thee on a j', and said,
2Sa 11: 10 Uriah, Camest thou not from thy j'?
1Ki 18: 27 or he is pursuing, or he is in a j',
19: 4 went a day's j' into the wilderness,
7 because the j' is too great for thee.
2Ki 3: 9 fetched a compass of seven days' j':
2Ch 1: 13 Solomon came from his j' to the high
Ne 2: 6 For how long shall thy j' be? and
Pr 7: 19 not at home, he is gone a long j':
Jon 3: 3 great city of three days' j'.
4 to enter into the city a day's j',
M't 10: 10 Nor scrip for your j', neither two
25: 15 ability; and straightway took his j'.
M'r 6: 8 should take nothing for their j',
13: 34 of man is as a man taking a far j',
Lu 2: 44 in the company, went a day's j';
9: 3 Take nothing for your j', neither
11: 6 a friend of mine in his j' is come
15: 13 and took his j' into a far country,
Joh 4: 6 therefore, being wearied with his j',
Ac 1: 12 from Jerusalem a sabbath day's j'.
10: 9 as they went on their j', and drew
22: 6 as I made my j', and was come
Ro 1: 10 I might have a prosperous j' by
15: 24 I take my j' into Spain, I will
24 I trust to see you in my j', and to
1Co 16: 6 may bring me on my j' whithersoever
Tit 3: 13 and Apollos on their j' diligently,
3Jo 6 if thou bring forward on their j'

journeyed
Ge 11: 2 to pass, as they j' from the east,
12: 9 Abram j', going on still toward the
13: 11 and Lot j' east: and they separated
20: 1 Abraham j' from thence toward the
33: 17 Jacob j' to Succoth, and built him
35: 5 And they j': and the terror of God
16 they j' from Beth-el; and there was
21 And Israel j', and spread his tent
Ex 12: 37 children of Israel j' from Rameses
17: 1 Israel j' from the wilderness of Sin,
40: 37 they j' not till the day that it was
Nu 9: 17 after that the children of Israel j':
18 of the Lord the children of Israel j',
19 the charge of the Lord, and j' not.
20 commandment of the Lord they j'.
21 up in the morning, then they j':
21 that the cloud was taken up, they j'
22 abode in their tents, and j' not:
22 but when it was taken up, they j'.
23 commandment of the Lord they j':
11: 35 people j' from Kibroth-hattaavah
12: 15 j' not till Miriam was brought in
20: 22 whole congregation, j' from Kadesh,
21: 4 And they j' from mount Hor by the
11 And they j' from Oboth, and pitched
33: 22 they j' from Rissah, and pitched in
De 10: 7 From thence they j' unto Gudgodah;
Jos 9: 17 children of Israel j', and came unto
J'g 17: 8 the house of Micah, as he j'.
Lu 10: 33 But a certain Samaritan, as he j',
Ac 9: 3 as he j', he came near Damascus:
7 the men which j' with him stood
26: 13 me and them which j' with me.

journeying See also JOURNEYINGS.
Nu 10: 2 and for the j' of the camps.
29 We are j' unto the place of which
Lu 13: 22 and j' toward Jerusalem.

journeyings
Nu 10: 28 the j' of the children of Israel
2Co 11: 26 in j' often, in perils of waters,

journeys
Ge 13: 3 he went on his j' from the south
Ex 17: 1 after their j', according to the
40: 36 Israel went onward in all their j':
38 of Israel, throughout all their j'.
Nu 10: 6 they shall blow an alarm for their j'
12 the children of Israel took their j'
33: 1 are the j' of the children of Israel,
2 goings out according to their j'
2 j' according to their goings out.

joy See also ENJOY; JOYED; JOYFUL; JOYING.
1Sa 18: 6 king Saul, with tabrets, with j',
1Ki 1: 40 rejoiced with great j', so that the
1Ch 12: 40 abundantly: for there was j' in Israel.
15: 16 by lifting up the voice with j'.
25 of the house of Obed-edom with j'.
29: 9 the king also rejoiced with great j'.
17 now have I seen with j' thy people,
2Ch 20: 27 to go again to Jerusalem with j';
30: 26 there was great j' in Jerusalem: for
Ezr 3: 12 and many shouted aloud for j':
13 discern the noise of the shout of j'
6: 16 of this house of God with j',
Ezr 6: 22 kept...bread seven days with j':
Ne 8: 10 the j' of the Lord is your strength.
12: 43 made them rejoice with great j':
43 that the j' of Jerusalem was heard
Es 8: 16 had light, and gladness, and j',
17 the Jews had j' and gladness, a
9: 22 turned unto them from sorrow to j',
22 make them days of feasting and j',
Job 8: 19 Behold, this is the j' of his way,
20: 5 and the j' of the hypocrite but for
29: 13 the widow's heart to sing for j'.
33: 26 he shall see his face with j': for he
38: 7 all the sons of God shouted for j'?
41: 22 sorrow is turned into j' before him.
Ps 5: 11 let them ever shout for j', because
16: 11 in thy presence is fullness of j';
21: 1 The king shall j' in thy strength,
27: 6 in his tabernacle sacrifices of j';
30: 5 but j' cometh in the morning.
32: 11 shout for j', all ye that are upright
35: 27 Let them shout for j', and be glad,
42: 4 with the voice of j' and praise,
43: 4 God, unto God my exceeding j':
48: 2 the j' of the whole earth, is mount
51: 8 Make me to hear j' and gladness;
12 unto me the j' of thy salvation;
65: 13 corn; they shout for j', they also sing.
67: 4 let the nations be glad and sing for j':
105: 43 brought forth his people with j',
126: 5 that sow in tears shall reap in j'.
132: 9 and let thy saints shout for j'.
16 her saints shall shout aloud for j'.
137: 6 not Jerusalem above my chief j'.
Pr 12: 20 but to the counsellors of peace is j'.
14: 10 doth not intermeddle with his j'.
15: 21 Folly is j' to him that is destitute of
23 man hath j' by the answer of his
17: 21 and the father of a fool hath no j'.
21: 15 It is j' to the just to do judgment:
23: 24 begetteth a wise child shall have j'
Ec 2: 10 withheld not my heart from any j';
26 wisdom, and knowledge, and j':
5: 20 answereth him in the j' of his heart.
9: 7 eat thy bread with j', and drink thy
Isa 9: 3 the nation, and not increased the j':
3 they j' before thee according to
3 according to the j' in harvest,
17 shall have no j' in their young men,
12: 3 with j' shall ye draw water out of
16: 10 and j' out of the plentiful field;
22: 13 j' and gladness, slaying oxen, and
24: 8 endeth, the j' of the harp ceaseth.
11 all j' is darkened, the mirth of the
29: 19 meek also shall increase their j'
32: 13 yea, upon all the houses of j' in the
14 a j' of wild asses, a pasture of
35: 2 rejoice even with j' and singing:
10 with songs and everlasting j' upon
10 they shall obtain j' and gladness,
51: 3 j' and gladness shall be found
11 everlasting j' shall be upon their
11 they shall obtain gladness and j';
52: 9 Break forth into j', sing together,
55: 12 For ye shall go out with j', and be
60: 15 a j' of many generations.
61: 3 the oil of j' for mourning, the
7 everlasting j' shall be unto them.
65: 14 servants shall sing for j' of heart,
18 a rejoicing, and her people a j'.
19 Jerusalem, and j' in my people:
66: 5 he shall appear to your j', and
10 love her: rejoice for j' with her,
Jer 15: 16 the j' and rejoicing of mine heart:
31: 13 I will turn their mourning into j',
33: 9 And it shall be to me a name of j',
11 The voice of j', and the voice of
48: 27 spakest of him, thou skippedst for j'.
33 j' and gladness is taken from the
49: 25 of praise not left, the city of my j'!
La 2: 15 beauty, The j' of the whole earth?
5: 15 The j' of our heart is ceased; our
Eze 24: 25 the j' of their glory, the desire of
36: 5 with the j' of all their heart,
Ho 9: 1 Rejoice not, O Israel, for j', as
Joe 1: 12 j' is withered away from the sons
16 j' and gladness from the house of
Hab 3: 18 I will j' in the God of my salvation.
Zep 3: 17 he will rejoice over thee with j';
17 he will j' over thee with singing.
Zec 8: 19 house of Judah j' and gladness,
M't 2: 10 rejoiced with exceeding great j'.
13: 20 word, and anon with j' receiveth it:
44 for j' thereof goeth and selleth all
25: 21, 23 enter thou into the j' of thy lord
28: 8 sepulchre with fear and great j';
Lu 1: 14 thou shalt have j' and gladness;
44 the babe leaped in my womb for j'.
2: 10 bring you good tidings of great j',
6: 23 ye in that day, and leap for j':
8: 13 they hear, receive the word with j';
10: 17 the seventy returned again with j',
15: 7 j' shall be in heaven over one sinner
10 is j' in the presence of the angels
24: 41 while they yet believed not for j',
52 returned to Jerusalem with great j':
Joh 3: 29 this my j' therefore is fulfilled.
15: 11 you, that my j' might remain in you,
11 and that your j' might be full.
16: 20 your sorrow shall be turned into j'.
21 for j' that a man is born into the
22 your j' no man taketh from you.
24 receive, that your j' may be full.
17: 13 have my j' fulfilled in themselves.
Ac 2: 28 thou shalt make me full of j' with
8: 8 And there was great j' in that city.
13: 52 the disciples were filled with j', and
Ac 15: 3 caused great j' unto all the brethren.
20: 24 I might finish my course with j',
Ro 5: 11 j' in God through our Lord Jesus
14: 17 peace, and j' in the Holy Ghost,
15: 13 fill you with all j' and peace in
32 That I may come unto you with j'
2Co 1: 24 faith, but are helpers of your j':
2: 3 in you all, that my j' is...of you all.
3 in you all, that...is the j' of you all.
7: 13 more joyed we for the j' of Titus,
8: 2 abundance of their j' and their deep
Ga 5: 22 fruit of the Spirit is love, j', peace,
Ph'p 1: 4 for you all making request with j',
25 for your furtherance and j' of faith;
2: 2 Fulfil ye my j', that ye be
17 faith, I j', and rejoice with you all.
18 For the same cause also do ye j',
4: 1 and longed for, my j' and crown,
1Th 1: 6 affliction, with j' of the Holy Ghost:
2: 19 what is our hope, or j', or crown of
20 For ye are our glory and j'.
3: 9 for all the j'...for your sakes before
9 wherewith we j' for your sakes
2Ti 1: 4 tears, that I may be filled with j';
Ph'm 7 we have great j' and consolation
20 let me have j' of thee in the Lord:
Heb 12: 2 who for the j' that was set before
13: 17 that they may do it with j', and not
Jas 1: 2 count it all j' when ye fall into
4: 9 mourning, and your j' to heaviness.
1Pe 1: 8 rejoice with j' unspeakable and full
4: 13 may be glad also with exceeding j'.
1Jo 1: 4 unto you, that your j' may be full.
2Jo 12 face to face, that our j' may be full.
3Jo 4 I have no greater j' than to hear
Jude 24 of his glory with exceeding j',

joyed
2Co 7: 13 the more j' we for the joy of Titus,

joyful
1Ki 8: 66 went unto their tents j' and glad of
Ezr 6: 22 for the Lord had made them j',
Es 5: 9 Haman went forth that day j' and
Job 3: 7 let no j' voice come therein.
Ps 5: 11 also that love thy name be j'
35: 9 my soul shall be j' in the Lord:
63: 5 mouth shall praise thee with j' lips:
66: 1 Make a j' noise unto God, all ye
81: 1 make a j' noise unto the God of
89: 15 the people that know the j' sound:
95: 1 let us make a j' noise to the rock
2 make a j' noise unto him with psalms.
96: 12 Let the field be j', and all that is
98: 4 Make a j' noise unto the Lord, all
6 make a j' noise before the Lord, the
8 hands: let the hills be j' together
100: 1 Make a j' noise unto the Lord, all
113: 9 and to be a j' mother of children.
149: 2 children of Zion be j' in their King.
5 Let the saints be j' in glory: let
Ec 7: 14 In the day of prosperity be j', but
Isa 49: 13 Sing, O heavens; and be j', O earth;
56: 7 them j' in my house of prayer:
61: 10 my soul shall be j' in my God;
2Co 7: 4 I am exceeding j' in all our

joyfully
Ec 9: 9 Live j' with the wife whom thou
Lu 19: 6 came down, and received him j'.
Heb 10: 34 took j' the spoiling of your

joyfulness
De 28: 47 not the Lord thy God with j',
Col 1: 11 and longsuffering with j';

joying
Col 2: 5 spirit, j' and beholding your order,

joyous
Isa 22: 2 stirs, a tumultuous city, a j' city:
23: 7 Is this your j' city, whose antiquity
32: 13 all the houses of joy in the j' city:
Heb 12: 11 for the present seemeth to be j',

Jozabad (*joz'-a-bad*) See also JEHOZABAD; JOSABAD.
1Ch 12: 20 J', and Jediael, and Michael, and
20 J', and Elihu, and Zilthai, captains
2Ch 31: 13 and Jerimoth, and J', and Eliel,
35: 9 Jeiel and J', chief of the Levites
Ezr 8: 33 with them was J' the son of Jeshua,
10: 22 Ishmael, Nethaneel, J', and Elasah.
23 Also of the Levites; J', and Shimei,
Ne 8: 7 Azariah, J', Hanan, Pelaiah, and
11: 16 Shabbethai and J', of the chief of

Jozachar (*joz'-a-kar*) See also ZABAD.
2Ki 12: 21 For J' the son of Shimeath, and

Jozadak (*joz'-a-dak*) See also JEHOZADAK; JOSEDECH.
Ezr 3: 2 stood up Jeshua the son of J',
8 and Jeshua the son of J', and the
5: 2 and Jeshua the son of J', and began
10: 18 of the sons of Jeshua the son of J',
Ne 12: 26 the son of Jeshua, the son of J',

Jubal (*ju'-bal*)
Ge 4: 21 And his brother's name was J': he

jubile (*ju'-bi-lee*)
Le 25: 9 the trumpet of the j' to sound on
10 it shall be a j' unto you; and ye
11 A j' shall that fiftieth year be unto
12 For it is the j'; it shall be holy unto
13 In the year of this j' ye shall return
15 after the j' thou shalt buy of thy
28 hath bought it until the year of j':
28 in the j' it shall go out, and he shall
30 it shall not go out in the j'.

Le 25:31 and they shall go out in the j.
33 shall go out in the year of j:
40 shall serve thee unto the year of j:
50 was sold to him unto the year of j:
52 but few years unto the year of j,
54 then he shall go out in the year of j,
27:17 sanctify his field from the year of j,
18 if he sanctify his field after the j,
18 remain, even unto the year of the j,
21 field, when it goeth out in the j,
23 even unto the year of the j:
24 year of the j the field shall return
Nu 36: 4 when the j of the children of Israel

jubilee See JUBILE.

Jucal (*ju'-kal*) See also JEHUCAL.
Jer 38: 1 and J· the son of Shelemiah, and

Juda (*ju'-dah*) See also JUDAH.
M't 2: 6 thou Bethlehem, in the land of J·,
6 the least among the princes of J·:
M'r 6: 3 of James, and Joses, and of J·,
Lu 1:39 with haste, into a city of J·;
3:26 of Joseph, which was the son of J·,
30 of Simeon, which was the son of J·,
33 Phares, which was the son of J·,
Heb 7:14 that our Lord sprang out of J·;
Re 5: 5 behold, the Lion of the tribe of J·,
7: 5 Of the tribe of J· were sealed

Judæa (*ju-de'-ah*) See also JEWRY; JUDAH; JUDEA.
M't 2: 1 Jesus was born in Bethlehem of J·
5 said unto him, In Bethlehem of J·:
22 heard that Archelaus did reign in J·
3: 1 preaching in the wilderness of J·,
5 out to him Jerusalem, and all J·,
4:25 and from Jerusalem, and from J·,
19: 1 the coasts of J· beyond Jordan;
24:16 be in J· flee into the mountains:
M'r 1: 5 out unto him all the land of J·,
3: 7 Galilee followed him, and from J·,
10: 1 and cometh into the coasts of J·
13:14 that be in J· flee to the mountains:
Lu 1: 5 the days of Herod, the king of J·,
65 all the hill country of J·.
2: 4 out of the city of Nazareth, into J·,
3: 1 Pontius Pilate being governor of J·,
5:17 out of every town of Galilee, and J·,
6:17 multitude of people out of all J·
7:17 him went forth throughout all J·,
21:21 are in J· flee to the mountains;
Joh 3:22 his disciples into the land of J·;
4: 3 He left J·, and departed again into
47 that Jesus was come out of J· into
54 he was come out of J· into Galilee.
7: 3 Depart hence, and go into J·, that
11: 7 disciples, Let us go into J· again.
Ac 1: 8 and in all J·, and in Samaria, and
2: 9 dwellers in Mesopotamia, and in J·,
14 Ye men of J·, and all ye that dwell
8: 1 the regions of J· and Samaria,
9:31 rest throughout all J· and Galilee
10:37 was published throughout all J·,
11: 1 and brethren that were in J· heard
29 unto the brethren which dwelt in J·:
12:19 he went down from J· to Cæsarea,
15: 1 men which came down from J·
21:10 there came down from J· a certain
26:20 and throughout all the coasts of J·,
28:21 neither received letters out of J·
Ro 15:31 from them that do not believe in J·;
2Co 1:16 be brought on my way toward J·.
Ga 1:22 by face unto the churches of J·
1Th 2:14 which in J· are in Christ Jesus:

Judah^ (*ju'-dah*) See also BETHLEHEM-JUDAH; JUDA; JUDAH'S; JUDAS; JUDÆA; JUDE.
Ge 29:35 therefore she called his name J·;
35:23 and Levi, and J·, and Issachar, and
37:26 And J· said unto his brethren, What
38: 1 J· went down from his brethren,
2 And J· saw there a daughter of a
6 J· took a wife for Er his firstborn,
8 J· said unto Onan, Go in unto thy
11 said J· to Tamar his daughter in
12 J· was comforted, and went up unto
15 When J· saw her, he thought her to
20 J· sent the kid by the hand of his
22 And he returned to J·, and said, I
23 J· said, Let her take it to her, lest
24 that it was told J·, saying, Tamar
24 J· said, Bring her forth, and let her
26 J· acknowledged them, and said,
43: 3 J· spake unto him, saying, The man
8 J· said unto Israel his father, Send
44:14 And J· and his brethren came to
16 J· said, What shall we say unto my
18 J· came near unto him, and said,
46:12 the sons of J·; Er, and Onan, and
28 he sent J· before him unto Joseph,
49: 8 J·, thou art he whom thy brethren
9 J· is a lion's whelp: from the prey,
10 sceptre shall not depart from J·,
Ex 1: 2 Reuben, Simeon, Levi, and J·,
31: 2 the son of Hur, of the tribe of J·:
35:30 the son of Hur, of the tribe of J·;
38:22 the son of Hur, of the tribe of J·,
Nu 1: 7 J·; Nahshon the son of Amminadab.
26 children of J·, by their generations,
27 of them, even of the tribe of J·,
2: 3 of the standard of the camp of J·
3 be captain of the children of J·
9 numbered in the camp of J· were an
7:12 of Amminadab, of the tribe of J·:
10:14 of the camp of the children of J·
13: 6 Of the tribe of J·, Caleb the son of
26:19 The sons of J· were Er and Onan:
20 sons of J· after their families were;
Nu 26:22 are the families of J· according to
34:19 Of the tribe of J·, Caleb the son of
De 27:12 and Levi, and J·, and Issachar, and
33: 7 this is the blessing of J·: and he
7 said, Hear, Lord, the voice of J·,
34: 2 all the land of J·, unto the utmost
Jos 7: 1 son of Zerah, of the tribe of J·, took
16 and the tribe of J· was taken:
17 he brought the family of J·; and he
18 Zerah, of the tribe of J·, was taken.
11:21 and from all the mountains of J·,
14: 6 of J· came unto Joshua in Gilgal:
15: 1 lot of the tribe of the children of J·
12 is the coast of the children of J·
13 a part among the children of J·,
20, 21 of the tribe of the children of J·
63 children of J· could not drive them
63 dwell with the children of J· unto
18: 5 J· shall abide in their coast on the
11 forth between the children of J·
14 a city of the children of J·:
19: 1 inheritance of the children of J·.
9 of the portion of the children of J·
9 part of the children of J· was too
34 and to J· upon Jordan toward the
20: 7 is Hebron, in the mountain of J·.
21: 4 had by lot out of the tribe of J·,
9 out of the tribe of the children of J·,
11 is Hebron, in the hill country of J·,
J'g 1: 2 And the Lord said, J· shall go up:
3 J· said unto Simeon his brother,
4 J· went up; and the Lord delivered
8 J· had fought against Jerusalem,
9 children of J· went down to fight
10 And J· went against the Canaanites
16 of J· into the wilderness of J·,
17 J· went with Simeon his brother,
18 J· took Gaza with the coast thereof,
19 Lord was with J·; and he drave out
10: 9 over Jordan to fight also against J·,
15: 9 Philistines went...and pitched in J·,
10 men of J· said, Why are ye come up
11 thousand men of J· went to the top
17: 7 Bethlehem-judah of the family of J·,
18:12 pitched in Kirjath-jearim, in J·:
20:18 the Lord said, J· shall go up first.
Ru 1: 7 way to return unto the land of J·.
4:12 Pharez, whom Tamar bare unto J·,
1Sa 11: 8 and the men of J· thirty thousand.
15: 4 and ten thousand men of J·.
17: 1 at Shochoh, which belongeth to J·,
52 the men of Israel and of J· arose,
18:16 But all Israel and J· loved David,
22: 5 and get thee into the land of J·.
23: 3 Behold, we be afraid here in J·:
23 throughout all the thousands of J·.
27: 6 pertaineth unto the kings of J·
10 David said, Against the south of J·,
30:14 the coast which belongeth to J·,
16 Philistines, and out of the land of J·
26 of the spoil unto the elders of J·,
2Sa 1:18 children of J· the use of the bow:
2: 1 I go up into any of the cities of J·?
4 the men of J· came, and there they
4 David king over the house of J·.
7 house of J· have anointed me king
10 But the house of J· followed David.
11 king in Hebron over the house of J·
3: 8 which against J· do shew kindness
10 of David over Israel and over J·,
5: 5 he reigned over J· seven years and
5 three years over all Israel and J·.
6: 2 were with him from Baale of J·,
11:11 and Israel, and J·, abide in tents;
12: 8 thee the house of Israel and of J·;
19:11 Speak unto the elders of J·, saying,
14 bowed the heart of all the men of J·,
15 J· came to Gilgal, to go to meet the
16 the men of J· to meet king David.
40 the people of J· conducted the king,
41 the men of J· stolen thee away,
42 all the men of J· answered the men
43 of Israel answered the men of J·,
43 words of the men of J· were fiercer
20: 2 the men of J· clave unto their king,
4 Assemble me the men of J· within
5 went to assemble the men of J·:
21: 2 zeal to the children of Israel and J·:
24: 1 to say, Go, number Israel and J·.
7 they went out to the south of J·,
9 of J· were five hundred thousand
1Ki 1: 9 the men of J· the king's servants:
35 to be ruler over Israel and over J·.
2:32 of Jether, captain of the host of J·.
4:20 J· and Israel were many, as the
25 J· and Israel dwelt safely, every
12:17 which dwelt in the cities of J·,
20 of David, but the tribe of J· only.
21 he assembled all the house of J·,
23 the son of Solomon, king of J·,
23 all the house of J· and Benjamin,
27 even unto Rehoboam king of J·,
27 go again to Rehoboam king of J·.
32 like unto the feast that is in J·,
13: 1 there came a man of God out of J·
12 of God went, which came from J·.
14 man of God that camest from J·?
21 the man of God that came from J·,
14:21 the son of Solomon reigned in J·.
22 J· did evil in the sight of the Lord,
29 of the chronicles of the kings of J·?
15: 1 of Nebat reigned Abijam over J·.
7 of the chronicles of the kings of J·?
9 king of Israel reigned Asa over J·.
17 king of Israel went up against J·,
17 go out or come in to Asa king of J·.
1Ki 15:22 a proclamation throughout all J·:
23 of the chronicles of the kings of J·?
25 the second year of Asa king of J·,
28, 33 the third year of Asa king of J·
16: 8 and sixth year of Asa king of J·
10 and seventh year of Asa king of J·,
15 and seventh year of Asa king of J·
23 and first year of Asa king of J·
29 and eighth year of Asa king of J·
19: 3 Beer-sheba, which belongeth to J·,
22: 2 king of J· came down to the king
10 and Jehoshaphat the king of J·
29 Jehoshaphat the king of J· went up
41 son of Asa began to reign over J·
45 of the chronicles of the kings of J·?
51 year of Jehoshaphat king of J·,
2Ki 1:17 the son of Jehoshaphat king of J·;
3: 1 year of Jehoshaphat king of J·,
7 sent to Jehoshaphat the king of J·,
9 of Israel went, and the king of J·,
14 of Jehoshaphat the king of J·,
8:16 Jehoshaphat being then king of J·,
16 son of Jehoshaphat king of J· began
19 Lord would not destroy J· for David
20 revolted from under the hand of J·,
22 revolted from under the hand of J·
23 of the chronicles of the kings of J·?
25 Jehoram king of J· begin to reign.
29 king of J· went down to see Joram
9:16 of J· was come down to see Joram.
21 and Ahaziah king of J· went out,
27 Ahaziah the king of J· saw this, he
29 began Ahaziah to reign over J·.
10:13 the brethren of Ahaziah king of J·,
12:18 Jehoash king of J· took all the
18 fathers, kings of J·, had dedicated,
19 of the chronicles of the kings of J·?
13: 1 Joash the son of Ahaziah king of J·
10 seventh year of Joash king of J·
12 fought against Amaziah king of J·,
14: 1 Amaziah the son of Joash king of J·.
9 Israel sent to Amaziah king of J·,
10 fall, even thou, and J· with thee?
11 he and Amaziah king of J· looked
11 which belongeth to J·.
12 And J· was put to the worse before
13 of Israel took Amaziah king of J·,
15 he fought with Amaziah king of J·,
17 the son of Joash king of J· lived
18 of the chronicles of the kings of J·?
21 all the people of J· took Azariah,
22 built Elath, and restored it to J·,
23 Amaziah the son of Joash king of J·
28 and Hamath, which belonged to J·,
15: 1 son of Amaziah king of J· to reign.
6 of the chronicles of the kings of J·?
8 eighth year of Azariah king of J·
13 thirtieth year of Uzziah king of J·;
17 thirtieth year of Azariah king of J·
23 fiftieth year of Azariah king of J·
27 fiftieth year of Azariah king of J·
32 son of Uzziah king of J· to reign.
36 of the chronicles of the kings of J·?
37 the Lord began to send against J·
16: 1 Jotham king of J· began to reign.
19 of the chronicles of the kings of J·?
17: 1 the twelfth year of Ahaz king of J·
13 against Israel, and against J·,
18 none left but the tribe of J· only.
19 Also J· kept not the commandments
18: 1 of Ahaz king of J· began to reign.
5 like him among all the kings of J·,
13 against all the fenced cities of J·,
14 Hezekiah king of J· sent to the king
14 appointed unto Hezekiah king of J·
16 Hezekiah king of J· had overlaid,
22 and hath said to J· and Jerusalem,
19:10 ye speak to Hezekiah king of J·,
30 that is escaped of the house of J·
20:20 of the chronicles of the kings of J·?
21:11 Manasseh king of J· hath done these
11 made J· also to sin with his idols:
12 such evil upon Jerusalem and J·,
16 sin wherewith he made J· to sin,
17, 25 the chronicles of the kings of J·?
22:13 for all J·, concerning the words of
16 book which the king of J· had read:
18 king of J· which sent you to inquire
23: 1 the elders of J· and of Jerusalem.
2 and all the men of J· and all the
5 kings of J· had ordained to burn
5 in the high places in the cities of J·,
8 the priests out of the cities of J·,
11 the horses that the kings of J· had
12 which the kings of J· had made,
17 man of God, which came from J·,
22 of Israel, nor of the kings of J·;
24 that were spied in the land of J·
26 his anger was kindled against J·,
27 will remove J· also out of my sight,
28 of the chronicles of the kings of J·?
24: 2 sent them against J· to destroy it,
3 of the Lord came this upon J·,
5 of the chronicles of the kings of J·?
12 Jehoiachin the king of J· went out
20 came to pass in Jerusalem and J·,
25:21 J· was carried away out of their
22 that remained in the land of J·,
27 captivity of Jehoiachin king of J·,
27 up the head of Jehoiachin king of J·
1Ch 2: 1 Simeon, Levi, and J·, Isaachar,
3 the sons of J·; Er, and Onan, and
3 Er, the firstborn of J·, was evil in
4 Zerah. All the sons of J· were five.
10 prince of the children of J·;
4: 1 The sons of J·; Pharez, Hezron,

1Ch 4:21 sons of Shelah the son of J' were,
27 multiply, like to the children of J'.
41 the days of Hezekiah king of J',
5: 2 J' prevailed above his brethren,
17 in the days of Jotham king of J',
6:15 Lord carried away J' and Jerusalem
55 gave them Hebron in the land of J',
65 of the tribe of the children of J',
9: 1 book of the kings of Israel and J'.
3 dwelt of the children of J', and of
4 children of Pharez the son of J'.
12:16 of the children of Benjamin and J'
24 children of J' that bare shield and
13: 6 which belonged to J', to bring up
21: 5 J' was four hundred threescore
27:18 Of J', Elihu, one of the brethren of
28: 4 he hath chosen J' to be the ruler;
4 of the house of J', the house of my
2Ch 2: 7 cunning men that are with me in J'
9:11 such seen before in the land of J'.
10:17 Israel that dwelt in the cities of J',
11: 1 of the house of J' and Benjamin
3 the son of Solomon, king of J',
3 to all Israel in J' and Benjamin,
5 and built cities for defence in J'.
10 Aijalon, and Hebron, which are in J'
12 having J' and Benjamin on his side.
14 their possession, and came to J'
17 strengthened the kingdom of J',
23 the countries of J' and Benjamin,
12: 4 fenced cities which pertained to J',
5 Rehoboam, and to the princes of J'.
12 and also in J' things went well.
13: 1 began Abijah to reign over J'.
13 so they were before J', and the
14 when J' looked back, behold, the
15 Then the men of J' gave a shout:
15 as the men of J' shouted, it came
15 and all Israel before Abijah and J'.
16 the children of Israel fled before J':
18 children of J' prevailed, because
14: 4 commanded J' to seek the Lord God
5 all the cities of J' the high places,
6 And he built fenced cities in J':
7 Therefore he said unto J', Let us
8 out of J' three hundred thousand;
12 before Asa, and before J'; and the
15: 2 me, Asa, and all J' and Benjamin;
8 idols out of all the land of J' and
9 he gathered all J' and Benjamin,
15 And all J' rejoiced at the oath:
16: 1 king of Israel came up against J',
1 go out or come in to Asa king of J'.
6 Asa the king took all J'; and they
7 the seer came to Asa king of J',
11 book of the kings of J' and Israel.
17: 2 forces in all the fenced cities of J',
2 set garrisons in the land of J', and
5 J' brought to Jehoshaphat presents;
6 high places and groves out of J'.
7 to teach in the cities of J'.
9 they taught in J', and had the book
9 throughout all the cities of J',
10 the lands that were round about J',
12 he built in J' castles, and cities of
13 much business in the cities of J':
14 Of J', the captains of thousands;
19 the fenced cities throughout all J'.
18: 3 said unto Jehoshaphat king of J',
9 Israel and Jehoshaphat king of J'
28 Jehoshaphat the king of J' went up
19: 1 Jehoshaphat king of J' returned to
5 all the fenced cities of J', city by
11 the ruler of the house of J', for all
20: 3 proclaimed a fast throughout all J'.
4 J' gathered themselves together, to
4 out of the cities of J' they came to
5 stood in the congregation of J' and
13 all J' stood before the Lord, with
15 he said, Hearken ye, all J', and ye
17 Lord with you, O J' and Jerusalem:
18 all J' and the inhabitants of
20 stood and said, Hear me, O J',
22 Seir, which were come against J';
24 when J' came toward the watch
27 every man of J' and Jerusalem,
31 Jehoshaphat reigned over J': he
35 Jehoshaphat king of J' join himself
21: 3 things, with fenced cities in J':
8 from under the dominion of J',
10 revolted from under the hand of J'
11 high places in the mountains of J',
11 and compelled J' thereto.
12 nor in the ways of Asa king of J',
13 hast made J' and the inhabitants
17 they came up into J', and brake
22: 1 son of Jehoram king of J' reigned.
6 Jehoram king of J' went down to
8 found the princes of J', and the
10 all the seed royal of the house of J'.
23: 2 they went about in J', and gathered
2 the Levites out of all the cities of J',
8 Levites and all J' did according to
24: 5 Go out unto the cities of J', and
6 the Levites to bring in out of J'
9 made a proclamation through J'
17 Jehoiada came the princes of J',
18 wrath came upon J' and Jerusalem
23 they came to J' and Jerusalem,
25: 5 Amaziah gathered J' together, and
5 of their fathers, throughout all J'
10 was greatly kindled against J',
12 children of J' carry away captive,
13 fell upon the cities of J', from
17 Amaziah king of J' took advice,
18 Israel sent to Amaziah king of J',

2Ch 25:19 fall, even thou, and J' with thee?
21 both he and Amaziah king of J',
21 which belongeth to J'.
22 J' was put to the worse before
23 of Israel took Amaziah king of J',
25 son of Joash king of J' lived after
26 book of the kings of J' and Israel?
28 with his fathers in the city of J'.
26: 1 all the people of J' took Uzziah,
2 built Eloth, and restored it to J',
27: 4 built cities in the mountains of J',
7 book of the kings of Israel and J'.
28: 6 slew in J' a hundred and twenty
9 of your fathers was wroth with J',
10 to keep under the children of J'
17 Edomites had come and smitten J',
18 low country, and of the south of J',
19 brought J' low because of Ahaz
19 he made J' naked, and transgressed
25 city of J' he made high places to
26 book of the kings of J' and Israel.
29: 8 the wrath of the Lord was upon J'
21 and for the sanctuary, and for J'.
30: 1 Hezekiah sent to all Israel and J',
6 throughout all Israel and J',
12 in J' the hand of God was to give
24 Hezekiah king of J' did give to the
25 the congregation of J', with the
25 and that dwelt in J', rejoiced.
31: 1 present went out to the cities of J',
1 places and the altars out of all J'
6 the children of Israel and J', that
6 dwelt in the cities of J', they also
20 did Hezekiah throughout all J',
32: 1 entered into J', and encamped
8 the words of Hezekiah king of J'.
9 unto Hezekiah king of J', and unto
9 unto all J' that were at Jerusalem,
12 commanded J' and Jerusalem,
23 presents to Hezekiah king of J':
25 was wrath upon him, and upon J'
32 book of the kings of J' and Israel.
33 all J' and the inhabitants of
33: 9 Manasseh made J' and the
14 war in all the fenced cities of J'.
16 commanded J' to serve the Lord
34: 3 twelfth year he began to purge J'
5 and cleansed J' and Jerusalem.
9 the remnant of Israel, and of all J'
11 which the kings of J' had destroyed.
21 that are left in Israel and in J',
24 have read before the king of J':
26 as for the king of J', who sent you
29 all the elders of J' and Jerusalem.
30 the Lord, and all the men of J',
35:18 all J' and Israel that was present,
21 to do with thee, thou king of J'?
24 all J' and Jerusalem mourned for
27 book of the kings of Israel and J'.
36: 4 Eliakim his brother king over J'
8 book of the kings of Israel and J':
10 Zedekiah his brother king over J'
23 house in Jerusalem, which is in J'.
Ezr 1: 2 house at Jerusalem, which is in J'.
3 go up to Jerusalem, which is in J',
5 rose up the chief of the fathers of J'
8 unto Sheshbazzar, the prince of J'.
2: 1 again unto Jerusalem and J',
3: 9 his sons, the sons of J', together,
4: 1 the adversaries of J' and Benjamin
4 the hands of the people of J',
6 against the inhabitants of J' and
5: 1 unto the Jews that were in J'
7:14 to enquire concerning J' and
9: 9 to give us a wall in J' and in
10: 7 made proclamation throughout J'
9 men of J' and Benjamin gathered
23 Kelita,) Pethahiah, J', and Eliezer.
Ne 1: 2 came, he and certain men of J';
2: 5 thou wouldest send me unto J',
7 convey me over till I come into J';
4:10 J' said, The strength of the bearers
16 were behind all the house of J'.
5:14 be their governor in the land of J',
6: 7 saying, There is a king in J':
17 nobles of J' sent many letters unto
18 were many in J' sworn unto him,
7: 6 came again to Jerusalem and to J',
11: 3 in the cities of J' dwelt every one
4 dwelt certain of the children of J',
4 the children of J'; Athaiah the son
9 J' the son of Senuah was second
20 Levites, were in all the cities of J',
24 the children of Zerah the son of J',
25 some of the children of J' dwelt at
36 the Levites were divisions in J',
12: 8 Sherebiah, J', and Mattaniah,
31 up the princes of J' upon the wall,
32 and half of the princes of J',
34 J', and Benjamin, and Shemaiah,
36 Nethaneel, and J', Hanani, with
44 J' rejoiced for the priests and for
13:12 brought all J' the tithe of the corn
15 days saw I in J' some treading
16 the sabbath unto the children of J',
17 contended with the nobles of J',
Es 2: 6 away with Jeconiah king of J',
Ps 48:11 let the daughters of J' be glad,
60: 7 of mine head; J' is my lawgiver;
63: *title* he was in the wilderness of J'.
68:27 the princes of J' and their council,
69:35 Zion, and will build the cities of J':
76: 1 In J' is God known: his name is
78:68 But chose the tribe of J', the
97: 8 the daughters of J' rejoiced
108: 8 of mine head; J' is my lawgiver;

Ps 114: 2 J' was his sanctuary, and Israel
Pr 25: 1 men of Hezekiah king of J' copied
Isa 1: 1 which he saw concerning J' and
1 Ahaz and Hezekiah, kings of J'.
2: 1 the son of Amoz saw concerning J'
3: 1 and from J' the stay and the staff,
8 Jerusalem is ruined, and J' is fallen:
5: 3 men of J', judge, I pray you,
7 the men of J' his pleasant plant:
7: 1 the son of Uzziah, king of J',
6 Let us go up against J', and vex it,
17 that Ephraim departed from J';
8: 8 he shall pass through J'; he shall
9:21 they together shall be against J'.
11:12 gather together the dispersed of J'
13 adversaries of J' shall be cut off:
13 Ephraim shall not envy J',
13 and J' shall not vex Ephraim.
19:17 the land of J' shall be a terror unto
22: 8 he discovered the covering of J',
21 Jerusalem, and to the house of J'.
26: 1 this song be sung in the land of J';
36: 1 against all the defenced cities of J',
7 said to J' and to Jerusalem, Ye
37:10 ye speak to Hezekiah king of J',
31 that is escaped of the house of J'
38: 9 The writing of Hezekiah king of J',
40: 9 say unto the cities of J', Behold
44:26 to the cities of J', Ye shall be built,
48: 1 come forth out of the waters of J',
65: 9 J' an inheritor of my mountains:
Jer 1: 2 Josiah the son of Amon king of J',
3 Jehoiakim...of Josiah king of J',
3 Zedekiah...of Josiah king of J',
15 and against all the cities of J'.
18 whole land, against the kings of J',
2:28 of thy cities are thy gods, O J'.
3: 7 her treacherous sister J' saw it.
8 treacherous sister J' feared not,
10 her treacherous sister J' hath not
11 herself more than treacherous J'.
18 the house of J' shall walk with the
4: 3 saith the Lord to the men of J'
4 Ye men of J' and inhabitants of
5 Declare ye in J', and publish in
16 their voice against the cities of J'.
5:11 the house of J' have dealt very
20 of Jacob, and publish it in J',
7: 2 the word of the Lord, all ye of J',
17 not what they do in the cities of J'
30 children of J' have done evil in my
34 cause to cease from the cities of J',
8: 1 out the bones of the kings of J',
9:11 will make the cities of J' desolate,
26 J', and Edom, and the children of
10:22 make the cities of J' desolate, and
11: 2 speak unto the men of J', and to
6 all these words in the cities of J',
9 is found among the men of J',
10 house of J' have broken...covenant
12 the cities of J' and inhabitants the
13 of thy cities were thy gods, O J';
17 of Israel and of the house of J',
12:14 pluck out the house of J' from
13: 9 manner will I mar the pride of J',
11 of Israel and the whole house of J',
19 J' shall be carried away captive all
14: 2 J' mourneth, and the gates thereof
19 Hast thou utterly rejected J'? hath
15: 4 the son of Hezekiah king of J',
17: 1 sin of J' is written with a pen of
19 the kings of J' come in, and by the
20 the Lord, ye kings of J', and all J',
25 their princes, the men of J', and
26 shall come from the cities of J',
18:11 go to, speak to the men of J',
19: 3 word of the Lord, O kings of J',
4 have known, nor the kings of J',
7 I will make void the counsel of J'
13 houses of the kings of J', shall be
20: 4 give all J' into the hand of the king
5 all the treasures of the kings of J'
21: 7 I will deliver Zedekiah king of J',
11 touching the house of the king of J',
22: 1 down to the house of the king of J',
2 O king of J', that sitteth upon the
6 Lord unto the king's house of J';
11 Shallum...of Josiah king of J',
18 Jehoiakim...of Josiah king of J';
24 the son of Jehoiakim king of J'
30 David, and ruling any more in J'.
23: 6 In his days J' shall be saved, and
24: 1 the son of Jehoiakim king of J',
1 and the princes of J', with the
5 that are carried away captive of J',
8 will I give Zedekiah the king of J',
25: 1 concerning all the people of J',
1 Jehoiakim...of Josiah king of J',
2 spake unto all the people of J'
3 Josiah the son of Amon king of J',
18 cities of J', and the kings thereof,
26: 1 Jehoiakim...of Josiah king of J'
2 and speak unto all the cities of J',
10 princes of J' heard these things,
18 in the days of Hezekiah king of J',
18 spake to all the people of J', saying,
19 Did Hezekiah king of J' and all
19 and all J' put him at all to death?
27: 1 Jehoiakim...of Josiah king of J'
3 come...unto Zedekiah king of J';
12 I spake also to Zedekiah king of J'
18 in the house of the king of J', and
20 the son of Jehoiakim king of J'
20 all the nobles of J' and Jerusalem;
21 in the house of the king of J' and
28: 1 of the reign of Zedekiah king of J'.

Jer 28: 4 the son of Jehoiakim king of J',
4 with all the captives of J', that went
29: 2 the princes of J' and Jerusalem,
3 (whom Zedekiah king of J' sent
22 up a curse by all the captivity of J'
30: 3 the captivity of my people...J',
4 spake concerning Israel and...J'.
31: 23 use this speech in the land of J'
24 there shall dwell in J' itself, and in
27 house of J' with the seed of man,
31 of Israel, and with the house of J':
32: 1 tenth year of Zedekiah king of J',
3 king of J' had shut him up, saying,
4 king of J' shall not escape out of
30 children of J' have only done evil
32 of Israel and of the children of J',
32 their prophets, and the men of J',
35 this abomination, to cause J' to sin.
44 Jerusalem, and in the cities of J',
33: 4 the houses of the kings of J',
7 And I will cause the captivity of J'
10 beast, even in the cities of J',
13 in the cities of J', shall the flocks
14 of Israel and to the house of J'.
16 In those days shall J' be saved, and
34: 2 speak to Zedekiah king of J', and
4 of the Lord, O Zedekiah king of J';
6 words unto Zedekiah king of J' in
7 against all the cities of J' that were
7 cities remained of the cities of J'.
19 princes of J', and the princes of
21 Zedekiah king of J' and his princes
22 make the cities of J' a desolation
35: 1 Jehoiakim...of Josiah king of J',
13 Go and tell the men of J' and the
17 I will bring upon J' and upon all
36: 1 Jehoiakim...of Josiah king of J',
2 thee against Israel, and against J',
3 be that the house of J' will hear all
6 shalt read them in the ears of all J'
9 Jehoiakim...of Josiah king of J',
9 that came from the cities of J' unto
28 which...the king of J' hath burned.
29 shalt say to Jehoiakim king of J',
30 the Lord of Jehoiakim king of J';
31 and upon the men of J', all the evil
32 Jehoiakim king of J' had burned
37: 1 Babylon made king in the land of J',
7 Thus shall ye say to the king of J',
39: 1 ninth year of Zedekiah king of J',
4 Zedekiah the king of J' saw them,
6 of Babylon slew all the nobles of J'.
10 which had nothing, in the land of J',
40: 1 away captive of Jerusalem and J',
5 made governor over the cities of J',
11 Babylon had left a remnant of J',
12 driven, and came to the land of J',
15 and the remnant in J' perish?
42: 15 word of the Lord, ye remnant of J';
19 concerning you, O ye remnant of J';
43: 4 the Lord, to dwell in the land of J'.
5 forces, took all the remnant of J',
5 driven, to dwell in the land of J';
9 in the sight of the men of J';
44: 2 and upon all the cities of J';
6 and was kindled in the cities of J'
7 child and suckling, out of J',
9 the wickedness of the kings of J',
9 have committed in the land of J',
11 you for evil, and to cut off all J'.
12 And I will take the remnant of J',
14 So that none of the remnant of J',
14 should return into the land of J',
17 and our princes, in the cities of J',
21 that ye burned in the cities of J',
24 all J' that are in the land of Egypt:
26 all J' that dwell in the land of Egypt;
26 in the mouth of any man of J' in all
27 all men of J' that are in the land of
28 land of Egypt into the land of J',
28 all the remnant of J', that are gone
30 I gave Zedekiah king of J' into the
45: 1 Jehoiakim...of Josiah king of J',
46: 2 Jehoiakim...of Josiah king of J'.
49: 34 of the reign of Zedekiah king of J',
50: 4 they and the children of J' together,
20 the sins of J', and they shall not be
33 the children of J' were oppressed
51: 5 been forsaken, nor J' of his God,
59 went with Zedekiah the king of J'
52: 3 came to pass in Jerusalem and J',
10 he slew also all the princes of J' in
27 J' was carried away captive out of
31 captivity of Jehoiachin king of J',
31 the head of Jehoiachin king of J',
La 1: 3 J' is gone into captivity because of
15 the virgin, the daughter of J', as in
2: 2 strong holds of the daughter of J';
5 increased in the daughter of J'
5: 11 and the maids in the cities of J'.
Eze 4: 6 bear the iniquity of the house of J'
8: 1 and the elders of J' sat before me,
17 Is it a light thing to the house of J'
9: 9 of Israel and J' is exceeding great,
21: 20 to J' in Jerusalem the defenced.
25: 3 and against the house of J', when
8 of J' is like unto all the heathen;
12 hath dealt against the house of J'
27: 17 J', and the land of Israel, they were
37: 16 For J', and for the children of Israel
19 with him, even with the stick of J',
48: 7 unto the west side, a portion for J'.
8 And by the border of J', from the
22 between the border of J' and the
31 one gate of J', one gate of Levi.
Da 1: 1 of the reign of Jehoiakim king of J'
Da 1: 2 gave Jehoiakim king of J' into his
6 these were of the children of J',
2: 25 found a man of the captives of J',
5: 13 the children of the captivity of J',
6: 13 the children of the captivity of J',
9: 7 to the men of J', and to the
Ho 1: 1 Ahaz, and Hezekiah, kings of J',
7 have mercy upon the house of J',
11 Then shall the children of J' and
4: 15 the harlot, yet let not J' offend;
5: 5 J' also shall fall with them.
10 princes of J' were like them that
12 to the house of J' as rottenness.
13 his sickness, and J' saw his wound,
14 as a young lion to the house of J':
6: 4 O J', what shall I do unto thee?
11 O J', he hath set an harvest for thee,
8: 14 J' hath multiplied fenced cities:
10: 11 J' shall plow, and Jacob shall break
11: 12 but J' yet ruleth with God, and is
12: 2 hath also a controversy with J',
Joe 3: 1 shall bring again the captivity of J'
6 children also of J' and the children
8 into the hand of the children of J',
18 rivers of J' shall flow with waters,
19 violence against the children of J',
20 But J' shall dwell forever, and
Am 1: 1 in the days of Uzziah king of J',
2: 4 For three transgressions of J', and
5 I will send a fire upon J', and it
7: 12 flee thee away into the land of J',
Ob 12 rejoiced over the children of J' in
Mic 1: 1 Ahaz, and Hezekiah, kings of J',
5 and what are the high places of J'?
9 is incurable; for it is come unto J';
5: 2 be little among the thousands of J',
Na 1: 15 O J', keep thy solemn feasts,
Zep 1: 1 Josiah the son of Amon, king of J',
4 also stretch out mine hand upon J',
2: 7 for the remnant of the house of J';
Hag 1: 1, 14 son of Shealtiel, governor of J',
2: 2 the son of Shealtiel, governor of J',
21 speak to Zerubbabel, governor of J',
Zec 1: 12 on Jerusalem and on the cities of J',
19, 21 horns which have scattered J',
21 horn over the land of J' to scatter
2: 12 the Lord shall inherit J' his portion
8: 13 among the heathen, O house of J',
15 Jerusalem and to the house of J':
19 to the house of J' joy and gladness,
9: 7 God, and he be as a governor in J',
13 have bent J' for me, filled the bow
10: 3 visited his flock the house of J',
6 I will strengthen the house of J',
11: 14 brotherhood between J' and Israel.
12: 2 be in the siege both against J' and
4 mine eyes upon the house of J',
5 governors of J' shall say in their
6 will I make the governors of J' like
7 also shall save the tents of J' first,
7 not magnify themselves against J'.
14: 5 in the days of Uzziah king of J':
14 J' also shall fight at Jerusalem;
21 every pot in Jerusalem and in J'
Mal 2: 11 J' hath dealt treacherously, and
11 for J' hath profaned the holiness
3: 4 shall the offering of J'...be pleasant
Heb 8: 8 of Israel and with the house of J':

Judah's (*ju'-dahs*)
Ge 38: 7 And Er, J' firstborn, was wicked
12 daughter of Shuah J' wife died;
Jer 32: 2 which was in the king of J' house.
38: 22 that are left in the king of J' house

Judas (*ju'-das*) See also BARSABAS; ISCARIOT; JUDAH; JUDE; LEBBÆUS; THADDÆUS.
M't 1: 2 Jacob begat J' and his brethren;
3 And J' begat Phares and Zara of
10: 4 J' Iscariot, who also betrayed him.
13: 55 and Joses, and Simon, and J'?
26: 14 twelve, called J' Iscariot, went
25 J', which betrayed him, answered
47 lo, J', one of the twelve, came,
27: 3 J', which had betrayed him, when
M'r 3: 19 J' Iscariot, which also betrayed
14: 10 J' Iscariot, one of the twelve, went
43 cometh J', one of the twelve, and
Lu 6: 16 And J' the brother of James, and
16 J' Iscariot, which...was the traitor.
22: 3 Satan into J' surnamed Iscariot,
47 and he that was called J', one of
48 J', betrayest thou the Son of man
Joh 6: 71 He spake of J' Iscariot the son of
12: 4 disciples, J' Iscariot, Simon's son,
13: 2 put into the heart of J' Iscariot,
26 the sop, he gave it to J' Iscariot,
29 thought, because J' had the bag,
14: 22 J' saith to him, not Iscariot, Lord,
18: 2 J' also, which betrayed him, knew
3 J' then, having received a band of
5 J' also, which betrayed him, stood
Ac 1: 13 and J' the brother of James.
16 David spake before concerning J',
25 from which J' by transgression fell,
5: 37 After this man rose up J' of Galilee
9: 11 the house of J' for one called Saul,
15: 22 J' surnamed Barsabas, and Silas,
27 have sent therefore J' and Silas,
32 J' and Silas, being prophets also

Judas-Iscariot See JUDAS and ISCARIOT.

Jude (*jood*) See also JUDAS.
Jude 1 J', the servant of Jesus Christ,

Judea (*ju-de'-ah*) See also JUDÆA.
Ezr 5: 8 we went into the province of J',

judge See also JUDGED; JUDGES; JUDGEST; JUDGETH; JUDGING.
Ge 15: 14 whom they shall serve, will I j':
16: 5 the Lord j' between me and thee.
18: 25 not the J' of all the earth do right?
19: 9 sojourn, and he will needs be a j':
31: 37 that they may j' betwixt us both.
53 God of their father, j' betwixt us.
49: 16 Dan shall j' his people, as one of
Ex 2: 14 thee a prince and a j' over us?
5: 21 The Lord look upon you, and j';
18: 13 that Moses sat to j' the people:
16 and I j' between one and another,
22 let them j' the people at all seasons:
22 every small matter they shall j':
Le 19: 15 shalt thou j' thy neighbour.
Nu 35: 24 the congregation shall j' between
De 1: 16 j' righteously between every man
16: 18 and they shall j' the people with just
17: 9 the j' that shall be in those days,
12 the Lord thy God, or unto the j',
25: 1 that the judges may j' them;
2 the j' shall cause him to lie down,
32: 36 For the Lord shall j' his people,
J'g 2: 18 Lord was with the j', and delivered
18 their enemies all the days of the j':
19 the j' was dead, that they returned,
11: 27 Lord the J' be j' this day between
1Sa 2: 10 Lord shall j' the ends of the earth;
25 against another, the j' shall...him:
25 against another, the...shall j' him:
3: 13 that I will j' his house for ever for
8: 5 make us a king to j' us like all the
6 they said, Give us a king to j' us.
20 that our king may j' us, and go out
24: 12 The Lord j' between me and thee,
15 The Lord therefore be j', and
15 and j' between me and thee, and
2Sa 15: 4 Oh that I were made j' in the land,
1Ki 3: 9 understanding heart to j' thy people,
9 for who is able to j' this thy so great
7: 7 for the throne where he might j',
8: 32 heaven, and do, and j' thy servants,
1Ch 16: 33 because he cometh to j' the earth.
2Ch 1: 10 who can j' this thy people, that is
11 that thou mayest j' my people,
6: 23 heaven, and do, and j' thy servants,
19: 6 ye j' not for man, but for the Lord,
20: 12 O our God, wilt thou not j' them?
Ezr 7: 25 which may j' all the people that
Job 9: 15 would make supplication to my j'.
22: 13 can he j' through the dark cloud?
23: 7 I be delivered for ever from my j'.
31: 28 iniquity to be punished by the j':
Ps 7: 8 The Lord shall j' the people:
8 j' me, O Lord, according to my
9: 8 shall j' the world in righteousness,
10: 18 j' the fatherless and the oppressed,
26: 1 J' me, O Lord; for I have walked
35: 24 J' me, O Lord my God, according
43: 1 J' me, O God, and plead my cause
50: 4 earth, that he may j' his people.
6 for God is j' himself.
54: 1 name, and j' me by thy strength.
58: 1 do ye j' uprightly, O ye sons of
67: 4 thou shalt j' the people righteously,
68: 5 a j' of the widows, is God in his
72: 2 j' thy people with righteousness,
4 He shall j' the poor of the people,
75: 2 congregation I will j' uprightly.
7 God is the j': he putteth down one,
82: 2 How long will ye j' unjustly, and
8 Arise, O God, j' the earth: for thou
94: 2 Lift up thyself, thou j' of the earth:
96: 10 he shall j' the people righteously.
13 for he cometh to j' the earth:
13 j' the world with righteousness,
98: 9 for he cometh to j' the earth:
9 righteousness shall he j' the world,
110: 6 He shall j' among the heathen, he
135: 14 Lord will j' his people, and he will
Pr 31: 9 Open thy mouth, j' righteously,
Ec 3: 17 God shall j' the righteous and the
Isa 1: 17 j' the fatherless, plead for the
23 they j' not the fatherless, neither
2: 4 he shall j' among the nations, and
3: 2 man of war, the j', and the prophet,
13 and standeth to j' the people.
5: 3 j', I pray you, betwixt me and
11: 3 not j' after the sight of his eyes,
4 righteousness shall he j' the poor,
33: 22 the Lord is our j', the Lord is our
51: 5 and mine arms shall j' the people;
Jer 5: 28 they j' not the cause, the cause of
28 right of the needy do they not j'.
La 3: 59 seen my wrong: j' thou my cause.
Eze 7: 3, 8 will j' thee according to thy ways,
27 to their deserts will I j' them;
11: 10 I will j' you in the border of Israel;
11 I will j' you in the border of Israel:
16: 38 I will j' thee, as women that break
18: 30 Therefore I will j' you, O house of
20: 4 Wilt thou j' them, son of man,
4 wilt thou j' them? cause them to
21: 30 I will j' thee in the place where thou
22: 2 Now, thou son of man, wilt thou j',
2 wilt thou j' the bloody city? yea,
23: 24 they shall j' thee according to their
36 Son of man, wilt thou j' Aholah and
45 they shall j' them after the manner
24: 14 to thy doings, shall they j' thee,
33: 20 I will j' you every one after his ways.
34: 17 I j' between cattle and cattle,
20 even I, will j' between the fat cattle
22 I will j' between cattle and cattle.
44: 24 j' it according to my judgments:

Joe 3:12 there will I sit to j' all the heathen
Am 2: 3 cut off the j' from the midst thereof,
Ob 21 Zion to j' the mount of Esau;
Mic 3:11 heads thereof j' for reward, and the
4: 3 And he shall j' among many people,
5: 1 shall smite the j' of Israel with a rod
7: 3 and the j' asketh for a reward;
Zec 3: 7 then thou shalt also j' my house,
M't 5:25 adversary deliver thee to the j',
25 the j' deliver thee to the officer,
7: 1 J' not, that ye be not judged.
2 with what judgment ye j', ye shall
Lu 6:37 J' not, and ye shall not be judged:
12:14 made me a j' or a divider over you?
57 yourselves j' ye not what is right?
58 him; lest he hale thee to the j',
58 and the j' deliver thee to the officer,
18: 2 There was in a city a j', which
6 said, Hear what the unjust j' saith.
19:22 of thine own mouth will I j' thee,
Joh 5:30 as I hear, I j': and my judgment
7:24 J' not according to the appearance,
24 but j' righteous judgment.
51 Doth our law j' any man, before it
8:15 Ye j' after the flesh; I j' no man.
16 And yet if I j', my judgment is true:
26 many things to say and to j' of you:
12:47 words, and believe not, I j' him not:
47 for I came not to j' the world, but to
48 the same shall j' him in the last day.
18:31 and j' him according to your law.
Ac 4:19 you more than unto God, j' ye.
7: 7 they shall be in bondage will I j',
27 made thee a ruler and j' over us?
35 Who made thee a ruler and a j'?
10:42 to be the J' of quick and dead.
13:46 j' yourselves unworthy of...life,
17:31 will j' the world in righteousness
18:15 for I will be no j' of such matters.
23: 3 sittest thou to j' me after the law,
24:10 thou hast been of many years a j'
Ro 2:16 God shall j' the secrets of men
27 if it fulfil the law, j' thee, who by
3: 6 then how shall God j' the world?
14: 3 which eateth not j' him that eateth:
10 But why dost thou j' thy brother?
13 Let us not therefore j' one another
13 but j' this rather, that no man put
1Co 4: 3 yea, I j' not mine own self.
5 j' nothing before the time, until
5:12 to j' them also that are without?
12 do not ye j' them that are within?
6: 2 that the saints shall j' the world?
2 are ye unworthy to j' the smallest
3 ye not that we shall j' angels?
4 them to j' who are least esteemed
5 be able to j' between his brethren?
10:15 as to wise men; j' ye what I say.
11:13 J' in yourselves: is it comely that
31 we would j' ourselves, we should
14:29 two or three, and let the others j'.
2Co 5:14 because we thus j', that if one
Col 2:16 Let no man therefore j' you in
2Ti 4: 1 who shall j' the quick and the dead
8 which the Lord, the righteous j',
Heb10:30 again, The Lord shall j' his people.
12:23 to God the J' of all, and to the
13: 4 and adulterers God will j'.
Jas 4:11 the law: but if thou j' the law,
11 art not a doer of the law, but a j'.
5: 9 the j' standeth before the door.
1Pe 4: 5 ready to j' the quick and the dead.
Re 6:10 thou not j' and avenge our blood
19:11 he doth j' and make war.

judged
Ge 30: 6 And Rachel said, God hath j' me,
Ex 18:26 they j' the people at all seasons:
26 small matter they j' themselves.
J'g 3:10 he j' Israel, and went out to war:
4: 4 Lapidoth, she j' Israel at that time.
10: 2 he j' Israel twenty and three years.
3 and j' Israel twenty and two years.
12: 7 And Jephthah j' Israel six years.
8 him Ibzan of Beth-lehem j' Israel.
9 sons. And he j' Israel seven years
11 him Elon, a Zebulonite, j' Israel;
11 and he j' Israel ten years.
13 of Hillel, a Pirathonite, j' Israel.
14 colts: and he j' Israel eight years.
15:20 And he j' Israel in the days of the
16:31 And he j' Israel twenty years.
1Sa 4:18 heavy. And he j' Israel forty years.
7: 6 Samuel j' the children of Israel in
15 Samuel j' Israel all the days of his
16 and j' Israel in all those places.
17 there he j' Israel; and there he
1Ki 3:28 judgment which the king had j';
2Ki 23:22 days of the judges that j' Israel,
Ps 9:19 let the heathen be j' in thy sight.
37:33 nor condemn him when he is j'.
109: 7 he shall be j', let him be condemned:
Jer 22:16 He j' the cause of the poor and
Eze 16:38 wedlock and shed blood are j';
52 also, which hast j' thy sisters,
28:23 the wounded shall be j' in the
35:11 among them, when I have j' thee.
36:19 according to their doings I j' them.
Da 9:12 and against our judges that j' us,
M't 7: 1 Judge not, that ye be not j'.
2 judgment ye judge, ye shall be j':
Lu 6:37 Judge not, and ye shall not be j':
7:43 said unto him, Thou hast rightly j'.
Joh 16:11 because the prince of this world is j'
Ac 16:15 If ye have j' me to be faithful to
24: 6 would have j' according to our law.
25: 9 be j' of these things before me?
Ac 25:10 seat, where I ought to be j': to the
20 and there be j' of these matters.
26: 6 now I stand and am j' for the hope
Ro 2:12 in the law shall be j' by the law;
3: 4 mightest overcome when thou art j'
7 why yet am I also j' as a sinner?
1Co 2:15 things, yet he himself is j' of no man.
4: 3 thing that I should be j' of you,
5: 3 present in spirit, have j' already,
6: 2 if the world shall be j' by you, are
10:29 why is my liberty j' of another
11:31 ourselves, we should not be j'.
32 when we are j', we are chastened
14:24 he is convinced of all, he is j' of all:
Heb11:11 she j' him faithful who had
Jas 2:12 as they that shall be j' by the law
1Pe 4: 6 they might be j' according to men
Re 11:18 of the dead, that they should be j',
16: 5 shalt be, because thou hast j' thus.
19: 2 for he hath j' the great whore,
20:12 the dead were j' out of those things
13 they were j' every man according to

judges^
Ex 21: 6 master shall bring him unto the j';
22 he shall pay as the j' determine.
22: 8 house shall be brought unto the j',
9 parties shall come before the j';
9 whom the j' shall condemn, he shall
Nu 25: 5 Moses said unto the j' of Israel,
De 1:16 And I charged your j' at that time,
16:18 J' and officers shalt thou make
19:17 before the priests and j', which
18 j' shall make diligent inquisition:
21: 2 elders and thy j' shall come forth,
25: 1 that the j' may judge them; then
32:31 our enemies themselves being j'.
Jos 8:33 their j', stood on this side the ark
23: 2 for their j', and for their officers,
24: 1 for their j', and for their officers;
J'g 2:16 Nevertheless the Lord raised up j',
17 would not hearken unto their j',
18 when the Lord raised them up j',
Ru 1: 1 pass in the days when the j' ruled,
1Sa 8: 1 that he made his sons j' over Israel
2 Abiah: they were j' in Beer-sheba.
2Sa 7:11 since the time that I commanded j'
2Ki 23:22 the days of the j' that judged Israel,
1Ch 17: 6 I a word to any of the j' of Israel,
10 since the time that I commanded j'
23: 4 six thousand were officers and j':
26:29 over Israel, for officers and j'.
2Ch 1: 2 to the j', and to every governor in
19: 5 he set j' in the land throughout all
6 said to the j', Take heed what ye do:
Ezr 7:25 thine hand, set magistrates and j',
10:14 of every city, and the j' thereof,
Job 9:24 covereth the faces of the j' thereof;
12:17 spoiled, and maketh the j' fools.
31:11 iniquity to be punished by the j'.
Ps 2:10 be instructed, ye j' of the earth.
141: 6 their j' are overthrown in...places;
148:11 princes, and all j' of the earth:
Pr 8:16 nobles, even all the j' of the earth.
Isa 1:26 I will restore thy j' as at the first,
40:23 maketh the j' of the earth as vanity.
Da 3: 2 governors, and the captains, the j',
3 the governors, and captains, the j',
9:12 against our j' that judged us, by
Hos 7: 7 oven, and have devoured their j';
13:10 thy j' of whom thou saidst, Give me
Zep 3: 3 her j' are evening wolves; they
M't 12:27 therefore they shall be your j'.
Lu 11:19 therefore shall they be your j'.
Ac 13:20 And after that he gave unto them j'
Jas 2: 4 And are become j' of evil thoughts?

judgest
Ps 51: 4 and be clear when thou j'.
Jer 11:20 O Lord of hosts, that j' righteously,
Ro 2: 1 O man, whosoever thou art that j':
1 for wherein thou j' another, thou
1 thou that j' doest the same things.
3 that j' them which do such things,
14: 4 Who art thou that j' another man's
Jas 4:12 who art thou that j' another?

judgeth
Job 21:22 seeing he j' those that are high.
36:31 by them j' he the people; he giveth
Ps 7:11 God j' the righteous, and God is
58:11 he is a God that j' in the earth.
82: 1 the mighty; he j' among the gods.
Pr 29:14 The king that faithfully j' the poor,
Joh 5:22 the Father j' no man, but hath
8:50 there is one that seeketh and j'.
12:48 not my words, hath one that j' him:
1Co 2:15 But he that is spiritual j' all things,
4: 4 but he that j' me is the Lord.
5:13 But them that are without God j'.
Jas 4:11 evil...brother, and j' his brother,
11 evil of the law, and j' the law:
1Pe 1:17 j' according to every man's work,
2:23 himself to him that j' righteously:
Re 18: 8 strong is the Lord God who j' her.

judging
2Ki 15: 5 house, j' the people of the land.
2Ch 26:21 house, j' the people of the land.
Ps 9: 4 thou satest in the throne j' right.
Isa 16: 5 of David, j', and seeking judgment,
M't 19:28 j' the twelve tribes of Israel.
Lu 22:30 thrones j' the twelve tribes of Israel.

judgment See also JUDGMENTS.
Ge 18:19 of the Lord, to do justice and j';
Ex 12:12 gods of Egypt I will execute j':
21:31 according to this j' shall it be done
Ex 23: 2 to decline after many to wrest j':
6 shalt not wrest the j' of thy poor
28:15 make the breastplate of j' with
29 the breastplate of j' upon his heart,
30 thou shalt put in the breastplate of j'
30 Aaron shall bear the j' of the
Le 19:15 shall do no unrighteousness in j':
35 shall do no unrighteousness in j',
Nu 27:11 the children of Israel a statute of j',
21 after the j' of Urim before the Lord:
35:12 stand before the congregation in j'.
29 shall be for a statute of j' unto you
De 1:17 ye shall not respect persons in j';
17 for the j' is God's: and the cause
10:18 He doth execute the j' of the
16:18 shall judge the people with just j'.
19 Thou shalt not wrest j'; thou shalt
17: 8 a matter too hard for thee in j',
9 shall shew thee the sentence of j':
11 according to the j' which they shall
24:17 not pervert the j' of the stranger,
25: 1 they come unto j', that the judges
27:19 perverteth the j' of the stranger,
32: 4 all his ways are j': a God of truth
41 and mine hand take hold on j';
Jos 20: 6 stand before the congregation for j',
J'g 4: 5 of Israel came up to her for j'.
5:10 ye that sit in j', and walk by the
1Sa 8: 3 and took bribes, and perverted j'.
2Sa 8:15 David executed j' and justice unto
15: 2 controversy came to the king for j',
6 Israel that came to the king for j':
1Ki 3:11 thyself understanding to discern j';
28 Israel heard of the j' which the king
28 wisdom of God was in him, to do j'.
7: 7 might judge, even the porch of j':
10: 9 he thee king, to do j' and justice.
20:40 said unto him, So shall thy j' be;
2Ki 25: 6 Riblah; and they gave j' upon him.
1Ch 18:14 executed j' and justice among all
2Ch 9: 8 king over them, to do j' and justice.
19: 6 who is with you in the j'.
8 for the j' of the Lord, and for
20: 9 j', or pestilence, or famine, we
22: 8 when Jehu was executing j' upon
24:24 So they executed j' against Joash.
Ezr 7:26 let j' be executed speedily upon
Es 1:13 toward all that knew law and j':
Job 8: 3 Doth God pervert j'? or doth the
9:19 and if of j', who shall set me a time
32 and we should come together in j'.
14: 3 and bringest me into j' with thee?
19: 7 I cry aloud, but there is no j'.
29 that ye may know there is a j'.
22: 4 will he enter with thee into j'?
27: 2 liveth, who hath taken away my j';
29:14 my j' was as a robe and a diadem.
32: 9 neither do the aged understand j'.
34: 4 Let us choose to us j': let us know
5 and God hath taken away my j'.
12 neither will the Almighty pervert j'.
23 he should enter into j' with God.
35:14 not see him, yet j' is before him;
36:17 hast fulfilled the j' of the wicked:
17 j' and justice take hold on thee.
37:23 he is excellent in power, and in j',
40: 8 Wilt thou also disannul my j'? wilt
Ps 1: 5 ungodly shall not stand in the j',
7: 6 to the j' that thou hast commanded.
9: 7 he hath prepared his throne for j'.
8 he shall minister j' to the people
16 by the j' which he executeth:
25: 9 The meek will he guide in j': and
33: 5 He loveth righteousness and j': the
35:23 awake to my j', even with my cause,
37: 6 the light, and thy j' as the noonday
28 Lord loveth j', and forsaketh not
30 wisdom, and his tongue talketh of j'.
72: 2 righteousness, and...poor with j'.
76: 8 didst cause j' to be heard from
9 God arose to j', to save all the
89:14 Justice and j' are the habitation
94:15 j' shall return unto righteousness:
97: 2 righteousness and j' are the
99: 4 The king's strength also loveth j';
4 executest j' and righteousness in
101: 1 I will sing of mercy and j': unto
103: 6 and j' for all that are oppressed.
106: 3 Blessed are they that keep j', and
30 up Phinehas, and executed j':
111: 7 of his hands are verity and j';
119:66 Teach me good j' and knowledge:
84 when wilt thou execute j' on them
121 I have done j' and justice: leave
149 quicken me according to thy j'.
122: 5 For there are set thrones of j', the
143: 2 enter not into j' with thy servant:
146: 7 executeth j' for the oppressed:
149: 9 execute upon them the j' written:
Pr 1: 3 wisdom, justice, and j', and equity;
2: 8 He keepeth the paths of j', and
9 understand righteousness, and j',
8:20 in the midst of the paths of j':
13:23 is that is destroyed for want of j'.
16:10 his mouth transgresseth not in j'.
17:23 the bosom to pervert the ways of j'.
18: 5 to overthrow the righteous in j'.
19:28 An ungodly witness scorneth j':
20: 8 that sitteth in the throne of j'
21: 3 To do justice and j' is more
7 them; because they refuse to do j'.
15 It is joy to the just to do j': but
24:23 to have respect of persons in j'.
28: 5 Evil men understand not j': but
29: 4 king by j' establisheth the land:
26 every man's j' cometh from the

Pr 31: 5 pervert the j' of any of the afflicted.
Ec 3:16 I saw under the sun the place of j',
5: 8 violent perverting of j' and justice
8: 5 heart discerneth both time and j'.
6 every purpose there is time and j',
11: 9 things God will bring thee into j'.
12:14 God shall bring every work into j',
Isa 1:17 well; seek j', relieve the oppressed,
21 it was full of j'; righteousness
27 Zion shall be redeemed with j', and
3:14 The Lord will enter into j' with the
4: 4 the midst thereof by the spirit of j',
5: 7 and he looked for j', but behold
16 Lord of hosts shall be exalted in j',
9: 7 to establish it with j' and with
10: 2 To turn aside the needy from j',
16: 3 Take counsel, execute j'; make
5 and seeking j', and hasting
28: 6 a spirit of j' to him that sitteth in j',
7 err in vision, they stumble in j'.
17 J' also will I lay to the line, and
30:18 you: for the Lord is a God of j':
32: 1 and princes shall rule in j'.
16 j' shall dwell in the wilderness,
33: 5 filled Zion with j' and righteousness.
34: 5 upon the people of my curse, to j'.
40:14 and taught him in the path of j',
27 my j' is passed over from my God?
41: 1 let us come near together to j'.
42: 1 shall bring forth j' to the Gentiles.
3 he shall bring forth j' unto truth.
4 till he have set j' in the earth:
49: 4 yet surely my j' is with the Lord,
51: 4 make my j' to rest for a light of the
53: 8 was taken from prison and from j':
54:17 that shall rise against thee in j'
56: 1 Keep ye j', and do justice: for my
59: 8 there is no j' in their goings: they
9 Therefore is j' far from us, neither
11 we look for j', but there is none;
14 j' is turned away backward, and
15 displeased him that there was no j'.
61: 8 I the Lord love j', I hate robbery
Jer 4: 2 in truth, in j', and in righteousness;
5: 1 if there be any that executeth j',
4 of the Lord, nor the j' of their God.
5 of the Lord, and the j' of their God:
7: 5 if ye thoroughly execute j' between
8: 7 people know not the j' of the Lord.
9:24 j', and righteousness, in the earth:
10:24 O Lord, correct me, but with j';
21:12 Execute j' in the morning, and
22: 3 Execute ye j' and righteousness,
15 eat and drink, and do j' and justice,
23: 5 execute j' and justice in the earth.
33:15 shall execute j' and righteousness
39: 5 where he gave j' upon him.
48:21 j' is come upon the plain country;
47 Lord: Thus far is the j' of Moab.
49:12 whose j' was not to drink of the cup
51: 9 her j' reacheth unto heaven, and is
47 will do j' upon the graven images
52 will do j' upon her graven images:
52: 9 where he gave j' upon him.
Eze 18: 8 executed true j' between man and
23:10 for they had executed j' upon her.
24 I will set j' before them, and they
34:16 the strong; I will feed them with j'.
39:21 heathen shall see my j' that I have
44:24 they shall stand in j';
45: 9 spoil, and execute j' and justice,
Da 4:37 works are truth, and his ways j':
7:10 the j' was set, and the books were
22 j' was given to the saints of the most
26 But the j' shall sit, and they shall
Ho 2:19 and in j', and in lovingkindness,
5: 1 j' is toward you, because ye have
11 is oppressed and broken in j',
10: 4 thus j' springeth up as hemlock in
12: 6 keep mercy and j', and wait on thy
Am 5: 7 Ye who turn j' to wormwood, and
15 good, and establish j' in the gate:
24 But let j' run down as waters, and
6:12 ye have turned j' into gall, and the
Mic 3: 1 Israel; Is it not for you to know j'?
8 and of j', and of might, to declare
9 that abhor j', and pervert all equity.
7: 9 my cause, and execute j' for me:
Hab 1: 4 slacked, and j' doth never go forth:
4 therefore wrong j' proceedeth.
7 j' and their dignity shall proceed
12 thou hast ordained them for j';
Zep 2: 3 earth, which have wrought his j';
3: 5 morning doth he bring his j' to light,
Zec 7: 9 Execute true j', and shew mercy
8:16 execute the j' of truth and peace in
Mal 2:17 them; or, Where is the God of j'?
3: 5 And I will come near to you to j';
M't 5:21 kill shall be in danger of the j':
22 a cause shall be in danger of the j':
7: 2 with what j' ye judge, ye shall be
10:15 and Gomorrha in the day of j',
11:22 for Tyre and Sidon at the day of j',
24 the land of Sodom in the day of j',
12:18 and he shall shew j' to the Gentiles.
20 till he send forth j' unto victory.
36 give account thereof in the day of j'.
41 The men of Nineveh shall rise in j'
42 of the south shall rise up in the j'
23:23 of the law, j', mercy, and faith:
27:19 he was set down on the j' seat,
M'r 6:11 and Gomorrah in the day of j',
Lu 10:14 for Tyre and Sidon at the j', than
11:31 of the south shall rise up in the j'
32 of Nineve shall rise up in the j'
42 pass over j' and the love of God:

Joh 5:22 hath committed all j' unto the Son:
27 him authority to execute j' also,
30 as I hear, I judge: and my j' is just;
7:24 appearance, but judge righteous j'.
8:16 And yet if I judge, my j' is true:
9:39 For j' I am come into this world,
12:31 Now is the j' of this world: now
16: 8 sin, and of righteousness, and of j':
11 Of j', because the prince of this
18:28 from Caiaphas unto the hall of j':
28 went not into the j' hall, lest they
33 Pilate entered into the j' hall
19: 9 And went again into the j' hall,
13 and sat down in the j' seat in a
Ac 8:33 humiliation his j' was taken away:
18:12 Paul, and brought him to the j' seat,
16 And he drave them from the j' seat.
17 and beat him before the j' seat.
23:35 him to be kept in Herod's j' hall.
24:25 temperance, and j' to come,
25: 6 the next day sitting on the j' seat
10 said Paul, I stand at Cæsar's j' seat,
15 desiring to have j' against him.
17 on the morrow I sat on the j' seat,
Ro 1:32 Who knowing the j' of God, that
2: 2 the j' of God is according to truth
3 that thou shalt escape the j' of God?
5 of the righteous j' of God;
5:16 the j' was by one to condemnation,
18 by the offence of one j' came upon all
14:10 all stand before the j' seat of Christ.
1Co 1:10 the same mind and in the same j'.
4: 3 be judged of you, or of man's j':
7:25 yet I give my j', as one that hath
40 happier if she so abide, after my j':
2Co 5:10 appear before the j' seat of Christ;
Ga 5:10 that troubleth you shall bear his j',
Ph'p 1: 9 more in knowledge and in all j';
2Th 1: 5 token of the righteous j' of God,
1Ti 5:24 open beforehand, going before to j';
Heb 6: 2 of the dead, and of eternal j'.
9:27 once to die, but after this the j':
10:27 certain fearful looking for of j' and
Jas 2: 6 and draw you before the j' seats?
13 For he shall have j' without mercy,
13 and mercy rejoiceth against j'.
1Pe 4:17 time is come that j' must begin
2Pe 2: 3 j' now of a long time lingereth
4 darkness, to be reserved unto j';
9 reserve the unjust unto the day of j'
3: 7 against the day of j' and perdition
1Jo 4:17 may have boldness in the day of j':
Jude 6 unto the j' of the great day.
15 To execute j' upon all, and to
Re 14: 7 him; for the hour of his j' is come:
17: 1 thee the j' of the great whore
18:10 for in one hour is thy j' come.
20: 4 them, and j' was given unto them:

judgment-hall See JUDGMENT and HALL.

judgments
Ex 6: 6 out arm, and with great j':
7: 4 out of the land of Egypt by great j'.
21: 1 are the j' which thou shalt set
24: 3 the words of the Lord, and all the j':
Le 18: 4 Ye shall do my j', and keep mine
5 keep my statutes, and my j':
26 keep my statutes and my j',
19:37 statutes, and all my j', and do them:
20:22 keep all my statutes, and all my j',
25:18 shall do my statutes, and keep my j',
26:15 statutes, or if your soul abhor my j',
43 because they despised my j', and
46 the statutes and j' and laws, which
Nu 33: 4 gods also the Lord executed j'.
35:24 of blood according to these j':
36:13 are the commandments and the j',
De 4: 1 unto the statutes and unto the j',
5 I have taught you statutes and j',
8 hath statutes and j' so righteous
14 time to teach you statutes and j',
45 the statutes, and the j', which Moses
5: 1 the statutes and j' which I speak in
31 and the j', which thou shalt teach
6: 1 and the j', which the Lord your God
20 and the j', which the Lord our God
7:11 and the j', which I command thee
12 if ye hearken to these j', and keep,
8:11 and his j', and his statutes, which I
11: 1 charge, and his statutes, and his j',
32 observe to do all the statutes and j'
12: 1 These are the statutes and j', which
26:16 thee to do these statutes and j':
17 and his commandments, and his j',
33:10 shall teach Jacob thy j', and Israel
21 of the Lord and his j' with Israel.
2Sa 22:23 For all his j' were before me: and as
1Ki 2: 3 and his j', and his testimonies,
6:12 and execute my j', and keep all my
8:58 and his j', which he commanded
9: 4 wilt keep my statutes and my j':
11:33 my statutes and my j', as did David
1Ch 16:12 wonders, and the j' of his mouth;
14 our God; his j' are in all the earth.
22:13 to fulfil the statutes and j' which
28: 7 do my commandments and my j',
2Ch 7:17 observe my statutes and my j':
19:10 and commandment, statutes and j',
Ezr 7:10 to teach in Israel statutes and j'.
Ne 1: 7 nor the statutes, nor the j', which
9:13 gavest them right j', and true laws,
29 but sinned against thy j', (which if a
10:29 Lord, and his j' and his statutes;
Ps 10: 5 thy j' are far above out of his sight:
18:22 For all his j' were before me, and I
19: 9 the j' of the Lord are true and

Ps 36: 6 thy j' are a great deep: O Lord,
48:11 Judah be glad, because of thy j'.
72: 1 Give the king thy j', O God, and thy
89:30 my law, and walk not in my j';
97: 8 of Judah rejoiced because of thy j',
105: 5 wonders, and the j' of his mouth;
7 our God: his j' are all in the earth.
119: 7 shall have learned thy righteous j'.
13 I declared all the j' of thy mouth.
20 that it hath unto thy j' at all times.
30 truth: thy j' have I laid before me.
39 which I fear: for thy j' are good.
43 mouth; for I have hoped in thy j'.
52 I remembered thy j' of old, O Lord;
62 thee because of thy righteous j'.
75 know, O Lord, that thy j' are right,
102 I have not departed from thy j':
106 that I will keep thy righteous j'.
108 mouth, O Lord, and teach me thy j'.
120 of thee; and I am afraid of thy j'.
137 O Lord, and upright are thy j'.
156 quicken me according to thy j'.
160 every one of thy righteous j'
164 thee because of thy righteous j'.
175 praise thee; and let thy j' help me.
147:19 his statutes and his j' unto Israel.
20 as for his j', they have not known
Pr 19:29 J' are prepared for scorners, and
Isa 26: 8 Yea, in the way of thy j', O Lord,
9 for when thy j' are in the earth,
Jer 1:16 And I will utter my j' against them
12: 1 yet let me talk with thee of thy j':
Eze 5: 6 she hath changed my j' into
6 for they have refused my j' and my
7 statutes, neither have kept my j',
7 have done according to the j' of
8 will execute j' in the midst of thee
10 and I will execute j' in thee,
15 when I shall execute j' in thee in
11: 9 and will execute j' among you.
12 statutes, neither executed my j',
14:21 my four sore j' upon Jerusalem,
16:41 execute j' upon thee in the sight of
18: 9 my statutes, and hath kept my j',
17 hath executed my j', hath walked in
20:11 my statutes, and shewed them my j',
13 statutes, and they despised my j',
16 they despised my j', and walked not
18 neither observe their j', nor defile
19 walk in my statutes, and keep my j',
21 neither kept my j' to do them,
24 they had not executed my j',
25 and j' whereby they should not live;
23:24 judge thee according to their j'.
25:11 And I will execute j' upon Moab;
28:22 when I shall have executed j' in her,
26 when I have executed j' upon all
30:14 in Zoan, and will execute j' in No.
19 Thus will I execute j' in Egypt:
36:27 ye shall keep my j', and do them.
37:24 also walk in my j', and observe my
44:24 shall judge it according to my j':
Da 9: 5 from thy precepts and from thy j':
Ho 6: 5 thy j' are as the light that goeth
Zep 3:15 the Lord hath taken away thy j',
Mal 4: 4 all Israel, with the statutes and j'.
Ro 11:33 how unsearchable are his j', and
1Co 6: 4 ye have j' of things pertaining to
Re 15: 4 thee; for thy j' are made manifest.
16: 7 true and righteous are thy j'.
19: 2 For true and righteous are his j':

judgment-seat See JUDGMENT and SEAT.

Judith (*ju'-dith*)
Ge 26:34 Esau...when he took to wife J'

juice
Ca 8: 2 wine of the j' of my pomegranate.

Julia (*ju'-le-ah*)
Ro 16:15 Salute Philologus, and J', Nereus,

Julius (*ju'-le-us*)
Ac 27: 1 unto one named J', a centurion of
3 And J' courteously entreated Paul,

jumping
Na 3: 2 horses, and of the j' chariots.

Junia (*ju'-ne-ah*)
Ro 16: 7 Salute Andronicus and J', my

Junias See JUNIA.

juniper
1Ki 19: 4 and sat down under a j' tree:
5 as he lay and slept under a j' tree,
Job 30: 4 bushes, and j' roots for their meat.
Ps 120: 4 of the mighty, with coals of j'.

Jupiter (*ju'-pit-ur*)
Ac 14:12 And they called Barnabas, J';
13 Then the priest of J', which was
19:35 image which fell down from J'?

jurisdiction
Lu 23: 7 that he belonged unto Herod's j',

Jushab-hesed (*ju''-shab-he'-sed*)
1Ch 3:20 and Berechiah, and Hasadiah, J',

just See also UNJUST.
Ge 6: 9 Noah was a j' man and perfect in
Le 19:36 J' balances, j' weights, a j' ephah,
36 and a j' hin, shall ye have; I am
De 16:18 judge the people with j' judgment.
20 is altogether j' shalt thou follow,
25:15 shalt have a perfect and j' weight,
15 a perfect and j' measure shalt thou
32: 4 without iniquity, j' and right is he.
2Sa 23: 3 He that ruleth over men must be j',
Ne 9:33 thou art j' in all that is brought

Job 4:17 mortal man be more *j'* than God?
9: 2 how should man be *j'* with God?
12: 4 the *j'* upright man is laughed to
27:17 prepare it, but the *j'* shall put it on,
33:12 in this thou art not *j'*: I will
34:17 thou condemn him that is most *j'*?
Ps 7: 9 establish the *j'*: for the righteous
37:12 The wicked plotteth against the *j'*.
Pr 3:33 he blesseth the habitation of the *j'*.
4:18 path of the *j'* is as the shining light,
9: 9 teach a *j'* man, and he will increase
10: 6 Blessings...upon the head of the *j'*:
7 The memory of the *j'* is blessed:
20 tongue of the *j'* is as choice silver:
31 The mouth of the *j'* bringeth forth
11: 1 but a *j'* weight is his delight.
9 shall the *j'* be delivered.
12:13 But the *j'* shall come out of trouble.
21 There shall no evil happen to the *j'*:
13:22 of the sinner is laid up for the *j'*.
16:11 A *j'* weight and balance are the
17:15 and he that condemneth the *j'*,
26 Also to punish the *j'* is not good,
18:17 is first in his own cause seemeth *j'*:
20: 7 The *j'* man walketh in his integrity:
21:15 It is joy to the *j'* to do judgment:
24:16 For a *j'* man falleth seven times,
29:10 upright: but the *j'* seek his soul.
27 man is an abomination to the *j'*:
Ec 7:15 there is a *j'* man that perisheth in
20 there is not a *j'* man upon earth,
8:14 that there be *j'* men, unto whom it
Isa 26: 7 The way of the *j'* is uprightness:
7 dost weigh the path of the *j'*.
29:21 aside the *j'* for a thing of nought.
45:21 a *j'* God and a Saviour; there is none
La 4:13 have shed the blood of the *j'* in the
Eze 18: 5 if a man be *j'*, and do that which is
9 he is *j'*, he shall surely live, saith
45:10 Ye shall have *j'* balances,
10 and a *j'* ephah, and a *j'* bath.
Ho 14: 9 right, and the *j'* shall walk in them:
Am 5:12 they afflict the *j'*, they take a bribe,
Hab 2: 4 but the *j'* shall live by his faith.
Zep 3: 5 The *j'* Lord is in the midst thereof;
Zec 9: 9 he is *j'*, and having salvation;
M't 1:19 her husband, being a *j'* man, and
5:45 rain on the *j'* and on the unjust.
13:49 sever the wicked from among the *j'*.
27:19 nothing to do with that *j'* man:
24 of the blood of this *j'* person:
M'r 6:20 that he was a *j'* man and an holy,
Lu 1:17 disobedient to the wisdom of the *j'*;
2:25 the same man was *j'* and devout,
14:14 at the resurrection of the *j'*.
15: 7 over ninety and nine *j'* persons,
20:20 should feign themselves *j'* men,
23:50 and he was a good man, and a *j'*:
Joh 5:30 I judge: and my judgment is *j'*;
Ac 3:14 ye denied the Holy One and the *J'*,
7:52 before of the coming of the *J'* One;
10:22 Cornelius the centurion, a *j'* man,
22:14 know his will, and see that *J'* One,
24:15 the dead, both of the *j'* and unjust.
Ro 1:17 written, The *j'* shall live by faith.
2:13 of the law are *j'* before God,
3: 8 may come? whose damnation is *j'*.
26 that he might be *j'*, and the justifier
7:12 commandment holy, and *j'*, and
Ga 3:11 for, The *j'* shall live by faith.
Ph'p 4: 8 honest, whatsoever things are *j'*,
Col 4: 1 servants that which is *j'* and equal;
Tit 1: 8 a lover of good men, sober, *j'*, holy,
Heb 2: 2 a *j'* recompence of reward;
10:38 Now the *j'* shall live by faith: but
12:23 the spirits of *j'* men made perfect,
Jas 5: 6 have condemned and killed the *j'*;
1Pe 3:18 for sins, the *j'* for the unjust, that
2Pe 2: 7 And delivered *j'* Lot, vexed with
1Jo 1: 9 and *j'* to forgive us our sins, and to
Re 15: 3 *j'* and true are thy ways, thou King

justice See also INJUSTICE.
Ge 18:19 the Lord, to do *j'* and judgment;
De 33:21 he executed the *j'* of the Lord,
2Sa 8:15 David executed judgment and *j'*
15: 4 unto me, and I would do him *j'*!
1Ki 10: 9 thee king, to do judgment and *j'*.
1Ch 18:14 executed judgment and *j'* among
2Ch 9: 8 over them, to do judgment and *j'*.
Job 8: 3 or doth the Almighty pervert *j'*?
36:17 judgment and *j'* take hold on thee.
37:23 in judgment, and in plenty of *j'*:
Ps 82: 3 do *j'* to the afflicted and needy.
89:14 *J'* and judgment are the
119:121 I have done judgment and *j'*:
Pr 1: 3 of wisdom, *j'*, and judgment, and
8:15 kings reign, and princes decree *j'*.
21: 3 To do *j'* and judgment is more
Ec 5: 8 perverting of judgment and *j'* in
Isa 9: 7 it with judgment and with *j'* from
56: 1 Lord, Keep ye judgment, and do *j'*:
58: 2 ask of me the ordinances of *j'*;
59: 4 None calleth for *j'*, nor any pleadeth
9 us, neither doth *j'* overtake us:
14 backward, and *j'* standeth afar off:
Jer 22:15 and drink, and do judgment and *j'*,
23: 5 shall execute judgment and *j'* in the
31:23 O habitation of *j'*, and mountain
50: 7 the habitation of *j'*, even the Lord,
Eze 45: 9 and execute judgment and *j'*, take

justification
Ro 4:25 and was raised again for our *j'*.
5:16 gift is of many offences unto *j'*.
18 came upon all men unto *j'* of life.

justified
Job 11: 2 should a man full of talk be *j'*?
13:18 cause; I know that I shall be *j'*.
25: 4 How then can man be *j'* with God?
32: 2 he *j'* himself rather than God.
Ps 51: 4 mighest be *j'* when thou speakest,
143: 2 thy sight shall no man living be *j'*.
Isa 43: 9 their witnesses, that they may be *j'*:
26 declare thou, that thou mayest be *j'*.
45:25 shall all the seed of Israel be *j'*,
Jer 3:11 backsliding Israel hath *j'* herself
Eze 16:51 and hast *j'* thy sisters in all thine
52 in that thou hast *j'* thy sisters.
M't 11:19 But wisdom is *j'* of her children.
12:37 For by thy words thou shalt be *j'*,
Lu 7:29 and the publicans, *j'* God, being
35 wisdom is *j'* of all her children.
18:14 this man went down to his house *j'*
Ac 13:39 that believe are *j'* from all things,
39 could not be *j'* by the law of Moses.
Ro 2:13 but the doers of the law shall be *j'*.
3: 4 thou mightest be *j'* in thy sayings,
20 shall no flesh be *j'* in his sight:
24 Being *j'* freely by his grace through
28 that a man is *j'* by faith without the
4: 2 For if Abraham were *j'* by works,
5: 1 being *j'* by faith, we have peace
9 then, being now *j'* by his blood,
8:30 whom he called, them he also *j'*:
30 whom he *j'*, them he also glorified.
1Co 4: 4 yet am I not hereby *j'*: but he that
6:11 *j'* in the name of the Lord Jesus,
Ga 2:16 is not *j'* by the works of the law,
16 might be *j'* by the faith of Christ,
16 works of the law shall no flesh be *j'*.
17 if, while we seek to be *j'* by Christ,
3:11 no man is *j'* by the law in the sight
24 Christ, that we might be *j'* by faith.
5: 4 whosoever of you are *j'* by the law;
1Ti 3:16 manifest in the flesh, *j'* in the Spirit,
Tit 3: 7 being *j'* by his grace, we should be
Jas 2:21 not Abraham our father *j'* by works
24 then how that by works a man is *j'*,
25 not Rahab the harlot *j'* by works,

justifier
Ro 3:26 *j'* of him which believeth in Jesus.

justifieth
Pr 17:15 He that *j'* the wicked, and he that
Isa 50: 8 He is near that *j'* me; who will
Ro 4: 5 on him that *j'* the ungodly,
8:33 of God's elect? It is God that *j'*.

justify See also JUSTIFIED; JUSTIFIETH; JUSTIFYING.
Ex 23: 7 not: for I will not *j'* the wicked.
De 25: 1 then they shall *j'* the righteous,
Job 9:20 I *j'* myself, mine own mouth shall
27: 5 God forbid that I should *j'* you: till
33:32 me: speak, for I desire to *j'* thee.
Isa 5:23 Which *j'* the wicked for reward,
53:11 shall my righteous servant *j'* many;
Lu 10:29 he, willing to *j'* himself, said unto
16:15 which *j'* yourselves before men.
Ro 3:30 shall *j'* the circumcision by faith,
Ga 3: 8 would *j'* the heathen through faith,

justifying
1Ki 8:32 and *j'* the righteous, to give him
2Ch 6:23 by *j'* the righteous, by giving him

justle
Na 2: 4 they shall *j'* one against another

justly See also UNJUSTLY.
Mic 6: 8 but to do *j'*, and to love mercy,
Lu 23:41 And we indeed *j'*; for we receive
1Th 2:10 how holily and *j'* and unblameably

Justus (*jus'-tus*) See also BARSABAS; JESUS.
Ac 1:23 Barsabas, who was surnamed *J'*,
18: 7 *J'*, one that worshipped God,
Col 4:11 And Jesus, which is called *J'*, who

Juttah (*jut'-tah*)
Jos 15:55 Maon, Carmel, and Ziph, and *J'*,
21:16 and *J'* with her suburbs, and

K.

Kabzeel (*kab'-ze-el*) See also JEKABZEEL.
Jos 15:21 coast of Edom southward were *K'*,
2Sa 23:20 the son of a valiant man, of *K'*,
1Ch 11:22 the son of a valiant man of *K'*,

Kadesh (*ka'-desh*) See also EN-MISHPAT; KADESH-BARNEA; KEDESH.
Ge 14: 7 came to En-mishpat, which is *K'*,
16:14 behold, it is between *K'* and Bered.
20: 1 dwelled between *K'* and Shur, and
Nu 13:26 the wilderness of Paran, to *K'*;
20: 1 the people abode in *K'*; and Miriam
14 Moses sent messengers from *K'*
16 behold, we are in *K'*, a city in the
22 congregation, journeyed from *K'*,
27:14 that is the water of Meribah in *K'*
33:36 the wilderness of Zin, which is *K'*.
37 they removed from *K'*, and pitched
De 1:46 abode in *K'* many days, according
J'g 11:16 unto the Red sea, and came to *K'*;
17 consent: and Israel abode in *K'*.
Ps 29: 8 Lord shaketh the wilderness of *K'*.
Eze 47:19 even to the waters of strife in *K'*,
48:28 unto the waters of strife in *K'*,

Kadesh-barnea (*ka''-desh-bar'-ne-ah*) See also KADESH.
Nu 32: 8 sent them from *K'* to see the land.
34: 4 shall be from the south to *K'*,
De 1: 2 by the way of mount Seir unto *K'*.)
19 commanded us; and we came to *K'*.
2:14 space in which we came from *K'*,
9:23 when the Lord sent you from *K'*,
Jos 10:41 Joshua smote them from *K'* even
14: 6 God concerning me and thee in *K'*.
7 servant of the Lord sent me from *K'*
15: 3 up on the south side unto *K'*,

Kadmiel (*kad'-me-el*)
Ezr 2:40 the children of Jeshua and *K'*,
3: 9 *K'* and his sons, the sons of Judah,
Neh 7:43 the children of Jeshua, of *K'*, and
9: 4 the Levites, Jeshua, and Bani, *K'*,
5 the Levites, Jeshua, and *K'*, Bani,
10: 9 Binnui of the sons of Henadad, *K'*;
12: 8 Binnui, *K'*, Sherebiah, Judah,
24 and Jeshua the son of *K'*, with their

Kadmonites (*kad'-mo-nites*)
Ge 15:19 and the Kennizzites, and the *K'*,

Kallai (*kal'-la-i*)
Neh 12:20 Of Sallai, *K'*; of Amok, Eber;

Kanah (*ka'-nah*)
Jos 16: 8 westward into the river *K'*;
17: 9 coast descended unto the river *K'*,
19:28 and *K'*, even unto great Zidon;

Kareah (*ka'-re-ah*) See also CAREAH.
Jer 40: 8 and Jonathan the sons of *K'*,
13 Johanan the son of *K'*, and all the
15 the son of *K'* spake to Gedaliah in
16 said unto Johanan the son of *K'*,
41:11 when Johanan the son of *K'*, and
13 Johanan the son of *K'*, and all the
14 went unto Johanan the son of *K'*.
16 took Johanan the son of *K'*, and all
42: 1 and Johanan the son of *K'*, and
8 called he Johanan the son of *K'*,
43: 2 Johanan the son of *K'*, and all the
4 So Johanan the son of *K'*, and all
5 But Johanan the son of *K'*, and all

Karkaa (*kar'-ka-ah*)
Jos 15: 3 and fetched a compass to *K'*:

Karkor (*kar'-kor*)
J'g 8:10 Zebah and Zalmunna were in *K'*,

Kartah (*kar'-tah*) See also KATTATH.
Jos 21:34 suburbs, and *K'* with her suburbs,

Kartan (*kar'-tan*) See also KIRJATHAIM.
Jos 21:32 *K'* with her suburbs; three cities.

Kattath (*kat'-tath*) See also KARTAH; KITRON.
Jos 19:15 And *K'*, and Nahallal, and

Kedar (*ke'-dar*)
Ge 25:13 of Ishmael, Nebajoth; and *K'*,
1Ch 1:29 of Ishmael, Nebaioth; then *K'*,
Ps 120: 5 that I dwell in the tents of *K'*!
Ca 1: 5 of Jerusalem, the tents of *K'*,
Isa 21:16 and all the glory of *K'* shall fail:
17 mighty men of the children of *K'*,
42:11 the villages that *K'* doth inhabit:
60: 7 the flocks of *K'* shall be gathered
Jer 2:10 and send unto *K'*, and consider
49:28 Concerning *K'*, and concerning the
28 go up to *K'*, and spoil the men of
Eze 27:21 Arabia, and all the princes of *K'*,

Kedemah (*ked'-e-mah*)
Ge 25:15 Tema, Jetur, Naphish, and *K'*:
1Ch 1:31 Jetur, Naphish, *K'*. These are the

Kedemoth (*ked'-e-moth*)
De 2:26 out of the wilderness of *K'* unto
Jos 13:18 Jahaza, and *K'*, and Mephaath,
21:37 *K'* with her suburbs, and Mephaath
1Ch 6:79 *K'* also with her suburbs, and

Kedesh (*ke'-desh*) See also KADESH; KEDESH-NAPHTALI; KISHION.
Jos 12:22 The king of *K'*, one; the king of
15:23 And *K'*, and Hazor, and Ithnan,
19:37 And *K'*, and Edrei, and En-hazor,
20: 7 And they appointed *K'* in Galilee
21:32 *K'* in Galilee with her suburbs,
J'g 4: 9 arose, and went with Barak to *K'*.
10 Zebulun and Naphtali to *K'*;
11 plain of Zaanaim, which is by *K'*.
2Ki 15:29 and *K'*, and Hazor, and Gilead, and
1Ch 6:72 *K'* with her suburbs, Daberath
76 *K'* in Galilee with her suburbs, and

Kedesh-naphtali (*ke''-desh-naf'-ta-li*)
J'g 4: 6 the son of Abinoam out of *K'*,

keep See also KEEPEST; KEEPETH; KEEPING; KEPT.
Ge 2:15 of Eden to dress it and to *k'* it.
3:24 way, to *k'* the way of the tree of life.
6:19 the ark, to *k'* them alive with thee;
20 come unto thee, to *k'* them alive.
7: 3 to *k'* seed alive upon the face of
17: 9 shalt *k'* my covenant therefore,
10 is my covenant, which ye shall *k'*,
18:19 they shall *k'* the way of the Lord,

Ge 28:15 will k' thee in all places whither
20 and will k' me in this way that I go,
30:31 I will again feed and k' thy flock.
33: 9 k' that thou hast unto thyself.
41:35 and let them k' food in the cities.
Ex 6: 5 whom the Egyptians k' in bondage:
12: 6 shall k' it up until the fourteenth
14 ye shall k' it a feast to the Lord
14 shall k' it a feast by an ordinance
25 that ye shall k' this service.
47 congregation of Israel shall k' it.
48 and will k' the passover to the Lord,
48 then let him come near and k' it;
13: 5 thou shalt k' this service in this
10 shalt therefore k' this ordinance
15:26 and k' all his statutes, I will put
16:28 refuse ye to k' my commandments
19: 5 voice indeed, and k' my covenant,
20: 6 love me, and k' my commandments.
8 the sabbath day, to k' it holy.
22: 7 neighbour money or stuff to k',
10 ox, or a sheep, or any beast, to k';
23: 7 K' thee far from a false matter;
14 Three times thou shalt k' a feast
15 Thou shalt k' the feast of...bread:
20 before thee, to k' thee in the way,
31:13 Verily my sabbaths ye shall k':
14 Ye shall k' the sabbath therefore;
16 of Israel shall k' the sabbath,
34:18 of unleavened bread shalt thou k'.
Le 6: 2 which was delivered him to k',
4 which was delivered him to k',
8:35 k' the charge of the Lord, that ye
18: 4 k' mine ordinances, to walk therein:
5 Ye shall therefore k' my statutes,
26 Ye shall therefore k' my statutes
30 shall ye k' mine ordinance, that
19: 3 and his father, and k' my sabbaths:
19 Ye shall k' my statutes. Thou shalt
30 Ye shall k' my sabbaths, and
20: 8 ye shall k' my statutes, and do
22 shall therefore k' all my statutes,
22: 9 shall therefore k' mine ordinance,
31 shall ye k' my commandments,
23:39 ye shall k' a feast unto the Lord
41 ye shall k' it a feast unto the Lord
25: 2 the land k' a sabbath unto the Lord.
18 k' my judgments, and do them;
26: 2 Ye shall k' my sabbaths, and
3 and k' my commandments, and do
Nu 1:53 k' the charge of the tabernacle of
3: 7 And they shall k' his charge, and
8 they shall k' all the instruments of
32 that k' the charge of the sanctuary.
6:24 The Lord bless thee, and k' thee;
8:26 to k' the charge, and shall do no
9: 2 of Israel also k' the passover at
3 shall k' it in his appointed season.
3 ceremonies thereof, shall ye k' it.
4 that they should k' the passover.
6 not k' the passover on that day:
10 yet he shall k' the passover unto
11 month at even they shall k' it,
12 of the passover they shall k' it.
13 and forbeareth to k' the passover,
14 will k' the passover unto the Lord:
18: 3 they shall k' thy charge, and the
4 k' the charge of the tabernacle of
5 shall k' the charge of the sanctuary,
7 with thee shall k' your priest's
29:12 ye shall k' a feast unto the Lord
31:18 with him, k' alive for yourselves.
30 k' the charge of the tabernacle
36: 7 k' himself to the inheritance
9 k' himself to his own inheritance.
De 4: 2 ye may k' the commandments of
6 K' therefore and do them; for this
9 and k' thy soul diligently, lest thou
40 shalt k' therefore his statutes, and
5: 1 learn them, and k', and do them.
10 love me and k' my commandments.
12 K' the sabbath day to sanctify it,
15 commanded thee to k' the sabbath
29 k' all my commandments always,
6: 2 God, to k' all his statutes and his
17 diligently k' the commandments of
7: 8 and because he would k' the oath
9 k' his commandments to a thousand
11 therefore k' the commandments,
12 judgments, and k', and do them,
12 shall k' unto thee the covenant
8: 2 wouldest k' his commandments, or
6 thou shalt k' the commandments
10:13 To k' the commandments of the
11: 1 and k' his charge, and his statutes,
8 shall ye k' all the commandments
22 For if ye shall diligently k' all these
13: 4 k' his commandments, and obey
18 to k' all his commandments which
16: 1 k' the passover unto the Lord
10 k' the feast of weeks unto the Lord
15 days shalt thou k' a solemn feast
17:19 to k' all the words of this law and
19: 9 shalt k' all these commandments
23: 9 k' thee from every wicked thing.
23 out of thy lips thou shalt k' and
26:16 k' and do them with all thine heart,
17 ways, and to k' his statutes, and his
18 shouldest k' all his commandments;
27: 1 K' all the commandments which I
28: 9 k' the commandments of the Lord
45 to k' his commandments and his
29: 9 K'...the words of this covenant,
30:10, 16 to k' his commandments and his
Jos 6:18 k' yourselves from the accursed
10:18 and set men by it for to k' them:

Jos 22: 5 to k' his commandments, and to
23: 6 to k' and to do all that is written in
J'g 2:22 will k' the way of the Lord to walk
22 as their fathers did k' it, or not.
3:19 thee, O king: who said, K' silence.
Ru 2:21 shalt k' fast by my young men,
1Sa 2: 9 will k' the feet of his saints, and
7: 1 his son to k' the ark of the Lord.
2Sa 8: 2 death, and with one full line to k' alive.
15:16 were concubines, to k' the house.
16:21 which he hath left to k' the house;
18:18 I have no son to k' my name in
20: 3 whom he had left to k' the house,
1Ki 2: 3 k' the charge of the Lord thy God,
3 walk in his ways, to k' his statutes,
3:14 walk in my ways, to k' my statutes
6:12 k' all my commandments to walk
8:25 k' with thy servant David my father
58 ways, and to k' his commandments,
61 and to k' his commandments, as at
9: 4 k' my statutes and my judgments:
6 and will not k' my commandments
11:33 to k' my statutes and my judgments,
38 in my sight, to k' my statutes and
20:39 unto me, and said, K' this man:
2Ki 11: 6 shall ye k' the watch of the house,
7 they shall k' the watch of the house
17:13 and k' my commandments and my
23: 3 to k' his commandments and his
21 K' the passover unto the Lord
1Ch 4:10 that thou wouldest k' me from evil,
12:33 thousand, which could k' rank:
38 men of war, that could k' rank,
22:12 mayest k' the law of the Lord thy
23:32 k' the charge of the tabernacle
28: 8 k' and seek for...the commandments
29:18 k' this for ever in the imagination
19 heart, to k' thy commandments,
2Ch 6:16 k' with thy servant David my father
13:11 we k' the charge of the Lord our
22: 9 no power to k' still the kingdom.
23: 6 shall k' the watch of the Lord.
28:10 to k' under the children of Judah
30: 1 to k' the passover unto the Lord
2 to k' the passover in the second
3 they could not k' it at that time,
5 to k' the passover unto the Lord
13 to k' the feast of unleavened bread
23 took counsel to k' other seven days:
34:31 Lord, and to k' his commandments,
35:16 the same day, to k' the passover,
18 kings of Israel k' such a passover
Ezr 8:29 and k' them, until ye weigh them
Ne 1: 9 and k' my commandments, and do
12:27 to k' the dedication with gladness,
13:22 they should come and k' the gates,
Es 3: 8 neither k' they the king's laws:
9:21 k' the fourteenth day of the month
27 would k' these two days according
Job 14:13 k' me secret, until thy wrath be
20:13 but k' it still within his mouth:
Ps 12: 7 Thou shalt k' them, O Lord, thou
17: 8 K' me as the apple of the eye,
19:13 K' back thy servant also from
22:29 and none can k' alive his own soul.
25:10 such as k' his covenant and his
20 O k' my soul, and deliver me: let
31:20 shalt k' them secretly in a pavilion
33:19 and to k' them alive in famine.
34:13 K' thy tongue from evil, and thy
35:22 hast seen, O Lord: k' not silence:
37:34 Wait on the Lord, and k' his way,
39: 1 I will k' my mouth with a bridle,
41: 2 preserve him, and k' him alive;
50: 3 come, and shall not k' silence:
78: 7 God, but k' his commandments:
83: 1 K' not thou silence, O God: hold not
89:28 My mercy will I k' for him for
31 and k' not my commandments;
91:11 over thee, to k' thee in all thy ways.
103: 9 neither will he k' his anger for
18 To such as k' his covenant, and to
105:45 his statutes, and k' his laws.
106: 3 are they that k' judgment, and he
113: 9 the barren woman to k' house,
119: 2 are they that k' his testimonies,
4 us to k' thy precepts diligently.
5 were directed to k' thy statutes!
8 I will k' thy statutes: O forsake
17 that I may live, and k' thy word.
33 and I shall k' it unto the end.
34 and I shall k' thy law;
44 So shall I k' thy law continually
57 said that I would k' thy words.
60 not to k' thy commandments.
63 and of them that k' thy precepts.
69 will k' thy precepts with my whole
88 I k' the testimony of thy mouth.
100 because I k' thy precepts.
101 way, that I might k' thy word.
106 I will k' thy righteous judgments.
115 I will k' the commandments of my
129 therefore doth my soul k' them.
134 of man: so will I k' thy precepts.
136 eyes, because they k' not thy law.
145 me, O Lord: I will k' thy statutes.
146 me, and I shall k' thy testimonies.
127: 1 except the Lord k' the city, the
132:12 If thy children will k' my covenant
140: 4 K' me, O Lord, from the hands of
141: 3 my mouth; k' the door of my lips.
9 K' me from the snares which they
Pr 2:11 thee, understanding shall k' thee:
20 and k' the paths of the righteous.
3: 1 thine heart k' my commandments:
21 k' sound wisdom and discretion:

Pr 3:26 shall k' thy foot from being taken.
4: 4 k' my commandments, and live.
6 love her, and she shall k' thee.
13 instruction; let her not go: k' her;
21 k' them in the midst of thine heart.
23 K' thy heart with all diligence;
5: 2 that thy lips may k' knowledge.
6:20 son, k' thy father's commandment
22 thou sleepest, it shall k' thee;
24 To k' thee from the evil woman,
7: 1 My son, k' my words, and lay up
2 K' my commandments, and live;
5 k' thee from the strange woman,
8:32 blessed are they that k' my ways.
22: 5 he that doth k' his soul shall be far
18 thing if thou k' them within thee;
28: 4 as k' the law contend with them.
Ec 3: 6 time to k', and a time to cast away;
7 time to k' silence, and a time to speak;
5: 1 K' thy foot when thou goest to the
8: 2 to k' the king's commandment,
12:13 God, and k' his commandments:
Ca 8:12 those that k' the fruit thereof two
Isa 26: 3 Thou wilt k' him in perfect peace,
27: 3 I the Lord do k' it; I will water it
3 hurt it, I will k' it night and day.
41: 1 K' silence before me, O islands;
42: 6 hold thine hand, and will k' thee,
43: 6 and to the south, K' not back;
56: 1 saith the Lord, K' ye judgment,
4 the eunuchs that k' my sabbaths,
62: 6 mention of the Lord, k' not silence,
65: 6 I will not k' silence, but will
Jer 3: 5 ever? will he k' it to the end?
12 and I will not k' anger for ever,
31:10 k' him, as a shepherd doth his
42: 4 I will k' nothing back from you.
La 2:10 sit upon the ground, and k' silence:
Eze 11:20 k' mine ordinances, and do them:
18:21 k' all my statutes, and do that which
20:19 k' my judgments, and do them;
36:27 ye shall k' my judgments, and do
43:11 that they may k' the whole form
44:16 me, and they shall k' my charge.
24 and they shall k' my laws and my
Da 9: 4 them that k' his commandments;
Ho 12: 6 k' mercy and judgment, and wait
Am 5:13 the prudent shall k' silence in that
Mic 7: 5 k' the doors of thy mouth from
Na 1:15 O Judah, k' thy solemn feasts,
2: 1 k' the munition, watch the way,
Hab 2:20 let all the earth k' silence before him.
Zec 3: 7 if thou wilt k' my charge, then
7 and shalt also k' my courts,
13: 5 man taught me to k' cattle from
14:16 to k' the feast of tabernacles.
18, 19 up to k' the feast of tabernacles.
Mal 2: 7 priest's lips should k' knowledge,
M't 19:17 into life, k' the commandments.
26:18 I will k' the passover at thy house
M'r 7: 9 that ye may k' your own tradition
Lu 4:10 charge over thee, to k' thee:
8:15 having heard the word, k' it.
11:28 hear the word of God, and k' it.
19:43 and k' thee in on every side,
Joh 8:51, 52 If a man k' my saying, he shall
55 but I know him, and k' his saying.
12:25 world shall k' it unto life eternal.
14:15 ye love me, k' my commandments.
23 a man love me, he will k' my words:
15:10 If ye k' my commandments, ye
20 my saying, they will k' yours also.
17:11 Holy Father, k' through thine own
15 shouldest k' them from the evil.
Ac 5: 3 to k' back part of the price of the
10:28 man that is a Jew to k' company,
12: 4 quaternions of soldiers to k' him;
15: 5 them to k' the law of Moses.
24 be circumcised, and k' the law:
29 from which if ye k' yourselves, ye
16: 4 deliver them the decrees for to k',
23 the jailor to k' them safely:
18:21 I must by all means k' this feast
21:25 only that they k' themselves from
24:23 a centurion to k' Paul, and
Ro 2:25 verily profiteth, if thou k' the law:
26 k' the righteousness of the law,
1Co 5: 8 Therefore let us k' the feast, not
11 unto you not to k' company,
7:37 heart that he will k' his virgin,
9:27 I k' under my body, and bring it
11: 2 k' the ordinances, as I delivered
14:28 let him k' silence in the church;
34 women k' silence in the churches:
15: 2 ye k' in memory what I preached
2Co 11: 9 unto you, and so will I k' myself.
Ga 6:13 who are circumcised k' the law;
Eph 4: 3 to k' the unity of the Spirit in the
Ph'p 4: 7 shall k' your hearts and minds
2Th 3: 3 stablish you, and k' you from evil.
1Ti 5:22 other men's sins: k' thyself pure.
6:14 k' this commandment without
20 k' that which is committed to thy
2Ti 1:12 k' that which I have committed
14 unto thee k' by the Holy Ghost
Jas 1:27 to k' himself unspotted from the
2:10 whosoever shall k' the whole law,
1Jo 2: 3 him, if we k' his commandments.
3:22 because we k' his commandments,
5: 2 God, and k' his commandments.
3 that we k' his commandments:
21 children, k' yourselves from idols.
Jude 21 K' yourselves in the love of God,
24 that is able to k' you from falling,
Re 1: 3 k' those things which are written
3:10 also will k' thee from the hour of

Re 12:17 which *k'* the commandments of
14:12 that *k'* the commandments of God,
22: 9 which *k'* the sayings of this book:
keeper See also DOORKEEPER; KEEPERS.
Ge 4: 2 Abel was a *k'* of the sheep, but
9 know not: Am I my brother's *k'*?
39:21 the sight of the *k'* of the prison.
22 the *k'* of the prison committed to
23 The *k'* of the prison looked not to
1Sa 17:20 and left the sheep with a *k'*,
22 carriage in the hand of the *k'* of
28: 2 make thee *k'* of mine head for ever
2Ki 22:14 son of Harhas, *k'* of the wardrobe;
2Ch 34:22 son of Hasrah, *k'* of the wardrobe;
Ne 2: 8 Asaph the *k'* of the king's forest,
3:29 Shemaiah...the *k'* of the east gate.
Es 2: 3 chamberlain, *k'* of the women;
8 custody of Hegai, *k'* of the women.
15 chamberlain, the *k'* of the women,
Job 27:18 and as a booth that the *k'* maketh
Ps 121: 5 The Lord is thy *k'*: the Lord is thy
Ca 1: 6 made me *k'* of the vineyards; but
Jer 35: 4 Maaseiah...the *k'* of the door:
Ac 16:27 the *k'* of the prison awaking out
36 the *k'* of the prison told this
keepers See also DOORKEEPERS.
2Ki 11: 5 even be *k'* of the watch of the
22: 4 which the *k'* of the door have
23: 4 the *k'* of the door, to bring forth
25:18 priest, and the three *k'* of the door
1Ch 9:19 *k'* of the gates of the tabernacle:
19 of the Lord, were *k'* of the entry.
Es 6: 2 chamberlains, the *k'* of the door,
Ec 12: 3 day when the *k'* of the house shall
Ca 5: 7 *k'* of the walls took away any veil
8:11 he let out the vineyard unto *k'*;
Jer 4:17 As *k'* of a field, are they against
52:24 and the three *k'* of the door:
Eze 40:45 the *k'* of the charge of the house.
46 the *k'* of the charge of the altar:
44: 8 ye have set *k'* of my charge in my
14 them *k'* of the charge of the house.
M't 28: 4 for fear of him the *k'* did shake,
Ac 5:23 *k'* standing without before the
12: 6 *k'* before the door kept the prison
19 him not, he examined the *k'*, and
Tit 2: 5 discreet, chaste, *k'* at home, good,
keepest
1Ki 8:23 who *k'* covenant and mercy with
2Ch 6:14 which *k'* covenant, and shewest
Ne 9:32 who *k'* covenant and mercy, let not
Ac 21:24 walkest orderly, and *k'* the law.
keepeth
Ex 21:18 and he die not, but *k'* his bed:
De 7: 9 *k'* covenant and mercy with them
1Sa 16:11 and, behold, he *k'* the sheep.
Ne 1: 5 that *k'* covenant and mercy for
Job 33:18 He *k'* back his soul from the pit,
Ps 34:20 He *k'* all his bones: not one of
121: 3 he that *k'* thee will not slumber.
4 he that *k'* Israel shall neither
146: 6 therein is: which *k'* truth for ever:
Pr 2: 8 He *k'* the paths of judgment, and
10:17 the way of life that *k'* instruction:
13: 3 He that *k'* his mouth...his life:
3 He that...his mouth *k'* his life:
6 *k'* him that is upright in the way:
16:17 he that *k'* his way preserveth his
19: 8 he that *k'* understanding shall
16 *k'* the commandment *k'* his own
21:23 Whoso *k'* his mouth and his
23 tongue *k'* his soul from troubles.
24:12 he that *k'* thy soul, doth not he
27:18 Whoso *k'* the fig tree shall eat the
28: 7 Whoso *k'* the law is a wise son: but
29: 3 he that *k'* company with harlots
11 a wise man *k'* it in till afterwards.
18 he that *k'* the law, happy is he.
Ec 8: 5 Whoso *k'* the commandment shall
Isa 26: 2 nation which *k'* the truth may enter
56: 2 that *k'* the sabbath from polluting
2 *k'* his hand from doing any evil.
6 that *k'* the sabbath from polluting
Jer 48:10 that *k'* back his sword from blood.
La 3:28 He sitteth alone and *k'* silence,
Hab 2: 5 he is a proud man, neither *k'* at home,
Lu 11:21 a strong man armed *k'* his palace,
Joh 7:19 and yet none of you *k'* the law?
9:16 because he *k'* not the sabbath day.
14:21 my commandments, and *k'* them,
24 loveth me not *k'* not my sayings:
1Jo 2: 4 and *k'* not his commandments,
5 whoso *k'* his word, in him verily is
3:24 And he that *k'* his commandments
5:18 that is begotten of God *k'* himself,
Re 2:26 and *k'* my works unto the end,
16:15 that watcheth, and *k'* his garments,
22: 7 blessed is he that *k'* the sayings of
keeping
Ex 34: 7 *K'* mercy for thousands, forgiving
Nu 3:28 *k'* the charge of the sanctuary.
38 *k'* the charge of the sanctuary for
De 8:11 God, in not *k'* his commandments,
1Sa 25:16 we were with them *k'* the sheep.
Ne 12:25 were porters *k'* the ward at the
Ps 19:11 in *k'* of them there is great reward.
Eze 17:14 by *k'* of his covenant it might stand.
Da 9: 4 *k'* the covenant and mercy to them
Lu 2: 8 *k'* watch over their flock by night.
1Co 7:19 *k'* of the commandments of God.
1Pe 4:19 commit the *k'* of their souls to him in
Kehelathah (*ke-hel'-a-thah*)
Nu 33:22 from Rissah, and pitched in *K'*.
23 they went from *K'*, and pitched in

Keilah (*ki'-lah*)
Jos 15:44 *K'*, and Achzib, and Mareshah;
1Sa 23: 1 the Philistines fight against *K'*,
2 smite the Philistines, and save *K'*.
3 much more then if we come to *K'*
4 and said, Arise, go down to *K'*;
5 So David and his men went to *K'*,
5 David saved the inhabitants of *K'*.
6 of Ahimelech fled to David to *K'*,
7 Saul that David was come to *K'*.
8 to go down to *K'*, to besiege David
10 that Saul seeketh to come to *K'*,
11 men of *K'* deliver me up into his
12 men of *K'* deliver me and my men
13 arose and departed out of *K'*,
13 that David was escaped from *K'*;
1Ch 4:19 the father of *K'* the Garmite,
Ne 3:17 the ruler of the half part of *K'*, in
18 the ruler of the half part of *K'*.
Kelaiah (*kel-ah'-yah*) See also KELITA.
Ezr 10:23 Jozabad, and Shimei, and *K'*,
Kelita (*kel'-i-tah*) See also KELAIAH.
Ezr 10:23 and Kelaiah, (the same is *K'*,)
Ne 8: 7 Maaseiah, *K'*, Azariah, Jozabad,
10:10 Hodijah, *K'*, Pelaiah, Hanan,
Kemuel (*kem-u'-el*)
Ge 22:21 and *K'* the father of Aram,
Nu 34:24 Ephraim, *K'* the son of Shiphtan.
1Ch 27:17 Levites, Hashabiah the son of *K'*:
Kenan (*ke'-nan*) See also CAINAN.
1Ch 1: 2 *K'*, Mahalaleel, Jered,
Kenath (*ke'-nath*) See also NOBAH.
Nu 32:42 And Nobah went and took *K'*,
1Ch 2:23 with *K'*, and the towns thereof,
Kenaz (*ke'-naz*) See also KENEZITE.
Ge 36:11 Omar, Zepho, and Gatam, and *K'*.
15 duke Omar, duke Zepho, duke *K'*,
42 Duke *K'*, duke Teman, duke
Jos 15:17 Othniel the son of *K'*, the brother
J'g 1:13 And Othniel the son of *K'*, Caleb's
3: 9 even Othniel the son of *K'*, Caleb's
11 And Othniel the son of *K'* died.
1Ch 1:36 Zephi, and Gatam, *K'*, and Timna,
53 Duke *K'*, duke Teman, duke
4:13 And the sons of *K'*; Othniel, and
15 and the sons of Elah, even *K'*.
Kenezite (*ken'-e-zite*) See also KENIZZITES.
Nu 32:12 the son of Jephunneh the *K'*,
Jos 14: 6, 14 the son of Jephunneh the *K'*
Kenite (*ken'-ite*) See also KENITES.
Nu 24:22 the *K'* shall be wasted, until
J'g 1:16 children of the *K'*, Moses' father
4:11 Now Heber the *K'*, which was of
17 of Jael the wife of Heber the *K'*:
17 and the house of Heber the *K'*.
5:24 Jael the wife of Heber the *K'* be,
Kenites (*ken'-ites*) See also MIDIANITES.
Ge 15:19 The *K'*, and the Kenizzites, and
Nu 24:21 he looked on the *K'*, and took up
J'g 4:11 had severed himself from the *K'*,
1Sa 15: 6 Saul said unto the *K'*, Go, depart,
6 So the *K'* departed from among
27:10 and against the south of the *K'*.
30:29 which were in the cities of the *K'*,
1Ch 2:55 These are the *K'* that came of
Kenizzites (*ken'-iz-zites*) See also KENEZITE.
Ge 15:19 The Kenites, and the *K'*, and the
kept
Ge 26: 5 *k'* my charge, my commandments,
29: 9 father's sheep: for she *k'* them.
39: 9 neither hath he *k'* back any thing
42:16 and ye shall be *k'* in prison, that
Ex 3: 1 Moses *k'* the flock of Jethro his
16:23 for you to be *k'* until the morning.
32 of it to be *k'* for your generations:
33 Lord, to be *k'* for your generations.
34 up before the Testimony, to be *k'*.
21:29 owner, and he hath not *k'* him in,
36 and his owner hath not *k'* him in;
Nu 5:13 of her husband, and be *k'* close,
9: 5 *k'* the passover on the fourteenth
7 wherefore are we *k'* back, that we
19 of Israel *k'* the charge of the Lord,
23 they *k'* the charge of the Lord, at
17:10 *k'* for a token against the rebels;
19: 9 it shall be *k'* for the congregation
24:11 hath *k'* thee back from honour.
31:47 *k'* the charge of the tabernacle
De 32:10 he *k'* him as the apple of his eye.
33: 9 thy word, and *k'* thy covenant.
Jos 5:10 *k'* the passover on the fourteenth
14:10 behold, the Lord hath *k'* me alive,
22: 2 have *k'* all that Moses the servant
3 *k'* the charge of the commandment
Ru 2:23 she *k'* fast by the maidens of Boaz
1Sa 9:24 this time hath it been *k'* for thee
13:13 hast not *k'* the commandment of
14 hast not *k'* that which the Lord
17:34 Thy servant *k'* his father's sheep,
21: 4 have *k'* themselves...from women.
6 women have been *k'* from us
25:21 vain have I *k'* all that this fellow
33 hast *k'* me this day from coming
34 *k'* me back from hurting thee,
39 and hath *k'* his servant from evil:
26:15 thou not *k'* thy lord the king?
16 because ye have not *k'* your master,
2Sa 13:34 And the young man that *k'* the watch
22:22 I have *k'* the ways of the Lord, and
24 have *k'* myself from mine iniquity.
44 *k'* me to be head of the heathen:
1Ki 2:43 Why then hast thou not *k'* the oath

1Ki 3: 6 hast *k'* for him this great kindness,
8:24 Who hast *k'* with thy servant David
11:10 but he *k'* not that which the Lord
11 thou hast not *k'* my covenant and
34 because he *k'* my commandments
13:21 and hast not *k'* the commandment
14: 8 who *k'* my commandments, and
27 *k'* the door of the king's house.
2Ki 9:14 (Now Joram had *k'* Ramoth-gilead,
12: 9 and the priests that *k'* the door put
17:19 Judah *k'* not the commandments of
18: 6 but *k'* his commandments, which
1Ch 10:13 word of the Lord, which he *k'* not,
12: 1 *k'* himself close because of Saul
29 part of them had *k'* the ward of
2Ch 6:15 hast *k'* with thy servant David
7: 8 Solomon *k'* the feast seven days,
9 they *k'* the dedication of the altar
12:10 *k'* the entrance of the king's house.
30:21 present at Jerusalem *k'* the feast
23 *k'* other seven days with gladness.
34: 9 the Levites that *k'* the doors had
21 our fathers have not *k'* the word of
35: 1 Moreover Josiah *k'* a passover
17 *k'* the passover at that time,
18 no passover like to that *k'* in Israel
18 keep such a passover as Josiah *k'*,
19 reign of Josiah was this passover *k'*
36:21 as she lay desolate she *k'* sabbath,
Ezr 3: 4 *k'* also the feast of tabernacles,
6:16 *k'* the dedication of this house of
19 of the captivity *k'* the passover
22 *k'* the feast of unleavened bread
Ne 1: 7 have not *k'* the commandments,
8:18 they *k'* the feast seven days; and
9:34 priests, nor our fathers, *k'* thy law,
11:19 brethren that *k'* the gates, were
12:45 singers and the porters *k'* the ward
Es 2:14 which *k'* the concubines:
21 of those which *k'* the door, were
9:28 days should be remembered and *k'*
Job 23:11 his way have I *k'*, and not
28:21 *k'* close from the fowls of the air.
29:21 waited, and *k'* silence at my counsel.
31:34 I *k'* silence, and went not out of the
Ps 17: 4 I have *k'* me from the paths of the
18:21 For I have *k'* the ways of the Lord,
23 and I *k'* myself from mine iniquity.
30: 3 hast *k'* me alive, that I should not
32: 3 When I *k'* silence, my bones
42: 4 with a multitude that *k'* holyday.
50:21 hast thou done, and I *k'* silence;
78:10 They *k'* not the covenant of God,
56 God, and *k'* not his testimonies:
99: 7 they *k'* his testimonies, and the
119:22 for I have *k'* thy testimonies.
55 in the night, and have *k'* thy law.
56 I had, because I *k'* thy precepts.
67 but now have I *k'* thy word.
158 because they *k'* not thy word.
167 My soul hath *k'* thy testimonies;
168 I have *k'* thy precepts and thy
Ec 2:10 eyes desired I *k'* not from them,
5:13 riches *k'* for the owners thereof to
Ca 1: 6 mine own vineyard have I not *k'*.
Isa 30:29 night when a holy solemnity is *k'*;
Jer 16:11 me, and have not *k'* my law;
35:18 your father, and *k'* all his precepts,
Eze 5: 7 neither have *k'* my judgments,
18: 9 and hath *k'* my judgments, to deal
19 hath *k'* all my statutes, and hath
20:21 neither *k'* my judgments to do them,
44: 8 ye have not *k'* the charge of mine
15 that *k'* the charge of my sanctuary
48:11 which have *k'* my charge, which
Da 5:19 whom he would he *k'* alive; and
7:28 but I *k'* the matter in my heart.
Ho 12:12 a wife, and for a wife he *k'* sheep.
Am 1:11 and he *k'* his wrath for ever:
2: 4 have not *k'* his commandments,
Mic 6:16 For the statutes of Omri are *k'*, and
Mal 2: 9 as ye have not *k'* my ways, but
3: 7 ordinances, and have not *k'* them.
14 is it that we have *k'* his ordinance,
M't 8:33 they that *k'* them fled, and went
13:35 things which have been *k'* secret
14: 6 But when Herod's birthday was *k'*,
19:20 things have I *k'* from my youth up:
M'r 4:22 neither was any thing *k'* secret,
9:10 *k'* that saying with themselves,
Lu 2:19 But Mary *k'* all these things, and
51 his mother *k'* all these sayings in
8:29 he was *k'* bound with chains and
9:36 they *k'* it close, and told no man
18:21 these have I *k'* from my youth up.
19:20 I have *k'* laid up in a napkin:
Joh 2:10 hast *k'* the good wine until now.
12: 7 of my burying hath she *k'* this.
15:10 even as I have *k'* my Father's
20 if they have *k'* my saying, they will
17: 6 me; and they have *k'* thy word.
12 the world, I *k'* them in thy name:
12 that thou gavest me I have *k'*,
18:16 and spake unto her that *k'* the door,
17 saith the damsel that *k'* the door
Ac 5: 2 *k'* back part of the price, his wife
7:53 of angels, and have not *k'* it.
9:33 which had *k'* his bed eight years.
12: 5 Peter therefore was *k'* in prison:
6 before the door *k'* the prison.
15:12 Then all the multitude *k'* silence,
20:20 how I *k'* back nothing that was
22: 2 them, they *k'* the more silence:
20 *k'* the raiment of them that slew
23:35 to be *k'* in Herod's judgment hall.
25: 4 Paul should be *k'* at Cæsarea, and

Ac 25:21 him to be *k* till I might send him to
27:43 Paul, *k* them from their purpose;
28:16 himself with a soldier that *k* him.
Ro 16:25 *k* secret since the world began,
2Co 11: 9 *k* myself from being burdensome
32 *k* the city of the Damascenes
Ga 3:23 we were *k* under the law, shut up
2Ti 4: 7 my course, I have *k* the faith:
Heb 11:28 Through faith he *k* the passover,
Jas 5: 4 which is of you *k* back by fraud,
1Pe 1: 5 *k* by the power of God through
2Pe 3: 7 by the same word are *k* in store,
Jude 6 which *k* not their first estate,
Re 3: 8 strength, and hast *k* my word,
10 hast *k* the word of my patience,

kerchiefs See also HANDKERCHIEFS.
Eze 13:18 make *k* upon the head of every
21 Your *k* also will I tear, and deliver

Keren-happuch (*ke''-ren-hap'-puk*)
Job 42:14 and the name of the third, *K*.

Kerioth (*ke'-re-oth*) See also ISCARIOT; KIRIOTH.
Jos 15:25 Hadattah, and *K*, and Hezron,
Jer 48:24 And upon *K*, and upon Bozrah,
41 *K* is taken, and the strong holds

kernels
Nu 6: 4 from the *k* even to the husk.

Keros (*ke'-ros*)
Ezr 2:44 The children of *K*, the children
Ne 7:47 The children of *K*, the children of

kettle
1Sa 2:14 he struck it into the pan, or *k*, or

Keturah (*ket-u'-rah*)
Ge 25: 1 took a wife, and her name was *K*.
4 All these were the children of *K*.
1Ch 1:32 Now the sons of *K*, Abraham's
33 All these are the sons of *K*.

key See also KEYS.
J'g 3:25 they took a *k*, and opened them:
Isa 22:22 the *k* of the house of David will I
Lu 11:52 taken away the *k* of knowledge:
Re 3: 7 true, he that hath the *k* of David,
9: 1 given the *k* of the bottomless pit.
20: 1 having the *k* of the bottomless pit

keys
M't 16:19 the *k* of the kingdom of heaven:
Re 1:18 have the *k* of hell and of death.

Kezia (*ke-zi'-ah*)
Job 42:14 and the name of the second, *K*;

Keziz (*ke'-ziz*)
Jos 18:21 Beth-hoglah, and the valley of *K*,

Kibroth-hattaavah (*kib''-roth-hat-ta'-a-vah*)
Nu 11:34 called the name of that place *K*:
35 journeyed from *K* unto Hazeroth;
33:16 desert of Sinai, and pitched at *K*.
17 And they departed from *K*, and
De 9:22 and at *K*, ye provoked the Lord to

Kibzaim (*kib-za'-im*) See also JOKMEAM.
Jos 21:22 And *K* with her suburbs, and

kick See also KICKED.
1Sa 2:29 Wherefore *k* ye at my sacrifice
Ac 9: 5 for thee to *k* against the pricks.
26:14 for thee to kick against the pricks.

kicked
De 32:15 Jeshurun waxed fat, and *k*: thou

kid See also KIDS.
Ge 37:31 killed a *k* of the goats, and dipped
38:17 send thee a *k* from the flock.
20 Judah sent the *k* by the hand
23 I sent this *k*, and thou hast not
Ex 23:19 seethe a *k* in his mother's milk.
34:26 seethe a *k* in his mother's milk.
Le 4:23 a *k* of the goats, a male without
28 his offering, a *k* of the goats,
5: 6 a *k* of the goats, for a sin offering;
9: 3 a *k* of the goats for a sin offering;
23:19 shall sacrifice one *k* of the goats
Nu 7:16, 22, 28, 34, 40, 46, 52, 58, 64, 70, 76, 82 One
k of the goats for a sin offering:
15:11 for one ram, or for a lamb, or a *k*.
24 one *k* of the goats for a sin
28:15 one *k* of the goats for a sin
30 one *k* of the goats to make an
29: 5 one *k* of the goats for a sin
11 One *k* of the goats for a sin
16, 19, 25 one *k* of the goats for a sin
De 14:21 seethe a *k* in his mother's milk.
J'g 6:19 went in, and made ready a *k*,
13:15 have made ready a *k* for thee.
19 took a *k* with a meat offering,
14: 6 him as he would have rent a *k*,
15: 1 visited his wife with a *k*;
1Sa 16:20 and a bottle of wine, and a *k*,
Isa 11: 6 leopard shall lie down with the *k*;
Eze 43:22 offer a *k* of the goats without
45:23 a *k* of the goats daily for a sin
Lu 15:29 thou never gavest me a *k*, that I

kidneys
Ex 29:13, 22 the two *k*, and the fat that is
Le 3: 4 the two *k*, and the fat that is on
4 caul above the liver, with the *k*,
10 the two *k*, and the fat that is upon
10 caul above the liver, with the *k*,
15 the two *k*, and the fat that is upon
15 caul above the liver, with the *k*,
4: 9 the two *k*, and the fat that is upon
9 caul above the liver, with the *k*,
7: 4 the two *k*, and the fat that is on
4 that is above the liver, with the *k*,
8:16, 25 above the liver, and the two *k*,

Le 9:10 the fat, and the *k*, and the caul
19 the *k*, and the caul above the liver:
De 32:14 goats, with the fat of *k* of wheat:
Isa 34: 6 goats, with the fat of the *k* of rams:

Kidron (*kid'-ron*) See also CEDRON.
2Sa 15:23 himself passed over the brook *K*,
1Ki 2:37 and passest over the brook *K*,
15:13 idol, and burnt it by the brook *K*.
2Ki 23: 4 Jerusalem in the fields of *K*,
6 Jerusalem, unto the brook *K*,
6 and burned it at the brook *K*, and
12 dust of them into the brook *K*.
2Ch 15:16 it, and burnt it at the brook *K*.
29:16 it out abroad into the brook *K*.
30:14 and cast them into the brook *K*.
Jer 31:40 all the fields unto the brook of *K*,

kids
Ge 27: 9 thence two good *k* of the goats;
16 put the skins of the *k* of the goats
Le 16: 5 two *k* of the goats for a sin
Nu 7:87 the *k* of the goats for sin offering
1Sa 10: 3 Beth-el, one carrying three *k*,
1Ki 20:27 them like two little flocks of *k*;
2Ch 35: 7 of the flock, lambs and *k*, all 1121,
Ca 1: 8 feed thy *k* beside the shepherds'

kill See also KILLED; KILLEST; KILLETH; KILLING.
Ge 4:15 any finding him should *k* him.
12:12 they will *k* me, but they will save
26: 7 place should *k* me for Rebekah;
27:42 himself, purposing to *k* thee.
37:21 and said, Let us not *k* him.
Ex 1:16 it be a son, then ye shall *k* him:
2:14 intendest thou to *k* me, as thou
4:24 met him, and sought to *k* him.
12: 6 Israel shall *k* it in the evening.
21 your families, and *k* the passover.
16: 3 to *k* this whole assembly with
17: 3 to *k* us and our children and our
20:13 Thou shalt not *k*.
22: 1 ox, or a sheep, and *k* it, or sell it;
24 and I will *k* you with the sword;
29:11 thou shalt *k* the bullock before
20 Then shalt thou *k* the ram, and
Le 1: 5 shall *k* the bullock before the Lord:
11 he shall *k* it on the side of the altar
3: 2 *k* it at the door of the tabernacle
8, 13 *k* it before the tabernacle of the
4: 4 and *k* the bullock before the Lord.
24 and *k* it in the place where they
24 *k* the burnt offering before the Lord:
33 where they *k* the burnt offering.
7: 2 where they *k* the burnt offering
2 shall they *k* the trespass offering:
14:13 where he shall *k* the sin offering
19 he shall *k* the burnt offering:
25 *k* the lamb of the trespass offering,
50 he shall *k* the one of the birds in
16:11 *k* the bullock of the sin offering
15 he *k* the goat of the sin offering,
20: 4 seed unto Molech, and *k* him not:
16 thou shalt *k* the woman, and the
22:28 ye shall not *k* it and her young
Nu 11:15 thus with me, *k* me, I pray thee,
14:15 thou shalt *k* all this people as one
16:13 to *k* us in the wilderness, except
22:29 hand, for now would I *k* thee.
31:17 *k* every male among the little ones,
17 *k* every woman that hath known
35:27 revenger of blood *k* the slayer;
De 4:42 should *k* his neighbour unawares,
5:17 Thou shalt not *k*.
12:15 *k* and eat flesh in all thy gates,
21 shalt *k* of thy herd and of thy
13: 9 thou shalt surely *k* him; thine
32:39 I *k*, and I make alive; I wound,
J'g 13:23 If the Lord were pleased to *k* us,
15:13 but surely we will not *k* thee.
16: 2 when it is day, we shall *k* him.
20:31 to smite of the people, and *k*,
39 smite and *k* of the men of Israel
1Sa 16: 2 if Saul hear it, he will *k* me. And
17: 9 fight with me, and to *k* me, then
9 prevail against him, and *k* him,
19: 1 that they should *k* David.
2 Saul my father seeketh to *k* thee:
17 Let me go; why should I *k* thee?
24:10 some bade me *k* thee: but mine
30:15 God, that thou wilt neither *k* me,
2Sa 13:28 Amnon; then *k* him, fear not:
14: 7 that we may *k* him, for the life of
32 any iniquity in me, let him *k* me.
21: 4 shalt thou *k* any man in Israel.
1Ki 11:40 sought therefore to *k* Jeroboam.
12:27 they shall *k* me, and go again to
2Ki 5: 7 Am I God, to *k* and make alive,
7: 4 and if they *k* us, we shall but die.
11:15 followeth her *k* with the sword.
2Ch 35: 6 So *k* the passover, and sanctify
Es 3:13 to *k*, and to cause to perish, all
Ps 59:*title* watched the house to *k* him.
Ec 3: 3 A time to *k*, and a time to heal;
Isa 14:30 I will *k* thy root with famine,
29: 1 to year; let them *k* sacrifices.
Eze 34: 3 the wool, ye *k* them that are fed:
M't 5:21 of old time, Thou shalt not *k*;
21 shall *k* shall be in danger of the
10:28 fear not them which *k* the body,
28 but are not able to *k* the soul:
17:23 they shall *k* him, and the third day
21:38 let us *k* him, and let us seize on his
23:34 some of them ye shall *k* and crucify;
24: 9 up to be afflicted, and shall *k* you:
26: 4 take Jesus by subtilty, and *k* him.
M'r 3: 4 or to do evil? to save life, or to *k*?

M'r 9:31 hands of men, and they shall *k* him;
10:19 Do not *k*, Do not steal, Do not
34 spit upon him, and shall *k* him:
12: 7 let us *k* him, and the inheritance
Lu 12: 4 not afraid of them that *k* the body,
13:31 depart hence: for Herod will *k* thee.
15:23 hither the fatted calf, and *k* it;
18:20 Do not commit adultery, Do not *k*,
20:14 is the heir: come, let us *k* him,
22: 2 sought how they might *k* him;
Joh 5:18 the Jews sought the more to *k* him,
7: 1 because the Jews sought to *k* him.
19 the law? Why go ye about to *k* me?
20 devil: who goeth about to *k* thee?
25 Is not this he, whom they seek to *k*?
8:22 said the Jews, Will he *k* himself?
37 ye seek to *k* me, because my word
40 now ye seek to *k* me, a man that
10:10 not, but for to steal, and to *k*, and
Ac 7:28 Wilt thou *k* me, as thou didst the
9:23 the Jews took counsel to *k* him:
24 the gates day and night to *k* him.
10:13 to him, Rise, Peter; *k*, and eat.
21:31 And as they went about to *k* him,
23:15 he come near, are ready to *k* him.
25: 3 laying wait in the way to *k* him.
26:21 temple, and went about to *k* me.
27:42 counsel was to *k* the prisoners,
Ro 13: 9 Thou shalt not *k*, Thou shalt not
Jas 2:11 adultery, said also, Do not *k*.
11 yet if thou *k*, thou art become a
4: 2 ye *k*, and desire to have, and
Re 2:23 I will *k* her children with death;
6: 4 that they should *k* one another:
8 to *k* with sword, and with hunger,
9: 5 given that they should not *k* them,
11: 7 shall overcome them, and *k* them.

killed See also KILLEDST.
Ge 37:31 *k* a kid of the goats, and dipped
Ex 21:29 him in, but that he hath *k* a man
Le 4:15 the bullock shall be *k* before the
6:25 place where the burnt offering is *k*
25 sin offering be *k* before the Lord:
8:19 And he *k* it; and Moses sprinkled
14: 5 one of the birds be *k* in an earthen
6 in the blood of the bird that was *k*
Nu 16:41 Ye have *k* the people of the Lord.
31:19 whosoever hath *k* any person,
1Sa 24:11 skirt of thy robe, and *k* thee not,
25:11 that I have *k* for my shearers,
28:24 hasted, and *k* it, and took flour,
2Sa 12: 9 hast *k* Uriah the Hittite with the
21:17 smote the Philistine, and *k* him.
1Ki 16: 7 Jeroboam; and because he *k* him.
10 in and smote him, and *k* him,
21:19 Hast thou *k*, and also taken
2Ki 15:25 *k* him, and reigned in his room.
1Ch 19:18 *k* Shophach the captain of the host.
2Ch 18: 2 Ahab *k* sheep and oxen for him
25: 3 servants that had *k* the king his
29:22 So they *k* the bullocks, and the
22 when they had *k* the rams, they
22 they *k* also the lambs, and they
24 And the priests *k* them, and they
30:15 *k* the passover on the fourteenth
35: 1 *k* the passover on the fourteenth
11 they *k* the passover, and the
Ezr 6:20 *k* the passover for all the children
Ps 44:22 for thy sake are we *k* all the day
Pr 9: 2 She hath *k* her beasts; she hath
La 2:21 anger; thou hast *k*, and not pitied.
M't 16:21 be *k*, and be raised again the third
21:35 beat one, and *k* another, and stoned
22: 4 my fatlings are *k*, and all things
23:31 of them which *k* the prophets.
M'r 6:19 him, and would have *k* him;
8:31 and be *k*, and after three days rise
9:31 after that he is *k*, he shall rise the
12: 5 and him they *k*, and many others;
8 they took him, and *k* him, and cast
14:12 when they *k* the passover,
Lu 11:47 prophets, and your fathers *k* them.
48 for they indeed *k* them, and ye build
12: 5 after he hath *k* hath power to cast
15:27 thy father hath *k* the fatted calf,
30 thou hast *k* for him the fatted calf.
20:15 out of the vineyard, and *k* him.
22: 7 when the passover must be *k*.
Ac 3:15 And *k* the Prince of life, whom God
12: 2 he *k* James the brother of John
16:27 sword, and would have *k* himself,
23:12 eat nor drink till they had *k* Paul.
21 eat nor drink till they have *k* him:
27 and should have been *k* of them:
Ro 8:36 For thy sake we are *k* all the day
11: 3 Lord, they have *k* thy prophets,
2Co 6: 9 we live; as chastened, and not *k*;
1Th 2:15 Who both *k* the Lord Jesus, and
Jas 5: 6 have condemned and *k* the just;
Re 6:11 should be *k* as they were, should
9:18 three was the third part of men *k*,
20 which were not *k* by these plagues
11: 5 them, he must in this manner be *k*.
13:10 sword must be *k* with the sword.
15 the image of the beast should be *k*.

killedst
Ex 2:14 kill me, as thou *k* the Egyptian?
1Sa 24:18 me into thine hand, thou *k* me not.

killest
M't 23:37 Jerusalem,...that *k* the prophets,
Lu 13:34 Jerusalem, which *k* the prophets,

killeth
Le 17: 3 of Israel, that *k* an ox, or lamb,
3 camp, or that *k* it out of the camp,

Le 24:17 he that *k*· any man shall surely
18 that *k*· a beast shall make it good;
21 he that *k*· a beast, he shall restore
21 he that *k*· a man, he shall be put to
Nu 35:11 which *k*· any person at unawares.
15 one that *k*· any person unawares
30 Whoso *k*· any person, the murderer
De 19: 4 Whoso *k*· his neighbour ignorantly,
Jos 20: 3 slayer that *k*· any person unawares
9 whosoever *k*· any...at unawares
1Sa 2: 6 The Lord *k*·, and maketh alive:
17:25 who *k*· him, the king will enrich
26 to the man that *k*· this Philistine,
27 it be done to the man that *k*· him.
Job 5: 2 For wrath *k*· the foolish man, and
24:14 the light *k*· the poor and needy,
Pr 21:25 The desire of the slothful *k*· him;
Isa 66: 3 He that *k*· an ox is as if he slew
Joh 16: 2 whosoever *k*· you will think that he
2Co 3: 6 letter *k*·, but the spirit giveth life.
Re 13:10 he that *k*· with the sword must be

killing
J'g 9:24 him in the *k*· of his brethren.
2Ch 30:17 charge of the *k*· of the passovers
Isa 22:13 slaying oxen, and *k*· sheep, eating
Ho 4: 2 By swearing, and lying, and *k*·,
M'r 12:5 others; beating some, and *k*· some.

kin See also KINSFOLK; KINSMAN; KINSWOMAN.
Le 18: 6 any that is near of *k*· to him,
20:19 for he uncovereth his near *k*·:
21: 2 for his *k*·, that is near unto him,
25:25 if any of his *k*· come to redeem it,
49 any that is nigh of *k*· unto him of
Ru 2:20 man is near of *k*· unto us, one of our
2Sa 19:42 Because the king is near of *k*· to us:
M'r 6: 4 country, and among his own *k*·,

Kinah (*ki'-nah*)
Jos 15:22 *K*·, and Dimonah, and Adadah,

kind See also KINDS; MANKIND; WOMANKIND.
Ge 1:11 tree yielding fruit after his *k*·,
12 and herb yielding seed after his *k*·,
12 seed was in itself, after his *k*·:
21 forth abundantly, after their *k*·,
21 every winged fowl after his *k*·:
24 the living creature after his *k*·,
24 beast of the earth after his *k*·: and
25 the beast of the earth after his *k*·,
25 and cattle after their *k*·, and every
25 creepeth upon the earth after his *k*·:
6:20 Of fowls after their *k*·,
20 and of cattle after their *k*·,
20 thing of the earth after his *k*·,
7:14 They, and every beast after his *k*·,
14 all the cattle after their *k*·, and
14 creepeth upon the earth after his *k*·,
14 and every fowl after his *k*·, every
Le 11:14 vulture, and the kite after his *k*·;
15 Every raven after his *k*·;
16 cuckow, and the hawk after his *k*·,
19 the stork, the heron after her *k*·,
22 ye may eat; the locust after his *k*·,
22 and the bald locust after his *k*·,
22 and the beetle after his *k*·,
22 and the grasshopper after his *k*·.
29 mouse, and the tortoise after his *k*·,
19:19 thy cattle gender with a diverse *k*·:
De 14:13 kite, and the vulture after his *k*·,
14 And every raven after his *k*·,
15 cuckow, and the hawk after his *k*·,
18 the stork, and the heron after her *k*·,
1Ch 28:14 instruments of every *k*· of service:
2Ch 10: 7 If thou be *k*· to this people, and
Ne 13:20 merchants and sellers of all *k*· of ware
Ec 2: 5 trees in them of all *k*· of fruits:
Eze 27:12 of the multitude of all *k*· of riches;
M't 13:47 the sea, and gathered of every *k*·:
17:21 this *k*· goeth not out but by prayer
M'r 9:29 This *k*· can come forth by nothing,
Lu 6:35 he is *k*· unto the unthankful and
1Co 13: 4 Charity suffereth long, and is *k*·;
15:39 but there is one *k*· of flesh of men,
Eph 4:32 And be ye *k*· one to another,
Jas 1:18 a *k*· of firstfruits of his creatures.
3: 7 For every *k*· of beasts, and of

kindle See also KINDLED; KINDLETH.
Ex 35: 3 shall *k*· no fire throughout your
Pr 26:21 is a contentious man to *k*· strife.
Isa 9:18 *k*· in the thickets of the forest,
10:16 *k*· a burning like the burning of a
30:33 a stream of brimstone, doth *k*· it.
43: 2 shall the flame *k*· upon thee.
50:11 all ye that *k*· a fire, that compass
Jer 7:18 wood, and the fathers *k*· the fire,
17:27 then will I *k*· a fire in the gates
21:14 I will *k*· a fire in the forest thereof,
33:18 and to *k*· meat offerings, and to do
43:12 *k*· a fire in the houses of the gods
49:27 *k*· a fire in the wall of Damascus,
50:32 and I will *k*· a fire in his cities,
Eze 20:47 God; Behold, I will *k*· a fire in thee,
24:10 *k*· the fire, consume the flesh,
Am 1:14 *k*· a fire in the wall of Rabbah,
Ob 18 they shall *k*· in them, and devour
Mal 1:10 neither do ye *k*· fire on mine altar

kindled
Ge 30: 2 And Jacob's anger was *k*· against
39:19 to me; that his wrath was *k*·,
Ex 4:14 of the Lord was *k*· against Moses,
22: 6 he that *k*· the fire shall surely
Le 10: 6 burning which the Lord hath *k*·.
Nu 11: 1 heard it; and his anger was *k*·;
10 anger of the Lord was *k*· greatly;
11:33 wrath of the Lord was *k*· against
12: 9 and the anger of the Lord was *k*·
Nu 22:22 And God's anger was *k*· because he
27 Balaam's anger was *k*·, and he
24:10 Balak's anger was *k*· against
25: 3 anger of the Lord was *k*· against
32:10 Lord's anger was *k*· the same time,
13 Lord's anger was *k*· against Israel,
De 6:15 anger of the Lord thy God be *k*·
7: 4 the anger of the Lord be *k*· against
11:17 Lord's wrath be *k*· against you,
29:27 anger of the Lord was *k*· against
31:17 my anger shall be *k*· against them
32:22 For a fire is *k*· in mine anger, and
Jos 7: 1 anger of the Lord was *k*· against
23:16 shall the anger of the Lord be *k*·
J'g 9:30 the son of Ebed, his anger was *k*·.
14:19 And his anger was *k*·, and he went
1Sa 11: 6 and his anger was *k*· greatly.
17:28 Eliab's anger was *k*· against David,
20:30 Saul's anger was *k*· against
2Sa 6: 7 anger of the Lord was *k*· against
12: 5 And David's anger was greatly *k*·
22: 9 devoured: coals were *k*· by it.
13 before him were coals of fire *k*·.
24: 1 anger of the Lord was *k*· against
2Ki 13: 3 anger of the Lord was *k*· against
22:13 wrath of the Lord that is *k*· against
17 my wrath shall be *k*· against this
23:26 his anger was *k*· against Judah,
1Ch 13:10 And the anger of the Lord was *k*·
2Ch 25:10 wherefore their anger was greatly *k*·
15 anger of the Lord was *k*· against
Job 19:11 hath also *k*· his wrath against me,
32: 2 Then was *k*· the wrath of Elihu the
2 against Job was his wrath *k*·,
3 his three friends was his wrath *k*·,
5 three men, then his wrath was *k*·.
42: 7 My wrath is *k*· against thee, and
Ps 2:12 when his wrath is *k*· but a little.
18: 8 devoured: coals were *k*· by it.
78:21 so a fire was *k*· against Jacob, and
106:18 a fire was *k*· in their company;
40 was the wrath of the Lord *k*·
124: 3 their wrath was *k*· against us:
Isa 5:25 is the anger of the Lord *k*· against
50:11 and in the sparks that ye have *k*·.
Jer 11:16 tumult he hath *k*· fire upon it,
15:14 a fire is *k*· in mine anger, which
17: 4 ye have *k*· a fire in mine anger,
44: 6 was *k*· in the cities of Judah and
La 4:11 hath *k*· a fire in Zion, and it hath
Eze 20:48 see that I the Lord have *k*· it:
Ho 8: 5 mine anger is *k*· against them:
11: 8 me, my repentings are *k*· together.
Zec 10: 3 was *k*· against the shepherds,
Lu 12:49 what will I, if it be already *k*·?
22:55 they had *k*· a fire in the midst of
Ac 28: 2 for they *k*· a fire, and received us

kindleth
Job 41:21 His breath *k*· coals, and a flame
Isa 44:15 yea, he *k*· it; and baketh bread;
Jas 3: 5 how great a matter a little fire *k*·!

kindly
Ge 24:49 if ye will deal *k*· and truly with
34: 3 and spake *k*· unto the damsel.
47:29 and deal *k*· and truly with me;
50:21 and spake *k*· unto them.
Jos 2:14 will deal *k*· and truly with thee.
Ru 1: 8 Lord deal *k*· with you, as ye have
1Sa 20: 8 shalt deal *k*· with thy servant;
2Ki 25:28 he spake *k*· to him, and set his
Jer 52:32 spake *k*· unto him, and set his
Ro 12:10 Be *k*· affectioned one to another

kindly-affectioned See KINDLY and AFFECTIONED.

kindness See also LOVINGKINDNESS.
Ge 20:13 is thy *k*· which thou shalt shew
21:23 to the *k*· that I have done unto thee,
24:12 shew *k*· unto my master Abraham.
14 hast shewed *k*· unto my master.
40:14 be well with thee, and shew *k*·,
Jos 2:12 Lord, since I have shewed you *k*·,
12 shew *k*· unto my father's house,
J'g 8:35 shewed they *k*· to the house of
Ru 2:20 not left off his *k*· to the living and
3:10 shewed more *k*· in the latter end
1Sa 15: 6 ye shewed *k*· to all the children of
20:14 I live shew me the *k*· of the Lord,
15 not cut off thy kindness from my
2Sa 2: 5 have shewed this *k*· unto your lord,
6 the Lord shew *k*· and truth unto
6 will requite you this *k*·, because
3: 8 Judah do shew *k*· this day unto
9: 1 shew him *k*· for Jonathan's sake?
3 may shew the *k*· of God unto him?
7 shew thee *k*· for Jonathan thy
10: 2 will shew *k*· unto Hanun the son of
2 as his father shewed *k*· unto me.
16:17 Hushai, Is this thy *k*· to thy friend?
1Ki 2: 7 shew *k*· unto the sons of Barzillai
3: 6 hast kept for him this great *k*·,
1Ch 19: 2 shew *k*· unto Hanun the son of
2 because his father shewed *k*· to me.
2Ch 24:22 king remembered not the *k*· which
Ne 9:17 slow to anger, and of great *k*·,
Es 2: 9 him, and she obtained *k*· of him;
Ps 31:21 hath shewed me his marvellous *k*·
117: 2 For his merciful *k*· is great toward
119:76 thy merciful *k*· be for my comfort,
141: 5 smite me; it shall be a *k*·:
Pr 19:22 The desire of a man is his *k*·: and
31:26 and in her tongue is the law of *k*·.
Isa 54: 8 with everlasting *k*· will I have
10 my *k*· shall not depart from thee,
Jer 2: 2 remember thee, the *k*· of thy youth,
Joe 2:13 slow to anger, and of great *k*·,
Jon 4: 2 slow to anger, and of great *k*·,
Ac 28: 2 people shewed us no little *k*·:
2Co 6: 6 by *k*·, by the Holy Ghost, by love
Eph 2: 7 in his *k*· toward us through Christ
Col 3:12 *k*·, humbleness of mind, meekness,
Tit 3: 4 after that the *k*· and love of God
2Pe 1: 7 to godliness brotherly *k*·; and to
7 and to brotherly *k*· charity.

kindred See also KINDREDS.
Ge 12: 1 of thy country, and from thy *k*·,
24: 4 go unto my country, and to my *k*·,
7 from the land of my *k*·, and which
38 my father's house, and to my *k*·;
40 take a wife for my son of my *k*·,
41 oath, when thou comest to my *k*·;
31: 3 land of thy fathers, and to thy *k*·;
13 return unto the land of thy *k*·.
32: 9 unto thy country, and to thy *k*·,
43: 7 straitly of our state, and of our *k*·,
Nu 10:30 to mine own land, and to my *k*·.
Jos 6:23 and they brought out all her *k*·,
Ru 2: 3 who was of the *k*· of Elimelech.
3: 2 And now is not Boaz of our *k*·,
1Ch 12:29 of Benjamin, the *k*· of Saul,
Es 2:10 not shewed her people nor her *k*·:
20 Esther had not yet shewed her *k*·
8: 6 to see the destruction of my *k*·?
Job 32: 2 the Buzite, of the *k*· of Ram:
Eze 11:15 thy brethren, the men of thy *k*·,
Lu 1:61 thy *k*· that is called by this name.
Ac 4: 6 were of the *k*· of the high priest,
7: 3 of thy country, and from thy *k*·,
13 Joseph's *k*· was made known unto
14 all his *k*·, threescore and fifteen
19 same dealt subtilly with our *k*·,
Re 5: 9 blood out of every *k*·, and tongue,
14: 6 every nation, and *k*·, and tongue,

kindreds
1Ch 16:28 unto the Lord, ye *k*· of the people,
Ps 22:27 all the *k*· of the nations shall
96: 7 O ye *k*· of the people, give unto the
Ac 3:25 all the *k*· of the earth be blessed.
Re 1: 7 all *k*· of the earth shall wail
7: 9 of all nations, and *k*·, and people,
11: 9 and *k*· and tongues and nations
13: 7 power was given him over all *k*·,

kinds
Ge 8:19 upon the earth, after their *k*·,
2Ch 16:14 odours and divers *k*· of spices
Jer 15: 3 I will appoint over them four *k*·,
Eze 47:10 fish shall be according to their *k*·,
Da 3: 5 dulcimer, and all *k*· of musick, ye
7 all *k*· of musick, all the people, the
10 and all *k*· of musick, shall fall down
15 all *k*· of musick, ye fall down and
1Co 12:10 another divers *k*· of tongues; to
14:10 so many *k*· of voices in the world,

kine See also cow.
Ge 32:15 forty *k*·, and ten bulls, twenty she
41: 2 river seven well favoured *k*· and
3 seven other *k*· came up after them
3 the other *k*· upon the brink of the
4 ill favoured and leanfleshed *k*·
4 the seven well favoured and fat *k*·.
18 came up out of the river seven *k*·,
19 seven other *k*· came up after them,
20 the lean and ill favoured *k*· did eat
20 did eat up the first seven fat *k*·:
26 The seven good *k*· are seven years;
27 the seven thin and ill favoured *k*·
De 7:13 increase of thy *k*·, and the flocks
28: 4, 18 increase of thy *k*·, and the flocks
51 increase of thy *k*·, or flocks of thy
32:14 Butter of *k*·, and milk of sheep,
1Sa 6: 7 new cart, and take two milch *k*·,
7 no yoke, and tie the *k*· to the cart,
10 and took two milch *k*·, and tied
12 the *k*· took the straight way to the
14 and offered the *k*· a burnt offering
2Sa 17:29 sheep, and cheese of *k*·, for David,
Am 4: 1 Hear this word, ye *k*· of Bashan,

king See also KING'S; KINGS.
Ge 14: 1 *k*· of Shinar, Arioch *k*· of Ellasar,
1 *k*· of Elam, and Tidal *k*· of nations;
2 made war with Bera *k*· of Sodom,
2 and with Birsha *k*· of Gomorrah,
2 Shinab *k*· of Admah, and Shemeber
2 *k*· of Zeboiim, and the *k*· of Bela.
8 *k*· of Sodom, and the *k*· of Gomorrah,
8 *k*· of Admah, and the *k*· of Zeboiim,
8 and the *k*· of Bela (the same is Zoar;)
9 With Chedorlaomer the *k*· of Elam,
9 and with Tidal *k*· of nations,
9 *k*· of Shinar, and Arioch *k*· of
17 *k*· of Sodom went out to meet him
18 *k*· of Salem brought forth bread
21 the *k*· of Sodom said unto Abram,
22 Abram said to the *k*· of Sodom,
20: 2 *k*· of Gerar sent, and took Sarah.
26: 1 *k*· of the Philistines unto Gerar.
8 *k*· of the Philistines looked out of
36:31 reigned any *k*· over the children
40: 1 butler of the *k*· of Egypt and his
1 offended their lord the *k*· of Egypt.
5 and the baker of the *k*· of Egypt,
41:46 stood before Pharaoh *k*· of Egypt.
Ex 1: 8 there arose up a new *k*· over Egypt,
15 *k*· of Egypt spake to the Hebrew
17 the *k*· of Egypt commanded them,
18 *k*· of Egypt called for the midwives,
2:23 of time that the *k*· of Egypt died:
3:18 of Israel, unto the *k*· of Egypt,
19 the *k*· of Egypt will not let you go,
5: 4 And the *k*· of Egypt said unto them,

Ex 6:11 speak unto Pharaoh k' of Egypt,
13 and unto Pharaoh k' of Egypt, to
27 which spake to Pharaoh k' of Egypt,
29 thou unto Pharaoh k' of Egypt
14: 5 it was told the k' of Egypt that the
8 the heart of Pharaoh k' of Egypt,
Nu 20:14 from Kadesh unto the k' of Edom,
21: 1 And when k' Arad the Canaanite,
21 unto Sihon k' of the Amorites,
26 city of Sihon the k' of the Amorites,
26 against the former k' of Moab,
29 unto Sihon k' of the Amorites.
33 and Og the k' of Bashan went out
34 didst unto Sihon k' of the Amorites,
22: 4 of Zippor was k' of the Moabites
10 k' of Moab, hath sent unto me,
23: 7 the k' of Moab hath brought me
21 the shout of a k' is among them.
24: 7 his k' shall be higher than Agag,
32: 33 kingdom of Sihon k' of the Amorites,
33 the kingdom of Og k' of Bashan,
33: 40 k' Arad the Canaanite, which dwelt
De 1: 4 slain Sihon the k' of the Amorites,
4 Og the k' of Bashan, which dwelt at
2: 24 Sihon the Amorite, k' of Heshbon,
26 Sihon k' of Heshbon with words of
30 Sihon k' of Heshbon would not let
3: 1 and Og the k' of Bashan came out
2 didst unto Sihon k' of the Amorites,
3 hands Og also, the k' of Bashan,
6 we did unto Sihon k' of Heshbon,
11 only Og k' of Bashan remained of
4: 46 land of Sihon k' of the Amorites,
47 and the land of Og k' of Bashan,
7: 8 the hand of Pharaoh k' of Egypt.
11: 3 unto Pharaoh the k' of Egypt,
17: 14 I will set a k' over me, like as all
15 set him k' over thee, whom the Lord
15 brethren shalt thou set k' over thee:
28: 36 k' which thou shalt set over thee,
29: 7 Sihon the k' of Heshbon, and Og
7 and Og the k' of Bashan, came out
33: 5 he was k' in Jeshurun, when the
Jos 2: 2 was told the k' of Jericho, saying,
3 the k' of Jericho sent unto Rahab,
6: 2 hand Jericho, and the k' thereof,
8: 1 into thy hand the k' of Ai, and his
2 thou shalt do to Ai and her k' as
2 thou didst unto Jericho and her k':
14 when the k' of Ai saw it, that they
23 k' of Ai they took alive, and brought
29 k' of Ai he hanged on a tree until
9: 10 Jordan, to Sihon k' of Heshbon,
10 and to Og k' of Bashan, which was
10: 1 k' of Jerusalem had heard how
1 he had done to Jericho and her k',
1 so he had done to Ai and her k';
3 Adoni-zedec k' of Jerusalem
3 sent unto Hoham k' of Hebron,
3 and unto Piram k' of Jarmuth,
3 and unto Japhia k' of Lachish,
3 and unto Debir k' of Eglon, saying,
5 k' of Jerusalem, the k' of Hebron,
5 k' of Jarmuth, the k' of Lachish,
5 k' of Eglon, gathered themselves
23 of the cave, the k' of Jerusalem,
23 k' of Hebron, the k' of Jarmuth,
23 k' of Lachish, and the k' of Eglon.
28 the k' thereof he utterly destroyed,
28 and he did to the k' of Makkedah
28 as he did unto the k' of Jericho.
30 delivered it also, and the k' thereof,
30 but did unto the k' thereof
30 as he did unto the k' of Jericho.
33 Horam k' of Gezer came up to help
37 and the k' thereof, and all the cities
39 And he took it, and the k' thereof,
39 did to Debir, and to the k' thereof;
39 done also to Libnah, and to her k'.
11: 1 k' of Hazor had heard those things,
1 that he sent to Jobab k' of Madon,
1 Madon, and to the k' of Shimron,
1 and to the k' of Achshaph,
10 Hazor, and smote the k' thereof
12: 2 Sihon k' of the Amorites, who
4 And the coast of Og k' of Bashan,
5 the border of Sihon k' of Heshbon.
9 The k' of Jericho, one;
9 the k' of Ai, which is beside Beth-el,
10 The k' of Jerusalem, one;
10 the k' of Hebron, one;
11 The k' of Jarmuth, one;
11 the k' of Lachish, one;
12 The k' of Eglon, one;
12 the k' of Gezer, one;
13 The k' of Debir, one;
13 the k' of Geder, one;
14 The k' of Hormah, one;
14 the k' of Arad, one;
15 The k' of Libnah, one;
15 the k' of Adullam, one;
16 The k' of Makkedah, one;
16 the k' of Beth-el, one;
17 The k' of Tappuah, one;
17 the k' of Hepher, one;
18 The k' of Aphek, one;
18 the k' of Lasharon, one;
19 The k' of Madon, one;
19 the k' of Hazor, one;
20 The k' of Shimron-meron, one;
20 the k' of Achshaph, one;
21 The k' of Taanach, one;
21 the k' of Megiddo, one;
22 The k' of Kedesh, one;
22 the k' of Jokneam of Carmel, one;
23 The k' of Dor in the coast of Dor,

Jos 12: 23 the k' of the nations of Gilgal, one;
24 The k' of Tirzah, one: all the kings
13: 10 cities of Sihon k' of the Amorites,
21 kingdom of Sihon k' of the Amorites,
27 the kingdom of Sihon k' of Heshbon,
30 all the kingdom of Og k' of Bashan,
24: 9 Balak the son of Zippor, k' of Moab,
J'g 3: 8 the hand of ... k' of Mesopotamia:
10 k' of Mesopotamia into his hand;
12 strengthened Eglon the k' of Moab
14 of Israel served the k' of Moab
15 present unto Eglon the k' of Moab.
17 the present unto Eglon k' of Moab:
19 a secret errand unto thee, O k':
4: 2 into the hand of Jabin k' of Canaan,
17 between Jabin the k' of Hazor and
23 on that day Jabin the k' of Canaan
24 against Jabin the k' of Canaan,
24 had destroyed Jabin k' of Canaan.
8: 18 one resembled the children of a k'.
9: 6 and made Abimelech k',
8 on a time to anoint a k' unto them;
15 If in truth ye anoint me k' over you,
16 that ye have made Abimelech k',
18 made...k' over the men of Shechem.
11: 12 sent messengers unto the k' of the
13 the k' of the children of Ammon
14 sent messengers again unto the k'
17 messengers unto the k' of Edom,
17 the k' of Edom would not hearken
17 they sent unto the k' of Moab:
19 Sihon k' of the Amorites, the k' of
25 Balak the son of Zippor, k' of Moab?
28 the k' of the children of Ammon,
17: 6 days there was no k' in Israel,
18: 1 days there was no k' in Israel:
19: 1 when there was no k' in Israel,
21: 25 days there was no k' in Israel:
1Sa 2: 10 he shall give strength unto his k',
8: 5 make us a k' to judge us like all
6 they said, Give us a k' to judge us.
9 manner of the k' that shall reign
10 the people that asked of him a k'.
11 manner of the k' that shall reign
18 your k' which ye shall have chosen
19 Nay; but we will have a k' over us;
20 that our k' may judge us, and go
22 voice, and make them a k'.
10: 19 unto him, Nay, but set a k' over us.
24 shouted, and said, God save the k'.
11: 15 they made Saul k' before the Lord
12: 1 and have made a k' over you.
2 behold, the k' walketh before you:
9 into the hand of the k' of Moab,
12 the k' of the children of Ammon
12 Nay; but a k' shall reign over us:
12 the Lord your God was your k'.
13 behold the k' whom ye have chosen,
13 the Lord hath set a k' over you.
14 also the k' that reigneth over you
17 sight of the Lord, in asking you a k'.
19 all our sins this evil, to ask us a k'.
25 be consumed, both ye and your k'.
15: 1 anoint thee to be k' over his people,
8 took Agag the k' of the Amalekites
11 that I have set up Saul to be k':
17 Lord anointed thee k' over Israel?
20 brought Agag the k' of Amalek,
23 also rejected thee from being k'.
26 thee from being k' over Israel.
32 me Agag the k' of the Amalekites.
35 he had made Saul k' over Israel.
16: 1 provided me a k' among his sons.
17: 25 k' will enrich him with great riches,
55 thy soul liveth, O k', I cannot tell.
56 the k' said, Enquire thou whose son
18: 6 and dancing, to meet k' Saul,
18 I should be son in law to the k'?
22 Behold, the k' hath delight in thee,
25 The k' desireth not any dowry,
27 they gave them in full tale to the k',
19: 4 not the k' sin against his servant,
20: 5 not fail to sit with the k' at meat:
24 the k' sat him down to eat meat.
25 the k' sat upon his seat, as at other
21: 2 k' hath commanded me a business,
10 and went to Achish the k' of Gath.
11 Is not this David the k' of the land?
12 sore afraid of Achish the k' of Gath.
22: 3 and he said unto the k' of Moab,
4 brought them before the k' of Moab:
11 k' sent to call Ahimelech the priest,
11 and they came all of them to the k'.
14 Then Ahimelech answered the k',
15 let not the k' impute any thing unto
16 the k' said, Thou shalt surely die,
17 k' said unto the footmen that stood
17 the servants of the k' would not put
18 k' said to Doeg, Turn thou, and fall
23: 17 and thou shalt be k' over Israel,
20 therefore, O k', come down
24: 8 after Saul, saying, My lord the k'.
14 After whom is the k' of Israel come
20 well that thou shalt surely be k',
25: 36 in his house, like the feast of a k';
26: 14 Who art thou that criest to the k'?
15 hast thou not kept thy lord the k'?
15 people in to destroy the k' thy lord.
17 said, It is my voice, my lord, O k'.
19 let my lord the k' hear the words of
20 the k' of Israel is come out to seek
27: 2 Achish, the son of Maoch, k' of Gath.
28: 13 the k' said unto her, Be not afraid:
29: 3 the servant of Saul the k' of Israel,
8 the enemies of my lord the k'?
2Sa 2: 4 David k' over the house of Judah.

2Sa 2: 7 of Judah have anointed me k' over
9 And made him k' over Gilead,
11 time that David was k' in Hebron
3: 3 daughter of Talmai k' of Geshur;
17 for David in times past to be k' over
21 gather all Israel unto my lord the k',
23 Abner the son of Ner came to the k',
24 Then Joab came to the k', and said,
31 k' David himself followed the bier.
32 the k' lifted up his voice, and wept
33 the k' lamented over Abner, and
36 whatsoever the k' did pleased all
37 it was not of the k' to slay Abner
38 And the k' said unto his servants,
39 this day weak, though anointed k';
4: 8 and said to the k', Behold the head
8 Lord hath avenged my lord the k'
5: 2 when Saul was k' over us, thou wast
3 the elders of Israel came to the k'
3 k' David made a league with them
3 they anointed David k' over Israel.
6 k' and his men went to Jerusalem
11 Hiram k' of Tyre sent messengers
12 had established him k' over Israel,
17 had anointed David k' over Israel,
6: 12 And it was told k' David, saying,
16 saw k' David leaping and dancing
20 How glorious was the k' of Israel
7: 1 pass, when the k' sat in his house,
2 the k' said unto Nathan the prophet,
3 And Nathan said to the k', Go, do all
18 Then went k' David in, and sat
8: 3 the son of Rehob, k' of Zobah,
5 to succour Hadadezer k' of Zobah,
8 k' David took...much brass.
9 When Toi k' of Hamath heard that
10 sent Joram his son unto k' David,
11 k' David did dedicate unto the Lord,
12 son of Rehob, k' of Zobah.
9: 2 the k' said unto him, Art thou Ziba?
3 And the k' said, Is there not yet any
3 Ziba said unto the k', Jonathan hath
4 the k' said unto him, Where is he?
4 Ziba said unto the k', Behold, he is
5 Then k' David sent, and fetched
9 Then the k' called to Ziba, Saul's
11 said Ziba unto the k', According
11 my lord the k' hath commanded his
11 As for Mephibosheth, said the k',
10: 1 k' of the children of Ammon died,
5 k' said, Tarry at Jericho until your
6 and of k' Maacah a thousand men,
11: 8 him a mess of meat from the k'.
19 the matters of the war unto the k',
12: 7 I anointed thee k' over Israel, and I
13: 6 when the k' was come to see him,
6 unto the k', I pray thee, let Tamar
13 I pray thee, speak unto the k';
21 when k' David heard of all these
24 Absalom came to the k', and said,
24 let the k', I beseech thee, and his
25 the k' said to Absalom, Nay, my son,
26 the k' said unto him, Why should
31 the k' arose, and tare his garments,
33 let not my lord the k' take the thing
35 Jonadab said unto the k', Behold,
36 the k' also and all his servants wept
37 the son of Ammihud, k' of Geshur.
39 soul of k' David longed to go forth
14: 3 come to the k', and speak on this
4 woman of Tekoah spake to the k',
4 did obeisance, and said, Help, O k'.
5 the k' said unto her, What aileth
8 the k' said unto the woman, Go to
9 woman of Tekoah said unto the k',
9 My lord, O k', the iniquity be on me,
9 the k' and his throne be guiltless.
10 the k' said, Whosoever saith ought
11 the k' remember the Lord thy God,
12 speak one word unto my lord the k'.
13 the k' doth speak this thing as one
13 k' doth not fetch home again his
15 of this thing unto my lord the k',
15 said, I will now speak unto the k';
16 For the k' will hear, to deliver his
17 The word of my lord the k' shall
17 so is my lord the k' to discern good
18 the k' answered and said unto the
18 said, Let my lord the k' now speak.
19 the k' said, Is not the hand of Joab
19 As thy soul liveth, my lord the k',
19 that my lord the k' hath spoken:
21 the k' said unto Joab, Behold now,
22 bowed himself, and thanked the k':
22 grace in thy sight, my lord, O k',
22 k' hath fulfilled the request of his
24 the k' said, Let him turn to his own
29 Joab, to have sent him to the k';
32 that I may send thee to the k', to
33 Joab came to the k', and told him:
33 came to the k', and bowed himself
33 face to the ground before the k':
33 and the k' kissed Absalom.
15: 2 came to the k' for judgment,
3 man deputed of the k' to hear thee.
6 that came to the k' for judgment:
7 Absalom said unto the k', I pray
9 the k' said unto him, Go in peace.
15 the king's servants said unto the k',
15 my lord the k' shall appoint.
16 And the k' went forth, and all his
16 the k' left ten women, which were
17 the k' went forth, and all the people
18 from Gath, passed on before the k'.
19 Then said the k' to Ittai the Gittite,
19 thy place, and abide with the k':

2Sa 15: 21 And Ittai answered the k', and said
21 liveth, and as my lord the k' liveth,
21 what place my lord the k' shall be,
23 the k' also himself passed over the
25 the k' said unto Zadok, Carry back
27 k' said also unto Zadok the priest,
34 Absalom, I will be thy servant, O k';
16: 2 k' said unto Ziba, What meanest
3 And the k' said, And where is thy
3 And Ziba said unto the k', Behold, he
4 Then said the k' to Ziba, Behold,
4 grace in thy sight, my lord, O k'.
5 when k' David came to Bahurim,
6 and at all the servants of k' David:
9 of Zeruiah unto the k', Why should
9 this dead dog curse my lord the k'?
10 And the k' said, What have I to do
14 And the k', and all the people that
16 God save the k', God save the k'.
17: 2 flee; and I will smite the k' only:
16 lest the k' be swallowed up, and all
17 and they went and told k' David.
21 well, and went and told k' David.
18: 2 the k' said unto the people, I will
4 k' said unto them, What seemeth
4 the k' stood by the gate side, and
5 And the k' commanded Joab and
5 the k' gave all the captains charge
12 in our hearing the k' charged thee
13 there is no matter hid from the k',
19 now run, and bear the k' tidings,
21 Go tell the k' what thou hast seen.
25 watchman cried, and told the k'.
26 k' said, He also bringeth tidings.
27 the k' said, He is a good man, and
28 and said unto the k', All is well.
28 earth upon his face before the k',
28 their hand against my lord the k'.
29 And the k' said, Is the young man
30 the k' said unto him, Turn aside,
31 Cushi said, Tidings, my lord the k':
32 the k' said unto Cushi, Is the young
32 enemies of my lord the k', and all
33 the k' was much moved, and went
19: 1 the k' weepeth and mourneth for
2 how the k' was grieved for his son.
4 But the k' covered his face,
4 and the k' cried with a loud voice,
5 Joab came into the house to the k',
8 the k' arose, and sat in the gate.
8 Behold, the k' doth sit in the gate.
8 all the people came before the k':
9 The k' saved us out of the hand of
10 not a word of bringing the k' back?
11 And k' David sent to Zadok and to
11 to bring the k' back to his house?
11 speech of...Israel is come to the k',
12 are ye the last to bring back the k'?
14 they sent this word unto the k',
15 So the k' returned, and came to
15 go to meet the k', to conduct the k'
16 the men of Judah to meet k' David.
17 they went over Jordan before the k'.
18 son of Gera fell down before the k',
19 said unto the k', Let not my lord
19 lord the k' went out of Jerusalem,
19 the k' should take it to his heart.
20 to go down to meet my lord the k'.
22 that I am this day k' over Israel?
23 k' said unto Shimei, Thou shalt not
23 die. And the k' sware unto him.
24 of Saul came down to meet the k',
24 from the day the k' departed until
25 come to Jerusalem to meet the k',
25 the k' said unto him, Wherefore
26 lord, O k', my servant deceived me:
26 may ride thereon, and go to the k';
27 thy servant unto my lord the k':
27 my lord the k' is as an angel of God:
28 dead men before my lord the k':
28 I yet to cry any more unto the k'?
29 the k' said unto him, Why speakest
30 And Mephibosheth said unto the k',
30 lord the k' is come again in peace
31 and went over Jordan with the k',
32 had provided the k' of sustenance
33 the k' said unto Barzillai, Come
34 Barzillai said unto the k', How long
34 go up with the k' unto Jerusalem?
35 yet a burden unto my lord the k'?
36 little way over Jordan with the k':
36 why should the k' recompense it me
37 let him go over with my lord the k';
38 the k' answered, Chimham shall go
39 And when the k' was come over,
39 the k' kissed Barzillai, and blessed
40 Then the k' went on to Gilgal, and
40 people of Judah conducted the k',
41 all the men of Israel came to the k',
41 and said unto the k', Why have our
41 brought the k', and his household,
42 Because the k' is near of kin to us:
43 said, We have ten parts in the k',
43 first had in bringing back our k'?
20: 2 men of Judah clave unto their k',
3 and the k' took the ten women his
4 said the k' to Amasa, Assemble me
21 lifted up his hand against the k',
22 returned to Jerusalem unto the k'.
21: 2 the k' called the Gibeonites, and
5 they answered the k', The man that
6 And the k' said, I will give them.
7 the k' spared Mephibosheth, the son
8 the k' took the two sons of Rizpah
14 all that the k' commanded.
22: 51 is the tower of salvation for his k':

2Sa 24: 2 the k' said to Joab the captain of
3 Joab said unto the k', Now the Lord
3 eyes of my lord the k' may see it:
3 doth my lord the k' delight in this
4 out from the presence of the k',
9 number of the people unto the k':
20 Araunah looked, and saw the k' and
20 bowed himself before the k' on his
21 lord the k' come to his servant?
22 Let my lord the k' take and offer up
23 Araunah, as a k', give unto the k'.
23 Araunah said unto the k', The Lord
24 And the k' said unto Araunah, Nay;
1Ki 1: 1 Now k' David was old and stricken
2 for my lord the k' a young virgin:
2 let her stand before the k', and let
2 that my lord the k' may get heat.
3 and brought her to the k'.
4 was very fair, and cherished the k',
4 to him: but the k' knew her not.
5 himself, saying, I will be k':
13 get thee in unto k' David, and say
13 Didst not thou, my lord, O k', swear
14 thou yet talkest there with the k',
15 in unto the k' into the chamber:
15 and the k' was very old; and
15 Shunammite ministered unto the k'.
16 and did obeisance unto the k'.
16 the k' said, What wouldest thou?
18 my lord the k', thou knowest it not:
19 hath called all the sons of the k',
20 O k', the eyes of Israel are upon
20 on the throne of my lord the k' after
21 the k' shall sleep with his fathers,
22 while she yet talked with the k',
23 told the k', saying, Behold Nathan
23 when he was come in before the k',
23 he bowed himself before the k' with
24 said, My lord, O k', hast thou said,
25 him, and say, God save k' Adonijah.
27 Is this thing done by my lord the k',
27 throne of my lord the k' after him?
28 k' David answered and said, Call
28 presence, and stood before the k'.
29 And the k' sware, and said, As the
31 earth, and did reverence to the k',
31 Let my lord k' David live for ever.
32 k' David said, Call me Zadok the
32 And they came before the k'.
33 The k' also said unto them, Take
34 anoint him there k' over Israel:
34 and say, God save k' Solomon.
35 he shall be k' in my stead: for I
36 son of Jehoiada answered the k',
36 Lord God of my lord the k' say so
37 Lord hath been with my lord the k',
37 than the throne of my lord k' David.
38 to ride upon k' David's mule,
39 people said, God save k' Solomon.
43 lord k' David hath made Solomon
43 David hath made Solomon k'.
44 the k' hath sent with him Zadok
45 have anointed him k' in Gihon:
47 came to bless our lord k' David,
47 the k' bowed himself upon the bed.
48 And also thus said the k', Blessed
51 Adonijah feareth k' Solomon:
51 k' Solomon swear unto me to day
53 k' Solomon sent, and they brought
53 and bowed himself to k' Solomon:
2: 17 I pray thee, unto Solomon the k',
18 I will speak for thee unto the k'.
19 therefore went unto k' Solomon,
19 And the k' rose up to meet her, and
20 the k' said unto her, Ask on, my
22 And k' Solomon answered and said
23 Then k' Solomon sware by the Lord,
25 And k' Solomon sent by the hand of
26 unto Abiathar the priest said the k',
29 it was told k' Solomon that Joab
30 him, Thus saith the k', Come forth.
30 Benaiah brought the k' word again,
31 the k' said unto him, Do as he hath
35 k' put Benaiah the son of Jehoiada
35 the k' put in the room of Abiathar.
36 the k' sent and called for Shimei,
38 Shimei said unto the k', The saying
38 as my lord the k' hath said, so will
39 Achish son of Maachah k' of Gath.
42 the k' sent and called for Shimei,
44 The k' said moreover to Shimei,
45 k' Solomon shall be blessed, and
46 the k' commanded Benaiah the son
3: 1 affinity with Pharaoh k' of Egypt,
4 the k' went to Gibeon to sacrifice
7 hast made thy servant k' instead of
16 that were harlots, unto the k',
22 son. Thus they spake before the k'.
23 Then said the k', The one saith,
24 And the k' said, Bring me a sword.
24 they brought a sword before the k'.
25 the k' said, Divide the living child
26 the living child was unto the k',
27 the k' answered and said, Give her
28 judgment which the k' had judged;
28 and they feared the k': for they saw
4: 1 k' Solomon was k' over all Israel.
7 provided victuals for the k' and his
19 in the country of Sihon k' of the
19 Amorites, and of Og k' of Bashan;
27 provided victual for k' Solomon,
27 that came unto k' Solomon's table.
5: 1 Hiram k' of Tyre sent his servants
1 anointed him k' in the room of his
13 k' Solomon raised a levy out of all
17 k' commanded, and they brought

1Ki 6: 2 house which k' Solomon built for
7: 13 k' Solomon sent and fetched Hiram
14 he came to k' Solomon, and wrought
40 work that he made k' Solomon for
45 which Hiram made to k' Solomon
46 plain of Jordan did the k' cast them,
51 work that k' Solomon made for the
8: 1 unto k' Solomon in Jerusalem,
2 themselves unto k' Solomon at the
5 And k' Solomon, and all the
14 the k' turned his face about, and
62 And the k', and all Israel with him,
63 the k' and all the children of Israel
64 did the k' hallow the middle of the
66 they blessed the k', and went unto
9: 11 Hiram the k' of Tyre had furnished
11 k' Solomon gave Hiram twenty
14 sent to the k' sixscore talents of
15 the levy which k' Solomon raised;
16 Pharaoh k' of Egypt had gone up,
26 k' Solomon made a navy of ships
28 and brought it to k' Solomon.
10: 3 was not any thing hid from the k',
6 And she said to the k', It was a true
9 for ever, therefore made he thee k',
10 And she gave the k' an hundred and
10 queen of Sheba gave to k' Solomon.
12 k' made of the almug trees pillars
13 k' Solomon gave unto the queen of
16 And k' Solomon made two hundred
17 the k' put them in the house of the
18 the k' made a great throne of ivory,
21 all k' Solomon's drinking vessels
22 k' had at sea a navy of Tharshish
23 k' Solomon exceeded all the kings
26 and with the k' at Jerusalem.
27 k' made silver to be in Jerusalem as
11: 1 But k' Solomon loved many strange
18 Egypt, unto Pharaoh k' of Egypt;
23 his lord Hadadezer k' of Zobah:
26 he lifted up his hand against the k'.
27 he lifted up his hand against the k':
37 and shalt be k' over Israel.
40 Egypt, unto Shishak k' of Egypt,
12: 1 come to Shechem to make him k'.
2 from the presence of k' Solomon,
6 k' Rehoboam consulted with the old
12 third day, as the k' had appointed,
13 the k' answered the people roughly,
15 k' hearkened not unto the people;
16 the k' hearkened not unto them,
16 the people answered the k', saying,
18 k' Rehoboam sent Adoram, who
18 k' Rehoboam made speed to get him
20 and made him k' over all Israel:
23 the son of Solomon, k' of Judah,
27 even unto Rehoboam k' of Judah,
27 go again to Rehoboam k' of Judah.
28 Whereupon the k' took counsel,
13: 4 when k' Jeroboam heard the saying
6 k' answered and said unto the man
7 the k' said unto the man of God,
8 the man of God said unto the k', If
11 which he had spoken unto the k',
14: 2 I should be k' over this people.
14 Lord shall raise him up a k' over
25 that Shishak k' of Egypt came up
27 k' Rehoboam made in their stead
28 k' went into the house of the Lord,
15: 1 eighteenth year of k' Jeroboam
9 year of Jeroboam k' of Israel
16 between Asa and Baasha k' of Israel
17 And Baasha k' of Israel went up
17 out or come in to Asa k' of Judah.
18 k' Asa sent them to Ben-hadad,
18 the son of Hezion, k' of Syria,
19 thy league with Baasha k' of Israel,
20 Ben-hadad hearkened unto k' Asa,
22 Then k' Asa made a proclamation
22 k' Asa built with them Geba of
25 the second year of Asa k' of Judah,
28 the third year of Asa k' of Judah
32 between Asa and Baasha k' of Israel
33 the third year of Asa k' of Judah
16: 8 and sixth year of Asa k' of Judah,
10 seventh year of Asa k' of Judah,
15 seventh year of Asa k' of Judah
16 and hath also slain the k':
16 Israel made Omri...k' over Israel
21 the son of Ginath, to make him k':
23 and first year of Asa k' of Judah
29 and eighth year of Asa k' of Judah
31 of Ethbaal k' of the Zidonians,
19: 15 anoint Hazael to be k' over Syria:
16 thou anoint to be k' over Israel:
20: 1 the k' of Syria gathered all his hosts
2 to Ahab k' of Israel into the city,
4 the k' of Israel answered and said,
4 My lord, O k', according to thy
7 the k' of Israel called all the elders
9 Tell my lord the k', All that thou
11 the k' of Israel answered and said,
13 a prophet unto Ahab k' of Israel,
20 the k' of Syria escaped on an horse
21 the k' of Israel went out, and smote
22 the prophet came to the k' of Israel,
22 year the k' of Syria will come up
23 servants of the k' of Syria said unto
28 and spake unto the k' of Israel,
31 and go out to the k' of Israel:
32 heads, and came to the k' of Israel,
38 and waited for the k' by the way,
39 And as the k' passed by, he cried
39 he cried unto the k': and he said,
40 k' of Israel said unto him, So shall
41 k' of Israel discerned him that he

1Ki 20:43 the *k'* of Israel went to his house
21: 1 the palace of Ahab *k'* of Samaria.
10 didst blaspheme God and the *k'*.
13 did blaspheme God and the *k'*.
18 go down to meet Ahab *k'* of Israel,
22: 2 *k'* of Judah came down to the *k'* of
3 *k'* of Israel said unto his servants,
3 out of the hand of the *k'* of Syria?
4 Jehoshaphat said to the *k'* of Israel,
5 said unto the *k'* of Israel, I enquire,
6 *k'* of Israel gathered the prophets
6 deliver it into the hand of the *k'*.
8 *k'* of Israel said unto Jehoshaphat,
8 said, Let not the *k'* say so.
9 the *k'* of Israel called an officer,
10 And the *k'* of Israel and
10 Jehoshaphat the *k'* of Judah sat
13 prophets declare good unto the *k'*
15 came to the *k'*. And the *k'* said
15 deliver it into the hand of the *k'*.
16 the *k'* said unto him, How many
18 the *k'* of Israel said unto Jehoshaphat,
26 And the *k'* of Israel said, Take
27 Thus saith the *k'*, Put this fellow
29 So the *k'* of Israel and
29 Jehoshaphat the *k'* of Judah went
30 *k'* of Israel said unto Jehoshaphat,
30 *k'* of Israel disguised himself, and
31 *k'* of Syria commanded his thirty
31 save only with the *k'* of Israel.
32 said, Surely it is the *k'* of Israel.
33 that it was not the *k'* of Israel, that
34 smote the *k'* of Israel between the
35 the *k'* was stayed up in his chariot
37 the *k'* died, and was brought to
37 and they buried the *k'* in Samaria.
41 the fourth year of Ahab *k'* of Israel.
44 made peace with the *k'* of Israel.
47 no *k'* in Edom: a deputy was *k'*.
51 year of Jehoshaphat *k'* of Judah,
2Ki 1: 3 messengers of the *k'* of Samaria,
6 again unto the *k'* that sent you,
9 Then the *k'* sent unto him a captain
9 Thou man of God, the *k'* hath said,
11 the *k'* said, Come down quickly.
15 went down with him unto the *k'*.
17 the son of Jehoshaphat *k'* of Judah;
3: 1 year of Jehoshaphat *k'* of Judah,
4 *k'* of Moab was a sheepmaster,
4 rendered unto the *k'* of Israel an
5 Ahab was dead, that the *k'* of Moab
5 rebelled against the *k'* of Israel.
6 *k'* Jehoram went out of Samaria
7 to Jehoshaphat the *k'* of Judah,
7 *k'* of Moab hath rebelled against
9 the *k'* of Israel went, and the *k'* of
9 the *k'* of Edom: and they fetched
10 *k'* of Israel said, Alas! that the
11 one of the *k'* of Israel's servants
12 the *k'* of Israel and Jehoshaphat
12 the *k'* of Edom went down to him.
13 Elisha said unto the *k'* of Israel,
13 And the *k'* of Israel said unto him,
14 of Jehoshaphat the *k'* of Judah,
26 the *k'* of Moab saw that the battle
26 through even unto the *k'* of Edom:
4:13 thou be spoken for to the *k'*,
5: 1 of the host of the *k'* of Syria,
5 And the *k'* of Syria said, Go to, go,
5 send a letter unto the *k'* of Israel.
6 the letter to the *k'* of Israel, saying,
7 when the *k'* of Israel had read the
8 the *k'* of Israel had rent his clothes,
8 that he sent to the *k'*, saying,
6: 8 *k'* of Syria warred against Israel,
9 of God sent unto the *k'* of Israel,
10 the *k'* of Israel sent to the place
11 the heart of the *k'* of Syria was sore
11 which of us is for the *k'* of Israel?
12 servants said, None, my lord, O *k'*:
12 telleth the *k'* of Israel the words
21 the *k'* of Israel said unto Elisha,
24 *k'* of Syria gathered all his host,
26 as the *k'* of Israel was passing by
26 him, saying, Help, my lord, O *k'*.
28 the *k'* said unto her, What aileth
30 when the *k'* heard the words of the
32 the *k'* sent a man from before him:
7: 2 lord on whose hand the *k'* leaned
6 the *k'* of Israel hath hired against
12 the *k'* arose in the night, and said
14 the *k'* sent after the host of the
15 returned, and told the *k'*.
17 the *k'* appointed the lord on whose
17 when the *k'* came down to him.
18 man of God had spoken to the *k'*,
8: 3 to cry unto the *k'* for her house
4 And the *k'* talked with Gehazi the
5 telling the *k'* how he had restored
5 cried to the *k'* for her house and for
5 My lord, O *k'*, this is the woman,
6 And when the *k'* asked the woman,
6 the *k'* appointed unto her a certain
7 Ben-hadad the *k'* of Syria was sick;
8 the *k'* said unto Hazael, Take a
9 *k'* of Syria hath sent me to thee,
13 that thou shalt be *k'* over Syria.
16 Joram the son of Ahab *k'* of Israel,
16 Jehoshaphat being...*k'* of Judah,
16 Jehoram *k'* of Judah began to reign.
20 and made a *k'* over themselves.
25 Joram the son of Ahab *k'* of Israel,
25 the son of Jehoram *k'* of Judah
26 the daughter of Omri *k'* of Israel.
28 *k'* of Syria in Ramoth-gilead;
29 *k'* Joram went back to be healed in

2Ki 8:29 fought against Hazael *k'* of Syria.
29 the son of Jehoram *k'* of Judah
9: 3 I have anointed thee *k'* over Israel.
6 I have anointed thee *k'* over the
12 I have anointed thee *k'* over Israel.
13 with trumpets, saying, Jehu is *k'*.
14 because of Hazael *k'* of Syria.
15 *k'* Joram was returned to be healed
15 he fought with Hazael *k'* of Syria.)
16 *k'* of Judah was come down to see
18, 19 Thus saith the *k'*, Is it peace?
21 *k'* of Israel and Ahaziah *k'* of Judah
27 Ahaziah the *k'* of Judah saw this,
10: 5 we will not make any *k'*: do thou
13 brethren of Ahaziah *k'* of Judah,
13 children of the *k'* and the children
11: 2 the daughter of *k'* Joram, sister of
7 the house of the Lord about the *k'*.
8 shall compass the *k'* round about,
8 be ye with the *k'* as he goeth out
10 give *k'* David's spears and shields,
11 in his hand, round about the *k'*,
12 and they made him *k'*, and anointed
12 hands, and said, God save the *k'*.
14 the *k'* stood by a pillar, as the
14 and the trumpeters by the *k'*, and
17 between the Lord and the *k'* and
17 between the *k'* also and the people.
19 they brought down the *k'* from the
12: 6 twentieth year of *k'* Jehoash the
7 *k'* Jehoash called for Jehoiada the
17 Hazael *k'* of Syria went up, and
18 Jehoash *k'* of Judah took all the
18 and sent it to Hazael *k'* of Syria:
13: 1 the son of Ahaziah *k'* of Judah
3 into the hand of Hazael *k'* of Syria,
4 the *k'* of Syria oppressed them.
7 the *k'* of Syria had destroyed them,
10 seventh year of Joash *k'* of Judah
12 against Amaziah *k'* of Judah,
14 Joash the *k'* of Israel came down
16 said to the *k'* of Israel, Put thine
18 he said unto the *k'* of Israel, Smite
22 Hazael *k'* of Syria oppressed Israel
24 So Hazael *k'* of Syria died; and
14: 1 son of Jehoahaz *k'* of Israel reigned
1 the son of Joash *k'* of Judah.
5 which had slain the *k'* his father.
8 Jehoahaz son of Jehu, *k'* of Israel,
9 And Jehoash the *k'* of Israel sent
9 sent to Amaziah *k'* of Judah, saying,
11 Jehoash *k'* of Israel went up;
11 Amaziah *k'* of Judah looked one
13 And Jehoash *k'* of Israel took
13 Amaziah *k'* of Judah, the son of
15 fought with Amaziah *k'* of Judah,
17 the son of Joash *k'* of Judah lived
17 son of Jehoahaz *k'* of Israel
21 made him *k'* instead of his father
22 that the *k'* slept with his fathers.
23 the son of Joash *k'* of Judah
23 the son of Joash *k'* of Israel began
15: 1 year of Jeroboam *k'* of Israel began
1 Azariah son of Amaziah *k'* of Judah
5 the Lord smote the *k'*, so that he
8 eighth year of Azariah *k'* of Judah
13 nine...year of Uzziah *k'* of Judah;
17 year of Azariah *k'* of Judah began
19 *k'* of Assyria came against the land:
20 of silver, to give to the *k'* of Assyria.
20 the *k'* of Assyria turned back, and
23 the fiftieth...of Azariah *k'* of Judah
27 and fiftieth...of Azariah *k'* of Judah
29 In the days of Pekah *k'* of Israel
29 Tiglath-pileser *k'* of Assyria, and
32 the son of Remaliah *k'* of Israel
32 son of Uzziah *k'* of Judah to reign.
37 against Judah Rezin the *k'* of Syria,
16: 1 Ahaz son of Jotham *k'* of Judah
5 Then Rezin *k'* of Syria and Pekah
5 son of Remaliah *k'* of Israel came
6 Rezin *k'* of Syria recovered Elath to
7 to Tiglath-pileser *k'* of Assyria,
7 me out of the hand of the *k'* of Syria,
7 out of the hand of the *k'* of Israel,
8 it for a present to the *k'* of Assyria.
9 *k'* of Assyria hearkened unto him:
9 the *k'* of Assyria went up against
10 And *k'* Ahaz went to Damascus to
10 meet Tiglath-pileser *k'* of Assyria,
10 *k'* Ahaz sent to Urijah the priest the
11 *k'* Ahaz had sent from Damascus:
11 *k'* Ahaz came from Damascus.
12 the *k'* was come from Damascus,
12 the *k'* saw the altar:
12 and the *k'* approached to the altar,
15 And *k'* Ahaz commanded Urijah the
16 to all that *k'* Ahaz commanded.
17 *k'* Ahaz cut off the borders of the
18 of the Lord for the *k'* of Assyria.
17: 1 the twelfth year of Ahaz *k'* of Judah
3 came up Shalmaneser *k'* of Assyria;
4 the *k'* of Assyria found conspiracy
4 sent messengers to So *k'* of Egypt,
4 no present to the *k'* of Assyria,
4 the *k'* of Assyria shut him up,
5 *k'* of Assyria came up throughout
6 the *k'* of Assyria took Samaria, and
7 the hand of Pharaoh *k'* of Egypt,
21 made Jeroboam the son of Nebat *k'*:
24 the *k'* of Assyria brought men from
26 they spake to the *k'* of Assyria,
27 Then the *k'* of Assyria commanded,
18: 1 of Hoshea son of Elah *k'* of Israel,
1 the son of Ahaz *k'* of Judah began
7 rebelled against the *k'* of Assyria,

2Ki 18: 9 in the fourth year of *k'* Hezekiah,
9 of Hoshea son of Elah *k'* of Israel,
9 Shalmaneser *k'* of Assyria came up
10 the ninth year of Hoshea *k'* of Israel,
11 *k'* of Assyria did carry away Israel
13 the fourteenth year of *k'* Hezekiah
13 Sennacherib *k'* of Assyria come up
14 *k'* of Judah sent to the *k'* of Assyria
14 the *k'* of Assyria appointed unto
14 Hezekiah *k'* of Judah three hundred
16 Hezekiah *k'* of Judah had overlaid,
16 and gave it to the *k'* of Assyria.
17 the *k'* of Assyria sent Tartan and
17 from Lachish to *k'* Hezekiah with
18 when they had called to the *k'*, there
19 saith the great *k'*, the *k'* of Assyria,
21 so is Pharaoh *k'* of Egypt unto all
23 pledges to my lord the *k'* of Assyria,
28 of the great *k'*, the *k'* of Assyria:
29 Thus saith the *k'*, Let not Hezekiah
30 into the hand of the *k'* of Assyria.
31 thus saith the *k'* of Assyria, Make an
33 out of the hand of the *k'* of Assyria?
19: 1 when *k'* Hezekiah heard it, that he
4 *k'* of Assyria his master hath sent
5 servants of *k'* Hezekiah came to
6 servants of the *k'* of Assyria have
8 the *k'* of Assyria warring against
9 heard say of Tirhakah *k'* of Ethiopia,
10 ye speak to Hezekiah *k'* of Judah,
10 into the hand of the *k'* of Assyria.
13 *k'* of Hamath, and the *k'* of Arpad,
13 and the *k'* of the city of Sepharvaim,
20 against Sennacherib *k'* of Assyria
32 Lord concerning the *k'* of Assyria,
36 Sennacherib *k'* of Assyria departed,
20: 6 out of the hand of the *k'* of Assyria;
12 *k'* of Babylon, sent letters and a
14 Isaiah the prophet unto *k'* Hezekiah,
18 in the palace of the *k'* of Babylon.
21: 3 a grove, as did Ahab *k'* of Israel;
11 Manasseh *k'* of Judah hath done
23 and slew the *k'* in his own house.
24 had conspired against *k'* Amon;
24 made Josiah his son *k'* in his stead.
22: 3 the eighteenth year of *k'* Josiah,
3 that the *k'* sent Shaphan the son of
9 Shaphan the scribe came to the *k'*,
9 brought the *k'* word again, and said,
10 Shaphan the scribe shewed the *k'*,
10 And Shaphan read it before the *k'*.
11 *k'* had heard the words of the book
12 *k'* commanded Hilkiah the priest,
16 which the *k'* of Judah hath read:
18 to the *k'* of Judah which sent you to
20 they brought the *k'* word again.
23: 1 the *k'* sent, and they gathered unto
2 the *k'* went up into the house of the
3 the *k'* stood by a pillar, and made a
4 the *k'* commanded Hilkiah the high
12 *k'* beat down, and brake them down
13 the *k'* of Israel had builded for
13 children of Ammon, did the *k'* defile.
21 the *k'* commanded all the people,
23 in the eighteenth year of *k'* Josiah,
25 unto him was there no *k'* before him,
29 Pharaoh-nechoh *k'* of Egypt went up
29 against the *k'* of Assyria to the river
29 *k'* Josiah went against him; and he
30 made him *k'* in his father's stead.
34 made Eliakim the son of Josiah *k'*
24: 1 *k'* of Babylon came up,
7 the *k'* of Egypt came not again any
7 the *k'* of Babylon had taken from
7 that pertained to the *k'* of Egypt.
10 of Nebuchadnezzar *k'* of Babylon
11 *k'* of Babylon came against the city,
12 Jehoiachin the *k'* of Judah went
12 went out to the *k'* of Babylon, he
12 the *k'* of Babylon took him in the
13 which Solomon *k'* of Israel had made
16 the *k'* of Babylon brought captive
17 the *k'* of Babylon made Mattaniah
17 made...his father's brother *k'* in
20 rebelled against the *k'* of Babylon.
25: 1 Nebuchadnezzar *k'* of Babylon came,
2 the eleventh year of *k'* Zedekiah.
4 *k'* went the way toward the plain.
5 the Chaldees pursued after the *k'*,
6 they took the *k'*, and brought him
6 up to the *k'* of Babylon to Riblah;
8 *k'* Nebuchadnezzar *k'* of Babylon,
8 a servant of the *k'* of Babylon, unto
11 that fell away to the *k'* of Babylon,
20 them to the *k'* of Babylon to Riblah:
21 And the *k'* of Babylon smote them,
22 Nebuchadnezzar *k'* of Babylon had
23 heard the *k'* of Babylon had made
24 the land, and serve the *k'* of Babylon;
27 captivity of Jehoiachin *k'* of Judah,
27 Evil-merodach *k'* of Babylon in the
27 the head of Jehoiachin *k'* of Judah
30 allowance given him of the *k'*,
1Ch 1:43 before any *k'* reigned over the
3: 2 daughter of Talmai *k'* of Geshur:
4:23 they dwelt with the *k'* for his work.
41 the days of Hezekiah *k'* of Judah,
5: 6 *k'* of Assyria carried away captive:
17 in the days of Jotham *k'* of Judah,
17 in the days of Jeroboam *k'* of Israel.
26 up the spirit of Pul *k'* of Assyria,
26 of Tilgath-pilneser *k'* of Assyria,
11: 2 when Saul was *k'*, thou wast he that
3 came all the elders of Israel to the *k'*
3 they anointed David *k'* over Israel,
10 with all Israel, to make him *k'*,

1Ch 12: 31 name, to come and make David k'.
38 to make David k' over all Israel:
38 were of one heart to make David k'.
14: 1 Hiram k' of Tyre sent messengers
2 had confirmed him k' over Israel,
8 was anointed k' over all Israel,
15: 29 saw k' David dancing and playing:
17: 16 David the k' came and sat before
18: 3 David smote Hadarezer k' of Zobah
5 came to help Hadarezer k' of Zobah,
9 when Tou k' of Hamath heard how
9 the host of Hadarezer k' of Zobah;
10 sent Hadoram his son to k' David,
11 k' David dedicated unto the Lord,
17 of David were chief about the k'.
19: 1 the k' of the children of Ammon
5 the k' said, Tarry at Jericho until
7 the k' of Maachah and his people;
20: 2 David took the crown of their k'
21: 3 my lord the k', are they not all my
23 let my lord the k' do that which is
24 k' David said to Ornan, Nay; but I
23: 1 made Solomon...k' over Israel.
24: 6 Levites, wrote them before the k',
31 in the presence of David the k',
25: 2 according to the order of the k'.
26: 26 David the k', and the chief fathers,
30 Lord, and in the service of the k'.
32 whom k' David made rulers over
32 to God, and affairs of the k'.
27: 1 and their officers that served the k'
24 account of the chronicles of k' David.
31 the substance which was k' David's.
28: 1 that ministered to the k' by course,
1 substance and possession of the k',
2 David the k' stood up upon his feet,
4 father to be k' over Israel for ever:
4 me to make me k' over all Israel:
29: 1 David the k' said unto all the
9 David the k' also rejoiced with great
20 and worshipped the Lord, and the k'.
22 made Solomon the son of David k'
23 sat on the throne of the Lord as k'
24 all the sons likewise of k' David,
24 themselves unto Solomon the k'.
25 been on any k' before him in Israel.
29 the acts of David the k', first and
2Ch 1: 9 hast made me k' over a people
11 over whom I have made thee k':
14 and with the k' at Jerusalem.
15 And the k' made silver and gold at
2: 3 sent to Huram the k' of Tyre,
11 Huram the k' of Tyre answered
11 he hath made thee k' over them.
12 given to David the k' a wise son,
4: 11 that he was to make for k' Solomon
16 make to k' Solomon for the house
17 plain of Jordan did the k' cast them,
5: 3 themselves unto the k' in the feast
6 k' Solomon, and all the congregation
6: 3 the k' turned his face, and blessed
7: 4 the k' and all the people offered
5 And k' Solomon offered a sacrifice
5 k' and all the people dedicated the
6 the k' had made to praise the Lord,
8: 10 the chief of k' Solomon's officers,
11 in the house of David k' of Israel,
15 the commandment of the k' unto
18 and brought them to k' Solomon.
9: 5 And she said to the k', It was a true
8 throne, to be k' for the Lord thy God:
8 therefore made he thee k' over them,
9 she gave the k' an hundred and
9 queen of Sheba gave k' Solomon.
11 the k' made of the algum trees
12 k' Solomon gave to the queen of
12 which she had brought unto the k'.
15 k' Solomon made two hundred
16 k' put them in the house of the forest
17 the k' made a great throne of ivory,
20 the drinking vessels of k' Solomon
22 k' Solomon passed all the kings of
25 cities, and with the k' at Jerusalem.
27 k' made silver in Jerusalem as
10: 1 all Israel come to make him k'.
2 the presence of Solomon the k',
6 k' Rehoboam took counsel with the
12 on the third day, as the k' bade,
13 And the k' answered them roughly;
13 k' Rehoboam forsook the counsel of
15 k' hearkened not unto the people:
16 the k' would not hearken unto them,
16 the people answered the k', saying,
18 Then k' Rehoboam sent Hadoram
18 k' Rehoboam made speed to get him
11: 3 the son of Solomon, k' of Judah,
22 for he thought to make him k'.
12: 2 in the fifth year of k' Rehoboam
2 Shishak k' of Egypt came up against
6 and the k' humbled themselves;
9 Shishak k' of Egypt came up against
10 k' Rehoboam made shields of brass,
11 k' entered into the house of the Lord,
13 k' Rehoboam strengthened himself
13: 1 the eighteenth year of k' Jeroboam
15: 16 Maachah the mother of Asa the k',
16: 1 Baasha k' of Israel came up against
1 out or come in to Asa k' of Judah.
2 and sent to Ben-hadad k' of Syria,
3 thy league with Baasha k' of Israel,
4 Ben-hadad hearkened unto k' Asa,
6 Then Asa the k' took all Judah;
7 the seer came to Asa k' of Judah,
7 thou hast relied on the k' of Syria,
7 the host of the k' of Syria escaped
17: 19 These waited on the k', beside

2Ch 17: 19 whom the k' put in the fenced cities?
18: 3 k' of Israel said unto Jehoshaphat
3 said unto Jehoshaphat k' of Judah,
4 said unto the k' of Israel, Enquire,
5 the k' of Israel gathered together
7 k' of Israel said unto Jehoshaphat,
7 said, Let not the k' say so.
8 k' of Israel called for one of his
9 the k' of Israel and Jehoshaphat
9 the k' of Judah sat either of them
11 deliver it into the hand of the k'.
12 the prophets declare good to the k'
14 come to the k', the k' said unto him,
15 the k' said to him, how many times
17 the k' of Israel said to Jehoshaphat,
19 Who shall entice Ahab k' of Israel,
25 k' of Israel said, Take ye Micaiah,
26 Thus saith the k', Put this fellow in
28 the k' of Israel and Jehoshaphat
28 the k' of Judah went up to
29 k' of Israel said unto Jehoshaphat,
29 the k' of Israel disguised himself;
30 the k' of Syria had commanded the
30 save only with the k' of Israel.
31 that they said, It is the k' of Israel.
32 that it was not the k' of Israel,
33 smote the k' of Israel between the
34 the k' of Israel stayed himself up in
19: 1 Jehoshaphat the k' of Judah
2 him, and said to k' Jehoshaphat,
20: 15 and thou k' Jehoshaphat, Thus
35 this did Jehoshaphat k' of Judah
35 himself with Ahaziah k' of Israel,
21: 2 sons of Jehoshaphat k' of Israel.
8 and made themselves a k'.
12 in the ways of Asa k' of Judah,
22: 1 made Ahaziah his...son k' in his
1 of Jehoram k' of Judah reigned.
5 the son of Ahab k' of Israel
5 to war against Hazael k' of Syria at
6 he fought with Hazael k' of Syria.
6 the son of Jehoram k' of Judah
11 the daughter of the k', took Joash
11 the daughter of k' Jehoram, the
23: 3 made a covenant with the k' in the
7 shall compass the k' round about,
7 be ye with the k' when he cometh
9 shields, that had been k' David's,
10 the temple, by the k' round about.
11 the testimony, and made him k'.
11 him, and said, God save the k'.
12 people running and praising the k',
13 k' stood at his pillar at the entering
13 princes and the trumpets by the k':
16 all the people, and between the k',
20 the k' from the house of the Lord:
20 k' upon the throne of the kingdom.
24: 6 the k' called for Jehoiada the chief,
12 the k' and Jehoiada gave it to such
14 the rest of the money before the k'
17 and made obeisance to the k'.
17 Then the k' hearkened unto them.
21 at the commandment of the k' in
22 k' remembered not the kindness
23 of them unto the k' of Damascus.
25: 3 that had killed the k' his father.
7 a man of God to him, saying, O k',
16 with him, that the k' said unto him,
17 Amaziah k' of Judah took advice,
17 the son of Jehu, k' of Israel,
18 Joash k' of Israel sent to Amaziah
18 to Amaziah k' of Judah, saying,
21 So Joash the k' of Israel went up;
21 both he and Amaziah k' of Judah,
23 And Joash the k' of Israel took
23 Amaziah k' of Judah, the son of
25 the son of Joash k' of Judah lived
25 Joash son of Jehoahaz k' of Israel
26: 1 sixteen years old, and made him k'
2 that the k' slept with his fathers.
13 to help the k' against the enemy.
18 And they withstood Uzziah the k',
21 Uzziah the k' was a leper unto the
27: 5 He fought also with the k' of the
28: 5 him into the hand of the k' of Syria;
5 into the hand of the k' of Israel,
7 Elkanah that was next to the k'.
16 k' Ahaz send unto the kings of
19 low because of Ahaz k' of Israel;
20 Tilgath-pilneser k' of Assyria came
21 out of the house of the k', and of
21 and gave it unto the k' of Assyria:
22 the Lord: this is that k' Ahaz.
29: 15 to the commandment of the k',
18 they went in to Hezekiah the k',
19 which k' Ahaz in his reign did cast
20 Then Hezekiah the k' rose early,
23 before the k' and the congregation;
24 the k' commanded that the burnt
27 ordained by David k' of Israel.
29 the k' and all that were present
30 Hezekiah the k' and the princes
30: 2 For the k' had taken counsel, and
4 the thing pleased the k' and all the
6 went with the letters from the k',
6 to the commandment of the k',
12 the commandment of the k' and of
24 Hezekiah k' of Judah did give to
26 the son of David k' of Israel their
31: 13 commandment of Hezekiah the k',
32: 1 Sennacherib k' of Assyria came,
7 nor dismayed for the k' of Assyria,
8 the words of Hezekiah k' of Judah.
9 k' of Assyria send his servants to
9 unto Hezekiah k' of Judah, and
10 saith Sennacherib, k' of Assyria,

2Ch 32: 11 of the hand of the k' of Assyria?
20 for this cause Hezekiah the k', and
21 in the camp of the k' of Assyria.
22 of Sennacherib the k' of Assyria,
23 presents to Hezekiah k' of Judah:
33: 11 of the host of the k' of Assyria,
25 had conspired against k' Amon;
25 made Josiah his son k' in his stead.
34: 16 Shaphan carried the book to the k',
16 brought the k' word back again,
18 Shaphan the scribe told the k',
18 And Shaphan read it before the k'.
19 when the k' had heard the words of
20 the k' commanded Hilkiah, and
22 they that the k' had appointed,
24 have read before the k' of Judah:
26 as for the k' of Judah, who sent you
28 So they brought the k' word again.
29 the k' sent and gathered together
30 the k' went up into the house of the
31 the k' stood in his place, and made
35: 3 son of David k' of Israel did build;
4 to the writing of David k' of Israel,
16 to the commandment of k' Josiah.
20 Necho k' of Egypt came up to fight
21 I to do with thee, thou k' of Judah?
23 the archers shot at k' Josiah;
23 k' said to his servants, Have me
36: 1 made him k' in his father's stead
3 the k' of Egypt put him down at
4 the k' of Egypt made Eliakim his
4 made Eliakim...k' over Judah
6 came up Nebuchadnezzar k' of
10 k' Nebuchadnezzar sent, and
10 made Zedekiah...k' over Judah
13 against k' Nebuchadnezzar,
17 upon them the k' of the Chaldees,
18 the treasures of the k', and of his
22 the first year of Cyrus k' of Persia,
22 up the spirit of Cyrus k' of Persia,
23 Thus saith Cyrus k' of Persia, All
Ezr 1: 1 the first year of Cyrus k' of Persia,
1 up the spirit of Cyrus k' of Persia,
2 Thus saith Cyrus k' of Persia, The
7 the k' brought forth the vessels
8 did Cyrus k' of Persia bring forth
2: 1 the k' of Babylon had carried away
3: 7 they had of Cyrus k' of Persia.
10 the ordinance of David k' of Israel.
4: 2 days of Esar-haddon k' of Assur,
3 as k' Cyrus the k' of Persia hath
5 all the days of Cyrus k' of Persia,
5 the reign of Darius k' of Persia.
7 unto Artaxerxes k' of Persia;
8 to Artaxerxes the k' in this sort:
11 him, even unto Artaxerxes the k';
12 Be it known unto the k', that the
13 Be it known now unto the k', that,
14 have we sent and certified the k';
16 We certify the k' that, if this city be
17 sent the k' an answer unto Rehum
23 of k' Artaxerxes' letter was read
24 of the reign of Darius k' of Persia.
5: 6 the river, sent unto Darius the k':
7 thus; Unto Darius the k', all peace.
8 known unto the k', that we went
11 which a great k' of Israel builded
12 Nebuchadnezzar the k' of Babylon,
13 first year of Cyrus the k' of Babylon
13 k' Cyrus made a decree to build
14 the k' take out of the temple of
17 therefore, if it seem good to the k',
17 decree was made of Cyrus the k' to
17 let the k' send his pleasure to us
6: 1 Darius the k' made a decree, and
3 In the first year of Cyrus the k' the
3 same Cyrus the k' made a decree
10 pray for the life of the k', and of his
13 that which Darius the k' had sent,
14 Darius, and Artaxerxes k' of Persia.
15 year of the reign of Darius the k',
22 heart of the k' of Assyria unto
7: 1 reign of Artaxerxes k' of Persia,
6 the k' granted him all his request,
7 seventh year of Artaxerxes the k'.
8 was in the seventh year of the k'.
11 the k' Artaxerxes gave unto Ezra
12 Artaxerxes, k' of kings, unto Ezra
14 as thou art sent of the k', and of his
15 k' and his counsellors have freely
21 And I, even I Artaxerxes the k', do
23 wrath against the realm of the k'
26 of thy God, and the law of the k',
28 mercy unto me before the k',
8: 1 in the reign of Artaxerxes the k'.
22 require of the k' a band of soldiers
22 we had spoken unto the k', saying,
25 which the k', and his counsellors,
Ne 2: 1 twentieth year of Artaxerxes the k',
1 the wine, and gave it unto the k'.
2 the k' said unto me, Why is thy
3 unto the k', Let the k' live for ever:
4 k' said unto me, For what dost thou
5 said unto the k', If it please the k',
6 the k' said unto me, (the queen also
6 it pleased the k' to send me; and I
7 said unto the k', If it please the k',
8 And the k' granted me, according
9 k' had sent captains of the army
19 ye do? will ye rebel against the k'?
5: 14 thirtieth year of Artaxerxes the k',
6: 6 thou mayest be their k', according
7 There is a k' in Judah: and now
7 reported to the k' according to
7: 6 the k' of Babylon had carried away,
9: 22 and the land of the k' of Heshbon,

Ne 9:22 and the land of Og k' of Bashan.
13: 6 and thirtieth year of Artaxerxes k'
6 of Babylon came I unto the k', and
6 days obtained I leave of the k':
26 k' of Israel sin by these things?
26 many nations were there no k' like
26 God made him k' over all Israel:
Es 1: 2 the k' Ahasuerus sat on the throne
5 the k' made a feast unto all the
7 according to the state of the k'.
8 for so the k' had appointed to all
9 which belonged to k' Ahasuerus.
10 the heart of the k' was merry with
10 the presence of Ahasuerus the k',
11 Vashti the queen before the k'
12 therefore was the k' very wroth, and
13 the k' said to the wise men, which
15 the commandment of the k'
16 Memucan answered before the k'
16 hath not done wrong to the k' only,
16 the provinces of the k' Ahasuerus.
17 The k' Ahasuerus commanded
19 If it please the k', let there go a
19 come no more before k' Ahasuerus;
19 let the k' give her royal estate unto
21 pleased the k' and the princes;
21 the k' did according to the word of
2: 1 the wrath of k' Ahasuerus was
2 young virgins sought for the k':
3 let the k' appoint officers in all the
4 maiden which pleaseth the k' be
4 the thing pleased the k'; and he
6 away with Jeconiah k' of Judah,
6 k' of Babylon had carried away.
12 was come to go in to k' Ahasuerus,
13 came every maiden unto the k';
14 she came in unto the k' no more,
14 except the k' delighted in her, and
15 was come to go in unto the k', she
16 was taken unto k' Ahasuerus into
17 the k' loved Esther above all the
18 the k' made a great feast unto all
18 according to the state of the k'.
21 to lay hand on the k' Ahasuerus.
22 Esther certified the k' thereof in
23 book of the chronicles before the k'.
3: 1 did k' Ahasuerus promote Haman
2 for the k' had so commanded
7 in the twelfth year of k' Ahasuerus,
8 And Haman said unto k' Ahasuerus,
9 If it please the k', let it be written
10 the k' took his ring from his hand,
11 k' said unto Haman, The silver is
12 in the name of k' Ahasuerus was it
15 k' and Haman sat down to drink;
4: 8 that she should go in unto the k',
11 unto the k' into the inner court,
11 k' shall hold out the golden sceptre,
11 been called to come in unto the k'
16 and so will I go in unto the k',
5: 1 the k' sat upon his royal throne in
2 k' saw Esther the queen standing
2 the k' held out to Esther the golden
3 said the k' unto her, What wilt thou,
4 If it seem good unto the k', let
4 the k' and Haman come this day
5 the k' said, Cause Haman to make
5 k' and Haman came to the banquet
6 k' said unto Esther at the banquet
8 found favour in the sight of the k',
8 please the k' to grant my petition,
8 k' and Haman come to the banquet
8 do to morrow as the king hath said.
11 wherein the k' had promoted him,
11 the princes and servants of the k'.
12 did let no man come in with the k'
12 I invited unto her also with the k'.
14 to morrow speak thou unto the k'
14 then go thou in merrily with the k'
6: 1 On that night could not the k' sleep,
1 and they were read before the k'.
2 to lay hand on the k' Ahasuerus.
3 k' said, What honour and dignity
4 And the k' said, Who is in the court?
4 speak unto the k' to hang Mordecai
5 And the k' said, Let him come in.
6 the k' said unto him, What shall be
6 whom the k' delighteth to honour?
6 would the k' delight to do honour
7 Haman answered the k', For the
7 whom the k' delighteth to honour,
8 brought which the k' useth to wear,
8 the horse that the k' rideth upon,
9 whom the k' delighteth to honour,
9 whom the k' delighteth to honour.
10 the k' said to Haman, Make haste,
11 whom the k' delighteth to honour.
7: 1 the k' and Haman came to banquet
2 the k' said again unto Esther on
3 have found favour in thy sight, O k',
3 and if it please the k', let my life be
5 the k' Ahasuerus answered and said
6 Haman was afraid before the k' and
7 k' arising from the banquet of wine
7 determined against him by the k'.
8 the k' returned out of the palace
8 said the k', Will he force the queen
9 chamberlains, said before the k',
9 who had spoken good for the k',
9 Then the k' said, Hang him thereon.
8: 1 did the k' Ahasuerus give the house
1 And Mordecai came before the k';
2 the k' took off his ring, which he
3 spake yet again before the k',
4 the k' held out the golden sceptre
4 arose, and stood before the k',
Es 8: 5 If it please the k', and if I have
5 the thing seem right before the k',
7 the k' Ahasuerus said unto Esther
10 he wrote in the k' Ahasuerus' name,
11 Wherein the k' granted the Jews
12 the provinces of the k' Ahasuerus,
15 went out from the presence of the k'
9: 2 the provinces of the k' Ahasuerus,
3 officers of the k', helped the Jews;
11 palace was brought before the k'.
12 the k' said unto Esther the queen,
13 If it please the k', let it be granted
14 the k' commanded it so to be done:
20 the provinces of the k' Ahasuerus,
25 when Esther came before the k', he
10: 1 And the k' Ahasuerus laid a tribute
2 whereunto the k' advanced him,
3 Jew was next unto k' Ahasuerus,
Job 15:24 him, as a k' ready to the battle.
18:14 shall bring him to the k' of terrors.
29:25 chief, and dwelt as a k' in the army,
34:18 fit to say to a k', Thou art wicked?
41:34 a k' over all the children of pride.
Ps 2: 6 Yet have I set my k' upon my holy
5: 2 voice of my cry, my K', and my God:
10:16 The Lord is K' for ever and ever:
18:50 deliverance giveth he to his k';
20: 9 let the k' hear us when we call.
21: 1 The k' shall joy in thy strength, O
7 For the k' trusteth in the Lord,
24: 7 and the K' of glory shall come in.
8 Who is this K' of glory? The Lord
9 and the K' of glory shall come in.
10 Who is this K' of glory? The Lord
10 Lord of hosts, he is the K' of glory.
29:10 yea, the Lord sitteth K' for ever.
33:16 no k' saved by the multitude of an
44: 4 Thou art my K', O God: command
45: 1 which I have made touching the k':
11 the k' greatly desire thy beauty:
14 be brought unto the k' in raiment
47: 2 he is a great K' over all the earth.
6 praises unto our K', sing praises.
7 For God is the K' of all the earth:
48: 2 the north, the city of the great K'.
63:11 But the k' shall rejoice in God;
68:24 the goings of my God, my K', in the
72: 1 Give the k' thy judgments, O God,
74:12 For God is my K' of old, working
84: 3 O Lord of hosts, my K', and my God.
89:18 and the Holy One of Israel is our k'.
95: 3 God, and a great K' above all gods.
98: 6 joyful noise before the Lord, the K'.
105:20 The k' sent and loosed him; even
135:11 Sihon k' of the Amorites, and Og k'
136:19 Sihon k' of the Amorites: for his
20 And Og the k' of Bashan: for his
145: 1 I will extol thee, my God, O k'; and
149: 2 children of Zion be joyful in their K'.
Pr 1: 1 the son of David, k' of Israel;
16:10 sentence is in the lips of the k':
14 The wrath of a k' is as messengers
20: 2 The fear of a k' is as the roaring of
8 A k' that sitteth in the throne of
26 A wise k' scattereth the wicked,
28 Mercy and truth preserve the k':
22:11 of his lips the k' shall be his friend.
24:21 son, fear thou the Lord and the k':
25: 1 of Hezekiah k' of Judah copied out.
5 away the wicked from before the k',
6 thyself in the presence of the k',
29: 4 The k' by judgment establisheth
14 k' that faithfully judgeth the poor,
30:27 The locusts have no k', yet go they
31 k' against whom there is no rising
31: 1 words of k' Lemuel, the prophecy
Ec 1: 1 the son of David, k' in Jerusalem.
12 I the Preacher was k' over Israel in
2:12 man do that cometh after the k'?
4:13 wise child than an old and foolish k',
5: 9 the k' himself is served by the field.
8: 4 Where the word of a k' is, there is
9:14 there came a great k' against it,
10:16 thee, O land, when thy k' is a child,
17 when thy k' is the son of nobles,
20 Curse not the k', no not in thy
Ca 1: 4 the k' hath brought me into his
12 While the k' sitteth at his table,
3: 9 K' Solomon made himself a chariot
11 behold k' Solomon with the crown
7: 5 the k' is held in the galleries.
Isa 6: 1 In the year that k' Uzziah died I saw
5 eyes have seen the K', the Lord of
7: 1 the son of Uzziah, k' of Judah,
1 Rezin the k' of Syria, and Pekah
1 the son of Remaliah, k' of Israel,
6 and set a k' in the midst of it, even
17 Judah; even the k' of Assyria.
20 the river, by the k' of Assyria,
8: 4 taken away before the k' of Assyria.
7 k' of Assyria, and all his glory:
21 and curse their k' and their God,
10:12 the stout heart of the k' of Assyria,
14: 4 proverb against the k' of Babylon,
28 In the year that k' Ahaz died was
19: 4 and a fierce k' shall rule over them,
20: 1 Sargon the k' of Assyria sent him,)
4 So shall the k' of Assyria lead away
6 be delivered from the k' of Assyria:
23:15 according to the days of one k':
30:33 old; yea, for the k' it is prepared;
32: 1 a k' shall reign in righteousness,
33:17 eyes shall see the k' in his beauty:
22 is our lawgiver, the Lord is our k';
36: 1 the fourteenth year of k' Hezekiah,
1 Sennacherib k' of Assyria came up
Isa 36: 2 the k' of Assyria sent Rabshakeh
2 unto k' Hezekiah with a great army.
4 saith the great k', the k' of Assyria,
6 so is Pharaoh k' of Egypt to all that
8 to my master the k' of Assyria, and
13 of the great k', the k' of Assyria.
14 Thus saith the k', Let not Hezekiah
15 into the hand of the k' of Assyria.
16 thus saith the k' of Assyria, Make
18 out of the hand of the k' of Assyria?
37: 1 when k' Hezekiah heard it, that he
4 k' of Assyria his master hath sent
5 the servants of k' Hezekiah came
6 servants of the k' of Assyria have
8 the k' of Assyria warring against
9 concerning Tirhakah k' of Ethiopia,
10 ye speak to Hezekiah k' of Judah,
10 into the hand of the k' of Assyria.
13 k' of Hamath, and the k' of Arphad,
13 and the k' of the city of Sepharvaim,
21 against Sennacherib k' of Assyria:
33 Lord concerning the k' of Assyria,
37 Sennacherib k' of Assyria departed,
38: 6 out of the hand of the k' of Assyria:
9 writing of Hezekiah k' of Judah,
39: 1 Baladan, k' of Babylon, sent letters
3 the prophet unto k' Hezekiah,
7 in the palace of the k' of Babylon.
41:21 reasons, saith the k' of Jacob.
43:15 One, the creator of Israel, your K'.
44: 6 saith the Lord the K' of Israel,
57: 9 wentest to the k' with ointment,
Jer 1: 2 Josiah the son of Amon k' of Judah,
3, 3 the son of Josiah k' of Judah,
3: 6 unto me in the days of Josiah the k',
4: 9 that the heart of the k' shall perish,
8:19 Lord in Zion? is not her k' in her?
10: 7 not fear thee, O K' of nations?
10 living God, and an everlasting k':
13:18 Say unto the k' and to the queen,
15: 4 the son of Hezekiah k' of Judah,
20: 4 into the hand of the k' of Babylon,
21: 1 when k' Zedekiah sent unto him
2 k' of Babylon maketh war against
4 ye fight against the k' of Babylon,
7 I will deliver Zedekiah k' of Judah,
7 of Nebuchadrezzar k' of Babylon,
10 into the hand of the k' of Babylon,
11 the house of the k' of Judah, say,
22: 1 to the house of the k' of Judah,
2 the word of the Lord, O k' of Judah,
11 the son of Josiah k' of Judah,
18 the son of Josiah k' of Judah;
24 the son of Jehoiakim k' of Judah
25 of Nebuchadrezzar k' of Babylon,
23: 5 and a K' shall reign and prosper,
24: 1 k' of Babylon had carried away
1 the son of Jehoiakim k' of Judah,
8 I give Zedekiah the k' of Judah,
25: 1 the son of Josiah k' of Judah,
1 of Nebuchadrezzar k' of Babylon;
3 Josiah the son of Amon k' of Judah,
9 the k' of Babylon, my servant, and
11 shall serve the k' of Babylon seventy
12 I will punish the k' of Babylon, and
19 Pharaoh k' of Egypt, and his
26 the k' of Sheshach shall drink after
26: 1 son of Josiah k' of Judah came this
18 the days of Hezekiah k' of Judah,
19 Did Hezekiah k' of Judah and all
21 when Jehoiakim the k', with all his
21 the k' sought to put him to death:
22 the k' sent men into Egypt, namely,
23 brought him unto Jehoiakim the k';
27: 1 the son of Josiah k' of Judah came
3 send them to the k' of Edom, and to
3 and to the k' of Moab, and to the
3 and to the k' of the Ammonites,
3 Ammonites, and to the k' of Tyrus,
3 and to the k' of Zidon, by the hand
3 unto Zedekiah k' of Judah;
6, 8 Nebuchadnezzar...k' of Babylon,
8 under the yoke of the k' of Babylon,
9 shall not serve the k' of Babylon:
11 under the yoke of the k' of Babylon,
12 spake also to Zedekiah k' of Judah
12 under the yoke of the k' of Babylon,
13 will not serve the k' of Babylon?
14 shall not serve the k' of Babylon:
17 serve the k' of Babylon, and live:
18 and in the house of the k' of Judah,
20 k' of Babylon took not, when he
20 k' of Judah from Jerusalem to
21 in the house of the k' of Judah and
28: 1 the reign of Zedekiah k' of Judah,
2 the yoke of the k' of Babylon.
3 k' of Babylon took away from this
4 k' of Judah, with all the captives of
4 break the yoke of the k' of Babylon.
11 of Nebuchadnezzar k' of Babylon
14 Nebuchadnezzar k' of Babylon;
29: 2 Jeconiah the k', and the queen, and
3 (whom Zedekiah k' of Judah sent
3 to Nebuchadnezzar k' of Babylon)
16 k' that sitteth upon the throne of
21 of Nebuchadrezzar k' of Babylon;
22 whom the k' of Babylon roasted in
30: 9 Lord their God, and David their k',
32: 1 tenth year of Zedekiah k' of Judah,
2 king of Babylon's army besieged
2 was in the k' of Judah's house.
3 Zedekiah k' of Judah had shut him
3 into the hand of the k' of Babylon,
4 k' of Judah shall not escape out of
4 into the hand of the k' of Babylon,
28 of Nebuchadrezzar k' of Babylon,

Jer 32: 36 into the hand of the k' of Babylon
34: 1 k' of Babylon, and all his army,
2 and speak to Zedekiah k' of Judah,
2 into the hand of the k' of Babylon,
3 behold the eyes of the k' of Babylon,
4 the Lord, O Zedekiah k' of Judah;
6 words unto Zedekiah k' of Judah in
7 the k' of Babylon's army fought
8 k' Zedekiah had made a covenant
21 And Zedekiah k' of Judah and his
21 hand of the k' of Babylon's army,
35: 1 the son of Josiah k' of Judah,
11 k' of Babylon came up into the land,
36: 1, 9 the son of Josiah k' of Judah,
16 We will surely tell the k' of all these
20 they went in to the k' into the court,
20 all the words in the ears of the k'.
21 the k' sent Jehudi to fetch the roll:
21 Jehudi read it in the ears of the k',
21 princes which stood beside the k'.
22 Now the k' sat in the winterhouse
24 the k', nor any of his servants that
25 intercession to the k' that he would
26 the k' commanded Jerahmeel the
27 that the k' had burned the roll,
28 the k' of Judah hath burned.
29 shalt say to Jehoiakim k' of Judah,
29 The k' of Babylon shall certainly
30 the Lord of Jehoiakim k' of Judah;
32 k' of Judah had burned in the fire:
37: 1 And k' Zedekiah the son of Josiah
1 Nebuchadrezzar k' of Babylon
1 made k' in the land of Judah.
3 Zedekiah the k' sent Jehucal the
7 Thus shall ye say to the k' of Judah,
17 Zedekiah the k' sent, and took him
17 and the k' asked him secretly in his
17 into the hand of the k' of Babylon.
18 Jeremiah said unto k' Zedekiah,
19 The k' of Babylon shall not come
20 now, I pray thee, O my lord the k':
21 Zedekiah the k' commanded that
38: 3 hand of the k' of Babylon's army,
4 the princes said unto the k', We
5 Zedekiah the k' said, Behold, he is in
5 for the k' is not he that can do any
7 the k' then sitting in the gate of
8 house, and spake to the k', saying,
9 My lord the k', these men have done
10 the k' commanded Ebed-melech
11 went into the house of the k' under
14 Then Zedekiah the k' sent, and took
14 the k' said unto Jeremiah, I will ask
16 Zedekiah the k' sware secretly unto
17 unto the k' of Babylon's princes,
18 forth to the k' of Babylon's princes,
19 Zedekiah the k' said unto Jeremiah,
22 are left in the k' of Judah's house
22 forth to the k' of Babylon's princes,
23 by the hand of the k' of Babylon:
25 what thou hast said unto the k',
25 also what the k' said unto thee:
26 my supplication before the k',
27 words that the k' had commanded.
39: 1 ninth year of Zedekiah k' of Judah,
1 Nebuchadrezzar k' of Babylon
3 princes of the k' of Babylon came
3 of the princes of the k' of Babylon.
4 Zedekiah the k' of Judah saw them,
5 to Nebuchadnezzar k' of Babylon
6 the k' of Babylon slew the sons of
6 the k' of Babylon slew all the nobles
11 Nebuchadrezzar k' of Babylon gave
13 and all the k' of Babylon's princes;
40: 5 k' of Babylon hath made governor
7 k' of Babylon had made Gedaliah
9 land, and serve the k' of Babylon,
11 k' of Babylon had left a remnant of
14 Baalis the k' of the Ammonites
41: 1 the princes of the k', even ten men
2 k' of Babylon had made governor
9 which Asa the k' had made for fear
9 for fear of Baasha k' of Israel
18 the k' of Babylon made governor
42: 11 Be not afraid of the k' of Babylon,
43: 10 Nebuchadrezzar the k' of Babylon,
44: 30 give Pharaoh-hophra k' of Egypt
30 Zedekiah k' of Judah into the hand
30 of Nebuchadrezzar k' of Babylon,
45: 1 the son of Josiah k' of Judah,
46: 2 army of Pharaoh-necho k' of Egypt,
2 Nebuchadrezzar k' of Babylon
2 the son of Josiah k' of Judah.
13 k' of Babylon should come and
17 Pharaoh k' of Egypt is but a noise;
18 As I live, saith the K', whose name
26 of Nebuchadrezzar k' of Babylon,
48: 15 the K', whose name is the Lord of
49: 1 why then doth their k' inherit Gad,
3 their k' shall go into captivity, and
28 k' of Babylon shall smite,
30 k' of Babylon hath taken counsel
34 the reign of Zedekiah k' of Judah,
38 thence the k' and the princes,
50: 17 k' of Assyria hath devoured him;
17 k' of Babylon hath broken his bones.
18 I will punish the k' of Babylon and
18 I have punished the k' of Assyria.
43 The k' of Babylon hath heard the
51: 31 shew the k' of Babylon that his city
34 the k' of Babylon hath devoured me,
57 the K', whose name is the Lord of
59 went with Zedekiah the k' of Judah
52: 3 rebelled against the k' of Babylon.
4 k' of Babylon came, he and all his
5 the eleventh year of k' Zedekiah.

Jer 52: 8 the Chaldeans pursued after the k',
9 they took the k', and carried him up
9 unto the k' of Babylon to Riblah in
10 the k' of Babylon slew the sons of
11 k' of Babylon bound him in chains,
12 of Nebuchadrezzar k' of Babylon,
12 which served the k' of Babylon,
15 that fell to the k' of Babylon, and
20 k' Solomon had made in the house
26 brought them to the k' of Babylon
27 the k' of Babylon smote them, and
31 captivity of Jehoiachin k' of Judah,
31 Evil-merodach k' of Babylon, in the
31 the head of Jehoiachin k' of Judah,
34 diet given him of the k' of Babylon,
La 2: 6 of his anger the k' and the priest.
9 her k' and her princes are among
Eze 1: 2 year of k' Jehoiachin's captivity,
7: 27 The k' shall mourn, and the prince
17: 12 k' of Babylon is come to Jerusalem,
12 and hath taken the k' thereof, and
16 surely in the place where the k'
16 dwelleth that made him k' whose
19: 9 brought him to the k' of Babylon:
21: 19 the sword of the k' of Babylon may
21 k' of Babylon stood at the parting
24: 2 k' of Babylon set himself against
26: 7 k' of Babylon, a k' of kings,
28: 12 a lamentation upon the k' of Tyrus,
29: 2 face against Pharaoh k' of Egypt,
3 against thee, Pharaoh k' of Egypt,
18 k' of Babylon caused his army to
19 Nebuchadrezzar k' of Babylon;
30: 10 of Nebuchadrezzar k' of Babylon.
21 the arm of Pharaoh k' of Egypt;
22 I am against Pharaoh k' of Egypt,
24, 25 the arms of the k' of Babylon,
25 into the hand of the k' of Babylon,
31: 2 speak unto Pharaoh k' of Egypt,
32: 2 lamentation for Pharaoh k' of Egypt,
11 The sword of the k' of Babylon shall
37: 22 and one k' shall be k' to them all:
24 David my servant shall be k' over
Da 1: 1 the reign of Jehoiakim k' of Judah
1 Nebuchadnezzar k' of Babylon
2 Lord gave Jehoiakim k' of Judah
3 k' spake unto Ashpenaz the master
5 k' appointed them a daily provision
5 they might stand before the k'.
10 unto Daniel, I fear my lord the k',
10 me endanger my head to the k'.
18 k' had said he should bring them in,
19 the k' communed with them; and
19 therefore stood they before the k'.
20 the k' enquired of them, he found
21 even unto the first year of k' Cyrus.
2: 2 Then the k' commanded to call the
2 for to shew the k' his dreams.
2 they came and stood before the k'.
3 k' said unto them, I have dreamed
4 Then spake the Chaldeans to the k'
4 O k', live for ever: tell thy servants
5 The k' answered and said to the
7 k' tell his servants the dream, and
8 The k' answered and said, I know of
10 Chaldeans answered before the k',
10 there is no k', lord, nor ruler,
11 is a rare thing that the k' requireth,
11 other that can shew it before the k',
12 For this cause the k' was angry and
15 is the decree so hasty from the k'?
16 desired of the k' that he would give
16 shew the k' the interpretation.
24 k' had ordained to destroy the wise
24 bring me in before the k', and I will
24 shew unto the k' the interpretation.
25 brought in Daniel before the k' in
25 will make known unto the k' the
26 The k' answered and said to Daniel,
27 answered in the presence of the k',
27 secret which the k' hath demanded
27 the soothsayers, shew unto the k';
28 known to the k' Nebuchadnezzar
29 As for thee, O k', thy thoughts
30 known the interpretation to the k',
31 Thou, O k', sawest, and behold a
36 interpretation thereof before the k'.
37 Thou, O k', art a k' of kings: for
45 known to the k' what shall come
46 the k' Nebuchadnezzar fell upon his
47 The k' answered unto Daniel, and
48 the k' made Daniel a great man,
49 Then Daniel requested of the k',
49 but Daniel sat in the gate of the k'.
3: 1 the k' made an image of gold,
2 Then Nebuchadnezzar the k' sent to
2 Nebuchadnezzar the k' had set up.
3 Nebuchadnezzar the k' had set up;
5 Nebuchadnezzar the k' hath set up:
7 Nebuchadnezzar the k' had set up.
9 They spake and said to the k'
9 Nebuchadnezzar, O k', live for ever.
10 Thou, O k', hast made a decree, that
12 men, O k', have not regarded thee:
13 brought these men before the k'.
16 said to the k', O Nebuchadnezzar,
17 deliver us out of thine hand, O k'.
18 if not, be it known unto thee, O k',
24 the k' was astonied, and rose up
24 and said unto the k', True, O k'.
30 k' promoted Shadrach, Meshach,
4: 1 Nebuchadnezzar the k', unto all
18 This dream I k' Nebuchadnezzar
19 k' spake, and said, Belteshazzar,
22 It is thou, O k', that art grown and
23 And whereas the k' saw a watcher

Da 4: 24 This is the interpretation, O k',
24 which is come upon my lord the k':
27 Wherefore, O k', let my counsel be
28 came upon the k' Nebuchadnezzar.
30 The k' spake, and said, Is not this
31 O k' Nebuchadnezzar, to thee it is
37 extol and honour the K' of heaven,
5: 1 Belshazzar the k' made a great
2 that the k', and his princes, his
3 and the k', and his princes, and
5 the k' saw the part of the hand that
7 The k' cried aloud to bring in the
7 the k' spake, and said to the wise
8 known to the k' the interpretation
9 was k' Belshazzar greatly troubled,
10 by reason of the words of the k'
10 and the queen spake and said, O k',
11 the k' Nebuchadnezzar thy father,
11 k', I say, thy father, made master
12 whom the k' named Belteshazzar:
13 Daniel brought in before the k'.
13 the k' spake and said unto Daniel,
13 k' my father brought out of Jewry?
17 answered and said before the k',
17 I will read the writing unto the k',
18 O thou k', the most high God gave
30 was...the k' of the Chaldeans slain.
6: 2 and the k' should have no damage.
3 the k' thought to set him over the
6 assembled together to the k',
6 unto him, K' Darius, live for ever.
7 save of thee, O k', he shall be cast
8 Now, O k', establish the decree, and
9 k' Darius signed the writing and
12 spake before the k' concerning the
12 save of thee, O k', shall be cast into
12 k' answered and said, The thing is
13 and said before the k', That Daniel,
13 regardeth not thee, O k', nor the
14 Then the k', when he heard these
15 these men assembled unto the k',
15 and said unto the k', Know, O k',
15 statute which the k' establisheth
16 k' commanded, and they brought
16 the k' spake and said unto Daniel,
17 the k' sealed it with his own signet,
18 Then the k' went to his palace, and
19 Then the k' arose very early in the
20 the k' spake and said to Daniel, O
21 unto the k', O k', live for ever.
22 before thee, O k', have I done no
23 was the k' exceeding glad for him
24 k' commanded, and they brought
25 k' Darius wrote unto all people,
7: 1 year of Belshazzar k' of Babylon
8: 1 year of the reign of k' Belshazzar
21 the rough goat is the k' of Grecia:
21 is between his eyes is the first k'.
23 the full, a k' of fierce countenance,
9: 1 was made k' over the realm of the
10: 1 third year of Cyrus k' of Persia
11: 3 And a mighty k' shall stand up, that
5 the k' of the south shall be strong,
6 shall come to the k' of the north
7 the fortress of the k' of the north,
8 more years than the k' of the north.
9 k' of the south shall come into his
11 the k' of the south shall be moved
11 him, even with the k' of the north:
13 For the k' of the north shall return,
14 up against the k' of the south:
15 k' of the north shall come, and cast
25 against the k' of the south with a
25 k' of the south shall be stirred up
36 k' shall do according to his will;
40 the k' of the south push at him:
40 k' of the north shall come against
Ho 1: 1 the son of Joash, k' of Israel.
3: 4 shall abide many days without a k',
5 Lord their God, and David their k';
5: 1 and give ye ear, O house of the k';
13 the Assyrian, and sent to k' Jareb:
7: 3 the k' glad with their wickedness,
5 In the day of our k' the princes
8: 10 for the burden of the k' of princes.
10: 3 We have no k', because we feared
3 what then should a k' do to us?
6 Assyria for a present to k' Jareb:
7 her k' is cut off as the foam upon
15 shall the k' of Israel utterly be cut
11: 5 Assyrian shall be his k', because
13: 10 I will be thy k': where is any other
10 saidst, Give me a k' and princes?
11 I gave thee a k' in mine anger, and
Am 1: 1 In the days of Uzziah k' of Judah,
1 the son of Joash k' of Israel,
15 their k' shall go into captivity, he
2: 1 burned the bones of the k' of Edom
7: 10 sent to Jeroboam k' of Israel,
Jon 3: 6 word came unto the k' of Nineveh,
7 the decree of the k' and his nobles,
Mic 2: 13 and their k' shall pass before them,
4: 9 no k' in thee? is thy counsellor
6: 5 what Balak k' of Moab consulted,
Na 3: 18 shepherds slumber, O k' of Assyria:
Zep 1: 1 the son of Amon, k' of Judah.
3: 15 the k' of Israel, even the Lord, is in
Hag 1: 1 in the second year of Darius the k',
15 in the second year of Darius the k'.
Zec 7: 1 pass in the fourth year of k' Darius,
9: 5 the k' shall perish from Gaza, and
9 behold, thy K' cometh unto thee:
11: 6 hand, and into the hand of his k':
14: 5 the days of Uzziah k' of Judah:
9 Lord shall be k' over all the earth:
16 to worship the K', the Lord of hosts,

Zec 14:17 unto Jerusalem to worship the K',
Mal 1:14 I am a great K', saith the Lord of
M't 1: 6 And Jesse begat David the k';
6 and David the k' begat Solomon
2: 1 Judæa in the days of Herod the k',
2 is he that is born K' of the Jews?
3 When Herod the k' had heard these
9 When they had heard the k', they
5:35 for it is the city of the great K'.
14: 9 the k' was sorry: nevertheless for
18:23 of heaven likened unto a certain k',
21: 5 Behold, thy K' cometh unto thee,
22: 2 of heaven is like unto a certain k',
7 when the k' heard thereof, he was
11 the k' came in to see the guests,
13 Then said the k' to the servants,
25:34 Then shall the K' say unto them
40 the K' shall answer and say unto
27:11 Art thou the K' of the Jews?
29 him, saying, Hail, K' of the Jews!
37 This Is Jesus The K' Of The Jews.
42 If he be the K' of Israel, let him
M'r 6:14 And k' Herod heard of him; (for his
22 him, the k' said unto the damsel,
25 straightway with haste unto the k',
26 the k' was exceeding sorry; yet for
27 the k' sent an executioner,
15: 2 him, Art thou the K' of the Jews?
9 release unto you the K' of the Jews?
12 whom ye call the K' of the Jews?
18 salute him, Hail, K' of the Jews?
26 written over, The K' Of The Jews.
32 Let Christ the K' of Israel descend
Lu 1: 5 the days of Herod, the k' of Judæa,
14:31 Or what k', going to make war
31 against another k', sitteth not down
19:38 Blessed be the K' that cometh in
23: 2 that he himself is Christ a K'.
3 Art thou the K' of the Jews?
37 If thou be the K' of the Jews, save
38 This Is The K' Of The Jews.
Joh 1:49 of God; thou art the K' of Israel.
6:15 take him by force, to make him a k',
12:13 Blessed is the K' of Israel that
15 thy K' cometh, sitting on an ass's
18:33 him, Art thou the K' of the Jews?
37 said unto him, Art thou a k' then?
37 Thou sayest that I am a k'. To this
39 unto you the K' of the Jews?
19: 3 said, Hail, K' of the Jews! and they
12 maketh himself a k' speaketh
14 unto the Jews, Behold your K'!
15 unto them, Shall I crucify your K'?
15 answered, We have no k' but Cæsar.
19 Jesus Of Nazareth The K' Of The
21 Write not, The K' of the Jews;
21 that he said, I am K' of the Jews.
Ac 7:10 the sight of Pharaoh k' of Egypt;
18 Till another k' arose, which knew
12: 1 Herod the k' stretched forth his
13:21 And afterward they desired a k':
22 unto them David to be their k';
17: 7 that there is another k', one Jesus.
25:13 days k' Agrippa and Bernice came
14 declared Paul's cause unto the k',
24 Festus said, K' Agrippa, and all
26 specially before thee, O k' Agrippa,
26: 2 I think myself happy, k' Agrippa,
7 For which hope's sake, k' Agrippa,
13 At midday, O k', I saw in the way a
19 O k' Agrippa, I was not disobedient
26 For the k' knoweth of these things,
27 K' Agrippa, believest thou the
30 the k' rose up, and the governor,
2Co 11:32 governor under Aretas the k' kept
1Ti 1:17 Now unto the K' eternal, immortal,
6:15 K' of kings, and Lord of lords;
Heb 7: 1 Melchisedec, k' of Salem, priest
2 interpretation K' of righteousness,
2 K' of Salem, which is, K' of peace;
11:27 not fearing the wrath of the k': for
1Pe 2:13 whether it be to the k', as supreme;
17 Fear God. Honour the k'.
Re 9:11 they had a k' over them, which is
15: 3 are thy ways, thou K' of saints.
17:14 is Lord of lords, and K' of kings:
19:16 K' Of Kings, And Lord Of Lords.
kingdom See also KINGDOMS.
Ge 10:10 the beginning of his k' was Babel,
20: 9 on me and on my k' a great sin?
Ex 19: 6 ye shall be unto me a k' of priests,
Nu 24: 7 Agag, and his k' shall be exalted.
32:33 k' of Sihon king of the Amorites,
33 and the k' of Og king of Bashan,
De 3: 4 of Argob, the k' of Og in Bashan.
10 cities of the k' of Og in Bashan.
13 being the k' of Og, gave I unto the
17:18 sitteth upon the throne of his k',
20 he may prolong his days in his k',
Jos 13:12 All the k' of Og in Bashan, which
21 k' of Sihon king of the Amorites,
27 the k' of Sihon king of Heshbon,
30 all the k' of Og king of Bashan,
31 cities of the k' of Og in Bashan,
1Sa 10:16 But of the matter of the k', whereof
25 the people the manner of the k',
11:14 to Gilgal, and renew the k' there.
13:13 Lord have established thy k' upon
14 But now thy k' shall not continue:
14:47 So Saul took the k' over Israel,
15:28 The Lord hath rent the k' of Israel
18: 8 can he have more but the k'?
20:31 not be established, nor thy k'.
24:20 k' of Israel shall be established
28:17 hath rent the k' out of thine hand,
2Sa 3:10 the k' from the house of Saul,
2Sa 3:28 I and my k' are guiltless before the
5:12 he had exalted his k' for his people
7:12 bowels, and I will establish his k'.
13 I will stablish the throne of his k'
16 and thy k' shall be established for
16: 3 restore me the k' of my father.
8 the k' into the hand of Absalom
1Ki 1:46 sitteth on the throne of the k'.
2:12 and his k' was established greatly.
15 Thou knowest that the k' was mine,
15 howbeit the k' is turned about,
22 ask for him the k' also; for he is
46 k' was established in the hand of
9: 5 the throne of thy k' upon Israel
10:20 was not the like made in any k'.
11:11 I will surely rend the k' from thee,
13 I will not rend away all the k'; but
31 I will rend the k' out of the hand
34 will not take the whole k' out of his
35 I will take the k' out of his son's
12:21 bring the k' again to Rehoboam
26 the k' return to the house of David
14: 8 rent the k' away from the house
18:10 God liveth, there is no nation or k',
10 he took an oath of the k' and
21: 7 thou now govern the k' of Israel?
2Ki 14: 5 the k' was confirmed in his hand,
15:19 him to confirm the k' in his hand.
1Ch 10:14 turned the k' unto David the son
11:10 themselves with him in his k',
12:23 to turn the k' of Saul to him,
14: 2 for his k' was lifted up on high,
16:20 from one k' to another people;
17:11 sons; and I will establish his k'.
14 mine house and in my k' for ever:
22:10 I will establish the throne of his k'
28: 5 the throne of the k' of the Lord
7 I will establish his k' for ever, if
29:11 thine is the k', O Lord, and thou
2Ch 1: 1 David was strengthened in his k',
2: 1 the Lord, and an house for his k'.
12 for the Lord, and an house for his k'.
7:18 will I stablish the throne of thy k',
9:19 was not the like made in any k'.
11: 1 bring the k' again to Rehoboam.
17 strengthened the k' of Judah,
12: 1 Rehoboam had established the k',
13: 5 gave the k' over Israel to David
8 withstand the k' of the Lord in the
14: 5 and the k' was quiet before him.
17: 5 the Lord stablished the k' in his
21: 3 the k' gave he to Jehoram; because
4 Jehoram was risen up to the k' of
22: 9 had no power to keep still the k'.
23:20 the king upon the throne of the k'.
25: 3 when the k' was established to him,
29:21 goats, for a sin offering for the k',
32:15 no god of any nation or k' was able
33:13 again to Jerusalem into his k'.
36:20 until the reign of the k' of Persia:
22 proclamation throughout all his k',
Ezr 1: 1 proclamation throughout all his k',
Ne 9:35 have not served thee in their k',
Es 1: 2 sat on the throne of his k', which
4 shewed the riches of his glorious k'
14 and which sat the first in the k';)
2: 3 in all the provinces of his k', that
3: 6 the whole k' of Ahasuerus,
8 people in all the provinces of thy k';
4:14 art come to the k' for such a time
5: 3 even given thee to the half of the k'.
6 even to the half of the k' it shall be
7: 2 performed, even to the half of the k'.
9:30 twenty and seven provinces of the k'
Ps 22:28 For the k' is the Lord's: and he
45: 6 sceptre of thy k' is a right sceptre.
103:19 heavens; and his k' ruleth over all.
105:13 from one k' to another people;
145:11 shall speak of the glory of thy k',
12 and the glorious majesty of his k'.
13 Thy k' is an everlasting k', and
Ec 4:14 is born in his k' becometh poor.
Isa 9: 7 upon his k', to order it, and to
17: 3 the k' from Damascus, and the
19: 2 city against city, and k' against k'.
34:12 call the nobles thereof to the k',
60:12 k' that will not serve thee shall
Jer 18: 7 concerning a k', to pluck up, and
9 concerning a k', to build and to
27: 8 nation and k' which will not serve
La 2: 2 hath polluted the princes and the k'
Eze 16:13 and thou didst prosper into a k'.
17:14 That the k' might be base, that it
29:14 and they shall be there a base k'.
Da 2:37 of heaven hath given thee a k',
39 shall arise another k' inferior to
39 and another third k' of brass, which
40 fourth k' shall be strong as iron:
41 part of iron, the k' shall be divided;
42 so the k' shall be partly strong,
44 shall the God of heaven set up a k',
44 the k' shall not be left to other
4: 3 his k' is an everlasting k', and his
17 most High ruleth in the k' of men,
18 the wise men of my k' are not able
25 most High ruleth in the k' of men,
26 thy k' shall be sure unto thee, after
29 in the palace of the k' of Babylon.
30 I have built for the house of the k'
31 The k' is departed from thee.
32 most High ruleth in the k' of men,
34 his k' is from generation to
36 for the glory of my k', mine honour
36 and I was established in my k',
5: 7 shall be the third ruler in the k'.
11 There is a man in thy k', in whom
Da 5:16 shalt be the third ruler in the k'.
18 Nebuchadnezzar thy father a k',
21 high God ruled in the k' of men,
26 Mene; God hath numbered thy k',
28 Peres; Thy k' is divided, and given
29 should be the third ruler in the k'.
31 And Darius the Median took the k',
6: 1 pleased Darius to set over the k'
1 which should be over the whole k';
4 against Daniel concerning the k';
7 All the presidents of the k', the
26 That in every dominion of my k'
26 his k' that which shall not be
7:14 him dominion, and glory, and a k',
14 his k' that which shall not be
18 of the most High shall take the k',
18 possess the k' for ever, even for ever
22 that the saints possessed the k'.
23 shall be the fourth k' upon earth,
24 out of this k' are ten kings that shall
27 And the k' and dominion, and the
27 greatness of the k' under the whole
27 High, whose k' is an everlasting k',
8:23 And in the latter time of their k',
10:13 But the prince of the k' of Persia
11: 4 stand up, his k' shall be broken,
4 for his k' shall be plucked up, even
9 of the south shall come into his k',
17 with the strength of his whole k',
20 of taxes in the glory of the k':
21 shall not give the honour of the k':
21 and obtain the k' by flatteries.
Ho 1: 4 cease the k' of the house of Israel.
Am 9: 8 Lord God are upon the sinful k',
Ob 21 and the k' shall be the Lord's.
Mic 4: 8 the k' shall come to the daughter
M't 3: 2 ye: for the k' of heaven is at hand.
4:17 for the k' of heaven is at hand.
23 and preaching the gospel of the k',
5: 3 spirit: for theirs is the k' of heaven.
10 sake: for theirs is the k' of heaven.
19 called the least in the k' of heaven:
19 be called great in the k' of heaven.
20 no case enter into the k' of heaven.
6:10 Thy k' come. Thy will be done in
13 For thine is the k', and the power,
33 seek ye first the k' of God, and his
7:21 shall enter into the k' of heaven,
8:11 Isaac, and Jacob, in the k' of heaven:
12 children of the k' shall be cast out
9:35 and preaching the gospel of the k',
10: 7 saying, The k' of heaven is at hand.
11:11 least in the k' of heaven is greater
12 the k' of heaven suffereth violence,
12:25 k' divided against itself is brought
26 how shall then his k' stand?
28 then the k' of God is come unto you.
13:11 the mysteries of the k' of heaven,
19 any one heareth the word of the k',
24 k' of heaven is likened unto a man
31 k' of heaven is like to a grain of
33 k' of heaven is like unto leaven,
38 good seed are the children of the k';
41 shall gather out of his k' all things
43 as the sun in the k' of their Father.
44 the k' of heaven is like unto treasure
45 k' of heaven is like unto a merchant
47 the k' of heaven is like unto a net,
52 is instructed unto the k' of heaven,
16:19 thee the keys of the k' of heaven:
28 see the Son of man coming in his k'.
18: 1 is the greatest in the k' of heaven?
3 shall not enter into the k' of heaven.
4 same is greatest in the k' of heaven.
23 k' of heaven likened unto a certain
19:12 eunuchs for the k' of heaven's sake.
14 me: for of such is the k' of heaven.
23 hardly enter into the k' of heaven.
24 for a rich man to enter into the k' of
20: 1 k' of heaven is like unto a man that
21 and the other on the left, in thy k'.
21:31 harlots go into the k' of God before
43 k' of God shall be taken from you,
22: 2 The k' of heaven is like unto a
23:13 ye shut up the k' of heaven against
24: 7 against nation, and k' against k':
14 gospel of the k' shall be preached
25: 1 k' of heaven be likened unto ten
14 k' of heaven is as a man travelling
34 inherit the k' prepared for you from
26:29 it new with you in my Father's k'.
M'r 1:14 preaching the gospel of the k' of God,
15 fulfilled, and the k' of God is at hand:
3:24 if a k' be divided against itself,
24 that k' cannot stand.
4:11 know the mystery of the k' of God:
26 So is the k' of God, as if a man
30 Whereunto shall we liken the k' of
6:23 give it thee, unto the half of my k'.
9: 1 have seen the k' of God come with
47 enter into the k' of God with one eye,
10:14 not: for of such is the k' of God.
15 shall not receive the k' of God as a
23 have riches enter into the k' of God!
24 in riches to enter into the k' of God!
25 rich man to enter into the k' of God.
11:10 Blessed be the k' of our father David,
12:34 Thou art not far from the k' of God.
13: 8 against nation, and k' against k':
14:25 that I drink it new in the k' of God
15:43 which also waited for the k' of God,
Lu 1:33 of his k' there shall be no end.
4:43 preach the k' of God to other cities
6:20 ye poor: for yours is the k' of God.
7:28 he that is least in the k' of God is
8: 1 the glad tidings of the k' of God:

Lu 8:10 know the mysteries of the k' of God:
9: 2 sent them to preach the k' of God,
11 spake unto them of the k' of God,
27 of death, till they see the k' of God.
60 go thou and preach the k' of God.
62 looking back, is fit for the k' of God.
10: 9 The k' of God is come nigh unto you.
11 the k' of God is come nigh unto you.
11: 2 Thy k' come. Thy will be done, as
17 Every k' divided against itself is
18 himself, how shall his k' stand?
20 no doubt the k' of God is come upon
12:31 But rather seek ye the k' of God;
32 good pleasure to give you the k'.
13:18 he, unto what is the k' of God like?
20 whereunto shall I liken the k' of God?
28 all the prophets, in the k' of God,
29 and shall sit down in the k' of God.
14:15 that shall eat bread in the k' of God.
16:16 that time the k' of God is preached,
17:20 when the k' of God should come, he
20 The k' of God cometh not with
21 behold, the k' of God is within you.
18:16 not: for of such is the k' of God.
17 shall not receive the k' of God as a
24 have riches enter into the k' of God!
25 rich man to enter into the k' of God.
29 or children, for the k' of God's sake,
19:11 they thought that the k' of God
12 to receive for himself a k', and to
15 was returned, having received the k',
21:10 against nation, and k' against k':
31 ye that the k' of God is nigh at hand.
22:16 until it be fulfilled in the k' of God.
18 vine, until the k' of God shall come.
29 I appoint unto you a k', as my
30 eat and drink at my table in my k',
23:42 me when thou comest into thy k'.
51 himself waited for the k' of God.
Joh 3: 3 again, he cannot see the k' of God.
5 he cannot enter into the k' of God.
18:36 answered, My k' is not of this world:
36 if my k' were of this world, then
36 but now is my k' not from hence.
Ac 1: 3 things pertaining to the k' of God:
6 time restore again the k' to Israel?
8:12 things concerning the k' of God,
14:22 tribulation enter into the k' of God.
19: 8 things concerning the k' of God.
20:25 have gone, preaching the k' of God,
28:23 and testified the k' of God,
31 Preaching the k' of God, and
Ro 14:17 For the k' of God is not meat and
1Co 4:20 the k' of God is not in word, but in
6: 9 shall not inherit the k' of God?
10 nor..., shall inherit the k' of God.
15:24 have delivered up the k' to God,
50 blood cannot inherit the k' of God;
Ga 5:21 shall not inherit the k' of God.
Eph 5: 5 any inheritance in the k' of Christ
Col 1:13 us into the k' of his dear Son:
4:11 fellow-workers unto the k' of God,
1Th 2:12 called you unto his k' and glory.
2Th 1: 5 be counted worthy of the k' of God,
2Ti 4: 1 dead at his appearing and his k':
18 preserve me unto his heavenly k':
Heb 1: 8 righteousness is the sceptre of thy k'.
12:28 we receiving a k' which cannot be
Jas 2: 5 heirs of the k' which he hath
2Pe 1:11 into the everlasting k' of our Lord
Re 1: 9 in the k' and patience of Jesus
12:10 strength, and the k' of our God,
16:10 his k' was full of darkness; and
17:12 which have received no k' as yet;
17 give their k' unto the beast, until

kingdoms
De 3:21 all the k' whither thou passest.
28:25 removed into all the k' of the earth.
Jos 11:10 was the head of all those k'.
1Sa 10:18 and out of the hand of all k',
1Ki 4:21 And Solomon reigned over all k'
2Ki 19:15 thou alone, of all the k' of the earth;
19 all the k' of the earth may know
1Ch 29:30 over all the k' of the countries.
2Ch 12: 8 service of the k' of the countries.
17:10 fell upon all the k' of the lands
20: 6 over all the k' of the heathen?
29 the fear of God was on all the k'
36:23 All the k' of the earth hath the Lord
Ezr 1: 2 given me all the k' of the earth;
Ne 9:22 thou gavest them k' and nations,
Ps 46: 6 heathen raged, the k' were moved:
68:32 Sing unto God, ye k' of the earth;
79: 6 and upon the k' that have not called
102:22 and the k', to serve the Lord.
135:11 Bashan, and all the k' of Canaan:
Isa 10:10 hand hath found the k' of the idols,
13: 4 tumultuous noise of the k' of nations
19 And Babylon, the glory of k',
14:16 earth to tremble, that did shake k';
23:11 over the sea, he shook the k':
17 commit fornication with all the k'
37:16 alone, of all the k' of the earth:
20 that all the k' of the earth may know
47: 5 no more be called, The lady of k'.
Jer 1:10 over the nations and over the k',
15 the families of the k' of the north,
10: 7 of the nations, and in all their k',
15: 4 be removed into all k' of the earth,
24: 9 be removed into the k' of the earth
25:26 another, and all the k' of the world,
28: 8 countries, and against great k',
29:18 be removed to all the k' of the earth,
34: 1 and all the k' of the earth of his
17 removed into all the k' of the earth.
49:28 and concerning the k' of Hazor,

Jer 51:20 and with thee will I destroy k';
27 against her the k' of Ararat,
Eze 29:15 It shall be the basest of the k';
37:22 divided into two k' any more at all:
Da 2:44 in pieces and consume all these k',
7:23 which shall be diverse from all k',
8:22 four k' shall stand up out of the
Am 6: 2 be they better than these k'?
Na 3: 5 nakedness, and the k' thy shame.
Zep 3: 8 nations, that I may assemble the k',
Hag 2:22 I will overthrow the throne of k',
22 I will destroy the strength of the k'
M't 4: 8 sheweth him all the k' of the world,
Lu 4: 5 unto him all the k' of the world in
Heb11:33 Who through faith subdued k',
Re 11:15 The k' of this world are become
15 the k' of our Lord, and of his Christ;

kingly
Da 5:20 was deposed from his k' throne,

king's
Ge 14:17 Shaveh, which is in the k' dale.
39:20 where the k' prisoners were bound:
Nu 20:17 we will go by the k' high way, we
21:22 we will go along by the k' high way,
1Sa 18:22 now therefore be the k' son in law.
23 a light thing to be a k' son in law,
25 to be avenged of the k' enemies.
26 David well to be the k' son in law:
27 that he might be the k' son in law.
20:29 he cometh not unto the k' table.
21: 8 the k' business required haste.
22:14 David, which is the k' son in law,
23:20 be to deliver him into the k' hand.
26:16 And now see where the k' spear is,
22 and said, Behold the k' spear!
2Sa 9:11 at my table, as one of the k' sons.
13 did eat continually at the k' table;
11: 2 upon the roof of the k' house:
8 Uriah departed out of the k' house,
9 slept at the door of the k' house
20 And if so be that the k' wrath arise,
24 some of the k' servants be dead,
12:30 he took their k' crown from off his
13: 4 Why art thou, being the k' son,
18 such robes were the k' daughters
23 Absalom invited all the k' sons.
27 and all the k' sons go with him.
29 Then all the k' sons arose, and
30 Absalom hath slain all the k' sons,
32 slain all the young men the k' sons;
33 think that all the k' sons are dead:
35 Behold, the k' sons come: as thy
36 the k' sons came, and lifted up
14: 1 the k' heart was toward Absalom.
24 house, and saw not the k' face.
26 hundred shekels after the k' weight.
28 Jerusalem, and saw not the k' face.
32 therefore let me see the k' face;
15:15 the k' servant said unto the king,
35 thou shalt hear out of the k' house,
16: 2 The asses be for the k' household
18:12 mine hand against the k' son:
18 pillar, which is in the k' dale:
20 because the k' son is dead.
29 When Joab sent the k' servant,
19:18 boat to carry over the k' household,
42 have we eaten at all of the k' cost?
24: 4 the k' word prevailed against Joab,
1Ki 1: 9 called all his brethren the k' sons,
9 the men of Judah the k' servants:
25 and hath called all the k' sons,
28 she came into the k' presence, and
44 him to ride upon the k' mule:
47 k' servants came to bless our lord
2:19 a seat to be set for the k' mother;
4: 5 principal officer, and the k' friend:
9: 1, 10 of the Lord, and the k' house,
10:12 of the Lord, and for the k' house,
28 the k' merchants received the linen
11:14 he was of the k' seed in Edom.
13: 6 k' hand was restored him again,
14:26 and the treasures of the k' house;
27 which kept the door of the k' house.
15:18 and the treasures of the k' house,
16:18 went into the palace of the k' house,
18 and burnt the k' house over him
22:12 shall deliver it into the k' hand.
26 of the city, and to Joash the k' son;
2Ki 7: 9 may go and tell the k' household.
11 they told it to the k' house within.
9:34 bury her: for she is a k' daughter.
10: 6 the k' sons, being seventy persons,
7 that they took the k' sons, and slew
8 brought the heads of the k' sons.
11: 2 stole him from among the k' sons
4 Lord, and shewed them the k' son.
5 of the watch of the k' house;
12 he brought forth the k' son, and put
16 the horses came into the k' house:
19 gate of the guard to the k' house.
20 with the sword beside the k' house.
12:10 the k' scribe and the high priest
18 of the Lord, and in the k' house,
13:16 put his hands upon the k' hands.
14:14 and in the treasures of the k' house,
15: 5 And Jotham the k' son was over the
25 in the palace of the k' house,
16: 8 and in the treasures of the k' house,
15 the k' burnt sacrifice, and his meat
18 the house, and the k' entry without,
18:15 and in the treasures of the k' house.
36 for the k' commandment was,
22:12 and Asahiah a servant of the k',
24:13 and the treasures of the k' house,
15 the k' mother, and the k' wives, and

2Ki 25: 4 walls, which is by the k' garden:
9 house of the Lord, and the k' house,
19 them that were in the k' presence,
1Ch 9:18 Who hitherto waited in the k' gate
21: 4 Nevertheless the k' word prevailed
6 k' word was abominable to Joab.
25: 5 Heman the k' seer in the words of
6 according to the k' order to Asaph,
27:25 over the k' treasures was Azmaveth
32 of Hachmoni was with the k' sons:
33 Ahithophel was the k' counsellor:
33 the Archite was the k' companion:
34 the general of the k' army was Joab.
29: 6 the rulers of the k' work, offered
2Ch 1:16 the k' merchants received the linen
7:11 house of the Lord, and the k' house:
9:11 of the Lord, and to the k' palace,
21 the k' ships went to Tarshish with
12: 9 and the treasures of the k' house;
10 kept the entrance of the k' house.
16: 2 of the Lord and of the k' house,
18: 5 God will deliver it into the k' hand.
25 the city, and to Joash the k' son;
19:11 of Judah, for all the k' matters:
21:17 that was found in the k' house,
22:11 stole him from among the k' sons
23: 3 Behold, the k' son shall reign, as
5 third part shall be at the k' house;
11 Then they brought out the k' son,
15 of the horse gate by the k' house,
20 the high gate into the k' house,
24: 8 at the k' commandment they made
11 chest was brought unto the k' office
11 the k' scribe and the high priest's
25:16 Art thou made of the k' counsel?
24 and the treasures of the k' house,
26:11 of Hananiah, one of the k' captains.
21 his son was over the k' house,
28: 7 Ephraim, slew Maaseiah the k' son,
29:25 of Gad the k' seer, and Nathan the
31: 3 He appointed also the k' portion of
34:20 Asaiah a servant of the k', saying,
35: 7 these were of the k' substance.
10 according to the k' commandment.
15 Heman, and Jeduthun the k' seer;
Ezr 4:14 maintenance from the k' palace,
14 meet for us to see the k' dishonour,
5:17 made in the k' treasure house,
6: 4 expences be given out of the k' house.
8 of the k' goods, even of the tribute
7:20 bestow it out of the k' treasure
27 such a thing as this in the k' heart,
28 before all the k' mighty princes.
8:36 they delivered the k' commissions
36 commissions unto the k' lieutenants,
Ne 1:11 man. For I was the k' cupbearer.
2: 8 Asaph the keeper of the k' forest,
9 river, and gave them the k' letters.
14 of the fountain, and to the k' pool:
18 the k' words that he had spoken
3:15 the pool of Siloah by the k' garden,
25 lieth out from the k' high house,
5: 4 borrowed money for the k' tribute,
11:23 k' commandment concerning them,
24 was at the k' hand in all matters
Es 1: 5 of the garden of the k' palace;
12 to come at the k' commandment
13 so was the k' manner toward all
14 which saw the k' face, and which
18 say this day unto all the k' princes,
20 the k' decree, which he shall make
22 sent letters into all the k' provinces,
2: 2 said the k' servants that ministered
3 Hege the k' chamberlain, keeper of
8 when the k' commandment and his
8 was brought also unto the k' house,
9 to be given her, out of the k' house:
13 of the women unto the k' house.
14 the k' chamberlain, which kept the
15 but what Hegai the k' chamberlain,
19 then Mordecai sat in the k' gate.
21 while Mordecai sat in the k' gate,
21 two of the k' chamberlains, Bigthan
3: 2 k' servants, that were in the k' gate,
3 k' servants, which were in the k' gate,
3 thou the k' commandment?
8 neither keep they the k' laws:
8 not for the k' profit to suffer them.
9 to bring it into the k' treasuries.
12 Then were the k' scribes called on
12 commanded unto the k' lieutenants,
12 written, and sealed with the k' ring.
13 by posts into all the k' provinces,
15 hastened by the k' commandment,
4: 2 And came even before the k' gate:
2 none might enter into the k' gate
3 whithersoever the k' commandment
5 one of the k' chamberlains, whom
6 city, which was before the k' gate.
7 promised to pay to the k' treasuries
11 All the k' servants, and the people
11 and the people of the k' provinces,
13 thou shalt escape in the k' house,
5: 1 in the inner court of the k' house,
1 house, over against the k' house:
9 Haman saw Mordecai in the k' gate,
13 Mordecai...sitting at the k' gate.
6: 2 Teresh, two of the k' chamberlains,
3 the k' servants that ministered unto
4 the outward court of the k' house,
5 k' servants said unto him, Behold,
9 of one of the k' most noble princes,
10 the Jew, that sitteth at the k' gate:
12 Mordecai came again to the k' gate.
14 with him, came the k' chamberlains,
7: 4 not countervail the k' damage.

Es 7: 8 the word went out of the k' mouth,
10 Then was the k' wrath pacified.
8: 5 which are in all the k' provinces:
8 as it liketh you, in the k' name,
8 name, and seal it with the k' ring:
8 which is written in the k' name,
8 name, and sealed with the k' ring,
9 the k' scribes called at that time
10 sealed it with the k' ring, and sent
14 pressed on by the k' commandment.
17 whithersoever the k' commandment
9: 1 k' commandment and his decree
4 Mordecai was great in the k' house,
12 done in the rest of the k' provinces?
16 Jews that were in the k' provinces
Ps 45: 5 sharp in the heart of the k' enemies;
13 k' daughter is all glorious within
15 they shall enter into the k' palace.
61: 6 Thou wilt prolong the k' life: and
72: 1 thy righteousness unto the k' son.
99: 4 k' strength also loveth judgment;
Pr 14: 28 multitude of people is the k' honour:
35 k' favour is toward a wise servant:
16: 15 In the light of the k' countenance
19: 12 The k' wrath is as the roaring of a
21: 1 The k' heart is in the hand of the
Ec 8: 2 thee to keep the k' commandment,
Isa 36: 21 for the k' commandment was,
Jer 22: 6 Lord unto the k' house of Judah;
26: 10 came up from the k' house unto the
36: 12 he went down into the k' house,
38: 7 eunuchs which was in the k' house,
8 went forth out of the k' house, and
39: 4 by the way of the k' garden, by the
8 the Chaldeans burned the k' house,
41: 10 even the k' daughters, and all the
43: 6 and children, and the k' daughters,
52: 7 walls, which was by the k' garden;
13 house of the Lord, and the k' house;
25 them that were near the k' person.
Eze 17: 13 hath taken of the k' seed, and
Da 1: 3 and of the k' seed, and of the
4 in them to stand in the k' palace.
5 a daily provision of the k' meat,
8 with the portion of the k' meat,
13 eat of the portion of the k' meat:
15 did eat the portion of the k' meat.
2: 10 earth that can shew the k' matter:
14 Arioch the captain of the k' guard,
15 and said to Arioch the k' captain,
23 made known unto us the k' matter.
3: 22 the k' commandment was urgent,
27 captains, and the k' counsellors,
28 him, and have changed the k' word,
4: 31 the word was in the k' mouth,
5: 5 plaister of the wall of the k' palace:
6 the k' countenance was changed,
8 Then came in all the k' wise men:
6: 12 the king concerning the k' decree;
8: 27 rose up, and did the k' business;
11: 6 the k' daughter of the south shall
Am 7: 1 latter growth after the k' mowings.
13 Beth-el: for it is the k' chapel,
13 chapel, and it is the k' court.
Zep 1: 8 the princes, and the k' children,
Zec 14: 10 Hananeel unto the k' winepresses.
Ac 12: 20 Blastus the k' chamberlain their
20 was nourished by the k' country.
Heb 11: 23 afraid of the k' commandment.
kings^ See also KINGS'.
Ge 14: 5 and the k' that were with him, and
9 king of Ellasar; four k' with five.
10 the k' of Sodom and Gomorrah fled,
17 of the k' that were with him, at the
17: 6 thee, and k' shall come out of thee.
16 nations; k' of people shall be of her.
35: 11 and k' shall come out of thy loins;
36: 31 the k' that reigned in the land of
Nu 31: 8 they slew the k' of Midian, beside
8 Hur, and Reba, five k' of Midian:
De 3: 8 hand of the two k' of the Amorites
21 God hath done unto these two k':
4: 47 of Bashan, two k' of the Amorites,
7: 24 deliver their k' into thine hand,
31: 4 Sihon and to Og, k' of the Amorites,
Jos 2: 10 unto the two k' of the Amorites,
5: 1 all the k' of the Amorites, which
1 and all the k' of the Canaanites,
9: 1 all the k' which were on this side
10 did to the two k' of the Amorites,
10: 5 the five k' of the Amorites, the
6 all the k' of the Amorites that dwell
16 these five k' fled, and hid themselves
17 The five k' are found hid in a cave
22 bring out those five k' unto me out
23 brought forth those five k' unto him
24 brought out those k' unto Joshua,
24 your feet upon the necks of these k'.
40 and of the springs, and all their k':
42 all these k' and their land did
11: 2 the k' that were on the north of the
5 all these k' were met together,
12 And all the cities of those k',
12 all the k' of them, did Joshua take,
17 their k' he took, and smote them,
18 war a long time with all those k'.
12: 1 these are the k' of the land, which
7 k' of the country which Joshua and
24 one: all the k' thirty and one.
24: 12 even the two k' of the Amorites;
J'g 1: 7 Threescore and ten k', having their
5: 3 Hear, O ye k'; give ear, O ye
19 The k' came and fought, then
19 fought the k' of Canaan in Taanach
8: 5 Zebah and Zalmunna, k' of Midian.
12 took the two k' of Midian, Zebah

J'g 8: 26 purple raiment that was on the k'
1Sa 14: 47 Edom, and against the k' of Zobah,
27: 6 pertaineth unto the k' of Judah
2Sa 10: 19 k' that were servants to Hadarezer
11: 1 the time when k' go forth to battle,
1Ki 3: 13 there shall not be any among the k'
4: 24 all the k' on this side the river:
34 from all k' of the earth, which had
10: 15 and of all the k' of Arabia, and of
23 king Solomon exceeded all the k'
29 and so for all the k' of the Hittites,
29 and for the k' of Syria, did they
14: 19 of the chronicles of the k' of Israel.
29 of the chronicles of the k' of Judah?
15: 7, 23 chronicles of the k' of Judah?
31 of the chronicles of the k' of Israel?
16: 5, 14, 20, 27 chronicles of...k' of Israel?
33 all the k' of Israel that were before
20: 1 were thirty and two k' with him,
12 he and the k' in the pavilions, that
16 in the pavilions, he and the k',
16 thirty and two k' that helped him.
24 Take the k' away, every man out of
31 have heard that the k' of the house
31 house of Israel are merciful k':
22: 39 the chronicles of the k' of Israel?
45 the chronicles of the k' of Judah?
2Ki 1: 18 the chronicles of the k' of Israel?
3: 10, 13 called these three k' together,
21 that the k' were come up to fight
23 k' are surely slain, and they have
7: 6 against us the k' of the Hittites,
6 the k' of the Egyptians, to come
8: 18 walked in the way of the k' of Israel,
23 the chronicles of the k' of Judah?
10: 4 two k' stood not before him: how
34 the chronicles of the k' of Israel?
11: 19 And he sat on the throne of the k'.
12: 18 k' of Judah, had dedicated, and his
19 the chronicles of the k' of Judah?
13: 8, 12 chronicles of the k' of Israel?
13 in Samaria with the k' of Israel.
14: 15 the chronicles of the k' of Israel?
16 in Samaria with the k' of Israel;
18 the chronicles of the k' of Judah?
28 the chronicles of the k' of Israel?
29 fathers, even with the k' of Israel;
15: 6 the chronicles of the k' of Judah?
11, 15 chronicles of the k' of Israel.
21 the chronicles of the k' of Israel?
26, 31 the chronicles of the k' of Israel.
36 the chronicles of the k' of Judah?
16: 3 walked in the way of the k' of Israel,
19 the chronicles of the k' of Judah?
17: 2 not as the k' of Israel that were
8 of Israel, and of the k' of Israel,
18: 5 him among all the k' of Judah,
19: 11 k' of Assyria have done to all lands,
17 k' of Assyria have destroyed the
20: 20 the chronicles of the k' of Judah?
21: 17, 25 chronicles of the k' of Judah?
23: 5 k' of Judah had ordained to burn
11 k' of Judah had given to the sun,
12 which the k' of Judah had made,
19 k' of Israel had made to provoke
22 in all the days of the k' of Israel,
22 nor of the k' of Judah;
28 the chronicles of the k' of Judah?
24: 5 of the chronicles of the k' of Judah?
25: 28 k' that were with him in Babylon;
1Ch 1: 43 k' that reigned in the land of Edom
9: 1 book of the k' of Israel and Judah,
16: 21 yea, he reproved k' for their sakes,
19: 9 and the k' that were come were by
20: 1 at the time that k' go out to battle,
2Ch 1: 12 such as none of the k' have had that
17 horses for all the k' of the Hittites,
17 and for the k' of Syria, by their
9: 14 all the k' of Arabia and governors of
22 passed all the k' of the earth in
23 k' of the earth sought the presence
26 And he reigned over all the k' from
16: 11 book of the k' of Judah and Israel.
20: 34 in the book of the k' of Israel.
21: 6, 13 in the way of the k' of Israel,
20 but not in the sepulchres of the k'.
24: 16 in the city of David among the k',
25 him not in the sepulchres of the k'.
27 in the story of the book of the k'.
25: 26 book of the k' of Judah and Israel?
26: 23 the burial which belonged to the k';
27: 7 book of the k' of Israel and Judah.
28: 2 in the ways of the k' of Israel,
16 Ahaz send unto the k' of Assyria
23 gods of the k' of Syria help them,
26 book of the k' of Judah and Israel.
27 the sepulchres of the k' of Israel:
30: 6 out of the hand of the k' of Assyria.
32: 4 Why should the k' of Assyria come,
32 book of the k' of Judah and Israel.
33: 18 in the book of the k' of Israel.
34: 11 which the k' of Judah had destroyed.
35: 18 the k' of Israel keep such a passover
27 book of the k' of Israel and Judah.
36: 8 book of the k' of Israel and Judah:
Ezr 4: 13 endamage the revenue of the k'.
15 and hurtful unto k' and provinces,
19 hath made insurrection against k',
20 been mighty k' also over Jerusalem,
22 damage grow to the hurt of the k'?
6: 12 there destroy all k' and people,
7: 12 Artaxerxes, king of k', unto Ezra
9: 7 have we, our k', and our priests,
7 into the hand of the k' of the lands,
9 us in the sight of the k' of Persia,
Ne 9: 24 with their k', and the people of the

Ne 9: 32 upon us, on our k', on our princes,
32 since the time of the k' of Assyria
34 Neither have our k', our princes,
37 the k' whom thou hast set over us
Es 10: 2 of the chronicles of the k' of Media
Job 3: 14 With k' and counsellors of the earth,
12: 18 He looseth the bond of k', and
36: 7 but with k' are they on the throne;
Ps 2: 2 k' of the earth set themselves, and
10 Be wise now therefore, O ye k': be
48: 4 For, lo, the k' were assembled, they
68: 12 K' of armies did flee apace: and she
14 Almighty scattered k' in it, it was
29 shall k' bring presents unto thee.
72: 10 k' of Tarshish and of the isles shall
10 k' of Sheba and Seba shall offer gifts.
11 all k' shall fall down before him:
76: 12 he is terrible to the k' of the earth.
89: 27 higher than the k' of the earth.
102: 15 and all the k' of the earth thy glory.
105: 14 yea, he reproved k' for their sakes;
30 in the chambers of their k'.
110: 5 shall strike through k' in the day of
119: 46 of thy testimonies also before k',
135: 10 great nations, and slew mighty k';
136: 17 To him which smote great k': for
18 And slew famous k': for his mercy
138: 4 the k' of the earth shall praise thee,
144: 10 is he that giveth salvation unto k':
148: 11 K' of the earth, and all people;
149: 8 To bind their k' with chains, and
Pr 8: 15 By me k' reign, and princes decree
16: 12 It is an abomination to k' to commit
13 Righteous lips are the delight of k';
22: 29 business? he shall stand before k';
25: 2 but the honour of k' is to search out
3 and the heart of k' is unsearchable.
31: 3 ways to that which destroyeth k'.
4 It is not for k', O Lemuel, it is not
4 it is not for k' to drink wine; nor for
Ec 2: 8 the peculiar treasure of k' and of
Isa 1: 1 Ahaz, and Hezekiah, k' of Judah.
7: 16 shall be forsaken of both her k'.
10: 8 Are not my princes altogether k'?
14: 9 thrones all the k' of the nations.
18 All the k' of the nations, even all of
19: 11 of the wise, the son of ancient k'?
24: 21 the k' of the earth upon the earth.
37: 11 heard what the k' of Assyria have
18 the k' of Assyria have laid waste all
41: 2 him, and made him ruler over k'?
45: 1 I will loose the loins of k', to open
49: 7 K' shall see and arise, princes also
23 And k' shall be thy nursing fathers,
52: 15 k' shall shut their mouths at him:
60: 3 k' to the brightness of thy rising.
10 their k' shall minister unto thee:
11 and that their k' may be brought.
16 and shalt suck the breast of k':
62: 2 righteousness, and all k' thy glory:
Jer 1: 18 whole land, against the k' of Judah,
2: 26 they, their k', their princes, and
8: 1 out the bones of the k' of Judah,
13: 13 the k' that sit upon David's throne,
17: 19 whereby the k' of Judah come in,
20 word of the Lord, ye k' of Judah,
25 city k' and princes sitting upon the
19: 3 the word of the Lord, O k' of Judah,
4 have known, nor the k' of Judah,
13 and the houses of the k' of Judah,
20: 5 all the treasures of the k' of Judah
22: 4 k' sitting upon the throne of David,
25: 14 great k' shall serve themselves of
18 cities of Judah, and the k' thereof,
20 and all the k' of the land of Uz,
20 the k' of the land of the Philistines,
22 k' of Tyrus, and all the k' of Zidon,
22 the k' of the isles which are beyond
24 And all the k' of Arabia,
24 and all the k' of the mingled people
25 k' of Zimri, and all the k' of Elam,
25 and all the k' of the Medes,
26 all the k' of the north, far and near,
27: 7 great k' shall serve themselves of
32: 32 they, their k', their princes, their
33: 4 the houses of the k' of Judah,
34: 5 former k' which were before thee,
44: 9 the wickedness of the k' of Judah,
17 fathers, our k', and our princes,
21 fathers, your k', and your princes,
46: 25 Egypt, with their gods, and their k';
50: 41 and many k' shall be raised up from
51: 11 up the spirit of the k' of the Medes:
28 nations with the k' of the Medes,
52: 32 k' that were with him in Babylon,
La 4: 12 The k' of the earth, and all the
Eze 26: 7 king of Babylon, a king of k',
27: 33 thou didst enrich the k' of the earth
35 and their k' shall be sore afraid,
28: 17 I will lay thee before k', that they
32: 10 k' shall be horribly afraid for thee,
29 Edom, her k', and all her princes,
43: 7 defile, neither they, nor their k',
7 carcases of their k' in their high
9 the carcases of their k', far from me,
Da 2: 21 he removeth k', and setteth up k':
37 Thou, O king, art a king of k': for
44 in the days of these k' shall the God
47 is a God of gods, and a Lord of k',
7: 17 beasts, which are four, are four k',
24 kingdom are ten k' that shall arise:
24 first, and he shall subdue three k'.
8: 20 are the k' of Media and Persia.
9: 6 which spake in thy name to our k',
8 to our k', to our princes, and to our
10: 13 remained there with the k' of Persia.

Da 11: 2 stand up yet three k· in Persia;
Ho 1: 1 Ahaz, and Hezekiah, k· of Judah,
7: 7 all their k· are fallen: there is
8: 4 They have set up k·, but not by me:
Mic 1: 1 Ahaz, and Hezekiah, k· of Judah,
14 shall be a lie to the k· of Israel.
Hab 1:10 they shall scoff at the k·, and the
M't 10:18 governors and k· for my sake,
17:25 of whom do the k· of the earth take
M'r 13: 9 before rulers and k· for my sake,
Lu 10:24 prophets and k· have desired to see
21:12 k· and rulers for my name's sake.
22:25 The k· of the Gentiles exercise
Ac 4:26 The k· of the earth stood up, and
9:15 my name before the Gentiles, and k·,
1Co 4: 8 ye have reigned as k· without us:
1Ti 2: 2 For k·, and for all that are in
6:15 the King of k·, and Lord of lords;
Heb 7: 1 returning from the slaughter of k·,
Re 1: 5 the prince of the k· of the earth.
6 hath made us k· and priests unto
5:10 us unto our God k· and priests:
6:15 the k· of the earth, and the great
10:11 and nations, and tongues, and k·.
16:12 the way of the k· of the east might
14 go forth unto the k· of the earth
17: 2 With whom the k· of the earth have
10 there are seven k·: five are fallen,
12 horns which thou sawest are ten k·,
12 receive power as k· one hour with
14 he is Lord of lords, and King of k·:
18 reigneth over the k· of the earth.
18: 3 the k· of the earth have committed
9 the k· of the earth, who have
19:16 King Of K·, And Lord Of Lords.
18 That ye may eat the flesh of k·,
19 the beast, and the k· of the earth,
21:24 the k· of the earth do bring their

kings'
Ps 45: 9 k· daughters were among thy
Pr 30:28 her hands, and is in k· palaces.
Da 11:27 both these k· hearts shall be to do
M't 11: 8 wear soft clothing are in k· houses.
Lu 7:25 and live delicately, are in k· courts.

King's-Dale See KING'S and DALE.

King's-Pool See KING'S and POOL.

kinsfolk See also KINSFOLKS.
Job 19:14 My k· have failed, and my familiar
Lu 2:44 they sought him among their k·

kinsfolks
1Ki 16:11 neither of his k·, nor of his
2Ki 10:11 his great men, and his k·, and his
Lu 21:16 and brethren, and k·, and friends

kinsman See also KINSMAN'S; KINSMEN.
Nu 5: 8 the man have no k· to recompence
27:11 give his inheritance unto his k·
Ru 2: 1 Naomi had a k· of her husband's,
3: 9 handmaid; for thou art a near k·.
12 it is true that I am thy near k·:
12 howbeit there is a k· nearer than I.
13 perform unto thee the part of a k·,
13 will not do the part of a k· to thee,
13 will I do the part of a k· to thee,
4: 1 the k· of whom Boaz spake came
3 he said unto the k·, Naomi, that is
6 the k· said, I cannot redeem it for
8 the k· said unto Boaz, Buy it for
14 not left thee this day without a k·,
Joh 18:26 being his k· whose ear Peter cut
Ro 16:11 Salute Herodion my k·. Greet them

kinsman's
Ru 3:13 let him do the k· part: but if he

kinsmen
Ru 2:20 of kin unto us, one of our next k·.
Ps 38:11 sore; and my k· stand afar off.
Lu 14:12 neither thy k·, nor thy rich
Ac 10:24 together his k· and near friends.
Ro 9: 3 my k· according to the flesh:
16: 7 Andronicus and Junia, my k·, and
21 and Jason, and Sosipater, my k·,

kinswoman See also KINSWOMEN.
Le 18:12 sister: she is thy father's near k·.
13 for she is thy mother's near k·.
Pr 7: 4 and call understanding thy k·:

kinswomen
Le 18:17 for they are her near k·: it is

Kir (kur) See also KIR-HARESH.
2Ki 16: 9 the people of it captive to K·,
Isa 15: 1 K· of Moab is laid waste,
22: 6 and K· uncovered the shield.
Am 1: 5 shall go into captivity unto K·,
9: 7 Caphtor, and the Syrians from K·?

Kir-haraseth (kur-har'-a-seth) See also KIR-HARESETH.
2Ki 3:25 in K· left they the stones thereof;

Kir-hareseth (kur-har'-e-seth) See also KIR-HARESH.
Isa 16: 7 foundations of K· shall ye mourn;

Kir-haresh (kur-ha'-resh) See also KIR-HARASETH; KIR-HARESETH; KIR-HERES.
Isa 16:11 and mine inward parts for K·.

Kir-heres (kur-he'-res) See also KIR-HARESH.
Jer 48:31 shall mourn for the men of K·.
36 sound like pipes for the men of K·:

Kiriathaim (kir-e-a-thay'-im) See also KARTAN; KIRJATHAIM.
Ge 14: 5 and the Emims in Shaveh K·,
Jer 48: 1 K· is confounded and taken:
23 upon K·, and upon Beth-gamul,
Eze 25: 9 Baal-meon, and K·,

Kirioth (kir'-e-oth) See also KERIOTH.
Am 2: 2 it shall devour the palaces of K·.

Kirjath (kur'-jath) See also KIRJATH-ARBA; KIRJATH-ARIM; KIRJATH-BAAL; KIRJATH-HUZOTH; KIRJATH-JEARIM; KIRJATH-SANNAH; KIRJATH-SEPHER.
Jos 18:28 Jerusalem, Gibeath, and K·;

Kirjathaim (kur''-jath-a'-im) See also KIRIATHAIM.
Nu 32:37 Heshbon, and Elealeh, and K·,
Jos 13:19 And K·, and Sibmah, and
1Ch 6:76 suburbs, and K· with her suburbs.

Kirjath-arba (kur''-jath-ar'-bah) See also HEBRON.
Ge 23: 2 And Sarah died in K·; the same
Jos 14:15 the name of Hebron before was K·;
15:54 and K·, which is Hebron, and Zior;
20: 7 and K·, which is Hebron, in the
J'g 1:10 name of Hebron before was K·:)
Ne 11:25 the children of Judah dwelt at K·,

Kirjath-arim (kur''-jath-a'-rim) See also KIRJATH-JEARIM.
Ezr 2:25 The children of K·, Chephirah,

Kirjath-baal (kur''-jath-ba'-al) See also BAALAH; KIRJATH-JEARIM.
Jos 15:60 K·, which is Kirjath-jearim, and
18:14 the goings out thereof were at K·,

Kirjath-huzoth (kur''-jath-hu'-zoth)
Nu 22:39 Balak, and they came unto K·.

Kirjath-jearim (kur''-jath-je'-a-rim) See also KIRJATH-SEPHER; KIRJATH-ARIM; KIRJATH-BAAL.
Jos 9:17 Chephirah, and Beeroth, and K·.
15: 9 was drawn to Baalah, which is K·:
60 Kirjath-baal, which is K·, and
18:14 K·, a city of the children of Judah:
15 quarter was from the end of K·,
J'g 18:12 they went up, and pitched in K·,
12 this day: behold, it is behind K·.
1Sa 6:21 sent...to the inhabitants of K·,
7: 1 the men of K· came, and fetched
2 to pass, while the ark abode in K·,
1Ch 2:50 Ephratah; Shobal the father of K·,
52 Shobal the father of K· had sons;
53 the families of K·; the Ithrites,
13: 5 to bring the ark of God from K·.
6 all Israel, to Baalah, that is, to K·,
2Ch 1: 4 had David brought up from K· to
Ne 7:29 The men of K·, Chephirah, and
Jer 26:20 Urijah the son of Shemaiah of K·,

Kirjath-sannah (kur''-jath-san'-nah) See also KIRJATH-SEPHER; SANSANNAH.
Jos 15:49 Dannah, and K·, which is Debir,

Kirjath-sepher (kur''-jath-se'-fer) See also DEBIR; KIRJATH-SANNAH.
Jos 15:15 the name of Debir before was K·.
16 He that smiteth K·, and taketh it,
J'g 1:11 the name of Debir before was K·:
12 He that smiteth K·, and taketh it,

Kish (kish) See also CIS.
1Sa 9: 1 of Benjamin, whose name was K·,
3 asses of K· Saul's father were lost.
3 K· said to Saul his son, Take now
10:11 that is come unto the son of K·?
21 and Saul the son of K· was taken:
14:51 K· was the father of Saul; and Ner
2Sa 21:14 in the sepulchre of K· his father:
1Ch 8:30 son Abdon, and Zur, and K·, and
33 Ner begat K·, and K· begat Saul,
9:36 son Abdon, then Zur, and K·, and
39 Ner begat K·; and K· begat Saul;
12: 1 because of Saul the son of K·:
23:21 the sons of Mahli; Eleazar, and K·.
22 brethren the sons of K· took them.
24:29 Concerning K·: the son of K· was
26:28 Saul the son of K·, and Abner the
2Ch 29:12 sons of Merari, K· the son of Abdi,
Es 2: 5 Shimei, the son of K·, a Benjamite;

Kishi (kish'-i) See also KUSHAIAH.
1Ch 6:44 Ethan the son of K·, the son of

Kishion (kish'-e-on) See also KEDESH; KISHON.
Jos 19:20 And Rabbith, and K·, and Abez,

Kishon (ki'-shon) See also KISHION; KISON.
Jos 21:28 of Issachar, K· with her suburbs,
J'g 4: 7 draw unto thee to the river K·
13 of the Gentiles unto the river of K·.
5:21 The river of K· swept them away,
21 that ancient river, the river K·.
1Ki 18:40 brought them down to the brook K·,

Kison (ki'-son) See also KISHON.
Ps 83: 9 as to Jabin, at the brook of K·:

kiss See also KISSED; KISSES.
Ge 27:26 near now, and k· me, my son.
31:28 to k· my sons and my daughters?
2Sa 20: 9 beard with the right hand to k· him.
1Ki 19:20 thee, k· my father and my mother,
Ps 2:12 K· the Son, lest he be angry, and
Pr 24:26 shall k· his lips that giveth a right
Ca 1: 2 Let him k· me with the kisses of his
8: 1 find thee without, I would k· thee;
Ho 13: 2 the men that sacrifice k· the calves.
M't 26:48 Whomsoever I shall k·, that same
M'r 14:44 Whomsoever I shall k·, that same
Lu 7:45 Thou gavest me no k·: but this
45 in hath not ceased to k· my feet.
22:47 drew near unto Jesus to k· him.
48 thou the Son of man with a k·?
Ro 16:16 Salute one another with an holy k·.
1Co 16:20 ye one another with an holy k·.
2Co 13:12 Greet one another with an holy k·.
1Th 5:26 all the brethren with an holy k·.
1Pe 5:14 ye one another with a k· of charity.

kissed
Ge 27:27 And he came near, and k· him:
29:11 Jacob k· Rachel, and lifted up his
13 him, and embraced him, and k· him,
31:55 and k· his sons and his daughters,
33: 4 and fell on his neck, and k· him:
45:15 Moreover he k· all his brethren,
48:10 he k· them, and embraced them.
50: 1 and wept upon him, and k· him.
Ex 4:27 in the mount of God, and k· him.
18: 7 law, and did obeisance, and k· him;
Ru 1: 9 Then she k· them; and they lifted up
14 and Orpah k· her mother in law;
1Sa 10: 1 poured it upon his head, and k· him,
20:41 they k· one another, and wept one
2Sa 14:33 the king: and the king k· Absalom.
15: 5 his hand, and took him, and k· him.
19:39 the king k· Barzillai, and blessed
1Ki 19:18 every mouth which hath not k· him.
Job 31:27 or my mouth hath k· my hand:
Ps 85:10 righteousness and peace have k·
Pr 7:13 So she caught him, and k· him, and
M't 26:49 said, Hail, master; and k· him.
M'r 14:45 saith, Master, master; and k· him.
Lu 7:38 and k· his feet, and anointed them
15:20 and fell on his neck, and k· him.
Ac 20:37 and fell on Paul's neck, and k· him,

kisses
Pr 27: 6 the k· of an enemy are deceitful.
Ca 1: 2 kiss me with the k· of his mouth:

kite
Le 11:14 vulture, and the k· after his kind;
De 14:13 the k·, and the vulture after his kind,

Kithlish (kith'-lish)
Jos 15:40 Cabbon, and Lahmam, and K·,

Kitron (ki'-tron) See also KATTAH.
J'g 1:30 drive out the inhabitants of K·,

Kittim (kit'-tim) See also CHITTIM.
Ge 10: 4 and Tarshish, K·, and Dodanim.
1Ch 1: 7 and Tarshish, K·, and Dodanim.

knead See also KNEADED; KNEADINGTROUGHS.
Ge 18: 6 of fine meal, k· it, and make cakes
Jer 7:18 and the women k· their dough, to

kneaded
1Sa 28:24 took flour, and k· it, and did bake
2Sa 13: 8 she took flour, and k· it, and made
Ho 7: 4 raising after he hath k· the dough,

kneadingtroughs
Ex 8: 3 into thine ovens, and into thy k·:
12:34 k· being bound up in their clothes

knee See also KNEES.
Ge 41:43 they cried before him, Bow the k·:
Isa 45:23 That unto me every k· shall bow,
M't 27:29 they bowed the k· before him, and
Ro 11: 4 have not bowed the k· to the image
14:11 the Lord, every k· shall bow to me,
Ph'p 2:10 name of Jesus every k· should bow,

kneel See also KNEELED; KNEELING.
Ge 24:11 he made his camels to k· down
Ps 95: 6 let us k· before the Lord our maker.

kneeled
2Ch 6:13 k· down upon his knees before
Da 6:10 he k· upon his knees three times
M'r 10:17 came one running, and k· to him,
Lu 22:41 cast, and k· down, and prayed,
Ac 7:60 he k· down, and cried with a
9:40 forth, and k· down, and prayed;
20:36 he k· down, and prayed with
21: 5 we k· down on the shore, and

kneeling
1Ki 8:54 from k· on his knees with his
M't 17:14 a certain man, k· down to him,
M'r 1:40 beseeching him, and k· down to him,

knees
Ge 30: 3 she shall bear upon my k·, that I
48:12 them out from between his k·,
50:23 were brought up upon Joseph's k·.
De 28:35 The Lord shall smite thee in the k·,
J'g 7: 5 boweth down upon his k· to drink.
6 down upon their k· to drink water.
16:19 made him sleep upon her k·; and
1Ki 8:54 kneeling on his k· with his hands
18:42 and put his face between his k·,
19:18 k· which have not bowed unto Baal,
2Ki 1:13 and fell on his k· before Elijah,
4:20 he sat on her k· till noon, and then
2Ch 6:13 kneeled down upon his k· before all
Ezr 9: 5 I fell upon my k·, and spread out
Job 3:12 Why did the k· prevent me? or why
4: 4 hast strengthened the feeble k·.
Ps 109:24 My k· are weak through fasting;
Isa 35: 3 hands, and confirm the feeble k·.
66:12 sides, and be dandled upon her k·.
Eze 7:17 and all k· shall be weak as water.
21: 7 and all k· shall be weak as water:
47: 4 waters; the waters were to the k·.
Da 5: 6 and his k· smote one against
6:10 kneeled upon his k· three times a
10:10 which set me upon my k· and upon
Na 2:10 and the k· smite together, and
M'r 15:19 bowing their k· worshipped him.
Lu 5: 8 he fell down at Jesus' k·, saying,
Eph 3:14 I bow my k· unto the Father of our
Heb 12:12 hang down, and the feeble k·;

knew See also FOREKNEW; KNEWEST.
Ge 3: 7 and they k· that they were naked;
4: 1 Adam k· Eve his wife; and she
17 Cain k· his wife; and she conceived,
25 Adam k· his wife again; and she

Ge 8:11 Noah *k*· that the waters were abated
9:24 *k*· what his younger son had done
28:16 Lord is in this place; and I *k*· it not.
31:32 *k*· not that Rachel had stolen them.
37:33 he *k*· it, and said, It is my son's
38: 9 Onan *k*· that the seed should not
16 he *k*· not that she was his daughter
26 son. And he *k*· her again no more.
39: 6 he *k*· not ought he had, save the
42: 7 saw his brethren, and he *k*· them,
8 Joseph *k*· his brethren, but they *k*·
23 they *k*· not that Joseph understood
Ex 1: 8 over Egypt, which *k*· not Joseph.
Nu 22:34 I *k*· not that thou stoodest in the
24:16 and *k*· the knowledge of the most
De 8:16 manna, which thy fathers *k*· not,
9:24 Lord from the day that I *k*· you.
29:26 gods whom they *k*· not, and whom
32:17 to gods whom they *k*· not, to new
33: 9 brethren, nor *k*· his own children:
34:10 whom the Lord *k*· face to face,
J'g 2:10 which *k*· not the Lord, nor yet the
3: 2 least such as before *k*· nothing
11:39 had vowed: and she *k*· no man.
13:16 Manoah *k*· not that he was an angel
21 *k*· that he was an angel of the Lord.
14: 4 mother *k*· not that it was of the
18: 3 they *k*· the voice of the young man
19:25 they *k*· her, and abused her all the
20:34 they *k*· not that evil was near them.
1Sa 1:19 Elkanah *k*· Hannah his wife; and
2:12 of Belial; they *k*· not the Lord.
3:20 *k*· that Samuel was established to
10:11 all that *k*· him beforetime saw that
14: 3 *k*· not that Jonathan was gone.
18:28 *k*· that the Lord was with David,
20: 9 If I *k*· certainly that evil were
33 Jonathan *k*· that it was determined
39 the lad *k*· not any thing: only
39 Jonathan and David *k*· the matter.
22:15 thy servant *k*· nothing of all this,
17 because they *k*· when he fled, and
22 I *k*· it that day, when Doeg the
23: 9 David *k*· that Saul secretly practised
26:12 and no man saw it, nor *k*· it, neither
17 Saul *k*· David's voice, and said,
2Sa 3:26 well of Sirah: but David *k*· it not.
11:16 where he *k*· that valiant men were.
20 *k*· ye not that they would shoot the
15:11 simplicity, and they *k*· not any thing.
18:29 tumult, but I *k*· not what it was.
22:44 which I *k*· not shall serve me.
1Ki 1: 4 to him: but the king *k*· her not.
18: 7 and he *k*· him, and fell on his face,
2Ki 4:39 of pottage: for they *k*· them not.
2Ch 33:13 *k*· that the Lord he was God.
Ne 2:16 the rulers *k*· not whither I went,
Es 1:13 the wise men, which *k*· the times,
13 all that *k*· law and judgment:
Job 2:12 and *k*· him not, they lifted up their
23: 3 I knew where I might find him!
29:16 cause which I *k*· not I searched out.
42: 3 wonderful for me, which I *k*· not.
Ps 35:11 my charge things that I *k*· not.
15 together against me, and I *k*· it not;
Pr 24:12 Behold, we *k*· it not; doth not he
Isa 42:16 blind by a way that they *k*· not;
25 on fire round about, yet he *k*· not;
48: 4 I *k*· that thou art obstinate, and
7 shouldest say, Behold, I *k*· them.
8 I *k*· that thou wouldest deal very
55: 5 nations that *k*· not thee shall run
Jer 1: 5 formed thee in the belly I *k*· thee;
2: 8 they that handle the law *k*· me not:
11:19 I *k*· not that they had devised
32: 8 Then I *k*· that this was the word
41: 4 slain Gedaliah, and no man *k*· it,
44: 3 serve other gods, whom they *k*· not,
15 the men which *k*· that their wives
Eze 10:20 I *k*· that they were the cherubims.
19: 7 And he *k*· their desolate palaces,
Da 5:21 he *k*· that the most high God ruled
6:10 when Daniel *k*· that the writing
11:38 his fathers *k*· not shall he honour
Ho 8: 4 have made princes, and I *k*· it not:
11: 3 but they *k*· not that I healed them.
Jon 1:10 the men *k*· that he fled from the
4: 2 I *k*· that thou art a gracious God,
Zec 7:14 all the nations whom they *k*· not.
11:11 *k*· that it was the word of the Lord.
M't 1:25 *k*· her not till she had brought
7:23 profess unto them, I never *k*· you:
12:15 But when Jesus *k*· it, he withdrew
25 Jesus *k*· their thoughts, and said
17:12 already, and they *k*· him not,
24:39 *k*· not until the flood came, and
25:24 I *k*· thee that thou art an...man,
27:18 For he *k*· that for envy they had
M'r 1:34 to speak, because they *k*· him.
6:33 them departing, and many *k*· him,
38 when they *k*·, they say, Five, and
54 of the ship, straightway they *k*· him,
8:17 when Jesus *k*· it, he saith unto
12:12 *k*· that he had spoken the parable
15:10 he *k*· that the chief priests had
45 when he *k*· it of the centurion, he
Lu 2:43 Joseph and his mother *k*· not of it.
4:41 for they *k*· that he was Christ.
6: 8 But he *k*· their thoughts, and said
7:37 when she *k*· that Jesus sat at meat
9:11 when they *k*· it, followed him:
12:47 servant, which *k*· his lord's will,
48 he that *k*· not, and did commit
18:34 neither *k*· they the things which
23: 7 as soon as he *k*· that he belonged
24:31 were opened, and they *k*· him;

Joh 1:10 by him, and the world *k*· him not.
31 I *k*· him not: but that he should
33 I *k*· him not: but he that sent me
2: 9 wine, and *k*· not whence it was:
9 servants which drew the water *k*·;)
24 unto them, because he *k*· all men,
25 of man: for he *k*· what was in man.
4: 1 the Lord *k*· how the Pharisees had
53 father *k*· that it was at the same
5: 6 *k*· that he had been now a long
6: 6 he himself *k*· what he would do.
61 When Jesus *k*· in himself that his
64 For Jesus *k*· from the beginning
11:42 I *k*· that thou hearest me always:
57 that, if any man *k*· where he were,
12: 9 the Jews therefore *k*· that he was
13: 1 Jesus *k*· that his hour was come
11 For he *k*· who should betray him;
28 *k*· for what intent he spake this
16:19 *k*· that they were desirous to ask
18: 2 which betrayed him, *k*· the place:
20: 9 For as yet they *k*· not the scripture,
14 and *k*· not that it was Jesus.
21: 4 disciples *k*· not that it was Jesus.
Ac 3:10 *k*·...it was he which sat for alms
7:18 king arose, which *k*· not Joseph.
9:30 Which when the brethren *k*·, they
12:14 And when she *k*· Peter's voice, she
13:27 because they *k*· him not, nor yet the
16: 3 *k*· all that his father was a Greek.
19:32 *k*· not wherefore they were come
34 when they *k*· that he was a Jew,
22:29 after he *k*· that he was a Roman,
26: 5 Which *k*· me from the beginning,
27:39 it was day, they *k*· not the land:
28: 1 *k*· that the island was called Melita.
Ro 1:21 when they *k*· God, they glorified
1Co 1:21 the world by wisdom *k*· not God,
2: 8 of the princes of this world *k*·:
2Co 5:21 him to be sin for us, who *k*· no sin
12: 2 *k*· a man in Christ above fourteen
3 I *k*· such a man, (whether in the
Ga 4: 8 when ye *k*· not God, ye did service
Col 1: 6 and *k*· the grace of God in truth:
2: 1 that ye *k*· what great conflict I
1Jo 3: 1 us not, because it *k*· him not.
Jude 5 though ye once *k*· this, how that
Re 19:12 a name written, that no man *k*·,

knewest
De 8: 3 with manna, which thou *k*· not,
Ru 2:11 people which thou *k*· not heretofore.
Ne 9:10 for thou *k*· that they dealt proudly
Ps 142: 3 within me, then thou *k*· my path.
Isa 48: 8 thou heardest not; yea, thou *k*· not;
Da 5:22 heart, though thou *k*· all this;
M't 25:26 thou *k*· that I reap where I sowed
Lu 19:22 Thou *k*· that I was an austere man,
44 *k*· not the time of thy visitation.
Joh 4:10 If thou *k*· the gift of God, and who

knife See KNIVES; PENKNIFE.
Ge 22: 6 took the fire in his hand, and a *k*·;
10 hand, and took the *k*· to slay his son.
J'g 19:29 he took a *k*·, and laid hold on his
Pr 23: 2 put a *k*· to thy throat, if thou be a
Eze 5: 1 take thee a sharp *k*·, take thee a
2 part, and smite about it with a *k*·:

knit
J'g 20:11 the city, *k*· together as one man.
1Sa 18: 1 Jonathan was *k*· with the soul of
1Ch 12:17 mine heart shall be *k*· unto you:
Ac 10:11 great sheet *k*· at the four corners,
Col 2: 2 being *k*· together in love, and unto
19 and *k*· together, increaseth with the

knives
Jos 5: 2 thee sharp *k*·, and circumcise
3 him sharp *k*·, and circumcised the
1Ki 18:28 their manner with *k*· and lancets,
Ezr 1: 9 of silver, nine and twenty *k*·,
Pr 30:14 swords, and their jaw teeth as *k*·,

knock See also KNOCKED; KNOCKETH; KNOCKING.
M't 7: 7 *k*·, and it shall be opened unto
Lu 11: 9 *k*·, and it shall be opened unto you.
13:25 stand without, and to *k*· at the door
Re 3:20 Behold, I stand at the door, and *k*·:

knocked
Ac 12:13 And as Peter *k*· at the door of the

knocketh
Ca 5: 2 is the voice of my beloved that *k*·,
M't 7: 8 to him that *k*· it shall be opened.
Lu 11:10 to him that *k*· it shall be opened.
12:36 that when he cometh and *k*·, they

knocking
Ac 12:16 But Peter continued *k*·: and when

knop See also KNOPS.
Ex 25:33 a *k*· and a flower in one branch;
33 branch, with a *k*· and a flower:
35, 35, 35 *k*· under two branches of the
37:19 in one branch, a *k*· and a flower;
19 in another branch, a *k*· and a flower:
21, 21, 21 *k*· under two branches of the

knops
Ex 25:31 his *k*·, and his flowers, shall be of
34 with their *k*· and their flowers.
36 *k*· and their branches shall be of
37:17 his *k*·, and his flowers, were of the
20 almonds, his *k*·, and his flowers:
22 *k*· and their branches were of the
1Ki 6:18 carved with *k*· and open flowers:
7:24 about there were *k*· compassing it,
24 the *k*· were cast in two rows, when

know See also FOREKNOW; KNEW; KNOWEST; KNOWETH; KNOWING; KNOWN.
Ge 3: 5 God doth *k*· that in the day ye eat

Ge 3:22 as one of us, to *k*· good and evil:
4: 9 I *k*· not: Am I my brother's keeper?
12:11 I *k*· that thou art a fair woman to
15: 8 shall I *k*· that I shall inherit it?
13 *K*· of a surety that thy seed shall
18:19 For I *k*· him, that he will command
21 come unto me; and if not, I will *k*·.
19: 5 out unto us, that we may *k*· them.
20: 6 Yea, I *k*· that thou didst this in the
7 *k*· thou that thou shalt surely die,
22:12 for now I *k*· that thou fearest God,
24:14 I *k*· that thou hast shewed kindness
27: 2 old, I *k*· not the day of my death:
29: 5 *K*· ye Laban the son of Nahor?
5 And they said, We *k*· him.
31: 6 And ye *k*· that with all my power I
37:32 *k*· now whether it be thy son's coat
42:33 shall I *k*· that ye are true men;
34 then shall I *k*· that ye are no spies,
43: 7 we certainly *k*· that he would say,
44:27 *k*· that my wife bare me two sons:
48:19 and said, I *k*· it, my son, I *k*· it:
Ex 3: 7 taskmasters; for I *k*· their sorrows;
4:14 I *k*· that he can speak well.
5: 2 I *k*· not the Lord, neither will I let
6: 7 ye shall *k*· that I am the Lord your
7: 5 shall *k*· that I am the Lord, when I
17 thou shalt *k*· that I am the Lord:
8:10 *k*· that there is none like unto the
22 end mayest *k*· that I am the Lord
9:14 *k*· that there is none like me in all
29 *k*· how that the earth is the Lord's.
30 *k*· that ye will not yet fear the Lord
10: 2 ye may *k*· how that I am the Lord.
26 we *k*· not with what we must serve
11: 7 may *k*· how that the Lord doth put
14: 4 may *k*· that I am the Lord.
18 shall *k*· that I am the Lord, when I
16: 6 shall *k*· that the Lord hath brought
12 ye shall *k*· that I am the Lord your
18:11 I *k*· that the Lord is greater than all
16 make them *k*· the statutes of God,
23: 9 for ye *k*· the heart of as tranger,
29:46 they shall *k*· that I am the Lord
31:13 that ye may *k*· that I am the Lord
33: 5 that I may *k*· what to do unto thee.
12 not let me *k*· whom thou wilt send
12 I *k*· thee by name, and thou hast
13 that I may *k*· thee, that I may find
17 in my sight, and I *k*· thee by name.
36: 1 *k*· how to work all manner of work
Le 23:43 That your generations may *k*· that
Nu 14:31 *k*· the land which ye have despised.
34 ye shall *k*· my breach of promise.
16:28 ye shall *k*· that the Lord hath sent
22:19 that I may *k*· what the Lord will say
De 3:19 (for I *k*· that ye have much cattle,)
4:35 mightest *k*· that the Lord he is God;
39 *K*· therefore this day, and consider
7: 9 *K*· therefore that the Lord thy God,
8: 2 to *k*· what was in thine heart,
3 not, neither did thy fathers *k*·;
3 thee *k*· that man doth not live by
11: 2 And *k*· ye this day: for I speak not
13: 3 to *k*· whether ye love the Lord your
18:21 How shall we *k*· the word which the
22: 2 if thou *k*· him not, then thou shalt
29: 6 that ye might *k*· that I am the Lord
16 ye *k*· how we have dwelt in the land
31:21 I *k*· their imagination which they
27 I *k*· thy rebellion, and thy stiff neck:
29 For I *k*· that after my death ye will
Jos 2: 9 *k*· that the Lord hath given you the
3: 4 *k*· the way by which ye must go:
7 may *k*· that, as I was with Moses,
10 *k*· that the living God is among you
4:22 Then ye shall let your children *k*·,
24 earth might *k*· the hand of the Lord,
22:22 he knoweth, and Israel he shall *k*·;
23:13 *K*· for a certainty that the Lord
14 *k*· in all your hearts and in all your
J'g 3: 2 Israel might *k*·, to teach them war,
4 to *k*· whether they would hearken
6:37 shall I *k*· that thou wilt save Israel
17:13 *k*· I that the Lord will do me good,
18: 5 *k*· whether our way which we go
14 *k*· that there is in these houses an
19:22 thine house, that we may *k*· him.
Ru 3:11 *k*· that thou art a virtuous woman.
14 up before one could *k*· another.
18 thou *k*· how the matter will fall:
4: 4 it, then tell me, that I may *k*·:
1Sa 3: 7 Samuel did not yet *k*· the Lord,
6: 9 *k*· that it is not his hand that smote
14:38 *k*· and see wherein this sin hath
17:28 I *k*· thy pride, and the naughtiness
46 may *k*· that there is a God in Israel.
47 *k*·...the Lord saveth not with sword
20: 3 Let not Jonathan *k*· this, lest he be
30 I *k*· that thou hast chosen the son
21: 2 no man *k*· any thing of the business
22: 3 till I *k*· what God will do for me.
23:22 *k*· and see his place where his haunt
24:11 *k*· thou and see that there is neither
20 I *k*·...that thou shalt surely be king,
25:11 whom I *k*· not whence they be?
17 *k*· and consider what thou wilt do;
28: 1 *K*· thou assuredly, that thou shalt
2 shalt *k*· what thy servant can do.
29: 9 I *k*· that thou art good in my sight,
2Sa 3:25 to *k*· thy going out and thy coming
25 in, and to *k*· all that thou doest.
38 *K*· ye not that there is a prince and
7:21 things, to make thy servant *k*· them.
14:20 *k*· all things that are in the earth.
19:20 servant doth *k*· that I have sinned:

2Sa 19: 22 do not I *k*' that I am this day king
24: 2 I may *k*' the number of the people.
1Ki 2: 37 *k*' for certain that thou shalt surely
42 *K*' for a certain, on the day thou
3: 7 I *k*' not how to go out or come in.
8: 38 which shall *k*' every man the plague
43 people of the earth may *k*' thy name,
43 that they may *k*' that this house,
60 earth may *k*' that the Lord is God,
17: 24 I *k*' that thou art a man of God,
18: 12 shall carry thee whither I *k*' not;
37 may *k*' that thou art the Lord God,
20: 13 thou shalt *k*' that I am the Lord.
28 and ye shall *k*' that I am the Lord.
22: 3 *K*' ye that Ramoth in Gilead is ours,
2Ki 2: 3, 5 Yea, I *k*' it; hold ye your peace.
5: 8 he shall *k*' that there is a prophet
15 I *k*' that there is no God in all the
7: 12 They *k*' that we be hungry;
8: 12 I *k*' the evil that thou wilt do unto
9: 11 he said unto them, Ye *k*' the man,
10: 10 *K*' now that there shall fall unto
17: 26 *k*' not the manner of the God of the
26 they *k*' not the manner of the God
19: 19 may *k*' that thou art the Lord God,
27 I *k*' thy abode, and thy going out,
1Ch 12: 32 to *k*' what Israel ought to do;
21: 2 of them to me, that I may *k*' it.
28: 9 son, *k*' thou the God of thy father,
29: 17 I *k*' also, my God, that thou triest
2Ch 2: 8 I *k*' that thy servants can skill to
6: 29 every one shall *k*' his own sore and
33 of the earth may *k*' thy name,
33 *k*' that this house which I have
12: 8 that they may *k*' my service, and
13: 5 Ought ye not to *k*' that the Lord
20: 12 neither *k*' we what to do: but our
25: 16 I *k*' that God hath determined to
32: 13 *K*' ye not what I and my fathers
31 might *k*' all that was in his heart.
Ezr 4: 15 and *k*' that this city is a rebellious
7: 25 all such as *k*' the laws of thy God;
25 teach ye them that *k*' them not.
Ne 4: 11 They shall not *k*', neither see, till
Es 2: 11 to *k*' how Esther did, and what
4: 5 to *k*' what it was, and why it was.
11 people of the king's provinces, do *k*',
Job 5: 24 thou shalt *k*' that thy tabernacle
25 shalt *k*' also that thy seed shall be
27 hear it, and *k*' thou it for thy good.
7: 10 shall his place *k*' him any more.
8: 9 but of yesterday, and *k*' nothing,
9: 2 I *k*' it is so of a truth: but how
5 the mountains, and they *k*' not:
21 perfect, yet would I not *k*' my soul:
28 I *k*' that thou wilt not hold me
10: 13 heart: I *k*' that this is with thee.
11: 6 *K*' therefore that God exacteth of
8 than hell; what canst thou *k*'?
13: 2 What ye *k*', the same do I...also:
2 What ye...the same do I *k*' also:
18 cause; I *k*' that I shall be justified.
23 make me to *k*' my transgression
15: 9 What knowest thou, that we *k*' not?
19: 6 *K*' now that God hath overthrown
25 For I *k*' that my redeemer liveth,
29 that ye may *k*' there is a judgment.
21: 19 rewardeth him, and he shall *k*' it.
27 Behold, I *k*' your thoughts, and
29 and do ye not *k*' their tokens,
22: 13 thou sayest, How doth God *k*'?
23: 5 I would *k*' the words which he
24: 1 they that *k*' him not see his days?
13 they *k*' not the ways thereof, nor
16 daytime: they *k*' not the light.
17 if one *k*' them, they are in the
30: 23 I *k*' that thou wilt bring...death,
31: 6 that God may *k*' mine integrity.
32: 22 I *k*' not to give flattering titles;
34: 4 *k*' among ourselves what is good.
36: 26 God is great, and we *k*' him not,
37: 7 man; that all men may *k*' his work.
15 Dost thou *k*' when God disposed
16 *k*' the balancings of the clouds,
38: 12 the dayspring to *k*' his place;
20 that thou shouldest *k*' the paths
42: 2 I *k*' that thou canst do every thing,
Ps 4: 3 But *k*' that the Lord hath set apart
9: 10 they that *k*' thy name will put their
20 nations may *k*' themselves...men.
20: 6 Now *k*' I that the Lord saveth his
36: 10 lovingkindness...them that *k*' thee;
39: 4 Lord, make me to *k*' mine end,
4 it is; that I may *k*' how frail I am.
41: 11 this I *k*' that thou favourest me,
46: 10 Be still, and *k*' that I am God:
50: 11 I *k*' all the fowls of the mountains:
51: 6 thou shalt make me to *k*' wisdom.
56: 9 back: this I *k*'; for God is for me.
59: 13 them *k*' that God ruleth in Jacob
71: 15 day; I *k*' not the numbers thereof.
73: 11 And they say, How doth God *k*'?
16 When I thought to *k*' this, it was
78: 6 generation to come might *k*' them,
82: 5 They *k*' not, neither will they
83: 18 That men may *k*' that thou, whose
87: 4 and Babylon to them that *k*' me:
89: 15 the people that *k*' the joyful sound:
94: 10 man knowledge, shall not he *k*'?
100: 3 *K*' ye that the Lord he is God: it
101: 4 me: I will not *k*' a wicked person.
103: 16 place thereof shall *k*' it no more.
109: 27 they may *k*' that this is thy hand;
119: 75 I *k*',...that thy judgments are right,
125 that I may *k*' thy testimonies.
135: 5 For I *k*' that the Lord is great,

Ps 139: 23 me, O God, and *k*' my heart:
23 heart: try me, and *k*' my thoughts:
140: 12 *k*' that the Lord will maintain the
142: 4 was no man that would *k*' me:
143: 8 cause me to *k*' the way wherein I
Pr 1: 2 To *k*' wisdom and instruction; to
4: 1 and attend to *k*' understanding.
19 they *k*' not at what they stumble.
5: 6 that thou canst not *k*' them.
10: 32 righteous *k*' what is acceptable:
22: 21 That I might make thee *k*' the
24: 12 keepeth thy soul, doth not he *k*' it?
25: 8 lest thou *k*' not what to do in the end
27: 23 diligent to *k*' the state of...flocks,
29: 7 the wicked regardeth not to *k*' it.
30: 18 for me, yea, four which I *k*' not:
Ec 1: 17 I gave my heart to *k*' wisdom,
17 and to *k*' madness and folly:
3: 12 I *k*' that there is no good in them,
14 I *k*' that, whatsoever God doeth, it
7: 25 I applied mine heart to *k*', and to
25 to *k*' the wickedness of folly, even
8: 12 yet surely I *k*' that it shall be well
16 I applied mine heart to *k*' wisdom,
17 though a wise man think to *k*' it,
9: 5 the living *k*' that they shall die: but
5 the dead *k*' not any thing, neither
11: 9 but *k*' thou, that for all these things
Ca 1: 8 If thou *k*' not, O thou fairest
Isa 1: 3 Israel doth not *k*', my people doth
5: 19 nigh and come, that we may *k*' it!
7: 15 that he may *k*' to refuse the evil,
16 the child shall *k*' to refuse the evil,
9: 9 And all the people shall *k*', even
19: 12 and let them *k*' what the Lord of
21 and the Egyptians shall *k*' the Lord
37: 20 all the kingdoms of the earth may *k*'
28 But I *k*' thy abode, and thy going
41: 20 That they may see, and *k*', and
22 them, and *k*' the latter end of them;
23 that we may *k*' that ye are gods:
26 the beginning, that we may *k*'?
43: 10 that ye may *k*' and believe me,
19 spring forth; shall ye not *k*' it?
44: 8 yea, there is no God; I *k*' not any.
9 own witnesses; they see not, nor *k*';
45: 3 that thou mayest *k*' that I, the
6 may *k*' from the rising of the sun,
47: 8 shall I *k*' the loss of children:
11 shalt not *k*' from whence it riseth:
11 suddenly, which thou shalt not *k*'.
48: 6 things, and thou didst not *k*' them.
49: 23 thou shalt *k*' that I am the Lord:
26 all flesh shall *k*' that I the Lord
50: 4 that I should *k*' how to speak a
7 I *k*' that I shall not be ashamed.
51: 7 unto me, ye that *k*' righteousness,
52: 6 my people shall *k*' my name:
6 they shall *k*' in that day that I am
58: 2 daily, and delight to *k*' my ways,
59: 8 The way of peace they *k*' not;
8 goeth therein shall not *k*' peace.
12 as for our iniquities, we *k*' them;
60: 16 and thou shalt *k*' that I the Lord
66: 18 I *k*' their works and their thoughts:
Jer 2: 19 *k*' therefore and see that it is an
23 valley, *k*' what thou hast done:
5: 1 of Jerusalem, and see now, and *k*',
4 for they *k*' not the way of the Lord,
6: 18 Therefore hear, ye nations, and *k*',
27 thou mayest *k*' and try their way.
7: 9 after other gods whom ye *k*' not;
8: 7 people *k*' not the judgment of the
9: 3 and they *k*' not me, saith the Lord.
6 through deceit they refuse to *k*' me,
10: 23 I *k*' that the way of man is not in
25 upon the heathen that *k*' thee not,
11: 18 me knowledge of it, and I *k*' it:
13: 12 *k*' that every bottle shall be filled
14: 18 about into a land that they *k*' not.
15: 15 *k*' that for thy sake I have suffered
16: 13 land into a land that ye *k*' not,
21 I will this once cause them to *k*',
21 shall *k*' that my name is The Lord.
17: 9 desperately wicked: who can *k*' it?
22: 16 was not this to *k*' me? saith the
28 into a land which they *k*' not?
24: 7 I will give them an heart to *k*' me,
26: 15 *k*' ye for certain, that if ye put me
29: 11 For I *k*' the thoughts that I think
16 *k*' that thus saith the Lord of the
23 even I *k*', and am a witness, saith
31: 34 his brother, saying, *K*' the Lord:
36: 19 and let no man *k*' where ye be.
38: 24 Let no man *k*' of these words, and
40: 14 Dost thou certainly *k*' that Baalis
15 Nethaniah, and no man shall *k*' it:
42: 19 *k*' certainly that I have admonished
22 *k*' certainly that ye shall die by the
44: 28 shall *k*' whose words shall stand,
29 *k*' that my words shall surely stand
48: 17 all ye that *k*' his name, say, How is
30 I *k*' his wrath, saith the Lord; but
Eze 2: 5 *k*' that there hath been a prophet
5: 13 *k*' that I the Lord have spoken it
6: 7 and ye shall *k*' that I am the Lord.
10 they shall *k*' that I am the Lord,
13 shall ye *k*' that I am the Lord,
14 they shall *k*' that I am the Lord.
7: 4 and ye shall *k*' that I am the Lord.
9 shall *k*' I am the Lord that smiteth.
27 they shall *k*' that I am the Lord.
11: 5 I *k*' the things that come into your
10 and ye shall *k*' that I am the Lord.
12 And ye shall *k*' that I am the Lord:
12: 15 they shall *k*' that I am the Lord,

Eze 12: 16 they shall *k*' that I am the Lord.
20 and ye shall *k*' that I am the Lord.
13: 9 ye shall *k*' that I am the Lord God.
14, 21, 23 shall *k*' that I am the Lord.
14: 8 and ye shall *k*' that I am the Lord.
23 *k*'...I have not done without cause
15: 7 and ye shall *k*' that I am the Lord,
16: 2 Jerusalem to *k*' her abominations,
62 thou shalt *k*' that I am the Lord:
17: 12 *K*' ye not what these things mean?
21 *k*' that I the Lord have spoken it.
24 of the field shall *k*' that I the Lord
20: 4 to *k*' the abominations of their
12 *k*' that I am the Lord that sanctify
20 *k*' that I am the Lord your God.
26 they might *k*' that I am the Lord.
38 and ye shall *k*' that I am the Lord.
42, 44 ye shall *k*' that I am the Lord.
21: 5 all flesh may *k*' that I the Lord have
22: 16 thou shalt *k*' that I am the Lord.
22 *k*' that I the Lord have poured out
23: 49 ye shall *k*' that I am the Lord God.
24: 24 ye shall *k*' that I am the Lord God.
27 they shall *k*' that I am the Lord.
25: 5 and ye shall *k*' that I am the Lord.
7 thou shalt *k*' that I am the Lord.
11 they shall *k*' that I am the Lord.
14 and they shall *k*' my vengeance,
17 they shall *k*' that I am the Lord.
26: 6 they shall *k*' that I am the Lord.
28: 19 they that *k*' thee among the people
22 they shall *k*' that I am the Lord,
23 they shall *k*' that I am the Lord.
24 they shall *k*' that I am the Lord God.
26 they shall *k*' that I am the Lord
29: 6 all the inhabitants of Egypt shall *k*'
9 they shall *k*' that I am the Lord:
16 they shall *k*' that I am the Lord God.
21 they shall *k*' that I am the Lord.
30: 8 they shall *k*' that I am the Lord,
19 they shall *k*' that I am the Lord.
25 they shall *k*' that I am the Lord,
26 they shall *k*' that I am the Lord.
32: 15 shall they *k*' that I am the Lord.
33: 29 shall they *k*' that I am the Lord,
33 they *k*' that a prophet hath been
34: 27 and shall *k*' that I am the Lord,
30 Thus shall they *k*' that I the Lord
35: 4 thou shalt *k*' that I am the Lord.
9 and ye shall *k*' that I am the Lord.
12 thou shalt *k*' that I am the Lord,
15 they shall *k*' that I am the Lord.
36: 11 and ye shall *k*' that I am the Lord.
23 heathen shall *k*' that I am the Lord,
36 *k*' that I the Lord build the ruined
38 they shall *k*' that I am the Lord.
37: 6 and ye shall *k*' that I am the Lord.
13 And ye shall *k*' that I am the Lord,
14 ye *k*' that I the Lord have spoken
28 heathen shall *k*' that I the Lord do
38: 14 dwelleth safely, shalt thou not *k*' it?
16 that the heathen may *k*' me, when
23 they shall *k*' that I am the Lord.
39: 6 they shall *k*' that I am the Lord.
7 heathen shall *k*' that I am the Lord,
22 Israel shall *k*' that I am the Lord
23 heathen shall *k*' that the house of
28 shall they *k*' that I am the Lord
Da 2: 3 spirit was troubled to *k*' the dream.
8 *k*' of certainty that ye would gain
9 I shall *k*' that ye can shew me the
21 to them that *k*' understanding:
30 *k*' the thoughts of thy heart.
4: 9 I *k*' that the spirit of the holy gods
17 intent that the living may *k*' that
25 till thou *k*' that the most High
32 until thou *k*' that the most High
5: 23 which see not, nor hear, nor *k*':
6: 15 *K*',...that the law of the Medes and
7: 16 and made me *k*' the interpretation
19 I would *k*' the truth of the fourth
8: 19 *k*' what shall be in the last end
9: 25 *K*' therefore and understand, that
11: 32 the people that do *k*' their God shall
Ho 2: 8 she did not *k*' that I gave her corn,
20 and thou shalt *k*' the Lord.
5: 3 I *k*' Ephraim, and Israel is not hid
6: 3 Then shall we *k*', if we follow on to
3 if we follow on to *k*' the Lord:
8: 2 cry unto me, My God, we *k*' thee.
9: 7 are come; Israel shall *k*' it:
13: 4 and thou shalt *k*' no god but me:
5 I did *k*' thee in the wilderness, in
14: 9 prudent, and he shall *k*' them?
Joe 2: 27 ye shall *k*' that I am in the midst
3: 17 So shall ye *k*' that I am the Lord
Am 3: 10 they *k*' not to do right, saith the
5: 12 I *k*' your manifold transgressions
Jon 1: 7 may *k*' for whose cause this evil is
12 *k*'...for my sake this great tempest
Mic 3: 1 Is it not for you to *k*' judgment?
4: 12 *k*' not the thoughts of the Lord,
6: 5 *k*' the righteousness of the Lord.
Zec 2: 9, 11 *k*'...the Lord of hosts hath sent
4: 9 *k*' that the Lord of hosts hath sent
6: 15 *k*' that the Lord of hosts hath sent
Mal 2: 4 *k*'...I have sent this commandment
M't 6: 3 left hand *k*' what thy right hand
7: 11 *k*' how to give good gifts unto your
16 Ye shall *k*' them by their fruits.
20 by their fruits ye shall *k*' them.
9: 6 *k*' that the Son of man hath power
30 saying, See that no man *k*' it.
13: 11 *k*' the mysteries of the kingdom of
20: 22 and said, Ye *k*' not what ye ask.
25 *k*' that the princes of the Gentiles

M't 22:16 Master, we k' that thou art true,
24:32 leaves, ye k' that summer is nigh:
33 all these things, k' that it is near,
42 for ye k' not what hour your Lord
43 But k' this, that if the goodman
25:12 Verily I say unto you, I k' you not.
13 ye k' neither the day nor the hour
26: 2 k' that after two days is the feast
70 saying, I k' not what thou sayest.
72 with an oath, I do not k' the man.
74 to swear, saying, I k' not the man.
28: 5 I k' that ye seek Jesus, which was
M'r 1:24 k' thee who thou art, the Holy One
2:10 k' that the Son of man hath power
4:11 to k' the mystery of the kingdom
13 K' ye not this parable? and how
13 how then will ye k' all parables?
5:43 straitly that no man should k' it;
7:24 house, and would have no man k' it:
9:30 would not that any man should k' it.
10:38 unto them, Ye k' not what ye ask:
42 k' that they which are accounted
12:14 Master, we k' that thou art true,
24 because ye k' not the scriptures,
13:28 leaves, ye k' that summer is near:
29 come to pass, k' that it is nigh, even
33 for ye k' not when the time is.
35 k' not when the master of the house
14:68 he denied, saying, I k' not, neither
71 I k' not this man of whom ye speak.
Lu 1: 4 mightest k' the certainty of those
18 the angel, Whereby shall I k' this?
34 shall this be, seeing I k' not a man?
4:34 I k' thee who thou art; the Holy
5:24 k' that the Son of man hath power
8:10 k' the mysteries of the kingdom of
9:55 Ye k' not what manner of spirit
11:13 k' how to give good gifts unto your
12:39 And this k', that if the goodman of
13:25 you, I k' you not whence ye are:
27 you, I k' you not whence ye are;
19:15 he might k' how much every man
20:21 k' that thou sayest and teachest
21:20 k' that the desolation thereof is
30 ye see and k' of your own selves
31 k' ye that the kingdom of God is
22:57 him, saying, Woman, I k' him not.
60 Man, I k' not what thou sayest.
23:34 them; for they k' not what they do.
24:16 that they should not k' him.
Joh 1:26 one among you, whom ye k' not;
3: 2 we k' that thou art a teacher come
11 We speak that we do k', and testify
4:22 Ye worship ye k' not what:
22 we k' what we worship: for
25 unto him, I k' that Messias cometh,
32 have meat to eat that ye k' not of.
42 k' that this is indeed the Christ,
5:32 and I k' that the witness which he
42 I k' you, that ye have not the love
6:42 whose father and mother we k'?
7:17 his will, he shall k' of the doctrine,
26 k' indeed...this is the very Christ?
27 we k' this man whence he is:
28 both k' me, and ye k' whence I am:
28 sent me is true, whom ye k' not,
29 But I k' him: for I am from him,
51 hear him, and k' what he doeth?
8:14 I k' whence I came, and whither I
19 Ye neither k' me, nor my Father:
28 man, then shall ye k' that I am he,
32 ye shall k' the truth, and the truth
37 I k' that ye are Abraham's seed;
52 Now we k' that thou hast a devil.
55 have not known him; but I k' him:
55 if I should say, I k' him not,
55 but I k' him, and keep his saying.
9:12 Where is he? He said, I k' not.
20 We k' that this is our son, and that
21 means he now seeth, we k' not;
21 hath opened his eyes, we k' not:
24 we k' that this man is a sinner.
25 he be a sinner or no, I k' not:
25 one thing I k', that, whereas I was
29 We k' that God spake unto Moses:
29 fellow, we k' not from whence he is.
30 that ye k' not from whence he is,
31 we k' that God heareth not sinners:
10: 4 follow him: for they k' his voice.
5 they k' not the voice of strangers.
14 good shepherd, and k' my sheep,
15 me, even so k' I the Father:
27 sheep hear my voice, and I k' them,
38 that ye may k', and believe, that
11:22 I k', that even now, whatsoever
24 I k' that he shall rise again in the
49 said unto them, Ye k' nothing at all,
12:50 I k' that his commandment is life
13: 7 now; but thou shalt k' hereafter.
12 K' ye what I have done to you?
17 If ye k' these things, happy are ye
18 you all: I k' whom I have chosen:
35 all men k' that ye are my disciples,
14: 4 And whither I go ye k', and the
4 whither I go..., and the way ye k'.
5 Lord, we k' not whither thou goest;
5 goest; and how can we k' the way?
7 and from henceforth ye k' him,
17 but ye k' him; for he dwelleth
20 ye shall k' that I am in my Father,
31 world may k' that I love the Father;
15:18 k' that it hated me before it hated
21 they k' not him that sent me.
17: 3 might k' thee the only true God,
23 may k' that thou hast sent me,
18:21 behold, they k' what I said.
Joh 19: 4 may k' that I find no fault in him.
20: 2 k' not where they have laid him.
13 I k' not where they have laid him.
21:24 we k' that his testimony is true.
Ac 1: 7 not for you to k' the times or the
2:22 you, as ye yourselves also know:
36 the house of Israel k' assuredly,
3:16 man strong, whom ye see and k':
10:28 Ye k' how that it is an unlawful
37 That word, I say, ye k', which was
12:11 Now I k' of a surety, that the Lord
15: 7 ye k' how that a good while ago
17:19 May we k' what this new doctrine,
20 k' therefore what these things mean.
19:15 and said, Jesus I k', and Paul
15 and Paul I k'; but who are ye?
25 ye k' that by this craft we have our
20:18 Ye k', from the first day that I came
25 I k' that ye all, among whom I
29 I k' this, that after my departing
34 ye yourselves k', that these hands
21:24 all may know that those things,
34 he could not k' the certainty for the
22:14 that thou shouldest k' his will, and
19 they k' that I imprisoned and beat
24 k' wherefore they cried so against
24:10 as I k' that thou hast been of many
22 k' the uttermost of your matter.
26: 3 I k' thee to be expert in all customs
4 at Jerusalem, k' all the Jews;
27 prophets? I k' that thou believest.
28:22 we k' that every where it is spoken
Ro 3:19 k' that what things soever the law
6: 3 K' ye not, that so many of us as
16 K' ye not, that to whom ye yield
7: 1 K' ye not, brethren, (for I speak to
1 speak to them that k' the law,)
14 For we k' that the law is spiritual:
18 For I k' that in me (that is, in my
8:22 For we k' that the whole creation
26 we k' not what we should pray for
28 we k' that all things work together
10:19 But I say, Did not Israel k'? First
14:14 k', and am persuaded by the Lord
1Co 1:16 k' not whether I baptized any other.
2: 2 not to k' any thing among you, save
12 might k' the things that are freely
14 neither can he k' them, because
3:16 K' ye not that ye are the temple
4: 4 For I k' nothing by myself; yet am
19 and will k', not the speech of them
5: 6 K' ye not that a little leaven
6: 2 ye not k' that the saints shall judge
3 K' ye not...we shall judge angels?
9 K' ye not that the unrighteous
15 K' ye not that your bodies are the
16 k' ye not that he which is joined to
19 k' ye not...your body is the temple
8: 1 we k' that we all have knowledge.
2 nothing yet as he ought to k'.
4 we k' that an idol is nothing in the
9:13 ye not k' that they which minister
24 K' ye not that they which run in a
11: 3 I would have you k', that the head
12: 2 Ye k' that ye were Gentiles, carried
13: 9 we k' in part, and we prophesy in
12 now I k' in part; but then shall I
12 shall I k' even as also I am known.
14:11 I k' not the meaning of the voice,
15:58 ye k' that your labour is not in vain
16:15 (ye k' the house of Stephanas, that
2Co 2: 4 ye might k' the love which I have
9 I might k' the proof of you, whether
5: 1 we k' that if our earthly house of
16 k' we no man after the flesh:
16 now henceforth k' we him no more.
8: 9 ye k' the grace of our Lord Jesus
9: 2 I k' the forwardness of your mind,
13: 5 K' ye not your own selves, how
6 k' that we are not reprobates.
Ga 3: 7 K' ye therefore that they which are
4:13 Ye k' how through infirmity of the
Eph 1:18 k' what is the hope of his calling,
3:19 And to k' the love of Christ, which
5: 5 this ye k', that no whoremonger,
6:21 But that ye also may k' my affairs,
22 that ye might k' our affairs,
Ph'p 1:19 For I k' that this shall turn to my
25 I k' that I shall abide and continue
2:19 good comfort, when I k' your state.
22 But ye k' the proof of him, that, as
3:10 That I may k' him, and the power
4:12 I k' both how to be abased, and
12 abased, and I k' how to abound:
15 Now ye Philippians k' also, that in
Col 4: 6 ye may k' how ye ought to answer
8 that he might k' your estate, and
1Th 1: 5 ye k' what manner of men we were
2: 1 k' our entrance in unto you, that it
2 were shamefully entreated, as ye k',
5 used we flattering words, as ye k',
11 k' how we exhorted and comforted
3: 3 yourselves k' that we are appointed
4 even as it came to pass, and ye k'.
5 forbear, I sent to k' your faith,
4: 2 k' what commandments we gave
4 should k' how to possess his vessel
5 as the Gentiles which k' not God:
5: 2 yourselves k' perfectly that the day
12 k' them which labour among you,
2Th 1: 8 vengeance on them that k' not God,
2: 6 now ye k' what withholdeth that he
3: 7 k' how ye ought to follow us:
1Ti 1: 8 But we k' that the law is good,
3: 5 a man k' not how to rule his own
15 k' how thou oughtest to behave
1Ti 4: 3 which believe and k' the truth.
2Ti 1:12 for I k' whom I have believed,
3: 1 This k' also, that in the last days
Tit 1:16 They profess that they k' God;
Heb 8:11 his brother, saying, K' the Lord:
11 for all shall k' me, from the least
10:30 k' him that hath said, Vengeance
12:17 For ye k' how that afterward,
13:23 K' ye that our brother Timothy is
Jas 2:20 wilt thou k', O vain man, that faith
4: 4 k' ye not that the friendship of the
14 k' not what shall be on the morrow.
5:20 him k', that he which converteth
1Pe 1:18 ye k' that ye were not redeemed
2Pe 1:12 of these things, though ye k' them,
3:17 seeing ye k' these things before,
1Jo 2: 3 hereby we do k' that we k' him,
4 He that saith, I k' him, and keepeth
5 hereby k' we that we are in him.
18 whereby we k' that it is the last time.
20 the Holy One, and ye k' all things.
21 you because ye k' not the truth,
21 but because ye k' it, and that no lie
29 If ye k' that he is righteous,
29 ye k' that every one that doeth
3: 2 we k' that, when he shall appear,
5 k' that he was manifested to take
14 We k' that we have passed from
15 ye k' that no murderer hath eternal
19 we k' that we are of the truth,
24 hereby we k' that he abideth in us,
4: 2 Hereby k' ye the Spirit of God:
6 Hereby k' we the spirit of truth,
13 Hereby k' we that we dwell in him,
5: 2 we k' that we love the children of
13 may k' that ye have eternal life,
15 if we k' that he hear us, whatsoever
15 we k' that we have the petitions
18 We k' that whosoever is born of God
19 we k' that we are of God, and the
20 we k' that the Son of God is come,
20 that we may k' him that is true,
3Jo 12 and ye k' that our record is true.
Jude 10 of those things which they k' not:
10 but what they k' naturally, as
Re 2: 2 I k' thy works, and thy labour,
9 I k' thy works, and tribulation,
9 I k' the blasphemy of them which say
13 I k' thy works, and where thou
19 I k' thy works, and charity, and
23 k' that I am he which searcheth
3: 1 I k' thy works, that thou hast a
3 shalt not k' what hour I will come
8 I k' thy works: behold, I have set
9 and to k' that I have loved thee.
15 I k' thy works, that thou art

knowest

Ge 30:26 thou k' my service which I have
29 Thou k' how I have served thee,
47: 6 and if thou k' any men of activity
Ex 10: 7 k' thou not...Egypt is destroyed?
32:22 thou k' the people, that they are set
Nu 10:31 as thou k' how we are to encamp
11:16 whom thou k' to be the elders of the
20:14 k' all the travel that hath befallen
De 7:15 diseases of Egypt, which thou k',
9: 2 of the Anakims, whom thou k', and
20:20 Only the trees which thou k' that
28:33 a nation which thou k' not eat up;
Jos 14: 6 Thou k' the thing that the Lord
J'g 15:11 K' thou not that the Philistines
1Sa 28: 9 thou k' what Saul hath done, how
2Sa 1: 5 How k' thou that Saul and Jonathan
2:26 k' thou not that it will be bitterness
3:25 Thou k' Abner the son of Ner, that
7:20 for thou, Lord God, k' thy servant.
17: 8 thou k' thy father and his men,
1Ki 1:18 my lord the king, thou k' it not:
2: 5 thou k' also what Joab the son of
9 k' what thou oughtest to do unto
15 Thou k' that the kingdom was mine,
44 Thou k' all the wickedness which
5: 3 Thou k' how that David my father
6 thou k' that there is not among us
8:39 to his ways, whose heart thou k';
39 k' the hearts of all the children of
2Ki 2: 3, 5 k' thou that the Lord will take
4: 1 thou k' that thy servant did fear
1Ch 17:18 servant? for thou k' thy servant.
2Ch 6:30 only k' the hearts of the children
Job 10: 7 Thou k' that I am not wicked;
15: 9 What k' thou, that we know not?
20: 4 K' thou not this of old, since man
34:33 therefore speak what thou k'.
38: 5 the measures thereof, if thou k'?
18 the earth? declare if thou k' it all.
21 K' thou it, because thou wast then
33 K' thou the ordinances of heaven?
39: 1 K' thou the time when the wild
2 k' thou the time when they bring
Ps 40: 9 refrained my lips, O Lord, thou k'.
69: 5 O God, thou k' my foolishness;
139: 2 Thou k' my downsitting and mine
4 lo, O Lord, thou k' it altogether.
Pro 27: 1 thou k' not what a day may bring
Ec 11: 2 thou k' not what evil shall be upon
5 thou k' not what is the way of the
5 so thou k' not the works of God
6 thou k' not whether shall prosper,
Isa 55: 5 shalt call a nation that thou k' not,
Jer 5:15 nation whose language thou k' not,
12: 3 But thou, O Lord, k' me: thou hast
15:14 into a land which thou k' not:
15 O Lord, thou k': remember me,
17: 4 in the land which thou k' not:
16 thou k': that which came out of

Jer 18:23 thou *k* all their counsel against me
33: 3 mighty things, which thou *k* not.
Eze 37: 3 I answered, O Lord God, thou *k*.
Da 10:20 *K*...wherefore I come unto thee?
Zec 4: 5 me, *K* thou not what these be?
13 said, *K* thou not what these be?
M't 15:12 *K* thou that the Pharisees were
M'r 10:19 Thou *k* the commandments, Do
Lu 18:20 Thou *k* the commandments, Do
22:34 shalt thrice deny that thou *k* me.
Joh 1:48 unto him, Whence *k* thou me?
3:10 of Israel, and *k* not these things?
13: 7 him, What I do thou *k* not now;
16:30 are we sure that thou *k* all things,
19:10 *k* thou not that I have power to
21:15, 16 Lord; thou *k* that I love thee.
17 unto him, Lord, thou *k* all things;
17 thou *k* that I love thee.
Ac 1:24 which *k* the hearts of all men,
25:10 no wrong, as thou very well *k*.
Ro 2:18 *k* his will, and approvest the
1Co 7:16 For what *k* thou, O wife, whether
16 or how *k* thou, O man, whether
2Ti 1:15 This thou *k*, that all they which
18 me at Ephesus, thou *k* very well.
Re 3:17 and *k* not that thou art wretched,
7:14 And I said unto him, Sir, thou *k*.

knoweth
Ge 33:13 *k* that the children are tender,
Le 5: 3, 4 when he *k* of it, then he shall be
De 2: 7 he *k* thy walking through this
34: 6 no man *k* of his sepulchre unto
Jos 22:22 gods, the Lord God of gods, he *k*,
1Sa 3:13 ever for the iniquity which he *k*;
20: 3 Thy father certainly *k* that I have
23:17 and that also Saul my father *k*.
2Sa 14:22 thy servant *k*...I have found grace
17:10 Israel *k* that thy father is a mighty
1Ki 1:11 reign, and David our lord *k* it not?
Es 4:14 who *k* whether thou art come to
Job 11:11 he *k* vain men: he seeth wickedness
12: 3 who *k* not such things as these?
9 Who *k* not in all these that the
14:21 come to honour, and he *k* it not;
15:23 he *k* that the day of darkness is
18:21 is the place of him that *k* not God.
23:10 he *k* the way that I take: when he
28: 7 There is a path which no fowl *k*,
13 Man *k* not the price thereof;
23 thereof, and he *k* the place thereof.
34:25 Therefore he *k* their works, and
35:15 yet he *k* it not in great extremity:
Ps 1: 6 Lord *k* the way of the righteous:
37:18 The Lord *k* the days of the upright:
39: 6 and *k* not who shall gather them.
44:21 for he *k* the secrets of the heart.
74: 9 among us any that *k* how long.
90:11 Who *k* the power of thine anger?
92: 6 A brutish man *k* not; neither doth
94:11 The Lord *k* the thoughts of man,
103:14 he *k* our frame; he remembereth
104:19 seasons: the sun *k* his going down.
138: 6 lowly: but the proud he *k* afar off.
139:14 and that my soul *k* right well.
Pro 7:23 and *k* not that it is for his life.
9:13 she is simple, and *k* nothing.
18 he *k* not that the dead are there;
14:10 The heart *k* his own bitterness;
24:22 and who *k* the ruin of them both?
Ec 2:19 who *k* whether he shall be a wise
3:21 Who *k* the spirit of man that
6: 8 that *k* to walk before the living?
12 who *k* what is good for man in this
7:22 also thine own heart *k* that thou
8: 1 who *k* the interpretation of a
7 For he *k* not that which shall be:
9: 1 no man *k* either love or hatred by
12 For man also *k* not his time: as the
10:15 he *k* not how to go to the city.
Isa 1: 3 The ox *k* his owner, and the ass
29:15 Who seeth us? and who *k* us?
Jer 8: 7 the heaven *k* her appointed times;
9:24 that he understandeth and *k* me,
Da 2:22 he *k* what is in the darkness, and
Ho 7: 9 his strength, and he *k* it not:
9 and there upon him, yet he *k* not.
Joe 2:14 Who *k* if he will return and repent,
Na 1: 7 and he *k* them that trust in him.
Zep 3: 5 not; but the unjust *k* no shame.
M't 6: 8 *k* what things ye have need of,
32 *k* that ye have need of all these
11:27 no man *k* the Son, but the Father;
27 neither *k* any man the Father,
24:36 of that day and hour *k* no man,
M'r 4:27 spring and grow up, he *k* not how.
13:32 that day and that hour *k* no man,
Lu 10:22 and no man *k* who the Son is,
12:30 *k* that ye have need of all these
16:15 men; but God *k* your hearts:
Joh 7:15 saying, How *k* this man letters,
27 cometh, no man *k* whence he is.
49 who *k* not the law are cursed.
10:15 As the Father *k* me, even so know
12:35 darkness *k* not whither he goeth.
14:17 it seeth him not, neither *k* him:
15:15 servant *k* not what his lord doeth:
19:35 he *k* that he saith true, that ye
Ac 15: 8 And God, which *k* the hearts, bare
19:35 there that *k* not how that the city
26:26 the king *k* of these things, before
Ro 8:27 *k* what is the mind of the Spirit,
1Co 2:11 what man *k* the things of a man,
11 the things of God *k* no man, but
3:20 Lord *k* the thoughts of the wise,
8: 2 man think that he *k* any thing,
2 he *k* nothing yet as he ought to
2Co 11:11 because I love you not? God *k*.
31 for evermore, *k* that I lie not.
12: 2, 3 of the body, I cannot tell: God *k*;)
2Ti 2:19 seal, The Lord *k* them that are his.
Jas 4:17 to him that *k* to do good, and
2Pe 2: 9 Lord *k* how to deliver the godly
1Jo 2:11 *k* not whither he goeth, because
3: 1 the world *k* us not, because it
20 than our heart, and *k* all things.
4: 6 he that *k* God heareth us; he that
7 loveth is born of God, and *k* God.
8 He that loveth not, *k* not God; for
Re 2:17 no man *k* saving he that receiveth
12:12 he *k*...he hath but a short time.

knowing
Ge 3: 5 shall be as gods, *k* good and evil.
1Ki 2:32 my father David not *k* thereof,
M't 9: 4 And Jesus *k* their thoughts said,
22:29 Ye do err, not *k* the scriptures, nor
M'r 5:30 *k* in himself that virtue had gone
33 *k* what was done in her, came
6:20 *k* that he was a just man and an
12:15 *k* their hypocrisy, said unto them,
Lu 8:53 him to scorn, *k* that she was dead.
9:33 one for Elias: not *k* what he said.
11:17 *k* their thoughts, said unto them,
Joh 13: 3 Jesus *k* that the Father had given
18: 4 *k* all things that should come upon
19:28 Jesus *k* that all things were now
21:12 art thou? *k* that it was the Lord.
Ac 2:30 *k* that God had sworn with an oath
5: 7 not *k* what was done, came in.
18:25 Lord, *k* only the baptism of John.
20:22 not *k* the things that shall befall
Ro 1:32 Who *k* the judgment of God, that
2: 4 not *k* that the goodness of God
5: 3 *k* that tribulation worketh
6: 6 *K* this, that our old man is
9 *K* that Christ being raised from
13:11 *k* the time, that now it is high time
2Co 1: 7 *k*, that as ye are partakers of the
4:14 *K* that he which raised up the Lord
5: 6 *k* that, whilst we are at home in
11 *K* therefore the terror of the Lord,
Ga 2:16 *K* that a man is not justified by
Eph 6: 8 *K* that whatsoever good thing any
9 *k* that your Master...is in heaven;
Ph'p 1:17 *k* that I am set for the defence of
Col 3:24 *K* that of the Lord ye shall receive
4: 1 *k* that ye...have a Master in heaven.
1Th 1: 4 *K*, brethren beloved, your election
1Ti 1: 9 *K* this, that the law is not made
6: 4 *k* nothing, but doting about
2Ti 2:23 *k* that they do gender strifes.
3:14 *k* of whom thou hast learned them;
Tit 3:11 *K* that he that is such is subverted,
Ph'm 21 *k* that thou wilt also do more than
Heb10:34 *k* in yourselves that ye have in
11: 8 went out, not *k* whither he went.
Jas 1: 3 *K* this, that the trying of your
3: 1 *k* that we shall receive the greater
1Pe 3: 9 *k* that ye are thereunto called,
5: 9 *k* that the same afflictions are
2Pe 1:14 *K* that shortly I must put off this
20 *K* this first, that no prophecy of
3: 3 *K* this first, that there shall come

knowledge See also ACKNOWLEDGE; FOREKNOWLEDGE.
Ge 2: 9 the tree of *k* of good and evil.
17 the tree of the *k* of good and evil,
Ex 31: 3 and in understanding, and in *k*,
35:31 in understanding, and in *k*,
Le 4:23, 28 he hath sinned, come to his *k*;
Nu 15:24 without the *k* of the congregation,
24:16 and knew the *k* of the most High,
De 1:39 had no *k* between good and evil,
Ru 2:10 that thou shouldest take *k* of me,
19 be he that did take *k* of thee.
1Sa 2: 3 the Lord is a God of *k*, and by
23:23 take *k* of all the lurking places
1Ki 9:27 shipmen that had *k* of the sea.
2Ch 1:10 Give me now wisdom and *k*, that
11 asked wisdom and *k* for thyself,
12 Wisdom and *k* is granted unto
8:18 servants that had *k* of the sea;
30:22 taught the good *k* of the Lord:
Ne 10:28 every one having *k*, and having
Job 15: 2 Should a wise man utter vain *k*,
21:14 for we desire not the *k* of thy ways.
22 Shall any teach God *k*? seeing he
33: 3 and my lips shall utter *k* clearly.
34: 2 give ear unto me, ye that have *k*.
35 Job hath spoken without *k*, and
35:16 he multiplieth words without *k*.
36: 3 I will fetch my *k* from afar,
4 that is perfect in *k* is with thee.
12 and they shall die without *k*.
37:16 of him which is perfect in *k*?
38: 2 counsel by words without *k*?
42: 3 he that hideth counsel without *k*?
Ps 14: 4 all the workers of iniquity no *k*?
19: 2 and night unto night sheweth *k*.
53: 4 the workers of iniquity no *k*?
73:11 and is there *k* in the Most High?
94:10 he that teacheth man *k*, shall not
119:66 Teach me good judgment and *k*:
139: 6 Such *k* is too wonderful for me;
144: 3 man, that thou takest *k* of him!
Pr 1: 4 the young man *k* and discretion.
7 the Lord is the beginning of *k*:
22 their scorning, and fools hate *k*?
29 For that they hated *k*, and did not
2: 3 Yea, if thou criest after *k*, and
5 the Lord, and find the *k* of God.
6 out of his mouth cometh *k* and
Pr 2:10 and *k* is pleasant unto thy soul;
3:20 By his *k* the depths are broken up,
5: 2 and that thy lips may keep *k*.
8: 9 and right to them that find *k*.
10 and *k* rather than choice gold.
12 and find out *k* of witty inventions.
9:10 the *k* of the holy is understanding.
10:14 Wise men lay up *k*: but the mouth
11: 9 but through *k* shall the just be
12: 1 Whoso loveth instruction loveth *k*:
23 A prudent man concealeth *k*:
13:16 Every prudent man dealeth with *k*:
14: 6 but *k* is easy unto him that
7 perceivest not in him the lips of *k*.
18 the prudent are crowned with *k*.
15: 2 tongue of the wise useth *k* aright:
7 The lips of the wise disperse *k*:
14 hath understanding seeketh *k*:
17:27 He that hath *k* spareth his words:
18:15 heart of the prudent getteth *k*;
15 and the ear of the wise seeketh *k*.
19: 2 Also, that the soul be without *k*,
25 and he will understand *k*.
27 causeth to err from the words of *k*.
20:15 the lips of *k* are a precious jewel.
21:11 wise is instructed, he receiveth *k*.
22:12 The eyes of the Lord preserve *k*,
17 and apply thine heart unto my *k*.
20 excellent things in counsels and *k*,
23:12 and thine ears to the words of *k*.
24: 4 by *k* shall the chambers be filled
5 a man of *k* increaseth strength.
14 So shall the *k* of wisdom be unto
28: 2 a man of understanding and *k*
30: 3 nor have the *k* of the holy.
Ec 1:16 great experience of wisdom and *k*.
18 increaseth *k* increaseth sorrow.
2:21 labour is in wisdom, and in *k*,
26 good in his sight wisdom, and *k*,
7:12 the excellency of *k* is, that wisdom
9:10 there is no work, nor device, nor *k*,
12: 9 wise, he still taught the people *k*;
Isa 5:13 captivity, because they have no *k*:
8: 4 the child shall have *k* to cry,
11: 2 the spirit of *k* and of the fear of
9 shall be full of the *k* of the Lord,
28: 9 Whom shall he teach *k*? and whom
32: 4 of the rash shall understand *k*,
33: 6 wisdom and *k* shall be the stability
40:14 taught him *k*, and shewed to him
44:19 there *k* nor understanding to say,
25 and maketh their *k* foolish;
45:20 have no *k* that set up the wood
47:10 thy *k*, it hath perverted thee;
53:11 by his *k* shall my righteous servant
58: 3 our soul, and thou takest no *k*?
Jer 3:15 which shall feed you with *k* and
4:22 but to do good they have no *k*.
10:14 Every man is brutish in his *k*:
11:18 the Lord hath given me *k* of it,
51:17 Every man is brutish by his *k*;
Da 1: 4 in all wisdom, and cunning in *k*,
17 God gave them *k* and skill in all
2:21 wise, and *k* to them that know
5:12 as an excellent spirit, and *k*, and
12: 4 and fro, and *k* shall be increased.
Ho 4: 1 nor mercy, nor *k* of God in the land.
6 people are destroyed for lack of *k*:
6 because thou hast rejected *k*, I will
6: 6 *k* of God more than burnt offerings.
Hab 2:14 be filled with the *k* of the glory of
Mal 2: 7 the priest's lips should keep *k*,
M't 14:35 men of that place had *k* of him,
Lu 1:77 give *k* of salvation unto his people
11:52 ye have taken away the key of *k*.
Ac 4:13 and they took *k* of them, that they
17:13 the Jews of Thessalonica had *k*
24: 8 mayest take *k* of all these things,
22 having more perfect *k* of that way,
Ro 1:28 not like to retain God in their *k*,
2:20 hast the form of *k* and of the truth
3:20 for by the law is the *k* of sin.
10: 2 zeal of God, but not according to *k*.
11:33 both of the wisdom and *k* of God!
15:14 full of goodness, filled with all *k*,
1Co 1: 5 him, in all utterance, and in all *k*;
8: 1 idols, we know that we all have *k*.
1 *K* puffeth up, but charity edifieth.
7 there is not in every man that *k*:
10 see thee which hast *k* sit at meat
11 And through thy *k* shall the weak
12: 8 the word of *k* by the same Spirit;
13: 2 understand all mysteries, and all *k*;
8 whether there be *k*, it shall vanish
14: 6 to you either by revelation, or by *k*,
15:34 for some have not the *k* of God:
2Co 2:14 manifest the savour of his *k* by us
4: 6 light of the *k* of the glory of God
6: 6 pureness, by *k*, by longsuffering,
8: 7 in faith, and utterance, and *k*, and
10: 5 exalteth itself against the *k* of God,
11: 6 I be rude in speech, yet not in *k*;
Eph 1:17 and revelation in the *k* of him:
3: 4 my *k* in the mystery of Christ)
19 love of Christ, which passeth *k*,
4:13 and of the *k* of the Son of God,
Ph'p 1: 9 abound yet more and more in *k*
3: 8 excellency of the *k* of Christ Jesus
Col 1: 9 be filled with the *k* of his will in
10 and increasing in the *k* of God;
2: 3 all the treasures of wisdom and *k*.
3:10 is renewed in *k* after the image of
1Ti 2: 4 and to come unto the *k* of the truth.
2Ti 3: 7 able to come to the *k* of the truth.
Heb10:26 have received the *k* of the truth,
Jas 3:13 and endued with *k* among you?

1Pe 3: 7 dwell with them according to k',
2Pe 1: 2 unto you through the k' of God,
3 the k' of him that hath called us
5 your faith virtue; and to virtue k';
6 And to k', temperance; and to
8 in the k' of our Lord Jesus Christ.
2: 20 in the k' of the Lord and Saviour
3: 18 in the k' of our Lord and Saviour

known See also UNKNOWN.
Ge 19: 8 daughters which have not k' man;
24: 16 virgin, neither had any man k' her:
41: 21 could not be k' that they had eaten
31 plenty shall not be k' in the land by
45: 1 Joseph made himself k' unto his
Ex 2: 14 and said, Surely this thing is k'.
6: 3 name Jehovah was I not k' to them.
21: 36 be k' that the ox hath used to push
33: 16 it be k' here that I and thy people
Le 4: 14 they have sinned against it, is k',
5: 1 whether he hath seen or k' of it;
Nu 12: 6 Lord will make myself k' unto him
31: 17 kill every woman that hath k' man
18 children, that have not k' a man by
35 of women that had not k' man by
De 1: 13 and k' among your tribes, and I will
15 wise men, and k', and made them
11: 2 your children which have not k',
28 other gods, which ye have not k'.
13: 2, 6 other gods, which thou hast not k',
13 other gods, which ye have not k';
21: 1 and it be not k' who hath slain him:
28: 36 neither thou nor thy fathers have k';
64 neither thou nor thy fathers have k',
31: 13 children, which have not k' any
Jos 24: 31 had k' all the works of the Lord,
J'g 3: 1 had not k' all the wars of Canaan;
16: 9 the fire. So his strength was not k'.
21: 12 young virgins, that had k' no man by
Ru 3: 3 make not thyself k' unto the man,
14 Let it not be k' that a woman came
1Sa 6: 3 it shall be k' to you why his hand is
28: 15 make k' unto me what I shall do.
2Sa 17: 19 thereon; and the thing was not k'.
1Ki 14: 2 be not k' to be the wife of Jeroboam;
18: 36 it be k' this day that thou art God
1Ch 16: 8 make k' his deeds among the
17: 19 in making k' all these great things.
Ezr 4: 12 it k' unto the king, that the Jews
13 Be it k' now unto the king, that, if
5: 8 it k' unto the king, that we went
Ne 4: 15 our enemies heard that it was k'
9: 14 And madest k' unto them thy holy
Es 2: 22 And the thing was k' to Mordecai,
Ps 9: 16 The Lord is k' by the judgment
18: 43 a people whom I have not k' shall
31: 7 thou hast k' my soul in adversities;
48: 3 God is k' in her palaces for a refuge.
67: 2 That thy way may be k' upon earth,
69: 19 Thou hast k' my reproach, and my
76: 1 In Judah is God k': his name is
77: 19 waters, and thy footsteps are not k'.
78: 3 Which we have heard and k', and
5 make them k' to their children:
79: 6 the heathen that have not k' thee,
79: 10 let him be k' among the heathen in
88: 12 Shall thy wonders be k' in the dark?
89: 1 will I make k' thy faithfulness to
91: 14 high, because he hath k' my name.
95: 10 and they have not k' my ways:
98: 2 Lord hath made k' his salvation:
103: 7 He made k' his ways unto Moses,
105: 1 make k' his deeds among the people.
106: 8 make his mighty power to be k'.
119: 79 those that have k' thy testimonies.
152 k' of old that thou hast founded
139: 1 thou hast searched me, and k' me.
145: 12 To make k' to the sons of men his
147: 20 judgments, they have not k' them.
Pr 1: 23 I will make k' my words unto you.
10: 9 that perverteth his ways shall be k'.
12: 16 A fool's wrath is presently k': but
14: 33 is in the midst of fools is made k'.
20: 11 Even a child is k' by his doings,
22: 19 I have made k' to thee this day,
31: 23 Her husband is k' in the gates,
Ec 5: 3 a fool's voice is k' by multitude of
6: 5 not seen the sun, nor k' any thing:
10 already, and it is k' that it is man:
Isa 12: 5 things: this is k' in all the earth.
19: 21 the Lord shall be k' to Egypt, and
38: 19 children shall make k' thy truth.
40: 21 Have ye not k'? have ye not heard?
28 Hast thou not k'? hast thou not
42: 16 them in paths that they have not k':
44: 18 They have not k' nor understood:
45: 4 thee, though thou hast not k' me.
5 thee, though thou hast not k' me:
61: 9 seed shall be k' among the Gentiles,
64: 2 thy name k' to thine adversaries,
66: 14 hand of the Lord shall be k' toward
Jer 4: 22 is foolish, they have not k' me;
5: 5 they have k' the way of the Lord,
9: 16 they nor their fathers have k':
19: 4 they nor their fathers have k',
28: 9 pass, then shall the prophet be k',
La 4: 8 they are not k' in the streets:
Eze 20: 5 and made myself k' unto them in
9 whose sight I made myself k' unto
32: 9 countries which thou hast not k'.
35: 11 I will make myself k' among them,
36: 32 the Lord God, be it k' unto you:
38: 23 be k' in the eyes of many nations
39: 7 So will I make my holy name k' in
Da 2: 5, 9 not make k' unto me the dream,
15 Arioch made the thing k' to Daniel.
17 and made the thing k' to Hananiah,
Da 2: 23 hast made k' unto me now what
23 thou hast now made k' unto us the
25 that will make k' unto the king the
26 able to make k' unto the dream
28 k' to the king Nebuchadnezzar
29 k' to thee what shall come to pass.
30 k' the interpretation to the king,
45 God hath made k' to the king what
3: 18 be it k' unto thee, O king, that we
4: 6, 7 k' unto me the interpretation
18 make k' unto me the interpretation:
26 have k' that the heavens do rule.
5: 8 nor make k' to the king the
15 make k' unto me the interpretation
16 make k' to me the interpretation
17 make k' to him the interpretation.
Ho 5: 4 and they have not k' the Lord.
9 made k' that which shall surely be.
Am 3: 2 You only have I k' of all the
Na 3: 17 their place is not k' where they are.
Hab 3: 2 in the midst of the years make k';
Zec 14: 7 day which shall be k' to the Lord,
M't 10: 26 and hid, that shall not be k'.
12: 7 if ye had k' what this meaneth,
16 that they should not make him k':
33 for the tree is k' by his fruit.
24: 43 had k' in what watch the thief
M'r 3: 12 that they should not make him k'.
Lu 2: 15 the Lord hath made k' unto us.
17 they made k' abroad the saying
6: 44 every tree is k' by his own fruit.
7: 39 k' who and what manner of woman
8: 17 shall not be k' and come abroad.
12: 2 neither hid, that shall not be k'.
39 had k' what hour the thief would
19: 42 Saying, If thou hadst k', even thou,
24: 18 hast not k' the things which are
35 k' of them in breaking of bread.
Joh 7: 4 he himself seeketh to be k' openly.
8: 19 nor my Father: if ye had k' me,
19 ye should have k' my Father also:
55 Yet ye have not k' him; but I
10: 14 know my sheep, and am k' of mine.
14: 7 k' me, ye should have k' my Father
9 yet hast thou not k' me, Philip?
15: 15 Father I have made k' unto you.
16: 3 they have not k' the Father, nor
17: 7 Now they have k' that all things
8 have k' surely that I came out from
25 Father, the world hath not k' thee:
25 but I have k' thee, and these
25 have k' that thou hast sent me.
18: 15 that disciple was k' unto the high
16 which was k' unto the high priest,
Ac 1: 19 it was k' unto all the dwellers at
2: 14 be this k' unto you, and hearken to
28 Thou hast made k' to me the ways
4: 10 Be it k' unto you all, and to all
7: 13 Joseph was made k' to his brethren;
13 Joseph's kindred was made k'
9: 24 their laying await was k' of Saul.
42 it was k' throughout all Joppa;
13: 38 Be it k' unto you therefore, men
15: 18 K' unto God are all his works from
19: 17 And this was k' to all the Jews
22: 30 he would have k' the certainty
23: 28 when I would have k' the cause
28: 28 Be it k' therefore unto you, that
Ro 1: 19 that which may be k' of God is
3: 17 way of peace have they not k':
7: 7 I had not k' sin, but by the law:
7 I had not k' lust, except the law
9: 22 wrath, and to make his power k',
23 that he might make k' the riches
11: 34 who hath k' the mind of the Lord?
16: 26 made k' to all nations for the
1Co 2: 8 for had they k' it, they would not
16 who hath k' the mind of the Lord,
8: 3 love God, the same is k' of him.
13: 12 shall I know even as also I am k'.
14: 7 it be k' what is piped or harped?
9 how shall it be k' what is spoken?
2Co 3: 2 our hearts, k' and read of all men:
5: 16 we have k' Christ after the flesh,
6: 9 As unknown, and yet well k';
Ga 4: 9 But now, after ye have k' God,
9 rather are k' of God, how turn ye
Eph 1: 9 made k' unto us the mystery of his
3: 3 he made k' unto me the mystery;
5 not made k' unto the sons of men,
10 be k' by the church the manifold
6: 19 make k' the mystery of the gospel,
21 shall make k' to you all things:
Ph'p 4: 5 moderation be k' unto all men.
6 requests be made k' unto God.
Col 1: 27 would make k' what is the riches
4: 9 shall make k' unto you all things
2Ti 3: 10 thou hast fully k' my doctrine,
15 thou hast k' the holy scriptures,
4: 17 the preaching might be fully k',
Heb 3: 10 and they have not k' my ways.
2Pe 1: 16 we made k' unto you the power
2: 21 for them not to have k' the way
21 than, after they have k' it, to turn
1Jo 2: 13 k' him that is from the beginning.
13 because ye have k' the Father.
14 k' him that is from the beginning.
3: 6 hath not seen him, neither k' him.
4: 16 have k' and believed the love that
2Jo 1 also all they that have k' the truth;
Re 2: 24 have not k' the depths of Satan,

Koa (*ko'-ah*)
Eze 23: 23 and Shoa, and K', and all the

Kohath (*ko'-hath*) See also KOHATHITES.
Ge 46: 11 the sons of Levi; Gershon, K',
Ex 6: 16 Gershon, K', and Merari;
18 And the sons of K'; Amram, and
18 and the years of the life of K' were
Nu 3: 17 by their names; Gershon, and K',
19 the sons of K' by their families;
27 of K' was the family of the
29 The families of the sons of K' shall
4: 2 sum of the sons of K' from among
4 be the service of the sons of K'
15 sons of K' shall come to bear it:
15 are the burden of the sons of K'
7: 9 unto the sons of K' he gave none:
16: 1 Izhar, the son of K', the son of
26: 57 of K', the family of the Kohathites:
58 Kohathites. And K' begat Amram.
Jos 21: 5 the rest of the children of K' had
20 the families of the children of K',
20 remained of the children of K',
26 the children of K' that remained.
1Ch 6: 1 sons of Levi; Gershon, K', and
2 sons of K'; Amram, Izhar, and
16 sons of Levi; Gershon, K', and
18 the sons of K' were, Amram, and
22 sons of K'; Amminadab his son,
38 The son of Izhar, the son of K',
61 unto the sons of K', which were
66 of the families of the sons of K'
70 of the remnant of the sons of K'.
15: 5 of the sons of K'; Uriel the chief,
23: 6 sons of Levi, namely, Gershon, K',
12 The sons of K'; Amram, Izhar,

Kohathites (*ko'-hath-ites*)
Nu 3: 27 these are the families of the K'.
30 father of the families of the K'
4: 18 the tribe of the families of the K'
34 numbered the sons of the K' after
37 numbered of the families of the K',
10: 21 K' set forward, bearing the
26: 57 of Kohath, the family of the K':
Jos 21: 4 came out for the families of the K':
10 being of the families of the K',
1Ch 6: 33 Of the sons of the K': Heman a
54 Aaron, of the families of the K':
9: 32 brethren, of the sons of the K',
2Ch 20: 19 Levites, of the children of the K',
29: 12 Azariah, of the sons of the K':
34: 12 Meshullam, of the sons of the K',

Kolaiah (*ko-la-i'-ah*)
Ne 11: 7 the son of Pedaiah, the son of K',
Jer 29: 21 of Israel, of Ahab the son of K',

Korah (*ko'-rah*) See also CORE; KORAHITE; KORE.
Ge 36: 5 bare Jeush, and Jaalam, and K'.
14 Esau Jeush, and Jaalam, and K'.
16 Duke K', duke Gatam, and duke
18 duke Jeush, duke Jaalam, duke K':
Ex 6: 21 And the sons of Izhar; K', and
24 And the sons of K'; Assir, and
Nu 16: 1 Now K', the son of Izhar, the son of
5 And he spake unto K' and unto all
6 censers, K', and all his company;
8 Moses said unto K', Hear, I pray
16 And Moses said unto K', Be thou
19 K' gathered all the congregation
24 from about the tabernacle of K',
27 gat up from the tabernacle of K',
32 the men that appertained unto K',
40 he be not as K', and as his
49 that died about the matter of K'.
26: 9 Aaron in the company of K',
10 them up together with K', when
11 the children of K' died not.
27: 3 the Lord in the company of K';
1Ch 1: 35 and Jeush, and Jaalam, and K'.
2: 43 the sons of Hebron; K', and
6: 22 Amminadab his son, K' his son,
37 son of Ebiasaph, the son of K',
9: 19 son of Ebiasaph, the son of K',
Ps 42: *title* Maschil, for the sons of K'.
44: *title* Musician for the sons of K',
45: *title* Shoshannim, for the sons of K',
46: *title* Musician for the sons of K',
47: *title* A Psalm for the sons of K'.
48: *title* and Psalm for the sons of K'.
49: *title* A Psalm for the sons of K'.
84: *title* A Psalm for the sons of K'.
85: *title* A Psalm for the sons of K'.
87: *title* Psalm or Song for the sons of K'.
88: *title* Song or Psalm for the sons of K'.

Korahite (*ko'-ra-hite*) See also KORAHITES; KORE.
1Ch 9: 31 the firstborn of Shallum the K',

Korahites (*ko'-ra-hites*) See also KORATHITES; KORHITES.
1Ch 9: 19 the K', were over the work of the

Korathites (*ko'-ra-thites*) See also KORAHITES.
Nu 26: 58 Mushites, the family of the K'.

Kore (*ko'-re*) See also KORAH; KORAHITE.
1Ch 9: 19 And Shallum the son of K',
26: 1 was Meshelemiah the son of K',
19 the porters among the sons of K',
2Ch 31: 14 K' the son of Imnah the Levite,

Korhites (*kor'-hites*) See also KORAHITES.
Ex 6: 24 these are the families of the K'.
1Ch 12: 6 Joezer, and Jashobeam, the K',
26: 1 K' was Meshelemiah the son of
2Ch 20: 19 and of the children of the K', stood

Koz (*coz*) See also HAKKOZ.
Ezr 2: 61 the children of K', the children
Ne 3: 4 the son of Urijah, the son of K'.
21 the son of K' another piece, from
7: 63 of Habaiah, the children of K',

Kushaiah (*cu-shah'-yah*) See also KISHI.
1Ch 15: 17 brethren, Ethan the son of K';

L.

Laadah (*la'-a-dah*)
1Ch 4:21 L' the father of Mareshah, and
Laadan (*la'-a-dan*) See also LIBNI.
1Ch 7:26 L' his son, Ammihud his son,
23: 7 Of the Gershonites were, L', and
8 The sons of L'; the chief was Jehiel,
9 were the chief of the fathers of L'.
26:21 As concerning the sons of L'; the
21 sons of the Gershonite L', chief
21 even of L' the Gershonite, were
Laban (*la'-ban*) See also LABAN'S; LIBNAH.
Ge 24:29 a brother, and his name was L':
29 and L' ran out unto the man, unto
50 L' and Bethuel answered and said,
25:20 the sister to L' the Syrian.
27:43 flee thou to L' my brother to Haran;
28: 2 from thence of the daughters of L'
5 and he went to Padan-aram unto L',
29: 5 them, Know ye L' the son of Nahor?
10 Jacob saw Rachel the daughter of L'
10 sheep of L' his mother's brother,
10 watered the flock of L' his mother's
13 when L' heard the tidings of Jacob
13 And he told L' all these things.
14 L' said to him, Surely thou art my
15 L' said unto Jacob, Because thou
16 L' had two daughters: the name of
19 L' said, It is better that I give her
21 And Jacob said unto L', Give me my
22 L' gathered together all the men of
24 L' gave unto his daughter Leah
25 he said to L', What is this thou hast
26 And L' said, It must not be so done
29 And L' gave to Rachel his daughter
30:25 Jacob said unto L', Send me away,
27 And L' said unto him, I pray thee,
34 L' said, Behold, I would it might be
40 and all the brown in the flock of L';
31: 2 beheld the countenance of L', and,
12 seen all that L' doeth unto thee.
19 And L' went to shear his sheep:
20 Jacob stole away unawares to L' the
22 told L' on the third day that Jacob
24 came to L' the Syrian in a dream
25 Then L' overtook Jacob. Now Jacob
25 L' with his brethren pitched in the
26 L' said to Jacob, What hast thou
31 Jacob answered and said to L',
33 L' went into Jacob's tent, and into
34 L' searched all the tent, but found
36 was wroth, and chode with L':
36 Jacob answered and said unto L',
43 L' answered and said unto Jacob,
47 And L' called it Jegar-sahadutha:
48 And L' said, This heap is a witness
51 L' said to Jacob, Behold this heap,
55 L' rose up, and kissed his sons and
55 L' departed, and returned unto his
32: 4 have sojourned with L', and stayed
46:18 whom L' gave to Leah his daughter;
25 which L' gave unto Rachel his
De 1: 1 Tophel, and L', and Hazeroth, and
Laban's (*la'-bans*)
Ge 30:36 and Jacob fed the rest of L' flocks.
40 and put them not unto L' cattle.
42 feebler were L', and the stronger
31: 1 heard the words of L' sons, saying,
labour See also LABOURED; LABOURETH; LABOURING; LABOURS.
Ge 31:42 affliction and the l' of my hands,
35:16 travailed, and she had hard l'.
17 when she was in hard l', that the
Ex 5: 9 the men, that they may l' therein;
20: 9 Six days shalt thou l', and do all
De 5:13 Six days thou shalt l', and do all
26: 7 and our l', and our oppression:
Jos 7: 3 not all the people to l' thither;
24:13 you a land for which ye did not l'.
Ne 4:22 be a guard to us, and l' on the day.
5:13 from his house, and from his l',
Job 9:29 be wicked, why then l' I in vain?
39:11 or wilt thou leave thy l' to him?
16 hers: her l' is in vain without fear;
Ps 78:46 gave also...their l' unto the locust.
90:10 yet is their strength l' and sorrow;
104:23 forth unto his work and to his l'
105:44 they inherited the l' of the people;
107:12 he brought down their heart with l';
109:11 and let the strangers spoil his l'.
127: 1 house, they l' in vain that build it:
128: 2 shalt eat the l' of thine hands:
144:14 our oxen may be strong to l';
Pr 10:16 l' of the righteous tendeth to life:
13:11 that gathereth by l' shall increase.
14:23 In all l' there is profit: but the
21:25 him; for his hands refuse to l'.
23: 4 L' not to be rich: cease from thine
Ec 1: 3 What profit hath a man of all his l'
8 All things are full of l'; man
2:10 for my heart rejoiced in all my l':
10 and this was my portion of all my l'
11 the l' that I had laboured to
18 I hated all my l' which I had taken
19 he have rule over all my l'
20 the l' which I took under the sun.
21 is a man whose l' is in wisdom, and
22 For what hath man of all his l', and
24 make his soul enjoy good in his l'.
3:13 and enjoy the good of all his l', it is
4: 8 yet is there no end of all his l';
Ec 4: 8 For whom do I l', and bereave my
9 have a good reward for their l'.
5:15 shall take nothing of his l', which
18 enjoy the good of all his l' that he
19 his portion, and to rejoice in his l';
6: 7 All the l' of man is for his mouth,
8:15 that shall abide with him of his l'
17 though a man l' to seek it out, yet
9: 9 and in thy l' which thou takest
10:15 l' of the foolish wearieth every one
Isa 22: 4 l' not to comfort me, because of the
45:14 The l' of Egypt, and merchandise
55: 2 your l' for that which satisfieth not?
65:23 They shall not l' in vain, nor bring
Jer 3:24 shame hath devoured the l' of our
20:18 forth out of the womb to see l' and
51:58 and the people shall l' in vain, and
La 5: 5 we l', and have no rest.
Eze 23:29 and shall take away all thy l', and
29:20 his l' wherewith he served against
Mic 4:10 and l' to bring forth, O daughter
Hab 2:13 the people shall l' in the very fire,
3:17 the l' of the olive shall fail, and
Hag 1:11 and upon all the l' of the hands.
M't 11:28 Come unto me, all ye that l' and
Joh 4:38 that whereon ye bestowed no l':
6:27 L' not for...meat which perisheth,
Ro 16: 6 who bestowed much l' on us.
12 and Tryphosa, who l' in the Lord.
1Co 3: 8 reward according to his own l'.
4:12 l', working with our own hands:
15:58 your l' is not in vain in the Lord.
2Co 5: 9 Wherefore we l', that, whether
Ga 4:11 have bestowed upon you l' in vain.
Eph 4:28 rather let him l', working with his
Ph'p 1:22 the flesh, this is the fruit of my l':
2:25 my brother, and companion in l',
Col 1:29 Whereunto I also l', striving
1Th 1: 3 your work of faith, and l' of love,
2: 9 brethren, our l' and travail:
3: 5 tempted you, and our l' be in vain.
5:12 to know them which l' among you,
2Th 3: 8 wrought with l' and travail night
1Ti 4:10 we both l' and suffer reproach,
5:17 who l' in the word and doctrine.
Heb 4:11 l' therefore to enter into that rest,
6:10 to forget your work and l' of love,
Re 2: 2 I know thy works, and thy l', and
laboured
Ne 4:21 So we l' in the work: and half of
Job 20:18 which he l' for shall he restore,
Ec 2:11 on the labour that I had l' to do:
19 all my labour wherein I have l',
21 to a man that hath not l' therein
22 wherein he hath l' under the sun?
5:16 hath he that hath l' for the wind?
Isa 47:12 thou hast l' from thy youth;
15 with whom thou hast l', even thy
49: 4 Then I said, I have l' in vain, I have
62: 8 thy wine, for the which thou hast l':
Da 6:14 he l' till the going down of the sun
Jon 4:10 for the which thou hast not l',
Joh 4:38 other men l', and ye are entered
Ro 16:12 Persis, which l' much in the Lord.
1Co 15:10 I l' more abundantly than they all:
Ph'p 2:16 not run in vain, neither l' in vain.
4: 3 which l' with me in the gospel,
Re 2: 3 and for my name's sake hast l',
labourer See also FELLOWLABOURER; LABOURERS.
Lu 10: 7 for the l' is worthy of his hire.
1Ti 5:18 And, The l' is worthy of his reward.
labourers See also FELLOWLABOURERS.
M't 9:37 is plenteous, but the l' are few;
38 will send forth l' into his harvest.
20: 1 morning to hire l' into his vineyard.
2 agreed with the l' for a penny a day,
8 Call the l', and give them their hire,
Lu 10: 2 truly is great, but the l' are few:
2 that he would send forth l' into his
1Co 3: 9 For we are l' together with God:
Jas 5: 4 the hire of the l' who have reaped
laboureth
Pr 16:26 He that l'...for himself; for
26 l' for himself; for his mouth
Ec 3: 9 he that worketh wherein he l'?
1Co 16:16 one that helpeth with us, and l'.
2Ti 2: 6 husbandman that l' must be first
labouring
Ec 5:12 The sleep of a l' man is sweet,
Ac 20:35 so l' ye ought to support the weak,
Col 4:12 l' fervently for you in prayers,
1Th 2: 9 for l' night and day, because we
labours
Ex 23:16 of harvest, the firstfruits of thy l',
16 gathered in thy l' out of the field.
De 28:33 The fruit of thy land, and all thy l',
Pr 5:10 l' be in the house of a stranger;
Isa 58: 3 pleasure, and exact all your l'.
Jer 20: 5 of this city, and all the l' thereof,
Ho 12: 8 my l' they shall find none iniquity
Hag 2:17 hail in all the l' of your hands;
Joh 4:38 and ye are entered into their l'.
2Co 6: 5 in imprisonments, in tumults, in l',
10:15 measure, that is, of other men's l';
11:23 in l' more abundant, in stripes
Re 14:13 that they may rest from their l';
lace
Ex 28:28 rings of the ephod with a l' of blue,
37 And thou shalt put it on a blue l',
Ex 39:21 rings of the ephod with a l' of blue,
31 And they tied unto it a l' of blue, to
Lachish (*la'-kish*)
Jos 10: 3 and unto Japhia king of L', and
5, 23 king of Jarmuth, the king of L',
31 and all Israel with him, unto L',
32 delivered L' into the hand of Israel,
33 king of Gezer came up to help L';
34 from L' Joshua passed unto Eglon,
35 to all that he had done to L'.
12:11 Jarmuth, one; the king of L', one;
15:39 L', and Bozkath, and Eglon,
2Ki 14:19 in Jerusalem: and he fled to L';
19 they sent after him to L', and slew
18:14 sent to the king of Assyria to L',
17 sent...from L' to king Hezekiah
19: 8 heard that he was departed from L'.
2Ch 11: 9 And Adoraim, and L', and Azekah,
25:27 in Jerusalem; and he fled to L':
27 they sent to L' after him, and slew
32: 9 he himself laid siege against L',
Ne 11:30 at L', and the fields thereof, at
Isa 36: 2 sent...from L' to Jerusalem unto
37: 8 heard that he was departed from L'.
Jer 34: 7 of Judah that were left, against L',
Mic 1:13 O thou inhabitant of L', bind the
lack See also LACKED; LACKEST; LACKETH; LACKING.
Ge 18:28 there shall l' five of the fifty
28 destroy all the city for l' of five?
Ex 16:18 he that gathered little had no l';
De 8: 9 thou shalt not l' any thing in it;
Job 4:11 old lion perisheth for l' of prey,
38:41 God, they wander for l' of meat.
Ps 34:10 The young lions do l', and suffer
Pr 28:27 giveth unto the poor shall not l':
Ec 9: 8 and let thy head l' no ointment.
Ho 4: 6 are destroyed for l' of knowledge:
M't 19:20 from my youth up: what l' I yet?
2Co 8:15 that had gathered little had no l'.
Ph'p 2:30 to supply your l' of service toward
1Th 4:12 that ye may have l' of nothing.
Jas 1: 5 If any of you l' wisdom, let him
lacked
De 2: 7 with thee; thou hast l' nothing.
2Sa 2:30 l' of David's servants nineteen
17:22 the morning light there l' not one
1Ki 4:27 man in his month: they l' nothing.
11:22 But what hast thou l' with me,
Ne 9:21 wilderness, so that they l' nothing;
Lu 8: 6 away, because it l' moisture.
22:35 scrip, and shoes, l' ye any thing?
Ac 4:34 was there any among them that l':
1Co 12:24 honour to that part which l':
Ph'p 4:10 also careful, but ye l' opportunity.
lackest
M'r 10:21 said unto him, One thing thou l':
Lu 18:22 unto him, Yet l' thou one thing:
lacketh
Nu 31:49 and there l' not one man of us.
2Sa 3:29 on the sword, or that l' bread.
Pr 6:32 with a woman l' understanding:
12: 9 honoureth himself, and l' bread.
2Pe 1: 9 that l' these things is blind,
lacking
Le 2:13 to be l' from thy meat offering:
22:23 thing superfluous or l' in his parts,
J'g 21: 3 be to day one tribe l' in Israel?
1Sa 30:19 And there was nothing l' to them,
Jer 23: 4 neither shall they be l', saith the
1Co 16:17 that which was l' on your part they
2Co 11: 9 that which was l' to me the brethren
1Th 3:10 that which is l' in your faith?
lad See also LAD'S; LADS.
Ge 21:12 in thy sight because of the l', and
17 And God heard the voice of the l';
17 God hath heard the voice of the l'
18 Arise, lift up the l', and hold him in
19 with water, and gave the l' drink.
20 God was with the l'; and he grew,
22: 5 and I and the l' will go yonder and
12 Lay not thy hand upon the l',
37: 2 the l' was with the sons of Bilhah,
43: 8 Send the l' with me, and we will
44:22 The l' cannot leave his father: for
30 father, and the l' be not with us;
31 he seeth that the l' is not with us,
32 thy servant became surety for the l'
33 thy servant abide instead of the l'
33 let the l' go up with his brethren.
34 father, and the l' be not with me?
J'g 16:26 Samson said unto the l' that held
1Sa 20:21 behold, I will send a l', saying, Go,
21 If I expressly say unto the l',
35 with David, and a little l' with him.
36 he said unto his l', Run, find out
36 And as the l' ran, he shot an arrow
37 when the l' was come to the place
37 Jonathan after the l', and said,
38 Jonathan cried after the l', Make
38 And Jonathan's l' gathered up the
39 But the l' knew not any thing: only
40 gave his artillery unto his l', and
41 as soon as the l' was gone, David
2Sa 17:18 Nevertheless a l' saw them, and told
2Ki 4:19 And he said to a l', Carry him to
Joh 6: 9 There is a l' here, which hath five
ladder
Ge 28:12 behold a l' set up on the earth,

lade See also LADED; LADEN; LADETH; LADING; UNLADE.
Ge 45:17 l' your beasts, and go, get you
1Ki 12:11 did l' you with a heavy yoke,
Lu 11:46 l' men with burdens grievous to

laded
Ge 42:26 they l' their asses with the corn,
44:13 and l' every man his ass, and
Ne 4:17 bare burdens, with those that l',
Ac 28:10 l' us with such things as were

laden See also LOADEN.
Ge 45:23 ten asses l' with the good things
23 ten she asses l' with corn and
1Sa 16:20 And Jesse took an ass l' with bread,
Isa 1: 4 people l' with iniquity, a seed of
M't 11:28 all ye that labour and are heavy l',
2Ti 3: 6 captive silly women l' with sins,

ladeth See also LOADETH.
Hab 2: 6 that l' himself with thick clay!

ladies
J'g 5:29 Her wise l' answered her, yea, she
Es 1:18 l' of Persia and Media say this day

lading
Ne 13:15 bringing in sheaves, and l' asses;
Ac 27:10 not only of the l' and ship, but

lad's
Ge 44:30 his life is bound up in the l' life;

lads
Ge 48:16 me from all evil, bless the l';

lady See also LADIES.
Isa 47: 5 be called, The l' of kingdoms.
7 thou saidst, I shall be a l' for ever:
2Jo 1 unto the elect l' and her children,
5 I beseech thee, l', not as though I

Lael (*la'-el*)
Nu 3:24 shall be Eliasaph the son of L'.

Lahad (*la'-had*)
1Ch 4: 2 Jahath begat Ahumai, and L'.

Lahai-roi (*la-hah'-ee-roy*) See also BEER-LAHAI-ROI.
Ge 24:62 came from the way of the well L';
25:11 and Isaac dwelt by the well L'.

Lahmam (*lah'-mam*)
Jos 15:40 And Cabbon, and L', and Kithlish,)

Lahmi (*lah'-mi*) See also BETHLEHEMITE.
1Ch 20: 5 the son of Jair slew L' the

laid See also LAIDST; OVERLAID.
Ge 9:23 l' it upon both their shoulders,
15:10 l' each piece one against another:
19:16 the men l' hold upon his hand,
22: 6 and l' it upon Isaac his son;
9 there, and l' the wood in order,
9 l' him on the altar upon the wood.
30:41 Jacob l' the rods before the eyes
38:19 l' by her vail from her, and put on
39:16 she l' up his garment by her, until
41:48 and l' up the food in the cities:
48 every city, l' he up in the same.
48:14 and l' it upon Ephraim's head,
17 l' his right hand upon the head of
Ex 2: 3 she l' it in the flags by the river's
5: 9 more work be l' upon the men,
16:24 l' up till the morning, as Moses
34 Aaron l' it up before the Testimony,
19: 7 l' before their faces all these
21:30 If...be l' on him a sum of money,
30 his life whatsoever is l' upon him.
24:11 of Israel he l' not his hand: also
Le 8:14, 18, 22 his sons l' their hands upon
Nu 16:18 l' incense thereon, and stood in
17: 7 Moses l' up the rods before the
21:30 l' them waste even unto Nophah,
27:23 he l' his hands upon him, and
De 26: 6 us, and l' upon us hard bondage:
29:22 which the Lord hath l' upon it;
32:34 Is not this l' up in store with me,
34: 9 Moses had l' his hands upon him:
Jos 2: 6 she had l' in order upon the roof.
8 before they were l' down, she came
4: 8 lodged, and l' them down there.
7:23 and l' them out before the Lord.
10:27 l' great stones in the cave's mouth,
J'g 9:24 blood be l' upon Abimelech their
34 l' wait against Shechem in four
43 and l' wait in the field, and looked,
48 took it, and l' it on his shoulder,
16: 2 l' wait for him all night in the gate
19:29 l' hold on his concubine, and divided
Ru 3: 7 uncovered his feet,...l' her down.
15 of barley, and l' it on her:
4:16 the child, and l' it in her bosom,
1Sa 3: 2 when Eli was l' down in his place,
3 and Samuel was l' down to sleep;
6:11 l' the ark of the Lord upon the
10:25 book, and l' it up before the Lord.
15: 2 how he l' wait for him in the way,
5 Amalek, and l' wait in the valley.
27 l' hold upon the skirt of his mantel,
19:13 took an image, and l' it in the bed,
21:12 David l' up these words in his
25:18 cakes of figs, and l' them on asses.
2Sa 13: 8 Amnon's house;...he was l' down.
19 her, and l' her hand on her head,
18:17 and l' a very great heap of stones
1Ki 3:20 slept, and l' it in her bosom,
20 l' her dead child in my bosom.
6:37 foundation of the house of the Lord l',
8:31 be l' upon him to cause him to
13:29 man of God, and l' it upon the ass,
30 he l' his carcase in his own grave;
15:27 and all Israel l' siege to Gibbethon.
16:34 he l' the foundation thereof in
1Ki 17:19 and l' him upon his own bed.
18:33 in pieces, and l' him on the wood,
19: 6 drink, and l' him down again.
21: 4 he l' him down upon his bed, and
2Ki 4:21 l' him on the bed of the man of
31 and l' the staff upon the face of
32 was dead, and l' upon his bed.
5:23 l' them upon two of his servants;
9:25 the Lord l' this burden upon him;
11:16 they l' hands on her; and she
12:11 they l' it out to the carpenters
12 l' out for the house to repair it.
20: 7 took and l' it on the boil, and he
17 thy fathers have l' up in store
2Ch 6:22 an oath be l' upon him to make
7:22 of Egypt, and l' hold on other gods,
16:14 l' him in the bed which was filled
23:15 So they l' hands on her; and
24: 9 the servant of God l' upon Israel
29:23 they l' their hands upon them:
31: 6 their God, and l' them by heaps.
32: 9 he himself l' siege against Lachish,
Ezr 3: 6 foundation of the temple...was not yet l'.
10 l' the foundation of the temple of
11 foundation of...house of Lord was l'.
12 foundation of this house was l'
5: 8 and timber is l' in the walls,
16 l' the foundation of the house of
6: 1 treasures were l' up in Babylon.
3 foundations thereof be strongly l';
Ne 3: 3 build, who also l' the beams thereof,
6 they l' the beams thereof, and set
13: 5 they l' the meat offerings,
Es 8: 7 he l' his hand upon the Jews.
9:10 on the spoil l' they not their hand.
15 on the prey they l' not their hand.
16 they l' not their hands on the prey,
10: 1 Ahasuerus l' a tribute upon the
Job 6: 2 and my calamity l' in the balances
18:10 snare is l' for him in the ground,
29: 9 and l' their hand on their mouth.
31: 9 l' wait at my neighbour's door;
38: 4 I l' the foundations of the earth?
5 Who hath l' the measures thereof,
6 or who l' the corner stone thereof;
Ps 3: 5 I l' me down and slept; I awaked;
21: 5 majesty hast thou l' upon him.
31: 4 net that they have l' privily for
19 hast l' up for them that fear thee;
35:11 l' to my charge things that I knew
49:14 Like sheep they are l' in the grave;
62: 9 to be l' in the balance, they are
79: 1 they have l' Jerusalem on heaps.
7 Jacob, and l' waste his dwelling place.
88: 6 Thou hast l' me in the lowest pit,
89:19 l' help upon one that is mighty;
102:25 thou l' the foundation of the earth:
104: 5 Who l' the foundations of the earth,
105:18 with fetters: he was l' in iron:
119:30 judgments have I l' before me.
110 wicked have l' a snare for me:
139: 5 before, and l' thine hand upon me.
141: 9 snares which they have l' for me,
142: 3 they privily l' a snare for me.
Pr 13:22 of the sinner is l' up for the just.
Ca 7:13 and old, which I have l' up for thee,
Isa 6: 7 he l' it upon my mouth, and said,
10:28 he hath l' up his carriages:
14: 8 Since thou art l' down, no feller is
15: 1 the night Ar of Moab is l' waste,
1 in the night Kir of Moab is l' waste,
7 that which they have l' up, shall
23: 1 for it is l' waste, so that there is
14 for your strength is l' waste.
18 it shall not be treasured nor l' up;
37:18 Assyria have l' waste all the nations,
39: 6 thy fathers have l' up in store until
42:25 him, yet he l' it not to heart.
44:28 temple, Thy foundation shall be l'.
47: 6 hast thou very heavily l' thy yoke.
48:13 hath l' the foundation of the earth,
51:13 and l' the foundations of the earth;
23 hast l' thy body as the ground,
53: 6 Lord hath l' on him the iniquity
57:11 me, nor laid it to thy heart?
64:11 all our pleasant things are l' waste.
Jer 4: 7 and thy cities shall be l' waste,
27:17 should this city be l' waste?
36:20 they l' up the roll in the chamber of
50:24 I have l' a snare for thee, and thou
La 4:19 they l' wait for us in the wilderness.
Eze 4: 5 I have l' upon thee the years of
6: 6 the cities shall be l' waste, and the
6 your altars may be l' waste and made
11: 7 Your slain whom ye have l' in the
12:20 that are inhabited shall be l' waste,
19: 7 palaces, and he l' waste their cities;
26: 2 be replenished, now she is l' waste:
29:12 the cities that are l' waste shall be
32:19 be thou l' with the uncircumcised.
27 have l' their swords under heads,
29 are l' by them that were slain
32 he shall be l' in the midst of the
33:29 I have l' the land most desolate
35:12 They are l' desolate, they are given us
39:21 my hand that I have l' upon them.
40:42 also they l' the instruments
Da 6:17 and l' upon the mouth of the den;
Ho 11: 4 jaws, and I l' meat unto them.
Joe 1: 7 He hath l' my vine waste, and
17 clods, the garners are l' desolate,
Am 2: 8 clothes l' to pledge by every altar,
7: 9 sanctuaries of Israel shall be l' waste;
Ob 7 eat thy bread have l' a wound
13 have l' hands on their substance
Jon 3: 6 and he l' his robe from him,
Mic 5: 1 he hath l' siege against us: they
Na 3: 7 thee, and say, Nineveh is l' waste:
Hab 2:19 it is l' over with gold and silver,
Hag 2:15 before a stone was l' upon a stone
18 foundation of the Lord's temple was l'.
Zec 3: 9 behold the stone that I have l'
4: 9 l' the foundation of this house;
7:14 they l' the pleasant land desolate.
8: 9 foundation of the house of...was l'.
Mal 1: 3 l' his mountains and his heritage
M't 3:10 axe is l' unto the root of the trees:
8:14 he saw his wife's mother l', and
14: 3 Herod had l' hold on John, and bound
18:28 he l' hands on him, and took him by
19:15 he l' his hands on them, and
26:50 came they, and l' hands on Jesus,
55 the temple, and ye l' no hold on me.
57 they that had l' hold on Jesus led him
27:60 l' it in his own new tomb, which
M'r 6: 5 he l' his hands upon a few sick
17 had sent forth and l' hold upon John,
29 up his corpse, and l' it in a tomb.
56 they l' the sick in the streets, and
7:30 and her daughter l' upon the bed.
14:46 they l' their hands on him, and
51 the young men l' hold on him: and
15:46 l' him in a sepulchre which was
47 of Joses beheld where he was l'.
16: 6 behold the place where they l' him.
Lu 1:66 them l' them up in their hearts,
2: 7 clothes, and l' him in a manger;
3: 9 axe is l' unto the root of the trees:
4:40 l' his hands on every one of them,
6:48 and l' the foundation on a rock:
12:19 much goods l' up for many years;
13:13 he l' his hands on her: and
14:29 he hath l' the foundation, and is not
16:20 Lazarus, which was l' at his gate,
19:20 which I have kept l' up in a napkin:
22 taking up that I l' not down, and
23:26 they l' hold upon one Simon, a
26 on him they l' the cross, that he
53 l' it in a sepulchre that was hewn
53 wherein never man before was l'.
55 and how his body was l'.
24:12 the linen clothes l' by themselves,
Joh 7:30 no man l' hands on him, because
44 him; but no man l' hands on him.
8:20 temple: and no man l' hands on him;
11:34 Where have ye l' him? They said
41 the place where the dead was l'.
13: 4 supper, and l' aside his garments:
19:41 wherein was never man yet l'.
42 There l' they Jesus therefore
20: 2 know not where they have l' him.
13 I know not where they have l' him.
15 tell me where thou hast l' him, and
21: 9 and fish l' thereon, and bread.
Ac 3: 2 l' daily at the gate of the temple
4: 3 they l' hands on them, and put
35 l' them down at the apostles' feet:
37 and l' it at the apostles' feet.
5: 2 part, and l' it at the apostles' feet.
15 and l' them on beds and couches,
18 l' their hands on the apostles, and
6: 6 they l' their hands on them.
7:16 l' in the sepulchre that Abraham
58 witnesses l' down their clothes at
8:17 Then l' they their hands on them,
9:37 they l' her in an upper chamber.
13: 3 and l' their hands on them, they
29 tree, and l' him in a sepulchre.
36 was l' unto his fathers, and saw
16:23 had l' many stripes upon them,
19: 6 Paul had l' his hands upon them,
20: 3 And when the Jews l' wait for him,
21:27 all the people, and l' hands on him,
23:29 nothing l' to his charge worthy of
30 that the Jews l' wait for the man,
25: 7 l' many and grievous complaints
16 the crime l' against him.
27 signify the crimes l' against him.
28: 3 of sticks, and l' them on the fire,
8 l' his hands on him, and healed
Ro 16: 4 my life l' down their own necks:
1Co 3:10 I have l' the foundation, and
11 can no man lay than that is l',
9:16 for necessity is l' upon me; yea,
Col 1: 5 hope which is l' up for you in
2Ti 4: 8 there is l' up for me a crown of
16 it may not be l' to their charge.
Heb 1:10 hast l' the foundation of the earth;
1Jo 3:16 because he l' down his life for us:
Re 1:17 he l' his right hand upon me,
20: 2 he l' hold on the dragon, that old

laidst See also LAYEDST.
Ps 66:11 thou l' affliction upon our loins.

lain See also LIEN.
Nu 5:19 If no man have l' with thee, and
20 some man have l' with thee
J'g 21:11 woman that hath l' by man.
Job 3:13 I have l' still and been quiet,
Joh 11:17 had l' in the grave four days already.
20:12 where the body of Jesus had l'.

Laish (*la'-ish*) See also DAN; LESHEM.
J'g 18: 7 men departed, and came to L',
14 went to spy out the country of L',
27 which he had, and came unto L',
29 the name of the city was L' at the
1Sa 25:44 David's wife, to Phalti the son of L',
2Sa 3:15 even from Phaltiel the son of L'.
Isa 10:30 cause it to be heard unto L',

lake
Lu 5: 1 God, stood by the l' of Gennesaret,

Lu 5: 2 saw two ships standing by the *l*:
8: 22 over unto the other side of the *l*.
23 down a storm of wind on the *l*;
33 down a steep place into the *l*,
Re 19: 20 both were cast alive into a *l* of fire
20: 10 them was cast into the *l* of fire
14 and hell were cast into the *l* of fire.
15 of life was cast into the *l* of fire.
21: 8 their part in the *l* which burneth

Lakum (*la'-kum*)
Jos 19: 33 Nekeb, and Jabneel, unto *L*;

lama (*la'-mah*)
M't 27: 46 saying, Eli, Eli, *l* sabachthani?
M'r 15: 34 saying, Eloi, Eloi, *l* sabachthani?

lamb See also LAMBS; LAMB'S.
Ge 22: 7 where is the *l* for a burnt offering?
8 God will provide himself a *l* for a
Ex 12: 3 shall take to them every man a *l*,
3 of their fathers, a *l* for an house:
4 the household be too little for the *l*,
4 shall make your count for the *l*.
5 Your *l* shall be without blemish, a
21 them, Draw out and take you a *l*
13: 13 an ass thou shalt redeem with a *l*;
29: 39 The one *l* thou shalt offer in the
39 the other *l* thou shalt offer at even:
40 with the one *l* a tenth deal of flour
41 the other *l* thou shalt offer at even,
34: 20 an ass thou shalt redeem with a *l*:
Le 3: 7 If he offer a *l* for his offering, then
4: 32 if he bring a *l* for a sin offering,
35 fat of the *l* is taken away from
5: 6 a *l* or a kid of the goats, for a sin
7 he be not able to bring a *l*, then he
9: 3 a calf and a *l*, both of the first
12: 6 she shall bring a *l* of the first year
8 she be not able to bring a *l*, then
14: 10 one ewe *l* of the first year without
12 priest shall take one he *l*, and
13 shall slay the *l* in the place where
21 take one *l* for a trespass offering
24 take the *l* of the trespass offering,
25 kill the *l* of the trespass offering,
17: 3 that killeth an ox, or *l*, or goat,
22: 23 *l* that hath any thing superfluous
23: 12 he *l* without blemish of the first
Nu 6: 12 shall bring a *l* of the first year for
14 one he *l* of the first year without
14 one ewe *l* of the first year without
7: 15, 21, 27, 33, 39, 45, 51, 57, 63, 69, 75, 81 one
l of the first year, for a burnt
15: 5 offering or sacrifice, for one *l*.
11 for one ram, or for a *l*, or a kid.
28: 4 The one *l* shalt thou offer in the
4 the other *l* shalt thou offer at even;
7 fourth part of an hin for the one *l*:
8 the other *l* shalt thou offer at even:
13 oil for a meat offering unto one *l*;
14 and a fourth part of an hin unto a *l*:
21 deal shalt thou offer for every *l*,
29 A several tenth deal unto one *l*,
29: 4 one tenth deal for one *l*, throughout
10 A several tenth deal for one *l*,
15 tenth deal to each *l* of the fourteen
1Sa 7: 9 And Samuel took a sucking *l*, and
17: 34 bear, and took a *l* out of the flock:
2Sa 12: 3 had nothing, save one little ewe *l*,
4 took the poor man's *l*, and dressed
6 And he shall restore the *l* fourfold,
Isa 11: 6 wolf also shall dwell with the *l*,
16: 1 Send ye the *l* to the ruler of the
53: 7 is brought as a *l* to the slaughter,
65: 25 wolf and the *l* shall feed together,
66: 3 he that sacrificeth a *l*, as if he
Jer 11: 19 But I was like a *l* or an ox that is
Eze 45: 15 one *l* out of the flock, out of two
46: 13 of a *l* of the first year without
15 Thus shall they prepare the *l*, and
Ho 4: 16 feed them as a *l* in a large place.
Joh 1: 29 and saith, Behold the *L* of God,
36 he saith, Behold the *L* of God!
Ac 8: 32 like a *l* dumb before his shearer, so
1Pe 1: 19 of Christ, as of a *l* without blemish
Re 5: 6 stood a *L* as it had been slain,
8 elders fell down before the *L*,
12 Worthy is the *L* that was slain to
13 the throne, and unto the *L* for ever
6: 1 when the *L* opened one of the seals,
16 and from the wrath of the *L*:
7: 9 before the throne, and before the *L*,
10 upon the throne, and unto the *L*.
14 them white in the blood of the *L*.
17 *L* which is in the midst of the throne
12: 11 overcame him by the blood of the *L*,
13: 8 written in the book of life of the *L*
11 and he had two horns like a *l*, and
14: 1 lo, a *L* stood on the mount Sion, and
4 These are they which follow the *L*
4 firstfruits unto God and to the *L*.
10 angels, and in the presence of the *L*:
15: 3 of God, and the song of the *L*,
17: 14 These shall make war with the *L*,
14 and the *L* shall overcome them:
19: 7 for the marriage of the *L* is come,
9 unto the marriage supper of the *L*.
21: 14 of the twelve apostles of the *L*.
22 Lord God Almighty and the *L* are
23 it, and the *L* is the light thereof.
22: 1 of the throne of God and of the *L*.
3 throne of God and of the *L* shall be

lamb's
Re 21: 9 shew thee the bride, the *L* wife.
27 are written in the *L* book of life.

lambs
Ge 21: 28 Abraham set seven ewe *l* of the
21: 29 What mean these seven ewe *l* which
30 these seven ewe *l* shalt thou take
30: 40 And Jacob did separate the *l*, and
Ex 29: 38 two *l* of the first year day by day
Le 14: 10 shall take two he *l* without blemish,
23: 18 the bread seven *l* without blemish
19 two *l* of the first year for a sacrifice
20 before the Lord, with the two *l*:
Nu 7: 17, 23, 29, 35, 41, 47, 53, 59, 65, 71, 77, 83 five
he goats, five *l* of the first year:
87 the *l* of the first year twelve,
88 sixty, the *l* of the first year sixty.
28: 3 two *l* of the first year without spot
9 two *l* of the first year without spot,
11 seven *l* of the first year without
19 ram, and seven *l* of the first year:
21 every lamb, throughout the seven *l*:
27 one ram, seven *l* of the first year;
29 one lamb, throughout the seven *l*;
29: 2 seven *l* of the first year without
4 one lamb, throughout the seven *l*:
8 ram, and seven *l* of the first year;
10 one lamb, throughout the seven *l*:
13 and fourteen *l* of the first year;
15 deal to each lamb of the fourteen *l*:
17 fourteen *l* of the first year without
18 bullocks, for the rams, and for the *l*,
20 fourteen *l* of the first year without
21 bullocks, for the rams, and for the *l*,
23 fourteen *l* of the first year without
24 bullocks, for the rams, and for the *l*,
26 fourteen *l* of the first year without
27 bullocks, for the rams, and for the *l*,
29 fourteen *l* of the first year without
30 bullocks, for the rams, and for the *l*,
32 fourteen *l* of the first year without
33 bullocks, for the rams, and for the *l*,
36 seven *l* of the first year without
37 bullock, for the ram, and for the *l*,
De 32: 14 with fat of *l*, and rams of the breed
1Sa 15: 9 and the *l*, and all that was good,
2Ki 3: 4 of Israel an hundred thousand *l*,
1Ch 29: 21 thousand rams, and a thousand *l*,
2Ch 29: 21 seven *l*, and seven he goats, for a
22 they killed also the *l*, and they
32 hundred rams, and two hundred *l*:
35: 7 the people, of the flock, *l* and kids,
Ezr 6: 9 young bullocks, and rams, and *l*,
17 two hundred rams, four hundred *l*;
7: 17 with this money bullocks, rams, *l*,
8: 35 and six rams, seventy and seven *l*,
Ps 37: 20 the Lord shall be as the fat of *l*:
114: 4 and the little hills like *l*.
6 rams; and ye little hills, like *l*?
Pr 27: 26 The *l* are for thy clothing, and
Isa 1: 11 blood of bullocks, or of *l*, or of he
5: 17 the *l* feed after their manner,
34: 6 and with the blood of *l* and goats,
40: 11 shall gather the *l* with his arm,
Jer 51: 40 them down like *l* to the slaughter,
Eze 27: 21 they occupied with thee in *l*, and
39: 18 princes of the earth, of rams, of *l*,
46: 4 six *l* without blemish, and a ram
5 and the meat offering for the *l* as he
6 blemish, and six *l*, and a ram:
7 and for the *l* according as his hand
11 and to the *l* as he is able to give,
Am 6: 4 eat the *l* out of the flock, and the
Lu 10: 3 send you forth as *l* among wolves.
Joh 21: 15 He saith unto him, Feed my *l*.

lame
Le 21: 18 a blind man, or a *l*, or he that hath
De 15: 21 as if it be *l*, or blind, or have any ill
2Sa 4: 4 had a son that was *l* of his feet.
4 to flee, that he fell, and became *l*.
5: 6 take away the blind and the *l*,
8 Jebusites, and the *l* and the blind,
8 the *l* shall not come into the house.
9: 3 yet a son, which is *l* on his feet.
13 table; and was *l* on both his feet.
19: 26 the king; because thy servant is *l*.
Job 29: 15 the blind, and feet was I to the *l*.
Pr 26: 7 The legs of the *l* are not equal: so
Isa 33: 23 spoil divided; the *l* take the prey.
35: 6 shall the *l* man leap as an hart,
Jer 31: 8 and with them the blind and the *l*,
Mal 1: 8 offer the *l* and sick, is it not evil?
13 was torn, and the *l*, and the sick;
M't 11: 5 *l* walk, the lepers are cleansed,
15: 30 with them those that were *l*, blind,
31 the *l* to walk, and the blind to see:
21: 14 the *l* came to him in the temple;
Lu 7: 22 *l* walk, the lepers are cleansed,
14: 13 poor, the maimed, the *l*, the blind:
Ac 3: 2 man *l* from his mother's womb
11 the *l* man which was healed held
8: 7 and that were *l*, were healed.
Heb 12: 13 which is *l* be turned out of the way;

Lamech (*la'-mek*)
Ge 4: 18 and Methusael begat *L*.
19 And *L* took unto him two wives:
23 And *L* said unto his wives, Adah
23 ye wives of *L*, harken unto my
24 truly *L* seventy and sevenfold.
5: 25 and seven years, and begat *L*:
26 Methuselah lived after he begat *L*
28 *L* lived an hundred eighty and two
30 *L* lived after he begat Noah five
31 the days of *L* were seven hundred
1Ch 1: 3 Henoch, Methuselah, *L*,
Lu 3: 36 Noe, which was the son of *L*,

lament See also LAMENTABLE; LAMENTED.
J'g 11: 40 to *l* the daughter of Jephthah
Isa 3: 26 And her gates shall *l* and mourn;
19: 8 cast angle into the brooks shall *l*,
32: 12 They shall *l* for the teats, for the
Jer 4: 8 you with sackcloth, *l* and howl:
16: 5 neither go to *l* nor bemoan them:
6 neither shall men *l* for them, nor
22: 18 They shall not *l* for him, saying,
18 they shall not *l* for him, saying,
34: 5 they will *l* thee, saying, Ah lord!
49: 3 *l*, and run to and fro by the hedges;
La 2: 8 the rampart and the wall to *l*;
Eze 27: 32 for thee, and *l* over thee, saying,
32: 16 wherewith they shall *l* her:
16 daughters of the nations shall *l* her:
16 shall *l* for her, even for Egypt,
Joe 1: 8 *L* like a virgin girded with
13 Gird yourselves, and *l*, ye priests:
Mic 2: 4 and *l* with a doleful lamentation,
Joh 16: 20 That ye shall weep and *l*, but the
Re 18: 9 shall bewail her, and *l* for her,

lamentable
Da 6: 20 cried with a *l* voice unto Daniel:

lamentation See also LAMENTATIONS.
Ge 50: 10 with a great and very sore *l*:
2Sa 1: 17 with this *l* over Saul and over
Ps 78: 64 and their widows made no *l*.
Jer 6: 26 as for an only son, most bitter *l*:
7: 29 and take up a *l* on high places;
9: 10 habitations of the wilderness a *l*,
20 and every one her neighbour *l*.
31: 15 in Ramah, *l*, and bitter weeping;
48: 38 There shall be *l* generally upon
La 2: 5 daughter of Judah mourning and *l*.
Eze 19: 1 up a *l* for the princes of Israel,
14 This is a *l*, and shall be for a *l*.
26: 17 they shall take up a *l* for thee, and
27: 2 son of man, take up a *l* for Tyrus;
32 they shall take up a *l* for thee, and
28: 12 take up a *l* upon the king of Tyrus,
32: 2 up a *l* for Pharaoh king of Egypt,
16 *l* wherewith they shall lament her:
Am 5: 1 you, even a *l*, O house of Israel.
16 such as are skilful of *l* to wailing.
8: 10 and all your songs into *l*;
Mic 2: 4 and lament with a doleful *l*, and
M't 2: 18 a voice heard, *l*, and weeping,
Ac 8: 2 burial, and made great *l* over him.

lamentations
2Ch 35: 25 women spake of Josiah in their *l*
25 behold, they are written in the *l*.
Eze 2: 10 there was written therein *l*, and

lamented
1Sa 6: 19 the people *l*, because the Lord had
7: 2 house of Israel *l* after the Lord.
25: 1 and *l* him, and buried him in his
28: 3 Israel had *l* him, and buried him
2Sa 1: 17 And David *l* with this lamentation
3: 33 the king *l* over Abner, and said,
2Ch 35: 25 And Jeremiah *l* for Josiah: and all
Jer 16: 4 they shall not be *l*; neither shall
25: 33 they shall not be *l*, neither gathered,
M't 11: 17 unto you, and ye have not *l*.
Lu 23: 27 which also bewailed and *l* him.

lamp See also LAMPS.
Ge 15: 17 burning *l* that passed between
Ex 27: 20 to cause the *l* to burn always.
1Sa 3: 3 *l* of God went out in the temple the
2Sa 22: 29 For thou art my *l*, O Lord: and the
1Ki 15: 4 his God give him a *l* in Jerusalem,
Job 12: 5 as a *l* despised in the thought of
Ps 119: 105 Thy word is a *l* unto my feet,
132: 17 ordained a *l* for mine anointed.
Pr 6: 23 For the commandment is a *l*; and
13: 9 the *l* of the wicked shall be put out.
20: 20 his *l* shall be put out in obscure
Isa 62: 1 the salvation thereof as a *l* that
Re 8: 10 heaven, burning as it were a *l*,

lamps
Ex 25: 37 shalt make the seven *l* thereof:
37 they shall light the *l* thereof, that
30: 7 when he dresseth the *l*, he shall
8 when Aaron lighteth the *l* at even,
35: 14 and his *l*, with the oil for the light,
37: 23 And he made his seven *l*, and his
39: 37 candlestick, with the *l* thereof,
37 even with the *l* to be set in order,
40: 4 candlestick, and light the *l* thereof,
25 he lighted the *l* before the Lord;
Le 24: 2 to cause the *l* to burn continually.
4 the *l* upon the pure candlestick
Nu 4: 9 the light, and his *l*, and his tongs,
8: 2 unto him, When thou lightest the *l*,
2 the seven *l* shall give light over
3 lighted the *l* thereof over against
J'g 7: 16 and *l* within the pitchers.
20 and held the *l* in their left hands,
1Ki 7: 49 and the *l*, and the tongs of gold,
1Ch 28: 15 and for their *l* of gold, by weight
15 candlestick, and for the *l* thereof:
15 and also for the *l* thereof,
2Ch 4: 20 the candlesticks with their *l*, that
21 flowers, and the *l*, and the tongs,
13: 11 of gold with the *l* thereof, to burn
29: 7 put out the *l*, and have not burned
Job 41: 19 Out of his mouth go burning *l*,
Eze 1: 13 fire, and like the appearance of *l*:
Da 10: 6 lightning, and his eyes as *l* of fire,
Zec 4: 2 top of it, and his seven *l* thereon,
2 and seven pipes to the seven *l*,
M't 25: 1 ten virgins, which took their *l*,
3 foolish took their *l*, and took no oil
4 took oil in their vessels with their *l*.
7 virgins arose, and trimmed their *l*.
8 of your oil; for our *l* are gone out.
Re 4: 5 seven *l* of fire burning before the

lance
Jer 50:42 shall hold the bow and the *l'*:
lancets
1Ki 18:28 their manner with knives and *l'*.
land See also ISLAND; LANDED; LANDING; LANDMARK; LANDS; OUTLANDISH.
Ge 1: 9 place, and let the dry *l'* appear:
10 and God called the dry *l'* Earth: and
2:11 compasseth the whole *l'* of Havilah,
12 the gold of that *l'* is good: there is
13 compasseth the whole *l'* of Ethiopia.
4:16 dwelt in the *l'* of Nod, on the east
7:22 of all that was in the dry *l'*, died.
10:10 and Calneh, in the *l'* of Shinar.
11 Out of that *l'* went forth Asshur,
11: 2 found a plain in the *l'* of Shinar;
28 Terah in the *l'* of his nativity,
31 Chaldees, to go into the *l'* of Canaan;
12: 1 unto a *l'* that I will shew thee:
5 forth to go into the *l'* of Canaan;
5 into the *l'* of Canaan they came.
6 Abram passed through the *l'* unto
6 the Canaanite was then in the *l'*.
7 said, Unto thy seed will I give this *l'*:
10 was a famine in the *l'*: and Abram
10 the famine was grievous in the *l'*.
13: 6 the *l'* was not able to bear them,
7 Perizzite dwelled then in the *l'*.
9 Is not the whole *l'* before thee?
10 like the *l'* of Egypt, as thou comest
12 Abram dwelled in the *l'* of Canaan,
15 For all the *l'* which thou seest, to
17 walk through the *l'* in the length of
15: 7 to give thee this *l'* to inherit it.
13 a stranger in a *l'* that is not theirs,
18 Unto thy seed have I given this *l'*,
16: 3 dwelt ten years in the *l'* of Canaan,
17: 8 the *l'* wherein thou art a stranger,
8 all the *l'* of Canaan, for...possession;
19:28 toward all the *l'* of the plain, and
20:15 my *l'* is before thee: dwell where it
21:21 him a wife out of the *l'* of Egypt.
23 *l'* wherein thou hast sojourned.
32 into the *l'* of the Philistines.
34 in the Philistines' *l'* many days.
22: 2 and get thee into the *l'* of Moriah;
23: 2 same is Hebron in the *l'* of Canaan:
7 bowed himself to the people of the *l'*,
12 himself before the people of the *l'*.
13 the audience of the people of the *l'*,
15 the *l'* is worth four hundred
19 same is Hebron in the *l'* of Canaan.
24: 5 be willing to follow me unto this *l'*:
5 the *l'* from whence thou camest?
7 from the *l'* of my kindred, and
7 Unto thy seed will I give this *l'*;
37 the Canaanites, in whose *l'* I dwell:
26: 1 there was a famine in the *l'*, beside
2 dwell in the *l'* which I shall tell thee
3 Sojourn in this *l'*, and I will be with
12 Then Isaac sowed in that *l'*, and
22 and we shall be fruitful in the *l'*.
27:46 which are of the daughters of the *l'*,
28: 4 inherit the *l'* wherein thou art a
13 *l'* whereon thou liest, to thee will I
15 will bring thee again into this *l'*;
29: 1 into the *l'* of the people of the east.
31: 3 Return unto the *l'* of thy fathers,
13 now arise, get thee out from this *l'*,
13 return unto the land of thy kindred.
18 Isaac his father in the *l'* of Canaan.
32: 3 Esau his brother unto the *l'* of Seir,
33:18 which is in the *l'* of Canaan,
34: 1 out to see the daughters of the *l'*.
10 us: and the *l'* shall be before you;
21 let them dwell in the *l'*, and trade
21 for the *l'*, behold, it is large enough
30 among the inhabitants of the *l'*.
35: 6 Luz, which is in the *l'* of Canaan,
12 *l'* which I gave Abraham and Isaac,
12 seed after thee will I give the *l'*.
22 to pass, when Israel dwelt in the *l'*,
36: 5 born unto him in the *l'* of Canaan.
6 which he had got in the *l'* of Canaan;
7 the *l'* wherein they were strangers
16 came of Eliphaz in the *l'* of Edom;
17 came of Reuel in the *l'* of Edom;
20 the Horite, who inhabited the *l'*;
21 children of Seir in the *l'* of Edom.
30 among their dukes in the *l'* of Seir.
31 kings that reigned in the *l'* of Edom,
34 Husham of the *l'* of Temani reigned
43 in the *l'* of their possession:
37: 1 Jacob dwelt in the *l'* wherein his
1 was a stranger, in the *l'* of Canaan.
40:15 I was stolen away out of the *l'* of
41:19 I never saw in all the *l'* of Egypt
29 plenty throughout all the *l'* of Egypt:
30 be forgotten in the *l'* of Egypt;
30 and the famine shall consume the *l'*;
31 plenty shall not be known in the *l'*.
33 and set him over the *l'* of Egypt.
34 let him appoint officers over the *l'*,
34 fifth part of the *l'* of Egypt in the
36 that food shall be for store to the *l'*
36 which shall be in the *l'* of Egypt;
41 have set thee over all the *l'* of Egypt.
43 him ruler over all the *l'* of Egypt.
44 hand or foot in all the *l'* of Egypt.
45 Joseph went out over all the *l'* of
46 went throughout all the *l'* of Egypt.
48 years, which were in the *l'* of Egypt,
52 be fruitful in the *l'* of my affliction.
53 that was in the *l'* of Egypt, were
54 in all the *l'* of Egypt...was bread.
Ge 41:55 all the *l'* of Egypt was famished,
56 famine waxed sore in the *l'* of Egypt.
42: 5 the famine was in the *l'* of Canaan.
6 Joseph was the governor over the *l'*,
6 that sold to all the people of the *l'*:
7 From the *l'* of Canaan to buy food.
9, 12 nakedness of the *l'* ye are come.
13 sons of one man in the *l'* of Canaan;
29 their father unto the *l'* of Canaan,
30 man, who is the lord of the *l'*, spake
32 with our father in the *l'* of Canaan.
34 and ye shall traffick in the *l'*.
43: 1 And the famine was sore in the *l'*.
11 take of the best fruits in the *l'* in
44: 8 unto thee out of the *l'* of Canaan:
45: 6 hath the famine been in the *l'*:
8 ruler throughout all the *l'* of Egypt.
10 thou shalt dwell in the *l'* of Goshen,
17 go, get you unto the *l'* of Canaan;
18 give you the good of the *l'* of Egypt,
18 and ye shall eat the fat of the *l'*.
19 you wagons out of the *l'* of Egypt
20 good of all the *l'* of Egypt is yours.
25 into the *l'* of Canaan unto Jacob
26 governor over all the *l'* of Egypt.
46: 6 they had gotten in the *l'* of Canaan,
12 and Onan died in the *l'* of Canaan.
20 unto Joseph in the *l'* of Egypt were
28 and they came into the *l'* of Goshen.
31 which were in the *l'* of Canaan, are
34 ye may dwell in the *l'* of Goshen;
47: 1 are come out of the *l'* of Canaan;
1 behold, they are in the *l'* of Goshen.
4 For to sojourn in the *l'* are we come;
4 famine is sore in the *l'* of Canaan:
4 servants dwell in the *l'* of Goshen.
6 *l'* of Egypt is before thee; in the
6 the best of the *l'* make thy father
6 in the *l'* of Goshen let them dwell:
11 them a possession in the *l'* of Egypt
11 best of the *l'*, in the *l'* of Rameses,
13 there was no bread in all the *l'*;
13 very sore, so that the *l'* of Egypt
13 and all the *l'* of Canaan fainted by
14 that was found in the *l'* of Egypt,
14 and in the *l'* of Canaan, for the corn
15 when money failed in the *l'* of Egypt,
15 and in the *l'* of Canaan, all the
19 thine eyes, both we and our *l'*?
19 buy us and our *l'* for bread, and we
19 and we and our *l'* will be servants
19 not die, that the *l'* be not desolate.
20 Joseph bought all the *l'* of Egypt
20 them: so the *l'* became Pharaoh's.
22 Only the *l'* of the priests bought he
23 bought you this day and your *l'* for
23 seed for you, and ye shall sow the *l'*.
26 made it a law over the *l'* of Egypt
26 except the *l'* of the priests only,
27 And Israel dwelt in the *l'* of Egypt,
28 Jacob lived in the *l'* of Egypt
48: 3 unto me at Luz in the *l'* of Canaan,
4 will give this *l'* to thy seed after
5 born unto thee in the *l'* of Egypt
7 Rachel died by me in the *l'* of Canaan
21 again unto the *l'* of your fathers.
49:15 and the *l'* that it was pleasant;
30 before Mamre, in the *l'* of Canaan,
50: 5 which I have digged for me in the *l'*
7 all the elders of the *l'* of Egypt,
8 herds, they left in the *l'* of Goshen.
11 And when the inhabitants of the *l'*,
13 carried him into the *l'* of Canaan,
24 you, and bring you out of this *l'*
24 the *l'* which he sware to Abraham,
Ex 1: 7 and the *l'* was filled with them.
10 and so get them up out of the *l'*.
2:15 and dwelt in the *l'* of Midian:
22 have been a stranger in a strange *l'*.
3: 8 them up out of that *l'* unto a good *l'*
8 a *l'* flowing with milk and honey;
17 Egypt unto the *l'* of the Canaanites,
17 a *l'* flowing with milk and honey.
4: 9 river, and pour it upon the dry *l'*:
9 shall become blood upon the dry *l'*.
20 and he returned to the *l'* of Egypt:
5: 5 the people of the *l'* now are many,
12 throughout all the *l'* of Egypt
6: 1 shall he drive them out of his *l'*.
4 them, to give them the *l'* of Canaan,
4 the *l'* of their pilgrimage, wherein
8 And I will bring you in unto the *l'*,
11 children of Israel go out of his *l'*.
13 of Israel out of the *l'* of Egypt.
26 of Israel from the *l'* of Egypt
28 spake unto Moses in the *l'* of Egypt,
7: 2 the children of Israel out of his *l'*.
3 and my wonders in the *l'* of Egypt.
4 out of the *l'* of Egypt by great
19 blood throughout all the *l'* of Egypt,
21 throughout all the *l'* of Egypt.
8: 5 to come up upon the *l'* of Egypt.
6 frogs came up, and covered the *l'*
7 up frogs upon the *l'* of Egypt.
14 upon heaps: and the *l'* stank.
16 rod, and smite the dust of the *l'*,
16 lice throughout all the *l'* of Egypt.
17 all the dust of the *l'* became lice
17 lice throughout all the *l'* of Egypt.
22 sever in that day the *l'* of Goshen,
24 houses, and into all the *l'* of Egypt:
24 *l'* was corrupted by reason of...flies.
25 ye, sacrifice to your God in the *l'*.
9: 5 Lord shall do this thing in the *l'*.
9 small dust in all the *l'* of Egypt,
9 beast, throughout all the *l'* of Egypt.
Ex 9:22 may be hail in all the *l'* of Egypt,
22 field, throughout the *l'* of Egypt.
23 rained hail upon the *l'* of Egypt.
24 none like it in all the *l'* of Egypt
25 hail smote throughout all the *l'* of
26 Only in the *l'* of Goshen, where the
10:12 over the *l'* of Egypt for the locusts,
12 may come upon the *l'* of Egypt,
12 and eat every herb of the *l'*, even
13 forth his rod over the *l'* of Egypt,
13 east wind upon the *l'* all that day,
14 And locusts went up over all the *l'*
15 earth, so that the *l'* was darkened;
15 and they did eat every herb of the *l'*,
15 field, through all the *l'* of Egypt.
21 be darkness over the *l'* of Egypt,
22 thick darkness in all the *l'* of Egypt
11: 3 Moses was...great in the *l'* of Egypt,
5 firstborn in the *l'* of Egypt shall die,
6 be a great cry throughout all the *l'*
9 be multiplied in the *l'* of Egypt.
10 children of Israel go out of his *l'*.
12: 1 Moses and Aaron in the *l'* of Egypt,
12 pass through the *l'* of Egypt this
12 will smite all the firstborn in the *l'*
13 you, when I smite the *l'* of Egypt.
17 your armies out of the *l'* of Egypt:
19 he be a stranger, or born in the *l'*.
25 the *l'* which the Lord will give you,
29 smote all the firstborn in the *l'* of
33 send them out of the *l'* in haste;
41 Lord went out from the *l'* of Egypt.
42 for bringing them out from the *l'* of
48 shall be as one that is born in the *l'*:
51 of Israel out of the *l'* of Egypt by
13: 5 thee into the *l'* of the Canaanites,
5 a *l'* flowing with milk and honey,
11 thee into the *l'* of the Canaanites,
15 all the firstborn in the *l'* of Egypt,
17 the way of the *l'* of the Philistines,
18 went up harnessed out of the *l'* of
14: 3 Israel, They are entangled in the *l'*,
21 made the sea dry *l'*, and the waters
29 Israel walked upon dry *l'* in the midst
15:19 children of Israel went on dry *l'* in
16: 1 after their departing out of the *l'* of
3 hand of the Lord in the *l'* of Egypt,
6 brought you out from the *l'* of Egypt:
32 you forth from the *l'* of Egypt.
35 until they came to a *l'* inhabited;
35 unto the borders of the *l'* of Canaan.
18: 3 have been an alien in a strange *l'*:
27 he went his way into his own *l'*.
19: 1 gone forth out of the *l'* of Egypt,
20: 2 brought thee out of the *l'* of Egypt,
12 thy days may be long upon the *l'*
22:21 were strangers in the *l'* of Egypt.
23: 9 were strangers in the *l'* of Egypt.
10 six years thou shalt sow thy *l'*, and
19 The first of the firstfruits of thy *l'*
26 young, nor be barren, in thy *l'*:
29 lest the *l'* become desolate, and the
30 thou be increased, and inherit the *l'*.
31 will deliver the inhabitants of the *l'*
33 They shall not dwell in thy *l'*, lest
29:46 them forth out of the *l'* of Egypt,
32: 1 brought us up out of the *l'* of Egypt,
4 brought thee up out of the *l'* of Egypt.
7 broughtest out of the *l'* of Egypt,
8 brought thee up out of the *l'* of Egypt.
11 brought forth out of the *l'* of Egypt
13 all this *l'* that I have spoken of will
23 brought us up out of the *l'* of Egypt,
33: 1 brought up out of the *l'* of Egypt,
1 the *l'* which I sware unto Abraham,
3 a *l'* flowing with milk and honey:
34:12 with the inhabitants of the *l'*
15 with the inhabitants of the *l'*,
24 neither shall any man desire thy *l'*,
26 The first of the firstfruits of thy *l'*
Le 11:45 you up out of the *l'* of Egypt,
14:34 ye be come into the *l'* of Canaan,
34 a house of the *l'* of your possession;
16:22 iniquities unto a *l'* not inhabited:
18: 3 After the doings of the *l'* of Egypt,
3 after the doings of the *l'* of Canaan,
25 And the *l'* is defiled: therefore I do
25 *l'* itself vomiteth out her inhabitants.
27 have the men of the *l'* done, which
27 before you, and the *l'* is defiled;)
28 That the *l'* spue not you out also,
19: 9 when ye reap the harvest of your *l'*,
23 when ye shall come into the *l'*, and
29 whore; lest the *l'* fall to whoredom,
29 and the *l'* become full of wickedness.
33 stranger sojourn with thee in your *l'*,
34 ye were strangers in the *l'* of Egypt:
36 brought you out of the *l'* of Egypt.
20: 2 the people of the *l'* shall stone him
4 if the people of the *l'* do any ways
22 that the *l'*, whither I bring you to
24 unto you, Ye shall inherit their *l'*,
24 *l'* that floweth with milk and honey:
22:24 make any offering thereof in your *l'*.
33 brought out of the *l'* of Egypt, to
23:10 When ye be come into the *l'* which
22 when ye reap the harvest of your *l'*,
39 have gathered in the fruit of the *l'*,
43 brought them out of the *l'* of Egypt:
24:16 as he that is born in the *l'*, when
25: 2 ye come into the *l'* which I give
2 shall the *l'* keep a sabbath unto the
4 shall be a sabbath of rest unto the *l'*,
5 for it is a year of rest unto the *l'*.
6 sabbath of the *l'* shall be meat for
7 and for the beast that are in thy *l'*,

Le 25: 9 sound throughout all your *l'*.
10 liberty throughout all the *l'* unto
18 ye shall dwell in the *l'* in safety.
19 And the *l'* shall yield her fruit, and
23 The *l'* shall not be sold for ever:
23 for the *l'* is mine; for ye are
24 And in all the *l'* of your possession
24 shall grant a redemption for the *l'*.
38 you forth out of the *l'* of Egypt,
38 to give you the *l'* of Canaan, and to
42 brought forth out of the *l'* of Egypt:
45 you, which they begat in your *l'*:
55 brought forth out of the *l'* of Egypt:
26: 1 up any image of stone in your *l'*,
4 and the *l'* shall yield her increase,
5 the full, and dwell in your *l'* safely.
6 And I will give peace in the *l'*, and
6 I will rid evil beasts out of the *l'*,
6 shall the sword go through your *l'*.
13 you forth out of the *l'* of Egypt,
20 your *l'* shall not yield her increase,
20 neither shall the trees of the *l'*
32 I will bring the *l'* into desolation:
33 and your *l'* shall be desolate, and
34 Then shall the *l'* enjoy her sabbaths,
34 and ye be in your enemies' *l'*; even
34 even then shall the *l'* rest, and
38 *l'* of your enemies shall eat you up.
41 them into the *l'* of their enemies;
42 and I will remember the *l'*.
43 The *l'* also shall be left of them,
44 they be in the *l'* of their enemies,
45 Brought forth out of the *l'* of Egypt
27: 24 the possession of the *l'* did belong.
30 And all the tithe of the *l'*, whether
30 whether of the seed of the *l'*, or of
Nu 1: 1 were come out of the *l'* of Egypt,
3: 13 I smote all the firstborn in the *l'*
8: 17 every firstborn in the *l'* of Egypt
9: 1 were come out of the *l'* of Egypt,
14 and for him that was born in the *l'*.
10: 9 if ye go to war in your *l'* against
30 but I will depart to mine own *l'*,
11: 12 *l'* which thou swearest unto their
13: 2 they may search the *l'* of Canaan,
16 which Moses sent to spy out the *l'*.
17 them to spy out the *l'* of Canaan,
18 see the *l'*, what it is; and the people
19 what the *l'* is that they dwell in,
20 what the *l'* is, whether it be fat or
20 and bring of the fruit of the *l'*.
21 they went up, and searched the *l'*
25 returned from searching of the *l'*
26 and shewed them the fruit of the *l'*.
27 unto the *l'* whither thou sentest us,
28 people be strong that dwell in the *l'*,
29 The Amalekites dwell in the *l'* of the
32 brought up an evil report of the *l'*
32 The *l'*, through which we have gone
32 is a *l'* that eateth up the inhabitants
14: 2 that we had died in the *l'* of Egypt!
3 the Lord brought us unto this *l'*,
6 were of them that searched the *l'*,
7 The *l'*, which we passed through to
7 to search it, is an exceeding good *l'*.
8 then he will bring us into this *l'*, and
8 a *l'* which floweth with milk and
9 neither fear ye the people of the *l'*;
14 tell it to the inhabitants of this *l'*:
16 able to bring this people into the *l'*
23 shall not see the *l'* which I sware
24 him will I bring into the *l'* whereinto
30 ye shall not come into the *l'*,
31 they shall know the *l'* which ye have
34 the days in which ye searched the *l'*,
36 which Moses sent to search the *l'*,
36 by bringing up a slander upon the *l'*,
37 bring up the evil report upon the *l'*,
38 of the men that went to search the *l'*,
15: 2 When ye be come into the *l'* of your
18 When ye come into the *l'* whither I
19 when ye eat of the bread of the *l'*,
30 whether he be born in the *l'*, or a
41 brought you out of the *l'* of Egypt,
16: 13 brought us up out of a *l'* that floweth
14 not brought us into a *l'* that floweth
18: 13 whatsoever is first ripe in the *l'*,
20 shalt have no inheritance in their *l'*
20: 12 bring this congregation into the *l'*
23 Hor, by the coast of the *l'* of Edom,
24 he shall not enter into the *l'* which
21: 4 Red sea, to compass the *l'* of Edom:
22 Let me pass through thy *l'*: we will
24 and possessed his *l'* from Arnon unto
26 taken all his *l'* out of his hand, even
31 Israel dwelt in the *l'* of the Amorites.
34 hand, and all his people, and his *l'*;
35 him alive: and they possessed his *l'*.
22: 5 river of the *l'* of the children of his
6 that I may drive them out of the *l'*:
13 Get you into your *l'*: for the Lord
26: 4 went forth out of the *l'* of Egypt.
19 Er and Onan died in the *l'* of Canaan.
53 Unto these the *l'* shall be divided
55 the *l'* shall be divided by lot:
27: 12 see the *l'* which I have given unto
32: 1 and when they saw the *l'* of Jazer,
1 and the *l'* of Gilead, that, behold, the
4 is a *l'* for cattle, and thy servants
5 let this *l'* be given unto thy servants
7 of Israel from going over into the *l'*
8 from Kadesh-barnea to see the *l'*.
9 and saw the *l'*, they discouraged the
9 that they should not go into the *l'*
11 *l'* which I sware unto Abraham,
17 because of the inhabitants of the *l'*.

Nu 32: 22 the *l'* be subdued before the Lord:
22 and this *l'* shall be your possession
29 the *l'* shall be subdued before you;
29 ye shall give them the *l'* of Gilead
30 among you in the *l'* of Canaan.
32 before the Lord into the *l'* of Canaan,
33 the *l'*, with the cities thereof in the
33: 1 went forth out of the *l'* of Egypt with
37 Hor, in the edge of the *l'* of Edom.
38 were come out of the *l'* of Egypt,
40 in the south in the *l'* of Canaan,
51 over Jordan into the *l'* of Canaan;
52 inhabitants of the *l'* from before you,
53 dispossess the inhabitants of the *l'*,
53 I have given you the *l'* to possess it.
54 ye shall divide the *l'* by lot for an
55 not drive out the inhabitants of the *l'*
55 shall vex you in the *l'* wherein ye
34: 2 When ye come into the *l'* of Canaan;
2 (this is the *l'* that shall fall unto you
2 even the *l'* of Canaan with the coasts
12 this shall be your *l'* with the coasts
13 This is the *l'* which ye shall inherit
17 which shall divide the *l'* unto you:
18 to divide the *l'* by inheritance.
29 children of Israel in the *l'* of Canaan.
35: 10 over Jordan into the *l'* of Canaan;
14 shall ye give in the *l'* of Canaan,
28 slayer shall return into the *l'* of his
32 should come again to dwell in the *l'*,
33 not pollute the *l'* wherein ye are:
33 ye are: for blood it defileth the *l'*:
33 *l'* cannot be cleansed of the blood
34 Defile not therefore the *l'* which ye
36: 2 to give the *l'* for an inheritance by
De 1: 5 this side Jordan, in the *l'* of Moab,
7 to the *l'* of the Canaanites, and unto
8 Behold, I have set the *l'* before you:
8 go in and possess the *l'* which the
21 thy God hath set the *l'* before thee:
22 they shall search us out the *l'*, and
25 they took of the fruit of the *l'* in their
25 is a good *l'* which the Lord our God
27 out of the *l'* of Egypt, to deliver us
35 this evil generation see that good *l'*,
36 to him will I give the *l'* that he hath
2: 5 I will not give you of their *l'*, no, not
9 I will not give thee of their *l'* for a
12 as Israel did unto the *l'* of his
19 not give thee of the *l'* of the children
20 also was accounted a *l'* of giants:
24 Sihon...king of Heshbon, and his *l'*:
27 Let me pass through thy *l'*: I will go
29 Jordan into the *l'* which the Lord
31 to give Sihon and his *l'* before thee:
31 that thou mayest inherit his *l'*.
37 unto the *l'* of the children of Ammon
3: 2 his people, and his *l'*, into thy hand;
8 the *l'* that was on this side Jordan,
12 this *l'*, which we possessed at that
13 which was called the *l'* of giants.
18 hath given you this *l'* to possess it:
20 also possess the *l'* which the Lord
25 the good *l'* that is beyond Jordan,
28 cause them to inherit the *l'* which
4: 1 in and possess the *l'* which the Lord
5 should do so in the *l'* whither ye go
14 might do them in the *l'* whither ye go
21 I should not go in unto that good *l'*,
22 But I must die in this *l'*, I must not
22 go over, and possess that good *l'*.
25 shall have remained long in the *l'*,
26 soon utterly perish from off the *l'*
38 give thee their *l'* for an inheritance,
46 the *l'* of Sihon king of the Amorites,
47 they possessed his *l'*, and the *l'* of Og
5: 6 brought thee out of the *l'* of Egypt,
15 wast a servant in the *l'* of Egypt,
16 *l'* which the Lord thy God giveth
31 may do them in the *l'* which I give
33 ye may prolong your days in the *l'*
6: 1 in the *l'* whither ye go to possess it:
3 *l'* that floweth with milk and honey.
10 thee into the *l'* which he sware unto
12 thee forth out of the *l'* of Egypt,
18 mayest go in and possess the good *l'*
23 give us the *l'* which he sware unto
7: 1 thy God shall bring thee into the *l'*
13 thy womb, and the fruit of thy *l'*,
13 *l'* which he sware unto thy fathers
8: 1 go in and possess the *l'* which the
7 into a good *l'*, a *l'* of brooks of water,
8 A *l'* of wheat, and barley, and vines,
8 a *l'* of oil olive, and honey;
9 A *l'* wherein thou shalt eat bread
9 a *l'* whose stones are iron, and out
10 the good *l'* which he hath given thee.
14 thee forth out of the *l'* of Egypt,
9: 4 brought me in to possess this *l'*:
5 dost thou go to possess their *l'*:
6 thy God giveth thee not this good *l'*
7 didst depart out of the *l'* of Egypt,
23 Go up and possess the *l'* which I
28 Lest the *l'* whence thou broughtest
28 into the *l'* which he promised them,
10: 7 to Jotbath, a *l'* of rivers of waters.
11 they may go in and possess the *l'*,
19 ye were strangers in the *l'* of Egypt.
11: 3 king of Egypt, and unto all his *l'*;
8 strong, and go in and possess the *l'*,
9 ye may prolong your days in the *l'*,
9 *l'* that floweth with milk and honey.
10 For the *l'*, whither thou goest in to
10 is not as the *l'* of Egypt, from whence
11 the *l'*, whither ye go to possess it,
11 is a *l'* of hills and valleys, and

De 11: 12 A *l'* which the Lord thy God careth
14 the rain of your *l'* in his due season,
17 and that the *l'* yield not her fruit;
17 perish quickly from off the good *l'*
21 the *l'* which the Lord sware unto
25 all the *l'* that ye shall tread upon,
29 unto the *l'* whither thou goest to
30 down, in the *l'* of the Canaanites,
31 to go in to possess the *l'* which the
12: 1 ye shall observe to do in the *l'*,
10 dwell in the *l'* which the Lord your
29 them, and dwellest in their *l'*;
13: 5 brought you out of the *l'* of Egypt,
10 brought thee out of the *l'* of Egypt,
15: 4 Lord shall greatly bless thee in the *l'*
7 within any of thy gates in thy *l'*
11 poor shall never cease out of the *l'*:
11 thy poor, and to thy needy, in thy *l'*.
15 wast a bondman in the *l'* of Egypt.
16: 3 forth out of the *l'* of Egypt in haste:
3 camest forth out of the *l'* of Egypt
20 inherit the *l'* which the Lord thy God
17: 14 When thou art come unto the *l'*
18: 9 when thou art come into the *l'*
19: 1 whose *l'* the Lord thy God giveth
2 cities for thee in the midst of thy *l'*,
3 divide the coasts of thy *l'*, which
8 give thee all the *l'* which he promised
10 innocent blood be not shed in thy *l'*,
14 which thou shalt inherit in the *l'*
20: 1 thee up out of the *l'* of Egypt.
21: 1 If one be found slain in the *l'* which
23 that thy *l'* be not defiled, which the
23: 7 thou wast a stranger in his *l'*.
20 in the *l'* whither thou goest to
24: 4 thou shalt not cause the *l'* to sin,
14 strangers that are in thy *l'* within
22 wast a bondman in the *l'* of Egypt:
25: 15 days may be lengthened in the *l'*
19 in the *l'* which the Lord thy God
26: 1 when thou art come in unto the *l'*
2 shalt bring of thy *l'* that the Lord
9 place, and hath given us this *l'*,
9 *l'* that floweth with milk and honey.
10 brought the firstfruits of the *l'*,
15 and the *l'* which thou hast given us,
15 *l'* that floweth with milk and honey.
27: 2 ye shall pass over Jordan unto the *l'*
3 that thou mayest go in unto the *l'*
3 *l'* that floweth with milk and honey;
28: 8 bless thee in the *l'* which the Lord
11 *l'* which the Lord sware unto thy
12 the rain unto thy *l'* in his season,
18 of thy body, and the fruit of thy *l'*,
21 have consumed thee from off the *l'*,
24 the rain of thy *l'* powder and dust:
33 fruit of thy *l'*, and all thy labours,
42 and fruit of thy *l'* shall the locust
51 of thy cattle, and the fruit of thy *l'*,
52 trustedst, throughout all thy *l'*:
52 all thy gates throughout all thy *l'*,
63 ye shall be plucked from off the *l'*
29: 1 children of Israel in the *l'* of Moab,
2 before your eyes in the *l'* of Egypt
2 all his servants, and unto all his *l'*;
8 we took their *l'*, and gave it for an
16 how we have dwelt in the *l'* of Egypt;
22 that shall come from a far *l'*,
22 when they see the plagues of that *l'*,
23 the whole *l'* thereof is brimstone,
24 the Lord done thus unto this *l'*?
25 them forth out of the *l'* of Egypt:
27 the Lord was kindled against this *l'*,
28 rooted them out of their *l'* in anger,
28 and cast them into another *l'*,
30: 5 thy God will bring thee into the *l'*
9 thy cattle, and in the fruit of thy *l'*,
16 thy God shall bless thee in the *l'*
18 not prolong your days upon the *l'*,
20 thou mayest dwell in the *l'* which
31: 4 Amorites, and unto the *l'* of them,
7 must go with this people unto the *l'*
13 as long as ye live in the *l'* whither
16 the gods of the strangers of the *l'*,
20 into the *l'* which I sware unto their
21 them into the *l'* which I sware.
23 into the *l'* which I sware unto them:
32: 10 He found him in a desert *l'*, and in
43 will be merciful unto his *l'*, and to
47 ye shall prolong your days in the *l'*,
49 Nebo, which is in the *l'* of Moab,
49 behold the *l'* of Canaan, which I
52 thou shalt see the *l'* before thee;
52 thither unto the *l'* which I give the
33: 13 Blessed of the Lord be his *l'*, for
28 shall be upon a *l'* of corn and wine;
34: 1 shewed him all the *l'* of Gilead,
2 the *l'* of Ephraim, and Manasseh,
2 all the *l'* of Judah, unto the utmost
4 the *l'* which I sware unto Abraham,
5 Lord died there in the *l'* of Moab,
6 him in a valley in the *l'* of Moab,
11 sent him to do in the *l'* of Egypt
11 to all his servants, and to all his *l'*,
Jos 1: 2 unto the *l'* which I do give to them,
4 all the *l'* of the Hittites, and unto
6 thou divide for an inheritance the *l'*,
11 to go in to possess the *l'*, which the
13 you rest, and hath given you this *l'*.
14 shall remain in the *l'* which Moses
15 they also have possessed the *l'*
15 return unto the *l'* of your possession,
2: 1 saying, Go view the *l'*, even Jericho.
9 that the Lord hath given you the *l'*,
9 inhabitants of the *l'* faint because of
14 when the Lord hath given us the *l'*,

Jos 2:18 we come into the l', thou shalt bind
24 delivered into our hands all the l';
4:18 feet were lifted up unto the dry l',
22 Israel came over this Jordan on dry l'.
5: 6 that he would not shew them the l',
6 l' that floweth with milk and honey.
11 eat of the old corn of the l' on the
12 had eaten of the old corn of the l';
12 they did eat of the fruit of the l' of
7: 9 the inhabitants of the l' shall hear
8: 1 his people, and his city, and his l':
9:24 servant Moses, to give you all the l',
24 destroy all the inhabitants of the l'
10:42 these kings and their l' did Joshua
11: 3 under Hermon in the l' of Mizpeh.
16 So Joshua took all that l', the hills,
16 all the l' of Goshen, and the valley,
22 none of the Anakims left in the l' of
23 Joshua took the whole l', according
23 tribes. And the l' rested from war.
12: 1 these are the kings of the l', which
1 possessed their l' on the other side
13: 1 yet very much l' to be possessed.
2 This is the l' that yet remaineth: all
4 all the l' of the Canaanites, and
5 And the l' of the Giblites, and all
7 divide this l' for an inheritance
25 half the l' of the children of Ammon,
14: 1 Israel inherited in the l' of Canaan,
4 no part unto the Levites in the l',
5 Israel did, and they divided the l'.
7 Kadesh-barnea to espy out the l';
9 l' whereon thy feet have trodden
15 And the l' had rest from war.
15:19 for thou hast given me a south l';
17: 5 beside the l' of Gilead and Bashan,
6 Manasseh's sons had the l' of Gilead.
8 Manasseh had the l' of Tappuah:
12 Canaanites would dwell in that l'.
15 l' of the Perizzites and of the giants,
16 that dwell in the l' of the valley
18: 1 and the l' was subdued before them.
3 are ye slack to go to possess the l',
4 they shall rise, and go through the l',
6 describe the l' into seven parts,
8 them that went to describe the l',
8 saying, Go and walk through the l',
9 men went and passed through the l',
10 there Joshua divided the l' unto the
19:49 dividing the l' for inheritance by
21: 2 them at Shiloh in the l' of Canaan,
43 the Lord gave unto Israel all the l'
22: 4 and unto the l' of your possession,
9 Shiloh, which is in the l' of Canaan,
9 l' of their possession, whereof they
10 that are in the l' of Canaan, the
11 altar over against the l' of Canaan,
13 of Manasseh, into the l' of Gilead,
15 of Manasseh, unto the l' of Gilead,
19 the l' of your possession be unclean,
19 then pass ye over unto the l' of the
32 of Gad, out of the l' of Gilead,
32 unto the l' of Canaan, to the children
33 destroy the l' wherein the children
23: 5 ye shall possess their l', as the Lord
13 until ye perish from off the good l'
15 destroyed you from off this good l'
16 perish quickly from off the good l'
24: 3 him throughout all the l' of Canaan,
8 you into the l' of the Amorites,
8 hand, that ye might possess their l';
13 you a l' for which ye did not labour,
15 the Amorites, in whose l' ye dwell:
17 our fathers out of the l' of Egypt,
18 the Amorites which dwelt in the l':
J'g 1: 2 have delivered the l' into his hand.
15 for thou hast given me a south l';
26 men went into the l' of the Hittites,
27 Canaanites would dwell in that l'.
32, 33 Canaanites,...inhabitants of the l':
2: 1 have brought you unto the l' which
2 with the inhabitants of this l';
6 his inheritance to possess the l'.
12 brought them out of the l' of Egypt,
3:11 And the l' had rest forty years.
30 And the l' had rest fourscore years.
5:31 And the l' had rest forty years.
6: 5 they entered into the l' to destroy it.
9 before you, and gave you their l';
10 the Amorites, in whose l' ye dwell:
9:37 people down by the middle of the l',
10: 4 day, which are in the l' of Gilead.
8 Jordan in the l' of the Amorites,
11: 3 brethren, and dwelt in the l' of Tob:
5 fetch Jephthah out of the l' of Tob:
12 come against me to fight in my l'?
13 Because Israel took away my l',
15 Israel took not away the l' of Moab,
15 nor the l' of the children of Ammon:
17 me, I pray thee, pass through thy l':
18 the l' of Edom, and the l' of Moab,
18 by the east side of the l' of Moab,
19 thee, through thy l' into my place.
21 possessed all the l' of the Amorites,
12:15 in Pirathon in the l' of Ephraim,
18: 2 to spy out the l', and to search it;
2 said unto them, Go, search the l':
7 there was no magistrate in the l',
9 for we have seen the l', and, behold,
9 to go, and to enter to possess the l'.
10 a people secure, and to a large l':
17 five men that went to spy out the l'
30 the day of the captivity of the l'.
19:30 Israel came up out of the l' of Egypt
20: 1 to Beer-sheba, with the l' of Gilead,
21:12 Shiloh, which is in the l' of Canaan.

J'g 21:21 Shiloh, and go to the l' of Benjamin.
Ru 1: 1 that there was a famine in the l'.
7 way to return unto the l' of Judah.
2:11 mother, and the l' of thy nativity,
4: 3 of Moab, selleth a parcel of l',
1Sa 6: 5 of your mice that mar the l';
5 off your gods, and from off your l'.
9: 4 passed through the l' of Shalisha,
4 passed through the l' of Shalim,
4 through the l' of the Benjamites,
5 they were come to the l' of Zuph,
16 thee a man out of the l' of Benjamin,
12: 6 your fathers up out of the l' of Egypt.
13: 3 the trumpet throughout all the l',
7 went over Jordan to the l' of Gad
17 to Ophrah, unto the l' of Shual:
19 throughout all the l' of Israel:
14:14 as it were an half acre of l', which
25 all they of the l' came to a wood;
29 My father hath troubled the l':
21:11 not this David the king of the l'?
22: 5 and get thee into the l' of Judah.
23:23 if he be in the l', that I will search
27 the Philistines have invaded the l'.
27: 1 escape into the l' of the Philistines;
8 were of old the inhabitants of the l',
8 to Shur, even unto the l' of Egypt.
9 David smote the l', and left neither
28: 3 and the wizards, out of the l'.
9 and the wizards, out of the l':
29:11 return into the l' of the Philistines.
30:16 out of the l' of the Philistines,
16 and out of the l' of Judah.
31: 9 sent into the l' of the Philistines
2Sa 3:12 his behalf, saying, Whose is the l'?
5: 6 Jebusites, the inhabitants of the l':
7:23 great things and terrible, for thy l',
9: 7 thee all the l' of Saul thy father;
10 thy servants, shall till the l' for him,
10: 2 into the l' of the children of Ammon.
15: 4 Oh that I were made judge in the l',
17:26 Absalom pitched in the l' of Gilead.
19: 9 he is fled out of the l' for Absalom.
29 said, Thou and Ziba divide the l'.
21:14 that God was intreated for the l'.
24: 6 and to the l' of Tahtim-hodshi;
8 they had gone through all the l',
13 of famine come unto thee in thy l'?
13 be three days' pestilence in thy l'?
25 So the Lord was intreated for the l',
1Ki 4:10 Sochoh, and all the l' of Hepher:
19 the only officer which was in the l'.
21 river unto the l' of the Philistines,
6: 1 were come out of the l' of Egypt,
8: 9 they came out of the l' of Egypt.
21 brought them out of the l' of Egypt.
34 unto the l' which thou gavest unto
36 give rain upon thy l', which thou
37 If there be in the l' famine, if there
37 besiege them in the l' of their cities;
40 all the days that they live in the l'
46 captives unto the l' of the enemy,
47 l' whither they were carried captives,
47 make supplication unto thee in the l'
48 in the l' of their enemies, which led
48 and pray unto thee toward their l',
9: 7 Then will I cut off Israel out of the l'
8 hath the Lord done thus unto this l',
9 their fathers out of the l' of Egypt,
11 twenty cities in the l' of Galilee.
13 And he called them the l' of Cabul
18 Tadmor in the wilderness, in the l',
19 and in all the l' of his dominion.
21 that were left after them in the l',
26 of the Red sea, in the l' of Edom.
10: 6 report that I heard in mine own l' of
11:18 him victuals, and gave him l'.
12:28 brought thee up out of the l' of Egypt.
14:15 root up Israel out of this good l',
24 there were also sodomites in the l':
15:12 took away the sodomites out of the l',
20 Cinneroth, with all the l' of Naphtali.
17: 7 there had been no rain in the l'.
18: 5 said unto Obadiah, Go into the l',
6 divided the l' between them to pass
20: 7 Israel called all the elders of the l',
22:46 his father Asa, he took out of the l'.
2Ki 2:21 thence any more death or barren l'.
3:19 mar every good piece of l' with stones.
25 on every good piece of l' cast every
27 him, and returned to their own l'.
4:38 and there was a dearth in the l'; and
5: 2 out of the l' of Israel a little maid;
4 the maid that is of the l' of Israel.
6:23 came no more into the l' of Israel.
8: 1 also come upon the l' seven years.
2 the l' of the Philistines seven years.
3 out of the l' of the Philistines: and
3, 5 king for her house and for her l'.
6 since the day that she left the l',
10:33 Jordan eastward, all the l' of Gilead,
11: 3 And Athaliah did reign over the l'.
14 all the people of the l' rejoiced, and
18 people of the l' went into the house
19 guard, and all the people of the l';
20 all the people of the l' rejoiced, and
13:20 bands of the Moabites invaded the l'
15: 5 house, judging the people of the l'.
19 king of Assyria came against the l':
20 back, and stayed not there in the l'.
29 all the l' of Naphtali, and carried
16:15 offering of all the people of the l',
17: 5 came up throughout all the l', and
7 them up out of the l' of Egypt, from
23 carried away out of their own l' to
26 not the manner of the God of the l':

2Ki 17:26 not the manner of the God of the l'.
27 them the manner of the God of the l'.
36 brought you up out of the l' of Egypt
18:25 said to me, Go up against this l', and
32 you away to a l' like your own l',
32 a l' of corn and wine,
32 a l' of bread and vineyards,
32 a l' of oil olive and of honey,
33 of the nations delivered at all his l'
19: 7 and shall return to his own l'; and
7 him to fall by the sword in his own l'.
37 they escaped into the l' of Armenia.
21: 8 Israel move any more out of the l'
24 people of the l' slew all them that
24 people of the l' made Josiah his son
23:24 that were spied in the l' of Judah
30 people of the l' took Jehoahaz the
33 bands at Riblah in the l' of Hamath,
33 put the l' to a tribute of an hundred
35 but he taxed the l' to give the money
35 and the gold of the people of the l',
24: 7 not again any more out of his l':
14 poorest sort of the people of the l'.
15 his officers, and the mighty of the l',
25: 3 was no bread for the people of the l'.
12 poor of the l' to be vinedressers and
19 which mustered the people of the l',
19 threescore men of the people of the l'
21 them at Riblah in the l' of Hamath.
21 was carried away out of their l'.
22 that remained in the l' of Judah,
24 dwell in the l', and serve the king of
1Ch 1:43 kings that reigned in the l' of Edom
45 Husham of the l' of the Temanites
2:22 and twenty cities in the l' of Gilead.
4:40 and the l' was wide, and quiet, and
5: 9 were multiplied in the l' of Gilead.
10 throughout all the east l' of Gilead.
11 in the l' of Bashan unto Salcah:
23 tribe of Manasseh dwelt in the l':
25 after the gods of the people of the l',
6:55 gave them Hebron in the l' of Judah,
7:21 Gath that were born in that l' slew,
10: 9 and sent into the l' of the Philistines
11: 4 Jebusites...the inhabitants of the l'.
13: 2 that are left in all the l' of Israel,
16:18 Unto thee will I give the l' of Canaan,
19: 2 into the l' of the children of Ammon
3 to overthrow, and to spy out the l'?
21:12 even the pestilence, in the l', and the
22: 2 the strangers...in the l' of Israel;
18 given the inhabitants of the l' into
18 the l' is subdued before the Lord,
28: 8 that ye may possess this good l',
2Ch 2:17 the strangers...in the l' of Israel,
6: 5 forth my people out of the l' of Egypt
25 bring them again unto the l' which
27 and send rain upon thy l', which
28 If there be dearth in the l', if there
28 besiege them in the cities of their l';
31 long as they live in the l' which
36 captives unto a l' far off or near;
37 in the l' whither they are carried
37 unto thee in the l' of their captivity,
38 their soul in the l' of their captivity,
38 captives, and pray toward their l',
7:13 command the locusts to devour the l',
14 their sin, and will heal their l'.
20 them up by the roots out of my l'
21 hath the Lord done thus unto this l',
22 them forth out of the l' of Egypt,
8: 6 throughout all the l' of his dominion.
8 who were left after them in the l',
17 at the sea side in the l' of Edom.
9: 5 report which I heard in mine own l'
11 such seen before in the l' of Judah.
12 turned, and went away to her own l',
26 even unto the l' of the Philistines,
14: 1 his days the l' was quiet ten years.
6 for the l' had rest, and he had no war
7 bars, while the l' is yet before us;
15: 8 idols out of all the l' of Judah and
17: 2 and set garrisons in the l' of Judah,
19: 3 taken away the groves out of the l',
5 he set judges in the l' throughout
20: 7 drive out the inhabitants of this l'
10 they came out of the l' of Egypt,
22:12 and Athaliah reigned over the l'.
23:13 all the people of the l' rejoiced, and
20 people, and all the people of the l',
21 And all the people of the l' rejoiced:
26:21 house, judging the people of the l'.
30: 9 they shall come again into this l':
25 that came out of the l' of Israel, and
32: 4 that ran through the midst of the l',
21 with shame of face to his own l'.
31 of the wonder that was done in the l',
33: 8 the foot of Israel from out of the l'
25 people of the l' slew all them that
25 people of the l' made Josiah his son
34: 7 idols throughout all the l' of Israel,
8 when he had purged the l', and the
36: 1 people of the l' took Jehoahaz the
3 and condemned the l' in an hundred
21 the l' had enjoyed her sabbaths:
Ezr 4: 4 people of the l' weakened the hands
6:21 the filthiness of the heathen of the l',
9:11 The l', unto which ye go to possess
11 is an unclean l' with the filthiness of
12 be strong, and eat the good of the l',
10: 2 strange wives of the people of the l':
11 yourselves from the people of the l',
Ne 4: 4 them for a prey in the l' of captivity:
5:14 be their governor in the l' of Judah,
16 this wall, neither bought we any l':
9: 8 to give the l' of the Canaanites, the

Ne 9:10 and on all the people of his l':
11 the midst of the sea on the dry l';
15 they should go in to possess the l'
22 so they possessed the l' of Sihon,
22 and the l' of the king of Heshbon,
22 and the l' of Og king of Bashan.
23 and broughtest them into the l',
24 children went in and possessed the l',
24 before them the inhabitants of the l',
24 their kings, and the people of the l',
25 they took strong cities, and a fat l',
35 large and fat l' which thou gavest
36 for the l' that thou gavest unto our
10:30 daughters unto the people of the l',
31 people of the l' bring ware or any
Es 8:17 of the people of the l' became Jews;
10: 1 Ahasuerus laid a tribute upon the l',
Job 1: 1 a man in the l' of Uz, whose name
10 his substance is increased in the l'.
10:21 to the l' of darkness and the shadow
22 A l' of darkness, as darkness itself;
28:13 is it found in the l' of the living.
31:38 If my l' cry against me, or that the
37:13 correction, or for his l', or for mercy.
39: 6 and the barren l' his dwellings.
42:15 the l' were no women found so fair
Ps 10:16 heathen are perished out of his l'.
27:13 of the Lord in the l' of the living.
35:20 against them that are quiet in the l'.
37: 3 shalt thou dwell in the l', and verily
29 The righteous shall inherit the l',
34 he shall exalt thee to inherit the l':
42: 6 remember thee from the l' of Jordan,
44: 3 they got not the l' in possession by
52: 5 root thee out of the l' of the living.
63: 1 for thee in a dry and thirsty l', where
66: 6 He turned the sea into dry l': they
68: 6 but the rebellious dwell in a dry l'.
74: 8 all the synagogues of God in the l'.
78:12 of their fathers, in the l' of Egypt, in
80: 9 to take deep root, and it filled the l'.
81: 5 he went out through the l' of Egypt:
10 brought thee out of the l' of Egypt:
85: 1 hast been favourable unto thy l':
9 him; that glory may dwell in our l'.
12 and our l' shall yield her increase.
88:12 in the l' of forgetfulness?
95: 5 it: and his hands formed the dry l'.
101: 6 shall be upon the faithful of the l',
8 early destroy all the wicked of the l';
105:11 thee will I give the l' of Canaan,
16 he called for a famine upon the l':
23 Jacob sojourned in the l' of Ham.
27 them, and wonders in the l' of Ham.
30 Their l' brought forth frogs in
32 for rain, and flaming fire in their l'.
35 did eat up all the herbs in their l',
36 smote also all the firstborn in their l',
106:22 Wondrous works in the l' of Ham,
24 they despised the pleasant l', they
38 and the l' was polluted with blood.
107:34 A fruitful l' into barrenness, for the
116: 9 before the Lord in the l' of the living.
135:12 And gave their l' for an heritage, an
136:21 And gave their l' for an heritage: for
137: 4 sing the Lord's song in a strange l'?
142: 5 my portion in the l' of the living.
143: 6 thirsteth after thee, as a thirsty l'.
10 lead me into the l' of uprightness.
Pr 2:21 For the upright shall dwell in the l',
12:11 that tilleth his l' shall be satisfied
28: 2 For the transgression of a l' many
19 that tilleth his l' shall have plenty
29: 4 by judgment establisheth the l':
31:23 he sitteth among the elders of the l'.
Ec 10:16 Woe to thee, O l', when thy king is
17 Blessed art thou, O l', when thy king
Ca 2:12 voice of the turtle is heard in our l';
Isa 1: 7 your l', strangers devour it in your
19 ye shall eat the good of the l':
2: 7 Their l' also is full of silver and gold,
7 their l' is also full of horses, neither
8 Their l' also is full of idols; they
5:30 look unto the l', behold darkness
6:11 man, and the l' be utterly desolate,
12 forsaking in the midst of the l'.
7:16 the l' that thou abhorrest shall be
18 the bee that is in the l' of Assyria.
22 every one eat that is left in the l'.
24 l' shall become briers and thorns.
8: 8 wings shall fill the breadth of thy l',
9: 1 he lightly afflicted the l' of Zebulun,
1 of Zebulun and the l' of Naphtali,
2 in the l' of the shadow of death,
19 the Lord of hosts is the l' darkened,
10:23 in the midst of all the l'.
11:16 he came up out of the l' of Egypt.
13: 5 indignation, to destroy the whole l'.
9 fierce anger, to lay the l' desolate:
14 and flee every one into his own l'.
14: 1 Israel, and set them in their own l':
2 possess them in the l' of the Lord
20 because thou hast destroyed thy l',
21 they do not rise, nor possess the l',
25 I will break the Assyrian in my l',
15: 9 and upon the remnant of the l'.
16: 1 ye the lamb to the ruler of the l'
4 oppressors...consumed out of the l'.
18: 1 Woe to the l' shadowing with wings,
2 whose l' the rivers have spoiled!
7 foot, whose l' the rivers have spoiled,
19:17 And the l' of Judah shall be a terror
18 five cities in the l' of Egypt speak
19 Lord in the midst of the l' of Egypt,
20 the Lord of hosts in the l' of Egypt:
24 even a blessing in the midst of the l'

Isa 21: 1 from the desert, from a terrible l'.
14 The inhabitants of the l' of Tema
23: 1 from the l' of Chittim it is revealed
10 Pass through thy l' as a river, O
13 Behold the l' of the Chaldeans; this
24: 3 The l' shall be utterly emptied, and
11 darkened, the mirth of the l' is gone.
13 shall be in the midst of the l' among
26: 1 this song be sung in the l' of Judah;
10 in the l' of uprightness will he deal
27:13 ready to perish in the l' of Assyria,
13 and the outcasts in the l' of Egypt,
30: 6 into the l' of trouble and anguish,
32: 2 shadow of a great rock in a weary l'.
13 Upon the l' of my people shall come
33:17 shall behold the l' that is very far off.
34: 6 great slaughter in the l' of Idumea.
7 their l' shall be soaked with blood,
9 l' thereof...become burning pitch.
35: 7 and the thirsty l' springs of water:
36:10 Lord against this l', to destroy it?
10 Go up against this l', and destroy it.
17 a l' like your own l', a l' of corn and
17 wine, a l' of bread and vineyards.
18 delivered his l' out of the hand of the
20 delivered their l' out of my hand,
37: 7 a rumour, and return to his own l';
7 to fall by the sword in his own l'.
38 they escaped into the l' of Armenia:
38:11 even the Lord, in the l' of the living:
41:18 and the dry l' springs of water.
49:12 west: and these from the l' of Sinim.
19 places, and the l' of thy destruction,
53: 8 was cut off out of the l' of the living:
57:13 his trust in me shall possess the l',
60:18 shall no more be heard in thy l',
21 they shall inherit the l' for ever, the
61: 7 in their l' they shall possess the
62: 4 thy l' any more be termed Desolate:
4 Hephzi-bah, and thy l' Beulah: for
4 in thee, and thy l' shall be married.
Jer 1: 1 in Anathoth in the l' of Benjamin:
14 upon all the inhabitants of the l'.
18 brasen walls against the whole l',
18 and against the people of the l'.
2: 2 wilderness, in a l' that was not sown.
6 brought us up out of the l' of Egypt,
6 through a l' of deserts and of pits,
6 through a l' of drought, and of the
6 a l' that no man passed through,
7 when ye entered, ye defiled my l',
15 yelled, and they made his l' waste:
31 a l' of darkness? wherefore say my
3: 1 shall not that l' be greatly polluted?
2 polluted the l' with thy whoredoms
9 she defiled the l', and committed
16 be multiplied and increased in the l',
18 together out of the l' of the north to
18 to the l' that I have given for an
19 and give thee a pleasant l', a goodly
4: 5 say, Blow ye the trumpet in the l':
7 his place to make thy l' desolate;
20 the whole l' is spoiled: suddenly are
27 said, The whole l' shall be desolate;
5:19 and served strange gods in your l',
19 ye serve strangers in a l' that is not
30 horrible thing is committed in the l';
6: 8 thee desolate, a l' not inhabited.
12 hand upon the inhabitants of the l',
7: 7 in the l' that I gave to your fathers,
22 brought them out of the l' of Egypt,
25 came forth out of the l' of Egypt
34 the bride: for the l' shall be desolate.
8:16 whole l' trembled at the sound of
16 have devoured the l', and all that is
9:12 l' perisheth and is burned up like a
19 because we have forsaken the l',
10:17 Gather up thy wares out of the l', O
18 sling out the inhabitants of the l' at
11: 4 them forth out of the l' of Egypt,
5 a l' flowing with milk and honey,
7 them up out of the l' of Egypt,
19 cut him off from the l' of the living,
12: 4 How long shall the l' mourn, and the
5 and if in the l' of peace, wherein
11 the whole l' is made desolate,
12 devour from the one end of the l'
12 even to the other end of the l':
14 I will pluck them out of their l',
15 heritage, and every man to his l'.
13:13 will fill all the inhabitants of this l',
14: 8 thou be as a stranger in the l', and
15 and famine shall not be in this l';
18 go about into a l' that they know not.
15: 7 with a fan in the gates of the l';
14 into a l' which thou knowest not:
16: 3 fathers that begat them in this l';
6 and the small shall die in this l':
13 will I cast you out of this l', into a
13 into a l' that ye know not, neither
14 of Israel out of the l' of Egypt;
15 of Israel from the l' of the north,
15 I will bring them again into their l'
18 because they have defiled my l',
17: 4 enemies in the l' which thou knowest
6 in a salt l' and not inhabited.
26 and from the l' of Benjamin, and
18:16 To make their l' desolate, and a
22:12 and shall see this l' no more.
27 But to the l' whereunto they desire
28 cast into a l' which they know not?
23: 7 of Israel out of the l' of Egypt;
8 and they shall dwell in their own l'.
10 For the l' is full of adulterers;
10 of swearing the l' mourneth;
15 profaneness gone forth into all the l'.

Jer 24: 5 place into the l' of the Chaldeans for
6 I will bring them again to this l':
8 of Jerusalem, that remain in this l',
8 them that dwell in the l' of Egypt:
10 they be consumed from off the l'
25: 5 dwell in the l' that the Lord hath
9 and will bring them against this l',
11 this whole l' shall be a desolation,
12 and the l' of the Chaldeans, and will
13 will bring upon that l' all my words
20 and all the kings of the l' of Uz, and
20 the kings of the l' of the Philistines,
38 for their l' is desolate because of the
26:17 rose up certain of the elders of the l',
20 against this city and against this l'
27: 7 until the very time of his l' come:
10 you, to remove you far from your l';
11 will I let remain still in their own l',
30: 3 to return to the l' that I gave to
10 seed from the l' of their captivity;
31:16 come again from the l' of the enemy.
23 use this speech in the l' of Judah
32 to bring them out of the l' of Egypt;
32:15 shall be possessed again in this l'.
20 signs and wonders in the l' of Egypt,
21 people Israel out of the l' of Egypt
22 hast given them this l', which thou
22 a l' flowing with milk and honey;
41 I will plant them in this l' assuredly
43 And fields shall be bought in this l',
44 take witnesses in the l' of Benjamin,
33:11 cause to return the captivity of the l',
13 and in the l' of Benjamin, and in the
15 judgment and righteousness in the l'.
34:13 them forth out of the l' of Egypt,
19 all the people of the l', which passed
35: 7 live many days in the l' where ye
11 king of Babylon came up into the l',
15 dwell in the l' which I have given
36:29 certainly come and destroy this l',
37: 1 made king in the l' of Judah,
2 nor the people of the l', did hearken
7 return to Egypt into their own l'.
12 to go into the l' of Benjamin,
19 come against you, nor against this l'?
39: 5 to Riblah in the l' of Hamath, where
10 which had nothing, in the l' of Judah,
40: 4 behold, all the l' is before thee:
6 the people that were left in the l'.
7 the son of Ahikam governor in the l',
7 children, and of the poor of the l',
9 dwell in the l', and serve the king of
12 driven, and came to the l' of Judah,
41: 2 had made governor over the l'.
18 of Babylon made governor in the l'.
42:10 If ye will still abide in this l', then
12 cause you to return to your own l'.
13 ye say, We will not dwell in this l',
14 but we will go into the l' of Egypt,
16 overtake you there in the l' of Egypt,
43: 4 the Lord, to dwell in the l' of Judah.
5 driven, to dwell in the l' of Judah;
7 they came into the l' of Egypt: for
11 he shall smite the l' of Egypt, and
12 array himself with the l' of Egypt,
13 that is in the l' of Egypt,
44: 1 Jews which dwell in the l' of Egypt,
8 unto other gods in the l' of Egypt,
9 have committed in the l' of Judah,
12 their faces to go into the l' of Egypt
12 consumed and fall in the l' of Egypt;
13 them that dwell in the l' of Egypt,
14 gone into the l' of Egypt to sojourn
14 should return into the l' of Judah,
15 people that dwelt in the l' of Egypt,
21 princes, and the people of the l',
22 therefore is your l' a desolation,
24 all Judah that are in the l' of Egypt:
26 Judah that dwell in the l' of Egypt;
26 man of Judah in all the l' of Egypt,
27 of Judah that are in the l' of Egypt
28 of the l' of Egypt into the l' of Judah,
28 gone into the l' of Egypt to sojourn
45: 4 I will pluck up, even this whole l'.
46:12 shame, and thy cry hath filled the l':
13 come and smite the l' of Egypt.
16 people, and to the l' of our nativity,
27 seed from the l' of their captivity;
47: 2 flood, and shall overflow the l', and
2 the inhabitants of the l' shall howl.
48:24 upon all the cities of the l' of Moab,
33 field, and from the l' of Moab;
50: 1 against the l' of the Chaldeans by
3 which shall make her l' desolate,
8 forth out of the l' of the Chaldeans,
12 a wilderness, a dry l', and a desert.
16 shall flee every one to his own l'.
18 punish the king of Babylon and his l',
21 Go up against the l' of Merathaim,
22 A sound of battle is in the l', and of
25 of hosts in the l' of the Chaldeans.
28 and escape out of the l' of Babylon,
34 that he may give rest to the l',
38 up: for it is the l' of graven images,
45 against the l' of the Chaldeans:
51: 2 shall fan her, and shall empty her l':
4 shall fall in the l' of the Chaldeans,
5 their l' was filled with sin against
27 Set ye up a standard in the l', blow
28 and all the l' of his dominion.
29 And the l' shall tremble and sorrow:
29 make the l' of Babylon a desolation
43 Her cities are a desolation, a dry l',
43 a l' wherein no man dwelleth,
46 rumour that shall be heard in the l';
46 come a rumour, and violence in the l',

Jer 51: 47 her whole l' shall be confounded,
52 through all her l' the wounded shall
54 from the l' of the Chaldeans:
52: 6 was no bread for the people of the l'.
9 to Riblah in the l' of Hamath; where
16 left certain of the poor of the l' for
25 who mustered the people of the l';
25 threescore men of the people of the l',
27 death in Riblah in the l' of Hamath.
27 carried away captive out of his...l'.
La 4: 21 Edom, that dwellest in the l' of Uz;
Eze 1: 3 the l' of the Chaldeans by the river
6: 14 them, and make the l' desolate, yea,
7: 2 the Lord God unto the l' of Israel;
2 come upon the four corners of the l'.
7 thee, O thou that dwellest in the l':
23 for the l' is full of bloody crimes,
27 people of the l' shall be troubled:
8: 17 they have filled the l' with violence,
9: 9 great, and the l' is full of blood, and
11: 15 unto us is this l' given in possession.
17 and I will give you the l' of Israel.
12: 13 Babylon to the l' of the Chaldeans;
19 say unto the people of the l', Thus
19 Jerusalem, and of the l' of Israel;
19 that her l' may be desolate from all
20 waste, and the l' shall be desolate;
22 that ye have in the l' of Israel,
13: 9 shall they enter into the l' of Israel;
14: 13 when the l' sinneth against me by
15 beasts to pass through the l',
16 delivered, but the l' shall be desolate.
17 Or if I bring a sword upon that l',
17 and say, Sword, go through the l';
19 Or if I send a pestilence into that l',
15: 8 I will make the l' desolate, because
16: 3 thy nativity is of the l' of Canaan;
29 thy fornication in the l' of Canaan
17: 4 and carried it into a l' of traffick;
5 He took also of the seed of the l',
13 hath also taken the mighty of the l':
18: 2 proverb concerning the l' of Israel,
19: 4 with chains unto the l' of Egypt.
7 the l' was desolate, and the fulness
20: 5 known unto them in the l' of Egypt,
6 forth of the l' of Egypt into a l' that I
8 them in the midst of the l' of Egypt.
9 them forth out of the l' of Egypt.
10 to go forth out of the l' of Egypt,
15 I would not bring them into the l',
28 when I had brought them into the l',
36 in the wilderness of the l' of Egypt,
38 shall not enter into the l' of Israel:
40 all of them in the l', serve me:
42 shall bring you into the l' of Israel,
21: 2 prophesy against the l' of Israel,
3 say to the l' of Israel, Thus saith
19 twain shall come forth out of one l':
30 wast created, in the l' of thy nativity.
32 blood shall be in the midst of the l';
22: 24 thou art the l' that is not cleansed,
29 of the l' have used oppression,
30 stand in the gap before me for the l',
23: 15 of Chaldea, the l' of their nativity:
19 played the harlot in the l' of Egypt.
27 brought from the l' of Egypt:
48 cause lewdness to cease out of the l',
25: 3 against the l' of Israel, when it was
6 thy despite against the l' of Israel;
26: 20 shall set glory in the l' of the living;
27: 17 and the l' of Israel, they were thy
29 ships, they shall stand upon the l';
28: 25 then shall they dwell in their l' that
29: 9 l' of Egypt shall be desolate and
10 make the l' of Egypt utterly waste
14 them to return into the l' of Pathros,
14 into the l' of their habitation; and
19 I will give the l' of Egypt unto
20 I have given him the l' of Egypt for
30: 5 the men of the l' that is in league,
11 shall be brought to destroy the l':
11 Egypt, and fill the l' with the slain.
12 sell the l' into the hand of the wicked:
12 I will make the l' waste, and all that
13 no more a prince of the l' of Egypt:
13 I will put a fear in the l' of Egypt.
25 stretch it out upon the l' of Egypt.
31: 12 are broken by all the rivers of the l';
32: 4 Then will I leave thee upon the l', I
6 will also water with thy blood the l'
8 thee, and set darkness upon thy l',
15 I shall make the l' of Egypt desolate,
23 caused terror in the l' of the living.
24 their terror in the l' of the living;
25 terror was caused in the l' of the
26 their terror in the l' of the living,
27 of the mighty in the l' of the living.
32 my terror in the l' of the living:
33: 2 When I bring the sword upon a l',
2 if the people of the l' take a man of
3 he seeth the sword come upon the l'
24 those wastes of the l' of Israel
24 was one, and he inherited the l':
24 the l' is given us for inheritance.
25 blood: and shall ye possess the l'?
26 wife: and shall ye possess the l'?
28 For I will lay the l' most desolate,
29 I have laid the l' most desolate,
34: 13 and will bring them to their own l',
25 the evil beasts to cease out of the l':
27 and they shall be safe in their l',
28 shall the beast of the l' devour
29 consumed with hunger in the l',
36: 5 my l' into their possession with
6 therefore concerning the l' of Israel,
13 unto you, Thou l' devourest up men,
Eze 36: 17 house of Israel dwelt in their own l',
18 blood that they had shed upon the l',
20 and are gone forth out of his l'.
24 and will bring you into your own l'.
28 ye shall dwell in the l' that I gave to
34 And the desolate l' shall be tilled,
35 This l' that was desolate is become
37: 12 and bring you into the l' of Israel.
14 and I shall place you in your own l':
21 and bring them into their own l':
22 in the l' upon the mountains of
25 they shall dwell in the l' that I have
38: 2 thy face against Gog, the l' of Magog,
8 thou shalt come into the l' that is
9 shalt be like a cloud to cover the l',
11 go up to the l' of unwalled villages:
12 that dwell in the midst of the l'.
16 of Israel, as a cloud to cover the l';
16 and I will bring thee against my l',
18 shall come against the l' of Israel,
19 a great shaking in the l' of Israel;
39: 12 them, that they may cleanse the l'.
13 Yea, all the people of the l' shall
14 passing through the l' to bury with
15 passengers that pass through the l',
16 Thus shall they cleanse the l'.
26 when they dwelt safely in their l',
28 gathered them unto their own l',
40: 2 brought he me into the l' of Israel,
45: 1 divide by lot the l' for inheritance,
1 the Lord, an holy portion of the l':
4 The holy portion of the l' shall be
8 In the l' shall be his possession in
8 the l' shall they give to the house of
16 the people of the l' shall give this
22 all the people of the l' a bullock for
46: 3 the people of the l' shall worship at
9 when the people of the l' shall come
47: 13 ye shall inherit the l' according to
14 and this l' shall fall unto you for
15 this shall be the border of the l'
18 and from the l' of Israel by Jordan,
21 So shall ye divide this l' unto you
48: 12 this oblation of the l' that is offered
14 nor alienate the firstfruits of the l':
29 This is the l' which ye shall divide by
Da 1: 2 he carried into the l' of Shinar to
8: 9 the east, and toward the pleasant l'.
9: 6 and to all the people of the l'.
15 people forth out of the l' of Egypt
11: 9 and shall return into his own l'.
16 he shall stand in the glorious l',
19 face toward the fort of his own l':
28 return into his l' with great riches;
28 do exploits, and return to his own l'.
39 and shall divide the l' for gain.
41 shall enter also into the glorious l',
42 and the l' of Egypt shall not escape.
Ho 1: 2 l' had committed great whoredom,
11 they shall come up out of the l':
2: 3 set her like a dry l', and slay her
15 she came up out of the l' of Egypt.
4: 1 with the inhabitants of the l',
1 nor knowledge of God in the l'.
3 Therefore shall the l' mourn, and
7: 16 their derision in the l' of Egypt.
9: 3 shall not dwell in the Lord's l';
10: 1 according to the goodness of his l'
11: 5 shall not return into the l' of Egypt,
11 as a dove out of the l' of Assyria:
12: 9 Lord thy God from the l' of Egypt
13: 4 Lord thy God from the l' of Egypt,
5 wilderness, in the l' of great drought.
Joe 1: 2 give ear, all ye inhabitants of the l'.
6 a nation is come up upon my l',
10 The field is wasted, the l' mourneth;
14 and all the inhabitants of the l'
2: 1 all the inhabitants of the l' tremble:
3 the l' is as the garden of Eden
18 will the Lord be jealous for his l',
20 him into a l' barren and desolate,
21 Fear not, O l'; be glad and rejoice:
3: 2 among the nations, and parted my l'.
19 have shed innocent blood in their l'.
Am 2: 10 brought you up from the l' of Egypt,
10 to possess the l' of the Amorite.
3: 1 I brought up from the l' of Egypt,
9 in the palaces in the l' of Egypt, and
11 shall be even round about the l';
5: 2 she is forsaken upon her l'; there
7: 2 an end of eating the grass of the l',
10 l' is not able to bear all his words.
11 led away captive out of their own l'.
12 flee thee away into the l' of Judah,
17 and thy l' shall be divided by line;
17 and thou shalt die in a polluted l':
17 go into captivity forth of his l'.
8: 4 to make the poor of the l' to fail,
8 Shall not the l' tremble for this, and
11 that I will send a famine in the l',
9: 5 of hosts is he that toucheth the l',
7 up Israel out of the l' of Egypt?
15 I will plant them upon their l', and
15 no more be pulled out of their l'
Jon 1: 9 which hath made the sea and dry l'.
13 men rowed hard to bring it to the l';
2: 10 it vomited out Jonah upon the dry l'.
Mic 5: 5 the Assyrian shall come into our l':
6 waste the l' of Assyria with the
6 l' of Nimrod in the entrances thereof:
6 when he cometh into our l',
11 And I will cut off the cities of thy l',
6: 4 thee up out of the l' of Egypt,
7: 13 the l' shall be desolate because of
15 of thy coming out of the l' of Egypt.
Na 3: 13 gates of thy l' shall be set wide open
Hab 1: 6 march through the breadth of the l',
2: 8, 17 and for the violence of the l',
3: 7 curtains of the l' of Midian did
12 march through the l' in indignation.
Zep 1: 2 consume all things from off the l',
3 I will cut off man from off the l',
18 whole l' shall be devoured by fire
18 all them that dwell in the l'.
2: 5 O Canaan, the l' of the Philistines,
3: 19 get them praise and fame in every l'
Hag 1: 11 I called for a drought upon the l',
2: 4 and be strong, all ye people of the l',
6 the earth, and the sea, and the dry l';
Zec 1: 21 their horn over the l' of Judah to
2: 6 and flee from the l' of the north,
12 Judah his portion in the holy l',
3: 9 I will remove the iniquity of that l'
5: 11 build it an house in the l' of Shinar:
7: 5 Speak unto all the people of the l',
14 Thus the l' was desolate after them,
14 they laid the pleasant l' desolate.
9: 1 of the Lord in the l' of Hadrach,
16 lifted up as an ensign upon his l'.
10: 10 bring them again also out of the l'
10 will bring them into the l' of Gilead
11: 6 more pity the inhabitants of the l',
6 his king: and they shall smite the l',
16 I will raise up a shepherd in the l',
12: 12 the l' shall mourn, every family
13: 2 off the names of the idols out of the l',
2 unclean spirit to pass out of the l',
8 shall come to pass, that in all the l',
14: 10 all the l' shall be turned as a plain
Mal 3: 12 for ye shall be a delightsome l',
M't 2: 6 thou Bethlehem in the l' of Juda,
20 mother, and go into the l' of Israel:
21 and came into the l' of Israel.
4: 15 The l' of Zabulon, and the
15 Zabulon, and the l' of Nephthalim,
9: 26 hereof went abroad into all that l'.
10: 15 for the l' of Sodom and Gomorrha
11: 24 more tolerable for the l' of Sodom
14: 34 they came into the l' of Gennesaret.
23: 15 ye compass sea and l' to make one
27: 45 there was darkness over all the l'
M'r 1: 5 out unto him all the l' of Judæa,
4: 1 multitude was by the sea on the l'.
6: 47 of the sea, and he alone on the l'.
53 they came into the l' of Gennesaret,
15: 33 there was darkness over the whole l'
Lu 4: 25 famine was throughout all the l';
5: 3 would thrust out a little from the l'.
11 they had brought their ships to l',
8: 27 when he went forth to l', there met
14: 35 It is neither fit for the l', nor yet for
15: 14 arose a mighty famine in that l';
21: 23 shall be great distress in the l',
Joh 3: 22 his disciples into the l' of Judæa;
6: 21 the ship was at the l' whither they
21: 8 were not far from l', but as it were
9 soon then as they were come to l',
11 drew the net to l' full of great fishes,
Ac 4: 37 Having l', sold it, and brought the
5: 3 back part of the price of the l'?
8 whether ye sold the l' for so much?
7: 3 come into the l' which I shall shew
4 he out of the l' of the Chaldæans,
4 he removed him into this l', wherein
6 seed should sojourn in a strange l';
11 dearth over all the l' of Egypt and
29 was a stranger in the l' of Madian,
36 and signs in the l' of Egypt, and in
40 brought us out of the l' of Egypt,
10: 39 did both in the l' of the Jews, and
13: 17 as strangers in the l' of Egypt,
19 seven nations in the l' of Chanaan,
19 he divided their l' to them by lot.
27: 39 it was day, they knew not the l':
43 first into the sea, and get to l':
44 pass, that they escaped all safe to l'.
Heb 8: 9 to lead them out of the l' of Egypt;
11: 9 he sojourned in the l' of promise,
29 through the Red sea as by dry l':
Jude 5 the people out of the l' of Egypt,

landed

Ac 18: 22 when he had l' at Cæsarea, and
21: 3 sailed into Syria, and l' at Tyre:

landing

Ac 28: 12 l' at Syracuse, we tarried there

landmark See also LANDMARKS.

De 19: 14 not remove thy neighbour's l',
27: 17 he that removeth his neighbour's l'.
Pr 22: 28 Remove not the ancient l', which
23: 10 Remove not the old l'; and enter

landmarks

Job 24: 2 Some remove the l'; they violently

lands

Ge 10: 5 of the Gentiles divided in their l';
31 after their tongues, in their l', after
41: 54 said: and the dearth was in all l';
57 that the famine was so sore in all l'.
47: 18 my lord, but our bodies, and our l':
22 wherefore they sold not their l'.
Le 26: 36 hearts in the l' of their enemies;
39 in their iniquity in your enemies' l';
J'g 11: 13 restore those l' again peaceably.
2Ki 19: 11 kings of Assyria have done to all l',
17 destroyed the nations and their l',
1Ch 14: 17 fame of David went out into all l';
2Ch 9: 28 horses out of Egypt, and out of all l'.
13: 9 manner of the nations of other l'?
17: 10 fell upon all the kingdoms of the l'
32: 13 done unto all the people of other l'?
13 the gods of the nations of those l'

2Ch32: 13 any ways able to deliver their l· out
17 As the gods of the nations of other l·
Ezr 9: 1 themselves from the people of the l·,
2 mingled...with the people of those l·:
7 into the hand of the kings of the l·,
11 the filthiness of the people of the l·.
Ne 5: 3 said, We have mortgaged our l·,
4 and that upon our l· and vineyards.
5 men have our l· and vineyards.
11 Restore,... their l·, their vineyards.
9: 30 into the hand of the people of the l·.
10: 28 themselves from the people of the l·
Ps 49: 11 call their l· after their own names.
66: 1 a joyful noise unto God, all ye l·:
100: 1 joyful noise unto the Lord, all ye l·.
105: 44 And gave them the l· of the heathen:
106: 27 nations, and to scatter them in the l·.
107: 3 gathered them out of the l·, from
Isa 36: 20 they among all the gods of these l·,
37: 11 have done to all l· by destroying
Jer 16: 15 the l· whither he had driven them:
27: 6 I given all these l· into the hand of
Eze 20: 6, 15 honey, which is the glory of all l·:
39: 27 them out of their enemies' l·,
M't 19: 29 children, or l·, for my name's sake,
M'r 10: 29 wife, or children, or l·, for my sake,
30 and mothers, and children, and l·,
Ac 4: 34 as were possessors of l· or houses

lanes
Lu 14: 21 into the streets and l· of the city,

language See also LANGUAGES.
Ge 11: 1 And the whole earth was of one l·,
6 is one, and they have all one l·;
7 down, and there confound their l·,
9 confound the l· of all the earth:
2Ki 18: 26 to thy servants in the Syrian l·;
26 and talk not with us in the Jews' l·
28 cried with a loud voice in the Jews' l·,
Ne 13: 24 and could not speak in the Jews' l·,
24 according to the l· of each people.
Es 1: 22 and to every people after their l·,
22 according to the l· of every people.
3: 12 and to every people after their l·;
8: 9 and unto every people after their l·,
9 writing, and according to their l·.
Ps 19: 3 There is no speech nor l·, where
81: 5 heard a l· that I understood not.
114: 1 Jacob from a people of strange l·;
Isa 19: 18 of Egypt speak the l· of Canaan,
36: 11 unto thy servants in the Syrian l·;
11 and speak not to us in the Jews' l·,
13 cried with a loud voice in the Jews' l·,
Jer 5: 15 nation whose l· thou knowest not,
Eze 3: 5, 6 strange speech and of an hard l·,
Da 3: 29 That every people, nation, and l·,
Zep 3: 9 will I turn to the people a pure l·,
Ac 2: 6 heard them speak in his own l·.

languages
Da 3: 4 O people, nations, and l·,
7 the people, the nations, and the l·,
4: 1 unto all people, nations, and l·, that
5: 19 people, nations, and l·, trembled
6: 25 unto all people, nations, and l·, that
7: 14 that all people, nations, and l·,
Zec 8: 23 hold out of all l· of the nations,

languish See also LANGUISHED; LANGUISHETH; LANGUISHING.
Isa 16: 8 For the fields of Heshbon l·, and
19: 8 spread nets upon the waters shall l·.
24: 4 the haughty people of the earth do l·.
Jer 14: 2 mourneth, and the gates thereof l·;
Ho 4: 3 one that dwelleth therein shall l·,

languished
La 2: 8 wall to lament; they l· together.

languisheth
Isa 24: 4 the world l· and fadeth away, the
7 The new wine mourneth, the vine l·,
33: 9 earth mourneth and l·: Lebanon is
Jer 15: 9 She that hath borne seven l·: she
Joe 1: 10 the new wine is dried up, the oil l·.
12 vine is dried up, and the fig tree l·;
Na 1: 4 rivers: Bashan l·, and Carmel,
4 and the flower of Lebanon l·.

languishing
Ps 41: 3 strengthen him upon the bed of l·:

lanterns
Joh 18: 3 cometh thither with l· and torches

Laodicea (*la-od-i-se'-ah*) See also LAODICEANS.
Col 2: 1 have for you, and for them at L·,
4: 13 for you, and them that are in L·,
15 Salute the brethren which are in L·,
16 ye likewise read the epistle from L·.
1Ti *subscr.* first to Timothy...written from L·
Re 1: 11 unto Philadelphia, and unto L·.

Laodiceans (*la-od-i-se'-uns*)
Col 4: 16 read also in the church of the L·;
Re 3: 14 angel of the church of the L· write;

lap See also LAPPED; LAPPETH; LAPPING.
2Ki 4: 39 thereof wild gourds his l· full, and
Ne 5: 13 Also I shook my l·, and said, So
Pr 16: 33 The lot is cast into the l·; but the

Lapidoth (*lap'-i-doth*)
J'g 4: 4 the wife of L·, she judged Israel

lapped
J'g 7: 6 And the number of them that l·,
7 By the three hundred men that l·

lappeth
J'g 7: 5 Every one that l· of the water with
5 water with his tongue, as a dog l·,

lapwing
Le 11: 19 heron after her kind, and the l·,
De 14: 18 heron after her kind, and the l·,

large See also ENLARGE.
Ge 34: 21 behold, it is l· enough for them;
Ex 3: 8 that land unto a good land and a l·,
J'g 18: 10 people secure, and to a l· land:
2Sa 22: 20 me forth also into a l· place:
Ne 4: 19 The work is great and l·, and we
7: 4 the city was l· and great: but
9: 35 in the l· and fat land which thou
Ps 18: 19 me forth also into a l· place;
31: 8 thou hast set my feet in a l· room.
118: 5 me, and set me in a l· place.
Isa 22: 18 like a ball into a l· country:
30: 23 shall thy cattle feed in l· pastures.
33 he hath made it deep and l·:
Jer 22: 14 me a wide house and l· chambers,
Eze 23: 32 of thy sister's cup deep and l·:
Hos 4: 16 feed them as a lamb in a l· place.
M't 28: 12 gave l· money unto the soldiers,
M'r 14: 15 he will shew you a l· upper room
Lu 22: 12 he shall shew you a l· upper room
Ga 6: 11 see how l· a letter I have written
Re 21: 16 the length is as l· as the breadth:

largeness
1Ki 4: 29 exceeding much, and l· of heart,

Lasæa See LASEA.

lasciviousness
M'r 7: 22 wickedness, deceit, l·, an evil eye,
2Co 12: 21 and l· which they have committed.
Ga 5: 19 fornication, uncleanness, l·,
Eph 4: 19 have given themselves over unto l·,
1Pe 4: 3 when we walked in l·, lusts, excess
Jude 4 turning the grace of our God into l·,

Lasea (*la-se'-ah*)
Ac 27: 8 nigh whereunto was the city of L·.

Lasha (*la'-shah*)
Ge 10: 19 Admah, and Zeboim, even unto L·.

Lasharon (*lash'-ar-on*)
Jos 12: 18 Aphek, one; the king of L·, one;

last See also LASTED; LASTING.
Ge 49: 1 shall befall you in the l· days.
19 but he shall overcome at the l·
Nu 23: 10 and let my l· end be like his!
2Sa 19: 11 ye the l· to bring the king back
12 are ye the l· to bring back the king?
23: 1 Now these be the l· words of David.
1Ch 23: 27 For by the l· words of David the
29: 29 acts of David the king, first and l·,
2Ch 9: 29 of the acts of Solomon, first and l·,
12: 15 the acts of Rehoboam, first and l·,
16: 11 behold, the acts of Asa, first and l·,
20: 34 acts of Jehoshaphat, first and l·,
25: 26 of the acts of Amaziah, first and l·,
26: 22 of the acts of Uzziah, first and l·,
28: 26 acts and of all his ways, first and l·,
35: 27 And his deeds, first and l·, behold,
Ezr 8: 13 And of the l· sons of Adonikam,
Ne 8: 18 from the first day unto the l· day,
Pr 5: 11 And thou mourn at the l·, when
23: 32 At the l· it biteth like a serpent,
Isa 2: 2 it shall come to pass in the l· days,
41: 4 Lord, the first, and with the l·;
44: 6 I am the first, and I am the l·; and
48: 12 he; I am the first, I also am the l·.
Jer 12: 4 said, He shall not see our l· end.
50: 17 and l· this Nebuchadrezzar king of
La 1: 9 she remembereth not her l· end;
Da 4: 8 at the l· Daniel came in before me,
8: 3 other, and the higher came up l·.
19 thee know what shall be in the l·
Am 9: 1 slay the l· of them with the sword:
Mic 4: 1 in the l· days it shall come to pass,
M't 12: 45 l· state of that man is worse than
19: 30 many that are first shall be l·;
30 and the l· shall be first.
20: 8 beginning from the l· unto the first.
12 These l· have wrought but one hour,
14 I will give unto this l·, even as unto
16 So the l· shall be first, and the first l·:
21: 37 But l· of all he sent unto them his
22: 27 And l· of all the woman died also.
26: 60 At the l· came two false witnesses,
27: 64 the l· error shall be worse than
M'r 9: 35 be first, the same shall be l· of all,
10: 31 are first shall be l·; and the l· first.
12: 6 he sent him also l· unto them,
22 seed: l· of all the woman died also.
Lu 11: 26 l· state of that man is worse than
12: 59 till thou hast paid the very l· mite.
13: 30 there are l· which shall be first,
30 there are first which shall be l·.
20: 32 L· of all the woman died also.
Joh 6: 39 raise it up again at the l· day.
40, 44, 54 raise him up at the l· day.
7: 37 In the l· day, that great day of the
8: 9 at the eldest, even unto the l·:
11: 24 in the resurrection at the l· day.
12: 48 same shall judge him in the l· day.
Ac 2: 17 it shall come to pass in the l· days,
1Co 4: 9 hath set forth us the apostles l·,
15: 8 And l· of all he was seen of me also,
26 l· enemy that shall be destroyed is
45 the l· Adam was made a quickening
52 twinkling of an eye, at the l· trump:
Ph'p 4: 10 at the l· your care of me hath
2Ti 3: 1 in the l· days perilous times shall
Heb 1: 2 Hath in the l· days spoken unto us
Jas 5: 3 treasure together for the l· days.
1Pe 1: 5 ready to be revealed in the l· time.
20 manifest in these l· times for you,
2Pe 3: 3 shall come in the l· days scoffers,
1Jo 2: 18 Little children, it is the l· time: and
18 we know that it is the l· time.
Jude 18 should be mockers in the l· time,
Re 1: 11 and Omega, the first and the l·:
17 Fear not; I am the first and the l·,
2: 8 things saith the first and the l·,
19 and the l· to be more than the first.
15: 1 angels having the seven l· plagues
21: 9 vials full of the seven l· plagues,
22: 13 and the end, the first and the l·.

lasted
J'g 14: 17 the seven days, while their feast l·:

lasting See also EVERLASTING.
De 33: 15 the precious things of the l· hills,

latchet See also SHOELACHET.
Isa 5: 27 nor the l· of their shoes be broken:
M'r 1: 7 l· of whose shoes I am not worthy
Lu 3: 16 l· of whose shoes I am not worthy
Joh 1: 27 shoe's l· I am not worthy to unloose.

late See also LAST; LATELY; LATTER.
Ps 127: 2 you to rise up early, to sit up l·,
Mic 2: 8 of l· my people is risen up as an
Joh 11: 8 Jews of l· sought to stone thee;

lately
Ac 18: 2 l· come from Italy, with his wife

Latin (*lat'-in*)
Lu 23: 38 in letters of Greek, and L·, and
Joh 19: 20 in Hebrew, and Greek, and L·.

latter
Ex 4: 8 will believe the voice of the l· sign.
Nu 24: 14 do to thy people in the l· days.
20 but his l· end shall be that he perish
De 4: 30 even in the l· days, if thou turn to
8: 16 thee, to do thee good at thy l· end;
11: 14 the first rain and the l· rain,
24: 3 if the l· husband hate her, and
3 or if the l· husband die, which took
31: 29 evil will befall you in the l· days;
32: 29 they would consider their l· end!
Ru 3: 10 shewed more kindness in the l· end
2Sa 2: 26 it will be bitterness in the l· end?
Job 8: 7 thy l· end should greatly increase.
19: 25 stand at the l· day upon the earth:
29: 23 their mouth wide as for the l· rain.
42: 12 the Lord blessed the l· end of Job
Pr 16: 15 favour is as a cloud of the l· rain.
19: 20 thou mayest be wise in thy l· end.
Isa 41: 22 and know the l· end of them; or
47: 7 didst remember the l· end of it.
Jer 3: 3 and there hath been no l· rain;
5: 24 rain, both the former and the l·,
23: 20 in the l· days ye shall consider it
30: 24 in the l· days ye shall consider it.
48: 47 the captivity of Moab in the l· days,
49: 39 it shall come to pass in the l· days,
Eze 38: 8 in the l· years thou shalt come into
16 the land: it shall be in the l· days,
Da 2: 28 what shall be in the l· days.
8: 23 And in the l· time of their kingdom,
10: 14 befall thy people in the l· days:
11: 29 not be as the former, or as the l·.
Ho 3: 5 and his goodness in the l· days.
6: 3 as the l· and former rain unto the
Joe 2: 23 and the l· rain in the first month.
Am 7: 1 the shooting up of the l· growth;
1 l· growth after the king's mowings.
Hag 2: 9 The glory of this l· house shall be
Zec 10: 1 rain in the time of the l· rain;
1Ti 4: 1 l· times some shall depart from
Jas 5: 7 he receive the early and l· rain.
2Pe 2: 20 l· end is worse with them than the

lattice
J'g 5: 28 window, and cried through the l·,
2Ki 1: 2 Ahaziah fell down through a l· in
Ca 2: 9 shewing himself through the l·.

laud
Ro 15: 11 Gentiles; and l· him, all ye people.

laugh See also LAUGHED; LAUGHETH; LAUGHING.
Ge 18: 13 Wherefore did Sarah l·, saying,
15 And he said, Nay; but thou didst l·.
21: 6 said, God hath made me to l·,
6 that all that hear will l· with me.
Job 5: 22 and famine thou shalt l·: neither
9: 23 will l· at the trial of the innocent.
22: 19 and the innocent l· them to scorn.
Ps 2: 4 sitteth in the heavens shall l·:
22: 7 they that see me l· me to scorn:
37: 13 The Lord shall l· at him: for he
52: 6 see, and fear, and shall l· at him:
59: 8 But thou, O Lord, shalt l· at them;
80: 6 our enemies l· among themselves.
Pr 1: 26 I also will l· at your calamity; I
29: 9 he rage or l·, there is no rest.
Ec 3: 4 A time to weep, and a time to l·;
Lu 6: 21 ye that weep now: for ye shall l·.
25 Woe unto you that l· now! for ye

laughed
Ge 17: 17 Abraham fell upon his face, and l·,
18: 12 Sarah l· within herself, saying,
15 Sarah denied, saying, I l· not; for
2Ki 19: 21 despised thee, and l· thee to scorn;
2Ch 30: 10 they l· them to scorn, and mocked
Ne 2: 19 heard it, they l· us to scorn, and
Job 12: 4 the just upright man is l· to scorn.
29: 24 If I l· on them, they believed it not:
Isa 37: 22 despised thee, and l· thee to scorn;
Eze 23: 32 be l· to scorn and had in derision;
M't 9: 24 And they l· him to scorn.
M'r 5: 40 they l· him to scorn. But when he
Lu 8: 53 they l· him to scorn, knowing that

laugheth
Job 41:29 he l' at the shaking of a spear.
laughing
Job 8:21 Till he fill thy mouth with l', and
laughter
Ps 126: 2 Then was our mouth filled with l',
Pr 14:13 Even in l' the heart is sorrowful;
Ec 2: 2 I said of l', It is mad: and of mirth,
7: 3 Sorrow is better than l': for by the
6 under a pot, so is the l' of the fool:
10:19 A feast is made for l', and wine
Jas 4: 9 let your l' be turned to mourning,
launch See also LAUNCHED.
Lu 5: 4 L' out into the deep, and let down
launched
Lu 8:22 of the lake. And they l' forth.
Ac 21: 1 were gotten from them, and had l'
27: 2 we l', meaning the sail by the
4 And when we l' from thence, we
laver See also LAVERS; LAVISH.
Ex 30:18 Thou shalt also make a l' of brass,
28 his vessels, and the l' and his foot.
31: 9 furniture, and the l' and his foot,
35:16 all his vessels, the l' and his foot,
38: 8 made the l' of brass, and the foot
39:39 all his vessels, the l' and his foot,
40: 7 shalt set the l' between the tent
11 shalt anoint the l' and his foot,
30 he set the l' between the tent of
Le 8:11 the l' and his foot, to sanctify them.
1Ki 7:30 under the l' were undersetters
38 one l' contained forty baths:
38 every l' was four cubits: and
38 every one of the ten bases one l'.
2Ki 16:17 and removed the l' from off them;
lavers
1Ki 7:38 Then made he ten l' of brass: one
40 Hiram made the l', and the shovels,
43 ten bases, and ten l' on the bases;
2Ch 4: 6 He made also ten l', and put five
14 and l' made he upon the bases;
lavish
Isa 46: 6 They l' gold out of the bag, and
law See also LAWFUL; LAWGIVER; LAWLESS; LAWS.
Ge 11:31 son, and Sarai his daughter in l',
19:12 son in l', and thy sons, and thy
14 out, and spake unto his sons in l',
14 that mocked unto his sons in l'.
38:11 Judah to Tamar his daughter in l',
13 father in l' goeth up to Timnath
16 that she was his daughter in l'.)
24 thy daughter in l' hath played the
25 forth, she sent to her father in l',
47:26 Joseph made it a l' over the land
Ex 3: 1 flock of Jethro his father in l',
4:18 returned to Jethro his father in l',
12:49 One l' shall be to him that is
13: 9 the Lord's l' may be in thy mouth:
16: 4 they will walk in my l', or no.
18: 1 of Midian, Moses' father in l',
2 Moses' father in l', took Zipporah,
5 Moses' father in l', came with his
6 I thy father in l' Jethro am come
7 went out to meet his father in l',
8 Moses told his father in l' all that
12 Moses' father in l', took a burnt
12 eat bread with Moses' father in l'
14 Moses' father in l' saw all that he
15 Moses said unto his father in l',
17 Moses' father in l' said unto him,
24 to the voice of his father in l',
27 Moses let his father in l' depart;
24:12 give thee tables of stone, and a l',
Le 6: 9 This is the l' of the burnt offering:
14 this is the l' of the meat offering:
25 This is the l' of the sin offering:
7: 1 is the l' of the trespass offering:
7 offering: there is one l' for them:
11 is the l' of the sacrifice of peace
37 This is the l' of the burnt offering,
11:46 the l' of the beasts, and of the fowl,
12: 7 This is the l' for her that hath born
13:59 is the l' of the plague of leprosy
14: 2 shall be the l' of the leper in the
32 the l' of him in whom is the plague
54 This is the l' for all manner of
57 is clean: this is the l' of leprosy.
15:32 the l' of him that hath an issue,
18:15 nakedness of thy daughter in l':
20:12 a man lie with his daughter in l',
24:22 Ye shall have one manner of l',
Nu 5:29 This is the l' of jealousies, when
30 shall execute upon her all this l'.
6:13 And this is the l' of the Nazarite,
21 This is the l' of the Nazarite who
21 do after the l' of his separation.
10:29 the Midianite, Moses' father in l',
15:16 One l' and one manner shall be for
29 have one l' for him that sinneth
19: 2 is the ordinance of the l' which the
14 This is the l', when a man dieth in
31:21 the ordinance of the l' which the
De 1: 5 Moses to declare this l', saying,
4: 8 so righteous as all this l', which
44 And this is the l' which Moses set
17:11 to the sentence of the l' which they
18 write him a copy of this l' in a book
19 keep all the words of this l' and
27: 3 upon them all the words of this l',
8 all the words of this l' very plainly.
23 he that lieth with his mother in l'.
De 27:26 all the words of this l' to do them.
28:58 do all the words of this l' that are
61 is not written in the book of this l',
29:21 are written in this book of the l':
29 we may do all the words of this l'.
30:10 are written in this book of the l',
31: 9 Moses wrote this l', and delivered
11 shalt read this l' before all Israel
12 to do all the words of this l':
24 the words of this l' in a book,
26 Take this book of the l', and put it
32:46 to do, all the words of this l'.
33: 2 right hand went a fiery l' for them.
4 Moses commanded us a l', even
10 thy judgments, and Israel thy l':
Jos 1: 7 observe to do according to all the l',
8 This book of the l' shall not depart
8:31 in the book of the l' of Moses,
32 the stones a copy of the l' of Moses,
34 he read all the words of the l',
34 that is written in the book of the l'.
22: 5 do the commandment and the l',
23: 6 in the book of the l' of Moses,
24:26 words in the book of the l' of God,
J'g 1:16 Moses' father in l', went up out of
4:11 of Hobab the father in l' of Moses,
15: 6 Samson, the son in l' of the Timnite,
19: 4 his father in l', the damsel's father,
5 father said unto his son in l',
7 depart, his father in l' urged him:
9 his servant, his father in l', the
Ru 1: 6 she arose with her daughters in l',
7 her two daughters in l' with her;
8 said unto her two daughters in l',
14 Orpah kissed her mother in l';
15 thy sister in l' is gone back unto her
15 return thou after thy sister in l'.
22 the Moabitess, her daughter in l',
2:11 hast done unto thy mother in l'
18 her mother in l' saw what she had
19 her mother in l' said unto her,
19 shewed her mother in l' with whom
20 said unto her daughter in l',
22 said unto Ruth her daughter in l',
23 and dwelt with her mother in l'.
3: 1 her mother in l' said unto her,
6 all that her mother in l' bade her.
16 when she came to her mother in l',
17 Go not empty unto thy mother in l'.
4:15 thy daughter in l', which loveth
1Sa 4:19 his daughter in l', Phinehas' wife,
19 her father in l' and her husband
21 because of her father in l' and her
18:18 I should be son in l' to the king?
21 Thou shalt this day be my son in l'
22 therefore be the king's son in l'.
23 a light thing to be a king's son in l',
26 David well to be the king's son in l':
27 he might be the king's son in l'.
22:14 which is the king's son in l', and
1Ki 2: 3 as it is written in the l' of Moses,
2Ki 8:27 the son in l' of the house of Ahab.
10:31 to walk in the l' of the Lord God
14: 6 in the book of the l' of Moses,
17:13 according to all the l' which I
34 or after the l' and commandment
37 and the l', and the commandment,
21: 8 to all the l' that my servant Moses
22: 8 I have found the book of the l' in
11 the words of the book of the l',
23:24 might perform the words of the l'
25 according to all the l' of Moses;
1Ch 2: 4 his daughter in l' bare him Pharez
16:17 the same to Jacob for a l', and
40 is written in the l' of the Lord,
22:12 thou mayest keep the l' of the Lord
2Ch 6:16 heed to their way to walk in my l',
12: 1 forsook the l' of the Lord, and all
14: 4 to do the l' and the commandment.
15: 3 a teaching priest, and without l'.
17: 9 had the book of the l' of the Lord
19:10 between l' and commandment,
23:18 as it is written in the l' of Moses,
25: 4 as it is written in the l' of the book
30:16 according to the l' of Moses the
31: 3 as it is written in the l' of the Lord.
4 encouraged in the l' of the Lord.
21 in the l', and in the commandments
33: 8 to the whole l' and the statutes
34:14 priest found a book of the l' of the
15 have found the book of the l' in the
19 king had heard the words of the l',
35:26 was written in the l' of the Lord,
Ezr 3: 2 as it is written in the l' of Moses
7: 6 a ready scribe in the l' of Moses,
10 his heart to seek the l' of the Lord,
12 a scribe of the l' of the God of
14 according to the l' of thy God which
21 the scribe of the l' of the God of
26 will not do the l' of thy God, and
26 the l' of the king, let judgment be
10: 3 let it be done according to the l'.
Ne 6:18 the son in l' of Shechaniah the son
8: 1 bring the book of the l' of Moses,
2 And Ezra the priest brought the l'
3 attentive unto the book of the l'.
7 the people to understand the l':
8 read in the book in the l' of God
9 when they heard the words of the l'.
13 to understand the words of the l'.
14 found written in the l' which the
18 read in the book of the l' of God.
9: 3 read in the book of the l' of the
26 cast thy l' behind their backs, and
29 bring them again unto thy l':
34 kept thy l', nor hearkened unto thy
Ne 10:28 of the lands unto the l' of God,
29 into an oath, to walk in God's l',
34 our God, as it is written in the l':
36 as it is written in the l', and the
12:44 the portions of the l' for the priests
13: 3 to pass, when they had heard the l',
28 was son in l' to Sanballat the
Es 1: 8 drinking was according to the l';
13 all that knew l' and judgment:
15 the queen Vashti according to l',
4:11 is one l' of his to put him to death,
16 which is not according to the l':
Job 22:22 I pray thee, the l' from his mouth,
Ps 1: 2 his delight is in the l' of the Lord;
2 in his l' doth he meditate day and
19: 7 The l' of the Lord is perfect,
37:31 The l' of his God is in his heart;
40: 8 God: yea, thy l' is within my heart.
78: 1 Give ear, O my people, to my l':
5 Jacob, and appointed a l' in Israel,
10 God, and refused to walk in his l';
81: 4 and a l' of the God of Jacob.
89:30 If his children forsake my l', and
94:12 and teachest him out of thy l';
20 which frameth mischief by a l'?
105:10 the same unto Jacob for a l', and
119: 1 who walk in the l' of the Lord.
18 wondrous things out of thy l'.
29 and grant me thy l' graciously.
34 and I shall keep thy l'; yea, I shall
44 So shall I keep thy l' continually
51 yet have I not declined from thy l'.
53 of the wicked that forsake thy l'.
55 in the night, and have kept thy l'.
61 but I have not forgotten thy l'.
70 as grease; but I delight in thy l'.
72 The l' of thy mouth is better unto
77 may live: for thy l' is my delight.
85 for me, which are not after thy l'.
92 Unless thy l' had been my delights,
97 O how love I thy l'! it is my
109 hand: yet do I not forget thy l'.
113 vain thoughts: but thy l' do I love.
126 for they have made void thy l'.
136 eyes, because they keep not thy l'.
142 and thy l' is the truth.
150 mischief: they are far from thy l'.
153 me: for I do not forget thy l'.
163 abhor lying: but thy l' do I love.
165 peace have they which love thy l':
174 O Lord; and thy l' is my delight.
Pr 1: 8 forsake not the l' of thy mother:
3: 1 My son, forget not my l'; but let
4: 2 doctrine, forsake ye not my l'.
6:20 forsake not the l' of thy mother:
23 is a lamp; and the l' is light;
7: 2 my l' as the apple of thine eye.
13:14 l' of the wise is a fountain of life,
28: 4 They that forsake the l' praise the
4 as keep the l' contend with them.
7 Whoso keepeth the l' is a wise son:
9 away his ear from hearing the l',
29:18 he that keepeth the l', happy is he.
31: 5 Lest they drink, and forget the l',
26 in her tongue is the l' of kindness.
Isa 1:10 give ear unto the l' of our God, ye
2: 3 for out of Zion shall go forth the l',
5:24 have cast away the l' of the Lord
8:16 seal the l' among my disciples.
20 To the l' and to the testimony:
30: 9 will not hear the l' of the Lord:
42: 4 and the isles shall wait for his l'.
21 he will magnify the l', and make it
24 were they obedient unto his l'.
51: 4 for a l' shall proceed from me, and
7 the people in whose heart is my l';
Jer 2: 8 that handle the l' knew me not:
6:19 unto my words, nor to my l',
8: 8 and the l' of the Lord is with us?
9:13 they have forsaken my l' which I
16:11 me, and have not kept my l';
18:18 for the l' shall not perish from the
26: 4 not hearken to me, to walk in my l',
31:33 will put my l' in their inward parts,
32:11 according to the l' and custom,
23 thy voice, neither walked in thy l';
44:10 they feared, nor walked in my l',
23 of the Lord, nor walked in his l',
La 2: 9 the l' is no more; her prophets also
Eze 7:26 the l' shall perish from the priest,
22:11 lewdly defiled his daughter in l';
26 Her priests have violated my l',
43:12 This is the l' of the house; upon
12 Behold, this is the l' of the house.
Da 6: 5 him concerning the l' of his God.
8, 12 l' of the Medes and Persians,
15 the l' of the Medes and Persians is,
9:11 Israel have transgressed thy l',
11 that is written in the l' of Moses the
13 As it is written in the l' of Moses,
Ho 4: 6 hast forgotten the l' of thy God,
8: 1 and trespassed against my l'.
12 to him the great things of my l',
Am 2: 4 have despised the l' of the Lord,
Mic 4: 2 for the l' shall go forth of Zion, and
7: 6 daughter in l' against her mother
6 daughter...against her mother in l';
Hab 1: 4 Therefore the l' is slacked, and
Zep 3: 4 they have done violence to the l'.
Hag 2:11 now the priests concerning the l',
Zec 7:12 stone, lest they should hear the l',
Mal 2: 6 The l' of truth was in his mouth,
7 should seek the l' at his mouth:
8 caused many to stumble at the l';
9 but have been partial in the l'.
4: 4 Remember ye the l' of Moses my

M't 5:17 that I am come to destroy the l'.
18 shall in no wise pass from the l', till
40 if any man will sue thee at the l',
7:12 for this is the l' and the prophets.
10:35 daughter in l' against her mother
35 daughter...against her mother in l'.
11:13 and the l' prophesied until John.
12: 5 have ye not read in the l', how that
22:36 the great commandment in the l'?
40 commandments hang all the l' and
23:23 the weightier matters of the l',
Lu 2:22 according to the l' of Moses were
23 it is written in the l' of the Lord,
24 which is said in the l' of the Lord,
27 for him after the custom of the l',
39 according to the l' of the Lord,
5:17 and doctors of the l' sitting by,
10:26 him, What is written in the l'?
12:53 mother in l' against her daughter
53 mother...against her daughter in l'
53 daughter in l' against her mother
53 daughter...against her mother in l'.
16:16 The l' and the prophets were until
17 pass, than one tittle of the l' to fail.
24:44 were written in the l' of Moses,
Joh 1:17 For the l' was given by Moses, but
45 found him, of whom Moses in the l',
7:19 Did not Moses give you the l', and
19 and yet none of you keepeth the l'?
23 l' of Moses should not be broken;
49 who knoweth not the l' are cursed.
51 Doth our l' judge any man, before
8: 5 Now Moses in the l' commanded us,
17 It is also written in your l', that
10:34 them, Is it not written in your l',
12:34 have heard out of the l' that Christ
15:25 be fulfilled that is written in their l',
18:13 for he was father in l' to Caiaphas,
31 judge him according to your l'.
19: 7 a l', and by our l' he ought to die,
Ac 5:34 named Gamaliel, a doctor of the l',
6:13 against this holy place, and the l':
7:53 received the l' by the disposition
13:15 after the reading of the l' and the
39 not be justified by the l' of Moses.
15: 5 them to keep the l' of Moses.
24 be circumcised, and keep the l';
18:13 to worship God contrary to the l'.
15 of words and names, and of your l',
19:38 l' is open, and there are deputies:
21:20 and they are all zealous of the l':
24 walkest orderly, and keepest the l'.
28 against the people, and the l', and
22: 3 to the perfect manner of the l' of
12 a devout man according to the l',
23: 3 sittest thou to judge me after the l',
3 to be smitten contrary to the l'?
29 be accused of questions of their l',
24: 6 have judged according to our l'.
14 all things which are written in the l'
25: 8 Neither against the l' of the Jews,
28:23 Jesus, both out of the l' of Moses,
Ro 2:12 as many as have sinned without l'
12 shall also perish without l':
12 as many as have sinned in the l'
12 shall be judged by the l';
13 not the hearers of the l' are just
13 the doers of the l' shall be justified.
14 the Gentiles, which have not the l',
14 do...the things contained in the l',
14 having not the l', are a l' unto
15 of the l' written in their hearts,
17 called a Jew, and restest in the l',
18 being instructed out of the l';
20 knowledge and of the truth in the l'.
23 that makest thy boast of the l',
23 through breaking the l' dishonorest
25 verily profiteth, if thou keep the l':
25 but if thou be a breaker of the l',
26 keep the righteousness of the l',
27 which is by nature, if it fulfil the l',
27 thee, who...dost transgress the l'?
3:19 that what things soever the l' saith,
19 saith to them who are under the l':
20 by the deeds of the l' there shall no
20 for by the l' is the knowledge of sin.
21 of God without the l' is manifested,
21 being witnessed by the l' and the
27 By what l'? of works? Nay: but by
27 Nay: but by the l' of faith.
28 by faith without the deeds of the l'.
31 make void the l' through faith?
31 God forbid: yea, we establish the l'.
4:13 or to his seed, through the l', but
14 if they which are of the l' be heirs,
15 Because the l' worketh wrath;
15 no l' is, there is no transgression.
16 not to that only which is of the l',
5:13 until the l' sin was in the world:
13 is not imputed where there is no l'.
20 Moreover the l' entered, that the
6:14 ye are not under the l', but under
15 we are not under the l', but under
7: 1 I speak to them that know the l',)
1 the l' hath dominion over a man as
2 is bound by the l' to her husband so
2 is loosed from the l' of her husband.
3 be dead she is free from that l';
4 become dead to the l' by the body
5 sins, which were by the l', did work
6 now we are delivered from the l',
7 say then, Is the l' sin? God forbid.
7 had not known sin, but by the l':
7 known lust, except the l' had said,
8 For without the l' sin was dead.
9 For I was alive without the l' once:
Ro 7:12 Wherefore the l' is holy, and the
14 For we know that the l' is spiritual:
16 I consent unto the l' that it is good.
21 I find then a l', that, when I would
22 I delight in the l' of God after the
23 I see another l' in my members,
23 warring against the l' of my mind,
23 me into captivity to the l' of sin
25 mind I myself serve the l' of God;
25 but with the flesh the l' of sin.
8: 2 the l' of the Spirit of life in Christ
2 me free from the l' of sin and death.
3 what the l' could not do, in that it
4 the righteousness of the l' might be
7 not subject to the l' of God, neither
9: 4 and the giving of the l', and the
31 after the l' of righteousness,
31 attained to the l' of righteousness.
32 as it were by the works of the l'.
10: 4 For Christ is the end of the l' for
5 the righteousness which is of the l',
13: 8 loveth another hath fulfilled the l'.
10 love is the fulfilling of the l'.
1Co 6: 1 go to l' before the unjust, and not
6 brother goeth to l' with brother,
7 ye go to l' one with another.
7:39 wife is bound by the l' as long as
9: 8 or saith not the l' the same also?
9 For it is written in the l' of Moses,
20 are under the l', as under the l',
20 gain them that are under the l';
21 that are without l', as without l',
21 (being not without l' to God,
21 but under the l' to Christ,)
21 might gain them that are without l'.
14:21 In the l' it is written, With men of
34 under obedience, as also saith the l'.
15:56 sin; and the strength of sin is the l'.
Ga 2:16 not justified by the works of the l',
16 and not by the works of the l': for
16 by the works of the l' shall no flesh
19 I through the l' am dead to the l',
21 for if righteousness come by the l',
3: 2 ye the Spirit by the works of the l',
5 doeth he it by the works of the l',
10 many as are of the works of the l'
10 are written in the book of the l' to
11 no man is justified by the l' in the
12 And the l' is not of faith: but, The
13 redeemed us from the curse of the l',
17 the l', which was four hundred and
18 For if the inheritance be of the l',
19 Wherefore then serveth the l'?
21 Is the l' then against the promises
21 if there had been a l' given which
21 righteousness...have been by the l'.
23 came, we were kept under the l',
24 the l' was our schoolmaster to bring
4: 4 of a woman, made under the l',
5 redeem them that were under the l',
21 be under the l', do ye not hear the l'?
5: 3 he is a debtor to do the whole l'.
4 of you are justified by the l';
14 all the l' is fulfilled in one word,
18 the Spirit, ye are not under the l'.
23 against such there is no l'.
6: 2 and so fulfil the l' of Christ.
13 who are circumcised keep the l';
Eph 2:15 l' of commandments contained
Ph'p 3: 5 as touching the l', a Pharisee;
6 the righteousness which is in the l',
9 righteousness, which is of the l',
1Ti 1: 7 Desiring to be teachers of the l';
8 But we know that the l' is good,
9 l' is not made for a righteous man,
Tit 3: 9 and strivings about the l';
Heb 7: 5 of the people according to the l',
11 under it the people received the l',)
12 necessity a change also of the l'.
16 the l' of a carnal commandment,
19 the l' made nothing perfect, but the
28 For the l' maketh men high priests
28 of the oath, which was since the l',
8: 4 that offer gifts according to the l':
9:19 to all the people according to the l',
22 are by the l' purged with blood;
10: 1 l' having a shadow of good things
8 therein; which are offered by the l';
28 He that despised Moses' l' died
Jas 1:25 into the perfect l' of liberty,
2: 8 If ye fulfil the royal l' according to
9 sin, and are convinced of the l' as
10 whosoever shall keep the whole l',
11 art become a transgressor of the l'
12 shall be judged by the l' of liberty.
4:11 evil of the l', and judgeth the l':
11 but if thou judge the l', thou art
11 not a doer of the l', but a judge.
1Jo 3: 4 sin transgresseth also the l':
4 for sin is the transgression of the l'.

lawful See also UNLAWFUL.
Ezr 7:24 it shall not be l' to impose toll,
Isa 49:24 mighty, or the l' captive delivered?
Eze 18: 5 and do that which is l' and right,
19 have done that which is l' and right,
21 and do that which is l' and right,
27 doeth that which is l' and right, he
33:14 and do that which is l' and right;
16 hath done that which is l' and right;
19 and do that which is l' and right, he
M't 12: 2 is not l' to do upon the sabbath day.
4 which was not l' for him to eat,
10 Is it l' to heal on the sabbath days?
12 l' to do well on the sabbath days.
14: 4 It is not l' for thee to have her.
19: 3 Is it l' for a man to put away his
M't 20:15 Is it not l' for me to do what I will
22:17 Is it l' to give tribute unto Cæsar,
27: 6 It is not l' for to put them into the
M'r 2:24 sabbath day that which is not l'?
26 is not l' to eat but for the priests,
3: 4 Is it l' to do good on the sabbath
6:18 It is not l'...to have thy brother's
10: 2 l' for a man to put away his wife?
12:14 Is it l' to give tribute to Cæsar, or
Lu 6: 2 which is not l' to do on the sabbath
4 is not l' to eat but for the priests
9 it l' on the sabbath days to do good,
14: 3 Is it l' to heal on the sabbath day?
20:22 l' for us to give tribute unto Cæsar,
Joh 5:10 it is not l' for thee to carry thy bed.
18:31 l' for us to put any man to death:
Ac 16:21 which are not l' for us to receive,
19:39 be determined in a l' assembly.
22:25 l' for you to scourge a man that is
1Co 6:12 All things are l' unto me, but all
12 all things are l' for me, but I will
10:23 All things are l' for me, but all
23 all things are l' for me, but all
2Co 12: 4 which it is not l' for a man to utter.

lawfully
1Ti 1: 8 the law is good, if a man use it l';
2Ti 2: 5 he not crowned, except he strive l'.

lawgiver
Ge 49:10 nor a l' from between his feet,
Nu 21:18 digged it, by the direction of the l',
De 33:21 a portion of the l', was he seated;
Ps 60: 7 of mine head; Judah is my l';
108: 8 of mine head; Judah is my l';
Isa 33:22 the Lord is our l', the Lord is our
Jas 4:12 There is one l', who is able to save

lawless
1Ti 1: 9 man, but for the l' and disobedient,

laws
Ge 26: 5 my statutes, and my l'.
Ex 16:28 keep my commandments and my l'?
18:16 know the statutes of God, and his l'.
20 shalt teach them ordinances and l',
Le 26:46 the statutes and judgments and l',
Ezr 7:25 such as know the l' of thy God;
Ne 9:13 them right judgments, and true l',
14 them precepts, statutes, and l',
Es 1:19 l' of the Persians and the Medes,
3: 8 their l' are diverse from all people;
8 neither keep they the king's l':
Ps 105:45 observe his statutes,...keep his l'.
Isa 24: 5 they have transgressed the l',
Eze 43:11 forms thereof, and all the l' thereof:
44: 5 of the Lord, and all the l' thereof;
24 they shall keep my l' and my
Da 7:25 and think to change times and l':
9:10 to walk in his l', which he set
Heb 8:10 I will put my l' into their mind,
10:16 I will put my l' into their hearts,

lawyer See also LAWYERS.
M't 22:35 was a l', asked him a question,
Lu 10:25 a certain l' stood up, and tempted
Tit 3:13 Bring Zenas the l' and Apollos on

lawyers
Lu 7:30 and l' rejected the counsel of God
11:45 answered one of the l', and said
46 he said, Woe unto you also, ye l'!
52 Woe unto you, l'! for ye have taken
14: 3 spake unto the l' and Pharisees,

lay See also LAID; LAIN; LAYEDST; LAYEST; LAYETH; LAYING; LIE; OVERLAY.
Ge 19: 4 before they l' down, the men of
33 went in, and l' with her father;
33 he perceived not when she l' down,
34 I l' yesternight with my father:
35 the younger arose, and l' with him;
35 he perceived not when she l' down.
22:12 L' not thine hand upon the lad,
28:11 and l' down in that place to sleep.
30:16 And he l' with her that night.
34: 2 he took her, and l' with her, and
35:22 Reuben went and l' with Bilhah his
37:22 l' no hand upon him; that he
41:35 and l' up corn under the hand of
Ex 5: 8 heretofore, ye shall l' upon them;
7: 4 I may l' my hand upon Egypt,
16:13 the dew l' round about the host.
14 when the dew that l' was gone up,
14 the wilderness there l' a small round
23 remaineth over l' up for you to
33 l' it up before the Lord, to be kept
21:22 woman's husband will l' upon him;
22:25 shalt thou l' upon him usury.
Le 1: 7 l' the wood in order upon the fire:
8 shall l' the parts,...in order upon
12 the priest shall l' them in order on
2:15 it, and l' frankincense thereon:
3: 2, 8, 13 he shall l' his hand upon the
4: 4 shall l' his hand upon the bullock's
15 shall l' their hands upon the head
24, 29, 33 he shall l' his hand upon the
6:12 l' the burnt offering in order upon
16:21 Aaron shall l' both his hands upon
24:14 him l' their hands upon his head,
Nu 8:12 Levites shall l' their hands upon
12:11 thee, l' not the sin upon us,
17: 4 shalt l' them up in the tabernacle
19: 9 l' them up without the camp in a
24: 9 He couched, he l' down as a lion,
27:18 and l' thine hand upon him;
De 7:15 will l' them upon all them that
11:18 shall ye l' up these my words in
25 your God shall l' the fear of you
14:28 shalt l' it up within thy gates:

De 21: 8 l' not innocent blood unto thy
19 his father and his mother l' hold
22:22 the man that l' with the woman,
25 man only that l' with her shall die:
28 and l' hold on her, and lie with her,
29 man that l' with her shall give
Jos 6:26 he shall l' the foundation thereof
8: 2 l' thee an ambush for the city
15:46 unto the sea, all that l' near Ashdod,
J'g 4:22 Sisera l' dead, and the nail was
5:27 feet he bowed, he fell, he l' down:
6:20 cakes, and l' them upon this rock,
7:12 children of the east l' along in the
13 overturned it, that the tent l' along.
14:17 her, because she l' sore upon him:
16: 3 Samson l' till midnight, and arose
18:19 l' thine hand upon thy mouth,
Ru 3: 4 uncover his feet, and l' thee down;
8 and, behold, a woman l' at his feet.
14 she l' at his feet until the morning:
1Sa 2:22 how they l' with the women that
3: 5 again. And he went and l' down.
9 Samuel went and l' down in his
15 And Samuel l' until the morning,
6: 8 the Lord, and l' it upon the cart;
11: 2 l' it for a reproach upon all Israel.
19:24 l' down naked all that day and all
26: 5 beheld the place where Saul l',
5 Saul l' in the trench, and the people
7 Saul l' sleeping within the trench,
7 and the people l' round about him.
2Sa 2:21 and l' thee hold on one of the young
4: 5 who l' on a bed at noon.
7 l' on his bed in his bedchamber,
11: 4 in unto him, and he l' with her;
12: 3 his own cup, and l' in his bosom,
16 and l' all night upon the earth.
24 went in unto her, and l' with her:
13: 5 L' thee down on thy bed, and make
6 Amnon l' down, and made himself
14 than she, forced her, and l' with her
31 his garments, and l' on the earth;
19:32 while he l' at Mahanaim; for he
1Ki 5:17 to l' the foundation of the house.
7: 3 l' on forty-five pillars, fifteen in a row.
13: 4 the altar, saying, L' hold on him.
31 l' my bones beside his bones:
18:23 cut it in pieces, and l' it on wood,
23 other bullock, and l' it on wood,
19: 5 l' and slept under a juniper tree,
21:27 fasted, and l' in sackcloth, and
2Ki 4:11 into the chamber, and l' there.
29 l' my staff upon the face of the
34 he went up, and l' upon the child,
9:16 went to Jezreel; for Joram l' there.
10: 8 L' ye them in two heaps at the
19:25 l' waste fenced cities into ruinous
2Ch 31: 7 l' the foundation of the heaps,
36:21 as long as she l' desolate she kept
Ezr 8:31 of such as l' in wait by the way.
Ne 13:21 do so again, I will l' hands on you.
Es 2:21 sought to l' hand on the king
3: 6 scorn to l' hands on Mordecai alone;
4: 3 many l' in sackcloth and ashes.
6: 2 who sought to l' hand on the king
9: 2 to l' hand on such as sought their
Job 9:33 might l' his hand upon us both.
17: 3 L' down now, put me in a surety
21: 5 l' your hand upon your mouth.
22:22 and l' up his words in thine heart.
24 Then shalt thou l' up gold as dust,
29:19 dew l' all night upon my branch.
34:23 he will not l' upon man more than
40: 4 I will l' mine hand upon my mouth.
41: 8 L' thine hand upon him, remember
Ps 4: 8 I will both l' me down in peace,
7: 5 and l' mine honour in the dust.
38:12 that seek after my life l' snares
71:10 they that l' wait for my soul take
84: 3 where she may l' her young,
104:22 and l' them down in their dens.
Pr 1:11 with us, let us l' wait for blood,
18 they l' wait for their own blood;
3:18 life to them that l' hold upon her:
7: 1 l' up my commandments with thee.
10:14 Wise men l' up knowledge: but the
24:15 L' not wait, O wicked man, against
30:32 evil, l' thine hand upon thy mouth.
Ec 2: 3 and to l' hold on folly, till I might see
7: 2 the living will l' it to his heart.
Isa 5: 6 And I will l' it waste: it shall not be
8 that l' field to field, till there be no
29 shall roar, and l' hold of the prey,
11:14 they shall l' their hand upon Edom
13: 9 anger, to l' the land desolate:
11 will l' low the haughtiness of the
22:22 key...will I l' upon his shoulder;
25:12 walls shall he bring down, l' low,
28:16 l' in Zion for a foundation a stone,
17 Judgment also will I l' to the line,
29: 3 l' siege against thee with a mount,
21 l' a snare for him that reproveth in
30:32 which the Lord shall l' upon him,
34:15 great owl make her nest, and l',
35: 7 where each l', shall be grass with
37:26 l' waste defenced cities into ruinous
38:21 and l' it for a plaister upon the boil,
47: 7 didst not l'...things to thy heart,
51:16 and l' the foundations of the earth,
54:11 will l' thy stones with fair colours,
11 and l' thy foundations with sapphires.
Jer 5:26 l' wait, as he that setteth snares;
6:21 will l' stumblingblocks before
23 shall l' hold on bow and spear;
Eze 3:20 I l' a stumblingblock before him,
4: 1 thee a tile, and l' it before thee,
2 l' siege against it, and build a fort
3 and thou shalt l' siege against it.
4 l' the iniquity of the house of
8 behold, I will l' bands upon thee,
6: 5 I will l' the dead carcases of the
19: 2 lioness: she l' down among lions,
23: 8 for in her youth they l' with her,
25:14 will l' my vengeance upon Edom
17 when I shall l' my vengeance upon
26:12 they shall l' thy stones and thy
16 l' away their robes, and put off
28:17 I will l' thee before kings, that
32: 5 will l' thy flesh upon the mountains,
33:28 I will l' the land most desolate,
35: 4 I will l' thy cities waste, and thou
36:29 it, and l' no famine upon you.
34 whereas it l' desolate in the sight of
37: 6 I will l' sinews upon you, and will
42:13 shall they l' the most holy things,
14 there they shall l' their garments
44:19 l' them in the holy chambers, and
Am 2: 8 they l' themselves down upon
Jon 1: 5 and he l', and was fast asleep.
14 and l' not upon us innocent blood:
Mic 1: 7 the idols thereof will I l' desolate:
7:16 l' their hand upon their mouth,
Zec 14:13 they shall l' hold every one on
Mal 2: 2 and if ye will not l' it to heart,
2 because ye do not l' it to heart.
M't 6:19 L' not up for yourselves treasures
20 l' up for yourselves treasures in
8:20 man hath not where to l' his head.
9:18 come and l' thy hand upon her,
12:11 will he not l' hold on it, and lift it
21:46 they sought to l' hands on him,
23: 4 and l' them on men's shoulders;
28: 6 see the place where the Lord l'.
M'r 1:30 Simon's wife's mother l' sick of a
2: 4 bed wherein the sick of the palsy l'.
3:21 it, they went out to l' hold on him:
5:23 come and l' thy hands on her, that
12:12 And they sought to l' hold on him,
15: 7 one named Barabbas, which l' bound
16:18 they shall l' hands on the sick,
Lu 5:18 him in, and to l' him before him.
25 and took up that whereon he l',
8:42 years of age, and she l' a dying.
9:58 man hath not where to l' his head.
19:44 shall l' thee even with the ground,
20:19 hour sought to l' hands on him;
21:12 they shall l' their hands on you,
Joh 5: 3 l' a great multitude of impotent
10:15 and I l' down my life for the sheep.
17 love me, because I l' down my life ,
18 from me, but I l' it down of myself.
18 I have power to l' it down, and I
11:38 was a cave, and a stone l' upon it.
13:37 I will l' down my life for thy sake.
38 Wilt thou l' down thy life for my
15:13 man l' down his life for his friends.
Ac 7:60 l' not this sin to their charge.
8:19 that on whomsoever I l' hands,
15:28 to l' upon you no greater burden
27:20 and no small tempest l' on us, all
28: 8 father of Publius l' sick of a fever
Ro 8:33 Who shall l' any thing to the charge
9:33 I l' in Sion a stumblingstone and
1Co 3:11 other foundation can no man l'
16: 2 every one of you l' by him in store,
2Co 12:14 ought not to l' up for the parents,
1Ti 5:22 L' hands suddenly on no man,
6:12 of faith, l' hold on eternal life,
19 they may l' hold on eternal life.
Heb 6:18 to l' hold upon the hope set before us:
12: 1 let us l' aside every weight, and the
Jas 1:21 Wherefore l' apart all filthiness
1Pe 2: 6 I l' in Sion a chief corner stone,
1Jo 3:16 we ought to l' down our lives for

layedst See also LAIDST.
Lu 19:21 takest up that thou l' not down,

layest
Nu 11:11 l' the burden of all this people
1Sa 28: 9 then l' thou a snare for my life, to

layeth
Job 21:19 God l' up his iniquity for his
24:12 out: yet God l' not folly to them.
41:26 sword of him that l' at him cannot
Ps 33: 7 he l' up the depth in storehouses.
104: 3 Who l' the beams of his chambers
Pr 2: 7 He l' up sound wisdom for the
13:16 but a fool l' open his folly.
26:24 lips, and l' up deceit within him;
31:19 She l' her hands to the spindle,
Isa 26: 5 high; the lofty city, he l' it low;
5 he l' it low, even to the ground;
56: 2 the son of man that l' hold on it;
57: 1 and no man l' it to heart: and
Jer 9: 8 mouth, but in heart he l' his wait.
12:11 because no man l' it to heart.
Zec 12: 1 l' the foundation of the earth, and
Lu 12:21 he that l' up treasure for himself,
15: 5 found it, he l' it on his shoulders,

laying See also OVERLAYING.
Nu 35:20 or hurl at him by l' of wait, that
22 him any thing without l' of wait,
Ps 64: 5 they commune of l' snares privily;
M'r 7: 8 l' aside the commandment of God,
Lu 11:54 L' wait for him, and seeking to
Ac 8:18 through l' on of the apostles' hands
9:24 their l' await was known of Saul,
25: 3 l' wait in the way to kill him.
1Ti 4:14 with the l' on of the hands of the
6:19 L' up in store for themselves a good
Heb 6: 1 not l' again the foundation of
2 baptisms, and of l' on of hands,
1Pe 2: 1 l' aside all malice, and all guile,

Lazarus (*laz'-a-rus*)
Lu 16:20 was a certain beggar named L',
23 afar off, and L' in his bosom.
24 have mercy on me, and send L',
25 things, and likewise L' evil things:
Joh 11: 1 a certain man was sick, named L',
2 her hair, whose brother L' was sick.)
5 Martha, and her sister, and L'.
11 unto them, Our friend L' sleepeth;
14 unto them plainly, L' is dead.
43 with a loud voice, L', come forth.
12: 1 where L' was which had been dead,
2 L' was one of them that sat at the
9 might see L' also, whom he had
10 they might put L' also to death;
17 when he called L' out of his grave,

leach See HORSELEACH.

lead See also LEADEST; LEADETH; LED.
Ge 33:14 I will l' on softly, according as the
Ex 13:21 of a cloud, to l' them the way;
15:10 sank as l' in the mighty waters.
32:34 l' the people unto the place of
Nu 27:17 which may l' them out, and which
31:22 brass, the iron, the tin, and the l',
De 4:27 whither the Lord shall l' you.
20: 9 of the armies to l' the people.
28:37 whither the Lord shall l' thee.
32:12 the Lord alone did l' him, and
J'g 5:12 and l' thy captivity captive, thou
1Sa 30:22 that they may l' them away, and
2Ch 30: 9 before them that l' them captive,
Ne 9:19 by day, to l' them in the way;
Job 19:24 graven with an iron pen and l'
Ps 5: 8 L' me, O Lord, in thy righteousness
25: 5 L' me in thy truth, and teach me:
27:11 l' me in a plain path, because of
31: 3 name's sake l' me, and guide me.
43: 3 let them l' me; let them bring me
60: 9 city? who will l' me into Edom?
61: 2 l' me to the rock that is higher
108:10 city? who will l' me into Edom?
125: 5 Lord shall l' them forth with the
139:10 Even there shall thy hand l' me,
24 and l' me in the way everlasting.
143:10 l' me into the land of uprightness.
Pr 6:22 When thou goest, it shall l' thee;
8:20 I l' in the way of righteousness,
Ca 8: 2 I would l' thee, and bring thee
Isa 3:12 they which l' thee cause thee to err,
11: 6 and a little child shall l' them.
20: 4 of Assyria l' away the Egyptians
40:11 shall gently l' those that are with
42:16 l' them in paths that they have not
49:10 hath mercy on them shall l' them,
57:18 I will l' him also, and restore
63:14 so didst thou l' thy people, to make
Jer 6:29 the l' is consumed of the fire;
31: 9 with supplications will I l' them:
32: 5 he shall l' Zedekiah to Babylon,
Eze 22:18 brass, and tin, and iron, and l',
20 silver, and brass, and iron, and l',
27:12 silver, iron, tin, and l', they
Na 2: 7 maids shall l' her as with the voice
Zec 5: 7 there was lifted up a talent of l':
8 the weight of l' upon the mouth
M't 6:13 And l' us not into temptation, but
15:14 if the blind l' the blind, both shall
M'r 13:11 when they shall l' you, and deliver
14:44 take him, and l' him away safely.
Lu 6:39 them, Can the blind l' the blind?
11: 4 And l' us not into temptation; but
13:15 stall, and l' him away to watering?
Ac 13:11 seeking some to l' him by the hand.
1Co 9: 5 we not power to l' about a sister,
1Ti 2: 2 may l' a quiet and peaceable life
2Ti 3: 6 l' captive silly women laden with
Heb 8: 9 to l' them out of the land of Egypt;
Re 7:17 shall l' them unto living fountains

leader See also LEADERS; RINGLEADER.
1Ch 12:27 was the l' of the Aaronites, and
13: 1 and hundreds, and with every l'.
Isa 55: 4 a l' and commander to the people.

leaders
2Ch 32:21 the l' and captains in the camp of
Isa 9:16 the l' of this people cause them to
M't 15:14 alone: they be blind l' of the blind.

leadest
Ps 80: 1 thou that l' Joseph like a flock;

leadeth
1Sa 13:17 turned unto the way that l' to Ophrah,
Job 12:17 He l' counsellors away spoiled,
19 He l' princes away spoiled, and
Ps 23: 2 he l' me beside the still waters.
3 l' me in...paths of righteousness
Pr 16:29 l'...into the way that is not good.
Isa 48:17 which l' thee by the way that thou
M't 7:13 is the way, that l' to destruction,
14 narrow is the way, which l' unto life,
M'r 9: 2 l' them up into an high mountain
Joh 10: 3 sheep by name, and l' them out.
Ac 12:10 the iron gate that l' unto the city;
Ro 2: 4 of God l' thee to repentance?
Re 13:10 He that l' into captivity shall go

leaf See also LEAVED; LEAVES.
Ge 8:11 lo, in her mouth was an olive l'
Le 26:36 the sound of a shaken l' shall chase
Job 13:25 thou break a l' driven to and fro?
Ps 1: 3 his l' also shall not wither; and
Isa 1:30 shall be as an oak whose l' fadeth,
34: 4 as the l' falleth off from the vine,
64: 6 rags; and we all do fade as a l';

Jer 8:13 on the fig tree, and the *l'* shall fade;
17: 8 cometh, but her *l'* shall be green;
Eze 47:12 whose *l'* shall not fade, neither shall
12 and the *l'* thereof for medicine.

league
Jos 9: 6 therefore make ye a *l'* with us.
7 how shall we make a *l'* with you?
11 therefore now make ye a *l'* with us.
15 them, and made a *l'* with them.
16 after they had made a *l'* with them.
J'g 2: 2 make no *l'* with the inhabitants of
1Sa 22: 8 made a *l'* with the son of Jesse,
2Sa 3:12 Make thy *l'* with me, and, behold,
13 Well; I will make a *l'* with thee:
21 that they may make a *l'* with thee,
5: 3 king David made a *l'* with them in
1Ki 5:12 and they two made a *l'* together.
15:19 There is a *l'* between me and thee,
19 break thy *l'* with Baasha king of
2Ch 16: 3 There is a *l'* between me and thee,
3 break thy *l'* with Baasha king of
Job 5:23 thou shalt be in *l'* with the stones
Eze 30: 5 and the men of the land that is in *l'*.
Da 11:23 after the *l'* made with him he shall

Leah (*le'-ah*) See also LEAH'S.
Ge 29:16 the name of the elder was *L'*, and
17 *L'* was tender eyed; but Rachel
23 that he took *L'* his daughter, and
24 gave unto his daughter *L'* Zilpah
25 in the morning, behold, it was *L'*:
30 he loved also Rachel more than *L'*,
31 the Lord saw that *L'* was hated, he
32 And *L'* conceived, and bare a son,
30: 9 *L'* saw that she had left bearing,
11 *L'* said, A troop cometh: and she
13 And *L'* said, Happy am I, for the
14 brought them unto his mother *L'*.
14 Rachel said to *L'*, Give me, I pray
16 and *L'* went out to meet him, and
17 God hearkened unto *L'*, and she
18 *L'* said, God hath given me my
19 *L'* conceived again, and bare Jacob
20 *L'* said, God hath endued me with
31: 4 Jacob sent and called Rachel and *L'*
14 Rachel and *L'* answered and said
33: 1 he divided the children unto *L'*,
2 and *L'* and her children after, and
7 And *L'* also with her children came
34: 1 Dinah the daughter of *L'*, which
35: 23 The sons of *L'*; Reuben, Jacob's
46:15 These be the sons of *L'*, which she
18 Laban gave to *L'* his daughter,
49:31 his wife; and there I buried *L'*.
Ru 4:11 house like Rachel and like *L'*,

Leah's (*le'-ahs*)
Ge 30:10 Zilpah *L'* maid bare Jacob a son.
12 Zilpah *L'* maid bare Jacob a second
31:33 into Jacob's tent, and into *L'* tent,
33 went he out of *L'* tent, and entered
35:26 the sons of Zilpah, *L'* handmaid;

lean See also LEANED; LEANETH; LEANFLESHED; LEANING.
Ge 41:20 *l'* and the ill favoured kine did eat
Nu 13:20 the land is, whether it be fat or *l'*,
J'g 16:26 standeth, that I may *l'* upon them.
2Sa 13: 4 the king's son, *l'* from day to day?
2Ki 18:21 on which if a man *l'*, it will go into
Job 8:15 He shall *l'* upon his house, but it
Pro 3: 5 *l'* not unto thine...understanding.
Isa 17: 4 fatness of his flesh shall wax *l'*.
36: 6 whereon if a man *l'*, it will go into
Eze 34:20 fat cattle and between the *l'* cattle.
Mic 3:11 yet will they *l'* upon the Lord, and

leaned
2Sa 1: 6 behold Saul *l'* upon his spear;
2Ki 7: 2 a lord on whose hand the king *l'*
17 the lord on whose hand he *l'* to have
Eze 29: 7 and when they *l'* upon thee, thou
Am 5:19 house, and *l'* his hand on the wall,
Joh 21:20 also *l'* on his breast at supper,

leaneth
2Sa 3:29 or that *l'* on a staff, or that falleth
2Ki 5:18 and he *l'* on my hand, and I bow

leanfleshed
Ge 41: 3 the river, ill favoured and *l'*;
4 ill favoured and *l'* kine did eat
19 and very ill favoured and *l'*,

leaning
Ca 8: 5 wilderness, *l'* upon her beloved?
Joh 13:23 there was *l'* on Jesus' bosom one
Heb 11:21 worshipped, *l'* upon the top of his staff.

leanness
Job 16: 8 and my *l'* rising up in me beareth
Ps 106:15 request but sent *l'* into their soul.
Isa 10:16 hosts, send among his fat ones *l'*;
24:16 I said, My *l'*, my *l'*, woe unto me!

Leannoth (*le-an'-noth*)
Ps 88: *title* Musician upon Mahalath *L'*,

leap See also LEAPED; LEAPING.
Ge 31:12 the rams which *l'* upon the cattle
Le 11:21 feet, to *l'* withal upon the earth;
De 33:22 whelp: he shall *l'* from Bashan.
Job 41:19 lamps, and sparks of fire *l'* out.
Ps 68:16 Why *l'* ye, ye high hills? this is
Isa 35: 6 Then shall the lame man *l'* as an
Joe 2: 5 the tops of mountains shall they *l'*,
Zep 1: 9 all those that *l'* on the threshold,
Lu 6:23 ye in that day, and *l'* for joy:

leaped
Ge 31:10 the rams which *l'* upon the cattle
2Sa 22:30 by my God have I *l'* over a wall.
1Ki 18:26 they *l'* upon the altar which was
Ps 18:29 by my God have I *l'* over a wall.
Lu 1:41 of Mary, the babe *l'* in her womb;
44 the babe *l'* in my womb for joy.
Ac 14:10 on thy feet. And he *l'* and walked.
19:16 the evil spirit was *l'* on them, and

leaping
2Sa 6:16 David *l'* and dancing before the
Ca 2: 8 he cometh *l'* upon the mountains,
Ac 3: 8 And he *l'* up stood, and walked,
8 walking, and *l'*, and praising God.

learn See also LEARNED; LEARNING.
De 4:10 that they may *l'* to fear me all the
5: 1 that ye may *l'* them, and keep, and
14:23 mayest *l'* to fear the Lord thy God
17:19 he may *l'* to fear the Lord his God,
18: 9 not *l'* to do after the abominations
31:12 that they may *l'*, and fear the Lord
13 and *l'* to fear the Lord your God, as
Ps 119:71 that I might *l'* thy statutes.
73 that I may *l'* thy commandments.
Pr 22:25 Lest thou *l'* his ways, and get a
Isa 1:17 *L'* to do well; seek judgment,
2: 4 neither shall they *l'* war any more.
26: 9 of the world will *l'* righteousness.
10 yet will he not *l'* righteousness:
29:24 that murmured shall *l'* doctrine.
Jer 10: 2 Lord, *L'* not the way of the heathen,
12:16 diligently *l'* the ways of my people,
Mic 4: 3 neither shall they *l'* war any more.
M't 9:13 go ye and *l'* what that meaneth,
11:29 my yoke upon you, and *l'* of me;
24:32 Now *l'* a parable of the fig tree;
M'r 13:28 Now *l'* a parable of the fig tree;
1Co 4: 6 might *l'* in us not to think of men
14:31 one by one, that all may *l'*, and all
35 And if they will *l'* any thing, let
Ga 3: 2 This only would I *l'* of you,
1Ti 1:20 they may *l'* not to blaspheme.
2:11 Let the woman *l'* in silence with
5: 4 them *l'* first to shew piety at home,
13 withal they *l'* to be idle, wandering
Tit 3:14 also *l'* to maintain good works for
Re 14: 3 no man could *l'* that song but the

learned See also UNLEARNED.
Ge 30:27 I have *l'* by experience that the
Ps 106:35 the heathen, and *l'* their works.
119: 7 have *l'* thy righteous judgments.
Pr 30: 3 I neither *l'* wisdom, nor have the
Isa 29:11 men deliver to one that is *l'*,
12 delivered to him that is not *l'*,
12 thee: and he saith, I am not *l'*.
50: 4 given me the tongue of the *l'*,
4 mine ear to hear as the *l'*.
Eze 19: 3 lion and it *l'* to catch the prey;
6 young lion, and *l'* to catch the prey,
Joh 6:45 heard, and hath *l'* of the Father,
7:15 this man letters, having never *l'*?
Ac 7:22 Moses was *l'* in all the wisdom
Ro 16:17 to the doctrine which ye have *l'*;
Eph 4:20 But ye have not so *l'* Christ;
Ph'p 4: 9 things, which ye have both *l'*, and
11 for I have *l'*, in whatsoever state I
Col 1: 7 As ye also *l'* of Epaphras our dear
2Ti 3:14 in the things which thou hast *l'* and
14 knowing of whom thou hast *l'* them;
Heb 5: 8 yet *l'* he obedience by the things

learning
Pr 1: 5 will hear, and will increase *l'*;
9: 9 just man, and he will increase in *l'*.
16:21 sweetness of the lips increaseth *l'*.
23 his mouth, and addeth *l'* to his lips.
Da 1: 4 whom they might teach the *l'* and
17 them knowledge and skill in all *l'*
Ac 26:24 much *l'* doth make thee mad.
Ro 15: 4 aforetime were written for our *l'*,
2Ti 3: 7 Ever *l'*, and never able to come to

leasing See also LYING.
Ps 4: 2 ye love vanity, and seek after *l'*?
5: 6 shalt destroy them that speak *l'*:

least
Ge 24:55 with us a few days, at the *l'* ten;
32:10 worthy of the *l'* of all the mercies,
Nu 11:32 gathered *l'* gathered ten homers:
J'g 3: 2 at the *l'* such as before knew
6:15 I am the *l'* in my father's house.
1Sa 9:21 my family the *l'* of all the families
21: 4 kept themselves at *l'* from women.
2Ki 18:24 of the *l'* of my master's servants,
1Ch 12:14 one of the *l'* was over an hundred,
Isa 36: 9 of the *l'* of my master's servants,
Jer 6:13 *l'* of them even unto the greatest
8:10 from the *l'* even unto the greatest
31:34 the *l'* of them unto the greatest
42: 1 from the *l'* even unto the greatest,
8 from the *l'* even to the greatest,
44:12 from the *l'* even unto the greatest.
49:20 the *l'* of the flock shall draw them
50:45 the *l'* of the flock shall draw them
Am 9: 9 not the *l'* grain fall upon the earth.
Jon 3: 5 of them even to the *l'* of them.
M't 2: 6 the *l'* among the princes of Juda:
5:19 one of these *l'* commandments,
19 the *l'* in the kingdom of heaven:
11:11 is *l'* in the kingdom of heaven is
13:32 Which indeed is the *l'* of all seeds:
25:40 one of the *l'* of these my brethren,
45 did it not to one of the *l'* of these,
Lu 7:28 that is *l'* in the kingdom of God
9:48 for he that is *l'* among you all, the
12:26 not able to do that thing which is *l'*,
16:10 that is faithful in that which is *l'*
10 he that is unjust in the *l'* is unjust
19:42 even thou, at *l'* in this thy day,
Ac 5:15 that at the *l'* the shadow of Peter
Ac 8:10 heed, from the *l'* to the greatest,
1Co 6: 4 to judge who are *l'* esteemed
15: 9 I am the *l'* of the apostles, that am
Eph 3: 8 who am less than the *l'* of all saints,
Heb 8:11 me, from the *l'* to the greatest.

leather
2Ki 1: 8 with a girdle of *l'* about his loins.

leathern
M't 3: 4 and a *l'* girdle about his loins;

leave See also LEAVETH; LEAVING; LEFT.
Ge 2:24 man *l'* his father and his mother,
28:15 I will not *l'* thee, until I have done
33:15 now *l'* with thee some of the folk
42:33 *l'* one of your brethren here with
44:22 The lad cannot *l'* his father:
22 for if he should *l'* his father, his
Ex 16:19 Let no man *l'* of it till the morning.
23:11 what they *l'* the beasts...shall eat.
Le 7:15 not *l'* any of it until the morning.
16:23 holy place, and shall *l'* them there:
19:10 *l'* them for the poor and stranger:
22:30 *l'* none of it until the morrow:
23:22 thou shalt *l'* them unto the poor,
Nu 9:12 *l'* none of it unto the morning,
10:31 he said, *L'* us not, I pray thee;
22:13 Lord refuseth to give me *l'* to go
32:15 again *l'* them in the wilderness;
De 28:51 shall not *l'* thee either corn, wine,
54 of his children which he shall *l'*:
Jos 4: 3 and *l'* them in the lodging place,
J'g 9: 9 unto them, Should I *l'* my fatness,
13 unto them, Should I *l'* my wine,
Ru 1:16 said, Intreat me not to *l'* thee, or
2:16 *l'* them, that she may glean them,
1Sa 9: 5 my father *l'* caring for the asses,
14:36 and let us not *l'* a man of them.
20: 6 asked *l'* of me that he might run
28 asked *l'* of me to go to Beth-lehem:
25:22 if I *l'* of all that pertain to him
2Sa 14: 7 not *l'* to my husband neither name
1Ki 8:57 let him not *l'* us, nor forsake us:
2Ki 2: 2, 4, 6 soul liveth, I will not *l'* thee.
4:30 as thy soul liveth, I will not *l'* thee.
43 They shall eat, and shall *l'* thereof.
13: 7 he *l'* of the people to Jehoahaz
1Ch 28: 8 *l'* it for an inheritance for your
Ezr 9: 8 *l'* us a remnant to escape, and to
12 *l'* it for an inheritance to your
Ne 5:10 I pray you, let us *l'* off this usury.
6: 3 the work cease, whilst I *l'* it,
10:31 we would *l'* the seventh year,
13: 6 days obtained I *l'* of the king:
Job 9:27 I will *l'* off my heaviness, and
10: 1 *l'* my complaint upon myself;
39:11 or wilt thou *l'* thy labour to him?
Ps 16:10 thou wilt not *l'* my soul in hell;
17:14 *l'* the rest of their substance to
27: 9 *l'* me not, neither forsake me, O
37:33 Lord will not *l'* him in his hand,
49:10 perish, and *l'* their wealth to others.
119:121 *l'* me not to mine oppressors.
141: 8 trust; *l'* not my soul destitute.
Pr 2:13 Who *l'* the paths of uprightness,
17:14 therefore *l'* off contention, before
Ec 2:18 *l'* it unto the man that shall be
21 shall he *l'* it for his portion.
10: 4 up against thee, *l'* not thy place;
Isa 10: 3 and where will ye *l'* your glory?
65:15 *l'* your name for a curse unto my
Jer 9: 2 that I might *l'* my people, and go
14: 9 are called by thy name; *l'* us not.
17:11 shall *l'* them in the midst of his
18:14 a man *l'* the snow of Lebanon
30:11 not *l'* thee altogether unpunished.
44: 7 Judah, to *l'* you none to remain;
46:28 I not *l'* thee wholly unpunished.
48:28 in Moab, *l'* the cities, and dwell
49: 9 they not *l'* some gleaning grapes?
11 *L'* thy fatherless children, I will
Eze 6: 8 Yet will I *l'* a remnant, that ye may
12:16 I will *l'* a few men of them from
16:39 and *l'* thee naked and bare.
22:20 I will *l'* you there, and melt you.
23:29 and shall *l'* thee naked and bare:
29: 5 *l'* thee thrown into the wilderness,
32: 4 Then will I *l'* thee upon the land, I
39: 2 and *l'* but the sixth part of thee,
Da 4:15 *l'* the stump of his roots in the
23 *l'* the stump of the roots thereof in
26 to *l'* the stump of the tree roots;
Ho 12:14 shall he *l'* his blood upon him,
Joe 2:14 and *l'* a blessing behind him;
Am 5: 3 by a thousand shall *l'* an hundred,
3 forth by an hundred shall *l'* ten,
7 *l'* off righteousness in the earth,
Ob 5 would they not *l'* some grapes?
Zep 3:12 *l'* in the midst of thee an afflicted
Mal 4: 1 *l'* them neither root nor branch.
M't 5:24 *L'* there thy gift before the altar,
18:12 doth he not *l'* the ninety and nine,
19: 5 shall a man *l'* father and mother,
23:23 and not to *l'* the other undone.
M'r 5:13 And forthwith Jesus gave them *l'*.
10: 7 a man *l'* his father and mother,
12:19 die, and *l'* his wife behind him,
19 and *l'* no children, that his brother
Lu 11:42 and not to *l'* the other undone.
15: 4 doth not *l'* the ninety and nine in
19:44 shall not *l'* in thee one stone upon
Joh 14:18 I will not *l'* you comfortless: I will
27 Peace I *l'* with you, my peace I give
16:28 I *l'* the world, and go to the Father.
32 to his own, and shall *l'* me alone:
19:38 of Jesus: and Pilate gave him *l'*.
Ac 2:27 thou wilt not *l'* my soul in hell,

Ac 6: 2 that we should l' the word of God,
18:18 then took his l' of the brethren,
21: 6 had taken our l' one of another,
1Co 7:13 dwell with her, let her not l' him.
2Co 2:13 taking my l' of them, I went from
Eph 5:31 a man l' his father and mother,
Heb13: 5 I will never l' thee, nor forsake
Rev11: 2 which is without the temple l' out,

leaved
Isa 45: 1 open before him the two l' gates;

leaven See also LEAVENED.
Ex 12:15 put away l' out of your houses:
19 be no l' found in your houses:
13: 7 shall there be l' seen with thee in
34:25 the blood of my sacrifice with l';
Le 2:11 No...offering...shall be made with l':
11 for ye shall burn no l',
6:17 It shall not be baked with l'. I
10:12 eat it without l' beside the altar:
23:17 they shall be baken with l'; they
Am 4: 5 sacrifice of thanksgiving with l',
M't 13:33 kingdom of heaven is like unto l',
16: 6, 11 beware of the l' of the Pharisees
12 not beware of the l' of bread,
M'r 8:15 beware of the l' of the Pharisees,
15 and of the l' of Herod.
Lu 12: 1 Beware ye of the l' of the Pharisees,
13:21 It is like l', which a woman took
1Co 5: 6 little l' leaveneth the whole lump?
7 Purge out therefore the old l', that
8 us keep the feast, not with old l',
8 neither with the l' of malice and
Ga 5: 9 little l' leaveneth the whole lump.

leavened See also UNLEAVENED; LEAVENETH.
Ex 12:15 whosoever eateth l' bread from
19 whosoever eateth that which is l',
20 Ye shall eat nothing l'; in all your
34 took their dough before it was l',
39 forth out of Egypt, for it was not l';
13: 3 there shall no l' bread be eaten.
7 shall no l' bread be seen with thee,
23:18 blood of my sacrifice with l' bread;
Le 7:13 shall offer for his offering l' bread
De 16: 3 Thou shalt eat no l' bread with it;
4 shall be no l' bread seen with thee
Ho 7: 4 kneaded the dough, until it be l'.
M't 13:33 of meal, till the whole was l'.
Lu 13:21 of meal, till the whole was l'.

leaveneth
1Co 5: 6 a little leaven l' the whole lump?
Ga 5: 9 A little leaven l' the whole lump.

leaves
Ge 3: 7 they sewed fig l' together, and
1Ki 6:34 the two l' of the one door were
34 the two l' of the other door were
Isa 6:13 is in them, when they cast their l':
Jer 36:23 Jehudi had read three or four l',
Eze17: 9 wither in all the l' of her spring,
41:24 had two l' apiece, two turning l';
24 two l' for the one door
24 and two l' for the other door.
Da 4:12 The l' thereof were fair, and the
14 off his branches, shake off his l',
21 Whose l' were fair, and the fruit
M't 21:19 found nothing thereon, but l' only,
24:32 yet tender, and putteth forth l',
M'r 11:13 seeing a fig tree afar off having l',
13 came to it, he found nothing but l';
13:28 yet tender, and putteth forth l',
Re 22: 2 l' of the trees were for the healing

leaveth
Job 39:14 Which l' her eggs in the earth,
Pr 13:22 A good man l' an inheritance to his
28: 3 like a sweeping rain which l' no food.
Zec 11:17 the idol shepherd that l' the flock!
M't 4:11 Then the devil l' him, and, behold,
Joh 10:12 coming, and l' the sheep, and fleeth:

leaving
M't 4:13 l' Nazareth, he came and dwelt
Lu 10:30 and departed, l' him half dead.
Ro 1:27 l' the natural use of the woman,
Heb 6: 1 l' the principles of the doctrine of
1Pe 2:21 suffered for us, l' us an example,

Lebana (*leb'-a-nah*) See also LEBANAH.
Ne 7:48 The children of L', the children

Lebanah (*leb'-a-nah*) See also LEBANA.
Ezr 2:45 The children of L', the children

Lebanon (*leb'-a-non*)
De 1: 7 unto L', unto the great river, the
3:25 that goodly mountain, and L'.
11:24 from the wilderness and L', from
Jos 1: 4 From the wilderness and this L'
9: 1 of the great sea over against L',
11:17 unto Baal-gad in the valley of L'
12: 7 in the valley of L' even unto the
13: 5 the land of the Giblites, and all L',
6 of the hill country from L' unto
J'g 3: 3 the Hivites that dwelt in mount L',
9:15 and devour the cedars of L'.
1Ki 4:33 from the cedar tree that is in L'
5: 6 they hew me cedar trees out of L';
9 shall bring them down from L'
14 he sent them to L', ten thousand
14 a month they were in L', and two
7: 2 also the house of the forest of L';
9:19 to build in Jerusalem, and in L',
10:17 in the house of the forest of L'.
21 of the house of the forest of L' were
2Ki 14: 9 The thistle that was in L' sent to
9 to the cedar that was in L', saying,
9 by a wild beast that was in L', and
19:23 of the mountains, to the sides of L',
2Ch 2: 8 trees, and algum trees, out of L':
8 can skill to cut timber in L';
16 we will cut wood out of L', as much
8: 6 to build in Jerusalem, and in L',
9:16 them in the house of the forest of L'.
20 of the house of the forest of L' were
25:18 The thistle that was in L' sent to
18 to the cedar that was in L', saying,
18 and by a wild beast that was in L',
Ezr 3: 7 cedar trees from L' to the sea of
Ps 29: 5 the Lord breaketh the cedars of L'.
6 L' and Sirion like a young unicorn.
72:16 the fruit thereof shall shake like L':
92:12 he shall grow like a cedar in L'.
104:16 cedars of L', which he hath planted;
Ca 3: 9 himself a chariot of the wood of L'.
4: 8 Come with me from L', my spouse,
8 with me from L': look from the top
11 thy garments is like the smell of L'.
15 living waters, and streams from L'.
5:15 his countenance is as L', excellent
7: 4 thy nose is as the tower of L' which
Isa 2:13 upon all the cedars of L', that are
10:34 and L' shall fall by a mighty one.
14: 8 at thee, and the cedars of L', saying,
29:17 L' shall be turned into a fruitful
33: 9 L' is ashamed and hewn down:
35: 2 the glory of L' shall be given unto
37:24 the mountains, to the sides of L';
40:16 L' is not sufficient to burn, nor the
60:13 The glory of L' shall come unto
Jer 18:14 leave the snow of L' which cometh
22: 6 Gilead unto me, and the head of L':
20 Go up to L', and cry; and lift up
23 O inhabitant of L', that makest thy
Eze 17: 3 came unto L', and took the highest
27: 5 cedars from L' to make masts
31: 3 the Assyrian was a cedar in L' with
15 and I caused L' to mourn for him,
16 of Eden, the choice and best of L',
Ho 14: 5 lily, and cast forth his roots as L'.
6 as the olive tree, and his smell as L'.
7 thereof shall be as the wine of L'.
Na 1: 4 and the flower of L' languisheth.
Hab 2:17 the violence of L' shall cover thee,
Zec 10:10 them into the land of Gilead and L';
11: 1 Open thy doors, O L', that the fire

Lebaoth (*leb'-a-oth*) See also BETH-LEBAOTH.
Jos 15:32 And L', and Shilhim, and Ain, and

Lebbæus (*leb-be'-us*) See also JUDAS; THADDÆUS.
M't 10: 3 James the son of Alphæus, and L',

Lebonah (*le-bo'-nah*)
J'g 21:19 Shechem, and on the south of L'.

Lecah (*le'-cah*)
1Ch 4:21 Er the father of L', and Laadah

led See also LEDDEST.
Ge 24:27 l' me to the house of my master's
48 which had l' me in the right way
Ex 3: 1 l' the flock to the backside of the
13:17 l' them not through the way of the
18 God l' the people about, through
15:13 thy mercy hast l' forth the people
De 8: 2 God l' thee these forty years in the
15 Who l' thee through that great and
29: 5 l' you forty years in the wilderness:
32:10 he l' him about, he instructed him,
Jos 24: 3 l' him throughout all the land of
1Ki 8:48 which l' them away captive,
2Ki 6:19 seek. But he l' them to Samaria.
1Ch 20: 1 l' forth the power of the army, and
2Ch 25:11 himself, and l' forth his people,
Ps 68:18 high, thou hast l' captivity captive:
78:14 also he l' them with a cloud,
53 And he l' them on safely so that
106: 9 so he l' them through the depths,
107: 7 he l' them forth by the right way,
136:16 which l' his people through the
Pr 4:11 I have l' thee in right paths.
Isa 9:16 that are l' of them are destroyed.
48:21 he l' them through the deserts:
55:12 joy, and be l' forth with peace:
63:12 l' them by the right hand of Moses
13 That l' them through the deep, as
Jer 2: 6 that l' us through the wilderness,
17 God, when he l' thee by the way?
22:12 whither they have l' him captive,
23: 8 l' the seed of the house of Israel
La 3: 2 He hath l' me, and brought me
Eze17:12 and l' them with him to Babylon;
39:28 caused them to be l' into captivity
47: 2 and l' me about the way without
Am 2:10 and l' you forty years through the
7:11 Israel shall surely be l' away captive
Na 2: 7 Huzzab shall be l' away captive,
M't 4: 1 Then was Jesus l' up of the spirit
26:57 had laid hold on Jesus l' him away
27: 2 had bound him, they l' him away,
31 him, and l' him away to crucify him.
M'r 8:23 hand, and l' him out of the town;
14:53 And they l' Jesus away to the high
15:16 the soldiers l' him away into the hall,
20 him, and l' him out to crucify him.
Lu 4: 1 l' by the spirit into the wilderness,
29 and l' him unto the brow of the hill
21:24 be l' away captive into all nations:
22:54 Then they took him, and l' him, and
66 and l' him into their council,
23: 1 of them arose, and l' him unto Pilate.
26 as they l' him away, they laid hold
32 l' with him to be put to death.
24:50 he l' them out as far as to Bethany,
Joh 18:13 And l' him away to Annas first; for
28 Then l' they Jesus from Caiaphas
Joh 19:16 they took Jesus, and l' him away.
Ac 8:32 was l' as a sheep to the slaughter;
9: 8 l' him by the hand, and brought
21:37 Paul was to be l' into the castle,
22:11 being l' by the hand of them that
Ro 8:14 many as are l' by the Spirit of God,
1Co 12: 2 these dumb idols, even as ye were l'.
Ga 5:18 But if ye be l' of the Spirit, ye are not
Eph 4: 8 up on high, he l' captivity captive,
2Ti 3: 6 with sins, l' away with divers lusts,
2Pe 3:17 being l' away with the error of

leddest
2Sa 5: 2 wast he that l' out and broughtest
1Ch 11: 2 wast he that l' out and broughtest
Ne 9:12 l' them in the day by a cloudy
Ps 77:20 Thou l' thy people like a flock by
Ac 21:38 and l' out into the wilderness four

ledges
1Ki 7:28 the borders were between the l':
29 the borders that were between the l'
29 upon the l' there was a base above:
35 the top of the base the l' thereof
36 on the plates of the l' thereof, and

leeks
Nu 11: 5 and the l', and the onions, and the

lees
Isa 25: 6 things, a feast of wines on the l',
6 of wines on the l' well refined.
Jer 48:11 hath settled on his l', and hath not
Zep 1:12 the men that are settled on their l':

left See also LEFTEST; LEFTHANDED.
Ge 11: 8 and they l' off to build the city.
13: 9 if thou wilt take the l' hand, then
9 right hand, then I will go to the l'.
14:15 is on the l' hand of Damascus.
17:22 And he l' off talking with him,
18:33 had l' communing with Abraham:
24:27 hath not l' destitute my master of
49 turn to the right hand, or to the l'.
29:35 his name Judah; and l' bearing.
30: 9 Leah saw that she had l' bearing,
32: 8 company which is l' shall escape.
24 And Jacob was l' alone; and there
39: 6 l' all that he had in Joseph's hand;
12 he l' his garment in her hand, and
13 she saw that he had l' his garment
15 that he l' his garment with me, and
18 l' his garment with me, and fled
41:49 very much, until he l' numbering;
42:38 brother is dead, and he is l' alone:
44:12 the eldest, and l' at the youngest:
20 brother is dead, and he alone is l'
47:18 is not ought l' in the sight of my
48:13 right hand toward Israel's l' hand,
13 Manasseh in his l' hand toward
14 his l' hand upon Manasseh's head,
50: 8 they l' in the land of Goshen.
Ex 2:20 why is it that ye have l' the man?
9:21 l' his servants and his cattle in the
10:12 land, even all that the hail hath l'.
15 of the trees which the hail had l':
26 shall not an hoof be l' behind;
14:22, 29 right hand, and on their l'.
16:20 of them l' of it until the morning,
34:25 passover be l' until the morning.
Le 2:10 which is l' of the meat offering
10:12 unto Ithamar, his sons that were l',
16 sons of Aaron which were l' alive,
14:15 into the palm of his own l' hand:
16 into the oil that is in his l' hand,
26 into the palm of his own l' hand:
27 some of the oil that is in his l' hand
26:36 upon them that are l' alive of you
39 they that are l' of you shall pine
43 The land also shall be l' of them,
Nu 20:17 to the right hand nor to the l',
21:35 until there was none l' him alive:
22:26 to the right hand or to the l'.
26:65 there was not l' a man of them,
De 2:27 unto the right hand nor to the l'.
34 every city, we l' none to remain:
3: 3 until none was l' to him remaining.
4:27 shall be l' few in number among
5:32 aside to the right hand or to the l'.
7:20 among them, until they that are l',
17:11 to the right hand, nor to the l'.
20 to the right hand, or to the l':
28:14 day, to the right hand, or to the l',
55 hath nothing l' him in the siege,
62 And ye shall be l' few in number,
32:36 and there is none shut up, or l'.
Jos 1: 7 it to the right hand or to the l',
6:23 l' them without the camp of
8:17 there was not a man l' in Ai or
17 l' the city open, and pursued after
10:33 until he had l' him none remaining.
37 he l' none remaining, according to
39 therein; he l' none remaining:
40 he l' none remaining, but utterly
11: 8 until they l' them none remaining.
11 there was not any l' to breathe:
14 neither l' they any to breathe.
15 l' nothing undone of all that the
22 There was none of the Anakims l'
19:27 goeth out to Cabul on the l' hand,
22: 3 not l' your brethren these many
23: 6 to the right hand or to the l';
J'g 2:21 of the nations which Joshua l'
23 the Lord l' those nations, without
3: 1 are the nations which the Lord l',
21 And Ehud put forth his l' hand,
4:16 sword; and there was not a man l'.
6: 4 and l' no sustenance for Israel,
7:20 held the lamps in their l' hands,

J'g 8:10 l' of all the hosts of the children
9: 5 youngest son of Jerubbaal was l';
16:29 hand, and of the other with his l'.
Ru 1: 3 and she was l', and her two sons.
5 woman was l' of her two sons and
18 then she l' speaking unto her.
2:11 hast l' thy father and thy mother,
14 did eat, and was sufficed, and l'.
20 not l' off his kindness to the living
4:14 hath not l' thee this day without a
1Sa 2:36 every one that is l' in thine house
5: 4 the stump of Dagon was l' to him.
6:12 aside to the right hand or to the l';
9:24 said, Behold that which is l'!
10: 2 father hath l' the care of the asses,
11:11 two of them were not l' together.
17:20 and l' the sheep with a keeper,
22 David l' his carriage in the hand of
28 whom hast thou l' those few sheep
25:34 had not been l' unto Nabal by the
27: 9 l' neither man nor woman alive.
30: 9 those that were l' behind stayed.
13 my master l' me, because three
2Sa 2:19 nor to the l' from following Abner.
21 aside to thy right hand or to thy l',
5:21 And there they l' their images,
9: 1 any that is l' of the house of Saul,
13:30 and there is not one of them l'.
14: 7 shall quench my coal which is l',
19 turn to the right hand or to the l'
15:16 the king l' ten women, which were
16: 6 on his right hand and on his l'.
21 he hath l' to keep the house;
17:12 shall not be l' so much as one.
20: 3 whom he had l' to keep the house,
1Ki 7:21 he set up the l' pillar, and called
39 five on the l' side of the house:
47 And Solomon l' all the vessels
49 the right side, and five on the l',
9:20 all the people that were l' of the
21 that were l' after them in the land,
14:10 him that is shut up and l' in Israel,
15:18 gold that were l' in the treasures
21 that he l' off building of Ramah,
29 he l' not to Jeroboam any that
16:11 he l' him not one that pisseth
17:17 that there was no breath l' in him.
19: 3 Judah, and l' his servant there.
10, 14 and I, even I only, am l'; and
18 Yet I have l' me seven thousand
20 And he l' the oxen, and ran after
20:30 thousand of the men that were l'.
21:21 him that is shut up and l' in Israel,
22:19 on his right hand and on his l'.
2Ki 3:25 in Kir-haraseth l' they the stones
4:44 and l' thereof, according to the
7: 7 in the twilight, and l' their tents,
13 remain, which are l' in the city,
13 multitude of Israel that are l' in it:
8: 6 since the day that she l' the land,
9: 8 him that is shut up and l' in Israel:
10:11 until he l' him none remaining.
14 men; neither l' he any of them.
21 was not a man l' that came not.
11:11 to the l' corner of the temple,
14:26 was not any shut up, nor any l',
17:16 l' all the commandments of the
18 none l' but the tribe of Judah only.
19: 4 prayer for the remnant that are l'.
20:17 into Babylon: nothing shall be l',
22: 2 aside to the right hand or to the l'.
23: 8 were on a man's l' hand at the gate
25:11 the people that were l' in the city,
12 captain of the guard l' of the poor
22 king of Babylon had l', even over
1Ch 6:44 sons of Merari stood on the l' hand:
61 were l' of the family of that tribe,
12: 2 hand and the l' in hurling stones
13: 2 that are l' in all the land of Israel,
14:12 when they had l' their gods there,
16:37 he l' there before the ark of the
2Ch 3:17 hand, and the other on the l';
17 the name of that on the l' Boaz.
4: 6 the right hand, and five on the l',
7 the right hand, and five on the l'.
8 on the right side, and five on the l'.
8: 7 people that were l' of the Hittites,
8 who were l' after them in the land,
11:14 the Levites l' their suburbs and
12: 5 also l' you in the hand of Shishak.
16: 5 that he l' off building of Ramah,
18:18 on his right hand and on his l'.
21:17 that there was never a son l' him,
23:10 temple to the l' side of the temple,
24:18 they l' the house of the Lord God
25 for they l' him in great diseases,)
25:12 And other ten thousand l' alive did the
28:14 armed men l' the captives and the
31:10 enough to eat, and have l' plenty:
10 that which is l' is this great store.
32:31 God l' him, to try him, that he
34: 2 to the right hand, nor to the l'.
21 that are l' in Israel and in Judah,
Ne 1: 2 which were l' of the captivity,
3 remnant that are l' of the captivity
6: 1 there was no breach l' therein;
8: 4 his l' hand, Pedaiah and Mishael,
Job 20:21 There shall none of his meat be l';
26 it shall go ill with him that is l' in
23: 9 On the l' hand, where he doth
32:15 no more: they l' off speaking.
Ps 36: 3 he hath l' off to be wise, and to do
106:11 there was not one of them l'.
Pr 3:16 in her l' hand riches and honour.
4:27 not to the right hand nor to the l':
29:15 a child l' to himself bringeth his

Ec 10: 2 hand; but a fool's heart at his l'.
Ca 2: 6 His l' hand is under my head, and
8: 3 His l' hand should be under my
Isa 1: 8 daughter of Zion is l' as a cottage
9 the Lord of hosts had l' unto us
4: 3 to pass, that he that is l' in Zion,
7:22 every one eat that is l' in the land.
9:20 and he shall eat on the l' hand,
10:14 as one gathereth eggs that are l',
11:11, 16, his people, which shall be l',
17: 6 Yet gleaning grapes shall be l' in it,
9 they l' because of the children of
18: 6 They shall be l' together unto the
24: 6 earth are burned, and few men l'.
12 In the city is l' desolation, and the
27:10 forsaken, and l' like a wilderness:
30:17 be l' as a beacon upon the top of a
21 hand, and when ye turn to the l'.
32:14 multitude of the city shall be l';
37: 4 prayer for the remnant that is l'.
39: 6 to Babylon: nothing shall be l'.
49:21 I was l' alone; these, where had
54: 3 on the right hand and on the l';
Jer 12: 7 house, I have l' mine heritage;
21: 7 are l' this city from the pestilence,
27:18 vessels which are l' in the house
31: 2 people which were l' of the sword
34: 7 all the cities of Judah that were l'.
38:22 women that are l' in the king of
27 they l' off speaking with him; for
39:10 captain of the guard l' of the poor
40: 6 the people that were l' in the land.
11 had l' a remnant of Judah, and
42: 2 (for we are l' but a few of many, as
43: 6 captain of the guard had l' with
44:18 l' off to burn incense to the queen
49:25 How is the city of praise not l', the
50:26 utterly: let nothing of her be l'.
52:16 captain of the guard l' certain of
Eze 1:10 the face of an ox on the l' side;
4: 4 Lie thou also upon thy l' side, and
9: 8 were slaying them, and I was l',
14:22 therein shall be l' a remnant that
16:46 daughters that dwell at thy l' hand:
21:16 on the right hand or on the l',
23: 8 Neither l' she her whoredoms
24:21 your daughters whom ye have l'
31:12 have cut him off, and have l' him:
12 from his shadow, and have l' him.
36:36 heathen that are l' round about
39: 3 smite thy bow out of thy l' hand,
28 l' none of them any more there.
41: 9 that which was l' was the place of
11 were toward the place that was l',
11 place that was l' was five cubits
48:15 that are l' in the breadth over
Da 2:44 kingdom shall not be l' to other
10: 8 I was l' alone, and saw this great
17 me, neither is there breath l' in me.
12: 7 hand and his l' hand unto heaven,
Ho 4:10 l' off to take heed to the Lord.
9:12 them, that there shall not be a man l':
Joe 1: 4 which the palmerworm hath l'
4 that which the locust hath l' hath
4 that which the cankerworm hath l'
Jon 4:11 their right hand and their l' hand;
Hag 2: 3 Who is l' among you that saw this
Zec 4: 3 the other upon the l' side thereof.
11 and upon the l' side thereof?
12: 6 on the right hand and on the l':
13: 8 but the third shall be l' therein.
14:16 one that is l' of all the nations
M't 4:20 they straightway l' their nets, and
22 they immediately l' the ship and
6: 3 let not thy l' hand know what thy
8: 15 her hand, and the fever l' her:
15:37 broken meat that was l' seven
16: 4 And he l' them, and departed.
20:21 the other on the l', in thy kingdom.
23 sit on my right hand, and on my l',
21:17 he l' them, and went out of the
22:22 and l' him, and went their way.
25 issue, l' his wife unto his brother:
23:38 your house is l' unto you desolate.
24: 2 shall not be l' here one stone upon
40, 41 shall be taken, and the other l'.
25:33 right hand, but the goats on the l'.
41 say also unto them on the l' hand,
26:44 he l' them, and went away again,
27:38 right hand, and another on the l'.
M'r 1: 20 and they l' their father Zebedee in
31 and immediately the fever l' her,
8: 8 meat that was l' seven baskets.
13 he l' them, and entering into the
10:28 we have l' all, and have followed
29 There is no man that hath l' house,
37 the other on thy l' hand, in thy
40 on my l' hand is not mine to give;
12:12 they l' him, and went their way.
20 took a wife, and dying l' no seed.
21 her, and died, neither l' he any seed:
22 the seven had her, and l' no seed:
13: 2 there shall not be l' one stone upon
34 a far journey, who l' his house,
14:52 he l' the linen cloth, and fled from
15:27 right hand, and the other on his l'.
Lu 4:39 rebuked the fever; and it l' her:
5: 4 when he had l' speaking, he said
28 And he l' all, rose up, and followed
10:40 my sister hath l' me to serve alone?
13:35 your house is l' unto you desolate:
17:34 be taken, and the other shall be l'.
35 shall be taken, and the other l'.
36 shall be taken, and the other l'.
18:28 Peter said, Lo, we have l' all, and
29 There is no man that hath l' house,

Lu 20:31 seven also: and they l' no children,
21: 6 not be l' one stone upon another,
23:33 right hand, and the other on the l'.
Joh 4: 3 He l' Judæa, and departed again
28 woman then l' her waterpot, and
52 at the seventh hour the fever l' him.
8: 9 Jesus was l' alone, and the woman
29 the Father hath not l' me alone;
Ac 2:31 his soul was not l' in hell, neither
14:17 he l' not himself without witness,
18:19 to Ephesus, and l' them there:
21: 3 we had discovered Cyprus, we l' it
3 it on the l' hand, and sailed into
32 soldiers, they l' beating of Paul.
23:32 l' the horsemen to go with him,
24:27 Jews a pleasure, l' Paul bound.
25:14 certain man l' in bonds by Felix:
Ro 9:29 Lord of Sabaoth had l' us a seed,
11: 3 and I am l' alone, and they seek
2Co 6: 7 on the right hand and on the l',
1Th 3: 1 thought it good to be l' at Athens
2Ti 4:13 cloke that I l' at Troas with Carpus,
20 Trophimus have I l' at Miletum sick.
Tit 1: 5 For this cause l' I thee in Crete,
Heb 2: 8 l' nothing that is not put under him.
4: 1 a promise being l' us of entering
Jude 6 estate, but l' their own habitation,
Re 2: 4 because thou hast l' thy first love.
10: 2 sea, and his l' foot on the earth.

leftest
Ne 9:28 therefore l' thou them in the hand

left-foot See LEFT and FOOT.

left-hand See LEFT and HAND; also LEFTHANDED.

lefthanded
J'g 3:15 a Benjamite, a man l':
20:16 hundred chosen men l';

left-side See LEFT and SIDE.

leg See also LEGS.
Isa 47: 2 make bare the l', uncover the

legion See also LEGIONS.
M'r 5: 9 My name is L': for we are many.
15 with the devil, and had the l',
Lu 8:30 What is thy name? And he said, L':

legions
M't 26:53 me more than twelve l' of angels?

legs
Ex 12: 9 his head with his l', and with the
29:17 wash the inwards of him, and his l',
Le 1: 9 inwards and his l' shall he wash in
13 he shall wash the inwards and the l'
4:11 flesh, with his head, and with his l'
8:21 he washed the inwards and the l'
9:14 he did wash the inwards and the l',
11:21 which have l' above their feet, to
De 28:35 thee in the knees, and in the l',
1Sa 17: 6 had greaves of brass upon his l',
Ps 147:10 not pleasure in the l' of a man.
Pr 26: 7 The l' of the lame are not equal: so
Ca 5:15 His l' are as pillars of marble, set
Isa 3:20 the ornaments of the l', and the
Da 2:33 His l' of iron, his feet part of iron
Am 3:12 out of the mouth of the lion two l',
Joh 19:31 that their l' might be broken, and
32 and brake the l' of the first, and of
33 dead already, they brake not his l':

Lehabim (*le'-ha-bim*)
Ge 10:13 Ludim, and Anamim, and L', and
1Ch 1:11 begat Ludim, and Anamim, and L',

Lehem See BETH-LEHEM; JESHUBI-LEHEM.

Lehi (*le'-hi*) See also RAMATH-LEHI.
J'g 15: 9 and spread themselves in L'.
14 And when he came unto L', the
19 which is in L' unto this day.

leisure
M'r 6:31 they had no l' so much as to eat.

Lemuel (*lem'-u-el*)
Pr 31: 1 words of king L', the prophecy
4 O L', it is not for kings to drink

lend See also LENDETH; LENT.
Ex 22:25 thou l' money to any of my people
Le 25:37 l' him thy victuals for increase.
De 15: 6 thou shalt l' unto many nations,
8 shalt surely l' him sufficient for his
23:19 Thou shalt not l' upon usury to
20 thou mayest l' upon usury;
20 thou shalt not l' upon usury:
24:10 When thou dost l' thy brother any
11 the man to whom thou dost l' shall
28:12 thou shalt l' unto many nations,
44 l' to thee, and thou shalt not l' to
Lu 6:34 if ye l' to them of whom ye hope to
34 sinners also l' to sinners, to receive
35 and l', hoping for nothing again;
11: 5 him, Friend, l' me three loaves;

lender
Pr 22: 7 the borrower is servant to the l'.
Isa 24: 2 as with the l', so with the borrower;

lendeth
De 15: 2 Every creditor that l' ought unto
Ps 37:26 He is ever merciful, and l'; and
112: 5 good man sheweth favour, and l':
Pr 19:17 pity upon the poor l' unto the Lord;

length
Ge 6:15 l' of the ark shall be three hundred
13:17 walk through the land in the l' of it
Ex 25:10, 17 cubits and a half shall be the l'
23 two cubits shall be the l' thereof,
26: 2 The l' of one curtain shall be eight
8 The l' of one curtain shall be thirty

Ex 26:13 remaineth in the l' of the curtains
16 Ten cubits shall be the l' of a board,
27:11 side in l' there shall be hangings
18 l' of the court shall be an hundred
28:16 a span shall be the l' thereof, and a
30: 2 A cubit shall be the l' thereof, and a
36: 9 The l' of one curtain was twenty
15 The l' of one curtain was thirty
21 The l' of a board was ten cubits, and
37: 1 two cubits and a half was the l' of it,
6 cubits and a half was the l' thereof,
10 two cubits was the l' thereof, and a
25 the l' of it was a cubit, and the
38: 1 five cubits was the l' thereof, and
18 and twenty cubits was the l', and the
39: 9 a span was the l' thereof, and a span
De 3:11 nine cubits was the l' thereof, and
30:20 he is thy life, and the l' of thy days:
J'g 3:16 which had two edges, of a cubit l';
1Ki 6: 2 the l' thereof was threescore cubits,
3 twenty cubits was the l' thereof,
20 the forepart was twenty cubits in l',
7: 2 the l' thereof was an hundred cubits,
6 the l' thereof was fifty cubits, and
27 four cubits was the l' of one base,
2Ch 3: 3 l' by cubits after the first measure
4 l' of it was according to the breadth
8 the l' thereof was according to the
4: 1 of brass, twenty cubits the l' thereof,
Job 12:12 and in l' of days understanding.
Ps 21: 4 even l' of days for ever and ever.
Pr 3: 2 For l' of days, and long life, and
16 L' of days is in her right hand; and
29:21 have him become his son at the l'.
Eze 31: 7 greatness, in the l' of his branches:
40:11 the l' of the gate, thirteen cubits.
18 over against the l' of the gates was
20 he measured the l' thereof, and the
21 the l' thereof was fifty cubits, and
25 windows: the l' was fifty cubits,
36 the l' was fifty cubits, and the
49 l' of the porch was twenty cubits,
41: 2 measured the l' thereof, forty cubits:
4 So he measured the l' thereof,
12 and the l' thereof ninety cubits.
15 he measured the l' of the building
22 high, and the l' thereof two cubits;
22 the l' thereof, and the walls thereof,
42: 2 the l' of an hundred cubits was the
7 the l' thereof was fifty cubits.
8 the l' of the chambers that were in
45: 1 the l' shall be the l' of five and
2 for the sanctuary five hundred in l',
3 measure shalt thou measure the l'
5 the five and twenty thousand of l',
7 the l' shall be over against one of
48: 8 and in l' as one of the other parts,
9 be of five and twenty thousand in l',
10 north five and twenty thousand in l',
10 south five and twenty thousand in l',
13 have five and twenty thousand in l',
13 l' shall be five and twenty thousand,
18 the residue in l' over against the
Zec 2: 2 thereof, and what is the l' thereof.
5: 2 the l' thereof is twenty cubits, and
Ro 1:10 at l' I might have a prosperous
Eph 3:18 what is the breadth, and l', and
Re 21:16 the l' is as large as the breadth:
16 l' and the breadth and the height

lengthen See also LENGTHENED; LENGTHENING.
1Ki 3:14 did walk then will I l' thy days.
Isa 54: 2 l' thy cords, and strengthen thy

lengthened
De 25:15 that thy days may be l' in the land

lengthening
Da 4:27 if it may be a l' of thy tranquillity.

lent
Ex 12:36 l' unto them such things as they
De 23:19 of any thing that is l' upon usury:
1Sa 1:28 also I have l' him to the Lord;
28 he liveth he shall be l' to the Lord.
2:20 the loan which is l' to the Lord.
Jer 15:10 I have neither l' on usury, nor
10 nor men have l' to me on usury;

lentiles
Ge 25:34 gave Esau bread and pottage of l';
2Sa 17:28 parched corn, and beans, and l',
23:11 was a piece of ground full of l':
Eze 4: 9 and beans, and l', and millet, and

leopard See also LEOPARDS.
Isa 11: 6 the l' shall lie down with the kid;
Jer 5: 6 a l' shall watch over their cities:
13:23 change his skin, or the l' his spots?
Da 7: 6 I beheld, and lo another, like a l',
Ho 13: 7 as a l' by the way will I observe
Re 13: 2 which I saw was like unto a l',

leopards
Ca 4: 8 from the mountains of the l'.
Hab 1: 8 horses also are swifter than the l',

leper See also LEPERS.
Le 13:45 And the l' in whom the plague is,
14: 2 this shall be the law of the l' in
3 plague of leprosy be healed in the l';
22: 4 soever of the seed of Aaron is a l',
Nu 5: 2 they put out of the camp every l',
2Sa 3:29 that hath an issue, or that is a l',
2Ki 5: 1 man in valour, but he was a l'.
11 over the place, and recover the l'.
27 he went out from his presence a l'
15: 5 was a l' unto the day of his death.
2Ch 26:21 Uzziah the king was a l' unto the
21 dwelt in a several house, being a l';
2Ch 26:23 the kings: for they said, He is a l':
M't 8: 2 there came a l' and worshipped
26: 6 in the house of Simon the l',
M'r 1:40 there came a l' to him, beseeching
14: 3 in the house of Simon the l', as he

lepers
2Ki 7: 8 l' came to the uttermost part of
M't 10: 8 sick, cleanse the l', raise the dead,
11: 5 the l' are cleansed, and the deaf
Lu 4:27 And many l' were in Israel in the
7:22 the l' are cleansed, the deaf hear,
17:12 there met him ten men that were l',

leprosy
Le 13: 2 of his flesh like the plague of l';
3 skin of his flesh, it is a plague of l':
8 pronounce him unclean: it is a l'.
9 When the plague of l' is in a man,
11 is an old l' in the skin of his flesh,
12 if a l' break out abroad in the skin,
12 and the l' cover all the skin of him
13 if the l' have covered all his flesh,
15 the raw flesh is unclean: it is a l'.
20 plague of l' broken out of the boil.
25 it is a l' broken out of the burning:
25, 27 unclean: it is the plague of l'.
30 even a l' upon the head or beard.
42 it is a l' sprung up in his bald head,
43 as the l' appeareth in the skin of the
47 garment...that the plague of l' is in,
49 a plague of l', and shall be shewed
51 plague is a fretting l'; it is unclean.
52 for it is a fretting l'; it shall be burnt
59 This is the law of the plague of l'
14: 3 plague of l' be healed in the leper;
7 him that is to be cleansed from l'
32 of him in whom is the plague of l',
34 I put the plague of l' in a house of
44 it is a fretting l' in the house: it is
54 law for all manner of plague of l',
55 And for the l' of a garment, and of
57 when it is clean: this is the law of l'.
De 24: 8 Take heed in the plague of l', that
2Ki 5: 3 for he would recover him of his l'.
6 thou mayest recover him of his l'.
7 unto me to recover a man of his l'?
27 The l' therefore of Naaman shall
2Ch 26:19 the l' even rose up in his forehead
M't 8: 3 immediately his l' was cleansed.
M'r 1:42 immediately the l' departed from
Lu 5:12 certain city, behold a man full of l':
13 immediately the l' departed from

leprous
Ex 4: 6 behold, his hand was l' as snow.
Le 13:44 He is a l' man, he is unclean:
Nu 12:10 Miriam became l', white as snow:
10 Miriam, and, behold, she was l'.
2Ki 7: 3 were four l' men at the entering in
2Ch 26:20 behold, he was l' in his forehead,

Leshem (*le'-shem*) See also LAISH.
Jos 19:47 Dan went up to fight against L',
47 dwelt therein, and called L', Dan,

less^ See also BLAMELESS; BOTTOMLESS; CAUSELESS; CHILDLESS; COMFORTLESS; DOUBTLESS; ENDLESS; FAITHLESS; FATHERLESS; FAULTLESS; HARMLESS; LAWLESS; LESSER; NEVERTHELESS; SHAMELESSLY; SPEECHLESS; UNLESS.
Ex 16:17 and gathered, some more, some l'.
30:15 the poor shall not give l' than half
Nu 22:18 the Lord my God, to do l' or more.
26:54 thou shalt give the l' inheritance:
33:54 ye shall give the l' inheritance:
1Sa 22:15 nothing of all this, l' or more.
25:36 she told him nothing, l' or more,
1Ki 8:27 how much l' this house that I have
2Ch 6:18 how much l' this house which I have
32:15 how much l' shall your God deliver
Ezr 9:13 punished us l' than our iniquities
Job 4:19 How much l' in them that dwell in
9:14 How much l' shall I answer him, and
11: 6 exacteth of thee l' than thine iniquity
25: 6 How much l' man, that is a worm?
Pr 17: 7 a fool: much l' do lying lips a prince.
19:10 much l' for a servant to have rule over
Isa 40:17 are counted to him l' than nothing,
M'r 4:31 l' than all the seeds that be in the
15:40 Mary the mother of James the l'
1Co 12:23 which we think to be l' honourable,
2Co 12:15 I love you, the l' I be loved.
Eph 3: 8 am l' than the least of all saints,
Ph'p 2:28 and that I may be the l' sorrowful.
Heb 7: 7 the l' is blessed of the better.

lesser
Ge 1:16 and the l' light to rule the night:
Isa 7:25 and for the treading of l' cattle.
Eze 43:14 and from the l' settle even to the

lest^
Ge 3: 3 neither shall ye touch it, l' ye die.
22 l' he put forth his hand, and take
4:15 l' any finding him should kill him.
11: 4 l' we be scattered abroad upon the
14:23 l' thou shouldest say, I have made
19:15 l' thou be consumed in the
17 mountain, l' thou be consumed.
19 l' some evil take me, and I die.
26: 7 l', said he, the men of the place
9 Because I said, L' I die for her.
32:11 him, l' he will come and smite me,
38: 9 l' that he should give seed to his
11 L' peradventure he die also, as his
23 her take it to her, l' we be shamed:
42: 4 L' peradventure mischief befall
44:34 l' peradventure I see the evil that
Ge 45:11 l' thou, and thy household, and all
Ex 1:10 l' they multiply, and it come to pass,
5: 3 l' he fall upon us with pestilence,
13:17 L' peradventure the people repent
19:21 l' they break through unto the Lord
22 l' the Lord break forth upon them.
24 Lord, l' he break forth upon them.
20:19 let not God speak with us, l' we die.
23:29 l' the land become desolate, and the
33 l' they make thee sin against me:
33: 3 l' I consume thee in the way.
34:12 l' thou make a covenant with the
12 l' it be for a snare in the midst of
15 L' thou make a covenant with the
Le 10: 6 neither rend your clothes; l' ye
6 l' wrath come upon all the people.
7 of the congregation, l' ye die:
9 of the congregation, l' ye die:
19:29 l' the land fall to whoredom, and
22: 9 l' they bear sin for it, and die
Nu 4:15 not touch any holy thing, l' they die.
20 the holy things are covered, l' they die.
16:26 l' ye be consumed in all their sins.
34 L' the earth swallow us up also.
18:22 congregation, l' they bear sin, and die.
32 of the children of Israel, l' ye die.
De 4: 9 l' thou forget the things which
9 l' they depart from thy heart all the
16 L' ye corrupt yourselves, and make
19 And l' thou lift up thine eyes unto
23 l' ye forget the covenant of the Lord
6:12 Then beware l' thou forget the Lord,
15 l' the anger of the Lord thy God be
7:22 l' the beasts of the field increase
25 unto thee, l' thou be snared therein.
26 l' thou be a cursed thing like it:
8:12 L' when thou hast eaten and art
9:28 L' the land whence thou broughtest
11:17 l' ye perish quickly from off the good
19: 6 L' the avenger of the blood pursue
20: 5, 6, 7 l' he die in the battle, and
8 l' his brethren's heart faint as well
22: 9 l' the fruit of thy seed which thou
24:15 l' he cry against thee unto the Lord,
25: 3 l', if he should exceed, and beat,
29:18 L' there should be among you man,
18 l' there should be among you a root
32:27 l' their adversaries should behave
27 and l' they should say, Our hand is
Jos 2:16 l' the pursuers meet you;
6:18 l' ye make yourselves accursed,
9:20 let them live, l' wrath be upon us,
24:27 unto you, l' ye deny your God.
J'g 7: 2 l' Israel vaunt themselves against
14:15 l' we burn thee and thy father's
18:25 l' angry fellows run upon thee, and
Ru 4: 6 l' I mar mine own inheritance:
1Sa 9: 5 l' my father leave caring for the
13:19 L' the Hebrews make them swords
15: 6 l' I destroy you with them: for ye
20: 3 know this, l' he be grieved:
27:11 L' they should tell on us, saying,
29: 4 l' in the battle he be an adversary
31: 4 l' these uncircumcised come and
2Sa 1:20 l' the daughters of the Philistines
20 rejoice, l' the daughters of the
12:28 l' I take the city, and it be called
13:25 go, l' we be chargeable unto thee.
14:11 any more, l' they destroy my son.
15:14 depart, l' he overtake us suddenly,
17:16 l' the king be swallowed up, and all
20: 6 l' he get him fenced cities, and
2Ki 2:16 l' peradventure the Spirit of the
1Ch 10: 4 l' these uncircumcised come and
Job 32:13 L' ye should say, We have found
34:30 reign not, l' the people be ensnared.
36:18 beware l' he take thee away with
42: 8 l' I deal with you after your folly,
Ps 2:12 Kiss the Son, l' he be angry, and
7: 2 L' he tear my soul like a lion,
13: 3 eyes, l' I sleep the sleep of death;
4 L' mine enemy say, I have prevailed
28: 1 l', if thou be silent to me, I become
32: 9 l' they come near unto thee.
38:16 l' otherwise they should rejoice
50:22 l' I tear you in pieces, and there be
59:11 Slay them not, l' my people forget:
106:23 his wrath, l' he should destroy them.
125: 3 l' the righteous put forth
140: 8 device; l' they exalt themselves.
143: 7 l' I be like unto them that go down
Pr 5: 6 L' thou shouldest ponder the
9 L' thou give thine honour unto
10 L' strangers be filled with thy
9: 8 not a scorner, l' he hate thee:
20:13 not sleep, l' thou come to poverty;
22:25 L' thou learn his ways, and get a
24:18 L' the Lord see it, and it displease
25: 8 l' thou know not what to do in the
10 L' he that heareth it put thee to
16 l' thou be filled therewith, and
17 l' he be weary of thee, and so hate
26: 4 folly, l' thou also be like unto him.
5 l' he be wise in his own conceit.
30: 6 l' he reprove thee, and thou be
9 L' I be full, and deny thee, and say,
10 l' he curse thee, and thou be found
31: 5 L' they drink, and forget the law,
Ec 7:21 l' thou hear thy servant curse
Isa 6:10 l' they see with their eyes, and
27: 3 l' any hurt it, I will keep it night
28:22 l' your bands be made strong: for
36:18 Beware l' Hezekiah persuade you,
48: 5 l' thou shouldest say, Mine idol
7 l' thou shouldest say, Behold, I
Jer 1:17 l' I confound thee before them.

Jer 4: 4 l' my fury come forth like fire, and
6: 8 l' my soul depart from thee;
8 l' I make thee desolate, a land not
10: 24 anger, l' thou bring me to nothing.
21: 12 l' my fury go out like fire, and burn
37: 20 Jonathan the scribe, l' I die there.
38: 19 l' they deliver me into their hand,
51: 46 And l' your heart faint, and ye fear
Ho 2: 3 L' I strip her naked, and set her as
Am 5: 6 l' he break out like fire in the house
Zec 7: 12 l' they should hear the law, and the
Mal 4: 6 l' I come and smite the earth with
M't 4: 6 l' at any time thou dash thy foot
5: 25 l' at any time the adversary deliver
7: 6 l' they trample them under their
13: 15 l' at any time they should see with
29 l' while ye gather up the tares, ye
15: 32 fasting, l' they faint in the way.
17: 27 l' we should offend them, go
25: 9 l' there be not enough for us and
26: 5 l' there be an uproar among
27: 64 l' his disciples come by night, and
M'r 3: 9 l' they should throng him.
4: 12 l'...time they should be converted,
13: 5 Take heed l' any man deceive you:
36 L' coming suddenly he find you
14: 2 l' there be an uproar of the people.
38 l' ye enter into temptation.
Lu 4: 11 l' at any time thou dash thy foot
8: 12 l' they should believe and be
12: 58 him; l' he hale thee to the judge,
14: 8 l' a more honourable man than
12 l' they also bid thee again, and a
29 L' haply, after he hath
16: 28 l' they also come into this
18: 5 l' by her continual coming she
21: 34 l' at any time your hearts be
22: 46 l' ye enter into temptation.
Joh 3: 20 l' his deeds should be reproved.
5: 14 l' a worse thing come unto thee.
12: 35 l' darkness come upon you:
42 l' they should be put out of the
18: 28 hall, l' they should be defiled;
Ac 5: 26 l' they should have been stoned.
39 l' haply ye be found even to fight
13: 40 therefore, l' that come upon you,
23: 10 fearing l' Paul should have been
27: 17 fearing l' they should fall into the
29 fearing l' we should have fallen
42 l' any of them should swim out,
28: 27 l' they should see with their eyes,
Ro 11: 21 take heed l' he also spare not thee.
25 l' ye should be wise in your
15: 20 l' I should build upon another
1Co 1: 15 L' any should say that I had
17 l' the cross of Christ should be
8: 9 heed l' by any means this liberty
13 l' I make my brother to offend.
9: 12 l' we should hinder the gospel
27 l' that by any means, when I have
10: 12 he standeth take heed l' he fall.
2Co 2: 3 l', when I came, I should have
7 l' perhaps such a one should be
11 L' Satan should get an
4: 4 l' the light of the glorious
9: 3 l' our boasting of you should
4 L' haply if they of Macedonia
11: 3 l' by any means, as the serpent
12: 6 l' any man should think of me
7 l' I should be...above measure,
7 l' I should be...above measure.
20 For I fear, l', when I come, I shall
20 l' there be debates, envyings,
21 l', when I come again, my God
13: 10 l' being present I should use
Ga 2: 2 l' by any means I should run, or
4: 11 l' I have bestowed upon you labour
6: 1 thyself, l' thou also be tempted.
12 only l' they should suffer
Eph 2: 9 l' any man should boast.
Ph'p 2: 27 l' I should have sorrow upon
Col 2: 4 l' any man should beguile
8 Beware l' any man spoil you
3: 21 l' they be discouraged.
1Th 3: 5 l' by some means the tempter have
1Ti 3: 6 l' being lifted up with pride
7 l' he fall into reproach and the
Heb 2: 1 l' at any time we should let them
3: 12 l' there be in any of you an evil
13 l' any of you be hardened
4: 1 fear, l', a promise being left us of
11 l' any man fall after the same
11: 28 l' he that destroyed the
12: 3 l' ye be wearied and faint in
13 l' that which is lame be
15 l' any man fail of the grace of God;
15 l' any root of bitterness springing
16 L' there be any fornicator, or
Jas 5: 9 l' ye be condemned: behold,
12 l' ye fall into condemnation.
2Pe 3: 17 beware l' ye also, being led
Re 16: 15 l' he walk naked, and they see

let^A See also LETTEST; LETTETH; LETTING.
Ge 1: 3 And God said, L' there be light: and
6 L' there be a firmament in the midst
9 L' the waters...the heaven be gathered
11 L' the earth bring forth grass, the
14 L' there be lights in the firmament of
14 l' them be for signs, and for seasons,
15 l' them be for lights in the firmament
20 L' the waters bring forth abundantly
22 seas, and l' fowl multiply in the earth.
24 L' the earth bring forth the living
26 L' us make man in our image, after
26 l' them have dominion over the fish
11: 3 to, l' us make brick, and burn them
Ge 11: 4 Go to, l' us build us a city and a tower,
4 and l' us make us a name, lest we be
7 Go to, l' us go down, and there
13: 8 L' there be no strife, I pray thee,
14: 24 Mamre; l' them take their portion.
18: 4 L' a little water, I pray you, be fetched,
30, 32 Oh l' not the Lord be angry, and I
19: 8 l' me, I pray you, bring them out unto
20 a little one: Oh, l' me escape thither,
32 l' us make our father drink wine,
34 l' us make him drink wine this night
21: 12 L' it not be grievous in thy sight
16 L' me not see the death of the child.
24: 14 And l' it come to pass, that the damsel
14 L' down thy pitcher, I pray thee,
14 l' the same be she that thou hast
17 L' me, I pray thee, drink a little
18 she hasted, and l' down her pitcher
44 l' the same be the woman whom the
45 unto her, L' me drink, I pray thee.
46 haste, and l' down her pitcher
51 and l' her be thy master's son's wife,
55 L' the damsel abide with us a few
60 l' thy seed possess the gate of those
26: 28 L' there be now an oath betwixt us,
28 and l' us make a covenant with thee;
27: 29 L' people serve thee, and nations bow
29 l' thy mother's sons bow down to thee:
31 L' my father arise, and eat of his son's
30: 26 whom I have served thee, and l' me go:
31: 32 thou findest thy gods, l' him not live:
35 L' it not displease my lord that I
44 l' us make a covenant, I and thou;
44 l' it be for a witness between me and
32: 26 L' me go, for the day breaketh.
26 I will not l' thee go, except thou
33: 12 L' us take our journey, and l' us go,
14 L' my lord, I pray thee, pass over
15 L' me now leave with thee some of
15 l' me find grace in the sight of my
34: 11 L' me find grace in your eyes, and
21 therefore l' them dwell in the land,
21 l' us take their daughters to us for
21 and l' us give them our daughters.
23 only l' us consent unto them, and they
35: 3 And l' us arise, and go up to Bethel;
37: 17 heard them say, L' us go to Dothan.
20 l' us slay him, and cast him into some
21 hands; and said, L' us not kill him.
27 and l' us sell him to the Ishmeelites,
27 and l' not our hand be upon him; for
38: 16 I pray thee, l' me come in unto thee;
23 L' her take it to her, lest we be
24 Bring her forth, and l' her be burnt.
41: 33 therefore l' Pharaoh look out a man
34 L' Pharaoh do this, and l' him appoint
35 l' them gather all the food of those
35 and l' them keep food in the cities.
42: 16 l' him fetch your brother, and ye shall
19 l' one of your brethren be bound in
43: 9 then l' me bear the blame forever.
44: 9 both l' him die, and we also will be
10 Now also l' it be according unto your
18 lord, l' thy servant, I pray thee, speak
18 l' not thine anger burn against thy
33 l' thy servant abide instead of the lad
33 and l' the lad go up with his brethren.
46: 30 Now l' me die, since I have seen thy
47: 4 l' thy servants dwell in the land of
6 in the land of Goshen l' them dwell:
25 l' us find grace in the sight of my
48: 16 l' my name be named on them, and the
16 l' them grow into a multitude in the
49: 21 Naphtali is a hind l' loose: he giveth
50: 5 Now therefore l' me go up, I pray thee,
Ex 1: 10 l' us deal wisely with them; lest they
3: 18 now l' us go, we beseech thee, three
19 king of Egypt will not l' you go,
20 and after that he will l' you go.
4: 18 L' me go, I pray thee, and return unto
21 that he shall not l' the people go.
23 L' my son go, that he may serve
23 and if thou refuse to l' him go,
26 So he l' him go: then she said: A
5: 1 L' my people go, that they may
2 obey his voice to l' Israel go?
2 Lord, neither will I l' Israel go.
3 l' us go, we pray thee, three days'
4 l' the people from their works?
7 l' them go and gather straw for
8 L' us go and sacrifice to our God.
9 L' there more work be laid upon the
9 and l' them not regard vain words.
17 L' us go and do sacrifice to the Lord.
6: 1 with a strong hand shall he l' them go,
11 he l' the children of Israel go out
7: 14 he refuseth to l' the people go.
16 L' my people go, that they may
8: 1 L' my people go, that they may
2 And if thou refuse to l' them go,
8 I will l' the people go, that they may
20 L' my people go, that they may
21 if thou wilt not l' my people go,
28 said, I will l' you go, that ye may
29 l' not Pharaoh deal deceitfully any
32 neither would he l' the people go.
9: 1 L' my people go, that they may
2 For if thou refuse to l' them go,
7 and he did not l' the people go.
8 l' Moses sprinkle it toward the heaven
13 L' my people go, that they may
17 that thou wilt not l' them go?
28 I will l' you go, and ye shall stay as
35 he l' the children of Israel go;
10: 3 l' my people go, that they may
4 if thou refuse to l' my people go,
Ex 10: 7 l' the men go, that they may serve
10 them, L' the Lord be so with you,
10 I will l' you go, and your little ones:
20 not l' the children of Israel go.
24 only l' your flocks and your herds be
24 l' your little ones also go with you.
27 and he would not l' them go.
11: 1 afterwards he will l' you go hence:
1 when he shall l' you go, he shall
2 l' every man borrow of his neighbour,
10 would not l' the children of Israel go
12: 4 l' him and his neighbour next...take it
10 shall l' nothing of it remain until the
48 Lord, l' all his males be circumcised,
48 then l' him come near and keep it;
13: 15 Pharaoh would hardly l' us go,
17 when Pharaoh had l' the people go,
14: 5 have l' Israel go from serving us?
12 L' us alone, that we may serve the
25 L' us flee from the face of Israel;
16: 19 L' no man leave of it till the morning.
29 l' no man go out of his place on the
17: 11 when he l' down his hand, Amalek
18: 22 l' them judge the people at all seasons:
27 Moses l' his father in law depart;
19: 10 morrow, and l' them wash their clothes,
22 And l' the priests also...sanctify
24 but l' not the priests and people break
20: 19 l' not God speak with us, lest we die.
21: 8 then shall he l' her be redeemed:
26 l' him go free for his eye's sake.
27 l' him go free for his tooth's sake.
22: 13 pieces, then l' him bring it for witness,
23: 11 thou shalt l' it rest and lie still;
13 neither l' it be heard out of thy mouth.
24: 14 matters to do, l' him come unto them.
25: 8 And l' them make me a sanctuary;
32: 10 Now therefore l' me alone, that
22 L' not the anger of my lord wax hot:
24 hath any gold, l' them break it off.
26 the Lord's side? l' him come unto me.
33: 12 l' me know whom thou wilt send
34: 3 neither l' any man be seen throughout
3 neither l' the flocks nor herds feed
9 Lord, l' my Lord, I pray thee, go among
35: 5 l' him bring it, an offering of the Lord;
36: 6 L' neither man nor woman make any
Le 1: 3 l' him offer a male without blemish:
4: 3 then l' him bring for his sin, which he
10: 6 but l' your brethren, the whole house
14: 7 shall l' the living bird loose into
53 l' go the living bird out of the city
16: 10 to l' him go for a scapegoat into the
22 l' go the goat in the wilderness.
26 l' go the goat for the scapegoat
18: 21 shalt not l' any of thy seed pass
19: 19 not l' thy cattle gender with a diverse
21: 17 l' him not approach to offer the bread
24: 14 l' all that heard him lay their hands
14 and l' all the congregation stone him.
25: 27 Then l' him count the years of the sale
Nu 5: 8 l' the trespass be recompensed unto
6: 5 shall l' the locks...of his head grow,
8: 7 them, and l' them shave all their flesh,
7 and l' them wash their clothes, and so
8 Then l' them take a young bullock
9: 2 L' the children of Israel also keep the
10: 35 and l' thine enemies be scattered;
35 l' them that hate thee flee before thee.
11: 15 and l' me not see my wretchedness.
31 l' them fall by the camp, as it were
12: 12 L' her not be as one dead, of whom
14 l' her be shut out from the camp seven
14 after that l' her be received in again.
13: 30 L' us go up at once, and possess it;
14: 4 L' us make a captain, and
4 and l' us return into Egypt.
17 l' the power of my Lord be great,
16: 38 l' them make them broad plates for a
20: 17 L' us pass, I pray thee, through thy
21: 22 L' me pass through thy land: we will
27 l' the city of Sihon be built and
22: 16 L' nothing, I pray thee, hinder thee
23: 10 L' me die the death of the righteous,
10 and l' my last end be like his!
27: 16 L' the Lord...set a man over the
31: 3 l' them go against the Midianites, and
32: 5 l' this land be given unto thy
33: 55 those which ye l' remain of them shall
36: 6 L' them marry to whom they think
De 2: 27 L' me pass through thy land: I will
30 Heshbon would not l' us pass by him:
3: 25 I pray thee, l' me go over, and see the
26 Lord said unto me, L' it suffice thee;
9: 14 L' me alone, that I may destroy
13: 2 L' us go after other gods, which thou
2 hast not known, and l' us serve them;
6, 13 L' us go and serve other gods,
15: 12 shalt l' him go free from thee.
13 shalt not l' him go away empty:
18: 16 L' me not hear again the voice of the
16 neither l' me see this great fire any
20: 3 l' not your hearts faint, fear not, and
5 l' him go and return to his house,
6 l' him also go and return unto his
7, 8 l' him go and return unto his
21: 14 shalt l' her go whither she will;
22: 7 shalt in any wise l' the dam go,
24: 1 l' him write her a bill of divorcement,
25: 7 l' his brother's wife go up to the gate
32: 38 l' them rise up and help you, and be
33: 6 L' Reuben live, and not die;
6 and l' not his men be few.
7 l' his hands be sufficient for him;
8 L' thy Thummim and thy Urim be
16 l' the blessing come upon the head of

De 33:24 L' Asher be blessed with children;
24 l' him be acceptable to his brethren,
24 and l' him dip his foot in oil.
Jos 2:15 Then she l' them down by a cord
18 which thou didst l' us down by:
4:22 ye shall l' your children know, saying,
6: 6 l' seven priests bear seven trumpets
7 l' him that is armed pass on before the
7: 3 unto him, L' not all the people go up;
3 but l' about two or three thousand
8:22 they l' none of them remain or escape.
9:15 a league with them, to l' them live:
20 we will even l' them live, lest wrath
21 said unto them, L' them live; but
21 but l' them be hewers of wood and
10:28 were therein; he l' none remain:
30 therein; he l' none remain in it;
22:23 thereon, l' the Lord himself require it;
26 L' us now prepare to build us an
24:28 So Joshua l' the people depart,
J'g 1:25 they l' go the man and all his family.
2: 6 when Joshua had l' the people go,
5:31 So l' all thine enemies perish, O Lord:
31 l' them that love him be as the sun
6:31 l' him be put to death whilst it is yet
31 he be a god, l' him plead for himself,
32 L' Baal plead against him, because
39 L' not thine anger be hot against me,
39 L' me prove, I pray thee, but this once
39 l' it now be dry only upon the fleece,
39 upon all the ground l' there be dew.
7: 3 l' him return and depart early
7 l' all the other people go every man
9:15 if not, l' fire come out of the bramble,
19 and l' him also rejoice in you:
20 if not, l' fire come out from Abimelech,
20 and l' fire come out from the men of
10:14 l' them deliver you in the time of your
11:17 L' me, I pray thee, pass through thy
19 L' us pass, we pray thee, through thy
37 father, L' this thing be done for me:
37 l' me alone two months, that I
12: 5 L' me go over; that the men of Gilead
13: 8 l' the man of God which thou didst
12 said, Now l' thy words come to pass.
13 I said unto the woman l' her beware.
14 neither l' her drink wine or strong
14 that I commanded her l' her observe.
15 thee, l' us detain thee, until we shall
15: 5 l' them go into the standing corn
16:30 said, L' me die with the Philistines.
18:25 L' not thy voice be heard among us,
19: 6 all night, and l' thine heart be merry.
11 and l' us turn in into this city of the
13 l' us draw near to one of these places
20 l' all thy wants lie upon me; only
25 day began to spring, they l' her go.
28 said unto her, Up, and l' us be going.
20:32 L' us flee, and draw them from the
Ru 2: 2 L' me now go to the field, and glean
7 l' me glean and gather after the
9 L' thine eyes be on the field that they
13 L' me find favour in thy sight, my
15 L' her glean even among the sheaves,
16 l' fall also some of the handfuls
3:13 l' him do the kinsman's part: but if he
14 L' it not be known that a woman came
4:12 And l' thy house be like the house of
1Sa 1:18 L' thine handmaid find grace in thy
2: 3 l' not arrogancy come out of your
16 L' them not fail to burn the fat
3:18 l' him do what seemeth him good.
19 did l' none of his words fall to the
4: 3 L' us fetch the ark of the covenant
5: 8 L' the ark of the God...be carried
11 and l' it go again to his own place,
6: 6 did they not l' the people go, and
9: 5 with him, Come, and l' us return;
6 now l' us go thither; peradventure he
9 Come, and l' us go to the seer: for he
10 his servant, Well said; come, l' us go.
19 to-morrow I will l' thee go, and
10: 7 And l' it be, when these signs are
11:14 Come, and l' us go to Gilgal, and
13: 3 land, saying, L' the Hebrews hear.
14: 1 and l' us go over to the Philistines'
6 and l' us go over unto the garrison of
36 L' us go down after the Philistines
36 and l' us not leave a man of them.
16:16 L' our lord now command thy
22 L' David, I pray thee, stand before
17: 8 you, and l' him come down to me.
32 L' no man's heart fail because of him;
18: 2 l' him go no more home to his
17 said, L' not mine hand be upon him,
17 l' the hand of the Philistines be upon
19: 4 L' not the king sin against his servant,
12 So Michal l' David down through
17 L' me go; why should I kill thee?
20: 3 L' not Jonathan know this, lest he be
5 l' me go, that I may hide myself
11 Come, and l' us go out into the field.
16 L' the Lord even require it at the
29 L' me go, I pray thee; for our
29 l' me get away, I pray thee, and
21: 2 L' no man know any thing of the
13 l' his spittle fall down upon his
22: 3 L' my father and my mother, I pray
15 l' not the king impute any thing unto
24:19 will he l' him go well away?
25: 8 l' the young men find favour in thine
24 my lord, upon me l' this iniquity be:
24 l' thine handmaid, I pray thee, speak
25 L' not my lord, I pray thee, regard
26 now l' thine enemies...be as Nabal.
27 l' it even be given unto the young

1Sa 25:41 l' thine handmaid be a servant to
26: 8 therefore l' me smite him, I pray thee,
11 and the cruse of water, and l' us go.
19 l' my lord the king hear the words of
19 against me, l' him accept an offering:
20 l' not my blood fall to the earth before
22 l' one of the young men come over
24 so l' my life be much set by in the
24 l' him deliver me out of all tribulation.
27: 5 l' them give me a place in some town
28:22 l' me set a morsel of bread before
29: 4 l' him not go down with us to
2Sa 1:21 of Gilboa, l' there be no dew,
21 neither l' there be rain upon you, nor
2: 7 now l' your hands be strengthened,
14 L' the young men now arise, and play
14 And Joab said, L' them arise.
3:29 L' it rest on the head of Joab, and on
29 l' there not fail from the house of
5:24 l' it be, when thou hearest the sound
7:26 And l' thy name be magnified for ever,
26 l' the house of...David be established
29 now l' it please thee to bless the house
29 l' the house of thy servant be blessed
10:12 and l' us play the men for our people,
11:12 to-morrow I will l' thee depart.
25 Joab, L' not this thing displease thee,
13: 5 l' my sister Tamar come, and give me
6 l' Tamar my sister come, and make
24 l' the king, I beseech thee, and his
25 Nay, my son, l' us not all now go,
26 l' my brother Amnon go with us.
27 l' Amnon and all the king's sons go
32 L' not my lord suppose that they have
33 l' not my lord the king take the thing
14:11 l' the king remember the Lord thy
12 L' thine handmaid, I pray thee, speak
18 said, L' my lord the king now speak.
24 said, L' him turn to his own house,
24 and l' him not see my face.
32 therefore l' me see the king's face;
32 be any iniquity in me, l' him kill me.
15: 7 pray thee, l' me go and pay my vow,
14 at Jerusalem, Arise, and l' us flee;
26 l' him do to me as seemeth good unto
16: 9 l' me go over, I pray thee, and take
10 so l' him curse, because the Lord hath
11 l' him alone, and l' him curse; for
17: 1 L' me now choose out twelve thousand
5 and l' us hear likewise what he saith.
18:19 L' me now run, and bear the king
22 l' me, I pray thee, also run after Cushi.
23 But howsoever, said he, l' me run.
19:19 L' not my lord impute iniquity unto
30 l' him take all, forasmuch as my lord
37 L' thy servant, I pray thee, turn back
37 l' him go over with my lord the king;
20:11 that is for David, l' him go after Joab.
21: 6 L' seven men of his sons be delivered
24:14 l' us fall now into the hand of the
14 l' me not fall into the hand of man.
17 l' thine hand, I pray thee, be against
22 L' my lord the king take and offer up
1Ki 1: 2 L' there be sought for my lord the
2 and l' her stand before the king,
2 before the king, and l' her cherish
2 and l' her lie in thy bosom, that my
12 l' me, I pray thee, give thee counsel,
31 L' my lord king David live for ever.
34 l' Zadok the priest and...anoint him
51 L' king Solomon swear unto me to
2: 6 l' not his hoar head go down to
7 l' them be of those that eat at thy
21 L' Abishag the Shunammite be given
3:26 L' it be neither mine nor thine, but
8:26 l' thy word, I pray thee, be verified,
57 l' him not leave us, nor forsake us:
59 And l' these my words...be nigh unto
61 L' your heart therefore be perfect
11:21 L' me depart, that I may go to
22 howbeit l' me go in any wise.
17:21 l' this child's soul come into him
18:23 L' them...give us two bullocks;
23 l' them choose one bullock for
24 that answereth by fire, l' him be God.
36 l' it be known this day that thou art
40 of Baal; l' not one of them escape.
19: 2 So l' the gods do to me, and more
20 L' me, I pray thee, kiss my father and
20:11 L' not him that girdeth on his harness
23 l' us fight against them in the plain,
31 l' us, I pray thee, put sackcloth on
32 saith, I pray thee, l' me live.
42 hast l' go out of thy hand a man
21: 7 bread, and l' thine heart be merry:
22: 8 said, L' not the king say so.
13 l' thy word, I pray thee, be like the
17 l' them return every man to his
49 L' my servants go with thy
2Ki 1:10, 12 l' fire come down from heaven,
13 l' my life, and the life...be precious in
14 l' my life now be precious in thy sight.
2: 9 l' a double portion of thy spirit be
16 l' them go, we pray thee, and seek
4:10 L' us make a little chamber, I pray
10 l' us set for him there a bed, and a
27 man of God said, L' her alone;
5: 8 l' him come now to me, and he shall
24 and he l' the men go, and they
6: 2 L' us go, we pray thee, unto
2 l' us make us a place there, where we
7: 4 l' us fall unto the host of the Syrians:
13 L' some take, I pray thee, five of the
13 consumed:) and l' us send and see.
9:15 l' none go forth nor escape out of the
17 meet them, and l' him say, Is it peace?

2Ki 10:19 all his priests; l' none be wanting:
25 and slay them; l' none come forth.
11: 8 within the ranges, l' him be slain:
15 L' her not be slain in the house of the
12: 5 L' the priests take it to them, every
5 l' them repair the breaches of the
13:21 when the man was l' down, and
14: 8 l' us look one another in the face.
17:27 and l' them go and dwell there,
27 l' him teach them the manner of the
18:29 the king, L' not Hezekiah deceive you:
30 Neither l' Hezekiah make you trust in
19:10 L' not thy God in whom thou trustest
20:10 but l' the shadow return backward
22: 5 l' them deliver it into the hand of
5 l' them give it to the doers of the
23:18 L' him alone; l' no man move his
18 So they l' his bones alone, with the
1Ch 13: 2 l' us send abroad unto our
3 l' us bring again the ark of our God to
16:10 l' the heart of them rejoice that seek
31 L' the heavens be glad, and l' the
31 and l' men say among the nations, the
32 L' the sea roar, and the fulness
32 l' the fields rejoice, and all that is
17:23 l' the thing that thou...be established
24 L' it even be established, that thy
24 l' the house of David...be established
27 l' it please thee to bless the house of
19:13 and l' us behave ourselves valiantly
13 and l' the Lord do that which is good
21:13 l' me fall now into the hand of the
13 but l' me not fall into the hand of man.
17 l' thine hand...O Lord my God, be on me
23 l' my lord the king do that which is
2Ch 1: 9 l' thy promise unto David my father
2:15 of, l' him send unto his servants:
6:17 God of Israel, l' thy word be verified,
40 l', I beseech thee, thine eyes be open,
40 l' thine ears be attent unto the prayer
41 l' thy priests, O Lord God, be clothed
41 and l' thy saints rejoice in goodness.
14: 7 unto Judah, L' us build these cities,
11 God; l' not man prevail against thee.
15: 7 and l' not your hands be weak:
16: 1 that he might l' none go out or
5 of Ramah, and l' his work cease.
18: 7 said, L' not the king say so.
12 l' thy word therefore, I pray thee, be like
16 l' them return therefore every man
19: 7 now l' the fear of the Lord be upon
20:10 thou wouldest not l' Israel invade,
23: 6 But l' none come into the house of the
14 her, l' him be slain with the sword.
25: 7 l' not the army of Israel go with thee;
17 l' us see one another in the face.
32:15 therefore l' not Hezekiah deceive you,
36:23 his God be with him, and l' him go up.
Ezr 1: 3 l' him go up to Jerusalem, which is in
4 l' the men of his place help him with
4: 2 L' us build with you: for we seek
5:15 l' the house of God be builded in his
17 l' there be search made in the king's
17 l' the king send his pleasure to us
6: 3 L' the house be builded, the place
3 l' the foundations thereof be strongly
4 l' the expences be given out of the
5 l' the golden and...vessels...be restored
7 L' the work of this house of God alone;
7 l' the governor of the Jews...build
9 l' it be given them day by day without
11 l' timber be pulled down from his
11 set up, l' him be hanged thereon;
11 and l' his house be made a dunghill for
12 a decree; l' it be done with speed.
7:23 l' it be diligently done for the house of
26 l' judgment be executed speedily
10: 3 l' us make a covenant with our God
3 and l' it be done according to the law.
14 L' now our rulers of all the...stand,
14 l' all them which have taken...come
Ne 1: 6 L' thine ear now be attentive, and
11 l' now thine ear be attentive to the
2: 3 the king, L' the king live for ever:
7 l' letters be given me to the
17 l' us build up the wall of Jerusalem,
18 And they said, L' us rise up and build.
4: 5 l' not their sin be blotted out from
22 L' every one with his servant lodge
5:10 I pray you, l' us leave off this usury.
6: 2 Come, l' us meet together in some one
7 and l' us take counsel together.
10 L' us meet together in the house of
10 and l' us shut the doors of the temple:
7: 3 L' not the gates of Jerusalem be
3 l' them shut the doors, and bar them:
9:32 l' not all the trouble seem little before
Es 1:19 l' there go a royal commandment
19 l' it be written among the laws of the
19 l' the king give her royal estate
2: 2 L' there be fair young virgins sought
3 And l' the king appoint officers in all
3 l' their things for purification be given
4 l' the maiden which pleaseth...be queen
3: 9 l' it be written that they may be
5: 4 l' the king and Haman come this day
8 l' the king and Haman come to the
12 the queen did l' no man come in with
14 L' a gallows be made of fifty cubits
6: 5 And the king said, L' him come in.
8 L' the royal apparel be brought which
9 l' this apparel and horse be delivered
10 l' nothing fail of all that thou hast
7: 3 l' my life be given me at my
8: 5 l' it be written to reverse the letters
9:13 l' it be granted to the Jews which

Es 9:13 l' Haman's ten sons be hanged upon
Job 3: 3 L' the day perish wherein I was born,
4 L' that day be darkness;
4 l' not God regard it from above,
4 neither l' the light shine upon it.
5 L' darkness and the shadow of death
5 stain it; l' a cloud dwell upon it;
5 l' the blackness of the day terrify it.
6 that night, l' darkness seize upon it;
6 l' it not be joined unto the days of the
6 l' it not come into the number of the
7 Lo, l' that night be solitary,
7 l' no joyful voice come therein.
8 L' them curse it that curse the day,
9 L' the stars of the twilight thereof be
9 l' it look for light, but have none;
9 neither l' it see the dawning of the
6: 9 he would l' loose his hand, and cut me
10 l' him not spare; for I have not
29 l' it not be iniquity; yea, return again,
7:16 not live alway: l' me alone; for
19 nor l' me alone till I swallow down
9:34 L' him take his rod away from me,
34 and l' not his fear terrify me:
10:20 and l' me alone, that I may take
11:14 and l' not wickedness dwell in thy
13:13 Hold your peace, l' me alone, that I
13 speak, and l' come on me what will.
21 and l' not thy dread make me afraid.
22 or l' me speak, and answer thou me.
15:31 L' not him that is deceived trust in
16:18 my blood, and l' my cry have no place.
21: 2 and l' this be your consolations.
27: 6 I hold fast, and will not l' it go:
7 L' my enemy be as the wicked, and he
30:11 have also l' loose the bridle before me.
31: 6 L' me be weighed in an even balance,
8 Then l' me sow, and l' another eat;
8 Yea, l' my offspring be rooted out.
10 Then l' my wife grind unto another,
10 and l' others bow down upon her.
22 l' mine arm fall from my shoulder
40 L' thistles grow instead of wheat, and
32:21 L' me not, I pray you, accept any
21 neither l' me give flattering titles
34: 4 L' us choose to us judgment:
4 l' us know among ourselves what is
34 L' men of understanding tell me,
34 and l' a wise man hearken unto me.
40: 2 reproveth God, l' him answer it.
Ps 2: 3 L' us break their bands asunder, and
5:10 l' them fall by their own counsels;
11 l' all those that put their trust...rejoice:
11 l' them ever shout for joy, because
11 l' them...that love thy name be joyful
6:10 L' all mine enemies be ashamed and
10 l' them return and be ashamed
7: 5 L' the enemy persecute my soul, and
5 l' him tread down my life upon the
9 l' the wickedness of the wicked come
9:19 Arise, O Lord; l' not man prevail:
19 l' the heathen be judged in thy sight.
10: 2 l' them be taken in the devices that
17: 2 L' my sentence come forth from thy
2 l' thine eyes behold the things that are
18:46 l' the God of my salvation be exalted.
19:13 l' them not have dominion over me:
14 L' the words of my...be acceptable
20: 9 l' the king hear us when we call.
22: 8 l' him deliver him, seeing he delighted
25: 2 trust in thee: l' me not be ashamed,
2 l' not mine enemies triumph over me.
3 l' none that wait on thee be ashamed:
3 l' them be ashamed which transgress
20 l' me not be ashamed; for I put my
21 L' integrity and uprightness preserve
31: 1 put my trust; l' me never be ashamed:
17 L' me not be ashamed, O Lord; for I
17 upon thee: l' the wicked be ashamed,
17 and l' them be silent in the grave.
18 L' the lying lips be put to silence;
33: 8 L' all the earth fear the Lord:
8 l' all the inhabitants...stand in awe
22 L' thy mercy, O Lord, be upon us,
34: 3 me, and l' us exalt his name together.
35: 4 L' them be confounded and put to
4 l' them be turned back and brought
5 L' them be as chaff before the wind:
5 l' the angel of the Lord chase them.
6 L' their way be dark and slippery:
6 l' the angel of the Lord persecute
8 L' destruction come upon him at
8 l' his net that he hath hid catch
8 into that very destruction l' him fall.
19 L' not them...mine enemies rejoice
19 neither l' them wink with the eye that
24 and l' them not rejoice over me.
25 L' them not say in their hearts, Ah, so
25 l' them not say, We have swallowed
26 L' them be ashamed and brought to
26 l' them be clothed with shame and
27 L' them shout for joy, and be glad,
27 cause: yea, l' them say continually,
27 L' the Lord be magnified, which hath
36:11 L' not the foot of pride come against
11 l' not the hand of the wicked remove
40:11 l' thy lovingkindness and...preserve me,
14 L' them be ashamed and confounded
14 l' them be driven backward and put to
15 L' them be desolate for a reward of
16 L' all those that seek thee rejoice
16 l' such as love thy salvation say
43: 3 light and thy truth: l' them lead me;
3 l' them bring me unto thy holy hill,
48:11 L' mount Zion rejoice,
11 l' the daughters of Judah be glad,

Ps 55:15 L' death seize upon them,
15 and l' them go down quick into hell:
57: 5, 11 l' thy glory be above all the earth.
58: 7 L' them melt away as waters which
7 his arrows, l' them be as cut in pieces.
8 l' every one of them pass away:
59:10 God shall l' me see my desire upon
12 l' them even be taken in their pride:
13 l' them know that God ruleth in Jacob
14 And at evening l' them return;
14 l' them make a noise like a dog, and
15 L' them wander up and down for
66: 7 l' not the rebellious exalt themselves.
67: 3 L' the people praise thee, O God;
3 l' all the people praise thee.
4 O l' the nations be glad and sing for
5 L' the people praise thee, O God;
5 l' all the people praise thee.
68: 1 L' God arise, l' his enemies be
1 l' them also that hate him flee before
2 so l' the wicked perish at the presence
3 But l' the righteous be glad;
3 l' them rejoice before God:
3 yea, l' them exceedingly rejoice.
69: 6 L' not them that wait on...be ashamed
6 l' not those that seek...be confounded
14 out of the mire, and l' me not sink:
14 l' me be delivered from them that hate
15 L' not the waterflood overflow me,
15 neither l' the deep swallow me up,
15 l' not the pit shut her mouth upon me.
22 L' their table become a snare before
22 for their welfare, l' it become a trap.
23 L' their eyes be darkened, that they
24 l' thy wrathful anger take hold of
25 L' their habitation be desolate;
25 and l' none dwell in their tents.
27 and l' them not come into thy
28 L' them be blotted out of the book of
29 l' thy salvation, O God, set me up on
34 L' the heaven and earth praise him,
70: 2 L' them be ashamed and confounded
2 l' them be turned backward, and put
3 L' them be turned back for a reward
4 L' all those that seek thee rejoice and
4 and l' such as love thy salvation say
4 say continually, L' God be magnified.
71: 1 trust: l' me never be put to confusion.
8 L' my mouth be filled with thy praise
13 L' them be confounded and consumed
13 l' them be covered with reproach and
72:19 l' the whole earth be filled with his
74: 8 hearts, L' us destroy them together:
21 O l' not the oppressed return ashamed:
21 l' the poor and needy praise thy name.
76:11 l' all that be round about him bring
78:28 he l' it fall in the midst of their camp,
79: 8 l' thy tender mercies speedily prevent
10 l' him be known among the heathen in
11 L' the sighing of the prisoner come
80:17 L' thy hand be upon the man of thy
83: 4 l' us cut them off from being a nation;
12 L' us take to ourselves the houses of
17 L' them be confounded and troubled
17 l' them be put to shame, and perish:
85: 8 l' them not turn again to folly.
88: 2 L' my prayer come before thee:
90:13 l' it repent thee concerning thy
16 L' thy work appear unto thy servants,
17 l' the beauty of the Lord our God be
95: 1 O come, l' us sing unto the Lord:
1 l' us make a joyful noise to the rock
2 L' us come before his presence with
6 O come, l' us worship and bow down:
6 l' us kneel before the Lord our maker.
96:11 L' the heavens rejoice, and l' the earth
11 l' the sea roar, and the fulness thereof.
12 L' the field be joyful, and all that is
97: 1 l' the earth rejoice; l' the multitude
98: 7 L' the sea roar, and the fulness
8 L' the floods clap their hands:
8 l' the hills be joyful together.
99: 1 Lord reigneth; l' the people tremble:
1 cherubims; l' the earth be moved.
3 L' them praise thy great and terrible
102: 1 O Lord, and l' my cry come unto thee.
104:35 L' the sinners be consumed out of the
35 and l' the wicked be no more. Bless
105: 3 l' the heart of them rejoice that seek
20 ruler of the people, and l' him go free.
106:48 and l' all the people say, Amen.
107: 2 L' the redeemed of the Lord say so,
22 And l' them sacrifice the sacrifices of
32 L' them exalt him also in the
109: 6 and l' Satan stand at his right hand.
7 be judged, l' him be condemned:
7 and l' his prayer become sin.
8 L' his days be few; and l' another
9 L' his children be fatherless, and his
10 L' his children be continually
10 l' them seek their bread also out of
11 L' the extortioner catch all that he
11 and l' the strangers spoil his labour.
12 L' there be none to extend mercy unto
12 neither l' there be any to favour his
13 L' his posterity be cut off; and in the
13 following l' their name be blotted out.
14 L' the iniquity of his fathers be
14 and l' not the sin of his mother be
15 L' them be before the Lord
17 loved cursing, so l' it come unto him:
17 not in blessing, so l' it be far from him.
18 so l' it come into his bowels like water,
19 L' it be unto him as the garment
20 L' this be the reward of mine
28 L' them curse, but bless thou: when

Ps 109:28 they arise, l' them be ashamed;
28 but l' thy servant rejoice.
29 L' mine adversaries be clothed with
29 l' them cover themselves with their
118: 2 L' Israel now say, that his mercy
3 L' the house of Aaron now say, that
4 L' them now that fear the Lord say,
119:10 O l' me not wander from thy
41 L' thy mercies come also unto me, O
76 L', I pray thee, thy merciful kindness
77 L' thy tender mercies come unto me,
78 L' the proud be ashamed; for they
79 L' those that fear thee turn unto me,
80 L' my heart be sound in thy statutes;
116 and l' me not be ashamed of my hope.
122 good: l' not the proud oppress me.
133 l' not any iniquity have dominion over
169 L' my cry come near before thee, O
170 L' my supplication come before thee:
173 L' thine hand help me; for I have
175 L' my soul live, and it shall praise
175 thee; and l' thy judgments help me.
122: 1 L' us go into the house of the Lord.
129: 5 L' them all be confounded and turned
6 L' them be as the grass upon the
130: 2 l' thine ears be attentive to the voice
7 L' Israel hope in the Lord: for with
131: 3 L' Israel hope in the Lord from
132: 9 L' thy priests be clothed with
9 and l' thy saints shout for joy.
137: 5 l' my right hand forget her cunning.
6 l' my tongue cleave to the roof of my
140: 9 l' the mischief of their own lips cover
10 L' burning coals fall upon them:
10 l' them be cast into the fire; into deep
11 L' not an evil speaker be established
141: 2 L' my prayer be set forth before thee
4 and l' me not eat of their dainties.
5 L' the righteous smite me; it shall be
5 l' him reprove me; it shall be an
10 L' the wicked fall into their own nets,
145:21 l' all flesh bless his holy name for ever
148: 5, 13 L' them praise the name of the Lord:
149: 2 L' Israel rejoice in him that made
2 l' the children of Zion be joyful in their
3 L' them praise his name in the dance:
3 l' them sing praises unto him with the
5 L' the saints be joyful in glory:
5 l' them sing aloud upon their beds.
6 L' the high praises of God be in their
150: 6 L' every thing that hath breath praise
Pr 1:11 Come with us, l' us lay wait for blood,
11 l' us lurk privily for the innocent
12 L' us swallow them up alive as the
14 among us; l' us all have one purse:
3: 1 l' thine heart keep my commandments:
3 L' not mercy and truth forsake thee:
21 l' not them depart from thine eyes:
4: 4 me, L' thine heart retain my words:
13 l' her not go: keep her; for she is
21 L' them not depart from thine eyes;
25 L' thine eyes look right on, and
25 L' thine eyelids look straight before
26 and l' all thy ways be established.
5:16 L' thy fountains be dispersed abroad,
17 L' them be only thine own, and not
18 L' thy fountain be blessed: and
19 L' her be as the loving hind and
19 l' her breasts satisfy thee at all times;
6:25 neither l' her take thee with her
7:18 l' us take our fill of love until the
18 l' us solace ourselves with loves.
25 L' not thine heart decline to her ways,
9: 4, 16 is simple, l' him turn in hither:
17:12 L' a bear robbed of her whelps meet a
19:18 l' not thy soul spare for his crying.
23:17 L' not thine heart envy sinners: but
26 and l' thine eyes observe my ways.
24:17 l' not thine heart be glad when he
27: 2 L' another man praise thee, and not
28:17 flee to the pit; l' no man stay him.
31: 7 L' him drink, and forget his poverty,
31 l' her own works praise her in the
Ec 5: 2 l' not thine heart be hasty to utter any
2 earth: therefore l' thy words be few.
9: 8 L' thy garments be always white;
8 and l' thy head lack no ointment.
11: 8 l' him remember the days of darkness;
9 l' thy heart cheer thee in the days of
12:13 L' us hear the conclusion of the whole
Ca 1: 2 L' him kiss me with the kisses of his
2:14 l' me see thy countenance, l' me hear
3: 4 held him, and would not l' him go,
4:16 L' my beloved come into his garden,
7:11 beloved, l' us go forth into the field;
11 l' us lodge in the villages.
12 L' us get up early to the vineyards;
12 l' us see if the vine flourish, whether
8:11 l' out the vineyards unto keepers;
Isa 1:18 Come now, and l' us reason together,
2: 3 l' us go up to the mountain of the
5 l' us walk in the light of the Lord.
3: 6 and l' this ruin be under thy hand:
4: 1 only l' us be called by thy name, to
5:19 L' him make speed and hasten his
19 l' the counsel of the Holy...draw nigh
7: 6 L' us go up against Judah, and vex it,
6 l' us make a breach therein for us,
8:13 hosts himself; and l' him be your fear,
13 and l' him be your dread.
16: 4 L' mine outcasts dwell with thee,
19:12 wise men? and l' them tell thee now,
12 l' them know what the Lord of hosts
21: 6 l' him declare what he seeth.
22:13 l' us eat and drink; for to-morrow we
26:10 L' favour be shewed to the wicked, yet

Isa 27: 5 Or l' him take hold of my strength,
29: 1 ye year to year; l' them kill sacrifices.
34: 1 l' the earth hear, and all that is
36: 14 king, L' not Hezekiah deceive you:
15 Neither l' Hezekiah make you trust in
37: 10 L' not thy God, in whom...deceive thee,
38: 21 had said, L' them take a lump of figs,
41: 1 l' the people renew their strength:
1 l' them come near; then l' them speak:
1 l' us come near together to judgment.
22 L' them bring them forth, and shew
22 l' them shew the former things, what
42: 11 L' the wilderness and the cities thereof
11 l' the inhabitants of the rock sing,
11 l' them shout from the top of the
12 L' them give glory unto the Lord,
43: 9 L' all the nations be gathered together,
9 and l' the people be assembled:
9 l' them bring forth their witnesses,
9 or l' them hear, and say, It is truth.
13 I will work, and who shall l' it?
26 in remembrance: l' us plead together:
44: 7 shall come, l' them shew unto them.
11 l' them all be gathered together,
11 l' them stand up; yet they shall fear,
45: 8 l' the skies pour down righteousness:
8 l' the earth open, and l' [*] them bring
8 l' righteousness spring up together;
9 L' the potsherd strive with the
13 he shall l' go my captives, not for
21 l' them take counsel together: who
47: 13 L' now the astrologers,...stand up,
50: 8 contend with me? l' us stand together:
8 adversary? l' him come near to me.
10 l' him trust in the name of the Lord,
54: 2 l' them stretch forth the curtains of
55: 2 l' your soul delight itself in fatness.
7 L' the wicked forsake his way, and
7 l' him return unto the Lord, and
56: 3 Neither l' the son of the...speak,
3 neither l' the eunuch say, Behold, I
57: 13 criest, l' thy companies deliver thee;
58: 6 to l' the oppressed go free, and
66: 5 L' the Lord be glorified: but he shall
Jer 2: 28 l' them arise, if they can save thee in
4: 5 and l' us go into the defenced cities.
5: 24 L' us now fear the Lord our God, that
6: 4 her; arise, and l' us go up at noon.
5 Arise, and l' us go by night,
5 and l' us destroy her palaces.
8: 14 l' us enter into the defenced cities,
14 and l' us be silent there: for the Lord
9: 18 And l' them make haste, and take up
20 and l' your ear receive the word of his
23 L' not the wise man glory in his
23 neither l' the mighty man glory in his
23 l' not the rich man glory in his riches:
24 But l' him that glorieth glory in this,
11: 19 L' us destroy the tree with the fruit
19 l' us cut him off from the land of the
20 l' me see thy vengeance on them:
12: 1 l' me talk with thee of thy judgments:
14: 17 L' mine eyes run down with tears
17 night and day, and l' them not cease:
15: 1 out of my sight, and l' them go forth.
19 l' them return unto thee; but
17: 15 the word of the Lord? l' it come now.
18 L' them be confounded that persecute
18 but l' not me be confounded:
18 l' them be dismayed,
18 but l' not me be dismayed:
18: 18 l' us devise devices against Jeremiah;
18 and l' us smite him with the tongue,
18 l' us not give heed to any of his words.
21 l' their wives be bereaved of their
21 and l' their men be put to death;
21 l' their young men be slain by the
22 L' a cry be heard from their houses,
23 but l' them be overthrown before thee;
20: 12 l' me see thy vengeance on them:
14 l' not the day wherein my mother bare
16 And l' that man be as the cities which
16 l' him hear the cry in the morning,
23: 28 that hath a dream, l' him tell a dream;
28 word, l' him speak my word faithfully.
27: 11 those will I l' remain still in their
18 l' them now make intercession to the
29: 8 L' not your prophets and your
31: 6 l' us go up to Zion unto the Lord our
34: 9 man should l' his manservant...go free;
10 one should l' his manservant...go free,
10 then they obeyed, and l' them go.
11 whom they had l' go free, to return,
14 l' ye go every man his brother an
14 thou shalt l' him go free from thee:
35: 11 and l' us go to Jerusalem for fear of
36: 19 and l' no man know where ye be.
37: 20 l' my supplication,...be accepted
38: 4 thee, l' this man be put to death:
6 they l' down Jeremiah with cords.
11 and l' them down by cords into the
24 L' no man know of these words, and
40: 1 captain of the guard had l' him go
5 victuals and a reward, and l' him go.
15 Mizpah secretly, saying, L' me go,
42: 2 L'...our supplication be accepted
46: 6 L' not the swift flee away, nor the
9 and l' the mighty men come forth;
16 l' us go again to our own people,
48: 2 l' us cut it off from being a nation.
49: 11 alive; and l' thy widows trust in me.
50: 5 and l' us join ourselves to the Lord
26 her utterly: l' nothing of her be left.
27 l' them go down to the slaughter:
29 about; l' none thereof escape:
33 them fast; they refused to l' them go.

Jer 51: 3 bendeth l' the archer bend his bow,
9 l' us go every one into his own
10 l' us declare in Zion the work of the
50 l' Jerusalem come into your mind.
La 1: 22 L' all their wickedness come before
2: 18 l' tears run down like a river day
18 l' not the apple of thine eye cease.
3: 40 L' us search and try our ways, and
41 L' us lift up our heart with our hands
Eze 1: 24 stood, they l' down their wings.
25 stood, and had l' down their wings.
3: 27 God; He that heareth, l' him hear;
27 and he that forbeareth, l' him forbear:
7: 12 l' not the buyer rejoice, nor the seller
9: 5 l' not your eye spare, neither have ye
11: 3 l' us build houses: this city is the*
13: 20 will l' the souls go, even the souls
21: 14 and l' the sword be doubled the third
24: 5 l' them seethe the bones of it therein.
6 piece by piece; l' no lot fall upon it.
10 spice it well,...l' the bones be burned.
39: 7 I will not l' them pollute my holy
43: 9 Now l' them put away their whoredom,
10 and l' them measure the pattern.
44: 6 Israel, l' it suffice you of all your
Da 1: 12 l' them give us pulse to eat, and water
13 l' our countenances be looked upon
2: 7 L' the king tell his servants the dream,
4: 14 l' the beasts get away from under it,
15 l' it be wet with the dew of heaven,
15 l' his portion be with the beasts in the
16 L' his heart be changed from man's,
16 l' a beast's heart be given unto him;
16 and l' seven times pass over him.
19 l' not the dream, or the...trouble thee.
23 l' it be wet with the dew of heaven,
23 l' his portion be with the beasts of the
27 l' my counsel be acceptable unto thee,
5: 10 ever: L' not thy thoughts trouble thee,
10 nor l' thy countenance be changed:
12 now l' Daniel be called, and he will
17 L' thy gifts be to thyself, and give thy
9: 16 l' thine anger and thy fury be turned
10: 19 said, L' my lord speak; for thou hast
Ho 2: 2 l' her therefore put away her
4: 4 Yet l' no man strive, nor reprove
15 the harlot, yet l' not Judah offend;
17 is joined to idols: l' him alone.
6: 1 and l' us return unto the Lord:
13: 2 L' the men that sacrifice kiss the
Joe 1: 3 l' your children tell their children, and
2: 1 l' all the inhabitants of the...tremble:
16 l' the bridegroom go forth of his
17 L' the priests...weep...l' them say,
3: 9 men, l' all the men of war draw near;
9 l' them come up:
10 spears: l' the weak say, I am strong.
12 L' the heathen be wakened, and come
Am 4: 1 their masters, Bring, and l' us drink.
5: 24 But l' judgment run down as waters,
Ob 1 and l' us rise up against her in battle.
Jon 1: 7 Come, and l' us cast lots, that we may
14 l' us not perish for this man's life, and
3: 7 L' neither man nor beast, herd...taste
7 l' them not feed, nor drink water:
8 But l' man and beast be covered with
8 l' them turn every one from his
Mic 1: 2 l' the Lord God be witness against
4: 2 and l' us go up to the mountain of the
11 L' her be defiled, and l' our eye look
6: 1 and l' the hills hear thy voice.
7: 14 l' them feed in Bashan and Gilead, as
Hab 2: 16 also, and l' thy foreskin be uncovered:
20 l' all the earth keep silence before
Zep 3: 16 to Zion, L' not thine hands be slack.
Zec 3: 5 L' them set a fair mitre upon his head.
7: 10 l' none of you imagine evil against his
8: 9 L' your hands be strong, ye that hear
13 fear not, but l' your hands be strong.
17 l' none of you imagine evil in your
21 L' us go speedily to pray before the
11: 9 not feed you: that that dieth, l' it die;
9 that that is to be cut off, l' it be cut off;
9 and l' the rest eat every one the flesh
Mal 2: 15 l' none deal treacherously against the
M't 5: 31 his wife, l' him give her a writing of
37 l' your communication be, Yea,
40 thy coat, l' him have thy cloke also.
7: 4 L' me pull out the mote out of thine
8: 22 me; and l' the dead bury their dead.
10: 13 be worthy, l' your peace come upon it:
13 worthy, l' your peace return to you.
11: 15 He that hath ears to hear, l' him hear.
13: 9 Who hath ears to hear, l' him hear.
30 L' both grow together until the
43 Who hath ears to hear, l' him hear.
15: 4 father or mother, l' him die the death.
14 L' them alone: they be blind
16: 24 l' him deny himself, and take up his
17: 4 l' us make here three tabernacles;
18: 17 l' him be unto thee as an heathen
19: 6 together, l' not man put asunder.
12 able to receive it, l' him receive it.
20: 26 you, l' him be your minister;
27 among you, l' him be your servant:
21: 19 L' no fruit grow on thee henceforward
33 l' it out to husbandmen, and went
38 This is the heir; come, l' us kill him,
41 will l' out his vineyard unto other
24: 15 (whoso readeth, l' him understand:)
16 l' them which be in Judæa flee into the
17 L' him which is on the housetop not
18 Neither l' him which is in the field
26: 39 be possible, l' this cup pass from me:
46 l' us be going: behold, he is at hand
27: 22 all say unto him, L' him be crucified.

M't 27: 23 the more, saying, L' him be crucified.
42 l' him now come down from the cross,
43 l' him deliver him now, if he will
49 The rest said, L' be,
49 l' us see whether Elias will come
M'r 1: 24 L' us alone; what have we to do
38 L' us go into the next towns, that I
2: 4 l' down the bed wherein the sick
4: 9 He that hath ears to hear, l' him hear.
23 man have ears to hear, l' him hear.
35 L' us pass over unto the other side.
7: 10 father or mother, l' him die the death:
16 man have ears to hear, l' him hear.
27 her, L' the children first be filled:
8: 34 l' him deny himself, and take up his
9: 5 and l' us make three tabernacles;
10: 9 together, l' not man put asunder.
11: 6 commanded: and they l' them go.
12: 1 l' it out to husbandmen, and went
7 This is the heir; come, l' us kill him,
13: 14 not, (l' him that readeth understand,)
14 l' them that be in Judæa flee to the
15 And l' him that is on the housetop not
16 And l' him that is in the field not turn
14: 6 And Jesus said, L' her alone; why
42 Rise up, l' us go; lo, he that betrayeth
15: 32 L' Christ the King of Israel descend
36 to drink, saying, L' alone;
36 l' us see whether Elias will come
Lu 2: 15 L' us now go even unto Bethlehem,
3: 11 l' him impart to him that hath none;
11 he that hath meat, l' him do likewise.
4: 34 Saying, L' us alone; what have
5: 4 l' your nets down for a draught.
5 at thy word I will l' down the net.
19 and l' him down through the tiling
6: 42 l' me pull out the mote that is in
8: 8 He that hath ears to hear, l' him hear.
22 L' us go over unto the other side of
9: 23 l' him deny himself, and take up his
33 l' us make three tabernacles; one for
44 L' these sayings sink down into your
60 him, L' the dead bury their dead:
61 l' me first go bid them farewell,
12: 35 L' your loins be girded about, and
13: 8 Lord, l' it alone this year also, till I
14: 4 him, and healed him, and l' him go;
35 He that hath ears to hear, l' him hear.
15: 23 kill it; and l' us eat, and be merry:
16: 29 and the prophets; l' them hear them.
17: 31 l' him not come down to take it away:
31 field, l' him likewise not return back.
20: 9 and l' it forth to husbandmen,
14 is the heir: come, l' us kill him,
21: 21 l' them which are in Judæa flee to
21 l' them which are in the midst...depart
21 l' not them...in the countries enter
22: 26 among you, l' him be as the younger;
36 l' him take it, and likewise his scrip:
36 l' him sell his garment, and buy one.
68 ye will not answer me, nor l' me go.
23: 22 therefore chastise him, and l' him go.
35 l' him save himself, if he be Christ, the
Joh 7: 37 thirst, l' him come unto me and drink.
8: 7 you, l' him first cast a stone at her.
11: 7 disciples, L' us go into Judæa again.
15 nevertheless l' us go unto him.
16 L' us also go, that we may die with
44 them, Loose him, and l' him go.
48 If we l' him thus alone, all men will
12: 7 said Jesus, L' her alone: against
26 any man serve me, l' him follow me;
14: 1 L' not your heart be troubled: ye
27 L' not your heart be troubled,
27 neither l' it be afraid.
31 even so I do. Arise, l' us go hence.
18: 8 ye seek me, l' these go their way:
19: 12 If thou l' this man go, thou art not
24 L' us not rend it, but cast lots for it,
Ac 1: 20 L' his habitation be desolate,
20 and l' no man dwell therein:
20 and his bishoprick l' another take.
2: 29 l' me freely speak unto you of the
36 l' all the house of Israel know
3: 13 he was determined to l' him go.
4: 17 l' us straitly threaten them, that they
21 threatened them, they l' them go,
23 And being l' go, they went to their own
5: 38 these men, and l' them alone:
40 in the name of Jesus, and l' them go.
9: 25 l' him down by the wall in a
10: 11 corners, and l' down to the earth:
11: 5 sheet, l' down from heaven by four
15: 33 they were l' go in peace from the
36 L' us go again and visit our brethren
16: 35 serjeants, saying, L' those men go.
36 magistrates have sent to l' you go:
37 l' them come themselves and fetch us
17: 9 and of the other, they l' them go.
19: 38 deputies: l' them implead one another.
23: 9 to him, l' us not fight against God.
22 then l' the young man depart,
24: 20 Or else l' these same here say, if they
23 keep Paul, and to l' him have liberty,
25: 5 L' them therefore,...go down with me,
27: 15 up into the wind, we l' her drive.
30 had l' down the boat into the sea,
32 ropes of the boat, and l' her fall off.
28: 18 examined me, would have l' me go.
Ro 1: 13 unto you, (but was l' hitherto,)
3: 4 yea, l' God be true, but every man a
8 L' us do evil, that good may come?
6: 12 L' not sin therefore reign in your
11: 9 L' their table be made a snare, and a
10 L' their eyes be darkened, that they
12: 6 l' us prophesy according to the

Ro 12: 7 ministry, *l'* us wait on our ministering:
8 giveth, *l'* him do it with simplicity;
9 *L'* love be without dissimulation.
13: 1 *L'* every soul be subject unto the
12 *l'* us therefore cast off the works of
12 and *l'* us put on the armour of light.
13 *L'* us walk honestly, as in the day;
14: 3 *L'* not him that eateth despise him
3 *l'* not him which eateth not judge him
5 *L'* every man be fully persuaded in
13 *L'* us not therefore judge one another
16 *L'* not then your good be evil spoken
19 *L'* us therefore follow after the things
15: 2 *L'* every one...please his neighbour
1Co 1: 31 that glorieth, *l'* him glory in the Lord.
3: 10 *l'* every man take heed how he buildeth
18 *L'* no man deceive himself. If any
18 *l'* him become a fool, that he may be
21 Therefore *l'* no man glory in men.
4: 1 *L'* a man so account of us, as of the
5: 8 Therefore *l'* us keep the feast, not
7: 2 *l'* every man have his own wife, and
2 *l'* every woman have her own husband.
3 *L'* the husband render unto the wife
9 if they cannot contain, *l'* them marry:
10 *L'* not the wife depart from her
11 she depart, *l'* her remain unmarried,
11 *l'* not the husband put away his wife.
12 with him, *l'* him not put her away.
13 to dwell with her, *l'* her not leave him.
15 the unbelieving depart, *l'* him depart.
17 hath called every one, so *l'* him walk.
18 *l'* him not become uncircumcised.
18 *l'* him not be circumcised.
20 *L'* every man abide in the same calling
24 *l'* every man, wherein he is...abide
36 need so require, *l'* him do what he will,
36 will he sinneth not: *l'* them marry.
10: 8 Neither *l'* us commit fornication, as
9 Neither *l'* us tempt Christ, as some of
12 *l'* him that...he standeth take heed
24 *L'* no man seek his own, but every
11: 6 be not covered, *l'* her also be shorn:
6 be shorn or shaven, *l'* her be covered.
28 But *l'* a man examine himself, and
28 so *l'* him eat of that bread, and drink
34 any man hunger, *l'* him eat at home;
14: 13 *l'* him that speaketh in an...pray
26 *L'* all things be done unto edifying.
27 *l'* it be by two, or at most by three,
27 that by course; and *l'* one interpret.
28 *l'* him keep silence in the church;
28 *l'* him speak to himself, and to God.
29 *L'* the prophets speak two or three,
29 two or three, and *l'* the other judge.
30 sitteth by, *l'* the first hold his peace.
34 *L'* your women keep silence in the
35 *l'* them ask their husbands at home:
37 *l'* him acknowledge that the things
38 man be ignorant, *l'* him be ignorant.
40 *L'* all things be done decently and in
15: 32 *l'* us eat and drink; for to morrow we
16: 2 *l'* every one of you lay by him in store,
11 *L'* no man therefore despise him: but
14 *L'* all your things be done with charity.
22 *l'* him be Anathema Maran-atha.
2Co 7: 1 *l'* us cleanse ourselves from all
9: 7 purposeth in his heart, so *l'* him give;
10: 7 *l'* him of himself think this again, that,
11 *L'* such an one think this, that, such
17 that glorieth, *l'* him glory in the Lord.
11: 16 say again, *L'* no man think me a fool;
33 basket was I *l'* down by the wall,
Ga 1: 8 unto you, *l'* him be accursed.
9 have received, *l'* him be accursed.
5: 25 the Spirit, *l'* us also walk in the Spirit.
26 *L'* us not be desirous of vain glory,
6: 4 But *l'* every man prove his own work,
6 *L'* him that is taught...communicate
9 *l'* us not be weary in well doing: for
10 *l'* us do good unto all men, especially
17 henceforth *l'* no man trouble me:
Eph 4: 26 *l'* not the sun go down upon your
28 *L'* him that stole steal no more: but
28 but rather *l'* him labour, working with
29 *L'* no corrupt communication proceed
31 *L'* all bitterness, and...be put away
5: 3 *l'* it not be once named among you, as
6 *L'* no man deceive you with vain
24 *l'* the wives be to their own husbands
33 *l'* every one of you in particular so love
Ph'p 1: 27 *l'* your conversation be as it becometh
2: 3 *L'* nothing be done through strife or
3 mind *l'* each esteem other better than
5 *L'* this mind be in you, which was also
3: 15 *L'* us therefore, as...be thus minded:
16 attained, *l'* us walk by the same rule,
16 *l'* us mind the same thing.
4: 5 *L'* your moderation be known unto all
6 *l'* your requests be made known unto
Col 2: 16 *L'* no man therefore judge you in
18 *L'* no man beguile you of your reward
3: 15 *l'* the peace of God rule in your hearts,
16 *L'* the word of Christ dwell in you
4: 6 *L'* your speech be alway with grace,
1Th 5: 6 Therefore *l'* us not sleep, as do others;
6 but *l'* us watch and be sober.
8 But *l'* us, who are of the day, be sober,
2Th 2: 3 *L'* no man deceive you by any means:
7 only he who now letteth will *l'*,
1Ti 2: 11 *L'* the woman learn in silence with all
3: 10 And *l'* these also first be proved; then
10 then *l'* them use the office of a deacon,
12 *L'* the deacons be the husbands of
4: 12 *L'* no man despise thy youth; but be
5: 4 *l'* them learn first to show piety at

1Ti 5: 9 *L'* not a widow be taken into the
16 have widows, *l'* them relieve them,
16 and *l'* not the church be charged; that
17 *L'* the elders that rule well be counted
6: 1 *L'* as many servants as are...count
2 masters, *l'* them not despise them,
8 raiment *l'* us be therewith content.
2Ti 2: 19 *L'* every one that nameth...depart
Tit 2: 15 authority. *L'* no man despise thee.
3: 14 *l'* ours also learn to maintain good
Ph'm 20 *l'* me have joy of thee in the Lord:
Heb 1: 6 *l'* all the angels of God worship him.
2: 1 at any time we should *l'* them slip.
4: 1 *L'* us therefore fear, lest, a promise
11 *L'* us labour therefore to enter into
14 of God, *l'* us hold fast our profession.
16 *L'* us therefore come boldly unto the
6: 1 of Christ, *l'* us go on unto perfection;
10: 22 *L'* us draw near with a true heart in
23 *L'* us hold fast the profession of our
24 *l'* us consider one another to provoke
12: 1 *l'* us lay aside every weight, and the
1 *l'* us run with patience the race that is
13 of the way; but *l'* it rather be healed.
28 *l'* us have grace, whereby we may
13: 1 *L'* brotherly love continue.
5 *L'* your conversation be without
13 *L'* us go forth therefore unto him
15 *l'* us offer the sacrifice of praise to God
Jas 1: 4 But *l'* patience have her perfect work,
5 you lack wisdom, *l'* him ask of God,
6 But *l'* him ask in faith, nothing
7 For *l'* not that man think that he shall
9 *L'* the brother of low degree rejoice
13 *L'* no man say when he is tempted, I
19 *l'* every man be swift to hear, slow to
3: 13 *l'* him shew out of a good conversation
4: 9 *l'* your laughter be turned to mourning,
5: 12 *l'* your yea be yea; and your nay, nay;
13 any among you afflicted? *l'* him pray.
13 Is any merry? *l'* him sing psalms.
14 *l'* him call for the elders of the church;
14 *l'* them pray over him, anointing him
20 *L'* him know, that he which converteth
1Pe 3: 3 *l'* it not be that outward adorning
4 But *l'* it be the hidden man of the
10 *l'* him refrain his tongue from evil,
11 *L'* him eschew evil, and do good,
11 *l'* him seek peace, and ensue it.
4: 11 *l'* him speak as the oracles of God;
11 *l'* him do it as of the ability which
15 *l'* none of you suffer as a murderer,
16 as a Christian, *l'* him not be ashamed;
16 but *l'* him glorify God on this behalf.
19 *l'* them that suffer according to the
1Jo 2: 24 *L'* that therefore abide in you, which
3: 7 Little children, *l'* no man deceive you:
18 little children, *l'* us not love in word,
4: 7 *l'* us love one another: for love is of
Re 2: 7, 11, 17, 29 *l'* him hear what the Spirit
3: 6, 13, 22 *l'* him hear what the Spirit saith
13: 9 If any man have an ear, *l'* him hear.
18 *L'* him that hath understanding count
19: 7 *L'* us be glad and rejoice, and give
22: 11 that is unjust, *l'* him be unjust still:
11 he which is filthy, *l'* him be filthy still:
11 is righteous, *l'* him be righteous still:
11 and he that is holy, *l'* him be holy still.
17 And *l'* him that heareth say, Come.
17 And *l'* him that is athirst come.
17 *l'* him take the water of life freely.

letter See also LETTERS.
2Sa 11: 14 David wrote a *l'* to Joab, and sent
15 And he wrote in the *l'*, saying, Set
2Ki 5: 5 and I will send a *l'* unto the king of
6 And he brought the *l'* to the king of
6 Now when this *l'* is come unto thee,
7 the king of Israel had read the *l'*,
10: 2 as soon as this *l'* cometh to you,
6 Then he wrote a *l'* the second time
7 to pass, when the *l'* came to them,
19: 14 And Hezekiah received the *l'* of the
Ezr 4: 7 writing of the *l'* was written in the
8 and Shimshai the scribe wrote a *l'*
11 the copy of the *l'* that they sent unto
18 The *l'* which ye sent unto us hath
23 the copy of king Artaxerxes' *l'* was
5: 5 returned answer by *l'* concerning
6 The copy of the *l'* that Tatnai,
7 They sent a *l'* unto him, wherein
7: 11 is the copy of the *l'* that the king
Ne 2: 8 And a *l'* unto Asaph the keeper of
6: 5 time with an open *l'* in his hand;
Es 9: 26 Therefore for all the words of this *l'*,
29 to confirm this second *l'* of Purim.
Isa 37: 14 Hezekiah received the *l'* from the
Jer 29: 1 words of the *l'* that Jeremiah the
29 the priest read this *l'* in the ears of
Ac 23: 25 he wrote a *l'* after this manner:
34 when the governor had read the *l'*,
Ro 2: 27 who by the *l'* and circumcision
29 heart, in the spirit, and not in the *l'*;
7: 6 and not in the oldness of the *l'*.
2Co 3: 6 not of the *l'*, but of the spirit:
6 the *l'* killeth, but the spirit giveth
7: 8 though I made you sorry with a *l'*,
Ga 6: 11 Ye see how large a *l'* I have
2Th 2: 2 nor by word, nor by *l'* as from us,
Heb 13: 22 I have written a *l'* unto you in few

letters
1Ki 21: 8 So she wrote *l'* in Ahab's name,
8 and sent the *l'* unto the elders and
9 And she wrote in the *l'*, saying,
11 as it was written in the *l'* which she
2Ki 10: 1 And Jehu wrote *l'*, and sent to

2Ki 20: 12 sent *l'* and a present unto Hezekiah:
2Ch 30: 1 and wrote *l'* also to Ephraim and
6 the posts went with the *l'* from the
32: 17 He wrote also *l'* to rail on the Lord
Ne 2: 7 let *l'* be given me to the governors
9 river, and gave them the king's *l'*.
6: 17 Judah sent many *l'* unto Tobiah,
17 the *l'* of Tobiah came unto them.
19 And Tobiah sent *l'* to put me in fear.
Es 1: 22 For he sent *l'* into all the king's
3: 13 the *l'* were sent by posts into all
8: 5 let it be written to reverse the *l'*
10 and sent *l'* by posts on horseback,
9: 20 sent *l'* unto all the Jews that were
25 he commanded by *l'* that his wicked
30 And he sent the *l'* unto all the Jews,
Isa 39: 1 sent *l'* and a present to Hezekiah:
Jer 29: 25 thou hast sent *l'* in thy name unto
Lu 23: 38 written over him in *l'* of Greek,
Joh 7: 15 How knoweth this man *l'*, having
Ac 9: 2 And desired of him *l'* to Damascus
15: 23 And they wrote *l'* by them after this
22: 5 I received *l'* unto the brethren,
28: 21 We neither received *l'* out of Judæa
1Co 16: 3 whomsoever...approve by your *l'*,
2Co 3: 1 you, or *l'* of commendation from you?
10: 9 seem as if I would terrify you by *l'*.
10 For his *l'*, say they, are weighty
11 in word by *l'* when we are absent,

lettest
Job 15: 13 *l'* such words go out of thy mouth?
41: 1 with a cord which thou *l'* down?
Lu 2: 29 now *l'* thou thy servant depart in

letteth
2Ki 10: 24 he that *l'* him go, his life shall be for
Pr 17: 14 strife is as when one *l'* out water:
2Th 2: 7 only he who now *l'* will let, until

letting
Ex 8: 29 in not *l'* the people go to sacrifice

Letushim (*le-tu'-shim*)
Ge 25: 3 of Dedan were Asshurim, and *L'*.

Leummim (*le-um'-mim*)
Ge 25: 3 Asshurim, and Letushim, and *L'*.

Levi (*le'-vi*) See also LEVITE; LEVITICAL; MATTHEW.
Ge 29: 34 therefore was his name called *L'*.
34: 25 the sons of Jacob, Simeon and *L'*,
30 And Jacob said to Simeon and *L'*,
35: 23 firstborn, and Simeon, and *L'*, and
46: 11 sons of *L'*; Gershon, Kohath, and
49: 5 Simeon and *L'* are brethren;
Ex 1: 2 Reuben, Simeon, *L'*, and Judah,
2: 1 there went a man of the house of *L'*,
1 and took to wife a daughter of *L'*.
6: 16 are the names of the sons of *L'*
16 life of *L'* were an hundred thirty
19 Mushi: these are the families of *L'*
32: 26 the sons of *L'* gathered themselves
28 of *L'* did according to the word of
Nu 1: 49 shalt not number the tribe of *L'*,
3: 6 Bring the tribe of *L'* near, and
15 Number the children of *L'* after the
17 were the sons of *L'* by their names;
4: 2 Kohath from among the sons of *L'*,
16: 1 the son of *L'*, and Dathan and
7 too much upon you, ye sons of *L'*.
8 Hear, I pray you, ye sons of *L'*:
10 brethren the sons of *L'* with thee:
17: 3 Aaron's name upon the rod of *L'*:
8 for the house of *L'* was budded,
18: 2 thy brethren also of the tribe of *L'*,
21 I have given the children of *L'* all
26: 59 was Jochebed, the daughter of *L'*,
59 her mother bare to *L'* in Egypt:
De 10: 8 the Lord separated the tribe of *L'*,
9 *L'* hath no part nor inheritance
18: 1 the Levites, and all the tribe of *L'*,
21: 5 the sons of *L'* shall come near:
27: 12 Simeon, and *L'*, and Judah, and
31: 9 it unto the priests the sons of *L'*,
33: 8 of *L'* he said, Let thy Thummim
Jos 13: 14 of *L'* he gave none inheritance;
33 *L'* Moses gave not any inheritance:
21: 10 who were of the children of *L'*, had:
1Ki 12: 31 which were not of the sons of *L'*.
1Ch 2: 1 Reuben, Simeon, *L'*, and Judah,
6: 1, 16 The sons of *L'*; Gershon,
38 the son of *L'*, the son of Israel.
43 the son of Gershom, the son of *L'*.
47 the son of Merari, the son of *L'*.
9: 18 the companies of the children of *L'*.
12: 26 Of the children of *L'* four thousand
21: 6 *L'* and Benjamin counted he not
23: 6 into courses among the sons of *L'*,
14 sons were named of the tribe of *L'*.
24 These were the sons of *L'* after the
24: 20 rest of the sons of *L'* were these:
Ezr 8: 15 found there none of the sons of *L'*.
18 the son of *L'*, the son of Israel;
Ne 10: 39 the children of *L'* shall bring the
12: 23 sons of *L'*, the chief of the fathers,
Ps 135: 20 Bless the Lord, O house of *L'*: ye
Eze 40: 46 sons of Zadok among the sons of *L'*,
48: 31 one gate of Judah, one gate of *L'*.
Zec 12: 13 The family of the house of *L'* apart,
Mal 2: 4 that my covenant might be with *L'*,
8 have corrupted the covenant of *L'*,
3: 3 he shall purify the sons of *L'*, and
M'r 2: 14 he saw *L'* the son of Alphæus
Lu 3: 24, 29 Matthat, which was the son of *L'*,
5: 27 saw a publican, named *L'*, sitting
29 *L'* made him a great feast in his
Heb 7: 5 they that are of the sons of *L'*,

Heb 7: 9 say, L· also, who receiveth tithes,
Re 7: 7 Of the tribe of L· were sealed twelve

leviathan (*le-vi'-ath-un*)
Job 41: 1 Canst thou draw out l· with an
Ps 74: 14 brakest the heads of l· in pieces,
104: 26 is that l·, whom thou hast made
Isa 27: 1 shall punish l· the piercing serpent,
1 even l· that crooked serpent; and he

Levite (*le'-vite*) See also LEVITES; LEVITICAL.
Ex 4: 14 Is not Aaron the L· thy brother?
De 12: 12 the L· that is within your gates;
18 and the L· that is within thy gates:
19 forsake not the L· as long as thou
14: 27 the L· that is within thy gates;
29 the L·, (because he hath no part
16: 11 and the L· that is within thy gates,
14 and the L·, the stranger, and the
18: 6 if a L· come from any of thy gates
26: 11 the L·, and the stranger that is
12 and hast given it unto the L·,
13 also have given them unto the L·,
J'g 17: 7 the family of Judah, who was a L·,
9 I am a L· of Beth-lehem-judah,
10 and thy victuals. So the L· went in.
11 the L· was content to dwell with
12 Micah consecrated the L·; and the
13 seeing I have a L· to my priest.
18: 3 the voice of the young man the L·:
15 the house of the young man the L·,
19: 1 there was a certain L· sojourning
20: 4 the L·, the husband of the woman
2Ch 20: 14 a L· of the sons of Asaph, came the
31: 12 which Cononiah the L· was ruler,
14 And Kore the son of Imnah the L·,
Ezr 10: 15 Shabbethai the L· helped them.
Lu 10: 32 likewise a L·, when he was at the
Ac 4: 36 The son of consolation,) a L·, and

Levites (*le'-vites*)
Ex 6: 25 the heads of the fathers of the L·
38: 21 of Moses for the service of the L·,
Le 25: 32 Notwithstanding the cities of the L·,
32 may the L· redeem at any time.
33 And if a man purchase of the L·,
33 for the houses of the cities of the L·
Nu 1: 47 L· after the tribe of their fathers
50 appoint the L· over the tabernacle
51 forward, the L· shall take it down:
51 to be pitched, the L· shall set it up:
53 the L· shall pitch round about the
53 the L· shall keep the charge of the
2: 17 with the camp of the L· in the midst
33 L· were not numbered among the
3: 9 shalt give the L· unto Aaron and to
12 I have taken the L· from among the
12 therefore the L· shall be mine;
20 These are the families of the L·
32 be chief over the chief of the L·,
39 All that were numbered of the L·,
41 And thou shalt take the L· for me
41 the cattle of the L· instead of all the
45 the L· instead of all the firstborn
45 the cattle of the L· instead of their
45 the L· shall be mine: I am the Lord.
46 Israel, which are more than the L·;
49 them that were redeemed by the L·;
4: 18 the Kohathites from among the L·:
46 that were numbered of the L·,
7: 5 thou shalt give them unto the L·,
6 oxen, and gave them unto the L·.
8: 6 Take the L· from among the
9 bring the L· before the tabernacle
10 shalt bring the L· before the Lord:
10 shall put their hands upon the L·:
11 shall offer the L· before the Lord
12 the L· shall lay their hands upon
12 to make an atonement for the L·.
13 thou shalt set the L· before Aaron,
14 thou separate the L· from among
14 of Israel: and the L· shall be mine.
15 shall the L· go in to do the service
18 taken the L· for all the firstborn
19 have given the L· as a gift to Aaron
20 did to the L· according unto all that
20 Moses concerning the L·, so did
21 And the L· were purified, and they
22 went the L· in to do their service
22 Moses concerning the L·, so did
24 is it that belongeth unto the L·:
26 Thus shalt thou do unto the L·
18: 6 I have taken your brethren the L·
23 the L· shall do the service of the
24 I have given to the L· to inherit:
26 Thus speak unto the L·, and say
30 counted unto the L· as the increase
26: 57 they that were numbered of the L·
58 These are the families of the L·:
31: 30 and give them unto the L·, which
47 and gave them unto the L·, which
35: 2 that they give also unto the L· of the
2 shall give also unto the L· suburbs
4 which ye shall give unto the L·,
6 which ye shall give unto the L·
7 cities which ye shall give to the L·
8 shall give of his cities unto the L·
De 17: 9 shalt come unto the priests the L·,
18 which is before the priests the L·:
18: 1 The priests the L·, and all the tribe
7 as all his brethren the L· do, which
24: 8 the priests the L· shall teach you:
27: 9 priests the L· spake unto all Israel,
14 the L· shall speak, and say unto all
31: 25 Moses commanded the L·, which
Jos 3: 3 the priests the L· bearing it, then
8: 33 that side before the priests the L·,
14: 3 the L· he gave none inheritance
Jos 14: 4 they gave no part unto the L· in
18: 7 the L· have no part among you;
21: 1 the heads of the fathers of the L·
3 children of Israel gave unto the L·
4 the priest, which were of the L·,
8 gave by lot unto the L· these cities
20 L· which remained of the children
27 of the families of the L·, out of the
34 the rest of the L·, out of the tribe
40 remaining of the families of the L·,
41 All the cities of the L· within the
1Sa 6: 15 L· took down the ark of the Lord,
2Sa 15: 24 also, and all the L· were with him,
1Ki 8: 4 did the priests and the L· bring up.
1Ch 6: 19 And these are the families of the L·
48 brethern also the L· were appointed
64 of Israel gave to the L· these cities
9: 2 the priests, L·, and the Nethinims.
14 And of the L·; Shemaiah the son of
26 For these L·, the four chief porters,
31 one of the L·, who was the firstborn
33 chief of the fathers of the L·, who
34 These chief fathers of the L· were
13: 2 with them also to the priests and L·
15: 2 carry the ark of God but the L·:
4 the children of Aaron, and the L·:
11 for the L·, for Uriel, Asaiah, and
12 the chief of the fathers of the L·:
14 and the L· sanctified themselves
15 the children of the L· bare the ark
16 David spake to the chief of the L·
17 the L· appointed Heman the son of
22 chief of the L·, was for song: he
26 when God helped the L· that bare
27 and all the L· that bare the ark,
16: 4 he appointed certain of the L· to
23: 2 Israel, with the priests and the L·.
3 Now the L· were numbered from
26 And also unto the L·; they shall no
27 L· were numbered from twenty
24: 6 Nethaneel the scribe, one of the L·,
6 the fathers of the priests and L·:
30 These were the sons of the L· after
31 the fathers of the priests and L·,
26: 17 Eastward were six L·, northward
20 And of the L·, Ahijah was over the
27: 17 Of the L·, Hashabiah the son of
28: 13, 21 courses of the priests and the L·,
2Ch 5: 4 came; and the L· took up the ark.
5 did the priests and the L· bring up.
12 Also the L· which were the singers,
7: 6 the L· also with instruments of
8: 14 the L· to their charges, to praise
15 of the king unto the priests and L·
11: 13 and the L· that were in all Israel
14 the L· left their suburbs and their
13: 9 the sons of Aaron, and the L·,
10 the L· wait upon their business:
17: 8 And with them he sent L·, even
8 Tobijah, and Tob-adonijah, L·;
19: 8 did Jehoshaphat set of the L·,
11 the L· shall be officers before you.
20: 19 And the L·, of the children of the
23: 2 gathered the L· out of all the cities
4 of the priests and of the L·, shall
6 and they that minister of the L·;
7 And the L· shall compass the king
8 the L· and all Judah did according
18 by the hand of the priests the L·,
24: 5 together the priests and the L·,
5 Howbeit the L· hastened it not.
6 hast thou not required of the L· to
11 king's office by the hand of the L·,
29: 4 brought in the priests and the L·,
5 And said unto them, hear me, ye L·,
12 Then the L· arose, Mahath the son
16 And the L· took it, to carry it out
25 he set the L· in the house of the
26 the L· stood with the instruments
30 commanded the L· to sing praise
34 their brethren the L· did help them,
34 the L· were more upright in heart
30: 15 priests and the L· were ashamed,
16 they received of the hand of the L·.
17 the L· had the charge of the killing
21 the L· and the priests praised the
22 spake comfortably unto all the L·
25 Judah, with the priests and the L·,
27 L· arose and blessed the people:
31: 2 and the L· after their courses,
2 L· for burnt offerings and for peace
4 portion of the priests and the L·,
9 with the priests and the L·
17 the L· from twenty years old and
19 by genealogies among the L·.
34: 9 which the L· that kept the doors had
12 were Jahath and Obadiah, the L·,
12 other of the L·, all that could skill
13 of the L· there were scribes, and
30 the priests, and the L·, and all the
35: 3 unto the L· that taught all Israel,
5 division of the families of the L·.
8 to the priests, and to the L·:
9 Jeiel and Jozabad, chief of the L·,
9 gave unto the L· for passover
10 place, and the L· in their courses,
11 their hands, and the L· flayed them.
14 the L· prepared for themselves,
15 brethren the L· prepared for them.
18 and the priests, and the L·, and all
Ezr 1: 5 and the priests, and the L·, with all
2: 40 The L·: the children of Jeshua
70 and the L·, and some of the people,
3: 8 brethren the priests and the L·,
8 appointed the L·, from twenty years
9 sons and their brethren the L·.
Ezr 3: 10 L· the sons of Asaph with cymbals,
12 of the priests and L· and chief of
6: 16 of Israel, the priests and the L·,
18 and the L· in their courses, for the
20 and the L· were purified together,
7: 7 the L·, and the singers, and the
13 and of his priests and L·, in my
24 touching any of the priests and L·,
8: 20 appointed for the service of the L·,
29 the chief of the priests of the L·,
30 So took the priests and the L· the
33 Noadiah the son of Binnui, L·;
9: 1 the priests, and the L·, have not
10: 5 chief priests, the L·, and all Israel,
23 of the L·; Jozabad, and Shimei,
Ne 3: 17 After him repaired the L·, Rehum
7: 1 singers and the L· were appointed,
43 The L·: the children of Jeshua,
73 So the priests, and the L·, and the
8: 7 and the L·, caused the people to
9 and the L· that taught the people,
11 the L· stilled all the people, saying,
13 and the L·, unto Ezra the scribe,
9: 4 upon the stairs, of the L·, Jeshua,
5 Then the L·, Jeshua, and Kadmiel,
38 princes, L·, and priests, seal unto it.
10: 9 And the L·: both Jeshua the son of
28 the priests, the L·, the porters, the
34 the lots among the priests, the L·,
37 tithes of our ground unto the L·,
37 L· might have the tithes in all the
38 with the L·, when the L· take tithes:
38 L· shall bring up the tithe of the
11: 3 wit, Israel, the priests, and the L·,
15 Also of the L·: Shemaiah the son
16 Jozabad, of the chief of the L·,
18 All the L· in the holy city were two
20 Israel, of the priests, and the L·,
22 overseer also of the L· at Jerusalem
36 of the L· were divisions in Judah,
12: 1 priests and the L· that went up
8 Moreover the L·: Jeshua, Binnui,
22 L· in the days of Eliashib, Joiada,
24 And the chief of the L·: Hashabiah,
27 sought the L· out of all their places,
30 and the L· purified themselves,
44 of the law for the priests and L·:
44 for the priests and for the L· that
47 sanctified holy things unto the L·;
47 the L· sanctified them unto the
13: 5 commanded to be given to the L·,
10 portions of the L· had not been given
10 the L· and the singers, that did the
13 the scribe, and of the L·, Pedaiah:
22 And I commanded the L· that they
29 of the priesthood, and of the L·,
30 the wards of the priests and the L·,
Isa 66: 21 take of them for priests and for L·,
Jer 33: 18 shall the priests the L· want a man
21 and with the L·, the priests, my
22 and the L· that minister unto me.
Eze 43: 19 thou shalt give to the priests the L·
44: 10 L· that are gone far away from me,
15 priests the L·, the sons of Zadok,
45: 5 shall also the L·, the ministers of
48: 11 went astray, as the L· went astray.
12 most holy by the border of the L·.
13 the L· shall have five and twenty
22 from the possession of the L·, and
Joh 1: 19 when the Jews sent priests and L·

Levitical
Heb 7: 11 were by the L· priesthood,

levy
Nu 31: 28 And l· a tribute unto the Lord of
1Ki 5: 13 king Solomon raised a l· out of all
13 and the l· was thirty thousand men.
14 and Adoniram was over the l·.
9: 15 the l· which king Solomon raised;
21 upon those did Solomon l· a tribute

lewd
Eze 16: 27 which are ashamed of thy l· way.
23: 44 and unto Aholibah, the l· women.
Ac 17: 5 certain l· fellows of the baser sort,

lewdly
Eze 22: 11 hath l· defiled his daughter in law;

lewdness
J'g 20: 6 committed l· and folly in Israel.
Jer 11: 15 she hath wrought l· with many,
13: 27 neighings, the l· of thy whoredom,
Eze 16: 43 shalt not commit this l· above all
58 Thou hast borne thy l· and thine
22: 9 in the midst of thee they commit l·.
23: 21 to remembrance the l· of thy youth,
27 Thus will I make thy l· to cease
29 both thy l· and thy whoredoms.
35 therefore bear thou also thy l· and
48 Thus will I cause l· to cease out of
48 be taught not to do after your l·.
49 shall recompense your l· upon you,
24: 13 In thy filthiness is l·: because I
Ho 2: 10 And now will I discover her l· in
6: 9 by consent: for they commit l·.
Ac 18: 14 a matter of wrong or wicked l·,

liar See also LIARS.
Job 24: 25 not so now, who will make me a l·,
Pr 17: 4 l· giveth ear to a naughty tongue.
19: 22 a poor man is better than a l·.
30: 6 thee, and thou be found a l·.
Jer 15: 18 thou be altogether unto me as a l·,
Joh 8: 44 for he is a l·, and the father of it.
55 him not, I shall be a l· like unto you:
Ro 3: 4 let God be true, but every man a l·;
1Jo 1: 10 have not sinned, we make him a l·,
2: 4 not his commandments, is a l·, and

1Jo 2:22 Who is a *l*' but he that denieth that
4:20 and hateth his brother, he is a *l*':
5:10 not God hath made him a *l*';

liars
De 33:29 shall be found *l*' unto thee;
Ps 116:11 I said in my haste, All men are *l*'.
Isa 44:25 frustrateth the tokens of the *l*', and
Jer 50:36 A sword is upon the *l*'; and they
1Ti 1:10 for *l*', for perjured persons, and if
Tit 1:12 said, The Cretians are alway *l*',
Re 2: 2 are not, and hast found them *l*':
21: 8 sorcerers, and idolaters, and all *l*',

liberal
Pr 11:25 The *l*' soul shall be made fat: and
Isa 32: 5 person shall be no more called *l*',
8 But the *l*' deviseth *l*' things; and
8 and by *l*' things shall he stand.
2Co 9:13 for your *l*' distribution unto them,

liberality
1Co 16: 3 to bring your *l*' unto Jerusalem.
2Co 8: 2 abounded unto the riches of their *l*'.

liberally
De 15:14 furnish him *l*' out of thy flock,
Jas 1: 5 ask of God, that giveth to all men *l*',

Libertines (*lib'-ur-tins*)
Ac 6: 9 is called the synagogue of the *L*',

liberty
Le 25:10 proclaim *l*' throughout all the land
Ps 119:45 And I will walk at *l*': for I seek thy
Isa 61: 1 to proclaim *l*' to the captives, and
Jer 34: 8 to proclaim *l*' unto them;
15 in proclaiming *l*' every man to his
16 he had set at *l*' at their pleasure,
17 in proclaiming *l*', every one to his
17 behold, I proclaim a *l*' for you, saith
Eze 46:17 then it shall be his to the year of *l*';
Lu 4:18 to set at *l*' them that are bruised,
Ac 24:23 to keep Paul, and to let him have *l*',
26:32 This man might have been set at *l*',
27: 3 gave him *l*' to go unto his friends
Ro 8:21 glorious *l*' of the children of God.
1Co 7:39 she is at *l*' to be married to whom
8: 9 any means this *l*' of yours become
10:29 for why is my *l*' judged of another
2Co 3:17 the Spirit of the Lord is, there is *l*'.
Ga 2: 4 to spy out our *l*' which we have in
5: 1 the *l*' wherewith Christ hath made
13 For...ye have been called unto *l*';
13 only use not *l*' for an occasion to
Heb 13:23 our brother Timothy is set at *l*';
Jas 1:25 looketh into the perfect law of *l*',
2:12 that shall be judged by the law of *l*'.
1Pe 2:16 and not using your *l*' for a cloke of
2Pe 2:19 While they promise them *l*', they

Libnah (*lib'-nah*) See also LABAN.
Nu 33:20 Rimmon-parez, and pitched in *L*'.
21 they removed from *L*', and pitched
Jos 10:29 unto *L*', and fought against *L*':
31 And Joshua passed from *L*', and all
32 to all that he had done to *L*'.
39 as he had done also to *L*', and to
12:15 The king of *L*', one; the king of
15:42 *L*', and Ether, and Ashan,
21:13 slayer; and *L*' with her suburbs,
2Ki 8:22 Then *L*' revolted at the same time.
19: 8 king of Assyria warring against *L*':
23:31 the daughter of Jeremiah of *L*'.
24:18 the daughter of Jeremiah of *L*'.
1Ch 6:57 of refuge, and *L*' with her suburbs,
2Ch 21:10 did *L*' revolt from under his hand;
Isa 37: 8 king of Assyria warring against *L*':
Jer 52: 1 the daughter of Jeremiah of *L*'.

Libnath See SHIHOR-LIBNATH.

Libni (*lib'-ni*) See also LAADAN; LIBNITES.
Ex 6:17 sons of Gershon; *L*', and Shimi,
Nu 3:18 Gershon by their families; *L*', and
1Ch 6:17 sons of Gershom; *L*', and Shimei.
20 Of Gershom; *L*' his son, Jahath his
29 *L*' his son, Shimei his son, Uzza his

Libnites (*lib'-nites*)
Nu 3:21 Gershon was the family of the *L*',
26:58 the family of the *L*', the family of

Libya (*lib'-e-ah*) See also LIBYANS.
Eze 30: 5 Ethiopia, and *L*', and Lydia, and
38: 5 Ethiopia, and *L*' with them;
Ac 2:10 and in the parts of *L*' about Cyrene,

Libyans (*lib'-e-uns*) See also LEHABIM.
Jer 46: 9 the Ethiopians and the *L*', that
Da 11:43 the *L*' and the Ethiopians shall be

lice
Ex 8:16 may become *l*' throughout all the
17 it became *l*' in man, and in beast;
17 all the dust of the land became *l*'
18 enchantments to bring forth *l*',
18 so there were *l*' upon man, and upon
Ps 105:31 of flies, and *l*' in all their coasts.

licence
Ac 21:40 when he had given him *l*', Paul
25:16 and have *l*' to answer for himself

lick See also LICKED; LICKETH.
Nu 22: 4 Now shall this company *l*' up all
1Ki 21:19 of Naboth shall dogs *l*' thy blood,
Ps 72: 9 and his enemies shall *l*' the dust.
Isa 49:23 and *l*' up the dust of thy feet;
Mic 7:17 They shall *l*' the dust like a serpent,

licked
1Ki 18:38 *l*' up the water that was in the
21:19 where dogs *l*' the blood of Naboth
22:38 and the dogs *l*' up his blood;
Lu 16:21 the dogs came and *l*' his sores.

licketh
Nu 22: 4 as the ox *l*' up the grass of the

lid See also EYELIDS.
2Ki 12: 9 and bored a hole in the *l*' of it,

lie^ See also LAIN; LAY; LIED; LIEN; LIES; LIEST; LIETH; LYING.
Ge 19:32 we will *l*' with him, that we may
34 go thou in, and *l*' with him, that
30:15 he shall *l*' with thee to night for
39: 7 Joseph; and she said, *L*' with me.
10 her, to *l*' by her, or to be with her.
12 by his garment, saying, *L*' with me:
14 he came in unto me to *l*' with me,
47:30 I will *l*' with my fathers, and thou
Ex 21:13 if a man *l*' not in wait, but God
22:16 is not betrothed, and *l*' with her,
23:11 thou shall let it rest and *l*' still;
Le 6: 2 and *l*' unto his neighbour in that
15:18 also with whom man shall *l*' with
24 And if any man *l*' with her at all,
18:20 thou shall not *l*' carnally with
22 Thou shalt not *l*' with mankind,
23 Neither shalt thou *l*' with any
23 before a beast to *l*' down thereto:
19:11 falsely, neither *l*' one to another.
20:12 if a man *l*' with his daughter in law,
13 If a man also *l*' with mankind, as
15 if a man *l*' with a beast, he
16 any beast, and *l*' down thereto,
18 if a man shall *l*' with a woman
20 man shall *l*' with his uncle's wife,
26: 6 ye shall *l*' down, and none shall
Nu 5:13 And a man *l*' with her carnally,
10: 5 camps that *l*' on the east parts
6 camps that *l*' on the south side
23:19 is not a man, that he should *l*';
24 *l*' down until he eat of the prey,
De 19:11 neighbour, and *l*' in wait for him,
22:23 her in the city, and *l*' with her;
25 the man force her, and *l*' with her:
28 lay hold on her, and *l*' with her,
25: 2 judge shall cause him to *l*' down,
28:30 and another man shall *l*' with her:
29:20 written in this book shall *l*' upon
Jos 8: 4 ye shall *l*' in wait against the city,
9 they went to *l*' in ambush, and abode
12 *l*' in ambush between Beth-el and
J'g 9:32 with thee, and *l*' in wait in the field:
19:20 let all thy wants *l*' upon me; only
21:20 Go and *l*' in wait in the vineyards;
Ru 3: 4 mark the place where he shall *l*',
7 he went to *l*' down at the end of the
13 liveth: *l*' down until the morning.
1Sa 3: 5 said, I called not; *l*' down again.
6 called not, my son; *l*' down again.
9 Eli said unto Samuel, Go, *l*' down:
15:29 of Israel will not *l*' nor repent:
22: 8, 13 me, to *l*' in wait, as at this day?
2Sa 11:11 to drink, and to *l*' with my wife?
13 at even he went out to *l*' on his bed
12:11 he shall *l*' with thy wives in the
13:11 her, Come *l*' with me, my sister.
1Ki 1: 2 him, and let her *l*' in thy bosom,
2Ki 4:16 do not *l*' unto thine handmaid.
Job 6:28 for it is evident unto you if I *l*'.
7: 4 When I *l*' down, I say, When shall
11:19 Also thou shalt *l*' down, and none
20:11 shall *l*' down with him in the dust.
21:26 They shall *l*' down alike in the dust,
27:19 The rich man shall *l*' down, but he
34: 6 Should I *l*' against my right? my
38:40 abide in the covert to *l*' in wait?
Ps 23: 2 me to *l*' down in green pastures:
57: 4 I *l*' even among them that are set
59: 3 For, lo, they *l*' in wait for my soul:
62: 9 and men of high degree are a *l*':
88: 5 like the slain that *l*' in the grave,
89:35 that I will not *l*' unto David.
119:69 The proud have forged a *l*' against
Pr 3:24 yea, thou shalt *l*' down, and thy
12: 6 wicked are to *l*' in wait for blood:
14: 5 A faithful witness will not *l*': but
Ec 4:11 if two *l*' together, then they have
Ca 1:13 *l*' all night betwixt my breasts.
Isa 11: 6 leopard shall *l*' down with the kid;
7 their young ones shall *l*' down
13:21 wild beasts of the desert shall *l*'
14:18 all of them, *l*' in glory, every one
30 the needy shall *l*' down in safety:
17: 2 be for flocks, which shall *l*' down,
27:10 and there shall he *l*' down, and
33: 8 The highways *l*' waste, the wayfaring
34:10 to generation it shall *l*' waste; none
43:17 they shall *l*' down together, they
44:20 Is there not a *l*' in my right hand?
50:11 hand; ye shall *l*' down in sorrow.
51:20 they *l*' at the head of all the streets,
63: 8 people, children that will not *l*':
65:10 a place for the herds to *l*' down in,
Jer 3:25 We *l*' down in our shame, and our
27:10 prophesy a *l*' unto you, to remove
14 for they prophesy a *l*' unto you,
15 they prophesy a *l*' in my name;
16 for they prophesy a *l*' unto you,
28:15 makest this people to trust in a *l*'.
29:21 prophesy a *l*' unto you in my name;
31 and he caused you to trust in a *l*':
33:12 causing their flocks to *l*' down.
La 2:21 young and the old *l*' on the ground
Eze 4: 4 *L*' thou also upon thy left side,
4 the days that thou shalt *l*' upon it
6 *l*' again on thy right side, and thou
9 days that thou shalt *l*' upon thy
21:29 Whiles they divine a *l*' unto thee,
31:18 *l*' in the midst of...uncircumcised
Eze 32:21 they *l*' uncircumcised, slain by the
27 they shall not *l*' with the mighty
28 shalt *l*' with them that are slain
29 shall *l*' with the uncircumcised,
30 they *l*' uncircumcised with them
34:14 there shall they *l*' in a good fold,
15 I will cause them to *l*' down, saith
Ho 2:18 will make them to *l*' down safely.
7: 6 like an oven, whiles they *l*' in wait:
Joe 1:13 *l*' all night in sackcloth,...ministers
Am 6: 4 That *l*' upon beds of ivory, and
Mic 1:14 shall be a *l*' to the kings of Israel.
2:11 in the spirit and falsehood do *l*',
7: 2 men: they all *l*' in wait for blood;
Hab 2: 3 the end it shall speak, and not *l*':
Zep 2: 7 shall they *l*' down in the evening:
14 flocks shall *l*' down in the midst of
15 a place for beasts to *l*' down in!
3:13 for they shall feed and *l*' down,
Hag 1: 4 houses, and this house *l*' waste?
Zec 10: 2 and the diviners have seen a *l*',
Joh 5: 6 When Jesus saw him *l*', and knew
8:44 When he speaketh a *l*', he
20: 6 and seeth the linen clothes *l*',
Ac 5: 3 hath Satan filled thine heart to *l*'
23:21 there *l*' in wait for him of them more
Ro 1:25 changed the truth of God into a *l*',
3: 7 through my *l*' unto his glory;
9: 1 I say the truth in Christ, I *l*' not,
2Co 11:31 evermore, knoweth that I *l*' not.
Ga 1:20 you, behold, before God, I *l*' not.
Eph 4:14 whereby they *l*' in wait to deceive;
Col 3: 9 *L*' not one to another, seeing that
2Th 2:11 that they should believe a *l*':
1Ti 2: 7 the truth in Christ, and *l*' not;)
Tit 1: 2 life, which God, that cannot *l*',
Heb 6:18 it was impossible for God to *l*',
Jas 3:14 not, and *l*' not against the truth.
1Jo 1: 6 darkness, we *l*', and do not the truth:
2:21 it, and that no *l*' is of the truth.
27 and is truth, and is no *l*', and even
Re 3: 9 are Jews, and are not, but do *l*';
21:27 abomination, or maketh a *l*':
22:15 whosoever loveth and maketh a *l*'.

lied See also BELIED.
1Ki 13:18 drink water. But he *l*' unto him.
Ps 78:36 *l*' unto him with their tongues.
Isa 57:11 or feared, that thou hast *l*', and
Ac 5: 4 thou hast not *l*' unto men, but unto

lien See also LAIN.
Ge 26:10 lightly have *l*' with thy wife,
Ps 68:13 Though ye have *l*' among the pots,
Jer 3: 2 where thou hast not been *l*' with.

liers
Jos 8:13 *l*' in wait on the west of the city,
14 were *l*' in ambush against him
J'g 9:25 of Shechem set *l*' in wait for him in
16:12 *l*' in wait abiding in the chamber.
20:29 set *l*' in wait round about Gibeah.
33 the *l*' in wait of Israel came forth
36 they trusted unto the *l*' in wait which
37 the *l*' in wait hasted, and rushed
37 the *l*' in wait drew themselves along,
38 the men of Israel and the *l*' in wait,

lies
J'g 16:10, 13 hast mocked me, and told me *l*':
Job 11: 3 thy *l*' make men hold their peace?
13: 4 But ye are forgers of *l*', ye are all
Ps 40: 4 proud, nor such as turn aside to *l*'.
58: 3 soon as they be born, speaking *l*'.
62: 4 they delight in *l*': they bless with
63:11 mouth of them that speak *l*' shall be
101: 7 telleth *l*' shall not tarry in my sight.
Pr 6:19 A false witness that speaketh *l*',
14: 5 lie: but a false witness will utter *l*'.
25 but a deceitful witness speaketh *l*'.
19: 5 he that speaketh *l*' shall not escape.
9 and he that speaketh *l*' shall perish.
29:12 If a ruler hearken to *l*', all his
30: 8 far from me vanity and *l*':
Isa 9:15 the prophet that teacheth *l*', he is
16: 6 wrath: but his *l*' shall not be so.
28:15 we have made *l*' our refuge, and
17 shall sweep away the refuge of *l*',
59: 3 your lips have spoken *l*', your
4 they trust in vanity, and speak *l*';
Jer 9: 3 their tongue like their bow for *l*':
5 taught their tongue to speak *l*',
14:14 prophets prophesy *l*' in my name:
16:19 Surely our fathers have inherited *l*',
20: 6 to whom thou hast prophesied *l*'.
23:14 commit adultery, and walk in *l*':
25 said, that prophesy *l*' in my name,
26 of the prophets that prophesy *l*'?
32 cause my people to err by their *l*',
48:30 be so; his *l*' shall not so effect it.
Eze 13: 8 ye have spoken vanity, and seen *l*',
9 that see vanity, and that divine *l*':
19 to my people that hear your *l*'?
22 with *l*' ye have made the heart of
22:28 vanity, and divining *l*' unto them,
24:12 She hath wearied herself with *l*',
Da 11:27 they shall speak *l*' at one table;
Ho 7: 3 and the princes with their *l*'.
13 they have spoken *l*' against me.
10:13 ye have eaten the fruit of *l*':
11:12 compasseth me about with *l*', and
12: 1 daily increaseth *l*' and desolation;
Am 2: 4 and their *l*' caused them to err,
Mic 6:12 inhabitants thereof have spoken *l*',
Na 3: 1 city! it is all full of *l*' and robbery;
Hab 2:18 molten image, and a teacher of *l*',
Zep 3:13 shall not do iniquity, nor speak *l*';
Zec 13: 3 speakest *l*' in the name of the Lord:
1Ti 4: 2 Speaking *l*' in hypocrisy; having

liest
Ge 28:13 land whereon thou l', to thee will
De 6: 7 when thou l' down, and when thou
11:19 when thou l' down, and when thou
Jos 7:10 l' thou thus upon thy face?
Pr 3:24 When thou l' down, thou shalt not

lieth
Ge 4: 7 doest not well, sin l' at the door.
49:25 blessings of the deep that l' under,
Ex 22:19 Whosoever l' with a beast shall
Le 6: 3 was lost, and l' concerning it,
14:47 he that l' in the house shall wash
15: 4 whereon he l' that hath the issue,
20 every thing that she l' upon in her
24 bed whereon he l' shall be unclean.
26 Every bed whereon she l' all the
33 him that l' with her that is unclean.
19:20 whosoever l' carnally with a woman,
20:11 man that l' with his father's wife
13 mankind, as he l' with a woman,
26:34 her sabbaths, as long as it l' desolate,
35 As long as it l' desolate it shall rest;
43 while she l' desolate without them:
Nu 21:15 and l' upon the border of Moab.
De 27:20 be he that l' with his father's wife;
21 that l' with any manner of beast.
22 Curse be he that l' with his sister,
23 he that l' with his mother in law.
Jos 15: 8 mountain that l' before the valley of
17: 7 Michmethah, that l' before Shechem;
18:13 the hill that l' on the south side of the
14 the hill that l' before Beth-horon
16 the mountain that l' before the valley
J'g 1:16 Judah, which l' in the south of Arad;
16: 5 and see wherein his great strength l',
6 thee, wherein thy great strength l',
15 told me wherein thy great strength l'.
18:28 in the valley that l' by Beth-rehob.
Ru 3: 4 when he l' down, that thou shalt
2Sa 2:24 that l' before Giah by the way of the
24: 5 city that l' in the midst of the river of
Ne 2: 3 of my fathers' sepulchres, l' waste,
17 Jerusalem l' waste, and the gates
3:25 tower which l' out from the king's
26 the east, and the tower that l' out.
27 against the great tower that l' out,
Job 14:12 So man l' down, and riseth not:
40:21 He l' under the shady trees, in the
Ps 10: 9 l' in wait secretly as a lion in his
9 he l' in wait to catch the poor: he
41: 8 now that he l' he shall rise up no
88: 7 Thy wrath l' hard upon me, and
Pr 7:12 and l' in wait at every corner.)
23:28 She also l' in wait as for a prey,
34 thou shall be as he that l' down in
34 as he that l' upon the top of a mast.
Eze 9: 2 gate, which l' toward the north,
29: 3 great dragon that l' in the midst
Mic 7: 5 from her that l' in thy bosom.
M't 8: 6 my servant l' at home sick of the
M'r 5:23 daughter l' at the point of death:
Ac 14: 6 unto the region that l' round about:
27:12 l' toward the south west and north
Ro 12:18 as much as l' in you, live peaceably
1Jo 5:19 the whole world l' in wickedness.
Re 21:16 And the city l' foursquare, and the

lieutenants
Ezr 8:36 commissions unto the king's l', and
Es 3:12 had commanded unto the king's l',
8: 9 unto the Jews, and to the l', and
9: 3 rulers of the provinces, and the l',

life See also LIFETIME; LIVES.
Ge 1:20 moving creature that hath l',
30 the earth, wherein there is l',
2: 7 into his nostrils the breath of l';
9 the tree of l' also in the midst of
3:14 shalt thou eat all the days of thy l':
17 thou eat of it all the days of thy l';
22 take also of the tree of l', and eat
24 to keep the way of the tree of l'.
6:17 flesh, wherein is the breath of l',
7:11 the six hundredth year of Noah's l',
15 flesh, wherein is the breath of l'.
22 whose nostrils was the breath of l',
9: 4 But flesh with the l' thereof, which
5 brother will I require the l' of man.
18:10 thee according to the time of l';
14 thee, according to the time of l',
19:17 Escape for thy l'; look not behind
19 shewed unto me in saving my l';
23: 1 were the years of the l' of Sarah.
25: 7 the years of Abraham's l' which he
17 are the years of the l' of Ishmael,
27:46 I am weary of my l' because of the
46 land, what good shall my l' do me?
32:30 to face, and my l' is preserved.
42:15 By the l' of Pharaoh ye shall not
16 by the l' of Pharaoh surely ye are
44:30 his l' is bound up in the lad's l';
45: 5 did send me before you to preserve l'.
47: 9 days of the years of my l' been,
9 of the years of the l' of my fathers
48:15 the God which fed me all my l' long
Ex 4:19 men are dead which sought thy l'.
6:16 the years of the l' of Levi were an
18 years of the l' of Kohath were an
20 the years of the l' of Amram were
21:23 then thou shalt give l' for l',
30 for the ransom of his l' whatsoever
Le 17:11 the l' of the flesh is in the blood:
14 For it is the l' of all flesh;
14 the blood of it is for the l' thereof:
14 l' of all flesh is the blood thereof:
18:18 beside the other in her l' time.
Nu 35:31 for the l' of a murderer, which is

De 4: 9 thy heart all the days of thy l':
6: 2 thy son's son, all the days of thy l';
12:23 the blood: for the blood is the l';
23 mayest not eat the l' with the flesh.
16: 3 land of Egypt all the days of thy l'.
17:19 read therein all the days of his l':
19:21 l' shall go for l', eye for eye, tooth
20:19 (for the tree of the field is man's l')
24: 6 for he taketh a man's l' to pledge.
28:66 And thy l' shall hang in doubt
66 shalt have none assurance of thy l':
30:15 set before thee this day l' and good,
19 I have set before you l' and death,
19 therefore choose l', that both thou
20 for he is thy l', and the length of
32:47 thing for you; because it is your l':
Jos 1: 5 before thee all the days of thy l':
2:14 Our l' for yours, if ye utter not
4:14 feared Moses, all the days of his l'.
J'g 9:17 for you, and adventured his l' far,
12: 3 I put my l' in my hands, and passed
16:30 than they which he slew in his l'.
18:25 run upon thee, and thou lose thy l',
Ru 4:15 be unto thee a restorer of thy l',
1Sa 1:11 unto the Lord all the days of his l',
7:15 judged Israel all the days of his l'.
18:18 and what is my l', or my father's
19: 5 For he did put his l' in his hand,
11 If thou save not thy l' to night,
20: 1 thy father, that he seeketh my l'?
22:23 he that seeketh my l' seeketh thy l':
23:15 Saul was come out to seek his l':
25:29 shall be bound in the bundle of l'
26:24 as thy l' was much set by this day
24 my l' be much set by in the eyes of
28: 9 then layest thou a snare for my l',
21 and I have put my l' in my hand,
2Sa 1: 9 because my l' is yet whole in me.
4: 8 thine enemy, which sought thy l';
14: 7 the l' of his brother whom he slew;
15:21 shall be, whether in death or l',
16:11 forth of my bowels, seeketh my l':
18:13 falsehood against mine own l': for
19: 5 which this day have saved thy l',
1Ki 1:12 that thou mayest save thine own l',
12 and the l' of thy son Solomon.
2:23 spoken this word against his own l'.
3:11 hast not asked for thyself long l';
11 hast asked the l' of thine enemies;
4:21 Solomon all the days of his l'.
11:34 him prince all the days of his l' for
15: 5 commanded...all the days of his l',
6 and Jeroboam all the days of his l'.
19: 2 if I make not thy l' as the l' of one
3 that, he arose, and went for his l',
4 now, O Lord, take away my l'; for
10, 14 they seek my l', to take it away.
20:31 peradventure he will save thy l'.
39 then shall thy l' be for his l', or else
42 therefore thy l' shall go for his l',
2Ki 1:13 let my l', and the l' of these fifty
14 my l' now be precious in thy sight.
4:16 season, according to the time of l',
17 unto her, according to the time of l'.
7: 7 camp as it was, and fled for their l'.
8: 1 whose son he had restored to l',
5 he had restored a dead body to l',
5 whose son he had restored to l',
5 her son, whom Elisha restored to l'.
10:24 go, his l' shall be for the l' of him.
25:29 before him all the days of his l'.
30 for every day, all the days of his l'.
2Ch 1:11 nor the l' of thine enemies,
11 neither yet hast asked long l'; but
Ezr 6:10 and pray for the l' of the king, and
Ne 6:11 go into the temple to save his l'?
Es 7: 3 king, let my l' be given me at my
7 stood up to make request for his l'
8:11 and to stand for their l', to destroy,
Job 2: 4 a man hath will he give for his l'.
6 he is in thine hand; but save his l'.
3:20 and l' unto the bitter in soul;
6:11 end, that I should prolong my l'?
7: 7 O remember that my l' is wind:
15 and death rather than my l'.
9:21 my soul: I would despise my l'.
10: 1 My soul is weary of my l'; I will
12 hast granted me l' and favour,
13:14 teeth, and put my l' in mine hand?
24:22 riseth up, and no man is sure of l'.
31:39 the owners thereof to lose their l':
33: 4 of the Almighty hath given me l'.
18 his l' from perishing by the sword.
20 So that his l' abhorreth bread, and
22 grave, and his l' to the destroyers.
28 the pit, and his l' shall see the light.
36: 6 preserveth not the l' of the wicked:
14 and their l' is among the unclean.
Ps 7: 5 tread down my l' upon the earth,
16:11 Thou wilt shew me the path of l':
17:14 which have their portion in this l',
21: 4 He asked l' of thee, and thou gavest
23: 6 follow me all the days of my l':
26: 9 sinners, nor my l' with bloody men:
27: 1 the Lord is the strength of my l';
4 of the Lord all the days of my l',
30: 5 but a moment; in his favour is l':
31:10 For my l' is spent with grief, and
13 they devised to take away my l'.
34:12 What man is he that desireth l',
36: 9 For with thee is the fountain of l':
38:12 They also that seek after my l'
42: 8 my prayer unto the God of my l'.
61: 6 wilt prolong the king's l':
63: 3 lovingkindness is better than l',
64: 1 preserve my l' from fear of the

Ps 66: 9 which holdeth our soul in l', and
78:50 gave their l' over to the pestilence;
88: 3 my l' draweth nigh unto the grave.
91:16 With long l' will I satisfy him, and
103: 4 redeemeth thy l' from destruction;
128: 5 of Jerusalem all the days of thy l'.
133: 3 the blessing, even l' for evermore.
143: 3 he hath smitten my l' down to the
Pr 1:19 taketh away the l' of the owners
2:19 take they hold of the paths of l'.
3: 2 For length of days, and long l',
18 She is a tree of l' to them that lay
22 So shall they be l' unto thy soul,
4:10 the years of thy l' shall be many.
13 not go: keep her; for she is thy l'.
22 are l' unto those that find them,
23 for out of it are the issues of l'.
5: 6 shouldest ponder the path of l',
6:23 of instruction are the way of l':
26 will hunt for the precious l'.
7:23 and knoweth not that it is for his l'.
8:35 For whoso findeth me findeth l',
9:11 years of thy l' shall be increased.
10:11 of a righteous man is a well of l':
16 of the righteous tendeth to l':
17 He is in the way of l' that keepeth
11:19 As righteousness tendeth to l': so
30 fruit of the righteous is a tree of l';
12:10 man regardeth the l' of his beast:
28 In the way of righteousness is l';
13: 3 keepeth his mouth keepeth his l':
8 ransom of a man's l' are his riches:
12 desire cometh, it is a tree of l'.
14 law of the wise is a fountain of l',
14:27 fear of the Lord is a fountain of l',
30 A sound heart is the l' of the flesh:
15: 4 A wholesome tongue is a tree of l':
24 The way of l' is above to the wise,
31 ear that heareth the reproof of l'
16:15 light of the king's countenance is l';
22 is a wellspring of l' unto him that
18:21 Death and l' are in the power of the
19:23 The fear of the Lord tendeth to l':
21:21 righteousness and mercy findeth l',
22: 4 Lord are riches, and honour, and l'.
31:12 and not evil all the days of her l'.
Ec 2: 3 the heaven all the days of their l'.
17 Therefore I hated l'; because the
3:12 to rejoice, and to do good in his l'.
5:18 under the sun all the days of his l',
20 much remember the days of his l';
6:12 what is good for man in this l', all
12 days of his vain l' which he spendeth
7:12 giveth l' to them that have it.
15 prolongeth his l' in his wickedness.
8:15 him of his labour the days of his l',
9: 9 lovest all the days of the l' of thy
9 for that is thy portion in this l',
Isa 15: 4 his l' shall be grievous unto him.
38:12 I have cut off like a weaver my l':
16 these things is the l' of my spirit:
20 all the days of our l' in the house
43: 4 men for thee, and people for thy l'.
57:10 hast found the l' of thine hand;
Jer 4:30 despise thee, they will seek thy l'.
8: 3 shall be chosen rather than l' by
11:21 men of Anathoth, that seek thy l',
21: 7 hand of those that seek their l':
8 I set before you the way of l', and
9 his l' shall be unto him for a prey.
22:25 the hand of them that seek thy l',
34:20 the hand of them that seek their l':
21 the hand of them that seek their l',
38: 2 he shall have his l' for a prey, and
16 hand of these men that seek thy l'.
39:18 thy l' shall be for a prey unto thee:
44:30 the hand of them that seek his l';
30 his enemy, and that sought his l'.
45: 5 thy l' will I give unto thee for a prey
49:37 and before them that seek their l':
52:33 before him all the days of his l'.
34 of his death, all the days of his l'.
La 2:19 for the l' of thy young children,
3:53 have cut off my l' in the dungeon,
58 soul; thou hast redeemed my l'.
Eze 3:18 from his wicked way, to save his l';
7:13 himself in the iniquity of his l'.
13:22 wicked way, by promising him l':
32:10 every man for his own l', in the
33:15 robbed, walk in the statutes of l',
Da 12: 2 awake, some to everlasting l',
Jon 1:14 let us not perish for this man's l',
2: 6 hast thou brought up my l' from
4: 3 take, I beseech thee, my l' from me;
Mal 2: 5 My covenant was with him of l'
M't 2:20 which sought the young child's l'.
6:25 Take no thought for your l', what
25 Is not the l' more than meat, and
7:14 is the way, which leadeth unto l',
10:39 He that findeth his l' shall lose it:
39 he that loseth his l' for my sake
16:25 will save his l' shall lose it:
25 will lose his l' for my sake shall
18: 8 better for thee to enter into l' halt
9 thee to enter into l' with one eye,
19:16 I do, that I may have eternal l'?
17 but if thou wilt enter into l', keep
29 and shall inherit everlasting l'.
20:28 to give his l' a ransom for many.
25:46 but the righteous into l' eternal.
M'r 3: 4 or to do evil? to save l', or to kill?
8:35 will save his l' shall lose it;
35 shall lose his l' for my sake and the
9:43 for thee to enter into l' maimed,
45 better for thee to enter halt into l',
10:17 I do that I may inherit eternal l'?

M'r 10:30 and in the world to come eternal l'.
45 to give his l' a ransom for many.
Lu 1:75 before him, all the days of our l'.
6: 9 evil? to save l', or to destroy it?
8:14 and riches and pleasures of this l',
9:24 will save his l' shall lose it:
24 will lose his l' for my sake, the
10:25 shall I do to inherit eternal l'?
12:15 for a man's l' consisteth not in the
22 Take no thought for your l', what
23 The l' is more than meat, and the
14:26 sisters, yea, and his own l' also,
17:33 seek to save his l' shall lose it;
33 shall lose his l' shall preserve it.
18:18 shall I do to inherit eternal l'?
30 in the world to come l' everlasting.
21:34 drunkenness, and cares of this l',
Joh 1: 4 In him was l'; and the l' was the
3:15 not perish, but have eternal l'.
16 not perish, but have everlasting l'.
36 on the Son hath everlasting l':
36 believeth not the Son shall not see l';
4:14 springing up into everlasting l'.
36 gathereth fruit unto l' eternal:
5:24 that sent me, hath everlasting l',
24 but is passed from death unto l'.
26 For as the Father hath l' in himself;
26 to the Son to have l' in himself;
29 good, unto the resurrection of l';
39 in them ye think ye have eternal l':
40 come to me, that ye might have l'.
6:27 which endureth unto everlasting l',
33 and giveth l' unto the world.
35 unto them, I am the bread of l':
40 on him, may have everlasting l':
47 believeth on me hath everlasting l'
48 I am that bread of l'.
51 I will give for the l' of the world.
53 his blood, ye have no l' in you.
54 drinketh my blood, hath eternal l';
63 you, they are spirit, and they are l'.
68 thou hast the words of eternal l'.
8:12 but shall have the light of l'.
10:10 I am come that they might have l',
11 giveth his l' for the sheep.
15 and I lay down my l' for the sheep.
17 because I lay down my l', that I
28 I give unto them eternal l'; and
11:25 I am the resurrection, and the l':
12:25 He that loveth his l' shall lose it;
25 hateth his l' in this world shall
25 shall keep it unto l' eternal.
50 his commandment is l' everlasting:
13:37 I will lay down my l' for thy sake.
38 thou lay down thy l' for my sake?
14: 6 am the way, the truth, and the l':
15:13 man lay down his l' for his friends.
17: 2 should give eternal l' to as many
3 this is l' eternal, that they might
20:31 ye might have l' through his name.
Ac 2:28 made known to me the ways of l';
3:15 And killed the Prince of l', whom
5:20 the people all the words of this l'.
8:33 for his l' is taken from the earth.
11:18 Gentiles granted repentance unto l'.
13:46 unworthy of everlasting l', lo, we
48 many as were ordained to eternal l'
17:25 seeing he giveth to all l', and breath,
20:10 not yourselves; for his l' is in him.
24 count I my l' dear unto myself,
26: 4 My manner of l' from my youth,
27:22 shall be no loss of any man's l'
Ro 2: 7 honour and immortality, eternal l':
5:10 we shall be saved by his l'.
17 reign in l' by one, Jesus Christ.)
18 upon all men unto justification of l'.
21 righteousness unto eternal l' by
6: 4 also should walk in newness of l'.
22 holiness, and the end everlasting l'.
23 but the gift of God is eternal l'
7:10 which was ordained to l', I found
8: 2 the law of the Spirit of l' in Christ
6 to be spiritually minded is l' and
10 Spirit is l' because of righteousness.
38 neither death, nor l', nor angels,
11: 3 am left alone, and they seek my l'.
15 of them be, but l' from the dead?
16: 4 have for my l' laid down their own
1Co 3:22 or l', or death, or things present,
6: 3 more things that pertain to this l'?
4 of things pertaining to this l', set
14: 7 even things without l' giving sound,
15:19 If in this l' only we have hope in
2Co 1: 8 that we despaired even of l':
2:16 the other the savour of l' unto l'.
3: 6 killeth, but the spirit giveth l'.
4:10, 11 the l' also of Jesus might be
12 death worketh in us, but l' in you.
5: 4 might be swallowed up of l'.
Ga 2:20 and the l' which I now live in the flesh
3:21 given which could have given l',
6: 8 of the Spirit reap l' everlasting.
Eph 4:18 being alienated from the l' of God
Ph'p 1:20 in my body, whether it be by l', or
2:16 Holding forth the word of l'; that
30 unto death, not regarding his l', to
4: 3 whose names are in the book of l'.
Col 3: 3 your l' is hid with Christ in God.
4 When Christ, who is our l', shall
1Ti 1:16 believe on him to l' everlasting.
2: 2 lead a quiet and peaceable l' in all
4: 8 promise of the l' that now is, and
6:12 lay hold on eternal l', whereunto
19 that they may lay hold on eternal l'.
2Ti 1: 1 promise of l' which is in Christ
10 hath brought l' and immortality to

2Ti 2: 4 himself with the affairs of this l';
3:10 known my doctrine, manner of l',
Tit 1: 2 In hope of eternal l', which God,
3: 7 according to the hope of eternal l'.
Heb 7: 3 beginning of days, nor end of l';
16 but after the power of an endless l'.
11:35 received their dead raised to l' again:
Jas 1:12 he shall receive the crown of l'.
4:14 For what is your l'? It is even a
1Pe 3: 7 heirs together of the grace of l';
10 For he that will love l', and see good
4: 3 time past of our l' may suffice us
2Pe 1: 3 that pertain unto l' and godliness,
1Jo 1: 1 have handled, of the Word of l';
2 the l' was manifested, and we have
2 and shew unto you that eternal l',
2:16 the pride of l', is not of the Father,
25 hath promised us, even eternal l'.
3:14 we have passed from death unto l',
15 hath eternal l' abiding in him.
16 he laid down his l' for us: and we
5:11 God hath given to us eternal l',
11 and this l' is in his Son.
12 He that hath the Son hath l';
12 hath not the Son of God hath not l'.
13 may know that ye have eternal l',
16 shall give him l' for them that sin
20 This is the true God, and eternal l'.
Jude 21 Lord Jesus Christ unto eternal l'.
Re 2: 7 will I give to eat of the tree of l',
10 and I will give thee a crown of l'.
3: 5 out his name out of the book of l',
8: 9 were in the sea, and had l', died;
11:11 Spirit of l' from God entered into
13: 8 are not written in the book of l'
15 power to give l' unto the image of
17: 8 were not written in the book of l'
20:12 was opened, which is the book of l':
15 not found written in the book of l'
21: 6 fountain of the water of l' freely.
27 written in the Lamb's book of l'.
22: 1 me a pure river of water of l',
2 was there the tree of l', which bare
14 may have right to the tree of l',
17 let him take the water of l' freely.
19 away his part out of the book of l',

lifetime
2Sa 18:18 Absalom in his l' had taken and
Lu 16:25 thou in thy l' receivedst thy good
Heb 2:15 all their l' subject to bondage.

lift See also LIFTED; LIFTEST; LIFTETH; LIFTING.
Ge 7:17 and it was l' up above the earth.
13:14 L' up now thine eyes, and look
14:22 I have l' up mine hand unto the
18: 2 And he l' up his eyes and looked,
21:16 him, and l' up her voice, and wept.
18 Arise, l' up the lad, and hold him in
31:12 L' up now thine eyes, and see, all
40:13 shall Pharaoh l' up thine head,
19 three days shall Pharaoh l' up thy
41:44 shall no man l' up his hand or foot
Ex 14:16 l' thou up thy rod, and stretch out
20:25 if thou l' up thy tool upon it, thou
Nu 6:26 The Lord l' up his countenance
16: 3 then l' ye up yourselves above the
23:24 and l' up himself as a young lion:
De 3:27 and l' up thine eyes westward, and
4:19 And lest thou l' up thine eyes unto
22: 4 help him to l' them up again.
27: 5 not l' up any iron tool upon them.
32:40 For I l' up my hand to heaven, and
Jos 8:31 which no man hath l' up any iron:
2Sa 23: 8 l' up his spear against eight hundred,
2Ki 19: 4 l' up thy prayer for the remnant
25:27 did l' up the head of Jehoiachin
1Ch 25: 5 the words of God, to l' up the horn.
Ezr 9: 6 and blush to l' up my face to thee,
Job 10:15 yet will I not l' up my head.
11:15 thou l' up thy face without spot;
22:26 and shalt l' up thy face unto God.
38:34 Canst thou l' up thy voice to the
Ps 4: 6 Lord, l' thou up the light of thy
7: 6 l' up thyself because of the rage of
10:12 O Lord; O God, l' up thine hand;
24: 7 L' up your heads, O ye gates;
7 be ye l' up, ye everlasting doors;
9 L' up your heads, O ye gates; even
9 l' them up, ye everlasting doors;
25: 1 thee, O Lord, do I l' up my soul.
28: 2 I l' up my hands toward thy holy
9 them also, and l' them up for ever.
63: 4 I will l' up my hands in thy name.
74: 3 L' up thy feet unto the perpetual
75: 4 to the wicked, L' not up the horn:
5 L' not up your horn on high: speak
86: 4 thee, O Lord, do I l' up my soul.
93: 3 voice; the floods l' up their waves.
94: 2 L' up thyself, thou judge of the
110: 7 therefore shall he l' up the head.
119:48 My hands also will I l' up unto thy
121: 1 I will l' up mine eyes unto the hills,
123: 1 Unto thee l' I up mine eyes, O thou
134: 2 L' up your hands in the sanctuary,
143: 8 walk; for I l' up my soul unto thee.
Ec 4:10 fall, the one will l' up his fellow:
Isa 2: 4 nation shall not l' up sword against
5:26 he will l' up an ensign to the nations
10:15 itself against them that l' it up.
15 if the staff should l' up itself, as if it
24 shall l' up his staff against thee,
26 so shall he l' it up after the manner
30 L' up thy voice, O daughter of
13: 2 L' ye up a banner upon the high
24:14 They shall l' up their voice, they

Isa 33:10 exalted; now will I l' up myself.
37: 4 wherefore l' up thy prayer for the
40: 9 l' up thy voice with strength;
9 l' it up, be not afraid; say unto the
26 L' up your eyes on high, and
42: 2 He shall not cry, nor l' up, nor
11 the cities thereof l' up their voice,
49:18 L' up thine eyes round about, and
22 will l' up mine hand to the Gentiles,
51: 6 L' up your eyes to the heavens, and
52: 8 watchmen shall l' up the voice;
58: 1 not, l' up thy voice like a trumpet,
59:19 the Lord shall l' up a standard
60: 4 L' up thine eyes round about, and
62:10 l' up a standard for the people.
Jer 3: 2 L' up thine eyes unto the high
7:16 neither l' up cry nor prayer for
11:14 neither l' up a cry or prayer for
13:20 L' up your eyes, and behold them
22:20 l' up thy voice in Bashan, and cry
51:14 they shall l' up a shout against
La 2:19 l' up thy hands toward him for the
3:41 Let us l' up our heart with our hands
Eze 8: 5 man, l' up thine eyes now the way
11:22 did the cherubims l' up their wings,
17:14 be base, that it might not l' itself up,
21:22 to l' up the voice with shouting, to
23:27 thou shalt not l' up thine eyes unto
26: 8 and l' up the buckler against thee.
33:25 l' up your eyes toward your idols,
Mic 4: 3 nation shall not l' up a sword
Zec 1:21 so that no man did l' up his head:
5: 5 L' up now thine eyes, and see what
M't 12:11 he not lay hold on it, and l' it out?
Lu 13:11 and could in no wise l' up herself.
16:23 in hell he l' up his eyes, being in
18:13 would not l' up so much as his eyes
21:28 then look up, and l' up your heads;
Joh 4:35 L' up your eyes, and look on the
Heb 12:12 l' up the hands which hang down,
Jas 4:10 of the Lord, and he shall l' you up.

lifted See also LIFT.
Ge 13:10 Lot l' up his eyes, and beheld all
22: 4 third day Abraham l' up his eyes,
13 Abraham l' up his eyes, and looked,
24:63 and he l' up his eyes, and saw, and,
64 Rebekah l' up her eyes, and when
27:38 And Esau l' up his voice, and wept.
29:11 Rachel, and l' up his voice, and wept.
31:10 that I l' up mine eyes, and saw in a
33: 1 Jacob l' up his eyes, and looked,
5 And he l' up his eyes, and saw the
37:25 they l' up their eyes and looked,
28 and l' up Joseph out of the pit,
39:15 that I l' up my voice and cried,
18 pass, as I l' up my voice and cried,
40:20 he l' up the head of the chief butler
43:29 And he l' up his eyes, and saw his
Ex 7:20 l' up the rod, and smote the waters
14:10 children of Israel l' up their eyes,
Le 9:22 Aaron l' up his hand toward the
Nu 14: 1 the congregation l' up their voice,
20:11 Moses l' up his hand, and with his
24: 2 Balaam l' up his eyes, and he saw
De 8:14 Then thine heart be l' up, and thou
17:20 That his heart be not l' up above
Jos 4:18 soles of the priests' feet were l' up
5:13 that he l' up his eyes and looked,
J'g 2: 4 people l' up their voice, and wept.
8:28 that they l' up their heads no more.
9: 7 and l' up his voice, and cried, and
19:17 when he had l' up his eyes, he saw
21: 2 l' up their voices, and wept sore;
Ru 1: 9 and they l' up their voice, and wept.
14 And they l' up their voice, and wept
1Sa 6:13 l' up their eyes, and saw the ark,
11: 4 people l' up their voices, and wept.
24:16 And Saul l' up his voice, and wept.
30: 4 with him l' up their voice and wept,
2Sa 3:32 the king l' up his voice, and wept at
13:34 that kept the watch l' up his eyes,
36 came, and l' up their voice and wept:
18:24 and l' up his eyes, and looked, and
28 men that l' up their hand against
20:21 l' up his hand against the king,
22:49 thou also hast l' me up on high
23:18 he l' up his spear against three
1Ki 11:26 he l' up his hand against the king.
27 he l' up his hand against the king:
2Ki 9:32 he l' up his face to the window,
14:10 and thine heart hath l' thee up:
19:22 and l' up thine eyes on high? even
1Ch 11:11 he l' up his spear against three
14: 2 for his kingdom was l' up on high,
21:16 David l' up his eyes, and saw the
2Ch 5:13 when they l' up their voice with the
17: 6 heart was l' up in the ways of the
26:16 heart was l' up to his destruction:
32:25 unto him; for his heart was l' up:
Job 2:12 when they l' up their eyes afar off,
12 they l' up their voice, and wept;
31:21 I have l' up my hand against the
29 l' up myself when evil found him:
Ps 24: 4 hath not l' up his soul unto vanity,
27: 6 head be l' up above mine enemies
30: 1 for thou hast l' me up, and hast
41: 9 hath l' up his heel against me.
74: 5 had l' up axes upon the thick trees.
83: 2 that hate thee have l' up the head.
93: 3 The floods have l' up, O Lord,
3 the floods have l' up their voice;
102:10 for thou hast l' me up, and cast me
106:26 he l' up his hand against them,
Pr 30:13 eyes! and their eyelids are l' up.
Isa 2:12 and upon every one that is l' up;
13 of Lebanon, that are high and l' up,

Isa 2:14 and upon all the hills that are l' up,
6: 1 upon a throne, high and l' up, and
26:11 when thy hand is l' up, they will
37:23 voice, and l' up thine eyes on high?
Jer 51: 9 heaven, and is l' up even to the skies.
52:31 l' up the head of Jehoiachin king of
Eze 1:19 when the living creatures were l' up
19 the earth, the wheels were l' up.
20 the wheels were l' up over against
21 those were l' up from the earth,
21 the wheels were l' up over against
3:14 So the spirit l' me up, and took me
8: 3 spirit l' me up between the earth
5 I l' up mine eyes the way toward
10:15 And the cherubims were l' up.
16 the cherubims l' up their wings
17 stood; and when they were l' up,
17 these l' up themselves also: for
19 the cherubims l' up their wings,
11: 1 the spirit l' me up, and brought me
18: 6 neither hath l' up his eyes to the
12 and hath l' up his eyes to the idols,
15 neither hath l' up his eyes to the
20: 5 and l' up mine hand unto the seed
5 when I l' up mine hand unto them,
6 that I l' up mine hand unto them,
15 Yet also I l' up my hand unto them
23 I l' up mine hand unto them also
28 I l' up mine hand to give it to them,
42 I l' up mine hand to give it to your
28: 2 Because thine heart is l' up, and
5 heart is l' up because of thy riches:
17 was l' up because of thy beauty,
31:10 thou hast l' up thyself in height,
10 and his heart is l' up in his height;
36: 7 I have l' up mine hand, Surely the
44:12 have I l' up mine hand against them,
47:14 the which I l' up mine hand to give
Da 4:34 I Nebuchadnezzar l' up mine eyes
5:20 when his heart was l' up, and his
23 hast l' up thyself against the Lord
7: 4 it was l' up from the earth, and
8: 3 Then I l' up mine eyes, and saw,
10: 5 Then I l' up mine eyes, and looked,
11:12 multitude, his heart shall be l' up;
Mic 5: 9 Thine hand shall be l' up upon thine
Hab 2: 4 soul which is l' up is not upright
3:10 voice, and l' up his hands on high.
Zec 1:18 Then l' I up mine eyes, and saw,
21 which l' up their horn over the land
2: 1 I l' up mine eyes again, and looked,
5: 1 Then I turned, and l' up mine eyes,
7 there was l' up a talent of lead: and
9 Then l' I up mine eyes, and looked,
9 l' up the ephah between the earth
6: 1 And I turned, and l' up mine eyes,
9:16 l' up as an ensign upon his land.
14:10 and it shall be l' up, and inhabited
M't 17: 8 when they had l' up their eyes,
M'r 1:31 her by the hand, and l' her up;
9:27 him by the hand, and l' him up;
Lu 6:20 he l' up his eyes on his disciples,
11:27 of the company l' up her voice,
17:13 they l' up their voices, and said,
24:50 and he l' up his hands, and blessed
Joh 3:14 as Moses l' up the serpent in the
14 so must the Son of man be l' up:
6: 5 When Jesus then l' up his eyes,
8: 7 l' up himself, and said unto them,
10 When Jesus had l' up himself, and
28 When ye have l' up the Son of man,
11:41 And Jesus l' up his eyes, and said,
12:32 And I, if I be l' up from the earth,
34 thou, The Son of man must be l' up?
13:18 me hath l' up his heel against me.
17: 1 Jesus, and l' up his eyes to heaven,
Ac 2:14 But Peter,...l' up his voice, and
3: 7 by the right hand, and l' him up:
4:24 l' up their voice to God with one
9:41 gave her his hand, and l' her up,
14:11 they l' up their voices, saying in
22:22 and then l' up their voices, and said,
1Ti 3: 6 lest being l' up with pride he fall
Re 10: 5 the earth l' up his hand to heaven,

lifter
Ps 3: 3 glory, and the l' up of mine head.

liftest
Job 30:22 Thou l' me up to the wind; thou
Ps 9:13 thou that l' me up from the gates
18:48 thou l' me up above those that rise
Pr 2: 3 l' up thy voice for understanding;

lifteth
1Sa 2: 7 rich: he bringeth low, and l' up.
8 l' up the beggar from the dunghill,
2Ch 25:19 thine heart l' thee up to boast:
Job 39:18 time she l' up herself on high, she
Ps 107:25 which l' up the waves thereof.
113: 7 l' the needy out of the dunghill;
147: 6 The Lord l' up the meek: he
Isa 18: 3 when he l' up an ensign on the
Jer 51: 3 l' himself up in his brigandine:
Na 3: 3 horseman l' up both the bright

lifting
1Ch 11:20 for l' up his spear against three
15:16 by l' up the voice with joy.
Ne 8: 6 Amen, with l' up their hands:
Job 22:29 thou shalt say, There is l' up;
Ps 141: 2 l' up of my hands as the evening
Pr 30:32 hast done foolishly in l' up thyself,
Isa 9:18 mount up like the l' up of smoke.
33: 3 at the l' up of thyself the nations
1Ti 2: 8 l' up holy hands, without wrath

light See also ALIGHT; DELIGHT; ENLIGHTEN; LIGHTED; LIGHTER; LIGHTEST; LIGHTETH; LIGHTING; LIGHTS; TWILIGHT.
Ge 1: 3 Let there be l': and there was l'.
4 God saw the l', that it was good:
4 divided the l' from the darkness.
5 And God called the l' Day, and the
15 heaven to give l' upon the earth:
16 the greater l' to rule the day,
16 and the lesser l' to rule the night:
17 heaven to give l' upon the earth,
18 to divide the l' from the darkness:
44: 3 As soon as the morning was l', the
Ex 10:23 of Israel had l' in their dwellings.
13:21 in a pillar of fire, to give them l';
14:20 but it gave l' by night to these:
25: 6 Oil for the l', spices for anointing
37 they shall l' the lamps thereof,
37 they may give l' over against it.
27:20 thee pure oil olive beaten for the l',
35: 8 oil for the l',...spices for anointing
14 The candlestick also for the l', and
14 and his lamps, with the oil for the l',
28 oil for the l', and for the anointing
39:37 vessels thereof, and the oil for l',
40: 4 in the candlestick, and l' the lamps
Le 24: 2 thee pure oil olive beaten for the l',
Nu 4: 9 cover the candlestick of the l', and
16 priest pertaineth the oil for the l',
8: 2 the seven lamps shall give l' over
21: 5 our soul loatheth this l' bread.
De 27:16 be he that setteth l' by his father
J'g 9: 4 hired vain and l' persons, which
19:26 where her lord was, till it was l'.
Ru 2: 3 hap was to l' on a part of the field
1Sa 14:36 spoil them until the morning l',
18:23 Seemeth it to you a l' thing to be
25:22 pertain to him by the morning l'
34 left unto Nabal by the morning l'
36 less or more, until the morning l'.
29:10 early in the morning, and have l',
2Sa 2:18 Asahel was as l' of foot as a wild
17:12 l' upon him as the dew falleth on
22 by the morning l' there lacked not
21:17 thou quench not the l' of Israel.
23: 4 shall be as the l' of the morning,
1Ki 7: 4, 5 l' was against l' in three ranks.
11:36 l' alway before me in Jerusalem,
16:31 had been a l' thing for him to walk
2Ki 3:18 is but a l' thing in the sight of the
7: 9 we tarry till the morning l', some
8:19 him to give him alway a l', and to
20:10 It is a l' thing for the shadow to
2Ch 21: 7 promised to give a l' to him and
Ne 9:12 l' in the way wherein they should
19 of fire by night, to shew them l',
Es 8:16 The Jews had l', and gladness, and
Job 3: 4 neither let the l' shine upon it.
9 let it look for l', but have none;
16 been; as infants which never saw l'.
20 is l' given to him that is in misery,
23 why is l' given to a man whose way is
10:22 and where the l' is as darkness.
12:22 out to l' the shadow of death.
25 They grope in the dark without l',
17:12 the l' is short because of darkness.
18: 5 the l' of the wicked shall be put out,
6 The l' shall be dark in his tabernacle,
18 shall be driven from l' into darkness,
22:28 the l' shall shine upon thy ways.
24:13 of those that rebel against the l';
14 murderer rising with the l' killeth
16 the daytime: they know not the l'.
25: 3 upon whom doth not his l' arise?
28:11 that is hid bringeth he forth to l'.
29: 3 by his l' I walked through darkness;
24 the l' of my countenance they cast
30:26 and when I waited for l', there came
33:28 the pit, and his life shall see the l'.
30 enlightened with the l' of the living.
36:30 Behold, he spreadeth his l' upon it,
32 With clouds he covereth the l';
37:15 caused the l' of his cloud to shine?
21 men see not the bright l' which is in
38:15 the wicked their l' is withholden,
19 Where is the way where l' dwelleth?
24 By what way is the l' parted, which
41:18 By his neesings a l' doth shine, and
Ps 4: 6 the l' of thy countenance upon us.
18:28 For thou wilt l' my candle: the Lord
27: 1 The Lord is my l' and my salvation;
36: 9 of life: in thy l' shall we see l'.
37: 6 forth thy righteousness as the l',
38:10 as for the l' of mine eyes, it also is
43: 3 O send out thy l' and thy truth: let
44: 3 arm, and the l' of thy countenance,
49:19 his fathers; they shall never see l'.
56:13 before God in the l' of the living?
74:16 hast prepared the l' and the sun.
78:14 and all the night with a l' of fire.
89:15 Lord, in the l' of thy countenance.
90: 8 sins in the l' of thy countenance.
97:11 L' is sown for the righteous, and
104: 2 coverest thyself with l' as with a
105:39 and fire to give l' in the night.
112: 4 Unto the upright there ariseth l' in
118:27 the Lord, which hath shewed us l':
119:105 my feet, and a l' unto my path.
130 entrance of thy words giveth l'; it
139:11 even the night shall be l' about me.
12 darkness and the l' are both alike
148: 3 moon: praise him, all ye stars of l'.
Pr 4:18 path of the just is as the shining l',
6:23 is a lamp; and the law is l'; and
13: 9 The l' of the righteous rejoiceth:
15:30 l' of the eyes rejoiceth the heart:
Pr 16:15 In the l' of the king's countenance
Ec 2:13 folly, as far as l' excelleth darkness.
11: 7 Truly the l' is sweet, and a pleasant
12: 2 While the sun, or the l', or the moon,
Isa 2: 5 let us walk in the l' of the Lord.
5:20 darkness for l', and l' for darkness;
30 the l' is darkened in the heavens
8:20 is because there is no l' in them.
9: 2 in darkness have seen a great l':
2 death, upon them hath the l' shined.
10:17 the l' of Israel shall be for a fire,
13:10 thereof shall not give their l':
10 moon shall not cause her l' to shine.
30:26 Moreover the l' of the moon shall
26 moon shall be as the l' of the sun,
26 the l' of the sun shall be sevenfold,
26 as the l' of seven days, in the day
42: 6 the people, for a l' of the Gentiles;
16 will make darkness l' before them,
45: 7 I form the l', and create darkness:
49: 6 It is a l' thing that thou shouldest
6 give thee for a l' to the Gentiles,
50:10 in darkness, and hath no l'? let
11 walk in the l' of your fire, and in
51: 4 to rest for a l' of the people.
58: 8 Then shall thy l' break forth as the
10 shall thy l' rise in obscurity, and thy
59: 9 we wait for l', but behold obscurity;
60: 1 Arise, shine; for thy l' is come, and
3 Gentiles shall come to thy l', and
19 sun shall be no more thy l' by day;
19 shall the moon give l' unto thee:
19 shall be unto thee an everlasting l',
20 Lord shall be thine everlasting l',
Jer 4:23 and the heavens, and they had no l'.
13:16 while ye look for l', he turn it into
25:10 millstones, and the l' of the candle.
31:35 which giveth the sun for a l' by day,
35 and of the stars for a l' by night,
La 3: 2 me into darkness, but not into l'.
Eze 8:17 Is it a l' thing to the house of Judah
22: 7 In thee have they set l' by father
32: 7 and the moon shall not give her l'.
Da 2:22 and the l' dwelleth with him.
5:11 of thy father l' and understanding
14 and that l' and understanding and
Ho 6: 5 thy judgments are as the l' that
Am 5:18 the Lord is darkness, and not l'.
20 the Lord be darkness, and not l'?
Mic 2: 1 when the morning is l', they practise
7: 8 the Lord shall be a l' unto me.
9 he will bring me forth to the l', and
Hab 3: 4 his brightness was as the l'; he had
11 at the l' of thine arrows they went,
Zep 3: 4 prophets are l' and treacherous
5 doth he bring his judgment to l',
Zec 14: 6 the l' shall not be clear, nor dark:
7 that at evening time it shall be l'.
M't 4:16 which sat in darkness saw great l';
16 shadow of death l' is sprung up.
5:14 Ye are the l' of the world. A city
15 Neither do men l' a candle, and
15 giveth l' unto all that are in the
16 Let your l' so shine before men,
6:22 The l' of the body is the eye: if
22 thy whole body shall be full of l'.
23 the l' that is in thee be darkness,
10:27 in darkness, that speak ye in l':
11:30 yoke is easy, and my burden is l'.
17: 2 his raiment was white as the l'.
22: 5 they made l' of it, and went their
24:29 and the moon shall not give her l',
M'r 13:24 and the moon shall not give her l',
Lu 1:79 give l' to them that sit in darkness
2:32 A l' to lighten the Gentiles, and
8:16 they which enter in may see the l'.
11:33 they which come in may see the l'.
34 The l' of the body is the eye:
34 thy whole body also is full of l';
35 that the l' which is in thee be not
36 whole body therefore be full of l',
36 dark, the whole shall be full of l',
36 of a candle doth give thee l'.
12: 3 darkness shall be heard in the l';
15: 8 doth not l' a candle, and sweep the
16: 8 wiser than the children of l'.
Joh 1: 4 and the life was the l' of men.
5 And the l' shineth in darkness; and
7 witness, to bear witness of the L',
8 He was not that L', but was sent
8 was sent to bear witness of that L'
9 That was the true L', which
3:19 that l' is come into the world, and
19 men loved darkness rather than l',
20 one that doeth evil hateth the l',
20 neither cometh to the l', lest his
21 that doeth truth cometh to the l',
5:35 was a burning and a shining l':
35 for a season to rejoice in his l'.
8:12 saying, I am the l' of the world:
12 but shall have the l' of life.
9: 5 the world, I am the l' of the world.
11: 9 because he seeth the l' of this world.
10 because there is no l' in him.
12:35 Yet a little while is the l' with you.
35 Walk while ye have the l', lest
36 While ye have the l', believe in the l',
36 that ye may be the children of l'.
46 I am come a l' into the world, that
Ac 9: 3 round about him a l' from heaven:
12: 7 him, and a l' shined in the prison:
13:47 set thee to be a l' of the Gentiles,
16:29 he called for a l', and sprang in,
22: 6 shone from heaven a great l' round
9 that were with me saw indeed the l',
11 could not see for the glory of that l',

Ac 26:13 I saw in the way a l' from heaven,
18 to turn them from darkness to l',
23 and should shew l' unto the people,
Ro 2:19 a l' of them which are in darkness,
13:12 and let us put on the armour of l'.
1Co 4: 5 will bring to l' the hidden things
2Co 4: 4 l' of the glorious gospel of Christ,
6 commanded the l' to shine out of
6 to give the l' of the knowledge of
17 our l' affliction, which is but for a
6:14 communion hath l' with darkness?
11:14 is transformed into an angel of l'.
Eph 5: 8 but now are ye l' in the Lord:
8 walk as children of l':
13 are made manifest by the l': for
13 whatsoever doth make manifest is l'.
14 and Christ shall give thee l'.
Col 1:12 the inheritance of the saints in l':
1Th 5: 5 Ye are all the children of l', and
1Ti 6:16 dwelling in the l' which no man
2Ti 1:10 brought life and immortality to l'
1Pe 2: 9 of darkness into his marvelous l':
2Pe 1:19 as unto a l' that shineth in a dark
1Jo 1: 5 declare unto you, that God is l',
7 if we walk in the l', as he is in the l',
2: 8 past, and the true l' now shineth.
9 He that saith he is in the l', and
10 loveth his brother abideth in the l',
Re 7:16 neither shall the sun l' on them,
18:23 l' of a candle shall shine no more
21:11 her l' was like unto a stone most
23 it, and the Lamb is the l' thereof.
24 saved shall walk in the l' of it:
22: 5 no candle, neither l' of the sun;
5 for the Lord God giveth them l':

lighted See also DELIGHTED.
Ge 24:64 she saw Isaac, she l' off the camel.
28:11 And he l' upon a certain place, and
Ex 40:25 he l' the lamps before the Lord; as
Nu 8: 3 he l' the lamps thereof over against
Jos 15:18 a field: and she l' off her ass; and
J'g 1:14 a field: and she l' from off her ass;
4:15 that Sisera l' down off his chariot,
1Sa 25:23 l' off the ass, and fell before David
2Ki 5:21 he l' down from the chariot to
10:15 l' on Jehonadab the son of Rechab
Isa 9: 8 Jacob, and it hath l' upon Israel.
Lu 8:16 No man, when he hath l' a candle,
11:33 No man, when he hath l' a candle,

lighten See also ENLIGHTEN; LIGHTENED; LIGHTENETH; LIGHTNING.
1Sa 6: 5 he will l' his hand from off you,
2Sa 22:29 and the Lord will l' my darkness.
Ezr 9: 8 that our God may l' our eyes, and
Ps 13: 3 l' mine eyes, lest I sleep the sleep
Jon 1: 5 ship into the sea, to l' it of them.
Lu 2:32 A light to l' the Gentiles, and the
Re 21:23 the glory of God did l' it, and the

lightened See also ENLIGHTENED.
Ps 34: 5 looked unto him, and were l':
77:18 the lightnings l' the world: the
Ac 27:18 the next day they l' the ship;
38 they l' the ship, and cast out the
Re 18: 1 the earth was l' with his glory.

lighteneth
Pr 29:13 the Lord l' both their eyes.
Lu 17:24 that l' out of the one part under

lighter
1Ki 12: 4 make...which he put upon us, l',
9 Make...father did put upon us l'?
10 heavy, but make thou it l' unto us;
2Ch 10:10 make thou it somewhat l' for us;
Ps 62: 9 they are altogether l' than vanity.

lightest
Nu 8: 2 unto him, When thou l' the lamps,

lighteth
Ex 30: 8 when Aaron l' the lamps at even,
De 19: 5 and l' upon his neighbour, that
Joh 1: 9 which l' every man that cometh

lighting
Isa 30:30 shall shew the l' down of his arm,
M't 3:16 like a dove, and l' upon him:

lightly
Ge 26:10 might l' have lien with thy wife,
De 32:15 and l' esteemed the Rock of his
1Sa 2:30 despise me shall be l' esteemed.
18:23 I am a poor man, and l' esteemed?
Isa 9: 1 he l' afflicted the land of Zebulun
Jer 4:24 trembled, and all the hills moved l'.
M'r 9:39 that can l' speak evil of me.

lightness
Jer 3: 9 through the l' of her whoredom,
23:32 err by their lies, and by their l';
2Co 1:17 was thus minded, did I use l'?

lightning See also LIGHTNINGS.
2Sa 22:15 them; l', and discomfited them.
Job 28:26 a way for the l' of the thunder:
37: 3 his l' unto the ends of the earth.
38:25 or a way for the l' of thunder;
Ps 144: 6 Cast forth l', and scatter them:
Eze 1:13 and out of the fire went forth l'.
14 as the appearance of a flash of l'.
Da 10: 6 his face as the appearance of l',
Zec 9:14 his arrow shall go forth as the l':
M't 24:27 For as the l' cometh out of the east,
28: 3 His countenance was like l', and
Lu 10:18 I beheld Satan as l' fall from heaven.
17:24 For as the l', that lighteneth out of

lightnings
Ex 19:16 that there were thunders and l',
20:18 saw the thunderings, and the l',
Job 38:35 Canst thou send l', that they may
Ps 18:14 and he shot out l', and discomfited
77:18 the l' lightened the world: the earth
97: 4 His l' enlightened the world: the
135: 7 he maketh l' for the rain; he
Jer 10:13 he maketh l' with rain, and bringeth
51:16 he maketh l' with rain, and bringeth
Na 2: 4 torches, they shall run like the l'.
Re 4: 5 out of the throne proceeded l' and
8: 5 were voices, and thunderings, and l',
11:19 and there were l', and voices, and
16:18 were voices, and thunders, and l';

lights See also DELIGHTS.
Ge 1:14 Let there be l' in the firmament of
15 let them be for l' in the firmament
16 God made two great l'; the greater
1Ki 6: 4 he made windows of narrow l'.
Ps 136: 7 To him that made great l': for his
Eze 32: 8 bright l' of heaven will I make
Lu 12:35 about, and your l' burning;
Ac 20: 8 there were many l' in the upper
Ph'p 2:15 whom ye shine as l' in the world;
Jas 1:17 cometh down from the Father of l',

lign
Nu 24: 6 as the trees of l' aloes which the Lord

lign-aloes See LIGN and ALOES.

ligure (*li'-gure*)
Ex 28:19 And the third row a l', an agate,
39:12 the third row, a l', an agate, and

like^ See also ALIKE; LIKED; LIKETH; LIKING; LIKEMINDED; LIKEWISE; LIONLIKE.
Ge 13:10 l' the land of Egypt, as thou comest
25:25 out red, all over l' an hairy garment;
Ex 7:11 also did in l' manner with their
9:14 there is none l' me in all the earth.
24 none l' it in all the land of Egypt
11: 6 none l' it, nor shall be l' it any more.
15:11 Who is l' unto thee, O Lord, among
11 who is l' thee, glorious in holiness,
16:31 and it was l' coriander seed, white;
31 the taste of it was l' wafers made with
23:11 l' manner thou shalt deal with thy
24:17 glory of the Lord was l' devouring fire
25:33 Three bowls made l' unto almonds,
33 three bowls made l' almonds in the
34 be four bowls made l' unto almonds,
28:11 l' the engravings of a signet, shalt
21 l' the engravings of a signet; every
36 upon it, l' the engravings of a signet,
30:32 shall ye make any other l' it, after
33 Whosoever compoundeth any l' it, or
34 of each shall there be a l' weight:
38 shall make l' unto that, to smell
34: 1 two tables of stone l' unto the first:
4 two tables of stone l' unto the first;
37:19 and three bowls made l' almonds in
20 were four bowls made l' almonds,
39: 8 work, l' the work of the ephod;
14 l' the engravings of a signet, every one
30 l' to the engravings of a signet,
Le 13: 2 his flesh l' the plague of leprosy;
Nu 23:10 and let my last end be l' his!
De 4:32 thing is, or hath been heard l' it?
7:26 lest thou be a cursed thing l' it:
10: 1, 3 two tables of stone l' unto the first,
17:14 l' as all the nations that are about me;
18: 8 They shall have l' portions to eat,
15 thee, of thy brethren, l' unto me;
18 among their brethren, l' unto thee.
22: 3 In l' manner shalt thou do with
25: 7 l' not to take his brother's wife,
8 to it, and say, I l' not to take her;
29:23 l' the overthrow of Sodom, and
33:17 glory is l' the firstling of his bullock,
17 his horns are l' the horns of unicorns:
26 is none l' unto the God of Jeshurun,
29 who is l' unto thee, O people saved
34:10 prophet since in Israel l' unto Moses,
Jos 10:14 no day l' that before it or after it,
J'g 7:12 lay along in the valley l' grasshoppers
11:17 in l' manner they sent unto the
13: 6 l' the countenance of an angel of God,
16:12 them from off his arms l' a thread.
17 become weak, and be l' any other man.
Ru 2:13 not l' unto one of thine handmaidens.
4:11 into thine house l' Rachel and l' Leah,
12 let thy house be l' the house of Pharez,
1Sa 2: 2 neither is there any rock l' our God.
4: 9 Be strong, and quit yourselves l' men,
9 quit yourselves l' men, and fight.
8: 5 us a king to judge us l' all the nations.
10:24 none l' him among all the people?
17: 7 his spear was l' a weaver's beam;
19:24 before Samuel in l' manner,
21: 9 David said, There is none l' that;
25:36 in his house, l' the feast of a king;
26:15 and who is l' to thee in Israel?
2Sa 7: 9 l' unto the name of the great men that
22 Lord God: for there is none l' thee,
23 earth is l' thy people, even l' Israel,
18:27 foremost is l' the running of Ahimaaz
21:19 whose spear was l' a weaver's beam.
22:34 He maketh my feet l' hinds' feet:
1Ki 3:12 there was none l' thee before thee,
12 after thee shall any arise l' unto thee.
13 be any among the kings l' unto thee
5: 6 to hew timber l' unto the Sidonians.
7: 8 the porch, which was of the l' work.
8 had taken to wife, l' unto this porch.
26 was wrought l' the brim of a cup,
33 was l' the work of a chariot wheel:
8:23 of Israel, there is no God l' thee,
10:20 not the l' made in any kingdom.
12:32 l' unto the feast that is in Judah, and
16: 3 thy house l' the house of Jeroboam
7 in being l' the house of Jeroboam;
18:44 cloud out of the sea, l' a man's hand.
20:25 army, l' the army that thou hast lost,
27 pitched before them l' two little flocks
21:22 thine house l' the house of Jeroboam
22 l' the house of Baasha the son of
25 But there was none l' unto Ahab,
22:13 thee, be l' the word of one of them,
2Ki 3: 2 not l' his father, and l' his mother:
9: 9 of Ahab l' the house of Jeroboam
9 l' the house of Baasha the son of
20 the driving is l' the driving of Jehu
13: 7 made them l' the dust by threshing.
14: 3 the Lord, yet not l' David his father:
16: 2 the Lord his God, l' David his father.
17:14 necks, l' to the neck of their fathers,
15 that they should not do l' them.
18: 5 none l' him among all the kings
32 you away to a land l' your own land,
23:25 And l' unto him was there no king
25 after him arose there any l' him.
25:17 l' unto these had the second pillar
1Ch 4:27 multiply, l' to the children of Judah.
11:23 hand was a spear l' a weaver's beam;
12: 8 whose faces were l' the faces of lions,
22 it was a great host, l' the host of God.
14:11 hand l' the breaking forth of waters:
17: 8 a name l' the name of the great men
20 O Lord, there is none l' thee,
21 in the earth is l' thy people Israel,
20: 5 spear staff was l' a weaver's beam.
27:23 would increase Israel l' to the stars of
2Ch 1: 9 a people l' the dust of the earth in
12 there any after thee have the l'.
9:19 not the l' made in any kingdom.
18:12 l' one of theirs, and speak thou good.
21: 6 of Israel, l' as did the house of Ahab:
13 l' to the whoredoms of the house of
19 for him, l' the burning of his fathers.
22: 4 sight of the Lord l' the house of Ahab:
28: 1 sight of the Lord, l' David his father:
30: 7 l' your fathers, and l' your brethren,
33: 2 l' unto the abominations of the
35:18 no passover l' to that kept in Israel
Ne 6: 5 his servant unto me in l' manner
13:26 nations was there no king l' him,
Es 2:20 l' as when she was brought up with
Job 1: 8 there is none l' him in the earth,
2: 3 there is none l' him in the earth,
3:24 roarings are poured out l' the waters.
5:26 l' as a shock of corn cometh in in his
7: 1 days also l' the days of an hireling?
8: 2 of thy mouth be l' a strong wind?
10:10 out as milk, and curdled me l' cheese?
11:12 man be born l' a wild ass's colt.
12:25 them to stagger l' a drunken man.
13:12 remembrances are l' unto ashes,
14: 2 forth l' a flower, and is cut down:
9 and bring forth boughs l' a plant.
15:16 man, which drinketh iniquity l' water?
16:14 beach, he runneth upon me l' a giant.
19:10 mine hope hath he removed l' a tree.
20: 7 shall perish for ever l' his own dung:
21:11 send forth their little ones l' a flock,
30:19 I am become l' dust and ashes.
32:19 it is ready to burst l' new bottles?
34: 7 l' Job, who drinketh up scorning l'
36:22 his power: who teacheth l' him?
40: 7 Gird up thy loins now l' a man: I will
9 Hast thou an arm l' God?
9 thou thunder with a voice l' him?
17 He moveth his tail l' a cedar: the
18 of brass; his bones are l' bars of iron.
41:18 eyes are l' the eyelids of the morning.
31 He maketh the deep to boil l' a pot:
31 he maketh the sea l' a pot of ointment.
33 Upon earth there is not his l', who 4915
42: 8 thing which is right, l' my servant Job.
Ps 1: 3 And he shall be l' a tree planted by the
4 are l' the chaff which the wind driveth
2: 9 dash them in pieces l' a potter's vessel.
7: 2 Lest he tear my soul l' a lion, rending
17:12 L' as a lion that is greedy of his
18:33 He maketh my feet l' hinds' feet, and
22:14 I am poured out l' water, and all my
14 my heart is l' wax; it is melted in the
15 my strength is dried up l' a potsherd;
28: 1 I become l' them that go down
29: 6 maketh them also to skip l' a calf;
35:10 who is l' unto thee, which deliverest
36: 6 Thy righteousness is l' the great
37: 2 shall soon be cut down l' the grass,
35 spreading himself l' a green bay tree.
39:11 his beauty to consume away l' a moth:
44:11 Thou hast given us l' sheep appointed
49:12 he is l' the beasts that perish.
14 L' sheep they are laid in the grave;
20 not, is l' the beasts that perish.
52: 2 l' a sharp razor, working deceitfully.
8 I am l' a green olive tree in the house
55: 6 said, Oh that I had wings l' a dove!
58: 4 Their poison is l' the poison of a
4 they are l' the deaf adder that
8 l' the untimely birth of a woman, that
59: 6 they make a noise l' a dog, and go
14 let them make a noise l' a dog, and go
64: 3 Who whet their tongue l' a sword,
71:19 O God, who is l' unto thee!
72: 6 down l' rain upon the mown grass:
16 fruit thereof shall shake l' Lebanon:
73: 5 are they plagued l' other men.
77:20 Thou leddest thy people l' a flock by
78:16 and caused waters to run down l' rivers.

Ps 78:27 feathered fowls l' as the sand of the
52 his own people to go forth l' sheep,
52 them in the wilderness l' a flock.
57 and dealt unfaithfully l' their fathers:
57 were turned aside l' a deceitful bow.
65 and l' a mighty man that shouteth by
69 he built his sanctuary l' high palaces,
69 l' the earth which he hath established
79: 3 Their blood have they shed l' water
5 ever? shall thy jealousy burn l' fire?
80: 1 thou that leadest Joseph l' a flock;
10 thereof were l' the goodly cedars.
82: 7 But ye shall die l' men,
7 and fall l' one of the princes.
83: 11 Make their nobles l' Oreb, and
11 Make their nobles...l' Zeeb:
13 O my God, make them l' a wheel; as
86: 8 the gods there is none l' unto thee, O
8 are there any works l' unto thy works.
88: 5 l' the slain that lie in the grave,
17 came round about me daily l' water;
89: 8 who is a strong Lord l' unto thee?
46 for ever? shall thy wrath burn l' fire?"
90: 5 they are l' grass which groweth up.
92: 10 thou exalt l' the horn of an unicorn:
12 shall flourish l' the palm tree:
12 he shall grow l' a cedar in Lebanon.
97: 5 hills melted l' wax at the presence of
102: 3 For my days are consumed l' smoke,
4 heart is smitten, and withered l' grass;
6 I am l' a pelican of the wilderness:
6 I am l' an owl of the desert.
9 For I have eaten ashes l' bread, and
11 days are l' a shadow that declineth;
11 and I am withered l' grass.
26 them shall wax old l' a garment;
103: 5 thy youth is renewed l' the eagle's.
13 L' as a father pitieth his children, so
104: 2 stretchest out the heavens l' a curtain:
107: 27 fro, and stagger l' a drunken man,
41 and maketh him families l' a flock.
109: 18 with cursing l' as with his garment,
18 so let it come into his bowels l' water,
18 water, and l' oil into his bones.
23 gone l' the shadow when it declineth:
113: 5 Who is l' unto the Lord our God, who
114: 4 The mountains skipped l' rams,
4 rams, and the little hills l' lambs.
6 mountains, that ye skipped l' rams;
6 rams; and ye little hills, l' lambs?
115: 8 make them are l' unto them;
118: 12 They compassed me about l' bees;
119: 83 I am become l' a bottle in the smoke;
176 I have gone astray l' a lost sheep:
126: 1 of Zion, we were l' them that dream.
128: 3 children l' olive plants round about
133: 2 It is l' the precious ointment upon the
135: 18 that make them are l' unto them:
140: 3 their tongues l' a serpent;
143: 7 lest I be l' unto them that go down
144: 4 Man is l' to vanity: his days are as
147: 16 He giveth snow l' wool:
16 he scattereth the hoarfrost l' ashes.
17 He casteth forth his ice l' morsels:
Pr 12: 18 speaketh l' the piercings of a sword:
17: 22 merry heart doeth good l' a medicine:
18: 19 contentions are l' the bars of a castle.
20: 5 in the heart of man is l' deep water;
23: 32 l' a serpent, and stingeth l' an adder.
25: 11 A word fitly spoken is l' apples of gold
14 of a false gift is l' clouds and wind
19 in time of trouble is l' a broken tooth,
28 spirit is l' a city that is broken down,
26: 4 lest thou also be l' unto him.
17 is l' one that taketh a dog by the ears.
23 and a wicked heart are l' a potsherd
28: 3 is l' a sweeping rain which leaveth no
31: 14 She is l' the merchants' ships; she
Ca 2: 9 My beloved is l' a roe or a young
17 and be thou l' a roe or a young hart"
3: 6 of the wilderness l' pillars of smoke,
4: 2 Thy teeth are l' a flock of sheep that
3 Thy lips are l' a thread of scarlet, and
3 are l' a piece of a pomegranate
4 Thy neck is l' the tower of David
5 Thy two breasts are l' two young roes
11 garments is l' the smell of Lebanon.
5: 13 his lips l' like lilies, dropping sweet
6: 12 me l' the chariots of Ammi-nadib.
7: 1 joints of thy thighs are l' jewels,
2 Thy navel is l' a round goblet, which
2 thy belly is l' an heap of wheat set
3 Thy two breasts are l' two young roes
4 thine eyes l' the fishpools in Heshbon,
5 Thine head upon thee is l' Carmel,
5 and the hair of thine head l' purple;
7 thy stature is l' to a palm tree,
8 and the smell of thy nose l' apples;
9 the roof of thy mouth l' the best wine
8: 10 I am a wall, and my breasts l' towers:
14 be thou l' to a roe or to a young
Isa 1: 9 have been l' unto Gomorrah.
18 though they be red l' crimson,
2: 6 and are soothsayers l' the Philistines,
3: 18 and their round tires l' the moon,
5: 28 horses' hoofs shall be counted l' flint,
28 and their wheels like a whirlwind:
29 Their roaring shall be l' a lion,
29 they shall roar l' young lions: yea,
30 against them l' the roaring of the sea:
9: 18 mount up l' the lifting up of smoke.
10: 6 to tread them down l' the mire of the
13 the inhabitants l' a valiant man:
16 a burning l' the burning of a fire.
11: 7 and the lion shall eat straw l' the ox.
14 l' as it was to Israel in the day that he
Isa 13: 4 mountains, l' as of a great people;
14: 10 as we? art thou become l' unto us?
14 clouds; I will be l' the most High.
19 of thy grave l' an abominable branch,
16: 11 shall sound l' an harp for Moab,
17: 12 make a noise l' the noise of the seas;
12 l' the rushing of mighty waters!
13 rush l' the rushing of many waters:
13 l' a rolling thing before the whirlwind.
18: 4 l' a cloud of dew in the heat of harvest.
19: 16 day shall Egypt be l' unto women:
20: 3 L' as my servant Isaiah hath walked
22: 18 toss thee l' a ball into a large country:
24: 20 shall reel to and fro l' a drunkard,
20 and shall be removed l' a cottage; for
26: 17 L' as a woman with child, that
27: 10 forsaken, and left l' a wilderness:
29: 5 thy strangers shall be l' small dust,
30: 33 of the Lord, l' a stream of brimstone,
31: 4 L' as the lion and the young lion
33: 9 Sharon is l' a wilderness; and Bashan
38: 12 I have cut off l' a weaver my life: he
14 L' a crane or a swallow, so did I
40: 11 He shall feed his flock l' a shepherd:
42: 13 shall stir up jealousy l' a man of war:
14 now will I cry l' a travailing woman;
46: 5 compare me, that we may be l'?
9 I am God, and there is none l' me,
48: 19 of thy bowels l' the gravel thereof;
49: 2 made my mouth l' a sharp sword;
50: 7 therefore have I set my face l' a flint,
51: 3 will make her wilderness l' Eden,
3 her desert l' the garden of the Lord;
6 heavens shall vanish away l' smoke,
6 the earth shall wax old l' a garment,
6 therein shall die in l' manner:
8 moth shall eat them up l' a garment,
8 and the worm shall eat them l' wool;
53: 6 All we l' sheep have gone astray;
57: 20 the wicked are l' the troubled sea,
58: 1 lift up thy voice l' a trumpet, and
11 thou shalt be l' a watered garden,
11 l' a spring of water, whose waters
59: 10 We grope for the wall l' the blind,
11 We roar all l' bears, and mourn sore
11 bears, and mourn sore l' doves:
19 the enemy shall come in l' a flood,
63: 2 thy garments l' him that treadeth in
64: 6 our iniquities, l' the wind, have taken
65: 25 the lion shall eat straw l' the bullock:
66: 12 I will extend peace to her l' a river,
12 of the Gentiles l' a flowing stream:
14 your bones shall flourish l' an herb:
15 and with his chariots l' a whirlwind,
Jer 2: 30 your prophets, l' a destroying lion.
4: 4 lest my fury come forth l' fire, and
5: 19 L' as ye have forsaken me, and served
6: 23 their voice roareth l' the sea; and
9: 3 they bend their tongues l' their bow
12 and is burned up l' a wilderness,
10: 6 as there is none l' unto thee, O
7 there is none l' unto thee.
16 The portion of Jacob is not l' them:
11: 19 But I was l' a lamb or an ox that is
12: 3 them out l' sheep for the slaughter,
14: 6 they snuffed up the wind l' dragons;
17: 6 he shall be l' the heath in the desert,
21: 12 lest my fury go out l' fire, and burn
23: 9 bones shake; I am l' a drunken man,
9 l' a man whom wine hath overcome,
29 Is not my word l' as a fire? saith
29 l' a hammer that breaketh the rock in
24: 2 even l' the figs that are first ripe:
5 L' these good figs, so will I
25: 34 and ye shall fall l' a pleasant vessel.
26: 6 Then will I make this house l' Shiloh,
9 This house shall be l' Shiloh, and this
18 Zion shall be plowed l' a field, and
29: 17 will make them l' vile figs, that cannot
22 make thee l' Zedekiah and l' Ahab,
30: 7 day is great, so that none is l' it:
31: 28 that l' as I have watched over them,
32: 42 L' as I have brought all this great evil
36: 32 besides unto them many l' words.
38: 9 he is l' to die for hunger in the place
46: 8 Egypt riseth up l' a flood, and
8 his waters are moved l' the rivers;
20 Egypt is l' a very fair heifer, but
21 in the midst of her l' fatted bullocks;
22 The voice thereof shall go l' a serpent;
48: 6 be l' the heath in the wilderness.
28 be l' the dove that maketh her nest in
36 heart shall sound for Moab l' pipes,
36 heart shall sound l' pipes for the men
49: 19 Behold, he shall come up l' a lion from
19 appoint over her? for who is l' me?
50: 42 their voice shall roar l' the sea, and
42 put in array, l' a man to the battle,
44 Behold, he shall come up l' a lion from
44 appoint over her? for who is l' me?
51: 19 The portion of Jacob is not l' them;
33 of Babylon is l' a threshingfloor,
34 he hath swallowed me up l' a dragon,
38 They shall roar together l' lions:
40 I will bring them down l' lambs to the
40 slaughter, l' rams with he goats.
55 her waves do roar l' great waters,
52: 22 the pomegranates were l' unto these.
La 1: 6 princes are become l' harts that find
12 be any sorrow l' unto my sorrow,
21 and they shall be l' unto me.
2: 3 burned against Jacob l' a flaming fire,
4 He hath bent his bow l' an enemy:
4 of Zion: he poured out his fury l' fire.
13 for thy breach is great l' the sea:
18 let tears run down l' a river day and
La 2: 19 pour out thine heart l' water before
3: 52 enemies chased me sore, l' a bird,
4: 3 l' the ostriches in the wilderness.
5: 10 Our skin was black l' an oven because
Eze 1: 7 feet was l' the sole of a calf's foot:
7 l' the colour of burnished brass.
13 appearance was l' burning coals of fire,
13 and l' the appearance of lamps:
16 work was l' unto the colour of a beryl:
24 wings, l' the noise of great waters,
2: 8 rebellious l' that rebellious house:
5: 9 I will not do any more the l',
7: 16 and shall be on the mountains l' doves
12: 11 l' as I have done, so shall it be done
13: 4 thy prophets are l' the foxes in the
16: 16 the l' things shall not come, neither
18: 10 doeth the l' to any one of these
14 considereth, and doeth not such l',
19: 10 Thy mother is l' a vine in thy blood,
20: 36 L' as I pleaded with your fathers in
22: 25 l' a roaring lion ravening the prey;
27 thereof are l' wolves ravening the prey,
23: 18 l' as my mind was alienated from her
20 whose issue is l' the issue of horses.
25: 8 of Judah is l' unto all the heathen;
26: 4 her, and make her l' the top of a rock.
14 I will make thee l' the top of a rock:
19 l' the cities that are not inhabited;
27: 32 over thee, saying, What city is l' Tyrus,
32 l' the destroyed in the midst of the
31: 2 Whom art thou l' in thy greatness?
8 the fir trees were not l' his boughs,
8 God was l' unto him in his beauty.
18 To whom art thou thus l' in glory
32: 2 art l' a young lion of the nations,
14 cause their rivers to run l' oil, saith
36: 35 is become l' the garden of Eden;
37 increase them with men l' a flock.
38: 9 shalt ascend and come l' a storm,
9 thou shalt be l' a cloud to cover the
40: 3 was l' the appearance of brass,
25 round about, l' those windows:
41: 25 trees, l' as were made upon the walls;
42: 11 was l' the appearance of the chambers
43: 2 voice was l' a noise of many waters:
3 visions were l' the vision that I saw
45: 25 he do the l' in the feast of the seven
Da 1: 19 them all was found none l' Daniel,
2: 35 became l' the chaff of the summer
3: 25 of the fourth is l' the Son of God.
4: 33 hairs were grown l' eagles' feathers,
33 and his nails l' birds' claws.
5: 11 wisdom, l' the wisdom of the gods,
21 his heart was made l' the beasts,
21 they fed him with grass l' oxen, and
7: 4 The first was l' a lion, and had eagles'
5 beast, a second, l' to a bear, and it
6 and lo another, l' a leopard, which had
8 horn were eyes l' the eyes of man,
9 the hair of his head l' the pure wool:
9 his throne was l' the fiery flame, and
13 one l' the Son of man came with the
10: 6 His body also was l' the beryl, and his
6 his feet l' in colour to polished brass,
6 his words l' the voice of a multitude.
18 me one l' the appearance of a man,
11: 40 shall come against him l' a whirlwind
Ho 2: 3 set her l' a dry land, and slay her with
4: 9 And there shall be, l' people, l' priest:
5: 10 were l' them that remove the bound:
10 out my wrath upon them l' water.
6: 7 l' men have transgressed the covenant:
7: 6 made ready their heart l' an oven,
11 Ephraim also is l' a silly dove without
16 they are l' a deceitful bow: their
9: 10 Israel l' grapes in the wilderness;
11 their glory shall fly away l' a bird,
11: 10 he shall roar l' a lion: when he shall
13: 8 there will I devour them l' a lion:
14: 8 I am l' a green fir tree. From me is
Joe 1: 8 Lament l' a virgin girded with
2: 2 there hath not been ever the l',
5 L' the noise of chariots on the tops of
5 l' the noise of a flame of fire that
7 They shall run l' mighty men; they
7 they shall climb the wall l' men of war;
9 shall enter in at the windows l' a thief.
Am 2: 9 height was l' the height of the cedars,
5: 6 lest he break out l' fire in the house of
6: 5 instruments of musick, l' David;
9: 5 and it shall rise up wholly l' a flood;
9 nations, l' as corn is sifted in a sieve,
Jon 1: 4 that the ship was l' to be broken.
Mic 1: 8 I will make a wailing l' the dragons,
4: 10 of Zion, l' a woman in travail:
7: 17 They shall lick the dust l' a serpent,
17 of their holes l' worms of the earth:
18 Who is a God l' unto thee, that
Na 1: 6 his fury is poured out l' fire, and the
2: 4 ways: they shall seem l' torches,
4 they shall run l' the lightnings.
8 Nineveh is of old l' a pool of water:
3: 12 thy strong holds shall be l' fig trees
15 it shall eat thee up l' the cankerworm:
Hab 3: 19 and he will make my feet l' hind's feet,
Zep 1: 17 men, that they shall walk l' blind men,
2: 13 a desolation, and dry l' a wilderness.
Zec 1: 6 L' as the Lord of hosts thought to do
5: 9 had wings l' the wings of a stork:
9: 15 and they shall be filled l' bowls, and as
10: 7 of Ephraim shall be l' a mighty man,
12: 6 governors of Judah l' a hearth of fire
6 wood, and l' a torch of fire in a sheaf;
14: 5 l' as ye fled from before the earthquake
20 shall be l' the bowls before the altar.
Mal 3: 2 l' a refiner's fire, and l' a fullers' sope:

M't 3:16 Spirit of God descending l' a dove,
6: 8 Be not ye therefore l' unto them:
29 was not arrayed l' one of these.
11:16 It is l' unto children sitting in the
12:13 was restored whole, l' as the other.
13:31 is l' to a grain of mustard seed,
33 kingdom of heaven is l' unto leaven,
44 is l' unto treasure hid in a field;
45 heaven is l' unto a merchant man,
47 kingdom of heaven is l' unto a net,
52 l' unto a man that is an householder,
20: 1 l' unto a man that is an householder,
21:24 I in l' wise will tell you by what
22: 2 of heaven is l' unto a certain king,
39 And the second is l' unto it, Thou
23:27 ye are l' unto whited sepulchres,
28: 3 His countenance was l' lightning,
M'r 1:10 and the Spirit l' a dove descending
4:31 It is l' a grain of mustard seed,
7: 8 many other such l' things ye do.
13 and many such l' things do ye.
12:31 And the second is l', namely this,
13:29 So ye in l' manner, when ye shall
Lu 3:22 descended...bodily shape l' a dove
6:23 in the l' manner did their fathers
47 I will shew you to whom he is l':
48 He is l' a man which built an house,
49 l' a man that without a foundation
7:31 generation? and to what are they l'?
32 They are l' unto children sitting in
12:27 was not arrayed l' one of these.
36 yourselves l' unto men that wait
13:18 Unto what is the kingdom of God l'?
19 It is l' a grain of mustard seed,
21 It is l' leaven, which a woman took
20:31 and in l' manner the seven also:
Joh 1:32 descending from heaven l' a dove,
7:46 Never man spake l' this man.
8:55 I shall be a liar l' unto you: but I
9: 9 is he: others said, He is l' him:
Ac 1:11 shall so come in l' manner as ye
2: 3 them cloven tongues l' as of fire,
3:22 you of your brethren, l' unto me;
7:37 you of your brethren, l' unto me;
8:32 l' a lamb dumb before his shearer,
11:17 God gave them the l' gift as he did
14:15 also are men of l' passions with you,
17:29 that the Godhead is l' unto gold,
19:25 with the workmen of l' occupation,
Ro 1:23 image made l' to corruptible man,
28 as they did not l' to retain God
6: 4 l' as Christ was raised up from
9:29 and been made l' unto Gomorrha.
1Co 16:13 the faith, quit you l' men, be strong.
Ga 5:21 revellings, and such l':
Ph'p 3:21 be fashioned l' unto his glorious
1Th 2:14 have suffered l' things of your own
1Ti 2: 9 In l' manner also, that women
Heb 2:17 to be made l' unto his brethren,
4:15 all points tempted l' as we are,
7: 3 but made l' unto the Son of God;
Jas 1: 6 wavereth is l' a wave of the sea
23 he is l' unto a man beholding his
5:17 a man subject to l' passions as we
1Pe 3:21 The l' figure whereunto even
2Pe 1: 1 that have obtained l' precious faith
1Jo 3: 2 shall appear, we shall be l' him;
Jude 7 cities about them in l' manner,
Re 1:13 candlesticks one l' unto the Son of
14 and his hairs were white l' wool,
15 his feet l' unto fine brass, as if
2:18 his eyes l' unto a flame of fire,
18 and his feet are l' fine brass;
4: 3 that sat was to look upon l' a jasper
3 throne, in sight l' unto an emerald.
6 was a sea of glass l' unto crystal:
7 And the first beast was l' a lion,
7 And the second beast l' a calf, and
7 the fourth beast was l' a flying eagle.
9: 7 of the locusts were l' unto horses
7 were as it were crowns l' gold,
10 they had tails l' unto scorpions, and
19 their tails were l' unto serpents,
11: 1 was given me a reed l' unto a rod:
13: 2 which I saw was l' unto a leopard,
4 Who is l' unto the beast? who is
11 he had two horns l' a lamb, and he
14:14 cloud one sat l' unto the Son of man,
16:13 I saw three unclean spirits l' frogs
18:18 What city is l' unto this great city!
21 up a stone l' a great millstone,
21:11 her light was l' unto a stone most
11 even l' a jasper stone, clear as
18 was pure gold, l' unto clear glass.

liked
1Ch 28: 4 he l' me to make me king over all

likeminded
Ro 15: 5 to be l' one toward another
Ph'p 2: 2 Fulfil ye my joy, that ye be l',
20 For I have no man l', who will

liken See also LIKENED.
Isa 40:18 To whom then will ye l' God? or
25 To whom then will ye l' me, or
46: 5 To whom will ye l' me, and make
La 2:13 what thing shall I l' to thee, O
M't 7:24 I will l' him unto a wise man,
11:16 whereunto shall I l' this generation?
M'r 4:30 shall we l' the kingdom of God?
Lu 7:31 then shall I l' the men of this
13:20 shall I l' the kingdom of God?

likened
Ps 89: 6 mighty can be l' unto the Lord?
Jer 6: 2 have l' the daughter of Zion to a
M't 7:26 shall be l' unto a foolish man,
13:24 of heaven is l' unto a man which
18:23 of heaven l' unto a certain king,
25: 1 of heaven be l' unto ten virgins,

likeness
Ge 1:26 man in our image, after our l':
5: 1 man, in the l' of God made he him;
3 begat a son in his own l', after his
Ex 20: 4 or any l' of any thing that is in
De 4:16 figure, the l' of male or female,
17 The l' of any beast that is on the
17 the l' of any winged fowl that flieth
18 The l' of any thing that creepeth on
18 the l' of any fish that is in the
23 image, or the l' of any thing,
25 graven image, or the l' of any thing,
5: 8 any l' of any thing that is in heaven
Ps 17:15 satisfied, when I awake, with thy l'.
Isa 40:18 what l' will ye compare unto him?
Eze 1: 5 came the l' of four living creatures.
5 they had the l' of a man.
10 As for the l' of their faces, they four
13 As for the l' of the living creatures,
16 a beryl: and they four had one l':
22 the l' of the firmament upon their
26 their heads was the l' of a throne,
26 and upon the l' of the throne was the
26 l' as the appearance of a man above
28 of the l' of the glory of the Lord.
8: 2 and lo a l' as the appearance of fire:
10: 1 the appearance of the l' of a throne.
10 appearances, they four had one l',
21 and the l' of the hands of a man
22 the l' of their faces was the same
Ac 14:11 come down to us in the l' of men.
Ro 6: 5 together in the l' of his death,
5 be also in the l' of his resurrection:
8: 3 his own Son in the l' of sinful flesh,
Ph'p 2: 7 and was made in the l' of men:

liketh
De 23:16 thy gates, where it l' him best:
Es 8: 8 ye also for the Jews, as it l' you,
Am 4: 5 for this l' you, O ye children of

likewise^ See also LIKE and WISE.
Ex 22:30 L' shalt thou do with thine oxen,
26: 4 l' shalt thou make in the uttermost
27:11 l' for the north side in length there
36:11 l' he made in the uttermost side of
Le 7: 1 L' this is the law of the trespass
De 9:23 L' when the Lord sent you from
12:30 their gods? even so will I do l'.
15:17 thy maidservant thou shalt do l'.
22: 3 thou hast found, shalt thou do l':
J'g 1: 3 I l' will go with thee into thy lot.
7: 5 l' every one that boweth down upon
17 unto them, Look on me, and do l':
8: 8 Penuel, and spake unto them l':
9:49 people l' cut down every man his
1Sa 14:22 L' all the men of Israel which had hid
19:21 and they prophesied l'.
31: 5 was dead, he fell l' upon his sword,
2Sa 1:11 l' all the men that were with him:
17: 5 and let us hear l' what he saith.
1Ki 11: 8 l' did he for all his strange wives,
1Ch 10: 5 was dead, he fell l' on the sword,
18: 8 L' from Tibhath, and from Chun,
19:15 l' fled before Abishai his brother,
23:30 praise the Lord, and l' at even;
24:31 These l' cast lots over against
27: 4 in his course l' were twenty and four
28:16 and l' silver for the tables of silver:
17 l' silver by weight for every bason of
29:24 and all the sons l' of king David,
2Ch 3:11 and the other wing was l' five cubits,
29:22 l', when they had killed the rams,
Ne 4:22 L' at the same time said I unto
5:10 I, l', and my brethren, and my
Es 1:18 L' shall the ladies of Persia and
4:16 I also and my maidens will fast l';
Job 31:38 the furrows l' thereof complain;
37: 6 l' to the small rain, and to the great
Ps 49:10 l' the fool and the brutish person
52: 5 God shall l' destroy thee for ever,
Ec 7:22 thou thyself l' hast cursed others.
Isa 30:24 The oxen l' and the young asses that
Jer 40:11 L' when all the Jews that were in
Eze 13:17 L', thou son of man, set thy face
40:16 round about, and l' to the arches:
46: 3 L' the people of the land shall worship
Na 1:12 they be quiet, and l' many, yet
M't 17:12 L' shall also the Son of man
18:35 So l' shall my heavenly Father do
20: 5 sixth and ninth hour, and did l'.
10 they l' received every man a penny.
21:30 he came to the second, and said l'.
36 the first: and they did unto them l'.
22:26 L' the second also, and the third,
24:33 So l' ye, when ye shall see all these
25:17 l' he that had received two, he also
26:35 thee. L' also said all the disciples.
27:41 L' also the chief priests mocking
M'r 4:16 these are they l' which are sown on
12:21 left he any seed: and the third l'.
14:31 in any wise. L' also said they all.
15:31 L' also the chief priests mocking
Lu 2:38 gave thanks l' unto the Lord, and
3:11 he that hath meat, let him do l'.
14 the soldiers l' demanded of him,
5:33 l' the disciples of the Pharisees;
6:31 do to you, do ye also to them l'.
10:32 And l' a Levite, when he was at the
37 Jesus unto him, Go, and do thou l'.
13: 3 ye repent, ye shall all l' perish.
5 ye repent, ye shall all l' perish.
14:33 So l', whosoever he be of you that
15: 7 that l' joy shall be in heaven over
10 L', I say unto you, there is joy in
16:25 things, and l' Lazarus evil things:
17:10 So l' ye, when ye shall have done
28 L' also as it was in the days of Lot;
31 the field, let him l' not return back.
19:19 And he said l' to him, Be thou also
21:31 So l' ye, when ye see these things
22:20 L' also the cup after supper,
36 let him take it, and l' his scrip:
Joh 5:19 doeth, these also doeth the Son l'.
6:11 l' of the fishes as much as they
21:13 bread and giveth them, and fish l'.
Ac 3:24 have l' foretold of these days.
Ro 1:27 And l' also the men, leaving the
6:11 L' reckon ye also yourselves to be
8:26 L' the Spirit also helpeth our
16: 5 L' greet the church that is in their
1Co 7: 3 l' also the wife unto the husband.
4 l' also the husband hath not power of
22 l' also he that is called, being free, is
14: 9 So l' ye, except ye utter by the
Ga 2:13 other Jews dissembled l' with him;
Col 4:16 that ye l' read the epistle from
1Ti 3: 8 L' must the deacons be grave, not
5:25 L' also the good works of some are
Tit 2: 3 The aged women l', that they be in
6 Young men l' exhort to be sober
Heb 2:14 himself l' took part of the same;
9:21 sprinkled [l'] with blood both the
Jas 2:25 L' also was not Rahab the harlot
1Pe 3: 1 L', ye wives, be in subjection to
7 L', ye husbands, dwell with them
4: 1 arm yourselves l' with the same
5: 5 L', ye younger, submit yourselves
Jude 8 L' also these filthy dreamers defile
Re 8:12 third part of it, and the night l'.

Likhi (*lik'-hi*)
1Ch 7:19 Ahian, and Shechem, and L', and

liking
Job 39: 4 Their young ones are in good l',
Da 1:10 should he see your faces worse l' than

lilies
1Ki 7:26 brim of a cup, with flowers of l':
2Ch 4: 5 brim of a cup, with flowers of l';
Ca 2:16 I am his: he feedeth among the l'.
4: 5 are twins, which feed among the l'.
5:13 his lips like l', dropping sweet
6: 2 in the gardens, and to gather l'.
3 is mine: he feedeth among the l'.
7: 2 an heap of wheat set about with l'.
M't 6:28 Consider the l' of the field, how
Lu 12:27 Consider the l' how they grow:

lily See LILIES.
1Ki 7:19 pillars were of l' work in the porch,
22 the top of the pillars was l' work:
Ca 2: 1 of Sharon, and the l' of the valleys.
2 As the l' among thorns, so is my
Ho 14: 5 he shall grow as the l', and cast

lily-work See LILY and WORK.

lime
Isa 33:12 shall be as the burnings of l':
Am 2: 1 bones of the king of Edom into l':

limit See also LIMITED; LIMITETH.
Eze 43:12 the whole l' thereof round about

limited
Ps 78:41 and l' the Holy One of Israel.

limiteth
Heb 4: 7 he l' a certain day, saying to David,

line See also LINES; PLUMBLINE.
Jos 2:18 shalt bind this l' of scarlet thread
21 bound the scarlet l' in the window.
2Sa 8: 2 and measured them with a l',
2 and with one full l' to keep alive.
1Ki 7:15 a l' of twelve cubits did compass
23 a l' of thirty cubits did compass
2Ki 21:13 over Jerusalem the l' of Samaria,
2Ch 4: 2 a l' of thirty cubits did compass it
Job 38: 5 who hath stretched the l' upon it?
Ps 19: 4 Their l' is gone out through all the
78:55 divided them an inheritance by l',
Isa 28:10,13 l' upon l', l' upon l'; here a
17 Judgment also will I lay to the l',
34:11 out upon it the l' of confusion,
17 hand hath divided it unto them by l':
44:13 he marketh it out with a l'; he
Jer 31:39 the measuring l' shall yet go forth
La 2: 8 he hath stretched out a l', he hath
Eze 40: 3 with a l' of flax in his hand, and
47: 3 man that had the l' in his hand
Am 7:17 thy land shall be divided by l';
Zec 1:16 a l' shall be stretched forth upon
2: 1 with a measuring l' in his hand.
2Co 10:16 not to boast in another man's l'

lineage
Lu 2: 4 was of the house and l' of David:)

linen
Ge 41:42 arrayed him in vestures of fine l',
Ex 25: 4 purple, and scarlet, and fine l',
26: 1 with ten curtains of fine twined l',
31 and fine twined l' of cunning work:
36 and scarlet, and fine twined l',
27: 9 for the court of fine twined l' of an
16 and scarlet, and fine twined l',
18 height five cubits of fine twined l',
28: 5 and purple, and scarlet, and fine l'.
6 purple, of scarlet, and fine twined l',
8 and scarlet, and fine twined l'.
15 and of scarlet, and of fine twined l',
39 shalt embroider the coat of fine l',
39 thou shalt make the mitre of fine l',
42 make them l' breeches to cover

Ex 35: 6, 23 purple, and scarlet, and fine l',
25 purple, and of scarlet, and of fine l'.
35 in purple, in scarlet, and in fine l',
36: 8 made ten curtains of fine twined l',
35 and scarlet, and fine twined l':
37 and scarlet, and fine twined l',
38: 9 of the court were of fine twined l',
16 round about were of fine twined l'.
18 and scarlet, and fine twined l':
23 purple, and in scarlet, and fine l'.
39: 2 and scarlet, and fine twined l'.
3 and in the scarlet, and in the fine l',
5 and scarlet, and fine twined l';
8 and scarlet, and fine twined l'.
24 and purple, and scarlet, and twined l'.
27 made coats of fine l' of woven work
28 fine l', and goodly bonnets of fine l',
28 and l' breeches of fine twined
28 and breeches of fine twined l',
29 And a girdle of fine twined l', and
Le 6: 10 priest shall put on his l' garment,
10 l' breeches shall he put upon his
13: 47 woollen garment, or a l' garment;
48 warp, or woof; of l', or of woollen;
52 warp or woof, in woollen or in l',
59 leprosy in a garment of woollen or l',
16: 4 He shall put on the holy l' coat,
4 have the l' breeches upon his flesh,
4 and shall be girded with a l' girdle,
4 with the l' mitre shall he be attired:
23 shall put off the l' garments, which
32 and shall put on the l' clothes, even
19: 19 garment mingled of l' and woollen
De 22: 11 divers sorts, as of woollen and l'
1Sa 2: 18 a child, girded with a l' ephod.
22: 18 persons that did wear a l' ephod.
2Sa 6: 14 David was girded with a l' ephod.
1Ki 10: 28 brought out of Egypt, and l' yarn:
28 received the l' yarn at a price.
1Ch 4: 21 house of them that wrought fine l',
15: 27 was clothed with a robe of fine l',
27 also had upon him an ephod of l'.
2Ch 1: 16 brought out of Egypt, and l' yarn:
16 received the l' yarn at a price.
2: 14 blue, and in fine l', and in crimson;
3: 14 and purple, and crimson, and fine l',
5: 12 brethren, being arrayed in white l',
Es 1: 6 hangings, fastened...cords of fine l'
8: 15 with a garment of fine l' and purple:
Pr 7: 16 carved works, with fine l' of Egypt.
31: 24 She maketh fine l', and selleth it;
Isa 3: 23 The glasses, and the fine l', and
Jer 13: 1 Go and get thee a l' girdle, and
Eze 9: 2 among them was clothed with l',
3 called to the man clothed with l',
11 behold, the man clothed with l',
10: 2 spake unto the man clothed with l',
6 commanded the man clothed with l',
7 of him that was clothed with l':
16: 10 I girded thee about with fine l',
13 thy raiment was of fine l', and silk,
27: 7 Fine l' with broidered work from
16 broidered work,...fine l', and coral,
44: 17 shall be clothed with l' garments;
18 have l' bonnets upon their heads,
18 have l' breeches upon their loins;
Da 10: 5 behold a certain man clothed in l',
12: 6 one said to the man clothed in l',
7 And I heard the man clothed in l',
M't 27: 59 he wrapped it in a clean l' cloth,
M'r 14: 51 l' cloth cast about his naked body;
52 And he left the l' cloth, and fled
15: 46 And he bought fine l', and took him
46 wrapped him in the l', and laid him
Lu 16: 19 was clothed in purple and fine l',
23: 53 took it down, and wrapped it in l',
24: 12 the l' clothes laid by themselves,
Joh 19: 40 of Jesus, and wound it in l' clothes
20: 5 looking in, saw the l' clothes lying;
6 and seeth the l' clothes lie,
7 not lying with the l' clothes, but
Re 15: 6 clothed in pure and white l', and
18: 12 pearls, and fine l', and purple,
16 city, that was clothed in fine l',
19: 8 that she should be arrayed in fine l',
8 for the fine l' is the righteousness
14 clothed in fine l', white and clean.

lines
2Sa 8: 2 even with two l' measured he to
Ps 16: 6 The l' are fallen unto me in pleasant

lingered See also LINGERETH.
Ge 19: 16 And while he l', the men laid hold
43: 10 For except we had l', surely now

lingereth See also LINGERED.
2Pe 2: 3 judgment now of a long time l' not,

lintel See also LINTELS.
Ex 12: 22 strike the l' and the two side posts
23 when he seeth the blood upon the l',
1Ki 6: 31 the l' and side posts were a fifth
Am 9: 1 he said, Smite the l' of the door,

lintels
Zep 2: 14 shall lodge in the upper l' of it;

Linus (*li'-nus*)
2Ti 4: 21 and L', and Claudia, and all the

lion See also LIONESS; LIONLIKE; LION'S; LIONS.
Ge 49: 9 stooped down, he couched as a l',
9 and as an old l'; who shall rouse
Nu 23: 24 people shall rise up as a great l',
24 and lift up himself as a young l':
24: 9 He couched, he lay down as a l',
9 and as a great l': who shall stir
De 33: 20 he dwelleth as a l', and teareth
J'g 14: 5 a young l' roared against him.
8 aside to see the carcase of the l':
J'g 14: 8 and honey in the carcase of the l'.
9 honey out of the carcase of the l'.
18 and what is stronger than a l'?
1Sa 17: 34 and there came a l', and a bear,
36 slew both the l' and the bear:
37 delivered me out of the paw of the l',
2Sa 17: 10 whose heart is as the heart of a l',
23: 20 slew a l' in the midst of a pit in time
1Ki 13: 24 l' met him by the way, and slew him:
24 the l' also stood by the carcase.
25 and the l' standing by the carcase:
26 Lord hath delivered him unto the l',
28 and the l' standing by the carcase:
28 the l' had not eaten the carcase, nor
20: 36 from me, a l' shall slay thee.
36 him, a l' found him, and slew him.
1Ch 11: 22 and slew a l' in a pit in a snowy day.
Job 4: 10 The roaring of the l', and the voice
10 the voice of the fierce l', and the
11 old l' perisheth for lack of prey,
10: 16 Thou huntest me as a fierce l':
28: 8 it, nor the fierce l' passed by it.
38: 39 Wilt thou hunt the prey for the l'?
Ps 7: 2 Lest he tear my soul like a l',
10: 9 in wait secretly as a l' in his den:
17: 12 Like as a l' that is greedy of his prey,
12 as it were a young l' lurking in
22: 13 as a ravening and a roaring l'.
91: 13 shalt tread upon the l' and adder:
13 the young l' and the dragon shalt
Pr 19: 12 king's wrath is as the roaring of a l';
20: 2 of a king is as the roaring of a l':
22: 13 There is a l' without, I shall be
26: 13 man saith, There is a l' in the way;
13 a l' is in the streets.
28: 1 but the righteous are bold as a l'.
15 As a roaring l', and a ranging bear;
30: 30 A l' which is strongest among
Ec 9: 4 living dog is better than a dead l'.
Isa 5: 29 Their roaring shall be like a l',
11: 6 young l' and the fatling together;
7 the l' shall eat straw like the ox.
21: 8 And he cried, A l': My lord, I stand
30: 6 whence come the young and old l',
31: 4 Like as the l' and the young
4 the young l' roaring on his prey,
35: 9 No l' shall be there, nor any
38: 13 as a l', so will he break all my bones:
65: 25 l' shall eat straw like the bullock:
Jer 2: 30 your prophets, like a destroying l'.
4: 7 The l' is come up from his thicket,
5: 6 a l' out of the forest shall slay them,
12: 8 Mine heritage is unto me as a l' in
25: 38 hath forsaken his covert, as the l':
49: 19 Behold, he shall come up like a l'
50: 44 Behold, he shall come up like a l'
La 3: 10 in wait, and as a l' in secret places.
Eze 1: 10 the face of a l', on the right side:
10: 14 man, and the third the face of a l',
19: 3 it become a young l', and it
5 whelps, and made him a young l'.
6 he became a young l', and learned
22: 25 like a roaring l' ravening the prey;
32: 2 art like a young l' of the nations,
41: 19 face of a young l' toward the palm
Da 7: 4 first was like a l', and had eagle's
Ho 5: 14 For I will be unto Ephraim as a l',
14 a young l' to the house of Judah:
11: 10 the Lord: he shall roar like a l':
13: 7 I will be unto them as a l':
8 there will I devour them like a l':
Joe 1: 6 whose teeth are the teeth of a l',
6 hath the cheek teeth of a great l'.
Am 3: 4 Will a l' roar in the forest, when he
4 will a young l' cry out of his den,
8 The l' hath roared, who will not
12 taketh out of the mouth of the l'
5: 19 As if a man did flee from a l', and a
Mic 5: 8 as a l' among the beasts of the forest,
8 as a young l' among the flocks of
Na 2: 11 of the young lions, where the l',
11 even the old l', walked, and the
12 The l' did tear in pieces enough
2Ti 4: 17 delivered out of the mouth of the l'.
1Pe 5: 8 adversary the devil, as a roaring l',
Re 4: 7 And the first beast was like a l',
5: 5 behold, the L' of the tribe of Juda,
10: 3 loud voice, as when a l' roareth:
13: 2 and his mouth as the mouth of a l':

lioness See also LIONESSES.
Eze 19: 2 What is thy mother? A l': she lay

lionesses
Na 2: 12 and strangled for his l', and filled

lionlike
2Sa 23: 20 acts, he slew two l' men of Moab:
1Ch 11: 22 acts; he slew two l' men of Moab:

lion's
Ge 49: 9 Judah is a l' whelp: from the prey,
De 33: 22 of Dan he said, Dan is a l' whelp:
Job 4: 11 the stout l' whelps are scattered
28: 8 The l' whelps have not trodden it,
Ps 22: 21 Save me from the l' mouth: for
Na 2: 11 old lion, walked, and the l' whelp,

lions See also LIONS'.
2Sa 1: 23 eagles, they were stronger than l'.
1Ki 7: 29 between the ledges were l', oxen, and
29 beneath the l' and oxen were certain
36 he graved cherubims, l', and palm
10: 19 and two l' stood beside the stays.
20 twelve l' stood there on the one side
2Ki 17: 25 the Lord sent l' among them, which
26 he hath sent l' among them, and,
1Ch 12: 8 whose faces were like the faces of l',
2Ch 9: 18 and two l' standing by the stays:
2Ch 9: 19 twelve l' stood there on the one side
Job 4: 10 teeth of the young l', are broken.
38: 39 or fill the appetite of the young l',
Ps 34: 10 The young l' do lack, and suffer
35: 17 destructions, my darling from the l'.
57: 4 My soul is among l': and I lie even
58: 6 out the great teeth of the young l',
104: 21 The young l' roar after their prey,
Isa 5: 29 lion, they shall roar like young l':
15: 9 l' upon him that escapeth of Moab,
Jer 2: 15 The young l' roared upon him, and
50: 17 the l' have driven him away: first
51: 38 They shall roar together like l':
Eze 19: 2 A lioness: she lay down among l',
2 her whelps among young l'.
6 he went up and down among the l',
38: 13 with all the young l' thereof, shall
Da 6: 7 he shall be cast into the den of l'.
12 king, shall be cast into the den of l'?
16 and cast him into the den of l'.
19 and went in haste unto the den of l'.
20 able to deliver thee from the l'?
24 they cast them into the den of l',
24 and the l' had the mastery of them,
27 Daniel from the power of the l'.
Na 2: 11 Where is the dwelling of the l', and
11 the feedingplace of the young l',
13 the sword shall devour thy young l':
Zep 3: 3 princes within her are roaring l';
Zec 11: 3 a voice of the roaring of young l';
Heb 11: 33 promises, stopped the mouths of l',
Re 9: 8 their teeth were as the teeth of l'.
17 the horses were as the heads of l';

lions'
Ca 4: 8 and Hermon, from the l' dens, from
Jer 51: 38 lions: they shall yell as l' whelps.
Da 6: 22 angel, and hath shut the l' mouths,

lip See also LIPS.
Le 13: 45 put a covering upon his upper l',
Ps 22: 7 they shoot out the l', they shake
Pr 12: 19 The l' of truth shall be established

lips
Ex 6: 12 me, who am of uncircumcised l'?
30 Behold, I am of uncircumcised l',
Le 5: 4 pronouncing with his l' to do evil
Nu 30: 6 vowed, or uttered ought out of her l',
8 that which she uttered with her l',
12 whatsoever proceeded out of her l'
De 23: 23 That which is gone out of thy l'
1Sa 1: 13 only her l' moved, but her voice
2Ki 19: 28 in thy nose, and my bridle in thy l',
Job 2: 10 all this did not Job sin with his l'.
8: 21 laughing, and thy l' with rejoicing.
11: 5 speak, and open his l' against thee;
13: 6 hearken to the pleadings of my l'.
15: 6 thine own l' testify against thee.
16: 5 the moving of my l' should asswage
23: 12 from the commandment of his l';
27: 4 My l' shall not speak wickedness,
32: 20 I will open my l' and answer.
33: 3 my l' shall utter knowledge clearly.
Ps 12: 2 with flattering l' and with a double
3 Lord shall cut off all flattering l',
4 our l' are our own: who is lord over
16: 4 nor take up their names into my l'.
17: 1 that goeth not out of feigned l'.
4 by the word of thy l' I have kept me
21: 2 not withholden the request of his l'.
31: 18 Let the lying l' be put to silence;
34: 13 evil, and thy l' from speaking guile.
40: 9 I have not refrained my l', O Lord,
45: 2 of men: grace is poured into thy l':
51: 15 O Lord, open thou my l'; and my
59: 7 their mouth: swords are in their l':
12 the words of their l' let them even
63: 3 than life, my l' shall praise thee.
5 shall praise thee with joyful l':
66: 14 Which my l' have uttered, and my
71: 23 My l' shall greatly rejoice when I
89: 34 the thing that is gone out of my l'.
106: 33 he spake unadvisedly with his l'.
119: 13 With my l' have I declared all the
171 My l' shall utter praise, when thou
120: 2 my soul, O Lord, from lying l',
140: 3 adders' poison is under their l'.
9 mischief of their own l' cover them.
141: 3 my mouth; keep the door of my l'.
Pr 4: 24 and perverse l' put far from thee.
5: 2 that thy l' may keep knowledge.
3 For the l' of a strange woman drop
7: 21 with the flattering of her l' she
8: 6 the opening of my l' shall be right
7 is an abomination to my l'.
10: 13 l' of him that hath understanding
18 He that hideth hatred with lying l',
19 but he that refraineth his l' is wise.
21 The l' of the righteous feed many:
32 The l' of the righteous know what
12: 13 snared by the transgression of his l':
22 Lying l' are abomination to the
13: 3 he that openeth wide his l' shall
14: 3 but the l' of the wise shall preserve
7 not in him the l' of knowledge.
23 talk of the l' tendeth only to penury.
15: 7 l' of the wise disperse knowledge:
16: 10 A divine sentence is in the l' of the
13 Righteous l' are the delight of kings;
21 the sweetness of the l' increaseth
23 mouth, and addeth learning to his l'.
27 in his l' there is as a burning fire.
30 moving his l' he bringeth evil to
17: 4 wicked doer giveth heed to false l';
7 fool: much less do lying l' a prince.
28 he that shutteth his l' is esteemed
18: 6 A fool's l' enter into contention,

Pr 18: 7 and his l' are the snare of his soul.
20 increase of his l' shall he be filled.
19: 1 he that is perverse in his l', and is a
20: 15 the l' of knowledge are a precious
19 with him that flattereth with his l'.
22: 11 the grace of his l' the king shall be
18 they shall withal be fitted in thy l'.
23: 16 when thy l' speak right things.
24: 2 and their l' talk of mischief.
26 Every man shall kiss his l' that
28 cause; and deceive not with thy l'.
26: 23 Burning l' and a wicked heart are
24 that hateth dissembleth with his l',
27: 2 a stranger, and not thine own l'.
Ec 10: 12 but the l' of a fool shall swallow up
Ca 4: 3 Thy l' are like a thread of scarlet,
11 Thy l', O my spouse, drop as the
5: 13 his l' like lilies, dropping sweet
7: 9 the l' of those that are asleep to
Isa 6: 5 because I am a man of unclean l',
5 the midst of a people of unclean l':
7 said, Lo, this hath touched thy l';
11: 4 with the breath of his l' shall he
28: 11 with stammering l' and another
29: 13 and with their l' do honour me,
30: 27 his l' are full of indignation, and
37: 29 thy nose, and my bridle in thy l',
57: 19 I create the fruit of the l'; Peace,
59: 3 your l' have spoken lies, your
Jer 17: 16 which came out of my l' was right
La 3: 62 The l' of those that rose up against
Eze 24: 17 cover not thy l', and eat not the
22 ye shall not cover your l', nor eat
36: 3 are taken up in the l' of talkers,
Da 10: 16 of the sons of men touched my l':
Ho 14: 2 will we render the calves of our l'.
Mic 3: 7 yea, they shall all cover their l';
Hab 3: 16 my l' quivered at the voice:
Mal 2: 6 and iniquity was not found in his l':
7 priest's l' should keep knowledge,
M't 15: 8 and honoureth me with their l';
M'r 7: 6 people honoureth me with their l',
Ro 3: 13 the poison of asps is under their l':
1Co 14: 21 men of other tongues and other l'
Heb 13: 15 the fruit of our l' giving thanks to
1Pe 3: 10 and his l' that they speak no guile:

liquor See also LIQUORS.
Nu 6: 3 shall he drink any l' of grapes,
Ca 7: 2 round goblet, which wanteth not l':

liquors
Ex 22: 29 of thy ripe fruits, and of thy l':

listed
M't 17: 12 done unto him whatsoever they l'.
M'r 9: 13 done unto him whatsoever they l',

listen
Isa 49 1 L', O isles, unto me; and hearken,

listeth
Joh 3: 8 The wind bloweth where it l', and
Jas 3: 4 whithersoever...governor l'.

litters
Isa 66: 20 horses, and in chariots, and in l',

little See also LEAST; LESS.
Ge 18: 4 a l' water, I pray you, be fetched,
19: 20 near to flee unto, and it is a l' one:
20 escape thither, (is it not a l' one?)
24: 17 drink a l' water of thy pitcher.
43 a l' water of thy pitcher to drink;
30: 30 l' which thou hadst before I came,
34: 29 all their l' ones, and their wives
35: 16 but a l' way to come to Ephrath:
43: 2 them, Go again, buy us a l' food.
8 we, and thou, and also our l' ones.
11 a present, a l' balm, and a l' honey,
44: 20 and a child of his old age, a l' one;
25 Go again, and buy us a l' food.
45: 19 the land of Egypt for your l' ones,
46: 5 and their l' ones, and their wives,
47: 24 and for food for your l' ones.
48: 7 a l' way to come unto Ephrath:
50: 8 only their l' ones, and their flocks,
21 will nourish you, and your l' ones.
Ex 10: 10 I will let you go, and your l' ones:
24 let your l' ones also go with you.
12: 4 household be too l' for the lamb,
16: 18 he that gathered l' had no lack;
23: 30 By l' and l' I will drive them out
Le 11: 17 And the l' owl, and the cormorant,
Nu 14: 31 But your l' ones, which ye said
16: 27 their sons, and their l' children.
31: 9 Midian captives, and their l' ones,
17 kill every male among the l' ones,
32: 16 our cattle, and cities for our l' ones:
17 our l' ones shall dwell in the fenced
24 Build you cities for your l' ones,
26 Our l' ones, our wives, our flocks,
De 1: 39 your l' ones, which ye said should
2: 34 the women, and the l' ones, of every
3: 19 your wives, and your l' ones, and
7: 22 nations before thee by l' and l':
14: 16 The l' owl, and the great owl, and
20: 14 the women, and the l' ones, and
28: 38 field, and shalt gather but l' in;
29: 11 Your l' ones, your wives, and thy
Jos 1: 14 Your wives, your l' ones, and your
8: 35 the women, and the l' ones, and the
19: 47 of Dan went out too l' for them:
22: 17 Is the iniquity of Peor too l' for us,
J'g 4: 19 I pray thee, a l' water to drink;
18: 21 put the l' ones and the cattle and
Ru 2: 7 that she tarried a l' in the house.
1Sa 2: 19 his mother made him a l' coat,
14: 29 because I tasted a l' of this honey.
43 I did but taste a l' honey with the
1Sa 15: 17 thou wast l' in thine own sight,
20: 35 with David, and a l' lad with him.
2Sa 12: 3 had nothing, save one l' ewe lamb,
8 and if that had been too l', I would
15: 22 all the l' ones that were with him.
16: 1 was a l' past the top of the hill,
19: 36 servant will go a l' way over Jordan
1Ki 3: 7 I am but a l' child: I know not how
8: 64 too l' to receive the burnt offerings,
11: 17 Egypt; Hadad being yet a l' child.
12: 10 My l' finger shall be thicker than
17: 10 Fetch me, I pray thee, a l' water
12 in a barrel, and a l' oil in a cruse:
13 but make me thereof a l' cake first,
18: 44 ariseth a l' cloud out of the sea,
20: 27 them like two l' flocks of kids;
2Ki 2: 23 forth l' children out of the city,
4: 10 Let us make a l' chamber, I pray
5: 2 out of the land of Israel a l' maid;
14 like unto the flesh of a l' child, and
19 So he departed from him a l' way.
10: 18 unto them, Ahab served Baal a l';
2Ch 10: 10 My l' finger shall be thicker than
20: 13 before the Lord, with their l' ones,
31: 18 the genealogy of all their l' ones,
Ezr 8: 21 way for us, and for our l' ones, and
9: 8 now for a l' space grace hath been
8 give us a l' reviving in our bondage.
Ne 9: 32 all the trouble seem l' before thee,
Es 3: 13 l' children and women, in one day,
8: 11 them, both l' ones and women,
Job 4: 12 and mine ear received a l' thereof.
10: 20 alone, that I may take comfort a l',
21: 11 forth their l' ones like a flock,
24: 24 They are exalted for a l' while,
26: 14 how l' a portion is heard of him?
36: 2 Suffer me a l', and I will shew
Ps 2: 12 when his wrath is kindled but a l'.
8: 5 made him a l' lower than the angels,
37: 10 For yet a l' while, and the wicked
16 A l' that a righteous man hath is
65: 12 the l' hills rejoice on every side.
68: 27 There is l' Benjamin with their
72: 3 and the l' hills, by righteousness.
114: 4 like rams, and the l' hills like lambs.
6 rams; and ye l' hills, like lambs?
137: 9 dasheth thy l' ones against the
Pr 6: 10 Yet a l' sleep, a l' slumber,
10 a l' folding of the hands to sleep:
10: 20 the heart of the wicked is l' worth.
15: 16 is l' with the fear of the Lord, than
16: 8 Better is a l' with righteousness,
24: 33 Yet a l' sleep, a l' slumber,
33 a l' folding of the hands to sleep:
30: 24 four things which are l' upon the
Ec 5: 12 sweet, whether he eat l' or much:
9: 14 There was a l' city, and few men
10: 1 so doth a l' folly him that is in
Ca 2: 15 Take us the foxes, the l' foxes,
3: 4 but a l' that I passed from them,
8: 8 We have a l' sister, and she hath
Isa 10: 25 For yet a very l' while, and the
11: 6 and a l' child shall lead them.
26: 20 thyself as it were for a l' moment,
28: 10 line; here a l', and there a l':
13 upon line; here a l', and there a l';
29: 17 Is it not yet a very l' while, and
40: 15 up the isles as a very l' thing.
54: 8 In a l' wrath I hid my face from
60: 22 A l' one shall become a thousand,
63: 18 have possessed it but a l' while:
Jer 14: 3 sent their l' ones to the waters:
48: 4 her l' ones have caused a cry to be
51: 33 yet a l' while, and the time of her
Eze 9: 6 maids, and l' children, and women:
11: 16 I be to them as a l' sanctuary in
16: 47 if that were a very l' thing, thou
31: 4 out her l' rivers unto all the trees
40: 7 every l' chamber was one reed
7 between the l' chambers were five
10 And the l' chambers of the gate
12 space also before the l' chambers
12 the l' chambers were six cubits on
13 from the roof of one l' chamber to
16 narrow windows to the l' chambers,
21 the l' chambers thereof were three
29, 33 the l' chambers thereof, and
36 The l' chambers thereof, the posts
Da 7: 8 up among them another l' horn,
8: 9 one of them came forth a l' horn,
11: 34 they shall be holpen with a l' help:
Ho 1: 4 for yet a l' while, and I will avenge
8: 10 shall sorrow a l' for the burden of
Am 6: 11 and the l' house with clefts.
Mic 5: 2 thou be l' among the thousands of
Hag 1: 6 have sown much, and bring in l';
9 for much, and, lo, it came to l';
2: 6 Yet once, it is a l' while, and I will
Zec 1: 15 I was but a l' displeased, and they
13: 7 turn mine hand upon the l' ones.
M't 6: 30 more clothe you, O ye of l' faith?
8: 26 Why are ye fearful, O ye of l' faith?
10: 42 to drink unto one of these l' ones
14: 31 O thou of l' faith, wherefore didst
15: 34 they said, Seven, and a few l' fishes.
16: 8 O ye of l' faith, why reason ye
18: 2 Jesus called a l' child unto him,
3 converted, and become as l' children,
4 humble himself as this l' child,
5 receive one such l' child in my
6 shall offend one of these l' ones
10 ye despise not one of these l' ones;
14 one of these l' ones should perish.
19: 13 brought unto him l' children, that
14 Jesus said, Suffer l' children, and
26: 39 went a l' farther, and fell on his
M'r 1: 19 he had gone a l' farther thence,
4: 36 were also with him other l' ships.
5: 23 My l' daughter lieth at the point
9: 42 shall offend one of these l' ones
10: 14 Suffer the l' children to come unto
15 the kingdom of God as a l' child,
14: 35 And he went forward a l', and fell
70 And a l' after, they that stood by
Lu 5: 3 would thrust out a l' from the land.
7: 47 l' is forgiven, the same loveth l'.
12: 28 will he clothe you, O ye of l' faith?
32 Fear not, l' flock; for it is your
17: 2 should offend one of these l' ones.
18: 16 Suffer l' children to come unto me,
17 the kingdom of God as a l' child
19: 3 press, because he was l' of stature.
17 thou hast been faithful in a very l',
22: 58 after a l' while another saw him,
Joh 6: 7 every one of them may take a l'.
7: 33 Yet a l' while am I with you, and
12: 35 Yet a l' while is the light with you.
13: 33 L' children, yet a...while I am with
33 children, yet a l' while I am with
14: 19 Yet a l' while, and the world seeth
16: 16 A l' while, and ye shall not see me:
16 a l' while, and ye shall see me:
17 A l' while, and ye shall not see me:
17 a l' while, and ye shall see me:
18 What is this that he saith, A l' while?
19 A l' while, and ye shall not see me:
19 a l' while, and ye shall see me?
21: 8 other disciples came in a l' ship;
Ac 5: 34 to put the apostles forth a l' space;
20: 12 alive, and were not a l' comforted.
27: 28 when they had gone a l' further,
28: 2 people shewed us no l' kindness:
1Co 5: 6 not that a l' leaven leaveneth the
2Co 8: 15 that had gathered l' had no lack.
11: 1 could bear with me a l' in my folly:
16 me, that I may boast myself a l'.
Ga 4: 19 My l' children, of whom I travail in
5: 9 A l' leaven leaveneth the whole
1Ti 4: 8 For bodily exercise profiteth l':
5: 23 a l' wine for thy stomach's sake
Heb 2: 7 him a l' lower than the angels;
9 made a l' lower than the angels for
10: 37 For yet a l' while, and he that shall
Jas 3: 5 Even so the tongue is a l' member,
5 great a matter a l' fire kindleth!
4: 14 vapour, that appeareth for a l' time,
1Jo 2: 1 My l' children, these things write
12 I write unto you, l' children,
13 I write unto you, l' children,
18 L' children, it is the last time: and
28 And now, l' children, abide in him;
3: 7 L' children, let no man deceive you:
18 My l' children, let us not love in
4: 4 Ye are of God, l' children, and have
5: 21 L' children, keep yourselves from
Re 3: 8 for thou hast a l' strength, and
6: 11 they should rest yet for a l' season,
10: 2 he had in his hand a l' book open:
8 take the l' book which is open in
9 said unto him, Give me the l' book.
10 the l' book out of the angel's hand,
20: 3 that he must be loosed a l' season.

little-owl See LITTLE and OWL.

live See also ALIVE; LIVED; LIVES; LIVEST; LIVETH; LIVING.
Ge 3: 22 tree of life, and eat, and l' for ever:
12: 13 my soul shall l' because of thee.
17: 18 unto God, O that Ishmael might l'
19: 20 not a little one?) and my soul shall l'.
20: 7 pray for thee, and thou shalt l':
27: 40 by thy sword shalt thou l', and shalt
31: 32 thou findest thy gods, let him not l':
42: 2 for us from thence; that we may l',
18 them the third day, This do, and l';
43: 8 that we may l', and not die, both we,
45: 3 am Joseph; doth my father yet l'?
47: 19 and give us seed, that we may l',
Ex 1: 16 if it be a daughter, then she shall l'.
19: 13 it be beast or man, it shall not l':
21: 35 they shall sell the l' ox, and divide
22: 18 Thou shalt not suffer a witch to l'.
33: 20 there shall no man see me, and l'.
Le 16: 20 altar, he shall bring the l' goat:
21 hands upon the head of the l' goat,
18: 5 if a man do, he shall l' in them:
25: 35 that he may l' with thee.
36 that thy brother may l' with thee.
Nu 4: 19 do unto them, that they may l',
14: 21 But as truly as I l', all the earth
28 As truly as I l', saith the Lord,
21: 8 when he looketh upon it, shall l'.
24: 23 who shall l' when God doeth this!
De 4: 1 ye may l', and go in and possess
10 all the days that they shall l' upon
33 the fire, as thou hast heard, and l'?
42 one of these cities he might l':
5: 33 that ye may l', and that it may be
8: 1 to do, that ye may l', and multiply,
3 that man doth not l' by bread only,
3 the mouth of the Lord doth man l'.
12: 1 the days that ye l' upon the earth.
16: 20 that thou mayest l', and inherit
19: 4 shall flee thither, that he may l':
5 flee unto one of those cities, and l':
30: 6 all thy soul, that thou mayest l'.
16 that thou mayest l' and multiply:
19 that both thou and thy seed may l':
31: 13 as long as ye l' in the land whither
32: 40 to heaven, and say, I l' for ever.
33: 6 Let Reuben l', and not die; and let
Jos 6: 17 only Rahab the harlot shall l', she

Jos 9:15 a league with them, to let them l':
20 we will even let them l', lest wrath
21 princes said unto them, Let them l';
1Sa 20:14 not only while yet I l' shew me the
2Sa 1:10 not l' after that he was fallen:
12:22 to me, that the child may l'?
19:34 How long have I to l', that I should
1Ki 1:31 Let my lord king David l' for ever.
8:40 all the days that they l' in the land
20:32 saith, I pray thee, let me l'. And
2Ki 4: 7 l' thou and thy children of the rest.
7: 4 if they save us alive, we shall l';
10:19 shall be wanting, he shall not l'.
18:32 honey, that ye may l', and not die:
20: 1 order; for thou shalt die, and not l'.
2Ch 6:31 so long as they l' in the land which
Ne 2: 3 the king, Let the king l' for ever:
5: 2 for them, that we may eat, and l'.
9:29 if a man do, he shall l' in them;)
Es 4:11 the golden sceptre, that he may l':
Job 7:16 I loathe it; I would not l' alway:
14:14 If a man die, shall he l' again?
21: 7 Wherefore do the wicked l', become
27: 6 not reproach me so long as I l'.
Ps 22:26 him: your heart shall l' for ever.
49: 9 That he should still l' for ever,
55:23 men shall not l' out half their days:
63: 4 I bless thee while I l': I will lift
69:32 your heart shall l' that seek God.
72:15 And he shall l', and to him shall
104:33 sing unto the Lord as long as I l':
116: 2 will I call upon him as long as I l'.
118:17 I shall not die, but l', and declare
119:17 that I may l', and keep thy word.
77 mercies come unto me, that I may l':
116 unto thy word, that I may l': and
144 me understanding, and I shall l'.
175 Let my soul l', and it shall praise
146: 2 While I l' will I praise the Lord:
Pr 4: 4 keep my commandments, and l'.
7: 2 Keep my commandments, and l';
9: 6 Forsake the foolish, and l'; and go
15:27 but he that hateth gifts shall l'.
Ec 6: 3 children, and l' many years, so that
6 Yea, though he l' a thousand years
9: 3 is in their heart while they l', and
9 L' joyfully with the wife whom
11: 8 But if a man l' many years, and
Isa 6: 6 me, having a l' coal in his hand,
26:14 They are dead, they shall not l';
19 Thy dead men shall l', together
38: 1 for thou shalt die, and not l'.
16 O Lord, by these things men l',
16 thou recover me, and make me to l'.
49:18 As I l', saith the Lord, thou shalt
55: 3 hear, and your soul shall l'; and I
Jer 21: 9 that besiege you, he shall l', and
22:24 As I l', saith the Lord, though
27:12 serve him and his people, and l'.
17 serve the king of Babylon, and l':
35: 7 that ye may l' many days in the
38: 2 forth to the Chaldeans shall l';
2 his life for a prey, and shall l'.
17 princes, then thy soul shall l',
17 and thou shalt l', and thine house:
20 unto thee, and thy soul shall l'.
46:18 As I l', saith the King, whose name
La 4:20 said, Under his shadow we shall l'
Eze 3:21 he doth not sin, he shall surely l',
5:11 as I l', saith the Lord God; Surely,
13:19 the souls alive that should not l',
14:16 as I l', saith the Lord God, they
18, 20 as I l', saith the Lord God,
16: 6 when thou wast in thy blood, L';
6 when thou wast in thy blood, L'.
48 As I l', saith the Lord God, Sodom
17:16 As I l', saith the Lord God, surely
19 As I l', surely mine oath that he
18: 3 As I l', saith the Lord God, ye shall
9 he is just, he shall surely l', saith
13 taken increase: shall he then l'?
13 shall he then...he shall not l':
17 of his father, he shall surely l'.
19 hath done them, he shall surely l'.
21 he shall surely l', he shall not die.
22 that he hath done he shall l'.
23 should return from his ways, and l'?
24 the wicked man doeth, shall he l'?
28 he shall surely l', he shall not die.
32 wherefore turn yourselves, and l' ye.
20: 3 As I l', saith the Lord God, I will
11 man do, he shall even l' in them.
13, 21 do, he shall even l' in them;
25 whereby they should not l';
31 As I l', saith the Lord God, I will
33 As I l', saith the Lord God, surely
33:10 in them, how should we then l'?
11 As I l', saith the Lord God, I have
11 wicked turn from his way and l':
12 shall the righteous be able to l' for
13 righteous, that he shall surely l';
15 he shall surely l', he shall not die.
16 lawful and right; he shall surely l'.
19 and right, he shall l' thereby.
27 As I l', surely they that are in the
34: 8 As I l', saith the Lord God, surely
35: 6, 11 as I l', saith the Lord God, I will
37: 3 Son of man, can these bones l'?
5 to enter into you, and ye shall l':
6 put breath in you, and ye shall l';
9 upon these slain, that they may l'.
14 put my spirit in you, and ye shall l',
47: 9 the rivers shall come, shall l':
9 thing shall l' whither the river
Da 2: 4 in Syriack, O king, l' for ever:
3: 9 Nebuchadnezzar, O king, l' for ever.

Da 5:10 spake and said, O king, l' for ever:
6: 6 unto him, King Darius, l' for ever.
21 unto the king, O king, l' for ever.
Ho 6: 2 us up, and we shall l' in his sight.
Am 5: 4 Israel, Seek ye me, and ye shall l':
6 Seek the Lord, and ye shall l'; lest
14 good, and not evil, that ye may l':
Jon 4: 3 is better for me to die than to l'.
8 It is better for me to die than to l'.
Hab 2: 4 but the just shall l' by his faith.
Zep 2: 9 as I l', saith the Lord of hosts,
Zec 1: 5 the prophets, do they l' for ever?
10: 9 they shall l' with their children,
13: 3 say unto him, Thou shalt not l';
M't 4: 4 Man shall not l' by bread alone,
9:18 thy hand upon her, and she shall l'.
M'r 5:23 she may be healed; and she shall l'.
Lu 4: 4 man shall not l' by bread alone, but
7:25 apparelled, and l' delicately, are
10:28 right: this do, and thou shalt l'.
20:38 of the living: for all l' unto him.
Joh 5:25 of God: and they that hear shall l'.
6:51 of this bread, he shall l' for ever:
57 hath sent me, and I l' by the Father:
57 eateth me, even he shall l' by me.
58 eateth of this bread shall l' for ever.
11:25 though he were dead, yet shall he l':
14:19 see me: because I l', ye shall l' also.
Ac 7:19 to the end they might not l'.
17:28 For in him we l', and move, and
22:22 for it is not fit that he should l'.
25:24 that he ought not to l' any longer.
28: 4 yet vengeance suffereth not to l'.
Ro 1:17 written, The just shall l' by faith.
6: 2 dead to sin, l' any longer therein?
8 that we shall also l' with him:
8:12 not to the flesh, to l' after the flesh.
13 For if ye l' after the flesh, ye shall
13 the deeds of the body, ye shall l'.
10: 5 doeth those things shall l' by them.
12:18 in you, l' peaceably with all men.
14: 8 whether we l', we l' unto the Lord;
8 whether we l' therefore, or die, we
11 As I l', saith the Lord, every knee
1Co 9:13 holy things l' of the things of the
14 the gospel should l' of the gospel.
2Co 4:11 For we which l' are alway delivered
5:15 he died for all, that they which l'
15 not henceforth l' unto themselves,
6: 9 as dying, and, behold, we l'; as
7: 3 our hearts to die and l' with you.
13: 4 we shall l' with him by the power
11 be of one mind, and l' in peace;
Ga 2:14 the Gentiles to l' as do the Jews?
19 the law, that I might l' unto God.
20 with Christ: nevertheless I l';
20 the life which I now l' in the flesh
20 I l' by the faith of the Son of God,
3:11 for, The just shall l' by faith.
12 that doeth them shall l' in them.
5:25 If we l' in the Spirit, let us also walk
Eph 6: 3 mayest l' long on the earth.
Ph'p 1:21 For to me to l' is Christ, and to
22 But if I l' in the flesh, this is the
1Th 3: 8 For now we l', if ye stand fast in the
5:10 we should l' together with him.
2Ti 2:11 with him, we shall also l' with him:
3:12 and all that will l' godly in Christ
Tit 2:12 we should l' soberly, righteously,
Heb 10:38 Now the just shall l' by faith: but
12: 9 unto the Father of spirits, and l'?
13:18 in all things willing to l' honestly.
Jas 4:15 If the Lord will, we shall l', and
1Pe 2:24 sins, should l' unto righteousness:
4: 2 longer should l' the rest of his time
6 l' according to God in the spirit.
2Pe 2: 6 those that after should l' ungodly;
18 escaped from them who l' in error.
1Jo 4: 9 that we might l' through him.
Re 13:14 the wound by a sword, and did l'.

lived See also OUTLIVED; OVERLIVED.
Ge 5: 3 Adam l' an hundred and thirty
5 And all the days that Adam l' were
6 Seth l' an hundred and five years,
7 Seth l' after he begat Enos eight
9 Enos l' ninety years, and begat
10 Enos l' after he begat Cainan eight
12 Cainan l' seventy years, and begat
13 Cainan l' after he begat Mahalaleel
15 Mahalaleel l' sixty and five years,
16 Mahalaleel l' after he begat Jared
18 Jared l' an hundred sixty and two
19 Jared l' after he begat Enoch eight
21 Enoch l' sixty and five years, and
25 Methuselah l' an hundred eighty
26 And Methuselah l' after he begat
28 Lamech l' an hundred eighty and
30 Lamech l' after he begat Noah five
9:28 And Noah l' after the flood three
11:11 Shem l' after he begat Arphaxad
12 Arphaxad l' five and thirty years,
13 Arphaxad l' after he begat Salah
14 Salah l' thirty years, and begat
15 Salah l' after he begat Eber four
16 Eber l' four and thirty years, and
17 Eber l' after he begat Peleg four
18 Peleg l' thirty years, and begat
19 Peleg l' after he begat Reu two
20 Reu l' two and thirty years, and
21 Reu l' after he begat Serug two
22 Serug l' thirty years, and begat
23 Serug l' after he begat Nahor two
24 Nahor l' nine and twenty years, and
25 Nahor l' after he begat Terah an
26 Terah l' seventy years, and begat
25: 6 Isaac his son, while he yet l',

Ge 25: 7 of Abraham's life which he l',
47:28 And Jacob l' in the land of Egypt
50:22 Joseph l' an hundred and ten years.
Nu 14:38 went to search the land, l' still.
21: 9 beheld the serpent of brass, he l'.
De 5:26 of the fire, as we have, and l'?
2Sa 19: 6 I perceive, that if Absalom had l',
1Ki 12: 6 Solomon his father while he yet l',
2Ki 14:17 the son of Joash king of Judah l'
2Ch 10: 6 Solomon his father while he yet l',
25:25 the son of Joash king of Judah l'
Job 42:16 After this l' Job an hundred and
Ps 49:18 while he l' he blessed his soul:
Eze 37:10 breath came into them, and they l',
Lu 2:36 and had l' with an husband seven
Ac 23: 1 I have l' in all good conscience
26: 5 sect of our religion I l' a Pharisee.
Col 3: 7 some time, when ye l' in them.
Jas 5: 5 have l' in pleasure on the earth,
Re 18: 7 glorified herself, and l' deliciously,
9 and l' deliciously with her, shall
20: 4 they l' and reigned with Christ a
5 rest of the dead l' not again until

lively
Ex 1:19 for they are l', and are delivered
Ps 38:19 But mine enemies are l', and they
Ac 7:38 the l' oracles to give unto us:
1Pe 1: 3 begotten us again unto a l' hope
2: 5 as l' stones, are built up a spiritual

liver
Ex 29:13 the caul that is above the l', and
22 the caul above the l', and the two
Le 3: 4, 10, 15 the caul above the l', with
4: 9 and the caul above the l', with the
7: 4 the caul that is above the l', with
8:16, 25 the caul above the l', and the
9:10 caul above the l' of the sin offering,
19 kidneys, and the caul above the l':
Pr 7:23 Till a dart strike through his l';
La 2:11 my l' is poured upon the earth,
Eze 21:21 with images, he looked in the l'.

lives
Ge 9: 5 your blood of your l' will I require;
45: 7 save your l' by a great deliverance.
47:25 they said, Thou hast saved our l':
Ex 1:14 their l' bitter with hard bondage,
Jos 2:13 and deliver our l' from death.
9:24 were sore afraid of our l' because
J'g 5:18 a people that jeoparded their l'
18:25 life, with the l' of thy household.
2Sa 1:23 lovely and pleasant in their l',
19: 5 and the l' of thy sons and of thy
5 l' of thy wives, and the l' of thy
23:17 that went in jeopardy of their l'?
1Ch 11:19 that have put their l' in jeopardy?
19 jeopardy of their l' they brought it.
Es 9:16 together, and stood for their l',
Pr 1:18 they lurk privily for their own l'.
Jer 19: 7 hands of them that seek their l':
9 they that seek their l', shall straiten
46:26 hand of those that seek their l',
48: 6 Flee, save your l', and be like the
La 5: 9 our bread with the peril of our l'
Da 7:12 yet their l' were prolonged for a
Lu 9:56 is not come to destroy men's l',
Ac 15:26 Men that have hazarded their l'
27:10 lading and ship, but also of our l'.
1Jo 3:16 to lay down our l' for the brethren.
Re 12:11 loved not their l' unto the death.

livest
De 12:19 as long as thou l' upon the earth.
2Sa 11:11 as thou l', and as thy soul liveth,
Ga 2:14 l' after the manner of Gentiles,
Re 3: 1 name that thou l', and art dead.

liveth
Ge 9: 3 Every moving thing that l' shall
De 5:24 God doth talk with man, and he l'.
J'g 8:19 as the Lord l', if ye had saved
Ru 3:13 a kinsman to thee, as I the Lord l':
1Sa 1:26 she said, Oh my Lord, as thy soul l',
28 as long as he l' he shall be lent to
14:39 For, as the Lord l', which saveth
45 as the Lord l', there shall not one
17:55 Abner said, As thy soul l', O king,
19: 6 Saul sware, As the Lord l', he shall
20: 3 as the Lord l', and as thy soul l',
21 thee, and no hurt; as the Lord l'.
31 long as the son of Jesse l' upon the
25: 6 ye say to him that l' in prosperity,
26 as the Lord l', and as thy soul l',
34 as the Lord God of Israel l', which
26:10 As the Lord l', the Lord shall smite
16 As the Lord l', ye are worthy to die,
28:10 saying, As the Lord l', there shall no
29: 6 unto him, Surely, as the Lord l',
2Sa 2:27 Joab said, As God l', unless thou
4: 9 and said unto them, As the Lord l',
11:11 thy soul l', I will not do this thing.
12: 5 said to Nathan, As the Lord l', the
14:11 As the Lord l', there shall not one
19 answered and said, As thy soul l',
15:21 the king, and said, As the Lord l',
21 and as my lord the king l', surely
22:47 The Lord l'; and blessed be my
1Ki 1:29 king sware, and said, As the Lord l',
2:24 Now therefore, as the Lord l', which
3:23 This is my son that l', and thy son
17: 1 Ahab, As the Lord God of Israel l',
12 she said, As the Lord thy God l',
23 and Elijah said, See, thy son l'.
18:10 As the Lord thy God l', there is no
15 Elijah said, As the Lord of hosts l',
22:14 Micaiah said, As the Lord l', what
2Ki 2: 2, 4, 6 the Lord l', and as thy soul l',
3:14 Elisha said, As the Lord of hosts l',

2Ki 4:30 As the Lord l', and as thy soul l', I
5:16 But he said, As the Lord l', before
20 As the Lord l', I will run after him,
2Ch 18:13 Micaiah said, As the Lord l', even
Job 19:25 For I know that my redeemer l',
27: 2 As God l', who hath taken away my
Ps 18:46 The Lord l'; and blessed be my
89:48 What man is he that l', and shall
Jer 4: 2 The Lord l', in truth, in judgment,
5: 2 And though they say, The Lord l';
12:16 to swear by my name, The Lord l';
16:14 shall no more be said, The Lord l',
15 The Lord l', that brought up the
23: 7 they shall no more say, The Lord l',
8 But, The Lord l', which brought up
38:16 As the Lord l', that made us this
44:26 of Egypt, saying, The Lord God l'.
Eze 47: 9 pass, that every thing that l',
Da 4:34 and honoured him that l' for ever,
12: 7 sware by him that l' for ever that it
Ho 4:15 Beth-aven, nor swear, The Lord l'.
Am 8:14 and say, Thy god, O Dan, l'; and
14 The manner of Beer-sheba l'; even
Joh 4:50 unto him, Go thy way; thy son l'.
51 and told him, saying, Thy son l'.
53 Jesus said unto him, Thy son l':
11:26 whosoever l' and believeth in me,
Ro 6:10 but in that he l', he l' unto God.
7: 1 over a man as long as he l'?
2 law to her husband so long as he l';
3 So then if, while her husband l', she
14: 7 For none of us l' to himself, and no
1Co 7:39 the law as long as her husband l';
2Co 13: 4 yet he l' by the power of God. For
Ga 2:20 live; yet not I, but Christ l' in me:
1Ti 5: 6 l' [*4684] in pleasure is dead while...l'.
Heb 7: 8 of whom it is witnessed that he l'.
25 he ever l' to make intercession
9:17 strength at all while the testator l'.
1Pe 1:23 by the word of God, which l' and
Re 1:18 I am he that l', and was dead; and,
4: 9 the throne, who l' for ever and ever,
10 him that l' for ever and ever,
5:14 him that l' for ever and ever.
10: 6 by him that l' for ever and ever,
15: 7 wrath of God, who l' for ever and

living See also QUICK.
Ge 1:21 and every l' creature that moveth,
24 bring forth the l' creature after his
28 over every l' thing that moveth
2: 7 of life; and man became a l' soul.
19 Adam called every l' creature,
3:20 because she was the mother of all l'.
6:19 of every l' thing of all flesh, two of
7: 4 and every l' substance that I have
23 And every l' substance was destroyed
8: 1 Noah, and every l' thing, and all
17 every l' thing that is with thee,
21 again smite any more every thing l',
9:10 with every l' creature that is with
12 and every l' creature that is with you,
15 and every l' creature of all flesh;
16 and every l' creature of all flesh
Le 11:10 any l' thing which is in the waters,
46 every l' creature that moveth in the
14: 6 As for the l' bird, he shall take it,
6 the l' bird in the blood of the bird
7 the l' bird loose into the open field.
51 and the l' bird, and dip them in the
52 running water, and with the l' bird,
53 shall let go the l' bird out of the city
20:25 any manner of l' thing that creepeth
Nu 16:48 stood between the dead and the l';
De 5:26 hath heard the voice of the l' God
Jos 3:10 know that the l' God is among you,
Ru 2:20 not left off his kindness to the l'
1Sa 17:26 defy the armies of the l' God?
36 defied the armies of the l' God.
2Sa 20: 3 of their death, l' in widowhood.
1Ki 3:22 said, Nay; but the l' is my son,
22 is thy son, and the l' is my son.
23 is the dead, and my son is the l'.
25 king said, Divide the l' child in two,
26 the woman whose the l' child was
26 said, O my lord, give her the l' child,
27 and said, Give her the l' child,
2Ki 19: 4 hath sent to reproach the l' God;
16 sent him to reproach the l' God.
Job 12:10 hand is the soul of every l' thing,
28:13 is it found in the land of the l'.
21 it is hid from the eyes of all l', and
30:23 to the house appointed for all l'.
33:30 enlightened with the light of the l'.
Ps 27:13 of the Lord in the land of the l'.
42: 2 thirsteth for God, for the l' God:
52: 5 root thee out of the land of the l'.
56:13 walk before God in the light of the l'?
58: 9 both l', and in his wrath.
69:28 be blotted out of the book of the l',
84: 2 my flesh crieth out for the l' God.
116: 9 before the Lord in the land of the l'.
142: 5 and my portion in the land of the l'.
143: 2 sight shall no man l' be justified.
145:16 satisfiest the desire of every l' thing.
Ec 4: 2 than the l' which are yet alive.
15 I considered all the l' which walk
6: 8 that knoweth to walk before the l'?
7: 2 and the l' will lay it to his heart.
9: 4 For to him that is joined to all the l'
4 a l' dog is better than a dead lion.
5 For the l' know that they shall die:
Ca 4:15 of gardens, a well of l' waters,
Isa 4: 3 written among the l' in Jerusalem:
8:19 their God? for the l' to the dead?
37: 4 hath sent to reproach the l' God,
17 hath sent to reproach the l' God.

Isa 38:11 even the Lord, in the land of the l':
19 The l', the l', he shall praise thee,
53: 8 was cut off out of the land of the l':
Jer 2:13 me the fountain of l' waters,
10:10 is the true God, he is the l' God,
11:19 cut him off from the land of the l',
17:13 the Lord, the fountain of l' waters.
23:36 perverted the words of the l' God,
La 3:39 Wherefore doth a l' man complain,
Eze 1: 5 the likeness of four l' creatures.
13 for the likeness of the l' creatures,
13 and down among the l' creatures;
14 the l' creatures ran and returned
15 as I beheld the l' creatures, behold
15 upon the earth by the l' creatures,
19 And when the l' creatures went, the
19 when the l' creatures were lifted up
20, 21 spirit of the l' creature was in
22 upon the heads of the l' creature
3:13 of the wings of the l' creatures that
10:15 This is the l' creature that I saw by
17 the spirit of the l' creature was in
20 This is the l' creature that I saw
26:20 shall set glory in the land of the l';
32:23 caused terror in the land of the l'.
24 their terror in the land of the l',
25 was caused in the land of the l',
26 their terror in the land of the l'.
27 of the mighty in the land of the l'.
32 my terror in the land of the l':
Da 2:30 that I have more than any l',
4:17 l' may know that the most High
6:20 Daniel, servant of the l' God, is thy
26 God of Daniel: for he is the l' God,
Ho 1:10 them, Ye are the sons of the l' God.
Zec 14: 8 that l' waters shall go out from
M't 16:16 the Christ, the Son of the l' God.
22:32 not the God of the dead, but of the l'.
26:63 him, I adjure thee by the l' God,
M'r 12:27 of the dead, but the God of the l':
44 in all that she had, even all her l'.
Lu 8:43 had spent all her l' upon physicians,
15:12 And he divided unto them his l'.
13 his substance with riotous l'.
30 hath devoured thy l' with harlots,
20:38 not a God of the dead, but of the l':
21: 4 hath cast in all the l' that she had.
24: 5 seek ye the l' among the dead?
Joh 4:10 he would have given thee l' water.
11 then hast thou that l' water?
6:51 I am the l' bread which came down
57 As the l' Father hath sent me, and
69 that Christ, the Son of the l' God.
7:38 belly shall flow rivers of l' water.
Ac 14:15 from these vanities unto the l' God,
Ro 9:26 be called the children of the l' God.
12: 1 present your bodies a l' sacrifice,
14: 9 be Lord both of the dead and l'.
1Co 15:45 first man Adam was made a l' soul;
2Co 3: 3 but with the Spirit of the l' God;
6:16 for ye are the temple of the l' God;
Col 2:20 why, as though l' in the world, are
1Th 1: 9 idols to serve the l' and true God;
1Ti 3:15 which is the church of the l' God,
4:10 because we trust in the l' God, who
6:17 uncertain riches, but in the l' God,
Tit 3: 3 pleasures, l' in malice and envy,
Heb 3:12 in departing from the l' God.
9:14 dead works to serve the l' God?
10:20 By a new and l' way, which he hath
31 to fall into the hands of the l' God.
12:22 and unto the city of the l' God,
1Pe 2: 4 whom coming, as unto a l' stone,
Re 7: 2 east, having the seal of the l' God:
17 them unto l' fountains of waters:
16: 3 and every l' soul died in the sea.

lizard
Le 11:30 and the chameleon, and the l',

lo^
Ge 8:11 l', in her mouth was an olive leaf
15: 3 l', one born in my house is mine
12 l', an horror of great darkness fell
18: 2 l', three men stood by him: and
10 l', Sarah thy wife shall have a son.
19:28 l', the smoke of the country went
29: 2 l', there were three flocks of sheep
7 And he said, L', it is yet high day,
37: 7 l', my sheaf arose, and also stood
42:28 l', it is even in my sack: and their
47:23 l', here is seed for you, and ye
48:11 l', God hath shewed me also thy
50: 5 made me swear, saying, L', I die:
Ex 8:20 l', he cometh forth to the water;
26 l',...we sacrifice the abomination
19: 9 L', I come unto thee in a thick
Nu 14:40 L', we be here, and will go up unto
22:38 Balak, L', I am come unto thee:
23: 6 l', he stood by his burnt sacrifice,
9 l', the people shall dwell alone,
24:11 l', the Lord hath kept thee back
De 22:17 l', he hath given occasions of speech
Jos 14:10 l', I am this day fourscore and five
J'g 7:13 l', a cake of barley bread tumbled
13: 5 l', thou shalt conceive, and bear a
1Sa 4:13 l', Eli sat upon a seat by the wayside
10: 2 l', thy father hath left the care of
14:43 in mine hand, and, l', I must die.
14 L', ye see the man is mad:
2Sa 1: 6 and, l', the chariots and horsemen
15:24 l' Zadok also, and all the Levites
1Ki 1:22 l', while she yet talked with the
51 l', he hath caught hold on the horns
3:12 l', I have given thee a wise and an
1Ch 21:23 l', I give thee the oxen also for
2Ch 16:11 l', they are written in the book of

2Ch 25:19 L', thou hast smitten the Edomites;
27: 7 l', they are written in the book of
29: 9 l', our fathers have fallen by the
Ne 5: 5 l', we bring into bondage our sons
6:12 l', I perceived that God had not
Job 3: 7 L', let that night be solitary, let no
5:27 L' this, we have searched it, so it
9:11 L', he goeth by me, and I see him
19 speak of strength, l', he is strong:
13: 1 L', mine eye hath seen all this,
21:16 L', their good is not in their hand:
26:14 L', these are parts of his ways: but
33:29 L', all these things worketh God
40:16 L' now, his strength is in his loins,
Ps 11: 2 For, l', the wicked bend their bow,
37:36 passed away, and, l', he was not:
40: 7 Then said I, L', I come: in the
9 l', I have not refrained my lips, O
48: 4 For, l', the kings were assembled,
52: 7 L', this is the man that made not
55: 7 L', then would I wander far off,
59: 3 For, l', they lie in wait for my soul:
68:33 l', he doth send out his voice, and
73:27 l', they that are far from thee shall
83: 2 l', thine enemies make a tumult:
92: 9 For, l', thine enemies, O Lord,
9 for, l', thine enemies shall perish;
127: 3 L', children are an heritage of the
132: 6 L', we heard of it at Ephratah: we
139: 4 but, l', O Lord, thou knowest it
Pr 24:31 And, l', it was all grown over with
Ec 1:16 L', I am come to great estate, and
7:29 L', this only have I found, that
Ca 2:11 l', the winter is past, the rain is
Isa 6: 7 said, L', this hath touched thy lips;
25: 9 said in that day, L', this is our God;
36: 6 L', thou trustest in the staff of this
49:12 l', these from the north and from
50: 9 l', they all shall wax old as a
Jer 1:15 l', I will call all the families of the
4:23 earth, and, l', it was without form,
24 mountains, and, l', they trembled,
25 I beheld, and, l', there was no man,
26 I beheld, and, l', the fruitful place
5:15 L', I will bring a nation upon you
8: 8 L', certainly in vain made he it;
9 l', they have rejected the word of
25:29 l', I begin to bring evil on the city
30: 3 l', the days come, saith the Lord,
10 l', I will save thee from afar, and
36:12 l', all the princes sat there, even
49:15 l', I will make thee small among
50: 9 l', I will raise and cause to come up
Eze 2: 9 and, l', a roll of a book was therein;
4:15 L', I have given thee cow's dung
8: 2 l' a likeness as the appearance of
17 l', they put the branch to their nose.
13:10 l', others daubed it with...morter:
12 L', when the wall is fallen, shall it
17:18 when, l', he had given his hand,
18:14 l', if he beget a son, that seeth all
18 l', even he shall die in his iniquity.
23:39 l', thus have they done in the midst
40 was sent; and, l', they came:
30: 9 the day of Egypt: for, l', it cometh.
21 l', it shall not be bound up to be
33:32 l', thou art unto them as a very
37: 2 valley; and, l', they were very dry.
8 l', the sinews and the flesh came
40:17 and, l', there were chambers, and a
42: 8 and, l', before the temple were an
Da 3:25 L', I see four men loose, walking
7: 6 and l' another, like a leopard,
10:13 but, l', Michael, one of the chief
20 l', the prince of Grecia shall come.
Ho 9: 6 For, l', they are gone because of
Am 4: 2 l', the days shall come upon you,
13 l', he that formeth the mountains,
7: 1 l', it was the latter growth after the
9: 9 l', I will command, and I will sift
Hab 1: 6 l', I raise up the Chaldeans, that
Hag 1: 9 for much, and, l', it came to little;
Zec 2:10 l', I come, and I will dwell in the
11: 6 l', I will deliver the men every one
16 l', I will raise up a shepherd in the
M't 2: 9 l', the star, which they saw in the
3:16 l', the heavens were opened unto
17 And l' a voice from heaven, saying,
24:23 L', here is Christ, or there; believe
25:25 l', there thou hast that is thine.
26:47 l', Judas, one of the twelve, came,
28: 7 ye see him: l', I have told you.
20 l', I am with you alway, even unto
M'r 10:28 say unto him, L', we have left all,
13:21 L', here is Christ; or, l', he is there;
14:42 l', he that betrayeth me is at hand.
Lu 1:44 For, l', as soon as the voice of thy
2: 9 l', the angel of the Lord came upon
9:39 And, l', a spirit taketh him, and he
13:16 l', these eighteen years, be loosed
15:29 L', these many years do I serve thee,
17:21 shall they say, L', here! or,...there!
21 here! or, l' there! for, behold,
18:28 Peter said, L', we have left all, and
23:15 l', nothing worthy of death is done
Joh 7:26 But, l', he speaketh boldly, and
16:29 him, L', now speakest thou plainly,
Ac 13:46 life, l', we turn to the Gentiles.
27:24 l', God hath given thee all them
Heb 10: 7 L', I come (in the volume of the
9 L', I come to do thy will, O God.
Re 5: 6 l', in the midst of the throne and
6: 5 And I beheld, and l' a black horse;
12 l', there was a great earthquake;
7: 9 l', a great multitude, which no man
14: 1 l', a Lamb stood on the mount Sion,

Lo See Lo-ammi; Lo-debar; Lo-ruhamah.
loaden See also laden.
Isa 46: 1 your carriages were heavy l';
loadeth See also ladeth.
Ps 68: 19 who daily l' us with benefits;
loaf See also loaves.
Ex 29: 23 And one l' of bread, and one cake
1Ch 16: 3 to every one a l' of bread, and a
M'r 8: 14 ship with them more than one l'.
Lo-ammi (*lo-am'-mi*).
Ho 1: 9 Then said God, Call his name L':
loan
1Sa 2: 20 the l' which is lent to the Lord.
loathe See also loatheth; loathsome; lothe.
Job 7: 16 I l' it; I would not live alway: let
loatheth See also lotheth.
Nu 21: 5 and our soul l' this light bread.
Pr 27: 7 The full soul l' an honeycomb; but
loathsome
Nu 11: 20 nostrils, and it be l' unto you:
Job 7: 5 my skin is broken, and become l'.
Ps 38: 7 loins are filled with a l' disease:
Pr 13: 5 a wicked man is l', and cometh to
loaves
Le 23: 17 two wave l' of two tenth deals:
J'g 8: 5 l' of bread unto the people that
1Sa 10: 3 another carrying three l' of bread,
4 thee, and give thee two l' of bread;
17: 17 this parched corn, and these ten l',
21: 3 give me five l' of bread in mine hand,
25: 18 haste, and took two hundred l',
2Sa 16: 1 upon them two hundred l' of bread,
1Ki 14: 3 take with thee ten l', and cracknels,
2Ki 4: 42 the firstfruits, twenty l' of barley,
M't 14: 17 We have here but five l', and two
19 took the five l', and the two fishes,
19 and gave the l' to his disciples, and
15: 34 unto them, How many l' have ye?
36 he took the seven l' and the fishes,
16: 9 remember the five l' of the five
10 Neither the seven l' of the four
M'r 6: 38 unto them, How many l' have ye?
41 when he had taken the five l' and
41 and blessed, and brake the l', and
44 they that did eat of the l' were about
52 not the miracle of the l': considered
8: 5 asked them, How many l' have ye?
6 took the seven l', and gave thanks,
19 When I brake the five l' among five
Lu 9: 13 We have no more but five l' and two
16 Then he took the five l' and the two
11: 5 unto him, Friend, lend me three l';
Joh 6: 9 lad here, which hath five barley l',
11 Jesus took the l'; and when he had
13 the fragments of the five barley l',
26 but because ye did eat of the l', and
lock See also locked; locks; wedlock.
Ca 5: 5 myrrh, upon the handles of the l'.
Eze 8: 3 and took me by a l' of mine head;
locked
J'g 3: 23 the parlour upon him, and l' them.
24 the doors of the parlour were l',
locks
Nu 6: 5 the l' of the hair of his head grow.
J'g 16: 13 weavest the seven l' of my head
19 to shave off the seven l' of his head;
Ne 3: 3, 6, 13, 14, 15 thereof, the l' thereof,
Ca 4: 1 thou hast doves' eyes within thy l':
3 of a pomegranate within thy l'.
5: 2 my l' with the drops of the night.
11 his l' are bushy, and black as a
6: 7 are thy temples within thy l'.
Isa 47: 2 uncover thy l', make bare the leg,
Eze 44: 20 nor suffer their l' to grow long;
locust See also locusts.
Ex 10: 19 not one l' in all the coasts of Egypt.
Le 11: 22 ye may eat; the l' after his kind,
22 and the bald l' after his kind, and
De 28: 38 little in; for the l' shall consume it.
42 of thy land shall the l' consume.
1Ki 8: 37 pestilence, blasting, mildew, l',
Ps 78: 46 and their labour unto the l'.
109: 23 I am tossed up and down as the l'.
Joe 1: 4 hath left hath the l' eaten; and
4 that which the l' hath left hath the
2: 25 you the years that the l' hath eaten,
locusts
Ex 10: 4 will I bring the l' into thy coast:
12 over the land of Egypt for the l',
13 the east wind brought the l'.
14 the l' went up over all the land of
14 them there were no such l' as they,
19 westwind, which took away the l',
2Ch 6: 28 there be blasting, or mildew, l', or
7: 13 command the l' to devour the land,
Ps 105: 34 He spake, and the l' came, and
Pr 30: 27 The l' have no king, yet go they
Isa 33: 4 as the running to and fro of l' shall
Na 3: 15 make thyself many as the l'.
17 Thy crowned are as the l', and thy
M't 3: 4 his meat was l' and wild honey.
M'r 1: 6 and he did eat l' and wild honey;
Re 9: 3 there came out of the smoke l' upon
7 of the l' were like unto horses
Lod (*lod*) See also Lydda.
1Ch 8: 12 Shamed, who built Ono, and L',
Ezr 2: 33 The children of L', Hadid, and Ono,
Ne 7: 37 The children of L', Hadid, and Ono,
11: 35 L', and Ono, the valley of craftsmen.

Lo-debar (*lo-de'-bar*)
2Sa 9: 4, 5 Machir, the son of Ammiel, in L'.
17: 27 Machir the son of Ammiel of L',
lodge See also lodged; lodgest; lodgeth; lodging.
Ge 24: 23 thy father's house for us to l' in?
25 and provender...and room to l' in.
Nu 22: 8 L' here this night, and I will bring
Jos 4: 3 place, where ye shall l' this night.
J'g 19: 9 the day groweth to an end, l' here,
11 city of the Jebusites, and l' in it.
13 one of these places to l' all night,
15 to go in and to l' in Gibeah:
20 upon me; only l' not in the street.
20: 4 Benjamin, I and my concubine, to l'.
Ru 1: 16 and where thou lodgest, I will l':
2Sa 17: 8 war, and will not l' with the people.
16 L' not this night in the plains of
Ne 4: 22 Let every one with his servant l'
13: 21 unto them, Why l' ye about the wall?
Job 24: 7 the naked to l' without clothing,
31: 32 stranger did not l' in the street:
Ca 7: 11 the field; let us l' in the villages.
Isa 1: 8 as a l' in a garden of cucumbers,
21: 13 In the forest in Arabia shall ye l',
65: 4 graves, and l' in the monuments,
Jer 4: 14 How long shall thy vain thoughts l'
Zep 2: 14 bittern shall l' in the upper lintels
M't 13: 32 and l' in the branches thereof.
M'r 4: 32 of the air may l' under the shadow
Lu 9: 12 and country round about, and l',
Ac 21: 16 disciple, with whom we should l'.
lodged
Ge 32: 13 And he l' there that same night;
21 himself l' that night in the company.
Jos 2: 1 house, named Rahab, and l' there.
3: 1 l' there before they passed over.
4: 8 them unto the place where they l',
6: 11 into the camp, and l' in the camp.
8: 9 Joshua l' that night among the
J'g 18: 2 the house of Micah, they l' there.
19: 4 they did eat and drink, and l' there.
7 him: therefore he l' there again.
1Ki 19: 9 thither unto a cave, and l' there;
1Ch 9: 27 l' round about the house of God,
Ne 13: 20 sellers of all kind of ware l' without
Isa 1: 21 Judgment; righteousness l' in it;
M't 21: 17 city into Bethany; and he l' there.
Lu 13: 19 fowls of the air l' in the branches
Ac 10: 18 was surnamed Peter, were l' there.
23 Then called he them in, and l' them.
32 he is l' in the house of one Simon
28: 7 and l' us three days courteously.
1Ti 5: 10 children, if she have l' strangers,
lodgest
Ru 1: 16 and where thou l', I will lodge:
lodgeth
Ac 10: 6 He l' with one Simon a tanner,
lodging See also lodgings.
Jos 4: 3 and leave them in the l' place,
J'g 19: 15 that took them into his house to l'.
Isa 10: 29 have taken up there l' at Geba;
Jer 9: 2 I had in the wilderness a l' place
Ac 28: 23 there came many to him into his l';
Ph'm 22 But withal prepare me also a l':
lodgings
2Ki 19: 23 enter into the l' of his borders,
loft^
1Ki 17: 19 carried him up into a l', where he
loftily
Ps 73: 8 oppression: they speak l'.
loftiness
Isa 2: 17 the l' of man shall be bowed down,
Jer 48: 29 his l', and his arrogancy, and his
lofty
Ps 131: 1 is not haughty, nor mine eyes l':
Pr 30: 13 generation, O how l' are their eyes!
Isa 2: 11 l' looks of man shall be humbled,
12 every one that is proud and l',
5: 15 eyes of the l' shall be humbled:
26: 5 high; the l' city, he layeth it low;
57: 7 Upon a l' and high mountain hast
15 l' One that inhabiteth eternity,
log
Le 14: 10 mingled with oil, and one l' of oil.
12 trespass offering, and the l' of oil,
15 priest shall take some of the l' of oil,
21 for a meat offering, and a l' of oil;
24 trespass offering, and the l' of oil,
loins
Ge 35: 11 and kings shall come out of thy l';
37: 34 and put sackcloth upon his l',
46: 26 which came out of his l', besides
Ex 1: 5 souls that came out of the l' of Jacob
12: 11 with your l' girded, your shoes on
28: 42 from the l' even unto the thighs
De 33: 11 smite through the l' of them that
2Sa 20: 8 with a sword fastened upon his l'
1Ki 2: 5 his girdle that was about his l',
8: 19 that shall come forth out of thy l',
12: 10 be thicker than my father's l'.
18: 46 and he girded up his l', and ran
20: 31 put sackcloth on our l', and ropes
32 So they girded sackcloth on their l',
2Ki 1: 8 with a girdle of leather about his l'.
4: 29 Gird up thy l', and take my staff in
9: 1 Gird up thy l', and take this box of
2Ch 6: 9 shall come forth out of thy l',
10: 10 be thicker than my father's l'.
Job 12: 18 and girdeth their l' with a girdle.
31: 20 If his l' have not blessed me, and

Job 38: 3 Gird up now thy l' like a man; for
40: 7 Gird up thy l' now like a man: I
16 his strength is in his l', and his
Ps 38: 7 my l' are filled with a loathsome
66: 11 thou laidst affliction upon our l'.
69: 23 make their l' continually to shake.
Pr 31: 17 She girdeth her l' with strength,
Isa 5: 27 the girdle of their l' be loosed,
11: 5 righteousness...the girdle of his l',
20: 2 loose the sackcloth from off thy l',
21: 3 Therefore are my l' filled with pain:
32: 11 and gird sackcloth upon your l'.
45: 1 I will loose the l' of kings, to open
Jer 1: 17 Thou therefore gird up thy l', and
13: 1 linen girdle, and put it upon thy l',
2 of the Lord, and put it on my l'.
4 thou hast got, which is upon thy l',
11 as the girdle cleaveth to the l' of a
30: 6 every man with his hands on his l',
48: 37 cuttings, and upon the l' sackcloth.
Eze 1: 27 appearance of his l' even upward,
27 appearance of his l' even downward,
8: 2 appearance of his l' even downward,
2 and from his l' even upward, as the
21: 6 of man, with the breaking of thy l';
23: 15 Girded with girdles upon their l',
29: 7 madest all their l' to be at a stand.
44: 18 have linen breeches upon their l';
47: 4 through; the waters were to the l'.
Da 5: 6 the joints of his l' were loosed,
10: 5 l' were girded with fine gold of
Am 8: 10 will bring up sackcloth upon all l',
Na 2: 1 watch the way, make thy l' strong,
10 together, and much pain is in all l',
M't 3: 4 and a leathern girdle about his l';
M'r 1: 6 with a girdle of a skin about his l';
Lu 12: 35 Let your l' be girded about, and
Ac 2: 30 to him, that of the fruit of his l',
Eph 6: 14 having your l' girt about with truth,
Heb 7: 5 they come out of the l' of Abraham:
10 For he was yet in the l' of his father,
1Pe 1: 13 gird up the l' of your mind, be sober,
Lois (*lo'-is*)
2Ti 1: 5 dwelt first in thy grandmother L',
long^ See also headlong; longed; longer; longeth; longing; longsuffering; longwinged; prolong.
Ge 26: 8 when he had been there a l' time,
48: 15 the God which fed me all my life l'
Ex 10: 3 How l' wilt thou refuse to humble
7 How l' shall this man be a snare
16: 28 How l' refuse ye to keep my
19: 13 when the trumpet soundeth l',
19 the voice of the trumpet sounded l',
20: 12 days may be l' upon the land which
27: 1 altar of shittim wood, five cubits l',
9 of an hundred cubits l' for one side:
11 be hangings of an hundred cubits l',
Le 18: 19 as l' as she is put apart for her
26: 34 sabbaths, as l' as it lieth desolate,
35 As l' as it lieth desolate it shall rest;
Nu 9: 18 as l' as the cloud abode upon the
19 And when the cloud tarried l' upon
14: 11 How l' will this people provoke me?
11 how l' will it be ere they believe me,
27 How l' shall I bear with this evil
20: 15 we have dwelt in Egypt a l' time;
De 1: 6 have dwelt l' enough in this mount:
2: 3 this mountain l' enough: turn you
4: 25 shall have remained l' in the land,
12: 19 as l' as thou livest upon the earth.
14: 24 if the way be too l' for thee, so that
19: 6 overtake him, because the way is l',
20: 19 thou shalt besiege a city a l' time,
28: 32 longing for them all the day l':
59 great plagues, and of l' continuance,
59 sicknesses, and of l' continuance.
31: 13 as l' as ye live in the land whither
33: 12 shall cover him all the day l', and he
Jos 6: 5 make a l' blast with the ram's horn,
9: 13 by reason of the very l' journey.
11: 18 made war a l' time with all those
18: 3 How l' are ye slack to go to possess
23: 1 a l' time after that the Lord had
24: 7 dwelt in the wilderness a l' season.
J'g 5: 28 Why is his chariot so l' in coming?
1Sa 1: 28 as l' as he liveth he shall be lent to
7: 2 Kirjath-jearim, that...time was l';
16: 1 How l' wilt thou mourn for Saul,
20: 31 as l' as the son of Jesse liveth upon
25: 15 l' as we were conversant with them,
29: 8 so l' as I have been with thee unto
2Sa 2: 26 how l' shall it be then, ere thou bid
3: 1 Now there was l' war between the
14: 2 be as a woman that had a l' time
19: 34 the king, How l' have I to live,
1Ki 3: 11 hast not asked for thyself l' life;
6: 17 temple before it, was forty cubits l'.
18: 21 How l' halt ye between two
2Ki 9: 22 so l' as the whoredoms of thy
19: 25 Hast thou not heard l' ago how I
2Ch 1: 11 neither yet hast asked l' life; but
3: 11 cherubims were twenty cubits l':
6: 13 a brasen scaffold, of five cubits l',
31 so l' as they live in the land which
15: 3 for a l' season Israel hath been
26: 5 as l' as he sought the Lord, God
30: 5 they had not done it of a l' time
36: 21 as l' as she lay desolate she kept
Es 5: 13 so l' as I see Mordecai the Jew
Job 3: 21 Which l' for death, but it cometh
6: 8 grant me the thing that I l' for!
7: 19 How l' wilt thou not depart from
8: 2 How l' wilt thou speak these
2 how l' shall the words of thy mouth

Job 18: 2 How l' will it be ere ye make
19: 2 How l' will ye vex my soul, and
27: 6 not reproach me so l' as I live.
Ps 4: 2 how l' will ye turn my glory into
2 how l' will ye love vanity, and seek
6: 3 vexed: but thou, O Lord, how l'?
13: 1 How l' wilt thou forget me, O Lord?
1 how l' wilt thou hide thy face from
2 How l' shall I take counsel in my soul,
2 how l' shall mine enemy be exalted
32: 3 old through my roaring all the day l'.
35: 17 Lord, how l' wilt thou look on?
28 and of thy praise all the day l'.
38: 6 greatly; I go mourning all the day l'.
12 and imagine deceits all the day l'.
44: 8 In God we boast all the day l', and
22 for thy sake are we killed all the day l'.
62: 3 How l' will ye imagine mischief
71: 24 of thy righteousness all the day l':
72: 5 as l' as the sun and moon endure,
7 peace so l' as the moon endureth.
17 be continued as l' as the sun:
73: 14 the day l' have I been plagued,
74: 9 among us any that knoweth how l'.
10 how l' shall the adversary reproach?
80: 4 how l' wilt thou be angry against the
82: 2 How l' will ye judge unjustly, and
89: 46 How l', Lord? wilt thou hide thyself
90: 13 Return, O Lord, how l'? and let it
91: 16 With l' life will I satisfy him, and
94: 3 Lord, how l' shall the wicked,
3 how l' shall the wicked triumph?
4 How l' shall they utter and speak
95: 10 Forty years l' was I grieved with this
104: 33 sing unto the Lord as l' as I live:
116: 2 will I call upon him as l' as I live.
120: 6 My soul hath l' dwelt with him
129: 3 back: they made l' their furrows.
143: 3 as those that have been l' dead.
Pr 1: 22 How l', ye simple ones, will ye love
3: 2 l' life, and peace, shall they add
6: 9 How l' wilt thou sleep, O sluggard?
7: 19 at home, he is gone a l' journey:
21: 26 He coveteth greedily all the day l':
23: 17 in the fear of the Lord all the day l'.
30 They that tarry l' at the wine; they
25: 15 By l' forbearing is a prince
Ec 12: 5 because man goeth to his l' home,
Isa 6: 11 Then said I, Lord, how l'? And he
22: 11 unto him that fashioned it l' ago.
37: 26 Hast thou not heard l' ago, how I
42: 14 I have l' time holden my peace; I
65: 22 elect shall l' enjoy the work of their
Jer 4: 14 How l' shall...vain thoughts lodge
21 How l' shall I see the standard, and
12: 4 How l' shall the land mourn, and
23: 26 How l' shall this be in the heart of
29: 28 This captivity is l': build ye houses,
31: 22 How l' wilt thou go about, O thou
47: 5 valley: how l' wilt thou cut thyself?
6 how l' will it be ere thou be quiet?
La 2: 20 their fruit, and children of a span l'?
5: 20 for ever, and forsake us so l' time?
Eze 31: 5 his branches became l' because of
40: 5 a measuring reed of six cubits l' by
7 little chamber was one reed l',
29 it was fifty cubits l', and five and
30 about were five and twenty cubits l',
33 it was fifty cubits l', and five and
42 of a cubit and an half l', and a cubit
47 the court, an hundred cubits l', and
41: 13 the house, a hundred cubits l'; and
13 walls thereof, an hundred cubits l';
42: 11 as l' as they, and as broad as they:
20 round about, five hundred reeds l',
43: 16 the altar shall be twelve cubits l',
17 the settle shall be fourteen cubits l'
44: 20 nor suffer their locks to grow l';
45: 6 and five and twenty thousand l',
46: 22 courts joined of forty cubits l' and
Da 8: 13 l' shall be the vision concerning
10: 1 but the time appointed was l':
12: 6 How l' shall it be to the end of these
Ho 8: 5 how l' will it be ere they attain to
13: 13 should not stay l' in the place of
Hab 1: 2 O Lord, how l' shall I cry, and thou
2: 6 that which is not his! how l'?
Zec 1: 12 how l' wilt thou not have mercy on
M't 9: 15 mourn, as l' as the bridegroom is
11: 21 repented l' ago in sackcloth and
17: 17 how l' shall I be with you?
17 how l' shall I suffer you? bring
23: 14 for a pretence make l' prayer:
25: 19 After a l' time the lord of those
M'r 2: 19 l' as they have the bridegroom
9: 19 how l' shall I be with you?
19 how l' shall I suffer you? bring
21 How l' is it ago since this came
12: 38 which love to go in l' clothing, and
40 for a pretence make l' prayers:
16: 5 side, clothed in a l' white garment;
Lu 1: 21 that he tarried so l' in the temple.
8: 27 man, which had devils l' time,
9: 41 how l' shall I be with you, and
18: 7 him, though he bear l' with them?
20: 9 into a far country for a l' time.
46 which desire to walk in l' robes,
47 and for a shew make l' prayers:
23: 8 to see him of a l' season,
Joh 5: 6 been now a l' time in that case,
9: 5 As l' as I am in the world, I am the
10: 24 How l' dost thou make us to
14: 9 Have I been so l' time with you,
Ac 8: 11 of l' time he had bewitched them
14: 3 L' time therefore abode they
28 they abode l' time with the
Ac 20: 9 as Paul was l' preaching, he
11 and talked a l' while, even till
27: 14 not l' after there arose against it
21 after l' abstinence Paul stood forth
Ro 1: 11 I l' to see you, that I may impart
7: 1 over a man as l' as he liveth?
2 law to her husband so l' as he liveth;
8: 36 thy sake we are killed all the day l';
10: 21 All day l' I have stretched forth my
1Co 7: 39 as l' as her husband liveth;
11: 14 if a man have l' hair, it is a shame
15 But if a woman have l' hair, it is a
13: 4 Charity suffereth l', and is kind;
2Co 9: 14 l' after you for the exceeding grace
Ga 4: 1 the heir, as l' as he is a child,
Eph 6: 3 thou mayest live l' on the earth.
Ph'p 1: 8 how greatly I l' after you all in
1Ti 3: 15 But if I tarry l', that thou mayest
Heb 4: 7 in David, To day, after so l' a time;
Jas 5: 7 earth, and hath l' patience for it,
1Pe 3: 6 daughters ye are, as l' as ye do well,
2Pe 1: 13 as l' as I am in this tabernacle, to stir
2: 3 now of a l' time lingereth not,
Re 6: 10 How l', O Lord, holy and true,

longed See also LONGEDST; PROLONGED.
2Sa 13: 39 David l' to go forth unto Absalom:
23: 15 And David l', and said, Oh that one
1Ch 11: 17 And David l', and said, Oh that one
Ps 119: 40 I have l' after thy precepts:
131 for I l' for thy commandments.
174 I have l' for thy salvation, O Lord;
Ph'p 2: 26 For he l' after you all, and was
4: 1 brethren dearly beloved and l' for,

longedst
Ge 31: 30 sore l' after thy father's house,

longer
Ex 2: 3 when she could not l' hide him,
9: 28 let you go, and ye shall stay no l'.
J'g 2: 14 any l' stand before their enemies.
2Sa 20: 5 he tarried l' than the set time which
2Ki 6: 33 should I wait for the Lord any l'?
Job 11: 9 measure thereof is l' than the earth,
Jer 44: 22 So that the Lord could no l' bear,
Lu 16: 2 for thou mayest be no l' steward.
Ac 18: 20 desired him to tarry l' time with
25: 24 that he ought not to live any l'.
Ro 6: 2 dead to sin, live any l' therein?
Ga 3: 25 we are no l' under a schoolmaster.
1Th 3: 1 we could no l' forbear, we thought
5 this cause, when I could no l' forbear,
1Ti 5: 23 Drink no l' water, but use a little
1Pe 4: 2 he no l' should live the rest of his
Re 10: 6 that there should be time no l':

longeth See also PROLONGETH.
Ge 34: 8 soul of my son Shechem l' for your
De 12: 20 because thy soul l' to eat flesh;
Ps 63: 1 my flesh l' for thee in a dry and
84: 2 My soul l', yea, even fainteth for

longing
De 28: 32 fail with l' for them all the day long:
Ps 107: 9 he satisfieth the l' soul, and filleth
119: 20 My soul breaketh for the l' that it

longsuffering
Ex 34: 6 merciful and gracious, l', and
Nu 14: 18 Lord is l', and of great mercy,
Ps 86: 15 l', and plenteous in mercy and
Jer 15: 15 take me not away in thy l':
Ro 2: 4 goodness and forbearance and l';
9: 22 endured with much l' the vessels
2Co 6: 6 by l', by kindness, by the Holy
Ga 5: 22 of the Spirit is love, joy, peace, l',
Eph 4: 2 with l', forbearing one another in
Col 1: 11 all patience and l' with joyfulness;
3: 12 humbleness of mind, meekness, l';
1Ti 1: 16 Christ might shew forth all l',
2Ti 3: 10 of life, purpose, faith, l', charity,
4: 2 exhort with all l' and doctrine.
1Pe 3: 20 the l' of God waited in the days of
2Pe 3: 9 but is l' to us-ward, not willing
3: 15 the l' of our Lord is salvation;

longwinged
Eze 17: 3 great eagle with great wings, l',

look See also LOOKED; LOOKEST; LOOKETH; LOOKING; LOOKS.
Ge 9: 16 and I will l' upon it, that I may
12: 11 thou art a fair woman to l' upon:
13: 14 l' from the place where thou art
15: 5 L' now toward heaven, and tell the
19: 17 l' not behind thee, neither stay thou
24: 16 damsel was very fair to l' upon,
26: 7 because she was fair to l' upon.
40: 7 Wherefore l' ye so sadly to day?
41: 33 l' out a man discreet and wise,
42: 1 Why do ye l' one upon another?
Ex 3: 6 for he was afraid to l' upon God.
5: 21 The Lord l' upon you, and judge;
10: 10 l' to it; for evil is before you.
25: 20 their faces shall l' one to another;
40 l' that thou make them after their
39: 43 And Moses did l' upon all the work,
Le 13: 3 the priest shall l' on the plague in
3 and the priest shall l' on him, and
5 And the priest shall l' on him the
6 the priest shall l' on him again the
21 But if the priest shall l' on it, and,
25 Then the priest shall l' upon it: and,
26 But if the priest l' on it, and, behold,
27 And the priest shall l' upon him the
31 priest l' on the plague of the scall,
32 the priest shall l' on the plague:
34 day the priest shall l' on the scall:
36 Then the priest shall l' on him: and,
39 Then the priest shall l': and,
Le 13: 43 Then the priest shall l' upon it:
50 the priest shall l' upon the plague,
51 And he shall l' on the plague on the
53 if the priest shall l', and, behold,
55 And the priest shall l' on the plague,
56 And if the priest l', and, behold,
14: 3 the priest shall l', and, behold, if
37 And he shall l' on the plague, and,
39 shall l': and, behold, if the plague
44 Then the priest shall come and l',
48 priest shall come in, and l' upon it,
Nu 15: 39 for a fringe, that ye may l' upon it,
De 9: 27 l' not unto the stubbornness of
26: 15 L' down from thy holy habitation,
28: 32 thine eyes shall l', and fail with
J'g 7: 17 them, L' on me, and do likewise:
1Sa 1: 11 l' on the affliction of thine handmaid.
16: 7 L' not on his countenance, or on
12 countenance, and goodly to l' to.
17: 18 and l' how thy brethren fare, and
2Sa 9: 8 l' upon such a dead dog as I am?
11: 2 was very beautiful to l' upon.
16: 12 the Lord will l' on mine affliction,
1Ki 18: 43 Go up now, l' toward the sea.
2Ki 3: 14 I would not l' toward thee, nor see
6: 32 l', when the messenger cometh,
9: 2 thither, l' out there Jehu the son of
10: 3 L' even out the best and meetest of
23 l' that there be here with you none
14: 8 let us l' one another in the face.
1Ch 12: 17 the God of our fathers l' thereon,
2Ch 24: 22 The Lord l' upon it, and require
Es 1: 11 for she was fair to l' on.
Job 3: 9 let it l' for light, but have none;
6: 28 therefore be content, l' upon me;
20: 21 shall no man l' for his goods.
35: 5 L' unto the heavens, and see; and
40: 12 L' on every one that is proud, and
Ps 5: 3 prayer unto thee, and will l' up.
22: 17 bones: they l' and stare upon me.
25: 18 L' upon mine affliction and my
35: 17 Lord, how long wilt thou l' on?
40: 12 me, so that I am not able to l' up;
80: 14 l' down from heaven, and behold,
84: 9 l' upon the face of thine anointed.
85: 11 righteousness shall l' down from
101: 5 hath an high l' and a proud heart
119: 132 L'...upon me, and be merciful
123: 2 eyes of servants l' unto the hand of
Pr 4: 25 Let thine eyes l' right on, and let
25 thine eyelids l' straight before thee.
6: 17 A proud l', a lying tongue, and
21: 4 An high l', and a proud heart, and
23: 31 L' not thou upon the wine when it
27: 23 flocks, and l' well to thy herds.
Ec 12: 3 those that l' out of the windows
Ca 1: 6 L' not upon me, because I am black,
4: 8 l' from the top of Amana, from the
6: 13 return, that we may l' upon thee.
Isa 5: 30 and if one l' unto the land, behold
8: 17 of Jacob, and I will l' for him.
21 and their God, and l' upward.
22 And they shall l' unto the earth;
14: 16 thee shall narrowly l' upon thee,
17: 7 day shall a man l' to his Maker,
8 And he shall not l' to the altars,
22: 4 L' away from me; I will weep
8 didst l' in that day to the armour
31: 1 they l' not unto the Holy One of
33: 20 L' upon Zion, the city of our
42: 18 and l', ye blind, that ye may see.
45: 22 L' unto me, and be ye saved, all
51: 1 l' unto the rock whence ye are
2 L' unto Abraham your father, and
6 and l' upon the earth beneath:
56: 11 they all l' to their own way, every
59: 11 l' for judgment, but there is none;
63: 15 L' down from heaven, and behold
66: 2 but to this man will I l', even to him
24 l' upon the carcases of the men
Jer 13: 16 while ye l' for light, he turn it into
39: 12 Take him, and l' well to him,
40: 4 and I will l' well unto thee:
46: 5 are fled apace, and l' not back:
47: 3 the fathers shall not l' back to their
La 3: 50 Till the Lord l' down, and behold
Eze 23: 15 heads, all of them princes to l' to,
29: 16 when they shall l' after them:
43: 17 his stairs shall l' toward the east.
Da 7: 20 whose l' was more stout than his
Ho 3: 1 of Israel, who l' to other gods,
Jon 2: 4 l' again toward thy holy temple.
Mic 4: 11 and let our eye l' upon Zion.
7: 7 Therefore I will l' unto the Lord;
Na 2: 8 they cry; but none shall l' back.
3: 7 all they that l' upon thee shall flee
Hab 1: 13 evil, and canst not l' on iniquity:
2: 15 thou mayest l' on their nakedness!
Zec 12: 10 shall l' upon me whom they have
M't 11: 3 come, or do we l' for another?
M'r 8: 25 upon his eyes, and made him l' up;
Lu 7: 19, 20 come? or l' we for another?
9: 38 I beseech thee, l' upon my son:
21: 28 then l' up, and lift up your heads;
Joh 4: 35 up your eyes, and l' on the fields;
7: 52 Search, and l': for out of
19: 37 shall l' on him whom they pierced.
Ac 3: 4 upon him with John, said, L' on us.
12 or why l' ye so earnestly on us, as
6: 3 l' ye out among you seven men of
18: 15 names, and of your law, l' ye to it;
1Co 16: 11 for I l' for him with the brethren.
2Co 3: 13 could not stedfastly l' to the end of
4: 18 l' not at the things which are seen,
10: 7 Do ye l' on things after the outward
Ph'p 2: 4 L' not every man on his own

Ph'p 3:20 whence also we l' for the Saviour,
Heb 9:28 unto them that l' for him shall he
1Pe 1:12 things the angels desire to l' into.
2Pe 3:13 l' for new heavens and a new
14 seeing that ye l' for such things,
2Jo 8 L' to yourselves, that we lose not
Re 4: 3 was to l' upon like a jasper and
5: 3 open the book, neither to l' thereon.
4 read the book, neither to l' thereon.

looked
Ge 6:12 And God l' upon the earth, and,
8:13 the covering of the ark, and l', and,
16:13 here l' after him that seeth me?
18: 2 he lift up his eyes and l', and, lo,
16 from thence, and l' toward Sodom:
19:26 But his wife l' back from behind
28 he l' toward Sodom and Gomorrah,
22:13 Abraham lifted up his eyes, and l',
26: 8 the Philistines l' out at a window,
29: 2 he l', and behold a well in the field,
32 Lord hath l' upon my affliction;
33: 1 Jacob lifted up his eyes, and l', and,
37:25 they lifted up their eyes and l', and,
39:23 The keeper of the prison l' not to
40: 6 in the morning, and l' upon them,
Ex 2:11 brethren, and l' on their burdens:
12 he l' this way and that way, and
25 God l' upon the children of Israel,
3: 2 he l', and, behold, the bush burned
4:31 he had l' upon their affliction,
14:24 in the morning watch the Lord l'
16:10 that they l' toward the wilderness,
33: 8 l' after Moses, until he was gone
Nu 12:10 and Aaron l' upon Miriam, and,
16:42 l' toward the tabernacle of the
17: 9 they l', and took every man his
24:20 when he l' on Amalek, he took up
21 he l' on the Kenites, and took up
De 9:16 And I l', and, behold, ye had sinned
26: 7 l' on our affliction, and our labour,
Jos 5:13 that he lifted up his eyes and l',
8:20 And when the men of Ai l' behind
J'g 5:28 of Sisera l' out at a window,
6:14 the Lord l' upon him, and said,
9:43 and laid wait in the field, and l',
13:19 and Manoah and his wife l' on.
20 and Manoah and his wife l' on it,
20:40 the Benjamites l' behind them,
1Sa 6:19 had l' into the ark of the Lord,
9:16 I have l' upon my people, because
14:16 of Saul in Gibeah of Benjamin l';
16: 6 they were come, that he l' on Eliab,
17:42 And when the Philistine l' about,
24: 8 And when Saul l' behind him, David
2Sa 1: 7 when he l' behind him, he saw me,
2:20 Then Abner l' behind him, and
6:16 daughter l' through a window,
13:34 watch lifted up his eyes, and l',
18:24 wall, and lifted up his eyes, and l',
22:42 They l', but there was none to
24:20 And Araunah l', and saw the king
1Ki 18:43 And he went up, and l', and said,
19: 6 And he l', and, behold, there was a
2Ki 2:24 he turned back, and l' on them,
6:30 by upon the wall, and the people l',
9:30 her head, and l' out at a window.
32 l' out to him two or three eunuchs.
11:14 And when she l', behold, the king
14:11 of Judah l' one another in the face
1Ch 21:21 Ornan, Ornan l' and saw David,
2Ch 13:14 when Judah l' back, behold, the
20:24 they l' unto the multitude, and,
23:13 she l', and, behold, the king stood
26:20 and all the priests, l' upon him,
Ne 4:14 I l', and rose up, and said unto the
Es 2:15 sight of all them that l' upon her.
Job 6:19 troops of Tema l', the companies
30:26 When I l' for good, then evil came
Ps 14: 2 Lord l' down from heaven upon
34: 5 They l' unto him, and were
53: 2 God l' down from heaven upon
69:20 I l' for some to take pity, but there
102:19 he hath l' down from the height of
109:25 when they l' upon me, they shaked
142: 4 I l' on my right hand,and beheld,
Pr 7: 6 house I l' through my casement,
24:32 it well: I l' upon it, and received
Ec 2:11 Then I l' on all the works that my
Ca 1: 6 because the sun hath l' upon me:
Isa 5: 2 he l' that it should bring forth
4 I l' that it should bring forth
7 and he l' for judgment, but behold
22:11 but ye have not l' unto the maker
63: 5 I l', and there was none to help;
64: 3 terrible things which we l' not for,
Jer 8:15 We l' for peace, but no good came;
14:19 we l' for peace, and there is no
La 2:16 this is the day that we l' for; we
Eze 1: 4 And I l', and, behold, a whirlwind
2: 9 and when I l', behold, an hand was
8: 7 when I l', behold a hole in the wall.
10: 1 I l', and, behold, in the firmament
9 when I l', behold the four wheels by
11 the head l' they followed it; they
16: 8 I passed by thee, and l' upon thee,
21:21 with images, he l' in the liver.
40:20 court that l' toward the north,
44: 4 I l', and, behold, the glory of the
46:19 priests, which l' toward the north:
Da 1:13 let our countenances be l' upon
10: 5 Then I lifted up mine eyes, and l',
12: 5 I Daniel l', and, behold, there stood
Ob 12 shouldest not have l' on the day
13 not have l' on their affliction in
Hag 1: 9 Ye l' for much, and, lo, it came to
Zec 2: 1 lifted up mine eyes again, and l',
Zec 4: 2 I have l', and behold a candlestick
5: 1 and lifted up mine eyes, and l',
9 Then lifted I up mine eyes, and l',
6: 1 and lifted up mine eyes, and l',
M'r 3: 5 when he had l' round about on
34 he l' round about on them which
5:32 he l' round about to see her that
6:41 he l' up to heaven, and blessed, and
8:24 he l' up, and said, I see men as trees,
33 about and l' on his disciples,
9: 8 when they had l' round about, they
10:23 And Jesus l' round about, and saith
11:11 when he had l' round about upon
14:67 warming himself, she l' upon him,
16: 4 And when they l', they saw that the
Lu 1:25 in the days wherein he l' on me,
2:38 to all them that l' for redemption
10:32 came and l' on him, and passed
19: 5 to the place, he l' up, and saw him,
21: 1 he l' up, and saw the rich men
22:56 the fire, and earnestly l' upon him,
61 Lord turned, and l' upon Peter.
Joh 13:22 the disciples l' one on another,
20:11 down, and l' into the sepulchre,
Ac 1:10 they l' stedfastly toward heaven
7:55 l' up stedfastly into heaven, and
10: 4 when he l' on him, he was afraid,
22:13 the same hour I l' up upon him.
28: 6 they l' when he should have
6 but after they had l' a great while,
Heb11:10 l' for a city which hath foundations,
1Jo 1: 1 which we have l' upon, and our
Re 4: 1 After this I l', and, behold, a door
6: 8 And I l', and behold a pale horse:
14: 1 I l', and, lo, a Lamb stood on the
14 I l', and behold a white cloud, and
15: 5 And after that I l', and, behold, the

lookest
Job 13:27 and l' narrowly unto all my paths;
Hab 1:13 wherefore l' thou upon them that

looketh
Le 13:12 wheresoever the priest l';
Nu 21: 8 when he l' upon it, shall live.
20 Pisgah, which l' toward Jeshimon.
23:28 of Peor, that l' toward Jeshimon.
Jos 15: 2 from the bay that l' southward:
1Sa 13:18 the border that l' to the valley of
16: 7 man l' on the outward appearance,
7 but the Lord l' on the heart.
Job 7: 2 an hireling l' for the reward of his
28:24 For he l' to the ends of the earth,
33:27 He l' upon men, and if any say,
Ps 33:13 The Lord l' from heaven; he
14 he l' upon all the inhabitants of
104:32 He l' on the earth, and it trembleth:
Pr 14:15 prudent man l' well to his going.
31:27 She l' well to the ways of her
Ca 2: 9 wall, he l' forth at the windows,
6:10 is she that l' forth as the morning,
7: 4 which l' toward Damascus.
Isa 28: 4 when he that l' upon it seeth,
Eze 8: 3 gate that l' toward the north;
11: 1 Lord's house, which l' eastward:
40: 6 the gate which l' toward the east,
22 of the gate that l' toward the east;
43: 1 the gate that l' toward the east:
44: 1 sanctuary which l' toward the east;
46: 1 inner court that l' toward the east
12 the gate that l' toward the east,
47: 2 gate by the way that l' eastward:
M't 5:28 l' on a woman to lust after her
24:50 in a day when he l' not for him,
Lu 12:46 in a day when he l' not for him,
Jas 1:25 l' into the perfect law of liberty,

looking See also LOOKINGGLASSES.
Jos 15: 7 so northward, l' toward Gilgal,
1Ki 7:25 oxen, three l' toward the north,
25 and three l' toward the west,
25 and three l' toward the south,
25 and three l' toward the east:
1Ch 15:29 l' out at a window saw king David
2Ch 4: 4 oxen three l' toward the north,
4 and three l' toward the west,
4 and three l' toward the south,
4 and three l' toward the east:
Job 37:18 strong, and as a molten l' glass?
Isa 38:14 dove: mine eyes fail with l' upward:
M't 14:19 and l' up to heaven, he blessed, and
M'r 7:34 And l' up to heaven, he sighed, and
10:27 Jesus l' upon them saith, With men
15:40 were also women l' on afar off:
Lu 6:10 l' round about upon them all, he
9:16 l' up to heaven, he blessed them,
62 his hand to the plough, and l' back,
21:26 and for l' after those things which
Joh 1:36 l' upon Jesus as he walked, he
20: 5 And he stooping down, and l' in, saw
Ac 6:15 l' stedfastly on him, saw his face as
23:21 ready, l' for a promise from thee.
Tit 2:13 L' for that blessed hope, and the
Heb10:27 a certain fearful l' for of judgment
12: 2 L' unto Jesus the author and
15 L' diligently lest any man fail of
2Pe 3:12 L' for and hasting unto the coming
Jude 21 l' for the mercy of our Lord Jesus

looking-glass See LOOKING and GLASS; also LOOKINGGLASSES.

lookingglasses
Ex 38: 8 the l' of the women assembling,

looks
Ps 18:27 but wilt bring down high l'.
Isa 2:11 lofty l' of man shall be humbled,
10:12 Assyria, and the glory of his high l'.
Eze 2: 6 words, nor be dismayed at their l',
3: 9 not, neither be dismayed at their l',

loops
Ex 26: 4 make l' of blue upon the edge of
5 Fifty l' shalt thou make in the one
5 fifty l' shalt thou make in the edge
5 the l' may take hold one of another.
10 make fifty l' on the edge of the one
10 and fifty l' in the edge of the curtain
11 and put the taches into the l', and
36:11 made l' of blue on the edge of one
12 Fifty l' made he in one curtain, and
12 fifty l' made he in the edge of the
12 the l' held one curtain to another.
17 fifty l' upon the uttermost edge of
17 fifty l' made he upon the edge of the

loose See also LOOSED; LOOSETH; LOOSING; UNLOOSE.
Ge 49:21 Naphtali is a bind let l': he giveth
Le 14: 7 living bird l' into the open field.
De 25: 9 and l' his shoe from off his foot,
Jos 5:15 L' thy shoe from off thy foot; for
Job 6: 9 that he would let l' his hand, and
30:11 also let l' the bridle before me.
38:31 Pleiades, or l' the bands of Orion?
Ps 102:20 l' those that are appointed to death;
Isa 20: 2 l' the sackcloth from off thy loins,
45: 1 I will l' the loins of kings, to open
52: 2 l' thyself from the bands of thy neck,
58: 6 to l' the bands of wickedness, to
Jer 40: 4 I l' thee this day from the chains
Da 3:25 Lo, I see four men l', walking in
M't 16:19 whatsoever thou shalt l' on earth
18:18 whatsoever ye shall l' on earth shall
21: 2 l' them, and bring them unto me.
M'r 11: 2 man sat; l' him, and bring him.
4 two ways met; and they l' him.
Lu 13:15 on the sabbath l' his ox or his ass
19:30 sat: l' him, and bring him thither.
31 any man ask you, Why do ye l' him?
33 said unto them, Why l' ye the colt?
Joh 11:44 unto them, L' him, and let him go.
Ac 13:25 of his feet I am not worthy to l'.
24:26 him of Paul, that he might l' him:
Re 5: 2 book, and to l' the seals thereof?
5 and to l' the seven seals thereof.
9:14 L' the four angels which are bound

loosed
Ex 28:28 the breastplate be not l' from the
39:21 the breastplate might not be l' from
De 25:10 house of him that hath his shoe l'.
J'g 15:14 his bands l' from off his hands.
Job 30:11 Because he hath l' my cord, and
39: 5 hath l' the bands of the wild ass?
Ps 105:20 The king sent and l' him; even
116:16 handmaid: thou hast l' my bonds.
Ec 12: 6 Or ever the silver cord be l', or the
Isa 5:27 shall the girdle of their loins be l',
33:23 Thy tacklings are l'; they could
51:14 exile hasteneth that he may be l',
Da 5: 6 that the joints of his loins were l',
M't 16:19 loose on earth shall be l' in heaven.
18:18 loose on earth shall be l' in heaven.
27 with compassion, and l' him, and
M'r 7:35 and the string of his tongue was l',
Lu 1:64 and his tongue l', and he spake, and
13:12 thou art l' from thine infirmity.
16 l' from this bond on the sabbath
Ac 2:24 up, having l' the pains of death:
13:13 and his company l' from Paphos,
16:26 and every one's bands were l'.
22:30 Jews, he l' him from his bands,
27:21 me, and not have l' from Crete,
40 l' the rudder bands, and hoised up
Ro 7: 2 is l' from the law of her husband.
1Co 7:27 unto a wife? seek not to be l'.
27 Art thou l' from a wife? seek not
Re 9:15 And the four angels were l', which
20: 3 that he must be l' a little season.
7 Satan shall be l' out of his prison,

looseth
Job 12:18 He l' the bond of kings, and
Ps 146: 7 hungry. The Lord l' the prisoners:

loosing
M'r 11: 5 unto them, What do ye, l' the colt?
Lu 19:33 And as they were l' the colt, the
Ac 16:11 Therefore l' from Troas, we came
27:13 l' thence, they sailed close by

lop
Isa 10:33 shall l' the bough with terror:

lord [or Lord]^ See also LORD'S [LORD'S]; LORDS.
Ge 2: 4 that the L' God made the earth
5 L' God had not caused it to rain
7 L' God formed man of the dust
8 And the L' God planted a garden
9 made the L' God to grow every
15 the L' God took the man, and put
16 the L' God commanded the man,
18 L' God said, It is not good that
19 the L' God formed every beast
21 L' God caused a deep sleep to fall
22 rib, which the L' God had taken
3: 1 field which the L' God had made.
8 heard the voice of the L' God
8 presence of the L' God amongst
9 L' God called unto Adam, and
13 the L' God said unto the woman,
14 the L' God said unto the serpent,
21 the L' God made coats of skins,
22 the L' God said, Behold, the man
23 L' God sent him forth from the
4: 1 I have gotten a man from the L'.
3 ground an offering unto the L'.
4 L' had respect unto Abel and to
6 L' said unto Cain, Why art thou

Ge 4: 9 L' said unto Cain, Where is Abel?
13 And Cain said unto the L', My
15 the L' said unto him, Therefore
15 L' set a mark upon Cain, lest any
16 out from the presence of the L',
26 to call upon the name of the L'.
5: 29 ground which the L' hath cursed.
6: 3 the L' said, My Spirit shall not
6 the L' that he had made man on
7 the L' said, I will destroy man
8 found grace in the eyes of the L'.
7: 1 And the L' said unto Noah, Come
5 all that the L' commanded him.
16 him: and the L' shut him in.
8: 20 builded an altar unto the L';
21 the L' smelled a sweet savour;
21 the L' said in his heart, I will not
9: 26 Blessed be the L' God of Shem;
10: 9 a mighty hunter before the L':
9 the mighty hunter before the L'.
11: 5 L' came down to see the city and
6 the L' said, Behold, the people
8 L' scattered them abroad from
9 the L' did there confound the
9 did the L' scatter them abroad
12: 1 Now the L' had said unto Abram,
4 as the L' had spoken unto him;
7 the L' appeared unto Abram, and
7 builded he an altar unto the L',
8 he builded an altar unto the L',
8 called upon the name of the L'.
17 the L' plagued Pharaoh and his
13: 4 called on the name of the L'.
10 before the L' destroyed Sodom
10 even as the garden of the L', like
13 sinners before the L' exceedingly.
14 the L' said unto Abram, after that
18 built there an altar unto the L'.
14: 22 lift up mine hand unto the L',
15: 1 word of the L' came unto Abram
2 said, L' God, what wilt thou give
4 the word of the L' came unto him,
6 And he believed in the L'; and he
7 L' that brought thee out of Ur of
8 L' God, whereby shall I know that
18 L' made a covenant with Abram,
16: 2 the L' hath restrained me from
5 L' judge between me and thee
7 the angel of the L' found her by
9, 10, 11 angel of the L' said unto
11 because the L' hath heard thy
13 And she called the name of the L'
17: 1 L' appeared to Abram, and said
18: 1 the L' appeared unto him in the
3 My L', if now I have found favour
12 have pleasure, my l' being old also?
13 And the L' said unto Abraham,
14 Is any thing too hard for the L'?
17 And the L' said, Shall I hide from
19 they shall keep the way of the L',
19 the L' may bring upon Abraham
20 the L' said, Because the cry of
22 Abraham stood yet before the L'.
26 the L' said, If I find in Sodom
27 upon me to speak unto the L',
30 Oh let not the L' be angry, and I
31 upon me to speak unto the L':
32 Oh let not the L' be angry, and I
33 the L' went his way, as soon as he
19: 13 great before the face of the L';
13 the L' hath sent us to destroy it.
14 for the L' will destroy this city.
16 the L' being merciful unto him:
18 unto them, Oh, not so, my L':
24 L' rained upon Sodom and upon
24 brimstone and fire from the L'
27 where he stood before the L':
20: 4 L', wilt thou slay also a righteous
18 the L' had fast closed up all the
21: 1 L' visited Sarah as he had said,
1 the L' did unto Sarah as he had
33 there on the name of the L', the
22: 11 angel of the L' called unto him
14 mount of the L' it shall be seen.
15 the angel of the L' called unto
16 myself have I sworn, saith the L',
23: 6 Hear us, my l': thou art a mighty
11 Nay, my l', hear me: the field give
15 My l', hearken unto me: the land is
24: 1 L' had blessed Abraham in all
3 I will make thee swear by the L',
7 The L' God of heaven, which took
12 O L' God of my master Abraham,
18 And she said, Drink, my l': and
21 wit whether the L' had made his
26 his head, and worshipped the L'.
27 L' God of my master Abraham,
27 the L' led me to the house of my
31 Come in, thou blessed of the L';
35 the L' hath blessed my master
40 The L', before whom I walk, will
42 O L' God of my master Abraham,
44 be the woman whom the L' hath
48 my head, and worshipped the L',
48 L' God of my master Abraham,
50 thing proceedeth from the L':
51 son's wife, as the L' hath spoken.
52 he worshipped the L', bowing
56 the L' hath prospered my way;
25: 21 And Isaac intreated the L' for his
21 the L' was intreated of him, and
22 And she went to enquire of the L'.
23 the L' said unto her, Two nations
26: 2 the L' appeared unto him, and
12 and the L' blessed him.
22 the L' hath made room for us,

Ge 26: 24 And the L' appeared unto him the
25 called upon the name of the L',
28 certainly that the L' was with
29 art now the blessed of the L'.
27: 7 bless thee before the L' before
20 the L' thy God brought it to me.
27 a field which the L' hath blessed:
29 be l' over thy brethren, and let
37 I have made him thy l', and all his
28: 13 behold, the L' stood above it, and
13 I am the L' God of Abraham thy
16 Surely the L' is in this place; and
21 then shall the L' be my God:
29: 31 the L' saw that Leah was hated,
32 the L' hath looked upon my
33 L' hath heard that I was hated,
35 she said, Now will I praise the L':
30: 24 L' shall add to me another son.
27 L' hath blessed me for thy sake.
30 the L' hath blessed thee since my
31: 3 the L' said unto Jacob, Return
35 Let it not displease my l' that I
49 The L' watch between me and
32: 4 shall ye speak unto my l' Esau;
5 I have sent to tell my l', that I may
9 the L' which saidst unto me,
18 is a present sent unto my l' Esau:
33: 8 to find grace in the sight of my l'.
13 My l' knoweth that the children are
14 Let my l', I pray thee, pass over
14 until I come unto my l' unto Seir.
15 me find grace in the sight of my l'.
38: 7 was wicked in the sight of the L';
7 and the L' slew him.
10 which he did displeased the L':
39: 2 the L' was with Joseph, and he
3 saw that the L' was with him,
3 that the L' made all that he did to
5 that the L' blessed the Egyptian's
5 blessing of the L' was upon all
16 by her, until his l' came home.
21 But the L' was with Joseph, and
23 because the L' was with him, and
23 he did, the L' made it to prosper.
40: 1 offended their l' the king of Egypt.
42: 10 And they said unto him, Nay, my l',
30 The man, who is the l' of the land,
33 the l' of the country, said unto us,
44: 5 not this it in which my l' drinketh,
7 Wherefore saith my l' these words?
16 What shall we say unto my l'?
18 Oh my l', let thy servant, I pray
19 My l' asked his servants, saying,
20 And we said unto my l', We have a
22 we said unto my l', The lad cannot
24 we told him the words of my l'.
33 of the lad a bondman to my l';
45: 8 and l' of all his house, and a ruler
9 God hath made me l' of all Egypt:
47: 18 We will not hide it from my l', how
18 my l' also hath our herds of cattle;
18 not ought left in the sight of my l',
25 us find grace in the sight of my l',
49: 18 waited for thy salvation, O L'.
Ex 3: 2 the angel of the L' appeared unto
4 L' saw that he turned aside to see,
7 the L' said, I have surely seen
15, 16 The L' God of your fathers,
18 The L' God of the Hebrews hath
18 may sacrifice to the L' our God.
4: 1 L' hath not appeared unto thee.
2 And the L' said unto him, What is
4 the L' said unto Moses, Put forth
5 they may believe in the L' God of
6 L' said furthermore unto him,
10 And Moses said unto the L',
10 O my L', I am not eloquent,
11 the L' said unto him, Who hath
11 or the blind? have not I the L'?
13 And he said, O my L', send, I pray
14 the anger of the L' was kindled
19 the L' said unto Moses in Midian,
21 L' said unto Moses, When thou
22 Thus saith the L', Israel is my
24 the L' met him, and sought to
27 the L' said to Aaron, Go into the
28 told Aaron all the words of the L'
30 the L' had spoken unto Moses,
31 heard that the L' had visited the
5: 1 Thus saith the L' God of Israel,
2 Pharaoh said, Who is the L', that
2 I know not the L', neither will I
3 and sacrifice unto the L' our God;
17 us go and do sacrifice to the L'.
21 The L' look upon you, and judge;
22 And Moses returned unto the L',
22 L', wherefore hast thou so evil
6: 1 Then the L' said unto Moses, Now
2 and said unto him, I am the L':
6 I am the L', and I will bring you
7 know that I am the L' your God,
8 you for an heritage: I am the L'.
10 the L' spake unto Moses, saying,
12 Moses spake before the L', saying,
13 L' spake unto Moses and Aaron,
26 and Moses, to whom the L' said,
28 L' spake unto Moses in the land
29 the L' spake unto Moses, saying,
29 I am the L': speak thou unto
30 Moses said before the L', Behold,
7: 1 And the L' said unto Moses, See, I
5 shall know that I am the L', when
6 did as the L' commanded them,
8 the L' spake unto Moses and unto
10 did so as the L' had commanded:
13 not unto them; as the L' had said.

Ex 7: 14 the L' said unto Moses, Pharaoh's
16 The L' God of the Hebrews hath
17 Thus saith the L', In this thou
17 thou shalt know that I am the L':
19 And the L' spake unto Moses, Say
20 did so, as the L' commanded;
22 unto them; as the L' had said.
25 that the L' had smitten the river.
8: 1 the L' spake unto Moses, Go unto
1 Thus saith the L', Let my people
5 And the L' spake unto Moses, Say
8 Intreat the L', that he may take
8 they may do sacrifice unto the L'.
10 is none like unto the L' our God.
12 Moses cried unto the L' because
13 L' did according to the word of
15 not unto them; as the L' had said.
16 the L' said unto Moses, Say unto
19 not unto them; as the L' had said.
20 the L' said unto Moses, Rise up
20 Thus saith the L', Let my people
22 I am the L' in the midst of the
24 the L' did so; and there came a
26 the Egyptians to the L' our God:
27 and sacrifice to the L' our God,
28 may sacrifice to the L' your God
29 intreat the L' that the swarms of
29 people go to sacrifice to the L'.
30 Pharaoh, and intreated the L'.
31 L' did according to the word of
9: 1 the L' said unto Moses, Go in
1 saith the L' God of the Hebrews,
3 hand of the L' is upon thy cattle
4 L' shall sever between the cattle
5 And the L' appointed a set time,
5 To morrow the L' shall do this
6 And the L' did that thing on the
8 the L' said unto Moses and unto
12 L' hardened the heart of Pharaoh,
12 as the L' had spoken unto Moses.
13 the L' said unto Moses, Rise up
13 saith the L' God of the Hebrews,
20 He that feared the word of the L'
21 regarded not the word of the L'
22 the L' said unto Moses, Stretch
23 and the L' sent thunder and hail,
23 the L' rained hail upon the land
27 the L' is righteous, and I and my
28 Intreat the L' (for it is enough)
29 abroad my hands unto the L';
30 ye will not yet fear the L' God.
33 abroad his hands unto the L':
35 as the L' had spoken by Moses.
10: 1 And the L' said unto Moses, Go in
2 may know how that I am the L'.
3 saith the L' God of the Hebrews,
7 they may serve the L' their God:
8 them, Go, serve the L' your God:
9 we must hold a feast unto the L'.
10 Let the L' be so with you, as I
11 that are men, and serve the L';
12 the L' said unto Moses, Stretch
13 the L' brought an east wind upon
16 sinned against the L' your God,
17 and intreat the L' your God, that
18 Pharaoh, and intreated the L'.
19 L' turned a mighty strong west
20 the L' hardened Pharaoh's heart,
21 the L' said unto Moses, Stretch
24 and said, Go ye, serve the L';
25 may sacrifice unto the L' our God.
26 we take to serve the L' our God;
26 with what we must serve the L',
27 the L' hardened Pharaoh's heart,
11: 1 the L' said unto Moses, Yet will I
3 the L' gave the people favour in
4 saith the L', About midnight will
7 L' doth put a difference between
9 the L' said unto Moses, Pharaoh
10 the L' hardened Pharaoh's heart,
12: 1 L' spake unto Moses and Aaron
12 execute judgment: I am the L'.
14 ye shall keep it a feast to the L'
23 the L' will pass through to smite
23 the L' will pass over the door,
25 land which the L' will give you,
28 did as the L' had commanded
29 the L' smote all the firstborn in the
31 go, serve the L', as ye have said.
36 the L' gave the people favour in
41 all the hosts of the L' went out
42 to be much observed unto the L'
42 this is that night of the L' to be
43 L' said unto Moses and Aaron,
48 will keep the passover to the L',
50 as the L' commanded Moses and
51 the L' did bring the children of
13: 1 the L' spake unto Moses, saying,
3 L' brought you out from this
5 when the L' shall bring thee into
6 day shall be a feast to the L'.
8 because of that which the L' did
9 hath the L' brought thee out of
11 L' shall bring thee into the land
12 thou shalt set apart unto the L'
14 L' brought us out from Egypt,
15 the L' slew all the firstborn in the
15 I sacrifice to the L' all that
16 L' brought us forth out of Egypt.
21 L' went before them by day in a
14: 1 And the L' spake unto Moses,
4 may know that I am the L'. And
8 L' hardened the heart of Pharaoh
10 of Israel cried out unto the L'.
13 and see the salvation of the L',
14 The L' shall fight for you, and ye

Ex 14:15 the L· said unto Moses, Wherefore
18 shall know that I am the L·, when
21 L· caused the sea to go back by a
24 the L· looked unto the host of the
25 L· fighteth for them against the
26 the L· said unto Moses, Stretch
27 L· overthrew the Egyptians in the
30 L· saved Israel that day out of
31 great work which the L· did upon
31 feared the L·, and believed the L·,
15: 1 of Israel this song unto the L·,
1 I will sing unto the L·, for he
2 The L· is my strength and song,
3 L· is a man of war; the L· is his
6 Thy right hand, O L·, is become
6 thy right hand, O L·, hath dashed
11 Who is like unto thee, O L·,
16 till thy people pass over, O L·,
17 in the place, O L·, which thou
17 Sanctuary, O L·, which thy hands
18 The L· shall reign for ever and
19 L· brought again the waters of
21 answered them, Sing ye to the L·,
25 And he cried unto the L·;
25 and the L· shewed him a tree,
26 hearken to the voice of the L· thy
26 for I am the L· that healeth thee.
16: 3 We had died by the hand of the L·
4 Then said the L· unto Moses,
6 ye shall know that the L· hath
7 ye shall see the glory of the L·;
7 your murmurings against the L·:
8 when the L· shall give you in the
8 the L· heareth your murmurings
8 against us, but against the L·.
9 Israel, Come near before the L·:
10 of the L· appeared in the cloud.
11 And the L· spake unto Moses,
12 ye shall know that I am the L·
15 bread which the L· hath given
16 which the L· hath commanded,
23 is that which the L· hath said,
23 of the holy sabbath unto the L·:
25 to day is a sabbath unto the L·:
28 the L· said unto Moses, How long
29 the L· hath given you the sabbath,
32 thing which the L· commandeth,
33 and lay it up before the L·, to be
34 As the L· commanded Moses, so
17: 1 to the commandment of the L·,
2 Wherefore do ye tempt the L·?
4 Moses cried unto the L·, saying,
5 And the L· said unto Moses, Go on
7 and because they tempted the L·,
7 Is the L· among us, or not?
14 the L· said unto Moses, Write
16 Because the L· hath sworn that
16 the L· will have war with Amalek
18: 1 the L· hath brought Israel out of
8 law all that the L· had done unto
8 and how the L· delivered them.
9 goodness which the L· had done
10 Jethro said, Blessed be the L·,
11 the L· is greater than all gods:
19: 3 the L· called unto him out of the
7 words which the L· commanded
8 the L· hath spoken we will do.
8 words of the people unto the L·.
9 And the L· said unto Moses, Lo, I
9 words of the people unto the L·.
10 the L· said unto Moses, Go unto
11 third day the L· will come down
18 the L· descended upon it in fire:
20 L· came down upon mount Sinai,
20 L· called Moses up to the top of
21 the L· said unto Moses, Go down,
21 they break through unto the L·
22 also, which come near to the L·,
22 the L· break forth upon them.
23 And Moses said unto the L·, The
24 the L· said unto him, Away, get
24 through to come up unto the L·,
20: 2 I am the L· thy God, which have
5 the L· thy God am a jealous God,
7 name of the L· thy God in vain;
7 the L· will not hold him guiltless
10 day is the sabbath of the L· thy
11 the L· made heaven and earth,
11 the L· blessed the sabbath day,
12 the land which the L· thy God
22 the L· said unto Moses, Thus
22:11 an oath of the L· be between
20 any god, save unto the L· only,
23:17 males shall appear before the L·
19 bring into the house of the L·.
25 ye shall serve the L· your God,
24: 1 Come up unto the L·, thou, and
2 alone shall come near the L·:
3 the people all the words of the L·,
3 All the words which the L· hath
4 wrote all the words of the L·,
5 offerings of oxen unto the L·.
7 All that the L· hath said will we
8 which the L· hath made with you
12 the L· said unto Moses, Come up
16 glory of the L· abode upon mount
17 glory of the L· was like devouring
25: 1 And the L· spake unto Moses,
27:21 evening to morning before the L·:
28:12 bear their names before the L·
29 before the L· continually.
30 when he goeth in before the L·:
30 heart before the L· continually.
35 unto the holy place before the L·,
36 of a signet, Holiness To The L·.
38 may be accepted before the L·.

Ex 29:11 kill the bullock before the L·,
18 it is a burnt offering unto the L·:
18 offering made by fire unto the L·.
23 bread that is before the L·:
24 for a wave offering before the L·.
25 for a sweet savour before the L·:
25 offering made by fire unto the L·.
26 for a wave offering before the L·:
28 their heave offering unto the L·.
41 offering made by fire unto the L·.
42 of the congregation before the L·:
46 know that I am the L· their God,
46 them: I am the L· their God.
30: 8 a perpetual incense before the L·
10 it is most holy unto the L·.
11 And the L· spake unto Moses,
12 ransom for his soul unto the L·,
13 shall be the offering of the L·.
14 shall give an offering unto the L·.
15 they give an offering unto the L·,
16 children of Israel before the L·,
17 And the L· spake unto Moses,
20 offering made by fire unto the L·:
22 the L· spake unto Moses, saying,
34 And the L· said unto Moses, Take
37 shall be unto thee holy for the L·.
31: 1, 12 And the L· spake unto Moses,
13 am the L· that doth sanctify you.
15 the sabbath of rest, holy to the L·:
17 the L· made heaven and earth,
32: 5 To morrow is a feast to the L·.
7 the L· said unto Moses, Go, get
9 the L· said unto Moses, I have
11 Moses besought the L· his God,
11 L·, Why doth thy wrath wax hot
14 L· repented of the evil which he
22 Let not the anger of my l· wax hot:
27 Thus saith the L· God of Israel,
29 yourselves to day to the L·, even
30 and now I will go up unto the L·;
31 Moses returned unto the L·, and
33 And the L· said unto Moses,
35 And the L· plagued the people,
33: 1 the L· said unto Moses, Depart,
5 the L· had said unto Moses, Say
7 every one which sought the L·
9 and the L· talked with Moses.
11 L· spake unto Moses face to face,
12 Moses said unto the L·, See, thou
17 the L· said unto Moses, I will do
19 will proclaim the name of the L·
21 And the L· said, Behold, there is a
34: 1 the L· said unto Moses, Hew thee
4 Sinai, as the L· had commanded
5 the L· descended in the cloud,
5 proclaimed the name of the L·.
6 the L· passed by before him, and
6 The L·, The L· God, merciful and
9 O L·, let my L·, I pray thee, go
10 art shall see the work of the L·:
14 for the L·, whose name is Jealous,
23 appear before the L· God,
24 the L· thy God thrice in the year.
26 bring unto the house of the L· thy
27 And the L· said unto Moses, Write
28 there with the L· forty days and
32 that the L· hath spoken with him
34 before the L· to speak with him,
35: 1 These are words which the L· hath
2 day, a sabbath of rest to the L·:
4 thing which the L· commanded,
5 you an offering unto the L·:
5 bring it, an offering of the L·;
10 all that the L· hath commanded;
22 an offering of gold unto the L·.
29 a willing offering unto the L·,
29 which the L· had commanded to
30 See, the L· hath called by name
36: 1 in whom the L· put wisdom and
1 all that the L· had commanded.
2 heart the L· had put wisdom,
5 which the L· commanded to make.
38:22 all that the L· commanded Moses.
39: 1,5,7,21,26,29 L· commanded Moses.
30 of a signet, Holiness To The L·.
31 as the L· commanded Moses.
32, 42 that the L· commanded Moses,
43 done it as the L· had commanded,
40: 1 And the L· spake unto Moses,
16 to all that the L· commanded him,
19, 21 as the L· commanded Moses.
23 in order upon it before the L·;
23 as the L· had commanded Moses.
25 he lighted the lamps before the L·:
25, 27, 29, 32 L· commanded Moses.
34, 35 the glory of the L· filled the
38 the cloud of the L· was upon the
Le 1: 1 And the L· called unto Moses,
2 you bring an offering unto the L·,
3 of the congregation before the L·.
5 shall kill the bullock before the L·:
9 of a sweet savour unto the L·.
11 the altar northward before the L·:
13 of a sweet savour unto the L·.
14 his offering to the L· be of fowls,
17 of a sweet savour unto the L·.
2: 1 offer a meat offering unto the L·,
2 of a sweet savour unto the L·:
3 offerings of the L· made by fire.
8 made of these things unto the L·:
9 of a sweet savour unto the L·.
10 offerings of the L· made by fire.
11 which ye shall bring unto the L·,
11 any offering of the L· made by fire.
12 ye shall offer them unto the L·:
14 of thy firstfruits unto the L·,

Le 2:16 offering made by fire unto the L·.
3: 1 it without blemish before the L·.
3 offering made by fire unto the L·;
5 of a sweet savour unto the L·.
6 offering unto the L· be of the flock;
7 then shall he offer it before the L·.
9 offering made by fire unto the L·;
11 offering made by fire unto the L·.
12 he shall offer it before the L·.
14 offering made by fire unto the L·;
4: 1 And the L· spake unto Moses,
2 of the commandments of the L·
3 bullock without blemish unto the L·
4 of the congregation before the L·;
4 and kill the bullock before the L·.
6 blood seven times before the L·,
7 of sweet incense before the L·,
13 of the commandments of the L·
15 head of the bullock before the L·:
15 bullock shall be killed before the L·.
17 it seven times before the L·,
18 of the altar which is before the L·,
22 of the commandments of the L·
24 the burnt offering before the L·:
27 of the commandments of the L·
31 for a sweet savour unto the L·;
35 offerings made by fire unto the L·:
5: 6 his trespass offering unto the L·
7 or two young pigeons, unto the L·;
12 offerings made by fire unto the L·:
14 And the L· spake unto Moses,
15 in the holy things of the L·;
15 bring for his trespass unto the L·
17 by the commandments of the L·;
19 certainly trespassed against the L·.
6: 1 And the L· spake unto Moses,
2 commit a trespass against the L·,
6 his trespass offering unto the L·,
7 atonement for him before the L·:
8 And the L· spake unto Moses,
14 of Aaron shall offer it before the L·,
15 the memorial of it, unto the L·.
18 offerings of the L· made by fire:
19 And the L· spake unto Moses,
20 offer unto the L· in the day when
21 for a sweet savour unto the L·.
22 it is a statute for ever unto the L·;
24 And the L· spake unto Moses,
25 sin offering be killed before the L·:
7: 5 offering made by fire unto the L·:
11 which he shall offer unto the L·.
14 for an heave offering unto the L·,
20 offerings that pertain unto the L·,
21 which pertain unto the L·,
22 And the L· spake unto Moses,
25 offering made by fire unto the L·,
28 And the L· spake unto Moses,
29 of his peace offerings unto the L·
29 shall bring his oblation unto the L·
30 offerings of the L· made by fire,
30 for a wave offering before the L·.
35 offerings of the L· made by fire,
35 minister unto the L· in the priest's
36 the L· commanded to be given
38 L· commanded Moses in mount
38 offer their oblations unto the L·,
8: 1 And the L· spake unto Moses,
4 Moses did as the L· commanded
5 the L· commanded to be done.
9, 13, 17 the L· commanded Moses.
21 offering made by fire unto the L·;
21 as the L· commanded Moses.
26 bread, that was before the L·,
27 for a wave offering before the L·.
28 offering made by fire unto the L·.
29 for a wave offering before the L·:
29 as the L· commanded Moses.
34 so the L· hath commanded to do,
35 keep the charge of the L·, that ye
36 the L· commanded by the hand of
9: 2 and offer them before the L·.
4 to sacrifice before the L·;
4 to day the L· will appear unto you.
5 drew near and stood before the L·.
6 L· commanded that ye should do:
6 glory of the L· shall appear unto
7 for them; as the L· commanded.
10 as the L· commanded Moses.
21 for a wave offering before the L·;
23 glory of the L· appeared unto all
24 came a fire out from before the L·,
10: 1 offered strange fire before the L·,
2 there went out fire from the L·,
2 and they died before the L·.
3 This is it that the L· spake,
6 burning...the L· hath kindled.
7 anointing oil of the L· is upon
8 the L· spake unto Aaron, saying,
11 statutes which the L· hath spoken
12 offerings of the L· made by fire,
13 sacrifices of the L· made by fire:
15 for a wave offering before the L·;
15 ever; as the L· hath commanded.
17 atonement for them before the L·?
19 their burnt offering before the L·;
19 accepted in the sight of the L·?
11: 1 L· spake unto Moses and to Aaron,
44 I am the L· your God: ye shall
45 I am the L· that bringeth you up
12: 1 And the L· spake unto Moses,
7 Who shall offer it before the L·,
13: 1 L· spake unto Moses and Aaron,
14: 1 And the L· spake unto Moses,
11 before the L·, at the door of the
12 for a wave offering before the L·:
16 finger seven times before the L·:

Le 14:18 atonement for him before the L'.
23 of the congregation, before the L'.
24 for a wave offering before the L':
27 hand seven times before the L':
29 atonement for him before the L'.
31 that is to be cleansed before the L'.
33 the L' spake unto Moses and unto
15: 1 L' spake unto Moses and to Aaron,
14 come before the L' unto the door
15 atonement for him before the L'
30 atonement for her before the L'
16: 1 And the L' spake unto Moses
1 when they offered before the L',
2 the L' said unto Moses, Speak
7 and present them before the L'
8 one lot for the L', and the other
10 be presented alive before the L',
12 from off the altar before the L',
13 upon the fire before the L', incense
18 the altar that is before the L',
30 from all your sins before the L'.
34 did as the L' commanded Moses.
17: 1 the L' spake unto Moses, saying,
2 which the L' hath commanded,
4 to offer an offering unto the L'
4 before the tabernacle of the L';
5 they may bring them unto the L',
5 for peace offerings unto the L'.
6 the blood upon the altar of the L'
6 for a sweet savour unto the L'.
9 to offer it unto the L'; even
18: 1 the L' spake unto Moses, saying,
2 unto them, I am the L' your God.
4 therein: I am the L' your God.
5 he shall live in them: I am the L'.
6 their nakedness: I am the L'.
21 the name of thy God: I am the L'.
30 therein: I am the L' your God.
19: 1 the L' spake unto Moses, saying,
2 for I the L' your God am holy.
3 sabbaths: I am the L' your God.
4 gods: I am the L' your God.
5 of peace offerings unto the L',
8 the hallowed thing of the L';
10 stranger: I am the L' your God.
12 the name of thy God: I am the L'.
14 shalt fear thy God: I am the L'.
16 of thy neighbour: I am the L'.
18 neighbour as thyself: I am the L'.
21 his trespass offering unto the L',
22 the trespass offering before the L'
24 be holy to praise the L' withal.
25 thereof: I am the L' your God.
28 any marks upon you: I am the L'.
30 my sanctuary: I am the L'.
31 by them: I am the L' your God.
32 and fear thy God: I am the L'.
34 of Egypt: I am the L' your God.
36 I am the L' your God, which
37 and do them: I am the L'.
20: 1 the L' spake unto Moses, saying,
7 ye holy: for I am the L' your God.
8 I am the L' which sanctify you.
24 I am the L' your God, which have
26 holy unto me: for I the L' am holy,
21: 1 the L' said unto Moses, Speak
6 offerings of the L' made by fire,
8 for I the L', which sanctify you,
12 his God is upon him: I am the L'.
15 for I the L' do sanctify him.
16 the L' spake unto Moses, saying,
21 offerings of the L' made by fire:
23 for I the L' do sanctify them.
22: 1 the L' spake unto Moses, saying,
2 they hallow unto me: I am the L'.
3 of Israel hallow unto the L',
3 from my presence: I am the L'.
8 himself therewith: I am the L'.
9 it: I the L' do sanctify them.
15 which they offer unto the L';
16 for I the L' do sanctify them.
17 the L' spake unto Moses, saying,
18 they will offer unto the L' for a
21 unto the L' to accomplish his vow,
22 shall not offer these unto the L',
22 them upon the altar unto the L'.
24 unto the L' that which is bruised,
26 the L' spake unto Moses, saying,
27 offering made by fire unto the L'.
29 of thanksgiving unto the L', offer
30 it until the morrow: I am the L'.
31 and do them: I am the L'.
32 I am the L' which hallow you,
33 to be your God: I am the L'.
23: 1 the L' spake unto Moses, saying,
2 Concerning the feasts of the L',
3 the sabbath of the L' in all your
4 These are the feasts of the L',
6 of unleavened bread unto the L':
8 offering made by fire unto the L':
9 the L' spake unto Moses, saying,
11 wave the sheaf before the L',
12 for a burnt offering unto the L'.
13 offering made by fire unto the L'
16 a new meat offering unto the L'.
17 they are the firstfruits unto the L'.
18 for a burnt offering unto the L',
18 fire, of sweet savour unto the L'.
20 for a wave offering before the L',
20 be holy to the L' for the priest.
22 stranger: I am the L' your God.
23 the L' spake unto Moses, saying,
25 offering made by fire unto the L'.
26 the L' spake unto Moses, saying,
27 offering made by fire unto the L'.
28 atonement for you before the L'

Le 23:33 the L' spake unto Moses, saying,
34 for seven days unto the L'.
36, 36 offering...by fire unto the L':
37 These are the feasts of the L',
37 offering made by fire unto the L',
38 Beside the sabbaths of the L',
38 offerings, which ye give unto the L'.
39 keep a feast unto the L' seven
40 rejoice before the L' your God
41 keep it a feast unto the L' seven
43 of Egypt: I am the L' your God.
44 of Israel the feasts of the L'.
24: 1 the L' spake unto Moses, saying,
3 before the L' continually: morning
4 the pure candlestick before the L'
6 upon the pure table before the L'.
7 offering made by fire unto the L'.
8 shall set it in order before the L'
9 offerings of the L' made by fire
11 blasphemed the name of the L',
12 mind of the L' might be shewed
13 the L' spake unto Moses, saying,
16 blasphemeth the name of the L',
22 for I am the L' your God.
23 did as the L' commanded Moses.
25: 1 L' spake unto Moses in mount
2 land keep a sabbath unto the L'.
4 the land, a sabbath for the L':
17 God: for I am the L' your God.
38 I am the L' your God, which
55 of Egypt: I am the L' your God.
26: 1 unto it: for I am the L' your God.
2 my sanctuary: I am the L'.
13 I am the L' your God, which
44 them: for I am the L' their God.
45 might be their God: I am the L'.
46 laws, which the L' made between
27: 1 the L' spake unto Moses, saying,
2 be for the L' by thy estimation.
9 men bring an offering unto the L',
9 man giveth of such unto the L'
11 not offer a sacrifice unto the L',
14 his house to be holy unto the L',
16 a man shall sanctify unto the L'
21 jubile, shall be holy unto the L',
22 man sanctify unto the L' a field
23 day, as a holy thing unto the L'.
28 devote unto the L' of all that he
28 thing is most holy unto the L'.
30 is the Lord's: it is holy unto the L'.
32 tenth shall be holy unto the L'.
34 which the L' commanded Moses
Nu 1: 1 the L' spake unto Moses in the
19 As the L' commanded Moses, so
48 L' had spoken unto Moses, saying,
54 all that the L' commanded Moses,
2: 1 the L' spake unto Moses and unto
33 as the L' commanded Moses.
34 all that the L' commanded Moses:
3: 1 L' spake with Moses in mount
4 and Abihu died before the L',
4 offered strange fire before the L',
5, 11 L' spake unto Moses, saying,
13 mine shall they be: I am the L'.
14 the L' spake unto Moses in the
16 according to the word of the L',
39 at the commandment of the L',
40 the L' said unto Moses, Number
41 the Levites for me (I am the L')
42 as the L' commanded him, all
44 the L' spake unto Moses, saying,
45 shall be mine: I am the L'.
51 according to the word of the L',
51 as the L' commanded Moses.
4: 1, 17 L' spake unto Moses and unto
21 the L' spake unto Moses, saying,
37 to the commandment of the L'
41 to the commandment of the L'.
45 according to the word of the L'
49 to the commandment of the L'
49 as the L' commanded Moses.
5: 1 the L' spake unto Moses, saying,
4 as the L' spake unto Moses, so
5 the L' spake unto Moses, saying,
6 to do a trespass against the L',
8 be recompensed unto the L', even
11 the L' spake unto Moses, saying,
16 near, and set her before the L':
18 shall set the woman before the L',
21 L' make thee a curse and an oath
21 L' doth make thy thigh to rot,
25 wave the offering before the L',
30 shall set the woman before the L',
6: 1 the L' spake unto Moses, saying,
2 separate themselves unto the L':
5 separateth himself unto the L',
6 separateth himself unto the L'
8 separation he is holy unto the L'.
12 consecrate unto the L' the days
14 shall offer his offering unto the L',
16 shall bring them before the L',
17 of peace offerings unto the L',
20 for a wave offering before the L':
21 of his offering unto the L' for his
22 the L' spake unto Moses, saying,
24 The L' bless thee, and keep thee:
25 L' make his face shine upon thee,
26 L' lift up his countenance upon
7: 3 their offering before the L',
4 the L' spake unto Moses, saying,
11 And the L' said unto Moses, They
8: 1 the L' spake unto Moses, saying,
3 as the L' commanded Moses.
4 pattern which the L' had shewed
5 the L' spake unto Moses, saying,
10 bring the Levites before the L':

Nu 8:11 offer the Levites before the L'
11 may execute the service of the L'.
12 for a burnt offering, unto the L',
13 them for an offering unto the L'.
20 all that the L' commanded Moses
21 them as an offering before the L';
22 as the L' had commanded Moses
23 the L' spake unto Moses, saying,
9: 1 the L' spake unto Moses in the
5 all that the L' commanded Moses,
7 of the L' in his appointed season
8 hear what the L' will command
9 the L' spake unto Moses, saying,
10 keep the passover unto the L'.
13 of the L' in his appointed season,
14 keep the passover unto the L';
18 At the commandment of the L'
18 at the commandment of the L'
19 Israel kept the charge of the L',
20, 20 to the commandment of the L'
23 At the commandment of the L'
23 at the commandment of the L'
23 they kept the charge of the L',
23 at the commandment of the L'
10: 1 the L' spake unto Moses, saying,
9 be remembered before the L'
10 your God: I am the L' your God.
13 to the commandment of the L' by
29 the place of which the L' said,
29 L' hath spoken good concerning
32 goodness the L' shall do unto us,
33 departed from the mount of the L'
33 the ark of the covenant of the L'
34 cloud of the L' was upon them
35 Rise up, L', and let thine enemies
36 Return, O L', unto the many
11: 1 complained, it displeased the L':
1 the L' heard it; and his anger
1 fire of the L' burnt among them,
2 when Moses prayed unto the L',
3 fire of the L' burnt among them.
10 the anger of the L' was kindled
11 Moses said unto the L', Wherefore
16 the L' said unto Moses, Gather
18 have wept in the ears of the L',
18 the L' will give you flesh, and ye
20 that ye have despised the L'
23 the L' said unto Moses, Is the
24 the people the words of the L',
25 And the L' came down in a cloud,
28 and said, My l' Moses, forbid them.
29 the L' would put his spirit upon
31 went forth a wind from the L',
33 the wrath of the L' was kindled
33 L' smote the people with a very
12: 2 Hath the L' indeed spoken only
2 also by us? And the L' heard it.
4 L' spake suddenly unto Moses,
5 L' came down in the pillar of the
6 I the L' will make myself known
8 the similitude of the L' shall he
9 the anger of the L' was kindled
11 Aaron said unto Moses, Alas, my l',
13 Moses cried unto the L', saying,
14 the L' said unto Moses, If her
13: 1 the L' spake unto Moses, saying,
3 by the commandment of the L'
14: 3 wherefore hath the L' brought us
8 If the L' delight in us, then he
9 Only rebel not ye against the L',
9 from them, and the L' is with us:
10 the glory of the L' appeared in
11 the L' said unto Moses, How long
13 Moses said unto the L', Then the
14 thou L' art among this people,
14 that thou L' art seen face to face,
16 the L' was not able to bring this
17 let the power of my L' be great,
18 The L' is longsuffering, and of
20 And the L' said, I have pardoned
21 be filled with the glory of the L'.
26 the L' spake unto Moses and
28 As truly as I live, saith the L', as
35 I the L' have said, I will surely
37 died by the plague before the L'.
40 place which the L' hath promised:
41 the commandment of the L'?
42 for the Lord is not among you;
43 ye are turned away from the L',
43 the L' will not be with you.
44 the ark of the covenant of the L',
15: 1 the L' spake unto Moses, saying,
3 offering by fire unto the L',
3 a sweet savour unto the L',
4 offereth his offering unto the L'
7 for a sweet savour unto the L'.
8 or peace offerings unto the L':
10, 13 of a sweet savour unto the L'.
14 of a sweet savour unto the L';
15 the stranger be before the L'.
17 the L' spake unto Moses, saying,
19 for an heave offering unto the L'.
21 give unto the L' a heave offering
22 the L' hath spoken unto Moses,
23 that the L' hath commanded you
23 that the L' commanded Moses,
24 for a sweet savour unto the L',
25 sacrifice made by fire unto the L',
25 their sin offering before the L',
28 by ignorance before the L', to
30 the same reproacheth the L';
31 hath despised the word of the L',
35 the L' said unto Moses, The man
36 as the L' commanded Moses.
37 the L' spake unto Moses, saying,
39 all the commandments of the L',

Nu 15:41 I am the L· your God, which
41 your God: I am the L· your God.
16: 3 them, and the L· is among them:
3 above the congregation of the L·?
5 the L· will shew who are his,
7 incense in them before the L·
7 man whom the L· doth choose,
9 service of the tabernacle of the L·,
11 gathered together against the L·:
15 very wroth, and said unto the L·,
16 all thy company before the L·,
17 bring ye before the L· every man
19 the glory of the L· appeared unto
20 the L· spake unto Moses and unto
23 the L· spake unto Moses, saying,
28 shall know that the L· hath sent
29 then the L· hath not sent me.
30 if the L· make a new thing, and
30 these men have provoked the L·.
35 there came out a fire from the L·,
36 the L· spake to Moses, saying,
38 they offered them before the L·,
40 to offer incense before the L·;
40 L· said to him by the hand of
41 have killed the people of the L·.
42 And the glory of the L· appeared.
44 the L· spake unto Moses, saying,
46 is wrath gone out from the L·;
17: 1 the L· spake unto Moses, saying,
7 laid up the rods before the L· in
9 all the rods from before the L·
10 And the L· said unto Moses, Bring
11 as the L· commanded him, so did
13 the tabernacle of the L· shall die:
18: 1 the L· said unto Aaron, Thou and
6 they are given as a gift for the L·,
8 the L· spake unto Aaron, Behold,
12 which they shall offer unto the L·,
13 which they shall bring unto the L·,
15 which they bring unto the L·,
17 for a sweet savour unto the L·.
19 children of Israel offer unto the L·,
19 of salt for ever before the L· unto
20 the L· spake unto Aaron, Thou
24 as an heave offering unto the L·,
25 the L· spake unto Moses, saying,
26 an heave offering of it for the L·,
28 an heave offering unto the L· of
29 every heave offering of the L·, of
19: 1 the L· spake unto Moses and unto
2 which the L· hath commanded,
13 defileth the tabernacle of the L·;
20 defiled the sanctuary of the L·:
20: 3 our brethren died before the L·!
4 up the congregation of the L· into
6 the glory of the L· appeared unto
7 the L· spake unto Moses, saying,
9 took the rod from before the L·,
12 L· spake unto Moses and Aaron,
13 of Israel strove with the L·, and
16 And when we cried unto the L·, he
23 L· spake unto Moses and Aaron
27 Moses did as the L· commanded:
21: 2 Israel vowed a vow unto the L·,
3 the L· hearkened to the voice of
6 L· sent fiery serpents among the
7 we have spoken against the L·,
7 pray unto the L·, that he take
8 And the L· said unto Moses, Make
14 in the book of the wars of the L·,
16 whereof the L· spake unto Moses,
34 the L· said unto Moses, Fear him
22: 8 as the L· shall speak unto me:
13 L· refuseth to give me leave to go
18 the word of the L· my God, to
19 I may know what the L· will say
22 angel of the L· stood in the way
23 saw the angel of the L· standing
24 angel of the L· stood in a path of
25 the ass saw the angel of the L·,
26 angel of the L· went further, and
27 the ass saw the angel of the L·,
28 L· opened the mouth of the ass,
31 L· opened the eyes of Balaam,
31 saw the angel of the L· standing
32 the angel of the L· said unto him,
34 said unto the angel of the L·,
35 angel of the L· said unto Balaam,
23: 3 the L· will come to meet me;
5 L· put a word in Balaam's mouth,
8 whom the L· hath not defied?
12 the L· hath put in my mouth?
15 while I meet the L· yonder.
16 And the L· met Balaam, and put
17 him, What hath the L· spoken?
21 the L· his God is with him, and
26 All that the L· speaketh, that I
24: 1 saw that it pleased the L· to bless
6 aloes which the L· hath planted,
11 the L· hath kept thee back from
13 the commandment of the L·,
13 but what the L· saith, that will I
25: 3 the anger of the L· was kindled
4 the L· said unto Moses, Take all
4 and hang them up before the L·
4 and fierce anger of the L· may be
10, 16 And the L· spake unto Moses,
26: 1 the L· spake unto Moses and unto
4 as the L· commanded Moses and
9 when they strove against the L·:
52 the L· spake unto Moses, saying,
61 offered strange fire before the L·.
65 For the L· had said of them, They
27: 3 against the L· in the company of
5 brought their cause before the L·.
6 the L· spake unto Moses, saying,

Nu 27:11 as the L· commanded Moses.
12 the L· said unto Moses, Get thee
15 Moses spake unto the L·, saying,
16 Let the L·, the God of the spirits
17 congregation of the L· be not as
18 the L· said unto Moses, Take thee
21 judgment of Urim before the L·:
22 Moses did as the L· commanded
23 L· commanded by the hand of
28: 1 the L· spake unto Moses, saying,
3 which ye shall offer unto the L·;
6 sacrifice made by fire unto the L·.
7 wine to be poured unto the L· for
8 of a sweet savour unto the L·.
11 offer a burnt offering unto the L·;
13 sacrifice made by fire unto the L·.
15 goats for a sin offering unto the L·
16 month is the passover of the L·.
19 for a burnt offering unto the L·;
24 of a sweet savour unto the L·:
26 a new meat offering unto the L·,
27 for a sweet savour unto the L·;
29: 2 for a sweet savour unto the L·;
6 sacrifice made by fire unto the L·.
8 offer a burnt offering unto the L·
12 a feast unto the L· seven days:
13 of a sweet savour unto the L·;
36 of a sweet savour unto the L·:
39 things ye shall do unto the L· in
40 all that the L· commanded Moses.
30: 1 which the L· hath commanded.
2 If a man vow a vow unto the L·, or
3 also vow a vow unto the L·,
5 the L· shall forgive her, because
8 and the L· shall forgive her.
12 void; and the L· shall forgive her.
16 which the L· commanded Moses,
31: 1 the L· spake unto Moses, saying,
3 and avenge the L· of Midian.
7 as the L· commanded Moses;
16 commit trespass against the L·
16 among the congregation of the L·.
21 the law which the L· commanded
25 the L· spake unto Moses, saying,
28 levy a tribute unto the L· of the
29 for an heave offering of the L·.
30 charge of the tabernacle of the L·.
31 priest did as the L· commanded
41 as the L· commanded Moses.
47 charge of the tabernacle of the L·;
47 as the L· commanded Moses.
50 brought an oblation for the L·,
50 for our souls before the L·.
52 that they offered up to the L·,
54 children of Israel before the L·.
32: 4 the country which the L· smote
7 the land which the L· hath given
9 the land which the L· had given
12 they have wholly followed the L·.
13 done evil in the sight of the L·,
14 anger of the L· toward Israel.
20 go armed before the L· to war,
21 armed over Jordan before the L·,
22 land be subdued before the L·:
22 and be guiltless before the L·,
22 be your possession before the L·.
23 ye have sinned against the L·:
25 will do as my l· commandeth.
27 for war, before the L· to battle,
27 to battle, as my l· saith.
29 armed to battle, before the L·,
31 the L· hath said unto thy servants,
32 will pass over armed before the L·
33: 2 by the commandment of the L·:
4 the L· had smitten among them:
4 also the L· executed judgments.
38 at the commandment of the L·,
50 L· spake unto Moses in the plains
34: 1 And the L· spake unto Moses,
13 which the L· commanded to give
16 And the L· spake unto Moses,
29 the L· commanded to divide the
35: 1 L· spake unto Moses in the plains
9 And the L· spake unto Moses,
34 I the L· dwell among the children
36: 2 L· commanded...to give the land
2 commanded my l· to give the land
2 my l· was commanded...to give the
2 was commanded by the L· to give
5 according to the word of the L·,
6 thing which the L· doth command
10 the L· commanded Moses, so did
13 the L· commanded by the hand of
De 1: 3 L· had given him in commandment
6 L· our God spake unto us in Horeb,
8 land which the L· sware unto your
10 L· your God hath multiplied you,
11 L· God of your fathers make you
19 as the L· our God commanded us;
20 which the L· our God doth give
21 the L· thy God hath set the land
21 L· God of thy fathers hath said
25 which the L· our God doth give
26 commandment of the L· your God.
27 Because the L· hated us, he hath
30 L· your God which goeth before
31 how that the L· thy God bare thee,
32 ye did not believe the L· your God,
34 L· heard the voice of your words,
36 he hath wholly followed the L·.
37 the L· was angry with me for your
41 We have sinned against the L·,
41 that the L· our God commanded
42 L· said unto me, Say unto them,
43 the commandment of the L·,
45 returned and wept before the L·;

De 1:45 the L· would not hearken to your
2: 1 Red sea, as the L· spake unto me:
2 the L· spake unto me, saying,
7 L· thy God hath blessed thee in all
7 L· thy God hath been with thee;
9 the L· said unto me, Distress not
12 which the L· gave unto them.
14 host, as the L· sware unto them.
15 hand of the L· was against them,
17 the L· spake unto me, saying,
21 L· destroyed them before them;
29 land which the L· our God giveth
30 L· thy God hardened his spirit,
31 the L· said unto me, Behold, I
33 L· our God delivered him before
36 L· our God delivered all unto us:
37 the L· our God forbad us.
3: 2 L· said unto me, Fear him not:
3 the L· our God delivered into our
18 L· your God hath given you this
20 the L· hath given rest unto your
20 which the L· your God hath given
21 all that the L· your God hath done
21 the L· do unto all the kingdoms
22 L· your God he shall fight for you.
23 I besought the L· at that time,
24 O L· God, thou hast begun to shew
26 L· was wroth with me for your
26 the L· said unto me, Let it suffice
4: 1 L· God of your fathers giveth
2 commandments of the L· your
3 eyes have seen what the L· did
3 L· thy God hath destroyed them
4 did cleave unto the L· your God
5 as the L· my God commanded me,
7 as the L· our God is in all things
10 stoodest before the L· thy God in
10 when the L· said unto me, Gather
12 the L· spake unto you out of the
14 L· commanded me at that time to
15 the L· spake unto you in Horeb
19 L· thy God hath divided unto all
20 L· hath taken you, and brought
21 the L· was angry with me for your
21 which the L· thy God giveth thee
23 forget the covenant of the L· your
23 L· thy God hath forbidden thee.
24 L· thy God is a consuming fire,
25 evil in the sight of the L· thy God,
27 L· shall scatter you among the
27 whither the L· shall lead you.
29 thou shalt seek the L· thy God,
30 if thou turn to the L· thy God,
31 the L· thy God is a merciful God;)
34 L· your God did for you in Egypt
35 know that the L· he is God;
39 that the L· he is God in heaven
40 which the L· thy God giveth thee,
5: 2 L· our God made a covenant with
3 L· made not this covenant with
4 L· talked with you face to face in
5 (I stood between the L· and you
5 to shew you the word of the L·;
6 am the L· thy God, which brought
9 the L· thy God am a jealous God,
11 name of the L· thy God in vain:
11 the L· will not hold him guiltless
12 L· thy God hath commanded thee.
14 is the sabbath of the L· thy God:
15 the L· thy God brought thee out
15 L· thy God commanded...to keep
16 the L· thy God hath commanded
16 land which the L· thy God giveth
22 L· spake unto all your assembly
24 L· our God hath shewed us his
25 hear the voice of the L· our God
27 all that the L· our God shall say:
27 all that the L· our God shall speak
28 L· heard the voice of your words,
28 the L· said unto me, I have heard
32, 33 L· your God hath commanded
6: 1 L· your God commanded to teach
2 thou mightest fear the L· thy God,
3 L· God of thy fathers...promised
4 Israel: The L· our God is one L·:
5 love the L· thy God with all thine
10 the L· thy God shall have brought
12 beware lest thou forget the L·,
13 Thou shalt fear the L· thy God,
15 the L· thy God is a jealous God
15 anger of the L· thy God be kindled
16 shall not tempt the L· your God,
17 keep the commandments of the L·
18 and good in the sight of the L·:
18 the good land which the L· sware
19 before thee, as the L· hath spoken.
20 L· our God hath commanded you?
21 L· brought us out of Egypt with
22 L· shewed signs and wonders,
24 L· commanded us to do all these
24 statutes, to fear the L· our God,
25 commandments before the L· our
7: 1 L· thy God shall bring thee into
2 the L· thy God shall deliver them
4 the anger of the L· be kindled
6 holy people unto the L· thy God:
6 L· thy God hath chosen thee to be
7 L· did not set his love upon you,
8 But because the L· loved you,
8 L· brought you out with a mighty
9 that the L· thy God, he is God,
12 L· thy God shall keep unto thee
15 L· will take away from thee all
16 which the L· thy God shall deliver
18 the L· thy God did unto Pharaoh,
19 the L· thy God brought thee out:

De 7:19 so shall the L' thy God do unto all
20 L' thy God will send the hornet
21 for the L' thy God is among you,
22 the L' thy God will put out those
23 L' thy God shall deliver them unto
25 an abomination to the L' thy God.
8: 1 land which the L' sware unto your
2 way which the L' thy God led thee
3 word...out of the mouth of the L'
5 son, so the L' thy God chasteneth
6 keep the commandments of the L'
7 L' thy God bringeth thee into a
10 shalt bless the L' thy God for the
11 thou forget not the L' thy God,
14 and thou forget the L' thy God,
18 shalt remember the L' thy God:
19 do at all forget the L' thy God,
20 nations which the L' destroyeth
20 unto the voice of the L' your God.
9: 3 L' thy God is he which goeth over
3 as the L' hath said unto thee.
4 the L' thy God hath cast them out
4 L' hath brought me in to possess
4 the L' doth drive them out from
5 L' thy God doth drive them out
5 the word which the L' sware unto
6 L' thy God giveth thee not this
7 provokedst the L' thy God to wrath
7 been rebellious against the L'.
8 ye provoked the L' to wrath, so
8 so that the L' was angry with you
9 covenant which the L' made with
10 L' delivered unto me two tables of
10 L' spake with you in the mount
11 L' gave me the two tables of stone,
12 L' said unto me, Arise, get thee
13 the L' spake unto me, saying, I
16 sinned against the L' your God,
16 out of the way which the L' had
18 I fell down before the L', as at the
18 wickedly in the sight of the L', to
19 the L' was wroth against you to
19 the L' hearkened unto me at that
20 L' was very angry with Aaron to
22 ye provoked the L' to wrath.
23 L' sent you from Kadesh-barnea,
23 commandment of the L' your God,
24 been rebellious against the L'
25 fell down before the L' forty days
25 L' had said he would destroy you.
26 I prayed therefore unto the L',
26 O L' God, destroy not thy people
28 the L' was not able to bring them
10: 1 that time the L' said unto me,
4 L' spake unto you in the mount
4 and the L' gave them unto me.
5 they be, as the L' commanded me.
8 the L' separated the tribe of Levi,
8 the ark of the covenant of the L',
8 before the L' to minister unto him,
9 the L' is his inheritance,
9 as the L' thy God promised him.
10 the L' hearkened unto me at that
10 and the L' would not destroy thee.
11 L' said unto me, Arise, take thy
12 what doth the L' thy God require
12 but to fear the L' thy God, to walk
12 to serve the L' thy God with all
13 the commandments of the L',
15 L' had a delight in thy fathers
17 the L' your God is God of gods,
17 L' of lords, a great God, a mighty,
20 Thou shalt fear the L' thy God;
22 L' thy God hath made thee as the
11: 1 love the L' thy God, and keep his
2 chastisement of the L' your God,
4 L' hath destroyed them unto this
7 great acts of the L' which he did.
9 the L' sware unto your fathers
12 land which the L' thy God careth
12 eyes of the L' thy God are always
13 to love the L' your God, and to
17 good land which the L' giveth you.
21 the L' sware unto your fathers
22 to love the L' your God, to walk
23 the L' drive out all these nations
25 L' your God shall lay the fear of
27, 28 obey...commandments of the L'
29 L' thy God hath brought thee in
31 the land which the L' your God
12: 1 L' God of thy fathers giveth thee
4 not do so unto the L' your God.
5 the L' your God shall choose out
7 shall eat before the L' your God,
7 the L' thy God hath blessed thee.
9 which the L' your God giveth you.
10 the land which the L' your God
11 the L' your God shall choose to
11 vows which ye vow unto the L':
12 rejoice before the L' your God,
14 place which the L' shall choose
15 to the blessing of the L' thy God
18 thou must eat them before the L'
18 which the L' thy God shall choose,
18 rejoice before the L' thy God in
20 the L' thy God shall enlarge thy
21 which the L' thy God hath chosen
21 which the L' hath given thee,
25 is right in the sight of the L'.
26 place which the L' shall choose:
27 upon the altar of the L' thy God:
27 upon the altar of the L' thy God,
28 and right in the sight of the L'
29 the L' thy God shall cut off the
31 not do so unto the L' thy God:
31 for every abomination to the L',

De 13: 3 for the L' your God proveth you,
3 ye love the L' your God with all
4 shall walk after the L' your God,
5 to turn you away from the L'
5 the L' thy God commanded thee
10 to thrust thee away from the L'
12 the L' thy God hath given thee to
16 every whit, for the L' thy God:
17 L' may turn from the fierceness
18 hearken to the voice of the L' thy
18 is right in the eyes of the L' which
14: 1 the children of the L' your God:
2 holy people unto the L' thy God,
2 the L' hath chosen thee to be a
21 holy people unto the L' thy God.
23 shalt eat before the L' thy God,
23 to fear the L' thy God always.
24 L' thy God shall choose to set his
24 the L' thy God hath blessed thee:
25 which the L' thy God shall choose:
26 eat there before the L' thy God,
29 L' thy God may bless thee in all
15: 4 L' shall greatly bless thee in the
4 land which the L' thy God giveth
5 unto the voice of the L' thy God,
6 For the L' thy God blesseth thee,
7 land which the L' thy God giveth
9 cry unto the L' against thee, and
10 L' thy God shall bless thee in all
14 the L' thy God hath blessed thee
15 the L' thy God redeemed thee:
18 L' thy God shall bless thee in all
19 shalt sanctify unto the L' thy God:
20 shalt eat it before the L' thy God
20 place which the L' shall choose,
21 not sacrifice unto the L' thy God.
16: 1 the passover unto the L' thy God:
1 L' thy God brought thee forth out
2 the passover unto the L' thy God,
2 place which the L' shall choose
5 which the L' thy God giveth thee:
6 which the L' thy God shall choose
7 which the L' thy God shall choose:
8 a solemn assembly to the L' thy
10 feast of weeks unto the L' thy God
10 shalt give unto the L' thy God,
10 the L' thy God hath blessed thee:
11 shalt rejoice before the L' thy God,
11 which the L' thy God hath chosen
15 solemn feast unto the L' thy God
15 place which the L' shall choose:
15 the L' thy God shall bless thee in
16 all thy males appear before the L'
16 not appear before the L' empty:
17 to the blessing of the L' thy God
18 which the L' thy God giveth thee,
20 land which the L' thy God giveth
21 unto the altar of the L' thy God,
22 which the L' thy God hateth.
17: 1 not sacrifice unto the L' thy God
1 abomination unto the L' thy God.
2 gates which the L' thy God giveth
2 wickedness in the sight of the L'
8 which the L' thy God shall choose;
10 place which the L' shall choose
12 to minister there before the L' thy
14 land which the L' thy God giveth
15 whom the L' thy God shall choose:
16 forasmuch as the L' hath said
19 may learn to fear the L' his God,
18: 1 offerings of the L' made by fire,
2 the L' is their inheritance, as he
5 L' thy God hath chosen him out
5 to minister in the name of the L',
6 place which the L' shall choose;
7 minister in the name of the L' his
7 which stand there before the L'.
9 land which the L' thy God giveth
12 are an abomination unto the L':
12 L' thy God doth drive them out
13 be perfect with the L' thy God.
14 L' thy God hath not suffered thee
15 L' thy God will raise up unto thee
16 thou desiredst of the L' thy God
16 again the voice of the L' my God,
17 L' said unto me, They have well
21 which the L' hath not spoken?
22 speaketh in the name of the L',
22 which the L' hath not spoken,
19: 1 L' thy God hath cut off the nations
1 whose land the L' thy God giveth
2 L' thy God giveth thee to possess
3 L' thy God giveth thee to inherit,
8 the L' thy God enlarge thy coast,
9 this day, to love the L' thy God,
10 land, which the L' thy God giveth
14 L' thy God giveth thee to possess
17 shall stand before the L', before
20: 1 for the L' thy God is with thee,
4 L' your God is he that goeth with
13 L' thy God hath delivered it into
14 the L' thy God hath given thee.
16 the L' thy God doth give thee for
17 L' thy God hath commanded thee:
18 so should ye sin against the L'
21: 1 land which the L' thy God giveth
5 them the L' thy God hath chosen
5 to bless in the name of the L';
8 Be merciful, O L', unto thy people
9 is right in the sight of the L'.
10 L' thy God hath delivered them
23 the L' thy God giveth thee for an
22: 5 do so are abominations unto the L'
23: 1 into the congregation of the L'.
2 into the congregation of the L';
2 into the congregation of the L'.

De 23: 3 into the congregation of the L';
3 into the congregation of the L'
5 L' thy God would not hearken
5 L' thy God turned the curse into
5 because the L' thy God loved thee.
8 into the congregation of the L'
14 L' thy God walketh in the midst
18 into the house of the L' thy God
18 are abomination unto the L' thy
20 L' thy God may bless thee in all
21 vow a vow unto the L' thy God,
21 L' thy God will surely require it
23 hast vowed unto the L' thy God,
24: 4 is abomination before the L':
4 the L' thy God giveth thee for an
9 the L' thy God did unto Miriam
13 unto thee before the L' thy God.
15 he cry against thee unto the L',
18 L' thy God redeemed thee thence:
19 L' thy God may bless thee in all
25: 15 land which the L' thy God giveth
16 abomination unto the L' thy God.
19 L' thy God hath given thee rest
19 land which the L' thy God giveth
26: 1 land which the L' thy God giveth
2 land that the L' thy God giveth
2 which the L' thy God shall choose
3 I profess this day unto the L' thy
3 country which the L' swear unto
4 before the altar of the L' thy God.
5 and say before the L' thy God,
7 we cried unto the L' God of our
7 L' heard our voice, and looked
8 L' brought us forth out of Egypt
10 which thou, O L', hast given me.
10 shalt set it before the L' thy God,
10 worship before the L' thy God:
11 which the L' thy God hath given
13 shalt say before the L' thy God,
14 to the voice of the L' my God,
16 the L' thy God hath commanded
17 avouched the L' this day to be thy
18 L' hath avouched thee this day to
19 holy people unto the L' thy God,
27: 2, 3 land which the L' thy God giveth
3 L' God of thy fathers...promised
5 build an altar unto the L' thy God,
6 build the altar of the L' thy God
6 offerings thereon unto the L' thy
7 and rejoice before the L' thy God.
9 the people of the L' thy God.
10 obey the voice of the L' thy God,
15 an abomination unto the L',
28: 1 unto the voice of the L' thy God,
1 L' thy God will set thee on high
2 unto the voice of the L' thy God.
7 L' shall cause thine enemies that
8 L' shall command the blessing
8 land which the L' thy God giveth
9 L' shall establish thee an holy
9 keep the commandments of the L'
10 art called by the name of the L';
11 L' shall make thee plenteous in
11 land which the L' sware unto thy
12 L' shall open unto thee his good
13 the L' shall make thee the head,
13 unto commandments of the L' thy
15 unto the voice of the L' thy God,
20 L' shall send upon thee cursing,
21 The L' shall make the pestilence
22 The L' shall smite thee with a
24 L' shall make the rain of thy land
25 L' shall cause thee to be smitten
27 L' will smite thee with the botch
28 L' shall smite thee with madness,
35 L' shall smite thee in the knees,
36 L' shall bring thee, and thy king
37 whither the L' shall lead thee.
45 not unto the voice of the L' thy
47 thou servedst not the L' thy God
48 enemies which the L' shall send
49 L' shall bring a nation against
52 the L' thy God hath given thee.
53 the L' thy God hath given thee,
58 fearful name, The L' Thy God;
59 Then the L' will make thy plagues
61 will the L' bring upon thee, until
62 not obey the voice of the L' thy
63 L' rejoiced over you to do you good,
63 L' will rejoice over you to destroy
64 L' shall scatter thee among all
65 L' shall give thee...a trembling
68 the L' shall bring thee into Egypt
29: 1 the L' commanded Moses to make
2 seen all that the L' did before your
4 L' hath not given you an heart to
6 know that I am the L' your God.
10 of you before the L' your God;
12 covenant with the L' thy God,
12 the L' thy God maketh with thee
15, 18 this day before the L' our God,
20 The L' will not spare him, but
20 anger of the L' and his jealousy
20 L' shall blot out his name from
21 L' shall separate him unto evil
22 sicknesses which the L' hath laid
23 the L' overthrew in his anger,
24 the L' done thus unto the land?
25 forsaken the covenant of the L'
27 the anger of the L' was kindled
28 L' rooted them out of their land
29 belong unto the L' our God:
30: 1 the L' thy God hath driven thee,
2 shalt return unto the L' thy God,
3 L' thy God will turn thy captivity,
3 L' thy God hath scattered thee.

De 30: 4 will the *L'* thy God gather thee,
5 *L'* thy God will bring thee into
6 *L'* thy God will circumcise thine
6 to love the *L'* thy God with all
7 the *L'* thy God will put all these
8 and obey the voice of the *L'*,
9 the *L'* thy God will make thee
9 *L'* will again rejoice over thee
10 unto the voice of the *L'* thy God,
10 turn unto the *L'* thy God with all
16 this day to love the *L'* thy God,
16 *L'* thy God shall bless thee in the
20 thou mayest love the *L'* thy God,
20 in the land which the *L'* sware
31: 2 the *L'* hath said unto me, Thou
3 The *L'* thy God, he will go over
3 before thee, as the *L'* hath said,
4 *L'* shall do unto them as he did
5 *L'* shall give them up before your
6 the *L'* thy God, he it is that doth
7 land which the *L'* hath sworn
8 And the *L'*, he it is that doth go
9 the ark of the covenant of the *L'*,
11 is come to appear before the *L'*
12 learn, and fear the *L'* your God,
13 learn to fear the *L'* your God, as
14 the *L'* said unto Moses, Behold,
15 the *L'* appeared in the tabernacle
16 the *L'* said unto Moses, Behold,
25 the ark of the covenant of the *L'*,
26 the ark of the covenant of the *L'*
27 been rebellious against the *L'*;
29 will do evil in the sight of the *L'*,
32: 3 will publish the name of the *L'*:
6 Do ye thus requite the *L'*, O
12 So the *L'* alone did lead him, and
19 when the *L'* saw it, he abhorred
27 and the *L'* hath not done all this.
30 and the *L'* hath shut them up?
36 For the *L'* shall judge his people,
48 And the *L'* spake unto Moses that
33: 2 he said, The *L'* came from Sinai,
7 Hear, *L'*, the voice of Judah, and
11 Bless, *L'*, his substance, and
12 The beloved of the *L'* shall dwell
12 the *L'* shall cover him all the day
13 Blessed of the *L'* be his land, for
21 he executed the justice of the *L'*,
23 full with the blessing of the *L'*,
29 O people saved by the *L'*, the
34: 1 the *L'* shewed him all the land of
4 And the *L'* said unto him, This is
5 the servant of the *L'* died there
5 according to the word of the *L'*.
9 did as the *L'* commanded Moses.
10 whom the *L'* knew face to face,
11 which the *L'* sent him to do in
Jos 1: 1 death of Moses...servant of the *L'*,
1 *L'* spake unto Joshua the son of
9 for the *L'* thy God is with thee
11 *L'* your God giveth you to possess
13 servant of the *L'* commanded you,
13 *L'* your God hath given you rest,
15 *L'* have given your brethren rest,
15 the land which the *L'* your God
17 only the *L'* thy God be with thee,
2: 9 the *L'* hath given you the land,
10 how the *L'* dried up the water of
11 for the *L'* your God, he is God in
12 you, swear unto me by the *L'*,
14 the *L'* hath given us the land,
24 *L'* hath delivered into our hands
3: 3 the ark of the covenant of the *L'*
5 *L'* will do wonders among you.
7 And the *L'* said unto Joshua,
9 hear the words of the *L'* your
11 the ark of the covenant of the *L'*
13 priests that bear the ark of the *L'*,
13 the *L'* of all the earth, shall rest
17 the ark of the covenant of the *L'*
4: 1 that the *L'* spake unto Joshua,
5 Pass over before the ark of the *L'*
7 the ark of the covenant of the *L'*;
8 as the *L'* spake unto Joshua,
10 finished that the *L'* commanded
11 the ark of the *L'* passed over,
13 for war passed over before the *L'*
14 that day the *L'* magnified Joshua
15 the *L'* spake unto Joshua, saying,
18 the ark of the covenant of the *L'*
23 *L'* your God dried up the waters
23 *L'* your God did to the Red sea,
24 might know the hand of the *L'*,
24 fear the *L'* your God for ever.
5: 1 the *L'* had dried up the waters of
2 time the *L'* said unto Joshua,
6 obeyed not the voice of the *L'*:
6 *L'* sware that he would not shew
6 the *L'* sware unto their fathers
9 the *L'* said unto Joshua, This
14 as captain of the host of the *L'*
14 What saith my *l'* unto his servant?
6: 2 the *L'* said unto Joshua, See, I
6 horns before the ark of the *L'*.
7 pass on before the ark of the *L'*.
8 horns passed on before the *L'*,
8 the ark of the covenant of the *L'*
11 So the ark of the *L'* compassed
12 priests took up the ark of the *L'*.
13 before the ark of the *L'* went on
13 came after the ark of the *L'*,
16 the *L'* hath given you the city.
17 and all that are therein, to the *L'*:
19 iron, are consecrated unto the *L'*:
19 come into the treasury of the *L'*.
24 treasury of the house of the *L'*.

Jos 6: 26 Cursed be the man before the *L'*,
27 So the *L'* was with Joshua; and
7: 1 the anger of the *L'* was kindled
6 face before the ark of the *L'* until
7 And Joshua said, Alas, O *L'* God,
8 O *L'*, what shall I say, when Israel
10 the *L'* said unto Joshua, Get thee
13 thus saith the *L'* God of Israel,
14 that the tribe which the *L'* taketh
14 the family which the *L'* shall take
14 household which the *L'* shall take
15 transgressed the covenant of the *L'*,
19 glory to the *L'* God of Israel,
20 have sinned against the *L'* God
23 and laid them out before the *L'*.
25 the *L'* shall trouble thee this day.
26 *L'* turned from the fierceness of
8: 1 the *L'* said unto Joshua, Fear not,
7 *L'* your God will deliver it into
8 to the commandment of the *L'*
18 the *L'* said unto Joshua, Stretch
27 unto the word of the *L'* which he
30 built an altar unto the *L'* God
31 the servant of the *L'* commanded
31 burnt offerings unto the *L'*,
33 the ark of the covenant of the *L'*,
33 servant of the *L'* had commanded
9: 9 of the name of the *L'* thy God:
14 counsel at the mouth of the *L'*.
18, 19 sworn unto them by the *L'* God
24 that the *L'* thy God commanded
27 and for the altar of the *L'*, even
10: 8 And the *L'* said unto Joshua, Fear
10 *L'* discomfited them before Israel,
11 *L'* cast down great stones from
12 Then spake Joshua to the *L'* in
12 the *L'* delivered up the Amorites
14 *L'* hearkened unto the voice of a
14 man: for the *L'* fought for Israel.
19 *L'* your God hath delivered them
25 shall the *L'* do to all your enemies
30 the *L'* delivered it also, and the
32 *L'* delivered Lachish into the hand
40 the *L'* God of Israel commanded.
42 *L'* God of Israel fought for Israel.
11: 6 the *L'* said unto Joshua, Be not
8 *L'* delivered them into the hand
9 did unto them as the *L'* bade him:
12 the servant of the *L'* commanded.
15 As the *L'* commanded Moses his
15 all that the *L'* commanded Moses.
20 of the *L'* to harden their hearts,
20 as the *L'* commanded Moses.
23 all that the *L'* said unto Moses;
12: 6 Moses the servant of the *L'* and
6 the servant of the *L'* gave it for a
13: 1 the *L'* said unto him, Thou art old
8 the servant of the *L'* gave them;
14 sacrifices of the *L'* God of Israel
33 the *L'* God of Israel was their
14: 2 the *L'* commanded by the hand of
5 As the *L'* commanded Moses, so
6 thing that the *L'* said unto Moses
7 servant of the *L'* sent me from
8 I wholly followed the *L'* my God.
9 wholly followed the *L'* my God.
10 behold, the *L'* hath kept me alive,
10 *L'* spake this word unto Moses,
12 whereof the *L'* spake in that day;
12 if so be the *L'* will be with me,
12 to drive them out, as the *L'* said.
14 followed the *L'* God of Israel.
15: 13 to the commandment of the *L'* to
17: 4 *L'* commanded Moses to give us
4 to the commandment of the *L'*
14 the *L'* hath blessed me hitherto?
18: 3 *L'* God of your fathers hath given
6 cast lots for you here before the *L'*
7 the priesthood of the *L'* is their
7 Moses the servant of the *L'* gave
8 cast lots for you before the *L'* in
10 for them in Shiloh before the *L'*:
19: 50 According to the word of the *L'*
51 by lot in Shiloh before the *L'*,
20: 1 The *L'* also spake unto Joshua,
21: 2 *L'* commanded by the hand of
3 at the commandment of the *L'*,
8 *L'* commanded by the hand of
43 *L'* gave unto Israel all the land
44 *L'* gave them rest round about,
44 the *L'* delivered all their enemies
45 *L'* had spoken unto the house of
22: 2 servant of the *L'* commanded you,
3 of the commandment of the *L'*
4 *L'* your God hath given rest unto
4 the servant of the *L'* gave you on
5 the servant of the *L'* charged you,
5 to love the *L'* your God, and to
9 the word of the *L'* by the hand of
16 the whole congregation of the *L'*,
16 this day from following the *L'*,
16 rebel this day against the *L'*?
17 in the congregation of the *L'*,
18 this day from following the *L'*?
18 ye rebel to day against the *L'*,
19 land of the possession of the *L'*,
19 but rebel not against the *L'*, nor
19 beside the altar of the *L'* our God.
22 The *L'* God of gods, the *L'* God
22 in transgression against the *L'*,
23 to turn from following the *L'*, or
23 let the *L'* himself require it;
24 What have ye to do with the *L'*
25 *L'* hath made Jordan a border
25 of Gad; ye have no part in the *L'*:
25 children cease from fearing the *L'*.

Jos 22: 27 do the service of the *L'* before
27 come, Ye have no part in the *L'*.
28 the pattern of the altar of the *L'*,
29 we should rebel against the *L'*,
29 this day from following the *L'*,
29 beside the altar of the *L'* our God
31 perceive that the *L'* is among us,
31 this trespass against the *L'*:
31 of Israel out of the hand of the *L'*.
34 between us that the *L'* is God.
23: 1 the *L'* had given rest unto Israel
3 all that the *L'* your God hath done
3 the *L'* your God is he that hath
5 And the *L'* your God, he shall
5 *L'* your God hath promised unto
8 But cleave unto the *L'* your God,
9 *L'* hath driven out from before
10 for the *L'* your God, he is that
11 that ye love the *L'* your God.
13 *L'* your God will no more drive
13 land which the *L'* your God hath
14 things which the *L'* your God
15 which the *L'* your God promised
15 *L'* bring upon you all evil things,
15 land which the *L'* your God hath
16 the covenant of the *L'* your God,
16 the anger of the *L'* be kindled
24: 2 Thus saith the *L'* God of Israel,
7 And when they cried unto the *L'*,
14 Now therefore fear the *L'*, and
14 in Egypt; and serve ye the *L'*.
15 evil unto you to serve the *L'*,
15 my house, we will serve the *L'*.
16 that we should forsake the *L'*, to
17 For the *L'* our God, he it is that
18 *L'* drave out from before us all
18 will we also serve the *L'*; for he
19 people, Ye cannot serve the *L'*:
20 If ye forsake the *L'*, and serve
21 Nay; but we will serve the *L'*.
22 that ye have chosen you the *L'*,
23 incline your heart unto the *L'* God
24 The *L'* our God will we serve,
26 was by the sanctuary of the *L'*.
27 hath heard all the words of the *L'*
29 son of Nun, the servant of the *L'*,
31 Israel served the *L'* all the days
31 had known all the works of the *L'*,
J'g 1: 1 children of Israel asked the *L'*,
2 the *L'* said, Judah shall go up:
4 the *L'* delivered the Canaanites
19 And the *L'* was with Judah; and
22 and the *L'* was with them.
2: 1 an angel of the *L'* came up from
4 the angel of the *L'* spake these
5 they sacrificed there unto the *L'*.
7 And the people served the *L'* all
7 seen all the great works of the *L'*,
8 son of Nun, the servant of the *L'*,
10 them, which knew not the *L'*, nor
11 did evil in the sight of the *L'*,
12 they forsook the *L'* God of their
12 and provoked the *L'* to anger.
13 forsook the *L'*, and served Baal
14 anger of the *L'* was hot against
15 hand of the *L'* was against them
15 *L'* had said,...as the *L'* had sworn
16 the *L'* raised up judges, which
17 the commandments of the *L'*;
18 the *L'* raised them up judges,
18 then the *L'* was with the judge,
18 repented the *L'* because of their
20 anger of the *L'* was hot against
22 will keep the way of the *L'* to
23 Therefore the *L'* left those nations,
3: 1 are the nations which the *L'* left,
4 the commandments of the *L'*,
7 did evil in the sight of the *L'*,
7 and forgat the *L'* their God, and
8 anger of the *L'* was hot against
9 children of Israel cried unto the *L'*
9 *L'* raised up a deliverer to the
10 Spirit of the *L'* came upon him,
10 *L'* delivered Chushan-rishathaim.
12 evil again in the sight of the *L'*:
12 *L'* strengthened Eglon the king
12 done evil in the sight of the *L'*.
15 children of Israel cried unto the *L'*
15 the *L'* raised them up a deliverer,
25 their *l'* was fallen down dead on
28 *L'* hath delivered your enemies
4: 1 did evil in the sight of the *L'*,
2 the *L'* sold them into the hand of
3 children of Israel cried unto the *L'*
6 the *L'* God of Israel commanded,
9 *L'* shall sell Sisera into the hand
14 the *L'* hath delivered Sisera into
14 is not the *L'* gone out before thee?
15 the *L'* discomfited Sisera, and all
18 him, Turn in, my *l'*, turn in to me;
5: 2 Praise ye the *L'* for the avenging
3 I, even I, will sing unto the *L'*;
3 I will sing praise to the *L'* God of
4 *L'*, when thou wentest out of Seir,
5 mountains melted...before the *L'*,
5 from before the *L'* God of Israel.
9 among the people. Bless ye the *L'*.
11 the righteous acts of the *L'*,
11 people of the *L'* go down to the
13 *L'* made me have dominion over
23 Meroz, said the angel of the *L'*,
23 came not to the help of the *L'*,
23 help of the *L'* against the mighty.
31 all thine enemies perish, O *L'*:
6: 1 did evil in the sight of the *L'*:
1 *L'* delivered them into the hand

J'g 6: 6 children of Israel cried unto the L'.
7 children of Israel cried unto the L'
8 L' sent a prophet unto the children
8 Thus saith the L' God of Israel,
10 unto you, I am the L' your God;
11 there came an angel of the L',
12 the angel of the L' appeared unto
12 The L' is with thee, thou mighty
13 Gideon said unto him, Oh my L',
13 if the L' be with us, why then is
13 the L' bring us up from Egypt?
13 now the L' hath forsaken us, and
14 the L' looked upon him, and said,
15 Oh my L', wherewith shall I save
16 And the L' said unto him, Surely
21 the angel of the L' put forth the
21 Then the angel of the L' departed
22 that he was an angel of the L',
22 Gideon said, Alas, O L' God! for
22 seen an angel of the L' face to
23 the L' said unto him, Peace be
24 build an altar there unto the L',
25 that the L' said unto him, Take
26 build an altar unto the L' thy God
27 did as the L' had said unto him:
34 Spirit of the L' came upon Gideon,
7: 2, 4 the L' said unto Gideon, The
5 the L' said unto Gideon, Every
7 the L' said unto Gideon, By the
9 the L' said unto him, Arise, get
15 L' hath delivered into your hand
18 and say, The sword of the L', and
20 they cried, The sword of the L',
22 L' set every man's sword against
8: 7 when the L' hath delivered Zebah
19 as the L' liveth, if ye had saved
23 you: the L' shall rule over you.
34 of Israel remembered not the L'
10: 6 evil again in the sight of the L',
6 Philistines, and forsook the L',
7 anger of the L' was hot against
10 children of Israel cried unto the L',
11 the L' said unto the children of
15 children of Israel said unto the L',
16 among them, and served the L':
11: 9 the L' deliver them before me,
10 The L' be witness between us,
11 uttered all his words before the L'
21 L' God of Israel delivered Sihon
23 L' God of Israel hath dispossessed
24 the L' our God shall drive out
27 the L' the Judge be judge this day
29 the Spirit of the L' came upon
30 Jephthah vowed a vow unto the L',
32 L' delivered them into his hands.
35 opened my mouth unto the L',
36 opened thy mouth unto the L',
36 as the L' hath taken vengeance
12: 3 L' delivered them into my hand:
13: 1 evil again in the sight of the L';
1 L' delivered them into the hand
3 angel of the L' appeared unto
8 Then Manoah entreated the L',
8 O my L', let the man of God which
13 angel of the L' said unto Manoah,
15 said unto the angel of the L',
16 angel of the L' said unto Manoah,
16 thou must offer it unto the L'.
16 that he was an angel of the L'.
17 said unto the angel of the L',
18 the angel of the L' said unto him,
19 offered it upon a rock unto the L':
20 the angel of the L' ascended in
21 the angel of the L' did no more
21 that he was an angel of the L'.
23 If the L' were pleased to kill us,
24 grew, and the L' blessed him.
25 the Spirit of the L' began to move
14: 4 knew not that it was of the L',
6 the Spirit of the L' came mightily
19 Spirit of the L' came upon him,
15: 14 the Spirit of the L' came mightily
18 sore athirst, and called on the L',
16: 20 wist not that the L' was departed
28 Samson called unto the L', and
28 O L' God, remember me, I pray
17: 2 said, Blessed be thou of the L',
3 dedicated the silver unto the L'
13 I that the L' will do me good,
18: 6 peace: before the L' is your way
19: 18 now going to the house of the L';
26 the man's house where her l' was,
27 And her l' rose up in the morning,
20: 1 Gilead, unto the L' in Mizpeh.
18 And the L' said, Judah shall go
23 went up and wept before the L'
23 even, and asked counsel of the L',
23 the L' said, Go up against him.)
26 and sat there before the L', and
26 and peace offerings before the L'.
27 of Israel enquired of the L',
28 And the L' said, Go up; for to
35 L' smote Benjamin before Israel:
21: 3 O L' God of Israel, Why is this
5 the congregation unto the L'?
5 came not up to the L' to Mizpeh,
7 seeing we have sworn by the L'
8 came not up to Mizpeh to the L'?
15 the L' had made a breach in the
19 there is a feast of the L' in Shiloh
Ru 1: 6 L' had visited his people in giving
8 the L' deal kindly with you, as ye
9 L' grant you that ye may find rest,
13 the hand of the L' is gone out
17 the L' do so to me, and more also,
21 L' hath brought me home again
Ru 1: 21 seeing the L'...testified against
2: 4 the reapers, The L' be with you.
4 answered him, The L' bless thee.
12 The L' recompense thy work,
12 reward be given thee of the L'
13 me find favour in thy sight, my l';
20 Blessed be he of the L', who hath
3: 10 Blessed be thou of the L' my
13 kinsman to thee, as the L' liveth:
4: 11 L' make the woman that is come
12 seed which the L' shall give thee
13 the L' gave her conception, and
14 Blessed be the L', which hath not
1Sa 1: 3 to sacrifice unto the L' of hosts
3 Phinehas, the priests of the L',
5, 6 the L' had shut up her womb.
7 went up to the house of the L',
9 by a post of the temple of the L'.
10 and prayed unto the L', and wept
11 O L' of hosts, if thou wilt indeed
11 give him unto the L' all the days
12 continued praying before the L',
15 answered and said, No, my l', I am
15 poured out my soul before the L'.
19 and worshipped before the L',
19 wife; and the L' remembered her.
20 I have asked him of the L'.
21 up to offer unto the L' the yearly
22 that he may appear before the L',
23 only the L' establish his word.
24 the house of the L' in Shiloh:
26 said, Oh my l', as thy soul liveth,
26 my l', I am the woman that stood
26 thee here, praying unto the L'.
27 the L' hath given me my petition
28 also I have lent him to the L';
28 liveth he shall be lent to the L'.
28 And he worshipped the L' there.
2: 1 said, My heart rejoiceth in the L',
1 mine horn is exalted in the L';
2 There is none holy as the L';
3 for the L' is a God of knowledge,
6 The L' killeth, and maketh alive:
7 The L' maketh poor, and maketh
10 adversaries of the L' shall be
10 the L' shall judge the ends of the
11 the child did minister unto the L'
12 of Belial; they knew not the L'.
17 men was very great before the L':
17 abhorred the offering of the L'.
18 Samuel ministered before the L',
20 L' give thee seed of this woman
20 the loan which is lent to the L'.
21 the L' visited Hannah, so that
21 child Samuel grew before the L'.
25 but if a man sin against the L',
25 because the L' would slay them.
26 was in favour both with the L',
27 Thus saith the L', Did I plainly
30 the L' God of Israel saith, I said
30 but now the L' saith, Be it far
3: 1 Samuel ministered unto the L'
1 the word of the L' was precious
3 went out in the temple of the L',
4 the L' called Samuel: and he
6 the L' called yet again, Samuel.
7 Samuel did not yet know the L',
7 the word of the L' yet revealed
8 L' called Samuel again the third
8 perceived that the L' had called
9 that thou shalt say, Speak, L';
10 And the L' came, and stood, and
11 the L' said to Samuel, Behold,
15 the doors of the house of the L'.
17 is the thing that the L' hath said
18 It is the L': let him do what
19 grew, and the L' was with him,
20 to be a prophet of the L'.
21 the L' appeared again in Shiloh:
21 L' revealed himself to Samuel
21 in Shiloh by the word of the L'.
4: 3 hath the L' smitten us to day
3, 4, 5 ark of the covenant of the L'
6 that the ark of the L' was come
5: 3 the earth before the ark of the L'.
4 ground before the ark of the L';
6 hand of the L' was heavy upon
9 hand of the L' was against the city
6: 1 ark of the L' was in the country
2 shall we do to the ark of the L'?
8 take the ark of the L', and lay it
11 laid the ark of the L' upon the cart,
14 kine a burnt offering unto the L'.
15 Levites took...the ark of the L',
15 offered...the same day unto the L'.
17 a trespass offering unto the L';
18 they set down the ark of the L':
19 had looked into the ark of the L',
19 L' had smitten many of the people
20 to stand before this holy L' God?
21 brought again the ark of the L';
7: 1 and fetched up the ark of the L',
1 his son to keep the ark of the L'.
2 of Israel lamented after the L'.
3 return unto the L' with all your
3 prepare your hearts unto the L',
4 Ashtaroth, and served the L' only.
5 I will pray for you unto the L'.
6 and poured it out before the L',
6 We have sinned against the L'.
8 Cease not to cry unto the L' our
9 burnt offering wholly unto the L':
9 and Samuel cried unto the L'
9 for Israel; and the L' heard him.
10 L' thundered with a great thunder
12 Hitherto hath the L' helped us.
1Sa 7: 13 hand of the L' was against the
17 there he built an altar unto the L'.
8: 6 And Samuel prayed unto the L'.
7 the L' said unto Samuel, Hearken
10 Samuel told all the words of the L'
18 L' will not hear you in that day.
21 rehearsed...in the ears of the L'.
22 the L' said to Samuel, Hearken
9: 15 L' had told Samuel in his ear a
17 L' said unto him, Behold the man
10: 1 because the L' hath anointed thee
6 Spirit of the L' will come upon
17 together unto the L' to Mizpeh;
18 Thus saith the L' God of Israel, I
19 present yourselves before the L'
22 they enquired of the L' further,
22 L' answered, Behold, he hath hid
24 him whom the L' hath chosen,
25 book, and laid it up before the L'.
11: 7 fear of the L' fell on the people,
13 the L' hath wrought salvation in
15 made Saul king before the L' in
15 of peace offerings before the L';
12: 3 witness against me before the L',
5 The L' is witness against you,
6 It is the L' that advanced Moses
7 may reason with you before the L'
7 of all the righteous acts of the L',
8 your fathers cried unto the L',
8 then the L' sent Moses and Aaron,
9 when they forgat the L' their God,
10 they cried unto the L', and said,
10 because we have forsaken the L',
11 the L' sent Jerubbaal, and Bedan,
12 the L' your God was your king.
13 the L' hath set a king over you.
14 If ye will fear the L', and serve
14 the commandment of the L',
14 continue following the L' your
15 will not obey the voice of the L',
15 the commandment of the L',
15 the hand of the L' be against you,
16 the L' will do before your eyes.
17 I will call unto the L', and he shall
17 have done in the sight of the L',
18 So Samuel called unto the L';
18 and the L' sent thunder and rain
18 greatly feared the L' and Samuel.
19 Pray for thy servants unto the L'
20 not aside from following the L',
20 serve the L' with all your heart;
22 L' will not forsake his people for
22 pleased the L' to make you his
23 that I should sin against the L'
24 Only fear the L', and serve him in
13: 12 made supplication unto the L':
13 kept the commandment of the L'
13 L' have established thy kingdom
14 L' hath sought him a man after
14 L'...commanded him to be captain
14 which the L' commanded thee.
14: 6 be that the L' will work for us:
6 is no restraint to the L' to save
10 L' hath delivered them into our
12 L' hath delivered them into the
23 So the L' saved Israel that day:
33 people sin against the L', in that
34 sin not against the L' in eating
35 Saul built an altar unto the L':
35 first altar that he built unto the L'.
39 For, as the L' liveth, which saveth
41 Saul said unto the L' God of Israel,
45 as the L' liveth, there shall not
15: 1 L' sent me to anoint thee to be
1 the voice of the words of the L'.
2 saith the L' of hosts, I remember
10 the word of the L' unto Samuel,
11 and he cried unto the L' all night.
13 him, Blessed be thou of the L':
13 the commandment of the L'.
15 to sacrifice unto the L' thy God;
16 what the L' hath said to me this
17 L' anointed thee king over Israel?
18 the L' sent thee on a journey, and
19 thou not obey the voice of the L',
19 didst evil in the sight of the L'?
20 I have obeyed the voice of the L',
20 gone the way which the L' sent me,
21 to sacrifice unto the L' thy God in
22 the L' as great delight in burnt
22 as in obeying the voice of the L'?
23 hast rejected the word of the L',
24 the commandment of the L',
25 with me, that I may worship the L'.
26 hast rejected the word of the L',
26 L' hath rejected thee from being
28 L' hath rent the kingdom of Israel
30 that I may worship the L' thy God.
31 Saul; and Saul worshipped the L'.
33 hewed Agag in pieces before the L'
35 L' repented that he had made Saul
16: 1 the L' said unto Samuel, How long
2 And the L' said, Take an heifer,
2 I am come to sacrifice to the L',
4 did that which the L' spake,
5 am come to sacrifice unto the L':
7 L' said unto Samuel, Look not on
7 L' seeth not as man seeth; for
7 but the L' looketh on the heart.
8, 9 Neither hath the L' chosen this.
10 The L' hath not chosen these.
12 the L' said, Arise, anoint him:
13 Spirit of the L' came upon David
14 Spirit of the L' departed from Saul,
14 an evil spirit from the L' troubled
16 our l' now command thy servants,

1Sa 16:18 person, and the L· is with him.
17:37 L· that delivered me out of the paw
37 Go, and the L· be with thee.
45 in the name of the L· of hosts,
46 This day will the L· deliver thee
47 the L· saveth not with sword and
18:12 because the L· was with him, and
14 ways; and the L· was with him.
28 knew that the L· was with David,
19: 5 L· wrought a great salvation for
6 As the L· liveth, he shall not be
9 evil spirit from the L· was upon
20: 3 as the L· liveth, and as thy soul
8 into a covenant of the L· with thee.
12 unto David, O L· God of Israel,
13 The L· do so and much more to
13 L· be with thee, as he hath been
14 shew me the kindness of the L·,
15 L· hath cut off...enemies of David
16 Let the L· even require it at the
21 and no hurt; as the L· liveth.
22 for the L· hath sent thee away.
23 L· be between thee and me for
42 both of us in the name of the L·,
42 The L· be between me and thee,
21: 6 that was taken from before the L·,
7 that day, detained before the L·;
22:10 he enquired of the L· for him,
12 And he answered, Here I am, my l·.
17 and slay the priests of the L·;
17 to fall upon the priests of the L·.
23: 2 David enquired of the L·, saying,
2 the L· said unto David, Go, and
4 David enquired of the L· yet
4 the L· answered him and said,
10 O L· God of Israel, thy servant
11 O L· God of Israel, I beseech thee,
11 the L· said, He will come down.
12 And the L· said, They will deliver
18 made a covenant before the L·:
21 Saul said, Blessed be ye of the L·;
24: 4 the day of which the L· said unto
6 L· forbid that I should do this
6 he is the anointed of the L·.
8 after Saul, saying, My l· the king.
10 the L· had delivered thee to day
10 put forth mine hand against my l·;
12 L· judge between me and thee,
12 and the L· avenge me of thee: but
15 The L· therefore be judge, and
18 L· had delivered me into thine
19 L· reward thee good for that thou
21 now therefore unto me by the L·,
25:24 Upon me, my l·, upon me let this
25 Let not my l·, I pray thee, regard
25 saw not the young men of my l·,
26 Now therefore, my l·, as the
26 as the L· liveth, and as thy soul
26 the L· hath withholden thee from
26 they that seek evil to my l·, be as
27 handmaid hath brought unto my l·,
27 the young men that follow my l·.
28 handmaid: for the L· will
28 certainly make my l· a sure house;
28 because my l· fighteth the battles
28 fighteth the battles of the L·, and
29 but the soul of my l· shall be bound
29 bundle of life with the L· thy God;
30 pass, when the L· shall have done
30 done to my l· according to all the
31 thee, nor offence of heart unto my l·,
31 or that my l· hath avenged himself:
31 when the L· shall have dealt well
31 have dealt well with my l·, then
32 Blessed be the L· God of Israel,
34 deed, as the L· God of Israel liveth,
38 that the L· smote Nabal, that he
39 said, Blessed be the L·, that hath
39 L· hath returned the wickedness
41 the feet of the servants of my l·.
26:10 said furthermore, As the L· liveth,
10 the L· shall smite him; or his day
11 L· forbid that I should stretch
12 deep sleep from the L· was fallen
15 hast thou not kept thy l· the king?
15 people in to destroy the king thy l·.
16 As the L· liveth, ye are worthy to
17 David said, It is my voice, my l·, O
18 doth my l· thus pursue after his
19 my l· the king hear the words of his
19 L· have stirred thee up against
19 men, cursed be they before the L·;
19 abiding in...inheritance of the L·,
20 earth before the face of the L·:
23 The L· render to every man his
23 L· delivered thee into my hand
24 much set by in the eyes of the L·,
28: 6 And when Saul enquired of the L·,
6 the L· answered him not, neither
10 And Saul sware to her by the L·,
10 As the L· liveth, there shall no
16 the L· is departed from thee, and
17 L· hath done to him, as he spake
17 L· hath rent the kingdom out of
18 obeyedst not the voice of the L·,
18 the L· done this thing unto thee
19 the L· will also deliver Israel with
19 L· also shall deliver the host of
29: 6 Surely, as the L· liveth, thou hast
8 the enemies of my l· the king?
30: 6 encouraged himself in the L· his
8 And David enquired at the Lord,
23 that which the L· hath given us,
26 the spoil of the enemies of the L·;
2Sa 1:10 brought them hither unto my l·.
12 and for the people of the L·; and

2Sa 2: 1 that David enquired of the L·,
1 And the L· said unto him, Go up.
5 them, Blessed be ye of the L·,
5 shewed this kindness unto your l·
6 L· shew kindness and truth unto
3: 9 as the L· hath sworn to David,
18 for the L· hath spoken of David,
21 will gather all Israel unto my l·
28 guiltless before the L· for ever
39 L· shall reward the doer of evil
4: 8 thy life; and the L· hath avenged
8 avenged my l· the king this day of
9 them, As the L· liveth, who hath
5: 2 L· said to thee, Thou shalt feed
3 them in Hebron before the L·:
10 the L· God of hosts was with him.
12 L· had established him king over
19 David enquired of the L·, saying,
19 the L· said unto David, Go up:
20 L· hath broken forth upon mine
23 David enquired of the L·, he said,
24 then shall the L· go out before
25 as the L· had commanded him;
6: 2 L· of hosts that dwelleth between
5 house of Israel played before the L·
7 anger of the L· was kindled against
8 L·...made a breach upon Uzzah:
9 David was afraid of the L· that
9 the ark of the L· come to me?
10 not remove the ark of the L· unto
11 the ark of the L· continued in the
11 L· blessed Obed-edom, and all his
12 The L· hath blessed the house of
13 they that bare the ark of the L·
14 David danced before the L· with
15 brought up the ark of the L· with
16 ark of the L· came into the city of
16 leaping and dancing before the L·:
17 they brought in the ark of the L·,
17 and peace offerings before the L·.
18 in the name of the L· of hosts.
21 unto Michal, It was before the L·,
21 me ruler over the people of the L·,
21 therefore will I play before the L·.
7: 1 L· had given him rest round about
3 heart; for the L· is with thee.
4 word of the L· came unto Nathan,
5 Thus saith the L·, Shalt thou
8 Thus saith the L· of hosts, I took
11 L· telleth thee that he will make
18 David in, and sat before the L·,
18 Who am I, O L· God? and what is
19 a small thing in thy sight, O L· God;
19 this the manner of man, O L· God?
20 thou, L· God, knowest thy servant.
22 thou art great, O L· God: for
24 thou, L·, art become their God.
25 O L· God, the word that thou hast
26 L· of hosts is the God over Israel:
27 thou, O L· of hosts, God of Israel,
28 now, O L· God, thou art that God,
29 for thou, O L· God, hast spoken it:
8: 6 L· preserved David whithersoever
11 David did dedicate unto the L·,
14 L· preserved David whithersoever
9:11 to all that my l· the king hath
10: 3 Ammon said unto Hanun their l·,
12 the L· do that which seemeth him
11: 9 house with all the servants of his l·,
11 and my l· Joab, and the servants of
11 servants of my l·, are encamped in
13 on his bed with the servants of his l·,
27 David had done displeased the L·.
12: 1 the L· sent Nathan unto David.
5 As the L· liveth, the man that hath
7 Thus saith the L· God of Israel, I
9 the commandment of the L·,
11 Thus saith the L·, Behold, I will
13 I have sinned against the L·.
13 L· also hath put away thy sin;
14 occasion to the enemies of the L·
15 L· struck the child that Uriah's
20 and came into the house of the L·,
24 Solomon: and the L· loved him.
25 name Jedidiah, because of the L·.
13:32 Let not my l· suppose that they
33 let not my l· the king take the thing
14: 9 My l·, O king, the iniquity be on me,
11 let the king remember the L· thy
11 As the L· liveth, there shall not one
12 speak one word unto my l· the king.
15 to speak of this thing unto my l· the
17 The word of my l· the king shall now
17 so is my l· the king to discern good
17 the L· thy God will be with thee.
18 said, Let my l· the king now speak.
19 As thy soul liveth, my l· the king,
19 that my l· the king hath spoken:
20 and my l· is wise, according to the
22 grace in thy sight, my l·, O king,
15: 7 which I have vowed unto the L·,
8 L· shall bring me again indeed to
8 Jerusalem, then I will serve the L·.
15 my l· the king shall appoint.
21 king, and said, As the L· liveth,
21 and as my l· the king liveth, surely
21 in what place my l· the king shall be,
25 find favour in the eyes of the L·,
31 And David said, O L·, I pray thee,
16: 4 grace in thy sight, my l·, O king.
8 L· hath returned upon thee all
8 L· hath delivered the kingdom into
9 this dead dog curse my l· the king?
10 the L· hath said unto him, Curse
11 for the L· hath bidden him.
12 the L· will look on mine affliction,

2Sa 16:12 the L· will requite me good for his
18 but whom the L·, and this people,
17:14 L·...appointed to defeat the good
14 L· might bring evil upon Absalom.
18:19 L· hath avenged him of his enemies.
28 Blessed be the L· thy God, which
28 their hand against my l· the king.
31 Cushi said, Tidings, my l· the king:
31 L· hath avenged thee this day of
32 The enemies of my l· the king, and
19: 7 I swear by the L·, if thou go not
19 Let not my l· impute iniquity unto
19 my l· the king went out of Jerusalem,
20 to go down to meet my l· the king.
26 My l·, O king, my servant deceived
27 slandered thy servant unto my l· the
27 my l· the king is as an angel of God:
28 but dead men before my l· the king:
30 my l· the king is come again in peace
35 be yet a burden unto my l· the king?
37 let him go over with my l· the king;
20:19 up the inheritance of the L·?
21: 1 and David enquired of the L·:
1 the L· answered, It is for Saul,
3 bless the inheritance of the L·?
6 we will hang them up unto the L·
6 of Saul, whom the L· did choose.
9 them in the hill before the L·:
22: 1 And David spake unto the L· the
1 day that the L· had delivered him
2 L· is my rock, and my fortress,
4 will call on the L·, who is worthy
7 my distress I called upon the L·,
14 The L· thundered from heaven,
16 at the rebuking of the L·,
19 but the L· was my stay.
21 L· rewarded me according to my
22 I have kept the ways of the L·,
25 L· hath recompensed me according
29 For thou art my lamp, O L·:
29 the L· will lighten my darkness.
31 the word of the L· is tried: he is
32 For who is God, save the L·? and
42 even unto the L·, but he answered
47 The L· liveth; and blessed be my
50 I will give thanks unto thee, O L·,
23: 2 The Spirit of the L· spake by me,
10 L· wrought a great victory that
12 the L· wrought a great victory.
16 but poured it out unto the L·.
17 Be it far from me, O L·, that I
24: 1 the anger of the L· was kindled
3 L· thy God add unto the people,
3 eyes of my l· the king may see it:
3 doth my l· the king delight in this
10 David said unto the L·, I have
10 O L·, take away the iniquity of
11 word of the L· came unto...Gad,
12 Thus saith the L·, I offer thee
14 us fall now into the hand of the L·;
15 L· sent a pestilence upon Israel
16 the L· repented him of the evil,
16 the angel of the L· was by the
17 David spake unto the L· when he
18 Go up, rear an altar unto the L·
19 went up as the L· commanded.
21 my l· the king come to his servant?
21 to build an altar unto the L·,
22 Let my l· the king take and offer up
23 king, The L· thy God accept thee.
24 offer burnt offerings unto the L·
25 built there an altar unto the L·,
25 the L· was intreated for the land,
1Ki 1: 2 for my l· the king a young virgin:
2 that my l· the king may get heat.
11 and David our l· knoweth it not?
13 Didst not thou, my l·, O king, swear
17 said unto him, My l·, thou swarest
17 thou swarest by the L· thy God
18 my l· the king, thou knowest it not:
20 my l·, O king, the eyes of all Israel
20 on the throne of my l· the king after
21 when my l· the king shall sleep with
24 Nathan said, My l·, O king, hast thou
27 Is this thing done by my l· the king,
27 on the throne of my l· the king after
29 sware, and said, As the L· liveth,
30 I sware unto thee by the L· God of
31 Let my l· king David live for ever.
33 Take with you the servants of your l·,
36 L· God of...the king say so too.
36 God of my l· the king say so too.
37 As the L· hath been with my
37 hath been with my l· the king,
37 than the throne of my l· king David.
43 l· king David hath made Solomon
47 came to bless our l· king David,
48 Blessed be the L· God of Israel,
2: 3 keep the charge of the L· thy God,
4 L· may continue his word which
8 and I sware to him by the L·,
15 brother's: for it was his from the L·.
23 Solomon sware by the L·, saying,
24 Now therefore, as the L· liveth,
26 thou barest the ark of the L· God
27 from being priest unto the L·;
27 he might fulfil the word of the L·,
28 fled unto the tabernacle of the L·,
29 fled unto the tabernacle of the L·;
30 came to the tabernacle of the L·,
32 L· shall return his blood upon his
33 there be peace for ever from the L·.
38 as my l· the king hath said, so will
42 not make thee to swear by the L·;
43 thou not kept the oath of the L·,
44 L· shall return thy wickedness

1Ki 2:45 established before the L· for ever.
3: 1 house, and the house of the L·,
2 house built unto the name of the L·,
3 Solomon loved the L·, walking in
5 the L· appeared to Solomon in a
7 O L· my God, thou hast made thy
10 And the speech pleased the L·, that
15 the ark of the covenant of the L·,
17 O my l·, I and this woman dwell
26 O my l·, give her the living child,
5: 3 unto the name of the L· his God
3 the L· put them under the soles
4 L· my God hath given me rest on
5 unto the name of the L· my God,
5 as the L· spake unto David my
7 Blessed be the L· this day, which
12 the L· gave Solomon wisdom, as
6: 1 began to build the house of the L·.
2 king Solomon built for the L·,
11 word of the L· came to Solomon,
19 the ark of the covenant of the L·.
37 foundation of the house of the L·
7:12 inner court of the house of the L·,
40 Solomon for the house of the L·:
45 Solomon for the house of the L·,
48 unto the house of the L·:
51 made for the house of the L·.
51 treasures of the house of the L·.
8: 1 the ark of the covenant of the L·
4 they brought up the ark of the L·,
6 the ark of the covenant of the L·
9 when the L· made a covenant
10 cloud filled the house of the L·,
11 glory of the L· had filled the
11 had filled the house of the L·.
12 The L· said that he would dwell
15 Blessed be the L· God of Israel,
17 the name of the L· God of Israel.
18 L· said unto David my father,
20 L· hath performed his word that
20 of Israel, as the L· promised,
20 the name of the L· God of Israel.
21 wherein is the covenant of the L·,
22 stood before the altar of the L·
23 L· God of Israel, there is no God
25 L· God of Israel, keep with thy
28 O L· my God, to hearken unto
44 pray unto the L· toward the city
53 our fathers out of Egypt, O L· God.
54 and supplication unto the L·,
54 from before the altar of the L·,
56 Blessed be the L·, that hath given
57 The L· our God be with us, as he
59 made supplication before the L·,
59 be nigh unto the L· our God day
60 may know that the L· is God,
61 be perfect with the L· our God,
62 offered sacrifice before the L·.
63 which he offered unto the L·,
63 dedicated the house of the L·.
64 was before the house of the L·:
64 altar that was before the L· was
65 before the L· our God, seven days
66 the goodness that the L· had done
9: 1 building of the house of the L·,
2 the L· appeared to Solomon the
3 And the L· said unto him, I have
8 Why hath the L· done this unto
9 they forsook the L· their God,
9 L· brought upon them all this
10 the house of the L·, and the king's
15 for to build the house of the L·,
25 altar which he built unto the L·,
25 the altar that was before the L·.
10: 1 concerning the name of the L·,
5 went up unto the house of the L·;
9 Blessed be the L· thy God, which
9 the L· loved Israel for ever,
12 pillars for the house of the L·,
11: 2 concerning which the L· said
4 not perfect with the L· his God,
6 did evil in the sight of the L·,
6 went not fully after the L·, as did
9 the L· was angry with Solomon,
9 heart was turned from the L· God
10 not that which the L· commanded.
11 the L· said unto Solomon,
14 L· stirred up an adversary unto
23 which fled from his l· Hadadezer
31 for thus saith the L·, the God of
12:15 for the cause was from the L·,
15 which the L· spake by Ahijah the
24 Thus saith the L·, Ye shall not go
24 therefore to the word of the L·,
24 according to the word of the L·.
27 sacrifice in the house of the L· at
27 people turn again unto their l·,
13: 1 Judah by the word of the L· unto
2 the altar in the word of the L·,
2 O altar, altar, thus saith the L·;
3 sign which the L· hath spoken;
5 had given by the word of the L·.
6 now the face of the L· thy God,
6 the man of God besought the L·,
9 charged me by the word of the L·,
17 said to me by the word of the L·,
18 unto me by the word of the L·,
20 the word of the L· came unto the
21 Judah, saying, Thus saith the L·,
21 disobeyed the mouth of the L·,
21 which the L· thy God commanded
22 the which the L· did say unto thee,
26 unto the word of the L·:
26 L· hath delivered him unto the
26 according to the word of the L·,
32 he cried by the word of the L·

1Ki 14: 5 the L· said unto Ahijah, Behold,
7 Thus saith the L· God of Israel,
11 eat: for the L· hath spoken it.
13 some good thing toward the L·
14 L· shall raise him up a king over
15 L· shall smite Israel, as a reed
15 groves, provoking the L· to anger.
18 according to the word of the L·,
21 the city which the L· did choose
22 did evil in the sight of the L·,
24 the nations which the L· cast out
26 treasures of the house of the L·,
28 went into the house of the L·,
15: 3 not perfect with the L· his God,
4 the L· his God give him a lamp
5, 11 was right in the eyes of the L·,
14 heart was perfect with the L· all
15 into the house of the L·, silver,
18 treasures of the house of the L·,
26 he did evil in the sight of the L·,
29 unto the saying of the L·, which
30 provoked the L· God of Israel to
34 he did evil in the sight of the L·,
16: 1 the word of the L· came to Jehu
7 word of the L· against Baasha,
7 that he did in the sight of the L·,
12 according to the word of the L·,
13 provoking the L· God of Israel to
19 doing evil in the sight of the L·,
25 wrought evil in the eyes of the L·,
26 to provoke the L· God of Israel
30 Omri did evil in the sight of the L·
33 provoke the L· God of Israel to
34 according to the word of the L·,
17: 1 As the L· God of Israel liveth,
2 the word of the L· came unto him,
5 according unto the word of the L·:
8 the word of the L· came unto him,
12 As the L· thy God liveth, I have
14 thus saith the L· God of Israel,
14 the day that the L· sendeth rain
16 according to the word of the L·,
20 he cried unto the L·, and said,
20 O L· my God, hast thou also
21 and cried unto the L·, and said,
21 O L· my God, I pray thee, let
22 the L· heard the voice of Elijah;
24 the word of the L· in thy mouth
18: 1 the word of the L· came to Elijah
3 Obadiah feared the L· greatly:
4 cut off the prophets of the L·,
7 said, Art thou that my l· Elijah?
8 go, tell thy l·, Behold, Elijah is
10 As the L· thy God liveth, there
10 whither my l· hath not sent to
11 Go, tell thy l·, Behold, Elijah is
12 Spirit of the L· shall carry thee
12 but I thy servant fear the L· from
13 Was it not told my l· what I did
13 slew the prophets of the L·,
14 Go, tell thy l·, Behold, Elijah is
15 said, As the L· of hosts liveth,
18 the commandments of the L·,
21 if the L· be God, follow him: but
22 only, remain a prophet of the L·;
24 I will call on the name of the L·:
30 repaired the altar of the L· that
31 unto whom the word of the L·
32 an altar in the name of the L·:
36 and said, L· God of Abraham,
37 Hear me, O L·, hear me, that this
37 know that thou art the L· God,
38 Then the fire of the L· fell, and
39 L·, he is the God; the L·, he is the
46 the hand of the L· was on Elijah;
19: 4 now, O L·, take away my life; for
7 the angel of the L· came again
9 the word of the L· came to him,
10 jealous for the L· God of hosts:
11 upon the mount before the L·.
11 the L· passed by, and a great and
11 in pieces the rocks before the L·;
11 but the L· was not in the wind:
11 L· was not in the earthquake:
12 but the L· was not in the fire:
14 jealous for the L· God of hosts:
15 the L· said unto him, Go, return
20: 4 Israel answered and said, My l·,
9 Tell my l· the king, All that thou
13 Thus saith the L·, Hast thou seen
13 thou shalt know that I am the L·.
14 Thus saith the L·, Even by the
28 Thus saith the L·, Because the
28 said, The L· is God of the hills,
28 ye shall know that I am the L·.
35 neighbour in the word of the L·,
36 not obeyed the voice of the L·,
42 Thus saith the L·, Because thou
21: 3 said to Ahab, The L· forbid it me,
17 the word of the L· came to Elijah
19 Thus saith the L·, Hast thou
19 Thus saith the L·, In the place
20 to work evil in the sight of the L·.
23 And of Jezebel also spake the L·,
25 wickedness in the sight of the L·,
26 Amorites, whom the L· cast out
28 the word of the L· came to Elijah
22: 5 thee, at the word of the L· to day.
6 L· shall deliver it into the hand of
7 there not here a prophet of the L·
8 whom we may enquire of the L·:
11 Thus saith the L·, With these
12 L· shall deliver it into the king's
14 Micaiah said, As the L· liveth,
14 what the L· saith unto me, that
15 L· shall deliver it into the hand of

1Ki 22:16 is true in the name of the L·?
17 L· said, These have no master:
19 thou therefore the word of the L·:
19 I saw the L· sitting on his throne,
20 the L· said, Who shall persuade
21 a spirit, and stood before the L·,
22 L· said unto him, Wherewith?
23 L· hath put a lying spirit in the
23 L· hath spoken evil concerning
24 went the Spirit of the L· from me
28 the L· hath not spoken by me.
38 according unto the word of the L·
43 was right in the eyes of the L·:
52 he did evil in the sight of the L·,
53 and provoked to anger the L· God
2Ki 1: 3 angel of the L· said to Elijah the
4 thus saith the L·, Thou shalt not
6 thus saith the L·, Is it not because
15 angel of the L· said unto Elijah,
16 Thus saith the L·, Forasmuch as
17 according to the word of the L·
2: 1 the L· would take up Elijah into
2 for the L· hath sent me to Beth-el.
2 said unto him, As the L· liveth,
3 the L· will take away thy master
4 for the L· hath sent me to Jericho.
4 said, As the L· liveth, and as thy
5 the L· will take away thy master
6 for the L· hath sent me to Jordan.
6 said, As the L· liveth, and as thy
14 Where is the L· God of Elijah?
16 Spirit of the L· hath taken him
19 this city is pleasant, as my l· seeth:
21 Thus saith the L·, I have healed
24 cursed them in the name of the L·.
3: 2 wrought evil in the sight of the L·;
10 L· hath called these three kings
11 there not here a prophet of the L·,
11 we may enquire of the L· by him?
12 The word of the L· is with him.
13 L· hath called these three kings
14 As the L· of hosts liveth, before
15 hand of the L· came upon him.
16 saith the L·, Make this valley
17 For thus saith the L·, Ye shall not
18 light thing in the sight of the L·:
4: 1 that thy servant did fear the L·:
16 said, Nay, my l·, thou man of God,
27 the L· hath hid it from me, and
28 said, Did I desire a son of my l·?
30 the child said, As the L· liveth,
33 twain, and prayed unto the L·.
43 thus saith the L·, They shall eat,
44 according to the word of the L·.
5: 1 the L· had given deliverance unto
3 God my l· were with the prophet
4 one went in, and told his l·, saying,
11 and call on the name of the L·
16 As the L· liveth, before whom I
17 unto other gods, but unto the L·.
18 thing the L· pardon thy servant,
18 the L· pardon thy servant in this
20 as the L· liveth, I will run after
6:12 servants said, None, my l·, O king:
17 L·, I pray thee, open his eyes,
17 L· opened the eyes of the young
18 Elisha prayed unto the L·, and
20 L·, open the eyes of these men,
20 And the L· opened their eyes, and
26 him, saying, Help, my l·, O king.
27 said, If the L· do not help thee,
33 said, Behold, this evil is of the L·;
33 I wait for the L· any longer?
7: 1 said, Hear ye the word of the L·;
1 Thus saith the L·, To morrow
2 l· on whose hand the king leaned
2 if the L· would make windows in
6 L· had made the host of Syrians
16 according to the word of the L·.
17 king appointed the l· on whose
19 that l· answered the man of God,
19 if the L· should make windows in
8: 1 the L· hath called for a famine;
5 Gehazi said, My l·, O king, this is
8 enquire of the L· by him, saying,
10 L· hath shewed me that he shall
12 Hazael said, Why weepeth my l·?
13 The L· hath shewed me that thou
18 he did evil in the sight of the L·.
19 L· would not destroy Judah for
27 and did evil in the sight of the L·,
9: 3 saith the L·, I have anointed
6 Thus saith the L· God of Israel,
6 king over the people of the L·,
7 blood of all the servants of the L·,
11 came forth to the servants of his l·:
12 Thus said the L·, I have anointed
25 the L· laid this burden upon him;
26 the blood of his sons, saith the L·;
26 thee in this plat, saith the L·.
26 according to the word of the L·.
36 This is the word of the L·, which
10:10 nothing of the word of the L·,
10 L· spake concerning the house of
10 L· hath done that which he spake
16 me, and see my zeal for the L·.
17 according to the saying of the L·,
23 none of the servants of the L·,
30 the L· said unto Jehu, Because
31 to walk in the law of the L· God
32 the L· began to cut Israel short:
11: 3 hid in the house of the L· six years.
4 to him into the house of the L·,
4 of them in the house of the L·,
7 the watch of the house of the L·
10 that were in the temple of the L·.

2Ki 11: 13 people into the temple of the *L*.
15 not be slain in the house of the *L*.
17 covenant between the *L* and the
18 officers over the house of the *L*.
19 the king from the house of the *L*.
12: 2 was right in the sight of the *L* all
4 brought into the house of the *L*.
4 to bring into the house of the *L*.
9 cometh into the house of the *L*:
9 brought into the house of the *L*.
10 was found in the house of the *L*.
11 oversight of the house of the *L*:
11 wrought upon the house of the *L*.
12 breaches of the house of the *L*.
13 not made for the house of the *L*
13 brought into the house of the *L*:
14 therewith the house of the *L*.
16 brought into the house of the *L*:
18 treasures of the house of the *L*.
13: 2 was evil in the sight of the *L*.
3 anger of the *L* was kindled
4 And Jehoahaz besought the *L*.
4 and the *L* hearkened unto him:
5 (And the *L* gave Israel a saviour,
11 was evil in the sight of the *L*;
23 the *L* was gracious unto them,
14: 3 was right in the sight of the *L*.
6 wherein the *L* commanded,
14 were found in the house of the *L*.
24 was evil in the sight of the *L*:
25 according to the word of the *L* God
26 the *L* saw the affliction of Israel,
27 *L* said not that he would blot out
15: 3 was right in the sight of the *L*.
5 the *L* smote the king, so that he
9 was evil in the sight of the *L*.
12 the word of the *L* which he spake
18, 24, 28 evil in the sight of the *L*:
34 was right in the sight of the *L*:
35 higher gate of the house of the *L*.
37 *L* began to send against Judah
16: 2 was right in the sight of the *L*
3 whom the *L* cast out from before
8 was found in the house of the *L*.
14 altar, which was before the *L*.
14 the altar and the house of the *L*.
18 he from the house of the *L* for
17: 2 was evil in the sight of the *L*.
7 sinned against the *L* their God,
8 heathen, whom the *L* cast out
9 that were not right against the *L*
11 whom the *L* carried away before
11 things to provoke the *L* to anger:
12 the *L* had said unto them, Ye
13 the *L* testified against Israel,
14 that did not believe in the *L* their
15 concerning whom the *L* had
16 all the commandments of the *L*
17 to do evil in the sight of the *L*.
18 the *L* was very angry with Israel,
19 not the commandments of the *L*
20 *L* rejected all the seed of Israel,
21 Israel from following the *L*.
23 *L* removed Israel out of his sight,
25 there, that they feared not the *L*:
25 the *L* sent lions among them,
28 how they should fear the *L*.
32 So they feared the *L*, and made
33 They feared the *L*, and served
34 they fear not the *L*, neither do
34 and commandment which the *L*
35 the *L* had made a covenant,
36 the *L*, who brought you up out
39 the *L* your God ye shall fear;
41 So these nations feared the *L*.
18: 3 was right in the sight of the *L*.
5 trusted in the *L* God of Israel;
6 he clave to the *L*, and departed
6 which the *L* commanded Moses.
7 And the *L* was with him; and he
12 obeyed not the voice of the *L*
12 the servant of the *L* commanded,
15 was found in the house of the *L*.
16 the doors of the temple of the *L*.
22 me, We trust in the *L* our God:
23 give pledges to my *l* the king of
25 Am I now come up without the *L*
25 The *L* said to me, Go up against
30 Hezekiah make you trust in the *L*.
30 The *L* will surely deliver us, and
32 saying, The *L* will deliver us.
35 *L* should deliver Jerusalem out
19: 1 and went into the house of the *L*.
4 *L* thy God will hear all the words
4 which the *L* thy God hath heard:
6 Thus saith the *L*, Be not afraid
14 went up into the house of the *L*.
14 and spread it before the *L*.
15 Hezekiah prayed before the *L*.
15 O *L* God of Israel, which dwellest
16 *L*, bow down thine ear, and hear:
16 open, *L*, thine eyes, and see:
17 Of a truth, *L*, the kings of Assyria
19 O *L* our God, I beseech thee, save
19 know that thou art the *L* God,
20 Thus saith the *L* God of Israel,
21 the word that the *L* hath spoken
23 thou hast reproached the *L*.
31 zeal of the *L* of hosts shall do
32 thus saith the *L* concerning the
33 come into this city, saith the *L*.
35 that the angel of the *L* went out,
20: 1 Thus saith the *L*, Set thine house
2 the wall, and prayed unto the *L*.
3 I beseech thee, O *L*, remember
4 the word of the *L* came to him,

2Ki 20: 5 Thus saith the *L*, the God of
5 go up unto the house of the *L*.
8 be the sign that the *L* will heal
8 go up into the house of the *L*
9 sign shalt thou have of the *L*.
9 *L* will do the thing that he hath
11 the prophet cried unto the *L*:
16 Hear the word of the *L*.
17 nothing shall be left, saith the *L*.
19 Good is the word of the *L* which
21: 2 was evil in the sight of the *L*.
2 *L* cast out before the children of
4 built altars in the house of the *L*.
5 two courts of the house of the *L*.
6 wickedness in the sight of the *L*.
7 of which the *L* said to David,
9 nations whom the *L* destroyed
10 the *L* spake by his servants the
12 thus saith the *L* God of Israel,
16 was evil in the sight of the *L*.
20 was evil in the sight of the *L*.
22 forsook the *L* God of his fathers,
22 walked not in the way of the *L*.
22: 2 was right in the sight of the *L*.
3 the scribe, to the house of the *L*.
4 brought into the house of the *L*.
5 oversight of the house of the *L*:
5 which is in the house of the *L*.
8 of the law in the house of the *L*.
9 oversight of the house of the *L*.
13 enquire of the *L* for me, and for
13 great is the wrath of the *L* that
15 Thus saith the *L* God of Israel,
16 Thus saith the *L*, Behold, I will
18 sent you to enquire of the *L*.
18 Thus saith the *L* God of Israel,
19 humbled thyself before the *L*.
19 have heard thee, saith the *L*.
23: 2 went up into the house of the *L*.
2 was found in the house of the *L*.
3 made a covenant before the *L*.
3 to walk after the *L*, and to keep
4 forth out of the temple of the *L*
6 grove from the house of the *L*
7 that were by the house of the *L*.
9 came not up to the altar of the *L*
11 entering in of the house of the *L*.
12 two courts of the house of the *L*.
16 according to the word of the *L*
19 made to provoke the *L* to anger,
21 Keep the passover unto the *L*
23 passover was holden to the *L* in
24 found in the house of the *L*.
25 that turned to the *L* with all his
26 *L* turned not from the fierceness
27 the *L* said, I will remove Judah
32, 37 was evil in the sight of the *L*.
24: 2 the *L* sent against him bands of
2 according to the word of the *L*.
3 at the commandment of the *L*
4 which the *L* would not pardon.
9 was evil in the sight of the *L*.
13 treasures of the house of the *L*.
13 had made in the temple of the *L*.
13 as the *L* had said.
19 was evil in the sight of the *L*.
20 For through the anger of the *L*
25: 9 he burnt the house of the *L*, and
13 that were in the house of the *L*.
13 that was in the house of the *L*.
16 made for the house of the *L*;
1Ch 2: 3 was evil in the sight of the *L*;
6: 15 when the *L* carried away Judah
31 of song in the house of the *L*.
32 had built the house of the *L* in
9: 19 being over the host of the *L*.
20 past, and the *L* was with him.
23 the gates of the house of the *L*.
10: 13 he committed against the *L*.
13 even against the word of the *L*.
14 enquired not of the *L*: therefore
11: 2 the *L* thy God said unto thee,
3 them in Hebron before the *L*;
3 the word of the *L* by Samuel.
9 for the *L* of hosts was with him.
10 word of the *L* concerning Israel.
14 and the *L* saved them by a great
18 of it, but poured it out to the *L*.
12: 23 according to the word of the *L*.
13: 2 and that it be of the *L* our God,
6 up thence the ark of God the *L*.
10 the anger of the *L* was kindled
11 *L* had made a breach upon Uzza:
14 And the *L* blessed the house of
14: 2 *L* had confirmed him king over
10 the *L* said unto him, Go up; for
17 *L* brought the fear of him upon
15: 2 them hath the *L* chosen to carry
3 bring up the ark of the *L* unto
12 up the ark of the *L* God of Israel
13 *L* our God made a breach upon
14 up the ark of the *L* God of Israel.
15 according to the word of the *L*.
25 the ark of the covenant of the *L*
26 the ark of the covenant of the *L*.
28, 29 ark of the covenant of the *L*
16: 2 the people in the name of the *L*.
4 minister before the ark of the *L*.
4 thank and praise the *L* God of
7 first this psalm to thank the *L*
8 Give thanks unto the *L*, call upon
10 of them rejoice that seek the *L*.
11 Seek the *L* and his strength,
14 He is the *L* our God; his
23 Sing unto the *L*, all the earth;
25 For great is the *L*, and greatly

1Ch 16: 26 but the *L* made the heavens.
28 Give unto the *L*, ye kindreds of
28 unto the *L* glory and strength.
29 Give unto the *L* the glory due
29 worship the *L* in the beauty of
31 the nations, The *L* reigneth.
33 sing out at the presence of the *L*.
34 O give thanks unto the *L*; for
36 Blessed be the *L* God of Israel
36 said, Amen, and praised the *L*.
37 the ark of the covenant of the *L*
39 before the tabernacle of the *L*
40 offer burnt offerings unto the *L*
40 that is written in the law of the *L*.
41 by name, to give thanks to the *L*.
17: 1 the ark of the covenant of the *L*
4 Thus saith the *L*, Thou shalt not
7 Thus saith the *L* of hosts, I took
10 the *L* will build thee an house.
16 king came and sat before the *L*.
16 Who am I, O *L* God, and what
17 a man of high degree, O *L* God.
19 O *L*, for thy servant's sake, and
20 O *L*, there is none like thee,
22 and thou, *L*, becamest their God.
23 Therefore now, *L*, let the thing
24 the *L* of hosts is the God of Israel,
26 And now, *L*, thou art God, and
27 for thou blessest, O *L*, and it shall
18: 6 Thus the *L* preserved David
11 king David dedicated unto the *L*.
13 Thus the *L* preserved David
19: 13 let the *L* do that which is good in
21: 3 *L* make his people an hundred
3 my *l* the king, are they not all my
3 why then doth my *l* require this
9 *L* spake unto Gad, David's seer,
10 Thus saith the *L*, I offer thee three
11 Thus saith the *L*, Choose thee
12 three days the sword of the *L*,
12 and the angel of the *L* destroying
13 fall now into the hand of the *L*;
14 *L* sent pestilence upon Israel:
15 the *L* beheld, and he repented
15 the angel of the *L* stood by the
16 and saw the angel of the *L* stand
17 hand, I pray thee, O *L* my God,
18 angel of the *L* commanded Gad
18 set up an altar unto the *L* in the
19 he spake in the name of the *L*.
22 build an altar therein unto the *L*:
23 my *l* the king do that which is good
24 take that which is thine for the *L*,
26 built there an altar unto the *L*,
26 offerings, and called upon the *L*;
27 And the *L* commanded the angel;
28 saw that the *L* had answered him
29 tabernacle of the *L*, which Moses
30 the sword of the angel of the *L*.
22: 1 This is the house of the *L* God,
5 *L* must be exceeding magnifical,
6 to build an house for the *L* God
7 unto the name of the *L* my God:
8 the word of the *L* came to me,
11 Now, my son, the *L* be with thee;
11 build the house of the *L* thy God,
12 Only the *L* give thee wisdom and
12 keep the law of the *L* thy God.
13 which the *L* charged Moses with
14 prepared for the house of the *L*
16 be doing, and the *L* be with thee.
18 Is not the *L* your God with you?
18 the land is subdued before the *L*,
19 your soul to seek the *L* your God;
19 ye the sanctuary of the *L* God,
19 the ark of the covenant of the *L*,
19 to be built in the name of the *L*.
23: 4 the work of the house of the *L*;
5 four thousand praised the *L* with
13 to burn incense before the *L*,
24 the service of the house of the *L*,
25 *L* God of Israel hath given rest
28 the service of the house of the *L*,
30 to thank and praise the *L*, and
31 all burnt sacrifices unto the *L* in
31 them, continually before the *L*:
32 the service of the house of the *L*.
24: 19 to come into the house of the *L*,
19 *L* God of Israel had commanded
25: 3 give thanks and to praise the *L*.
6 for song in the house of the *L*,
7 instructed in the songs of the *L*,
26: 12 to minister in the house of the *L*
22 treasures of the house of the *L*.
27 to maintain the house of the *L*.
30 in all the business of the *L*, and
27: 23 the *L* had said he would increase
28: 2 the ark of the covenant of the *L*,
4 *L* God of Israel chose me before
5 the *L* hath given me many sons,)
5 throne of the kingdom of the *L*
8 Israel the congregation of the *L*,
8 all the commandments of the *L*
9 the *L* searcheth all hearts, and
10 *L* hath chosen thee to build an
12 the courts of the house of the *L*,
13 the service of the house of the *L*,
13 of service in the house of the *L*.
18 the ark of the covenant of the *L*.
19 *L* made me understand in writing
20 for the *L* God, even my God, will
20 the service of the house of the *L*.
29: 1 is not for man, but for the *L* God.
5 his service this day unto the *L*?
8 treasure of the house of the *L*,
9 they offered willingly to the *L*:

1Ch 29: 10 David blessed the L' before all
10 be thou, L' God of Israel our father,
11 Thine, O L', is the greatness, and
11 thine is the kingdom, O L', and
16 O L' our God, all this store that
18 O L' God of Abraham, Isaac, and
20 Now bless the L' your God.
20 congregation blessed the L' God
20 worshipped the L', and the king.
21 sacrificed sacrifices unto the L',
21 offered burnt offerings unto the L',
22 did eat and drink before the L'
22 anointed him unto the L' to be
23 sat on the throne of the L' as king
25 And the L' magnified Solomon
2Ch 1: 1 the L' his God was with him, and
3 Moses the servant of the L' had
5 before the tabernacle of the L':
6 to the brasen altar before the L',
9 Now, O L' God, let thy promise
2: 1 an house for the name of the L',
4 to the name of the L' my God,
4 solemn feasts of the L' our God.
11 the L' hath loved his people,
12 Blessed be the L' God of Israel,
12 might build an house for the L',
14 the cunning men of my l' David thy
15 wine, which my l' hath spoken of,
3: 1 began to build the house of the L'
1 where the L' appeared unto David
4: 16 Solomon for the house of the L'
5: 1 the house of the L' was finished:
2, 7 the ark of the covenant of the L
10 the L' made a covenant with the
13 in praising and thanking the L';
13 musick, and praised the L', saying,
13 cloud, even the house of the L';
14 glory of the L' had filled the house
6: 1 L' hath said that he would dwell
4 Blessed be the L' God of Israel,
7 house for the name of the L' God
8 the L' said to David my father,
10 The L' therefore hath performed
10 of Israel, as the L' promised,
10 house for the name of the L' God
11 wherein is the covenant of the L',
12 he stood before the altar of the L'
14 O L' God of Israel, there is no God
16 O L' God of Israel, keep with thy
17 O L' God of Israel, let thy word
19 O L' my God, to hearken unto the
41 arise, O L' God, into thy resting
41 thy priests, O L' God, be clothed
42 O L' God, turn not away the face
7: 1 glory of the L' filled the house.
2 not enter into the house of the L',
2 glory of the L' had filled the Lord's
3 glory of the L' upon the house,
3 and praised the L', saying, For he
4 offered sacrifices before the L'.
6 instruments of musick of the L',
6 king had made to praise the L',
7 was before the house of the L':
10 goodness that the L' had shewed
11 finished the house of the L', and
11 to make in the house of the L',
12 L' appeared to Solomon by night,
21 Why hath the L' done thus unto
22 they forsook the L' God of their
8: 1 had built the house of the L', and
11 the ark of the L' hath come.
12 unto the L' on the altar of the L',
16 foundation of the house of the L',
16 the house of the L' was perfected.
9: 4 went up into the house of the L';
8 Blessed be the L' thy God, which
8 to be king for the L' thy God:
11 terraces to the house of the L',
10: 15 the L' might perform his word,
11: 2 word of the L' came to Shemaiah
4 Thus saith the L', Ye shall not
4 they obeyed the words of the L',
14 the priest's office unto the L':
16 set their hearts to seek the L' God
16 sacrifice unto the L' God of their
12: 1 he forsook the law of the L', and
2 had transgressed against the L',
5 saith the L', Ye have forsaken
6 and they said, the L' is righteous.
7 the L' saw that they humbled
7 word of the L' came to Shemaiah,
9 treasures of the house of the L',
11 entered into the house of the L',
12 wrath of the L' turned from him,
13 city which the L' had chosen out
14 not his heart to seek the L'.
13: 5 L' God of Israel gave the kingdom
6 and hath rebelled against his l'.
8 withstand the kingdom of the L'
9 not cast out the priests of the L',
10 as for us, the L' is our God, and
10 which minister unto the L',
11 burn unto the L' every morning
11 the charge of the L' our God;
12 fight ye not against the L' God of
14 they cried unto the L', and the
18 they relied upon the L' God of
20 the L' struck him, and he died.
14: 2 right in the eyes of the L' his God:
4 Judah to seek the L' God of their
6 because the L' had given him rest.
7 we have sought the L' our God,
11 And Asa cried unto the L' his God,
11 L', it is nothing with thee to help,
11 help us, O L' our God; for we
11 O L', thou art our God; let not

2Ch 14: 12 L' smote the Ethiopians before
13 they were destroyed before the L',
14 fear of the L' came upon them:
15: 2 The L' is with you, while ye be
4 trouble did turn unto the L' God
8 and renewed the altar of the L',
8 was before the porch of the L'.
9 that the L' his God was with him.
11 they offered unto the L' the same
12 seek the L' God of their fathers
13 not seek the L' God of Israel
14 sware unto the L' with a loud
15 L' gave them rest round about.
16: 2 treasures of the house of the L'
7 and not relied on the L' thy God,
8 because thou didst rely on the L',
9 the eyes of the L' run to and fro
12 his disease he sought not the L',
17: 3 And the L' was with Jehoshaphat,
5 the L' stablished the kingdom in
6 lifted up in the ways of the L':
9 had the book of the law of the L'
10 the fear of the L' fell upon all the
16 offered himself unto the L':
18: 4 I pray thee, at the word of the L'
6 there not here a prophet of the L'
7 whom we may enquire of the L':
10 Thus saith the L', With these
11 L' shall deliver it into the hand of
13 Micaiah said, As the L' liveth,
15 truth to me in the name of the L'?
16 and the L' said, These have no
18 Therefore hear the word of the L';
18 saw the L' sitting upon his throne,
19 And the L' said, Who shall entice
20 a spirit, and stood before the L',
20 the L' said unto him, Wherewith?
21 And the L' said, Thou shalt entice
22 the L' hath put a lying spirit in
22 L' hath spoken evil against thee.
23 went the Spirit of the L' from me
27 hath not the L' spoken by me.
31 cried out, and the L' helped him;
19: 2 and love them that hate the L'?
2 upon thee from before the L'.
4 back unto the L' God of their
6 but for the L', who is with you in
7 the fear of the L' be upon you;
7 no iniquity with the L' our God,
8 for the judgment of the L', and
9 do in the fear of the L', faithfully,
10 they trespass not against the L',
11 over you in all matters of the L';
11 and the L' shall be with the good.
20: 3 and set himself to seek the L',
4 together, to ask help of the L':
4 Judah, they came to seek the L'.
5 in the house of the L', before the
6 O L' God of our fathers, art not
13 all Judah stood before the L',
14 Spirit of the L' in the midst of the
15 Thus saith the L' unto you, Be not
17 the salvation of the L' with you,
17 them: for the L' will be with you.
18 before the L', worshipping the L'.
19 up to praise the L' God of Israel.
20 Believe in the L' your God, so
21 he appointed singers unto the L',
21 say, Praise the L'; for his mercy
22 L' set ambushments against the
26 for there they blessed the L':
27 L' had made them to rejoice over
28 trumpets unto the house of the L'.
29 heard that the L' fought against
32 was right in the sight of the L'.
37 the L' hath broken thy works.
21: 6 was evil in the eyes of the L'.
7 L' would not destroy the house of
10 he had forsaken the L' God of his
12 Thus saith the L' God of David
14 will the L' smite thy people, and
16 L' stirred up against Jehoram
18 L' smote him in his bowels with
22: 4 evil in the sight of the L' like the
7 the L' had anointed to cut off the
9 sought the L' with all his heart.
23: 3 L' hath said of the sons of David.
5 the courts of the house of the L'.
6 come into the house of the L',
6 shall keep the watch of the L'.
12 people into the house of the L':
14 her not in the house of the L'.
18 the offices of the house of the L'
18 distributed in the house of the L',
18 offer the burnt offerings of the L',
19 at the gates of the house of the L',
20 the king from the house of the L':
24: 2 was right in the sight of the L'
4 to repair the house of the L'.
6 of Moses the servant of the L',
7 things of the house of the L' did
8 at the gate of the house of the L'.
9 bring in to the L' the collection
12 the service of the house of the L',
12 to repair the house of the L', and
12 brass to mend the house of the L'.
14 vessels for the house of the L',
14 offerings in the house of the L'
18 left the house of the L' God of
19 to bring them again unto the L';
20 ye the commandments of the L',
20 because ye have forsaken the L',
21 in the court of the house of the L'.
22 The L' look upon it, and require
24 the L' delivered a very great host
24 had forsaken the L' God of their

2Ch 25: 2 was right in the sight of the L',
4 Moses, where the L' commanded,
7 for the L' is not with Israel, to wit,
9 L' is able to give thee much more
15 the anger of the L' was kindled
27 turn away from following the L'
26: 4 was right in the sight of the L',
5 as long as he sought the L', God
16 for he transgressed against the L'
16 into the temple of the L' to burn
17 him fourscore priests of the L',
18 to burn incense unto the L',
18 for thine honour from the L' God.
19 the priests in the house of the L',
20 because the L' had smitten him.
21 cut off from the house of the L':
27: 2 was right in the sight of the L',
2 not into the temple of the L'.
3 high gate of the house of the L',
6 prepared his ways before the L'
28: 1 was right in the sight of the L',
3 heathen whom the L' had cast out
5 L' his God delivered him into the
6 had forsaken the L' God of their
9 a prophet of the L' was there,
9 L' God of your fathers was wroth
10 sins against the L' your God?
11 fierce wrath of the L' is upon you.
13 offended against the L' already,
19 L' brought Judah low because of
19 transgressed sore against the L'.
21 portion out of the house of the L',
22 trespass yet more against the L':
24 the doors of the house of the L',
25 provoked to anger the L' God of
29: 2 was right in the sight of the L',
3 the doors of the house of the L',
5 sanctify the house of the L' God
6 evil in the eyes of the L' our God,
6 from the habitation of the L',
8 wrath of the L' was upon Judah
10 a covenant with the L' God of
11 the L' hath chosen you to stand
15 the king, by the words of the L',
15 to cleanse the house of the L'.
16 inner part of the house of the L',
16 they found in the temple of the L'
16 the court of the house of the L'.
17 came they to the porch of the L':
17 sanctified the house of the L' in
18 cleansed all the house of the L',
19 they are before the altar of the L'.
20 went up to the house of the L'.
21 offer them on the altar of the L'.
25 the Levites in the house of the L'
25 was the commandment of the L'
27 the song of the L' began also with
30 Levites to sing praise unto the L'
31 consecrated yourselves unto the L',
31 offerings into the house of the L'
32 for a burnt offering to the L'.
35 house of the L' was set in order.
30: 1 come to the house of the L' at
1, 5 to keep the passover unto the L'
6 turn again unto the L' God of
7 trespassed against the L' God of
8 but yield yourselves unto the L',
8 and serve the L' your God, that
9 For if ye turn again unto the L',
9 for the L' your God is gracious
12 princes, by the word of the L'.
15 offerings into the house of the L'.
17 to sanctify them unto the L'.
18 The good L' pardon every one
19 God, the L' God of his fathers,
20 the L' hearkened to Hezekiah,
21 priests praised the L' day by day,
21 loud instruments unto the L'.
22 the good knowledge of the L':
22 making confession to the L' God
31: 2 in the gates of the tents of the L'.
3 it is written in the law of the L'.
4 encouraged in the law of the L'.
6 consecrated unto the L' their God,
8 blessed the L', and his people
10 offerings into the house of the L',
10 for the L' hath blessed his people;
11 chambers in the house of the L';
14 distribute the oblations of the L',
16 entereth into the house of the L',
20 and truth before the L' his God.
32: 8 with us is the L' our God to help
11 The L' our God shall deliver us
16 yet more against the L' God,
17 also letters to rail on the L' God
21 the L' sent an angel, which cut off
22 Thus the L' saved Hezekiah and
23 many brought gifts unto the L' to
24 death, and prayed unto the L':
26 the wrath of the L' came not upon
33: 2 was evil in the sight of the L',
2 heathen, whom the L' had cast out
4 built altars in the house of the L',
4 the L' had said, In Jerusalem
5 two courts of the house of the L'.
6 much evil in the sight of the L',
9 whom the L' had destroyed before
10 the L' spake to Manasseh, and to
11 the L' brought upon them the
12 in affliction, he besought the L',
13 knew that the L' he was God.
15 the idol out of the house of the L',
15 the mount of the house of the L',
16 he repaired the altar of the L',
16 to serve the L' God of Israel.
17 yet unto the L' their God only.

2Ch 33:18 the name of the L' God of Israel.
22 was evil in the sight of the L',
23 humbled not himself before the L',
34: 2 was right in the sight of the L',
8 repair the house of the L' his God.
10 oversight of the house of the L',
10 wrought in the house of the L',
14 brought into the house of the L',
14 found a book of the law of the L'
15 of the law in the house of the L'.
17 was found in the house of the L',
21 Go, enquire of the L' for me, and
21 great is the wrath of the L' that
21 have not kept the word of the L',
23 Thus saith the L' God of Israel,
24 Thus said the L', Behold, I will
26 who sent you to enquire of the L',
26 Thus saith the L' God of Israel
27 even heard thee also, saith the L'.
30 went up into the house of the L',
30 was found in the house of the L'.
31 made a covenant before the L',
31 to walk after the L', and to keep
33 even to serve the L' their God.
33 departed not from following the L'
35: 1 Josiah kept a passover unto the L'
2 the service of the house of the L',
3 which were holy unto the L',
3 serve now the L' your God, and
6 according to the word of the L'
12 the people, to offer unto the L',
16 service of the L' was prepared the
16 offerings upon the altar of the L',
26 was written in the law of the L',
36: 5 evil in the sight of the L' his God.
7 the vessels of the house of the L'
9 was evil in the sight of the L'.
10 vessels of the house of the L',
12 evil in the sight of the L' his God,
12 speaking from the mouth of the L'.
13 his heart from turning unto the L'
14 and polluted the house of the L'
15 the L' God of their fathers sent to
16 wrath of the L' arose against his
18 treasures of the house of the L',
21 To fulfill the word of the L' by the
22 the word of the L' spoken by the
22 L' stirred up the spirit of Cyrus
23 the L' God of heaven given me;
23 The L' his God be with him, and
Ezr 1: 1 word of the L' by the mouth of
1 L' stirred up the spirit of Cyrus
2 L' God of heaven hath given me
3 build the house of the L' God of
5 build the house of the L' which is
7 the vessels of the house of the L',
2:68 they came to the house of the L'
3: 3 offerings thereon unto the L',
5 of all the set feasts of the L' that
5 a freewill offering unto the L'.
6 offer burnt offerings unto the L'.
6 foundation of the temple of the L'
8 the work of the house of the L'.
10 foundation of the temple of the L',
10 with cymbals, to praise the L',
11 and giving thanks unto the L';
11 shout, when they praised the L',
11 foundation of the house of the L'
4: 1 builded the temple unto the L'
3 build unto the L' God of Israel,
6:21 to seek the L' God of Israel, did
22 the L' had made them joyful, and
7: 6 the L' God of Israel had given:
6 hand of the L' his God upon him.
10 heart to seek the law of the L',
11 of the commandments of the L',
27 Blessed be the L' God of our
27 to beautify the house of the L'
28 hand of the L' my God was upon
8:28 them, Ye are holy unto the L';
28 freewill offering unto the L' God
29 chambers of the house of the L'.
35 was a burnt offering unto the L'.
9: 5 spread out my hands unto the L'
8 grace...been shewed from the L'
15 O L' God of Israel, thou art
10: 3 according to the counsel of my l',
11 make confession unto the L' God
Ne 1: 5 O L' God of heaven, the great and
11 O L', I beseech thee, let now thine
3: 5 their necks to the work of their L'.
4:14 remember the L', which is great
5:13 said, Amen, and praised the L'.
8: 1 which the L' had commanded to
6 Ezra blessed the L', the great God.
6 and worshipped the L' with their
9 This day is holy unto the L' your
10 for this day is holy unto our L':
10 the joy of the L' is your strength.
14 law which the L' had commanded
9: 3 book of the law of the L' their
3 and worshipped the L' their God.
4 with a loud voice unto the L'
5 Stand up and bless the L' your
6 Thou, even thou, art L' alone;
7 Thou art the L' the God, who
10:29 all the commandments of the L',
29 all the commandments of...our L',
34 to burn upon the altar of the L'
35 by year, unto the house of the L':
Job 1: 6 present themselves before the L',
7 the L' said unto Satan, Whence
7 Satan answered the L', and said,
8 the L' said unto Satan, Hast thou
9 Satan answered the L', and said,
12 the L' said unto Satan, Behold, all

Job 1:12 forth from the presence of the L'.
21 L' gave, and the L' hath taken
21 blessed be the name of the L'.
2: 1 present themselves before the L',
1 to present himself before the L'.
2 And the L' said unto Satan, From
2 Satan answered the L', and said,
3 And the L' said unto Satan, Hast
4 Satan answered the L', and said,
6 the L' said unto Satan, Behold,
7 forth from the presence of the L',
12: 9 hand of the L' hath wrought this?
28:28 the fear of the L', that is wisdom;
38: 1 the L' answered Job out of the
40: 1 the L' answered Job, and said,
3 Job answered the L', and said,
6 Then answered the L' unto Job
42: 1 Job answered the L', and said,
7 L' had spoken these words unto
7 L' said to Eliphaz the Temanite,
9 according as the L' commanded
9 them: the L' also accepted Job.
10 L' turned the captivity of Job,
10 L' gave Job twice as much as he
11 evil that the L' had brought upon
12 L' blessed the latter end of Job
Ps 1: 2 his delight is in the law of the L';
6 the L' knoweth the way of the
2: 2 against the L', and against his
4 L' shall have them in derision.
7 L' hath said unto me, Thou art
11 Serve the L' with fear, and rejoice
3: 1 L', how are they increased that
3 But thou, O L', art a shield for
4 I cried unto the L' with my voice,
5 awaked; for the L' sustained me.
7 Arise, O L'; save me, O my God:
8 Salvation belongeth unto the L':
4: 3 the L' hath set apart him that is
3 the L' will hear when I call unto
5 and put your trust in the L'.
6 L', lift thou up the light of thy
8 for thou, L', only makest me
5: 1 Give ear to my words, O L',
3 thou hear in the morning, O L';
6 the L' will abhor the bloody and
8 Lead me, O L', in...righteousness
12 thou, L', wilt bless the righteous;
6: 1 O L', rebuke me not in thine
2 Have mercy upon me, O L'; for
2 O L', heal me; for my bones are
3 vexed: but thou, O L', how long?
4 Return, O L', deliver my soul: oh
8 the L' hath heard the voice of my
9 L' hath heard my supplication;
9 the L' will receive my prayer.
7: *title* David, which he sang unto the L',
1 O L' my God, in thee do I put my
3 O L' my God, if I have done this;
6 Arise, O L', in thine anger, lift up
8 The L' shall judge the people:
8 L', according to my righteousness,
17 will praise the L' according to his
17 sing praise to the name of the L'
8: 1 O L'...how excellent is thy name
1 our L', how excellent is thy name
9 O L'...how excellent is thy name
9 our L', how excellent is thy name
9: 1 I will praise thee, O L', with my
7 But the L' shall endure for ever:
9 L' also will be a refuge for the
10 thou, L', hast not forsaken them
11 Sing praises to the L', which
13 Have mercy upon me, O L';
16 The L' is known by the judgment
19 Arise, O L'; let not man prevail:
20 Put them in fear, O L': that the
10: 1 Why standest thou afar off, O L'?
3 covetous, whom the L' abhorreth.
12 Arise, O L'; O God, lift up thine
16 The L' is King for ever and ever:
17 L', thou hast heard the desire of
11: 1 In the L' put I my trust: how say
4 The L' is in his holy temple, the
5 The L' trieth the righteous: but
7 righteous L' loveth righteousness;
12: 1 Help, L'; for the godly man
3 L' shall cut off all flattering lips,
4 lips are our own: who is l' over us?
5 now will I arise, saith the L';
6 words of the L' are pure words:
7 Thou shalt keep them, O L', thou
13: 1 long wilt thou forget me, O L'?
3 and hear me, O L' my God:
6 I will sing unto the L', because
14: 2 The L' looked down from heaven
4 bread, and call not upon the L'.
6 poor, because the L' is his refuge.
7 L' bringeth back the captivity of
15: 1 L', who shall abide in thy
4 honoureth them that fear the L'.
16: 2 soul, thou hast said unto the L',
2 Thou art my L': my goodness
5 The L' is the portion of mine
7 I will bless the L', who hath given
8 have set the L' always before me:
17: 1 Hear the right, O L', attend unto
13 Arise, O L', disappoint him, cast
14 men which are thy hand, O L',
18: *title* of David, the servant of the L',
title who spake unto the L' the words
title the day that the L' delivered him
1 I will love thee, O L', my strength.
2 L' is my rock, and my fortress,
3 I will call upon the L', who is
6 my distress I called upon the L',

Ps 18:13 L' also thundered in the heavens,
15 discovered at thy rebuke, O L',
18 calamity: but the L' was my stay.
20 L' rewarded me according to my
21 I have kept the ways of the L',
24 hath the L' recompensed me
28 the L' my God will enlighten my
30 the word of the L' is tried:
31 For who is God save the L'? or
41 even unto the L', but he answered
46 The L' liveth; and blessed be my
49 will I give thanks unto thee, O L',
19: 7 The law of the L' is perfect,
7 the testimony of the L' is sure,
8 The statutes of the L' are right,
8 commandment of the L' is pure,
9 The fear of the L' is clean,
9 the judgments of the L' are true
14 be acceptable in thy sight, O L',
20: 1 L' hear thee in the day of trouble;
5 the L' fulfil all thy petitions.
6 I that the L' saveth his anointed;
7 will remember the name of the L'
9 Save, L': let the king hear us
21: 1 shall joy in thy strength, O L';
7 For the king trusteth in the L',
9 L' shall swallow them up in his
13 Be thou exalted, L', in thine own
22: 8 trusted on the L' that he would
19 But be not thou far from me, O L':
23 Ye that fear the L', praise him;
26 shall praise the L' that seek him:
27 remember and turn unto the L':
30 it shall be accounted to the L' for a
23: 1 The L' is my shepherd; I shall
6 in the house of the L' for ever.
24: 3 shall ascend into the hill of the L'?
5 receive the blessing from the L',
8 The L' strong and mighty,
8 the L' mighty in battle.
10 The L' of hosts, he is the King of
25: 1 Unto thee, O L', do I lift up my
4 Shew me thy ways, O L'; teach
6 Remember, O L', thy tender
7 me for thy goodness' sake, O L'.
8 Good and upright is the L':
10 the paths of the L' are mercy and
11 For thy name's sake, O L', pardon
12 man is he that feareth the L'?
14 secret of the L' is with them that
15 Mine eyes are ever toward the L';
26: 1 Judge me, O L'; for I have walked
1 I have trusted also in the L';
2 Examine me, O L', and prove me;
6 will I compass thine altar, O L':
8 L', I have loved the habitation of
12 congregations will I bless the L'.
27: 1 L' is my light and my salvation;
1 the L' is the strength of my life;
4 One thing have I desired of the L',
4 may dwell in the house of the L'
4 to behold the beauty of the L',
6 I will sing praises unto the L'.
7 Hear, O L', when I cry with my
8 thee, Thy face, L', will I seek.
10 me, then the L' will take me up.
11 Teach me thy way, O L', and lead
13 goodness of the L' in the land of
14 Wait on the L': be of good
14 thine heart: wait, I say, on the L'.
28: 1 thee will I cry, O L' my rock;
5 regard not the works of the L',
6 Blessed be the L', because he
7 The L' is my strength and my
8 The L' is their strength, and he
29: 1 Give unto the L', O ye mighty,
1 give unto the L' glory and
2 Give unto the L' the glory due
2 worship the L' in the beauty of
3 voice of the L' is upon the waters:
3 the L' is upon many waters.
4 The voice of the L' is powerful;
4 voice of the L' is full of majesty.
5 voice of the L' breaketh the cedars;
5 L' breaketh the cedars of Lebanon.
7 voice of the L' divideth the flames
8 The voice of the L' shaketh the
8 the L' shaketh the wilderness of
9 voice of the L' maketh the hinds
10 The L' sitteth upon the flood;
10 yea, the L' sitteth King for ever.
11 The L' will give strength unto his
11 L' will bless his people with peace.
30: 1 I will extol thee, O L'; for thou
2 O L' my God, I cried unto thee,
3 O L', thou hast brought up my soul
4 Sing unto the L', O ye saints of his,
7 L', by thy favour thou hast made
8 I cried to thee, O L'; and unto
8 unto the L' I made supplication.
10 Hear, O L', and have mercy upon
10 upon me: L', be thou my helper.
12 O L' my God, I will give thanks
31: 1 In thee, O L', do I put my trust;
5 redeemed me, O L' God of truth.
6 vanities: but I trust in the L'.
9 Have mercy upon me, O L', for I
14 But I trusted in thee, O L': I said,
17 Let me not be ashamed, O L'; for
21 Blessed be the L': for he hath
23 O love the L', all ye his saints:
23 for the L' preserveth the faithful,
24 heart, all ye that hope in the L'.
32: 2 the L' imputeth not iniquity,
5 my transgressions unto the L';
10 but he that trusteth in the L',

Ps 32:11 Be glad in the *L'*, and rejoice, ye
33: 1 Rejoice in the *L'*, O ye righteous:
2 Praise the *L'* with harp: sing unto
4 For the word of the *L'* is right;
5 is full of the goodness of the *L'*.
6 word of the *L'* were the heavens
8 Let all the earth fear the *L'*: let
10 The *L'* bringeth the counsel of the
11 counsel of the *L'* standeth for ever,
12 is the nation whose God is the *L'*;
13 The *L'* looketh from heaven; he
18 eye of the *L'* is upon them that fear
20 Our soul waiteth for the *L'*: he is
22 Let thy mercy, O *L'*, be upon us,
34: 1 I will bless the *L'* at all times:
2 shall make her boast in the *L'*:
3 O magnify the *L'* with me, and
4 I sought the *L'*, and he heard me,
6 man cried, and the *L'* heard him,
7 angel of the *L'* encampeth round
8 taste and see that the *L'* is good:
9 O fear the *L'*, ye his saints: for
10 that seek the *L'* shall not want any
11 I will teach you the fear of the *L'*.
15 The eyes of the *L'* are upon the
16 face of the *L'* is against them that
17 the *L'* heareth, and delivereth
18 *L'* is nigh unto them that are of
19 *L'* delivereth him out of them all.
22 The *L'* redeemeth the soul of his
35: 1 Plead my cause, O *L'*, with them
5 the angel of the *L'* chase them.
6 angel of the *L'* persecute them.
9 my soul shall be joyful in the *L'*:
10 All my bones shall say, *L'*, who is
17 *L'*, how long wilt thou look on?
22 This thou hast seen, O *L'*: keep
22 silence: O *L'*, be not far from me.
23 unto my cause, my God and my *L'*.
24 Judge me, O *L'* my God,
27 Let the *L'* be magnified, which
36: *title* of David the servant of the *L'*.
5 mercy, O *L'*, is in the heavens;
6 O *L'*, thou preservest man and
37: 3 Trust in the *L'*, and do good; so
4 Delight thyself also in the *L'*;
5 Commit thy way unto the *L'*;
7 Rest in the *L'*, and wait patiently
9 but those that wait upon the *L'*,
13 the *L'* shall laugh at him; for he
17 the *L'* upholdeth the righteous.
18 The *L'* knoweth the days of the
20 enemies of the *L'* shall be as the
23 good man are ordered by the *L'*:
24 *L'* upholdeth him with his hand.
28 For the *L'* loveth judgment, and
33 *L'* will not leave him in his hand,
34 Wait on the *L'*, and keep his way,
39 of the righteous is of the *L'*:
40 *L'* shall help them, and deliver
38: 1 O *L'*, rebuke me not in thy wrath:
9 *L'*, all my desire is before thee;
15 For in thee, O *L'*, do I hope:
15 thou wilt hear, O *L'* my God.
21 Forsake me not, O *L'*: O my God,
22 to help me, O *L'* my salvation.
39: 4 *L'*, make me to know mine end,
7 *L'*, what wait I for? my hope is in
12 Hear my prayer, O *L'*, and give
40: 1 I waited patiently for the *L'*; and
3 and fear, and shall trust in the *L'*.
4 man that maketh the *L'* his trust,
5 Many, O *L'* my God, are thy
9 have not refrained my lips, O *L'*,
11 tender mercies from me, O *L'*:
13 Be pleased, O *L'*, to deliver me:
13 O *L'*, make haste to help me.
16 continually, The *L'* be magnified.
17 yet the *L'* thinketh upon me: thou
41: 1 the *L'* will deliver him in time of
2 The *L'* will preserve him, and
3 *L'* will strengthen him upon the
4 I said, *L'*, be merciful unto me:
10 But thou, O *L'*, be merciful unto
13 Blessed be the *L'* God of Israel
42: 8 *L'* will command...lovingkindness
44: 23 Awake, why sleepest thou, O *L'*?
45: 11 for he is thy *L'*; and worship thou
46: 7 The *L'* of hosts is with us; the
8 Come, behold the works of the *L'*,
11 The *L'* of hosts is with us; the
47: 2 For the *L'* most high is terrible;
5 *L'* with the sound of a trumpet.
48: 1 Great is the *L'*, and greatly to be
8 seen in the city of the *L'* of hosts,
50: 1 The mighty God, even the *L'*,
51: 15 O *L'*, open thou my lips; and my
54: 4 *L'* is with them that uphold my
6 I will praise thy name, O *L'*; for
55: 9 Destroy, O *L'*, and divide their
16 God; and the *L'* shall save me.
22 Cast thy burden upon the *L'*, and
56: 10 in the *L'* will I praise his word.
57: 9 I will praise thee, O *L'*, among the
58: 6 teeth of the young lions, O *L'*.
59: 3 transgression, nor for my sin, O *L'*.
5 O *L'* God of hosts, the God of
8 But thou, O *L'*, shalt laugh at
11 bring them down, O *L'* our shield.
62: 12 unto thee, O *L'*, belongeth mercy:
64: 10 righteous shall be glad in the *L'*,
66: 18 my heart, the *L'* will not hear me:
68: 11 The *L'* gave the word: great was
16 the *L'* will dwell in it for ever.
17 the *L'* is among them, as in Sinai,
19 Blessed be the *L'*, who daily loadeth

Ps 68: 20 unto God the *L'* belong the issues
22 The *L'* said, I will bring again from
26 even the *L'*, from the fountain of
32 earth; O sing praises unto the *L'*;
69: 6 wait on thee, O *L'* God of hosts,
13 my prayer is unto thee, O *L'*,
16 Hear me, O *L'*; for thy
31 please the *L'* better than an ox
33 For the *L'* heareth the poor, and
70: 1 me; make haste to help me, O *L'*.
5 O *L'*, make no tarrying.
71: 1 In thee, O *L'*, do I put my trust:
5 thou art my hope, O *L'* God: thou
16 go in the strength of the *L'* God:
72: 18 Blessed be the *L'* God, the God
73: 20 so, O *L'*, when thou awakest, thou
28 I have put my trust in the *L'* God,
74: 18 the enemy hath reproached, O *L'*,
75: 8 the hand of the *L'* there is a cup,
76: 11 and pay unto the *L'* your God:
77: 2 day of my trouble I sought the *L'*:
7 Will the *L'* cast off for ever? and
11 remember the works of the *L'*:
78: 4 to come the praises of the *L'*,
21 the *L'* heard this, and was wroth:
65 *L'* awaked as one out of a sleep,
79: 5 How long, *L'*? wilt thou be angry
12 they have reproached thee, O *L'*.
80: 4 O *L'* God of hosts, how long wilt
19 Turn us again, O *L'* God of hosts,
81: 10 I am the *L'* thy God, which brought
15 The haters of the *L'* should have
83: 16 they may seek thy name, O *L'*.
84: 1 thy tabernacles, O *L'* of hosts!
2 fainteth for the courts of the *L'*:
3 even thine altars, O *L'* of hosts,
8 O *L'* God of hosts, hear my prayer:
11 the *L'* God is a sun and shield:
11 the *L'* will give grace and glory:
12 O *L'* of hosts, blessed is the man
85: 1 *L'*, thou hast been favourable
7 Shew us thy mercy, O *L'*, and
8 hear what God the *L'* will speak:
12 *L'* shall give that which is good;
86: 1 Bow down thine ear, O *L'*, hear
3 Be merciful unto me, O *L'*: for I
4 unto thee, O *L'*, do I lift up my
5 For thou, *L'*, art good, and ready
6 Give ear, O *L'*, unto my prayer;
8 there is none like unto thee, O *L'*;
9 and worship before thee, O *L'*;
11 Teach me thy way, O *L'*; I will
12 I will praise thee, O *L'* my God,
15 But thou, O *L'*, art a God full of
17 because thou, *L'*, hast holpen me,
87: 2 *L'* loveth the gates of Zion more
6 The *L'* shall count, when he
88: 1 O *L'* God of my salvation, I have
9 *L'*, I have called daily upon thee,
13 But unto thee have I cried, O *L'*;
14 *L'*, why castest thou off my soul?
89: 1 I will sing of the mercies of the *L'*
5 shall praise thy wonders, O *L'*:
6 can be compared unto the *L'*?
6 can be likened unto the *L'*?
8 O *L'* God of hosts, who is a strong
8 who is a strong *L'* like unto thee?
15 shall walk, O *L'*, in the light of thy
18 For the *L'* is our defence; and the
46 How long, *L'*? wilt thou hide
49 *L'*, where are thy former
50 Remember, *L'*, the reproach of thy
51 enemies have reproached, O *L'*;
52 Blessed be the *L'* for evermore.
90: 1 *L'*, thou hast been our dwelling
13 Return, O *L'*, how long? and let it
17 let the beauty of the *L'* our God be
91: 2 will say of the *L'*, He is my refuge
9 Because thou hast made the *L'*,
92: 1 thing to give thanks unto the *L'*,
4 For thou, *L'*, hast made me glad
5 O *L'*, how great are thy works!
8 But thou, *L'*, art most high for
9 O *L'*, for, lo, thine enemies shall
13 be planted in the house of the *L'*
15 To shew that the *L'* is upright:
93: 1 The *L'* reigneth, he is clothed
1 the *L'* is clothed with strength,
3 The floods have lifted up, O *L'*,
4 *L'* on high is mightier than the
5 becometh thine house, O *L'*,
94: 1 O *L'* God, to whom vengeance
3 *L'*, how long shall the wicked,
5 break in pieces thy people, O *L'*,
7 they say, The *L'* shall not see,
11 *L'* knoweth the thoughts of man,
12 man whom thou chastenest, O *L'*,
14 the *L'* will not cast off his people,
17 Unless the *L'* had been my help,
18 thy mercy, O *L'*, held me up.
22 But the *L'* is my defence; and my
23 the *L'* our God shall cut them off.
95: 1 O come, let us sing unto the *L'*:
3 For the *L'* is a great God, and a
6 us kneel before the *L'* our maker.
96: 1 O sing unto the *L'* a new song:
1 sing unto the *L'*, all the earth.
2 Sing unto the *L'*, bless his name;
4 For the *L'* is great, and greatly to
5 but the *L'* made the heavens.
7 Give unto the *L'*, O ye kindreds
7 give unto the *L'* glory and
8 Give unto the *L'* the glory due
9 O worship the *L'* in the beauty of
10 the heathen that the *L'* reigneth:
13 Before the *L'*: for he cometh, for

Ps 97: 1 The *L'* reigneth; let the earth
5 like wax at the presence of the *L'*,
5 the presence of the *L'* of the whole
8 because of thy judgments, O *L'*.
9 For thou, *L'*, art high above all the
10 Ye that love the *L'*, hate evil: he
12 Rejoice in the *L'*, ye righteous;
98: 1 O sing unto the *L'* a new song;
2 *L'* hath made known his salvation:
4 Make a joyful noise unto the *L'*,
5 Sing unto the *L'* with the harp;
6 make a joyful noise before the *L'*,
9 Before the *L'*; for he cometh to
99: 1 The *L'* reigneth; let the people
2 The *L'* is great in Zion; and he is
5 Exalt ye the *L'* our God, and
6 they called upon the *L'*, and he
8 answeredst them, O *L'* our God:
9 Exalt the *L'* our God, and worship
9 hill; for the *L'* our God is holy.
100: 1 Make a joyful noise unto the *L'*,
2 Serve the *L'* with gladness: come
3 Know ye that the *L'* he is God:
5 For the *L'* is good; his mercy is
101: 1 unto thee, O *L'*, will I sing.
8 doers from the city of the *L'*.
102: *title* out his complaint before the *L'*.
1 Hear my prayer, O *L'*, and let my
12 thou, O *L'*, shalt endure for ever:
15 shall fear the name of the *L'*, and
16 When the *L'* shall build up Zion,
18 be created shall praise the *L'*.
19 from heaven did the *L'* behold
21 declare the name of the *L'* in Zion,
22 and the kingdoms, to serve the *L'*.
103: 1 Bless the *L'*, O my soul: and all
2 Bless the *L'*, O my soul, and forget
6 The *L'* executeth righteousness
8 The *L'* is merciful and gracious,
13 the *L'* pitieth them that fear him.
17 mercy of the *L'* is from everlasting
19 *L'* hath prepared his throne in the
20 Bless the *L'*, ye his angels, that
21 Bless ye the *L'*, all ye his hosts;
22 Bless the *L'*, all his works in all
22 bless the *L'*, O my soul.
104: 1 Bless the *L'*, O my soul.
1 O *L'* my God, thou art very great;
16 The trees of the *L'* are full of sap;
24 O *L'*, how manifold are thy works!
31 The glory of the *L'* shall endure
31 the *L'* shall rejoice in his works.
33 I will sing unto the *L'* as long as
34 be sweet: I will be glad in the *L'*.
35 Bless thou the *L'*, O my soul.
35 Praise ye the *L'*.
105: 1 O give thanks unto the *L'*; call
3 of them rejoice that seek the *L'*.
4 Seek the *L'*, and his strength:
7 He is the *L'* our God: his
19 came: the word of the *L'* tried him.
21 He made him *l'* of his house, and
45 keep his laws. Praise ye the *L'*.
106: 1 Praise ye the *L'*. O give thanks
1 O give thanks unto the *L'*; for he
2 utter the mighty acts of the *L'*?
4 Remember me, O *L'*, with the
16 and Aaron the saint of the *L'*.
25 not unto the voice of the *L'*.
34 whom the *L'* commanded them:
40 was the wrath of the *L'* kindled
47 Save us, O *L'* our God, and gather
48 Blessed be the *L'* God of Israel
48 say, Amen. Praise ye the *L'*.
107: 1 O give thanks unto the *L'*, for he
2 Let the redeemed of the *L'* say so,
6 cried unto the *L'* in their trouble,
8 praise the *L'* for his goodness,
13 cried unto the *L'* in their trouble,
15 praise the *L'* for his goodness,
19 cry unto the *L'* in their trouble,
21 praise the *L'* for his goodness,
24 These see the works of the *L'*,
28 cry unto the *L'* in their trouble,
31 praise the *L'* for his goodness,
43 the lovingkindness of the *L'*.
108: 3 I will praise thee, O *L'*, among the
109: 14 be remembered with the *L'*;
15 them be before the *L'* continually,
20 of mine adversaries from the *L'*,
21 But do thou for me, O God the *L'*, for
26 Help me, O *L'* my God: O save
27 hand; that thou, *L'*, hast done it.
30 praise the *L'* with my mouth;
110: 1 The *L'* said...Sit thou at my right
1 said unto my *L'*, Sit thou at my
2 The *L'* shall send the rod of thy
4 The *L'* hath sworn, and will not
5 *L'* at thy right hand shall strike
111: 1 Praise ye the *L'*. I will praise
1 will praise the *L'* with my whole
2 The works of the *L'* are great,
4 the *L'* is gracious and full of
10 The fear of the *L'* is the beginning
112: 1 Praise ye the *L'*. Blessed is the
1 is the man that feareth the *L'*,
7 heart is fixed, trusting in the *L'*.
113: 1 Praise ye the *L'*. Praise, O ye
1 Praise, O ye servants of the *L'*,
1 praise the name of the *L'*.
2 Blessed be the name of the *L'*
4 The *L'* is high above all nations,
5 Who is like unto the *L'* our God,
9 of children. Praise ye the *L'*.
114: 7 thou earth, at the presence of the *L'*,
115: 1 Not unto us, O *L'*, not unto us,

Ps 115: 9 O Israel, trust thou in the L·: he
10 O house of Aaron, trust in the L·:
11 Ye that fear the L·, trust in the L·:
12 The L· hath been mindful of us:
13 He will bless them that fear the L·,
14 L· shall increase you more and
15 are blessed of the L· which made
17 The dead praise not the L·,
18 we will bless the L· from this time
18 and for evermore. Praise the L·.
116: 1 I love the L·, because he hath
4 called I upon the name of the L·;
4 O L·, I beseech thee, deliver my
5 Gracious is the L·, and righteous;
6 The L· preserveth the simple:
7 the L· hath dealt bountifully with
9 will walk before the L· in the land
12 What shall I render unto the L·
13 and call upon the name of the L·.
14 I will pay my vows unto the L·
15 Precious in the sight of the L· is
16 O L·, truly I am thy servant; I am
17 will call upon the name of the L·.
18 I will pay my vows unto the L·
19 O Jerusalem. Praise ye the L·.
117: 1 O praise the L·, all ye nations:
2 truth of the L· endureth for ever.
2 for ever. Praise ye the L·.
118: 1 O give thanks unto the L·; for he
4 Let them now that fear the L· say,
5 I called upon the L· in distress:
5 the L· answered me, and set me in
6 The L· is on my side; I will not
7 L· taketh my part with them that
8, 9 It is better to trust in the L· than
10, name of the L· will I destroy them.
11, 12 name of the L· I will destroy
13 might fall: but the L· helped me.
14 The L· is my strength and song,
15 hand of the L· doeth valiantly.
16 right hand of the L· is exalted:
16 hand of the L· doeth valiantly.
17 and declare the works of the L·.
18 The L· hath chastened me sore:
19 into them, and I will praise the L·:
20 This gate of the L·, into which
24 the day which the L· hath made;
25 Save now, I beseech thee, O L·:
25 O L·, I beseech thee, send now
26 that cometh in the name of the L·:
26 you out of the house of the L·.
27 God is the L·, which hath shewed
29 O give thanks unto the L·; for he
119: 1 who walk in the law of the L·.
12 Blessed art thou, O L·: teach me
31 O L·, put me not to shame.
33 Teach me, O L·, the way of thy
41 mercies come also unto me, O L·,
52 thy judgments of old, O L·;
55 remembered thy name, O L·, in
57 Thou art my portion, O L·: I
64 The earth, O L·, is full of thy
65 dealt well with thy servant, O L·,
75 O L·, that thy judgments are
89 For ever, O L·, thy word is settled
107 quicken me, O L·, according unto
108 offerings of my mouth, O L·,
126 It is time for thee, L·, to work:
137 Righteous art thou, O L·, and
145 hear me, O L·: I will keep thy
149 O L·, quicken me according to
151 Thou art near, O L·; and all thy
156 are thy tender mercies, O L·:
159 quicken me, O L·, according to
166 L·, I have hoped for thy salvation,
169 cry come near before thee, O L·:
174 longed for thy salvation, O L·;
120: 1 my distress I cried unto the L·,
2 Deliver my soul, O L·, from lying
121: 2 My help cometh from the L·,
5 The L· is thy keeper: the
5 L· is thy shade upon thy right
7 L· shall preserve thee from all
8 L· shall preserve thy going out
122: 1 us go into the house of the L·.
4 tribes go up, the tribes of the L·,
4 thanks unto the name of the L·.
9 of the house of the L· our God
123: 2 so our eyes wait upon the L· our
3 Have mercy upon us, O L·, have
124: 1, 2 the L· who was on our side,
6 Blessed be the L·, who hath not
8 Our help is in the name of the L·,
125: 1 trust in the L· shall be as mount
2 L· is round about his people from
4 Do good, O L·, unto those that be
5 L· shall lead them forth with the
126: 1 L· turned again the captivity of
2 L· hath done great things for
3 L· hath done great things for us;
4 Turn again our captivity, O L·,
127: 1 Except the L· build the house,
1 except the L· keep the city, the
3 children are an heritage of the L·:
128: 1 is every one that feareth the L·;
4 be blessed that feareth the L·.
5 L· shall bless thee out of Zion:
129: 4 The L· is righteous: he hath cut
8 blessing of the L· be upon you:
8 bless you in the name of the L·.
130: 1 have I cried unto thee, O L·.
2 L·, hear my voice: let thine ears
3 L·, shouldest mark iniquities,
3 O L·, who shall stand?
5 I wait for the L·, my soul doth
6 My soul waiteth for the L· more

Ps 130: 7 Let Israel hope in the L·: for
7 with the L· there is mercy, and
131: 1 L·, my heart is not haughty, nor
3 Let Israel hope in the L· from
132: 1 L·, remember David, and all his
2 How he sware unto the L·, and
5 Until I find out a place for the L·,
8 Arise, O L·, into thy rest; thou
11 The L· hath sworn in truth unto
13 For the L· hath chosen Zion; he
133: 3 the L· commanded the blessing,
134: 1 Behold, bless ye the L·,
1 all ye servants of the L·, which
1 night stand in the house of the L·.
2 the sanctuary, and bless the L·.
3 L· that made heaven and earth
135: 1 Praise ye the L·. Praise ye the
1 Praise ye the name of the L·;
1 him, O ye servants of the L·.
2 that stand in the house of the L·,
3 Praise the L·; for...is good:
3 for the L· is good: sing praises
4 the L· hath chosen Jacob unto
5 For I know that the L· is great,
5 and that our L· is above all gods.
6 Whatsoever the L· pleased, that
13 Thy name, O L·, endureth for
13 thy memorial, O L·, throughout
14 For the L· will judge his people,
19 Bless the L·, O house of Israel:
19 bless the L·, O house of Aaron:
20 Bless the L·, O house of Levi:
20 ye that fear the L·, bless the L·.
21 Blessed be the L· out of Zion,
21 at Jerusalem. Praise ye the L·.
136: 1 O give thanks unto the L·; for
3 O give thanks to the L· of lords:
137: 7 Remember, O L·, the children of
138: 4 the earth shall praise thee, O L·,
5 shall sing in the ways of the L·:
5 for great is the glory of the L·.
6 Though the L· be high, yet hath
8 The L· will perfect that which
8 thy mercy, O L·, endureth for
139: 1 O L·, thou hast searched me,
4 O L·, thou knowest it altogether.
21 hate them, O L·, that hate thee?
140: 1 Deliver me, O L·, from the evil
4 Keep me, O L·, from the hands of
6 I said unto the L·, Thou art my
6 voice of my supplications, O L·.
7 O God the L·, the strength of my
8 Grant not, O L·, the desires of
12 L· will maintain the cause of the
141: 1 L·, I cry unto thee: make haste
3 watch, O L·, before my mouth;
8 eyes are unto thee, O God the L·:
142: 1 cried unto the L· with my voice;
1 my voice unto the L· did I make
5 I cried unto thee O L·: I said,
143: 1 Hear my prayer, O L·, give ear to
7 Hear me speedily, O L·: my spirit
9 Deliver me, O L·, from mine
11 Quicken me, O L·, for thy name's
144: 1 Blessed be the L· my strength,
3 L·, what is man, that thou takest
5 Bow thy heavens, O L·, and come
15 that people, whose God is the L·.
145: 3 Great is the L·, and greatly to be
8 The L· is gracious, and full of
9 The L· is good to all: and his
10 thy works shall praise thee, O L·;
14 The L· upholdeth all that fall,
17 The L· is righteous in all his ways,
18 L· is nigh unto all them that call
20 L· preserveth all them that love
21 shall speak the praise of the L·:
146: 1 Praise ye the L·. Praise the
1 Praise the L·, O my soul.
2 While I live will I praise the L·: I
5 whose hope is in the L· his God:
7 The L· looseth the prisoners:
8 L· openeth the eyes of the blind:
8 L· raiseth them that are bowed
8 the L· loveth the righteous:
9 The L· preserveth the strangers;
10 The L· shall reign for ever, even
10 generations. Praise ye the L·.
147: 1 Praise ye the L·: for it is good
2 L· doth build up Jerusalem: he
5 Great is our L·, and of great
6 The L· lifteth up the meek: he
7 unto the L· with thanksgiving;
11 L· taketh pleasure in them that
12 Praise the L·, O Jerusalem;
20 known them. Praise ye the L·.
148: 1 Praise ye the L·. Praise ye the
1 Praise ye the L· from the
5 them praise the name of the L·:
7 Praise the L· from the earth, ye
13 them praise the name of the L·:
14 near unto him. Praise ye the L·.
149: 1 Praise ye the L·. Sing unto the
1 Sing unto the L· a new song,
4 L· taketh pleasure in his people:
9 all his saints. Praise ye the L·.
150: 1 Praise ye the L·. Praise God in
6 that hath breath praise the L·.
6 Praise ye the L·.
Pr 1: 7 fear of the L· is the beginning of
29 did not choose the fear of the L·:
2: 5 understand the fear of the L·,
6 For the L· giveth wisdom: out of
3: 5 Trust in the L· with all thine
7 fear the L·, and depart from evil.
9 Honour the L· with thy substance,

Pr 3: 11 not the chastening of the L·;
12 whom the L· loveth he correcteth;
19 L· by wisdom hath founded the
26 For the L· shall be thy confidence,
32 froward is abomination to the L·:
33 curse of the L· is in the house of
5: 21 man are before the eyes of the L·,
6: 16 These six things doth the L· hate:
8: 13 The fear of the L· is to hate evil:
22 L· possessed me in the beginning
35 and shall obtain favour of the L·.
9: 10 fear of the L· is the beginning of
10: 3 L· will not suffer the soul of the
22 The blessing of the L·, it maketh
27 fear of the L· prolongeth days:
29 The way of the L· is strength to
11: 1 balance is abomination to the L·:
20 heart are abomination to the L·:
12: 2 man obtaineth favour of the L·:
22 lips are abomination to the L·:
14: 2 his uprightness feareth the L·:
26 fear of the L· is strong confidence:
27 fear of the L· is a fountain of life,
15: 3 eyes of the L· are in every place,
8 is an abomination to the L·:
9 is an abomination unto the L·:
11 and destruction are before the L·:
16 little with the fear of the L· than
25 L· will destroy the house of the
26 are an abomination to the L·:
29 The L· is far from the wicked:
33 fear of the L· is the instruction
[illegible] 1 of the tongue, is from the L·.
2 but the L· weigheth the spirits.
3 Commit thy works unto the L·,
[illegible] The L· hath made all things for
[illegible] is an abomination to the L·:
[illegible] fear of the L· men depart from
[illegible] When a man's ways please the L·,
9 but the L· directeth his steps.
20 and whoso trusteth in the L·,
33 disposing thereof is of the L·.
17: 3 gold: but the L· trieth the hearts.
15 both are abomination to the L·.
18: 10 name of the L· is a strong tower:
22 and obtaineth favour of the L·.
19: 3 his heart fretteth against the L·.
14 and a prudent wife is from the L·.
17 upon the poor lendeth unto the L·;
21 the counsel of the L·, that shall
23 The fear of the L· tendeth to life:
20: 10 are alike abomination to the L·.
12 L· hath made even both of them.
22 wait on the L·, and he shall save
23 are an abomination unto the L·;
24 Man's goings are of the L·; how
27 of man is the candle of the L·,
21: 1 heart is in the hand of the L·,
2 but the L· pondereth the hearts.
3 is more acceptable to the L· than
30 nor counsel against the L·.
31 of battle: but safety is of the L·.
22: 2 the L· is the maker of them all.
4 and the fear of the L· are riches,
12 eyes of the L· preserve knowledge,
14 is abhorred of the L· shall fall
19 That thy trust may be in the L·, I
23 For the L· will plead their cause,
23: 17 fear of the L· all the day long.
24: 18 Lest the L· see it, and it displease
21 fear thou the L· and the king:
25: 22 and the L· shall reward thee.
28: 5 seek the L· understand all things.
25 he that putteth his trust in the L·
29: 13 the L· lighteneth both their eyes.
25 whoso putteth his trust in the L·
26 judgment cometh from the L·.
30: 9 deny thee, and say, Who is the L·?
31: 30 a woman that feareth the L·, she
Isa 1: 2 for the L· hath spoken, I have
4 have forsaken the L·, they have
9 the L· of hosts had left unto us a
10 Hear the word of the L·, ye
11 sacrifices unto me? saith the L·:
18 us reason together, saith the L·:
20 mouth of the L· hath spoken it.
24 Therefore saith the L·,...the
24 the L· of hosts, the mighty One
28 they that forsake the L· shall be
2: 3 go up to the mountain of the L·,
3 word of the L· from Jerusalem.
5 let us walk in the light of the L·.
10 in the dust, for fear of the L·,
11 L· alone shall be exalted in that
12 L· of hosts shall be upon every
17 L· alone shall be exalted in that
19 of the earth, for fear of the L·,
21 ragged rocks, for fear of the L·,
3: 1 For, behold, the L·,...doth take
1 the L· of hosts, doth take away
8 their doings are against the L·,
13 The L· standeth up to plead, and
14 L· will enter into judgment with
15 poor? saith the L· God of hosts.
16 Moreover the L· saith, Because
17 the L· will smite with a scab the
17 L· will discover their secret parts.
18 the L· will take away the bravery
4: 2 branch of the L· be beautiful and
4 L· shall have washed away the
5 And the L· will create upon every
5: 7 vineyard of the L· of hosts is the
9 In mine ears said the L· of hosts,
12 regard not the work of the L·,
16 the L· of hosts shall be exalted in
24 cast away the law of the L· of

Isa 5:25 anger of the L' kindled against
6: 1 also the L' sitting upon a throne,
3 Holy, holy, holy, is the L' of
5 seen the king, the L' of hosts.
8 I heard the voice of the L', saying,
11 Then said I, L', how long? And he
12 L' have removed men far away,
7: 3 Then said the L' unto Isaiah, Go
7 Thus saith the L' God, It shall not
10 the L' spake again unto Ahaz,
11 Ask thee a sign of the L' thy God;
12 ask, neither will I tempt the L'.
14 L' himself shall give you a sign;
17 The L' shall bring upon thee, and
18 the L' shall hiss for the fly that is
20 day shall the L' shave with a rasor
8: 1 the L' said unto me, Take thee a
3 Then said the L' to me, Call his
5 The L' spake also unto me again,
7 the L' bringeth up upon them the
11 the L' spake thus to me with a
13 Sanctify the L' of hosts himself;
17 I will wait upon the L', that hideth
18 children whom the L' hath given
18 wonders in Israel from the L' of
9: 7 zeal of the L' of hosts will perform
8 The L' sent a word into Jacob, and
11 L' shall set up the adversaries of
13 neither do they seek the L' of
14 L' will cut off from Israel head and
17 L' shall have no joy in their young
19 the wrath of the L' of hosts is the
10:12 L' hath performed his whole work
16 shall the L',...send among his fat
16 the L' of hosts, send among his fat
20 stay upon the L', the Holy One of
23 the L' God of hosts shall make a
24 thus saith the L' God of hosts,
26 L' of hosts shall stir up a scourge
33 the L',...shall lop the bough with
33 the L' of hosts, shall lop the
11: 2 the spirit of the L' shall rest upon
2 and of the fear of the L';
3 quick...in the fear of the L':
9 full of the knowledge of the L',
11 the L' shall set his hand again the
15 the L' shall utterly destroy the
12: 1 shalt say, O L', I will praise thee:
2 L' Jehovah is my strength and
4 day shall ye say, Praise the L',
5 Sing unto the L'; for he hath
13: 4 L' of hosts mustereth the host of
5 even the L', and the weapons of
6 for the day of the L' is at hand;
9 Behold, the day of the L' cometh,
13 in the wrath of the L' of hosts,
14: 1 the L' will have mercy on Jacob,
2 them in the land of the L' for
3 L' shall give thee rest from thy
5 L' hath broken the staff of the
22 against them, saith the L' of hosts,
22 and son, and nephew, saith the L'.
23 destruction, saith the L' of hosts.
24 The L' of hosts hath sworn,
27 the L' of hosts hath purposed,
32 That the L' hath founded Zion,
16:13 L' hath spoken concerning Moab
14 But now the L' hath spoken,
17: 3 of Israel, saith the L' of hosts.
6 saith the L' God of Israel.
18: 4 For so the L' said unto me, I will
7 be brought unto the L' of hosts
7 of the name of the L' of hosts,
19: 1 the L' rideth upon a swift cloud,
4 over into the hand of a cruel l';
4 shall rule over them, saith the L',
4 over them, saith...the L' of hosts.
12 L' of hosts hath purposed upon
14 L' hath mingled a perverse spirit
16 of the hand of the L' of hosts,
17 of the counsel of the L' of hosts,
18 and swear to the L' of hosts;
19 shall there be an altar to the L'
19 at the border thereof to the L'.
20 for a witness unto the L' of hosts
20 for they shall cry unto the L'
21 the L' shall be known to Egypt,
21 the Egyptians shall know the L'
21 they shall vow a vow unto the L',
22 And the L' shall smite Egypt: he
22 they shall return even to the L',
25 Whom the L' of hosts shall bless,
20: 2 same time spake the L' by Isaiah
3 L' said, Like as my servant Isaiah
21: 6 For thus hath the L' said unto me,
8 My l', I stand continually upon the
10 I have heard of the L' of hosts,
16 For thus hath the L' said unto me,
17 the L' God of Israel hath spoken
22: 5 perplexity by the L' God of hosts
12 the L' God of hosts call to weeping,
14 in mine ears by the L' of hosts,
14 ye die, saith the L' God of hosts.
15 Thus saith the L' God of hosts, Go,
17 the L' will carry thee away with a
25 In that day, saith the L' of hosts,
25 cut off: for the L' hath spoken it.
23: 9 The L' of hosts hath purposed it,
11 L' hath given a commandment
17 years, that the L' will visit Tyre,
18 hire shall be holiness to the L':
18 for them that dwell before the L',
24: 1 the L' maketh the earth empty,
3 for the L' hath spoken this word.
14 sing for the majesty of the L',
15 glorify ye the L' in the fires, even

Isa 24:15 the name of the L' God of Israel
21 L' shall punish the host of the
23 L' of hosts shall reign in mount
25: 1 O L', thou art my God; I will exalt
6 L' of hosts make unto all people
8 L' God will wipe away tears from
8 earth: for the L' hath spoken it.
9 this is the L'; we have waited for
10 shall the hand of the L' rest,
26: 4 Trust ye in the L' forever: for
4 in the L' Jehovah is everlasting
8 in the way of thy judgments, O L',
10 not behold the majesty of the L'.
11 L', when thy hand is lifted up, they
12 L', thou wilt ordain peace for us:
13 O L' our God, other lords beside
15 hast increased the nation, O L',
16 L', in trouble have they visited
17 so have we been in thy sight, O L'.
21 the L' cometh out of his place to
27: 1 the L' with his sore and great and
3 I the L' do keep it; I will water it
12 L' shall beat off from the channel
13 worship the L' in the holy mount
28: 2 L' hath a mighty and strong one,
5 L' of hosts be for a crown of glory,
13 the word of the L' was unto them
14 hear the word of the L', ye scornful
16 Therefore thus saith the L' God,
21 the L' shall rise up as in mount
22 have heard from the L' God of hosts
29 cometh forth from the L' of hosts,
29: 6 shalt be visited of the L' of hosts
10 L' hath poured out upon you the
13 Wherefore the L' said, Forasmuch
15 to hide their counsel from the L',
19 shall increase their joy in the L',
22 thus saith the L', who redeemed
30: 1 rebellious children, saith the L',
9 will not hear the law of the L':
15 thus saith the L' God, the Holy One
18 And therefore will the L' wait,
18 for the L' is a God of judgment:
20 L' give you the bread of adversity,
26 L' bindeth up the breach of his
27 name of the L' cometh from far,
29 come into the mountain of the L',
30 L' shall cause his glorious voice
31 through the voice of the L' shall
32 which the L' shall lay upon him,
33 the breath of the L', like a stream
31: 1 One of Israel, neither seek the L'!
3 the L' shall stretch out his hand,
4 thus hath the L' spoken unto me,
4 the L' of hosts come down to fight
5 the L' of hosts defend Jerusalem;
9 afraid of the ensign, saith the L',
32: 6 and to utter error against the L',
33: 2 O L', be gracious unto us; we
5 The L' is exalted; for he dwelleth
6 the fear of the L' is his treasure.
10 Now will I rise, saith the L'; now
21 glorious L' will be unto us a place
22 For the L' is our judge,
22 the L' is our lawgiver,
22 the L' is our king; he will save us.
34: 2 indignation of the L' is upon all
6 sword of the L' is filled with blood,
6 the L' hath a sacrifice in Bozrah,
16 Seek ye out of the book of the L',
35: 2 they shall see the glory of the L',
10 ransomed of the L' shall return,
36: 7 to me, We trust in the L' our God:
10 am I now come up without the L'
10 L' said unto me, Go up against
15 make you trust in the L', saying,
15 The L' will surely deliver us:
18 saying, The L' will deliver us.
20 the L' should deliver Jerusalem
37: 1 and went into the house of the L'.
4 L' thy God will hear the words of
4 which the L' thy God hath heard:
6 Thus saith the L', Be not afraid
14 went up unto the house of the L',
14 and spread it before the L'.
15 And Hezekiah prayed unto the L',
16 O L' of hosts, God of Israel, that
17 Incline thine ear, O L', and hear;
17 open thine eyes, O L', and see:
18 L', the kings of Assyria have laid
20 O L' our God, save us from his
20 may know that thou art the L',
21 Thus saith the L' God of Israel,
22 word which the L' hath spoken
24 hast thou reproached the L', and
32 zeal of the L' of hosts shall do
33 thus saith the L' concerning the
34 come into this city, saith the L'.
36 the angel of the L' went forth,
38: 1 Thus saith the L', Set thine house
2 the wall, and prayed unto the L',
3 Remember now, O L', I beseech
4 came the word of the L' to Isaiah,
5 saith the L', the God of David
7 be a sign unto thee from the L',
7 that the L' will do this thing that
11 shall not see the L', even the L',
14 O L', I am oppressed; undertake
16 O L', by these things men live, and
20 The L' was ready to save me:
20 of our life in the house of the L'.
22 I shall go up to the house of the L'?
39: 5 Hear the word of the L' of hosts:
6 nothing shall be left, saith the L'.
8 Good is the word of the L' which
40: 3 Prepare ye the way of the L',

Isa 40: 5 glory of the L' shall be revealed,
5 mouth of the L' hath spoken it.
7 spirit of the L' bloweth upon it:
10 L' God will come with strong hand,
13 hath directed the Spirit of the L',
27 My way is hid from the L', and
28 the L', the Creator of the ends of
31 that wait upon the L' shall renew
41: 4 I the L', the first, and with the
13 I the L' thy God will hold thy right
14 I will help thee, saith the L', and
16 and thou shalt rejoice in the L',
17 I the L' will hear them, I the God
20 the hand of the L' hath done this,
21 Produce your cause, saith the L';
42: 5 saith God the L', he that created
6 I the L' have called thee in
8 I am the L': that is my name:
10 Sing unto the L' a new song, and
12 Let them give glory unto the L',
13 L' shall go forth as a mighty man,
21 The L' is well pleased for his
24 did not the L', he against whom
43: 1 thus saith the L' that created thee,
3 I am the L' thy God, the Holy One
10 Ye are my witnesses, saith the L',
11 I, even I, am the L'; and beside
12 ye are my witnesses, saith the L',
14 Thus saith the L', your redeemer,
15 I am the L', your Holy One, the
16 Thus saith the L', which maketh
44: 2 Thus saith the L' that made thee,
5 with his hand unto the L',
6 saith the L' the King of Israel,
6 and his redeemer the L' of hosts;
23 heavens; for the L' hath done it:
23 for the L' hath redeemed Jacob,
24 saith the L', thy redeemer, and
24 am the L' that maketh all things;
45: 1 Thus saith the L' to his anointed,
3 know that I, the L', which call
5 I am the L', and there is none else,
6 I am the L', and there is none else.
7 evil: I the L' do all these things.
8 together; I the L' have created it.
11 Thus saith the L', the Holy One
13 nor reward, saith the L' of hosts.
14 saith the L', The labour of Egypt,
17 But Israel shall be saved in the L'
18 the L' that created the heavens;
18 I am the L'; and there is none else.
19 I the L' speak righteousness,
21 from that time? have not I the L'?
24 in the L' have I righteousness and
25 In the L' shall all the seed of Israel
47: 4 the L' of hosts is his name, the
48: 1 swear by the name of the L', and
2 The L' of hosts is his name.
14 The L' hath loved him: he will
16 the L' God, and his Spirit, hath
17 Thus saith the L', thy Redeemer,
17 L' thy God which teacheth thee
20 The L' hath redeemed his servant
22 There is no peace, saith the L',
49: 1 L' hath called me from the womb;
4 my judgment is with the L', and
5 saith the L' that formed me from
5 be glorious in the eyes of the L',
7 Thus saith the L', the Redeemer
7 because of the L' that is faithful,
8 Thus saith the L', In an acceptable
13 the L' hath comforted his people,
14 said, The L' hath forsaken me,
14 and my L' hath forgotten me.
18 saith the L', thou shalt surely
22 Thus saith the L' God, Behold, I
23 thou shalt know that I am the L':
25 But thus saith the L', Even the
26 I the L' am thy Saviour and thy
50: 1 saith the L', Where is the bill of
4 L' God hath given me the tongue
5 L' God hath opened mine ear, and
7 For the L' God will help me;
9 the L' God will help me; who is
10 is among you that feareth the L',
10 trust in the name of the L', and
51: 1 righteousness, ye that seek the L':
3 For the L' shall comfort Zion:
3 desert like the garden of the L';
9 put on strength, O arm of the L';
11 redeemed of the L' shall return,
13 forgettest the L' thy maker, that
15 I am the L' thy God, that divided
15 The L' of hosts is his name.
17 drunk at the hand of the L' the cup
20 they are full of the fury of the L',
22 Thus saith thy L'...and thy God
22 Thus saith...the L', and thy God
52: 3 thus saith the L', Ye have sold
4 thus saith the L' God, My people
5 what have I here, saith the L',
5 make them to howl, saith the L';
8 when the L' shall bring again Zion.
9 the L' hath comforted his people,
10 L' hath made bare his holy arm
11 that bear the vessels of the L'.
12 for the L' will go before you; and
53: 1 is the arm of the L' revealed?
6 L' hath laid on him the iniquity
10 it pleased the L' to bruise him;
10 pleasure of the L' shall prosper in
54: 1 of the married wife, saith the L'.
5 the L' of hosts is his name; and
6 L' hath called thee as a woman
8 thee, saith the L' thy Redeemer.
10 the L' that hath mercy on thee.

Isa 54:13 children shall be taught of the L';
17 heritage of the servants of the L',
17 righteousness is of me, saith the L'.
55: 5 thee because of the L' thy God,
6 Seek ye the L' while he may be
7 and let him return unto the L',
8 your ways my ways, saith the L'.
13 it shall be to the L' for a name,
56: 1 saith the L', Keep ye judgment,
3 that hath joined himself to the L',
3 L' hath utterly separated me from
4 saith the L' unto the eunuchs
6 that join themselves to the L', to
6 love the name of the L', to be his
8 The L' God which gathereth the
57:19 to him that is near, saith the L';
58: 5 and an acceptable day to the L'?
8 the glory of the L' shall be thy
9 thou call, and the L' shall answer;
11 the L' shall guide thee continually,
13 the holy of the L', honourable;
14 thou delight thyself in the L';
14 mouth of the L' hath spoken it.
59:13 and lying against the L', and
15 the L' saw it, and it displeased
19 fear the name of the L' from the
19 the Spirit of the L' shall lift up a
20 transgression in Jacob, saith the L'.
21 covenant with them, saith the L';
21 of thy seed's seed, saith the L',
60: 1 glory of the L' is risen upon thee.
2 the L' shall arise upon thee, and
6 shew forth the praises of the L'.
9 unto the name of the L' thy God,
14 shall call thee, The city of the L',
16 I the L' am thy Saviour and thy
19 but the L' shall be unto thee an
20 the L' shall be thine everlasting
22 I the L' will hasten it in his time.
61: 1 Spirit of the L' God is upon me;
1 the L' hath anointed me to preach
2 the acceptable year of the L', and
3 planting of the L', that he might
6 be named the Priests of the L':
8 I the L' love judgment, I hate
9 seed which the L' hath blessed.
10 I will greatly rejoice in the L',
11 L' God will cause righteousness
62: 2 the mouth of the L' shall name.
3 of glory in the hand of the L',
4 for the L' delighteth in thee, and
6 ye that make mention of the L',
8 L' hath sworn by his right hand,
9 it shall eat it, and praise the L';
11 L' hath proclaimed unto the end
12 people, The redeemed of the L':
63: 7 the lovingkindnesses of the L',
7 and the praises of the L',
7 that the L' hath bestowed on us,
14 Spirit of the L' caused him to rest:
16 thou, O L', art our father, our
17 O L', why hast thou made us to err
64: 8 now, O L', thou art our father;
9 Be not wroth very sore, O L',
12 thyself for these things, O L'?
65: 7 your fathers together, saith the L',
8 saith the L', As the new wine is
11 ye are they that forsake the L',
13 thus saith the L' God, Behold, my
15 the L' God shall slay thee, and
23 the seed of the blessed of the L',
25 my holy mountain, saith the L'.
66: 1 saith the L', The heaven is my
2 things have been, saith the L':
5 Hear the word of the L', ye that
5 sake, said, Let the L' be glorified:
6 a voice of the L' that rendereth
9 to bring forth? saith the L':
12 thus saith the L', Behold, I will
14 the hand of the L' shall be known
15 behold, the L' will come with fire,
16 will the L' plead with all flesh:
16 the slain of the L' shall be many.
17 consumed together, saith the L'.
20 for an offering unto the L' out of
20 mountain Jerusalem, saith the L',
20 vessel into the house of the L'.
21 and for Levites, saith the L'.
22 remain before me, saith the L',
23 worship before me, saith the L'.
Jer 1: 2 To whom the word of the L' came
4 the word of the L' came unto me,
6 Ah, L' God! behold, I cannot speak:
7 But the L' said unto me, Say not,
8 thee to deliver thee, saith the L'.
9 the L' put forth his hand, and
9 And the L' said unto me, Behold
11 the word of the L' came unto me,
12 Then said the L' unto me, Thou
13 word of the L' came unto me the
14 Then the L' said unto me, Out of
15 kingdoms of the north, saith the L';
19 for I am with thee, saith the L',
2: 1 the word of the L' came to me,
2 Thus saith the L'; I remember
3 Israel was holiness unto the L',
3 come upon them, saith the L'.
4 Hear ye the word of the L', O
5 Thus saith the L', What iniquity
6 Where is the L' that brought us
8 priests said not, Where is the L'?
9 yet plead with you, saith the L',
12 be ye very desolate, saith the L'.
17, 19 hast forsaken the L' thy God,
19 not in thee, saith the L' God of hosts.
22 marked before me, saith the L' God.

Jer 2:29 against me, saith the L'.
31 see ye the word of the L'. Have I
37 L' hath rejected thy confidences,
3: 1 return again to me, saith the L'.
6 L' said also unto me in the days
10 heart, but feignedly, saith the L'.
11 L' said unto me, The backsliding
12 backsliding Israel, saith the L';
12 I am merciful, saith the L', and
13 transgressed against the L' thy
13 not obeyed my voice, saith the L'.
14 backsliding children, saith the L';
16 saith the L', they shall say no more,
16 The ark of the covenant of the L':
17 call Jerusalem the throne of the L';
17 unto it, to the name of the L', to
20 me, O house of Israel, saith the L'.
21 have forgotten the L' their God.
22 thee; for thou art the L' our God.
23 in the L' our God is the salvation
25 we have sinned against the L' our
25 not obeyed the voice of the L' our
4: 1 wilt return, O Israel, saith the L',
2 L' liveth, in truth, in judgment,
3 thus saith the L' to the men of
4 Circumcise yourselves to the L',
8 anger of the L' is not turned back
9 to pass at that day, saith the L',
10 L' God! surely thou hast greatly
17 rebellious against me, saith the L'.
26 down at the presence of the L',
27 thus hath the L' said, The whole
5: 2 though they say, The L' liveth;
3 O L', are not thine eyes upon the
4 they know not the way of the L',
5 they have known the way of the L',
9 for these things? saith the L':
11 very treacherously...saith the L'.
12 They have belied the L', and said,
14 thus saith the L' God of hosts,
15 O house of Israel, saith the L':
18 saith the L', I will not make a full
19 Wherefore doeth the L' our God
22 Fear ye not me? saith the L': will
24 Let us now fear the L' our God,
29 for these things? saith the L':
6: 6 For thus hath the L' of hosts said,
9 Thus saith the L' of hosts, They
10 the word of the L' is unto them a
11 I am full of the fury of the L';
12 inhabitants of...land, saith the L'.
15 shall be cast down, saith the L'.
16 Thus saith the L', Stand ye in the
21 thus saith the L', Behold, I will lay
22 Thus saith the L', Behold, a people
30 because the L' hath rejected them.
7: 1 came to Jeremiah from the L',
2 Hear the word of the L', all ye of
2 at these gates to worship the L'.
3 saith the L' of hosts, the God of
4 The temple of the L', The temple
4 of the L', The temple of the L',
11 even I have seen it, saith the L'.
13 done all these works, saith the L',
19 provoke me to anger? saith the L':
20 thus saith the L' God; Behold, mine
21 the L' of hosts, the God of Israel;
28 that obeyeth not the voice of the L'
29 L' hath rejected and forsaken the
30 done evil in my sight, saith the L':
32 saith the L', that it shall no more
8: 1 saith the L', they shall bring out
3 driven them, saith the L' of hosts.
4 Thus saith the L'; Shall they fall,
7 know not the judgment of the L'.
8 and the law of the L' is with us?
9 have rejected the word of the L';
12 shall be cast down, saith the L'.
13 surely consume them, saith the L':
14 L' our God hath put us to silence,
14 we have sinned against the L'.
17 they shall bite you, saith the L'.
19 Is not the L' in Zion? is not her
9: 3 they know not me, saith the L'.
6 refuse to know me, saith the L'.
7 thus saith the L' of hosts, Behold,
9 for these things? saith the L':
12 the mouth of the L' hath spoken,
13 the L' saith, Because they have
15 the L' of hosts, the God of Israel;
17 saith the L' of hosts, Consider
20 Yet hear the word of the L', O ye
22 Speak, Thus saith the L', Even
23 Thus saith the L', Let not the wise
24 L' which exercise lovingkindness
24 these things I delight, saith the L'.
25 the days come, saith the L', that
10: 1 the word which the L' speaketh
2 Thus saith the L', Learn not the
6 there is none like unto thee, O L';
10 the L' is the true God, he is the
16 The L' of hosts is his name.
18 For thus saith the L', Behold, I
21 and have not sought the L':
23 O L', I know that the way of man
24 L', correct me, but with judgment;
11: 1 that came to Jeremiah from the L',
3 Thus saith the L' God of Israel;
5 answered I, and said, So be it, O L'.
6 the L' said unto me, Proclaim
9 L' said unto me, A conspiracy
11 thus saith the L', Behold, I will
16 The L' called thy name, A green
17 For the L' of hosts, that planted
18 L' hath given me knowledge of it,
20 But, O L' of hosts, that judgest

Jer 11:21 thus saith the L' of the men of
21 prophesy not in the name of the L',
22 thus saith the L' of hosts, Behold,
12: 1 Righteous art thou, O L', when I
3 But thou, O L', knowest me: thou
12 sword of the L' shall devour from
13 because of the fierce anger of the L'.
14 saith the L' against all mine evil
16 swear by my name, The L' liveth;
17 destroy that nation, saith the L'.
13: 1 saith the L' unto me, Go and get
2 according to the word of the L',
3 the word of the L' came unto me
5 Euphrates, as the L' commanded
6 the L' said unto me, Arise, go to
8 the word of the L' came unto me,
9 saith the L', After this manner
11 whole house of Judah, saith the L';
12 Thus saith the L' God of Israel,
13 Thus saith the L', Behold, I will
14 the sons together, saith the L':
15 not proud: for the L' hath spoken.
16 Give glory to the L' your God,
25 measures from me, saith the L';
14: 1 The word of the L' that came to
7 O L', though our iniquities testify
9 thou, O L', art in the midst of us,
10 Thus saith the L' unto this people,
10 the L' doth not accept them;
11 Then said the L' unto me, Pray
13 Ah, L' God! behold, the prophets
14 L' said unto me, The prophets
15 thus saith the L' concerning the
20 We acknowledge, O L', our
22 art not thou he, O L' our God?
15: 1 Then said the L' unto me, Though
2 Thus saith the L'; Such as are for
3 over them four kinds, saith the L':
6 hast forsaken me, saith the L',
9 before their enemies, saith the L'.
11 The L' said, Verily it shall be well
15 O L', thou knowest: remember
16 by thy name, O L' God of hosts.
19 thus saith the L', If thou return,
20 and to deliver thee, saith the L'.
16: 1 The word of the L' came also unto
3 saith the L' concerning the sons
5 thus saith the L', Enter not into
5 from this people, saith the L',
9 the L' of hosts, the God of Israel;
10 L' pronounced all this great evil
10 have committed against the L' our
11 have forsaken me, saith the L',
14 the days come, saith the L', that
14, 15 The L' liveth, that brought up
16 send for many fishers, saith the L',
19 L', my strength, and my fortress,
21 shall know that my name is The L'.
17: 5 Thus saith the L'; Cursed be the
5 whose heart departeth from the L'.
7 the man that trusteth in the L',
7 and whose hope the L' is.
10 I the L' search the heart, I try the
13 O L', the hope of Israel, all that
13 forsaken the L', the fountain of
14 Heal me, O L', and I shall be
15 Where is the word of the L'? let it
19 said the L' unto me; Go and stand
20 Hear ye the word of the L', ye
21 Thus saith the L'; Take heed to
24 hearken unto me, saith the L',
26 praise, unto the house of the L'.
18: 1 came to Jeremiah from the L',
5 the word of the L' came to me,
6 you as this potter? saith the L'.
11 saith the L'; Behold, I frame
13 thus saith the L'; Ask ye now
19 Give heed to me, O L', and hearken
23 L', thou knowest all their counsel
19: 1 Thus saith the L', Go and get a
3 say, Hear ye the word of the L', O
3 Thus saith the L' of hosts, the
6 the days come, saith the L', that
11 them, Thus saith the L' of hosts;
12 I do unto this place, saith the L',
14 the L' had sent him to prophesy;
15 Thus saith the L' of hosts, the
20: 1 governor in the house of the L',
2 which was by the house of the L'.
3 The L' hath not called thy name
4 thus saith the L', Behold, I will
7 O L', thou hast deceived me, and
8 word of the L' was made a reproach
11 L' is with me as a mighty terrible
12 But, O L' of hosts, that triest the
13 Sing unto the L', praise ye the L':
16 the cities which the L' overthrew,
21: 1 came unto Jeremiah from the L',
2 Enquire, I pray thee, of the L' for
2 L' will deal with us according to
4 Thus saith the L' God of Israel;
7 And afterward, saith the L', I will
8 Thus saith the L'; Behold, I set
10 and not for good, saith the L':
11 say, Hear ye the word of the L';
12 saith the L'; Execute judgment
13 and rock of the plain, saith the L';
14 fruit of your doings, saith the L':
22: 1 Thus saith the L'; Go down to
2 Hear the word of the L', O king
3 Thus saith the L'; Execute ye
5 I swear by myself, saith the L',
6 thus saith the L' unto the king's
8 L' done thus unto this great city?
9 forsaken the covenant of the L'
11 saith the L' touching Shallum the

Jer 22: 16 not this to know me? saith the *L'*.
18 saith the *L'* concerning Jehoiakim
18 saying, Ah *l'*! or, Ah his glory!
24 As I live, saith the *L'*, though
29 earth, hear the word of the *L'*.
30 Thus saith the *L'*, Write ye this
23: 1 sheep of my pasture! saith the *L'*.
2 thus saith the *L'* God of Israel
2 evil of your doings, saith the *L'*.
4 shall they be lacking, saith the *L'*.
5 the days come, saith the *L'*, that
6 called, The *L'* Our Righteousness.
7 the days come, saith the *L'*, that
7, 8 The *L'* liveth, which brought up
9 hath overcome, because of the *L'*,
11 their wickedness, saith the *L'*.
12 of their visitation, saith the *L'*.
15 saith the *L'* of hosts concerning
16 saith the *L'* of hosts, Hearken
16 and not out of the mouth of the *L'*.
17 The *L'* hath said, Ye shall have
18 hath stood in the counsel of the *L'*,
19 whirlwind of the *L'* is gone forth
20 anger of the *L'* shall not return,
23 Am I a God at hand, saith the *L'*,
24 I shall not see him? saith the *L'*.
24 heaven and earth? saith the *L'*.
28 chaff to the wheat? saith the *L'*.
29 word like as a fire? saith the *L'*;
30, 31 the prophets, saith the *L'*,
32 prophesy false dreams, saith the *L'*,
32 this people at all, saith the *L'*.
33 What is the burden of the *L'*?
33 will even forsake you, saith the *L'*.
34 The burden of the *L'*, I will even
35 What hath the *L'* answered?
35 and, What hath the *L'* spoken?
36 burden of the *L'* shall ye mention
36 God, of the *L'* of hosts our God.
37 What hath the *L'* answered thee?
37 and, What hath the *L'* spoken?
38 ye say, The burden of the *L'*;
38 therefore thus saith the *L'*;
38 this word, The burden of the *L'*,
38 not say, The burden of the *L'*;
24: 1 The *L'* shewed me, and, behold,
1 set before the temple of the *L'*,
3 said the *L'* unto me, What seest
4 the word of the *L'* came unto me,
5 saith the *L'*, the God of Israel;
7 to know me, that I am the *L'*:
8 surely thus saith the *L'*, So will I
25: 3 word of the *L'* hath come unto me,
4 the *L'* hath sent unto you all his
5 in the land that the *L'* hath given
7 hearkened unto me, saith the *L'*;
8 thus saith the *L'* of hosts; Because
9 of the north, saith the *L'*, and
12 and that nation, saith the *L'*, for
15 For thus saith the *L'* God of Israel
17 unto whom the *L'* had sent me:
27 Thus saith the *L'* of hosts, the God
28 Thus saith the *L'* of hosts; Ye shall
29 of the earth, saith the *L'* of hosts.
30 The *L'* shall roar from on high,
31 the *L'* hath a controversy with the
31 wicked to the sword, saith the *L'*.
32 Thus saith the *L'* of hosts, Behold,
33 slain of the *L'* shall be at that day
36 the *L'* hath spoiled their pasture.
37 because of the fierce anger of the *L'*.
26: 1 Judah came this word from the *L'*,
2 saith the *L'*; Stand in the court
4 Thus saith the *L'*; If ye will not
7 these words in the house of the *L'*.
8 all that the *L'* had commanded
9 prophesied in the name of the *L'*,
9 Jeremiah in the house of the *L'*.
10 house unto the house of the *L'*,
12 *L'* sent me to prophesy against
13 obey the voice of the *L'* your God;
13 *L'* will repent him of the evil that
15 for of a truth the *L'* hath sent me
16 us in the name of the *L'* our God.
18 saith the *L'* of hosts; Zion shall
19 fear the *L'*, and besought the *L'*,
19 *L'* repented him of the evil which
20 prophesied in the name of the *L'*,
27: 1 word unto Jeremiah from the *L'*,
2 saith the *L'* to me; Make thee
4 saith the *L'* of hosts, the God of
8 nation will I punish, saith the *L'*,
11 in their own land, saith the *L'*;
13 as the *L'* hath spoken against the
15 I have not sent them, saith the *L'*,
16 Thus saith the *L'*; Hearken not to
18 the word of the *L'* be with them,
18 intercession to the *L'* of hosts,
18 are left in the house of the *L'*,
19 saith the *L'* of hosts concerning
21 saith the *L'* of hosts, the God of
21 remain in the house of the *L'*,
22 day that I visit them, saith the *L'*;
28: 1 unto me in the house of the *L'*,
2 speaketh the *L'* of hosts, the God
4 went into Babylon, saith the *L'*:
5 that stood in the house of the *L'*,
6 the *L'* do so: the *L'* perform thy
9 that the *L'* hath truly sent him.
11 Thus saith the *L'*; Even so will I
12 word of the *L'* came unto Jeremiah
13 saith the *L'*; Thou hast broken
14 saith the *L'* of hosts, the God of
15 The *L'* hath not sent thee; but
16 saith the *L'*; Behold, I will cast
16 taught rebellion against the *L'*.

Jer 29: 4 saith the *L'* of hosts, the God of
7 and pray unto the *L'* for it: for in
8 saith the *L'* of hosts, the God of
9 have not sent them, saith the *L'*.
10 saith the *L'*, That after seventy
11 I think toward you, saith the *L'*,
14 will be found of you, saith the *L'*:
14 I have driven you, saith the *L'*;
15 The *L'* hath raised us up prophets
16 that thus saith the *L'* of the king
17 saith the *L'* of hosts; Behold, I
19 hearkened to my words,...the *L'*,
19 ye would not hear, saith the *L'*.
20 Hear ye...the word of the *L'*, all
21 saith the *L'* of hosts, the God of
22 *L'* make thee like Zedekiah and
23 and am a witness, saith the *L'*.
25 Thus speaketh the *L'* of hosts, the
26 *L'* hath made thee priest in the
26 be officers in the house of the *L'*,
30 the word of the *L'* unto Jeremiah,
31 saith the *L'* concerning Shemaiah
32 thus saith the *L'*; Behold, I will
32 will do for my people, saith the *L'*;
32 taught rebellion against the *L'*.
30: 1 that came to Jeremiah from the *L'*,
2 speaketh the *L'* God of Israel,
3 the days come, saith the *L'*, that
3 Israel and Judah, saith the *L'*:
4 are the words that the *L'* spake
5 thus saith the *L'*; We have heard
8 saith the *L'* of hosts, that I will
9 shall serve the *L'* their God, and
10 O my servant Jacob, saith the *L'*;
11 For I am with thee, saith the *L'*,
12 thus saith the *L'*, Thy bruise is
17 thee of thy wounds, saith the *L'*;
18 Thus saith the *L'*; Behold, I will
21 approach unto me? saith the *L'*.
23 whirlwind of the *L'* goeth forth
24 anger of the *L'* shall not return,
31: 1 saith the *L'*, will I be the God of
2 saith the *L'*, The people which
3 *L'* hath appeared of old unto me,
6 us go up to Zion unto the *L'* our
7 saith the *L'*; Sing with gladness
7 and say, O *L'*, save thy people,
10 Hear the word of the *L'*, O ye
11 For the *L'* hath redeemed Jacob,
12 to the goodness of the *L'*, for
14 with my goodness, saith the *L'*.
15 saith the *L'*; A voice was heard
16 saith the *L'*; Refrain thy voice
16 shall be rewarded, saith the *L'*;
17 is hope in thine end, saith the *L'*,
18 for thou art the *L'* my God.
20 mercy upon him, saith the *L'*.
22 *L'* hath created a new thing in the
23 saith the *L'* of hosts, the God of
23 The *L'* bless thee, O habitation
27 the days come, saith the *L'*, that
28 build, and to plant, saith the *L'*.
31 the days come, saith the *L'*, that
32 husband unto them, saith the *L'*:
33 After those days, saith the *L'*, I
34 Know the *L'*: for they shall all
34 the greatest of them, saith the *L'*:
35 Thus saith the *L'*, which giveth
35 The *L'* of hosts is his name:
36 from before me, saith the *L'*,
37 saith the *L'*; If heaven above can
37 that they have done, saith the *L'*.
38 the days come, saith the *L'*, that
38 city shall be built to the *L'* from
40 east, shall be holy unto the *L'*;
32: 1 came to Jeremiah from the *L'* in
3 Thus saith the *L'*, Behold, I will
5 until I visit him, saith the *L'*:
6 The word of the *L'* came unto me,
8 according to the word of the *L'*,
8 that this was the word of the *L'*.
14 saith the *L'* of hosts, the God of
15 For thus saith the *L'* of hosts,
16 I prayed unto the *L'*, saying,
17 Ah *L'* God! behold, thou hast made
18 God, The *L'* of hosts, is his name,
25 thou hast said unto me, O *L'* God,
26 the word of the *L'* unto Jeremiah,
27 Behold, I am the *L'*, the God of
28 Therefore thus saith the *L'*;
30 work of their hands, saith the *L'*.
36 therefore thus saith the *L'*, the
42 For thus saith the *L'*; Like as I
44 captivity to return, saith the *L'*.
33: 1 the word of the *L'* came unto
2 saith the *L'* the maker thereof,
2 the *L'* that formed it, to establish
2 establish it; The *L'* is his name;
4 For thus saith the *L'*, the God of
10 Thus saith the *L'*; again there
11 shall say, Praise the *L'* of hosts:
11 for the *L'* is good; for his mercy
11 of praise into the house of the *L'*.
11 land, as at the first, saith the *L'*.
12 Thus saith the *L'* of hosts; Again
13 that telleth them, saith the *L'*.
14 saith the *L'*, that I will perform
16 called, The *L'* our righteousness.
17 For thus saith the *L'*; David shall
19 And the word of the *L'* came unto
20 Thus saith the *L'*; If ye can break
23 word of the *L'* came to Jeremiah,
24 two families which the *L'* hath
25 Thus saith the *L'*; If my covenant
34: 1 came unto Jeremiah from the *L'*,
2 Thus saith the *L'*, the God of

Jer 34: 2 and tell him, Thus saith the *L'*;
4 Yet hear the word of the *L'*, O
4 Thus saith the *L'* of thee, Thou
5 will lament thee, saying, Ah *l'*!
5 pronounced the word, saith the *L'*.
8 came unto Jeremiah from the *L'*,
12 word of the *L'* came to Jeremiah
12 came to Jeremiah from the *L'*,
13 Thus saith the *L'*, the God of
17 thus saith the *L'*; Ye have not
17 a liberty for you, saith the *L'*,
22 I will command, saith the *L'*, and
35: 1 came unto Jeremiah from the *L'*,
2, 4 them into the house of the *L'*,
12 the word of the *L'* unto Jeremiah,
13 Thus saith the *L'* of hosts, the
13 to my words? saith the *L'*.
17 thus saith the *L'* God of hosts,
18 Thus saith the *L'* of hosts, the
19 thus saith the *L'* of hosts; the
36: 1 came unto Jeremiah from the *L'*,
4 Jeremiah all the words of the *L'*,
5 go into the house of the *L'*:
6 words of the *L'* in the ears of the
7 their supplication before the *L'*,
7 fury that the *L'* hath pronounced
8 in the book the words of the *L'* in
9 proclaimed a fast before the *L'*
10 Jeremiah in the house of the *L'*,
11 the book all the words of the *L'*,
26 the prophet: but the *L'* hid them.
27 word of the *L'* came to Jeremiah,
29 Thus saith the *L'*; Thou hast
30 saith the *L'* of Jehoiakim king of
37: 2 hearken unto the words of the *L'*,
3 Pray now unto the *L'* our God
6 word of the *L'* unto the prophet
7 Thus saith the *L'*, the God of
9 Thus saith the *L'*; Deceive not
17 Is there any word from the *L'*?
20 I pray thee, O my *l'* the king:
38: 2 Thus saith the *L'*, He that
3 Thus saith the *L'*, This city shall
9 My *l'* the king, these men have
14 that is in the house of the *L'*:
16 As the *L'* liveth, that made us this
17 unto Zedekiah, Thus saith the *L'*,
20 I beseech thee, the voice of the *L'*,
21 the word that the *L'* hath shewed
39: 15 the word of the *L'* came unto
16 saith the *L'* of hosts, the God of
17 thee in that day, saith the *L'*:
18 put thy trust in me, saith the *L'*.
40: 1 came to Jeremiah from the *L'*,
2 *L'* thy God hath pronounced this
3 Now the *L'* hath brought it, and
3 ye have sinned against the *L'*,
41: 5 bring them to the house of the *L'*.
42: 2 pray for us unto the *L'* thy God,
3 *L'* thy God may shew us the way
4 I will pray unto the *L'* your God
4 thing the *L'* shall answer you, I
5 *L'* be a true and faithful witness
5 *L'* thy God shall send thee to us.
6 will obey the voice of the *L'* our
6 we obey the voice of the *L'* our
7 the word of the *L'* came unto
9 saith the *L'*, the God of Israel,
11 not afraid of him, saith the *L'*:
13 neither obey the voice of the *L'*
15 therefore hear the word of the *L'*,
15, 18 saith the *L'* of hosts, the God
19 The *L'* hath said concerning you,
20 ye sent me unto the *L'* your God,
20 Pray for us unto the *L'* our God;
20 all that the *L'* our God shall say,
21 not obeyed the voice of the *L'*
43: 1 all the words of the *L'* their God,
1 the *L'* their God had sent him
2 *L'* our God hath not sent thee to
4 obeyed not the voice of the *L'*,
7 obeyed not the voice of the *L'*:
8 the word of the *L'* unto Jeremiah
10 saith the *L'* of hosts, the God of
44: 2 saith the *L'* of hosts, the God of
7 thus saith the *L'*, the God of hosts,
11 saith the *L'* of hosts, the God of
16 unto us in the name of the *L'*,
21 did not the *L'* remember them,
22 that the *L'* could no longer bear,
23 ye have sinned against the *L'*,
23 not obeyed the voice of the *L'*,
24 Hear the word of the *L'*, all Judah
25 saith the *L'* of hosts, the God of
26 hear ye the word of the *L'*, all
26 by my great name, saith the *L'*,
26 Egypt, saying, The *L'* God liveth.
29 be a sign unto you, saith the *L'*,
30 Thus saith the *L'*; Behold, I will
45: 2 saith the *L'*, the God of Israel,
3 *L'* hath added grief to my sorrow;
4 The *L'* saith thus; Behold, that
5 evil upon all flesh, saith the *L'*:
46: 1 The word of the *L'* which came to
5 was round about, saith the *L'*.
10 is the day of the *L'* God of hosts,
10 *L'* God of hosts hath a sacrifice in
13 The word that the *L'* spake to
15 because the *L'* did drive them.
18 whose name is the *L'* of hosts,
23 cut down her forest, saith the *L'*,
25 The *L'* of hosts, the God of Israel,
26 in the days of old, saith the *L'*.
28 O Jacob my servant, saith the *L'*:
47: 1 The word of the *L'* that came to
2 Thus saith the *L'*; Behold, waters

Jer 47: 4 the L' will spoil the Philistines,
6 O thou sword of the L', how long
7 seeing the L' hath given it a
48: 1 Against Moab thus saith the L'
8 destroyed, as the L' hath spoken.
10 he that doeth the work of the L'
12 the days come, saith the L', that
15 whose name is the L' of hosts.
25 his arm is broken, saith the L'.
26 magnified himself against the L':
30 I know his wrath, saith the L';
35 to cease in Moab, saith the L',
38 is no pleasure, saith the L'.
40 thus saith the L'; Behold, he shall
42 magnified himself against the L'.
43 inhabitant of Moab, saith the L'.
44 of their visitation, saith the L'.
47 in the latter days, saith the L'.
49: 1 the Ammonites, thus saith the L';
2 saith the L', that I will cause an
2 that were his heirs, saith the L'.
5 a fear upon thee, saith the L'
6 children of Ammon, saith the L'.
7 Concerning Edom, thus saith the L'
12 For thus saith the L'; Behold,
13 sworn by myself, saith the L',
14 have heard a rumour from the L',
16 down from thence, saith the L'.
18 saith the L', no man shall abide
20 hear the counsel of the L', that he
26 cut off in that day, saith the L' of
28 shall smite, thus saith the L';
30 inhabitants of Hazor, saith the L';
31 without care, saith the L', which
32 all sides thereof, saith the L'.
34 The word of the L' that came to
35 Thus saith the L' of hosts, Behold,
37 even my fierce anger, saith the L';
38 and the princes, saith the L'.
39 captivity of Elam, saith the L'.
50: 1 word that the L' spake against
4 saith the L', the children of Israel
4 go, and seek the L' their God.
5 and let us join ourselves to the L'
7 they have sinned against the L',
7 even the L', the hope of their
10 her shall be satisfied, saith the L'.
13 Because of the wrath of the L' it
14 she hath sinned against the L'.
15 for it is the vengeance of the L':
18 saith the L' of hosts, the God of
20 saith the L', the iniquity of Israel
21 destroy after them, saith the L',
24 thou hast striven against the L'.
25 The L' hath opened his armoury,
25 for this is the work of the L' God
28 the vengeance of the L' our God,
29 hath been proud against the L',
30 cut off in that day, saith the L'.
31 most proud, saith the L' God of
33 Thus saith the L' of hosts; The
34 The L' of hosts is his name: he
35 upon the Chaldeans, saith the L',
40 cities thereof, saith the L';
45 hear ye the counsel of the L', that
51: 1 Thus saith the L'; Behold, I will
5 of his God, of the L' of hosts;
10 The L' hath brought forth our
10 declare in Zion the work of the L'
11 the L' hath raised up the spirit
11 it is the vengeance of the L',
12 L' hath both devised and done
14 L' of hosts hath sworn by himself,
19 The L' of hosts is his name.
24 Zion in your sight, saith the L'.
25 destroying mountain, saith the L',
26 be desolate for ever, saith the L'.
29 every purpose of the L' shall be
33 saith the L' of hosts, the God of
36 thus saith the L'; Behold, I will
39 and not awake, saith the L'.
45 from the fierce anger of the L'.
48 her from the north, saith the L'.
50 remember the L' afar off, and let
52 the days come, saith the L', that
53 come unto her, saith the L'.
55 the L' hath spoiled Babylon, and
56 the L' God of recompenses shall
57 whose name is the L' of hosts.
58 Thus saith the L' of hosts; The
62 O L', thou hast spoken against
52: 2 was evil in the eyes of the L',
3 through the anger of the L' it
13 burned the house of the L', and
17 that were in the house of the L',
17 that was in the house of the L',
20 had made in the house of the L':
La 1: 5 the L' hath afflicted her for the
9 O L', behold my affliction: for
11 see, O L', and consider; for I am
12 wherewith the L' hath afflicted
14 the L' hath delivered me into their
15 L' hath trodden under foot all my
15 the L' hath trodden the virgin, the
17 the L' hath commanded...Jacob,
18 The L' is righteous; for I have
20 Behold, O L'; for I am in distress:
2: 1 hath the L' covered the daughter
2 The L' hath swallowed up all the
5 The L' was as an enemy: he hath
6 L' hath caused the solemn feasts
7 the L' hath cast off his altar, he
7 a noise in the house of the L',
8 The L' hath purposed to destroy
9 also find no vision from the L'.
17 L' hath done that which he had

La 2: 18 Their heart cried unto the L', O
19 water before the face of the L':
20 Behold, O L', and consider to
20 be slain in the sanctuary of the L'?
3: 18 my hope is perished from the L':
24 The L' is my portion, saith my
25 L' is good unto them that wait
26 wait for the salvation of the L'.
31 For the L' will not cast off for ever:
36 in his cause, the L' approveth not.
37 when the L' commandeth it not?
40 ways, and turn again to the L'.
50 Till the L' look down, and behold
55 I called upon thy name, O L', out
58 O L', thou hast pleaded the causes
59 O L', thou hast seen my wrong:
61 hast heard their reproach, O L',
64 unto them a recompense, O L',
66 from under the heavens of the L'.
4: 11 L' hath accomplished his fury;
16 The anger of the L' hath divided
20 nostrils, the anointed of the L',
5: 1 Remember, O L', what is come
19 Thou, O L', remainest for ever;
21 Turn thou us unto thee, O L',
Eze 1: 3 The word of the L' came expressly
3 the hand of the L' was there upon
28 likeness of the glory of the L'.
2: 4 unto them, Thus saith the L' God.
3: 11 tell them, Thus saith the L' God;
12 Blessed be the glory of the L'
14 hand of the L' was strong upon
16 the word of the L' came unto me,
22 hand of the L' was there upon me;
23 the glory of the L' stood there,
27 Thus saith the L' God; He that
4: 13 And the L' said, Even thus shall
14 said I, Ah L' God! behold, my soul
5: 5 Thus saith the L' God; This is
7, 8 Therefore thus saith the L' God;
11 as I live, saith the L' God; Surely,
13 the L' have spoken it in my zeal,
15 rebukes. I the L' have spoken it.
17 thee. I the L' have spoken it.
6: 1 the word of the L' came unto me,
3 hear the word of the L' God; Thus
3 Thus saith the L' God to the
7 ye shall know that I am the L'.
10 they shall know that I am the L',
11 Thus saith the L' God; Smite with
13 shall ye know that I am the L',
14 they shall know that I am the L'.
7: 1 the word of the L' came unto me,
2 saith the L' God unto the land of
4 ye shall know that I am the L'.
5 Thus saith the L' God; An evil,
9 that I am the L' that smiteth.
19 in the day of the wrath of the L':
27 they shall know that I am the L'.
8: 1 hand of the L' God fell there upon
12 they say, The L' seeth us not;
12 the L' hath forsaken the earth.
16 at the door of the temple of the L',
16 backs toward the temple of the L',
9: 4 the L' said unto him, Go through
8 Ah L' God! wilt thou destroy all
9 The L' hath forsaken the earth,
9 the earth, and the L' seeth not.
10: 4 the glory of the L' went up from
18 the glory of the L' departed from
11: 5 the Spirit of the L' fell upon me,
5 Thus saith the L'; Thus have ye
7 thus saith the L' God; Your slain
8 sword upon you, saith the L' God.
10 ye shall know that I am the L'.
12 ye shall know that I am the L':
13 Ah L' God! wilt thou make a full
14 the word of the L' came unto me,
15 have said, Get you far from the L':
16, 17 say, Thus saith the L' God;
21 their own heads, saith the L' God.
23 the glory of the L' went up from
25 things that the L' had shewed me.
12: 1 word of the L' also came unto me,
8 came the word of the L' unto me,
10 unto them, Thus saith the L' God;
15 they shall know that I am the L',
16 they shall know that I am the L'.
17 the word of the L' came to me,
19 saith the L' God of the inhabitants
20 ye shall know that I am the L'.
21 the word of the L' came unto me,
23 Thus saith the L' God; I will make
25 I am the L': I will speak, and the
25 will perform it, saith the L' God.
26 the word of the L' came to me,
28 saith the L' God; There shall
28 shall be done, saith the L' God.
13: 1 the word of the L' came unto me,
2 Hear ye the word of the L';
3 Thus saith the L' God; Woe unto
5 in the battle in the day of the L'.
6 The L' saith: and the L' hath not
7 whereas ye say, The L' saith it;
8 thus saith the L' God; Because
8 I am against you, saith the L' God.
9 ye shall know that I am the L' God.
13 saith the L' God; I will even rend
14 ye shall know that I am the L'.
16 there is no peace, saith the L' God.
18 Thus saith the L' God; Woe to the
20 Thus saith the L' God; Behold, I
21, 23 ye shall know that I am the L'.
14: 2 the word of the L' came unto me,
4 Thus saith the L' God; Every man
4 L' will answer him that cometh

Eze 14: 6 of Israel, Thus saith the L' God;
7 L' will answer him by myself:
8 ye shall know that I am the L'.
9 L' have deceived that prophet,
11 may be their God, saith the L' God.
12 word of the L' came again to me,
14 righteousness, saith the L' God.
16, 18, 20 as I live, saith the L' God, they
21 thus saith the L' God; How much
23 I have done in it, saith the L' God.
15: 1 the word of the L' came unto me,
6 thus saith the L' God; As the vine
7 ye shall know that I am the L',
8 a trespass, saith the L' God.
16: 1 the word of the L' came unto me,
3 saith the L' God unto Jerusalem;
8 covenant with thee, saith the L' God,
14 had put upon thee, saith the L' God.
19 and thus it was, saith the L' God.
23 woe unto thee! saith the L' God,)
30 weak is thine heart, saith the L' God,
35 O harlot, hear the word of the L':
36 Thus saith the L' God; Because
43 upon thine head, saith the L' God:
48 saith the L' God, Sodom thy sister
58 thine abominations, saith the L'.
59 thus saith the L' God; I will even
62 thou shalt know that I am the L':
63 thou hast done, saith the L' God.
17: 1 the word of the L' came unto me,
3 saith the L' God; A great eagle
9 saith the L' God; Shall it prosper?
11 the word of the L' came unto me,
16 As I live, saith the L' God, surely
19 Therefore thus saith the L' God; As
21 know that I the L' have spoken it.
22 Thus saith the L' God; I will also
24 I the L' have brought down the
24 L' have spoken and have done it.
18: 1 The word of the L' came unto me
3 As I live, saith the L' God, ye shall
9 shall surely live, saith the L' God.
23 wicked should die? saith the L' God:
25 ye say, The way of the L' is not equal.
29 Israel, The way of the L' is not equal.
30 to his ways, saith the L' God.
32 of him that dieth, saith the L' God:
20: 1 Israel came to enquire of the L',
2 came the word of the L' unto me,
3 saith the L' God; Are ye come to
3 As I live, saith the L' God, I will not
5 Thus saith the L' God; In the day
5 saying, I am the L' your God;
7 of Egypt: I am the L' your God.
12 I am the L' that sanctify them.
19 I am the L' your God; walk in my
20 know that I am the L' your God.
26 they might know that I am the L'.
27 saith the L' God; Yet in this your
30 saith the L' God; Are ye polluted
31 As I live, saith the L' God, I will not
33 As I live, saith the L' God, surely
36 I plead with you, saith the L' God.
38 ye shall know that I am the L'.
39 saith the L' God; Go ye, serve ye
40 the height of Israel, saith the L' God,
42, 44 shall know that I am the L',
44 ye house of Israel, saith the L' God.
45 the word of the L' came unto me,
47 the south, Hear the word of the L';
47 Thus saith the L' God; Behold, I
48 see that I the L' have kindled it:
49 Ah L' God! they say of me, Doth he
21: 1 the word of the L' came unto me,
3 Thus saith the L'; Behold, I am
5 I the L' have drawn forth my sword
7 brought to pass, saith the L' God.
8 the word of the L' came unto me,
9 Thus saith the L'; Say, A sword,
13 shall be no more, saith the L' God.
17 fury to rest: I the L' have said it.
18 word of the L' came unto me again,
24 thus saith the L' God; Because ye
26 thus saith the L' God; Remove the
28 thus saith the L' God concerning the
32 for I the L' have spoken it.
22: 1 the word of the L' came unto me,
3 Thus saith the L' God; The city
12 hast forgotten me, saith the L' God.
14 I the L' have spoken it, and will
16 thou shalt know that I am the L'.
17 the word of the L' came unto me,
19 Therefore thus saith the L' God;
22 I the L' have poured out my fury
23 the word of the L' came unto me,
28 saying, Thus saith the L' God,
28 when the L' hath not spoken.
31 upon their heads, saith the L' God.
23: 1 word of the L' came again unto
22 O Aholibah, thus saith the L' God;
28 For thus saith the L' God; Behold, I
32 Thus saith the L' God; Thou shalt
34 I have spoken it, saith the L' God.
35 Therefore thus saith the L' God;
36 L' said moreover unto me; Son of
46 thus saith the L' God; I will bring
49 ye shall know that I am the L' God.
24: 1 the word of the L' came unto me,
3 Thus saith the L' God; Set on a pot,
6, 9 saith the L' God; Woe to the bloody
14 I the L' have spoken it: it shall
14 they judge thee, saith the L' God.
15 the word of the L' came unto me,
20 The word of the L' came unto me,
21 Thus saith the L' God; Behold, I
24 ye shall know that I am the L' God.

Eze 24:27 they shall know that I am the L·.
25: 1 word of the L· came again unto
3 Hear the word of the L· God;
3 Thus saith the L· God; Because
5 ye shall know that I am the L·.
6 For thus saith the L· God; Because
7 thou shalt know that I am the L·.
8 Thus saith the L· God; Because
11 they shall know that I am the L·.
12 Thus saith the L· God; Because
13 Therefore thus saith the L· God;
14 my vengeance, saith the L· God.
15 Thus saith the L· God; Because
16 Therefore thus saith the L· God;
17 they shall know that I am the L·.
26: 1 the word of the L· came unto me,
3 Therefore thus saith the L· God;
5 I have spoken it, saith the L· God:
6 they shall know that I am the L·.
7 For thus saith the L· God; Behold,
14 for I the L· have spoken it, saith
14 I...have spoken it, saith the L· God.
15 Thus saith the L· God to Tyrus;
19 thus saith the L· God; When I shall
21 be found again, saith the L· God.
27: 1 word of the L· came again unto
3 Thus saith the L· God; O Tyrus,
28: 1 word of the L· came again unto
2 Thus saith the L· God; Because
6 thus saith the L· God; Because thou
10 I have spoken it, saith the L· God.
11 the word of the L· came unto me,
12 Thus saith the L· God; Thou sealest
20 the word of the L· came unto me,
22 Thus saith the L· God; Behold, I
22 they shall know that I am the L·,
23 they shall know that I am the L·.
24 shall know that I am the L· God.
25 Thus saith the L· God; When I shall
26 know that I am the L· their God.
29: 1 the word of the L· came unto me,
3 Thus saith the L· God; Behold, I
6 Egypt shall know that I am the L·,
8 Therefore thus saith the L· God;
9 they shall know that I am the L·:
13 thus saith the L· God; At the end
16 they shall know that I am the L· God.
17 the word of the L· came unto me,
19 Therefore thus saith the L· God;
20 wrought for me, saith the L· God.
21 they shall know that I am the L·.
30: 1 word of the L· came again unto
2 Thus saith the L· God; Behold, I
3 even the day of the L· is near,
6 Thus saith the L·; They also that
6 in it by the sword, saith the L· God.
8 they shall know that I am the L·,
10 Thus saith the L· God; I will also
12 strangers: I the L· have spoken it.
13 Thus saith the L· God; I will also
19 they shall know that I am the L·.
20 the word of the L· came unto me,
22 Therefore thus saith the L· God;
25 they shall know that I am the L·,
26 they shall know that I am the L·.
31: 1 the word of the L· came unto me,
10 Therefore thus saith the L· God;
15 Thus saith the L· God; In the day
18 all his multitude, saith the L· God.
32: 1 the word of the L· came unto me,
3 saith the L· God; I will therefore
8 upon thy land, saith the L· God.
11 thus saith the L· God; The sword
14 to run like oil, saith the L· God.
15 shall they know that I am the L·.
16 all her multitude, saith the L· God.
17 the word of the L· came unto me,
31 by the sword, saith the L· God.
32 all his multitude, saith the L· God.
33: 1 the word of the L· came unto me,
11 As I live, saith the L· God, I have
17 say, The way of the L· is not equal:
20 say, The way of the L· is not equal.
22 the hand of the L· was upon me
23 the word of the L· came unto me,
25 Thus saith the L· God; Ye eat with
27 saith the L· God; As I live, surely
29 shall they know that I am the L·,
30 the word that cometh from the L·.
34: 1 the word of the L· came unto me,
2 Thus saith the L· God unto the
7 hear the word of the L·;
8 As I live, saith the L· God, surely
9 hear the word of the L·;
10 Thus saith the L· God; Behold, I
11 For thus saith the L· God; Behold,
15 them to lie down, saith the L· God.
17 O my flock, thus saith the L· God;
20 thus saith the L· God unto them;
24 And I the L· will be their God,
24 them; I the L· have spoken it.
27 and shall know that I am the L·,
30 I the L· their God am with them,
30 are my people, saith the L· God.
31 and I am your God, saith the L· God.
35: 1 the word of the L· came unto me,
3 say unto it, Thus saith the L· God;
4 thou shalt know that I am the L·.
6 live, saith the L· God, I will prepare
9 ye shall know that I am the L·.
10 it; whereas the L· was there:
11 I live, saith the L· God, I will even
12 thou shalt know that I am the L·,
14 Thus saith the L· God; When the
15 they shall know that I am the L·.
36: 1 of Israel, hear the word of the L·:

Eze 36: 2 Thus saith the L· God; Because the
3 Thus saith the L· God; Because they
4 Israel, hear the word of the L· God;
4 saith the L· God to the mountains,
5 saith the L· God; Surely in the fire
6 Thus saith the L· God; Behold, I
7 thus saith the L· God; I have lifted
11 ye shall know that I am the L·.
13 Thus saith the L· God; Because
14 nations any more, saith the L· God.
15 to fall any more, saith the L· God.
16 the word of the L· came unto me,
20 These are the people of the L·, and
22 Thus saith the L· God; I do not this
23 heathen shall know...I am the L·,
23 saith the L· God, when I shall be
32 your sakes do I this, saith the L·,
33 Thus saith the L· God; In the day
36 I the L· build the ruined places,
36 I the L· have spoken it, and I will
37 saith the L· God; I will yet for this
38 they shall know that I am the L·.
37: 1 The hand of the L· was upon me,
1 me out in the spirit of the L·, and
3 answered, O L· God, thou knowest.
4 bones, hear the word of the L·.
5 saith the L· God unto these bones;
6 ye shall know that I am the L·.
9 Thus saith the L· God; Come from
12 Thus saith the L· God; Behold, O my
13 ye shall know that I am the L·,
14 know that I the L· have spoken it,
14 it, and performed it, saith the L·.
15 word of the L· came again unto
19, 21 Thus saith the L· God; Behold, I
28 that I the L· do sanctify Israel,
38: 1 the word of the L· came unto me,
3 Thus saith the L· God; Behold, I
10 Thus saith the L· God; It shall also
14 Thus saith the L· God; In that day
17 Thus saith the L· God; Art thou he
18 saith the L· God, that my fury shall
21 all my mountains, saith the L· God:
23 they shall know that I am the L·.
39: 1 Thus saith the L· God; Behold, I
5 for I have spoken it, saith the L· God.
6 they shall know that I am the L·.
7 heathen shall know...I am the L·,
8 and it is done, saith the L· God;
10 that robbed them, saith the L· God.
13 shall be glorified, saith the L· God.
17 son of man, thus saith the L· God;
20 all men of war, saith the L· God.
22 Israel shall know that I am the L·
25 Therefore thus saith the L· God;
28 know that I am the L· their God,
29 house of Israel, saith the L· God.
40: 1 the hand of the L· was upon me,
46 come near to the L· to minister
41:22 is the table that is before the L·.
42:13 priests that approach unto the L·
43: 4 glory of the L· came into the house
5 the glory of the L· filled the house.
18 Son of man, thus saith the L· God;
19 minister unto me, saith the L· God,
24 shalt offer them before the L·,
24 up for a burnt offering unto the L·.
27 I will accept you, saith the L· God.
44: 2 Then said the L· unto me; This
2 because the L·, the God of Israel,
3 sit in it to eat bread before the L·;
4 of the L· filled the house of the L·:
5 the L· said unto me, Son of man,
5 ordinances of the house of the L·,
6 Thus saith the L· God; O ye house
9 Thus saith the L· God; No stranger,
12 hand against them, saith the L· God,
15 fat and the blood, saith the L· God:
27 his sin offering, saith the L· God.
45: 1 shall offer an oblation unto the L·,
4 come near to minister unto the L·:
9 saith the L· God; Let it suffice you,
9 from my people, saith the L· God.
15 reconciliation...saith the L· God.
18 Thus saith the L· God; In the first
23 prepare a burnt offering to the L·,
46: 1 Thus saith the L· God; The gate of
3 door of this gate before the L·
4 the prince shall offer unto the L·
9 of the land shall come before the L·
12 offerings voluntarily unto the L·,
13 a burnt offering unto the L· of a
14 a perpetual ordinance unto the L·.
16 Thus saith the L· God; If the prince
47:13 Thus saith the L· God; This shall be
23 his inheritance, saith the L· God.
48: 9 that ye shall offer unto the L·
10 sanctuary of the L· shall be in
14 the land: for it is holy unto the L·.
29 are their portions, saith the L· God.
35 that day shall be, The L· is there.
Da 1: 2 L· gave Jehoiakim king of Judah
10 I fear my l· the king, who hath
2:10 there is no king, l·, nor ruler, that
47 a God of gods, and a L· of kings,
4:19 My l·, the dream be to them that
24 which is come upon my l· the king:
5:23 thyself against the L· of heaven;
9: 2 word of the L· came to Jeremiah
3 And I set my face unto the L· God,
4 I prayed unto the L· my God,
4 O L·, the great and dreadful God,
7 O L·, righteousness belongeth unto
8 O L·, to us belongeth confusion of
9 To the L· our God belong mercies
10 we obeyed the voice of the L· our

Da 9:13 not our prayer before the L· our
14 hath the L· watched upon the evil,
14 L· our God is righteous in all his
15 O L· our God, thou hast brought
16 O L·, according to all thy
19 O L·, hear; O L·, forgive;
19 O L·, hearken and do; defer not,
20 my supplication before the L· my
10:16 O my l·, by the vision my sorrows
17 of this my l· talk with this my l·?
19 Let my l· speak; for thou hast
12: 8 O my L·, what shall be the end of
Ho 1: 1 The word of the L· that came
2 of the word of the L· by Hosea.
2 the L· said to Hosea, Go, take
2 whoredom, departing from the L·.
4 L· said unto him, Call his name
7 will save them by the L· their
2:13 and forgat me, saith the L·.
16 saith the L·, that thou shalt call
20 and thou shalt know the L·.
21 that day, I will hear, saith the L·,
3: 1 Then said the L· unto me, Go yet,
1 according to the love of the L·
5 return, and seek the L· their God,
5 shall fear the L· and his goodness
4: 1 Hear the word of the L·, ye
1 the L· hath a controversy with
10 left off to take heed to the L·.
15 nor swear, The L· liveth.
16 the L· will feed them as a lamb
5: 4 and they have not known the L·.
6 with their herds to seek the L·;
7 treacherously against the L·:
6: 1 and let us return unto the L·:
3 if we follow on to know the L·:
7:10 not return to the L· their God,
8: 1 eagle against the house of the L·,
13 but the L· accepteth them not;
9: 4 not offer wine offerings to the L·,
4 not come into the house of the L·.
5 in the day of the feast of the L·?
14 Give them, O L·: what wilt thou
10: 3 because we feared not the L·;
12 for it is time to seek the L·, till
11:10 They shall walk after the L·: he
11 them in their houses, saith the L·.
12: 2 L· hath also a controversy with
5 Even the L· God of hosts;
5 the L· is his memorial.
9 I that am the L· thy God from the
13 L· brought Israel out of Egypt,
14 reproach shall his L· return unto
13: 4 yet I am the L· thy God from the
15 the wind of the L· shall come up
14: 1 return unto the L· thy God; for
2 you words, and turn to the L·:
9 for the ways of the L· are right,
Joe 1: 1 word of the L· that came to Joel
9 cut off from the house of the L·;
14 into the house of the L· your God,
14 your God, and cry unto the L·,
15 for the day of the L· is at hand,
19 O L·, to thee will I cry: for the
2: 1 for the day of the L· cometh, for
11 L· shall utter his voice before his
11 for the day of the L· is great and
12 also now, saith the L·, turn ye
13 and turn unto the L· your God:
14 drink offering unto the L· your
17 the ministers of the L·, weep
17 Spare thy people, O L·, and give
18 the L· be jealous for his land,
19 L· will answer and say unto his
21 for the L· will do great things.
23 and rejoice in the L· your God:
26 and praise the name of the L·
27 and that I am the L· your God,
31 the terrible day of the L· come.
32 shall call on the name of the L·
32 deliverance, as the L· hath said,
32 remnant whom the L· shall call.
3: 8 far off: for the L· hath spoken it.
11 mighty ones to come down, O L·.
14 day of the L· is near in the valley
16 The L· also shall roar out of Zion,
16 L· will be the hope of his people,
17 know that I am the L· your God
18 come forth of the house of the L·,
21 for the L· dwelleth in Zion.
Am 1: 2 The L· will roar from Zion, and
3 Thus saith the L·; For three
5 captivity unto Kir, saith the L·.
6 Thus saith the L·; For three
8 shall perish, saith the L· God.
9, 11, 13 Thus saith the L·; For three
15 his princes together, saith the L·.
2: 1 Thus saith the L·; For three
3 thereof with him, saith the L·.
4 Thus saith the L·; For three
4 have despised the law of the L·,
6 Thus saith the L·; For three
11 children of Israel? saith the L·.
16 naked in that day, saith the L·.
3: 1 this word that the L· hath spoken
6 city, and the L· hath not done it?
7 Surely the L· God will do nothing,
8 the L· God hath spoken, who can
10 know not to do right, saith the L·,
11 Therefore thus saith the L· God;
12 Thus saith the L·; As the
13 house of Jacob, saith the L· God,
15 shall have an end, saith the L·.
4: 2 L· God hath sworn by his holiness,
3 then into the palace, saith the L·.
5 of Israel, saith the L· God.

Am 4: 6, 8, 9, 10, 11 unto me, saith the L'.
13 The L', The God of hosts, is his
5: 3 For thus saith the L' God; The
4 the L' unto the house of Israel,
6 Seek the L', and ye shall live;
8 of the earth: The L' is his name:
14 so the L', the God of hosts, shall
15 that the L' God of hosts will be
16 Therefore the L', the God of hosts,
16 the L', saith thus; Wailing shall
17 pass through thee, saith the L'.
18 you that desire the day of the L'!
18 the day of the L' is darkness, and
20 not the day of the L' be darkness,
27 saith the L', whose name is The
6: 8 The L' God hath sworn by himself,
8 saith the L' the God of hosts, I
10 mention of the name of the L'.
11 the L' commandeth, and he will
14 saith the L' the God of hosts;
7: 1 hath the L' God shewed unto me:
2 O L' God, forgive, I beseech thee:
3 The L' repented for this: It shall
3 this: It shall not be, saith the L'.
4 hath the L' God shewed unto me:
4 the L' God called to contend by fire,
5 I, O L' God, cease, I beseech thee:
6 The L' repented for this: This
6 also shall not be, saith the L' God.
7 the L' stood upon a wall made by a
8 the L' said unto me, Amos, what
8 Then said the L', Behold, I will set
15 L' took me as I followed the flock,
15 the L' said unto me, Go, prophesy
16 hear thou the word of the L':
17 thus saith the L'; Thy wife shall
8: 1 hath the L' God shewed unto me:
2 Then said the L' unto me, The
3 howlings in that day, saith the L'
7 L' hath sworn by the excellency
9 pass in that day, saith the L' God,
11 the days come, saith the L' God,
11 of hearing the words of the L':
12 and fro to seek the word of the L',
9: 1 saw the L' standing upon the altar:
5 L' God of hosts is he that toucheth
6 of the earth: The L' is his name.
7 O children of Israel? saith the L'.
8 the eyes of the L' God are upon the
8 the house of Jacob, saith the L'.
12 called by my name, saith the L'
13 the days come, saith the L', that
15 given them, saith the L' thy God.
Ob 1 Thus saith the L' God concerning
1 have heard a rumour from the L',
4 I bring thee down, saith the L'.
8 I not in that day, saith the L',
15 the day of the L' is near upon all
18 Esau; for the L' hath spoken it.
Jon 1: 1 word of the L' came unto Jonah
3 from the presence of the L', and
3 from the presence of the L'.
4 L' sent out a great wind into the
9 I am an Hebrew; and I fear the L',
10 fled from the presence of the L',
14 they cried unto the L', and said,
14 O L', we beseech thee, let us not
14 thou, O L', hast done as it pleased
16 the men feared the L' exceedingly,
16 and offered a sacrifice unto the L',
17 the L' had prepared a great fish to
2: 1 Jonah prayed unto the L' his God
2 of mine affliction unto the L',
6 my life from corruption, O L' my
7 within me I remembered the L':
9 have vowed. Salvation is of the L'.
10 the L' spake unto the fish, and it
3: 1 word of the L' came unto Jonah
3 according to the word of the L'.
4: 2 he prayed unto the L', and said, I
2 I pray thee, O L', was not this my
3 O L', take, I beseech thee, my life
4 said the L', Doest thou well to be
6 the L' God prepared a gourd, and
10 Then said the L', Thou hast had
Mic 1: 1 The word of the L' that came to
2 the L' God be witness against you,
2 the L' from his holy temple.
3 L' cometh forth out of his place,
12 evil came down from the L' unto
2: 3 Therefore thus saith the L';
5 lot in the congregation of the L'.
7 is the spirit of the L' straitened?
13 and the L' on the head of them.
3: 4 Then shall they cry unto the L',
5 Thus saith the L' concerning the
8 of power by the spirit of the L',
11 yet will they lean upon the L',
11 Is not the L' among us? none evil
4: 1 house of the L' shall be established
2 us go up to the mountain of the L',
2 word of the L' from Jerusalem.
4 of the L' of hosts hath spoken it.
5 walk in the name of the L' our God
6 In that day, saith the L', will I
7 the L' shall reign over them in
10 the L' shall redeem thee from the
12 know not the thoughts of the L',
13 consecrate their gain unto the L',
13 unto the L' of the whole earth.
5: 4 and feed in the strength of the L',
4 the majesty of the name of the L'
7 many people as a dew from the L',
10 to pass in that day, saith the L',
6: 1 Hear ye now what the L' saith;
2 the L' hath a controversy with his
Mic 6: 5 know the righteousness of the L'.
6 shall I come before the L', and
7 the L' be pleased with thousands
8 what doth the L' require of thee,
7: 7 Therefore I will look unto the L';
8 the L' shall be a light unto me.
9 will bear the indignation of the L',
10 unto me, Where is the L' thy God?
17 shall be afraid of the L' our God,
Na 1: 2 is jealous, and the L' revengeth;
2 the L' revengeth, and is furious;
2 the L' will take vengeance on his
3 The L' is slow to anger, and great
3 L' hath his way in the whirlwind
7 The L' is good, a strong hold in
9 do ye imagine against the L'?
11 that imagineth evil against the L',
12 Thus saith the L'; Though they
14 the L' hath given a commandment
2: 2 For the L' hath turned away the
13 against thee, saith the L' of hosts,
3: 5 against thee, saith the L' of hosts;
Hab 1: 2 O L', how long shall I cry, and
12 not from everlasting, O L' my God,
12 O L', thou hast ordained them for
2: 2 And the L' answered me, and said,
13 is it not of the L' of hosts that the
14 knowledge of the glory of the L',
20 But the L' is in his holy temple:
3: 2 O L', I have heard thy speech, and
2 O L', revive thy work in the midst
8 Was the L' displeased against the
18 Yet I will rejoice in the L', I will
19 The L' God is my strength, and he
Zep 1: 1 word of the L' which came unto
2, 3 from off the land, saith the L'.
5 worship and that swear by the L',
6 that are turned back from the L';
6 those that have not sought the L',
7 at the presence of the L' God:
7 for the day of the L' is at hand:
7 the L' hath prepared a sacrifice,
10 to pass in that day, saith the L',
12 The L' will not do good, neither
14 The great day of the L' is near, it
14 even the voice of the day of the L':
17 they have sinned against the L':
2: 2 fierce anger of the L' come upon
3 Seek ye the L', all ye meek of the
5 the word of the L' is against you;
7 the L' their God shall visit them,
9 saith the L' of hosts, the God of
10 the people of the L' of hosts.
11 The L' will be terrible unto them:
3: 2 she trusted not in the L'; she
5 The just L' is in the midst thereof;
8 wait ye upon me, saith the L',
9 all call upon the name of the L',
12 shall trust in the name of the L'.
15 L' hath taken away thy judgments,
15 even the L', is in the midst of thee:
17 L' thy God in the midst of thee is
20 before your eyes, saith the L'.
Hag 1: 1 the word of the L' by Haggai the
2 speaketh the L' of hosts, saying,
3 the word of the L' by Haggai the
5, 7 saith the L' of hosts; Consider
8 and I will be glorified, saith the L'.
9 it. Why? saith the L' of hosts.
12 obeyed the voice of the L' their
12 as the L' their God had sent him,
12 the people did fear before the L'.
13 saying, I am with you, saith the L'.
14 And the L' stirred up the spirit of
14 did work in the house of the L' of
2: 1 the word of the L' by the prophet
4 strong, O Zerubbabel, saith the L';
4 ye people of the land, saith the L',
4 am with you, saith the L' of hosts:
6 For thus saith the L' of hosts;
7 with glory, saith the L' of hosts.
8 gold is mine, saith the L' of hosts.
9 the former, saith the L' of hosts:
9 I give peace, saith the L' of hosts.
10 the word of the L' by Haggai the
11 Thus saith the L' of hosts; Ask
14 nation before me, saith the L';
15 a stone in the temple of the L':
17 ye turned not to me, saith the L'.
20 word of the L' came unto Haggai
23 In that day, saith the L' of hosts,
23 will I take thee,...saith the L', and
23 chosen thee, saith the L' of hosts.
Zec 1: 1 the word of the L' unto Zechariah,
2 L' hath been sore displeased with
3 them, Thus saith the L' of hosts;
3 ye unto me, saith the L' of hosts,
3 unto you, saith the L' of hosts.
4 Thus saith the L' of hosts; Turn
4 hearken unto me, saith the L'.
6 Like as the L' of hosts thought
7 the word of the L' unto Zechariah,
9 said I, O my l', what are these?
10 are they whom the L' hath sent
11 they answered the angel of the L'
12 the angel of the L' answered and
12 O L' of hosts, how long wilt thou
13 L' answered the angel that talked
14 Thus saith the L' of hosts; I am
16 thus saith the L'; I am returned
16 be built in it, saith the L' of hosts,
17 Thus saith the L' of hosts; My
17 the L' shall yet comfort Zion, and
20 L' shewed me four carpenters.
2: 5 For I, saith the L', will be unto
6 land of the north, saith the L'.
Zec 2: 6 winds of the heaven, saith the L'.
8 thus saith the L' of hosts; After
9 that the L' of hosts hath sent me.
10 in the midst of thee, saith the L'.
11 nations shall be joined to the L'
11 that the L' of hosts hath sent me
12 L' shall inherit Judah his portion
13 silent, O all flesh, before the L':
3: 1 priest...before the angel of the L',
2 And the L' said unto Satan,
2 The L' rebuke thee, O Satan;
2 L' that hath chosen Jerusalem
5 And the angel of the L' stood by.
6 the angel of the L' protested unto
7 Thus saith the L' of hosts; If thou
9 the graving thereof, saith the L'
10 In that day, saith the L' of hosts,
4: 4 me, saying, What are these, my l'?
5 these be? And I said, No, my l'.
6 word of the L' unto Zerubbabel,
6 by my Spirit, saith the L' of hosts.
8 the word of the L' came unto me,
9 that the L' of hosts hath sent me
10 they are the eyes of the L', which
13 these be? And I said, No, my l'.
14 stand by the L' of the whole earth.
5: 4 it forth, saith the L' of hosts,
6: 4 with me, What are these, my l'?
5 before the L' of all the earth.
9 the word of the L' came unto me,
12 Thus speaketh the L' of hosts,
12 shall build the temple of the L':
13 shall build the temple of the L';
14 memorial in the temple of the L'.
15 and build in the temple of the L',
15 that the L' of hosts hath sent me
15 diligently obey the voice of the L'
7: 1 word of...L' came unto Zechariah
2 their men, to pray before the L',
3 were in the house of the L' of
4 word of the L' of hosts unto me,
7 the words which the L' hath cried
8 word of...L' came unto Zechariah,
9 Thus speaketh the L' of hosts,
12 words which the L' of hosts hath
12 came a great wrath from the L'
13 not hear, saith the L' of hosts:
8: 1 word of the L' of hosts came to me,
2 Thus saith the L' of hosts; I was
3 Thus saith the L'; I am returned
3 the mountain of the L' of hosts
4 Thus saith the L' of hosts; There
6 Thus saith the L' of hosts; If it be
6 mine eyes? saith the L' of hosts.
7 Thus saith the L' of hosts;
9 Thus saith the L' of hosts; Let
9 foundation of the house of the L'
11 former days, saith the L' of hosts.
14 thus saith the L' of hosts; As I
14 me to wrath, saith the L' of hosts,
17 things that I hate, saith the L'.
18 the word of the L' of hosts came
19 Thus saith the L' of hosts; The
20 saith the L' of hosts; It shall yet
21 go speedily to pray before the L',
21 and to seek the L' of hosts: I will
22 shall come to seek the L' of hosts
22 and to pray before the L'.
23 saith the L' of hosts; In those
9: 1 The burden of the word of the L'
1 of Israel, shall be toward the L'.
4 Behold, the L' will cast her out,
14 the L' shall be seen over them,
14 the L' God shall blow the trumpet,
15 the L' of hosts shall defend them;
16 L' their God shall save them in
10: 1 Ask ye of the L' rain in the time
1 the L' shall make bright clouds,
3 L' of hosts hath visited his flock
5 because the L' is with them, and
6 I am the L' their God, and will
7 their heart shall rejoice in the L'.
12 will strengthen them in the L';
12 down in his name, saith the L'.
11: 4 Thus saith the L' my God; Feed
5 sell them say, Blessed be the L';
6 inhabitants of...land, saith the L':
11 that it was the word of the L'.
13 the L' said unto me, Cast it unto
13 the potter in the house of the L'.
15 the L' said unto me, Take unto
12: 1 burden of the word of the L' for
1 saith the L', which stretcheth
4 In that day, saith the L', I will
5 be my strength in the L' of hosts
7 The L' also shall save the tents of
8 the L' defend the inhabitants of
8 the angel of the L' before them.
13: 2 in that day, saith the L' of hosts,
3 lies in the name of the L':
7 is my fellow, saith the L' of hosts:
8 that in all the land, saith the L',
9 they shall say, The L' is my God.
14: 1 Behold, the day of the L' cometh,
3 Then shall the L' go forth, and
5 and the L' my God shall come,
7 which shall be known to the L',
9 L' shall be king over all the earth:
9 in that day shall there be one L',
12 the L' shall smite all the people
13 a great tumult from the L' shall
16, 17 to worship the King, the L' of
18 the L' will smite the heathen
20 horses, Holiness Unto The L';
21 be holiness unto the L' of hosts:
21 in the house of the L' of hosts.

Mal 1: 1 The burden of the word of the *L*'
2 I have loved you, saith the *L*'.
2 Jacob's brother? saith the *L*':
4 thus saith the *L*' of hosts, They
4 people against whom the *L*' hath
5 The *L*' will be magnified from
6 saith the *L*' of hosts unto you,
7 The table of the *L*' is contemptible.
8 thy person? saith the *L*' of hosts.
9 persons? saith the *L*' of hosts.
10 in you, saith the *L*' of hosts,
11 the heathen, saith the *L*' of hosts.
12 The table of the *L*' is polluted;
13 snuffed at it, saith the *L*' of hosts;
13 this of your hand? saith the *L*'.
14 unto the *L*' a corrupt thing:
14 great King, saith the *L*' of hosts,
2: 2 my name, saith the *L*' of hosts,
4 with Levi, saith the *L*' of hosts.
7 the messenger of the *L*' of hosts.
8 of Levi, saith the *L*' of hosts.
11 profaned the holiness of the *L*'
12 The *L*' will cut off the man that
12 offereth an offering unto the *L*'
13 the altar of the *L*' with tears,
14 the *L*' hath been witness between
16 For the *L*', the God of Israel, saith
16 garment, saith the *L*' of hosts:
17 wearied the *L*' with your words.
17 evil is good in the sight of the *L*',
3: 1 and the *L*', whom ye seek, shall
1 shall come, saith the *L*' of hosts.
3 may offer unto the *L*' an offering
4 Jerusalem be pleasant unto the *L*',
5 fear not me, saith the *L*' of hosts.
6 For I am the *L*', I change not;
7 unto you, saith the *L*' of hosts.
10 herewith, saith the *L*' of hosts,
11 in the field, saith the *L*' of hosts.
12 land, saith the *L*' of hosts.
13 stout against me, saith the *L*'.
14 walked mournfully before the *L*'
16 that feared the *L*' spake often one
16 and the *L*' hearkened, and heard
16 him for them that feared the *L*',
17 they shall be mine, saith the *L*'
4: 1 shall burn them up, saith the *L*'
3 that I shall do this, saith the *L*'
5 great and dreadful day of the *L*':
M't 1: 20 angel of the *L*' appeared unto him
22 spoken of the *L*' by the prophet,
24 angel of the *L*' had bidden him,
2: 13 angel of the *L*' appeareth to Joseph
15 spoken of the *L*' by the prophet,
19 an angel of the *L*' appeareth in a
3: 3 Prepare ye the way of the *L*', make
4: 7 shalt not tempt the *L*' thy God.
10 Thou shalt worship the *L*' thy God,
5: 33 perform unto the *L*' thine oaths:
7: 21 every one that saith unto me, *L*', *L*',
22 *L*', *L*', have we not prophesied in
8: 2 *L*', if thou wilt, thou canst make
6 *L*', my servant lieth at home sick
8 said, *L*', I am not worthy that thou
21 *L*', suffer me first to go and bury
25 awoke him, saying, *L*', save us:
9: 28 this? They said unto him, Yea, *L*'.
38 ye therefore the *L*' of the harvest,
10: 24 master, nor the servant above his *l*'.
25 master, and the servant as his *l*'.
11: 25 O Father, *L*' of heaven and earth,
12: 8 man is *L*' even of the sabbath day.
13: 51 things? They say unto him, Yea, *L*'.
14: 28 *L*', if it be thou, bid me come unto
30 sink, he cried, saying, *L*', save me.
15: 22 Have mercy on me, O *L*', thou son
25 worshipped him, saying, *L*', help me.
27 Truth, *L*': yet the dogs eat of the
16: 22 him, saying, Be it far from thee, *L*':
17: 4 *L*', it is good for us to be here: if
15 *L*', have mercy on my son: for he
18: 21 *L*', how oft shall my brother sin
25 his *l*' commanded him to be sold,
26 *L*', have patience with me, and I
27 *l*' of that servant was moved with
31 told unto their *l*' all that was done.
32 Then his *l*', after that he had called
34 And his *l*' was wroth, and delivered
20: 8 the *l*' of the vineyard saith unto his
30, 31 Have mercy on us, O *L*', thou
33 *L*', that our eyes may be opened.
21: 3 say, The *L*' hath need of them; and
9 that cometh in the name of the *L*';
40 *l*' therefore of the vineyard cometh,
22: 37 love the *L*' thy God with all thy
43 then doth David in spirit call him *L*',
44 The *L*' said...Sit thou on my right
44 unto my *L*', Sit thou on my right
45 If David then call him *L*', how is he
23: 39 that cometh in the name of the *L*'.
24: 42 not what hour your *L*' doth come.
45 whom his *l*' hath made ruler over
46 his *l*' when he cometh shall find so
48 heart, My *l*' delayeth his coming;
50 *l*' of that servant shall come in a
25: 11 virgins, saying, *L*', *L*', open to us.
19 time the *l*' of those servants cometh,
20 *L*', thou deliveredst unto me five
21 His *l*' said unto him, Well done, thou
21 enter thou into the joy of thy *l*'.
22 *L*', thou deliveredst unto me two
23 His *l*' said unto him, Well done, good
23 enter thou into the joy of thy *l*'.
24 *L*', I knew thee that thou art an
26 His *l*' answered and said unto him,
37, 44 *L*', when saw we thee an hungred,
M't 26: 22 of them to say unto him, *L*', is it I?
27: 10 potter's field, as the *L*' appointed
28: 2 the angel of the *L*' descended from
6 Come, see the place where the *L*' lay.
M'r 1: 3 Prepare ye the way of the *L*', make
2: 28 Son of man is *L*' also of the sabbath.
5: 19 how great things the *L*' hath done
7: 28 and said unto him, Yes, *L*': yet the
9: 24 *L*', I believe; help thou mine
10: 51 *L*', that I might receive my sight.
11: 3 ye that the *L*' hath need of him;
9 that cometh in the name of the *L*':
10 that cometh in the name of the *L*':
12: 9 therefore the *l*' of the vineyard do?
29 Israel; The *L*' our God is one *L*':
30 love the *L*' thy God with all thy
36 The *L*' said...Sit thou on my right
36 said to my *L*', Sit thou on my right
37 therefore himself calleth him *L*';
13: 20 the *L*' had shortened those days,
16: 19 after the *L*' had spoken unto them,
20 the *L*' working with them, and
Lu 1: 6 and ordinances of the *L*' blameless.
9 he went into the temple of the *L*'.
11 appeared unto him an angel of the *L*'
15 shall be great in the sight of the *L*',
16 shall he turn to the *L*' their God.
17 ready a people prepared for the *L*'.
25 Thus hath the *L*' dealt with me in
28 highly favoured, the *L*' is with thee:
32 the *L*' God shall give unto him the
38 Behold the handmaid of the *L*'; be
43 mother of my *L*' should come to me?
45 which were told her from the *L*'.
46 said, My soul doth magnify the *L*',
58 how the *L*' had shewed great mercy
66 the hand of the *L*' was with him.
68 Blessed be the *L*' God of Israel; for
76 shalt go before the face of the *L*' to
2: 9 the angel of the *L*' came upon them,
9 glory of the *L*' shone round about
11 a Saviour, which is Christ the *L*'.
15 which the *L*' hath made known unto
22 Jerusalem, to present him to the *L*';
23 (As it is written in the law of the *L*',
23 womb shall be called holy to the *L*';)
24 which is said in the law of the *L*',
29 *L*', now lettest thou thy servant
38 gave thanks likewise unto the *L*',
39 according to the law of the *L*', they
3: 4 Prepare ye the way of the *L*', make
4: 8 Thou shalt worship the *L*' thy God,
12 shalt not tempt the *L*' thy God.
18 Spirit of the *L*' is upon me, because
19 preach the acceptable year of the *L*'.
5: 8 me; for I am a sinful man, O *L*'.
12 *L*', if thou wilt, thou canst make me
17 power of the *L*' was present to heal
6: 5 Son of man is *L*' also of the sabbath.
46 why call ye me, *L*', *L*', and do not
7: 6 unto him, *L*', trouble not thyself:
13 And when the *L*' saw her, he had
31 the *L*' said, Whereunto then shall
9: 54 *L*', wilt thou that we command fire
57 *L*', I will follow thee whithersoever
59 *L*', suffer me first to go and bury my
61 also said, *L*', I will follow thee; but
10: 1 the *L*' appointed other seventy also,
2 ye therefore the *L*' of the harvest,
17 *L*', even the devils are subject unto
21 O Father, *L*' of heaven and earth,
27 love the *L*' thy God with all thy
40 said, *L*', dost thou not care that my
11: 1 *L*', teach us to pray, as John also
39 the *L*' said unto him, Now do ye
12: 36 like unto men that wait for their *l*',
37 the *l*' when he cometh shall find
41 *L*', speakest thou this parable unto
42 *L*' said, Who then is that faithful
42 whom his *l*' shall make ruler over
43 his *l*' when he cometh shall find so
45 heart, My *l*' delayeth his coming;
46 *l*' of that servant will come in a day
13: 8 *L*', let it alone this year also, till I
15 *L*' then answered him, and said,
23 *L*', are there few that be saved?
25 *L*',...open unto us; and he shall
25 *L*', open unto us; and he shall
35 that cometh in the name of the *L*'.
14: 21 and shewed his *l*' these things.
22 said, *L*', it is done as thou hast
23 the *l*' said unto the servant, Go out
16: 3 for my *l*' taketh away from me the
5 How much owest thou unto my *l*'?
8 *l*' commended the unjust steward,
17: 5 apostles said unto the *L*', Increase
6 *L*' said, If ye had faith as a grain
37 Where, *L*'? And he said unto them,
18: 6 *L*' said, Hear what the unjust judge
41 *L*', that I may receive my sight.
19: 8 Zacchæus...and said unto the *L*';
8 *L*', the half of my goods I give to
16 *L*', thy pound hath gained ten
18 *L*', thy pound hath gained five
20 *L*', behold, here is thy pound, which
25 unto him, *L*', he hath ten pounds.)
31 Because the *L*' hath need of him.
34 they said, The *L*' hath need of him.
38 that cometh in the name of the *L*':
20: 13 said the *l*' of the vineyard, What
15 *l*' of the vineyard do unto them?
37 calleth the *L*' the God of Abraham,
42 The *L*' said...Sit thou on my right
42 unto my *L*', Sit thou on my right
44 David therefore calleth him *L*',
22: 31 the *L*' said, Simon, Simon, behold,
Lu 22: 33 *L*', I am ready to go with thee,
38 *L*', behold, here are two swords.
49 *L*', shall we smite with the sword?
61 *L*' turned, and looked upon Peter.
61 remembered the word of the *L*',
23: 42 *L*', remember me when thou comest
24: 3 found not the body of the *L*' Jesus.
34 The *L*' is risen indeed, and hath
Joh 1: 23 Make straight the way of the *L*', as
4: 1 the *L*' knew how the Pharisees had
6: 23 after that the *L*' had given thanks:)
34 *L*', evermore give us this bread.
68 him, *L*', to whom shall we go?
8: 11 She said, No man, *L*'. And Jesus
9: 36 Who is he, *L*', that I might believe
38 *L*', I believe. And he worshipped
11: 2 anointed the *L*' with ointment,
3 *L*', behold, he whom thou lovest is
12 *L*', if he sleep, he shall do well.
21 Jesus, *L*', if thou hadst been here,
27 Yea, *L*': I believe that thou art the
32 *L*', if thou hadst been here, my
34 said unto him, *L*', come and see.
39 *L*', by this time he stinketh: for he
12: 13 that cometh in the name of the *L*'.
38 *L*', who hath believed our report?
38 the arm of the *L*' been revealed?
13: 6 him, *L*', dost thou wash my feet?
9 *L*', not my feet only, but also my
13 Ye call me Master and *L*': and ye
14 If I then, your *L*' and Master, have
16 servant is not greater than his *l*';
25 saith unto him, *L*', who is it?
36 unto him, *L*', whither goest thou?
37 *L*', why cannot I follow thee now?
14: 5 *L*', we know not whither thou goest;
8 him, *L*', shew us the Father, and it
22 *L*', how is it that thou wilt manifest
15: 15 knoweth not what his *l*' doeth: but
20 servant is not greater than his *l*'.
20: 2 away the *L*' out of the sepulchre,
13 they have taken away my *L*', and I
18 disciples that she had seen the *L*',
20 disciples glad, when they saw the *L*'.
25 said unto him, We have seen the *L*'.
28 said unto him, My *L*' and my God.
21: 7 loved saith unto Peter, It is the *L*'.
7 Peter heard that it was the *L*', he
12 thou? knowing that it was the *L*'.
15, 16 *L*'; thou knowest that I love
17 *L*', thou knowest all things; thou
20 *L*', which is he that betrayeth thee?
21 *L*', and what shall this man do?
Ac 1: 6 *L*', wilt thou at this time restore
21 time that the *L*' Jesus went in and
24 Thou, *L*', which knowest the hearts
2: 20 and notable day of the *L*' come:
21 the name of the *L*' shall be saved.
25 the *L*' always before my face; for
34 The *L*' said...Sit thou on my right
34 unto my *L*', Sit thou on my right
36 have crucified, both *L*' and Christ.
39 many as the *L*' our God shall call.
47 *L*' added to the church daily such
3: 19 come from the presence of the *L*';
22 prophet shall the *L*' your God raise
4: 24 *L*', thou art God, which hast made
26 gathered together against the *L*',
29 now, *L*', behold their threatenings:
33 of the resurrection of the *L*' Jesus:
5: 9 to tempt the Spirit of the *L*'?
14 believers were...added to the *L*',
19 the angel of the *L*' by night opened
7: 30 angel of the *L*' in a flame of fire in
31 the voice of the *L*' came unto him,
33 Then said the *L*' to him, Put off thy
37 prophet shall the *L*' your God raise
49 will ye build me? saith the *L*': or
59 saying, *L*' Jesus, receive my spirit.
60 *L*', lay not this sin to their charge.
8: 16 in the name of the *L*' Jesus.)
24 Pray ye to the *L*' for me, that none
25 and preached the word of the *L*',
26 angel of the *L*' spake unto Philip,
39 Spirit of the *L*' caught away Philip,
9: 1 against the disciples of the *L*',
5 And he said, Who art thou, *L*'?
5 And the *L*' said, I am Jesus whom
6 *L*', what wilt thou have me to do?
6 *L*' said unto him, Arise, and go
10 said the *L*' in a vision, Ananias.
10 And he said, Behold, I am here, *L*'.
11 the *L*' said unto him, Arise, and go
13 *L*', I have heard by many of this
15 the *L*' said unto him, Go thy way:
17 the *L*', even Jesus, that appeared
27 how he had seen the *L*' in the way,
29 boldly in the name of the *L*' Jesus,
31 walking in the fear of the *L*', and in
35 saw him and turned to the *L*'.
42 and many believed in the *L*'.
10: 4 was afraid, and said, What is it, *L*'?
14 Not so, *L*'; for I have never eaten
36 by Jesus Christ: (he is *L*' of all:)
48 be baptized in the name of the *L*'.
11: 8 Not so, *L*': for nothing common or
16 remembered I the word of the *L*',
17 who believed on the *L*' Jesus Christ;
20 Grecians, preaching the *L*' Jesus.
21 the hand of the *L*' was with them:
21 believed, and turned unto the *L*'.
23 they would cleave unto the *L*'.
24 much people was added unto the *L*'.
12: 7 the angel of the *L*' came upon him,
11 that the *L*' hath sent his angel, and
17 how the *L*' had brought him out of

Ac 12:23 the angel of the L· smote him,
13: 2 As they ministered to the L·, and
10 to pervert the right ways of the L·?
11 the hand of the L· is upon thee, and
12 astonished at the doctrine of the L·.
47 For so hath the L· commanded us,
48 and glorified the word of the L·:
49 the word of the L· was published
14: 3 they speaking boldly in the L·,
23 they commended them to the L·,
15:11 the grace of the L· Jesus Christ
17 of men might seek after the L·,
17 saith the L·, who doeth all these
26 for the name of our L· Jesus Christ.
35 and preaching the word of the L·,
36 have preached the word of the L·,
16:10 the L· had called us for to preach
14 whose heart the L· opened, that she
15 judged me to be faithful to the L·,
31 Believe on the L· Jesus Christ, and
32 spake unto him the word of the L·,
17:24 that he is L· of heaven and earth,
27 That they should seek the L·, if
18: 8 believed on the L· with all his house;
9 spake the L· to Paul in the night by
25 was instructed in the way of the L·:
25 diligently the things of the L·,
19: 5 baptized in the name of the L· Jesus.
10 Asia heard the word of the L· Jesus,
13 spirits the name of the L· Jesus,
17 name of the L· Jesus was magnified.
20:19 Serving the L· with all humility of
21 faith toward our L· Jesus Christ.
24 I have received of the L· Jesus, to
35 remember the words of the L· Jesus,
21:13 for the name of the L· Jesus.
14 saying, The will of the L· be done.
20 they heard it, they glorified the L·,
22: 8 And I answered, Who art thou, L·?
10 And I said, What shall I do, L·?
10 And the L· said unto me, Arise, and
16 sins, calling on the name of the L·.
19 L·, they know that I imprisoned and
23:11 night following the L· stood by him,
25:26 no certain thing to write unto my l·.
26:15 And I said, Who art thou, L·? And
28:31 which concern the L· Jesus Christ,
Ro 1: 3 his Son Jesus Christ our L·, which
7 our Father, and the L· Jesus Christ.
4: 8 to whom the L· will not impute sin.
24 that raised up Jesus our L· from the
5: 1 God through our L· Jesus Christ:
11 in God through our L· Jesus Christ,
21 eternal life by Jesus Christ our L·.
6:11 God through Jesus Christ our L·.
23 life through Jesus Christ our L·.
7:25 God through Jesus Christ our L·.
8:39 God, which is in Christ Jesus our L·.
9:28 a short work will the L· make upon
29 the L· of Sabaoth had left us a seed,
10: 9 confess with thy mouth the L· Jesus,
12 the same L· over all is rich unto all
13 shall call upon the name of the L·
16 L·, who hath believed our report?
11: 3 L·, they have killed thy prophets,
34 who hath known the mind of the L·?
12:11 fervent in spirit; serving the L·;
19 is mine; I will repay, saith the L·.
13:14 But put ye on the L· Jesus Christ,
14: 6 the day, regardeth it unto the L·;
6 day, to the L· he doth not regard it.
6 He that eateth, eateth to the L·, for
6 eateth not, to the L· he eateth not,
8 whether we live, we live unto the L·;
8 whether we die, we die unto the L·:
9 be L· both of the dead and living.
11 As I live, saith the L·, every knee
14 and am persuaded by the L· Jesus,
15: 6 the Father of our L· Jesus Christ.
11 again, Praise the L·, all ye Gentiles;
30 for the L· Jesus Christ's sake, and
16: 2 That ye receive her in the L·, as
8 Greet Amplias my beloved in the L·.
11 of Narcissus, which are in the L·.
12 and Tryphosa, who labour in the L·.
12 which laboured much in the L·.
13 Salute Rufus chosen in the L·, and
18 such serve not our L· Jesus Christ,
20 grace of our L· Jesus Christ be with
22 this epistle, salute you in the L·.
24 grace of our L· Jesus Christ be with
1Co 1: 2 the name of Jesus Christ our L·,
3 and from the L· Jesus Christ.
7 the coming of our L· Jesus Christ:
8 in the day of our L· Jesus Christ.
9 of his Son Jesus Christ our L·.
10 by the name of our L· Jesus Christ,
31 that glorieth, let him glory in the L·.
2: 8 not have crucified the L· of glory.
16 who hath known the mind of the L·,
3: 5 even as the L· gave to every man?
20 L· knoweth the thoughts of the wise,
4: 4 but he that judgeth me is the L·.
5 before the time, until the L· come,
17 beloved son, and faithful in the L·,
19 come to you shortly, if the L· will,
5: 4 In the name of our L· Jesus Christ,
4 the power of our L· Jesus Christ.
5 be saved in the day of the L· Jesus.
6:11 justified in the name of the L· Jesus,
13 not for fornication, but for the L·;
13 and the L· for the body.
14 God hath both raised up the L·, and
17 is joined unto the L· is one spirit.
7:10 I command, yet not I, but the L·,
12 But to the rest speak I, not the L·:

1Co 7:17 as the L· hath called every one, as
22 For he that is called in the L·, being
25 I have no commandment of the L·:
25 that hath obtained mercy of the L·
32 for the things that belong to the L·,
32 how he may please the L·:
34 careth for the things of the L·, that
35 ye may attend upon the L· without
39 to whom she will; only in the L·.
8: 6 and one L· Jesus Christ, by whom
9: 1 have I not seen Jesus Christ our L·?
1 are not ye my work in the L·?
2 of mine apostleship are ye in the L·.
5 and as the brethren of the L·, and
14 Even so hath the L· ordained that
10:21 Ye cannot drink the cup of the L·,
22 Do we provoke the L· to jealousy?
11:11 woman without the man, in the L·.
23 I have received of the L· that which
23 That the L· Jesus the same night
27 bread, and drink this cup of the L·,
27 of the body and blood of the L·.
32 judged, we are chastened of the L·,
12: 3 no man can say that Jesus is the L·,
5 administrations, but the same L·.
14:21 will they not hear me, saith the L·.
37 are the commandments of the L·.
15:31 which I have in Christ Jesus our L·,
47 second man is the L· from heaven.
57 victory through our L· Jesus Christ.
58 abounding in the work of the L·,
58 your labour is not in vain in the L·.
16: 7 a while with you, if the L· permit.
10 for he worketh the work of the L·,
19 Priscilla salute you much in the L·,
22 man love not the L· Jesus Christ,
23 grace of our L· Jesus Christ be with
2Co 1: 2 and from the L· Jesus Christ.
3 the Father of our L· Jesus Christ,
14 are ours in the day of the L· Jesus.
2:12 door was opened unto me of the L·,
3:16 when it shall turn to the L·, the vail
17 Now the L· is that Spirit: and where
17 where the Spirit of the L· is, there
18 as in a glass the glory of the L·,
18 glory even as by the Spirit of the L·.
4: 5 ourselves, but Christ Jesus the L·;
10 the body the dying of the L· Jesus,
14 he which raised up the L· Jesus
5: 6 body, we are absent from the L·:
8 body, and to be present with the L·.
11 Knowing...the terror of the L·, we
6:17 and be ye separate, saith the L·,
18 daughters, saith the L· Almighty.
8: 5 gave their own selves to the L·, and
9 ye know the grace of our L· Jesus
19 by us to the glory of the same L·,
21 not only in the sight of the L·, but
10: 8 the L· hath given us for edification,
17 glorieth, let him glory in the L·.
18 but whom the L· commendeth.
11:17 I speak, I speak it not after the L·,
31 and Father of our L· Jesus Christ,
12: 1 visions and revelations of the L·.
8 this thing I besought the L· thrice,
13:10 power which the L· hath given me
14 The grace of the L· Jesus Christ,
Ga 1: 3 and from our L· Jesus Christ,
4: 1 a servant, though he be l· of all;
5:10 confidence in you through the L·,
6:14 in the cross of our L· Jesus Christ,
17 my body the marks of the L· Jesus.
18 grace of our L· Jesus Christ be with
Eph 1: 2 and from the L· Jesus Christ.
3 and Father of our L· Jesus Christ,
15 heard of your faith in the L· Jesus,
17 That the God of our L· Jesus Christ,
2:21 unto an holy temple in the L·:
3:11 he purposed in Christ Jesus our L·:
14 the Father of our L· Jesus Christ,
4: 1 I therefore, the prisoner of the L·,
5 One L·, one faith, one baptism,
17 I say therefore, and testify in the L·,
5: 8 but now are ye light in the L·: walk
10 what is acceptable unto the L·.
17 what the will of the L· is.
19 melody in your heart to the L·;
20 in the name of our L· Jesus Christ;
22 your own husbands, as unto the L·.
29 it, even as the L· the church:
6: 1 obey your parents in the L·: for
4 nurture and admonition of the L·.
7 good will doing service, as to the L·,
8 the same shall he receive of the L·,
10 my brethren, be strong in the L·,
21 and faithful minister in the L·,
23 the Father and the L· Jesus Christ.
24 them that love our L· Jesus Christ
Ph'p 1: 2 and from the L· Jesus Christ.
14 And many of the brethren in the L·,
2:11 confess that Jesus Christ is L·, to
19 But I trust in the L· Jesus to send
24 I trust in the L· that I also myself
29 Receive him therefore in the L· with
3: 1 my brethren, rejoice in the L·.
8 knowledge of Christ Jesus my L·:
20 for the Saviour, the L· Jesus Christ:
4: 1 and crown, so stand fast in the L·,
2 they be of the same mind in the L·.
4 Rejoice in the L· alway: and again
5 unto all men. The L· is at hand.
10 But I rejoiced in the L· greatly, that
23 grace of our L· Jesus Christ be with
Col 1: 2 our Father and the L· Jesus Christ.
3 the Father of our L· Jesus Christ,
10 That ye might walk worthy of the L·

Col 2: 6 received Christ Jesus the L·, so
3:16 with grace in your hearts to the L·.
17 do all in the name of the L· Jesus,
18 own husbands, as it is fit in the L·.
20 for this is well pleasing unto the L·.
23 ye do, do it heartily, as to the L·,
24 of the L· ye shall receive the reward
24 for ye serve the L· Christ.
4: 7 and fellowservant in the L·:
17 which thou hast received in the L·,
1Th 1: 1 Father and in the L· Jesus Christ:
1 Father, and the L· Jesus Christ.
3 of hope in our L· Jesus Christ,
6 followers of us, and of the L·,
8 you sounded out the word of the L·
2:15 Who both killed the L· Jesus, and
19 the presence of our L· Jesus Christ
3: 8 we live, if ye stand fast in the L·.
11 our Father, and our L· Jesus Christ,
12 L· make you to increase and abound
13 the coming of our L· Jesus Christ
4: 1 and exhort you by the L· Jesus,
2 we gave you by the L· Jesus.
6 the L· is the avenger of all such,
15 say unto you by the word of the L·,
15 remain unto the coming of the L·
16 the L· himself shall descend from
17 the clouds, to meet the L· in the air:
17 and so shall we ever be with the L·.
5: 2 day of the L· so cometh as a thief
9 salvation by our L· Jesus Christ,
12 you, and are over you in the L·, and
23 the coming of our L· Jesus Christ.
27 I charge you by the L· that this
28 grace of our L· Jesus Christ be with
2Th 1: 1 our Father and the L· Jesus Christ:
2 our Father and the L· Jesus Christ.
7 the L· Jesus shall be revealed from
8 the gospel of our L· Jesus Christ:
9 from the presence of the L·, and
12 name of our L· Jesus Christ may be
12 of our God and the L· Jesus Christ.
2: 1 the coming of our L· Jesus Christ,
8 whom the L· shall consume with the
13 for you, brethren beloved of the L·,
14 of the glory of our L· Jesus Christ.
16 Now our L· Jesus Christ himself,
3: 1 the word of the L· may have free
3 L· is faithful, who shall stablish
4 confidence in the L· touching you,
5 L· direct your hearts into the love
6 in the name of our L· Jesus Christ,
12 and exhort by our L· Jesus Christ,
16 L· of peace himself give you peace
16 all means. The L· be with you all.
18 grace of our L· Jesus Christ be with
1Ti 1: 1 our Saviour, and L· Jesus Christ,
2 our Father, and Jesus Christ our L·.
12 And I thank Christ Jesus our L·,
14 the grace of our L· was exceeding
5:21 before God, and the L· Jesus Christ,
6: 3 even the words of our L· Jesus,
14 appearing of our L· Jesus Christ:
15 the King of kings, and L· of lords;
2Ti 1: 2 the Father and Christ Jesus our L·.
8 ashamed of the testimony of our L·,
16 The L· give mercy unto the house of
18 L· grant unto him that he may find
18 find mercy of the L· in that day:
2: 7 L· give thee understanding in all
14 charging them before the L· that
19 The L· knoweth them that are his.
22 call on the L· out of a pure heart.
24 servant of the L· must not strive;
3:11 out of them all the L· delivered me.
4: 1 before God, and the L· Jesus Christ,
8 which the L·, the righteous judge,
14 the L· reward him according to his
17 L· stood with me, and strengthened
18 L· shall deliver me from every evil
22 L· Jesus Christ be with thy spirit.
Tit 1: 4 the L· Jesus Christ our Saviour.
Ph'm 3 our Father and the L· Jesus Christ.
5 which thou hast toward the L· Jesus,
16 both in the flesh, and in the L·?
20 let me have joy of thee in the L·:
20 refresh my bowels in the L·.
25 grace of our L· Jesus Christ be with
Heb 1:10 Thou, L·, in the beginning hast
2: 3 first began to be spoken by the L·,
7:14 that our L· sprang out of Juda;
21 The L· sware and will not repent,
8: 2 tabernacle, which the L· pitched,
8 the days come, saith the L·, when
9 I regarded them not, saith the L·.
10 Israel after those days, saith the L·;
11 his brother, saying, Know the L·:
10:16 them after those days, saith the L·:
30 me, I will recompense, saith the L·,
30 The L· shall judge his people.
12: 5 not thou the chastening of the L·,
6 whom the L· loveth he chasteneth,
14 which no man shall see the L·:
13: 6 boldly say, The L· is my helper,
20 again from the dead our L· Jesus,
Jas 1: 1 of God and of the L· Jesus Christ,
7 shall receive any thing of the L·.
12 which the L· hath promised to them
2: 1 not the faith of our L· Jesus Christ,
1 L· of glory, with respect of persons.
4:10 yourselves in the sight of the L·,
15 that ye ought to say, If the L· will,
5: 4 into the ears of the L· of Sabaoth.
7 brethren unto the coming of the L·.
8 the coming of the L· draweth nigh.
10 have spoken in the name of the L·.

Jas 5:11 and have seen the end of the L';
11 that the L' is very pitiful, and of
14 him with oil in the name of the L':
15 sick, and the L' shall raise him up;
1Pe 1: 3 and Father of our L' Jesus Christ,
25 word of the L' endureth for ever.
2: 3 have tasted that the L' is gracious.
3: 6 obeyed Abraham, calling him l':
12 For the eyes of the L' are over the
12 the face of the L' is against them
15 sanctify the L' God in your hearts:
2Pe 1: 2 of God, and of Jesus our L',
8 knowledge of our L' Jesus Christ.
11 kingdom of our L' and Saviour
14 L' Jesus Christ hath shewed me.
16 and coming of our L' Jesus Christ,
2: 1 denying the L' that bought them,
9 The L' knoweth how to deliver the
11 against them before the L'.
20 knowledge of the L' and Saviour
3: 2 the apostles of the L' and Saviour:
8 one day is with the L' as a thousand
9 The L' is not slack concerning his
10 day of the L' will come as a thief
15 that the longsuffering of our L' is
18 knowledge of our L' and Saviour
2Jo 3 and from the L' Jesus Christ, the
Jude 4 and denying the only L' God,
4 God, and our L' Jesus Christ.
5 how that the L', having saved the
9 but said, The L' rebuke thee.
14 the L' cometh with ten thousands
17 of the apostles of our L' Jesus
21 for the mercy of our L' Jesus Christ
Re 1: 8 and the ending, saith the L', which
4: 8 Holy, holy, holy, L' God Almighty,
11 Thou art worthy, O L', to receive
6:10 How long, O L', holy and true, dost
11: 8 where also our L' was crucified.
15 are become the kingdoms of our L',
17 thee thanks, O L' God Almighty,
14:13 are the dead which die in the L'.
15: 3 are thy works, L' God Almighty;
4 Who shall not fear thee, O L', and
16: 5 Thou art righteous, O L', which
7 Even so, L' God Almighty, true and
17:14 for he is L' of lords, and King of
18: 8 strong is the L' God who judgeth
19: 1 and power, unto the L' our God:
6 the L' God omnipotent reigneth.
16 King Of Kings, And L' Of Lords.
21:22 for the L' God Almighty and the
22: 5 the L' God giveth them light: and
6 the L' God of the holy prophets
20 Amen. Even so, come, L' Jesus.
21 grace of our L' Jesus Christ be with

lordly
J'g 5:25 brought forth butter in a l' dish.

lord's [or Lord's]^
Ge 40: 7 him in the ward of his l' house
44: 8 we steal out of thy l' house silver
9 and we also will be my l' bondmen.
16 behold, we are my l' servants, both
18 speak a word in my l' ears, and let
Ex 9:29 know how that the earth is the L'.
12:11 it in haste: it is the L' passover.
27 is the sacrifice of the L' passover,
13: 9 the L' law may be in thy mouth:
12 hast; the male shall be the L'.
32:26 Who is on the L' side? let him
35:21 they brought the L' offering to
24 and brass brought the L' offering:
Le 3:16 sweet savour: all the fat is the L'.
16: 9 goat upon which the L' lot fell,
23: 5 month at even is the L' passover.
27:26 which should be the L' firstling,
26 it be ox, or sheep: it is the L'.
Nu 11:23 Is the L' hand waxed short?
29 all the L' people were prophets,
18:28 the L' heave offering to Aaron
31:37 the L' tribute of the sheep was
38, 39 the L' tribute was three score
40 the L' tribute was thirty and two
41 which was the L' heave offering,
32:10 L' anger was kindled the same
13 the L' anger was kindled against
De 10:14 of heavens is the L' thy God,
11:17 L' wrath be kindled against you,
15: 2 because it is called the L' release.
32: 9 For the L' portion is his people;
Jos 1:15 Moses the L' servant gave you
5:15 captain of the L' host said unto
22:19 wherein the L' tabernacle
J'g 11:31 Ammon, shall surely be the L',
1Sa 2: 8 the pillars of the earth are the L',
24 make the L' people to transgress.
14: 3 son of Eli, the L' priest in Shiloh,
16: 6 the L' anointed is before him.
17:47 for the battle is the L', and he will
18:17 for me, and fight the L' battles.
22:21 that Saul had slain the L' priests.
24: 6 unto my master, the L' anointed,
10 lord; for he is the L' anointed.
26: 9 his hand against the L' anointed,
11 hand against the L' anointed:
16 your master, the L' anointed.
23 hand against the L' anointed.
2Sa 1:14 hand to destroy the L' anointed?
16 I have slain the L' anointed.
19:21 because he cursed the L' anointed?
20: 6 take thou thy l' servants, and
21: 7 L' oath that was between them,
1Ki 18:13 an hundred men of the L' prophets
2Ki 11:17 that they should be the L' people;
13:17 The arrow of the L' deliverance,
1Ch 21: 3 are they not all my l' servants?
2Ch 7: 2 glory...had filled the L' house.
23:16 that they should be the L' people.
Ps 11: 4 the L' throne is in heaven: his
22:28 For the kingdom is the L': and
24: 1 earth is the L', and the fulness
113: 3 the L' name is to be praised.
115:16 even the heavens, are the L':
116:19 In the courts of the L' house, in
118:23 This is the L' doing; it is
137: 4 How shall we sing the L' song in
Pr 16:11 weight and balance are the L':
Isa 2: 2 that the mountain of the L' house
22:18 shall be the shame of thy l' house.
34: 8 is the day of the L' vengeance,
40: 2 received of the L' hand double
42:19 and blind as the L' servant?
44: 5 One shall say, I am the L'; and
59: 1 the L' hand is not shortened, that
Jer 5:10 for they are not the L'.
7: 2 Stand in the gate of the L' house,
13:17 L' flock is carried away captive.
19:14 stood in the court of the L' house;
25:17 took I the cup at the L' hand,
26: 2 Stand in the court of the L' house,
2 come to worship in the L' house,
10 of the new gate of the L' house.
27:16 the vessels of the L' house shall
28: 3 all the vessels of the L' house,
6 again the vessels of the L' house,
36: 6 ears of the people in the L' house
8 words of the Lord in the L' house.
10 of the new gate of the L' house,
51: 6 is the time of the L' vengeance;
7 been a golden cup in the L' hand,
51 the sanctuaries of the L' house.
La 2:22 day of the L' anger none escaped
3:22 of the L' mercies that we are not
Eze 8:14 door of the gate of the L' house
16 the inner court of the L' house,
10: 4 of the brightness of the L' glory.
19 of the east gate of the L' house;
11: 1 unto the east gate of the L' house,
Da 9:17 that is desolate, for the L' sake.
Ho 9: 3 shall not dwell in the L' land;
Joe 1: 9 priests, the L' ministers, mourn.
Ob 21 and the kingdom shall be the L'.
Mic 6: 2 O mountains, the L' controversy,
9 The L' voice crieth unto the city,
Hab 2:16 the cup of the L' right hand shall
Zep 1: 8 pass in the day of the L' sacrifice,
18 them in the day of the L' wrath;
2: 2 before the day of the L' anger
3 be hid in the day of the L' anger.
Hag 1: 2 that the L' house should be built.
13 spake Haggai the L' messenger
13 in the L' message unto the people,
2:18 the foundation of the L' temple
Zec 14:20 pots in the L' house shall be like
M't 21:42 this is the L' doing, and it is
25:18 in the earth, and hid his l' money.
M'r 12:11 This was the L' doing, and it is
Lu 2:26 before he had seen the L' Christ.
12:47 that servant, which knew his l' will,
16: 5 he called every one of his l' debtors
Ro 14: 8 live therefore, or die, we are the L'.
1Co 7:22 being a servant, is the L' freeman:
10:21 cannot be partakers of the L' table,
26 the earth is the L', and the fulness
28 earth is the L', and the fulness
11:20 this is not to eat the L' supper.
26 do shew the L' death till he come.
29 himself, not discerning the L' body.
Ga 1:19 none, save James the L' brother.
1Pe 2:13 ordinance of man for the L' sake:
Re 1:10 I was in the Spirit on the L' day,

lords
Ge 19: 2 he said, Behold now, my l', turn in,
Nu 21:28 the l' of the high places of Arnon.
De 10:17 God is God of gods, and Lord of l',
Jos 13: 3 five l' of the Philistines; the
J'g 3: 3 five l' of the Philistines, and all the
16: 5 l' of the Philistines came up unto
8 l' of the Philistines brought up to
18 called for the l' of the Philistines,
18 l' of the Philistines came up unto
23 the l' of the Philistines gathered
27 l' of the Philistines were there;
30 the house fell upon the l', and upon
1Sa 5: 8 gathered all the l' of the Philistines
11 together all the l' of the Philistines,
6: 4 number of the l' of the Philistines:
4 was on you all, and on your l'.
12 l' of the Philistines went after them
16 five l' of the Philistines had seen it,
18 Philistines belonging to the five l',
7: 7 l' of the Philistines went up against
29: 2 the l' of the Philistines passed on
6 nevertheless the l' favour thee not.
7 displease not the l' of the Philistines.
1Ch 12:19 for the l' of the Philistines upon
Ezr 8:25 his l', and all Israel there present,
Ps 136: 3 O give thanks to the Lord of l':
Isa 16: 8 l' of the heathen have broken down
26:13 other l' beside thee have had
Jer 2:31 say my people, We are l';
Eze 23:23 and rulers, great l' and renowned,
Da 4:36 and my l' sought unto me; and
5: 1 a great feast to a thousand of his l',
9 in him, and his l' were astonied.
10 of the words of the king and his l'
23 thou, and thy l', thy wives, and thy
6:17 and with the signet of his l';
M'r 6:21 birthday made a supper to his l',
1Co 8: 5 there be gods many, and l' many,)
1Ti 6:15 the King of kings, and Lord of l';
1Pe 5: 3 as being l' over God's heritage,
Re 17:14 is Lord of l', and King of kings:
19:16 King Of Kings, And Lord Of L'.

lordship
M'r 10:42 Gentiles exercise l' over them;
Lu 22:25 Gentiles exercise l' over them;

Lo-ruhamah (*lo-ru-ha'-mah*)
Ho 1: 6 said unto him, Call her name L':
8 Now when she had weaned L', she

lose See also LOSETH; LOST.
J'g 18:25 and thou l' thy life, with the lives
1Ki 18: 5 alive, that we l' not all the beasts.
Job 31:39 the owners thereof to l' their life:
Pr 23: 8 vomit up, and l' thy sweet words.
Ec 3: 6 A time to get, and a time to l'; a
M't 10:39 He that findeth his life shall l' it:
42 he shall in no wise l' his reward.
16:25 will save his life shall l' it:
25 will l' his life for my sake shall find
26 whole world, and l' his own soul?
M'r 8:35 will save his life shall l' it;
35 shall l' his life for my sake and
36 whole world, and l' his own soul?
9:41 unto you, he shall not l' his reward.
Lu 9:24 will save his life shall l' it:
24 will l' his life for my sake, the
25 gain the whole world, and l' himself,
15: 4 hundred sheep, if he l' one of them,
8 if she l' one piece, doth not light a
17:33 shall seek to save his life shall l' it;
33 shall l' his life shall preserve it.
Joh 6:39 hath given me I should l' nothing,
12:25 He that loveth his life shall l' it;
2Jo 8 l' not those things which we have

loseth
M't 10:39 l' his life for my sake shall find it.

loss
Ge 31:39 not unto thee; I bare the l' of it;
Ex 21:19 he shall pay for the l' of his time,
Isa 47: 8 shall I know the l' of children:
9 in one day, the l' of children, and
Ac 27:21 to have gained this harm and l'.
22 be no l' of any man's life among
1Co 3:15 shall be burned, he shall suffer l':
Ph'p 3: 7 me, those I counted l' for Christ.
8 I count all things but l' for the
8 I have suffered the l' of all things,

lost
Ex 22: 9 or for any manner of l' thing, which
Lev 6: 3 Or have found that which was l', and
4 keep, or the l' thing which he found,
Nu 6:12 days that were before shall be l',
De 22: 3 with all l' thing of thy brother's,
3 which he hath l', and thou hast
1Sa 9: 3 the asses of Kish Saul's father were l'.
20 as for thine asses that were l' three
1Ki 20:25 like the army that thou hast l',
Ps 119:176 I have gone astray like a l' sheep;
Isa 49:20 have, after thou hast l' the other,
21 seeing I have l' my children, and
Jer 50: 6 My people hath been l' sheep: their
Eze 19: 5 she had waited, and her hope was l',
34: 4 have ye sought that which was l';
16 I will seek that which was l', and
37:11 bones are dried, and our hope is l':
M't 5:13 but if the salt have l' his savour,
10: 6 the l' sheep of the house of Israel.
15:24 the l' sheep of the house of Israel.
18:11 is come to save that which was l'.
M'r 9:50 if the salt have l' his saltness,
Lu 14:34 but if the salt have l' his savour,
15: 4 and go after that which is l', until
6 I have found my sheep which was l'.
9 I have found the piece which I had l'.
24 alive again; he was l', and is found.
32 alive again; and was l', and is found.
19:10 to seek and to save that which was l'.
Joh 6:12 that remain, that nothing be l'.
17:12 and none of them is l', but the son
18: 9 which thou gavest me have I l' none.
2Co 4: 3 be hid, it is hid to them that are l':

lot See also LOTS.
Le 16: 8 the two goats; one l' for the Lord,
8 and the other l' for the scapegoat.
9 goat upon which the Lord's l' fell,
10 which the l' fell to be the scapegoat,
Nu 26:55 the land shall be divided by l':
56 According to the l' shall the
33:54 ye shall divide the land by l' for an
54 be in the place where his l' falleth;
34:13 the land which ye shall inherit by l',
36: 2 give the land for an inheritance by l'
3 taken from the l' of our inheritance.
De 32: 9 Jacob is the l' of his inheritance.
Jos 13: 6 divide thou it by l' unto the Israelites
14: 2 By l' was their inheritance, as the
15: 1 was the l' of the tribe of...Judah
16: 1 the l' of the children of Joseph fell
17: 1 also a l' for the tribe of Manasseh;
2 also a l' for the rest of the children
14 Why hast thou given me but one l'
17 thou shalt not have one l' only:
18:11 the l' of the tribe of the children of
11 coast of their l' came forth between
19: 1 the second l' came forth to Simeon,
10 third l' came up for the children of
17 the fourth l' came out to Issachar,
24 the fifth l' came out for the tribe of
32 sixth l' came out to the children of
40 seventh l' came out for the tribe
51 for an inheritance by l' in Shiloh
21: 4 the l' came out for the families of

Jos 21: 4 had by l' out of the tribe of Judah,
5, 6 had by l' out of the families of the
8 Israel gave by l' unto the Levites
10 Levi, had: for theirs was the first l'.
20 they had cities of their l' out of the
40 were by their l' twelve cities.
23: 4 divided unto you by l' these nations
J'g 1: 3 Come up with me into my l', that
3 and I...will go with thee into thy l'.
20: 9 we will go up by l' against it;
1Sa 14: 41 Lord God of Israel, Give a perfect l'.
1Ch 6: 54 Kohathites: for theirs was the l'.
61 tribe of Manasseh, by l', ten cities.
63 the sons of Merari were given by l',
65 And they gave by l' out of the tribe
16: 18 Canaan, the l' of your inheritance;
24: 5 Thus were they divided by l', one
7 the first l' came forth to Jehoiarib,
25: 9 the first l' came forth for Asaph to
26: 14 the l' eastward fell to Shelemiah.
14 and his l' came out northward.
16 Hosah the l' came forth westward,
Es 3: 7 they cast Pur, that is, the l',
9: 24 and had cast Pur, that is, the l', to
Ps 16: 5 of my cup: thou maintainest my l'.
105: 11 Canaan, the l' of your inheritance:
125: 3 rest upon the l' of the righteous;
Pr 1: 14 Cast in thy l' among us; let us all
16: 33 The l' is cast into the lap; but the
18: 18 The l' causeth contentions to cease,
Isa 17: 14 and the l' of them that rob us.
34: 17 And he hath cast the l' for them,
57: 6 thy portion; they, they are thy l':
Jer 13: 25 This is thy l', the portion of thy
Eze 24: 6 piece by piece; let no l' fall upon it.
45: 1 when ye shall divide by l' the land for
47: 22 shall divide it by l' for an inheritance
48: 29 ye shall divide by l' unto the tribes
Da 12: 13 and stand in thy l' at the end of
Jon 1: 7 cast lots, and the l' fell upon Jonah.
Mic 2: 5 none that shall cast a cord by l' in
Lu 1: 9 his l' was to burn incense when
Ac 1: 26 and the l' fell upon Matthias;
8: 21 neither part nor l' in this matter:
13: 19 he divided their land to them by l'.

Lot (*lot*) See also LOT'S.
Ge 11: 27 and Haran; and Haran begat L'.
31 L' the son of Haran his son's son,
12: 4 and L' went with him: and Abram
5 his wife, and L' his brother's son,
13: 1 and L' with him, into the south,
5 L' also, which went with Abram,
8 Abram said unto L', Let there be no
10 L' lifted up his eyes, and beheld all
11 Then L' chose him all the plain of
11 of Jordan; and L' journeyed east:
12 L' dwelled in the cities of the plain,
14 after...L' was separated from him,
14: 12 they took L', Abram's brother's son,
16 also brought again his brother L',
19: 1 and L' sat in the gate of Sodom:
1 and L' seeing them rose up to meet
5 they called unto L', and said unto
6 L' went out at the door unto them,
9 pressed sore upon the man, even L',
10 pulled L' into the house to them,
12 men said unto L', Hast thou here
14 L' went...and spake unto his sons
15 then the angels hastened L', saying,
18 And L' said unto them, Oh, not so,
23 earth when L' entered into Zoar.
29 and sent L' out of the midst of the
29 the cities in the which L' dwelt.
30 L' went up out of Zoar, and dwelt in
36 both the daughters of L' with child
De 2: 9 given Ar unto the children of L' for
19 given it unto the children of L' for
Ps 83: 8 they have holpen the children of L'.
Lu 17: 28 also as it was in the days of L';
29 same day that L' went out of Sodom
2Pe 2: 7 And delivered just L', vexed with

Lotan (*lo'-tan*) See also LOTAN'S.
Ge 36: 20 L', and Shobal, and Zibeon, and
22 the children of L' were Hori and
29 that came of the Horites; duke L',
1Ch 1: 38 L', and Shobal, and Zibeon, and
39 the sons of L'; Hori, and Homan:

Lotan's (*lo'-tans*)
Ge 36: 22 Hemam; and L' sister was Timna.
1Ch 1: 39 Homam: and Timna was L' sister.

lothe See also LOATHE; LOTHED; LOTHETH; LOTHING.
Ex 7: 18 Egyptians shall l' to drink of the
Eze 6: 9 shall l' themselves for the evils
20: 43 l' yourselves in your own sight for
36: 31 l' yourselves in your own sight for

lothed See also LOATHED.
Jer 14: 19 hath thy soul l' Zion? why hast
Eze 16: 45 which l' their husbands and their
Zec 11: 8 my soul l' them, and their soul

lotheth See also LOATHETH.
Eze 16: 45 l' her husband and her children;

lothing
Eze 16: 5 open field, to the l' of thy person,

Lot's (*lots*)
Ge 13: 7 and the herdman of L' cattle:
Lu 17: 32 Remember L' wife.

lots
Le 16: 8 shall cast l' upon the two goats;
Jos 18: 6 cast l' for you here before the Lord
8 here cast l' for you before the Lord
10 Joshua cast l' for them in Shiloh
1Sa 14: 42 Cast l' between me and Jonathan my
1Ch 24: 31 cast l' over against their brethren
25: 8 they cast l', ward against ward, as
26: 13 they cast l', as well the small as the
14 son, a wise counsellor, they cast l';
Ne 10: 34 we cast the l' among the priests, the
11: 1 the rest of the people also cast l', to
Ps 22: 18 them, and cast l' upon my vesture.
Joe 3: 3 they have cast l' for my people; and
Ob 11 gates, and cast l' upon Jerusalem,
Jon 1: 7 Come, and let us cast l', that we
7 So they cast l', and the lot fell upon
Na 3: 10 they cast l' for her honourable men,
M't 27: 35 parted his garments, casting l':
35 upon my vesture did they cast l'.
M'r 15: 24 garments, casting l' upon them,
Lu 23: 34 they parted his raiment, and cast l'.
Joh 19: 24 Let us not rend it, but cast l' for it,
24 and for my vesture they did cast l'.
Ac 1: 26 they gave forth their l'; and the lot

loud See also LOUDER.
Ge 39: 14 me, and I cried with a l' voice:
Ex 19: 16 voice of the trumpet exceeding l';
De 27: 14 the men of Israel with a l' voice,
1Sa 28: 12 Samuel, she cried with a l' voice:
2Sa 15: 23 all the country wept with a l' voice,
19: 4 and the king cried with a l' voice,
1Ki 8: 55 congregation of Israel with a l' voice,
2Ki 18: 28 cried with a l' voice in the Jews'
2Ch 15: 14 sware unto the Lord with a l' voice,
20: 19 Lord God of Israel with a l' voice
30: 21 singing with l' instruments unto
32: 18 cried with a l' voice in the Jews'
Ezr 3: 12 their eyes, wept with a l' voice;
13 the people shouted with a l' shout,
10: 12 answered and said with a l' voice.
Ne 9: 4 cried with a l' voice unto the Lord
12: 42 the singers sang l', with Jezrahiah
Es 4: 1 cried with a l' and a bitter cry;
Ps 33: 3 song: play skilfully with a l' noise.
98: 4 make a l' noise, and rejoice, and sing
150: 5 Praise him upon the l' cymbals:
Pr 7: 11 (She is l' and stubborn; her feet
27: 14 blesseth his friend with a l' voice,
Isa 36: 13 cried with a l' voice in the Jews'
Eze 8: 18 they cry in mine ears with a l' voice,
9: 1 also in mine ears with a l' voice,
11: 13 my face, and cried with a l' voice,
M't 27: 46 Jesus cried with a l' voice, saying,
50 he had cried again with a l' voice,
M'r 1: 26 torn him, and cried with a l' voice,
5: 7 And cried with a l' voice, and said,
15: 34 Jesus cried with a l' voice, saying,
37 And Jesus cried with a l' voice, and
Lu 1: 42 she spake out with a l' voice, and
4: 33 devil, and cried out with a l' voice,
8: 28 and with a l' voice said, What have
17: 15 and with a l' voice glorified God,
19: 37 and praise God with a l' voice for
23: 23 they were instant with l' voices,
46 Jesus had cried with a l' voice,
Joh 11: 43 he cried with a l' voice, Lazarus,
Ac 7: 57 Then they cried out with a l' voice,
60 and cried with a l' voice, Lord, lay
8: 7 unclean spirits, crying with l' voice,
14: 10 Said with a l' voice, Stand upright
16: 28 Paul cried with a l' voice, saying,
26: 24 Festus said with a l' voice, Paul,
Re 5: 2 angel proclaiming with a l' voice,
12 Saying with a l' voice, Worthy is
6: 10 they cried with a l' voice, saying,
7: 2 with a l' voice to the four angels,
10 and cried with a l' voice, saying,
8: 13 saying with a l' voice, Woe, woe,
10: 3 cried with a l' voice, as when a lion
12: 10 I heard a l' voice saying in heaven,
14: 7 Saying with a l' voice, Fear God,
9 saying with a l' voice, If any man
15 crying with a l' voice to him that
18 cried with a l' voice to him that had
19: 17 he cried with a l' voice, saying to all

louder
Ex 19: 19 sounded long, and waxed l' and l'.

love See also LOVED; LOVE'S; LOVES; LOVEST; LOVETH; LOVING.
Ge 27: 4 make me savoury meat, such as I l',
29: 20 few days, for the l' he had to her.
32 therefore my husband will l' me.
Ex 20: 6 unto thousands of them that l' me,
21: 5 I l' my master, my wife, and my
Le 19: 18 but thou shalt l' thy neighbour as
34 and thou shalt l' him as thyself; for
De 5: 10 unto thousands of them that l' me
6: 5 thou shalt l' the Lord thy God with
7: 7 Lord did not set his l' upon you,
9 mercy with them that l' him and
13 he will l' thee, and bless thee, and
10: 12 walk in all his ways, and to l' him,
15 a delight in thy fathers to l' them,
19 L' ye therefore the stranger: for ye
11: 1 Therefore thou shalt l' the Lord thy
13 you this day, to l' the Lord your God,
22 to l' the Lord your God, to walk in
13: 3 whether ye l' the Lord your God
19: 9 to l' the Lord thy God, and to walk
30: 6 to l' the Lord thy God with all thine
16 thee this day to l' the Lord thy God,
20 thou mayest l' the Lord thy God,
Jos 22: 5 to l' the Lord your God, and to walk
23: 11 selves, that ye l' the Lord your God.
J'g 5: 31 let them that l' him be as the sun
16: 15 How canst thou say, I l' thee, when
1Sa 18: 22 in thee, and all his servants l' thee:
2Sa 1: 26 me; thy l' to me was wonderful,
2Sa 1: 26 wonderful, passing the l' of women.
13: 4 Amnon said unto him, I l' Tamar,
15 greater than the l' wherewith he had
1Ki 11: 2 Solomon clave unto these in l'.
2Ch 19: 2 and l' them that hate the Lord?
Ne 1: 5 and mercy for them that l' him and
Ps 4: 2 how long will ye l' vanity, and seek
5: 11 let them also that l' thy name be
18: 1 I will l' thee, O Lord, my strength.
31: 23 O l' the Lord, all ye his saints: for
40: 16 let such as l' thy salvation say
69: 36 they that l' his name shall dwell
70: 4 and let such as l' thy salvation say
91: 14 Because he hath set his l' upon me,
97: 10 Ye that l' the Lord, hate evil: he
109: 4 For my l' they are my adversaries:
5 evil for good, and hatred for my l'.
116: 1 I l' the Lord, because he hath heard
119: 97 O how l' I thy law! it is my
113 vain thoughts: but thy law do I l'.
119 dross: therefore I l' thy testimonies.
127 Therefore I l' thy commandments
132 to do unto those that l' thy name.
159 Consider how I l' thy precepts:
163 and abhor lying: but thy law do I l'.
165 peace have they which l' thy law:
167 and I l' them exceedingly.
122: 6 they shall prosper that l' thee.
145: 20 Lord preserveth all them that l' him:
Pr 1: 22 ye simple ones, will ye l' simplicity?
4: 6 thee: l' her, and she shall keep thee.
5: 19 thou ravished always with her l'.
7: 18 let us take our fill of l' until the
8: 17 I l' them that l' me; and those that
21 cause those that l' me to inherit
36 soul: all they that hate me l' death.
9: 8 a wise man, and he will l' thee.
10: 12 up strifes: but l' covereth all sins.
15: 17 is a dinner of herbs where l' is, than
16: 13 and they l' him that speaketh right.
17: 9 covereth a transgression seeketh l';
18: 21 and they that l' it shall eat the fruit
20: 13 L' not sleep, lest thou come to
27: 5 rebuke is better than secret l'.
Ec 3: 8 A time to l', and a time to hate; a
9: 1 man knoweth either l' or hatred by
6 Also their l', and their hatred, and
Ca 1: 2 for thy l' is better than wine.
3 therefore do the virgins l' thee.
4 remember thy l' more than wine:
4 than wine: the upright l' thee.
9 I have compared thee, O my l', to
15 Behold, thou art fair, my l'; behold,
2: 2 so is my l' among the daughters.
4 and his banner over me was l'.
5 me with apples: for I am sick of l'.
7 up, nor awake my l', till he please.
10 Rise up, my l', my fair one, and
13 Arise, my l', my fair one, and come
3: 5 up, nor awake my l', till he please.
10 midst thereof being paved with l',
4: 1 Behold, thou art fair, my l';
7 Thou art all fair, my l'; there is no
10 How fair is thy l', my sister, my
10 how much better is thy l' than wine!
5: 2 to me, that my sister, my l', my dove,
8 that ye tell him, I am sick of l'.
6: 4 Thou art beautiful, O my l', as
7: 6 and how pleasant art thou, O l', for
8: 4 that ye stir not up, nor awake my l',
6 for l' is strong as death; jealousy
7 Many waters cannot quench l',
7 all the substance of his house for l',
Isa 38: 17 but thou hast in l' to my soul
56: 6 to l' the name of the Lord, to be
61: 8 For I the Lord l' judgment, I hate
63: 9 in his l' and in his pity he redeemed
66: 10 be glad with her, all ye that l' her:
Jer 2: 2 the l' of thine espousals, when thou
33 trimmest thou thy way to seek l'?
5: 31 and my people l' to have it so: and
31: 3 loved thee with an everlasting l':
Eze 16: 8 behold, thy time was the time of l';
23: 11 more corrupt in her inordinate l'
17 came to her into the bed of l', and
33: 31 their mouth they shew much l',
Da 1: 9 Daniel into favour and tender l'
9: 4 and mercy to them that l' him,
Ho 3: 1 l' a woman beloved of her friend,
1 according to the l' of the Lord
1 other gods, and l' flagons of wine.
4: 18 her rulers with shame do l', Give
9: 15 mine house, I will l' them no more:
11: 4 cords of a man, with bands of l':
14: 4 backsliding, I will l' them freely:
Am 5: 15 Hate the evil, and l' the good, and
Mic 3: 2 Who hate the good, and l' the evil;
6: 8 but to do justly, and to l' mercy,
Zep 3: 17 he will rest in his l', he will joy over
Zec 8: 17 l' no false oath: for all these are
19 therefore l' the truth and peace.
M't 5: 43 Thou shalt l' thy neighbour, and hate
44 But I say unto you, L' your enemies,
46 For if ye l' them which l' you, what
6: 5 for they l' to pray standing in the
24 he will hate the one, and l' the other;
19: 19 shalt l' thy neighbour as thyself.
22: 37 Thou shalt l' the Lord thy God with
39 shalt l' thy neighbour as thyself.
23: 6 l' the uppermost rooms at feasts,
24: 12 the l' of many shall wax cold.
M'r 12: 30 thou shalt l' the Lord thy God with
31 shalt l' thy neighbour as thyself.
33 to l' him with all the heart, and with
33 and to l' his neighbour as himself,
38 the scribes, which l' to go in long

M'r 12:38 *l'* salutations in the marketplaces,
Lu 6:27 *L'* your enemies, do good to them
32 For if ye *l'* them which *l'* you, what
32 for sinners also *l'* those that *l'* them.
35 But *l'* ye your enemies, and do good,
7:42 which of them will *l'* him most?
10:27 Thou shalt *l'* the Lord thy God with
11:42 pass over judgment and the *l'* of God:
43 for ye *l'* the uppermost seats in the
16:13 he will hate the one, and *l'* the other;
20:46 and *l'* greetings in the markets,
Joh 5:42 that ye have not the *l'* of God in you.
8:42 were your Father, ye would *l'* me:
10:17 Therefore doth my Father *l'* me,
13:34 give unto you, That ye *l'* one another;
34 loved you, that ye also *l'* one another.
35 disciples, if ye have *l'* one to another.
14:15 If ye *l'* me, keep my commandments.
21 and I will *l'* him, and will manifest
23 a man *l'* me, he will keep my words:
23 my Father will *l'* him, and we will
31 may know that I *l'* the Father; and
15: 9 I loved you: continue ye in my *l'*.
10 ye shall abide in my *l'*; even as I
10 commandments, and abide in his *l'*.
12 That ye *l'* one another, as I have
13 Greater *l'* hath no man than this,
17 command you, that ye *l'* one another.
19 world, the world would *l'* his own:
17:26 *l'* wherewith thou hast loved me
21:15, 16, 17 thou knowest that I *l'* thee.
Ro 5: 5 because the *l'* of God is shed abroad
8 God commendeth his *l'* toward us,
8:28 together for good to them that *l'* God,
35 separate us from the *l'* of Christ?
39 able to separate us from the *l'* of God,
12: 9 Let *l'* be without dissimulation.
10 one to another with brotherly *l'*;
13: 8 any thing, but to *l'* one another:
9 Thou shalt *l'* thy neighbour as
10 *L'* worketh no ill to his neighbour:
10 therefore *l'* is the fulfilling of the law.
15:30 sake, and for the *l'* of the Spirit,
1Co 2: 9 hath prepared for them that *l'* him.
4:21 come unto you with a rod, or in *l'*;
8: 3 if any man *l'* God, the same is known
16:22 If any man *l'* not the Lord Jesus
24 My *l'* be with you all in Christ Jesus.
2Co 2: 4 ye might know the *l'* which I have
8 would confirm your *l'* toward him.
5:14 For the *l'* of Christ constraineth us;
6: 6 by the Holy Ghost, by *l'* unfeigned,
8: 7 in all diligence, and in your *l'* to us,
8 and to prove the sincerity of your *l'*.
24 the churches, the proof of your *l'*,
11:11 because I *l'* you not? God knoweth.
12:15 though the more abundantly I *l'* you,
13:11 God of *l'* and peace shall be with you.
14 the *l'* of God, and the communion
Ga 5: 6 but faith which worketh by *l'*.
13 flesh, but by *l'* serve one another.
14 shalt *l'* thy neighbour as thyself.
22 the fruit of the Spirit is *l'*, joy, peace,
Eph 1: 4 and without blame before him in *l'*:
15 Jesus, and *l'* unto all the saints.
2: 4 great *l'* wherewith he loved us.
3:17 ye, being rooted and grounded in *l'*,
19 And to know the *l'* of Christ, which
4: 2 forbearing one another in *l'*;
15 speaking the truth in *l'*, may grow
16 body unto the edifying of itself in *l'*.
5: 2 And walk in *l'*, as Christ also hath
25 Husbands, *l'* your wives, even as
28 So ought men to *l'* their wives as
33 so *l'* his wife even as himself; and
6:23 be to the brethren, and *l'* with faith,
24 with all them that *l'* our Lord Jesus
Ph'p 1: 9 your *l'* may abound yet more and
17 the other of *l'*, knowing that I am
2: 1 in Christ, if any comfort of *l'*, if any
2 be likeminded, having the same *l'*,
Col 1: 4 and of the *l'* which ye have to all the
8 Who also declared unto us your *l'* in
2: 2 comforted, being knit together in *l'*,
3:19 Husbands, *l'* your wives, and be not
1Th 1: 3 your work of faith, and labour of *l'*,
3:12 abound in *l'* one toward another,
4: 9 as touching brotherly *l'* ye need
9 are taught of God to *l'* one another.
5: 8 on the breastplate of faith and *l'*.
13 highly in *l'* for their work's sake.
2Th 2:10 they received not the *l'* of the truth,
3: 5 direct your hearts into the *l'* of God,
1Ti 1:14 faith and *l'* which is in Christ Jesus.
6:10 *l'* of money is the root of all evil:
11 faith, *l'*, patience, meekness.
2Ti 1: 7 and of *l'*, and of a sound mind.
13 faith and *l'* which is in Christ Jesus.
4: 8 all them also that *l'* his appearing.
Tit 2: 4 to be sober, to *l'* their husbands,
4 to be sober,...to *l'* their children,
3: 4 that the kindness and *l'* of God
15 Greet them that *l'* us in the faith.
Ph'm 5 Hearing of thy *l'* and faith, which
7 great joy and consolation in thy *l'*,
Heb 6:10 to forget your work and labour of *l'*,
10:24 to provoke unto *l'* and to good works:
13: 1 Let brotherly *l'* continue.
Jas 1:12 hath promised to them that *l'* him.
2: 5 hath promised to them that *l'* him?
8 shalt *l'* thy neighbour as thyself,
1Pe 1: 8 Whom having not seen, ye *l'*; in
22 unto unfeigned *l'* of the brethren,
22 ye *l'* one another with a pure heart
2:17 *L'* the brotherhood. Fear God.
3: 8 one to another, *l'* as brethren, be
1Pe 3:10 For he that will *l'* life, and see good
1Jo 2: 5 him verily is the *l'* of God perfected:
15 *L'* not the world, neither the things
15 If any man *l'* the world,
15 the *l'* of the Father is not in him.
3: 1 what manner of *l'* the Father hath
11 that we should *l'* one another.
14 unto life, because we *l'* the brethren.
16 Hereby perceive we the *l'* of God,
17 how dwelleth the *l'* of God in him?
18 little children, let us not *l'* in word,
23 Son Jesus Christ, and *l'* one another,
4: 7 Beloved, let us *l'* one another:
7 for *l'* is of God; and every one that
8 not knoweth not God; for God is *l'*.
9 manifested the *l'* of God toward us,
10 Herein is *l'*, not that we loved God,
11 us, we ought also to *l'* one another.
12 If we *l'* one another, God dwelleth in
12 in us, and his *l'* is perfected in us.
16 believed the *l'* that God hath to us.
16 God is *l'*; and he that dwelleth in
16 that dwelleth in *l'* dwelleth in God,
17 Herein is our *l'* made perfect, that
18 There is no fear in *l'*; but perfect
18 but perfect *l'* casteth out fear:
18 that feareth is not made perfect in *l'*.
19 We *l'* him, because he first loved us.
20 If a man say, I *l'* God, and hateth
20 how can he *l'* God whom he hath not
21 who loveth God *l'* his brother also.
5: 2 know that we *l'* the children of God,
2 when we *l'* God, and keep his
3 this is the *l'* of God, that we keep
2Jo 1 her children, whom I *l'* in the truth;
3 the Son of the Father, in truth and *l'*.
5 beginning, that we *l'* one another.
6 And this is *l'*, that we walk after his
3Jo 1 unto...Gaius, whom I *l'* in the truth.
Jude 2 Mercy unto you, and peace, and *l'*,
21 Keep yourselves in the *l'* of God,
Re 2: 4 because thou hast left thy first *l'*.
3:19 As many as I *l'*, I rebuke and

loved See also BELOVED; LOVEDST.
Ge 24:67 she became his wife; and he *l'* her:
25:28 And Isaac *l'* Esau, because he did
28 his venison: but Rebekah *l'* Jacob.
27:14 savoury meat, such as his father *l'*.
29:18 Jacob *l'* Rachel; and said, I will
30 he *l'* also Rachel more than Leah.
34: 3 he *l'* the damsel, and spake kindly
37: 3 Now Israel *l'* Joseph more than all
4 saw that their father *l'* him more
De 4:37 because he *l'* thy fathers, therefore
7: 8 But because the Lord *l'* you, and
23: 5 because the Lord thy God *l'* thee.
33: 3 Yea, he *l'* the people; all his
J'g 16: 4 *l'* a woman in the valley of Sorek,
1Sa 1: 5 he *l'* Hannah: but the Lord had
16:21 before him: and he *l'* him greatly;
18: 1 and Jonathan *l'* him as his own soul.
3 because he *l'* him as his own soul.
16 But all Israel and Judah *l'* David,
20 Michal Saul's daughter *l'* David:
28 that Michal Saul's daughter *l'* him.
20:17 to swear again, because he *l'* him:
17 for he *l'* him as he...his own soul.
17 for he...him as he *l'* his own soul.
2Sa 12:24 name Solomon: and the Lord *l'* him.
13: 1 and Amnon the son of David *l'* her.
15 the love wherewith he had *l'* her.
1Ki 3: 3 And Solomon *l'* the Lord, walking
10: 9 because the Lord *l'* Israel for ever,
11: 1 Solomon *l'* many strange women,
2Ch 2:11 Because the Lord hath *l'* his people,
9: 8 thy God: because thy God *l'* Israel,
11:21 And Rehoboam *l'* Maachah the
26:10 and in Carmel: for he *l'* husbandry.
Es 2:17 And the king *l'* Esther above all the
Job 19:19 they whom I *l'* are turned against
Ps 26: 8 Lord, I have *l'* the habitation of thy
47: 4 the excellency of Jacob whom he *l'*.
78:68 Judah, the mount Zion which he *l'*.
109:17 As he *l'* cursing, so let it come unto
119:47 thy commandments, which I have *l'*.
48 thy commandments, which I have *l'*;
Isa 43: 4 been honourable, and I have *l'* thee:
48:14 The Lord hath *l'* him: he will do his
Jer 2:25 I have *l'* strangers, and after them
8: 2 host of heaven, whom they have *l'*,
14:10 Thus have they *l'* to wander, they
31: 3 I have *l'* thee with an everlasting
Eze 16:37 all them that thou hast *l'*, with all
Ho 9: 1 *l'* a reward upon every cornfloor.
10 were according as they *l'*.
11: 1 Israel was a child, then I *l'* him, and
Mal 1: 2 I have *l'* you, saith the Lord.
2 Yet ye say, Wherein hast thou *l'* us?
2 saith the Lord: yet I *l'* Jacob,
2:11 the holiness of the Lord which he *l'*,
M'r 10:21 Jesus beholding him *l'* him, and said
Lu 7:47 many, are forgiven; for she *l'* much:
Joh 3:16 For God so *l'* the world, that he
19 men *l'* darkness rather than light,
11: 5 Now Jesus *l'* Martha, and her sister,
36 the Jews, Behold how he *l'* him!
12:43 they *l'* the praise of men more than
13: 1 having *l'* his own which were in the
1 the world, he *l'* them unto the end.
23 one of his disciples, whom Jesus *l'*.
34 as I have *l'* you, that ye also love one
14:21 loveth me shall be *l'* of my Father,
28 If ye *l'* me, ye would rejoice, because
15: 9 As the Father hath *l'* me, so have I
9 me, so have I *l'* you: continue ye in
12 ye love one another, as I have *l'* you.
Joh 16:27 because ye have *l'* me, and have
17:23 and hast *l'* them, as thou hast *l'* me.
26 the love wherewith thou hast *l'* me
19:26 the disciple standing by, whom he *l'*,
20: 2 the other disciple, whom Jesus *l'*,
21: 7 that disciple whom Jesus *l'* saith
20 the disciple whom Jesus *l'* following;
Ro 8:37 conquerors through him that *l'* us.
9:13 As it is written, Jacob have I *l'*, but
2Co 12:15 abundantly I love you, the less I be *l'*.
Ga 2:20 faith of the Son of God, who *l'* me,
Eph 2: 4 his great love wherewith he *l'* us,
5: 2 in love, as Christ also hath *l'* us,
25 even as Christ also *l'* the church,
2Th 2:16 even our Father, which hath *l'* us,
2Ti 4:10 me, having *l'* this present world,
Heb 1: 9 hast *l'* righteousness, and hated
2Pe 2:15 who *l'* the wages of unrighteousness;
1Jo 4:10 Herein is love, not that we *l'* God,
10 but that he *l'* us, and sent his Son to
11 Beloved, if God so *l'* us, we ought
19 We love him, because he first *l'* us.
Re 1: 5 Unto him that *l'* us, and washed us
3: 9 feet, and to know that I have *l'* thee.
12:11 they *l'* not their lives unto the death.

lovedst
Isa 57: 8 *l'* their bed where thou sawest it.
Joh 17:24 *l'* me before the foundation of the

lovely
2Sa 1:23 and Jonathan were *l'* and pleasant
Ca 5:16 sweet: yea, he is altogether *l'*.
Eze 33:32 art unto them as a very *l'* song of
Ph'p 4: 8 are pure, whatsoever things are *l'*,

lover See also LOVERS.
1Ki 5: 1 for Hiram was ever a *l'* of David.
Ps 88:18 *L'* and friend hast thou put far from
Tit 1: 8 But a *l'* of hospitality,...of good
8 a *l'* of good men, sober, just, holy,

lovers
Ps 38:11 My *l'* and my friends stand aloof
Jer 3: 1 played the harlot with many *l'*;
4:30 thy *l'* will despise thee, they will
22:20 for all thy *l'* are destroyed.
22 and thy *l'* shall go into captivity:
30:14 All thy *l'* have forgotten thee; they
La 1: 2 among all her *l'* she hath none to
19 I called for my *l'*, but they deceived
Eze 16:33 but thou givest thy gifts to all thy *l'*,
36 through thy whoredoms with thy *l'*,
37 therefore I will gather all thy *l'*,
23: 5 doted on her *l'*, on the Assyrians
9 delivered her into the hand of her *l'*,
22 I will raise up thy *l'* against thee,
Ho 2: 5 I will go after my *l'*, that give me my
7 she shall follow after her *l'*, but she
10 her lewdness in the sight of her *l'*,
12 rewards that my *l'* have given me:
13 she went after her *l'*, and forgat me,
8: 9 by himself: Ephraim hath hired *l'*.
2Ti 3: 2 men shall be *l'* of their own selves,
4 highminded, *l'* of pleasures more
4 of pleasures more than *l'* of God;

love's
Ph'm 9 for *l'* sake I rather beseech thee,

loves
Ps 45: *title* of Korah, Maschil, A Song of *l'*.
Pr 7:18 let us solace ourselves with *l'*.
Ca 7:12 forth: there will I give thee my *l'*.

lovest
Ge 22: 2 thine only son Isaac, whom thou *l'*,
J'g 14:16 dost but hate me, and *l'* me not:
2Sa 19: 6 In that thou *l'* thine enemies, and
Ps 45: 7 Thou *l'* righteousness, and hatest
52: 3 Thou *l'* evil more than good; and
4 Thou *l'* all devouring words, O thou
Ec 9: 9 joyfully with the wife whom thou *l'*
Joh 11: 3 behold, he whom thou *l'* is sick.
21:15 Jonas, *l'* thou me more than these?
16 Simon, son of Jonas, *l'* thou me?
17 Simon, son of Jonas, *l'* thou me?
17 him the third time, *L'* thou me?

loveth
Ge 27: 9 meat for thy father, such as he *l'*:
44:20 of his mother, and his father *l'* him.
De 10:18 *l'* the stranger, in giving him food
15:16 because he *l'* thee and thine house,
Ru 4:15 thy daughter in law, which *l'* thee,
Ps 11: 5 him that *l'* violence his soul hateth.
7 the righteous Lord *l'* righteousness;
33: 5 He *l'* righteousness and judgment:
34:12 that desireth life, and *l'* many days,
37:28 The Lord *l'* judgment, and forsaketh
87: 2 The Lord *l'* the gates of Zion more
99: 4 king's strength also *l'* judgment;
119:140 pure: therefore thy servant *l'* it.
146: 8 down: the Lord *l'* the righteous:
Pr 3:12 for whom the Lord *l'* he correcteth;
12: 1 Whoso *l'* instruction *l'* knowledge:
13:24 that *l'* him chasteneth him betimes.
15: 9 but he *l'* him that followeth after
12 A scorner *l'* not one that reproveth
17:17 friend *l'* at all times, and a brother
19 He *l'* transgression that *l'* strife:
19: 8 that getteth wisdom *l'* his own soul:
21:17 that *l'* pleasure shall be a poor man:
17 that *l'* wine and oil shall not be rich.
22:11 He that *l'* pureness of heart, for the
29: 3 Whoso *l'* wisdom rejoiceth his
Ec 5:10 that *l'* silver shall not be satisfied
10 he that *l'* abundance with increase:
Ca 1: 7 Tell me, O thou whom my soul *l'*,
3: 1 bed I sought him whom my soul *l'*:
2 I will seek him whom my soul *l'*:
3 I said, Saw ye him whom my soul *l'*?
4 but I found him whom my soul *l'*:

Isa 1:23 every one l' gifts, and followeth after
Ho 10:11 taught, and l' to tread out the corn;
12: 7 are in his hand: he l' to oppress.
M't 10:37 l' father or mother more than me
37 l' son or daughter more than me
Lu 7: 5 he l' our nation, and he hath built
47 little is forgiven, the same l' little.
Joh 3:35 Father l' the Son, and hath given
5:20 Father l' the Son, and sheweth
12:25 He that l' his life shall lose it; and
14:21 keepeth them, he it is that l' me:
21 l' me shall be loved by my Father,
24 l' me not keepeth not my sayings:
16:27 the Father himself l' you, because
Ro 13: 8 that l' another hath fulfilled the law.
2Co 9: 7 necessity: for God l' a cheerful giver.
Eph 5:28 bodies. He that l' his wife l' himself.
Heb12: 6 For whom the Lord l' he chasteneth,
1Jo 2:10 l' his brother abideth in the light,
3:10 neither he that l' not his brother.
14 l' not his brother abideth in death.
4: 7 and every one that l' is born of God,
8 He that l' not knoweth not God; for
20 l' not his brother whom he hath seen,
21 he who l' God love his brother also.
5: 1 and every one that l' him that begat
1 l' him also that is begotten of him.
3Jo 9 l' to have the preeminence among
Re 22:15 and whosoever l' and maketh a lie.

loving See also LOVINGKINDNESS.
Pr 5:19 be as the l' hind and pleasant roe;
22: 1 l' favour rather than silver and
Isa 56:10 sleeping, lying down, l' to slumber.

lovingkindness See also LOVINGKINDNESSES.
Ps 17: 7 Shew thy marvellous l', O thou
26: 3 For thy l' is before mine eyes: and
36: 7 How excellent is thy l', O God!
10 continue thy l' unto them that know
40:10 I have not concealed thy l' and thy
11 let thy l' and thy truth continually
42: 8 Yet the Lord will command his l'
48: 9 We have thought of thy l', O God,
51: 1 upon me, O God, according to thy l':
63: 3 Because thy l' is better than life,
69:16 Hear me, O Lord; for thy l' is good:
88:11 Shall thy l' be declared in the grave?
89:33 my l' will I not utterly take from
92: 2 To shew forth thy l' in the morning,
103: 4 crowneth thee with l' and tender
107:43 shall understand the l' of the Lord.
119:88 Quicken me after thy l'; so shall I
149 my voice according unto thy l':
159 me, O Lord, according to thy l'.
138: 2 name for thy l' and for thy truth:
143: 8 me to hear thy l' in the morning;
Jer 9:24 I am the Lord which exercise l',
16: 5 saith the Lord, even l' and mercies.
31: 3 therefore with l' have I drawn thee.
32:18 Thou shewest l' unto thousands,
Ho 2:19 judgment, and in l', and in mercies.

lovingkindnesses
Ps 25: 6 thy tender mercies and thy l';
89:49 Lord, where are thy former l',
Isa 63: 7 I will mention the l' of the Lord,
7 according to the multitude of his l'.

low See also LOWER; LOWEST; LOWETH; LOWING.
De 28:43 and thou shalt come down very l'.
J'g 11:35 thou hast brought me very l', and
1Sa 2: 7 rich: he bringeth l', and lifteth up.
1Ch 27:28 trees that were in the l' plains
2Ch 9:27 trees that are in the l' plains in
26:10 much cattle, both in the l' country,
28:18 invaded the cities of the l' country,
19 the Lord brought Judah l' because
Job 5:11 To set up on high those that be l';
14:21 and they are brought l', but he
24:24 but are gone and brought l'; they
40:12 that is proud, and bring him l';
Ps 49: 2 Both l' and high, rich and poor,
62: 9 Surely men of l' degree are vanity,
79: 8 us: for we are brought very l'.
106:43 were brought l' for their iniquity.
107:39 they are minished and brought l'
116: 6 I was brought l', and he helped me.
136:23 remembered us in our l' estate:
142: 6 my cry; for I am brought very l':
Pr 29:23 A man's pride shall bring him l':
Ec 10: 6 dignity, and the rich sit in l' place.
12: 4 the sound of the grinding is l', and
4 of musick shall be brought l';
Isa 2:12 up; and he shall be brought l':
17 haughtiness of men shall be made l':
13:11 will lay l' the haughtiness of the
25: 5 terrible ones shall be brought l'.
12 lay l', and bring to the ground,
26: 5 high; the lofty city, he layeth it l';
5 he layeth it l', even to the ground;
29: 4 speech shall be l' out of the dust,
32:19 the forest; and the city shall be l'
19 and the city shall be...in a l' place.
40: 4 mountain and hill shall be made l':
La 3:55 O Lord, out of the l' dungeon.
Eze 17: 6 a spreading vine of l' stature,
24 have exalted the l' tree, have dried
21:26 exalt him that is l', and abase him
26:20 thee in the l' parts of the earth,
Lu 1:48 hath regarded the l' estate of his
52 and exalted them of l' degree.
3: 5 and hill shall be brought l';
Ro 12:16 but condescend to men of l' estate.
Jas 1: 9 brother of l' degree rejoice in that
10 the rich, in that he is made l':

lower See also LOWRING.
Ge 6:16 with l', second, and third stories
Le 13:20 it be in sight l' than the skin, and
21 if it be not l' than the skin, but be
26 and it be no l' than the other skin,
14:37 which in sight are l' than the wall;
Ne 4:13 set I in the l' places behind the
Ps 8: 5 him a little l' than the angels,
63: 9 go into the l' parts of the earth.
Pr 25: 7 l' in the presence of the prince
Isa 22: 9 together the waters of the l' pool.
44:23 shout, ye l' parts of the earth:
Eze 40:18 of the gates was the l' pavement.
19 from the forefront of the l' gate
42: 5 were higher than these, than the l',
43:14 the ground even to the l' settle
Eph 4: 9 descended first into the l' parts
Heb 2: 7 madest him a little l' than...angels;
9 was made a little l' than the angels

lowering See LOWRING.

lowest
De 32:22 and shall burn unto the l' hell,
1Ki 12:31 priests of the l' of the people,
13:33 again of the l' of the people priests
2Ki 17:32 of the l' of them priests of the high
Ps 86:13 delivered my soul from the l' hell.
88: 6 Thou hast laid me in the l' pit, in
139:15 wrought in the lowest parts of the
Eze 41: 7 increased from the l' chamber to
42: 6 was straitened more than the l'
Lu 14: 9 with shame to take the l' room.
10 go and sit down in the l' room;

loweth
Job 6: 5 grass? or l' the ox over his fodder?

lowing
1Sa 6:12 l' as they went, and turned not
15:14 the l' of the oxen which I hear?

lowliness
Eph 4: 2 With all l' and meekness, with
Ph'p 2: 3 in l' of mind let each esteem other

lowly
Ps 138: 6 yet hath he respect unto the l':
Pr 3:34 but he giveth grace unto the l'.
11: 2 shame: but with the l' is wisdom.
16:19 be of an humble spirit with the l',
Zec 9: 9 l', and riding upon an ass, and upon
M't 11:29 me; for I am meek and l' in heart:

lowring
M't 16: 3 to-day: for the sky is red and l'.

Lubim (*lu'-bim*) See also LUBIMS.
Na 3: 9 Put and L' were thy helpers.

Lubims (*lu'-bims*) See also LEHABIM; LUBIM.
2Ch 12: 3 the L', the Sukkiims, and the
16: 8 Ethiopians and the L' a huge host,

Lucas (*lu'-cas*) See also LUKE.
2Co *subscr.* of Macedonia, by Titus and L'.
Ph'm 24 Demas, L', my fellowlabourers,

Lucifer (*lu'-sif-ur*)
Isa 14:12 O L', son of the morning! how

Lucius (*lu'-she-us*)
Ac 13: 1 and L' of Cyrene, and Manaen,
Ro 16:21 Timotheus my workfellow, and L',

lucre See also LUCRE'S.
1Sa 8: 3 but turned aside after l', and took
1Ti 3: 3 no striker, not greedy of filthy l';
8 much wine, not greedy of filthy l';
Tit 1: 7 no striker, not given to filthy l';
1Pe 5: 2 not for filthy l', but of a ready

lucre's
Tit 1:11 they ought not, for filthy l' sake.

Lud (*lud*) See also LUDIM; LYDIA.
Ge 10:22 Asshur, and Arphaxad, and L',
1Ch 1:17 and L', and Aram, and Uz, and
Isa 66:19 Pul, and L', that draw the bow,
Eze 27:10 They of Persia and of L' and of

Ludim (*lu'-dim*) See also LUD.
Ge 10:13 Mizraim begat L', and Anamim,
1Ch 1:11 Mizraim begat L', and Anamim,

Luhith (*lu'-hith*)
Isa 15: 5 mounting up of L' with weeping
Jer 48: 5 going up of L' continual weeping

Luke[A] (*luke*) See also LUCAS.
Col 4:14 L', the beloved physician, and
2Ti 4:11 Only L' is with me. Take Mark,

lukewarm
Re 3:16 So then because thou art l', and

lump
2Ki 20: 7 And Isaiah said, Take a l' of figs.
Isa 38:21 had said, Let them take a l' of figs,
Ro 9:21 same l' to make one vessel unto
11:16 firstfruit be holy, the l' is also holy:
1Co 5: 6 little leaven leaveneth the whole l'?
7 old leaven, that ye may be a new l',
Ga 5: 9 little leaven leaveneth the whole l'.

lunatick
M't 4:24 and those which were l', and those
17:15 son: for he is l', and sore vexed:

lure See ALLURE.

lurk See also LURKING.
Pr 1:11 let us l' privily for the innocent
18 they l' privily for their own lives.

lurking
1Sa 23:23 take knowledge of all the l' places
Ps 10: 8 in the l' places of the villages:
17:12 a young lion l' in secret places.

lurking-places See LURKING and PLACES.

lust See also LUSTED; LUSTETH; LUSTING; LUSTS.
Ex 15: 9 my l' shall be satisfied upon them;
Ps 78:18 heart by asking meat for their l'.
30 were not estranged from their l'.
81:12 them up unto their own hearts' l':
Pr 6:25 L' not after her beauty in thine
M't 5:28 looketh on a woman to l' after her
Ro 1:27 burned in their l' one toward
7: 7 for I had not known l', except the
1Co 10: 6 should not l' after evil things,
Ga 5:16 shall not fulfil the l' of the flesh.
1Th 4: 5 Not in the l' of concupiscence,
Jas 1:14 he is drawn away of his own l',
15 Then when l' hath conceived, it
4: 2 Ye l', and have not: ye kill, and
2Pe 1: 4 that is in the world through l'.
2:10 the flesh in the l' of uncleanness,
1Jo 2:16 l' of the flesh, and the l' of the eyes,
17 passeth away, and the l' thereof:

lusted
Nu 11:34 there they buried the people that l'.
Ps 106:14 But l' exceedingly in the wilderness,
1Co 10: 6 after evil things, as they also l'.
Re 18:14 the fruits that thy soul l' after are

lusteth
De 12:15 eat...whatsoever thy soul l' after,
20 flesh, whatsoever thy soul l' after.
21 gates whatsoever thy soul l' after.
14:26 for whatsoever thy soul l' after,
Ga 5:17 For the flesh l' against the Spirit,
Jas 4: 5 that dwelleth in us l' to envy?

lusting
Nu 11: 4 that was among them fell a l':

lusts
M'r 4:19 the l' of other things entering in,
Joh 8:44 and the l' of your father ye will do:
Ro 1:24 through the l' of their own hearts, to
6:12 ye should obey it in the l' thereof.
13:14 for the flesh, to fulfil the l' thereof.
Ga 5:24 the flesh with the affections and l'.
Eph 2: 3 in times past in the l' of our flesh,
4:22 corrupt according to the deceitful l';
1Ti 6: 9 and into many foolish and hurtful l',
2Ti 2:22 Flee also youthful l': but follow
3: 6 with sins, led away with divers l',
4: 3 after their own l' shall they heap
Tit 2:12 denying ungodliness and worldly l',
3: 3 serving divers l' and pleasures,
Jas 4: 1 your l' that war in your members?
3 ye may consume it upon your l'.
1Pe 1:14 to the former l' in your ignorance:
2:11 abstain from fleshly l', which war
4: 2 time in the flesh to the l' of men,
3 walked in lasciviousness, l', excess
2Pe 2:18 allure through the l' of the flesh,
3: 3 scoffers, walking after their own l',
Jude 16 walking after their own l';
18 walk after their own ungodly l'.

lusty
J'g 3:29 men, all l', and all men of valour;

Luz (*luz*) See also BETH-EL.
Ge 28:19 the name of that city was called L'
35: 6 So Jacob came to L', which is in the
48: 3 Almighty appeared unto me at L'
Jos 16: 2 And goeth out from Beth-el to L',
18:13 thence toward L', to the side of L',
J'g 1:23 the name of the city before was L'.)
26 and called the name thereof L':

Lycaonia (*li-ca-o'-ne-ah*)
Ac 14: 6 Lystra and Derbe, cities of L', and
11 voices, saying in the speech of L',

Lycia (*lish'-e-ah*)
Ac 27: 5 we came to Myra, a city of L'.

Lydda (*lid'-dah*) See also LOD.
Ac 9:32 to the saints which dwelt at L'.
35 And all that dwelt at L' and Saron
38 forasmuch as L' was nigh to Joppa,

Lydia (*lid'-e-ah*) See also LUDIM; LYDIANS.
Eze 30: 5 Ethopia, and Libya, and L', and
Ac 16:14 And a certain woman named L',
40 and entered into the house of L':

Lydians (*lid'-e-uns*) See also LUDIMS.
Jer 46: 9 L', that handle and bend the bow.

lying See also LEASING.
Ge 29: 2 were three flocks of sheep l' by it;
34: 7 Israel in l' with Jacob's daughter;
Ex 23: 5 hateth thee l' under his burden,
Nu 31:17 hath known man by l' with him.
18 not known a man by l' with him,
35 not known a man by l' with him.
De 21: 1 l' in the field, and it be not known
22:22 a man be found l' with a woman
J'g 9:35 were with him, from l' in wait.
16: 9 Now there were men l' in wait,
21:12 known no man by l' with any male:
1Ki 22:22 be a l' spirit in the mouth of all his
23 Lord hath put a l' spirit in the mouth
2Ch 18:21 be a l' spirit in the mouth of all his
22 Lord hath put a l' spirit in the mouth
Ps 31: 6 them that regard l' vanities:
18 Let the l' lips be put to silence;
52: 3 and l' rather than...righteousness.
59:12 and for cursing and l', which they
109: 2 against me with a l' tongue.
119:29 Remove from me the way of l':
163 I hate and abhor l': but thy law
120: 2 Deliver my soul, O Lord, from l' lips,
139: 3 Thou compassest...my l' down,
Pr 6:17 proud look, a l' tongue, and hands
10:18 He that hideth hatred with l' lips,
12:19 but a l' tongue is but for a moment.
22 L' lips are abomination to the Lord:
13: 5 A righteous man hateth l': but

Pr 17: 7 fool: much less do l' lips a prince.
21: 6 getting of treasures by a l' tongue
26:28 A l' tongue hateth those that are
Isa 30: 9 is a rebellious people, l' children,
32: 7 to destroy the poor with l' words,
56:10 l' down, loving to slumber.
59:13 and l' against the Lord, and
Jer 7: 4 Trust ye not in l' words, saying,
8 ye trust in l' words, that cannot
29:23 have spoken l' words in my name,
La 3:10 He was unto me as a bear l' in wait.
Eze 13: 6 have seen vanity and l' divination,
7 have ye not spoken a l' divination,
19 by your l' to my people that hear
Da 2: 9 prepared l' and corrupt words to
Ho 4: 2 By swearing, and l', and killing,
Jon 2: 8 that observe l' vanities forsake
M't 9: 2 a man sick of the palsy, l' on a bed:
M'r 5:40 entereth in where...damsel was l'.
Lu 2:12 swaddling clothes, l' in a manger.
16 Joseph, and the babe l' in a manger.
Joh 13:25 He then l' on Jesus' breast saith
20: 5 looking in, saw the linen clothes l';
7 not l' with the linen clothes, but
Ac 20:19 me by the l' in wait of the Jews:
23:16 sister's son heard of their l' in wait,
Eph 4:25 Wherefore putting away l', speak
2Th 2: 9 all power and signs and l' wonders,

Lysanias (*li-sa'-ne-as*)
Lu 3: 1 and L' the tetrarch of Abilene,

Lysias (*lis'-e-as*)
Ac 23:26 Claudius L' unto...Felix sendeth
24: 7 the chief captain L' came upon us,
22 L' the chief captain shall come

Lystra (*lis'-trah*)
Ac 14: 6 fled unto L' and Derbe, cities of
8 And there sat a certain man at L',
21 they returned again to L', and to
16: 1 Then came he to Derbe and L':
2 by the brethren that were at L' and
2Ti 3:11 me at Antioch, at Iconium, at L';

M.

Maacah (*ma'-a-kah*) See also MAACHAH.
2Sa 3: 3 son of M' the daughter of Talmai
10: 6 and of king M' a thousand men,
8 and M', were by themselves in

Maachah (*ma'-a-kah*) See also BETH-MAACHAH; MAACAH; MAACHATHITE; SYRIA-MAACHAH.
Ge 22:24 and Gaham, and Thahash, and M'.
1Ki 2:39 Achish son of M' king of Gath.
15: 2, 10 his mother's name was M', the
13 And also M' his mother, even her
1Ch 2:48 M', Caleb's concubine, bare
3: 2 son of M' the daughter of Talmai
7:15 whose sister's name was M',)
16 M' the wife of Machir bare a son,
8:29 whose wife's name was M':
9:35 Jehiel, whose wife's name was M':
11:43 Hanan the son of M', and
19: 7 and the king of M' and his people;
27:16 Shephatiah the son of M':
2Ch 11:20 took M' the daughter of Absalom;
21 Rehoboam loved M' the daughter
22 Abijah the son of M' the chief,
15:16 concerning M' the mother of Asa

Maachathi (*ma-ak'-a-thi*) See also MAACHATHITE.
De 3:14 the coasts of Geshuri and M';

Maachathite (*ma-ak'-a-thite*) See also MAACHATHI; MAACHATHITES.
2Sa 23:34 son of Ahasbai, the son of the M',
2Ki 25:23 Jaazaniah the son of a M', they
1Ch 4:19 Garmite, and Eshtemoa the M'.
Jer 40: 8 and Jezaniah the son of a M',

Maachathites (*ma-ak'-a-thites*)
Jos 12: 5 of the Geshurites and the M',
13:11 border of the Geshurites and M',
13 not the Geshurites, nor the M':
13 M' dwell among the Israelites

Maadai (*ma'-a-dahee*)
Ezr 10:34 of Bani; M', Amram, and Uel,

Maadiah (*ma-a-di'-ah*) See also MOADIAH.
Ne 12: 5 Miamin, M', Bilgah,

Maai (*ma'-ahee*)
Ne 12:36 Milalai, Gilalai, M', Nethaneel,

Maaleh-acrabbim (*ma''-a-leh-ac-rab'-bim*) See also AKRABBIM.
Jos 15: 3 went out to the south side to M',

Maarath (*ma'-a-rath*)
Jos 15:59 And M', and Beth-anoth, and

Maaseiah (*ma-a-si'-ah*)
1Ch 15:18 Eliab, and Benaiah, and M', and
20 M', and Benaiah, with psalteries
2Ch 23: 1 Obed, and M' the son of Adaiah,
26:11 Jeiel the scribe and M' the ruler,
28: 7 a mighty man of Ephraim, slew M'
34: 8 and M' the governor of the city,
Ezr 10:18 M', and Eliezer, and Jarib, and
21 And of the sons of Harim; M', and
22 the sons of Pashur; Elioenai, M',
30 Chelal, Benaiah, M', Mattaniah,
Ne 3:23 repaired Azariah the son of M' the
8: 4 and M', on his right hand; and
7 Hodijah, M', Kelita, Azariah,
10:25 Rehum, Hashabnah, M',
11: 5 And M' the son of Baruch, the son
7 the son of M', the son of Ithiel, the
12:41 the priests; Eliakim, M', Miniamin,
42 M', and Shemaiah, and Eleazar,
Jer 21: 1 Zephaniah the son of M' the priest,
29:21 Zedekiah the son of M', which
25 to Zephaniah the son of M' the
32:12 the son of M', in the sight of
35: 4 was above the chamber of M'
37: 3 Zephaniah the son of M' the
51:59 the son of M', when he went with

Maasiai (*ma-a'-see-ahee*)
1Ch 9:12 and M' the son of Adiel, the son

Maath (*ma'-ath*)
Lu 3:26 Which was the son of M', which was

Maaz (*ma'-az*)
1Ch 2:27 firstborn of Jerahmeel were, M',

Maaziah (*ma-a-zi'-ah*)
1Ch 24:18 the four and twentieth to M'.
Ne 10: 8 M', Bilgai, Shemaiah: these were

Macedonia (*mas-e-do'-nee-ah*) See also MACEDONIAN.
Ac 16: 9 stood a man of M', and prayed
9 Come over into M', and help us.
10 we endeavoured to go into M',
12 is the chief city of that part of M',
18: 5 and Timotheus were come from M',
Ac 19:21 when he had passed through M' and
22 he sent into M' two of them that
29 men of M', Paul's companions in
20: 1 and departed for to go into M'.
3 he purposed to return through M'.
Ro 15:26 it hath pleased them of M' and
1Co 16: 5 when I shall pass through M':
5 for I do pass through M'.
2Co 1:16 to pass by you into M', and to
16 come again out of M' unto you,
2:13 them, I went from thence into M'.
7: 5 when we were come into M', our
8: 1 bestowed on the churches of M';
9: 2 I boast of you to them of M', that
4 Lest haply if they of M' come with
11: 9 the brethren which came from M'
subscr. from Philippi, a city of M'.
Ph'p 4:15 when I departed from M', no
1Th 1: 7 ensamples to all that believe in M'
8 word of the Lord not only in M'
4:10 the brethren which are in all M':
1Ti 1: 3 at Ephesus, when I went into M',
Tit *subscr.* Cretians, from Nicopolis of M'.

Macedonian (*mas-e-do'-nee-an*)
Ac 27: 2 Aristarchus,...being with a M' of

Machbanai (*mak'-ba-nahee*)
1Ch 12:13 the tenth, M' the eleventh.

Machbenah (*mak'-be-nah*)
1Ch 2:49 Sheva the father of M', and the

Machi (*ma'-ki*)
Nu 13:15 tribe of Gad, Geuel the son of M'.

Machir (*ma'-kur*) See also MACHIRITE.
Ge 50:23 also of M' the son of Manasseh
Nu 26:29 of M', the family of the Machirites:
29 M' begat Gilead: of Gilead come
27: 1 son of M', the son of Manasseh,
32:39 children of M' the son of Manasseh
40 unto M' the son of Manasseh,
36: 1 children of Gilead, the son of M',
De 3:15 And I gave Gilead unto M'.
Jos 13:31 pertaining unto the children of M'
31 to the one half of the children of M
17: 1 for M' the firstborn of Manasseh,
3 son of M', the son of Manasseh,
J'g 5:14 out of M' came down governors,
2Sa 9: 4 he is in the house of M', the son of
5 fetched him out of the house of M',
17:27 M' the son of Ammiel of Lo-debar,
1Ch 2:21 went in to the daughter of M' the
23 these belonged to the sons of M'.
7:14 concubine the Aramitess bare M'
15 And M' took to wife the sister of
16 the wife of M' bare a son, and
17 son of M', the son of Manasseh.

Machirites (*ma'-kur-ites*)
Nu 26:29 of Machir, the family of the M':

Machnadebai (*mak-nad'-e-bahee*)
Ezr 10:40 M', Shashai, Sharai,

Machpelah (*mak-pe'-lah*)
Ge 23: 9 he may give me the cave of M',
17 field of Ephron, which was in M',
19 wife in the cave of the field of M'
25: 9 buried him in the cave of M', in
49:30 In the cave that is in the field of M',
50:13 him in the cave of the field of M',

mad
De 28:34 be m' for the sight of thine eyes
1Sa 21:13 feigned himself m' in their hands,
14 servants, Lo, ye see the man is m':
15 Have I need of m' men, that ye
15 to play the m' man in my presence?
2Ki 9:11 came this m' fellow to thee? And
Ps 102: 8 m' against me are sworn against
Pr 26:18 a m' man who casteth firebrands,
Ec 2: 2 I said of laughter, It is m': and of
7: 7 oppression maketh a wise man m';
Isa 44:25 the liars, and maketh diviners m';
Jer 25:16 drink, and be moved, and be m',
29:26 every man that is m', and maketh
50:38 and they are m' upon their idols.
51: 7 wine; therefore the nations are m'.
Hos 9: 7 is a fool, the spiritual man is m',
Joh 10:20 said, He hath a devil, and is m';
Ac 12:15 they said unto her, Thou art m'.
26:11 exceedingly m' against them,
24 learning doth make thee m'.
25 I am not m', most noble Festus;
1Co 14:23 will they not say that ye are m'?

Madai (*ma'-dahee*) See also MEDE; MEDIA.
Ge 10: 2 Magog, and M', and Javan, and
1Ch 1: 5 Magog, and M', and Javan, and

made See also MADEST.
Ge 1: 7 And God m' the firmament, and
16 God made two great lights; the
16 to rule the night: he m' the stars also.
25 And God m' the beast of the earth
31 God saw every thing that he had m',
2: 2 ended his work which he had m';
2 from all his work which he had m'.
3 work which God created and m'.
4 the Lord God m' the earth and the
9 of the ground m' the Lord God to grow
22 taken from man, m' he a woman,
3: 1 beast...which the Lord God had m'.
7 together, and m' themselves aprons.
5: 1 in the likeness of God m' he him;
6: 6 the Lord that he had m' man on
7 repenteth me that I have m' them.
7: 4 living substance that I have m' will
8: 1 God m' a wind to pass over the earth,
6 window of the ark which he...m':
9: 6 for in the image of God m' he man.
13: 4 which he had m' there at the first:
14: 2 m' war with Bera king of Sodom,
23 shouldest say, I have m' Abram rich:
15:18 Lord m' a covenant with Abram,
17: 5 of many nations have I m' thee.
19: 3 he m' them a feast, and did bake
33, 35 they m' their father drink wine
21: 6 God hath m' me to laugh, so that all
8 and Abraham m' a great feast the
27 and both of them m' a covenant.
32 they m' a covenant at Beer-sheba:
23:17 borders round about, were m' sure
20 cave that is therein, were m' sure
24:11 And he m' his camels to kneel down
21 had m' his journey prosperous
37 And my master m' me swear, saying,
46 And she m' haste, and let down
46 and she m' the camels drink also.
26:22 now the Lord hath m' room for us,
30 And he m' them a feast, and they
27:14 and his mother m' savoury meat,
30 had m' an end of blessing Jacob,
31 And he also had m' savoury meat,
37 I have m' him thy lord, and all his
29:22 men of the place, and m' a feast.
30:37 m' the white appear which was in the
31:46 they took stones, and m' an heap:
33:17 house, and m' booths for his cattle:
37: 3 he m' him a coat of many colours.
7 and m' obeisance to my sheaf.
9 and the eleven stars m' obeisance
39: 3 the Lord m' all that he did to prosper
4 he m' him overseer over his house,
5 had m' him overseer in his house,
23 he did, the Lord m' it to prosper.
40:20 m' a feast unto all his servants:
41:43 he m' him to ride in the second chariot
43 he m' him ruler over all the land
51 said he, hath m' me forget all my toil,
42: 7 but m' himself strange unto them,
43:25 they m' ready the present against
28 their heads, and m' obeisance.
30 Joseph m' haste; for his bowels
45: 1 Joseph m' himself known unto his
8 hath m' me a father to Pharaoh,
9 God hath m' me lord of all Egypt:
46:29 And Joseph m' ready his chariot,
47:26 Joseph m' it a law over the land
49:24 arms of his hands were m' strong
33 had m' an end of commanding his
50: 5 My father m' me swear, saying, Lo, I
6 according as he m' thee swear.
10 he m' a mourning for his father
Ex 1:13 m' the children of Israel to serve
14 and they m' their lives bitter with
14 service, wherein they m' them serve,
21 God, that he m' them houses.
2:14 Who m' thee a prince and a judge
4:11 him, Who hath m' man's mouth?
5:21 ye have m' our savour to be abhorred
7: 1 I have m' thee a god to Pharaoh:
9:20 m' his servants and his cattle flee into
14: 6 he m' ready his chariot, and took
21 and m' the sea dry land, and the
15:17 thou hast m' for thee to dwell in;
25 waters, the waters were m' sweet:
25 he m' for them a statute and an
16:31 of it was like wafers m' with honey.
18:25 m' them heads over the people,
20:11 the Lord m' heaven and earth,
24: 8 which the Lord hath m' with you
25:31 work shall the candlestick be m':
33 Three bowls m' like unto almonds,
33 and three bowls m' like almonds in
34 be four bowls m' like unto almonds,

Ex 26: 31 with cherubims shall it be *m'*:
29: 18, 25 offering *m'* by fire unto the Lord.
33 wherewith the atonement was *m'*,
36 thou hast *m'* an atonement for it,
41 an offering *m'* by fire unto the Lord.
30: 20 offering *m'* by fire unto the Lord:
31: 17 the Lord *m'* heaven and earth,
18 had *m'* an end of communing with
32: 4 after he had *m'* it a molten calf:
5 Aaron *m'* proclamation, and said,
8 they have *m'* them a molten calf,
20 he took the calf which they had *m'*,
20 *m'* the children of Israel drink of it.
25 Aaron had *m'* them naked unto
31 and have *m'* them gods of gold.
35 they *m'* the calf, which Aaron *m'*.
34: 8 And Moses *m'* haste, and bowed his
27 I have *m'* a covenant with thee and
35: 21 every one whom his spirit *m'* willing,
29 whose heart *m'* them willing to bring
29 to be *m'* by the hand of Moses.
36: 4 man from his work which they *m'*;
8 *m'* ten curtains of fine twined linen,
8 of cunning work *m'* he them.
11 And he *m'* loops of blue on the edge
11 he *m'* in the uttermost side of
12 Fifty loops *m'* he in one curtain,
12 fifty loops *m'* he in the edge of the
13 And he *m'* fifty taches of gold, and
14 And he *m'* curtains of goats' hair
14 eleven curtains he *m'* them.
17 he *m'* fifty loops upon the uttermost
17 and fifty loops *m'* he upon the edge
18 he *m'* fifty taches of brass to couple
19 And he *m'* a covering for the tent of
20 he *m'* boards for the tabernacle of
23 he *m'* boards for the tabernacle;
24 forty sockets of silver he *m'* under
25 north corner, he *m'* twenty boards,
27 westward he *m'* six boards.
28 two boards *m'* he for the corners of
31 And he *m'* bars of shittim wood;
33 *m'* the middle bar to shoot through
34 *m'* their rings of gold to be places
35 he *m'* a vail of blue, and purple,
35 cherubims *m'* he it of cunning work.
36 *m'* thereunto four pillars of shittim
37 *m'* an hanging for the tabernacle
37: 1 Bezaleel *m'* the ark of shittim
2 and *m'* a crown of gold to it round
4 And he *m'* staves of shittim wood,
6 he *m'* the mercy seat of pure gold:
7 And he *m'* two cherubims of gold,
7 beaten out of one piece *m'* he them,
8 mercy seat *m'* he the cherubims
10 And he *m'* the table of shittim wood:
11 and *m'* thereunto a crown of gold
12 Also he *m'* thereunto a border of an
12 *m'* a crown of gold for the border
15 he *m'* the staves of shittim wood,
16 *m'* the vessels which were upon the
17 he *m'* the candlestick of pure gold:
17 beaten work *m'* he the candlestick;
19 *m'* after the fashion of almonds in
19 and three bowls *m'* like almonds in
20 were four bowls *m'* like almonds,
23 he *m'* his seven lamps, and his
24 Of a talent of pure gold *m'* he it,
25 he *m'* the incense altar of shittim
26 he *m'* unto it a crown of gold round
27 he *m'* two rings of gold for it under
28 *m'* the staves of shittim wood, and
29 he *m'* the holy anointing oil, and
38: 1 he *m'* the altar of burnt offering of
2 he *m'* the horns thereof on the four
3 *m'* all the vessels of the altar, the
3 the vessels thereof *m'* he of brass.
4 he *m'* for the altar a brasen grate of
6 *m'* the staves of shittim wood, and
7 he *m'* the altar hollow with boards.
8 And he *m'* the laver of brass, and
9 And he *m'* the court: on the south
22 *m'* all that the Lord commanded
28 shekels he *m'* hooks for the pillars,
30 he *m'* the sockets to the door of the
39: 1 *m'* cloths of service, to do service
1 *m'* the holy garments for Aaron;
2 he *m'* the ephod of gold, blue, and
4 They *m'* shoulderpieces for it, to
8 *m'* the breastplate of cunning work,
9 they *m'* the breastplate double: a
15 *m'* upon the breastplate chains at
16 they *m'* two ouches of gold, and
19 And they *m'* two rings of gold, and
20 And they *m'* two other golden rings,
22 *m'* the robe of the ephod of woven
24 they *m'* upon the hems of the robe
25 And they *m'* bells of pure gold, and
27 *m'* coats of fine linen of woven work
30 *m'* the plate of the holy crown of
42 children of Israel *m'* all the work.
Le 1: 9, 13, 17 an offering *m'* by fire, of a sweet
2: 2 to be an offering *m'* by fire, of a sweet
3 of the offerings of the Lord *m'* by fire.
7 it shall be *m'* of fine flour with oil.
8 offering that is *m'* of these things
9 it is an offering *m'* by fire, of a sweet
10 of the offerings of the Lord *m'* by fire.
11 the Lord, shall be *m'* with leaven:
11 in any offering of the Lord *m'* by fire.
16 is an offering *m'* by fire unto the Lord.
3: 3 an offering *m'* by fire unto the Lord;
5 it is an offering *m'* by fire, of a sweet
9 an offering *m'* by fire unto the Lord;
11 it is the food of the offering *m'* by fire
14 an offering *m'* by fire unto the Lord;
Le 3: 16 it is the food of the offering *m'* by fire
4: 35 the offerings *m'* by fire unto the Lord:
5: 12 the offerings *m'* by fire unto the Lord:
6: 17 portion of my offerings *m'* by fire;
18 the offerings of the Lord *m'* by fire:
21 In a pan it shall be *m'* with oil;
7: 5 an offering *m'* by fire unto the Lord:
25 an offering *m'* by fire unto the Lord,
30, 35 offerings of the Lord *m'* by fire,
8: 21 an offering *m'* by fire unto the Lord;
28 is an offering *m'* by fire unto the Lord.
10: 12 of the offerings of the Lord *m'* by fire,
13 of the sacrifices of the Lord *m'* by fire:
15 with the offerings *m'* by fire of the fat,
13: 48 a skin, or in any thing *m'* of skin;
51 or in any work that is *m'* of skin;
14: 11 the man that is to be *m'* clean,
36 in the house be not *m'* unclean:
16: 17 have *m'* an atonement for himself,
20 he hath *m'* an end of reconciling
21: 6 the offerings of the Lord *m'* by fire,
21 the offerings of the Lord *m'* by fire:
22: 5 whereby he may be *m'* unclean,
27 an offering *m'* by fire unto the Lord.
23: 8, 13 offering *m'* by fire unto the Lord
18 even an offering *m'* by fire, of sweet
25, 27 offering *m'* by fire unto the Lord.
36, 36 offering *m'* by fire unto the Lord:
37 an offering *m'* by fire unto the Lord,
43 I *m'* the children of Israel to dwell
24: 7 an offering *m'* by fire unto the Lord.
9 Lord *m'* by fire by a perpetual statute.
26: 13 of your yoke, and *m'* you go upright.
46 which the Lord *m'* between him
Nu 4: 15 have *m'* an end of covering the
26 service, and all that is *m'* for them:
5: 8 an atonement shall be *m'* for him.
27 he hath *m'* her to drink the water,
6: 4 nothing that is *m'* of the vine tree,
8: 4 Moses, so he *m'* the candlestick.
21 Aaron *m'* an atonement for them
11: 8 baked it in pans, and *m'* cakes of
14: 36 *m'* all the congregation to murmur
15: 10, 13, 14 an offering *m'* by fire, of a
25 a sacrifice *m'* by fire unto the Lord,
16: 31 as he had *m'* an end of speaking
39 they were *m'* broad plates for a
47 *m'* an atonement for the people.
18: 17 an offering *m'* by fire, for a sweet
20: 5 ye *m'* us to come up out of Egypt,
21: 9 Moses *m'* a serpent of brass, and
25: 13 *m'* an atonement for the children
28: 2 my bread for my sacrifices *m'* by fire,
3 This is the offering *m'* by fire which
6 a sacrifice *m'* by fire unto the Lord.
8 a sacrifice *m'* by fire, of a sweet savour
13 a sacrifice *m'* by fire unto the Lord.
19 ye shall offer a sacrifice *m'* by fire for
24 meat of the sacrifice *m'* by fire, of a
29: 6 a sacrifice *m'* by fire unto the Lord.
13, 36 offering, a sacrifice *m'* by fire,
30: 12 hath utterly *m'* them void on the day
12 her husband hath *m'* them void; and
31: 20 and all that is *m'* of skins, and all
20 goats' hair, and all things *m'* of wood.
32: 13 *m'* them wander in the wilderness
De 1: 15 and *m'* them heads over you,
2: 30 and *m'* his heart obstinate, that he
4: 23 covenant...which he *m'* with you,
36 heaven he *m'* thee to hear his voice,
5: 2 our God *m'* a covenant with us in
3 The Lord *m'* not this covenant with
9: 9 covenant which the Lord *m'* with
12 have *m'* them a molten image.
16 had *m'* you a molten calf: ye had
21 the calf which ye had *m'*, and burnt
10: 3 I *m'* an ark of shittim wood, and
5 tables in the ark which I had *m'*;
22 thy God hath *m'* thee as the stars
11: 4 *m'* the water of the Red sea to overflow
18: 1 of the offerings of the Lord *m'* by fire,
20: 9 officers have *m'* an end of speaking
26: 12 *m'* an end of tithing all the tithes
19 all nations which he hath *m'*,
29: 1 covenant which he *m'* with them
25 he *m'* with them when he brought
31: 16 my covenant which I have *m'* with
24 Moses had *m'* an end of writing
32: 6 not *m'* thee, and established thee
13 *m'* him ride on the high places of the
13 *m'* him to suck honey out of the rock,
15 he forsook God which *m'* him,
45 Moses *m'* an end of speaking all
Jos 2: 17 oath which thou hast *m'* us swear.
20 oath which thou hast *m'* us to swear.
5: 3 And Joshua *m'* him sharp knives,
8: 15 all Israel *m'* as if they were beaten
24 Israel had *m'* an end of slaying
28 Ai, and *m'* it an heap for ever,
9: 4 *m'* as if they had been ambassadors,
15 And Joshua *m'* peace with them,
15 and *m'* a league with them, to let
16 they had *m'* a league with them,
27 Joshua *m'* them that day hewers
10: 1 Gibeon had *m'* peace with Israel,
4 it hath *m'* peace with Joshua and
5 before Gibeon; and *m'* war against it.
20 Israel had *m'* an end of slaying
11: 18 Joshua *m'* war a long time with
19 not a city that *m'* peace with the
13: 14 sacrifices...of Israel *m'* by fire
14: 8 me *m'* the heart of the people melt:
19: 49 had *m'* an end of dividing the land
51 *m'* an end of dividing the country.
22: 25 hath *m'* Jordan a border between
28 of the Lord, which our fathers *m'*,
Jos 24: 25 *m'* a covenant with the people that
J'g 2: 1 *m'* you to go up out of Egypt, and have
3: 16 *m'* him a dagger which had two
18 had *m'* an end to offer the present,
5: 13 he *m'* him that remaineth have
13 Lord *m'* me have dominion over the
6: 2 of Israel *m'* them the dens which
19 went in, and *m'* ready a kid, and
8: 27 Gideon *m'* an ephod thereof, and
33 and *m'* Baal-berith their god.
9: 6 and went, and *m'* Abimelech king,
16 in that ye have *m'* Abimelech king,
18 and have *m'* Abimelech, the son...king
27 and *m'* merry, and went into the
11: 4 of Ammon *m'* war against Israel.
5 of Ammon *m'* war against Israel,
11 people *m'* him head and captain
13: 10 the woman *m'* haste, and ran, and
15 shall have *m'* ready a kid for thee.
14: 10 and Samson *m'* there a feast; for
15: 17 he had *m'* an end of speaking,
16: 19 And she *m'* him sleep upon her knees;
25 prison house; and he *m'* them sport:
27 that beheld while Samson *m'* sport.
17: 4 who *m'* thereof a graven image
5 and *m'* an ephod, and teraphim,
18: 24 taken away my gods which I *m'*,
27 took the things which Micah had *m'*,
31 Micah's graven image, which he *m'*,
21: 5 had *m'* a great oath concerning him
15 Lord had *m'* a breach in the tribes
1Sa 2: 19 his mother *m'* him a little coat,
28 father all the offerings *m'* by fire
3: 13 his sons *m'* themselves vile, and
4: 18 when he *m'* mention of the ark of God,
8: 1 he *m'* his sons judges over Israel.
9: 22 *m'* them sit in the chiefest place
10: 13 he had *m'* an end of prophesying,
11: 15 they *m'* Saul king before the Lord
12: 1 me, and have *m'* a king over you.
8 Egypt, and *m'* them dwell in this place.
13: 10 as he had *m'* an end of offering
12 I have not *m'* supplication unto
14: 14 and his armourbearer *m'*, was
15: 17 wast thou not *m'* the head of the
33 sword hath *m'* woman childless,
35 he had *m'* Saul king over Israel.
16: 8 and *m'* him pass before Samuel.
9 Then Jesse *m'* Shammah to pass by.
10 Jesse *m'* seven of his sons to pass
18: 1 he had *m'* an end of speaking unto
3 and David *m'* a covenant, because
13 and *m'* him his captain over a
20: 16 So Jonathan *m'* a covenant with
22: 8 *m'* a league with the son of Jesse,
23: 18 two *m'* a covenant before the Lord:
26 David *m'* haste to get away for
24: 16 David had *m'* an end of speaking
25: 18 Abigail *m'* haste, and took two
27: 10 said, Whither have ye *m'* a road to day?
12 *m'* his people Israel utterly to abhor
30: 11 eat; and they *m'* him drink water;
14 We *m'* an invasion upon the south
21 whom they had *m'* also to abide at the
25 he *m'* it a statute and an ordinance
2Sa 2: 9 *m'* him king over Gilead, and over
3: 6 Abner *m'* himself strong for the
20 David *m'* Abner and the men that
4: 4 she *m'* haste to flee, that he fell,
5: 3 king David *m'* a league with them
6: 5 manner of instruments *m'* of fir wood,
8 Lord had *m'* a breach upon Uzzah:
18 David had *m'* an end of offering
7: 9 have *m'* thee a great name, like
10: 19 they *m'* peace with Israel, and
11: 13 before him; and he *m'* him drunk:
19 thou hast *m'* an end of telling
12: 31 *m'* them pass through the brickkiln:
13: 6 lay down, and *m'* himself sick:
8 and *m'* cakes in his sight, and did
10 took the cakes which she had *m'*,
36 as he had *m'* an end of speaking,
14: 15 the people have *m'* me afraid:
15: 4 that I were *m'* judge in the land,
17: 25 Absalom *m'* Amasa captain of the
22: 5 of ungodly men *m'* me afraid;
12 he *m'* darkness pavilions round
36 thy gentleness hath *m'* me great.
23: 5 he hath *m'* with me an everlasting
1Ki 1: 41 as they had *m'* an end of eating.
43 king David hath *m'* Solomon king.
2: 24 who hath *m'* me an house, as he
3: 1 Solomon *m'* affinity with Pharaoh king
1 had *m'* an end of building his own
7 hast *m'* thy servant king instead of
15 and *m'* a feast to all his servants.
4: 7 his month in a year *m'* provision.
5: 12 and they two *m'* a league together.
6: 4 he *m'* windows of narrow lights.
5 and he *m'* chambers round about:
6 house he *m'* narrowed rests round
7 of stone *m'* ready before it was
21 *m'* a partition by the chains of gold
23 the oracle he *m'* two cherubims
31 the oracle he *m'* doors of olive tree:
33 *m'* he for the door of the temple
7: 6 And he *m'* a porch of pillars; the
7 *m'* a porch for the throne where he
8 *m'* also an house for Pharaoh's
16 *m'* two chapiters of molten brass,
18 And he *m'* the pillars, and two rows
23 he *m'* a molten sea, ten cubits from
27 *m'* ten bases of brass; four cubits
29 certain additions *m'* of thin work.
37 this manner he *m'* the ten bases:
38 *m'* he ten lavers of brass: one laver

1Ki 7:40 And Hiram *m'* the lavers, and the
40 *m'* an end of doing all the work
40 *m'* king Solomon for the house
45 Hiram *m'* to king Solomon for the
48 And Solomon *m'* all the vessels that
51 work that king Solomon *m'* for the
8: 9 the Lord *m'* a covenant with the
21 Lord, which he *m'* with our fathers,
38 supplication soever be *m'* by any man,
54 Solomon had *m'* an end of praying
59 have *m'* supplication before the Lord,
9: 3 supplication, that thou hast *m'* before
26 king Solomon *m'* a navy of ships
10: 9 therefore *m'* he thee king, to do
12 king *m'* of the almug trees pillars
16 *m'* two hundred targets of beaten
17 he *m'* three hundred shields of beaten
18 king *m'* a great throne of ivory,
20 was not the like *m'* in any kingdom.
27 king *m'* silver to be in Jerusalem
27 cedars *m'* he to be as the sycomore
11: 28 *m'* him ruler over all the charge of
12: 4 Thy father *m'* our yoke grievous: now
10 Thy father *m'* our yoke heavy, but
14 My father *m'* your yoke heavy, and I
18 *m'* speed to get him up to his chariot,
20 and *m'* him king over all Israel:
28 counsel, and *m'* two calves of gold,
31 And he *m'* an house of high places,
31 *m'* priests of the lowest of...people,
32 unto the calves that he had *m'*:
32 of the high places which he had *m'*.
33 upon the altar which he had *m'* in
13: 33 *m'* again of the lowest of the people
14: 7 and *m'* thee prince over my people
15 because they have *m'* their groves,
16 who did sin, and who *m'* Israel to sin.
26 shields...which Solomon had *m'*.
27 *m'* in their stead brasen shields,
15: 12 all the idols that his fathers had *m'*.
13 she had *m'* an idol in a grove;
22 Then king Asa *m'* a proclamation
26 his sin wherewith he *m'* Israel to sin.
30 sinned, and which he *m'* Israel to sin,
34 his sin wherewith he *m'* Israel to sin.
16: 2 and *m'* thee prince over my people
2 hast *m'* my people Israel to sin, to
13 and by which they *m'* Israel to sin,
16 all Israel *m'* Omri...king
26 his sin wherewith he *m'* Israel to sin,
33 Ahab *m'* a grove; and Ahab did
18: 26 upon the altar which was *m'*.
32 he *m'* a trench about the altar, as
20: 34 as my father *m'* in Samaria. Then
34 So he *m'* a covenant with him, and
21: 22 me to anger, and *m'* Israel to sin.
22: 11 son of Chenaanah *m'* him horns of
39 the ivory house which he *m'*, and
44 Jehoshaphat *m'* peace with the
48 *m'* ships of Tarshish to go to
52 the son of Nebat, who *m'* Israel to sin:
2Ki 3: 2 of Baal that his father had *m'*.
3 son of Nebat, which *m'* Israel to sin;
7: 6 had *m'* the host of the Syrians to hear
8: 20 and *m'* a king over themselves.
9: 21 And his chariot was *m'* ready.
10: 16 So they *m'* him ride in his chariot.
25 as he had *m'* an end of offering the
27 *m'* it a draught house unto this
29 the son of Nebat, who *m'* Israel to sin,
31 of Jeroboam, which *m'* Israel to sin.
11: 4 and *m'* a covenant with them, and
12 they *m'* him king, and anointed
17 Jehoiada *m'* a covenant between
12: 13 not *m'* for the house of the Lord
20 servants arose, and *m'* a conspiracy,
13: 2 son of Nebat, which *m'* Israel to sin;
6 house of Jeroboam, who *m'* Israel sin,
7 and had *m'* them like the dust by
11 the son of Nebat, who *m'* Israel sin:
14: 19 they *m'* a conspiracy against him
21 *m'* him king instead of his father
24 the son of Nebat, who *m'* Israel to sin.
15: 9 the son of Nebat, who *m'* Israel to sin.
15 and his conspiracy which he *m'*,
18, 24, 28 Nebat, who *m'* Israel to sin.
30 the son of Elah *m'* a conspiracy
16: 3 *m'* his son to pass through the fire,
11 the priest *m'* it against king Ahaz
17: 8 kings of Israel, which they had *m'*.
15 his covenant that he *m'* with their
16 *m'* them molten images, even two
16 and *m'* a grove, and worshipped all
19 statutes of Israel which they *m'*.
21 and they *m'* Jeroboam...king:
21 the Lord, and *m'* them sin a great sin.
29 every nation *m'* gods of their own,
29 which the Samaritans had *m'*,
30 men of Babylon *m'* Succoth-benoth,
30 and the men of Cuth *m'* Nergal,
30 and the men of Hamath *m'* Ashima,
31 the Avites *m'* Nibhaz and Tartak,
32 *m'* unto themselves of the lowest of
35 whom the Lord had *m'* a covenant,
38 covenant that I have *m'* with you
18: 4 brasen serpent that Moses had *m'*:
19: 15 thou hast *m'* heaven and earth.
20: 20 how he *m'* a pool, and a conduit,
21: 3 up altars for Baal, and *m'* a grove,
6 he *m'* his son pass through the fire,
7 grove that he had *m'* in the house,
11 *m'* Judah also to sin with his idols:
16 his sin wherewith he *m'* Judah to sin,
24 of the land *m'* Josiah his son king
22: 7 no reckoning *m'* with them of the
23: 3 and *m'* a covenant before the Lord,

2Ki 23: 4 all the vessels that were *m'* for Baal,
12 which the kings of Judah had *m'*,
12 altars which Manasseh had *m'* in
15 the son of Nebat, who *m'* Israel to sin,
15 which Jeroboam the son...had *m'*,
19 Israel had *m'* to provoke the Lord
30 *m'* him king in his father's stead.
34 *m'* Eliakim the son of Josiah king
24: 13 had *m'* in the temple of the Lord,
17 *m'* Mattaniah his father's brother king
25: 16 Solomon had *m'* for the house of
22 over them he *m'* Gedaliah...ruler.
23 Babylon had *m'* Gedaliah governor,
1Ch 5: 10, 19 they *m'* war with the Hagarites.
9: 30 of the priests *m'* the ointment of
31 things that were *m'* in the pans.
11: 3 David *m'* a covenant with them in
12: 18 and *m'* them captains of the band.
13: 11 Lord had *m'* a breach upon Uzza:
15: 1 David *m'* him houses in the city of
13 Lord our God *m'* a breach upon us,
16: 2 David had *m'* an end of offering
5 Asaph *m'* a sound with cymbals;
16 which he *m'* with Abraham, and
26 but the Lord *m'* the heavens.
17: 8 *m'* thee a name like the name of
18: 8 Solomon *m'* the brasen sea, and
19: 6 had *m'* themselves odious to David,
19 they *m'* peace with David, and
21: 29 which Moses *m'* in the wilderness,
22: 8 abundantly, and hast *m'* great wars:
23: 1 he *m'* Solomon his son king over
5 with the instruments which I *m'*.
26: 10 yet his father *m'* him the chief;)
32 whom king David *m'* rulers over the
28: 19 the Lord *m'* me understand in writing
29: 2 the gold for things to be *m'* of gold,
5 manner of work to be *m'* by the hands
19 for the which I have *m'* provision.
22 they *m'* Solomon the son of David king
2Ch 1: 3 the servant of the Lord had *m'* in
5 brasen altar, that Bezaleel...had *m'*,
8 hast *m'* me to reign in his stead.
9 thou hast *m'* me king over a people
11 over whom I have *m'* thee king:
15 And the king *m'* silver and gold at
15 cedar trees *m'* he as the sycomore
2: 11 he hath *m'* thee king over them.
12 Israel, that *m'* heaven and earth,
3: 8 And he *m'* the most holy house, the
10 he *m'* two cherubims of image work,
14 he *m'* the vail of blue, and purple,
15 he *m'* before the house two pillars
16 And he *m'* chains, as in the oracle,
16 and *m'* an hundred pomegranates,
4: 1 Moreover he *m'* an altar of brass,
2 he *m'* a molten sea of ten cubits
6 He *m'* also ten lavers, and put five
7 And he *m'* ten candlesticks of gold
8 He *m'* also ten tables, and placed
8 he *m'* an hundred basons of gold.
9 he *m'* the court of the priests, and
11 Huram *m'* the pots, and the shovels,
14 He *m'* also bases, and lavers *m'* he
18 Thus Solomon *m'* all these vessels
19 And Solomon *m'* all the vessels that
21 lamps, and the tongs, *m'* he of gold,
5: 1 all the work that Solomon *m'* for
10 when the Lord *m'* a covenant with
6: 11 that he *m'* with the children of
13 Solomon had *m'* a brasen scaffold,
29 supplication soever shall be *m'* of any
40 the prayer that is *m'* in this place.
7: 1 Solomon had *m'* an end of praying,
6 the king had *m'* to praise the Lord,
7 brasen altar which Solomon had *m'*
9 day they *m'* a solemn assembly:
15 the prayer that is *m'* in this place.
9: 8 therefore *m'* he thee king over
11 king *m'* of the algum trees terraces
15 Solomon *m'* two hundred targets
16 hundred shields *m'* he of beaten gold:
17 king *m'* a great throne of ivory,
19 not the like *m'* in any kingdom.
27 the king *m'* silver in Jerusalem as
27 cedar trees *m'* he as the sycomore
10: 4 Thy father *m'* our yoke grievous:
10 Thy father *m'* our yoke heavy, but
14 My father *m'* your yoke heavy, but
18 Rehoboam *m'* speed to get him up to
11: 12 and *m'* them exceeding strong,
15 for the calves which he had *m'*.
17 *m'* Rehoboam...son of Solomon strong
22 *m'* Abijah the son...to be ruler among
12: 9 of gold which Solomon had *m'*.
10 king Rehoboam *m'* shields of brass,
13: 8 which Jeroboam *m'* you for gods.
9 *m'* you priests after the manner of
15: 16 she had *m'* an idol in a grove: and
16: 14 *m'* for himself in the city of David,
14 *m'* a very great burning for him.
17: 10 they *m'* no war against Jehoshaphat.
18: 10 Chenaanah had *m'* him horns of
20: 23 had *m'* an end of the inhabitants
27 *m'* them to rejoice over their enemies.
36 they *m'* the ships in Ezion-gaber.
21: 7 covenant...he had *m'* with David,
8 Judah, and *m'* themselves a king.
11 *m'* high places in the mountains of
13 hast *m'* Judah and the inhabitants of
19 his people *m'* no burning for him,
22: 1 *m'* Ahaziah his youngest son king
23: 3 congregation *m'* a covenant with
11 the testimony, and *m'* him king.
16 Jehoiada *m'* a covenant between
24: 8 commandment they *m'* a chest,

2Ch 24: 9 *m'* a proclamation through Judah
10 the chest, until they had *m'* an end.
14 were *m'* vessels for the house of
17 and *m'* obeisance to the king.
25: 5 *m'* them captains over thousands,
16 Art thou *m'* of the king's counsel?
27 they *m'* a conspiracy against him
26: 1 and *m'* him king in the room of his
5 the Lord, God *m'* him to prosper.
13 that *m'* war with mighty power, to
15 And he *m'* in Jerusalem engines,
28: 2 *m'* also molten images for Baalim.
19 for he *m'* Judah naked, and
24 he *m'* him altars in every corner
25 he *m'* high places to burn incense
29: 17 of the first month they *m'* an end.
24 they *m'* reconciliation with their
24 offering should be *m'* for all Israel.
29 they had *m'* an end of offering,
32: 5 *m'* darts and shields in abundance.
27 he *m'* himself treasuries for silver,
33: 3 up altars for Baalim, and *m'* groves,
7 the idol which he had *m'*, in the
9 Manasseh *m'* Judah and the...to err,
22 which Manasseh his father had *m'*,
25 the land *m'* Josiah his son king
34: 4 brake in pieces, and *m'* dust of them,
31 and *m'* a covenant before the Lord,
33 *m'* all that were...in Israel to serve,
35: 14 they *m'* ready for themselves, and
25 *m'* them an ordinance in Israel:
36: 1 *m'* him king in his father's stead
4 Egypt *m'* Eliakim his brother king
10 *m'* Zedekiah his brother king over
13 who had *m'* him swear by God:
22 *m'* a proclamation throughout all his
Ezr 1: 1 *m'* a proclamation throughout all his
4: 15 search may be *m'* in the book of
19 and search hath been *m'*, and it is
19 hath *m'* insurrection against kings,
19 and sedition have been *m'* therein.
23 and *m'* them to cease by force and
5: 13 Cyrus *m'* a decree to build this
14 whom he had *m'* governor;
17 be search *m'* in the king's treasure
17 decree was *m'* of Cyrus the king to
6: 1 Darius the king *m'* a decree, and
1 search was *m'* in the house of the
3 same Cyrus the king *m'* a decree
11 have *m'* a decree, that whosoever
11 let his house be *m'* a dunghill for
12 I Darius have *m'* a decree; let it
22 for the Lord had *m'* them joyful,
10: 5 *m'* the chief priests, the Levites...swear
7 *m'* proclamation throughout Judah
17 *m'* an end with all the men that
Ne 3: 16 to the pool that was *m'*, and unto
4: 7 walls of Jerusalem were *m'* up,
9 Nevertheless we *m'* our prayer
6: 9 For they all *m'* us afraid, saying,
8: 4 pulpit of wood, which they had *m'*
16 them, and *m'* themselves booths,
17 *m'* booths, and sat under the booths:
9: 6 thou hast *m'* heaven, the heaven of
18 they had *m'* them a molten calf,
10: 32 Also we *m'* ordinances for us, to
12: 43 God had *m'* them rejoice with great joy:
13: 13 I *m'* treasurers over the treasuries,
25 their hair, and *m'* them swear by God,
26 God *m'* him king over all Israel:
Es 1: 3 he *m'* a feast unto all his princes
5 king *m'* a feast unto all the people
9 Vashti the queen *m'* a feast for the
2: 17 *m'* her queen instead of Vashti.
18 Then the king *m'* a great feast
18 he *m'* a release to the provinces,
23 inquisition was *m'* of the matter,
5: 14 Let a gallows be *m'* of fifty cubits
14 and he caused the gallows to be *m'*.
7: 9 which Haman had *m'* for Mordecai,
9: 17, 18 and *m'* it a day of feasting and
19 *m'* the fourteenth day of the month
Job 1: 10 not thou *m'* an hedge about him,
17 The Chaldeans *m'* out three bands,
2: 11 had *m'* an appointment together
4: 14 which *m'* all my bones to shake.
7: 3 am I *m'* to possess months of vanity,
10: 8 Thine hands have *m'* me and
9 that thou hast *m'* me as the clay;
15: 7 or wast thou *m'* before the hills?
16: 7 But now he hath *m'* me weary:
7 hast *m'* desolate all my company.
17: 6 *m'* me also a byword of the people:
13 have *m'* my bed in the darkness.
28: 18 No mention shall be *m'* of coral, or of
26 When he *m'* a decree for the rain,
31: 1 I *m'* a covenant with mine eyes;
15 *m'* me in the womb make him?
24 If I have *m'* gold my hope, or have
33: 4 The Spirit of God hath *m'* me, and
38: 9 *m'* the cloud the garment thereof,
39: 6 house I have *m'* the wilderness,
40: 15 behemoth, which I *m'* with thee;
19 *m'* him can make his sword to
41: 33 not his like, who is *m'* without fear.
Ps 7: 12 hath bent his bow, and *m'* it ready.
15 He *m'* a pit, and digged it, and
15 fallen into the ditch which he *m'*.
8: 5 thou hast *m'* him a little lower
9: 15 sunk down in the pit that they *m'*:
18: 4 of ungodly men *m'* me afraid.
11 He *m'* darkness his secret place;
35 thy gentleness hath *m'* me great.
43 *m'* me the head of the heathen:
21: 6 *m'* him most blessed for ever:
6 thou hast *m'* him exceeding glad

Ps 30: 1 hast not *m'* my foes to rejoice over me.
7 *m'* my mountain to stand strong:
8 unto the Lord I *m'* supplication and
33: 6 of the Lord were the heavens *m'*;
39: 5 *m'* my days as an handbreadth;
45: 1 things which I have *m'* touching
8 whereby they have *m'* thee glad.
46: 8 he hath *m'* in the earth.
49: 16 thou afraid when one is *m'* rich,
50: 5 that have *m'* a covenant with me
52: 7 man that *m'* not God his strength;
60: 2 Thou hast *m'* the earth to tremble;
3 hast *m'* us to drink the wine of
69: 11 I *m'* sackcloth also my garment;
72: 15 prayer also shall be *m'* for him
74: 17 thou hast *m'* summer and winter.
77: 6 and my spirit *m'* diligent search.
78: 13 *m'* the waters to stand as an heap.
50 He *m'* a way to his anger; he
52 *m'* his own people to go forth like
55 *m'* the tribes of Israel to dwell in their
64 their widows *m'* no lamentation.
86: 9 nations whom thou hast *m'* shall
88: 8 hast *m'* me an abomination unto
89: 3 *m'* a covenant with my chosen,
39 Thou hast *m'* void the covenant of thy
42 thou hast *m'* all his enemies to rejoice.
43 hast not *m'* him to stand in the battle.
44 Thou hast *m'* his glory to cease, and
47 hast thou *m'* all men in vain?
91: 9 *m'* the Lord, which is my refuge,
92: 4 *m'* me glad through thy work:
95: 5 The sea is his, and he *m'* it: and
96: 5 idols: but the Lord *m'* the heavens.
98: 2 Lord hath *m'* known his salvation:
100: 3 he is God: it is he that hath *m'* us,
103: 7 He *m'* known his ways unto Moses,
104: 24 in wisdom hast thou *m'* them all:
26 thou hast *m'* to play therein.
105: 9 covenant he *m'* with Abraham,
21 He *m'* him lord of his house, and
24 and *m'* them stronger than their
28 He sent darkness, and *m'* it dark;
106: 19 They *m'* a calf in Horeb, and
46 He *m'* them also to be pitied of all
111: 4 He hath *m'* his wonderful works
115: 15 Lord which *m'* heaven and earth.
118: 24 the day which the Lord hath *m'*;
119: 60 I *m'* haste, and delayed not to
73 Thy hands have *m'* me and
98 hast *m'* me wiser than mine enemies:
126 work; for they have *m'* void thy law.
121: 2 Lord, which *m'* heaven and earth.
124: 8 Lord, who *m'* heaven and earth.
129: 3 back: they *m'* long their furrows.
134: 3 Lord that *m'* heaven and earth
136: 5 that by wisdom *m'* the heavens:
7 To him that *m'* great lights: for
14 *m'* Israel to pass through the midst of
139: 14 for I am fearfully and wonderfully *m'*:
15 when I was *m'* in secret, and
143: 3 he hath *m'* me to dwell in darkness,
146: 6 Which *m'* heaven, and earth, the
148: 6 *m'* a decree which shall not pass.
149: 2 Israel rejoice in him that *m'* him:
Pr 8: 26 as yet he had not *m'* the earth, nor
11: 25 The liberal soul shall be *m'* fat:
13: 4 soul of the diligent shall be *m'* fat.
14: 33 is in the midst of fools is *m'* known.
15: 19 way of the righteous is *m'* plain.
16: 4 hath *m'* all things for himself:
20: 9 can say, I have *m'* my heart clean,
12 Lord hath *m'* even both of them.
21: 11 is punished, the simple is *m'* wise:
22: 19 I have *m'* known to thee this day, even
28: 25 trust in the Lord shall be *m'* fat.
Ec 1: 15 is crooked cannot be *m'* straight:
2: 4 I *m'* me great works; I builded me
5 I *m'* me gardens and orchards,
6 I *m'* me pools of water, to water
3: 11 He hath *m'* every thing beautiful in
7: 3 countenance the heart is *m'* better.
13 which he hath *m'* crooked?
29 that God hath *m'* man upright;
10: 19 A feast is *m'* for laughter, and wine
Ca 1: 6 *m'* me the keeper of the vineyards;
3: 9 Solomon *m'* himself a chariot of
10 He *m'* the pillars thereof of silver,
6: 12 my soul *m'* me like the chariots of
Isa 2: 8 which their own fingers have *m'*:
17 haughtiness...shall be *m'* low:
20 they *m'* each one for himself to
5: 2 and also *m'* a winepress therein:
14: 3 wherein thou wast *m'* to serve,
16 man that *m'* the earth to tremble,
17 That *m'* the world as a wilderness,
16: 10 *m'* their vintage shouting to cease.
17: 4 the glory of Jacob shall be *m'* thin,
8 that which his fingers have *m'*,
21: 2 sighing thereof have I *m'* to cease.
22: 11 *m'* also a ditch between the two
25: 2 thou hast *m'* of a city an heap;
26: 14 and *m'* all their memory to perish.
27: 11 that *m'* them will not have mercy
28: 15 have *m'* a covenant with death,
15 for we have *m'* lies our refuge,
22 lest your bands be *m'* strong:
25 hath *m'* plain the face thereof,
29: 16 of him that *m'* it, He *m'* me not?
30: 33 he hath *m'* it deep and large:
31: 7 idols of God, own hands have *m'*
34: 6 it is *m'* fat with fatness, and with
7 and their dust *m'* fat with fatness.
37: 16 thou hast *m'* heaven and earth.
40: 4 mountain and hill shall be *m'* low:
4 the crooked shall be *m'* straight, and

Isa 41: 2 him, and *m'* him rule over kings?
43: 7 formed him; yea, I have *m'* him.
24 hast *m'* me to serve with thy sins,
44: 2 Thus saith the Lord that *m'* thee,
45: 12 have *m'* the earth, and created man
18 that formed the earth and *m'* it; he
46: 4 I have *m'*, and I will bear; even I
49: 1 hath he *m'* mention of my name.
2 *m'* my mouth like a sharp sword;
2 hid me, and *m'* me a polished shaft;
17 that *m'* thee waste shall go forth of
51: 10 hath *m'* the depths of the sea a way
12 man which shall be *m'* as grass;
52: 10 Lord hath *m'* bare his holy arm
53: 9 he *m'* his grave with the wicked,
12 many, and *m'* intercession for the
57: 8 and *m'* thee a covenant with them;
16 me, and the souls which I have *m'*.
59: 8 they have *m'* them crooked paths:
63: 17 hast thou *m'* us to err from thy ways,
66: 2 those things hath mine hand *m'*,
8 the earth be *m'* to bring forth in one
Jer 1: 18 I have *m'* thee this day a defenced
2: 7 *m'* mine heritage an abomination.
15 yelled, and they *m'* his land waste:
28 thy gods that thou hast *m'* thee?
5: 3 *m'* their faces harder than a rock;
8: 8 Lo, certainly in vain *m'* he it;
10: 11 gods that have not *m'* the heavens
12 He hath *m'* the earth by his power,
25 have *m'* his habitation desolate.
11: 10 broken my covenant which I *m'*
12: 10 they have *m'* my pleasant portion
11 They have *m'* it desolate, and being
11 the whole land is *m'* desolate,
13: 22 discovered, and thy heels *m'* bare.
27 Jerusalem! wilt thou not be *m'* clean?
14: 22 for thou hast *m'* all these things.
17: 23 but *m'* their neck stiff, that they might
18: 4 the vessel that he *m'* of clay was
4 so he *m'* it again another vessel, as
19: 11 that cannot be *m'* whole again:
20: 8 word of the Lord was *m'* a reproach
25: 17 and *m'* all the nations to drink,
26: 8 Jeremiah had *m'* an end of speaking
27: 5 I have *m'* the earth, the man and
29: 26 The Lord hath *m'* thee priest in
31: 32 according to the covenant that I *m'*
32: 17 hast *m'* the heaven and the earth
20 and hast *m'* thee a name, as at this
34: 8 king Zedekiah had *m'* a covenant
13 I *m'* a covenant with your fathers
15 ye had *m'* a covenant before me in
18 covenant which they had *m'* before
36: 25 Gemariah had *m'* intercession to
37: 1 *m'* king in the land of Judah.
15 for they had *m'* that the prison.
38: 16 the Lord liveth, that *m'* us this soul,
40: 5 king of Babylon hath *m'* governor
7 had *m'* Gedaliah...governor in
41: 2 king of Babylon had *m'* governor
9 which Asa the king had *m'* for fear
18 the king of Babylon *m'* governor
43: 1 Jeremiah had *m'* an end of speaking
46: 10 and *m'* drunk with their blood:
16 He *m'* many to fall, yea, one fell
49: 10 But I have *m'* Esau bare, I have
51: 7 that *m'* all the earth drunken:
15 He hath *m'* the earth by his power,
34 he hath *m'* me an empty vessel, he
63 thou hast *m'* an end of reading this
52: 20 Solomon had *m'* in the house of
La 1: 13 he hath *m'* me desolate and faint
14 he hath *m'* my strength to fall, the
2: 7 *m'* a noise in the house of the Lord,
8 *m'* the rampart and the wall to lament;
3: 4 flesh and my skin hath he *m'* old;
7 out: he hath *m'* my chain heavy.
9 he hath *m'* my paths crooked.
11 in pieces: he hath *m'* me desolate.
15 *m'* me drunken with wormwood.
45 Thou hast *m'* us as the offscouring
Eze 3: 8 I have *m'* thy face strong against
9 than flint have I *m'* thy forehead:
17 *m'* thee a watchman unto the house
6: 6 may be laid waste and *m'* desolate,
7: 20 *m'*...images of their abominations
13: 5 *m'* up the hedge for the house
6 have *m'* others to hope that they
22 *m'* the heart of the righteous sad,
22 sad, whom I have not *m'* sad; and
16: 24 hast *m'* thee an high place in every
25 hast *m'* thy beauty to be abhorred, and
17: 13 and *m'* a covenant with him, and
16 king dwelleth that *m'* him king,
24 and have *m'* the dry tree to flourish:
19: 5 whelps, and *m'* him a young lion.
20: 5 and *m'* myself known unto them in the
9 sight I *m'* myself known unto them,
28 also they *m'* their sweet savour,
21: 15 it is *m'* bright, it is wrapped up for the
21 *m'* his arrows bright, he consulted
24 *m'* your iniquity to be remembered,
22: 4 thine idols which thou hast *m'*;
4 have I *m'* thee a reproach unto the
13 dishonest gain which thou hast *m'*,
25 have *m'* her many widows in the midst
26: 10 into a city wherein is *m'* a breach.
15 slaughter is *m'* in the midst of thee?
27: 5 *m'* all thy ship boards of fir trees
6 Bashan have they *m'* thine oars;
6 have *m'* thy benches of ivory,
11 they have *m'* thy beauty perfect.
24 bound with cords, and *m'* of cedar,
25 replenished, and *m'* very glorious
29: 3 own, and I have *m'* it for myself.

Eze 29: 9 The river is mine, and I have *m'* it.
18 every head was *m'* bald, and every
31: 4 The waters *m'* him great, the deep
6 heaven *m'* their nests in his boughs,
9 *m'* him fair by the multitude of his
16 I *m'* the nations to shake at the
36: 3 they have *m'* you desolate, and
39: 26 land, and none *m'* them afraid.
40: 14 *m'* also posts of threescore cubits,
17 a pavement *m'* for the court round
41: 18 it was *m'* with cherubims and palm
19 was *m'* through all the house round
20 were cherubims and palm trees *m'*,
25 there were *m'* on them, on the doors
25 like as were *m'* upon the walls;
42: 15 he had *m'* an end of measuring
43: 23 thou hast *m'* an end of cleansing it,
46: 23 it was *m'* with boiling places under
Da 2: 5 houses shall be *m'* a dunghill.
15 Arioch *m'* the thing known to Daniel.
17 *m'* the thing known to Hananiah,
23 hast *m'* known unto me now what we
23 hast now *m'* known unto us the king's
38 and hath *m'* thee ruler over them all.
45 God hath *m'* known to the king what
48 the king *m'* Daniel a great man,
48 *m'* him ruler over the whole province
3: 1 the king *m'* an image of gold,
10 Thou, O king, hast *m'* a decree,
15 the image which I have *m'*;
29 houses shall be *m'* a dunghill:
4: 5 saw a dream which *m'* me afraid,
6 Therefore *m'* I a decree to bring
5: 1 the king *m'* a great feast to a
11 father, *m'* master of the magicians,
21 his heart was *m'* like the beasts,
29 and *m'* a proclamation concerning
7: 4 *m'* stand upon the feet as a man,
16 *m'* me know the interpretation of
21 same horn *m'* war with the saints,
9: 1 was *m'* king over the realm of the
4 my God, and *m'* my confession,
13 yet *m'* we not our prayer before
11: 23 after the league *m'* with him he shall
12: 10 shall be purified, and *m'* white,
Ho 5: 9 *m'* known that which shall surely
7: 5 the princes have *m'* him sick with
6 they have *m'* ready their heart like
8: 4 they have *m'* princes, and I knew
4 gold have they *m'* them idols,
6 the workman *m'* it; therefore it is
11 Ephraim hath *m'* many altars to sin,
10: 1 land they have *m'* goodly images.
12: 4 and *m'* supplication unto him:
13: 2 *m'* them molten images of their
Joe 1: 7 he hath *m'* it clean bare, and cast
7 the branches thereof are *m'* white.
18 the flocks of sheep are *m'* desolate.
Am 4: 10 *m'* the stink of your camp to come
5: 26 god, which ye *m'* to yourselves.
7: 2 had *m'* an end of eating the grass
7 stood upon a wall *m'* by a plumbline,
Ob 2 *m'* thee small among the heathen:
Jon 1: 9 hath *m'* the sea and the dry land.
16 unto the Lord, and *m'* vows.
4: 5 city, and there *m'* him a booth,
6 and *m'* it to come up over Jonah,
Na 2: 3 shield of his mighty men is *m'* red,
11 whelp, and none *m'* them afraid?
Hab 2: 17 of beasts, which *m'* them afraid,
3: 9 Thy bow was *m'* quite naked,
Zep 3: 6 I *m'* their streets waste, that none
Zec 7: 12 *m'* their hearts as an adamant
9: 13 *m'* thee as the sword of a mighty
10: 3 *m'* them as his goodly horse in the
11: 10 covenant which I had *m'* with all
Mal 2: 9 have I also *m'* you contemptible
M't 4: 3 that these stones be *m'* bread.
9: 16 garment, and the rent is *m'* worse.
22 thy faith hath *m'* thee whole.
22 the woman was *m'* whole from that
11: 1 had *m'* an end of commanding his
14: 36 touched were *m'* perfectly whole.
15: 6 *m'* the commandment...none effect
28 her daughter was *m'* whole from
18: 25 that he had, and payment to be *m'*.
19: 4 read, that he which *m'* them at the
4 beginning *m'* them male and female.
12 which were *m'* eunuchs of men:
12 have *m'* themselves eunuchs for the
20: 12 thou hast *m'* them equal unto us,
21: 13 but ye have *m'* it a den of thieves.
22: 2 which *m'* a marriage for his son,
5 they *m'* light of it, and went their
23: 15 when he is *m'*, ye make him
24: 45 his lord hath *m'* ruler over his
25: 6 at midnight there was a cry *m'*,
16 and *m'* them other five talents.
26: 19 and they *m'* ready the passover.
27: 24 but that rather a tumult was *m'*,
64 sepulchre be *m'* sure until the third
66 they went, and *m'* the sepulchre sure,
M'r 2: 21 the old, and the rent is *m'* worse.
27 The sabbath was *m'* for man, and
5: 34 thy faith hath *m'* thee whole; go
6: 21 birthday *m'* a supper to his lords,
56 as touched him were *m'* whole.
8: 25 upon his eyes, and *m'* him look up:
10: 6 God *m'* them male and female.
52 way; thy faith hath *m'* thee whole.
11: 17 but ye have *m'* it a den of thieves.
14: 4 was this waste of the ointment *m'*?
16 and they *m'* ready the passover.
58 this temple that is *m'* with hands,
58 build another *m'* without hands.
15: 7 that had *m'* insurrection with him,

Lu 1:62 they m· signs to his father, how
2: 2 taxing was first m· when Cyrenius
15 the Lord hath m· known unto us.
17 they m· known abroad the saying
3: 5 the crooked shall be m· straight,
5 the rough ways shall be m· smooth:
4: 3 this stone that it be m· bread.
5:29 Levi m· him a great feast in his
8:17 that shall not be m· manifest;
48 thy faith hath m· thee whole; go
50 believe only, she shall be m· whole.
9:15 did so, and m· them all sit down.
11:40 he that m· that which is without
12:14 m· me a judge or a divider over
13:13 immediately she was m· straight,
14:12 and a recompense be m· thee.
16 A certain man m· a great supper,
17:19 way: thy faith hath m· thee whole.
19: 6 and he m· haste, and came down,
46 but ye have m· it a den of thieves.
22:13 and they m· ready the passover.
23:12 Pilate and Herod were m· friends
19 a certain sedition m· in the city,
24:22 of our company m· us astonished,
28 m· as though he would have gone
Joh 1: 3 All things were m· by him; and
3 was not anything m· that was m·.
10 the world was m· by him, and the
14 the Word was m· flesh, and dwelt
2: 9 tasted the water that was m· wine,
15 had m· a scourge of small cords,
3:21 that his deeds may be m· manifest,
4: 1 that Jesus m· and baptized more
46 Galilee, where he m· the water wine.
5: 4 water stepped in was m· whole of
6 unto him, Wilt thou be m· whole?
9 immediately the man was m· whole,
11 He that m· me whole, the same
14 him, Behold, thou art m· whole:
15 Jesus, which had m· him whole.
7:23 I have m· a man every whit whole
8:33 sayest thou, Ye shall be m· free?
9: 3 of God should be m· manifest in him.
6 and m· clay of the spittle, and he
11 man that is called Jesus m· clay,
14 sabbath day when Jesus m· the clay,
39 they which see might be m· blind.
12: 2 There they m· him a supper; and
15:15 Father I have m· known unto you.
17:23 that they may be m· perfect in one;
18:18 had m· a fire of coals, for it was
19: 7 he m· himself the Son of God.
23 his garments, and m· four parts,
Ac 1: 1 The former treatise have I m·, O
2:28 m· known to me the ways of life;
36 hath m· that same Jesus...Lord
3:12 we had m· this man to walk?
16 name hath m· this man strong,
25 which God m· with our fathers,
4: 9 by what means he is m· whole;
24 which hast m· heaven, and earth,
35 distribution was m· unto every man
7:10 he m· him governor over Egypt
13 Joseph was m· known to his
13 Joseph's kindred was m· known
27 Who m· thee a ruler and a judge
35 Who m· thee a ruler and a judge?
41 they m· a calf in those days, and
43 which ye m· to worship them:
48 not in temples m· with hands; as
50 not my hand m· all these things?
8: 2 m· great lamentation over him.
9:39 and garments which Dorcas m·,
10:10 they m· ready, he fell into a trance,
17 had m· enquiry for Simon's house,
12: 5 prayer was m· without ceasing of
20 m· Blastus the king's...their friend,
21 and m· an oration unto them.
13:32 which was m· unto the fathers,
14: 2 and m· their minds evil affected
5 an assault m· both of the Gentiles,
15 God, which m· heaven, and earth,
15: 7 ago God m· choice among us,
16:13 where prayer was wont to be m·;
24 and m· their feet fast in the stocks.
17:24 m· the world and all things therein,
24 not in temples m· with hands;
26 m· of one blood all nations of men
18:12 Jews m· insurrection with one
19:24 which m· silver shrines for Diana,
26 no gods, which are m· with hands:
33 have m· his defence unto the people.
20:28 Holy Ghost hath m· you overseers,
21:40 when there was m· a great silence,
22: 6 as I m· my journey, and was come
23:13 forty which had m· this conspiracy.
26: 6 the hope of the promise m· of God
27:40 to the wind, and m· toward shore.
Ro 1: 3 which was m· of the seed of David
20 by the things that are m·, even
23 an image m· like to corruptible man,
2:25 circumcision...m· uncircumcision.
4:14 of the law be heirs, faith is m· void,
14 and the promise m· of none effect:
17 m· thee a father of many nations,)
5:19 disobedience...were m· sinners,
19 of one shall many be m· righteous.
6:18 Being then m· free from sin, ye
22 But now being m· free from sin,
7:13 which is good m· death unto me?
8: 2 hath m· me free from the law of
20 creature was m· subject to vanity,
9:20 it, Why hast thou m· me thus?
29 and been m· like unto Gomorrha.
10:10 confession is m· unto salvation.
20 I was m· manifest unto them that
Ro 11: 9 Let their table be m· a snare, and a
14:21 or is offended, or is m· weak.
15: 8 the promises m· unto the fathers:
27 Gentiles have been m· partakers
16:26 now is m· manifest, and by the
26 m· known to all nations for the
1Co 1:17 Christ should be m· of none effect.
20 not God m· foolish the wisdom of
30 who of God is m· unto us wisdom,
3:13 man's work shall be m· manifest:
4: 9 are m· a spectacle unto the world,
13 we are m· as the filth of the world,
7:21 if thou mayest be m· free, use it
9:19 have I m· myself servant unto all,
22 I am m· all things to all men, that
11:19 may be m· manifest among you.
12:13 been all m· to drink into one Spirit.
14:25 secrets of his heart m· manifest;
15:22 so in Christ shall all be m· alive.
45 man Adam was m· a living soul;
45 Adam was m· a quickening spirit.
2Co 2: 2 the same which is m· sorry by me?
3: 6 Who also hath m· us able ministers
10 was m· glorious had no glory in
4:10 might be m· manifest in our body.
11 be m· manifest in our mortal flesh.
5: 1 God, an house not m· with hands,
11 but we are m· manifest unto God;
11 m· manifest in your consciences.
21 For he hath m· him to be sin for us,
21 be m· the righteousness of God in
7: 8 though I m· you sorry with a letter,
8 the same epistle hath m· you sorry,
9 I rejoice, not that ye were m· sorry,
9 were m· sorry after a godly manner,
14 boasting, which I m· before Titus, is
10:16 of things m· ready to our hand.
11: 6 have been thoroughly m· manifest
12: 9 strength is m· perfect in weakness.
Ga 3: 3 are ye now m· perfect by the flesh?
13 the law, being m· a curse for us:
16 his seed were the promises m·.
19 come to whom the promise was m·;
4: 4 m· of a woman, m· under the law,
5: 1 wherewith Christ hath m· us free,
Eph 1: 6 m· us accepted in the beloved:
9 Having m· known unto us the
2: 6 and m· us sit together in heavenly
11 Circumcision in...flesh m· by hands;
13 are m· nigh by the blood of Christ.
14 our peace, who hath m· both one,
3: 3 m· known unto me the mystery;
5 was not m· known unto the sons of
7 Whereof I was m· a minister,
5:13 reproved are m· manifest by...light:
Ph'p 2: 7 But m· himself of no reputation,
7 and was m· in the likeness of men:
3:10 m· conformable unto his death;
4: 6 requests be m· known unto God.
Col 1:12 hath m· us meet to be partakers of
20 having m· peace through the blood
23 whereof I Paul am m· a minister;
25 Whereof I am m· a minister,
26 now is m· manifest to his saints:
2:11 circumcision m· without hands,
15 he m· a shew of them openly,
1Ti 1: 9 law is not m· for a righteous man,
19 faith have m· shipwreck:
2: 1 giving of thanks, be m· for all men;
2Ti 1:10 now m· manifest by the appearing
Tit 3: 7 m· heirs according to the hope of
Heb 1: 2 by whom also he m· the worlds;
4 Being m· so much better than the
2: 9 m· a little lower than the angels
17 to be m· like unto his brethren,
3:14 For we are m· partakers of Christ,
5: 5 not himself to be m· an high priest;
9 And being m· perfect, he became
6: 4 and were m· partakers of the Holy
13 when God m· promise to Abraham,
20 Jesus, m· an high priest for ever
7: 3 but m· like unto the Son of God;
12 is m· of necessity a change also of
16 Who is m·, not after the law of a
19 For the law m· nothing perfect, but
20 not without an oath he was m· priest:
21 priests were m· without an oath;
22 was Jesus m· a surety of a better
26 and m· higher than the heavens;
8: 9 the covenant that I m· with their
13 covenant, he hath m· the first old.
9: 2 For there was a tabernacle m·;
8 holiest...was not yet m· manifest,
11 tabernacle, not m· with hands,
24 into the holy places m· with hands,
10: 3 is a remembrance again m· of sins
13 till his enemies be m· his footstool.
33 whilst ye were m· a gazingstock
11: 3 not m· of things which do appear.
22 m· mention of the departing of the
34 out of weakness were m· strong,
40 without us should not be m· perfect.
12:23 to the spirits of just men m· perfect,
27 shaken, as of things that are m·,
Jas 1:10 But the rich, in that he is m· low:
2:22 and by works was faith m· perfect?
3: 9 are m· after the similitude of God.
1Pe 2: 7 same is m· the head of the corner,
3:22 powers being m· subject unto him.
2Pe 1:16 we m· known unto you the power
2:12 m· to be taken and destroyed,
1Jo 2:19 that they might be m· manifest that
4:17 Herein is our love m· perfect, that
18 that feareth is not m· perfect in love.
5:10 not God hath m· him a liar;
Re 1: 6 m· us kings and priests unto God
Re 5:10 hast m· us unto our God kings and
7:14 and m· them white in the blood of
8:11 because they were m· bitter.
14: 7 worship him that m· heaven, and
8 she m· all nations drink of the wine
15: 4 for thy judgments are m· manifest.
17: 2 have been m· drunk with the wine
18:15 things, which were m· rich by her,
19 were m· rich all that had ships in
19 for in one hour is she m· desolate.
19: 7 his wife hath m· herself ready.

madest
Ne 9: 8 m· a covenant with him to give
14 And m· known unto them thy holy
Ps 8: 6 Thou m· him to have dominion over
80:15 that thou m· strong for thyself.
17 whom thou m· strong for thyself.
Eze 16:17 m· to thyself images of men, and
29: 7 m· all their loins to be at a stand.
Jon 4:10 not laboured, neither m· it grow;
Ac 21:38 before these days m· an uproar,
Heb 2: 7 m· him a little lower than the

Madian (*ma'-de-an*) See also MIDIAN.
Ac 7:29 was a stranger in the land of M·,

madman See MAD and MAN.

Madmannah (*mad-man'-nah*)
Jos 15:31 Ziklag, and M·, and Sansannah,
1Ch 2:49 bare also Shaaph the father of M·,

Madmen (*mad'-men*) See also MADMENAH.
Jer 48: 2 thou shalt be cut down, O M·;

Madmenah (*mad-me'-nah*) See also MADMEN.
Isa 10:31 M· is removed; the inhabitants of

madness
De 28:28 The Lord shall smite thee with m·,
Ec 1:17 wisdom, and to know m· and folly:
2:12 behold wisdom, and m·, and folly:
7:25 of folly, even of foolishness and m·:
9: 3 m· is in their heart while they live,
10:13 end of his talk is mischievous m·.
Zec 12: 4 and his rider with m·:
Lu 6:11 And they were filled with m·; and
2Pe 2:16 voice forbad the m· of the prophet.

Madon (*ma'-don*)
Jos 11: 1 that he sent to Jobab king of M·,
12:19 The king of M·, one; the king of

Mag See RAB-MAG.

Magbish (*mag'-bish*)
Ezr 2:30 The children of M·, an hundred

Magdala (*mag'-da-lah*) See also MAGDALENE.
M't 15:39 and came into the coasts of M·.

Magdalene (*mag'-da-leen*)
M't 27:56 Among which was Mary M·, and
61 there was Mary M·, and the other
28: 1 came Mary M· and the other Mary
M'r 15:40 among whom was Mary M·, and
47 Mary M· and Mary the mother of
16: 1 Mary M·, and Mary the mother of
9 week, he appeared first to Mary M·,
Lu 8: 2 Mary called M·, out of whom went
24:10 It was Mary M·, and Joanna, and
Joh 19:25 the wife of Cleophas, and Mary M·.
20: 1 day of the week cometh Mary M·
18 Mary M· came and told...disciples

Magdiel (*mag'-de-el*)
Ge 36:43 Duke M·, duke Iram: these be
1Ch 1:54 Duke M·, duke Iram. These are

magician See also MAGICIANS.
Da 2:10 that asked such things at any m·,

magicians
Ge 41: 8 and called for all the m· of Egypt,
24 I told this unto the m·; but there
Ex 7:11 now the m· of Egypt, they also did
22 the m· of Egypt did so with their
8: 7 m· did so with their enchantments,
18 m· did so with their enchantments
19 Then the m· said unto Pharaoh,
9:11 m· could not stand before Moses
11 the boil was upon the m·, and upon
Da 1:20 ten times better than all the m· and
2: 2 the king commanded to call the m·,
27 wise men, the astrologers, the m·,
4: 7 came in the m·, the astrologers,
9 O Belteshazzar, master of the m·,
5:11 thy father, made master of the m·,

magistrate See also MAGISTRATES.
J'g 18: 7 there was no m· in the land,
Lu 12:58 with thine adversary to the m·,

magistrates
Ezr 7:25 set m· and judges, which may
Lu 12:11 unto the synagogues, and unto m·,
Ac 16:20 brought them to the m·, saying,
22 and the m· rent off their clothes,
35 the m· sent the serjeants, saying,
36 The m· have sent to let you go:
38 told these words unto the m·:
Tit 3: 1 to obey m·, to be ready to every

magnifical
1Ch 22: 5 the Lord must be exceeding m·,

magnificence
Ac 19:27 and her m· should be destroyed,

magnified
Ge 19:19 and thou hast m· thy mercy,
Jos 4:14 m· Joshua in the sight of all Israel;
2Sa 7:26 And let thy name be m· for ever,
1Ch 17:24 that thy name may be m· for ever,
29:25 the Lord m· Solomon exceedingly
2Ch 1: 1 with him, and m· him exceedingly.

2Ch 32:23 was m· in the sight of all nations
Ps 35:27 Let the Lord be m·, which hath
40:16 say continually, The Lord be m·.
70: 4 say continually, Let God be m·.
138: 2 m· thy word above all thy name.
Jer 48:26 for he m· himself against the Lord:
42 hath m· himself against the Lord.
La 1: 9 for the enemy hath m· himself.
Da 8:11 he m· himself even to the prince
Zep 2: 8 m· themselves against their border.
10 m· themselves against the people
Mal 1: 5 Lord will be m· from the border of
Ac 5:13 to them: but the people m· them.
19:17 the name of the Lord Jesus was m·.
Ph'p 1:20 also Christ shall be m· in my body.

magnify See also MAGNIFIED.
Jos 3: 7 begin to m· thee in the sight of all
Job 7:17 man, that thou shouldest m· him?
19: 5 ye will m· yourselves against me,
36:24 Remember that thou m· his work,
Ps 34: 3 O m· the Lord with me, and let us
35:26 that m· themselves against me.
38:16 they m· themselves against me.
55:12 me that did m· himself against me;
69:30 and will m· him with thanksgiving.
Isa 10:15 the saw m· itself against him that
42:21 he will m· the law, and make it
Eze 38:23 Thus will I m· myself, and sanctify
Da 8:25 he shall m· himself in his heart,
11:36 and m· himself above every god,
37 for he shall m· himself above all.
Zec 12: 7 not m· themselves against Judah.
Lu 1:46 said, My soul doth m· the Lord,
Ac 10:46 speak with tongues, and m· God.
Ro 11:13 of the Gentiles, I m· mine office:

Magog (*ma'-gog*)
Ge 10: 2 sons of Japheth; Gomer, and M·,
1Ch 1: 5 sons of Japheth; Gomer, and M·,
Eze 38: 2 face against Gog, the land of M·,
39: 6 I will send a fire on M·, and among
Re 20: 8 quarters of the earth, Gog and M·,

Magor-missabib (*ma"-gor-mis'-sa-bib*)
Jer 20: 3 called thy name Pashur, but M·.

Magpiash (*mag'-pe-ash*)
Ne 10:20 M·, Meshullam, Hezir,

Mahalah (*ma'-ha-lah*) See also MAHLAH.
1Ch 7:18 bare Ishod, and Abiezer, and M·.

Mahalaleel (*ma-hal'-a-le-el*) See also MALELEEL.
Ge 5:12 lived seventy years, and begat M·:
13 Cainan lived after he begat M·
15 And M· lived sixty and five years,
16 M· lived after he begat Jared eight
17 And all the days of M· were eight
1Ch 1: 2 Kenan, M·, Jered,
Ne 11: 4 son of M·, of the children of Perez;

Mahalath (*ma'-ha-lath*) See also BASHEMATH.
Ge 28: 9 had M· the daughter of Ishmael
2Ch 11:18 Rehoboam took him M· the
Ps 53: *title* To the chief Musician upon M·,
88: *title* to the chief Musician upon M·

Mahali (*ma'-ha-li*) See also MAHLI.
Ex 6:19 sons of Merari; M· and Mushi:

Mahanaim (*ma-ha-na'-im*)
Ge 32: 2 called the name of that place M·.
Jos 13:26 from M· unto the border of Debir;
30 And their coast was from M·, all
21:38 slayer; and M· with her suburbs,
2Sa 2: 8 Saul, and brought him over to M·;
12 Saul, went out from M· to Gibeon.
29 all Bithron, and they came to M·.
17:24 Then David came to M·. And
27 pass, when David was come to M·,
19:32 of sustenance while he lay at M·;
1Ki 2: 8 in the day when I went to M·:
4:14 Ahinadab the son of Iddo had M·:
1Ch 6:80 suburbs, and M· with her suburbs,

Mahaneh-dan (*ma'-ha-neh-dan*)
J'g 18:12 they called that place M· unto

Maharai (*ma'-ha-rahee*)
2Sa 23:28 the Ahohite, M· the Netophathite,
1Ch 11:30 M· the Netophathite, Heled the son
27:13 captain for the tenth month was M·

Mahath (*ma'-hath*) See also AHIMOTH.
1Ch 6:35 the son of M·, the son of Amasai,
2Ch 29:12 arose, M· the son of Amasai,
31:13 M·, and Benaiah, were overseers

Mahavite (*ma'-ha-vite*)
1Ch 11:46 Eliel the M·, and Jeribai, and

Mahazioth (*ma-ha'-ze-oth*)
1Ch 25: 4 Mallothi, Hothir, and M·:
30 three and twentieth to M·, he, his

Maher-shalal-hash-baz (*ma"-her-sha"-lal-hash'-baz*)
Isa 8: 1 with a man's pen concerning M·.
3 the Lord to me, Call his name M·.

Mahlah (*mah'-lah*) See also MAHALAH.
Nu 26:33 daughters of Zelophehad were M·,
27: 1 M·, Noah, and Hoglah, and Milcah,
36:11 For M·, Tirzah, and Hoglah, and
Jos 17: 3 the names of his daughters, M·,

Mahli (*mah'-li*) See also MAHALI; MAHLITES.
Nu 3:20 of Merari by their families; M·,
1Ch 6:19 sons of Merari; M·, and Mushi.
29 sons of Merari; M·, Libni his son,
47 The son of M·, the son of Mushi,
23:21 sons of Merari; M·, and Mushi.
23 sons of Mushi; M·, and Eder, and
24:26 sons of Merari were M· and Mushi:
1Ch 24:28 Of M· came Eleazar, who had no
30 sons also of Mushi; M·, and Eder,
Ezr 8:18 understanding, of the sons of M·,

Mahlites (*mah'-lites*)
Nu 3:33 Merari was the family of the M·,
26:58 the family of the M·, the family of

Mahlon (*mah'-lon*) See also MAHLON'S.
Ru 1: 2 of his two sons M· and Chilion,
5 M· and Chilion died also both of
4:10 Ruth the Moabitess, the wife of M·,

Mahlon's (*mah'-lons*)
Ru 4: 9 and all that was Chilion's and M·,

Mahol (*ma'-hol*)
1Ki 4:31 and Darda, the sons of M·:

maid See also BONDMAID; HANDMAID; MAIDEN; MAID'S; MAIDS; MAIDSERVANT.
Ge 16: 2 I pray thee, go in unto my m·; it
3 took Hagar her m· the Egyptian,
5 I have given my m· into thy bosom;
6 Behold, thy m· is in thy hand; do
8 Sarai's m·, Whence camest thou?
29:24 Zilpah his m· for an handmaid.
29 Bilhah his handmaid to be her m·.
30: 3 Behold my m· Bilhah, go in unto
7 Rachel's m· conceived again, and
9 she took Zilpah her m·, and gave
10 Zilpah Leah's m· bare Jacob a son.
12 Leah's m· bare Jacob a second son.
Ex 2: 5 flags, she sent her m· to fetch it.
8 the m· went and called the child's
21:20 a man smite his servant, or his m·,
26 or the eye of his m·, that it perish;
22:16 if a man entice a m· that is not
Le 12: 5 if she bear a m· child, then she
25: 6 and for thy servant, and for thy m·,
De 22:14 came to her, I found her not a m·:
17 I found not thy daughter a m·;
2Ki 5: 2 of the land of Israel a little m·;
4 Thus and thus said the m· that is of
Es 2: 7 and the m· was fair and beautiful;
Job 31: 1 then should I think upon a m·?
Pr 30:19 and the way of a man with a m·.
Isa 24: 2 master; as with the m·, so with her
Jer 2:32 Can a m· forget her ornaments, or
51:22 pieces the young man and the m·;
Am 2: 7 father will go in unto the same m·,
M't 9:24 the m· is not dead, but sleepeth.
25 her by the hand, and the m· arose.
26:71 into the porch, another m· saw him,
M'r 14:69 a m· saw him again, and began to
Lu 8:54 hand, and called, saying, M·, arise.
22:56 a certain m· beheld him as he sat

maiden See also HANDMAIDEN; MAIDENS.
Ge 30:18 have given my m· to my husband:
J'g 19:24 Behold, here is my daughter a m·,
2Ch 36:17 compassion upon young man or m·,
Es 2: 4 let the m· which pleaseth the king
9 m· pleased him, and she obtained
13 thus came every m· unto the king;
Ps 123: 2 eyes of a m· unto the hand of her
Lu 8:51 father and the mother of the m·.

maidens See also HANDMAIDENS.
Ex 2: 5 her m· walked along by the river's
Ru 2: 8 but abide here fast by my m·:
22 that thou go out with his m·, that
23 So she kept fast by the m· of Boaz
3: 2 kindred, with those m· thou wast?
1Sa 9:11 found young m· going out to draw
Es 2: 8 many m· were gathered together
9 as belonged to her, and seven m·,
4:16 I also and my m· will fast likewise;
Job 41: 5 or wilt thou bind him for thy m·?
Ps 78:63 m· were not given to marriage.
148:12 Both young men, and m·; old men,
Pr 9: 3 She hath sent forth her m·: she
27:27 and for the maintenance for thy m·.
31:15 household, and a portion to her m·.
Ec 2: 7 I got me servants and m·, and had
Eze 44:22 they shall take m· of the seed of
Lu 12:45 to beat the menservants and m·,

maid-child See MAID and CHILD.

maid's
Es 2:12 when every m· turn was come to

maids See also BONDMAIDS.
Ezr 2:65 Beside their servants and their m·,
Es 2: 9 he preferred her and her m· unto
4: 4 So Esther's m· and...chamberlains
Job 19:15 my m·, count me for a stranger:
La 5:11 and the m· in the cities of Judah.
Eze 9: 6 utterly old and young, both m·, and
Na 2: 7 her m· shall lead her as with the
Zec 9:17 cheerful, and new wine the m·.
M'r 14:66 one of the m· of the high priest:

maidservant See also MAIDSERVANT'S; MAIDSERVANTS.
Ex 11: 5 unto the firstborn of the m· that is
20:10 thy manservant, nor thy m·, nor thy
17 his manservant, nor his m·, nor his
21: 7 a man sell his daughter to be a m·,
32 ox shall push a manservant or a m·;
De 5:14 nor thy manservant, nor thy m·, nor
14 and thy m· may rest as well as thou.
21 or his manservant, or his m·, his ox,
12:18 thy manservant, and thy m·, and the
15:17 unto thy m· thou shalt do likewise.
16:11, 14 thy manservant, and thy m·, and
J'g 9:18 made Abimelech, the son of his m·,
Job 31:13 cause of my manservant or of my m·,
Jer 34: 9 manservant, and every man his m·,
10 manservant, and every one his m·,

maidservant's
Ex 21:27 manservant's tooth, or his m· tooth;

maidservants See also MAIDSERVANTS'.
Ge 12:16 asses, and menservants, and m·,
20:17 Abimelech, and his wife, and his m·;
24:35 menservants, and m·, and camels,
30:43 cattle, and m·, and menservants,
De 12:12 menservants, and your m·, and the
1Sa 8:16 menservants, and your m·, and
2Sa 6:22 of the m· which thou hast spoken
2Ki 5:26 oxen, and menservants, and m·?
Ne 7:67 their manservants and their m·, of

maidservants'
Ge 31:33 tent, and into the two m· tents;

mail
1Sa 17: 5 he was armed with a coat of m·;
38 also he armed him with a coat of m·.

maimed
Le 22:22 Blind, or broken, or m·, or having
M't 15:30 that were lame, blind, dumb, m·,
31 dumb to speak, the m· to be whole,
18: 8 thee to enter into life halt or m·,
M'r 9:43 better for thee to enter into life m·,
Lu 14:13 a feast, call the poor, the m·, the
21 bring in hither the poor, and the m·,

mainsail
Ac 27:40 and hoised up the m· to the wind,

maintain See also MAINTAINED; MAINTAINEST.
1Ki 8:45 supplication, and m· their cause.
49 dwelling place, and m· their cause,
59 that he m· the cause of his servant,
1Ch 26:27 to m· the house of the Lord.
2Ch 6:35 supplication, and m· their cause.
39 supplications, and m· their cause,
Job 13:15 I will m· mine own ways before
Ps 140:12 will m· the cause of the afflicted,
Tit 3: 8 might be careful to m· good works.
14 let ours also learn to m· good works

maintained
Ps 9: 4 hast m· my right and my cause;

maintainest
Ps 16: 5 and of my cup: thou m· my lot.

maintenance
Ezr 4:14 have m· from the king's palace,
Pr 27:27 and for the m· for thy maidens.

majesty
1Ch 29:11 glory, and the victory, and the m·:
25 bestowed upon him such royal m·
Es 1: 4 and the honour of his excellent m·
Job 37:22 the north: with God is terrible m·.
40:10 Deck thyself now with m· and
Ps 21: 5 honour and m· hast thou laid upon
29: 4 the voice of the Lord is full of m·.
45: 3 mighty, with thy glory and thy m·.
4 And in thy m· ride prosperously
93: 1 reigneth, he is clothed with m·;
96: 6 Honour and m· are before him:
104: 1 thou art clothed with honour and m·.
145: 5 of the glorious honour of thy m·,
12 the glorious m· of his kingdom.
Isa 2:10 Lord, and for the glory of his m·.
19, 21 Lord, and for the glory of his m·,
24:14 shall sing for the m· of the Lord,
26:10 will not behold the m· of the Lord.
Eze 7:20 of his ornament, he set it in m·:
Da 4:30 and for the honour of my m·?
36 excellent m· was added unto me.
5:18 and m·, and glory, and honour:
19 And for the m· that he gave him,
Mic 5: 4 in the m· of the name of the Lord
Heb 1: 3 the right hand of the M· on high;
8: 1 throne of the M· in the heavens;
2Pe 1:16 but were eyewitnesses of his m·.
Jude 25 be glory and m·, dominion and

Makaz (*ma'-kaz*)
1Ki 4: 9 The son of Dekar, in M·, and in

make See also MADE; MAKEST; MAKETH; MAKING.
Ge 1:26 said, Let us m· man in our image,
2:18 I will m· him an help meet for him.
3: 6 a tree to be desired to m· one wise,
21 did the Lord m· coats of skins,
6:14 M· thee an ark of gopher wood:
14 rooms shalt thou m· in the ark, and
15 fashion which thou shalt m· it of:
16 window shalt thou m· to the ark,
16 and third stories shalt thou m· it.
9:12 covenant which I m· between me
11: 3 let us m· brick, and burn them
4 and let us m· us a name, lest we be
12: 2 And I will m· of thee a great nation,
2 bless thee, and m· thy name great;
13:16 I will m· thy seed as the dust of
17: 2 will m· my covenant between me
6 I will m· thee exceeding fruitful,
6 and I will m· nations of thee, and
20 him, and will m· him fruitful, and will
20 and I will m· him a great nation.
18: 6 M· ready quickly three measures of
6 it, and m· cakes upon the hearth.
19:32 let us m· our father drink wine,
34 let us m· him drink wine this night
21:13 the bondwoman will I m· a nation,
18 for I will m· him a great nation.
24: 3 And I will m· thee swear by the Lord,
26: 4 I will m· thy seed to multiply as
28 let us m· a covenant with thee;
27: 4 m· me savoury meat, such as I
7 venison, and m· me savoury meat,
9 I will m· them savoury meat for thy
28: 3 bless thee, and m· thee fruitful,
31:44 come thou, let us m· a covenant,
32:12 m· thy seed as the sand of the sea,
34: 9 m· ye marriages with us, and give
30 have troubled me to m· me to stink

Ge 35: 1 and m' there an altar unto God,
3 I will m' there an altar unto God,
40:14 and m' mention of me unto Pharaoh,
43:16 men home, and slay, and m' ready;
46: 3 there m' of thee a great nation:
47: 6 m' thy father and brethren to dwell;
6 m' them rulers over my cattle.
48: 4 me, Behold, I will m' thee fruitful,
4 m' of thee a multitude of people;
20 God m' thee as Ephraim and as
Ex 5: 5 ye m' them rest from their burdens.
7 give the people straw to m' brick,
8 which they did m' heretofore,
16 and they say to us, M' brick: and,
12: 4 shall m' your count for the lamb.
18:16 m' them know the statutes of God,
20: 4 m' unto thee any graven image,
23 shall not m' with me gods of silver,
23 shall ye m' unto you gods of gold.
24 An altar of earth thou shalt m'
25 thou wilt m' me an altar of stone,
21:34 owner of the pit shall m' it good,
22: 3 for he should m' full restitution;
5 vineyard, shall he m' restitution.
6 the fire shall surely m' restitution.
11 thereof, and he shall not m' it good.
12 shall m' restitution unto the owner
13 he shall not m' good that which
14 with it, he shall surely m' it good.
15 be with it, he shall not m' it good:
23:13 m' no mention of the name of other
27 I will m' all thine enemies turn
32 Thou shalt m' no covenant with
33 land, lest they m' thee sin against me:
25: 8 And let them m' me a sanctuary;
9 thereof, even so shall ye m' it.
10 shall m' an ark of shittim wood:
11 and shalt m' upon it a crown of gold
13 shalt m' staves of shittim wood,
17 shalt m' a mercy seat of pure gold:
18 thou shalt m' two cherubims of gold,
18 of beaten work shalt thou m' them,
19 And m' one cherub on the one end,
19 ye m' the cherubims on the two ends
23 also m' a table of shittim wood:
24 m' thereto a crown of gold round
25 thou shalt m' unto it a border of an
25 thou shalt m' a golden crown to
26 shalt m' for it four rings of gold,
28 shalt m' the staves of shittim wood,
29 thou shalt m' the dishes thereof,
29 of pure gold shalt thou m' them.
31 shalt m' a candlestick of pure gold:
37 shalt m' the seven lamps thereof:
39 a talent of pure gold shall he m' it,
40 thou m' them after their pattern,
26: 1 thou shalt m' the tabernacle with
1 of cunning work shalt thou m' them.
4 thou shalt m' loops of blue upon the
4 shalt thou m' in the uttermost edge
5 Fifty loops shalt thou m' in the one
5 and fifty loops shalt thou m' in the
6 thou shalt m' fifty taches of gold,
7 thou shalt m' curtains of goats' hair
7 eleven curtains shalt thou m'.
10 thou shalt m' fifty loops on the edge
11 thou shalt m' fifty taches of brass,
14 shalt m' a covering for the tent of
15 shalt m' boards for the tabernacle,
17 thou m' for all the boards of the
18 m' the boards for the tabernacle,
19 thou shalt m' forty sockets of silver
22 westward thou shalt m' six boards.
23 two boards shalt thou m' for the
26 thou shalt m' bars of shittim wood;
29 m' their rings of gold for places for
31 And thou shalt m' a vail of blue,
36 And thou shalt m' an hanging for
37 m' for the hanging five pillars
27: 1 shalt m' an altar of shittim wood,
2 thou shalt m' the horns of it upon
3 m' his pans to receive his ashes,
3 vessels...thou shalt m' of brass.
4 shalt m' for it a grate of network of
4 shalt thou m' four brasen rings in
6 thou shalt m' staves for the altar,
8 Hollow with boards shalt thou m' it:
8 in the mount, so shall they m' it.
9 shalt m' the court of the tabernacle:
28: 2 shalt m' holy garments for Aaron
3 they may m' Aaron's garments to
4 the garments which they shall m';
4 shall m' holy garments for Aaron
6 they shall m' the ephod of gold,
11 m' them to be set in ouches of gold.
13 And thou shalt m' ouches of gold;
14 wreathen work shalt thou m' them,
15 m' the breastplate of judgment
15 work of the ephod thou shalt m' it;
15 fine twined linen, shalt thou m' it.
22 m' upon the breastplate chains at
23 m' upon the breastplate two rings
26 And thou shalt m' two rings of gold,
27 other rings of gold thou shalt m',
31 m' the robe of the ephod all of blue.
33 shalt m' pomegranates of blue, and
36 thou shalt m' a plate of pure gold,
39 shalt m' the mitre of fine linen, and
39 shalt m' the girdle of needlework.
40 Aaron's sons thou shalt m' coats,
40 m' for them girdles, and bonnets
40 and bonnets shalt thou m' for them,
42 m' them linen breeches to cover
29: 2 wheaten flour shalt thou m' them.
37 m' an atonement for the altar, and
30: 1 m' an altar to burn incense upon:

Ex 30: 1 of shittim wood shalt thou m' it.
3 m' unto it a crown of gold round
4 two golden rings shalt thou m' to it
4 the two sides of it shalt thou m' it;
5 shalt m' the staves of shittim wood,
10 Aaron shall m' an atonement upon
10 in the year shall he m' atonement
15, 16 to m' an atonement for your souls.
18 shalt also m' a laver of brass, and
25 shalt m' it an oil of holy ointment,
32 neither shall ye m' any other like it,
35 And thou shalt m' it a perfume, a
37 the perfume which thou shalt m',
37 not m' to yourselves according to
38 Whosoever shall m' like unto that,
31: 6 m' all that I have commanded thee;
32: 1 m' us gods, which shall go before
10 and I will m' of thee a great nation.
23 M' us gods, which shall go before
30 shall m' an atonement for your sin.
33:19 m' all my goodness pass before thee,
34:10 Behold, I m' a covenant: before
12, 15 m' a covenant with...inhabitants
16 m' thy sons go a whoring after their
17 Thou shalt m' thee no molten gods.
35:10 and m' all that the Lord hath
33 to m' any manner of cunning work.
36: 3 of the sanctuary, to m' it withal.
5 which the Lord commanded to m'.
6 man nor woman m' any more work
7 sufficient for all the work to m' it,
22 did he m' for all the boards of the
Le 1: 4 for him to m' atonement for him.
4:20, 26, 31, 35 priest shall m' an atonement
5: 6, 10, 13 priest shall m' an atonement
16 he shall m' amends for the harm
16, 18 priest shall m' an atonement for
6: 7 the priest shall m' an atonement for
8:15 it, to m' reconciliation upon it.
34 to do, to m' an atonement for you.
9: 7 and m' an atonement for thyself,
7 and m' an atonement for them; as
10:17 m' atonement for them before the
11:43 not m' yourselves abominable
43 ye m' yourselves unclean with
47 m' a difference between the unclean
12: 7 and m' an atonement for her; and
8 priest shall m' an atonement for
14:18 priest shall m' an atonement for him
19 m' an atonement for him that is to
20 priest shall m' an atonement for him,
21 waved, to m' an atonement for him,
29 to m' an atonement for him before
31 priest shall m' an atonement for
53 and m' an atonement for the house:
15:15, 30 priest shall m' an atonement for
16: 6 m' an atonement for himself, and for
10 to m' an atonement with him, and
11 shall m' an atonement for himself,
16 shall m' an atonement for the holy
17 in to m' an atonement in the holy
18 Lord, and m' an atonement for it;
24 m' an atonement for himself, and for
27 to m' atonement in the holy place,
30 the priest m' an atonement for you,
32 shall m' the atonement, and shall
33 shall m' an atonement for the holy
33 he shall m' an atonement for the
33 m' an atonement for the priests,
34 m' an atonement for the children of
17:11 to m' an atonement for your souls:
19: 4 nor m' to yourselves molten gods:
22 priest shall m' an atonement for him
28 not m' any cuttings in your flesh
20:25 m' your souls abominable by beast,
21: 5 not m' baldness upon their head,
5 nor m' any cuttings in their flesh.
22:22 nor m' an offering by fire of them
24 shall ye m' any offering thereof in
23:22 shalt not m' clean riddance of the
28 to m' an atonement for you before
24:18 killeth a beast shall m' it good;
25: 9 ye m' the trumpet sound throughout
26: 1 shall m' you no idols nor graven
6 and none shall m' you afraid:
9 unto you, and m' you fruitful, and
19 and I will m' your heaven as iron,
22 cattle, and m' you few in number;
31 And I will m' your cities waste,
27: 2 When a man shall m' a singular vow,
Nu 5:21 The Lord m' thee a curse and an
21 the Lord doth m' thy thigh to rot,
22 thy bowels, to m' thy belly to swell,
6: 7 shall not m' himself unclean for
11 and m' an atonement for him, for
25 the Lord m' his face shine upon thee,
8: 7 and so m' themselves clean.
12 m' an atonement for the Levites.
19 to m' an atonement for the children
10: 2 M' thee two trumpets of silver; of
2 a whole piece shalt thou m' them:
12: 6 I the Lord will m' myself known
14: 4 Let us m' a captain, and let us
12 will m' of thee a greater nation
30 which I sware to m' you dwell therein,
15: 3 will m' an offering by fire unto the
3 to m' a sweet savour unto the Lord,
25, 28 priest shall m' an atonement for
28 Lord, to m' an atonement for him;
38 m' them fringes in the borders
16:13 m' thyself altogether a prince over
30 But if the Lord m' a new thing,
38 m' them broad plates for a covering
46 and m' an atonement for them:
17: 5 and I will m' to cease from me the
21: 8 M' thee a fiery serpent, and set it

Nu 23:19 spoken, and shall he not m' it good?
28:22, 30 to m' an atonement for you.
29: 5 to m' an atonement for you:
30: 8 shall m' her vow which she vowed,
13 it, or her husband may m' it void.
15 shall any ways m' them void after that
31:23 ye shall m' it go through the fire,
23 ye shall m' go through the water.
50 to m' an atonement for our souls
De 1:11 m' you a thousand times so many more
13 and I will m' them rulers over you.
4:10 and I will m' them hear my words,
16, 23, 25 and m' you a graven image,
5: 8 shalt not m' thee any graven image,
7: 2 shalt m' no covenant with them,
3 thou m' marriages with them;
8: 3 might m' thee know that man doth not
9:14 I will m' of thee a nation mightier
10: 1 mount, and m' thee an ark of wood.
13:14 enquire, and m' search, and ask
14: 1 nor m' any baldness between your
15: 1 years thou shalt m' a release.
16:18 and officers shalt thou m' thee in
21 thy God, which thou shalt m' thee.
19:18 shall m' diligent inquisition: and,
20: 9 they shall m' captains of the armies
11 if it m' thee answer of peace, and open
12 if it will m' no peace with thee, but will
21:14 shalt not m' merchandise of her,
16 m' the son of the beloved firstborn
22: 8 shalt m' a battlement for thy roof,
12 Thou shalt m' thee fringes upon the
26:19 to m' thee high above all nations
28:11 the Lord shall m' thee plenteous
13 the Lord shall m' thee the head,
21 m' the pestilence cleave unto thee,
24 The Lord shall m' the rain of thy
59 Then the Lord will m' thy plagues
29: 1 the Lord commanded Moses to m'
14 I m' this covenant and this oath;
30: 9 thy God will m' thee plenteous in
32:26 m' the remembrance of them to cease
35 that shall come upon them m' haste.
39 I kill, and I m' alive; I wound, and
42 m' mine arrows drunk with blood,
Jos 1: 8 thou shalt m' thy way prosperous,
5: 2 Joshua, M' thee sharp knives, and
6: 5 when they m' a long blast with the
10 shall not shout, nor m' any noise
18 ye m' yourselves accursed, when
18 and m' the camp of Israel a curse,
7: 3 and m' not all the people to labour
19 and m' confession unto him; and
9: 6 therefore m' ye a league with us.
7 how shall we m' a league with you?
11 now m' ye a league with us.
22:25 m' our children cease from fearing
23: 7 neither m' mention of the name of their
12 and shall m' marriages with them.
J'g 2: 2 m' no league with the inhabitants
9:48 m' haste, and do as I have done.
16:25 for Samson, that he may m' us sport.
17: 3 m' a graven image and a molten
20:38 should m' a great flame with smoke
Ru 3: 3 but m' not thyself known unto the
4:11 Lord m' the woman...like Rachel
1Sa 1: 6 her sore, for to m' her fret, because
2: 8 to m' them inherit the throne of
24 m' the Lord's people to transgress.
29 m' yourselves fat with the chiefest
3:12 when I begin, I will also m' an end.
6: 5 shall m' images of your emerods,
7 Now therefore m' a new cart, and
8: 5 m' us a king to judge us like all
12 and to m' his instruments of war,
22 their voice, and m' them a king.
9:12 m' haste now, for he came to day
11: 1 M' a covenant with us, and we
2 will I m' a covenant with you,
12:22 the Lord to m' you his people.
13:19 Lest the Hebrews m' them swords
17:25 m' his father's house free in Israel.
18:25 Saul thought to m' David fall by
20:38 cried after the lad, M' speed, haste,
22: 7 m' you all captains of thousands,
25:28 certainly m' my lord a sure house;
28: 2 I m' thee keeper of mine head for
15 the Philistines m' war against me,
15 m' known unto me what I shall do.
29: 4 M' this fellow return, that he may
2Sa 3:12 also, M' thy league with me, and,
13 Well; I will m' a league with thee:
21 they may m' a league with thee,
7:11 thee that he will m' thee an house.
21 to m' thy servant know them.
23 to himself, and to m' him a name,
11:25 m' thy battle more strong against
13: 5 on thy bed, and m' thyself sick:
6 and m' me a couple of cakes in my
15:14 m' speed to depart, lest he overtake us
20 m' thee go up and down with us?
17: 2 handed, and will m' him afraid:
21: 3 shall I m' the atonement, that
23: 5 although he m' it not to grow.
1Ki 1:37 m' his throne greater than the throne
47 m' the name of Solomon better than
47 m' his throne greater than thy throne.
2:42 I not m' thee to swear by the Lord,
8:29 prayer which thy servant shall m'
33, 47 and m' supplication unto thee
9:22 did Solomon m' no bondmen: but
11:34 I will m' him prince all the days
12: 1 come to Shechem to m' him king.
4 m' thou the grievous service of
9 M' the yoke which thy father...lighten?
10 but m' thou it lighter unto us;

1Ki 16: 3 m' thy house like the house of
19 which he did, to m' Israel to sin.
21 the son of Ginath, to m' him king;
17:13 m' me thereof a little cake first,
13 after m' for thee and for thy son.
19: 2 m' not thy life as the life of one of
20:34 m' streets for thee in Damascus,
21:22 m' thine house like the house of
2Ki 3:16 M' this valley full of ditches.
4:10 Let us m' a little chamber, I pray
5: 7 Am I God, to kill and to m' alive,
6: 2 let us m' us a place there, where
7: 2 Lord would m' windows in heaven,
19 Lord should m' windows in heaven,
9: 2 and m' him arise up from among his
9 And I will m' the house of Ahab
21 And Joram said, M' ready. And his
10: 5 bid us; we will not m' any king:
18:30 let Hezekiah m' you trust in the Lord,
31 M' an agreement with me by a
21: 8 will I m' the feet of Israel move
23:10 might m' his son...pass through the
1Ch 6:49 and to m' an atonement for Israel,
11:10 with all Israel, to m' him king,
12:31 name, to come and m' David king.
38 to m' David king over all Israel:
38 were of one heart to m' David king.
16: 8 name, m' known his deeds among
42 for those that should m' a sound,
17:21 to m' thee a name of greatness
22 didst thou m' thine own people
21: 3 Lord m' his people an hundred...more
22: 5 will therefore now m' preparation
28: 4 me to m' me king over all Israel:
29:12 and in thine hand it is to m' great,
2Ch 4:11 work that he was to m' for king
16 his father m' to king Solomon for
5:13 to m' one sound to be heard in
6:21 supplication...they shall m' toward
22 be laid upon him to m' him swear,
24 pray and m' supplication before
7:11 came into Solomon's heart to m'
20 and will m' it to be a proverb and
8: 8 did Solomon m' to pay tribute
9 m' no servants for his work; but
10: 1 all Israel come to m' him king.
10 m' thou it somewhat lighter for us;
11:22 for he thought to m' him king.
14: 7 m' about them walls, and towers,
20:36 joined himself with him to m' ships
25: 8 shall m' thee fall before the enemy:
29:10 m' a covenant with the Lord God
24 to m' an atonement for all Israel:
30: 5 m' proclamation throughout all Israel,
35:21 God commanded me to m' haste:
Ezr 5: 3 house, and to m' up this wall?
4 of the men that m' this building?
9 house, and to m' up these walls?
6: 8 I m' a decree what ye shall do to
7:13 I m' a decree, that all they of the
21 do m' a decree to all the treasurers
10: 3 let us m' a covenant with our God
11 m' confession unto the Lord God
Ne 2: 4 me, For what dost thou m' request?
8 timber to m' beams for the gates
4: 2 will they m' an end in a day? will
8:12 portions, and to m' great mirth,
15 of thick trees, to m' booths, as it
9:38 of all this we m' a sure covenant,
10:33 to m' an atonement for Israel,
Es 1:20 king's decree which he shall m'
4: 8 to m' supplication unto him, and
8 to m' request before him for her
5: 5 said, Cause Haman to m' haste,
6:10 M' haste, and take the apparel and
7: 7 Haman stood up to m' request for his
9:22 should m' them days of feasting
Job 5:18 and his hands m' whole.
8: 5 and m' thy supplication to the
6 m' the habitation of thy...prosperous.
9:15 I would m' supplication to my judge.
30 and m' my hands never so clean;
11: 3 thy lies m' men hold their peace?
3 shall no man m' thee ashamed?
19 and none shall m' thee afraid;
19 yea, many shall m' suit unto thee.
13:11 not his excellency m' you afraid?
21 and let not thy dread m' me afraid.
23 m' me to know my transgression
15:24 and anguish shall m' him afraid;
18: 2 it be ere ye m' an end of words?
11 Terrors shall m' him afraid on
19: 3 ye m' yourselves strange to me.
20: 2 to answer, and for this I m' haste.
22:27 shalt m' thy prayer unto him, and
24:11 Which m' oil within their walls,
25 not so now, who will m' me a liar,
25 and m' my speech nothing worth?
28:25 To m' the weight for the winds;
31:15 made me in the womb m' him?
33: 7 my terror shall not m' thee afraid,
34:29 who then can m' trouble? and
35: 9 they m' the oppressed to cry:
39:20 m' him afraid as a grasshopper?
27 and m' her nest on high?
40:19 can m' his sword to approach unto
41: 3 Will he m' many supplications
4 Will he m' a covenant with thee?
Ps 5: 8 m' thy way straight before my face.
6: 6 all the night m' I my bed to swim;
11: 2 they m' ready their arrow upon
21: 9 shalt m' them as a fiery oven in
12 shalt thou m' them turn their back,
12 thou shalt m' ready thine arrows
22: 9 didst m' me hope when I was upon
31:16 M' thy face to shine upon thy

Ps 34: 2 shall m' her boast in the Lord:
36: 8 shalt m' them drink of the river of
38:22 M' haste to help me, O Lord my
39: 4 Lord, m' me to know mine end,
8 m' me not the reproach of the
40:13 me: O Lord, m' haste to help me.
17 deliverer; m' no tarrying, O my God.
41: 3 wilt m' all his bed in his sickness.
45:16 mayest m' princes in all the earth.
17 m' thy name to be remembered in all
46: 4 shall m' glad the city of God,
51: 6 thou shalt m' me to know wisdom.
8 M' me to hear joy and gladness;
55: 2 in my complaint, and m' a noise;
57: 1 of thy wings will I m' my refuge,
59: 6 they m' a noise like a dog, and go
14 them m' a noise like a dog, and go
64: 8 shall m' their own tongue to fall
66: 1 M' a joyful noise unto God, all ye
2 his name: m' his praise glorious.
8 m' the voice of his praise to be heard:
69:23 m' their loins continually to shake.
70: 1 M' haste, O God, to deliver me;
1 m' haste to help me, O Lord.
5 needy: m' haste unto me, O God:
5 my deliverer; O Lord, m' no tarrying.
71:12 O my God, m' haste for my help.
16 will m' mention of thy righteousness,
78: 5 m' them known to their children:
81: 1 m' a joyful noise unto the God of
83: 2 For, lo, thine enemies m' a tumult:
11 M' their nobles like Oreb, and like
13 O my God, m' them like a wheel; as
15 and m' them afraid with thy storm.
84: 6 the valley of Baca m' it a well;
87: 4 will m' mention of Rahab and Babylon
89: 1 will I m' known thy faithfulness to all
27 I will m' him my firstborn, higher
29 His seed also will I m' to endure
90:15 M' us glad according to the days
95: 1 us m' a joyful noise to the rock of
2 and m' a joyful noise unto him with
98: 4 M' a joyful noise unto the Lord, all
4 m' a loud noise, and rejoice, and
6 m' a joyful noise before the Lord,
100: 1 M' a joyful noise unto the Lord, all
104:15 oil to m' his face to shine, and bread
17 Where the birds m' their nests: as
105: 1 m' known his deeds among the people.
106: 8 m' his mighty power to be known.
110: 1 I m' thine enemies thy footstool.
115: 8 that m' them are like unto them;
119:27 M' me to understand the way of thy
35 M' me to go in the path of thy
135 M' thy face to shine upon thy servant;
135:18 They that m' them are like unto
139: 8 if I m' my bed in hell, behold, thou
141: 1 cry unto thee: m' haste unto me;
142: 1 the Lord did I m' my supplication.
145:12 To m' known to the sons of men his
Pr 1:16 evil, and m' haste to shed blood.
23 I will m' known my words unto you.
6: 3 thyself, and m' sure thy friend.
14: 9 Fools m' a mock at sin: but
20:18 and with good advice m' war.
25 holy, and after vows to m' enquiry.
22:21 might m' thee know the certainty
24 M' no friendship with an angry
23: 5 certainly m' themselves wings;
24: 6 wise counsel thou shalt m' thy war:
27 and m' it fit for thyself in the field;
27:11 be wise, and m' my heart glad,
30:26 m' they their houses in the rocks;
Ec 2:24 and that he should m' his soul enjoy
7:13 who can m' that straight, which
16 much; neither m' thyself over wise:
Ca 1:11 We will m' thee borders of gold
8:14 M' haste, my beloved, and be thou
Isa 1:15 when ye m' many prayers, I will not
16 Wash you, m' you clean; put away
3: 7 m' me not a ruler of the people.
5:19 Let him m' speed, and hasten his work,
6:10 M' the heart of this people fat,
10 m' their ears heavy, and shut their
7: 6 let us m' a breach therein for us,
10:23 of hosts shall m' a consumption,
11: 3 m' him of quick understanding in
15 and m' men go over dryshod.
12: 4 m' mention that his name is exalted.
13:12 m' a man more precious than fine
20 the shepherds m' their fold there.
14:23 m' it a possession for the bittern,
16: 3 m' thy shadow as the night in the
17: 2 and none shall m' them afraid.
11 day shalt thou m' thy plant to grow,
11 shalt thou m' thy seed to flourish:
12 m' a noise like the noise of the seas;
12 m' a rushing like the rushing of
19:10 that m' sluices and ponds for fish.
23:16 m' sweet melody, sing many songs,
25: 6 m' unto all people a feast of fat
26:13 only will we m' mention of thy name.
27: 5 that he may m' peace with me;
5 and he shall m' peace with me.
28: 9 shall he m' to understand doctrine?
16 that believeth shall not m' haste.
29:21 That m' a man an offender for a word,
32: 6 m' empty the soul of the hungry,
11 strip you, and m' you bare, and
33: 1 m' an end to deal treacherously,
34:15 shall the great owl m' her nest,
36:15 let Hezekiah m' you trust in the Lord,
16 M' an agreement with me by a
37: 9 He is come forth to m' war with thee.
38:12, 13 wilt thou m' an end of me.
16 thou recover me, and m' me to live.

Isa 38:19 the children shall m' known thy truth.
40: 3 m'...in the desert a highway for
41:15 I will m'...a new sharp threshing
15 and shalt m' the hills as chaff.
18 m' the wilderness a pool of water,
42:15 I will m' waste mountains and hills,
15 and I will m' the rivers islands, and
16 will m' darkness light before them,
21 the law, and m' it honourable.
43:19 even m' a way in the wilderness,
44: 9 They that m' a graven image are
19 shall I m' the residue thereof an
45: 2 m' the crooked places straight:
7 I m' peace, and create evil: I the
14 they shall m' supplication unto thee
46: 5 will ye liken me, and m' me equal,
47: 2 m' bare the leg, uncover the thigh,
48: 1 and m' mention of the God of Israel,
15 he shall m' his way prosperous.
49:11 I will m' all my mountains a way,
17 Thy children shall m' haste: thy
50: 2 sea, I m' the rivers a wilderness:
3 and I m' sackcloth their covering.
51: 3 will m' her wilderness like Eden.
4 m' my judgment to rest for a light of
52: 5 rule over them m' them to howl,
53:10 thou shalt m' his soul an offering
54: 3 m' the desolate cities to be inhabited.
12 I will m' thy windows of agates,
55: 3 I will m' an everlasting covenant
56: 7 m' them joyful in my house of
57: 4 against whom m' ye a wide mouth,
58: 4 m' your voice to be heard on high.
11 in drought, and m' fat thy bones:
59: 7 m' haste to shed innocent blood:
60:13 m' the place of my feet glorious.
15 will m' thee an eternal excellency,
17 I will also m' thy officers peace,
61: 8 I will m' an everlasting covenant
62: 6 ye that m' mention of the Lord, keep
7 till he m' Jerusalem a praise in
63: 6 and m' them drunk in my fury, and
12 m' himself an everlasting name?
14 to m' thyself a glorious name.
64: 2 to m' thy name known to thine
66:22 and the new earth, which I will m',
Jer 4: 7 his place to m' thy land desolate;
16 M' ye mention to the nations; behold,
27 yet will I not m' a full end.
30 in vain shalt thou m' thyself fair;
5:10 and destroy; but m' not a full end:
14 m' my words in thy mouth fire,
18 I will not m' a full end with you.
6: 8 lest I m' thee desolate, a land not
26 m' thee mourning, as for an only
7:16 neither m' intercession to me: for
18 dough, to m' cakes to the queen
9:11 And I will m' Jerusalem heaps,
11 will m' the cities of Judah desolate,
18 let them m' haste, and take up a
10:22 to m' the cities of Judah desolate,
13:16 of death, and m' it gross darkness.
15:14 I will m' thee to pass with thine
20 And I will m' thee unto this people
16: 6 nor m' themselves bald for them:
20 Shall a man m' gods unto himself,
18: 4 seemed good to the potter to m' it.
11 m' your ways and your doings good.
16 To m' their land desolate, and a
19: 7 I will m' void the counsel of Judah
8 And I will m' this city desolate,
12 and even m' this city as Tophet:
20: 4 I will m' thee a terror to thyself,
9 I will not m' mention of him, nor
22: 6 surely I will m' thee a wilderness,
23:15 and m' them drink the water of gall:
16 prophesy unto you: they m' you vain:
25: 9 and m' them an astonishment, and
12 and will m' it perpetual desolations.
18 thereof, to m' them a desolation,
26: 6 will I m' this house like Shiloh,
6 and will m' this city a curse to all
27: 2 M' thee bonds and yokes, and put
18 now m' intercession to the Lord of
28:13 shalt m' for them yokes of iron.
29:17 and will m' them like vile figs, that
22 The Lord m' thee like Zedekiah
30:10 and none shall m' him afraid.
11 I m' a full end of all nations
11 yet will I not m' a full end of thee:
19 the voice of them that m' merry.
31: 4 the dances of them that m' merry.
13 m' them rejoice from their sorrow.
21 waymarks, m' thee high heaps:
31 m' a new covenant with the house
33 the covenant that I will m' with the
32:40 I will m' an everlasting covenant
34:17 I will m' you to be removed into all
22 and I will m' the cities of Judah a
44:19 we m' her cakes to worship her,
46:27 ease, and none shall m' him afraid.
28 will m' a full end of all the nations
28 I will not m' a full end of thee, but
48:26 M' ye him drunken: for he
49:15 m' thee small among the heathen,
16 m' thy nest as high as the eagle,
19 will...m' him run away from her:
20 shall m' their habitations desolate
50: 3 which shall m' her land desolate,
44 will m' them...run away from her:
45 shall m' their habitation desolate
51:11 M' bright the arrows; gather the
12 m' the watch strong, set up the
25 will m' thee a burnt mountain.
29 m' the land of Babylon a desolation
36 her sea, and m' her springs dry.

Jer 51:39 In their heat I will *m'* their feasts,
39 and I will *m'* them drunken, that
57 And I will *m'* drunk her princes,
La 4:21 and shalt *m'* thyself naked.
Eze 3:26 *m'* thy tongue cleave to the roof
4: 9 vessel, and *m'* thee bread thereof,
5:14 Moreover I will *m'* thee waste,
6:14 them, and *m'* the land desolate,
7:14 the trumpet, even to *m'* all ready;
23 *M'* a chain: for the land is full of
24 *m'* the pomp of the strong to cease:
11:13 *m'* a full end of the remnant of
12:23 I will *m'* this proverb to cease, and
13:18 and *m'* kerchiefs upon the head of
20 hunt the souls to *m'* them fly,
20 souls that ye hunt to *m'* them fly.
14: 8 will *m'* him a sign and a proverb,
15: 8 And I will *m'* the land desolate,
16:42 I *m'* my fury toward thee to rest,
17:17 company *m'* for him in the war,
18:31 and *m'* you a new heart and a new
20:17 neither did I *m'* an end of them in
26 that I might *m'* them desolate, to
31 ye *m'* your sons to pass through the
21:10 sharpened to *m'* a sore slaughter;
10 glitter: should we then *m'* mirth?
22:30 them, that should *m'* up the hedge,
23:27 will I *m'* thy lewdness to cease
24: 5 bones under it, and *m'* it boil well,
9 will even *m'* the pile for fire great.
17 cry, *m'* no mourning for the dead,
25: 4 and *m'* their dwellings in thee:
5 *m'* Rabbah a stable for camels,
13 I will *m'* it desolate from Teman;
26: 4 and *m'* her like the top of a rock.
8 and he shall *m'* a fort against thee,
12 they shall *m'* a spoil of thy riches,
12 *m'* a prey of thy merchandise: and
14 I will *m'* thee like the top of a rock:
19 shall *m'* thee a desolate city, like
21 I will *m'* thee a terror, and thou
27: 5 cedars from Lebanon to *m'* masts
31 shall *m'* themselves utterly bald
29:10 *m'* the land of Egypt utterly waste
12 will *m'* the land of Egypt desolate
30: 9 *m'* the careless Ethiopians afraid,
10 *m'* the multitude of Egypt to cease
12 And I will *m'* the rivers dry, and
12 and I will *m'* the land waste, and all
14 And I will *m'* Pathros desolate,
21 to *m'* it strong to hold the sword.
32: 7 and *m'* the stars thereof dark; I
8 heaven will I *m'* dark over thee.
10 *m'* many people amazed at thee,
14 Then will I *m'* their waters deep,
15 shall *m'* the land of Egypt desolate,
34:25 *m'* with them a covenant of peace,
26 will *m'* them and the places round
28 and none shall *m'* them afraid.
35: 3 and I will *m'* thee most desolate,
7 will I *m'* mount Seir most desolate,
9 will *m'* thee perpetual desolations,
14 rejoiceth, I will *m'* thee desolate.
37:19 of Judah, and *m'* them one stick,
22 will *m'* them one nation in the land
26 I will *m'* a covenant of peace with
39: 7 So will I *m'* my holy name known
42:20 to *m'* a separation between the
43:18 in the day when they shall *m'* it,
27 the priests shall *m'* your burnt
44:14 I will *m'* them keepers of the charge
45:15 to *m'* reconciliation for them,
17 to *m'* reconciliation for the house of
Da 1:10 shall ye *m'* me endanger my head
2: 5, 9 *m'* known unto me the dream,
25 will *m'* known unto the king the
26 able to *m'* known unto me the dream
30 shall *m'* known the interpretation
3:29 Therefore I *m'* a decree, that
4: 6 might *m'* known...the interpretation
7 not *m'* known...the interpretation
18 *m'* known unto me the interpretation:
25, 32 shall *m'* thee to eat grass as oxen,
5: 8 nor *m'* known to the king the
15 *m'* known unto me the interpretation
16 thou canst *m'* interpretations, and
16 *m'* known to me the interpretation
17 *m'* known to him the interpretation.
6: 7 statute, and to *m'* a firm decree,
26 I *m'* a decree, That in every
8:16 *m'* this man to understand the vision.
19 *m'* thee know what shall be in the last
9:24 and to *m'* an end of sins, and to
24 to *m'* reconciliation for iniquity,
27 he shall *m'* it desolate, even until
10:14 *m'* thee understand what shall befall
11: 6 of the north to *m'* an agreement:
35 to purge, and to *m'* them white,
44 and utterly to *m'* away many.
Ho 2: 3 and *m'* her as a wilderness, and
6 and *m'* a wall, that she shall not
12 and I will *m'* them a forest, and
18 day will I *m'* a covenant for them
18 and will *m'* them to lie down safely.
5: 2 are profound to *m'* slaughter,
7: 3 They *m'* the king glad with their
10:11 I will *m'* Ephraim to ride; Judah shall
11: 8 how shall I *m'* thee as Admah?
12: 1 *m'* a covenant with the Assyrians,
9 yet *m'* thee to dwell in tabernacles,
Joe 2:19 no more *m'* you a reproach among
Am 6:10 *m'* mention of the name of the Lord.
8: 4 even to *m'* the poor of the land to fail,
10 I will *m'* it as the mourning of an
9:14 they shall also *m'* gardens, and
Mic 1: 6 I will *m'* Samaria as an heap of

Mic 1: 8 will *m'* a wailing like the dragons,
16 *M'* thee bald, and poll thee for thy
2:12 they shall *m'* great noise by reason
3: 5 the prophets that *m'* my people err,
4: 4 none shall *m'* them afraid: for the
7 will *m'* her that halted a remnant,
13 Zion: for I will *m'* thine horn iron,
13 I will *m'* thy hoofs brass: and thou
6:13 also will I *m'* thee sick in smiting
16 that I should *m'* thee a desolation,
Na 1: 8 will *m'* an utter end of the place
9 he will *m'* an utter end: affliction
14 I will *m'* thy grave; for thou art
2: 1 *m'* thy loins strong, fortify thy
5 shall *m'* haste to the wall thereof,
3: 6 filth upon thee, and *m'* thee vile,
14 morter, *m'* strong the brickkiln.
15 *m'* thyself many as the cankerworm,
15 *m'* thyself many as the locusts.
Hab 2: 2 and *m'* it plain upon the tables,
18 trusteth therein, to *m'* dumb idols?
3: 2 in the midst of the years *m'* known;
19 he will *m'* my feet like hinds' feet,
19 he will *m'* me to walk upon mine high
Zep 1:18 he shall *m'* even a speedy riddance
2:13 will *m'* Nineveh a desolation, and
3:13 and none shall *m'* them afraid.
20 I will *m'* you a name and a praise
Hag 2:23 will *m'* thee as a signet: for I have
Zec 6:11 silver and gold, and *m'* crowns,
9:15 and *m'* a noise as through wine;
17 shall *m'* the young men cheerful,
10: 1 Lord shall *m'* bright clouds, and
12: 2 *m'* Jerusalem a cup of trembling
3 *m'* Jerusalem a burdensome stone
6 *m'* the governors of Judah like an
Mal 2:15 And did not he *m'* one? Yet had he
3:17 that day when I *m'* up my jewels;
M't 1:19 to *m'* her a publick example, was
3: 3 of the Lord, *m'* his paths straight.
4:19 and I will *m'* you fishers of men.
5:36 canst not *m'* one hair white or black.
8: 2 thou wilt, thou canst *m'* me clean.
12:16 they should not *m'* him known:
33 Either *m'* the tree good, and his
33 or else *m'* the tree corrupt, and his
17: 4 let us *m'* here three tabernacles;
22:44 I *m'* thine enemies thy footstool?
23: 5 they *m'* broad their phylacteries,
14 and for a pretence *m'* long prayer:
15 sea and land to *m'* one proselyte,
15 *m'* him twofold more the child of
25 *m'* clean the outside of the cup and
24:47 *m'* him ruler over all his goods.
25:21, 23 *m'* thee ruler over many things:
27:65 your way, *m'* it as sure as ye can.
M'r 1: 3 of the Lord, *m'* his paths straight.
17 *m'* you to become fishers of men.
40 thou wilt, thou canst *m'* me clean.
3:12 they should not *m'* him known.
5:39 Why *m'* ye this ado, and weep? the
6:39 *m'* all sit down by companies upon
9: 5 let us *m'* three tabernacles; one
12:36 I *m'* thine enemies thy footstool.
40 for a pretence *m'* long prayers:
42 in two mites, which *m'* a farthing.
14:15 prepared: there *m'* ready for us.
Lu 1:17 *m'* ready a people prepared for the
3: 4 of the Lord, *m'* his paths straight.
5:12 thou wilt, thou canst *m'* me clean.
33 of John fast often, and *m'* prayers,
34 *m'* the children of the bridechamber
9:14 *M'* them sit down by fifties in a
33 let us *m'* three tabernacles; one
52 Samaritans, to *m'* ready for him.
11:39 ye Pharisees *m'* clean the outside
40 *m'* that which is within also?
12:37 and *m'* them to sit down to meat,
42 whom his lord shall *m'* ruler over
44 that he will *m'* him ruler over all
14:18 one consent began to *m'* excuse.
31 to *m'* war against another king,
15:19 *m'* me as one of thy hired servants.
29 I might *m'* merry with my friends:
32 was meet that we should *m'* merry,
16: 9 *M'* to yourself friends of the
17: 8 *M'* ready wherewith I may sup,
19: 5 Zacchæus, *m'* haste, and come
20:43 I *m'* thine enemies thy footstool.
47 and for a shew *m'* long prayers:
22:12 room furnished: there *m'* ready.
Joh 1:23 *M'* straight the way of the Lord,
2:16 *m'* not my Father's house an house
6:10 Jesus said, *M'* the men sit down.
15 take him by force, to *m'* him a king,
8:32 and the truth shall *m'* you free.
36 the Son therefore shall *m'* you free,
10:24 long dost thou *m'* us to doubt?
14:23 him, and *m'* our abode with him.
Ac 2:28 shalt *m'* me full of joy with thy
35 Until I *m'* thy foes thy footstool.
7:40 Aaron, *M'* us gods to go before us:
44 *m'* it according to the fashion
9:34 thee whole: arise, and *m'* thy bed.
22: 1 my defence which I *m'* now unto you.
18 *M'* haste, and get thee quickly out
23:23 *M'* ready two hundred soldiers to
26:16 *m'* thee a minister and a witness
24 much learning doth *m'* thee mad.
Ro 1: 9 *m'* mention of you always in my
3: 3 *m'* the faith of God without effect?
31 then *m'* void the law through faith?
9:21 to *m'* one vessel unto honour,
22 wrath, and to *m'* his power known,
23 *m'* known the riches of his glory
28 short work will the Lord *m'* upon

Ro 13:14 and *m'* not provision for the flesh,
14: 4 for God is able to *m'* him stand.
19 the things which *m'* for peace,
15:18 *m'* the Gentiles obedient, by word
26 to *m'* a certain contribution for the
1Co 4: 5 will *m'* manifest the counsels of the
6:15 *m'* them the members of an harlot?
8:13 if meat *m'* my brother to offend,
13 lest I *m'* my brother to offend.
9:15 man should *m'* my glorying void.
18 *m'* the gospel of Christ without
10:13 temptation...*m'* a way to escape,
2Co 2: 2 For if I *m'* you sorry, who is he
9: 5 *m'* up beforehand your bounty,
8 God is able to *m'* all grace abound
10:12 dare not *m'* ourselves of the number,
12:17 Did I *m'* a gain of you by any of
18 Did Titus *m'* a gain of you? walked
Ga 2:18 I *m'* myself a transgressor.
3:17 *m'* the promise of none effect.
6:12 to *m'* a fair shew in the flesh,
Eph 2:15 to *m'* in himself of twain one new
3: 9 to *m'* all men see...the fellowship
6:19 to *m'* known the mystery of the
21 shall *m'* known to you all things:
Col 1:27 *m'* known what is the riches of the
4: 4 That I may *m'* it manifest, as I
9 *m'* known unto you all things
1Th 3:12 *m'* you to increase and abound in
2Th 3: 9 to *m'* ourselves an ensample unto
2Ti 3:15 able to *m'* thee wise unto salvation
4: 5 *m'* full proof of thy ministry.
Heb 1:13 I *m'* thine enemies thy footstool?
2:10 *m'* the captain of...salvation perfect
17 to *m'* reconciliation for the sins of
7:25 he ever liveth to *m'* intercession
8: 5 he was about to *m'* the tabernacle:
5 thou *m'* all things according to the
8 *m'* a new covenant with the house
10 this is the covenant that I will *m'*
9: 9 *m'* him that did the service perfect,
10: 1 *m'* the comers thereunto perfect.
16 This is the covenant that I will *m'*
12:13 *m'* straight paths for your feet,
13:21 *M'* you perfect in every good work
Jas 3:18 in peace of them that *m'* peace.
1Pe 5:10 *m'*...perfect, stablish, strengthen,
2Pe 1: 8 they *m'* you that ye shall neither
10 *m'* your calling and election sure:
2: 3 words *m'* merchandise of you:
1Jo 1:10 have not sinned, we *m'* him a liar,
Re 3: 9 I will *m'* them of the synagogue
9 will *m'* them to come and worship
12 will I *m'* a pillar in the temple of
10: 9 and it shall *m'* thy belly bitter,
11: 7 pit shall *m'* war against them,
10 rejoice over them, and *m'* merry,
12:17 went to *m'* war with the remnant
13: 4 who is able to *m'* war with him?
7 to *m'* war with the saints, and to
14 should *m'* an image to the beast,
17:14 These shall *m'* war with the Lamb,
16 shall *m'* her desolate and naked,
19:11 he doth judge and *m'* war.
19 to *m'* war against him that sat on
21: 5 said, Behold, I *m'* all things new.

maker See also MAKERS.
Job 4:17 a man be more pure than his *m'*?
32:22 my *m'* would soon take me away.
35:10 Where is God my *m'*, who giveth
36: 3 ascribe righteousness to my *M'*.
Ps 95: 6 us kneel before the Lord our *M'*.
Pr 14:31 the poor reproacheth his *M'*:
17: 5 the poor reproacheth his *M'*:
22: 2 the Lord is the *m'* of them all.
Isa 1:31 tow, and the *m'* of it as a spark,
17: 7 day shall a man look to his *M'*,
22:11 not looked unto the *m'* thereof,
45: 9 him that striveth with his *M'*!
11 the Holy One of Israel, and his *M'*,
51:13 And forgettest the Lord thy *m'*,
54: 5 For thy *M'* is thine husband; The
Jer 33: 2 Thus saith the Lord the *m'* thereof,
Ho 8:14 For Israel hath forgotten his *M'*,
Hab 2:18 the *m'* thereof hath graven it;
18 the *m'* of his work trusteth therein.
Heb 11:10 whose builder and *m'* is God.

makers See also PEACEMAKERS; TENTMAKERS.
Isa 45:16 together that are *m'* of idols.

makest
J'g 18: 3 and what *m'* thou in this place?
Job 13:26 *m'* me to possess the iniquities of
22: 3 him, that thou *m'* thy ways perfect?
Ps 4: 8 Lord, only *m'* me dwell in safety.
39:11 *m'* his beauty to consume away
44:10 Thou *m'* us to turn back from the
13 Thou *m'* us a reproach to our
14 Thou *m'* us a byword among the
65: 8 thou *m'* the outgoings of...to rejoice
10 thou *m'* it soft with showers:
80: 6 Thou *m'* us a strife unto our
104:20 Thou *m'* darkness, and it is night:
144: 3 man, that thou *m'* account of him!
Ca 1: 7 thou *m'* thy flock to rest at noon:
Isa 45: 9 that fashioned it, What *m'* thou?
Jer 22:23 that *m'* thy nest in the cedars,
28:15 thou *m'* this people to trust in a lie.
Eze 16:31 and *m'* thine high place in every
Hab 1:14 And *m'* men as the fishes of the sea,
2:15 to him, and *m'* him drunken also,
Lu 14:12 When thou *m'* a dinner or a supper,
13 when thou *m'* a feast, call the poor,
Joh 8:53 are dead: whom *m'* thou thyself?
10:33 thou, being a man, *m'* thyself God.

Ro 2:17 the law, and *m'* thy boast of God,
23 Thou that *m'* thy boast of the law,

maketh
Ex 4:11 who *m'* the dumb, or deaf, or the
Le 7: 7 the priest that *m'* atonement
14:11 the priest that *m'* him clean shall
17:11 blood that *m'* an atonement for the
De 18:10 *m'* his son or his daughter to pass
20:20 the city that *m'* war with thee,
21:16 *m'* his sons to inherit that which
24: 7 and *m'* merchandise of him, or
27:15 man that maketh any graven or
18 be he that *m'* the blind to wander out
29:12 the Lord thy God *m'* with thee this
1Sa 2: 6 The Lord killeth, and *m'* alive:
7 The Lord *m'* poor, and *m'* rich:
2Sa 22:33 power: and he *m'* my way perfect.
34 He *m'* my feet like hinds' feet: and
Job 5:18 For he *m'* sore, and bindeth up: he
9: 9 Which *m'* Arcturus, Orion, and
12:17 spoiled, and *m'* the judges fools.
25 *m'* them to stagger like a drunken
15:27 *m'* collops of fat on his flanks.
23:16 For God *m'* my heart soft, and the
25: 2 he *m'* peace in his high places.
27:18 and as a booth that the keeper *m'*.
35:11 and *m'* us wiser than the fowls of
36:27 he *m'* small the drops of water:
41:31 He *m'* the deep to boil like a pot: he
31 *m'* the sea like a pot of ointment.
32 He *m'* a path to shine after him; one
Ps 9:12 When he *m'* inquisition for blood,
18:32 strength, and *m'* my way perfect.
33 He *m'* my feet like hinds' feet, and
23: 2 He *m'* me to lie down in green
29: 6 He *m'* them also to skip like a calf;
9 voice of the Lord *m'* the hinds to calve,
33:10 *m'* the devices of the people of none
40: 4 man that *m'* the Lord his trust,
46: 9 He *m'* wars to cease unto the end
104: 3 who *m'* the clouds his chariot:
4 Who *m'* his angels spirits; his
15 wine that *m'* glad the heart of
107:29 He *m'* the storm a calm, so that
36 there he *m'* the hungry to dwell,
41 and *m'* him families like a flock.
113: 9 He *m'* the barren woman to keep
135: 7 he *m'* lightnings for the rain;
147: 8 who *m'* grass to grow upon the
14 He *m'* peace in thy borders, and
Pr 10: 1 A wise son *m'* a glad father: but a
4 the hand of the diligent *m'* rich.
22 The blessing of the Lord, it *m'* rich,
12: 4 she that *m'* ashamed is as rottenness
25 in the heart of man *m'* it stoop:
25 but a good word *m'* it glad.
13: 7 There is that *m'* himself rich, yet
7 there is that *m'* himself poor, yet
12 Hope deferred *m'* the heart sick:
15:13 A merry heart *m'* a cheerful
20 A wise son *m'* a glad father: but a
30 a good report *m'* the bones fat.
16: 7 he *m'* even his enemies to be at peace
18:16 A man's gift *m'* room for him, and
19: 4 Wealth *m'* many friends; but the
28:20 he that *m'* haste to be rich shall not
31:22 She *m'* herself coverings of
24 She *m'* fine linen, and selleth it;
Ec 3:11 can find out the work that God *m'*
7: 7 oppression *m'* a wise man mad;
8: 1 man's wisdom *m'* his face to shine,
10:19 made for laughter, and wine *m'* merry:
11: 5 not the works of God who *m'* all.
Isa 19:17 every one that *m'* mention thereof
24: 1 the Lord *m'* the earth empty,
1 and *m'* it waste, and turneth it upside
27: 9 he *m'* all the stones of the altar
40:23 he *m'* the judges of the earth as
43:16 Lord, which *m'* a way in the sea,
44:13 *m'* it after the figure of a man,
15 he *m'* a god, and worshippeth it;
15 he *m'* it a graven image, and
17 the residue thereof he *m'* a god,
24 I am the Lord that *m'* all things;
25 of the liars, and *m'* diviners mad;
25 and *m'* their knowledge foolish;
46: 6 a goldsmith; and he *m'* it a god:
55:10 *m'* it bring forth and bud, that it
59:15 departeth from evil *m'* himself a prey:
Jer 4:19 my heart *m'* a noise in me;
10:13 he *m'* lightnings with rain, and
17: 5 trusteth in man, and *m'* flesh his arm,
21: 2 king of Babylon *m'* war against us;
29:26 that is mad, and *m'* himself a prophet,
27 which *m'* himself a prophet to you?
48:28 dove that *m'* her nest in the sides
51:16 he *m'* lightnings with rain, and
Eze 22: 3 *m'* idols against herself to defile
Da 2:28 and *m'* known to the king
29 *m'* known to thee what shall come
6:13 *m'* his petition three times a day.
11:31 the abomination that *m'* desolate.
12:11 the abomination that *m'* desolate set
Am 4:13 that *m'* the morning darkness,
5: 8 that *m'* the seven stars and Orion,
8 and *m'* the day dark with night:
Na 1: 4 He rebuketh the sea, and *m'* it dry,
M't 5:45 for he *m'* his son to rise on the evil
M'r 7:37 he *m'* both the deaf to hear, and
Lu 5:36 then both the new *m'* a rent, and
Joh 19:12 whosoever *m'* himself a king
Ac 9:34 Jesus Christ *m'* thee whole:
Ro 5: 5 hope *m'* not ashamed; because
8:26 Spirit itself *m'* intercession for us
27 he *m'* intercession for the saints
34 who also *m'* intercession for us.
Ro 11: 2 he *m'* intercession to God against
1Co 4: 7 For who *m'* thee to differ from
2Co 2: 2 who is he then that *m'* me glad,
14 and *m'* manifest the savour of his
Ga 2: 6 they were, it *m'* no matter to me:
Eph 4:16 *m'* increase of the body unto the
Heb 1: 7 Who *m'* his angels spirits, and his
7:28 law *m'* men high priests which
28 *m'* the Son, who is consecrated for
Re 13:13 he *m'* fire come down from heaven
21:27 worketh abomination, or *m'* a lie:
22:15 and whosoever loveth and *m'* a lie.

Makheloth (*mak'-he-loth*)
Nu 33:25 from Haradah, and pitched in *M'*.
26 And they removed from *M'*, and

making
Ex 5:14 not fulfilled your task in *m'* brick
De 20:19 time, in *m'* war against it to take it,
J'g 19:22 they were *m'* their hearts merry,
1Ki 4:20 and drinking, and *m'* merry.
1Ch 15:28 *m'* a noise with psalteries and
17:19 *m'* known all these great things.
2Ch 30:22 *m'* confession to the Lord God of
Ps 19: 7 Lord is sure, *m'* wise the simple.
Ec 12:12 *m'* many books there is no end;
Isa 3:16 and *m'* a tinkling with their feet:
Jer 20:15 born unto thee; *m'* him very glad.
Eze 27:16 multitude of the wares of thy *m'*:
18 multitude of the wares of thy *m'*,
Da 6:11 and *m'* supplication before his God.
Ho 10: 4 swearing falsely in *m'* a covenant:
Am 8: 5 *m'* the ephah small, and the shekel
Mic 6:13 in *m'* thee desolate because of thy
M't 9:23 and the people *m'* a noise,
M'r 7:13 *M'* the word of God of none effect
Joh 5:18 Father, *m'* himself equal with God.
Ro 1:10 *M'* request, if by any means now
2Co 6:10 as poor, yet *m'* many rich; as
Eph 1:16 *m'* mention of you in my prayers;
2:15 twain one new man, so *m'* peace;
5:19 and *m'* melody in your heart to the
Ph'p 1: 4 for you all *m'* request with joy,
1Th 1: 2 *m'* mention of you in our prayers;
Ph'm 4 *m'* mention of thee always in my
2Pe 2: 6 *m'* them an ensample unto those
Jude 22 have compassion, *m'* a difference:

Makkedah (*mak'-ke-dah*)
Jos 10:10 them to Azekah, and unto *M'*.
16 and hid themselves in a cave at *M'*.
17 kings are found hid in a cave at *M'*.
21 the camp to Joshua at *M'* in peace:
28 And that day Joshua took *M'*, and
28 he did to the king of *M'* as he did
29 Then Joshua passed from *M'*, and
12:16 The king of *M'*, one; the king of
15:41 Beth-dagon, and Naamah, and *M'*;

Maktesh (*mak'-tesh*)
Zep 1:11 Howl, ye inhabitants of *M'*, for all

Malachi (*mal'-a-ki*)
Mal 1: 1 word of the Lord to Israel by *M'*.

Malcham (*mal'-kam*) See also MILCOM.
1Ch 8: 9 and Zibia, and Mesha, and *M'*,
Zep 1: 5 the Lord, and that swear by *M'*;

Malchiah (*mal-ki'-ah*) See also MALCHIJAH; MELCHIAH.
1Ch 6:40 son of Baaseiah, the son of *M'*,
Ezr 10:25 and Jeziah, and *M'*, and Miamin,
31 Eliezer, Ishijah, *M'*, Shemaiah,
Ne 3:14 the dung gate repaired *M'* the son
31 him repaired *M'* the goldsmith's
8: 4 Pedaiah, and Mishael, and *M'*,
11:12 the son of Pashur, the son of *M'*,
Jer 38: 1 and Pashur the son of *M'*, heard
6 and cast him into the dungeon of *M'*

Malchiel (*mal'-ke-el*) See also MALCHIELITES.
Ge 46:17 sons of Beriah; Heber, and *M'*.
Nu 26:45 *M'*, the family of the Malchielites.
1Ch 7:31 sons of Beriah; Heber, and *M'*,

Malchielites (*mal'-ke-el-ites*)
Nu 26:45 Malchiel, the family of the *M'*.

Malchijah (*mal-ki'-jah*) See also MALCHIAH.
1Ch 9:12 the son of Pashur, the son of *M'*,
24: 9 The fifth to *M'*, the sixth to
Ezr 10:25 and Eleazar, and *M'*, and Benaiah.
Ne 3:11 *M'* the son of Harim, and Hashub
10: 3 Pashur, Amariah, *M'*,
12:42 Jehohanan, and *M'*, and Elam, and

Malchiram (*mal'-ki-ram*)
1Ch 3:18 *M'* also, and Pedaiah, and

Malchi-shua (*mal''-ki-shu'-ah*) See also MELCHI-SHUA.
1Ch 8:33 Saul begat Jonathan, and *M'*,
9:39 Saul begat Jonathan, and *M'*,
10: 2 and Abinadab, and *M'*, the sons of

Malchus (*mal'-kus*)
Joh 18:10 ear. The servant's name was *M'*.

male See also MALES.
Ge 1:27 *m'* and female created he them.
5: 2 *M'* and female created he them;
6:19 thee; they shall be *m'* and female.
7: 2 by sevens, the *m'* and his female:
2 clean by two, the *m'* and his female.
3 by sevens, the *m'* and the female;
9 into the ark, the *m'* and the female,
16 went in *m'* and female of all flesh,
17:23 every *m'* among the men of
34:15 every *m'* of you be circumcised;
22 every *m'* among us be circumcised,
24 and every *m'* was circumcised, all
Ex 12: 5 blemish, a *m'* of the first year:
Ex 34:19 whether ox or sheep, that is *m'*.
Le 1: 3 him offer a *m'* without blemish:
10 shall bring it a *m'* without blemish.
3: 1 whether it be a *m'* or a female, he
6 Lord be of the flock; *m'* or female,
4:23 the goats, a *m'* without blemish:
7: 6 Every *m'* among the priests shall
12: 7 her that hath born a *m'* or a female.
22:19 own will a *m'* without blemish,
27: 3 of the *m'* from twenty years old
5 shall be of the *m'* twenty shekels,
6 be of the *m'* five shekels of silver,
7 if it be a *m'*, then thy estimation
Nu 1: 2 names, every *m'* by their polls;
20, 22 every *m'* from twenty years old
3:15 every *m'* from a month old and
5: 3 Both *m'* and female shall be put
18:10 every *m'* shall eat it: it shall be
31:17 kill every *m'* among the little ones,
De 4:16 figure, the likeness of *m'* or female,
7:14 be *m'* or female barren among you,
20:13 shalt smite every *m'* thereof with
Jos 17: 2 *m'* children of Manasseh the son
J'g 21:11 Ye shall utterly destroy every *m'*,
12 no man by lying with any *m'*:
1Ki 11:15 he had smitten every *m'* in Edom;
16 he had cut off every *m'* in Edom:)
Mal 1:14 which hath in his flock a *m'*, and
M't 19: 4 made them *m'* and female,
M'r 10: 6 God made them *m'* and female.
Lu 2:23 Every *m'* that openeth the womb
Ga 3:28 free, there is neither *m'* nor female:

malefactor See also MALEFACTORS.
Joh 18:30 If he were not a *m'*, we would not

malefactors
Lu 23:32 *m'*, led with him to be put to death.
33 they crucified him, and the *m'*,
39 one of the *m'* which were hanged

Maleleel (*mal'-e-le-el*) See also MAHALALEEL.
Lu 3:37 which was the son of *M'*, which

males
Ge 34:25 the city boldly, and slew all the *m'*.
Ex 12:48 let all his *m'* be circumcised, and
13:12 hast; the *m'* shall be the Lord's.
15 that openeth the matrix, being *m'*;
23:17 all thy *m'* shall appear before the
Le 6:18 All the *m'* among the children of
29 the *m'* among the priests shall eat
Nu 3:22 to the number of all the *m'*, from a
28 In the number of all the *m'*, from a
34 to the number of all the *m'*, from a
39 *m'* from a month old and upward,
40 Number all the firstborn of the *m'*
43 the firstborn *m'* by the number of
26:62 *m'* from a month old and upward:
31: 7 Moses; and they slew all the *m'*.
De 15:19 firstling *m'* that come of thy herd
16:16 all thy *m'* appear before the Lord
Jos 5: 4 came out of Egypt, that were *m'*,
2Ch 31:16 Beside their genealogy of *m'*, from
19 to give portions to all the *m'* among
Ezr 8: 3 reckoned by genealogy of the *m'* an
4 and with him two hundred *m'*.
5 and with him three hundred *m'*.
6 of Jonathan, and with him fifty *m'*.
7 Athaliah, and with him seventy *m'*.
8 Michael, and with him fourscore *m'*.
9 him two hundred and eighteen *m'*.
10 him an hundred and threescore *m'*.
11 and with him twenty and eight *m'*.
12 with him an hundred and ten *m'*.
13 and with him threescore *m'*.
14 Zabbud, and with him seventy *m'*.

malice
1Co 5: 8 the leaven of *m'* and wickedness;
14:20 howbeit in *m'* be ye children, but in
Eph 4:31 be put away from you, with all *m'*;
Col 3: 8 anger, wrath, *m'*, blasphemy,
Tit 3: 3 living in *m'* and envy, hateful, and
1Pe 2: 1 laying aside all *m'*, and all guile,

malicious
3Jo 10 prating against us with *m'* words:

maliciousness
Ro 1:29 wickedness, covetousness, *m'*;
1Pe 2:16 using your liberty for a cloke of *m'*,

malignity
Ro 1:29 envy, murder, debate, deceit, *m'*;

Mallothi (*mal'-lo-thi*)
1Ch 25: 4 Romamti-ezer, Joshbekashah, *M'*,
26 The nineteenth to *M'*, he, his sons,

mallows
Job 30: 4 Who cut up *m'* by the bushes,

Malluch (*mal'-luk*) See also MELICU.
1Ch 6:44 the son of Abdi, the son of *M'*,
Ezr 10:29 the sons of Bani; Meshullam, *M'*,
32 Benjamin, *M'*, and Shemariah.
Ne 10: 4 Hattush, Shebaniah, *M'*,
27 *M'*, Harim, Baanah.
12: 2 Amariah, *M'*, Hattush,

mammon (*mam'-mon*)
M't 6:24 Ye cannot serve God and *m'*.
Lu 16: 9 friends of the *m'* of unrighteousness;
11 been faithful in the unrighteous *m'*,
13 other. Ye cannot serve God and *m'*.

Mamre (*mam'-re*)
Ge 13:18 came and dwelt in the plain of *M'*,
14:13 in the plain of *M'* the Amorite,
24 with me, Aner, Eshcol, and *M'*;
18: 1 unto him in the plains of *M'*:
23:17 Machpelah, which was before *M'*,
19 of the field of Machpelah before *M'*

Ge 25: 9 the Hittite, which is before M':
35: 27 came unto Isaac his father unto M',
49: 30 Machpelah, which is before M',
50: 13 of Ephron the Hittite, before M'.

man^A See also BONDMAN; CRAFTSMAN; DAYSMAN; FREEMAN; HARVESTMAN; HERDMAN; HORSEMAN; HUSBANDMAN; KINSMAN; MAN'S; MANSERVANT; MANSLAYER; MANKIND; MEN; NOBLEMAN; PLOWMAN; SPOKESMAN; WATCHMAN; WOMAN; WORKMAN.

Ge 1: 26 said, Let us make m' in our image,
27 So God created m' in his own image,
2: 5 there was not a m' to till the ground.
7 Lord God formed m' of the dust of
7 of life; and m' became a living soul.
8 he put the m' whom he had formed.
15 the Lord God took the m', and put
16 the Lord God commanded the m',
18 good that the m' should be alone;
22 the Lord God had taken from m',
22 woman, and brought her unto the m'.
23 because she was taken out of M'.
24 shall a m' leave his father and his
25 both naked, the m' and his wife,
3: 12 the m' said, The woman whom thou
22 m' is become as one of us, to know
24 So he drove out the m'; and he
4: 1 I have gotten a m' from the Lord.
23 I have slain a m' to my wounding,
23 and a young m' to my hurt.
5: 1 In the day that God created m', in
6: 3 shall not always strive with m',
5 that the wickedness of m' was great,
6 repented the Lord...he had made m'
7 will destroy m' whom I have created
7 both m', and beast, and the creeping
9 Noah was a just m' and perfect in
7: 21 upon the earth, and every m':
23 both m', and cattle, and the creeping
9: 5 I require it, and at the hand of m';
5 brother will I require the life of m'.
6 blood, by m' shall his blood be shed:
6 for in the image of God made he m'.
13: 16 if a m' can number the dust of the
16: 12 And he will be a wild m'; his hand
12 his hand will be against every m', and
17: 10 Every m' child among you shall
12 every m' child in your generations,
14 the uncircumcised m' child whose
18: 7 good, and gave it unto a young m';
19: 8 which have not known m';
9 And they pressed sore upon the m',
31 not a m' in the earth to come in unto
20: 7 therefore restore the m' his wife;
24: 16 neither had any m' known her:
21 m' wondering at her held his peace,
22 the m' took a golden earring of half
26 And the m' bowed down his head,
29 and Laban ran out unto the m', unto
30 saying, Thus spake the m' unto me;
30 that he came unto the m'; and,
32 And the m' came into the house:
58 unto her, Wilt thou go with this m'?
61 the camels, and followed the m':
65 m' is this that walketh in the field
25: 8 old age, an old m', and full of years;
27 a cunning hunter, a m' of the field;
27 and Jacob was a plain m', dwelling
26: 11 He that toucheth this m' or his wife
13 m' waxed great, and went forward,
27: 11 is a hairy m', and I am a smooth m':
29: 19 that I should give her to another m':
30: 43 And the m' increased exceedingly,
31: 50 my daughters, no m' is with us;
32: 24 there wrestled a m' with him until
34: 19 the young m' deferred not to do the
25 brethren, took each m' his sword,
37: 15 And a certain m' found him, and,
15 and the m' asked him, saying, What
17 And the m' said, They are departed
38: 25 By the m', whose these are, am I
39: 2 Joseph, and he was a prosperous m';
40: 5 them, each m' his dream in one night,
5 m' according to the interpretation
41: 11 m' according to the interpretation
12 there was there with us a young m',
12 each m' according to his dream he
33 look out a m' discreet and wise,
38 a m' in whom the Spirit of God is?
44 shall no m' lift up his hand or foot in
42: 13 twelve brethren, the sons of one m'
30 The m', who is the lord of the land,
33 the m', the lord of the country, said
43: 3 The m' did solemnly protest unto us,
5 the m' said unto us, Ye shall not see
6 as to tell the m' whether ye had yet a
7 m' asked us straitly of our state,
11 carry down the m' a present, a little
13 and arise, go again unto the m':
14 God...give you mercy before the m',
17 And the m' did as Joseph bade;
17, 24 m' brought the men into Joseph's
27 well, the old m' of whom ye spake?
44: 11 took down every m' his sack to the
11 and opened every m' his sack.
13 clothes, and laded every m' his ass,
15 such a m' as I can certainly divine?
17 but the m' in whose hand the cup is
20 We have a father, an old m', and a
45: 1 Cause every m' to go out from me.
1 there stood no m' with him, while
22 he gave each m' changes of raiment;
47: 20 Egyptians sold every m' his field,
49: 6 for in their anger they slew a m',
Ex 1: 1 every m' and his household came
2: 1 there went a m' of the house of Levi,

Ex 2: 12 when he saw that there was no m',
20 why is it that ye have left the m'?
21 was content to dwell with the m':
7: 12 For they cast down every m' his rod,
8: 17 it became lice in m', and in beast;
18 were lice upon m', and upon beast.
9: 9, 10 forth with blains upon m', and
19 for upon every m' and beast which
22 hail in all the land of Egypt, upon m',
25 was in the field, both m' and beast;
10: 7 long shall this m' be a snare unto us?
11: 2 every m' borrow of his neighbour,
3 m' Moses was very great in the land
7 a dog move his tongue, against m' or
12: 3 shall take to them every m' a lamb,
4 m' according to his eating shall
12 firstborn...both m' and beast;
16 save that which every m' must eat,
13: 2 both of m' and of beast: it is mine.
13 firstborn of m' among thy children
15 of Egypt, both the firstborn of m',
15: 3 The Lord is a m' of war: the Lord
16: 16 it every m' according to his eating,
16 an omer for every m', according
16 take ye every m' for them which are
18 every m' according to his eating.
19 no m' leave of it till the morning.
21 every m' according to his eating:
22 much bread, two omers for one m':
29 m' in his place, let no m' go out of
19: 13 whether it be beast or m', it shall
21: 7 And if a m' sell his daughter to be a
12 He that smiteth a m', so that he die,
13 And if a m' lie not in wait, but God
14 a m' come presumptuously upon his
16 he that stealeth a m', and selleth
20 And if a m' smite his servant, or his
26 if a m' smite the eye of his servant,
28 If an ox gore a m' or a woman, that
29 that he hath killed a m' or a woman;
33 And if a m' shall open a pit, or if
33 a m' shall dig a pit, and not cover it,
22: 1 If a m' shall steal an ox, or a sheep,
5 If a m' shall cause a field or
7 If a m'...deliver unto his neighbour
10 If a m' deliver unto his neighbour
10 hurt, or driven away, no m' seeing it:
14 And if a m' borrow ought of his
16 And if a m' entice a maid that is not
23: 3 shalt thou countenance a poor m' in
24: 14 if any m' have any matters to do,
25: 2 of every m' that giveth it willingly
30: 12 give every m' a ransom for his soul
32: 1, 23 the m' that brought us up out of
27 Put every m' his sword by his side,
27 camp, and slay every m' his brother,
27 and every m' his companion,
27 and every m' his neighbour.
29 every m' upon his son, and upon his
33: 4 no m' did put on him his ornaments.
8 stood every m' at his tent door, and
10 worshipped, every m' in his tent door.
11 as a m' speaketh unto his friend.
11 the son of Nun, a young m', departed
20 face: for there shall no m' see me,
34: 3 And no m' shall come up with thee,
3 neither let...m' be seen throughout
24 neither shall any m' desire thy land,
35: 22 every m' that offered offered an
23, 24 every m', with whom was found
29 every m' and woman, whose heart
36: 1 every wise hearted m', in whom the
2 and every wise hearted m', in whose
4 came every m' from his work which
6 Let neither m' nor woman make any
8 every wise hearted m' among them
38: 26 A bekah for every m', that is, half
Le 1: 2 m' of you bring an offering unto
5: 3 Or if he touch the uncleanness of m',
3 be that a m' shall be defiled withal,
4 a m' shall pronounce with an oath,
6: 3 of all these that a m' doeth, sinning
7: 21 as the uncleanness of m', or any
12: 2 conceived seed,...born a m' child:
13: 2 a m' shall have in the skin of his
9 the plague of leprosy is in a m', then
29 If a m' or woman have a plague
38 If a m' also or a woman have in the
40 m' whose hair is fallen off his head,
44 He is a leprous m', he is unclean:
14: 11 present the m' that is to be clean,
15: 2 When any m' hath a running issue
18 The woman also with whom m' shall
24 if any m' lie with her at all, and her
33 of the m', and of the woman, and
16: 17 shall be no m' in the tabernacle of
21 away by the hand of a fit m' in the
17: 3 What m' soever there be of the house
4 shall be imputed unto that m'; he
4 that m' shall be cut off from among
8 Whatsoever m' there be of the house
9 even that m' shall be cut off from
10 whatsoever m' there be of the house
13 And whatsoever m' there be of the
18: 5 which if a m' do, he shall live in
19: 3 Ye shall fear every m' his mother,
32 honour the face of the old m', and
20: 3 I will set my face against that m',
4 ways hide their eyes from the m',
5 I will set my face against that m',
10 m' that committeth adultery with
11 m' that lieth with his father's wife
12 if a m' lie with his daughter in law,
13 If a m' also lie with mankind, as he
14 if a m' take a wife and her mother,
15 And if a m' lie with a beast, he shall

Le 20: 17 And if a m' shall take his sister, his
18 if a m' shall lie with a woman having
20 if a m' shall lie with his uncle's wife,
21 if a m' shall take his brother's wife,
27 A m' also or woman that hath a
21: 4 being a chief m' among his people,
18 m' he be that hath a blemish, he
18 a blind m', or a lame, or he that hath
19 Or a m' that is brokenfooted, or
21 No m' that hath a blemish of the
22: 4 What m' soever of the seed of Aaron
4 or a m' whose seed goeth from him;
5 or a m' of whom he may take
14 And if a m' eat of the holy thing
24: 10 a m' of Israel strove together in the
17 And he that killeth any m' shall 5315,
19 m' cause a blemish in his
20 he hath caused a blemish in a m',
21 he that killeth a m', he shall be put
25: 10 return every m' unto his possession,
10 return every m' unto his family;
13 return every m' unto his possession.
26 And if the m' have none to redeem it,
27 restore the overplus unto the m' to
29 And if a m' sell a dwelling house in a
33 And if a m' purchase of the Levites,
27: 2 a m' shall make a singular vow, the
9 all that any m' giveth of such unto
14 when a m' shall sanctify his house
16 if a m' shall sanctify unto the Lord
20 he have sold the field to another m',
22 And if a m' sanctify unto the Lord a
26 firstling, no m' shall sanctify it;
28 that a m' shall devote unto the Lord
28 that he hath, both of m' and beast,
31 m' will at all redeem ought of his
Nu 1: 4 there shall be a m' of every tribe;
52 tents, every m' by his own camp,
52 and every m' by his own standard,
2: 2 Every m' of the children of Israel
17 m' in his place by their standards.
3: 13 in Israel, both m' and beast:
5: 6 m' or woman shall commit any sin
8 But if the m' have no kinsman to
10 whatsoever any m' giveth the priest,
13 a m' lie with her carnally, and it be
15 the m' bring his wife unto the priest,
19 If no m' have lain with thee, and if
20 some m' have lain with thee beside
31 the m' be guiltless from iniquity,
6: 2 either m' or woman shall separate
9 if any m' die very suddenly by him,
7: 5 every m' according to his service.
8: 17 Israel are mine, both m' and beast:
9: 6 defiled by the dead body of a m',
7 are defiled by the dead body of a m':
10 if any m' of you or of your posterity
13 But the m' that is clean, and is not
13 season, that m' shall bear his sin.
11: 10 every m' in the door of his tent:
27 there ran a young m', and told Moses,
12: 3 the m' Moses was very meek, above
13: 2 of their fathers shall ye send a m',
14: 15 shalt kill all this people as one m',
15: 32 a m' that gathered sticks upon the
35 The m' shall be surely put to death:
16: 7 the m' whom the Lord doth choose,
17 take every m' his censer, and put
17 before the Lord every m' his censer,
18 they took every m' his censer, and
22 shall one m' sin, and wilt thou be
17: 9 looked, and took every m' his rod.
18: 15 firstborn of m' shalt thou surely
19: 9 a m' that is clean shall gather up the
11 the dead body of any m' shall be
13 dead body of any m' that is dead,
14 the law, when a m' dieth in a tent:
16 or a dead body, or a bone of a m',
20 But the m' that shall be unclean,
21: 9 if a serpent had bitten any m',
23: 19 God is not a m', that he should lie;
19 neither the son of m', that he should
24: 3, 15 the m' whose eyes are open hath1
25: 8 he went after the m' of Israel into
8 the m' of Israel, and the woman
26: 64 there was not a m' of them whom
65 there was not left a m' of them, save
27: 8 If a m' die, and have no son, then ye
16 flesh, set a m' over the congregation,
18 a m' in whom is the spirit, and lay
30: 2 If a m' vow a vow unto the Lord, or
16 Moses, between a m' and his wife,
31: 17 hath known m' by lying with 376,
18 not known a m' by lying with him,
26 was taken, both of m' and of beast,
35 not known m' by lying with him.
47 both of m' and of beast, and gave
49 and there lacketh not one m' of us.
50 what every m' hath gotten, of jewels
53 taken spoil, every m' for himself.)
32: 18 inherited every m' his inheritance.
27 pass over, every m' armed for war,
29 every m' armed to battle, before the
35: 23 any stone, wherewith a m' may die,
36: 8 enjoy every m' the inheritance of his
De 1: 16 between every m' and his brother,
17 shall not be afraid of the face of m';
31 as a m' doth bear his son, in all the
41 had girded on every m' his weapons
3: 11 breadth of it, after the cubit of a m'.
20 return every m' unto his possession,
4: 32 the day that God created m' upon
5: 24 that God doth talk with m', and he
7: 24 shall no m' be able to stand before
8: 3 m' doth not live by bread only, but
3 the mouth of the Lord doth m' live.

De 8: 5 as a *m'* chasteneth his son, so the
11: 25 shall no *m'* be able to stand before
12: 8 every *m'* whatsoever is right in his
15: 7 If there be among you a poor *m'*
12 if thy brother, an Hebrew *m'*, or an
16: 17 Every *m'* shall give as he is able,
17: 2 *m'* or woman, that hath wrought
5 bring forth that *m'* or that woman,
5 even that *m'* or that woman, and
12 the *m'* that will do presumptuously,
12 the judge, even that *m'* shall die:
19: 5 As when a *m'* goeth into the wood with
11 But if any *m'* hate his neighbour,
15 rise up against a *m'* for any iniquity,
16 false witness rise up against any *m'*
20: 5 What *m'* is there that hath built a
5 battle, and another *m'* dedicate it.
6 what *m'* is he that hath planted a
6 the battle, and another *m'* eat of it.
7 what *m'* is there that hath betrothed
7 the battle, and another *m'* take her.
8 What *m'* is there that is fearful and
21: 3 city which is next unto the slain *m'*,
6 city, that are next unto the slain *m'*,
15 If a *m'* have two wives, one beloved,
18 *m'* have a stubborn and rebellious
22 If a *m'* have committed a sin worthy
22: 5 that which pertaineth unto a *m'*,
5 a *m'* put on a woman's garment:
8 house, if any *m'* fall from thence.
13 If any *m'* take a wife, and go in unto
16 my daughter unto this *m'* to wife,
18 shall take that *m'* and chastise him;
22 If a *m'* be found lying with a woman
22 the *m'* that lay with the woman, and
23 *m'* find her in the city, and lie with
24 the *m'*, because he hath humbled his
25 a *m'* find a betrothed damsel in the
25 the *m'* force her, and lie with her:
25 *m'* only that lay with her shall die:
26 a *m'* riseth against his neighbour,
28 a *m'* find a damsel that is a virgin,
29 *m'* that lay with her shall give unto
30 A *m'* shall not take his father's wife,
23: 10 among you any *m'*, that is not clean
24: 1 a *m'* hath taken a wife, and married
5 When a *m'* hath taken a new wife,
6 No *m'* shall take the nether or the
7 If a *m'* be found stealing any of his
11 *m'* to whom thou dost lend shall
12 And if the *m'* be poor, thou shalt not
16 every *m'* shall be put to death for his
25: 2 the wicked *m'* be worthy to be beaten,
7 *m'* like not to take his brother's wife,
9 be done unto that *m'* that will not
27: 15 Cursed be the *m'* that maketh any
28: 26 earth, and no *m'* shall fray them away.
29 evermore, and no *m'* shall save thee.
30 and another *m'* shall lie with her:
54 the *m'* that is tender among you,
68 bondwomen, and no *m'* shall buy you.
29: 18 Lest there should be among you *m'*,
20 shall smoke against that *m'*, and
32: 25 destroy both the young *m'* and the
25 also with the *m'* of gray hairs.
33: 1 *m'* of God blessed the children of
34: 6 but no *m'* knoweth of his sepulchre
Jos 1: 5 shall not any *m'* be able to stand
2: 11 remain any more courage in any *m'*,
3: 12 of Israel, out of every tribe a *m'*.
4: 2 the people, out of every tribe a *m'*,
4 of Israel, out of every tribe a *m'*:
5 take ye up every *m'* of you a stone
5: 13 stood a *m'* over against him with a
6: 5 up every *m'* straight before him.
20 every *m'* straight before him, and
21 was in the city, both *m'* and woman,
26 Cursed be the *m'* before the Lord,
7: 14 shall take shall come *m'* by *m'*.
17 family of the Zarhites *m'* by *m'*;
18 he brought his household *m'* by *m'*;
8: 17 And there was not a *m'* left in Ai or
31 which no *m'* hath lifted up any iron:
10: 8 there shall not a *m'* of them stand
14 hearkened unto the voice of a *m'*:
11: 14 every *m'* they smote with the edge
14: 6 Lord said unto Moses the *m'* of God
15 was a great *m'* among the Anakims.
17: 1 he was a *m'* of war, therefore he
21: 44 stood not a *m'* of all their enemies
22: 20 and that *m'* perished not alone in
23: 9 no *m'* hath been able to stand before
10 One *m'* of you...chase a thousand:
24: 28 every *m'* unto his inheritance.
J'g 1: 24 spies saw a *m'* come forth out of the
25 they let go the *m'* and all his family.
26 And the *m'* went into the land of the
2: 6 went every *m'* unto his inheritance
3: 15 Gera, a Benjamite, a *m'* lefthanded:
17 Moab: and Eglon was a very fat *m'*.
28 and suffered not a *m'* to pass over.
29 valour; and there escaped not a *m'*.
4: 16 sword; and there was not a *m'* left.
20 when any *m'* doth come and enquire
20 say, Is there any *m'* here? that thou
22 I will shew thee the *m'* whom thou
5: 30 to every *m'* a damsel or two; to
6: 12 is with thee, thou mighty *m'* of valour.
16 smite the Midianites as one *m'*.
7: 7 people go every *m'* unto his place.
8 rest of Israel every *m'* unto his tent,
13 was a *m'* that told a dream unto his
14 the son of Joash, a *m'* of Israel:
21 stood every *m'* in his place round
8: 14 a young *m'* of the men of Succoth,
21 for as the *m'* is, so is his strength.
J'g 8: 24 give me every *m'* the earrings of his
25 cast therein every *m'* the earrings
9: 9 by me they honour God and *m'*,
13 my wine, which cheereth God and *m'*,
49 cut down every *m'* his bough, and
54 unto the young *m'* his armourbearer,
54 And his young *m'* thrust him through,
55 departed every *m'* unto his place.
10: 1 the son of Dodo, a *m'* of Issachar;
18 What *m'* is he that will begin to
11: 1 Gileadite was a mighty *m'* of valour,
39 had vowed: and she knew no *m'*.
13: 2 there was a certain *m'* of Zorah, of
6 saying, A *m'* of God came unto me,
8 the *m'* of God which thou didst send
10 the *m'* hath appeared unto me, that
11 came to the *m'*, and said unto him,
11 Art thou the *m'* that spakest unto
16: 7, 11 be weak, and be as another *m'*.
17 weak, and be like any other *m'*.
19 she called for a *m'*, and she caused
17: 1 there was a *m'* of mount Ephraim,
5 the *m'* Micah had an house of gods,
6 every *m'* did that which was right
7 a young *m'* out of Beth-lehem-judah
8 And the *m'* departed out of the city
11 was content to dwell with the *m'*;
11 the young *m'* was unto him as one of
12 and the young *m'* became his priest,
18: 3 they knew the voice of the young *m'*
7 and had no business with any *m'*.
15 came to the house of the young *m'*
19 a priest unto the house of one *m'*,
28 they had no business with any *m'*;
19: 6 damsel's father...said unto the *m'*,
7, 9 when the *m'* rose up to depart,
10 the *m'* would not tarry that night,
15 no *m'* that took them into his house
16 there came an old *m'* from his work
17 saw a wayfaring *m'* in the street of
17 and the old *m'* said, Whither goest
18 is no *m'* that receiveth me to house.
19 for the young *m'* which is with thy
20 And the old *m'* said, Peace be with
22 the master of the house, the old *m'*,
22 the *m'* that came into thine house,
23 And the *m'*, the master of the house,
23 this *m'* is come into mine house,
24 unto this *m'* do not so vile a thing.
25 so the *m'* took his concubine, and
28 the *m'* took her up upon an ass,
28 the *m'* rose up, and gat him unto his
20: 1 was gathered together as one *m'*,
8 And all the people arose as one *m'*,
11 the city, knit together as one *m'*.
21: 11 every woman that hath lain by *m'*.
12 had known no *m'* by lying with any
21 catch you every *m'* his wife of the
22 not to each *m'* his wife in the war:
24 every *m'* to his tribe and to his
24 thence every *m'* to his inheritance.
25 every *m'* did that which was right in
Ru 1: 1 a certain *m'* of Beth-lehem-judah
2 the name of the *m'* was Elimelech,
2: 1 husband's, a mighty *m'* of wealth,
20 The *m'* is near of kin unto us, one of
3: 3 make not thyself known unto the *m'*,
8 that the *m'* was afraid, and turned
16 told her all that the *m'* had done to
18 for the *m'* will not be in rest, until
4: 7 a *m'* plucked off his shoe, and gave
1Sa 1: 1 Now there was a certain *m'* of
3 And this *m'* went up out of his city
11 unto thine handmaid a *m'* child,
21 the *m'* Elkanah, and all his house,
2: 9 for by strength shall no *m'* prevail.
13 when any *m'* offered sacrifice, the
15 said to the *m'* that sacrificed, Give
16 if any *m'* said unto him, Let them
25 If one *m'* sin against another, the
25 but if a *m'* sin against the Lord, who
27 there came a *m'* of God unto Eli,
31 shall not be an old *m'* in thine house.
32 not be an old *m'* in thine house for
33 And the *m'* of thine, whom I shall
4: 10 and they fled every *m'* into his tent:
12 ran a *m'* of Benjamin out of the army,
13 when the *m'* came into the city, and
14 And the *m'* came in hastily, and told
16 the *m'* said unto Eli, I am he that
18 for he was an old *m'*, and heavy.
8: 22 Israel, Go ye every *m'* unto his city.
9: 1 Now there was a *m'* of Benjamin,
1 a Benjamite, a mighty *m'* of power.
2 was Saul, a choice young *m'*, and a
6 there is in this city a *m'* of God,
6 he is an honourable *m'*; all that he
7 if we go, what shall we bring the *m'*?
7 a present to bring to the *m'* of God:
8 that will I give to the *m'* of God, to
9 when a *m'* went to enquire of God,
10 the city where the *m'* of God was.
16 I will send thee a *m'* out of the land
17 the *m'* whom I spake to thee of!
10: 6 and shalt be turned into another *m'*.
22 if the *m'* should yet come thither.
25 people away, every *m'* to his house.
27 said, How shall this *m'* save us?
11: 3 if there be no *m'* to save us, we will
13 shall not be a *m'* put to death this
13: 2 people he sent every *m'* to his tent.
14 sought him a *m'* after his own heart,
20 to sharpen every *m'* his share, and
14: 1 the son of Saul said unto the young *m'*
6 Jonathan said to the young *m'* that
24 Cursed be the *m'* that eateth any
1Sa 14: 26 but no *m'* put his hand to his mouth:
28 Cursed be the *m'* that eateth any
34 *m'* his ox, and every *m'* his sheep,
34 brought every *m'* his ox with him
36 and let us not leave a *m'* of them.
39 was not a *m'* among all the people
52 and when Saul saw any strong *m'*,
52 or any valiant *m'*, he took him
15: 3 slay both *m'* and woman, infant and
29 for he is not a *m'*, that he should
16: 7 for the Lord seeth not as *m'* seeth;
7 for *m'* looketh on the outward
16 to seek out a *m'*, who is a cunning
17 Provide me now a *m'* that can play
18 in playing, and a mighty valiant *m'*,
18 and a *m'* of war, and prudent in
17: 8 choose you a *m'* for you, and let him
10 give me a *m'*, that we may fight
12 the *m'* went among men for an old
12 went among men for an old *m'* in the
24 when they saw the *m'*, fled from him,
25 ye seen this *m'* that is come up?
25 the *m'* who killeth him, the king
26 be done to the *m'* that killeth this
27 be done to the *m'* that killeth him.
33 and he a *m'* of war from his youth.
41 *m'* that bare the shield went before
58 Whose son art thou, thou young *m'*?
18: 23 am a poor *m'*, and lightly esteemed?
20: 22 if I say thus unto the young *m'*,
21: 1 thou alone, and no *m'* with thee?
2 Let no *m'* know any thing of the
7 a certain *m'* of the servants of Saul
14 Lo, ye see the *m'* is mad: wherefore
15 this fellow to play the mad *m'* in my
24: 19 if a *m'* find his enemy, will he let
25: 2 And there was a *m'* in Maon, whose
2 and the *m'* was very great, and he
3 Now the name of the *m'* was Nabal;
3 the *m'* was churlish and evil in his
10 away every *m'* from his master.
13 men, Gird ye on every *m'* his sword.
13 they girded on every *m'* his sword;
17 Belial, that a *m'* cannot speak to him.
25 pray thee, regard this *m'* of Belial,
29 Yet a *m'* is risen to pursue thee,
26: 12 they gat them away, and no *m'* saw it,
15 Abner, Art not thou a valiant *m'*?
23 The Lord render to every *m'* his
27: 3 every *m'* with his household, even
9 and left neither *m'* nor woman alive,
11 saved neither *m'* nor woman alive,
28: 14 An old *m'* cometh up; and he is
30: 6 every *m'* for his sons and for his
13 I am a young *m'* of Egypt, servant
17 there escaped not a *m'* of them,
22 save to every *m'* his wife and his
2Sa 1: 2 a *m'* came out of the camp from Saul
5 said unto the young *m'* that told him,
6 the young *m'* that told him said, As I
13 said unto the young *m'* that told him,
2: 3 up, every *m'* with his household:
3: 34 as a *m'* falleth before wicked men,
38 a great *m'* fallen this day in Israel?
7: 19 is this the manner of *m'*, O Lord
12: 2 rich *m'* had exceeding many flocks
3 But the poor *m'* had nothing, save one
4 came a traveller unto the rich *m'*,
4 to dress for the wayfaring *m'* that
4 dressed it for the *m'* that was come
5 was greatly kindled against the *m'*;
5 *m'* that hath done this thing shall
7 said to David, Thou art the *m'*.
13: 3 and Jonadab was a very subtil *m'*.
9 they went out every *m'* from him.
29 every *m'* gat him up upon his mule,
34 And the young *m'* that kept the watch
14: 16 out of the hand of the *m'* that would
21 bring the young *m'* Absalom again.
15: 2 any *m'* that had a controversy came
3 is no *m'* deputed of the king to hear
4 every *m'* which hath any suit or
5 that when any *m'* came nigh to him
30 with him covered every *m'* his head,
16: 5 thence came out a *m'* of the family
7 thou bloody *m'*, and thou *m'* of Belial:
8 because thou art a bloody *m'*.
23 as if a *m'* had enquired at the oracle
17: 3 the *m'* whom thou seekest is as if all
8 thy father is a *m'* of war, and will
10 that thy father is a mighty *m'*, and
18: 5 gently for my sake with the young *m'*,
10 a certain *m'* saw it, and told Joab,
11 Joab said unto the *m'* that told him,
12 And the *m'* said unto Joab, Though I
12 none touch the young *m'* Absalom.
24 and behold a *m'* running alone.
26 watchman saw another *m'* running:
26 Behold another *m'* running alone.
27 He is a good *m'*, and cometh with
29 said, Is the young *m'* Absalom safe?
32 Cushi, Is the young *m'* Absalom safe?
32 do thee hurt, be as that young *m'* is.
19: 8 Israel had fled every *m'* to his tent.
14 Judah, even as the heart of one *m'*;
22 any *m'* be put to death this day in
32 Barzillai was a very aged *m'*, even
32 for he was a very great *m'*.
20: 1 happened to be there a *m'* of Belial,
1 every *m'* to his tents, O Israel.
2 So every *m'* of Israel went up from
12 when the *m'* saw that all the people
21 a *m'* of mount Ephraim, Sheba the
22 from the city, every *m'* to his tent.
21: 4 for us shalt thou kill any *m'* in Israel.
5 The *m'* that consumed us, and that

2Sa 21:20 was a m' of great stature, that had
22:26 upright m' thou wilt shew thyself
49 delivered me from the violent m'.
23: 1 the m' who was raised up on high,
7 m' that shall touch them must be
20 the son of a valiant m', of Kabzeel,
21 he slew an Egyptian, a goodly m':
24:14 let me not fall into the hand of m'.
1Ki 1: 6 and he also was a very goodly m';
42 thou art a valiant m', and bringest
49 rose up, and went every m' his way.
52 he will shew himself a worthy m',
2: 2 therefore, and shew thyself a m';
4 a m' on the throne of Israel.
9 for thou art a wise m', and knowest
4: 7 each m' his month in a year made
25 every m' under his vine and under
27 table, every m' in his month:
28 every m' according to his charge.
7:14 and his father was a m' of Tyre, a
8:25 shall not fail thee a m' in my sight
31 m' trespass against his neighbour,
38 supplication...be made by any m',
38 shall know every m' the plague of
39 give to every m' according to his
46 (for there is no m' that sinneth not,)
9: 5 not fail thee a m' upon the throne
10:25 they brought every m' his present,
11:28 And the m' Jeroboam was a mighty
28 Jeroboam was a mighty m' of valour.
28 young m' that he was industrious,
12:22 came unto Shemaiah the m' of God,
24 return every m' to his house; for
13: 1 there came a m' of God out of Judah,
4 heard the saying of the m' of God,
5 sign which the m' of God had given
6 said unto the m' of God, Intreat
6 the m' of God besought the Lord,
7 the king said unto the m' of God,
8 the m' of God said unto the king,
11 works that the m' of God had done
12 seen what way the m' of God went,
14 went after the m' of God, and found
14 Art thou the m' of God that camest
21 cried unto the m' of God that came
26 he said, It is the m' of God, who was
29 took up the carcase of the m' of God,
31 wherein the m' of God is buried;
14:10 as a m' taketh away dung, till it be all
17:18 to do with thee, O thou m' of God?
24 I know that thou art a m' of God,
20: 7 and see how this m' seeketh mischief:
20 And they slew every one his m':
24 every m' out of his place, and put
28 there came a m' of God, and spake
35 m' of the sons of the prophets said
35 And the m' refused to smite him.
37 Then he found another m', and said,
37 the m' smote him, so that in smiting
39 and, behold, a m' turned aside,
39 and brought a m' unto me, and said,
39 Keep this m': if by any means he be
42 hand a m' whom I appointed to utter
22: 8 There is yet one m', Micaiah the son
17 them return every m' to his house in
34 certain m' drew a bow at a venture,
36 Every m' to his city, and every m' to
2Ki 1: 6 came a m' up to meet us, and said
7 What manner of m' was he which
8 He was an hairy m', and girt with
9 Thou m' of God, the king hath said,
10 If I be a m' of God, then let fire come
11 O m' of God, thus hath the king said,
12 I be a m' of God, let fire come down
13 O m' of God, I pray thee, let my life,
3:25 of land cast every m' his stone,
4: 7 she came and told the m' of God.
9 that this is an holy m' of God,
16 Nay, my lord, thou m' of God, do not
21 laid him on the bed of the m' of God,
22 that I may run to the m' of God,
25 came unto the m' of God to mount
25 when the m' of God saw her afar off,
27 when she came to the m' of God to
27 the m' of God said, Let her alone;
29 if thou meet any m', salute him not;
40 O thou m' of God, there is death in
42 came a m' from Baal-shalisha,
42 and brought the m' of God bread of
5: 1 was a great m' with his master,
1 he was also a mighty m' in valour,
7 that this m' doth send unto me to
7 me to recover a m' of his leprosy?
8 Elisha the m' of God had heard that
14 to the saying of the m' of God:
15 he returned to the m' of God, he and
20 the servant of Elisha the m' of God,
26 m' turned again from his chariot
6: 2 take thence every m' a beam, and
6 the m' of God said, Where fell it?
9 the m' of God sent unto the king of
10 which the m' of God told him and
15 servant of the m' of God was risen
17 opened the eyes of the young m';
19 bring you to the m' whom ye seek.
32 the king sent a m' from before him:
7: 2 king leaned answered the m' of God,
5 Syria, behold, there was no m' there.
10 and, behold, there was no m' there,
10 neither voice of m', but horses tied,
17 he died, as the m' of God had said,
18 as the m' of God had spoken to the
19 that lord answered the m' of God,
8: 2 after the saying of the m' of God:
4 Gehazi the servant of the m' of God,
7 saying, The m' of God is come hither.
2Ki 8: 8 meet the m' of God, and enquire of
11 ashamed: and the m' of God wept.
9: 4 So the young m', even the young m'
11 said unto them, Ye know the m',
13 took every m' his garment, and put
10:21 was not a m' left that came not.
11: 8 every m' with his weapons in his
9 and they took every m' his men that
11 every m' with his weapons in his
12: 4 the money that every m' is set at,
5 every m' of his acquaintance:
13:19 the m' of God was wroth with him,
21 to pass, as they were burying a m',
21 they cast the m' into the sepulchre of
21 and when the m' was let down, and
14: 6 every m' shall be put to death for
12 and they fled every m' to their tents.
15:20 of each m' fifty shekels of silver,
18:21 on which if a m' lean, it will go into
31 eat ye every m' of his own vine, and
21:13 wipe Jerusalem as a m' wipeth a dish,
22:15 Tell the m' that sent you to me,
23:10 that no m' might make his son or
16 which the m' of God proclaimed,
17 It is the sepulchre of the m' of God,
18 alone; let no m' move his bones.
1Ch 11:22 the son of a valiant m' of Habzeel,
23 Egyptian, a m' of great stature, five
12: 4 a mighty m' among the thirty, and
28 Zadok, a young m' mighty of valour,
16: 3 both m' and woman, to every one a
21 He suffered no m' to do them wrong:
43 departed every m' to his house:
17:17 to the estate of a m' of high degree,
20: 6 where was a m' of great stature,
21:13 let me not fall into the hand of m'.
22: 9 to thee, who shall be a m' of rest;
23: 3 number by their polls, m' by m',
14 concerning Moses the m' of God,
27:32 counsellor, a wise m', and a scribe:
28: 3 because thou hast been a m' of war,
21 workmanship every willing skilful m',
29: 1 for the palace is not for m', but for
2Ch 2: 7 Send...a m' cunning to work in gold,
13 And now I have sent a cunning m',
14 his father was a m' of Tyre, skilful
6: 5 chose I any m' to be ruler over my
16 not fail thee a m' in my sight to sit
22 If a m' sin against his neighbour,
29 soever shall be made of any m',
30 m' according unto all his ways,
36 there is no m' which sinneth not,)
7:18 shall not fail thee a m' to be ruler
8:14 David the m' of God commanded.
9:24 they brought every m' his present,
10:16 every m' to your tents, O Israel: and
11: 2 came to Shemaiah the m' of God,
4 return every m' to his house: for
14:11 let not m' prevail against thee.
15:13 or great, whether m' or woman.
17:17 Eliada a mighty m' of valour, and
18: 7 There is yet one m', by whom we
16 every m' to his house in peace.
33 certain m' drew a bow at a venture,
33 therefore he said to his chariot m',
19: 6 for ye judge not for m', but for the
20:27 every m' of Judah and Jerusalem,
23: 7 every m' with his weapons in his
8 took every m' his men that were to
10 every m' having his weapon in his
25: 4 every m' shall die for his own sin.
7 But there came a m' of God to him,
9 Amaziah said to the m' of God, But
9 the m' of God answered, The Lord is
22 and they fled every m' to his tent.
28: 7 And Zichri, a mighty m' of Ephraim,
30:16 to the law of Moses the m' of God:
31: 1 returned, every m' to his possession,
2 every m' according to his service,
32:19 were the work of the hands of m'.
34:23 Tell ye the m' that sent you to me,
36:17 no compassion upon young m' or
17 or maiden, old m', or him that stooped
Ezr 3: 1 together as one m' to Jerusalem.
2 in the law of Moses the m' of God.
8:18 brought us a m' of understanding,
Ne 1:11 him mercy in the sight of this m'.
2:10 was come a m' to seek the welfare
12 told I any m' what my Lord had put
5:13 shake out every m' from his house
6:11 I said, Should such a m' as I flee?
7: 2 for he was a faithful m', and feared
8: 1 themselves together as one m' into
9:29 (which if a m' do, he shall live in
12:24 of David the m' of God, ward over
36 instruments of David the m' of God,
Es 1:22 every m' should bear rule in his own
4:11 whether m' or woman, shall come
5:12 did let no m' come in with the king
6: 6, 7 the m' whom the king delighteth
9 they may array the m' withal whom
9 Thus shall it be done to the m'
11 Thus shall it be done unto the m'
8: 8 the king's ring, may no m' reverse.
9: 2 no m' could withstand them; for
4 this m' Mordecai waxed greater and
Job 1: 1 was a m' in the land of Uz, whose
1 and that m' was perfect and upright,
3 this m' was the greatest of all the
8 a perfect and an upright m', one
2: 3 perfect and an upright m', one that
4 all that a m' hath will he give for his
3: 3 said, There is a m' child conceived.
23 given to a m' whose way is hid,
4:17 Shall mortal m' be more just than
17 shall a m' be more pure than his
Job 5: 2 For wrath killeth the foolish m', and
7 Yet m' is born unto trouble, as the
17 Behold, happy is the m' whom God
7: 1 appointed time to m' upon earth?
17 What is m', that thou shouldest
8:20 God will not cast away a perfect m',
9: 2 how should m' be just with God?
32 For he is not a m', as I am, that I
10: 4 of flesh? or seest thou as m' seeth?
5 Are thy days as the days of m'?
11: 2 should a m' full of talk be justified?
3 shall no m' make thee ashamed?
12 For vain m' would be wise, though
12 m' be born like a wild ass's colt.
12: 4 just upright m' is laughed to scorn.
14 he shutteth up a m', and there can
25 them to stagger like a drunken m'.
13: 9 or as one m' mocketh another, do
14: 1 M' that is born of a woman is of
10 But m' dieth, and wasteth away:
10 m' giveth up the ghost, and where
12 So m' lieth down, and riseth not:
14 If a m' die, shall he live again? all
19 and thou destroyest the hope of m'.
15: 2 a wise m' utter vain knowledge,
7 thou the first m' that was born? or
14 What is m', that he should be
16 more abominable and filthy is m',
20 The wicked m' travaileth with pain
28 houses which no m' inhabiteth, which
16:21 one might plead for a m' with God,
21 as a m' pleadeth for his neighbour!
17:10 I cannot find one wise m' among you.
20: 4 old, since m' was placed upon earth,
21 shall no m' look for his goods.
29 the portion of a wicked m' from God,
21: 4 As for me, is my complaint to m'?
33 every m' shall draw after him, as
22: 2 Can a m' be profitable unto God,
8 But as for the mighty m', he had
8 and the honourable m' dwelt in it.
24:22 he riseth up, and no m' is sure of life.
25: 4 then can m' be justified with God?
6 How much less m', that is a worm?
6 the son of m', which is a worm?
27:13 the portion of a wicked m' with God,
19 The rich m' shall lie down, but he
28:13 M' knoweth not the price thereof;
28 unto m' he said, Behold, the fear of
32: 8 But there is a spirit in m': and the
13 God thrusteth him down, not m'.
21 let me give flattering titles unto m'.
33:12 thee, that God is greater than m'.
14 yea twice, yet m' perceiveth it not.
17 may withdraw m' from his purpose,
17 purpose, and hide pride from m'.
23 to shew unto m' his uprightness:
26 render unto m' his righteousness.
29 worketh God oftentimes with m',
34: 7 What m' is like Job, who drinketh
9 It profiteth a m' nothing that he
11 work of a m' shall he render unto
11 cause every m' to find according
14 If he set his heart upon m', if he
15 and m' shall turn again unto dust.
21 his eyes are upon the ways of m',
23 not lay upon m' more than right;
29 a nation, or against a m' only:
34 let a wise m' hearken unto me.
35: 8 Thy wickedness may hurt a m' as
8 may profit the son of m'.
36:25 Every m' may see it;
25 m' may behold it afar off.
28 clouds do drop and distil upon m'
37: 7 He sealeth up the hand of every m';
20 if a m' speak, surely he shall be
38: 3 Gird up now thy loins like a m';
26 rain on the earth, where no m' is;
26 wilderness, wherein there is no m';
40: 7 Gird up thy loins now like a m':
42:11 every m' also gave him a piece of
Ps 1: 1 Blessed is the m' that walketh not
5: 6 abhor the bloody and deceitful m'.
8: 4 What is m', that thou art mindful
4 son of m', that thou visitest him?
9:19 Arise, O Lord; let not m' prevail:
10:15 arm of the wicked and the evil m':
18 m' of the earth...no more oppress.
18:25 with an upright m' thou wilt shew
48 delivered me from the violent m'.
19: 5 rejoiceth as a strong m' to run a race.
22: 6 But I am a worm, and no m'; a
25:12 What m' is he that feareth the Lord?
31:12 forgotten as a dead m' out of mind:
20 thy presence from the pride of m':
32: 2 Blessed is the m' unto whom the
33:16 mighty m' is not delivered by much
34: 6 poor m' cried, and the Lord heard
8 blessed is the m' that trusteth in
12 What m' is he that desireth life,
36: 6 Lord, thou preservest m' and beast.
37: 7 m' who bringeth wicked devices to
16 little that a righteous m' hath is better
23 steps of a good m' are ordered by
37 Mark the perfect m', and behold the
37 for the end of that m' is peace.
38:13 But I, as a deaf m', heard not; and I
13 I was as a dumb m' that openeth not
14 I was as a m' that heareth not, and
39: 5 m' at his best state is altogether
6 every m' walketh in a vain shew:
11 rebukes dost correct m' for iniquity,
11 a moth: surely every m' is vanity.
40: 4 Blessed is that m' that maketh the
43: 1 from the deceitful and unjust m'.
49:12 m' being in honour abideth not:

Ps 49:20 M' that is in honour, and
52: 1 thyself in mischief, O mighty m'?
7 this is the m' that made not God
55:13 But it was thou, a m' mine equal,
56: 1 God: for m' would swallow me up;
11 I will not be afraid what m' can do
58:11 So that a m' shall say, Verily there
60:11 trouble: for vain is the help of m'.
62: 3 ye imagine mischief against a m'?
12 to every m' according to his work.
65: 4 Blessed is the m' whom thou choosest,
71: 4 hand of the unrighteous and cruel m'.
74: 5 A m' was famous according as he had
22 the foolish m' reproacheth thee daily.
76:10 the wrath of m' shall praise thee:
78:25 M' did eat angels' food: he sent
65 and like a mighty m' that shouteth
80:17 be upon the m' of thy right hand,
17 the son of m' whom thou madest
84: 5 Blessed is the m' whose strength is
12 blessed is the m' that trusteth in
87: 4 Ethiopia; this m' was born there.
5 This and that m' was born in her:
6 people, that this m' was born there.
88: 4 am as a m' that hath no strength: 1
89:48 What m' is he that liveth, and shall
90: title A Prayer of Moses the m' of God.
3 Thou turnest m' to destruction;
92: 6 A brutish m' knoweth not; neither
94:10 he that teacheth m' knowledge,
11 Lord knoweth the thoughts of m',
12 is the m' whom thou chastenest,
103:15 As for m', his days are as grass:
104:14 and herb for the service of m':
15 that maketh glad the heart of m',
23 M' goeth forth unto his work and
105:14 He suffered no m' to do them wrong:
17 He sent a m' before them, even
107:27 fro, and stagger like a drunken m',
108:12 trouble: for vain is the help of m'.
109: 6 Set thou a wicked m' over him: and
16 persecuted the poor and needy m',
112: 1 Blessed is the m' that feareth the
5 A good m' sheweth favour, and
118: 6 not fear: what can m' do unto me?
8 Lord than to put confidence in m'.
119: 9 shall a young m' cleanse his way?
134 me from the oppression of m':
127: 4 are in the hand of a mighty m';
5 Happy is the m' that hath his
128: 4 shall the m' be blessed that feareth
135: 8 of Egypt, both of m' and beast.
140: 1 me, O Lord, from the evil m':
1, 4 preserve me from the violent m';
11 evil shall hunt the violent m' to
142: 4 there was no m' that would know me:
4 failed me; no m' cared for my soul.
143: 2 sight shall no m' living be justified.
144: 3 is m', that thou takest knowledge
3 or the son of m', that thou makest
4 M' is like to vanity: his days are
146: 3 son of m', in whom there is no help.
147:10 not pleasure in the legs of a m'.
Pr 1: 4 to the young m' knowledge and
5 wise m' will hear, and will increase
5 m' of understanding shall attain
24 out my hand, and no m' regarded;
2:12 thee from the way of the evil m',
12 m' that speaketh froward things;
3: 4 favour...in the sight of God and m'.
13 Happy is the m' that findeth wisdom,
13 the m' that getteth understanding.
30 Strive not with a m' without cause,
5:21 ways of m' are before the eyes of
6:11 and thy want as an armed m'.
12 A naughty person, a wicked m',
26 a m' is brought to a piece of bread:
27 Can a m' take fire in his bosom,
34 For jealousy is the rage of a m':
7: 7 a young m' void of understanding,
8: 4 and my voice is to the sons of m'.
34 Blessed is the m' that heareth me,
9: 7 he that rebuketh a wicked m' getteth
8 rebuke a wise m', and he will love
9 Give instruction to a wise m', and he
9 teach a just m', and he will increase
10:11 mouth of a righteous m' is a well of
23 m' of understanding hath wisdom.
11: 7 When a wicked m' dieth, his
12 m' of understanding holdeth his
17 merciful m' doeth good to his own
12: 2 A good m' obtaineth favour of the
2 but a m' of wicked devices will he
3 A m' shall not be established by
8 m' shall be commended according
10 A righteous m' regardeth the life of
14 A m' shall be satisfied with good
16 but a prudent m' covereth shame.
23 prudent m' concealeth knowledge:
25 Heaviness in the heart of m'
27 slothful m' roasteth not that which he
27 the substance of a diligent m' is
13: 2 m' shall eat good by the fruit of
5 A righteous m' hateth lying: but a
5 but a wicked m' is loathsome, and
16 prudent m' dealeth with knowledge:
22 A good m' leaveth an inheritance to
14: 7 from the presence of a foolish m',
12 way which seemeth right unto a m',
14 a good m' shall be satisfied from
15 prudent m' looketh well to his going.
16 A wise m' feareth, and departeth
17 a m' of wicked devices is hated.
15:18 A wrathful m' stirreth up strife: but
19 way of the slothful m' is as an hedge
20 a foolish m' despiseth his mother.
Pr 15:21 but a m' of understanding walketh
23 A m' hath joy by the answer of his
16: 1 The preparations of the heart in m',
2 ways of a m' are clean in his own
14 death: but a wise m' will pacify it.
25 way that seemeth right unto a m',
27 An ungodly m' diggeth up evil: and
28 A froward m' soweth strife: and a
29 A violent m' enticeth his neighbour,
17:10 a wise m' than an hundred stripes
11 An evil m' seeketh only rebellion:
12 robbed of her whelps meet a m',
18 A m' void of understanding striketh
23 A wicked m' taketh a gift out of the
27 and a m' of understanding is of an
28 shutteth his lips is esteemed a m' of
18: 1 Through desire a m', having
12 the heart of m' is haughty, and
14 The spirit of a m' will sustain his
24 A m' that hath friends must shew
19: 3 The foolishness of m' perverteth
6 and every m' is a friend to him that
11 The discretion of a m' deferreth his
19 A m' of great wrath shall suffer
22 The desire of a m' is his kindness:
22 and a poor m' is better than a liar.
24 A slothful m' hideth his hand in his
20: 3 honour for a m' to cease from strife:
5 in the heart of m' is like deep water;
5 a m' of understanding will draw it
6 but a faithful m' who can find?
7 The just m' walketh in his integrity:
17 Bread of deceit is sweet to a m';
24 how can a m' then understand his
25 is a snare to the m' who devoureth
27 spirit of m' is the candle of the Lord,
21: 2 way of a m' is right in his own
8 way of m' is froward and strange:
12 The righteous m' wisely considereth
16 The m' that wandereth out of the
17 loveth pleasure shall be a poor m':
20 but a foolish m' spendeth it up.
22 A wise m' scaleth the city of the
28 but the m' that heareth speaketh
29 A wicked m' hardeneth his face:
22: 3 A prudent m' foreseeth the evil, and
13 The slothful m' saith, There is a lion
24 no friendship with an angry m';
24 with a furious m' thou shalt not go:
29 thou a m' diligent in his business?
23: 2 if thou be a m' given to appetite.
21 drowsiness shall clothe a m' with rags.
24: 5 A wise m' is strong; yea,
5 yea, a m' of knowledge increaseth
12 to every m' according to his works?
16 For a just m' falleth seven times, and
20 shall be no reward to the evil m';
26 Every m' shall kiss his lips that
29 to the m' according to his work.
30 of the m' void of understanding;
34 and thy want as an armed m'.
25:18 A m' that beareth false witness
19 Confidence in an unfaithful m' in
26 A righteous m' falleth down before
26:12 thou a m' wise in his own conceit?
13 The slothful m' saith, There is a lion
18 As a mad m' who casteth firebrands,
19 m' that deceiveth his neighbour,
21 is a contentious m' to kindle strife.
27: 2 Let another m' praise thee, and not
8 m' that wandereth from his place.
12 A prudent m' foreseeth the evil, and
17 so a m' sharpeneth the countenance
19 to face, so the heart of m' to m'.
20 the eyes of m' are never satisfied.
21 for gold; so is a m' to his praise.
28: 1 The wicked flee when no m' pursueth:
2 but by a m' of understanding and
3 poor m' that oppresseth the poor
11 rich m' is wise in his own conceit;
12 the wicked rise, a m' is hidden.
14 Happy is the m' that feareth alway:
17 m' that doeth violence to the blood
20 A faithful m' shall abound with
21 of bread that m' will transgress.
23 He that rebuketh a m' afterwards
29: 5 m' that flattereth his neighbour
6 transgression of an evil m' there
9 m' contendeth with a foolish m',
11 wise m' keepeth it in till afterwards.
13 The poor and the deceitful m' meet
20 a m' that is hasty in his words?
22 An angry m' stirreth up strife, and
22 and a furious m' aboundeth in
25 fear of m' bringeth a snare: but
27 An unjust m' is an abomination to
30: 1 the m' spake unto Ithiel, even
2 I am more brutish than any m',
2 have not the understanding of a m'.
19 and the way of a m' with a maid.
Ec 1: 3 What profit hath a m' of all his
8 full of labour; m' cannot utter it:
13 God given to the sons of m' to be
2:12 what can the m' do that cometh
16 And how dieth the wise m'? as the
18 I should leave it unto the m' that
19 he shall be a wise m' or a fool? yet
21 is a m' whose labour is in wisdom,
21 yet to a m' that hath not laboured
22 For what hath m' of all his labour,
24 There is nothing better for a m',
26 to a m' that is good in his sight
3:11 no m' can find out the work that God
12 but for a m' to rejoice, and to do good
13 that every m' should eat and drink,
19 so that a m' hath no preeminence
Ec 3:21 Who knoweth the spirit of m' 1121,
22 a m' should rejoice in his own works;
4: 4 a m' is envied of his neighbour.
5:12 The sleep of a labouring m' is sweet,
19 m' also to whom God hath given
6: 2 m' to whom God hath given riches,
3 If a m' beget an hundred children,
7 labour of m' is for his mouth, and
10 already, and it is known that it is m':
11 vanity, what is m' the better?
12 what is good for m' in this life, all
12 who can tell a m' what shall be after
7: 5 for a m' to hear the song of fools.
7 oppression maketh a wise m' mad;
14 m' should find nothing after him.
15 there is a just m' that perisheth in
15 wicked m' that prolongeth his life in
20 there is not a just m' upon earth,
28 one m' among a thousand have I
29 that God hath made m' upright; but
8: 6 the misery of m' is great upon him.
8 is no m' that hath power over the
9 m' ruleth over another to his hurt.
15 a m' hath no better thing under the
17 a m' cannot find out the work that
17 though a m' labour to seek it out,
17 a wise m' think to know it, yet shall
9: 1 m' knoweth either love or hatred
12 For m' also knoweth not his time:
15 was found in it a poor wise m',
15 yet no m' remembered that same
15 remembered that same poor m'.
10:14 a m' cannot tell what shall be;
11: 8 But if a m' live many years, and
9 Rejoice, O young m', in thy youth; and
12: 5 because m' goeth to his long home,
13 for this is the whole duty of m'.
Ca 3: 8 every m' hath his sword upon his
8: 7 if a m' would give all the substance
Isa 2: 9 And the mean m' boweth down,
9 and the great m' humbleth himself:
11 lofty looks of m' shall be humbled,
17 loftiness of m' shall be bowed down,
20 In that day a m' shall cast his idols
22 Cease ye from m', whose breath is
3: 2 The mighty m', and the...of war,
2 The mighty..., and the m' of war,
3 the honourable m', and the counsellor,
6 a m' shall take hold of his brother
4: 1 women shall take hold of one m',
5:15 the mean m' shall be brought down,
15 the mighty m' shall be humbled,
6: 5 because I am a m' of unclean lips,
11 and the houses without m', and the
7:21 a m' shall nourish a young cow,
9:19 fire: no m' shall spare his brother.
20 eat every m' the flesh of his own
10:13 down the inhabitants like a valiant m':
13:12 I will make a m' more precious
12 even a m' than the golden wedge of
14 and as a sheep that no m' taketh up:
14 every m' turn to his own people,
14:16 m' that made the earth to tremble,
17: 7 day shall a m' look to his Maker,
19:14 drunken m' staggereth in his vomit.
24:10 is shut up, that no m' may come in.
29: 8 be as when an hungry m' dreameth,
8 or as when a thirsty m' dreameth, and,
21 make a m' an offender for a word,
31: 7 every m' shall cast away his idols
8 with the sword, not of a mighty m'.
8 the sword, not of a mean m', shall
32: 2 a m' shall be as an hiding place
33: 8 lie waste, the wayfaring m' ceaseth:
8 the cities, he regardeth no m'.
35: 6 shall the lame m' leap as an hart, and
36: 6 whereon if a m' lean, it will go into
38:11 I shall behold m' no more with the
41: 2 Who raised up the righteous m' from
28 For I beheld, and there was no m';
42:13 Lord shall go forth as a mighty m',
13 stir up jealousy like a m' of war:
44:13 maketh it after the figure of a m',
13 according to the beauty of a m';
15 Then shall it be for a m' to burn: for
45:12 the earth, and created m' upon it:
46:11 the m' that executeth my counsel
47: 3 and I will not meet thee as a m'.
49: 7 One, to him whom m' despiseth,
50: 2 when I came, was there no m'?
51:12 be afraid of a m' that shall die,
12 son of m' which shall be made as
52:14 was so marred more than any m',
53: 3 a m' of sorrows, and acquainted with
55: 7 the unrighteous m' his thoughts:
56: 2 Blessed is the m' that doeth this,
2 the son of m' that layeth hold on it;
57: 1 and no m' layeth it to heart:
58: 5 a day for a m' to afflict his soul?
59:16 he saw that there was no m', and
60:15 hated, so that no m' went through thee,
62: 5 For as a young m' marrieth a virgin,
65:20 an old m' that hath not filled his days:
66: 2 but to this m' will I look, even to him
3 killeth an ox is as if he slew a m';
7 she was delivered of a m' child.
Jer 2: 6 a land that no m' passed through,
6 through, and where no m' dwelt?
3: 1 If a m' put away his wife, and she
4:25 I beheld, and, lo, there was no m',
29 and not a m' dwell therein.
5: 1 if ye can find a m', if there be any
7: 5 between a m' and his neighbour;
20 this place, upon m', and upon beast,
8: 6 no m' repented...of his wickedness,
9:12 is the wise m', that may understand

Jer 9:23 not the wise *m'* glory in his wisdom,
23 let the mighty *m'* glory in his might,
23 let not the rich *m'* glory in his riches:
10:14 *m'* is brutish in his knowledge:
23 that the way of *m'* is not in himself:
23 it is not in *m'* that walketh to direct
11: 3 Cursed be the *m'* that obeyeth not
12:11 because no *m'* layeth it to heart.
15 them again, every *m'* to his heritage,
15 heritage, and every *m'* to his land.
13:11 girdle cleaveth to the loins of a *m'*,
14: 8 as a wayfaring *m'* that turneth aside
9 shouldest thou be as a *m'* astonied,
9 as a mighty *m'* that cannot save?
15:10 hast borne me a *m'* of strife and a
10 *m'* of contention to the whole earth!
16:20 Shall a *m'* make gods unto himself,
17: 5 Cursed be the *m'* that trusteth in
5 that trusteth in *m'*, and maketh
7 is the *m'* that trusteth in the Lord,
10 to give every *m'* according to his
18:14 Will a *m'* leave the snow of Lebanon
20:15 the *m'* who brought tidings to my
15 A *m'* child is born unto thee;
16 let that *m'* be as the cities which
21: 6 of this city, both *m'* and beast:
22: 8 shall say every *m'* to his neighbour,
28 Is this *m'* Coniah a despised broken
30 the Lord, Write ye this *m'* childless,
30 a *m'* that shall not prosper in his
30 for no *m'* of his seed shall prosper,
23: 9 I am like a drunken *m'*, and like
9 a *m'* whom wine hath overcome,
27 they tell every *m'* to his neighbour,
34 even punish that *m'* and his house.
26: 3 turn every *m'* from his evil way, that
11 This *m'* is worthy to die; for he hath
16 This *m'* is not worthy to die: for he
20 there was also a *m'* that prophesied
27: 5 the earth, the *m'* and the beast that
29:26 every *m'* that is mad, and maketh
32 shall not have a *m'* to dwell among
30: 6 see whether a *m'* doth travail with
6 *m'* with his hands on his loins,
17 is Zion, whom no *m'* seeketh after.
31:22 A woman shall compass a *m'*.
27 with the seed of *m'*, and with the
30 every *m'* that eateth the sour grape,
34 shall teach no more every *m'* his
34 neighbour, and every *m'* his brother.
32:43 It is desolate without *m'* or beast;
33:10 be desolate without *m'* and without
10 desolate, without *m'*, and without
12 is desolate without *m'* and without
17 David shall never want a *m'* to sit
18 Levites want a *m'* before me to offer
34: 9 every *m'* should let his manservant,
9 and every *m'* his maidservant, being
14 years let ye go every *m'* his brother
15 liberty every *m'* to his neighbour;
16 and caused every *m'* his servant,
16 and every *m'* his handmaid, whom
17 and every *m'* to his neighbour:
35: 4 son of Igdaliah, a *m'* of God, which
15 ye now every *m'* from his evil way,
19 not want a *m'* to stand before me
36: 3 return every *m'* from his evil way;
19 and let no *m'* know where ye be.
29 to cease from thence *m'* and beast?
37:10 they rise up every *m'* in his tent,
38: 4 thee, let this *m'* be put to death:
4 this *m'* seeketh not the welfare of
24 Let no *m'* know of these words, and
40:15 Nethaniah, and no *m'* shall know it:
41: 4 slain Gedaliah, and no *m'* knew it,
44: 2 and no *m'* dwelleth therein,
7 to cut off from you *m'* and woman,
26 be named in the mouth of any *m'* of
46: 6 flee away, nor the mighty *m'* escape;
12 the mighty *m'* hath stumbled against
49: 5 and ye shall be driven out every *m'*
18 the Lord, no *m'* shall abide there,
18 neither shall a son of *m'* dwell in it.
19 who is a chosen *m'*, that I may appoint
33 ever: there shall no *m'* abide there,
33 nor any son of *m'* dwell in it.
50: 3 they shall depart, both *m'* and beast.
9 shall be as of a mighty expert *m'*;
40 Lord; so shall no *m'* abide there,
40 shall any son of *m'* dwell therein.
42 put in array, like a *m'* to the battle,
44 who is a chosen *m'*, that I may appoint
51: 6 and deliver every *m'* his soul:
17 *m'* is brutish by his knowledge;
22 I break in pieces *m'* and woman;
22 in pieces the young *m'* and the maid;
43 a land wherein no *m'* dwelleth,
43 doth any son of *m'* pass thereby.
45 deliver ye every *m'* his soul from
62 remain in it, neither *m'* nor beast,
La 3: 1 I am the *m'* that hath seen affliction
26 It is good that a *m'* should both hope
27 good for a *m'* that he bear the yoke I
35 turn aside the right of a *m'* before
36 subvert a *m'* in his cause, the Lord
39 doth a living *m'* complain, a
39 *m'* for the punishment of his sins?
4: 4 and no *m'* breaketh it unto them.
Eze 1: 5 they had the likeness of a *m'*.
8 hands of a *m'* under their wings
10 faces, they four had the face of a *m'*,
26 appearance of a *m'* above upon it.
2: 1 Son of *m'*, stand upon thy feet, and
3 Son of *m'*, I send thee to the children
6 son of *m'*, be not afraid of them,
8 son of *m'*, hear what I say unto thee;

Eze 3: 1 Son of *m'*, eat that thou findest;
3 Son of *m'*, cause thy belly to eat,
4 Son of *m'*, go, get thee unto the house
10 Son of *m'*, all my words that I shall
17 Son of *m'*, I have made thee a
18 wicked *m'* shall die in his iniquity;
20 When a righteous *m'* doth turn from
21 if thou warn the righteous *m'*, that the
25 O son of *m'*, behold, they shall put
4: 1 son of *m'*, take thee a tile, and lay it
12 it with dung that cometh out of *m'*,
16 Son of *m'*, behold, I will break the
5: 1 son of *m'*, take thee a sharp knife,
6: 2 Son of *m'*, set thy face toward the
7: 2 thou son of *m'*, thus saith the Lord
8: 5 Son of *m'*, lift up thine eyes now the
6 Son of *m'*, seest thou what they do?
8 Son of *m'*, dig now in the wall: and
11 every *m'* his censer in his hand;
12 Son of *m'*, hast thou seen what the
12 every *m'* in the chambers of his
15, 17 thou seen this, O son of *m'*?
9: 1 *m'* with his destroying weapon in
2 every *m'* a slaughter weapon in his
2 and one *m'* among them was clothed
3 called to the *m'* clothed with linen,
6 come not near any *m'* upon whom
11 behold, the *m'* clothed with linen,
10: 2 spake unto the *m'* clothed with linen,
3 of the house, when the *m'* went in;
6 had commanded the *m'* clothed with
14 second face was the face of a *m'*,
21 the likeness of the hands of a *m'*
11: 2 Then said he unto me, Son of *m'*,
4 against them, prophesy, O son of *m'*.
15 Son of *m'*, thy brethren, even thy
12: 2 Son of *m'*, thou dwellest in the midst
3 thou son of *m'*, prepare thee stuff
9 Son of *m'*, hath not the house of
18 Son of *m'*, eat...bread with quaking,
22 Son of *m'*, what is that proverb that
27 Son of *m'*, behold, they of the house
13: 2 Son of *m'*, prophesy against the
17 thou son of *m'*, set thy face against
14: 3 Son of *m'*, these men have set up
4 Every *m'* of the house of Israel
8 I will set my face against that *m'*,
13 Son of *m'*, when the land sinneth
13 will cut off *m'* and beast from it:
15 no *m'* may pass through because of
17 that I cut off *m'* and beast from it:
19 to cut off from it *m'* and beast:
21 to cut off from it *m'* and beast?
15: 2 Son of *m'*, What is the vine tree
16: 2 Son of *m'*, cause Jerusalem to know
17: 2 Son of *m'*, put forth a riddle, and
18: 5 But if a *m'* be just, and do that
8 true judgment between *m'* and *m'*,
24 abominations that the wicked *m'* doeth,
26 a righteous *m'* turneth away from his
27 when the wicked *m'* turneth away from
20: 3 Son of *m'*, speak unto the elders of
4 Wilt thou judge them, son of *m'*,
7 ye away every *m'* the abominations
8 did not every *m'* cast away the
11, 13, 21 which if a *m'* do, he shall even
27 son of *m'*, speak unto the house of
46 Son of *m'*, set thy face toward the
21: 2 Son of *m'*, set thy face toward
6 Sigh therefore, thou son of *m'*, with
9 Son of *m'*, prophesy, and say, Thus
12 Cry and howl, son of *m'*: for it shall
14 Thou therefore, son of *m'*, prophesy,
19 thou son of *m'*, appoint thee two
28 And thou, son of *m'*, prophesy and
22: 2 Now, thou son of *m'*, wilt thou judge,
18 Son of *m'*, the house of Israel is to
24 Son of *m'*, say unto her, Thou art
30 I sought for a *m'* among them, that
23: 2 Son of *m'*, there were two women,
36 Son of *m'*, wilt thou judge Aholah
24: 2 Son of *m'*, write thee the name of
16 Son of *m'*, behold, I take away from
25 thou son of *m'*, shall it not be in the
25: 2 Son of *m'*, set thy face against the
13 will cut off *m'* and beast from it;
26: 2 Son of *m'*, because that Tyrus hath
27: 2 son of *m'*, take up a lamentation
28: 2 Son of *m'*, say unto the prince of
2 yet thou art a *m'*, and not God,
9 thou shalt be a *m'*, and no God, in
12 Son of *m'*, take up a lamentation
21 Son of *m'*, set thy face against
29: 2 Son of *m'*, set thy face against
8 and cut off *m'* and beast out of thee.
11 No foot of *m'* shall pass through it,
18 Son of *m'*, Nebuchadrezzar king of
30: 2 Son of *m'*, prophesy and say, Thus
21 Son of *m'*, I have broken the arm of
24 groanings of a deadly wounded *m'*.
31: 2 Son of *m'*, speak unto Pharaoh king
32: 2 Son of *m'*, take up a lamentation
10 every *m'* for his own life, in the day
13 shall the foot of *m'* trouble them
18 Son of *m'*, wail for the multitude of
33: 2 Son of *m'*, speak to the children of
2 the land take a *m'* of their coasts,
7 O Son of *m'*, I have set thee a
8 O wicked *m'*, thou shalt surely die;
8 wicked *m'* shall die in his iniquity;
10 O thou son of *m'*, speak unto the
12 thou son of *m'*, say unto the children
24 Son of *m'*, they that inhabit those
30 thou son of *m'*, the children of thy
34: 2 Son of *m'*, prophesy against the
35: 2 Son of *m'*, set thy face against

Eze 36: 1 thou son of *m'*, prophesy unto the
11 multiply upon you *m'* and beast;
17 Son of *m'*, when the house of Israel
37: 3 Son of *m'*, can these bones live?
9 prophesy, son of *m'*, and say to the
11 Son of *m'*, these bones are the whole
16 thou son of *m'*, take thee one stick,
38: 2 Son of *m'*, set thy face against Gog,
14 son of *m'*, prophesy and say unto
39: 1 thou son of *m'*, prophesy against
17 thou son of *m'*, thus saith the Lord
40: 3 there was a *m'*, whose appearance
4 And the *m'* said unto me,
4 Son of *m'*, behold with thine eyes,
41:19 the face of a *m'* was toward the palm
43: 6 the house; and the *m'* stood by me.
7 Son of *m'*, the place of my throne,
10 Thou son of *m'*, shew the house to
18 Son of *m'*, thus saith the Lord God;
44: 2 and no *m'* shall enter in by it;
5 Son of *m'*, mark well, and behold
46:18 every *m'* from his possession.
47: 3 when the *m'* that had the line in his
6 me, Son of *m'*, hast thou seen this?
20 till a *m'* come over against Hamath.
Da 2:10 There is not a *m'* upon the earth
25 I have found a *m'* of the captives
48 the king made Daniel a great *m'*,
3:10 every *m'* that shall hear the sound
5:11 There is a *m'* in thy kingdom, in
6: 7 ask a petition of any God or *m'* for
12 every *m'* that shall ask a petition
12 a petition of any God or *m'* within
7: 4 made stand upon the feet as a *m'*,
8 horn were eyes like the eyes of *m'*
13 one like the Son of *m'* came with the
8:15 me as the appearance of a *m'*.
16 make this *m'* to understand the vision.
17 Understand, O Son of *m'*: for at the
9:21 even the *m'* Gabriel, whom I had
10: 5 a certain *m'* clothed in linen, whose
11 me, O Daniel, a *m'* greatly beloved,
18 one like the appearance of a *m'*,
19 O *m'* greatly beloved, fear not:
12: 6 one said to the *m'* clothed in linen,
7 And I heard the *m'* clothed in linen,
Ho 3: 3 thou shalt not be for another *m'*:
4: 4 Yet let no *m'* strive, nor reprove
6: 9 as troops of robbers wait for a *m'*,
9: 7 is a fool, the spiritual *m'* is mad,
12 that there shall not be a *m'* left:
11: 4 I drew them with cords of a *m'*,
9 for I am God, and not *m'*; the Holy
Am 2: 7 and a *m'* and his father will go in
4:13 unto *m'* what is his thought, that
5:19 As if a *m'* did flee from a lion, and
Jon 1: 5 and cried every *m'* unto his god, and
3: 7 Let neither *m'* nor beast, herd nor
8 But let *m'* and beast be covered
Mic 2: 2 they oppress a *m'* and his house,
2 house, even a *m'* and his heritage.
11 If a *m'* walking in the spirit and
4: 4 shall sit every *m'* under his vine and
5: 5 this *m'* shall be the peace, when the
7 the grass, that tarrieth not for *m'*,
6: 8 shewed thee, O *m'*, what is good;
9 the *m'* of wisdom shall see thy name:
7: 2 The good *m'* is perished out of the
2 they hunt every *m'* his brother
3 and the great *m'* he uttereth his
Na 3:18 mountains, and no *m'* gathereth them.
Hab 1:13 the wicked devoureth the *m'* that is
2: 5 he is a proud *m'*, neither keepeth
Zep 1: 3 I will consume *m'* and beast; I
3 I will cut off *m'* from off the land,
14 the mighty *m'* shall cry there bitterly.
3: 6 destroyed, so that there is no *m'*,
Hag 1: 9 ye run every *m'* unto his own house.
Zec 1: 8 a *m'* riding upon a red horse, and
10 the *m'* that stood among the myrtle
21 so that no *m'* did lift up his head:
2: 1 behold a *m'* with a measuring line
4 Run, speak to this young *m'*, saying,
3:10 shall ye call every *m'* his neighbour
4: 1 as a *m'* that is wakened out of his
6:12 the *m'* whose name is The Branch;
7: 9 compassions every *m'* to his brother:
14 no *m'* passed through nor returned:
8: 4 every *m'* with his staff in his hand
10 days there was no hire for *m'*, nor
16 Speak ye every *m'* the truth to his
9: 1 the eyes of *m'*, as of all the tribes
13 thee as the sword of a mighty *m'*.
10: 7 of Ephraim shall be like a mighty *m'*,
12: 1 and formeth the spirit of *m'* within
13: 5 for *m'* taught me to keep cattle
7 against the *m'* that is my fellow,
Mal 2:10 deal treacherously every *m'* against
12 will cut off the *m'* that doeth this,
3: 8 Will a *m'* rob God? Yet ye have
17 as a *m'* spareth his own son that
M't 1:19 her husband, being a just *m'*, and
4: 4 *M'* shall not live by bread alone,
5:40 And if any *m'* will sue thee at the law,
6:24 No *m'* can serve two masters: for
7: 9 what *m'* is there of you, whom if
24 I will liken him unto a wise *m'*,
26 shall be likened unto a foolish *m'*,
8: 4 See thou tell no *m'*; but go thy
9 For I am a *m'* under authority,
9 I say to this *m'*, Go, and he goeth; and
20 the Son of *m'* hath not where to lay
27 What manner of *m'* is this, that even
28 that no *m'* might pass by that way.
9: 2 brought to him a *m'* sick of the palsy,
3 themselves, This *m'* blasphemeth.

M't 9: 6 know that the Son of *m'* hath power
9 he saw a *m'*, named Matthew, sitting
16 No *m'* putteth a piece of new cloth
30 saying, See that no *m'* know it.
32 they brought to him a dumb *m'*
10: 23 of Israel, till the Son of *m'* be come.
35 I am come to set a *m'* at variance
41 he that receiveth a righteous *m'* in
41 in the name of a righteous *m'* shall
11: 8 see? A *m'* clothed in soft raiment?
19 The Son of *m'* came eating and
19 Behold a *m'* gluttonous, and a
27 no *m'* knoweth the Son, but the
27 neither knoweth any *m'* the Father,
12: 8 the Son of *m'* is Lord even of the
10 there was a *m'* which had his hand
11 What *m'* shall there be among you,
12 then is a *m'* better than a sheep?
13 to the *m'*, Stretch forth thine hand.
19 shall any *m'* hear his voice in the
29 except he first bind the strong *m'*?
32 a word against the Son of *m'*,
35 A good *m'* out of the good treasure
35 an evil *m'* out of the evil treasure
40 so shall the Son of *m'* be three days
43 unclean spirit is gone out of a *m'*,
45 last state of that *m'* is worse than
13: 24 of heaven is likened unto a *m'* which
31 of mustard seed, which a *m'* took,
37 the good seed is the Son of *m'*;
41 The Son of *m'* shall send forth his
44 the which when a *m'* hath found, he
45 of heaven is like unto a merchant *m'*,
52 unto a *m'* that is an householder,
54 Whence hath this *m'* this wisdom,
56 then hath this *m'* all these things?
15: 11 goeth into the mouth defileth a *m'*;
11 out of the mouth, this defileth a *m'*.
18 the heart; and they defile the *m'*.
20 are the things which defile a *m'*:
20 unwashen hands defileth not a *m'*.
16: 13 do men say that I the Son of *m'* am?
20 tell no *m'* that he was Jesus the
24 If any *m'* will come after me, let him
26 For what is a *m'* profited, if he shall
26 a *m'* give in exchange for his soul?
27 Son of *m'* shall come in the glory of
27 shall reward every *m'* according to his
28 till they see the Son of *m'* coming
17: 8 they saw no *m'*, save Jesus only.
9 saying, Tell the vision to no *m'*,
9 until the Son of *m'* be risen again
12 shall also the Son of *m'* suffer of
14 came to him a certain *m'*, kneeling
22 The Son of *m'* shall be betrayed into
18: 7 woe to that *m'* by whom the offence
11 For the Son of *m'* is come to save
12 if a *m'* have an hundred sheep, and
17 let him be unto thee as an heathen *m'*
19: 3 lawful for a *m'* to put away his wife
5 this cause shall a *m'* leave father
6 together, let not *m'* put asunder.
10 case of the *m'* be so with his wife,
20 The young *m'* saith unto him, All
22 the young *m'* heard that saying,
23 a rich *m'* shall hardly enter into the
24 than for a rich *m'* to enter into the
28 when the Son of *m'* shall sit in the
20: 1 unto a *m'* that is an householder,
7 him, Because no *m'* hath hired us.
9 hour, they received every *m'* a penny.
10 likewise received every *m'* a penny.
18 Son of *m'* shall be betrayed unto
28 Even as the Son of *m'* came not to
21: 3 And if any *m'* say ought unto you,
28 A certain *m'* had two sons; and he
22: 11 a *m'* which had not on a wedding
16 neither carest thou for any *m'*: for
24 If a *m'* die, having no children, his
46 no *m'* was able to answer him a
46 neither durst any *m'* from that day
23: 9 And call no *m'* your father upon the
24: 4 Take heed that no *m'* deceive you.
23 Then if any *m'* shall say unto you,
27 also the coming of the Son of *m'* be.
30 the sign of the Son of *m'* in heaven:
30 see the Son of *m'* coming in the clouds
36 that day and hour knoweth no *m'*,
37, 39 the coming of the Son of *m'* be.
44 ye think not the Son of *m'* cometh.
25: 13 hour wherein the Son of *m'* cometh.
14 as a *m'* travelling into a far country,
15 every *m'* according to his...ability;
24 knew thee that thou art an hard *m'*,
31 Son of *m'* shall come in his glory,
26: 2 and the Son of *m'* is betrayed to be
18 Go into the city to such a *m'*, and say
24 Son of *m'* goeth as it is written of
24 but woe unto that *m'* by whom the
24 by whom the Son of *m'* is betrayed!
24 been good for that *m'* if he had not
45 Son of *m'* is betrayed into the hands
64 ye see the Son of *m'* sitting on the
72 with an oath, I do not know the *m'*.
74 to swear, saying, I know not the *m'*.
27: 19 thou nothing to do with that just *m'*:
32 they found a *m'* of Cyrene, Simon
47 that, said, This *m'* calleth for Elias.
57 there came a rich *m'* of Arimathæa,
M'r 1: 23 a *m'* with an unclean spirit; and
44 See thou say nothing to any *m'*:
2: 7 doth this *m'* thus speak blasphemies?
10 know that the Son of *m'* hath power
21 No *m'* also seweth a piece of new
22 no *m'* putteth new wine into old
27 The sabbath was made for *m'*,

M'r 2: 27 and not *m'* for the sabbath:
28 the Son of *m'* is Lord also of the
3: 1 was a *m'* there which had a withered
3 the *m'* which had the withered hand,
5 unto the *m'*, Stretch forth thine hand.
27 No *m'* can enter into a strong
27 he will first bind the strong *m'*;
4: 23 If any *m'* have ears to hear, let him
26 as if a *m'* should cast seed into the
41 What manner of *m'* is this, that even
5: 2 tombs a *m'* with an unclean spirit,
3 no *m'* could bind him, no, not with
4 neither could any *m'* tame him.
8 Come out of the *m'*, thou unclean
37 he suffered no *m'* to follow him,
43 that no *m'* should know it; and
6: 2 whence hath this *m'* these things?
20 knowing that he was a just *m'* and
7: 11 If a *m'* shall say to his father or
15 There is nothing from without a *m'*,
15 those are they that defile the *m'*.
16 If any *m'* have ears to hear, let him
18 from without entereth into the *m'*,
20 out of the *m'*, that defileth the *m'*.
23 come from within, and defile the *m'*.
24 and would have no *m'* know it:
36 them that they should tell no *m'*:
8: 4 can a *m'* satisfy these men with
22 and they bring a blind *m'* unto him,
23 And he took the blind *m'* by the hand,
25 restored, and saw every *m'* clearly.
30 that they should tell no *m'* of him.
31 Son of *m'* must suffer many things,
36 For what shall it profit a *m'*, if he
37 a *m'* give in exchange for his soul?
38 also shall the Son of *m'* be ashamed,
9: 8 saw no *m'* any more, save Jesus
9 them that they should tell no *m'*
9 till the Son of *m'* were risen from
12 how it is written of the Son of *m'*,
30 not that any *m'* should know it.
31 The Son of *m'* is delivered into the
35 If any *m'* desire to be first, the same
39 is no *m'* which shall do a miracle
10: 2 lawful for a *m'* to put away his wife?
7 cause shall a *m'* leave his father and
9 together, let not *m'* put asunder.
25 for a rich *m'* to enter into the kingdom
29 is no *m'* that hath left house, or
33 Son of *m'* shall be delivered unto
45 For even the Son of *m'* came not to
49 And they call the blind *m'*, saying
51 The blind *m'* said unto him, Lord,
11: 2 a colt tied, whereon never *m'* sat;
3 if any *m'* say unto you, Why do ye
14 No *m'* eat fruit of thee hereafter
16 any *m'* should carry any vessel
12: 1 A certain *m'* planted a vineyard,
14 thou art true, and carest for no *m'*:
34 no *m'* after that durst ask him any
13: 5 Take heed lest any *m'* deceive you:
21 then if any *m'* shall say to you, Lo,
26 shall they see the Son of *m'* coming
32 day and that hour knoweth no *m'*,
34 For the Son of *m'* is as a...taking a
34 is as a *m'* taking a far journey,
34 servants, and to every *m'* his work,
14: 13 meet you a *m'* bearing a pitcher
21 The Son of *m'* indeed goeth, as it is
21 woe to that *m'* by whom the Son of
21 by whom the Son of *m'* is betrayed!
21 were it for that *m'* if he had never
41 Son of *m'* is betrayed into the hands
51 followed him a certain young *m'*,
62 ye shall see the Son of *m'* sitting on
71 know not this *m'* of whom ye speak.
15: 24 upon them, what every *m'* should take.
39 Truly this *m'* was the Son of God.
16: 5 they saw a young *m'* sitting on the
8 said they any thing to any *m'*;
Lu 1: 18 for I am an old *m'*, and my wife well
27 to a *m'* whose name was Joseph,
34 shall this be, seeing I know not a *m'*?
2: 25 there was a *m'* in Jerusalem, whose
25 the same *m'* was just and devout,
52 and in favour with God and *m'*.
3: 14 Do violence to no *m'*, neither
4: 4 *m'* shall not live by bread alone,
33 in the synagogue there was a *m'*,
5: 8 me; for I am a sinful *m'*, O Lord.
12 city; behold a *m'* full of leprosy:
14 And he charged him to tell no *m'*:
18 brought in a bed a *m'* which was
20 him, *M'*, thy sins are forgiven thee.
24 Son of *m'* hath power upon earth to
36 No *m'* putteth a piece of a new
37 No *m'* putteth new wine into old
39 No *m'* also having drunk old wine
6: 5 the Son of *m'* is Lord also of the
6 a *m'* whose right hand was withered.
8 the *m'* which had the withered hand,
10 he said unto the *m'*, Stretch forth
30 Give to every *m'* that asketh of thee;
45 good *m'* out of the good treasure
45 an evil *m'* out of the evil treasure of
48 He is like a *m'* which built an house,
49 like a *m'* that without a foundation
7: 8 I also am a *m'* set under authority,
12 there was a dead *m'* carried out,
14 Young *m'*, I say unto thee, Arise.
25 see? A *m'* clothed in soft raiment?
34 The Son of *m'* is come eating and
34 Behold a gluttonous *m'*, and a
39 This *m'*, if he were a prophet, would
8: 16 No *m'*, when he hath lighted a
25 What manner of *m'* is this! for he

Lu 8: 27 a certain *m'*, which had devils long
29 unclean spirit to come out of the *m'*.
33 Then went the devils out of the *m'*,
35 found the *m'*, out of whom the devils
38 the *m'* out of whom the devils were
41 there came a *m'* named Jairus,
51 he suffered no *m'* to go in, save
56 should tell no *m'* what was done.
9: 21 commanded them to tell no *m'* that
22 The Son of *m'* must suffer many
23 If any *m'* will come after me, let him
25 For what is a *m'* advantaged, if he
26 him shall the Son of *m'* be ashamed,
36 and told no *m'* in those days any of
38 a *m'* of the company cried out,
44 for the Son of *m'* shall be delivered
56 Son of *m'* is not come to destroy
57 a certain *m'* said unto him, Lord,
58 Son of *m'* hath not where to lay his
62 No *m'*, having put his hand to the
10: 4 and salute no *m'* by the way.
22 no *m'* knoweth who the Son is,
30 *m'* went down from Jerusalem to
11: 21 a strong *m'* armed keepeth his
24 unclean spirit is gone out of a *m'*,
26 last state of that *m'* is worse than
30 Son of the *m'* be to this generation.
33 No *m'*, when he hath lighted a
12: 8 him shall the Son of *m'* also confess
10 speak a word against the Son of *m'*,
14 unto him, *M'*, who made me a judge
16 ground of a certain rich *m'* brought
40 Son of *m'* cometh at an hour when
13: 6 A certain *m'* had a fig tree planted in
19 of mustard seed, which a *m'* took,
14: 2 a certain *m'* before him which had
8 art bidden of any *m'* to a wedding,
8 lest a more honourable *m'* than thou
9 and say to thee, Give this *m'* place;
16 certain *m'* made a great supper, and
26 If any *m'* come to me, and hate not his
30 This *m'* began to build, and was
15: 2 This *m'* receiveth sinners, and eateth
4 What *m'* of you, having an hundred
11 he said, A certain *m'* had two sons:
16 did eat: and no *m'* gave unto him.
16: 1 There was a certain rich *m'*, which
16 preached, and every *m'* presseth into
19 There was a certain rich *m'*, which
22 the rich *m'* also died, and was buried;
17: 22 one of the days of the Son of *m'*,
24 so shall also the Son of *m'* be in his
26 be also in the days of the Son of *m'*.
30 day when the Son of *m'* is revealed.
18: 2 feared not God, neither regarded *m'*:
4 I fear not God, nor regard *m'*;
8 when the Son of *m'* cometh, shall he
14 this *m'* went down to his house justified
25 a rich *m'* to enter into the kingdom
29 is no *m'* that hath left house, or
31 prophets concerning the Son of *m'*
35 blind *m'* sat by the wayside begging:
19: 2 was a *m'* named Zacchæus, which
7 be guest with a *m'* that is a sinner.
8 have taken any thing from any *m'*
10 the Son of *m'* is come to seek and
14 will not have this *m'* to reign over us.
15 how much every *m'* had gained by
21 because thou art an austere *m'*:
22 knewest that I was an austere *m'*,
30 colt tied, whereon yet never *m'* sat:
31 if any *m'* ask you, Why do ye loose
20: 9 A certain *m'* planted a vineyard,
21: 27 see the Son of *m'* coming in a cloud
36 and to stand before the Son of *m'*.
22: 10 a *m'* meet you, bearing a pitcher
22 And truly the Son of *m'* goeth, as it
22 that *m'* by whom he is betrayed!
48 betrayest thou the Son of *m'* with a
56 and said, This *m'* was also with him.
58 And Peter said, *M'*, I am not.
60 *M'*, I know not what thou sayest.
69 Hereafter shall the Son of *m'* sit on
23: 4 the people, I find no fault in this *m'*.
6 whether the *m'* were a Galilæan.
14 Ye have brought this *m'* unto me, as
14 I,...have found no fault in this *m'*
18 Away with this *m'*, and release unto
41 but this *m'* hath done nothing amiss.
47 Certainly this was a righteous *m'*.
50 there was a *m'* named Joseph, a
50 and he was a good *m'*, and a just:
52 This *m'* went unto Pilate, and begged
53 wherein never *m'* before was laid.
24: 7 The Son of *m'* must be delivered
Joh 1: 6 There was a *m'* sent from God, whose
9 lighteth every *m'* that cometh into
13 nor of the will of *m'*, but of God.
18 No *m'* hath seen God at any time;
30 me cometh a *m'* which is preferred
51 and descending upon the Son of *m'*.
2: 10 Every *m'* at the beginning doth set
25 not that any should testify of *m'*:
25 for he knew what was in *m'*.
3: 1 There was a *m'* of the Pharisees,
2 for no *m'* can do these miracles
3 Except a *m'* be born again, he
4 How can a *m'* be born when he is
5 Except a *m'* be born of water and
13 no *m'* hath ascended up to heaven,
13 the Son of *m'* which is in heaven.
14 so must the Son of *m'* be lifted up:
27 A *m'* can receive nothing, except it
32 and no *m'* receiveth his testimony.
4: 27 no *m'* said, What seekest thou? or,
29 Come, see a *m'*, which told me all

Joh 4:33 any m' brought him ought to eat?
50 the m' believed the word that Jesus
5: 5 certain m' was there, which had an
7 The impotent m' answered him, Sir,
7 I have no m', when the water is
9 immediately the m' was made whole,
12 What m' is that which said unto
15 m' departed, and told the Jews that
22 the Father judgeth no m', but hath
27 also, because he is the Son of m'.
34 But I receive not testimony from m':
6:27 the Son of m' shall give unto you:
44 No m' can come to me, except the
45 Every m' therefore that hath heard,
46 that any m' hath seen the Father,
50 a m' may eat thereof, and not die.
51 if any m' eat of this bread, he shall
52 can this m' give us his flesh to eat?
53 ye eat the flesh of the Son of m',
62 if ye shall see the Son of m' ascend
65 no m' can come unto me, except
7: 4 is no m' that doeth any thing in
12 some said, He is a good m': others
13 no m' spake openly of him for fear
15 How knoweth this m' letters, having
17 If any m' will do his will, he shall
22 on the sabbath day circumcise a m'.
23 If a m' on the sabbath day receive
23 made a m' every whit whole on the
27 we know this m' whence he is: but
27 no m' knoweth whence he is.
30 him: but no m' laid hands on him,
31 than these which this m' hath done?
37 If any m' thirst, let him come unto
44 him; but no m' laid hands on him.
46 answered, Never m' spake like this
46 Never...spake like this m'.
51 Doth our law judge any m', before
53 And every m' went unto his own house.
8:10 hath no m' condemned thee?
11 She said, No m', Lord. And Jesus
15 judge after the flesh; I judge no m'.
20 and no m' laid hands on him; for
28 ye have lifted up the Son of m',
33 and were never in bondage to any m':
40 a m' that hath told you the truth,
51, 52 If a m' keep my saying, he shall5
9: 1 he saw a m' which was blind from
2 who did sin, this m', or his parents,
3 hath this m' sinned, nor his parents:
4 cometh, when no m' can work.
6 he anointed the eyes of the blind m'
11 A m' that is called Jesus made clay,
16 This m' is not of God, because he
16 said, How can a m' that is a sinner
17 say unto the blind m' again, What
22 if any m' did confess that he was
24 called they the m' that was blind,
24 we know that this m' is a sinner.
30 m' answered and said unto them,
31 but if any m' be a worshipper of God,
32 that any m' opened the eyes of one
33 If this m' were not of God, he could do
10: 9 by me if any m' enter in, he shall be
18 No m' taketh it from me, but I lay
28 any m' pluck them out of my hand.
29 no m' is able to pluck them out of
33 being a m', makest thyself God.
41 that John spake of this m' were true.
11: 1 a certain m' was sick, named Lazarus,
9 If any m' walk in the day, he stumbleth
10 But if a m' walk in the night, he
37 Could not this m', which opened the
37 even this m' should not have died?
47 for this m' doeth many miracles.
50 one m' should die for the people,
57 if any m' knew where he were, he
12:23 the Son of m' should be glorified.
26 If any m' serve me, let him follow
26 if any m' serve me, him will my
34 The Son of m' must be lifted up?
34 who is this Son of m'?
47 And if any m' hear my words, and
13:28 no m' at the table knew for what
31 said, Now is the Son of m' glorified,
14: 6 no m' cometh unto the Father, but
23 If a m' love me, he will keep my
15: 6 If a m' abide not in me, he is cast
13 Greater love hath no m' than this,
13 that a m' lay down his life for his
24 the works which none other m' did,
16:21 joy that a m' is born into the world.
22 your joy no m' taketh from you.
30 not that any m' should ask thee:
32 shall be scattered, every m' to his own,
18:14 one m' should die for the people.
29 accusation bring ye against this m'?
31 lawful for us to put any m' to death:
19: 5 saith unto them, Behold the m'!
41 wherein was never m' yet laid.
21:21 Jesus, Lord, and what shall this m' do?
Ac 1:18 this m' purchased a field with the
20 desolate, and let no m' dwell therein:
2: 6 m' heard them speak in his own
8 we every m' in our own tongue,
22 a m' approved of God among you
45 to all men, as every m' had need.
3: 2 m' lame from his mother's womb
11 lame m' which was healed held Peter
12 holiness we had made this m' to walk?
16 his name hath made this m' strong,
4: 9 good deed done to the impotent m',
10 doth this m' stand here before you
14 the m' which was healed standing
17 henceforth to no m' in this name.
22 the m' was above forty years old,

Ac 4:35 every m' according as he had need.
5: 1 a certain m' named Ananias, with
13 durst no m' join himself to them:
23 had opened, we found no m' within.
37 After this m' rose up Judas of Galilee
6: 5 a m' full of faith and of the Holy
13 said, This m' ceaseth not to speak
7:56 Son of m' standing on the right hand
8: 9 was a certain m', called Simon,
10 This m' is the great power of God.
27 behold, a m' of Ethiopia, an eunuch
31 I, except some m' should guide me?
34 this? of himself, or of some other m'?
9: 7 hearing a voice, but seeing no m'.
8 eyes were opened, he saw no m':
12 in a vision a m' named Ananias
13 heard by many of this m', how much
33 he found a certain m' named Æneas,
10: 1 m' in Cæsarea called Cornelius,
2 A devout m', and one that feared God
22 just m', and one that feareth God,
26 Stand up; I myself also am a m'.
28 a m' that is a Jew to keep company,
28 should not call any m' common or
30 a m' stood before me in bright
47 Can any m' forbid water, that
11:24 he was a good m', and full of the
29 every m' according to his ability,
12:22 the voice of a god, and not of a m'.
13: 7 Sergius Paulus, a prudent m'; who
21 of Cis, a m' of the tribe of Benjamin,
22 of Jesse, a m' after mine own heart,
38 through this m' is preached unto you
41 though a m' declare it unto you.
14: 8 there sat a certain m' at Lystra,
16: 9 There stood a m' of Macedonia, and
17:31 by that m' whom he hath ordained;
18:10 and no m' shall set on thee to hurt
24 an eloquent m', and mighty in the
25 This m' was instructed in the way of
19:16 the m' in whom the evil spirit was
24 For a certain m' named Demetrius,
35 what m' is there that knoweth not
38 have a matter against any m', the law
20: 9 sat in a window a certain young m'
12 And they brought the young m' alive,
21: 9 And the same m' had four daughters,
11 bind the m' that owneth this girdle
28 This is the m', that teacheth all men
39 I am a m' which am a Jew of Tarsus,
22: 3 I am verily a m' which am a Jew,
12 a devout m' according to the law,
25 to scourge a m' that is a Roman,
26 thou doest: for this m' is a Roman.
23: 9 saying, We find no evil in this m':
17 Bring this young m' unto the chief
18 to bring this young m' unto thee,
22 captain...let the young m' depart,
22 tell no m' that thou hast shewed
27 This m' was taken of the Jews, and
30 that the Jews laid wait for the m',
24: 5 have found this m' a pestilent fellow,
12 the temple disputing with any m',
25: 5 down with me, and accuse this m',
11 no m' may deliver me unto them.
14 a certain m' left in bonds by Felix:
16 the Romans to deliver any m' to die,
17 commanded the m' to be brought
22 I would also hear the m' myself.
24 ye see this m', about whom all the
26:31 This m' doeth nothing worthy of
32 This m' might have been set at
28: 4 No doubt this m' is a murderer,
7 possessions of the chief m' of the island,
31 all confidence, no m' forbidding him.
Ro 1:23 image made like to corruptible m',
2: 1 inexcusable, O m', whosoever thou
3 And thinkest thou this, O m', that
6 to every m' according to his deeds:
9 every soul of m' that doeth evil,
10 to every m' that worketh good,
21 that preachest a m' should not steal,
22 that sayest a m' should not commit
3: 4 let God be true, but every m' a liar;
5 taketh vengeance? (I speak as a m')
28 a m' is justified by faith without the
4: 6 describeth the blessedness of the m',
8 Blessed is the m' to whom the Lord
5: 7 for a righteous m' will one die:
7 good m' some would even dare to die.
12 as by one m' sin entered into the
15 gift by grace, which is by one m',
6: 6 our old m' is crucified with him,
7: 1 law hath dominion over a m' as long
3 liveth, she be married to another m',
3 though she be married to another m'.
22 the law of God after the inward m':
24 O wretched m' that I am! who shall
8: 9 if any m' have not the Spirit of Christ,
24 for what a m' seeth, why doth he
9:20 O m', who art thou that repliest
10: 5 the m' which doeth those things
10 For with the heart m' believeth unto
12: 3 to every m' that is among you, not to
3 dealt to every m' the measure of
17 Recompense to no m' evil for evil.
13: 8 Owe no m' any thing, but to love
14: 5 One m' esteemeth one day above
5 Let every m' be fully persuaded in
7 himself, and no m' dieth to himself.
13 that no m' put a stumblingblock
20 for that m' who eateth with offence.
1Co 2: 9 have entered into the heart of m',
11 For what m' knoweth the things
11 knoweth the things of a m', save
11 the spirit of m' which is in him?

1Co 2:11 the things of God knoweth no m',
14 natural m' receiveth not the things
15 yet he himself is judged of no m'.
3: 5 as the Lord gave to every m'?
8 and every m' shall receive his own
10 every m' take heed how he buildeth
11 can no m' lay than that is laid,
12 if any m' build upon this foundation
17 If any m' defile the temple of God,
18 Let no m' deceive himself.
18 any m' among you seemeth to be wise
21 Therefore let no m' glory in men.
4: 1 Let a m' so account of us, as of the
2 that a m' be found faithful.
5 shall every m' have praise of God.
5:11 if any m' that is called a brother be
6: 5 that there is not a wise m' among you?
18 Every sin that a m' doeth is without
7: 1 good for a m' not to touch a woman.
2 let every m' have his own wife, and
7 But every m' hath his proper gift
16 how knowest thou, O m', whether
17 God hath distributed to every m',
18 any m' called being circumcised?
20 every m' abide in the same calling
24 let every m', wherein he is called,
26 say, that it is good for a m' so to be.
36 But if any m' think that he behaveth
8: 2 if any m' think that he knoweth any
3 But if any m' love God, the same is
7 not in every m' that knowledge:
10 For if any m' see thee which hast
9: 8 Say I these things as a m'? or saith
15 any m' should make my glorying
25 And every m' that striveth for the
10:13 you but such as is common to m':
24 Let no m' seek his own,
24 but every m' another's wealth.
28 But if any m' say unto you, This
11: 3 that the head of every m' is Christ;
3 the head of the woman is the m';
4 Every m' praying or prophesying,
7 a m' indeed ought not to cover his
7 the woman is the glory of the m'.
8 For the m' is not of the woman;
8 woman; but the woman of the m'.
9 was the m' created for the woman;
9 woman; but the woman for the m'.
11 neither is the m' without the woman,
11 neither the woman without the m',
12 For as the woman is of the m', even
12 so is the m' also by the woman;
14 if a m' have long hair, it is a shame
16 if any m' seem to be contentious, we
28 But let a m' examine himself, and
34 if any m' hunger, let him eat at home;
12: 3 no m' speaking by the Spirit of God
3 that no m' can say that Jesus is the
7 given to every m' to profit withal.
11 dividing to every m' severally as he
13:11 when I became a m', I put away
14: 2 for no m' understandeth him;
27 any m' speak in an unknown tongue,
37 any m' think himself to be a prophet,
38 But if any m' be ignorant, let him be
15:21 For since by m' came death,
21 by m' came also the resurrection of
23 But every m' in his own order:
35 some m' will say, How are the dead
45 first m' Adam was made a living
47 The first m' is of the earth, earthy:
47 second m' is the Lord from heaven.
16:11 Let no m' therefore despise him:
22 If any m' love not the Lord Jesus
2Co 2: 6 Sufficient to such a m' is this
4:16 but though our outward m' perish,
16 the inward m' is renewed day by day.
5:16 know we no m' after the flesh:
17 Therefore if any m' be in Christ, he is
7: 2 us; we have wronged no m',
2 we have corrupted no m',
2 we have defrauded no m'.
8:12 is...according to that a m' hath,
20 that no m' should blame us in this
9: 7 Every m' according as he purposeth
10: 7 If any m' trust to himself that he is
11: 9 I was chargeable to no m': for
10 no m' shall stop me of this boasting
16 again, let no m' think me a fool; if
20 if a m' bring you into bondage,
20 if a m' devour you, if a m' take of
20 a m' exalt himself, if a m' smite
12: 2 I knew a m' in Christ above
3 I knew such a m', (whether in the
4 it is not lawful for a m' to utter.
6 any m' should think of me above
Ga 1: 1 men, neither by m', but by Jesus
9 any m' preach any other gospel unto
11 was preached of me is not after m'.
12 I neither received it of m', neither
2:16 knowing that a m' is not justified by
3:11 no m' is justified by the law in the
12 m' that doeth them shall live in
15 no m' disannulleth, or addeth
5: 3 I testify again to every m' that is
6: 1 if a m' be overtaken in a fault, ye
3 For if a m' think himself to be
4 let every m' prove his own work,
5 every m' shall bear his own burden.
7 whatsoever a m' soweth, that shall
17 henceforth let no m' trouble me:
Eph 2: 9 works, lest any m' should boast.
15 in himself of twain one new m',
3:16 might by his Spirit in the inner m';
4:13 the Son of God, unto a perfect m',
22 former conversation the old m',

Eph 4:24 that ye put on the new *m*·, which
25 every *m*· truth with his neighbour:
5: 6 Let no *m*· deceive you with vain
29 For no *m*· ever yet hated his own
31 cause shall a *m*· leave his father
6: 8 whatsoever good thing any *m*· doeth,
Ph'p 2: 4 Look not every *m*· on his own
4 but every *m*· also on the things of
8 being found in fashion as a man,
20 I have no *m*· likeminded, who will
3: 4 If any other *m*· thinketh that he hath
Col 1:28 we preach, warning every *m*·, and
28 teaching every *m*· in all wisdom;
28 we may present every *m*· perfect in
2: 4 lest any *m*· should beguile you
8 Beware lest any *m*· spoil you
16 Let no *m*· therefore judge you in
18 Let no *m*· beguile you of your
3: 9 put off the old *m*· with his deeds;
10 And have put on the new *m*·, which is
13 any *m*· have a quarrel against any:
4: 6 how ye ought to answer every *m*·.
1Th 3: 3 no *m*· should be moved by these
4: 6 That no *m*· go beyond and defraud his
8 despiseth not *m*·, but God, who
5:15 none render evil for evil unto any *m*·;
2Th 2: 3 Let no *m*· deceive you by any
3 that *m*· of sin be revealed, the son
3:14 if any *m*· obey not our word by this
14 note that *m*·, and have no company
1Ti 1: 8 is good, if a *m*· use it lawfully;
9 the law is not made for a righteous *m*·,
2: 5 God and men, the *m*· Christ Jesus;
12 nor to usurp authority over the *m*·,
3: 1 a *m*· desire the office of a bishop,
5 if a *m*· know not how to rule his
4:12 no *m*· despise thy youth; but be
5: 9 having been the wife of one *m*·,
16 If any *m*· or woman that believeth
22 Lay hands suddenly on no *m*·,
6: 3 If any *m*· teach otherwise, and
11 O *m*· of God, flee these things; and
16 the light which no *m*· can approach
16 whom no *m*· hath seen, nor can see:
2Ti 2: 4 No *m*· that warreth entangleth
5 if a *m*· also strive for masteries,
21 If a *m*· therefore purge himself
3:17 That the *m*· of God may be perfect,
4:16 first answer no *m*· stood with me,
Tit 2:15 authority. Let no *m*· despise thee.
3: 2 To speak evil of no *m*·, to be no
4 God our Saviour toward *m*· appeared,
10 A *m*· that is an heretick, after the
Heb 2: 6 What is *m*·, that thou art mindful
6 son of *m*·, that thou visitest him?
9 God should taste death for every *m*·.
3: 3 this *m*· was counted worthy of more
4 every house is builded by some *m*·;
4:11 lest any *m*· fall after the same example
5: 4 And no *m*· taketh this honour unto
7: 4 consider how great this *m*· was,
13 no *m*· gave attendance at the altar.
24 But this *m*·, because he continueth
8: 2 which the Lord pitched, and not *m*·.
3 this *m*· have somewhat also to offer.
11 shall not teach every *m*· his neighbour,
11 and every *m*· his brother, saying,
10:12 this *m*·, after he had offered one
38 but if any *m*· draw back, my soul
12:14 which no *m*· shall see the Lord:
15 any *m*· fail of the grace of God;
13: 6 not fear what *m*· shall do unto me.
Jas 1: 7 that *m*· think that he shall receive
8 double minded *m*· is unstable in
11 the rich *m*· fade away in his ways.
12 Blessed is the *m*· that endureth
13 no *m*· say when he is tempted,
13 evil, neither tempteth he any *m*·:
14 every *m*· is tempted, when he is
19 let every *m*· be swift to hear, slow
20 For the wrath of *m*· worketh not the
23 unto a *m*· beholding his natural face
24 forgetteth what manner of *m*· he was.
25 this *m*· shall be blessed in his deed.
26 any *m*· among you seem to be religious,
2: 2 assembly a *m*· with a gold ring,
2 come in also a poor *m*· in vile raiment;
14 though a *m*· say he hath faith, and
18 a *m*· may say, Thou hast faith, and
20 O vain *m*·, that faith without works
24 how that by works a *m*· is justified,
3: 2 any *m*· offend not in word, the same
2 the same is a perfect *m*·, and able
8 the tongue can no *m*· tame; it is an
13 Who is a wise *m*· and endued with
5:16 fervent prayer of a righteous *m*·
17 *m*· subject to like passions as we
1Pe 1:24 glory of *m*· as the flower of grass.
2:13 ordinance of *m*· for the Lord's sake:
19 if a *m*· for conscience toward God
3: 4 it be the hidden *m*· of the heart,
15 answer to every *m*· that asketh
4:10 As every *m*· hath received the gift,
11 If any *m*· speak, let him speak as the
11 if any *m*· minister, let him do it as of
16 if any *m*· suffer as a Christian, let him
2Pe 1:21 not in old time by the will of *m*·:
2: 8 that righteous *m*· dwelling among
19 of whom a *m*· is overcome, of the
1Jo 2: 1 if any *m*· sin, we have an advocate
15 If any *m*· love the world, the love
27 ye need not that any *m*· teach you:
3: 3 And every *m*· that hath this hope
7 children, let no *m*· deceive you:
4:12 No *m*· hath seen God at any time.
20 If any *m*· say, I love God, and
1Jo 5:16 If any *m*· see his brother sin a sin
Re 1:13 one like unto the Son of *m*·, clothed
2:17 which no *m*· knoweth saving he
3: 7 that openeth, and no *m*· shutteth;
7 and shutteth, and no *m*· openeth;
8 open door, and no *m*· can shut it:
11 hast, that no *m*· take thy crown.
20 if any *m*· hear my voice, and open
4: 7 the third beast had a face as a *m*·,
5: 3 And no *m*· in heaven, nor in earth,
4 no *m*· was found worthy to open
6:15 every bondman, and every free *m*·,
7: 9 multitude,...no *m*· could number,
9: 5 a scorpion, when he striketh a *m*·.
11: 5 And if any *m*· will hurt them, fire
5 and if any *m*· will hurt them, he must
12: 5 And she brought forth a *m*· child,
13 which brought forth the *m*· child.
13: 9 If any *m*· have an ear, let him hear.
17 And that no *m*· might buy or sell,
18 for it is the number of a *m*·; and
14: 3 no *m*· could learn that song but
9 If any *m*· worship the beast and his
14 cloud one sat like unto the Son of *m*·,
15: 8 no *m*· was able to enter into the
16: 3 it became as the blood of a dead *m*·:
18:11 no *m*· buyeth their merchandise
19:12 a name written, that no *m*· knew,
20:13 every *m*· according to their works.
21:17 according to the measure of a *m*·,
22:12 every *m*· according as his work
18 every *m*· that heareth the words
18 If any *m*· shall add unto these
19 if any *m*· shall take away from the

Manaen *(man'-a-en)*
Ac 13: 1 and Lucius of Cyrene, and *M*·,

Manahath *(man'-a-hath)*
Ge 36:23 Alvan, and *M*·, and Ebal, Shepho,
1Ch 1:40 Alian, and *M*·, and Ebal, Shephi,
8: 6 and they removed them to *M*·:

Manahethites *(man'-a-heth-ites)*
1Ch 2:52 sons; Haroeh, and half of the *M*·.
54 and half of the *M*·, the Zorites.

Manasseh *(ma-nas'-seh)* See also MANASSEH'S; MANASSES; MANASSITES.
Ge 41:51 the name of the firstborn *M*·:
46:20 Egypt were born *M*· and Ephraim,
48: 1 him his two sons, *M*· and Ephraim.
5 now thy two sons, Ephraim and *M*·,
13 *M*· in his left hand toward Israel's
14 wittingly; for *M*· was the firstborn.
20 make thee as Ephraim and as *M*·:
20 and he set Ephraim before *M*·.
50:23 also of Machir the son of *M*· were
Nu 1:10 the son of Ammihud: of *M*·;
34 Of the children of *M*·, by their
35 even of the tribe of *M*·, were thirty
2:20 by him shall be the tribe of *M*·:
20 the captain of the children of *M*·
7:54 prince of the children of *M*·:
10:23 of the tribe of the children of *M*·
13:11 Joseph, namely, of the tribe of *M*·,
26:28 after their families were *M*· and
29 Of the sons of *M*·: of Machir, the
34 These are the families of *M*·, and
27: 1 son of *M*·, of the families of *M*·
32:33 unto half the tribe of *M*· the son
39 children of Machir the son of *M*·
40 Gilead unto Machir the son of *M*·;
41 Jair the son of *M*· went and took
34:14 the tribe of *M*· have received their
23 for the tribe of the children of *M*·,
36: 1 the son of *M*·, of the families of the
12 into the families of the sons of *M*·
De 3:13 gave I unto the half tribe of *M*·;
14 Jair the son of *M*· took all the
29: 8 Gadites, and to the half tribe of *M*·.
33:17 and they are the thousands of *M*·.
34: 2 and the land of Ephraim, and *M*·,
Jos 1:12 and to half the tribe of *M*·, spake
4:12 half the tribe of *M*·, passed over
12: 6 Gadites, and the half tribe of *M*·.
13: 7 tribes, and the half tribe of *M*·,
29 unto the half tribe of *M*·: and this
29 the half tribe of the children of *M*·
31 children of Machir the son of *M*·,
14: 4 of Joseph were two tribes, *M*· and
16: 4 *M*· and Ephraim, took their
9 inheritance of the children of *M*·,
17: 1 was also a lot for the tribe of *M*·;
1 for Machir the firstborn of *M*·, the
2 for the rest of the children of *M*·
2 these were the male children of *M*·
3 the son of *M*·, had no sons, but
5 And there fell ten portions to *M*·,
6 Because the daughters of *M*· had an
7 the coast of *M*· was from Asher
8 Now *M*· had the land of Tappuah:
8 but Tappuah on the border of *M*·
9 are among the cities of *M*·: the
9 coast of *M*· also was on the north
11 *M*· had in Issachar and in Asher
12 children of *M*· could not drive out
17 and to *M*·, saying, Thou art a great
18: 7 half the tribe of *M*·, have received
20: 8 in Bashan out of the tribe of *M*·.
21: 5 Dan, and out of the half tribe of *M*·,
6 of the half tribe of *M*· in Bashan,
25 And out of the half tribe of *M*·,
27 out of the other half tribe of *M*·
22: 1 Gadites, and the half tribe of *M*·,
7 to the one half of the tribe of *M*·
9, 10, 11 Gad and the half tribe of *M*·
13, 15 Gad, and to the half tribe of *M*·,
Jos 22:21 of Gad and the half tribe of *M*·
30 Gad and the children of *M*· spake,
31 of Gad, and to the children of *M*·,
J'g 1:27 did *M*· drive out the inhabitants
6:15 my family is poor in *M*·, and I am
35 messengers throughout all *M*·;
7:23 out of Asher, and out of all *M*·,
11:29 he passed over Gilead, and *M*·, and
18:30 the son of Gershom, the son of *M*·,
1Ki 4:13 the towns of Jair the son of *M*·,
2Ki 20:21 and *M*· his son reigned in his stead.
21: 1 *M*· was twelve years old when he
9 *M*· seduced them to do more evil
11 *M*· king of Judah hath done these
16 *M*· shed innocent blood very much,
17 the rest of the acts of *M*·, and all
18 *M*· slept with his fathers, and was
20 of the Lord, as his father *M*· did.
23:12 the altars which *M*· had made in
26 provocations that *M*· had provoked
24: 3 for the sins of *M*·, according to all
1Ch 3:13 son, Hezekiah his son, *M*· his son,
5:18 Gadites, and half the tribe of *M*·,
23 the children of the half tribe of *M*·
26 Gadites, and the half tribe of *M*·,
6:61 out of the half tribe of *M*·, by lot,
62 out of the tribe of *M*· in Bashan,
70 And out of the half tribe of *M*·;
71 the family of the half tribe of *M*·,
7:14 The sons of *M*·; Ashriel, whom she
17 Gilead, son of Machir, the son of *M*·.
29 the borders of the children of *M*·,
9: 3 the children of Ephraim, and *M*·;
12:19 And there fell some of *M*· to David,
20 there fell to him of *M*·, Adnah, and
20 of the thousands that were of *M*·.
31 of the half tribe of *M*· eighteen
37 and of the half tribe of *M*·, with all
26:32 and the half tribe of *M*·, for every
27:20 the half tribe of *M*·, Joel the son of
21 Of the half tribe of *M*· in Gilead,
2Ch 15: 9 with them out of Ephraim and *M*·,
30: 1 letters also to Ephraim and *M*·,
10 the country of Ephraim and *M*·
11 and *M*· and of Zebulun humbled
18 even many of Ephraim and *M*·,
31: 1 in Ephraim also and *M*·, until they
32:33 *M*· his son reigned in his stead.
33: 1 *M*· was twelve years old when he
9 So *M*· made Judah and the
10 the Lord spake to *M*·, and to his
11 which took *M*· among the thorns,
13 *M*· knew that the Lord he was God.
18 the rest of the acts of *M*·, and his
20 So *M*· slept with his fathers, and
22 of the Lord, as did *M*· his father:
22 images which *M*· his father had
23 as *M*· his father had humbled
34: 6 And so did he in the cities of *M*·,
9 had gathered of the hand of *M*· and
Ezr 10:30 Bezaleel, and Binnui, and *M*·.
33 Eliphelet, Jeremai, *M*·, and Shimei.
Ps 60: 7 Gilead is mine, and *M*· is mine;
80: 2 and *M*· stir up thy strength, and
108: 8 Gilead is mine; *M*· is mine;
Isa 9:21 *M*·, Ephraim; and Ephraim, *M*·:
Jer 15: 4 of *M*· the son of Hezekiah king of
Eze 48: 4 unto the west side, a portion for *M*·.
5 by the border of *M*·, from the east

Manasseh's *(ma-nas'-sez)*
Ge 48:14 and his left hand upon *M*· head,
17 Ephraim's head unto *M*· head.
Jos 17: 6 the rest of *M*· sons had the lands
10 northward it was *M*·, and the sea

Manasses *(ma-nas'-seez)* See also MANASSEH.
M't 1:10 And Ezekias begat *M*·; and
10 *M*· begat Amon; and Amon begat
Re 7: 6 the tribe of *M*· were sealed twelve

Manassites *(ma-nas'-sites)*
De 4:43 and Golan in Bashan, of the *M*·.
J'g 12: 4 Ephraimites, and among the *M*·.
2Ki 10:33 and the Reubenites, and the *M*·,

mandrakes
Ge 30:14 found *m*· in the field, and brought
14 Give me, I pray thee, of thy son's *m*·.
15 thou take away my son's *m*· also?
15 with thee to night for thy son's *m*·.
16 have hired thee with my son's *m*·.
Ca 7:13 The *m*· give a smell, and our gates

maneh *(ma'-neh)*
Eze 45:12 fifteen shekels, shall be your *m*·.

manger
Lu 2: 7 clothes, and laid him in a *m*·;
12 in swaddling clothes, lying in a *m*·.
16 and the babe lying in the *m*·.

manifest See also MANIFESTED.
Ec 3:18 that God might *m*· them, and that
Lu 8:17 secret, that shall not be made *m*·;
Joh 1:31 he should be made *m*· to Israel,
3:21 that his deeds may be made *m*·,
9: 3 works of God should be made *m*·.
14:21 him, and will *m*· myself to him.
22 that thou wilt *m*· thyself unto us,
Ac 4:16 is *m*· to all them that dwell in
Ro 1:19 be known of God is *m*· in them;
10:20 I was made *m*· unto them that
16:26 But now is made *m*·, and by the
1Co 3:13 man's work shall be made *m*·: for
4: 5 make *m*· the counsels of the hearts:
11:19 may be made *m*· among you.
14:25 the secrets of his heart made *m*·;
15:27 him, it is *m*· that he is excepted,
2Co 2:14 and maketh *m*· the savour of his
4:10 of Jesus...be made *m*· in our body.

2Co 4:11 of Jesus might be made *m·* in our
5:11 but we are made *m·* unto God; and
11 I trust also are made *m·* in your
11: 6 we have been thoroughly made *m·*
Ga 5:19 Now the works of the flesh are *m·*,
Eph 5:13 reproved are made *m·* by the light:
13 whatsoever doth make *m·* is light.
Ph'p 1:13 my bonds in Christ are *m·* in all
Col 1:26 but now is made *m·* to his saints:
4: 4 I may make it *m·*, as I ought to
2Th 1: 5 a *m·* token of the righteous judgment
1Ti 3:16 God was *m·* in the flesh, justified
5:25 the good works of some are *m·*
2Ti 1:10 is now made *m·* by the appearing
3: 9 folly shall be *m·* unto all men, as
Heb 4:13 creature that is not *m·* in his sight:
9: 8 holiest of all was not yet made *m·*,
1Pe 1:20 was *m·* in these last times for you,
1Jo 2:19 they might be made *m·* that they
3:10 In this the children of God are *m·*,
Re 15: 4 for thy judgments are made *m·*.

manifestation
Ro 8:19 for the *m·* of the sons of God.
1Co 12: 7 But the *m·* of the Spirit is given to
2Co 4: 2 by *m·* of the truth commending

manifested
M'k 4:22 nothing hid, which shall not be *m·*;
Joh 2:11 of Galilee, and *m·* forth his glory;
17: 6 I have *m·* thy name unto the men
Ro 3:21 of God without the law is *m·*, being
Tit 1: 3 But hath in due times *m·* his word
1Jo 1: 2 the life was *m·*, and we have seen
2 the Father, and was *m·* unto us;)
3: 5 that he was *m·* to take away our
8 purpose the Son of God was *m·*.
4: 9 In this was *m·* the love of God

manifestly
2Co 3: 3 *m·* declared to be the epistle of

manifold
Ne 9:19 thou in thy *m·* mercies forsookest
27 according to thy *m·* mercies thou
Ps 104:24 O Lord, how *m·* are thy works! in
Am 5:12 I know your *m·* transgressions
Lu 18:30 Who shall not receive *m·* more in
Eph 3:10 the church the *m·* wisdom of God,
1Pe 1: 6 through *m·* temptations:
4:10 stewards of the *m·* grace of God.

mankind See also WOMANKIND.
Le 18:22 Thou shalt not lie with *m·*, as with
20:13 If a man also lie with *m·*, as he
Job 12:10 thing, and the breath of all *m·*.
1Co 6: 9 nor abusers of themselves with *m·*,
1Ti 1:10 them that defile themselves with *m·*,
Jas 3: 7 and hath been tamed of *m·*:

manna (*man'-nah*)
Ex 16:15 it, said one to another, It is *m·*:
31 Israel called the name thereof *M·*:
33 and put an omer full of *m·* therein,
35 children of Israel did eat *m·* forty
35 they did eat *m·*, until they came
Nu 11: 6 is nothing at all, besides this *m·*,
7 And the *m·* was as coriander seed,
9 in the night, the *m·* fell upon it.
De 8: 3 and fed thee with *m·*, which thou
16 fed thee in the wilderness with *m·*,
Jos 5:12 And the *m·* ceased on the morrow
12 the children of Israel *m·* any more;
Ne 9:20 withheldest not thy *m·* from their
Ps 78:24 rained down *m·* upon them to eat,
Joh 6:31 Our fathers did eat *m·* in the
49 Your fathers did eat *m·* in the
58 not as your fathers did eat *m·*, and
Heb 9: 4 was the golden pot that had *m·*,
Re 2:17 will I give to eat of the hidden *m·*,

manner^ See also MANNERS.
Ge 18:11 with Sarah after the *m·* of women.
25 far from thee to do after this *m·*,
19:31 us after the *m·* of all the earth:
25:23 two *m·* of people shall be separated
32:19 this *m·* shall ye speak unto Esau,
39:19 After this *m·* did thy servant to me;
40:13 the former *m·* when thou wast his
17 of all *m·* of bakemeats for Pharaoh;
45:23 to his father he sent after this *m·*;
Ex 1:14 and in all *m·* of service in the field:
7:11 like *m·* with their enchantments.
12:16 no *m·* of work shall be done in them,
21: 9 with her after the *m·* of daughters.
22: 9 For all *m·* of trespass, whether it
9 or for any *m·* of lost thing, which
23:11 In like *m·* thou shalt deal with thy
31: 3 and in all *m·* of workmanship,
5 to work in all *m·* of workmanship.
35:29 willing to bring for all *m·* of work,
31 in all *m·* of workmanship; and
33 to make any *m·* of cunning work.
35 all *m·* of work, of the engraver,
36: 1 all *m·* of work for the service of the
Le 5:10 offering, according to the *m·*:
7:23 Ye shall eat no *m·* of fat, of ox, or of
26 Moreover ye shall eat no *m·* of blood,
27 soul it be that eateth any *m·* of blood,
9:16 and offered it according to the *m·*.
11:27 among all *m·* of beasts that go on all
44 with any *m·* of creeping thing
14:54 law for all *m·* of plague of leprosy,
17:10 you, that eateth any *m·* of blood;
14 shall eat the blood of no *m·* of flesh:
19:23 have planted all *m·* of trees for food,
20:25 any *m·* of living thing that creepeth
23:31 Ye shall do no *m·* of work: it shall be
24:22 Ye shall have one *m·* of law, as
Nu 5:13 her, neither she be taken with the *m·*;
9:14 and according to the *m·* thereof,
Nu 15:13 shall do these things after this *m·*,
16 One law and one *m·* shall be for
24 drink offering, according to the *m·*,
28:18 ye shall do no *m·* of servile work
24 After this *m·* ye shall offer daily,
29: 6 offerings, according unto their *m·*,
18, 21, 24, 27, 30, 33, 37 according to their
number, after the *m·*:
31:30 and of the flocks, of all *m·* of beasts,
De 4:15 ye saw no *m·* of similitude on the day
15: 2 And this is the *m·* of the release:
22: 3 like *m·* shalt thou do with his ass;
27:21 be he that lieth with any *m·* of beast.
Jos 6:15 after the same *m·* seven times:
J'g 8:18 *m·* of men were they whom ye slew at
11:17 in like *m·* they sent unto the king of
18: 7 after the *m·* of the Zidonians,
Ru 4: 7 this was the *m·* in former time in
1Sa 8: 9, 11 *m·* of the king that shall reign
10:25 the people the *m·* of the kingdom,
17:27 people answered him after this *m·*,
30 and spake after the same *m·*: and
30 him again after the former *m·*.
18:24 saying, On this *m·* spake David.
19:24 before Samuel in like *m·*, and
21: 5 the bread is in a *m·* common, yea,
27:11 so will be his *m·* all the while he
2Sa 6: 5 *m·* of instruments made of fir wood,
7:19 And is this the *m·* of man, O Lord
14: 3 and speak on this *m·* unto him.
15: 6 And on this *m·* did Absalom to all
17: 6 hath spoken after this *m·*: shall
1Ki 7:28 the work of the bases was on this *m·*:
37 After this *m·* he made the ten bases:
18:28 cut themselves after their *m·* with
22:20 And one said on this *m·*, and
20 and another said on that *m·*.
2Ki 1: 7 What *m·* of man was he which
11:14 stood by a pillar, as the *m·* was,
17:26 not the *m·* of the God of the land:
26 not the *m·* of the God of the land.
27 them the *m·* of the God of the land.
33 after the *m·* of the nations whom
40 but they did after their former *m·*.
1Ch 6:48 appointed unto all *m·* of service of
12:37 with all *m·* of instruments of war for
18:10 all *m·* of vessels of gold and silver and
22:15 and timber, and all *m·* of cunning men
15 cunning men for every *m·* of work.
23:29 and for all *m·* of measure and size;
24:19 of the Lord, according to their *m·*,
28:14 for all instruments of all *m·* of service;
21 with thee for all *m·* of workmanship
21 skilful man, for any *m·* of service:
29: 2 and all *m·* of precious stones, and
5 *m·* of work to be made by the hands
2Ch 2:14 also to grave any *m·* of graving, and
4:20 should burn after the *m·* before
13: 9 priests after the *m·* of the nations of
18:19 one spake saying after this *m·*,
19 and another saying after that *m·*.
30:16 stood in their place after their *m·*,
32:27 and for all *m·* of pleasant jewels;
28 stalls for all *m·* of beasts, and cotes
34:13 wrought the work in any *m·* of service:
Ezr 5: 4 Then said we unto them after this *m·*,
Ne 6: 4 answered them after the same *m·*.
5 unto me in like *m·* the fifth time
8:18 assembly, according unto the *m·*.
10:37 the fruit of all *m·* of trees, of wine and
13:15 grapes, and figs, and all *m·* of burdens,
16 brought fish, and all *m·* of ware, and
Es 1:13 king's *m·* toward all that knew law
2:12 according to the *m·* of the women,
Ps 107:18 Their soul abhorreth all *m·* of meat;
144:13 be full, affording all *m·* of store:
Ca 7:13 our gates are all *m·* of pleasant fruits,
Isa 5:17 the lambs feed after their *m·*,
10:24 against thee, after the *m·* of Egypt.
26 he lift it up after the *m·* of Egypt.
51: 6 dwell therein shall die in like *m·*:
Jer 13: 9 After this *m·* will I mar the pride
22:21 hath been thy *m·* from thy youth,
30:18 shall remain after the *m·* thereof.
Eze 20:30 after the *m·* of your fathers?
23:15 after the *m·* of the Babylonians of
45 them after the *m·* of adulteresses,
45 the *m·* of women that shed blood;
Da 6:23 no *m·* of hurt was found upon him,
Am 4:10 pestilence after the *m·* of Egypt:
8:14 The *m·* of Beer-sheba liveth; even
M't 4:23 and healing all *m·* of sickness and
23 all *m·* of disease among the people.
5:11 shall say all *m·* of evil against you
6: 9 After this *m·* therefore pray ye:
8:27 What *m·* of man is this, that even
10: 1 and to heal all *m·* of sickness and
1 of sickness and all *m·* of disease.
12:31 All *m·* of sin and blasphemy shall
M'r 4:41 What *m·* of man is this, that
13: 1 Master, see what *m·* of stones and
29 So ye in like *m·*, when ye shall see
Lu 1:29 what *m·* of salutation this should
66 What *m·* of child shall this be!
6:23 in the like *m·* did their fathers
7:39 who and what *m·* of woman this is
8:25 What *m·* of man is this! for he
9:55 not what *m·* of spirit ye are of.
11:42 mint and rue and all *m·* of herbs,
20:31 and in like *m·* the seven also: and
24:17 What *m·* of communications are
Joh 2: 6 the *m·* of the purifying of the Jews,
7:36 What *m·* of saying is this that he said,
19:40 as the *m·* of the Jews is to bury.
Ac 1:11 like *m·* as ye have seen him go
10:12 were all *m·* of fourfooted beasts of
Ac 15: 1 circumcised after the *m·* of Moses,
23 letters by them after this *m·*;
17: 2 And Paul, as his *m·* was, went
20:18 after what *m·* I have been with you
22: 3 to the perfect *m·* of the law of the
23:25 And he wrote a letter after this *m·*:
25:16 It is not the *m·* of the Romans to
20 doubted of such *m·* of questions,
26: 4 My *m·* of life from my youth, which
Ro 6:19 I speak after the *m·* of men because
7: 8 in me all *m·* of concupiscence.
1Co 7: 7 one after this *m·*, and another
11:25 the same *m·* also he took the cup,
15:32 If after the *m·* of men I have fought
2Co 7: 9 ye were made sorry after a godly *m·*,
Ga 2:14 livest after the *m·* of Gentiles,
3:15 I speak after the *m·* of men;
1Th 1: 5 ye know what *m·* of men we were
9 what *m·* of entering in we had
1Ti 2: 9 In like *m·* also, that women adorn
2Ti 3:10 known my doctrine, *m·* of life,
Heb 10:25 together, as the *m·* of some is;
Jas 1:24 forgetteth what *m·* of man he was.
1Pe 1:11 what *m·* of time the Spirit of
15 ye holy in all *m·* of conversation;
3: 5 For after this *m·* in the old time
2Pe 3:11 what *m·* of persons ought ye to be
1Jo 3: 1 what *m·* of love the Father hath
Jude 7 cities about them in like *m·*,
Re 11: 5 them, he must in this *m·* be killed.
18:12 wood, and all *m·* vessels of ivory,
12 and all *m·* vessels of most precious
21:19 with all *m·* of precious stones.
22: 2 of life, which bare twelve *m·* of fruits,

manners
Le 20:23 not walk in the *m·* of the nation,
2Ki 17:34 day they do after the former *m·*:
Eze 11:12 done after the *m·* of the heathen
Ac 13:18 he their *m·* in the wilderness.
1Co 15:33 communications corrupt good *m·*.
Heb 1: 1 and in divers *m·* spake in time past

Manoah (*ma-no'-ah*)
J'g 13: 2 the Danites, whose name was *M·*;
8 Then *M·* intreated the Lord, and
9 God hearkened to the voice of *M·*;
9 *M·* her husband was not with her.
11 *M·* arose, and went after his wife,
12 *M·* said, Now let thy words come to
13 the angel of the Lord said unto *M·*,
15 *M·* said unto the angel of the Lord,
16 the angel of the Lord said unto *M·*,
16 *M·* knew not that he was an angel
17 *M·* said unto the angel of the Lord,
19 *M·* took a kid with a meat offering,
19 and *M·* and his wife looked on.
20 *M·* and his wife looked on it, and
21 the Lord did no more appear to *M·*
21 Then *M·* knew that he was an angel
22 And *M·* said unto his wife, We shall
16:31 the buryingplace of *M·* his father.

man's See also WOMAN'S.
Ge 8:21 the ground any more for *m·* sake;
21 the imagination of *m·* heart is evil
9: 5 at the hand of every *m·* brother will
6 Whoso sheddeth *m·* blood, by man
20: 3 hast taken; for she is a *m·* wife.
42:11 We are all one *m·* sons; we are true
25 to restore every *m·* money into his
35 every *m·* bundle of money was in his
43:21 every *m·* money was in the mouth of
44: 1 every *m·* money in his sack's mouth.
26 we may not see the *m·* face, except
Ex 4:11 him, Who hath made *m·* mouth?
12:44 But every *m·* servant that is bought
21:35 if one *m·* ox hurt another's, that he
22: 5 and shall feed in another *m·* field;
7 and it be stolen out of the *m·* house;
30:32 Upon *m·* flesh shall it not be
Le 7: 8 that offereth any *m·* burnt offering,
15:16 if any *m·* seed of copulation go out
20:10 adultery with another *m·* wife,
Nu 5:10 every *m·* hallowed things shall be
12 If any *m·* wife go aside, and commit
17: 2 write...every *m·* name upon his rod.
5 the *m·* rod, whom I shall choose,
33:54 every *m·* inheritance shall be in the
De 20:19 (for the tree of the field is *m·* life)
24: 2 she may go and be another *m·* wife.
6 for he taketh a *m·* life to pledge.
J'g 7:16 he put a trumpet in every *m·* hand,
22 every *m·* sword against his fellow,
19:26 down at the door of the *m·* house
Ru 2:19 The *m·* name with whom I wrought
1Sa 12: 4 thou taken ought of any *m·* hand.
14:20 every *m·* sword...against his fellow
17:32 Let no *m·* heart fail because of him;
2Sa 12: 4 took the poor *m·* lamb, and dressed
17:18 came to a *m·* house in Bahurim,
25 which Amasa was a *m·* son, whose
1Ki 18:44 cloud out of the sea, like a *m·* hand.
2Ki 12: 4 money that cometh into any *m·* heart
23: 8 which were on a *m·* left hand at the
25: 9 great *m·* house burnt he with fire.
Es 1: 8 do according to every *m·* pleasure.
Job 10: 5 of man? are thy years as *m·* days,
32:21 I pray you, accept any *m·* person,
Ps 104:15 which strengtheneth *m·* heart.
Pr 10:15 The rich *m·* wealth is his strong city:
12:14 recompence of a *m·* hands shall be
13: 8 ransom of a *m·* life are his riches:
16: 7 When a *m·* ways please the Lord, he
9 A *m·* heart deviseth his way: but
18: 4 words of a *m·* mouth are as deep
11 The rich *m·* wealth is his strong city,
16 A *m·* gift maketh room for him, and

Pr 18:20 A m' belly shall be satisfied with
19:21 are many devices in a m' heart;
20:24 M' goings are of the Lord; how
27: 9 so doth the sweetness of a m' friend
29:23 A m' pride shall bring him low: but
26 m' judgment cometh from the Lord.
Ec 2:14 The wise m' eyes are in his head; but
8: 1 a m' wisdom maketh his face to
5 wise m' heart discerneth both time
9:16 the poor m' wisdom is despised, and
10: 2 A wise m' heart is at his right hand;
12 The words of a wise m' mouth are
Isa 8: 1 roll, and write in it with a m' pen
13: 7 faint, and every m' heart shall melt:
Jer 3: 1 from him, and become another m',
23:36 every m' word shall be his burden;
Eze 4:15 given thee cow's dung for m' dung,
10: 8 form of a m' hand under their wings.
38:21 every m' sword shall be against his
39:15 when any seeth a m' bone, then
40: 5 in the m' hand a measuring reed of
Da 4:16 Let his heart be changed from m',
5: 5 hour came forth fingers of a m' hand,
7: 4 man, and a m' heart was given to it.
8:16 heard a m' voice between the banks
Am 6:10 And a m' uncle shall take him up, and
Jon 1:14 let us not perish for this m' life,
Mic 7: 6 a m' enemies are the men of his own
M't 10:36 a m' foes shall be they of his own
41 shall receive a righteous m' reward.
12:29 can one enter into a strong m' house,
M'r 3:27 man can enter into a strong m' house,
12:19 If a m' brother die, and leave his
Lu 6:22 as evil, for the Son of m' sake.
12:15 for a m' life consisteth not in the
16:12 in that which is another m', who
21 which fell from the rich m' table:
20:28 If any m' brother die, having a
Joh 18:17 thou also one of this m' disciples?
Ac 5:28 to bring this m' blood upon us.
7:58 their clothes at a young m' feet,
11:12 and we entered into the m' house:
13:23 Of this m' seed hath God according
17:29 stone, graven by art and m' device.
18: 7 and entered into a certain m' house,
20:33 I have coveted no m' silver, or
27:22 be no loss of any m' life among you,
Ro 5:17 For if by one m' offence death reigned
19 by one m' disobedience many were
14: 4 that judgest another m' servant?
15:20 build upon another m' foundation:
1Co 2: 4 with enticing words of m' wisdom,
13 words which m' wisdom teacheth,
3:13 Every m' work...be made manifest:
13 fire shall try every m' work of what
14 If any m' work abide which he hath
15 If any m' work shall be burned, he
4: 3 judged of you, or of m' judgment:
10:29 judged of another m' conscience?
2Co 4: 2 every m' conscience in the sight of
10:16 boast in another m' line of things
Ga 2: 6 me: God accepteth no m' person:)
3:15 Though it be but a m' covenant, yet
2Th 3: 8 we eat any m' bread for nought;
Jas 1:26 his own heart, this m' religion is vain.
1Pe 1:17 according to every m' work,
2Pe 2:16 dumb ass speaking with m' voice

manservant See also MANSERVANT'S; MANSERVANTS.
Ex 20:10 thy son, nor thy daughter, thy m',
17 thy neighbour's wife, nor his m',
21:32 If the ox shall push a m' or a)
De 5:14 son, nor thy daughter, nor thy m',
14 that thy m' and thy maidservant
21 house, his field, or his m', or his
12:18 son, and thy daughter, and thy m',
16:11, 14 and thy daughter, and thy m',
Job 31:13 If I did despise the cause of my m'
Jer 34: 9 That every man should let his m',
10 that every one should let his m',

manservant's
Ex 21:27 And if he smite out his m' tooth,

manservants
Ne 7:67 Besides their m' and their

mansions
Joh 14: 2 my Father's house are many m':

manslayer See also MANSLAYERS.
Nu 35: 6 which ye shall appoint for the m',
12 that the m' die not, until he stand

manslayers
1Ti 1: 9 and murderers of mothers, for m',

mantle See also MANTLES.
J'g 4:18 tent, she covered him with a m'.
1Sa 15:27 hold upon the skirt of his m', and
28:14 up; and he is covered with a m'.
1Ki 19:13 that he wrapped his face in his m',
19 by him, and cast his m' upon him.
2Ki 2: 8 Elijah took his m', and wrapped it
13 He took up also the m' of Elijah that
14 took the m' of Elijah that fell from
Ezr 9: 3 I rent my garment and my m',
5 rent my garment and my m', I
Job 1:20 Then Job arose, and rent his m',
2:12 they rent every one his m', and
Ps 109:29 their own confusion, as with a m'.

mantles
Isa 3:22 suits of apparel, and the m', and

many^ See also MANIFOLD.
Ge 17: 4 shalt be a father of m' nations.
5 father of m' nations have I made
21:34 in the Philistines' land m' days.
37: 3 and he made him a coat of m' colours.
Ge 37:23 his coat of m' colours that was on him;
32 And they sent the coat of m' colours,
34 and mourned for his son m' days.
Ex 5: 5 the people of the land now are m',
19:21 to gaze, and m' of them perish.
23: 2 decline after m' to wrest judgment:
35:22 as m' as were willing hearted, and
Le 15:25 issue of her blood m' days out of
25:51 If there be yet m' years behind,
Nu 9:19 long upon the tabernacle m' days,
10:36 unto the m' thousands of Israel.
13:18 they be strong or weak, few or m';
22: 3 the people, because they were m':
24: 7 his seed shall be in m' waters, and
26:54 To m' thou shalt give the more
56 be divided between m' and few.
35: 8 that have m' ye shall give
8 that have... ye shall give m':
De 1:11 thousand times as m' more as ye are,
46 So ye abode in Kadesh m' days,
2: 1 we compassed mount Seir m' days.
10, 21 and m', and tall, as the Anakims;
3: 5 beside unwalled towns a great m'.
7: 1 cast out m' nations before thee, the
15: 6 thou shalt lend unto m' nations,
6 thou shalt reign over m' nations,
25: 3 him above these with m' stripes,
28:12 thou shalt lend unto m' nations,
31:17 m' evils and troubles shall befall
21 when m' evils and troubles are
32: 7 consider the years of m' generations:
Jos 11: 4 with horses and chariots very m'.
22: 3 left your brethren these m' days
J'g 3: 1 even as m' of Israel as had not known
7: 2 are with thee are too m' for me to
4 The people are yet too m'; bring
8:30 begotten: for he had m' wives.
9:40 m' were overthrown and wounded,
16:24 our country, which slew m' of us.
1Sa 2: 5 hath m' children is waxed feeble.
6:19 Lord had smitten m' of the people
14: 6 the Lord to save by m' or by few.
25:10 be m' servants now a days that
2Sa 1: 4 m' of the people also are fallen
2:23 as m' as came to the place where
12: 2 exceeding m' flocks and herds:
22:17 me; he drew me out of m' waters;
23:20 who had done m' acts, he slew two
24: 3 the people, how m' soever they be,
1Ki 2:38 dwelt in Jerusalem m' days.
4:20 Judah and Israel were m', as the
7:47 because they were exceeding m':
11: 1 Solomon loved m' strange women,
17:15 he, and her house, did eat m' days.
18: 1 it came to pass after m' days, that
25 for ye are m'; and call on the name
22:16 How m' times shall I adjure thee that
2Ki 9:22 Jezebel and...witchcrafts are so m'?
1Ch 4:27 his brethren had not m' children,
5:22 there fell down m' slain, because
7: 4 for they had m' wives and sons.
22 Ephraim...mourned m' days, and
8:40 had m' sons, and sons' sons, an
11:22 Kabzeel, who had done m' acts;
21: 3 an hundred times so m' more as they
23:11 and Beriah had not m' sons;
17 the sons of Rehabiah were very m'.
28: 5 the Lord hath given me m' sons,)
2Ch 11:23 And he desired m' wives.
14:11 whether with m', or with them
16: 8 very m' chariots and horsemen?
18:15 How m' times shall I adjure thee that
26:10 the desert, and digged m' wells:
29:31 and as m' as were of a free heart
30:17 m' in the congregation that were
18 m' of Ephraim, and Manasseh, and
32:23 m' brought gifts unto the Lord to
Ezr 3:12 But m' of the priests and Levites
12 voice; and m' shouted aloud for joy:
5:11 was builded these m' years ago,
10:13 But the people are m', and it is a
13 we are m' that have transgressed
Ne 5: 2 sons, and our daughters, are m':
6:17 the nobles of Judah sent m' letters
18 there were m' in Judah sworn unto
7: 2 man, and feared God above m'.
9:28 m' times didst thou deliver them
30 m' years didst thou forbear them,
13:26 among m' nations was there no
Es 1: 4 of his excellent majesty m' days,
2: 8 when m' maidens were gathered
4: 3 and m' lay in sackcloth and ashes.
8:17 m' of the people of the land became
Job 4: 3 Behold, thou hast instructed m',
11:19 yea, m' shall make suit unto thee.
13:23 How m' are mine iniquities and sins?
16: 2 I have heard m' such things:
23:14 and m' such things are with him.
41: 3 Will he make m' supplications
Ps 3: 1 m' are they that rise up against
2 M' there be which say of my soul,
4: 6 m' that say, Who will show us any
18:16 me, he drew me out of m' waters.
22:12 M' bulls have compassed me:
25:19 mine enemies; for they are m';
29: 3 the Lord is upon m' waters.
31:13 I have heard the slander of m':
32:10 M' sorrows shall be to the wicked:
34:12 loveth m' days, that he may see good?
19 M' are the afflictions of the
37:16 better than the riches of m' wicked.
40: 3 m' shall see it, and fear, and shall
5 M', O Lord my God, are thy
55:18 me: for there were m' with me.
56: 2 they be m' that fight against me,
61: 6 life: and his years as m' generations.
Ps 71: 7 I am as a wonder unto m'; but
78:38 yea, m' a time turned he his anger
93: 4 than the noise of m' waters, yea,
106:43 M' times did he deliver them; but
110: 6 wound the heads over m' countries.
119:84 How m' are the days of thy servant?
157 M' are my persecutors and mine
129: 1, 2 M' a time have they afflicted me
Pr 4:10 the years of thy life shall be m'.
6:35 though thou givest m' gifts.
7:26 she hath cast down m' wounded:
26 m' strong men have been slain by
10:21 The lips of the righteous feed m':
14:20 but the rich hath m' friends.
19: 4 Wealth maketh m' friends; but the
6 M' will intreat the favour of the
21 are m' devices in a man's heart;
28: 2 of a land m' are the princes thereof:
27 his eyes shall have m' a curse.
29:26 M' seek the ruler's favour; but
31:29 M' daughters have done virtuously.
Ec 5: 7 multitude of dreams and m' words
6: 3 and live m' years, so that the
3 so that the days of his years be m',
11 be m' things that increase vanity,
7:29 have sought out m' inventions.
11: 1 thou shalt find it after m' days.
8 But if a man live m' years, and
8 of darkness; for they shall be m'.
12: 9 out, and set in order m' proverbs.
12 of making m' books there is no end;
Ca 8: 7 M' waters cannot quench love,
Isa 1:15 when ye make m' prayers, I will
2: 3 And m' people shall go and say,
4 and shall rebuke m' people: and
5: 9 truth m' houses shall be desolate,
8: 7 waters of the river, strong and m',
15 And m' among them shall stumble,
17:12 Woe to the multitude of m' people,
13 rush like the rushing of m' waters:
22: 9 the city of David, that they are m':
23:16 sweet melody, sing m' songs,
24:22 after m' days...they be visited.
31: 1 in chariots, because they are m';
32:10 M' days and years shall ye be troubled,
42:20 Seeing m' things, but thou
52:14 As m' were astonied at thee; his
15 So shall he sprinkle m' nations;
53:11 my righteous servant justify m';
12 and he bare the sin of m', and made
58:12 up the foundations of m' generations;
60:15 excellency, a joy of m' generations.
66:16 the slain of the Lord shall be m'.
Jer 3: 1 played the harlot with m' lovers;
5: 6 their transgressions are m', and
11:15 hath wrought lewdness with m',
12:10 M' pastors have destroyed my
13: 6 And it came to pass after m' days,
14: 7 for our backslidings are m'; we
16:16 I will send for m' fishers, saith
16 after will I send for m' hunters,
20:10 For I heard the defaming of m',
22: 8 m' nations shall pass by this city,
25:14 m' nations and great kings shall
27: 7 m' nations and great kings shall
28: 8 both against m' countries, and
32:14 that they may continue m' days.
35: 7 that ye may live m' days in the land
36:32 besides unto them m' like words.
37:16 had remained there m' days;
42: 2 (for we are left but a few of m', as
46:11 vain shalt thou use m' medicines;
16 He made m' to fall, yea, one fell
50:41 m' kings shall be raised up from
51:13 thou that dwellest upon m' waters,
La 1:22 for my sighs are m', and my heart
Eze 3: 6 Not to m' people of a strange speech
12:27 he seeth is for m' days to come,
16:41 upon thee in the sight of m' women:
17: 7 with great wings and m' feathers:
9 m' people to pluck it up by the roots
17 building forts, to cut off m' persons:
19:10 of branches by reason of m' waters.
22:25 they have made her m' widows
26: 3 m' nations to come up against
27: 3 merchant of the people for m' isles,
15 m' isles were the merchandise of
33 of the seas, thou filledst m' people;
32: 3 thee with a company of m' people;
9 also vex the hearts of m' people,
10 make m' people amazed at thee,
33:24 but we are m'; the land is given us
37: 2 were very m' in the open valley;
38: 6 bands: and m' people with thee.
8 After m' days thou shalt be visited:
8 and is gathered out of m' people,
9 thy bands, and m' people with thee.
15 thou, and m' people with thee, all
17 prophesied in those days m' years
22 the m' people that are with him,
23 be known in the eyes of m' nations,
39:27 in them in the sight of m' nations;
43: 2 voice was like a noise of m' waters:
47: 7 very m' trees on the one side and
10 fish of the great sea, exceeding m'.
Da 2:48 and gave him m' great gifts, and
8:25 and by peace shall destroy m':
26 vision; for it shall be for m' days.
9:27 shall confirm the covenant with m'
10:14 days: for yet the vision is for m' days.
11:12 he shall cast down m' ten thousands:
14 there shall m' stand up against
18 unto the isles, and shall take m':
26 and m' shall fall down slain.
33 among the people shall instruct m':
33 by captivity, and by spoil, m' days.

Da 11:34 but *m'* shall cleave to them with
39 shall cause them to rule over *m'*,
40 with horsemen, and with *m'* ships;
41 *m'* countries shall be overthrown:
44 and utterly to make away *m'*.
12: 2 *m'* of them that sleep in the dust
3 they that turn *m'* to righteousness
4 of the end: *m'* shall run to and fro,
10 *M'* shall be purified, and made
Ho 3: 3 Thou shalt abide for me *m'* days;
4 Israel shall abide *m'* days without
8:11 Ephraim hath made *m'* altars to
Joe 2: 2 it, even to the years of *m'* generations.
Am 8: 3 be *m'* dead bodies in every place;
Mic 4: 2 *m'* nations shall come, and say,
3 he shall judge among *m'* people,
11 Now also *m'* nations are gathered
13 thou shalt beat in pieces *m'* people:
5: 7 shall be in the midst of *m'* people
8 Gentiles in the midst of *m'* people
Na 1:12 they be quiet, and likewise *m'*,
3:15 thyself *m'* as the cankerworm,
15 make thyself *m'* as the locusts.
Hab 2: 8 thou hast spoiled *m'* nations, all
10 thy house by cutting off *m'* people,
Zec 2:11 *m'* nations shall be joined to the
7: 3 as I have done these so *m'* years?
8:20 and the inhabitants of *m'* cities:
22 *m'* people and strong nations shall
Mal 2: 6 did turn *m'* away from iniquity.
8 caused *m'* to stumble at the law;
M't 3: 7 when he saw *m'* of the Pharisees
7:13 *m'* there be which go in thereat:
22 *M'* will say to me in that day, Lord,
22 thy name done *m'* wonderful works?
8:11 *m'* shall come from the east and
16 *m'* that were possessed with devils:
30 them an herd of *m'* swine feeding.
9:10 *m'* publicans and sinners came and
10:31 of more value than *m'* sparrows.
13: 3 he spake *m'* things...in parables,
17 *m'* prophets and righteous men
58 he did not *m'* mighty works there
14:36 *m'* as touched were made perfectly
15:30 dumb, maimed, and *m'* others,
34 them, How *m'* loaves have ye?
16: 9, 10 and how *m'* baskets ye took up?
21 suffer *m'* things of the elders and
19:30 *m'* that are first shall be last; and
20:16 for *m'* be called, but few chosen.
28 and to give his life a ransom for *m'*.
22: 9 as *m'* as ye shall find, bid to the
10 together all as *m'* as they found,
14 *m'* are called, but few are chosen.
24: 5 *m'* shall come in my name, saying,
5 I am Christ; and shall deceive *m'*.
10 then shall *m'* be offended, and shall
11 And *m'* false prophets shall rise,
11 shall rise, and shall deceive *m'*.
12 the love of *m'* shall wax cold.
25:21, 23 make thee ruler over *m'* things:
26:28 shed for *m'* for the remission of sins.
60 though *m'* false witnesses came,
27:13 not how *m'* things they witness
19 I have suffered *m'* things this day
52 *m'* bodies of the saints which slept
53 holy city, and appeared unto *m'*.
55 *m'* women were there beholding
M'r 1:34 healed *m'* that were sick of divers
34 and cast out *m'* devils; and suffered
2: 2 *m'* were gathered together,
15 *m'* publicans and sinners sat also
15 for there were *m'*, and they followed
3:10 For he had healed *m'*; insomuch
10 to touch him, as *m'* as had plagues.
4: 2 he taught...*m'* things by parables,
33 with *m'* such parables spake he the
5: 9 My name is Legion: for we are *m'*.
26 suffered *m'* things of *m'* physicians,
6: 2 *m'* hearing him were astonished,
13 And they cast out *m'* devils, and
13 anointed with oil *m'* that were sick,
20 he did *m'* things, and heard him
31 there were *m'* coming and going,
33 *m'* knew him, and ran afoot thither
34 he began to teach them *m'* things.
38 them, How *m'* loaves have ye?
56 as *m'* as touched him were made
7: 4 *m'* other things there be, which
8 and *m'* other such like things ye do.
13 and *m'* such like things do ye.
8: 5 them, How *m'* loaves have ye?
19, 20 how *m'* baskets full of fragments
31 Son of man must suffer *m'* things,
9:12 that he must suffer *m'* things, and
26 insomuch that *m'* said, He is dead.
10:31 But *m'* that are first shall be last;
45 and to give his life a ransom for *m'*.
48 And *m'* charged him that he should
11: 8 *m'* spread their garments in the
12: 5 and him they killed, and *m'* others;
41 and *m'* that were rich cast in much.
13: 6 *m'* shall come in my name, saying,
6 I am Christ; and shall deceive *m'*.
14:24 testament, which is shed for *m'*.
56 *m'* bare false witness against him,
15: 3 priests accused him of *m'* things:
4 *m'* things they witness against
41 *m'* other women which came up
Lu 1: 1 as *m'* have taken in hand to set
14 and *m'* shall rejoice at his birth.
16 *m'* of the children of Israel shall he
2:34 and rising again of *m'* in Israel;
35 the thoughts of *m'* hearts may be
3:18 *m'* other things in his exhortation
4:25 *m'* widows were in Israel in the

Lu 4:27 And *m'* lepers were in Israel in the
41 devils also came out of *m'*, crying
7:11 *m'* of his disciples went with him,
21 cured *m'* of their infirmities and
21 *m'* that were blind he gave sight.
47 thee, Her sins, which are *m'*, are
8: 3 *m'* others, which ministered unto
30 *m'* devils were entered into him.
32 there an herd of *m'* swine feeding
9:22 Son of man must suffer *m'* things,
10:24 *m'* prophets and kings have desired
41 and troubled about *m'* things:
11: 8 and give him as *m'* as he needeth.
53 provoke him to speak of *m'* things:
12: 7 of more value than *m'* sparrows.
19 much goods laid up for *m'* years;
47 shall be beaten with *m'* stripes.
13:24 *m'*, I say unto you, will seek to enter
14:16 made a great supper, and bade *m'*:
15:13 not *m'* days after the younger son
17 *m'* hired servants of my father's
29 Lo, these *m'* years do I serve thee,
17:25 first must he suffer *m'* things, and
21: 8 *m'* shall come in my name, saying,
22:65 And *m'* other things blasphemously
23: 8 he had heard *m'* things of him;
9 questioned with him in *m'* words;
Joh 1:12 But as *m'* as received him, to them
2:12 they continued there not *m'* days.
23 *m'* believed in his name, when they
4:39 *m'* of the Samaritans of that city
41 *m'* more believed because of his
6: 9 but what are they among so *m'*?
60 *M'* therefore of his disciples, when
66 time *m'* of his disciples went back,
7:31 *m'* of the people believed on him,
40 *M'* of the people therefore, when
8:26 *m'* things to say and to judge of
30 these words, *m'* believed on him.
10:20 *m'* of them said, He hath a devil,
32 *M'* good works have I shewed you
41 *m'* resorted unto him, and said,
42 And *m'* believed on him there.
11:19 *m'* of the Jews came to Martha and
45 *m'* of the Jews which came to Mary,
47 for this man doeth *m'* miracles.
55 *m'* went out of the country up to
12:11 of him *m'* of the Jews went away,
37 done so *m'* miracles before them,
42 rulers also *m'* believed on him;
14: 2 Father's house are *m'* mansions:
16:12 I have yet *m'* things to say unto you,
17: 2 give eternal life to as *m'* as thou hast
19:20 This title then read *m'* of the Jews:
20:30 *m'* other signs truly did Jesus in
21:11 for all there were so *m'*, yet was
25 And there are also *m'* other things
Ac 1: 3 his passion by *m'* infallible proofs,
5 the Holy Ghost not *m'* days hence.
2:39 as *m'* as the Lord our God shall call.
40 with *m'* other words did he testify
43 *m'* wonders and signs were done
3:24 as *m'* as have spoken, have likewise
4: 4 *m'* of them which heard the word
6 as *m'* as were of the kindred of the
34 for as *m'* as were possessors of lands
5:11 upon as *m'* as heard these things.
12 *m'* signs and wonders wrought
36 *m'* as obeyed him, were scattered,
37 as *m'* as obeyed him, were dispersed.
8: 7 came out of *m'* that were possessed
7 and *m'* taken with palsies, and that
25 in *m'* villages of the Samaritans.
9:13 I have heard by *m'* of this man,
23 after that *m'* days were fulfilled,
42 and *m'* believed in the Lord.
43 tarried *m'* days in Joppa with one
10:27 found *m'* that were come together.
45 as *m'* as came with Peter,
12:12 *m'* were gathered together praying.
13:31 And he was seen *m'* days of them
43 *m'* of the Jews and religious
48 as *m'* as were ordained to eternal
14:21 to that city, and had taught *m'*,
15:32 the brethren with *m'* words, and
35 of the Lord, with *m'* others also.
16:18 And this did she *m'* days. But Paul,
23 they had laid *m'* stripes upon them,
17:12 Therefore *m'* of them believed;
18: 8 and *m'* of the Corinthians hearing
19:18 And *m'* that believed came, and
19 *M'* of them...which used curious
20: 8 were *m'* lights in the upper chamber,
19 with *m'* tears, and temptations,
21:10 as we tarried there *m'* days, there
20 how *m'* thousands of Jews there
24:10 thou hast been of *m'* years a judge
17 after *m'* years I came to bring
25: 7 laid *m'* and grievous complaints
14 when they had been there *m'* days,
26: 9 do *m'* things contrary to the name
10 and *m'* of the saints did I shut up
27: 7 when we had sailed slowly *m'* days,
20 nor stars in *m'* days appeared,
28:10 honoured us with *m'* honours:
23 came *m'* to him into his lodging;
Ro 2:12 as *m'* as have sinned without law
12 as *m'* as have sinned in the law
4:17 made thee a father of *m'* nations,)
18 become the father of *m'* nations,
5:15 the offence of one *m'* be dead,
15 Christ, hath abounded unto *m'*.
16 is of *m'* offences unto justification.
19 disobedience *m'* were made sinners,
19 of one shall *m'* be made righteous.
6: 3 as *m'* of us as were baptized into

Ro 8:14 as *m'* as are led by the Spirit of God,
29 the firstborn among *m'* brethren.
12: 4 we have *m'* members in one body,
5 So we, being *m'*, are one body in
15:23 these *m'* years to come unto you;
16: 2 for she hath been a succourer of *m'*,
1Co 1:26 that not *m'* wise men after the flesh,
26 not *m'* mighty, not *m'* noble, are
4:15 Christ, yet have ye not *m'* fathers:
8: 5 (as there be gods *m'*, and lords *m'*,)
10: 5 with *m'* of them God was not well
17 we being *m'* are one bread, and
33 own profit, but the profit of *m'*.
11:30 For this cause *m'* are weak and
30 sickly among you, and *m'* sleep.
12:12 body is one, and hath *m'* members,
12 members of that one body, being *m'*,
14 the body is not one member, but *m'*.
20 But now are they *m'* members, yet
14:10 so *m'* kinds of voices in the world,
16: 9 me, and there are *m'* adversaries.
2Co 1:11 upon us by the means of *m'* persons
11 thanks may be given by *m'* on our
2: 4 I wrote unto you with *m'* tears;
6 which was inflicted of *m'*.
17 we are not as *m'*, which corrupt
4:15 through the thanksgiving of *m'*
6:10 as poor, yet making *m'* rich; as
8:22 proved diligent in *m'* things, but
9: 2 your zeal hath provoked very *m'*.
12 by *m'* thanksgivings unto God;
11:18 Seeing that *m'* glory after the flesh,
12:21 shall bewail *m'* which have sinned
Ga 1:14 Jews' religion above *m'* my equals
3: 4 ye suffered so *m'* things in vain?
10 as *m'* as are of the works of the law
16 saith not, And to seeds, as of *m'*;
27 as *m'* of you as have been baptized
4:27 desolate hath *m'* more children
6:12 As *m'* as desire to make a fair shew
16 as *m'* as walk according to this rule,
Ph'p 1:14 *m'* of the brethren in the Lord,
3:15 us therefore, as *m'* as be perfect,
18 (For *m'* walk, of whom I have told
Col 2: 1 as *m'* as have not seen my face in
1Ti 6: 1 Let as *m'* servants as are under the
9 into *m'* foolish and hurtful lusts,
10 pierced...through with *m'* sorrows.
12 good profession before *m'* witnesses.
2Ti 1:18 in how *m'* things he ministered
2: 2 heard of me among *m'* witnesses,
Tit 1:10 there are *m'* unruly and vain talkers
He 2:10 in bringing *m'* sons unto glory, to
5:11 Of whom we have *m'* things to say,
7:23 And they truly were *m'* priests,
9:28 once offered to bear the sins of *m'*;
11:12 so *m'* as the stars of the sky in
12:15 you, and thereby *m'* be defiled;
Jas 3: 1 My brethren, be not *m'* masters,
2 For in *m'* things we offend all. If
2Pe 2: 2 And *m'* shall follow their pernicious
1Jo 2:18 even now are there *m'* antichrists;
4: 1 *m'* false prophets are gone out into
2Jo 7 For *m'* deceivers are entered into
12 Having *m'* things to write unto you,
3Jo 13 I had *m'* things to write, but I will
Re 1:15 his voice as the sound of *m'* waters.
2:24 as *m'* as have not this doctrine, and
3:19 As *m'* as I love, I rebuke and chasten:
5:11 and I heard the voice of *m'* angels
8:11 and *m'* men died of the waters,
9: 9 of *m'* horses running to battle.
10:11 prophesy again before *m'* peoples,
13:15 as *m'* as would not worship the
14: 2 heaven, as the voice of *m'* waters,
17: 1 whore that sitteth upon *m'* waters:
18:17 sailors, and as *m'* as trade by sea,
19: 6 and as the voice of *m'* waters, and
12 and on his head were *m'* crowns;

Maoch (*ma'-ok*)
1Sa 27: 2 the son of *M'*, king of Gath.

Maon (*ma'-on*) See also MAONITES.
Jos 15:55 *M'*, Carmel, and Ziph, and Juttah,
1Sa 23:24 men were in the wilderness of *M'*,
25 and abode in the wilderness of *M'*.
25 after David in the wilderness of *M'*.
25: 2 And there was a man in *M'*, whose
1Ch 2:45 And the son of Shammai was *M'*:
45 and *M'* was the father of Beth-zur.

Maonites (*ma'-on-ites*) See also MEHUNIM.
J'g 10:12 and the *M'*, did oppress you;

mar See also MARRED.
Le 19:27 thou *m'* the corners of thy beard.
Ru 4: 6 lest I *m'* mine own inheritance:
1Sa 6: 5 of your mice that *m'* the land;
2Ki 3:19 and *m'* every good piece of land
Job 30:13 They *m'* my path, they set forward
Jer 13: 9 will I *m'* the pride of Judah, and

Mara (*ma'-rah*)
Ru 1:20 Call me not Naomi, call me *M'*:

Marah (*ma'-rah*)
Ex 15:23 when they came to *M'*, they could
23 could not drink of the waters of *M'*,
23 the name of it was called *M'*.
Nu 33: 8 of Etham, and pitched in *M'*.
9 they removed from *M'*, and came

Maralah (*mar'-a-lah*)
Jos 19:11 went up toward the sea, and *M'*.

Maran-atha (*mar-an-a'-thah*)
1Co 16:22 Christ, let him be Anathema *M'*.

marble
1Ch 29: 2 and *m'* stones in abundance.
Es 1: 6 to silver rings and pillars of *m'*:

Es 1: 6 and blue, and white, and black, *m'*.
Ca 5:15 His legs are as pillars of *m'*, set
Re 18:12 and of brass, and iron, and *m'*,

Marcaboth See BETH-MARCABOTH.

march See also MARCHED; MARCHEDST.
Ps 68: 7 didst *m'* through the wilderness;
Jer 46:22 for they shall *m'* with an army,
Joe 2: 7 they shall *m'* every one on his ways,
Hab 1: 6 shall *m'* through the breadth of
3:12 Thou didst *m'* through the land in

marched See also MARCHEDST.
Ex 14:10 the Egyptians *m'* after them;

marchedst
J'g 5: 4 thou *m'* out of the field of Edom,

Marcus (*mar'-cus*) See also MARK.
Col 4:10 and *M'*, sister's son to Barnabas,
Ph'm 24 *M'*, Aristarchus, Demas, Lucas,
1Pe 5:13 you; and so doth *M'* my son.

Mareshah (*mar'-e-shah*)
Jos 15:44 And Keilah, and Achzib, and *M'*;
1Ch 2:42 sons of *M'* the father of Hebron.
4:21 and Laadah the father of *M'*, and
2Ch 11: 8 And Gath, and *M'*, and Ziph,
14: 9 chariots; and came unto *M'*.
10 in the valley of Zephathah at *M'*.
20:37 Eliezer the son of Dodavah of *M'*
Mic 1:15 heir unto thee, O inhabitant of *M'*:

mariners
Eze 27: 8 of Zidon and Arvad were thy *m'*:
9 the ships of the sea with their *m'*
27 thy *m'*, and thy pilots, thy calkers,
29 the *m'*, and all the pilots of the sea,
Jon 1: 5 Then the *m'* were afraid, and cried

marishes
Eze 47:11 *m'* thereof shall not be healed;

mark See also LANDMARK; MARKED; MARKEST; MARKETH; MARKS.
Ge 4:15 the Lord set a *m'* upon Cain, lest
Ru 3: 4 *m'* the place where he shall lie,
1Sa 20:20 thereof, as though I shot at a *m'*.
2Sa 13:28 *M'* ye now when Amnon's heart
1Ki 20: 7 *M'*, I pray you, and see how this
22 and *m'*, and see what thou doest:
Job 7:20 thou set me as a *m'* against thee,
16:12 pieces, and set me up for his *m'*.
18: 2 *m'*, and afterwards we will speak.
21: 5 *M'* me, and be astonished, and lay
33:31 *M'* well, O Job, hearken unto me:
39: 1 thou *m'* when the hinds do calve?
Ps 37:37 *M'* the perfect man, and behold
48:13 *M'* ye well her bulwarks, consider
56: 6 they *m'* my steps, when they wait
130: 3 thou, Lord, shouldest *m'* iniquities,
La 3:12 and set me as a *m'* for the arrow.
Eze 9: 4 *m'* upon the foreheads of the men
6 any man upon whom is the *m'*;
44: 5 Son of man, *m'* well, and behold
5 *m'* well the entering in of the
Ro 16:17 *m'* them which cause divisions and
Ph'p 3:14 press toward the *m'* for the prize
17 *m'* them which walk so as ye have
Re 13:16 to receive a *m'* in their right hand,
17 save he that had the *m'*, or the
14: 9 and receive his *m'* in his forehead,
11 receiveth the *m'* of his name.
15: 2 over his image, and over his *m'*,
16: 2 upon the men which had the *m'* of
19:20 had received the *m'* of the beast,
20: 4 had received his *m'* upon their

Mark (*mark*) See also MARCUS.
Ac 12:12 of John, whose surname was *M'*;
25 John, whose surname was *M'*.
15:37 John, whose surname was *M'*.
39 and so Barnabas took *M'*, and
2Ti 4:11 Take *M'*, and bring him with thee:

marked
1Sa 1:12 the Lord, and Eli *m'* her mouth.
Job 22:15 Hast thou *m'* the old way which
24:16 *m'* for themselves in the daytime:
Jer 2:22 yet thine iniquity is *m'* before me,
23:18 who hath *m'* his word, and heard
Lu 14: 7 when he *m'* how they chose out

markest
Job 10:14 If I sin, then thou *m'* me, and

market See also MARKETPLACE; MARKETS.
Eze 27:13 and vessels of brass in thy *m'*.
17 they traded in thy *m'* wheat of
19 and calamus, were in thy *m'*.
25 Tarshish did sing of thee in thy *m'*:
M'r 7: 4 And when they come from the *m'*,
Joh 5: 2 at Jerusalem by the sheep *m'* a pool,
Ac 17:17 in the *m'* daily with them that met

marketh
Job 33:11 in the stocks, he *m'* all my paths.
Isa 44:13 *m'* it out with a line; he fitteth it
13 *m'* it out with the compass, and

marketplace
M't 20: 3 saw others standing idle in the *m'*,
Lu 7:32 like unto children sitting in the *m'*,
Ac 16:19 them into the *m'* unto the rulers,

marketplaces
M'r 12:38 and love salutations in the *m'*,

markets
M't 11:16 like unto children sitting in the *m'*,
23: 7 greetings in the *m'*, and to be called
Lu 11:43 synagogues, and greetings in the *m'*.
20:46 robes, and love greetings in the *m'*,

marks See also WAYMARKS.
Le 19:28 dead, nor print any *m'* upon you:
Ga 6:17 my body the *m'* of the Lord Jesus.

Maroth (*ma'-roth*)
Mic 1:12 inhabitant of *M'* waited carefully

marred
Isa 52:14 his visage was so *m'* more than
Jer 13: 7 the girdle was *m'*, it was profitable
18: 4 vessel that he made of clay was *m'*
Na 2: 2 out, and *m'* their vine branches.
M'r 2:22 spilled, and the bottles will be *m'*:

marriage See also MARRIAGES.
Ex 21:10 her raiment, and her duty of *m'*,
Ps 78:63 maidens were not given to *m'*.
M't 22: 2 king which made a *m'* for his son,
4 are ready: come unto the *m'*.
9 many as ye shall find, bid to the *m'*.
30 neither marry, nor are given in *m'*,
24:38 marrying and giving in *m'*, until
25:10 ready went in with him to the *m'*:
M'r 12:25 neither marry, nor are given in *m'*;
Lu 17:27 they were given in *m'*, until the
20:34 world marry, and are given in *m'*:
35 neither marry, nor are given in *m'*:
Jo 2: 1 there was a *m'* in Cana of Galilee;
2 called, and his disciples, to the *m'*.
1Co 7:38 that giveth her in *m'* doeth well;
38 giveth her not in *m'* doeth better.
Heb 13: 4 *M'* is honourable in all, and the
Re 19: 7 for the *m'* of the Lamb is come,
9 unto the *m'* supper of the Lamb.

marriages
Ge 34: 9 make ye *m'* with us, and give your
De 7: 3 Neither shalt thou make *m'* with
Jos 23:12 shall make *m'* with them, and go

married See also UNMARRIED.
Ge 19:14 in law, which *m'* his daughters,
Ex 21: 3 if he were *m'*, then his wife
Le 22:12 If the priest's daughter also be *m'*
Nu 12: 1 of the...woman whom he had *m'*:
1 he had *m'* an Ethiopian woman.
36: 3 And if they be *m'* to any of the sons
11 *m'* unto their father's brother's sons:
12 were *m'* into the families of the sons
De 22:22 with a woman *m'* to an husband.
24: 1 hath taken a wife, and *m'* her,
1Ch 2:21 he *m'* when he was threescore
2Ch 13:21 mighty, and *m'* fourteen wives,
Ne 13:23 that had *m'* wives of Ashdod,
Pr 30:23 odious woman when she is *m'*;
Isa 54: 1 than the children of the *m'* wife,
62: 4 in thee, and thy land shall be *m'*.
Jer 3:14 the Lord; for I am *m'* unto you:
Mal 2:11 *m'* the daughter of a strange god.
M't 22:25 the first, when he had *m'* a wife,
M'r 6:17 Philip's wife: for he had *m'* her.
10:12 husband, and be *m'* to another,
Lu 14:20 another said, I have *m'* a wife,
17:27 did eat, they drank, they *m'* wives.
Ro 7: 3 liveth, she be *m'* to another man,
3 though she be *m'* to another man.
4 that ye should be *m'* to another,
1Co 7:10 unto the *m'* I command, yet not I,
33 he that is *m'* careth for the things
34 she that is *m'* careth for the things
39 liberty to be *m'* to whom she will;

marrieth
Isa 62: 5 For as a young man *m'* a virgin,
M't 19: 9 whoso *m'* her which is put away
Lu 16:18 away his wife, and *m'* another,
18 whosoever *m'* her that is put away

marrow
Job 21:24 his bones are moistened with *m'*.
Ps 63: 5 satisfied as with *m'* and fatness;
Pr 3: 8 to thy navel, and *m'* to thy bones.
Isa 25: 6 of fat things full of *m'*, of wines
Heb 4:12 spirit, and of the joints and *m'*,

marry See also MARRIED; MARRIETH; MARRYING.
Ge 38: 8 thy brother's wife, and *m'* her,
Nu 36: 6 them *m'* to whom they think best;
6 tribe of their father shall they *m'*.
De 25: 5 not *m'* without unto a stranger:
Isa 62: 5 virgin, so shall thy sons *m'* thee:
M't 5:32 shall *m'* her that is divorced
19: 9 *m'* another, committeth adultery:
10 with his wife, it is not good to *m'*.
22:24 his brother shall *m'* his wife, and
30 in the resurrection they neither *m'*,
M'r 10:11 put away his wife, and *m'* another,
12:25 they neither *m'*, nor are given in
Lu 20:34 The children of this world *m'*, and
35 the dead, neither *m'*, nor are given
1Co 7: 9 they cannot contain, let them *m'*:
9 for it is better to *m'* than to burn.
28 if thou *m'*, thou hast not sinned;
28 if a virgin *m'*, she hath not sinned.
36 will, he sinneth not: let them *m'*.
1Ti 4: 3 Forbidding to *m'*, and commanding
5:11 wanton against Christ, they will *m'*;
14 that the younger women *m'*, bear

marrying
Ne 13:27 our God in *m'* strange wives?
M't 24:38 *m'* and giving in marriage, until

Mars' (*marz*)
Ac 17:22 Paul stood in the midst of *M'* hill,

Marsena (*mar'-se-nah*)
Es 1:14 *M'*, and Memucan, the seven

marshes See MARISHES.

Mars'-Hill See MARS' and HILL; also AREOPAGUS.

mart
Isa 23: 3 and she is a *m'* of nations.

Martha (*mar'-thah*)
Lu 10:38 and a certain woman named *M'*
40 But *M'* was cumbered about much
41 *M'*, *M'*, thou art careful and
Joh 11: 1 the town of Mary and her sister *M'*.
5 Jesus loved *M'*, and her sister,
19 the Jews came to *M'* and Mary, to
20 Then *M'*, as soon as she heard that
21 Then said *M'* unto Jesus, Lord, if
24 *M'* saith unto him, I know that he
30 in that place where *M'* met him.
39 *M'*, the sister of him that was dead,
12: 2 made him a supper; and *M'* served:

martyr See also MARTYRS.
Ac 22:20 blood of thy *m'* Stephen was shed,
Re 2:13 Antipas was my faithful *m'*, who

martyrs
Re 17: 6 with the blood of the *m'* of Jesus:

marvel See also MARVELLED; MARVELS.
Ec 5: 8 in a province, *m'* not at the matter:
M'r 5:20 done for him: and all men did *m'*.
Joh 3: 7 *M'* not that I said unto thee, Ye
5:20 works than these, that ye may *m'*.
28 *M'* not at this: for the hour is
7:21 have done one work, and ye all *m'*.
Ac 3:12 men of Israel, why *m'* ye at this?
2Co 11:14 And no *m'*; for Satan himself is
Ga 1: 6 I *m'* that ye are so soon removed
1Jo 3:13 *M'* not, my brethren, if the world
Re 17: 7 unto me, Wherefore didst thou *m'*?

marvelled
Ge 43:33 and the men *m'* one at another.
Ps 48: 5 They saw it, and so they *m'*; they
M't 8:10 When Jesus heard it, he *m'*, and
27 the men *m'*, saying, What manner
9: 8 when the multitudes saw it, they *m'*,
33 the multitudes *m'*, saying, It was
21:20 when the disciples saw it, they *m'*,
22:22 had heard these words, they *m'*,
27:14 that the governor *m'* greatly.
M'r 6: 6 he *m'* because of their unbelief.
12:17 are God's. And they *m'* at him.
15: 5 answered nothing; so that Pilate *m'*.
44 Pilate *m'* if he were already dead:
Lu 1:21 and *m'* that he tarried so long in the
63 name is John. And they *m'* all.
2:33 And Joseph and his mother *m'* at
7: 9 heard these things, he *m'* at him,
11:38 he *m'* that he had not first washed
20:26 and they *m'* at his answer, and held
Joh 4:27 *m'* that he talked with the woman:
7:15 the Jews *m'*, saying, How knoweth
Ac 2: 7 they were all amazed and *m'*,
4:13 and ignorant men, they *m'*; and

marvellous
1Ch 16:12 Remember his *m'* works that he
24 his *m'* works among all nations.
Job 5: 9 *m'* things without number:
10:16 thou shewest thyself *m'* upon me.
Ps 9: 1 I will shew forth all thy *m'* works.
17: 7 Shew thy *m'* lovingkindness, O
31:21 hath shewed me his *m'* kindness
78:12 *M'* things did he in the sight of
98: 1 for he hath done *m'* things: his
105: 5 Remember his *m'* works that he
118:23 Lord's doing; it is *m'* in our eyes.
139:14 *m'* are thy works; and that my soul
Isa 29:14 I will proceed to do a *m'* work
14 even a *m'* work and a wonder:
Da 11:36 speak *m'* things against the God of
Mic 7:15 will I shew unto him *m'* things.
Zec 8: 6 it be *m'* in the eyes of the remnant
6 should it also be *m'* in mine eyes?
M't 21:42 doing, and it is *m'* in our eyes?
M'r 12:11 doing, and it is *m'* in our eyes?
Joh 9:30 Why herein is a *m'* thing, that ye
1Pe 2: 9 out of darkness into his *m'* light:
Re 15: 1 sign in heaven, great and *m'*, seven
3 Great and *m'* are thy works, Lord

marvellously
2Ch 26:15 for he was *m'* helped, till he was
Job 37: 5 God thundereth *m'* with his voice;
Hab 1: 5 and regard, and wonder *m'*;

marvels
Ex 34:10 before all thy people I will do *m'*.

Mary (*ma'-ry*) See also MIRIAM.
M't 1:16 begat Joseph the husband of *M'*,
18 mother *M'* was espoused to Joseph,
20 fear not to take unto thee *M'* thy
2:11 young child with *M'* his mother,
13:55 son? is not his mother called *M'*?
27:56 Among which was *M'* Magdalene,
56 *M'* the mother of James and Joses,
61 And there was *M'* Magdalene, and
61 the other *M'*, sitting over against
28: 1 came *M'* Magdalene and the other
1 the other *M'* to see the sepulchre.
M'r 6: 3 this the carpenter, the son of *M'*,
15:40 among whom was *M'* Magdalene,
40 *M'* the mother of James the less
47 *M'* Magdalene and...the mother of
47 and *M'* the mother of Joses beheld
16: 1 sabbath was past, *M'* Magdalene,
1 and *M'* the mother of James, and
9 he appeared first to *M'* Magdalene,
Lu 1:27 and the virgin's name was *M'*.
30 angel said unto her, Fear not, *M'*:
34 Then said *M'* unto the angel, How
38 And *M'* said, Behold the handmaid
39 *M'* arose in those days, and went
41 heard the salutation of *M'*, the
46 And *M'* said, My soul doth magnify
56 And *M'* abode with her about three
2: 5 be taxed with *M'* his espoused wife.

Lu 2:16 haste, and found *M'*, and Joseph,
19 But *M'* kept all these things, and
34 said unto *M'* his mother, Behold,
8: 2 *M'* called Magdalene, out of whom
10:39 And she had a sister called *M'*,
42 and *M'* hath chosen that good part,
24:10 It was *M'* Magdalene, and Joanna,
10 *M'* the mother of James, and other
Joh 11: 1 town of *M'* and her sister Martha.
2 that *M'* which anointed the Lord
19 the Jews came to Martha and *M'*,
20 him: but *M'* sat still in the house.
28 and called *M'* her sister secretly,
31 when they saw *M'*, that she rose up
32 *M'* was come where Jesus was,
45 of the Jews which came to *M'*, and
12: 3 Then took *M'* a pound of ointment
19:25 *M'* the wife of Cleophas, and
25 wife of Cleophas, and *M'* Magdalene.
20: 1 week cometh *M'* Magdalene early,
11 *M'* stood without at the sepulchre
16 Jesus saith unto her, *M'*. She
18 *M'* Magdalene came and told the
Ac 1:14 and *M'* the mother of Jesus, and
12:12 house of *M'* the mother of John,
Ro 16: 6 Greet *M'*, who bestowed much

Maschil (*mas'-kil*)
Ps 32: *title* A Psalm of David, *M'*.
42: *title* To the chief Musician, *M'*, for the
44: *title* for the sons of Korah, *M'*.
45: *title* for the sons of Korah, *M'*, A Song
52: *title* To the chief Musician, *M'*, A
53: *title* Musician upon Mahalath, *M'*, A
54: *title* chief Musician on Neginoth, *M'*,
55: *title* chief Musician on Neginoth, *M'*,
74: *title* *M'* of Asaph.
78: *title* *M'* of Asaph.
88: *title* *M'* of Heman the Ezrahite.
89: *title* *M'* of Ethan the Ezrahite.
142: *title* *M'* of David; A Prayer when he

Mash (*mash*)
Ge 10:23 Uz, and Hul, and Gether, and *M'*.

Mashal (*ma'-shal*)
1Ch 6:74 *M'* with her suburbs, and Abdon

masons
2Sa 5:11 trees, and carpenters, and *m'*:
2Ki 12:12 And to *m'*, and hewers of stone,
22: 6 carpenters, and builders, and *m'*,
1Ch 14: 1 with *m'* and carpenters, to
22: 2 he set *m'* to hew wrought stones
2Ch 24:12 hired *m'* and carpenters to repair
Ezr 3: 7 They gave money also unto the *m'*,

Masrekah (*mas'-re-kah*)
Ge 36:36 Samlah of *M'* reigned in his stead.
1Ch 1:47 Samlah of *M'* reigned in his stead.

Massa (*mas'-sah*)
Ge 25:14 And Mishma, and Dumah, and *M'*,
1Ch 1:30 Dumah, *M'*, Hadad, and Tema,

Massah (*mas'-sah*) See also MERIBAH.
Ex 17: 7 called the name of the place *M'*,
De 6:16 your God, as ye tempted him in *M'*.
9:22 at *M'*, and at Kibroth-hattaavah,
33: 8 whom thou didst prove at *M'*, and

mast See also MASTS.
Pr 23:34 he that lieth upon the top of a *m'*.
Isa 33:23 not well strengthen their *m'*,

master See also MASTERBUILDER; MASTER'S; MASTERS; MISTRESS; SCHOOLMASTERS; SHEEPMASTER; SHIPMASTER; TASKMASTERS.
Ge 24: 9 under the thigh of Abraham his *m'*,
10 ten camels of the camels of his *m'*,
10 goods of his *m'* were in his hand:
12 said, O Lord God of my *m'* Abraham,
12 shew kindness unto my *m'* Abraham.
14 hast shewed kindness unto my *m'*.
27 be the Lord God of my *m'* Abraham,
27 hath not left destitute my *m'* of his
35 Lord hath blessed my *m'* greatly;
36 bare a son to my *m'* when she was
37 my *m'* made me swear, saying, Thou
39 I said unto my *m'*, Peradventure
42 O Lord God of my *m'* Abraham, if
48 the Lord God of my *m'* Abraham,
49 deal kindly and truly with my *m'*,
54 he said, Send me away unto my *m'*.
56 me away that I may go to my *m'*:
65 the servant had said, It is my *m'*:
39: 2 in the house of his *m'* the Egyptian.
3 And his *m'* saw that the Lord was
8 my *m'* wotteth not what is with me
19 his *m'* heard the words of his wife,
20 And Joseph's *m'* took him, and put
Ex 21: 4 If his *m'* have given him a wife, and
5 say, I love my *m'*, my wife, and my
6 *m'* shall bring him unto the judges;
6 his *m'* shall bore his ear through
8 If she please not her *m'*, who hath
32 give unto their *m'* thirty shekels of
22: 8 *m'* of the house shall be brought
De 23:15 not deliver unto his *m'* the servant
15 is escaped from his *m'* unto thee:
J'g 19:11 the servant said unto his *m'*, Come,
12 And his *m'* said unto him, We will
22 and spake to the *m'* of the house,
23 the *m'* of the house, went out unto
1Sa 20:38 up the arrows, and came to his *m'*.
24: 6 I should do this thing unto my *m'*,
25:10 break away every man from his *m'*.
14 of the wilderness to salute our *m'*;
17 evil is determined against our *m'*,
26:16 ye have not kept your *m'*, the Lord's
29: 4 he reconcile himself unto his *m'*?
30:13 my *m'* left me, because three days
1Sa 30:15 deliver me into the hands of my *m'*,
2Sa 2: 7 your *m'* Saul is dead, and also the
1Ki 22:17 the Lord said, These have no *m'*:
2Ki 2: 3, 5 that the Lord will take away thy *m'*
16 go, we pray thee, and seek thy *m'*:
5: 1 was a great man with his *m'*, and
18 when my *m'* goeth into the house of
20 my *m'* hath spared Naaman this
22 well. My *m'* hath sent me, saying,
25 he went in, and stood before his *m'*.
6: 5 said, Alas, *m'*! for it was borrowed.
15 him, Alas, my *m'*! how shall we do?
22 eat and drink, and go to their *m'*.
23 away, and they went to their *m'*.
8:14 from Elisha, and came to his *m'*;
9: 7 smite the house of Ahab thy *m'*,
31 Had Zimri peace, who slew his *m'*?
10: 9 I conspired against my *m'*, and slew
18:27 Hath my *m'* sent me to thy *m'*, and
19: 4 the king of Assyria his *m'* hath sent
6 them, Thus shall ye say to your *m'*,
1Ch 12:19 He will fall to his *m'* Saul to the
15:27 and Chenaniah the *m'* of the song
2Ch 18:16 These have no *m'*; let them return
Job 3:19 and the servant is free from his *m'*.
Pr 27:18 he that waiteth on his *m'* shall be
30:10 Accuse not a servant unto his *m'*,
Isa 24: 2 as with the servant, so with his *m'*;
36: 8 thee, to my *m'* the king of Assyria,
12 Hath my *m'* sent me to thy *m'* and to
37: 4 the king of Assyria his *m'* hath sent
6 Thus shall ye say unto your *m'*,
Da 1: 3 Ashpenaz the *m'* of his eunuchs,
4: 9 Belteshazzar, *m'* of the magicians,
5:11 father, made *m'* of the magicians,
Mal 1: 6 his father, and a servant his *m'*:
6 and if I be a *m'*, where is my fear?
2:12 doeth this, the *m'* and the scholar,
M't 8:19 unto him, *M'*, I will follow thee
9:11 Why eateth your *M'* with publicans
10:24 The disciple is not above his *m'*,
25 for the disciple that he be as his *m'*,
25 they have called the *m'* of the house
12:38 *M'*, we would see a sign from thee.
17:24 said, Doth not your *m'* pay tribute?
19:16 Good *M'*, what good thing shall I
22:16 *M'*, we know that thou art true,
24 *M'*, Moses said, If a man die,
36 *M'*, which is...great commandment
23: 8 for one is your *M'*, even Christ;
10 for one is your *M'*, even Christ.
26:18 The *M'* saith, My time is at hand;
25 answered and said, *M'*, is it I?
49 and said, Hail, *m'*; and kissed him.
M'r 4:38 him, *M'*, carest thou not that we
5:35 troublest thou the *M'* any further?
9: 5 *M'*, it is good for us to be here:
17 *M'*, I have brought unto thee my
38 *M'*, we saw one casting out devils
10:17 Good *M'*, what shall I do that I
20 *M'*, all these have I observed from
35 *M'*, we would that thou shouldest
11:21 *M'*, behold, the fig tree which thou
12:14 *M'*, we know that thou art true,
19 *M'*, Moses wrote unto us, If a man's
32 Well, *M'*, thou hast said the truth:
13: 1 *M'*, see what manner of stones and
35 when the *m'* of the house cometh,
14:14 to the goodman...The *M'* saith,
45 saith, *M'*, *m'*; and kissed him.
Lu 3:12 unto him, *M'*, what shall we do?
5: 5 *M'*, we have toiled all the night,
6:40 The disciple is not above his *m'*:
40 that is perfect shall be as his *m'*.
7:40 thee. And he saith, *M'*, say on.
8:24 him, saying, *M'*, *m'*, we perish.
45 *M'*, the multitude throng thee and
49 is dead; trouble not the *M'*.
9:33 *M'*, it is good for us to be here:
38 *M'*, I beseech thee, look upon my
49 *M'*, we saw one casting out devils
10:25 *M'*, what shall I do to inherit
11:45 *M'*, thus saying thou reproachest
12:13 *M'*, speak to my brother, that he
13:25 When once the *m'* of the house is
14:21 *m'* of the house being angry said
17:13 said, Jesus, *M'*, have mercy on us.
18:18 Good *M'*, what shall I do to inherit
19:39 unto him, *M'*, rebuke thy disciples.
20:21 *M'*, we know that thou sayest and
28 *M'*, Moses wrote unto us, If any
39 said, *M'*, thou hast well said.
21: 7 *M'*, but when shall these things be?
22:11 The *M'* saith unto thee, Where is
Joh 1:38 is to say, being interpreted, *M'*,)
3:10 Art thou a *m'* of Israel, and knowest
4:31 prayed him, saying, *M'*, eat.
8: 4 *M'*, this woman was taken in
9: 2 *M'*, who did sin, this man, or his
11: 8 *M'*, the Jews of late sought to stone
28 The *M'* is come, and calleth for
13:13 Ye call me *M'* and Lord: and ye
14 If I then, your Lord and *M'*, have
20:16 him, Rabboni; which is to say, *M'*.
Ac 27:11 the *m'* and the owner of the ship,
Ro 14: 4 to his own *m'* he standeth or
Eph 6: 9 that your *M'* also is in heaven;
Col 4: 1 that ye also have a *M'* in heaven.

masterbuilder
1Co 3:10 is given unto me, as a wise *m'*,

master's
Ge 24:27 me to the house of my *m'* brethren.
36 And Sarah my *m'* wife bare a son to
44 hath appointed out for my *m'* son.
48 to take my *m'* brother's daughter
Ge 24:51 and let her be thy *m'* son's wife, as
39: 7 *m'* wife cast her eyes upon Joseph;
8 said unto his *m'* wife, Behold, my
Ex 21: 4 and her children shall be her *m'*,
1Sa 29:10 thy *m'* servants that are come with
2Sa 9: 9 have given unto thy *m'* son all that
10 that thy *m'* son may have food to
10 thy *m'* son shall eat bread alway
12: 8 I gave thee thy *m'* house, and thy
8 thy *m'* wives into thy bosom, and
16: 3 said, And where is thy *m'* son?
2Ki 6:32 the sound of his *m'* feet behind him?
10: 2 seeing your *m'* sons are with you,
3 best and meetest of your *m'* sons,
3 throne, and fight for your *m'* house.
6 the heads of the men your *m'* sons,
18:24 of the least of my *m'* servants,
Isa 1: 3 his owner, and the ass his *m'* crib:
36: 9 of the least of my *m'* servants, and
2Ti 2:21 and meet for the *m'* use, and

masters See also MASTERS'; TASKMASTERS.
Ps 123: 2 look unto the hand of their *m'*,
Pr 25:13 for he refresheth the soul of his *m'*.
Ec 12:11 fastened by the *m'* of assemblies,
Jer 27: 4 command them to say unto their *m'*,
4 Thus shall ye say unto your *m'*;
Am 4: 1 which say to their *m'*, Bring, and
M't 6:24 No man can serve two *m'*: for
23:10 Neither be ye called *m'*: for one is
Lu 16:13 No servant can serve two *m'*: for
Ac 16:16 which brought her *m'* much gain
19 when her *m'* saw that the hope of
Eph 6: 5 obedient to them that are your *m'*
9 ye *m'*, do the same things unto
Col 3:22 Servants, obey in all things your *m'*
4: 1 *M'*, give unto your servants that
1Ti 6: 1 their own *m'* worthy of all honour,
2 And they that have believing *m'*,
Tit 2: 9 to be obedient unto their own *m'*,
Jas 3: 1 My brethren, be not many *m'*,
1Pe 2:18 subject to your *m'* with all fear;

masters'
Zep 1: 9 fill their *m'* houses with violence
M't 15:27 which fall from their *m'* table.

masteries
2Ti 2: 5 And if a man also strive for *m'*, yet

mastery See also MASTERIES.
Ex 32:18 voice of them that shout for *m'*,
Da 6:24 and the lions had the *m'* of them,
1Co 9:25 every man that striveth for the *m'*

masts
Eze 27: 5 cedars from Lebanon to make *m'*

mate
Isa 34:15 gathered, every one with her *m'*.
16 shall fail, none shall want her *m'*:

Mathusala (*ma-thu'-sa-lah*) See also METHUSELAH.
Lu 3:37 Which was the son of *M'*, which

Matred (*ma'-tred*)
Ge 36:39 Mehetabel, the daughter of *M'*,
1Ch 1:50 Mehetabel, the daughter of *M'*,

Matri (*ma'-tri*)
1Sa 10:21 the family of *M'* was taken, and

matrix
Ex 13:12 the Lord all that openeth the *m'*,
15 to the Lord all that openeth the *m'*,
34:19 All that openeth the *m'* is mine;
Nu 3:12 the firstborn that openeth the *m'*
18:15 that openeth the *m'* in all flesh,

Mattan (*mat'-tan*)
2Ki 11:18 slew *M'* the priest of Baal before
2Ch 23:17 slew *M'* the priest of Baal before
Jer 38: 1 Then Shephatiah the son of *M'*,

Mattanah (*mat'-ta-nah*)
Nu 21:18 the wilderness they went to *M'*:
19 And from *M'* to Nahaliel: and from

Mattaniah (*mat-ta-ni'-ah*) See also ZEDEKIAH.
2Ki 24:17 made *M'* his father's brother king
1Ch 9:15 and *M'* the son of Micah, the son of
25: 4 the sons of Heman; Bukkiah, *M'*,
16 The ninth to *M'*, he, his sons, and
2Ch 20:14 the son of *M'*, a Levite of the sons
29:13 sons of Asaph; Zechariah, and *M'*:
Ezr 10:26 sons of Elam; *M'*, Zechariah,
27 of Zattu; Elioenai, Eliashib, *M'*,
30 *M'*, Bezaleel, and Binnui, and
37 *M'*, Mattenai, and Jaasau,
Ne 11:17 *M'* the son of Micha, the son of
22 son of Hashabiah, the son of *M'*,
12: 8 Judah, and *M'*, which was over the
25 *M'*, and Bakbukiah, Obadiah,
35 the son of *M'*, the son of Michaiah,
13:13 the son of Zaccur, the son of *M'*:

Mattatha (*mat'-ta-thah*) See also MATTATHAH.
Lu 3:31 which was the son of *M'*, which

Mattathah (*mat'-ta-thah*) See also MATTATHA.
Ezr 10:33 Mattenai, *M'*, Zabad, Eliphelet,

Mattathias (*mat-ta-thi'-as*) See also MATTITHIAH.
Lu 3:25 Which was the son of *M'*, which
26 of Maath, which was the son of *M'*,

Mattenai (*mat'-te-nahee*)
Ezr 10:33 sons of Hashum; *M'*, Mattathah,
37 Mattaniah, *M'*, and Jaasau,
Ne 12:19 And of Joiarib, *M'*; of Jedaiah,

matter See also MATTERS.
Ge 24: 9 sware to him concerning that *m'*.
30:15 Is it a small *m'* that thou hast taken
Ex 18:16 When they have a *m'*, they come

Ex 18:22 every great m' they shall bring
22 but every small m' they shall judge:
26 but every small m' they judged
23: 7 Keep thee far from a false m'; and
Nu 16:49 that died about the m' of Korah.
25:18 in the m' of Peor, and in the m' of
31:16 against the Lord in the m' of Peor,
De 3:26 speak no more unto me of this m'.
17: 8 If there arise a m' too hard for thee
19:15 shall the m' be established.
22:26 and slayeth him, even so is this m':
Ru 3:18 thou know how the m' will fall:
1Sa 10:16 But of the m' of the kingdom,
20:23 as touching the m' which thou and
39 Jonathan and David knew the m'.
30:24 will hearken unto you in this m'?
2Sa 1: 4 said unto him, How went the m'?
18:13 there is no m' hid from the king,
19:42 then be ye angry for this m'?
20:18 at Abel: and so they ended the m'.
21 The m' is not so: but a man of
1Ki 8:59 all times, as the m' shall require:
15: 5 only in the m' of Uriah the Hittite.
1Ch 26:32 for every m' pertaining to God, and
27: 1 the king in any m' of the courses,
2Ch 8:15 and Levites concerning any m', or
24: 5 year, and see that ye hasten the m'.
Ezr 5: 5 to cease, till the m' came to Darius:
5 answer by letter concerning this m'.
17 pleasure to us concerning this m'.
10: 4 for this m' belongeth unto thee:
9 trembling because of this m', and
14 fierce wrath of our God for this m'
15 Tikvah were employed about this m':
16 tenth month to examine the m'.
Ne 6:13 they might have m' for an evil report,
Es 2:23 inquisition was made of the m',
9:26 they had seen concerning this m',
Job 19:28 the root of the m' is found in me?
32:18 I am full of m', the spirit within
Ps 45: 1 My heart is inditing a good m':
64: 5 encourage themselves in an evil m':
Pr 11:13 a faithful spirit concealeth the m'.
16:20 He that handleth a m' wisely shall
17: 9 he that repeateth a m' separateth
18:13 answereth a m' before he heareth
25: 2 of kings is to search out a m'.
Ec 5: 8 a province, marvel not at the m':
10:20 hath wings shall tell the m'.
12:13 the conclusion of the whole m':
Jer 38:27 him; for the m' was not perceived.
Eze 9:11 by his side, reported the m', saying,
16:20 this of thy whoredoms a small m',
Da 1:14 he consented to them in this m',
2:10 earth that can shew the king's m':
23 made known unto us the king's m'.
3:16 careful to answer thee in this m'.
4:17 This m' is by the decree of the
7:28 Hitherto is the end of the m'.
28 me: but I kept the m' in my heart.
9:23 understand the m', and consider
M'r 1:45 much, and to blaze abroad the m',
10:10 asked him again of the same m'.
Ac 8:21 neither part nor lot in this m':
11: 4 rehearsed the m' from the beginning,
15: 6 together for to consider of this m'.
17:32 We will hear thee again of this m'.
18:14 a m' of wrong or wicked lewdness,
19:38 him, have a m' against any man,
24:22 know the uttermost of your m'.
1Co 6: 1 you, having a m' against another,
2Co 7:11 yourselves to be clear in this m'.
9: 5 might be ready, as a m' of bounty,
Gal 2: 6 they were, it maketh no m' to me:
1Th 4: 6 and defraud his brother in any m':
Jas 3: 5 great a m' a little fire kindleth!

matters
Ex 24:14 if any man have any m' to do, let
De 17: 8 m' of controversy within thy gates:
1Sa 16:18 a man of war, and prudent in m',
2Sa 11:19 an end of telling the m' of the war
15: 3 See, thy m' are good and right;
19:29 speakest thou any more of thy m'?
2Ch 19:11 is over you in all m' of the Lord;
11 house of Judah, for all the king's m':
Ne 11:24 in all m' concerning the people.
Es 3: 4 whether Mordecai's m' would stand:
9:31 the m' of the fastings and their cry.
32 confirmed these m' of Purim;
Job 33:13 giveth not account of any of his m'.
Ps 35:20 devise deceitful m' against them
131: 1 do I exercise myself in great m',
Da 1:20 m' of wisdom and understanding,
7: 1 dream, and told the sum of the m'.
M't 23:23 omitted the weightier m' of the law,
Ac 18:15 to it: for I will be no judge of such m'.
19:39 enquire any thing concerning other m',
25:20 and there be judged of these m'.
1Co 6: 2 ye unworthy to judge the smallest m'?
1Pe 4:15 or as a busybody in other men's m'.

Matthan (*mat'-than*)
M't 1:15 Eleazar begat M'; and M' begat

Matthat (*mat'-that*)
Lu 3:24 Which was the son of M', which
29 which was the son of M', which

Matthew^ (*math'-ew*) See also LEVI.
M't 9: 9 he saw a man, named M', sitting
10: 3 Thomas, and M' the publican;
M'r 3:18 Bartholomew, and M', and Thomas,
Lu 6:15 M' and Thomas, James the son of
Ac 1:13 Thomas, Bartholomew, and M',

Matthias (*mat'-thias*)
Ac 1:23 was surnamed Justus, and M'.
26 their lots; and the lot fell upon M';

Mattithiah (*mat-tith-i'-ah*) See also MATTATHIAS.
1Ch 9:31 M', one of the Levites, who was
15:18 And M', and Elipheleh, and
21 and M', and Elipheleh, and Mikneiah,
16: 5 Shemiramoth, and Jehiel, and M',
25: 3 Jeshaiah, Hashabiah, and M',
21 fourteenth to M', he, his sons, and
Ezr 10:43 Jeiel, M', Zabad, Zebina, Jadau,
Ne 8: 4 and beside him stood M', and

mattock See also MATTOCKS.
1Sa 13:20 coulter, and his axe, and his m'.
Isa 7:25 that shall be digged with the m',

mattocks
1Sa 13:21 they had a file for the m', and for
2Ch 34: 6 with their m' round about.

maul
Pr 25:18 against his neighbour is a m', and

maw
De 18: 3 and the two cheeks, and the m'.

may^ See also MAYEST; MIGHT.
Ge 1:20 fowl that m' fly above the earth in the
3: 2 We m' eat of the fruit of the trees of
8:17 they m' breed abundantly in the earth,
9:16 that I m' remember the everlasting
11: 4 whose top m' reach unto heaven;
7 that they m' not understand one
12:13 it m' be well with me for thy sake;
16: 2 it m' be that I...obtain children by
2 be that I m' obtain children by her
18:19 the Lord m' bring upon Abraham
19: 5 out unto us, that we m' know them.
32, 34 we m' preserve seed of our father.
21:30 that they m' be a witness unto me,
23: 4 I m' bury my dead out of my sight.
9 That he m' give me the cave of
24:14 pitcher, I pray thee, that I m' drink;
49 that I m' turn to the right hand, or to
56 me away that I m' go to my master.
27: 4 and bring it to me, that I m' eat;
4 my soul m' bless thee before I die.
7 make me savoury meat, that I m' eat,
10 bring it to thy father, that he m' eat,
10 that he m' bless thee before his death.
19 my venison, that thy soul m' bless me.
21 I pray thee, that I m' feel thee, my
25 venison, that my soul m' bless thee.
31 venison, that thy soul m' bless me.
29:21 are fulfilled, that I m' go in unto her.
30: 3 that I m' also have children by her.
25 that I m' go unto mine own place,
31:37 that they m' judge betwixt us both.
32: 5 that I m' find grace in thy sight.
42: 2 thence; that we m' live, and not die.
16 that your words m' be proved,
43: 8 that we m' live, and not die, both we,
14 he m' send away your other brother,
18 that he m' seek occasion against us,
44:21 that I m' set mine eyes upon him.
26 for we m' not see the man's face,
46:34 that ye m' dwell in the land of Goshen;
47:19 us seed, that we m' live, and not die,
49: 1 I m' tell you that which shall befall
Ex 2: 7 that she m' nurse the child for thee?
20 man? call him, that he m' eat bread.
3:18 we m' sacrifice to the Lord our God.
4: 5 they m' believe that the Lord God
23 Let my son go, that he m' serve me:
5: 1 people go, that they m' hold a feast
9 men, that they m' labour therein;
7: 4 that I m' lay my hand upon Egypt,
16 they m' serve me in the wilderness:
19 water, that they m' become blood;
19 there m' be blood throughout all the
8: 1 my people go, that they m' serve me.
8 that he m' take away the frogs from
8 they m' do sacrifice unto the Lord.
9 they m' remain in the river only?
16 that it m' become lice throughout all
20 my people go, that they m' serve me.
28 that ye m' sacrifice to the Lord your
29 the swarms of flies m' depart from
9: 1, 13 people go, that they m' serve me.
15 that I m' smite thee and thy people
16 my name m' be declared throughout
22 m' be hail in all the land of Egypt,
10: 2 ye m' know how that I am the Lord.
3 my people go, that they m' serve me.
7 men go, that they m' serve the Lord
12 m' come up upon the land of Egypt,
17 he m' take away from me this death
21 m' be darkness over the land of Egypt,
21 Egypt, even darkness which m' be felt.
25 m' sacrifice unto the Lord our God.
11: 7 ye m' know how that the Lord doth
9 my wonders m' be multiplied in the
12:16 must eat, that only m' be done of you.
13: 9 the Lord's law m' be in thy mouth:
14: 4 m' know that I am the Lord.
12 that we m' serve the Egyptians?
26 the waters m' come again upon the
16: 4 that I may prove them, whether they
32 m' see the bread wherewith I have fed
17: 2 said, Give us water that we m' drink.
6 out of it, that the people m' drink.
19: 9 people m' hear when I speak with
20:12 thy days m' be long upon the land
20 that his fear m' be before your faces,
21:14 him from mine altar, that he m' die.
23:11 that the poor of thy people m' eat:
12 that thine ox and thine ass m' rest, and
12 and thy stranger, m' be refreshed.
25: 8 that I m' dwell among them.
14 that the ark m' be borne with them.
28 that the table m' be borne with them.
Ex 25:37 that they m' give light over against it.
26: 5 loops m' take hold one of another.
11 the tent together, that it m' be one.
27: 5 net m' be even to the midst of the
28: 1 m' minister unto me in the priest's
3 they m' make Aaron's garments to
3, 4 m' minister unto me in the priest's
28 it m' be above the curious girdle of
37 blue lace, that it m' be upon the mitre;
38 Aaron m' bear the iniquity of the holy
38 they m' be accepted before the Lord.
41 m' minister unto me in the priest's
29:46 Egypt, that I m' dwell among them:
30:16 m' be a memorial unto the children
29 them, that they m' be most holy:
30 m' minister unto me in the priest's
31:13 m' know that I am the Lord that doth
15 Six days m' work be done; but in the
32:10 my wrath m' wax hot against them,
10 and that I m' consume them: and I
29 m' bestow upon you a blessing this
33: 5 that I m' know what to do unto thee.
13 now thy way, that I m' know thee,
13 that I m' find grace in thy sight:
35:34 put in his heart that he m' teach,
40:13, 15 m' minister unto me in the
Le 7:24 beasts, m' be used in any other use:
30 m' be waved for a wave offering
10:10 m' put difference between holy and
11 m' teach the children of Israel all the
11:21 m' ye eat of every flying creeping
22 Even these of them ye m' eat; the
34 Of all meat which m' be eaten, that on
34 all drink that m' be drunk in every
47 between the beast that m' be eaten
47 and the beast that m' not be eaten.
14: 8 himself in water, that he m' be clean:
16:13 the incense m' cover the mercy seat
30 m' be clean from all your sins before
17: 5 of Israel m' bring their sacrifices,
5 they m' bring them unto the Lord.
19:25 m' yield unto you the increase thereof:
21: 3 no husband; for her m' he be defiled.
22: 5 whereby he m' be made unclean,
5 man of whom he m' take uncleanness,
12 m' not eat of an offering of the holy
23:21 it m' be a holy convocation unto you:
43 That your generations m' know that I
24: 7 it m' be on the bread for a memorial,
25:27 that he m' return unto his possession.
29 then he m' redeem it within a whole
29 within a full year m' he redeem it.
31 they m' be redeemed, and they shall
32 m' the Levites redeem at any time.
34 suburbs of their cities m' not be sold;
35 a sojourner; that he m' live with thee.
36 that thy brother m' live with thee.
48 that he is sold he m' be redeemed
48 one of his brethren m' redeem him:
49 or his uncle's son, m' redeem him,
49 him of his family m' redeem him;
49 if he be able, he m' redeem himself.
Nu 3: 6 priest, that they m' minister unto him.
4:19 thus do unto them, that they m' live,
6:20 after that the Nazarite m' drink wine.
7: 5 they m' be to do the service of the
8:11 that they m' execute the service of the
9: 7 that we m' not offer an offering of the
10:10 m' be to you for a memorial before
11:13 saying, Give us flesh, that we m' eat.
16 that they m' stand there with thee.
21 flesh, that they m' eat a whole month.
13: 2 they m' search the land of Canaan,
15:39 that ye m' look upon it, and remember
40 That ye m' remember, and do all my
16:21, 45 I m' consume them in a moment.
18: 2 thee, that they m' be joined unto thee,
19: 3 he m' bring her forth without the
22: 6 shall prevail, that we m' smite them,
6 that I m' drive them out of the land:
19 I m' know what the Lord will say unto
25: 4 Lord m' be turned away from Israel.
27:17 Which m' go out before them, and
17 which m' go in before them, and
17 and which m' lead them out, and
17 which m' bring them in; that the
30:13 the soul, her husband m' establish it,
13 it, or her husband m' make it void.
31:23 Every thing that m' abide the fire, ye
32:32 on this side Jordan m' be ours.
35: 6 manslayer, that he m' flee thither:
11 that the slayer m' flee thither, which
15 killeth any person unawares m' flee
17 a stone, wherewith he m' die, and
18 weapon of wood, wherewith he m' die,
23 any stone, wherewith a man m' die,
36: 8 m' enjoy every man the inheritance
De 2: 6 of them for money, that ye m' eat;
6 of them for money, that ye m' drink.
28 sell me meat for money, that I m' eat;
28 me water for money, that I m' drink:
4: 1 you, for to do them, that ye m' live,
2 ye m' keep the commandments of the
10 they m' learn to fear me all the days
10 and that they m' teach their children.
40 this day, that it m' go well with thee,
5: 1 m' learn them, and keep, and do them.
14 maidservant m' rest as well as thou.
16 that thy days m' be prolonged,
16 and that it m' go well with thee,
31 shall teach them, that they m' do them
33 hath commanded you, that ye m' live,
33 that it m' be well with you, and that
33 ye m' prolong your days in the land
6: 2 and that thy days m' be prolonged.
3 to do it; that it m' be well with thee,

De 6: 3 that ye *m'* increase mightily, as the
18 that it *m'* be well with thee, and that
7: 4 me, that they *m'* serve other gods:
8: 1 shall ye observe to do, that ye *m'* live,
18 *m'* establish his covenant which he
9: 5 and that he *m'* perform the word
14 that I *m'* destroy them, and blot out
10: 11 they *m'* go in and possess the land,
11: 8 that ye *m'* be strong, and go in and
9 ye *m'* prolong your days in the land,
18 *m'* be as frontlets between your eyes.
21 That your days *m'* be multiplied,
12: 15 unclean and the clean *m'* eat thereof,
25, 28 that it *m'* go well with thee, and
13: 17 Lord *m'* turn from the fierceness of
14: 10 hath not fins and scales ye *m'* not eat;
20 But of all clean fowls ye *m'* eat.
21 that is in thy gates, that he *m'* eat it;
17: 19 he *m'* learn to fear the Lord his God,
20 *m'* prolong his days in his kingdom,
19: 3 parts, that every slayer *m'* flee thither.
4 shall flee thither, that he *m'* live:
12 of the avenger of blood, that he *m'* die.
13 Israel, that it *m'* go well with thee.
21: 16 *m'* not make the son of the beloved
22: 7 that it *m'* be well with thee, and that
19, 29 he *m'* not put her away all his
23: 20 that the Lord thy God *m'* bless thee
24: 2 she *m'* go and be another man's wife.
4 *m'* not take her again to be his
13 that he *m'* sleep in his own raiment,
19 that the Lord thy God *m'* bless thee in
25: 1 that the judges *m'* judge them;
3 Forty stripes he *m'* give him, and not
15 thy days *m'* be lengthened in the land
26: 12 they *m'* eat within thy gates, and be
29: 9 that ye *m'* prosper in all that ye do.
13 he *m'* establish thee to day for a people
13 and that he *m'* be unto thee a God, as
29 we *m'* do all the words of this law.
30: 12, 13 us, that we *m'* hear it, and do it?
19 that both thou and thy seed *m'* live:
31: 5 that ye *m'* do unto them according
12 within thy gates, that they *m'* hear,
12 and that they *m'* learn, and fear the
13 have not known any thing, *m'* hear,
14 that I *m'* give him a charge.
19 that this song *m'* be a witness for me
26 it *m'* be there for a witness against
28 *m'* speak these words in their ears,
Jos 2: 16 and afterward *m'* ye go your way.
3: 4 that ye *m'* know the way by which ye
7 that they *m'* know that, as I was with
4: 6 That this *m'* be a sign among you,
9: 19 therefore we *m'* not touch them.
10: 4 and help me, that we *m'* smite Gibeon:
18: 6 that I *m'* cast lots for you here before
8 that I *m'* here cast lots for you before
20: 3 and unwittingly *m'* flee thither:
4 a place, that he *m'* dwell among them.
22: 27 But that it *m'* be a witness between us,
27 children *m'* not say to our children
28 we *m'* say again, Behold the pattern
J'g 1: 3 my lot, that we *m'* fight against the
2: 22 That through them I *m'* prove Israel,
6: 30 Bring out thy son, that he *m'* die:
9: 7 that God *m'* hearken unto you.
11: 6 *m'* fight with the children of Ammon.
37 that I *m'* go up and down upon the
13: 14 *m'* not eat of any thing that cometh
17 come to pass we *m'* do thee honour?
14: 13 Put forth thy riddle, that we *m'* hear it.
15 that he *m'* declare unto us the riddle,
15: 12 *m'* deliver thee into the hand of the
16: 5 means we *m'* prevail against him,
5 that we *m'* bind him to afflict him:
25 for Samson, that he *m'* make us sport.
26 Suffer me that I *m'* feel the pillars
26 standeth, that I *m'* lean upon them.
28 that I *m'* be at once avenged of the
17: 9 go to sojourn where I *m'* find a place.
18: 5 *m'* know whether our way which we
9 Arise, that we *m'* go up against them:
19: 9 here, that thine heart *m'* be merry;
22 thine house, that we *m'* know him.
20: 10 for the people, that they *m'* do,
13 that we *m'* put them to death, and put
21: 18 we *m'* not give them wives of our
Ru 1: 9 Lord grant you that ye *m'* find rest.
11 womb, that they *m'* be your husbands?
2: 16 leave them, that she *m'* glean them,
3: 1 for thee, that it *m'* be well with thee?
4: 4 it, then tell me, that I *m'* know:
14 that his name *m'* be famous in Israel.
1Sa 1: 22 that he *m'* appear before the Lord,
2: 36 offices, that I *m'* eat a piece of bread.
4: 3 it *m'* save us out of the hand of our
6: 8 and send it away, that it *m'* go.
20 and that our king *m'* judge us, and
8: 20 we also *m'* be like all the nations;
9: 16 he *m'* save my people out of the hand
26 saying, Up, that I *m'* send thee away.
27 that I *m'* shew thee the word of God.
11: 2 that I *m'* thrust out all your right eyes,
3 that we *m'* send messengers unto all
12 men, that we *m'* put them to death.
12: 7 *m'* reason with you before the Lord
17 that ye *m'* perceive and see that your
14: 6 it *m'* be that the Lord will work for us:
24 that I *m'* be avenged on mine enemies.
15: 25 with me, that I *m'* worship the Lord.
30 that I *m'* worship the Lord thy God.
17: 10 me a man, that we *m'* fight together.
46 earth *m'* know that there is a God in
18: 21 him her, that she *m'* be a snare to him,
21 of the Philistines *m'* be against him.
1Sa 19: 15 to me in the bed, that I *m'* slay him.
20: 5 that I *m'* hide myself in the field unto
27: 5 in the country, that I *m'* dwell there:
28: 7 I *m'* go to her, and enquire of her.
29: 4 that he *m'* go again to his place which
8 I *m'* not go fight against the enemies
30: 22 *m'* lead them away, and depart.
2Sa 3: 21 that they *m'* make a league with thee,
7: 10 they *m'* dwell in a place of their own,
29 it *m'* continue for ever before thee:
9: 1 that I *m'* shew him kindness for
3 *m'* shew the kindness of God unto him?
10 thy master's son *m'* have food to eat:
11: 15 him, that he *m'* be smitten, and die.
12: 22 to me, that the children *m'* live?
13: 5 the meat in my sight, that I *m'* see it,
6 in my sight, that I *m'* eat at her hand.
10 chamber, that I *m'* eat of thine hand.
14: 7 *m'* kill him, for the life of his brother
15 *m'* be that the king will perform the
32 that I *m'* send thee to the king, to say,
15: 20 seeing I go whither I *m'*, return thou,
16: 2 as be faint in the wilderness *m'* drink.
4 thee that I *m'* find grace in thy sight,
11 more now *m'* this Benjamite do it?
12 It *m'* be that the Lord will look on
19: 26 me an ass, that I *m'* ride thereon,
37 again, that I *m'* die in mine own city,
20: 16 near hither, that I *m'* speak with thee.
21: 3 ye *m'* bless the inheritance of the
24: 2 *m'* know the number of the people.
3 the eyes of my lord the king *m'* see it:
12 one of them, that I *m'* do it unto thee.
21 plague *m'* be stayed from the people.
1Ki 1: 2 that my lord the king *m'* get heat.
35 that he *m'* come and sit upon my
2: 4 That the Lord *m'* continue his word
3: 9 I *m'* discern between good and bad:
8: 29 That thine eyes *m'* be open toward
40 they *m'* fear thee all the days that
43 people of the earth *m'* know thy name,
43 that they *m'* know that this house,
50 they *m'* have compassion on them:
52 eyes *m'* be open unto the supplication
58 he *m'* incline our hearts unto him,
60 earth *m'* know that the Lord is God,
11: 21 that I *m'* go to mine own country.
36 David my servant *m'* have a light
12: 6 advise that I *m'* answer this people?
9 give ye that we *m'* answer this people,
13: 6 my hand *m'* be restored me again.
16 I *m'* not return with thee, nor go
18 that he *m'* eat bread and drink water.
15: 19 of Israel, that he *m'* depart from me.
17: 10 water in a vessel, that I *m'* drink.
12 that I *m'* go in and dress it for me
12 and my son, that we *m'* eat it, and die.
18: 5 we *m'* find grass to save the horses
37 people *m'* know that thou art the Lord
20: 9 will do: but this thing I *m'* not do.
21: 2 that I *m'* have it for a garden of herbs,
10 out, and stone him, that he *m'* die.
22: 8 by whom we *m'* enquire of the Lord:
20 *m'* go up and fall at Ramoth-gilead?
2Ki 3: 11 we *m'* enquire of the Lord by him?
17 ye *m'* drink, both ye, and your cattle,
4: 22 I *m'* run to the man of God, and come
41 out for the people, that they *m'* eat.
42 Give unto the people, that they *m'* eat.
43 Give the people, that they *m'* eat:
5: 12 *m'* I not wash in them, and be clean?
6: 2 us a place there, where we *m'* dwell.
13 he is, that I *m'* send and fetch him.
17 thee, open his eyes, that he *m'* see.
20 eyes of these men, that they *m'* see.
22 they *m'* eat and drink, and go to their
28 thy son, that we *m'* eat him to day,
29 Give thy son, that we *m'* eat him: and
7: 9 *m'* go and tell the king's household.
9: 7 *m'* avenge the blood of my servants
18: 27 that they *m'* eat their own dung, and
32 of honey, that ye *m'* live, and not die:
19: 4 It *m'* be the Lord thy God will hear
19 earth *m'* know that thou art the Lord
22: 4 that he *m'* sum the silver which is
1Ch 4: 10 from evil, that it *m'* not grieve me!
13: 2 they *m'* gather themselves unto us:
15: 12 ye *m'* bring up the ark of the Lord God
16: 35 we *m'* give thanks to thy holy name,
17: 24 thy name *m'* be magnified for ever,
27 that it *m'* be before thee for ever:
21: 2 of them to me, that I *m'* know it.
10 one of them, that I *m'* do it unto thee.
22 that I *m'* build an altar therein unto
22 plague *m'* be stayed from the people.
23: 25 they *m'* dwell in Jerusalem for ever:
28: 8 that ye *m'* possess this good land, and
2Ch 1: 10 I *m'* go out and come in before this
6: 20 That thine eyes *m'* be open upon this
31 That they *m'* fear thee, to walk in thy
33 people of the earth *m'* know thy name,
33 *m'* know that this house which I have
7: 16 that my name *m'* be there for ever:
10: 9 we *m'* return answer to this people,
12: 8 that they *m'* know my service, and the
13: 9 the same *m'* be a priest of them that
16: 3 of Israel, that he *m'* depart from me.
18: 7 by whom we *m'* enquire of the Lord:
19 *m'* go up and fall at Ramoth-gilead?
28: 23 to them, that they *m'* help me.
29: 10 fierce wrath *m'* turn away from us.
30: 8 of his wrath *m'* turn away from you.
35: 6 *m'* do according to the word of the
Ezr 4: 15 search *m'* be made in the book of the
6: 10 *m'* offer sacrifices of sweet savours
7: 25 which *m'* judge all the people that are
Ezr 9: 8 our God *m'* lighten our eyes, and give
12 that ye *m'* be strong, and eat the good
Ne 2: 5 fathers' sepulchres, that I *m'* build it.
7 they *m'* convey me over till I come
8 he *m'* give me timber to make beams
4: 22 in the night they *m'* be a guard to us,
5: 2 take up corn for them, that we *m'* eat.
Es 2: 3 they *m'* gather together all the fair
3: 9 be written that they *m'* be destroyed:
4: 11 the golden sceptre, that he *m'* live:
5: 5 that he *m'* do as Esther hath said.
14 that Mordecai *m'* be hanged thereon:
6: 9 they *m'* array the man withal whom
8: 8 the king's ring, *m'* no man reverse.
Job 1: 5 It *m'* be that my sons have sinned,
5: 11 which mourn *m'* be exalted to safety.
10: 20 alone, that I *m'* take comfort a little,
13: 13 peace, let me alone, that I *m'* speak,
14: 6 Turn from him, that he *m'* rest, till he
19: 29 that ye *m'* know there is a judgment.
21: 3 Suffer me that I *m'* speak; and after
22: 2 he that is wise *m'* be profitable unto
27: 17 He *m'* prepare it, but the just shall
31: 6 that God *m'* know mine integrity.
32: 20 I will speak, that I *m'* be refreshed:
33: 17 *m'* withdraw man from his purpose,
34: 22 the workers of iniquity *m'* hide
36 is that Job *m'* be tried unto the end
35: 8 wickedness *m'* hurt a man as thou
8 righteousness *m'* profit the son of
36: 25 Every man *m'* see it;
25 man *m'* behold it afar off.
37: 7 man; that all men *m'* know his work.
12 *m'* do whatsoever he commandeth
38: 34 abundance of waters *m'* cover thee?
35 that they *m'* go, and say unto thee,
39: 15 that the foot *m'* crush them, or
15 that the wild beast *m'* break them.
Ps 9: 14 That I *m'* shew forth all thy praise in
20 *m'* know themselves to be but men.
10: 10 the poor *m'* fall by his strong ones.
18 man of the earth *m'* no more oppress.
11: 2 they *m'* privily shoot at the upright in
22: 17 I *m'* tell all my bones: they look and
26: 7 That I *m'* publish with the voice of
27: 4 I *m'* dwell in the house of the Lord
30: 5 weeping *m'* endure for a night, but joy
12 that my glory *m'* sing praise to thee,
34: 12 loveth many days, that he *m'* see good?
39: 4 it is; that I *m'* know how frail I am.
13 that I *m'* recover strength, before I go
41: 10 raise me up, that I *m'* requite them.
48: 13 that ye *m'* tell it to the generation
50: 4 the earth, that he *m'* judge his people.
51: 8 bones...thou hast broken *m'* rejoice.
56: 13 I *m'* walk before God in the light of
58: 8 woman, that they *m'* not see the sun.
59: 13 consume them, that they *m'* not be:
60: 4 *m'* be displayed because of the truth.
5 That thy beloved *m'* be delivered;
61: 7 and truth, which *m'* preserve him.
8 that I *m'* daily perform my vows.
64: 4 they *m'* shoot in secret at the perfect:
65: 4 thee, that he *m'* dwell in thy courts:
67: 2 That thy way *m'* be known upon earth,
68: 23 thy foot *m'* be dipped in the blood
69: 35 that they *m'* dwell there, and have it
71: 3 whereunto I *m'* continually resort:
73: 28 God, that I *m'* declare all thy works.
76: 7 and who *m'* stand in thy sight when
83: 4 the name of Israel *m'* be no more in
16 that they *m'* seek thy name, O Lord.
18 That men *m'* know that thou, whose
84: 3 nest...where she *m'* lay her young,
85: 6 that thy people *m'* rejoice in thee?
9 him; that glory *m'* dwell in our land.
86: 17 that they which hate me *m'* see it, and
90: 12 we *m'* apply our hearts unto wisdom.
14 we *m'* rejoice and be glad all our days.
101: 6 the land, that they *m'* dwell with me:
8 I *m'* cut off all wicked doers from the
104: 9 set a bound that they *m'* not pass over,
14 *m'* bring forth food out of the earth;
106: 5 That I *m'* see the good of thy chosen,
5 that I *m'* rejoice in the gladness of thy
5 that I *m'* glory with thine inheritance.
107: 36 they *m'* prepare a city for habitation;
37 which *m'* yield fruits of increase.
108: 6 That thy beloved *m'* be delivered:
109: 15 he *m'* cut off the memory of them from
27 they *m'* know that this is thy hand;
111: 6 he *m'* give them the heritage of the
113: 8 he *m'* set him with princes, even with
119: 17 that I *m'* live, and keep thy word.
18 I *m'* behold wondrous things out of
73 that I *m'* learn thy commandments.
77 mercies come unto me, that I *m'* live;
116 according unto thy word, that I *m'* live:
125 that I *m'* know thy testimonies.
124: 1 was on our side, now *m'* Israel say;
129: 1 me from my youth, *m'* Israel now say:
142: 7 of prison, that I *m'* praise thy name:
144: 12 our sons *m'* be as plants grown up in
12 our daughters *m'* be as corner stones,
13 That our garners *m'* be full, affording
13 our sheep *m'* bring forth thousands
14 That our oxen *m'* be strong to labour;
Pr 5: 2 and that thy lips *m'* keep knowledge.
7: 5 *m'* keep thee from the strange woman,
8: 11 all things that *m'* be desired are not to
21 I *m'* cause those that love me to inherit
15: 24 that he *m'* depart from hell beneath.
18: 2 but that his heart *m'* discover itself.
20: 21 An inheritance *m'* be gotten hastily at
22: 19 That thy trust *m'* be in the Lord, I
27: 1 knowest not what a day *m'* bring forth.

Pr 27:11 I m· answer him that reproacheth me.
Ec 1:10 there any thing whereof it m· be said,
2:26 m· give to him that is good before God.
5:15 which he m· carry away in his hand.
6:10 neither m· he contend with him
8: 4 and who m· say unto him, What doest
Ca 4:16 that the spices thereof m· flow out.
6: 1 aside? that we m· seek him with thee.
13 return, that we m· look upon thee.
Isa 5: 8 m· be placed alone in the midst of the
11 that they m· follow strong drink;
19 hasten his work, that we m· see it:
19 nigh and come, that we m· know it!
7:15 he m· know to refuse the evil, and
10: 2 people, that widows m· be their prey,
2 and that they m· rob the fatherless!
19 be few, that a child m· write them.
13: 2 they m· go into the gates of the nobles.
19:15 the head or tail, branch or rush, m· do.
24:10 is shut up, that no man m· come in.
26: 2 which keepeth the truth m· enter in.
27: 5 that he m· make peace with me;
28:12 ye m· cause the weary to rest;
21 that he m· do his work, his strange
30: 1 my spirit, that they m· add sin to sin:
8 it m· be for the time to come for ever
18 wait, that he m· be gracious unto you,
18 that he m· have mercy upon you:
36:12 wall, that they m· eat their own dung,
37: 4 It m· be the Lord thy God will hear the
20 all the kingdoms of the earth m· know
41:20 they m· see, and know, and consider,
22 that we m· consider them, and know
23 that we m· know that ye are gods:
23 that we m· be dismayed, and behold it
26 from the beginning, that we m· know?
26 that we m· say, He is righteous?
42:18 and look, ye blind, that ye m· see.
43: 9 witnesses, that they m· be justified:
10 that ye m· know and believe me, and
44: 9 nor know; that they m· be ashamed.
13 a man; that it m· remain in the house.
45: 6 m· know from the rising of the sun,
46: 5 and compare me, that we m· be like?
49:15 yea, they m· forget, yet will I not forget
20 me: give place to me that I m· dwell.
51:14 exile hasteneth that he m· be loosed.
16 that I m· plant the heavens, and lay
23 soul, Bow down, that we m· go over:
55: 6 Seek ye the Lord while he m· be found,
10 bud, that it m· give seed to the sower,
60:11 that men m· bring unto thee the forces
11 and that their kings m· be brought.
21 of my hands, that I m· be glorified.
64: 2 nations m· tremble at thy presence!
65: 8 sakes, that I m· not destroy them all.
66:11 That ye m· suck, and be satisfied with
11 that ye m· milk out, and be delighted
Jer 6:10 and give warning, that they m· hear?
7:18 that they m· provoke me to anger.
23 you, that it m· be well unto you.
9:12 wise man, that m· understand this?
12 hath spoken, that he m· declare it,
17 mourning women, that they m· come;
17 cunning women, that they m· come:
18 that our eyes m· run down with tears,
10:18 distress them, that they m· find it so.
11: 5 I m· perform the oath which I have
19 his name m· be no more remembered.
13:23 then m· ye also do good, that are
26 thy face, that thy shame m· appear.
16:12 that they m· not hearken unto me:
21: 2 works, that he m· go up from us.
26: 3 that I m· repent me of the evil, which
28:14 they m· serve Nebuchadnezzar king
29: 6 that they m· bear sons and daughters;
6 that ye m· be increased there, and not
32:14 that they m· continue many days.
39 one way, that they m· fear me for ever,
33:21 Then m· also my covenant be broken
35: 7 that ye m· live many days in the land
36: 3 It m· be that the house of Judah will
3 they m· return every man from his evil
3 I m· forgive their iniquity and their
7 It m· be they will present their
42: 3 the Lord thy God m· shew us the way
3 shew us the way wherein we m· walk,
3 walk, and the thing that we m· do.
6 that it m· be well with us, when we
12 that he m· have mercy upon you, and
44:29 ye m· know that my words shall surely
48: 9 Moab, that it m· flee and get away:
49:19 man, that I m· appoint over her?
50:34 that he m· give rest to the land, and
44 man that I m· appoint over her?
51: 8 for her pain, if so be she m· be healed.
39 that they m· rejoice, and sleep a
La 2:13 that I m· comfort thee, O virgin
3:29 in the dust; if so be there m· be hope.
Eze 4:17 That they m· want bread and water,
6: 6 that your altars m· be laid waste and
6 and your idols m· be broken and cease,
6 and your images m· be cut down,
6 and your works m· be abolished.
8 ye m· have some that shall escape the
11:20 That they m· walk in my statutes, and
12: 3 it m· be they will consider, though
16 they m· declare all their abominations
19 that her land m· be desolate from all
14: 5 I m· take the house of Israel in their
11 That the house of Israel m· go no more
11 but that they m· be my people, and I
11 I m· be their God, saith the Lord God.
15 no man m· pass through because of
16:33 they m· come unto thee on every side
37 that they m· see all thy nakedness.

Eze 20:20 m· know that I am the Lord your God.
21: 5 all flesh m· know that I the Lord
10 it is furbished that it m· glitter:
11 to be furbished, that it m· be handled:
15 that their heart m· faint, and their
19 sword of the king of Babylon m· come:
20 that the sword m· come to Rabbath
23 the iniquity, that they m· be taken.
22: 3 midst of it, that her time m· come,
23:48 all women m· be taught not to do after
24:11 the brass of it m· be hot, and m· burn,
11 the filthiness of it m· be molten in it,
11 it, that the scum of it m· be consumed.
25:10 the Ammonites m· not be remembered
28:17 before kings, that they m· behold thee.
37: 9 upon these slain, that they m· live.
38:16 that the heathen m· know me, when I
39:12 of them, that they m· cleanse the land.
17 that ye m· eat flesh, and drink blood.
43:10 they m· be ashamed of their iniquities:
11 they m· keep the whole form thereof,
44:25 no husband, they m· defile themselves.
30 m· cause the blessing to rest in thine
45:11 the bath m· contain the tenth part of
Da 4:17 the living m· know that the Most High
27 m· be a lengthening of thy tranquillity.
6:15 the king establisheth m· be changed.
Ho 8: 4 them idols, that they m· be cut off.
13:10 that m· save thee in all thy cities?
Am 5:14 good, and not evil, that ye m· live:
15 it m· be that the Lord God of hosts
6:10 we m· not make mention of the name
8: 5 moon be gone, that we m· sell corn?
5 that we m· set forth wheat, making
6 That we m· buy the poor for silver,
9: 1 of the door, that the posts m· shake:
12 they m· possess the remnant of Edom,
Ob 9 of Esau m· be cut off by slaughter.
Jon 1: 7 m· know for whose cause this evil is
11 thee, that the sea m· be calm unto us?
Mic 6: 5 ye m· know the righteousness of the
7: 3 m· do evil with both hands earnestly,
Hab 2: 2 tables, that he m· run that readeth it.
9 house, that he m· set his rest on high,
9 m· be delivered from the power of evil!
Zep 2: 3 it m· be ye shall be hid in the day of
3: 8 that I m· assemble the kingdoms, to
9 m· all call upon the name of the Lord,
Zec 11: 1 that the fire m· devour thy cedars.
Mal 3: 2 who m· abide the day of his coming?
3 m· offer unto the Lord an offering
10 that there m· be meat in mine house,
M't 2: 8 that I m· come and worship him also.
5:16 that they m· see your good works, and
45 ye m· be the children of your Father
6: 2 that they m· have glory of men.
4 That thine alms m· be in secret: and
5 streets, that they m· be seen of men.
16 that they m· appear unto men to fast.
9: 6 that ye m· know that the Son of man
21 If I m· but touch his garment, I shall
14:15 away, that they m· go into the villages,
18:16 witnesses every word m· be established.
19:16 shall I do, that I m· have eternal life?
20:21 Grant that these my two sons m· sit,
33 him, Lord, that our eyes m· be opened.
23:26 the outside of them m· be clean also.
35 you m· come all the righteous blood
26:42 if this cup m· not pass away from
M'r 1:38 next towns, that I m· preach there also:
2:10 that ye m· know that the Son of man
4:12 That seeing they m· see, and not
12 and hearing they m· hear, and not
32 fowls of the air m· lodge under the
5:12 the swine, that we m· enter into them.
23 hands on her, that she m· be healed;
28 If I m· touch but his clothes, I shall
6:36 m· go into the country round about,
7: 9 that ye m· keep your own tradition.
10:17 shall I do that I m· inherit eternal life?
37 Grant unto us that we m· sit, one on
11:25 also which is in heaven m· forgive you
12:15 me? bring me a penny, that I m· see it.
14: 7 ye will ye m· do them good: but
15:32 the cross, that we m· see and believe.
Lu 2:35 thoughts of many hearts m· be revealed.
5:24 that ye m· know that the Son of man
8:16 they which enter in m· see the light.
9:12 they m· go into the towns and country
11:33 they which come in m· see the light.
50 m· be required of this generation.
12:36 they m· open unto him immediately.
14:10 he m· say unto thee, Friend, go up
23 to come in, that my house m· be filled.
16: 4 they m· receive me into their houses.
9 they m· receive you into everlasting
24 he m· dip the tip of his finger in water,
28 that he m· testify unto them, lest they
17: 8 Make ready wherewith I m· sup, and
18:41 said, Lord, that I m· receive my sight.
20:13 it m· be they will reverence him
14 him, that the inheritance m· be ours.
21:22 which are written m· be fulfilled.
36 ye m· be accounted worthy to escape
22: 8 prepare us the passover, that we m· eat.
30 That ye m· eat and drink at my table
31 you, that he m· sift you as wheat:
Joh 1:22 that we m· give an answer to them
3:21 that his deeds m· be made manifest,
4:36 he that reapeth m· rejoice together.
5:20 works than these, that ye m· marvel.
6: 5 shall we buy bread, that these m· eat?
7 that every one of them m· take a little.
30 shewest thou then, that we m· see,
40 on him, m· have everlasting life: and
50 that a man m· eat thereof, and not die.

Joh 7: 3 that thy disciples also m· see the works
10:38 that ye m· know, and believe, that the
11:11 I go, that I m· awake him out of sleep.
15 there, to the intent that ye m· believe;
16 us also go, that we m· die with him.
42 they m· believe that thou hast sent me.
12:36 that ye m· be the children of light.
13:18 but that the scripture m· be fulfilled,
19 to pass, ye m· believe that I am he.
14: 3 that where I am, there ye m· be also.
13 the Father m· be glorified in the Son.
16 that he m· abide with you for ever;
31 world m· know that I love the Father;
15: 2 it, that it m· bring forth more fruit.
16 Father in my name, he m· give it you.
16: 4 ye m· remember that I told you of
24 shall receive, that your joy m· be full.
17: 1 Son, that thy Son also m· glorify thee:
11 me, that they m· be one, as we are.
21 That they all m· be one; as thou,
21 in thee, that they also m· be one in us:
21 that the world m· believe that thou
22 that they m· be one, even as we are
23 that they m· be made perfect in one;
23 that the world m· know that thou hast
24 that they m· behold my glory, which
26 thou hast loved me m· be in them,
19: 4 that ye m· know I find no fault in him.
Ac 1:25 That they m· take part of this ministry
3:19 that your sins m· be blotted out, when
4:29 all boldness they m· speak thy word.
30 signs and wonders m· be done by the
6: 3 wisdom, whom we m· appoint over
8:19 hands, he m· receive the Holy Ghost.
20 the gift of God m· be purchased with
22 thought of thine heart m· be forgiven
17:19 M· we know what this new doctrine,
19:40 whereby we m· give an account of
21:24 them, that they m· shave their heads:
24 and all m· know that those things,
37 captain, M· I speak unto thee?
23:24 them beasts, that they m· set Paul on,
25:11 no man m· deliver me unto them.
26:18 that they m· receive forgiveness of
Ro 1:11 I m· impart to you some spiritual gift,
11 gift, to the end ye m· be established;
12 that I m· be comforted together with
19 that which m· be known of God is
3: 8 Let us do evil, that good m· come?
19 that every mouth m· be stopped, and
19 world m· become guilty before God.
6: 1 continue in sin, that grace m· abound?
8:17 that we m· be also glorified together.
11:10 be darkened, that they m· not see,
14 any means I m· provoke to emulation
31 your mercy they also m· obtain mercy.
12: 2 that ye m· prove what is that good, and
14: 2 believeth that he m· eat all things:
19 wherewith one m· edify another,
15: 6 ye m· with one mind and one mouth
13 m· abound in hope, through the power
17 I m· glory through Jesus Christ in
31 That I m· be delivered from them that
31 I have for Jerusalem m· be accepted
32 That I m· come unto you with joy by
32 of God, and m· with you be refreshed.
1Co 1: 8 m· be blameless in the day of our Lord
2:16 of the Lord, that he m· instruct him?
3:18 him become a fool, that he m· be wise.
5: 5 the spirit m· be saved in the day of the
7 old leaven, that ye m· be a new lump,
7: 5 that ye m· give yourselves to fasting
32 the Lord, how he m· please the Lord:
33 the world, how he m· please his wife.
34 that she m· be holy both in body and
34 world, how she m· please her husband.
35 not that I m· cast a snare upon you,
35 and that ye m· attend upon the Lord
9:18 I m· make the gospel of Christ without
24 the prize? So run, that ye m· obtain.
10:13 to escape, that ye m· be able to bear it.
33 profit of many, that they m· be saved.
11:19 m· be made manifest among you.
14: 1 gifts, but rather that ye m· prophesy.
5 that the church m· receive edifying.
10 There are, it m· be, so many kinds of
12 seek that ye m· excel to the edifying
13 tongue pray that he m· interpret.
31 For ye m· all prophesy one by one,
31 all m· learn, and all m· be comforted.
15:28 under him, that God m· be all in all.
37 it m· chance of wheat, or of some
16: 6 And it m· be that I will abide, yea, and
6 that ye m· bring me on my journey
10 that he m· be with you without fear:
11 in peace, that he m· come unto me:
2Co 1: 4 that we m· be able to comfort them
11 thanks m· be given by many on our
2: 5 part: that I m· not overcharge you all.
4: 7 excellency of the power m· be of God,
5: 9 or absent, we m· be accepted of him.
10 that every one m· receive the things
12 that ye m· have somewhat to answer
8:11 so there m· be a performance also out
14 your abundance m· be a supply for
14 their abundance also m· be a supply
14 want: that there m· be equality:
9: 3 that, as I said, ye m· be ready:
8 things, m· abound to every good work:
10: 2 I m· not be bold when I am present
9 I m· not seem as if I would terrify you
11: 2 I m· present you as a chaste virgin to
12 I m· cut off occasion from them which
12 glory, they m· be found even as we.
16 me, that I m· boast myself a little.
12: 9 the power of Christ m· rest upon me.

Ga 6:13 that they *m*' glory in your flesh.
Eph 1:17 *m*' give unto you the spirit of wisdom
18 *m*' know what is the hope of his calling,
3: 4 ye *m*' understand my knowledge
17 Christ *m*' dwell in your hearts by faith;
18 *M*' be able to comprehend with all
4:15 *m*' grow up into him in all things,
28 that he *m*' have to give to him that
29 it *m*' minister grace unto the hearers.
6: 3 That it *m*' be well with thee, and thou
11 *m*' be able to stand against the wiles
13 ye *m*' be able to withstand in the evil
19 that utterance *m*' be given unto me,
19 that I *m*' open my mouth boldly, to
20 that therein I *m*' speak boldly, as I
21 But that ye also *m*' know my affairs,
Ph'p 1: 9 love *m*' abound yet more and more
10 *m*' approve things that are excellent;
10 ye *m*' be sincere and without offence
26 your rejoicing *m*' be more abundant in
27 I *m*' hear of your affairs, that ye
2:15 ye *m*' be blameless and harmless, the
16 that I *m*' rejoice in the day of Christ,
19 I also *m*' be of good comfort, when I
28 when ye see him again, ye *m*' rejoice,
28 and that I *m*' be the less sorrowful.
3: 8 them but dung, that I *m*' win Christ,
10 That I *m*' know him, and the power of
12 I *m*' apprehend that for which also I
21 that it *m*' be fashioned like unto his
4:17 fruit that *m*' abound to your account.
Col 1:28 we *m*' present every man perfect in
4: 4 I *m*' make it manifest, as I ought to
6 ye *m*' know how ye ought to answer
12 that ye *m*' stand perfect and complete
1Th 3:13 To the end he *m*' stablish your hearts
4:12 ye *m*' walk honestly toward them that
12 and that ye *m*' have lack of nothing.
2Th 1: 5 that ye *m*' be counted worthy of the
12 our Lord Jesus Christ *m*' be glorified
3: 1 word of the Lord *m*' have free course,
2 we *m*' be delivered from unreasonable
14 with him, that he *m*' be ashamed.
1Ti 1:20 that they *m*' learn not to blaspheme.
2: 2 we *m*' lead a quiet and peaceable life
4:15 that thy profiting *m*' appear to all.
5: 7 in charge, that they *m*' be blameless.
16 it *m*' relieve them that are widows
20 before all, that others also *m*' fear.
6:19 that they *m*' lay hold on eternal life.
2Ti 1: 4 thy tears, that I *m*' be filled with joy;
18 grant unto him that he *m*' find mercy
2: 4 he *m*' please him who hath chosen
10 *m*' also obtain the salvation which is
26 And that they *m*' recover themselves
3:17 That the man of God *m*' be perfect,
4:16 that it *m*' not be laid to their charge.
Tit 1: 9 that he *m*' be able by sound doctrine
13 that they *m*' be sound in the faith;
2: 4 they *m*' teach the young women to be
8 is of the contrary part *m*' be ashamed,
10 they *m*' adorn the doctrine of God our
Ph'm 6 of thy faith *m*' become effectual by
Heb 4:16 we *m*' obtain mercy, and find grace
5: 1 he *m*' offer both gifts and sacrifices for
7: 9 And as I *m*' so say, Levi also, who
10: 9 first, that he *m*' establish the second.
12:27 which cannot be shaken *m*' remain.
28 whereby we *m*' serve God acceptably
13: 6 So that we *m*' boldly say, The Lord is
17 that they *m*' do it with joy, and not
19 I *m*' be restored to you the sooner.
Jas 1: 4 ye *m*' be perfect and entire, wanting
2:18 Yea, a man *m*' say, Thou hast faith,
3: 3 horses' mouths, that they *m*' obey us;
4: 3 ye *m*' consume it upon your lusts.
5:16 one for another, that ye *m*' be healed.
1Pe 2: 2 of the word, that ye *m*' grow thereby:
12 they *m*' by your good works, which
15 with well doing ye *m*' put to silence
3: 1 they also *m*' without the word be won
16 *m*' be ashamed that falsely accuse
4: 3 *m*' suffice us to have wrought the will
11 that God in all things *m*' be glorified
13 ye *m*' be glad also with exceeding
5: 6 God, that he *m*' exalt you in due time:
8 about, seeking whom he *m*' devour:
2Pe 1:15 that ye *m*' be able after my decease
3: 2 That ye *m*' be mindful of the words
14 be diligent that ye *m*' be found of him
1Jo 1: 3 ye also *m*' have fellowship with us:
4 we unto you, that your joy *m*' be full.
2:28 we *m*' have confidence, and not be
4:17 that we *m*' have boldness in the day of
5:13 ye *m*' know that ye have eternal life,
13 ye *m*' believe on the name of the Son
20 that we *m*' know him that is true;
2Jo 12 face to face, that our joy *m*' be full.
Re 2:10 of you into prison, that ye *m*' be tried;
14:13 that they *m*' rest from their labours;
19:18 That ye *m*' eat the flesh of kings, and
22:14 they *m*' have right to the tree of life,
14 *m*' enter in through the gates into the

mayest
Ge 2:16 tree of the garden thou *m*' freely eat:
23: 6 but that thou *m*' bury thy dead.
28: 3 that thou *m*' be a multitude of people;
4 thou *m*' inherit the land wherein thou
38:16 me, that thou *m*' come in unto me?
Ex 3:10 that thou *m*' bring forth my people
8:10 *m*' know that there is none like unto
22 thou *m*' know that I am the Lord in
9:14 *m*' know that there is none like me
29 *m*' know...that the earth is the Lord's,
10: 2 thou *m*' tell in the ears of thy son, and
18:19 thou *m*' bring the causes unto God:
Ex 24:12 written; that thou *m*' teach them.
26:33 *m*' bring in thither within the vail
Le 22:23 *m*' thou offer for a free will offering;
Nu 10: 2 thou *m*' use them for the calling of
31 and thou *m*' be to us instead of eyes.
23:13 place, from whence thou *m*' see them:
27 thou *m*' curse me them from thence.
De 2:31 possess, that thou *m*' inherit his land.
4:40 that thou *m*' prolong thy days upon
6:18 *m*' go in and possess the good land
7:22 thou *m*' not consume them at once,
8: 9 out of whose hills thou *m*' dig brass.
11:14 thou *m*' gather in thy corn, and thy
15 cattle, that thou *m*' eat and be full.
12:15 thou *m*' kill and eat flesh in all thy
17 Thou *m*' not eat within thy gates
20 thou *m*' eat flesh, whatsoever thy soul
23 thou *m*' not eat the life with the flesh.
14:21 eat it; or thou *m*' sell it unto an alien:
23 thou *m*' learn to fear the Lord thy God
15: 3 Of a foreigner thou *m*' exact it again:
16: 3 thou *m*' remember the day when thou
5 Thou *m*' not sacrifice the passover
20 that thou *m*' live, and inherit the land
17:15 *m*' not set a stranger over thee,
20:19 for thou *m*' eat of them, and thou shalt
22: 3 likewise: thou *m*' not hide thyself.
7 and that thou *m*' prolong thy days.
23:20 a stranger thou *m*' lend upon usury:
24 *m*' eat grapes thy fill at thine own
25 *m*' pluck the ears with thine hand;
26:19 that thou *m*' be an holy people unto the
27: 3 thou *m*' go in unto the land which
28:58 *m*' fear this glorious and fearful name,
30: 6 with all thy soul, that thou *m*' live.
14 and in thy heart, that thou *m*' do it.
16 that thou *m*' live and multiply: and
20 That thou *m*' love the Lord thy God,
20 and that thou *m*' obey his voice, and
20 and that thou *m*' cleave unto him:
20 thou *m*' dwell in the land which the
Jos 1: 7 thou *m*' observe to do according to all
7 *m*' prosper wheresoever thou goest.
8 *m*' observe to do according to all that
J'g 9:33 *m*' thou do to them as thou shalt find
11: 8 that thou *m*' go with us, and fight
19: 9 on your way, that thou *m*' go home.
1Sa 20:13 thee away, that thou *m*' go in peace:
24: 4 *m*' do to him as it shall seem good
28:15 *m*' make known unto me what I shall
22 *m*' have strength, when thou goest on
2Sa 3:21 *m*' reign over all that thine heart
15:34 *m*' thou for me defeat the counsel of
22:28 that thou *m*' bring them down.
1Ki 1:12 thou *m*' save thine own life, and the
2: 3 *m*' prosper in all that thou doest, and
31 thou *m*' take away the innocent blood,
8:29 *m*' hearken unto the prayer which thy
2Ki 5: 6 thou *m*' recover him of his leprosy.
8:10 unto him, Thou *m*' certainly recover:
1Ch 22:12 *m*' keep the law of the Lord thy God.
14 I prepared; and thou *m*' add thereto.
2Ch 1:11 thyself, that thou *m*' judge my people,
18:33 that thou *m*' carry me out of the host;
Ezr 7:17 thou *m*' buy speedily with this money
Ne 1: 6 that thou *m*' hear the prayer of thy
6: 6 that thou *m*' be their king, according
Job 40: 8 me, that thou *m*' be righteous?
Ps 32: 6 thee in a time when thou *m*' be found:
45:16 thou *m*' make princes in all the earth.
94:13 That thou *m*' give him rest from the
104:27 thou *m*' give them their meat in due
130: 4 with thee, that thou *m*' be feared.
Pr 2:20 thou *m*' walk in the way of good men,
5: 2 That thou *m*' regard discretion, and
19:20 that thou *m*' be wise in thy latter end.
Isa 23:16 songs, that thou *m*' be remembered.
43:26 declare thou, that thou *m*' be justified.
45: 3 that thou *m*' know that I, the Lord,
47:12 able to profit, if so be thou *m*' prevail.
49: 6 thou *m*' be my salvation unto the end
9 That thou *m*' say to the prisoners, Go
Jer 4:14 wickedness, that thou *m*' be saved.
6:27 that thou *m*' know and try their way.
30:13 thy cause, that thou *m*' be bound up:
Eze 16:54 That thou *m*' bear thine own shame,
54 *m*' be confounded in all that thou hast
63 That thou *m*' remember, and be
Hab 2:15 that thou *m*' look on their nakedness!
M'r 14:12 prepare that thou *m*' eat the passover?
Lu 12:58 that thou *m*' be delivered from him;
16: 2 for thou *m*' be no longer steward.
Ac 8:37 with all thine heart, thou *m*'.
24: 8 *m*' take knowledge of all these things,
11 Because that thou *m*' understand,
1Co 7:21 but if thou *m*' be made free, use
Eph 6: 3 and thou *m*' live long on the earth.
1Ti 3:15 that thou *m*' know how thou oughtest
3Jo 2 that thou *m*' prosper and be in health,
Re 3:18 tried in the fire, that thou *m*' be rich;
18 that thou *m*' be clothed, and that the
18 eyes with eyesalve, that thou *m*' see.

maze See AMAZE.

Mazzaroth (*maz'-za-roth*)
Job 38:32 thou bring forth *M*' in his season?

meadow See also MEADOWS.
Ge 41: 2 fatfleshed; and they fed in a *m*'.
18 well favoured; and they fed in a *m*'.

meadows
J'g 20:33 even out of the *m*' of Gibeah.

Meah (*me'-ah*)
Ne 3: 1 the tower of *M*' they sanctified it,
12:39 the tower of *M*', even unto the

meal See also MEALTIME.
Ge 18: 6 three measures of fine *m*',
Nu 5:15 part of an ephah of barley *m*';
1Ki 4:22 and threescore measures of *m*',
17:12 but an handful of *m*' in a barrel,
14 barrel of *m*' shall not waste, neither
16 the barrel of *m*' wasted not, neither
2Ki 4:41 But he said, Then bring *m*'. And
1Ch 12:40 meat, *m*', cakes of figs, and bunches
Isa 47: 2 Take the millstones, and grind *m*':
Ho 8: 7 stalk: the bud shall yield no *m*':
M't 13:33 and hid in three measures of *m*',
Lu 13:21 and hid in three measures of *m*',

mealtime
Ru 2:14 her, At *m*' come thou hither,

mean^ See also MEANEST; MEANETH; MEANING; MEANS; MEANT.
Ex 12:26 unto you, What *m*' ye by this service?
De 6:20 What *m*' the testimonies, and the
Jos 4: 6 saying, What *m*' ye by these stones?
21 to come, saying, What *m*' these stones?
1Ki 18:45 came to pass in the *m*' while,
Pr 22:29 he shall not stand before *m*' men.
Isa 2: 9 the *m*' man boweth down, and the
3:15 *m*' ye that ye beat my people to pieces,
5:15 the *m*' man shall be brought down,
31: 8 the sword, not of a *m*' man, shall
Eze 17:12 Know ye not what these things *m*'?
18: 2 What *m*' ye, that ye use this proverb
M'r 9:10 rising from the dead should *m*'.
Lu 12: 1 In the *m*' time, when there were
Joh 4:31 the *m*' while his disciples prayed
Ac 10:17 vision...he had seen should *m*'.
17:20 know...what these things *m*'.
21:13 What *m*' ye to weep and to break
39 in Cilicia, a citizen of no *m*' city:
Ro 2:15 thoughts the *m*' while accusing
2Co 8:13 I *m*' not that other men be eased, and

meanest
Ge 33: 8 What *m*' thou by all this drove which
2Sa 16: 2 unto Ziba, What *m*' thou by these?
Eze 37:18 not shew us what thou *m*' by these?
Jon 1: 6 unto him, What *m*' thou, O sleeper?

meaneth
De 29:24 what *m*' the heat of this great anger?
1Sa 4: 6 What *m*' the noise of this great shout
14 What *m*' the noise of this tumult?
15:14 *m*' then this bleating of the sheep
Isa 10: 7 Howbeit he *m*' not so, neither
M't 9:13 But go ye and learn what that *m*',
12: 7 But if ye had known what this *m*',
Ac 2:12 one to another, What *m*' this?

meaning
Da 8:15 the vision, and sought for the *m*',
Ac 27: 2 *m*' to sail by the coasts of Asia;
1Co 14:11 if I know not the *m*' of the voice,

means
Ex 34: 7 that will by no *m*' clear the guilty;
Nu 14:18 and by no *m*' clearing the guilty,
J'g 5:22 broken by *m*' of the pransings, the
16: 5 by what *m*' we may prevail against
2Sa 14:14 yet doth he devise *m*', that his
1Ki 10:29 they bring them out by their *m*'.
20:39 if by any *m*' he be missing, then shall
2Ch 1:17 for the kings of Syria, by their *m*'.
Ezr 4:16 by this *m*' thou shalt have no
Ps 49: 7 can by any *m*' redeem his brother,
Pr 6:26 For by *m*' of a whorish woman a
Jer 5:31 the priests bear rule by their *m*';
Mal 1: 9 this hath been by your *m*': will he
M't 5:26 Thou shalt by no *m*' come out
Lu 5:18 and they sought *m*' to bring him in,
8:36 by what *m*' he that was possessed
10:19 nothing shall by any *m*' hurt you.
Joh 9:21 But by what *m*' he now seeth, we
Ac 4: 9 by what *m*' he is made whole;
18:21 I must by all *m*' keep this feast
27:12 if by any *m*' they might attain to
Ro 1:10 if by any *m*' now at length I might
11:14 If by any *m*' I may provoke to
1Co 8: 9 heed lest by any *m*' this liberty of
9:22 that I might by all *m*' save some.
27 lest that by any *m*', when I have
2Co 1:11 upon us by the *m*' of many persons
11: 3 lest by any *m*', as the serpent
Ga 2: 2 lest by any *m*' I should run, or had
Ph'p 3:11 If by any *m*' I might attain unto
1Th 3: 5 lest by some *m*' the tempter have
2Th 2: 3 no man deceive you by any *m*':
3:16 give you peace always by all *m*'.
Heb 9:15 testament, that by *m*' of death,
Re 13:14 by the *m*' of those miracles which he

meant
Ge 50:20 God *m*' it unto good, to bring to
Lu 15:26 and asked what these things *m*'.
18:36 pass by, he asked what it *m*'.

meanwhile See MEAN and WHILE.

Mearah (*me'-a-rah*)
Jos 13: 4 *M*' that is beside the Sidonians,

measure See also MEASURED; MEASURES; MEASURING.
Ex 26: 2 the curtains shall have one *m*'.
8 curtains shall be all of one *m*'.
Le 19:35 in meteyard, in weight, or in *m*'.
Nu 35: 5 ye shall *m*' from without the city
De 21: 2 they shall *m*' unto the cities which
25:15 and just *m*' shalt thou have: that
Jos 3: 4 about two thousand cubits by *m*':
1Ki 6:25 were of one *m*' and one size.
7:37 one casting, one *m*', and one size.

2Ki 7: 1 shall a *m*· of fine flour be sold for
16 So a *m*· of fine flour was sold for a
18 a *m*· of fine flour for a shekel, shall
1Ch 23: 29 and for all manner of *m*· and size;
2Ch 3: 3 first *m*· was threescore cubits,
Job 11: 9 The *m*· thereof is longer than the
28: 25 he weigheth the waters by *m*·.
Ps 39: 4 and the *m*· of my days, what it is;
80: 5 them tears to drink in great *m*·.
Isa 5: 14 opened her mouth without *m*·:
27: 8 In *m*·, when it shooteth forth,
40: 12 the dust of the earth in a *m*·, and
65: 7 I *m*· their former work into their
Jer 30: 11 but I will correct thee in *m*·, and
46: 28 end of thee, but correct thee in *m*·;
51: 13 and the *m*· of thy covetousness.
Eze 4: 11 Thou shalt drink also water by *m*·,
16 and they shall drink water by *m*·,
40: 10 side; they three were of one *m*·:
10 the posts had one *m*· on this side
21 were after the *m*· of the first gate:
22 were after the *m*· of the gate that
41: 17 about within and without, by *m*·.
43: 10 and let them *m*· the pattern.
45: 3 of this *m*· shalt thou...the length
3 of this...shalt thou *m*· the length
11 and the bath shall be of one *m*·,
11 the *m*· thereof shall be after the
46: 22 these four corners were of one *m*·.
47: 18 east side ye shall *m*· from Hauran,
Mic 6: 10 the scant *m*· that is abominable?
Zec 2: 2 To *m*· Jerusalem, to see what is
M't 7: 2 and with what *m*· ye mete, it shall
23: 32 Fill ye up then the *m*· of your
M'r 4: 24 With what *m*· ye mete, it shall be
6: 51 in themselves beyond *m*·, and
7: 37 And were beyond *m*· astonished,
10: 26 they were astonished out of *m*·,
Lu 6: 38 good *m*·, pressed down, and
38 For with the same *m*· that ye mete
Joh 3: 34 not the Spirit by *m*· unto him.
Ro 12: 3 dealt to every man the *m*· of faith.
2Co 1: 8 we were pressed out of *m*·,
10: 13 not boast of things without our *m*·,
13 but according to the *m*· of the rule
13 to us, a *m*· to reach even unto you.
14 stretch not ourselves beyond our *m*·,
15 boasting of things without our *m*·,
11: 23 in stripes above *m*·, in prisons
12: 7 lest I should be exalted above *m*·
7 lest I should be exalted above *m*·.
Ga 1: 13 beyond *m*· I persecuted the
Eph 4: 7 to the *m*· of the gift of Christ.
13 the *m*· of the stature of the fulness
16 working in the *m*· of every part,
Re 6: 6 A *m*· of wheat for a penny, and
11: 1 Rise, and *m*· the temple of God,
2 temple leave out, and *m*· it not;
21: 15 had a golden reed to *m*· the city,
17 according to the *m*· of a man, that

measured
Ru 3: 15 it, he *m*· six measures of barley,
2Sa 8: 2 Moab, and *m*· them with a line,
2 even with two lines *m*· he to put to
Isa 40: 12 hath *m*· the waters in the hollow
Jer 31: 37 If heaven above can be *m*·, and the
33: 22 neither the sand of the sea *m*·:
Eze 40: 5 he *m*· the breadth of the building,
6 and *m*· the threshold of the gate,
8 He *m*· also the porch of the gate
9 Then *m*· he the porch of the gate,
11 And he *m*· the breadth of the entry
13 He *m*· then the gate from the roof
19 Then he *m*· the breadth from the
20 he *m*· the length thereof, and the
23 *m*· from gate to gate an hundred
24 and he *m*· the posts thereof and the
27 and he *m*· from gate to gate toward
28 and he *m*· the south gate according
32 and he *m*· the gate according to
35 gate, and *m*· it according to these
47 So he *m*· the court, an hundred
48 and *m*· each post of the porch, five
41: 1 and *m*· the posts, six cubits broad
2 and he *m*· the length thereof, forty
3 inward, and *m*· the post of the door,
4 So he *m*· the length thereof, twenty
5 After he *m*· the wall of the house,
13 So he *m*· the house, an hundred
15 And he *m*· the length of the building
42: 15 the east, and *m*· it round about.
16 He *m*· the east side with the
17 He *m*· the north side, five hundred
18 He *m*· the south side, five hundred
19 and *m*· five hundred reeds with the
20 He *m*· it by the four sides: it had a
47: 3 eastward he *m*· a thousand cubits,
4, 4 Again he *m*· a thousand, and
5 Afterward he *m*· a thousand; and
Ho 1: 10 which cannot be *m*· nor numbered;
Hab 3: 6 He stood, and *m*· the earth: he
M't 7: 2 mete, it shall be *m*· to you again.
M'r 4: 24 ye mete, it shall be *m*· to you:
Lu 6: 38 withal it shall be *m*· to you again.
Re 21: 16 and he *m*· the city with the reed,
17 he *m*· the wall thereof, an hundred

measures
Ge 18: 6 quickly three *m*· of fine meal,
De 25: 14 not have in thine house divers *m*·,
Ru 3: 15 he measured six *m*· of barley, and
17 These six *m*· of barley gave he me;
1Sa 25: 18 five *m*· of parched corn, and an
1Ki 4: 22 one day was thirty *m*· of fine flour,
22 flour, and threescore *m*· of meal,
5: 11 Hiram twenty thousand *m*· of wheat
1Ki 5: 11 and twenty *m*· of pure oil:
7: 9 to the *m*· of hewed stones,
11 after the *m*· of hewed stones, and
18: 32 as would contain two *m*· of seed.
2Ki 7: 1, 16 and two *m*· of barley for a shekel,
18 Two *m*· of barley for a shekel, and
2Ch 2: 10 thousand *m*· of beaten wheat, and
10 twenty thousand *m*· of barley, and
27: 5 ten thousand *m*· of wheat, and ten
Ezr 7: 22 and to an hundred *m*· of wheat, and
Job 38: 5 Who hath laid the *m*· thereof, if
Pr 20: 10 Divers weights, and divers *m*·,
Jer 13: 25 the portion of thy *m*· from me,
Eze 40: 24 thereof according to these *m*·.
28 south gate according to these *m*·;
29 thereof, according to these *m*·:
32 the gate according to these *m*·.
33 thereof, were according to these *m*·:
35 measured it according to these *m*·;
43: 13 these are the *m*· of the altar after
48: 16 And these shall be the *m*· thereof;
30 four thousand and five hundred *m*·.
33 four thousand and five hundred *m*·:
35 round about eighteen thousand *m*·:
Hag 2: 16 one came to an heap of twenty *m*·,
M't 13: 33 took, and hid in three *m*· of meal,
Lu 13: 21 took and hid in three *m*· of meal,
16: 6 And he said, An hundred *m*· of oil.
7 he said, An hundred *m*· of wheat.
Re 6: 6 three *m*· of barley for a penny;

measuring
Jer 31: 39 the *m*· line shall yet go forth over
Eze 40: 3 of flax in his hand, and a *m*· reed;
5 in the man's hand a *m*· reed of six
42: 15 made an end of *m*· the inner house,
16 the east side with the *m*· reed,
16, 17 with the *m*· reed round about.
18 hundred reeds, with the *m*· reed.
19 hundred reeds with the *m*· reed.
Zec 2: 1 a man with a *m*· line in his hand.
2Co 10: 12 they *m*· themselves by themselves,

measuring-line See MEASURING and LINE.

meat^ See also MEATS.
Ge 1: 29 seed; to you it shall be for *m*·.
30 have given every green herb for *m*·:
9: 3 that liveth shall be *m*· for you;
27: 4 make me savoury *m*·, such as I
7 make me savoury *m*·, that I may
9 make them savoury *m*· for thy
14 and his mother made savoury *m*·,
17 she gave the savoury *m*· and the
31 And he also had made savoury *m*·,
45: 23 laden with corn and bread and *m*·
Ex 29: 41 to the *m*· offering of the morning,
30: 9 nor burnt sacrifice, nor *m*· offering;
40: 29 burnt offering and the *m*· offering;
Le 2: 1 when any will offer a *m*· offering
3 remnant of the *m*· offering shall be
4 bring an oblation of a *m*· offering
5 And if thy oblation be a *m*· offering
6 oil thereon: it is a *m*· offering.
7 And if thy oblation be a *m*· offering
8 thou shalt bring the *m*· offering
9 shall take from the *m*· offering
10 that which is left of the *m*· offering
11 No *m*· offering, which ye shall bring
13 every oblation of thy *m*· offering
13 to be lacking from thy *m*· offering:
14 offer a *m*· offering of thy firstfruits
14 thou shalt offer for the *m*· offering
15 thereon: it is a *m*· offering.
5: 13 be the priest's, as a *m*· offering.
6: 14 this is the law of the *m*· offering:
15 of the flour of the *m*· offering,
15 which is upon the *m*· offering,
20 flour for a *m*· offering perpetual,
21 the baken pieces of the *m*· offering
23 every *m*· offering for the priest
7: 9 And all the *m*· offering that is baken
10 every *m*· offering, mingled with oil,
37 burnt offering, of the *m*· offering,
9: 4 and a *m*· offering mingled with oil:
17 he brought the *m*· offering, and took
10: 12 Take the *m*· offering that remaineth
11: 34 Of all *m*· which may be eaten, that
14: 10 deals of fine flour for a *m*· offering,
20 and the *m*· offering upon the altar:
21 mingled with oil for a *m*· offering,
31 offering, with the *m*· offering:
22: 11 house: they shall eat of his *m*·.
13 she shall eat of her father's *m*·:
23: 13 the *m*· offering thereof shall be
16 shall offer a new *m*· offering unto
18 the Lord, with their *m*· offering,
37 a burnt offering, and a *m*· offering,
25: 6 of the land shall be *m*· for you;
7 all the increase thereof be *m*·.
Nu 4: 16 and the daily *m*· offering,
6: 15 and their *m*· offering, and their
17 shall offer also his *m*· offering,
7: 13, 19, 25, 31, 37, 43, 49, 55, 61, 67, 73, 79 flour
mingled with oil for a *m*· offering:
87 twelve, with their *m*· offering:
8: 8 young bullock with his *m*· offering,
15: 4 bring a *m*· offering of a tenth deal
6 shalt prepare for a *m*· offering
9 a *m*· offering of three tenth deals of
24 with his *m*· offering, and his drink
18: 9 every *m*· offering of theirs, and
28: 5 ephah of flour for a *m*· offering,
8 as the *m*· offering of the morning,
9, 12, 12 of flour for a *m*· offering,
13 mingled with oil for a *m*· offering
20 their *m*· offering shall be of flour
Nu 28: 24 *m*· of the sacrifice made by fire,
26 when ye bring a new *m*· offering
28 *m*· offering of flour mingled with
31 offering, and his *m*· offering,
29: 3 their *m*· offering shall be of flour
6 his *m*· offering, and the daily burnt
6 and his *m*· offering, and their drink
9 their *m*· offerings shall be of flour
11 and the *m*· offering of it, and their
14 their *m*· offering shall be of flour
16 his *m*· offering, and his drink
18 their *m*· offering and their drink
19 the *m*· offering thereof, and their
21 their *m*· offering and their drink
22 burnt offering, and his *m*· offering,
24 Their *m*· offering and their drink
25 burnt offering, his *m*· offering, and
27 their *m*· offering and their drink
28 and his *m*· offering, and his drink
30 their *m*· offering and their drink
31 his *m*· offering, and his drink
33 their *m*· offering and their drink
34 his *m*· offering, and his drink
37 Their *m*· offering and their drink
38 and his *m*· offering, and his drink
39 for your *m*· offerings, and for your
De 2: 6 Ye shall buy *m*· of them for money,
28 Thou shalt sell me *m*· for money,
20: 20 that they be not trees for *m*·, thou
28: 26 thy carcase shall be *m*· unto all
Jos 22: 23 burnt offering or *m*· offering,
29 burnt offerings, for *m*· offerings, or
J'g 1: 7 off, gathered their *m*· under my table:
13: 19 took a kid with a *m*· offering, and
23 and a *m*· offering at our hands,
14: 14 Out of the eater came forth *m*·,
1Sa 20: 5 not fail to sit with the king at *m*·:
24 the king sat him down to eat *m*·.
27 cometh not the son of Jesse to *m*·,
34 did eat no *m*· the second day of the
2Sa 3: 35 to eat *m*· while it was yet day,
11: 8 him a mess of *m*· from the king.
12: 3 it did eat of his own *m*·, and drank
13: 5 Tamar come, and give me *m*·,
5 dress the *m*· in my sight, that I
7 Amnon's house, and dress him *m*·.
10 Bring the *m*· into the chamber,
1Ki 8: 64, 64 offerings, and *m*· offerings,
10: 5 the *m*· of his table, and the sitting
19: 8 the strength of that *m*· forty days
2Ki 3: 20 when the *m*· offering was offered,
16: 13 burnt offering, and his *m*· offering,
15 evening *m*· offering, and the king's
15 and his *m*· offering, with the burnt
15 their *m*· offering, and their drink
1Ch 12: 40 on oxen, and *m*·, meal, cakes of
21: 23 and the wheat for the *m*· offering;
23: 29 fine flour for *m*· offering, and for
2Ch 7: 7 and the *m*· offerings, and the fat.
9: 4 And the *m*· of his table, and the
Ezr 3: 7 and *m*·, and drink, and oil, unto
7: 17 their *m*· offerings and their drink
Ne 10: 33 for the continual *m*· offering, and
13: 5 aforetime they laid the *m*· offerings,
9 *m*· offering and the frankincense,
Job 6: 7 to touch are as my sorrowful *m*·.
12: 11 words? and the mouth taste his *m*·?
20: 14 his *m*· in his bowels is turned, it
21 There shall none of his *m*· be left;
30: 4 and juniper roots for their *m*·.
33: 20 bread, and his soul dainty *m*·.
34: 3 words, as the mouth tasteth *m*·.
36: 31 people; he giveth *m*· in abundance.
38: 41 God, they wander for lack of *m*·.
Ps 42: 3 My tears have been my *m*· day
44: 11 us like sheep appointed for *m*·;
59: 15 them wander up and down for *m*·,
69: 21 They gave me also gall for my *m*·;
74: 14 gavest him to be *m*· to the people
78: 18 heart by asking *m*· for their lust.
25 food: he sent them *m*· to the full.
30 their *m*· was yet in their mouths,
79: 2 servants have they given to be *m*·
104: 21 prey, and seek their *m*· from God.
27 give them their *m*· in due season.
107: 18 soul abhorreth all manner of *m*·;
111: 5 hath given *m*· unto them that fear
145: 15 givest them their *m*· in due season.
Pr 6: 8 Provideth her *m*· in the summer,
23: 3 dainties: for they are deceitful *m*·.
30: 22 and a fool when he is filled with *m*·;
25 prepare their *m*· in the summer;
31: 15 giveth *m*· to her household, and a
Isa 57: 6 thou hast offered a *m*· offering.
62: 8 no more give thy corn to be *m*·
65: 25 dust shall be the serpent's *m*·.
Jer 7: 33 carcases of this people shall be *m*·
16: 4 carcases shall be *m*· for the fowls
17: 26 and *m*· offerings, and incense, and
19: 7 will I give to be *m*· for the fowls
33: 18 to kindle *m*· offerings, and to do
34: 20 dead bodies shall be for *m*· unto
La 1: 11 given their pleasant things for *m*·
19 they sought their *m*· to relieve
4: 10 were their *m*· in the destruction
Eze 4: 10 thy *m*· which thou shalt eat shall
16: 19 My *m*· also which I gave thee,
29: 5 given thee for *m*· to the beasts of
34: 5 became *m*· to all the beasts of the
8 flock became *m*· to every beast of
10 that they may not be *m*· for them.
42: 13 holy things, and the *m*· offering,
44: 29 They shall eat the *m*· offering, and
45: 15 for a *m*· offering, and for a burnt
17 burnt offerings, and *m*· offerings,
17 and the *m*· offering, and the burnt

Eze 45: 24 he shall prepare a *m'* offering of an
25 according to the *m'* offering, and
46: 5 *m'* offering shall be an ephah for
5 the *m'* offering for the lambs as he
7 he shall prepare a *m'* offering, an
11 the *m'* offering shall be an ephah
14 shalt prepare a *m'* offering for it
14 a *m'* offering continually by a
15 the *m'* offering, and the oil, every
20 they shall bake the *m'* offering;
47: 12 shall grow all trees for *m'*, whose
12 the fruit thereof shall be for *m'*,
Da 1: 5 a daily provision of the king's *m'*,
8 with the portion of the king's *m'*,
10 hath appointed your *m'* and your
13 eat of the portion of the king's *m'*:
15 eat the portion of the king's *m'*.
16 took away the portion of their *m'*,
4: 12 much, and in it was *m'* for all:
21 much, and in it was *m'* for all;
11: 26 feed of the portion of his *m'* shall
Ho 11: 4 their jaws, and I laid *m'* unto them.
Joel 1: 9 The *m'* offering and the drink
13 for the *m'* offering and the drink
16 Is not the *m'* cut off before our
2: 14 a *m'* offering and a drink offering
Am 5: 22 offerings and your *m'* offerings,
Hab 1: 16 is fat, and their *m'* plenteous.
3: 17 and the fields shall yield no *m'*;
Hag 2: 12 pottage, or wine, or oil, or any *m'*,
Mal 1: 12 even his *m'*, is contemptible.
3: 10 there may be *m'* in mine house,
M't 3: 4 his *m'* was locusts and wild honey.
6: 25 Is not the life more than *m'*, and
9: 10 as Jesus sat at *m'* in the house,
10: 10 the workman is worthy of his *m'*.
14: 9 and them which sat with him at *m'*,
15: 37 broken *m'* that was left seven baskets
24: 45 to give them *m'* in due season?
25: 35 an hungred, and ye gave me *m'*:
42 hungred, and ye gave me no *m'*:
26: 7 poured it on his head, as he sat at *m'*.
M'r 2: 15 as Jesus sat at *m'* in his house,
8: 8 broken *m'* that was left seven baskets.
14: 3 as he sat at *m'*, there came a woman
16: 14 unto the eleven as they sat at *m'*,
Lu 3: 11 and he that hath *m'*, let him do
7: 36 Pharisee's house, and sat down to *m'*.
37 sat at *m'* in the Pharisee's house,
49 they that sat at *m'* with him began to
8: 55 and he commanded to give her *m'*.
9: 13 go and buy *m'* for all this people.
11: 37 and he went in, and sat down to *m'*.
12: 23 The life is more than *m'*, and the
37 and make them to sit down to *m'*,
42 their portion of *m'* in due season?
14: 10 of them that sit at *m'* with thee.
15 them that sat at *m'* with him heard
17: 7 from the field, Go and sit down to *m'*?
22: 27 is greater, he that sitteth at *m'*, or
27 serveth? is not he that sitteth at *m'*?
24: 30 as he sat at *m'* with them, he took
41 unto them, Have ye here any *m'*?
Joh 4: 8 away unto the city to buy *m'*.)
32 have *m'* to eat that ye know not of.
34 My *m'* is to do the will of him that
6: 27 not for the *m'* which perisheth,
27 *m'* which endureth unto everlasting
55 For my flesh is *m'* indeed, and my
21: 5 them, Children, have ye any *m'*?
Ac 2: 46 did eat their *m'* with gladness and
9: 19 received *m'*, he was strengthened.
16: 34 set *m'* before them, and rejoiced,
27: 33 besought them all to take *m'*,
34 I pray you to take some *m'*: for
36 cheer, and they also took some *m'*.
Ro 14: 15 brother be grieved with thy *m'*,
15 Destroy not him with thy *m'*, for
17 the kingdom of God is not *m'* and
20 *m'* destroy not the work of God.
1Co 3: 2 fed you with milk, and not with *m'*:
8: 8 But *m'* commendeth us not to God:
10 sit at *m'* in the idol's temple,
13 if *m'* make my brother to offend,
10: 3 did all eat the same spiritual *m'*;
Col 2: 16 no man therefore judge you in *m'*,
Heb 5: 12 of milk, and not of strong *m'*.
14 strong *m'* belongeth to them that
12: 16 morsel of *m'* sold his birthright.

meat-offering See MEAT and OFFERING.

meats See also BAKEMEATS.
Pr 23: 6 neither desire thou his dainty *m'*:
M'r 7: 19 into the draught, purging all *m'*?
Ac 15: 29 abstain from *m'* offered to idols,
1Co 6: 13 *M'* for the belly, and the belly for
13 and the belly for *m'*: but God shall
1Ti 4: 3 commanding to abstain from *m'*,
Heb 9: 10 Which stood only in *m'* and drinks,
13: 9 not with *m'*, which have not

Mebunnai (*me-bun'-nahee*) See also SIBBECHAI.
2Sa 23: 27 Anethothite, *M'* the Hushathite,

Mecherathite (*me-ker'-ath-ite*)
1Ch 11: 36 Hepher the *M'*, Ahijah the

Medad (*me'-dad*)
Nu 11: 26 and the name of the other *M'*:
27 Eldad and *M'* do prophesy in the

Medan (*me'-dan*)
Ge 25: 2 Zimran, and Jokshan, and *M'*,
1Ch 1: 32 *M'*, and Midian, and Ishbak, and

meddle See also INTERMEDDLE; MEDDLED; MEDDLETH; MEDDLING.
De 2: 5 *M'* not with them; for I will not
19 them not, nor *m'* with them:
2Ki 14: 10 why shouldest thou *m'* to thy hurt,
2Ch 25: 19 shouldest thou *m'* to thine hurt,
Pr 20: 19 *m'* not with him that flattereth
24: 21 *m'* not with them that are given to

meddled
Pr 17: 14 contention, before it be *m'* with.

meddleth See also INTERMEDDLETH.
Pr 26: 17 *m'* with strife belonging not to

meddling
2Ch 35: 21 forbear thee from *m'* with God, who
Pr 20: 3 strife: but every fool will be *m'*.

Mede (*meed*) See also MEDES; MEDIAN.
Da 11: 1 in the first year of Darius the *M'*,

Medeba (*med'-e-bah*)
Nu 21: 30 Nophah, which reacheth unto *M'*.
Jos 13: 9 and all the plain of *M'* unto Dibon;
16 the river, and all the plain by *M'*;
1Ch 19: 7 who came and pitched before *M'*.
Isa 15: 2 shall howl over Nebo, and over *M'*:

Medes (*meeds*)
2Ki 17: 6 Gozan, and in the cities of the *M'*.
18: 11 Gozan, and in the cities of the *M'*:
Ezr 6: 2 that is in the province of the *M'*,
Es 1: 19 laws of the Persians and the *M'*,
Isa 13: 17 I will stir up the *M'* against them,
Jer 25: 25 Elam, and all the kings of the *M'*,
51: 11 up the spirit of the kings of the *M'*:
28 nations with the kings of the *M'*,
Da 5: 28 is divided, and given to the *M'* and
6: 8, 12 according to the law of the *M'*
15 O king, that the law of the *M'* and
9: 1 Ahasuerus, of the seed of the *M'*,
Ac 2: 9 Parthians, and *M'*, and Elamites,

Media (*me'-de-ah*) See also MADAI; MEDE; MEDIAN.
Es 1: 3 power of Persia and *M'*, the nobles
14 the seven princes of Persia and *M'*,
18 shall the ladies of Persia and *M'*
10: 2 of the chronicles of the kings of *M'*
Isa 21: 2 Go up, O Elam: besiege, O *M'*; all
Da 8: 20 two horns are the kings of *M'* and

Median (*me'-de-an*) See also MEDE.
Da 5: 31 Darius the *M'* took the kingdom,

mediator
Ga 3: 19 by angels in the hand of a *m'*.
20 a *m'* is not...of one, but God is one.
20 is not a *m'* of one, but God is one.
1Ti 2: 5 and one *m'* between God and men,
Heb 8: 6 he is the *m'* of a better covenant,
9: 15 he is the *m'* of the new testament,
12: 24 Jesus the *m'* of the new covenant,

medicine See also MEDICINES.
Pr 17: 22 merry heart doeth good like a *m'*:
Eze 47: 12 meat, and the leaf thereof for *m'*.

medicines
Jer 30: 13 up: thou hast no healing *m'*.
46: 11 in vain shalt thou use many *m'*;

meditate See also PREMEDITATE.
Ge 24: 63 went out to *m'* in the field at the
Jos 1: 8 shalt *m'* therein day and night,
Ps 1: 2 his law doth he *m'* day and night.
63: 6 *m'* on thee in the night watches.
77: 12 I will *m'* also of all thy work, and
119: 15 I will *m'* in thy precepts, and have
23 thy servant did *m'* in thy statutes.
48 loved; and I will *m'* in thy statutes.
78 cause: but I will *m'* in thy precepts.
148 that I might *m'* in thy word.
143: 5 I *m'* on all thy works; I muse on
Isa 33: 18 Thine heart shall *m'* terror. Where
Lu 21: 14 not to *m'* before what ye shall
1Ti 4: 15 *M'* upon these things; give thyself

meditation
Ps 5: 1 words, O Lord, consider my *m'*.
19: 14 the *m'* of my heart, be acceptable
49: 3 *m'* of my heart...be understanding.
104: 34 My *m'* of him shall be sweet: I will
119: 97 I thy law! it is my *m'* all the day.
99 for thy testimonies are my *m'*.

meek
Nu 12: 3 man Moses was very *m'*, above all
Ps 22: 26 The *m'* shall eat and be satisfied:
25: 9 The *m'* will he guide in judgment:
9 and the *m'* will he teach his way.
37: 11 But the *m'* shall inherit the earth;
76: 9 to save all the *m'* of the earth.
147: 6 The Lord lifteth up the *m'*: he
149: 4 will beautify the *m'* with salvation.
Isa 11: 4 with equity for the *m'* of the earth:
29: 19 The *m'* also shall increase their joy
61: 1 preach good tidings unto the *m'*;
Am 2: 7 and turn aside the way of the *m'*:
Zep 2: 3 ye the Lord, all ye *m'* of the earth,
M't 5: 5 Blessed are the *m'*: for they shall
11: 29 for I am *m'* and lowly in heart:
21: 5 thee, *m'*, and sitting upon an ass,
1Pe 3: 4 ornament of a *m'* and quiet spirit,

meekness
Ps 45: 4 truth and *m'* and righteousness;
Zep 2: 3 seek righteousness, seek *m'*: it
1Co 4: 21 or in love, and in the spirit of *m'*?
2Co 10: 1 by the *m'* and gentleness of Christ,
Ga 5: 23 *M'*, temperance: against such
6: 1 such an one in the spirit of *m'*;
Eph 4: 2 With all lowliness and *m'*, with
Col 3: 12 of mind, *m'*, longsuffering;
1Ti 6: 11 godliness, faith, love, patience, *m'*.
2Ti 2: 25 In *m'* instructing those that oppose
Tit 3: 2 gentle, shewing all *m'* unto all men.
Jas 1: 21 and receive with *m'* the engrafted
3: 13 his works with *m'* of wisdom.
1Pe 3: 15 that is in you with *m'* and fear:

meet See also MEETEST; MEETETH; MEETING, MET.
Ge 2: 18 will make him an help *m'* for him.
20 was not found an help *m'* for him.
14: 17 king of Sodom went out to *m'* him,
18: 2 he ran to *m'* them from the tent
19: 1 seeing them rose up to *m'* them;
24: 17 servant ran to *m'* her, and said, Let
65 that walketh in the field to *m'* us?
29: 13 he ran to *m'* him, and embraced
30: 16 Leah went out to *m'* him, and said,
32: 6 and also he cometh to *m'* thee, and
33: 4 Esau ran to *m'* him, and embraced
46: 29 went up to *m'* Israel his father, to
Ex 4: 14 behold, he cometh forth to *m'* thee:
27 Go into the wilderness to *m'* Moses.
8: 26 Moses said, It is not *m'* so to do;
18: 7 went out to *m'* his father in law,
19: 17 out of the camp to *m'* with God;
23: 4 If thou *m'* thine enemy's ox or his
25: 22 there I will *m'* with thee, and I
29: 42 where I will *m'* you, to speak there
43 I will *m'* with the children of Israel,
30: 6 testimony, where I will *m'*...thee:
36 where I will *m'* with thee: it
Nu 17: 4 testimony, where I will *m'* with you.
22: 36 he went out to *m'* him unto a city
23: 3 the Lord will come to *m'* me: and
15 while I *m'* the Lord yonder.
31: 13 to *m'* them without the camp.
De 3: 18 Israel, all that are *m'* for the war.
Jos 2: 16 lest the pursuers *m'* you; and
9: 11 and go to *m'* them, and say unto
J'g 4: 18 Jael went out to *m'* Sisera, and said
22 Jael came out to *m'* him, and said
5: 30 *m'* for the necks of them that take the
6: 35 and they came up to *m'* them.
11: 31 of the doors of my house to *m'* me,
34 came out to *m'* him with timbrels
19: 3 saw him, he rejoiced to *m'* him.
Ru 2: 22 that they *m'* thee not in any other
1Sa 10: 3 and there shall *m'* thee three men
5 that thou shalt *m'* a company of
13: 10 Saul went out to *m'* him, that he
15: 12 Samuel rose early to *m'* Saul in the
17: 48 drew nigh to *m'* David, that David
48 the army to *m'* the Philistine.
18: 6 to *m'* king Saul, with tabrets, with
25: 32 which sent thee this day to *m'* me:
34 hadst hasted and come to *m'* me,
30: 21 they went forth to *m'* David, and to
21 *m'* the people that were with him:
2Sa 6: 20 of Saul came out to *m'* David,
10: 5 he sent to *m'* them, because the
15: 32 the Archite came to *m'* him with his
19: 15 came to Gilgal, to go to *m'* the king,
16 the men of Judah to *m'* king David.
20 to go down to *m'* my lord the king.
24 of Saul came down to *m'* the king,
25 come to Jerusalem to *m'* the king,
1Ki 2: 8 he came down to *m'* me at Jordan,
19 And the king rose up to *m'* her, and
18: 16 Obadiah went to *m'* Ahab, and told
16 him: and Ahab went to *m'* Elijah.
21: 18 go down to *m'* Ahab king of Israel,
2Ki 1: 3 go up to *m'* the messengers of the
6 There came a man up to *m'* us, and
7 was he which came up to *m'* you,
2: 15 they came to *m'* him, and bowed
4: 26 Run now, I pray thee, to *m'* her,
29 if thou *m'* any man, salute him not;
31 he went again to *m'* him, and told
5: 21 down from the chariot to *m'* him,
26 again from his chariot to *m'* thee?
8: 8 hand, and go, *m'* the man of God,
9 Hazael went to *m'* him, and took a
9: 17 send to *m'* them, and let him say, Is
18 went one on horseback to *m'* him,
10: 15 son of Rechab coming to *m'* him:
16: 10 to Damascus to *m'* Tiglath-pileser
1Ch 12: 17 And David went out to *m'* them,
19: 5 he sent to *m'* them: for the men
2Ch 15: 2 he went out to *m'* Asa, and said
19: 2 Hanani the seer went out to *m'* him,
Ezr 4: 14 was not *m'* for us to see the king's
Ne 6: 2 let us *m'* together in some one of
10 us *m'* together in the house of God,
Es 2: 9 which were *m'* to be given her,
Job 5: 14 They *m'* with darkness in the
34: 31 it is *m'* to be said unto God, I have
39: 21 he goeth on to *m'* the armed men.
Pr 7: 15 came I forth to *m'* thee, diligently
11: 24 that withholdeth more than is *m'*,
17: 12 robbed of her whelps *m'* a man,
22: 2 The rich and poor *m'* together: the
29: 13 and the deceitful man *m'* together:
Isa 7: 3 Isaiah, Go forth now to *m'* Ahaz,
14: 9 is moved for thee to *m'* thee at thy
34: 14 beasts of the desert shall also *m'*
47: 3 and I will not *m'* thee as a man.
Jer 26: 14 as seemeth good and *m'* unto you.
27: 5 unto whom it seemed *m'* unto me.
41: 6 forth from Mizpah to *m'* them,
51: 31 One post shall run to *m'* another,
31 and one messenger to *m'* another,
Eze 15: 4 burned. Is it *m'* for any work?
5 was whole, it was *m'* for no work:
5 less shall it be *m'* yet for any work,
Ho 13: 8 I will *m'* them as a bear that is
Am 4: 12 prepare to *m'* thy God, O Israel.
Zec 2: 3 another angel went out to *m'* him,
M't 3: 8 therefore fruits *m'* for repentance:
8: 34 city came out to *m'* Jesus:
15: 26 not *m'* to take the children's bread,
25: 1 forth to *m'* the bridegroom.
6 cometh; go ye out to *m'* him.

M'r 7:27 not *m'* to take the children's bread,
14:13 *m'* you a man bearing a pitcher of
Lu 14:31 to *m'* him that cometh against him
15:32 *m'* that we should make merry,
22:10 a man *m'* you, bearing a pitcher
Joh 12:13 and went forth to *m'* him,
Ac 26:20 and do works *m'* for repentance.
28:15 to *m'* us as far as Appii forum,
Ro 1:27 that recompence...which was *m'*.
1Co 15: 9 am not *m'* to be called an apostle,
16: 4 if it be *m'* that I go also, they shall
Ph'p 1: 7 is *m'* for me to think this of you
Col 1:12 hath made us *m'* to be partakers
1Th 4:17 to *m'* the Lord in the air:
2Th 1: 3 always for you, brethren, as it is *m'*,
2Ti 2:21 and *m'* for the master's use, and
Heb 6: 7 forth herbs *m'* for them by whom
2Pe 1:13 I think it *m'*, as long as I am in

meetest
2Ki 10: 3 the best and *m'* of your master's
Isa 64: 5 Thou *m'* him that rejoiceth and

meeteth
Ge 32:17 When Esau my brother *m'* thee,
Nu 35:19 when he *m'* him, he shall slay him.
21 slay the murderer, when he *m'* him.

meeting
1Sa 21: 1 was afraid at the *m'* of David,
Isa 1:13 it is iniquity, even the solemn *m'*.

Megiddo (*me-ghid'-do*) See also MEGIDDON.
Jos 12:21 one; the king of *M'*, one;
17:11 inhabitants of *M'* and her towns,
J'g 1:27 inhabitants of *M'* and her towns:
5:19 in Taanach by the waters of *M'*;
1Ki 4:12 to him pertained Taanach and *M'*,
9:15 and Hazor, and *M'*, and Gezer.
2Ki 9:27 And he fled to *M'*, and died there.
23:29 slew him at *M'*, when he had seen
30 him in a chariot dead from *M'*,
1Ch 7:29 *M'* and her towns, Dor and her
2Ch 35:22 came to fight in the valley of *M'*.

Megiddon (*me-ghid'-don*) See also ARMAGEDDON; MEGIDDO.
Zec 12:11 mourning...in the valley of *M'*.

Mehetabeel (*me-het'-a-be-el*) See also MEHETABEL.
Ne 6:10 son of Delaiah the son of *M'*,

Mehetabel (*me-het'-a-bel*) See also MEHETABEEL
Ge 36:39 wife's name was *M'*, the daughter
1Ch 1:50 wife's name was *M'*, the daughter

Mehida (*me-hi'-dah*)
Ezr 2:52 of Bazluth, the children of *M'*,
Neh 7:54 of Bazlith, the children of *M'*,

Mehir (*me'-hur*)
1Ch 4:11 the brother of Shuah begat *M'*,

Meholah See ABEL-BETH-MEHOLAH; MEHOLATHITE.

Meholathite (*me-ho'-lath-ite*)
1Sa 18:19 given unto Adriel the *M'* to wife.
2Sa 21: 8 Adriel the son of Barzillai the *M'*:

Mehujael (*me-hu'-ja-el*)
Ge 4:18 and Irad begat *M'*: and *M'* begat

Mehuman (*me-hu'-man*)
Es 1:10 with wine, he commanded *M'*,

Mehunim (*me-hu'-nim*) See also MAONITE; MEHUNIMS; MEUNIM.
Ezr 2:50 of Asnah, the children of *M'*,

Mehunims (*me-hu'-nims*) See also MEHUNIM.
2Ch 26: 7 dwelt in Gur-baal, and the *M'*.

Me-jarkon (*me-jar'-kon*)
Jos 19:46 *M'*, and Rakkon, with the border

Mekonah (*me-ko'-nah*)
Ne 11:28 and at *M'*, and in the villages

Melatiah (*mel-a-ti'-ah*)
Ne 3: 7 them repaired *M'* the Gibeonite,

Melchi (*mel'-ki*) See also MELCHI-SHUA; MELCHIZEDEK.
Lu 3:24 which was the son of *M'*, which
28 Which was the son of *M'*, which

Melchiah (*mel-ki'-ah*) See also MALCHIAH.
Jer 21: 1 unto him Pashur the son of *M'*,

Melchisedec (*mel-kis'-e-dek*) See also MELCHIZEDEK.
Heb 5: 6 for ever after the order of *M'*.
10 high priest after the order of *M'*.
6:20 for ever after the order of *M'*.
7: 1 For this *M'*, king of Salem, priest
10 of his father, when *M'* met him.
11 should rise after the order of *M'*,
15 for that after the similitude of *M'*
17 for ever after the order of *M'*.
21 for ever after the order of *M'*:)

Melchi-shua (*mel''-ki-shu'-ah*) See also MALCHI-SHUA.
1Sa 14:49 Jonathan, and Ishui, and *M'*:
31: 2 Jonathan, and Abinadab, and *M'*,

Melchizedek (*mel-kiz'-e-dek*) See also MELCHISEDEC.
Ge 14:18 *M'* king of Salem brought forth
Ps 110: 4 for ever after the order of *M'*.

Melea (*mel'-e-ah*)
Lu 3:31 Which was the son of *M'*, which

Melech (*me'-lek*) See also EBED-MELECH; HAMMELECH; NATHAN-MELECH; REGEM-MELECH.
1Ch 8:35 of Micah were, Pithon, and *M'*,
9:41 sons of Micah were, Pithon, and *M'*,

Melicu (*mel'-i-cu*) See also MALLUCH.
Ne 12:14 Of *M'*, Jonathan; of Shebaniah,

Melita (*mel'-i-tah*)
Ac 28: 1 that the island was called *M'*.

melody
Isa 23:16 make sweet *m'*, sing many songs,
51: 3 thanksgiving, and the voice of *m'*.
Am 5:23 I will not hear the *m'* of thy viols.
Eph 5:19 making *m'* in your heart to the

melons
Nu 11: 5 the *m'*, and the leeks, and the onions,

melt See also MELTED; MELTETH; MELTING; MOLTEN.
Ex 15:15 inhabitants of Caanan shall *m'*
Jos 2:11 these things, our hearts did *m'*,
14: 8 made the heart of the people *m'*:
2Sa 17:10 heart of a lion, shall utterly *m'*:
Ps 58: 7 Let them *m'* away as waters which
112:10 gnash with his teeth, and *m'* away:
Isa 13: 7 and every man's heart shall *m'*:
19: 1 heart of Egypt shall *m'* in the midst
Jer 9: 7 I will *m'* them, and try them;
Eze 21: 7 every heart shall *m'*, and all hands
22:20 to blow the fire upon it, to *m'* it;
20 I will leave you there, and *m'* you.
Am 9: 5 toucheth the land, and it shall *m'*,
13 wine, and all the hills shall *m'*.
Na 1: 5 the hills *m'*, and the earth is burned
2Pe 3:10 elements shall *m'* with fervent
12 elements shall *m'* with fervent

melted See also MOLTEN.
Ex 16:21 when the sun waxed hot, it *m'*.
Jos 5: 1 that their heart *m'*, neither was
7: 5 the hearts of the people *m'*, and
J'g 5: 5 The mountains *m'* from before
1Sa 14:16 the multitude *m'* away, and they
Ps 22:14 is *m'* in the midst of my bowels.
46: 6 he uttered his voice, the earth *m'*.
97: 5 hills *m'* like wax at the presence
107:26 their soul is *m'* because of trouble.
Isa 34: 3 mountains...*m'* with their blood.
Eze 22:21 and ye shall be *m'* in the midst
22 As silver is *m'* in the midst of the
22 so shall ye be *m'* in the midst

melteth
Ps 58: 8 As a snail which *m'*, let every one
68: 2 as wax *m'* before the fire, so let
119:28 My soul *m'* for heaviness:
147:18 out this word, and *m'* them: he
Isa 40:19 The workman *m'* a graven image,
Jer 6:29 the founder *m'* in vain: for the
Na 2:10 and the heart *m'*, and the knees

melting
Isa 64: 2 As when the *m'* fire burneth, the

Melzar (*mel'-zar*)
Da 1:11 Then said Daniel to *M'*, whom
16 *M'* took away the portion of their

member See also MEMBERS.
De 23: 1 or hath his privy *m'* cut off, shall not
1Co 12:14 For the body is not one *m'*, but
19 And if they were all one *m'*, where
26 And whether one *m'* suffer, all the
26 or one *m'* be honoured, all the
Jas 3: 5 Even so the tongue is a little *m'*,

members
Job 17: 7 and all my *m'* are as a shadow.
Ps 139:16 in thy book all my *m'* were written,
M't 5:29, 30 one of thy *m'* should perish,
Ro 6:13 Neither yield ye your *m'* as
13 and your *m'* as instruments of
19 as ye have yielded your *m'* servants
19 so now yield your *m'* servants to
7: 5 did work in our *m'* to bring forth
23 But I see another law in my *m'*,
23 to the law of sin which is in my *m'*.
12: 4 as we have many *m'* in one body,
4 all *m'* have not the same office:
5 and every one *m'* one of another.
1Co 6:15 your bodies are the *m'* of Christ?
15 shall I then take the *m'* of Christ,
15 and make them the *m'* of a harlot?
12:12 the body is one, and hath many *m'*,
12 and all the *m'* of that one body,
18 now hath God set the *m'* every one
20 But now are they many *m'*, yet but
22 much more those *m'* of the body,
23 And those *m'* of the body, which we
25 that the *m'* should have the same
26 suffer, all the *m'* suffer with it;
26 honoured, all the *m'* rejoice with it.
27 body of Christ, and *m'* in particular.
Eph 4:25 for we are *m'* one of another.
5:30 For we are *m'* of his body, of his
Col 3: 5 Mortify therefore your *m'* which
Jas 3: 6 so is the tongue among our *m'*, that
4: 1 of your lusts that war in your *m'*?

memorial
Ex 3:15 is my *m'* unto all generations.
12:14 day shall be unto you for a *m'*;
13: 9 and for a *m'* between thine eyes,
17:14 Write this for a *m'* in a book, and
28:12 the ephod for stones of *m'* unto the
12 upon his two shoulders for a *m'*.
29 for a *m'* before the Lord continually.
30:16 it may be a *m'* unto the children
39: 7 stones for a *m'* to the children of
Le 2: 2 the priest shall burn the *m'* of it
9 from the meat offering a *m'* thereof,
16 the priest shall burn the *m'* of it,
5:12 even a *m'* thereof, and burn it on the
6:15 even the *m'* of it, unto the Lord.
Le 23:24 a *m'* of blowing of trumpets, an
24: 7 it may be on the bread for a *m'*,
Nu 5:15 an offering of *m'*, bringing iniquity
18 put the offering of *m'* in her hands,
26 the *m'* thereof, and burn it upon
10:10 that they may be to you for a *m'*
16:40 be a *m'* unto the children of Israel,
31:54 for a *m'* for the children of Israel
Jos 4: 7 these stones shall be for a *m'* unto
Ne 2:20 nor right, nor *m'*, in Jerusalem.
Es 9:28 the *m'* of them perish from their
Ps 9: 6 their *m'* is perished with them.
135:13 and thy *m'*, O Lord, throughout all
Ho 12: 5 God of hosts; the Lord is his *m'*.
Zec 6:14 for a *m'* in the temple of the Lord.
M't 26:13 hath done, be told for a *m'* of her.
M'r 14: 9 shall be spoken of for a *m'* of her.
Ac 10: 4 thine alms are come up for a *m'*

memory
Ps 109:15 cut off the *m'* of them from the
145: 7 utter the *m'* of thy great goodness,
Pr 10: 7 The *m'* of the just is blessed: but
Ec 9: 5 for the *m'* of them is forgotten.
Isa 26:14 and made all their *m'* to perish.
1Co 15: 2 if ye keep in *m'* what I preached unto

Memphis (*mem'-fis*) See also NOPH.
Ho 9: 6 them up, *M'* shall bury them:

Memucan (*mem-u'-can*)
Es 1:14 Meres, Marsena, and *M'*, the
16 *M'* answered before the king and
21 did according to the word of *M'*:

men^ See also BONDMEN; BOWMEN; CHAPMEN; COUNTRYMEN; CRAFTSMEN; FISHERMEN; FOOTMEN; HERDMEN; HORSEMEN; HUSBANDMEN; KINSMEN; MENCHILDREN; MENPLEASERS; MEN'S; MENSERVANTS; MENSTEALERS; MERCHANTMEN; PLOWMEN; SHIPMEN; SPEARMEN; WATCHMEN; WORKMEN; WOMEN.
Ge 6: 1 *m'* began to multiply on the face
2 daughters of *m'* that they were fair;
4 came in unto the daughters of *m'*,
4 the same became mighty *m'* which
4 which were of old, *m'* of renown.
11: 5 which the children of *m'* builded.
12:20 commanded his *m'* concerning
13:13 the *m'* of Sodom were wicked and
14:24 that which the young *m'* have eaten,
24 of the *m'* which went with me, by
17:23 male among the *m'* of Abraham's
27 all the *m'* of his house, born in the
18: 2 and, lo, three *m'* stood by him:
16 the *m'* rose up from thence, and
22 *m'* turned their faces from thence,
19: 4 the *m'* of the city, even the *m'* of
5 Where are the *m'* which came in to
8 only unto these *m'* do nothing; for
10 But the *m'* put forth their hand, and
11 smote the *m'* that were at the door
12 the *m'* said unto Lot, Hast thou here
16 the *m'* laid hold upon his hand, and
20: 8 ears: and the *m'* were sore afraid.
22: 3 took two of his young *m'* with him,
5 And Abraham said unto his young *m'*,
19 Abraham returned unto his young *m'*,
24:13 the daughters of the *m'* of the city
54 he and the *m'* that were with him,
59 and Abraham's servant, and his *m'*.
26: 7 the *m'* of the place asked him of his
7 the *m'* of the place should kill me
29:22 together all the *m'* of the place,
32: 6 and four hundred *m'* with him.
28 thou power with God and with *m'*,
33: 1 and with him four hundred *m'*.
13 if *m'* should overdrive them one day,
34: 7 the *m'* were grieved, and they were
20 communed with the *m'* of their city,
21 These *m'* are peaceable with us;
22 Only herein will the *m'* consent unto
38:21 Then he asked the *m'* of that place,
22 also the *m'* of the place said, that
39:11 none of the *m'* of the house there
14 she called unto the *m'* of her house,
41: 8 of Egypt, and all the wise *m'* thereof:
42:11 we are true *m'*; thy servants are no
19 If ye be true *m'*, let one of your
31 him, We are true *m'*; we are no spies:
33 shall I know that ye are true *m'*;
34 are no spies, but that ye are true *m'*:
43:15 *m'* took that present, and they took
16 Bring these *m'* home, and slay, and
16 these *m'* shall dine with me at noon.
17 brought the *m'* into Joseph's house.
18 the *m'* were afraid, because they
24 brought the *m'* into Joseph's house,
33 and the *m'* marvelled one at another.
44: 3 *m'* were sent away, they and their
4 his steward, Up, follow after the *m'*;
46:32 And the *m'* are shepherds, for their
47: 2 some of his brethren, even five *m'*,
6 any *m'* of activity among them,
Ex 1:17 them, but saved the *m'* children alive.
18 and have saved the *m'* children alive?
2:13 two *m'* of the Hebrews strove
4:19 *m'* are dead which sought thy life.
5: 9 more work be laid upon the *m'*,
7:11 Pharaoh also called the wise *m'* and
10: 7 let the *m'* go, that they may serve
11 go now ye that are *m'*, and serve
12:33 haste; for they said, We be all dead *m'*.
37 thousand on foot that were *m'*,
15:15 the mighty *m'* of Moab, trembling
17: 9 said unto Joshua, Choose us out *m'*,
18:21 the people able *m'*, such as fear God,
21 *m'* of truth, hating covetousness;

Ex 18:25 chose able *m'* out of all Israel, and
21:18 if *m'* strive together, and one smite
22 If *m'* strive, and hurt a woman with
22:31 And ye shall be holy *m'* unto me:
24: 5 sent young *m'* of the children of Israel,
32:28 that day about three thousand *m'*.
35:22 they came, both *m'* and women, as
36: 4 And all the wise *m'*, that wrought all
38:26 thousand and five hundred and fifty *m'*.
Le 7:25 *m'* offer an offering made by fire
18:27 have the *m'* of the land done, which
27: 9 *m'* bring an offering unto the Lord,
29 which shall be devoted of *m'*, shall
Nu 1: 5 these are the names of the *m'* that
17 And Moses and Aaron took these *m'*
44 princes of Israel, being twelve *m'*:
5: 6 commit any sin that *m'* commit, to
9: 6 there were certain *m'*, who were
7 And those *m'* said unto him, We are
11:16 Gather unto me seventy *m'* of the
24 and gathered the seventy *m'* of the
26 remained two of the *m'* in the camp,
28 servant of Moses, one of his young *m'*,
12: 3 above all the *m'* which were upon
13: 2 Send thou *m'*, that they may search
3 all those *m'* were heads of the
16 names of the *m'* which Moses sent
21 unto Rehob, as *m'* come to Hamath.
31 the *m'* that went up with him said,
32 saw in it are *m'* of a great stature.
14:22 those *m'* which have seen my glory,
36 the *m'*, which Moses sent to search
37 those *m'* that did bring up the evil
38 the *m'* that went to search the land,
16: 1 of Peleth, sons of Reuben, took *m'*:
2 in the congregation, *m'* of renown:
14 thou put out the eyes of these *m'*?
26 from the tents of these wicked *m'*,
29 If these *m'* die the common death
29 die the common death of all *m'*,
29 visited after the visitation of all *m'*;
30 these *m'* have provoked the Lord.
32 the *m'* that appertained unto Korah,
35 the two hundred and fifty *m'* that
18:15 be of *m'* or beasts, shall be thine:
22: 9 said, What *m'* are these with thee?
20 If the *m'* come to call thee, rise up,
35 said unto Balaam, Go with the *m'*:
25: 5 Slay ye every one his *m'* that were
26:10 devoured two hundred and fifty *m'*:
31:11 the prey, both of *m'* and of beasts.
21 the priest said unto the *m'* of war
28 *m'* of war which went out to battle:
42 divided from the *m'* that warred,
49 have taken the sum of the *m'* of war
53 the *m'* of war had taken spoil, every
32:11 Surely none of the *m'* that came up
14 an increase of sinful *m'*, to augment
34:17 names of the *m'* which shall divide
19 And the names of the *m'* are these:
De 1:13 you wise *m'*, and understanding,
15 the chief of your tribes, wise *m'*, and
22 We will send *m'* before us, and they
23 and I took twelve *m'* of you, one of
35 shall not one of these *m'* of this evil
2:14 all the generation of the *m'* of war
16 *m'* of war were consumed and dead
34 utterly destroyed the *m'*, and the
3: 6 utterly destroying the *m'*, women,
4: 3 all the *m'* that followed Baal-peor,
13:13 Certain *m'*, the children of Belial,
19:17 Then both the *m'*, between whom
21:21 all the *m'* of his city shall stone him
22:21 *m'* of her city shall stone her with
25: 1 there be a controversy between *m'*,
11 When *m'* strive together one with
27:14 say unto all the *m'* of Israel with a
29:10 officers, with all the *m'* of Israel,
25 Then *m'* shall say, Because they have
31:12 Gather the people together, *m'*, and
32:26 of them to cease from among *m'*:
33: 6 not die; and let not his *m'* be few.
Jos 1:14 all the mighty *m'* of valour, and help
2: 1 sent out of Shittim two *m'* to spy
2 came *m'* in hither to night of the
3 Bring forth the *m'* that are come to
4 the woman took the two *m'*, and hid
4 There came *m'* unto me, but I wist
5 it was dark, that the *m'* went out:
5 whither the *m'* went I wot not:
7 the *m'* pursued after them the way
9 she said unto the *m'*, I know that
14 *m'* answered her, Our life for yours,
17 And the *m'* said unto her, We will be
23 the two *m'* returned, and descended
3:12 take you twelve *m'* out of the tribes
4: 2 twelve *m'* out of the people, out of
4 Joshua called the twelve *m'*, whom
5: 4 even all the *m'* of war, died in the
6 all the people that were *m'* of war,
6: 2 thereof, and the mighty *m'* of valour.
3 compass the city, all ye *m'* of war,
9 the armed *m'* went before the priests
13 and the armed *m'* went before them;
22 Joshua had said unto the two *m'*
23 the young *m'* that were spies went in,
7: 2 Joshua sent *m'* from Jericho to Ai,
2 And the *m'* went up and viewed Ai.
3 two or three thousand *m'* go up
4 people about three thousand *m'*:
4 and they fled before the *m'* of Ai.
5 the *m'* of Ai smote of them about
5 of them about thirty and six *m'*:
8: 3 chose out thirty thousand mighty *m'*
12 he took about five thousand *m'*, and
14 the *m'* of the city went out against

Jos 8:20 the *m'* of Ai looked behind them,
21 turned again, and slew the *m'* of Ai.
25 that day, both of *m'* and women,
25 thousand, even all the *m'* of Ai.
9: 6 unto him, and to the *m'* of Israel,
7 And the *m'* of Israel said unto the
14 the *m'* took of their victuals, and
10: 2 and all the *m'* thereof were mighty.
6 the *m'* of Gibeon sent unto Joshua
7 him, and all the mighty *m'* of valour.
18 and set *m'* by it for to keep them:
24 called for all the *m'* of Israel, and
24 said unto the captains of the *m'* of war
18: 4 from among you three *m'* for each
8 the *m'* arose, and went away: and
9 the *m'* went and passed through the
24:11 *m'* of Jericho fought against you,
J'g 1: 4 of them in Bezek ten thousand *m'*.
3:29 at that time about ten thousand *m'*,
29 all lusty, and all *m'* of valour; and
31 of the Philistines six hundred *m'*
4: 6 take with thee ten thousand *m'* of
10 up with ten thousand *m'* at his feet:
14 and ten thousand *m'* after him.
6:27 Gideon took ten *m'* of his servants,
27 household, and the *m'* of the city,
28 the *m'* of the city arose early in the
30 the *m'* of the city said unto Joash,
7: 6 mouth, were three hundred *m'*:
7 By the three hundred *m'* that lapped
8 retained those three hundred *m'*:
11 of the armed *m'* that were in the host.
16 the three hundred *m'* into three
19 the hundred *m'* that were with him,
23 the *m'* of Israel gathered themselves
24 *m'* of Ephraim gathered themselves
8: 1 the *m'* of Ephraim said unto him,
4 three hundred *m'* that were with
5 And he said unto the *m'* of Succoth,
8 and the *m'* of Penuel answered him
8 *m'* of Succoth had answered him.
9 he spake also unto the *m'* of Penuel,
10 with them, about fifteen thousand *m'*,
10 thousand *m'* that drew sword.
14 a young man of the *m'* of Succoth,
14 even threescore and seventeen *m'*.
15 he came unto the *m'* of Succoth,
15 bread unto thy *m'* that are weary?
16 them he taught the *m'* of Succoth.
17 Penuel, and slew the *m'* of the city.
18 What manner of *m'* were they whom
22 the *m'* of Israel said unto Gideon,
9: 2 the ears of all the *m'* of Shechem,
3 in the ears of all the *m'* of Shechem
6 *m'* of Shechem gathered together,
7 unto me, ye *m'* of Shechem, that
18 king over the *m'* of Shechem,
20 devour the *m'* of Shechem, and the
20 come out from the *m'* of Shechem,
23 Abimelech and the *m'* of Shechem;
23 *m'* of Shechem dealt treacherously
24 and upon the *m'* of Shechem, which
25 the *m'* of Shechem set liers in wait
26 *m'* of Shechem put their confidence
28 *m'* of Hamor...father of Shechem:
36 of the mountains as if they were *m'*.
39 went out before the *m'* of Shechem,
46, 47 the *m'* of the tower of Shechem
49 the *m'* of the tower of Shechem died
49 about a thousand *m'* and women.
51 thither fled all the *m'* and women,
54 that *m'* say not of me, A woman slew
55 the *m'* of Israel saw that Abimelech
57 evil of the *m'* of Shechem did God
11: 3 were gathered vain *m'* to Jephthah,
12: 1 *m'* of Ephraim gathered themselves
4 together all the *m'* of Gilead,
4 the *m'* of Gilead smote Ephraim,
5 the *m'* of Gilead said unto him, Art
14:10 feast; for so used the young *m'* to do.
18 the *m'* of the city said unto him on
19 slew thirty *m'* of them, and took
15:10 And the *m'* of Judah said, Why are
11 three thousand *m'* of Judah went to
15 and slew a thousand *m'* therewith.
16 of an ass have I slain a thousand *m'*.
16: 9 there were *m'* lying in wait, abiding
27 house was full of *m'* and women;
27 three thousand *m'* and women,
18: 2 five *m'* from their coasts,
2 *m'* of valour, from Zorah, and
7 the five *m'* departed, and came to
11 six hundred *m'* appointed with
14 Then answered the five *m'* that
16 the six hundred *m'* appointed with
17 the five *m'* that went to spy out the
17 with the six hundred *m'* that were
22 the *m'* that were in the houses near
19:16 the *m'* of the place were Benjamites.
22 *m'* of the city, certain sons of Belial,
25 the *m'* would not hearken to him: so
20: 5 the *m'* of Gibeah rose against me,
10 we will take ten *m'* of an hundred
11 all the *m'* of Israel were gathered
12 Israel sent *m'* through all the tribe
13 Now therefore deliver us the *m'*, the
15 six thousand *m'* that drew sword,
15 numbered seven hundred chosen *m'*.
16 seven hundred chosen *m'* lefthanded;
17 *m'* of Israel, beside Benjamin, were
17 four hundred thousand *m'* that drew
17 sword: all these were *m'* of war.
20 the *m'* of Israel went out to battle
20 *m'* of Israel put themselves in array
21 day twenty and two thousand *m'*.
22 people the *m'* of Israel encouraged

J'g 20:25 again eighteen thousand *m'*; all
31 in the field, about thirty *m'* of Israel.
33 all the *m'* of Israel rose up out of
34 thousand chosen *m'* out of all Israel,
35 five thousand and an hundred *m'*:
36 for the *m'* of Israel gave place to the
38 sign between the *m'* of Israel and
39 the *m'* of Israel retired in the battle,
39 to smite and kill of the *m'* of Israel
41 when the *m'* of Israel turned again,
41 the *m'* of Benjamin were amazed:
42 their backs before the *m'* of Israel
44 fell...eighteen thousand *m'*;
44 all these were *m'* of valour.
45 in the highways five thousand *m'*;
45 and slew two thousand *m'* of them.
46 thousand *m'* that drew the sword;
46 all these were *m'* of valour.
47 six hundred *m'* turned and fled to
48 the *m'* of Israel turned again upon
48 as well the *m'* of every city, as the
21: 1 *m'* of Israel had sworn in Mizpeh,
10 sent thither twelve thousand *m'* of
Ru 2: 9 have I not charged the young *m'* that
9 that which the young *m'* have drawn.
15 Boaz commanded his young *m'*,
21 Thou shalt keep fast by my young *m'*,
3:10 as thou followedst not young *m'*,
4: 2 took ten *m'* of the elders of the city,
1Sa 2: 4 The bows of the mighty *m'* are broken,
17 the sin of the young *m'* was very great
17 for *m'* abhorred the offering of the
26 both with the Lord, and also with *m'*.
4: 2 in the field about four thousand *m'*.
9 strong, and quit yourselves like *m'*,
9 quit yourselves like *m'*, and fight.
5: 7 the *m'* of Ashdod saw that it was so,
9 smote the *m'* of the city, both small
12 *m'* that died not were smitten with
6:10 the *m'* did so; and took two milch
15 *m'* of Beth-shemesh offered burnt
19 he smote the *m'* of Beth-shemesh,
19 thousand and threescore and ten *m'*:
20 the *m'* of Beth-shemesh said, Who
7: 1 And the *m'* of Kirjath-jearim came,
11 the *m'* of Israel went out of Mizpeh,
8:16 your goodliest young *m'*, and your
22 Samuel said unto the *m'* of Israel,
10: 2 find two *m'* by Rachel's sepulchre
3 there shall meet thee three *m'* going
26 there went with him a band of *m'*,
11: 1 the *m'* of Jabesh said unto Nahash,
5 him the tidings of the *m'* of Jabesh.
8 the *m'* of Judah thirty thousand.
9 say unto the *m'* of Jabesh-gilead,
9 and shewed it to the *m'* of Jabesh;
10 Therefore the *m'* of Jabesh said,
12 bring the *m'*, that we may put them
15 Saul and all the *m'* of Israel rejoiced
13: 2 Saul chose him three thousand *m'* of
6 When the *m'* of Israel saw that they
15 with him, about six hundred *m'*:
14: 2 with him were about six hundred *m'*;
8 we will pass over unto these *m'*,
12 the *m'* of the garrison answered
14 slaughter,...was about twenty *m'*,
22 all the *m'* of Israel which had hid
24 the *m'* of Israel were distressed that
15: 4 and ten thousand *m'* of Judah.
17: 2 And Saul and the *m'* of Israel were
12 man went among *m'* for an old man
19 and they, and all the *m'* of Israel,
24 all the *m'* of Israel, when they saw
25 the *m'* of Israel said, Have ye seen
26 David spake to the *m'* that stood
28 heard when he spake unto the *m'*;
52 the *m'* of Israel and of Judah arose,
18: 5 and Saul set him over the *m'* of war,
27 arose and went, he and his *m'*, and
27 of the Philistines two hundred *m'*;
21: 4 if the young *m'* have kept themselves
5 the vessels of the young *m'* are holy,
15 Have I need of mad *m'*, that ye have
22: 2 with him about four hundred *m'*.
6 and the *m'* that were with him,
19 both *m'* and women, children and
23: 3 David's *m'* said unto him, Behold,
5 So David and his *m'* went to Keilah,
8 Keilah, to besiege David and his *m'*.
11 Will the *m'* of Keilah deliver me up
12 Will the *m'* of Keilah deliver me and
12 and my *m'* into the hand of Saul?
13 David and his *m'*, which were about
24 and his *m'* were in the wilderness
25 also and his *m'* went to seek him.
26 his *m'* on that side of the mountain:
26 for Saul and his *m'* compassed David
26 compassed David and his *m'* round
24: 2 Saul took three thousand chosen *m'*
2 and went to seek David and his *m'*
3 David and his *m'* remained in the
4 And the *m'* of David said unto him,
6 he said unto his *m'*, The Lord forbid
22 David and his *m'* gat them up unto
25: 5 And David sent out ten young *m'*, and
5 David said unto the young *m'*, Get you
8 Ask thy young *m'*, and they will shew
8 let the young *m'* find favour in thine
9 when David's young *m'* came, they
11 give it unto *m'*, whom I know not
12 So David's young *m'* turned their way,
13 David said unto his *m'*, Gird ye on
13 after David about four hundred *m'*;
14 But one of the young *m'* told Abigail.
15 But the *m'* were very good unto us,
20 David and his *m'* came down against

1Sa 25: 25 thine handmaid saw not the young m'
27 unto the young m' that follow my lord.
26: 2 three thousand chosen m' of Israel
19 if they be the children of m', cursed
22 and let one of the young m' come over
27: 2 passed over with the six hundred m'
3 with Achish at Gath, he and his m',
8 And David and his m' went up, and
28: 1 with me to battle, thou and thy m'.
8 he went, and two m' with him, and
29: 2 David and his m' passed on in the
4 it not be with the heads of these m'?
11 So David and his m' rose up early
30: 1 David and his m' were come to Ziklag
3 David and his m' came to the city,
9 six hundred m' that were with him,
10 pursued, he and four hundred m':
17 save four hundred young m', which
21 David came to the two hundred m',
22 Then answered all the wicked m'
22 all the wicked...and m' of Belial,
31 and his m' were wont to haunt.
31: 1 the m' of Israel fled from before the
6 his armourbearer, and all his m',
7 the m' of Israel...on the other side
7 saw that the m' of Israel fled, and
12 All the valiant m' arose, and went
2Sa 1: 11 all the m' that were with him:
15 And David called one of the young m',
2: 3 m' that were with him did David
4 And the m' of Judah came, and there
4 m' of Jabesh-gilead were they that
5 sent...unto the m' of Jabesh-gilead,
14 Let the young m' now arise, and play
17 was beaten, and the m' of Israel,
21 lay thee hold on one of the young m',
29 Abner and his m' walked all that
30 of David's servants nineteen m'
31 of Benjamin, and of Abner's m',
31 hundred and threescore m' died.
32 Joab and his m' went all night, and
3: 20 to Hebron, and twenty m' with him.
20 the m' that were with him a feast.
34 as a man falleth before wicked m',
39 these m' the sons of Zeruiah be too
4: 2 son had two m' that were captains
11 wicked m' have slain a righteous
12 David commanded his young m', and
5: 6 king and his m' went to Jerusalem
21 and David and his m' burned them.
6: 1 together all the chosen m' of Israel,
19 Israel, as well to the women as m',
7: 9 like unto the name of the great m'
14 chasten him with the rod of m',
14 the stripes of the children of m':
8: 5 two and twenty thousand m'.
13 of salt, being eighteen thousand m'.
10: 5 the m' were greatly ashamed:
6 and of king Maacah a thousand m',
6 and of Ish-tob twelve thousand m'.
7 and all the host of the mighty m'.
9 chose of all the choice m' of Israel, and
12 let us play the m' for our people,
18 David slew the m' of seven hundred
11: 16 where he knew...valiant m' were.
17 the m' of the city went out, and
23 Surely the m' prevailed against us,
12: 1 There were two m' in one city; the
13: 9 said, Have out all m' from me.
32 slain all the young m' the king's sons;
15: 1 and fifty m' to run before him.
6 stole the hearts of the m' of Israel.
11 with Absalom went two hundred m'
13 hearts of the m' of Israel are after
18 six hundred m' which came after
22 Gittite passed over, and all his m',
16: 2 summer fruit for the young m' to eat;
6 all the mighty m' were on his right
13 David and his m' went by the way,
15 the m' of Israel, came to Jerusalem,
18 this people, and all the m' of Israel,
17: 1 now choose out twelve thousand m',
8 knowest thy father and his m',
8 that they be mighty m', and they be
10 which be with him are valiant m'.
12 and of all the m' that are with him
14 Absalom and all the m' of Israel
24 he and all the m' of Israel with him.
18: 7 that day of twenty thousand m'.
15 young m' that bare Joab's armour
28 which hath delivered up the m'
19: 14 the heart of all the m' of Judah,
16 came down wiih the m' of Judah
17 were a thousand m' of Benjamin
28 father's house were but dead m'
41 all the m' of Israel came to the
41 our brethren the m' of Judah stolen
41 David's m' with him, over Jordan?
42 the m' of Judah answered the m' of
43 the m' of Israel answered the m' of
43 the words of the m' of Judah were
43 than the words of the m' of Israel.
20: 2 m' of Judah clave unto their king,
4 Assemble me the m' of Judah within
5 went to assemble the m' of Judah:
7 went out after him Joab's m', and
7 the Pelethites, and all the mighty m':
11 and one of Joab's m' stood by him,
21: 6 seven m' of his sons be delivered
12 son from the m' of Jabesh-gilead,
17 the m' of David sware unto him,
22: 5 floods of ungodly m' made me afraid;
23: 3 that ruleth over m' must be just,
8 the names of the mighty m' whom
9 of the three mighty m' with David,
9 the m' of Israel were gone away:

2Sa 23: 16 three mighty m' brake through the
17 the blood of the m' that went in
17 things did these three mighty m'.
20 acts, he slew two lionlike m' of Moab:
22 the name among three mighty m'.
24: 9 valiant m' that draw the sword;
9 the m' of Judah were five hundred
9 were five hundred thousand m'.
15 to Beer-sheba seventy thousand m'.
1Ki 1: 5 and fifty m' to run before him.
8 mighty m' which belonged to David,
9 m' of Judah the king's servants:
10 and the mighty m', and Solomon his
2: 32 two m' more righteous and better
4: 31 For he was wiser than all m'; than
5: 13 the levy was thirty thousand m'.
8: 2 m' of Israel assembled themselves
39 the hearts of all the children of m';)
9: 22 but they were m' of war, and his
10: 8 Happy are thy m', happy are these
11: 18 took m' with them out of Paran,
24 And he gathered m' unto him, and
12: 6 Rehoboam consulted with the old m',
8 he forsook the counsel of the old m',
8 and consulted with the young m' that
10 the young m' that were grown up with
14 after the counsel of the young m',
21 and fourscore thousand chosen m',
13: 25 m' passed by, and saw the carcase
18: 13 hundred m' of the Lord's prophets
22 are four hundred and fifty m'.
20: 14 by the young m' of the princes of the
15 he numbered the young m' of the
17 the young m' of the princes of the
17 There are m' come out of Samaria.
19 So these young m' of the princes of
30 and seven thousand of the m' that
33 Now the m' did diligently observe
21: 10 And set two m', sons of Belial, before
11 And the m' of his city, even the elders
13 there came in two m', children of
13 the m' of Belial witnessed against
22: 6 together, about four hundred m',
2Ki 2: 7 fifty m' of the sons of the prophets
16 thy servants fifty strong m';
17 They sent therefore fifty m'; and
19 the m' of the city said unto Elisha,
3: 26 him seven hundred m' that drew
4: 22 me, I pray thee, one of the young m',
40 they poured out for the m' to eat.
43 I set this before an hundred m'?
5: 22 two young m' of the sons of the
24 he let the m' go, and they departed.
6: 20 open the eyes of these m', that they
7: 3 there were four leprous m' at the
8: 12 and their young m' wilt thou slay
10: 6 heads of the m' your master's sons,
6 were with the great m' of the city,
11 all his great m', and his kinsfolks, and
14 house, even two and forty m';
24 appointed fourscore m' without,
24 any of the m' whom I have brought
11: 9 and they took every man his m' that
12: 15 they reckoned not with the m', into
13: 21 that, behold, they spied a band of m';
15: 20 of all the mighty m' of wealth, of each
25 with him fifty m' of the Gileadites:
17: 24 of Assyria brought m' from Babylon,
30 And the m' of Babylon made
30 the m' of Cuth made Nergal, and the
30 the m' of Hamath made Ashima,
18: 27 me to the m' which sit on the wall,
20: 14 said unto him, What said these m'?
23: 2 and all the m' of Judah and all the
14 their places with the bones of m'.
17 the m' of the city told him, It is the
24: 14 all the mighty m' of valour, even ten
16 And all the m' of might, even seven
25: 4 all the m' of war fled by night by the
19 that was set over the m' of war, and
19 and five m' of them that were in the
19 threescore m' of the people of the
23 they and their m', heard that the
23 of a Maachathite, they and their m'.
24 and to their m', and said unto them,
25 royal, came, and ten m' with him.
1Ch 4: 12 These are the m' of Rechah.
22 the m' of Chozeba, and Joash, and
42 the sons of Simeon, five hundred m',
5: 18 the tribe of Manasseh, of valiant m',
18 m' able to bear buckler and sword,
21 of m' an hundred thousand.
24 and Jahdiel, mighty m' of valour,
24 famous m', and heads of the house
7: 2 were valiant m' of might in their
3 Joel, Ishiah, five: all of them chief m'.
4 for war, six and thirty thousand m':
5 of Issachar were valiant m' of might,
7, 9 fathers, mighty m' of valour;
11 their fathers, mighty m' of valour,
21 whom the m' of Gath that were born
40 choice and mighty m' of valour,
40 was twenty and six thousand m'.
8: 28 fathers, by their generations, chief m'.
40 of Ulam were mighty m' of valour,
9: 9 these m' were chief of the fathers
13 very able m' for the work of the
10: 1 the m' of Israel fled from before the
7 m' of Israel that were in the valley
12 They arose, all the valiant m', and
11: 10 of the mighty m' whom David had,
11 of the mighty m' whom David had;
19 shall I drink the blood of these m'
26 the valiant m' of the armies were,
12: 1 and they were among the mighty m',
8 to the wilderness m' of might,

1Ch 12: 8 and m' of war fit for the battle,
21 for they were all mighty m' of valour,
25 mighty m' of valour for the war,
30 mighty m' of valour, famous
38 All these m' of war, that could keep
16: 31 and let m' say among the nations,
17: 8 like the name of the great m' that are
18: 5 two and twenty thousand m'.
19: 5 told David how the m' were served.
5 for the m' were greatly ashamed.
8 and all the host of the mighty m'.
18 seven thousand m' which fought in
21: 5 thousand m' that drew sword: and
5 ten thousand m' that drew sword.
14 fell of Israel seventy thousand m'.
22: 15 all manner of cunning m' for every
24: 4 there were more chief m' found of
4 of Eleazar there were sixteen chief m'
26: 6 for they were mighty m' of valour.
7 whose brethren were strong m',
8 able m' for strength for the service,
9 had sons and brethren, strong m',
12 porters, even among the chief m',
30 and his brethren, m' of valour,
31 among them mighty m' of valour at
32 And his brethren, m' of valour,
28: 1 the officers, and with the mighty m',
1 and with all the valiant m', unto
29: 24 all the princes, and the mighty m',
2Ch 2: 2 ten thousand m' to bear burdens,
7 cunning m' that are with me in Judah
14 be put to him, with thy cunning m',
14 with the cunning m' of my lord David
5: 3 m' of Israel assembled themselves
6: 18 God in very deed dwell with m' on
30 the hearts of the children of m':)
8: 9 but they were m' of war, and chief
9: 7 Happy are thy m', and happy are
10: 6 Rehoboam took counsel with the old m'
8 the counsel which the old m' gave him,
8 and took counsel with the young m'
10 young m' that were brought up with
13 forsook the counsel of the old m',
14 them after the advice of the young m',
11: 1 chosen m', which were warriors, to
13: 3 with an army of valiant m' of war,
3 four hundred thousand chosen m':
3 eight hundred thousand chosen m',
3 being mighty m' of valour.
7 are gathered unto him vain m', the
15 Then the m' of Judah gave a shout:
15 and as the m' of Judah shouted, it
17 five hundred thousand chosen m'.
14: 8 And Asa had an army of m' that bare
8 all these were mighty m' of valour.
17: 13 and the m' of war, mighty...of
13 mighty m' of valour were in Jerusalem.
14 mighty m' of valour three hundred
16 thousand mighty m' of valour.
17 him armed m' with bow and shield
18: 5 of prophets four hundred m', and
23: 8 and took every man his m' that
24: 24 came with a small company of m',
25: 5 three hundred thousand choice m',
6 thousand mighty m' of valour out of
26: 11 Uzziah had an host of fighting m',
12 the fathers of the mighty m' of valour
15 engines, invented by cunning m', to be
17 of the Lord, that were valiant m':
28: 6 one day, which were all valiant m';
14 So the armed m' left the captives and
15 m' which were expressed by name
31: 19 the m' that were expressed by name,
32: 3 and his mighty m' to stop the waters
21 cut off all the mighty m' of valour,
34: 12 And the m' did the work faithfully:
30 the Lord, and all the m' of Judah,
35: 25 all the singing m' and the singing
36: 17 slew their young m' with the sword
Ezr 1: 4 m' of his place help him with silver,
2: 2 of the m' of the people of Israel:
22 The m' of Netophah, fifty and six.
23 The m' of Anathoth, an hundred
27 The m' of Michmas, an hundred
28 m' of Beth-el and Ai, two hundred
3: 12 of the fathers, who were ancient m',
4: 11 the m' on this side of the river,
21 to cause these m' to cease, and
5: 4 the names of the m' that make this
10 names of the m' that were the chief
6: 8 expences be given unto these m',
8: 16 and for Meshullam, chief m'; also
10: 1 very great congregation of m' and
9 all the m' of Judah and Benjamin
17 the m' that had taken strange wives
Neh 1: 2 came, he and certain m' of Judah;
2: 12 night, I and some few m' with me;
3: 2 unto him builded the m' of Jericho.
7 the m' of Gibeon, and of Mizpah,
22 the priests, the m' of the plain.
4: 23 servants, nor the m' of the guard
5: 5 for other m' have our lands and
7: 7 m' of the people of Israel was this;
26 The m' of Beth-lehem and Netophah,
27 The m' of Anathoth, an hundred
28 The m' of Beth-azmaveth, forty and
29 m' of Kirjath-jearim, Chephirah,
30 The m' of Ramah and Gaba, six
31 The m' of Michmas, an hundred and
32 m' of Beth-el and Ai, an hundred
33 The m' of the other Nebo, fifty and
67 forty and five singing m' and singing
8: 2 congregation both of m' and women,
3 before the m' and the women, and
11: 2 And the people blessed all the m',
6 threescore and eight valiant m'.

Neh 11:14 their brethren, mighty m' of valour,
14 the son of one of the great m'.
Es 1:13 Then the king said to the wise m',
6:13 said his wise m' and Zeresh his wife
9: 6 slew and destroyed five hundred m'.
12 and destroyed five hundred m' in
15 slew three hundred m' at Shushan:
Job 1: 3 greatest of all the m' of the east.
19 it fell upon the young m', and they are
4:13 night, when deep sleep falleth on m',
7:20 unto thee, O thou preserver of m'?
11: 3 thy lies make m' hold their peace?
11 For he knoweth vain m': he seeth
15:10 the grayheaded and very aged m',
18 Which wise m' have told from their
17: 8 Upright m' shall be astonied at this,
22:15 which wicked m' have trodden?
29 When m' are cast down, then thou
24:12 M' groan from out of the city, and
27:23 M' shall clap their hands at him, and
28: 4 up, they are gone away from m'.
29: 8 The young m' saw me, and hid
21 Unto me m' gave ear, and waited,
30: 5 were driven forth from among m',
8 of fools, yea, children of base m':
31:31 the m' of my tabernacle said not,
32: 1 So these three m' ceased to answer
5 in the mouth of these three m',
9 Great m' are not always wise: neither
33:15 when deep sleep falleth upon m',
16 Then he openeth the ears of m', and
27 He looketh upon m', and if any say,
34: 2 Hear my words, O ye wise m'; and
8 and walketh with wicked m'.
10 unto me, ye m' of understanding:
24 He shall break in pieces mighty m'
26 He striketh them as wicked m' in the
34 Let m' of understanding tell me,
36 of his answers for wicked m'.
35:12 because of the pride of evil m'.
36:24 magnify his work, which m' behold.
37: 7 that all m' may know his work.
21 And now m' see not the bright light
24 M' do therefore fear him: he
39:21 he goeth on to meet the armed m'.
Ps 4: 2 O ye sons of m', how long will ye
9:20 may know themselves to be but m'.
11: 4 his eyelids try, the children of m'.
12: 1 fail from among the children of m'.
8 when the vilest m' are exalted.1121,
14: 2 from heaven upon the children of m',
17: 4 Concerning the works of m', by the
14 From m' which are thy hand, O
14 from m' of the world, which have
18: 4 floods of ungodly m' made me afraid.
21:10 seed from among the children of m'.
22: 6 a reproach of m', and despised of
26: 9 sinners, nor my life with bloody m':
31:19 trust in thee before the sons of m'!
33:13 he beholdeth all the sons of m'.
36: 7 children of m' put their trust under
45: 2 art fairer than the children of m':
49:10 For he seeth that wise m' die, likewise
18 and m' will praise thee, when thou
53: 2 from heaven upon the children of m',
55:23 deceitful m' shall not live out half
57: 4 are set on fire, even the sons of m',
58: 1 ye judge uprightly, O ye sons of m'?
59: 2 and save me from bloody m'.
62: 9 m' of low degree are vanity,
9 m' of high degree are a lie: to be"
64: 9 all m' shall fear, and shall declare
66: 5 his doing toward the children of m'.
12 caused m' to ride over our heads;
68:18 thou hast received gifts for m'; yea,
72:17 sun: and m' shall be blessed in him:
73: 5 They are not in trouble as other m';
5 are they plagued like other m'.
76: 5 m' of might have found their hands.
78:31 smote down the chosen m' of Israel.
60 the tent which he placed among m';
63 The fire consumed their young m';
82: 7 But ye shall die like m', and fall like
83:18 That m' may know that thou, whose
86:14 violent m' have sought after my soul;
89:47 hast thou made all m' in vain?
90: 3 and sayest, Return, ye children of m'.
105:12 they were but a few m' in number;
107: 8 Oh that m' would praise the Lord for
8 works to the children of m'!
15 Oh that m' would praise the Lord for
15 works to the children of m'!
21 Oh that m' would praise the Lord for
21 works to the children of m'!
31 Oh that m' would praise the Lord for
31 works to the children of m'!
115:16 hath he given to the children of m'.
116:11 I said in my haste, All m' are liars.
124: 2 side, when m' rose up against us:
139:19 from me therefore, ye bloody m'.
141: 4 works with m' that work iniquity:
145: 6 m' shall speak of the might of thy
12 To make known to the sons of m'
148:12 Both young m', and maidens;
12 and maidens; old m', and children:
Pr 2:20 mayest walk in the way of good m',
4:14 and go not in the way of evil m'.
6:30 M' do not despise a thief, if he steal to
8: 4 Unto you, O m', I call; and my
31 delights were with the sons of m'.
10:14 Wise m' lay up knowledge: but the
11: 7 and the hope of unjust m' perisheth.
16 honour: and strong m' retain riches.
12:12 The wicked desireth the net of evil m':
13:20 walketh with wise m' shall be wise:
15:11 the hearts of the children of m'?

Pr 16: 6 fear of the Lord m' depart from evil.
17: 6 children are the crown of old m';
18:16 and bringeth him before great m'.
20: 6 Most m' will proclaim every one
29 glory of young m' is their strength:
29 the beauty of old m' is the gray head.
22:29 he shall not stand before mean m'.
23:28 the transgressors among m'.
24: 1 not thou envious against evil m',
9 scorner is an abomination to m'.
19 Fret not thyself because of evil m',
25: 1 the m' of Hezekiah king of Judah
6 and stand not in the place of great m':
27 for m' to search their own glory is not
26:16 seven m' that can render a reason.
28: 5 Evil m' understand not judgment:
7 that is a companion of riotous m'
12 When righteous m' do rejoice, there is
28 wicked rise, m' hide themselves:
29: 8 Scornful m' bring a city into a
8 snare: but wise m' turn away wrath.
30:14 and the needy from among m'.
Ec 2: 3 was that good for the sons of m',
8 me m' singers and women singers,
8 and the delights of the sons of m',
3:10 God hath given to the sons of m'
18 the estate of the sons of m', that God
19 that which befalleth the sons of m'
6: 1 sun, and it is common among m':
7: 2 for that is the end of all m'; and the
19 ten mighty m' which are in the city.
8:11 heart of the sons of m' is fully set
14 that there be just m', unto whom it
14 again, there be wicked m', to whom it
9: 3 heart of the sons of m' is full of evil,
11 nor yet riches to m' of understanding,
11 nor yet favour to m' of skill; but time
12 so are the sons of m' snared in an
14 a little city, and few m' within it;
17 words of wise m' are heard in quiet
12: 3 strong m' shall bow themselves,
Ca 3: 7 threescore valiant m' are about it,
4: 4 bucklers, all shields of mighty m'.
Isa 2:11 haughtiness of m' shall be bowed
17 haughtiness of m' shall be made low:
3:25 Thy m' shall fall by the sword, and
5: 3 and m' of Judah, judge, I pray you,
7 the m' of Judah his pleasant plant:
13 their honourable m' are famished,
22 and m' of strength to mingle strong
6:12 Lord have removed m' far away,
7:13 a small thing for you to weary m',
24 and with bows shall m' come thither;
9: 3 m' rejoice when they divide the spoil.
17 shall have no joy in their young m',
11:15 streams, and make m' go over dryshod.
13:18 shall dash the young m' to pieces;
19:12 where are thy wise m'? and let them
21: 9 here cometh a chariot of m', with
17 mighty m' of the children of Kedar,
22: 2 slain m' are not slain with the sword,
6 with chariots of m' and horsemen,
23: 4 neither do I nourish up young m', nor
24: 6 earth are burned, and few m' left.
26:19 Thy dead m' shall live, together with
28:14 word of the Lord, ye scornful m',
29:11 which m' deliver to one that is learned,
13 me is taught by the precept of m':
14 wisdom of their wise m' shall perish,
14 the understanding of their prudent m'
19 the poor among m' shall rejoice in
31: 3 the Egyptians are m', and not God;
8 and his young m' shall be discomfited.
36:12 me to the m' that sit upon the wall,
38:16 O Lord, by these things m' live, and in
39: 3 What said these m'? and from
40:30 and the young m' shall utterly fall:
41: 9 called thee from the chief m' thereof,
14 worm Jacob, and ye m' of Israel;
43: 4 therefore will I give m' for thee,
44:11 and the workmen, they are of m': let
25 that turneth wise m' backward, and
45:14 and of the Sabeans, m' of stature,
24 even to him shall m' come; and all that
46: 8 this, and shew yourselves m':
51: 7 fear ye not the reproach of m',
52:14 his form more than the sons of m':
53: 3 He is despised and rejected of m';
57: 1 merciful m' are taken away, none
59:10 we are in desolate places as dead m'.
60:11 that m' may bring unto thee the forces
61: 6 m' shall call you the Ministers of our
64: 4 m' have not heard, nor perceived by
66:24 look upon the carcases of the m'
Jer 4: 3 saith the Lord to the m' of Judah
4 ye m' of Judah and inhabitants of
5: 5 I will get me unto the great m', and
16 sepulchre, they are all mighty m'.
26 my people are found wicked m': they
26 they set a trap, they catch m'.
6:11 and upon the assembly of young m'
23 set in array as m' for war against
30 Reprobate silver shall m' call them,
8: 9 The wise m' are ashamed, they are
9: 2 a lodging place of wayfaring m'; that
2 an assembly of treacherous m'.
10 can m' hear the voice of the cattle;
21 and the young m' from the streets.
22 Even the carcases of m' shall fall
10: 7 among all the wise m' of the nations,
9 they are all the work of cunning m'.
11: 2 speak unto the m' of Judah, and
9 is found among the m' of Judah,
21 the Lord of the m' of Anathoth,
22 the young m' shall die by the sword;
23 bring evil upon the m' of Anathoth,

Jer 15: 8 against the mother of the young m' a
10 nor m' have lent to me on usury; yet
16: 6 neither shall m' lament for them, nor
7 shall m' tear themselves for them in
7 m' give them the cup of consolation
17:25 m' of Judah, and the inhabitants of
18:11 speak to the m' of Judah, and to
21 and let their m' be put to death;
21 young m' be slain by the sword in
19:10 sight of the m' that go with thee,
26:21 the king, with all his mighty m',
22 the king sent m' into Egypt,
22 and certain m' with him into Egypt.
31:13 both young m' and old together:
32:19 upon all the ways of the sons of m':
20 and in Israel, and among other m';
32 prophets, and the m' of Judah, and
44 M' shall buy fields for money, and
33: 5 them with the dead bodies of m',
34:18 give the m' that have transgressed
35:13 Go and tell the m' of Judah and
36:31 and upon the m' of Judah, all the
37:10 there remained but wounded m'
38: 4 weakeneth the hands of the m' of
9 m' have done evil in all that they
10 from hence thirty m' with thee, and
11 Ebed-melech took the m' with him,
16 give thee into the hand of these m'
39: 4 saw them, and all the m' of war,
17 not be given into the hand of the m'
40: 7 and their m', heard that the king
7 had committed unto him m', and
8 a Maachathite, they and their m'.
9 sware unto them and to their m',
41: 1 of the king, even ten m' with him,
2 and the ten m' that were with him,
3 were found there, and the m' of war.
5 from Samaria, even fourscore m',
7 he, and the m' that were with him.
8 ten m' were found among them that
9 cast all the dead bodies of the m',
12 Then they took all the m', and went
15 from Johanan with eight m', and
16 even mighty m' of war, and the
42:17 shall it be with all the m' that set
43: 2 Johanan...and all the proud m',
6 Even m', and women, and the
9 in the sight of the m' of Judah;
44:15 Then all the m' which knew that
19 offerings unto her, without our m'?
20 to the m', and to the women, and
27 all the m' of Judah that are in the
46: 9 and let the mighty m' come forth;
15 Why are thy valiant m' swept away?
21 Also her hired m' are in the midst of
47: 2 then the m' shall cry, and all the
48:14 mighty and strong m' for the war?
15 his chosen young m' are gone down to
31 mourn for the m' of Kir-heres.
36 like pipes for the m' of Kir-heres.
49:15 heathen, and despised among m'.
22 the heart of the mighty m' of Edom be
26 her young m' shall fall in her streets,
26 all the m' of war shall be cut off
28 and spoil the m' of the east.
50:30 shall her young m' fall in her streets,
30 all her m' of war shall be cut off in
35 her princes, and upon her wise m'.
36 a sword is upon her mighty m'; and
51: 3 spare ye not her young m'; destroy ye
14 Surely I will fill thee with m', as
30 mighty m' of Babylon have forborn
32 and the m' of war are affrighted.
56 her mighty m' are taken, every one
57 drunk her princes, and her wise m'
57 and her rulers, and her mighty m':
52: 7 all the m' of war fled, and went
13 all houses of the great m', burned he
25 had the charge of the m' of war;
25 and seven m' of them that were near
25 m' of the people of the land, that
La 1:15 trodden under foot all my mighty m'
15 against me to crush my young m':
18 my young m' are gone into captivity.
2:15 the city that m' call The perfection
21 my young m' are fallen by the sword;
3:33 nor grieve the children of m'.
4:14 wandered as blind m' in the streets,
14 m' could not touch their garments.
5:13 They took the young m' to grind, and
14 gate, the young m' from their musick.
Eze 6: 4 cast down your slain m' before your
13 slain m' shall be among their idols
8:11 there stood before them seventy m'
16 about five and twenty m', with their
9: 2 six m' came from the way of the
4 mark upon the foreheads of the m'
6 they began at the ancient m' which
11: 1 door of the gate five and twenty m';
2 are the m' that devise mischief,
15 thy brethren, the m' of thy kindred,
12:16 a few m' of them from the sword,
14: 3 these m' have set up their idols in
14 these three m', Noah, Daniel, and
16, 18 these three m' were in it, as I
15: 3 will m' take a pin of it to hang any
16:17 madest to thyself images of m',
19: 3 to catch the prey; it devoured m'.
6 to catch the prey, and devoured m'.
21:14 is the sword of the great m' that are
31 thee into the hand of brutish m',
22: 9 In thee are m' that carry tales to
23: 6 rulers, all of them desirable young m',
7 were the chosen m' of Assyria,
12 horses, all of them desirable young m'.
14 she saw m' pourtrayed upon the

Eze 23: 23 all of them desirable young *m'*,
40 have sent for *m'* to come from far,
42 and with the *m'* of the common sort
45 the righteous *m'*, they shall judge
24: 17 thy lips, and eat not the bread of *m'*.
22 your lips, nor eat the bread of *m'*.
25: 4 deliver thee to the *m'* of the east
10 *m'* of the east with the Ammonites,
26: 10 as *m'* enter into a city wherein is made
17 that wast inhabited of seafaring *m'*,
27: 8 thy wise *m'*, O Tyrus, that were in
9 the wise *m'* thereof were in thee thy
10 were in thine army, thy *m'* of war:
11 The *m'* of Arvad with thine army
13 they traded the persons of *m'* and
15 *m'* of Dedan were thy merchants;
27 all thy *m'* of war, that are in thee,
30: 5 *m'* of the land that is in league,
17 The young *m'* of Aven...shall fall
31: 14 in the midst of the children of *m'*,
34: 31 the flock of my pasture, are *m'*, and
35: 8 fill his mountains with his slain *m'*:
36: 10 And I will multiply *m'* upon you,
12 I will cause *m'* to walk upon you,
12 more henceforth bereave them of *m'*.
13 Thou land devourest up *m'*, and
14 thou shalt devour *m'* no more,
15 Neither will I cause *m'* to hear in thee
37 increase them with *m'* like a flock.
38 cities be filled with flocks of *m'*:
38: 20 all the *m'* that are upon the face of
39: 14 they shall sever out *m'* of continual
20 horses and chariots, with mighty *m'*,
20 and with all *m'* of war, saith the
47: 15 way of Hethlon, as *m'* go to Zedad;
Da 2: 12 to destroy all the wise *m'* of Babylon.
13 forth that the wise *m'* should be slain;
14 forth to slay the wise *m'* of Babylon:
18 with the rest of the wise *m'* of Babylon.
24 to destroy the wise *m'* of Babylon: he
24 Destroy not the wise *m'* of Babylon:
27 hath demanded cannot the wise *m'*,
38 the children of *m'* dwell, the
43 themselves with the seed of *m'*:
48 over all the wise *m'* of Babylon.
3: 12 these *m'*, O king, have not
13 brought these *m'* before the king.
20 commanded the most mighty *m'*
21 these *m'* were bound in their coats,
22 the fire slew those *m'* that took up
23 these three *m'*, Shadrach, Meshach,
24 Did not we cast three *m'* bound
25 Lo, I see four *m'* loose, walking in
27 saw these *m'*, upon whose bodies
4: 6 to bring in all the wise *m'* of Babylon
17 High ruleth in the kingdom of *m'*,
17 setteth up over it the basest of *m'*.
18 wise *m'* of my kingdom are not able
25 they shall drive thee from *m'*, and
25 High ruleth in the kingdom of *m'*,
32 they shall drive thee from *m'*, and
32 High ruleth in the kingdom of *m'*,
33 he was driven from *m'*, and did eat
5: 7 and said to the wise *m'* of Babylon,
8 Then came in all the king's wise *m'*:
15 And now the wise *m'*, the astrologers,
21 he was driven from the sons of *m'*;
21 God ruled in the kingdom of *m'*,
6: 5 Then said these *m'*, We shall not
11 Then these *m'* assembled, and found
15 Then these *m'* assembled unto the
24 *m'* which had accused Daniel,
26 *m'* tremble and fear before the God of
9: 7 *m'* of Judah, and to the inhabitants
10: 7 *m'* that were with me saw not the
16 like the similitude of the sons of *m'*
Ho 6: 7 But they like *m'* have transgressed
10: 13 in the multitude of thy mighty *m'*.
13: 2 *m'* that sacrifice kiss the calves.
Joe 1: 2 Hear this, ye old *m'*, and give ear, all
12 withered away from the sons of *m'*.
2: 7 shall run like mighty *m'*; they shall
7 shall climb the wall like *m'* of war;
28 your old *m'* shall dream dreams,
28 your young *m'* shall see visions:
3: 9 war, wake up the mighty *m'*, let
9 let all the *m'* of war draw near; let
Am 2: 11 and of your young *m'* for Nazarites.
4: 10 your young *m'* have I slain with the
6: 9 there remain ten *m'* in one house,
8: 13 virgins and young *m'* faint for thirst.
Ob 7 *m'* of thy confederacy have brought
7 the *m'* that were at peace with thee
8 even destroy the wise *m'* out of Edom,
9 And thy mighty *m'*, O Teman, shall be
Jon 1: 10 were the *m'* exceedingly afraid,
10 For the *m'* knew that he fled from
13 Nevertheless the *m'* rowed hard to
16 the *m'* feared the Lord exceedingly,
Mic 2: 8 by securely as *m'* averse from war.
12 by reason of the multitude of *m'*.
5: 5 shepherds, and eight principal *m'*.
7 man, nor waiteth for the sons of *m'*.
6: 12 rich *m'* thereof are full of violence,
7: 2 there is none upright among *m'*:
6 enemies are...*m'* of his own house.
Na 2: 3 shield of his mighty *m'* is made red,
3 red, the valiant *m'* are in scarlet:
3: 10 they cast lots for her honourable *m'*,
10 all her great *m'* were bound in chains.
Hab 1: 14 makest *m'* as the fishes of the sea,
Zep 1: 12 punish the *m'* that are settled on
17 I will bring distress upon *m'*, that
17 that they shall walk like blind *m'*,
2: 11 and *m'* shall worship him, every
Hag 1: 11 and upon *m'*, and upon cattle, and

Zec 2: 4 for the multitude of *m'* and cattle
3: 8 for they are *m'* wondered at: for,
7: 2 their *m'*, to pray before the Lord,
7 when *m'* inhabited the south and the
8: 4 There shall yet old *m'* and old women
10 I set all *m'* every one against his
23 that ten *m'* shall take hold out of
9: 17 shall make the young *m'* cheerful,
10: 5 And they shall be as mighty *m'*, which
11: 6 I will deliver the *m'* every one into
14: 11 And *m'* shall dwell in it, and there
M't 2: 1 there came wise *m'* from the east to
7 he had privily called the wise *m'*,
16 saw that he was mocked of the wise *m'*,
16 had diligently enquired of the wise *m'*.
4: 19 and I will make you fishers of *m'*.
5: 11 are ye, when *m'* shall revile you,
13 and to be trodden under foot of *m'*.
15 Neither do *m'* light a candle, and put
16 Let your light so shine before *m'*,
19 and shall teach *m'* so, he shall be
6: 1 that ye do not your alms before *m'*,
2 that they may have glory of *m'*.
5 streets, that they may be seen of *m'*.
14 For if ye forgive *m'* their trespasses,
15 if ye forgive not *m'* their trespasses,
16 they may appear unto *m'* to fast.
18 thou appear not unto *m'* to fast, but
7: 12 ye would that *m'* should do to you,
16 Do *m'* gather grapes of thorns, or figs
8: 27 the *m'* marvelled, saying, What
9: 8 had given such power unto *m'*.
17 Neither do *m'* put new wine into old
27 two blind *m'* followed him, crying, and
28 the house, the blind *m'* came to him:
10: 17 beware of *m'*: for they will deliver
22 be hated of all *m'* for my name's
32 shall confess me before *m'*, him
33 whosoever shall deny me before *m'*,
12: 31 blasphemy shall be forgiven unto *m'*:
31 Ghost shall not be forgiven unto *m'*.
36 every idle word that *m'* shall speak,
41 The *m'* of Nineveh shall rise in
13: 17 righteous *m'* have desired to see those
25 while *m'* slept, his enemy came and
14: 21 eaten were about five thousand *m'*,
35 the *m'* of that place had knowledge
15: 9 doctrines the commandments of *m'*.
38 that did eat were four thousand *m'*,
16: 13 Whom do *m'* say that I the Son of
23 be of God, but those that be of *m'*.
17: 22 be betrayed into the hands of *m'*:
19: 11 All *m'* cannot receive this saying, save
12 which were made eunuchs of *m'*:
26 With *m'* this is impossible; but with
20: 30 two blind *m'* sitting by the way side,
21: 25 was it? from heaven, or of *m'*?
26 if we shall say, Of *m'*; we fear the
22: 16 thou regardest not the person of *m'*.
23: 5 works they do for to be seen of *m'*:
7 and to be called of *m'*, Rabbi, Rabbi.
13 the kingdom of heaven against *m'*:
28 appear righteous unto *m'*, but
34 send unto you prophets, and wise *m'*
26: 33 Though all *m'* shall be offended
28: 4 did shake, and became as dead *m'*.
M'r 1: 17 make you to become fishers of *m'*.
37 said unto him, All *m'* seek for thee.
3: 28 be forgiven unto the sons of *m'*,
5: 20 done for him: and all *m'* did marvel.
6: 12 and preached that *m'* should repent.
44 loaves were about five thousand *m'*.
7: 7 doctrines the commandments of *m'*.
8 ye hold the tradition of *m'*, as the
21 out of the heart of *m'*, proceed evil
8: 4 man satisfy these *m'* with bread here
24 and said, I see *m'* as trees, walking.
27 them, Whom do *m'* say that I am?
33 of God, but the things that be of *m'*.
9: 31 is delivered into the hands of *m'*,
10: 27 With *m'* it is impossible, but not with
11: 30 John, was it from heaven, or of *m'*?
32 if we shall say, Of *m'*; they feared
32 for all *m'* counted John, that he was a
12: 14 regardest not the person of *m'*, but
13: 13 be hated of all *m'* for my name's sake:
14: 51 and the young *m'* laid hold on him:
Lu 1: 25 take away my reproach among *m'*.
2: 14 on earth peace, good will toward *m'*.
3: 15 all *m'* mused in their hearts of John,
5: 10 from henceforth thou shalt catch *m'*.
18 *m'* brought in a bed a man which
6: 22 are ye, when *m'* shall hate you, and
26 when all *m'* shall speak well of you!
31 ye would that *m'* should do to you,
38 over, shall *m'* give into your bosom.
44 For of thorns *m'* do not gather figs,
7: 20 When the *m'* were come unto him,
31 I liken the *m'* of this generation?
9: 14 they were about five thousand *m'*.
30 behold, there talked with him two *m'*,
32 and the two *m'* that stood with him.
44 be delivered into the hands of *m'*.
11: 31 with the *m'* of this generation, and
32 *m'* of Nineve shall rise up in the
44 the *m'* that walk over them are not
46 ye lade *m'* with burdens grievous to
12: 8 shall confess me before *m'*, him shall
9 he that denieth me before *m'* shall
36 like unto *m'* that wait for their lord,
48 to whom *m'* have committed much,
13: 4 that they were sinners above all *m'*
14 six days in which *m'* ought to work:
14: 24 none of those *m'* which were bidden
35 yet for the dunghill; but *m'* cast it out.
16: 15 which justify yourselves before *m'*;

Lu 16: 15 esteemed among *m'* is abomination
17: 12 met him ten *m'* that were lepers,
34 there shall be two *m'* in one bed;
36 Two *m'* shall be in the field; the one
18: 1 that *m'* ought always to pray, and not
10 Two *m'* went up into the temple to
11 thee, that I am not as other *m'* are,
27 impossible with *m'* are possible with
20: 4 John, was it from heaven, or of *m'*?
6 if we say, Of *m'*; all the people will
20 which should feign themselves just *m'*,
21: 1 rich *m'* casting their gifts into the
17 be hated of all *m'* for my name's sake.
22: 63 the *m'* that held Jesus mocked him,
23: 11 his *m'* of war set him at nought,
24: 4 two *m'* stood by them in shining
7 delivered into the hands of sinful *m'*,
Joh 1: 4 and the life was the light of *m'*.
7 that all *m'* through him might believe.
2: 10 and when *m'* have well drunk, then
24 unto them, because he knew all *m'*,
3: 19 *m'* loved darkness rather than light,
26 baptizeth, and all *m'* come to him.
4: 20 the place where *m'* ought to worship.
28 into the city, and saith to the *m'*,
38 other *m'* laboured, and ye are
5: 23 That all *m'* should honour the Son,
41 I receive not honour from *m'*.
6: 10 Jesus said, Make the *m'* sit down.
10 the *m'* sat down, in number about
14 Then those *m'*, when they had seen
8: 17 that the testimony of two *m'* is true.
11: 48 thus alone, all *m'* will believe on him:
12: 32 the earth, will draw all *m'* unto me.
43 For they loved the praise of *m'* more
13: 35 this shall all *m'* know that ye are my
15: 6 *m'* gather them, and cast them into the
17: 6 manifested thy name unto the *m'*
18: 3 having received a band of *m'* and
Ac 1: 10 two *m'* stood by them in white
11 *m'* of Galilee, why stand ye gazing
16 *M'* and brethren, this scripture
21 these *m'* which have companied with
24 which knowest the hearts of all *m'*,
2: 5 Jews, devout *m'*, out of every nation
13 said, These *m'* are full of new wine.
14 Ye *m'* of Judæa, and all ye that
17 your young *m'* shall see visions,
17 and your old *m'* shall dream dreams:
22 Ye *m'* of Israel, hear these words:
29 *M'* and brethren, let me freely
37 *M'* and brethren, what shall we do?
45 parted them to all *m'*, as every man
3: 12 Ye *m'* of Israel, why marvel ye at
4: 4 the number of the *m'* was about five
12 under heaven given among *m'*,
13 they were unlearned and ignorant *m'*,
16 What shall we do to these *m'*? for
21 all *m'* glorified God for that which was
5: 4 thou hast not lied unto *m'*, but unto
6 the young *m'* arose, wound him up,
10 the young *m'* came in, and found
14 multitudes both of *m'* and women.)
25 the *m'* whom ye put in prison are
29 ought to obey God rather than *m'*.
35 *m'* of Israel, take heed to yourselves
35 intend to do as touching these *m'*.
36 to whom a number of *m'*, about
38 Refrain from these *m'*, and let them
38 if this counsel or this work be of *m'*,
6: 3 among you seven *m'* of honest
11 Then they suborned *m'*, which said,
7: 2 *M'*, brethren, and fathers, hearken;
8: 2 *m'* carried Stephen to his burial, and
3 *m'* and women committed them to
12 were baptized, both *m'* and women.
9: 2 whether they were *m'* or women, he
7 the *m'* which journeyed with him
38 there, they sent unto him two *m'*,
10: 5 send *m'* to Joppa, and call for one
17 *m'* which were sent from Cornelius
19 unto him, Behold, three *m'* seek thee.
21 went down to the *m'* which were sent
11: 3 wentest in to *m'* uncircumcised, and
11 there were three *m'* already come
13 Send *m'* to Joppa, and call for
20 them were *m'* of Cyprus and Cyrene,
13: 15 Ye *m'* and brethren, if ye have any
16 *M'* of Israel, and ye that fear God,
26 *M'* and brethren, children of the
38 unto you therefore, *m'* and brethren,
50 women, and the chief *m'* of the city,
14: 11 down to us in the likeness of *m'*.
15 We also are *m'* of like passions with
15: 1 certain *m'* which came...from Judæa
7 *M'* and brethren, ye know how
13 *M'* and brethren, hearken unto me:
17 the residue of *m'* might seek after
22 send chosen *m'* of their...company
22 Silas, chief *m'* among the brethren:
25 to send chosen *m'* unto you with our
26 *M'* that have hazarded their lives
16: 17 *m'* are the servants of the most high
20 saying, These *m'*, being Jews, do
35 serjeants, saying, Let those *m'* go.
17: 12 were Greeks, and of *m'*, not a few.
22 Ye *m'* of Athens, I perceive that in
26 made of one blood all nations of *m'*
30 all *m'* every where to repent:
31 he hath given assurance unto all *m'*,
34 Howbeit certain *m'* clave unto him,
18: 13 persuadeth *m'* to worship God
19: 7 And all the *m'* were about twelve.
19 and burned them before all *m'*:
29 and Aristarchus, *m'* of Macedonia,
35 Ye *m'* of Ephesus, what man is there

Ac 19:37 ye have brought hither these *m'*.
20:26 I am pure from the blood of all *m'*.
30 of your own selves shall *m'* arise,
21:23 We have four *m'* which have a vow
26 Then Paul took the *m'*, and the next
28 Crying out, *M'* of Israel, help: This
28 man, that teacheth all *m'* every where
38 thousand *m'* that were murderers?
22: 1 *M'*, brethren, and fathers, hear ye
4 into prisons both *m'* and women.
15 thou shalt be his witness unto all *m'*
23: 1 *M'* and brethren, I have lived in
6 *M'* and brethren, I am a Pharisee,
21 for him of them more than forty *m'*,
24:16 offence toward God, and toward *m'*.
25:23 and principal *m'* of the city,
24 all *m'* which are here present with
28:17 *M'* and brethren, though I have
Ro 1:18 unrighteousness of *m'*, who hold
27 also the *m'*, leaving the natural use
27 *m'* with *m'* working that which is
2:16 God shall judge the secrets of *m'*
29 whose praise is not of *m'*, but of
5:12 so death passed upon all *m'*, for
18 judgment came upon all *m'* to
18 the free gift came upon all *m'* unto
6:19 I speak after the manner of *m'*
11: 4 reserved...seven thousand *m'*,
12:16 but condescend to *m'* of low estate.
17 things honest in the sight of all *m'*.
18 in you, live peaceably with all *m'*.
14:18 to God, and approved of *m'*.
16:19 obedience is come abroad unto all *m'*.
1Co 1:25 foolishness of God is wiser than *m'*;
25 weakness of God is stronger than *m'*.
26 that not many wise *m'* after the flesh,
2: 5 not stand in the wisdom of *m'*, but
3: 3 are ye not carnal, and walk as *m'*?
21 Therefore let no man glory in *m'*:
4: 6 not to think of *m'* above that which is
9 the world, and to angels, and to *m'*.
7: 7 that all *m'* were even as I myself.
23 price; be not ye the servants of *m'*.
9:19 For though I be free from all *m'*, yet
22 I am made all things to all *m'*, that I
10:15 I speak as to wise *m'*; judge ye what I
33 Even as I please all *m'* in all things,
13: 1 the tongues of *m'* and of angels,
14: 2 speaketh not unto *m'*, but unto God:
3 speaketh unto *m'* to edification, and
20 but in understanding be *m'*.
21 With *m'* of other tongues and other
15:19 we are of all *m'* most miserable.
32 after the manner of *m'* I have fought
39 but there is one kind of flesh of *m'*,
16:13 faith, quit you like *m'*, be strong.
2Co 3: 2 hearts, known and read of all *m'*:
5:11 terror of the Lord, we persuade *m'*;
8:13 mean not that other *m'* be eased, and
21 Lord, but also in the sight of *m'*.
9:13 unto them, and unto all *m'*;
Ga 1: 1 apostle, (not of *m'*, neither by man,
10 For do I now persuade *m'*, or God?
10 or do I seek to please *m'*? for if I yet
10 if I yet pleased *m'*, I should not be
3:15 I speak after the manner of *m'*;
6:10 let us do good unto all *m'*, especially
Eph 3: 5 made known unto the sons of *m'*,
9 make all *m'* see what is the fellowship
4: 8 captive, and gave gifts unto *m'*.
14 by the sleight of *m'*, and cunning
5:28 So ought *m'* to love their wives as
6: 7 as to the Lord, and not to *m'*:
Ph'p 2: 7 and was made in the likeness of *m'*:
4: 5 moderation be known unto all *m'*.
Col 2: 8 vain deceit, after the tradition of *m'*,
22 commandments and doctrines of *m'*?
3:23 as to the Lord, and not unto *m'*;
1Th 1: 5 what manner of *m'* we were among
2: 4 not as pleasing *m'*, but God, which
6 Nor of *m'* sought we glory, neither
13 ye received it not as the word of *m'*,
15 not God, and are contrary to all *m'*:
5:14 the weak, be patient toward all *m'*.
15 both among yourselves, and to all *m'*.
2Th 3: 2 from unreasonable and wicked *m'*:
2 for all *m'* have not faith.
1Ti 2: 1 of thanks, be made for all *m'*;
4 Who will have all *m'* to be saved,
5 one mediator between God and *m'*,
8 I will...that *m'* pray every where,
4:10 God, who is the Saviour of all *m'*,
5:24 and some *m'* they follow after.
6: 5 disputings of *m'* of corrupt minds,
9 which drown *m'* in destruction and
2Ti 2: 2 the same commit thou to faithful *m'*,
24 be gentle unto all *m'*, apt to teach,
3: 2 For *m'* shall be lovers of their own
8 *m'* of corrupt minds, reprobate
9 folly shall be manifest unto all *m'*,
13 But evil *m'* and seducers shall wax
4:16 stood with me, but all *m'* forsook me:
Tit 1: 8 of hospitality, a lover of good *m'*,
14 fables, and commandments of *m'*,
2: 2 That the aged *m'* be sober, grave,
6 Young *m'* likewise exhort to be sober
11 salvation hath appeared to all *m'*,
3: 2 shewing all meekness unto all *m'*.
8 are good and profitable unto *m'*.
Heb 5: 1 high priest taken from among *m'* is
1 for *m'* in things pertaining to God,
6:16 For *m'* verily swear by the greater:
7: 8 And here *m'* that die receive tithes;
28 For the law maketh *m'* high priests
9:17 is of force after *m'* are dead:
27 it is appointed unto *m'* once to die.
Heb12:14 Follow peace with all *m'*, and holiness,
Jas 2: 6 Do not rich *m'* oppress you, and draw
3: 9 Therewith curse we *m'*, which are
5: 1 Go to now, ye rich *m'*, weep and howl
1Pe 2: 4 disallowed indeed of *m'*, but chosen
15 silence the ignorance of foolish *m'*:
17 Honour all *m'*. Love the brotherhood.
4: 2 time in the flesh to the lusts of *m'*,
6 judged according to *m'* in the flesh,
2Pe 1:21 holy *m'* of God spake as they were
3: 7 and perdition of ungodly *m'*.
9 promise, as some *m'* count slackness;
1Jo 2:13 I write unto you, young *m'*,
14 I have written unto you, young *m'*,
5: 9 If we receive the witness of *m'*,
3Jo 12 Demetrius hath good report of all *m'*,
Jude 4 are certain *m'* crept in unawares,
4 ungodly *m'*, turning the grace of
Re 6:15 the great *m'*, and the rich *m'*, and the
15 the chief captains, and the mighty *m'*,
8:11 and many *m'* died of the waters,
9: 4 *m'* which have not the seal of God
6 in those days shall *m'* seek death,
7 their faces were as the faces of *m'*.
10 power was to hurt *m'* five months.
15 year, for to slay the third part of *m'*.
18 three was the third part of *m'* killed,
20 rest of the *m'* which were not killed
11:13 were slain of *m'* seven thousand:
13:13 on the earth in the sight of *m'*,
14: 4 These were redeemed from among *m'*,
16: 2 grievous sore upon the *m'* which had
8 unto him to scorch *m'* with fire.
9 *m'* were scorched with great heat,
18 not since *m'* were upon the earth,
21 there fell upon *m'* a great hail out of
21 *m'* blasphemed God because of the
18:13 chariots, and slaves, and souls of *m'*.
23 were the great *m'* of the earth;
19:18 the flesh of mighty *m'*, and the flesh of
18 the flesh of all *m'*, both free and bond,
21: 3 the tabernacle of God is with *m'*,

Menahem (*men'-a-hem*)
2Ki 15:14 *M'* the son of Gadi went up from
16 *M'* smote Tiphsah, and all that
17 began *M'* the son of Gadi to reign
19 *M'* gave Pul a thousand talents of
20 *M'* exacted the money of Israel,
21 the rest of the acts of *M'*, and all
22 And *M'* slept with his father; and
23 the son of *M'* began to reign over

Menan (*me'-nan*)
Lu 3:31 which was the son of *M'*, which

menchildren See also MEN and CHILDREN.
Ex 34:23 the year shall all your *m'* appear

mend See also AMEND; MENDING.
2Ch 24:12 brass to *m'* the house of the Lord.

mending
M't 4:21 with...their father, *m'* their nets;
M'r 1:19 also were in the ship *m'* their nets.

Mene (*me'-ne*)
Da 5:25 written, *M'*, *M'*, Tekel, Upharsin.
26 *M'*; God hath numbered thy

menpleasers
Eph 6: 6 Not with eyeservice, as *m'*; but as
Col 3:22 not with eyeservice, as *m'*; but in

men's
Ge 24:32 and the *m'* feet that were with him.
44: 1 Fill the *m'* sacks with food, as much
De 4:28 serve gods, the work of *m'* hands,
1Sa 24: 9 Wherefore hearest thou *m'* words,
1Ki 12:13 forsook the old *m'* counsel that they
13: 2 *m'* bones shall be burnt upon thee.
2Ki 19:18 no gods, but the work of *m'* hands,
23:20 and burned *m'* bones upon them,
Ps 115: 4 and gold, the work of *m'* hands.
135:15 and gold, the work of *m'* hands.
Isa 37:19 no gods, but the work of *m'* hands.
Jer 48:41 the mighty *m'* hearts in Moab at that
Hab 2: 8, 17 because of *m'* blood, and for the
M't 23: 4 and lay them on *m'* shoulders; but
27 but are within full of dead *m'* bones,
Lu 9:56 is not come to destroy *m'* lives,
21:26 *M'* hearts failing them for fear, and
Ac 17:25 Neither is worshiped with *m'* hands,
2Co 10:15 measure, that is, of other *m'* labours;
1Ti 5:22 neither be partaker of other *m'* sins:
24 Some *m'* sins are open beforehand,
1Pe 4:15 or as a busy body in other *m'* matters.
Jude 16 having *m'* persons in admiration

menservants
Ge 12:16 and oxen, and he asses, and *m'*,
20:14 took sheep, and oxen, and *m'*, and
24:35 herds, and silver, and gold, and *m'*,
30:43 cattle, and maidservants, and *m'*,
32: 5 oxen, and asses, flocks, and *m'*, and
Ex 21: 7 she shall not go out as the *m'* do.
De 12:12 your *m'*, and your maidservants,
1Sa 8:16 he will take your *m'*, and your
2Ki 5:26 and sheep, and oxen, and *m'*, and
Lu 12:45 shall begin to beat the *m'* and

menstealers
1Ti 1:10 with mankind, for *m'*, for liars,

menstruous
Isa 30:22 cast them away as a *m'* cloth;
La 1:17 Jerusalem is as a *m'* woman
Eze 18: 6 hath come near to a *m'* woman,

mention See also MENTIONED.
Ge 40:14 and make *m'* of me unto Pharaoh,
Ex 23:13 make no *m'* of the name of other
Jos 23: 7 make *m'* of the name of their gods,
1Sa 4:18 when he made *m'* of the ark of God,
Job 28:18 No *m'* shall be made of coral, or of
Ps 71:16 will make *m'* of thy righteousness,
87: 4 make *m'* of Rahab and Babylon to
Isa 12: 4 make *m'* that his name is exalted.
19:17 every one that maketh *m'* thereof
26:13 only will we make *m'* of thy name.
48: 1 and make *m'* of the God of Israel,
49: 1 hath he made *m'* of my name.
62: 6 ye that make *m'* of the Lord, keep
63: 7 *m'* the lovingkindness of the Lord,
Jer 4:16 Make ye *m'* to the nations; behold,
20: 9 I said, I will not make *m'* of him,
23:36 burden of the Lord shall ye *m'* no
Am 6:10 make *m'* of the name of the Lord.
Ro 1: 9 *m'* of you always in my prayers;
Eph 1:16 making *m'* of you in my prayers;
1Th 1: 2 making *m'* of you in our prayers;
Ph'm 4 *m'* of thee always in my prayers,
Heb11:22 died, made *m'* of the departing of

mentioned
Jos 21: 9 these cities which are here *m'* by
1Ch 4:38 *m'* by their names were princes.
2Ch 20:34 who is *m'* in the book of the kings
Eze 16:56 For thy sister Sodom was not *m'*
18:22 they shall not be *m'* unto him:
24 that he hath done shall not be *m'*:
33:16 hath committed shall be *m'* unto

Meon See BAAL-MEON; BETH-MEON.

Meonenim (*me-on'-e-nim*)
J'g 9:37 come along by the plain of *M'*.

Meonothai (*me-on'-o-thahee*)
1Ch 4:14 *M'* begat Ophrah: and Seraiah

Mephaath (*mef'-a-ath*)
Jos 13:18 Jahaza, and Kedemoth, and *M'*,
21:37 *M'* with her suburbs; four cities.
1Ch 6:79 suburbs, and *M'* with...suburbs;
Jer 48:21 and upon Jahazah, and upon *M'*,

Mephibosheth (*me-fib'-o-sheth*) See also MERIB-BAAL.
2Sa 4: 4 lame. And his name was *M'*.
9: 6 Now when *M'*, the son of Jonathan,
6 And David said, *M'*. And he
10 *M'* thy master's son shall eat bread
11 As for *M'*, said the king, he shall
12 *M'* had a young son, whose name
12 of Ziba were servants unto *M'*.
13 So *M'* dwelt in Jerusalem: for he
16: 1 Ziba the servant of *M'* met him,
4 are all that pertained unto *M'*.
19:24 *M'* the son of Saul came down to
25 wentest not thou with me, *M'*?
30 *M'* said unto the king, Yea, let him
21: 7 But the king spared *M'*, the son of
8 bare unto Saul, Armoni and *M'*;

Merab (*me'-rab*)
1Sa 14:49 the name of the firstborn *M'*, and
18:17 Behold my elder daughter *M'*, her
19 pass at the time when *M'* Saul's

Meraiah (*mer-a-i'-ah*)
Ne 12:12 of the fathers: of Seraiah, *M'*; of

Meraioth (*me-rah'-yoth*) See also MEREMOTH.
1Ch 6: 6 Zerahiah, and Zerahiah begat *M'*,
7 *M'* begat Amariah, and Amariah
52 *M'* his son, Amariah his son,
9:11 the son of *M'*, the son of Ahitub,
Ezr 7: 3 the son of Azariah, the son of *M'*,
Ne 11:11 the son of Zadok, the son of *M'*, the
12:15 Of Harim, Adna; of *M'*, Helkai;

Merari (*me-ra'-ri*) See also MERARITES.
Ge 46:11 Levi; Gershon, Kohath, and *M'*.
Ex 6:16 Gershon, and Kohath, and *M'*:
19 the sons of *M'*; Mahali and Mushi:
Nu 3:17 Gershon, and Kohath, and *M'*.
20 the sons of *M'* by their families;
33 *M'* was the family of the Mahlites,
33 these are the families of *M'*.
35 of the families of *M'* was Zuriel the
36 custody and charge of the sons of *M'*
4:29 the sons of *M'*, thou shalt number
33, 42, 45 the families of the sons of *M'*,
7: 8 oxen he gave unto the sons of *M'*,
10:17 sons of *M'* set forward, bearing the
26:57 of *M'*, the family of the Merarites.
Jos 21: 7 The children of *M'* by their families
34 the families of the children of *M'*,
40 all the cities for the children of *M'*
1Ch 6: 1 of Levi; Gershon, Kohath, and *M'*.
16 of Levi; Gershom, Kohath, and *M'*.
19 The sons of *M'*; Mahli, and Mushi.
29 The sons of *M'*; Mahli; Libni his
44 sons of *M'* stood on the left hand:
47 the son of Mushi, the son of *M'*,
63 Unto the sons of *M'* were given by
77 Unto the rest of the children of *M'*
9:14 of Hashabiah, of the sons of *M'*;
15: 6 Of the sons of *M'*; Asaiah the chief,
17 of the sons of *M'* their brethren,
23: 6 namely, Gershon, Kohath, and *M'*,
21 The sons of *M'*; Mahli, and Mushi.
24:26 sons of *M'* were Mahli and Mushi:
27 The sons of *M'* by Jaaziah; Beno,
26:10 Hosah, of the children of *M'*, had
19 Kore, and among the sons of *M'*.
2Ch 29:12 and of the sons of *M'*; Kish the son
34:12 the Levites, of the sons of *M'*;
Ezr 8:19 him Jeshaiah of the sons of *M'*,

Merarites (*me-ra'-rites*)
Nu 26:57 of Merari, the family of the *M'*.

Merathaim (*mer-a-tha'-im*)
Jer 50:21 Go up against the land of *M'*.

merchandise
De 21:14 thou shalt not make m' of her,
24: 7 maketh m' of him, or selleth him;
Pr 3:14 For the m' of it is better than the
14 is better than the m' of silver,
31:18 perceiveth that her m' is good:
Isa 23:18 m' and her hire shall be holiness
18 her m' shall be for them that dwell
45:14 m' of Ethiopia and of the Sabeans,
Eze 26:12 riches, and make a prey of thy m':
27: 9 were in thee to occupy thy m'.
15 isles were the m' of thine hand:
24 and made of cedar, among thy m'.
27 and thy fairs, thy m', thy mariners,
27 calkers, and the occupiers of thy m',
33 multitude of thy riches and of thy m'.
34 thy m' and all thy company in the
28:16 By the multitude of thy m' they
M't 22: 5 one to his farm, another to his m':
Joh 2:16 my Father's house an house of m'.
2Pe 2: 3 with feigned words make m' of you:
Re 18:11 no man buyeth their m' any more:
12 m' of gold, and silver, and precious

merchant See also MERCHANTMEN; MERCHANTS.
Ge 23:16 silver, current money with the m'.
Pr 31:24 delivereth girdles unto the m'.
Ca 3: 6 with all powders of the m'?
Isa 23:11 against the m' city, to destroy
Eze 27: 3 a m' of the people for many isles,
12 Tarshish was thy m' by reason of
16 Syria was thy m' by reason of the
18 Damascus was thy m' in the
20 Dedan was thy m' in precious
Ho 12: 7 He is a m', the balances of deceit
Zep 1:11 for all the m' people are cut down;
M't 13:45 of heaven is like unto a m' man,

merchantmen See also MERCHANT and MEN.
Ge 37:28 there passed by Midianites m';
1Ki 10:15 Besides that he had of the m',

merchants See also MERCHANTS'.
1Ki 10:15 and of the traffick of the spice m',
28 king's m' received the linen yarn
2Ch 1:16 king's m' received the linen yarn at
9:14 which chapmen and m' brought.
Ne 3:31 of the Nethinims, and of the m',
32 repaired the goldsmiths and the m'.
13:20 m' and sellers of all kind of ware
Job 41: 6 shall they part him among the m'?
Isa 23: 2 the m' of Zidon, that pass over
8 crowning city, whose m' are princes,
47:15 thou hast laboured, even thy m',
Eze 17: 4 traffick; he set it in a city of m'.
27:13 and Mesech, they were thy m':
15 The men of Dedan were thy m';
17 land of Israel, they were thy m':
21 goats: in these were they thy m'.
22 The m' of Sheba and Raamah,
22 they were thy m': they occupied in
23 Canneh, and Eden, the m' of Sheba,
23 Asshur, and Chilmad, were thy m'.
24 were thy m' in all sorts of things,
36 m' among the people shall hiss at
38:13 and Dedan, and the m' of Tarshish,
Na 3:16 multiplied thy m' above the stars
Re 18: 3 the m' of the earth are waxed rich
11 the m' of the earth shall weep and
15 The m' of these things, which were
23 m' were the great men of the earth;

merchants'
Pr 31:14 She is like the m' ships; she

mercies See also MERCIES'.
Ge 32:10 worthy of the least of all the m',
2Sa 24:14 of the Lord, for his m' are great:
1Ch 21:13 the Lord; for very great are his m':
2Ch 6:42 remember the m' of David thy
Ne 9:19 thou in thy manifold m' forsookest
27 according to thy manifold m' thou
28 deliver them according to thy m';
Ps 25: 6 O Lord, thy tender m' and thy
40:11 not thou thy tender m' from me,
51: 1 unto the multitude of thy tender m'
69:16 to the multitude of thy tender m'.
77: 9 he in anger shut up his tender m'?
79: 8 let thy tender m' speedily prevent
89: 1 I will sing of the m' of the Lord
103: 4 lovingkindness and tender m';
106: 7 not the multitude of thy m';
45 according to the multitude of his m'.
119:41 thy m' come also unto me, O Lord,
77 Let thy tender m' come unto me,
156 Great are thy tender m', O Lord:
145: 9 his tender m' are over all his works.
Pr 12:10 tender m' of the wicked are cruel.
Isa 54: 7 with great m' will I gather thee.
55: 3 you, even the sure m' of David.
63: 7 on them according to his m', and
15 of thy bowels and of thy m' toward
Jer 16: 5 Lord, even lovingkindness and m'.
42:12 I will shew m' unto you, that ye may
La 3:22 It is of the Lord's m' that we are
32 according...the multitude of his m'.
Da 2:18 they would desire m' of the God
9: 9 To the Lord our God belong m'
18 righteousnesses,...for thy great m'.
Ho 2:19 and in lovingkindness, and in m'.
Zec 1:16 I am returned to Jerusalem with m':
Ac 13:34 will give you the sure m' of David.
Ro 12: 1 by the m' of God, that ye present
2Co 1: 3 the Father of m', and the God of all
Ph'p 2: 1 of the Spirit, if any bowels and m',
Col 3:12 bowels of m', kindness, humbleness

mercies'
Ne 9:31 Nevertheless for thy great m' sake
Ps 6: 4 soul: oh save me for thy m' sake.
31:16 servant: save me for thy m' sake.
44:26 help, and redeem us for thy m' sake.

merciful
Ge 19:16 the Lord being m' unto him: and
Ex 34: 6 The Lord God, m' and gracious,
De 4:31 (For the Lord thy God is a m' God;)
21: 8 Be m', O Lord, unto thy people
32:43 and will be m' unto his land, and
2Sa 22:26 With the m' thou wilt shew thyself
26 wilt shew thyself m', and with the
1Ki 20:31 the house of Israel are m' kings:
2Ch 30: 9 Lord your God is gracious and m',
Ne 9:17 ready to pardon, gracious and m',
31 for thou art a gracious and m' God.
Ps 18:25 With the m' thou wilt shew thyself
25 shew thyself m'; with an upright
26:11 redeem me, and be m' unto me.
37:26 He is ever m', and lendeth; and his
41: 4 Lord, be m' unto me: heal my soul;
10 But thou, O Lord, be m' unto me,
56: 1 Be m' unto me, O God: for man
57: 1 Be m' unto me, O God, be m' unto
59: 5 be not m' to...wicked transgressors.
67: 1 God be m' unto us, and bless us;
86: 3 Be m' unto me, O Lord: for I cry
103: 8 the Lord is m' and gracious, slow
116: 5 and righteous; yea, our God is m'.
117: 2 his m' kindness is great toward
119:58 be m' unto me according to thy
76 m' kindness be for my comfort,
132 be m' unto me, as thou usest to do
Pr 11:17 The m' man doeth good to his own
Isa 57: 1 and m' man are taken away, none
Jer 3:12 for I am m', saith the Lord, and
Joe 2:13 for he is gracious and m', slow to
Jon 4: 2 art a gracious God, and m', slow to
M't 5: 7 Blessed are the m': for they shall
Lu 6:36 m', as your Father also is m'.
18:13 saying, God be m' to me a sinner.
Heb 2:17 be a m' and faithful high priest
8:12 be m' to their unrighteousness,

Mercurius (*mer-cu'-re-us*)
Ac 14:12 Barnabas, Jupiter; and Paul, M',

mercy See also MERCIES; MERCIFUL; MERCYSEAT.
Ge 19:19 and thou hast magnified thy m',
24:27 left destitute my master of his m'
39:21 with Joseph, and shewed him m',
43:14 Almighty give you m' before the
Ex 15:13 Thou in thy m' hast led forth the
20: 6 shewing m' unto thousands of them
25:17 shalt make a m' seat of pure gold:
18 them, in the two ends of the m' seat.
19 of the m' seat shall ye make the
20 covering...m' seat with their wings,
20 toward the m' seat shall the faces of
21 put the m' seat above upon the ark;
22 with thee from above the m' seat,
26:34 put the m' seat upon the ark of the
30: 6 m' seat that is over the testimony,
31: 7 the m' seat that is thereupon, and
33:19 shew m' on whom I will shew m'.
34: 7 Keeping m' for thousands,
35:12 staves thereof, with the m' seat,
37: 6 he made the m' seat of pure gold:
7 on the two ends of the m' seat;
8 out of the m' seat made he the
9 with their wings over the m' seat,
9 to the m' seatward were the faces
39:35 the staves thereof, and the m' seat,
40:20 put the m' seat above upon the ark:
Le 16: 2 within the vail before the m' seat,
2 appear in the cloud upon the m' seat.
13 the incense may cover the m' seat
14 finger upon the m' seat eastward;
14 before the m' seat shall he sprinkle
15 and sprinkle it upon the m' seat,
15 and before the m' seat:
Nu 7:89 unto him from off the m' seat that
14:18 is longsuffering, and of great m',
19 unto the greatness of thy m', and
De 5:10 shewing m' unto thousands of them
7: 2 with them, nor shew m' unto them:
9 covenant and m' with them that
12 and the m' which he sware unto
13:17 of his anger, and shew thee m',
J'g 1:24 city, and we will shew thee m'.
2Sa 7:15 But my m' shall not depart away
15:20 m' and truth be with thee.
22:51 sheweth m' to his anointed, unto
1Ki 3: 6 servant David my father great m',
8:23 covenant and m' with thy servants
1Ch 16:34 good; for his m' endureth for ever.
41 because his m' endureth for ever;
17:13 not take my m' away from him, as
28:11 and of the place of the m' seat,
2Ch 1: 8 hast shewed great m' unto David
5:13 good; for his m' endureth for ever:
6:14 shewest m' unto thy servants, that
7: 3 good; for his m' endureth for ever.
6 because his m' endureth for ever,
20:21 Lord; for his m' endureth for ever.
Ezr 3:11 his m' endureth for ever toward
7:28 hath extended m' unto me before
9: 9 hath extended m' unto us in the
Ne 1: 5 keepeth covenant and m' for them
11 and grant him m' in the sight of
9:32 who keepest covenant and m', let
13:22 to the greatness of thy m'.
Job 37:13 or for his land, or for m'.
Ps 4: 1 have m' upon me, and hear my
5: 7 house in the multitude of thy m':
6: 2 Have m' upon me, O Lord; for I
9:13 Have m' upon me, O Lord; consider
13: 5 But I have trusted in thy m'; my
18:50 and sheweth m' to his anointed, to
21: 7 through the m' of the most High
23: 6 goodness and m' shall follow me
25: 7 according to thy m' remember thou
10 paths of the Lord are m' and truth
16 unto me, and have m' upon me;
27: 7 have m' also upon me, and answer
30:10 O Lord, and have m' upon me:
31: 7 will be glad and rejoice in thy m':
9 Have m' upon me, O Lord, for I am
32:10 Lord, m' shall compass him about.
33:18 upon them that hope in his m';
22 Let thy m', O Lord, be upon us,
36: 5 Thy m', O Lord, is in the heavens:
37:21 but the righteous sheweth m',
51: 1 Have m' upon me, O God, according
52: 8 I trust in the m' of God for ever
57: 3 God shall send forth his m' and his
10 thy m' is great unto the heavens,
59:10 The God of my m' shall prevent
16 I will sing aloud of thy m' in the
17 my defence, and the God of my m'.
61: 7 O prepare m' and truth, which may
62:12 unto thee, O Lord, belongeth m':
66:20 my prayer, nor his m' from me.
69:13 in the multitude of thy m' hear me,
77: 8 Is his m' clean gone for ever? doth
85: 7 Shew us thy m', O Lord, and grant
10 M' and truth are met together;
86: 5 plenteous in m' unto all them that
13 For great is thy m' toward me: and
15 and plenteous in m' and truth.
16 unto me, and have m' upon me;
89: 2 said, M' shall be built up for ever:
14 m' and truth shall go before thy
24 and my m' shall be with him: and
28 My m' will I keep for him for
90:14 O satisfy us early with thy m'; that
94:18 thy m', O Lord, held me up.
98: 3 He hath remembered his m' and
100: 5 is good; his m' is everlasting;
101: 1 I will sing of m' and judgment: unto
102:13 arise, and have m' upon Zion: for
103: 8 to anger, and plenteous in m'.
11 great is his m' toward them that
17 But the m' of the Lord is from
106: 1 good: for his m' endureth for ever.
107: 1 good: for his m' endureth for ever.
108: 4 thy m' is great above the heavens:
109:12 be none to extend m' unto him:
16 he remembered not to shew m',
21 because thy m' is good, deliver thou
26 O save me according to thy m':
115: 1 for thy m', and for thy truth's sake.
118: 1 because his m' endureth for ever.
2, 3, 4 that his m' endureth for ever.
29 good: for his m' endureth for ever.
119:64 The earth, O Lord, is full of thy m':
124 thy servant according unto thy m',
123: 2 God, until that he have m' upon us.
3 Have m' upon us, O Lord, have m'
130: 7 for with the Lord there is m', and
136: 1, 2, 3, 4, 5, 6 his m' endureth for ever.
7, 8 for his m' endureth for ever:
9 for his m' endureth for ever.
10, 11 for his m' endureth for ever:
12 arm: for his m' endureth for ever.
13, 14 for his m' endureth for ever:
15, 16 for his m' endureth for ever.
17, 18, 19, 20, 21 for his m' endureth for
22 for his m' endureth for ever.
23 for his m' endureth for ever:
24, 25, 26 for his m' endureth for ever.
138: 8 thy m', O Lord, endureth for ever:
143:12 And of thy m' cut off mine enemies,
145: 8 slow to anger, and of great m'.
147:11 him, in those that hope in his m'.
Pr 3: 3 Let not m' and truth forsake thee:
14:21 but he that hath m' on the poor,
22 m' and truth shall be to them that
31 honoureth him hath m' on the
16: 6 m' and truth iniquity is purged:
20:28 M' and truth preserve the king:
28 and his throne is upholden by m'.
21:21 righteousness and m' findeth life,
28:13 and forsaketh them shall have m'.
Isa 9:17 shall have m' on their fatherless
14: 1 the Lord will have m' on Jacob,
16: 5 And in m' shall the throne be
27:11 them will not have m' on them,
30:18 that he may have m' upon you:
47: 6 thou didst shew them no m'; upon
49:10 he that hath m' on them shall lead
13 and will have m' upon his afflicted.
54: 8 kindness will I have m' on thee,
10 saith the Lord that hath m' on thee.
55: 7 and he will have m' upon him; and
60:10 in my favour have I had m' on thee.
Jer 6:23 they are cruel, and have no m';
13:14 not pity, nor spare, nor have m',
21: 7 neither have pity, nor have m'.
30:18 and have m' on his dwellingplaces;
31:20 I will surely have m' upon him,
33:11 for his m' endureth for ever: and
26 to return, and have m' on them.
42:12 that he may have m' upon you, and
50:42 are cruel, and will not shew m':
Eze 39:25 and have m' upon the whole house
Da 4:27 by shewing m' to the poor; if it
9: 4 and m' to them that love him,
Ho 1: 6 no more have m' upon the house
7 have m' upon the house of Judah.
2: 4 will not have m' upon her children;
23 earth; and I will have m' upon her
23 upon her that had not obtained m';
4: 1 because there is no truth, nor m',
6: 6 For I desired m', and not sacrifice;

Ho 10:12 in righteousness, reap in *m*·; break
12: 6 keep *m*· and judgment, and wait
14: 3 in thee the fatherless findeth *m*·.
Jon 2: 8 vanities forsake their own *m*·.
Mic 6: 8 but to do justly, and to love *m*·,
7:18 ever, because he delighteth in *m*·.
20 the *m*· to Abraham, which thou
Hab 3: 2 known; in wrath remember *m*·.
Zec 1:12 thou not have *m*· on Jerusalem and
7: 9 and shew *m*· and compassions
10: 6 for I have *m*· upon them: and they
M't 5: 7 merciful: for they shall obtain *m*·.
9:13 I will have *m*·, and not sacrifice:
27 Thou son of David, have *m*· on us.
12: 7 I will have *m*·, and not sacrifice,
15:22 Have *m*· on me, O Lord, thou son
17:15 Lord, have *m*· on my son: for he is
20:30, 31 Have *m*· on us, O Lord, thou son
23:23 the law, judgment, *m*·, and faith:
M'r 10:47, 48 son of David, have *m*· on me.
Lu 1:50 his *m*· is on them that fear him
54 Israel, in remembrance of his *m*·;
58 Lord had shewed great *m*· upon her;
72 To perform the *m*· promised to our
78 Through the tender *m*· of our God;
10:37 he said, He that shewed *m*· on him.
16:24 Father Abraham, have *m*· on me,
17:13 said, Jesus, Master, have *m*· on us.
18:38, 39 thou son of David, have *m*· on me.
Ro 9:15 have *m*· on whom I will have *m*·,
16 but of God that sheweth *m*·.
18 Therefore hath he *m*· on whom he
18 on whom he will have *m*·, and on
23 of his glory on the vessels of *m*·,
11:30 yet have now obtained *m*· through
31 that through your *m*· they also
31 they also may obtain *m*·.
32 that he might have *m*· upon all.
12: 8 that sheweth *m*·, with cheerfulness.
15: 9 might glorify God for his *m*·;
1Co 7:25 that hath obtained *m*· of the Lord
2Co 4: 1 as we have received *m*·, we faint not;
Ga 6:16 rule, peace be on them, and *m*·,
Eph 2: 4 But God, who is rich in *m*·, for his
Ph'p 2:27 but God had *m*· on him; and not on
1Ti 1: 2 Grace, *m*·, and peace, from God
13 but I obtained *m*·, because I did it
16 for this cause I obtained *m*·, that
2Ti 1: 2 Grace, *m*·, and peace, from God
16 The Lord give *m*· unto the house
18 that he may find *m*· of the Lord in
Tit 1: 4 Grace, *m*·, and peace, from God
3: 5 but according to his *m*· he saved us,
Heb 4:16 that we may obtain *m*·, and find
10:28 Moses' law died without *m*· under
Jas 2:13 he shall have judgment without *m*·,
13 that hath shewed no *m*·;
13 and *m*· rejoiceth against judgment.
3:17 full of *m*· and good fruits, without
5:11 is very pitiful, and of tender *m*·.
1Pe 1: 3 according to his abundant *m*· hath
2:10 of God: which had not obtained *m*·,
10 but now have obtained *m*·.
2Jo 3 Grace be with you, *m*·, and peace,
Jude 2 *M*· unto you, and peace, and love,
21 for the *m*· of our Lord Jesus Christ

mercyseat See also MERCY and SEAT.
Heb 9: 5 of glory shadowing the *m*·;

Mered (*me'-red*)
1Ch 4:17 sons of Ezra were, Jether, and *M*·,
18 daughter of Pharaoh, which *M*· took.

Meremoth (*mer'-e-moth*) See also MERAIOTH.
Ezr 8:33 by the hand of *M*· the son of Uriah
10:36 Vaniah, *M*·, Eliashib,
Ne 3: 4 them repaired *M*· the son of Urijah,
21 him repaired *M*· the son of Urijah
10: 5 Harim, *M*·, Obadiah,
12: 3 Shechaniah, Rehum, *M*·,

Meres (*me'-res*)
Es 1:14 *M*·, Marsena, and Memucan,

Meribah (*mer'-i-bah*) See also MASSAH; MERIBAH-KADESH.
Ex 17: 7 name of the place Massah, and *M*·,
Nu 20:13 This is the water of *M*·; because
24 against my word at the water of *M*·.
27:14 that is the water of *M*· in Kadesh
De 33: 8 didst strive at the waters of *M*·;
Ps 81: 7 I proved thee at the waters of *M*·.

Meribah-Kadesh (*mer''-i-bah-ka'-desh*)
De 32:51 of Israel at the waters of *M*·,

Merib-baal (*me-rib'-ba-al*) See also MEPHIBOSHETH.
1Ch 8:34 And the son of Jonathan was *M*·;
34 and *M*· begat Micah.
9:40 And the son of Jonathan was *M*·:
40 and *M*· begat Micah.

Merodach (*mer'-o-dak*) See also BERODACH; EVIL-MERODACH; MERODACH-BALADAN.
Jer 50: 2 *M*· is broken in pieces;

Merodach-baladan (*mer''-o-dak-bal'-a-dan*) See also BERODACH-BALADAN.
Isa 39: 1 that time *M*·, the son of Baladan,

Merom (*me'-rom*)
Jos 11: 5 together at the waters of *M*·,
7 against them by the waters of *M*·

Meron See SHIMRON-MERON; MERONOTHITE.

Meronothite (*me-ron'-o-thite*)
1Ch 27:30 the asses was Jehdeiah the *M*·:
Ne 3: 7 the Gibeonite, and Jadon the *M*·,

Meroz (*me'-roz*)
J'g 5:23 Curse ye *M*·, said the angel of the

merrily
Es 5:14 then go thou in *m*· with the king

merry See also MERRYHEARTED.
Ge 43:34 they drank, and were *m*· with him.
J'g 9:27 trode the grapes, and made *m*·,
16:25 pass, when their hearts were *m*·,
19: 6 all night, and let thine heart be *m*·.
9 here, that thine heart may be *m*·;
22 they were making their hearts *m*·,
Ru 3: 7 and drunk, and his heart was *m*·,
1Sa 25:36 Nabal's heart was *m*· within him,
2Sa 13:28 Amnon's heart is *m*· with wine,
1Ki 4:20 and drinking, and making *m*·.
21: 7 bread, and let thine heart be *m*·:
2Ch 7:10 their tents, glad and *m*· in heart
Es 1:10 when the heart of the king was *m*·
Pr 15:13 A *m*· heart maketh a cheerful
15 but he that is of a *m*· heart hath a
17:22 A *m*· heart doeth good like a
Ec 8:15 to eat, and to drink, and to be *m*·:
9: 7 drink thy wine with a *m*· heart;
10:19 for laughter, and wine maketh *m*·:
Jer 30:19 the voice of them that make *m*·:
31: 4 in the dances of them that make *m*·.
Lu 12:19 thine ease, eat, drink, and be *m*·.
15:23 and kill it; and let us eat, and be *m*·:
24 is found. And they began to be *m*·.
29 I might make *m*· with my friends:
32 was meet that we should make *m*·,
Jas 5:13 Is any *m*·? let him sing psalms.
Re 11:10 rejoice over them, and make *m*·,

merryhearted
Isa 24: 7 languisheth, all the *m*· do sigh.

Mesech (*me'-sek*) See also MESHECH.
Ps 120: 5 Woe is me, that I sojourn in *M*·,

Mesha (*me'-shah*)
Ge 10:30 And their dwelling was from *M*·,
2Ki 3: 4 *M*·...of Moab was a sheepmaster,
1Ch 2:42 *M*· his firstborn, which was the
8: 9 and Zibia, and *M*·, and Malcham,

Meshach (*me'-shak*)
Da 1: 7 Shadrach; and to Mishael, of *M*·;
2:49 set Shadrach, *M*·, and Abed-nego,
3:12 Shadrach, *M*·, and Abed-nego;
13 bring Shadrach, *M*·, and Abed-nego.
14 O Shadrach, *M*·, and Abed-nego,
16 Shadrach, *M*·, and Abed-nego,
19 was changed against Shadrach, *M*·,
20 bind Shadrach, *M*·, and Abed-nego,
22 men that took up Shadrach, *M*·,
23 Shadrach, *M*·, and Abed-nego, fell
26 spake, and said, Shadrach, *M*·, and
26 Shadrach, *M*·, and Abed-nego,
28 be the God of Shadrach, *M*·, and
29 against the God of Shadrach, *M*·,
30 the king promoted Shadrach, *M*·,

Meshech (*me'-shek*) See also MESECH.
Ge 10: 2 and Tubal, and *M*·, and Tiras.
1Ch 1: 5 and Tubal, and *M*·, and Tiras.
17 Uz, and Hul, and Gether, and *M*·.
Eze 27:13 and *M*·, they were thy merchants:
32:26 There is *M*·, Tubal, and all her
38: 2 the chief prince of *M*· and Tubal,
3 the chief prince of *M*· and Tubal:
39: 1 the chief prince of *M*· and Tubal:

Meshelemiah (*me-shel-e-mi'-ah*) See also MESHULLAM; SHELEMIAH; SHALLUM.
1Ch 9:21 son of *M*· was porter of the
26: 1 Korhites was *M*· the son of Kore,
2 the sons of *M*· were, Zechariah the
9 *M*· had sons and brethren, strong

Meshezabeel (*me-shez'-a-be-el*)
Ne 3: 4 son of Berechiah, the son of *M*·.
10:21 *M*·, Zadok, Juddua,
11:24 And Pethahiah the son of *M*·, of

Meshillemith (*me-shil'-le-mith*) See also MESHILLEMOTH.
1Ch 9:12 son of Meshullam, the son of *M*·,

Meshillemoth (*me-shil'-le-moth*) See also MESHILLEMITH.
2Ch 28:12 Berechiah the son of *M*·, and
Ne 11:13 the son of Ahasai, the son of *M*·,

Meshobab (*me-sho'-bab*)
1Ch 4:34 And *M*·, and Jamlech, and Joshah

Meshullam (*me-shul'-lam*) See also MESHELLEMIAH.
2Ki 22: 3 son of *M*·, the scribe, to the house
1Ch 3:19 *M*·, and Hananiah, and Shelomith
5:13 and *M*·, and Sheba, and Jorai, and
8:17 And Zebadiah, and *M*·, and Hezeki,
9: 7 Sallu the son of *M*·, the son of
8 *M*· the son of Shephathiah, the son
11 the son of Hilkiah, the son of *M*·,
12 son of *M*·, the son of Meshillemith,
2Ch 34:12 *M*·, of the sons of the Kohathites,
Ezr 8:16 and for Zechariah, and for *M*·, chief
10:15 and *M*· and Shabbethai the Levite
29 of the sons of Bani; *M*·, Malluch,
Ne 3: 4 And next unto them repaired *M*·
6 and *M*· the son of Besodeiah; they
30 repaired *M*· the son of Berechiah
6:18 had taken the daughter of *M*· the
8: 4 Hashbadana, Zechariah, and *M*·.
10: 7 *M*·, Abijah, Mijamin,
20 Magpiash, *M*·, Hezir,
11: 7 Sallu the son of *M*·, the son of Joed,
11 the son of Hilkiah, the son of *M*·,
12:13 Of Ezra, *M*·; of Amariah,
16 Iddo, Zechariah; of Ginnethon, *M*·;
25 and Bakbukiah, Obadiah, *M*·,
33 And Azariah, Ezra, and *M*·,

Meshullemeth (*me-shul'-le-meth*)
2Ki 21:19 And his mother's name was *M*·,

Mesobaite (*me-so'-ba-ite*)
1Ch 11:47 Eliel, and Obed, and Jasiel the *M*·.

Mesopotamia (*mes-o-po-ta'-me-ah*) See also ARAM and NAHARAIM.
Ge 24:10 and he arose, and went to *M*·, unto
De 23: 4 the son of Beor of Pethor of *M*·,
J'g 3: 8 of Chushan-rishathaim king of *M*·:
10 Chushan-rishathaim king of *M*·
1Ch 19: 6 chariots and horsemen out of *M*·,
Ac 2: 9 the dwellers in *M*·, and in Judæa,
7: 2 father Abraham, when he was in *M*·,

mess See also MESSES.
Ge 43:34 Benjamin's *m*· was five times so
2Sa 11: 8 there followed him a *m*· of meat

message
J'g 3:20 I have a *m*· from God unto thee.
1Ki 20:12 when Ben-hadad heard this *m*·, as
Pr 26: 6 He that sendeth a *m*· by the hand
Hag 1:13 in the Lord's *m*· unto the people,
Lu 19:14 him, and sent a *m*· after him,
1Jo 1: 5 is the *m*· which we have heard of
3:11 is the *m*· that ye heard from the

messenger See also MESSENGERS.
Ge 50:16 And they sent a *m*· unto Joseph,
1Sa 4:17 the *m*· answered and said, Israel
23:27 But there came a *m*· unto Saul,
2Sa 11:19 And charged the *m*·, saying, When
22 So the *m*· went, and came and
23 the *m*· said unto David, Surely the
25 David said unto the *m*·, Thus shalt
15:13 there came a *m*· to David, saying,
1Ki 19: 2 Jezebel sent a *m*· unto Elijah,
22:13 And the *m*· that was gone to call
2Ki 5:10 Elisha sent a *m*· unto him, saying,
6:32 ere the *m*· came to him, he said to
32 when the *m*· cometh, shut the door,
33 the *m*· came down unto him: and
9:18 The *m*· came to them, but he
10: 8 And there came a *m*·, and told him,
2Ch 18:12 the *m*· that went to call Micaiah
Job 1:14 And there came a *m*· unto Job, and
33:23 If there be a *m*· with him, an
Pr 13:17 A wicked *m*· falleth into mischief:
17:11 a cruel *m*· shall be sent against
25:13 is a faithful *m*· to them that send
Isa 42:19 or deaf, as my *m*· that I sent?
Jer 51:31 and one *m*· to meet another, to
Eze 23:40 unto whom a *m*· was sent; and,
Hag 1:13 spake Haggai the Lord's *m*· in the
Mal 2: 7 he is the *m*· of the Lord of hosts.
3: 1 I will send my *m*·, and he shall
1 even the *m*· of the covenant, whom
M't 11:10 I send my *m*· before thy face, which
M'r 1: 2 I send my *m*· before thy face, which
Lu 7:27 I send my *m*· before thy face, which
2Co 12: 7 the *m*· of Satan to buffet me, lest I
Ph'p 2:25 your *m*·, and he that ministered

messengers
Ge 32: 3 Jacob sent *m*· before him to Esau
6 the *m*· returned to Jacob, saying,
Nu 20:14 And Moses sent *m*· from Kadesh
21:21 Israel sent *m*· unto Sihon king of
22: 5 He sent *m*· therefore unto Balaam
24:12 Spake I not also to thy *m*· which
De 2:26 And I sent *m*· out of the wilderness
Jos 6:17 because he hid the *m*· that we sent.
25 she hid the *m*·, which Joshua sent
7:22 So Joshua sent *m*·, and they ran
J'g 6:35 sent *m*· throughout all Manasseh;
35 he sent *m*· unto Asher, and unto
7:24 And Gideon sent *m*· throughout all
9:31 he sent *m*· unto Abimelech privily,
11:12 Jephthah sent *m*· unto the king
13 answered unto the *m*· of Jephthah,
14 Jephthah sent *m*· again unto the
17 Israel sent *m*· unto the king of
19 Israel sent *m*· unto Sihon king of
1Sa 6:21 And they sent *m*· to the inhabitants
11: 3 may send *m*· unto all the coasts of
4 Then came the *m*· to Gibeah of
7 coasts of Israel by the hands of *m*·,
9 they said unto the *m*· that came
9 *m*· came and shewed it to the men
16:19 Wherefore Saul sent *m*· unto Jesse,
19:11 also sent *m*· unto David's house,
14 when Saul sent *m*· to take David,
15 Saul sent the *m*· again to see David,
16 when the *m*· were come in, behold,
20 And Saul sent *m*· to take David:
20 Spirit of God was upon the *m*· of
21 it was told Saul, he sent other *m*·,
21 Saul sent *m*· again the third time,
25:14 David sent *m*· out of the wilderness
42 and she went after the *m*· of David,
2Sa 2: 5 And David sent *m*· unto the men
3:12 And Abner sent *m*· to David on his
14 And David sent *m*· to Ish-bosheth
26 he sent *m*· after Abner, which
5:11 king of Tyre sent *m*· to David,
11: 4 And David sent *m*·, and took her;
12:27 Joab sent *m*· to David, and said,
1Ki 20: 2 he sent *m*· to Ahab king of Israel
5 And the *m*· came again, and said,
9 he said unto the *m*· of Ben-hadad,
9 the *m*· departed, and brought him
2Ki 1: 2 he sent *m*· and said unto them, Go,
3 meet the *m*· of the king of Samaria,
5 when the *m*· turned back unto him,
16 as thou hast sent *m*· to enquire of
7:15 the *m*· returned, and told the king.
14: 8 Then Amaziah sent *m*· to Jehoash,
16: 7 So Ahaz sent *m*· to Tiglath-pileser

2Ki 17: 4 he had sent *m'* to So king of Egypt,
19: 9 he sent *m'* again unto Hezekiah,
14 the letter of the hand of the *m'*, and
23 By thy *m'* thou hast reproached the
1Ch 14: 1 king of Tyre sent *m'* to David,
19: 2 And David sent *m'* to comfort him
16 worse before Israel, they sent *m'*,
2Ch 36: 15 their father sent to them by his *m'*,
16 But they mocked the *m'* of God, and
Ne 6: 3 I sent *m'* unto them, saying, I am
Pr 16: 14 wrath of a king is as *m'* of death:
Isa 14: 32 then answer the *m'* of the nation?
18: 2 saying, Go, ye swift *m'*, to a nation
37: 9 he heard it, he sent *m'* to Hezekiah,
14 the letter from the hand of the *m'*,
44: 26 performeth the counsel of his *m'*;
57: 9 didst send thy *m'* far off, and didst
Jer 27: 3 by the hand of the *m'* which come
Eze 23: 16 and sent *m'* unto them into Chaldea.
30: 9 that day shall *m'* go forth from me
Na 2: 13 the voice of thy *m'* shall no more be
Lu 7: 24 when the *m'* of John were departed,
9: 52 And sent *m'* before his face: and
2Co 8: 23 they are the *m'* of the churches,
Jas 2: 25 she had received the *m'*, and had

messes
Ge 43: 34 sent *m'* unto them from before

Messiah (*mes-si'-ah*) See also MESSIAS.
Da 9: 25 and build Jerusalem unto the *M'*
26 and two weeks shall *M'* be cut off,

Messias (*mes-si'-as*) See also MESSIAH.
Joh 1: 41 unto him, We have found the *M'*,
4: 25 I know that *M'* cometh, which is

met
Ge 32: 1 and the angels of God *m'* him.
33: 8 thou by all this drove which I *m'*?
Ex 3: 18 of the Hebrews hath *m'* with us:
4: 24 that the Lord *m'* him, and sought
27 and *m'* him in the mount of God,
5: 3 of the Hebrews hath *m'* with us:
20 And they *m'* Moses and Aaron,
Nu 23: 4 And God *m'* Balaam: and he said
16 Lord *m'* Balaam, and put a word
De 23: 4 they *m'* you not with bread and
25: 18 How he *m'* thee by the way, and
Jos 11: 5 all these kings were *m'* together,
17: 10 *m'* together in Asher on the north,
1Sa 10: 10 a company of prophets *m'* him;
25: 20 against her; and she *m'* them.
2Sa 2: 13 *m'* together by the pool of Gibeon:
16: 1 servant of Mephibosheth *m'* him,
18: 9 Absalom *m'* the servants of David.
1Ki 13: 24 a lion *m'* him by the way, and slew
18: 7 in the way, behold, Elijah *m'* him:
2Ki 9: 21 *m'* him in the portion of Naboth
10: 13 *m'* with the brethren of Ahaziah
Ne 13: 2 *m'* not the children of Israel with
Ps 85: 10 Mercy and truth are *m'* together
Pr 7: 10 *m'* him a woman with the attire
Jer 41: 6 as he *m'* them, he said unto them,
Am 5: 19 flee from a lion, and a bear *m'* him;
M't 8: 28 *m'* him two possessed with devils,
28: 9 Jesus *m'* them, saying, All hail.
M'r 5: 2 there *m'* him out of the tombs a man
11: 4 in a place where two ways *m'*;
Lu 8: 27 *m'* him out of the city a certain
9: 37 from the hill, much people *m'* him.
17: 12 *m'* him ten men that were lepers,
Joh 4: 51 his servants *m'* him, and told him,
11: 20 was coming, went and *m'* him:
30 in that place where Martha *m'* him.
12: 18 this cause the people also *m'* him,
Ac 10: 25 was coming in, Cornelius *m'* him,
16: 16 with a spirit of divination *m'* us,
17: 17 daily with them that *m'* with him.
20: 14 when he *m'* with us at Assos, we
27: 41 falling into a place where two seas *m'*,
Heb 7: 1 who *m'* Abraham returning from
10 father, when Melchisedec *m'* him.

mete See also METED; METEYARD.
Ex 16: 18 when they did *m'* it with an omer,
Ps 60: 6 and *m'* out the valley of Succoth.
108: 7 and *m'* out the valley of Succoth.
M't 7: 2 with what measure ye *m'*, it shall
M'r 4: 24 with what measure ye *m'*, it shall
Lu 6: 38 with the same measure that ye *m'*

meted
Isa 18: 2 a nation *m'* out and trodden down,
7 a nation *m'* out and trodden under
40: 12 and *m'* out heaven with the span,

meteyard
Le 19: 35 in *m'*, in weight, or in measure.

Metheg-ammah (*me''-theg-am'-mah*)
2Sa 8: 1 David took *M'* out of the hand of

Methoar See REMMON-METHOAR.

Methusael (*me-thu'-sa-el*)
Ge 4: 18 Mehujael begat *M'*: and *M'* begat

Methuselah (*me-thu'-se-lah*) See also MATHUSALA.
Ge 5: 21 and five years, and begat *M'*:
22 walked with God after he begat *M'*
25 *M'* lived an hundred eighty and
26 *M'* lived after he begat Lamech
27 the days of *M'* were nine hundred
1Ch 1: 3 Henoch, *M'*, Lamech,

Meunim (*me-u'-nim*) See also MEHUNIM.
Ne 7: 52 the children of *M'*, the children

Mezahab (*mez'-a-hab*)
Ge 36: 39 of Matred, the daughter of *M'*.
1Ch 1: 50 of Matred, the daughter of *M'*.

Miamin (*mi'-a-min*) See also MIJAMIN; MINIAMIN.
Ezr 10: 25 Malchiah, and *M'*, and Eleazar,
Ne 12: 5 *M'*, Maadiah, Bilgah,

Mibhar (*mib'-har*)
1Ch 11: 38 Nathan, *M'* the son of Haggeri,

Mibsam (*mib'-sam*)
Ge 25: 13 and Kedar, and Adbeel, and *M'*,
1Ch 1: 29 then Kedar, and Adbeel, and *M'*,
4: 25 Shallum his son, *M'* his son,

Mibzar (*mib'-zar*)
Ge 36: 42 Kenaz, duke Teman, duke *M'*,
1Ch 1: 53 Kenaz, duke Teman, duke *M'*,

Micah[A] (*mi'-cah*) See also MICAIAH; MICAH'S; MICHAH.
J'g 17: 1 Ephraim, whose name was *M'*.
4 and they were in the house of *M'*.
5 the man *M'* had an house of gods,
8 mount Ephraim to the house of *M'*,
9 *M'* said unto him, Whence comest
10 *M'* said unto him, Dwell with me,
12 *M'* consecrated the Levite; and
12 priest, and was in the house of *M'*.
13 said *M'*, Now know I that the Lord
18: 2 mount Ephraim, to the house of *M'*,
3 they were by the house of *M'*, they
4 Thus and thus dealeth *M'* with me,
13 and come unto the house of *M'*.
15 even unto the house of *M'*, and
22 a good way from the house of *M'*,
23 said unto *M'*, What aileth thee,
26 when *M'* saw that they were too
27 the things which *M'* had made,
1Ch 5: 5 *M'* his son, Reaia his son, Baal his
8: 34 and Merib-baal begat *M'*.
35 the sons of *M'* were, Pithon, and
9: 15 Mattaniah the son of *M'*, the son
40 and Merib-baal begat *M'*.
41 the sons of *M'* were, Pithon, and
23: 20 Of the sons of Uzziel; *M'* the first,
2Ch 34: 20 Abdon the son of *M'*, and Shaphan
Jer 26: 18 *M'* the Morashite prophesied in
Mic 1: 1 word of the Lord that came to *M'*

Micah's (*mi'-cahs*)
J'g 18: 18 And these went into *M'* house, and
22 in the houses near to *M'* house
31 they set them up *M'* graven image,

Micaiah (*mi-ka-i'-ah*) See also MICHA; MICHAIAH.
1Ki 22: 8 yet one man, *M'* the son of Imlah,
9 said, Hasten hither *M'* the son of
13 messenger that was gone to call *M'*
14 *M'* said, As the Lord liveth, what
15 unto him *M'*, shall we go against
24 and smote *M'* on the cheek, and
25 *M'* said, Behold, thou shalt see in
26 Take *M'*, and carry him back unto
28 And *M'* said, If thou return at all in
2Ch 18: 7 the same is *M'* the son of Imla.
8 Fetch quickly *M'* the son of Imla.
12 the messenger that went to call *M'*
13 *M'* said, As the Lord liveth, even
14 king said unto him, *M'*, shall we
23 and smote *M'* upon the cheek, and
24 *M'* said, Behold, thou shalt see on
25 Take ye *M'*, and carry him back to
27 *M'* said, If thou certainly return in

mice
1Sa 6: 4 and five golden *m'*, according to the
5 images of your *m'* that mar the
11 the coffer with the *m'* of gold and
18 the golden *m'*, according to the

Micha (*mi'-cah*) See also MICAH; MICAIAH.
2Sa 9: 12 young son, whose name was *M'*.
Ne 10: 11 *M'*, Rehob, Hashabiah,
11: 17 And Mattaniah the son of *M'*, the
22 son of Mattaniah, the son of *M'*.

Michael (*mi'-ka-el*)
Nu 13: 13 of Asher, Sethur the son of *M'*.
1Ch 5: 13 house of their fathers were, *M'*,
14 the son of *M'*, the son of Jeshishai,
6: 40 son of *M'*, the son of Baaseiah, the
7: 3 *M'*, and Obadiah, and Joel, Ishiah,
8: 16 *M'*, and Ispah, and Joha, the sons
12: 20 *M'*, and Jozabad, and Elihu, and
27: 18 of Issachar, Omri the son of *M'*:
2Ch 21: 2 Zechariah, and Azariah, and *M'*,
Ezr 8: 8 Zebadiah the son of *M'*, and with
Da 10: 13 *M'*, one of the chief princes, came
21 in these things, but *M'* your prince.
12: 1 at that time shall *M'* stand up,
Jude 9 Yet *M'* the archangel, when
Re 12: 7 *M'* and his angels fought against

Michah (*mi'-cah*) See also MICAH; MICHAIAH.
1Ch 24: 24 Of the sons of Uzziel; *M'*: of the
24 of the sons of *M'*; Shamir.
25 The brother of *M'* was Isshiah: of

Michaiah (*mi-ka-i'-ah*) See also MICAH; MICAIAH.
2Ki 22: 12 and Achbor the son of *M'*, and
2Ch 13: 2 His mother's name also was *M'*
17: 7 and to *M'*, to teach in the cities of
Ne 12: 35 the son of *M'*, the son of Zaccur,
41 Eliakim, Maaseiah, Miniamin, *M'*,
Jer 36: 11 When *M'* the son of Gemariah,
13 *M'* declared unto them all the

Michal (*mi'-kal*) See also EGLAH.
1Sa 14: 49 and the name of the younger *M'*:
18: 20 *M'* Saul's daughter loved David:
27 Saul gave him *M'* his daughter to
28 that *M'* Saul's daughter loved him.
19: 11 *M'* David's wife told him, saying,
12 So *M'* let David down through a
13 *M'* took an image, and laid it in
17 Saul said unto *M'*, Why hast thou
17 *M'* answered Saul, He said unto
25: 44 Saul had given *M'* his daughter,
2Sa 3: 13 first bring *M'* Saul's daughter,
14 Deliver me my wife *M'*, which I
6: 16 *M'* Saul's daughter looked through
20 *M'* the daughter of Saul came out
21 David said unto *M'*, It was before
23 *M'* the daughter of Saul had no
21: 8 sons of *M'* the daughter of Saul,
1Ch 15: 29 *M'* the daughter of Saul looking

Michmas (*mik'-mas*) See also MICHMASH.
Ezr 2: 27 The men of *M'*, an hundred
Ne 7: 31 The men of *M'*, an hundred

Michmash (*mik'-mash*) See also MICHMAS.
1Sa 13: 2 thousand were with Saul in *M'*
5 they came up, and pitched in *M'*,
11 themselves together at *M'*;
16 the Philistines encamped in *M'*.
23 went out to the passage of *M'*.
14: 5 situate northward over against *M'*,
31 the Philistines that day from *M'*
Ne 11: 31 Benjamin from Geba dwelt at *M'*,
Isa 10: 28 at *M'* he had laid up his carriages:

Michmethah (*mik'-me-thah*)
Jos 16: 6 went out toward the sea to *M'*
17: 7 Manasseh was from Asher to *M'*,

Michri (*mik'-ri*)
1Ch 9: 8 the son of Uzzi, the son of *M'*,

Michtam (*mik'-tam*)
Ps 16: *title* *M'* of David.
56: *title* *M'* of David, when the Philistines
57: *title* *M'* of David, when he fled from
58: *title* Al-taschith, *M'* of David.
59: *title* *M'* of David; when Saul sent,
60: *title* *M'* of David, to teach; when he

midday
1Ki 18: 29 came to pass, when *m'* was past,
Ne 8: 3 from the morning until *m'*,
Ac 26: 13 At *m'*, O king, I saw in the

Middin (*mid'-din*)
Jos 15: 61 the wilderness, Beth-arabah, *M'*,

middle See also MIDDLEMOST; MIDST.
Ex 26: 28 *m'* bar in the midst of the boards
36: 33 And he made the *m'* bar to shoot
Jos 12: 2 from the *m'* of the river, and from
J'g 7: 19 in the beginning of the *m'* watch;
9: 37 people down by the *m'* of the land,
16: 29 took hold of the two *m'* pillars
1Sa 25: 29 out, as out of the *m'* of a sling.
2Sa 10: 4 cut off their garments in the *m'*,
1Ki 6: 6 and the *m'* was six cubits broad,
8 door for the *m'* chamber was in the
8 winding stairs into the *m'* chamber,
8 and out of the *m'* into the third.
8: 64 the king hallow the *m'* of the court
2Ki 20: 4 was gone out into the *m'* court,
2Ch 7: 7 hallowed the *m'* of the court that
Jer 39: 3 came in, and sat in the *m'* gate,
Eze 1: 16 were a wheel in the *m'* of a wheel.
Eph 2: 14 hath broken down the *m'* wall of

middlemost
Eze 42: 5 and the *m'* of the building.
6 lowest and the *m'* from the ground.

Midian (*mid'-e-an*) See also MADIAN; MIDIANITE.
Ge 25: 2 and Medan, and *M'*, and Ishbak,
4 sons of *M'*; Ephah, and Epher, and
36: 35 who smote *M'* in the field of Moab,
Ex 2: 15 and dwelt in the land of *M'*: and
16 priest of *M'* had seven daughters:
3: 1 his father in law, the priest of *M'*:
4: 19 the Lord said unto Moses in *M'*, Go,
18: 1 When Jethro, the priest of *M'*,
Nu 22: 4 Moab said unto the elders of *M'*,
7 and the elders of *M'* departed with
25: 15 people, and of a chief house in *M'*.
18 the daughter of a prince of *M'*,
31: 3 and avenge the Lord of *M'*.
8 they slew the kings of *M'*, beside
8 Hur, and Reba, five kings of *M'*:
9 took all the women of *M'* captives,
Jos 13: 21 Moses smote with the princes of *M'*,
J'g 6: 1 delivered them into the hand of *M'*
2 the hand of *M'* prevailed against
7: 8 host of *M'* was beneath him in the
13 bread tumbled into the host of *M'*,
14 his hand hath God delivered *M'*,
15 into your hand the host of *M'*.
25 and pursued *M'*, and brought the
8: 3 into your hands the princes of *M'*,
5 Zebah and Zalmunna, kings of *M'*.
12 them, and took the two kings of *M'*,
22 delivered us from the hand of *M'*.
26 that was on the kings of *M'*, and
28 *M'* subdued before the children of
9: 17 you out of the hand of *M'*:
1Ki 11: 18 they arose out of *M'*, and came to
1Ch 1: 32 and Medan, and *M'*, and Ishbak,
33 the sons of *M'*; Ephah, and Epher,
46 smote *M'* in the field of Moab,
Isa 9: 4 his oppressor, as in the days of *M'*.
10: 26 to the slaughter of *M'* at the rock
60: 6 the dromedaries of *M'* and Ephah;
Hab 3: 7 the curtains of the land of *M'* did

Midianite (*mid'-e-an-ite*) See also MIDIANITES; MIDIANITISH.
Nu 10: 29 Hobab, the son of Raguel the *M'*,

Midianites (*mid'-e-an-ites*) See also KENITES.
Ge 37:28 there passed by *M'* merchantmen;
36 the *M'* sold him into Egypt unto
Nu 25:17 Vex the *M'*, and smite them:
31: 2 the children of Israel of the *M'*:
3 and let them go against the *M'*,
7 And they warred against the *M'*,
J'g 6: 2 because of the *M'* the children of
3 had sown, that the *M'* came up,
6 impoverished because of the *M'*;
7 unto the Lord because of the *M'*,
11 winepress, to hide it from the *M'*.
13 us into the hands of the *M'*.
14 Israel from the hand of the *M'*:
16 thou shalt smite the *M'* as one man.
33 Then all the *M'* and the Amalekites
7: 1 host of the *M'* were on the north
2 me to give the *M'* into their hands,
7 deliver the *M'* into thine hand:
12 And the *M'* and the Amalekites and
23 Manasseh,...pursued after the *M'*.
24 saying, Come down against the *M'*,
25 they took two princes of the *M'*,
8: 1 thou wentest to fight with the *M'*?
Ps 83: 9 Do unto them as unto the *M'*; as

Midianitish (*mid''-e-an-i'-tish*)
Nu 25: 6 a *M'* woman in the sight of Moses,
14 that was slain with the *M'* woman,
15 the name of the *M'* woman that

midnight
Ex 11: 4 About *m'* will I go out into
12:29 at *m'* the Lord smote all the
J'g 16: 3 lay till *m'*, and arose at *m'*,
Ru 3: 8 it came to pass at *m'*, that the
1Ki 3:20 she arose at *m'*, and took my
Job 34:20 people shall be troubled at *m'*,
Ps 119:62 At *m'* I will rise to give thanks
M't 25: 6 at *m'* there was a cry made,
M'r 13:35 or at *m'*, or at the cockcrowing, or
Lu 11: 5 and shall go unto him at *m'*, and
Ac 16:25 at *m'* Paul and Silas prayed, and
20: 7 and continued his speech until *m'*.
27:27 about *m'* the shipmen deemed

midst See also MIDDLE.
Ge 1: 6 firmament in the *m'* of the waters,
2: 9 tree of life...in the *m'* of the garden,
3: 3 which is in the *m'* of the garden,
15:10 and divided them in the *m'*, and laid
19:29 Lot out of the *m'* of the overthrow,
48:16 multitude in the *m'* of the earth.
Ex 3: 2 of fire out of the *m'* of a bush:
4 unto him out of the *m'* of the bush,
20 which I will do in the *m'* thereof:
8:22 am the Lord in the *m'* of the earth.
11: 4 will I go out into the *m'* of Egypt:
14:16 ground through the *m'* of the sea.
22 of Israel went into the *m'* of the sea
23 in after them to the *m'* of the sea,
27 the Egyptians in the *m'* of the sea.
29 upon dry land in the *m'* of the sea;
15:19 on dry land in the *m'* of the sea.
23:25 sickness away from the *m'* of thee.
24:16 Moses out of the *m'* of the cloud.
18 Moses went into the *m'* of the cloud,
26:28 middle bar in the *m'* of the boards
27: 5 may be even to the *m'* of the altar.
28:32 in the top of it, in the *m'* thereof:
33: 3 I will not go up in the *m'* of thee;
5 I will come up into the *m'* of thee
34:12 it be for a snare in the *m'* of thee:
38: 4 thereof beneath unto the *m'* of it.
39:23 was an hole in the *m'* of the robe,
Le 16:16 them in the *m'* of their uncleanness.
Nu 2:17 the Levites in the *m'* of the camp:
5: 3 camps, in the *m'* whereof I dwell.
16:47 ran into the *m'* of the congregation;
19: 6 into the *m'* of the burning of the
33: 8 passed through the *m'* of the sea
35: 5 and the city shall be in the *m'*: this
De 4:11 with fire unto the *m'* of heaven,
12 unto you out of the *m'* of the fire:
15 in Horeb out of the *m'* of the fire:
33 speaking out of the *m'* of the fire,
34 from the *m'* of another nation, by
36 his words out of the *m'* of the fire.
5: 4, 22 mount out of the *m'* of the fire,
23 voice out of the *m'* of the darkness,
24 his voice out of the *m'* of the fire:
26 speaking out of the *m'* of the fire,
9:10 out of the *m'* of the fire in the day
10: 4 out of the *m'* of the fire in the day
11: 3 did in the *m'* of Egypt unto Pharaoh
6 possession, in the *m'* of all Israel:
13: 5 the evil away from the *m'* of thee.
16 spoil of it into the *m'* of the street
17:20 his children, in the *m'* of Israel.
18:15 thee a Prophet from the *m'* of thee,
19: 2 for thee in the *m'* of thy land,
23:14 walketh in the *m'* of thy camp,
32:51 in the *m'* of the children of Israel.
Jos 3:17 on dry ground in the *m'* of Jordan,
4: 3 you hence out of the *m'* of Jordan,
5 your God into the *m'* of Jordan,
8 stones out of the *m'* of Jordan, as
9 twelve stones in the *m'* of Jordan,
10 the ark stood in the *m'* of Jordan,
18 come up out of the *m'* of Jordan,
7:13 accursed thing in the *m'* of thee,
21 in the earth in the *m'* of my tent,
23 took them out of the *m'* of the tent,
8:13 that night into the *m'* of the valley.
22 so they were in the *m'* of Israel,
10:13 sun stood still in the *m'* of heaven,
13:9, 16 city that is in the *m'* of the river,
J'g 15: 4 put a firebrand in the *m'* between
J'g 18:20 and went in the *m'* of the people.
20:42 they destroyed in the *m'* of them.
1Sa 11:11 they came into the *m'* of the host
16:13 him in the *m'* of his brethren: and
18:10 prophesied in the *m'* of the house:
2Sa 1:25 mighty fallen in the *m'* of the battle!
4: 6 thither into the *m'* of the house,
6:17 in the *m'* of the tabernacle that
18:14 was yet alive in the *m'* of the oak.
20:12 in blood in the *m'* of the highway.
23:12 he stood in the *m'* of the ground,
20 slew a lion in the *m'* of a pit in time
24: 5 city that lieth in the *m'* of the river
1Ki 3: 8 thy servant is in the *m'* of thy people
6:27 one another in the *m'* of the house.
8:51 from the *m'* of the furnace of iron:
20:39 went out into the *m'* of the battle;
22:35 wound into the *m'* of the chariot.
2Ki 6:20 they were in the *m'* of Samaria.
1Ch 11:14 themselves in the *m'* of that parcel,
16: 1 and set it in the *m'* of the tent that
19: 4 their garments in the *m'* hard by
2Ch 6:13 had set it in the *m'* of the court:
20:14 Lord in the *m'* of the congregation;
32: 4 that ran through the *m'* of the land,
Ne 4:11 till we come in the *m'* among them,
9:11 through the *m'* of the sea on dry
Es 4: 1 and went out into the *m'* of the city,
Job 21:21 of his months is cut off in the *m'*?
Ps 22:14 is melted in the *m'* of my bowels.
22 in the *m'* of the congregation will I
46: 2 be carried into the *m'* of the sea;
5 God is in the *m'* of her; she shall
48: 9 O God, in the *m'* of thy temple.
55:10 also and sorrow are in the *m'* of it.
11 Wickedness is in the *m'* thereof:
57: 6 into the *m'* whereof they are fallen
74: 4 roar in the *m'* of thy congregation;
12 salvation in the *m'* of the earth.
78:28 he let it fall in the *m'* of their camp,
102:24 me not away in the *m'* of my days:
110: 2 thou in the *m'* of thine enemies.
116:19 Lord's house, in the *m'* of thee, O.
135: 9 and wonders in the *m'* of thee,
136:14 Israel to pass through the *m'* of it:
137: 2 upon the willows in the *m'* thereof.
138: 7 Though I walk in the *m'* of trouble,
Pro 4:21 keep them in the *m'* of thine heart.
5:14 all evil in the *m'* of the congregation
8:20 in the *m'* of the paths of judgment:
14:33 that which is in the *m'* of fools is
23:34 he lieth down in the *m'* of the sea,
30:19 way of a ship in the *m'* of the sea;
Ca 3:10 *m'* thereof being paved with love,
Isa 4: 4 the blood of Jerusalem from the *m'*
5: 2 and built a tower in the *m'* of it,
8 be...alone in the *m'* of the earth!
25 were torn in the *m'* of the streets.
6: 5 I dwell in the *m'* of a people of
12 forsaking in the *m'* of the land.
7: 6 and set a king in the *m'* of it, even
10:23 even...in the *m'* of all the land.
12: 6 Holy One of Israel in the *m'* of thee.
16: 3 night in the *m'* of the noonday;
19: 1 of Egypt shall melt in the *m'* of it.
3 Egypt shall fail in the *m'* thereof;
14 a perverse spirit in the *m'* thereof:
19 Lord in the *m'* of the land of Egypt,
24 a blessing in the *m'* of the land:
24:13 it shall be in the *m'* of the land
18 cometh up out of the *m'* of the pit
25:11 forth his hand in the *m'* of them,
29:23 of mine hands, in the *m'* of him,
30:28 shall reach to the *m'* of the neck,
41:18 fountains in the *m'* of the valleys:
52:11 go ye out of the *m'* of her; be ye
58: 9 thou take away from the *m'* of thee
66:17 gardens behind one tree in the *m'*,
Jer 6: 1 flee out of the *m'* of Jerusalem,
6 wholly oppression in the *m'* of her.
9: 6 habitation is in the *m'* of deceit;
12:16 they be built in the *m'* of my people.
14: 9 thou, O Lord, art in the *m'* of us,
17:11 leave them in the *m'* of his days,
21: 4 them into the *m'* of this city.
29: 8 that be in the *m'* of you, deceive
30:21 shall proceed from the *m'* of them;
37:12 thence in the *m'* of the people.
41: 7 they came into the *m'* of the city,
7 and cast them into the *m'* of the pit.
46:21 her hired men are in the *m'* of her
48:45 flame from the *m'* of Sihon, and shall
50: 8 Remove out of the *m'* of Babylon,
37 people that are in the *m'* of her;
51: 1 them that dwell in the *m'* of them
6 Flee out of the *m'* of Babylon, and
45 people, go ye out of the *m'* of her,
47 her slain shall fall in the *m'* of her.
63 cast it into the *m'* of Euphrates:
52:25 that were found in the *m'* of the city.
La 1:15 my mighty men in the *m'* of me:
3:45 and refuse in the *m'* of the people.
4:13 blood of the just in the *m'* of her,
Eze 1: 4 and out of the *m'* thereof as the
4 of amber, out of the *m'* of the fire.
5 Also out of the *m'* thereof came the
5: 2 fire a third part in the *m'* of the city,
4 and cast them into the *m'* of the fire,
5 I have set it in the *m'* of the nations
8 judgments in the *m'* of thee in the
10 shall eat the sons in the *m'* of thee,
12 they be consumed in the *m'* of thee:
6: 7 the slain shall fall in the *m'* of you,
7: 4 abominations shall be in the *m'* of
9 abominations that are in the *m'* of
8:11 in the *m'* of them stood Jaazaniah
Eze 9: 4 him, Go through the *m'* of the city,
4 through the *m'* of Jerusalem, and
4 that be done in the *m'* thereof.
10:10 wheel had been in the *m'* of a wheel.
11: 7 whom ye have laid in the *m'* of it,
7 bring you forth out of the *m'* of it.
9 will bring you out of the *m'* thereof,
11 ye be the flesh in the *m'* thereof;
23 went up from the *m'* of the city,
12: 2 in the *m'* of a rebellious house,
13:14 be consumed in the *m'* thereof:
14: 8 him off from the *m'* of my people;
9 from the *m'* of my people Israel.
15: 4 ends of it, and the *m'* of it is burned.
16:53 of thy captives in the *m'* of them:
17:16 in the *m'* of Babylon he shall die.
20: 8 them in the *m'* of the land of Egypt.
21:32 blood shall be in the *m'* of the land;
22: 3 city sheddeth blood in the *m'* of it,
7 in the *m'* of thee have they dealt by
9 *m'* of thee they commit lewdness.
13 which hath been in the *m'* of thee.
18 and lead, in the *m'* of the furnace;
19 gather you into the *m'* of Jerusalem
20 and tin, into the *m'* of the furnace,
21 ye shall be melted in the *m'* thereof.
22 is melted in the *m'* of the furnace,
22 shall ye be melted in the *m'* thereof;
25 of her prophets in the *m'* thereof,
25 her many widows in the *m'* thereof.
27 Her princes in the *m'* thereof are
23:39 they done in the *m'* of mine house.
24: 7 For her blood is in the *m'* of her;
26: 5 of nets in the *m'* of the sea:
12 and thy dust in the *m'* of the water.
15 slaughter is made in the *m'* of thee?
27: 4 borders are in the *m'* of the seas,
25 very glorious in the *m'* of the seas.
26 broken thee in the *m'* of the seas.
27 company which is in the *m'* of thee
27 shall fall into the *m'* of the seas
32 the destroyed in the *m'* of the sea?
34 company in the *m'* of thee shall fall.
28: 2 seat of God, in the *m'* of the seas;
8 that are slain in the *m'* of the seas.
14 in the *m'* of the stones of fire.
16 filled the *m'* of thee with violence,
16 from the *m'* of the stones of fire.
18 forth a fire from the *m'* of thee,
22 I will be glorified in the *m'* of thee:
23 shall be judged in the *m'* of her by
29: 3 that lieth in the *m'* of his rivers,
4 thee up out of the *m'* of thy rivers,
12 the *m'* of the countries are desolate,
21 of the mouth in the *m'* of them;
30: 7 the *m'* of the countries are desolate,
7 the *m'* of the cities that are wasted.
31:14 in the *m'* of the children of men,
17 shadow in the *m'* of the heathen.
18 lie in the *m'* of the uncircumcised
32:20 fall in the *m'* of them that are slain
21 speak to him out of the *m'* of hell
25 set her a bed in the *m'* of the slain
25 put in the *m'* of them that be slain.
28 in the *m'* of the uncircumcised,
32 laid in the *m'* of the uncircumcised
36:23 ye have profaned in the *m'* of them;
37: 1 set me down in the *m'* of the valley
26 set my sanctuary in the *m'* of them
28 sanctuary shall be in the *m'* of them
38:12 that dwell in the *m'* of the land.
39: 7 in the *m'* of my people Israel.
41: 7 chamber to the highest by the *m'*.
43: 7 in the *m'* of the children of Israel
9 and I will dwell in the *m'* of them
46:10 And the prince in the *m'* of them,
48: 8 sanctuary shall be in the *m'* of it.
10 the Lord shall be in the *m'* thereof.
15 the city shall be in the *m'* thereof.
21 the house shall be in the *m'* thereof.
22 the *m'* of that which is the prince's,
Da 3: 6, 11 *m'* of a burning fiery furnace.
15 the *m'* of a burning fiery furnace;
21, 23 *m'* of the burning fiery furnace.
24 men bound into the *m'* of the fire?
25 loose, walking in the *m'* of the fire,
26 came forth of the *m'* of the fire.
4:10 behold a tree in the *m'* of the earth,
7:15 in my spirit in the *m'* of my body,
9:27 *m'* of the week he shall cause the
Ho 5: 4 of whoredoms is in the *m'* of them,
11: 9 man; the Holy One in the *m'* of thee:
Joe 2:27 know that I am in the *m'* of Israel,
Am 2: 3 off the judge from the *m'* thereof,
3: 9 great tumults in the *m'* thereof,
9 the oppressed in the *m'* thereof.
6: 4 the calves out of the *m'* of the stall;
7: 8 plumbline in the *m'* of my people
10 in the *m'* of the house of Israel:
Jon 2: 3 the deep, in the *m'* of the seas;
Mic 2:12 as the flock in the *m'* of their fold:
5: 7 in the *m'* of many people as a dew
8 in the *m'* of many people as a lion
10 off thy horses out of the *m'* of thee,
13 images out of the *m'* of thee;
14 up thy groves out of the *m'* of thee:
6:14 down shall be in the *m'* of thee;
7:14 in the wood, in the *m'* of Carmel:
Na 3:13 people in the *m'* of thee are women:
Hab 2:19 is no breath at all in the *m'* of it.
3: 2 thy work in the *m'* of the years,
2 in the *m'* of the years make known;
Zep 2:14 shall lie down in the *m'* of her,
3: 5 The just Lord is in the *m'* thereof;
11 will take away out of the *m'* of thee
12 leave in the *m'* of thee an afflicted

Zep 3:15 even the Lord, is in the m' of thee:
17 thy God in the m' of thee is mighty;
Zec 2: 5 will be the glory in the m' of her.
10, 11 and I will dwell in the m' of thee,
5: 4 shall remain in the m' of his house,
7 that sitteth in the m' of the ephah.
8 he cast it into the m' of the ephah;
8: 3 will dwell in the m' of Jerusalem:
8 shall dwell in the m' of Jerusalem:
14: 1 shall be divided in the m' of thee.
4 shall cleave in the m' thereof
M't 10:16 forth as sheep in the m' of wolves:
14:24 ship was now in the m' of the sea,
18: 2 him, and set him in the m' of them,
20 name, there am I in the m' of them.
M'r 6:47 the ship was in the m' of the sea,
7:31 the m' of the coasts of Decapolis.
9:36 child, and set him in the m' of them:
14:60 the high priest stood up in the m',
Lu 2:46 sitting in the m' of the doctors,
4:30 he passing through the m' of them
35 the devil had thrown him in the m',
5:19 his couch into the m' before Jesus.
6: 8 Rise up, and stand forth in the m'.
17:11 passed through the m' of Samaria
21:21 which are in the m' of it depart out;
22:55 kindled a fire in the m' of the hall,
23:45 of the temple was rent in the m'.
24:36 Jesus...stood in the m' of them,
Joh 7:14 the m' of the feast Jesus went up
8: 3 when they had set her in the m',
9 and the woman standing in the m'.
59 going through the m' of them, and
19:18 either side one, and Jesus in the m'.
20:19 came Jesus and stood in the m',
26 stood in the m', and said, Peace be
Ac 1:15 stood up in the m' of the disciples,
18 he burst asunder in the m', and all
2:22 God did by him in the m' of you,
4: 7 when they had set them in the m',
17:22 Paul stood in the m' of Mars' hill,
27:21 Paul stood forth in the m' of them,
Ph'p 2:15 in the m' of a crooked and perverse
Heb 2:12 m' of the church will I sing praise
Re 1:13 in the m' of the seven candlesticks
2: 1 m' of the seven golden candlesticks;
7 is in the m' of the paradise of God.
4: 6 in the m' of the throne, and round
5: 6 in the m' of the throne and of the
6 in the m' of the elders, stood a Lamb
6: 6 a voice in the m' of the four beasts
7:17 which is in the m' of the throne
8:13 flying through the m' of heaven,
14: 6 angel fly in the m' of heaven,
19:17 fowls that fly in the m' of heaven,
22: 2 In the m' of the street of it, and on

midwife See also MIDWIVES.
Ge 35:17 labour, that the m' said unto her,
38:28 m' took and bound upon his hand a
Ex 1:16 When ye do the office of a m' to the

midwives
Ex 1:15 of Egypt spake to the Hebrew m',
17 the m' feared God, and did not as
18 the king of Egypt called for the m',
19 the m' said unto Pharaoh, Because
19 ere the m' come in unto them.
20 God dealt well with the m': and the
21 to pass because the m' feared God,

Migdal-el (mig'-dal-el)
Jos 19:38 And Iron, and M', Horem, and

Migdal-gad (mig'-dal-gad)
Jos 15:37 Zenan, and Hadashah, and M',

Migdol (mig'-dol)
Ex 14: 2 between M' and the sea, over
Nu 33: 7 and they pitched before M'.
Jer 44: 1 land of Egypt, which dwelt at M',
46:14 ye in Egypt, and publish in M', and

might^ See also MIGHTEST.
Ge 12:19 so I m' have taken her to me to wife:
13: 6 them, that they m' dwell together:
17:18 O that Ishmael m' live before thee!
26:10 m' lightly have lien with thy wife,
30:34 would it m' be according to thy word.
41 that they m' conceive among the rods.
31:27 I m' have sent thee away with mirth,
36: 7 than that they m' dwell together;
37:22 that he m' rid him out of their hands,
43:32 Egyptians m' not eat bread with
49: 3 thou art my firstborn, my m', and
Ex 10: 1 I m' shew these my signs before him:
12:33 m' send them out of the land in haste;
36:18 the tent together, that it m' be one.
39:21 m' be above the curious girdle of the
21 that the breastplate m' not be loosed
Le 24:12 mind of the Lord m' be shewed them.
26:45 the heathen, that I m' be their God:
Nu 4:37, 41 that m' do service in the tabernacle
14:13 broughtest up this people in thy m'
22:41 m' see the utmost part of the people.
De 2:30 that he m' deliver him into thy hand,
3:24 works, and according to thy m'?
4:14 m' do them in the land whither ye go
36 his voice, that he m' instruct thee:
42 That the slayer m' flee thither, which
42 unto one of these cities he m' live:
5:29 that it m' be well with them, and with
6: 1 m' do them in the land whither ye go
5 all thy soul, and with all thy m'
23 that he m' bring us in, to give us the
24 that he m' preserve us alive, as it is at
8: 3 he m' make thee know that man doth
16 m' humble thee, and that he m' prove
17 the m' of mine hand hath gotten
28:32 there shall be no m' in thine hand.
De 29: 6 ye m' know that I am the Lord your
32:13 he m' eat the increase of the fields;
Jos 4:24 people of the earth m' know the hand
24 ye m' fear the Lord your God for ever.
11:20 that he m' destroy them utterly, and
20 and that they m' have no favour,
20 but that he m' destroy them, as the
20: 9 killeth any person at unawares m' flee
22:16 ye m' rebel this day against the Lord?
24 your children m' speak unto our
27 that we m' do the service of the Lord
24: 8 hand, that ye m' possess their land;
J'g 3: 2 of Israel m' know, to teach them war,
5:31 sun when he goeth forth in his m'.
6:14 Go in this thy m', and thou shalt
9:24 ten sons of Jerubbaal m' come, and
16:30 he bowed himself with all his m';
18: 7 m' put them to shame in any thing;
Ru 1: 6 m' return from the country of Moab:
1Sa 4: 4 they m' bring from thence the ark of
13:10 to meet him, that he m' salute him.
14:14 of land, which a yoke of oxen m' plow.
18:27 that he m' be the king's son in law.
20: 6 of me that he m' run to Beth-lehem
2Sa 6:14 before the Lord with all his m';
10:10 that he m' put them in array against
15: 4 any suit or cause m' come unto me,
17:14 the Lord m' bring evil upon Absalom.
17 they m' not be seen to come into
22:41 that I m' destroy them that hate me.
1Ki 2:27 that he m' fulfil the word of the Lord,
7: 7 for the throne where he m' judge,
8: 1 that they m' bring up the ark of the
16 an house, that my name m' be therein;
12:15 that he m' perform his saying, which
15:17 that he m' not suffer any to go out or
23 all the acts of Asa, and all his m',
16: 5 what he did, and his m', are they
27 he did, and his m' that he shewed,
19: 4 requested for himself that he m' die;
22: 7 besides, that we m' enquire of him?
45 and his m' that he shewed, and
2Ki 7: 2 windows in heaven, m' this thing be?
19 in heaven, m' such a thing be?
10:19 he m' destroy the worshippers of Baal.
34 and all that he did, and all his m',
13: 8 and all that he did, and his m', are
12 and all that he did, and his m'
14:15 Jehoash which he did, and his m',
28 and all that he did, and his m', how
15:19 his hand m' be with him to confirm
20:20 acts of Hezekiah, and all his m',
22:17 that they m' provoke me to anger with
23:10 man m' make his son or his daughter
24 he m' perform the words of the law
25 all his soul, and with all his m',
33 that he m' not reign in Jerusalem;
24:16 And all the men of m', even seven
1Ch 4:10 that thine hand m' be with me, and
7: 2 men of m' in the generations;
5 Issachar were valiant men of m',
12: 8 hold to the wilderness men of m',
13: 8 before God with all their m', and
29: 2 prepared with all my m' for the
12 and in thine hand is power and m';
30 With all his reign and his m', and
2Ch 2:12 that m' build an house for the Lord,
6: 5 an house in, that my name m' be there;
6 Jerusalem, that my name m' be there;
10:15 that the Lord m' perform his word,
11: 1 he m' bring the kingdom again to
16: 1 he m' let none go out or come in to
18: 6 besides, that we m' enquire of him?
20: 6 hand is there not power and m',
12 no m' against this great company
25:20 m' deliver them into the hand of their
31: 4 m' be encouraged in the law of the
32:18 them; that they m' take the city.
31 he m' know all that was in his heart.
34:25 they m' provoke me to anger with all
35:12 they m' give according to the divisions
15 they m' not depart from their service;
22 he m' fight with him, and hearkened
36:22 of Jeremiah m' be accomplished,
Ezr 1: 1 mouth of Jeremiah m' be fulfilled,
5:10 m' write the names of the men that
8:21 we m' afflict ourselves before our God,
Ne 5: 3 that we m' buy corn, because of the
10 m' exact of them money and corn:
6:13 m' have matter for an evil report,
13 evil report, that they m' reproach me.
7: 5 they m' be reckoned by genealogy.
9:24 they m' do with them as they would.
10:37 the same Levites m' have the tithes
Es 4: 2 for none m' enter into the king's gate
10: 2 the acts of his power and of his m',
Job 6: 8 that I m' have my request; and that
9:33 us, that m' lay his hand upon us both.
16:21 that one m' plead for a man with God,
23: 3 Oh that I knew where I m' find him!
3 that I m' come even to his seat!
7 the righteous m' dispute with him;
30: 2 whereto m' the strength of their
38:13 m' take hold of the ends of the earth,
13 that the wicked m' be shaken out of it?
Ps 18:40 that I m' destroy them that hate me.
68:18 the Lord God m' dwell among them.
76: 5 none of the men of m' have found
78: 6 the generation to come m' know them,
7 That they m' set their hope in God,
8 m' not be as their fathers, a stubborn
105:45 That they m' observe his statutes, and
106: 8 he m' make his mighty power to be
107: 7 that they m' go to a city of habitation.
109:16 he m' even slay the broken in heart.
118:13 hast thrust sore at me that I m' fall:
Ps 119:11 heart, that I m' not sin against thee.
71 afflicted; that I m' learn thy statutes.
101 evil way, that I m' keep thy word.
148 that I m' meditate in thy word.
145: 6 speak of the m' of thy terrible acts:
Pr 22:21 I m' make thee know the certainty
Ec 2: 3 I m' see what was that good for the
3:18 of men, that God m' manifest them,
18 they m' see that they themselves are
9:10 findeth to do, do it with thy m';
Isa 11: 2 the spirit of counsel and m', the
28:13 that they m' go, and fall backward,
33:13 that are near, acknowledge my m'.
40:26 names by the greatness of his m',
29 have no m' he increaseth strength.
61: 3 m' be called trees of righteousness,
3 of the Lord, that he m' be glorified.
64: 1 m' flow down at thy presence,
Jer 9: 1 I m' weep day and night for the slain
2 I m' leave my people, and go from
23 let the mighty man glory in his m',
10: 6 great, and thy name is great in m'.
13:11 that they m' be unto me for a people,
16:21 to know mine hand and my m';
17:23 their neck stiff, that they m' not hear,
19:15 necks, that they m' not hear my words.
20:17 my mother m' have been my grave,
25: 7 ye m' provoke me to anger with the
26:19 m' we procure great evil against our
27:15 in my name; that I m' drive you out,
15 that ye m' perish, ye, and the prophets
43: 3 that they m' put us to death, and carry
44: 8 that ye m' cut yourselves off, and that
8 that ye m' be a curse and a reproach
49:35 bow of Elam, the chief of their m'.
51:30 their m' hath failed; they became
Eze 17: 7 that he m' water it by the furrows of
8 that it m' bring forth branches, and
8 branches, and that it m' bear fruit,
8 bear fruit, that it m' be a goodly vine.
14 That the kingdom m' be base, that
14 that it m' not lift itself up, but that
14 by keeping of his covenant it m' stand.
15 they m' give him horses and much
20:12 that they m' know that I am the Lord
26 that I m' make them desolate, to the
26 that they m' know that I am the Lord.
24: 8 That it m' cause fury to come up to
32:29 with their m' are laid by them that
30 terror they are ashamed of their m';
36: 3 ye m' be a possession unto the residue
40: 4 intent that I m' shew them unto thee
41: 6 that they m' have hold, but they had
Da 1: 4 whom they m' teach the learning and
5 thereof they m' stand before the king.
8 eunuchs that he m' not defile himself.
2:20 ever: for wisdom and m' are his:
23 who hast given me wisdom and m',
3:28 m' not serve nor worship any god,
4: 6 that they m' make known unto me the
30 kingdom by the m' of my power,
5: 2 and his concubines, m' drink therein.
6: 2 princes m' give accounts unto them,
17 that the purpose m' not be changed
8: 4 so that no beasts m' stand before him,
9:11 that they m' not obey thy voice;
13 that we m' turn from our iniquities,
Joe 3: 3 sold a girl for wine, that they m' drink.
6 ye m' remove them far from their
Am 1:13 that they m' enlarge their border:
Jon 4: 5 m' see what would become of the city.
6 that it m' be a shadow over his head,
Mic 3: 8 of judgment, and of m', to declare
7:16 and be confounded at all their m':
Hab 3:16 that I m' rest in the day of trouble:
Zec 4: 6 Not by m', nor by power, but by
6: 7 to go that they m' walk to and fro
8: 9 was laid, that the temple m' be built.
11:10 m' break my covenant which I had
14 I m' break the brotherhood between
Mal 2: 4 that my covenant m' be with Levi,
15 one? That he m' seek a godly seed.
M't 1:22 it m' be fulfilled which was spoken
2:15, 23 it m' be fulfilled which was spoken
4:14 it m' be fulfilled which was spoken
8:17 it m' be fulfilled which was spoken
28 that no man m' pass by that way.
12:10 days? that they m' accuse him.
14 him, how they m' destroy him.
17 it m' be fulfilled which was spoken
13:35 it m' be fulfilled which was spoken
14:36 they m' only touch the hem of his
21: 4 it m' be fulfilled which was spoken by
32 not afterward, that ye m' believe him.
34 that they m' receive the fruits of it.
22:15 how they m' entangle him in his talk.
26: 4 that they m' take Jesus by subtilty,
9 this ointment m' have been sold for
56 of the prophets m' be fulfilled.
27:35 it m' be fulfilled which was spoken by
M'r 3: 2 day; that they m' accuse him.
6 against him, how they m' destroy him.
14 that he m' send them forth to preach,
5:18 prayed him that he m' be with him.
6:56 they m' touch if it were but the border
10:51 him, Lord, that I m' receive my sight.
11:13 if haply he m' find any thing thereon:
18 and sought how they m' destroy him:
12: 2 he m' receive from the husbandmen
14: 1 scribes sought how they m' take him
5 For it m' have been sold for more
11 how he m' conveniently betray him.
35 possible, the hour m' pass from him.
16: 1 that they m' come and anoint him.
Lu 1:74 enemies m' serve him without fear,
4:29 that they m' cast him down headlong.

Lu 5:19 by what way they *m'* bring him in
6: 7 *m'* find an accusation against him.
11 another what they *m'* do to Jesus.
8: 9 saying, What *m'* this parable be?
10 parables; that seeing they *m'* not see,
10 and hearing they *m'* not understand.
38 besought him that he *m'* be with him:
11:54 of his mouth, that they *m'* accuse him.
15:29 that I *m'* make merry with my friends:
17: 6 ye *m'* say unto this sycamine tree,
19:15 *m'* know how much every man had
23 I *m'* have required mine own with
48 And could not find what they *m'* do:
20:20 that they *m'* take hold of his words,
20 *m'* deliver him unto the power and
22: 2 scribes sought how they *m'* kill him;
4 how he *m'* betray him unto them.
23:23 requiring that he *m'* be crucified.
26 cross, that he *m'* bear it after Jesus.
24:45 they *m'* understand the scriptures,
Joh 1: 7 that all men through him *m'* believe.
3:17 the world through him *m'* be saved.
5:34 things I say, that ye *m'* be saved.
40 not come to me, that ye *m'* have life.
6:28 that we *m'* work the works of God?
8: 6 him, that they *m'* have to accuse him.
9:36 is he, Lord, that I *m'* believe on him?
39 world, that they which see not *m'* see;
39 that they which see *m'* be made blind.
10:10 I am come that they *m'* have life,
10 that they *m'* have it more abundantly.
17 down my life, that I *m'* take it again.
11: 4 that the Son of God *m'* be glorified
57 should shew it, that they *m'* take him.
12: 9 that they *m'* see Lazarus also, whom
10 they *m'* put Lazarus also to death;
38 of Esaias the prophet *m'* be fulfilled,
14:29 when it is come to pass, ye *m'* believe.
15:11 you, that my joy *m'* remain in you,
11 in you, and that your joy *m'* be full.
25 that the word *m'* be fulfilled that is
16:33 unto you, that in me ye *m'* have peace.
17: 3 they *m'* know thee the only true God,
12 that the scripture *m'* be fulfilled.
13 that they *m'* have my joy fulfilled in
19 that they also *m'* be sanctified
18: 9 That the saying *m'* be fulfilled, which
28 but that they *m'* eat the passover.
32 the saying of Jesus *m'* be fulfilled,
19:24, 36 that the scripture *m'* be fulfilled,
31 Pilate that their legs *m'* be broken,
31 and that they *m'* be taken away.
35 that he saith true, that ye *m'* believe.
38 he *m'* take away the body of Jesus:
20:31 ye *m'* believe that Jesus is the Christ,
31 ye *m'* have life through his name.
Ac 1:25 fell, that he *m'* go to his own place.
4:21 nothing how they *m'* punish them,
5:15 Peter passing by *m'* overshadow some
7:19 children, to the end they *m'* not live.
8:15 that they *m'* receive the Holy Ghost:
9: 2 *m'* bring them bound unto Jerusalem.
12 on him, that he *m'* receive his sight.
21 that he *m'* bring them bound unto
13:42 that these words *m'* be preached to
15:17 residue of men *m'* seek after the Lord,
17:27 if haply they *m'* feel after him, and
20:24 so that I *m'* finish my course with joy,
22:24 that he *m'* know wherefore they cried
24:26 him of Paul, that he *m'* loose him:
25:21 be kept till I *m'* send him to Cæsar.
26 had, I *m'* have somewhat to write.
26:32 man *m'* have been set at liberty, if
27:12 means they *m'* attain to Phenice,
Ro 1:10 length I *m'* have a prosperous journey
13 I *m'* have some fruit among you also,
3:26 that he *m'* be just, and the justifier of
4:11 that he *m'* be the father of all them
11 righteousness *m'* be imputed unto
16 it is of faith, that it *m'* be by grace;
16 the promise *m'* be sure to all the seed;
18 *m'* become the father of many nations,
5:20 entered, that the offence *m'* abound.
21 *m'* grace reign through righteousness
6: 6 that the body of sin *m'* be destroyed,
7:13 But sin, that it *m'* appear sin, working
13 that sin...*m'* become exceeding sinful.
8: 4 the law *m'* be fulfilled in us, who walk
29 he *m'* be the firstborn among many
9:11 of God according to election *m'* stand,
17 up, that I *m'* shew my power in thee,
17 my name *m'* be declared throughout
23 that he *m'* make known the riches of
10: 1 for Israel is, that they *m'* be saved.
11:14 my flesh, and *m'* save some of them.
19 broken off, that I *m'* be graffed in.
32 that he *m'* have mercy upon all.
14: 9 that he *m'* be Lord both of the dead
15: 4 comfort of the scriptures *m'* have hope.
9 Gentiles *m'* glorify God for his mercy;
16 up of the Gentiles *m'* be acceptable,
1Co 2:12 that we *m'* know the things that are
4: 6 ye *m'* learn in us not to think of men
8 reign, that we also *m'* reign with you.
5: 2 hath done this deed *m'* be taken away
9:19 unto all, that I *m'* gain the more.
20 as a Jew, that I *m'* gain the Jews;
20 I *m'* gain them that are under the
21 I *m'* gain them that are without law.
22 I as weak, that I *m'* gain the weak:
22 that I *m'* by all means save some.
23 that I *m'* be partaker thereof with you.
14:19 by my voice I *m'* teach others also,
2Co 1:15 that ye *m'* have a second benefit;
2: 4 that ye *m'* know the love which I have
9 that I *m'* know the proof of you,

2Co 4:10, 11 also of Jesus *m'* be made manifest
15 grace *m'* through the thanksgiving of
5: 4 mortality *m'* be swallowed up of life.
21 *m'* be made the righteousness of God
7: 9 ye *m'* receive damage by us in nothing.
12 in the sight of God *m'* appear unto you.
8: 9 that ye through his poverty *m'* be rich.
9: 5 that the same *m'* be ready, as a matter
11: 4 not accepted, ye *m'* well bear with him.
7 abasing myself that ye *m'* be exalted,
12: 8 Lord thrice, that it *m'* depart from me.
Ga 1: 4 he *m'* deliver us from this present evil
16 I *m'* preach him among the heathen;
2: 4 that they *m'* bring us into bondage:
5 truth of the gospel *m'* continue with
16 *m'* be justified by the faith of Christ,
19 to the law, that I *m'* live unto God.
3:14 blessing of Abraham *m'* come on the
14 we *m'* receive the promise of the Spirit
22 *m'* be given to them that believe.
24 Christ, that we *m'* be justified by faith.
4: 5 we *m'* receive the adoption of sons.
17 exclude you, that ye *m'* affect them
Eph 1:10 he *m'* gather together in one all things
21 principality, and power, and *m'*,
2: 7 he *m'* shew the exceeding riches of
16 *m'* reconcile both unto God in one
3:10 places *m'* be known by the church
16 to be strengthened with *m'* by his
19 *m'* be filled with all the fulness of
4:10 all heavens, that he *m'* fill all things,)
5:26 he *m'* sanctify and cleanse it with the
27 he *m'* present it to himself a glorious
6:10 Lord, and in the power of his *m'*.
22 purpose, that ye *m'* know our affairs,
22 and that he *m'* comfort your hearts.
Ph'p 3: 4 I *m'* also have confidence in the flesh.
4 hath whereof he *m'* trust in the flesh,
11 I *m'* attain unto the resurrection of
Col 1: 9 *m'* be filled with the knowledge of his
10 That ye *m'* walk worthy of the Lord
11 Strengthened with all *m'*,
18 all things he *m'* have the preeminence.
2: 2 their hearts *m'* be comforted, being
4: 8 he *m'* know your estate, and comfort
1Th 2: 6 we *m'* have been burdensome, as
16 to the Gentiles that they *m'* be saved,
3:10 exceedingly that we *m'* see your face,
10 *m'* perfect that which is lacking in
2Th 2: 6 that he *m'* be revealed in his time.
10 of the truth, that they *m'* be saved.
12 all *m'* be damned who believed not
3: 8 *m'* not be chargeable to any of you:
1Ti 1:16 Christ *m'* shew forth all longsuffering,
2Ti 4:17 me the preaching *m'* be fully known,
17 and that all the Gentiles *m'* hear:
Tit 2:14 *m'* redeem us from all iniquity, and
3: 8 God *m'* be careful to maintain good
Ph'm 13 stead he *m'* have ministered unto me
Heb 2:14 through death he *m'* destroy him that
17 he *m'* be a merciful and faithful high
6:18 we *m'* have a strong consolation, who
9:15 are called *m'* receive the promise of
10:36 of God, ye *m'* receive the promise.
11:15 they *m'* have had an opportunity to
35 they *m'* obtain a better resurrection:
12:10 that we *m'* be partakers of his holiness.
18 unto the mount that *m'* be touched,
13:12 he *m'* sanctify the people with his own
Jas 5:17 prayed earnestly that it *m'* not rain:
1Pe 1: 7 *m'* be found unto praise and honour
21 your faith and hope *m'* be in God.
3:18 unjust, that he *m'* bring us to God,
4: 6 that they *m'* be judged according to
2Pe 1: 4 *m'* be partaker of the divine nature,
2:11 which are greater in power and *m'*,
1Jo 2:19 they *m'* be made manifest that they
3: 8 he *m'* destroy the works of the devil.
4: 9 world, that we *m'* live through him.
3Jo 8 we *m'* be fellowhelpers to the truth.
Re 7:12 power, and *m'*, be unto our God
12:14 that she *m'* fly into the wilderness,
15 he *m'* cause her to be carried away
13:17 that no man *m'* buy or sell, save
16:12 the kings of the east *m'* be prepared.

mightest
De 4:35 thou *m'* know that the Lord he is God;
6: 2 That thou *m'* fear the Lord thy God,
J'g 16: 6 thou *m'* be bound to afflict thee.
10 thee, wherewith thou *m'* be bound.
13 tell me wherewith thou *m'* be bound.
1Sa 17:28 come down that thou *m'* see the battle.
Ne 9:29 that thou *m'* bring them again unto
Ps 8: 2 that thou *m'* still the enemy and the
51: 4 *m'* be justified when thou speakest,
Pr 22:21 thou *m'* answer the words of truth
Da 2:30 that thou *m'* know the thoughts of
M't 15: 5 whatsoever thou *m'* be profited by me;
M'r 7:11 whatsoever thou *m'* be profited by me;
Lu 1: 4 thou *m'* know the certainty of those
Ac 9:17 that thou *m'* receive thy sight, and
Ro 3: 4 thou *m'* be justified in thy sayings,
4 *m'* overcome when thou art judged.
1Ti 1: 3 thou *m'* charge some that they teach
18 thou by them *m'* war a good warfare;

mightier
Ge 26:16 for thou are much *m'* than we.
Ex 1: 9 of Israel are more and *m'* than we:
Nu 14:12 a greater nation and *m'* than they.
De 4:38 thee greater and *m'* than thou art,
7: 1 nations greater and *m'* than thou;
9: 1 greater and *m'* than thyself, cities
14 a nation *m'* and greater than they.
11:23 nations and *m'* than yourselves.
Ps 93: 4 Lord on high is *m'* than the noise

Ec 6:10 with him that is *m'* than he.
M't 3:11 that cometh after me is *m'* than I,
M'r 1: 7 cometh one *m'* than I after me,
Lu 3:16 one *m'* than I cometh, the lachet of

mighties
1Ch 11:12 who was one of the three *m'*.
24 had the name among the three *m'*.

mightiest
1Ch 11:19 These things did these three *m'*.

mightily
De 6: 3 that ye may increase *m'*, as the
J'g 4: 3 twenty years he *m'* oppressed the
14: 6 Spirit of the Lord came *m'* upon him,
15:14 Spirit of the Lord came *m'* upon him,
Jer 25:30 he shall *m'* roar upon his habitation;
Jon 3: 8 sackcloth, and cry *m'* unto God:
Na 2: 1 loins strong, fortify thy power *m'*.
Ac 18:28 For he *m'* convinced the Jews, and
19:20 *m'* grew the word of God and
Col 1:29 which worketh in me *m'*.
Re 18: 2 cried *m'* with a strong voice,

mighty See also ALMIGHTY; MIGHTIER; MIGHTIES; MIGHTIEST.
Ge 6: 4 the same became *m'* men which
10: 8 began to be a *m'* one in the earth.
9 was a *m'* hunter before the Lord:
9 the *m'* hunter before the Lord.
18:18 become a great and *m'* nation,
23: 6 thou art a *m'* prince among us:
49:24 strong by the hands of the *m'* God
Ex 1: 7 and waxed exceeding *m'*; and the
20 multiplied, and waxed very *m'*.
3:19 let you go, no, not by a *m'* hand.
9:28 be no more *m'* thunderings and hail;
10:19 turned a *m'* strong west wind,
15:10 they sank as lead in the *m'* waters.
15 the *m'* men of Moab, trembling
32:11 great power, and with a *m'* hand?
Le 19:15 nor honour the person of the *m'*:
Nu 22: 6 people; for they are too *m'* for me:
De 3:24 thy greatness, and thy *m'* hand:
4:34 and by war, and by a *m'* hand,
37 in his sight with his *m'* power out
5:15 out thence through a *m'* hand, and
6:21 us out of Egypt with a *m'* hand:
7: 8 brought you out with a *m'* hand,
19 *m'* hand, and the stretched out arm,
21 among you, a *m'* God and terrible.
23 destroy them with a *m'* destruction,
9:26 forth out of Egypt with a *m'* hand.
29 broughtest out by thy *m'* power
10:17 a great God, a *m'*, and a terrible,
11: 2 God, his greatness, his *m'* hand,
26: 5 nation, great, *m'*, and populous:
8 forth out of Egypt with a *m'* hand,
34:12 in all that *m'* hand, and in all the
Jos 1:14 armed, all the *m'* men of valour,
4:24 the hand of the Lord, that it is *m'*:
6: 2 thereof, and the *m'* men of valour.
8: 3 thirty thousand *m'* men of valour,
10: 2 and all the men thereof were *m'*.
7 him, and all the *m'* men of valour.
J'g 5:13 me have dominion over the *m'*.
22 the pransings of their *m'* ones.
23 help of the Lord against the *m'*.
6:12 with thee, thou *m'* men of valour.
11: 1 Gileadite was a *m'* man of valour,
Ru 2: 1 a *m'* man of wealth, of the family of
1Sa 2: 4 bows of the *m'* men are broken,
4: 8 out of the hand of these *m'* Gods?
9: 1 a Benjamite, a *m'* man of power.
16:18 in playing, and a *m'* valiant man,
2Sa 1:19 high places: how are the *m'* fallen!
21 shield of the *m'* is vilely cast away,
22 from the fat of the *m'*, the bow of
25 How are the *m'* fallen in the midst
27 How are the *m'* fallen, and the
10: 7 and all the host of the *m'* men.
16: 6 the *m'* men were on his right hand
17: 8 that they be *m'* men, and they be
10 knoweth that thy father is a *m'* man,
20: 7 the Pelethites, and all the *m'* men:
23: 8 be the names of the *m'* men whom
9 one of the three *m'* men with David,
16 the three *m'* men brake through the
17 things did these three *m'* men.
22 had the name among three *m'* men.
1Ki 1: 8 *m'* men which belonged to David,
10 and the *m'* men, and Solomon his
11:28 Jeroboam was a *m'* man of valour:
2Ki 5: 1 he was also a *m'* man in valour, but
15:20 even of all the *m'* men of wealth, of
24:14 and all the *m'* men of valour, even
15 the *m'* of the land, those carried he
1Ch 1:10 he began to be *m'* upon the earth.
5:24 *m'* men of valour, famous men, and
7: 7 their fathers, *m'* men of valour;
9, 11 their fathers, *m'* men of valour,
40 choice and *m'* men of valour, chief
8:40 of Ulam were *m'* men of valour,
11:10 of the *m'* men whom David had,
11 of the *m'* men whom David had;
12: 1 were among the *m'* men, helpers of
4 a *m'* man among the thirty, and
21 for they were all *m'* men of valour,
25 *m'* men of valour for the war, seven
28 Zadok, a young man *m'* of valour,
30 eight hundred, *m'* men of valour,
19: 8 and all the host of the *m'* men.
26: 6 for they were *m'* men of valour.
31 them *m'* men of valour at Jazer of
27: 6 who was *m'* among the thirty, and
28: 1 the officers, and with the *m'* men,
29:24 all the princes, and the *m'* men, and

2Ch 6:32 thy m' hand, and thy stretched out
13: 3 men, being m' men of valour.
21 But Abijah waxed m', and married
14: 8 all these were m' men of valour.
17:13 m' men of valour, were in Jerusalem.
14 m' men of valour three hundred
16 hundred thousand m' men of valour.
17 Eliada a m' man of valour, and with
25: 6 m' men of valour out of Israel for
26:12 the fathers of the m' men of valour
13 that made war with m' power, to
27: 6 So Jotham became m', because he
28: 7 And Zichri, a m' man of Ephraim,
32: 3 and his m' men to stop the waters
21 cut off all the m' men of valour, and
Ezr 4:20 been m' kings also over Jerusalem,
7:28 before all the king's m' princes.
Ne 3:16 and unto the house of the m'.
9:11 as a stone into the m' waters.
32 our God, the great, the m', and the
11:14 their brethren, m' men of valour,
Job 5:15 and from the hand of the m'.
6:23 me from the hand of the m'?
9: 4 wise in heart, and m' in strength:
12:19 spoiled, and overthroweth the m'.
21 weakeneth the strength of the m'.
21: 7 become old, yea, are m' in power?
22: 8 But as for the m' man, he had the
24:22 draweth also the m' with his power:
34:20 the m' shall be taken away without
24 break in pieces m' men without
35: 9 out by reason of the arm of the m'.
36: 5 God is m', and despiseth not any:
5 he is m' in strength and wisdom.
41:25 up himself, the m' are afraid: by
Ps 24: 8 strong and m', the Lord m' in battle
29: 1 Give unto the Lord, O ye m', 1121.
33:16 a m' man is not delivered by much
45: 3 sword upon thy thigh, O most m',
50: 1 The m' God, even the Lord, hath
52: 1 thou thyself in mischief, O m' man?
59: 3 the m' are gathered against me;
68:33 out his voice, and that a m' voice.
69: 4 mine enemies wrongfully, are m':
74:15 the flood: thou driedst up m' rivers.
78:65 m' man that shouteth by reason of
82: 1 in the congregation of the m'; he
89: 6 who among the sons of the m' can
13 Thou hast a m' arm: strong is thy
19 have laid help upon one that is m';
50 the reproach of all the m' people;
93: 4 yea, than the m' waves of the sea.
106: 2 can utter the m' acts of the Lord?
8 make his m' power to be known.
112: 2 His seed shall be m' upon earth:
120: 4 Sharp arrows of the m', with coals
127: 4 arrows are in the hand of a m' man;
132: 2 vowed unto the m' God of Jacob;
5 habitation for the m' God of Jacob.
135:10 great nations, and slew m' kings;
145: 4 and shall declare thy m' acts.
12 to the sons of men his m' acts,
150: 2 Praise him for his m' acts: praise
Pr 16:32 to anger is better than the m';
18:18 cease, and parteth between the m'.
21:22 man scaleth the city of the m', and
23:11 For their redeemer is m'; he shall
Ec 7:19 more than ten m' men which are
Ca 4: 4 bucklers, all shields of m' men.
Isa 1:24 Lord of hosts, the m' One of Israel,
3: 2 The m' man, and the man of war,
25 the sword, and thy m' in the war.
5:15 and the m' man shall be humbled,
22 them that are m' to drink wine,
9: 6 Wonderful, Counsellor, The m' God,
10:21 remnant of Jacob, unto the m' God.
34 and Lebanon shall fall by a m' one.
11:15 with his m' wind shall he shake
13: 3 called my m' ones for mine anger,
17:12 like the rushing of m' waters!
21:17 m' men of the children of Kedar,
22:17 thee away with a m' captivity,
28: 2 Lord hath a m' and strong one,
2 as a flood of m' waters overflowing,
30:29 the Lord, to the m' One of Israel.
31: 8 with the sword, not of a m' man;
42:13 Lord shall go forth as a m' man,
43:16 sea, and a path in the m' waters;
49:24 the prey be taken from the m', or
25 the captives of the m' shall be taken
26 thy Redeemer, the m' One of Jacob.
60:16 thy Redeemer, the m' One of Jacob.
63: 1 speak in righteousness, m' to save.
Jer 5:15 it is a m' nation, it is an ancient
16 sepulchre, they are all m' men.
9:23 let the m' man glory in his might,
14: 9 as a m' man that cannot save?
20:11 Lord is with me as a m' terrible one:
26:21 the king, with all his m' men, and all
32:18 the Great, the M' God, the Lord
19 Great in counsel, and m' in work:
33: 3 shew thee great and m' things,
41:16 m' men of war, and the women,
46: 5 their m' ones are beaten down,
6 flee away, nor the m' man escape;
9 and let the m' men come forth; the
12 m' man...stumbled against the m',
48:14 are m' and strong men for the war?
41 the m' men's hearts in Moab at that
49:22 heart of the m' men of Edom be as
50: 9 shall be as of a m' expert man;
36 a sword is upon her m' men; and
51:30 The m' men of Babylon have forborn
56 Babylon, and her m' men are taken,
57 and her rulers, and her m' men:
La 1:15 trodden under foot all my m' men

Eze 17:13 hath also taken the m' of the land:
17 shall Pharaoh with his m' army
20:33, 34 with a m' hand, and with a
31:11 hand of the m' one of the heathen:
32:12 By the swords of the m' will I cause
21 strong among the m' shall speak
27 not lie with the m' that are fallen
27 terror of the m' in the land of the
38:15 a great company, and a m' army:
39:18 Ye shall eat the flesh of the m',
20 with m' men, and with all men of
Da 3:20 he commanded the most m' men
4: 3 and how m' are his wonders!
8:24 And his power shall be m', but not
24 the m' and the holy people.
9:15 the land of Egypt with a m' hand,
11: 3 And a m' king shall stand up, that
25 with a very great and m' army;
Ho 10:13 in the multitude of thy m' men.
Joe 2: 7 They shall run like m' men; they
3: 9 Prepare war, wake up the m' men,
11 thy m' ones to come down, O Lord.
Am 2:14 neither shall the m' deliver himself:
16 he that is courageous among the m'
5:12 transgressions and your m' sins:
24 and righteousness as a m' stream.
Ob 9 thy m' men, O Teman, shall be
Jon 1: 4 there was a m' tempest in the sea,
Na 2: 3 shield of his m' men is made red,
Hab 1:12 O m' God, thou hast established
Zep 1:14 m' man shall cry there bitterly.
3:17 thy God in the midst of thee is m';
Zec 9:13 made thee as the sword of a m' man.
10: 5 And they shall be as m' men, which
7 of Ephraim shall be like a m' man,
11: 2 because the m' are spoiled: howl,
M't 11:20 most of his m' works were done,
21 if the m' works, which were done
23 if the m' works, which have been
13:54 this wisdom, and these m' works?
58 he did not many m' works there
14: 2 m' works do shew forth themselves
M'r 6: 2 such m' works are wrought by his
5 he could there do no m' work, save
14 m' works do shew forth themselves
Lu 1:49 he that is m' hath done to me great
52 put down the m' from their seats,
9:43 all amazed at the m' power of God.
10:13 if the m' works had been done in
15:14 arose a m' famine in that land;
19:37 the m' works that they had seen;
24:19 was a prophet m' in deed and word
Ac 2: 2 heaven as of a rushing m' wind,
7:22 and was m' in words and in deeds.
18:24 man, and m' in the scriptures,
Ro 15:19 Through m' signs and wonders,
1Co 1:26 not many m', not many noble, are
27 confound the things which are m';
2Co 10: 4 but m' through God to the pulling
12:12 signs, and wonders, and m' deeds.
13: 3 is not weak, but is m' in you.
Ga 2: 8 m' in me toward the Gentiles:)
Eph 1:19 to the working of his m' power,
2Th 1: 7 from heaven with his m' angels,
1Pe 5: 6 under the m' hand of God, that he
Re 6:13 when she is shaken of a m' wind.
15 chief captains, and the m' men,
10: 1 saw another m' angel come down
16:18 so m' an earthquake, and so great.
18:10 great city Babylon, that m' city!
21 a m' angel took up a stone like a
19: 6 and as the voice of m' thunderings,
18 captains, and the flesh of m' men,

Migron (mi'-gron)
1Sa 14: 2 pomegranate tree which is in M':
Isa 10:28 come to Aiath, he is passed to M';

Mijamin (mij'-a-min) See also Miamin.
1Ch 24: 9 fifth to Malchijah, the sixth to M',
Ne 10: 7 Meshullam, Abijah, M',

Mikloth (mik'-loth)
1Ch 8:32 And M' begat Shimeah. And
9:37 and Ahio, and Zechariah, and M'.
38 And M' begat Shimeam. And they
27: 4 his course was M' also the ruler:

Mikneiah (mik-ne-i'-ah)
1Ch 15:18, 21 M', and Obed-edom, and Jeiel,

Milalai (mil'-a-lahee)
Ne 12:36 and Azarael, M', Gilalai, Maai,

Milcah (mil'-cah)
Ge 11:29 and the name of Nahor's wife, M',
29 the father of M', and the father of
22:20 M', she hath also borne children
23 these eight M' did bear to Nahor,
24:15 who was born to Bethuel, son of M',
24 daughter of Bethuel the son of M',
47 son, whom M' bare unto him:
Nu 26:33 and Noah, Hoglah, M', and Tirzah.
27: 1 and Hoglah, and M', and Tirzah.
36:11 Tirzah, and Hoglah, and M', and
Jos 17: 3 and Noah, Hoglah, M', and Tirzah.

milch See also milk.
Ge 32:15 Thirty m' camels with their colts,
1Sa 6: 7 new cart, and take two m' kine,
10 took two m' kine, and tied them to

Milcom (mil'-com) See also Malcham; Molech.
1Ki 11: 5 after M' the abomination of the
33 and M' the god of the children of
2Ki 23:13 M' the abomination of the children

mildew
De 28:22 and with blasting, and with m';
1Ki 8:37 if there be pestilence, blasting, m',
2Ch 6:28 pestilence, if there be blasting, or m',

Am 4: 9 smitten you with blasting and m':
Hag 2:17 smote you with blasting and with m'

mile
M't 5:41 shall compel thee to go a m', go

Miletum (mi-le'-tum) See also Miletus.
2Ti 4:20 Trophimus have I left at M' sick.

Miletus (mi-le'-tus) See also Miletum.
Ac 20:15 and the next day we came to M'.
17 from M' he sent to Ephesus, and

milk See also milch.
Ge 18: 8 he took butter, and m', and the
49:12 wine, and his teeth white with m'.
Ex 3: 8 a land flowing with m' and honey;
17 a land flowing with m' and honey.
13: 5 a land flowing with m' and honey,
23:19 not seethe a kid in his mother's m'.
33: 3 a land flowing with m' and honey:
34:26 not seethe a kid in his mother's m'.
Le 20:24 that floweth with m' and honey:
Nu 13:27 it floweth with m' and honey; and
14: 8 which floweth with m' and honey.
16:13, 14 that floweth with m' and honey,
De 6: 3 that floweth with m' and honey.
11: 9 that floweth with m' and honey.
14:21 not seethe a kid in his mother's m'.
26: 9, 15 that floweth with m' and honey.
27: 3 that floweth with m' and honey;
31:20 that floweth with m' and honey;
32:14 Butter of kine, and m' of sheep,
Jos 5: 6 that floweth with m' and honey.
J'g 4:19 she opened a bottle of m', and gave
5:25 asked water, and she gave him m';
Job 10:10 thou not poured me out as m', and
21:24 His breasts are full of m', and his
Pr 27:27 have goats' m' enough for thy food,
30:33 the churning of m' bringeth forth
Ca 4:11 honey and m' are under thy tongue;
5: 1 I have drunk my wine with my m':
12 rivers of waters, washed with m',
Isa 7:22 abundance of m' that they shall
28: 9 them that are weaned from the m',
55: 1 buy wine and m' without money
60:16 also suck the m' of the Gentiles,
66:11 that ye may m' out, and be
Jer 11: 5 a land flowing with m' and honey,
32:22 a land flowing with m' and honey;
La 4: 7 than snow, they were whiter than m',
Eze 20: 6, 15 flowing with m' and honey,
25: 4 fruit, and they shall drink thy m'.
Joe 3:18 and the hills shall flow with m', and
1Co 3: 2 I have fed you with m', and not
9: 7 eateth not of the m' of the flock?
Heb 5:12 become such as have need of m',
13 every one that useth m' is unskilful
1Pe 2: 2 desire the sincere m' of the word,

mill See also mills; millstone.
Ex 11: 5 maidservant that is behind the m';
M't 24:41 shall be grinding at the m'; the

millet
Eze 4: 9 and lentiles, and m', and fitches,

millions
Ge 24:60 the mother of thousands of m',

Millo (mil'-lo)
J'g 9: 6 together, and all the house of M',
20 of Shechem, and the house of M';
20 and from the house of M', and
2Sa 5: 9 David built round about from M'
1Ki 9:15 and M', and the wall of Jerusalem,
24 built for her: then did he build M'.
11:27 Solomon built M', and repaired
2Ki 12:20 and slew Joash in the house of M',
1Ch 11: 8 about, even from M' round about:
2Ch 32: 5 repaired M' in the city of David,

mills
Nu 11: 8 and ground it in m', or beat it in a

millstone See also millstones.
De 24: 6 nether or the upper m' to pledge:
J'g 9:53 of a m' upon Abimelech's head,
2Sa 11:21 woman cast a piece of a m' upon him
Job 41:24 as hard as a piece of the nether m'.
M't 18: 6 a m' were hanged about his
M'r 9:42 a m' were hanged about his
Lu 17: 2 a m' were hanged about his
Re 18:21 took up a stone like a great m',
22 the sound of a m' shall be heard no

millstones
Isa 47: 2 Take the m', and grind meal:
Jer 25:10 sound of the m', and the light of

mincing
Isa 3:16 walking and m' as they go, and

mind See also minded; mindful; minding; minds.
Ge 23: 8 if it be your m' that I should bury
26:35 were a grief of m' unto Isaac and
Le 24:12 m' of the Lord might be shewed
Nu 16:28 not done them of mine own m'.
24:13 either good or bad of mine own m';
De 18: 6 come with all the desire of his m'
28:65 failing of eyes, and sorrow of m':
30: 1 thou shalt call them to m' among
1Sa 2:35 is in mine heart and in my m':
9:20 days ago, set not thy m' on them;
1Ch 22: 7 was in my m' to build an house
28: 9 heart and with a willing m': for
Ne 4: 6 for the people had a m' to work.
Job 23:13 he is in one m', and who can turn him?
34:33 Should it be according to thy m'?
Ps 31:12 forgotten as a dead man out of m':
Pr 21:27 he bringeth it with a wicked m'?
29:11 A fool uttereth all his m': but a

Isa 26: 3 peace, whose m' is stayed on thee:
46: 8 men: bring it again to m', O ye
65: 17 be remembered, nor come into m'.
Jer 3: 16 Lord: neither shall it come to m':
15: 1 yet my m' could not be toward this
19: 5 it, neither came it into my m':
32: 35 neither came it into my m', that
44: 21 them, and came it not into his m'?
51: 50 let Jerusalem come into your m'.
La 3: 21 This I recall to my m', therefore
Eze 11: 5 the things that come into your m',
20: 32 that which cometh into your m'
23: 17 her m' was alienated from them.
18 then my m' was alienated from her,
18 m' was alienated from her sister.
22 from whom thy m' is alienated, and
28 from whom thy m' is alienated:
38: 10 shall things come into thy m',
Da 2: 29 came into thy m' upon thy bed,
5: 20 up, and his m' hardened in pride,
Hab 1: 11 Then shall his m' change, and he
M't 22: 37 all thy soul, and with all thy m'.
M'r 5: 15 and clothed, and in his right m':
12: 30 all thy soul, and with all thy m',
14: 72 Peter called to m' the word that
Lu 1: 29 and cast in her m' what manner of
8: 35 Jesus, clothed, and in his right m':
10: 27 thy strength, and with all thy m';
12: 29 neither be ye of doubtful m'.
Ac 17: 11 the word with all readiness of m',
20: 19 the Lord with all humility of m',
Ro 1: 28 gave them over to a reprobate m',
7: 23 warring against the law of my m',
25 then with the m' I myself serve the
8: 5 flesh do m' the things of the flesh:
7 carnal m' is enmity against God:
27 knoweth what is the m' of the Spirit,
11: 34 hath known the m' of the Lord?
12: 2 by the renewing of your m', that
16 the same m' one toward another.
16 M' not high things, but condescend
14: 5 be fully persuaded in his own m'.
15: 6 may with one m' and one mouth
15 as putting you in m', because of
1Co 1: 10 joined together in the same m'
2: 16 who hath known the m' of the Lord,
16 him? But we have the m' of Christ.
2Co 7: 7 mourning, your fervent m' toward me:
8: 12 if there be first a willing m', it is
19 and declaration of your ready m':
9: 2 I know the forwardness of your m',
13: 11 be of one m', live in peace; and
Eph 2: 3 desires of the flesh and of the m';
4: 17 walk, in the vanity of the m',
23 renewed in the spirit of your m';
Ph'p 1: 27 with one m' striving together for
2: 2 being of one accord, of one m'.
3 in lowliness of m' let each esteem
5 Let this m' be in you, which was
3: 16 rule, let us m' the same thing.
19 shame, who m' earthly things.)
4: 2 they be of the same m' in the Lord.
Col 1: 21 enemies in your m' by wicked
2: 18 vainly puffed up by his fleshly m',
3: 12 humbleness of m', meekness,
2Th 2: 2 That ye be not soon shaken in m',
2Ti 1: 7 and of love, and of sound m'.
Tit 1: 15 their m' and conscience is defiled.
3: 1 Put them in m' to be subject to
Ph'm 14 But without thy m' would I do
Heb 8: 10 I will put my laws into their m',
1Pe 1: 13 gird up the loins of your m', be
3: 8 be ye all of one m', having
4: 1 likewise with the same m': for
5: 2 for filthy lucre, but of a ready m';
Re 17: 9 here is the m' which hath wisdom.
13 These have one m', and shall give

minded See also FEEBLEMINDED; HIGHMINDED; LIKEMINDED
Ru 1: 18 she was steadfastly m' to go with her.
2Ch 24: 4 was m' to repair the house
Ezr 7: 13 are m' of their own freewill to go up
M't 1: 19 was m' to put her away privily.
Ac 27: 39 shore, into the which they were m',
Ro 8: 6 to be carnally m' is death;
6 spiritually m' is life and peace.
2Co 1: 15 I was m' to come unto you before,
17 When I therefore was thus m', did
Gal 5: 10 that ye will be none otherwise m':
Ph'p 3: 15 as many as be perfect, be thus m':
15 if in any thing ye be otherwise m',
Ti 2: 6 likewise exhort to be sober m'.
Jas 1: 8 A double m' man is unstable in all
4: 8 purify your hearts, ye double m'.

mindful See also UNMINDFUL.
1Ch 16: 15 Be ye m' always of his covenant;
Ne 9: 17 neither were m' of thy wonders that
Ps 8: 4 is man, that thou art m' of him?
111: 5 he will ever be m' of his covenant.
115: 12 The Lord hath been m' of us: he
Isa 17: 10 hast not been m' of the rock of thy
2Ti 1: 4 being m' of thy tears, that I may
Heb 2: 6 is man, that thou art m' of him?
11: 15 they had been m' of that country
2Pe 3: 2 That ye may be m' of the words

minding
Ac 20: 13 appointed, m' himself to go afoot.

minds
J'g 19: 30 of it, take advice, and speak your m'.
2Sa 17: 8 they be chafed in their m', as a
2Ki 9: 15 If it be your m', then let none go
Eze 24: 25 whereupon they set their m', their
36: 5 all their heart, with despiteful m',
Ac 14: 2 made their m' evil affected against
28: 6 changed their m', and said that he
2Co 3: 14 But their m' were blinded: for until
4: 4 hath blinded the m' of them which
11: 3 so your m' should be corrupted
Ph'p 4: 7 keep your hearts and m' through
1Ti 6: 5 disputings of men of corrupt m',
2Ti 3: 8 men of corrupt m', reprobate
Heb 10: 16 and in their m' will I write them;
12: 3 be wearied and faint in your m'.
2Pe 3: 1 I stir up your pure m' by way of

mine[^] See also MY.
Ge 14: 22 I have lifted up m' hand unto the
15: 3 lo, one born in my house is m' heir.
24: 33 not eat, until I have told m' errand.
45 I had done speaking in m' heart,
30: 25 that I may go unto m' own place,
30 shall I provide for m' own house also?
31: 10 that I lifted up m' eyes, and saw in a
40 and my sleep departed from m' eyes.
42 God hath seen m' affliction and the
43 cattle, and all that thou seest is m':
41: 13 me he restored unto m' office, and
44: 21 me, that I may set m' eyes upon him.
48: 5 came unto thee into Egypt, are m';
5 Reuben and Simeon, they shall be m'.
Ex 7: 4 bring forth m' armies, and my people
5 I stretch forth m' hand upon Egypt,
17 with the rod that is in m' hand upon
13: 2 both of man and of beast: it is m'.
17: 9 hill with the rod of God in m' hand.
18: 4 of my father, said he, was m' help,
19: 5 all people: for all the earth is m':
20: 26 shalt thou go up by steps unto m' altar,
21: 14 shalt take him from m' altar, that he
23: 23 For m' Angel shall go before thee, and
32: 34 behold, m' Angel shall go before thee:
33: 23 And I will take away m' hand, and
34: 19 All that open the matrix is m'; and
Le 18: 4 keep m' ordinances, to walk therein:
30 Therefore shall ye keep m' ordinance,
20: 26 other people, that ye should be m'.
22: 9 shall therefore keep m' ordinance,
25: 23 be sold for ever: for the land is m';
Nu 3: 12 therefore the Levites shall be m';
13 Because all the first born are m';
13 m' shall they be: I am the Lord.
45 and the Levites shall be m': I am the
8: 14 of Israel: and the Levites shall be m'.
10: 30 but I will depart to m' own land, and
12: 7 not so, who is faithful in all m' house.
14: 28 as ye have spoken in m' ears, so will I
16: 28 I have not done them of m' own mind.
18: 8 thee the charge of m' heave offerings
22: 29 would there were a sword in m' hand,
23: 11 I took thee to curse m' enemies, and
24: 10 I called thee to curse m' enemies, and,
13 do either good or bad of m' own mind;
De 8: 17 My power and the might of m' hand
10: 3 having the two tables in m' hand.
26: 13 the hallowed things out of m' house,
29: 19 I walk in the imagination of m' heart,
32: 22 For a fire is kindled in m' anger, and
23 I will spend m' arrows upon them.
41 and m' hand take hold on judgment;
41 will render vengeance to m' enemies,
42 make m' arrows drunk with blood,
Jos 14: 7 him word again as it was in m' heart.
J'g 6: 36 If thou wilt save Israel by m' hand, as
37 that thou wilt save Israel by m' hand.
7: 2 saying, M' own hand hath saved me.
8: 7 Zebah and Zalmunna unto m' hand,
11: 30 the children of Ammon into m' hands,
16: 17 hath not come a rasor upon m' head;
17: 2 and spakest of also in m' ears, behold,
19: 23 that this man is come into m' house,
Ru 4: 6 myself, lest I mar m' own inheritance:
1Sa 2: 1 Lord, m' horn is exalted in the Lord:
1 mouth is enlarged over m' enemies;
28 be my priest, to offer upon m' altar,
29 ye at my sacrifice and at m' offering,
33 whom I shall not cut off from m' altar,
35 according to that which is in m' heart
35 shall walk before m' anointed for ever.
12: 3 I received any bribe to blind m' eyes
14: 24 that I may be avenged on m' enemies.
29 how m' eyes have been enlightened,
43 end of the rod that was in m' hand,
15: 14 this bleating of the sheep in m' ears,
17: 46 the Lord deliver thee into m' hand;
18: 17 said, Let not m' hand be upon him,
19: 17 me so, and sent away m' enemy,
20: 1 what is m' iniquity? and what is my
21: 3 give me five loaves of bread in m' hand,
4 is no common bread under m' hand,
23: 7 have delivered him into m' hand;
24: 6 to stretch forth m' hand against him,
10 delivered thee to day into m' hand
10 me kill thee: but m' eye spared thee;
10 not put forth m' hand against my
11 evil nor transgression in m' hand,
12, 13 but m' hand shall not be upon thee,
25: 33 avenging myself with m' own hand.
26: 11 m' hand against the Lord's anointed:
18 I done? or what evil is in m' hand?
23 m' hand against the Lord's anointed.
24 was much set by this day in m' eyes,
28: 2 make thee keeper of m' head for ever.
2Sa 5: 19 wilt thou deliver them into m' hand?
20 hath broken forth upon m' enemies
6: 22 and will be base in m' own sight:
11: 11 shall I then go into m' house, to eat
14: 5 woman, and m' husband is dead.
30 See, Joab's field is near m', and he
16: 12 the Lord will look on m' affliction,
18: 12 thousand shekels of silver in m' hand,
12 would I not put forth m' hand against
2Sa 18: 13 wrought falsehood against m' own life:
19: 37 that I may die in m' own city, and be
22: 4 so shall I be saved from m' enemies.
24 and have kept myself from m' iniquity.
35 a bow of steel is broken by m' arms.
38 I have pursued m' enemies, and
41 also given me the necks of m' enemies,
49 bringeth me forth from m' enemies:
1Ki 1: 33 my son to ride upon m' own mule,
48 throne this day, m' eyes even seeing it.
2: 22 for he is m' elder brother; even for
3: 26 Let it be neither m' nor thine, but
9: 3 m' eyes and m' [†] heart shall be there
10: 6 report that I heard in m' own land of
7 until I came, and m' eyes had seen it:
11: 21 that I may go to m' own country.
33 to do that which is right in m' eyes,
14: 8 that only which was right in m' eyes;
20: 3 Thy silver and thy gold is m'; thy
3 children, even the goodliest, are m'.
21: 20 Hast thou found me, O m' enemy?
2Ki 4: 13 I dwell among m' own people.
5: 26 Went not m' heart with thee, when
6: 32 hath sent to take away m' head?
10: 6 If ye be m', and if ye will hearken unto
30 that which is right in m' eyes, and
30 according to all that was in m' heart,
18: 34 delivered Samaria out of m' hand?
35 delivered their country out of m' hand,
35 deliver Jerusalem out of m' hand?
19: 28 thy tumult is come up into m' ears,
34 for m' own sake, and for my servant
20: 6 will defend this city for m' own sake,
15 All the things that are in m' house
21: 14 forsake the remnant of m' inheritance,
1Ch 12: 17 me, m' heart shall be knit unto you:
17 ye be come to betray me to m' enemies,
17 seeing there is no wrong in m' hands,
14: 10 wilt thou deliver them into m' hand?
11 in upon m' enemies by m' hand like
16: 22 Touch not m' anointed, and do my
17: 14 I will settle him in m' house and in
16 and what is m' house, that thou hast
22: 18 inhabitants of the land into m' hand;
28: 2 I had in m' heart to build an house of
29: 3 I have of m' own proper good, of gold
17 in the uprightness of m' heart I have
2Ch 7: 15 Now m' eyes shall be open, and
15 m' ears attent unto the prayer that is
16 m' eyes and...heart shall be there
16 eyes and m' heart shall be there
9: 5 report which I heard in m' own land
6 until I came, and m' eyes had seen it:
29: 10 it is in m' heart to make a covenant
32: 13 to deliver their lands out of m' hand?
14 deliver his people out of m' hand,
14 be able to deliver you out of m' hand?
15 to deliver his people out of m' hand,
15 your God deliver you out of m' hand?
17 delivered their people out of m' hand,
17 deliver his people out of m' hand.
Job 3: 10 womb, nor hid sorrow from m' eyes.
4: 12 and m' ear received a little thereof.
16 an image was before m' eyes, there
6: 11 and what is m' end, that I should
7: 7 wind: m' eye shall no more see good.
21 and take away m' iniquity? for now
9: 20 m' own mouth shall condemn me:
31 and m' own clothes shall abhor me.
10: 6 That thou enquirest after m' iniquity,
14 wilt not acquit me from m' iniquity.
15 therefore see thou m' affliction;
13: 1 Lo, m' eye hath seen all this,
1 m' ear hath heard and understood it.
14 my teeth, and put my life in m' hand?
15 I will maintain m' own ways before
23 How many are m' iniquities and sins?
14: 17 a bag, and thou sewest up m' iniquity.
16: 4 against you, and shake m' head at you.
9 m' enemy sharpeneth his eyes upon
17 Not for any injustice in m' hands: also
20 but m' eye poureth out tears unto God.
17: 2 and doth not m' eye continue in their
7 M' eye also is dim by reason of
13 If I wait, the grave is m' house: I
19: 4 erred, m' error remaineth with myself.
10 m' hope hath he removed like a tree.
13 m' acquaintance are verily estranged
15 They that dwell in m' house, and my
17 for the children's sake of m' own body.
27 m' eyes shall behold, and not another;
27: 5 till I die I will not remove m' integrity
7 Let m' enemy be as the wicked, and
31: 1 I made a covenant with m' eyes; why
6 that God may know m' integrity.
7 and m' heart walked after m' eyes,
7 if any blot hath cleaved to m' hands;
9 If m' heart have been deceived by a
12 and would root out all m' increase.
22 Then let m' arm fall from my shoulder
22 and m' arm be broken from the bone.
25 because m' hand hath gotten much;
33 by hiding m' iniquity in my bosom:
35 that m' adversary had written a book.
32: 6 and durst not shew you m' opinion.
10 to me; I also will shew m' opinion.
17 my part; I also will shew m' opinion.
33: 8 thou hast spoken in m' hearing, and
40: 4 I will lay m' hand upon my mouth.
41: 11 is under the whole heaven is m'.
42: 5 of the ear: but now m' eye seeth thee.
Ps 3: 3 my glory, and the lifter up of m' head.
7 for thou hast smitten all m' enemies
5: 8 righteousness because of m' enemies;
6: 7 M' eye is consumed because of grief;
7 waxeth old because of all m' enemies.

Ps 6:10 Let all m' enemies be ashamed and
7: 4 him that without cause is m' enemy:
5 earth, and lay m' honour in the dust.
6 because of the rage of m' enemies:
8 according to m' integrity that is in me.
9: 3 When m' enemies are turned back,
13: 2 how long shall m' enemy be exalted
3 lighten m' eyes, lest I sleep the sleep
4 Lest m' enemy say, I have prevailed
16: 5 Lord is the portion of m' inheritance
17: 3 Thou hast proved m' heart; thou hast
18: 3 so shall I be saved from m' enemies.
23 and I kept myself from m' iniquity.
34 a bow of steel is broken by m' arms.
37 I have pursued m' enemies, and
40 given me the necks of m' enemies;
48 He delivereth me from m' enemies:
23: 5 me in the presence of m' enemies:
25: 2 let not m' enemies triumph over me.
11 O Lord, pardon m' iniquity; for it is
15 M' eyes are ever toward the Lord; for
18 Look upon m' affliction and my pain;
19 Consider m' enemies; for they are
26: 1 for I have walked in m' integrity: I
3 thy lovingkindness is before m' eyes:
6 I will wash m' hands in innocency: so
11 as for me, I will walk in m' integrity:
27: 2 even m' enemies and my foes, came
6 now shall m' head be lifted up above
6 above m' enemies round about me:
11 in a plain path, because of m' enemies.
12 not over unto the will of m' enemies:
31: 9 m' eye is consumed with grief, yea,
10 faileth because of m' iniquity, and my
11 was a reproach among all m' enemies,
11 and a fear to m' acquaintance:
15 me from the hand of m' enemies, and
32: 5 thee, and m' iniquity have I not hid.
8 go: I will guide thee with m' eye.
35: 2 and buckler, and stand up for m' help.
13 prayer returned into m' own bosom.
15 But in m' adversity they rejoiced, and†
19 m' enemies wrongfully rejoice over
26 together that rejoice at m' hurt:
38: 4 For m' iniquities are gone over m' head:
10 as for the light of m' eyes, it also is
18 For I will declare m' iniquity; I will
19 But m' enemies are lively, and they
20 evil for good are m' adversaries;
39: 4 Lord, make me to know m' end, and
5 and m' age is as nothing before thee:
40: 6 desire; m' ears hast thou opened:
12 m' iniquities have taken hold upon me,
12 are more than the hairs of m' head:
41: 5 M' enemies speak evil of me, When
9 m' own familiar friend, in whom I
11 m' enemy doth not triumph over me.
12 thou upholdest me in m' integrity, and
42: 10 my bones, m' enemies reproach me;
49: 4 I will incline m' ear to a parable: I
50: 10 For every beast of the forest is m',
11 the wild beasts of the field are m'.
12 for the world is m', and the fulness
51: 2 Wash me throughly from m' iniquity,
9 my sins, and blot out all m' iniquities.
54: 4 Behold, God is m' helper: the Lord is
5 He shall reward evil unto m' enemies:
7 m' eye hath seen his desire upon m'
55: 13 But it was thou, a man m' equal, my
13 my guide, and m' acquaintance.
56: 2 M' enemies would daily swallow me
9 thee, then shall m' enemies turn back:
59: 1 Deliver me from m' enemies, O my
10 me see my desire upon m' enemies.
60: 7 Gilead is m', and Manasseh is m';
7 also is the strength of m' head;
69: 3 m' eyes fail while I wait for my God.
4 are more than the hairs of m' head:
4 me, being m' enemies wrongfully,
18 it: deliver me because of m' enemies.
19 m' adversaries are all before thee.
71: 10 For m' enemies speak against me;
77: 4 Thou holdest m' eyes waking: I am
6 I commune with m' own heart: and
88: 8 Thou hast put away m' acquaintance
9 M' eye mourneth by reason of
18 and m' acquaintance into darkness.
89: 21 m' arm also shall strengthen him.
92: 11 M' eye also shall see my desire on
11 shall see my desire on m' enemies,
11 and m' ears shall hear my desire of
101: 3 set no wicked thing before m' eyes:
6 M' eyes shall be upon the faithful of
102: 8 M' enemies reproach me all the day;
105: 15 Touch not m' anointed, and do my
108: 8 Gilead is m'; Manasseh is m';
8 also is the strength of m' head;
109: 20 this be the reward of m' adversaries
29 Let m' adversaries be clothed with
116: 8 soul from death, m' eyes from tears,
119: 11 Thy word have I hid in m' heart, that
18 Open thou m' eyes, that I may behold
37 Turn away m' eyes from beholding
82 M' eyes fail for thy word, saying,
92 then have perished in m' affliction.
98 made me wiser than m' enemies: for
112 I have inclined m' heart to perform
121 justice: leave me not to m' oppressors.
123 M' eyes fail for thy salvation, and for
136 Rivers of waters run down m' eyes,
139 m' enemies have forgotten thy words.
148 M' eyes prevent the night watches,
153 Consider m' affliction, and deliver me:
157 are my persecutors and m' enemies;
121: 1 I will lift up m' eyes unto the hills,
123: 1 Unto thee lift I up m' eyes, O thou that

Ps 131: 1 heart is not haughty, nor m' eyes lofty:
132: 4 I will not give sleep to m' eyes,
4 or slumber to m' eyelids,
17 have ordained a lamp for m' anointed.
139: 2 my downsitting and m' uprising,
22 hatred: I count them m' enemies.
141: 8 But m' eyes are unto thee, O God the
143: 9 Deliver me, O Lord, from m' enemies:
12 And of thy mercy cut off m' enemies,
Pr 5:13 inclined m' ear to them that instructed
23:15 my heart shall rejoice, even m'.
Ec 1:16 I communed with m' own heart,
2: 1 I said in m' heart, Go to now, I will
3 in m' heart to give myself unto wine,
3 acquainting m' heart with wisdom;
10 whatsoever m' eyes desired I kept not
3:17 I said in m' heart, God shall judge the
18 I said in m' heart concerning the
7:25 I applied m' heart to know, and to
8:16 I applied m' heart to know wisdom,
Ca 1: 6 but m' own vineyard have I not kept.
2:16 My beloved is m', and I am his: he
6: 3 my beloved's, and my beloved is m':
8:12 My vineyard, which is m', is before
Isa 1:15 hands, I will hide m' eyes from you:
16 of your doings from before m' eyes;
24 Ah, I will ease me of m' adversaries,
24 and avenge me of m' enemies:
5: 9 In m' ears said the Lord of hosts, Of a
6: 5 m' eyes have seen the King, the Lord
10: 5 O Assyrian, the rod of m' anger, and
5 staff in their hand is m' indignation.
25 and m' anger in their destruction.
13: 3 called my mighty ones for m' anger,
16: 4 Let m' outcasts dwell with thee,
11 and m' inward parts for Kir-haresh.
19:25 my hands, and Israel m' inheritance.
22:14 it was revealed in m' ears by the Lord
29:23 his children, the work of m' hands,
37:29 and thy tumult, is come into m' ears,
35 this city to save it for m' own sake,
38:12 M' age is departed, and is removed
14 m' eyes fail with looking upward: O
39: 4 All that is in m' house have they seen:
42: 1 m' elect, in whom my soul delighteth;
43: 1 called thee by thy name; thou art m'.
25 thy transgressions for m' own sake,
45: 4 my servant's sake, and Israel m' elect,
47: 6 I have polluted m' inheritance, and
48: 5 say, M' idol hath done them; and my
9 my name's sake will I defer m' anger,
11 For m' own sake, even for m' own sake,
13 M' hand also hath laid the foundation
49:22 I will lift up m' hand to the Gentiles,
50: 4 he wakeneth m' ear to hear as the
5 The Lord God hath opened m' ear,
8 who is m' adversary? let him come
11 This shall ye have of m' hand; ye
51: 5 and m' arms shall judge the people;
5 me, and on m' arm shall they trust.
16 covered thee in the shadow of m' hand,
56: 5 unto them will I give in m' house and
7 shall be accepted upon m' altar;
7 m' house shall be called an house of
60: 7 come up with acceptance on m' altar,
63: 3 for I will tread them in m' anger, and
4 the day of vengeance is in m' heart,
5 m' own arm brought salvation unto
6 tread down the people in m' anger,
65: 9 and m' elect shall inherit it, and my
12 but did evil before m' eyes, and did
16 and because they are hid from m' eyes.
22 m' elect shall long enjoy the work of
66: 2 all those things hath m' hand made,
4 but they did evil before m' eyes, and
Jer 2: 7 and made m' heritage an abomination.
3:12 not cause m' anger to fall upon you:
15 give you pastors according to m' heart,
7:20 m' anger and my fury shall be poured
9: 1 and m' eyes a fountain of tears, that I
11:15 hath my beloved to do in m' house,
12: 3 me, and tried m' heart toward thee:
7 I have forsaken m' house, I have left
7 I have left m' heritage; I have given
8 M' heritage is unto me as a lion in the
9 M' heritage is unto me as a speckled
14 Lord against all m' evil neighbours,
13:17 and m' eye shall weep sore, and run
14:17 Let m' eyes run down with tears night
15:14 for a fire is kindled in m' anger, which
16 me the joy and rejoicing of m' heart:
16:17 For m' eyes are upon all their ways:
17 is their iniquity hid from m' eyes.
18 they have filled m' inheritance with
21 them to know m' hand and my might;
17: 4 for ye have kindled a fire in m' anger,
18: 6 potter's hand, so are ye in m' hand, O
20: 9 his word was in m' heart as a burning
23: 9 M' heart within me is broken because
24: 6 I will set m' eyes upon them for good,
32: 8 Hanameel m' uncle's son came to me
12 the sight of Hanameel m' uncle's son,
31 been to me a provocation of m' anger
37 I have driven them in m' anger, and
33: 5 whom I have slain in m' anger and in
42:18 As m' anger and my fury hath been
44: 6 my fury and m' anger was poured
28 words shall stand, m', or theirs,
48:31 m' heart shall mourn for the men of
36 m' heart shall sound for Moab like
36 and m' heart shall sound like pipes for
50:11 O ye destroyers of m' heritage,
51:25 I will stretch out m' hand upon thee,
La 1:16 m' eye, m' eye runneth down with
19 and m' elders gave up the ghost in
20 m' heart is turned within me; for I

La 1:21 m' enemies have heard of my trouble,
2:11 M' eyes do fail with tears, my bowels
22 brought up hath m' enemy consumed.
3:19 Remembering m' affliction and my
48 M' eye runneth down with rivers of
49 M' eye trickleth down, and ceaseth
51 M' eye affecteth m' heart because of
52 M' enemies chased me sore, like a
54 Waters flowed over m' head; then I
Eze 5:11 neither shall m' eye spare, neither will
13 Thus shall m' anger be accomplished,
7: 3 I will send m' anger upon thee, and
4 m' eye shall not spare thee, neither
8 and accomplish m' anger upon thee:
9 And m' eye shall not spare, neither
8: 1 as I sat in m' house, and the elders of
3 and took me by a lock of m' head;
5 up m' eyes the way toward the north,
18 m' eye shall not spare, neither will I
18 they cry in m' ears with a loud voice,
9: 1 He cried also in m' ears with a loud
5 to the others he said in m' hearing,
10 m' eye shall not spare, neither will I
11:20 and keep m' ordinances, and do them:
12: 7 digged through the wall with m' hand;
13: 9 m' hand shall be upon the prophets
13 be an overflowing shower in m' anger,
14:13 then will I stretch out m' hand upon it,
16: 8 the Lord God, and thou becamest m'.
18 hast set m' oil and m' incense before
17:19 surely m' oath that he hath despised,
18: 4 Behold, all souls are m'; as the soul
4 so also the soul of the son is m':
20: 5 lifted up m' hand unto the seed of the
5 when I lifted up m' hand unto them,
6 that I lifted up m' hand unto them,
17 m' eye spared them from destroying
22 Nevertheless I withdrew m' hand,
23 I lifted up m' hand unto them also in
28 I lifted up m' hand to give it to them,
40 For in m' holy mountain, in the
42 I lifted up m' hand to give it to your
21:17 I will also smite m' hands together,
31 I will pour out m' indignation upon
22: 8 Thou hast despised m' holy things,
13 smitten m' hand at thy dishonest
20 so will I gather you in m' anger and
26 and have profaned m' holy things:
31 I poured out m' indignation upon
23: 4 and they were m', and they bare sons
5 played the harlot when she was m';
39 they done in the midst of m' house.
41 thou hast set m' incense and m' oil.
25: 7 I will stretch out m' hand upon thee,
13 also stretch out m' hand upon Edom,
14 shall do in Edom according to m' anger
16 out m' hand upon the Philistines,
29: 3 My river is m' own, and I have made it
9 The river is m', and I have made it.
35: 3 I will stretch out m' hand against thee,
10 and these two countries shall be m',
36: 7 I have lifted up m' hand, Surely the
21 But I had pity for m' holy name, which
22 but for m' holy name's sake, which ye
37:19 and they shall be one in m' hand.‡
43: 8 I have consumed them in m' anger.
44: 8 not kept the charge of m' holy things:
12 have I lifted up m' hand against them,
24 and my statutes in all m' assemblies;
47:14 I lifted up m' hand to give it unto your
Da 4: 4 I Nebuchadnezzar was...in m' house,
10 the visions of m' head in my bed;
34 lifted up m' eyes unto heaven, and
34 m' understanding returned unto me,
36 m' honour and brightness returned
8: 3 Then I lifted up m' eyes, and saw, and
10: 5 Then I lifted up m' eyes, and looked,
Ho 2: 5 wool and my flax, m' oil and my drink.
10 none shall deliver her out of m' hand.
8: 5 m' anger is kindled against them:
13 flesh for the sacrifices of m' offerings,
9:15 I will drive them out of m' house,
11: 8 m' heart is turned within me, my
9 not execute the fierceness of m' anger,
13:11 I gave thee a king in m' anger, and
14 repentance shall be hid from m' eyes.
14: 4 for m' anger is turned away from him.
Am 1: 8 I will turn m' hand against Ekron:
9: 2 hell, thence shall m' hand take them;
4 I will set m' eyes upon them for evil,
Jon 2: 2 I cried by reason of m' affliction unto
Mic 7: 8 Rejoice not against me, O m' enemy:
10 Then she that is m' enemy shall see it,
10 m' eyes shall behold her: now shall
Hab 1:12 O Lord my God, m' Holy One? we shall
3:19 make me to walk upon m' high places.
Zep 1: 4 also stretch out m' hand upon Judah,
3: 8 pour upon them m' indignation, even
10 my dispersed, shall bring m' offering.
Hag 1: 9 Because of m' house that is waste, and
2: 8 The silver is m', and the gold is m',
Zec 1:18 Then lifted I up m' eyes, and saw, and
2: 1 I lifted up m' eyes again, and looked,
9 I will shake m' hand upon them, and
5: 1 and lifted up m' eyes, and looked, and
9 Then lifted I up m' eyes, and looked,
6: 1 and lifted up m' eyes, and looked, and
8: 6 it also be marvellous in m' eyes?
9: 8 I will encamp about m' house because
8 for now have I seen with m' eyes.
10: 3 M' anger was kindled against the
11:14 I cut asunder m' other staff, even
12: 4 open m' eyes upon the house of Judah,
13: 7 will turn m' hand upon the little ones.
Mal 1: 6 I be a father, where is m' honour?
7 Ye offer polluted bread upon m' altar;

Mal 1:10 ye kindle fire on m' altar for nought.
3: 7 are gone away from m' ordinances,
10 that there may be meat in m' house,
17 shall be m', saith the Lord of hosts,
M't 7:24, 26 heareth these sayings of m',
20:15 me to do what I will with m' own?
23 not m' to give, but it shall be given
25:27 have received m' own with usury.
M'r 9:24 I believe; help thou m' unbelief.
10:40 and on my left hand is not m' to give;
Lu 1:44 thy salutation sounded in m' ears,
2:30 m' eyes have seen thy salvation.
9:38 my son: for he is m' only child.
11: 6 friend of m' in his journey is come
18: 3 saying, Avenge me of m' adversary.
19:23 have required m' own with usury?
27 those m' enemies, which would
Joh 2: 4 with thee? m' hour is not yet come.
5:30 I can of m' own self do nothing;
30 I seek not m' own will, but the will
6:38 not to do m' own will, but the will of
7:16 My doctrine is not m', but his that
8:50 I seek not m' own glory: there is
9:11 made clay, and anointed m' eyes,
15 He put clay upon m' eyes, and I
30 is, and yet he hath opened m' eyes.
10:14 my sheep, and am known of m'.
14:24 word which ye hear is not m', but
16:14 for he shall receive of m', and shall
15 things that the Father hath are m';
15 that he shall take of m', and shall
17:10 And all m' are thine, and thine, m';
Ac 11: 6 which when I had fastened m' eyes,
13:22 a man after m' own heart, which
21:13 ye to weep and to break m' heart?
26: 4 at the first among m' own nation
Ro 11:13 of the Gentiles, I magnify m' office:
12:19 Vengeance is m'; I will repay, saith
16:13 the Lord, and his mother and m'.
23 Gaius m' host, and of the whole
1Co 1:15 I had baptized in m' own name.
4: 3 yea, I judge not m' own self.
9: 2 for the seal of m' apostleship are
3 M' answer to them that do examine
10:33 not seeking m' own profit, but the
16:21 of me Paul with m' own hand.
2Co 11:26 in perils by m' own countrymen, in
30 which concern m' infirmities.
12: 5 will not glory, but in m' infirmities.
Ga 1:14 many my equals in m' own nation,
6:11 unto you with m' own hand.
Ph'p 1: 4 in every prayer of m' for you all
3: 9 not having m' own righteousness,
2Th 3:17 of Paul with m' own hand, which
Tit 1: 4 m' own son after the common faith:
Ph'm 12 him, that is, m' own bowels:
18 thee ought, put that on m' account;
19 Paul have written it with m' own hand,
Re 22:16 sent m' angel to testify unto you

mingle See also MINGLED.
Isa 5:22 of strength to m' strong drink:
Da 2:43 m' themselves with the seed of

mingled
Ex 9:24 was hail, and fire m' with the hail,
29:40 of flour m' with the fourth part of
Le 2: 4 cakes of fine flour m' with oil, or
5 fine flour unleavened, m' with oil.
7:10 every meat offering, m' with oil,
12 unleavened cakes m' with oil, and
12 and cakes m' with oil, of fine flour,
9: 4 and a meat offering m' with oil: for
14:10 flour for a meat offering m' with oil.
21 flour m' with oil for a meat offering,
19:19 not sow thy field with m' seed:
19 a garment m' of linen and woollen
23:13 tenth deals of fine flour m' with oil,
Nu 6:15 cakes of fine flour m' with oil, and
7:13, 19, 25, 31, 37, 43, 49, 55, 61, 67, 73,
79 full of fine flour m' with oil for a
8: 8 even fine flour m' with oil, and
15: 4 m' with the fourth part of an hin of
6 m' with the third part of an hin of
9 of flour m' with half a hin of oil.
28: 5 m' with the fourth part of an hin of
9, 12, 12 a meat offering, m' with oil,
13 tenth deal of flour m' with oil for a
20 offering shall be of flour m' with oil:
28 meat offering of flour m' with oil,
29: 3 offering shall be of flour m' with oil,
9, 14 shall be of flour m' with oil,
Ezr 9: 2 the holy seed have m' themselves
Ps 102: 9 and m' my drink with weeping,
106:35 were m' among the heathen, and
Pr 9: 2 she hath m' her wine; she hath
5 drink the wine which I have m'.
Isa 19:14 The Lord hath m' a perverse spirit
Jer 25:20 And all the m' people, and all the
24 all the kings of the m' people that
50:37 upon all the m' people that are in the
Ezr 30: 5 all the m' people, and Chub, and
M't 27:34 him vinegar to drink m' with gall:
M'r 15:23 him to drink wine m' with myrrh:
Lu 13: 1 Pilate had m' with their sacrifices.
Re 8: 7 followed hail and fire m' with blood,
15: 2 it were a sea of glass m' with fire:

Miniamin (*min'-e-a-min*) See also MIAMIN.
2Ch 31:15 were Eden, and M', and Jeshua,
Ne 12:17 Of Abijah, Zichri; of M',...Moadiah,
41 the priests; Eliakim, Maaseiah, M',

minish See also DIMINISH; MINISHED.
Ex 5:19 not m' ought from your bricks of

minished See also DIMINISHED.
Ps 107:39 they are m' and brought low

minister See also ADMINISTER; MINISTERED; MINISTERETH; MINISTERING; MINISTERS.
Ex 24:13 rose up, and his m' Joshua: and
28: 1 may m' unto me in the priest's office,
3, 4 m' unto me in the priest's office.
35 And it shall be upon Aaron to m':
41 may m' unto me in the priest's office.
43 the altar to m' in the holy place;
29: 1 to m' unto me in the priest's office:
30 cometh...to m' in the holy place.
44 sons, to m' to me in the priest's office.
30:20 they come near to the altar to m',
30 may m' unto me in the priest's office.
31:10 his sons, to m' in the priest's office,
35:19 sons, to m' in the priest's office.
39:26 about the hem of the robe to m' in;
41 to m' in the priest's office.
40:13 may m' unto me in the priest's office.
15 may m' unto me in the priest's office:
Le 7:35 to m' unto the Lord in the priest's
16:32 consecrate to m' in the priest's office
Nu 1:50 and they shall m' unto it, and shall
3: 3 consecrated to m' in the priest's office.
6 priest, that they may m' unto him.
31 the sanctuary wherewith they m',
4: 9 thereof, wherewith they m' unto it:
12 wherewith they m' in the sanctuary,
14 wherewith they m' about it, even
8:26 But shall m' with their brethren in
16: 9 the congregation to m' unto them?
18: 2 joined unto thee, and m' unto thee:
2 thou and thy sons with thee shall m'
De 10: 8 before the Lord to m' unto him,
17:12 that standeth to m' there before the
18: 5 stand to m' in the name of the Lord,
7 he shall m' in the name of the Lord
21: 5 God hath chosen to m' unto him,
Jos 1: 1 Joshua the son of Nun, Moses' m',
1Sa 2:11 And the child did m' unto the Lord
1Ki 8:11 the priests could not stand to m'
1Ch 15: 2 of God, and to m' unto him for ever.
16: 4 Levites to m' before the ark of the
37 to m' before ark continually, as
23:13 before the Lord, to m' unto him, and
26:12 to m' in the house of the Lord.
2Ch 5:14 the priests could not stand to m' by
8:14 to praise and m' before the priests,
13:10 the priests, which m' unto the Lord,
23: 6 and they that m' of the Levites;
24:14 even vessels to m', and to offer
29:11 ye should m' unto him, and burn
31: 2 to m', and to give thanks, and to
Ne 10:36 that m' in the house of our God:
39 priests that m', and the porters,
Ps 9: 8 shall m' judgment to the people in
Isa 60: 7 rams of Nebaioth...m' unto thee:
10 and their kings shall m' unto thee:
Jer 33:22 and the Levites that m' unto me.
Eze 40:46 near to the Lord to m' unto him.
42:14 lay their garments wherein they m';
43:19 approach unto me, to m' unto me,
44:11 stand before them to m' unto them.
15 come near to me to m' unto me,
16 near to my table, to m' unto me,
17 m' in the gates of the inner court,
27 inner court, to m' in the sanctuary,
45: 4 shall come near to m' unto the Lord:
M't 20:26 among you, let him be your m';
28 to be ministered unto, but to m',
25:44 prison, and did not m' unto thee?
M'r 10:43 among you, shall be your m':
45 to be ministered unto, but to m',
Lu 4:20 he gave it again to the m', and sat
Ac 13: 5 and they had also John to their m'.
24:23 none...to m' or come unto him.
26:16 to make thee a m' and a witness
Ro 13: 4 is the m' of God to thee for good.
4 he is the m' of God, a revenger to
15: 8 a m' of the circumcision for the
16 I should be the m' of Jesus Christ
25 Jerusalem to m' unto the saints.
27 to m' unto them in carnal things.
1Co 9:13 they which m' about holy things
2Co 9:10 sower both m' bread for your food,
Ga 2:17 is therefore Christ the m' of sin?
Eph 3: 7 Whereof I was made a m', according
4:29 it may m' grace unto the hearers.
6:21 a beloved brother and faithful m'
Col 1: 7 is for you a faithful m' of Christ;
23 whereof I Paul am made a m';
25 Whereof I am made a m', according
4: 7 a faithful m' and fellowservant in
1Th 3: 2 our brother, and m' of God, and our
1Ti 1: 4 m' questions, rather than godly
4: 6 shalt be a good m' of Jesus Christ,
Heb 1:14 sent forth to m' for them who shall
6:10 ministered to the saints, and do m'.
8: 2 A m' of the sanctuary, and of the
1Pe 1:12 but unto us they did m' the things,
4:10 even so m' the same one to another,
11 if any man m', let him do it as of

ministered
Nu 3: 4 Ithamar m' in the priest's office
De 10: 6 his son m' in the priest's office in
1Sa 2:18 Samuel m' before the Lord, being
3: 1 the child Samuel m' unto the Lord
2Sa 13:17 called his servant that m' unto him,
1Ki 1: 4 cherished the king, and m' to him:
15 the Shunammite m' unto the king.
19:21 went after Elijah, and m' unto him.
2Ki 25:14 vessels of brass wherewith they m',
1Ch 6:32 m' before the dwelling place of the
28: 1 companies that m' to the king by
2Ch 22: 8 of Ahaziah, that m' to Ahaziah, he
Es 2: 2 king's servants that m' unto him,
6: 3 king's servants that m' unto him,

Jer 52:18 vessels of brass wherewith they m',
Eze 44:12 they m' unto them before their idols,
19 their garments wherein they m',
Da 7:10 thousand thousands m' unto him,
M't 4:11 angels came and m' unto him.
8:15 and she arose, and m' unto them.
20:28 Son of man came not to be m' unto,
M'r 1:13 beasts; and the angels m' unto him.
31 left her, and she m' unto them.
10:45 Son of man came not to be m' unto,
15:41 followed him, and m' unto him;)
Lu 4:39 she arose and m' unto them.
8: 3 m' unto him of their substance.
Ac 13: 2 As they m' to the Lord, and fasted,
19:22 two of them that m' unto him,
20:34 hands have m' unto my necessities,
2Co 3: 3 to be the epistle of Christ m' by us,
Ph'p 2:25 and he that m' to my wants.
Col 2:19 and bands having nourishment m',
2Ti 1:18 things he m' unto me at Ephesus,
Ph'm 13 might have m' unto me in the bonds
Heb 6:10 m' to the saints, and do minister.
2Pe 1:11 an entrance shall be m' unto you

ministereth
2Co 9:10 Now he that m' seed to the sower
Ga 3: 5 therefore that m' to you the Spirit,

ministering
1Ch 9:28 had the charge of the m' vessels,
Eze 44:11 of the house, and m' to the house:
M't 27:55 Jesus from Galilee, m' unto him:
Ro 12: 7 Or ministry, let us wait on our m':
15:16 the Gentiles, m' the gospel of God,
2Co 8: 4 fellowship of the m' to the saints.
9: 1 as touching the m' to the saints,
Heb 1:14 Are they not all m' spirits, sent
10:11 every priest standeth daily m' and

ministers
1Ki 10: 5 attendance of his m', and their
2Ch 9: 4 attendance of his m', and their
Ezr 7:24 or m' of this house of God,
8:17 that they should bring unto us m'
Ps 103:21 ye m' of his, that do his pleasure.
104: 4 angels spirits; his m' a flaming fire:
Isa 61: 6 shall call you the M' of our God:
Jer 33:21 with the Levites the priests, my m'.
Eze 44:11 they shall be m' in my sanctuary,
45: 4 the priests the m' of the sanctuary,
5 the Levites, the m' of the house,
46:24 with the m' of the house shall boil
Joe 1: 9 the priests, the Lord's m', mourn.
13 howl, ye m' of the altar: come, lie
13 night in sackcloth, ye m' of my God:
2:17 Let the priests, the m' of the Lord,
Lu 1: 2 eyewitnesses, and m' of the word;
Ro 13: 6 for they are God's m', attending
1Co 3: 5 m' by whom ye believed, even as
4: 1 account of us, as of...m' of Christ,
2Co 3: 6 hath made us able m' of the new
6: 4 approving ourselves as...m' of God,
11:15 thing if his m' also be transformed
15 as the m' of righteousness; whose
23 Are they m' of Christ? (I speak as a
Heb 1: 7 spirits, and his m' a flame of fire.

ministration
Lu 1:23 days of his m' were accomplished,
Ac 6: 1 were neglected in the daily m'.
2Co 3: 7 But if the m' of death, written and
8 m' of the spirit be rather glorious?
9 if the m' of condemnation be glory,
9 m' of righteousness exceed in glory.
9:13 Whiles by the experiment of this m'

ministry
Nu 4:12 take all the instruments of m',
47 came to do the service of the m',
2Ch 7: 6 when David praised by their m';
Ho 12:10 by the m' of the prophets.
Ac 1:17 and had obtained part of this m'.
25 That he may take part of this m'
6: 4 prayer, and to the m' of the word.
12:25 when they had fulfilled their m',
20:24 and the m', which I have received
21:19 among the Gentiles by his m'.
Ro 12: 7 Or m', let us wait on...ministering;
1Co 16:15 addicted...to the m' of the saints,)
2Co 4: 1 Therefore seeing we have this m',
5:18 given to us the m' of reconciliation;
6: 3 thing, that the m' be not blamed:
Eph 4:12 for the work of the m', for the
Col 4:17 Take heed to the m' which thou hast
1Ti 1:12 faithful, putting me into the m';
2Ti 4: 5 evangelist, make full proof of thy m'.
11 for he is profitable to me for the m'.
Heb 8: 6 he obtained a more excellent m',
9:21 and all the vessels of the m'.

Minni (*min'-ni*)
Jer 51:27 the kingdoms of Ararat, M', and

Minnith (*min'-nith*)
J'g 11:33 Aroer, even till thou come to M',
Eze 27:17 traded in thy market wheat of M',

minstrel See also MINSTRELS.
2Ki 3:15 But now bring me a m'. And it
15 came to pass, when the m' played,

minstrels
M't 9:23 m' and the people making a noise,

mint
M't 23:23 ye pay the tithe of m' and anise
Lu 11:42 ye tithe m' and rue and all manner

Miphkad (*mif'-kad*)
Ne 3:31 over against the gate M',

miracle See also MIRACLES.
Ex 7: 9 you, saying, Shew a *m'* for you:
M'r 6:52 considered not the *m'* of the loaves:
9:39 which shall do a *m'* in my name,
Lu 23: 8 hoped to have seen some *m'* done
Joh 4:54 again the second *m'* that Jesus did,
6:14 they had seen the *m'* that Jesus did,
10:41 him, and said, John did no *m'*:
12:18 heard that he had done this *m'*.
Ac 4:16 notable *m'* hath been done by them
22 this *m'* of healing was shewed.

miracles
Nu 14:22 and my *m'*, which I did in Egypt
De 11: 3 his *m'*, and his acts, which he did
29: 3 the signs, and those great *m'*:
J'g 6:13 and where be all his *m'* which our
Joh 2:11 beginning of *m'* did Jesus in Cana
23 they saw the *m'* which he did.
3: 2 can do these *m'* that thou doest,
6: 2 because they saw his *m'* which he
26 seek me, not because ye saw the *m'*,
7:31 will he do more *m'* than these
9:16 man that is a sinner do such *m'*?
11:47 we? for this man doeth many *m'*.
12:37 though he had done so many *m'*
Ac 2:22 approved of God among you by *m'*
6: 8 did great wonders and *m'* among
8: 6 and seeing the *m'* which he did.
13 the *m'* and signs which were done.
15:12 *m'* and wonders God had wrought
19:11 special *m'* by the hands of Paul:
1Co 12:10 To another the working of *m'*; to
28 after that *m'*, then gifts of healings,
29 all teachers? are all workers of *m'*?
Ga 3: 5 worketh *m'* among you, doeth he it
Heb 2: 4 and wonders, and with divers *m'*,
Re 13:14 those *m'* which he had power to do
16:14 the spirits of devils, working *m'*,
19:20 the false prophet that wrought *m'*

mire
2Sa 22:43 them as the *m'* of the street, and
Job 8:11 Can the rush grow up without *m'*?
30:19 He hath cast me into the *m'*, and
41:30 sharp pointed things upon the *m'*.
Ps 69: 2 I sink in deep *m'*, where there is
14 Deliver me out of the *m'*, and let
Isa 10: 6 down like the *m'* of the streets.
57:20 whose waters cast up *m'* and dirt.
Jer 38: 6 there was no water, but *m'*:
6 so Jeremiah sunk in the *m'*.
22 thy feet are sunk in the *m'*, and
Mic 7:10 down as the *m'* of the streets.
Zec 9: 3 fine gold as the *m'* of the streets.
10: 5 enemies in the *m'* of the streets in
2Pe 2:22 washed to her wallowing in the *m'*.

Miriam (*mir'-e-am*) See also MARY.
Ex 15:20 *M'* the prophetess, the sister of
21 *M'* answered them, Sing ye to the
Nu 12: 1 *M'* and Aaron spake against Moses
4 unto *M'*, Come out ye three unto
5 and called Aaron and *M'*: and they
10 *M'* became leprous, white as snow:
10 Aaron looked upon *M'*, and, behold,
15 *M'* was shut out from the camp
15 not till *M'* was brought in again.
20: 1 and *M'* died there, and was buried
26:59 and Moses, and *M'* their sister.
De 24: 9 what the Lord thy God did unto *M'*
1Ch 4:17 and she bare *M'*, and Shammai,
6: 3 Aaron, and Moses, and *M'*. The
Mic 6: 4 before thee Moses, Aaron, and *M'*.

Mirma (*mur'-mah*)
1Ch 8:10 And Jeuz, and Shachia, and *M'*.

mirth
Ge 31:27 have sent thee away with *m'*, and
Ne 8:12 portions, and to make great *m'*,
Ps 137: 3 that wasted us required of us *m'*,
Pr 14:13 and the end of that *m'* is heaviness.
Ec 2: 1 to now, I will prove thee with *m'*,
2 is mad: and of *m'*, What doeth it?
7: 4 heart of fools is in the house of *m'*.
8:15 Then I commended *m'*, because a
Isa 24: 8 The *m'* of tabrets ceaseth, the
11 the *m'* of the land is gone.
Jer 7:34 the voice of *m'*, and the voice of
16: 9 and in your days, the voice of *m'*,
25:10 will take from them the voice of *m'*,
Eze 21:10 glitter: should we then make *m'*?
Ho 2:11 will also cause all her *m'* to cease,

miry
Ps 40: 2 an horrible pit, out of the *m'* clay,
Eze 47:11 But the *m'* places thereof and the
Da 2:41 the iron mixed with *m'* clay.
43 sawest iron mixed with *m'* clay,

miscarrying
Ho 9:14 give them a *m'* womb and dry

mischief See also MISCHIEFS.
Ge 42: 4 Lest peradventure *m'* befall him.
38 if *m'* befall him by the way in the
44:29 this also from me, and *m'* befall him,
Ex 21:22 from her, and yet no *m'* follow:
23 if any *m'* follow, then thou shalt
32:12 For *m'* did he bring them out, to
22 the people, that they are set on *m'*.
1Sa 23: 9 secretly practised *m'* against him;
2Sa 16: 8 thou art taken in thy *m'*, because
1Ki 11:25 beside the *m'* that Hadad did: and
20: 7 and see how this man seeketh *m'*:
2Ki 7: 9 light, some *m'* will come upon us:
Ne 6: 2 But they thought to do me *m'*.
Es 8: 3 tears to put away the *m'* of Haman
Job 15:35 They conceive *m'*, and bring forth
Ps 7:14 iniquity, and hath conceived *m'*,
16 His *m'* shall return upon his own
10: 7 under his tongue is *m'* and vanity.
14 for thou beholdest *m'* and spite, to
26:10 In whose hands is *m'*, and their
28: 3 but *m'* is in their hearts.
36: 4 He deviseth *m'* upon his bed; he
52: 1 Why boastest thou thyself in *m'*,
55:10 *m'* also and sorrow are in the midst
62: 3 will ye imagine *m'* against a man?
94:20 thee, which frameth *m'* by a law?
119:150 draw nigh that follow after *m'*:
140: 9 *m'* of their own lips cover them.
Pr 4:16 not, except they have done *m'*;
6:14 he deviseth *m'* continually; he
18 feet that be swift in running to *m'*,
10:23 It is as sport to a fool to do *m'*:
11:27 he that seeketh *m'*, it shall come
12:21 the wicked shall be filled with *m'*.
13:17 wicked messenger falleth into *m'*:
17:20 a perverse tongue falleth into *m'*.
24: 2 and their lips talk of *m'*.
16 but the wicked shall fall into *m'*.
28:14 his heart shall fall into *m'*.
Isa 47:11 *m'* shall fall upon thee; thou shalt
59: 4 they conceive *m'*, and bring forth
Eze 7:26 *M'* shall come upon *m'*, and
11: 2 these are the men that devise *m'*,
Da 11:27 king's hearts shall be to do *m'*,
Ho 7:15 do they imagine *m'* against me.
Ac 13:10 O full of all subtilty and all *m'*,

mischiefs
De 32:23 I will heap *m'* upon them; I will
Ps 52: 2 Thy tongue deviseth *m'*; like a
140: 2 Which imagine *m'* in their hearts;

mischievous
Ps 21:11 they imagined a *m'* device, which
38:12 that seek my hurt speak *m'* things,
Pr 24: 8 evil shall be called a *m'* person.
Ec 10:13 the end of his talk is *m'* madness.
Mic 7: 3 man, he uttereth his *m'* desire:

miserable
Job 16: 2 things: *m'* comforters are ye all.
1Co 15:19 Christ, we are of all men most *m'*.
Re 3:17 that thou art wretched, and *m'*,

miserably
M't 21:41 will *m'* destroy those wicked men,

miseries
La 1: 7 days of her affliction and of her *m'*
Jas 5: 1 weep and howl for your *m'* that

misery See also MISERABLE; MISERIES.
J'g 10:16 was grieved for the *m'* of Israel.
Job 3:20 is light given to him that is in *m'*,
11:16 Because thou shalt forget thy *m'*,
Pr 31: 7 and remember his *m'* no more.
Ec 8: 6 the *m'* of man is great upon him.
La 3:19 mine affliction and my *m'*, the
Ro 3:16 and *m'* are in their ways:

Misgab (*mis'-gab*)
Jer 48: 1 *M'* is confounded and dismayed.

Mishael (*mish'-a-el*) See also MISHAL.
Ex 6:22 And the sons of Uzziel; *M'*, and
Lev 10: 4 Moses called *M'* and Elzaphan,
Ne 8: 4 on his left hand, Pedaiah, and *M'*,
Da 1: 6 of Judah, Daniel, Hananiah, *M'*,
7 and to *M'*, of Meshach; and to
11 had set over Daniel, Hananiah, *M'*,
19 none like Daniel, Hananiah, *M'*,
2:17 the thing known to Hananiah, *M'*,

Mishal (*mi'-shal*) See also MISHAEL.
Jos 21:30 of Asher, *M'* with her suburbs,

Misham (*mi'-sham*)
1Ch 8:12 and *M'*, and Shamed, who built

Misheal (*mish'-e-al*)
Jos 19:26 Alammelech, and Amad, and *M'*;

Mishma (*mish'-mah*)
Ge 25:14 And *M'*, and Dumah, and Massa,
1Ch 1:30 *M'*, and Dumah, Massa, Hadad,
4:25 son, Mibsam his son, *M'* his son.
26 And the sons of *M'*; Hamuel his

Mishmannah (*mish-man'-nah*)
1Ch 12:10 *M'* the fourth, Jeremiah the fifth,

Mishpat See EN-MISHPAT.

Mishraites (*mish'-ra-ites*)
1Ch 2:53 and the Shumathites, and the *M'*;

Mispereth (*mis-pe'-reth*) See also MIZPAR.
Ne 7: 7 Bilshan, *M'*, Bigvai, Nehum,

Misrephoth-maim (*mis"-re-foth-mah'-yim*) See also ZAREPHATH.
Jos 11: 8 unto great Zidon, and unto *M'*,
13: 6 country from Lebanon unto *M'*,

miss See also AMISS; MISSED; MISSING; MISCARRYING; MISUSED.
J'g 20:16 at an hair breadth, and not *m'*.
1Sa 20: 6 If thy father at all *m'* me, then

missed
1Sa 20:18 and thou shalt be *m'*, because thy
25:15 not hurt, neither *m'* we any thing,
21 nothing was *m'* of all that pertained

missing
1Sa 25: 7 neither was there ought *m'* unto
1Ki 20:39 if by any means he be *m'*, then shall

mist
Ge 2: 6 there went up a *m'* from the earth,
Ac 13:11 fell on him a *m'* and a darkness;
2Pe 2:17 the *m'* of darkness is reserved for

mistress
Ge 16: 4 her *m'* was despised in her eyes.
8 flee from the face of my *m'* Sarai.
9 said unto her, Return to thy *m'*,
1Ki 17:17 the *m'* of the house, fell sick; and
2Ki 5: 3 And she said unto her *m'*, Would
Ps 123: 2 maiden unto the hand of her *m'*;
Pr 30:23 handmaid that is heir to her *m'*.
Isa 24: 2 as with the maid, so with her *m'*;
Na 3: 4 the *m'* of witchcrafts, that selleth

misused
2Ch 36:16 and *m'* his prophets, until the

mite See also MITES.
Lu 12:59 till thou hast paid the very last *m'*.

mites
M'r 12:42 and she threw in two *m'*, which
Lu 21: 2 widow casting in thither two *m'*.

Mithcah (*mith'-cah*)
Nu 33:28 from Tarah, and pitched in *M'*.
29 they went from *M'*, and pitched in

Mithnite (*mith'-nite*)
1Ch 11:43 Maachah, and Joshaphat the *M'*,

Mithredath (*mith'-re-dath*)
Ezr 1: 8 by the hand of *M'* the treasurer,
4: 7 Artaxerxes wrote Bishlam, *M'*,

mitre
Ex 28: 4 broidered coat, a *m'*, and a girdle:
37 lace, that it may be upon the *m'*;
37 the forefront of the *m'* it shall be.
39 shalt make the *m'* of fine linen, and
29: 6 shalt put the *m'* upon his head, and
6 put the holy crown upon the *m'*.
39:28 And a *m'* of fine linen, and goodly
31 to fasten it on high upon the *m'*;
Le 8: 9 And he put the *m'* upon his head;
9 also upon the *m'*, even upon his
16: 4 and with the linen *m'* shall he be
Zec 3: 5 them set a fair *m'* upon his head.
5 So they set a fair *m'* upon his head,

Mitylene (*mit-i-le'-ne*)
Ac 20:14 we took him in, and came to *M'*.

mixed See also MIXT.
Ex 12:38 a *m'* multitude went up also with
Ne 13: 3 from Israel all the *m'* multitude.
Pr 23:30 wine; they that go to seek *m'* wine.
Isa 1:22 dross, thy wine *m'* with water:
Da 2:41 sawest the iron *m'* with miry clay.
43 thou sawest iron *m'* with miry clay,
43 even as iron is not *m'* with clay.
Ho 7: 8 he hath *m'* himself among the
Heb 4: 2 not being *m'* with faith in them

mixt See also MIXED
Nu 11: 4 the *m'* multitude that was among them

mixture
Ps 75: 8 the wine is red; it is full of *m'*;
Joh 19:39 brought a *m'* of myrrh and aloes,
Re 14:10 is poured out without *m'* into the

Mizar (*mi'-zar*)
Ps 42: 6 the Hermonites, from the hill *M'*.

Mizpah (*miz'-pah*) See also MIZPEH.
Ge 31:49 *M'*; for he said, the Lord watch
1Ki 15:22 them Geba of Benjamin, and *M'*.
2Ki 25:23 there came to Gedaliah to *M'*, even
25 Chaldees that were with him at *M'*.
2Ch 16: 6 he built therewith Geba and *M'*.
Ne 3: 7 and of *M'*, unto the throne of the
15 Col-hozeh, the ruler of part of *M'*;
19 the son of Jeshua, the ruler of *M'*,
Jer 40: 6 Gedaliah the son of Ahikam to *M'*;
8 they came to Gedaliah to *M'*, even
10 for me, behold, I will dwell at *M'*,
12 land of Judah, to Gedaliah, unto *M'*,
13 the fields, came to Gedaliah to *M'*,
15 spake to Gedaliah in *M'* secretly,
41: 1 Gedaliah the son of Ahikam to *M'*;
1 they did eat bread together in *M'*.
3 at *M'*, and the Chaldeans that were
6 went forth from *M'* to meet them,
10 of the people that were in *M'*,
10 all the people that remained in *M'*,
14 had carried away captive from *M'*
16 from *M'*, after that he had slain
Ho 5: 1 ye have been a snare on *M'*,

Mizpar (*miz'-par*) See also MISPERETH.
Ezr 2: 2 Bilshan, *M'*, Bigvai, Rehum,

Mizpeh (*miz'-peh*) See also MIZPAH; RAMATHAIM-ZOPHIM.
Jos 11: 3 under Hermon in the land of *M'*.
8 unto the valley of *M'* eastward;
15:38 And Dilean, and *M'*, and Joktheel,
18:26 *M'*, and Chephirah, and Mozah,
J'g 10:17 together, and encamped in *M'*.
11:11 all his words before the Lord in *M'*.
29 and passed over *M'* of Gilead, and
29 from *M'* of Gilead he passed over
34 came to *M'* unto his house, and,
20: 1 land of Gilead, unto the Lord in *M'*.
3 of Israel were gone up to *M'*.)
21: 1 the men of Israel had sworn in *M'*,
5 came not up to the Lord to *M'*,
8 of Israel that came not up to *M'* to
1Sa 7: 5 said, Gather all Israel to *M'*, and
6 they gathered together to *M'*,
6 Samuel judged...of Israel in *M'*.
7 were gathered together to *M'*,
11 the men of Israel went out of *M'*,
12 and set it between *M'* and Shen,
16 to Beth-el, and Gilgal, and *M'*, and
10:17 together unto the Lord to *M'*
22: 3 David went thence to *M'* of Moab:

Mizraim (*miz'-ra-im*) See also ABEL-MIZRAIM; EGYPT.
Ge 10: 6 sons of Ham; Cush, and *M'*, and
13 And *M'* begat Ludim, and Anamim,
1Ch 1: 8 The sons of Ham; Cush, and *M'*,
11 And *M'* begat Ludim, and Anamim,

Mizzah (*miz'-zah*)
Ge 36: 13 and Zerah, Shammah, and *M'*:
17 Zerah, duke Shammah, duke *M'*:
1Ch 1: 37 Nahath, Zerah, Shammah, and *M'*.

Mnason (*na'-son*)
Ac 21: 16 with them one *M'* of Cyprus, an

Moab (*mo'-ab*) See also MOABITE; PAHATH-MOAB.
Ge 19: 37 a son, and called his name *M'*:
36: 35 who smote Midian in the field of *M'*,
Ex 15: 15 the mighty men of *M'*, trembling
Nu 21: 11 the wilderness which is before *M'*,
13 for Arnon is the border of *M'*,
13 between *M'* and the Amorites.
15 Ar, and lieth upon the border of *M'*.
20 in the country of *M'*, to the top of
26 against the former king of *M'*, and
28 it hath consumed Ar of *M'*, and the
29 Woe to thee, *M'*! thou art undone,
22: 1 pitched in the plains of *M'* on this
3 *M'* was sore afraid of the people,
3 *M'* was distressed because of the
4 *M'* said unto the elders of Midian,
7 the elders of *M'* and the elders of
8 princes of *M'* abode with Balaam.
10 king of *M'*, hath sent unto me,
14 the princes of *M'* rose up, and they
21 and went with the princes of *M'*.
36 out to meet him unto a city of *M'*,
23: 6 he, and all the princes of *M'*.
7 king of *M'* hath brought me from
17 and the princes of *M'* with him.
24: 17 and shall smite the corners of *M'*,
25: 1 whoredom with the daughters of *M'*.
26: 3 spake with them in the plains of *M'*
63 children of Israel in the plains of *M'*
31: 12 unto the camp at the plains of *M'*,
33: 44 in Ije-abarim, in the border of *M'*.
48 and pitched in the plains of *M'* by
49 Abel-shittim in the plains of *M'*.
50 spake unto Moses in...plains of *M'*
35: 1 spake unto Moses in the plains of *M'*
36: 13 children of Israel in the plains of *M'*
De 1: 5 this side Jordan, in the land of *M'*,
2: 8 by the way of the wilderness of *M'*.
18 over through Ar, the coast of *M'*,
29: 1 children of Israel in the land of *M'*,
32: 49 which is in the land of *M'*, that is
34: 1 went up from the plains of *M'* unto
5 Lord died there in the land of *M'*,
6 him in a valley in the land of *M'*,
8 wept for Moses in the plains of *M'*
Jos 13: 32 for inheritance in the plains of *M'*,
24: 9 the son of Zippor, king of *M'*, arose
J'g 3: 12 strengthened Eglon the king of *M'*
14 Israel served Eglon the king of *M'*
15 present unto Eglon the king of *M'*.
17 the present unto Eglon king of *M'*:
28 took the fords of Jordan toward *M'*,
29 slew of *M'* at that time about ten
30 *M'* was subdued that day under
10: 6 gods of Zidon, and the gods of *M'*,
11: 15 Israel took not away the land of *M'*,
17 they sent unto the king of *M'*: but
18 land of Edom, and the land of *M'*,
18 by the east side of the land of *M'*,
18 came not within the border of *M'*:
18 for Arnon was the border of *M'*.
25 the son of Zippor, king of *M'*?
Ru 1: 1 to sojourn in the country of *M'*, he,
2 they came into the country of *M'*,
4 them wives of the women of *M'*;
6 return from the country of *M'*:
6 had heard in the country of *M'* how
22 returned out of the country of *M'*:
2: 6 Naomi out of the country of *M'*:
4: 3 come again out of the country of *M'*,
1Sa 12: 9 and into the hand of the king of *M'*,
14: 47 enemies on every side, against *M'*,
22: 3 David went thence to Mizpeh of *M'*:
3 and he said unto the king of *M'*,
4 brought them before the king of *M'*:
2Sa 8: 2 he smote *M'*, and measured them
12 and of *M'*, and of the children of
23: 20 he slew two lionlike men of *M'*: he
1Ki 11: 7 for Chemosh, the abomination of *M'*,
2Ki 1: 1 *M'* rebelled against Israel after the
3: 4 king of *M'* was a sheepmaster, and
5 the king of *M'* rebelled against the
7 king of *M'* hath rebelled against
7 go with me against *M'* to battle?
10 to deliver them into the hand of *M'*!
13 to deliver them into the hand of *M'*.
23 now therefore, *M'*, to the spoil.
26 king of *M'* saw that the battle
1Ch 1: 46 smote Midian in the field of *M'*,
4: 22 who had the dominion in *M'*, and
8: 8 begat children in the country of *M'*,
11: 22 he slew two lionlike men of *M'*:
18: 2 And he smote *M'*; and the Moabites
11 from *M'*, and from the children of
2Ch 20: 1 that the children of *M'*, and the
10 the children of Ammon and *M'* and
22 against the children of Ammon, *M'*,
23 children of Ammon and *M'* stood up
Ne 13: 23 of Ashdod, of Ammon, and of *M'*:
Ps 60: 8 *M'* is my washpot; over Edom will
83: 6 of *M'*, and the Hagarenes;
108: 9 *M'* is my washpot; over Edom will
Isa 11: 14 lay their hand upon Edom and *M'*;
15: 1 The burden of *M'*. Because in the
1 in the night Ar of *M'* is laid waste,
1 in the night Kir of *M'* is laid waste,
2 *M'* shall howl over Nebo, and over
4 armed soldiers of *M'* shall cry out;
5 My heart shall cry out for *M'*; his
8 round about the borders of *M'*;
9 lions upon him that escapeth of *M'*,
16: 2 the daughters of *M'* shall be at the
4 mine outcasts dwell with thee, *M'*;
6 We have heard of the pride of *M'*;
7 Therefore shall *M'* howl for *M'*,
11 shall sound like an harp for *M'*, and
12 that *M'* is weary on the high place,
13 Lord hath spoken concerning *M'*
14 the glory of *M'* shall be contemned,
25: 10 *M'* shall be trodden down under
Jer 9: 26 *M'*, and all that are in the utmost
25: 21 and *M'*, and the children of Ammon,
27: 3 of Edom, and to the king of *M'*,
40: 11 when all the Jews that were in *M'*,
48: 1 Against *M'* thus saith the Lord of
2 There shall be no more praise of *M'*:
4 *M'* is destroyed; her little ones
9 Give wings unto *M'*, that it may
11 *M'*...been at ease from his youth,
13 *M'* shall be ashamed of Chemosh,
15 *M'* is spoiled, and gone up out of
16 The calamity of *M'* is near to come,
18 the spoiler of *M'* shall come upon
20 *M'* is confounded; for it is broken
20 ye it in Arnon, that *M'* is spoiled,
24 upon all the cities of the land of *M'*,
25 The horn of *M'* is cut off, and his
26 *M'* also shall wallow in his vomit,
28 O ye that dwell in *M'*, leave the
29 We have heard the pride of *M'*, (he
31 Therefore will I howl for *M'*, and I
31 and I will cry out for all *M'*; mine
33 field, and from the land of *M'*;
35 I will cause to cease in *M'*, saith
36 heart shall sound for *M'* like pipes,
38 upon all the housetops of *M'*, and in
38 for I have broken *M'* like a vessel
39 *M'* turned the back with shame!
39 *M'* be a derision and a dismaying
40 and shall spread his wings over *M'*.
41 mighty men's hearts in *M'* at that
42 *M'* shall be destroyed from being
43 be upon thee, O inhabitant of *M'*,
44 I will bring upon it, even upon *M'*,
45 and shall devour the corner of *M'*,
46 Woe be unto thee, O *M'*! the people
47 I bring again the captivity of *M'*
47 Thus far is the judgment of *M'*.
Eze 25: 8 Because that *M'* and Seir do say,
9 open the side of *M'* from the cities,
11 I will execute judgments upon *M'*;
Da 11: 41 even Edom, and *M'*, and the chief
Am 2: 1 For three transgressions of *M'*,
2 But I will send a fire upon *M'*, and
2 and *M'* shall die with tumult, with
Mic 6: 5 what Balak king of *M'* consulted,
Zep 2: 8 I have heard the reproach of *M'*,
9 Surely *M'* shall be as Sodom, and

Moabite (*mo'-ab-ite*) See also MOABITES; MOABITESS; MOABITISH.
De 23: 3 Ammonite or *M'* shall not enter
1Ch 11: 46 sons of Elnaam, and Ithmah the *M'*,
Ne 13: 1 and the *M'* shall not come into the

Moabites (*mo'-ab-ites*)
Ge 19: 37 the same is the father of the *M'*
Nu 22: 4 son of Zippor was king of the *M'*
De 2: 9 Distress not the *M'*, neither
11 but the *M'* call them Emims.
29 *M'* which dwell in Ar, did unto me;)
J'g 3: 28 delivered your enemies the *M'* into
2Sa 8: 2 so the *M'* became David's servants,
1Ki 11: 1 of Pharaoh, women of the *M'*,
33 Chemosh the god of the *M'*, and
2Ki 3: 18 deliver the *M'* also into your hand.
21 *M'* heard that the kings were come
22 the *M'* saw the water on the other
24 rose up and smote the *M'*, so that
24 they went forward smiting the *M'*,
13: 20 bands of the *M'* invaded the land
23: 13 Chemosh the abomination of...*M'*,
24: 2 the Syrians, and bands of the *M'*,
1Ch 18: 2 the *M'* became David's servants,
Ezr 9: 1 the *M'*, the Egyptians, and the

Moabitess (*mo'-ab-i-tess*)
Ru 1: 22 and Ruth the *M'*, her daughter in
2: 2 And Ruth the *M'* said unto Naomi,
21 Ruth the *M'* said, He said unto me
4: 5 must buy it also of Ruth the *M'*,
10 Moreover Ruth the *M'*, the wife of
2Ch 24: 26 the son of Shimrith a *M'*.

Moabitish (*mo'-ab-i-tish*)
Ru 2: 6 It is the *M'* damsel that came back

Moadiah (*mo-ad-i'-ah*) See also MAADIAH.
Ne 12: 17 Zichri; of Miniamin, of *M'*, Piltai;

moan See BEMOAN.

mock See also MOCKED; MOCKEST; MOCKETH; MOCKING.
Ge 39: 14 in an Hebrew unto us to *m'* us;
17 unto us, came in unto me to *m'* me:
Job 13: 9 mocketh another, do ye so *m'* him?
21: 3 after that I have spoken, *m'* on.
Pr 1: 26 I will *m'* when your fear cometh;
14: 9 Fools make a *m'* at sin: but among
Jer 38: 19 into their hand, and they *m'* me.
La 1: 7 her, and did *m'* at her sabbaths.
Eze 22: 5 be far from thee, shall *m'* thee,
M't 20: 19 deliver him to the Gentiles to *m'*,
M'r 10: 34 they shall *m'* him, and shall scourge
Lu 14: 29 all that behold it begin to *m'* him,

mocked
Ge 19: 14 one that *m'* unto his sons in law.
Nu 22: 29 the ass, Because thou hast *m'* me:
J'g 16: 10, 13 hast *m'* me, and told me lies:
15 thou hast *m'* me these three times,
1Ki 18: 27 pass at noon, that Elijah *m'* them,
2Ki 2: 23 children out of the city, and *m'* him,
2Ch 30: 10 them to scorn, and *m'* them.
36: 16 But they *m'* the messengers of God,
Ne 4: 1 great indignation, and *m'* the Jews.
Job 12: 4 I am as one *m'* of his neighbour,
M't 2: 16 that he was *m'* of the wise men,
27: 29 the knee before him, and *m'* him,
31 after that they had *m'* him, they
M'r 15: 20 And when they had *m'* him, they
Lu 18: 32 shall be *m'*, and spitefully entreated,
22: 63 and the men that held Jesus *m'* him,
23: 11 war set him at nought, and *m'* him,
36 the soldiers also *m'* him, coming
Ac 17: 32 resurrection of the dead, some *m'*:
Ga 6: 7 Be not deceived; God is not *m'*: for

mocker See also MOCKERS.
Pr 20: 1 Wine is a *m'*, strong drink is

mockers
Job 17: 2 Are there not *m'* with me? and
Ps 35: 16 With hypocritical *m'* in feasts, they
Isa 28: 22 therefore be ye not *m'*, lest your
Jer 15: 17 sat not in the assembly of the *m'*,
Jude 18 there should be *m'* in the last time,

mockest
Job 11: 3 when thou *m'*, shall no man make

mocketh
Job 13: 9 or as one man *m'* another, do ye so
39: 22 He *m'* at fear, and is not affrighted;
Pr 17: 5 Whoso *m'* the poor reproacheth
30: 17 The eye that *m'* at his father, and
Jer 20: 7 in derision daily, every one *m'* me.

mocking See also MOCKINGS.
Ge 21: 9 she had born unto Abraham, *m'*.
Eze 22: 4 heathen, and a *m'* to all countries.
M't 27: 41 Likewise also the chief priests *m'*
M'r 15: 31 Likewise also the chief priests *m'*
Ac 2: 13 Others *m'* said, These men are full

mockings
Heb 11: 36 trial of cruel *m'* and scourgings,

moderately
Joe 2: 23 given you the former rain *m'*,

moderation
Ph'p 4: 5 Let your *m'* be known unto all

modest
1Ti 2: 9 adorn themselves in *m'* apparel,

moist
Nu 6: 3 nor eat *m'* grapes, or dried.

moistened
Job 21: 24 his bones are *m'* with marrow.

moisture
Ps 32: 4 my *m'* is turned into the drought of
Lu 8: 6 it withered...because it lacked *m'*.

Moladah (*mo-la'-dah*)
Jos 15: 26 Amam, and Shema, and *M'*,
19: 2 Beer-sheba, and Sheba, and *M'*,
1Ch 4: 28 they dwelt at Beer-sheba, and *M'*,
Ne 11: 26 And at Jeshua, and at *M'*, and at

mole See also MOLES.
Le 11: 30 lizard, and the snail, and the *m'*.

Molech (*mo'-lek*) See also MALCHAM; MOLOCH.
Le 18: 21 seed pass through the fire to *M'*,
20: 2 that giveth any of his seed unto *M'*;
3 he hath given of his seed unto *M'*,
4 when he giveth of his seed unto *M'*,
5 to commit whoredom with *M'*, from
1Ki 11: 7 is before Jerusalem, and for *M'*,
2Ki 23: 10 to pass through the fire to *M'*.
Jer 32: 35 to pass through the fire unto *M'*;

moles
Isa 2: 20 worship, to the *m'* and to the bats;

Molid (*mo'-lid*)
1Ch 2: 29 and she bare him Ahban, and *M'*.

mollified
Isa 1: 6 up, neither *m'* with ointment.

Moloch (*mo'-loch*) See also MILCHOM; MOLECH.
Am 5: 26 borne the tabernacle of your *M'*
Ac 7: 43 ye took up the tabernacle of *M'*,

molten See also MELTED.
Ex 32: 4 after he had made it a *m'* calf:
8 they have made them a *m'* calf, and
34: 17 Thou shalt make thee no *m'* gods.
Le 19: 4 nor make to yourselves *m'* gods: I
Nu 33: 52 and destroy all their *m'* images, and
De 9: 12 they have made them a *m'* image.
16 God, and had made you a *m'* calf:
27: 15 maketh any graven or *m'* image, an
J'g 17: 3, 4 a graven image and a *m'* image:
18: 14 a graven image, and a *m'* image?
17 the teraphim, and the *m'* image:
18 the teraphim, and the *m'* image.
1Ki 7: 16 made two chapiters of *m'* brass,
23 he made a *m'* sea, ten cubits from
30 the laver were undersetters *m'*, at
33 and their spokes, were all *m'*.
14: 9 thee other gods, and *m'* images,
2Ki 17: 16 made them *m'* images, even two

2Ch 4: 2 made a m' sea of ten cubits from
28: 2 made also m' images for Baalim.
34: 3 carved images, and the m' images.
4 carved images, and the m' images,
Ne 9:18 they had made them a m' calf,
Job 28: 2 and brass is m' out of the stone.
37:18 strong, and as a m' looking glass?
Ps 106:19 and worshipped the m' image.
Isa 30:22 ornament of thy m' images of gold:
41:29 m' images are wind and confusion.
42:17 say to the m' images, Ye are our
44:10 god, or m' a graven image that is
48: 5 my m' image, hath commanded
Jer 10:14 for his m' image is falsehood, and
51:17 for his m' image is falsehood, and
Eze 24:11 the filthiness of it may be m' in it,
Ho 13: 2 them m' images of their silver,
Mic 1: 4 mountains shall be m' under him,
Na 1:14 graven image and the m' image:
Hab 2:18 the m' image, and a teacher of lies,

moment
Ex 33: 5 up into the midst of thee in a m',
Nu 16:21 that I may consume them in a m'.
45 I may consume them as in a m'.
Job 7:18 morning, and try him every m'?
20: 5 joy of the hypocrite but for a m'?
21:13 and in a m' go down to the grave.
34:20 In a m' shall they die, and the
Ps 30: 5 For his anger endureth but a m';
73:19 brought into desolation, as in a m'!
Pr 12:19 but a lying tongue is but for a m'.
Isa 26:20 thyself as it were for a little m',
27: 3 I will water it every m': lest any
47: 9 things shall come to thee in a m' in
54: 7 a small m' have I forsaken thee;
8 I hid my face from thee for a m';
Jer 4:20 spoiled, and my curtains in a m'.
La 4: 6 that was overthrown as in a m', and
Eze 26:16 and shall tremble at every m', and
32:10 shall tremble at every m', and they
Lu 4: 5 kingdoms of the world in a m' of
1Co 15:52 In a m', in the twinkling of an eye,
2Co 4:17 affliction, which is but for a m',

money^ See also MONEYCHANGERS.
Ge 17:12 or bought with m' of any stranger,
13 he that is bought with thy m', must
23 all that were bought with his m',
27 and bought with m' of the stranger,
23: 9 for as much m' as it is worth he
13 I will give thee m' for the field;
31:15 hath quite devoured also our m'.
33:19 for an hundred pieces of m'.
42:25 to restore every man's m' into his
27 he espied his m'; for, behold, it was
28 My m' is restored; and, lo, it is
35 man's bundle of m' was in his sack:
35 their father saw the bundles of m',
43:12 And take double m' in your hand;
12 the m' that was brought again in
15 they took double m' in their hand,
18 m' that was returned in our sacks
21 m' was in the mouth of his sack,
21 of his sack, our m' in full weight:
22 other m' have we brought down in
22 tell who put our m' in our sacks.
23 in your sacks: I had your m'.
44: 1 every man's m' in his sack's mouth.
2 of the youngest, and his corn m'.
8 Behold, the m', which we found in
47:14 Joseph gathered up all the m' that
14 Joseph brought...m' into Pharaoh's
15 when m' failed in the land of Egypt,
15 in thy presence? for the m' faileth.
16 give you for your cattle, if m' fail.
18 my lord, how that our m' is spent;
Ex 12:44 man's servant that is bought for m',
21:11 shall she go out free without m'.
21 not be punished: for he is his m'.
30 If there be laid on him a sum of m',
34 give m' unto the owner of them;
35 the live ox, and divide the m' of it;
22: 7 deliver unto his neighbour m' or
17 pay m' according to the dowry of
25 If thou lend m' to any of my people
30:16 thou shalt take the atonement m'
Le 22:11 priest buy any soul with his m',
25:37 not give him thy m' upon usury,
51 out of the m' that he was bought
27:15 fifth part of the m' of thy estimation
18 priest shall reckon unto him the m'
19 fifth part of the m' of thy estimation
Nu 3:48 thou shalt give the m', wherewith
49 Moses took the redemption m' of
50 children of Israel took he the m';
51 And Moses gave the m' of them that
18:16 for the m' of five shekels, after the
De 2: 6 Ye shall buy meat of them for m',
6 shall also buy water of them for m',
28 Thou shalt sell me meat for m',
28 give me water for m', that I may
14:25 Then shalt thou turn it into m',
25 and bind up the m' in thine hand,
26 And thou shalt bestow that m' for
21:14 thou shalt not sell her at all for m',
23:19 usury of m', usury of victuals, usury
J'g 5:19 Megiddo; they took no gain of m'.
16:18 her, and brought m' in their hand.
17: 4 he restored the m' unto his mother;
1Ki 21: 2 will give thee the worth of it in m'.
6 him, Give me thy vineyard for m';
15 he refused to give thee for m': for
2Ki 5:26 Is it a time to receive m', and to
12: 4 All the m' of the dedicated things
4 the m' of every one that passeth the
4 the m' that every man is set at, and

2Ki 12: 4 the m' that cometh into any man's
7 no more m' of your acquaintance,
8 receive no more m' of the people,
9 the m' that was brought into the
10 there was much m' in the chest,
10 the m' that was found in the house
11 And they gave the m', being told,
13 m' that was brought into the house
15 the m' to be bestowed on workmen:
16 The trespass m' and sin m' was not
15:20 Menahem exacted the m' of Israel,
22: 7 made with them of the m' that
9 Thy servants have gathered the m'
23:35 but he taxed the land to give the m'
2Ch 24: 5 of all Israel m' to repair the house
11 they saw that there was much m',
11 and gathered m' in abundance.
14 brought the rest of the m' before
34: 9 delivered the m' that was brought
14 when they brought out the m' that
17 they have gathered together the m'
Ezr 3: 7 They gave m' also unto the masons,
7:17 mayest buy speedily with this m'
Ne 5: 4 have borrowed m' for the king's
10 might exact of them m' and corn:
11 also the hundredth part of the m',
Es 4: 7 the m' that Haman had promised
Job 31:39 eaten the fruits thereof without m',
42:11 man also gave him a piece of m',
Ps 15: 5 putteth not out his m' to usury,
Pro 7:20 hath taken a bag of m' with him,
Ec 7:12 is a defence, and m' is a defence:
10:19 merry: but m' answereth all things.
Isa 43:24 bought me no sweet cane with m',
52: 3 ye shall be redeemed without m'.
55: 1 the waters, and he that hath no m';
1 milk without m' and without price.
2 do ye spend m' for that which is not
Jer 32: 9 weighed him the m', even seventeen
10 weighed him the m' in the balances.
25 Buy thee the field for m', and take
44 Men shall buy fields for m', and
La 5: 4 We have drunken our water for m';
Mic 3:11 the prophets thereof divine for m':
M't 17:24 that received tribute m' came to
27 thou shalt find a piece of m': that
22:19 Shew me the tribute m'. And they
25:18 in the earth, and hid his lord's m'.
27 have put my m' to the exchangers,
28:12 they gave large m' unto the soldiers,
15 So they took the m', and did as they
M'r 6: 8 no bread, no m' in their purse:
12:41 the people cast m' into the treasury:
14:11 glad, and promised to give him m'.
Lu 9: 3 nor scrip, neither bread, neither m';
19:15 to whom he had given the m', that
23 not thou my m' into the bank, that
22: 5 glad, and covenanted to give him m'.
Joh 2:14 and the changers of m' sitting:
15 poured out the changers' m', and
Ac 4:37 land, sold it, and brought the m',
7:16 Abraham bought for a sum of m' of
8:18 was given, he offered them m',
20 Thy m' perish with thee, because
20 of God may be purchased with m'.
24:26 hoped also that m' should have
1Ti 6:10 the love of m' is the root of all evil:

moneychangers
M't 21:12 and overthrew the tables of the m',
M'r 11:15 and overthrew the tables of the m',

monsters
La 4: 3 the sea m' draw out the breast,

month See also MONTHS.
Ge 7:11 m', the seventeenth day of the m',
8: 4 the ark rested in the seventh m',
4 the seventeenth day of the m', upon
5 continually until the tenth m':
5 in the tenth m', on the first day of the
5 on the first day of the m', were the
13 first year, in the first m', the first
13 the first day of the m', the waters
14 And in the second m', on the seven
14 seven and twentieth day of the m',
29:14 abode with him the space of a m'.
Ex 12: 2 This m' shall be unto you the
2 be the first m' of the year to you.
3 the tenth day of this m' they shall
6 the fourteenth day of the same m':
18 In the first m', on the fourteenth day
18 fourteenth day of the m' at even,
18 one and twentieth day of the m' at
13: 4 This day came ye out in the m' Abib.
5 shalt keep this service in this m'.
16: 1 on the fifteenth day of the second m'
19: 1 In the third m', when the children
23:15 the time appointed of the m' Abib;
34:18 thee, in the time of the m' Abib:
18 the m' Abib thou camest out from
40: 2 first day of the first m' shalt thou
17 in the first m' in the second year,
17 on the first day of the m', that the
Lev 16:29 seventh m', on...tenth day of the m',
23: 5 the fourteenth day of the first m' at
6 on the fifteenth day of the same m'
24 seventh m', in...first day of the m',
27 tenth day of this seventh m' there
32 in the ninth day of the m' at even,
34 The fifteenth day of this seventh m'
39 the fifteenth day of the seventh m',
41 shall celebrate it in the seventh m'.
25: 9 on the tenth day of the seventh m',
27: 6 from a m' old even unto five years
Nu 1: 1, 18 on the first day of the second m',
3:15 every male from a m' old and

Nu 3:22, 28, 34, 39 from a m' old and upward
40 children of Israel from a m' old and
43 names, from a m' old and upward,
9: 1 in the first m' of the second year
3 In the fourteenth day of this m', at
5 on the fourteenth day of the first m'
11 The fourteenth day of the second m'
22 or a m', or a year, that the cloud
10:11 the twentieth day of the second m',
11:20 even a whole m', until it come out
21 flesh, that they may eat a whole m'.
18:16 from a m' old shalt thou redeem,
20: 1 the desert of Zion in the first m':
26:62 males from a m' old and upward:
28:14 is the burnt offering of every m'
16 the fourteenth day of the first m'
17 in the fifteenth day of this m' is the
29: 1 And in the seventh m', on the first
1 first day of the m', ye shall have an
6 Beside the burnt offering of the m',
7 on the tenth day of this seventh m'
12 the fifteenth day of the seventh m'
33: 3 from Rameses in the first m',
3 on the fifteenth day of the first m';
38 in the first day of the fifth m'.
De 1: 3 eleventh m', on...first day of the m',
16: 1 Observe the m' of Abib, and keep
1 for in the m' of Abib the Lord thy
21:13 her father and her mother a full m':
Jos 4:19 on the tenth day of the first m',
5:10 on the fourteenth day of the m' at
1Sa 20:27 was the second day of the m', that
34 no meat the second day of the m':
1Ki 4: 7 each man his m' in a year made
27 table, every man in his m': they
5:14 ten thousand a m' by courses:
14 a m' they were in Lebanon, and two
6: 1 the m' Zif, which is the second m',
37 of the Lord laid, in the m' Zif:
38 in the eleventh year, in the m' Bul,
38 Bul, which is the eighth m',
8: 2 at the feast of the m' Ethanim,
2 Ethanim, which is the seventh m'.
12:32 ordained a feast in the eighth m',
32 on the fifteenth day of the m', like
33 the fifteenth day of the eighth m',
33 even in the m' which he had devised
2Ki 15:13 he reigned a full m' in Samaria.
25: 1 tenth m', in...tenth day of the m',
3 on the ninth day of the fourth m'
8 fifth m', on...seventh day of the m',
25 it came to pass in the seventh m',
27 king of Judah, in the twelfth m',
27 seven and twentieth day of the m',
1Ch 12:15 went over Jordan in the first m',
27: 1 came in and went out m' by m'
2 for the first m' was Jashobeam the
3 captains of the host for the first m'.
4 course of the second m' was Dodai
5 host for the third m' was Benaiah
7 for the fourth m' was Asahel the
8 for the fifth m' was Shamhuth the
9 captain for the sixth m' was Ira the
10 for the seventh m' was Helez the
11 for the eighth m' was Sibbecai the
12 captain for the ninth m' was Abiezer
13 for the tenth m' was Maharai the
14 for the eleventh m' was Benaiah
15 for the twelfth m' was Heldai the
2Ch 3: 2 in the second day of the second m',
5: 3 feast which was in the seventh m'.
7:10 and twentieth day of the seventh m'
15:10 at Jerusalem in the third m', in
29: 3 year of his reign, in the first m',
17 first day of the first m' to sanctify,
17 on the eighth day of the m' came
17 sixteenth day of the first m' they
30: 2 keep the passover in the second m'.
13 unleavened bread in the second m',
15 fourteenth day of the second m':
31: 7 the third m' they began to lay the
7 finished them in the seventh m'.
35: 1 the fourteenth day of the first m'.
Ezr 3: 1 when the seventh m' was come, and
6 first day of the seventh m' began
8 second m', began Zerubbabel the
6:15 on the third day of the m' Adar,
19 the fourteenth day of the first m'.
7: 8 came to Jerusalem in the fifth m',
9 first day of the first m' began he to
9 first day of the fifth m' came he to
8:31 on the twelfth day of the first m',
10: 9 the ninth m', on the twentieth day
9 twentieth day of the m'; and all the
16 down in the first day of the tenth m'
17 wives by the first day of the first m'.
Ne 1: 1 it came to pass in the m' Chisleu, in
2: 1 it came to pass in the m' Nisan, in
6:15 twenty and fifth day of the m' Elul,
7:73 and when the seventh m' came, the
8: 2 upon the first day of the seventh m'.
14 in the feast of the seventh m':
9: 1 twenty and fourth day of this m'
Es 2:16 tenth m', which is the m' Tebeth,
3: 7 the first m', that is, the m' Nisan,
7 from day to day, and from m' to m',
7 to the twelfth m', that is,...Adar.
7 the twelfth...that is, the m' Adar.
12 the thirteenth day of the first m',
13 twelfth m', which is the m' Adar,
8: 9 the third m', that is, the m' Sivan,
12 twelfth m', which is the m' Adar.
9: 1 the twelfth m', that is, the m' Adar,
15 fourteenth day also of the m' Adar,
17 the thirteenth day of the m' Adar;
19 fourteenth day of the m' Adar a day

Es 9:21 the fourteenth day of the m' Adar,
22 the m' which was turned unto them
Jer 1: 3 Jerusalem captive in the fifth m'.
2:24 in her m' they shall find her.
28: 1 the fourth year, and in the fifth m',
17 the same year in the seventh m'.
36: 9 the ninth m', that they proclaimed a
22 in the winterhouse in the ninth m':
39: 1 the tenth m', came Nebuchadrezzar
2 fourth m', the ninth day of the m',
41: 1 it came to pass in the seventh m',
52: 4 tenth m', in the tenth day of the m',
6 fourth m',...the ninth day of the m',
12 fifth m', in the tenth day of the m',
31 in the twelfth m', in the five and
31 five and twentieth day of the m',
Eze 1: 1 in the thirtieth year, the fourth m',
1 in the fifth day of the m', as I was
2 In the fifth day of the m', which
8: 1 in the sixth year, in the sixth m',
1 in the fifth day of the m', as I sat
20: 1 in the seventh year, in the fifth m',
1 tenth day of the m', that certain
24: 1 in the ninth year, in the tenth m',
1 in the tenth day of the m', the word
26: 1 eleventh year,...first day of the m',
29: 1 In the tenth year, in the tenth m',
1 in the twelfth day of the m', the
17 and twentieth year, in the first m',
17 in the first day of the m', the word
30:20 in the eleventh year, in the first m',
20 in the seventh day of the m', that
31: 1 the eleventh year, in the third m',
1 in the first day of the m', that the
32: 1 the twelfth year, in the twelfth m',
1 in the first day of the m', that the
17 year, in the fifteenth day of the m',
33:21 of our captivity, in the tenth m',
21 in the fifth day of the m', that one
40: 1 the year, in the tenth day of the m',
45:18 saith the Lord God; in the first m',
18 in the first day of the m', thou shalt
20 shalt do the seventh day of the m'
21 In the first m', in the fourteenth
21 in the fourteenth day of the m', ye
25 In the seventh m', in the fifteenth
25 in the fifteenth day of the m', shall
Da 10: 4 and twentieth day of the first m',
Ho 5: 7 now shall a m' devour them with
Joe 2:23 and the latter rain in the first m'.
Hag 1: 1 sixth m', in the first day of the m',
15 and twentieth day of the sixth m',
2: 1 In the seventh m', in the one and
1 twentieth day of the m', came the
10, 18 and twentieth day of the ninth m',
20 four and twentieth day of the m',
Zec 1: 1 In the eighth m', in the second year
7 twentieth day of the eleventh m',
7 which is the m' Sebat, in the second
7: 1 in the fourth day of the ninth m',
3 Should I weep in the fifth m',
5 in the fifth and seventh m', even
8:19 The fast of the fourth m', and the fast
11: 8 shepherds also I cut off in one m';
Lu 1:26 in the sixth m' the angel Gabriel
36 this is the sixth m' with her, who
Re 9:15 and a day, and a m', and a year, for
22: 2 and yielded her fruit every m':

monthly
Isa 47:13 the m' prognosticators, stand up,

months
Ge 38:24 came to pass about three m' after,
Ex 2: 2 child, she hid him three m'.
12: 2 be unto you the beginning of m':
Nu 10:10 the beginnings of your m', ye shall
28:11 the beginnings of your m' ye shall
14 throughout the m' of the year.
J'g 11:37 let me alone two m', that I may go
38 And he sent her away for two m':
39 it came to pass at the end of two m',
19: 2 and was there four whole m'.
20:47 abode in the rock Rimmon four m'.
1Sa 6: 1 country of the Philistines seven m'.
27: 7 was a full year and four m'.
2Sa 2:11 Judah was seven years and six m'.
5: 5 Judah seven years and six m',
6:11 of Obed-edom the Gittite three m':
24: 8 to Jerusalem at the end of nine m'
13 flee three m' before thine enemies,
1Ki 5:14 in Lebanon, and two m' at home:
11:16 (For six m' did Joab remain there
2Ki 15: 8 reign over Israel in Samaria six m'.
23:31 he reigned three m' in Jerusalem.
24: 8 he reigned in Jerusalem three m'.
1Ch 3: 4 he reigned seven years and six m':
13:14 Obed-edom in his house three m'.
21:12 three m' to be destroyed before thy
27: 1 throughout all the m' of the year,
2Ch 36: 2 he reigned three m' in Jerusalem.
9 he reigned three m' and ten days
Es 2:12 after that she had been twelve m',
12 to wit, six m' with oil of myrrh, and
12 six m' with sweet odours, and with
Job 3: 6 come into the number of the m'.
7: 3 am I made to possess m' of vanity,
14: 5 number of his m' are with thee,
21:21 the number of his m' is cut off in
29: 2 Oh that I were as in m' past, as in
39: 3 Canst thou number the m' that they
Eze 39:12 seven m' shall the house of Israel
14 after the end of seven m' shall they
47:12 forth new fruit according to his m',
Da 4:29 At the end of twelve m' he walked
Am 4: 7 were yet three m' to the harvest:
Lu 1:24 conceived, and hid herself five m',
1:56 abode with her about three m',
4:25 was shut up three years and six m',
Joh 4:35 Say not ye, There are yet four m',
Ac 7:20 up in his father's house three m':
18:11 he continued a year and six m',
19: 8 boldly for the space of three m',
20: 3 there abode three m'. And when
28:11 after three m' we departed in a ship
Ga 4:10 Ye observe days, and m', and times,
Heb 11:23 was hid three m' of his parents,
Jas 5:17 space of three years and six m'.
Re 9: 5 they should be tormented five m':
10 power was to hurt men five m'.
11: 2 tread under foot forty and two m'.
13: 5 him to continue forty and two m'.

monuments
Isa 65: 4 the graves, and lodge in the m',

moon See also MOONS.
Ge 37: 9 sun...the m' and the eleven stars
De 4:19 the sun, and the m', and the stars,
17: 3 either the sun, or m', or any of the
33:14 things put forth by the m',
Jos 10:12 thou, M', in the valley of Ajalon.
13 sun stood still, and the m' stayed,
1Sa 20: 5 Behold, to morrow is the new m',
18 To morrow is the new m': and thou
24 and when the new m' was come,
2Ki 4:23 it is neither new m', nor sabbath.
23: 5 to the sun, and to the m', and to
Job 25: 5 even to the m', and it shineth not;
31:26 or the m' walking in brightness;
Ps 8: 3 m' and the stars, which thou hast
72: 5 as long as the sun and m' endure,
7 of peace so long as the m' endureth.
81: 3 Blow up the trumpet in the new m',
89:37 be established for ever as the m',
104:19 He appointed the m' for seasons:
121: 6 thee by day, nor the m' by night.
136: 9 The m' and stars to rule by night:
148: 3 Praise ye him, sun and m': praise
Ec 12: 2 m', or the stars, be not darkened,
Ca 6:10 fair as the m', clear as the sun,
Isa 3:18 and their round tires like the m',
13:10 the m' shall not cause her light to
24:23 Then the m' shall be confounded,
30:26 light of the m' shall be as the light
60:19 shall the m' give light unto thee:
20 neither shall thy m' withdraw
66:23 that from one new m' to another,
Jer 8: 2 before the sun, and the m', and all
31:35 ordinances of the m' and of the stars
Eze 32: 7 and the m' shall not give her light.
46: 1, 6 in the day of the new m' it shall
Joe 2:10 the sun and the m' shall be dark,
31 darkness, and the m' into blood,
3:15 sun and the m' shall be darkened,
Am 8: 5 When will the new m' be gone,
Hab 3:11 The sun and m' stood still in their
M't 24:29 and the m' shall not give her light,
M'r 13:24 and the m' shall not give her light,
Lu 21:25 be signs in the sun, and in the m',
Ac 2:20 darkness, and the m' into blood,
1Co 15:41 sun, and another glory of the m',
Col 2:16 or of the new m', or of the sabbath
Re 6:12 hair, and the m' became as blood;
8:12 and the third part of the m', and the
12: 1 the sun, and the m' under her feet,
21:23 need of the sun, neither of the m',

moons
1Ch 23:31 the new m', and on the set feasts,
2Ch 2: 4 on the new m', and on the solemn
8:13 on the new m', and on the solemn
31: 3 the new m', and for the set feasts,
Ezr 3: 5 both of the new m', and of all the set
Ne 10:33 of the sabbaths, of the new m', for
Isa 1:13 the new m' and sabbaths, the
14 new m' and your appointed feasts
Eze 45:17 in the feasts, and in the new m',
46: 3 in the sabbaths and in the new m',
Ho 2:11 her feast days, her new m', and her

Morasthite (*mo'-ras-thite*)
Jer 26:18 Micah the M' prophesied in the
Mic 1: 1 Lord that came to Micah the M'

Mordecai (*mor'-de-cahee*) See also MORDECAI'S.
Ezr 2: 2 Nehemiah, Seraiah, Reelaiah, M',
Ne 7: 7 Nahamani, M', Bilshan, Mispereth,
Es 2: 5 a certain Jew, whose name was M',
7 whom M',...took for his own
10 M' had charged her that she should
11 M' walked every day before the
15 daughter of Abihail the uncle of M',
19 then M' sat in the king's gate.
20 her people; as M' had charged her:
20 Esther did the commandment of M',
21 while M' sat in the king's gate,
22 And the thing was known to M',
3: 2 But M' bowed not, nor did him
3 said unto M', Why transgressest
5 Haman saw that M' bowed not,
6 scorn to lay hands on M' alone;
6 had shewed him the people of M':
6 Ahasuerus, even the people of M'.
4: 1 M' perceived all that was done,
1 M' rent his clothes, and put on
4 and she sent raiment to clothe M',
5 gave him a commandment to M',
6 Hatach went forth to M' unto the
7 M' told him of all that had happened
9 and told Esther the words of M'.
10 gave him commandment unto M';
12 And they told to M' Esther's words.
13 M' commanded to answer Esther,
15 bade them return M' this answer,
17 M' went his way, and did according
Es 5: 9 Haman saw M' in the king's gate,
9 was full of indignation against M'.
13 so long as I see M' the Jew sitting
14 that M' may be hanged thereon:
6: 2 that M' had told of Bigthana and
3 and dignity hath been done to M'
4 the king to hang M' on the gallows
10 and do even so to M' the Jew, that
11 arrayed M', and brought him on
12 M' came again to the king's gate.
13 If M' be of the seed of the Jews,
7: 9 which Haman had made for M',
10 that he had prepared for M'. Then
8: 1 And M' came before the king; for
2 from Haman, and gave it unto M'.
2 Esther set M' over the house of
7 unto Esther...and to M' the Jew,
9 that M' commanded unto the Jews,
15 M' went out from the presence of
9: 3 the fear of M' fell upon them.
4 M' was great in the king's house,
4 man M' waxed greater and greater.
20 M' wrote these things, and sent
23 and as M' had written unto them;
29 and M' the Jew, wrote with all
31 M' the Jew and Esther the queen
10: 2 declaration of the greatness of M,
3 For M' the Jew was next unto king

Mordecai's (*mor'-de-cahees*)
Es 2:22 the king thereof in M' name.
3: 4 whether M' matters would stand:

more^ See also EVERMORE; FURTHERMORE; MOREOVER.
Ge 3: 1 Now the serpent was m' subtil than
8:12 returned not...unto him any m'.
21 curse the ground any m' for man's
21 smite any m' everything living, as
9:11 shall all flesh be cut off any m' by
11 shall there any m' be a flood to
15 waters shall no m' become a flood
17: 5 thy name any m' be called Abram,
29:30 he loved also Rachel m' than Leah,
32:28 name shall be called no m' Jacob,
34:19 m' honourable than all the house
35:10 shall not be called any m' Jacob,
36: 7 For their riches were m' than that
37: 3 loved Joseph m' than all his children,
4 loved him m' than all his brethren,
5 and they hated him yet the m'.
8 they hated him yet the m' for his
9 I have dreamed a dream m'; and,
38:26 She hath been m' righteous than I;
26 And he knew her again no m'.
44:23 you, ye shall see my face no m'.
Ex 1: 9 of Israel are m' and mightier than
12 But the m' they afflicted them,
12 the m' they multiplied and grew.
5: 7 shall no m' give the people straw
9 there m' work be laid upon the men.
8:29 Pharaoh deal deceitfully any m'
9:28 be no m' mighty thunderings and
29 neither shall there be any m' hail;
34 he sinned yet m', and hardened
10:28 heed to thyself, see my face no m';
29 I will see thy face again no m'.
11: 1 I bring one plague m' upon Pharaoh,
6 like it, nor shall be like it any m'.
14:13 see them again no m' for ever.
16:17 and gathered, some m', some less,
30:15 The rich shall not give m', and
36: 5 people bring much m' than enough
6 man nor woman make any m' work
Le 6: 5 and shall add the fifth part m'
11:42 hath m' feet among all creeping
13: 5 shall shut him up seven days m':
33 that hath the scall seven days m':
54 he shall shut it up seven days m';
17: 7 shall no m' offer their sacrifices
26:18 will punish you seven times m' for
21 bring seven times m' plagues upon
27:20 it shall not be redeemed any m'.
Nu 3:46 which are m' than the Levites;
8:25 thereof, and shall serve no m':
18: 5 no wrath any m' upon the children
22:15 Balak sent yet again princes, m',
15 princes...m' honourable than they.
18 the Lord my God, to do less or m'.
19 the Lord will say unto me m'.
26:54 thou shalt give the m' inheritance,
33:54 and to the m' ye shall give the
54 ye shall give the m' inheritance.
De 1:11 thousand times so many m' as ye
3:26 speak no m' unto me of this
5:22 great voice: and he added no m'.
25 voice of the Lord our God any m',
7: 7 ye were m' in number than any
17 These nations are m' than I; how
10:16 heart, and be no m' stiffnecked.
13:11 do no m' any such wickedness as
17:13 and do no m' presumptuously.
16 henceforth return no m' that way.
18:16 let me see this great fire any m',
19: 9 thou add three cities m' for thee,
20 commit no m' any such evil among
20: 1 and a people m' than thou, be not
28:68 Thou shalt see it no m' again:
31: 2 I can no m' go out and come in:
27 and how much m' after my death?
Jos 2:11 neither did there remain any m'
5: 1 was there spirit in them any m',
12 children of Israel manna any m';
7:12 neither will I be with you any m',
10:11 they were m' which died with
23:13 will no m' drive out any of these
J'g 2:19 themselves m' than their fathers,
2:28 they lifted up their heads no m'.

J'g 10:13 wherefore I will deliver you no *m*.
13:21 angel of the Lord did no *m*. appear
15: 3 shall I be *m*. blameless than the
16:30 which he slew at his death were *m*.
18:24 gone away: and what have I *m*.?
Ru 1:11 are there yet any *m*. sons in my womb,
17 the Lord do so to me, and *m*. also,
3:10 thou hast shewed *m*. kindness in the
1Sa 1:18 her countenance was no *m*. sad.
2: 3 Talk no *m*. so exceeding proudly;
3:17 God do so to thee, and *m*. also,
7:13 came no *m*. into the coast of 3254.
14:30 How much *m*., if haply the people
44 answered, God do so and *m*. also:
15:35 And Samuel came no *m*. to see Saul
18: 2 go no *m*. home to his father's house.
8 can he have *m*. but the kingdom?
29 was yet the *m*. afraid of David;
30 that David behaved himself *m*. wisely
20:13 do so and much *m*. to Jonathan:
22:15 knew nothing of all this, less or *m*.
23: 3 much *m*. then if we come to Keilah
24:17 Thou art *m*. righteous than I: for thou
25:22 *m*. also do God unto the enemies
36 she told him nothing, less or *m*.
26:21 for I will no *m*. do thee harm,
27: 1 to seek me any *m*. in any coast of
4 he sought no *m*. again for him.
28:15 and answereth me no *m*., neither by
30: 4 until they had no *m*. power to weep.
2Sa 2:28 and pursued after Israel no *m*.,
28 neither fought they any *m*.
3: 9 So do God to Abner, and *m*. also,
35 So do God to me, and *m*. also, if I
4:11 How much *m*., when wicked men
5:13 David took him *m*. concubines
6:22 And I will yet be *m*. vile than thus,
7:10 place of their own, and move no *m*.;
10 of wickedness afflict them any *m*.,
20 what can David say *m*. unto thee?
10:19 help the children of Ammon any *m*.
11:25 thy battle *m*. strong against the city,
14:10 shall not touch thee any *m*.
11 revengers of blood to destroy...*m*.,
16:11 much *m*. now may this Benjamite do it?
18: 8 and the wood devoured *m*. people
19:13 God do so to me, and *m*. also, if
28 I yet to cry any *m*. unto the king?
29 Why speakest thou any *m*. of thy
35 I hear any *m*. the voice of singing
43 have also *m*. right in David than ye:
20: 6 do us *m*. harm than did Absalom:
21:17 Thou shalt go no *m*. out with us
23:23 He was *m*. honourable than the thirty,
1Ki 2:23 God do so to me, and *m*. also, if
32 who fell upon two men *m*. righteous
10: 5 there was no *m*. spirit in her.
10 no *m*. such abundance of spices
16:33 Ahab did *m*. to provoke the Lord
19: 2 let the gods do to me, and *m*. also,
20:10 gods do so unto me, and *m*. also, if
2Ki 2:12 And he saw him no *m*.: and he
21 thence any *m*. death or barren land.
4: 6 unto her, There is not a vessel *m*.
6:16 they that be with us are *m*. than
23 came no *m*. into the...of Israel.
31 God do so and *m*. also to me, if the
9:35 they found no *m*. of her than the
12: 7 now therefore receive no *m*. money of
8 consented to receive no *m*. money of
21: 8 make the feet of Israel move any *m*.
9 seduced them to do *m*. evil than did
24: 7 Egypt came not again any *m*. out
1Ch 4: 9 And Jabez was *m*. honourable than
11:21 he was *m*. honourable than the two;
14: 3 David took *m*. wives at Jerusalem:
3 David begat *m*. sons and daughters.
17: 9 place, and shall be moved no *m*.;
9 of wickedness waste them any *m*.,
18 can David speak *m*. to thee
19:19 help the children of Ammon any *m*.
21: 3 hundred times so many *m*. as they
23:26 they shall no *m*. carry the tabernacle,
24: 4 there were *m*. chief men found of
2Ch 9: 4 there was no *m*. spirit in her.
10:11 you, I will put *m*. to your yoke:
15:19 there was no *m*. war unto the five and
20:25 *m*. than they could carry away:
25: 9 is able to give thee much *m*. than
28:13 ye intend to add *m*. to our sins
22 trespass yet *m*. against the Lord:
29:34 the Levites were *m*. upright in heart
32: 7 there be *m*. with us than with him:
16 spake yet *m*. against the Lord God,
33: 8 will I any *m*. remove the foot of Israel
23 himself; but Amon trespassed *m*.
23 but Amon trespassed...and *m*.
Ezr 7:20 whatsoever *m*. shall be needful
Ne 2:17 that we be no *m*. a reproach.
13:18 yet ye bring *m*. wrath upon Israel
21 forth came they no *m*. on the sabbath.
Es 1:19 Vashti come no *m*. before king
2:14 she came in unto the king no *m*.,
17 in his sight *m*. than all the virgins;
4:13 the king's house, *m*. than all the Jews.
6: 6 to do honour *m*. than to myself?
Job 3:21 dig for it *m*. than for hid treasures;
4:17 mortal man be *m*. just than God?
17 a man be *m*. pure than his maker?
7: 7 mine eye shall no *m*. see good.
8 that hath seen me shall see me no *m*.;
9 down to the grave shall come up no *m*.
10 shall return no *m*. to his house,
10 shall his place know him any *m*.
14:12 till the heavens be no *m*., they shall
15:16 *m*. abominable and filthy is man,

Job 20: 9 saw him shall see him no *m*.;
9 shall his place any *m*. behold him.
23:12 his mouth *m*. than my necessary food.
24:20 he shall be no *m*. remembered;
32:15 were amazed, they answered no *m*.:
16 stood still, and answered no *m*.;)
34:19 regardeth...rich *m*. than the poor?
23 not lay upon man *m*. than right;
31 chastisement, I will not offend any *m*.
32 have done iniquity, I will do no *m*.
35: 2 My righteousness is *m*. than God's?
11 Who teacheth us *m*. than the beasts of
41: 8 remember the battle, do no *m*.
42:12 end of Job *m*. than his beginning:
Ps 4: 7 *m*. than in the time that their corn and
10:18 the earth may no *m*. oppress.
19:10 *M*. to be desired are they than gold,
39:13 before I go hence, and be no *m*.
40: 5 are *m*. than can be numbered.
12 are *m*. than the hairs of mine head:
41: 8 he lieth he shall rise up no *m*.
52: 3 Thou lovest evil *m*. than good; and
69: 4 *m*. than the hairs of mine head:
71:14 and will yet praise thee *m*. and *m*.
73: 7 have *m*. than heart could wish.
74: 9 there is no *m*. any prophet:
76: 4 Thou art *m*. glorious and excellent
77: 7 will he be favourable no *m*.?
78:17 they sinned yet *m*. against him by
83: 4 may be no *m*. in remembrance.
87: 2 *m*. than all the dwellings of Jacob.
88: 5 whom thou rememberest no *m*.:
103:16 place thereof shall know it no *m*.
104:35 earth, and let the wicked be no *m*.
115:14 Lord shall increase you *m*. and *m*.,
119:99 *m*. understanding than all my teachers:
100 I understand *m*. than the ancients,
130: 6 *m*. than they that watch for...morning:
6 *m*. than they that watch for...morning.
139:18 are *m*. in number than the sand:
Pr 3:15 She is *m*. precious than rubies: and
4:18 that shineth *m*. and *m*. unto the
10:25 passeth, so is the wicked no *m*.:
11:24 is that withholdeth *m*. than is meet,
31 much *m*. the wicked and the sinner.
12:26 is *m*. excellent than his neighbour:
15:11 how much *m*. then the hearts of the
17:10 A reproof entereth *m*. into a wise man
19: 7 how much *m*. do his friends go far
21: 3 justice and judgment is *m*. acceptable
27 how much *m*., when he bringeth it
26:12 there is *m*. hope of a fool than of him.
28:23 rebuketh a man...shall find *m*. favour
29:20 there is *m*. hope of a fool than of him.
30: 2 Surely I am *m*. brutish than any man,
31: 7 and remember his misery no *m*.
Ec 1:16 and have gotten *m*. wisdom than all
2: 9 and increased *m*. than all that were
15 me; and why was I then *m*. wise?
16 of the wise *m*. than of the fool
25 can hasten hereunto, *m*. than I?
4: 2 *m*. than the living which are yet
13 who will no *m*. be admonished.
5: 1 and be *m*. ready to hear, than to
6: 5 this hath *m*. rest than the other.
8 hath the wise *m*. than the fool?
7:19 *m*. than ten mighty men which are
26 I find *m*. bitter than death the woman.
9: 5 neither have they any *m*. a reward;
6 neither have they any *m*. a portion
17 *m*. than the cry of him that ruleth
10:10 edge, then must he put to *m*. strength:
Ca 1: 4 will remember thy love *m*. than wine:
5: 9, 9 thy beloved *m*. than another beloved,
Isa 1: 5 Why should ye be stricken any *m*.?
5 ye will revolt *m*. [3254] and *m*.: the
13 Bring no *m*. vain oblations; incense
2: 4 shall they learn war any *m*.
5: 4 have been done *m*. to my vineyard,
9: 1 did *m*. grievously afflict her by the
10:20 shall no *m*. again stay upon him
13:12 make a man *m*. precious than fine gold;
15: 9 for I will bring *m*. upon Dimon,
19: 7 wither, be driven away, and be no *m*.
23:10 Tarshish: there is no *m*. strength.
12 Thou shalt no *m*. rejoice, O thou
26:21 and shall no *m*. cover her slain.
30:19 thou shalt weep no *m*.: he will be
20 be removed into a corner any *m*.,
32: 5 shall be no *m*. called liberal, nor
38:11 I shall behold man no *m*. with the
47: 1 thou shalt no *m*. be called tender
5 thou shalt no *m*. be called, The lady
51:22 thou shalt no *m*. drink it again:
52: 1 shall no *m*. come into thee
14 was so marred *m*. than any man,
14 and his form *m*. than the sons of men:
54: 1 *m*. are the children of the desolate
4 reproach of...widowhood any *m*.
9 should no *m*. go over the earth;
56:12 this day, and much *m*. abundant.
60:18 Violence shall no *m*. be heard in
19 sun shall be no *m*. thy light by day;
20 Thy sun shall no *m*. go down;
62: 4 shalt no *m*. be termed Forsaken;
4 land any *m*. be termed Desolate:
8 will no *m*. give thy corn to be meat
65:19 weeping shall be no *m*. heard in her,
20 be no *m*. thence an infant of days,
Jer 2:31 we will come no *m*. unto thee?
3:11 herself *m*. than treacherous Judah.
16 they shall say no *m*., The ark of
16 neither shall that be done any *m*.
17 walk any *m*. after the imagination
7:32 it shall no *m*. be called Tophet, nor
10:20 to stretch forth my tent any *m*.,

Jer 11:19 name may be no *m*. remembered.
16:14 that it shall no *m*. be said, The
19: 6 that this place shall no *m*. be called
20: 9 him, nor speak any *m*. in his name.
22:10 he shall return no *m*., nor see his
11 He shall not return thither any *m*.:
12 and shall see this land no *m*.
30 David, and ruling any *m*. in Judah.
23: 4 and they shall fear no *m*., nor be
7 that they shall no *m*. say, The Lord
36 the Lord shall ye mention no *m*.:
25:27 and spue, and fall, and rise no *m*.,
30: 8 no *m*. serve themselves of him.
31:12 shall not sorrow any *m*. at all.
29 In those days they shall say no *m*.,
34 they shall teach no *m*. every man
34 I will remember their sin no *m*.
40 nor thrown down any *m*. for ever.
33:24 be no *m*. a nation before them.
34:10 serve themselves of them any *m*.
38: 9 for there is no *m*. bread in the city.
42:18 and ye shall see this place no *m*.
44:26 my name shall no *m*. be named in
46:23 they are *m*. than the grasshoppers,
48: 2 shall be no *m*. praise of Moab:
49: 7 Is wisdom no *m*. in Teman? is
50:39 and it shall be no *m*. inhabited for
51:44 not flow together any *m*. unto him:
La 2: 9 the law is no *m*.; her prophets also
4: 7 they were *m*. ruddy in body than
15 They shall no *m*. sojourn there.
16 them; he will no *m*. regard them:
22 he will no *m*. carry thee away into
Eze 5: 6 my judgments into wickedness *m*.
6 my statutes *m*. than the countries
7 Because ye multiplied *m*. than the
9 I will not do any *m*. the like,
6:14 *m*. desolate than the wilderness
12:23 shall no *m*. use it as a proverb in
24 shall be no *m*. any vain vision nor
25 it shall be no *m*. prolonged: for in
28 of my words be prolonged any *m*.,
13:15 the wall is no *m*., neither they that
21 shall be no *m*. in your hand to be
23 shall see no *m*. vanity, nor divine
14:11 may go no *m*. astray from me,
11 polluted any *m*. with all their
21 How much *m*. when I send my four
15: 2 is the vine tree *m*. than any tree, or
16:41 also shalt give no hire any *m*.
42 be quiet, and will be no *m*. angry.
47 thou wast corrupted *m*. than they in
51 thine abominations *m*. than they,
52 committed *m*. abominable than
52 they are *m*. righteous than thou: yea,
63 and never open thy mouth any *m*.
18: 3 not have occasion any *m*. to use this
19: 9 that his voice should no *m*. be heard
20:39 pollute ye my holy name no *m*. with
21: 5 sheath: it shall not return any *m*.
13 it shall be no *m*., saith the Lord God.
27 and it shall be no *m*., until he come
32 thou shalt be no *m*. remembered: for
23:11 was *m*. corrupt in her inordinate love
11 *m*. than her sister in her whoredoms.
27 nor remember Egypt any *m*.
24:13 purged from thy filthiness any *m*.,
27 shalt speak, and be no *m*. dumb:
26:13 of thy harps shall be no *m*. heard.
14 thou shalt be built no *m*.: for I the
21 thee a terror, and thou shalt be no *m*.:
27:36 terror, and never shalt be any *m*.
28:19 and never shalt thou be any *m*.
24 shall be no *m*. a pricking brier
29:15 itself any *m*. above the nations:
15 that they shall no *m*. rule over the
16 shall be no *m*. the confidence of
30:13 shall be no *m*. a prince of the land
32:13 foot of man trouble them any *m*.,
33:22 opened, and I was no *m*. dumb.
34:10 shepherds feed themselves any *m*.;
22 they shall no *m*. be a prey; and I
28 they shall no *m*. be a prey to the
29 they shall no *m*. be consumed with
29 the shame of the heathen any *m*.
36:12 shalt no *m*. henceforth bereave
14 thou shalt devour men no *m*.,
14 neither bereave thy nations any *m*.,
15 the shame of the heathen any *m*.,
15 the reproach of the people any *m*.,
15 cause thy nations to fall any *m*.,
30 ye shall receive no *m*. reproach of
37:22 they shall be no *m*. two nations,
22 into two kingdoms any *m*. at all.
23 defile themselves any *m*. with their
39: 7 them pollute my holy name any *m*.:
28 left none of them any *m*. there.
29 I hide my face any *m*. from them:
42: 6 was straitened *m*. than the lowest
43: 7 the house of Israel no *m*. defile,
45: 8 shall no *m*. oppress my people;
Da 2:30 that I have *m*. than any living,
3:19 seven times *m*. than it was wont
7:20 whose look was *m*. stout than his
11: 8 continue *m*. years than the king of
Ho 1: 6 I will no *m*. have mercy upon the
2:16 and shalt call me no *m*. Baali.
17 they shall no *m*. be remembered
6: 6 of God *m*. than burnt offerings.
9:15 house, I will love them no *m*.:
13: 2 And now they sin *m*. [3254] and *m*., and
14: 3 will we say any *m*. to the work of
8 have I to do any *m*. with idols?
Joe 2: 2 neither shall be any *m*. after it,
19 I will no *m*. make you a reproach
3:17 strangers pass through her any *m*.

Am 5: 2 is fallen; she shall no *m'* rise:
7: 8 will not again pass by them any *m'*:
13 prophesy not...any *m'* at Bethel:
8: 2 will not again pass by them any *m'*.
9:15 they shall no *m'* be pulled up out
Jon 4:11 wherein are *m'* than sixscore
Mic 4: 3 shall they learn war any *m'*.
5:12 thou shalt have no *m'* soothsayers:
13 shalt no *m'* worship the work of
Na 1:12 thee, I will afflict thee no *m'*.
14 that no *m'* of thy name be sown:
15 the wicked shall no *m'* pass
2:13 messengers shall no *m'* be heard.
Hab 1: 8 are *m'* fierce than the evening wolves:
13 the man that is *m'* righteous than he?
Zep 3:11 thou shalt no *m'* be haughty
15 thee: thou shalt not see evil any *m'*.
Zec 9: 8 shall pass through them any *m'*:
11: 6 For I will no *m'* pity the inhabitants
13: 2 they shall no *m'* be remembered:
14:11 shall be no *m'* utter destruction;
21 shall be no *m'* the Canaanite in the
Mal 2:13 regardeth not the offering any *m'*,
M't 5:37 is *m'* than these cometh of evil.
47 only, what do ye *m'* than others?
6:25 Is not the life *m'* than meat, and
30 shall he not much *m'* clothe you,
7:11 how much *m'* shall your Father
10:15 It shall be *m'* tolerable for the land
25 how much *m'* shall they call them
31 are of *m'* value than many sparrows.
37 father or mother *m'* than me is
37 loveth son or daughter *m'* than me
11: 9 unto you, and *m'* than a prophet.
22 be *m'* tolerable for Tyre and Sidon
24 it shall be *m'* tolerable for the land
12:45 seven other spirits *m'* wicked than
13:12 and he shall have *m'* abundance:
18:13 he rejoiceth *m'* of that sheep, than
16 take with thee one or two *m'*, that
19: 6 they are no *m'* twain, but one flesh
20:10 they should have received *m'*; and
31 but they cried the *m'*, saying,
21:36 other servants *m'* than the first:
22:46 forth ask him any *m'* questions.
23:15 make him twofold *m'* the child of hell
25:20 gained besides them five talents *m'*.
26:53 give me *m'* than twelve legions
27:23 But they cried out the *m'*, saying,
M'r 1:45 Jesus could no *m'* openly enter
4:24 you that hear shall *m'* be given.
6:11 It shall be *m'* tolerable for Sodom
7:12 suffer him no *m'* to do ought for
36 but the *m'* he charged them, so
36 much the *m'* a great deal they
8:14 ship with them *m'* than one loaf.
9: 8 they saw no man any *m'*, save Jesus
25 out of him, and enter no *m'* into
10: 8 they are no *m'* twain, but one flesh.
48 he cried the *m'* a great deal, Thou
12:33 *m'* than all whole burnt offerings
43 this poor widow hath cast *m'* in,
14: 5 sold for *m'* than three hundred
25 drink no *m'* of the fruit of the vine,
31 But he spake the *m'* vehemently,
15:14 cried out...*m'* exceedingly, Crucify
Lu 3:13 Exact no *m'* than that which is
5:15 But so much the *m'* went there a
7:26 you, and much *m'* than a prophet.
9:13 We have no *m'* but five loaves and
10:12 it shall be *m'* tolerable in that day
14 it shall be *m'* tolerable for Tyre and
35 whatsoever thou spendest *m'*, when
11:13 how much *m'* shall your heavenly
26 seven other spirits *m'* wicked than
12: 4 that have no *m'* that they can do.
7 of *m'* value than many sparrows.
23 The life is *m'* than meat,
23 and the body is *m'* than raiment.
24 how much *m'* are ye better than
28 how much *m'* will he clothe you,
48 much, of him they will ask the *m'*.
14: 8 lest a *m'* honourable man than thou
15: 7 *m'* than over ninety and nine just
19, 21 am no *m'* worthy to be called
18:30 receive manifold *m'* in this present
39 cried so much the *m'*, Thou Son
20:36 Neither can they die any *m'*: for
21: 3 poor widow hath cast in *m'* than
22:16 I will not any *m'* eat thereof, until
44 an agony he prayed *m'* earnestly:
23: 5 they were the *m'* fierce, saying, He
Joh 4: 1 made and baptized *m'* disciples
41 many *m'* believed because of his
5:14 sin no *m'*, lest a worse thing come
18 Jews sought the *m'* to kill him,
6:66 back, and walked no *m'* with him.
7:31 will he do *m'* miracles than these
8:11 I condemn thee: go, and sin no *m'*.
10:10 that they might have it *m'* abundantly.
11:54 Jesus...walked no *m'* openly
12:43 praise of men *m'* than the praise
14:19 and the world seeth me no *m'*;
15: 2 that it may bring forth *m'* fruit.
4 *m'* can ye, except ye abide in me
16:10 my Father, and ye see me no *m'*;
21 remembereth no *m'* the anguish,
25 I shall no *m'* speak unto you in
17:11 now I am no *m'* in the world, but
19: 8 that saying, he was the *m'* afraid;
21:15 lovest thou me *m'* than these?
Ac 4:19 unto you *m'* than unto God, judge
5:14 were the *m'* added to the Lord,
8:39 that the eunuch saw him no *m'*:
9:22 Saul increased the *m'* in strength,
13:34 now no *m'* to return to corruption,

Ac 17:11 *m'* noble than those in Thessalonica,
18:26 him the way of God *m'* perfectly.
19:32 *m'* part knew not wherefore they
20:25 of God, shall see my face no *m'*.
35 *m'* blessed to give than to receive.
38 that they should see his face no *m'*.
22: 2 to them, they kept the *m'* silence:
23:13 *m'* than forty which had made
15 something *m'* perfectly concerning
20 somewhat of him *m'* perfectly.
21 for him of them *m'* than forty men,
24:10 *m'* cheerfully answer for myself:
22 *m'* perfect knowledge of that way,
25: 6 among them *m'* than ten days,
27:11 *m'* than those things which were
12 *m'* part advised to depart thence
Ro 1:25 the creature *m'* than the Creator,
2:18 the things that are *m'* excellent,
3: 7 if the truth of God hath *m'* abounded
5: 9 Much *m'* then, being now justified
10 much *m'*, being reconciled, we shall
15 much *m'* the grace of God, and the
17 *m'* they which receive abundance
20 abounded, grace did much *m'* abound:
6: 9 raised from the dead dieth no *m'*;
9 death hath no *m'* dominion over
7:17 Now then it is no *m'* I that do it,
20 it is no *m'* I that do it, but sin that
8:37 *m'* than conquerors through him
11: 6 by grace, then is it no *m'* of works:
6 otherwise grace is no *m'* grace.
6 of works, then is it no *m'* grace:
6 otherwise work is no *m'* work.
12 how much *m'* their fulness?
24 how much *m'* shall these, which be
12: 3 *m'* highly than he ought to think;
14:13 therefore judge one another any *m'*:
15:15 I have written the *m'* boldly unto
23 having no *m'* place in these parts,
1Co 6: 3 how much *m'* things that pertain to
9:19 unto all, that I might gain the *m'*.
12:22 much *m'* those members of the
23 we bestow *m'* abundant honour;
24 having given *m'* abundant honour to
31 unto you a *m'* excellent way.
14:18 speak with tongues *m'* than ye all:
15:10 laboured *m'* abundantly than they
2Co 1:12 and *m'* abundantly to you-ward.
2: 4 the love which I have *m'* abundantly
3: 9 much *m'* doth the ministration of
11 much *m'* that which remaineth is
4:17 for us a far *m'* exceeding and
5:16 henceforth know we him no *m'*.
7: 7 me; so that I rejoiced the *m'*.
13 and exceedingly the *m'* joyed we
15 his inward affection is *m'* abundant
8:17 but being *m'* forward, of his own
22 but now much *m'* diligent, upon the
10: 8 somewhat *m'* of our authority,
11:23 ministers of Christ?...I am *m'*;
23 in labors *m'* abundant, in stripes
23 in prisons *m'* frequent, in deaths
12:15 the *m'* abundantly I love you, the
Ga 1:14 being *m'* exceedingly zealous of the
3:18 of the law, it is no *m'* of promise:
4: 7 thou art no *m'* a servant, but a son;
27 the desolate hath many *m'* children
Eph 2:19 are no *m'* strangers and foreigners,
4:14 we henceforth be no *m'* children,
28 Let him that stole steal no *m'*: but
Ph'p 1: 9 love may abound yet *m'* and *m'* in
14 are much *m'* bold to speak the
24 to abide in the flesh is *m'* needful for
26 your rejoicing may be *m'* abundant
2:12 but now much *m'* in my absence,
3: 4 he might trust in the flesh, I *m'*:
1Th 2:17 endeavoured the *m'* abundantly to
4: 1 so ye would abound *m'* and *m'*.
10 that ye increase *m'* and *m'*;
2Ti 2:16 will increase unto *m'* ungodliness.
3: 4 pleasures *m'* than lovers of God;
Ph'm 16 me, but how much *m'* unto thee,
21 thou wilt also do *m'* than I say.
Heb 1: 4 obtained a *m'* excellent name than
2: 1 ought to give the *m'* earnest heed
3: 3 worthy of *m'* glory than Moses,
3 the house hath *m'* honour than the
6:17 willing *m'* abundantly to shew unto
7:15 it is yet far *m'* evident: for that
8: 6 obtained a *m'* excellent ministry,
12 iniquities will I remember no *m'*.
9:11 a greater and *m'* perfect tabernacle,
14 How much *m'* shall the blood of
10: 2 have had no *m'* conscience of sins.
17 iniquities will I remember no *m'*.
18 is, there is no *m'* offering for sin.
25 so much the *m'*, as ye see the day
26 remaineth no *m'* sacrifice for sins,
11: 4 unto God a *m'* excellent sacrifice
32 what shall I *m'* say? for the time
12:19 not be spoken to them any *m'*:
25 much *m'* shall not we escape, if
26 once *m'* I shake not the earth only,
27 And this word, Yet once *m'*, signifieth
Jas 4: 6 But he giveth *m'* grace. Wherefore
1Pe 1: 7 being much *m'* precious than of gold
2Pe 1:19 have also a *m'* sure word of prophecy;
Re 2:19 and the last to be *m'* than the first.
3:12 God, and he shall go no *m'* out:
7:16 hunger no *m'*, neither thirst any *m'*;
9:12 there come two woes *m'* hereafter.
12: 8 their place found any *m'* in heaven.
18:11 buyeth their merchandise any *m'*:
14 and thou shalt find them no *m'* at all.
21 and shall be found no *m'* at all.
22 shall be heard no *m'* at all in thee;

Re 18:22 be, shall be found any *m'* in thee;
22 shall be heard no *m'* at all in thee;
23 of a candle shall shine no *m'* at all
23 shall be heard no *m'* at all in thee:
20: 3 should deceive the nations no *m'*,
21: 1 away; and there was no *m'* sea.
4 there shall be no *m'* death, neither
4 neither shall there be any *m'* pain:
22: 3 there shall be no *m'* curse: but

Moreh (*mo'-reh*)
Ge 12: 6 of Sichem, unto the plain of *M'*.
De 11:30 Gilgal, beside the plains of *M'*?
J'g 7: 1 by the hill of *M'*, in the valley.

moreover ^
Ge 32:20 say ye *m'*, Behold, thy servant
45:15 *M'* he kissed all his brethren, and
47: 4 They said *m'* unto Pharaoh, For to
48:22 *M'* I have given to thee one portion
Ex 3:15 God said *m'* unto Moses, Thus
18:21 *M'* thou shalt provide out of all the
26: 1 *M'* thou shalt make the tabernacle
30:22 *M'* the Lord spake unto Moses, saying,
Le 7:21 *M'* the soul that shall touch any
26 *M'* ye shall eat no manner of blood,
14:46 *M'* he that goeth into the house all
18:20 *M'* thou shalt not lie carnally with thy
25:45 *M'* of the children of the strangers
Nu 13:28 and *m'* we saw the children of Anak
16:14 *M'* thou hast not brought us into a
33:56 *M'* it shall come to pass, that I
35:31 *M'* ye shall take no satisfaction for
De 1:28 *m'* we have seen the sons of the
39 *M'* your little ones, which ye said
7:20 *M'* the Lord thy God will send the
28:45 *M'* all these curses shall come upon
60 *M'* he will bring upon thee all the
J'g 10: 9 *M'* the children of Ammon passed
Ru 4:10 *M'* Ruth the Moabitess, the wife of
1Sa 2:19 *M'* his mother made him a little
12:23 *M'* as for me, God forbid that I
14:21 *M'* the Hebrews that were with the
17:37 David said *m'*, The Lord that
20: 3 And David sware *m'*, and said, Thy
24:11 *M'*, my father, see, yea, see the skirt
28:19 *M'* the Lord will also deliver
2Sa 7:10 *M'* I will appoint a place for my people
12: 8 *m'* have given unto thee such and
15: 4 Absalom said *m'*, Oh that I were made
17: 1 *M'* Ahithophel said unto Absalom,
13 *M'*, if he be gotten into a city, then
21:15 *M'* the Philistines had yet war again
1Ki 2: 5 *M'* thou knowest also what Joab
14 He said *m'*, I have somewhat to say
44 The king said *m'* to Shimei, Thou
8:41 *M'* concerning a stranger, that is
10:18 *M'* the king made a great throne of
14:14 *M'* the Lord shall raise him up a king
2Ki 12:15 *M'* they reckoned not with the men,
21:16 *M'* Manasseh shed innocent blood
23:15 *M'* the altar that was at Beth-el,
24 *M'* the workers with familiar
1Ch 11: 2 *m'* in time past, even when Saul
12:40 *M'* they that were nigh them, even
17:10 *M'* I will subdue all thine enemies.
18:12 *M'* Abishai the son of Zeruiah slew
22:15 *M'* there are workmen with thee in
23: 5 *M'* four thousand were porters; and
25: 1 *M'* David and the captains of the host
26: 4 *M'* the sons of Obed-edom were,
28: 7 *M'* I will establish his kingdom
29: 3 *M'*, because I have set my
2Ch 1: 5 *M'* the brasen altar, that Bezaleel
2:12 Huram said *m'*, Blessed be the Lord
4: 1 *M'* he made an altar of brass, twenty
20 *M'* the candlesticks with their lamps,
6:32 *M'* concerning the stranger, which
7: 7 *M'* Solomon hallowed the middle of
9:17 *M'* the king made a great throne of
17: 6 *m'* he took away the high places
19: 8 *M'* in Jerusalem did Jehoshaphat
21:11 *M'* he made high places in the
16 *M'* the Lord stirred up against
23: 9 *M'* Jehoiada the priest delivered to
25: 5 *M'* Amaziah gathered Judah
26: 9 *M'* Uzziah built towers in Jerusalem
11 *M'* Uzziah had an host of fighting
27: 4 *M'* he built cities in the mountains
28: 3 *M'* he burnt incense in the valley
29:19 *M'* all the vessels, which king Ahaz
30 *M'* Hezekiah the king and the princes
31: 4 *M'* he commandeth the people that
32:29 *M'* he provided him cities, and
35: 1 *M'* Josiah kept a passover unto the
36:14 *M'* all the chief of the priests, and
Ezr 6: 8 *M'* I make a decree what ye shall do
10:25 *M'* of Israel: of the sons of Parosh;
Ne 2: 7 *M'* I said unto the king, If it please
3: 6 *M'* the old gate repaired Jehoiada
26 *M'* the Nethinims dwelt in Ophel,
5:14 *M'* from the time that I was
17 *M'* there were at my table an hundred
6:17 *M'* in those days the nobles of
9:12 *M'* thou leddest them in the day by
22 *M'* thou gavest them kingdoms and
11:19 *M'* the porters, Akkub, Talmon, and
Es 5:12 Haman said *m'*, Yea, Esther the
Job 27: 1 *M'* Job continued his parable, and
29: 1 *M'* Job continued his parable, and
35: 1 Elihu spake *m'*, and said,
40: 1 *M'* the Lord answered Job, and said,
Ps 19:11 *M'* by them is...servant warned:
78:66 *M'* he refused the tabernacle of
105:16 *M'* he called for a famine upon the
Ec 3:16 *m'* I saw under the sun the place
5: 9 *M'* the profit of the earth is for all:

Ec 6: 5 *M'* he hath not seen the sun, nor
12: 9 *m'*, because the preacher was
Isa 3:16 *M'* the Lord saith, Because the
7:10 *M'* the Lord spake again unto Ahaz,
19: 9 *M'* they that work in fine flax, and
29: 5 *M'* the multitude of thy strangers
30:26 *M'* the light of the moon shall be as
39: 8 He said *m'*, For there shall be peace
Jer 1:11 *M'* the word of the Lord came unto
2: 1 *M'* the word of the Lord came to me,
8: 4 *M'* thou shalt say unto them, Thus
20: 5 *M'* I will deliver all the strength of
25:10 *M'* I will take from them the voice of
33: 1 *M'* the word of the Lord came unto
23 *M'* the word of the Lord came to
37:18 *M'* Jeremiah said unto king Zedekiah,
39: 7 *M'* he put out Zedekiah's eyes, and
40:13 *M'* Johanan the son of Kareah, and
44:24 *M'* Jeremiah said unto all the people,
48:35 *M'* I will cause to cease in Moab,
Eze 3: 1 *M'* he said unto me, Son of man, eat
10 *M'* he said unto me, Son of man, all
4: 3 *M'* take thou unto thee an iron pan,
16 *M'* he said unto me, Son of man,
5:14 *M'* I will make thee waste, and a
7: 1 *M'* the word of the Lord came unto
11: 1 *M'* the spirit lifted me up, and
12:17 *M'* the word of the Lord came to me,
16:20 *M'* thou hast taken thy sons and thy
29 hast *m'* multiplied thy fornication
17:11 *M'* the word of the Lord came unto
19: 1 *M'* take thou up a lamentation for
20:12 *M'* also I gave them my sabbaths,
45 *M'* the word of the Lord came unto
22: 1 *M'* the word of the Lord came unto
23:36 The Lord said *m'* unto me; Son of
38 *M'* this they have done unto me:
28:11 *M'* the word of the Lord came unto
36:16 *M'* the word of the Lord came unto
37:16 *M'*, thou son of man, take thee one
26 *M'* I will make a covenant of peace
45: 1 *M'*, when ye shall divide by lot the
46:18 *M'* the prince shall not take of the
48:22 *M'* from the possession of the Levites,
Zec 4: 8 *M'* the word of the Lord came unto
5: 6 He said *m'*, This is their resemblance
M't 6:16 *M'* when ye fast, be not, as the
18:15 *M'* if thy brother shall trespass
Lu 16:21 *m'* the dogs came and licked
Ac 2:26 *m'* also my flesh shall rest in hope:
11:12 *M'* these...brethren accompanied
19:26 *M'* ye see and hear, that not alone
Ro 5:20 *M'* the law entered, that...offence
8:30 *M'* whom he did predestinate, them
1Co 4: 2 *M'*...required...stewards,
10: 1 *M'*, brethren, I would not that ye
15: 1 *M'*, brethren, I declare unto you
2Co 1:23 *M'* I call God for a record upon my
8: 1 *M'*, brethren, we do you to wit of
1Ti 3: 7 *M'* he must have a good report of
Heb 9:21 *M'* he sprinkled with blood
11:36 *m'* of bonds and imprisonments:
2Pe 1:15 *M'* I will endeavour that ye

Moresheth-gath (*mor'-e-sheth-gath*) See also MORASTHITE.
Mic 1:14 shalt thou give presents to *M'*:

Moriah (*mo-ri'-ah*)
Ge 22: 2 and get thee into the land of *M'*:
2Ch 3: 1 Lord at Jerusalem in mount *M'*,

morning
Ge 1: 5 evening and the *m'* were the first
8 evening and the *m'* were the second
13 evening and the *m'* were the third
19 evening and the *m'* were the fourth
23 evening and the *m'* were the fifth
31 evening and the *m'* were the sixth
19:15 And when the *m'* arose, then the
27 Abraham gat up early in the *m'*
20: 8 Abimelech rose early in the *m'*,
21:14 Abraham rose up early in the *m'*,
22: 3 Abraham rose up early in the *m'*,
24:54 they rose up in the *m'*, and he said,
26:31 they rose up betimes in the *m'*,
28:18 Jacob rose up early in the *m'*, and
29:25 that in the *m'*, behold, it was Leah:
31:55 early in the *m'* Laban rose up, and
40: 6 Joseph came in unto them in the *m'*,
41: 8 it came to pass in the *m'* that his
44: 3 soon as the *m'* was light, the men
49:27 in the *m'* he shall devour the prey,
Ex 7:15 Get thee unto Pharaoh in the *m'*;
8:20 Rise up early in the *m'*, and stand
9:13 Rise up early in the *m'*, and stand
10:13 and when it was *m'*, the east wind
12:10 nothing of it remain until the *m'*;
10 which remaineth of it until the *m'*
22 the door of his house until the *m'*.
14:24 *m'* watch the Lord looked unto the
27 his strength when the *m'* appeared;
16: 7 And in the *m'*, then ye shall see the
8 and in the *m'* bread to the full; for
12 and in the *m'* ye shall be filled with
13 in the *m'* the dew lay round about
19 Let no man leave of it till the *m'*,
20 some of them left of it until the *m'*,
21 they gathered it every *m'*, every
23 up for you to be kept until the *m'*.
24 they laid it up till the *m'*, as Moses
18:13 from the *m'* unto the evening.
14 stand by thee from *m'* unto even?
19:16 to pass on the third day in the *m'*,
23:18 of my sacrifice remain until the *m'*.
24: 4 and rose up early in the *m'*, and
27:21 from evening to *m'* before the Lord:
29:34 remain unto the *m'*, then thou shalt
Ex 29:39 one lamb thou shalt offer in the *m'*;
41 to the meat offering of the *m'*, and
30: 7 thereon sweet incense every *m'*:
34: 2 be ready in the *m'*, and come up in
2 and come up in the *m'* unto mount
4 and Moses rose up early in the *m'*,
25 of the passover be left unto the *m'*.
36: 3 unto him free offerings every *m'*.
Le 6: 9 upon the altar all night unto the *m'*,
12 shall burn wood on it every *m'*, and
20 perpetual, half of it in the *m'*, and
7:15 shall not leave any of it until the *m'*.
9:17 beside the burnt sacrifice of the *m'*.
19:13 with thee all night until the *m'*.
24: 3 it from the evening unto the *m'*
Nu 9:12 shall leave none of it unto the *m'*,
15 the appearance of fire, until the *m'*.
21 cloud abode from even unto the *m'*,
21 the cloud was taken up in the *m'*,
14:40 they rose up early in the *m'*, and
22:13, 21 Balaam rose up in the *m'*, and
28: 4 one lamb shalt thou offer in the *m'*,
8 as the meat offering of the *m'*, and
23 beside the burnt offering in the *m'*,
De 16: 4 even, remain all night until the *m'*.
7 thou shalt turn in the *m'*, and go
28:67 In the *m'* thou shalt say, Would God
67 shalt say, Would God it were *m'*!
Jos 3: 1 Joshua rose early in the *m'*; and
6:12 Joshua rose early in the *m'*, and
7:14 In the *m'* therefore ye shall be
16 So Joshua rose up early in the *m'*,
8:10 And Joshua rose up early in the *m'*,
J'g 6:28 of the city arose early in the *m'*,
31 be put to death whilst it is yet *m'*:
9:33 it shall be, that in the *m'*, as soon
16: 2 In the *m'*, when it is day, we shall
19: 5 when they arose early in the *m'*,
8 And he arose early in the *m'* on the
25 abused her all...night until the *m'*:
27 And her lord rose up in the *m'*, and
20:19 children of Israel rose up in the *m'*,
Ru 2: 7 even from the *m'* until now, that
3:13 it shall be in the *m'*, that if he will
13 Lord liveth: lie down until the *m'*.
14 And she lay at his feet until the *m'*:
1Sa 1:19 they rose up in the *m'* early, and
3:15 And Samuel lay until the *m'*, and
5: 4 they arose early on the morrow *m'*,
11:11 midst of the host in the *m'* watch,
14:36 and spoil them until the *m'* light,
15:12 rose early to meet Saul in the *m'*,
17:16 drew near *m'* and evening, and
20 David rose up early in the *m'*, and
19: 2 take heed to thyself until the *m'*,
11 him, and to slay him in the *m'*:
20:35 And it came to pass in the *m'*, that
25:22 that pertain to him by the *m'* light
34 been left unto Nabal by the *m'* light
36 less or more, until the *m'* light.
37 it came to pass in the *m'*, when the
29:10 now rise up early in the *m'* with
10 as soon as ye be up early in the *m'*,
11 rose up early to depart in the *m'*,
2Sa 2:27 then in the *m'* the people had gone
11:14 And it came to pass in the *m'*, that
17:22 by the *m'* light there lacked not one
23: 4 he shall be as the light of the *m'*,
4 riseth, even a *m'* without clouds;
24:11 For when David was up in the *m'*,
15 upon Israel from the *m'* even to the
1Ki 3:21 I rose in the *m'* to give my child
21 when I had considered it in the *m'*,
17: 6 him bread and flesh in the *m'*, and
18:26 of Baal from *m'* even until noon,
2Ki 3:20 it came to pass in the *m'*, when the
22 they rose up early in the *m'*, and the
7: 9 if we tarry till the *m'* light, some
10: 8 entering in of the gate until the *m'*,
9 it came to pass in the *m'*, that he
16:15 altar burn the *m'* burnt offering,
19:35 and when they arose early in the *m'*,
1Ch 9:27 and the opening thereof every *m'*
16:40 offering continually *m'* and evening,
23:30 every *m'* to thank and praise the
2Ch 2: 4 the burnt offerings *m'* and evening,
13:11 every *m'* and every evening burnt
20:20 they rose early in the *m'*, and went
31: 3 the *m'* and evening burnt offerings,
Ezr 3: 3 burnt offerings *m'* and evening.
Neh 4:21 the rising of the *m'* till the stars
8: 3 water gate from the *m'* until midday,
Job 1: 5 and rose up early in the *m'*, and
4:20 are destroyed from *m'* to evening:
7:18 thou shouldest visit him every *m'*,
21 thou shalt seek me in the *m'*, but
11:17 shine forth, thou shalt be as the *m'*.
24:17 For the *m'* is to them even as the
38: 7 When the *m'* stars sang together,
12 Hast thou commanded the *m'* since
41:18 eyes are like the eyelids of the *m'*.
Ps 5: 3 voice shalt thou hear in the *m'*,
3 in the *m'* will I direct my prayer
30: 5 a night, but joy cometh in the *m'*.
49:14 have dominion over them in the *m'*;
55:17 and *m'*, and at noon, will I pray,
59:16 sing aloud of thy mercy in the *m'*:
65: 8 of the *m'* and evening to rejoice.
73:14 plagued, and chastened every *m'*.
88:13 in the *m'* shall my prayer prevent
90: 5 in the *m'* they are like grass which
6 In the *m'* it flourisheth, and groweth
92: 2 forth thy lovingkindness in the *m'*,
110: 3 holiness from the womb of the *m'*:
119:147 prevented the dawning of the *m'*, and
130: 6 than they that watch for the *m'*:
Ps 130: 6 than they that watch for the *m'*.
139: 9 If I take the wings of the *m'*, and
143: 8 hear thy lovingkindness in the *m'*;
Pr 7:18 us take our fill of love until the *m'*:
27:14 rising early in the *m'*, it shall be
Ec 10:16 and thy princes eat in the *m'*!
11: 6 In the *m'* sow thy seed, and in the
Ca 6:10 is she that looketh forth as the *m'*,
Isa 5:11 them that rise up early in the *m'*,
14:12 heaven, O Lucifer, son of the *m'*!
17:11 in the *m'* shalt thou make thy seed
14 and before the *m'* he is not.
21:12 The *m'* cometh, and also the night:
28:19 for *m'* by *m'* shall it pass over, by
33: 2 be thou their arm every *m'*, our
37:36 when they arose early in the *m'*,
38:13 I reckoned till *m'*, that, as a lion, so
50: 4 he wakeneth *m'* by *m'*, he wakeneth
58: 8 thy light break forth as the *m'*,
Jer 5: 8 They were as fed horses in the *m'*:
20:16 and let him hear the cry in the *m'*,
21:12 Execute judgment in the *m'*, and
La 3:23 They are new every *m'*: great is thy
Eze 7: 7 The *m'* is come unto thee, O thou
10 the *m'* is gone forth; the rod hath
12: 8 the *m'* came the word of the Lord
24:18 I spake unto the people in the *m'*:
18 I did in the *m'* as I was commanded.
33:22 until he came to me in the *m'*;
46:13 thou shalt prepare it every *m'*.
14 a meat offering for it every *m'*,
15 every *m'* for a continual...offering.
Da 6:19 king arose very early in the *m'*,
8:26 vision of the evening and the *m'*
Ho 6: 3 going forth is prepared as the *m'*;
4 your goodness is as a *m'* cloud,
7: 6 the *m'* it burneth as a flaming fire.
10:15 in a *m'* shall the king of Israel
13: 3 they shall be as the *m'* cloud, and
Joe 2: 2 *m'* spread upon the mountains:
Am 4: 4 bring your sacrifices every *m'*,
13 that maketh the *m'* darkness, and
5: 8 the shadow of death into the *m'*,
Jon 4: 7 when the *m'* rose the next day,
Mic 2: 1 when the *m'* is light, they practise
Zep 3: 5 every *m'* doth he bring his judgment
M't 16: 3 in the *m'*, It will be foul weather
20: 1 out early in the *m'* to hire labourers
21:18 Now in the *m'* as he returned into
27: 1 When the *m'* was come, all the chief
M'r 1:35 in the *m'*, rising up a great while
11:20 And in the *m'*, as they passed by,
13:35 or at the cockcrowing, or in the *m'*:
15: 1 in the *m'* the chief priests held
16: 2 very early in the *m'*, the first day
Lu 21:38 all the people came early in the *m'*
24: 1 very early in the *m'*, they came unto
Joh 8: 2 early in the *m'* he came again into
21: 4 But when the *m'* was now come,
Ac 5:21 into the temple early in the *m'*,
28:23 the prophets, from *m'* till evening.
Re 2:28 And I will give him the *m'* star.
22:16 David, and the bright and *m'* star.

morning-cloud See MORNING and CLOUD.

morning-light See MORNING and LIGHT.

morning-star See MORNING and STAR.

morning-watch See MORNING and WATCH.

morrow
Ge 19:34 it came to pass on the *m'*, that the
Ex 8:10 And he said, To *m'*. And he said,
23 thy people: to *m'* shall this sign be.
29 servants, and from his people, to *m'*:
9: 5 To *m'* the Lord shall do this thing
6 the Lord did that thing on the *m'*,
18 to *m'* about this time I will cause
10: 4 to *m'* will I bring the locusts into
16:23 To *m'* is the rest of the holy sabbath
17: 9 to *m'* I will stand on the top of the
18:13 pass on the *m'*, that Moses sat to
19:10 sanctify them to day and to *m'*,
32: 5 said, To *m'* is a feast to the Lord.
6 And they rose up early on the *m'*,
30 to pass on the *m'*, that Moses said
Le 7:16 on the *m'* also the remainder of it
19: 6 same day ye offer it, and on the *m'*:
22:30 shall leave none of it until the *m'*:
23:11 on the *m'* after the sabbath the
15 you from the *m'* after the sabbath,
16 Even unto the *m'* after the seventh
Nu 11:18 Sanctify yourselves against to *m'*,
14:25 To *m'* turn you, and get you into
16: 5 to *m'* the Lord will shew who are
7 in them before the Lord to *m'*:
16 thou, and they, and Aaron, to *m'*:
41 But on the *m'* all the congregation
17: 8 that on the *m'* Moses went into the
22:41 to pass on the *m'*, that Balak
33: 3 on the *m'* after the passover the
Jos 3: 5 for to *m'* the Lord will do wonders
5:11 land on the *m'* after the passover,
12 the manna ceased on the *m'* after
7:13 Sanctify yourselves against to *m'*:
11: 6 to *m'* about this time will I deliver
22:18 the Lord, that to *m'* he will be wroth
J'g 6:38 for he rose up early on the *m'*, and
9:42 to pass on the *m'*, that the people
19: 9 to *m'* get you early on your way,
20:28 to *m'* I will deliver them into
21: 4 to pass on the *m'*, that the people
1Sa 5: 3 of Ashdod arose early on the *m'*,
4 they arose early on the *m'* morning,
9:16 To *m'* about this time I will send
19 to *m'* I will let thee go, and will
11: 9 To *m'*, by that time the sun be hot,

1Sa 11: 10 To *m'* we will come out unto you,
11 it was so on the *m'*, that Saul put
18: 10 to pass on the *m'*, that the evil
19: 11 to night, to *m'* thou shalt be slain.
20: 5 to *m'* is the new moon, and I should
12 sounded my father about to *m'* any
18 to David, To *m'* is the new moon:
27 came to pass on the *m'*, which was
28: 19 to *m'* shalt thou and thy sons be
31: 8 on the *m'*, when the Philistines
2Sa 11: 12 and to *m'* I will let thee depart.
12 in Jerusalem that day, and the *m'*.
1Ki 19: 2 of them by to *m'* about this time.
20: 6 send my servants unto thee to *m'*
2Ki 6: 28 day, and we will eat my son to *m'*.
7: 1 To *m'* about this time...a measure
18 be to *m'* about this time in the gate
8: 15 it came to pass on the *m'*, that he
10: 6 me to Jezreel by to *m'* this time.
1Ch 10: 8 on the *m'*, when the Philistines
29: 21 on the *m'* after that day, even a
2Ch 20: 16 To *m'* go ye down against them:
17 to *m'* go out against them: for the
Es 2: 14 on the *m'* she returned into the
5: 8 will do to *m'* as the king hath said.
12 and to *m'* am I invited unto her also
14 to *m'* speak thou unto the king
9: 13 to do to *m'* also according unto
Pr 3: 28 come again, and to *m'* I will give;
27: 1 Boast not thyself of to *m'*; for thou
Isa 22: 13 and drink; for to *m'* we shall die.
56: 12 to *m'* shall be as this day, and much
Jer 20: 3 to pass on the *m'*, that Pashur
Zep 3: 3 they gnaw not the bones till the *m'*.
M't 6: 30 is, and to *m'* is cast into the oven,
34 therefore no thought for the *m'*:
34 for the *m'* shall take thought for the
M'r 11: 12 on the *m'*, when they were come
Lu 10: 35 And on the *m'* when he departed,
12: 28 field, and to *m'* is cast into the oven;
13: 32 and I do cures to day and to *m'*,
33 and to *m'*, and the day following:
Ac 4: 5 to pass on the *m'*, that their rulers,
10: 9 On the *m'*, as they went on their
23 And on the *m'* Peter went away with
24 And the *m'* after they entered into
20: 7 them, ready to depart on the *m'*;
22: 30 On the *m'*, because he would have
23: 15 he bring him down unto you to *m'*,
20 down Paul to *m'* into the council,
32 On the *m'* they left the horsemen
25: 17 on the *m'* I sat on the judgment
22 To *m'*, said he, thou shalt hear him.
23 And on the *m'*, when Agrippa was
1Co 15: 32 us eat and drink; for to *m'* we die.
Jas 4: 13 To day or to *m'* we will go into such
14 ye know not what shall be on the *m'*.

morsel See also MORSELS.
Ge 18: 5 And I will fetch a *m'* of bread, and
J'g 19: 5 thine heart with a *m'* of bread, and
Ru 2: 14 bread, and dip thy *m'* in the vinegar.
1Sa 2: 36 piece of silver and a *m'* of bread,
28: 22 let me set a *m'* of bread before
1Ki 17: 11 Bring me, I pray thee, a *m'* of bread
Job 31: 17 Or have eaten my *m'* myself alone,
Pr 17: 1 Better is a dry *m'*, and quietness
23: 8 The *m'* which thou hast eaten shalt
Heb 12: 16 one *m'* of meat sold his birthright.

morsels
Ps 147: 17 He casteth forth his ice like *m'*:

mortal See also IMMORTAL.
Job 4: 17 *m'* man be more just than God?
Ro 6: 12 therefore reign in your *m'* body,
8: 11 also quicken your *m'* bodies by his
1Co 15: 53 this *m'* must put on immortality.
54 *m'* shall have put on immortality,
2Co 4: 11 be made manifest in our *m'* flesh.

mortality See also IMMORTALITY.
2Co 5: 4 *m'* might be swallowed up of life.

mortally
De 19: 11 and smite him *m'* that he die, and

mortar See also MORTER.
Nu 11: 8 or beat it in a *m'*, and baked it in
Pr 27: 22 thou shouldest bray a fool in a *m'*

morter See also MORTAR.
Ge 11: 3 stone, and slime had they for *m'*.
Ex 1: 14 hard bondage, in *m'*, and in brick,
Le 14: 42 and he shall take other *m'*, and
45 and all the *m'* of the house;
Isa 41: 25 come upon princes as upon *m'*,
Eze 13: 10 others daubed it with untempered *m'*:
11 which daub it with untempered *m'*,
14 ye have daubed with untempered *m'*,
15 have daubed it with untempered *m'*,
22: 28 daubed them with untempered *m'*.
Na 3: 14 go into clay, and tread the *m'*,

mortgaged
Ne 5: 3 We have *m'* our lands, vineyards,

mortify
Ro 8: 13 the Spirit do *m'* the deeds of the
Col 3: 5 *M'* therefore your members which

Mosera (*mo-se'-rah*) See also MOSEROTH.
De 10: 6 of the children of Jaakan to *M'*:

Moseroth (*mo-se'-roth*) See also MOSERA.
Nu 33: 30 Hashmonah,...encamped at *M'*.
31 they departed from *M'*, and pitched

Moses (*mo'-zez*) See also MOSES'.
Ex 2: 10 she called his name *M'*: and she
11 in those days, when *M'* was grown,
14 *M'* feared, and said, Surely this
15 this thing, he sought to slay *M'*.
15 *M'* fled from the face of Pharaoh,
Ex 2: 17 *M'* stood up and helped them, and
21 *M'* was content to dwell with the
21 he gave *M'* Zipporah his daughter.
3: 1 Now *M'* kept the flock of Jethro his
3 *M'* said, I will now turn aside, and
4 midst of the bush, and said, *M'*, *M'*.
6 *M'* hid his face; for he was afraid to
11 *M'* said unto God, Who am I, that I
13 *M'* said unto God, Behold, when I
14 God said unto *M'*, I Am That I Am:
15 God said moreover unto *M'*, Thus
4: 1 And *M'* answered and said, But,
3 serpent; and *M'* fled from before it.
4 Lord said unto *M'*, Put forth thine
10 *M'* said unto the Lord, O my Lord,
14 the Lord was kindled against *M'*,
18 *M'* went and returned to Jethro his
18 And Jethro said to *M'*, Go in peace.
19 Lord said unto *M'* in Midian, Go,
20 *M'* took his wife and his sons, and
20 *M'* took the rod of God in his hand.
21 the Lord said unto *M'*, When thou
27 Go into the wilderness to meet *M'*.
28 *M'* told Aaron all the words of the
29 *M'* and Aaron went and gathered
30 the Lord had spoken unto *M'*, and
5: 1 afterward *M'* and Aaron went in,
4 *M'* and Aaron, let the people from
20 they met *M'* and Aaron, who stood
22 *M'* returned unto the Lord, and
6: 1 the Lord said unto *M'*, Now shalt
2 God spake unto *M'*, and said unto
9 *M'* spake so unto the children of
9 they hearkened not unto *M'* for
10 the Lord spake unto *M'*, saying,
12 *M'* spake unto the Lord, saying,
13 the Lord spake unto *M'* and unto
20 and she bare him Aaron and *M'*:
26 These are that Aaron and *M'*, to
27 these are that *M'* and Aaron.
28 the Lord spake unto *M'* in the land
29 the Lord spake unto *M'*, saying, I
30 *M'* said before the Lord, Behold, I
7: 1 The Lord said unto *M'*, See, I have
6 And *M'* and Aaron did as the Lord
7 *M'* was fourscore years old, and
8 the Lord spake unto *M'* and unto
10 *M'*...Aaron went in unto Pharaoh,
14 Lord said unto *M'*, Pharaoh's heart
19 the Lord spake unto *M'*, Say unto
20 *M'* and Aaron did so, as the Lord
8: 1 the Lord spake unto *M'*, Go unto
5 the Lord spake unto *M'*, Say unto
8 Pharaoh called for *M'* and Aaron,
9 *M'* said unto Pharaoh, Glory over
12 And *M'* and Aaron went out from
12 *M'* cried unto the Lord because of
13 did according to the word of *M'*;
16 Lord said unto *M'*, Say unto Aaron,
20 Lord said unto *M'*, Rise up early
25 called for *M'* and for Aaron, and
26 *M'* said, It is not meet so to do; for
29 And *M'* said, Behold, I go out from
30 *M'* went out from Pharaoh, and
31 did according to the word of *M'*;
9: 1 the Lord said unto *M'*, Go in unto
8 Lord said unto *M'* and unto Aaron,
8 *M'* sprinkle it toward the heaven
10 *M'* sprinkled it up toward heaven;
11 could not stand before *M'* because
12 as the Lord had spoken unto *M'*.
13 Lord said unto *M'*, Rise up early
22 Lord said unto *M'*, Stretch forth
23 *M'* stretched forth his rod toward
27 sent, and called for *M'* and Aaron,
29 *M'* said unto him, As soon as I am
33 And *M'* went out of the city from
35 go; as the Lord had spoken by *M'*.
10: 1 the Lord said unto *M'*, Go in unto
3 And *M'* and Aaron came in unto
8 *M'* and Aaron were brought again
9 *M'* said, We will go with our young
12 the Lord said unto *M'*, Stretch out
13 *M'* stretched forth his rod over the
16 Pharaoh called for *M'* and Aaron
21 Lord said unto *M'*, Stretch out
22 *M'* stretched forth his hand toward
24 Pharaoh called unto *M'*, and said,
25 *M'* said, Thou must give us also
29 *M'* said, Thou hast spoken well, I
11: 1 Lord said unto *M'*, Yet will I bring
3 *M'* was very great in the land of
4 And *M'* said, Thus saith the Lord,
9 Lord said unto *M'*, Pharaoh shall
10 *M'* and Aaron did all these wonders
12: 1 unto *M'* and Aaron in the land of
21 *M'* called for all the elders of Israel,
28 Lord had commanded *M'*...Aaron,
31 called for *M'* and Aaron by night,
35 did according to the word of *M'*;
43 the Lord said unto *M'* and Aaron,
50 Lord commanded *M'* and Aaron,
13: 1 the Lord spake unto *M'*, saying,
3 *M'* said unto the people, Remember
19 *M'* took the bones of Joseph with
14: 1 the Lord spake unto *M'*, saying,
11 they said unto *M'*, Because there
13 *M'* said unto the people, Fear ye
15 the Lord said unto *M'*, Wherefore
21 *M'* stretched out his hand over the
26 unto *M'*, Stretch out thine hand
27 *M'* stretched forth his hand over
31 the Lord, and his servant *M'*.
15: 1 Then sang *M'* and the children of
22 *M'* brought Israel from the Red
24 the people murmured against *M'*,
Ex 16: 2 murmured against *M'* and Aaron
4 unto *M'*, Behold, I will rain bread
6 *M'* and Aaron said unto all the
8 *M'* said, This shall be, when the
9 *M'* spake unto Aaron, Say unto all
11 the Lord spake unto *M'*, saying,
15 And *M'* said unto them, This is the
19 *M'* said, Let no man leave of it till
20 they hearkened not unto *M'*; but
20 and *M'* was wroth with them.
22 the congregation came and told *M'*.
24 it up till the morning, as *M'* bade:
25 And *M'* said, Eat that to day; for
28 the Lord said unto *M'*, How long
32 *M'* said, This is the thing which
33 *M'* said unto Aaron, Take a pot,
34 As the Lord commanded *M'*, so
17: 2 the people did chide with *M'*, and
2 *M'* said unto them, Why chide ye
3 people murmured against *M'*, and
4 *M'* cried unto the Lord, saying,
5 Lord said unto *M'*, Go on before
6 *M'* did so in the sight of the elders
9 *M'* said unto Joshua, Choose us
10 Joshua did as *M'* had said to him,
10 *M'*, Aaron, and Hur went up to the
11 when *M'* held up his hand, that
14 the Lord said unto *M'*, Write this
15 *M'* built an altar, and called the
18: 1 of all that God had done for *M'*,
5 wife unto *M'* in the wilderness,
6 he said unto *M'*, I thy father in law
7 *M'* went out to meet his father in
8 *M'* told his father in law all that
13 that *M'* sat to judge the people:
13 stood by *M'* from the morning unto
15 And *M'* said unto his father in law,
24 *M'* hearkened to the voice of his
25 *M'* chose able men out of all Israel,
26 hard causes they brought unto *M'*,
27 *M'* let his father in law depart;
19: 3 And *M'* went up unto God, and the
7 *M'* came and called for the elders
8 And *M'* returned the words of the
9 the Lord said unto *M'*, Lo, I come
9 *M'* told the words of the people
10 Lord said unto *M'*, Go unto the
14 And *M'* went down from the mount
17 *M'* brought forth the people out of
19 *M'* spake, and God answered him
20 Lord called *M'* up to the top of the
20 top of the mount; and *M'* went up.
21 the Lord said unto *M'*, Go down,
23 *M'* said unto the Lord, The people
25 *M'* went down unto the people, and
20: 19 said unto *M'*, Speak thou with us,
20 *M'* said unto the people, Fear not:
21 and *M'* drew near unto the thick
22 the Lord said unto *M'*, Thus thou
24: 1 unto *M'*, Come up unto the Lord,
2 *M'* alone shall come near the Lord:
3 *M'* came and told the people all
4 *M'* wrote all the words of the Lord,
6 *M'* took half of the blood, and put
8 *M'* took the blood, and sprinkled it
9 Then went up *M'*, and Aaron, and
12 Lord said unto *M'*, Come up to me
13 And *M'* rose up, and his minister
13 *M'* went up into the mount of God.
15 *M'* went up into the mount, and a
16 he called unto *M'* out of the midst
18 *M'* went into the midst of the cloud,
18 *M'* was in the mount forty days
25: 1 the Lord spake unto *M'*, saying,
30: 11, 17 the Lord spake unto *M'*, saying,
22 the Lord spake unto *M'*, saying,
34 the Lord said unto *M'*, Take unto
31: 1, 12 the Lord spake unto *M'*, saying,
18 And he gave unto *M'*, when he had
32: 1 the people saw that *M'* delayed to
1 for as for this *M'*, the man that
7 Lord said unto *M'*, Go, get thee
9 the Lord said unto *M'*, I have seen
11 *M'* besought the Lord his God, and
17 as they shouted, he said unto *M'*,
21 And *M'* said unto Aaron, What did
23 for as for this *M'*, the man that
25 when *M'* saw that the people were
26 *M'* stood in the gate of the camp,
28 did according to the word of *M'*:
29 *M'* had said, Consecrate yourselves
30 *M'* said unto the people, Ye have
31 *M'* returned unto the Lord, and
33 the Lord said unto *M'*, Whosoever
33: 1 Lord said unto *M'*, Depart, and go
5 Lord had said unto *M'*, Say unto
7 And *M'* took the tabernacle, and
8 *M'* went out unto the tabernacle,
8 his tent door, and looked after *M'*,
9 *M'* entered into the tabernacle, the
9 and the Lord talked with *M'*.
11 Lord spake unto *M'* face to face,
12 *M'* said unto the Lord, See, thou
17 Lord said unto *M'*, I will do this
34: 1 Lord said unto *M'*, Hew thee two
4 *M'* rose up early in the morning,
8 *M'* made haste, and bowed his
27 the Lord said unto *M'*, Write thou
29 *M'* came down from mount Sinai
29 *M'* wist not that the skin of his face
30 all the children of Israel saw *M'*,
31 *M'* called unto them; and Aaron
31 him: and *M'* talked with them.
33 *M'* had done speaking with them,
34 when *M'* went in before the Lord
35 of Israel saw the face of *M'*, that

Ex 34:35 M' put the vail upon his face again.
35: 1 M' gathered all the congregation
4 M' spake unto all the congregation
20 departed from the presence of M'.
29 to be made by the hand of M'.
30 M' said unto the children of Israel,
36: 2 M' called Bezaleel and Aholiab,
3 they received of M' all the offering,
5 they spake unto M', saying, The
6 M' gave commandment, and they
38:21 to the commandment of M', for
22 all that the Lord commanded M'.
39: 1, 5, 7, 21, 26, 29, 31 as the Lord commanded M'.
32 all that the Lord commanded M',
33 brought the tabernacle unto M',
42 all that the Lord commanded M',
43 M' did look upon all the work, and,
43 they done it: and M' blessed them.
40: 1 the Lord spake unto M', saying,
16 Thus did M': according to all that
18 M' reared up the tabernacle, and
19 it; as the Lord commanded M'.
21 as the Lord commanded M'.
23 as the Lord had commanded M'.
25, 27, 29 the Lord commanded M'.
31 M' and Aaron and his sons washed
32 as the Lord commanded M'.
33 gate. So M' finished the work.
35 M' was not able to enter into the
Le 1: 1 the Lord called unto M', and spake
4: 1 the Lord spake unto M', saying,
5:14 the Lord spake unto M', saying,
6: 1, 8, 19, 24 the Lord spake unto M',
7:22, 28 the Lord spake unto M', saying,
38 Which the Lord commanded M' in
8: 1 the Lord spake unto M', saying,
4 M' did as the Lord commanded
5 M' said unto the congregation,
6 M' brought Aaron and his sons,
9 as the Lord commanded M'.
10 And M' took the anointing oil, and
13 M' brought Aaron's sons, and put
13 them; as the Lord commanded M'.
15 M' took the blood, and put it upon
16 and M' burned it upon the altar.
17 camp; as the Lord commanded M'.
19 and M' sprinkled the blood upon the
20 M' burnt the head, and the pieces,
21 M' burnt the whole ram upon the
21 Lord; as the Lord commanded M'.
23 M' took of the blood of it, and put
24 M' put of the blood upon the tip of
24 and M' sprinkled the blood upon the
28 M' took them from off their hands,
29 M' took the breast, and waved it
29 part; as the Lord commanded M'.
30 M' took of the anointing oil, and of
31 M' said unto Aaron and to his sons,
36 Lord commanded by the hand of M'.
9: 1 that M' called Aaron and his sons,
5 brought that which M' commanded
6 M' said, This is the thing which the
7 M' said unto Aaron, Go unto the
10 altar; as the Lord commanded M'.
21 before the Lord; as M' commanded.
23 And M' and Aaron went into the
10: 3 M' said unto Aaron, This is it that
4 M' called Mishael and Elzaphan,
5 out of the camp; as M' had said.
6 And M' said unto Aaron, and unto
7 did according to the word of M'.
11 unto them by the hand of M'.
12 And M' spake unto Aaron, and unto
16 M' diligently sought the goat of the
19 Aaron said unto M', Behold, this
20 And when M' heard that, he was
11: 1 Lord spake unto M' and to Aaron,
12: 1 the Lord spake unto M', saying,
13: 1 the Lord spake unto M' and Aaron,
14: 1 the Lord spake unto M', saying,
33 the Lord spake unto M' and unto
15: 1 Lord spake unto M' and to Aaron,
16: 1 Lord spake unto M' after the death
2 And the Lord said unto M', Speak
34 did as the Lord commanded M'.
17: 1 the Lord spake unto M', saying,
18: 1 the Lord spake unto M', saying,
19: 1 the Lord spake unto M', saying,
20: 1 the Lord spake unto M', saying,
21: 1 And the Lord said unto M', Speak
16 the Lord spake unto M', saying,
24 M' told it unto Aaron, and to his
22: 1, 17, 26 Lord spake unto M', saying,
23: 1, 9, 23, 26, 33 spake unto M', saying,
44 M' declared unto the children of
24: 1 the Lord spake unto M', saying,
11 they brought him unto M': (and his
13 the Lord spake unto M', saying,
23 And M' spake unto the children of
23 did as the Lord commanded M'.
25: 1 Lord spake unto M' in mount Sinai,
26:46 in mount Sinai by the hand of M'.
27: 1 the Lord spake unto M', saying,
34 which the Lord commanded M' for
Nu 1: 1 And the Lord spake unto M' in the
17 And M' and Aaron took these men
19 As the Lord commanded M', so he
44 which M' and Aaron numbered,
48 For the Lord had spoken unto M',
54 all that the Lord commanded M',
2: 1 the Lord spake unto M' and unto
33 Israel; as the Lord commanded M'.
34 all that the Lord commanded M':
3: 1 the generations of Aaron and M'
5, 11 the Lord spake unto M', saying,

Nu 3:14 And the Lord spake unto M' in the
16 M' numbered them according to
38 congregation eastward, shall be M',
39 which M' and Aaron numbered at
40 the Lord said unto M', Number all
42 And M' numbered, as the Lord
44 the Lord spake unto M', saying,
49 M' took the redemption money of
51 M' gave the money of them that
51 Lord, as the Lord commanded M'.
4: 1, 17 Lord spake unto M' and unto
21 the Lord spake unto M', saying,
34 M' and Aaron and the chief of the
37 which M' and Aaron did number
37 of the Lord by the hand of M'.
41 whom M' and Aaron did number
45 whom M' and Aaron numbered
45 word of the Lord by the hand of M'.
46 whom M' and Aaron and the chief
49 were numbered by the hand of M',
49 him, as the Lord commanded M'.
5: 1 the Lord spake unto M', saying,
4 as the Lord spake unto M', so did
5, 11 the Lord spake unto M', saying,
6: 1, 22 the Lord spake unto M', saying,
7: 1 M' had fully set up the tabernacle,
4 the Lord spake unto M', saying,
6 M' took the wagons and the oxen,
11 the Lord said unto M', They shall
89 M' was gone into the tabernacle of
8: 1 the Lord spake unto M', saying,
3 as the Lord commanded M'.
4 which the Lord had shewed M', so
5 the Lord spake unto M', saying,
20 And M', and Aaron, and all the
20 Lord commanded M' concerning
22 had commanded M' concerning the
23 the Lord spake unto M', saying,
9: 1 And the Lord spake unto M' in the
4 And M' spake unto the children of
5 all that the Lord commanded M',
6 came before M' and before Aaron
8 M' said unto them, Stand still, and
9 the Lord spake unto M', saying,
23 of the Lord by the hand of M'.
10: 1 the Lord spake unto M', saying,
13 of the Lord by the hand of M'.
29 And M' said unto Hobab, the son of
35 that M' said, Rise up, Lord, and let
11: 2 And the people cried unto M'; and
2 M' prayed unto the Lord, the fire
10 Then M' heard the people weep
10 greatly; M' also was displeased.
11 M' said unto the Lord, Wherefore
16 the Lord said unto M', Gather unto
21 M' said, The people, among whom
23 said unto M', Is the Lord's hand
24 M' went out, and told the people the
27 ran a young man, and told M', and
28 the son of Nun, the servant of M',
28 answered and said, My lord M',
29 M' said unto him, Enviest thou for
30 M' gat him into the camp, he and
12: 1 Aaron spake against M' because of
2 Lord indeed spoken only by M'?
3 the man M' was very meek, above
4 the Lord spake suddenly unto M',
7 My servant M' is not so, who is
8 to speak against my servant M'?
11 And Aaron said unto M', Alas, my
13 M' cried unto the Lord, saying,
14 And the Lord said unto M', If her
13: 1 the Lord spake unto M', saying,
3 M' by the commandment of the
16 which M' sent to spy out the land.
16 M' called Oshea the son of Nun
17 M' sent them to spy out the land
26 And they went and came to M', and
30 Caleb stilled the people before M',
14: 2 Israel murmured against M' and
5 M' and Aaron fell on their faces
11 the Lord said unto M', How long
13 And M' said unto the Lord, Then
26 the Lord spake unto M' and unto
36 the men, which M' sent to search
39 M' told these sayings unto all the
41 And M' said, Wherefore now do ye
44 M', departed not out of the camp.
15: 1, 17 the Lord spake unto M', saying,
22 the Lord hath spoken unto M',
23 commanded you by the hand of M',
23 day that the Lord commanded M',
33 brought him unto M' and Aaron,
35 the Lord said unto M', The man
36 died; as the Lord commanded M'.
37 the Lord spake unto M', saying,
16: 2 And they rose up before M', with
3 themselves together against M' and
4 when M' heard it, he fell upon his
8 M' said unto Korah, Hear, I pray
12 And M' sent to call Dathan and
15 M' was very wroth, and said unto
16 M' said unto Korah, Be thou and
18 of the congregation with M' and
20 the Lord spake unto M' and unto
23 the Lord spake unto M', saying,
25 M' rose up and went unto Dathan
28 M' said, Hereby ye shall know that
36 the Lord spake unto M', saying,
40 Lord said to him by the hand of M'.
41 murmured against M' and against
42 gathered against M' and against
43 And M' and Aaron came before the
44 the Lord spake unto M', saying,
46 M' said unto Aaron, Take a censer,
47 Aaron took as M' commanded, and

Nu 16:50 returned unto M' unto the door of
17: 1 the Lord spake unto M', saying,
6 And M' spake unto the children of
7 M' laid up the rods before the Lord
8 M' went into the tabernacle of
9 M' brought out all the rods from
10 Lord said unto M', Bring Aaron's
11 M' did so: as the Lord commanded
12 children of Israel spake unto M',
18:25 the Lord spake unto M', saying,
19: 1 the Lord spake unto M' and unto
20: 2 together against M' and against
3 And the people chode with M', and
6 And M' and Aaron went from the
7 the Lord spake unto M', saying,
9 M' took the rod from before the
10 And M' and Aaron gathered the
11 M' lifted up his hand, and with his
12 the Lord spake unto M' and Aaron,
14 M' sent messengers from Kadesh
23 spake unto M' and Aaron in mount
27 M' did as the Lord commanded:
28 M' stripped Aaron of his garments,
28 M' and Eleazar came down from
21: 5 spake against God, and against M',
7 Therefore the people came to M',
7 And M' prayed for the people.
8 the Lord said unto M', Make thee
9 M' made a serpent of brass, and
16 whereof the Lord spake unto M',
32 M' sent to spy out Jaazer, and they
34 Lord said unto M', Fear him not:
25: 4 the Lord said unto M', Take all the
5 M' said unto the judges of Israel,
6 woman in the sight of M', and in
10, 16 the Lord spake unto M', saying,
26: 1 the Lord spake unto M' and unto
3 M' and Eleazar the priest spake
4 as the Lord commanded M' and the
9 who strove against M' and against
52 the Lord spake unto M', saying,
59 bare unto Amram Aaron and M',
63 they that were numbered by M' and
64 was not a man of them whom M'
27: 2 they stood before M', and before
5 M' brought their cause before the
6 the Lord spake unto M', saying,
11 as the Lord commanded M'.
12 said unto M', Get thee up into this
15 M' spake unto the Lord, saying,
18 the Lord said unto M', Take thee
22 M' did as the Lord commanded him:
23 commanded by the hand of M'.
28: 1 the Lord spake unto M', saying,
29:40 And M' told the children of Israel
40 all that the Lord commanded M'.
30: 1 And M' spake unto the heads of the
16 which the Lord commanded M',
31: 1 the Lord spake unto M', saying,
3 M' spake unto the people, saying,
6 And M' sent them to the war, a
7 as the Lord commanded M'; and
12 the prey, and the spoil, unto M',
13 M', and Eleazar the priest, and all
14 M' was wroth with the officers of
15 M' said unto them, Have ye saved
21 which the Lord commanded M';
25 the Lord spake unto M', saying,
31 M' and Eleazar the priest did as the
31 did as the Lord commanded M'.
41 M' gave the tribute, which was the
41 priest, as the Lord commanded M'.
42 which M' divided from the men that
47 M' took one portion of fifty, both of
47 Lord; as the Lord commanded M'.
48 of hundreds, came near unto M':
49 they said unto M', Thy servants
51, 54 M' and Eleazar the priest took
32: 2 Reuben came and spake unto M',
6 M' said unto the children of Gad
20 M' said unto them, If ye will do
25 children of Reuben spake unto M',
28 M' commanded Eleazar the priest,
29 M' said unto them, If the children
33 M' gave unto them, even to the
40 M' gave Gilead unto Machir the son
33: 1 their armies under the hand of M'
2 And M' wrote their goings out
50 Lord spake unto M' in the plains of
34: 1 the Lord spake unto M', saying,
13 And M' commanded the children of
16 the Lord spake unto M', saying,
35: 1 Lord spake unto M' in the plains of
9 the Lord spake unto M', saying,
36: 1 came near, and spake before M',
5 And M' commanded the children of
10 Even as the Lord commanded M',
13 commanded by the hand of M' unto
De 1: 1 which M' spake unto all Israel on
3 that M' spake unto the children
5 Moab, began M' to declare this law,
4:41 M' severed three cities on this side
44 M' set before the children of Israel:
45 which M' spake unto the children
46 M' and the children of Israel smote,
5: 1 M' called all Israel, and said unto
27: 1 And M' with the elders of Israel
9 And M' and the priests the Levites
11 M' charged the people the same
29: 1 which the Lord commanded M' to
2 M' called unto all Israel, and said
31: 1 And M' went and spake these words
7 M' called unto Joshua, and said
9 M' wrote this law, and delivered it
10 And M' commanded them, saying,
14 the Lord said unto M', Behold, thy

De 31:14 And M' and Joshua went, and
16 the Lord said unto M', Behold, thou
22 M' therefore wrote this song the
24 M' had made an end of writing the
25 That M' commanded the Levites,
30 And M' spake in the ears of all the
32:44 M' came and spake all the words of
45 M' made an end of speaking all
48 And the Lord spake unto M' that
33: 1 M' the man of God blessed the
4 M' commanded us a law, even the
34: 1 And M' went up from the plains of
5 So M' the servant of the Lord died
7 M' was an hundred and twenty
8 the children of Israel wept for M'
8 and mourning for M' were ended.
9 M' had laid his hands upon him:
9 and did as the Lord commanded M'.
10 prophet since in Israel like unto M'.
12 terror which M' shewed in the
Jos 1: 1 after the death of M' the servant of
2 M' my servant is dead; now
3 given unto you, as I said unto M'.
5 as I was with M', so I will be with
7 which M' my servant commanded
13 Remember the word which M' the
14 in the land which M' gave you on
15 which M' the Lord's servant gave
17 we hearkened unto M' in all things,
17 be with thee, as he was with M'.
3: 7 as I was with M', so I will be with
4:10 to all that M' commanded Joshua:
12 of Israel, as M' spake unto them:
14 they feared him, as they feared M',
8:31 As M' the servant of the Lord
31 written in the book of the law of M',
32 the stones a copy of the law of M',
33 as M' the servant of the Lord had
35 a word of all that M' commanded,
9:24 commanded his servant M' to give
11:12 as M' the servant of the Lord
15 As the Lord commanded M' his
15 so did M' command Joshua, and so
15 of all that the Lord commanded M'.
20 them, as the Lord commanded M'.
23 to all that the Lord said unto M';
12: 6 did M' the servant of the Lord and
6 M' the servant of the Lord gave it
13: 8 inheritance, which M' gave them,
8 as M' the servant of the Lord gave
12 for these did M' smite, and cast
15 And M' gave unto the tribe of the
21 whom M' smote with the princes of
24 M' gave inheritance unto the tribe
29 M' gave inheritance unto the half
32 countries which M' did distribute
33 Levi M' gave not any inheritance:
14: 2 commanded by the hand of M', for
3 M' had given the inheritance of two
5 As the Lord commanded M', so
6 the thing that the Lord said unto M'
7 M' the servant of the Lord sent me
9 And M' sware on that day, saying,
10 the Lord spake this word unto M',
11 I was in the day that M' sent me:
17: 4 Lord commanded M' to give us an
18: 7 M' the servant of the Lord gave
20: 2 spake unto you by the hand of M':
21: 2 commanded by the hand of M' to
8 commanded by the hand of M'.
22: 2 all that M' the servant of the Lord
4 M' the servant of the Lord gave
5 M' the servant of the Lord charged
7 M' had given possession in Bashan:
9 word of the Lord by the hand of M'.
23: 6 written in the book of the law of M',
24: 5 I sent M' also and Aaron, and I
J'g 1:20 Hebron unto Caleb, as M' said:
3: 4 their fathers by the hand of M'.
4:11 of Hobab the father in law of M',
1Sa 12: 6 Lord that advanced M' and Aaron,
8 then the Lord sent M' and Aaron,
1Ki 2: 3 as it is written in the law of M',
8: 9 stone, which M' put there at Horeb,
53 as thou spakest by the hand of M'
56 he promised by the hand of M' his
2Ki 14: 6 in the book of the law of M',
18: 4 brasen serpent that M' had made:
6 which the Lord commanded M'.
12 that M' the servant of the Lord
21: 8 that my servant M' commanded
23:25 according to all the law of M';
1Ch 6: 3 children of Amram; Aaron, and M',
49 to all that M' the servant of God
15:15 as M' commanded according to
21:29 which M' made in the wilderness,
22:13 which the Lord charged M' with
23:13 sons of Amram; Aaron and M':
14 concerning M' the man of God,
15 The sons of M' were, Gershom, and
26:24 the son of Gershom, the son of M',
2Ch 1: 3 M'...servant of the Lord had made
5:10 two tables which M' put therein
8:13 to the commandment of M',
23:18 as it is written in the law of M',
24: 6 commandment of M' the servant of
9 that M' the servant of God laid upon
25: 4 written in the law in the book of M',
30:16 to the law of M' the man of God;
33: 8 the ordinances by the hand of M'.
34:14 of the law of the Lord given by M'.
35: 6 word of the Lord by the hand of M'.
12 as it is written in the book of M'.
Ezr 3: 2 in the law of M' the man of God.
6:18 as it is written in the book of M'.
7: 6 a ready scribe in the law of M',
Ne 1: 7 thou commandest thy servant M'.
8 thou commandest thy servant M',
8: 1 to bring the book of the law of M',
14 the Lord had commanded by M',
9:14 by the hand of M' thy servant:
10:29 was given by M' the servant of God,
13: 1 that day they read in the book of M'
Ps 77:20 flock by the hand of M' and Aaron.
90: *title* A Prayer of M' the man of God.
99: 6 M' and Aaron among his priests,
103: 7 He made known his ways unto M',
105:26 He sent M' his servant; and Aaron
106:16 They envied M' also in the camp,
23 had not M' his chosen stood before
32 it went ill with M' for their sakes:
Isa 63:11 the days of old, M', and his people,
12 led them by the right hand of M'
Jer 15: 1 M' and Samuel stood before me,
Da 9:11 in the law of M' the servant of God,
13 As it is written in the law of M',
Mic 6: 4 I sent before thee M', Aaron, and
Mal 4: 4 ye the law of M' my servant, which
M't 8: 4 offer the gift that M' commanded,
17: 3 appeared unto them M' and Elias
4 one for thee, and one for M', and
19: 7 Why did M' then command to give
8 M' because of the hardness of your
22:24 M' said, If a man die, having no
M'r 1:44 those things which M' commanded,
7:10 M' said, Honour thy father and thy
9: 4 appeared unto them Elias with M':
5 one for thee, and one for M', and
10: 3 them, What did M' command you?
4 M' suffered...a bill of divorcement,
12:19 M' wrote...If a man's brother die,
26 have ye not read in the book of M',
Lu 2:22 the law of M' were accomplished,
5:14 according as M' commanded, for a
9:30 two men, which were M' and Elias:
33 one for thee, and one for M', and
16:29 They have M' and the prophets;
31 they hear not M' and the prophets,
20:28 M' wrote...If any man's brother die,
37 even M' shewed at the bush, when
24:27 And beginning at M' and all the
44 which were written in the law of M',
Joh 1:17 For the law was given by M', but
45 found him, of whom M' in the law,
3:14 as M' lifted up the serpent in the
5:45 you, even M', in whom ye trust.
46 For had ye believed M', ye would
6:32 M' gave you not that bread from
7:19 Did not M' give you the law, and
22 M'...gave unto you circumcision;
22 (not because it is of M', but of the
23 the law of M' should not be broken:
8: 5 M' in the law commanded us, that
9:29 We know that God spake unto M':
Ac 3:22 For M' truly said unto the fathers,
6:11 blasphemous words against M',
14 the customs which M' delivered us.
7:20 In which time M' was born, and
22 M' was learned in all the wisdom
29 Then fled M' at this saying, and
31 When M' saw it, he wondered at
32 Then M' trembled, and durst not
35 This M' whom they refused, saying,
37 This is that M', which said unto the
40 for as for this M', which brought us
44 had appointed, speaking unto M',
13:39 not be justified by the law of M'.
15: 1 circumcised after the manner of M',
5 command...to keep the law of M'.
21 M' of old time hath in every city
21:21 among the Gentiles to forsake M',
26:22 the prophets and M' did say should
28:23 both out of the law of M', and out
Ro 5:14 death reigned from Adam to M',
9:15 he saith to M', I will have mercy
10: 5 M' describeth the righteousness
19 First M' saith, I will provoke you
1Co 9: 9 For it is written in the law of M',
10: 2 all baptized unto M' in the cloud
2Co 3: 7 not stedfastly behold the face of M'
13 not as M', which put a vail over his
15 unto this day, when M' is read,
2Ti 3: 8 Jannes and Jambres withstood M',
Heb 3: 2 as also M' was faithful in all his
3 worthy of more glory than M',
5 And M' verily was faithful in all his
16 all that came out of Egypt by M'.
7:14 of which tribe M' spake nothing
8: 5 as M' was admonished of God when
9:19 when M' had spoken every precept
11:23 By faith M', when he was born, was
24 By faith M', when he was come to
12:21 that M' said, I exceedingly fear and
Jude 9 he disputed about the body of M',
Re 15: 3 sing the song of M' the servant of

Moses' (*mo'-zez*)
Ex 17:12 M' hands were heavy; and they
18: 1 priest of Midian, M' father in law,
2 Then Jethro, M' father in law, took
2 took Zipporah, M' wife, after he
5 M' father in law, came with his
12 M' father in law, took a burnt
12 to eat bread with M' father in law
14 M' father in law saw all that he did
17 And M' father in law said unto him,
32:19 M' anger waxed hot, and he cast
34:29 two tables of testimony in M' hand,
35 that the skin of M' face shone: and
Le 8:29 ram of consecration it was M' part;
Nu 10:29 the Midianite, M' father in law,
Jos 1: 1 Joshua the son of Nun, M' minister,
J'g 1:16 of the Kenite, M' father in law,
M't 23: 2 and the Pharisees sit in M' seat:
Joh 9:28 disciple; but we are M' disciples.
Heb 10:28 that despised M' law died without

most^ See also ALMOST; FOREMOST; HINDERMOST; HINDMOST; INNERMOST; MIDDLEMOST; NETHERMOST; OUTMOST; UTMOST; UTTERMOST.
Ge 14:18 was the priest of the m' high God.
19 be Abram of the m' high God,
20 blessed be the m' high God, which
22 unto the Lord, the m' high God,
Ex 26:33 the holy place and the m' holy.
34 the testimony in the m' holy place.
29:37 and it shall be an altar m' holy:
30:10 it is m' holy unto the Lord.
29 them, that they may be m' holy:
36 thee: it shall be unto you m' holy.
40:10 and it shall be an altar m' holy.
Le 2: 3, 10 a thing m' holy of the offerings
6:17 it is m' holy, as is the sin offering,
25 killed before the Lord: it is m' holy
29 shall eat thereof: it is m' holy.
7: 1 the trespass offering: it is m' holy.
6 eaten in the holy place: it is m' holy.
10:12 beside the altar: for it is m' holy.
17 the holy place, seeing it is m' holy,
14:13 the trespass offering: it is m' holy:
21:22 both of the m' holy, and of the holy.
24: 9 is m' holy unto him of the offerings
27:28 every devoted thing is m' holy unto
Nu 4: 4 about the m' holy things:
19 approach unto the m' holy things:
18: 9 shall be thine of the m' holy things,
9 be m' holy for thee and thy sons.
10 In the m' holy place shalt thou eat
24:16 knew the knowledge of the m' High,
De 32: 8 When the m' High divided to the
2Sa 22:14 and the m' High uttered his voice.
23:19 Was he not m' honourable of three?
1Ki 6:16 oracle, even for the m' holy place.
7:50 the inner house, the m' holy place,
8: 6 of the house, to the m' holy place,
1Ch 6:49 all the work of the place m' holy,
23:13 should sanctify the m' holy things,
2Ch 3: 8 And he made the m' holy house,
10 in the m' holy house he made two
4:22 doors thereof for the m' holy place,
5: 7 into the m' holy place, even under
31:14 the Lord, and the m' holy things.
Ne 7:65 should not eat of the m' holy things,
Es 6: 9 one of the king's m' noble princes,
Job 34:17 thou condemn him that is m' just?
Ps 7:17 to the name of the Lord m' high.
9: 2 to thy name, O thou m' High.
21: 6 hast made him m' blessed for ever:
7 the mercy of the m' High he shall
45: 3 sword upon thy thigh, O m' mighty,
46: 4 of the tabernacles of the m' High.
47: 2 For the Lord m' high is terrible; he
50:14 pay thy vows unto the m' High:
56: 2 against me, O thou m' High.
57: 2 I will cry unto God m' high; unto
73:11 there knowledge in the m' High?
77:10 of the right hand of the m' High.
78:17 by provoking the m' High in the
56 and provoked the m' high God, and
83:18 art the m' High over all the earth.
91: 1 in the secret place of the m' High
9 even the m' High, thy habitation;
92: 1 praises unto thy name, O m' High:
8 thou, Lord, art m' high for evermore.
107:11 the counsel of the m' High:
Pr 20: 6 M' men will proclaim every one
Ca 5:11 His head is as the m' fine gold,
16 His mouth is m' sweet: yea, he is
8: 6 which hath a m' vehement flame.
Isa 14:14 clouds; I will be like the m' High.
26: 7 m' upright, dost weigh the path of the
Jer 6:26 an only son, m' bitter lamentation:
50:31 I am against thee, O thou m' proud,
32 the m' proud shall stumble and fall,
La 3:35 man before the face of the m' High,
38 Out of the mouth of the m' High
4: 1 how is the m' fine gold changed!
Eze 2: 7 forbear: for they are m' rebellious.
23:12 and rulers clothed m' gorgeously,
33:28 For I will lay the land m' desolate,
29 when I have laid the land m' desolate
35: 3 and I will make thee m' desolate.
7 I make mount Seir m' desolate,
41: 4 unto me, This is the m' holy place.
42:13 Lord shall eat the m' holy things:
13 shall they lay the m' holy things,
43:12 round about shall be m' holy.
44:13 holy things, in the m' holy place:
45: 3 sanctuary and the m' holy place.
48:12 be unto them a thing m' holy
Da 3:20 commanded the m' mighty men
26 ye servants of the m' high God,
4:17 may know that the m' High ruleth
24 this is the decree of the m' High,
25, 32 know that the m' High ruleth in
34 and I blessed the m' High, and I
5:18 m' high God gave Nebuchadnezzar
21 knew that the m' high God ruled
7:18 saints of the m' High shall take
22 given to the saints of the m' High;
25 great words against the m' High,
25 wear out the saints of the m' High,
27 of the saints of the m' High, whose
9:24 and to anoint the m' Holy
11:15 mount, and take the m' fenced cities:
39 he do in the m' strong holds with
Ho 7:16 return, but not to the m' High:
11: 7 they called them to the m' High,
12:14 provoked him to anger m' bitterly:
Mic 7: 4 the m' upright is sharper than a thorn

M't 11: 20 m' of his mighty works were done,
M'r 5: 7 thou Son of the m' high God? I
Lu 1: 1 are m' surely believed among us,
3 in order, m' excellent Theophilus,
7: 42 which of them will love him m'?
43 that he, to whom he forgave m'.
8: 28 Jesus, thou Son of God m' high?
Ac 7: 48 m' High dwelleth not in temples
16: 17 the servants of the m' high God,
20: 38 Sorrowing m' of all for the words
23: 26 unto the m' excellent governor
24: 3 and in all places, m' noble Felix,
26: 5 that after the m' straitest sect of our
25 I am not mad, m' noble Festus;
1Co 14: 27 let it be by two, or at the m' by three,
15: 19 we are of all men m' miserable.
2Co 12: 9 M' gladly therefore will I rather
Heb 7: 1 Salem, priest of the m' high God,
Jude 20 yourselves on your m' holy faith,
Re 18: 12 manner vessels of m' precious wood,
21: 11 was like unto a stone m' precious,

Most-High See MOST and HIGH.

Most-Holy See MOST and HOLY.

mote
M't 7: 3 the m' that is in thy brother's eye,
4 me pull out the m' out of thine eye;
5 out the m' out of thy brother's eye.
Lu 6: 41 the m' that is in thy brother's eye,
42 pull out the m' that is in thine eye,
42 the m' that is in thy brother's eye.

moth See also MOTHEATEN.
Job 4: 19 which are crushed before the m.?
13: 28 garment...m'eaten[*some eds.* MOTH-EATEN]
27: 18 He buildeth his house as a m', and
Ps 39: 11 beauty to consume away like a m':
Isa 50: 9 garment; the m' shall eat them up.
51: 8 For the m' shall eat them up like a
Ho 5: 12 will I be unto Ephraim as a m',
M't 6: 19 where m' and rust doth corrupt,
20 where neither m' nor rust doth
Lu 12: 33 approacheth, neither m' corrupteth.

motheaten [*some eds.* MOTH-EATEN] See also MOTH and EATEN.
Jas 5: 2 and your garments are m'.

mother See also GRANDMOTHER; MOTHER'S; MOTHERS.
Ge 2: 24 a man leave his father and his m',
3: 20 because she was the m' of all living.
17: 16 and she shall be a m' of nations;
20: 12 but not the daughter of my m'; and
21: 21 his m' took him a wife out of the
24: 53 and to her m' precious things.
55 her m' said, Let the damsel abide
60 be thou the m' of thousands of
67 her into his m' Sarah's tent, and
27: 11 And Jacob said to Rebekah his m',
13 his m' said unto him, Upon me be
14 and brought them to his m': and
14 and his m' made savoury meat, such
28: 5 of Rebekah, Jacob's and Esau's m'.
7 Jacob obeyed his father and his m',
30: 14 and brought them unto his m' Leah.
32: 11 me, and the m' with the children.
37: 10 I and thy m' and thy brethren indeed
44: 20 he alone is left of his m', and his
Ex 2: 8 maid went and called the child's m'.
20: 12 Honour thy father and thy m': that
21: 15 that smiteth his father, or his m',
17 he that curseth his father, or his m',
Le 18: 7 father, or the nakedness of thy m',
7 she is thy m'; thou shalt not
9 of thy father, or daughter of thy m',
19: 3 Ye shall fear every man his m', and
20: 9 that curseth his father or his m'
9 he hath cursed his father or his m';
14 If a man take a wife and her m', it is
21: 2 for his m', and for his father, and for
11 himself for his father, or for his m';
Nu 6: 7 unclean for his father, or for his m',
26: 59 whom her m' bare to Levi in Egypt:
De 5: 16 Honour thy father and thy m', as
13: 6 the son of thy m', or thy son, or thy
21: 13 bewail her father and her m' a full
18 of his father, or the voice of his m',
19 father and his m' lay hold on him,
22: 15 father of the damsel, and her m',
27: 16 setteth light by his father or his m'.
22 father, or the daughter of his m'.
23 he that lieth with his m' in law.
33: 9 said unto his father and to his m',
Jos 2: 13 save alive my father, and my m',
18 shalt bring thy father, and thy m',
6: 23 and her father, and her m', and her
J'g 5: 7 arose, that I arose a m' in Israel.
28 The m' of Sisera looked out at a
8: 19 brethren, even the sons of my m':
14: 2 up, and told his father and his m',
3 Then his father and his m' said unto
4 But his father and his m' knew not
5 his father and his m', to Timnath,
6 he told not...his m' what he had done.
9 came to his father and m', and he
16 have not told it my father nor my m',
17: 2 he said unto his m', The eleven
2 his m' said, Blessed be thou of the
3 hundred shekels of silver to his m',
3 his m' said, I had wholly dedicated
4 he restored the money unto his m';
4 his m' took two hundred shekels of
Ru 1: 14 and Orpah kissed her m' in law;
2: 11 hast done unto thy m' in law since
11 hast left thy father and thy m',
18 her m' in law saw what she had
19 And her m' in law said unto her,
19 And she shewed her m' in law with
Ru 2: 23 and dwelt with her m' in law.
3: 1 Naomi her m' in law said unto her,
6 to all that her m' in law bade her.
16 when she came to her m' in law,
17 Go not empty unto thy m' in law.
1Sa 2: 19 his m' made him a little coat, and
15: 33 so shall thy m' be childless among
22: 3 Let my father and my m', I pray
2Sa 17: 25 sister to Zeruiah Joab's m'.
19: 37 grave of my father and of my m'.
20: 19 to destroy a city and a m' in Israel:
1Ki 1: 6 and his m' bare him after Absalom.
11 unto Bath-sheba the m' of Solomon,
2: 13 to Bath-sheba the m' of Solomon.
19 a seat to be set for the king's m';
20 king said unto her, Ask on, my m':
22 answered and said unto his m',
3: 27 no wise slay it: she is the m' thereof.
15: 13 And also Maachah his m', even her
17: 23 and delivered him unto his m':
19: 20 pray thee, kiss my father and my m',
22: 52 his father, and in the way of his m',
2Ki 3: 2 not like his father, and like his m':
13 and to the prophets of thy m'. And
4: 19 said to a lad, Carry him to his m'.
20 and brought him to his m', he sat
30 And the m' of the child said, As the
9: 22 thy m' Jezebel and her witchcrafts
11: 1 Athaliah the m' of Ahaziah saw
24: 12 his m', and his servants, and his
15 and the king's m', and the king's
1Ch 2: 26 Atarah; she was the m' of Onam.
4: 9 and his m' called his name Jabez,
2Ch 15: 16 Maachah the m' of Asa the king, he
22: 3 for his m' was his counsellor to do
10 Athaliah the m' of Ahaziah saw that
Es 2: 7 she had neither father nor m', and
7 when her father and m' were dead,
Job 17: 14 Thou art my m', and my sister.
Ps 27: 10 my father and my m' forsake me,
35: 14 as one that mourneth for his m'.
51: 5 and in sin did my m' conceive me.
109: 14 not the sin of his m' be blotted out.
113: 9 and to be a joyful m' of children.
131: 2 as a child that is weaned of his m':
Pr 1: 8 and forsake not the law of thy m':
4: 3 only beloved in the sight of my m'.
6: 20 and forsake not the law of thy m':
10: 1 foolish son is the heaviness of his m'.
15: 20 but a foolish man despiseth his m'.
19: 26 chaseth away his m', is a son that
20: 20 Whoso curseth his father or his m',
23: 22 despise not thy m' when she is old.
25 Thy father and thy m' shall be glad,
28: 24 Whoso robbeth his father or his m',
29: 15 to himself bringeth his m' to shame.
30: 11 father, and doth not bless their m'.
17 despiseth to obey his m', the ravens
31: 1 prophecy that his m' taught him.
Ca 3: 11 wherewith his m' crowned him in
6: 9 she is the only one of her m', she is
8: 1 that sucked the breasts of my m'!
5 there thy m' brought thee forth:
Isa 8: 4 to cry, My father, and my m', the
49: 1 from the bowels of my m' hath he
50: 1 transgressions is your m' put away.
66: 13 As one whom his m' comforteth, so
Jer 15: 8 against the m' of the young men a
10 Woe is me, my m', that thou hast
16: 7 for their father or for their m'.
20: 14 not the day wherein my m' bare me
17 my m' might have been my grave,
22: 26 thee out, and thy m' that bare thee,
50: 12 Your m' shall be sore confounded;
Eze 16: 3 an Amorite, and thy m' an Hittite.
44 As is the m', so is her daughter.
45 your m' was an Hittite, and your
19: 2 And say, What is thy m'? A lioness:
10 Thy m' is like a vine in thy blood,
22: 7 they set light by father and m': in
23: 2 women, the daughters of one m':
44: 25 but for father, or for m', or for son,
Ho 2: 2 Plead with your m', plead: for she
5 For their m' hath played the harlot:
4: 5 the night, and I will destroy thy m'.
10: 14 m' was dashed in pieces upon her
Mic 7: 6 daughter riseth up against her m',
6 in law against her m' in law;
Zec 13: 3, 3 father and his m' that begat him
M't 1: 18 as his m' Mary was espoused to
2: 11 the young child with Mary his m',
13 take the young child and his m',
14 took the young child and his m' by
20 take the young child and his m',
21 took the young child and his m',
8: 14 he saw his wife's m' laid, and sick
10: 35 and the daughter against her m',
35 in law against her m' in law.
37 that loveth father or m' more than
12: 46 his m' and his brethren stood
47 thy m' and thy brethren stand
48 Who is my m'? and who are my
49 behold my m' and my brethren!
50 is my brother, and sister, and m'.
13: 55 son? is not his m' called Mary?
14: 8 being before instructed of her m',
11 and she brought it to her m'.
15: 4 saying, Honour thy father and m':
4 that curseth father or m', let him
5 shall say to his father or his m',
6 honour not his father or his m',
19: 5 shall a man leave father and m',
19 Honour thy father and thy m': and,
29 father, or m', or wife, or children,
20: 20 to him the m' of Zebedee's children
27: 56 Mary the m' of James and Joses,
M't 27: 56 and the m' of Zebedee's children.
M'r 1: 30 But Simon's wife's m' lay sick of a
3: 31 then his brethren and his m',
32 thy m' and thy brethren without
33 Who is my m', or my brethren?
34 Behold my m' and my brethren!
35 my brother, and my sister, and m'.
5: 40 father and the m' of the damsel,
6: 24 said unto her m', What shall I ask?
28 and the damsel gave it to her m'.
7: 10 Honour thy father and thy m':
10 Whoso curseth father or m', let him
11 man shall say to his father or m',
12 do ought for his father or his m';
10: 7 shall a man leave his father and m',
19 not, Honour thy father and m'.
29 or sisters, or father, or m', or wife,
15: 40 Mary the m' of James the less and
47 Mary the m' of Joses beheld where he
16: 1 Mary the m' of James, and Salome
Lu 1: 43 the m' of my Lord should come to
60 his m' answered and said, Not so;
2: 33 Joseph and his m' marvelled at
34 and said unto Mary his m', Behold,
43 Joseph and his m' knew not of it.
48 and his m' said unto him, Son, why
51 his m' kept all these sayings in her
4: 38 Simon's wife's m' was taken with
7: 12 the only son of his m', and she
15 and he delivered him to his m'.
8: 19 Then came to him his m' and his
20 Thy m' and thy brethren stand
21 My m' and my brethren are these
51 father and the m' of the maiden.
12: 53 the m' against the daughter, and
53 and the daughter against the m';
53 m' in law against the daughter
53 in law against the m' in law.
14: 26 hate not his father, and m', and
18: 20 Honour thy father and thy m'.
24: 10 Joanna, and Mary the m' of James,
Joh 2: 1 and the m' of Jesus was there:
3 m' of Jesus saith unto him, They
5 His m' saith unto the servants,
12 and his m', and his brethren, and
6: 42 whose father and m' we know? how
19: 25 stood by the cross of Jesus his m',
26 When Jesus therefore saw his m',
26 he saith unto his m', Woman,
27 he to the disciple, Behold thy m'!
Ac 1: 14 and Mary the m' of Jesus, and with
12: 12 the house of Mary the m' of John,
Ro 16: 13 in the Lord, and his m' and mine.
Ga 4: 26 is free, which is the m' of us all.
Eph 5: 31 shall a man leave his father and m',
6: 2 Honour thy father and m'; which
2Ti 1: 5 Lois, and thy m' Eunice; and I
Heb 7: 3 Without father, without m', without
Re 17: 5 Great, The M' Of Harlots And

mother-in-law See MOTHER and LAW.

mother's
Ge 24: 28 told them of her m' house these
67 was comforted after his m' death.
27: 29 let thy m' sons bow down to thee:
28: 2 the house of Bethuel thy m' father;
2 daughters of Laban thy m' brother.
29: 10 daughter of Laban his m' brother,
10 the sheep of Laban his m' brother,
10 the flock of Laban his m' brother.
43: 29 his brother Benjamin, his m' son,
Ex 23: 19 shalt not seethe a kid in his m' milk.
34: 26 shalt not seethe a kid in his m' milk.
Le 18: 13 the nakedness of thy m' sister:
13 for she is thy m' near kinswoman.
20: 17 or his m' daughter, and see her
19 the nakedness of thy m' sister, nor
24: 11 (and his m' name was Shelomith,
Nu 12: 12 he cometh out of his m' womb.
De 14: 21 shalt not seethe a kid in his m' milk.
J'g 9: 1 to Shechem unto his m' brethren,
1 family of the house of his m' father,
3 his m' brethren spake of him in the
16: 17 unto God from my m' womb: if I
Ru 1: 8 Go, return each to her m' house:
1Sa 20: 30 the confusion of thy m' nakedness?
1Ki 11: 26 whose m' name was Zeruah, a
14: 21, 31 And his m' name was Naamah
15: 2, 10 And his m' name was Maachah,
22: 42 And his m' name was Azubah the
2Ki 8: 26 And his m' name was Athaliah, the
12: 1 m' name was Zibiah of Beer-sheba.
14: 2 And his m' name was Jehoaddan of
15: 2 And his m' name was Jecholiah of
33 And his m' name was Jerusha, the
18: 2 m' name also was Abi, the daughter
21: 1 And his m' name was Hephzi-bah.
19 his m' name was Meshullemeth,
22: 1 And his m' name was Jedidah, the
23: 31 And his m' name was Hamutal, the
36 And his m' name was Zebudah, the
24: 8 And his m' name was Nehushta, the
18 And his m' name was Hamutal, the
2Ch 12: 13 And his m' name was Naamah an
13: 2 His m' name also was Michaiah the
20: 31 And his m' name was Azubah the
22: 2 His m' name also was Athaliah the
24: 1 His m' name also was Zibiah of
25: 1 And his m' name was Jehoaddan of
26: 3 His m' name also was Jecoliah of
27: 1 His m' name also was Jerushah, the
29: 1 And his m' name was Abijah, the
Job 1: 21 Naked came I out of my m' womb,
3: 10 shut not up the doors of my m' womb,
31: 18 guided her from my m' womb;)
Ps 22: 9 when I was upon my m' breasts.

Ps 22:10 thou art my God from my m' belly.
50:20 thou slanderest thine own m' son.
69: 8 and an alien unto my m' children.
71: 6 that took me out of my m' bowels:
139:13 hast covered me in my m' womb.
Ec 5:15 As he came forth of his m' womb,
Ca 1: 6 my m' children were angry with me;
3: 4 had brought him into my m' house,
8: 2 and bring thee into my m' house,
Isa 50: 1 is the bill of your m' divorcement,
Jer 52: 1 And his m' name was Hamutal the
Eze 16:45 Thou art thy m' daughter, that
M't 19:12 were so born from their m' womb:
Lu 1:15 Ghost, even from his m' womb.
Joh 3: 4 the second time into his m' womb,
19:25 And his m' sister, Mary the wife of
Ac 3: 2 man lame from his m' womb was
14: 8 being a cripple from his m' womb,
Ga 1:15 separated me from my m' womb,

mothers See also MOTHERS'.
Isa 49:23 and their queens thy nursing m':
Jer 16: 3 concerning their m' that bare them,
La 2:12 They say to their m', Where is corn
5: 3 fatherless, our m' are as widows.
M'r 10:30 and sisters, and m', and children,
1Ti 1: 9 of fathers and murderers of m',
5: 2 The elder women as m'; the

mothers'
La 2:12 poured out into their m' bosom.

motions
Ro 7: 5 the m' of sin, which were by the

mouldy
Jos 9: 5 their provision was dry and m'.
12 now, behold, it is dry, and it is m':

mount See also MOUNTAIN; MOUNTED; MOUNTING; MOUNTS.
Ge 10:30 unto Sephar a m' of the east.
14: 6 And the Horites in their m' Seir,
22:14 in the m' of the Lord it shall be
31:21 set his face toward the m' Gilead.
23 they overtook him in the m' Gilead.
25 had pitched his tent in the m':
25 Laban...pitched in the m' of Gilead.
54 Jacob offered sacrifice upon the m',
54 and tarried all night in the m'.
36: 8 Thus dwelt Esau in m' Seir: Esau
9 father of the Edomites in m' Seir:
Ex 4:27 went, and met him in the m' of God,
18: 5 he encamped at the m' of God:
19: 2 there Israel camped before the m'.
11 sight of all the people upon m' Sinai.
12 that ye go not up into the m', or
12 whosoever toucheth the m' shall be
13 long, they shall come up to the m'.
14 Moses went down from the m' unto
16 and a thick cloud upon the m', and
17 stood at the nether part of the m'.
18 m' Sinai was altogether on a smoke,
18 and the whole m' quaked greatly.
20 the Lord came down upon m' Sinai,
20 on the top of the m': and the Lord
20 called Moses up to the top of the m';
23 people cannot come up to m' Sinai:
23 us, saying, Set bounds about the m',
24:12 Moses, Come up to me into the m',
13 Moses went up into the m' of God.
15 And Moses went up into the m',
15 and a cloud covered the m'.
16 of the Lord abode upon m' Sinai,
17 devouring fire on the top of the m'
18 cloud, and gat him up into the m':
18 Moses was in the m' forty days and
25:40 which was shewed thee in the m'.
26:30 which was shewed thee in the m'.
27: 8 as it was shewed thee in the m', so
31:18 communing with him upon m' Sinai,
32: 1 delayed to come down out of the m',
15 turned, and went down from the m',
19 and brake them beneath the m'.
33: 6 of their ornaments by the m' Horeb.
34: 2 up in the morning unto m' Sinai,
2 there to me in the top of the m'.
3 man be seen throughout all the m';
3 flocks nor herds feed before that m'.
4 and went up unto m' Sinai, as
29 Moses came down from m' Sinai
29 when he came down from the m',
32 had spoken with him in m' Sinai.
Le 7:38 Lord commanded Moses in m' Sinai,
25: 1 Lord spake unto Moses in m' Sinai,
26:46 in m' Sinai by the hand of Moses.
27:34 for the children of Israel in m' Sinai.
Nu 3: 1 Lord spake with Moses in m' Sinai.
10:33 departed from the m' of the Lord
20:22 Kadesh, and came unto m' Hor.
23 unto Moses and Aaron in m' Hor,
25 and bring them up unto m' Hor:
27 and they went up into m' Hor in the
28 died there in the top of the m':
28 Eleazar came down from the m'.
21: 4 they journeyed from m' Hor by the
27:12 Get thee up into this m' Abarim,
28: 6 ordained in m' Sinai for a sweet
33:23 and pitched in m' Shapher.
24 And they removed from m' Shapher,
37 Kadesh, and pitched in m' Hor,
38 the priest went up into m' Hor at
39 years old when he died in m' Hor.
41 they departed from m' Hor, and
34: 7 ye shall point out for you m' Hor:
8 From m' Hor ye shall point out
De 1: 2 from Horeb by the way of m' Seir
6 have dwelt long enough in this m':
7 go to the m' of the Amorites, and

De 2: 1 we compassed m' Seir many days.
5 I have given m' Seir unto Esau for
3: 8 the river of Arnon unto m' Hermon;
12 the river Arnon, and half m' Gilead,
4:48 unto m' Sion, which is Hermon,
5: 4 with you face to face in the m' out
5 fire, and went not up into the m';)
22 unto all your assembly in the m'
9: 9 When I was gone up into the m' to
9 I abode in the m' forty days and
10 the Lord spake with you in the m'
15 turned and came down from the m',
15 and the m' burned with fire: and
21 brook that descended out of the m'.
10: 1 and come up unto me into the m',
3 the first, and went up into the m',
4 the Lord spake unto you in the m'
5 came down from the m', and put
10 I stayed in the m', according to the
11:29 put the blessing upon m' Gerizim,
29 and the curse upon m' Ebal.
27: 4 in m' Ebal, and thou shalt plaister
12 stand upon m' Gerizim to bless the
13 shall stand upon m' Ebal to curse;
32:49 unto m' Nebo, which is in the land
50 die in the m' whither thou goest up,
50 Aaron thy brother died in m' Hor,
33: 2 he shined forth from m' Paran, and
Jos 8:30 the Lord God of Israel in m' Ebal,
33 of them over against m' Gerizim,
33 half of them over against m' Ebal;
11:17 from the m' Halak, that goeth up
17 of Lebanon under m' Hermon:
12: 1 the river Arnon unto m' Hermon,
5 And reigned in m' Hermon, and in
7 Lebanon even unto the m' Halak,
13: 5 from Baal-gad under m' Hermon
11 all m' Hermon, and all Bashan unto
19 Zareth-Shahar in...m' of the valley,
15: 9 went out to the cities of m' Ephron;
10 from Baalah westward unto m' Seir,
10 along unto the side of m' Jearim,
11 And passed along to m' Baalah, and
16: 1 Jericho throughout m' Beth-el,
17:15 if m' Ephraim be too narrow for
19:50 Timnath-serah in m' Ephraim:
20: 7 Kedesh in Galilee in m' Naphtali,
7 and Shechem in m' Ephraim, and
21:21 with her suburbs in m' Ephraim,
24: 4 I gave unto Esau m' Seir, to possess
30 which is in m' Ephraim, on the
33 was given him in m' Ephraim.
J'g 1:35 Amorites would dwell in m' Heres
2: 9 in the m' of Ephraim, on the north
3: 3 Hivites that dwell in m' Lebanon,
3 from m' Baal-hermon unto the
27 went down with him from the m',
4: 5 Ramah and Beth-el in m' Ephraim:
6 Go and draw toward m' Tabor, and
12 Abinoam was gone up to m' Tabor.
14 Barak went down from m' Tabor,
7: 3 and depart early from m' Gilead.
24 throughout all m' Ephraim, saying,
9: 7 and stood in the top of m' Gerizim,
48 gat him up to m' Zalmon, he and
10: 1 he dwelt in Shamir in m' Ephraim.
12:15 in the m' of the Amalekites.
17: 1 there was a man of m' Ephraim,
8 and he came to m' Ephraim to the
18: 2 when they came to m' Ephraim, to
13 passed thence unto m' Ephraim,
19: 1 on the side of m' Ephraim, who
16 which was also of m' Ephraim;
18 toward the side of m' Ephraim;
1Sa 1: 1 of m' Ephraim, and his name was
9: 4 he passed through m' Ephraim,
13: 2 in Michmash and in m' Beth-el, and
14:22 had hid themselves in m' Ephraim,
31: 1 and fell down slain in m' Gilboa.
8 his three sons fallen in m' Gilboa.
2Sa 1: 6 by chance upon m' Gilboa, behold,
15:30 went up by the ascent of m' Olivet,
32 David was come to the top of the m',
20:21 but a man of m' Ephraim, Sheba
1Ki 4: 8 The son of Hur, in m' Ephraim:
12:25 built Shechem in m' Ephraim, and
18:19 to me all Israel unto m' Carmel,
20 prophets together unto m' Carmel.
19: 8 nights unto Horeb the m' of God.
11 stand upon the m' before the Lord.
2Ki 2:25 he went from thence to m' Carmel,
4:25 unto the man of God to m' Carmel.
5:22 from m' Ephraim two young men
19:31 and they that escape out of m' Zion:
23:13 right hand of the m' of corruption,
16 sepulchres...were there in the m',
1Ch 4:42 five hundred men, went to m' Seir,
5:23 and Senir, and unto m' Hermon.
6:67 Shechem in m' Ephraim with her
10: 1 and fell down slain in m' Gilboa.
8 and his sons fallen in m' Gilboa.
2Ch 3: 1 the Lord at Jerusalem in m' Moriah,
13: 4 Abijah stood up upon m' Zemaraim,
4 which is in m' Ephraim, and said,
15: 8 he had taken from m' Ephraim,
19: 4 from Beer-sheba to m' Ephraim,
20:10 of Ammon and Moab and m' Seir,
22 of Ammon, Moab, and m' Seir,
23 against the inhabitants of m' Seir,
33:15 altars that he had built in the m' of
Ne 8:15 Go forth unto the m', and fetch
9:13 camest down also upon m' Sinai,
Job 20: 6 excellency m' up to the heavens,
39:27 the eagle m' up at thy command,
Ps 48: 2 joy of the whole earth, is m' Zion,
11 m' Zion rejoice, let the daughters

Ps 74: 2 m' Zion, wherein thou hast dwelt.
78:68 Judah, the m' Zion which he loved.
107:26 They m' up to the heaven, they go
125: 1 in the Lord shall be as m' Zion,
Ca 4: 1 goats, that appear from m' Gilead.
Isa 4: 5 every dwelling place of m' Zion,
8:18 of hosts, which dwelleth in m' Zion.
9:18 m' up like the lifting up of smoke.
10:12 his whole work upon m' Zion and
32 the m' of the daughter of Zion,
14:13 upon the m' of the congregation,
16: 1 unto the m' of the daughter of Zion.
18: 7 of the Lord of hosts, the m' Zion.
24:23 Lord of hosts shall reign in m' Zion,
27:13 Lord in the holy m' at Jerusalem.
28:21 shall rise up as in m' Perazim, he
29: 3 lay siege against thee with a m',
8 be, that fight against m' Zion.
31: 4 come down to fight for m' Zion, and
37:32 they that escape out of m' Zion:
40:31 shall m' up with wings as eagles;
Jer 4:15 affliction from m' Ephraim.
6: 6 and cast a m' against Jerusalem:
31: 6 upon the m' Ephraim shall cry,
50:19 upon m' Ephraim and Gilead.
51:53 Babylon should m' up to heaven,
Eze 4: 2 against it, and cast a m' against it:
10:16 wings to m' up from the earth, the
21:22 to cast a m', and to build a fort.
26: 8 cast a m' against thee, and lift up
35: 2 man, set thy face against m' Seir,
3 Behold, O m' Seir, I am against
7 will I make m' Seir most desolate,
15 thou shalt be desolate, O m' Seir,
Da 11:15 north shall come, and cast up a m',
Joe 2:32 in m' Zion and in Jerusalem shall
Ob 8 understanding out of the m' of
9 every one of the m' of Esau may be
17 upon m' Zion shall be deliverance,
19 south shall possess the m' of Esau;
21 saviours shall come up on m' Zion
21 to judge the m' of Esau; and the
Mic 4: 7 shall reign over them in m' Zion
Hab 3: 3 and the Holy One from m' Paran.
Zec 14: 4 in that day upon the m' of Olives,
4 the m' of Olives shall cleave in the
M't 21: 1 Bethphage, unto the m' of Olives,
24: 3 as he sat upon the m' of Olives, the
26:30 they went out into the m' of Olives.
M'r 11: 1 and Bethany, at the m' of Olives,
13: 3 And as he sat upon the m' of Olives
14:26 they went out into the m' of Olives.
Lu 19:29 Bethany, at the m' called...Olives,
29 at...the m' of Olives, he sent two
37 at the descent of the m' of Olives,
21:37 he went out, and abode in the m'
37 out, and abode in...the m' of Olives.
22:39 as he was wont, to the m' of Olives;
Joh 8: 1 Jesus went unto the m' of Olives.
Ac 1:12 from the m' called Olivet, which is
7:30 to him in the wilderness of m' Sina
38 which spake to him in the m' Sina,
Ga 4:24 the one from the m' Sinai, which
25 For this Agar is m' Sinai in Arabia,
Heb 8: 5 the pattern shewed to thee in the m'.
12:18 unto the m' that might be touched,
22 ye are come unto m' Sion, and unto
2Pe 1:18 we were with him in the holy m'.
Re 14: 1 lo, a Lamb stood on the m' Sion,

mountain See also MOUNTAINS.
Ge 12: 8 unto a m' on the east of Beth-el,
14:10 they that remained fled to the m'.
19:17 escape to the m', lest thou be
19 I cannot escape to the m', lest some
30 and dwelt in the m', and his two
Ex 3: 1 and came to the m' of God, even to
12 ye shall serve God upon this m'.
15:17 in the m' of thine inheritance, in
19: 3 Lord called unto him out of the m',
20:18 of the trumpet, and the m' smoking:
Nu 13:17 southward, and go up into the m':
14:40 gat them up into the top of the m'.
De 1:19 the way of the m' of the Amorites,
20 come unto the m' of the Amorites,
24 turned and went up into the m',
44 Amorites, which dwelt in that m',
2: 3 Ye have compassed this m' long
3:25 that goodly m', and Lebanon.
4:11 came near and stood under the m';
11 and the m' burned with fire unto the
5:23 (for the m' did burn with fire,) that
32:49 Get thee up into this m' Abarim,
33:19 shall call the people unto the m';
34: 1 plains of Moab unto the m' of Nebo,
Jos 2:16 Get you to the m', lest the pursuers
22 came unto the m', and abode there
23 descended from the m', and passed
11:16 and the plain, and the m' of Israel,
14:12 therefore give me this m', whereof
15: 8 border went up to the top of the m'
17:18 But the m' shall be thine; for it is
18:16 came down to the end of the m'
20: 7 which is Hebron, in the m' of Judah.
J'g 1: 9 Canaanites, that dwelt in the m',
19 drave out the inhabitants of the m';
34 the children of Dan into the m':
3:27 a trumpet in the m' of Ephraim,
1Sa 17: 3 the Philistines stood on a m' on the
3 Israel stood on a m' on the other
23:14 remained in a m' in the wilderness
26 Saul went on this side of the m',
26 and his men on that side of the m':
2Ki 2:16 cast him upon some m', or into
6:17 behold, the m' was full of horses
2Ch 2: 2 thousand to hew in the m', and
18 thousand to be hewers in the m',

Job 14: 18 the *m'* falling cometh to nought.
Ps 11: 1 my soul, Flee as a bird to your *m'*?
30: 7 hast made my *m'* to stand strong:
48: 1 our God, in the *m'* of his holiness.
78: 54 to this *m'*, which his right hand had
Ca 4: 6 I will get me to the *m'* of myrrh,
Isa 2: 2 the *m'* of the Lord's house shall be
3 let us go up to the *m'* of the Lord,
11: 9 hurt nor destroy in all my holy *m'*:
13: 2 ye up a banner upon the high *m'*,
25: 6 in this *m'* shall the Lord of hosts
7 he will destroy in this *m'* the face
10 For in this *m'* shall the hand of the
30: 17 as a beacon upon the top of a *m'*,
25 there shall be upon every high *m'*,
29 to come into the *m'* of the Lord,
40: 4 and every *m'* and hill shall be made
9 get thee up into the high *m'*: O
56: 7 them will I bring to my holy *m'*,
57: 7 Upon a lofty and high *m'* hast thou
13 land, and shall inherit my holy *m'*;
65: 11 that forget my holy *m'*, that
25 hurt nor destroy in all my holy *m'*,
66: 20 beasts, to my holy *m'* Jerusalem,
Jer 3: 6 she is gone up upon every high *m'*
16: 16 they shall hunt them from every *m'*,
17: 3 O my *m'* in the field, I will give thy
26: 18 the *m'* of the house as the high
31: 23 of justice, and *m'* of holiness.
50: 6 they have gone from *m'* to hill, they
51: 25 I am against thee, O destroying *m'*,
25 and will make thee a burnt *m'*.
La 5: 18 Because of the *m'* of Zion, which
Eze 11: 23 stood upon the *m'* which is on the
17: 22 will plant it upon an high *m'* and
23 In the *m'* of the height of Israel
20: 40 For in mine holy *m'* in the
40 in the *m'* of the height of Israel,
28: 14 thou wast upon the holy *m'* of God;
16 as profane out of the *m'* of God:
40: 2 and set me upon a very high *m'*,
43: 12 Upon the top of the *m'* the whole
Da 2: 35 the image became a great *m'*,
45 cut out of the *m'* without hands,
9: 16 thy city Jerusalem, thy holy *m'*:
20 my God for the holy *m'* of my God;
11: 45 the seas in the glorious holy *m'*;
Joe 2: 1 and sound an alarm in my holy *m'*:
3: 17 God dwelling in Zion, my holy *m'*:
Am 4: 1 that are in the *m'* of Samaria,
6: 1 and trust in the *m'* of Samaria,
Ob 16 as ye have drunk upon my holy *m'*,
Mic 3: 12 and the *m'* of the house as the high
4: 1 that the *m'* of the house of the Lord
2 let us go up to the *m'* of the Lord,
7: 12 from sea to sea, and from *m'* to *m'*.
Zep 3: 11 be haughty because of my holy *m'*.
Hag 1: 8 Go up to the *m'*, and bring wood,
Zec 4: 7 Who art thou, O great *m'*? before
8: 3 *m'* of the Lord of hosts the holy *m'*.
14: 4 half of the *m'* shall remove toward
M't 4: 8 up into an exceeding high *m'*,
5: 1 multitudes, he went up into a *m'*:
8: 1 he was come down from the *m'*,
14: 23 went up into a *m'* apart to pray:
15: 29 went up into a *m'*, and sat down
17: 1 them up into an high *m'* apart,
9 as they came down from the *m'*,
20 ye shall say unto this *m'*, Remove
21: 21 but also if ye shall say unto this *m'*,
28: 16 Galilee, into a *m'* where Jesus had
M'r 3: 13 And he goeth up into a *m'*, and
6: 46 he departed into a *m'* to pray.
9: 2 leadeth them up into an high *m'*
9 as they came down from the *m'*, he
11: 23 whosoever shall say unto this *m'*,
Lu 3: 5 every *m'* and hill shall be brought
4: 5 taking him up into an high *m'*,
6: 12 that he went out into a *m'* to pray,
8: 32 of many swine feeding on the *m'*:
9: 28 and went up into a *m'* to pray.
Joh 4: 20 Our fathers worshipped in this *m'*;
21 when ye shall neither in this *m'*,
6: 3 And Jesus went up into a *m'*, and
15 again into a *m'* himself alone.
Heb 12: 20 if so much as a beast touch the *m'*,
Re 6: 14 every *m'* and island were moved
8: 8 as it were a great *m'* burning with
21: 10 in the spirit to a great and high *m'*,

mountains
Ge 7: 20 prevail; and the *m'* were covered.
8: 4 the month, upon the *m'* of Ararat.
5 month, were the tops of the *m'* seen.
22: 2 burnt offering upon one of the *m'*
Ex 32: 12 them out, to slay them in the *m'*,
Nu 13: 29 and the Amorites, dwell in the *m'*:
23: 7 Aram, out of the *m'* of the east,
33: 47 and pitched in the *m'* of Abarim,
48 departed from the *m'* of Abarim,
De 2: 37 nor unto the cities in the *m'*, nor
12: 2 their gods, upon the high *m'*, and
32: 22 on fire the foundations of the *m'*.
33: 15 the chief things of the ancient *m'*,
Jos 10: 6 the Amorites that dwell in the *m'*
11: 2 that were on the north of the *m'*,
3 and the Jebusite in the *m'*, and to
21 cut off the Anakims from the *m'*,
21 and from all the *m'* of Judah, and
21 and from all the *m'* of Israel:
12: 8 In the *m'*, and in the valleys, and
15: 48 And in the *m'*, Shamir, and Jattir,
18: 12 went up through the *m'* westward;
J'g 5: 5 *m'* melted from before the Lord,
6: 2 them the dens which are in the *m'*,
9: 25 in wait for him in the top of the *m'*,
36 people down from the top of the *m'*.
J'g 9: 36 Thou seest the shadow of the *m'* as
11: 37 may go up and down upon the *m'*,
38 bewailed her virginity upon the *m'*.
1Sa 26: 20 doth hunt a partridge in the *m'*.
2Sa 1: 21 Ye *m'* of Gilboa, let there be no
1Ki 5: 15 thousand hewers in the *m'*;
19: 11 great and strong wind rent the *m'*,
2Ki 19: 23 come up to the height of the *m'*, to
1Ch 12: 8 as swift as the roes upon the *m'*;
2Ch 18: 16 all Israel scattered upon the *m'*,
21: 11 high places in the *m'* of Judah,
26: 10 and vine dressers in the *m'*, and in
27: 4 he built cities in the *m'* of Judah,
Job 9: 5 Which removeth the *m'*, and they
24: 8 are wet with the showers of the *m'*,
28: 9 he overturneth the *m'* by the roots.
39: 8 The range of the *m'* is his pastures,
40: 20 Surely the *m'* bring him forth food,
Ps 36: 6 righteousness is like the great *m'*;
46: 2 the *m'* be carried into the midst
3 *m'* shake with the swelling thereof.
50: 11 I know all the fowls of the *m'*: and
65: 6 by his strength setteth fast the *m'*;
72: 3 The *m'* shall bring peace to the
16 in the earth upon the top of the *m'*;
76: 4 and excellent than the *m'* of prey.
83: 14 as the flame setteth the *m'* on fire;
87: 1 His foundation is in the holy *m'*.
90: 2 Before the *m'* were brought forth,
104: 6 the waters stood above the *m'*.
8 They go up by the *m'*; they go down
114: 4 The *m'* skipped like rams, and the
6 Ye *m'*, that ye skipped like rams;
125: 2 the *m'* are round about Jerusalem,
133: 3 descended upon the *m'* of Zion:
144: 5 touch the *m'*, and they shall
147: 8 maketh grass to grow upon the *m'*.
148: 9 *M'*, and all hills; fruitful trees, and
Pr 8: 25 Before the *m'* were settled, before
27: 25 and herbs of the *m'* are gathered.
Ca 2: 8 he cometh leaping upon the *m'*,
17 young hart upon the *m'* of Bether.
4: 8 dens, from the *m'* of the leopards.
8: 14 young hart upon the *m'* of spices.
Isa 2: 2 established in the top of the *m'*,
14 upon all the high *m'*, and upon all
13: 4 noise of a multitude in the *m'*, like
14: 25 upon my *m'* tread him under foot:
17: 13 shall be chased as the chaff of the *m'*
18: 3 he lifteth up an ensign on the *m'*;
6 together unto the fowls of the *m'*,
22: 5 the walls, and of crying to the *m'*.
34: 3 the *m'* shall be melted with their
37: 24 I come up to the height of the *m'*,
40: 12 weighed the *m'* in scales, and the
41: 15 thou shalt thresh the *m'*, and beat
42: 11 them shout from the top of the *m'*.
15 I will make waste *m'* and hills, and
44: 23 break forth into singing, ye *m'*, O
49: 11 I will make all my *m'* a way, and
13 break forth into singing, O *m'*: for
52: 7 How beautiful upon the *m'* are the
54: 10 For the *m'* shall depart, and the
55: 12 the *m'* and the hills shall break
64: 1 that the *m'* might flow down at thy
3 the *m'* flowed down at thy presence.
65: 7 have burned incense upon the *m'*,
9 out of Judah an inheritor of my *m'*:
Jer 3: 23 hills, and from the multitude of *m'*:
4: 24 I beheld the *m'*, and, lo, they
9: 10 For the *m'* will I take up a weeping
13: 16 your feet stumble upon the dark *m'*,
17: 26 and from the *m'*, and from the
31: 5 vines upon the *m'* of Samaria:
32: 44 Judah, and in the cities of the *m'*,
33: 13 In the cities of the *m'*, in the cities
46: 18 Surely as Tabor is among the *m'*,
50: 6 have turned them away on the *m'*:
La 4: 19 they pursued us upon the *m'*, they
Eze 6: 2 thy face toward the *m'* of Israel,
3 Ye *m'* of Israel, hear the word of
3 Thus saith the Lord God to the *m'*,
13 in all the tops of the *m'*, and under
7: 7 not the sounding again of the *m'*.
16 and shall be on the *m'* like doves
18: 6 And hath not eaten upon the *m'*,
11 but even hath eaten upon the *m'*,
15 That hath not eaten upon the *m'*,
19: 9 be heard upon the *m'* of Israel.
22: 9 and in thee they eat upon the *m'*:
31: 12 upon the *m'* and in all the valleys
32: 5 I will lay thy flesh upon the *m'*,
6 thou swimmest, even to the *m'*;
33: 28 the *m'* of Israel shall be desolate,
34: 6 sheep wandered through all the *m'*,
13 feed them upon the *m'* of Israel
14 upon the high *m'* of Israel shall
14 they feed upon the *m'* of Israel.
35: 8 will fill his *m'* with his slain men:
12 spoken against the *m'* of Israel,
36: 1 prophesy unto the *m'* of Israel, and
1, 4 Ye *m'* of Israel, hear the word
4 Thus saith the Lord God to the *m'*,
6 say unto the *m'*, and to the hills,
8 O *m'* of Israel, ye shall shoot forth
37: 22 in the land upon the *m'* of Israel;
38: 8 people, against the *m'* of Israel,
20 and the *m'* shall be thrown down,
21 against him throughout all my *m'*,
39: 2 bring thee upon the *m'* of Israel:
4 shalt fall upon the *m'* of Israel,
17 sacrifice upon the *m'* of Israel, that
Ho 4: 13 sacrifice upon the tops of the *m'*,
10: 8 they shall say to the *m'*, Cover us;
Joe 2: 2 the morning spread upon the *m'*:
5 noise of chariots on the tops of *m'*
Joe 3: 18 the *m'* shall drop down new wine,
Am 3: 9 yourselves upon the *m'* of Samaria,
4: 13 For, lo, he that formeth the *m'*, and
9: 13 and the *m'* shall drop sweet wine,
Jon 2: 6 went down to the bottoms of the *m'*;
Mic 1: 4 the *m'* shall be molten under him,
4: 1 be established in the top of the *m'*,
6: 1 Arise, contend thou before the *m'*,
2 Hear ye, O *m'*, the Lord's
Na 1: 5 The *m'* quake at him, and the hills
15 Behold upon the *m'* the feet of him
3: 18 thy people is scattered upon the *m'*,
Hab 3: 6 the everlasting *m'* were scattered,
10 *m'* saw thee, and they trembled:
Hag 1: 11 upon the land, and upon the *m'*,
Zec 6: 1 chariots out from between two *m'*;
1 and the *m'* were *m'* of brass.
14: 5 ye shall flee to the valley of the *m'*;
5 for the valley of the *m'* shall reach
Mal 1: 3 laid his *m'* and his heritage waste
M't 18: 12 goeth into the *m'*, and seeketh
24: 16 which be in Judæa flee into the *m'*:
M'r 5: 5 night and day, he was in the *m'*,
11 there nigh unto the *m'* a great herd
13: 14 them that be in Judæa flee to the *m'*:
Lu 21: 21 which are in Judæa flee to the *m'*;
23: 30 begin to say to the *m'*, Fall on us;
1Co 13: 2 faith, so that I could remove *m'*,
Heb 11: 38 wandered in deserts, and in *m'*,
Re 6: 15 dens and in the rocks of the *m'*;
16 said to the *m'* and rocks, Fall on us,
16: 20 away, and the *m'* were not found.
17: 9 The seven heads are seven *m'*, on

mounted
Eze 10: 19 *m'* up from the earth in my sight:

mounting
Isa 15: 5 for by the *m'* up of Luhith with

mounts
Jer 32: 24 the *m'*, they are come unto the
33: 4 which are thrown down by the *m'*,
Eze 17: 17 by casting up *m'*, and building

mourn See also MOURNED; MOURNETH; MOURNFULLY; MOURNING.
Ge 23: 2 Abraham came to *m'* for Sarah,
1Sa 16: 1 How long wilt thou *m'* for Saul,
2Sa 3: 31 sackcloth, and *m'* before Abner.
1Ki 13: 29 to the city, to *m'* and to bury him.
14: 13 And all Israel shall *m'* for him, and
Ne 8: 9 Lord your God; *m'* not, nor weep.
Job 2: 11 together to come to *m'* with him
5: 11 those which *m'* may be exalted
14: 22 and his soul within him shall *m'*.
Ps 55: 2 I *m'* in my complaint, and make a
Pr 5: 11 And thou *m'* at the last, when they
29: 2 wicked beareth rule, the people *m'*.
Ec 3: 4 a time to *m'*, and a time to dance;
Isa 3: 26 her gates shall lament and *m'*; and
16: 7 of Kir-hareseth shall ye *m'*;
19: 8 The fishers also shall *m'*, and all
38: 14 I did *m'* as a dove: mine eyes fail
59: 11 like bears, and *m'* sore like doves:
61: 2 of our God; to comfort all that *m'*;
3 To appoint unto them that *m'* in
66: 10 joy with her, all ye that *m'* for her:
Jer 4: 28 For this shall the earth *m'*, and the
12: 4 How long shall the land *m'*, and the
48: 31 shall *m'* for the men of Kir-heres.
La 1: 4 The ways of Zion do *m'*, because
Eze 7: 12 the buyer rejoice, nor the seller *m'*:
27 The king shall *m'*, and the prince
24: 16 neither shalt thou *m'* nor weep,
23 ye shall not *m'* nor weep; but ye
23 and *m'* one toward another.
31: 15 I caused Lebanon to *m'* for him,
Ho 4: 3 Therefore shall the land *m'*, and
10: 5 the people thereof shall *m'* over it,
Joe 1: 9 the priests, the Lord's ministers, *m'*.
Am 1: 2 habitations of the shepherds shall *m'*,
8: 8 every one *m'* that dwelleth therein?
9: 5 and all that dwell therein shall *m'*:
Zec 12: 10 and they shall *m'* for him, as one
12 land shall *m'*, every family apart;
M't 5: 4 Blessed are they that *m'*: for they
9: 15 children of the bridechamber *m'*,
24: 30 shall all the tribes of the earth *m'*,
Lu 6: 25 now! for ye shall *m'* and weep.
Jas 4: 9 Be afflicted, and *m'*, and weep: let
Re 18: 11 earth shall weep and *m'* over her;

mourned
Ge 37: 34 loins, and *m'* for his son many days.
50: 3 Egyptians *m'* for him threescore
10 there they *m'* with a great and
Ex 33: 4 heard these evil tidings, they *m'*:
Nu 14: 39 of Israel: and the people *m'* greatly.
20: 29 they *m'* for Aaron thirty days,
1Sa 15: 35 nevertheless Samuel *m'* for Saul:
2Sa 1: 12 And they *m'*, and wept, and fasted
11: 26 was dead, she *m'* for her husband.
13: 37 And David *m'* for his son every day.
14: 2 that had a long time *m'* for the dead:
1Ki 13: 30 and they *m'* over him, saying,
14: 18 and all Israel *m'* for him, according
1Ch 7: 22 Ephraim their father *m'* many days,
2Ch 35: 24 Judah and Jerusalem *m'* for Josiah.
Ezr 10: 6 he *m'* because of the transgression of
Ne 1: 4 I...wept, and *m'* certain days, and
Zec 7: 5 When ye fasted and *m'* in the
M't 11: 17 we have *m'* unto you, and ye have
M'r 16: 10 with him, as they *m'* and wept.
Lu 7: 32 we have *m'* to you, and ye have
1Co 5: 2 and have not rather *m'*, that he

mourner See also MOURNERS.
2Sa 14: 2 I pray thee, feign thyself to be a *m'*,

mourners
Job 29: 25 army, as one that comforteth the *m*'.
Ec 12: 5 and the *m*' go about the streets:
Isa 57: 18 comforts unto him and to his *m*'.
Hos 9: 4 be unto them as the bread of *m*';

mourneth
2Sa 19: 1 king weepeth and *m*' for Absalom.
Ps 35: 14 as one that *m*' for his mother.
88: 9 Mine eye *m*' by reason of
Isa 24: 4 The earth *m*' and fadeth away, the
7 new wine *m*', the vine languisheth,
33: 9 The earth *m*' and languisheth:
Jer 12: 11 and being desolate it *m*' unto me;
14: 2 Judah *m*', and the gates thereof
23: 10 for because of swearing the land *m*';
Joe 1: 10 The field is wasted, the land *m*'; for
Zec 12: 10 for him, as one *m*' for his only son,

mournfully
Mal 3: 14 that we have walked *m*' before the

mourning
Ge 27: 41 The days of *m*' for my father are at
37: 35 down into the grave unto my son *m*'.
50: 4 when the days of his *m*' were past,
10 made a *m*' for his father seven days.
11 saw the *m*' in the floor of Atad, they
11 is a grievous *m*' to the Egyptians:
De 26: 14 I have not eaten thereof in my *m*',
34: 8 and *m*' for Moses were ended.
2Sa 11: 27 when the *m*' was past, David sent
14: 2 put on now *m*' apparel, and anoint
19: 2 that day was turned into *m*' unto all
Es 4: 3 great *m*' among the Jews,...fasting,
6: 12 Haman hasted to his house *m*', and
9: 22 to joy, and from *m*' into a good day:
Job 3: 8 who are ready to raise up their *m*'.
30: 28 I went *m*' without the sun: I stood
31 My harp also is turned to *m*', and my
Ps 30: 11 turned for me my *m*' into dancing:
38: 6 greatly; I go *m*' all the day long.
42: 9 go I *m*' because of the oppression
43: 2 go I *m*' because of the oppression
Ec 7: 2 better to go to the house of *m*', than
4 of the wise is in the house of *m*';
Isa 22: 12 hosts call to weeping, and to *m*',
51: 11 and sorrow and *m*' shall flee away.
60: 20 the days of thy *m*' shall be ended.
61: 3 beauty for ashes, the oil of joy for *m*',
Jer 6: 26 make thee *m*', as for an only son,
9: 17 call for the *m*' women, that they
16: 5 not into the house of *m*', neither
7 men tear themselves for them in *m*',
31: 13 I will turn their *m*' into joy, and will
La 2: 5 in the daughter of Judah *m*' and
5: 15 ceased; our dance is turned into *m*'.
Eze 2: 10 lamentations, and *m*', and woe.
7: 16 all of them *m*', every one for his
24: 17 to cry, make no *m*' for the dead,
31: 15 down to the grave I caused a *m*':
Da 10: 2 I Daniel was *m*' three full weeks.
Joe 2: 12 and with weeping, and with *m*':
Am 5: 16 shall call the husbandman to *m*',
8: 10 And I will turn your feasts into *m*',
10 will make it as the *m*' of an only son,
Mic 1: 8 like the dragons, and *m*' as the owls.
11 not forth in the *m*' of Beth-ezel;
Zec 12: 11 there be a great *m*' in Jerusalem,
11 as the *m*' of Hadadrimmon in the
M't 2: 18 and great *m*', Rachel weeping for
2Co 7: 7 your *m*', your fervent mind toward
Jas 4: 9 laughter be turned to *m*', and your
Re 18: 8 day, death, and *m*', and famine;

mouse See also MICE.
Le 11: 29 the weasel, and the *m*', and the
Isa 66: 17 and the *m*', shall be consumed

mouth See also MOUTHS.
Ge 4: 11 hath opened her *m*' to receive thy
8: 11 in her *m*' was an olive leaf pluckt
24: 57 the damsel, and enquire at her *m*'.
29: 2 great stone was upon the well's *m*'.
3 rolled the stone from the well's *m*',
3 the stone again upon the well's *m*',
8 roll the stone from the well's *m*';
10 rolled the stone from the well's *m*',
42: 27 for, behold, it was in his sack's *m*'.
43: 12 again in the *m*' of your sacks, carry
21 money was in the *m*' of his sack,
44: 1 every man's money in his sack's *m*'.
2 in the sack's *m*' of the youngest,
45: 12 it is my *m*' that speaketh unto you.
Ex 4: 11 him, Who hath made man's *m*'? or
12 and I will be with thy *m*', and teach
15 unto him, and put words in his *m*':
15 will be with thy *m*', and with his *m*',
16 he shall be to thee instead of a *m*',
13: 9 the Lord's law may be in thy *m*':
23: 13 neither let it be heard out of thy *m*'.
Nu 12: 8 With him will I speak *m*' to *m*', even
16: 30 thing, and the earth open her *m*',
32 earth opened her *m*', and swallowed
22: 28 the Lord opened the *m*' of the ass,
38 the word that God putteth in my *m*',
23: 5 the Lord put a word in Balaam's *m*',
12 which the Lord hath put in my *m*'?
16 Balaam, and put a word in his *m*',
26: 10 earth opened her *m*', and swallowed
30: 2 to all that proceedeth out of his *m*'.
32: 24 hath proceeded out of your *m*'.
35: 30 put to death by the *m*' of witnesses:
De 8: 3 of the *m*' of the Lord doth man live.
11: 6 earth opened her *m*', and swallowed
17: 6 At the *m*' of two witnesses, or three
6 at the *m*' of one witness he shall not
18: 18 and will put my words in his *m*';
De 19: 15 sinneth: at the *m*' of two witnesses,
15 or at the *m*' of three witnesses, shall
23: 23 thou hast promised with thy *m*'.
30: 14 is very nigh unto thee, in thy *m*',
32: 1 hear, O earth, the words of my *m*'.
Jos 1: 8 law shall not depart out of thy *m*'; and
6: 10 any word proceed out of your *m*',
9: 14 not counsel at the *m*' of the Lord.
10: 18 stones upon the *m*' of the cave, and
22 Open the *m*' of the cave, and bring
27 laid great stones in the cave's *m*',
J'g 7: 6 putting their hand to their *m*', were
9: 38 Where is now thy *m*', wherewith
11: 35 I have opened my *m*' unto the Lord,
36 hast opened thy *m*' unto the Lord,
36 hath proceeded out of thy *m*';
18: 19 lay thine hand upon thy *m*', and go
1Sa 1: 12 the Lord, that Eli marked her *m*'.
2: 1 my *m*' is enlarged over mine
3 not arrogancy come out of your *m*':
14: 26 but no man put his hand to his *m*':
27 honeycomb,...put his hand to his *m*';
17: 35 him, and delivered it out of his *m*':
2Sa 1: 16 thy *m*' hath testified against thee,
14: 3 So Joab put the words in her *m*'.
19 words in the *m*' of thine handmaid:
17: 19 spread a covering over the well's *m*',
18: 25 be alone, there is tidings in his *m*'.
22: 9 and fire out of his *m*' devoured:
1Ki 7: 31 And the *m*' of it within the chapiter
31 but the *m*' thereof was round after
31 also upon the *m*' of it were gravings
8: 15 spake with his *m*' unto David my
24 thou spakest also with thy *m*', and
13: 21 hast disobeyed the *m*' of the Lord,
17: 24 word of the Lord in thy *m*' is truth.
19: 18 every *m*' which hath not kissed him.
22: 13 good unto the king with one *m*':
22 spirit in the *m*' of all his prophets.
23 in the *m*' of all these thy prophets,
2Ki 4: 34 child, and put his *m*' upon his *m*',
1Ch 16: 12 and the judgments of his *m*';
2Ch 6: 4 he spake with his *m*' to my father
15 and spakest with thy *m*', and hast
18: 21 spirit in the *m*' of all his prophets.
22 in the *m*' of these thy prophets, and
35: 22 words of Necho from the *m*' of God,
36: 12 speaking from the *m*' of the Lord.
21 of the Lord by the *m*' of Jeremiah,
22 Lord spoken by the *m*' of Jeremiah
Ezr 1: 1 of the Lord by the *m*' of Jeremiah
Ne 9: 20 not thy manna from their *m*', and
Es 7: 8 word went out of the king's *m*', they
Job 3: 1 After this opened Job his *m*', and
5: 15 from their *m*', and from the hand of
16 hope, and iniquity stoppeth her *m*'.
7: 11 Therefore I will not refrain my *m*';
8: 2 the words of thy *m*' be like a strong
21 Till he fill thy *m*' with laughing,
9: 20 mine own *m*' shall condemn me:
12: 11 words? and the *m*' taste his meat?
15: 5 For thy *m*' uttereth thine iniquity,
6 Thine own *m*' condemneth thee,
13 lettest such words go out of thy *m*'?
30 by the breath of his *m*' shall he go
16: 5 would strengthen you with my *m*',
10 have gaped upon me with their *m*';
19: 16 I intreated him with my *m*'.
20: 12 wickedness be sweet in his *m*',
13 not; but keep it still within his *m*':
21: 5 and lay your hand upon your *m*'.
22: 22 I pray thee, the law from his *m*',
23: 4 and fill my *m*' with arguments.
12 have esteemed the words of his *m*'
29: 9 and laid their hand on their *m*'.
10 cleaved to the roof of their *m*'.
23 they opened their *m*' wide as for
31: 27 or my *m*' hath kissed my hand:
30 have I suffered my *m*' to sin by
32: 5 no answer in the *m*' of these three
33: 2 Behold, now I have opened my *m*',
2 my tongue hath spoken in my *m*'.
34: 3 trieth words, as the *m*' tasteth meat.
35: 16 doth Job open his *m*' in vain;
37: 2 the sound that goeth out of his *m*'.
40: 4 I will lay mine hand upon my *m*'.
23 he can draw up Jordan into his *m*'.
41: 19 Out of his *m*' go burning lamps,
21 and a flame goeth out of his *m*'.
Ps 5: 9 there is no faithfulness in their *m*';
8: 2 Out of...*m*' of babes and sucklings
10: 7 His *m*' is full of cursing and deceit
17: 3 that my *m*' shall not transgress.
10 with their *m*' they speak proudly.
18: 8 and fire out of his *m*' devoured:
19: 14 Let the words of my *m*', and the
22: 21 Save me from the lion's *m*': for
32: 9 whose *m*' must be held in with bit
33: 6 of them by the breath of his *m*'.
34: 1 shall continually be in my *m*'.
35: 21 they opened their *m*' wide against
36: 3 The words of his *m*' are iniquity
37: 30 The *m*' of the righteous speaketh
38: 13 dumb man that openeth not his *m*'.
14 and in whose *m*' are no reproofs.
39: 1 I will keep my *m*' with a bridle,
9 I was dumb, I opened not my *m*';
40: 3 he hath put a new song in my *m*',
49: 3 My *m*' shall speak of wisdom; and
50: 16 that...take my covenant in thy *m*'?
19 Thou givest thy *m*' to evil, and thy
51: 15 my *m*' shall shew forth thy praise.
54: 2 give ear to the words of my *m*'.
55: 21 The words of his *m*' were smoother
58: 6 Break their teeth, O God, in their *m*':
59: 7 they belch out with their *m*':
Ps 59: 12 the sin of their *m*' and the words
62: 4 they bless with their *m*', but they
63: 5 my *m*' shall praise thee with joyful
11 the *m*' of them that speak lies shall
66: 14 and my *m*' hath spoken, when I was
17 I cried unto him with my *m*', and
69: 15 not the pit shut her *m*' upon me.
71: 8 Let my *m*' be filled with thy praise
15 My *m*' shall shew forth thy
73: 9 set their *m*' against the heavens,
78: 1 your ears to the words of my *m*'.
2 I will open my *m*' in a parable: I
36 they did flatter him with their *m*',
81: 10 open thy *m*' wide, and I will fill it.
89: 1 with my *m*' will I make known thy
103: 5 satisfieth thy *m*' with good things;
105: 5 and the judgments of his *m*';
107: 42 and all iniquity shall stop her *m*'.
109: 2 For the *m*' of the wicked and the
2 the *m*' of the deceitful are opened
30 greatly praise the Lord with my *m*';
119: 13 all the judgments of thy *m*'.
43 word of truth utterly out of my *m*';
72 The law of thy *m*' is better unto me
88 shall I keep the testimony of thy *m*'.
103 yea, sweeter than honey to my *m*'!
108 the freewill offerings of my *m*', O
131 I opened my *m*', and panted: for I
126: 2 was our *m*' filled with laughter,
137: 6 tongue cleave to the roof of my *m*';
138: 4 they hear the words of thy *m*'.
141: 3 Set a watch, O Lord, before my *m*';
7 are scattered at the grave's *m*',
144: 8 Whose *m*' speaketh vanity, and
11 whose *m*' speaketh vanity, and
145: 21 My *m*' shall speak the praise of the
149: 6 high praises of God be in their *m*',
Pr 2: 6 out of his *m*' cometh knowledge
4: 5 decline from the words of my *m*'.
24 put away from thee a froward *m*',
5: 3 and her *m*' is smoother than oil:
7 not from the words of my *m*'.
6: 2 snared with the words of thy *m*',
2 art taken with the words of thy *m*'.
12 man, walketh with a froward *m*'.
7: 24 and attend to the words of my *m*'.
8: 7 For my *m*' shall speak truth; and
8 All the words of my *m*' are in
13 way, and the froward *m*', do I hate.
10: 6 covereth the *m*' of the wicked.
11 The *m*' of a righteous man is a well
11 covereth the *m*' of the wicked.
14 but the *m*' of the foolish is near
31 The *m*' of the just bringeth forth
32 but the *m*' of the wicked speaketh
11: 9 An hypocrite with his *m*' destroyeth
11 overthrown by the *m*' of the wicked.
12: 6 the *m*' of the upright shall deliver
14 with good by the fruit of his *m*':
13: 2 shall eat good by the fruit of his *m*':
3 He that keepeth his *m*' keepeth his
14: 3 In the *m*' of the foolish is a rod of
15: 2 but the *m*' of fools poureth out
14 but the *m*' of fools feedeth on
23 hath joy by the answer of his *m*':
28 the *m*' of the wicked poureth out
16: 10 king: his *m*' transgresseth not in
23 heart of the wise teacheth his *m*',
26 for his *m*' craveth it of him.
18: 4 The words of a man's *m*' are as
6 and his *m*' calleth for strokes.
7 A fool's *m*' is his destruction, and
20 satisfied with the fruit of his *m*';
19: 24 much as bring it to his *m*' again.
28 and the *m*' of the wicked devoureth
20: 17 his *m*' shall be filled with gravel.
21: 23 Whoso keepeth his *m*' and his
22: 14 The *m*' of strange women is a deep
24: 7 he openeth not his *m*' in the gate.
26: 7, 9 so is a parable in the *m*' of fools.
15 him to bring it again to his *m*'.
28 and a flattering *m*' worketh ruin.
27: 2 praise thee, and not thine own *m*';
30: 20 she eateth, and wipeth her *m*', and
32 evil, lay thine hand upon thy *m*'.
31: 8 Open thy *m*' for the dumb in the
9 Open thy *m*', judge righteously,
26 She openeth her *m*' with wisdom;
Ec 5: 2 Be not rash with thy *m*', and let not
6 Suffer not thy *m*' to cause thy flesh
6: 7 All the labour of man is for his *m*',
10: 12 The words of a wise man's *m*' are
13 beginning of the words of his *m*'
Ca 1: 2 kiss me with the kisses of his *m*':
5: 16 His *m*' is most sweet: yea, he is
7: 9 And the roof of thy *m*' like the best
Isa 1: 20 the *m*' of the Lord hath spoken it.
5: 14 opened her *m*' without measure:
6: 7 he laid it upon my *m*', and said, Lo,
9: 12 shall devour Israel with open *m*'.
17 and every *m*' speaketh folly. For
10: 14 wing, or opened the *m*', or peeped.
11: 4 the earth with the rod of his *m*',
19: 7 by the *m*' of the brooks, and every
29: 13 people draw near me with their *m*',
30: 2 and have not asked at my *m*'; to
34: 16 for my *m*' it hath commanded, and
40: 5 the *m*' of the Lord hath spoken it.
45: 23 the word is gone out of my *m*' in
48: 3 and they went forth out of my *m*',
49: 2 made my *m*' like a sharp sword;
51: 16 I have put my words in thy *m*',
53: 7 afflicted, yet he opened not his *m*':
7 is dumb, so he openeth not his *m*'.
9 neither was any deceit in his *m*'.
55: 11 be that goeth forth out of my *m*':

Isa 57: 4 against whom make ye a wide m',
58: 14 the m' of the Lord hath spoken it.
59: 21 words, which I have put in thy m',
21 shall not depart out of thy m', nor
21 nor out of the m' of thy seed, nor
21 nor out of the m' of thy seed's seed,
62: 2 the m' of the Lord shall name.
Jer 1: 9 forth his hand, and touched my m'.
9 I have put my words in thy m'.
5: 14 I will make my words in thy m' fire,
7: 28 and is cut off from their m'.
9: 8 to his neighbour with his m', but
12 the m' of the Lord hath spoken,
20 your ear receive the word of his m',
12: 2 thou art near in their m', and far
15: 19 the vile, thou shalt be as my m':
23: 16 and not out of the m' of the Lord.
32: 4 and shall speak with him m' to m',
34: 3 he shall speak with thee m' to m',
36: 4 wrote from the m' of Jeremiah all
6 thou hast written from my m', the
17 write all these words at his m'?
18 these words unto me with his m',
27 wrote at the m' of Jeremiah,
32 therein from the m' of Jeremiah
44: 17 thing goeth forth out of our own m',
26 be named in the m' of any man of
45: 1 in a book at the m' of Jeremiah,
48: 28 nest in the sides of the hole's m'.
51: 44 bring forth out of his m' that which
La 2: 16 have opened their m' against thee:
3: 29 He putteth his m' in the dust; if so
38 Out of the m' of the most High
4: 4 cleaveth to the roof of his m' for
Eze 2: 8 open thy m', and eat that I give
3: 2 So I opened my m', and he caused
3 and it was in my m' as honey for
17 hear the word at my m', and give
26 tongue cleave to the roof of thy m',
27 I will open thy m', and thou shalt
4: 14 there abominable flesh into my m'.
16: 56 was not mentioned by thy m' in
63 and never open thy m' any more
21: 22 open the m' in the slaughter, to lift
24: 27 thy m' be opened to him which is
29: 21 the opening of the m' in the midst
33: 7 thou shalt hear the word at my m',
22 had opened my m', until he came
22 my m' was opened, and I was no
31 with their m' they shew much love,
34: 10 will deliver my flock from their m',
35: 13 Thus with your m' ye have boasted
Da 3: 26 near to the m' of the burning fiery
4: 31 the word was in the king's m',
6: 17 and laid upon the m' of the den;
7: 5 and it had three ribs in the m' of it
8 and a m' speaking great things.
20 a m' that spake very great things.
10: 3 came flesh nor wine in my m',
16 then I opened my m', and spake,
Ho 2: 17 the names of Baalim out of her m',
6: 5 slain them by the words of my m':
8: 1 Set the trumpet to thy m'. He
Joe 1: 5 for it is cut off from your m'.
Am 3: 12 out of the m' of the lion two legs,
Mic 4: 4 m' of the Lord of hosts hath spoken
6: 12 tongue is deceitful in their m'.
7: 5 keep the doors of thy m' from her
16 shall lay their hand upon their m',
Na 3: 12 even fall into the m' of the eater.
Zep 3: 13 tongue be found in their m': for
Zec 5: 8 weight of lead upon the m' thereof.
8: 9 words by the m' of the prophets,
9: 7 take away his blood out of his m',
14: 12 shall consume away in their m'.
Mal 2: 6 The law of truth was in his m', and
7 they should seek the law at his m':
M't 4: 4 proceedeth out of the m' of God.
5: 2 he opened his m', and taught them,
12: 34 of the heart the m' speaketh.
13: 35 I will open my m' in parables; I will
15: 8 draweth nigh unto me with their m',
11 which goeth into the m' defileth a
11 but that which cometh out of the m',
17 entereth in at the m' goeth into the
18 which proceed out of the m' come
17: 27 and when thou hast opened his m',
18: 16 in the m' of two or three witnesses
21: 16 Out of the m' of babes and sucklings
Lu 1: 64 his m' was opened immediately, and
70 spake by the m' of his holy prophets,
4: 22 which proceeded out of his m'. And
6: 45 of the heart his m' speaketh.
11: 54 to catch something out of his m',
19: 22 of thine own m' will I judge thee,
21: 15 I will give you a m' and wisdom,
22: 71 ourselves have heard of his own m'.
Joh 19: 29 upon hyssop, and put it to his m'.
Ac 1: 16 the Holy Ghost by the m' of David
3: 18 by the m' of all his prophets, that
21 by the m' of all his holy prophets
4: 25 by the m' of thy servant David hast
8: 32 shearer, so opened he not his m':
35 Philip opened his m', and began at
10: 34 Then Peter opened his m', and said,
11: 8 hath at any time entered into my m'.
15: 7 the Gentiles by my m' should hear
27 tell you the same things by m'.
18: 14 was now about to open his m',
22: 14 shouldest hear the voice of his m'.
23: 2 by him to smite him on the m'.
Ro 3: 14 Whose m' is full of cursing and
19 that every m' may be stopped, and
10: 8 word is nigh thee, even in thy m',
9 confess with thy m' the Lord Jesus,
10 and with the m' confession is made

Ro 15: 6 one mind and one m' glorify God,
1Co 9: 9 shalt not muzzle the m' of the ox
2Co 6: 11 our m' is open unto you, our
13: 1 In the m' of two or three witnesses
Eph 4: 29 proceed out of your m', but that
6: 19 that I may open my m' boldly, to
Col 3: 8 communication out of your m'.
2Th 2: 8 consume with the spirit of his m',
2Ti 4: 17 delivered out of the m' of the lion.
Jas 3: 10 of the same m' proceedeth blessing
1Pe 2: 22 neither was guile found in his m':
Jude 16 m' speaketh great swelling words,
Re 1: 16 and out of his m' went a sharp
2: 16 them with the sword of my m'.
3: 16 hot, I will spue thee out of my m'.
9: 19 For their power is in their m', and
10: 9 shall be in thy m' sweet as honey.
10 it was in my m' sweet as honey:
11: 5 fire proceedeth out of their m', and
12: 15 cast out of his m' water as a flood
16 earth opened her m', and swallowed
16 which the dragon cast out of his m'.
13: 2 and his m' as the m' of a lion: and
5 him a m' speaking great things and
6 And he opened his m' in blasphemy
14: 5 And in their m' was found no guile:
16: 13 come out of the m' of the dragon,
13 and out of the m' of the beast,
13 out of the m' of the false prophet.
19: 15 out of his m' goeth a sharp sword.
21 sword proceeded out of his m':

mouths
Ge 44: 8 which we found in our sacks' m',
De 31: 19 put it in their m', that this song
21 out of the m' of their seed: for I
Ps 22: 13 They gaped upon me with their m',
78: 30 their meat was yet in their m',
115: 5 They have m', but they speak not:
135: 16 They have m', but they speak not;
17 is there any breath in their m'.
Isa 52: 15 the kings shall shut their m' at him:
Jer 44: 25 have both spoken with your m', and
La 3: 46 our enemies have opened their m'
Da 6: 22 angel, and hath shut the lions' m',
Mic 3: 5 he that putteth not into their m',
Tit 1: 11 Whose m' must be stopped, who
Heb11: 33 promises, stopped the m' of lions,
Jas 3: 3 we put bits in the horses' m', that
Re 9: 17 and out of their m' issued fire and
18 which issued out of their m'.

move See also MOVEABLE; MOVED; MOVETH; MOVING; REMOVE.
Ex 11: 7 shall not a dog m' his tongue,
Le 11: 10 of all that m' in the waters, and of
De 23: 25 thou shalt not m' a sickle unto thy
32: 21 I will m' them to jealousy with those
J'g 13: 25 Spirit of the Lord began to m' him
2Sa 7: 10 of their own, and m' no more;
2Ki 21: 8 will I make the feet of Israel m'
23: 18 alone; let no man m' his bones.
Jer 10: 4 and with hammers, that it m' not.
Mic 7: 17 they shall m' out of their holes
M't 23: 4 will not m' them with one of their
Ac 17: 28 in him we live, and m', and have
20: 24 none of these things m' me,

moveable See also UNMOVEABLE.
Pr 5: 6 her ways are m', that thou canst

moved See also MOVEDST; REMOVED.
Ge 1: 2 the Spirit of God m' upon the face
7: 21 And all flesh died that m' upon the
De 32: 21 They have m' me to jealousy with that
Jos 10: 21 none m' his tongue against any of
15: 18 she m' him to ask of her father a
J'g 1: 14 she m' him to ask of her father a
Ru 1: 19 all the city was m' about them,
1Sa 1: 13 only her lips m', but her voice was
2Sa 18: 33 the king was much m', and went
22: 8 the foundations of heaven m' and
24: 1 he m' David against them to say,
1Ch 16: 30 shall be stable, that it be not m'.
17: 9 place, and shall be m' no more;
2Ch 18: 31 God m' them to depart from him.
Ezr 4: 15 they have m' sedition within the
Es 5: 9 he stood not up, nor m' for him,
Job 37: 1 my heart...is m' out of his place.
41: 23 in themselves; they cannot be m'.
Ps 10: 6 said in his heart, I shall not be m':
13: 4 trouble me rejoice when I am m'.
15: 5 doeth these things shall never be m'.
16: 8 at my right hand, I shall not be m'.
18: 7 foundations also of the hills m'
21: 7 the most High he shall not be m'.
30: 6 I said, I shall never be m'.
46: 5 she shall not be m': God shall help
6 raged, the kingdoms were m': he
55: 22 never suffer the righteous to be m'.
62: 2 defence; I shall not be greatly m'.
6 he is my defence; I shall not be m'.
66: 9 and suffereth not our feet to be m'.
68: 8 Sinai itself was m' at the presence of
78: 58 m' him to jealousy with their graven
93: 1 is stablished, that it cannot be m'.
96: 10 established that it shall not be m':
99: 1 cherubims; let the earth be m'.
112: 6 Surely he shall not be m' for ever:
121: 3 He will not suffer thy foot to be m':
Pr 12: 3 of the righteous shall not be m'.
Ca 5: 4 and my bowels were m' for him.
Isa 6: 4 posts of the door m' at the voice
7: 2 his heart was m', and the heart of
2 the trees of the wood are m' with
10: 14 there was none that m' the wing,
14: 9 Hell from beneath is m' for thee
19: 1 the idols of Egypt shall be m' at
24: 19 the earth is m' exceedingly.

Isa 40: 20 graven image, that shall not be m'.
41: 7 with nails, that it should not be m'.
Jer 4: 24 and all the hills m' lightly.
25: 16 And they shall drink, and be m',
46: 7 whose waters are m' as the rivers?
8 his waters are m' like the rivers;
49: 21 The earth is m' at the noise of
50: 46 taking of Babylon the earth is m',
Da 8: 7 he was m' with choler against him,
11: 11 of the south shall be m' with choler,
M't 9: 36 was m' with compassion on them,
14: 14 m' with compassion toward them,
18: 27 servant was m' with compassion,
20: 24 were m' with indignation against
21: 10 all the city was m', saying, Who is
M'r 1: 41 Jesus, m' with compassion, put
6: 34 and was m' with compassion toward
15: 11 But the chief priests m' the people,
Ac 2: 25 hand, that I should not be m':
7: 9 the patriarchs, m' with envy, sold
17: 5 Jews which believed not, m' with
21: 30 And all the city was m', and the
Col 1: 23 and be not m' away from the hope
1Th 3: 3 no man should be m' by these
Heb11: 7 By faith Noah,...m' with fear,
12: 28 a kingdom which cannot be m',
2Pe 1: 21 they were m' by the Holy Ghost.
Re 6: 14 every mountain and island were m'

movedst
Job 2: 3 thou m' me against him, to destroy

mover
Ac 24: 5 and a m' of sedition among all the

moveth See also REMOVETH.
Ge 1: 21 and every living creature that m',
28 over every living thing that m' upon
9: 2 upon all that m' upon the earth, and
Le 11: 46 living creature that m' in the waters,
Job 40: 17 He m' his tail like a cedar: the
Ps 69: 34 seas,...every thing that m' therein.
Pr 23: 31 the cup, when it m' itself aright.
Eze 47: 9 every thing that liveth, which m',

moving See also REMOVING.
Ge 1: 20 the m' creature that hath life,
9: 3 Every m' thing that liveth shall be
Job 16: 5 the m' of my lips should asswage
Pr 16: 30 m' his lips he bringeth evil to
Joh 5: 3 waiting for the m' of the water.

mower
Ps 129: 7 the m' filleth not his hand: nor

mowings
Am 7: 1 latter growth after the king's m'.

mown
Ps 72: 6 down like rain upon the m' grass:

Moza (*mo'-zah*)
1Ch 2: 46 concubine, bare Haran, and M',
8: 36 and Zimri; and Zimri begat M',
37 M' begat Binea: Rapha was his
9: 42 and Zimri; and Zimri begat M';
43 And M' begat Binea; and Rephaiah

Mozah (*mo'-zah*)
Jos 18: 26 Mizpeh, and Chephirah, and M',

much^A See also INASMUCH; FORASMUCH; FORSOMUCH.
Ge 26: 16 for thou art m' mightier than we.
30: 43 had m' cattle, and maidservants,
34: 12 Ask me never so m' dowry
41: 49 corn as the sand of the sea, very m',
43: 34 mess was five times so m' as any of
44: 1 with food, as m' as they can carry,
50: 20 this day, to save m' people alive.
Ex 12: 38 and herds, even very m' cattle.
42 a night to be m' observed unto the
14: 28 remained not so m' as one of them.
16: 5 be twice as m' as they gather daily.
18 gathered m' had nothing over, and
22 day they gathered twice as m' bread,
30: 23 of sweet cinnamon half so m', even
36: 5 The people bring m' more than
7 the work to make it, and too m'.
Le 7: 10 of Aaron have, one as m' as another.
13: 7 But if the scab spread m' abroad
22 if it spread m' abroad in the skin,
27 it be spread m' abroad in the skin,
35 if the scall spread m' in the skin
14: 21 if he be poor, and cannot get so m';
Nu 16: 3 Ye take too m' upon you, seeing
7 Ye take too m' upon you, ye sons of
20: 20 out against him with m' people.
21: 4 of the people was m' discouraged
6 and m' people of Israel died.
De 2: 5 land,...not so m' as a foot breadth;
3: 19 (for I know that ye have m' cattle,)
28: 38 carry m' seed out into the field,
Jos 11: 4 m' people, even as the sand that is
13: 1 yet very m' land to be possessed.
19: 9 of Judah was too m' for them:
22: 8 with m' riches unto your tents, and
8 with very m' cattle, with silver, and
8 iron, and with very m' raiment:
Ru 1: 13 it grieveth me m' for your sakes
1Sa 2: 16 then take as m' as thy soul desireth;
14: 30 How m' more, if haply the people
30 m' greater slaughter among the
18: 30 so that his name was m' set by.
19: 2 Saul's son delighted m' in David:
20: 13 do so and m' more to Jonathan:
23: 3 how m' more then if we come to
26: 24 as thy life was m' set by this day
24 so let my life be m' set by in the
2Sa 4: 11 How m' more, when wicked men
8: 8 David took exceeding m' brass.

2Sa 13:34 there came *m'* people by the way
14:25 to be so *m'* praised as Absalom for
16:11 *m'* more now may this Benjamite
17:12 there shall not be left so *m'* as one.
18:33 the king was *m'* moved, and went up
1Ki 4:29 and understanding exceeding *m'*,
8:27 how *m'* less this house that I have
10: 2 very *m'* gold, and precious stones:
12:28 It is too *m'* for you to go up to
2Ki 5:13 how *m'* rather then, when he
10:18 little; but Jehu shall serve him *m'*.
12:10 there was *m'* money in the chest,
21: 6 he wrought *m'* wickedness in the
16 shed innocent blood very *m'*, till he
1Ch 18: 8 brought David very *m'* brass,
20: 2 brought also exceeding *m'* spoil
22: 4 brought *m'* cedar wood to David.
8 thou hast shed *m'* blood upon the
2Ch 2:16 Lebanon, as *m'* as thou shalt need:
6:18 how *m'* less this house which I have
14:13 they carried away very *m'* spoil.
14 was exceeding *m'* spoil in them.
17:13 *m'* business in the cities of Judah:
20:25 gathering of the spoil, it was so *m'*.
24:11 they saw that there was *m'* money,
25: 9 Lord is able to give thee *m'* more
13 of them, and took *m'* spoil.
26:10 he had *m'* cattle, both in the low
27: 3 on the wall of Ophel he built *m'*.
5 So *m'*...the children of Ammon pay
28: 8 took also away *m'* spoil from them,
30:13 assembled at Jerusalem *m'* people
32: 4 was gathered *m'* people together,
4 Assyria come, and find *m'* water?
15 how *m'* less shall your God
27 Hezekiah had exceeding *m'* riches
29 had given him substance very *m'*.
33: 6 wrought *m'* evil in the sight of the
36:14 transgressed very *m'* after all the
Ezr 10:13 it is a time of *m'* rain, and we are
Ne 4:10 decayed, and there is *m'* rubbish;
6:16 *m'* cast down in their own eyes:
9:37 it yieldeth *m'* increase unto the
Es 1:18 shall there arise too *m'* contempt
Job 4:19 How *m'* less in them that dwell in
9:14 How *m'* less shall I answer him,
15:10 men, *m'* elder than thy father.
25: 6 How *m'* less man, that is a worm?
31:25 because mine hand had gotten *m'*;
34:19 How *m'* less to him that accepteth not
42:10 gave Job twice as *m'* as he...before.
Ps 19:10 than gold, yea, than *m'* fine gold:
33:16 is not delivered by *m'* strength.
35:18 will praise thee among *m'* people.
119:14 thy testimonies, as *m'* as in all riches.
107 I am afflicted very *m'*: quicken
Pr 7:21 With...*m'* fair speech she caused
11:31 *m'* more the wicked and the sinner.
13:23 *M'* food is in the tillage of the
14: 4 *m'* increase is by the strength of
15: 6 of the righteous is *m'* treasure:
11 how *m'* more then the hearts of the
16:16 How *m'* better is it to get wisdom than
17: 7 fool: *m'* less do lying lips a prince.
19: 7 how *m'* more do his friends go far
10 *m'* less for a servant to have rule
24 not so *m'* as bring it to his mouth
21:27 how *m'* more, when he bringeth it
25:16 eat so *m'* as is sufficient for thee,
27 It is not good to eat *m'* honey:
Ec 1:18 in *m'* wisdom is *m'* grief: and he
5:12 sweet, whether he eat little or *m'*:
17 he hath *m'* sorrow and wrath with
20 he shall not *m'* remember the days
7:16 Be not righteous over *m'*; neither
17 Be not over *m'* wicked, neither be
9:18 but one sinner destroyeth *m'* good.
10:18 By *m'* slothfulness the building
12:12 and *m'* study is a weariness of the
Ca 4:10 how *m'* better is thy love than wine!
Isa 21: 7 hearkened diligently with *m'* heed:
30:33 pile thereof is fire and *m'* wood,
56:12 this day, and *m'* more abundant.
Jer 2:22 with nitre, and take thee *m'* sope,
36 Why gaddest thou about so *m'* to
40:12 wine and summer fruits very *m'*.
Eze 14:21 How *m'* more when I send my four
17:15 give him horses and *m'* people.
22: 5 which art infamous and *m'* vexed.
23:32 had in derision; it containeth *m'*.
26: 7 and companies, and *m'* people.
33:31 their mouth they shew *m'* love,
Da 4:12, 21 fair, and the fruit thereof *m'*,
7: 5 thus unto it, Arise, devour *m'* flesh.
28 my cogitations *m'* troubled me, and
11:13 with a great army and with *m'* riches.
Joe 2: 6 the people shall be *m'* pained:
Jon 4:11 their left hand; and also *m'* cattle?
Na 2:10 and *m'* pain is in all loins,
Hag 1: 6 Ye have sown *m'*, and bring in
9 Ye looked for *m'*, and lo, it came to
Mal 3:13 have we spoken so *m'* against thee?
M't 6: 7 be heard for their *m'* speaking.
26 Are ye not *m'* better than they?
30 shall he not *m'* more clothe you, O
7:11 how *m'* more shall your Father
10:25 how *m'* more shall they call them
12:12 How *m'* then is a man better than a
13: 5 where they had not *m'* earth: and
15:33 so *m'* bread in the wilderness, as
26: 9 might have been sold for *m'*, and
M'r 1:45 out, and began to publish it *m'*,
2: 2 no, not so *m'* as about the door:
3:20 they could not so *m'* as eat bread.
4: 5 ground, where it had not *m'* earth;
5:10 he besought him *m'* that he would

M'r 5:21 side, *m'* people gathered unto him:
24 and *m'* people followed him, and
6:31 they had no leisure so *m'* as to eat.
34 when he came out, saw *m'* people,
7:36 so *m'* the more a great deal they
10:14 Jesus saw it, he was *m'* displeased,
41 they began to be *m'* displeased with
12:41 and many that were rich cast in *m'*.
Lu 5:15 so *m'* the more went there a fame
6: 3 Have ye not read so *m'* as this,
34 to sinners, to receive as *m'* again.
7:11 went with him, and *m'* people.
12 *m'* people of the city was with her.
26 you, and *m'* more than a prophet.
47 are forgiven; for she loved *m'*:
8: 4 *m'* people were gathered together,
9:37 from the hill, *m'* people met him.
10:40 was cumbered about *m'* serving,
11:13 how *m'* more shall your heavenly
12:19 *m'* goods laid up for many years;
24 how *m'* more are ye better than
28 *m'* more will he clothe you, O ye of
48 unto whomsoever *m'* is given, of
48 given, of him shall be *m'* required:
48 to whom men have committed *m'*,
16: 5 How *m'* owest thou unto my lord?
7 another, And how *m'* owest thou?
10 is least is faithful also in *m'*:
10 in the least is unjust also in *m'*.
18:13 not lift up so *m'* as his eyes unto
39 but he cried so *m'* the more, Thou
19:15 how *m'* every man had gained by
24: 4 were *m'* perplexed thereabout,
Joh 3:23 because there was *m'* water there:
6:10 there was *m'* grass in the place.
11 of the fishes as *m'* as they would.
7:12 *m'* murmuring among the people
12: 9 *M'* people of the Jews therefore
12 *m'* people that were come to the
24 if it die, it bringeth forth *m'* fruit.
14:30 I will not talk *m'* with you: for the
15: 5 the same bringeth forth *m'* fruit:
8 glorified, that ye bear *m'* fruit;
Ac 5: 8 whether ye sold the land for so *m'*?
8 And she said, Yea, for so *m'*.
37 drew away *m'* people after him:
7: 5 it, no, not so *m'* as to set his foot on:
9:13 how *m'* evil he hath done to thy
10: 2 which gave *m'* alms to the people,
11:24 and *m'* people was added unto the
26 the church, and taught *m'* people.
14:22 through *m'* tribulation enter into
15: 7 when there had been *m'* disputing,
16:16 brought her masters *m'* gain by
18:10 for I have *m'* people in this city.
27 helped them *m'* which had believed
19: 2 have not so *m'* as heard whether
26 and turned away *m'* people, saying
20: 2 had given them *m'* exhortation, he
26:24 *m'* learning doth make thee mad.
27: 9 Now when *m'* time was spent, and
10 will be with hurt and *m'* damage,
16 had *m'* work to come by the boat:
Ro 1:15 So, as *m'* as in me is, I am ready
3: 2 *M'* every way: chiefly, because
5: 9 *M'* more then, being now justified
10 *m'* more, being reconciled, we shall
15 *m'* more the grace of God, and the
17 *m'* more they which receive...grace
20 grace did *m'* more abound:
9:22 endured with *m'* longsuffering the
11:12 how *m'* more their fulness?
24 how *m'* more shall these, which be
12:18 as *m'* as lieth in you, live peaceably
15:22 I have been *m'* hindered from
16: 6 who bestowed *m'* labour on us.
12 which laboured *m'* in the Lord.
1Co 2: 3 and in fear, and in *m'* trembling.
5: 1 fornication as is not so *m'* as
6: 3 *m'* more things that pertain to this
12:22 *m'* more those members of the
16:19 Priscilla salute you *m'* in the Lord,
2Co 2: 4 out of *m'* affliction and anguish of
3: 9 *m'* more doth the ministration of
11 *m'* more that which remaineth is
6: 4 in *m'* patience, in afflictions, in
8: 4 Praying us with *m'* intreaty that
15 had gathered *m'* had nothing over;
22 things, but now *m'* more diligent,
Ph'p 1:14 *m'* more bold to speak the word
2:12 but now *m'* more in my absence,
1Th 1: 5 Holy Ghost, and in *m'* assurance;
6 received the word in *m'* affliction,
2: 2 gospel of God with *m'* contention.
1Ti 3: 8 not given to *m'* wine, not greedy of
2Ti 4:14 the coppersmith did me *m'* evil:
Tit 2: 3 false accusers, not given to *m'* wine,
Ph'm 8 though I might be *m'* bold in Christ
16 how *m'* more unto thee, both in the
Heb 1: 4 made so *m'* better than the angels,
7:22 By so *m'* was Jesus made a surety
8: 6 by how *m'* also he is the mediator
9:14 How *m'* more shall the blood of
10:25 so *m'* the more, as ye see the day
29 how *m'* sorer punishment, suppose
12: 9 we not *m'* rather be in subjection
20 if so *m'* as a beast touch the
25 *m'* more shall not we escape, if we
Jas 5:16 of a righteous man availeth *m'*.
1Pe 1: 7 being *m'* more precious than of gold
2Pe 2:18 the flesh, through *m'* wantonness.
Re 5: 4 I wept *m'*, because no man was
8: 3 was given unto him *m'* incense.
18: 7 How *m'* she hath glorified herself,
7 so *m'* torment and sorrow give her:
19: 1 I heard a great voice of *m'* people

mufflers
Isa 3:19 and the bracelets, and the *m'*,

mulberry
2Sa 5:23 them over against the *m'* trees.
24 a going in the tops of the *m'* trees,
1Ch 14:14 them over against the *m'* trees.
15 of going in the tops of the *m'* trees,

mulberry-trees See MULBERRY and TREES.

mule See also MULES.
2Sa 13:29 every man gat him up upon his *m'*,
18: 9 And Absalom rode upon a *m'*, and
9 the *m'* went under the thick boughs
9 *m'* that was under him went away.
1Ki 1:33 my son to ride upon mine own *m'*,
38 to ride upon king David's *m'*,
44 him to ride upon the king's *m'*:
Ps 32: 9 ye not as the horse, or as the *m'*,
Zec 14:15 the plague of the horse, of the *m'*,

mules See also MULES'.
Ge 36:24 found the *m'* in the wilderness,
1Ki 10:25 armour, and spices, horses, and *m'*,
18: 5 to save the horses and the *m'* alive,
1Ch 12:40 on asses, and on camels, and on *m'*,
2Ch 9:24 harness, and spices, horses, and *m'*,
Ezr 2:66 their *m'*, two hundred forty and
Ne 7:68 their *m'*, two hundred forty and
Es 8:10 on horseback, and riders on *m'*,
14 posts that rode upon *m'* and camels
Isa 66:20 and in litters, and upon *m'*, and
Eze 27:14 with horses and horsemen and *m'*.

mules'
2Ki 5:17 servant two *m'* burden of earth?

multiplied See also MULTIPLIEDST.
Ge 47:27 and grew, and *m'* exceedingly.
Ex 1: 7 *m'*, and waxed exceeding mighty;
12 them, the more they *m'* and grew.
20 people *m'*, and waxed very mighty.
11: 9 my wonders may be *m'* in the land
De 1:10 The Lord your God hath *m'* you,
8:13 and thy silver and thy gold is *m'*,
13 and all that thou hast is *m'*;
11:21 That your days may be *m'*, and the
Jos 24: 3 *m'* his seed, and gave him Isaac.
1Ch 5: 9 their cattle were *m'* in the land of
Job 27:14 If his children be *m'*, it is for the
35: 6 or if thy transgressions be *m'*,
Ps 16: 4 Their sorrows shall be *m'* that
38:19 that hate me wrongfully are *m'*.
107:38 also, so that they are *m'* greatly;
Pr 9:11 For by me thy days shall be *m'*,
29:16 When the wicked are *m'*,
Isa 9: 3 Thou hast *m'* the nation, and not
59:12 our transgressions are *m'* before
Jer 3:16 when ye be *m'* and increased in
Eze 5: 7 ye *m'* more than the nations that
11: 6 Ye have *m'* your slain in this city,
16:25 passed by, and *m'* thy whoredoms.
29 hast moreover *m'* thy fornication
51 thou hast *m'* thine abominations
21:15 may faint, and their ruins be *m'*:
23:19 she *m'* her whoredoms, in calling
31: 5 boughs were *m'*, and his branches
35:13 have *m'* your words against me:
Da 4: 1 the earth; Peace be *m'* unto you.
6:25 the earth; Peace be *m'* unto you.
Ho 2: 8 and oil, and *m'* her silver and gold,
8:14 and Judah hath *m'* fenced cities:
12:10 *m'* visions, and used similitudes,
Na 3:16 *m'* thy merchants above the stars
Ac 6: 1 number of the disciples was *m'*,
7 of the disciples *m'* in Jerusalem
7:17 the people grew and *m'* in Egypt,
9:31 comfort of the Holy Ghost, were *m'*.
12:24 But the word of God grew and *m'*.
1Pe 1: 2 Grace unto you, and peace, be *m'*.
2Pe 1: 2 Grace and peace be *m'* unto you
Jude 2 unto you, and peace, and love, be *m'*.

multipliedst
Ne 9:23 children also *m'* thou as stars

multiplieth
Job 9:17 and *m'* my wounds without cause.
34:37 us, and *m'* his words against God.
35:16 he *m'* words without knowledge.

multiply See also MULTIPLIED; MULTIPLIETH; MULTIPLYING.
Ge 1:22 Be fruitful, and *m'*, and fill the
22 seas, and let fowl *m'* in the earth.
28 Be fruitful, and *m'*, and replenish
3:16 I will greatly *m'* thy sorrow and thy
6: 1 men began to *m'* on the face of the
8:17 be fruitful, and *m'* upon the earth.
9: 1 Be fruitful, and *m'*, and replenish
7 be ye fruitful, and *m'*; bring forth
7 in the earth, and *m'* therein.
16:10 I will *m'* thy seed exceedingly, that
17: 2 thee, and will *m'* thee exceedingly.
20 and will *m'* him exceedingly;
22:17 I will *m'* thy seed as the stars of the
26: 4 make thy seed to *m'* as the stars of
24 and *m'* thy seed for my servant
28: 3 and make thee fruitful, and *m'* thee,
35:11 be fruitful and *m'*; a nation and a
48: 4 will make thee fruitful, and *m'* thee,
Ex 1:10 lest they *m'*, and it come to pass,
7: 3 *m'* my signs and my wonders in the
23:29 beast of the field *m'* against thee.
32:13 I will *m'* your seed as the stars of
Le 26: 9 and make you fruitful, and *m'* you,
De 7:13 thee, and bless thee, and *m'* thee:
8: 1 that ye may live, and *m'*, and go in
13 when thy herds and thy flocks *m'*,

De 13:17 compassion upon thee, and *m'* thee,
17:16 he shall not *m'* horses to himself,
16 to the end that he should *m'* horses:
17 Neither shall he *m'* wives to himself,
17 *m'* to himself silver and gold.
28:63 you to do you good, and to *m'* you;
30: 5 good, and *m'* thee above thy fathers.
16 that thou mayest live and *m'*:
1Ch 4:27 neither did all their family *m'*, like
Job 29:18 and I shall *m'* my days as the sand.
Jer 30:19 I will *m'* them, and they shall not
33:22 so will I *m'* the seed of David my
Eze 16: 7 I have caused thee to *m'* as the bud
36:10 And I will *m'* men upon you, all
11 I will *m'* upon you man and beast;
30 And I will *m'* the fruit of the tree,
37:26 and I will place them, and *m'* them,
Am 4: 4 at Gilgal *m'* transgression; and
2Co 9:10 *m'* your seed sown, and increase
Heb 6:14 and multiplying I will *m'* thee.

multiplying
Ge 22:17 in *m'* I will multiply thy seed as
Heb 6:14 thee, and *m'* I will multiply thee.

multitude See also MULTITUDES.
Ge 16:10 it shall not be numbered for *m'*.
28: 3 thou mayest be a *m'* of people;
30:30 and it is now increased unto a *m'*;
32:12 which cannot be numbered for *m'*.
48: 4 I will make of thee a *m'* of people;
16 let them grow into a *m'* in the midst
19 seed shall become a *m'* of nations.
Ex 12:38 mixed *m'* went up also with them;
23: 2 shalt not follow a *m'* to do evil;
Le 25:16 According to the *m'* of years thou
Nu 11: 4 the mixt *m'* that was among them
32: 1 Gad had a very great *m'* of cattle:
De 1:10 day as the stars of heaven for *m'*.
10:22 thee as the stars of heaven for *m'*.
28:62 were as the stars of heaven for *m'*;
Jos 11: 4 that is upon the sea shore in *m'*,
J'g 4: 7 army, with his chariots and his *m'*;
6: 5 they came as grasshoppers for *m'*;
7:12 valley like grasshoppers for *m'*;
12 as the sand by the sea side for *m'*.
1Sa 13: 5 sand which is on the sea shore in *m'*:
14:16 and, behold, the *m'* melted away,
2Sa 6:19 even among the whole *m'* of Israel,
17:11 the sand that is by the sea for *m'*;
1Ki 3: 8 be numbered nor counted for *m'*.
4:20 the sand which is by the sea in *m'*,
8: 5 not be told nor numbered for *m'*.
20:13 Hast thou seen all this great *m'*?
28 deliver all this great *m'* into thine
2Ki 7:13 they are as all the *m'* of Israel that
13 even as all the *m'* of the Israelites
19:23 With the *m'* of my chariots I am
25:11 with the remnant of the *m'*, did
2Ch 1: 9 like the dust of the earth in *m'*.
5: 6 not be told nor numbered for *m'*.
13: 8 and ye be a great *m'*, and there are
14:11 in thy name we go against this *m'*.
20: 2 cometh a great *m'* against thee
15 dismayed by reason of this great *m'*;
24 wilderness, they looked unto the *m'*,
28: 5 and carried away a great *m'* of them
30:18 For a *m'* of the people, even many
32: 7 nor for all the *m'* that is with him:
Ne 13: 3 from Israel all the mixed *m'*.
Es 5:11 riches, and the *m'* of his children,
10: 3 accepted of the *m'* of his brethren,
Job 11: 2 not the *m'* of words be answered?
31:34 Did I fear a great *m'*, or did the
32: 7 *m'* of years should teach wisdom.
33:19 *m'* of his bones with strong pain:
35: 9 By reason of the *m'* of oppressions
39: 7 He scorneth the *m'* of the city,
Ps 5: 7 thy house in the *m'* of thy mercy:
10 in the *m'* of their transgressions;
33:16 no king saved by the *m'* of an host:
42: 4 for I had gone with the *m'*, I went
4 praise, with a *m'* that kept holyday.
49: 6 in the *m'* of their riches;
51: 1 unto the *m'* of thy tender mercies
68:30 of spearmen, the *m'* of the bulls,
69:13 in the *m'* of thy mercy hear me,
16 to the *m'* of thy tender mercies:
74:19 unto the *m'* of the wicked: forget
94:19 In the *m'* of my thoughts within
97: 1 let the *m'* of isles be glad thereof.
106: 7 not the *m'* of thy mercies; but
45 according to the *m'* of his mercies.
109:30 I will praise him among the *m'*.
Pr 10:19 In the *m'* of words there wanteth
11:14 in the *m'* of counsellors there is
14:28 In the *m'* of people is the king's
15:22 in the *m'* of counsellors they are
20:15 There is gold, and a *m'* of rubies:
24: 6 in *m'* of counsellors there is safety.
Ec 5: 3 cometh through the *m'* of business;
3 a fool's voice is known by *m'* of
7 For in the *m'* of dreams and many
Isa 1:11 the *m'* of your sacrifices unto me?
5:13 and their *m'* dried up with thirst.
14 their glory, and their *m'*, and their
13: 4 The noise of a *m'* in the mountains,
16:14 contemned, with all that great *m'*;
17:12 Woe to the *m'* of many people,
29: 5 Moreover the *m'* of thy strangers
5 the *m'* of the terrible ones shall be
7 the *m'* of all the nations that fight
8 So shall the *m'* of all the nations be,
31: 4 a *m'* of shepherds is called forth
32:14 the *m'* of the city shall be left; the
37:24 By the *m'* of my chariots am I
47: 9 and for the *m'* of thy sorceries,
Isa 47:12 and with the *m'* of thy sorceries,
13 wearied in the *m'* of thy counsels.
60: 6 The *m'* of camels shall cover thee,
63: 7 and according to the *m'* of his
Jer 3:23 and from the *m'* of mountains:
10:13 is a *m'* of waters in the heavens,
12: 6 they have called a *m'* after thee:
30:14 one, for the *m'* of thine iniquity;
15 for the *m'* of thine iniquity:
44:15 a great *m'*, even all the people
46:25 I will punish the *m'* of No, and
49:32 and the *m'* of their cattle a spoil:
51:16 is a *m'* of waters in the heavens;
42 covered with the *m'* of the waves
52:15 of Babylon, and the rest of the *m'*.
La 1: 5 for the *m'* of her transgressions:
3:32 according to the *m'* of his mercies.
Eze 7:11 shall remain, nor of their *m'*, nor
12 wrath is upon all the *m'* thereof.
13 is touching the whole *m'* thereof,
14 wrath is upon all the *m'* thereof.
14: 4 according to the *m'* of his idols;
19:11 height with the *m'* of her branches.
23:42 a voice of a *m'* being at ease was
27:12 of the *m'* of all kind of riches;
16 by reason of the *m'* of the wares
18 thy merchant in the *m'* of the wares
18 making, for the *m'* of all riches;
33 the earth with the *m'* of thy riches
28:16 By the *m'* of thy merchandise they
18 by the *m'* of thine iniquities, by
29:19 he shall take her *m'*, and take her
30: 4 and they shall take away her *m'*,
10 make the *m'* of Egypt to cease by
15 and I will cut off the *m'* of No.
31: 2 king of Egypt, and to his *m'*; Whom
5 long because of the *m'* of waters,
9 him fair by the *m'* of his branches:
18 This is Pharaoh and all his *m'*,
32:12 mighty will I cause thy *m'* to fall,
12 all the *m'* thereof shall be destroyed.
16 even for Egypt, and for all her *m'*,
18 of man, wail for the *m'* of Egypt,
24 There is Elam and all her *m'* round
25 midst of the slain with all her *m'*:
26 is Meshech, Tubal, and all her *m'*:
31 shall be comforted over all his *m'*,
32 even Pharaoh and all his *m'*, saith
39:11 shall they bury Gog and all his *m'*:
47: 9 there shall be a very great *m'* of fish,
Da 10: 6 of his words like the voice of a *m'*.
11:10 shall assemble a *m'* of great forces:
11 and he shall set forth a great *m'*;
11 the *m'* shall be given into his hand.
12 when he hath taken away the *m'*,
13 shall set forth a *m'* greater than
Hos 9: 7 mad, for the *m'* of thine iniquity,
10: 1 according to the *m'* of his fruit he
13 way, in the *m'* of thy mighty men.
Mic 2:12 noise by reason of the *m'* of men.
Na 3: 3 and there is a *m'* of slain, and a
4 Because of the *m'* of the whoredoms
Zec 2: 4 the *m'* of m n and cattle therein:
M't 13: 2 the whole *m'* stood on the shore.
34 things spake Jesus unto the *m'* in
36 Then Jesus sent the *m'* away, and
14: 5 put him to death, he feared the *m'*,
14 went forth, and saw a great *m'*,
15 send the *m'* away, that they may
19 he commanded the *m'* to sit down
19 disciples, and...disciples to the *m'*.
15:10 And he called the *m'*, and said unto
31 Insomuch that the *m'* wondered,
32 said, I have compassion on the *m'*,
33 wilderness, as to fill so great a *m'*?
35 he commanded the *m'* to sit down
36 disciples, and...disciples to the *m'*.
39 And he sent away the *m'*, and took
17:14 And when they were come to the *m'*,
20:29 Jericho, a great *m'* followed him.
31 And the *m'* rebuked them, because
21: 8 And a very great *m'* spread their
11 And the *m'* said, This is Jesus the
46 hands on him, they feared the *m'*.
22:33 And when the *m'* heard this, they
23: 1 Then spake Jesus to the *m'*, and to
26:47 with him a great *m'* with swords
27:20 *m'* that they should ask Barabbas,
24 washed his hands before the *m'*,
M'r 2:13 and all the *m'* resorted unto him,
3: 7 a great *m'* from Galilee followed
8 a great *m'*, when they had heard
9 wait on him because of the *m'*,
20 And the *m'* cometh together again,
32 And the *m'* sat about him, and they
4: 1 was gathered unto him a great *m'*,
1 and the whole *m'* was by the sea on
36 when they had sent away the *m'*,
5:31 Thou seest the *m'* thronging thee,
7:33 And he took him aside from the *m'*,
8: 1 those days the *m'* being very great,
2 I have compassion on the *m'*,
9:14 he saw a great *m'* about them, and
17 one of the *m'* answered and said,
14:43 with him a great *m'* with swords
15: 8 the *m'* crying aloud began to desire
Lu 1:10 *m'* of the people were praying
2:13 a *m'* of the heavenly host praising
3: 7 *m'* that came forth to be baptized
5: 6 they inclosed a great *m'* of fishes:
19 bring him in because of the *m'*,
6:17 and a great *m'* of people out of all
19 the whole *m'* sought to touch him:
8:37 Then the whole *m'* of the country
45 the *m'* throng thee and press thee,
9:12 Send the *m'* away, that they may
Lu 9:16 the disciples to set before the *m'*.
12: 1 an innumerable *m'* of people,
18:36 hearing the *m'* pass by, he asked
19:37 whole *m'* of the disciples began to
39 the Pharisees from among the *m'*
22: 6 unto them in the absence of the *m'*.
47 while he yet spake, behold a *m'*,
23: 1 And the whole *m'* of them arose,
Joh 5: 3 lay a great *m'* of impotent folk,
13 away, a *m'* being in that place.
6: 2 a great *m'* followed him, because
21: 6 able to draw it for the *m'* of fishes.
Ac 2: 6 abroad, the *m'* came together, and
4:32 the *m'* of them that believed were
5:16 came also a *m'* out of the cities
6: 2 called the *m'* of the disciples unto
5 the saying pleased the whole *m'*:
14: 1 that a great *m'* both of the Jews
4 But the *m'* of the city was divided:
15:12 Then all the *m'* kept silence, and
30 they had gathered the *m'* together,
16:22 *m'* rose up together against them:
17: 4 of the devout Greeks a great *m'*,
19: 9 spake evil of that way before the *m'*,
33 they drew Alexander out of the *m'*,
21:22 the *m'* must needs come together:
34 thing, some another, among...*m'*:
36 the *m'* of the people followed after,
23: 7 Sadducees: and the *m'* was divided.
24:18 neither with *m'*, nor with tumult,
25:24 about whom all the *m'* of the Jews
Heb 11:12 many as the stars of the sky in *m'*,
Jas 5:20 death, and shall hide a *m'* of sins.
1Pe 4: 8 for charity shall cover a *m'* of sins.
Re 7: 9 a great *m'*, which no man could
19: 6 as it were the voice of a great *m'*,

multitudes
Eze 32:20 the sword: draw her and all her *m'*.
Joe 3:14 *M'*, *m'* in the valley of decision:
M't 4:25 followed him great *m'* of people
5: 1 And seeing the *m'*, he went up into
8: 1 mountain, great *m'* followed him.
18 Jesus saw great *m'* about him,
9: 8 But when the *m'* saw it, they
33 and the *m'* marvelled, saying, It
36 But when he saw the *m'*, he was
11: 7 Jesus began to say unto the *m'*,
12:15 and great *m'* followed him, and he
13: 2 great *m'* were gathered together
14:22 side, while he sent the *m'* away.
23 when he had sent the *m'* away, he
15:30 great *m'* came unto him, having
19: 2 And great *m'* followed him; and he
21: 9 And the *m'* that went before, and
26:55 same hour said Jesus to the *m'*,
Lu 5:15 great *m'* came together to hear,
14:25 there went great *m'* with him: and
Ac 5:14 Lord, *m'* both of men and women.)
13:45 when the Jews saw the *m'*, they
Re 17:15 are peoples, and *m'*, and nations,

munition See also MUNITIONS.
Isa 29: 7 that fight against her and her *m'*,
Na 2: 1 keep the *m'*, watch the way, make

munitions
Isa 33:16 defence shall be the *m'* of rocks:

Muppim (*mup'-pim*) See also SHUPPIM.
Ge 46:21 and Rosh, *M'*, and Huppim, and

murder See also MURDERS.
Ps 10: 8 places doth he *m'* the innocent:
94: 6 stranger, and *m'* the fatherless.
Jer 7: 9 Will ye steal, *m'*, and commit
Ho 6: 9 company of priests *m'* in the way
M't 19:18 Jesus said, Thou shalt do no *m'*,
M'r 15: 7 committed *m'* in the insurrection.
Lu 23:19 and for *m'*, was cast into prison.)
25 and *m'* was cast into prison, whom
Ro 1:29 full of envy, *m'*, debate, deceit,

murderer See also MURDERERS.
Nu 35:16 of iron, so that he die, he is a *m'*:
16 the *m'* shall surely be put to death.
17 he may die, and he die, he is a *m'*:
17 the *m'* shall surely be put to death.
18 he may die, and he die, he is a *m'*:
18 the *m'* shall surely be put to death.
19 of blood himself shall slay the *m'*:
21 for he is a *m'*: the revenger of blood
21 shall slay the *m'*, when he meeteth
30 the *m'* shall be put to death by the
31 no satisfaction for the life of a *m'*,
2Ki 6:32 this son of a *m'* hath sent to take
Job 24:14 *m'* rising with the light killeth the
Ho 9:13 bring forth his children to the *m'*.
Joh 8:44 He was a *m'* from the beginning,
Ac 3:14 desired a *m'* to be granted unto
28: 4 No doubt this man is a *m'*, whom,
1Pe 4:15 let none of you suffer as a *m'*, or as
1Jo 3:15 hateth his brother is a *m'*: and ye
15 know that no *m'* hath eternal life

murderers
2Ki 14: 6 children of the *m'* he slew not:
Isa 1:21 lodged in it; but now *m'*.
Jer 4:31 my soul is wearied because of *m'*.
M't 22: 7 armies, and destroyed those *m'*,
Ac 7:52 been now the betrayers and *m'*:
21:38 four thousand men that were *m'*?
1Ti 1: 9 and profane, for *m'* of fathers
9 and *m'* of mothers, for manslayers,
Re 21: 8 and the abominable, and *m'*, and
22:15 and whoremongers, and *m'*, and

murders
M't 15:19 heart proceed evil thoughts, *m'*,
M'r 7:21 adulteries, fornications, *m'*,

Ga 5:21 Envyings, m', drunkenness,
Re 9:21 Neither repented they of their m',

murmur See also MURMURED; MURMURING.
Ex 16: 7 are we, that ye m' against us?
8 which ye m' against him: and
Nu 14:27 congregation which m' against me?
27 Israel, which they m' against me.
36 congregation to m' against him,
16:11 is Aaron, that ye m' against him?
17: 5 whereby they m' against you.
Joh 6:43 them, M' not among yourselves.
1Co 10:10 Neither m' ye, as some of them also

murmured
Ex 15:24 And the people m' against Moses,
16: 2 children of Israel m' against Moses
17: 3 and the people m' against Moses,
Nu 14: 2 children of Israel m' against Moses
29 upward, which have m' against me,
16:41 children of Israel m' against Moses
De 1:27 And ye m' in your tents, and said,
Jos 9:18 And all...m' against the princes.
Ps 106:25 But m' in their tents, and
Isa 29:24 they that m' shall learn doctrine.
M't 20:11 they m' against the goodman of
M'r 14: 5 poor. And they m' against her.
Lu 5:30 Pharisees m' against his disciples,
15: 2 And the Pharisees and scribes m',
19: 7 And when they saw it, they all m',
Joh 6:41 The Jews then m' at him, because
61 himself that his disciples m' at it,
7:32 that the people m' such things
1Co 10:10 as some of them also m', and were

murmurers
Jude 16 These are m', complainers,

murmuring See also MURMURINGS.
Joh 7:12 was much m' among the people
Ac 6: 1 there arose a m' of the Grecians

murmurings
Ex 16: 7 heareth your m' against the Lord:
8 for that the Lord heareth your m'
8 your m' are not against us, but
9 Lord: for he hath heard your m'.
12 have heard the m' of the children of
Nu 14:27 have heard the m' of the children of
17: 5 me the m' of the children of Israel,
10 quite take away their m' from me.
Ph'p 2:14 Do all things without m' and

murrain
Ex 9: 3 there shall be a very grievous m'.

muse See also MUSED; MUSING.
Ps 143: 5 I m' on the work of thy hands.

mused
Lu 3:15 all men m' in their hearts of John,

Mushi (*mu'-shi*) See also MUSHITES.
Ex 6:19 sons of Merari; Mahali and M':
Nu 3:20 by their families; Mahli, and M'.
1Ch 6:19 The sons of Merari; Mahli, and M'.
47 the son of M', the son of Merari,
23:21 sons of Merari; Mahli, and M'.
23 sons of M'; Mahli, and Eder, and
24:26 sons of Merari were Mahli and M':
30 sons also of M'; Mahli, and Eder,

Mushites (*mu'-shites*)
Nu 3:33 and the family of the M': these
26:58 family of the M', the family of the

music See MUSICK.

musical
1Ch 16:42 and with m' instruments of God.
Ne 12:36 with the m' instruments of David
Ec 2: 8 as m' instruments, and that of all

musician See also MUSICIANS.
Ps 4: *title* To the chief M' on Neginoth,
5: *title* To the chief M' upon Nehiloth,
6: *title* To the chief M' on Neginoth
8: *title* To the chief M' upon Gittith,
9: *title* To the chief M' upon Muth-labben,
11: *title* To the chief M', A Psalm of
12: *title* To the chief M' upon Sheminith,
13: *title* To the chief M', A Psalm of
14: *title* To the chief M', A Psalm of
18: *title* To the chief M', A Psalm of
19: *title* To the chief M', A Psalm of
20: *title* To the chief M', A Psalm of
21: *title* To the chief M', A Psalm of
22: *title* To the chief M' upon Aijeleth
31: *title* To the chief M', A Psalm of
36: *title* To the chief M', A Psalm of
39: *title* To the chief M', even to
40: *title* To the chief M', A Psalm of
41: *title* To the chief M', A Psalm of
42: *title* To the chief M', Maschil, for
44: *title* To the chief M' for the sons of
45: *title* To the chief M' upon Shoshannim,
46: *title* To the chief M' for the sons of
47: *title* To the chief M', A Psalm for
49: *title* To the chief M', A Psalm for
51: *title* To the chief M', A Psalm of
52: *title* To the chief M', Maschil, A
53: *title* To the chief M' upon Mahalath,
54: *title* To the chief M' on Neginoth,
55: *title* To the chief M' on Neginoth,
56: *title* To the chief M' upon Jonath-...
57: *title* To the chief M', Al-taschith,
58: *title* To the chief M', Al-taschith,
59: *title* To the chief M', Al-taschith,
60: *title* To the chief M' upon Shushan-...
61: *title* To the chief M' upon Neginah,
62: *title* To the chief M', to Jeduthun,
64: *title* To the chief M', A Psalm of
65: *title* To the chief M', A Psalm and
66: *title* To the chief M', A Song or
Ps 67: *title* To the chief M' on Neginoth.
68: *title* To the chief M', a Psalm or
69: *title* To the chief M' upon Shoshannim,
70: *title* To the chief M', A Psalm of
75: *title* To the chief M', Al-taschith,
76: *title* To the chief M' on Neginoth,
77: *title* To the chief M', to Jeduthun,
80: *title* To...chief M' upon Shoshannim-...
81: *title* To the chief M' upon Gittith,
84: *title* To the chief M' upon Gittith,
85: *title* To the chief M', A Psalm for
88: *title* to the chief M' upon Mahalath
109: *title* To the chief M', A Psalm of
139: *title* To the chief M', A Psalm of
140: *title* To the chief M', A Psalm of

musicians
Re 18:22 of harpers, and m', and of pipers,

musick
1Sa 18: 6 with joy, and with instruments of m'.
1Ch 15:16 singers with instruments of m',
2Ch 5:13 cymbals and instruments of m',
7: 6 instruments of m' of the Lord,
23:13 the singers with instruments of m',
34:12 could skill of instruments of m'.
Ec 12: 4 all the daughters of m' shall be
La 3:63 their rising up; I am their m'.
5:14 gate, the young men from their m'
Da 3: 5 dulcimer, and all kinds of m', ye
7 psaltery, and all kinds of m', all
10, 15 dulcimer, and all kinds of m',
6:18 neither were instruments of m'
Am 6: 5 to themselves instruments of m',
Lu 15:25 house, he heard m' and dancing.

musing
Ps 39: 3 while I was m' the fire burned:

must^
Ge 29:26 Laban said, It m' not be so done in
30:16 Thou m' come in unto me; for surely
43:11 If it m' be so now, do this; take of the
47:29 the time drew nigh that Israel m' die:
Ex 10: 9 for we m' hold a feast unto the Lord.
25 Thou m' give us also sacrifices and
26 thereof m' we take to serve the Lord
26 not with what we m' serve the Lord,
12:16 save that which every man m' eat,
18:20 m' walk, and the work that they m' do.
Le 11:32 it m' be put into water, and it shall be
23: 6 days ye m' eat unleavened bread.
Nu 6:21 so he m' do after the law of his
18:22 Neither m' the children of Israel
20:10 m' we fetch you water out of this
23:12 M' I not take heed to speak that
26 that the Lord speaketh, that I m' do?
De 1:22 again by what way we m' go up,
4:22 But I m' die in this land,
22 I m' not go over Jordan: but ye
12:18 m' eat them before the Lord thy God
31: 7 thou m' go with this people unto the
14 thy days approach that thou m' die:
Jos 3: 4 know the way by which ye m' go:
22:18 that ye m' turn away this day from
J'g 13:16 thou m' offer it unto the Lord.
21:17 There m' be an inheritance for them
Ru 4: 5 thou m' buy it also of Ruth the
1Sa 14:43 was in mine hand, and, lo, I m' die.
2Sa 14:14 we m' needs die, and are as water
23: 3 that ruleth over men m' be just,
7 touch them m' be fenced with iron
1Ki 18:27 he sleepeth, and m' be awaked.
1Ch 22: 5 Lord m' be exceedingly magnifical,
Ps 32: 9 mouth m' be held in with bit and
Pr 18:24 hath friends m' shew himself friendly:
19:19 deliver him, yet thou m' do it again.
Ec 10:10 edge, then m' he put to more strength:
Ca 8:12 O Solomon, m' have a thousand, and
Jer 10: 5 they m' needs be borne, because thy
19 Truly this is a grief, and I m' bear it.
Eze 34:18 but ye m' tread down with your feet
18 ye m' foul the residue with your feet?
M't 16:21 that he m' go unto Jerusalem,
17:10 scribes that Elias m' first come?
18: 7 it m' needs be that offences come;
24: 6 all these things m' come to pass,
26:54 be fulfilled, that thus it m' be?
M'r 2:22 new wine m' be put into new bottles.
8:31 Son of man m' suffer many things,
9:11 the scribes that Elias m' first come?
12 man, that he m' suffer many things,
13: 7 for such things m' needs be; but
10 the gospel m' first be published
14:49 but the scriptures m' be fulfilled.
Lu 2:49 that I m' be about my Father's
4:43 I m' preach the kingdom of God to
5:38 new wine m' be put into new bottles;
9:22 Son of man m' suffer many things,
13:33 Nevertheless I m' walk to-day, and
14:18 and I m' needs go and see it:
17:25 first m' he suffer many things, and
19: 5 for to day I m' abide at thy house.
21: 9 these things m' first come to pass;
22: 7 when the passover m' be killed.
37 m' yet be accomplished in me,
23:17 (he m' release one unto them at
24: 7 Son of man m' be delivered into
44 that all things m' be fulfilled, which
Joh 3: 7 unto thee, Ye m' be born again.
14 so m' the Son of man be lifted up:
30 He m' increase, but I...decrease.
30 He...increase, but I m' decrease.
4: 4 he m' needs go through Samaria.
24 m' worship him in spirit and in
9: 4 I m' work the works of him that
10:16 them also I m' bring, and they
12:34 The Son of man m' be lifted up?
Joh 20: 9 he m' rise again from the dead.
Ac 1:16 m' needs have been fulfilled,
22 m' one be ordained to be a witness
3:21 Whom the heaven m' receive until
4:12 men, whereby we m' be saved.
9: 6 shall be told thee what thou m' do.
16 he m' suffer for my name's sake.
14:22 m' through much tribulation enter
15:24 souls, saying, Ye m' be circumcised,
16:30 Sirs, what m' I do to be saved?
17: 3 Christ m' needs have suffered,
18:21 I m' by all means keep this feast
19:21 been there, I m' also see Rome.
21:22 the multitude m' needs come
23:11 so m' thou bear witness also at
27:24 thou m' be brought before Cæsar:
26 m' be cast upon a certain island.
Ro 13: 5 ye m' needs be subject, not only
1Co 5:10 for then m' ye needs go out of the
11:19 there m' be also heresies among
15:25 For he m' reign, till he hath put all
53 corruptible m' put on incorruption,
53 this mortal m' put on immortality.
2Co 5:10 For we m' all appear before the
11:30 If I m' needs glory, I will glory of
1Ti 3: 2 A bishop then m' be blameless, the
7 Moreover he m' have a good report
8 Likewise m' the deacons be grave, not
11 Even so m' their wives be grave, not
2Ti 2: 6 laboureth m' be first partaker of
24 servant of the Lord m' not strive;
Tit 1: 7 For a bishop m' be blameless, as
11 Whose mouths m' be stopped, who
Heb 4: 6 remaineth that some m' enter therein,
9:16 there m' also of necessity be the
26 For then m' he often have suffered
11: 6 he that cometh to God m' believe
13:17 as they that m' give account, that
1Pe 4:17 judgment m' begin at the house of
2Pe 1:14 shortly I m' put off this my tabernacle,
Re 1: 1 which m' shortly come to pass;
4: 1 thee things which m' be hereafter.
10:11 Thou m' prophesy again before
11: 5 he m' in this manner be killed.
13:10 sword m' be killed with the sword.
17:10 he m' continue a short space.
20: 3 after that he m' be loosed a little
22: 6 things which m' shortly be done.

mustard
M't 13:31 heaven is like a grain of m' seed,
17:20 ye have faith as a grain of m' seed,
M'r 4:31 It is like a grain of m' seed, which
Lu 13:19 It is like a grain of m' seed, which
17: 6 ye had faith as a grain of m' seed,

mustard-seed See MUSTARD and SEED.

mustered
2Ki 25:19 which m' the people of the land,
Jer 52:25 host, who m' the people of the land;

mustereth
Isa 13: 4 the Lord of hosts m' the host of

mutability See IMMUTABILITY.

mutable See IMMUTABLE.

Muth-labben (*muth-lab'-ben*)
Ps 9: *title* To the chief Musician upon M'.

mutter See also MUTTERED.
Isa 8:19 wizards that peep, and that m':

muttered
Isa 59: 3 your tongue hath m' perverseness.

mutual
Ro 1:12 m' faith both of you and me.

muzzle
De 25: 4 not m' the ox when he treadeth
1Co 9: 9 not m' the mouth of the ox that
1Ti 5:18 not m' the ox that treadeth out

Myra (*mi'-rah*)
Ac 27: 5 we came to M', a city of Lycia.

myrrh
Ge 37:25 bearing spicery and balm and m',
43:11 spices, and m', nuts, and almonds:
Ex 30:23 of pure m' five hundred shekels,
Es 2:12 six months with oil of m', and six
Ps 45: 8 thy garments smell of m', and aloes,
Pr 7:17 I have perfumed my bed with m',
Ca 1:13 A bundle of m' is my wellbeloved
3: 6 of smoke, perfumed with m' and
4: 6 will get me to the mountain of m',
14 m' and aloes, with all the chief
5: 1 gathered my m' with my spice; I
5 my hands dropped with m', and my
5 my fingers with sweet smelling m',
13 lilies, dropping sweet smelling m'.
M't 2:11 gold, and frankincense, and m'.
M'r 15:23 to drink wine mingled with m':
Joh 19:39 a mixture of m' and aloes, about

myrtle
Ne 8:15 m' branches, and palm branches,
Isa 41:19 the shittah tree, and the m' tree,
55:13 brier shall come up the m' tree:
Zec 1: 8 he stood among the m' trees that
10 man that stood among the m' trees
11 that stood among the m' trees, and

myrtle-tree See MYRTLE and TREE.

myself
Ge 3:10 because I was naked; and I hid m'.
22:16 By m' have I sworn, saith the Lord,
Ex 19: 4 wings, and brought you unto m'.
Nu 8:17 land of Egypt I sanctified them for m'.
12: 6 I the Lord will make m' known unto
De 1: 9 I am not able to bear you m' alone:

De 1:12 How can I m· alone bear your
10: 5 I turned m· and came down from the
J'g 16:20 at other times before, and shake m·.
Ru 4: 6 I cannot redeem it for m·, lest I mar
1Sa 13:12 I forced m· therefore, and offered a
20: 5 that I may hide m· in the field unto
25:33 avenging m· with mine own hand.
2Sa 18: 2 surely go forth with you m· also.
22:24 and have kept m· from mine iniquity.
1Ki 18:15 I will surely show m· unto him to-day.
22:30 I will disguise m·, and enter into the
2Ki 5:18 and I bow m· in the house of Rimmon:
18 when I bow down m· in the house of
2Ch 7:12 place to m· for a house of sacrifice.
18:29 I will disguise m·, and will go to the
Es 5:12 banquet that she had prepared but m·.
6: 6 delight to do honour more than to m·?
Job 6:10 I would harden m· in sorrow: let him
7:20 thee, so that I am a burden to m·?
9:20 If I justify m·, mine own mouth shall
27 off my heaviness, and comfort m·.
30 If I wash m· with snow water, and
10: 1 I will leave my complaint upon m·;
13:20 then will I not hide m· from thee.
19: 4 erred, mine error remaineth with m·.
27 Whom I shall see for m·, and mine
31:17 have eaten my morsel m· alone, and
29 or lifted up m· when evil found him:
42: 6 I abhor m·, and repent in dust and
Ps 18:23 and I kept m· from mine iniquity.
35:14 I behaved m· as though he had been
55:12 then I would have hid m· from him:
57: 8 and harp: I m· will awake early.
101: 2 behave m· wisely in a perfect way.
108: 2 and harp: I m· will awake early.
109: 4 adversaries: but I give m· unto prayer.
119:16 I will delight m· in thy statutes: I will
47 will delight m· in thy commandments,
52 old, O Lord; and I have comforted m·.
131: 1 do I exercise m· in great matters,
2 I have behaved and quieted m·,
Ec 2: 3 in mine heart to give m· unto wine,
12 I turned m· to behold wisdom, and
14 I m· perceived also that one event
19 I have shewed m· wise under the sun.
Isa 33:10 I be exalted; now will I lift up m·.
42:14 I have been still, and refrained m·:
43:21 This people have I formed for m·; they
Isa 44:24 spreadeth abroad the earth by m·;
45:23 I have sworn by m·, the word is gone
Jer 8:18 I would comfort m· against sorrow,
21: 5 I m· will fight against you with an
22: 5 words, I swear by m·, saith the Lord,
49:13 I have sworn by m·, saith the Lord,
Eze 14: 7 I the Lord will answer him by m·:
20: 5 made m· known unto them in the land
9 sight I made m· known unto them,
29: 3 mine own, and I have made it for m·.
35:11 I will make m· known among them,
38:23 will I magnify m·, and sanctify m·;
Da 10: 3 neither did I anoint m· at all, till
Mic 6: 6 and bow m· before the high God?
Hab 3:16 I trembled in m·, that I might rest
Zec 7: 3 separating m·, as I have done these
Lu 7: 7 I m· worthy to come unto thee:
24:39 my hands and my feet, that it is I m·:
Joh 5:31 If I bear witness of m·, my witness
7:17 be of God, or whether I speak of m·.
28 I am not come of m·, but he that
8:14 Though I bear record of m·, yet my
18 I am one that bear witness of m·,
28 am he, and that I do nothing of m·;
42 neither came I of m·, but he sent
54 If I honour m·, my honour is
10:18 it from me, but I lay it down of m·.
12:49 For I have not spoken of m·; but
14: 3 again, and receive you unto m·;
10 speak unto you I speak not of m·:
21 him, and will manifest m· to him.
17:19 for their sakes I sanctify m·, that
Ac 10:26 saying, Stand up; I m· also am a man.
20:24 count I my life dear unto m·, so
24:10 the more cheerfully answer for m·:
16 And herein do I exercise m·, to have
25:22 Festus, I would also hear the man m·.
26: 2 I think m· happy, king Agrippa,
2 I shall answer for m· this day before
9 I verily thought with m·, that I
Ro 7:25 the mind I m· serve the law of God;
9: 3 could wish that m· were accursed
11: 4 reserved to m· seven thousand
15:14 I m· also am persuaded of you, my
16: 2 succourer of many, and of m· also.
1Co 4: 4 For I know nothing by m·; yet am
6 I have in a figure transferred to m·
7: 7 that all men were even as I m·.
1Co 9:19 I made m· servant unto all, that I
27 to others, I m· should be a castaway.
2Co 2: 1 But I determined this with m·,
10: 1 Now I Paul m· beseech you by the
11: 7 an offence in abasing m· that ye
9 kept m· from being burdensome
9 unto you, and so will I keep m·.
16 me, that I may boast m· a little.
12: 5 of m· I will not glory, but in mine
13 it be that I m· was not burdensome
Ga 2:18 I make m· a transgressor.
Ph'p 2:24 that I also m· shall come shortly.
3:13 I count not m· to have apprehended:
Ph'm 17 a partner, receive him as m·.

Mysia (*miz'-ye-ah*)
Ac 16: 7 After they were come to M·, they
8 passing by M· came down to Troas.

mysteries
M't 13:11 the m· of the kingdom of heaven,
Lu 8:10 the m· of the kingdom of God:
1Co 4: 1 and stewards of the m· of God.
13: 2 and understand all m·, and all
14: 2 in the spirit he speaketh m·.

mystery See also MYSTERIES.
M'k 4:11 the m· of the kingdom of God:
Ro 11:25 ye should be ignorant of this m·,
16:25 to the revelation of the m·, which
1Co 2: 7 speak the wisdom of God in a m·,
15:51 I shew you a m·; We shall not all
Eph 1: 9 known unto us the m· of his will,
3: 3 he made known unto me the m·;
4 my knowledge in the m· of Christ)
9 what is the fellowship of the m·,
5:32 This is a great m·: but I speak
6:19 make known the m· of the gospel,
Col 1:26 even the m· which hath been hid
27 glory of this m· among the Gentiles;
2: 2 acknowledgment of the m· of God,
4: 3 to speak the m· of Christ, for which
2Th 2: 7 m· of iniquity doth already work:
1Ti 3: 9 Holding the m· of the faith in a
16 great is the m· of godliness:
Re 1:20 The m· of the seven stars which
10: 7 the m· of God should be finished,
17: 5 written, M·, Babylon The Great,
7 will tell thee the m· of the woman,

N.

Naam (*na'-am*)
1Ch 4:15 of Jephunneh; Iru, Elah, and N·:

Naamah (*na'-a-mah*) See also NAAMATHITE.
Ge 4:22 the sister of Tubal-cain was N·.
Jos 15:41 Gederoth, Beth-dagon, and N·,
1Ki 14:21, 31 And his mother's name was N·
2Ch 12:13 And his mother's name was N· an

Naaman (*na'-a-man*) See also NAAMAN'S; NAAMITES.
Ge 46:21 N·, Ehi, and Rosh, Muppim, and
Nu 26:40 the sons of Bela were Ard and N·:
40 Ardites: and of N·, the family of
2Ki 5: 1 Now N·, captain of the host of the
6 sent N· my servant to thee, that
9 So N· came with his horses and
11 But N· was wroth, and went away,
17 And N· said, Shall there not then,
20 master hath spared N· this Syrian,
21 So Gehazi followed after N·. And
21 when N· saw him running after
23 And N· said, Be content, take two
27 leprosy therefore of N· shall cleave
1Ch 8: 4 And Abishua, and N·, and Ahoah,
7 And N·, and Ahiah, and Gera, he
Lu 4:27 cleansed, saving N· the Syrian.

Naaman's (*na'-a-mans*)
2Ki 5: 2 maid; and she waited on N· wife.

Naamathite (*na'-a-math-ite*)
Job 2:11 the Shuhite, and Zophar the N·:
11: 1 Then answered Zophar the N·,
20: 1 Then answered Zophar the N·,
42: 9 Shuhite and Zophar the N· went,

Naamites (*na'-a-mites*)
Nu 26:40 of Naaman, the family of the N·.

Naarah (*na'-a-rah*) See also NAARAN; NAARATH.
1Ch 4: 5 had two wives, Helah and N·.
6 And N· bare him Ahuzam, and
6 These were the sons of N·.

Naarai (*na'-a-rahee*) See also PAARAI.
1Ch 11:37 Carmelite, N· the son of Ezbai,

Naaran (*na'-a-ran*) See also NAARATH.
1Ch 7:28 eastward N·, and westward Gezer,

Naarath (*na'-a-rath*) See also NAARAH; NAARAN.
Jos 16: 7 and to N·, and came to Jericho,

Naashon (*na'-a-shon*) See also NAHSHON.
Ex 6:23 Amminadab, sister of N·, to wife;

Naasson (*na'-as-son*) See also NAASHON.
M't 1: 4 Aminadab begat N·; and N·
Lu 3:32 Salmon, which was the son of N·,

Nabal (*na'-bal*) See also NABAL'S.
1Sa 25: 3 Now the name of the man was N·;
4 that N· did shear his sheep.
5 and go to N·, and greet him in my
9 they spake to N· according to all
10 N· answered David's servants, and
19 But she told not her husband N·.
25 regard this man of Belial, even N·:
1Sa 25:25 N· is his name, and folly is with
26 that seek evil to my lord, be as N·.
34 there had not been left unto N· by
36 Abigail came to N·; and, behold,
37 when the wine was gone out of N·,
38 the Lord smote N·, that he died.
39 David heard that N· was dead,
39 my reproach from the hand of N·,
39 the wickedness of N· upon his own
30: 5 the wife of N· the Carmelite.
2Sa 3: 3 the wife of N· the Carmelite;

Nabal's (*na'-balz*)
1Sa 25:14 young men told Abigail, N· wife,
36 N· heart was merry within him,
27: 3 Abigail the Carmelitess, N· wife.
2Sa 2: 2 Abigail N· wife the Carmelite.

Nabas See BARNABAS.

Naboth (*na'-both*)
1Ki 21: 1 N· the Jezreelite had a vineyard,
2 Ahab spake unto N·, saying, Give
3 N· said to Ahab, The Lord forbid it
4 which N· the Jezreelite had spoken
6 I spake unto N· the Jezreelite, and
7 the vineyard of N· the Jezreelite.
8 were in his city, dwelling with N·.
9 set N· on high among the people:
12 set N· on high among the people.
13 against him, even against N·, in
13 N· did blaspheme God and the
14 saying, N· is stoned, and is dead.
15 Jezebel heard that N· was stoned,
15 possession of the vineyard of N· the
15 for N· is not alive, but dead.
16 when Ahab heard that N· was dead,
16 to go down to the vineyard of N·
18 he is in the vineyard of N·, whither
19 where dogs licked the blood of N·
2Ki 9:21 in the portion of N· the Jezreelite.
25 in the portion of the field of N· the
26 seen yesterday the blood of N·,

Nachon's (*na'-kons*) See also CHIDON.
2Sa 6: 6 they came to N· threshingfloor,

Nachor (*na'-kor*) See also NAHOR.
Jos 24: 2 Abraham, and the father of N·:
Lu 3:34 Thara, which was the son of N·,

Nadab (*na'-dab*)
Ex 6:23 to wife; and she bare him N·, and
24: 1 the Lord, thou, and Aaron, N·, and
9 went up Moses, and Aaron, N·, and
28: 1 office, even Aaron, N· and Abihu,
Le 10: 1 N· and Abihu, the sons of Aaron,
Nu 3: 2 the names of the sons of Aaron; N·
4 N· and Abihu died before the Lord,
26:60 And unto Aaron was born N·, and
61 And N· and Abihu died, when they
1Ki 14:20 N· his son reigned in his stead.
15:25 N· the son of Jeroboam began to
27 for N· and all Israel laid siege to
31 the rest of the acts of N·, and all
1Ch 2:28 sons of Shammai; N·, and Abishur.
30 sons of N·; Seled, and Appaim:
6: 3 sons also of Aaron; N·, and Abihu,
8:30 Zur, and Kish, and Baal, and N·,
9:36 Kish, and Baal, and Ner, and N·,
24: 1 The sons of Aaron; N·, and Abihu,
2 N· and Abihu died before their

Nadib See AMMI-NADIB.

Naggæ See NAGGE.

Nagge (*nag'-e*) See also NEARIAH.
Lu 3:25 of Esli, which was the son of N·,

Nahalal (*na'-ha-lal*) See also NAHALLAL; NAHALOL.
Jos 21:35 N· with her suburbs; four cities.

Nahaliel (*na-ha'-le-el*)
Nu 21:19 And from Mattanah to N·:
19 and from N· to Bamoth:

Nahallal (*na'-hal-el*) See also NAHALAL.
Jos 19:15 Kattath, and N·, and Shimron,

Nahalol (*na'-ha-lol*) See also NAHALAL.
J'g 1:30 Kitron, nor the inhabitants of N·;

Naham (*na'-ham*) See also ISHBAH.
1Ch 4:19 the sister of N·, the father of

Nahamani (*na-ham'-a-ni*)
Ne 7: 7 Azariah, Raamiah, N·, Mordecai,

Naharai (*na'-ha-rahee*) See also NAHARI.
1Ch 11:39 the Ammonite, N· the Berothite,

Naharaim See ARAM-NAHARAIM.

Nahari (*na'-ha-ri*) See also NAHARAI.
2Sa 23:37 N· the Beerothite, armourbearer

Nahash (*na'-hash*) See also IR-NAHASH.
1Sa 11: 1 Then N· the Ammonite came up,
1 the men of Jabesh said unto N·,
2 N· the Ammonite answered them.
12:12 that N· the king of the children of
2Sa 10: 2 kindness unto Hanun the son of N·,
17:25 in to Abigail the daughter of N·,
27 that Shobi the son of N· of Rabbah
1Ch 19: 1 that N· the king of the children of
2 kindness unto Hanun the son of N·,

Nahath (*na'-hath*) See also TOHU.
Ge 36:13 the sons of Reuel; N·, and Zerah,
17 duke N·, duke Zerah, duke
1Ch 1:37 N·, Zerah, Shammah, and Mizzah.
6:26 Zophai his son, and N· his son,
2Ch 31:13 and Azaziah, and N·, and Asahel,

Nahbi (*nah'-bi*)
Nu 13:14 of Naphtali, N· the son of Vophsi.

Nahor (*na'-hor*) See also NACHOR; NAHOR'S.
Ge 11:22 lived thirty years, and begat N·:
23 Serug lived after he begat N· two
24 N· lived nine and twenty years,
25 N· lived after he begat Terah an
26 and begat Abram, N·, and Haran.
27 begat Abram, N·, and Haran; and

Ge 11:29 Abram and *N'* took them wives:
22:20 born children unto thy brother *N'*;
23 these eight Milcah did bear to *N'*.
24:10 Mesopotamia, unto the city of *N'*.
15 the wife of *N'*, Abraham's brother,
24 of Milcah, which she bare unto *N'*.
29: 5 Know ye Laban the son of *N'*?
31:53 God of *N'*, the God of their father,
1Ch 1:26 Serug, *N'*, Terah,

Nahor's (*na'-hors*)
Ge 11:29 and the name of *N'* wife, Milcah.
24:47 The daughter of Bethuel, *N'* son,

Nahshon (*nah'-shon*) See also NAASHON; NAASSON.
Nu 1: 7 *N'* the son of Amminadab.
2: 3 *N'* the son of Amminadab shall be
7:12 his offering the first day was *N'*
17 of *N'* the son of Amminadab.
10:14 was *N'* the son of Amminadab.
Ru 4:20 begat *N'*, and *N'* begat Salmon,
1Ch 2:10 and Amminadab begat *N'*, prince
11 *N'* begat Salma, and Salma begat

Nahum^ (*na'-hum*) See also NAUM.
Na 1: 1 the vision of *N'* the Elkoshite.

nail See also NAILING; NAILS.
J'g 4:21 Heber's wife took a *n'* of the tent,
21 and smote the *n'* into his temples,
22 dead, and the *n'* was in his temples.
5:26 She put her hand to the *n'*, and her
Ezr 9: 8 to give us a *n'* in his holy place,
Isa 22:23 fasten him as a *n'* in a sure place;
25 *n'* that is fastened in the sure place
Zec 10: 4 out of him the *n'*, out of him the

nailing
Col 2:14 out of the way, *n'* it to his cross;

nails
De 21:12 shave her head, and pare her *n'*;
1Ch 22: 3 iron in abundance for the *n'* for
2Ch 3: 9 weight of the *n'* was fifty shekels
Ec 12:11 as *n'* fastened by the masters of
Isa 41: 7 and he fastened it with *n'*, that it
Jer 10: 4 it with *n'* and with hammers, that
Da 4:33 and his *n'* like birds' claws.
7:19 were of iron, and his *n'* of brass;
Joh 20:25 in his hands the print of the *n'*,
25 my finger into the print of the *n'*,

Nain (*nane*)
Lu 7:11 that he went into a city called *N'*;

Naioth (*nah'-yoth*)
1Sa 19:18 Samuel went and dwelt in *N'*.
19 Behold, David is at *N'* in Ramah.
22 Behold, they be at *N'* in Ramah.
23 he went thither to *N'* in Ramah:
23 until he came to *N'* in Ramah.
20: 1 David fled from *N'* in Ramah, and

naked
Ge 2:25 they were both *n'*, the man and
3: 7 knew that they were *n'*; and they
10 I was afraid, because I was *n'*;
11 Who told thee that thou wast *n'*?
Ex 32:25 saw that the people were *n'*,
25 had made them *n'* unto their shame
1Sa 19:24 lay down *n'* all that day and all
2Ch 28:15 all that were *n'* among them, and
19 Israel; for he made Judah *n'*,
Job 1:21 *N'* came I out of my mother's
21 and *n'* shall I return thither: the
22: 6 stripped the *n'* of their clothing.
24: 7 the *n'* to lodge without clothing,
10 him to go *n'* without clothing, and
26: 6 Hell is *n'* before him, and
Ec 5:15 *n'* shall he return to go as he came,
Isa 20: 2 he did so, walking *n'* and barefoot.
3 servant Isaiah hath walked *n'* and
4 young and old, *n'* and barefoot,
58: 7 when thou seest the *n'*, that thou
La 4:21 and shalt make thyself *n'*.
Eze 16: 7 whereas thou wast *n'* and bare.
22 youth, when thou wast *n'* and bare,
39 jewels, and leave thee *n'* and bare.
18: 7 hath covered the *n'* with a garment;
16 hath covered the *n'* with a garment,
23:29 and shall leave thee *n'* and bare:
Ho 2: 3 Lest I strip her *n'*, and set her as
Am 2:16 the mighty shall flee away *n'* in
Mic 1: 8 howl, I will go stripped and *n'*:
11 of Saphir, having thy shame *n'*:
Hab 3: 9 Thy bow was made quite *n'*,
M't 25:36 *N'*, and ye clothed me: I was sick
38 thee in? or *n'*, and clothed thee?
43 *n'*, and ye clothed me not: sick,
44 or *n'*, or sick, or in prison, and did
M'r 14:51 linen cloth cast about his *n'* body;
52 linen cloth, and fled from them *n'*.
Joh 21: 7 coat unto him, (for he was *n'*,) and
Ac 19:16 out of that house *n'* and wounded.
1Co 4:11 hunger, and thirst, and are *n'*,
2Co 5: 3 clothed we shall not be found *n'*.
Heb 4:13 all things are *n'* and opened unto
Jas 2:15 If a brother or sister be *n'*, and
Re 3:17 and poor, and blind, and *n'*:
16:15 lest he walk *n'*, and they see his
17:16 and shall make her desolate and *n'*,

nakedness
Ge 9:22 Canaan, saw the *n'* of his father,
23 and covered the *n'* of their father;
23 and they saw not their father's *n'*.
42: 9, 12 to see the *n'* of the land ye are
Ex 20:26 thy *n'* be not discovered thereon.
28:42 them linen breeches to cover their *n'*;
Le 18: 6 of kin to him, to uncover their *n'*:
7 *n'* of thy father, or the *n'* of thy
Le 18: 7 thou shalt not uncover her *n'*.
8 The *n'* of thy father's wife shalt
8 not uncover: it is thy father's *n'*.
9 The *n'* of thy sister, the daughter
9 their *n'* thou shalt not uncover.
10 The *n'* of thy son's daughter, or of
10 their *n'* thou shalt not uncover:
10 uncover: for theirs is thine own *n'*.
11 *n'* of thy father's wife's daughter,
11 sister, thou shalt not uncover her *n'*.
12 uncover the *n'* of thy father's sister:
13 the *n'* of thy mother's sister:
14 the *n'* of thy father's brother,
15 the *n'* of thy daughter in law:
15 wife; thou shalt not uncover her *n'*.
16 uncover the *n'* of thy brother's wife:
16 brother's wife: it is thy brother's *n'*.
17 not uncover the *n'* of a woman and
17 daughter, to uncover her *n'*; for
18 vex her, to uncover her *n'*, besides
19 unto a woman to uncover her *n'*;
20:11 uncovered his father's *n'*: both of
17 and see her *n'*, and she see his *n'*;
17 he hath uncovered his sister's *n'*;
18 sickness, and shall uncover her *n'*;
19 the *n'* of thy mother's sister, nor
20 he hath uncovered his uncle's *n'*:
21 he hath uncovered his brother's *n'*:
De 28:48 hunger, and in thirst, and in *n'*,
1Sa 20:30 the confusion of thy mother's *n'*?
Isa 47: 3 Thy *n'* shall be uncovered, yea, thy
La 1: 8 because they have seen her *n'*: yea,
Eze 16: 8 skirt over thee, and covered thy *n'*:
36 and thy *n'* discovered through thy
37 and will discover thy *n'* unto them,
37 them, that they may see all thy *n'*.
22:10 they discovered their father's *n'*:
23:10 These discovered her *n'*: they took
18 discovered her *n'*: then my mind
29 the *n'* of thy whoredoms shall be
Ho 2: 9 and my flax given to cover her *n'*.
Na 3: 5 and I will shew the nations thy *n'*,
Hab 2:15 that thou mayest look on their *n'*!
Ro 8:35 famine, or *n'*, or peril, or sword?
2Co 11:27 in fastings often, in cold and *n'*.
Re 3:18 the shame of thy *n'* do not appear;

name^ See also NAMED; NAME'S; NAMES; NAMETH; SURNAME.
Ge 2:11 *n'* of the first is Pison: that is it
13 the *n'* of the second river is Gihon:
14 the *n'* of the third river is Hiddekel:
19 creature, that was the *n'* thereof.
3:20 And Adam called his wife's *n'* Eve;
4:17 *n'* of the city, after the *n'* of his son,
19 wives: the *n'* of the one was Adah,
19 Adah, and the *n'* of the other Zillah.
21 his brother's *n'* was Jubal: he was
25 bare a son, and called his *n'* Seth:
26 a son; and he called his *n'* Enos:
26 men to call upon the *n'* of the Lord.
5: 2 and called their *n'* Adam, in the
3 his image; and called his *n'* Seth:
29 And he called his *n'* Noah, saying,
10:25 two sons: the *n'* of one was Peleg;
25 and his brother's *n'* was Joktan.
11: 4 and let us make us a *n'*, lest we be
9 is the *n'* of it called Babel; because
29 the *n'* of Abram's wife was Sarai;
29 the *n'* of Nahor's wife, Milcah, the
12: 2 bless thee, and make thy *n'* great;
8 and called upon the *n'* of the Lord.
13: 4 Abram called on the *n'* of the Lord.
16: 1 an Egyptian, whose *n'* was Hagar.
11 son, and shalt call his *n'* Ishmael;
13 she called the *n'* of the Lord that
15 Abram called his son's *n'*, which
17: 5 thy *n'* any more be called Abram,
5 but thy *n'* shall be Abraham;
15 thou shalt not call her *n'* Sarai,
15 Sarai, but Sarah shall her *n'* be.
19 and thou shalt call his *n'* Isaac:
19:22 the *n'* of the city was called Zoar.
37 bare a son, and called his *n'* Moab:
38 a son, and called his *n'* Ben-ammi:
21: 3 Abraham called the *n'* of his son
33 called there on the *n'* of the Lord,
22:14 the *n'* of that place Jehovah-jireh:
24 concubine, whose *n'* was Reumah,
24:29 a brother, and his *n'* was Laban:
25: 1 a wife, and her *n'* was Keturah.
25 and they called his *n'* Esau.
26 his *n'* was called Jacob: and Isaac
30 therefore was his *n'* called Edom.
26:20 he called the *n'* of the well Esek;
21 and he called the *n'* of it Sitnah.
22 he called the *n'* of it Rehoboth; and
25 called upon the *n'* of the Lord, and
33 the *n'* of the city is Beer-sheba
28:19 called the *n'* of that place Beth-el:
19 *n'* of that city was called Luz at the
29:16 the *n'* of the elder was Leah, and
16 the *n'* of the younger was Rachel.
32 a son, and she called his *n'* Reuben:
33 also: and she called his *n'* Simeon.
34 therefore was his *n'* called Levi.
35 she called his *n'* Judah; and left
30: 6 son: therefore called she his *n'* Dan.
8 and she called his *n'* Naphtali.
11 cometh: and she called his *n'* Gad.
13 blessed: and she called his *n'* Asher.
18 and she called his *n'* Issachar.
20 sons: and she called his *n'* Zebulun.
21 daughter, and called her *n'* Dinah.
24 she called his *n'* Joseph; and said,
31:48 was the *n'* of it called Galeed;
32: 2 the *n'* of that place Mahanaim.
Ge 32:27 What is thy *n'*? And he said, Jacob.
28 *n'* shall be called no more Jacob,
29 said, Tell me, I pray thee, thy *n'*.
29 it that thou dost ask after my *n'*?
30 called the *n'* of the place Peniel:
33:17 *n'* of the place is called Succoth.
35: 8 the *n'* of it was called Allon-bachuth.
10 said unto him, Thy *n'* is Jacob:
10 thy *n'* shall not be called any more
10 Jacob, but Israel shall be thy *n'*:
10 and he called his *n'* Israel.
15 And Jacob called the *n'* of the place
18 she called his *n'* Ben-oni: but his
36:32 the *n'* of his city was Dinhabah.
35 and the *n'* of his city was Avith.
39 stead: and the *n'* of his city was Pau;
39 and his wife's *n'* was Mehetabel, the
38: 1 Adullamite, whose *n'* was Hirah.
2 Canaanite, whose *n'* was Shuah;
3 bare a son; and he called his *n'* Er.
4 a son; and she called his *n'* Onan.
5 bare a son; and called his *n'* Shelah:
6 his firstborn, whose *n'* was Tamar.
29 therefore his *n'* was called Pharez.
30 hand: and his *n'* was called Zarah.
41:45 And Pharaoh called Joseph's *n'*
51 Joseph called the *n'* of the firstborn
52 *n'* of the second called he Ephraim:
48: 6 called after the *n'* of their brethren
16 and let my *n'* be named on them,
16 the *n'* of my fathers Abraham and
50:11 the *n'* of it was called Abel-mizraim,
Ex 1:15 which the *n'* of the one was Shiphrah,
15 and the *n'* of the other Puah:
2:10 son. And she called his *n'* Moses:
22 son, and he called his *n'* Gershom:
3:13 shall say to me, What is his *n'*?
15 this is my *n'* for ever, and this is
5:23 I came to Pharaoh to speak in thy *n'*,
6: 3 Jacob, by the *n'* of God Almighty,
3 by my *n'* Jehovah was I not known
9:16 and that my *n'* may be declared
15: 3 is a man of war: the Lord is his *n'*.
23 the *n'* of it was called Marah.
16:31 Israel called the *n'* thereof Manna:
17: 7 called the *n'* of the place Massah,
15 called the *n'* of it Jehovah-nissi:
18: 3 the *n'* of the one was Gershom; for
4 And the *n'* of the other was Eliezer;
20: 7 the *n'* of the Lord thy God in vain;
7 guiltless that taketh his *n'* in vain.
24 in all places where I record my *n'* I
23:13 no mention of the *n'* of other gods,
21 transgressions: for my *n'* is in him.
28:21 every one with his *n'* shall they be
31: 2 called by *n'* Bezaleel the son of Uri,
33:12 I know thee by *n'*, and thou hast
17 in my sight, and I know thee by *n'*.
19 proclaim the *n'* of the Lord before
34: 5 and proclaimed the *n'* of the Lord.
14 the Lord, whose *n'* is Jealous, is a
35:30 the Lord hath called by *n'* Bezaleel
39:14 of a signet, every one with his *n'*,
Le 18:21 shalt thou profane the *n'* of thy God:
19:12 ye shall not swear by my *n'* falsely,
12 shalt thou profane the *n'* of thy God:
20: 3 and to profane my holy *n'*.
21: 6 and not profane the *n'* of their God:
22: 2 that they profane not my holy *n'* in
32 Neither shall ye profane my holy *n'*;
24:11 son blasphemed the *n'* of the Lord,
11 his mother's *n'* was Shelomith, the
16 that blasphemeth the *n'* of the Lord,
16 he blasphemeth the *n'* of the Lord,
Nu 4:32 *n'* ye shall reckon the instruments
6:27 shall put my *n'* upon the children of
11: 3 called the *n'* of the place Taberah:
26 camp, the *n'* of the one was Eldad,
26 and the *n'* of the other Medad:
34 *n'* of that place Kibroth-hattaavah:
17: 2 thou every man's *n'* upon his rod.
3 Aaron's *n'* upon the rod of Levi:
21: 3 called the *n'* of the place Hormah.
25:14 the *n'* of the Israelite that was slain,
15 And the *n'* of the Midianitish woman
26:46 the *n'* of the daughter of Asher was
59 *n'* of Amram's wife was Jochebed,
27: 4 the *n'* of our father be done away
32:42 and called it Nobah, after his own *n'*.
De 3:14 and called them after his own *n'*,
5:11 the *n'* of the Lord thy God in vain:
11 guiltless that taketh his *n'* in vain.
6:13 serve him, and shalt swear by his *n'*.
7:24 destroy their *n'* from under heaven:
9:14 blot out their *n'* from under heaven:
10: 8 and to bless in his *n'*, unto this day.
20 thou cleave, and swear by his *n'*.
12: 5 of all your tribes to put his *n'* there,
11 to cause his *n'* to dwell there;
21 God hath chosen to put his *n'* there
14:23 he shall choose to place his *n'* there,
24 God shall choose to set his *n'* there,
16: 2 shall choose to place his *n'* there.
6 God shall choose to place his *n'* in,
11 hath chosen to place his *n'* there.
18: 5 to minister in the *n'* of the Lord,
7 shall minister in the *n'* of the Lord
19 words which he shall speak in my *n'*,
20 presume to speak a word in my *n'*,
20 shall speak in the *n'* of other gods,
22 speaketh in the *n'* of the Lord, if
21: 5 and to bless in the *n'* of the Lord;
22:14 bring up an evil *n'* upon her, and
19 hath brought up an evil *n'* upon a
25: 6 shall succeed in the *n'* of his brother
6 that his *n'* be not put out of Israel.

De 25: 7 up unto his brother a n' in Israel,
10 And his n' shall be called in Israel,
26: 2 shall choose to place his n' there.
19 in praise, and in n', and in honour;
28: 10 thou art called by the n' of the Lord;
58 fear this glorious and fearful n',
29: 20 blot out his n' from under heaven.
32: 3 I will publish the n' of the Lord:
Jos 5: 9 the n' of the place is called Gilgal
7: 9 and cut off our n' from the earth:
9 what wilt thou do unto thy great n'?
26 the n' of that place was called, The
9: 9 of the n' of the Lord thy God: for
14: 15 And the n' of Hebron before was
15: 15 and the n' of Debir before was
19: 47 Dan, after the n' of Dan their father.
21: 9 which are here mentioned by n',
23: 7 make mention of the n' of their gods,
J'g 1: 10 (now the n' of Hebron before was
11 and the n' of Debir before was
17 the n' of the city was called Hormah.
23 the n' of the city before was Luz.)
26 city, and called the n' thereof Luz:
26 which is the n' thereof unto this day.
2: 5 called the n' of that place Bochim:
8: 31 son, whose n' he called Abimelech.
13: 2 the Danites, whose n' was Manoah;
6 he was, neither told he me his n':
17 What is thy n', that when thy sayings
18 Why askest thou thus after my n',
24 a son, and called his n' Samson:
15: 19 wherefore he called the n' thereof
16: 4 of Sorek, whose n' was Delilah.
17: 1 Ephraim, whose n' was Micah.
18: 29 they called the n' of the city Dan,
29 after the n' of Dan their father, who
29 howbeit the n' of the city was Laish
Ru 1: 2 the n' of the man was Elimelech,
2 and the n' of his wife Naomi, and
2 the n' of his two sons Mahlon and
4 Moab; the n' of the one was Orpah,
4 and the n' of the other Ruth: and
2: 1 of Elimelech; and his n' was Boaz.
19 The man's n' with whom I wrought
4: 5, 10 to raise up the n' of the dead upon
10 the n' of the dead be not cut off from
14 that his n' may be famous in Israel.
17 women her neighbours gave it a n',
17 Naomi; and they called his n' Obed:
1Sa 1: 1 and his n' was Elkanah, the son of
2 the n' of the one was Hannah, and
2 the n' of the other Peninnah:
20 bare a son, and called his n' Samuel,
7: 12 and called the n' of it Eben-ezer,
8: 2 Now the n' of his firstborn was Joel;
2 and the n' of his second, Abiah:
9: 1 whose n' was Kish, the son of Abiel,
2 he had a son, whose n' was Saul, a
14: 4 and the n' of the one was Bozez,
4 and the n' of the other Seneh.
49 these; the n' of the firstborn Merab,
49 and the n' of the younger Michal:
50 the n' of Saul's wife was Ahinoam,
50 the n' of the captain of his host was
16: 3 unto me him whom I n' unto thee.
17: 12 whose n' was Jesse; and he had
23 the Philistine of Gath, Goliath by n',
45 to thee in the n' of the Lord of hosts,
18: 30 Saul; so that his n' was much set by.
20: 42 both of us in the n' of the Lord,
21: 7 and his n' was Doeg, an Edomite,
24: 21 wilt not destroy my n' out of my
25: 3 Now the n' of the man was Nabal;
3 and the n' of his wife Abigail: and
5 go to Nabal, and greet him in my n':
9 to all those words in the n' of David,
25 even Nabal: for as his n' is, so is he;
25 Nabal is his n', and folly is with him:
28: 8 him up, whom I shall n' unto thee.
2Sa 3: 7 a concubine, whose n' was Rizpah,
4: 2 the n' of the one was Baanah, and
2 and the n' of the other Rechab, the
4 lame. And his n' was Mephibosheth.
5: 20 the n' of that place Baal-perazim.
6: 2 n' is called by the n' of the Lord of
18 the people in the n' of the Lord of
7: 9 and have made thee a great n',
9 like unto the n' of the great men
13 He shall build an house for my n',
23 to make him a n', and to do for you
26 thy n' be magnified for ever, saying,
8: 13 And David gat him a n' when he
9: 2 Saul a servant whose n' was Ziba.
12 a young son, whose n' was Micha.
12: 24 a son, and he called his n' Solomon:
25 and he called his n' Jedidiah,
28 the city, and it be called after my n'.
13: 1 a fair sister, whose n' was Tamar;
3 had a friend, whose n' was Jonadab,
14: 7 not leave to my husband neither n'
27 one daughter, whose n' was Tamar:
16: 5 whose n' was Shimei, the son of Gera:
17: 25 whose n' was Ithra an Israelite,
18: 18 I have no son to keep my n' in
18 he called the pillar after his own n':
20: 1 man of Belial, whose n' was Sheba,
21 Sheba the son of Bichri by n', hath
22: 50 and I will sing praises unto thy n'.
23: 18 them, and had the n' among three.
22 had the n' among three mighty men.
1Ki 1: 47 God make the n' of Solomon better
47 of Solomon better than thy n', and
3: 2 house built unto the n' of the Lord,
5: 3 house unto the n' of the Lord his
5 house unto the n' of the Lord my
5 he shall build an house unto my n'.

1Ki 7: 21 and called the n' thereof Jachin:
21 pillar, and called the n' thereof Boaz.
8: 16 house, that my n' might be therein:
17 an house for the n' of the Lord God
18 heart to build an house unto my n',
19 he shall build the house unto my n'.
20 an house for the n' of the Lord God
29 thou hast said, My n' shall be there:
33 thee, and confess thy n', and pray,
35 confess thy n', and turn from their
42 (For they shall hear of thy great n',
43 people of the earth may know thy n',
43 I have builded, is called by thy n'.
44 house that I have built for thy n':
48 house which I have built for thy n':
9: 3 built, to put my n' there for ever;
7 which I have hallowed for my n',
10: 1 concerning the n' of the Lord, she
11: 26 whose mother's n' was Zeruah, a
36 have chosen me to put my n' there.
13: 2 the house of David, Josiah by n';
14: 21 tribes of Israel, to put his n' there.
21, 31 his mother's n' was Naamah an
15: 2, 10 his mother's n' was Maachah, the
16: 24 the n' of the city which he built,
24 after the n' of Shemer, owner of the
18: 24 And call ye on the n' of your gods,
24 and I will call on the n' of the Lord:
25 call on the n' of your gods, but put
26 and called on the n' of Baal from
31 came, saying, Israel shall be thy n':
32 built an altar in the n' of the Lord:
21: 8 So she wrote letters in Ahab's n',
22: 16 which is true in the n' of the Lord?
42 And his mother's n' was Azubah
2Ki 2: 24 cursed them in the n' of the Lord.
5: 11 call on the n' of the Lord his God,
8: 26 And his mother's n' was Athaliah,
12: 1 And his mother's n' was Zibiah of
14: 2 his mother's n' was Jehoaddan of
7 called the n' of it Joktheel unto this
27 he would blot out the n' of Israel
15: 2 his mother's n' was Jecholiah of
33 And his mother's n' was Jerusha,
18: 2 His mother's n' also was Abi, the
21: 1 his mother's n' was Hephzi-bah.
4 said, In Jerusalem will I put my n'.
7 of Israel, will I put my n' for ever:
19 his mother's n' was Meshullemeth,
22: 1 And his mother's n' was Jedidah,
23: 27 which I said, My n' shall be there.
31 And his mother's n' was Hamutal,
34 and turned his n' to Jehoiakim, and
36 And his mother's n' was Zebudah,
24: 8 And his mother's n' was Nehushta,
17 and changed his n' to Zedekiah.
18 And his mother's n' was Hamutal,
1Ch 1: 19 sons: the n' of the one was Peleg;
19 and his brother's n' was Joktan.
43 and the n' of his city was Dinhabah.
46 and the n' of his city was Avith.
50 and the n' of his city was Pai;
50 and his wife's n' was Mehetabel,
2: 26 wife, whose n' was Atarah; she was
29 the n' of the wife of Abishur was
34 an Egyptian, whose n' was Jarha.
4: 3 n' of their sister was Hazelelponi:
9 and his mother called his n' Jabez,
41 these written by n' came in the days
7: 15 whose sister's n' was Maachah;)
15 the n' of the second...Zelophehad:
16 son, and she called his n' Peresh;
16 the n' of his brother was Sheresh;
23 he called his n' Beriah, because it
8: 29 whose wife's n' was Maachah:
9: 35 whose wife's n' was Maachah:
11: 20 them, and had a n' among the three.
24 the n' among the three mighties.
12: 31 which were expressed by n', to
13: 6 cherubims, whose n' is called on it.
14: 11 the n' of that place Baal-perazim.
16: 2 the people in the n' of the Lord.
8 call upon his n', make known his
10 Glory ye in his holy n': let the heart
29 the Lord the glory due unto his n':
35 we may give thanks to thy holy n',
41 who were expressed by n', to give
17: 8 thee a n' like the n' of the great men
21 to make thee a n' of greatness and
24 thy n' may be magnified for ever,
21: 19 he spake in the n' of the Lord.
22: 7 unto the n' of the Lord my God:
8 shalt not build an house unto my n',
9 for his n' shall be Solomon, and I
10 He shall build an house for my n';
19 is to be built to the n' of the Lord.
23: 13 him, and to bless in his n' for ever.
28: 3 shalt not build an house for my n',
29: 13 thee, and praise thy glorious n'.
16 build thee an house for thine holy n'
2Ch 2: 1 an house for the n' of the Lord,
4 build an house to the n' of the Lord
3: 17 n' of that on the right hand Jachin,
17 and the n' of that on the left Boaz.
6: 5 house in, that my n' might be there;
6 Jerusalem,...my n' might be there;
7 an house for the n' of the Lord God
8 heart to build an house for my n',
9 he shall build the house for my n'.
10 the house for the n' of the Lord God
20 that thou wouldest put thy n' there;
24 and shall return and confess thy n',
26 and confess thy n', and turn from
33 people of the earth may know thy n',
33 I have built is called by thy n'.
34 house which I have built for thy n';

2Ch 6: 38 house which I have built for thy n':
7: 14 people, which are called by my n',
16 that my n' may be there for ever:
20 which I have sanctified for my n',
12: 13 tribes of Israel, to put his n' there.
13 And his mother's n' was Naamah
13: 2 His mother's n' also was Michaiah
14: 11 and in thy n' we go against this
18: 15 truth to me in the n' of the Lord?
20: 8 thee a sanctuary therein for thy n',
9 presence, (for thy n' is in this house,)
26 the n' of the same place was called,
31 And his mother's n' was Azubah
22: 2 His mother's n' also was Athaliah
24: 1 His mother's n' also was Zibiah of
25: 1 And his mother's n' was Jehoaddan
26: 3 His mother's n' also was Jecoliah of
8 his n' spread abroad even to the
15 And his n' spread far abroad; for
27: 1 His mother's n' also was Jerushah,
28: 9 Lord was there, whose n' was Oded:
15 which were expressed by n' rose up,
29: 1 And his mother's n' was Abijah,
31: 19 the men that were expressed by n',
33: 4 Jerusalem shall my n' be for ever.
7 of Israel, will I put my n' for ever:
18 spake to him in the n' of the Lord
36: 4 and turned his n' to Jehoiakim.
Ezr 2: 61 Gileadite,...was called after their n':
5: 1 in the n' of the God of Israel, even
14 one, whose n' was Sheshbazzar,
6: 12 hath caused his n' to dwell there
8: 20 all of them were expressed by n'.
Ne 1: 9 I have chosen to set my n' there.
11 servants, who desire to fear thy n':
7: 63 to wife, and was called after their n'.
9: 5 and blessed be thy glorious n',
7 and gavest him the n' of Abraham;
10 So didst thou get thee a n', as it is
Es 2: 5 whose n' was Mordecai, the son of
14 her, and that she were called by n'.
22 the king thereof in Mordecai's n'.
3: 12 in the n' of king Ahasuerus was it
8: 8 as it liketh you, in the king's n',
8 which is written in the king's n',
10 he wrote in the king Ahasuerus' n',
9: 26 days Purim after the n' of Pur.
Job 1: 1 whose n' was Job; and that man
21 away; blessed be the n' of the Lord.
18: 17 he shall have no n' in the street.
42: 14 called the n' of the first, Jemima;
14 and the n' of the second, Kezia;
14 the n' of the third, Keren-happuch.
Ps 5: 11 them also that love thy n' be joyful
7: 17 will sing praise to the n' of the Lord
8: 1, 9 excellent is thy n' in all the earth!
9: 2 I will sing praise to thy n', O thou
5 thou hast put out their n' for ever
10 they that know thy n' will put their
18: 49 and sing praises unto thy n'.
20: 1 n' of the God of Jacob defend thee;
5 in the n' of our God we will set up
7 we will remember the n' of the Lord
22: 22 declare thy n' unto my brethren:
29: 2 the Lord the glory due unto his n';
33: 21 we have trusted in his holy n'.
34: 3 me, and let us exalt his n' together.
41: 5 When shall he die, and his n' perish?
44: 5 through thy n' will we tread them
8 day long, and praise thy n' for ever.
20 we have forgotten the n' of our God,
45: 17 will make thy n' to be remembered
48: 10 According to thy n', O God, so is
52: 9 I will wait on thy n'; for it is good
54: 1 Save me, O God, by thy n', and
6 I will praise thy n', O Lord; for it is
61: 5 heritage of those that fear thy n'.
8 I sing praise unto thy n' for ever,
63: 4 I will lift up my hands in thy n'.
66: 2 Sing forth the honour of his n':
4 unto thee; they shall sing to thy n'.
68: 4 unto God, sing praises to his n':
4 upon the heavens by his n' Jah,
69: 30 will praise the n' of God with a song,
36 that love his n' shall dwell therein.
72: 17 His n' shall endure for ever:
17 his n' shall be continued as long as
19 blessed be his glorious n' for ever:
74: 7 the dwelling place of thy n' to the
10 enemy blaspheme thy n' for ever?
18 people have blasphemed thy n'.
21 let the poor and needy praise thy n'.
75: 1 thy n' is near thy wondrous works
76: 1 God known: his n' is great in Israel.
79: 6 that have not called upon thy n'.
9 salvation, for the glory of thy n':
80: 18 us, and we will call upon thy n'.
83: 4 that the n' of Israel be no more in
16 shame; that they may seek thy n',
18 thou, whose n' alone is Jehovah,
86: 9 O Lord; and shall glorify thy n'.
11 truth: unite my heart to fear thy n'.
12 I will glorify thy n' for evermore.
89: 12 and Hermon shall rejoice in thy n'.
16 In thy n' shall they rejoice all the
24 in my n' shall his horn be exalted.
91: 14 high, because he hath known my n'.
92: 1 to sing praises unto thy n', O most
96: 2 Sing unto the Lord, bless his n';
8 the Lord the glory due unto his n':
99: 3 praise thy great and terrible n';
6 among them that call upon his n';
100: 4 thankful unto him, and bless his n'.
102: 15 shall fear the n' of the Lord, and
21 declare the n' of the Lord in Zion,
103: 1 that is within me, bless his holy n'.

Ps 105: 1 call upon his n': make known his
3 Glory ye in his holy n': let the
106:47 to give thanks unto thy holy n', and
109:13 following let their n' be blotted out.
111: 9 ever: holy and reverend is his n'.
113: 1 Lord, praise the n' of the Lord.
2 Blessed be the n' of the Lord from
3 same the Lord's n' is to be praised.
115: 1 but unto thy n' give glory, for thy
116: 4 called I upon the n' of the Lord;
13 and call upon the n' of the Lord.
17 and will call upon the n' of the Lord.
118:10 in the n' of the Lord will I destroy
11, 12 the n' of the Lord I will destroy
26 that cometh in the n' of the Lord:
119:55 I have remembered thy n', O Lord,
132 to do unto those that love thy n'.
122: 4 give thanks unto the n' of the Lord.
124: 8 Our help is in the n' of the Lord,
129: 8 we bless you in the n' of the Lord.
135: 1 Praise ye the n' of the Lord; praise
3 sing praises unto his n': for it is
13 Thy n', O Lord, endureth for ever;
138: 2 praise thy n' for thy lovingkindness
2 magnified thy word above all thy n'.
139:20 and thine enemies take thy n' in vain.
140:13 shall give thanks unto thy n':
142: 7 of prison, that I may praise thy n':
145: 1 I will bless thy n' for ever and ever.
2 and I will praise thy n' for ever and
21 let all flesh bless his holy n' for ever
148: 5, 13 them praise the n' of the Lord:
13 for his n' alone is excellent; his
149: 3 Let them praise his n' in the dance:
Pr 10: 7 but the n' of the wicked shall rot.
18:10 n' of the Lord is a strong tower:
21:24 Proud and haughty scorner is his n',
22: 1 A good n' is rather to be chosen
30: 4 is his n', and what is his son's n',
9 and take the n' of my God in vain.
Ec 6: 4 and his n' shall be covered with
7: 1 A good n' is better than precious
Ca 1: 3 thy n' is as ointment poured forth,
Isa 4: 1 only let us be called by thy n', to
7:14 son, and shall call his n' Immanuel.
8: 3 Call his n' Maher-shalal-hash-baz.
9: 6 his n' shall be called Wonderful,
12: 4 Praise the Lord, call upon his n',
4 mention that his n' is exalted.
14:22 cut off from Babylon the n', and
18: 7 to the place of the n' of the Lord
24:15 even the n' of the Lord God of
25: 1 I will exalt thee, I will praise thy n';
26: 8 the desire of our soul is to thy n',
13 will we make mention of thy n'.
29:23 of him, they shall sanctify my n',
30:27 the n' of the Lord cometh from far,
41:25 the sun shall he call upon my n':
42: 8 I am the Lord: that is my n': and
43: 1 thee, I have called thee by thy n';
7 every one that is called by my n':
44: 5 shall call himself by the n' of Jacob;
5 himself by the n' of Israel.
45: 3 the Lord, which call thee by thy n',
4 I have even called thee by thy n':
47: 4 the Lord of hosts is his n', the
48: 1 are called by the n' of Israel, and
1 which swear by the n' of the Lord,
2 Israel; The Lord of hosts is his n'.
11 for how should my n' be polluted? and
19 his n' should not have been cut off
49: 1 hath he made mention of my n'.
50:10 let him trust in the n' of the Lord,
51:15 roared: The Lord of hosts is his n'.
52: 5 and my n' continually every day is
6 my people shall know my n':
54: 5 the Lord of hosts is his n'; and thy
55:13 and it shall be to the Lord for a n',
56: 5 and a n' better than of sons and of
5 I will give them an everlasting n',
6 him, and to love the n' of the Lord,
57:15 eternity, whose n' is Holy; I dwell
59:19 shall they fear the n' of the Lord
60: 9 unto the n' of the Lord thy God,
62: 2 thou shalt be called by a new n',
2 the mouth of the Lord shall n'.
63:12 to make himself an everlasting n'?
14 to make thyself a glorious n'.
16 redeemer; thy n' is from everlasting.
19 they were not called by thy n'.
64: 2 thy n' known to thine adversaries,
7 is none that calleth upon thy n',
65: 1 nation that was not called by my n'.
15 leave your n' for a curse unto my
15 and call his servants by another n':
66:22 shall your seed and your n' remain.
Jer 3:17 unto it, to the n' of the Lord, to
7:10, 11 house, which is called by my n',
12 where I set my n' at the first, and
14 house, which is called by my n',
30 the house which is called by my n',
10: 6 great, and thy n' is great in might.
16 The Lord of hosts is his n'.
25 the families that call not on thy n':
11:16 The Lord called thy n', A green
19 his n' may be no more remembered.
21 Prophesy not in the n' of the Lord,
12:16 of my people, to swear by my n',
13:11 unto me for a people, and for a n',
14: 9 and we are called by thy n'; leave
14 prophets prophesy lies in my n':
15 prophets that prophesy in my n',
15:16 for I am called by thy n', O Lord
16:21 shall know that my n' is The Lord.
20: 3 Lord hath not called thy n' Pashur,
9 him, nor speak any more in his n'.

Jer 23: 6 his n' whereby he shall be called,
25 that prophesy lies in my n', saying,
27 to forget my n' by their dreams
27 have forgotten my n' for Baal.
25:29 the city which is called by my n',
26: 9 prophesied in the n' of the Lord,
16 spoken to us in the n' of the Lord
20 prophesied in the n' of the Lord,
27:15 yet they prophesy a lie in my n';
29: 9 prophesy falsely unto you in my n':
21 prophesy a lie unto you in my n';
23 have spoken lying words in my n',
25 hast sent letters in thy n' unto all
31:35 roar; The Lord of hosts is his n':
32:18 God, The Lord of hosts, is his n',
20 and hast made thee a n', as at this
34 the house which is called by my n',
33: 2 to establish it; the Lord is his n';
9 it shall be to me a n' of joy, a praise
16 is the n' wherewith she shall be called,
34:15 house which is called by my n':
16 But ye turned and polluted my n',
37:13 was there, whose n' was Irijah,
44:16 unto us in the n' of the Lord, we
26 I have sworn by my great n', saith
26 that my n' shall no more be named
46:18 King, whose n' is the Lord of hosts,
48:15 King, whose n' is the Lord of hosts,
17 all ye that know his n', say, How is
50:34 strong; the Lord of hosts is his n':
51:19 the Lord of hosts is his n'.
57 King, whose n' is the Lord of hosts.
52: 1 his mother's n' was Hamutal the
La 3:55 I called upon thy n', O Lord, out of
Eze 20:29 And the n' thereof is called Bamah
39 but pollute ye my holy n' no more
24: 2 man, write thee the n' of the day,
36:20 they went, they profaned my holy n',
21 But I had pity for mine holy n',
23 I will sanctify my great n', which
39: 7 So will I make my holy n' known in
7 them pollute my holy n' any more:
16 n' of the city shall be Hamonah.
25 and will be jealous for my holy n';
43: 7 my holy n', shall the house of Israel
8 even defiled my holy n' by their
48:35 n' of the city from that day shall be
Da 1: 7 unto Daniel the n' of Belteshazzar;
2:20 Blessed be the n' of God for ever
26 Daniel, whose n' was Belteshazzar,
4: 8 me, whose n' was Belteshazzar,
8 according to the n' of my god, and
19 Daniel, whose n' was Belteshazzar,
9: 6 spake in thy n' to our kings, our
18 the city which is called by thy n':
19 and thy people are called by thy n'.
10: 1 whose n' was called Belteshazzar;
Ho 1: 4 said unto him, Call his n' Jezreel;
6 unto him, Call her n' Lo-ruhamah:
9 said God, Call his n' Lo-ammi:
2:17 more be remembered by their n'.
Joe 2:26 praise the n' of the Lord your God,
32 shall call on the n' of the Lord shall
Am 2: 7 same maid, to profane my holy n':
4:13 Lord, The God of hosts, is his n'.
5: 8 of the earth: The Lord is his n':
27 Lord, whose n' is the God of hosts.
6:10 make mention of the n' of the Lord.
9: 6 of the earth: The Lord is his n'.
12 heathen, which are called by my n',
Mic 4: 5 walk every one in the n' of his god,
5 we will walk in the n' of the Lord
5: 4 in the majesty of the n' of the Lord
6: 9 the man of wisdom shall see thy n':
Na 1:14 that no more of thy n' be sown: out
Zep 1: 4 the n' of the Chemarims with the
3: 9 all call upon the n' of the Lord,
12 shall trust in the n' of the Lord.
20 I will make you a n' and a praise
Zec 5: 4 him that sweareth falsely by my n':
6:12 the man whose n' is The Branch;
10:12 shall walk up and down in his n',
13: 3 speakest lies in the n' of the Lord:
9 they shall call on my n', and I will
14: 9 there be one Lord, and his n' one.
Mal 1: 6 you, O priests, that despise my n'.
6 Wherein have we despised thy n'?
11 same my n' shall be great among
11 incense shall be offered unto my n',
11 for my n' shall be great among the
14 and my n' is dreadful among the
2: 2 to heart, to give glory unto my n',
5 me, and was afraid before my n'.
3:16 Lord, and that thought upon his n'.
4: 2 But unto you that fear my n' shall
M't 1:21 and thou shalt call his n' Jesus:
23 they shall call his n' Emmanuel,
25 son: and he called his n' Jesus.
6: 9 art in heaven, Hallowed be thy n'.
7:22 have we not prophesied in thy n'?
22 and in thy n' have cast out devils?
22 and in thy n' done many wonderful
10:41 a prophet in the n' of a prophet
41 man in the n' of a righteous man
42 water only in the n' of a disciple,
12:21 in his n' shall the Gentiles trust.
18: 5 one such little child in my n'
20 are gathered together in my n',
21: 9 that cometh in the n' of the Lord;
23:39 that cometh in the n' of the Lord.
24: 5 many shall come in my n', saying,
27:32 a man of Cyrene, Simon by n': him
28:19 them in the n' of the Father, and of
M'r 5: 9 What is thy n'? And he answered,
9 My n' is Legion: for we are many.
22 of the synagogue, Jairus by n';

M'r 6:14 (for his n' was spread abroad:) and
9:37 one of such children in my n',
38 saw one casting out devils in thy n',
39 which shall do a miracle in my n',
41 a cup of water to drink in my n',
11: 9 that cometh in the n' of the Lord:
10 that cometh in the n' of the Lord:
13: 6 many shall come in my n', saying,
16:17 In my n' shall they cast out devils;
Lu 1: 5 of Aaron, and her n' was Elisabeth.
13 son, and thou shalt call his n' John.
27 to a man whose n' was Joseph, of
27 David; and the virgin's n' was Mary.
31 a son, and shalt call his n' Jesus.
49 me great things; and holy is his n'.
59 Zacharias, after the n' of his father.
61 thy kindred that is called by this n'.
63 and wrote, saying, His n' is John.
2:21 the child, his n' was called Jesus,
25 Jerusalem, whose n' was Simeon;
6:22 and cast out your n' as evil, for the
8:30 asked him, saying, What is thy n'?
9:48 receive this child in my n' receiveth
49 saw one casting out devils in thy n';
10:17 are subject unto us through thy n'.
11: 2 art in heaven, Hallowed be thy n'.
13:35 that cometh in the n' of the Lord.
19:38 that cometh in the n' of the Lord:
21: 8 many shall come in my n', saying,
24:18 one of them, whose n' was Cleopas,
47 be preached in his n' among all
Joh 1: 6 sent from God, whose n' was John.
12 even to them that believe on his n':
2:23 feast day, many believed in his n',
3:18 not believed in the n' of the only
5:43 I am come in my Father's n', and
43 if another shall come in his own n',
10: 3 he calleth his own sheep by n', and
25 works that I do in my Father's n',
12:13 that cometh in the n' of the Lord.
28 Father, glorify thy n'. Then came
14:13 whatsoever ye shall ask in my n',
14 If ye shall ask any thing in my n',
26 whom the Father will send in my n',
15:16 ye shall ask of the Father in my n',
16:23 ye shall ask the Father in my n', he
24 have ye asked nothing in my n':
26 At that day ye shall ask in my n':
17: 6 manifested thy n' unto the men
11 keep through thine own n' those
12 in the world, I kept them in thy n':
26 I have declared unto them thy n',
18:10 ear. The servant's n' was Malchus.
20:31 ye might have life through his n'.
Ac 2:21 shall call on the n' of the Lord shall
38 one of you in the n' of Jesus Christ
3: 6 the n' of Jesus Christ of Nazareth
16 his n' through faith in his n' hath
4: 7 or by what n', have ye done this?
10 the n' of Jesus Christ of Nazareth,
12 there is none other n' under heaven
17 henceforth to no man in this n'.
18 at all nor teach in the n' of Jesus.
30 by the n' of thy holy child Jesus.
5:28 that ye should not teach in this n'?
40 should not speak in the n' of Jesus,
41 worthy to suffer shame for his n'.
7:58 man's feet, whose n' was Saul.
8:12 of God, and the n' of Jesus Christ,
16 baptized in the n' of the Lord Jesus.)
9:14 to bind all that call on thy n'.
15 to bear my n' before the Gentiles,
21 called on this n' in Jerusalem,
27 at Damascus in the n' of Jesus.
29 boldly in the n' of the Lord Jesus,
10:43 that through his n' whosoever
48 to be baptized in the n' of the Lord.
13: 6 a Jew, whose n' was Bar-jesus:
8 (for so is his n' by interpretation)
15:14 take out of them a people for his n'.
17 upon whom my n' is called, saith
26 lives for the n' of our Lord Jesus
16:18 in the n' of Jesus Christ to come out
19: 5 baptized in the n' of the Lord Jesus.
13 spirits the n' of the Lord Jesus,
17 n' of the Lord Jesus was magnified.
21:13 Jerusalem for the n' of the Lord
22:16 sins, calling on the n' of the Lord.
26: 9 things contrary to the n' of Jesus of
28: 7 the island, whose n' was Publius;
Ro 1: 5 faith among all nations, for his n':
2:24 the n' of God is blasphemed among
9:17 and that my n' might be declared
10:13 shall call upon the n' of the Lord
15: 9 the Gentiles, and sing unto thy n'.
1Co 1: 2 call upon the n' of Jesus Christ
10 by the n' of our Lord Jesus Christ,
13 were ye baptized in the n' of Paul?
15 that I had baptized in mine own n'.
5: 4 In the n' of our Lord Jesus Christ,
6:11 in the n' of the Lord Jesus, and by
Eph 1:21 and every n' that is named, not
5:20 in the n' of our Lord Jesus Christ;
Ph'p 2: 9 him a n' which is above every n':
10 That at the n' of Jesus every knee
Col 3:17 do all in the n' of the Lord Jesus,
2Th 1:12 That the n' of our Lord Jesus
3: 6 in the n' of our Lord Jesus Christ,
1Ti 6: 1 that the n' of God and his doctrine
2Ti 2:19 one that nameth the n' of Christ
Heb 1: 4 a more excellent n' than they.
2:12 declare thy n' unto my brethren,
6:10 which ye have shewed toward his n',
13:15 of our lips giving thanks to his n'.
Jas 2: 7 n' by the which ye are called?
5:10 have spoken in the n' of the Lord,

Jas 5:14 him with oil in the *n*· of the Lord:
1Pe 4:14 be reproached for the *n*· of Christ,
1Jo 3:23 believe on the *n*· of his Son Jesus
5:13 believe on the *n*· of the Son of God;
13 believe on the *n*· of the Son of God.
3Jo 14 thee. Greet the friends by *n*·.
Re 2:13 thou holdest fast my *n*·, and hast
17 and in the stone a new *n*· written,
3: 1 that thou hast a *n*· that thou livest,
5 not blot out his *n*· out of the book
5 will confess his *n*· before my Father,
8 word, and hast not denied my *n*·.
12 *n*· of my God, and the *n*· of the city
12 I will write upon him my new *n*·.
6: 8 his *n*· that sat on him was Death,
8:11 *n*· of the star is called Wormwood:
9:11 whose *n*· in the Hebrew tongue is
11 Greek tongue hath his *n*· Apollyon.
11:18 and them that fear thy *n*·, small and
13: 1 upon his heads the *n*· of blasphemy.
6 against God, to blaspheme his *n*·,
17 had the mark, or the *n*· of the beast,
17 the beast, or the number of his *n*·.
14: 1 having his Father's *n*· written in
11 receiveth the mark of his *n*·.
15: 2 and over the number of his *n*·,
4 O Lord, and glorify thy *n*·? for thou
16: 9 and blasphemed the *n*· of God,
17: 5 upon her forehead was a *n*· written,
19:12 and he had a *n*· written, that no
13 his *n*· is called The Word of God.
16 and on his thigh a *n*· written, King
22: 4 his *n*· shall be in their foreheads.

named See also SURNAMED.
Ge 23:16 which he had *n*· in the audience
27:36 Is not he rightly *n*· Jacob?
48:16 and let my name be *n*· on them,
Jos 2: 1 into an harlot's house, *n*· Rahab,
1Sa 4:21 And she *n*· the child I-chabod,
17: 4 *n*· Goliath, of Gath, whose height
22:20 the son of Ahitub, *n*· Abiathar,
2Ki 17:34 of Jacob, whom he *n*· Israel;
1Ch 23:14 sons were *n*· of the tribe of Levi.
Ec 6:10 which hath been is *n*· already,
Isa 61: 6 shall be *n*· the Priests of the Lord:
Jer 44:26 my name shall no more be *n*· in the
Da 5:12 whom the king *n*· Belteshazzar:
Am 6: 1 which are *n*· chief of the nations,
Mic 2: 7 thou that art *n*· the house of Jacob,
M't 9: 9 a man, *n*· Matthew, sitting at the
27:57 a rich man of Arimathæa, *n*· Joseph,
M'r 14:32 a place which was *n*· Gethsemane:
15: 7 there was one *n*· Barabbas, which
Lu 1: 5 a certain priest *n*· Zacharias, of
26 unto a city of Galilee, *n*· Nazareth,
2:21 which was so *n*· of the angel
5:27 forth, and saw a publican, *n*· Levi,
6:13 twelve, whom also he *n*· apostles;
14 Simon, (whom he also *n*· Peter,)
8:41 there came a man *n*· Jairus, and he
10:38 woman *n*· Martha received him into
16:20 was a certain beggar *n*· Lazarus,
19: 2 there was a man *n*· Zacchæus,
23:50 behold, there was a man *n*· Joseph,
Joh 3: 1 of the Pharisees, *n*· Nicodemus,
11: 1 a certain man was sick, *n*· Lazarus,
49 And one of them, *n*· Caiaphas, being
Ac 5: 1 But a certain man *n*· Ananias,
34 a Pharisee, *n*· Gamaliel, a doctor
9:10 disciple at Damascus, *n*· Ananias;
12 vision a man *n*· Ananias coming in,
33 he found a certain man *n*· Æneas,
36 Joppa a certain disciple *n*· Tabitha,
11:28 stood up one of them *n*· Agabus,
12:13 damsel came to hearken, *n*· Rhoda.
16: 1 disciple was there, *n*· Timotheus,
14 woman *n*· Lydia, a seller of purple,
17:34 a woman *n*· Damaris, and others
18: 2 Jew *n*· Aquila, born in Pontus,
7 a certain man's house, *n*· Justus,
24 And a certain Jew *n*· Apollos, born
19:24 man *n*· Demetrius, a silversmith,
20: 9 a certain young man *n*· Eutychus,
21:10 Judæa a certain prophet, *n*· Agabus.
24: 1 with a certain orator *n*· Tertullus,
27: 1 other prisoners unto one *n*· Julius,
Ro 15:20 gospel, not where Christ was *n*·,
1Co 5: 1 so much as *n*· among the Gentiles,
Eph 1:21 and every name that is *n*·, not only
3:15 family in heaven and earth is *n*·,
5: 3 let it not be once *n*· among you,

namely^
Le 1:10 be of the flocks, *n*·, of the sheep,
Nu 1:32 Of the children of Joseph, *n*·, of the
9:15 *n*·, the tent of the testimony:
31: 8 that were slain; *n*·, Evi, and Rekem,
De 4:43 *N*·, Bezer in the wilderness, in the
13: 7 *N*·, of the gods of the people which
20:17 *n*·, the Hittites, and the Amorites, the
J'g 3: 3 *N*·, five lords of the Philistines, and
8:35 to the house of Jerubbaal, *n*·, Gideon,
1Ch 6:57 they gave the cities of Judah, *n*·,
61 tribe, *n*·, out of the half tribe of
9:23 *n*·, the house of the tabernacle, by
23: 6 the sons of Levi, *n*·, Gershon, Kohath,
Ezr 10:18 *n*·, of the sons of Jeshua the son of
Ne 12:35 *n*·, Zechariah the son of Jonathan, the
Es 8:12 *n*·, upon the thirteenth day of the
Ec 5:13 *n*·, riches kept for the owners thereof
Isa 7:20 *n*·, by them beyond the river, by
Jer 26:22 *n*·, Elnathan the son of Achbor, and
M'r 12:31 And the second is like, *n*· this, Thou
Ac 15:22 *n*·, Judas surnamed Barsabas, and
Ro 13: 9 *n*·, Thou shalt love thy neighbour

name's
1Sa 12:22 his people for his great *n*· sake:
1Ki 8:41 out of a far country for thy *n*· sake;
2Ch 6:32 a far country for thy great *n*· sake,
Ps 23: 3 of righteousness for his *n*· sake.
25:11 For thy *n*· sake, O Lord, pardon
31: 3 therefore for thy *n*· sake lead me,
79: 9 away our sins, for thy *n*· sake.
106: 8 he saved them for his *n*· sake, that
109:21 O God the Lord, for thy *n*· sake:
143:11 Quicken me, O Lord, for thy *n*· sake:
Isa 48: 9 For my *n*· sake will I defer mine
66: 5 cast you out for my *n*· sake, said,
Jer 14: 7 us, do thou it for thy *n*· sake:
21 Do not abhor us, for thy *n*· sake,
Eze 20: 9, 14 But I wrought for my *n*· sake,
22 and wrought for my *n*· sake, that it
44 wrought with you for my *n*· sake,
36:22 but for mine holy *n*· sake, which ye
M't 10:22 hated of all men for my *n*· sake:
19:29 children, or lands, for my *n*· sake,
24: 9 hated of all nations for my *n*· sake.
M'k 13:13 be hated of all men for my *n*· sake:
Lu 21:12 kings and rulers for my *n*· sake.
17 be hated of all men for my *n*· sake.
Joh 15:21 they do unto you for my *n*· sake,
Ac 9:16 he must suffer for my *n*· sake.
1Jo 2:12 are forgiven you for his *n*· sake.
3Jo 7 that for his *n*· sake they went forth,
Re 2: 3 and for my *n*· sake hast laboured,

names
Ge 2:20 Adam gave *n*· to all cattle, and to
25:13 are the *n*· of the sons of Ishmael,
13 by their *n*·, according to their
16 of Ishmael, and these are their *n*·,
26:18 called their *n*· after the *n*· by which
36:10 are the *n*· of Esau's sons; Eliphaz
40 the *n*· of the dukes that came of
40 after their places, by their *n*·; Duke
46: 8 are the *n*· of the children of Israel,
Ex 1: 1 are the *n*· of the children of Israel,
6:16 these are the *n*· of the sons of Levi
28: 9 them the *n*· of the children of Israel:
10 Six of their *n*· on one stone, and the
10 six *n*· of the rest on the other stone,
11 with the *n*· of the children of Israel:
12 shall bear their *n*· before the Lord
21 with the *n*· of the children of Israel,
21 twelve, according to their *n*·, like
29 bear the *n*· of the children of Israel
39: 6 with the *n*· of the children of Israel.
14 to the *n*· of the children of Israel,
14 twelve, according to their *n*·, like
Nu 1: 2 with the number of their *n*·, every
5 *n*· of the men that shall stand with
17 which are expressed by their *n*·:
18, 20, 22, 24, 26, 28, 30, 32, 34, 36, 38, 40,
42 according to the number of the *n*·,
3: 2 are the *n*· of the sons of Aaron;
3 are the *n*· of the sons of Aaron, the
17 were the sons of Levi by their *n*·;
18 are the *n*· of the sons of Gershon
40 and take the number of their *n*·.
43 firstborn males by the number of *n*·,
13: 4 these were their *n*·: of the tribe
16 *n*· of the men which Moses sent
26:33 and the *n*· of the daughters of
53 according to the number of *n*·.
55 the *n*· of the tribes of their fathers
27: 1 these are the *n*· of his daughters;
32:38 (their *n*· being changed,) and
38 gave other *n*· unto the cities which
34:17 These are the *n*· of the men which
19 the *n*· of the men are these: of the
De 12: 3 the *n*· of them out of that place.
Jos 17: 3 these are the *n*· of his daughters,
1Sa 14:49 the *n*· of his two daughters were
17:13 the *n*· of his three sons that went
2Sa 5:14 *n*· of those that were born unto him
23: 8 These be the *n*· of the mighty men
1Ki 4: 8 And these are their *n*·: The son of
1Ch 4:38 mentioned by their *n*· were princes
6:17 be the *n*· of the sons of Gershom;
65 cities, which are called by their *n*·.
8:38 had six sons, whose *n*· are these,
9:44 had six sons, whose *n*· are these,
14: 4 are the *n*· of his children which he
23:24 by number of *n*· by their polls, that
Ezr 5: 4 What are the *n*· of the men that
10 We asked their *n*· also, to certify
10 we might write the *n*· of the men
8:13 whose *n*· are these, Eliphelet,
10:16 and all of them by their *n*·, were
Ps 16: 4 nor take up their *n*· into my lips.
49:11 call their lands after their own *n*·.
147: 4 he calleth them all by their *n*·.
Isa 40:26 he calleth them all by *n*· by the
Eze 23: 4 the *n*· of them were Aholah the
4 were their *n*·; Samaria is Aholah,
48: 1 Now these are the *n*· of the tribes.
31 after the *n*· of the tribes of Israel:
Da 1: 7 the prince of the eunuchs gave *n*·:
Ho 2:17 I will take away the *n*· of Baalim
Zec 13: 2 will cut off the *n*· of the idols out of
M't 10: 2 the *n*· of the twelve apostles are
Lu 10:20 your *n*· are written in heaven.
Ac 1:15 (the number of the *n*· together were
18:15 if it be a question of words and *n*·,
Ph'p 4: 3 whose *n*· are in the book of life.
Re 3: 4 hast a few *n*· even in Sardis which
13: 8 whose *n*· are not written in the
17: 3 full of *n*· of blasphemy, having
8 whose *n*· were not written in the
21:12 angels, and *n*· written thereon,
12 are the *n*· of the twelve tribes of the
14 them the *n*· of the twelve apostles

nameth
2Ti 2:19 one that *n*· the name of Christ

Nangæ See NAGGE.

Naomi (*na'-o-mee*) See also NAOMI'S.
Ru 1: 2 and the name of his wife *N*·, and
8 *N*· said unto her two daughters in
11 *N*. said, Turn again, my daughters:
19 them, and they said, Is this *N*·?
20 them, Call me not *N*·, call me Mara:
21 why then call ye me *N*·, seeing the
22 So *N*· returned, and Ruth the
2: 1 *N*· had a kinsman of her husband's,
2 Ruth the Moabitess said unto *N*·,
6 damsel that came back with *N*·
20 *N*· said unto her daughter in law,
20 *N*· said unto her, The man is near
22 *N*· said unto Ruth, her daughter in
3: 1 *N*· her mother in law said unto her
4: 3 he said unto the kinsman, *N*·, that
5 buyest the field of the hand of *N*·,
9 and Mahlon's, at the hand of *N*·.
14 women said unto *N*·, Blessed be
16 *N*· took the child, and laid it in her
17 saying, There is a son born to *N*·;

Naomi's (*na'-o-meze*)
Ru 1: 3 And Elimelech *N*· husband died;

Naphish (*na'-fish*) See also NEPHISH.
Ge 25:15 Tema, Jetur, *N*·, and Kedemah:
1Ch 1:31 Jetur, *N*·, and Kedemah. These

Naphtali (*naf'-ta-li*) See also KEDESH-NAPHTALI; NEPHTHALIM.
Ge 30: 8 and she called his name *N*·.
35:25 Rachel's handmaid; Dan, and *N*·:
46:24 And the sons of *N*·; Jahzeel, and
49:21 *N*· is a hind let loose: he giveth
Ex 1: 4 Dan, and *N*·, Gad, and Asher.
Nu 1:15 Of *N*·; Ahira the son of Enan.
42 Of the children of *N*·, throughout
43 of them, even of the tribe of *N*·,
2:29 Then the tribe of *N*·: and the
29 captain of the children of *N*· shall
7:78 Ahira...prince of the children of *N*·,
10:27 of the children of *N*· was Ahira
13:14 Of the tribe of *N*·, Nahbi the son of
26:48 the sons of *N*· after their families:
50 These are the families of *N*·
34:28 of the tribe of the children of *N*·,
De 27:13 Asher, and Zebulun, Dan, and *N*·.
33:23 of *N*· he said, O *N*·, satisfied with
34: 2 all *N*·, and the land of Ephraim,
Jos 19:32 lot came out to the children of *N*·,
32 for the children of *N*· according to
39 children of *N*· according to their
20: 7 Kedesh in Galilee in mount *N*·,
21: 6 and out of the tribe of *N*·, and out
32 out of the tribe of *N*·, Kedesh in
J'g 1:33 did *N*· drive out the inhabitants
4: 6 thousand men of the children of *N*·
10 called Zebulun and *N*· to Kedesh;
5:18 Zebulun and *N*· were a people that
6:35 and unto Zebulun, and unto *N*·;
7:23 themselves together out of *N*·, and
1Ki 4:15 Ahimaaz was in *N*·; he also took
7:14 a widow's son of the tribe of *N*·,
15:20 Cinneroth, with all the land of *N*·.
2Ki 15:29 all the land of *N*·, and carried them
1Ch 2: 2 Joseph, and Benjamin, *N*·, Gad,
6:62 and out of the tribe of *N*·, and out
76 And out of the tribe of *N*·; Kedesh
7:13 The sons of *N*·; Jahziel, and Guni,
12:34 And of *N*· a thousand captains, and
40 unto Issachar and Zebulun and *N*·,
27:19 of *N*·, Jerimoth the son of Azriel:
2Ch 16: 4 and all the store cities of *N*·.
34: 6 and Simeon, even unto *N*·, with
Ps 68:27 of Zebulun, and the princes of *N*·.
Isa 9: 1 land of Zebulun and the land of *N*·,
Eze 48: 3 unto the west side, a portion for *N*·.
4 And by the border of *N*·, from the
34 one gate of Asher, one gate of *N*·.

Naphtuhim (*naf'-too-him*)
Ge 10:13 Anamim, and Lehabim, and *N*·.
1Ch 1:11 Anamim, and Lehabim, and *N*·.

napkin
Lu 19:20 which I have kept laid up in a *n*·:
Joh 11:44 face was bound about with a *n*·.
20: 7 And the *n*·, that was about his head,

Narcissus (*nar-sis'-sus*)
Ro 16:11 that be of the household of *N*·.

nard See SPIKENARD.

narrow See also NARROWED; NARROWER.
Nu 22:26 further, and stood in a *n*· place,
Jos 17:15 mount Ephraim be too *n*· for thee.
1Ki 6: 4 he made windows of *n*· lights.
Pr 23:27 and a strange woman is a *n*· pit.
Isa 49:19 even now be too *n*· by reason of
Eze 40:16 *n*· windows to the little chambers,
41:16 posts, and the *n*· windows, and the
26 were *n*· windows and palm trees
M't 7:14 is the gate, and *n*· is the way,

narrowed
1Ki 6: 6 he made *n*· rests round about,

narrower
Isa 28:20 covering *n*· than that he can wrap

narrowly
Job 13:27 and lookest *n*· unto all my paths;
Isa 14:16 that see thee shall *n*· look upon thee,

Nathan (*na'-than*) See also NATHAN-MELECH.
2Sa 5:14 Shammuah, and Shobab, and *N*·,
7: 2 the king said unto *N*· the prophet,
3 And *N*· said unto the king, Go, do

2Sa 7: 4 the word of the Lord came unto N',
17 vision, so did N' speak unto David.
12: 1 And the Lord sent N' unto David.
5 he said to N', As the Lord liveth,
7 And N' said to David, Thou art the
13 David said unto N', I have sinned
13 N' said unto David, The Lord also
15 And N' departed unto his house.
25 sent by the hand of N' the prophet;
23: 36 Igal the son of N' of Zobah, Bani
1Ki 1: 8 N' the prophet, and Shimei, and
10 N' the prophet, and Benaiah, and
11 N' spake unto Bath-sheba the
22 king, N' the prophet also came in.
23 saying, Behold N' the prophet.
24 And N' said, My lord, O king, hast
32 the priest, and N' the prophet, and
34 priest and N' the prophet anoint
38, 44 the priest, and N' the prophet,
45 N' the prophet have anointed him
4: 5 the son of N' was over the officers:
5 Zabud the son of N' was principal
1Ch 2: 36 Attai begat N', and N' begat
3: 5 Shimea, and Shobab, and N', and
11: 38 Joel the brother of N', Mibhar the
14: 4 and Shobab, N', and Solomon.
17: 1 that David said to N' the prophet,
2 N' said unto David, Do all that is
3 word of God came to N', saying,
15 vision, so did N' speak unto David.
29: 29 and in the book of N' the prophet,
2Ch 9: 29 in the book of N' the prophet, and
29: 25 king's seer, and N' the prophet:
Ezr 8: 16 for N', and for Zechariah, and for
10: 39 Shelemiah, and N', and Adaiah,
Ps 51: *title* N' the prophet came unto him,
Zec 12: 12 the family of the house of N' a part,
Lu 3: 31 which was the son of N', which

Nathanael (*na-than'-a-el*) See also BARTHOLOMEW.
Joh 1: 45 Philip findeth N', and saith unto
46 N' said unto him, Can there any
47 Jesus saw N' coming to him, and
48 N' saith unto him, Whence knowest
49 N' answered and saith unto him,
21: 2 Didymus, and N' of Cana in Galilee,

Nathan-melech (*na''-than-me'-lek*)
2Ki 23: 11 chamber of N' the chamberlain,

nation See also NATIONS.
Ge 12: 2 I will make of thee a great n', and
15: 14 also that n', whom they shall serve,
17: 20 and I will make him a great n'.
18: 18 become a great and mighty n', and
20: 4 wilt thou slay also a righteous n'?
21: 13 of the bondwoman will I make a n',
18 for I will make him a great n'.
35: 11 a n' and a company of nations shall
46: 3 I will there make of thee a great n':
Ex 9: 24 land of Egypt since it became a n'.
19: 6 kingdom of priests, and an holy n'.
21: 8 to sell her unto a strange n' he
32: 10 and I will make of thee a great n'.
33: 13 consider that this n' is thy people.
34: 10 done in all the earth, nor in any n':
Le 18: 26 neither any of your own n', nor any
20: 23 not walk in the manners of the n',
Nu 14: 12 and will make of thee a greater n'
De 4: 6 Surely this great n' is a wise and
7 what n' is there so great, who hath
8 what n' is there so great, that hath
34 a n' from the midst of another n',
9: 14 I will make of thee a n' mightier
26: 5 with a few, and became there a n',
28: 33 shall a n' which thou knowest not
36 unto a n' which neither thou nor
49 Lord shall bring a n' against thee
49 a n' whose tongue thou shalt not
50 A n' of fierce countenance, which
32: 21 them to anger with a foolish n'.
28 For they are a n' void of counsel,
2Sa 7: 23 what one n' in the earth is like thy
1Ki 18: 10 there is no n' or kingdom, whither
10 took an oath of the kingdom and n',
2Ki 17: 29 every n' made gods of their own,
29 every n' in their cities wherein they
1Ch 16: 20 And when they went from n' to n',
17: 21 what one n' in the earth is like thy
2Ch 15: 6 n' was destroyed of n', and city of
32: 15 for no god of any n' or kingdom was
Job 34: 29 done against a n', or against a man
Ps 33: 12 Blessed is the n' whose God is the
43: 1 my cause against an ungodly n':
83: 4 let us cut them off from being a n';
105: 13 they went from one n' to another,
106: 5 rejoice in the gladness of thy n',
147: 20 He hath not dealt so with any n':
Pr 14: 34 Righteousness exalteth a n': but
Isa 1: 4 Ah sinful n', a people laden with
2: 4 n' shall not lift up sword against n',
9: 3 Thou hast multiplied the n', and
10: 6 send him against an hypocritical n',
14: 32 answer the messengers of the n'?
18: 2 to a n' scattered and peeled, to a
2 a n' meted out and trodden down,
7 a n' meted out and trodden under
26: 2 that the righteous n' which keepeth
15 Thou hast increased the n', O Lord,
15 O Lord, thou hast increased the n':
49: 7 to him whom the n' abhorreth, to
51: 4 and give ear unto me, O my n':
55: 5 shalt call a n' that thou knowest
58: 2 as a n' that did righteousness, and
60: 12 n' and kingdom that will not serve
22 and a small one a strong n': I the
65: 1 n' that was not called by my name.
Isa 66: 8 or shall a n' be born at once? for as
Jer 2: 11 Hath a n' changed their gods, which
5: 9 my soul be avenged on such a n' as
15 I will bring a n' upon you from far,
15 it is a mighty n', it is an ancient n',
15 a n' whose language thou knowest
29 my soul be avenged on such a n' as
6: 22 a great n' shall be raised from the
7: 28 is a n' that obeyeth not the voice of
9: 9 my soul be avenged on such a n' as
12: 17 pluck up and destroy that n', saith
18: 7 I shall speak concerning a n', and
8 If that n', against whom I have
9 I shall speak concerning a n', and
25: 12 the king of Babylon, and that n',
32 evil shall go forth from n' to n', and
27: 8 the n' and kingdom which will not
8 that n' will I punish, saith the Lord,
13 against the n' that will not serve
31: 36 shall cease from being a n' before
33: 24 that they should be no more a n'
48: 2 and let us cut it off from being a n'.
49: 31 get you up unto the wealthy n',
36 shall be no n' whither the outcasts
50: 3 there cometh up a n' against her,
41 a great n', and many kings shall be
La 4: 17 watched for a n' that could not save
Eze 2: 3 a rebellious n' that hath rebelled
37: 22 I will make them one n' in the land
Da 3: 29 every people, n', and language,
8: 22 shall stand up out of the n',
12: 1 as never was since there was a n'
Joe 1: 6 For a n' is come up upon my land,
Am 6: 14 I will raise up against you a n', O
Mic 4: 3 n' shall not lift...sword against n',
7 that was cast far off a strong n':
Hab 1: 6 Chaldeans, that bitter and hasty n',
Zep 2: 1 gather together, O n' not desired;
5 sea coast, the n' of the Cherethites!
Hag 2: 14 So is this people, and so is this n'
Mal 3: 9 have robbed me, even this whole n'.
M't 21: 43 to a n' bringing forth the fruits
24: 7 For n' shall rise against n', and
M'r 7: 26 a Greek, a Syrophenician by n';
13: 8 For n' shall rise against n', and
Lu 7: 5 he loveth our n', and he hath built
21: 10 unto them, N' shall rise against n',
23: 2 found this fellow perverting the n',
Joh 11: 48 take away both our place and n'.
50 and that the whole n' perish not.
51 that Jesus should die for that n';
52 And not for that n' only, but that
18: 35 Thine own n' and the chief priests
Ac 2: 5 men, out of every n' under heaven.
7: 7 n' to whom they shall be in bondage
10: 22 report among all the n' of the Jews,
28 or come unto one of another n';
35 in every n' he that feareth him,
24: 2 worthy deeds are done unto this n'
10 of many years a judge unto this n',
17 I came to bring alms to my n', and
26: 4 among mine own n' at Jerusalem,
28: 19 that I had ought to accuse my n' of.
Ro 10: 19 and by a foolish n' I will anger you.
Ga 1: 14 many my equals in mine own n',
Ph'p 2: 15 of a crooked and perverse n',
1Pe 2: 9 an holy n', a peculiar people;
Re 5: 9 and tongue, and people, and n';
14: 6 every n', and kindred, and tongue,

nations
Ge 10: 5 after their families, in their n'.
20 in their countries, and in their n'.
31 in their lands, after their n'.
32 after their generations, in their n':
32 were the n' divided in the earth
14: 1 king of Elam, and Tidal king of n';
9 Elam, and with Tidal king of n',
17: 4 thou shalt be a father of many n'.
5 father of many n' have I made thee.
6 I will make n' of thee, and kings
16 and she shall be a mother of n';
18: 18 the n' of the earth shall be blessed
22: 18 all the n' of the earth be blessed;
25: 16 twelve princes according to their n'.
23 Two n' are in thy womb, and two
26: 4 all the n' of the earth be blessed;
27: 29 thee, and n' bow down to thee:
35: 11 a company of n' shall be of thee,
48: 19 seed shall become a multitude of n'.
Ex 34: 24 I will cast out the n' before thee,
Le 18: 24 for in all these the n' are defiled
28 spued out the n' that were before
Nu 14: 15 the n' which have heard the fame
23: 9 shall not be reckoned among the n'.
24: 8 he shall eat up the n' his enemies,
20 Amalek was the first of the n';
De 2: 25 the n' that are under the whole
4: 6 understanding...the sight of the n',
19 unto all n' under the whole heaven.
27 shall scatter you among the n',
38 To drive out n' from before thee
7: 1 hath cast out many n' before thee,
1 seven n' greater and mightier than
17 These n' are more than I; how can
22 God will put out those n' before thee
8: 20 As the n' which the Lord destroyeth
9: 1 possess n' greater and mightier than
4, 5 but for the wickedness of these n'
11: 23 will the Lord drive out all these n'
23 possess greater n' and mightier than
12: 2 the n' which ye shall possess served
29 God shall cut off the n' from before
30 How did these n' serve their gods?
14: 2 all the n' that are upon the earth.
15: 6 and thou shalt lend unto many n',
6 and thou shalt reign over many n',
De 17: 14 like as all the n' that are about me:
18: 9 after the abominations of those n'.
14 these n', which thou shalt possess,
19: 1 Lord thy God hath cut off the n',
20: 15 are not of the cities of these n'.
26: 19 And to make thee high above all n'
28: 1 on high above all n' of the earth:
12 and thou shalt lend unto many n',
37 all n' whither the Lord shall lead
65 among these n' shalt thou find no
29: 16 and how we came through the n'
18 to go and serve the gods of these n';
24 Even all n' shall say, Wherefore
30: 1 call them to mind among all the n',
3 and gather thee from all the n',
31: 3 destroy these n' from before thee,
32: 8 the Most High divided to the n' their
43 Rejoice, O ye n', with his people:
Jos 12: 23 one; the king of the n' of Gilgal,
23: 3 God hath done unto all these n'
4 divided unto you by lot these n' that
4 with all the n' that I have cut off,
7 That ye come not among these n',
9 from before you great n' and strong:
12 cleave unto the remnant of these n',
13 no more drive out any of these n'
J'g 2: 21 n' which Joshua left when he died:
23 Therefore the Lord left those n',
3: 1 these are the n' which the Lord left,
1Sa 8: 5 a king to judge us like all the n'.
20 That we also may be like all the n';
27: 8 those n' were of old the inhabitants
2Sa 7: 23 Egypt, from the n' and their gods?
8: 11 dedicated of all n' which he subdued;
1Ki 4: 31 his fame was in all n' round about.
11: 2 n' concerning which the Lord said
14: 24 to all the abominations of the n'
2Ki 17: 26 The n' which thou hast removed,
33 manner of the n' whom they carried
41 So these n' feared the Lord, and
18: 33 of the gods of the n' delivered at all
19: 12 Have the gods of the n' delivered
17 destroyed the n' and their lands,
21: 9 to do more evil than did the n'
1Ch 14: 17 brought the fear of him upon all n'.
16: 24 marvellous works among all n'.
31 and let men say among the n', The
17: 21 by driving out n' from before thy
18: 11 that he brought from all these n':
2Ch 7: 20 and a byword among all n'.
13: 9 manner of the n' of other lands?
32: 13 the gods of the n' of those lands
14 there among all the gods of those n'
17 the gods of the n' of other lands
23 was magnified in the sight of all n'
Ezr 4: 10 the rest of the n' whom the great
Ne 1: 8 scatter you abroad among the n':
9: 22 gavest them kingdoms and n',
13: 26 among many n' was there no king
Job 12: 23 He increaseth the n', and destroyeth
23 he enlargeth the n', and straiteneth
Ps 9: 17 hell, and all the n' that forget God.
20 n' may know themselves to be but
22: 27 the kindreds of the n' shall worship
28 he is the governor among the n'.
47: 3 us, and the n' under our feet.
57: 9 I will sing unto thee among the n'.
66: 7 for ever; his eyes behold the n':
67: 2 thy saving health among all n'.
4 let the n' be glad and sing for joy:
4 and govern the n' upon earth.
72: 11 before him: all n' shall serve him.
17 in him: all n' shall call him blessed.
82: 8 earth: for thou shalt inherit all n'.
86: 9 All n'...thou hast made shall come
96: 5 all the gods of the n' are idols:
106: 27 their seed also among the n', and
34 They did not destroy the n',
108: 3 praises unto thee among the n'.
113: 4 The Lord is high above all n', and
117: 1 O praise the Lord, all ye n': praise
118: 10 All n' compassed me about: but in
135: 10 smote great n', and slew mighty
Pr 24: 24 people curse, n' shall abhor him:
Isa 2: 2 hills; and all n' shall flow unto it.
4 And he shall judge among the n',
5: 26 lift up an ensign to the n' from far,
9: 1 beyond Jordan, in Galilee of the n'.
10: 7 to destroy and cut off n' not a few.
11: 12 he shall set up an ensign for the n',
13: 4 kingdoms of n' gathered together:
14: 6 he that ruled the n' in anger, is
9 their thrones all the kings of the n'.
12 ground, which didst weaken the n'!
18 the kings of the n', even all of them,
26 is stretched out upon all the n'.
17: 12 and to the rushing of n', that make
13 The n' shall rush like the rushing of
23: 3 revenue; and she is a mart of n'.
25: 3 city of the terrible n' shall fear thee.
7 the vail that is spread over all n'.
29: 7 the multitude of all the n' that fight
8 shall the multitude of all the n' be,
30: 28 sift the n' with the sieve of vanity:
33: 3 up of thyself the n' were scattered.
34: 1 Come near, ye n', to hear; and
2 of the Lord is upon all n', and his
36: 18 any of the gods of the n' delivered
37: 12 Have the gods of the n' delivered
18 Assyria have laid waste all the n',
40: 15 the n' are as a drop of a bucket,
17 All n' before him are as nothing;
41: 2 to his foot, gave the n' before him,
43: 9 Let all the n' be gathered together,
45: 1 holden, to subdue n' before him;
20 ye that are escaped of the n': they

Isa 52:10 holy arm in the eyes of all the n';
15 So shall he sprinkle many n'; the
55: 5 n' that knew not thee shall run
60:12 those n' shall be utterly wasted.
61:11 to spring forth before all the n'.
64: 2 the n' may tremble at thy presence!
66:18 I will gather all n' and tongues;
19 that escape of them unto the n',
20 the Lord out of all n' upon horses,
Jer 1: 5 ordained thee a prophet unto the n'.
10 have this day set thee over the n'
3:17 all the n' shall be gathered unto it,
19 goodly heritage of the hosts of n'?
4: 2 and the n' shall bless themselves in
16 Make ye mention to the n'; behold,
6:18 Therefore hear, ye n', and know,
9:26 for all these n' are uncircumcised,
10: 7 would not fear thee, O King of n'?
7 among all the wise men of the n',
10 and the n' shall not be able to abide
22: 8 And many n' shall pass by this city
25: 9 against all these n' round about,
11 and these n' shall serve the king
13 hath prophesied against all the n'.
14 many n' and great kings shall serve
15 and cause all the n', to whom I send
17 and made all the n' to drink, unto
31 Lord hath a controversy with the n',
26: 6 a curse to all the n' of the earth.
27: 7 all n' shall serve him, and his son,
7 many n' and great kings shall serve
11 the n' that bring their neck under
28:11 of Babylon from the neck of all n'
14 iron upon the neck of all these n',
29:14 I will gather you from all the n',
18 among all the n' whither I have
30:11 I make a full end of all n' whither I
31: 7 shout among the chief of the n':
10 Hear the word of the Lord, O ye n',
33: 9 honour before all the n' of the earth,
36: 2 Judah, and against all the n', from
43: 5 that were returned from all n',
44: 8 among all the n' of the earth?
46:12 The n' have heard of thy shame,
28 I will make a full end of all the n'
50: 2 Declare ye among the n',...publish,
9 an assembly of great n' from the
12 the hindermost of the n' shall be a
23 become a desolation among the n'!
46 and the cry is heard among the n'.
51: 7 the n' have drunken of her wine;
7 her wine; therefore the n' are mad.
20 thee will I break in pieces the n',
27 blow the trumpet among the n',
27 prepare the n' against her, call
28 Prepare against her the n' with the
41 an astonishment among the n'!
44 the n' shall not flow together any
La 1: 1 that she was great among the n',
Eze 5: 5 I have set it in the midst of the n'
6 into wickedness more than the n',
7 multiplied more than the n' that
7 according to the judgments of the n'
8 midst of thee in the sight of the n'.
14 a reproach among the n' that are
15 unto the n' that are round about
6: 8 escape the sword among the n',
9 shall remember me among the n'
12:15 I shall scatter them among the n',
19: 4 The n' also heard of him; he was
8 the n' set against him on every
25:10 not be remembered among the n'.
26: 3 and will cause many n' to come up
5 and it shall become a spoil to the n'.
28: 7 upon thee, the terrible of the n':
29:12 scatter the Egyptians among the n',
15 exalt itself any more above the n':
15 they shall no more rule over the n'.
30:11 the terrible of the n', shall be
23, 26 scatter...Egyptians among...n',
31: 6 under his shadow dwelt all great n'.
12 And strangers, the terrible of the n',
16 I made the n' to shake at the sound
32: 2 Thou art like a young lion of the n',
9 bring thy destruction among the n',
12 the terrible of the n', all of them:
16 the daughters of the n' shall lament
18 and the daughters of the famous n',
35:10 said, These two n' and these two
36:13 up men, and hast bereaved thy n';
14 neither bereave thy n' any more,
15 thou cause thy n' to fall any more,
37:22 and they shall be no more two n',
38: 8 but it is brought forth out of the n',
12 that are gathered out of the n',
23 be known in the eyes of many n',
39:27 in them in the sight of many n';
Da 3: 4 O people, n', and languages,
7 the people, the n',...the languages,
4: 1 unto all people, n', and languages,
5:19 him, all people, n', and languages,
6:25 Darius wrote unto all people, n',
7:14 that all people, n', and languages,
Ho 8:10 they have hired among the n',
9:17 shall be wanderers among the n'.
Joe 3: 2 I will also gather all n', and will
2 they have scattered among the n',
Am 6: 1 which are named chief of the n', to
9: 9 the house of Israel among all n',
Mic 4: 2 many n' shall come, and say, Come,
3 people,...rebuke strong n' afar off;
11 many n' are gathered against thee,
7:16 n' shall see and be confounded at
Na 3: 4 selleth n' through her whoredoms,
5 I will shew the n' thy nakedness,
Hab 1:17 not spare continually to slay the n'?
Hab 2: 5 but gathereth unto him all n', and
8 thou hast spoiled many n', all the
3: 6 beheld, and drove asunder the n';
Zep 2:14 midst of her, all the beasts of the n':
3: 6 I have cut off the n': their towers
8 determination is to gather the n',
Hag 2: 7 And I will shake all n', and the
7 and the desire of all n' shall come:
Zec 2: 8 me unto the n' which spoiled you:
11 many n' shall be joined to the Lord
7:14 all the n' whom they knew not.
8:22 n' shall come to seek the Lord of
23 hold out of all languages of the n',
12: 9 n' that come against Jerusalem.
14: 2 gather all n' against Jerusalem to
3 go forth, and fight against those n',
16 n' which came against Jerusalem
19 punishment of all n' that come not
Mal 3:12 all n' shall call you blessed: for ye
M't 24: 9 ye shall be hated of all n' for my
14 the world for a witness unto all n';
25:32 before him shall be gathered all n':
28:19 Go ye therefore, and teach all n',
M'r 11:17 called of all n' the house of prayer?
13:10 first be published among all n'.
Lu 12:30 do the n' of the world seek after:
21:24 shall be led away captive into all n':
25 and upon the earth distress of n',
24:47 preached in his name among all n',
Ac 13:19 when he had destroyed seven n' in
14:16 all n' to walk in their own ways.
17:26 made of one blood all n' of men
Ro 1: 5 obedience to the faith among all n',
4:17 made thee a father of many n',)
18 become the father of many n',
16:26 known to all n' for the obedience
Ga 3: 8 In thee shall all n' be blessed.
Re 2:26 him will I give power over the n':
7: 9 no man could number, of all n',
10:11 many peoples, and n', and tongues,
11: 9 people...kindreds...tongues and n'
18 the n' were angry, and thy wrath
12: 5 was to rule all n' with a rod of iron:
13: 7 all kindreds, and tongues, and n'.
14: 8 she made all n' drink of the wine
15: 4 for all n' shall come and worship
16:19 parts, and the cities of the n' fell:
17:15 peoples, and multitudes, and n',
18: 3 For all n' have drunk of the wine
23 thy sorceries were all n' deceived.
19:15 that with it he should smite the n':
20: 3 he should deceive the n' no more,
8 and shall go out to deceive the n'
21:24 And the n' of them which are saved
26 glory and honour of the n' into it.
22: 2 tree were for the healing of the n'.

native
Jer 22:10 no more, nor see his n' country.

nativity
Ge 11:28 father Terah in the land of his n',
Ru 2:11 thy mother, and the land of thy n',
Jer 46:16 people and to the land of our n',
Eze 16: 3 and thy n' is of the land of Canaan;
4 as for thy n', in the day thou wast
21:30 wast created, in the land of thy n'.
23:15 of Chaldea, the land of their n':

natural
De 34: 7 not dim, nor his n' force abated.
Ro 1:26 women did change the n' use into
27 leaving the n' use of the woman,
31 without n' affection, implacable,
11:21 spared not the n' branches,
24 these, which be the n' branches,
1Co 2:14 But the n' man receiveth not the
15:44 It is sown a n' body; it is raised a
44 There is a n' body, and there is a
46 is spiritual, but that which is n';
2Ti 3: 3 Without n' affection, trucebreakers,
Jas 1:23 beholding his n' face in a glass:
2Pe 2:12 But these, as n' brute beasts, made

naturally
Ph'p 2:20 who will n' care for your state.
Jude 10 what they know n', as brute beasts,

nature
Ro 1:26 use into that which is against n':
2:14 do by n' the things contained in the
27 not uncircumcision which is by n',
11:24 of the olive tree which is wild by n',
24 and wert graffed contrary to n' into
1Co 11:14 Doth not even n' itself teach you,
Ga 2:15 We who are Jews by n', and not
4: 8 unto them which by n' are no gods.
Eph 2: 3 were by n' the children of wrath,
Heb 2:16 he took not on him the n' of angels;
Jas 3: 6 and setteth on fire the course of n';
2Pe 1: 4 be partakers of the divine n',

naught See also NOUGHT.
2Ki 2:19 water is n', and the ground barren.
Pr 20:14 It is n', it is n', saith the buyer:

naughtiness
1Sa 17:28 pride, and the n' of thine heart;
Pr 11: 6 shall be taken in their own n'.
Jas 1:21 all filthiness and superfluity of n',

naughty
Pr 6:12 A n' person, a wicked man,
17: 4 a liar giveth ear to a n' tongue.
Jer 24: 2 the other basket had very n' figs,

Naum (*na'-um*) See also NAHUM.
Lu 3:25 of Amos, which was the son of N',

navel
Job 40:16 his force is in the n' of his belly.
Pr 3: 8 It shall be health to thy n', and
Ca 7: 2 Thy n' is like a round goblet,
Eze 16: 4 thou wast born thy n' was not cut,

naves
1Ki 7:33 axletrees, and their n', and their

navy
1Ki 9:26 King Solomon made a n' of ships
27 Hiram sent in the n' his servants,
10:11 the n' also of Hiram, that brought
22 a n' of Tharshish with the n' of
22 once in three years came the n' of

nay^ See also NO.
Ge 18:15 he said, N'; but thou didst laugh.
23:11 N', my lord, hear me: the field give
33:10 Jacob said, N', I pray thee, if now
42:10 N', my lord, but to buy food are
12 N', but to see the nakedness of
Nu 22:30 do so unto thee? And he said, N'.
Jos 5:14 said, N'; but as captain of the host
24:21 said unto Joshua, N'; but we will
J'g 12: 5 thou an Ephraimite? If he said, N';
19:23 N', my brethren,...I pray you, do
23 n', I pray you, do not so wickedly;
Ru 1:13 n', my daughters; for it grieveth me
1Sa 2:16 N'; but thou shalt give it me now:
24 N', my sons; for it is no good
8:19 N'; but we will have a king over
10:19 unto him, N', but set a king over us.
12:12 N'; but a king shall reign over us:
2Sa 13:12 N', my brother, do not force me;
25 N', my son, let us not all now go,
16:18 Hushai said unto Absalom, N';
24:24 the king said unto Araunah, N';
1Ki 2:17 (for he will not say thee n',) that he give
20 I pray thee, say me not n'. And
20 my mother: for I will not say thee n'.
2:30 he said, N'; but I will die here.
3:22 And the other woman said, N'; but
23 saith, N'; but thy son is the dead,
2Ki 3:13 king of Israel said unto him, N':
4:16 said, N', my lord, thou man of God,
20:10 n', but let the shadow return
1Ch 21:24 And king David said to Ornan, N';
Jer 6:15 n', they were not at all ashamed,
8:12 n', they were not at all ashamed,
M't 5:37 communication be, Yea, yea; N', n':
13:29 he said, N'; lest while ye gather
Lu 12:51 I tell you, N'; but rather division:
13: 3, 5 tell you, N': but, except ye repent,
16:30 And he said, N', father Abraham:
Joh 7:12 N'; but he deceiveth the people.
Ac 16:37 n' verily; but let them come
Ro 3:27 works? N': but by the law of faith.
7: 7 N', I had not known sin, but by the
8:37 N', in all these things we are more
9:20 N' but, O man, who art thou that
1Co 6: 8 N', ye do wrong, and defraud, and
12:22 N', much more those members of the
2Co 1:17 there should be yea yea, and n' n'?
18 word toward you was not yea and n'.
19 was not yea and n', but in him was
Jas 5:12 your yea be yea; and your n', n';

Nazarene (*naz-a-reen'*) See also NAZARENES.
M't 2:23 prophets, He shall be called a N'.

Nazarenes (*naz-a-reens'*)
Ac 24: 5 a ringleader of the sect of the N':

Nazareth (*naz'-a-reth*) See also NAZARENE.
M't 2:23 came and dwelt in a city called N':
4:13 And leaving N', he came and dwelt
21:11 Jesus the prophet of N' of Galilee.
26:71 fellow was also with Jesus of N'.
M'r 1: 9 that Jesus came from N' of Galilee,
24 to do with thee, thou Jesus of N'?
10:47 he heard that it was Jesus of N',
14:67 thou also wast with Jesus of N'.
16: 6 Ye seek Jesus of N', which was
Lu 1:26 unto a city of Galilee, named N',
2: 4 from Galilee, out of the city of N',
39 into Galilee, to their own city N'.
51 down with them, and came to N',
4:16 he came to N', where he had been
34 to do with thee, thou Jesus of N'?
18:37 told him, that Jesus of N' passeth by.
24:19 Concerning Jesus of N', which was
Joh 1:45 Jesus of N', the son of Joseph.
46 any good thing come out of N'?
18: 5 They answered him, Jesus of N'.
7 seek ye? And they said, Jesus of N'.
19:19 Jesus Of N' The King Of The Jews.
Ac 2:22 Jesus of N', a man approved of God
3: 6 In the name of Jesus Christ of N'
4:10 by the name of Jesus Christ of N',
6:14 this Jesus of N' shall destroy this
10:38 How God anointed Jesus of N' with
22: 8 me, I am Jesus of N', whom thou
26: 9 contrary to the name of Jesus of N'.

Nazarite (*naz'-a-rite*) See also NAZARITES.
Nu 6: 2 themselves to vow a vow of a N',
13 And this is the law of the N', when
18 the N' shall shave the head of his
19 put them upon the hands of the N',
20 after that the N' may drink wine.
21 the law of the N' who hath vowed,
J'g 13: 5 the child shall be a N' unto God
7 for the child shall be a N' to God
16:17 I have been a N' unto God from my

Nazarites (*naz'-a-rites*)
La 4: 7 Her N' were purer than snow,
Am 2:11 and of your young men for N'.
12 But ye gave the N' wine to drink;

Neah (*ne'-ah*)
Jos 19:13 out to Remmon-methoar to N';

Neapolis (*ne-ap'-o-lis*)
Ac 16:11 and the next day to N';
near^ See also NEARER; NEXT; NIGH.
Ge 12:11 was come n' to enter into Egypt,
18:23 Abraham drew n', and said, Wilt
19: 9 Lot, and came n' to break the door.
20 this city is n' to flee unto, and it is
20: 4 Abimelech had not come n' her:
27:21 unto Jacob, Come n', I pray thee,
22 Jacob went n' unto Isaac his father;
25 Bring it n' to me, and I will eat of
25 he brought it n' to him, and he did
26 Come n' now, and kiss me, my son.
27 he came n', and kissed him: and he
29:10 Jacob went n', and rolled the stone
33: 3 until he came n' to his brother.
6 Then the handmaidens came n',
7 Leah also with her children came n',
7 after came Joseph n' and Rachel,
37:18 even before he came n' unto them,
43:19 came n' to the steward of Joseph's
44:18 Then Judah came n' unto him, and
45: 4 brethren, Come n' to me, I pray you.
4 they came n'. And he said, I am
10 and thou shalt be n' unto me, thou,
48:10 And he brought them n' unto him;
13 and brought them n' unto him.
Ex 12:48 then let him come n' and keep it;
13:17 Philistines, although that was n';
14:20 the one came not n' the other all
16: 9 of Israel, Come n' before the Lord:
19:22 also, which come n' to the Lord,
20:21 drew n' unto the thick darkness
24: 2 Moses alone shall come n' the Lord:
28:43 come n' unto the altar to minister
30:20 come n' to the altar to minister,
40:32 when they came n' unto the altar,
Le 9: 5 all the congregation drew n' and
10: 4 Come n', carry your brethren from
5 So they went n', and carried them
18: 6 to any that is n' of kin to him, to
12 she is thy father's n' kinswoman.
13 she is thy mother's n' kinswoman.
17 for they are her n' kinswomen:
20:19 he uncovereth his n' kin: they
21: 2 for his kin, that is n' unto him,
Nu 3: 6 Bring the tribe of Levi n', and
5:16 the priest shall bring her n', and
16: 5 cause him to come n' unto him:
5 will he cause to come n' unto him.
9 to bring you n' to himself to do
10 he hath brought thee n' to him,
40 come n' to offer incense before
17:13 cometh any thing n' unto the
26: 3 of Moab by Jordan n' Jericho, saying.
63 plains of Moab by Jordan n' Jericho,
31:12 Moab, which are by Jordan n' Jericho.
48 of hundreds, came n' unto Moses;
32:16 they came n' unto him, and said,
33:50 plains of Moab by Jordan n' Jericho,
34:15 this side Jordan n' Jericho eastward,
36: 1 came n', and spake before Moses,
13 plains of Moab by Jordan n' Jericho.
De 1:22 ye came n' unto me every one of
4:11 ye came n' and stood under the
5:23 that ye came n' unto me, even all
27 Go thou n', and hear all that the
16:21 any trees n' unto the altar of the
21: 5 the sons of Levi shall come n';
25:11 the wife of the one draweth n' for
Jos 3: 4 come not n' unto it, that ye may
10:24 Come n', put your feet upon the
24 they came n', and put their feet
15:46 all that lay n' Ashdod, with their
17: 4 they came n' before Eleazar the
18:13 n' the hill that lieth on the south
21: 1 Then came n' the heads of the
J'g 18:22 were in the houses n' to Micah's
19:13 and let us draw n' to one of these
20:24 And the children of Israel came n'
34 knew not that evil was n' them.
Ru 2:20 The man is n' of kin unto us, one
3: 9 handmaid; for thou art a n' kinsman.
12 it is true that I am thy n' kinsman:
1Sa 4:19 was with child, n' to be delivered:
7:10 the Philistines drew n' to battle
9:18 then Saul drew n' to Samuel in the
10:20 all the tribes of Israel to come n',
21 the tribe of Benjamin to come n' by
14:36 Let us draw n' hither unto God.
38 Draw ye n' hither, all the chief of
17:16 the Philistine drew n' morning and
40 and he drew n' to the Philistine.
41 Philistine came on and drew n'
30:21 when David came n' to the people,
2Sa 1:15 and said, Go n', and fall upon him.
14:30 See Joab's field is n' mine, and he
18:25 And he came apace, and drew n'.
19:42 the king is n' of kin to us:
20:16 Come n' hither, that I may speak
17 And when he was come n' unto her,
1Ki 8:46 the land of the enemy, far or n';
18:30 all the people, Come n' unto me.
30 all the people came n' unto him.
36 Elijah the prophet came n', and
21: 2 because it is n' unto my house:
22:24 the son of Chenaanah went n', and
2Ki 4:27 Gehazi came n' to thrust her away.
5:13 And his servants came n', and
2Ch 6:36 captives unto a land far off or n';
18:23 the son of Chenaanah came n',
21:16 that were n' the Ethiopians:
29:31 come n' and bring sacrifices and
Es 5: 2 So Esther drew n', and touched
9: 1 drew n' to be put in execution,
Job 31:37 a prince would I go n' unto him.
Job 33:22 his soul draweth n' unto the grave,
41:16 One is so n' to another, that no air
Ps 22:11 not far from me; for trouble is n';
32: 9 bridle, lest they come n' unto thee.
73:28 is good for me to draw n' to God:
75: 1 name is n' thy wondrous works
107:18 draw n' unto the gates of death.
119:151 Thou art n', O Lord; and all thy
169 Let my cry come n' before thee,
148:14 of Israel, a people n' unto him.
Pr 7: 8 through the street n' her corner;
10:14 of the foolish is n' destruction.
27:10 for better is a neighbour that is n'
Isa 13:22 and her time is n' to come, and her
26:17 n' the time of her delivery, is in
29:13 draw n' me with their mouth, and
33:13 ye that are n', acknowledge my
34: 1 Come n', ye nations, to hear; and
41: 1 let them come n'; then let them
1 let us come n' together to
5 of the earth were afraid, drew n',
45:20 draw n' together, ye that are
21 Tell ye, and bring them n'; yea, let
46:13 I bring n' thy righteousness; it
48:16 Come ye n' unto me, hear ye this;
50: 8 He is n' that justifieth me; who
8 adversary? let him come n' to me.
51: 5 My righteousness is n'; my
54:14 for it shall not come n' thee.
55: 6 call ye upon him while he is n':
56: 1 for my salvation is n' to come, and
57: 3 But draw n' hither, ye sons of the
19 is far off, and to him that is n',
65: 5 come not n' to me; for I am holier
Jer 12: 2 thou art n' in their mouth, and
25:26 the kings of the north, far and n',
30:21 will cause him to draw n', and he
42: 1 even unto the greatest, came n',
46: 3 and shield, and draw n' to battle.
48:16 calamity of Moab is n' to come,
24 cities of the land of Moab, far or n'.
52:25 that were n' the king's person,
La 3:57 Thou drewest n' in the day that I
4:18 our end is n', our days are fulfilled;
Eze 6:12 that is n' shall fall by the sword;
7: 7 is come, the day of trouble is n',
12 time is come, the day draweth n':
9: 1 charge over the city to draw n',
6 come not n' any man upon whom
11: 3 Which say, It is not n'; let us
18: 6 come n' to a menstruous woman,
22: 4 hast caused thy days to draw n',
5 Those that be n', and those that
30: 3 For the day is n', even the day of
3 the day of the Lord is n', a cloudy
40:46 n' to the Lord to minister unto
44:13 they shall not come n' unto me,
13 come n' to any of my holy things,
15 n' to me to minister unto me,
16 and they shall come n' to my table,
45: 4 come n' to minister unto the Lord:
Da 3: 8 time certain Chaldeans came n',
26 n' to the mouth of the burning
6:12 came n', and spake before the king
7:13 they brought him n' before him.
16 I came n' unto one of them that
8:17 So he came n' where I stood: and
9: 7 and unto all Israel, that are n',
Joe 3: 9 let all the men of war draw n';
14 the day of the Lord is n' in the
Am 6: 3 the seat of violence to come n';
Ob 15 day of the Lord is n' upon all the
Zep 1:14 great day of the Lord is n', it is n',
3: 2 Lord; she drew not n' to her God.
Mal 3: 5 I will come n' to you to judgment;
M't 21:34 when the time of the fruit drew n',
24:33 these things, know that it is n',
M'r 13:28 leaves, ye know that summer is n':
Lu 15: 1 Then drew n' unto him all the
18:40 when he was come n', he asked him,
19:41 when he was come n', he beheld
21: 8 the time draweth n': go ye not
22:47 drew n' unto Jesus to kiss him.
24:15 Jesus himself drew n', and went
Joh 3:23 baptizing in Ænon n' to Salim,
4: 5 n' to the parcel of ground that
11:54 a country n' to the wilderness,
Ac 7:31 and as he drew n' to behold it, the
8:29 Philip, Go n', and join thyself to this
9: 3 journeyed, he came n' Damascus:
10:24 together his kinsmen and n' friends.
21:33 chief captain came n', and took him,
23:15 ever he come n', are ready to kill him.
27:27 that they drew n' to some country;
Heb10:22 Let us draw n' with a true heart
nearer
Ru 3:12 there is a kinsman n' than I.
Ro 13:11 is our salvation n' than when we
Neariah (*ne-a-ri'-ah*) See also NAGGE.
1Ch 3:22 and Bariah, and N', and Shaphat,
23 And the sons of N'; Elioenai, and
4:42 and N', and Rephaiah, and Uzziel,
neath See BENEATH; UNDERNEATH.
Nebai (*ne'-bahee*)
Ne 10:19 Hariph, Anathoth, N',
Nebaioth (*ne-bah'-yoth*) See also NEBAJOTH.
1Ch 1:29 The firstborn of Ishmael, N';
Isa 60: 7 the rams of N' shall minister unto
Nebajoth (*ne-ba'-joth*) See also NEBAIOTH.
Ge 25:13 the firstborn of Ishmael, N'; and
28: 9 son, the sister of N', to be his wife.
36: 3 Ishmael's daughter, sister of N'.
Neballat (*ne-bal'-lat*)
Ne 11:34 Hadid, Zeboim, N',
Nebat (*ne'-bat*)
1Ki 11:26 And Jeroboam the son of N', an
12: 2 when Jeroboam the son of N', who
15 unto Jeroboam the son of N'.
15: 1 of king Jeroboam the son of N'
16: 3 house of Jeroboam the son of N'.
26 the way of Jeroboam the son of N',
31 the sins of Jeroboam the son of N',
21:22 house of Jeroboam the son of N',
22:52 the way of Jeroboam the son of N',
2Ki 3: 3 the sins of Jeroboam the son of N',
9: 9 house of Jeroboam the son of N',
10:29 the sins of Jeroboam the son of N',
13: 2, 11 sins of Jeroboam the son of N',
14:24 the sins of Jeroboam the son of N',
15: 9, 18, 24, 28 of Jeroboam the son of N',
17:21 made Jeroboam the son of N' king:
23:15 which Jeroboam the son of N', who
2Ch 9:29 against Jeroboam the son of N'?
10: 2 when Jeroboam the son of N', who
15 spake...to Jeroboam the son of N'.
13: 6 Yet Jeroboam the son of N', the
Nebo (*ne'-bo*) See also PISGAH; SAMGAR-NEBO.
Nu 32: 3 and Shebam, and N', and Beon,
38 N', and Baal-meon, (their names
33:47 mountains of Abarim, before N'.
De 32:49 mount N', which is in the land of
34: 1 of Moab unto the mountain of N',
1Ch 5: 8 dwelt in Aroer, even unto N' and
Ezr 2:29 The children of N', fifty and two.
10:43 the sons of N'; Jeiel, Mattithiah,
Ne 7:33 men of the other N', fifty and two.
Isa 15: 2 Moab shall howl over N', and over
46: 1 Bel boweth down, N' stoopeth,
Jer 48: 1 Woe unto N'! for it is spoiled:
22 upon N', and upon Beth-diblathaim,
Nebuchadnezzar (*neb-u-kad-nez'-zar*) See also NEBUCHADREZZAR.
2Ki 24: 1 N' king of Babylon came up, and
10 servants of N' king of Babylon
11 N' king of Babylon came against
25: 1 that N' king of Babylon came, he,
8 is the nineteenth year of king N'
22 whom N' king of Babylon had left,
1Ch 6:15 and Jerusalem by the hand of N'.
2Ch 36: 6 Against him came up N' king of
7 N' also carried of the vessels of the
10 king N' sent, and brought him to
13 he also rebelled against king N',
Ezr 1: 7 which N' had brought forth out of
2: 1 whom N' the king of Babylon had
5:12 he gave them into the hand of N'
14 which N' took out of the temple
6: 5 N' took forth out of the temple
Ne 7: 6 N' the king of Babylon had carried
Es 2: 6 N' the king of Babylon had carried
Jer 27: 6 all these lands into the hand of N.
8 which will not serve the same N'
20 Which N' king of Babylon took not,
28: 3 that N' king of Babylon took away
11 Even so will I break the yoke of N'
14 they may serve N' king of Babylon;
29: 1 whom N' had carried away captive
3 of Judah sent unto Babylon to N'
34: 1 when N' king of Babylon, and all
39: 5 up to N' king of Babylon to Riblah
Da 1: 1 came N' king of Babylon unto
18 eunuchs brought them in before N'.
2: 1 the second year of the reign of N',
1 N' dreamed dreams, wherewith
28 maketh known to the king N'
46 the king N' fell upon his face, and
3: 1 N' the king made an image of gold,
2 N' the king sent to gather together
2 the image which N' the king had
3 image that N' the king had set up;
3 the image that N' had set up.
5 image that N' the king hath set up:
7 image that N' the king had set up.
9 They spake and said to the king N',
13 N' in his rage and fury commanded
14 N' spake and said unto them, Is it
16 O N', we are not careful to answer
19 Then was N' full of fury, and the
24 Then N' the king was astonied,
26 N' came near to the mouth of the
28 N' spake, and said, Blessed be the
4: 1 N' the king, unto all people,
4 I N' was at rest in mine house, and
18 This dream I king N' have seen.
28 All this came upon the king N'.
31 O king N', to thee it is spoken; The
33 was the thing fulfilled upon N':
34 days I N' lifted up mine eyes unto
37 I N' praise and extol and honour
5: 2 which his father N' had taken out
11 whom the king N' thy father, the
18 God gave N' thy father a kingdom,
Nebuchadrezzar (*neb-u-kad-rez'-zar*) See also NEBUCHADNEZZAR.
Jer 21: 2 N' king of Babylon maketh war
7 the hand of N' king of Babylon,
22:25 the hand of N' king of Babylon,
24: 1 that N' king of Babylon had carried
25: 1 the first year of N' king of Babylon;
9 N' the king of Babylon, my servant,
29:21 deliver them into the hand of N'
32: 1 which was the eighteenth year of N'
28 Chaldeans, and into the hand of N'
35:11 when N' king of Babylon came up
37: 1 whom N' king of Babylon made
39: 1 came N' king of Babylon and all
11 N' king of Babylon gave charge
43:10 I will send and take N' the king of

Jer 44:30 king of Judah into the hand of N·
46: 2 N· king of Babylon smote in the
13 N· king of Babylon should come
26 into the hand of N· king of Babylon,
49:28 N· king of Babylon shall smite,
30 for N· king of Babylon hath taken
50:17 N· king of Babylon hath broken
51:34 N· the king of Babylon hath
52: 4 N· king of Babylon came, he and
12 the nineteenth year of N· king of
28 the people whom N· carried away
29 In the eighteenth year of N· he
30 the three and twentieth year of N·
Eze 26: 7 I will bring upon Tyrus N· king of
29:18 N· king of Babylon caused his army
19 will give the land of Egypt unto N·
30:10 to cease by the hand of N· king of

Nebushasban (*neb-u-shas'-ban*)
Jer 39:13 captain of the guard sent, and N·,

Nebuzar-adan (*neb-u-zar'-a-dan*)
2Ki 25: 8 came N·, captain of the guard, a
11 did N· the captain of the guard
20 N· captain of the guard took these,
Jer 39: 9 Then N· the captain of the guard
10 N· the captain of the guard left of
11 to N· the captain of the guard,
13 So N· the captain of the guard sent,
40: 1 that N· the captain of the guard
41:10 whom N· the captain of the guard
43: 6 that N· the captain of the guard
52:12 came N·, captain of the guard,
15 N· the captain of the guard carried
16 But N· the captain of the guard left
26 N· the captain of the guard took
30 N· the captain of the guard carried

necessary
Job 23:12 his mouth more than my n· food.
Ac 13:46 It was n· that the word of God
15:28 burden than these n· things;
28:10 such things as were n·.
1Co 12:22 seem to be more feeble, are n·:
2Co 9: 5 Therefore I thought it n· to exhort
Ph'p 2:25 Yet I supposed it n· to send to you
Tit 3:14 maintain good works for n· uses,
Heb 9:23 was therefore n· that the patterns

necessities
Ac 20:34 hands have ministered unto my n·,
2Co 6: 4 much patience, in affliction, in n·,
12:10 reproaches, in n·, in persecutions,

necessity See also NECESSITIES.
Lu 23:17 (For of n· he must release one
Ro 12:13 Distributing to the n· of saints;
1Co 7:37 stedfast in his heart, having no n·,
9:16 for n· is laid upon me; yea, woe is
2Co 9: 7 not grudgingly, or of n·: for God
Ph'p 4:16 sent once and again unto my n·.
Ph'm 14 not be as it were of n·, but willingly.
Heb 7:12 there is made of n· a change also
8: 3 wherefore it is of n· that this man
9:16 there must also of n· be the death

Necho (*ne'-ko*) See also PHARAOH-NECHOH.
2Ch 35:20 N· king of Egypt came up to fight
22 the words of N· from the mouth of
36: 4 N· took Jehoahaz his brother, and

Nechoh See NECHO.

neck See also NECKS; STIFFNECKED.
Ge 27:16 and upon the smooth of his n·:
40 shalt break his yoke from off thy n·.
33: 4 and fell on his n·, and kissed him:
41:42 and put a gold chain about his n·;
45:14 fell upon his brother Benjamin's n·,
14 and Benjamin wept upon his n·.
46:29 fell on his n·, and he wept on his n·
49: 8 shall be in the n· of thine enemies;
Ex 13:13 it, then thou shalt break his n·:
34:20 not, then shalt thou break his n·.
Le 5: 8 and wring off his head from his n·,
De 21: 4 shall strike off the heifer's n· there
28:48 put a yoke of iron upon thy n·,
31:27 thy rebellion, and thy stiff n·:
1Sa 4:18 and his n· brake, and he died: for
2Ki 17:14 like to the n· of their fathers, that
2Ch 36:13 he stiffened his n·, and hardened
Ne 9:29 hardened their n·, and would not
Job 15:26 runneth upon him, even on his n·,
16:12 he hath also taken me by my n·,
39:19 thou clothed his n· with thunder?
41:22 In his n· remaineth strength, and
Ps 75: 5 on high: speak not with a stiff n·.
Pr 1: 9 thy head, and chains about thy n·.
3: 3 bind them about thy n·; write
22 unto thy soul, and grace to thy n·.
6:21 heart, and tie them about thy n·.
29: 1 often reproved hardeneth his n·,
Ca 1:10 jewels, thy n· with chains of gold.
4: 4 Thy n· is like the tower of David
9 eyes, with one chain of thy n·.
7: 4 Thy n· is as a tower of ivory;
Isa 8: 8 over, he shall reach even to the n·;
10:27 and his yoke from off thy n·, and
30:28 shall reach to the midst of the n·,
48: 4 and thy n· is an iron sinew, and
52: 2 thyself from the bands of thy n·,
66: 3 a lamb, as if he cut off a dog's n·;
Jer 7:26 their ear, but hardened their n·:
17:23 their ear, but made their n· stiff,
27: 2 yokes, and put them upon thy n·,
8 will not put their n· under the yoke
11 that bring their n· under the yoke
28:10 from off the prophet Jeremiah's n·,
11 n· of all nations within the space
12 off the n· of the prophet Jeremiah,

Jer 28:14 a yoke of iron upon the n· of all
30: 8 will break his yoke from off thy n·,
La 1:14 wreathed, and come up upon my n·:
Eze 16:11 thy hands, and a chain on thy n·.
Da 5: 7, 16, 29 chain of gold about his n·,
Hos 10:11 but I passed over upon her fair n·:
Hab 3:13 the foundation unto the n·. Selah.
M't 18: 6 were hanged about his n·, and that
M'r 9:42 were hanged about his n·, and he
Lu 15:20 and fell on his n·, and kissed him.
17: 2 were hanged about his n·, and he
Ac 15:10 a yoke upon the n· of the disciples,
20:37 and fell on Paul's n·, and kissed him,

necks
Jos 10:24 feet upon the n· of these kings.
24 put their feet upon the n· of them.
J'g 5:30 the n· of them that take the spoil?
8:21 that were on their camels' n·.
26 that were about their camels' n·.
2Sa 22:41 given me the n· of mine enemies,
2Ki 17:14 not hear, but hardened their n·,
Ne 3: 5 put not their n· to the work of
9:16 proudly, and hardened their n·,
17 but hardened their n·, and in their
Ps 18:40 given me the n· of mine enemies;
Isa 3:16 walk with stretched forth n· and
Jer 19:15 they have hardened their n·, that
27:12 Bring your n· under the yoke of
La 5: 5 Our n· are under persecution: we
Eze 21:29 upon the n· of them that are slain,
Mic 2: 3 which ye shall not remove your n·;
Ro 16: 4 for my life laid down their own n·:

necromancer
De 18:11 spirits, or a wizard, or a n·.

Nedabiah (*ned-a-bi'-ah*)
1Ch 3:18 Jecamiah, Hoshama, and N·.

need See also NEEDED; NEEDEST; NEEDETH; NEEDFUL; NEEDS.
De 15: 8 lend him sufficient for his n·, in
1Sa 21:15 Have I n· of mad men, that ye
2Ch 2:16 Lebanon, as much as thou shalt n·:
20:17 Ye shall not n· to fight in this battle:
Ezr 6: 9 that which they have n· of, both
Pr 31:11 that he shall have no n· of spoil.
M't 3:14 I have n· to be baptized of thee,
6: 8 knoweth what things ye have n· of,
32 that ye have n· of all these things.
9:12 be whole n· not a physician,
14:16 They n· not depart; give ye them
21: 3 shall say The Lord hath n· of them;
26:65 further n· have we of witnesses?
M'r 2:17 whole have no n· of the physician,
25 what David did, when he had n·,
11: 3 ye that the Lord hath n· of him;
14:63 n· we any further witnesses?
Lu 5:31 that are whole n· not a physician;
9:11 healed them that had n· of healing.
12:30 that ye have n· of these things.
15: 7 which n· no repentance.
19:31 Because the Lord hath n· of him.
34 they said, The Lord hath n· of him.
22:71 What n· we any further witness?
Joh 13:29 that we have n· of against the feast;
Ac 2:45 to all men, as every man had n·.
4:35 every man according as he had n·.
Ro 16: 2 business she hath n· of you: for
1Co 7:36 and n· so require, let him do what
12:21 the hand, I have no n· of thee:
21 to the feet, I have no n· of you.
24 For our comely parts have no n·:
2Co 3: 1 or n· we, as some others, epistles
Ph'p 4:12 both to abound and to suffer n·.
19 my God shall supply all your n·
1Th 1: 8 we n· not to speak any thing.
4: 9 love ye n· not that I write unto you:
5: 1 ye have no n· that I write unto you.
Heb 4:16 and find grace to help in time of n·.
5:12 ye have n· that one teach you
12 are become such as have n· of milk,
7:11 further n· was there that another
10:36 For ye have n· of patience, that,
1Pe 1: 6 though now for a season, if n· be,
1Jo 2:27 n· not that any man teach you:
3:17 and seeth his brother have n·, and
Re 3:17 with goods, and have n· of nothing;
21:23 And the city had no n· of the sun,
22: 5 they n· no candle, neither light

needed
Joh 2:25 n· not that any should testify
Ac 17:25 hands, as though he n· any thing,

needest
Joh 16:30 n· not that any man should ask

needeth
Ge 33:15 And he said, What n· it? let me find
Lu 11: 8 and give him as many as he n·.
Joh 13:10 n· not save to wash his feet,
Eph 4:28 he may have to give to him that n·.
2Ti 2:15 workman that n· not to be ashamed,
Heb 7:27 Who n· not daily, as those high

needful
Ezr 7:20 be n· for the house of thy God,
Lu 10:42 But one thing is n·: and Mary hath
Ac 15: 5 That it was n· to circumcise them,
Ph'p 1:24 abide in the flesh is more n· for you.
Jas 2:16 things which are n· to the body;
Jude 3 it was n· for me to write unto you,

needle See also NEEDLE'S; NEEDLEWORK.
M't 19:24 camel to go through the eye of a n·,
M'r 10:25 camel to go through the eye of a n·,

needle's
Lu 18:25 for a camel to go through a n· eye,

needlework
Ex 26:36 linen, wrought with n·.
27:16 twined linen, wrought with n·:
28:39 shalt make the girdle of n·.
36:37 and fine twined linen, of n·;
38:18 for the gate of the court was n·,
39:29 and purple, and scarlet, of n·;
J'g 5:30 a prey of divers colours of n·,
30 divers colours of n· on both sides,
Ps 45:14 unto the king in raiment of n·:

needs^
Ge 31:30 though thou wouldest n· be gone,
2Sa 14:14 For we must n· die, and are as
Jer 10: 5 they must n· be borne, because
M't 18: 7 for it must n· be that offences
M'r 13: 7 for such things must n· be; but the
Lu 14:18 and I must n· go and see it:
Joh 4: 4 he must n· go through Samaria.
Ac 1:16 this scripture must n· have been
17: 3 that Christ must n· have suffered,
21:22 the multitude must n· come
Ro 13: 5 ye must n· be subject, not only
1Co 5:10 then must ye n· go out of the world.
2Co 11:30 If I must n· glory, I will glory of

needy
De 15:11 to thy poor, and to thy n·, in thy land.
24:14 an hired servant that is poor and n·,
Job 24: 4 They turn the n· out of the way:
14 with the light killeth the poor and n·,
Ps 9:18 the n· shall not alway be forgotten:
12: 5 of the poor, for the sighing of the n·,
35:10 the n· from him that spoileth him?
37:14 to cast down the poor and n·, and to
40:17 But I am poor and n·; yet the Lord
70: 5 I am poor and n·: make haste unto
72: 4 he shall save the children of the n·,
12 shall deliver the n· when he crieth;
13 He shall spare the poor and n·, and
13 and shall save the souls of the n·.
74:21 let the poor and n· praise thy name.
82: 3 do justice to the afflicted and n·.
4 Deliver the poor and n·: rid them
86: 1 Lord, hear me: for I am poor and n·.
109:16 but persecuted the poor and n· man,
22 For I am poor and n·, and my heart
113: 7 and lifteth the n· out of the dunghill;
Pr 30:14 earth, and the n· from among men.
31: 9 plead the cause of the poor and n·.
20 forth her hands to the n·.
Isa 10: 2 turn aside the n· from judgment,
14:30 and the n· shall lie down in safety:
25: 4 a strength to the n· in his distress,
26: 6 the poor, and the steps of the n·.
32: 7 even when the n· speaketh right.
41:17 When the poor and n· seek water,
Jer 5:28 the right of the n· do they not judge.
22:16 judged the cause of the poor and n·;
Eze 16:49 the hand of the poor and n·.
18:12 Hath oppressed the poor and n·,
22:29 and have vexed the poor and n·:
Am 4: 1 oppress the poor, which crush the n·,
8: 4 this, O ye that swallow up the n·,
6 and the n· for a pair of shoes;

neesings
Job 41:18 By his n· a light doth shine, and

Neginah (*neg'-i-nah*) See also NEGINOTH.
Ps 61: *title* To the chief Musician upon N·,

Neginoth (*neg'-i-noth*) See also NEGINAH.
Ps 4: *title* To the chief Musician on N·,
6: *title* To the chief Musician on N·,
54: *title* To the chief Musician on N·,
55: *title* To the chief Musician on N·,
67: *title* To the chief Musician on N·,
76: *title* To the chief Musician on N·,

neglect See also NEGLECTED; NEGLECTING.
M't 18:17 And if he shall n· to hear them,
17 but if he n· to hear the church, let
1Ti 4:14 N· not the gift that is in thee,
Heb 2: 3 escape, if we n· so great salvation;

neglected
Ac 6: 1 were n· in the daily ministration.

neglecting
Col 2:23 and humility, and n· of the body;

negligent
2Ch 29:11 My sons, be not now n·: for the
2Pe 1:12 I will not be n· to put you always

Nego See ABED-NEGO.

Nehelamite (*ne-hel'-am-ite*)
Jer 29:24 also speak to Shemaiah the N·,
31 Lord concerning Shemaiah the N·;
32 I will punish Shemaiah the N·,

Nehemiah^ (*ne-he-mi'-ah*)
Ezr 2: 2 with Zerubbabel: Jeshua, N·,
Ne 1: 1 words of N· the son of Hachaliah.
3:16 him repaired N· the son of Azbuk,
7: 7 came with Zerubbabel, Jeshua, N·,
8: 9 N·, which is the Tirshatha, and
10: 1 that sealed were, N·, the Tirshatha,
12:26 and in the days of N· the governor,
47 in the days of N·, gave the portions

Nehiloth (*ne'-hi-loth*)
Ps 5: *title* To the chief Musician upon N·,

Nehum (*ne'-hum*) See also REHUM.
Ne 7: 7 Bilshan, Mispereth, Bigvai, N·,

Nehushta (*ne-hush'-tah*)
2Ki 24: 8 And his mother's name was N·,

Nehushtan (*ne-hush'-tan*)
2Ki 18: 4 incense to it: and he called it N·.

Neiel (*ne-i'-el*)'
Jos 19:27 and *N'*, and goeth out to Cabul

neighbour See also NEIGHBOUR'S; NEIGHBOURS.
Ex 3:22 woman shall borrow of her *n'*,
11: 2 let every man borrow of his *n'*,
2 and every woman of her *n'*, jewels
12: 4 him and his *n'* next unto his house
20:16 bear false witness against thy *n'*.
21:14 come presumptuously upon his *n'*,
22: 7 man shall deliver unto his *n'* money
9 he shall pay double unto his *n'*.
10 If a man deliver unto his *n'* an ass,
14 if a man borrow ought of his *n'*,
32:27 companion, and every man his *n'*.
Le 6: 2 and lie unto his *n'* in that which
2 violence, or hath deceived his *n'*;
19:13 Thou shalt not defraud thy *n'*,
15 shalt thou judge thy *n'*.
16 stand against the blood of thy *n'*:
17 shalt in any wise rebuke thy *n'*,
18 thou shalt love thy *n'* as thyself:
24:19 a man cause a blemish in his *n'*;
25:14 And if thou sell ought unto thy *n'*,
15 the jubile thou shalt buy of thy *n'*,
De 4:42 which should kill his *n'* unawares,
5:20 bear false witness against thy *n'*.
15: 2 that lendeth ought unto his *n'* shall
2 he shall not exact it of his *n'*, or of
19: 4 Whoso killeth his *n'* ignorantly,
5 man goeth into the wood with his *n'*
5 lighteth upon his *n'*, that he die;
11 But if any man hate his *n'*, and lie
22:26 when a man riseth against his *n'*,
23:25 into the standing corn of thy *n'*,
27:24 be he that smiteth his *n'* secretly.
Jos 20: 5 because he smote his *n'* unwittingly,
Ru 4: 7 off his shoe, and gave it to his *n'*:
1Sa 15:28 and hath given it to a *n'* of thine,
28:17 given it to thy *n'*, even to David:
2Sa 12:11 and give them unto thy *n'*, and he
1Ki 8:31 If any man trespass against his *n'*,
20:35 said unto his *n'* in the word of the
2Ch 6:22 If a man sin against his *n'*, and an
Job 12: 4 I am as one mocked of his *n'*, who
16:21 God, as a man pleadeth for his *n'*!
Ps 12: 2 speak vanity every one with his *n'*:
15: 3 his tongue, nor doeth evil to his *n'*,
3 up a reproach against his *n'*.
101: 5 Whoso privily slandereth his *n'*,
Pr 3:28 Say not unto thy *n'*, Go, and come
29 Devise not evil against thy *n'*,
11: 9 with his mouth destroyeth his *n'*:
12 is void of wisdom despiseth his *n'*:
12:26 is more excellent than his *n'*:
14:20 poor is hated even of his own *n'*:
21 He that despiseth his *n'* sinneth:
16:29 A violent man enticeth his *n'*, and
18:17 his *n'* cometh and searcheth him.
19: 4 the poor is separated from his *n'*.
21:10 his *n'* findeth no favour in his eyes.
24:28 Be not a witness against thy *n'*
25: 8 when thy *n'* hath put thee to shame.
9 Debate thy cause with thy *n'*
18 beareth false witness against his *n'*
26:19 So is the man that deceiveth his *n'*,
27:10 better is a *n'* that is near than a
29: 5 that flattereth his *n'* spreadeth a
Ec 4: 4 for this a man is envied of his *n'*.
Isa 3: 5 by another, and every one by his *n'*:
19: 2 and every one against his *n'*;
41: 6 They helped every one his *n'*; and
Jer 6:21 the *n'* and his friend shall perish.
7: 5 between a man and his *n'*;
9: 4 Take ye heed every one of his *n'*,
4 every *n'* will walk with slanders.
5 they will deceive every one his *n'*,
8 speaketh peaceably to his *n'* with
20 and every one her *n'* lamentation.
22: 8 they shall say every man to his *n'*,
23:27 which they tell every man to his *n'*,
30 my words every one from his *n'*.
35 shall ye say every one to his *n'*, and
31:34 teach no more every man his *n'*,
34:15 liberty every man to his *n'*; and ye
17 brother, and every man to his *n'*:
49:18 Gomorrah and the *n'* cities thereof,
50:40 Gomorrah and the *n'* cities thereof,
Hab 2:15 unto him that giveth his *n'* drink,
Zec 3:10 ye call every man his *n'* under the
8:10 all men every one against his *n'*.
16 ye every man the truth to his *n'*;
17 evil in your hearts against his *n'*;
14:13 every one on the hand of his *n'*, and
13 rise up against the hand of his *n'*.
M't 5:43 been said, Thou shalt love thy *n'*,
19:19 Thou shalt love thy *n'* as thyself.
22:39 Thou shalt love thy *n'* as thyself.
M'r 12:31 Thou shalt love thy *n'* as thyself.
33 and to love his *n'* as himself, is
Lu 10:27 all thy mind; and thy *n'* as thyself.
29 said unto Jesus, And who is my *n'*?
36 was *n'* unto him that fell among
Ac 7:27 he that did his *n'* wrong thrust him
Ro 13: 9 Thou shalt love thy *n'* as thyself.
10 Love worketh no ill to his *n'*:
15: 2 Let every one of us please his *n'*
Gal 5:14 Thou shalt love thy *n'* as thyself.
Eph 4:25 speak every man truth with his *n'*:
Heb 8:11 shall not teach every man his *n'*,
Jas 2: 8 Thou shalt love thy *n'* as thyself,

neighbour's
Ex 20:17 Thou shalt not covet thy *n'* house,
17 thou shalt not covet thy *n'* wife,
17 his ass, nor any thing that is thy *n'*.
22: 8 have put his hand unto his *n'* goods.
Ex 22:11 not put his hand unto his *n'* goods;
26 If thou at all take thy *n'* raiment
Le 18:20 not lie carnally with thy *n'* wife, to
20:10 adultery with his *n'* wife,
25:14 or buyest ought of thy *n'* hand, ye
De 5:21 shalt thou desire thy *n'* wife,
21 shalt thou covet thy *n'* house, his
21 his ass, or any thing that is thy *n'*.
19:14 shalt not remove thy *n'* landmark,
22:24 he hath humbled his *n'* wife:
23:24 thou comest into thy *n'* vineyard,
25 a sickle unto thy *n'* standing corn.
27:17 he that removeth his *n'* landmark.
Job 31: 9 or if I have laid wait at my *n'* door;
Pr 6:29 So he that goeth in to his *n'* wife;
25:17 thy foot from thy *n'* house; lest he
Jer 5: 8 every one neighed after his *n'* wife.
22:13 useth his *n'* service without wages,
Eze 18: 6 neither hath defiled his *n'* wife,
11 mountains, and defiled his *n'* wife,
15 Israel, hath not defiled his *n'* wife,
22:11 abomination with his *n'* wife; and
33:26 and ye defile every one his *n'* wife:
Zec 11: 6 the men every one into his *n'* hand,

neighbours See also NEIGHBOURS'.
Jos 9:16 they heard that they were their *n'*,
Ru 4:17 the women her *n'* gave it a name,
2Ki 4: 3 vessels abroad of all thy *n'*, even
Ps 28: 3 which speak peace to their *n'*, but
31:11 but especially among my *n'*, and
44:13 makest us a reproach to our *n'*, a
79: 4 We are become a reproach to our *n'*,
12 And render unto our *n'* sevenfold
80: 6 Thou makest us a strife unto our *n'*:
89:41 him: he is a reproach to his *n'*.
Jer 12:14 against all mine evil *n'*, that touch
49:10 his brethren, and his *n'*, and he is
Eze 16:26 the Egyptians thy *n'*, great of flesh;
22:12 thou hast greedily gained of thy *n'*
23: 5 her lovers, on the Assyrians her *n'*,
12 doted upon the Assyrians her *n'*,
Lu 1:58 And her *n'* and her cousins heard
14:12 thy kinsmen, nor thy rich *n'*; lest
15: 6 calleth together his friends and *n'*,
9 she calleth her friends and her *n'*
Joh 9: 8 The *n'* therefore, and they which

neighbours'
Jer 29:23 adultery with their *n'* wives, and

neighed
Jer 5: 8 every one *n'* after his neighbour's

neighing See also NEIGHINGS.
Jer 8:16 sound of the *n'* of his strong ones;

neighings
Jer 13:27 seen thine adulteries, and thy *n'*.

neither^
Ge 9:11 *n'* shall all flesh be cut off any more
11 *n'* shall there any more be a flood
17: 5 *N'* shall thy name any more be
19:17 thee, *n'* stay thou in all the plain;
21:26 this thing: *n'* didst thou tell me,
26 me, *n'* yet heard I of it, but to day.
22:12 *n'* do thou any thing unto him:
24:16 *n'* had any man known her: and
29: 7 *n'* is it time that the cattle should
39: 9 *n'* hath he kept back any thing from
45: 6 there shall *n'* be earing nor harvest.
Ex 4: 8 *n'* hearken to the voice of the first
9 signs, *n'* hearken unto thy voice,
10 *n'* heretofore, nor since thou hast
5: 2 Lord, *n'* will I let Israel go.
23 *n'* hast thou delivered thy people
7:22 *n'* did he hearken unto them; as
23 *n'* did he set his heart to this also.
8:32 also, *n'* would he let the people go.
9:29 *n'* shall there be any more hail;
35 *n'* would he let the children of
10: 6 *n'* thy fathers, nor thy fathers'
14 as they, *n'* after them shall be such.
23 *n'* rose any from his place for three
12:39 *n'* had...prepared...victual.
46 *n'* shall ye break a bone thereof.
13: 7 *n'* shall there be leaven seen with
16:24 *n'* was there any worm therein.
20:23 *n'* shall ye make unto you gods of
26 *N'* shalt thou go up by steps unto
22:21 *n'* vex a stranger, nor oppress him:
25 *n'* shalt thou lay upon him usury.
31 *n'* shall ye eat any flesh that is torn
23: 2 *n'* shalt thou speak in a cause to
2 *N'* shalt thou countenance a poor
13 *n'* let it be heard out of thy mouth.
18 *n'* shall the fat of my sacrifice
24: 2 *n'* shall the people go up with him.
30: 9 *n'* shall ye pour drink offering
32 *n'* shall ye make any other like it,
32:18 *n'* is it the voice of them that cry for
34: 3 *n'* let any man be seen throughout
3 *n'* let the flocks nor herds feed
24 *n'* shall any man desire thy land,
28 he did *n'* eat bread, nor drink water.
36: 6 Let *n'* man nor woman make any
Le 2:13 *n'* shalt thou suffer the salt of the
3:17 that ye eat *n'* fat nor blood.
5:11 *n'* shall he put any frankincense
7:18 *n'* shall it be imputed unto him that
10: 6 *n'* rend your clothes; lest ye die, and
11:43 *n'* shall ye make yourselves unclean
44 *n'* shall ye defile yourselves with
17:12 *n'* shall any stranger...eat blood.
18: 3 *n'* shall ye walk in their ordinances.
17 *n'* shalt thou take her son's
18 *N'* shalt thou take a wife to her
21 *n'* shalt thou profane the name of
23 *N'* shalt thou lie with any beast to
Le 18:23 *n'* shall any woman stand before a
26 *n'* any of your own nation, nor any
19: 9 *n'* shalt thou gather the gleanings of
10 *n'* shalt thou gather every grape of
11 Ye shall not steal, *n'* deal falsely,
11 deal falsely, *n'* lie one to another.
12 *n'* shalt thou profane the name of thy
13 not defraud thy neighbour, *n'* rob
16 *n'* shalt thou stand against the
19 *n'* shall a garment mingled of linen
26 *n'* shall ye use enchantment, nor
27 *n'* shalt thou mar the corners of thy
31 *n'* seek after wizards, to be defiled
21: 5 *n'* shall they shave off the corner
7 *n'* shall they take a woman put away
11 *N'* shall he go in to any dead body,
12 *N'* shall he go out of the sanctuary,
15 *N'* shall he profane his seed among
22:24 *n'* shall ye make any offering
25 *N'* from a stranger's hand shall ye
32 *N'* shall ye profane my holy name;
23:14 ye shall eat *n'* bread, nor parched
22 *n'* shalt thou gather any gleaning
25: 4 thou shalt *n'* sow thy field, nor
5 *n'* gather the grapes of thy vine
11 *n'* reap that which groweth of itself
26: 1 *n'* rear you up a standing image,
1 *n'* shall ye set up any image of
6 *n'* shall the sword go through your
20 *n'* shall the trees of the land yield
44 them away, *n'* will I abhor them,
27:33 good or bad, *n'* shall he change it:
Nu 1:49 *n'* take the sum of them among the
5:13 *n'* she be taken with the manner;
11:19 days, *n'* ten days, nor twenty days;
14: 9 *n'* fear ye the people of the land;
23 *n'* shall any of them that provoked
16:15 them, *n'* have I hurt one of them.
18: 3 that *n'* they, nor ye also, die.
20 *n'* shalt thou have any part among
22 *N'* must the children of Israel
32 *n'* shall ye pollute the holy things
20: 5 *n'* is there any water to drink.
17 *n'* will we drink of the water of thy
21: 5 is no bread, *n'* is there any water;
23:19 *n'* the son of man, that he should
21 *n'* hath he seen perverseness in
23 *n'* is there any divination against
25 *N'* curse them at all, nor bless
35:23 not his enemy, *n'* sought his harm:
36: 9 *N'* shall the inheritance remove
De 1:21 thee; fear not, *n'* be discouraged.
29 Dread not, *n'* be afraid of them.
42 unto them, Go not up, *n'* fight;
2: 9 *n'* contend with them in battle:
27 I will *n'* turn unto the right hand
4: 2 *n'* shall ye diminish ought from it,
28 *n'* see, nor hear, nor eat, nor smell.
31 not forsake thee, *n'* destroy thee,
5:18 *N'* shalt thou commit adultery.
19 *N'* shalt thou steal.
20 *N'* shalt thou bear false witness
21 *N'* shalt thou desire thy neighbour's
21 *n'* shalt thou covet thy neighbour's
7: 3 *N'* shalt thou make marriages with
16 them: *n'* shalt thou serve their gods;
26 *N'* shalt thou bring an abomination
8: 3 not, *n'* did thy fathers know;
4 old upon thee, *n'* did thy foot swell,
9: 9 I *n'* did eat bread nor drink water:
18 I did *n'* eat bread, nor drink water,
13: 8 *n'* shall thine eye pity him,
8 eye pity him, *n'* shalt thou spare,
8 spare, *n'* shalt thou conceal him:
16: 4 *n'* shall there any thing of the flesh,
19 not respect persons, *n'* take a gift:
22 *N'* shalt thou set thee up any image;
17:17 *N'* shall he multiply wives to
17 *n'* shall he greatly multiply...silver
18:16 *n'* let me see this great fire any more,
20: 3 *n'* be ye terrified because of them;
21: 4 valley, which is *n'* eared nor sown,
7 this blood, *n'* have our eyes seen it.
22: 5 *n'* shall a man put on a woman's
24: 5 *n'* shall he be charged with any
15 *n'* shall the sun go down upon it;
16 *n'* shall the children be put to death
26:13 commandments, *n'* have I forgotten
14 *n'* have I taken away ought thereof
28:36 *n'* thou nor thy fathers have known;
39 *n'* drink of the wine, nor gather the
64 *n'* thou nor thy fathers have known,
65 *n'* shall...sole of thy foot have rest:
29: 6 *n'* have ye drunk wine or strong
14 *N'* with you only do I make this
30:11 not hidden from thee, *n'* is it far off.
13 *N'* is it beyond the sea, that thou
31: 8 he will not fail thee, *n'* forsake thee:
8 thee: fear not, *n'* be dismayed.
32:28 *n'* is there any understanding in
39 *n'* is there any that can deliver out of
33: 9 *n'* did...acknowledge his brethren,
Jos 1: 9 be not afraid, *n'* be thou dismayed:
2:11 *n'* did...remain any more courage
5: 1 *n'* was there spirit in them any more,
12 *n'* had the children of Israel manna
6:10 *n'* shall any word proceed out of your
7:12 *n'* will I be with you any more,
8: 1 Fear not, *n'* be thou dismayed:
11:14 them, *n'* left they any to breathe.
23: 7 *n'* make mention of the name of
7 *n'* serve them, nor bow yourselves
J'g 1:27 *N'* did Manasseh drive out the
29 *N'* did Ephraim drive out the
30 *N'* did Zebulun drive out the
31 *N'* did Asher drive out the

J'g 1:33 *N'* did Naphtali drive out the
2:23 *n'* delivered he them into the hand
6: 4 for Israel, *n'* sheep, nor ox, nor ass.
8:23 you, *n'* shall my son rule over you:
35 *N'* shewed they kindness to the
11:34 her he had *n'* son nor daughter.
13: 6 he was, *n'* told he me his name:
7 drink, *n'* eat any unclean thing:
14 *n'* let her drink wine or strong drink,
23 *n'* would he have shewed us all
20: 8 *n'* will we any of us turn into his
Ru 2: 8 *n'* go from hence, but abide
1Sa 1:15 I have drunk *n'* wine nor strong
2: 2 *n'* is there any rock like our God.
3: 7 *n'* was the word of the Lord yet
4:20 answered not, *n'* did she regard it.
5: 5 *n'* the priests of Dagon, nor any
12: 4 *n'* hast thou taken ought of any
13:22 was *n'* sword nor spear found in the
16: 8, 9 *N'* hath the Lord chosen
20:27 to meat, *n'* yesterday, nor to-day?
21: 8 *n'* brought my sword nor my
24:11 is *n'* evil nor transgression in mine
25: 7 *n'* was there ought missing unto
15 not hurt, *n'* missed we any thing,
26:12 man saw it, nor knew it, *n'* awaked:
27: 9 and left *n'* man nor woman alive,
11 saved *n'* man nor woman alive,
28: 6 *n'* by dreams, nor by Urim, nor by
15 *n'* by prophets, nor by dreams:
30:15 that thou wilt *n'* kill me, nor deliver
19 *n'* small nor great, *n'* sons nor
19 *n'* spoil, nor anything that they had
2Sa 1:21 dew, *n'* let there be rain, upon you,
2:28 no more, *n'* fought they any more.
7:10 *n'* shall the children of wickedness
22 *n'* is there any God beside thee,
12:17 not, *n'* did he eat bread with them.
13:22 his brother Amnon *n'* good nor bad:
14: 7 *n'* name nor remainder upon the
14 *n'* doth God respect any person:
18: 3 *n'* if half of us died, will they care
19: 6 regardest *n'* princes nor servants:
19 *n'* do thou remember that which thy
24 *n'* dressed his feet, nor trimmed
20: 1 *n'* have we inheritance in the son of
21: 4 *n'* for us shalt thou kill any man in
10 *n'* the birds of the air to rest on
24:24 *n'* will I offer burnt offerings unto
1Ki 3:11 *n'* hast asked riches for thyself,
26 Let it be *n'* mine nor thine,
5: 4 that there is *n'* adversary nor evil
6: 7 there was *n'* hammer nor axe nor
7:47 *n'* was the weight of the brass found
11: 2 *n'* shall they come in unto you:
12:16 *n'* have we inheritance in the son of
13: 8, 16 *n'* will I eat bread nor drink water
16:11 *n'* of his kinsfolks, nor of his friends.
17:14 waste, *n'* shall the cruse of oil fail,
16 not, *n'* did the cruse of oil fail,
18:29 was *n'* voice, nor any to answer,
22:31 Fight *n'* with small nor great, save
2Ki 3:17 not see wind, *n'* shall ye see rain;
4:23 it is *n'* new moon, nor sabbath.
31 but there was *n'* voice, nor hearing.
5:17 offer *n'* burnt offering nor sacrifice
6:19 is not the way, *n'* is this the city:
7:10 was no man there, *n'* voice of man,
10:14 forty men; *n'* left he any of them.
12: 8 *n'* to repair the breaches of the
13: 7 *N'* did he leave of the people to
23 *n'* cast he them from his presence
17:34 *n'* do they after their statutes, or
38 forget; *n'* shall ye fear other gods.
18:30 *N'* let Hezekiah make you trust in
21: 8 *N'* will I make the feet of Israel
23:25 *n'* after him arose there any like
1Ch 4:27 *n'* did all their family multiply, like
17: 9 *n'* shall the children of wickedness
20 *n'* is there any God beside thee,
19:19 *n'* would the Syrians help the
27:24 *n'* was the number put in the
2Ch 1:11 enemies, *n'* yet hast asked long life;
12 *n'* shall there any after thee have
6: 5 *n'* chose I any man to be a ruler
9: 9 *n'* was there any such spice as the
13:20 *N'* did Jeroboam recover strength
20:12 *n'* know we what to do: but our
25: 4 *n'* shall the children die for the
26:18 *n'* shall it be for thine honour from
30: 3 *n'* had the people gathered
32:15 on this manner, *n'* yet believe him:
33: 8 *N'* will I any more remove the foot
34: 2 declined *n'* to the right hand, nor
28 *n'* shall thine eyes see all the evil
35:18 *n'* did all the kings of Israel keep
Ezr 9:12 *n'* take their daughters unto your
10:13 *n'* is this a work of one day or two:
Ne 2:12 *n'* told I any man what my God had
12 *n'* was there any beast with me,
16 *n'* had I as yet told it to the Jews,
4:11 They shall not know, *n'* see, till we
23 So *n'* I, nor my brethren, nor my
5: 5 *n'* is it in our power to redeem them;
16 this wall, *n'* bought we any land:
8:10 *n'* be ye sorry; for the joy of the
11 for the day is holy; *n'* be ye grieved.
9:17 *n'* were mindful of thy wonders
19 *n'* the pillar of fire by night, to shew
34 *N'* have our kings, our princes,
35 *n'* turned they from their wicked
Es 2: 7 for she had *n'* father nor mother,
3: 8 people; *n'* keep they the king's laws:
4:16 *n'* eat nor drink three days, night
Job 3: 4 *n'* let the light shine upon it.
9 *n'* let it see the dawning of the day:

Job 3:26 I was not in safety, *n'* had I rest,
26 *n'* was I quiet; yet trouble came.
5: 4 *n'* is there any to deliver them.
6 *n'* doth trouble spring out of the
21 *n'* shalt...be afraid of destruction
22 *n'* shalt thou be afraid of the beasts
7:10 *n'* shall his place know him any
8:20 man, *n'* will he help the evil doers:
9:33 *N'* is there any daysman betwixt
15:29 *n'* shall his substance continue,
29 *n'* shall he prolong the perfection
18:19 He shall *n'* have son nor nephew
20: 9 *n'* shall his place any more behold
21: 9 *n'* is the rod of God upon them.
23:12 *N'* have I gone back from the
17 *n'* hath he covered the darkness from
28:13 *n'* is it found in the land of the
15 *n'* shall silver be weighed for the
19 *n'* shall it be valued with pure gold.
31:30 *N'* have I suffered my mouth to sin
32: 9 *n'* do the aged understand judgment.
14 *n'*...answer him with...speeches.
21 *n'* let me give flattering titles unto
33: 7 *n'* shall my hand be heavy upon
9 innocent; *n'* is there iniquity in me.
34:12 *n'*...the Almighty pervert judgment.
35:13 *n'* will the Almighty regard it.
36:26 *n'* can the number of his years be
39: 7 *n'* regardeth he the crying of the
17 *n'*...imparted to her understanding.
22 *n'* turneth he back from the sword.
24 *n'* believeth he that it is the sound
Ps 5: 4 *n'* shall evil dwell with thee.
16:10 *n'* wilt thou suffer thine Holy One
18:37 *n'* did I turn again till they were
22:24 *n'* hath he hid his face from him;
26: 4 *n'* will I go in with dissemblers.
27: 9 leave me not, *n'* forsake me, O God
33:17 *n'*...deliver any by...great strength.
35:19 *n'* let them wink with the eye that hate
37: 1 *n'* be thou envious against the
38: 1 *n'* chasten me in thy hot displeasure.
3 *n'* is there any rest in my bones
44: 3 *n'* did their own arm save them:
6 my bow, *n'* shall my sword save me.
17 *n'* have we dealt falsely in thy
18 *n'* have our steps declined from thy
55:12 *n'* was it he that hated me that
69:15 *n'* let the deep swallow me up, and
73: 5 *n'* are they plagued like other men.
74: 9 *n'* is there among us any that
75: 6 promotion cometh *n'* from the east,
78:37 *n'* were...steadfast in his covenant.
81: 9 *n'* shalt thou worship any strange
82: 5 know not, *n'* will they understand;
86: 8 *n'* are there any works like unto
91:10 *n'* shall any plague come nigh thy
92: 6 not; *n'* doth a fool understand this.
94: 7 *n'* shall the God of Jacob regard it.
14 *n'* will he forsake his inheritance.
103: 9 *n'* will he keep his anger for ever.
109:12 *n'* let there be any to favour his
115: 7 *n'* speak they through their throat.
17 *n'* any that go down into silence.
121: 4 Israel shall *n'* slumber nor sleep.
129: 8 *N'* do they which go by say, The
131: 1 *n'* do I exercise myself in great
135:17 *n'* is there any breath in their
Pr 2:19 *n'* take they hold of the paths of life.
3:11 *n'* be weary of his correction:
25 *n'* of the desolation of the wicked,
4: 5 *n'* decline from the words of my
6:25 *n'* let her take thee with her eyelids.
35 *n'* will he rest content, though
15:12 him: *n'* will he go unto the wise.
22:22 *n'* oppress the afflicted in the gate:
23: 6 *n'* desire thou his dainty meats:
24: 1 evil men, *n'* desire to be with them:
19 *n'* be thou envious at the wicked;
27:10 *n'* go into thy brother's house in the
30: 3 I *n'* learned wisdom, nor have the
8 give me *n'* poverty nor riches; feed
Ec 1:11 *n'* shall there be any remembrance
4: 8 he hath *n'* child nor brother:
8 *n'* is his eye satisfied with riches;
8 *n'* saith he, For whom do I labour,
5: 6 *n'* say thou before the angel, that
6:10 *n'* may he contend with him that
7:16 much; *n'* make thyself over wise:
17 much wicked, *n'* be thou foolish:
8: 8 *n'* hath...power in the day of death:
8 *n'* shall wickedness deliver those
13 *n'* shall he prolong his days, which
16 there is that *n'* day nor night
9: 5 *n'* have they any more a reward; for
6 *n'* have they any more a portion for
11 *n'* yet bread to the wise, nor yet
Ca 8: 7 love, *n'* can the floods drown it:
Isa 1: 6 *n'* bound up, *n'* mollified with
23 *n'* doth the cause of the widow
2: 4 *n'* shall they learn war any more.
7 *n'* is there...end of their treasures;
7 *n'* is there any end of their chariots;
3: 7 my house is *n'* bread nor clothing:
5:12 *n'* consider the operation of his
27 *n'* shall the girdle of their loins be
7: 4 *n'* be fainthearted for the two tails
7 stand, *n'* shall it come to pass.
12 not ask, *n'* will I tempt the Lord.
8:12 *n'* fear ye their fear, nor be afraid.
9:13 *n'* do they seek the Lord of hosts.
17 *n'*...have mercy on their fatherless
10: 7 not so, *n'* doth his heart think so;
11: 3 *n'* reprove after the hearing of his
13:20 *n'* shall it be dwelt in from
20 *n'* shall the Arabian pitch tent

Isa 13:20 *n'* shall the shepherds make their
16:10 singing, *n'* shall there be shouting;
17: 8 *n'* shall respect that which his
19:15 *N'* shall there be any work for
22:11 *n'* had respect unto him that
23: 4 *n'* do I nourish up young men, nor
26:18 *n'* have the inhabitants of the
28:27 *n'* is a cart wheel turned about upon
29:22 *n'* shall his face now wax pale.
31: 1 One of Israel, *n'* seek the Lord!
33:20 *n'* shall any of the cords thereof
21 *n'* shall gallant ship pass thereby.
36:15 *N'* let Hezekiah make you trust in
40:28 earth, fainteth not, *n'* is weary?
42: 8 *n'* my praise to graven images.
24 *n'* were they obedient unto his law.
43: 2 *n'* shall the flame kindle upon thee.
10 formed, *n'* shall there be after me.
18 things, *n'* consider the things of old.
23 *n'* hast thou honoured me with
24 *n'* hast thou filled me with the fat
44: 8 Fear ye not, *n'* be afraid: have not
19 heart, *n'* is there knowledge nor
47: 7 *n'* didst remember the latter end
8 *n'* shall I know the loss of children:
49:10 *n'* shall the heat nor sun smite
50: 5 not rebellious, *n'* turned away back.
51: 7 *n'* be ye afraid of their revilings.
18 *n'* is there any that taketh her by
53: 9 *n'* was any deceit in his mouth.
54: 4 *n'* be thou confounded; for thou
10 *n'* shall the covenant of my peace
55: 8 *n'* are your ways my ways, saith
56: 3 *N'* let the son of the strangers,
3 *n'* let the eunuch say, Behold, I am
57:16 *n'* will I be always wroth: for the
59: 1 *n'* his ear heavy, that it cannot hear.
6 *n'* shall they cover themselves with
9 from us, *n'* doth justice overtake us:
60:19 *n'* for brightness shall the moon
20 *n'* shall thy moon withdraw itself:
62: 4 *n'*...thy land any more be termed
64: 4 *n'* hath the eye seen, O God, besides
9 *n'* remember iniquity for ever:
66:19 my fame, *n'* have seen my glory;
24 die, *n'* shall their fire be quenched;
Jer 2: 6 *N'* said they, Where is the Lord
3:16 the Lord: *n'* shall it come to mind:
16 *n'* shall they remember it;
16 *n'* shall they visit it;
16 *n'* shall that be done any more.
17 *n'* shall they walk any more after
4:28 repent, *n'* will I turn back from it.
5:12 not he; *n'* shall evil come upon us;
12 *n'* shall we see sword nor famine:
15 *n'* understandest what they say.
24 *N'* say they in their heart, Let us
6:15 ashamed, *n'* could they blush:
7: 6 *n'* walk after other gods to your
16 *n'* lift up cry nor prayer for them,
16 them, *n'* make intercession to me:
31 them not, *n'* came it into my heart.
8:12 all ashamed, *n'* could they blush:
9:10 *n'* can men hear the voice of the
13 obeyed my voice, *n'* walked therein;
16 *n'* they nor their fathers have
23 *n'* let the mighty man glory in his
10: 5 *n'* also is it in them to do good.
11:14 *n'* lift up a cry or prayer for them:
14:13 sword, *n'* shall ye have famine;
14 not, *n'* have I commanded them,
14 them, *n'* spake unto them:
15:10 I have *n'* lent on usury, nor men
16: 2 a wife, *n'* shalt thou have sons or
4 lamented; *n'* shall they be buried;
5 *n'* go to lament nor bemoan them:
6 *n'* shall men lament for them, nor
7 *N'* shall men tear themselves for
7 *n'* shall men give them the cup of
13 know not, *n'* ye nor your fathers;
17 *n'* is their iniquity hid from mine
17: 8 *n'* shall cease from yielding fruit.
16 *n'* have I desired the woeful day;
22 *N'* carry forth a burden out of your
22 the sabbath day, *n'* do ye any work,
23 obeyed not, *n'* inclined their ear,
18:23 *n'* blot out their sin from thy sight,
19: 4 *n'* they nor their fathers have
5 spake it, *n'* came it into my mind:
21: 7 them, *n'* have pity, nor have mercy.
22: 3 *n'* shed innocent blood in this place.
10 ye not for the dead, *n'* bemoan him:
23: 4 *n'* shall they be lacking, saith the
25:33 lamented, *n'* gathered, nor buried;
29: 8 *n'* hearken to your dreams which
32 *n'* shall he behold the good that I
30:10 *n'* be dismayed, O Israel: for, lo, I
32:23 thy voice, *n'* walked in thy law;
35 them not, *n'* came it into my mind,
33:18 *N'* shall the priests the Levites
22 *n'* the sand of the sea measured:
34:14 not unto me, *n'* inclined their ear.
35: 6 drink no wine, *n'* ye nor your sons
7 *N'* shall ye build house, nor sow
9 *n'* have we vineyard, nor field, nor
36:24 *n'* the king, nor any of his servants
37: 2 *n'* he, nor his servants, nor the
38:16 *n'* will I give thee into the hand of
42:13 *n'* obey the voice of the Lord your
44: 3 knew not, *n'* they, ye, nor your fathers.
10 *n'* have they feared, nor walked in
48:11 *n'* hath he gone into captivity:
49:18 *n'* shall a son of man dwell in it.
31 which have *n'* gates nor bars
50:39 *n'* shall it be dwelt in from
40 *n'* shall any son of man dwell

Jer 51:43 n' doth any son of man pass
62 remain in it, n' man nor beast.
Eze 2: 6 them, n' be afraid of their words,
3: 9 not, n' be dismayed at their looks,
4:14 n' came there abominable flesh into
5: 7 n' have kept my judgments,
7 n' have done according to the
11 thee; n' shall mine eye spare,
11 eye spare, n' will I have any pity.
7: 4 not spare thee, n' will I have pity:
9 shall not spare, n' will I have pity:
11 n' shall there be wailing for them.
13 n' shall any strengthen himself in
19 their souls, n' fill their bowels:
8:18 shall not spare, n' will I have pity:
9: 5 not your eye spare, n' have ye pity:
10 shall not spare, n' will I have pity,3
11:11 n' shall ye be the flesh in the midst
12 n' executed my judgments, but
13: 5 n' made up the hedge for the house of
9 n' shall they be written in the
9 n' shall they enter into the land of
15 is no more, n' they that daubed it;
14:11 n' be polluted any more with all
16 shall deliver n' sons nor daughters;
18 shall deliver n' sons nor daughters,
20 shall deliver n' son nor daughter;
16: 4 n' wast thou washed in water to
16 shall not come, n' shall it be so.
49 n' did she strengthen the hand of
51 N' hath Samaria committed half of
17:17 N' shall Pharaoh with his mighty
18: 6 n' hath lifted up his eyes to the
6 n' hath defiled his neighbour's
6 n' hath come near to a menstruous
8 usury, n' hath taken any increase,
15 n' hath lifted up his eyes to the
16 N' hath oppressed any, hath not
16 pledge, n' hath spoiled by violence,
20 n' shall the father bear the iniquity
20: 8 n' did they forsake the idols of
17 n' did I make an end of them in the
18 n' observe their judgments, nor
21 n' kept my judgments to do them,
22:26 n' have they shewed difference
23: 8 N' left she her whoredoms brought
24:14 n' will I spare, n' will I repent;
16 yet n' shalt thou mourn nor weep,
16 weep, n' shall thy tears run down.
29:11 n' shall it be inhabited forty years.
15 n' shall it exalt itself any more
31:14 n' shoot up their top among the
14 n' their trees stand up in their
32:13 n' shall the foot of man trouble
33:12 n' shall the righteous be able to live
34: 4 n' have ye healed that which was
4 n' have ye bound up that which was
4 n' have ye brought again that which
4 n' have ye sought that which was
8 n' did my shepherds search for my
10 flock; n' shall the shepherds feed
28 n' shall the beast of the land devour
29 n' bear the shame of the heathen
36:14 n' bereave thy nations any more,
15 N' will I cause men to hear in thee
15 n' shalt thou bear the reproach of
15 n' shalt thou cause thy nations to
37:22 n' shall they be divided into two
23 N' shall they defile themselves any
38:11 walls, and having n' bars nor gates,
39:10 n' cut down any out of the forests;
29 N' will I hide my face any more
43: 7 more defile, n' they, nor their kings,
44:20 N' shall they shave their heads,
21 N' shall any priest drink wine,
22 N' shall they take for their wives a
47:12 fade, n' shall the fruit thereof be
48:14 they shall not sell of it, n' exchange,
Da 3:27 n' were their coats changed, nor
6: 4 n' was there any error or fault found
18 n' were instruments of musick
8: 4 n' was there any that could deliver
9: 6 N' have we hearkened unto thy
10 N' have we obeyed the voice of the
10: 3 n' came flesh nor wine in my mouth,
3 n' did I anoint myself at all, till
17 in me, n' is there breath left in me.
11: 6 n' shall he stand, nor his arm: but
15 withstand, n' his chosen people,
15 n' shall there be any strength to
17 not stand on his side, n' be for him.
20 destroyed, n' in anger, nor in battle.
37 N' shall he regard the God of his
Ho 2: 2 not my wife, n' am I her husband:
4:15 Gilgal, n' go ye up to Beth-aven,
9: 4 n' shall they be pleasing unto him:
14: 3 n' will we say any more to the work
Joe 2: 2 like, n' shall be any more after it,
8 N' shall one thrust another; they
Am 2:14 n' shall the mighty deliver himself:
15 N' shall he stand that handleth the
15 n' shall he that rideth the horse
5:22 n' will I regard the peace offerings
7:14 prophet, n' was I a prophet's son;
Ob 12 n' shouldest thou have rejoiced
12 n' shouldest thou have spoken
14 N' shouldest thou have stood in the
14 n' shouldest thou have delivered up
Jon 3: 7 Let n' man nor beast, herd nor
4:10 not laboured, n' madest it grow;
Mic 2: 3 your necks; n' shall ye go haughtily:
4: 3 n' shall they learn war any more.
12 n' understand they his counsel:
Hab 2: 5 a proud man, n' keepeth at home,
3:17 n' shall fruit be in the vines;
Zep 1:12 will not do good, n' will he do evil.
Zep 1:18 N' their silver nor their gold shall
3:13 n' shall a deceitful tongue be found
Zec 8:10 n' was there any peace to him that
11:16 n' shall seek the young one, nor
13: 4 n' shall they wear a rough garment
Mal 1:10 n' do ye kindle fire on mine altar
10 n' will I accept an offering at your
3:11 n' shall your vine cast her fruit
4: 1 shall leave them n' root nor branch.
M't 5:15 N' do men light a candle, and put
34 n' by heaven; for it is God's throne:
35 n' by Jerusalem; for it is the city
36 N' shalt thou swear by thy head,
6:15 n' will your Father forgive your
20 n' moth nor rust doth corrupt, and
26 n' do they reap, nor gather into
28 grow; they toil not, n' do they spin:
7: 6 n' cast ye your pearls before swine,
18 n' can a corrupt tree bring forth
9:17 N' do men put new wine into old
10: 9 Provide n' gold, nor silver, nor
10 journey, n' two coats, n' [*] shoes,
11:18 John came n' eating nor drinking,
27 n' knoweth any man the Father,
12: 4 n' for them which were with him,
19 n' shall any man hear his voice in
32 be forgiven him, n' in this world,
32 world, n' in the world to come.
13:13 hear not, n' do they understand.
16: 9 n' remember the five loaves of the
10 N' the seven loaves of the four
21:27 N' tell I you by what authority I do
22:16 n' carest thou for any man:
30 n' marry, nor...given in marriage,
46 n' durst any man from that day
23:10 N' be ye called masters: for one
13 men: for ye n' go in yourselves,
13 n' suffer ye them that are entering
24:18 N' let him which is in the field
20 the winter, n' on the sabbath day:
25:13 ye know n' the day nor the hour
M'r 4:22 n' was any thing kept secret, but
5: 4 n' could any man tame him.
8:14 n' had they in the ship with
17 perceive ye not yet, n' understand?
26 N' go into the town, nor tell it to
11:26 N' will your Father which is in
33 N' do I tell you by what authority
12:21 her, and died, n' left he any seed:
24 scriptures, n' the power of God?
25 n' marry, nor...given in marriage;
13:11 shall speak, n' do ye premeditate:
15 n' enter therein, to take any thing
19 unto this time, n' shall be.
32 heaven, n' the Son, but the Father.
14:40 n' wist they what to answer
59 But n' so did their witness agree
68 n' understand I what thou sayest.
16: 8 n' said they any thing to any
13 residue: n' believed they them.
Lu 1:15 n' wine nor strong drink;
3:14 to no man, n' accuse any falsely;
6:43 n' doth a corrupt tree bring forth
7: 7 n' thought I myself worthy to come
33 came n' eating bread nor drinking
8:17 n' any thing hid, that shall not be
27 n' abode in any house, but in
43 n' could be healed of any,
9: 3 journey, n' staves, nor scrip,
3 nor scrip, n' bread, n' money;
3 money; n' have two coats apiece.
10: 4 Carry n' purse, nor scrip, nor
11:33 secret place, n' under a bushel,
12: 2 n' hid, that shall not be known.
22 n' for the body, what ye shall put
24 ravens: for they n' sow nor reap;
24 which n' have storehouse nor barn;
29 drink, n' be ye of doubtful mind.
33 approacheth, n' moth corrupteth.
47 n' did according to his will, shall
14:12 thy brethren, n' thy kinsmen, nor
35 It is n' fit for the land, nor yet for
15:29 n' transgressed I at any time thy
16:26 n' can they pass to us, that would
31 n' will they be persuaded, though
17:21 N' shall they say, Lo here! or, lo
18: 2 feared not God, n' regarded man:
34 n' knew they the things which
20: 8 N' tell I you by what authority I
21 n' acceptest thou the person
35 n' marry, nor...given in marriage:
36 N' can they die any more: for
Joh 1:25 Christ, nor Elias, n' that prophet?
3:20 light, n' cometh to the light,
4:15 thirst not, n' come hither to draw.
21 shall n' in this mountain, nor yet
5:37 n' heard his voice at any time, nor
6:24 was not there, n' his disciples,
7: 5 n' did his brethren believe in him.
8:11 N' do I condemn thee: go, and sin
19 Ye n' know me, nor my Father: if
42 n' came I of myself, but he sent
9: 3 N' hath this man sinned, nor his
10:28 n' shall any man pluck them
13:16 n' he that is sent greater than he
14:17 it seeth him not, n' knoweth him:
27 be troubled, n' let it be afraid.
17:20 N' pray I for these alone, but for
Ac 2:27 n' wilt thou suffer thine Holy One
31 n' his flesh did see corruption.
4:12 N' is there salvation in any
32 n' said any of them that ought of
34 N' was there any among them
8:21 Thou hast n' part nor lot in this
9: 9 sight, and n' did eat nor drink.
15:10 n' our fathers nor we were able to
Ac 16:21 us to receive, n' to observe, being
17:25 N' is worshipped with men's
19:37 which are n' robbers of churches,
20:24 n' count I my life dear unto
21:21 n' to walk after the customs.
23: 8 resurrection, n' angel, nor spirit:
12 they would n' eat nor drink till
21 they will n' eat nor drink till they
24:12 they n' found me in the temple
12 any man, n' raising up the people,
12 n' in the synagogue, nor in the
13 N' can they prove the things
18 in the temple, n' with multitude,
25: 8 N' against the law of the Jews,
8 n' against the temple, nor yet
27:20 when n' sun nor stars in many
28:21 We n' received letters out of Judæa
21 n' any of the brethren that came
Ro 1:21 him not as God, n' were thankful;
2:28 n' is that circumcision, which is
4:19 n' yet the deadness of Sarah's womb:
6:13 N' yield ye your members as
8: 7 to the law of God, n' indeed can be.
38 n' death, nor life, nor angels, nor
9: 7 N', because they are the seed of
11 n' having done any good or evil,
14:21 It is good n' to eat flesh, nor to
1Co 2: 9 n' have entered into the heart
14 n' can he know them, because
3: 2 bear it, n' yet now are ye able.
7 n' is he that planteth any thing,
7 n' he that watereth; but God that
5: 8 n' with the leaven of malice and
6: 9 n' fornicators, nor idolaters, nor
8: 8 for n', if we eat, are we the better;
8 n', if we eat not, are we the worse.
9:15 n' have I written these things, that it
10: 7 N' be ye idolaters, as were some
8 N' let us commit fornication, as
9 N' let us tempt Christ, as some of
10 N' murmur ye, as some of them
32 n' to the Jews, nor to the Gentiles,
11: 9 N' was the man created for
11 n' is the man without the woman,
11 n' the woman without the man,
16 custom, n' the churches of God.
15:50 of God; n' doth corruption inherit
Ga 1: 1 n' by man, but by Jesus Christ, and
12 For I n' received it of man,
12 n' was I taught it, but by the Lord
17 N' went I up to Jerusalem to them
2: 3 N' Titus, who was with me, being a
3:28 There is n' Jew nor Greek, there
28 there is n' bond nor free, there is
28 there is n' male nor female: for ye
5: 6 n' circumcision availeth any thing,
6:13 For n' they themselves who are
15 n' circumcision availeth any thing,
Eph 4:27 N' give place to the devil.
5: 4 N' filthiness, nor foolish
6: 9 n' is there respect of persons
Ph'p 2:16 run in vain, n' laboured in vain.
Col 3:11 Where there is n' Greek nor Jew,
1Th 2: 5 n' at any time used we flattering
6 glory, n' of you, nor yet of others,
2Th 2: 2 n' by spirit, nor by word, nor by
3: 8 N' did we eat any man's bread for
10 would not work, n' should he eat.
1Ti 1: 4 N' give heed to fables and endless
7 understanding n' what they say,
5:22 n' be partaker of other men's sins:
Heb 4:13 N' is there any creature that
7: 3 n' beginning of days, nor end of
9:12 N' by the blood of goats and
18 n' the first testament was dedicated
10: 8 not, n' hadst pleasure therein;
Jas 1:13 evil, n' tempteth he any man:
17 variableness, n' shadow of turning.
5:12 brethren, swear not, n' by heaven,
12 n' by earth, n' by any other oath:
1Pe 2:22 n' was guile found in his mouth:
3:14 of their terror, n' be troubled;
5: 3 N' as being lords over God's
2Pe 1: 8 shall n' be barren nor unfruitful
1Jo 2:15 n' the things that are in the world.
3: 6 hath not seen him, n' known him.
10 God, n' he that loveth not his brother.
18 us not love in word, n' in tongue;
2Jo 10 your house, n' bid him God speed:
3Jo 10 n' doth he himself receive the
Re 3:15 works, that thou art n' cold nor hot:
16 art lukewarm, and n' cold nor hot.
5: 3 nor in earth, n' under the earth,
3 to open the book, n' to look thereon.
4 read the book, n' to look thereon.
7: 3 Hurt not the earth, n' the sea, nor
16 no more, n' thirst any more;
16 n' shall the sun light on them, nor
9: 4 n' any green thing, n' any tree; but
20 which n' can see, nor hear, nor
21 N' repented they of their
12: 8 n' was there place found any more
20: 4 worshipped the beast, n' his image,
4 n'...received his mark upon
21: 4 more death, n' sorrow, nor crying,
4 n' shall there be any more pain: for
23 sun, n' of the moon, to shine in it:
27 n' whatsoever worketh abomination,
22: 5 need no candle, n' light of the sun;

Nekeb (*ne'-keb*)
Jos 19:33 N', and Jabneel, unto Lakum;

Nekoda (*ne-ko'-dah*)
Ezr 2:48 of Rezin, the children of N',
60 children of N', six hundred fifty

Ne 7:50 of Rezin, the children of *N*·.
62 children of *N*·, six hundred forty

Nemuel (*ne-mu'-el*) See also JEMUEL; NEMUELITES.
Nu 26: 9 sons of Eliab; *N*·, and Dathan,
12 of *N*·, the family of the Nemuelites:
1Ch 4:24 sons of Simeon were, *N*· and Jamin,

Nemuelites (*ne-mu'-el-ites*)
Nu 26:12 of Nemuel, the family of the *N*·:

Nepheg (*ne'-feg*)
Ex 6:21 sons of Izhar; Korah, and *N*·, and
2Sa 5:15 Ibhar also, and Elishua, and *N*·,
1Ch 3: 7 And Nogah, and *N*·, and Japhia,
14: 6 And Nogah, and *N*·, and Japhia,

nephew See also NEPHEWS.
Job 18:19 neither have son nor *n*· among
Isa 14:22 and son, and *n*·, saith the Lord.

nephews
J'g 12:14 he had forty sons and thirty *n*·,
1Ti 5: 4 if any widow have children or *n*·,

Nephish (*ne'-fish*) See also NAPHISH.
1Ch 5:19 Hagarites, with Jetur, and *N*·,

Nephishesim (*ne-fish'-e-sim*) See also NEPHUSIM.
Ne 7:52 of Meunim, the children of *N*·,

Nephthalim (*nef'-tha-lim*) See also NAPHTALI.
M't 4:13 in the borders of Zabulon and *N*·:
15 and the land of *N*·, by the way of
Re 7: 6 *N*· were sealed twelve thousand.

Nephtoah (*nef-to'-ah*)
Jos 15: 9 the fountain of the water of *N*·,
18:15 went out to the well of waters of *N*·:

Nephusim (*ne-fu'-sim*) See also NEPHISHESIM.
Ezr 2:50 of Mehunim, the children of *N*·,

Ner (*nur*)
1Sa 14:50 Abner, the son of *N*·, Saul's uncle.
51 *N*· the father of Abner was the son
26: 5 Abner the son *N*·, the captain of
14 and to Abner the son of *N*·, saying,
2Sa 2: 8 Abner the son of *N*·, captain of
12 And Abner the son of *N*·, and the
3:23 son of *N*· came to the king, and he
25 Thou knowest Abner the son of *N*·,
28 the blood of Abner the son of *N*·:
37 king to slay Abner the son of *N*·.
1Ki 2: 5 unto Abner the son of *N*·, and unto
32 Abner the son of *N*·, captain of the
1Ch 8:33 *N*· begat Kish, and Kish begat Saul,
9:36 Kish, and Baal, and *N*·, and Nadab,
39 *N*· begat Kish; and Kish begat
26:28 and Abner the son of *N*·, and Joab

Nereus (*ne'-re-us*)
Ro 16:15 Salute Philologus, and Julia, *N*·,

Nergal (*nur'-gal*) See also NERGAL-SHAREZER.
2Ki 17:30 and the men of Cuth made *N*·, and

Nergal-sharezer (*nur''-gal-sha-re'-zur*)
Jer 39: 3 sat in the middle gate, even *N*·,
3 *N*·, Rab-mag, with all the residue
13 *N*·, Rab-mag, and all the king of

Neri (*ne'-ri*)
Lu 3:27 Salathiel, which was the son of *N*·,

Neriah (*ne-ri'-ah*)
Jer 32:12, 16 unto Baruch the son of *N*·,
36: 4 called Baruch the son of *N*·: and
8 Baruch the son of *N*· did according
14 the son of *N*· took the roll in his
32 to Baruch the scribe, the son of *N*·;
43: 3 son of *N*· setteth thee on against us,
6 prophet, and Baruch the son of *N*·.
45: 1 spake unto Baruch the son of *N*·,
51:59 commanded Seraiah the son of *N*·,

Nero (*ne'-ro*)
2Ti *subscr.* when Paul was brought before *N*·

nest See also NESTS.
Nu 24:21 and thou puttest thy *n*· in a rock.
Du 22: 6 If a bird's *n*· chance to be before
32:11 As an eagle stirreth up her *n*·,
Job 29:18 Then I said, I shall die in my *n*·,
39:27 command, and make her *n*· on high?
Ps 84: 3 the swallow a *n*· for herself, where
Pr 27: 8 a bird that wandereth from her *n*·,
Isa 10:14 as a *n*· the riches of the people:
16: 2 a wandering bird cast out of the *n*·,
34:15 shall the great owl make her *n*·,
Jer 22:23 that makest thy *n*· in the cedars,
48:28 like the dove that maketh her *n*· in
49:16 make thy *n*· as high as the eagle,
Ob 4 thou set thy *n*· among the stars,
Hab 2: 9 that he may set his *n*· on high, that

nests
Ps 104:17 Where the birds make their *n*·: as
Eze 31: 6 heaven made their *n*· in his boughs,
M't 8:20 and the birds of the air have *n*·;
Lu 9:58 holes, and birds of the air have *n*·;

net See also NETS; NETWORK.
Ex 27: 4 upon the *n*· shalt thou make four
5 the *n*· may be even to the midst of
Job 18: 8 he is cast into a *n*· by his own feet,
19: 6 hath compassed me with his *n*·.
Ps 9:15 in the *n*· which they hid is their
10: 9 when he draweth him into his *n*·.
25:15 he shall pluck my feet out of the *n*·.
31: 4 me out of the *n*· that they have laid
35: 7 they hid for me their *n*· in a pit,
8 *n*· that he hath hid catch himself:
57: 6 have prepared a *n*· for my steps;
66:11 Thou broughtest us into the *n*·;
140: 5 have spread a *n*· by the wayside;
Pr 1:17 *n*· is spread in the sight of any bird.
12:12 wicked desireth the *n*· of evil men:
29: 5 spreadeth a *n*· for his feet.
Ec 9:12 fishes that are taken in an evil *n*·,
Isa 51:20 the streets, as a wild bull in a *n*·:
La 1:13 he hath spread a *n*· for my feet, he
Eze 12:13 My *n*· also will I spread upon him,
17:20 And I will spread my *n*· upon him,
19: 8 and spread their *n*· over him: he
32: 3 I will therefore spread out my *n*·
3 they shall bring thee up in my *n*·.
Ho 5: 1 and a *n*· spread upon Tabor.
7:12 go, I will spread my *n*· upon them;
Mic 7: 2 every man his brother with a *n*·.
Hab 1:15 they catch them in their *n*·, and
16 they sacrifice unto their *n*·, and
17 Shall they therefore empty their *n*·,
M't 4:18 brother, casting a *n*· into the sea:
13:47 the kingdom of heaven is like a *n*·,
M'r 1:16 brother, casting a *n*· into the sea:
Lu 5: 5 at thy word I will let down the *n*·.
6 of fishes: and their *n*· break.
Joh 21: 6 Cast the *n*· on the right side of the
8 cubits,) dragging the *n*· with fishes.
11 drew the *n*· to the land full of fishes,
11 many, yet was not the *n*· broken.

Nethaneel (*ne-than'-e-el*)
Nu 1: 8 of Issachar; *N*· the son of Zuar.
2: 5 *N*· the son of Zuar shall be captain
7:18 the second day *N*· the son of Zuar,
23 the offering of *N*· the son of Zuar.
10:15 Issachar was *N*· the son of Zuar.
1Ch 2:14 *N*· the fourth, Raddai the fifth,
15:24 *N*·, and Amasai, and Zechariah,
24: 6 Shemaiah the son of *N*· the scribe,
26: 4 Sacar the fourth, and *N*· the fifth,
2Ch 17: 7 to *N*·, and to Michaiah, to teach in
35: 9 and Shemaiah and *N*·, his brethren,
Ezr 10:22 Ishmael, *N*·, Jozabad, and Elasah.
Ne 12:21 Hashabiah; of Jedaiah, *N*·.
36 *N*·, and Judah, Hanani, with the

Nethaniah (*neth-a-ni'-ah*)
2Ki 25:23 even Ishmael the son of *N*·, and
25 month, that Ishmael the son of *N*·,
1Ch 25: 2 and *N*·, and Asarelah, the sons of
12 The fifth to *N*·, he, his sons, and
2Ch 17: 8 Levites, even Shemaiah, and *N*·,
Jer 36:14 princes sent Jehudi the son of *N*·,
40: 8 Mizpah, even Ishmael the son of *N*·,
14 Ishmael the son of *N*· to slay thee?
15 I will slay Ishmael the son of *N*·,
41: 1 Ishmael the son of *N*· the son of
2 arose Ishmael the son *N*·, and the
6 Ishmael the son of *N*· went forth
7 Ishmael the son of *N*· slew them,
9 Ishmael the son of *N*· filled it with
10 Ishmael the son of *N*· carried them
11 Ishmael the son of *N*· had done,
12 to fight with Ishmael the son of *N*·,
15 But Ishmael the son of *N*· escaped
16 from Ishmael the son of *N*·, from
18 the son of *N*· had slain Gedaliah

nether See also NETHERMOST.
Ex 19:17 stood at the *n*· part of the mount.
De 24: 6 take the *n*· or the upper millstone
Jos 15:19 upper springs, and the *n*· springs.
16: 3 the coast of Beth-horon the *n*·,
18:13 the south side of the *n*· Beth-horon.
J'g 1:15 upper springs and the *n*· springs.
1Ki 9:17 Gezer, and Beth-horon the *n*·,
1Ch 7:24 who built Beth-horon the *n*·, and
2Ch 8: 5 the upper, and Beth-horon the *n*·,
Job 41:24 hard as a piece of the *n*· millstone.
Eze 31:14 death, to the *n*· parts of the earth,
16 in the *n*· parts of the earth.
18 Eden unto the *n*· parts of the earth:
32:18 unto the *n*· parts of the earth, with
24 into the *n*· parts of the earth, which

nethermost
1Ki 6: 6 *n*· chamber was five cubits broad,

Nethinims (*neth'-in-ims*)
1Ch 9: 2 the priests, Levites, and the *N*·.
Ezr 2:43 The *N*·: the children of Ziha, the
58 All the *N*·, and the children of
70 and the *N*·, dwelt in their cities,
7: 7 and the *N*·, unto Jerusalem, in the
24 *N*·, or ministers of this house of
8:17 his brethren the *N*·, at the place
20 Also of the *N*·, whom David and
20 two hundred and twenty *N*·: all
Ne 3:26 Moreover the *N*· dwelt in Ophel,
31 Malchiah...unto the place of the *N*·,
7:46 The *N*·: the children of Ziha, the
60 All the *N*·, and the children of
73 people, and the *N*·, and all Israel,
10:28 the porters, the singers, the *N*·,
11: 3 and the *N*·, and the children of
21 But the *N*· dwelt in Ophel: and
21 Ziha and Gispa were over the *N*·.

Netophah (*ne-to'-fah*) See also NETOPHATHITE.
Ezr 2:22 The men of *N*·, fifty and six.
Ne 7:26 The men of Beth-lehem and *N*·,

Netophathi (*ne-to'-fa-thi*) See also NETOPHATHITE.
Ne 12:28 and from the village of *N*·;

Netophathite (*ne-to'-fa-thite*) See also NETOPHATHI; NETOPHATHITES.
2Sa 23:28 the Ahohite, Maharai the *N*·,
29 Heleb the son of Baanah, a *N*·,
2Ki 25:23 the son of Tanhumeth the *N*·,
1Ch 11:30 Maharai the *N*·, Heled the son
30 Heled the son of Baanah the *N*·,
1Ch 27:13 tenth month was Maharai the *N*·,
15 twelfth month was Heldai the *N*·,
Jer 40: 8 sons of Ephai the *N*·, and Jezaniah

Netophathites (*ne-to'-fa-thites*)
1Ch 2:54 of Salma; Beth-lehem, and the *N*·,
9:16 dwelt in the villages of the *N*·.

nets
1Ki 7:17 *n*· of checker work, and wreaths
Ps 141:10 the wicked fall into their own *n*·,
Ec 7:26 whose heart is snares and *n*·, and
Isa 19: 8 that spread *n*· upon the waters
Eze 26: 5 be a place for the spreading of *n*·
14 shalt be a place to spread *n*· upon;
47:10 shall be a place to spread forth *n*·;
M't 4:20 they straightway left their *n*·, and
21 their father, mending their *n*·; and
M'r 1:18 straightway they forsook their *n*·,
19 were in the ship mending their *n*·.
Lu 5: 2 them, and were washing their *n*·.
4 and let down your *n*· for a draught.

nettles
Job 30: 7 under the *n*· they were gathered
Pr 24:31 *n*· have covered the face thereof,
Isa 34:13 *n*· and brambles in the fortresses
Ho 9: 6 their silver, *n*· shall possess them:
Zep 2: 9 the breeding of *n*·, and saltpits,

network See also NETWORKS.
Ex 27: 4 for it a grate of *n*· of brass;
38: 4 for the altar a brasen grate of *n*·,
1Ki 7:18 rows round about upon the one *n*·,
20 the belly which was by the *n*·: and
42 rows of pomegranates for one *n*·,
Jer 52:22 *n*· and pomegranates upon the
23 all the pomegranates upon the *n*·

networks
1Ki 7:41 the two *n*·, to cover the two bowls
42 pomegranates for the two *n*·, even
Isa 19: 9 and they that weave *n*·, shall be

never^ See also NEVERTHELESS.
Ge 34:12 Ask me *n*· so much dowry and gift,
41:19 such as I *n*· saw in all the land of
Le 6:13 upon the altar; it shall *n*· go out.
Nu 19: 2 and upon which *n*· came yoke:
De 15:11 poor shall *n*· cease out of the land:
J'g 2: 1 *n*· break my covenant with
14: 3 *n*· a woman among the daughters
16: 7 green withs that were *n*· dried,
11 new ropes that were *n*· occupied,
2Sa 12:10 sword shall *n*· depart
2Ch 18: 7 he *n*· prophesied good unto me,
Job 3:16 as infants which *n*· saw light.
9:30 and make my hands *n*· so clean;
21:25 soul, and *n*· eateth with pleasure.
Ps 10: 6 for I shall *n*· be in adversity.
11 his face; he will *n*· see it.
15: 5 these things shall *n*· be moved.
30: 6 I said, I shall *n*· be moved.
31: 1 let me *n*· be ashamed:
49:19 they shall *n*· see light.
55:22 *n*· suffer the righteous to be
58: 5 of charmers, charming *n*· so wisely.
71: 1 trust: let me *n*· be put to
119:93 I will *n*· forget thy precepts:
Pr 10:30 righteous shall *n*· be removed:
27:20 Hell and destruction are *n*· full;
20 the eyes of man are *n*· satisfied.
30:15 three things that are *n*· satisfied,
Isa 13:20 It shall *n*· be inhabited,
14:20 seed of evildoers shall *n*· be
25: 2 be no city; it shall *n*· be built.
56:11 dogs which can *n*· have enough,
62: 6 shall *n*· hold their peace day nor
63:19 thou *n*· barest rule over them;
Jer 33:17 shall *n*· want a man to sit upon
Eze 16:63 and *n*· open thy mouth any more
26:21 shalt thou *n*· be found again,
27:36 and *n*· shalt be any more.
28:19 and *n*· shalt thou be any
Da 2:44 which shall *n*· be destroyed:
12: 1 such as *n*· was since there was a
Joe 2:26, 27 and my people shall *n*· be
Am 8: 7 *n*· forget any of their works.
14 shall fall, and *n*· rise up again.
Hab 1: 4 judgment doth *n*· go forth:
M't 7:23 I *n*· knew you: depart from me,
9:33 saying, It was *n*· so seen in Israel.
21:16 have ye *n*· read, Out of the mouth
42 Did ye *n*· read in the scriptures,
26:33 of thee, yet I will *n*· be offended.
27:14 answered him to *n*· a word;
M'r 2:12 We *n*· saw it on this fashion.
25 Have ye *n*· read what David did,
3:29 hath *n*· forgiveness,
9:43, 45 fire that *n*· shall be quenched:
11: 2 colt tied, whereon *n*· man sat;
14:21 that man if he had *n*· been born.
Lu 15:29 and yet thou *n*· gavest me a kid,
19:30 tied, whereon yet *n*· man sat:
23:29 and the wombs that *n*· bare,
29 and the paps which *n*· gave suck.
53 wherein *n*· man before was laid.
Joh 4:14 give...shall *n*· thirst;
6:35 that cometh to me shall *n*· hunger;
35 believeth on me shall *n*· thirst.
7:15 man letters, having *n*· learned?
46 *N*· man spake like this man.
8:33 *n*· in bondage to any man:
51 saying,...shall *n*· see
52 shall *n*· taste of death.
10:28 shall *n*· perish, neither
11:26 believeth in me shall *n*·
13: 8 Thou shalt *n*· wash my
19:41 wherein was *n*· man yet laid.
Ac 10:14 *n*· eaten any thing that is common

Ac 14: 8 mother's womb, who *n'* had walked:
1Co 13: 8 Charity *n'* faileth: but whether
2Ti 3: 7 *n'* able to come to the knowledge
Heb 10: 1 can *n'* with those sacrifices which
11 which can *n'* take away sins:
13: 5 I will *n'* leave thee, nor forsake
2Pe 1: 10 these things, ye shall *n'* fall:

nevertheless
Ex 32: 34 *N'* in the day when I visit I will
Le 11: 4 *N'* these shall ye not eat of them
36 *N'* a fountain or pit, wherein there
Nu 13: 28 *N'* the people be strong that dwell
14: 44 *n'* the ark of the covenant of the
18: 15 *n'* the firstborn of man shalt thou
24: 22 *N'* the Kenite shall be wasted,
31: 23 *n'* it shall be purified with the
De 14: 7 *N'* these ye shall not eat of them
23: 5 *N'* the Lord thy God would not
Jos 13: 13 *N'* the children of Israel expelled not
14: 8 *N'* my brethren that went up with
J'g 1: 33 *n'* the inhabitants of Beth-shemesh
2: 16 *N'* the Lord raised up judges, which
1Sa 8: 19 *N'* the people refused to obey the
15: 35 *n'* Samuel mourned for Saul: and
20: 26 *N'* Saul spake not any thing that
29: 6 day: *n'* the lords favour thee not.
2Sa 5: 7 *N'* David took the strong hold of
17: 18 *N'* a lad saw them, and told Absalom:
23: 16 *n'* he would not drink thereof,
1Ki 8: 19 *N'* thou shalt not build the house;
15: 4 *N'* for David's sake did the Lord
14 *n'* Asa's heart was perfect with
23 *N'* in the time of his old age he
22: 43 *n'* the high places were not taken
2Ki 2: 10 *n'*, if thou see me when I am taken
3: 3 *N'* he cleaved unto the sins of
13: 6 *N'* they departed not from the sins
23: 9 *N'* the priests of the high places
1Ch 11: 5 *N'* David took the castle of Zion,
21: 4 *N'* the king's word prevailed against
2Ch 12: 8 *N'* they shall be his servants;
15: 17 *n'* the heart of Asa was perfect all
19: 3 *N'* there are good things found in
30: 11 *N'* divers of Asher and Manasseh
33: 17 *N'* the people did sacrifice still in
35: 22 *N'* Josiah would not turn his face
Ne 4: 9 *N'* we made our prayer unto our God,
9: 26 *N'* they were disobedient, and
31 *N'* for thy great mercies' sake thou
13: 26 *n'* even him did outlandish women
Es 5: 10 *N'* Haman refrained himself: and
Ps 31: 22 *n'* thou heardest the voice of my
49: 12 *N'* man being in honour abideth
73: 23 *N'* I am continually with thee:
78: 36 *N'* they did flatter him with their
89: 33 *N'* my lovingkindness will I not
106: 8 *N'* he saved them for his name's
44 *N'* he regarded their affliction, when
Pr 19: 21 *n'* the counsel of the Lord, that
Ec 9: 16 *n'* the poor man's wisdom is despised,
Isa 9: 1 *N'* the dimness shall not be such
Jer 5: 18 *N'* in those days, saith the Lord,
26: 24 *N'* the hand of Ahikam the son of
28: 7 *N'* hear thou now this word that I
36: 25 *N'* Elnathan and Delaiah and
Eze 16: 60 *N'* I will remember my covenant
20: 17 *N'* mine eye spared them from
22 *N'* I withdrew mine hand, and
33: 9 *N'*, if thou warn the wicked of his
Da 4: 15 *N'* leave the stump of his roots in
Jon 1: 13 *N'* the men rowed hard to bring it to
M't 14: 9 *n'* for the oath's sake, and them
26: 39 *n'* not as I will, but as thou wilt.
64 *n'* I say unto you, Hereafter shall
M'r 14: 36 *n'* not what I will, but what thou
Lu 5: 5 *n'* at thy word I will let down the
13: 33 *N'* I must walk to day, and
18: 8 *N'* when the Son of man cometh,
22: 42 *n'* not my will, but thine, be done.
Joh 11: 15 may believe; *n'* let us go unto him.
12: 42 *N'* among the chief rulers
16: 7 *N'* I tell you the truth; It is
Ac 14: 17 *N'* he left not himself without
27: 11 *N'* the centurion believed the
Ro 5: 14 *N'* death reigned from Adam to
15: 15 *N'*, brethren, I have written the
1Co 7: 2 *N'*, to avoid fornication, let every
28 *N'* such shall have trouble in the
37 *N'* he that standeth stedfast in his
9: 12 *N'* we have not used this power;
11: 11 *N'* neither is the man without the
2Co 3: 16 *N'*, when it shall turn to the Lord,
7: 6 *N'* God, that comforteth those that
12: 16 *n'*, being crafty, I caught you with
Ga 2: 20 *n'* I live; yet not I, but Christ
4: 30 *N'* what saith the scripture? Cast
Eph 5: 33 *N'*, let every one of you...so love
Ph'p 1: 24 *N'* to abide in the flesh is more
3: 16 *N'*, whereto we have already
2Ti 1: 12 *n'* I am not ashamed: for I know
2: 19 *N'* the foundation of God standeth
Heb 12: 11 *n'* afterward it yieldeth the
2Pe 3: 13 *N'* we, according to his promise,
Re 2: 4 *N'* I have somewhat against thee,

new See also NEWBORN; NEWS; RENEW.
Ex 1: 8 arose up a *n'* king over Egypt,
Le 23: 16 a *n'* meat offering unto the Lord.
26: 10 forth the old because of the *n'*.
Nu 16: 30 But if the Lord make a *n'* thing,
28: 26 a *n'* meat offering unto the Lord,
De 20: 5 is there that hath built a *n'* house,
22: 8 When thou buildest a *n'* house,
24: 5 When a man hath taken a *n'* wife,
32: 17 not, to *n'* gods that came newly up,
Jos 9: 13 of wine, which we filled, were *n'*;
J'g 5: 8 They chose *n'* gods; then was war
15: 13 they bound him with two *n'* cords,
15 he found a *n'* jawbone of an ass,
16: 11 If they bind me fast with *n'* ropes
12 Delilah therefore took *n'* ropes,
1Sa 6: 7 Now therefore make a *n'* cart, and
20: 5 Behold, to morrow is the *n'* moon,
18 To morrow is the *n'* moon: and
24 and when the *n'* moon was come,
2Sa 6: 3 set the ark of God upon a *n'* cart,
3 sons of Abinadab, drave the *n'* cart.
21: 16 he being girded with a *n'* sword,
1Ki 11: 29 had clad himself with a *n'* garment;
30 Ahijah caught the *n'* garment that
2Ki 2: 20 Bring me a *n'* cruse, and put salt
4: 23 it is neither *n'* moon, nor sabbath.
1Ch 13: 7 carried the ark of God in a *n'* cart
23: 31 in the *n'* moons, and on the set
2Ch 2: 4 on the *n'* moons, and on the solemn
8: 13 on the *n'* moons, and on the solemn
20: 5 of the Lord, before the *n'* court,
31: 3 and for the *n'* moons, and for the
Ezr 3: 5 offering, both of the *n'* moons, and
6: 4 stones, and a row of *n'* timber:
Ne 10: 33 of the sabbaths, of the *n'* moons,
39 offering of the corn, of the *n'* wine,
13: 5 the tithes of the corn, the *n'* wine,
12 tithe of the corn and the *n'* wine
Job 32: 19 it is ready to burst like *n'* bottles.
Ps 33: 3 Sing unto him a *n'* song; play
40: 3 hath put a *n'* song in my mouth,
81: 3 up the trumpet in the *n'* moon,
96: 1 O sing unto the Lord a *n'* song:
98: 1 O sing unto the Lord a *n'* song; for
144: 9 I will sing a *n'* song unto thee, O
149: 1 Sing unto the Lord a *n'* song, and
Pr 3: 10 presses...burst out with *n'* wine.
Ec 1: 9 there is no *n'* thing under the sun.
10 it may be said, See, this is *n'*? it
Ca 7: 13 of pleasant fruits, *n'* and old, which
Isa 1: 13 the *n'* moons and sabbaths, the
14 Your *n'* moons and your appointed
24: 7 The *n'* wine mourneth, the vine
41: 15 a *n'* sharp threshing instrument
42: 9 to pass, and *n'* things do I declare:
10 Sing unto the Lord a *n'* song, and
43: 19 Behold, I will do a *n'* thing; now it
48: 6 shewed thee *n'* things from this
62: 2 thou shalt be called by a *n'* name,
65: 8 the *n'* wine is found in the cluster,
17 create *n'* heavens and a *n'* earth:
66: 22 as the *n'* heavens and the *n'* earth,
23 that from one *n'* moon to another,
Jer 26: 10 down in the entry of the *n'* gate
31: 22 hath created a *n'* thing in the earth,
31 I will make a *n'* covenant with the
36: 10 at the entry of the *n'* gate of the
La 3: 23 They are *n'* every morning: great
Eze 11: 19 I will put a *n'* spirit within you;
18: 31 make you a *n'* heart and a *n'* spirit:
36: 26 A *n'* heart also will I give you, and
26 a *n'* spirit will I put within you:
45: 17 in the feasts, and in the *n'* moons,
46: 1 day of the *n'* moon it shall be opened.
3 the sabbaths and in the *n'* moons.
6 in the day of the *n'* moon it shall be
47: 12 shall bring forth *n'* fruit according
Ho 2: 11 her feast days, her *n'* moons, and
4: 11 and *n'* wine take away the heart.
9: 2 and the *n'* wine shall fail in her.
Joe 1: 5 because of the *n'* wine; for it is cut
10 the *n'* wine is dried up, the oil
3: 18 mountains shall drop down *n* wine,
Am 8: 5 When will the *n'* moon be gone,
Hag 1: 11 upon the *n'* wine,...upon the oil,
Zec 9: 17 cheerful, and *n'* wine the maids.
M't 9: 16 of *n'* cloth unto an old garment, for
17 men put *n'* wine into old bottles:
17 they put *n'* wine into...bottles,
17 they put...wine into *n'* bottles,
13: 52 of his treasure things *n'* and old.
26: 28 this is my blood of the *n'* testament,
29 that day when I drink it *n'* with you
27: 60 And laid it in his own *n'* tomb, which
M'r 1: 27 is this? What *n'* doctrine is this?
2: 21 piece of *n'* cloth on an old garment:
21 else the *n'* piece that filled it up
22 putteth *n'* wine into old bottles:
22 else the *n'* wine doth burst...bottles,
22 *n'* wine must be put into...bottles,
22 wine must be put into *n'* bottles.
14: 24 is my blood of the *n'* testament,
25 I drink it *n'* in the kingdom of God.
16: 17 they shall speak with *n'* tongues;
Lu 5: 36 piece of a *n'* garment upon an old;
36 then both the *n'* maketh a rent, and
36 of the *n'* agreeth not with the old.
37 putteth *n'* wine into old bottles;
37 else the *n'* wine will burst...bottles,
38 *n'* wine must be put into...bottles;
38 wine must be put into *n'* bottles;
39 old wine straightway desireth *n'*:
22: 20 This cup is the *n'* testament in my
Joh 13: 34 A *n'* commandment I give unto you,
19: 41 and in the garden a *n'* sepulchre,
Ac 2: 13 These men are full of *n'* wine.
17: 19 we know what this *n'* doctrine,
21 to tell, or to hear some *n'* thing.)
1Co 5: 7 that ye may be a *n'* lump, as ye
11: 25 This cup is the *n'* testament in my
2Co 3: 6 able ministers of the *n'* testament;
5: 17 be in Christ, he is a *n'* creature:
17 behold, all things are become *n'*.
Ga 6: 15 uncircumcision, but a *n'* creature.
Eph 2: 15 in himself of twain one *n'* man,
4: 24 that ye put on the *n'* man, which
Col 2: 16 or of the *n'* moon, or of the sabbath
3: 10 have put on the *n'* man, which is
Heb 8: 8 I will make a *n'* covenant with the
13 A *n'* covenant, he hath made the
9: 15 the mediator of the *n'* testament,
10: 20 By a *n'* and living way, which he
12: 24 the mediator of the *n'* covenant,
2Pe 3: 13 look for *n'* heavens and a *n'* earth,
1Jo 2: 7 I write no *n'* commandment unto
8 *n'* commandment I write unto you,
2Jo 5 I wrote a *n'* commandment unto
Re 2: 17 and in the stone a *n'* name written,
3: 12 city of my God,...is *n'* Jerusalem,
12 I will write upon him my *n'* name.
5: 9 they sung a *n'* song, saying, Thou
14: 3 And they sung as it were a *n'* song
21: 1 I saw a *n'* heaven and a *n'* earth:
2 I...saw the holy city, *n'* Jerusalem,
5 said, Behold, I make all things *n'*.

newborn
1Pe 2: 2 As *n'* babes, desire the sincere

newly
De 32: 17 new gods that came *n'* up, whom
J'g 7: 19 they had but *n'* set the watch:

new-moon See NEW and MOON.

newness
Ro 6: 4 we also should walk in *n'* of life.
7: 6 that we should serve in *n'* of spirit,

news
Pr 25: 25 so is good *n'* from a far country.

next
Ge 17: 21 thee at this set time in the *n'* year.
Ex 12: 4 his neighbour *n'* unto his house
Nu 2: 5 those that do pitch *n'* unto him shall
11: 32 all that night, and all the *n'* day,
27: 11 his kinsman that is *n'* to him of
De 21: 3 city which is *n'* unto the slain man,
6 city, that are *n'* unto the slain man,
Ru 2: 20 of kin unto us, one of our *n'* kinsmen.
1Sa 17: 13 *n'* unto him Abinadab, and the
23: 17 Israel, I shall be *n'* unto thee;
30: 17 unto the evening of the *n'* day:
2Ki 6: 29 I said unto her on the *n'* day, Give
1Ch 5: 12 Joel the chief,...Shapham the *n'*,
16: 5 the chief, and *n'* to him Zechariah,
2Ch 17: 15 And *n'* to him was Jehohanan
16 *n'* him was Amasiah the son of
18 And *n'* him was Jehozabad, and
28: 7 Elkanah that was *n'* to the king.
31: 12 and Shimei his brother was the *n'*.
15 and *n'* him were Eden, and
Ne 3: 2 *n'* unto him builded the men of
2 *n'* to them builded Zaccur the
4 *n'*...them repaired Meremoth
4 *n'*...them repaired Meshullam
4 *n'* unto them repaired Zadok
5 *n'* unto them the Tekoites
7 *n'* unto them repaired Melatiah
8 *N'* unto him repaired Uzziel the
8 *N'*...also repaired Hananiah
9 *n'*...them repaired Rephaiah
10 *n'* unto them repaired Jedaiah
10 *n'* unto him repaired Hattush
12 *n'* unto him repaired Shallum
17 *N'*...him repaired Hashabiah,
19 And *n'* to him repaired Ezer the
13: 13 *n'* to them was Hanan...son of
Es 1: 14 the *n'* unto him was Carshena,
10: 3 Jew was *n'* unto king Ahasuerus,
Jon 4: 7 when the morning rose the *n'* day,
M't 27: 62 Now the *n'* day, that followed the
M'r 1: 38 Let us go into the *n'* towns, that I
Lu 9: 37 that on the *n'* day, when they were
Joh 1: 29 *n'* day John seeth Jesus coming
35 the *n'* day after John stood, and
12: 12 On the *n'* day much people that
Ac 4: 3 put them in hold unto the *n'* day:
7: 26 the *n'* day he shewed himself unto
13: 42 preached to them the *n'* sabbath.
44 the *n'* sabbath day came almost
14: 20 *n'* day he departed with Barnabas
16: 11 Samothracia,...*n'* day to Neapolis;
20: 15 came the *n'* day over against Chios;
15 the *n'* day we arrived at Samos,
15 and the *n'* day we came to Miletus.
21: 8 the *n'* day we that were of Paul's
26 the *n'* day purifying himself with
25: 6 the *n'* day sitting on the judgment
27: 3 the *n'* day we touched at Sidon.
18 the *n'* day they lightened the ship;
28: 13 we came the *n'* day to Puteoli:

Neziah (*ne-zi'-ah*)
Ezr 2: 54 children of *N'*, the children of
Ne 7: 56 children of *N'*, the children of

Nezib (*ne'-zib*)
Jos 15: 43 Jiphtah, and Ashnah, and *N'*,

Nibhaz (*nib'-haz*)
2Ki 17: 31 the Avites made *N'* and Tartak,

Nibshan (*nib'-shan*)
Jos 15: 62 And *N'*, and the city of Salt, and

Nicanor (*ni-ca'-nor*)
Ac 6: 5 Prochorus, and *N'*, and Timon,

Nicodemus (*nic-o-de'-mus*)
Joh 3: 1 a man of the Pharisees, named *N'*,
4 *N'* saith unto him, How can a man
9 *N'* answered and said unto him,
7: 50 *N'* saith unto them, (he that came
19: 39 And there came also *N'*, which at

Nicolaitanes (*nic-o-la'-i-tans*)
Re 2: 6 thou hatest the deeds of the *N'*,
15 that hold the doctrine of the *N'*,

Nicolas (*nic'-o-las*)
Ac 6: 5 and *N*' a proselyte of Antioch:
Nicopolis (*ni-cop'-o-lis*)
Tit 3:12 diligent to come unto me to *N*':
subscr. Cretians, from *N*' of Macedonia.
Niger (*ni'-jur*) See also SIMEON.
Ac 13: 1 and Simeon that was called *N*',
nigh See also NEAR.
Ge 47:29 time drew *n*' that Israel must die:
Ex 3: 5 Draw not *n*' hither: put off thy
14:10 when Pharaoh drew *n*', the children
24: 2 Lord: but they shall not come *n*':
32:19 soon as he came *n*' unto the camp,
34:30 they were afraid to come *n*' him.
32 all the children of Israel came *n*':
Le 10: 3 be sanctified in them that come *n*'
21: 3 sister a virgin, that is *n*' unto him,
21 shall come *n*' to offer the offerings
21 not come *n*' to offer the bread of
23 nor come *n*' unto the altar, because
25:49 any that is *n*' of kin unto him of
Nu 1:51 stranger that cometh *n*' shall be
3:10, 38 stranger that cometh *n*' shall be
8:19 children of Israel come *n*' unto
18: 3 they shall not come *n*' the vessels
4 a stranger shall not come *n*' unto
7 stranger that cometh *n*' shall be
22 come *n*' the tabernacle of the
24:17 I shall behold him, but not *n*': there
De 1: 7 unto all the places *n*' thereunto,
2:19 when thou comest *n*' over against
4: 7 who hath God so *n*' unto them, as
13: 7 *n*' unto thee, or far off from thee,
20: 2 when ye are come *n*' unto the battle,
10 thou comest *n*' unto a city to fight
22: 2 if thy brother be not *n*' unto thee,
30:14 But the word is very *n*' unto thee,
Jos 8:11 went up, and drew *n*', and came
1Sa 17:48 came and drew *n*' to meet David,
2Sa 10:13 Joab drew *n*', and the people that
11:20 approached ye so *n*' unto the city
21 why went ye *n*' the wall? then say
15: 5 any man came *n*' to him to do him
1Ki 2: 1 the days of David drew *n*' that he
8:59 be *n*' unto the Lord our God day and
1Ch 12:40 Moreover they that were *n*' them,
19:14 drew *n*' before the Syrians unto
Es 9:20 king Ahasuerus, both *n*' and far,
Ps 32: 6 they shall not come *n*' unto him.
34:18 *n*' unto them that are of a broken
69:18 Draw *n*' unto my soul, and
73: 2 gone; my steps had well *n*' slipped.
85: 9 his salvation is *n*' them that fear
88: 3 my life draweth *n*' unto the grave.
91: 7 but it shall not come *n*' thee.
10 any plague come *n*' thy dwelling.
119:150 draw *n*' that follow after mischief:
145:18 *n*' unto all them that call upon him,
Pr 5: 8 come not *n*' the door of her house:
Ec 12: 1 nor the years draw *n*', when thou
Isa 5:19 of the Holy One of Israel draw *n*'
Joe 2: 1 Lord cometh, for it is *n*' at hand;
M't 15: 8 draweth *n*' unto me with their
29 came *n*' unto the sea of Galilee;
21: 1 when they drew *n*' unto Jerusalem,
24:32 ye know that summer is *n*':
M'r 2: 4 not come *n*' unto him for the press,
5:11 there was *n*' unto the mountains
21 him: and he was *n*' unto the sea.
11: 1 And when they came *n*' to Jerusalem,
13:29 come to pass, know that it is *n*',
Lu 7:12 when he came *n*' to the gate of
10: 9, 11 kingdom of God is come *n*' unto
15:25 as he came and drew *n*' to the house,
18:35 as he was come *n*' unto Jericho,
19:11 because he was *n*' to Jerusalem,
29 when he was come *n*' to Bethphage
37 when he was come *n*', even now at
21:20 that the desolation thereof is *n*'.
28 for your redemption draweth *n*'.
30 that summer is now *n*' at hand.
31 the kingdom of God is *n*' at hand.
22: 1 feast of unleavened bread drew *n*',
24:28 And they drew *n*' unto the village,
Joh 6: 4 a feast of the Jews, was *n*'.
19 sea, and drawing *n*' unto the ship:
23 *n*' unto the place where they did
11:18 Bethany was *n*' unto Jerusalem,
55 the Jews' passover was *n*' at hand:
19:20 Jesus was crucified...*n*' to the city:
42 for the sepulchre was *n*' at hand.
Ac 7:17 the time of the promise drew *n*',
9:38 as Lydda was *n*' to Joppa, and the
10: 9 drew *n*' unto the city, Peter went
22: 6 was come *n*' unto Damascus about
27: 8 *n*' whereunto was the city of Lasea.
Ro 10: 8 The word is *n*' thee, even in thy
Eph 2:13 are made *n*' by the blood of Christ.
17 afar off, and to them that were *n*'.
Ph'p 2:27 indeed he was sick *n*' unto death:
30 work of Christ he was *n*' unto death,
Heb 6: 8 rejected, and is *n*' unto cursing;
7:19 by the which we draw *n*' unto God.
Jas 4: 8 Draw *n*' to God, and he will draw *n*'
5: 8 the coming of the Lord draweth *n*'.
night^ See also MIDNIGHT; NIGHTS; YESTERNIGHT.
Ge 1: 5 and the darkness he called *N*'.
14 to divide the day from the *n*'; and
16 the lesser light to rule the *n*': he
18 to rule over the day and over the *n*',
8:22 and day and *n*' shall not cease.
14:15 he and his servants, by *n*', and smote
19: 2 tarry all *n*', and wash your feet, and ye
2 but we will abide in the street all *n*'.
Ge 19: 5 men which came in to thee this *n*'?
33 made their father drink wine that *n*':
34 make him drink wine this *n*' also;
35 made their father drink wine that *n*'
20: 3 came to Abimelech in a dream by *n*',
24:54 that were with him, and tarried all *n*';
26:24 appeared unto him the same *n*',
28:11 tarried there all *n*', because the sun
30:15 Therefore he shall lie with thee to *n*'
16 And he lay with her that *n*'.
31:24 Laban the Syrian in a dream by *n*',
39 stolen by day, or stolen by *n*'.
40 consumed me, and the frost by *n*';
54 bread, and tarried all *n*' in the mount.
32:13 And he lodged there that same *n*';
21 lodged that *n*' in the company.
22 he rose up that *n*', and took his two
40: 5 each man his dream in one *n*', each
41:11 And we dreamed a dream in one *n*',
46: 2 God spake...in the visions of the *n*',
49:27 and at *n*' he shall divide the spoil.
Ex 10:13 land all that day, and all that *n*';
12: 8 they shall eat the flesh in that *n*',
12 through the land of Egypt this *n*',
30 And Pharaoh rose up in the *n*', he,
31 called for Moses and Aaron by *n*',
42 It is a *n*' to be much observed unto
42 that *n*' of the Lord to be observed
13:21 by *n*' in a pillar of fire, to give
21 them light; to go by day and *n*':
22 by day, nor the pillar of fire by *n*',
14:20 it gave light by *n*' to these: so that
20 came not near the other all the *n*'.
21 by a strong east wind all that *n*',
40:38 and fire was on it by *n*', in the sight
Le 6: 9 the burning upon the altar all *n*'
20 morning, and half thereof at *n*'.
8:35 day and *n*' seven days, and keep
11:16 And the owl, and the *n*' hawk, and
19:13 abide with thee all *n*' until...morning.
Nu 9:16 and the appearance of fire by *n*'.
21 whether it was by day or by *n*' that
11: 9 dew fell upon the camp in the *n*',
32 up all that day, and all that *n*', and
14: 1 cried; and the people wept that *n*'.
14 cloud, and in a pillar of fire by *n*'.
22: 8 said unto them, Lodge here this *n*',
19 tarry ye also here this *n*', that I
20 And God came unto Balaam at *n*',
De 1:33 in fire by *n*', to shew you by what
14:15 the owl, and the *n*' hawk, and the
16: 1 thee forth out of Egypt by *n*'.
4 even, remain all *n*' until the morning.
21:23 shall not remain all *n*' upon the tree,
23:10 that chanceth him by *n*', then
28:66 and thou shalt fear day and *n*', and
Jos 1: 8 shalt meditate therein day and *n*',
2: 2 there came men in hither to *n*' of
4: 3 place, where ye shall lodge this *n*'.
8: 3 valour, and sent them away by *n*'.
9 Joshua lodged that *n*' among the
13 Joshua went that *n*' into the midst
10: 9 and went up from Gilgal all *n*'.
J'g 6:25 And it came to pass the same *n*',
27 do it by day, that he did it by *n*'.
40 And God did so that *n*': for it was
7: 9 And it came to pass the same *n*',
9:32 Now therefore up by *n*', thou and
34 people that were with him, by *n*',
16: 2 laid wait for him all *n*' in the gate
2 and were quiet all the *n*', saying,
19: 6 content, I pray thee, and tarry all *n*',
9 evening, I pray you tarry all *n*':
10 But the man would not tarry that *n*',
13 to one of these places to lodge all *n*',
25 and abused her all the *n*' until
20: 5 house round about upon me by *n*',
Ru 1:12 I should have an husband also to *n*',
3: 2 he winnoweth barley to *n*' in the
13 Tarry this *n*', and it shall be in
1Sa 14:34 every man his ox with him that *n*',
36 go down after the Philistines by *n*',
15:11 and he cried unto the Lord all *n*'.
16 the Lord hath said to me this *n*'.
19:10 and David fled, and escaped that *n*'.
11 If thou save not thy life to *n*', to
24 naked all that day and all that *n*'.
25:16 a wall unto us both by *n*' and day,
26: 7 Abishai came to the people by *n*':
28: 8 and they came to the woman by *n*':
20 no bread all the day, nor all the *n*'.
25 rose up, and went away that *n*'.
31:12 valiant men arose, and went all *n*',
2Sa 2:29 and his men walked all that *n*'
32 And Joab and his men went all *n*',
4: 7 them away through the plain all *n*'.
7: 4 And it came to pass that *n*', that
12:16 went in, and lay all *n*' upon the earth.
17: 1 and pursue after David this *n*':
16 Lodge not this *n*' in the plains of
19: 7 not tarry one with thee this *n*':
21:10 day, nor the beasts of the field by *n*'.
1Ki 3: 5 to Solomon in a dream by *n*': and
19 this woman's child died in the *n*';
8:29 open toward this house *n*' and day,
59 unto the Lord our God day and *n*',
2Ki 6:14 they came by *n*', and compassed
7:12 the king arose in the *n*', and said
8:21 and he arose by *n*', and smote the
19:35 it came to pass that *n*', that the
25: 4 all the men of war fled by *n*' by the
1Ch 9:33 employed in that work day and *n*'.
17: 3 it came to pass the same *n*', that
2Ch 1: 7 In that *n*' did God appear unto
6:20 open upon this house day and *n*',
7:12 Lord appeared to Solomon by *n*',
2Ch 21: 9 he rose up by *n*', and smote the
35:14 burnt offerings and the fat until *n*';
Ne 1: 6 I pray before thee now, day and *n*',
2:12 I arose in the *n*', I and some few
13 I went out by *n*' by the gate of the
15 went I up in the *n*' by the brook,
4: 9 a watch against them day and *n*',
22 in the *n*' they may be a guard to us,
6:10 in the *n*' will they come to slay
9:12 in the *n*' by a pillar of fire, to give
19 neither the pillar of fire by *n*', to
Es 4:16 eat nor drink three days, *n*' or day:
6: 1 On that *n*' could not the king sleep,
Job 3: 3 the *n*' in which it was said, There
6 As for that *n*', let darkness seize
7 let that *n*' be solitary, let no joyful
4:13 thoughts from the visions of the *n*',
5:14 grope in the noonday as in the *n*'.
7: 4 shall I arise, and the *n*' be gone?
17:12 They change the *n*' into day: the
20: 8 chased away as a vision of the *n*'.
24:14 needy, and in the *n*' is as a thief.
26:10 the day and *n*' come to an end.
27:20 stealeth him away in the *n*'.
29:19 the dew lay all *n*' upon my branch.
30:17 bones are pierced in me in the *n*'
33:15 In a dream, in a vision of the *n*',
34:25 and he overturneth them in the *n*',
35:10 maker, who giveth songs in the *n*';
36:20 Desire not the *n*', when people are
Ps 1: 2 law doth he meditate day and *n*'.
6: 6 all the *n*' make I my bed to swim;
16: 7 also instruct me in the *n*' seasons.
17: 3 thou hast visited me in the *n*'; thou
19: 2 and *n*' unto *n*' sheweth knowledge.
22: 2 and in the *n*' season, and am not
30: 5 weeping may endure for a *n*', but
32: 4 day and *n*' thy hand was heavy
42: 3 have been my meat day and *n*',
8 in the *n*' his song shall be with
55:10 Day and *n*' they go about it upon
74:16 day is thine, the *n*' also is thine:
77: 2 my sore ran in the *n*', and ceased
6 to remembrance my song in the *n*':
78:14 and all the *n*' with a light of fire.
88: 1 I have cried day and *n*' before thee:
90: 4 is past, and as a watch in the *n*'.
91: 5 not be afraid for the terror by *n*';
92: 2 and thy faithfulness every *n*',
104:20 Thou makest darkness, and it is *n*':
105:39 and fire to give light in the *n*'.
119:55 O Lord, in the *n*', and have kept
148 Mine eyes prevent the *n*' watches,
121: 6 thee by day, nor the moon by *n*'.
134: 1 which by *n*' stand in the house of
136: 9 The moon and stars to rule by *n*':
139:11 even the *n*' shall be light about me.
12 thee; but the *n*' shineth as the day:
Pr 7: 9 evening, in the black and dark *n*':
31:15 She riseth also while it is yet *n*',
18 her candle goeth not out by *n*'.
Ec 2:23 his heart taketh not rest in the *n*'.
8:16 neither day nor *n*' seeth sleep with
Ca 1:13 he shall lie all *n*' betwixt my breasts.
3: 1 By *n*' on my bed I sought him
8 his thigh because of fear in the *n*'.
5: 2 my locks with the drops of the *n*'.
Isa 4: 5 the shining of a flaming fire by *n*':
5:11 that continue until *n*', till wine
15: 1 in the *n*' Ar of Moab is laid waste,
1 in the *n*' Kir of Moab is laid waste,
16: 3 make thy shadow as the *n*' in the
21: 4 the *n*' of my pleasure hath he
11, 11 Watchman, what of the *n*'?
12 morning cometh, and also the *n*':
26: 9 soul have I desired thee in the *n*';
27: 3 hurt it, I will keep it *n*' and day.
28:19 it pass over, by day and by *n*':
29: 7 shall be as a dream of a *n*' vision.
30:29 Ye shall have a song, as in the *n*'
34:10 shall not be quenched *n*' nor day;
38:12, 13 from day even to *n*' wilt thou
59:10 stumble at noon day as in the *n*';
60:11 they shall not be shut day nor *n*';
62: 6 never hold their peace day nor *n*':
Jer 6: 5 Arise, and let us go by *n*', and let
9: 1 that I might weep day and *n*' for
14: 8 that turneth aside to tarry for a *n*'?
17 run down with tears *n*' and day,
16:13 shall ye serve other gods day and *n*';
31:35 and of the stars for a light by *n*',
33:20 and my covenant of the *n*', and that
20 not be day and *n*' in their seasons;
25 my covenant be not with day and *n*',
36:30 the heat, and in the *n*' to the frost.
39: 4 and went forth out of the city by *n*',
49: 9 if thieves by *n*', they will destroy
52: 7 went forth out of the city by *n*' by
La 1: 2 She weepeth sore in the *n*', and her
2:18 run down like a river day and *n*':
19 Arise, cry out in the *n*': in the
Da 2:19 revealed unto Daniel in a *n*' vision.
5:30 In that *n*' was Belshazzar the king
6:18 palace, and passed the *n*' fasting:
7: 2 I was in my vision by *n*', and,
7 After this I saw in the *n*' visions, and,
13 I saw in the *n*' visions, and, behold,
Ho 4: 5 also shall fall with thee in the *n*',
7: 6 their baker sleepeth all the *n*'; in
Joe 1:13 lie all *n*' in sackcloth, ye ministers of
Am 5: 8 and maketh the day dark with *n*':
Ob 5 thieves came to thee, if robbers by *n*',
Jon 4:10 up in a *n*', and perished in a *n*':
Mic 3: 6 Therefore *n*' shall be unto you,
Zec 1: 8 I saw by *n*', and behold a man
14: 7 not day, nor *n*': but it shall come

M't 2:14 young child and his mother by *n'*.
14:25 in the fourth watch of the *n'* Jesus
26:31 be offended because of me this *n'*:
34 That this *n'*, before the cock crow.
27:64 his disciples come by *n'*, and steal
28:13 Say ye, His disciples came by *n'*,
M'r 4:27 should sleep, and rise *n'* and day,
5: 5 always, *n'* and day, he was in the
6:48 about the fourth watch of the *n'* he
14:27 be offended because of me this *n'*:
30 thee, That this day, even in this *n'*,
Lu 2: 8 keeping watch over their flock by *n'*.
37 fastings and prayers *n'* and day.
5: 5 we have toiled all the *n'*, and have
6:12 continued all *n'* in prayer to God.
12:20 this *n'* thy soul shall be required
17:34 in that *n'* there shall be two men
18: 7 which cry day and *n'* unto him,
21:37 at *n'* he went out, and abode in the
Joh 3: 2 same came to Jesus by *n'*, and said
7:50 (he that came to Jesus by *n'*, being
9: 4 the *n'* cometh, when no man can
11:10 But if a man walk in the *n'*, he
13:30 immediately out: and it was *n'*.
19:39 at the first came to Jesus by *n'*, and
21: 3 and that *n'* they caught nothing.
Ac 5:19 angel...by *n'* opened the prison
9:24 watched the gates day and *n'* to
25 Then the disciples took him by *n'*,
12: 6 the same *n'* Peter was sleeping
16: 9 vision appeared to Paul in the *n'*;
33 took them the same hour of the *n'*,
17:10 sent away Paul and Silas by *n'* unto
18: 9 spake the Lord to Paul in the *n'* by
20:31 not to warn every one *n'* and day
23:11 the *n'* following the Lord stood by
23 hundred, at the third hour of the *n'*;
31 brought him by *n'* to Antipatris.
26: 7 serving God day and *n'*, hope to
27:23 there stood by me this *n'* the angel
27 when the fourteenth *n'* was come,
Ro 13:12 The *n'* is far spent, the day is at
1Co 11:23 same *n'* in which he was betrayed
2Co 11:25 a *n'* and a day I have been in the
1Th 2: 9 labouring *n'* and day, because we
3:10 *N'* and day praying exceedingly
5: 2 Lord so cometh as a thief in the *n'*.
5 we are not of the *n'*, nor of darkness.
7 For they that sleep sleep in the *n'*;
7 be drunken are drunken in the *n'*.
2Th 3: 8 with labour and travail *n'* and day,
1Ti 5: 5 supplications and prayers *n'* and
2Ti 1: 3 of thee in my prayers *n'* and day;
2Pe 3:10 Lord will come as a thief in the *n'*;
Re 4: 8 they rest not day and *n'*, saying,
7:15 serve him day and *n'* in his temple:
8:12 third part of it, and the *n'* likewise.
12:10 them before our God day and *n'*.
14:11 they have no rest day nor *n'*, who
20:10 be tormented day and *n'* for ever
21:25 day: for there shall be no *n'* there.
22: 5 And there shall be no *n'* there; and

night-hawk See NIGHT and HAWK.

nights
Ge 7: 4 the earth forty days and forty *n'*;
12 the earth forty days and forty *n'*.
Ex 24:18 the mount forty days and forty *n'*.
34:28 the Lord forty days and forty *n'*;
De 9: 9 the mount forty days and forty *n'*,
11 the end of forty days and forty *n'*,
18 at the first, forty days and forty *n'*:
25 the Lord forty days and forty *n'*,
10:10 first time, forty days and forty *n'*;
1Sa 30:12 any water, three days and three *n'*.
1Ki 19: 8 of that meat forty days and forty *n'*
Job 2:13 ground seven days and seven *n'*,
7: 3 wearisome *n'* are appointed to me.
Isa 21: 8 and I am set in my ward whole *n'*:
Jon 1:17 of the fish three days and three *n'*.
M't 4: 2 had fasted forty days and forty *n'*,
12:40 and three *n'* in the whale's belly;
40 three *n'* in the heart of the earth.

night-vision See NIGHT and VISION.

night-watches See NIGHT and WATCHES.

Nimrah (*nim'-rah*) See also BETH-NIMRAH.
Nu 32: 3 *N'*, and Heshbon, and Elealeh,

Nimrim (*nim'-rim*)
Isa 15: 6 the waters of *N'* shall be desolate:
Jer 48:34 waters also of *N'* shall be desolate.

Nimrod (*nim'-rod*)
Ge 10: 8 Cush begat *N'*: he began to be a
9 *N'* the mighty hunter before the
1Ch 1:10 Cush begat *N'*: he began to be
Mic 5: 6 land of *N'* in the entrances thereof:

Nimshi (*nim'-shi*)
1Ki 19:16 the son of *N'* shalt thou anoint
2Ki 9: 2 son of Jehoshaphat the son of *N'*,
14 son of Jehoshaphat the son of *N'*
20 the driving of Jehu the son of *N'*;
2Ch 22: 7 against Jehu the son of *N'*, whom

nine See also NINETEEN.
Ge 5: 5 that Adam lived were *n'* hundred
8 of Seth were *n'* hundred and twelve
11 of Enos were *n'* hundred and five
14 of Cainan were *n'* hundred and ten
20 of Jared were *n'* hundred sixty and
27 were *n'* hundred sixty and *n'* years:
9:29 of Noah were *n'* hundred and fifty
11:19 Reu two hundred and *n'* years, and
24 Nahor lived *n'* and twenty years,
17: 1 Abram was ninety years old and *n'*,
24 Abraham was ninety years...and *n'*,
Ex 38:24 offering, was twenty and *n'* talents,
Le 25: 8 be unto thee forty and *n'* years.
Nu 1:23 Simeon, were fifty and *n'* thousand
2:13 fifty and *n'* thousand and three
29:26 And on the fifth day *n'* bullocks,
34:13 to give unto the *n'* tribes, and to
De 3:11 *n'* cubits was the length thereof,
Jos 13: 7 an inheritance unto the *n'* tribes,
14: 2 for the *n'* tribes, and for the half
15:32 the cities are twenty and *n'*, with
44 *n'* cities with their villages.
54 Zior; *n'* cities with their villages.
21:16 *n'* cities out of those two tribes.
J'g 4: 3 he had *n'* hundred chariots of iron;
13 even *n'* hundred chariots of iron.
2Sa 24: 8 Jerusalem at the end of *n'* months
2Ki 14: 2 and reigned twenty and *n'* years in
15:13 the *n'* and thirtieth year of Uzziah
17 *n'* and thirtieth year of Azariah
17: 1 in Samaria over Israel *n'* years.
18: 2 he reigned twenty and *n'* years in
1Ch 3: 8 and Eliada, and Eliphelet, *n'*.
9: 9 *n'* hundred and fifty and six.
2Ch 25: 1 he reigned twenty and *n'* years in
29: 1 he reigned *n'* and twenty years in
Ezr 1: 9 of silver, *n'* and twenty knives,
2: 8 of Zattu, *n'* hundred forty and five.
36 *n'* hundred seventy and three.
42 in all an hundred thirty and *n'*.
Ne 7:38 thousand *n'* hundred and thirty.
39 *n'* hundred seventy and three.
11: 1 and *n'* parts to dwell in other cities.
8 Sallai, *n'* hundred twenty and eight.
M't 18:12 he not leave the ninety and *n'*, and
13 and *n'* which went not astray.
Lu 15: 4 ninety and *n'* in the wilderness,
7 over ninety and *n'* just persons,
17:17 ten cleansed? but where are the *n'*?

nine-hundred See NINE and HUNDRED.

nineteen
Ge 11:25 an hundred and *n'* years,
Jos 19:38 *n'* cities with their villages.
2Sa 2:30 of David's servants *n'* men and

nineteenth
2Ki 25: 8 which is the *n'* year of king
1Ch 24:16 The *n'* to Pethahiah, the
25:26 The *n'* to Mallothi, he, his sons,
Jer 52:12 the *n'* year of Nebuchadrezzar

ninety
Gen 5: 9 Enos lived *n'* years, and begat
17 eight hundred *n'* and five years:
30 Noah five hundred *n'* and five years,
17: 1 when Abram was *n'* years old and
17 Sarah, that is *n'* years old, bear?
24 Abraham was *n'* years old and nine,
1Sa 4:15 Now Eli was *n'* and eight years old;
1Ch 9: 6 their brethren, six hundred and *n'*.
Ezr 2:16 of Ater of Hezekiah, *n'* and eight.
20 The children of Gibbar, *n'* and five.
58 were three hundred *n'* and two.
8:35 for all Israel, *n'* and six rams,
Ne 7:21 of Ater of Hezekiah, *n'* and eight.
25 The children of Gibeon, *n'* and five.
60 were three hundred *n'* and two.
Jer 52:23 there were *n'* and six pomegranates
Eze 4: 5 days, three hundred and *n'* days:
9 hundred and *n'* days shalt thou eat
41:12 and the length thereof *n'* cubits.
Da 12:11 thousand two hundred and *n'* days.
M't 18:12 doth he not leave the *n'* and nine,
13 *n'* and nine which went not astray.
Lu 15: 4 doth not leave the *n'* and nine in
7 than over *n'* and nine just persons,

Nineve (*nin'-e-ve*) See also NINEVEH; NINEVITES.
Lu 11:32 The men of *N'* shall rise up in

Nineveh (*nin'-e-veh*) See also NINEVE.
Ge 10:11 forth Asshur, and builded *N'*, and
12 And Resen between *N'* and Calah:
2Ki 19:36 and returned, and dwelt at *N'*.
Isa 37:37 and returned, and dwelt at *N'*.
Jon 1: 2 go to *N'*, that great city, and cry
3: 2 Arise, go unto *N'*, that great city,
3 So Jonah arose, and went unto *N'*,
3 *N'* was an exceeding great city of
4 days, and *N'* shall be overthrown.
5 So the people of *N'* believed God,
6 word came unto the king of *N'*, and
7 published through *N'* by the decree
4:11 should not I spare *N'*, that great
Na 1: 1 The burden of *N'*. The book of the
2: 8 *N'* is of old like a pool of water:
3: 7 thee, and say, *N'* is laid waste:
Zep 2:13 will make *N'* a desolation, and dry
M't 12:41 men of *N'* shall rise in judgment

Ninevites (*nin'-e-vites*)
Lu 11:30 as Jonas was a sign unto the *N'*.

ninth
Le 23:32 in the *n'* day of the month at even,
25:22 yet of old fruit until the *n'* year;
Nu 7:60 On the *n'* day Abidan the son of
2Ki 17: 6 In the *n'* year of Hoshea the king
18:10 is the *n'* year of Hoshea king of
25: 1 to pass in the *n'* year of his reign,
3 on the *n'* day of the fourth month
1Ch 12:12 the eighth, Elzabad the *n'*,
24:11 The *n'* to Jeshuah, the tenth to
25:16 The *n'* to Mattaniah, he, his sons,
27:12 The *n'* captain for the *n'* month was
2Ch 16:12 Asa in the thirty and *n'* year of
Ezr 10: 9 It was the *n'* month, on the
Jer 36: 9 king of Judah, in the *n'* month,
Jer 36:22 in the winterhouse in the *n'* month:
39: 1 In the *n'* year of Zedekiah king of
2 the *n'* day of the month, the city
52: 4 to pass in the *n'* year of his reign,
6 in the *n'* day of the month, the
Eze 24: 1 Again in the *n'* year, in the tenth
Hag 2:10, 18 twentieth day of the *n'* month,
Zec 7: 1 in the fourth day of the *n'* month,
M't 20: 5 out about the sixth and *n'* hour,
27:45 over all the land unto the *n'* hour.
46 the *n'* hour Jesus cried with a loud
M'r 15:33 the whole land until the *n'* hour.
34 the *n'* hour Jesus cried with a loud
Lu 23:44 over all the earth until the *n'* hour.
Ac 3: 1 hour of prayer, being the *n'* hour.
10: 3 vision evidently about the *n'* hour
30 and at the *n'* hour I prayed in my
Re 21:20 the eighth, beryl; the *n'*, a topaz;

Nisan (*ni'-san*) See also ABIB.
Ne 2: 1 it came to pass in the month *N'*,
Es 3: 7 first month, that is, the month *N'*.

Nisroch (*nis'-rok*)
2Ki 19:37 worshipping in the house of *N'*
Isa 37:38 worshipping in the house of *N'*

Nissi See JEHOVAH-NISSI.

nitre
Pr 25:20 as vinegar upon *n'*, so is he that
Jer 2:22 though thou wash thee with *n'*,

no^ See also NAY; NONE; NOTHING.
Ge 8: 9 dove found *n'* rest for the sole of
9:15 waters shall *n'* more become a flood
11:30 Sarai was barren; she had *n'* child.
13: 8 unto Lot, Let there be *n'* strife,
15: 3 to me thou hast given *n'* seed: and,
16: 1 Abram's wife bare him *n'* children:
26:29 That thou wilt do us *n'* hurt, as we
30: 1 that she bare Jacob *n'* children,
31:50 my daughters, *n'* man is with us;
32:28 name shall be called *n'* more Jacob,
37:22 said unto them, Shed *n'* blood, but
22 and lay *n'* hand upon him; that he
24 was empty, there was *n'* water in it.
32 whether it be thy son's coat or *n'*.
38:21 There was *n'* harlot in this place.
22 there was *n'* harlot in this place.
26 And he knew her again *n'* more.
40: 8 and there is *n'* interpreter of it.
41:44 thee shall *n'* man lift up his hand
42:11 true men, thy servants are *n'* spies.
31 We are true men; we are *n'* spies:
34 shall I know that ye are *n'* spies,
44:23 you, ye shall see my face *n'* more.
45: 1 there stood *n'* man with him, while
47: 4 have *n'* pasture for their flocks;
13 there was *n'* bread in all the land;
Ex 2:12 when he saw that there was *n'* man,
3:19 you go, *n'*, not by a mighty hand.
5: 7 *n'* more give the people straw to
16 is *n'* straw given unto thy servants,
18 there shall *n'* straw be given you,
8:22 that *n'* swarms of flies shall be
9:26 of Israel were, was there *n'* hail.
28 be *n'* more mighty thunderings and
28 you go, and ye shall stay *n'* longer.
10:14 there were *n'* such locusts as they,
28 heed to thyself, see my face *n'* more;
29 I will see thy face again *n'* more.
12:16 *n'* manner of work shall be done in
19 be *n'* leaven found in your houses:
43 there shall *n'* stranger eat thereof:
48 *n'* uncircumcised person shall eat
13: 3 shall *n'* leavened bread be eaten.
7 *n'* leavened bread be seen with thee,
14:11 there were *n'* graves in Egypt, hast
13 see them again *n'* more for ever.
15:22 wilderness, and found *n'* water.
16: 4 they will walk in my law, or *n'*.
18 he that gathered little had *n'* lack;
19 *n'* man leave of it till the morning.
29 *n'* man go out of his place on the
17: 1 *n'* water for the people to drink.
20: 3 have *n'* other gods before me.
21: 8 strange nation...shall have *n'* power,
22 her, and yet *n'* mischief follow:
22: 2 there shall *n'* blood be shed for him.
10 or driven away, *n'* man seeing it:
23: 8 And thou shalt take *n'* gift: for
13 make *n'* mention of the name of
32 shalt make *n'* covenant with them,
30: 9 offer *n'* strange incense thereon,
12 there be *n'* plague among them,
33: 4 and *n'* man did put on him his
20 for there shall *n'* man see me, and
34: 3 *n'* man shall come up with thee,
7 will by *n'* means clear the guilty;
14 thou shalt worship *n'* other god:
17 shalt make thee *n'* molten gods.
35: 3 shall kindle *n'* fire throughout your
Le 2:11 *N'* meat offering, which ye shall
11 for ye shall burn *n'* leaven, nor any
5:11 he shall put *n'* oil upon it, neither
6:30 And *n'* sin offering, whereof any of
7:23 ye shall eat *n'* manner of fat, of ox,
24 use: but ye shall in *n'* wise eat of it.
26 ye shall eat *n'* manner of blood,
11:12 Whatsoever hath *n'* fins or scales
12: 4 she shall touch *n'* hallowed thing,
13:21 there be *n'* white hairs therein, and
26 be *n'* white hair in the bright spot,
26 it be *n'* lower than the other skin,
31 and that there is *n'* black hair in it;
32 and there be in it *n'* yellow hair,
16:17 shall be *n'* man in the tabernacle
29 do *n'* work at all, whether it be one

Le 17: 7 shall *n'* more offer their sacrifices
12 *N'* soul of you shall eat blood,
14 eat the blood of *n'* manner of flesh:
19:15, 35 Ye shall do *n'* unrighteousness
20:14 there be *n'* wickedness among you.
21: 3 him, which hath had *n'* husband:
22:10 *n'* stranger eat of the holy thing:
13 or divorced, and have *n'* child, and
13 there shall *n'* stranger eat thereof.
21 there shall be *n'* blemish therein.
23: 3 ye shall do *n'* work therein: it is the
7, 8, 21 ye shall do *n'* servile work
25 Ye shall do *n'* servile work
28 shall do *n'* work in that same day:
31 Ye shall do *n'* manner of work: it
35, 36 ye shall do *n'* servile work
25:31 which have *n'* wall round about
36 Take thou *n'* usury of him, or
26: 1 you *n'* idols nor graven image,
37 have *n'* power to stand before your
27:26 firstling, *n'* man shall sanctify it;
28 *n'* devoted thing,...shall be sold
Nu 1:53 be *n'* wrath upon the congregation
3: 4 of Sinai, and they had *n'* children:
5: 8 have *n'* kinsmen to recompense the
13 and there be *n'* witness against her.
15 he shall pour *n'* oil upon it, nor
19 If *n'* man have lain with thee, and
6: 3 shall drink *n'* vinegar of wine, or
5 shall *n'* rasor come upon his head:
6 Lord...shall come at *n'* dead body.
8:19 be *n'* plague among the children of
25 thereof, and shall serve *n'* more:
26 the charge, and shall do *n'* service.
14:18 by *n'* means clearing the guilty,
16:40 that *n'* stranger, which is not of the
18: 5 be *n'* wrath any more upon the
20 have *n'* inheritance in their land,
23 of Israel they have *n'* inheritance.
24 they shall have *n'* inheritance.
32 ye shall bear *n'* sin by reason of it,
19: 2 without spot, wherein is *n'* blemish,
15 hath *n'* covering bound upon it, is
20: 5 it is *n'* place of seed, or of figs, or
21: 5 there is *n'* bread, neither is there
22:26 where was *n'* way to turn either to
23:23 there is *n'* enchantment against
26:33 the son of Hepher had *n'* sons, but
62 was *n'* inheritance given them
27: 3 in his own sin, and had *n'* sons.
4 family, because he hath *n'* son?
8 If a man die, and have *n'* son, then
9 And if he have *n'* daughter, then ye
10 And if he have *n'* brethren, then ye
11 And if his father have *n'* brethren,
17 as sheep which have *n'* shepherd.
28:18 shall do *n'* manner of servile work
25 ye shall do *n'* servile work.
26 ye shall do *n'* servile work:
29: 1 ye shall do *n'* servile work: it is
12 ye shall do *n'* servile work, and
35 ye shall do *n'* servile work
33:14 was *n'* water for the people to drink.
35:31 shall take *n'* satisfaction for the life
32 ye shall take *n'* satisfaction for him
De 1:39 *n'* knowledge between good and evil,
2: 5 *n'*, not so much as a foot breadth;
3:26 speak *n'* more unto me of this
4:12 the words, but saw *n'* similitude;
15 ye saw *n'* manner of similitude on
5:22 great voice: and he added *n'* more.
7: 2 shalt make *n'* covenant with them,
16 eye shall have *n'* pity upon them:
24 there shall *n'* man be able to stand
8: 2 keep his commandments, or *n'*.
15 drought, where there was *n'* water;
10: 9 Levi hath *n'* part nor inheritance
16 heart, and be *n'* more stiffnecked.
11:17 that there be *n'* rain, and that the
25 *n'* man shall be able to stand before
12:12 as he hath *n'* part nor inheritance
13:11 do *n'* more any such wickedness
14:27, 29 he hath *n'* part nor inheritance
15: 4 there shall be *n'* poor among you;
19 do *n'* work with the firstling of thy
16: 3 Thou shalt eat *n'* leavened bread
4 shall be *n'* leavened bread seen
8 God: thou shalt do *n'* work therein.
17:13 and do *n'* more presumptuously.
16 henceforth return *n'* more that way.
18: 1 the tribe of Levi, shall have *n'* part
2 they have *n'* inheritance among
19:20 commit *n'* more any such evil
20:12 if it will make *n'* peace with thee,
21:14 be, if thou have *n'* delight in her,
22:26 the damsel *n'* sin worthy of death:
23:14 he see *n'* unclean thing in thee,
17 be *n'* whore of the daughters of
22 to vow, it shall be *n'* sin in thee.
24: 1 that she find *n'* favour in his eyes,
6 *N'* man shall take the nether or the
25: 5 one of them die, and have *n'* child,
28:26 and *n'* man shall fray them away.
29 and *n'* man shall save thee.
32 shall be *n'* might in thine hand.
65 nations shalt thou find *n'* ease,
68 Thou shalt see it *n'* more again:
68 and *n'* man shall buy you.
31: 2 I can *n'* more go out and come in:
32:12 there was *n'* strange god with him.
20 children in whom is *n'* faith.
39 am he, and there is *n'* god with me:
34: 6 *n'* man knoweth of his sepulchre
Jos 8:20 they had *n'* power to flee this way
31 which *n'* man hath lift up any iron:
10:14 there was *n'* day like that before it

Jos 11:20 that they might have *n'* favour,
14: 4 they gave *n'* part unto the Levites
17: 3 the son of Manasseh, had *n'* sons,
18: 7 Levites have *n'* part among you:
22:25 Gad; ye have *n'* part in the Lord:
27 come, Ye have *n'* part in the Lord.
23: 9 *n'* man hath been able to stand
13 God will *n'* more drive out any of
J'g 2: 2 *n'* league with the inhabitants of
4:20 man here? that thou shalt say, *N'*.
5:19 they took *n'* gain of money.
6: 4 and left *n'* sustenance for Israel,
8:28 they lifted up their heads *n'* more.
10:13 I will deliver you *n'* more.
11:39 had vowed; and she knew *n'* man.
13: 5 *n'* rasor shall come on his head:
7 now drink *n'* wine nor strong drink,
21 of the Lord did *n'* more appear
15:13 they spake unto him, saying, *N'*;
17: 6 days there was *n'* king in Israel,
18: 1 there was *n'* king in Israel: and in
7 was *n'* magistrate in the land, that
7 and had *n'* business with any man.
10 where there is *n'* want of any thing
28 And there was *n'* deliverer, because
28 had *n'* business with any man; and
19: 1 when there was *n'* king in Israel,
15 was *n'* man that took them into his
18 *n'* man that receiveth me to house.
19 there is *n'* want of any thing.
30 *n'* such deed done nor seen from
21:12 virgins, that had known *n'* man by
25 days there was *n'* king in Israel;
1Sa 1: 2 but Hannah had *n'* children.
11 shall *n'* rasor come upon his head.
15 answered and said, *N'*, my lord,
18 her countenance was *n'* more sad.
2: 3 Talk *n'* more so exceeding proudly;
9 by strength shall *n'* man prevail.
24 for it is *n'* good report that I hear:
3: 1 days; there was *n'* open vision.
6: 7 on which there hath come *n'* yoke,
7:13 *n'* more into the coast of Israel:
10:14 we saw that they were *n'* where,
27 him, and brought him *n'* presents.
11: 3 then, if there be *n'* man to save us,
13:19 Now there was *n'* smith found
14: 6 is *n'* restraint to the Lord to save
26 *n'* man put his hand to his mouth:
15:35 Samuel came *n'* more to see Saul
17:32 Let *n'* man's heart fail because of
50 was *n'* sword in the hand of David.
18: 2 would let him go *n'* more home to
20:15 *n'*, not when the Lord hath cut off
21 there is peace to thee, and *n'* hurt;
34 eat *n'* meat the second day of the
21: 1 thou alone, and *n'* man with thee?
2 Let *n'* man know any thing of the
4 *n'* common bread under mine hand,
6 *n'* bread there but the shewbread,
9 for there is *n'* other save that here.
25:31 this shall be *n'* grief unto thee,
26:12 gat them away, and *n'* man saw it,
21 for I will *n'* more do thee harm,
27: 4 he sought *n'* more again for him.
28:10 there shall *n'* punishment happen
15 me, and answereth me *n'* more,
20 and there was *n'* strength in him;
20 he had eaten *n'* bread all the day,
29: 3 found *n'* fault in him since he fell
30: 4 they had *n'* more power to weep.
12 he had eaten *n'* bread, nor drunk
2Sa 1:21 let there be *n'* dew, neither let
2:28 and pursued after Israel *n'* more,
6:23 the daughter of Saul had *n'* child
7:10 of their own, and move *n'* more;
12: 6 thing, and because he had *n'* pity.
13:12 *n'* such thing ought to be done in
16 said unto him, There is *n'* cause:
14:25 head there was *n'* blemish in him.
15: 3 there is *n'* man deputed of the king
26 I have *n'* delight in thee; behold,
18:13 there is *n'* matter hid from the king,
18 I have *n'* son to keep my name in
20 day thou shalt bear *n'* tidings,
22 that thou hast *n'* tidings ready?
20: 1 We have *n'* part in David, neither
10 Amasa took *n'* heed to the sword
21: 4 will have *n'* silver nor gold of Saul,
17 go *n'* more out with us to battle,
1Ki 1: 1 with clothes, but he gat *n'* heat.
3: 2 was *n'* house built unto the name
18 *n'* stranger with us in the house,
22 said, *N'*; but the dead is thy son,
26 living child, and in *n'* wise slay it.
27 living child, and in *n'* wise slay it:
6:18 was cedar; there was *n'* stone seen.
8:16 I chose *n'* city out of all the tribes
23 Israel, there is *n'* God like thee,
35 is shut up, and there is *n'* rain,
46 there is *n'* man that sinneth not,)
9:22 did Solomon make *n'* bondmen:
10: 5 there was *n'* more spirit in her.
10 there came *n'* more such abundance
12 there came *n'* such almug trees, nor
13: 9 Eat *n'* bread, nor drink water, nor
17 shalt eat *n'* bread nor drink water
22 Eat *n'* bread, and drink *n'* water;
17: 7 there had been *n'* rain in the land.
17 that there was *n'* breath left in him.
18:10 there is *n'* nation or kingdom,
23, 23 on wood, and put *n'* fire under:
25 your gods, but put *n'* fire under.
26 there was *n'* voice, nor any that
21: 4 his face, and would eat *n'* bread.
5 so sad, that thou eatest *n'* bread?

1Ki 22:17 These have *n'* master: let them
18 prophesy *n'* good concerning me,
47 There was then *n'* king in Edom:
2Ki 1:16 is *n'* God in Israel to inquire of his
17 of Judah; because he had *n'* son.
2:12 And he saw him *n'* more: and he
3: 9 there was *n'* water for the host, and
4:14 she hath *n'* child, and her husband
41 And there was *n'* harm in the pot.
5:15 that there is *n'* God in all the earth,
25 Thy servant went *n'* whither.
6:23 came *n'* more into the land of Israel.
7: 5 behold, there was *n'* man there.
10 there was *n'* man there, neither
9:35 *n'* more of her than the skull, and
10:31 Jehu took *n'* heed to walk in the law
12: 7 receive *n'* more money of your
8 to receive *n'* more money of the
17: 4 *n'* present to the king of Assyria,
19:18 were *n'* gods, but the work of men's
22: 7 was *n'* reckoning made with them
23:10 that *n'* man might make his son or
18 alone; let *n'* man move his bones.
25 him was there *n'* king before him,
25: 3 *n'* bread for the people of the land.
1Ch 2:34 Now Sheshan had *n'* sons, but
12:17 there is *n'* wrong in mine hands,
16:21 suffered *n'* man to do them wrong:
22 and do my prophets *n'* harm.
17: 9 place, and shall be moved *n'* more;
22:16 and the iron, there is *n'* number.
23:22 Eleazar died, and had *n'* sons, but
26 shall *n'* more carry the tabernacle,
24: 2 their father, and had *n'* children:
28 came Eleazar, who had *n'* sons.
2Ch 6: 5 I chose *n'* city among all the tribes
14 is *n'* God like thee in the heaven,
26 is shut up, and there is *n'* rain,
36 there is *n'* man which sinneth not,)
7:13 up heaven that there be *n'* rain,
8: 9 Solomon make *n'* servants for his
9: 4 there was *n'* more spirit in her.
13: 9 a priest of them that are *n'* gods.
14: 6 and he had *n'* war in those years;
11 or with them that have *n'* power:
15: 5 was *n'* peace to him that went out,
19 was *n'* more war unto the five and
17:10 made *n'* war against Jehoshaphat.
18:16 sheep that have *n'* shepherd: and
16 These have *n'* master; let them
19: 7 *n'* iniquity with the Lord our God,
20:12 *n'* might against this great company
21:19 people made *n'* burning for him,
22: 9 *n'* power to keep still the kingdom.
32:15 *n'* good of any nation or kingdom
35:18 was *n'* passover like to that kept
36:16 people, till there was *n'* remedy.
17 *n'* compassion upon young man or
Ezr 4:16 *n'* portion on this side of the river.
9:14 should be *n'* remnant nor escaping?
10: 6 he did eat *n'* bread, nor drink
Ne 2:14 there was *n'* place for the beast
17 that we be *n'* more a reproach.
20 ye have *n'* portion, nor right, nor
6: 1 there was *n'* breach left therein;
8 *n'* such things done as thou sayest,
13:19 there should *n'* burden be brought
21 came they *n'* more on the Sabbath.
26 was there *n'* king like him, who was
Es 1:19 Vashti come *n'* more before king
2:14 came in unto the king *n'* more,
5:12 let *n'* man come in with the king
8: 8 king's ring, may *n'* man reverse.
9: 2 and *n'* man could withstand them;
Job 3: 7 let *n'* joyful voice come therein.
4:18 he put *n'* trust in his servants;
5:19 seven there shall *n'* evil touch thee.
7: 7 mine eye shall *n'* more see good.
8 hath seen me shall see me *n'* more.
9 the grave shall come up *n'* more.
10 shall return *n'* more to his house,
9:25 they flee away, they see *n'* good.
10:18 the ghost, and *n'* eye had seen me!
11: 3 shall *n'* man make thee ashamed?
12: 2 *N'* doubt but ye are the people,
14 man, and there can be *n'* opening.
24 a wilderness where there is *n'* way.
13: 4 ye are all physicians of *n'* value.
14:12 till the heavens be *n'* more, they
15: 3 wherewith he can do *n'* good?
15 he putteth *n'* trust in his saints;
19 *n'* stranger passed among them.
28 in houses which *n'* man inhabiteth,
16:18 blood, and let my cry have *n'* place.
18:17 shall have *n'* name in the street.
19: 7 aloud, but there is *n'* judgment.
16 servant, and he gave me *n'* answer;
20: 9 saw him shall see him *n'* more;
21 shall *n'* man look for his goods.
23: 6 *N'*; but he would put strength in
24: 7 they have *n'* covering in the cold.
15 saying, *N'* eye shall see me: and
20 he shall be *n'* more remembered;
22 riseth up, and *n'* man is sure of life.
26: 2 thou the arm that hath *n'* strength?
3 counselled him that hath *n'* wisdom?
6 and destruction hath *n'* covering.
28:18 *N'* mention shall be made of coral,
30:13 my calamity, they have *n'* helper.
17 season: and my sinews take *n'* rest.
32: 3 because they had found *n'* answer,
5 there was *n'* answer in the mouth
15 amazed, they answered *n'* more:
16 stood still, and answered *n'* more;)
19 belly is as wine which hath *n'* vent;
34:22 is *n'* darkness, nor shadow of death,

Job 34: 32 done iniquity, I will do n' more.
36: 16 place, where there is n' straitness;
19 n' not gold, nor all the forces of
38: 11 shalt thou come, but n' further:
26 on the earth, where n' man is; on
26 wilderness, wherein there is n' man;
40: 5 twice; but I will proceed n' further.
41: 8 remember the battle, do n' more.
16 that n' air can come between them.
42: 2 that n' thought can be withholden
15 all the land were n' women found
Ps 3: 2 There is n' help for him in God.
5: 9 is n' faithfulness in their mouth;
6: 5 in death there is n' remembrance of
10: 18 man of...earth may n' more oppress.
14: 1 said in his heart, There is n' God.
3 is none that doeth good, n', not one.
4 workers of iniquity n' knowledge?
19: 3 There is n' speech nor language,
22: 6 But I am a worm, and n' man; a
23: 4 I will fear n' evil: for thou art with
32: 2 and in whose spirit there is n' guile.
9 mule, which have n' understanding:
33: 16 is n' king saved by the multitude of
34: 9 is n' want to them that fear him.
36: 1 is n' fear of God before his eyes.
38: 3 There is n' soundness in my flesh
7 there is n' soundness in my flesh.
14 and in whose mouth are n' reproofs.
39: 13 before I go hence, and be n' more.
40: 17 make n' tarrying, O my God.
41: 8 he lieth he shall rise up n' more.
50: 9 will take n' bullock out of thy house,
53: 1 said in his heart, There is n' God.
3 is none that doeth good, n', not one.
4 workers of iniquity n' knowledge?
5 in great fear, where n' fear was:
55: 19 Because they have n' changes,
63: 1 thirsty land, where n' water is;
69: 2 mire, where there is n' standing:
70: 5 O Lord, make n' tarrying.
72: 12 also, and him that hath n' helper.
73: 4 there are n' bands in their death:
74: 9 signs: there is n' more any prophet:
77: 7 and will he be favourable n' more?
78: 64 their widows made n' lamentation.
81: 9 shall n' strange god be in thee;
83: 4 may be n' more in remembrance.
84: 11 n' good thing will he withhold from
88: 4 am as a man that hath n' strength:
5 whom thou rememberest n' more:
91: 10 There shall n' evil befall thee,
92: 15 there is n' unrighteousness in him.
101: 3 n' wicked thing before mine eyes:
102: 27 and thy years shall have n' end.
103: 16 thereof shall know it n' more.
104: 35 and let the wicked be n' more.
105: 14 suffered n' man to do them wrong:
15 and do my prophets n' harm.
107: 4 way; they found n' city to dwell in.
40 wilderness, where there is n' way.
119: 3 They also do n' iniquity: they walk
142: 4 was n' man that would know me:
4 failed me; n' man cared for my soul.
143: 2 shall n' man living be justified.
144: 14 that there be n' breaking in, nor
14 be n' complaining in our streets.
146: 3 son of man, in whom there is n' help.
Pr 1: 24 out my hand, and n' man regarded;
3: 30 if he have done thee n' harm.
6: 7 Which having n' guide, overseer,
8: 24 When there were n' depths, I was
24 n' fountains abounding with water.
10: 22 and he addeth n' sorrow with it.
25 passeth, so is the wicked n' more:
11: 14 Where n' counsel is, the people fall:
12: 21 shall n' evil happen to the just:
28 pathway thereof there is n' death.
14: 4 Where n' oxen are, the crib is
17: 16 seeing he hath n' heart to it?
20 a froward heart findeth n' good:
21 and the father of a fool hath n' joy.
18: 2 hath n' delight in understanding,
21: 10 findeth n' favour in his eyes.
30 is n' wisdom nor understanding nor
22: 24 Make n' friendship with an angry
24: 20 be n' reward to the evil man; the
25: 28 hath n' rule over his own spirit is
26: 20 Where n' wood is, there the fire
20 so where there is n' talebearer, the
28: 1 wicked flee when n' man pursueth:
3 sweeping rain which leaveth n' food.
17 flee to the pit; let n' man stay him.
24 and saith, It is n' transgression;
29: 9 he rage or laugh, there is n' rest.
18 Where there is n' vision, the people
30: 20 saith, I have done n' wickedness.
27 The locusts have n' king, yet go
31 against whom there is n' rising up.
31: 7 and remember his misery n' more.
11 that he shall have n' need of spoil.
Ec 1: 9 there is n' new thing under the sun.
11 is n' remembrance of former things;
2: 11 there was n' profit under the sun.
16 there is n' remembrance of the wise
3: 11 n' man can find out the work that
12 know that there is n' good in them,
19 a man hath n' preeminence above a
4: 1 and they had n' comforter; and on
1 power; but they had n' comforter.
8 yet is there n' end of all his labour;
13 who will n' more be admonished.
16 There is n' end of all the people,
5: 4 for he hath n' pleasure in fools:
6: 3 and also that he have n' burial;
6 told, yet he hath seen n' good:

Ec 7: 21 Also take n' heed unto all words
8: 5 commandment shall feel n' evil
8 There is n' man that hath power
8 there is n' discharge in that war;
15 hath n' better thing under the sun,
9: 1 n' man knoweth either love or
8 and let thy head lack n' ointment.
10 for there is n' work, nor device, nor
15 yet n' man remembered that same
10: 11 and a babbler is n' better.
20 not the king, n' not in thy thought;
12: 1 say, I have n' pleasure in them;
12 making many books there is n' end;
Ca 4: 7 my love; there is n' spot in thee.
5: 6 him, but he gave me n' answer.
8: 8 sister, and she hath n' breasts:
Isa 1: 6 head there is n' soundness in it;
13 Bring n' more vain oblations;
30 and as a garden that hath n' water.
5: 6 clouds that they rain n' rain upon it.
8 field to field, till there be n' place,
13 because they have n' knowledge:
8: 20 because there is n' light in them.
9: 7 and peace there shall be n' end,
17 have n' joy in their young men,
19 fire: n' man shall spare his brother.
10: 15 lift up itself, as if it were n' wood.
20 shall n' more again stay upon him
13: 14 as a sheep that n' man taketh up:
18 shall have n' pity on the fruit of
14: 8 n' feller is come up against us.
15: 6 faileth, there is n' green thing.
16: 10 vineyards there shall be n' singing,
10 tread out n' wine in their presses;
19: 7 be driven away, and be n' more.
23: 1 that there is n' house, n' entering in:
10 Tarshish: there is n' more strength.
12 Thou shalt n' more rejoice, O thou
12 there also shalt thou have n' rest.
24: 10 is shut up, that n' man may come in.
25: 2 a palace of strangers to be n' city;
26: 21 and shall n' more cover her slain.
27: 11 it is a people of n' understanding:
11 them will shew them n' favour.
28: 8 so that there is n' place clean.
29: 16 it, He had n' understanding?
30: 7 help in vain, and to n' purpose:
16 ye said, N'; for we will flee upon
19 thou shalt weep n' more: he will
32: 5 shall be n' more called liberal, nor
33: 8 the cities, he regardeth n' man.
21 shall go n' galley with oars,
34: 16 n' one of these shall fail, none
35: 9 N' lion shall be there, nor any
37: 19 they were n' gods, but the work of
38: 11 I shall behold man n' more with the
40: 20 impoverished...he hath n' oblation
28 n' searching of his understanding.
29 n' might he increaseth strength.
41: 28 I beheld, and there was n' man;
28 and there was n' counsellor, that,
43: 10 me there was n' God formed,
11 and beside me there is n' saviour.
12 was n' strange god among you:
24 me n' sweet cane with money,
44: 6 last; and beside me there is n' God.
8 yea, there is n' God; I know not any.
12 he drinketh n' water, and is faint.
45: 5 else, there is n' God besides me:
9 or thy work, He hath n' hands?
14 there is none else, there is n' God.
20 have n' knowledge that set up the
21 and there is n' God else beside me;
47: 1 there is n' throne, O daughter of the
1 thou shalt n' more be called tender
5 thou shalt n' more be called, The
6 thou didst shew them n' mercy;
48: 22 There is n' peace, saith the Lord,
50: 2 when I came, was there n' man?
2 or have I n' power to deliver? behold,
2 stinketh, because there is n' water,
10 in darkness, and hath n' light? let
51: 22 thou shalt n' more drink it again:
52: 1 there shall n' more come unto thee
11 thence, touch n' unclean thing;
53: 2 he hath n' form nor comeliness;
2 n' beauty that we should desire him.
9 because he had done n' violence,
54: 9 waters of Noah should n' more go over
17 N' weapon that is formed against
55: 1 and he that hath n' money; come
57: 1 and n' man layeth it to heart: and
10 saidst thou not, There is n' hope:
21 There is n' peace, saith my God, to
58: 3 and thou takest n' knowledge?
59: 8 is n' judgment in their goings:
10 and we grope as if we had n' eyes:
15 him that there was n' judgment.
16 And he saw that there was n' man,
16 that there was n' intercessor:
60: 15 so that n' man went through thee,
18 Violence shall n' more be heard in
19 The sun shall be n' more thy light
20 Thy sun shall n' more go down;
62: 4 shalt n' more be termed Forsaken;
7 give him n' rest, till he establish,
8 n' more give thy corn to be meat
65: 19 of weeping shall be n' more heard
20 shall be n' more thence an infant
Jer 2: 6 a land that n' man passed through,
6 and where n' man dwelt?
11 their gods, which are yet n' gods?
13 cisterns, that can hold n' water.
25 but thou saidst, There is n' hope:
25 n'; for I have loved strangers, and
30 they received n' correction: your

Jer 2: 31 we will come n' more unto thee?
3: 3 and there hath been n' latter rain;
16 the Lord, they shall say n' more,
4: 22 to do good they have n' knowledge.
23 the heavens, and they had n' light.
25 and, lo, there was n' man, and all
5: 7 sworn by them that are n' gods:
6: 10 reproach; they have n' delight in it.
14 peace; when there is n' peace.
23 they are cruel, and have n' mercy;
7: 32 it shall n' more be called Tophet,
32 in Tophet, till there be n' place.
8: 6 n' man repented...of his wickedness,
11 Peace, peace; when there is n' peace.
13 there shall be n' grapes on the vine,
15 looked for peace, but n' good came;
22 Is there n' balm in Gilead? is there
22 is there n' physician there? why
10: 14 and there is n' breath in them.
11: 19 name may be n' more remembered:
23 there shall be n' remnant of them:
12: 11 because n' man layeth it to heart.
12 the land: n' flesh shall have peace.
14: 3 to the pits, and found n' water;
4 for there was n' rain in the earth,
5 it, because there was n' grass.
6 did fail, because there was n' grass.
19 us, and there is n' healing for us?
19 for peace, and there is n' good; and
16: 14 that it shall n' more be said, The
19 things, wherein there is n' profit.
20 himself, and they are n' gods?
17: 21 bear n' burden on the sabbath day,
24 in n' burden through the gates of
24 sabbath day, to do n' work therein;
18: 12 There is n' hope: but we will walk
19: 6 shall n' more be called Tophet,
11 till there be n' place to bury.
22: 3 do n' wrong, do n' violence to the
10 for he shall return n' more, nor
12 and shall see this land n' more.
28 he a vessel wherein is n' pleasure?
30 n' man of his seed shall prosper,
23: 4 and they shall fear n' more, nor be
7 shall n' more say, The Lord liveth,
17 heart, N' evil shall come upon you.
36 the Lord shall ye mention n' more;
25: 6 hands; and I will do you n' hurt.
27 and spue, and fall, and rise n' more,
35 shepherds shall have n' way to flee,
30: 8 and strangers shall n' more serve
13 up: thou hast n' healing medicines.
17 Zion, whom n' man seeketh after.
31: 29 those days they shall say n' more,
34 shall teach n' more every man his
34 I will remember their sin n' more.
33: 24 be n' more a nation before them.
35: 6 they said, We will drink n' wine:
6 Ye shall drink n' wine, neither ye,
8 us, to drink n' wine all our days,
36: 19 and let n' man know where ye be.
38: 6 the dungeon there was n' water,
9 there is n' more bread in the city.
24 Let n' man know of these words,
39: 12 well to him, and do him n' harm;
40: 15 and n' man shall know it:
41: 4 Gedaliah, and n' man knew it,
42: 14 Saying, N', but we will go into the
14 where we shall see n' war, nor hear
18 and ye shall see this place n' more.
44: 2 and n' man dwelleth therein,
5 burn n' incense unto other gods.
17 and were well, and saw n' evil.
22 that the Lord could n' longer bear.
26 my name shall n' more be named
45: 3 in my sighing, and I find n' rest.
48: 2 shall be n' more praise of Moab:
8 city, and n' city shall escape:
33 their shouting shall be n' shouting.
38 like a vessel wherein is n' pleasure.
49: 1 Hath Israel n' sons? hath he n' heir?
7 Is wisdom n' more in Teman? is
18 n' man shall abide there, neither
33 there shall n' man abide there, nor
36 there shall be n' nation whither the
50: 14 shoot at her, spare n' arrows: for
39 be n' more inhabited for ever;
40 so shall n' man abide there, neither
51: 17 and there is n' breath in them.
43 a land wherein n' man dwelleth,
52: 6 there was n' bread for the people
La 1: 3 the heathen, she findeth n' rest:
6 like harts that find n' pasture, and
9 wonderfully: she had n' comforter.
2: 9 the Gentiles: the law is n' more;
9 also find n' vision from the Lord,
18 give thyself n' rest; let not the
4: 4 and n' man breaketh it unto them.
6 and n' hands stayed on her.
15 They shall n' more sojourn there.
16 he will n' more regard them: they
22 will n' more carry thee away into
5: 5 we labour, and have n' rest.
Eze 12: 23 shall n' more use it as a proverb in
24 shall be n' more any vain vision
25 it shall be n' more prolonged: for
13: 10 and there was n' peace; and one
15 The wall is n' more, neither they
16 and there is n' peace, saith the Lord
21 shall be n' more in your hand to
23 ye shall see n' more vanity, nor
14: 11 of Israel may go n' more astray
15 n' man may pass through because
15: 5 whole, it was meet for n' work:
16: 34 and n' reward is given unto thee:
41 also shalt give n' hire any more.

Eze 16:42 quiet, and will be n' more angry.
18:32 I have n' pleasure in the death of
19: 9 voice should n' more be heard upon
14 hath n' strong rod to be a sceptre
20:39 pollute ye my holy name n' more
21:13 it shall be n' more, saith the Lord
27 it shall be n' more, until he come
32 thou shalt be n' more remembered:
22:26 put n' difference between the holy
24: 6 by piece; let n' lot fall upon it.
17 make n' mourning for the dead,
27 speak, and shall be n' more dumb:
26:13 thy harps shall be n' more heard.
14 thou shalt be built n' more: for I
21 terror, and thou shalt be n' more:
28: 3 there is n' secret...they can hide
9 thou shalt be a man, and n' God,
24 shall be n' more a pricking brier
29:11 N' foot of man shall pass through
15 shall n' more rule over the nations.
16 shall be n' more the confidence of
18 yet had he n' wages, nor his army,
30:13 there shall be n' more a prince of
33:11 I have n' pleasure in the death of
22 opened, and I was n' more dumb.
34: 5 because there is n' shepherd: and
8 because there was n' shepherd,
22 they shall n' more be a prey; and
28 they shall n' more be a prey to the
29 shall be n' more consumed with
36:12 shalt n' more henceforth bereave
14 thou shalt devour men n' more,
29 it, and lay n' famine upon you.
30 receive n' more reproach of famine
37: 8 but there was n' breath in them.
22 they shall be n' more two nations,
39:10 shall take n' wood out of the field,
43: 7 the house of Israel n' more defile,
44: 2 n' man shall enter in by it; because
9 N' stranger, uncircumcised in
17 and n' wool shall come upon them,
25 come at n' dead person to defile
25 sister that hath had n' husband,
28 give them n' possession in Israel:
45: 8 shall n' more oppress my people;
Da 1: 4 Children in whom was n' blemish,
2:10 therefore there is n' king,
35 n' place was found for them:
3:25 of the fire, and they have n' hurt;
27 whose bodies the fire had n' power,
29 is n' other God that can deliver
4: 9 and n' secret troubleth thee,
6: 2 the king should have n' damage.
15 is, That n' decree nor statute
22 O king, have I done n' hurt.
23 n' manner of hurt was found
8: 4 n' beasts might stand before him,
7 was n' power in the ram to stand
10: 3 I ate n' pleasant bread, neither
8 there remained n' strength in me:
8 corruption,...I retained n' strength.
16 and I have retained n' strength.
17 there remained n' strength in me,
Ho 1: 6 I will n' more have mercy upon the
2:16 and shalt call me n' more Baali.
17 shall n' more be remembered by
4: 1 there is n' truth, nor mercy, nor
4 Yet let n' man strive, nor reprove
6 that thou shalt be n' priest to me:
8: 7 the whirlwind: it hath n' stalk:
7 the bud shall yield n' meal: if so be
8 as a vessel wherein is n' pleasure.
9:15 I will love them n' more: all their
16 dried up, they shall bear n' fruit:
10: 3 We have n' king, because we feared
13: 4 thou shalt know n' god but me:
4 for there is n' saviour beside me.
Joe 1:18 because they have n' pasture; yea,
2:19 will n' more make you a reproach
3:17 shall n' strangers pass through her
Am 3: 4 in the forest, when he hath n' prey?
5 the earth, where n' gin is for him:
5: 2 is fallen; she shall n' more rise:
20 very dark, and n' brightness in it?
6:10 and he shall say, N'. Then shall
7:14 I was n' prophet, neither was I a
9:15 they shall n' more be pulled up out
Mic 3: 7 lips; for there is n' answer of God.
4: 9 is there n' king in thee? is thy
5:12 shalt have n' more soothsayers:
13 shalt n' more worship the work of
7: 1 there is n' cluster to eat: my soul
Na 1:12 thee, I will afflict thee n' more.
14 that n' more of thy name be sown:
15 wicked shall n' more pass through
2:13 messengers shall n' more be heard,
3:18 and n' man gathereth them.
19 There is n' healing of thy bruise;
Hab 1:14 that have n' ruler over them?
2:19 is n' breath at all in the midst of it.
3:17 fields shall yield n' meat; and the
17 there shall be n' herd in the stalls:
Zep 2: 5 that there shall be n' inhabitant.
3: 5 but the unjust knoweth n' shame.
6 so that there is n' man, that there
11 thou shalt n' more be haughty
Hag 2:12 the priests answered and said, N'.
Zec 1:21 so that n' man did lift up his head:
4: 5, 13 these be? And I said, N', my lord.
7:14 that n' man passed through nor
8:10 there was n' hire for man, nor any
17 neighbour; and love n' false oath:
9: 8 n' oppressor shall pass through
11 out of the pit wherein is n' water.
10: 2 because there was n' shepherd.
11: 6 I will n' more pity the inhabitants

Zec 13: 2 they shall n' more be remembered:
5 he shall say, I am n' prophet, I am
14:11 shall be n' more utter destruction;
17 even upon them shall be n' rain.
18 and come not, that have n' rain;
21 shall be n' more the Canaanite in
Mal 1:10 I have n' pleasure in you, saith
M't 5:18 shall in n' wise pass from the law,
20 in n' case enter into the kingdom
26 shalt by n' means come out thence,
6: 1 otherwise ye have n' reward of
24 N' man can serve two masters:
25 Take n' thought for your life,
31 Therefore take n' thought, saying,
34 Take...n' thought for the morrow:
8: 4 unto him, See thou tell n' man;
10 so great faith, n', not in Israel.
28 n' man might pass by that way.
9:16 N' man putteth a piece of new
30 saying, See that n' man know it.
36 as sheep having n' shepherd.
10:19 n' thought how or what ye shall
42 shall in n' wise lose his reward.
11:27 n' man knoweth the Son, but the
12:39 there shall n' sign be given to it,
13: 5 they had n' deepness of earth:
6 they had n' root, they withered
16: 4 there shall n' sign be given unto it,
7 is because we have taken n' bread.
8 because ye have brought n' bread?
20 tell n' man that he was Jesus the
17: 8 they saw n' man, save Jesus only.
9 Tell the vision to n' man, until the
19: 6 are n' more twain, but one flesh.
18 Thou shalt do n' murder, Thou
20: 7 Because n' man hath hired us.
13 said, Friend, I do thee n' wrong:
21:19 unto it, Let n' fruit grow on thee
22:23 say that there is n' resurrection,
24 If a man die, having n' children,
25 having n' issue, left his wife unto
46 n' man was able to answer him a
23: 9 And call n' man your father upon
24: 4 Take heed that n' man deceive you.
21 to this time, n', nor ever shall be.
22 there should n' flesh be saved:
36 that day and hour knoweth n' man,
36 n', not the angels of heaven, but
25: 3 lamps, and took n' oil with them:
42 an hungred, and ye gave me n' meat:
42 thirsty, and ye gave me n' drink:
26:55 temple, and ye laid n' hold on me.
M'r 1:45 could n' more openly enter into
2: 2 was n' room to receive them,
2 n', not so much as about the door:
17 have n' need of the physician, but
21 N' man also seweth a piece of
22 n' man putteth new wine into old
3:27 N' man can enter into a strong
4: 5 because it had n' depth of earth:
6 because it had n' root, it withered
7 choked it, and it yielded n' fruit.
17 have n' root in themselves, and so
40 how is it that ye have n' faith?
5: 3 and n' man could bind him,
3 bind him, n', not with chains,
37 he suffered n' man to follow him,
43 that n' man should know it; and
6: 5 he could there do n' mighty work,
8 n' scrip, n' bread, n' money in
31 had n' leisure so much as to eat.
7:12 suffer him n' more to do ought for
24 and would have n' man know it:
36 them that they should tell n' man:
8:12 shall n' sign be given unto this
16 It is because we have n' bread.
17 ye, because ye have n' bread?
30 they should tell n' man of him.
9: 3 n' fuller on earth can white them.
8 saw n' man any more, save Jesus
9 tell n' man what things they had
25 him, and enter n' more into him.
39 n' man which shall do a miracle
10: 8 are n' more twain, but one flesh.
29 is n' man that hath left house, or
11:14 N' man eat fruit of thee hereafter
12:14 art true, and carest for n' man:
18 which say there is n' resurrection;
19 behind him, and leave n' children,
20 took a wife, and dying left n' seed.
22 the seven had her, and left n' seed:
34 n' man after that durst ask him
13:11 take n' thought beforehand what
20 days, n' flesh should be saved:
32 and that hour knoweth n' man,
32 n', not the angels which are in heaven,
14:25 I will drink n' more of the fruit of
Lu 1: 7 they had n' child, because that
33 his kingdom there shall be n' end.
2: 7 was n' room for them in the inn.
3:13 Exact n' more than that which is
14 Do violence to n' man, neither
4:24 N' prophet is accepted in his own
5:14 he charged him to tell n' man: but
36 N' man putteth a piece of a new
37 n' man putteth new wine into old
39 N' man also having drunk old wine
7: 9 so great faith, n', not in Israel.
44 gavest me n' water for my feet:
45 Thou gavest me n' kiss: but this
8:13 and these have n' root, which for a
14 and bring n' fruit to perfection.
16 N' man, when he hath lighted a
27 and ware n' clothes, neither abode
51 he suffered n' man to go in, save
56 should tell n' man what was done.

Lu 9:13 We have n' more but five loaves
21 them to tell n' man that thing;
36 and told n' man in those days any
62 N' man, having put his hand to the
10: 4 and salute n' man by the way.
22 n' man knoweth who the Son is,
11:20 n' doubt the kingdom of God is
29 and there shall n' sign be given it,
33 N' man, when he hath lighted a
36 of light, having n' part dark,
12: 4 have n' more that they can do.
11 ye n' thought how or what thing
17 I have n' room where to bestow
22 Take n' thought for your life,
33 not, where n' thief approacheth,
13:11 and could in n' wise lift up herself.
15: 7 persons, which need n' repentance.
16 eat: and n' man gave unto him.
19, 21 am n' more worthy to be called
16: 2 thou mayest be n' longer steward.
13 N' servant can serve two masters:
18:17 child shall in n' wise enter therein.
29 is n' man that hath left house, or
20:22 to give tribute unto Cæsar, or n'?
31 and they left n' children, and died.
22:36 and he that hath n' sword, let him
53 forth n' hands against me:
23: 4 people, I find n' fault in this man.
14 have found n' fault in this man
15 N', nor yet Herod: for I sent
22 found n' cause of death in him:
Joh 1:18 N' man hath seen God at any time;
21 prophet? And he answered, N'.
47 Israelite...in whom is n' guile!
2: 3 saith unto him, They have n' wine.
3: 2 for n' man can do these miracles
13 n' man hath ascended up to heaven,
32 n' man receiveth his testimony.
4: 9 n' dealings with the Samaritans.
17 and said, I have n' husband.
17 hast well said, I have n' husband:
27 n' man said, What seekest thou?
38 whereon ye bestowed n' labour:
44 hath n' honour in his own country.
5: 7 I have n' man, when the water is
14 sin n' more, lest a worse thing
22 For the Father judgeth n' man,
6:37 to me I will in n' wise cast out.
44 N' man can come to me, except
53 his blood, ye have n' life in you.
65 that n' man can come unto me,
66 and walked n' more with him.
7: 4 n' man...doeth any thing in secret,
13 n' man spake openly of him for fear
18 and n' unrighteousness is in him.
27 n' man knoweth whence he is.
30 but n' man laid hands on him,
44 but n' man laid hands on him.
52 out of Galilee ariseth n' prophet.
8:10 hath n' man condemned thee?
11 She said, N' man, Lord. And
11 condemn thee: go, and sin n' more.
15 after the flesh; I judge n' man.
20 and n' man laid hands on him; for
37 my word hath n' place in you.
44 because there is n' truth in him.
9: 4 cometh, when n' man can work.
25 Whether he be a sinner or n', I know
41 were blind, ye should have n' sin:
10:18 N' man taketh it from me, but I
29 n' man is able to pluck them out
41 and said, John did n' miracle:
11:10 because there is n' light in him.
54 walked n' more openly among
13: 8 not, thou hast n' part with me.
28 n' man at the table knew for what
14: 6 n' man cometh unto the Father,
19 and the world seeth me n' more;
15: 4 n' more can ye, except ye abide
13 Greater love hath n' man than
22 they have n' cloke for their sin.
16:10 Father, and ye see me n' more;
21 remembereth n' more the anguish,
22 your joy n' man taketh from you.
25 shall n' more speak...in proverbs,
29 plainly, and speakest n' proverb.
17:11 now I am n' more in the world,
18:38 them, I find in him n' fault at all.
19: 4 know that I find n' fault in him.
6 him: for I find n' fault in him.
9 But Jesus gave him n' answer.
11 have n' power at all against me,
15 We have n' king but Cæsar.
21: 5 any meat? They answered him, N'.
Ac 1:20 and let n' man dwell therein:
4:17 spread n' further among the people,
17 henceforth to n' man in this name.
5:13 durst n' man join himself to them:
23 opened, we found n' man within.
7: 5 n', not so much as to set his foot on:
5 him, when as yet he had n' child.
11 and our fathers found n' sustenance.
8:39 that the eunuch saw him n' more:
9: 7 hearing a voice, but seeing n' man.
8 eyes were opened, he saw n' man:
10:34 God is n' respecter of persons:
12:18 n' small stir among the soldiers,
13:28 found n' cause of death in him,
34 n' more to return to corruption,
37 raised again, saw n' corruption.
41 which ye shall in n' wise believe,
15: 2 Barnabas had n' small dissension
9 n' difference between us and them,
24 we gave n' such commandment:
28 you n' greater burden than these
16:28 Do thyself n' harm: for we are all

Ac 18:10 n· man shall set on thee to hurt
15 I will be n· judge of such matters.
19:23 arose n· small stir about that way.
24 n· small gain unto the craftsmen;
26 saying that they be n· gods, which
40 n· cause whereby we may give
20:25 ye all,...shall see my face n· more.
33 I have coveted n· man's silver, or
38 they should see his face n· more.
21:25 that they observe n· such thing,
39 Cilicia, a citizen of n· mean city:
23: 8 say that there is n· resurrection,
9 We find n· evil in this man: but if
22 See thou tell n· man that thou hast
25:10 to the Jews have I done n· wrong,
11 n· man may deliver me unto them.
26 I have n· certain thing to write
27:20 and n· small tempest lay on us,
22 shall be n· loss of any man's life
28: 2 people shewed us n· little kindness:
4 N· doubt this man is a murderer,
5 into the fire, and felt n· harm.
6 and saw n· harm come to him,
18 there was n· cause of death in me.
31 confidence, n· man forbidding him.
Ro 2:11 is n· respect of person with God.
3: 9 are we better than they? N·,
9 we better than they?...in n· wise:
10 There is none righteous, n·, not one:
12 is none that doeth good, n·, not one.
18 There is n· fear of God before
20 n· flesh be justified in his
22 believe: for there is n· difference:
4:15 wrath: for where n· law is, there
15 law is, there is n· transgression.
5:13 not imputed when there is n· law.
6: 9 from the dead dieth n· more;
9 hath n· more dominion over him.
7: 3 so that she is n· adulteress, though
17 Now then it is n· more I that do it,
18 my flesh) dwelleth n· good thing:
20 it is n· more I that do it, but sin
8: 1 therefore now n· condemnation
10:12 is n· difference between the Jew
19 jealousy by them that are n· people,
11: 6 grace, then is it n· more of works:
6 otherwise grace is n· more grace.
6 of works, then is it n· more grace:
6 otherwise work is n· more work.
12:17 Recompense to n· man evil for evil.
13: 1 For there is n· power but of God:
8 Owe n· man any thing, but to love
10 worketh n· ill to his neighbour:
14: 7 and n· man dieth to himself.
13 that n· man put a stumblingblock
15:23 now having n· more place in these
1Co 1: 7 So that ye come behind in n· gift;
10 there be n· divisions among you;
29 n· flesh...glory in his presence.
2:11 things of God knoweth n· man,
15 yet he himself is judged of n· man.
3:11 other foundation can n· man lay
18 Let n· man deceive himself. If
21 Therefore let n· man glory in men.
4: 6 that n· one of you be puffed up for
11 and have n· certain dwellingplace;
5:11 with such an one n· not to eat.
6: 5 n·, not one that shall be able to
7:25 virgins I have n· commandment
37 in his heart, having n· necessity,
8:13 I will eat n· flesh while the world
9:10 For our sakes, n· doubt, this is
10:13 hath n· temptation taken you but
24 Let n· man seek his own, but
25, 27 asking n· question for conscience
11:16 we have n· such custom, neither
12: 3 that n· man speaking by the Spirit
3 that n· man can say that Jesus is
21 to the hand, I have n· need of thee:
21 to the feet, I have n· need of you.
24 For our comely parts have n· need:
25 should be n· schism in the body;
13: 5 easily provoked, thinketh n· evil;
14: 2 for n· man understandeth him;
28 But if there be n· interpreter, let
15:12 there is n· resurrection of the dead?
13 there be n· resurrection of the dead,
16: 2 there be n· gatherings when I come.
11 Let n· man therefore despise him:
2Co 2:13 I had n· rest in my spirit, because
3:10 had n· glory in this respect, by
5:16 know we n· man after the flesh:
16 henceforth know we him n· more.
21 to be sin for us, who knew n· sin;
6: 3 Giving n· offence in any thing,
7: 2 us; we have wronged n· man,
2 we have corrupted n· man; we have
2 man, we have defrauded n· man.
5 our flesh had n· rest, but we were
8:15 had gathered little had n· lack.
20 that n· man should blame us in
11: 9 I was chargeable to n· man:
10 n· man shall stop me of this
14 And n· marvel; for Satan himself
15 it is n· great thing if his ministers
16 again, Let n· man think me a fool;
13: 7 pray to God that ye do n· evil;
Ga 2: 5 by subjection, n·, not for an hour;
6 were, it maketh n· matter to me:
6 God accepteth n· man's person:)
16 law shall n· flesh be justified.
3:11 that n· man is justified by the law
15 n· man disannulleth, or addeth
18 the law, it is n· more of promise:
25 are n· longer under a schoolmaster.
4: 7 art n· more a servant, but a son;

Ga 4: 8 them which by nature are n· gods.
5: 4 Christ is become of n· effect unto
23 against such there is n· law.
6:17 henceforth let n· man trouble me:
Eph 2:12 having n· hope, and without God
19 therefore ye are n· more strangers
4:14 we henceforth be n· more children,
28 Let him that stole steal n· more:
29 Let n· corrupt communication
5: 5 ye know, that n· whoremonger,
6 Let n· man deceive you with vain
11 n· fellowship with the unfruitful
29 For n· man ever yet hated his own
Ph'p 2: 7 But made himself of n· reputation,
20 For I have n· man likeminded,
3: 3 have n· confidence in the flesh.
4:15 n· church communicated with me
Col 2:16 Let n· man therefore judge you in
18 n· man beguile you of your reward
3:25 and there is n· respect of persons.
1Th 3: 1 when we could n· longer forbear,
3 n· man should be moved by these
5 when I could n· longer forbear,
4: 6 n· man go beyond and defraud his
13 even as others which have n· hope.
5: 1 have n· need that I write unto you.
2Th 2: 3 Let n· man deceive you by any
3:14 have n· company with him, that
1Ti 1: 3 that they teach n· other doctrine,
3: 3 Not given to wine, n· striker, not
4:12 Let n· man despise thy youth; but
5:22 Lay hands suddenly on n· man,
23 Drink n· longer water, but use a
6:16 which n· man can approach unto;
16 whom n· man hath seen, nor can see:
2Ti 2: 4 N· man that warreth entangleth
14 strive not about words to n· profit,
3: 9 they shall proceed n· further: for
4:16 answer n· man stood with me,
Tit 1: 7 not given to wine, n· striker, not
2: 8 having n· evil thing to say of you.
15 authority. Let n· man despise thee.
3: 2 To speak evil of n· man, to be
2 man, to be n· brawlers, but gentle,
Heb 5: 4 n· man taketh this honour unto
6:13 he could sware by n· greater, he
7:13 of which n· man gave attendance
8: 7 should n· place have been sought
12 will I remember n· more.
9:17 otherwise it is of n· strength at all
22 shedding of blood is n· remission.
10: 2 had n· more conscience of sins.
6 for sin thou hast had n· pleasure.
17 iniquities will I remember n· more.
18 there is n· more offering for sin.
26 remaineth n· more sacrifice for sins,
38 soul shall have n· pleasure in him.
12:11 Now n· chastening for the
14 without which n· man shall see the
17 for he found n· place of repentance,
13:10 whereof they have n· right to eat
14 here we have n· continuing city,
Jas 1:11 the sun is n· sooner risen with a
13 Let n· man say when he is tempted,
17 with whom is n· variableness,
2:11 Now if thou commit n· adultery,
13 mercy, that hath shewed n· mercy;
3: 8 the tongue can n· man tame; it is
12 so can n· fountain both yield salt
1Pe 2:22 Who did n· sin, neither was guile
3:10 his lips that they speak n· guile:
4: 2 That he n· longer should live the
2Pe 1:20 n· prophecy of the scripture
1Jo 1: 5 and in him is n· darkness at all.
8 If we say that we have n· sin, we
2: 7 I write n· new commandment unto
19 n· doubt have continued with us:
21 and that n· lie is of the truth.
27 and his truth, and is n· lie, and
3: 5 our sins; and in him is n· sin.
7 children, let n· man deceive you:
15 n· murderer hath eternal life
4:12 N· man hath seen God at any
18 There is n· fear in love; but
3Jo 4 n· greater joy than to hear that my
Re 2:17 which n· man knoweth saving he
3: 7 openeth, and n· man shutteth,
7 and shutteth, and n· man openeth;
8 open door, and n· man can shut it:
11 hast, that n· man take thy crown.
12 and he shall go n· more out: and I
5: 3 n· man in heaven, nor in earth,
4 because n· man was found worthy
7: 9 which n· man could number, of all
16 They shall hunger n· more,
10: 6 that there should be time n· longer:
13:17 And that n· man might buy or sell,
14: 3 and n· man could learn that song
5 in their mouth was found n· guile:
11 they have n· rest day nor night,
15: 8 and n· man was able to enter into
17:12 have received n· kingdom as yet;
18: 7 I sit a queen, and am n· widow,
7 widow, and shall see n· sorrow.
11 n· man buyeth their merchandise
14 thou shalt find them n· more at all.
21 and shall be found n· more at all.
22 shall be heard n· more at all in thee;
22 n· craftsman, of whatsoever
22 shall be heard n· more at all in thee:
23 shall shine n· more at all in thee;
23 bride shall be heard n· more at all
19:12 name written, that n· man knew,
20: 3 should deceive the nations n· more,
6 the second death hath n· power,
11 there was found n· place for them.

Re 21: 1 away; and there was n· more sea.
4 and there shall be n· more death,
22 And I saw n· temple therein: for
23 And the city had n· need of the sun,
25 for there shall be n· night there.
27 there shall in n· wise enter into it
22: 3 And there shall be n· more curse:
5 And there shall be n· night there;

No (*no*) See also POPULOUS.
Jer 46:25 will punish the multitude of N·.
Eze 30:14 and will execute judgments in N·.
15 I will cut off the multitude of N·.
16 pain, and N· shall be rent asunder,
Na 3: 8 Art thou better than populous N·,

Noadiah (*no-a-di'-ah*)
Ezr 8:33 Jeshua, and N· the son of Binnui,
Ne 6:14 and on the prophetess N·, and the

Noah (*no'-ah*) See also NOAH'S; NOE.
Ge 5:29 he called his name N·, saying,
30 after he begat N· five hundred
32 And N· was five hundred years old:
32 N· begat Shem, Ham, and Japheth.
6: 8 N· found grace in the eyes of the
9 These are the generations of N·:
9 N· was a just man and perfect in
9 and N· walked with God.
10 N· begat three sons, Shem, Ham,
13 And God said unto N·, The end of
22 Thus did N·; according to all that
7: 1 the Lord said unto N·, Come thou
5 N· did according unto all that the
6 N· was six hundred years old when
7 N· went in, and his sons, and his
9 two and two unto N· into the ark,
9 female, as God had commanded N·.
13 In the selfsame day entered N·,
13 Ham, and Japheth, the sons of N·,
15 they went in unto N· into the ark,
23 N· only remained alive, and they
8: 1 God remembered N·, and every
6 N· opened the window of the ark
11 so N· knew that the waters were
13 N· removed the covering of the ark,
15 And God spake unto N·, saying,
18 N· went forth, and his sons, and
20 N· builded an altar unto the Lord;
9: 1 God blessed N· and his sons, and
8 God spake unto N·, and to his sons
17 God said unto N·, This is the token
18 the sons of N·, that went forth of
19 These are the three sons of N·: and
20 N· began to be an husbandman,
24 N· awoke from his wine, and knew
28 And N· lived after the flood three
29 the days of N· were nine hundred
10: 1 the generations of the sons of N·,
32 are the families of the sons of N·,
Nu 26:33 Zelophehad were Mahlah, and N·,
27: 1 of his daughters; Mahlah, N·,
36:11 N·, the daughters of Zelophehad,
Jos 17: 3 of his daughters, Mahlah, and N·,
1Ch 1: 4 N·, Shem, Ham, and Japheth.
Isa 54: 9 is as the waters of N· unto me:
9 waters of N· should no more go
Eze 14:14 three men, N·, Daniel, and Job,
20 Though N·, Daniel, and Job, were
Heb 11: 7 By faith N·, being warned of God
1Pe 3:20 of God waited in the days of N·,
2Pe 2: 5 but saved N· the eighth person, a

Noah's (*no'-ahz*)
Ge 7:11 the six hundredth year of N· life,
13 and N· wife, and three wives of his

Nob (*nob*)
1Sa 21: 1 came David to N· to Abimelech
22: 9 I saw the son of Jesse coming to N·,
11 house, the priests that were in N·:
19 And N·, the city of the priests, smote
Ne 11:32 And at Anathoth, N·, Ananiah,
Isa 10:32 yet shall he remain at N· that day:

Nobah (*no'-bah*) See also KENAH; NOPHAH.
Nu 32:42 And N· went and took Kenath,
42 called it N·, after his own name.
J'g 8:11 dwelt in tents on the east of N·

noble See also NOBLEMAN; NOBLES.
Ezr 4:10 whom the great and n· Asnapper
Es 6: 9 one of the king's most n· princes,
Jer 2:21 Yet I had planted thee a n· vine, wholly
Ac 17:11 These were more n· than those in
24: 3 and in all places, most n· Felix,
26:25 said, I am not mad, most n· Festus;
1Co 1:26 mighty, not many n·, are called:

nobleman
Lu 19:12 A certain n· went into a far
Joh 4:46 there was a certain n·, whose son
49 The n· saith unto him, Sir, come

nobles
Ex 24:11 the n· of the children of Israel
Nu 21:18 the n· of the people digged it, by
J'g 5:13 have dominion over the n· among
1Ki 21: 8 to the n· that were in his city,
11 the elders and the n· who were the
2Ch 23:20 captains of hundreds, and the n·,
Ne 2:16 nor to the priests, nor to the n·,
3: 5 but their n· put not their necks to
4:14 rose up, and said unto the n·, and
19 And I said unto the n·, and to the
5: 7 I rebuked the n·, and the rulers, and
6:17 the n· of Judah sent many letters
7: 5 heart to gather together the n·,
10:29 clave to their brethren, their n·,
13:17 I contended with the n· of Judah,
Es 1: 3 n· and princes of the provinces,
Job 29:10 The n· held their peace, and their

Ps 83:11 Make their *n'* like Oreb, and like
149: 8 and their *n'* with fetters of iron;
Pr 8:16 By me princes rule, and *n'*, even
Ec 10:17 when thy king is the son of *n'*, and
Isa 13: 2 may go into the gates of the *n'*.
34:12 call the *n'* thereof to the kingdom,
43:14 have brought down all their *n'*,
Jer 14: 3 their *n'* have sent their little ones to
27:20 the *n'* of Judah and Jerusalem;
30:21 their *n'* shall be of themselves,
39: 6 Babylon slew all the *n'* of Judah.
Jon 3: 7 the decree of the king and his *n'*,
Na 3:18 thy *n'* shall dwell in the dust: thy

Nod (*nod*)
Ge 4:16 dwelt in the land of *N'*, on the

Nodab (*no'-dab*)
1Ch 5:19 with Jetur, and Nephish, and *N'*.

Noe (*no'-e*) See also NOAH.
M't 24:37 as the days of *N'* were, so shall
38 day that *N'* entered into the ark,
Lu 3:36 which was the son of *N'*, which
17:26 as it was in the days of *N'*, so shall
27 day that *N'* entered into the ark,

Nogah (*no'-gah*)
1Ch 3: 7 And *N'*, and Nepheg, and Japhia,
14: 6 And *N'*, and Nepheg, and Japhia,

Nohah (*no'-hah*)
1Ch 8: 2 *N'* the fourth, and Rapha the fifth.

noise See also NOISED.
Ex 20:18 and the *n'* of the trumpet, and the
32:17 Joshua heard the *n'* of the people
17 There is a *n'* of war in the camp.
18 the *n'* of them that sing do I hear.
Jos 6:10 nor make any *n'* with your voice,
J'g 5:11 delivered from the *n'* of archers
1Sa 4: 6 heard the *n'* of the shout, they
6 meaneth the *n'* of this great shout
14 when Eli heard the *n'* of the crying,
14 What meaneth the *n'* of this tumult?
14:19 the *n'* that was in the host of the
1Ki 1:41 *n'* of the city being in an uproar?
45 This is the *n'* that ye have heard.
2Ki 7: 6 the Syrians to hear a *n'* of chariots,
6 *n'* of horses, even the *n'* of a great
11:13 Athaliah heard the *n'* of the guard
1Ch 15:28 making a *n'* with psalteries and
2Ch 23:12 when Athaliah heard the *n'* of the
Ezr 3:13 discern the *n'* of the shout of joy
13 the *n'* of the weeping of the people:
13 shout, and the *n'* was heard afar off.
Job 36:29 or the *n'* of his tabernacle?
33 *n'* thereof sheweth concerning it,
37: 2 Hear attentively the *n'* of his voice,
Ps 33: 3 song; play skilfully with a loud *n'*.
42: 7 deep at the *n'* of thy waterspouts:
55: 2 in my complaint, and make a *n'*;
59: 6 they make a *n'* like a dog, and go
14 let them make a *n'* like a dog,
65: 7 Which stilleth the *n'* of the seas,
7 *n'* of their waves, and the tumult of
66: 1 Make a joyful *n'* unto God, all ye
81: 1 make a joyful *n'* unto the God of
93: 4 than the *n'* of many waters, yea,
95: 1 let us make a joyful *n'* to the rock of
2 a joyful *n'* unto him with psalms.
98: 4 Make a joyful *n'* unto the Lord, all
4 make a loud *n'*, and rejoice, and
6 make a joyful *n'* before the Lord, the
100: 1 Make a joyful *n'* unto the Lord, all ye
Isa 9: 5 of the warrior is with confused *n'*,
13: 4 *n'* of a multitude in the mountains,
4 tumultuous *n'* of the kingdoms of
14:11 the grave, and the *n'* of thy viols:
17:12 make a *n'* like the *n'* of the seas;
24: 8 the *n'* of them that rejoice endeth,
18 who fleeth from the *n'* of the fear
25: 5 bring down the *n'* of strangers, as
29: 6 and with earthquake, and great *n'*,
31: 4 abase himself for the *n'* of them:
33: 3 At the *n'* of the tumult the people
66: 6 A voice of *n'* from the city, a voice
Jer 4:19 my heart maketh a *n'* in me; I
29 flee for the *n'* of the horsemen
10:22 Behold, the *n'* of the bruit is come,
11:16 with the *n'* of a great tumult he
25:31 A *n'* shall come even to the ends of
46:17 Pharaoh king of Egypt is but a *n'*;
47: 3 the *n'* of the stamping of the hoofs
49:21 is moved at the *n'* of their fall;
21 at the cry the *n'* thereof was heard
50:46 At the *n'* of the taking of Babylon
51:55 a *n'* of their voice is uttered:
La 2: 7 a *n'* in the house of the Lord,
Eze 1:24 went, I heard the *n'* of their wings,
24 like the *n'* of great waters, as the
24 of speech, as the *n'* of an host:
3:13 I heard also the *n'* of the wings of
13 the *n'* of the wheels over against
13 them, and a *n'* of a great rushing.
19: 7 thereof, by the *n'* of his roaring.
26:10 shake at the *n'* of the horsemen,
13 cause the *n'* of thy songs to cease;
37: 7 as I prophesied, there was a *n'*,
43: 2 voice was like a *n'* of many waters:
Joe 2: 5 Like the *n'* of chariots on the tops of
5 like the *n'* of a flame of fire that
Am 5:23 away from me the *n'* of thy songs;
Mic 2:12 make a great *n'* by reason of the
Na 3: 2 The *n'* of a whip, and the *n'* of the
Zep 1:10 the *n'* of a cry from the fish gate,
Zec 9:15 and make a *n'* as through wine;
M't 9:23 minstrels and...people make a *n'*,
2Pe 3:10 shall pass away with a great *n'*,
Re 6: 1 heard, as it were the *n'* of thunder,

noised
Jos 6:27 his fame was *n'* throughout all the
M'r 2: 1 it was *n'* that he was in the house.
Lu 1:65 all these sayings were *n'* abroad
Ac 2: 6 when this was *n'* abroad, the

noisome
Ps 91: 3 fowler, and from the *n'* pestilence.
Eze 14:15 I cause *n'* beasts to pass through
21 the *n'* beast, and the pestilence,
Re 16: 2 fell a *n'* and grievous sore upon the

Non (*non*) See also NUN.
1Ch 7:27 *N'* his son, Jehoshuah his son.

none^ See also NO and ONE.
Ge 23: 6 *n'* of us shall withhold from
28:17 is *n'* other but the house of God,
39: 9 is *n'* greater in this house than I;
11 there was *n'* of the men of the house
41: 8 there was *n'* that could interpret
15 and there is *n'* that can interpret it:
24 was *n'* that could declare it to me.
39 there is *n'* so discreet and wise as
Ex 8:10 is *n'* like unto the Lord our God.
9:14 there is *n'* like me in all the earth.
24 *n'* like it in all the land of Egypt
11: 6 such as there was *n'* like it, nor
12:22 *n'* of you shall go out at the door of
15:26 put *n'* of these diseases upon thee,
16:26 the sabbath, in it there shall be *n'*.
27 for to gather, and they found *n'*.
23:15 *n'* shall appear before me empty:)
34:20 *n'* shall appear before me empty.
Le 18: 6 *N'* of you shall approach to any
21: 1 shall *n'* be defiled for the dead
22:30 leave *n'* of it until the morrow:
25:26 if the man have *n'* to redeem it, and
26: 6 down, and *n'* shall make you afraid:
17 ye shall flee when *n'* pursueth you.
36 they shall fall when *n'* pursueth.
37 before a sword, when *n'* pursueth:
27:29 *N'* devoted, which shall be
Nu 7: 9 the sons of Kohath he gave *n'*:
9:12 leave *n'* of it unto the morning, nor
21:35 until there was *n'* left him alive:
30: 8 she bound her soul, of *n'* effect:
32:11 Surely *n'* of the men that came up
De 2:34 of every city, we left *n'* to remain:
3: 3 smote him until *n'* was left to him
4:35 God; there is *n'* else beside him.
39 the earth beneath: there is *n'* else.
5: 7 shalt have *n'* other gods before me.
7:15 *n'* of the evil diseases of Egypt,
22:27 cried, and there was *n'* to save her.
28:31 thou shalt have *n'* to rescue them.
66 have *n'* assurance of thy life:
32:36 and there is *n'* shut up, or left.
33:26 is *n'* like unto the God of Jeshurun,
Jos 6: 1 Israel: *n'* went out, and *n'* came in.
8:22 let *n'* of them remain or escape.
9:23 *n'* of you be freed from being
10:21 *n'* moved his tongue against any
28 were therein; he let *n'* remain:
30 therein; he let *n'* remain in it;
33 he had left him *n'* remaining.
37 he left *n'* remaining, according
39 therein; he left *n'* remaining: as
40 he left *n'* remaining, but utterly
11: 8 they left them *n'* remaining.
13 Israel burned *n'* of them, save
22 *n'* of the Anakims left in the land
13:14 of Levi he gave *n'* inheritance;
14: 3 gave *n'* inheritance among them.
J'g 19:28 let us be going. But *n'* answered.
21: 8 came *n'* to the camp from
9 were *n'* of the inhabitants of
Ru 4: 4 is *n'* to redeem it beside thee; and
1Sa 2: 2 There is *n'* holy as the Lord: for
2 for there is *n'* besides thee: neither
3:19 *n'* of his words fall to the ground.
10:24 *n'* like him among all the people?
14:24 *n'* of the people tasted any food.
21: 9 David said, There is *n'* like that;
22: 8 is *n'* that sheweth me that my son
8 is *n'* of you that is sorry for me, or
2Sa 7:22 for there is *n'* like thee, neither is
14: 6 and there was *n'* to part them, but
19 *n'* can turn to the right hand or to
25 was *n'* to be so much praised
18:12 Beware that *n'* touch the young man
22:42 looked, but there was *n'* to save;
1Ki 3:12 there was *n'* like thee before thee,
8:60 is God, and that there is *n'* else.
10:21 were of pure gold: *n'* were of silver:
12:20 was *n'* that followed the house of
15:22 all Judah; *n'* was exempted:
21:25 But there was *n'* like unto Ahab,
2Ki 5:16 I will receive *n'*. And he urged him
6:12 his servants said, *N'*, my lord, O
9:10 and there shall be *n'* to bury her.
15 let *n'* go forth nor escape out of the
10:11 until he left him *n'* remaining.
19 his priests; let *n'* be wanting:
23 be here with you *n'* of the servants
25 and slay them; let *n'* come forth.
17:18 was *n'* left but the tribe of Judah
18: 5 after him was *n'* like him among
24:14 *n'* remained, save the poorest sort
1Ch 15: 2 *N'* ought to carry the ark of God
17:20 O Lord, there is *n'* like thee,
23:17 Eliezer had *n'* other sons; but
29:15 a shadow, and there is *n'* abiding.
2Ch 1:12 such as *n'* of the kings have had
9:11 *n'* such seen before in the land of
20 were of pure gold: *n'* were of silver:
10:16 we have *n'* inheritance in the son
16: 1 let *n'* go out or come in to Asa

2Ch 20: 6 that *n'* is able to withstand thee?
24 fallen to the earth, and *n'* escaped.
23: 6 let *n'* come into the house of the
19 that *n'* which was unclean in any
Ezr 8:15 found there *n'* of the sons of Levi.
Ne 4:23 *n'* of us put off our clothes, saving
Es 1: 8 *n'* did compel: for so the king had
4: 2 *n'* might enter into the king's gate
Job 1: 8 there is *n'* like him in the earth,
2: 3 there is *n'* like him in the earth,
13 and *n'* spake a word unto him: for
3: 9 dark; let it look for light but have *n'*,
10: 7 there is *n'* that can deliver out of
11:19 down, and *n'* shall make thee afraid;
18:15 tabernacle, because it is *n'* of his:
20:21 There shall *n'* of his meat be left;
29:12 and him that had *n'* to help him.
32:12 was *n'* of you that convinced Job,
35:10 *n'* saith, Where is God my maker,
12 they cry, but *n'* giveth answer,
41:10 *N'* is so fierce that dare stir him up:
Ps 7: 2 pieces, while there is *n'* to deliver.
10:15 his wickedness till thou find *n'*.
14: 1 works, there is *n'* that doeth good.
3 is *n'* that doeth good, no, not one.
18:41 cried, but there was *n'* to save them:
22:11 is near; for there is *n'* to help.
29 and *n'* can keep alive his own soul.
25: 3 *n'* that wait on thee be ashamed:
33:10 devices of the people of *n'* effect.
34:22 *n'* of them that trust in him shall
37:31 heart; *n'* of his steps shall slide.
49: 7 *N'* of them can by any means
50:22 pieces, and there be *n'* to deliver.
53: 1 iniquity: there is *n'* that doeth good.
3 there is *n'* that doeth good, no, not
69:20 some to take pity, but there was *n'*;
20 and for comforters, but I found *n'*.
25 and let *n'* dwell in their tents.
71:11 him; for there is *n'* to deliver him.
73:25 is *n'* upon earth that I desire
76: 5 *n'* of the men of might have found
79: 3 and there was *n'* to bury them.
81:11 voice; and Israel would *n'* of me.
86: 8 the gods there is *n'* like unto thee,
107:12 fell down, and there was *n'* to help.
109:12 be *n'* to extend mercy unto him:
Pr 1:25 and would *n'* of my reproof:
30 They would *n'* of my counsel: they
2:19 *N'* that go unto her return again,
3:31 and choose *n'* of his ways.
Ca 4: 2 twins, and *n'* is barren among them.
Isa 1:31 together, and *n'* shall quench them.
5:27 *N'* shall be weary nor stumble
27 them; *n'* shall slumber nor sleep;
29 away safe, and *n'* shall deliver it.
10:14 there was *n'* that moved the wing,
14: 6 is persecuted, and *n'* hindereth.
31 *n'* shall be alone in his appointed
17: 2 down, and *n'* shall make them afraid.
22:22 so he shall open, and *n'* shall shut;
22 and he shall shut, and *n'* shall open.
34:10 *n'* shall pass through it for ever and
12 the kingdom, but *n'* shall be there,
16 fail, *n'* shall want her mate:
41:17 needy seek water, and there is *n'*,
26 yea, there is *n'* that sheweth,
26 yea, there is *n'* that declareth,
26 there is *n'* that heareth your words.
42:22 are for a prey, and *n'* delivereth;
22 for a spoil, and *n'* saith, Restore.
43:13 is *n'* that can deliver out of my hand:
44:19 And *n'* considereth in his heart,
45: 5 I am the Lord, and there is *n'* else,
6 west, that there is *n'* beside me.
6 I am the Lord, and there is *n'* else.
14 and there is *n'* else, there is no God.
18 I am the Lord; and there is *n'* else.
21 a Saviour; there is *n'* beside me.
22 for I am God, and there is *n'* else.
46: 9 for I am God, and there is *n'* else;
9 I am God, and there is *n'* like me,
47: 8 heart, I am, and *n'* else besides me;
10 thou hast said, *n'* seeth me. Thy
10 heart, I am, and *n'* else besides me.
15 to his quarter; *n'* shall save thee.
50: 2 I called, was there *n'* to answer?
51:18 is *n'* to guide her among all the sons
57: 1 *n'* considering that the righteous is
59: 4 *n'* calleth for justice, nor any
11 look for judgment, but there is *n'*;
63: 3 people there was *n'* with me;
5 looked, and there was *n'* to help;
5 that there was *n'* to uphold:
64: 7 is *n'* that calleth upon thy name,
66: 4 when I called, *n'* did answer;
Jer 4: 4 fire, and burn that *n'* can quench it,
22 and they have *n'* understanding:
7:33 and *n'* shall fray them away.
9:10 *n'* can pass through them;
12 that *n'* passeth through?
22 and *n'* shall gather them.
10: 6 as there is *n'* like unto thee, O Lord
7 kingdoms, there is *n'* like unto thee.
20 there is *n'* to stretch forth my tent
13:19 be shut up, and *n'* shall open them:
14:16 they shall have *n'* to bury them,
21:12 and burn that *n'* can quench it,
23:14 *n'* doth return from...wickedness:
30: 7 day is great, so that *n'* is like it:
10 quiet, and *n'* shall make him afraid.
13 There is *n'* to plead thy cause, that
34: 9 *n'* should serve himself of them,
10 *n'* should serve themselves of them
35:14 for unto this day they drink *n'*,
36:30 shall have *n'* to sit upon the throne

Jer 42:17 *n'* of them shall remain or escape
44: 7 Judah, to leave you *n'* to remain;
14 that *n'* of the remnant of Judah,
14 *n'* shall return but such as shall
46:27 ease, and *n'* shall make him afraid.
48:33 *n'* shall tread with shouting;
49: 5 and *n'* shall gather up him that
50: 3 and *n'* shall dwell therein; they
9 man; *n'* shall return in vain.
20 sought for, and there shall be *n'*;
29 round about; let *n'* thereof escape:
32 and fall, and *n'* shall raise him up:
51:62 that *n'* shall remain in it, neither
La 1: 2 lovers she hath *n'* to comfort her:
4 *n'* come to the solemn feasts: all
7 of the enemy, and *n'* did help her:
17 and there is *n'* to comfort her: the
21 I sigh: there is *n'* to comfort me:
2:22 of the Lord's anger *n'* escaped
5: 8 is *n'* that doth deliver us out of
Eze 7:11 *n'* of them shall remain, nor of
14 ready; but *n'* goeth to the battle:
25 seek peace, and there shall be *n'*.
12:28 *n'* of my words be prolonged any
16: 5 *N'* eye pitied thee, to do any of
34 *n'* followeth thee to commit
18: 7 pledge, hath spoiled *n'* by violence,
22:30 not destroy it: but I found *n'*.
31:14 end that *n'* of all the trees by the
33:16 *N'* of his sins...he hath committed
28 that *n'* shall pass through.
34: 6 *n'* did search or seek after them.
28 and *n'* shall make them afraid.
39:26 land, and *n'* made them afraid.
28 left *n'* of them any more there.
Da 1:19 them all was found *n'* like Daniel,
2:11 *n'* other that can shew it before
4:35 *n'* can stay his hand, or say unto
6: 4 could find *n'* occasion nor fault;
8: 7 *n'* that could deliver the ram out
27 at the vision, but *n'* understood it.
10:21 is *n'* that holdeth with me in these
11:16 and *n'* shall stand before him: and
45 to his end, and *n'* shall help him.
12:10 *n'* of the wicked shall understand;
Ho 2:10 and *n'* shall deliver her out of mine
5:14 take away and *n'* shall rescue him.
7: 7 *n'* among them that calleth unto
11: 7 High, *n'* at all would exalt him.
12: 8 *n'* iniquity in me that were sin.
Joe 2:27 the Lord your God, and *n'* else:
Am 5: 2 land; there is *n'* to raise her up.
6 there be *n'* to quench it in Beth-el.
Ob 7 there is *n'* understanding in him.
Mic 2: 5 *n'* that shall cast a cord by lot in
3:11 us? *n'* evil can come upon us.
4: 4 *n'* shall make them afraid: for the
5: 8 in pieces, and *n'* can deliver.
7: 2 and there is *n'* upright among men:
Na 2: 8 they cry; but *n'* shall look back.
9 for there is *n'* end of the store and
11 whelp, and *n'* make them afraid?
3: 3 and there is *n'* end of their corpses;
Zep 2:15 I am, and there is *n'* beside me:
3: 6 streets waste, that *n'* passeth by:
6 man, that there is *n'* inhabitant.
13 and *n'* shall make them afraid.
Hag 1: 6 ye clothe you, but there is *n'* warm;
Zec 7:10 let *n'* of you imagine evil against
8:17 let *n'* of you imagine evil in your
Mal 2:15 let *n'* deal treacherously against
M't 12:43 places, seeking rest, and findeth *n'*.
15: 6 commandment of God of *n'* effect
19:17 there is *n'* good but one, that is,
26:60 But found *n'*: yea, though many
60 witnesses came, yet found they *n'*.
M'r 7:13 Making...word of God of *n'* effect
10:18 is *n'* good but one, that is, God.
12:31 is *n'* other commandment greater
32 God; and there is *n'* other but he:
14:55 to put him to death; and found *n'*.
Lu 1:61 is *n'* of thy kindred that is called
3:11 him impart to him that hath *n'*;
4:26 unto *n'* of them was Elias sent,
27 *n'* of them was cleansed, saving
11:24 seeking rest; and finding *n'*, he
13: 6 sought fruit thereon, and found *n'*,
7 fruit on this fig tree, and find *n'*:
14:24 *n'* of those men which were bidden
18:19 *n'* is good, save one, that is, God.
34 they understood *n'* of these things:
Joh 6:22 that there was *n'* other boat there,
7:19 *n'* of you keepeth the law? Why go
8:10 saw *n'* but the woman, he said
15:24 the works which *n'* other man did,
16: 5 *n'* of you asketh me, Whither goest
17:12 and *n'* of them is lost, but the son
18: 9 thou gavest me have I lost *n'*.
21:12 *n'* of the disciples durst ask him,
Ac 3: 6 said, Silver and gold have I *n'*;
4:12 is *n'* other name under heaven
7: 5 he gave him *n'* inheritance in it,
8:16 yet he was fallen upon *n'* of them:
24 *n'* of these things which ye have
11:19 word to *n'* but unto the Jews only.
18:17 Gallio cared for *n'* of these things.
20:24 But *n'* of these things move
24:23 forbid *n'* of his acquaintance to
25:11 but if there be *n'* of these things
18 they brought *n'* accusation of such
26:22 saying *n'* other things than those
26 persuaded that *n'* of these
Ro 3:10 there is *n'* righteous, no, not one:
11 There is *n'* that understandeth,
11 there is *n'* that seeketh after God.
12 there is *n'* that doeth good, no, not

Ro 4:14 and the promise made of *n'* effect:
8: 9 the Spirit of Christ, he is *n'* of his.
9: 6 word of God hath taken *n'* effect.
14: 7 For *n'* of us liveth to himself, and
1Co 1:14 thank God that I baptized *n'* of you,
17 cross...should be made of *n'* effect.
2: 8 *n'* of the princes of this world
7:29 wives be as though they had *n'*;
8: 4 there is *n'* other God but one.
9:15 But I have used *n'* of these things:
10:32 Give *n'* offence, neither to...Jews,
14:10 *n'* of them is without signification.
2Co 1:13 we write *n'* other things unto you,
Ga 1:19 But other of the apostles saw I *n'*,
3:17 make the promise of *n'* effect.
5:10 ye will be *n'* otherwise minded:
1Th 5:15 *n'* render evil for evil unto any
1Ti 5:14 give *n'* occasion to the adversary
1Pe 4:15 let *n'* of you suffer as a murderer,
1Jo 2:10 is *n'* occasion of stumbling in him.
Re 2:10 Fear *n'* of those things which thou
24 put upon you *n'* other burden.

noon See also AFTERNOON; NOONDAY; NOONTIDE.
Ge 43:16 men shall dine with me at *n'*.
25 present against Joseph came at *n'*:
2Sa 4: 5 Ish-bosheth, who lay on a bed at *n'*.
1Ki 18:26 Baal from morning even until *n'*,
27 it came to pass at *n'*, that Elijah
20:16 And they went out at *n'*. But
2Ki 4:20 he sat on her knees till *n'*, and then
Ps 55:17 Evening, and morning, and at *n'*,
Ca 1: 7 thou makest thy flock to rest at *n'*:
Isa 58:10 and thy darkness be as the *n'* day:
59:10 we stumble at *n'* day as in the
Jer 6: 4 her; arise, and let us go up at *n'*.
Am 8: 9 will cause the sun to go down at *n'*,
Zep 2: 4 shall drive out Ashdod at the *n'* day,
Ac 22: 6 nigh unto Damascus about *n'*,

noonday See also NOON and DAY.
De 28:29 And thou shalt grope at *n'*, as the
Job 5:14 and grope in the *n'* as in the night.
11:17 age shall be clearer than the *n'*;
Ps 37: 6 light, and thy judgment as the *n'*.
91: 6 the destruction that wasteth at *n'*.
Isa 16: 3 as the night in the midst of the *n'*;
Jer 15: 8 of the young men a spoiler at *n'*:

noontide
Jer 20:16 and the shouting at *n'*;

Noph (*nof*) See also MEMPHIS.
Isa 19:13 the princes of *N'* are deceived;
Jer 2:16 the children of *N'* and Tahapanes
44: 1 and at Tahpanhes, and at *N'*, and
46:14 publish in *N'* and in Tahpanhes:
19 for *N'* shall be waste and desolate
Eze 30:13 their images to cease out of *N'*;
16 and *N'* shall have distresses daily.

Nophah (*no'-fah*) See also NOBAH.
Nu 21:30 them waste even unto *N'*, which

nor
Ge 21:23 me, *n'* with my son, *n'* with my son's
45: 5 grieved, *n'* angry with yourselves,
6 shall neither be earing *n'* harvests.
49:10 Judah, *n'* a lawgiver from between
Ex 4: 1 me, *n'* hearken unto my voice:
10 *n'* since thou hast spoken unto thy
10: 6 thy fathers, *n'* thy father's fathers
11: 6 none like it, *n'* be like it any more.
12: 9 of it raw, *n'* sodden at all with water,
13:22 by day, *n'* the pillar of fire by night,
20: 5 thyself to them, *n'* serve them:
10 thou, *n'* thy son, *n'* thy daughter,
10 thy manservant, *n'* thy maidservant,
10 *n'* thy cattle, *n'* thy stranger that is
17 *n'* his manservant, *n'* his maidservant,
17 *n'* his ox, *n'* his ass, *n'* any thing that is
22:21 vex a stranger, *n'* oppress him:
28 *n'* curse the ruler of thy people.
23:24 gods, *n'* serve them, *n'* do after their
26 nothing cast their young, *n'* be barren,
32 covenant with them, *n'* with their gods.
30: 9 *n'* burnt sacrifice, *n'* meat offering;
34: 3 *n'* herds feed before that mount.
10 in all the earth, *n'* in any nation:
28 neither eat bread, *n'* drink water.
36: 6 *n'* woman make any more work
Le 2:11 shall burn no leaven, *n'* any honey,
3:17 that ye eat neither fat *n'* blood.
10: 9 Do not drink wine *n'* strong drink,
9 *n'* thy sons with thee, when ye go
11:12 hath no fins *n'* scales in the waters,
26 clovenfooted, *n'* cheweth the cud,
12: 4 thing, *n'* come into the sanctuary,
13:34 *n'* be in sight deeper than the skin;
17:16 wash them not, *n'* bathe his flesh;
18:26 your own nation, *n'* any stranger that
19: 4 *n'* make to yourselves molten
14 *n'* put a stumblingblock before the
15 *n'* honour the person of the mighty:
18 *n'* bear any grudge against the
20 redeemed, *n'* freedom given her;
26 use enchantment, *n'* observe times.
28 dead, *n'* print any marks upon you:
20:19 sister, *n'* of thy father's sister:
21: 5 *n'* make...cuttings in their flesh.
10 his head, *n'* rend his clothes;
11 *n'* defile himself for his father, or
12 *n'* profane the sanctuary of his God;
23 vail, *n'* come nigh unto the altar,
22:22 *n'* make an offering by fire of them
23:14 *n'* parched corn, *n'* green ears, until
25: 4 thy field, *n'* prune thy vineyard.
11 *n'* gather the grapes in it of thy vine
20 not sow, *n'* gather in our increase.
37 *n'* lend him thy victuals for increase.

Le 26: 1 shall make no idols *n'* graven image,
27:10 shall not alter it, *n'* change it, a
Nu 5:15 it, *n'* put frankincense thereon;
6: 3 *n'* eat moist grapes, or dried.
9:12 morning, *n'* break any bone of it:
11:19 one day, *n'* two days, *n'* five days,
19 neither ten days, *n'* twenty days;
18: 3 that neither they, *n'* ye also, die.
20:17 turn to the right hand, *n'* to the left,
23:25 them at all, *n'* bless them at all.
De 1:45 your voice, *n'* give ear unto you.
2:19 them not, *n'* meddle with them:
27 turn unto the right hand *n'* to the left.
37 *n'* unto any place of the river Jabbok,
37 *n'* unto the cities in the mountains,
37 *n'* unto whatsoever the Lord our God
4:28 see, *n'* hear, *n'* eat, *n'* smell.
31 thee, *n'* forget the covenant of thy
5: 9 thyself unto them, *n'* serve them:
14 work, thou, *n'* thy son, *n'* thy daughter,
14 *n'* thy manservant, *n'* thy maidservant,
14 *n'* thine ox, *n'* thine ass, *n'* any of thy
14 *n'* thy servant that is within thy gates;
7: 2 them, *n'* shew mercy unto them:
3 *n'* his daughter shalt thou take
7 his love upon you, *n'* choose you,
25 *n'* take it unto thee, lest thou be
9: 9 did eat bread *n'* drink water:
18 neither eat bread, *n'* drink water,
23 him not, *n'* hearkened to his voice.
27 *n'* to their wickedness, *n'* to their sin:
10:17 not persons, *n'* taketh reward:
12:12 hath no part *n'* inheritance with you.
17 *n'* any of thy vows which thou vowest,
17 *n'* thy freewill offerings, or heave
32 add thereto, *n'* diminish from it.
13: 6 hast not known, thou, *n'* thy fathers;
8 unto him, *n'* hearken unto him;
14: 1 *n'* make any baldness between your
8 flesh, *n'* touch their dead carcase.
27 hath no part *n'* inheritance with thee.
29 hath no part *n'* inheritance with thee,)
15: 7 *n'* shut thine hand from thy poor
19 *n'* shear the firstling of thy sheep.
17:11 thee, to the right hand, *n'* to the left.
16 *n'* cause the people to return to
18: 1 no part *n'* inheritance with Israel:
22 thing follow not, *n'* come to pass,
21: 4 which is neither eared *n'* sown, and
22:30 wife, *n'* discover his father's skirt.
23: 6 seek their peace *n'* their prosperity
17 *n'* a sodomite of the sons of Israel.
24:17 the stranger, *n'* of the fatherless;
17 *n'* take a widow's raiment to
26:14 *n'* given ought thereof for the dead:
28:36 neither thou *n'* thy father have known;
39 of the wine, *n'* gather the grapes;
50 old, *n'* shew favour to the young:
64 neither thou *n'* thy fathers have known,
29:23 *n'* beareth, *n'* any grass groweth
31: 6 fear not, *n'* be afraid of them: for
6 will not fail thee, *n'* forsake thee.
33: 9 brethren, *n'* knew his own children:
34: 7 dim, *n'* his natural force abated.
Jos 1: 5 I will not fail thee, *n'* forsake thee.
6:10 shall not shout, *n'* make any noise
10:25 Fear not, *n'* be dismayed, be strong
13:13 Geshurites, *n'* the Maachathites:
22:19 the Lord, *n'* rebel against us, in
26 for burnt offering, *n'* for sacrifice:
28 for burnt offerings, *n'* for sacrifices;
23: 7 gods, *n'* cause to swear by them,
7 them, *n'* bow yourselves unto them:
24:12 with thy sword, *n'* with thy bow.
19 your transgressions *n'* your sins.
J'g 1:27 her towns, *n'* Taanach and her towns,
27 *n'* the inhabitants of Dor and her
27 *n'* the inhabitants of Ibleam and her
27 *n'* the inhabitants of Megiddo and her
30 *n'* the inhabitants of Nahalol; but the
31 *n'* the inhabitants of Zidon, *n'* of Ahlab,
31 *n'* of Achzib, *n'* of Helbah,
31 *n'* of Aphik, *n'* of Rehob:
33 *n'* the inhabitants of Beth-anath;
2:10 not the Lord, *n'* yet the works
19 doings, *n'* from their stubborn way.
6: 4 Israel, neither sheep, *n'* ox, *n'* ass.
11:15 *n'* the land of the children of Ammon:
34 he had neither son *n'* daughter.
13: 4 and drink not wine *n'* strong drink,
7 now drink no wine *n'* strong drink,
14 drink, *n'* eat any unclean thing:
23 *n'* would as at this time have told
14:16 not told it my father *n'* my mother,
19:30 was no such deed done *n'* seen from
1Sa 1:15 drunk neither wine *n'* strong drink,
3:14 with sacrifice *n'* offering for ever.
5: 5 *n'* any that come into Dagon's house,
12: 4 not defrauded us, *n'* oppressed us,
21 which cannot profit *n'* deliver; for
13:22 *n'* spear found in the hand of any of
15:29 of Israel will not lie *n'* repent:
20:27 meat, neither yesterday, *n'* to day?
31 not be established, *n'* thy kingdom.
21: 8 my sword *n'* my weapons with me,
22:15 *n'* to all the house of my father:
24:11 there is neither evil *n'* transgression
25:31 thee, *n'* offence of heart unto my lord,
26:12 no man saw it, *n'* knew it, neither
27: 9 and left neither man *n'* woman alive,
11 saved neither man *n'* woman alive,
28: 6 dreams, *n'* by Urim, *n'* by prophets.
15 neither by prophets, *n'* by dreams:
18 *n'* executedst his fierce wrath
20 no bread all the day, *n'* all the night.
30:12 no bread, *n'* drunk any water,

1Sa 30:15 n' deliver me into the hands of my
19 small n' great, neither sons n'
19 n' any thing that they had taken
2Sa 1:21 rain, upon you, n' fields of offerings:
2:19 not to the right hand n' to the left
3:34 bound, n' thy feet put into fetters:
13:22 brother Amnon neither good n' bad:
14: 7 name n' remainder upon the earth.
19: 6 regardest neither princes n' servants:
24 n' trimmed his beard, n' washed
21: 4 n' gold of Saul, n' of his house;
10 n' the beasts of the field by night.
1Ki 3: 8 numbered n' counted for multitude.
11 n' hast asked the life of thine
26 Let it be neither mine n' thine, but
5: 4 neither adversary n' evil occurrent.
6: 7 that there was neither hammer n' axe
7 n' any tool of iron heard in the house,
8: 5 told n' numbered for multitude.
57 let him not leave us, n' forsake us:
10:12 trees, n' were seen unto this day.
12:24 up, n' fight against your brethren
13: 8 will I eat bread n' drink water in
9 Eat no bread, n' drink water,
9 n' turn again by the same way
16 return with thee, n' go in with thee:
16 bread n' drink water with thee in
17 eat no bread n' drink water there,
17 n' turn again to go by the way that
28 eaten the carcase, n' torn the ass.
16:11 of his kinsfolks, n' of his friends.
17: 1 shall not be dew n' rain these years,
18:26 was no voice, n' any that answered.
29 n' any to answer, n' any that
20: 8 Hearken not unto him, n' consent.
22:31 Fight neither with small n' great,
2Ki 3:14 not look toward thee, n' see thee.
4:23 is neither new moon, n' Sabbath.
31 there was neither voice, n' hearing.
5:17 offering n' sacrifice unto other gods,
6:10 himself there, not once n' twice.
9:15 go forth n' escape out of the city
14: 6 n' the children be put to death for
26 n' [657] any left, n' any helper for
17:35 gods, n' bow yourselves to them,
35 n' serve them, n' sacrifice to them:
18: 5 Judah, n' any that were before him.
12 would not hear them, n' do them.
19:32 this city, n' shoot an arrow there,
32 n' come before it with shield,
32 with shield, n' cast a bank against it.
20:13 in his house, n' in all his dominion.
23:22 Israel, n' in all the days of the kings
22 of Israel, n' of the kings of Judah;
1Ch 21:24 n' offer burnt offerings without cost.
22:13 courage; dread not, n' be dismayed.
23:26 n' any vessels of it for the service
28:20 fear not, n' be dismayed: for the
20 will not fail thee, n' forsake thee,
2Ch 1:11 or honour, n' the life of thine enemies,
5: 6 told n' numbered for multitude.
6:14 thee in the heaven, n' in the earth;
11: 4 up, n' fight against your brethren:
15: 5 that went out, n' to him that came in,
19: 7 n' respect of persons, n' taking of gifts.
20:15 afraid n' dismayed by reason of
17 fear not, n' be dismayed; to morrow
21:12 n' in the ways of Asa king of Judah,
29: 7 incense n' offered burnt offerings
32: 7 n' dismayed for the king of Assyria,
7 n' for all the multitude that is with
15 n' persuade you on this manner,
34: 2 to the right hand, n' to the left.
Ezr 9:12 n' seek their peace or their wealth
14 should be no remnant n' escaping?
10: 6 did eat no bread, n' drink water:
Ne 1: 7 n' the statutes, n' the judgments,
2:16 Jews, n' to the priests, n' to the nobles,
16 n' to the rulers, n' to the rest that did
20 no portion, n' right, n' memorial, in
4:23 I, n' my brethren, n' my servants,
23 n' the men of the guard which
7:61 their father's house, n' their seed,
8: 9 your God; mourn not, n' weep.
9:31 consume them, n' forsake them:
34 priests, n' our fathers, kept thy law,
34 thy law, n' hearkened unto thy
10:30 n' take their daughters for our
13:25 n' take their daughters unto your
Es 2: 7 for she had neither father n' mother,
10 not shewed her people n' her kindred:
20 yet shewed her kindred n' her people;
3: 2 bowed not, n' did him reverence.
5 bowed not, n' did him reverence,
4:16 neither eat n' drink three days,
5: 9 stood not up, n' moved for him,
9:28 n' the memorial of them perish
Job 1:22 not, n' charged God foolishly.
3:10 womb, n' hid sorrow from mine eyes.
7:19 n' let me alone till I swallow
14:12 n' be raised out of their sleep.
18:19 son n' nephew among his people,
19 n' any remaining in his dwellings.
24:13 n' abide in the paths thereof.
27: 4 n' my tongue utter deceit.
28: 8 it, n' the fierce lion passed by it.
34:19 n' regardeth the rich more than
22 no darkness, n' shadow of death,
36:19 gold, n' all the forces of strength.
41:12 n' his power, n' his comely proportion.
26 spear, the dart, n' the habergeon.
Ps 1: 1 n' standeth in the way of sinners,
1 n' sitteth in the seat of the scornful.
5 n' sinners in the congregation of the
15: 3 n' doeth evil to his neighbour,
3 n' taketh up a reproach against his

Ps 15: 5 n' taketh reward against the
16: 4 n' take up their names into my
19: 3 There is no speech n' language,
22:24 despised n' abhored the affliction
24: 4 unto vanity, n' sworn deceitfully.
25: 7 of my youth, n' my transgression:
26: 9 sinners, n' my life with bloody men:
28: 5 Lord, n' the operation of his hands,
37:25 forsaken, n' his seed begging bread.
33 n' condemn him when he is
40: 4 proud, n' such as turn aside to lies.
49: 7 n' give to God a ransom for him:
50: 9 thy house, n' he goats out of thy folds.
59: 3 my transgression, n' for my sin,
66:20 my prayer, n' his mercy from me.
75: 6 n' from the west, n' from the south,
78:42 n' the day when he delivered them
89:22 n' the son of wickedness afflict him.
33 n' suffer my faithfulness to fail.
34 n' alter the thing that is gone out of
91: 5 n' for the arrow that flieth by day;
6 N' for the pestilence that walketh
6 n' for the destruction that wasteth at
103:10 n' rewarded us according to our
121: 4 Israel shall neither slumber n' sleep.
6 thee by day, n' the moon by night.
129: 7 n' he that bindeth sheaves his bosom.
131: 1 not haughty, n' mine eyes lofty:
132: 3 of my house, n' go up into my bed;
144:14 be no breaking in, n' going out;
146: 3 trust in princes, n' in the son of man,
Pr 4:27 not to the right hand n' to the left:
5:13 n' inclined mine ear to them that
6: 4 thine eyes, n' slumber to thine eyelids.
8:26 had not made the earth, n' the fields,
26 n' the highest part of the dust of the
17:26 good, n' to strike princes for equity.
21:30 no...n' understanding n' counsel
30: 3 n' have the knowledge of the holy.
8 give me neither poverty n' riches;
31: 3 n' thy ways to that which destroyeth
4 wine; n' for princes strong drink:
Ec 1: 8 n' the ear filled with hearing.
3:14 to it, n' any thing taken from it:
4: 8 yea, he hath neither child n' brother:
5:10 n' he that loveth abundance with
6: 5 seen the sun, n' known any thing:
8:16 neither day n' night seeth sleep
9:10 n' device, n' knowledge, n' wisdom,
11 swift, n' the battle to the strong,
11 n'...riches to men of understanding,
11 n' yet favour to men of skill;
11: 5 n' how the bones do grow in the womb
12: 1 n' the years draw nigh, when thou
2 n' the clouds return after the rain:
Ca 2: 7 n' awake my love, till he please.
3: 5 n' awake my love, till he please.
8: 4 n' awake my love, until he please.
Isa 3: 7 house is neither bread n' clothing:
5: 6 it shall not be pruned, n' digged;
27 be weary n' stumble among them;
27 none shall slumber n' sleep;
27 n' the latchet of their shoes be
8:12 fear ye their fear, n' be afraid.
11: 9 not hurt n' destroy in all my holy
14:21 they do not rise, n' possess the land,
21 n' fill the face of the world with cities.
22: 2 with the sword, n' dead in battle.
23: 4 travail not, n' bring forth children,
4 up young men, n' bring up virgins.
18 shall not be treasured n' laid up;
28:28 n' break it with the wheel of his cart
28 n' bruise it with his horsemen.
30: 5 not profit them, n' be an help
5 be an help n' profit, but a shame,
31: 4 n' abase himself for the noise of
32: 5 n' the churl said to be bountiful.
34:10 It shall not be quenched night n' day;
35: 9 n' any ravenous beast shall go up
37:33 this city, n' shoot an arrow there,
33 n' come before it with shields,
33 n' cast a bank against it.
39: 2 in his house, n' in all his dominion.
40:16 n' the beasts thereof sufficient for
42: 2 He shall not cry, n' lift up,
2 n' cause his voice to be heard in the
4 He shall not fail n' be discouraged,
43:23 n' wearied thee with incense.
44: 9 witnesses; they see not, n' know;
19 knowledge n' understanding to
20 n' say, Is there not a lie in my right
45:13 captives, not for price n' reward,
17 shall not be ashamed n' confounded
46: 7 n' save him out of his trouble.
47:14 coal to warm at, n' fire to sit before it.
48: 1 not in truth, n' in righteousness.
19 cut off n' destroyed from before me.
49:10 They shall not hunger n' thirst;
10 shall the heat n' sun smite them:
51:14 pit, n' that his bread should fail.
52:12 go out with haste, n' go by flight:
53: 2 he hath no form n' comeliness; and
54: 9 not be wroth with thee, n' rebuke thee.
57:11 me, n' laid it to thy heart?
58:13 ways, n' finding thine own pleasure,
13 n' speaking thine own words:
59: 4 justice, n' any pleadeth for truth:
21 mouth, n' out of the mouth of thy seed,
21 n' out of the mouth of thy seed's seed,
60:11 they shall not be shut day n' night;
18 wasting n' destruction within thy
62: 6 never hold their peace day n' night:
64: 4 not heard, n' perceived by the ear,
65:17 be remembered, n' come into mind.
19 heard in her, n' the voice of crying.
20 n' an old man that hath not filled his

Isa 65:23 in vain, n' bring forth for trouble:
25 not hurt n' destroy in all my holy
Jer 4:11 my people, not to fan, n' to cleanse,
5: 4 Lord, n' the judgment of their God.
12 neither shall we see sword n' famine:
6:19 my words, n' to my law, but rejected it.
20 n' your sacrifices sweet unto me.
25 into the field, n' walk by the way;
7:16 lift up cry n' prayer for them,
22 n' commanded them in the day
24 hearkened not, n' inclined their ear,
26 not unto me, n' inclined their ear,
28 their God, n' receiveth correction:
32 n' the valley of the son of Hinnom,
8: 2 not be gathered, n' be buried;
13 on the vine, n' figs on the fig tree,
9:16 they n' their fathers have known:
11: 8 obeyed not, n' inclined their ear,
13:14 not pity, n' spare, n' have mercy,
14:16 wives, n' their sons, n' their daughters:
15:10 n' men have lent to me on usury;
17 assembly of the mockers, n' rejoiced;
16: 2 shalt thou have sons [n'] daughters
5 go to lament n' bemoan them: for
6 lament for them, n' cut themselves,
6 n' make themselves bald for them:
13 know not, neither ye n' your fathers;
17:21 n' bring it in by the gates of
23 not hear, n' receive instruction.
18:18 the priest, n' counsel from the wise,
18 the wise, n' the word from the prophet.
19: 4 they n' their fathers have known,
4 have known, n' the kings of Judah,
5 I commanded not, n' spake it,
6 n' The valley of the son of Hinnom,
20: 9 n' speak any more in his name.
21: 7 neither have pity, n' have mercy.
22: 3 stranger, the fatherless, n' the widow,
10 no more, n' see his native country.
23: 4 shall fear no more, n' be dismayed,
32 sent them not, n' commanded them:
25: 4 n' inclined your ear to hear.
33 neither gathered, n' buried;
35 n' the principal of the flock to escape.
27: 9 n' to your diviners, n' to...dreamers,
9 n' to...enchanters, n' to...sorcerers,
31:40 n' thrown down any more for ever.
35: 6 wine, neither ye, n' your sons for ever:
7 shall ye build house, n' sow seed,
7 n' plant vineyard, n' have any:
8 our wives, our sons, n' our daughters;
9 N' to build houses for us to dwell
9 have we vineyard, n' field, n' seed:
15 your ear, n' hearkened unto me.
36:24 not afraid, n' rent their garments,
24 the king, n' any of his servants that
37: 2 he, n' his servants, n' the people of the
19 come against you, n' against this land?
42:14 n' hear the sound of the trumpet,
14 trumpet, n' have hunger of bread;
21 n' any thing for the which he hath
44: 3 not, neither they, ye, n' your fathers.
5 n' inclined their ear to turn from
10 have they feared, n' walked in my
10 in my law, n' in my statutes,
23 voice of the Lord, n' walked in...law,
23 n' in his statutes, n' in his testimonies;
46: 6 away, n' the mighty man escape;
49:31 which have neither gates n' bars
33 n' any son of man dwell in it.
51: 5 been forsaken, n' Judah of his God,
26 a corner, n' a stone for foundations;
62 remain in it, neither man n' beast,
La 2:22 anger none escaped n' remained:
3:33 n' grieve the children of men.
Eze 2: 6 n' be dismayed at their looks,
3:18 n' speakest to warn the wicked
19 wickedness, n' from his wicked way,
7:11 n' of their multitude, n' of any of
12 buyer rejoice, n' the seller mourn:
12:24 any vain vision n' flattering divination
13:23 more vanity, n' divine divinations:
14:16 deliver neither sons n' daughters;
18 shall deliver neither sons n' daughters,
20 deliver neither son n' daughter;
16: 4 not salted at all, n' swaddled at all.
47 n' done after their abominations:
48 hath not done, she n' her daughters,
18:17 hath not received usury n' increase,
20:18 n' defile yourselves with their idols:
44 n' according to your corrupt doings,
22:24 cleansed, n' rained upon in the day
23:27 n' remember Egypt any more.
24:16 neither shalt thou mourn n' weep,
22 your lips, n' eat the bread of men.
23 ye shall not mourn n' weep; but ye
28:24 n' any grieving thorn of all that are
29: 5 be brought together, n' gathered:
11 n' foot of beast shall pass through
18 yet had he no wages, n' his army,
32:13 n' the hoofs of beasts trouble them.
37:23 idols, n' with their detestable things,
23 n' with any of their transgressions:
38:11 walls, and having neither bars n' gates,
43: 7 defile, neither they, n' their kings,
7 n' by the carcases of their kings in
44: 9 in heart, n' uncircumcised in flesh,
13 n' to come near to any of my holy
20 n' suffer their locks to grow long;
22 a widow, n' her that is put away:
48:14 n' alienate the firstfruits of the
Da 1: 8 n' with the wine which he drank:
2:10 there is no king, lord, n' ruler,
3:12,14,18, n' worship the golden image
27 n' was an hair of their head singed,
27 n' the smell of fire had passed on

Da 3:28 n' worship any god, except their
5: 8 n' make known to the king the
30 n' let thy countenance be changed:
23 which see not, n' hear, n' know:
6: 4 could find none occasion n' fault;
13 n' the decree that thou hast signed,
15 n' statute which the king establisheth
10: 3 came flesh n' wine in any mouth,
11: 4 n' according to his dominion which
6 neither shall he stand, n' his arm:
20 neither in anger, n' in battle.
24 have not done, n' his fathers' fathers;
37 of his fathers, n' the desire of women,
37 n' regard any god: for he shall
Ho 1: 7 by bow, n' by sword, n' by battle,
7 battle, by horses, n' by horsemen.
10 cannot be measured n' numbered;
4: 1 because there is no truth, n' mercy,
1 n' knowledge of God in the land.
4 no man strive, n' reprove another:
14 n' your spouses when they commit
15 n' swear, the Lord liveth.
5:13 you, n' cure you of your wound.
7:10 their God, n' seek him for all this.
Am 5: 5 not Beth-el, n' enter into Gilgal,
8:11 of bread, n' a thirst for water, but
9:10 evil shall not overtake n' prevent us.
Ob 13 n'...laid hands on their substance
Jon 3: 7 man n' beast, herd n' flock, taste any
7 let them not feed, n' drink water:
Mic 5: 7 n' waiteth for the sons of men.
Zep 1: 6 the Lord, n' enquired for him.
18 silver n' their gold shall be able to
3:13 not do iniquity, n' speak lies;
Zec 1: 4 did not hear, n' hearken unto me,
4: 6 Not by might, n' by power, but by
7:10 not the widow, n' the fatherless, the
10 the stranger, n' the poor; and let
14 no man passed through n' returned:
8:10 hire for man, n' any hire for beast;
11:16 one, n' heal that that is broken,
16 n' feed that that standeth still: but
14: 6 the light shall not be clear, n' dark:
7 to the Lord, not day, n' night:
Mal 4: 1 leave them neither root n' branch.
M't 5:35 N' by the earth; for it is his
6:20 neither moth n' rust doth corrupt,
20 do not break through n' steal:
25 n' yet for your body, what ye shall
26 do they reap, n' gather into barns;
10: 9 neither gold, n' silver, n' brass in
10 N' scrip for your journey, neither
10 coats, neither shoes, n' yet staves:
14 receive you, n' hear your words,
24 n' the servant above his lord.
11:18 came neither eating n' drinking,
12:19 He shall not strive, n' cry; neither
22:29 scriptures, n' the power of God.
30 marry, n' are given in marriage,
24:21 this time, no, n' ever shall be.
25:13 day n' the hour wherein the Son of
M'r 6:11 shall not receive you, n' hear you,
8:26 town, n' tell it to any in the town.
12:25 marry, n' are given in marriage;
Lu 1:15 drink neither wine n' strong drink;
6:44 n' of a bramble bush gather they
7:33 eating bread n' drinking wine;
9: 3 staves, n' scrip, neither bread,
10: 4 neither purse, n' scrip, n' shoes:
12:24 for they neither sow n' reap;
24 neither have storehouse n' barn;
14:12 not thy friends, n' thy brethren,
12 kinsmen, n' thy rich neighbours;
35 for the land, n' yet for the dunghill;
17:23 go not after them, n' follow them.
18: 4 I fear not God, n' regard man;
20:35 marry, n' are given in marriage:
21:15 not be able to gainsay n' resist.
22:68 will not answer me, n' let me go.
23:15 No, n' yet Herod: for I sent you to
Joh 1:13 of blood, n' of the will of the flesh,
13 n' of the will of man, but of God.
25 thou be not that Christ, n' Elias,
4:21 this mountain, n' yet at Jerusalem,
5:37 at any time, n' seen his shape.
8:19 neither know me, n' my Father:
9: 3 this man sinned, n' his parents:
11:50 N' consider that it is expedient
12:40 n' understand with their hearts,
16: 3 have not known the Father, n' me.
Ac 4:18 all n' teach in the name of Jesus.
8:21 neither part n' lot in this matter:
9: 9 sight, and neither did eat n' drink.
13:27 n' yet the voices of the prophets
15:10 fathers n' we were able to bear?
19:37 n' yet blasphemers of your goddess.
23: 8 neither angel, n' spirit: but the
12, 21 neither eat n' drink till they had
24:12 in the synagogues, n' in the city:
18 with multitude, n' with tumult.
25: 8 the temple, n' yet against Cæsar,
27:20 neither sun n' stars in many days
Ro 8:38 neither death, n' life, n' angels,
38 n' principalities, n' powers,
38 n' things present, n' things to come,
39 N' height, n' depth, n' any other
9:16 willeth, n' of him that runneth,
14:21 to eat flesh, n' to drink wine,
21 n' any thing whereby thy brother
1Co 2: 6 n' of the princes of this world, that
9 hath not seen, n' ear heard,
6: 9 n' idolaters, n' adulterers,
9 n' effeminate, n' abusers of
10 N' thieves, n' covetous,
10 n' drunkards, n' revilers,
10 n' extortioners, shall inherit the
1Co 10:32 n' to the Gentiles, n' to the church
12:21 n' again the head to the feet, I
2Co 4: 2 n' handling the word of God
7:12 n' for his cause...suffered wrong,
Ga 3:28 There is neither Jew n' Greek,
28 there is neither bond n' free,
28 there is neither male n' female:
4:14 flesh ye despised not, n' rejected;
5: 6 any thing, n' uncircumcision;
6:15 any thing, n' uncircumcision, but
Eph 5: 4 Neither filthiness, n' foolish talking,
4 n' jesting, which are not
5 n' unclean person, n' covetous man,
Col 3:11 there is neither Greek n' Jew,
11 circumcision n' uncircumcision,
11 Barbarian, Scythian, bond n' free:
1Th 2: 3 not of deceit, n' of uncleanness,
3 of uncleanness, n' of guile,
5 know, n' a cloke of covetousness;
6 N' of men sought we glory, neither
6 n' yet of others, when we might have
5: 5 not of the night, n' of darkness.
2Th 2: 2 n' by word, n' by letter as from us,
1Ti 1: 7 they say, n' whereof they affirm.
2:12 n' to usurp authority over the
6:16 no man hath seen, n' can see: to
17 n' trust in uncertain riches, but
2Ti 1: 8 of our Lord, n' of me his prisoner:
Heb 7: 3 beginning of days, n' end of life;
9:25 N' yet that he should offer himself
12: 5 n' faint when thou art rebuked of
18 n' unto blackness, and darkness,
13: 5 never leave thee, n' forsake
2Pe 1: 8 neither be barren n' unfruitful in
Re 3:15 that thou art neither cold n' hot:
16 lukewarm, and neither cold n' hot,
5: 3 no man in heaven, n' in earth,
7: 1 n' on the sea, n' on any tree.
3 neither the sea, n' the trees, till
16 the sun light on them, n' any heat.
9:20 neither can see, n' hear, n' walk:
21 their murders, n' of their sorceries,
21 sorceries, n' of their fornication,
21 their fornication, n' of their thefts.
14:11 and they have no rest day n' night,
21: 4 death, neither sorrow, n' crying,

north See also NORTHERN; NORTHWARD.
Ge 28:14 and to the n', and to the south:
Ex 26:20 n' side there shall be twenty boards:
35 shalt put the table on the n' side.
27:11 for the n' side in length there shall
36:25 which is toward the n' corner,
38:11 for the n' side the hangings were an
Nu 2:25 camp of Dan shall be on the n' side
34: 7 And this shall be your n' border:
9 this shall be your n' border:
35: 5 on the n' side two thousand cubits;
Jos 8:11 and pitched on the n' side of Ai:
13 host that was on the n' of the city,
11: 2 were on the n' of the mountains,
15: 5 their border in the n' quarter was
6 along by the n' of Beth-arabah;
10 which is Chesalon, on the n' side,
16: 6 sea to Michmethah on the n' side;
17: 9 also was on the n' side of the river,
10 met together in Asher on the n',
18: 5 shall abide in their coasts on the n'.
12 their border on the n' side was from
12 to the side of Jericho on the n' side,
16 in the valley of the giants on the n',
17 And was drawn from the n', and
19 were at the n' bay of the salt sea
19:14 compasseth it on the n' side to
27 toward the n' side of Beth-emek,
24:30 on the n' side of the hill of Gaash.
J'g 2: 9 on the n' side of the hill Gaash.
7: 1 Midianites were on the n' side
21:19 which is on the n' side of Beth-el,
1Ki 7:25 oxen, three looking toward the n',
2Ki 16:14 put it on the n' side of the altar.
1Ch 9:24 toward the east, west, n', and south.
2Ch 4: 4 oxen, three looking toward the n',
Job 26: 7 He stretcheth out the n' over the
37: 9 whirlwind: and cold out of the n'.
22 Fair weather cometh out of the n':
Ps 48: 2 mount Zion, on the sides of the n',
89:12 n' and the south thou hast created
107: 3 from the n', and from the south.
Pr 25:23 The n' wind driveth away rain:
Ec 1: 6 and turneth about unto the n';
11: 3 toward the south, or toward the n',
Ca 4:16 Awake, O n' wind; and come, thou
Isa 14:13 congregation, in the sides of the n':
31 shall come from the n' a smoke,
41:25 I have raised up one from the n',
43: 6 I will say to the n', Give up; and to
49:12 these from the n' and from the west;
Jer 1:13 the face thereof is toward the n'.
14 Out of the n' an evil shall break
15 families of the kingdoms of the n',
3:12 proclaim these words toward the n',
18 out of the land of the n' to the land
4: 6 for I will bring evil from the n', and
6: 1 for evil appeareth out of the n', and
22 people cometh from the n' country,
10:22 commotion out of the n' country,
13:20 behold them that come from the n':
16:15 of Israel from the land of the n',
23: 8 of Israel out of the n' country,
25: 9 and take all the families of the n',
26 all the kings of the n', far and near,
31: 8 will bring them from the n' country,
46: 6 stumble, and fall toward the n' by
10 hath a sacrifice in the n' country
20 cometh; it cometh out of the n'.
24 into the hand of the people of the n'.
Jer 47: 2 Behold, waters rise up out of the n',
50: 3 out of the n'....cometh up a nation
9 great nations from the n' country:
41 a people shall come from the n',
51:48 shall come unto her from the n',
Eze 1: 4 a whirlwind came out of the n',
8: 3 gate that looketh toward the n';
5 eyes now the way toward the n',
5 mine eyes the way toward the n',
14 house which was toward the n';
9: 2 gate, which lieth toward the n',
20:47 all faces from the south to the n'
21: 4 all flesh from the south to the n':
26: 7 a king of kings, from the n', with
32:30 There be the princes of the n', all
38: 6 of Togarmah of the n' quarters,
15 from thy place out of the n' parts,
39: 2 cause thee to come up from n' parts,
40:20 court that looked toward the n',
23 over against the gate toward the n',
35 And he brought me to the n' gate,
40 goeth up to the entry of the n' gate,
44 which was at the side of the n' gate;
44 having the prospect toward the n'.
46 whose prospect is toward the n'
41:11 one door toward the n', and another
42: 1 utter court, the way toward the n':
1 before the building toward the n'.
2 an hundred cubits was the n' door,
4 cubit; and their doors toward the n'.
11 chambers which were toward the n',
13 The n' chambers and the south
17 measured the n' side, five hundred
44: 4 brought...me the way of the n' gate
46: 9 entering in by the way of the n' gate
9 go forth by the way of the n' gate:
19 priests, which looked toward the n':
47:15 of the land toward the n' side, from
17 Damascus, and the n' northward,
17 of Hamath. And this is the n' side.
48: 1 From the n' end to the coast of the
10 toward the n' five and twenty
16 the n' side four thousand and five
17 toward the n' two hundred and
30 goings out of the city on the n' side,
Da 11: 6 shall come to the king of the n' to
7 the fortress of the king of the n',
8 more years than the king of the n'.
11 him, even with the king of the n':
13 For the king of the n' shall return,
15 So the king of the n' shall come,
40 and the king of the n' shall come
44 tidings...out of the n' shall trouble
Am 8:12 and from the n' even to the east,
Zep 2:13 stretch out his hand against the n',
Zec 2: 6 and flee from the land of the n',
6: 6 therein go forth into the n' country;
8 these that go toward the n' country
8 quieted my spirit in the n' country.
14: 4 half...shall remove toward the n',
Lu 13:29 from the n', and from the south,
Ac 27:12 toward the south west and n' west.
Re 21:13 on the n' three gates; on the south

northern
Jer 15:12 Shall iron break the n' iron and
Joe 2:20 far off from you the n' army,

northward See also NORTH and TOWARD.
Ge 13:14 from the place where thou art n',
Ex 40:22 upon the side of the tabernacle n',
Le 1:11 shall kill it on the side of the altar n'
Nu 3:35 pitch on the side of the tabernacle n'.
De 2: 3 mountain long enough: turn you n'.
3:27 lift up thine eyes westward, and n',
Jos 13: 3 even unto the borders of Ekron n',
15: 7 and so n', looking toward Gilgal,
8 end of the valley of the giants n':
11 went out unto the side of Ekron n':
17:10 n' it was Manasseh's, and the sea
18:18 the side over against Arabah n',
19 along to the side of Beth-hoglah n':
J'g 12: 1 themselves together, and went n',
1Sa 14: 5 situate n' over against Michmash,
1Ch 26:14 cast lots; and his lot came out n'.
17 n' four a day, southward four a day,
Eze 8: 5 behold n' at the gate of the altar
40:19 an hundred cubits eastward and n'.
47: 2 he me out of the way of the gate n',
17 of Damascus, and the north n',
48: 1 the border of Damascus n', to the
31 three gates n'; one gate of Reuben,
Da 8: 4 the ram pushing westward, and n',

north-west See NORTH and WEST.

nose See also NOSES.
Le 21:18 or a lame, or he that hath a flat n',
2Ki 19:28 I will put my hook in thy n', and
Job 40:24 eyes: his n' pierceth through snares.
41: 2 Canst thou put an hook into his n'?
Pr 30:33 the wringing of the n' bringeth forth
Ca 7: 4 thy n' is as the tower of Lebanon
8 and the smell of thy n' like apples;
Isa 3:21 The rings, and n' jewels.
37:29 therefore will I put my hook in thy n',
65: 5 These are a smoke in my n', a fire
Eze 8:17 lo, they put the branch to their n'.
23:25 they shall take away thy n' and thine

nose-jewels See NOSE and JEWELS.

noses
Ps 115: 6 n' have they, but they smell not:
Eze 39:11 it shall stop the n' of the passengers:

nostrils
Ge 2: 7 into his n' the breath of life; and
7:22 in whose n' was the breath of life,
Ex 15: 8 with the blast of thy n' the waters
Nu 11:20 month, until it come out at your n',

2Sa 22: 9 There went up a smoke out of his n'.
16 at the blast of the breath of his n'.
Job 4: 9 by the breath of his n' are they
27: 3 and the spirit of God is in my n';
39: 20 the glory of his n' is terrible.
41: 20 Out of his n' goeth smoke, as out
Ps 18: 8 went up a smoke out of his n',
15 at the blast of the breath of thy n'.
Isa 2: 22 from man, whose breath is in his n':
La 4: 20 The breath of our n', the anointed
Am 4: 10 your camps to come up unto your n':

notable
Da 8: 5 goat had a n' horn between his
8 and for it came up four n' ones
M't 27: 16 a n' prisoner, called Barabbas.
Ac 2: 20 great and n' day of the Lord come:
4: 16 indeed a n' miracle hath been done

note See also NOTABLE; NOTED.
Isa 30: 8 in a table, and n' it in a book,
Ro 16: 7 who are of n' among the apostles,
2Th 3: 14 n' that man, and have no company

noted
Da 10: 21 is n' in the scripture of truth:

nothing See also NAUGHT.
Ge 11: 6 n' will be restrained from
19: 8 only unto these men do n'; for
26: 29 have done unto thee n' but good,
40: 15 and here also have I done n'
Ex 9: 4 n' die of all that is the children's
12: 10 ye shall let n' of it remain until
20 Ye shall eat n' leavened; in all your
16: 18 that gathered much had n' over,
21: 2 seventh he shall go out free for n'.
22: 3 if he have n', then he shall be sold
23: 26 There shall n' cast their young,
Nu 6: 4 eat n' that is made of the vine tree,
11: 6 is n' at all, beside this manna,
16: 26 and touch n' of theirs, lest ye
22: 16 Let n', I pray thee, hinder thee
De 2: 7 with thee; thou hast lacked n'.
20: 16 save alive n' that breatheth:
22: 26 the damsel thou shalt do n';
28: 55 he hath n' left him in the siege
Jos 11: 15 left n' undone of all that the
J'g 3: 2 such as before knew n' thereof;
7: 14 is n' else save the sword of Gideon
14: 6 and he had n' in his hand:
1Sa 3: 18 every whit, and hid n' from him.
20: 2 father will do n' either great
22: 15 thy servant knew n' of all this,
25: 21 so that n' was missed of all that
36 she told him n', less or more,
27: 1 there is n' better for me than that
30: 19 And there was n' lacking to them,
2Sa 12: 3 But the poor man had n', save
24: 24 offer...that which doth cost me n'.
1Ki 4: 27 in his month: they lacked n'.
8: 9 There was n' in the ark save the
10: 21 n' accounted of in the days of
11: 22 country? And he answered, N':
18: 43 looked, and said, There is n'.
22: 16 tell me n' but that which is true
2Ki 10: 10 fall unto the earth n' of the word of
20: 13 there was n' in his house, nor
15 there is n' among my treasures
17 n' shall be left, saith the Lord.
2Ch 5: 10 There was n' in the ark save the
9: 2 n' hid from Solomon which
18: 15 thou say n' but the truth to me
Ne 2: 2 this is n' else but sorrow of heart.
5: 8 peace, and found n' to answer.
12 them, and will require n' of them;
8: 10 unto them for whom n' is prepared:
9: 21 wilderness, so that they lacked n';
Es 2: 15 required n' but what Hegai
5: 13 Yet all this availeth me n', so long
6: 3 There is n' done for him.
10 n' fail of all that thou hast spoken.
Job 6: 18 aside; they go to n', and perish.
21 now ye are n'; ye see my casting
8: 9 are but of yesterday, and know n',
24: 25 liar, and make my speech n' worth?
26: 7 and hangeth the earth upon n'.
34: 9 It profiteth a man n' that he
Ps 19: 6 is n' hid from the heat thereof.
39: 5 and mine age is as n' before thee:
49: 17 dieth he shall carry n' away:
119: 165 law: and n' shall offend them.
Pr 8: 8 is n' froward or perverse in them.
9: 13 is simple, and knoweth n'.
10: 2 Treasures of wickedness profit n':
13: 4 the sluggard desireth, and hath n':
7 himself rich, yet hath n':
20: 4 shall he beg in harvest and have n'.
22: 27 If thou hast n' to pay, why should
Ec 2: 24 There is n' better for a man, than
3: 14 n' can be put to it, nor any thing
22 is n' better, than that a man should
5: 14 and there is n' in his hand.
15 and shall take n' of his labour, "
6: 2 so that he wanteth n' for his soul
7: 14 man should find n' after him.
Isa 34: 12 and all her princes shall be n'.
39: 2 there was n' in his house, nor
4 is n' among my treasures that
6 n' shall be left, saith the Lord.
40: 17 All nations before him are as n';
17 counted to him less than n',
41: 11 confounded: they shall be as n';
12 that war against thee shall be as n',
24 Behold, ye are of n', and your work
29 are all vanity; their works are n':
Isa 44: 10 image that is profitable for n'?
Jer 10: 24 anger, lest thou bring me to n'.
13: 7 it was profitable for n'.
10 girdle, which is good for n'.
32: 17 there is n' too hard for thee:
23 n' of all that thou commandedst
38: 14 thee a thing; hide n' from me.
39: 10 of the people, which had n',
42: 4 I will keep n' back from you.
50: 26 her utterly: let n' of her be left.
La 1: 12 Is it n' to you, all ye that pass by?
Eze 13: 3 their own spirit, and have seen n'!
Da 4: 35 of the earth are reputed as n':
Joe 2: 3 yea, and n' shall escape them.
Am 3: 4 out of his den, if he have taken n'?
5 earth, and have taken n' at all?
7 the Lord God will do n', but
Hag 2: 3 your eyes in comparison of it as n'?
M't 5: 13 it is thenceforth good for n', but to
10: 26 there is n' covered, that shall not
15: 32 three days, and have n' to eat:
17: 20 n' shall be impossible unto you.
21: 19 found n' thereon, but leaves only,
23: 16 shall swear by the temple, it is n';
18 shall swear by the altar, it is n';
26: 62 said unto him, Answerest thou n'?
27: 12 priests and elders, he answered n'.
19 thou n' to do with that just man:
24 Pilate saw that he could prevail n',
M'r 1: 44 See thou say n' to any man: but
4: 22 there is n' hid, which shall not
5: 26 was n' bettered, but rather grew
6: 8 should take n' for their journey,
36 for they have n' to eat.
7: 15 There is n' from without a man,
8: 1 and having n' to eat, Jesus called
2 three days, and have n' to eat:
9: 29 This kind can come forth by n',
11: 13 came to it, he found n' but leaves;
14: 60 Jesus, saying, Answerest thou n'?
61 he held his peace, and answered n'.
15: 3 things: but he answered n'.
4 again, saying, Answerest thou n'?
5 But Jesus yet answered n'; so that
Lu 1: 37 n' shall be impossible.
4: 2 And in those days he did eat n':
5: 5 all the night, and have taken n':
6: 35 and lend, hoping for n' again;
7: 42 And when they had n' to pay, he
8: 17 n' is secret, that shall not be made
9: 3 Take n' for your journey, neither
10: 19 n' shall by any means hurt you.
11: 6 I have n' to set before him?
12: 2 there is n' covered, that shall not
22: 35 ye any thing? And they said, N'.
23: 9 words; but he answered him n'.
15 n' worthy of death is done unto him.
41 but this man hath done n' amiss.
Joh 3: 27 A man can receive n', except it be
4: 11 Sir, thou hast n' to draw with,
5: 19 The Son can do n' of himself, but
30 I can of mine own self do n':
6: 12 that remain, that n' be lost.
39 hath given me I should lose n',
63 quickeneth; the flesh profiteth n':
7: 26 boldly, and they say n' unto him.
8: 28 I am he, and that I do n' of myself;
54 I honour myself, my honour is n':
9: 33 man were not of God, he could do n'.
11: 49 unto them, Ye know n' at all,
12: 19 Perceive ye how ye prevail n'?
14: 30 world cometh, and hath n' in me.
15: 5 fruit: for without me ye can do n'.
16: 23 And in that day ye shall ask me n'.
24 have ye asked n' in my name:
18: 20 resort; and in secret have I said n'.
21: 3 and that night they caught n'.
Ac 4: 14 them, they could say n' against it.
21 finding n' how they might punish
10: 20 and go with them, doubting n':
11: 8 n' common or unclean hath
12 me go with them, n' doubting.
17: 21 spent their time in n' else, but
19: 36 to be quiet, and to do n' rashly.
20: 20 kept back n' that was profitable
21: 24 informed concerning thee, are n';
23: 14 will eat n' until we have slain Paul.
29 to have n' laid to his charge worthy
25: 25 had committed n' worthy of death,
26: 31 This man doeth n' worthy of death
27: 33 continued fasting, having taken n'.
28: 17 committed n' against the people,
Ro 14: 14 that there is n' unclean of itself:
1Co 1: 19 will bring to n' the understanding
4: 4 For I know n' by myself; yet am I
5 Therefore judge n' before the time.
7: 19 Circumcision is n', and
19 and uncircumcision is n', but the
8: 2 he knoweth n' yet as he ought to
4 that an idol is n' in the world,
9: 16 the gospel, I have n' to glory of:
13: 2 and have not charity, I am n'.
3 not charity, it profiteth me n'.
2Co 6: 10 as having n', and yet possessing
7: 9 might receive damage by us in n'.
8: 15 had gathered much had n' over;
12: 11 for in n' am I behind the very
11 chiefest apostles, though I be n'.
13: 8 we can do n' against the truth,
Ga 2: 6 in conference added n' to me:
4: 1 a child, differeth n' from a servant,
5: 2 Christ shall profit you n'.
6: 3 to be something, when he is n',
Ph'p 1: 20 that in n' I shall be ashamed,
28 in n' terrified by your adversaries:
2: 3 Let n' be done through strife or
Ph'p 4: 6 Be careful for n'; but in every thing
1Th 4: 12 and that ye may have lack of n'.
1Ti 4: 4 God is good, and n' to be refused,
5: 21 another, doing n' by partiality.
6: 4 He is proud, knowing n', but doting
7 For we brought n' into this world,
7 certain we can carry n' out.
Tit 1: 15 defiled and unbelieving is n' pure;
3: 13 that n' be wanting unto them.
Ph'm 14 without thy mind would I do n';
Heb 2: 8 he left n' that is not put under him.
7: 14 of which tribe Moses spake n'
19 For the law made n' perfect, but the
Jas 1: 4 be perfect and entire, wanting n'.
6 let him ask in faith, n' wavering:
3Jo 7 forth, taking n' of the Gentiles.
Re 3: 17 with goods, and have need of n';

notice
2Sa 3: 36 all the people took n' of it, and it
2Co 9: 5 bounty, whereof ye had n' before,

notwithstanding
Ex 16: 20 N' they hearkened not unto Moses;
21: 21 N', if he continue a day or two, he
Le 25: 32 N' the cities of the Levites, and
27: 28 N' no devoted thing, that a man
Nu 26: 11 N' the children of Korah died not.
55 N' the land shall be divided by lot:
De 1: 26 N' ye would not go up, but rebelled
12: 15 N' thou mayest kill and eat flesh
Jos 22: 19 N', if the land of your possession
J'g 4: 9 n' the journey that thou takest shall
9: 5 n' yet Jotham the youngest son
1Sa 2: 25 N' they hearkened not unto the
20: 8 n', if there be in me iniquity, slay
29: 9 n' the princes of the Philistines
2Sa 24: 4 N' the king's word prevailed against
1Ki 11: 12 N' in thy days I will not do it for
2Ki 17: 14 N' they would not hear, but
23: 26 N' the Lord turned not from the
2Ch 6: 9 N' thou shalt not build the house;
32: 26 N' Hezekiah humbled himself for
Jer 35: 14 n' I have spoken unto you, rising
Eze 20: 21 N' the children rebelled against me:
Mic 7: 13 N' the land shall be desolate
M't 2: 22 n', being warned of God in a dream,
11: 11 n' he that is least in the kingdom
17: 27 N', lest we should offend them,
Lu 10: 11 n' be ye sure of this, that the
20 N' in this rejoice not, that the
Ac 15: 34 N' it pleased Silas to abide there
24: 4 N', that I be not further tedious
Ph'p 1: 18 n', every way, whether in
4: 14 N' ye have well done, that ye did
1Ti 2: 15 N' she shall be saved in childbearing,
2Ti 4: 17 N' the Lord stood with me, and
Jas 2: 16 n' ye give them not those things
Re 2: 20 N' I have a few things against thee,

nought See also NAUGHT; NOTHING.
Ge 29: 15 thou therefore serve me for n'?
De 13: 17 cleave n' of the cursed thing
15: 9 brother, and thou givest him n';
28: 63 destroy you, and to bring you to n';
Ne 4: 15 had brought their counsel to n',
Job 1: 9 said, Doth Job fear God for n'?
8: 22 place of the wicked shall come to n'.
14: 18 the mountain falling cometh to n',
22: 6 a pledge from thy brother for n',
Ps 33: 10 the counsel of the heathen to n':
44: 12 Thou sellest thy people for n',
Pr 1: 25 ye have set at n' all my counsel,
Isa 8: 10 together, and it shall come to n';
29: 20 the terrible one is brought to n',
21 turn aside the just for a thing of n'.
41: 12 be as nothing, and as a thing of n'.
24 of nothing, and your work of n':
49: 4 I have spent my strength for n',
52: 3 Ye have sold yourselves for n';
5 my people is taken away for n'?
Jer 14: 14 and a thing of n', and the deceit of
Am 5: 5 and Beth-el shall come to n'.
6: 13 which rejoice in a thing of n',
Mal 1: 10 you that would shut the doors for n'?
10 ye kindle fire on mine altar for n'.
M'r 9: 12 many things, and be set at n'.
Lu 23: 11 with his men of war set him at n',
Ac 4: 11 is the stone which was set at n' of
5: 36 were scattered, and brought to n'.
38 work be of men, it will come to n':
19: 27 craft is in danger to be set at n';
Ro 14: 10 why dost thou set at n' thy brother?
1Co 1: 28 not, to bring to n' things that are:
2: 6 of this world, that come to n':
2Th 3: 8 did we eat any man's bread for n';
Re 18: 17 hour so great riches is come to n'.

nourish See also NOURISHED; NOURISHETH; NOURISHING.
Ge 45: 11 And there will I n' thee; for yet
50: 21 I will n' you, and your little ones.
Isa 7: 21 a man shall n' a young cow, and
23: 4 neither do I n' up young men, nor
44: 14 an ash, and the rain doth n' it.

nourished
Ge 47: 12 And Joseph n' his father, and his
2Sa 12: 3 which he had bought and n' up:
Isa 1: 2 I have n' and brought up children,
Eze 19: 2 n' her whelps among young lions.
Ac 7: 20 n' up in his father's house three
21 him up, and n' him for her own son.
12: 20 their country was n' by the king's
1Ti 4: 6 n' up in the words of faith and of
Jas 5: 5 ye have n' your hearts, as in a day
Re 12: 14 her place, where she is n' for a time.

nourisher
Ru 4: 15 thy life, and a n' of thine old age:

nourisheth
Eph 5:29 n' and cherisheth it, even as the
nourishing
Da 1: 5 so n' them three years, that at the
nourishment
Col 2:19 having n' ministered, and knit
novice
1Ti 3: 6 Not a n', lest being lifted up with
now^
Ge 2:23 This is n' bone of my bones, and
3: 1 N' the serpent was more subtil than
22 and n', lest he put forth his hand,
4:11 n' art thou cursed from the earth,
10: 1 N' these are the generations of the
11: 6 n' nothing will be restrained from
27 N' these are the generations of
12: 1 N' the Lord had said unto Abram, Get
11 Behold n', I know...thou art a fair
19 n' therefore behold thy wife, take
13:14 Lift up n' thine eyes, and look from
15: 5 Look n' toward heaven, and tell
16: 1 N' Sarai, Abram's wife, bare him no
2 n', the Lord hath restrained me
18: 3 if n' I have found favour in thy
11 N' Abraham and Sarah were old and
21 I will go down n', and see whether
27, 31 Behold n', I have taken upon me
19: 2 Behold n', my lords, turn in, I pray
8 Behold n', I have two daughters
9 n' will we deal worse with thee,
19 Behold n', thy servant hath found
20 Behold n', this city is near to flee
20: 7 N'...restore the man his wife;
21:23 N' therefore swear unto me here
22:12 for n' I know that thou fearest God,
24:49 n' if ye will deal kindly and truly
25:12 N' these are the generations of
26:22 n' the Lord hath made room for us,
28 Let there be n' an oath betwixt us,
29 thou art n' the blessed of the Lord.
27:26 Come near n', and kiss me, my son.
36 n' he hath taken...my blessing.
37 shall I do n' unto thee, my son?
43 N' therefore, my son, obey my
29:32 n' therefore my husband will love
34 N' this time will my husband
35 said, N' will I praise the Lord:
30:20 n' will my husband dwell with me,
30 it is n' increased unto a multitude;
30 n' when shall I provide for mine
31:12 Lift up n' thine eyes, and see, all
13 n' arise, get thee out from this
16 n' then, whatsoever God hath said
25 N' Jacob had pitched his tent in the
28 hast n' done foolishly in so doing.
30 n', though thou wouldest needs be
34 N' Rachel had taken the images, and
42 hadst sent me away n' empty.
44 N' therefore come thou, let us
32: 4 Laban, and stayed there until n':
10 and n' I am become two bands.
33:10 n' I have found grace in thy sight,
15 Let me n' leave with thee some of
34: 5 n' his sons were with his cattle in the
35:22 N' the sons of Jacob were twelve:
36: 1 N' these are the generations of Esau,
37: 3 N' Israel loved Joseph more than all
20 Come n' therefore, and let us slay
32 know n' whether it be thy son's
42: 1 N' when Jacob saw that there was
43:10 surely n' we had returned this
11 If it must be so n', do this; take of
44:10 N' also let it be according unto
30 N' therefore when I come to thy
33 N' therefore, I pray thee, let thy
45: 5 N' therefore be not grieved, nor
8 So n' it was not you that sent me
19 N' thou art commanded, this do ye;
46:30 N' let me die, since I have seen
34 from our youth even until n', both
47: 4 n' therefore, we pray thee, let thy
48: 5 And n' thy two sons, Ephraim and
10 N' the eyes of Israel were dim for age,
50: 4 n' I have found grace in your eyes,
5 N' therefore let me go up, I pray
17 Forgive, I pray...n', the trespass
17 n', we pray...forgive the trespass
21 N' therefore fear ye not: I will
Ex 1: 1 N' these are the names of the children
8 N' there arose up a new king over
2:15 N' when Pharaoh heard this thing,
16 N' the priest of Midian had seven
3: 1 N' Moses kept the flock of Jethro
3 I will n' turn aside, and see this
9 N' therefore, behold, the cry of
10 Come n' therefore, and I will send
18 n' let us go, we beseech thee, three
4: 6 Put n' thine hand into thy bosom.
12 N' therefore go, and I will be with
5: 5 the people of the land n' are many,
18 Go therefore n', and work: for
6: 1 N' shalt thou see what I will do to
9:15 For n' I will stretch out my hand,
18 foundation thereof even until n'.
19 Send therefore n', and gather thy
10:17 N' therefore forgive, I pray thee,
11: 2 Speak n' in the ears of the people,
12:40 N' the sojourning of the children of
16:36 N' an omer is the tenth part of an
18:11 N' I know that the Lord is greater
19 Hearken n' unto my voice, I will
19: 5 N' therefore, if ye will obey my
21: 1 N' these are the judgments which
29:38 N' this is that which thou shalt offer
Ex 32:10 N' therefore let me alone, that my
30 and n' I will go up unto the Lord;
32 n', if thou wilt forgive their sin—;
34 Therefore n' go, lead the people
33: 5 n' put off thy ornaments from thee,
13 N' therefore, I pray thee, if I have
13 shew me n' thy way, that I may
34: 9 n' I have found grace in thy sight,
Nu 11: 6 But n' our soul is dried away:
23 shalt see n' whether my word shall
12: 3 (N' the man Moses was very meek,
6 Hear n' my words: If there be a
13 Heal her n', O God, I beseech thee.
13:20 N' the time was the time of the
22 (N' Hebron was built seven years
14:15 N' if thou shalt kill all this people as
17 n', I beseech thee, let the power of
19 people, from Egypt even until n'.
22 tempted me n' these ten times,
25 (N' the Amalekites and the Canaanites
41 Wherefore n' do ye transgress the
16: 1 N' Korah, the son of Izhar, the son of
49 N' they that died in the plague were
20:10 Hear n', ye rebels; must we fetch
22: 4 N' shall this company lick up all
6 Come n' therefore, I pray thee,
11 the earth: come n', curse me them;
19 N' therefore, I pray you, tarry ye
22 N' he was riding upon his ass, and his
29 hand, for n' would I kill thee.
33 surely n' also I had slain thee, and
34 n' therefore, if it displease thee, I
38 have I n' any power at all to say
24:11 Therefore n' flee thou to thy place:
14 n', behold, I go unto my people:
17 I shall see him, but not n': I shall
25:14 N' the name of the Israelite that was
31:17 N' therefore kill every male
43 (N' the half that pertained unto the
32: 1 N' the children of Reuben and the
De 2:13 N' rise up, said I, and get you
4: 1 N' therefore hearken, O Israel,
32 ask n' of the days that are past,
5:25 N' therefore why should we die?
6: 1 N' these are the commandments, the
10:12 n', Israel, what doth the Lord thy
22 n' the Lord thy God hath made thee
26:10 And n', behold, I have brought the
31:19 N' therefore write ye this song for
21 even n', before I have brought
32:39 See n' that I, even I, am he, and
Jos 1: 1 N' after the death of Moses the
2 n' therefore arise, go over this
2:12 N' therefore, I pray you, swear
3:12 N' therefore take you twelve men
5: 5 N' all the people that came out
14 the host of the Lord am I n' come.
6: 1 N' Jericho was straitly shut up
7:19 tell me n' what thou hast done;
8:11 n' there was a valley between them
9: 6 n' therefore make ye a league
11 n' make ye a league with us.
12 but n', behold, it is dry, and it is
17 N' their cities were Gibeon, and
19 n' therefore we may not touch
23 N' therefore ye are cursed, and
25 n', behold, we are in thine hand;
10: 1 N' it came to pass, when Adoni-zedec
12: 1 N' these are the kings of the land,
13: 1 N' Joshua was old and stricken in
7 N' therefore divide this land for
14:10 n', behold, the Lord hath kept me
10 n', lo, I am this day fourscore and
11 even so is my strength n', for war,
12 N' therefore give me this mountain,
17: 8 N' Manasseh had the land of
18:21 N' the cities of the tribe of the children
22: 4 n' the Lord your God hath given
4 n' return ye, and get you unto your
7 N' to the one half of the tribe of
26 Let us n' prepare to build us an
31 n' ye have delivered the children of
24:14 N' therefore fear the Lord, and
23 N' therefore put away, said he, the
J'g 1: 1 N' after the death of Joshua it came
8 N' the children of Judah had fought
10 (n' the name of Hebron before was
23 (N' the name of the city before was
3: 1 N' these are the nations which the
4:11 N' Heber the Kenite, which was of
6:13 n' the Lord hath forsaken us, and
17 If n' I have found grace in thy
39 it n' be dry only upon the fleece;
7: 3 N' therefore go to, proclaim in
8: 2 I done n' in comparison of you?
6 and Zalmunna n' in thine hand,
10 N' Zebah and Zalmunna were in
15 and Zalmunna n' in thine hand,
9:16 N' therefore, if ye have done truly
32 N' therefore up by night, thou and
38 Where is n' thy mouth, wherewith
38 go out, I pray n', and fight with
11: 1 N' Jephthah the Gileadite was a
7 and why are ye come unto me n'
8 Therefore we turn again to thee n',
13 n' therefore restore those lands
23 So n' the Lord God of Israel hath
25 n' art thou anything better than
12: 6 they unto him, Say n' Shibboleth:
13: 3 Behold n', thou art barren, and
4 N' therefore beware, I pray thee,
7 n' drink no wine nor strong drink,
12 said, N' let thy words come to pass.
14: 2 n' therefore get her for me to wife.
12 I will n' put forth a riddle unto
15: 3 N' shall I be more blameless than
J'g 15:18 n' shall I die for thirst, and fall
16: 9 N' there were men lying in wait,
10 n' tell me, I pray thee, wherewith
27 N' the house was full of men and
17: 3 n' therefore I will restore it unto
13 N' know I that the Lord will do me
18:14 n' therefore consider what ye have
19: 9 n' the day draweth toward evening,
18 am n' going to the house of the Lord;
22 N' as they were making their hearts
24 them I will bring out n', and
20: 3 (N' the children of Benjamin heard
9 n' this shall be the thing which
13 N' therefore deliver us the men,
38 N' there was an appointed sign
21: 1 N' the men of Israel had sworn in
Ru 1: 1 N' it came to pass in the days when
2: 2 Let me n' go to the field, and
7 even from the morning until n',
3: 2 and n' is not Boaz of our kindred,
11 n', my daughter, fear not; I will do
12 n' it is true...I am thy near kinsman:
4: 7 N' this was the manner in former time
18 n' these are the generations of Pharez:
1Sa 1: 1 N' there was a certain man of
9 N' Eli the priest sat upon a seat by a
13 N' Hannah, she spake in her heart;
2:12 N' the sons of Eli were the sons of
16 but thou shalt give it me n':
22 N' Eli was very old, and heard all that
30 n' the Lord saith, Be it far from
3: 7 N' Samuel did not yet know the Lord,
4: 1 n' Israel went out against the
15 N' Eli was ninety and eight years old;
6: 7 N' therefore make a new cart, and
8: 2 N' the name of his firstborn was Joel;
5 n' make us a king to judge us like
9 N' therefore hearken unto their
9: 1 N' there was a man of Benjamin,
3 Take n' one of the servants with
6 Behold n', there is in this city a
9 he that is n' called a prophet was
12 make haste n', for he came to day
13 N' therefore get you up; for about
15 N' the Lord had told Samuel in his
10:19 N' therefore present yourselves
12: 2 n', behold, the king walketh before
7 N' therefore stand still, that I may
10 n' deliver us out of the hand of our
13 N' therefore behold the king whom
16 N'...stand and see this great thing,
13:12 come down n' upon me to Gilgal,
13 n' would the Lord have established
14 n' thy kingdom shall not continue:
19 N' there was no smith found
14: 1 N' it came to pass upon a day, that
17 Number n', and see who is gone
30 there not been n' a much greater
49 N' the sons of Saul were Jonathan,
15: 1 n' therefore hearken thou unto
3 N' go and smite Amalek, and
25 N' therefore, I pray thee, pardon
30 yet honour me n', I pray thee,
16:12 N' he was ruddy, and withal of a
15 Behold n', an evil spirit from God
16 our Lord n' command thy servants,
17 Provide me n' a man that can play
17: 1 N' the Philistines gathered together
12 N' David was the son of that
17 Take n' for thy brethren an ephah
19 N' Saul, and they, and all the men of
29 David said, What have I n' done?
18:22 n' therefore be the king's son in
19: 2 n' therefore, I pray thee, take heed
20:29 and n', if I have found favour in
31 n' send and fetch him unto me,
36 Run, find out n' the arrows which I
21: 3 N'...what is under thine hand?
7 N' a certain man of the servants of
22: 6 (n' Saul abode in Gibeah under a tree
7 Hear n', ye Benjamites; will the
12 said, Hear n', thou son of Ahitub.
23:20 N' therefore, O king, come down
24:20 And n', behold, I know well that
21 Swear n' therefore unto me by the
25: 3 N' the name of the man was Nabal:
7 n' I have heard that thou hast
7 n' thy shepherds which were with us,
10 be many servants n' a days that break
17 N' therefore know and consider
21 N' David had said, Surely in vain have
26 N' therefore, my lord, as the Lord
26 n' let thine enemies, and they that
27 And n' this blessing which thine
26: 8 n' therefore let me smite him, I
11 take thou n' the spear that is at his
16 n' see where the king's spear is,
19 N' therefore, I pray thee, let my
20 N' therefore, let not my blood fall
27: 1 I shall n' perish one day by the
5 have n' found grace in thine eyes,
28: 3 N' Samuel was dead, and all Israel
22 N' therefore, I pray thee, hearken
29: 1 N' the Philistines gathered together
7 Wherefore n' return, and go in
10 n' rise up early in the morning
31: 1 N' the Philistines fought against
2Sa 1: 1 N' it came to pass after the death of
2: 6 n' the Lord shew kindness and
7 n' let your hands be strengthened,
14 Let the young men n' arise, and
3: 1 N' there was long war between the
18 N' then do it: for the Lord hath
4:11 not therefore n' require his blood
7: 2 See n', I dwell in an house of
8 N' therefore so shalt thou say

2Sa 7:25 *n*·, O Lord God, the word that thou
28 *n*·, O Lord God, thou art that God,
9: 6 *N*· when Mephibosheth, the son of
10 *N*· Ziba had fifteen sons and twenty
12:10 *N*· therefore the sword shall
23 *n*· he is dead, wherefore should
28 *N*· therefore gather the rest of the
13: 7 Go *n*· to thy brother Amnon's
13 *N*· therefore, I pray thee, speak
17 Put *n*· this woman out from me,
20 but hold *n*· thy peace, my sister:
24 said, Behold *n*·, thy servant hath
25 Nay, my son, let us not all *n*· go,
28 *N*· Absalom had commanded his
28 *n*· when Amnon's heart is merry
33 *N*· therefore let not my lord the
14: 1 *N*· Joab the son of Zeruiah perceived
2 and put on *n*· mourning apparel,
15 *N*· therefore that I am come to
15 I will *n*· speak unto the king; it
17 the king shall *n*· be comfortable:
18 said, Let my lord the king *n*· speak.
21 Behold *n*·, I have done this thing:
32 *n*·...let me see the king's face;
15:34 so will I *n*· also be thy servant:
16:11 more *n*· may this Benjamite do it?
17: 1 Let me *n*· choose out twelve
5 Call *n*· Hushai the Archite also,
9 he is hid *n*· in some pit, or in some
16 *N*· therefore send quickly, and tell
17 *N*· Jonathan and Ahimaaz stayed by
18: 3 *n*· thou art worth ten thousand of
3 therefore *n*· it is better that than
18 *N*· Absalom in his lifetime had taken
19 Let me *n*· run, and fear the king
19: 7 *N*· therefore arise, go forth, and
7 befell thee from thy youth until *n*·.
9 and *n*· he is fled out of the land for
10 *N*· therefore why speak ye not a
32 *N*· Barzillai was a very aged man,
20: 6 *N*· shall Sheba the son of Bichri
23 *N*· Joab was over all the host of
21: 2 (*n*· the Gibeonites were not of the
23: 1 *N*· these be the last words of David.
24: 2 go *n*· through all the tribes of
3 *N*· the Lord thy God add unto the
10 and *n*·, I beseech thee, O Lord,
13 *n*· advise, and see what answer I
14 fall *n*· into the hand of the Lord;
16 is enough: stay *n*· thine hand.
1Ki 1: 1 *N*· king David was old and stricken
12 *N*· therefore come, let me, I pray
18 And *n*·, behold, Adonijah reigneth;
18 *n*·, my lord the king, thou knowest
2: 1 *N*· the days of David drew nigh that
9 *N*·...hold him not guiltless: for
16 *n*· I ask one petition of thee, deny
24 *N*· therefore, as the Lord liveth,
3: 7 And *n*·, O Lord my God, thou hast
5: 4 *n*· the Lord my God hath given me
6 *N*· therefore command thou that
8:25 Therefore *n*·, Lord God of Israel,
9:11 (*N*· Hiram the king of Tyre had
10:14 *N*· the weight of gold that came to
12: 4 *n*· therefore make thou the
11 *n*· whereas my father did lade you
16 *n*· see to thine own house, David.
26 *N*· shall the kingdom return to the
13: 6 Intreat *n*· the face of the Lord
11 *N*· there dwelt an old prophet in
14:14 that day: but what? even *n*·.
29 *N*· the rest of the acts of Rehoboam,
15: 1 *N*· in the eighteenth year of king
7 *N*· the rest of the acts of Abijam, and
31 *N*· the rest of the acts of Nadab, and
16: 5 *N*· the rest of the acts of Baasha,
14 *N*· the rest of the acts of Elah, and
20 *N*· the rest of the acts of Zimri, and
27 *N*· the rest of the acts of Omri which
17:24 *N*· by this I know that thou art a
18: 3 (*N*· Obadiah feared the Lord greatly:
11, 14 *n*· thou sayest, Go, tell thy
19 *N*· therefore send, and gather to
43 And said to his servant, Go up *n*·.
19: 4 *n*·, O Lord, take away my life;
20:31 Behold *n*·, we have heard that the
33 *N*· the men did diligently observe
21: 7 Dost thou *n*· govern the kingdom
22:13 Behold *n*·, the words of the
23 *N*· therefore, behold, the Lord
39 *N*· the rest of the acts of Ahab, and
45 *N*· the rest of the acts of Jehoshaphat,
2Ki 1: 4 *N*· therefore thus saith the Lord,
5 Why are ye *n*· turned back?
14 my life *n*· be precious in thy sight.
18 *N*· the rest of the acts of Ahaziah
2:16 *n*·, there be with thy servants
3: 1 *N*· Jehoram the son of Ahab began to
15 But *n*· bring me a minstrel. And
23 *n*· therefore, Moab, to the spoil.
4: 1 *N*· there cried a certain woman of
9 Behold *n*·, I perceive that this is
13 Say *n*· unto her, Behold, thou hast
26 Run *n*·, I pray thee, to meet her,
5: 1 *N*· Naaman, captain of the host of
6 *N*· when this letter is come unto
8 let him come *n*· to me, and he
15 *n*· I know that there is no god in
15 *n*· therefore, I pray thee, take a
22 even *n*· there be come to me from
6: 1 Behold *n*·, the place where we
7: 4 *N*· therefore come, and let us fall
9 *n*· therefore come, that we may go
12 will *n*· shew you what the Syrians
19 *N*·, behold, if the Lord should make
8: 6 she left the land, even until *n*·.

2Ki 9:12 they said, It is false; tell us *n*·.
14 (*N*· Joram had kept Ramoth-gilead,
26 *N*· therefore take and cast him·
34 Go, see *n*· this cursed woman, and
10: 2 *N*· as soon as this letter cometh
6 *N*· the king's sons, being seventy
10 Know *n*· that there shall fall unto
19 *N*· therefore call unto me all the
34 *N*· the rest of the acts of Jehu, and all
12: 7 *n*· therefore receive no more
13:14 *N*· Elisha was fallen sick of his
19 *n*· thou shalt smite Syria...thrice.
14:15 *N*· the rest of the acts of Jehoash
19 *N*· they made a conspiracy against
28 *N*· the rest of the acts of Jeroboam,
15:36 *N*· the rest of the acts of Jotham,
16:19 *N*· the rest of the acts of Ahaz which
18: 1 *N*· it came to pass in the third year
13 *N*· in the fourteenth year of king
19 them, Speak ye *n*· to Hezekiah,
20 *N*· on whom dost thou trust, that
21 *N*·, behold, thou trustest upon the
23 *N*· therefore, I pray thee, give
25 Am I *n*· come up without the Lord
19:19 *N*· therefore, O Lord our God, I
25 *n*· have I brought it to pass, that
20: 3 remember *n*· how I have walked
21:17 *N*· the rest of the acts of Manasseh,
25 *N*· the rest of the acts of Amon which
22:14 (*n*· she dwelt in Jerusalem in the
23:28 *N*· the rest of the acts of Josiah, and
24: 5 *N*· the rest of the acts of Jehoiakim,
25: 4 (*n*· the Chaldees were against the
11 *N*· the rest of the people that were
1Ch 1:32 *N*· the sons of Keturah, Abraham's
43 *N*· these are the kings that reigned
2:34 *N*· Sheshan had no sons, but
42 *N*· the sons of Caleb the brother of
3: 1 *N*· these were the sons of David,
5: 1 *N*· the sons of Reuben the firstborn
6:54 *N*· these are their dwelling places
7: 1 *N*· the sons of Issachar were, Tola,
8: 1 *N*· Benjamin begat Bela his firstborn,
9: 2 *N*· the first inhabitants that dwelt in
10: 1 *N*· the Philistines fought against
11:15 *N*· three of the thirty captains went
12: 1 *N*· these are they that came to David
14: 1 *N*· Hiram king of Tyre sent
4 *N*· these are the names of his
17: 1 *N*· it came to pass, as David sat in
7 *N*· therefore thus shalt thou say
23 Therefore *n*·, Lord, let the thing
26 And *n*·, Lord, thou art God, and
27 *N*· therefore let it please thee to
18: 1 *N*· after this it came to pass, that
9 *N*· when Tou king of Hamath heard
19: 1 *N*· it came to pass after this, that
10 *N*· when Joab saw that the battle
21: 8 but *n*·, I beseech thee, do away
12 *N*· therefore advise thyself what
13 let me fall *n*· into the hand of the
15 is enough, stay *n*· thine hand.
20 *N*· Ornan was threshing wheat.
22: 5 *n*· make preparations for it. So
11 *N*·, my son, the Lord be with
14 *N*·, behold, in my trouble I have
19 *N*· set your heart and your soul
23: 3 *N*· the Levites were numbered from
14 *N*· concerning Moses the man of God,
24: 1 *N*· these are the divisions of the sons
7 *N*· the first lot came forth to
25: 9 *N*· the first lot came forth for Asaph
27: 1 *N*· the children of Israel after their
28: 8 *N*· therefore in the sight of all
10 Take heed *n*·; for the Lord hath
29: 2 *N*· I have prepared with all my might
13 *N*· therefore, our God, we thank
17 *n*· have I seen with joy thy people,
20 *N*· bless the Lord your God. And
29 *N*· the acts of David the king, first
2Ch 1: 9 *N*·, O Lord God, let thy promise
10 me *n*· wisdom and knowledge,
2: 7 Send me *n*· therefore a man cunning
13 And *n*· I have sent a cunning man,
15 *N*· therefore the wheat, and the
3: 3 *N*· these are the things wherein
6: 7 *N*· it was in the heart of David my
16 *N*· therefore, O Lord God of Israel,
17 *N*· then, O Lord God of Israel, let
40 *N*·, my God, let, I beseech thee,
41 *N*· therefore arise, O Lord God,
7: 1 *N*· when Solomon had made an end
15 *N*· mine eyes shall be open, and
16 For *n*· have I chosen and sanctified
8:16 *N*· all the work of Solomon was
9:13 *N*· the weight of gold that came to
29 *N*· the rest of the acts of Solomon,
10: 4 *n*· therefore ease thou somewhat
16 *n*·, David, see to thine own house.
12:15 *N*· the acts of Rehoboam, first and
13: 1 *N*· in the eighteenth year of king
8 And *n*· ye think to withstand the
15: 3 *N*· for a long season Israel hath been
18: 1 *N*· Jehoshaphat had riches and
22 *N*· therefore, behold, the Lord
30 *N*· the king of Syria had commanded
19: 7 *n*· let the fear of the Lord be
20:10 *n*·, behold, the children of Ammon
34 *N*· the rest of the acts of Jehoshaphat.
21: 1 *N*· Jehoshaphat slept with his fathers,
4 *N*· when Jehoram was risen up to
23:12 *N*· when Athaliah heard the noise of
24:11 *N*· it came to pass, that at what time
17 *N*· after the death of Jehoiada came
27 *N*· concerning his sons, and the
25: 3 *N*· it came to pass, when the

2Ch 25:14 *N*· it came to pass, after that
19 abide *n*· at home; why shouldest
26 *N*· the rest of the acts of Amaziah,
27 *N*· after the time that Amaziah did
26:22 *N*· the rest of the acts of Uzziah, first
27: 7 *N*· the rest of the acts of Jotham, and
28:10 And *n*· ye purpose to keep under
11 *N*· hear me therefore, and deliver
26 *N*· the rest of his acts and of all his
29: 5 Levites, sanctify *n*· yourselves,
10 *N*· it is in mine heart to make a
11 My sons, be not *n*· negligent: for
17 *N*· they began on the first day of the
31 *N*·...have consecrated yourselves
30: 8 *N*· be ye not stiffnecked, as your
31: 1 *N*· when all this was finished, all
32:15 *N*· therefore let not Hezekiah
32 *N*· the rest of the acts of Hezekiah,
33:14 *N*· after this he built a wall without
18 *N*· the rest of the acts of Manasseh,
34: 8 *N*· in the eighteenth year of his reign,
22 (*n*· she dwelt in Jerusalem in the
35: 3 serve *n*· the Lord your God, and
26 *N*· the rest of the acts of Josiah, and
36: 8 *N*· the rest of the acts of Jehoiakim,
22 *N*· in the first year of Cyrus king of
Ezr 1: 1 *N*· in the first year of Cyrus king of
2: 1 *N*· these are the children of the
3: 8 *N*· in the second year of their coming
4: 1 *N*· when the adversaries of Judah and
13 Be it known *n*· unto the king, that,
14 *N*· because we have maintenance
21 Give ye *n*· commandment to cause
22 Take heed *n*· that ye fail not to do
23 *N*· when the copy of king
5:16 until *n*· hath it been in building,
17 *N*· therefore, if it seem good to the
6: 6 *N*· therefore, Tatnai, governor
7: 1 *N*· after these things, in the reign of
11 *N*· this is the copy of the letter that
8: 1 These are *n*· the chief of their fathers,
33 *N*· on the fourth day was the silver
9: 1 *N*· when these things were done, the
8 And *n*· for a little space grace hath
10 *n*·, O our God, what shall we say
12 *N*·...give not your daughters unto
10: 1 *N*· when Ezra had prayed, and when
2 land: yet *n*· there is hope in Israel
3 *N*·...let us make a covenant with
11 *N*· therefore make confession unto
14 Let *n*· our rulers of all the
Ne 1: 6 Let thine ear *n*· be attentive, and
6 which I pray before thee *n*·, day
10 *N*· these are thy servants and thy
11 let *n*· thine ear be attentive to the
2: 1 *N*· I had not been beforetime sad in
9 *N*· the king had sent captains of the
4: 3 *N*· Tobiah the Ammonite was by him,
5: 5 *n*· our flesh is as the flesh of our
18 *N*· that which was prepared for me
6: 1 *N*· it came to pass, when Sanballat,
7 *n*· shall it be reported to the king
6 Come *n*· therefore, and let us take
9 *N*· therefore, O God, strengthen my
7: 1 *N*· it came to pass, when the wall was
4 *N*· the city was large and great: but
9: 1 *N*· in the twenty and fourth day of
32 *N*· therefore, our God, the great,
10: 1 *N*· those that sealed were, Nehemiah,
11: 3 *N*· these are the chief of the province
12: 1 *N*· these are the priests and the
13: 3 *N*· it came to pass, when they had
Es 1: 1 *N*· it came to pass in the days of
2: 5 *N*· in Shushan the palace there was a
12 *N*· when every maid's turn was come
15 *N*· when the turn of Esther, the
3: 4 *N*· it came to pass, when they spake
5: 1 *N*· it came to pass on the third day,
6: 4 *N*· Haman was come into the outward
6 *N*· Haman thought in his heart, To
9: 1 *N*· in the twelfth month, that is, the
12 *n*· what is thy petition? and it shall
Job 1: 6 *N*· there was a day when the sons of
11 But put forth thine hand *n*·, and
2: 5 But put forth thine hand *n*·, and
11 *N*· when Job's three friends heard of
3:13 For *n*· should I have lain still and
4: 5 But *n*· it is come upon thee, and
12 *N*· a thing was secretly brought to me,
5: 1 Call *n*·, if there be any that will
6: 3 For *n*· it would be heavier than the
21 For *n*· ye are nothing; ye see my
28 *N*· therefore be content, look upon
7:21 for *n*· shall I sleep in the dust; and
8: 6 surely *n*· he would awake for thee,
9:25 *N*· my days are swifter than a post:
12: 7 But ask *n*· the beasts, and they
13: 6 Hear *n*· my reasoning, and hearken
18 Behold *n*·, I have ordered my cause;
19 for *n*·, if I hold my tongue, I shall
14:16 For *n*· thou numberest my steps:
16: 7 But *n*· he hath made me weary:
19 Also *n*·, behold, my witness is in
17: 3 Lay down *n*·, put me in a surety
10 you all, do ye return, and come *n*·:
15 And where is *n*· my hope? as for
19: 6 Know *n*· that God hath overthrown
23 Oh that my words were *n*· written!
22:21 Acquaint *n*· thyself with him, and
24:25 if it be not so *n*·, who will make
30: 1 *n*· they that are younger than I
9 And *n*· am I their song, yea, I am
16 *n*· my soul is poured out upon me;
32:14 *N*· he hath not directed his words
33: 2 *n*· I have opened my mouth, my
34:16 If *n*· thou hast understanding, hear

Job 35:15 But n', because it is not so, he hath
37:21 And n' men see not the bright light
38: 3 Gird up n' thy loins like a man;
40: 7 Gird up thy loins n' like a man: I
10 Deck thyself n' with majesty and
15 Behold n' behemoth, which I made
16 Lo n', his strength is in his loins,
42: 5 ear: but n' mine eye seeth thee.
8 take unto you n' seven bullocks
Ps 2:10 Be wise n' therefore, O ye kings: be
12: 5 sighing of the needy, n' will I arise,
17:11 have n' compassed us in our steps:
20: 6 N' know I that the Lord saveth his
27: 6 And n' shall mine head be lifted up
37:25 I have been young, and n' am old; yet
39: 7 And n', Lord, what wait I for? my
41: 8 and n' that he lieth he shall rise up no
50:22 N' consider this, ye that forget
71:18 N' also when I am old and
74: 6 n' they break down the carved
115: 2 say, Where is n' their God?
116:14, 18 pay my vows unto the Lord n' in
118: 2 Let Israel n' say, that his mercy
3 Let the house of Aaron n' say, that
4 Let them n' that fear the Lord say,
25 Save n', I beseech thee, O Lord: O
25 I beseech thee, send n' prosperity.
119:67 astray: but n' have I kept thy word.
122: 8 I will n' say, Peace be within thee.
124: 1 was on our side, n' may Israel say;
129: 1 from my youth, may Israel n' say:
Pr 5: 7 Hear me n' therefore, O ye
6: 3 Do this n', my son, and deliver
7:12 N' is she without, n' in the streets,
24 Hearken unto me n' therefore, O
8:32 N' therefore hearken unto me, O
Ec 2: 1 Go to n', I will prove thee with
16 which n' is in the days to come
3:15 That which hath been is n'; and
9: 6 and their envy, is n' perished;
7 for God n' accepteth thy works.
15 N' there was found in it a poor wise
12: 1 Remember n' thy Creator in the days
Ca 3: 2 I will rise n', and go about the
7: 8 N' also thy breasts shall be as
Isa 1:18 Come n', and let us reason
21 lodged in it; but n' murderers.
5: 1 N' will I sing to my wellbeloved
3 n', O inhabitants of Jerusalem,
5 n' go to; I will tell you what I will
7: 3 Go forth n' to meet Ahaz, thou,
8: 7 N' therefore, behold, the Lord
16:14 n' the Lord hath spoken, saying,
19:12 men? and let them tell thee n',
22: 1 What aileth thee n', that thou art
28:22 N' therefore be ye not mockers,
29:22 Jacob shall not n' be ashamed,
30: 8 N' go, write it before them in a
31: 3 N' the Egyptians are men, and not
33:10 N' will I rise, saith the Lord;
10 the Lord; n' will I be exalted;
10 be exalted; n' will I lift up myself.
36: 1 N' it came to pass in the fourteenth
4 Say ye n' to Hezekiah, Thus saith
5 n', on whom dost thou trust, that
8 N' therefore give pledges, I pray
10 And am I n' come up without the
37:20 N' therefore, O Lord our God, save
38: 3 Remember n', O Lord, I beseech
42:14 n' will I cry like a travailing woman;
43: 1 n' thus saith the Lord that created
19 n' it shall spring forth; shall ye not
44: 1 Yet n' hear, O Jacob my servant;
47: 8 hear n' this, thou that art given to
12 Stand n' with thine enchantments,
13 Let n' the astrologers, the
48: 7 They are created n', and not from
16 and n' the Lord God, and his Spirit,
49: 5 n', saith the Lord that formed me
19 even n' be too narrow by reason
51:21 hear n' this, thou afflicted, and
52: 5 N' therefore, what have I here,
64: 8 n', O Lord, thou art our father; we
Jer 2:18 n' what hast thou to do in the way
4:12 n' also will I give sentence against
31 Woe is me n'! for my soul is
5: 1 and see n', and know, and seek in
21 Hear n' this, O foolish people, and
24 Let us n' fear the Lord our God,
7:12 But go ye n' unto my place which
13 n', because ye have done all these
14:10 he will n' remember their iniquity,
17:15 the word of the Lord? let it come n'.
18:11 N' therefore go to, speak to the
11 return...n' every one from his evil
13 Ask ye n' among the heathen, who
20: 1 N' Pashur the son of Immer the
25: 5 Turn ye again n' every one from
26: 8 N' it came to pass, when Jeremiah
13 Therefore n' amend your ways
27: 6 And n' have I given all these lands
16 shall n' shortly be brought again
18 n' make intercession to the Lord
28: 7 hear thou n' this word that I speak
15 Hear n', Hananiah; The Lord hath
29: 1 N' these are the words of the letter
30: 6 Ask ye n', and see whether a man
32:16 N' when I had delivered the evidence
36 n' therefore thus saith the Lord,
34:10 N' when all the princes, and all the
15 ye were n' turned, and had done
35:15 Return ye n' every man from his
36:15 Sit down n', and read it in our ears.
16 N' it came to pass, when they had
17 Tell us n', How didst thou write
22 N' the king sat in the winterhouse in
Jer 37: 3 Pray n' unto the Lord our God for
4 N' Jeremiah came in and went out
19 Where are n' your prophets which
20 hear n', I pray thee, O my lord the
38: 7 N' when Ebed-melech the Ethiopian,
12 Put n' these old cast clouts and
25 Declare unto us n' what thou hast
39:11 N' Nebuchadrezzar king of Babylon
15 N' the word of the Lord came unto
40: 3 N' the Lord hath brought it, and
4 n', behold, I loose thee this day
5 N' while he was not yet gone back, he
7 N' when all the captains of the forces
41: 1 N' it came to pass in the seventh
9 N' the pit wherein Ishmael had cast
13 N' it came to pass, that when all the
42:15 n' therefore hear the word of the
21 n' I have this day declared it to you;
22 N' therefore know certainly that
44: 7 Therefore n' thus saith the Lord,
45: 3 Woe is me n'! for the Lord hath
52: 7 (n' the Chaldeans were by the city
12 N' in the fifth month, in the tenth day
Eze 1: 1 N' it came to pass in the thirtieth
15 N' as I beheld the living creatures,
7: 3 N' is the end come upon thee,
8 N' will I shortly pour out my fury
8: 5 Son of man, lift up thine eyes n'
8 me, Son of man, dig n' in the wall:
10: 3 N' the cherubims stood on the right
16: 8 N' when I passed by thee, and looked
17:12 Say n' to the rebellious house,
18:14 N', lo, if he beget a son, that seeth all
25 Hear n', O house of Israel; Is not
19: 5 N' when she saw that she had waited,
13 n' she is planted in the wilderness,
22: 2 N', thou son of man, wilt thou judge,
23:43 Will they n' commit whoredoms
26: 2 be replenished, n' she is laid waste:
18 N' shall the isles tremble in the
27: 2 N', thou son of man, take up a
33:22 N' the hand of the Lord was upon me
38:12 desolate places that are n' inhabited,
39:25 N' will I bring again the captivity
41:12 N' the building that was before the
42: 5 N' the upper chambers were shorter:
15 N' when he had made an end of
43: 9 N' let them put away their
46:12 N' when the prince shall prepare
47: 7 N' when I had returned, behold, at
48: 1 N' these are the names of the tribes.
Da 1: 6 N' among these were of the children
9 N' God had brought Daniel into favour
18 N' at the end of the days that the king
2:23 made known unto me n' what we
23 n' made known unto us the king's
3:15 N' if ye be ready that at what time
4:18 N' thou, O Belteshazzar, declare
37 N' I Nebuchadnezzar praise and
5:10 N' the queen by reason of the words
12 n' let Daniel be called, and he will
15 n' the wise men, the astrologers,
16 n' if thou canst read the writing,
6: 8 N', O king, establish the decree,
10 N' when Daniel knew that the
16 N' the king spake and said unto
8:18 N' as he was speaking with me, I was
22 N' that being broken, whereas four
9:15 And n', O Lord our God, that hast
17 N' therefore, O our God, hear the
22 I am n' come forth to give thee skill
10:11 for unto thee am I n' sent:
14 N' I am come to make thee
20 n' will I return to fight with the
11: 2 And n' will I shew thee the truth.
34 N' when they shall fall, they shall be
Ho 1: 8 N' when she had weaned Lo-ruhamah,
2: 7 then was it better with me than n'.
10 n' will I discover her lewdness in
4:16 n' the Lord will feed them as a lamb
5: 3 for n', O Ephraim, thou committest
7 n' shall a month devour them
7: 2 n' their own doings have beset them
8: 8 n' shall they be among the Gentiles as
10 n' will I gather them, and they
13 n' will he remember their iniquity,
10: 2 n' shall they be found faulty: he
3 n' they shall say, We have no king,
13: 2 And n' they sin more and more, and
Am 6: 7 Therefore n' shall they go captive
7:16 N' therefore hear thou the word
Jon 1: 1 N' the word of the Lord came unto
17 N' the Lord...prepared a great fish
3: 3 N' Nineveh was an exceeding great
4: 3 n', O Lord, take, I beseech thee,
Mic 4: 9 N' why dost thou cry out aloud? is
10 n' shalt thou go...out of the city,
11 N' also many nations are gathered
5: 1 N' gather thyself in troops, O
4 n' shall he be great unto the ends
6: 1 Hear ye n' what the Lord saith;
5 remember n' what Balak king of
7: 4 n' shall be their perplexity.
10 n' shall she be trodden down as the
Na 1:13 n' will I break his yoke from off
Hag 1: 5 N' therefore thus saith the Lord of
2: 2 Speak n' to Zerubbabel the son of
3 and how do ye see it n'? is it not
4 Yet n' be strong, O Zerubbabel,
11 Ask n' the priests concerning the
15 n', I pray...consider from this day
18 Consider n' from this day and
Zec 1: 4 Turn ye n' from your evil ways,
3: 3 N' Joshua was clothed with filthy
8 Hear n', O Joshua the high priest,
5: 5 Lift up n' thine eyes, and see what
Zec 8:11 n' I will not be unto the residue
9: 8 for n' have I seen with mine eyes.
Mal 1: 8 offer it n' unto thy governor; will
9 n', I pray you, beseech God that
2: 1 n', O ye priests, this commandment
3:10 and prove me n' herewith, saith
15 And n' we call the proud happy;
M't 1:18 N' the birth of Jesus Christ was on
22 N' all this was done, that it might
2: 1 N' when Jesus was born in
3:10 n' also the ax is laid unto the root
15 Suffer it to be so n': for thus it
4:12 N' when Jesus had heard that
8:18 N' when Jesus saw great
9:18 saying, My daughter is even n' dead:
10: 2 N' the names of the twelve
11: 2 N' when John had heard in the
12 until n' the kingdom of heaven
14:15 place, and the time is n' past;
24 But the ship was n' in the midst of
15:32 continue with me n' three days,
21:18 N' in the morning as he returned
22:25 N' there were with us seven
24:32 N' learn a parable of the fig tree;
26: 6 N' when Jesus was in Bethany, in
17 N' the first day of the feast of
20 N' when the even was come, he sat
45 Sleep on n', and take your rest:
48 N' he that betrayed him gave
53 that I cannot n' pray to my Father,
65 n' ye have heard his blasphemy.
69 N' Peter sat without in the palace:
27:15 N' at that feast the governor was
42 him n' come down from the cross,
43 let him deliver him n', if he will
45 N' from the sixth hour there was
54 N' when the centurion, and they
62 N' the next day, that followed the
28:11 N' when they were going, behold,
M'r 1:14 N' after that John was put in
16 N' as he walked by the sea of Galilee,
4:37 into the ship, so that it was n' full.
5:11 N' there was there nigh unto the
6:35 when the day was n' far spent,
35 place, and n' the time is far passed:
8: 2 have n' been with me three days,
14 N' the disciples had forgotten to
10:30 an hundredfold n' in this time,
11:11 n' the eventide was come, he went
12:20 N' there were seven brethren: and
13:12 N' the brother shall betray the
28 N' learn a parable of the fig tree;
14:41 Sleep on n', and take your rest: it
15: 6 N' at that feast he released unto
32 Christ...descend n' from the cross,
42 And n' when the even was come,
16: 9 N' when Jesus was risen early the
Lu 1: 7 both were n' well stricken in years.
57 N' Elisabeth's full time came that
2:15 Let us n' go even unto Bethlehem,
29 n' lettest thou thy servant depart
41 N' his parents went to Jerusalem
3: 1 N' in the fifteenth year of the reign
9 n' also the axe is laid unto the root
21 N' when all the people were
4:40 N' when the sun was setting, all
5: 4 N' when he had left speaking, he
6:21 Blessed are ye that hunger n': for
21 Blessed are ye that weep n': for ye
25 Woe unto you that laugh n'! for ye
7: 1 N' when he had ended all his
6 he was n' not far from the house,
12 N' when he came nigh to the gate
39 N' when the Pharisee which had
8:11 N' the parable is this: The seed is
22 N' it came to pass on a certain day,
38 N' the man out of whom the devils
9: 7 N' Herod the tetrarch heard of all
10:36 which n' of these three, thinkest
38 N' it came to pass, as they went,
11: 7 the door is n' shut, and my
39 N' do ye Pharisees make clean the
14:17 Come; for all things are n' ready.
15:25 N' his elder son was in the field:
16:25 n' he is comforted, and thou art
18:22 N' when Jesus heard these things,
19:37 even n' at the descent of the mount
42 n' they are hid from thine eyes.
20:37 N' that the dead are raised, even
21:30 when they n' shoot forth, ye see
30 that summer is n' nigh at hand.
22: 1 N' the feast of unleavened bread
36 But n', he that hath a purse, let
23:47 N' when the centurion saw what
24: 1 N' upon the first day of the week,
Joh 1:44 N' Philip was of Bethsaida, the
2: 8 Draw out n', and bear unto the
10 hast kept the good wine until n'.
23 N' when he was in Jerusalem at
4: 6 N' Jacob's well was there. Jesus
18 he whom thou n' hast is not thy
23 the hour cometh, and n' is, when
42 N' we believe, not because of thy
43 N' after two days he departed
51 And as he was n' going down, his
5: 2 N' there is at Jerusalem by the
6 been n' a long time in that case,
25 The hour is coming, and n' is,
6:10 N' there was much grass in the
16 And when even was n' come, his
17 it was n' dark, and Jesus was not
7: 2 N' the Jews' feast of tabernacles
14 N' about the midst of the feast
8: 5 N' Moses in the law commanded
40 But n' ye seek to kill me, a man
52 N' we know that thou hast a devil.

Joh 9:19 blind? how then doth he *n*' see?
21 by what means he *n*' seeth, we
25 that, whereas I was blind, *n*' I see.
31 *N*' we know that God heareth not
41 *n*' ye say, We see; therefore your
11: 1 *N*' a certain man was sick, named
5 *N*' Jesus loved Martha, and her
18 *N*' Bethany was nigh...Jerusalem,
22 that even *n*', whatsoever thou wilt
30 *N*' Jesus was not yet come into the
57 *N*' both the chief priests and the
12:27 *N*' is my soul troubled; and what
31 *N*' is the judgment of this world:
31 *n*' shall the prince of this world be
13: 1 *N*' before the feast of the passover,
2 devil having *n*' put into the heart
7 What I do thou knowest not *n*';
19 *N*' I tell you before it come, that,
23 *N*' there was leaning on Jesus'
28 *N*' no man at the table knew for
31 *N*' is the Son of man glorified,
33 ye cannot come; so *n*' I say to you.
36 go, thou canst not follow me *n*';
37 Lord, why cannot I follow thee *n*'?
14:29 *n*' I have told you before it come
15: 3 *N*' ye are clean through the word
22 *n*' they have no cloke for their sin.
24 *n*' have they both seen and hated
16: 5 *n*' I go my way to him that sent me;
12 you, but ye cannot bear them *n*'.
19 *N*' Jesus knew that they were
22 ye *n*' therefore have sorrow: but I
29 Lo, *n*' speakest thou plainly, and
30 *N*' are we sure that thou knowest
31 answered them, Do ye *n*' believe?
32 the hour cometh, yea, is *n*' come,
17: 5 *n*', O Father, glorify thou me with
7 *N*' they have known that all things
11 And *n*' I am no more in the world,
13 And *n*' come I to thee; and these
18:14 *N*' Caiaphas was he, which gave
24 *N*' Annas had sent him bound
36 *n*' is my kingdom not from hence.
40 *N*' Barabbas was a robber.
19:23 *n*' the coat was without seam, woven
25 *N*' there stood by the cross of Jesus
28 all things were *n*' accomplished,
29 *N*' there was set a vessel full of
41 *N*' in the place where he was
21: 4 when the morning was *n*' come,
6 *n*' they were not able to draw it
7 *N*' when Simon Peter heard
10 the fish which ye have *n*' caught.
14 This is *n*' the third time that Jesus
Ac 1:18 *N*' this man purchased a field
2: 6 *N*' when this was noised abroad,
33 this, which ye *n*' see and hear.
37 *N*' when they heard this they were
3: 1 *N*' Peter and John went up together
17 *n*', brethren, I wot that through
4: 3 next day: for it was *n*' eventide.
13 *N*', when they saw the boldness of
29 *n*', Lord, behold their threatenings:
5:24 *N*' when the high priest and the
38 *n*' I say unto you, Refrain from
7: 4 into this land, wherein ye *n*' dwell.
11 *N*' there came a dearth all over
34 *n*' come, I will send thee into
52 whom ye have been *n*' the betrayers
8:14 *N*' when the apostles which were
9:36 *N*' there was at Joppa a certain
10: 5 *n*' send men to Joppa, and call for
17 *N*' while Peter doubted in himself
33 *N*' therefore are we all here
11:19 *N*' they which were scattered
12: 1 *N*' about that time Herod the king
11 *N*' I know of a surety, that the
18 *N*' as soon as it was day, there
13: 1 *N*' there were in the church that
11 *n*', behold, the hand of the Lord is
13 *N*' when Paul and his company
34 *n*' no more to return to corruption, he
43 *N*' when the congregation was
15:10 *N*' therefore why tempt ye God, to
16:36 *n*' therefore depart, and go in peace.
37 *n*' do they thrust us out privily?
17: 1 *N*' when they had passed through
16 *N*' while Paul waited for them at
30 *n*' commandeth all men everywhere
18:14 was *n*' about to open his mouth,
20:22 *n*', behold, I go bound in the spirit
25 And *n*', behold, I know that ye all,
32 *n*', brethren, I commend you to God,
21: 3 *N*' when we had discovered
22: 1 ye my defence which I make *n*'
16 *n*' why tarriest thou? arise, and
23:15 *N*' therefore ye with the counsel
21 and *n*' are they ready, looking for a
24:13 things whereof they *n*' accuse me.
17 *N*' after many years I came to
25: 1 *N*' when Festus was come into
26: 6 *n*' I stand and am judged for the
17 Gentiles, unto whom *n*' I send thee,
27: 9 *N*' when much time was spent, and
9 when sailing was *n*' dangerous,
9 the fast was *n*' already past,
22 And *n*' I exhort you to be of good
Ro 1:10 if by any means *n*' at length I
13 *N*' I would not have you ignorant,
3:19 *N*' we know that what things soever
21 But *n*' the righteousness of God
4: 4 *N*' to him that worketh is the
19 not his own body *n*' dead, when
23 *N*' it was not written for his sake
5: 9 being *n*' justified by his blood,
11 we have *n*' received the atonement.
Ro 6:19 even so *n*' yield your members
21 things whereof ye are *n*' ashamed?
22 But *n*' being made free from sin,
7: 6 *n*' we are delivered from the law,
17 *N*' then it is no more I that do it,
20 *N*' if I do that I would not, it is no
8: 1 therefore *n*' no condemnation to
9 *N*' if any man have not the Spirit
22 in pain together until *n*'.
11:12 *N*' if the fall of them be the riches
30 God, yet have *n*' obtained mercy
31 so have these also *n*' not believed,
13:11 *n*' it is high time to awake out of
11 for *n*' is our salvation nearer than
14:15 *n*' walkest thou not charitably.
15: 5 *N*' the God of patience and
8 *N*' I say that Jesus Christ was a
13 *N*' the God of hope fill you with all
23 *n*' having no more place in these
25 *n*' I go unto Jerusalem to minister
30 *N*' I beseech you, brethren, for the
33 *N*' the God of peace be with you all.
16:17 *N*' I beseech you, brethren, mark
25 *N*' to him that is of power to stablish
26 But *n*' is made manifest, and by
1Co 1:10 *N*' I beseech you, brethren, by the
12 *N*' this I say, that every one of you
2:12 *N*' we have received, not the spirit
3: 2 bear it, neither yet *n*' are ye able.
8 *N*' he that planteth and he that
12 *N*' if any man build upon this
4: 7 *n*' if thou didst receive it, why
8 *N*' ye are full, *n*' ye are rich, ye
18 *N*' some are puffed up, as though I
5:11 *n*' I have written unto you not to
6: 7 *N*' therefore there is utterly a
13 *N*' the body is not for fornication,
7: 1 *N*' concerning the things whereof ye
14 unclean; but *n*' are they holy.
8: 1 *N*' as touching things offered unto
9:25 *N*' they do it to obtain a...crown;
10: 6 *N*' these things were our examples,
11 *N*' all these things happened unto
11: 2 *N*' I praise you, brethren, that ye
17 *N*' in this that I declare unto you I
12: 1 *N*' concerning spiritual gifts,
4 *N*' there are diversities of gifts, but
18 *n*' hath God set the members every
20 But *n*' are they many members,
27 *N*' ye are the body of Christ, and
13:12 *n*' we see through a glass, darkly;
12 *N*' I know in part; but then shall I
13 And *n*' abideth faith, hope, charity,
14: 6 *N*', brethren, if I come unto you
15:12 *N*' if Christ be preached that he
20 *n*' is Christ risen from the dead,
50 *N*' this I say, brethren, that flesh
16: 1 *N*' concerning the collection for the
5 *N*' I will come unto you, when I
7 I will not see you *n*' by the way;
10 *N*' if Timotheus come, see that he
2Co 1:21 *N*' he which stablisheth us with you
2:14 *N*' thanks be unto God, which
3:17 *N*' the Lord is that Spirit: and
5: 5 *N*' he that hath wrought us for the
16 yet *n*' henceforth know we him no
20 *N*' then we are ambassadors for
6: 2 behold, *n*' is the accepted time;
2 behold, *n*' is the day of salvation.)
13 *N*' for a recompence in the same,
7: 9 *N*' I rejoice, not that ye were made
8:11 *N*' therefore perform the doing of
14 *n*' at this time your abundance
22 but *n*' much more diligent, upon
9:10 *N*' he that ministereth seed to
10: 1 *N*' I Paul myself beseech you by the
12: 6 but *n*' I forbear, lest any man should
13: 2 being absent *n*' I write to them
7 *N*' I pray to God that ye do no evil;
Ga 1: 9 As we said before, so say I *n*' again,
10 For do I *n*' persuade men, or God?
20 *N*' the things which I write unto
23 *n*' preacheth the faith which once
2:20 the life which I *n*' live in the flesh
3: 3 are ye *n*' made perfect by the flesh?
16 *N*' to Abraham and his seed were
20 *N*' a mediator is not a mediator of
4: 1 *N*' I say, That the heir, as long as
9 But *n*', after that ye have known
20 I desire to be present with you *n*',
25 to Jerusalem which *n*' is, and is
28 *N*' we, brethren, as Isaac was, are
29 after the Spirit, even so it is *n*'.
5:19 *N*' the works of the flesh are
Eph 2: 2 the spirit that *n*' worketh in the
13 But *n*' in Christ Jesus ye who
19 *N*'...ye are no more strangers
3: 5 *n*' revealed unto his holy apostles
10 *n*' unto the principalities and
20 *N*' unto him that is able to do
4: 9 (*N*' that he ascended, what is it but
5: 8 but *n*' are ye light in the Lord:
Ph'p 1: 5 gospel from the first day until *n*';
20 so *n*' also Christ shall be magnified
30 saw in me, and *n*' hear to be in me.
2:12 but *n*' much more in my absence,
3:18 *n*' tell you even weeping, that they
4:10 *n*' at the last your care of me hath
15 *N*' ye Philippians know also, that
20 *N*' unto God and our Father be glory
Col 1:21 works, yet *n*' hath he reconciled
24 *n*' rejoice in my sufferings for you,
26 *n*' is made manifest to his saints:
3: 8 *n*' ye also put off all these; anger,
1Th 3: 6 *n*' when Timotheus came from you
8 For *n*' we live, if ye stand fast in
1Th 3:11 *N*' God himself and our Father, and
5:14 *N*' we exhort you, brethren, warn
2Th 2: 1 *N*' we beseech you, brethren, by the
6 And *n*' ye know what withholdeth
7 only he who *n*' letteth will let,
16 *N*' our Lord Jesus Christ himself,
3: 6 *N*' we command you, brethren, in
12 *N*' them that are such we command
16 *N*' the Lord of peace himself give
1Ti 1: 5 *N*' the end of the commandment is
17 *N*' unto the King eternal, immortal,
4: 1 *N*' the Spirit speaketh expressly,
8 promise of the life that *n*' is, and
5: 5 *N*' she that is a widow indeed, and
2Ti 1:10 But is *n*' made manifest by the
3: 8 *N*' as Jannes and Jambres
4: 6 For I am *n*' ready to be offered,
Ph'm 9 *n*' also a prisoner of Jesus Christ.
11 but *n*' profitable to thee and to me:
16 Not *n*' as a servant, but above a
Heb 2: 8 *n*' we see not yet all things put
7: 4 *N*' consider how great this man
8: 1 *N*' of the things which we have
6 But *n*' hath he obtained a more
13 *N*' that which decayeth and
9: 5 we cannot *n*' speak particularly.
6 *N*' when these things were thus
24 *n*' to appear in the presence of
26 *n*' once in the end of the world hath
10:18 *N*' where remission of these is,
38 *N*' the just shall live by faith: but
11: 1 *N*' faith is the substance of things
16 *n*' they desire a better country,
12:11 *N*' no chastening for the present
26 *n*' he hath promised, saying, Yet
13:20 *N*' the God of peace, that brought
Jas 4:13 Go to *n*', ye that say, To day or
16 *n*' ye rejoice in your boastings: all
5: 1 Go to *n*', ye rich men, weep and
1Pe 1: 6 though *n*' for a season, if need be,
8 in whom, though *n*' ye see him not,
12 which are *n*' reported unto you by
2:10 people, but are *n*' the people of God:
10 mercy, but *n*' have obtained mercy.
25 are *n*' returned unto the Shepherd
3:21 even baptism doth also *n*' save us
2Pe 2: 3 *n*' of a long time lingereth not,
3: 1 beloved, I *n*' write unto you; in
7 and the earth, which are *n*',
18 him be glory both *n*' and for ever.
1Jo 2: 8 past, and the true light *n*' shineth.
9 brother, is in darkness even until *n*'.
18 even *n*' are there many antichrists;
28 *n*', little children, abide in him;
3: 2 Beloved, *n*' are we the sons of God,
4: 3 even *n*' already is it in the world.
2Jo 5 And *n*' I beseech thee, lady, not as
Jude 24 *N*' unto him that is able to keep
25 and power, both *n*' and ever.
Re 12:10 *N*' is come salvation, and strength,

now-a-days See NOW and DAYS.

no-wise See NO and WISE.

number See also NUMBERED; NUMBERETH; NUMBERING; NUMBERS.
Ge 13:16 man can *n*' the dust of the earth,
15: 5 stars, if thou be able to *n*' them:
34:30 being few in *n*', they shall gather
41:49 numbering; for it was without *n*'.
Ex 12: 4 it according to the *n*' of the souls;
16:16 according to the *n*' of your persons;
23:26 land: the *n*' of thy days I will fulfil.
30:12 children of Israel after their *n*',
Le 15:13 he shall *n*' to himself seven days
28 she shall *n*' to herself seven days,
23:16 seventh sabbath shall ye *n*' fifty
25: 8 thou shalt *n*' seven sabbaths of
15 to the *n*' of years after the jubile
15 unto the *n*' of years of the fruits
16 to the *n*' of the years of the fruits
50 be according unto the *n*' of years,
26:22 your cattle, and make you few in *n*';
Nu 1: 2 fathers, with the *n*' of their names,
3 shall *n*' them by their armies.
18, 20, 22, 24, 26, 28, 30, 32, 34, 36, 38, 40,
42 according to the *n*' of the names,
49 thou shalt not *n*' the tribe of Levi,
3:15 *N*' the children of Levi after the
15 old and upward shalt thou *n*' them.
22 according to the *n*' of all the males,
28 In the *n*' of all the males, from a
34 according to the *n*' of all the males,
40 *N*' all the firstborn of the males of
40 and take the *n*' of their names.
43 firstborn males by the *n*' of names,
48 odd *n*' of them is to be redeemed,
4:23 fifty years old shalt thou *n*' them;
29 shalt *n*' them after their families,
30 fifty years old shalt thou *n*' them,
37 which Moses and Aaron did *n*'
41 whom Moses and Aaron did *n*'
14:29 of you, according to your whole *n*',
34 *n*' of the days in which ye searched
15:12 According to the *n*'...ye...prepare,
12 do to every one according to their *n*'.
23:10 the *n*' of the fourth part of Israel?
26:53 according to the *n*' of names.
29:18, 21, 24, 27, 30, 33, 37 shall be according to their *n*', after the
31:36 was in *n*' three hundred thousand
De 4:27 be left few in *n*' among the heathen,
7: 7 ye were more in *n*' than any people:
16: 9 Seven weeks shalt thou *n*' unto
9 begin to *n*' the seven weeks from
25: 2 to his fault, by a certain *n*'.
28:62 And ye shall be left few in *n*', whereas

De 32: 8 the n· of the children of Israel.
Jos 4: 5, 8 n· of the tribes of the children of
J'g 6: 5 and their camels were without n·:
7: 6 the n· of them that lapped, putting
12 and their camels were without n·,
21: 23 them wives, according to their n·,
1Sa 6: 4 n· of the lords of the Philistines:
18 n· of all the cities of the Philistines
14: 17 N· now, and see who is gone from
2Sa 2: 15 over by n· twelve of Benjamin,
21: 20 foot six toes, four and twenty in n·:
24: 1 to say, Go, n· Israel and Judah.
2 Beer-sheba, and n· ye the people,
2 I may know the n· of the people.
4 the king, to n· the people of Israel.
9 the sum of the n· of the people
1Ki 18: 31 to the n· of the tribes of the sons of
20: 25 And n· thee an army, like the army
1Ch 7: 2 whose n· was in the days of David
9 And the n· of them, after their
40 n· throughout the genealogy
11: 11 n· of the mighty men whom David
21: 1 and provoked David to n· Israel.
2 Go, n· Israel from Beer-sheba even
2 and bring the n· of them to me,
5 the sum of the n· of the people
22: 16 brass, and the iron, there is no n·.
23: 3 their n· by their polls, man by man,
24 counted by n· of names by their
31 feasts, by n·, according to the order
25: 1 the n· of the workmen according to
7 the n· of them, with their brethren
27: 1 the children of Israel after their n·,
23 But David took not the n· of them
24 the son of Zeruiah began to n·,
24 was the n· put in the account of
2Ch 12: 3 people were without n· that came
26: 11 according to the n· of their account
12 whole n· of the chief of the fathers
29: 32 And the n· of the burnt offerings,
30: 24 n· of priests sanctified themselves.
35: 7 to the n· of thirty thousand, and
Ezr 1: 9 And this is the n· of them: thirty
2: 2 the n· of the men of the people of
3: 4 the daily burnt offerings by n·,
6: 17 to the n· of the tribes of Israel.
8: 34 By n· and by weight of every one:
Ne 7: 7 n·, I say, of the men of the people
Es 9: 11 day the n· of those that were slain
Job 1: 5 according to the n· of them all.
3: 6 not come into the n· of the months.
5: 9 marvellous things without n·:
9: 10 out; yea, and wonders without n·.
14: 5 the n· of his months are with thee,
15: 20 and the n· of years is hidden to the
21: 21 the n· of his months is cut off in the
25: 3 Is there any n· of his armies? and
31: 37 unto him the n· of my steps; as a
34: 24 in pieces mighty men without n·,
36: 26 can the n· of his years be searched
38: 21 because the n· of thy days is great?
37 Who can n· the clouds in wisdom?
39: 2 Canst thou n· the months that they
Ps 90: 12 So teach us to n· our days, that
105: 12 they were but a few men in n·;
34 caterpillars, and that without n·,
139: 18 they are more in n· than the sand:
147: 4 He telleth the n· of the stars; he
Ca 6: 8 concubines, and virgins without n·.
Isa 21: 17 the residue of the n· of archers,
40: 26 that bringeth out their host by n·:
65: 11 the drink offering unto that n·.
12 will I n· you to the sword, and ye
Jer 2: 28 according to the n· of thy cities
32 have forgotten me days without n·.
11: 13 For according to the n· of thy cities
13 according to the n· of the streets
44: 28 a small n· that escape the sword
Eze 4: 4 according to the n· of the days that
5 according to the n· of the days,
9 according to the n· of the days that
5: 3 shalt also take thereof a few in n·,
Da 9: 2 by books the n· of the years,
Ho 1: 10 the n· of the children of Israel shall
Joe 1: 6 my land, strong, and without n·,
Na 3: 3 of slain, and a great n· of carcases:
M'r 10: 46 disciples and a great n· of people,
Lu 22: 3 being of the n· of the twelve.
Joh 6: 10 sat down, in n· about five thousand.
Ac 1: 15 (the n· of names together were
4: 4 the n· of the men was about five
5: 36 to whom a n· of men, about four
6: 1 the n· of the disciples was multiplied,
7 the n· of the disciples multiplied in
11: 21 and a great n· believed, and turned
16: 5 the faith, and increased in n· daily.
Ro 9: 27 the n· of the children of Israel be
2Co 10: 12 dare not make ourselves of the n·,
1Ti 5: 9 not a widow be taken into the n·
Re 5: 11 the n· of them was ten thousand
7: 4 I heard the n· of them which were
9 multitude, which no man could n·,
9: 16 the n· of the army of the horsemen
16 and I heard the n· of them.
13: 17 of the beast, or the n· of his name.
18 count the n· of the beast: for it is
18 the beast: for it is the n· of a man;
18 his n· is Six hundred threescore
15: 2 mark, and over the n· of his name,
20: 8 n· of whom is as the sand of the sea.

numbered
Ge 13: 16 then shall thy seed also be n·.
16: 10 it shall not be n· for multitude.
32: 12 which cannot be n· for multitude.
Ex 30: 13, 14 among them that are n·,
38: 25 And the silver of them that were n·
26 for every one that went to be n·,
Nu 1: 19 so he n· them in the wilderness of
21 Those that were n· of them, even
22 fathers, those that were n· of them,
23, 25, 27, 29, 31, 33, 35, 37, 39, 41, 43
Those that were n· of them,
44 These are those that were n·,
44 which Moses and Aaron n·, and the
45 So were all those that were n· of
46 they that were n· were six hundred
47 fathers were not n· among them.
2: 4 and those that were n· of them,
6, 8 and those that were n· thereof,
9 that were n· in the camp of Judah
11 and those that were n· thereof,
13, 15 and those that were n· of them,
16 that were n· in the camp of Reuben
19, 21, 23 those that were n· of them,
24 All that were n· of the camp of
26, 28, 30 those that were n· of them,
31 that were n· in the camp of Dan
32 were n· of the children of Israel by
32 all those that were n· of the camps
33 the Levites were not n· among the
3: 16 And Moses n· them according to the
22 that were n· of them, according to
22 that were n· of them were seven
34 And those that were n· of them,
39 that were n· of the Levites, which
39 Levites, which Moses and Aaron n·
42 Moses n·, as the Lord commanded
43 of those that were n· of them, were
4: 34 n· the sons of the Kohathites after
36 those that were n· of them by their
37 they that were n· of the families
38 And those that were n· of the sons
40 Even those that were n· of them,
41 they that were n· of the families of
42 those that were n· of the families of
44 Even those that were n· of them
45 those that were n· of the families
45 Moses and Aaron n· according to
46 those that were n· of the Levites,
46 Aaron and the chief of Israel n·,
48 Even those that were n· of them,
49 they were n· by the hand of Moses,
49 thus were they n· of him, as the
7: 2 and were over them that were n·,
14: 29 all that were n· of you, according
26: 7 that were n· of them were forty and
18, 22, 25, 27, 34 that were n· of them,
37 according to those that were n· of
41 that were n· of them were forty
43 to those that were n· of them,
47 to those that were n· of them;
50 and they that were n· of them were
51 the n· of the children of Israel, six
54 to those that were n· of him.
57 are they that were n· of the Levites
62 that were n· of them were twenty
62 were not n· among the children of
63 are they that were n· by Moses and
63 who n· the children of Israel in the
64 Moses and Aaron the priest n·,
64 when they n· the children of Israel
Jos 8: 10 and n· the people, and went up, he
J'g 20: 15 the children of Benjamin were n·
15 were n· seven hundred chosen men.
17 were n· four hundred thousand
21: 9 For the people were n·, and, behold,
1Sa 11: 8 And when he n· them in Bezek, the
13: 15 Saul n· the people that were present
14: 17 when they had n·, behold, Jonathan
15: 4 together, and n· them in Telaim,
2Sa 18: 1 David n· the people that were with
24: 10 after that he had n· the people.
1Ki 3: 8 be n· nor counted for multitude.
8: 5 not be told nor n· for multitude.
20: 15 he n· the young men of the princes
15 after them he n· all the people,
26 year, that Ben-hadad n· the Syrians,
27 children of Israel were n·, and were
2Ki 3: 6 the same time, and n· all Israel.
1Ch 21: 17 commanded the people to be n·?
23: 3 the Levites were n· from the age
27 the Levites were n· from twenty
2Ch 2: 17 Solomon n· all the strangers that
17 David his father had n· them; and
5: 6 not be told nor n· for multitude.
25: 5 he n· them from twenty years old
Ezr 1: 8 and n· them unto Sheshbazzar, the
Ps 40: 5 them, they are more than can be n·.
Ec 1: 15 which is wanting cannot be n·.
Isa 22: 10 have n· the houses of Jerusalem.
53: 12 he was n· with the transgressors;
Jer 33: 22 the host of heaven cannot be n·,
Da 5: 26 God hath n· thy kingdom, and
Ho 1: 10 which cannot be measured nor n·;
M't 10: 30 very hairs of your head are all n·.
M'r 15: 28 he was n· with the transgressors.
Lu 12: 7 very hairs of your head are all n·.
Ac 1: 17 For he was n· with us, and had
26 he was n· with the eleven apostles.

numberest
Ex 30: 12 the Lord, when thou n· them;
12 among them, when thou n· them.
Job 14: 16 For now thou n· my steps: dost

numbering
Ge 41: 49 sea, very much, until he left n·:
2Ch 2: 17 after the n· wherewith David his

numbers
1Ch 12: 23 the n· of the bands that were
2Ch 17: 14 the n· of them according to the
Ps 71: 15 for I know not the n· thereof.

Nun *(nun)* See also Non.
Ex 33: 11 his servant Joshua, the son of N·.
Nu 11: 28 Joshua the son of N·, the servant
13: 8 of Ephraim, Oshea the son of N·.
16 Moses called Oshea the son of N·
14: 6 Joshua the son of N·, and Caleb
30 Jephunneh,...Joshua the son of N·.
38 Joshua the son of N·, and Caleb
26: 65 Jephunneh,...Joshua the son of N·.
27: 18 Take thee Joshua the son of N·, a
32: 12 Kenezite, and Joshua the son of N·:
28 Joshua the son of N·, and the chief
34: 17 priest, and Joshua the son of N·.
De 1: 38 But Joshua the son of N·, which
31: 23 gave Joshua the son of N· a charge,
32: 44 he, and Hoshea the son of N·.
34: 9 the son of N· was full of the spirit
Jos 1: 1 spake unto Joshua the son of N·,
2: 1 Joshua the son of N· sent out of
23 and came to Joshua the son of N·,
6: 6 the son of N· called the priests,
14: 1 priest, and Joshua the son of N·,
17: 4 before Joshua the son of N·, and
19: 49 inheritance to Joshua the son of N·
51 priest, and Joshua the son of N·,
21: 1 and unto Joshua the son of N·,
24: 29 Joshua the son of N·, the servant
J'g 2: 8 Joshua the son of N·, the servant of
1Ki 16: 34 he spake by Joshua the son of N·.
Ne 8: 17 the days of Jeshua the son of N·

nurse See also nursed; nursing.
Ge 24: 59 Rebekah their sister, and her n·,
35: 8 But Deborah Rebekah's n· died, and
Ex 2: 7 to thee a n· of the Hebrew women,
7 that she may n· the child for thee?
9 this child away, and n· it for me,
Ru 4: 16 her bosom, and became n· unto it.
2Sa 4: 4 and his n· took him up, and fled:
2Ki 11: 2 they hid him, even him and his n·,
2Ch 22: 11 him and his n· in a bedchamber.
1Th 2: 7 as a n· cherisheth her children:

nursed
Ex 2: 9 woman took the child, and n· it.
Isa 60: 4 daughters shall be n· at thy side.

nursing
Nu 11: 12 as a n· father beareth the sucking
Isa 49: 23 And kings shall be thy n· fathers,
23 and their queens thy n· mothers:

nurture
Eph 6: 4 n· and admonition of the Lord.

nuts
Ge 43: 11 spices, and myrrh, n·, and almonds:
Ca 6: 11 went down into the garden of n· to

Nymphas *(nim'-fas)*
Col 4: 15 which are in Laodicea, and N·,

O.

oak See also oaks.
Ge 35: 4 Jacob hid them under the o· which
8 buried beneath Beth-el under an o·:
Jos 24: 26 set it up there under an o·, that was
J'g 6: 11 under an o· which was in Ophrah,
19 brought it out unto him under the o·,
2Sa 18: 9 under the thick boughs of a great o·,
9 and his head caught hold of the o·,
10 I saw Absalom hanged in an o·.
14 was yet alive in the midst of the o·.
1Ki 13: 14 and found him sitting under an o·:
1Ch 10: 12 buried their bones under the o· in
Isa 1: 30 shall be as an o· whose leaf fadeth,
6: 13 and as an o·, whose substance is in
44: 14 taketh the cypress and the o·, which
Eze 6: 13 and under every thick o·, the place

oaks
Isa 1: 29 be ashamed of the o· which ye have
2: 13 up, and upon all the o· of Bashan,
Eze 27: 6 Of the o· of Bashan have they made
Ho 4: 13 hills, under o· and poplars and elms,
Am 2: 9 and he was strong as the o·; yet I
Zec 11: 2 howl, O ye o· of Bashan; for the

oar See also oars.
Eze 27: 29 And all that handle the o·, the

oars
Isa 33: 21 wherein shall go no galley with o·,
Eze 27: 6 Bashan have they made thine o·;

oath See also oath's; oaths.
Ge 24: 8 shalt be clear from this my o·:
41 shalt thou be clear from this my o·,
41 one, thou shalt be clear from my o·.
26: 3 I will perform the o· which I
28 Let there be now an o· betwixt us,
50: 25 Joseph took an o· of the children
Ex 22: 11 an o· of the Lord be between them
Le 5: 4 a man shall pronounce with an o·,
Nu 5: 19 priest shall charge her by an o·,

Nu 5:21 the woman with an *o'* of cursing,
21 Lord make thee a curse and an *o'*
30: 2 swear an *o'* to bind his soul with a
10 her soul by a bond with an *o'*;
13 every binding *o'* to afflict the soul,
De 7: 8 he would keep the *o'* which he had
29:12 into his *o'*, which the Lord thy God
14 do I make this covenant and this *o'*;
Jos 2:17 will be blameless of this thine *o'*
20 then we will be quit of thine *o'*
9:20 because of the *o'* which we sware
J'g 21: 5 had made a great *o'* concerning him
1Sa 14:26 mouth: for the people feared the *o'*.
27 charged the people with the *o'*:
28 straitly charged...people with an *o'*.
2Sa 21: 7 Lord's *o'* that was between them,
1Ki 2:43 thou not kept the *o'* of the Lord,
8:31 an *o'* be laid upon him to cause him
31 *o'* come before thine altar in this
18:10 he took an *o'* of the kingdom and
2Ki 11: 4 took an *o'* of them in the house of
1Ch 16:16 Abraham, and of his *o'* unto Isaac;
2Ch 6:22 an *o'* be laid upon him to make him
22 the *o'* come before the altar in this
15:15 And all Judah rejoiced at the *o'*:
Ne 5:12 priests, and took an *o'* of them,
10:29 entered into a curse, and into an *o'*,
Ps 105: 9 Abraham, and his *o'* unto Isaac;
Ec 8: 2 and that in regard of the *o'* of God.
9: 2 sweareth, as he that feareth an *o'*.
Jer 11: 5 That I may perform the *o'* which I
Eze 16:59 despised the *o'* in breaking the
17:13 him, and hath taken an *o'* of him:
16 whose *o'* he despised, and whose
18 he despised the *o'* by breaking the
19 surely mine *o'* that he hath despised,
Da 9:11 the *o'* that is written in the law of
Zec 8:17 his neighbour; and love no false *o'*:
M't 14: 7 he promised with an *o'* to give her
26:72 he denied with an *o'*, I do not know
Lu 1:73 *o'* which he sware to our father
Ac 2:30 God had sworn with an *o'* to him,
23:21 have bound themselves with an *o'*,
Heb 6:16 an *o'* for confirmation is to them
17 his counsel, confirmed it by an *o'*:
7:20 without an *o'* he was made priest:
21 priests were made without an *o'*;
21 but this with an *o'* by him that said
28 the word of the *o'*, which was since
Jas 5:12 the earth, neither by any other *o'*:

oath's
M't 14: 9 nevertheless for the *o'* sake, and
M'r 6:26 yet for his *o'* sake, and for their

oaths
Eze 21:23 sight, to them that have sworn *o'*:
Hab 3: 9 according to the *o'* of the tribes,
M't 5:33 perform unto the Lord thine *o'*:

Obadiah^ (*o-ba-di'-ah*)
1Ki 18: 3 And Ahab called *O'*, which was the
3 (Now *O'* feared the Lord greatly:
4 *O'* took an hundred prophets, and
5 And Ahab said unto *O'*, Go into the
6 *O'* went another way by himself.
7 And as *O'* was in the way, behold,
16 So *O'* went to meet Ahab, and told
1Ch 3:21 the sons of Arnan, the sons of *O'*,
7: 3 Michael, and *O'*, and Joel, Ishiah,
8:38 and Sheariah, and *O'*, and Hanan.
9:16 *O'* the son of Shemaiah, the son of
44 and Sheariah, and *O'*, and Hanan:
12: 9 Ezer the first, *O'* the second, Eliab
27:19 Of Zebulun, Ishmaiah the son of *O'*:
2Ch 17: 7 and to *O'*, and to Zechariah, and to
34:12 overseers...were Jahath and *O'*,
Ezr 8: 9 *O'* the son of Jehiel, and with him
Ne 10: 5 Harim, Meremoth, *O'*,
12:25 *O'*, Meshullam, Talmon, Akkub,
Ob 1 The vision of *O'*. Thus saith the

Obal (*o'-bal*)
Ge 10:28 And *O'*, and Abimael, and Sheba,

Obed (*o'-bed*) See also OBED-EDOM.
Ru 4:17 and they called his name *O'*: he
21 begat Boaz, and Boaz begat *O'*,
22 *O'* begat Jesse, and Jesse begat
1Ch 2:12 Boaz begat *O'*, and *O'* begat Jesse,
37 begat Ephlal, and Ephlal begat *O'*,
38 And *O'* begat Jehu, and Jehu begat
11:47 and *O'*, and Jasiel the Mesobaite.
26: 7 and *O'*, Elzabad, whose brethren
2Ch 23: 1 and Azariah the son of *O'*, and
M't 1: 5 begat *O'* of Ruth; and *O'* begat
Lu 3:32 of Jesse, which was the son of *O'*,

Obed-edom (*o''-bed-e'-dom*)
2Sa 6:10 into the house of *O'* the Gittite.
11 continued in the house of *O'* the
11 the Lord blessed *O'*, and all his
12 Lord hath blessed the house of *O'*,
12 from the house of *O'* into the city of
1Ch 13:13 carried it aside into the house of *O'*
14 God remained with the family of *O'*
14 the Lord blessed the house of *O'*,
15:18 and *O'*, and Jeiel, the porters.
21 and *O'*, and Jeiel, and Azaziah, with
24 *O'* and Jehiah were doorkeepers
25 Lord out of the house of *O'* with joy.
16: 5 and Eliab, and Benaiah, and *O'*:
38 *O'* with their brethren, threescore
38 *O'* also the son of Jeduthun and
26: 4 Moreover the sons of *O'* were,
8 All these of the sons of *O'*: they and
8 were threescore and two of *O'*.
15 To *O'* southward; and to his sons
2Ch 25:24 found in the house of God with *O'*,

obedience See also DISOBEDIENCE.
Ro 1: 5 *o'* to the faith among all nations,
5:19 so by the *o'* of one shall many be
6:16 death, or of *o'* unto righteousness?
16:19 For your *o'* is come abroad unto all
26 to all nations for the *o'* of faith:
1Co 14:34 are commanded to be under *o'*,
2Co 7:15 he remembereth the *o'* of you all,
10: 5 every thought to the *o'* of Christ;
6 when your *o'* is fulfilled.
Ph'm 21 Having confidence in thy *o'* I wrote
Heb 5: 8 yet learned he *o'* by the things
1Pe 1: 2 unto *o'* and sprinkling of the blood

obedient See also DISOBEDIENT.
Ex 24: 7 Lord...said will we do, and be *o'*.
Nu 27:20 the children of Israel may be *o'*.
De 4:30 and shalt be *o'* unto his voice;
8:20 ye would not be *o'* unto the voice
2Sa 22:45 they hear, they shall be *o'* unto me.
Pr 25:12 so is a wise reprover upon an *o'* ear.
Isa 1:19 If ye be willing and *o'*, ye shall eat
42:24 neither were they *o'* unto his law.
Ac 6: 7 of the priests were *o'* to the faith.
Ro 15:18 to make the Gentiles *o'*, by word
2Co 2: 9 whether ye be *o'* in all things.
Eph 6: 5 *o'* to them that are your masters
Ph'p 2: 8 and became *o'* unto death, even
Tit 2: 5 good, *o'* to their own husbands,
9 to be *o'* unto their own masters,
1Pe 1:14 As *o'* children, not fashioning

obeisance
Ge 37: 7 about, and made *o'* to my sheaf.
9 moon and the eleven stars made *o'*
43:28 down their heads, and made *o'*.
Ex 18: 7 meet his father in law, and did *o'*,
2Sa 1: 2 that he fell to the earth, and did *o'*.
14: 4 her face to the ground, and did *o'*,
15: 5 man came nigh to him to do him *o'*,
1Ki 1:16 Bath-sheba bowed, and did *o'* unto
2Ch 24:17 of Judah, and made *o'* to the king.

obey See also DISOBEYED; OBEYED; OBEYETH; OBEYING.
Ge 27: 8 my son, *o'* my voice according to
13 only *o'* my voice, and go fetch me
43 my son, *o'* my voice; and arise, flee
Ex 5: 2 should *o'* his voice to let Israel go?
19: 5 if ye will *o'* my voice indeed, and
23:21 Beware of him, and *o'* his voice,
22 if thou shalt indeed *o'* his voice,
De 11:27 if ye *o'* the commandments of the
28 if ye will not *o'* the commandments
13: 4 commandments, and *o'* his voice,
21:18 will not *o'* the voice of his father,
20 rebellious, he will not *o'* our voice;
27:10 *o'* the voice of the Lord thy God,
28:62 wouldest not *o'* the voice of the
30: 2 shalt *o'* his voice according to all
8 return and *o'* the voice of the Lord,
20 and that thou mayest *o'* his voice,
Jos 24:24 we serve, and his voice will we *o'*.
1Sa 8:19 refused to *o'* the voice of Samuel;
12:14 serve him, and *o'* his voice, and not
15 ye will not *o'* the voice of the Lord,
15:19 didst thou not *o'* the voice of the
22 to *o'* is better than sacrifice, and to
Ne 9:17 refused to *o'*, neither were mindful
Job 36:11 If they *o'* and serve him, they shall
12 But if they *o'* not, they shall perish
Ps 18:44 they hear of me, they shall *o'* me:
Pr 30:17 and despiseth to *o'* his mother,
Isa 11:14 children of Ammon shall *o'* them.
Jer 7:23 *O'* my voice, and I will be your
11: 4 *O'* my voice, and do them, according
7 and protesting, saying, *O'* my voice.
12:17 if they will not *o'*, I will utterly
18:10 in my sight, that it *o'* not my voice,
26:13 *o'* the voice of the Lord your God;
35:14 but *o'* their father's commandment:
38:20 *O'*, I beseech thee, the voice of the
42: 6 we will *o'* the voice of the Lord our
6 when we *o'* the voice of the Lord
13 neither *o'* the voice of the Lord your
Da 7:27 dominions shall serve and *o'* him.
9:11 that they might not *o'* thy voice;
Zec 6:15 diligently *o'* the voice of the Lord
M't 8:27 even the winds and the sea *o'* him!
M'r 1:27 unclean spirits, and they do *o'* him.
4:41 even the wind and the sea *o'* him?
Lu 8:25 winds and water, and they *o'* him.
17: 6 in the sea; and it should *o'* you.
Ac 5:29 ought to *o'* God rather than men.
32 God hath given to them that *o'* him.
7:39 our fathers would not *o'*,
Ro 2: 8 and do not *o'* the truth, but
8 the truth, but *o'* unrighteousness,
6:12 ye should *o'* it in the lusts thereof.
16 yield yourselves servants to *o'*,
16 his servants ye are to whom ye *o'*;
Ga 3: 1 that ye should not *o'* the truth,
5: 7 that ye should not *o'* the truth?
Eph 6: 1 Children, *o'* your parents in the
Col 3:20 Children, *o'* your parents in all
22 *o'* in all things your masters
2Th 1: 8 that *o'* not the gospel of our Lord
3:14 if any man *o'* not our word by this
Tit 3: 1 to *o'* magistrates, to be ready to
Heb 5: 9 salvation unto all them that *o'*
13:17 *O'* them that have the rule over
Jas 3: 3 horses' mouths, that they may *o'*
1Pe 3: 1 if any *o'* not the word, they also
4:17 them that *o'* not the gospel of God?

obeyed See also DISOBEYED; OBEYEDST.
Ge 22:18 because thou hast *o'* my voice.
26: 5 Because that Abraham *o'* my voice,
28: 7 Jacob *o'* his father and his mother,
Jos 5: 6 they *o'* not the voice of the Lord:
22: 2 *o'* my voice in all that I commanded
J'g 2: 2 but ye have not *o'* my voice: why
6:10 dwell: but ye have not *o'* my voice.
1Sa 15:20 Yea, I have *o'* the voice of the Lord,
24 the people, and *o'* their voice.
28:21 thine handmaid hath *o'* thy voice,
1Ki 20:36 hast not *o'* the voice of the Lord,
2Ki 18:12 they *o'* not the voice of the Lord
1Ch 29:23 prospered; and all Israel *o'* him.
2Ch 11: 4 they *o'* the words of the Lord, and
Pr 5:13 have not *o'* the voice of my teachers,
Jer 3:13 ye have not *o'* my voice, saith the
25 have not *o'* the voice of the Lord our
9:13 and have not *o'* my voice, neither
11: 8 Yet they *o'* not, nor inclined their
17:23 they *o'* not, neither inclined their
32:23 but they *o'* not thy voice, neither
34:10 more, then they *o'*, and let them go.
35: 8 we *o'* the voice of Jonadab the son
10 we have dwelt in tents, and have *o'*,
18 *o'* the commandment of Jonadab
40: 3 the Lord, and have not *o'* his voice,
42:21 not *o'* the voice of the Lord your
43: 4 *o'* not the voice of the Lord, to dwell
7 they *o'* not the voice of the Lord:
44:23 have not *o'* the voice of the Lord,
Da 9:10 Neither have we *o'* the voice of the
14 he doeth: for we *o'* not his voice.
Zep 3: 2 She *o'* not the voice; she received
Hag 1:12 *o'* the voice of the Lord their God,
Ac 5:36 as many as *o'* him, were scattered,
37 as many as *o'* him, were dispersed.
Ro 6:17 have *o'* from the heart that form
10:16 they have not all *o'* the gospel.
Ph'p 2:12 my beloved, as ye have always *o'*,
Heb 11: 8 By faith Abraham,...*o'*;
1Pe 3: 6 Even as Sara *o'* Abraham, calling

obeyedst
1Sa 28:18 thou *o'* not the voice of the Lord,
Jer 22:21 youth, that thou *o'* not my voice.

obeyeth
Isa 50:10 that *o'* the voice of his servant,
Jer 7:28 a nation that *o'* not the voice of the
11: 3 Cursed be the man that *o'* not the

obeying
J'g 2:17 *o'* the commandments of the Lord;
1Sa 15:22 as in *o'* the voice of the Lord?
1Pe 1:22 purified your souls in *o'* the truth

Obil (*o'-bil*)
1Ch 27:30 Over the camels also was *O'* the

object
Ac 24:19 *o'*, if they had ought against me.

oblation See also OBLATIONS.
Le 2: 4 thou bring an *o'* of a meat offering
5, 7 if thy *o'* be a meat offering baken
12 for the *o'* of the firstfruits, ye shall
13 every *o'* of thy meat offering shalt
3: 1 And if his *o'* be a sacrifice of peace
7:14 one out of the whole *o'* for an heave
29 shall bring his *o'* unto the Lord of
22:18 that will offer his *o'* for all his vows,
Nu 18: 9 every *o'* of theirs, every meat
31:50 We have therefore brought an *o'*
Isa 19:21 and shall do sacrifice and *o'*; yea,
40:20 so impoverished that he hath no *o'*
66: 3 he that offereth an *o'*, as if he
Jer 14:12 they offer burnt offering and an *o'*,
Eze 44:30 every *o'* of all, of every sort of
45: 1 ye shall offer an *o'* unto the Lord,
6 against the *o'* of the holy portion:
7 side of the *o'* of the holy portion,
7 before the *o'* of the holy portion,
13 This is the *o'* that ye shall offer;
16 give this *o'* for the prince in Israel.
48: 9 The *o'* that ye shall offer unto the
10 for the priests, shall be this holy *o'*;
12 this *o'* of the land that is offered
18 against the *o'* of the holy portion
20 All the *o'* shall be five and twenty
20 shall offer the holy *o'* foursquare,
21 and on the other of the holy *o'*,
21 five and twenty thousand of the *o'*
21 and it shall be the holy *o'*; and the
Da 2:46 should offer an *o'* and sweet odours
9:21 about the time of the evening *o'*.
27 the sacrifice and the *o'* to cease,

oblations
Le 7:38 children of Israel to offer their *o'*
2Ch 31:14 to distribute the *o'* of the Lord,
Isa 1:13 Bring no more vain *o'*; incense is
Eze 20:40 and the firstfruits of your *o'*,
44:30 of every sort of your *o'*, shall be

Oboth (*o'-both*)
Nu 21:10 set forward, and pitched in *O'*.
11 they journeyed from *O'*, and pitched
33:43 from Punon, and pitched in *O'*.
44 they departed from *O'*, and pitched

obscure
Pr 20:20 shall be put out in *o'* darkness.

obscurity
Isa 29:18 eyes of the blind shall see out of *o'*,
58:10 then shall thy light rise in *o'*, and
59: 9 we wait for light, but behold *o'*;

observation
Lu 17:20 of God cometh not with *o'*:

observe See also OBSERVED; OBSERVEST; OBSERVETH.
Ex 12:17 *o'* the feast of unleavened bread;
17 ye *o'* this day in your generations
24 shall *o'* this thing for an ordinance

Ex 31:16 o' the sabbath throughout their
34:11 O' thou that which I command
22 thou shalt o' the feast of weeks,
Le 19:26 ye use enchantment, nor o' times.
37 shall ye o' all my statutes, and
Nu 28: 2 shall ye o' to offer unto me in their
De 5:32 shall o' to do therefore as the Lord
6: 3 O Israel, and o' to do it; that it
25 o' to do all these commandments
8: 1 commandments...shall ye o' to do,
11:32 ye shall o' to do all the statutes
12: 1 which ye shall o' to do in the land,
28 O' and hear all these words which
32 soever I command you, o' to do it:
15: 5 to o' to do all these commandments
16: 1 O' the month of Abib, and keep the
12 thou shalt o' and do these statutes.
13 shalt o' the feast of tabernacles
17:10 thou shalt o' to do according to all
24: 8 of leprosy, that thou o' diligently,
8 them, so ye shall o' to do.
28: 1 to o' and to do...his commandments
13 thee this day, to o' and to do them:
15 to o' to do all his commandments
58 wilt not o' to do all the words of
31:12 o' to do all the words of this law:
32:46 command your children to o' to do,
Jos 1: 7, 8 thou mayest o' to do according to
J'g 13:14 all that I commanded her let her o'.
1Ki 20:33 Now the men did diligently o'
2Ki 17:37 ye shall o' to do for evermore;
21: 8 only if they will o' to do according
2Ch 7:17 and shalt o' my statutes and my
Ne 1: 5 him and o' his commandments:
10:29 to o' and do all the commandments
Ps 105:45 That they might o' his statutes,
107:43 is wise, and will o' these things,
119:34 I shall o' it with my whole heart.
Pr 23:26 and let thine eyes o' my ways.
Jer 8: 7 the swallow o' the time of their
Eze 20:18 neither o' their judgments, nor
37:24 and o' my statutes, and do them.
Ho 13: 7 as a leopard by the way will I o'
Jon 2: 8 They that o' lying vanities forsake
M't 23: 3 whatsoever they bid you o', that
3 that o' and do; but do not ye
28:20 Teaching them to o' all things
Ac 16:21 to receive, neither to o', being
21:25 that they o' no such thing, save
Ga 4:10 Ye o' days, and months, and
1Ti 5:21 that thou o' these things without

observed
Ge 37:11 him; but his father o' the saying.
Ex 12:42 is a night to be much o' unto the
42 is that night of the Lord to be o' of
Nu 15:22 not o' all these commandments,
De 33: 9 they have o' thy word, and kept
2Sa 11:16 to pass, when Joab o' the city,
2Ki 21: 6 through the fire, and o' times,
2Ch 33: 6 also he o' times, and used
Ho 14: 8 I have heard him, and o' him: I
M'r 6:20 just man and a holy, and o' him;
10:20 all these have I o' from my youth.

observer See also OBSERVERS.
De 18:10 an o' of times, or an enchanter,

observers
De 18:14 hearkened unto o' of times, and

observest
Isa 42:20 many things, but thou o' not;

observeth
Ec 11: 4 He that o' the wind shall not sow;

obstinate
De 2:30 his spirit, and made his heart o',
Isa 48: 4 Because I knew that thou art o',

obtain See also OBTAINED; OBTAINETH; OBTAINING.
Ge 16: 2 be that I may o' children by her.
Pr 8:35 and shall o' favour of the Lord.
Isa 35:10 they shall o' joy and gladness, and
51:11 they shall o' gladness and joy; and
Da 11:21 and o' the kingdom by flatteries.
M't 5: 7 merciful: for they shall o' mercy.
Lu 20:35 accounted worthy to o' that world,
Ro 11:31 mercy they also may o' mercy.
1Co 9:24 the prize? So run, that ye may o'.
25 do it to o' a corruptible crown;
1Th 5: 9 to o' salvation by our Lord Jesus
2Ti 2:10 that they may also o' the salvation
Heb 4:16 that we may o' mercy, and find
11:35 might o' a better resurrection:
Jas 4: 2 and desire to have, and cannot o':

obtained
Ne 13: 6 certain days o' I leave of the king:
Es 2: 9 him, and she o' kindness of him;
15 Esther o' favour in the sight of all
17 she o' grace and favour in his
5: 2 that she o' favour in his sight:
Ho 2:23 upon her that had not o' mercy;
Ac 1:17 and had o' part of this ministry.
22:28 With a great sum o' I this freedom.
26:22 Having therefore o' help of God, I
27:13 that they had o' their purpose,
Ro 11: 7 Israel hath not o' that which he
7 but the election hath o' it, and the
30 o' mercy through their unbelief:
1Co 7:25 one that hath o' mercy of the Lord
Eph 1:11 also we have o' an inheritance,
1Ti 1:13 but I o' mercy, because I did it
16 Howbeit for this cause I o' mercy,
Heb 1: 4 by inheritance o' a more excellent
6:15 endured, he o' the promise.
8: 6 he o' a more excellent ministry.
Heb 9:12 o' eternal redemption for us.
11: 2 by it the elders o' a good report.
4 o' witness that he was righteous,
33 o' promises, stopped the mouths of
39 o' a good report through faith,
1Pe 2:10 of God: which had not o' mercy,
10 but now have o' mercy.
2Pe 1: 1 that have o' like precious faith

obtaineth
Pr 12: 2 A good man o' favour of the Lord:
18:22 thing, and o' favour of the Lord.

obtaining
2Th 2:14 to the o' of the glory of our Lord

occasion See also OCCASIONED; OCCASIONS.
Ge 43:18 that he may seek o' against us, and
J'g 9:33 do to them as thou shalt find o'.
14: 4 sought an o' against...Philistines:
1Sa 10: 7 thee, that thou do as o' serve thee;
2Sa 12:14 given great o' to the enemies of the
Ezr 7:20 which thou shalt have o' to bestow,
Jer 2:24 in her o' who can turn her away?
Eze 18: 3 have o' any more to use this proverb
Da 6: 4 sought to find o' against Daniel
4 they could find none o' nor fault;
5 not find any o' against this Daniel,
Ro 7: 8, 11 taking o' by the commandment,
14:13 or an o' to fall in his brother's way.
2Co 5:12 give you o' to glory on our behalf,
8: 8 by o' of the forwardness of others,
11:12 cut off o' from them which desire o';
Ga 5:13 use not liberty for an o' to the flesh,
1Ti 5:14 give none o' to the adversary to
1Jo 2:10 is none o' of stumbling in him.

occasioned
1Sa 22:22 o' the death of all the persons

occasions
De 22:14 And give o' of speech against her,
17 hath given o' of speech against her,
Job 33:10 Behold, he findeth o' against me,

occupation
Ge 46:33 and shall say, What is your o'?
47: 3 unto his brethren, What is your o'?
Jon 1: 8 What is thine o'? and whence
Ac 18: 3 by their o' they were tentmakers.
19:25 together with the workmen of like o',

occupied
Ex 38:24 the gold that was o' for the work
J'g 16:11 new ropes that never were o',
Eze 27:16 they o' in thy fairs with emeralds,
19 going to and fro o' in thy fairs:
21 they o' with thee in lambs, and
22 they o' in thy fairs with chief of
Heb 13: 9 them that have been o' therein.

occupiers
Eze 27:27 and the o' of thy merchandise,

occupieth
1Co 14:16 that o' the room of unlearned

occupy See also OCCUPIED; OCCUPIETH.
Eze 27: 9 in thee to o' thy merchandise.
Lu 19:13 and said unto them, O' till I come.

occurrent
1Ki 5: 4 is neither adversary nor evil o'.

Ocran (*o'-cran*)
Nu 1:13 Of Asher; Pagiel the son of O'.
2:27 Asher shall be Pagiel the son of O'.
7:72 Pagiel the son of O', prince of the
77 the offering of Pagiel the son of O'.
10:26 of Asher was Pagiel the son of O'.

odd
Nu 3:48 the o' number...is to be redeemed,

Oded (*o'-ded*)
2Ch 15: 1 came upon Azariah the son of O':
8 and the prophecy of O' the prophet,
28: 9 Lord was there, whose name was O':

odious
1Ch 19: 6 had made themselves o' to David,
Pr 30:23 o' woman when she is married;

odour See also ODOURS.
Joh 12: 3 filled with the o' of the ointment.
Ph'p 4:18 an o' of a sweet smell, a sacrifice

odours
Le 26:31 smell the savour of your sweet o'.
2Ch 16:14 bed which was filled with sweet o'
Es 2:12 and six months with sweet o', and
Jer 34: 5 thee, so shall they burn o' for thee;
Da 2:46 an oblation and sweet o' unto him.
Re 5: 8 golden vials full of o', which are
18:13 cinnamon, and o', and ointments,

off See also OFFSCOURING; OFFSPRING.
Ge 7: 4 from o' the face of the earth.
8: 3 waters returned from o' the earth
7 were dried up from o' the earth.
8 from o' the face of the ground;
11 mouth was an olive leaf pluckt o':
11 were abated from o' the earth.
13 were dried up from o' the earth:
9:11 shall all flesh be cut o' any more by
11: 8 and they left o' to build the city.
17:14 soul shall be cut o' from his people;
22 he left o' talking with him, and God
21:16 down over against him a good way o',
22: 4 up his eyes, and saw the place afar o'.
24:64 saw Isaac, she lighted o' the camel.
27:40 break his yoke from o' thy neck.
37:18 And when they saw him afar o' even
Ge 38:14 her widow's garments o' from her,
40:19 lift up thy head from o' thee,
19 shall eat thy flesh from o' thee.
41:42 took o' his ring from his hand,
44: 4 out of the city, and not yet far o',
Ex 2: 4 his sister stood afar o', to wit what
3: 5 put o' thy shoes from o' thy feet; for
4:25 and cut o' the foreskin of her son,
9:15 thou shalt be cut o' from the earth.
12:15 that soul shall be cut o' from Israel.
19 shall be cut o' from the congregation
14:25 And took o' their chariot wheels, that
20:18 saw it, they removed, and stood afar o'.
21 the people stood afar o', and Moses
23:23 the Jebusites; and I will cut them o'.
24: 1 of Israel; and worship ye afar o'.
30:33, 38 shall even be cut o' from his people.
31:14 shall be cut o' from among his people.
32: 2 Break o' the golden earrings, which are
3 people brake o' the golden earrings
24 hath any gold, let them break it o'.
33: 5 now put o' thy ornaments from thee,
7 the camp, afar o' from the camp.
34:34 he took the vail o', until he came out.
Le 1:15 and wring o' his head, and burn it on
3: 9 he take o' hard by the backbone;
4: 8 take o' from it...the fat of the bullock
10 As it was taken o' from the bullock
31 fat is taken away from o' the sacrifice
5: 8 and wring o' his head from his neck,
6:11 And he shall put o' his garments, and
7:20, 21 soul shall be cut o' from his people.
25 it shall be cut o' from his people.
27 soul shall be cut o' from his people.
34 from o' the sacrifices of their peace
8:28 took them from o' their hands,
13:40 man whose hair is fallen o' his head,
41 hair fallen o' from the part of his head
14: 8 shave o' all his hair, and wash himself
9 he shall shave all his hair o' his head
9 even all his hair he shall shave o':
41 that they scrape o' without the city
16:12 coals of fire from o' the altar
23 shall put o' the linen garments, which
17: 4 shall be cut o' from among his people:
9 shall be cut o' from among his people.
10 will cut him o' from among his people.
14 whosoever eateth it shall be cut o'.
18:29 be cut o' from among their people.
19: 8 shall be cut o' from among his people.
20: 3 will cut him o' from among his people;
5 against his family, and will cut him o',
6 will cut him o' from among his people.
17 be cut o' in the sight of their people:
18 be cut o' from among their people.
21: 5 they shave o' the corner of their beard,
22: 3 shall be cut o' from my presence:
23:29 shall be cut o' from among his people.
Nu 2: 2 far o' about the tabernacle of the
4:18 Cut ye not o' the tribe of the families
7:89 unto him from o' the mercy seat
9:10 or be in a journey afar o', yet he shall
13 shall be cut o' from among his people:
10:11 taken up from o' the tabernacle
12:10 departed from o' the tabernacle;
15:30 shall be cut o' from among his people.
31 that soul shall utterly be cut o';
16:46 put fire therein from o' the altar,
19:13 that soul shall be cut o' from Israel:
20 cut o' from among the congregation,
De 4:26 utterly perish from o' the land
6:15 thee from o' the face of the earth.
12:29 shall cut o' the nations from before
13: 7 nigh unto thee, or far o' from thee,
19: 1 Lord thy God hath cut o' the nations,
20:15 cities which are very far o' from thee,
21: 4 strike o' the heifer's neck there in the
13 of her captivity from o' her,
23: 1 or hath his privy member cut o',
25: 9 loose his shoe from o' his foot,
12 Then thou shalt cut o' her hand, thine
28:21 consumed thee from o' the land,
63 shall be plucked from o' the land
30:11 hidden from thee, neither is it far o'.
Jos 3:13 the waters of Jordan shall be cut o'
16 the salt sea, failed, and were cut o':
4: 7 the waters of Jordan were cut o'
7 the waters of Jordan were cut o':
5: 9 the reproach of Egypt from o' you.
15 loose thy shoe from o' thy foot; for
7: 9 and cut o' our name from the earth:
10:27 they took them down o' the trees,
11:21 and cut o' the Anakims from the
15:18 and she lighted o' her ass; and
23: 4 with all the nations that I have cut o',
13 ye perish from o' this good land
15 you from o' this good land which
16 quickly from o' the good land
J'g 1: 6 caught him, and cut o' his thumbs
7 thumbs and their great toes cut o',
14 and she lighted from o' her ass;
4:15 lighted down from o' his chariot,
5:26 smote Sisera, she smote o' his head,
13:20 toward heaven from o' the altar,
15:14 his bands loosed from o' his hands.
16:12 from o' his arms like a thread.
19 caused him to shave o' the seven locks
21: 6 is one tribe cut o' from Israel this day.
Ru 2:20 Lord, who hath not left o' his kindness
4: 7 a man plucked o' his shoe, and gave it
8 it for thee. So he drew o' his shoe.
10 that the name of the dead be not cut o'
1Sa 2:31 come, that I will cut o' thine arm,
33 I shall not cut o' from mine altar,
4:18 fell from o' the seat backward by
5: 4 hands were cut o' upon the threshold;

1Sa 6: 5 will lighten his hand from o' you,
5 and from o' your gods,
5 and from o' your land.
17: 39 them. And David put them o' him.
51 him, and cut o' his head therewith.
19: 24 And he stripped o' his clothes also,
20: 15 cut o' thy kindness from my house
15 when the Lord hath cut o' the enemies
24: 4 and cut o' the skirt of Saul's robe
5 because he had cut o' Saul's skirt.
11 for in that I cut o' the skirt of thy robe,
21 thou wilt not cut o' my seed after me,
25: 23 lighted o' the ass, and fell before
26: 13 and stood on the top of an hill afar o';
28: 9 hath cut o' those that have familiar
31: 9 And they cut o' his head, and
9 and stripped o' his armour, and
2Sa 4: 12 and cut o' their hands and their feet,
7: 9 have cut o' all thine enemies out of
10: 4 shaved o' the one half of their beards,
4 cut o' their garments in the middle,
11: 2 that David arose from o' his bed,
24 shooters shot from o' the wall upon
12: 30 their king's crown from o' his head,
15: 17 and tarried in a place that was far o'.
16: 9 over, I pray thee, and take o' his head.
20: 22 cut o' the head of Sheba the son of
1Ki 9: 7 will I cut o' Israel out of the land
11: 16 he had cut o' every male in Edom:)
13: 34 house of Jeroboam, even to cut it o',
34 it from o' the face of the earth.
14: 10 will cut o' from Jeroboam him that
14 cut o' the house of Jeroboam that day:
15: 21 that he left o' building of Ramah, and
18: 4 Jezebel cut o' the prophets of the Lord,
20: 11 boast himself as he that putteth it o'.
21: 21 and will cut o' from Ahab him that
2Ki 1: 16 shalt not come down o' that bed on
2: 7 went, and stood to view afar o':
4: 25 man of God saw her afar o', that he
9: 8 and I will cut o' from Ahab him that
16: 17 Ahaz cut o' the borders of the bases,
17 removed the laver from o' them;
17 the sea from o' the brasen oxen
18: 16 cut o' the gold from the doors of the
23: 27 and will cast o' this city Jerusalem
1Ch 17: 8 have cut o' all thine enemies from
19: 4 and cut o' their garments in the midst
20: 2 of their king from o' his head,
28: 9 forsake him, he will cast thee o' for ever.
2Ch 6: 36 captives unto a land far o' or near;
11: 14 cast them o' from executing the
16: 5 he left o' building of Ramah, and let
20: 25 which they stripped o' for themselves,
22: 7 anointed to cut o' the house of Ahab.
26: 21 was cut o' from the house of the Lord:
32: 21 angel, which cut o' all the mighty men
Ezr 3: 13 and the noise was heard afar o'.
9: 3 plucked o' the hair of my head and of
Ne 4: 23 none of us put o' our clothes, saving
23 every one put them o' for washing.
5: 10 I pray you, let us leave o' this usury.
12: 43 joy of Jerusalem was heard...afar o'.
13: 25 and plucked o' their hair, and made
Es 8: 2 And the king took o' his ring, which
Job 2: 12 lifted up their eyes afar o', and knew
4: 7 or where were the righteous cut o'?
6: 9 let loose his hand, and cut me o'!
8: 14 Whose hope shall be cut o', and whose
9: 27 I will leave o' my heaviness, and
11: 10 If he cut o', and shut up, or gather
15: 4 Yea, thou castest o' fear, and
33 shake o' his unripe grape as the vine,
33 shall cast o' his flower as the olive.
17: 11 my purposes are broken o', even the
18: 16 and above shall his branch be cut o'.
21: 21 of his months is cut o' in the midst?
23: 17 I was not cut o' before the darkness,
24: 24 cut o' as the tops of the ears of corn.
32: 15 no more: they left o' speaking.
36: 20 when people are cut o' in their place.
25 may see it; man may behold it afar o'.
39: 25 and he smelleth the battle afar o',
29 the prey, and her eyes behold afar o'.
Ps 10: 1 Why standest thou afar o', O Lord?
12: 3 Lord shall cut o' all flattering lips,
30: 11 thou hast put o' my sackcloth, and
31: 22 I am cut o' from before thine eyes:
34: 16 cut o' the remembrance of them from
36: 3 he hath left o' to be wise, and to do
37: 9 For evildoers shall be cut o': but
22 that be cursed of him shall be cut o'.
28 the seed of the wicked shall be cut o'.
34 when the wicked are cut o', thou shalt
38 the end of the wicked shall be cut o'.
38: 11 sore; and my kinsman stand afar o'.
43: 2 why dost thou cast me o'? why go I
44: 9 But thou hast cast o', and put us to
23 O Lord? arise, cast us not o' for ever.
54: 5 enemies: cut them o' in thy truth.
55: 7 Lo, then would I wander far o', and
60: 1 O God, thou hast cast us o', thou hast
10 thou, O God, which hadst cast us o'?
65: 5 of them that are afar o' upon the sea:
71: 9 Cast me not o' in the time of old age;
74: 1 why hast thou cast us o' for ever?
75: 10 horns of the wicked also will I cut o';
76: 12 He shall cut o' the spirit of princes:
77: 7 Will the Lord cast o' for ever? and will
83: 4 let us cut them o' from being a nation;
88: 5 and they are cut o' from thy hand.
14 why castest thou o' my soul? why
16 over me; thy terrors have cut me o'.
89: 38 But thou hast cast o' and abhorred,
90: 10 for it is soon cut o', and we fly away.
94: 14 the Lord will not cast o' his people,

Ps 94: 23 cut them o' in their...wickedness;
23 the Lord our God shall cut them o'.
101: 5 his neighbour, him will I cut o':
8 I may cut o' all the wicked doers from
108: 11 not thou, O God, who hast cast us o'?
109: 13 Let his posterity be cut o'; and in the
15 he may cut o' the memory of them
138: 6 but the proud he knoweth afar o'.
139: 2 understandest my thought afar o'.
143: 12 of thy mercy cut o' mine enemies,
Pr 2: 22 wicked shall be cut o' from the earth,
17: 14 leave o' contention, before it be
23: 18 thine expectation shall not be cut o'.
24: 14 and thy expectation shall not be cut o'.
26: 6 the hand of a fool cutteth o' the feet,
27: 10 that is near than a brother far o'.
30: 14 to devour the poor from o' the earth,
Ec 7: 24 That which is far o', and exceeding
Ca 5: 3 I have put o' my coat; how shall I put
Isa 6: 6 with the tongs from o' the altar:
9: 14 will cut o' from Israel head and tail,
10: 7 heart to destroy and cut o' nations
27 taken away from o' thy shoulder,
27 and his yoke from o' thy neck,
11: 13 adversaries of Judah shall be cut o':
14: 22 cut o' from Babylon the name, and
25 shall his yoke depart from o' them,
25 depart from o' their shoulders.
15: 2 be baldness, and every beard cut o'.
17: 13 rebuke them, and they shall flee far o',
18: 5 cut o' the sprigs with pruning hooks,
20: 2 the sackcloth from o' thy loins,
2 and put o' thy shoe from thy foot.
22: 25 that was upon it shall be cut o':
23: 7 feet shall carry her afar o' to sojourn.
25: 8 wipe away tears from o' all faces;
8 he take away from o' all the earth:
27: 11 withered, they shall be broken o':
12 beat o' from the channel of the river
29: 20 all that watch for iniquity are cut o':
33: 9 and Carmel shake o' their fruits.
13 Hear, ye that are far o', what I have
17 behold the land that is very far o'.
34: 4 as the leaf falleth o' from the vine, and
38: 10 I said in the cutting o' of my days,
12 cut o' like a weaver my life: he will
12 he will cut me o' with pining sickness:
46: 13 it shall not be far o', and my salvation
47: 11 thou shalt not be able to put it o':
48: 9 refrain for thee, that I cut thee not o'.
19 his name should not have been cut o'
50: 6 to them that plucked o' the hair:
53: 8 for he was cut o' out of the land of the
55: 13 everlasting sign...shall not be cut o'.
56: 5 everlasting name,...shall not be cut o'.
57: 9 and didst send thy messengers far o',
19 Peace, peace to him that is far o', and
59: 11 for salvation, but it is far o' from us.
14 backward, and justice standeth afar o':
66: 3 a lamb, as if he cut o' a dog's neck;
19 to the isles afar o', that have not heard
Jer 7: 28 perished,...is cut o' from their mouth.
29 Cut o' thine hair, O Jerusalem,...cast
9: 21 to cut o' the children from without,
11: 19 cut him o' from the land of the living,
23: 23 saith the Lord, and not a God afar o'?
24: 10 they be consumed from o' the land
28: 10 o' the prophet Jeremiah's neck,
12 o' the neck of the prophet Jeremiah,
16 thee from o' the face of the earth;
30: 8 break his yoke from o' thy neck,
31: 10 and declare it in the isles afar o', and
37 I will also cast o' all the seed of Israel
33: 24 he hath even cast them o'? thus they
38: 27 So they left o' speaking with him; for
44: 7 to cut o' from you man and woman,
8 that ye might cut yourselves o', and
11 you for evil, and to cut o' all Judah.
18 since we left o' to burn incense to the
46: 27 behold, I will save thee from afar o',
47: 4 And to cut o' from Tyrus and Zidon
5 Askelon is cut o' with the remnant of
48: 2 let us cut it o' from being a nation.
25 The horn of Moab is cut o', and his
49: 26 men of war shall be cut o' in that day,
30 Flee, get you far o', dwell deep, O ye
50: 16 Cut o' the sower from Babylon, and
30 men of war shall be cut o' in that day,
51: 6 be not cut o' in her iniquity; for this is
50 remember the Lord afar o', and let
62 to cut it o', that none shall remain in
La 2: 3 He hath cut o' in his fierce anger all
7 The Lord hath cast o' his altar, he
3: 17 removed my soul far o' from peace:
31 For the Lord will not cast o' for ever:
53 have cut o' my life in the dungeon,
54 mine head; then I said, I am cut o'.
Eze 6: 12 that is far o' shall die of the pestilence;
8: 6 I should go far o' from my sanctuary?
10: 18 departed from o' the threshold of
11: 16 cast them far o' among the heathens,
12: 27 of the times that are afar o'.
14: 8 will cut him o' from the midst of my
13 and will cut o' man and beast from it:
17 so that I cut o' man and beast from it:
19 blood, to cut o' from it man and beast:
21 to cut o' from it man and beast?
17: 4 cropped o' the top of his young twigs,
9 and cut o' the fruit thereof, that it
17 building forts, to cut o' many persons:
22 I will crop o' from the top of his young
18: 17 hath taken o' his hand from the poor,
21: 3 will cut o' from thee the righteous and
4 I will cut o' from thee the righteous
26 the diadem, and take o' the crown:
23: 34 thereof,...pluck o' thine own breasts:

Eze 25: 7 and I will cut thee o' from the people,
13 and will cut o' man and beast from it;
16 and I will cut o' the Cherethims, and
26: 16 and put o' their broidered garments:
29: 8 and cut o' man and beast out of thee.
30: 15 and I will cut o' the multitude of No.
31: 12 terrible of the nations, have cut him o',
35: 7 will cut o' from him that passeth out
37: 11 is lost: we are cut o' for our parts.
44: 19 shall put o' their garments wherein
Da 4: 14 down the tree, and cut o' his branches,
27 and break o' thy sins by righteousness,
9: 7 that are near, and that are far o',
26 two weeks shall Messiah be cut o',
Ho 4: 10 have left o' to take heed to the Lord.
8: 3 hath cast o' the thing that is good:
4 them idols, that they may be cut o'.
5 Thy calf, O Samaria, hath cast thee o';
10: 7 Samaria, her king is cut o' as the foam
15 the king of Israel utterly be cut o'.
11: 4 take o' the yoke on their jaws,
Joe 1: 5 wine; for it is cut o' from your mouth.
9 is cut o' from the house of the Lord;
16 Is not the meat cut o' before our eyes,
2: 20 far o' from you the northern army,
3: 8 to the Sabeans, to a people far o':
Am 1: 5 cut o' the inhabitant from the plain of
8 cut o' the inhabitant from Ashdod,
11 and did cast o' all pity, and his anger
2: 3 I will cut o' the judge from the midst
3: 14 the horns of the altar shall be cut o',
5: 7 leave o' righteousness in the earth,
9: 8 it from o' the face of the earth;
Ob 5 (how art thou cut o'!) would they not
9 of Esau may be cut o' by slaughter.
10 and thou shalt be cut o' for ever.
14 to cut o' those of his that did escape;
Mic 2: 8 ye pull o' the robe with the garment
3: 2 who pluck o' the skin from o' them,
2 their flesh from o' their bones;
3 and flay their skin from o' them;
4: 3 rebuke strong nations afar o'; and
7 that was cast far o' a strong nation:
5: 9 and all thine enemies shall be cut o'.
10 cut o' thy horses out of the midst of
11 And I will cut o' the cities of thy land,
12 cut o' witchcrafts out of thine hand;
13 Thy graven images also will I cut o',
Na 1: 13 will I break his yoke from o' thee,
14 thy gods will I cut o' the graven image
15 through thee; he is utterly cut o'.
2: 13 I will cut o' thy prey from the earth,
3: 15 the sword shall cut thee o', it shall eat
Hab 2: 10 thy house by cutting o' many people,
3: 17 the flock shall be cut o' from the fold,
Zep 1: 2 all things from o' the land,
3 cut o' [] man from o' the land,
4 I will cut o' the remnant of Baal from
11 all they that bear silver are cut o'.
3: 6 I have cut o' the nations: their towers
7 their dwelling should not be cut o',
Zec 5: 3 every one that stealeth shall be cut o'
3 every one that sweareth shall be cut o'
6: 15 that are far o' shall come and build
9: 6 will cut o' the pride of the Philistines.
10 I will cut o' the chariot from Ephraim,
10 and the battle bow shall be cut o';
10: 6 be as though I had not cast them o':
11: 8 Three shepherds also I cut o' in one
9 that is to be cut o', let it be cut o';
16 shall not visit those that be cut o',
13: 2 cut o' the names of the idols out of the
8 parts therein shall be cut o' and die;
14: 2 shall not be cut o' from the city.
Mal 2: 12 will cut o' the man that doeth this,
M't 5: 30 thy right hand offend thee, cut it o',
8: 30 a good way o' from them a herd
10: 14 city, shake o' the dust of your feet.
18: 8 or thy foot offend thee, cut them o',
26: 51 high priest's, and smote o' his ear.
58 Peter followed him afar o' unto the
27: 31 they took the robe o' from him,
55 women were...beholding afar o',
M'r 5: 6 when he saw Jesus afar o', he ran
6: 11 shake o' the dust under your feet
9: 43 And if thy hand offend thee, cut it o':
45 And if thy foot offend thee, cut it o':
11: 8 cut down branches o' the trees
13 seeing a fig tree afar o' having leaves,
14: 47 of the high priest, and cut o' his ear,
54 Peter followed him afar o', even
15: 20 they took o' the purple from him,
40 were also women looking on afar o':
Lu 10: 11 on us, we do wipe o' against you:
14: 32 while the other is yet a great way o',
15: 20 But when he was yet a great way o',
16: 23 and seeth Abraham afar o', and
17: 12 that were lepers, which stood afar o':
18: 13 publican, standing afar o', would not
22: 50 high priest, and cut o' his right ear.
54 house. And Peter followed afar o'.
23: 49 him from Galilee, stood afar o',
Joh 11: 18 Jerusalem, about fifteen furlongs o'.
18: 10 servant, and cut o' his right ear.
26 his kinsman whose ear Peter cut o',
Ac 2: 39 to all that are afar o', even as many
7: 33 Put o' thy shoes from thy feet:
12: 7 his chains fell o' from his hands.
13: 51 shook o' the dust of their feet
16: 22 the magistrates rent o' their clothes,
22: 23 cried out, and cast o' their clothes,
27: 32 soldiers cut o' the ropes of the boat,
32 ropes of the boat, and let her fall o'.
28: 5 he shook o' the beast into the fire,
Ro 11: 17 if some of the branches be broken o',
19 The branches were broken o', that I

Ro 11:20 of unbelief they were broken *o'*,
22 otherwise thou also shalt be cut *o'*.
13:12 let us...cast *o'* the works of darkness,
2Ch 11:12 I may cut *o'* occasion from them
Ga 5:12 were even cut *o'* which trouble you.
Eph 2:13 were far *o'* are made nigh by the
17 peace to you which were afar *o'*, and
4:22 ye put *o'* concerning the former
Col 2:11 putting *o'* the body of the sins of the
3: 8 But now ye also put *o'* all these;
9 put *o'* the old man with his deeds;
1Ti 5:12 they have cast *o'* their first faith.
Heb 11:13 but having seen them afar *o'*, and were
2Pe 1: 9 things is blind, and cannot see afar *o'*,
14 I must put *o'* this my tabernacle,
Re 18:10 Standing afar *o'* for the fear of her
15 shall stand afar *o'* for the fear of
17 many as trade by sea, stood afar *o'*,

offence See also OFFENCES.
1Sa 25:31 thee, nor *o'* of heart unto my lord,
Isa 8:14 a rock of *o'* to both the houses of
Ho 5:15 till they acknowledge their *o'*, and
M't 16:23 Satan: thou art an *o'* unto me:
18: 7 that man by whom the *o'* cometh!
Ac 24:16 conscience void of *o'* toward God,
Ro 5:15 not as the *o'*, so also is the free
15 through...*o'* of one many be dead,
17 if by one man's *o'* death reigned
18 as by the *o'* of one judgment came
20 entered, that the *o'* might abound.
9:33 a stumblingstone and rock of *o'*:
14:20 for that man who eateth with *o'*.
1Co 10:32 Give none *o'*, neither to the Jews,
2Co 6: 3 Giving no *o'* in any thing, that the
11: 7 committed an *o'* in abasing myself
Ga 5:11 then is the *o'* of the cross ceased.
Ph'p 1:10 and without *o'* till the day of Christ;
1Pe 2: 8 of stumbling, and a rock of *o'*,

offences
Ec 10: 4 for yielding pacifieth great *o'*.
M't 18: 7 Woe unto the world because of *o'*!
7 for it must needs be that *o'* come;
Lu 17: 1 impossible but that *o'* will come:
Ro 4:25 Who was delivered for our *o'*, and
5:16 the free gift is of many *o'* unto
16:17 them which cause divisions and *o'*

offend See also OFFENDED.
Job 34:31 I will not *o'* any more:
Ps 73:15 I should *o'* against the generation
119:165 law: and nothing shall *o'* them.
Jer 2: 3 all that devour him shall *o'*; evil
50: 7 We *o'* not, because they have sinned
Ho 4:15 play the harlot, yet let not Judah *o'*;
Hab 1:11 he shall pass over, and *o'*, imputing
M't 5:29 if thy right eye *o'* thee, pluck it
30 if thy right hand *o'* thee, cut it off,
13:41 of his kingdom all things that *o'*,
17:27 lest we should *o'* them, go thou to
18: 6 shall *o'* one of these little ones
8 if thy hand or thy foot *o'* thee, cut
9 And if thine eye *o'* thee, pluck it
M'r 9:42 shall *o'* one of these little ones
43 And if thy hand *o'* thee, cut it off:
45 And if thy foot *o'* thee, cut it off:
47 And if thine eye *o'* thee, pluck it
Lu 17: 2 should *o'* one of these little ones.
Joh 6:61 said unto them, Doth this *o'* you?
1Co 8:13 if meat make my brother to *o'*,
13 lest I make my brother to *o'*.
Jas 2:10 the whole law, yet *o'* in one point,
3: 2 For in many things we *o'* all.
2 If any man *o'* not in word, the

offended
Ge 20: 9 what have I *o'* thee, that thou
40: 1 baker had *o'* their lord the king of
2Ki 18:14 saying, I have *o'*; return from me:
2Ch 28:13 have *o'* against the Lord already,
Pr 18:19 A brother *o'* is harder to be won
Jer 37:18 What have I *o'* against thee, or
Eze 25:12 and hath greatly *o'*, and revenged
Ho 13: 1 but when he *o'* in Baal, he died.
M't 11: 6 whosoever shall not be *o'* in me.
13:21 of the word, by and by he is *o'*.
57 And they were *o'* in him. But Jesus
15:12 thou that the Pharisees were *o'*,
24:10 And then shall many be *o'*, and
26:31 All ye shall be *o'* because of me
33 Though all men shall be *o'* because
33 of thee, yet will I never be *o'*.
M'r 4:17 sake, immediately they are *o'*.
6: 3 with us? And they were *o'* at him.
14:27 All ye shall be *o'* because of me
29 Although all shall be *o'*, yet will not
Lu 7:23 whosoever shall not be *o'* in me.
Joh 16: 1 unto you, that ye should not be *o'*.
Ac 25: 8 Cæsar, have I *o'* any thing at all.
Ro 14:21 brother stumbleth, or is *o'*, or
2Co 11:29 weak? who is *o'*, and I burn not?

offender See also OFFENDERS.
Isa 29:21 That make a man an *o'* for a word,
Ac 25:11 if I be an *o'*, or have committed

offenders
1Ki 1:21 son Solomon shall be counted *o'*.

offer See also OFFERED; OFFERETH; OFFERING.
Ge 22: 2 *o'* him there for a burnt offering
Ex 22:29 not delay to *o'* the first of thy ripe
23:18 not *o'* the blood of my sacrifice
29:36 thou shalt *o'* every day a bullock
38 which thou shalt *o'* upon the altar;
39 lamb thou shalt *o'* in the morning;
39 other lamb thou shalt *o'* at even:
41 other lamb thou shalt *o'* at even,
30: 9 *o'* no strange incense thereon,
34:25 not *o'* the blood of my sacrifice
35:24 that did *o'* an offering of silver
Le 1: 3 him *o'* a male without blemish:
3 shall *o'* it of his own voluntary will
2: 1 when any will *o'* a meat offering
12 ye shall *o'* them unto the Lord:
13 thine offerings thou shalt *o'* salt.
14 *o'* a meat offering of thy firstfruits
14 thou shalt *o'* for the meat offering
3: 1 offering, if he *o'* it of the herd;
1 he shall *o'* it without blemish before
3 shall *o'* of the sacrifice of the peace
6 he shall *o'* it without blemish.
7 If he *o'* a lamb for his offering, then
7 then shall he *o'* it before the Lord.
9 *o'* of the sacrifice of the peace
12 then he shall *o'* it before the Lord.
14 he shall *o'* thereof his offering,
4:14 shall *o'* a young bullock for the sin,
5: 8 who shall *o'* that which is for the sin
10 *o'* the second for a burnt offering,
6:14 Aaron shall *o'* it before the Lord,
20 which they shall *o'* unto the Lord in
21 shalt thou *o'* for a sweet savour
22 is anointed in his stead shall *o'* it:
7: 3 he shall *o'* of it all the fat thereof;
11 which he shall *o'* unto the Lord.
12 If he *o'* it for a thanksgiving, then
12 *o'* with the sacrifice of thanksgiving
13 *o'* for his offering leavened bread
14 *o'* one out of the whole oblation
25 men *o'* an offering made by fire unto
38 to *o'* their oblations unto the Lord,
9: 2 and *o'* them before the Lord.
7 *o'* thy sin offering, and thy burnt
7 *o'* the offering of the people, and
12: 7 Who shall *o'* it before the Lord,
14:12 *o'* him for a trespass offering, and
19 the priest shall *o'* the sin offering,
20 priest shall *o'* the burnt offering
30 shall *o'* the one of the turtledoves,
15:15 And the priest shall *o'* them, the
30 shall *o'* the one for a sin offering,
16: 6 *o'* his bullock of the sin offering,
9 fell, and *o'* him for a sin offering.
24 forth, and *o'* his burnt offering,
17: 4 to *o'* an offering unto the Lord
5 which they *o'* in the open field,
5 *o'* them for peace offerings unto
7 *o'* their sacrifices unto devils,
9 to *o'* it unto the Lord; even that
19: 5 ye *o'* a sacrifice of peace offerings
5 Lord, ye shall *o'* it at your own will.
6 be eaten the same day ye *o'* it,
21: 6 bread of their God, they do *o'*:
17 approach to *o'* the bread of his God.
21 nigh to *o'* the offerings of the Lord
21 nigh to *o'* the bread of his God.
22:15 Israel, which they *o'* unto the Lord;
18 that will *o'* his oblation for all his
18 will *o'* unto the Lord for a burnt
19 Ye shall *o'* at your own will a male
20 a blemish, that shall ye not *o'*:
22 ye shall not *o'* these unto the Lord,
23 thou *o'* for a freewill offering;
24 not *o'* unto the Lord that which
25 shall ye *o'* the bread of your God
29 when ye will *o'* a sacrifice of
29 the Lord, *o'* it at your own will.
23: 8 shall *o'* an offering made by fire
12 ye shall *o'* that day when ye wave
16 shall *o'* a new meat offering unto
18 shall *o'* with the bread seven lambs
25, 27, 36, 36, 37 *o'* an offering...by fire
27:11 do not *o'* a sacrifice unto the Lord,
Nu 5:25 the Lord, and *o'* it upon the altar:
6:11 shall *o'* the one for a sin offering,
14 shall *o'* his offering unto the Lord,
16 shall *o'* his sin offering, and his
17 shall *o'* the ram for a sacrifice of
17 shall *o'* also his meat offering, and
7:11 They shall *o'* their offering, each
18 of Zuar, prince of Issachar, did *o'*:
24 of the children of Zebulun, did *o'*:
30 of the children of Reuben, did *o'*:
36 of the children of Simeon, did *o'*:
8:11 Aaron shall *o'* the Levites before
12 shalt *o'* the one for a sin offering,
13 *o'* them for an offering unto the
15 them, and *o'* them for an offering.
9: 7 not *o'* an offering of the Lord in
15: 7 *o'* the third part of an hin of wine,
14 will *o'* an offering made by fire,
19 ye shall *o'* up an heave offering
20 *o'* up a cake of the first of your
24 shall *o'* one young bullock for a
16:40 come near to *o'* incense before
18:12 which they shall *o'* unto the Lord,
19 children of Israel *o'* unto the Lord,
24 they *o'* as an heave offering unto
26 shall *o'* up an heave offering of it
28 ye also shall *o'* an heave offering
29 ye shall *o'* every heave offering of
28: 2 *o'* unto me in their due season.
3 which ye shall *o'* unto the Lord;
4 lamb shalt thou *o'* in the morning,
4 other lamb shalt thou *o'* at even;
8 other lamb shalt thou *o'* at even:
8 thou shalt *o'* it, a sacrifice made by
11 ye shall *o'* a burnt offering unto
19 ye shall *o'* a sacrifice made by fire
20 tenth deals shall ye *o'* for a bullock,
21 A several tenth deal shalt thou *o'* for
23 *o'* these beside the burnt offering
24 this manner ye shall *o'* daily,
27 ye shall *o'* the burnt offering for
31 shall *o'* them beside the continual
Nu 29: 2 shall *o'* a burnt offering for a sweet
8 shall *o'* a burnt offering unto the
13 And ye shall *o'* a burnt offering, a
17 shall *o'* twelve young bullocks, two
36 But ye shall *o'* a burnt offering,
De 12:13 thou *o'* not thy burnt offerings in
14 thou shalt *o'* thy burnt offerings,
27 thou shalt *o'* thy burnt offerings,
18: 3 from them that *o'* a sacrifice,
27: 6 *o'* burnt offerings thereon unto
7 thou shalt *o'* peace offerings, and
33:19 shall *o'* sacrifices of righteousness:
Jos 22:23 *o'* thereon burnt offering or meat
23 if to *o'* peace offerings thereon, let
J'g 3:18 made an end to *o'* the present,
6:26 *o'* a burnt sacrifice with the wood
11:31 I will *o'* it up for a burnt offering.
13:16 if thou wilt *o'* a burnt offering,
16 thou must *o'* it unto the Lord.
16:23 *o'* a great sacrifice unto Dagon
1Sa 1:21 went up to *o'* unto the Lord the
2:19 husband to *o'* the yearly sacrifice.
28 to *o'* upon mine altar, to burn
10: 8 unto thee, to *o'* burnt offerings,
2Sa 24:12 the Lord, I *o'* thee three things;
22 take and *o'* up what seemeth good
24 will I *o'* burnt offerings unto the
1Ki 3: 4 did Solomon *o'* upon that altar.
9:25 did Solomon *o'* burnt offerings
13: 2 upon thee shall he *o'* the priests
2Ki 5:17 *o'* neither burnt offering nor
10:24 to *o'* sacrifices and burnt offerings,
1Ch 16:40 *o'* burnt offerings unto the Lord
21:10 the Lord, I *o'* thee three things:
24 nor *o'* burnt offerings without
23:31 *o'* all burnt sacrifices unto the
29:14 should be able to *o'* so willingly
17 here, to *o'* willingly unto thee.
2Ch 23:18 *o'* the burnt offerings of the Lord,
24:14 to minister, and to *o'* withal, and
29:21 to *o'* them on the altar of the Lord.
27 to *o'* the burnt offering upon the
35:12 *o'* unto the Lord, as it is written
16 *o'* burnt offerings upon the altar
Ezr 3: 2 to *o'* burnt offerings thereon, as it
6 *o'* burnt offerings unto the Lord.
6:10 may *o'* sacrifices of sweet savours
7:17 and *o'* them upon the altar of the
Job 42: 8 and *o'* up for yourselves a burnt
Ps 4: 5 *O'* the sacrifices of righteousness,
16: 4 offerings of blood will I not *o'*,
27: 6 *o'* in his tabernacle sacrifices of
50:14 *O'* unto God thanksgiving; and
51:19 they *o'* bullocks upon thine altar.
66:15 will *o'* unto thee burnt sacrifices of
15 I will *o'* bullocks with goats.
72:10 Sheba and Seba shall *o'* gifts.
116:17 I will *o'* to thee the sacrifice of
Isa 57: 7 wentest thou up to *o'* sacrifice.
Jer 11:12 gods unto whom they *o'* incense:
14:12 *o'* burnt offering and an oblation,
33:18 before me to *o'* burnt offerings,
Eze 6:13 where they did *o'* sweet savour
20:31 For when ye *o'* your gifts, when
43:18 *o'* burnt offerings thereon, and to
22 second day thou shalt *o'* a kid
23 thou shalt *o'* a young bullock
24 thou shalt *o'* them before the Lord,
24 *o'* them up for a burnt offering
44: 7 *o'* my bread, the fat and the blood,
15 *o'* unto me the fat and the blood,
27 he shall *o'* his sin offering, saith
45: 1 shall *o'* an oblation unto the Lord,
13 is the oblation that ye shall *o'*;
14 ye shall *o'* the tenth part of a bath
46: 4 offering that the prince shall *o'*
48: 8 be the offering which ye shall *o'*
9 oblation that ye shall *o'* unto the
20 *o'* the holy oblation foursquare,
Da 2:46 *o'* an oblation and sweet odours
Ho 9: 4 not *o'* wine offerings to the Lord,
Am 4: 5 And *o'* a sacrifice of thanksgiving
5:22 Though ye *o'* me burnt offerings
Hag 2:14 which they *o'* there is unclean.
Mal 1: 7 Ye *o'* polluted bread upon mine
8 if ye *o'* the blind for sacrifice, is it
8 if ye *o'* the lame and sick, is it not
8 *o'* it now unto thy governor; will
3: 3 may *o'* unto the Lord an offering
M't 5:24 and then come and *o'* thy gift.
8: 4 *o'* the gift that Moses commanded,
M'r 1:44 *o'* for thy cleansing those things
Lu 2:24 to *o'* a sacrifice according to that
5:14 *o'* for thy cleansing, according as
6:29 on the one cheek *o'* also the other;
11:12 an egg, will he *o'* him a scorpion?
Heb 5: 1 *o'* both gifts and sacrifices
3 so also for himself, to *o'* for sins.
7:27 to *o'* up sacrifice, first for his own
8: 3 ordained to *o'* gifts and sacrifices:
3 man have somewhat also to *o'*.
4 that *o'* gifts according to the law:
9:25 that he should *o'* himself often,
13:15 let us *o'* the sacrifice of praise to
1Pe 2: 5 to *o'* up spiritual sacrifices,
Re 8: 3 *o'* it with the prayers of all saints

offered
Ge 8:20 *o'* burnt offerings on the altar.
22:13 and *o'* him up for a burnt offering
31:54 *o'* sacrifice upon the mount, and
46: 1 and *o'* sacrifices unto the God of his
Ex 24: 5 of Israel, which *o'* burnt offerings,
32: 6 *o'* burnt offerings, and brought
35:22 man that *o'*...an offering of gold
22 every man...*o'* an offering of gold
40:29 *o'* upon it the burnt offering and

Le 7: 8 burnt offering which he hath *o*'.
15 eaten the same day that it is *o*';
9:15 slew it, and *o*' it for sin, as the
16 and *o*' it according to the manner.
10: 1 *o*' strange fire before the Lord,
19 day have they *o*' their sin offering
16: 1 when they *o*' before the Lord, and
Nu 3: 4 they *o*' strange fire before the Lord,
7: 2 over them that were numbered, *o*':
10 *o*' for dedicating of the altar in
10 *o*' their offering before the altar.
12 he that *o*' his offering the first day
19 He *o*' for his offering one silver
42 prince of the children of Gad, *o*':
48 prince of the children of Ephraim, *o*':
54 On the eighth day *o*' Gamaliel the
60 prince of the children of Benjamin, *o*':
66 prince of the children of Dan, *o*':
72 prince of the children of Asher, *o*':
78 prince of the children of Naphtali, *o*':
8:21 and Aaron *o*' them as an offering
16:35 and fifty men that *o*' incense.
38 for they *o*' them before the Lord,
39 they that were burnt had *o*'; and
22:40 And Balak *o*' oxen and sheep,
23: 2 and Balaam *o*' on every altar a
4 *o*' upon every altar a bullock and
14, 30 *o*' a bullock and a ram on every
26:61 *o*' strange fire before the Lord.
28:15 offering unto the Lord shall be *o*',
24 *o*' beside the continual burnt
31:52 gold of the offering that they *o*'
Jos 8:31 they *o*' thereon burnt offerings
J'g 5: 2 the people willingly *o*' themselves.
9 *o*' themselves willingly among the
6:28 bullock was *o*' upon the altar
13:19 *o*' it upon a rock unto the Lord:
20:26 and *o*' burnt offerings and peace
21: 4 and *o*' burnt offerings and peace
1Sa 1: 4 the time was that Elkanah *o*',
2:13 that, when any man *o*' sacrifice,
6:14 *o*' the kine a burnt offering unto
15 of Beth-shemesh *o*' burnt offerings
7: 9 lamb, and *o*' it for a burnt offering
13: 9 And he *o*' the burnt offering.
12 therefore, and *o*' a burnt offering.
2Sa 6:17 David *o*' burnt offerings and peace
15:12 from Giloh, while he *o*' sacrifices.
24:25 and *o*' burnt offerings and peace
1Ki 3:15 Lord, and *o*' up burnt offerings,
15 *o*' peace offerings, and made a
8:62 him, *o*' sacrifice before the Lord.
63 And Solomon *o*' a sacrifice of peace
63 he *o*' unto the Lord, two and twenty
64 there he *o*' burnt offerings, and
12:32 in Judah, and he *o*' upon the altar.
33 So he *o*' upon the altar which he
33 he *o*' upon the altar, and burnt
22:43 the people *o*' and burnt incense
2Ki 3:20 when the meat offering was *o*',
27 *o*' him for a burnt offering upon
16:12 to the altar, and *o*' thereon.
1Ch 6:49 his sons *o*' upon the altar of the
15:26 they *o*' seven bullocks and seven
16: 1 they *o*' burnt sacrifices and peace
21:26 and *o*' burnt offerings and peace
29: 6 of the king's work, *o*' willingly,
9 rejoiced, for that they *o*' willingly,
9 with perfect heart they *o*' willingly
17 have willingly *o*' all these things:
21 *o*' burnt offerings unto the Lord,
2Ch 1: 6 *o*' a thousand burnt offerings upon
4: 6 such things as they *o*' for the
7: 4 *o*' sacrifices before the Lord.
5 And king Solomon *o*' a sacrifice of
7 there he *o*' burnt offerings, and the
8:12 Solomon *o*' burnt offerings unto
15:11 *o*' unto the Lord the same time,
17:16 willingly *o*' himself unto the Lord;
24:14 And they *o*' burnt offerings in the
29: 7 incense nor *o*' burnt offerings
Ezr 1: 6 beside all that was willingly *o*'.
2:68 *o*' freely for the house of God to
3: 3 they *o*' burnt offerings thereon
4 *o*' the daily burnt offerings by number,
5 *o*' the continual burnt offering,
5 willingly *o*' a freewill offering
6: 3 the place where they *o*' sacrifices,
17 *o*' at the dedication of this house
7:15 freely *o*' unto the God of Israel,
8:25 all Israel there present, had *o*':
35 *o*' burnt offerings unto the God of
10:19 they *o*' a ram of the flock for their
Ne 11: 2 willingly *o*' themselves to dwell at
12:43 that day they *o*' great sacrifices,
Job 1: 5 *o*' burnt offerings according to
Isa 57: 6 thou hast *o*' a meat offering.
66: 3 oblation, as if he *o*' swine's blood;
Jer 32:29 they have *o*' incense unto Baal,
Eze 20:28 and they *o*' there their sacrifices,
48:12 this oblation of the land that is *o*'
Da 11:18 the reproach *o*' by him to cease;
Am 5:25 Have ye *o*' unto me sacrifices and
Jon 1:16 *o*' a sacrifice unto the Lord, and
Mal 1:11 in every place incense shall be *o*'
Ac 7:41 and *o*' sacrifice unto the idol, and
42 have ye *o*' to me slain beasts and
8:18 was given, he *o*' them money,
15:29 ye abstain from meats *o*' to idols,
21:25 themselves from things *o*' to idols,
26 until that an offering should be *o*'
1Co 8: 1 as touching things *o*' unto idols,
4 are *o*' in sacrifice unto idols,
7 eat it as a thing *o*' unto an idol;
10 those things which are *o*' to idols;
10:19 *o*' in sacrifice to idols is any thing?
1Co 10:28 This is *o*' in sacrifice unto idols,
Ph'p 2:17 and if I be *o*' upon the sacrifice
2Ti 4: 6 For I am now ready to be *o*', and
Heb 5: 7 when he had *o*' up prayers and
7:27 he did once, when he *o*' up himself.
9: 7 which he *o*' for himself, and for
9 were *o*' both gifts and sacrifices,
14 *o*' himself without spot to God,
28 once *o*' to bear the sins of many;
10: 1 they *o*' year by year continually
2 they not have ceased to be *o*'?
8 therein; which are *o*' by the law;
12 he had *o*' one sacrifice for sins
11: 4 By faith Abel *o*' unto God a more
17 when he was tried, *o*' up Isaac:
17 *o*' up his only begotten son,
Jas 2:21 when he had *o*' Isaac his son upon

offereth
Le 6:26 The priest that *o*' it for sin shall
7: 8 that *o*' any man's burnt offering
9 shall be the priest's that *o*' it.
16 same day that he *o*' his sacrifice:
18 it be imputed unto him that *o*' it:
29 He that *o*' the sacrifice of his peace
33 *o*' the blood of the peace offerings,
17: 8 that *o*' a burnt offering or sacrifice,
21: 8 for he *o*' the bread of thy God: he
22:21 *o*' a sacrifice of peace offerings unto
Nu 15: 4 that *o*' his offering unto the Lord
Ps 50:23 Whoso *o*' praise glorifieth me:
Isa 66: 3 he that *o*' an oblation, as if he
Jer 48:35 him that *o*' in the high places, and
Mal 2:12 that *o*' an offering unto the Lord

offering See also OFFERINGS.
Ge 4: 3 the ground an *o*' unto the Lord.
4 respect unto Abel and to his *o*':
5 and to his *o*' he had not respect.
22: 2 and offer him there for a burnt *o*'
3 and clave the wood for the burnt *o*',
6 took the wood of the burnt *o*', and
7 where is the lamb for a burnt *o*'?
8 himself a lamb for a burnt *o*': so
13 a burnt *o*' in the stead of his son.
35:14 and he poured a drink *o*' thereon,
Ex 18:12 took a burnt *o*' and sacrifices for
25: 2 Israel, that they bring me an *o*':
2 with his heart ye shall take my *o*'.
3 the *o*' which ye shall take of them;
29:14 without the camp: it is a sin *o*'.
18 it is a burnt *o*' unto the Lord: it is
18 an *o*' made by fire unto the Lord.
24 for a wave *o*' before the Lord.
25 them upon the altar for a burnt *o*',
25 an *o*' made by fire unto the Lord.
26 wave it for a wave *o*' before the Lord:
27 sanctify the breast of the wave *o*',
27 shoulder of the heave *o*', which is
28 of Israel; for it is an heave *o*':
28 be an heave *o*' from the children
28 even their heave *o*' unto the Lord.
36 every day a bullock for a sin *o*'
40 of an hin of wine for a drink *o*'.
41 to the meat *o*' of the morning,
41 according to the drink *o*' thereof,
41 an *o*' made by fire unto the Lord.
42 This shall be a continual burnt *o*'
30: 9 nor burnt sacrifice, nor meat *o*';
9 neither shall ye pour drink *o*'
10 year with the blood of the sin *o*'
13 shekel shall be the *o*' of the Lord.
14 shall give an *o*' unto the Lord.
15 when they give an *o*' unto the Lord,
20 minister, to burn *o*' made by fire
28 altar of burnt *o*' with all his vessels,
31: 9 the altar of burnt *o*' with all his
35: 5 among you an *o*' unto the Lord:
5 let him bring it, an *o*' of the Lord;
16 The altar of burnt *o*', with his
21 they brought the Lord's *o*' to the
22 that offered offered an *o*' of gold
24 did offer an *o*' of silver and brass
24 and brass brought the Lord's *o*':
29 of Israel brought a willing *o*' unto
36: 3 they received of Moses all the *o*',
6 work for the *o*' of the sanctuary.
38: 1 altar of burnt *o*' of shittim wood:
24 holy place, even the gold of the *o*',
29 the brass of the *o*' was seventy
40: 6 set the altar of the burnt *o*' before
10 anoint the altar of the burnt *o*',
29 the altar of burnt *o*' by the door
29 offered upon it the burnt *o*' and the
29 and offered upon it...the meat *o*';
Le 1: 2 of you bring an *o*' unto the Lord,
2 ye shall bring your *o*' of the cattle,
3 If his *o*' be a burnt sacrifice of the
4 upon the head of the burnt *o*';
6 he shall flay the burnt *o*', and cut
9 an *o*' made by fire, of a sweet
10 if his *o*' be of the flocks, namely,
13 an *o*' made by fire, of a sweet
14 for his *o*' to the Lord be of fowls,
14 he shall bring his *o*' of turtledoves,
17 an *o*' made by fire, of a sweet
2: 1 will offer a meat *o*' unto the Lord,
1 Lord, his *o*' shall be of fine flour;
2 to be an *o*' made by fire, of a sweet
3 of the meat *o*' shall be Aaron's
4 of a meat *o*' baken in the oven,
5 be a meat *o*' baken in a pan, it
6 pour oil thereon: it is a meat *o*'.
7 be a meat *o*' baken in a fryingpan,
8 thou shalt bring the meat *o*' that is
9 priest shall take from the meat *o*'
9 it is an *o*' made by fire, of a sweet
Le 2:10 is left of the meat *o*' shall be
11 No meat *o*', which ye shall bring
11 in any *o*' of the Lord made by fire.
13 thy meat *o*' shalt thou season
13 to be lacking from thy meat *o*':
14, 14 offer a meat *o*' of thy firstfruits
15 thereon: it is a meat *o*'.
16 is an *o*' made by fire unto the Lord.
3: 1 oblation be a sacrifice of peace *o*',
2 his hand upon the head of his *o*',
3 offer of the sacrifice of the peace *o*',
3 an *o*' made by fire unto the Lord;
5 it is an *o*' made by fire, of a sweet
6 if his *o*' for a sacrifice of peace
6 sacrifice of peace *o*' unto the Lord
7 If he offer a lamb for his *o*', then
8 his hand upon the head of his *o*',
9 offer of the sacrifice of the peace *o*'
9 an *o*' made by fire unto the Lord;
11 it is the food of the *o*' made by fire
12 if his *o*' be a goat, then he shall
14 And he shall offer thereof his *o*',
14 an *o*' made by fire unto the Lord;
16 it is the food of the *o*' made by fire
4: 3 blemish unto the Lord for a sin *o*.'
7 bottom of the altar of the burnt *o*',
8 fat of the bullock for the sin *o*';
10 upon the altar of the burnt *o*'.
18 bottom of the altar of the burnt *o*',
20 did with the bullock for a sin *o*',
21 it is a sin *o*' for the congregation.
23 he shall bring his *o*', a kid of the
24 where they kill the burnt *o*' before
24 before the Lord: it is a sin *o*'.
25 take of the blood of the sin *o*' with
25 the horns of the altar of burnt *o*',
25 bottom of the altar of burnt *o*'.
28 he shall bring his *o*', a kid of the
29 hand upon the head of the sin *o*',
29 and slay the sin *o*' in the place of
29 in the place of the burnt *o*'.
30 the horns of the altar of burnt *o*',
32 And if he bring a lamb for a sin *o*',
33 hand upon the head of the sin *o*',
33 and slay it for a sin *o*', in the
33 place where they kill the burnt *o*'.
34 blood of the sin *o*' with his finger,
34 the horns of the altar of burnt *o*',
5: 6 bring his trespass *o*' unto the Lord
6 or a kid of the goats, for a sin *o*';
7 one for a sin *o*', and the other
7 and the other for a burnt *o*'.
8 that which is for the sin *o*' first,
9 sprinkle of the blood of the sin *o*'
9 bottom of the altar: it is a sin *o*'.
10 offer the second for a burnt *o*',
11 that sinned shall bring for his *o*'
11 an ephah of fine flour for a sin *o*';
11 thereon: for it is a sin *o*'.
12 fire unto the Lord: it is a sin *o*'.
13 shall be the priest's, as a meat *o*'.
15 of the sanctuary, for a trespass *o*':
16 him with the ram of the trespass *o*',
18 thy estimation, for a trespass *o*', unto
19 It is a trespass *o*': he hath certainly
6: 5 in the day of his trespass *o*'.
6 bring his trespass *o*' unto the Lord,
6 with thy estimation, of a trespass *o*',
9 This is the law of the burnt *o*':
9 It is the burnt *o*', because of the
10 with the burnt *o*' on the altar, and
12 lay the burnt *o*' in order upon it;
14 And this is the law of the meat *o*':
15 the flour of the meat *o*', and of the
15 which is upon the meat *o*', and
17 it is most holy, as is the sin *o*',
17 most holy, as is...the trespass *o*'.
20 is the *o*' of Aaron and of his sons,
20 fine flour for a meat *o*' perpetual,
21 and the baken pieces of the meat *o*' "
23 every meat *o*' for the priest shall be"
25 saying, This is the law of the sin *o*':
25 place where the burnt *o*' is killed
25 the sin *o*' be killed before the Lord:
30 no sin *o*', whereof any of the blood
7: 1 this is the law of the trespass *o*':
2 place where they kill the burnt *o*'
2 shall they kill the trespass *o*': and
5 upon the altar for an *o*' made by fire
5 fire unto the Lord: it is a trespass *o*'.
7 As the sin *o*' is, so is the trespass
7 so is the trespass *o*': there is one
8 that offereth any man's burnt *o*',
8 the burnt *o*' which he hath offered.
9 meat *o*' that is baken in the oven,
10 every meat *o*', mingled with oil,
13 offer for his *o*' leavened bread
14 for an heave *o*' unto the Lord, and
16 if the sacrifice of his *o*' be a vow,
16 or a voluntary *o*', it shall be eaten the
25 offer an *o*' made by fire unto the Lord,
30 waved for a wave *o*' before the Lord.
32 for an heave *o*' of the sacrifices of
37 This is the law of the burnt *o*',
37 This is the law of...the meat *o*',
37 This is the law of...the sin *o*',
37 This is the law of...the trespass *o*',
8: 2 and a bullock for the sin *o*', and
14 brought the bullock for the sin *o*':
14 head of the bullock for the sin *o*'.
18 brought the ram for the burnt *o*':
21 an *o*' made by fire unto the Lord;
27 them for a wave *o*' before the Lord.
28 on the altar upon the burnt *o*':
28 an *o*' made by fire unto the Lord.
29 waved it for a wave *o*' before the Lord:

Le 9: 2 Take thee a young calf for a sin *o'*,
2 and a ram for a burnt *o'*, without
3 ye a kid of the goats for a sin *o'*;
3 without blemish, for a burnt *o'*;
4 and a meat *o'* mingled with oil:
7 unto the altar, and offer thy sin *o'*,
7 and thy burnt *o'*, and make an
7 and offer the *o'* of the people, and
8 slew the calf of the sin *o'*, which
10 caul above the liver of the sin *o'*,
12 he slew the burnt *o'*; and Aaron's
13 presented the burnt *o'* unto him,
14 them upon the burnt *o'* on the altar.
15 And he brought the people's *o'*,
15 took the goat, which was the sin *o'*
16 he brought the burnt *o'*, and offered it
17 he brought the meat *o'*, and took
21 waved for a wave *o'* before the Lord;
22 and came down from *o'* of the sin
22 of the sin *o'*, and the burnt
22 and the burnt *o'*, and peace offerings.
24 upon the altar the burnt *o'* and
10: 12 Take the meat *o'* that remaineth
15 wave it for a wave *o'* before the Lord;
16 sought the goat of the sin *o'*, and,
17 have ye not eaten the sin *o'* in the
19 day have they offered their sin *o'*
19 and their burnt *o'* before the Lord;
19 if I had eaten the sin *o'* to day,
12: 6 of the first year for a burnt *o'*,
6 or a turtledove, for a sin *o'*, unto
8 pigeons; the one for the burnt *o'*,
8 and the other for a sin *o'*: and
14: 10 deals of fine flour for a meat *o'*,
12 lamb, and offer him for a trespass *o'*,
12 them for a wave *o'* before the Lord:
13 place where he shall kill the sin *o'*
13 and the burnt *o'*, in the holy place:
13 for as the sin *o'* is the priest's,
13 so is the trespass *o'*: it is most holy:
14 some of the blood of the trespass *o'*,
17 upon the blood of the trespass *o'*:
19 the priest shall offer the sin *o'*,
19 he shall kill the burnt *o'*:
20 the priest shall offer the burnt *o'*
20 and the meat *o'* upon the altar:
21 lamb for a trespass *o'* to be waved,
21 mingled with oil for a meat *o'*,
22 and the one shall be a sin *o'*,
22 and the other a burnt *o'*.
24 take the lamb of the trespass *o'*,
24 them for a wave *o'* before the Lord:
25 shall kill the lamb of the trespass *o'*,
25 some of the blood of the trespass *o'*,
28 place of the blood of the trespass *o'*:
31 is able to get, the one for a sin *o'*,
31 and the other for a burnt *o'*, with
31 with the meat *o'*: and the priest
15: 15 offer them, the one for a sin *o'*,
15 and the other for a burnt *o'*; and
30 shall offer the one for a sin *o'*,
30 and the other for a burnt *o'*; and
16: 3 with a young bullock for a sin *o'*,
3 and a ram for a burnt *o'*.
5 two kids of the goats for a sin *o'*,
5 and one ram for a burnt *o'*.
6 shall offer his bullock of the sin *o'*,
9 lot fell, and offer him for a sin *o'*.
11 bring the bullock of the sin *o'*,
11 kill the bullock of the sin *o'* which
15 shall he kill the goat of the sin *o'*,
24 come forth, and offer his burnt *o'*,
24 and the burnt *o'* of the people, and
25 fat of the sin *o'* shall he burn upon
27 And the bullock for the sin *o'*, and
27 and the goat for the sin *o'*, whose
17: 4 to offer an *o'* unto the Lord before
8 offereth a burnt *o'* or sacrifice,
19: 21 bring his trespass *o'* unto the Lord,
21 even a ram for a trespass *o'*.
22 with the ram of the trespass *o'* before
22: 12 not eat of an *o'* of the holy things.
18 offer unto the Lord for a burnt *o'*;
21 or a freewill *o'* in beeves or sheep,
22 nor make an *o'* by fire of them
23 mayest thou offer for a freewill *o'*;
24 neither shall ye make any *o'* thereof
27 an *o'* made by fire unto the Lord.
23: 8 an *o'* made by fire unto the Lord
12 year for a burnt *o'* unto the Lord.
13 meat *o'* thereof shall be two tenth
13 an *o'* made by fire unto the Lord for a
13 drink *o'* thereof shall be of wine,
14 have brought an *o'* unto your God:
15 ye brought the sheaf of the wave *o'*;
16 offer a new meat *o'* unto the Lord.
18 be for a burnt *o'* unto the Lord,
18 with their meat *o'*, and their
18 even an *o'* made by fire, of sweet
19 one kid of the goats for a sin *o'*,
20 for a wave *o'* before the Lord,
25, 27 an *o'* made by fire unto the Lord.
36, 36 an *o'* made by fire unto the Lord:
37 an *o'* made by fire unto the Lord,
37 unto the Lord, a burnt *o'*,
37 and a meat *o'*, a sacrifice,
24: 7 even an *o'* made by fire unto the Lord.
27: 9 men bring an *o'* unto the Lord,
Nu 4: 16 incense, and the daily meat *o'*,
5: 9 every *o'* of all the holy things of
15 and he shall bring her *o'* for her,
15 thereon; for it is an *o'* of jealousy,
15 *o'* of memorial, bringing iniquity
18 the *o'* of memorial in her hands,
18 which is the jealousy *o'*: and the
25 jealousy *o'* out of a woman's hand,

Nu 5: 25 shall wave the *o'* before the Lord,
26 shall take an handful of the *o'*,
6: 11 shall offer the one for a sin *o'*,
11 and the other for a burnt *o'*, and
12 of the first year for a trespass *o'*:
14 shall offer his *o'* unto the Lord,
14 without blemish for a burnt *o'*, and
14 year without blemish for a sin *o'*,
15 and their meat *o'*, and their drink
16 Lord, and shall offer his sin *o'*,
16 offer his sin...and his burnt *o'*:
17 priest shall offer also his meat *o'*,
17 also his meat...and his drink *o'*.
20 them for a wave *o'* before the Lord:
21 *o'* unto the Lord for...separation,
7: 3 brought their *o'* before the Lord,
10 offered their *o'* before the altar.
11 They shall offer their *o'*, each
12 he that offered his *o'* the first day
13 his *o'* was one silver charger, the
13 mingled with oil for a meat *o'*:
15 of the first year, for a burnt *o'*:
16 One kid of the goats for a sin *o'*:
17 this was the *o'* of Nahshon the
19 for his *o'* one silver charger, the
19 mingled with oil for a meat *o'*:
21 of the first year, for a burnt *o'*:
22 One kid of the goats for a sin *o'*:
23 was the *o'* of Nethaneel the son
25 His *o'* was one silver charger, the
25 mingled with oil for a meat *o'*:
27 of the first year, for a burnt *o'*:
28 One kid of the goats for a sin *o'*:
29 the *o'* of Eliab the son of Helon.
31 His *o'* was one silver charger of
31 mingled with oil for a meat *o'*:
33 of the first year, for a burnt *o'*:
34 One kid of the goats for a sin *o'*:
35 this was the *o'* of Elizur the son of
37 His *o'* was one silver charger,
37 mingled with oil for a meat *o'*:
39 of the first year, for a burnt *o'*:
40 One kid of the goats for a sin *o'*:
41 this was the *o'* of Shelumiel the
43 His *o'* was one silver charger of the
43 mingled with oil for a meat *o'*:
45 of the first year, for a burnt *o'*:
46 One kid of the goats for a sin *o'*:
47 this was the *o'* of Eliasaph the
49 His *o'* was one silver charger, the
49 mingled with oil for a meat *o'*:
51 of the first year, for a burnt *o'*:
52 One kid of the goats for a sin *o'*:
53 this was the *o'* of Elishama the
55 His *o'* was one silver charger of
55 mingled with oil for a meat *o'*:
57 of the first year, for a burnt *o'*:
58 One kid of the goats for a sin *o'*:
59 this was the *o'* of Gamaliel the
61 His *o'* was one silver charger, the
61 mingled with oil for a meat *o'*:
63 of the first year, for a burnt *o'*:
64 One kid of the goats for a sin *o'*:
65 this was the *o'* of Abidan the son
67 His *o'* was one silver charger, the
67 mingled with oil for a meat *o'*:
69 of the first year, for a burnt *o'*:
70 One kid of the goats for a sin *o'*:
71 this was the *o'* of Ahiezer the son
73 His *o'* was one silver charger, the
73 mingled with oil for a meat *o'*:
75 of the first year, for a burnt *o'*:
76 One kid of the goats for a sin *o'*:
77 this was the *o'* of Pagiel the son
79 His *o'* was one silver charger, the
79 mingled with oil for a meat *o'*:
81 of the first year, for a burnt *o'*:
82 One kid of the goats for a sin *o'*:
83 this was the *o'* of Ahira the son of
87 the burnt *o'* were twelve bullocks,
87 year twelve, with their meat *o'*:
87 kids of the goats for sin *o'* twelve.
8: 8 a young bullock with his meat *o'*,
8 bullock shalt thou take for a sin *o'*.
11 for an *o'* of the children of Israel,
12 shalt offer the one for a sin *o'*,
12 other for a burnt *o'*, unto the Lord,
13 offer them for an *o'*, unto the Lord.
15 them, and offer them for an *o'*.
21 them as an *o'* before the Lord; and
9: 7 we may not offer an *o'* of the Lord
13 he brought not the *o'* of the Lord
15: 3 will make an *o'* by fire unto the Lord
3 Lord, a burnt *o'*, or a sacrifice in
3 or in a freewill *o'*, or in your
4 that offereth his *o'* unto the Lord
4 bring a meat *o'* of a tenth deal of
5 of an hin of wine for a drink *o'* shalt
5 with the burnt *o'* or sacrifice, for one
6 prepare for a meat *o'* two tenth
7 for a drink *o'* thou shalt offer the
8 preparest a bullock for a burnt *o'*,
9 a meat *o'* of three tenth deals of
10 for a drink *o'* half an hin of wine,
10 *o'* made by fire, of a sweet savour
13 after this manner, in *o'*...by fire,
13, 14 an *o'* made by fire, of a sweet
19 offer up an heave *o'* unto the Lord.
20 first of your dough for an heave *o'*:
20 the heave *o'* of the threshingfloor,
21 an heave *o'* in your generations.
24 one young bullock for a burnt *o'*,
24 unto the Lord, with his meat *o'*,
24 and his drink *o'*, according to the
24 One kid of the goats for a sin *o'*.
25 and they shall bring their *o'*, a

Nu 15: 25 and their sin *o'* before the Lord,
27 goat of the first year for a sin *o'*.
16: 15 Respect not thou their *o'*: I have
18: 9 of theirs, every meat *o'* of theirs,
9 and every sin *o'* of theirs, and
9 every trespass *o'* of theirs, which they
11 the heave *o'* of their gift, with all
17 their fat for an *o'* made by fire,
24 they offer as an heave *o'* unto the
26 ye shall offer up an heave *o'* of it
27 your heave *o'* shall be reckoned
28 offer an heave *o'* unto the Lord
28 Lord's heave *o'* to Aaron the priest.
29 offer every heave *o'* of the Lord,
23: 3 unto Balak, Stand by thy burnt *o'*,
15 Balak, Stand here by thy burnt *o'*,
17 he stood by his burnt *o'*, and the
28: 2 My *o'*, and my bread for my
3 This is the *o'* made by fire which ye
3 by day, for a continual burnt *o'*.
5 of an ephah of flour for a meat *o'*,
6 a continual burnt *o'*, which was
7 the drink *o'* thereof shall be the
7 unto the Lord for a drink *o'*.
8 as the meat *o'* of the morning,
8 and as the drink *o'* thereof, thou
9 tenth deals of flour for a meat *o'*,
9 with oil, and the drink *o'* thereof:
10 is the burnt *o'* of every sabbath,
10 beside the continual burnt *o'*,
10 and his drink *o'*.
11 offer a burnt *o'* unto the Lord;
12, 12 tenth deals of flour...a meat *o'*,
13 oil for a meat *o'* unto one lamb;
13 for a burnt *o'* of a sweet savour, a
14 is the burnt *o'* of every month
15 one kid of the goats for a sin *o'*
15 beside the continual burnt *o'*,
15 and his drink *o'*.
19 made by fire for a burnt *o'* unto
20 meat *o'* shall be of flour mingled
22 one goat for a sin *o'*, to make an
23 the burnt *o'* in the morning,
23 which is for a continual burnt *o'*.
24 beside the continual burnt *o'*,
24 and his drink *o'*.
26 when ye bring a new meat *o'* unto
27 the burnt *o'* for a sweet savour
28 meat *o'* of flour mingled with oil,
31 beside the continual burnt *o'*,
31 and his meat *o'*, (they shall be
29: 2 offer a burnt *o'* for a sweet savour
3 meat *o'* shall be of flour mingled
5 one kid of the goats for a sin *o'*,
6 Beside the burnt *o'* of the month,
6 and his meat *o'*,
6 and the daily burnt *o'*,
6 and his meat *o'*,
8 offer a burnt *o'* unto the Lord for a
9 meat *o'* shall be of flour mingled
11 One kid of the goats for a sin *o'*;
11 beside the sin *o'* of atonement,
11 and the continual burnt *o'*,
11 and the meat *o'* of it, and their
13 offer a burnt *o'*, a sacrifice made
14 meat *o'* shall be of flour mingled
16 And one kid of the goats for a sin *o'*;
16 beside the continual burnt *o'*,
16 his meat *o'*,
16 and his drink *o'*.
18 And their meat *o'* and their drink
19 one kid of the goats for a sin *o'*;
19 beside the continual burnt *o'*, and
19 and the meat *o'* thereof, and their
21 And their meat *o'* and their drink
22 And one goat for a sin *o'*; beside
22 beside the continual burnt *o'*,
22 and his meat *o'*,
22 and his drink *o'*.
24 Their meat *o'* and their drink
25 And one kid of the goats for a sin *o'*;
25 beside the continual burnt *o'*,
25 his meat *o'*,
25 and his drink *o'*.
27 And their meat *o'* and their drink
28 And one goat for a sin *o'*; beside
28 beside the continual burnt *o'*,
28 and his meat *o'*,
28 and his drink *o'*.
30 and their meat *o'* and their drink
31 And one goat for a sin *o'*; beside
31 beside the continual burnt *o'*,
31 his meat *o'*,
31 and his drink *o'*.
33 And their meat *o'* and their drink
34 And one goat for a sin *o'*; beside
34 beside the continual burnt *o'*,
34 his meat *o'*,
34 and his drink *o'*.
36 ye shall offer a burnt *o'*, a sacrifice
37 Their meat *o'* and their drink
38 And one goat for a sin *o'*; beside
38 beside the continual burnt *o'*,
38 and his meat *o'*,
38 and his drink *o'*.
31: 29 for an heave *o'* of the Lord.
41 which was the Lord's heave *o'*,
52 the gold of the *o'* that they offered
De 12: 11 and the heave *o'* of your hand, and
17 offerings, or heave *o'* of thine hand:
16: 10 with a tribute of a freewill *o'*
23: 23 a freewill *o'*, according as thou hast
Jos 22: 23 to offer thereon burnt *o'* or meat
23 offer thereon burnt...or meat *o'*,
26 an altar, not for burnt *o'*, nor for
J'g 11: 31 and I will offer it up for a burnt *o'*.

J'g 13:16 and if thou wilt offer a burnt *o'*.
19 Manoah took a kid with a meat *o'*.
23 would not have received a burnt *o'*
23 and a meat *o'* at our hands.
1Sa 2:17 for men abhorred the *o'* of the Lord.
29 ye at my sacrifice and at mine *o'*.
3:14 purged with sacrifice nor *o'* for ever.
6: 3 in any wise return him a trespass *o'*:
4 What shall be the trespass *o'* which
8 which ye return him for a trespass *o'*,
14 offered the kine a burnt *o'* unto
17 returned for a trespass *o'* unto the
7: 9 lamb, and offered it for a burnt *o'*
10 as Samuel was *o'* up the burnt
10 the burnt *o'*, the Philistines drew
13: 9 said, Bring hither a burnt *o'* to me,
9 And he offered the burnt *o'*.
10 soon as he had made an end of *o'*
10 the burnt *o'*, behold, Samuel
12 therefore, and offered a burnt *o'*.
26:19 against me, let him accept an *o'*:
2Sa 6:18 as David had made an end of *o'*
1Ki 18:29, 36 the *o'* of the evening sacrifice,
2Ki 3:20 when the meat *o'* was offered,
27 offered him for a burnt *o'* upon
5:17 offer neither burnt *o'* nor sacrifice
10:25 soon as he had made an end of *o'*
25 the burnt *o'*, that Jehu said to the
16:13 And he burnt his burnt *o'*, and his
13 and his meat *o'*, and poured his
13 and poured his drink *o'*, and
15 altar burn the morning burnt *o'*,
15 and the evening meat *o'*, and the
15 burnt sacrifice, and his meat *o'*,
15 with the burnt *o'* of all the people
15 meat *o'*, and their drink offerings;
15 it all the blood of the burnt *o'*,
1Ch 6:49 upon the altar of the burnt *o'*,
16: 2 when David had made an end of *o'*
29 bring an *o'*, and come before him:
40 upon the altar of the burnt *o'*
21:23 and the wheat for the meat *o'*;
26 by fire upon the altar of burnt *o'*.
29 and the altar of the burnt *o'*, were at
22: 1 this is the altar of the burnt *o'* for
23:29 and for the fine flour for meat *o'*,
2Ch 4: 6 as they offered for the burnt *o'*
7: 1 and consumed the burnt *o'* and the
8:13 *o'* according to the commandment
29:18 and the altar of burnt *o'*, with all the
21 goats, for a sin *o'* for the kingdom,
23 goats for the sin *o'* before the king
24 king commanded that the burnt *o'*
24 and the sin *o'* should be made for
27 offer the burnt *o'* upon the altar.
27 And when the burnt *o'* began, the
28 until the burnt *o'* was finished.
29 when they had made an end of *o'*,
32 all these were for a burnt *o'* to the
35 drink offerings for every burnt *o'*.
30:22 *o'* peace offerings, and making
35:14 Aaron were busied in *o'* of burnt
Ezr 1: 4 freewill *o'* for the house of God
3: 5 offered the continual burnt *o'*,
5 that willingly offered a freewill *o'*
6:17 for a sin *o'* for all Israel, twelve
7:16 with the freewill *o'* of the people,
16 *o'* willingly for the house of their God
8:25 even the *o'* of the house of our God,
28 silver and the gold are a freewill *o'*
35 twelve he goats for a sin *o'*:
35 this was a burnt *o'* unto the Lord.
Ne 10:33 and for the continual meat *o'*,
33 and for the continual burnt *o'* of the
34 for the wood *o'*, to bring it into
39 shall bring the *o'* of the corn,
13: 9 the meat *o'* and the frankincense.
31 And for the wood *o'*, at times
Job 42: 8 offer up for yourselves a burnt *o'*;
Ps 40: 6 and *o'* thou didst not desire;
6 burnt *o'*...hast thou not required.
6 and sin *o'* hast thou not required.
51:16 thou delightest not in burnt *o'*.
19 with burnt *o'* and whole burnt *o'*:
96: 8 bring an *o'*, and come into his
Isa 40:16 beasts sufficient for a burnt *o'*.
43:23 caused thee to serve with an *o'*,
53:10 shalt make his soul an *o'* for sin,
57: 6 them hast thou poured a drink *o'*,
6 thou hast offered a meat *o'*.
61: 8 I hate robbery for burnt *o'*;
65:11 furnish the drink *o'* unto that number.
66:20 brethren for an *o'* unto the Lord
20 bring an *o'* in a clean vessel into
Jer 11:17 me to anger in *o'* incense unto Baal.
14:12 when they offer burnt *o'* and an
Eze 20:28 the provocation of their *o'*:
40:38 where they washed the burnt *o'*.
39 side, to slay thereon the burnt *o'* and
39 to slay thereon...the sin *o'* and
39 to slay thereon...the trespass *o'*.
42 of hewn stone for the burnt *o'*,
42 slew the burnt *o'* and the sacrifice.
43 the tables was the flesh of the *o'*.
42:13 most holy things, and the meat *o'*,
13 and the sin *o'*, and the
13 and the trespass *o'*; for the place
43:19 a young bullock for a sin *o'*.
21 take the bullock also of the sin *o'*,
22 goats without blemish for a sin *o'*;
24 shall offer them up for a burnt *o'*
25 every day a goat for a sin *o'*:
44:11 they shall slay the burnt *o'* and
27 he shall offer his sin *o'*, saith the
29 They shall eat the meat *o'*, and
29 They shall eat...the sin *o'*, and

Eze 44:29 They shall eat...the trespass *o'*;
45:15 pastures of Israel; for a meat *o'*,
15 and for a burnt *o'*, and for peace
17 he shall prepare the sin *o'*,
17 he shall prepare...the meat *o'*,
17 he shall prepare...the burnt *o'*,
19 shall take of the blood of the sin *o'*,
22 of the land a bullock for a sin *o'*.
23 prepare a burnt *o'* to the Lord,
23 kid of the goats daily for a sin *o'*.
24 he shall prepare a meat *o'* of an
25 seven days, according to the sin *o'*,
25 and according to the burnt *o'*, and
25 and according to the meat *o'*, and
46: 2 priests shall prepare his burnt *o'*
4 the burnt *o'* that the prince shall offer
5 the meat *o'* shall be an ephah for
5 and the meat *o'* for the lambs as he
7 And he shall prepare a meat *o'*, an
11 the meat *o'* shall be an ephah to a
12 shall prepare a voluntary burnt *o'*
12 he shall prepare his burnt *o'* and
13 Thou shalt daily prepare a burnt *o'*
14 And thou shalt prepare a meat *o'*
14 a meat *o'* continually by a perpetual
15 prepare the lamb, and the meat *o'*,
15 morning for a continual burnt *o'*.
20 priests shall boil the trespass *o'*
20 priests shall boil...the sin *o'*,
20 where they shall bake the meat *o'*:
48: 8 be the *o'* which ye shall offer of
Joe 1: 9 The meat *o'* and the
9 drink *o'* is cut off from the house
13 my God: for the meat *o'* and the
13 drink *o'* is withholden from the
2:14 behind him; even a meat *o'* and a
14 drink *o'* unto the Lord your God.
Zep 3:10 my dispersed, shall bring mine *o'*.
Mal 1:10 neither will I accept an *o'* at your
11 unto my name, and a pure *o'*:
13 thus ye brought an *o'*: should I
2:12 and him that offereth an *o'* unto the
13 he regardeth not the *o'* any more,
3: 3 the Lord an *o'* in righteousness.
4 the *o'* of Judah and Jerusalem be
Lu 23:36 coming to him, and *o'* him vinegar,
Ac 21:26 until that an *o'* should be offered
Ro 15:16 the *o'* up of the Gentiles might be
Eph 5: 2 hath given himself for us an *o'* and
Heb 10: 5 Sacrifice and *o'* thou wouldest not,
8 Sacrifice and *o'* and burnt offerings
8 and *o'* for sin thou wouldest not,
10 through the *o'* of the body of Jesus
11 *o'* oftentimes the same sacrifices,
14 by one *o'* he hath perfected for ever
18 these is, there is no more *o'* for sin.

offerings
Ge 8:20 and offered burnt *o'* on the altar.
Ex 10:25 give us also sacrifices and burnt *o'*,
20:24 shalt sacrifice thereon thy burnt *o'*,
24 thy peace *o'*, thy sheep, and thine
24: 5 Israel, which offered burnt *o'*, and
5 sacrificed peace *o'* of oxen unto
29:28 of the sacrifice of their peace *o'*,
32: 6 the morrow, and offered burnt *o'*,
6 and brought peace *o'*; and the people
36: 3 brought yet unto him free *o'* every
Le 2: 3, 10 the *o'* of the Lord made by fire.
13 with all thine *o'*...shalt offer salt.
4:10 bullock of the sacrifice of peace *o'*:
26 the fat of the sacrifice of peace *o'*:
31 from off the sacrifice of peace *o'*;
35 from the sacrifice of the peace *o'*;
35 the *o'* made by fire unto the Lord:
5:12 the *o'* made by fire unto the Lord:
6:12 thereon the fat of the peace *o'*.
17 their portion of my *o'* made by fire;
18 the *o'* of the Lord made by fire:
7:11 the law of the sacrifice of peace *o'*,
13 of thanksgiving of his peace *o'*.
14 sprinkleth the blood of the peace *o'*.
15, 18 of the sacrifice of his peace *o'*
20, 21 flesh of the sacrifice of peace *o'*,
29 offereth the sacrifice of his peace *o'*
29 of the sacrifice of his peace *o'*.
30 the *o'* of the Lord made by fire,
32 of the sacrifices of your peace *o'*.
33 offereth the blood of the peace *o'*,
34 off the sacrifices of their peace *o'*,
35 out of the *o'* of the Lord made by fire,
37 of the sacrifice of the peace *o'*;
9: 4 a bullock and a ram for peace *o'*,
18 the ram for a sacrifice of peace *o'*,
22 the burnt offering, and peace *o'*.
10:12 the *o'* of the Lord made by fire,
14 out of the sacrifices of peace *o'* of the
15 with the *o'* made by fire of the fat,
17: 5 offer them for peace *o'* unto the
19: 5 offer a sacrifice of peace *o'* unto
21: 6 for the *o'* of the Lord made by fire,
21 the *o'* of the Lord made by fire:
22:18 vows, and for all his freewill *o'*, which
21 offereth a sacrifice of peace *o'* unto
23:18 and their drink *o'*, even an
19 year for a sacrifice of peace *o'*.
37 offering, a sacrifice, and drink *o'*,
38 and beside all your freewill *o'*,
24: 9 of the *o'* of the Lord made by fire
Nu 6:14 ram without blemish for peace *o'*.
15 meat offering, and their drink *o'*.
17 the ram for a sacrifice of peace *o'*
18 under the sacrifice of the peace *o'*.
7:17, 23, 29, 35, 41, 47, 53, 59, 65, 71, 77,
83 And for a sacrifice of peace *o'*,
88 oxen for the sacrifice of the peace *o'*
10:10 the trumpets over your burnt *o'*,

Nu 10:10 over the sacrifices of your peace *o'*;
15: 8 a vow, or peace *o'* unto the Lord:
18: 8 mine heave *o'* of all the hallowed
11 the wave *o'* of the children of Israel:
19 All the heave *o'* of the holy things,
28:14 their drink *o'* shall be half an hin
31 without blemish) and their drink *o'*.
29: 6 meat offering, and their drink *o'*,
11 offering of it, and their drink *o'*.
18 and their drink *o'* for the bullocks, for
19 offering thereof, and their drink *o'*.
21, 24, 27, 30, 33 and their drink *o'* for
the bullocks,
37 and their drink *o'* for the bullock,
39 your vows, and your freewill *o'*,
39 for your burnt *o'*, and for your
39 for your meat *o'*, and for your
39 and for your drink *o'*, and for your
39 and for your peace *o'*.
De 12: 6 ye shall bring your burnt *o'*, and
6 tithes, and heave *o'* of your hand,
6 your vows, and your freewill *o'*,
11 your burnt *o'*, and your sacrifices,
13 offer not thy burnt *o'* in every place
14 there thou shalt offer thy burnt *o'*,
17 thou vowest, freewill *o'*, or heave
27 And thou shalt offer thy burnt *o'*,
18: 1 eat the *o'* of the Lord made by fire,
27: 6 shalt not offer burnt *o'* thereon
7 thou shalt offer peace *o'*, and shalt
32:38 drank the wine of their drink *o'*?
Jos 8:31 they offered thereon burnt *o'* unto
31 unto the Lord, and sacrificed peace *o'*.
22:23 or if to offer peace *o'* thereon, let
27 Lord before him with our burnt *o'*,
27 sacrifices, and with our peace *o'*;
28 not for burnt *o'*, nor for sacrifices;
29 to build an altar for burnt *o'*, for
29 for meat *o'*, or for sacrifices,
J'g 20:26 until even, and offered burnt *o'*
26 and peace *o'* before the Lord.
21: 4 an altar, and offered burnt *o'* and
4 an altar, and offered...peace *o'*.
1Sa 2:28 thy father all the *o'* made by fire of
29 chiefest of all the *o'* of Israel my
6:15 of Beth-shemesh offered burnt *o'*
10: 8 down unto thee, to offer burnt *o'*,
8 to sacrifice sacrifices of peace *o'*:
11:15 sacrificed sacrifices of peace *o'*
13: 9 burnt offering to me, and peace *o'*.
15:22 Lord as great delight in burnt *o'*
2Sa 1:21 be rain, upon you, nor fields of *o'*:
6:17 for it: and David offered burnt *o'*
17 and peace *o'* before the Lord.
18 made an end of offering burnt *o'*
18 and peace *o'*, he blessed the people
24:24 neither will I offer burnt *o'* unto
25 unto the Lord, and offered burnt *o'*
25 and peace *o'*. So the Lord was
1Ki 3: 4 a thousand burnt *o'* did Solomon
15 the Lord, and offered up burnt *o'*,
15 and offered peace *o'*, and made a
8:63 offered a sacrifice of peace *o'*,
64 for there he offered burnt *o'*,
64 for there he offered...and meat *o'*,
64 and the fat of the peace *o'*:
64 too little to receive the burnt *o'*,
64 too little to receive the...meat *o'*,
64 and the fat of the peace *o'*.
9:25 year did Solomon offer burnt *o'*
25 and peace *o'* upon the altar which he
2Ki 10:24 in to offer sacrifices and burnt *o'*,
16:13 sprinkled the blood of his peace *o'*
15 meat offering, and their drink *o'*;
1Ch 16: 1 sacrifices and peace *o'* before God.
2 an end of offering the burnt *o'* and
2 and the peace *o'*, he blessed the people
40 To offer burnt *o'* unto the Lord
21:23 give thee the oxen also for burnt *o'*,
24 nor offer burnt *o'* without cost.
26 unto the Lord, and offered burnt *o'*
26 and peace *o'*, and called upon the
29:21 and offered burnt *o'* unto the Lord,
21 with their drink *o'*, and sacrifices
2Ch 1: 6 a thousand burnt *o'* upon it.
2: 4 the burnt *o'* morning and evening,
7: 7 Lord: for there he offered burnt *o'*,
7 and the fat of the peace *o'*, because
7 was not able to receive the burnt *o'*,
7 and the meat *o'*, and the fat.
8:12 Then Solomon offered burnt *o'*
23:18 to offer the burnt *o'* of the Lord
24:14 And they offered burnt *o'* in the house
29: 7 nor offered burnt *o'* in the holy place
31 bring sacrifices and thank *o'* into the
31 brought in sacrifices and thank *o'*;
31 as were of a free heart burnt *o'*.
32 And the number of the burnt *o'*,
34 they could not flay all the burnt *o'*:
35 the burnt *o'* were in abundance,
35 with the fat of the peace *o'*, and
35 drink *o'* for every burnt offering.
30:15 and brought in the burnt *o'* into the
22 feast seven days, offering peace *o'*,
31: 2 the priests and Levites for burnt *o'*
2 and for peace *o'*, to minister, and
3 of his substance for the burnt *o'*,
3 the morning and evening burnt *o'*,
3 and the burnt *o'* for the sabbaths,
10 the people began to bring the *o'*
12 brought in the *o'* and the tithes
14 was over the freewill *o'* of God,
33:16 and sacrificed thereon peace *o'*
16 and thank *o'*, and commanded
35: 7 and kids, all for the passover *o'*,
8 unto the priests for the passover *o'*

2Ch 35: 9 gave unto the Levites for passover o'
12 they removed the burnt o', that they
13 but the other holy o' sod they in pots,
14 were busied in offering of burnt o'
16 to offer burnt o' upon the altar of
Ezr 3: 2 to offer burnt o' thereon, as it is
3 they offered burnt o' thereon unto
3 even burnt o' morning and evening.
4 and offered the daily burnt o' by
6 they to offer burnt o' unto the Lord.
6: 9 for the burnt o' of the God of heaven,
7: 17 rams, lambs, with their meat o'
17 and their drink o', and offer them
8: 35 offered burnt o' unto the God of Israel,
Ne 10: 33 for the sin o' to make an atonement
37 firstfruits of our dough, and our o',
12: 44 for the treasures, for the o', for
13: 5 aforetime they laid the meat o',
5 porters; and the o' of the priests.
Job 1: 5 offered burnt o' according to the
Ps 16: 4 their drink o' of blood will I not offer,
20: 3 Remember all thy o', and accept
50: 8 for thy sacrifices or thy burnt o',
66: 13 go into thy house with burnt o':
119: 108 thee, the freewill o' of my mouth,
Pro 7: 14 I have peace o' with me; this day
Isa 1: 11 I am full of the burnt o' of rams,
43: 23 me the small cattle of thy burnt o';
56: 7 their burnt o' and their sacrifices
Jer 6: 20 your burnt o' are not acceptable,
7: 18 pour out drink o' unto other gods,
21 Put your burnt o' unto your
22 concerning burnt o' or sacrifices:
17: 26 from the south, bringing burnt o',
26 and sacrifices, and meat o', and
19: 5 sons with fire for burnt o' unto
13 out drink o' unto other gods.
32: 29 out drink o' unto other gods,
33: 18 a man before me to offer burnt o',
18 and to kindle meat o', and to do
41: 5 with o' and incense in their hand,
44: 17, 18 to pour out drink o' unto her,
19 and poured out drink o' unto her,
19 and pour out drink o' unto her,
25 and to pour out drink o' unto her:
Eze 20: 28 poured out there their drink o'.
40 and there will I require your o',
43: 18 make it, to offer burnt o' thereon,
27 the priests shall make your burnt o'
27 upon the altar, and your peace o';
45: 15 burnt offering, and for peace o', to
17 the prince's part to give burnt o',
17 and meat o',
17 and drink o', in the feasts, and in
17 the peace o', to make reconciliation
46: 2 burnt offering and his peace o', and
12 or peace o' voluntarily unto the
12 burnt offering and his peace o', as he
Hos 6: 6 of God more than burnt o'.
8: 13 flesh for the sacrifices of mine o',
9: 4 shall not offer wine o' to the Lord,
Am 4: 5 proclaim and publish the free o':
5: 22 Though ye offer me burnt o' and
22 meat o', I will not accept them:
22 the peace o' of your fat beasts.
25 o' in the wilderness forty years,
Mic 6: 6 I come before him with burnt o',
Mal 3: 8 we robbed thee? In tithes and o'.
M'r 12: 33 all whole burnt o' and sacrifices.
Lu 21: 4 cast in unto the o' of God:
Ac 24: 17 bring alms to my nation, and o'.
Heb 10: 6 In burnt o' and sacrifices for sin
8 and burnt o' and offering for sin

office See also OFFICES.
Ge 41: 13 me he restored unto mine o', and
Ex 1: 16 the o' of a midwife to the Hebrew
28: 1 minister unto me in the priest's o',
3, 4, 41 unto me in the priest's o'.
29: 1 minister unto me in the priest's o':
9 and the priest's o' shall be theirs for
44 minister to me in the priest's o'.
30: 30 minister unto me in the priest's o'.
31: 10 sons, to minister in the priest's o',
35: 19 sons, to minister in the priest's o'.
39: 41 to minister in the priest's o'.
40: 13 minister unto me in the priest's o'.
15 minister unto me in the priest's o':
Le 7: 35 unto the Lord in the priest's o';
16: 32 in the priest's o' in his father's
Nu 3: 3 to minister in the priest's o'.
4 ministered in the priest's o' in the
10 they shall wait on their priest's o':
4: 16 And to the o' of Eleazar the son of
18: 7 keep your priest's o' for everything
7 I have given your priest's o' unto you
De 10: 6 in the priest's o' in his stead.
1Ch 6: 10 priest's o' in the temple that
32 waited on their o' according to
9: 22 the seer did ordain in their set o'.
26 were in their set o', and were over
31 had the set o' over the things that
23: 28 their o' was to wait on the sons of
24: 2 Ithamar executed the priest's o'.
2Ch 11: 14 from executing the priest's o' unto
24: 11 was brought unto the king's o' by
31: 15 the cities of the priests, in their set o',
18 for in their set o' they sanctified
Ne 13: 13 and their o' was to distribute unto
Ps 109: 8 few; and let another take his o'.
Eze 44: 13 to do the o' of a priest unto me,
Lu 1: 8 while he executed the priest's o'
9 to the custom of the priest's o',
Ro 11: 13 of the Gentiles, I magnify mine o':
12: 4 all members have not the same o':
1Ti 3: 1 If a man desire the o' of a bishop,
10 let them use the o' of a deacon,
1Ti 3: 13 that have used the o' of a deacon
Heb 7: 5 receive the o' of the priesthood,

officer See also OFFICERS.
Ge 37: 36 unto Potiphar, an o' of Pharaoh's,
39: 1 and Potiphar, an o' of Pharaoh,
J'g 9: 28 of Jerubbaal? and Zebul his o'?
1Ki 4: 5 the son of Nathan was principal o',
19 the only o' which was in the land.
22: 9 the king of Israel called an o', and
2Ki 8: 6 appointed unto her a certain o',
25: 19 he took an o' that was set over the
2Ch 24: 11 priest's o' came and emptied the
M't 5: 25 the judge deliver thee to the o',
Lu 12: 58 the judge deliver thee to the o',
58 and the o' cast thee into prison.

officers
Ge 40: 2 was wroth against two of his o',
7 asked Pharaoh's o' that were with
41: 34 let him appoint o' over the land,
Ex 5: 6 of the people, and their o', saying,
10 of the people went out, and their o',
14 And the o' of the children of Israel,
15 the o' of the children of Israel came
19 the o' of the children of Israel did
Nu 11: 16 of the people, and o' over them;
31: 14 was wroth with the o' of the host,
48 o' which were over thousands of
De 1: 15 tens, and o' among your tribes.
16: 18 Judges and o' shalt thou make thee
20: 5 the o' shall speak unto the people,
8 the o' shall speak further unto the
9 when the o' have made an end of
29: 10 your o', with all the men of Israel,
31: 28 elders of your tribes, and your o',
Jos 1: 10 Joshua commanded the o' of the
3: 2 that the o' went through the host;
8: 33 all Israel, and their elders, and o',
23: 2 for their judges, and for their o',
24: 1 for their judges, and for their o';
1Sa 8: 15 give to his o', and to his servants.
1Ki 4: 5 the son of Nathan was over the o':
7 had twelve o' over all Israel, which
27 those o' provided victual for king
28 they unto the place where the o' were,
5: 16 the chief of Solomon's o' which
9: 23 o' that were over Solomon's work,
2Ki 11: 15 the hundreds, the o' of the host,
18 priest appointed o' over the house
24: 12 and his princes, and his o': and
15 king's wives, and his o', and the
1Ch 23: 4 six thousand were o' and judges:
26: 29 over Israel, for o' and judges.
30 o' among them of Israel on this
27: 1 their o' that served the king in
28: 1 with the o', and with the mighty
2Ch 8: 10 the chief of king Solomon's o',
18: 8 of Israel called for one of his o',
19: 11 the Levites shall be o' before you.
34: 13 there were scribes, and o', and
Es 1: 8 to all the o' of his house, that
2: 3 king appoint o' in all the provinces
9: 3 o' of the king, helped the Jews;
Isa 60: 17 I will also make thy o' peace, and
Jer 29: 26 be o' in the house of the Lord,
Joh 7: 32 chief priests sent o' to take him.
45 came the o' of the chief priests and
46 The o' answered, Never man spake
18: 3 received a band of men and o' from
12 and o' of the Jews took Jesus, and
18 the servants and o' stood there,
22 one of the o' which stood by struck
19: 6 priests therefore and o' saw him,
Ac 5: 22 But when the o' came, and found
26 Then went the captain with the o',

offices
1Sa 2: 36 pray thee, into one of the priest's o',
1Ch 24: 3 according to their o' in their
2Ch 7: 6 And the priests waited on their o':
23: 18 the o' of the house of the Lord
Ne 13: 14 of my God, and for the o' thereof.

offscouring
La 3: 45 made us as the o' and refuse in
1Co 4: 13 the o' of all things unto this day.

offspring
Job 5: 25 thine o' as the grass of the earth.
21: 8 and their o' before their eyes.
27: 14 o' shall not be satisfied with bread.
31: 8 eat; yea, let my o' be rooted out.
Isa 22: 24 o' and the issue, all vessels of small
44: 3 and my blessing upon thine o':
48: 19 the o' of thy bowels like the gravel
61: 9 and their o' among the people:
65: 23 the Lord, and their o' with them.
Ac 17: 28 have said, For we are also his o'.
29 then as we are the o' of God, we
Re 22: 16 I am the root and the o' of David,

oft See also OFTEN; OFTTIMES.
2Ki 4: 8 as o' as he passed by, he turned
Job 21: 17 How o' is the candle of...wicked put out!
17 how o' cometh their destruction upon
Ps 78: 40 How o' did they provoke him in
M't 9: 14 do we and the Pharisees fast o',
17: 15 into the fire, and o' into the water.
18: 21 how o' shall my brother sin against
M'r 7: 3 they wash their hands o', eat not,
Ac 26: 11 And I punished them o' in every
1Co 11: 25 this do ye, as o' as ye drink it, in
2Co 11: 23 more frequent, in deaths o'.
2Ti 1: 16 he o' refreshed me, and was not
Heb 6: 7 in the rain that cometh o' upon it,

often See also OFTENER; OFTENTIMES.
Pr 29: 1 He, that being o' reproved hardeneth
Mal 3: 16 they that feared the Lord spake o' one
M't 23: 37 how o' would I have gathered thy
M'r 5: 4 been o' bound with fetters and
Lu 5: 33 the disciples of John fast o', and
13: 34 how o' would I have gathered thy
1Co 11: 26 For as o' as ye eat this bread, and
2Co 11: 26 In journeyings o', in perils of
27 watchings o', in hunger and thirst,
27 fastings o', in cold and nakedness.
Ph'p 3: 18 walk, of whom I have told you o',
1Ti 5: 23 sake and thine o' infirmities.
Heb 9: 25 that he should offer himself o', as
26 For then must he o' have suffered
Re 11: 6 with all plagues, as o' as they will.

oftener
Ac 24: 26 wherefore he sent for him the o',

oftentimes See also OFTTIMES.
Job 33: 29 these things worketh God o'
Ec 7: 22 For o' also thine own heart
Lu 8: 29 o' it had caught him: and he
Ro 1: 13 o' I purposed to come unto you,
2Co 8: 22 o' proved diligent in many things,
Heb 10: 11 and offering o' the same sacrifices,

ofttimes
M't 17: 15 for o' he falleth into the fire, and
M'r 9: 22 o' it hath cast him into the fire,
Joh 18: 2 Jesus o' resorted thither with his

Og (*og*)
Nu 21: 33 *O'* the king of Bashan went out
32: 33 the kingdom of *O'* king of Bashan,
De 1: 4 and *O'* the king of Bashan, which
3: 1 *O'* the king of Bashan came out
3 God delivered into our hands *O'*
4 the kingdom of *O'* in Bashan.
10 of the kingdom of *O'* in Bashan.
11 only *O'* king of Bashan remained
13 Bashan, being the kingdom of *O'*,
4: 47 and the land of *O'* king of Bashan,
29: 7 and *O'* the king of Bashan, came
31: 4 as he did to Sihon and to *O'*, kings
Jos 2: 10 Sihon and *O'*, whom ye utterly
9: 10 and to *O'* king of Bashan, which
12: 4 the coast of *O'* king of Bashan,
13: 12 All the kingdom of *O'* in Bashan,
30 the kingdom of *O'* king of Bashan,
31 of the kingdom of *O'* in Bashan,
1Ki 4: 19 and of *O'* king of Bashan; and he
Ne 9: 22 and the land of *O'* king of Bashan.
Ps 135: 11 and *O'* king of Bashan, and all the
136: 20 And *O'* the king of Bashan: for his

oh
Ge 18: 30, 32 *O'* let not the Lord be angry,
19: 18 unto them, *O'*, not so, my Lord:
20 *O'*, let me escape thither, (is it not
44: 18 *O'* my lord, let thy servant, I pray
Ex 32: 31 *O'*, this people have sinned a great
J'g 6: 13 *O'* my Lord, if the Lord be with us,
15 *O'* my Lord, wherewith shall I save
1Sa 1: 26 *O'* my lord, as thy soul liveth, my
2Sa 15: 4 *O'* that I were made judge in the land,
23: 15 *O'* that one would give me drink of the
1Ch 4: 10 *O'* that thou wouldest bless me
11: 17 *O'* that one would give me drink of the
Job 6: 2 *O'* that my grief were thoroughly
8 *O'* that I might have my request; and
10: 18 *O'* that I had given up the ghost, and
11: 5 o' that God would speak, and open his
19: 23 *O'* that my words were now written!
23 o' that they were printed in a book!
23: 3 *O'* that I knew where I might find him!
29: 2 *O'* that I were as in months past, as in
31: 31 *O'* that we had of his flesh! we cannot
35 o' that one would hear me! behold,
Ps 6: 4 o' save me for thy mercies' sake.
7: 9 *O'* let the wickedness of the
14: 7 *O'* that the salvation of Israel were
31: 19 *O'* how great is thy goodness, which
53: 6 *O'* that the salvation of Israel were
55: 6 *O'* that I had wings like a dove! for
81: 13 *O'* that my people had hearkened
107: 8, 15, 21, 31 *O'* that men would praise
Isa 64: 1 *O'* that thou wouldest rend the
Jer 9: 1 *O'* that my head were waters, and
2 *O'* that I had in the wilderness a
44: 4 *O'*, do not this abominable thing

Ohad (*o'-had*)
Ge 46: 10 Jemuel, and Jamin, and *O'*, and
Ex 6: 15 Jemuel, and Jamin, and *O'*, and

Ohel (*o'-hel*)
1Ch 3: 20 And Hashubah, and *O'*, and

oil See also OILED.
Ge 28: 18 and poured o' upon the top of it.
35: 14 thereon, and he poured o' thereon.
Ex 25: 6 *O'* for the light, spices for
6 spices for anointing o', and for
27: 20 pure o' olive beaten for the light,
29: 2 cakes unleavened tempered with o',
2 wafers unleavened anointed with o':
7 shalt thou take the anointing o',
21 the altar, and of the anointing o',
40 fourth part of an hin of beaten o';
30: 24 sanctuary, and of o' olive an hin:
25 make it an o' of holy ointment, an
25 it shall be an holy anointing o'.
31 be an holy anointing o' unto me
31: 11 the anointing o', and sweet incense
35: 8 And o' for the light, and spices for
8 and spices for anointing o', and for
14 his lamps, with the o' for the light,
15 and the anointing o', and the sweet
28 And spice, and o' for the light,
28 and for the anointing o', and for
37: 29 And he made the holy anointing o',

Ex 39:37 vessels thereof, and the o' for light,
38 and the anointing o', and the sweet
40: 9 thou shalt take the anointing o',
Le 2: 1 he shall pour o' upon it, and put
2 and of the o' thereof, with all the
4 cakes of fine flour mingled with o',
4 unleavened wafers anointed with o'.
5 flour unleavened, mingled with o'.
6 it in pieces, and pour o' thereon:
7 shall be made of fine flour with o'.
15 And thou shalt put o' upon it, and
16 thereof, and part of the o' thereof,
5:11 he shall put no o' upon it, neither
6:15 meat offering, and of the o' thereof,
21 In a pan it shall be made with o';
7:10 meat offering, mingled with o',
12 unleavened cakes mingled with o',
12 unleavened wafers anointed with o',
12 and cakes mingled with o', of fine
8: 2 the garments, and the anointing o',
10 Moses took the anointing o', and
12 he poured of the anointing o' upon
30 Moses took of the anointing o', and
9: 4 meat offering mingled with o': for
10: 7 anointing o' of the Lord is upon you.
14:10 mingled with o', and one log of o'.
12 trespass offering, and the log of o',
15 shall take some of the log of o', and
16 shall dip his right finger in the o'
16 sprinkle of the o' with his finger
17 the rest of the o' that is in his hand
18 the remnant of the o' that is in the
21 deal of fine flour mingled with o'
21 for a meat offering, and a log of o';
24 trespass offering, and the log of o',
26 priest shall pour of the o' into the
27 some of the o' that is in his left
28 priest shall put of the o' that is in
29 rest of the o' that is in the priest's
21:10 head the anointing o' was poured,
12 the crown of the anointing o' of his
23:13 deals of fine flour mingled with o',
24: 2 pure o' olive beaten for the light,
Nu 4: 9 snuffdishes, and all the o' vessels
16 pertaineth the o' for the light,
16 meat offering, and the anointing o'
5:15 he shall pour no o' upon it, nor put
6:15 cakes of fine flour mingled with o',
15 unleavened bread anointed with o',
7:13, 19, 25, 31, 37, 43, 49, 55, 61, 67, 73, 79
mingled with o' for a meat offering:
8: 8 even fine flour mingled with o', and
11: 8 of it was as the taste of fresh o'.
15: 4 with the fourth part of an hin of o'.
6 with the third part of an hin of o'.
9 flour mingled with half an hin of o'.
18:12 the best of the o', and all the best of
28: 5 fourth part of an hin of beaten o'.
9, 12, 12 meat offering, mingled with o',
13 tenth deal of flour mingled with o'
20 shall be of flour mingled with o':
28 offering of flour mingled with o',
29: 3, 9, 14 be of flour mingled with o',
35:25 was anointed with the holy o'.
De 7:13 corn, and thy wine, and thine o',
8: 8 a land of o' olive, and honey;
11:14 corn, and thy wine, and thine o'.
12:17 thy corn, or of thy wine, or of thy o',
14:23 corn, of thy wine, and of thine o',
18: 4 corn, of thy wine, and of thine o',
28:40 not anoint thyself with the o';
51 leave thee either corn, wine, or o',
32:13 rock, and o' out of the flinty rock;
33:24 and let him dip his foot in o'.
1Sa 10: 1 Samuel took a vial of o', and poured
16: 1 fill thine horn with o', and go, I will
13 Then Samuel took the horn of o',
2Sa 1:21 he had not been anointed with o'.
14: 2 anoint not thyself with o', but be as
1Ki 1:39 the priest took an horn of o' out of
5:11 and twenty measures of pure o':
17:12 in a barrel, and a little o' in a cruse:
14 neither shall the cruse of o' fail,
16 not, neither did the cruse of o' fail,
2Ki 4: 2 thing in the house, save a pot of o'.
6 a vessel more. And the o' stayed.
7 Go, sell the o', and pay thy debt,
9: 1 take this box of o' in thine hand,
3 Then take the box of o', and pour it
6 and he poured the o' on his head,
18:32 a land of o' olive and of honey,
1Ch 9:29 flour, and the wine, and the o',
12:40 bunches of raisins, and wine, and o',
27:28 over the cellars of o' was Joash:
2Ch 2:10 and twenty thousand baths of o'.
15 the barley, the o', and the wine,
11:11 store of victual, and of o' and wine.
31: 5 of corn, wine, and o', and honey,
32:28 increase of corn, and wine, and o';
Ezr 3: 7 meat, and drink, and o', unto them
6: 9 salt, wine, and o', according to
7:22 to an hundred baths of o', and salt
Neh 5:11 the corn, the wine, and the o', that
10:37 of wine and of o', unto the priests,
39 the new wine, and the o', unto the
13: 5 new wine, and the o', which was
12 wine and the o' unto the treasuries,
Es 2:12 wit, six months with o' of myrrh,
Job 24:11 Which make o' within their walls,
29: 6 rock poured me out rivers of o';
Ps 23: 5 thou anointest my head with o';
45: 7 anointed thee with...o' of gladness
55:21 his words were softer than o', yet
89:20 with my holy o' have I anointed him:
92:10 I shall be anointed with fresh o'.
104:15 o' to make his face to shine, and
Ps 109:18 water, and like o' into his bones.
141: 5 it shall be an excellent o', which
Pr 5: 3 and her mouth is smoother than o':
21:17 he that loveth wine and o' shall not
20 and o' in the dwelling of the wise;
Isa 41:19 and the myrtle, and the o' tree;
61: 3 ashes, the o' of joy for mourning,
Jer 31:12 for wine, and for o', and for the
40:10 wine, and summer fruits, and o',
41: 8 of barley, and of o', and of honey.
Eze 16: 9 thee, and I anointed thee with o'.
13 eat fine flour, and honey, and o':
18 hast set mine o' and mine incense
19 thee, fine flour, and o', and honey,
23:41 hast set mine incense and mine o'.
27:17 and honey, and o', and balm.
32:14 and cause their rivers to run like o',
45:14 the ordinance of o', the bath of o',
24 ram, and an hin of o' for an ephah.
25 offering, and according to the o'.
46: 5, 7, 11 and an hin of o' to an ephah.
14 and the third part of an hin of o', to
15 and the meat offering, and the o',
Ho 2: 5 and my flax, mine o' and my drink.
8 I gave her corn, and wine, and o',
22 the corn, and the wine, and the o';
12: 1 and o' is carried into Egypt.
Joe 1:10 is dried up, the o' languisheth.
2:19 send you corn, and wine, and o',
24 shall overflow with wine and o'.
Mic 6: 7 with ten thousands of rivers of o'?
15 thou shalt not anoint thee with o';
Hag 1:11 the new wine and upon the o',
2:12 bread or pottage, or wine, or o', or
Zec 4:12 empty the golden o' out of themselves?
M't 25: 3 lamps, and took no o' with them:
4 wise took o' in their vessels with
8 Give us of your o'; for our lamps
M'r 6:13 anointed with o' many that were
Lu 7:46 My head with o' thou didst not
10:34 his wounds, pouring in o' and wine,
16: 6 he said, An hundred measures of o'.
Heb 1: 9 anointed thee with...o' of gladness
Jas 5:14 anointing him with o' in the name
Re 6: 6 thou hurt not the o' and the wine.
18:13 and wine, and o', and fine flour, and

oiled
Ex 29:23 bread, and one cake of o' bread,
Le 8:26 a cake of o' bread, and one wafer,

oil-olive See OIL and OLIVE.

oil-tree See OIL and TREE.

ointment See also OINTMENTS.
Ex 30:25 shalt make it an oil of holy o', an o'
25 an o' compound after the art
2Ki 20:13 the spices, and the precious o',
1Ch 9:30 sons of the priests made the o' of
Job 41:31 he maketh the sea like a pot of o'.
Ps 133: 2 like the precious o' upon the head,
Pr 27: 9 O' and perfume rejoice the heart:
16 and the o' of his right hand, which
Ec 7: 1 name is better than precious o';
9: 8 white; and let thy head lack no o'.
10: 1 flies cause the o' of the apothecary
Ca 1: 3 thy name is as o' poured forth,
Isa 1: 6 bound up, neither mollified with o'.
39: 2 and the spices, and the precious o',
57: 9 thou wentest to the king with o',
M't 26: 7 alabaster box of very precious o',
9 For this o' might have been sold for
12 she hath poured this o' on my body,
M'r 14: 3 alabaster box of o' of spikenard
4 Why was this waste of the o' made?
Lu 7:37 brought an alabaster box of o',
38 feet, and anointed them with the o'.
46 hath anointed my feet with o'.
Joh 11: 2 which anointed the Lord with o',
12: 3 Mary a pound of o' of spikenard,
3 was filled with the odour of the o'.
5 Why was not this o' sold for three

ointments
Ca 1: 3 of the savour of thy good o' thy
4:10 the smell of thine o' than all spices!
Am 6: 6 anoint themselves with the chief o':
Lu 23:56 and prepared spices and o'; and
Re 18:13 cinnamon, and odours, and o', and

old See also ELDER; ELDEST.
Ge 5:32 Noah was five hundred years o':
6: 4 mighty men which were of o',
7: 6 Noah was six hundred years o'
11:10 Shem was an hundred years o',
12: 4 Abram was seventy and five years o'
15: 9 Take...an heifer of three years o',
9 and a she goat of three years o',
9 and a ram of three years o', and a
15 shalt be buried in a good o' age.
16:16 was fourscore and six years o',
17: 1 when Abram was ninety years o'
12 he that is eight days o' shall be
17 him that is an hundred years o'?
17 Sarah, that is ninety years o', bear?
24 Abraham was ninety years o' and
25 Ishmael...was thirteen years o',
18:11 Now Abraham and Sarah were o'
12 After I am waxed o' shall I have
12 pleasure, my lord being o' also?
13 a surety bear a child, which am o'?
19: 4 house round, both o' and young,
31 unto the younger, Our father is o',
21: 2 bare Abraham a son in his o' age,
4 his son Isaac being eight days o',
5 Abraham was an hundred years o',
7 have born him a son in his o' age.
23: 1 and seven and twenty years o':
24: 1 Abraham was o', and well stricken
Ge 24:36 son to my master when she was o':
25: 8 ghost, and died in a good o' age,
8 an o' man, and full of years; and
20 Isaac was forty years o' when he
26 Isaac was threescore years o' when
26:34 Esau was forty years o' when he
27: 1 when Isaac was o', and his eyes
2 I am o', I know not the day of my
35:29 people, being o' and full of days:
37: 2 Joseph, being seventeen years o',
3 he was the son of his o' age:
41:46 Joseph was thirty years o' when
43:27 well, the o' man of whom ye spake?
44:20 We have a father, an o' man, and
20 a child of his o' age, a little one;
47: 8 Jacob, How o' art thou?
49: 9 as a lion, and as an o' lion;
50:26 being an hundred and ten years o':
Ex 7: 7 Moses was fourscore years o', and
7 Aaron fourscore and three years o',
10: 9 go with our young and with our o',
30:14 from twenty years o' and above,
38:26 from twenty years o' and upward,
Le 13:11 It is an o' leprosy in the skin of
19:32 and honour the face of the o' man,
25:22 eat yet of o' fruit until the ninth
22 come in ye shall eat of the o' store.
26:10 And ye shall eat o' store, and bring
10 forth the o' because of the new.
27: 3 years o' even unto sixty years o',
5 years o' even unto twenty years o',
6 a month o' even unto five years o',
7 it be from sixty years o' and above;
Nu 1: 3 From twenty years o' and upward,
18, 20, 22, 24, 26, 28, 30, 32, 34, 36, 38, 40,
42, 45 from twenty years o' and
3:15 male from a month o' and upward
22, 28, 34, 39, 40, 43 from a month o'
and upward,
4: 3 From thirty years o' and upward
3 even unto fifty years o', all that
23 From thirty years o' and upward
23 until fifty years o' shalt thou
30 From thirty years o' and upward
30 even unto fifty years o' shalt thou
35 From thirty years o' and upward
35 even unto fifty years o', every one
39 From thirty years o' and upward
39 even unto fifty years o', every one
43 From thirty years o' and upward
43 even unto fifty years o', every one
47 From thirty years o' and upward
47 even unto fifty years o', every one
8:24 from twenty and five years o' and
14:29 from twenty years o' and upward,
18:16 from a month o' shalt thou redeem,
26: 2 from twenty years o' and upward,
4 from twenty years o' and upward;
62 males from a month o' and upward:
32:11 from twenty years o' and upward,
33:39 and twenty and three years o'
De 2:20 giants dwelt therein in o' time;
8: 4 raiment waxed not o' upon thee,
19:14 they of o' time have set in thine
28:50 not regard the person of the o',
29: 5 clothes are not waxen o' upon you,
5 shoe is not waxen o' upon thy foot.
31: 2 an hundred and twenty years o'
32: 7 Remember the days of o', consider
34: 7 an hundred and twenty years o'
Jos 5:11 did eat of the o' corn of the land
12 after they had eaten of the o' corn
6:21 man and woman, young and o',
9: 4 and took o' sacks upon their asses,
4 and wine bottles, o', and rent, and
5 And o' shoes and clouted upon their
5 feet, and o' garments upon them;
13 shoes are become o' by reason of
13: 1 Now Joshua was o' and stricken in
1 Thou art o' and stricken in years,
14: 7 Forty years o' was I when Moses
10 this day fourscore and five years o'.
23: 1 that Joshua waxed o' and stricken
2 them, I am o' and stricken in age:
24: 2 the other side of the flood in o' time,
29 being an hundred and ten years o'.
J'g 2: 8 being an hundred and ten years o'.
6:25 the second bullock of seven years o',
8:32 Gideon...died in a good o' age,
19:16 came an o' man from his work
17 and the o' man said, Whither goest
20 And the o' man said, Peace be with
22 the master of the house, the o' man,
Ru 1:12 I am too o' to have an husband.
4:15 and a nourisher of thine o' age:
1Sa 2:22 Now Eli was very o', and heard
31 not be an o' man in thine house.
32 not be an o' man in thine house for
4:15 Eli was ninety and eight years o';
18 for he was an o' man, and heavy.
8: 1 came to pass, when Samuel was o',
5 Behold, thou art o', and thy sons
12: 2 and I am o' and grayheaded; and,
17:12 man went among men for an o' man
27: 8 nations were of o' inhabitants
28:14 she said, An o' man cometh up;
2Sa 2:10 Saul's son was forty years o' when
4: 4 was five years o' when the tidings
5: 4 David was thirty years o' when he
19:32 aged man, even fourscore years o':
35 I am this day fourscore years o':
20:18 They were wont to speak in o' time,
1Ki 1: 1 king David was o' and stricken in
15 chamber: and the king was very o':
11: 4 to pass, when Solomon was o',
12: 6 consulted with the o' men, that

1Ki 12: 8 forsook the counsel of the o· men,
13 forsook the o· men's counsel that
13: 11 dwelt an o· prophet in Beth-el;
25 the city where the o· prophet dwelt.
29 and the o· prophet came to the city,
14: 21 was forty and one years o· when
15: 23 time of his o· age he was diseased
22: 42 was thirty and five years o· when
2Ki 4: 14 no child, and her husband is o·.
8: 17 Thirty and two years o· was he
26 and twenty years o· was Ahaziah
11: 21 Seven years o· was Jehoash when
14: 2 He was twenty and five years o·
21 Azariah, which was sixteen years o·.
15: 2 Sixteen years o· was he when he
33 Five and twenty years o· was he
16: 2 Twenty years o· was Ahaz when he
18: 2 Twenty and five years o· was he
21: 1 Manasseh was twelve years o· when
19 Amon was twenty and two years o·
22: 1 Josiah was eight years o· when he
23: 31 was twenty and three years o· when
36 was twenty and five years o· when
24: 8 Jehoiachin was eighteen years o·
18 was twenty and one years o· when
1Ch 2: 21 when he was threescore years o·;
4: 40 they of Ham had dwelt there of o·.
23: 1 So when David was o· and full of
27 from twenty years o· and above:
27: 23 from twenty years o· and under;
29: 28 And he died in a good o· age, full
2Ch 10: 6 took counsel with the o· men that
8 the counsel which the o· men gave
13 forsook the counsel of the o· men,
12: 13 was one and forty years o· when
20: 31 was thirty and five years o· when
21: 5 was thirty and two years o· when
20 Thirty and two years o· was he
22: 2 Forty and two years o· was Ahaziah
24: 1 Joash was seven years o· when he
15 But Jehoiada waxed o·, and was
15 an hundred and thirty years o·
25: 1 was twenty and five years o· when
5 from twenty years o· and above,
26: 1 Uzziah, who was sixteen years o·,
3 Sixteen years o· was Uzziah when
27: 1 was twenty and five years o· when
8 was five and twenty years o· when
28: 1 was twenty years o· when he began
29: 1 he was five and twenty years o·,
31: 16 from three years o· and upward,
17 from twenty years o· and upward,
33: 1 Manasseh was twelve years o·
21 Amon was two and twenty years o·
34: 1 Josiah was eight years o· when he
36: 2 was twenty and three years o· when
5 was twenty and five years o· when
9 Jehoiachin was eight years o· when
11 was one and twenty years o· when
17 o· man, or him that stooped for
Ezr 3: 8 from twenty years o· and upward,
4: 15 within the same of o· time:
19 this city of o· time hath made
Ne 3: 6 o· gate repaired Jehoiada the son
9: 21 their clothes waxed not o·, and
12: 39 Ephraim, and above the o· gate,
46 the days of David and Asaph of o·
Es 3: 13 all Jews, both young and o·, little
Job 4: 11 o· lion perisheth for lack of prey,
14: 8 root thereof wax o· in the earth,
20: 4 Knowest thou not this of o·, since
21: 7 do the wicked live, become o·, yea,
22: 15 the o· way which wicked men have
30: 2 me, in whom o· age was perished?
32: 6 I am young, and ye are very o·;
42: 17 died, being o· and full of days.
Ps 6: 7 it waxeth o· because of all mine
25: 6 for they have been ever of o·.
32: 3 my bones waxed o· through my
37: 25 have been young, and now am o·;
44: 1 in their days, in the times of o·.
55: 19 them, even he that abideth of o·.
68: 33 of heavens, which were of o·;
71: 9 me not off in the time of o· age;
18 when I am o· and grayheaded, O
74: 2 which thou hast purchased of o·;
12 For God is my King of o·, working
77: 5 I have considered the days of o·,
11 will remember thy wonders of o·.
78: 2 I will utter dark sayings of o·:
92: 14 still bring forth fruit in o· age;
93: 2 Thy throne is established of o·:
102: 25 Of o· hast thou laid the foundation
26 them shall wax o· like a garment;
119: 52 remembered thy judgments of o·,
152 have known of o· that thou hast
143: 5 I remember the days of o·; I
148: 12 maidens; o· men, and children:
Pro 8: 22 of his way, before his works of o·.
17: 6 children are the crown of o· men;
20: 29 beauty of o· men is the gray head.
22: 6 when he is o·, he will not depart
23: 10 Remove not the o· landmark; and
22 not thy mother when she is o·.
Ec 1: 10 it hath been already of o· time,
4: 13 child than an o· and foolish king,
Ca 7: 13 of pleasant fruits, new and o·,
Isa 15: 5 Zoar, an heifer of three years o·:
20: 4 Ethiopians captives, young and o·,
22: 11 walls for the water of the o· pool:
25: 1 thy counsels of o· are faithfulness
30: 6 whence come...young and o· lion,
33 For Tophet is ordained of o·; yea,
43: 18 neither consider the things of o·.
46: 4 And even to your o· age I am he;
9 Remember the former things of o·:

Isa 50: 9 all shall wax o· as a garment;
51: 6 earth shall wax o· like a garment,
9 days, in the generations of o·.
57: 11 not I held my peace even of o·, and
58: 12 shall build the o· waste places:
61: 4 they shall build the o· wastes,
63: 9 and carried them all the days of o·.
11 Then he remembered the days of o·,
65: 20 an o· man that hath not filled his
20 shall die an hundred years o·;
20 sinner being an hundred years o·
Jer 2: 20 of o· time I have broken thy yoke,
6: 16 and see, and ask for the o· paths,
28: 8 been before me and before thee of o·
31: 3 The Lord hath appeared of o· unto
13 both young men and o· together:
38: 11 o· cast clouts and o· rotten rags,
12 Put now these o· cast clouts and
46: 26 be inhabited, as in the days of o·.
48: 34 as an heifer of three years o·:
51: 22 I break in pieces o· and young;
52: 1 was one and twenty years o· when
La 1: 7 that she had in the days of o·,
2: 17 had commanded in the days of o·:
21 The young and the o· lie on the
3: 4 and my skin hath he made o·;
6 places, as they that be dead of o·.
5: 21 turned; renew our days as of o·.
Eze 9: 6 Slay utterly o· and young, both
23: 43 her that was o· in adulteries,
25: 15 to destroy it for the o· hatred;
26: 20 the pit, with the people of o· time,
20 the earth, in places desolate of o·,
36: 11 settle you after your o· estates,
38: 17 of whom I have spoken in o· time
Da 5: 31 about threescore and two years o·.
Joe 1: 2 Hear this, ye o· men, and give ear,
2: 28 your o· men shall dream dreams,
Am 9: 11 I will build it as in the days of o·:
Mic 5: 2 goings forth have been from of o·,
6: 6 offerings, with calves of a year o·?
7: 14 and Gilead, as in the days of o·.
20 our fathers from the days of o·.
Na 2: 8 But Nineveh is of o· like a pool of
11 the lion, even the o· lion, walked,
Zec 8: 4 yet o· men and o· women dwell in
Mal 3: 4 as in the days of o·, and as in
M't 2: 16 from two years o· and under,
5: 21 that it was said by them of o· time,
27 that it was said by them of o· time,
33 hath been said by them of o· time,
9: 16 of new cloth unto an o· garment,
17 men put new wine into o· bottles:
13: 52 of his treasure things new and o·.
M'r 2: 21 of new cloth on an o· garment;
21 filled it up taketh away from the o·,
22 putteth new wine into o· bottles:
Lu 1: 18 for I am an o· man, and my wife
36 also conceived a son in her o· age:
2: 42 And when he was twelve years o·,
5: 36 of a new garment upon an o·;
36 the new agreeth not with the o·.
37 putteth new wine into o· bottles;
39 No man also having drunk o· wine
39 new: for he saith, The o· is better.
9: 8 one of the o· prophets was risen
19 one of the o· prophets is risen again.
12: 33 yourselves bags which wax not o·,
Joh 3: 4 can a man be born when he is o·?
8: 57 Thou art not yet fifty years o·, and
21: 18 when thou shalt be o·, thou shalt
Ac 2: 17 your o· men shall dream dreams:
4: 22 For the man was above forty years o·,
7: 23 when he was full forty years o·, it
15: 21 Moses of o· time hath in every city
21: 16 Mnason of Cyprus, an o· disciple,
Ro 4: 19 he was about an hundred years o·,
6: 6 our o· man is crucified with him,
1Co 5: 7 Purge out therefore the o· leaven,
8 not with o· leaven, neither with the
2Co 3: 14 in the reading of the o· testament;
5: 17 creature: o· things are past away;
Eph 4: 22 That ye put off...the o· man, which
Col 3: 9 that ye have put off the o· man
1Ti 4: 7 refuse profane and o· wives' fables,
5: 9 number under threescore years o·,
Heb 1: 11 shall wax o· as doth a garment;
8: 13 covenant, he hath made the first o·.
13 that which decayeth and waxeth o·
1Pe 3: 5 in the o· time the holy women
2Pe 1: 9 he was purged from his o· sins.
21 came not in o· time by the will of
2: 5 spared not the o· world, but saved
3: 5 word of God the heavens were of o·,
1Jo 2: 7 an o· commandment which ye had
7 The o· commandment is the word
Jude 4 who were before of o· ordained to
Re 12: 9 that o· serpent, called the Devil,
20: 2 that o· serpent, which is the Devil,

old age See OLD and AGE.

oldness
Ro 7: 6 and not in the o· of the letter.

olive See also OLIVES; OLIVEYARDS.
Ge 8: 11 in her mouth was an o· leaf pluckt
Ex 27: 20 that they bring thee pure oil o·
30: 24 the sanctuary, and of oil o· an hin:
Le 24: 2 they bring unto thee pure oil o·
De 6: 11 o· trees, which thou plantedst not;
8: 8 a land of oil o·, and honey;
24: 20 When thou beatest thine o· tree,
28: 40 Thou shalt have o· trees throughout
40 for thine o· shall cast his fruit.
J'g 9: 8 they said unto the o· tree, Reign
9 But the o· tree said unto them,
1Ki 6: 23 he made two cherubims of o· tree.

1Ki 6: 31 the oracle he made doors of o· tree:
32 The two doors also were of o· tree;
33 door of the temple posts of o· tree,
2Ki 18: 32 a land of oil o· and of honey,
1Ch 27: 28 over the o· trees and the sycomore
Ne 8: 15 and fetch o· branches, and pine
Job 15: 33 shall cast off his flower as the o·.
Ps 52: 8 am like a green o· tree in the house
128: 3 thy children like o· plants round
Isa 17: 6 in it, as the shaking of an o· tree,
24: 13 shall be as the shaking of an o· tree,
Jer 11: 16 called thy name, A green o· tree,
Hos 14: 6 his beauty shall be as the o· tree,
Am 4: 9 trees and your o· trees increased,
Hab 3: 17 the labour of the o· shall fail, and
Hag 2: 19 the pomegranate, and the o· tree,
Zec 4: 3 two o· trees by it, one upon the right
11 What are these two o· trees upon
12 What be these two o· branches
Ro 11: 17 and thou, being a wild o· tree, wert
17 the root and fatness of the o· tree;
24 if thou wert cut out of the o· tree
24 to nature into a good o· tree:
24 be graffed into their own o· tree?
Jas 3: 12 tree, my brethren, bear o· berries?
Re 11: 4 These are the two o· trees, and the

olive-berries See OLIVE and BERRIES.

olive-branches See OLIVE and BRANCHES.

olive-leaf See OLIVE and LEAF.

olives
J'g 15: 5 corn, with the vineyards and o·.
Mic 6: 15 thou shalt tread the o·, but thou
Zec 14: 4 in that day upon the mount of O·,
4 the mount of O· shall cleave in the
M't 21: 1 Bethphage, unto the mount of O·,
24: 3 And as he sat upon the mount of O·,
26: 30 they went out into the mount of O·.
M'r 11: 1 and Bethany, at the mount of O·,
13: 3 And as he sat upon the mount of O·
14: 26 they went out into the mount of O·.
Lu 19: 29 the mount called the mount of O·,
37 at the descent of the mount of O·,
21: 37 that is called the mount of O·.
22: 39 as he was wont, to the mount of O·;
Joh 8: 1 Jesus went unto the mount of O·.

Olivet See also MOUNT and OLIVES.
2Sa 15: 30 up by the ascent of mount O·,
Ac 1: 12 from the mount called O·, which

olive-tree See OLIVE and TREE.

oliveyard See also OLIVEYARDS.
Ex 23: 11 with thy vineyard and with thy o·.

oliveyards
Jos 24: 13 vineyard and o· which ye planted
1Sa 8: 14 and your o·, even the best of them,
2Ki 5: 26 and to receive garments, and o·,
Ne 5: 11 vineyards, their o·, and their houses,
9: 25 o·, and fruit trees in abundance:

Olympas (*o-lim'-pas*)
Ro 16: 15 and O·, and all the saints which

Omar (*o'-mar*)
Ge 36: 11 sons of Eliphaz were Teman, O·,
15 duke Teman, duke O·, duke Zepho,
1Ch 1: 36 The sons of Eliphaz; Teman, and O·,

Omega (*o'-me-gah*)
Re 1: 8 I am Alpha and O·, the beginning
11 I am Alpha and O·, the first and
21: 6 I am Alpha and O·, the beginning
22: 13 I am Alpha and O·, the beginning

omer See also OMERS.
Ex 16: 16 an o· for every man, according to
18 when they did mete it with an o·,
32 Fill an o· of it to be kept for your
33 a pot, and put an o· full of manna
36 an o· is the tenth part of an ephah.

omers
Ex 16: 22 much bread, two o· for one man:

omitted
M't 23: 23 o·...weightier matters of the law.

omnipotent
Re 19: 6 for the Lord God o· reigneth.

Omri (*om'-ri*)
1Ki 16: 16 made O·...captain of the host, king
17 O· went up from Gibbethon, and all
21 him king; and half followed O·.
22 people that followed O· prevailed
22 so Tibni died, and O· reigned.
23 began O· to reign over Israel, twelve
25 O· wrought evil in the eyes of the
27 rest of the acts of O· which he did
28 O· slept with his fathers, and was
29 began Ahab the son of O· to reign
29 Ahab the son of O· reigned over
30 Ahab the son of O· did evil in the
2Ki 8: 26 Athaliah, the daughter of O· king
1Ch 7: 8 and O·, and Jerimoth, and Abiah,
9: 4 the son of Ammihud, the son of O·,
27: 18 of Issachar, O· the son of Michael:
2Ch 22: 2 was Athaliah the daughter of O·.
Mic 6: 16 the statutes of O· are kept, and all

on^ See also ANON; ONWARD; THEREON; UPON; WHEREON.
Ge 2: 2 o· the seventh day God ended his work
2 he rested o· the seventh day from all
4: 15 Cain, vengeance shall be taken o· him
16 in the land of Nod, o· the east of Eden
6: 1 multiply o· the face of the earth,
6 that he had made man o· the earth,
8: 4 o· the seventeenth day of the month,
5 month, o· the first day of the month,

Ge 8: 9 *o'* the face of the whole earth:
14 *o'* the seven and twentieth day of the
20 offered burnt offerings *o'* the altar.
12: 8 unto a mountain *o'* the east of Beth-el,
8 Beth-el *o'* the west, and Hai *o'* the east:
9 going *o'* still toward the south.
13: 3 he went *o'* his journeys from the south
4 Abram called *o'* the name of the Lord.
14: 15 which is *o'* the left hand of Damascus.
17: 3 Abram fell *o'* his face: and God
18: 5 your hearts; after that ye shall pass *o'*:
16 with them to bring them *o'* the way.
19: 2 rise up early, and go *o'* your ways.
34 And it came to pass *o'* the morrow,
20: 9 brought *o'* me and *o'* my kingdom
21: 14 Hagar, putting it *o'* her shoulder,
33 called there *o'* the name of the Lord,
22: 4 Then *o'* the third day Abraham lifted
9 him *o'* the altar upon the wood.
24: 33 mine errand. And he said, Speak *o'*.
45 with her pitcher *o'* her shoulder;
25: 26 and his hand took hold *o'* Esau's heel;
28: 12 behold a ladder set up *o'* the earth,
12 of God ascending and descending *o'* it.
20 bread to eat, and raiment to put *o'*,
29: 1 Then Jacob went *o'* his journey, and
31: 22 it was told Laban *o'* the third day that
32: 1 Jacob went *o'* his way, and the angels
19 *O'* this manner shall ye speak unto
33: 4 fell *o'* his neck, and kissed him:
14 and I will lead *o'* softly, according as
16 Esau returned that day *o'* his way
34: 25 And it came to pass *o'* the third day,
37: 23 of many colours that was *o'* him;
38: 9 wife, that he spilled it *o'* the ground,
19 put *o'* the garments of her widowhood.
40: 14 think *o'* me when it shall be well with
16 three white baskets *o'* my head:
19 thee, and shall hang thee *o'* a tree;
43: 31 himself, and said, Set *o'* bread.
32 And they set *o'* for him by himself,
44: 14 they fell before him *o'* the ground.
34 evil that shall come *o'* my father.
46: 29 fell *o'* his neck, and wept *o'* his neck
48: 16 and let my name be named *o'* them,
49: 26 they shall be *o'* the head of Joseph,
26 and *o'* the crown of the head of him
Ex 1: 10 Come *o'*, let us deal wisely with them;
2: 6 And she had compassion *o'* him,
11 brethren, and looked *o'* their burdens:
4: 3 And he said, Cast it *o'* the ground.
3 he cast it *o'* the ground, and it became
6: 28 came to pass *o'* the day when the Lord
8: 4 the frogs shall come up both *o'* thee,
12: 7 and strike it *o'* the two side posts
7 *o'* the upper door post of the houses,
11 your shoes *o'* your feet, and your staff
18 *o'* the fourteenth day of the month at
23 lintel, and *o'* the two side posts,
29 of Pharaoh that sat *o'* his throne
37 six hundred thousand *o'* foot that
14: 16 Israel shall go *o'* dry ground through
22, 29 *o'* their right hand, and *o'* their
15: 14 hold *o'* the inhabitants of Palestina.
19 children of Israel went *o'* dry land in
16: 1 *o'* the fifteenth day of the second
5 *o'* the sixth day they shall prepare
14 as the hoar frost *o'* the ground.
22 *o'* the sixth day they gathered twice
26 but *o'* the seventh day, which is the
27 some of the people *o'* the seventh day
29 he giveth you *o'* the sixth day the
29 go out of his place *o'* the seventh day.
17: 5 Moses, Go *o'* before the people,
9 I will stand *o'* the top of the hill
12 up his hands, the one *o'* the one side,
12 and the other *o'* the other side; and
18: 13 it came to pass *o'* the morrow, that
19: 4 how I bare you *o'* eagles' wings,
16 to pass *o'* the third day in the morning,
18 mount Sinai was altogether *o'* a smoke,
20 Sinai, *o'* the top of the mount:
21: 30 be laid *o'* him a sum of money,
22: 30 *o'* the eighth day thou shalt give it me.
23: 12 *o'* the seventh day thou shalt rest:
24: 6 the blood he sprinkled *o'* the altar.
8 and sprinkled it *o'* the people, and
17 devouring fire *o'* the top of the mount
25: 19 And make one cherub *o'* the one end,
19 and the other cherub *o'* the other end:
19 the cherubims *o'* the two ends thereof.
20 stretch forth their wings *o'* high,
26 that are *o'* the four feet thereof.
26: 10 loops *o'* the edge of the one curtain
13 And a cubit *o'* the one side,
13 and a cubit *o'* the other side of that
13 *o'* this side and *o'* that side, to cover
18 boards *o'* the south side southward.
20 *o'* the north side there shall be
35 table *o'* the side of the tabernacle
35 put the table *o'* the north side.
27: 12 breadth of the court *o'* the west side
13 *o'* the east side eastward shall be fifty
15 *o'* the other side shall be hangings
28: 9 grave *o'* them the names of the
10 Six of their names *o'* one stone,
10 names of the rest *o'* the other stone,
23 put the two rings *o'* the two ends
24 two rings which are *o'* the ends of
25 put them *o'* the shoulderpieces of
27 them *o'* the two sides of the ephod
37 thou shalt put it *o'* a blue lace, that
29: 9 sons, and put the bonnets *o'* them:
30 shall put them *o'* seven days,
31: 17 and *o'* the seventh day he rested, and
32: 6 And they rose up early *o'* the morrow,

Ex 32: 15 tables were written *o'* both their sides;
15 *o'* the one side and *o'* the other were
22 people, that they are set *o'* mischief.
26 Who is *o'* the Lord's side? let him
30 And it came to pass *o'* the morrow,
33: 4 man did put *o'* him his ornaments.
19 will shew mercy *o'* whom I will shew
34: 21 but *o'* the seventh day thou shalt rest:
33 them, he put a vail *o'* his face.
35: 2 *o'* the seventh day there shall be to
36: 11 he made loops of blue *o'* the edge
37: 7 *o'* the two ends of the mercy seat;
8 One cherub *o'* the end *o'* this side, and
8 cherub *o'* the other end *o'* that side:
8 the cherubims *o'* the two ends thereof.
9 spread out their wings *o'* high,
38: 2 horns thereof *o'* the four corners
7 the rings *o'* the sides of the altar,
9 *o'* the south side southward the
15 *o'* this hand and that hand, were
39: 7 *o'* the shoulders of the ephod,
17 *o'* the ends of the breastplate.
18 put them *o'* the shoulderpieces of
19 *o'* the two ends of the breastplate,
19 *o'* the side of the ephod inward.
20 them *o'* the two sides of the ephod
31 fasten it *o'* high upon the mitre;
40: 2 *O'* the first day of the first month
17 *o'* the first day of the month, that the
20 set the staves *o'* the ark, and put
24 *o'* the side of the tabernacle
38 by day, and fire was *o'* it by night,
Le 1: 8 *o'* the fire which is upon the altar:
9 the priest shall burn all *o'* the altar,
11 shall kill it *o'* the side of the altar
12 order *o'* the wood that is *o'* the fire
15 off his head, and burn it *o'* the altar;
16 it beside the altar *o'* the east part,
2: 12 not be burnt *o'* the altar for a sweet
3: 4 kidneys, and the fat that is *o'* them,
5 Aaron's sons shall burn it *o'* the altar
5 upon the wood that is *o'* the fire:
4: 12 burn him *o'* the wood with fire:
5: 12 thereof, and burn it *o'* the altar,
6: 10 shall put *o'* his linen garment,
10 the burnt offering *o'* the altar,
11 and put *o'* other garments, and
12 priest shall burn wood *o'* it every
7: 4 and the fat that is *o'* them, which
16 *o'* the morrow also the remainder of it
17 sacrifice *o'* the third day shall be burnt
18 be eaten at all *o'* the third day,
8: 26 wafer, and put them *o'* the fat,
28 *o'* the altar upon the burnt offering:
9: 1 came to pass *o'* the eighth day, that
14 upon the burnt offering *o'* the altar.
24 shouted, and fell *o'* their faces.
11: 2 all the beasts that are *o'* the earth.
27 manner of beasts that go *o'* all four,
34 *o'* which such water cometh shall
13: 3 priest shall look *o'* the plague in
3 the priest shall look *o'* him, and
5 shall look *o'* him the seventh day:
6 look *o'* him again the seventh day:
21, 26 But if the priest look *o'* it, and,
31 look *o'* the plague of the scall, and,
32 the priest shall look *o'* the plague:
34 the priest shall look *o'* the scall:
36 Then the priest shall look *o'* him:
51 look *o'* the plague *o'* the seventh
55 the priest shall look *o'* the plague,
14: 9 it shall be *o'* the seventh day, that
10 *o'* the eighth day he shall take two
37 he shall look *o'* the plague, and,
15: 6 And he that sitteth *o'* any thing
14 *o'* the eighth day he shall take to him
23 if it be *o'* her bed, or *o'* any thing
29 *o'* the eighth day she shall take unto
16: 4 He shall put *o'* the holy linen coat,
4 flesh in water, and so put them *o'*.
10 goat, *o'* which the lot fell to be
23 put *o'* when he went into the holy
24 and put *o'* his garments, and come
29 *o'* the tenth day of the month, ye shall
30 *o'* that day shall the priest make an
32 shall put *o'* the linen clothes, even
19: 6 day ye offer it, and *o'* the morrow:
7 if it be eaten at all *o'* the third day,
20: 25 thing that creepeth *o'* the ground,
21: 10 consecrated to put *o'* the garments,
22: 30 *O'* the same day it shall be eaten up;
23: 6 *o'* the fifteenth day of the same
11 *o'* the morrow after the sabbath the
21 shall proclaim *o'* the selfsame day,
27 *o'* the tenth day of this seventh month
35 *O'* the first day shall be an holy
36 *o'* the eighth day shall be an holy
39 *o'* the first day shall be a sabbath,
39 *o'* the eighth day shall be a sabbath.
40 take you *o'* the first day the boughs
24: 6 set them in two rows, six *o'* a row,
7 it may be *o'* the bread for a memorial,
25: 9 of the jubile to sound *o'* the tenth
Nu 1: 1 *o'* the first day of the second month, in
18 congregation together *o'* the first day
2: 3 *o'* the east side toward the rising of
10 *O'* the south side shall be the
18 *O'* the west side shall be the standard
3: 10 shall wait *o'* their priest's office:
13 *o'* the day that I smote all the firstborn
29, 35 pitch *o'* the side of the tabernacle
4: 12 skins, and shalt put them *o'* a bar:
6: 9 *o'* the seventh day shall he shave it.
10 *o'* the eighth day he shall bring two
23 *O'* this wise ye shall bless the
7: 1 it came to pass *o'* the day that Moses

Nu 7: 11 their offering, each prince *o'* his day,
18 *O'* the second day Nathaneel the son
24 *O'* the third day Eliab the son of
30 *O'* the fourth day Elizur the son of
36 *O'* the fifth day Shelumiel the son of
42 *O'* the sixth day Eliasaph the son of
48 *O'* the seventh day Elishama the son
54 *O'* the eighth day offered Gamaliel the
60 *O'* the ninth day Abidan the son of
66 *O'* the tenth day Ahiezer the son of
72 *O'* the eleventh day Pagiel the son of
78 *O'* the twelfth day Ahira the son of
8: 17 *o'* the day that I smote every firstborn
9: 5 kept the passover *o'* the fourteenth
6 not keep the passover *o'* that day:
6 Moses and before Aaron *o'* that day:
15 *o'* the day that the tabernacle was
10: 5 the camps that lie *o'* the east parts
6 the camps that lie *o'* the south side
11 it came to pass *o'* the twentieth day
11: 31 it were a day's journey *o'* this side,
31 were a day's journey *o'* the other side,
14: 5 Moses and Aaron fell *o'* their faces
16: 27 Dathan, and Abiram, *o'* every side:
41 *o'* the morrow all the congregation
46 off the altar, and put *o'* incense,
47 he put *o'* incense, and made an
17: 8 *o'* the morrow Moses went into the
19: 12 *o'* the seventh day he shall be clean:
12 purify himself with it *o'* the third day,
19 *o'* the third day, and *o'* the seventh
19 *o'* the seventh day he shall purify
20: 19 any thing else, go through *o'* my feet.
21: 13 and pitched *o'* the other side of Arnon,
22: 1 Moab *o'* this side Jordan by Jericho.
24 vineyards, a wall being *o'* this side,
24 this side, and a wall *o'* that side.
31 down his head, and fell flat *o'* his face.
41 it came to pass *o'* the morrow, that
23: 2 *o'* every altar a bullock and a ram.
14, 30 a bullock and a ram *o'* every altar.
24: 20 And when he looked *o'* Amalek,
21 he looked *o'* the Kenites, and took
28: 9 *o'* the sabbath day two lambs of the
25 *o'* the seventh day ye shall have an holy
29: 1 *o'* the first day of the month, ye shall
7 shall have *o'* the tenth day of this
12 *o'* the fifteenth day of the seventh
17 *o'* the second day ye shall offer twelve
20 And *o'* the third day eleven bullocks,
23 And *o'* the fourth day ten bullocks, two
26 And *o'* the fifth day nine bullocks, two
29 And *o'* the sixth day eight bullocks,
32 *o'* the seventh day seven bullocks, two
35 *O'* the eighth day ye shall have a
30: 12 them void *o'* the day he heard them;
31: 19 and your captives *o'* the third day,
19 third day, and *o'* the seventh day
24 wash your clothes *o'* the seventh day,
32: 19 with them *o'* yonder side Jordan,
19 to us *o'* this side Jordan eastward.
32 of our inheritance *o'* this side Jordan
33: 3 *o'* the fifteenth day of the first month;
3 *o'* the morrow after the passover the
34: 4 of Akrabbim, and pass *o'* to Zin:
4 and shall go *o'* to Hazar-addar,
4 and pass *o'* to Azmon:
9 And the border shall go *o'* to Ziphron,
11 to Riblah, *o'* the east side of Ain;
15 their inheritance *o'* this side Jordan
35: 5 city *o'* the east side two thousand
5 and *o'* the south side two thousand
5 and *o'* the west side two thousand
5 and *o'* the north side two thousand
14 give three cities *o'* this side Jordan,
De 1: 1 unto all Israel *o'* this side Jordan
3 month, *o'* the first day of the month,
5 *O'* this side Jordan, in the land of
41 *o'* every man his weapons of war,
2: 28 only I will pass through *o'* my feet;
3: 8 the land that was *o'* this side Jordan,
4: 15 *o'* the day that the Lord spake unto
17 of any beast that is *o'* the earth,
18 any thing that creepeth *o'* the ground,
41 severed three cities *o'* this side Jordan
46 *O'* this side Jordan, in the valley over
47 were *o'* this side Jordan toward the
49 the plain *o'* this side Jordan eastward,
6: 9 posts of thy house, and *o'* thy gates.
7: 25 the silver or gold that is *o'* them,
9: 10 *o'* them was written according to
10: 2 I will write *o'* the tables the words
4 he wrote *o'* the tables, according to
11: 30 they not *o'* the other side Jordan, by
16: 8 *o'* the seventh day shall be a solemn
21: 19 father and his mother lay hold *o'* him,
22 and thou hang him *o'* a tree:
22: 5 man put *o'* a woman's garment:
6 way in any tree, or *o'* the ground,
28 and lay hold *o'* her, and lie with her,
23: 11 shall be, when evening cometh *o'*,
26: 7 voice, and looked *o'* our affliction,
27: 2 *o'* the day when ye shall pass over
28: 1 set thee *o'* high above all nations
2 these blessings shall come *o'* thee,
30: 7 and *o'* them that hate thee, which
32: 11 them, beareth them *o'* her wings:
13 ride *o'* the high places of the earth,
22 set *o'* fire the foundations of the
41 mine hand take hold *o'* judgment;
33: 26 help, and in his excellency *o'* the sky.
Jos 1: 14 Moses gave you *o'* this side Jordan;
15 servant gave you *o'* this side Jordan
2: 10 that were *o'* the other side Jordan,
19 his blood shall be *o'* our head, if any
3: 17 of the Lord stood firm *o'* dry ground

Jos 3:17 Israelites passed over o' dry ground,
4:14 O' that day the Lord magnified
19 up out of Jordan o' the tenth day
22 came over this Jordan o' dry land.
5: 1 were o' the side of Jordan westward,
10 kept the passover o' the fourteenth
11 the old corn of the land o' the morrow
12 And the manna ceased o' the morrow
14 Joshua fell o' his face to the earth,
6: 7 Pass o', and compass the city, and
7 armed pass o' before the ark of the
8 horns passed o' before the Lord,
9 the priests going o', and blowing
13 before the ark of the Lord went o'
13 priests going o', and blowing with
15 And it came to pass o' the seventh day,
15 o' that day they compassed the city
7: 2 Beth-aven, o' the east side of Beth-el,
7 and dwelt o' the other side Jordan!
8: 8 city, that ye shall set the city o' fire:
9 Beth-el and Ai, o' the west side of Ai:
11 and pitched o' the north side of Ai:
12 and Ai, o' the west side of the city.
13 host that was o' the north of the city,
13 liers in wait o' the west of the city,
19 and hasted and set the city o' fire.
22 some o' this side, and some o' that
24 all fallen o' the edge of the sword,
29 he hanged o' a tree until eventide:
33 stood o' this side the ark and o' that
9: 1 kings which were o' this side Jordan,
12 of our houses o' the day we came forth
17 came unto their cities o' the third day.
10:26 and hanged them o' five trees:
32 Israel, which took it o' the second day,
35 they took it o' that day, and smote
11: 2 were o' the north of the mountains,
2 and in the borders of Dor o' the west,
3 Canaanite o' the east and o' the west,
12: 1 their land o' the other side Jordan
1 Hermon, and all the plain o' the east:
3 to the sea of Chinneroth o' the east,
3 the plain, even the salt sea o' the east,
7 smote o' this side Jordan o' the west,
13:16 is o' the bank of the river Arnon,
27 sea of Chinnereth o' the other side
32 of Moab, o' the other side Jordan,
14: 3 an half tribe o' the other side Jordan:
9 And Moses sware o' that day, saying,
15: 3 and ascended up o' the south side
7 which is o' the south side of the river:
10 which is Chesalon, o' the north side,
10 and passed o' to Timnah:
16: 1 unto the water of Jericho o' the east,
5 inheritance o' the east side was
6 the sea to Michmethah o' the north
6 passed by it o' the east to Janohah;
17: 5 which were o' the other side Jordan;
7 went along o' the right hand unto
8 Tappuah o' the border of Manasseh
9 also was o' the north side of the river,
10 met together in Asher o' the north,
10 and in Issachar o' the east.
18: 5 shall abide in their coast o' the south,
5 shall abide in their coasts o' the north.
7 inheritance beyond Jordan o' the east,
12 border o' the north side was from
12 to the side of Jericho o' the north side,
13 lieth o' the south side of the nether
15 and the border went out o' the west,
16 in the valley of the giants o' the north,
16 to the side of Jebusi o' the south,
20 was the border of it o' the east side.
19:13 passeth o' along o' the east to
14 it o' the north side to Hannathon:
27 goeth out to Cabul o' the left hand,
34 reacheth to Zebulun o' the south side,
34 reacheth to Asher o' the west side,
20: 8 o' the other side Jordan by Jericho
22: 4 gave you o' the other side Jordan.
7 brethren o' this side Jordan westward.
20 o' all the congregation of Israel?
24: 2 dwelt o' the other side of the flood
8 which dwelt o' the other side Jordan;
14 served o' the other side of the flood,
15 were o' the other side of the flood,
30 o' the north side of the hill of Gaash.
J'g 1: 8 of the sword, and set the city o' fire.
2: 9 o' the north side of the hill Gaash.
3:25 lord was fallen down dead o' the earth.
4:15 his chariot, and fled away o' his feet.
17 fled away o' his feet to the tent of
23 God subdued o' that day Jabin the
5: 1 Barak the son of Abinoam o' that day,
10 Speak, ye that ride o' white asses, ye
15 he was sent o' foot into the valley.
17 Asher continued o' the sea shore, and
30 colours of needlework o' both sides,
6:32 o' that day he called him Jerubbaal,
37 if the dew be o' the fleece only,
38 for he rose up early o' the morrow,
40 there was dew o' all the ground.
7: 1 were o' the north side of them, by
17 them, Look o' me, and do likewise:
18 also o' every side of all the camp,
25 to Gideon o' the other side Jordan.
8:11 dwelt in tents o' the east of Nobah
21 that were o' their camels' necks.
26 that was o' the kings of Midian,
34 of all their enemies o' every side:
9: 8 went forth o' a time to anoint a king
42 And it came to pass o' the morrow,
48 took it, and laid it o' his shoulder,
49 and set the hold o' fire upon them;
10: 4 sons that rode o' thirty ass colts,
8 that were o' the other side Jordan
J'g 11:18 pitched o' the other side of Arnon,
12:14 o' threescore and ten ass colts:
13: 5 no rasor shall come o' his head:
19 and Manoah and his wife looked o'.
20 And Manoah and his wife looked o' it,
20 and fell o' their faces to the
14: 9 in his hands, and went o' eating,
15, 17 came to pass o' the seventh day,
18 of the city said unto him o' the seventh
15: 5 when he had set the brands o' fire,
18 and called o' the Lord, and said,
16:29 and o' which it was borne up,
19: 1 o' the side of mount Ephraim,
5 o' the fourth day, when they arose
8 early in the morning o' the fifth day
9 to morrow get you early o' your way,
14 they passed o' and went their way;
29 a knife, and laid hold o' his concubine,
20:30 the children of Benjamin o' the third
48 also they set o' fire all the cities that
21: 4 And it came to pass o' the morrow,
19 which is o' the north side of Beth-el,
19 o' the east side of the highway that
19 Shechem, and o' the south of Lebonah.
Ru 1: 7 went o' the way to return unto the
2: 3 hap was to light o' a part of the field
9 Let thine eyes be o' the field that they
10 she fell o' her face, and bowed
3:15 of barley, and laid it o' her:
1Sa 1:11 look o' the affliction of thine handmaid,
2:26 And the child Samuel grew o', and
34 two sons, o' Hophni and Phinehas;
5: 3 of Ashdod arose early o' the morrow,
4 arose early o' the morrow morning,
5 tread o' the threshold of Dagon
6: 4 plague was o' you all, and o' your lords.
7 o' which there hath come no yoke,
15 and put them o' the great stone:
7: 6 before the Lord, and fasted o' that day,
10 with a great thunder o' that day
9:20 days ago, set not thy mind o' them;
20 o' whom is all the desire of Israel?
27 Is it not o' thee, and o' all thy father's
27 o' before us, (and he passed o',)
10: 3 thou go o' forward from thence,
11: 2 O' this condition will I make a
7 fear of the Lord fell o' the people,
11 And it was so o' the morrow, that Saul
12:11 hand of your enemies o' every side,
13: 5 sand which is o' the sea shore in
14: 1 garrison, that is o' the other side.
4 there was a sharp rock o' the one side,
4 and a sharp rock o' the other side:
16 they went o' beating down one
19 Philistines went o' and increased:
24 I may be avenged o' mine enemies.
32 calves, and slew them o' the ground:
40 he unto all Israel, Be ye o' one side,
40 my son will be o' the other side.
47 against all his enemies o' every side,
15:12 is gone about, and passed o', and
16 And he said unto him, Say o'.
18 the Lord sent thee o' a journey, and
16: 6 were come, that he looked o' Eliab,
7 Look not o' his countenance, or
7 or o' the height of his stature;
7 looketh o' the outward appearance,
7 but the Lord looketh o' the heart.
16 who is a cunning player o' an harp:
17: 3 stood o' a mountain o' the one side,
3 stood o' a mountain o' the other
41 Philistine came o' and drew near
18:10 And it came to pass o' the morrow,
24 saying, O' this manner spake David.
19:23 and he went o', and prophesied,
20:20 shoot three arrows o' the side thereof,
21 the arrows are o' this side of thee,
27 And it came to pass o' the morrow,
41 fell o' his face to the ground, and
21:13 scrabbled o' the doors of the gate,
22:18 and slew o' that day fourscore and five
23:19 which is o' the south of Jeshimon?
21 Lord; for ye have compassion o' me.
24 the plain o' the south of Jeshimon.
26 Saul went o' this side of the mountain,
26 his men o' that side of the mountain:
24: 7 out of the cave, and went o' his way.
25:13 men, Gird ye o' every man his sword.
13 they girded o' every man his sword;
13 and David also girded o' his sword:
14 our master; and he railed o' them.
18 of figs, and laid them o' asses.
19 Go o' before me; behold, I come
20 it was so, as she rode o' the ass,
23 and fell before David o' her face,
41 bowed herself o' her face to the earth,
26:13 and stood o' the top of an hill afar
25 So David went o' his way, and Saul
27:11 Lest they should tell o' us, saying,
28: 8 himself, and put o' other raiment,
20 fell straightway all along o' the earth,
22 strength, when thou goest o' thy way.
29: 2 Philistines passed o' by hundreds,
2 his men passed o' in the rereward
30: 1 were come to Ziklag o' the third day,
2 them away, and went o' their way.
31: 7 were o' the other side of the valley,
7 that were o' the other side Jordan,
8 And it came to pass o' the morrow,
2Sa 1: 2 It came even to pass o' the third day,
10 the bracelet that was o' his arm,
11 Then David took hold o' his clothes,
24 who put o' ornaments of gold upon
2:13 the one o' the one side of the pool,
13 other o' the other side of the pool.
21 lay thee hold o' one of the young men,
2Sa 2:25 and stood o' the top of an hill.
3:12 sent messengers to David o' his behalf,
29 Let it rest o' the head of Joab,
29 Joab, and o' all his father's house;
29 is a leper, or that leaneth o' a staff,
29 or that falleth o' the sword, or that
4: 5 who lay o' a bed at noon.
7 lay o' his bed in his bedchamber,
5: 8 David said o' that day, Whosoever
10 And David went o', and grew great,
6: 5 o' all manner of instruments made of
5 even o' harps, and o' psalteries, and
5 o' timbrels,...o' cornets,...o' cymbals.
8: 7 were o' the servants of Hadadezer,
9: 3 yet a son, which is lame o' his feet.
6 come unto David, he fell o' his face,
13 table; and was lame o' both his feet.
11:13 at even he went out to lie o' his bed
12:18 And it came to pass o' the seventh day,
30 and it was set o' David's head.
13: 5 Lay thee down o' thy bed, and make
19 Tamar put ashes o' her head, and
19 of divers colours that was o' her,
19 and laid her hand o' her head,
19 her head, and went o' crying.
31 his garments, and lay o' the earth;
14: 2 and put o' now mourning apparel,
3 and speak o' this manner unto him.
4 she fell o' her face to the ground,
9 be o' me, and o' my father's house:
12 lord the king. And he said, Say o'.
14 and are as water spilt o' the ground,
22 Joab fell to the ground o' his face,
26 because the hair was heavy o' him,
30 hath barley there; go and set it o' fire.
30 Absalom's servants set the field o' fire.
31 have thy servants set my field o' fire?
33 bowed himself o' his face to the
15: 6 And o' this manner did Absalom to all
18 his servants passed o' beside him;
18 Gath, passed o' before the king.
33 If thou passest o' with me, then
16: 2 be for the king's household to ride o';
6 were o' his right hand and o' his left.
12 the Lord will look o' mine affliction,
13 Shimei went along o' the hill's side
17:12 as the dew falleth o' the ground:
19:40 Then the king went o' to Gilgal,
40 and Chimham went o' with him:
20: 8 Joab's garment that he had put o'
13 all the people went o' after Joab,
21:10 birds of the air to rest o' them
20 that had o' every hand six fingers,
20 and o' every foot six toes, four and
22: 4 I will call o' the Lord, who is worthy
49 also hast lifted me up o' high
23: 1 man who was raised up o' high,
24: 5 in Aroer, o' the right side of the city
20 servants coming o' toward him:
20 the king o' his face upon the ground.
1Ki 1:20 shall sit o' the throne of my lord
27 who should sit o' the throne of my lord
46 Solomon sitteth o' the throne of
48 hath given one to sit o' my throne
50 caught hold o' the horns of the altar.
51 caught hold o' the horns of the altar,
2: 4 a man o' the throne of Israel.
5 and in his shoes that were o' his feet.
14 unto thee. And she said, Say o'.
15 that all Israel set their faces o' me,
16 And she said unto him, Say o'.
19 her, and sat down o' his throne,
19 and she sat o' his right hand.
20 said unto her, Ask o', my mother:
24 o' the throne of David my father,
28 caught hold o' the horns of the altar.
37 be, that o' the day thou goest out,
42 certain, o' the day thou goest out,
3: 6 him a son to sit o' his throne, as
4:24 all the region o' this side the river,
24 all the kings o' this side the river:
24 peace o' all sides round about him.
29 the sand that is o' the sea shore.
5: 3 which were about him o' every side,
4 God hath given me rest o' every side,
6:10 o' the house with timber of cedar,
15 covered them o' the inside with wood,
16 twenty cubits o' the sides of the house,
7: 3 beams, that lay o' forty five pillars,
9 so o' the outside toward the great
28 work of the bases was o' this manner:
29 o' the borders that were between
35 o' the top of the base the ledges
36 o' the plates of the ledges thereof,
36 o' the borders thereof, he graved
39 bases o' the right side of the house,
39 five o' the left side of the house:
39 he set the sea o' the right side of the
41 were o' the top of the two pillars;
43 bases, and ten lavers o' the bases;
49 of pure gold, five o' the right side,
49 and five o' the left; before the oracle,
8:20 and sit o' the throne of Israel,
23 heaven above, or o' earth beneath,
25 sight to sit o' the throne of Israel;
27 will God indeed dwell o' the earth?
50 they may have compassion o' them:
54 arose...from kneeling o' his knees
66 O' the eighth day he sent the people
9:26 o' the shore of the Red sea, in the
10: 9 to set thee o' the throne of Israel:
19 and there were stays o' either side
19 o' the place of the seat, and two
20 twelve lions stood there o' the one side
20 and o' the other upon the six steps:
11:30 the new garment that was o' him,

1Ki 12: 32 o' the fifteenth day of the month, like
13: 4 from the altar, saying, Lay hold o' him.
14: 23 o' every high hill, and under
16: 11 soon as he sat o' his throne, that he
24 and built o' the hill, and called the
18: 7 he knew him, and fell o' his face,
23, 23 and lay it o' wood, and put no fire
24 And call ye o' the name of your gods,
24 and I will call o' the name of the Lord:
25 and call o' the name of your gods, but
26 and called o' the name of Baal from
33 pieces, and laid him o' the wood,
33 pour it o' the burnt sacrifice and on
39 people saw it, they fell o' their faces:
46 the hand of the Lord was o' Elijah;
19: 6 there was a cake baken o' the coals,
15 Go, return o' thy way to the wilderness
20: 11 Let not him that girdeth o' his harness
20 king of Syria escaped o' an horse
31 put sackcloth o' our loins, and rope
32 So they girded sackcloth o' their loins,
32 and put ropes o' their heads, and
21: 9, 12 set Naboth o' high among the
22: 10 of Judah sat each o' his throne,
10 having put o' their robes,
19 I saw the Lord sitting o' his throne,
19 standing by him o' his right hand and
19 his right hand and o' his left.
20 And one said o' this manner,
20 and another said o' that manner.
24 and smote Micaiah o' the cheek,
30 battle; but put thou o' thy robes.
2Ki 1: 4, 6 that bed o' which thou art gone up.
9 behold, he sat o' the top of an hill.
13 and fell o' his knees before Elijah,
16 that bed o' which thou art gone up,
2: 6 leave thee. And they two went o'.
8 they two went over o' dry ground.
11 as they still went o', and talked,
15 spirit of Elijah doth rest o' Elisha.
24 he turned back, and looked o' them,
3: 11 water o' the hands of Elijah.
21 that were able to put o' armour,
22 water o' the other side as red as
25 o' every good piece of land cast every
4: 8 And it fell o' a day, that Elisha passed
10 little chamber, I pray thee, o' the wall;
11 it fell o' a day, that he came thither
18 it fell o' a day, that he went out to his
20 he sat o' her knees till noon, and
21 him o' the bed of the man of God,
31 Gehazi passed o' before them, and
38 Set o' the great pot, and seethe
5: 2 and she waited o' Naaman's wife.
11 and call o' the name of the Lord his
18 and he leaneth o' my hand, and I
6: 29 I said unto her o' the next day, Give
31 head of Elisha...shall stand o' him
7: 2 lord o' whose hand the king leaned
17 the lord o' whose hand he leaned to
8: 12 their strong holds wilt thou set o' fire,
15 And it came to pass o' the morrow,
15 in water, and spread it o' his face,
9: 3 box of oil, and pour it o' his head,
6 and he poured the oil o' his head,
13 it under him o' the top of the stairs,
17 watchman o' the tower in Jezreel,
18 went one o' horseback to meet him,
19 sent out a second o' horseback, which
32 and said, Who is o' my side? who?
33 o' the wall, and o' the horses.
10: 3 and set him o' his father's throne,
15 he lighted o' Jehonadab the son of
30 shall sit o' the throne of Israel.
11: 5 of you that enter in o' the sabbath shall
7 of all you that go forth o' the sabbath,
9 that were to come in o' the sabbath,
9 that should go out o' the sabbath,
16 they laid hands o' her; and she went
19 he sat o' the throne of the kings.
12: 9 o' the right side as one cometh into
15 money to be bestowed o' workmen:
13: 21 revived, and stood up o' his feet.
23 had compassion o' them, and had
14: 4 and burnt incense o' the high places.
20 And they brought him o' horses:
15: 4 burnt incense still o' the high places.
12 shall sit o' the throne of Israel
16: 4 o' the hills, and under every green
14 put it o' the north side of the altar.
18: 14 which thou puttest o' me will I bear.
20 o' whom dost thou trust, that thou
21 o' which if a man lean, it will go into
21 of Egypt unto all that trust o' him.
23 be able o' thy part to set riders upon
24 put thy trust o' Egypt for chariots
26 of the people that are o' the wall.
27 me to the men which sit o' the wall,
19: 22 and lifted up thine eyes o' high?
26 as the grass o' the house tops, and as
20: 5 o' the third day thou shalt go up unto
7 laid it o' the boil, and he recovered.
23: 8 which were o' a man's left hand at
12 were o' the top of the upper chamber
13 were o' the right hand of the mount
25: 3 o' the ninth day of the fourth month
8 o' the seventh day of the month,
27 o' the seven and twentieth day of the
1Ch 4: 10 And Jabez called o' the God of Israel,
6: 32 then they waited o' their office
39 Asaph, who stood o' his right hand,
44 of Merari stood o' the left hand:
49 offering, and o' the altar of incense,
78 o' the other side Jordan by Jericho,
78 o' the east of Jordan, were given them
10: 5 fell likewise o'...sword, and died.

1Ch 10: 8 And it came to pass o' the morrow,
12: 18 Thine are we, David, and o' thy side,
37 And o' the other side of Jordan, of the
40 brought bread o' asses, and o' camels,
40 and o' mules, and o' oxen, and meat,
13: 6 Lord,...whose name is called o' it.
14: 2 his kingdom was lifted up o' high,
15: 20 with psalteries o' Alamoth;
21 harps o' the Sheminith to excel.
16: 7 o' that day David delivered first this
18: 7 were o' the servants of Hadarezer,
20: 6 six o' each hand, and six o' each foot:
21: 17 be o' me and o' my father's house:
17 not o' thy people, that they should be
22: 18 he not given you rest o' every side?
23: 28 was to wait o' the sons of Aaron
31 the new moons, and o' the set feasts,
26: 30 them of Israel o' this side Jordan
29: 15 our days o' the earth are as a
21 the Lord, o' the morrow after that day,
22 and drink before the Lord o' that day
23 Solomon sat o' the throne of the
25 o' any king before him in Israel.
2Ch 2: 4 o' the sabbaths, and o' the new moons,
4 and o' the solemn feasts of the Lord
3: 7 and graved cherubims o' the walls.
13 they stood o' their feet, and their
15 chapiter that was o' the top of each
16 put them o' the heads of the pillars;
16 and put them o' the chains.
17 the pillars...one o' the right hand,
17 and the other o' the left; and called
17 name of that o' the right hand Jachin,
17 and the name of that o' the left Boaz.
4: 6 lavers, and put five o' the right hand,
6 and five o' the left, to wash in them:
7 candlesticks...five o' the right hand,
7 and five o' the left.
8 ten tables,...five o' the right side,
8 and five o' the left.
10 he set the sea o' the right side of the
12 were o' the top of the two pillars,
12 which were o' the top of the pillars;
13 pomegranates o' the two wreaths;
13 rows of pomegranates o' each wreath,
6: 10 and am set o' the throne of Israel,
18 deed dwell with men o' the earth?
7: 6 the priests waited o' their offices:
10 o' the three and twentieth day of the
22 of Egypt, and laid hold o' other gods,
8: 12 offerings unto the Lord o' the altar
13 o' the sabbaths, and o' the new moons,
13 and o' the solemn feasts, three times
9: 8 in thee to set thee o' his throne,
18 stays o' each side of the sitting place,
19 twelve lions stood there o' the one side
19 and o' the other upon the six steps.
10: 12 came to Rehoboam o' the third day,
12 Come again to me o' the third day.
11: 12 strong, having Judah...o' his side.
14: 7 he hath given us rest o' every side.
11 for we rest o' thee, and in thy
16: 7 thou hast relied o' the king of Syria,
7 and not relied o' the Lord thy God,
8 because thou didst rely o' the Lord,
17: 19 These waited o' the king, beside
18: 9 sat either of them o' his throne,
18 o' [5921] his right hand and o' his left.
24 Behold, thou shalt see o' that day
29 battle; but put thou o' thy robes.
20: 2 from beyond the sea o' this side Syria;
19 of Israel with a loud voice o' high.
26 And o' the fourth day they assembled
29 of God was o' all the kingdoms
23: 4 part of you entering o' the sabbath,
8 that were to come in o' the sabbath,
8 that were to go out o' the sabbath:
15 So they laid hands o' her; and when
24: 25 slew him o' his bed, and he died:
26: 15 o' the towers and upon the bulwarks,
27: 3 o' the wall of Ophel he built much.
28: 4 o' the hills, and under every green
29: 17 began o' the first day of the first month
17 o' the eighth day of the month came
21 offer them o' the altar of the Lord.
22 the blood, and sprinkled it o' the altar:
30: 15 o' the fourteenth day of the second
32: 15 nor persuade you o' this manner,
17 to rail o' the Lord God of Israel,
18 of Jerusalem that were o' the wall,
22 other, and guided them o' every side.
33: 14 o' the west side of Gihon, in the valley,
34: 4 that were o' high above them,
35: 1 o' the fourteenth day of the first
36: 15 o' his people, and o' his dwelling
Ezr 4: 10 the rest that are o' this side the river,
11 the men o' this side the river, and
16 have no portion o' this side the river.
5: 3, 6 governor o' this side the river, and
6 which were o' this side the river, sent
8 the walls, and this work goeth fast o',
6: 13 Tatnai, governor o' this side the river,
15 o' the third day of the month Adar,
7: 9 and o' the first day of the fifth month
8: 31 o' the twelfth day of the first month,
33 Now o' the fourth day was the silver
36 the governors o' this side the river:
10: 9 o' the twentieth day of the month;
Ne 2: 14 went o' to the gate of the fountain,
3: 7 of the governor o' this side the river.
13 cubits o' the wall unto the dung gate.
4: 13 the wall, and o' the higher places,
17 They which builded o' the wall, and
22 a guard to us, and labour o' the day.
6: 14 and o' the prophetess Noadiah, and
8: 4 and Maaseiah, o' his right hand;

Ne 8: 4 and o' his left hand, Pedaiah, and
13 And o' the second day were gathered
18 and o' the eighth day was a solemn
9: 10 Pharaoh, and o' all his servants,
10 and o' all the people of his land:
11 the midst of the sea o' the dry land;
32 that hath come upon us, o' our kings,
32 o' our princes, and o' our priests, and
32 o' our prophets, and o' our fathers,
32 and o' all thy people, since the time
10: 31 victuals o' the sabbath day to sell,
31 o' the sabbath, or o' the hold day:
12: 31 went o' the right hand upon the wall
13: 1 O' that day they read in the book of
15 treading wine presses o' the sabbath,
15 into Jerusalem o' the sabbath day:
16 sold o' the sabbath unto the children
19 be brought in o' the sabbath day.
21 ye do so again, I will lay hands o' you.
21 came they no more o' the sabbath.
Es 1: 2 Ahasuerus sat o' the throne of his
10 O' the seventh day, when the heart of
11 beauty: for she was fair to look o'.
2: 14 o' the morrow she returned into the
21 to lay hand o' the king Ahasuerus.
23 they were both hanged o' a tree:
3: 6 scorn to lay hands o' Mordecai alone;
12 o' the thirteenth day of the first
4: 1 and put o' sackcloth with ashes,
5: 1 Now it came to pass o' the third day,
1 Esther put o' her royal apparel,
6: 1 O' that night could not the king sleep.
2 to lay hand o' the king Ahasuerus.
4 to hang Mordecai o' the gallows
9 bring him o' horseback through
11 brought him o' horseback through
7: 2 said unto Esther o' the second day
10 hanged Haman o' the gallows
8: 1 O' that day did the king Ahasuerus
9 Sivan, o' the three and twentieth day
10 sent letters by posts o' horseback,
10 riders o' mules, camels, and young
13 avenge themselves o' their enemies.
14 hastened and pressed o' by the king's
9: 1 o' the thirteenth day of the same,
2 to lay hand o' such as sought their
10 o' the spoil laid they not their hand.
11 O' that day the number of those that
15 o' the fourteenth day also of the
15 o' the prey they laid not their hand.
16 they laid not their hands o' the prey.
17 O' the thirteenth day of the month
17 o' the fourteenth day of the same
18 together o' the thirteenth day thereof,
18 and o' the fourteenth day thereof;
18 and o' the fifteenth day of the same
25 should be hanged o' the gallows.
Job 1: 10 about all that he hath o' every side?
4: 13 when deep sleep falleth o' men,
5: 11 set up o' high those that be low;
9: 11 he passeth o' also, but I perceive
13: 13 and let come o' me what will.
15: 26 runneth upon him, even o' his neck,
27 maketh collops of fat o' his flanks.
16: 16 and o' my eyelids is the shadow of
19 heaven, and my record is o' high.
17: 9 righteous also shall hold o' his way,
18: 11 shall make him afraid o' every side,
19: 10 He hath destroyed me o' every side,
21: 3 and after that I have spoken, mock o'.
6 trembling taketh hold o' my flesh.
23: 9 O' the left hand, where he doth work,
9 he hideth himself o' the right hand,
24: 20 the worm shall feed sweetly o' him;
27: 17 but the just shall put it o', and the
20 Terrors take hold o' him as waters,
29: 9 and laid their hand o' their mouth.
14 I put o' righteousness, and it
24 If I laughed o' them, they believed
31: 2 of the Almighty from o' high?
36: 2 I have yet to speak o' God's behalf.
7 with kings are they o' the throne;
16 which should be set o' thy table
17 judgment and justice take hold o' thee.
37: 6 to the snow, Be thou o' the earth;
39: 18 time she lifteth up herself o' high,
21 goeth o' to meet the armed men.
27 command, and make her nest o' high?
28 She dwelleth and abideth o' the rock,
40: 12 Look o' every one that is proud, and
Ps 4: *title* To the chief Musician o' Neginoth,
6: *title* To the chief Musician o' Neginoth
7: 7 therefore return thou o' high.
12: 8 The wicked walk o' every side, when
21: 3 a crown of pure gold o' his head.
22: 8 He trusted o' the Lord that he
25: 3 that wait o' thee be ashamed:
5 o' thee do I wait all the day.
21 preserve me; for I wait o' thee.
27: 14 Wait o' the Lord: be of good
14 heart: wait, I say, o' the Lord.
31: 13 fear was o' every side: while they took
35: 17 Lord, how long wilt thou look o'?
37: 34 Wait o' the Lord, and keep his
48: 2 mount Zion, o' the sides of the north,
49: 14 the grave; death shall feed o' them;
52: 9 and I will wait o' thy name: for
54: *title* To the chief Musician o' Neginoth,
55: *title* To the chief Musician o' Neginoth,
57: 4 even among them that are set o' fire,
63: 6 meditate o' thee in the night watches.
65: 12 the little hills rejoice o' every side.
66: 6 went through the flood o' foot:
67: *title* To the chief Musician o' Neginoth,
68: 18 Thou hast ascended o' high, thou
21 one as goeth o' still in his trespasses.

Ps 68:25 the players o' instruments followed
69: 6 Let not them that wait o' thee, O
29 salvation, O God, set me up o' high.
71:21 and comfort me o' every side.
75: 5 Lift not up your horn o' high:
76: *title* To the chief Musician o' Neginoth,
78:53 And he led them o' safely so that
79: 1 they have laid Jerusalem o' heaps.
81: 3 appointed, o' our solemn feast day.
82: 5 they walk o' in darkness: all the
83:14 the flame setteth the mountains o' fire:
87: 7 players o' instruments shall be there:
91:14 I will set him o' high, because he hath
92:11 shall see my desire o' mine enemies,
93: 4 The Lord o' high is mightier than
104:32 He looketh o' the earth, and it
107:41 Yet setteth he the poor o' high from
113: 5 Lord our God, who dwelleth o' high,
118: 6 The Lord is o' my side; I will not fear:
119:59 I thought o' my ways, and turned my
84 thou execute judgment o' them that
143 and anguish have taken hold o' me:
124: 1, 2 been the Lord who was o' our side,
142: 4 I looked o' my right hand, and beheld,
143: 5 I meditate o' all thy works;
5 I muse o' the work of thy hands.
Pr 4:25 Let thine eyes look right o', and let
5: 5 to death; her steps take hold o' hell.
9:14 o' a seat in the high places of the
15 who go right o' their ways:
14:21 he that hath mercy o' the poor, happy
31 honoureth him hath mercy o' the poor.
15:14 mouth of fools feedeth o' foolishness.
20:22 but wait o' the Lord, and he shall
22: 3 simple pass o', and are punished.
27:12 simple pass o', and are punished.
18 he that waiteth o' his master
Ec 2: 3 and to lay hold o' folly, till I might see
11 I looked o' all the works that my hands
11 o' the labour that I had laboured to do:
4: 1 o' the side of their oppressors there
Ca 2:12 The flowers appear o' the earth; the
3: 1 By night o' my bed I sought him
5: 3 off my coat; how shall I put it o'?
Isa 7:25 o' all hills that shall be digged with
9:17 have mercy o' their fatherless and
20 he shall snatch o' the right hand,
20 and he shall eat o' the left hand,
10:12 upon mount Zion and o' Jerusalem,
11: 8 shall play o' the hole of the asp,
8 put his hand o' the cockatrice' den.
13:18 have no pity o' the fruit of the womb;
14: 1 the Lord will have mercy o' Jacob,
15: 2 o' all their heads shall be baldness,
3 o' the tops of their houses, and in
16:12 Moab is weary o' the high place,
18: 3 the world, and dwellers o' the earth,
3 lifteth up an ensign o' the mountains;
22:16 him out a sepulchre o' high,
24:18 the windows from o' high are open,
21 of the high ones that are o' high,
25: 6 fat things, a feast of wine o' the lees,
6 of wines o' the lees well refined.
26: 3 peace, whose mind is stayed o' thee:
5 down them that dwell o' high;
27:11 the women come, and set them o' fire:
11 them will not have mercy o' them,
28: 1 are o' the head of the fat valleys of
4 is o' the head of the fat valley,
20 that a man can stretch himself o' it:
30:17 and as an ensign o' an hill.
31: 1 and stay o' horses, and trust in
4 the young lion roaring o' his prey,
32:15 be poured upon us from o' high,
19 shall hail, coming down o' the forest;
33: 5 exalted; for he dwelleth o' high:
16 He shall dwell o' high: his place of
36: 5 now o' whom dost thou trust, that
6 of this broken reed, o' Egypt;
8 be able o' thy part to set riders upon
9 put thy trust o' Egypt for chariots
11 of the people that are o' the wall.
37:23 and lifted up thine eyes o' high?
27 as the grass o' the housetops, and as
40:26 Lift up your eyes o' high, and
42:25 it hath set him o' fire round about,
44:20 He feedeth o' ashes: a deceived heart
47: 1 of Babylon, sit o' the ground:
48:14 he will do his pleasure o' Babylon, and
14 and his arm shall be o' the Chaldeans.
49:10 hath mercy o' them shall lead them,
15 compassion o' the son of her womb?
18 bind them o' thee, as a bride doeth.
51: 5 and o' mine arm shall they trust.
9 put o' strength, O arm of the Lord;
52: 1 awake; put o' thy strength, O Zion;
1 put o' thy beautiful garments, O
53: 6 hath laid o' him the iniquity of us all.
54: 3 forth o' the right hand and o' the left;
8 kindness will I have mercy o' thee,
10 the Lord that hath mercy o' thee.
56: 2 the son of man that layeth hold o' it;
57:17 he went o' frowardly in the way
58: 4 your voice to be heard o' high.
13 doing thy pleasure o' my holy day;
59:17 For he put o' righteousness as a
17 put o' the garments of vengeance
60: 7 up with acceptance o' mine altar,
10 in my favour have I had mercy o' thee.
63: 7 all that the Lord hath bestowed o' us,
7 which he hath bestowed o' them
Jer 4: 7 destroyer of the Gentiles is o' his way;
5: 9, 29 soul be avenged o' such a nation
6:23 They shall lay hold o' bow and spear;
25 of the enemy and fear is o' every side.
7:29 up a lamentation o' high places;

Jer 8:13 there shall be no grapes o' the vine,
13 nor figs o' the fig tree, and the leaf
21 astonishment hath taken hold o' me.
9: 9 my soul be avenged o' such a nation
10:25 the families that call not o' thy name:
11:20 let me see thy vengeance o' them: for
12:15 and have compassion o' them, and will
13: 2 girdle...and put it o' my loins.
27 thine abominations o' the hills in
15:10 I have neither lent o' usury, nor men
10 nor men have lent to me o' usury; yet
17:11 As the partridge sitteth o' eggs, and
21 bear no burden o' the sabbath day,
22 out of your houses o' the sabbath day,
24 gates of this city o' the sabbath day,
25 riding in chariots and o' horses, they,
27 gates of Jerusalem o' the sabbath day;
18: 3 he wrought a work o' the wheels.
20: 3 And it came to pass o' the morrow,
10 defaming of many, fear o' every side.
10 and we shall take our revenge o' him.
12 let me see thy vengeance o' them:
22: 4 riding in chariots and o' horses, he,
23:12 they shall be driven o', and fall
25:29 to bring evil o' the city which is called
30 The Lord shall roar from o' high,
30: 6 man with his hands o' his loins,
18 and have mercy o' his dwellingplaces;
31:29 children's teeth are set o' edge.
30 grape, his teeth shall be set o' edge.
32:29 shall come and set fire o' this city,
33:26 to return, and have mercy o' them.
36:22 there was a fire o' the hearth burning
23 into the fire that was o' the hearth.
23 in the fire that was o' the hearth.
38:22 Thy friends have set thee o', and
43: 3 of Neriah setteth thee o' against us,
12 as a shepherd putteth o' his garment;
46: 4 spears, and put o' the brigandines.
48:11 and he hath settled o' his lees, and
49:23 there is sorrow o' the sea; it cannot be
24 flee, and fear hath seized o' her:
29 cry unto them, Fear is o' every side.
50: 6 turned them away o' the mountains:
19 he shall feed o' Carmel and Bashan,
52:23 and six pomegranates o' a side;
La 1: 2 and her tears are o' her cheeks:
2:21 young and the old lie o' the ground in
4: 6 moment, and no hands stayed o' her.
Eze 1: 8 their wings o' their four sides;
10 the face of a lion, o' the right side:
10 had the face of an ox o' the left side;
23 two, which covered o' this side,
23 two, which covered o' that side,
3:23 of Chebar: and I fell o' my face.
4: 6 lie again o' thy right side, and thou
7:16 and shall be o' the mountains like
11:23 which is o' the east side of the city.
16:11 thy hands, and a chain o' thy neck.
12 I put a jewel o' thy forehead, and
15 fornications o' every one that passed
33 they may come unto thee o' every side
18: 2 children's teeth are set o' edge?
19: 8 nations set against him o' every side
21:16 o' the right hand, or o' the left,
23: 5 doted o' her lovers, o' the Assyrians
7 and with all o' whom she doted:
22 bring them against thee o' every side;
24: 3 Set o' a pot, set it o', and also pour
10 Heap o' wood, kindle the fire, consume
17 put o' thy shoes upon thy feet, and
25: 9 his cities which are o' his frontiers,
26:17 their terror to be o' all that haunt it!
28:23 by the sword upon her o' every side;
31: 4 the deep set him o' high with her rivers
33:32 and can play well o' an instrument:
36: 3 and swallowed you up o' every side,
37:21 and will gather them o' every side,
39: 6 I will send a fire o' Magog, and among
9 shall set o' fire and burn the weapons,
11 the passengers o' the east of the sea:
17 gather yourselves o' every side to my
40: 2 was as the frame of a city o' the south.
5 a wall o' the outside of the house
10 three o' this side, and three o' that.
10 measure o' this side and o' that side.
12 was one cubit o' this side, and the
12 space was one cubit o' that side:
12 chambers were six cubits o' this side,
12 and six cubits o' that side.
21 three o' this side and three o' that side;
26 it had palm trees, one o' this side,
26 and another o' that side, upon the
34, 37 o' this side, and o' that side:
39 the gate were two tables o' this side,
39 and two tables o' that side, to slay
40 o' the other side, which was at the
41 Four tables were o' this side, and four
41 tables o' that side, by the side of the
48 of the porch, five cubits o' this side,
48 and five cubits o' that side:
48 the gate was three cubits o' this side,
48 and three cubits o' that side.
49 pillars by the posts, one o' this side,
49 and another o' that side.
41: 1 posts, six cubits broad o' the one side,
1 and six cubits broad o' the other side,
2 door were five cubits o' the one side,
2 and five cubits o' the other side: and
5, 10 round about the house o' every side.
15 o' the one side and o' the other side,
16 round about o' their three stories,
19 toward the palm tree o' the one side,
19 toward the palm tree o' the other side:
20 made, and o' the wall of the temple.
25 o' them, o' the doors of the temple,

Eze 41:26 o' the one side and o' the other side,
26 o' the sides of the porch, and upon
42: 7 court o' the forepart of the chambers,
9 was the entry o' the east side, as one
14 and shall put o' other garments,
43:20 and put it o' the four horns of it,
20 and o' the four corners of the settle,
22 o' the second day thou shalt offer a kid
44:19 they shall put o' other garments;
45: 7 o' the one side and o' the other side of
46: 1 but o' the sabbath it shall be opened,
12 offerings, as he did o' the sabbath day:
19 was a place o' the two sides westward.
47: 2 there ran out waters o' the right side.
2 trees o' the one side and o' the other.
12 o' this side and o' that side, shall
48:16 o' the east side four thousand and
30 goings out of the city o' the north side,
Da 3:27 the smell of fire had passed o' them.
6:14 set his heart o' Daniel to deliver
7: 5 it raised up itself o' one side, and it
8: 5 west o' the face of the whole earth,
18 I was in a deep sleep o' my face
10: 9 was I in a deep sleep o' my face, and
11:17 she shall not stand o' his side, neither
31 And arms shall stand o' his part, and
12: 5 one o' this side of the bank of the
5 o' that side of the bank of the river.
Ho 4: 8 set their heart o' their iniquity.
5: 1 ye have been a snare o' Mizpah, and
6: 3 if we follow o' to know the Lord:
10: 5 priests thereof that rejoiced o' it,
8 thistle shall come up o' their altars;
8 Cover us; and to the hills, Fall o' us.
11: 4 that take off the yoke o' their jaws,
6 the sword shall abide o' his cities,
12: 1 Ephraim feedeth o' wind, and
6 and wait o' thy God continually.
Joe 2: 5 chariots o' the tops of mountains
7 shall march every one o' his ways,
32 shall call o' the name of the Lord
Am 1: 7 I will send a fire o' the wall of Gaza,
10 I will send a fire o' the wall of Tyrus,
2: 7 of the earth o' the head of the poor,
5:19 leaned his hand o' the wall, and a
Ob 11 that thou stoodest o' the other side,
12 have looked o' the day of thy brother
13 not have looked o' their affliction
13 have laid hands o' their substance
21 saviours shall come up o' mount Zion
Jon 3: 5 put o' sackcloth, from the greatest
4: 5 and sat o' the east side of the city, and
10 Thou hast had pity o' the gourd,
Mic 2:13 and the Lord o' the head of them.
Na 1: 2 will take vengeance o' his adversaries,
Hab 1:13 evil, and canst not look o' iniquity:
2: 9 that he may set his nest o' high,
15 mayest look o' their nakedness!
16 spewing shall be o' thy glory.
3:10 and lifted up his hands o' high.
19 singer o' my stringed instruments.
Zep 1: 9 those that leap o' the threshold,
12 men that are settled o' their lees:
Zec 1:12 thou not have mercy o' Jerusalem
12 and o' the cities of Judah,
5: 3 cut off as o' this side according to it;
3 cut off as o' that side according to it.
10: 5 riders o' horses shall be confounded.
12: 6 o' the right hand and o' the left:
13: 9 they shall call o' my name, and I will
14: 4 which is before Jerusalem o' the east,
13 every one o' the hand of his neighbour,
Mal 1:10 kindle fire o' mine altar for nought.
M't 1:18 of Jesus Christ was o' this wise.
20 while he thought o' these things,
4: 5 him o' a pinnacle of the temple,
21 And going o' from thence, he saw
5:14 A city that is set o' an hill cannot
15 a bushel, but o' a candlestick;
28 whosoever looketh o' a woman to
39 shall smite thee o' thy right cheek,
45 to rise o' the evil and...the good,
45 the evil and o' the good, and sendeth
45 rain o' the just and...the unjust.
45 the just and o' the unjust.
6:25 your body, what ye shall put o'.
9: 2 sick of the palsy, lying o' a bed:
6 hath power o' earth to forgive sins,
27 Thou son of David, have mercy o' us.
36 moved with compassion o' them,
10:29 them shall not fall o' the ground
34 I am come to send peace o' earth:
12: 1 that time Jesus went o' the sabbath
5 that o' the sabbath days the priests
10 it lawful to heal o' the sabbath days?
11 if it fall into a pit o' the sabbath day,
11 will he not lay hold o' it, and lift it out?
12 lawful to do well o' the sabbath days.
13: 2 whole multitude stood o' the shore.
14: 3 For Herod had laid hold o' John,
13 followed him o' foot out of...cities.
19 multitude to sit down o' the grass,
25 went unto them, walking o' the sea.
26 disciples saw him walking o' the sea.
28 bid me come unto thee o' the water.
29 walked o' the water, to go to Jesus.
15:22 Have mercy o' me, O Lord, thou son
32 have compassion o' the multitude,
35 multitude to sit down o' the ground.
16:19 whatsoever thou shalt bind o' earth
19 whatsoever thou shalt loose o' earth
17: 6 they fell o' their face, and were sore
15 Lord, have mercy o' my son: for he is
18:18 Whatsoever ye shall bind o' earth,
18 whatsoever ye shall loose o' earth,
19 if two of you shall agree o' earth as

M't 18:28 and he laid hands o' him, and took
33 had compassion o' thy fellow servant,
33 even as I had pity o' thee?
19:13 he should put his hands o' them,
15 And he laid his hands o' them, and
20:21 sit, the one o' thy right hand,
21 and the other o' the left, in thy
23 sit o' my right hand, and o' my left,
30, 31 Have mercy o' us, O Lord, thou
34 So Jesus had compassion o' them, and
21: 7 and put o' them their clothes, and
19 fruit grow o' thee henceforward
38 and let us seize o' his inheritance.
44 whosoever shall fall o' this stone
44 o' whomsoever it shall fall, it will
46 when they sought to lay hands o' him,
22:11 had not o' a wedding garment:
40 O' these two commandments hang
44 Sit thou o' my right hand, till I
23: 4 and lay them o' men's shoulders;
24:17 is o' the housetop not come down
20 winter, neither o' the sabbath day:
25:33 set the sheep o' his right hand,
33 right hand, but the goats o' the left.
34 say unto them o' his right hand,
41 say also unto them o' the left hand,
26: 5 Not o' the feast day, lest there be
7 poured it o' his head, as he sat at
12 poured this ointment o' my body,
39 and fell o' his face, and prayed,
45 Sleep o' now, and take your rest:
50 they, and laid hands o' Jesus,
55 the temple, and ye laid no hold o' me.
57 they that had laid hold o' Jesus led
64 sitting o' the right hand of power,
27:19 was set down o' the judgment seat,
25 blood be o' us, and o' our children.
28 him, and put o' him a scarlet robe.
30 reed, and smote him o' the head.
31 and put his own raiment o' him,
38 with him, one o' the right hand,
38 right hand, and another o' the left.
48 vinegar, and put it o' a reed, and
M'r 1:21 o' the sabbath day he entered into
2:10 hath power o' earth to forgive sins,
12 We never saw it o' this fashion.
21 of new cloth o' an old garment:
23 the corn fields o' the sabbath day;
24 why do they o' the sabbath day that
3: 2 would heal him o' the sabbath day;
4 lawful to do good o' the sabbath days,
5 had looked round about o' them with
9 that a small ship should wait o' him
21 of it, they went out to lay hold o' him:
34 looked round about o' them which sat
4: 1 was by the sea o' the land.
5 And some fell o' stony ground,
8 And other fell o' good ground,
16 which are sown o' stony ground;
20 which are sown o' good ground;
21 and not to be set o' a candlestick?
38 part of the ship, asleep o' a pillow:
5:19 and hath had compassion o' thee.
23 thee, come and lay thy hands o' her,
6: 9 sandals; and not put o' two coats.
21 Herod o' his birthday made a supper
47 the sea, and he alone o' the land.
8: 2 I have compassion o' the multitude,
6 people to sit down o' the ground:
23 when he had spit o' his eyes, and
33 about and looked o' his disciples,
9: 3 no fuller o' earth can white them.
20 he fell o' the ground, and wallowed
22 have compassion o' us, and help us.
40 is not against us is o' our part.
10:37 we may sit, one o' thy right hand,
37 other o' thy left hand, in thy glory.
40 But to sit o' my right hand and
40 o' my left hand is not mine to give;
47 thou son of David, have mercy o' me.
48 Thou son of David, have mercy o' me.
11: 7 and cast their garments o' him;
12 o' the morrow, when they were come
12:12 And they sought to lay hold o' him,
36 Sit thou o' my right hand, till I
13:15 that is o' the housetop not go down
14: 2 Not o' the feast day, lest there be
3 box, and poured it o' his head.
6 hath wrought a good work o' me.
35 and fell o' the ground, and prayed
41 Sleep o' now, and take your rest:
46 they laid their hands o' him, and
51 and the young men laid hold o' him:
62 sitting o' the right hand of power,
65 And some began to spit o' him, and
15:19 they smote him o' the head with a reed,
20 and put his own clothes o' him, and
27 thieves; the one o' his right hand,
27 hand, and the other o' his left.
29 that passed by railed o' him, wagging
36 of vinegar, and put it o' a reed, and
40 were also women looking o' afar off:
16: 5 young man sitting o' the right side,
18 they shall lay hands o' the sick,
19 and sat o' the right hand of God.
Lu 1:11 standing o' the right side of the altar
25 the days wherein he looked o' me,
50 his mercy is o' them that fear him
59 o' the eighth day they came to
65 fear came o' all that dwelt round
78 the dayspring from o' high hath visited
2:14 o' earth peace, good will toward
4: 9 set him o' a pinnacle of the temple,
16 the synagogue o' the sabbath day,
20 the synagogue were fastened o' him.
31 taught them o' the sabbath days.

Lu 5:12 who seeing Jesus fell o' his face,
17 it came to pass o' a certain day,
6: 1 came to pass o' the second sabbath
2 lawful to do o' the sabbath days?
6 to pass also o' another sabbath,
7 he would heal o' the sabbath day;
9 lawful o' the sabbath days to do good,
20 lifted up his eyes o' his disciples,
29 him smiteth thee o' the one cheek
48 and laid the foundation o' a rock:
7:13 saw her, he had compassion o' her,
16 And there came a fear o' all: and they
40 thee. And he saith, Master, say o'.
8: 8 And other fell o' good ground, and
13 They o' the rock are they, which,
15 that o' the good ground are they,
16 but setteth it o' a candlestick,
22 it came to pass o' a certain day,
23 down a storm of wind o' the lake;
32 swine feeding o' the mountain:
9:37 came to pass, that o' the next day,
10:11 which cleaveth o' us, we do wipe off
19 tread o' serpents and scorpions,
31 him, he passed by o' the other side.
32 at the place, came and looked o' him,
32 and passed by o' the other side.
33 saw him, he had compassion o' him,
34 and set him o' his own beast, and
35 o' the morrow when he departed,
37 He that shewed mercy o' him.
11:33 a bushel, but o' a candlestick,
12:22 for the body, what ye shall put o'.
49 am come to send fire o' the earth;
51 I am come to give peace o' earth?
13: 7 come seeking fruit o' this fig tree,
10 of the synagogues o' the sabbath.
13 And he laid his hands o' her: and
14 that Jesus had healed o' the sabbath
14 be healed, and not o' the sabbath day.
15 o' the sabbath loose his ox or his ass
16 from this bond o' the sabbath day?
14: 1 Pharisees to eat bread o' the sabbath
3 Is it lawful to heal o' the sabbath day?
5 pull him out o' the sabbath day?
15: 5 he layeth it o' his shoulders,
20 and fell o' his neck, and kissed him.
22 the best robe, and put it o' him;
22 o' his hand, and shoes o' his feet:
16:24 Father Abraham, have mercy o' me,
17:13 said, Jesus, Master, have mercy o' us.
16 fell down o' his face at his feet,
18: 8 shall he find faith o' the earth?
32 spitefully entreated,...spitted o':
38 thou son of David, have mercy o' me.
39 Thou Son of David, have mercy o' me.
19:43 and keep thee in o' every side,
20: 1 to pass, that o' one of those days,
18 o' whomsoever it shall fall, it will
19 hour sought to lay hands o' him;
42 my Lord, Sit thou o' my right hand,
21:12 they shall lay their hands o' you,
26 which are coming o' the earth.
35 dwell o' the face of the whole earth.
22:21 betrayeth me is with me o' the table.
30 o' thrones judging the twelve tribes
64 they struck him o' the face, and
69 sit o' the right hand of the power
23:26 and o' him they laid the cross, that
30 say to the mountains, Fall o' us;
33 malefactors, one o' the right hand,
33 right hand, and the other o' the left.
39 which were hanged railed o' him,
54 preparation,...the sabbath drew o'.
24:49 be endued with power from o' high.
Joh 1:12 to them that believe o' his name:
33 descending, and remaining o' him,
2:11 and his disciples believed o' him.
3:18 believeth o' him is not condemned:
36 believeth o' the Son hath everlasting
36 the wrath of God abideth o' him.
4: 6 his journey, sat thus o' the well:
35 up your eyes, and look o' the fields;
39 the Samaritans...believed o' him
5: 9 o' the same day was the sabbath.
16 these things o' the sabbath day.
24 and believeth o' him that sent me,
6: 2 he did o' them that were diseased.
19 they see Jesus walking o' the sea,
22 which stood o' the other side of the sea
25 found him o' the other side of the sea,
29 believe o' him whom he hath sent.
35 believeth o' me shall never thirst.
40 seeth the Son, and believeth o' him,
47 believeth o' me hath everlasting
7:22 ye o' the sabbath day circumcise
23 a man o' the sabbath day receive
23 whit whole o' the sabbath day?
30 but no man laid hands o' him,
31 of the people believed on him,
38 He that believeth o' me, as the
39 that believe o' him should receive:
44 but no man laid hands o' him.
48 of the Pharisees believed o' him?
8: 6 with his finger wrote o' the ground,
8 down, and wrote o' the ground.
20 and no man laid hands o' him; for his
30 these words, many believed o' him.
31 to those Jews which believed o' him,
9: 6 spat o' the ground, and made clay
35 thou believe o' the Son of God?
36 Lord, that I might believe o' him?
10:42 And many believed o' him there.
11:45 which Jesus did, believed o' him.
48 alone, all men will believe o' him:
12:11 went away, and believed o' Jesus.
12 O' the next day much people that

Joh 12:15 cometh, sitting o' an ass's colt.
37 them, yet they believed not o' him:
42 rulers also many believed o' him;
44 and said, He that believeth o' me,
44 believeth not o' me, but o' him that
46 believeth o' me should not abide in
13:22 the disciples looked one o' another,
23 leaning o' Jesus' bosom one of his
25 He then lying o' Jesus' breast
14:12 He that believeth o' me, the works
16: 9 sin, because they believe not o' me;
17: 4 I have glorified thee o' the earth:
20 believe o' me through their word;
19: 2 of thorns, and put it o' his head,
2 and they put o' him a purple robe,
18 other with him, o' either side one,
19 a title, and put it o' the cross.
31 upon the cross o' the sabbath day,
37 look o' him whom they pierced.
20:22 had said this, he breathed o' them,
21: 1 and o' this wise shewed he himself.
4 come, Jesus stood o' the shore:
6 net o' the right side of the ship,
20 also leaned o' his breast at supper,
Ac 2:18 And o' my servants and
18 o' my handmaidens I will pour
21 shall call o' the name of the Lord
25 for he is o' my right hand, that I
30 up Christ to sit o' his throne;
34 Lord, Sit thou o' my right hand,
3: 4 him with John, said, Look o' us.
12 or why look ye so earnestly o' us,
4: 3 they laid hands o' them, and put
5 And it came to pass o' the morrow,
22 o' whom this miracle of healing
5: 5 great fear came o' all them that
15 and laid them o' beds and couches,
18 laid their hands o' the apostles,
30 whom ye slew and hanged o' a tree.
6: 6 prayed, they laid...hands o' them.
15 council, looking stedfastly o' him,
7: 5 no, not so much as to set his foot o':
6 And God spake o' this wise, That his
54 gnashed o' him with their teeth.
55 standing o' the right hand of God,
56 standing o' the right hand of God.
8:17 laid they their hands o' them,
18 laying o' of the apostles' hands
19 o' whomsoever I lay hands, he may
36 And as they went o' their way,
39 and he went o' his way rejoicing.
9:12 putting his hand o' him, that he
14 to bind all that call o' thy name.
17 and putting his hands o' him said,
21 called o' this name in Jerusalem,
10: 4 And when he looked o' him, he was
7 soldier of them that waited o' him
9 O' the morrow, as they went o' their
19 While Peter thought o' the vision,
23 o' the morrow Peter went away with
39 they slew and hanged o' a tree:
44 Holy Ghost fell o' all them which
45 o' the Gentiles also was poured out
11:15 Holy Ghost fell o' them, as o' us at
17 us, who believed o' the Lord Jesus
12: 7 he smote Peter o' the side, and raised
8 thyself, and bind o' thy sandals.
10 out, and passed o' through one street;
13: 3 and laid their hands o' them,
9 Holy Ghost, set his eyes o' him,
11 fell o' him a mist and a darkness;
14 into the synagogue o' the sabbath day,
15 exhortation for the people, say o'.
34 he said o' this wise, I will give you
36 fell o' sleep, and was laid unto his
14:10 voice, Stand upright o' thy feet.
23 the Lord, o' whom they believed.
15: 3 being brought o' their way by the
16:13 o' the sabbath we went out of the city
31 Believe o' the Lord Jesus Christ,
17: 5 and set all the city o' an uproar,
26 to dwell o' all the face of the earth,
18: 8 believed o' the Lord with all his
10 man shall set o' thee to hurt thee:
19: 4 believe o' him which should come
4 after him, that is, o' Christ Jesus.
6 the Holy Ghost came o' them; and
16 the evil spirit was leaped o' them,
17 fear fell o' them all, and the name
20: 7 them, ready to depart o' the morrow;
10 Paul went down, and fell o' him,
37 wept sore, and fell o' Paul's neck,
21: 3 Cyprus, we left it o' the left hand,
5 brought us o' our way, with wives
5 we kneeled down o' the shore, and
23 men which have a vow o' them;
27 the people, and laid hands o' him,
40 licence Paul stood o' the stairs,
22:16 calling o' the name of the Lord.
19 them that believed o' thee:
30 O' the morrow, because he would
23: 2 by him to smite him o' the mouth.
24 beasts, that they may set Paul o',
32 O' the morrow they left the horsemen
25: 6 day sitting o' the judgment seat
17 any delay o' the morrow I sat
17 I sat o' the judgment seat,
23 o' the morrow, when Agrippa was
27:20 and no small tempest lay o' us,
33 while the day was coming o', Paul
44 And the rest, some o' boards,
44 some o' broken pieces of the ship.
28: 3 of sticks, and laid them o' the fire,
3 the heat, and fastened o' his hand.
4 venomous beast hang o' his hand,
8 laid his hands o' him, and healed

Ro 4: 5 believeth o' him that justifieth the
24 if we believe o' him that raised up
9: 15 I will have mercy o' whom I will
15 will have compassion o' whom I will
18 hath he mercy o' whom he will have
23 his glory o' the vessels of mercy,
33 whosoever believeth o' him shall
10: 6 is of faith speaketh o' this wise, Say
11 Whosoever believeth o' him shall
14 they call o' him in whom they have
11: 22 God: o' them which fell, severity;
12: 7 let us wait o' our ministering:
7 or he that teacheth, o' teaching;
8 he that exhorteth, o' exhortation:
20 shalt heap coals of fire o' his head.
13: 12 let us put o' the armour of light.
14 put ye o' the Lord Jesus Christ,
15: 3 that reproached thee fell o' me.
24 be brought o' my way thitherward
16: 6 who bestowed much labour o' us.
19 am glad therefore o' your behalf:
1Co 1: 4 my God always o' your behalf, for
11: 10 woman to have power o' her head
14: 25 so falling down o' his face he will
15: 53 must put o' incorruption,
53 this mortal must put o' immortality.
54 shall have put o' incorruption,
54 mortal shall have put o' immortality,
16: 6 bring me o' my journey whithersoever
17 that which was lacking o' your part
2Co 1: 11 be given by many o' our behalf.
16 be brought o' my way toward Judæa.
4: 8 We are troubled o' every side, yet
5: 12 occasion to glory o' our behalf,
6: 7 o' the right hand and o' the left,
7: 5 but we were troubled o' every side;
8: 1 o' the churches of Macedonia;
24 and of our boasting o' your behalf.
10: 7 ye look o' things after the outward
11: 20 if a man smite you o' the face.
Ga 3: 13 is every one that hangeth o' a tree:
14 might come o' the Gentiles
27 into Christ have put o' Christ.
6: 16 peace be o' them, and mercy, and
Eph 1: 10 in heaven, and which are o' earth;
4: 8 When he ascended up o' high, he
24 And that ye put o' the new man,
6: 3 thou mayest live long o' the earth.
11 Put o' the whole armour of God,
14 o' the breastplate of righteousness;
Ph'p 1: 29 not only to believe o' him, but also
2: 4 not every man o' his own things, but
4 every man also o' the things of others.
27 mercy o' him; and not o' him only,
27 o' me also, lest I should have sorrow
4: 8 be any praise, think o' these things.
Col 3: 1 sitteth o' the right hand of God.
2 affection o' things above, not o' things
2 things above, not...o' the earth.
6 o' the children of disobedience:
10 And have put o' the new man, which
12 Put o' therefore, as the elect of God,
14 above all these things put o' charity,
1Th 5: 8 putting o' the breastplate of faith
2Th 1: 8 vengeance o' them that know not God,
1Ti 1: 16 believe o' him to life everlasting.
18 prophecies...went before o' thee,
3: 16 believed o' in the world, received up
5: 22 Lay hands suddenly o' no man,
6: 12 lay hold o' eternal life, whereunto
19 they may lay hold o' eternal life.
2Ti 1: 6 thee by the putting o' of my hands.
2: 22 call o' the Lord out of a pure heart.
Tit 3: 6 Which he shed o' us abundantly
13 lawyer and Apollos o' their journey
Ph'm 18 ought, put that o' mine account;
Heb 1: 3 sat down o' the right hand of the
3 right hand of the Majesty o' high;
13 Sit o' my right hand, until I make
2: 16 not o' him the nature of angels;
16 took o' him the seed of Abraham.
4: 4 place of the seventh day o' this wise,
5: 2 can have compassion o' the ignorant,
2 and o' them that are out of the way;
6: 1 let us go o' unto perfection; not
2 baptisms, and of laying o' of hands,
8: 1 o' the right hand of the throne of
4 if he were o' the earth, he should
9: 10 carnal ordinances, imposed o' them
10: 12 sat down o' the right hand of God;
11: 13 strangers and pilgrims o'...earth.
12: 25 refused him that spoke o' earth,
Jas 3: 6 and setteth o' fire the cause of nature;
6 of nature; and it is set o' fire of hell.
4: 14 know not what shall be o' the morrow.
5: 5 have lived in pleasure o' the earth,
17 and it rained not o' the earth by the
1Pe 1: 17 And if ye call o' the Father, who
2: 6 that believeth o' him shall not be
24 our sins in his own body o' the tree,
3: 3 of gold, or of putting o' of apparel;
22 and is o' the right hand of God;
4: 14 o' their part he is evil spoken of,
14 but o' your part he is glorified.
16 let him glorify God o' this behalf.
2Pe 3: 12 being o' fire shall be dissolved,
1Jo 3: 23 should believe o' the name of his Son
5: 10 He that believeth o' the Son of God
13 13 believe o' the name of the Son
3Jo 6 if thou bring forward o' their journey
Jude 20 up yourselves o' your most holy faith,
Re 1: 10 was in the Spirit o' the Lord's day,
3: 3 I will come o' thee as a thief, and
4: 2 heaven, and one sat o' the throne.
4 had o' their heads crowns of gold.
9 thanks to him that sat o' the throne,

Re 4: 10 before him that sat o' the throne,
5: 1 hand of him that sat o' the throne
1 written within and o' the backside,
10 and we shall reign o' the earth.
13 is in heaven, and o' the earth, and
6: 2 and he that sat o' him had a bow;
5 he that sat o' him had a pair of
8 name that sat o' him was Death,
10 o' [575] them that dwell o'...earth?
16 the mountains and rocks, Fall o' us,
16 of him that sitteth o' the throne,
7: 1 angels standing o' the four corners
1 wind should not blow o' the earth,
1 the earth, nor o' the sea, nor
1 the sea, nor o' any tree.
11 before the throne o' their faces,
15 he that sitteth o' the throne shall
16 neither shall the sun light o' them,
9: 7 and o' their heads were as it were
17 and them that sat o' them, having
10: 2 sea, and his left foot o' the earth,
11: 10 them that dwelt o' the earth.
16 which sat before God o' their seats,
13: 13 down from heaven o' the earth in
14 them that dwell o' the earth by
14 to them that dwell o' the earth,
14: 1 a Lamb stood o' the mount Sion,
6 unto them that dwell o' the earth,
14 having o' his head a golden crown,
15 voice to him that sat o' the cloud,
16 And he that sat o' the cloud thrust
16 thrust in his sickle o' the earth;
15: 2 stand o' the sea of glass, having
17: 8 dwell o' the earth shall wonder,
9 o' which the woman sitteth.
18: 19 they cast dust o' their heads, and
20 for God hath avenged you o' her.
19: 4 God that sat o' the throne, saying,
12 and o' his head were many crowns;
16 hath o' his vesture and o' his thigh
18 and of them that sit o' them, and
19 against him that sat o' the horse,
20: 2 he laid hold o' the dragon, that old
6 o' such the second death hath no
9 up o' the breadth of the earth,
11 white throne, and him that sat o' it,
21: 13 O' the east three gates;
13 o' the north three gates;
13 o' the south three gates;
13 and o' the west three gates.
22: 2 and o' either side of the river, was

On (*on*)
Ge 41: 45 daughter of Poti-pherah priest of O'.
50 daughter of Poti-pherah priest of O'
46: 20 daughter of Poti-pherah priest of O'
Nu 16: 1 and O', the son of Peleth, sons of

Onam (*o'-nam*)
Ge 36: 23 and Ebal, Shepho, and O'.
1Ch 1: 40 and Ebal, Shephi, and O'.
2: 26 Atarah; she was the mother of O'.
28 the sons of O' were, Shammai, and

Onan (*o'-nan*)
Ge 38: 4 a son; and she called his name O'.
8 Judah said unto O', Go in unto thy
9 O' knew that the seed should not be
46: 12 the sons of Judah; Er, and O', and
12 and O' died in the land of Canaan.
Nu 26: 19 The sons of Judah were Er and O':
19 and O' died in the land of Canaan.
1Ch 2: 3 The sons of Judah; Er, and O', and

once
Ge 18: 32 and I will speak yet but this o':
Ex 10: 17 I pray thee, my sin only this o',
30: 10 upon the horns of it o' in a year
10 o' in the year shall he make
Le 16: 34 of Israel for all their sins o' a year.
Nu 13: 30 Let us go up at o', and possess it;
De 7: 22 mayest not consume them at o',
Jos 6: 3 and go round about the city o'.
11 compassed the city, going about it o':
14 day they compassed the city o',
J'g 6: 39 me, and I will speak but this o':
39 prove,...but this o' with the fleece;
16: 18 Come up this o', for he hath shewed
28 me, I pray thee, only this o', O God,
28 be at o' avenged of the Philistines
1Sa 26: 8 spear even to the earth at o',
1Ki 10: 22 o' in three years came the navy of
2Ki 6: 10 saved himself there, not o' nor twice.
2Ch 9: 21 every three years o' came the ships
Ne 5: 18 and o' in ten days store of all sorts
13: 20 lodged without Jerusalem o' or
Job 33: 14 For God speaketh o', yea twice, yet
40: 5 O' have I spoken; but I will not
Ps 62: 11 God hath spoken o'; twice have I
74: 6 carved work thereof at o' with axes
76: 7 in thy sight when o' thou art angry?
89: 35 O' have I sworn by my holiness that
Pr 28: 18 perverse in his ways shall fall at o'.
Isa 42: 14 I will destroy and devour at o'.
66: 8 or shall a nation be born at o'?
Jer 10: 18 inhabitants of the land at this o',
13: 27 made clean? when shall it o' be?
16: 21 I will this o' cause them to know,
Hag 2: 6 Yet o', it is a little while, and I will
Lu 13: 25 When o' the master of the house is risen
23: 18 they cried out all at o', saying,
Ro 6: 10 that he died, he died unto sin o':
7: 9 I was alive without the law o': but
1Co 15: 6 above five hundred brethren at o';
2Co 11: 25 I beaten with rods, o' was I stoned,
Ga 1: 23 the faith which o' he destroyed.
Eph 5: 3 let it not be o' named among you,
Ph'p 4: 16 o' and again unto my necessity.
1Th 2: 18 unto you, even I Paul, o' and again;

Heb 6: 4 for those who were o' enlightened,
7: 27 for this he did o', when he offered
9: 7 the high priest alone o' every year,
12 he entered in o' into the holy place,
26 o' in the end of the world hath he
27 it is appointed unto men o' to die,
28 So Christ was o' offered to bear the
10: 2 worshippers o' purged should have
10 the body of Jesus Christ o' for all.
12: 26 o' more I shake not the earth only,
27 this word, Yet o' more, signifieth the
1Pe 3: 18 Christ also hath o' suffered for sins,
20 when o' the longsuffering of God
Jude 3 faith which was o' delivered unto the
5 though ye o' knew this, how that the

one^ See also NONE; ONE'S; ONES.
Ge 1: 9 be gathered together unto o' place,
2: 21 he took o' of his ribs, and closed up
24 his wife: and they shall be o' flesh.
3: 6 a tree to be desired to make o' wise,
22 the man is become as o' of us, to
4: 14 every o' that findeth me shall slay
19 the name of the o' was Adah, and
10: 5 every o' after his tongue, after their
8 began to be a mighty o' in the earth.
25 sons: the name of o' was Peleg;
11: 1 was of o' language, and of o' speech.
3 they said o' to another, Go to, let us
6 Lord said, Behold, the people is o',
6 and they have all o' language; and
7 not understand o' another's speech.
13: 11 themselves the o' from the other.
14: 13 And there came o' that had escaped,
15: 3 lo, o' born in my house is mine heir.
10 laid each piece o' against another:
19: 9 This o' fellow came in to sojourn,
14 But he seemed as o' that mocked
20 to flee unto, and it is a little o':
20 escape thither, (is it not a little o'?)
21: 15 cast the child under o' of the shrubs.
22: 2 upon o' of the mountains which I
25: 23 the o' people shall be stronger than
26: 10 o' of the people might lightly have
26 and Ahuzzath o' of his friends, and
31 morning, and sware o' to another:
27: 29 cursed be every o' that curseth thee,
38 Hast thou but o' blessing, my
45 deprived also of you both in o' day?
30: 33 every o' that is not speckled and
35 and every o' that had some white in it,
31: 49 when we are absent o' from another.
32: 8 If Esau come to the o' company,
33: 13 if men should overdrive them o' day,
34: 14 sister to o' that is uncircumcised;
16 you, and we will become o' people.
22 dwell with us, to be o' people,
37: 19 they said o' to another, Behold, this
38: 28 that the o' put out his hand: and
40: 5 each man his dream in o' night,
41: 5 ears of corn came up upon o' stalk,
11 And we dreamed a dream in o' night,
22 seven ears came up in o' stalk, full
25 The dream of Pharaoh is o': God
26 are seven years: the dream is o'.
38 Can we find such a o' as this is, a man
42: 1 sons, Why do ye look o' upon another?
11 We are all o' man's sons; we are
13 the sons of o' man in the land of
13 day with our father, and o' is not.
16 Send o' of you, and let him fetch
19 let o' of your brethren be bound in
21 And they said o' to another, We are
27 And as o' of them opened his sack
28 saying o' to another, What is this
32 o' is not, and the youngest is this
33 leave o' of your brethren here with
43: 33 the men marvelled o' at another.
44: 20 and a child of his old age, a little o';
28 And the o' went out from me, and
47: 21 to cities from o' end of the borders
48: 1 o' told Joseph, Behold, thy father is
2 o' told Jacob, and said, Behold, thy son
22 given to thee o' portion above thy
49: 16 people, as o' of the tribes of Israel.
28 every o' according to his blessing
Ex 1: 15 the name of the o' was Shiphrah,
2: 6 This is o' of the Hebrews' children.
11 smiting an Hebrew, o' of his brethren.
6: 25 o' of the daughters of Putiel to wife;
8: 31 his people; there remained not o'.
9: 6 of the children of Israel died not o'.
7 not o' of the cattle of the Israelites
10: 5 o' cannot be able to see the earth:
19 remained not o' locust in all the
23 They saw not o' another, neither
11: 1 o' plague more upon Pharaoh,
12: 18 until the o' and twentieth day of the
30 house where there was not o' dead.
46 In o' house shall it be eaten; thou
48 shall be as o' that is born in the land:
49 O' law shall be to him that is
14: 7 and captains over every o' of them.
20 o' came not near the other all the
28 remained not so much as o' of them.
16: 15 they said o' to another, It is manna:
22 much bread, two omers for o' man:
17: 12 o' [259] on the o' side, and the other
18: 3 the name of the o' was Gershom;
16 I judge between o' and another,
21: 18 and o' smite another with a stone, or
35 And if o' man's ox hurt another's,
23: 29 out from before thee in o' year;
24: 3 the people answered with o' voice,
25: 12 two rings shall be in the o' side of it,
19 make o' [259] cherub on the o' end,
20 their faces shall look o' to another;

Ex 25:32 of the candlestick out of the o' side,
33 a knop and a flower in o' branch;
36 shall be o' beaten work of pure gold.
26: 2 length of o' curtain shall be eight
2 breadth of o' curtain four cubits:
2 every o' of the curtains shall have
2 the curtains shall have o' measure.
3 be coupled together o' to another;
3 shall be coupled o' to another.
4 blue upon the edge of the o' curtain
5 shalt thou make in the o' curtain,
5 loops may take hold o' of another.
6 taches: and it shall be o' tabernacle.
8 length of o' curtain shall be thirty
8 breadth of o' curtain four cubits:
8 curtains shall be all of o' measure.
10 loops on the edge of the o' curtain
11 the tent together, that it may be o'.
13 And a cubit on the o' side, and a cubit
16 shall be the breadth of o' board.
17 tenons shall there be in o' board.
17 set in order o' against another:
19 two sockets under o' board for his
21 two sockets under o' board, and two
24 above the head of it unto o' ring:
25 two sockets under o' board, and two
26 of the o' side of the tabernacle,
27: 9 an hundred cubits long for o' side:
14 The hangings of o' side of the gate
28:10 Six of their names on o' stone, and
21 every o' with his name shall they be
29: 1 Take o' young bullock, and two
3 thou shalt put them into o' basket,
15 Thou shalt also take o' ram; and
23 o' loaf of bread, and o' cake of oiled
23 and o' wafer out of the basket of the
39 The o' lamb thou shalt offer in the
40 And with the o' lamb a tenth deal of
30:13 every o' that passeth among them that
14 Every o' that passeth among them
31:14 every o' that defileth it shall surely be
32:15 on the o' side and on the other were
33: 7 that every o' which sought the Lord
34:15 and o' call thee, and thou eat of his
35:21 every o' whose heart stirred him up,
21 and every o' whom his spirit made
24 Every o' that did offer an offering of
36: 2 even every o' whose heart stirred him
9 length of o' curtain was twenty and
9 breadth of o' curtain four cubits:
9 the curtains were all of o' size.
10 the five curtains o' unto another:
10 curtains he coupled o' unto another.
11 loops of blue on the edge of o' curtain
12 Fifty loops made he in o' curtain,
12 the loops held o' curtain to another.
13 coupled the curtains o' unto another
13 taches: so it became o' tabernacle.
15 of o' curtain was thirty cubits,
15 cubits was the breadth of o' curtain:
15 the eleven curtains were of o' size.
18 the tent together, that it might be o'.
21 breadth of a board o' cubit and a half.
22 O' board had two tenons, equally
22 equally distant o' from another:
24 under o' board for his two tenons,
26 silver; two sockets under o' board,
29 at the head thereof, to o' ring:
31 of the o' side of the tabernacle,
33 boards from the o' end to the other.
37: 3 even two rings upon the o' side of it,
6 o' cubit and half the breadth thereof.
7 beaten out of o' piece made he them,
8 O' cherub on the end on this side,
9 seat, with their faces o' to another;
18 candlestick out of the o' side thereof,
19 fashion of almonds in o' branch,
22 it was o' beaten work of pure gold.
38:14 The hangings of the o' side of the gate
26 every o' that went to be numbered,
39:14 of a signet, every o' with his name,
Le 4:27 if any o' of the common people sin
5: 4 then he shall be guilty in o' of these.
5 shall be guilty in o' of these things,
7 o' for a sin offering, and the other
13 sin that he hath sinned in o' of these,
6:18 every o' that toucheth them shall be
7: 7 there is o' law for them: the priest
10 Aaron have, o' as much as another.
14 offer o' out of the whole oblation
8:26 he took o' unleavened cake, and a
26 a cake of oiled bread, and o' wafer,
12: 8 the o' for the burnt offering, and the
13: 2 or unto o' of his sons the priests:
14: 5 that o' of the birds be killed
10 and o' ewe lamb of the first year
10 mingled with oil, and o' log of oil.
12 And the priest shall take o' he lamb,
21 take o' lamb for a trespass offering
21 o' tenth deal of fine flour mingled
22 the o' shall be a sin offering, and the
30 shall offer the o' of the turtledoves,
31 the o' for a sin offering, and the
50 And he shall kill the o' of the birds
15:15 the o' for a sin offering, and the
30 shall offer the o' for a sin offering,
16: 5 and o' ram for a burnt offering.
8 o' lot for the Lord, and the other lot
27 o' carry forth without the camp;
29 whether it be o' of your own country,
17:15 whether it be o' of your own country,
18:30 any o' of these abominable customs,
19: 8 every o' that eateth it shall bear his
11 falsely, neither lie o' to another.
34 be unto you as o' born among you,
20: 9 every o' that curseth his father or
Le 22:28 kill it and her young both in o' day.
23:18 and o' young bullock, and two rams:
19 ye shall sacrifice o' kid of the goats
24: 5 two tenth deals shall be in o' cake.
22 Ye shall have o' manner of law, as
22 stranger, as for o' of your own country:
25:14 ye shall not oppress o' another:
17 not therefore oppress o' another;
46 shall not rule o' over another with
48 o' of his brethren may redeem him:
26:26 shall bake your bread in o' oven,
37 And they shall fall o' upon another,
Nu 1: 4 every o' head of the house of his
41 were forty and o' thousand and
44 each o' was for the house of his
2:16 fifty and o' thousand and four
28 forty and o' thousand and five
34 every o' after their families,
4:19 appoint them every o' to his service
30, 35, 39, 43 every o' that entereth into
47 every o' that came to do the service
49 every o' according to his service,
5: 2 and every o' that hath an issue, and
6:11 shall offer the o' for a sin offering,
14 o' he lamb of the first year without
14 o' ewe lamb of the first year without
14 o' ram without blemish for peace
19 and o' unleavened cake out of the
19 and o' unleavened wafer, and shall
7: 3 of the princes, and for each o' an ox:
13 his offering was o' silver charger,
13 o' silver bowl of seventy shekels,
14 O' spoon of ten shekels of gold, full
15 O' young bullock, o' ram, o' lamb
16 O' kid of the goats for a sin offering:
19 for his offering o' silver charger,
19 o' silver bowl of seventy shekels,
20 O' spoon of gold of ten shekels, full
21 O' young bullock, o' ram, o' lamb
22 O' kid of the goats for a sin offering:
25 His offering was o' silver charger,
25 o' silver bowl of seventy shekels,
26 O' golden spoon of ten shekels, full
27 O' young bullock, o' ram, o' lamb
28 O' kid of the goats for a sin offering:
31 His offering was o' silver charger of
31 o' silver bowl of seventy shekels,
32 O' golden spoon of ten shekels, full
33 O' young bullock, o' ram, o' lamb
34 O' kid of the goats for a sin offering:
37 His offering was o' silver charger,
37 o' silver bowl of seventy shekels,
38 O' golden spoon of ten shekels, full
39 O' young bullock, o' ram, o' lamb
40 O' kid of the goats for a sin offering:
43 His offering was o' silver charger
44 O' golden spoon of ten shekels, full
45 O' young bullock, o' ram, o' lamb
46 O' kid of the goats for a sin offering:
49 His offering was o' silver charger
49 o' silver bowl of seventy shekels,
50 O' golden spoon of ten shekels, full
51 O' young bullock, o' ram, o' lamb
52 O' kid of the goats for a sin offering:
55 His offering was o' silver charger of
55 o' silver bowl of seventy shekels,
56 O' golden spoon of ten shekels, full
57 O' young bullock, o' ram, o' lamb
58 O' kid of the goats for a sin offering:
61 His offering was o' silver charger,
61 o' silver bowl of seventy shekels,
62 O' golden spoon of ten shekels, full
63 O' young bullock, o' ram, o' lamb
64 O' kid of the goats for a sin offering:
67 His offering was o' silver charger,
67 o' silver bowl of seventy shekels,
68 O' golden spoon of ten shekels, full
69 O' young bullock, o' ram, o' lamb
70 O' kid of the goats for a sin offering:
73 His offering was o' silver charger,
73 o' silver bowl of seventy shekels,
74 O' golden spoon of ten shekels, full
75 O' young bullock, o' ram, o' lamb
76 O' kid of the goats for a sin offering:
79 His offering was o' silver charger,
79 o' silver bowl of seventy shekels,
80 O' golden spoon of ten shekels, full
81 O' young bullock, o' ram, o' lamb
82 O' kid of the goats for a sin offering:
89 the voice of o' speaking unto him
8:12 shalt offer the o' for a sin offering,
9:14 ye shall have o' ordinance, both for
10: 4 if they blow but with o' trumpet,
11:19 Ye shall not eat o' day, nor two days,
26 the name of the o' was Eldad, and
28 o' of his young men, answered and
12:12 Let her not be as o' dead, of whom
13: 2 man, every o' a ruler among them.
23 a branch with o' cluster of grapes,
14: 4 And they said o' to another, Let us
15 shalt kill all this people as o' man,
15: 5 offering or sacrifice, for o' lamb.
11 be done for o' bullock, or for o' ram,
12 ye do to every o' according to their
15 O' ordinance shall be both for you
16 O' law and o' manner shall be for
24 o' young bullock for a burnt offering,
24 o' kid of the goats for a sin offering.
29 o' law for him that sinneth through
16: 3 the congregation are holy, every o'
15 I have not taken o' ass from them,
15 neither have I hurt o' of them.
22 shall o' man sin, and wilt thou be
17: 3 o' rod shall be for the head of the
6 every o' of their princes gave him a
6 a rod apiece, for each prince o',
Nu 18:11 every o' that is clean in thy house
13 every o' that is clean in thine house
19: 3 and o' shall slay her before his face:
5 o' shall burn the heifer in his sight;
16 whosoever toucheth o' that is slain
18 bone, or o' slain, or o' dead, or a grave:
21: 8 that every o' that is bitten, when he
25: 5 Slay ye every o' his men that were
6 o' of the children of Israel came and
26:54 to every o' shall his inheritance be
28: 4 The o' lamb shalt thou offer in the
7 fourth part of an hin for the o' lamb:
11 and o' ram, seven lambs of the first
12 mingled with oil, for o' bullock;
12 mingled with oil, for o' ram;
13 for a meat offering unto o' lamb;
15 o' kid of the goats for a sin offering
19 o' ram, and seven lambs of the first
22 o' goat for a sin offering, to make
27 o' ram, seven lambs of the first year;
28 three tenth deals unto o' bullock,
28 two tenth deals unto o' ram,
29 A several tenth deal unto o' lamb,
30 And o' kid of the goats, to make an
29: 2 o' young bullock, o' ram, and seven
4 And o' tenth deal for
4 tenth deal for o' lamb, throughout
5 o' kid of the goats for a sin offering,
8 o' young bullock, o' ram, and seven
9 and two tenth deals to o' ram,
10 A several tenth deal for o' lamb,
11 O' kid of the goats for a sin offering;
16, 19 And o' kid of the goats for a sin
22 o' goat for a sin offering; beside the
25 o' kid of the goats for a sin offering;
28, 31, 34 And o' goat for a sin offering;
36 o' bullock, o' ram, seven lambs of
38 o' goat for a sin offering; beside the
31:28 o' soul of five hundred, both of the
30 thou shalt take o' portion of fifty, of
34 threescore and o' thousand asses,
39 Lord's tribute was threescore and o'.
47 Moses took o' portion of fifty, both
49 and there lacketh not o' man of us,
34:18 shall take o' prince of every tribe,
35: 8 every o' shall give of his cities unto
15 o' that killeth any person unawares
30 o' witness shall not testify against
36: 7 for every o' of the children of Israel
8 be wife unto o' of the family of the
9 remove from o' tribe to another tribe;
9 every o' of the tribes of the children
De 1:22 ye came near unto me every o' of you,
23 twelve men of you, o' of a tribe:
35 there shall not o' of these men of
2:36 there was not o' city too strong for us:
4: 4 are alive every o' of you this day.
32 from the o' side of heaven unto the
42 that fleeing unto o' of these cities he
6: 4 Israel: The Lord our God is o' Lord:
12:14 Lord shall choose in o' of thy tribes,
13: 7 from the o' end of the earth even unto
12 shalt hear say in o' of thy cities,
15: 7 a poor man of o' of thy brethren
17: 6 at the mouth of o' witness he shall
15 o' from among thy brethren shalt thou
18:10 any o' that maketh his son or his
19: 5 he shall flee unto o' of those cities,
11 die, and fleeth into o' of these cities:
15 O' witness shall not rise up against
21:15 two wives, o' beloved, and another
23:16 he shall choose in o' of thy gates,
24: 5 but he shall be free at home o' year,
25: 5 dwell together, and o' of them die,
11 men strive together o' with another,
11 and the wife of the o' draweth near
28: 7 shall come out against thee o' way,
25 shalt go out o' way against them,
57 And toward her young o' that cometh
32:30 How should o' chase a thousand,
33: 3 every o' shall receive of thy words.
8 and thy Urim be with thy holy o',
Jos 9: 2 and with Israel, with o' accord.
10: 2 a great city, as o' of the royal cities,
42 land did Joshua take at o' time,
12: 9 The king of Jericho, o';
9 of Ai, which is beside Beth-el, o';
10 The king of Jerusalem, o';
10 the king of Hebron, o';
11 The king of Jarmuth, o';
11 the king of Lachish, o';
12 The king of Eglon, o';
12 the king of Gezer, o';
13 The king of Debir, o';
13 the king of Geder, o';
14 The king of Hormah, o';
14 the king of Arad, o';
15 The king of Libnah, o';
15 the king of Adullam, o';
16 The king of Makkedah, o';
16 the king of Beth-el, o';
17 The king of Tappuah, o';
17 the king of Hepher, o';
18 The king of Aphek, o';
18 the king of Lasharon, o';
19 The king of Madon, o';
19 the king of Hazor, o';
20 The king of Shimron-meron, o';
20 the king of Achshaph, o';
21 The king of Taanach, o';
21 the king of Megiddo, o';
22 The king of Kedesh, o';
22 the king of Jokneam of Carmel, o';
23 king of Dor in the coast of Dor, o';
23 the king of the nations of Gilgal, o';
24 The king of Tirzah, o';

Jos 12:24 all the kings thirty and o'.
13:31 to the o' half of the children of Machir
17:14 Why hast thou given me but o' lot
14 and o' portion to inherit, seeing I
17 thou shalt not have o' lot only:
20: 4 that doth flee unto o' of those cities
21:42 cities were every o' with their suburbs
22: 7 the o' half of the tribe of Manasseh
14 each o' was an head of the house of
23:10 O' man of you shall chase a
14 not o' thing hath failed of all the
14 and not o' thing hath failed thereof.
J'g 6:16 smite the Midianites as o' man.
29 they said o' to another, Who hath
31 because o' hath cast down his altar.
7: 5 Every o' that lappeth of the water
5 every o' that boweth down upon his
8:18 each o' resembled the children of a
9: 2 over you, or that o' reign over you?
5 and ten persons, upon o' stone:
18 and ten persons, upon o' stone,
10:18 princes of Gilead said o' to another,
11:35 thou art o' of them that trouble me:
12: 7 was buried in o' of the cities of Gilead.
16: 5 will give thee every o' of us eleven
29 of the o' with his right hand, and of
17: 5 and consecrated o' of his sons, who
11 man was unto him as o' of his sons.
18:19 be a priest unto the house of o' man,
19:13 let us draw near to o' of these places
20: 1 was gathered together as o' man,
8 And all the people arose as o' man,
11 the city, knit together as o' man.
16 every o' could sling stones at an hair
31 o' goeth up to the house of God,
21: 3 be to day o' tribe lacking in Israel?
6 o' tribe cut off from Israel this day.
8 What o' is there of the tribes of
Ru 1: 4 the name of the o' was Orpah, and
2:13 like unto o' of thine handmaidens.
20 kin unto us, o' of our next kinsmen.
3:14 rose up before o' could know another.
4: 1 Ho, such a o'! turn aside, sit down
1Sa 1: 2 the name of the o' was Hannah,
24 and o' ephah of flour, and a bottle of
2:25 If o' man sin against another, the
34 in o' day they shall die both of them.
36 every o' that is left in thine house
36 thee, into o' of the priests' offices,
3:11 every o' that heareth it shall tingle.
6: 4 for o' plague was on you all, and on
17 the Lord; for Ashdod o', for Gaza o',
17 Askelon o', for Gath o', for Ekron o';
9: 3 now o' of the servants with thee,
10: 3 o' carrying three kids, and another
11 people said o' to another, What is
12 o' of the same place answered and
11: 7 and they came out with o' consent.
13: 1 Saul reigned o' year; and when he had
17 o' company turned unto the way
14: 4 was a sharp rock on the o' side,
4 the name of the o' was Bozez, and
5 The forefront of the o' was situate
16 they went on beating down o' another.
28 Then answered o' of the people, and
40 Be ye on o' side, and I and Jonathan
45 there shall not o' hair of his head fall
16:18 Then answered o' of the servants,
17: 3 stood on a mountain on the o' side,
7 o' bearing a shield went before him.
36 Philistine shall be as o' of them,
18: 7 women answered o' another as they
21 my son in law in the o' of the twain.
19:22 And o' said, Behold, they be at Naioth
20:15 every o' from the face of the earth.
41 times: and they kissed o' another,
41 wept o' with another, until David
21:11 did they not sing o' to another of him
22: 2 And every o' that was in distress,
2 and every o' that was in debt, and
2 and every o' that was discontented,
7 son of Jesse give every o' of you fields
20 o' of the sons of Ahimelech the son
25:14 o' of the young men told Abigail,
26:15 came o' of the people in to destroy
22 let o' of the young men come over
27: 1 perish o' day by the hand of Saul:
29: 5 they sang o' to another in dances,
2Sa 1:15 David called o' of the young men,
2:13 the o'[428] on the o' side of the pool,
16 And they caught every o' his fellow
21 thee hold on o' of the young men,
25 and became o' troop, and stood on
27 every o' from following his brother.
3:13 o' thing I require of thee, that is,
29 house of Joab o' that hath an issue,
4: 2 the name of the o' was Baanah,
10 When o' told me, saying, Behold, Saul
6:19 as men, to every o' a cake of bread,
19 departed every o' to his house.
20 o' of the vain fellows shamelessly
7:23 what o' nation in the earth is like
8: 2 and with o' full line to keep alive.
9:11 at my table, as o' of the king's sons.
10: 4 and shaved off o' half of their beards,
11: 3 o' said, Is not this Bath-sheba, the
25 the sword devoureth o' as well as
12: 1 There were two men in o' city; the
1 city; the o' rich, and the other poor.
3 had nothing, save o' little ewe lamb,
13:13 shalt be as o' of the fools in Israel.
30 sons, and there is not o' of them left.
14: 6 but the o' smote the other, and slew
11 not o' hair of thy son fall to the earth.
12 speak o' word unto my lord the king.
13 speak this thing as o' which is faulty,

2Sa 14:27 and o' daughter, whose name was
15: 2 Thy servant is o' of the tribes of
31 And o' told David, saying, Ahithophel
17:12 there shall not be left so much as o'.
13 be not o' small stone found there.
22 lacked not o' of them that was not
18:17 all Israel fled every o' to his tent.
19: 7 not tarry o' with thee this night:
14 Judah, even as the heart of o' man;
20:11 And o' of Joab's men stood by him,
12 every o' that came by him stood still.
19 I am o' of them that are peaceable and
23: 8 hundred, whom he slew at o' time.
9 o' of the three mighty men with David,
15 Oh that o' would give me drink of the
24 brother of Joab was o' of the thirty;
24:12 choose thee o' of them, that I may
1Ki 1:48 hath given o' to sit on my throne this
2:16 I ask o' petition of thee, deny me
20 I desire o' small petition of thee;
3:17 And the o' woman said, O my lord,
17 I and this woman dwell in o' house;
23 The o' saith, This is my son that
25 half to the o', and half to the other.
4:22 Solomon's provision for o' day was
6:24 five cubits was the o' wing of the
24 from the uttermost part of the o' wing
25 were of o' measure and o' size.
26 of the o' cherub was ten cubits, and
27 so that the wing of the o' touched
27 touched the o' wall, and the wing
27 touched o' another in the midst of
34 leaves of the o' door were folding,
7: 7 from o' side of the floor to the other.
16 of the o' chapiter was five cubits,
17 seven for the o' chapiter, and seven
18 round about upon the o' network,
23 cubits from the o' brim to the other:
27 cubits was the length of o' base,
34 to the four corners of o' base: and
36 to the proportion of every o',
37 o' casting, o' measure, and o' size.
38 o' laver contained forty baths: and
38 upon every o' of the ten bases o' laver.
42 of pomegranates for o' network,
44 o' sea, and twelve oxen under the
8:56 o' word of all his good promise,
9: 8 every o' that passeth by it shall be
10:14 that came to Solomon in o' year
16 shekels of gold went to o' target.
17 pound of gold went to o' shield:
20 twelve lions stood...on the o' side
11:13 give o' tribe to thy son for David my
32 have o' tribe for my servant David's
36 And unto his son will I give o' tribe,
12:29 And he set the o' in Beth-el, and the
30 went to worship before the o', even
13:33 and he became o' of the priests of the
14:21 was forty and o' years old when he
15:10 And forty and o' years reigned he in
16:11 left him not o' that pisseth against a
18: 6 Ahab went o' way by himself, and
23 choose o' bullock for themselves,
25 you o' bullock for yourselves, and
40 of Baal; let not o' of them escape.
19: 2 not thy life as the life of o' of them
20:20 And they slew every o' his man:
29 thousand footmen in o' day.
22: 8 There is yet o' man, Micaiah the
13 good unto the king with o' mouth:
13 thee, be like the word of o' of them,
20 And o' said on this manner, and
28 Hearken, O people, every o' of you.
38 o' washed the chariot in the pool of
2Ki 3:11 o' of the king of Israel's servants
23 and they have smitten o' another:
4:22 o' of the young men, and o' of the
39 o' went out into the field to gather
5: 4 o' went in, and told his lord, saying,
6: 3 o' said, Be content, I pray thee, and
5 as o' was felling a beam, the axe
12 o' of his servants said, None, my
7: 3 they said o' to another, Why sit we
6 and they said o' to another, Lo, the
8 they went into o' tent, and did eat
9 they said o' to another, We do not
13 o' of his servants answered and
8:26 he reigned o' year in Jerusalem.
9: 1 prophet called o' of the children of
11 and o' said unto him, Is all well?
18 went o' on horseback to meet him,
10:21 was full from o' end to another.
12: 4 of every o' that passeth the account,
9 side as o' cometh into the house of
14: 8 let us look o' another in the face.
11 looked o' another in the face at
23 and reigned forty and o' years.
17:27 Carry thither o' of the priests whom
28 Then o' of the priests whom they
18:24 turn away the face of o' captain of
31 vine, and every o' of his fig tree,
31 drink ye every o' the waters of his
21:16 Jerusalem from o' end to another;
22: 1 thirty and o' years in Jerusalem.
23:35 every o' according to his taxation,
24:18 was twenty and o' years old when he
25:16 two pillars, o' sea, and the bases
17 height of the o' pillar was eighteen
1Ch 1:19 sons: the name of the o' Peleg;
9:31 Mattithiah, o' of the Levites,
10:13 of o' that had a familiar spirit,
11:11 hundred slain by him at o' time.
12 who was o' of the three mighties.
17 o' would give me drink of the water
12:14 o' of the least was over an hundred,
25 war, seven thousand and o' hundred.

1Ch 12:38 of o' heart to make David king.
16: 3 And he dealt to every o' of Israel,
3 to every o' a loaf of bread, and a
20 from o' kingdom to another people;
17: 5 and from o' tabernacle to another.
21 what o' nation in the earth is like
21:10 things: choose thee o' of them, that
23:11 therefore they were in o' reckoning,
24: 5 divided by lot, o' sort with another;
6 o' of the Levites, wrote them before
6 o' principal household being taken
6 Eleazar, and o' taken for Ithamar.
17 The o' and twentieth to Jachin, the
25:28 The o' and twentieth to Hothir, he,
26:12 having wards o' against another,
27:18 Elihu, o' of the brethren of David:
29: 7 o' hundred thousand talents of iron.
2Ch 3:11 o' wing of the...cherub was five
11 wing of the o' cherub was five cubits,
12 o' wing of the other cherub was five
17 o' on the right hand, and the other
4:15 O' sea, and twelve oxen under it.
5:13 trumpeters and singers were as o',
13 o' sound to be heard in praising and
6:29 every o' shall know his own sore
7:21 to every o' that passeth by it; so
9: 6 o' half of the greatness of thy wisdom
13 that came to Solomon in o' year
15 of beaten gold went to o' target.
16 shekels of gold went to o' shield.
19 twelve lions stood there on the o' side
12:13 was o' and forty years old when he
16:13 died in the o' and fortieth year of
18: 7 There is yet o' man, by whom we
8 Israel called for o' of his officers,
12 good to the king with o' assent;
12 be like o' of theirs, and speak thou
19 o' spake saying after this manner, and
20:23 every o' helped to destroy another.
22: 2 he reigned o' year in Jerusalem.
25:17 Come, let us see o' another in the face.
21 and they saw o' another in the face,
26:11 Hananiah, o' of the king's captains.
28: 6 and twenty thousand in o' day,
30:12 was to give them o' heart to do the
17 for every o' that was not clean,
18 saying, The good Lord pardon every o'
31:16 every o' that entereth into the house
32:12 Ye shall worship before o' altar,
34: 1 in Jerusalem o' and thirty years.
35:24 in o' of the sepulchres of his fathers.
36:11 Zedekiah was o' and twenty years
Ezr 2: 1 and Judah, every o' unto his city;
26 Gaba, six hundred twenty and o'.
69 and o' thousand drams of gold,
69 and o' hundred priests' garments.
3: 1 together as o' man to Jerusalem.
5 every o' that willingly offered a
5:14 and they were delivered unto o',
6: 5 every o' to his place, and place them
8:34 By number and by weight of every o':
9: 4 every o' that trembled at the words of
11 filled it from o' end to another with
10: 2 o' of the sons of Elam, answered and
13 is this a work of o' day or two: for
Ne 1: 2 Hanani, o' of my brethren, came, he
3: 8 the son of o' of the apothecaries,
28 every o' over against his house.
4:15 to the wall, every o' unto his work.
17 every o' with...hands wrought in
17 with o' of his hands wrought in the
18 every o' had his sword girded by
19 upon the wall, o' far from another.
22 Let every o' with his servant lodge
23 every o' put them off for washing.
5: 7 exact usury, every o' of his brother.
18 prepared for me daily was o' ox and
6: 2 together in some o' of the villages
7: 3 every o' in his watch, and every o'
6 and to Judah, every o' unto his city;
30 Gaba, six hundred twenty and o'.
37 Ono, seven hundred twenty and o'.
63 took o' of the daughters of Barzillai
8: 1 themselves together as o' man
16 every o' upon the roof of his house,
9: 3 their God o' fourth part of the day;
10:28 every o' having knowledge, and having
11: 1 cast lots, to bring o' of ten to dwell
3 dwelt every o' in his possession in
14 Zabdiel, the son of o' of the great men.
20 Judah, every o' in his inheritance.
12:31 o' went on the right hand upon the
13:10 work, were fled every o' to his field.
30 Levites, every o' in his business;
Es 1: 7 being diverse o' from another,)
3:13 children and women, in o' day, even
4: 5 Hatach, o' of the king's chamberlains,
11 is o' law of his to put him to death,
6: 9 to the hand of o' of the king's most
7: 9 o' of the chamberlains, said before
8:12 o' day in all the provinces of king
9:19 of sending portions o' to another.
22 of sending portions o' to another,
Job 1: 1 o' that feared God, and eschewed evil.
4 in their houses, every o' his day;
8 o' that feareth God, and escheweth
2: 3 o' that feareth God, and escheweth
10 Thou speakest as o' of the foolish
11 came every o' from his own place;
12 they rent every o' his mantle, and
5: 2 man, and envy slayeth the silly o'.
6:10 concealed the words of the Holy O'.
26 and the speeches of o' that is desperate,
9: 3 cannot answer him o' of a thousand.
22 This is o' thing, therefore I said it.
12: 4 I am as o' mocked of his neighbour,

Job 13: 9 as o· mocketh another, do ye so mock
14: 3 open thine eyes upon such an o·,
4 thing out of an unclean? not o·.
16: 21 o· might plead for a man with God,
17: 10 I cannot find o· wise man among you.
19: 11 me unto him as o· of his enemies.
21: 23 O· dieth in his full strength, being
23: 13 he is in o· mind, and who can turn
24: 6 They reap every o· his corn in the
17 if o· know them, they are in the terrors
29: 25 as o· that comforteth the mourners.
31: 15 did not o· fashion us in the womb?
35 Oh that o· would hear me! behold,
33: 23 interpreter, o· among a thousand,
40: 11 and behold every o· that is proud, and
12 Look on every o· that is proud,
41: 9 shall not o· be cast down even at the
16 O· is so near to another, that no air
17 They are joined o· to another, they
32 o· would think the deep to be hoary.
42: 11 and every o· an earring of gold.
Ps 12: 2 They speak vanity every o· with his
14: 3 is none that doeth good, no, not o·.
16: 10 thine Holy O· to see corruption.
27: 4 O· thing have I desired of the Lord,
29: 9 doth every o· speak of his glory.
32: 6 For this shall every o· that is godly
34: 20 bones: not o· of them is broken.
35: 14 as o· that mourneth for his mother.
49: 16 thou afraid when o· is made rich,
50: 21 I was altogether such an o· as thyself:
53: 3 Every o· of them is gone back: they
3 is none that doeth good, no, not o·.
58: 8 let every o· of them pass away:
63: 11 every o· that sweareth by him shall
64: 6 inward thought of every o· of them,
68: 21 hairy scalp of such an o· as goeth on
30 every o· submit himself with pieces of
71: 18 thy power to every o· that is to come.
22 the harp, O thou Holy O· of Israel.
73: 20 As a dream when o· awaketh; so,
75: 7 he putteth down o· and setteth up
78: 41 and limited the Holy O· of Israel.
65 the Lord awaked as o· out of sleep,
82: 7 men, and fall like o· of the princes.
83: 5 consulted together with o· consent:
84: 7 every o· of them in Zion appeareth
89: 10 Rahab in pieces, as o· that is slain;
18 the Holy O· of Israel is our king.
19 spakest in vision to thy holy o·,
19 laid help upon o· that is mighty;
19 exalted o· chosen out of the people.
105: 13 they went from o· nation to another,
13 from o· kingdom to another people;
37 not o· feeble person among their
106: 11 there was not o· of them left.
115: 8 so is every o· that trusteth in them.
119: 160 every o· of thy righteous judgments
162 thy word, as o· that findeth great spoil.
128: 1 Blessed is every o· that feareth the
135: 18 so is every o· that trusteth in them.
137: 3 saying, Sing us o· the songs of Zion.
141: 7 as when o· cutteth and cleaveth wood
145: 4 O· generation shall praise thy works
Pr 1: 14 among us; let us all have o· purse:
19 the ways of every o· that is greedy of
3: 18 happy is every o· that retaineth her.
6: 11 thy poverty come as o· that travelleth,
28 Can o· go upon hot coals, and his
8: 30 by him, as o· brought up with him:
15: 12 scorner loveth not o· that reproveth
16: 5 Every o· that is proud in heart is an
17: 14 strife is as when o· letteth out water:
19: 25 reprove o· that hath understanding,
20: 6 proclaim every o· his own goodness:
21: 5 every o· that is hasty only to want.
22: 26 Be not thou o· of them that strike
24: 34 poverty come as o· that travelleth;
26: 17 like o· that taketh a dog by the ears.
Ec 1: 4 O· generation passeth away, and
2: 14 o· event happeneth to them all.
3: 19 even o· thing befalleth them: as
19 as the o· dieth, so dieth the other;
19 they have all o· breath; so that a
20 All go unto o· place; all are of the
4: 8 There is o· alone, and there is not a
9 Two are better than o·; because
10 they fall, the o· will lift up his fellow:
11 heat: but how can o· be warm alone?
12 if o· prevail against him, two shall
5: 18 and comely for o· to eat and to drink,
6: 6 no good: do not all go to o· place?
7: 14 set the o· over against the other,
27 counting o· by o· [*], to find out the
28 o· man among a thousand have I
8: 9 a time wherein o· man ruleth over
9: 2 there is o· event to the righteous,
3 that there is o· event unto all: yea,
18 but o· sinner destroyeth much good.
10: 3 he saith to every o· that he is a fool.
15 labour of the foolish wearieth every o·
12: 11 which are given from o· shepherd.
Ca 1: 7 as o· that turneth aside by the flocks
2: 10 Rise up, my love, my fair o·, and come
13 Arise, my love, my fair o·, and come
4: 2 whereof every o· bear twins, and none
9 my heart with o· of thine eyes,
9 thine eyes, with o· chain of thy neck.
6: 6 whereof every o· beareth twins,
6 there is not o· barren among them.
9 My dove, my undefiled is but o·;
9 she is the only o· of her mother,
9 choice o· of her that bare her.
8: 10 in his eyes as o· that found favour.
11 every o· for the fruit thereof was to
Isa 1: 4 provoked the Holy O· of Israel

Isa 1: 23 every o· loveth gifts, and followeth
24 Lord of hosts, the mighty O· of Israel,
2: 12 shall be upon every o· that is proud
12 and upon every o· that is lifted up;
20 made each o· for himself to worship,
3: 5 be oppressed, every o· by another,
5 and every o· by his neighbour: the
4: 1 women shall take hold of o· man,
3 even every o· that is written among
5: 10 acres of vineyard shall yield o· bath,
19 counsel of the Holy O· of Israel
24 the word of the Holy O· of Israel.
30 and if o· look unto the land, behold
6: 2 seraphims: each o· had six wings;
3 o· cried unto another, and said, Holy,
6 Then flew o· of the seraphims unto
7: 22 every o· eat that is left in the land.
9: 14 and tail, branch and rush, in o· day.
17 every o· is an hypocrite and an evildoer,
10: 17 fire, and his Holy O· for a flame:
17 his thorns and his briers in o· day;
20 Lord, the Holy O· of Israel, in truth.
34 and Lebanon shall fall by a mighty o·.
12: 6 for great is the Holy O· of Israel
13: 8 they shall be amazed o· at another;
14 and flee every o· into his own land.
15 Every o· that is found shall be thrust
15 every o· that is joined unto them
14: 18 in glory, every o· in his own house.
32 shall o· then answer the messengers
15: 3 and in their streets, every o· shall howl,
16: 7 howl for Moab, every o· shall howl: for
17: 7 respect to the Holy O· of Israel.
19: 2 fight every o· against his brother,
2 and every o· against his neighbour;
17 every o· that maketh mention thereof
18 o· shall be called, The city of
20 send them a saviour, and a great o·,
23: 15 according to the days of o· king:
27: 12 ye shall be gathered o· by o·, O ye
28: 2 the Lord hath a mighty and strong o·,
29: 4 be, as of o· that hath a familiar spirit,
11 men deliver to o· that is learned,
19 rejoice in the Holy O· of Israel.
20 terrible o· is brought to nought,
23 and sanctify the Holy O· of Jacob,
30: 11 cause the Holy O· of Israel to cease
12 thus saith the Holy O· of Israel,
15 Lord God, the Holy O· of Israel;
17 O· thousand shall flee at the rebuke
17 shall flee at the rebuke of o·; at the
29 when o· goeth with a pipe to come
29 to the mighty O· of Israel.
31: 1 not unto the Holy O· of Israel,
33: 20 not o· of the stakes thereof shall ever
34: 15 be gathered, every o· with her mate.
16 no o· of these shall fail, none shall
36: 9 turn away the face of o· captain of
16 and eat ye every o· of his vine,
16 and every o· of his fig tree, and
16 drink ye every o· the waters of his
37: 23 even against the Holy O· of Israel.
40: 25 shall I be equal? saith the Holy O·.
26 is strong in power; not o· faileth.
41: 6 They helped every o· his neighbour;
6 every o· said to his brother, Be of
14 redeemer, the Holy O· of Israel.
16 shalt glory in the Holy O· of Israel.
20 the Holy O· of Israel hath created it.
25 I have raised up o· from the north,
43: 3 the Holy O· of Israel, thy Saviour:
7 every o· that is called by my name:
14 redeemer, the Holy O· of Israel;
15 I am the Lord, your Holy O·, the
44: 5 O· shall say, I am the Lord's; and
45: 11 the Lord, the Holy O· of Israel,
24 Surely, shall o· say, in the Lord have
46: 7 o· shall cry unto him, yet can he not
47: 4 is his name, the Holy O· of Israel.
9 come to thee in a moment in o· day,
15 wander every o· to his quarter;
48: 17 Redeemer, the Holy O· of Israel;
49: 7 Redeemer of Israel, and his Holy O·,
7 the Holy O· of Israel, and he shall
26 thy Redeemer, the Mighty O· of Jacob.
53: 6 turned every o· to his own way;
54: 5 Redeemer the Holy O· of Israel;
55: 1 Ho, every o· that thirsteth, come ye
5 and for the Holy O· of Israel; for
56: 6 every o· that keepeth the sabbath
11 their own way, every o· for his gain,
57: 2 each o· walking in his uprightness.
15 lofty O· that inhabiteth eternity,
60: 9 God, and to the Holy O· of Israel,
14 The Zion of the Holy O· of Israel.
16 thy Redeemer, the mighty O· of Jacob.
22 A little o· shall become a thousand,
22 and a small o· a strong nation:
65: 8 and o· saith, Destroy it not; for a
66: 8 be made to bring forth in o· day?
13 As o· whom his mother comforteth,
17 in the gardens, behind o· tree in the
23 that from o· new moon to another,
23 and from o· sabbath to another,
Jer 1: 15 shall set every o· his throne at the
3: 14 I will take you o· of a city, and two
5: 6 every o· that goeth out thence shall be
8 morning: every o· neighed after his
6: 3 they shall feed every o· in his place.
13 them every o· is given to covetousness;
13 the priest every o· dealeth falsely.
8: 6 every o· turned to his course, as the
10 for every o· from the least even unto
10 the priest every o· dealeth falsely.
9: 4 ye heed every o· of his neighbour,
5 will deceive every o· his neighbour,

Jer 9: 8 o· speaketh peaceably to his
20 every o· her neighbour lamentation.
10: 3 for o· cutteth a tree out of the forest,
11: 8 walked every o· in the imagination
12: 12 devour from the o· end of the land
13: 14 will dash them o· against another,
15: 10 yet every o· of them doth curse me.
16: 12 walk every o· after the imagination
18: 11 return ye now every o· from his evil
12 we will every o· do the imagination
16 every o· that passeth thereby shall be
19: 8 every o· that passeth thereby shall be
9 eat every o· the flesh of his friend
11 as o· breaketh a potter's vessel, that
20: 7 in derision daily, every o· mocketh me.
11 is with me as a mighty terrible o·:
22: 7 thee, every o· with his weapons:
23: 17 they say unto every o· that walketh
30 steal my words every o· from his
35 ye say every o· to his neighbour,
35 and every o· to his brother, What
24: 2 O· basket had very good figs, even
25: 5 now every o· from his evil way,
26 north, far and near, o· with another,
33 at that day from o· end of the earth
30: 14 with the chastisement of a cruel o·, for
31: 30 But every o· shall die for his own
32: 19 give every o· according to his ways,
39 will give them o· heart, and o· way,
34: 10 every o· should let his manservant,
10 every o· his maidservant, go free,
17 liberty, every o· to his brother, and
35: 2 into o· of the chambers, and give
36: 7 will return every o· from his evil way:
16 they were afraid both o· and other,
38: 7 o· of the eunuchs which was in the
46: 16 to fall, yea, o· fell upon another:
49: 17 Every o· that goeth by it shall be
50: 13 every o· that goeth by Babylon shall
16 shall turn every o· to his people,
16 shall flee every o· to his own land.
29 Lord, against the Holy O· of Israel.
42 every o· put in array, like a man to the
51: 5 sin against the Holy O· of Israel.
9 go every o· into his own country:
31 O· post shall run to meet another, and
31 and o· messenger to meet another, to
31 that his city is taken at o· end,
46 a rumour shall both come o· year, and
56 every o· of their bows is broken: for
52: 1 Zedekiah was o· and twenty years
20 o· sea, and twelve brasen bulls that
21 of o· pillar was eighteen cubits;
22 height of o· chapiter was five cubits,
Eze 1: 6 And every o· had four faces, and
6 faces, and every o· had four wings.
9 wings were joined o· to another;
9 they went every o· straight forward.
11 wings of every o· were joined o· to
12 they went every o· straight forward:
15 behold o· wheel upon the earth by
16 and they four had o· likeness: and
23 straight, the o· toward the other:
23, 23 every o· had two, which covered
28 and I heard a voice of o· that spake.
3: 13 creatures that touched o· another,
4: 8 turn thee from o· side to another,
9 fitches, and put them in o· vessel,
17 and be astonied o· with another,
7: 16 mourning, every o· for his iniquity.
9: 2 o· man among them was clothed
10: 7 o· cherub stretched forth his hand
9 o· wheel by...cherub, and another
10 wheel by o· cherub, and another
10 they four had o· likeness, as if a
14 every o· had four faces: the first face
19 every o· stood at the door of the east
21 Every o· had four faces apiece, and
21 faces apiece, and every o· four wings;
22 they went every o· straight forward.
11: 5 into your mind, every o· of them.
19 And I will give them o· heart, and
13: 10 and o· built up a wall, and, lo, others
14: 7 For every o· of the house of Israel,
15: 7 they shall go out from o· fire, and
16: 15 on every o· that passed by; his it was.
25 thy feet to every o· that passed by,
44 Behold, every o· that useth proverbs
17: 22 top of his young twigs a tender o·,
18: 10 the like to any o· of these things,
30 every o· according to his ways,
19: 3 she brought up o· of her whelps:
20: 39 Go ye, serve ye every o· his idols,
21: 16 Go thee o· way or other, either on the
19 shall come forth out of o· land:
22: 6 every o· were in thee to their power
11 And o· hath committed abomination
23: 2 women, the daughters of o· mother:
13 defiled, that they took both o· way,
24: 23 and mourn o· toward another.
31: 11 hand of the mighty o· of the heathen;
33: 20 judge...every o· after his own ways.
21 o· that had escaped out of Jerusalem
24 Abraham was o·, and he inherited
26 ye defile every o· his neighbour's
30 houses, and speak o· to another,
30 every o· to his brother, saying,
32 song of o· that hath a pleasant voice,
34: 23 will set up o· shepherd over them,
37: 16 son of man, take thee o· stick, and
17 join them o· to another into o· stick;
17 they shall become o· in thine hand.
19 of Judah, and make them o· stick,
19 and they shall be o· in mine hand.
22 make them o· nation in the land
22 o· king shall be king to them all:

Eze 37: 24 and they all shall have o' shepherd:
39: 7 am the Lord, the Holy O' in Israel.
40: 5 the breadth of the building, o' reed;
5 and the height, o' reed.
6 the gate, which was o' reed broad;
6 the gate, which was o' reed broad.
7 little chamber was o' reed long,
7 and o' reed broad; and between the
7 of the gate within was o' reed.
8 porch of the gate within, o' reed.
10 they three were of o' measure: and
10 posts had o' measure on this side
12 the little chamber was o' cubit on
12 and the space was o' cubit on that side;
13 from the roof of o' little chamber to
26 it had palm trees, o' on this side,
42 an half broad, and o' cubit high:
44 o' at the side of the east gate having
49 o' on this side, and another on that
41: 1 six cubits broad on the o' side,
2 were five cubits on the o' side, and
6 o' over another, and thirty in order;
11 was left, o' door toward the north,
15 the galleries thereof on the o' side
19 toward the palm tree on the o' side,
21 the appearance of the o' as the
24 two leaves for the o' door, and two
26 and palm trees on the o' side and on
42: 4 breadth inward, a way of o' cubit;
9 as o' goeth into them from the utter
12 the east, as o' entereth into them.
43: 14 two cubits, and the breadth o' cubit.
14 four cubits, and the breadth o' cubit;
45: 7 be for the prince on the o' side and
7 be over against o' of the portions,
11 and the bath shall be of o' measure,
15 o' lamb out of the flock, out of two
20 the month for every o' that erreth,
46: 12 o' shall then open him the gate that
12 his going forth o' shall shut the gate.
17 his inheritance to o' of his servants,
22 four corners were of o' measure.
47: 7 many trees on the o' side and on the
14 inherit it, o' as well as another:
48: 1 of Hethlon, as o' goeth to Hamath,
8 in length as o' of the other parts,
21 on the o' side and on the other of the
31 gates northward; o' gate of Reuben,
31 o' gate of Judah, o' gate of Levi.
32 three gates; and o' gate of Joseph,
32 o' gate of Benjamin, o' gate of Dan.
33 and three gates; o' gate of Simeon,
33 o' gate of Issachar, o' gate of Zebulun.
34 their three gates; o' gate of Gad,
34 o' gate of Asher, o' gate of Naphtali.
Da 2: 9 there is but o' decree for you:
43 they shall not cleave o' to another,
3: 19 heat the furnace o' seven times
4: 13 and an holy o' came down from
19 was astonied for o' hour, and his
23 and an holy o' coming down from
5: 6 knees smote o' against another.
7: 3 the sea, diverse o' from another.
5 and it raised up itself on o' side,
13 o' like the Son of man came with the
16 near unto o' of them that stood
8: 3 but o' was higher than the other,
9 out of o' of them came forth a little
13 Then I heard o' saint speaking, and
9: 27 the covenant with many for o' week:
10: 13 withstood me o' and twenty days:
13 lo, Michael, o' of the chief princes,
16 o' like the similitude of the sons of
18 touched me o' like the appearance
11: 5 shall be strong, and o' of his princes;
7 roots shall o' stand up in his estate,
10 and o' shall certainly come, and
27 they shall speak lies at o' table;
12: 1 every o' that shall be found written in
5 the o' on this side of the bank of
6 o' said to the man clothed in linen,
Ho 1: 11 and appoint themselves o' head,
4: 3 every o' that dwelleth therein shall
11: 9 and Holy O' in the midst of thee:
Joe 2: 7 shall march every o' on his ways,
8 Neither shall o' thrust another;
8 shall walk every o' in his path:
Am 3: 5 o' take up a snare from the earth,
4: 7 I caused it to rain upon o' city, and
7 o' piece was rained upon, and the
8 three cities wandered unto o' city,
6: 9 if there remain ten men in o' house,
12 rock? will o' plow there with oxen?
8: 8 every o' mourn that dwelleth therein?
Ob 9 every o' of the mount of Esau may
11 even thou wast as o' of them.
Jon 1: 7 And they said every o' to his fellow,
3: 8 turn every o' from his evil way, and
Mic 2: 4 shall o' take up a parable against you,
4: 5 every o' in the name of his god,
Na 1: 11 There is o' come out of thee, that
2: 4 shall justle o' against another in the
Hab 1: 12 O Lord my God, mine Holy O'?
3: 3 and the Holy O' from mount Paran.
Zep 2: 11 every o' from his place, even all
15 every o' that passeth by her shall hiss,
3: 9 Lord, to serve him with o' consent.
Hag 2: 1 and twentieth day of the month,
12 If o' bear holy flesh in the skirt of
13 If o' that is unclean by a dead body
16 o' came to an heap of twenty measures,
16 o' came to the pressfat for to draw
22 every o' by the sword of his brother.
Zec 3: 9 upon o' stone shall be seven eyes:
9 the iniquity of that land in o' day.
4: 3 o' upon the right side of the bowl,

Zec 5: 3 every o' that stealeth shall be cut off
3 every o' that sweareth shall be cut off
8: 10 men every o' against his neighbour.
21 the inhabitants of o' city shall go to
10: 1 rain, to every o' grass in the field.
11: 6 every o' into his neighbour's hand,
7 two staves; the o' I called Beauty,
8 shepherds...I cut off in o' month;
9 rest eat every o' the flesh of another.
16 neither shall seek the young o', nor
12: 10 as o' mourneth for his only son, and
10 as o' that is in bitterness for his
13: 4 be ashamed every o' of his vision,
6 And o' shall say unto him, What are
14: 7 But it shall be o' day which shall be
9 there be o' Lord, and his name o'.
13 lay hold every o' on the hand of his
16 that every o' that is left of all the
Mal 2: 3 and o' shall take you away with it.
10 Have we not all o' father? hath
10 hath not o' God created us? why do
15 And did not he make o'? Yet had he
15 And wherefore o'? That he might
16 for o' covereth violence with his
17 Every o' that doeth evil is good in the
3: 16 the Lord spake often o' to another:
M't 3: 3 voice of o' crying in the wilderness,
5: 18 heaven and earth pass, o' jot or
18 o' tittle shall in no wise pass
19 shall break o' of these least
29, 30 o' of thy members should perish,
36 not make o' hair whiter or black.
6: 24 for either he will hate the o', and
24 or else he will hold to the o', and
27 can add o' cubit unto his stature?
29 was not arrayed like o' of these.
7: 8 every o' that asketh receiveth; and
21 Not every o' that saith unto me,
26 every o' that heareth these sayings
29 he taught them as o' having authority,
10: 29 o' of them shall not fall on the
42 o' of these little ones a cup of cold
12: 6 place is o' greater than the temple.
11 that shall have o' sheep, and if it
22 unto him o' possessed with a devil,
29 can o' enter into a strong man's
47 Then o' said unto him, Behold, thy
13: 19 When any o' heareth the word of
19 then cometh the wicked o', and
38 are the children of the wicked o';
46 had found o' pearl of great price,
16: 14 Jeremias, or o' of the prophets.
17: 4 here three tabernacles, o' for thee,
4 and o' for Moses, and o' for Elias.
18: 5 shall receive o' such little child in
6 shall offend o' of these little ones
9 for thee to enter into life with o' eye,
10 despise not o' of these little ones;
12 o' of them be gone astray, doth he
14 o' of these little ones should perish.
16 then take with thee o' or two more,
24 o' was brought unto him, which
28 and found o' of his fellowservants,
35 forgive not every o' his brother
19: 5 and they twain shall be o' flesh?
6 they are no more twain, but o' flesh.
16 o' came and said unto him, Good
17 is none good but o', that is, God:
29 And every o' that hath forsaken
20: 12 last have wrought but o' hour, and
13 he answered o' of them, and said,
21 may sit, the o' on thy right hand,
21: 24 I also will ask you o' thing, which if
35 took his servants, and beat o', and
22: 5 went their ways, o' to his farm,
35 o' of them, which was a lawyer,
23: 4 not move them with o' of their fingers.
8 for o' is your Master, even Christ;
9 for o' is your Father, which is in
10 for o' is your Master, even Christ.
15 sea and land to make o' proselyte,
24: 2 not be left here o' stone upon another,
10 and shall betray o' another,
10 another, and shall hate o' another.
31 from o' end of heaven to the other.
40, 41 o' shall be taken, and the other
25: 15 unto o' he gave five talents,
15 to another two, and to another o';
18 he that had received o' went and
24 he which had received the o' talent
29 every o' that hath shall be given,
32 separate them o' from another, as
40 it unto o' of the least of these my
45 did it not to o' of the least of these,
26: 14 Then o' of the twelve, called Judas
21 you, that o' of you shall betray me.
22 every o' of them to say unto him,
40 ye not watch with me o' hour?
47 lo, Judas, o' of the twelve, came,
51 o' of them which were with Jesus
73 Peter, Surely thou also art o' of them;
27: 38 o' on the right hand, and another
48 And straightway o' of them ran,
M'r 1: 3 voice of o' crying in the wilderness,
7 cometh o' mightier than I after me,
22 taught them as o' that had authority,
24 who thou art, the Holy O' of God.
2: 3 bringing o' sick of the palsy, which
4: 41 said o' to another, What manner
5: 22 o' of the rulers of the synagogue,
6: 15 prophet, or as o' of the prophets.
7: 14 Hearken unto me every o' of you,
32 bring unto him o' that was deaf,
8: 14 ship with them more than o' loaf.
28 and others, O' of the prophets.
9: 5 three tabernacles; o' for thee,

M'r 9: 5 and o' for Moses, and o' for Elias.
10 questioning o' with another what
17 o' of the multitude answered and
26 and he was as o' dead; insomuch
37 receive o' of such children in my
38 o' casting out devils in thy name,
42 shall offend o' of these little ones
47 into the kingdom of God with o'
49 every o' shall be salted with fire,
50 and have peace o' with another.
10: 8 And they twain shall be o' flesh:
8 are no more twain, but o' flesh.
17 came o' running, and kneeled to
18 is none good but o', that is, God.
21 O' thing thou lackest: go thy way,
37 we may sit, o' on thy right hand,
11: 29 I will also ask of you o' question,
12: 6 Having yet therefore o' son, his
28 o' of the scribes came, and having
29 The Lord our God is o' Lord:
32 there is o' God; and there is none
13: 1 o' of his disciples saith unto him,
2 not be left o' stone upon another,
14: 10 Judas Iscariot, o' of the twelve,
18 O' of you which eateth with me
19 to say unto him o' by o', Is it I?
20 It is o' of the twelve, that dippeth
37 couldest thou not watch o' hour?
43 cometh Judas, o' of the twelve,
47 o' of them that stood by drew a
66 o' of the maids of the high priest:
69 that stood by, This is o' of them.
70 to Peter, Surely thou art o' of them:
15: 6 he released unto them o' prisoner,
7 And there was o' named Barabbas,
21 they compel o' Simon a Cyrenian,
27 the o' on his right hand, and the
36 o' ran and filled a sponge full of
Lu 2: 3 taxed, every o' into his own city.
15 the shepherds said o' to another,
36 there was o' Anna, a prophetess,
3: 4 voice of o' crying in the wilderness,
16 but o' mightier than I cometh, the
4: 34 who thou art; the Holy O' of God.
40 laid his hands on every o' of them,
5: 3 And he entered into o' of the ships,
6: 9 unto them, I will ask you o' thing;
11 communed o' with another what
29 on the o' cheek offer also the other;
40 every o' that is perfect shall be as
7: 8 I say unto o', Go, and he goeth;
32 calling o' to another, and saying,
36 o' of the Pharisees desired him
41 the o' owed five hundred pence,
8: 25 wondered, saying o' to another,
42 For he had o' only daughter, about
49 cometh o' from the ruler of the
9: 8 o' of the old prophets was risen
19 that o' of the old prophets is risen
33 three tabernacles; o' for thee,
33 and o' for Moses, and o' for Elias:
43 wondered every o' at all things
49 o' casting out devils in thy name;
10: 42 But o' thing is needful: and Mary
11: 1 o' of his disciples said unto him,
4 forgive every o' that is indebted
10 every o' that asketh receiveth: and
45 Then answered o' of the lawyers,
46 burdens with o' of your fingers.
12: 1 that they trode o' upon another, he
6 not o' of them is forgotten before
13 o' of the company said unto him,
25 can add to his stature o' cubit?
27 was not arrayed like o' of these.
52 shall be five in o' house divided,
13: 10 teaching in o' of the synagogues
15 not each o' of you on the sabbath
23 Then said o' unto him, Lord, are
14: 1 house of o' of the chief Pharisees
15 o' of them that sat at meat with
18 o' consent began to make excuse.
15: 4 he lose o' of them, doth not leave
7 over o' sinner that repenteth, more
8 if she lose o' piece, doth not light
10 God over o' sinner that repenteth.
19 make me as o' of thy hired servants.
26 he called o' of the servants, and
16: 5 called every o' of his lord's debtors
13 either he will hate the o', and love
13 or else he will hold to the o', and
17 than o' tittle of the law to fail.
30 if o' went unto them from the dead,
31 though o' rose from the dead.
17: 2 should offend o' of these little ones.
15 And o' of them, when he saw that
22 shall desire to see o' of the days of
24 out of the o' part under heaven,
34 there shall be two men in o' bed;
34 the o' shall be taken, and the
35 the o' shall be taken, and the
36 the o' shall be taken, and the
18: 10 the o' a Pharisee, and the other a
14 for every o' that exalteth himself
19 none is good, save o', that is, God.
22 Yet lackest thou o' thing: sell all
19: 26 unto every o' which hath shall be
44 leave in thee o' stone upon another;
20: 1 on o' of those days, as he taught
3 I will also ask you o' thing: and
21: 6 shall not be left o' stone upon another,
22: 36 him sell his garment, and buy o'.
47 was called Judas, o' of the twelve,
50 o' of them smote the servant of the
59 about the space of o' hour after
23: 14 as o' that perverteth the people: and
17 release o' unto them at the feast.)

Lu 23:26 away, they laid hold upon o· Simon,
33 o· on the right hand, and the
39 o· of the malefactors which were
24:17 these that ye have o· to another,
18 the o· of them, whose name was
32 they said o· to another, Did not our
Joh 1:23 voice of o· crying in the wilderness,
26 there standeth o· among you, whom
40 O· of the two which heard John
3: 8 so is every o· that is born of the
20 every o· that doeth evil hateth the
4:33 said the disciples o· to another,
37 O· soweth, and another reapeth.
5:44 which receive honour o· of another,
45 there is o· that accuseth you, even
6: 7 every o· of them may take a little.
8 O· of his disciples, Andrew, Simon
22 save that o· whereinto his disciples
40 every o· which seeth the Son, and
70 you twelve, and o· of you is a devil?
71 betray him, being o· of the twelve.
7:21 unto them, I have done o· work,
50 Jesus by night, being o· of them,)
8: 9 went out o· by o·, beginning at the
18 am o· that bear witness of myself,
41 we have o· Father, even God.
50 there is o· that seeketh and judgeth.
9:25 o· thing I know, that, whereas I
32 the eyes of o· that was born blind.
10:16 there shall be o· fold, and
16 there shall be...o· shepherd.
30 I and my Father are o·.
11:49 o· of them, named Caiaphas, being
50 o· man should die for the people,
52 together in o· the children of God
12: 2 Lazarus was o· of them that sat at
4 o· of his disciples, Judas Iscariot,
48 my words, hath o· that judgeth him:
13:14 also ought to wash o· another's feet.
21 you, that o· of you shall betray me.
22 the disciples looked o· on another,
23 on Jesus' bosom o· of his disciples,
34 unto you, That ye love o· another;
34 you, that ye also love o· another.
35 if ye have love o· to another.
15:12 That ye love o· another, as I have
17 you, that ye love o· another.
17:11 me, that they may be o·, as we are.
21 That they all may be o·; as thou,
21 thee, that they also may be o· in us:
22 they may be o·, even as we are o·:
23 they may be made perfect in o·;
18:14 o· man should die for the people.
17 thou also o· of this man's disciples?
22 o· of the officers which stood by
25 Art not thou also o· of his disciples?
26 O· of the servants of the high
37 Every o· that is of the truth
39 release unto you o· at the passover:
19:18 on either side o·, and Jesus in the
34 But o· of the soldiers with a spear
20:12 the o· at the head, and the other at
24 Thomas, o· of the twelve, called
21:25 if they should be written every o·,
Ac 1:14 continued with o· accord in prayer
22 must o· be ordained to be a witness
2: 1 they were all with o· accord in
1 all with...accord in o· place.
7 marvelled, saying o· to another,
12 in doubt, saying o· to another,
27 thine Holy O· to see corruption.
38 and be baptized every o· of you in
46 daily with o· accord in the temple,
3:14 ye denied the Holy O· and the Just,
26 turning away every o· of you from
4:24 their voice to God with o· accord,
32 were of o· heart and of...soul:
32 were of...heart and of o· soul:
5:12 with o· accord in Solomon's porch.
16 and they were healed every o·.
25 came o· and told them, saying,
34 stood there up o· in the council, a
7:24 seeing o· of them suffer wrong, he
26 would have set them at o· again,
26 why do ye wrong o· to another?
52 before of the coming of the Just O·; of
57 and ran upon him with o· accord,
8: 6 the people with o· accord gave heed
9 that himself was some great o·:
9:11 the house of Judas for o· called Saul,
43 in Joppa with o· Simon a tanner.
10: 2 o· that feared God with all his house,
5 men to Joppa, and call for o· Simon,
6 lodgeth with o· Simon a tanner,
22 a just man, and o· that feareth God,
28 or come unto o· of another nation;
32 the house of o· Simon a tanner by the
11:28 stood up o· of them named Agabus,
12:10 and passed on through o· street;
20 they came with o· accord to him,
13:25 there cometh o· after me, whose
35 thine Holy O· to see corruption.
15:25 being assembled with o· accord,
39 departed asunder o· from the other:
17: 7 that there is another king, o· Jesus.
26 hath made of o· blood all nations
27 he be not far from every o· of us:
18: 7 o· that worshipped God, whose house
12 made insurrection with o· accord
19: 9 daily in the school of o· Tyrannus.
14 there were seven sons of o· Sceva, a
29 with o· accord into the theatre.
32 cried o· thing, and some another:
34 all with o· voice about the space of
38 let them implead o· another.
20:31 ceased not to warn every o· night

Ac 21: 6 had taken our leave o· of another,
7 and abode with them o· day.
8 evangelist, which was o· of the seven;
16 with them o· Mnason of Cyprus,
26 be offered for every o· of them.
34 some cried o· thing, and some another,
22:12 And o· Ananias, a devout man
14 know his will, and see that Just O·,
23: 6 that the o· part were Sadducees,
17 Paul called o· of the centurions
24:21 Except it be for this o· voice, that
25:19 and of o· Jesus, which was dead,
27: 1 other prisoners unto o· named Julius,
2 o· Aristarchus, a Macedonian of
28: 2 a fire, and received us every o·,
13 after o· day the south wind blew,
25 that Paul had spoken o· word,
Ro 1:16 salvation to every o· that believeth;
27 in their lust o· toward another;
2:15 accusing or...excusing o· another;)
28 is not a Jew, which is o· outwardly;
29 But he is a Jew, which is o· inwardly;
3:10 There is none righteous, no, not o·:
12 is none that doeth good, no, not o·.
30 Seeing it is o· God, which shall
5: 7 for a righteous man will o· die:
12 as by o· man sin entered into the
15 the offence of o· many be dead,
15 which is by o· man, Jesus Christ,
16 not as it was by o· that sinned, so
16 was by o· to condemnation, but the
17 by o· man's offence death reigned
17 man's offence death reigned by o·;
17 reign in life by o·, Jesus Christ.)
18 by the offence of o· judgment came
18 the righteousness of o· the free gift
19 as by o· man's disobedience many
19 by the obedience of o· shall many be
9:10 Rebecca also had conceived by o·,
21 lump to make o· vessel unto honour,
10: 4 law for righteousness to every o·
12: 4 have many members in o· body,
5 being many, are o· body in Christ,
5 every o· members...of another.
5 members o· of another.
10 kindly affectioned o· to another
10 in honour preferring o· another;
16 of the same mind o· toward another.
13: 8 any thing, but to love o· another:
14: 5 O· man esteemeth...day above
5 man esteemeth o· day above another:
12 every o· of us shall give account of
13 not...judge o· another any more:
19 wherewith o· may edify another.
15: 2 every o· of us please his neighbour
5 be likeminded o· toward another
6 That ye may with o· mind...mouth
6 with...mind and o· mouth glorify
7 Wherefore receive ye o· another,
14 able also to admonish o· another.
16:16 Salute o· another with an holy kiss.
1Co 1:12 that every o· of you saith, I am of
3: 4 For while o· saith, I am of Paul;
8 and he that watereth are o·:
4: 6 no o· of you be puffed up for o·
5: 1 o· should have his father's wife.
5 To deliver such an o· unto Satan
11 with such an o· no not to eat.
6: 5 not o· that shall be able to judge
7 ye go to law with o· another.
16 is joined to an harlot is o· body?
16 two, saith he, shall be o· flesh.
17 is joined unto the Lord is o· spirit.
7: 5 Defraud ye not o· the other, except
7 o· after this manner, and
17 as the Lord hath called every o·, so
25 as o· that hath obtained mercy of the
8: 4 there is none other God but o·.
6 But to us there is but o· God, the
6 o· Lord Jesus Christ, by whom are
9:24 run all, but o· receiveth the prize?
26 fight I, not as o· that beateth the air:
10: 8 and fell in o· day three and twenty
17 many are o· bread, and o· body:
17 are all partakers of that o· bread.
11: 5 is even all o· as if she were shaven.
20 come together...into o· place,
21 eating every o· taketh before other
21 o· is hungry, and another is
33 together to eat, tarry o· for another.
12: 8 For to o· is given by the Spirit
11 that o· and the selfsame Spirit,
12 as the body is o·, and hath many
12 the members of that o· body, being
12 many, are o· body: so also is Christ.
13 For by o· Spirit are we all baptized
13 into o· body, whether we be Jews or
13 been all made to drink o· Spirit.
14 For the body is not o· member, but
18 every o· of them in the body, as it
19 if they were all o· member, where
20 many members, yet but o· body.
25 have the same care o· for another.
26 whether o· member suffer, all the
26 or o· member be honoured, all the
14:23 be come together into o· place,
24 come in o· that believeth not, or
24 or o· unlearned, he is convinced of
26 every o· of you hath a psalm, hath
27 by course; and let o· interpret.
31 For ye may all prophesy o· by
31 ye may all prophesy...by o·,
15: 8 of me also, as of o· born out of due time.
39 there is o· kind of flesh of men,
40 the glory of the celestial is o·, and
41 There is o· glory of the sun, and

1Co 15:41 o· star differeth from another star in
16: 2 every o· of you lay by him in store,
16 to every o· that helpeth with us,
20 ye o· another with an holy kiss.
2Co 2: 7 such a o· should be swallowed up
5:10 every o· may receive the things done
14 that if o· died for all, then were all
10:11 Let such an o· think this, that,
11: 2 have espoused you to o· husband,
24 received I forty stripes save o·.
12: 2 o· caught up to the third heaven.
5 Of such an o· will I glory: yet of
13:11 be of o· mind, live in peace;
12 Greet o· another with an holy kiss.
Ga 3:10 Cursed is every o· that continueth
13 Cursed is every o· that hangeth on
16 as of o·, And to thy seed, which is
20 not a mediator of o·, but God is o·.
28 for ye are all o· in Christ Jesus.
4:22 o· by a bondmaid, the other by a
24 the o· from the mount Sinai, which
5:13 flesh, but by love serve o· another.
14 all the law is fulfilled in o· word,
15 if ye bite and devour o· another,
15 ye be not consumed o· of another.
17 are contrary the o· to the other: so
26 o· another, envying o· another.
6: 1 restore such an o· in the spirit of
2 Bear ye o· another's burdens, and
Eph 1:10 gather together in o· all things
2:14 who hath made both o·, and hath
15 in himself of twain o· new man, so
16 both unto God in o· body by the
18 access by o· Spirit unto the Father.
4: 2 forbearing o· another in love;
4 There is o· body, and o· Spirit, even
4 called in o· hope of your calling;
5 O· Lord,...faith, o· baptism,
5 Lord, o· faith,...baptism,
6 O· God and Father of all, who is
7 unto every o· of us is given grace
25 for we are members o· of another.
32 And be ye kind o· to another,
32 forgiving o· another, even as God
5:21 Submitting yourselves o· to another
31 wife, and they two shall be o· flesh.
33 let every o· of you in particular
Ph'p 1:16 The o· preach Christ of contention,
27 that ye stand fast in o· spirit, with
27 with o· mind striving together
2: 2 the same love, being of o· accord,
2 love, being...of o· mind.
3:13 this o· thing I do, forgetting those
Col 3: 9 Lie not o· to another, seeing that
13 Forbearing o· another, and
13 forgiving o· another, if any man
15 also ye are called in o· body; and
16 and admonishing o· another in
4: 9 and beloved brother, who is o· of you.
12 Epaphras, who is o· of you, a servant
1Th 2:11 and charged every o· of you, as a
3:12 abound in love o· toward another,
4: 4 every o· of you should know how
9 taught of God to love o· another.
18 comfort o· another with these words.
5:11 edify o· another, even as also ye
2Th 1: 3 charity of every o· of you all toward
1Ti 2: 5 there is o· God, and o· mediator
3: 2 husband of o· wife, vigilant, sober,
12 deacons be the husbands of o· wife,
5: 9 having been the wife of o· man,
21 without preferring o· before another,
2Ti 2:19 every o· that nameth the name of
Tit 1: 6 blameless, the husband of o· wife,
12 O· of themselves, even a prophet
3: 3 envy, hateful, and hating o· another.
Ph'm 9 being such an o· as Paul the aged,
Heb 2: 6 But o· in a certain place testified,
11 who are sanctified are all of o·:
3:13 exhort o· another daily, while it
5:12 ye have need that o· teach you again
13 For every o· that useth milk is
6:11 every o· of you do shew the same
10:12 he had offered o· sacrifice for sins
14 by o· offering he hath perfected for
24 us consider o· another to provoke
25 but exhorting o· another: and so much
11:12 Therefore sprang there even of o·,
12:16 who for o· morsel of meat sold his
13:14 continuing city,...we seek o· to come.
Jas 2:10 yet offend in o· point, he is guilty
16 o· of you say unto them, Depart in
19 believest that there is o· God; thou
4:11 Speak not evil o· of another,
12 There is o· lawgiver, who is able to
5: 9 Grudge not o· against another,
16 Confess your faults o· to another,
16 pray o· for another, that ye may be
19 the truth, and o· convert him;
1Pe 1:22 love o· another with a pure heart
3: 8 Finally, be ye all of o· mind, having
8 having compassion o· for another,
4: 9 hospitality o· to another without
10 minister the same o· to another,
5: 5 all of you be subject o· to another,
14 Greet ye o· another with a kiss of
2Pe 3: 8 be not ignorant of this o· thing,
8 that o· day is with the Lord as a
8 and a thousand years as o· day.
1Jo 1: 7 have fellowship o· with another,
2:13 ye have overcome the wicked o·.
14 and ye have overcome the wicked o·.
20 ye have an unction from the Holy O·,
29 every o· that doeth righteousness
3:11 that we should love o· another.
12 Not as Cain, who was of that wicked o·,

1Jo 3:23 and love o' another, as he gave us
4: 7 Beloved, let us love o' another: for
7 every o' that loveth is born of God,
11 ye ought also to love o' another.
12 If we love o' another, God dwelleth
5: 1 every o' that loveth him that begat
7 Ghost: and these three are o'.
8 blood: and these three agree in o'.
18 and that wicked o' toucheth him not.
2Jo 5 beginning, that we love o' another.
Re 1:13 midst...o' like unto the Son of man,
2:23 I will give unto every o' of you
4: 2 in heaven, and o' sat on the throne.
5: 5 And o' of the elders saith unto me,
8 having every o' of them harps, and
6: 1 the Lamb opened o' of the seals,
1 o' of the four beasts saying, Come
4 that they should kill o' another:
11 robes were given unto every o' of
7:13 o' of the elders answered, saying
9:12 O' woe is past; and, behold, there
11:10 and shall send gifts o' to another;
13: 3 I saw o' of his heads as it were
14:14 cloud o' sat like unto the Son of man,
15: 7 o' of the four beasts gave unto the
17: 1 there came o' of the seven angels
10 five are fallen, and o' is, and the
12 as kings o' hour with the beast.
13 These have o' mind, and shall give
18: 8 shall her plagues come in o' day,
10 in o' hour is thy judgment come.
17 in o' hour so great riches is come
19 for in o' hour is she made desolate.
21: 9 unto me o' of the seven angels
21 every several gate was of o' pearl:

one's^
Ac 16:26 and every o' bands were loosed.

ones^
Ge 34:29 all their little o', and their wives took
43: 8 we, and thou, and also our little o'.
45:19 the land of Egypt for your little o',
46: 5 their little o', and their wives, in the
47:24 and for food for your little o'.
50: 8 only their little o', and their flocks,
21 I will nourish you, and your little o'.
Ex 10:10 as I will let you go, and your little o':
24 let your little o' also go with you.
Nu 14:31 But your little o', which ye said should
31: 9 of Midian captives, and their little o',
17 kill every male among the little o',
32:16 our cattle, and cities for our little o':
17 little o' shall dwell in the fenced cities
24 Build your cities for your little o', and
26 Our little o', our wives, our flocks, and
De 1:39 your little o', which ye said should be a
2:34 women, and the little o', of every city,
3:19 But your wives, and your little o', and
20:14 But the women, and the little o', and
22: 6 whether they be young o', or eggs, and
29:11 Your little o', your wives, and thy
Jos 1:14 Your wives, your little o', and your
8:35 with the women, and the little o', and
J'g 5:22 the pransings of their mighty o'.
18:21 and put the little o' and the cattle
2Sa 15:22 and all the little o' that were with him.
1Ch 16:13 ye children of Jacob, his chosen o'.
Ezr 8:21 and for our little o', and for all our
Es 8:11 assault them, both little o' and women,
Job 21:11 send forth their little o' like a flock,
38:41 when his young o' cry unto God, they
39: 3 bring forth their young o', they cast
4 Their young o' are in good liking, they
16 She is hardened against her young o',
30 Her young o' also suck up blood: and
Ps 10:10 that the poor may fall by his strong o'.
137: 9 dasheth thy little o' against the stones.
Pr 1:22 How long, ye simple o', will ye love
7: 7 among the simple o', I discerned
Isa 5:17 the waste places of the fat o' shall
10:16 hosts, send among his fat o' leanness;
33 high o' of stature shall be hewn down;
11: 7 their young o' shall lie down together:
13: 3 I have commanded my sanctified o', I
3 called my mighty o' for mine anger,
14: 9 thee, even all the chief o' of the earth;
24:21 shall punish the host of the high o'
25: 4 the blast of the terrible o' is as a storm
5 of the terrible o' shall be brought low.
29: 5 of the terrible o' shall be as chaff that
32:11 be troubled, ye careless o': strip you,
33: 7 valiant o' shall cry without: their
57:15 to revive the heart of the contrite o'.
Jer 2:33 also taught the wicked o' thy ways.
8:16 sound of the neighing of his strong o';
14: 3 have sent their little o' to the waters:
48: 4 her little o' have caused a cry to be
45 of the head of the tumultuous o'.
La 4: 3 they give suck to their young o':
Da 4:17 the demand by the word of the holy o':
8: 8 for it came up four notable o'
11:17 and upright o' with him; thus shall he
Joe 3:11 cause thy mighty o' to come down,
Zec 4:14 These are the two anointed o', that
13: 7 will turn mine hand upon the little o'.
M't 10:42 of these little o' a cup of cold water
18: 6 shall offend one of these little o' which
10 ye despise not one of these little o';
14 one of these little o' should perish.
M'r 9:42 shall offend one of these little o' that
10:42 their great o' exercise authority upon

Onesimus (*o-nes'-i-mus*)
Col 4: 9 O', a faithful and beloved brother,
subscr. Colossians by Tychicus and O'.
Ph'm 10 I beseech thee for my son O',
subscr. to Philemon, by O' a servant.

Onesiphorus (*o-ne-sif'-o-rus*)
2Ti 1:16 give mercy unto the house of O';
4:19 Aquila, and the household of O'.

Oni See BEN-ONI.

onions
Nu 11: 5 leeks, and the o', and the garlick:

only^
Ge 6: 5 his heart was o' evil continually.
7:23 Noah o' remained alive, and they
22: 2 now thy son, thine o' son Isaac,
12 thy son, thine o' son from me
16 withheld thy son, thine o' son:
34:22 O' herein will the men consent
23 o' let us consent unto them, and
41:40 o' in the throne will I be greater
47:22 O' the land of the priests bought
26 except the land of the priests o',
50: 8 o' their little ones, and their
Ex 8:11 they shall remain in the river o'.
9:26 O' in the land of Goshen, where
21:19 o' he shall pay for the loss of his
22:20 unto any god, save unto the Lord o',
27 For that is his covering o', it is his
Le 21:23 O' he shall not go in unto the vail,
27:26 O' the firstling of the beasts, which
Nu 1:49 O' thou shalt not number the tribe
12: 2 indeed spoken o' by Moses?
14: 9 O' rebel not ye against the Lord,
18: 3 o' they shall not come nigh the
20:19 I will o', without doing any thing
22:35 o' the word that I shall speak unto
31:22 O' the gold, and the silver, the
36: 6 o' to the family of the tribe of their
De 2:28 o' I will pass through on my feet;
35 O' the cattle we took for a prey
37 O' unto the land of the children of
3:11 o' Og king of Bashan remained of
4: 9 O' take heed to thyself, and keep
12 similitude; o' ye heard a voice.
8: 3 that man doth not live by bread o',
10:15 O' the Lord had a delight in thy
12:16 O' ye shall not eat the blood; ye
23 O' be sure that thou eat not the
26 O' thy holy things which thou hast,
15: 5 O' if thou carefully hearken unto
23 O' thou shalt not eat the blood
20:20 O' the trees which thou knowest
22:25 man o' that lay with her shall die:
28:13 and thou shalt be above o', and
29, 33 thou shalt be o' oppressed and
29:14 with you o' do I make this covenant
Jos 1: 7 O' be thou strong and very
17 o' the Lord thy God be with thee,
18 o' be strong and of a good courage.
6:15 o' on that day they compassed the
17 o' Rahab the harlot shall live, she
24 o' the silver, and the gold, and the
8: 2 o' the spoil thereof, and the cattle
27 O' the cattle and the spoil of that
11:13 none of them, save Hazor o';
22 o' in Gaza, in Gath, and in Ashdod,
13: 6 o' divide thou it by lot unto the
14 O' unto the tribe of Levi he gave
17:17 thou shalt not have one lot o':
J'g 3: 2 O' that the generations of the
6:37 and if the dew be on the fleece o',
39 it now be dry o' upon the fleece,
40 for it was dry upon the fleece o',
10:15 deliver us o', we pray thee, this
11:34 she was his o' child; beside her
16:28 and strengthen me,...o' this once,
19:20 me; o' lodge not in the street.
1Sa 1:13 o' her lips moved, but her voice
23 o' the Lord establish his word.
5: 4 o' the stump of Dagon was left to
7: 3 unto the Lord, and serve him o':
4 Ashtaroth, and served the Lord o'.
12:24 O' fear the Lord, and serve him in
18:17 o' be thou valiant for me, and fight
20:14 shalt not o' while yet I live shew me
39 o' Jonathan and David knew the
2Sa 13:32 king's sons; for Amnon o' is dead:
33 are dead: for Amnon o' is dead.
17: 2 flee; and I will smite the king o':
23:10 returned after him o' to spoil.
1Ki 3: 2 O' the people sacrificed in high
3 o' he sacrificed and burnt incense
4:19 o' officer which was in the land.
8:39 (for thou, even thou o', knowest
12:20 David, but the tribe of Judah o'.
14: 8 to do that o' which was right in
13 he o' of Jeroboam shall come to
15: 5 save o' in the matter of Uriah the
18:22 even I o', remain a prophet of the
19:10, 14 and I, even I o', am left; and
22:31 save o' with the king of Israel.
2Ki 3:25 o' in Kir-haraseth left they the stones
10:23 but the worshippers of Baal o'.
17:18 none left but the tribe of Judah o'.
19:19 thou art the Lord God, even thou o'.
21: 8 o' if they will observe to do
1Ch 22:12 O' the Lord give thee wisdom and
2Ch 2: 6 save o' to burn sacrifice before him?
18:30 save o' with the king of Israel.
33:17 yet unto the Lord their God o'.
Ezr 10:15 O' Jonathan the son of Asahel and
Es 1:16 not done wrong to the king o',
Job 1:12 o' upon himself put not forth
15, 16, 17, 19 I o' am escaped alone
13:20 O' do not two things unto me:
34:29 a nation, or against a man o':
Ps 4: 8 Lord, o' makest me dwell in safety.
51: 4 Against thee, thee o', have I sinned,
62: 2 He o' is my rock and my salvation;
4 They o' consult to cast him down

Ps 62: 5 My soul, wait thou o' upon God;
6 He o' is my rock and my salvation:
71:16 thy righteousness, even of thine o'.
72:18 who o' doeth wonderful things.
91: 8 O' with thine eyes shalt thou
Pr 4: 3 tender and o' beloved in the sight
11:23 desire of the righteous is o' good:
13:10 O' by pride cometh contention:
14:23 of the lips tendeth o' to penury.
17:11 An evil man seeketh o' rebellion:
21: 5 diligent tend o' to plenteousness;
5 every one that is hasty o' to want.
Ec 7:29 this o' have I found, that God hath
Ca 6: 9 she is the o' one of her mother, she
Isa 4: 1 o' let us be called by thy name, to
26:13 by thee o' will we make mention
28:19 o' to understand the report.
37:20 thou art the Lord, even thou o'.
Jer 3:13 O' acknowledge thine iniquity,
6:26 thee mourning, as for an o' son,
32:30 children of Judah have o' done evil
30 have o' provoked me to anger with
Eze 7: 5 God; An evil, an o' evil, behold, is
14:16 they o' shall be delivered, but the
18 o' shall be delivered themselves.
44:20 they shall o' poll their heads.
Am 3: 2 You o' have I known of all the
8:10 it as the mourning of an o' son,
Zec 12:10 one mourneth for his o' son, and
M't 4:10 God, and him o' shalt thou serve.
5:47 And if ye salute your brethren o',
8: 8 speak the word o', and my servant
10:42 a cup of cold water o' in the name
12: 4 with him, but o' for the priests?
14:36 o' touch the hem of his garment:
17: 8 they saw no man, save Jesus o'.
21:19 nothing thereon, but leaves o',
21 not o' do this which is done to the
24:36 of heaven, but my Father o'.
M'r 2: 7 who can forgive sins but God o'?
5:36 Be not afraid, o' believe.
6: 8 for their journey, save a staff o';
9: 8 save Jesus o' with themselves.
Lu 4: 8 God, and him o' shalt thou serve.
7:12 the o' son of his mother, and she
8:42 For he had one o' daughter, about
50 Fear not: believe o', and she shall
9:38 my son: for he is mine o' child.
24:18 thou o' a stranger in Jerusalem,
Joh 1:14 as of the o' begotten of the Father,)
18 the o' begotten Son, which is in the
3:16 he gave his o' begotten Son, that
18 name of the o' begotten Son of God.
5:18 he not o' had broken the sabbath,
44 honour that cometh from God o'?
11:52 And not for that nation o', but
12: 9 they came not for Jesus' sake o',
13: 9 Lord, not my feet o', but also my
17: 3 might know thee the o' true God,
Ac 8:16 o' they were baptized in the name
11:19 word to none but unto the Jews o'.
18:25 knowing o' the baptism of John.
19:27 not o' this our craft is in danger to
21:13 I am ready not to be bound o', but
25 save o' that they keep themselves from
26:29 not o' thou, but also all that hear
27:10 not o' of the lading and ship, but
Ro 1:32 not o' do the same, but have
3:29 Is he the God of the Jews o'? is he
4: 9 then upon the circumcision o', or
12 who are not of the circumcision o',
16 not to that o' which is of the law,
5: 3 And not o' so, but we glory in
11 not o' so, but we also joy in God
8:23 And not o' they, but ourselves also,
9:10 And not o' this; but when Rebecca
24 not of the Jews o', but also of the
13: 5 needs be subject, not o' for wrath,
16: 4 unto whom not o' I give thanks,
27 To God o' wise, be glory through
1Co 7:39 to whom she will; o' in the Lord.
9: 6 Or I o' and Barnabas, have not we
14:36 from you? or came it unto you o'?
15:19 If in this life o' we have hope in
2Co 7: 7 And not by his coming o', but by
8:10 not o' to do, but also to be forward
19 And not that o', but who was also
21 not o' in the sight of the Lord, but
9:12 not o' supplieth the want of the
Ga 1:23 they had heard o', That he which
2:10 O' they would that we should
3: 2 This o' would I learn of you
4:18 not o' when I am present with you.
5:13 o' use not liberty for an occasion to
6:12 o' lest they...suffer persecution
Eph 1:21 not o' in this world, but also in that
Phil 1:27 O' let your conversation be as it
29 not o' to believe on him, but also to
2:12 obeyed, not as in my presence o',
27 and not on him o', but on me also,
4:15 giving and receiving, but ye o'.
Col 4:11 These o' are my fellowworkers
1Th 1: 5 came not unto you in word o', but
8 not o' in Macedonia and Achaia,
2: 8 not the gospel of God o', but also
2Th 2: 7 o' he who now letteth will let, until
1Ti 1:17 the o' wise God, be honour and
5:13 not o' idle, but tattlers also and
6:15 is the blessed and o' Potentate,
16 Who o' hath immortality, dwelling
2Ti 2:20 there are not o' vessels of gold and
4: 8 and not to me o', but unto all them
11 O' Luke is with me. Take Mark,
Heb 9:10 stood o' in meats and drinks, and
11:17 offered up his o' begotten son,
12:26 once more I shake not the earth o',

Jas 1:22 of the word, and not hearers o'.
2:24 man is justified, and not by faith o'.
1Pe 2:18 not o' to the good and gentle, but
1Jo 2: 2 and not for ours o', but also for
4: 9 God sent his o' begotten Son into
5: 6 not by water o', but by water and
2Jo 1: 1 and not I o', but also all they that
Jude 4 denying the o' Lord God, and our
25 To the o' wise God our Saviour, be
Re 9: 4 o' those men which have not the
15: 4 for thou o' art holy: for all nations

only-begotten See ONLY and BEGOTTEN.

Ono (o'-no)
1Ch 8:12 who built O', and Lod, with the
Ezr 2:33 The children of Lod, Hadid, and O',
Ne 6: 2 one of the villages in the plain of O'.
7:37 The children of Lod, Hadid, and O',
11:35 Lod, and O', the valley of craftsmen.

onward
Ex 40:36 of Israel went o' in all their journeys:

onycha (*on'-e-kah*)
Ex 30:34 stacte, and o', and galbanum;

onyx (*o'-nix*)
Ge 2:12 there is bdellium and the o' stone.
Ex 25: 7 O' stones, and stones to be set in
28: 9 And thou shalt take two o' stones,
20 the fourth row a beryl, and an o',
35: 9 o' stones, and stones to be set for
27 And the rulers brought o' stones,
39: 6 they wrought o' stones inclosed in
13 row, a beryl, an o', and a jasper:
1Ch 29: 2 o' stones, and stones to be set,
Job 28:16 gold of Ophir, with the precious o',
Eze 28:13 the beryl, the o', and the jasper,

open See also OPENED; OPENEST; OPENETH; OPENING.
Ge 1:20 in the o' firmament of heaven.
38:14 sat in an o' place, which is by the
Ex 21:33 if a man shall o' a pit, or if a man
Le 14: 7 living bird loose into the o' field.
53 bird out of the city into the o' fields,
17: 5 which they offer in the o' field, even
Nu 8:16 instead of such as o' every womb,
16:30 and the earth o' her mouth, and
19:15 And every o' vessel, which hath no
16 slain with a sword in the o' fields,
24: 3 man whose eyes are o' hath said:
4 a trance, but having his eyes o':
15 man whose eyes are o' hath said:
16 a trance, but having his eyes o':
De 15: 8 shalt o' thine hand wide unto him,
11 shalt o' thine hand wide unto thy
20:11 answer of peace, and o' unto thee,
28:12 shall o' unto thee his good treasure,
Jos 8:17 they left the city o', and pursued
10:22 O' the mouth of the cave, and bring
1Sa 3: 1 those days; there was no o' vision.
2Sa 11:11 lord, are encamped in the o' fields;
1Ki 6:18 carved with knops and o' flowers:
29 palm trees and o' flowers, within
32 and palm trees and o' flowers, and
35 and palm trees and o' flowers:
8:29 thine eyes may be o' toward this
52 That thine eyes may be o' unto the
2Ki 6:17 Lord, I pray thee, o' his eyes, that
20 Lord, o' the eyes of these men,
9: 3 Then o' the door, and flee, and
13:17 he said, O' the window eastward.
19:16 o', Lord, thine eyes, and see: and
2Ch 6:20 That thine eyes may be o' upon
40 let, I beseech thee, thine eyes be o',
7:15 Now mine eyes shall be o', and
Ne 1: 6 and thine eyes o', that thou mayest
6: 5 time with an o' letter in his hand;
Job 11: 5 speak, and o' his lips against thee;
14: 3 dost thou o' thine eyes upon such
32:20 I will o' my lips and answer.
34:26 men in the o' sight of others;
35:16 doth Joab o' his mouth in vain;
41:14 Who can o' the doors of his face?
Ps 5: 9 their throat is an o' sepulchre; they
34:15 and his ears are o' unto their cry.
49: 4 I will o' my dark saying upon the
51:15 O Lord, o' thou my lips; and my
78: 2 I will o' my mouth in a parable:
81:10 o' thy mouth wide, and I will fill it.
118:19 O'...the gates of righteousness:
119:18 O' thou mine eyes, that I may
Pr 13:16 but a fool layeth o' his folly.
20:13 o' thine eyes, and thou shalt be
27: 5 O' rebuke is better than secret
31: 8 O' thy mouth for the dumb in the
9 O' thy mouth, judge righteously,
Ca 5: 2 O' to me, my sister, my love, my
5 I rose up to o' to my beloved; and
Isa 9:12 shall devour Israel with o' mouth.
22:22 so he shall o', and none shall shut;
22 and he shall shut, and none shall o'.
24:18 the windows from on high are o',
26: 2 O' ye the gates, that the righteous
28:24 doth he o' and break the clods of
37:17 o' thine eyes, O Lord, and see: and
41:18 I will o' rivers in high places, and
42: 7 To o' the blind eyes, to bring out
45: 1 to o' before him the two leaved
8 let the earth o', and let them bring
60:11 thy gates shall be o' continually;
Jer 5:16 Their quiver is as an o' sepulchre,
9:22 fall as dung upon the o' field, and
13:19 shut up, and none shall o' them:
32:11 custom, and that which was o':
14 and this evidence which is o'; and
19 thine eyes are o' upon all the ways
50:26 utmost border, o' her storehouses:
Eze 2: 8 o' thy mouth, and eat that I give
3:27 I will o' thy mouth, and thou shalt
16: 5 thou wast cast out in the o' field,
63 and never o' thy mouth any more
21:22 to o' the mouth in the slaughter,
25: 9 I will o' the side of Moab from the
29: 5 thou shalt fall upon the o' fields;
32: 4 cast thee forth upon the o' field,
33:27 him that is in the o' field will I give
37: 2 were very many in the o' valley;
12 I will o' your graves, and cause
39: 5 Thou shalt fall upon the o' field:
46:12 one shall then o' him the gate that
Da 6:10 and his windows being o' in his
9:18 o' thine eyes, and behold our
Na 3:13 set wide o' unto thine enemies:
Zec 11: 1 O' thy doors, O Lebanon, that the
12: 4 I will o' mine eyes upon the house
Mal 3:10 I will not o' you the windows of
M't 13:35 I will o' my mouth in parables; I
25:11 virgins, saying, Lord, Lord, o' to us.
Lu 12:36 they may o' unto him immediately.
13:25 door, saying, Lord, Lord, o' unto us;
Joh 1:51 Hereafter ye shall see heaven o',
10:21 Can a devil o' the eyes of the blind?
Ac 16:27 sleep, and seeing the prison doors o',
18:14 Paul was now about to o' his mouth,
19:38 the law is o', and there are deputies:
26:18 To o' their eyes, and to turn them
Ro 3:13 Their throat is an o' sepulchre;
2Co 3:18 with o' face beholding as in a glass
6:11 our mouth is o' unto you, our heart
Eph 6:19 that I may o' my mouth boldly,
Col 4: 3 that God would o' unto us a door of
1Ti 5:24 men's sins are o' beforehand,
Heb 6: 6 afresh, and put him to an o' shame.
1Pe 3:12 and his ears are o' unto their prayers:
Re 3: 8 I have set before thee an o' door,
20 man hear my voice, and o' the door,
5: 2 Who is worthy to o' the book, and to
3 no man...was able to o' the book,
4 worthy to o' and to read the book,
5 hath prevailed to o' the book, and
9 the book, and to o' the seals thereof:
10: 2 he had in his hand a little book o':
8 and take the little book which is o'

opened
Ge 3: 5 thereof, then your eyes shall be o',
7 And the eyes of them both were o',
4:11 which hath o' her mouth to receive
7:11 the windows of heaven were o'.
8: 6 that Noah o' the window of the ark
21:19 God o' her eyes, and she saw a
29:31 Leah was hated, he o' her womb:
30:22 hearkened to her, and o' her womb.
41:56 Joseph o' all the storehouses, and
42:27 as one of them o' his sack to give
43:21 we o' our sacks, and, behold, every
44:11 ground, and o' every man his sack.
Ex 2: 6 she had o' it, she saw the child:
Nu 16:32 earth o' her mouth, and swallowed
22:28 the Lord o' the mouth of the ass,
31 the Lord o' the eyes of Balaam,
26:10 earth o' his mouth, and swallowed
De 11: 6 earth o' her mouth, and swallowed
J'g 3:25 he o' not the doors of the parlour;
25 they took a key, and o' them:
4:19 she o' a bottle of milk, and gave
11:35 I have o' my mouth unto the Lord,
36 hast o' thy mouth unto the Lord,
19:27 o' the doors of the house, and went
1Sa 3:15 o' the doors of the house of the Lord.
2Ki 4:35 times, and the child o' his eyes.
6:17 Lord o' the eyes of the young man;
20 Lord o' their eyes, and they saw;
9:10 And he o' the door and fled.
13:17 window eastward. And he o' it.
15:16 because they o' not to him,
2Ch 29: 3 o' the doors of the house of the Lord,
Ne 7: 3 Let not the gates of Jerusalem be o'
8: 5 Ezra o' the book in the sight of all
5 when he o' it, all the people stood
13:19 that they should not be o' till after
Job 3: 1 After this o' Job his mouth, and
29:23 they o' their mouth wide as for the
31:32 but I o' my doors to the traveller.
33: 2 Behold, now I have o' my mouth,
38:17 Have the gates of death been o'
Ps 35:21 they o' their mouth wide against
39: 9 I was dumb, I o' not my mouth;
40: 6 mine ears hast thou o': burnt
78:23 above, and o' the doors of heaven,
105:41 He o' the rock, and the waters
106:17 earth o' and swallowed up Dathan,
109: 2 the mouth of the deceitful are o'
119:131 I o' my mouth, and panted:
Ca 5: 6 I o' to my beloved; but my beloved
Isa 5:14 o' her mouth without measure:
10:14 moved the wing or o' the mouth,
14:17 o' not the house of his prisoners?
35: 5 the eyes of the blind shall be o',
48: 8 time that thine ear was not o':
50: 5 The Lord God hath o' mine ear,
53: 7 afflicted, yet he o' not his mouth:
Jer 20:12 for unto thee have I o' my cause.
50:25 The Lord hath o' his armoury,
La 2:16 enemies have o' their mouths
3:46 our enemies have o' their mouths
Eze 1: 1 the heavens were o', and I saw
3: 2 I o' my mouth, and he caused me to
16:25 and hast o' thy feet to every one
24:27 In that day shall thy mouth be o'
33:22 had o' my mouth, until he came to
22 and my mouth was o', and I was no
37:13 when I have o' your graves, O my
44: 2 gate shall be shut, it shall not be o',
Eze 46: 1 on the sabbath it shall be o', and in
1 day of the new moon it shall be o'.
Da 7:10 was set, and the books were o'.
10:16 then I o' my mouth, and spake,
Na 2: 6 The gates of the rivers shall be o',
Zec 13: 1 shall be a fountain o' to the house
M't 2:11 when they had o' their treasures,
3:16 the heavens were o' unto him, and
5: 2 he o' his mouth, and taught them,
7: 7 knock, and it shall be o' unto you:
8 to him that knocketh it shall be o'.
9:30 their eyes were o'; and Jesus straitly
17:27 and when thou hast o' his mouth,
20:33 him, Lord, that our eyes may be o'.
27:52 graves were o'; and many bodies
M'r 1:10 he saw the heavens o', and the
7:34 him, Ephphatha, that is, Be o'.
35 straightway his ears were o', and
Lu 1:64 his mouth was o' immediately,
3:21 and praying, the heaven was o',
4:17 And when he had o' the book, he
11: 9 knock, and it shall be o' unto you.
10 to him that knocketh it shall be o'.
24:31 their eyes were o', and they knew
32 while he o' to us the scriptures?
45 Then o' he their understanding,
Joh 9:10 unto him, How were thine eyes o'?
14 Jesus made the clay, and o' his eyes.
17 of him, that he hath o' thine eyes?
21 who hath o' his eyes, we know not:
26 did he to thee? how o' he thine eyes?
30 he is, and yet he hath o' mine eyes.
32 that any man o' the eyes of one that
11:37 man, which o' the eyes of the blind,
Ac 5:19 Lord by night o' the prison doors,
23 when we had o', we found no man
7:56 Behold, I see the heavens o', and
8:32 his shearer, so o' he not his mouth:
35 Then Philip o' his mouth, and began
9: 8 when his eyes were o', he saw no
40 she o' her eyes: and when she saw
10:11 saw heaven o', and a certain vessel
34 Then Peter o' his mouth, and said,
12:10 which o' to them of his own accord:
14 she o' not the gate for gladness, but
16 and when they had o' the door, and
14:27 o' the door of faith unto the Gentiles.
16:14 whose heart the Lord o', that she
26 immediately all the doors were o',
1Co 16: 9 door and effectual is o' unto me,
2Co 2:12 a door was o' unto me of the Lord,
Heb 4:13 all things are naked and o' unto
Re 4: 1 behold, a door was o' in heaven:
6: 1 when the Lamb o' one of the seals,
3 And when he had o' the second seal,
5 And when he had o' the third seal,
7 And when he had o' the fourth seal,
9 And when he had o' the fifth seal,
12 when he had o' the sixth seal,
8: 1 And when he had o' the seventh seal,
9: 2 And he o' the bottomless pit; and
11:19 the temple of God was o' in heaven,
12:16 earth o' her mouth, and swallowed
13: 6 o' his mouth in blasphemy against
15: 5 of the testimony in heaven was o':
19:11 And I saw heaven o', and behold a
20:12 before God; and the books were o':
12 another book was o', which is the

openest
Ps 104:28 thou o' thine hand, they are filled
145:16 Thou o' thine hand, and satisfiest

openeth
Ex 13: 2 whatsoever o' the womb among
12 unto the Lord all that o' the matrix,
15 to the Lord all that o' the matrix,
34:19 All that o' the matrix is mine; and
Nu 3:12 all the firstborn that o' the matrix
18:15 thing that o' the matrix in all flesh,
Job 27:19 he o' his eyes, and he is not.
33:16 he o' the ears of men, and sealeth
36:10 He o' also their ear to discipline,
15 and o' their ears in oppression.
Ps 38:13 dumb man that o' not his mouth.
146: 8 The Lord o' the eyes of the blind:
Pr 13: 3 he that o' wide his lips shall have
24: 7 he o' not his mouth in the gate.
31:26 She o' her mouth with wisdom;
Isa 53: 7 is dumb, so he o' not his mouth.
Eze 20:26 the fire all that o' the womb,
Lu 2:23 Every male that o' the womb shall
Joh 10: 3 To him the porter o'; and the sheep
Re 3: 7 he that o', and no man shutteth;
7 and shutteth, and no man o';

opening See also OPENINGS.
1Ch 9:27 and the o' thereof every morning
Job 12:14 up a man, and there can be no o'.
Pr 8: 6 o' of my lips shall be right things.
Isa 42:20 o' the ears, but he heareth not.
61: 1 o' of the prison to them that are
Eze 29:21 will give thee the o' of the mouth
Ac 17: 3 O' and alleging, that Christ must

openings
Pr 1:21 concourse, in the o' of the gates:

openly
Ge 38:21 that was o' by the way side?
Ps 98: 2 righteousness hath he o' shewed in
M't 6: 4 shall reward thee o'.
6 secret shall reward thee o'.
18 secret, shall reward thee o'.
M'r 1:45 no more o' enter into the city,
8:32 And he spake that saying o'.
Joh 7: 4 himself seeketh to be known o'.
10 not o', but as it were in secret.

Joh 7:13 no man spake o· of him for fear of
11:54 walked no more o· among the Jews;
18:20 I spake o· to the world; I ever
Ac 10:40 the third day, and shewed him o·;
16:37 have beaten us o· uncondemned,
Col 2:15 he made a shew of them o·,

operation See also OPERATIONS.
Ps 28: 5 the Lord, nor the o· of his hands,
Isa 5:12 neither consider the o· of his hands.
Col 2:12 through the faith of the o· of God,

operations
1Co 12: 6 there are diversities of o·, but it is

Ophel (*o'-fel*)
2Ch 27: 3 on the wall of O· he built much.
33:14 and compassed about O·, and raised
Ne 3:26 the Nethinims dwelt in O·, unto
27 lieth out, even unto the wall of O·.
11:21 But the Nethinims dwelt in O·:

Ophir (*o'-fur*)
Ge 10:29 And O·, and Havilah, and Jobab:
1Ki 9:28 they came to O·, and fetched from
10:11 Hiram, that brought gold from O·,
11 brought in from O· great plenty of
22:48 ships of Tharshish to go to O· for
1Ch 1:23 And O·, and Havilah, and Jobab.
29: 4 talents of gold, of the gold of O·,
2Ch 8:18 with the servants of Solomon to O·,
9:10 which brought gold from O·, brought
Job 22:24 the gold of O· as the stones of the
28:16 cannot be valued with the gold of O·,
Ps 45: 9 did stand the queen in gold of O·.
Isa 13:12 man than the golden wedge of O·.

Ophni (*of'-ni*)
Jos 18:24 Chephar-haammonai, and O·, and

Ophrah (*of'-rah*) See also APHRAH.
Jos 18:23 And Avim, and Parah, and O·,
J'g 6:11 sat under an oak which was in O·,
24 it is yet in O· of the Abi-ezrites.
8:27 and put it in his city, even in O·:
32 sepulchre of Joash his father, in O·
9: 5 went unto his father's house at O·,
1Sa 13:17 unto the way that leadeth to O·,
1Ch 4:14 And Meonothai begat O·: and

opinion See also OPINIONS.
Job 32: 6 and durst not shew you mine o·.
10 to me; I also will shew mine o·.
17 my part, I also will shew mine o·.

opinions
1Ki 18:21 How long halt ye between two o·?

opportunity
M't 26:16 time he sought o· to betray him.
Lu 22: 6 sought o· to betray him unto them
Ga 6:10 As we have therefore o·, let us do
Ph'p 4:10 were also careful, but ye lacked o·.
Heb 11:15 have had o· to have returned.

oppose See also OPPOSED; OPPOSEST; OPPOSETH.
2Ti 2:25 instructing those that o· themselves;

opposed
Ac 18: 6 And when they o· themselves, and

opposest
Job 30:21 hand thou o· thyself against me.

opposeth
2Th 2: 4 Who o· and exalteth himself above

oppositions
1Ti 6:20 and o· of science falsely so called:

oppress See also OPPRESSED; OPPRESSETH; OPPRESSING.
Ex 3: 9 wherewith the Egyptians o· them.
22:21 neither vex a stranger, nor o· him:
23: 9 Also thou shalt not o· a stranger:
Le 25:14 hand, ye shall not o· one another:
17 shall not therefore o· one another;
De 23:16 him best: thou shalt not o· him.
24:14 Thou shalt not o· an hired servant
J'g 10:12 and the Maonites, did o· you;
Job 10: 3 unto thee that thou shouldest o·,
Ps 10:18 man of the earth may no more o·.
17: 9 From the wicked that o· me, from
119:122 for good: let not the proud o· me.
Pr 22:22 neither o· the afflicted in the gate:
Isa 49:26 I will feed them that o· thee with
Jer 7: 6 If ye o· not the stranger, the
30:20 and I will punish all that o· them.
Eze 45: 8 shall no more o· my people; and
Ho 12: 7 are in his hand: he loveth to o·.
Am 4: 1 which o· the poor, which crush the
Mic 2: 2 so they o· a man and his house,
Zec 7:10 o· not the widow, nor the fatherless,
Mal 3: 5 that o· the hireling in his wages,
Jas 2: 6 Do not rich men o· you, and draw

oppressed
De 28:29 thou shalt be only o· and spoiled
33 thou shalt be only o· and crushed
J'g 2:18 by reason of them that o· them
4: 3 mightily o· the children of Israel.
6: 9 out of the hand of all that o· you,
10: 8 and o· the children of Israel:
1Sa 10:18 kingdoms, and of them that o· you:
12: 3 whom have I o·? or of whose hand
4 hast not defrauded us, nor o· us,
2Ki 13: 4 because the king of Syria o· them.
22 But Hazael king of Syria o· Israel
2Ch 16:10 And Asa o· some of the people
Job 20:19 o· and hath forsaken the poor;
35: 9 they make the o· to cry: they cry out
Ps 9: 9 also will be a refuge for the o·,
10:18 To judge the fatherless and the o·,
74:21 O let not the o· return ashamed:
103: 6 and judgment for all that are o·.
106:42 Their enemies also o· them, and
146: 7 executeth judgment for the o·:
Ec 4: 1 the tears of such as were o·,
Isa 1:17 seek judgment, relieve the o·,
3: 5 And the people shall be o·, every
23:12 no more rejoice, O thou o· virgin,
38:14 O Lord, I am o·; undertake for me.
52: 4 Assyrian o· them without cause.
53: 7 He was o·, and he was afflicted,
58: 6 to let the o· go free, and that ye
Jer 50:33 and the children of Judah were o·
Eze 18: 7 hath not o· any, but hath restored
12 Hath o· the poor and needy, hath
16 Neither hath o· any, hath not
18 because he cruelly o·, spoiled his
22:29 have o· the stranger wrongfully.
Ho 5:11 Ephraim is o· and broken in
Am 3: 9 and the o· in the midst thereof.
Ac 7:24 and avenged him that was o·, and
10:38 all that were o· of the devil;

oppresseth
Nu 10: 9 against the enemy that o· you,
Ps 56: 1 me up; he fighting daily o· me.
Pr 14:31 He that o· the poor reproacheth
22:16 He that o· the poor to increase his
28: 3 A poor man that o· the poor is like

oppressing
Jer 46:16 our nativity, from the o· sword.
50:16 for fear of the o· sword they shall
Zep 3: 1 filthy and polluted, to the o· city!

oppression See also OPPRESSIONS.
Ex 3: 9 the o· wherewith the Egyptians
De 26: 7 and our labour, and our o·:
2Ki 13: 4 he saw the o· of Israel, because the
Job 36:15 and openeth their ears in o·.
Ps 12: 5 For the o· of the poor, for the
42: 9 because of the o· of the enemy?
43: 2 because of the o· of the enemy?
44:24 forgettest our affliction and our o·?
55: 3 because of the o· of the wicked:
62:10 Trust not in o·, and become not
73: 8 and speak wickedly concerning o·:
107:39 brought low through o·, affliction,
119:134 Deliver me from the o· of man:
Ec 5: 8 If thou seest the o· of the poor,
7: 7 Surely o· maketh a wise man mad;
Isa 5: 7 for judgment, but behold o·;
30:12 despise this word, and trust in o·
54:14 thou shalt be far from o·; for thou
59:13 speaking o· and revolt, concerning
Jer 6: 6 she is wholly o· in the midst of her.
22:17 and for o·, and for violence, to do it.
Eze 22: 7 they dealt by o· with the stranger:
29 people of the land have used o·,
46:18 of the people's inheritance by o·,

oppressions
Job 35: 9 By reason of the multitude of o·
Ec 4: 1 the o· that are done under the sun:
Isa 33:15 he that despiseth the gain of o·,

oppressor See also OPPRESSORS.
Job 3:18 they hear not the voice of the o·.
15:20 number of years is hidden to the o·.
Ps 72: 4 and shall break in pieces the o·.
Pr 3:31 Envy thou not the o·, and
28:16 understanding is also a great o·:
Isa 9: 4 of his shoulder, the rod of his o·,
14: 4 and say, How hath the o· ceased!
51:13 day because of the fury of the o·,
13 and where is the fury of the o·?
Jer 21:12 spoiled out of the hand of the o·,
22: 3 spoiled out of the hand of the o·:
25:38 because of the fierceness of the o·,
Zec 9: 8 no o· shall pass through them
10: 4 bow, out of him every o· together.

oppressors
Job 27:13 and the heritage of o·, which they
Ps 54: 3 and o· seek after my soul: they
119:121 justice: leave me not to mine o·.
Ec 4: 1 side of their o· there was power;
Isa 3:12 children are their o·, and women
14: 2 and they shall rule over their o·.
16: 4 o· are consumed out of the land.
19:20 unto the Lord because of the o·,

or^ See also NOR.
Ge 13: 9 o· if thou depart to the right hand,
17:12 o· bought with money of any stranger,
24:21 his journey prosperous o· not.
49 to the right hand, o· to the left.
50 cannot speak unto thee bad o· good.
26:11 that toucheth this man o· his wife
27:21 thou be my very son Esau o· not.
30: 1 Give me children, o· else I die.
31:14 yet any portion o· inheritance for us
24, 29 to Jacob either good o· bad.
39 stolen by day, o· stolen by night.
43 daughters, o· unto their children
50 o· if thou shalt take other wives
37: 8 o· shalt thou indeed have dominion
32 whether it be thy son's coat o· no.
39:10 her, to lie by her, o· to be with her.
41:44 no man lift up his hand o· foot in
42:16 o· else by the life of Pharaoh
44: 8 of thy lord's house silver o· gold?
16 speak? o· how shall we clear ourselves?
19 Have ye a father, o· a brother?
Ex 4:11 mouth? o· who maketh the dumb,
11 o· deaf, o· the seeing, o· the blind?
5: 3 with pestilence, o· with the sword.
10:15 the trees, o· in the herbs of the field,
11: 7 his tongue, against man o· beast:
12: 5 out from the sheep, o· from the goats:
Ex 12:19 he be a stranger, o· born in the land.
16: 4 they will walk in my law, o· no.
17: 7 Is the Lord among us, o· not?
19:12 the mount, o· touch the border of it:
13 whether it be beast o· man, it shall
13 surely be stoned, o· shot through;
20: 4 o· any likeness of any thing that is
4 o· that is in the earth beneath, o· that
21: 4 have born him sons o· daughters;
6 to the door, o· unto the door post;
15 that smiteth his father, o· his mother,
16 him, o· if he be found in his hand,
17 that curseth his father, o· his mother,
18 with a stone, o· with his fist, and
20 man smite his servant, o· his maid,
21 if he continue a day o· two, he
26 his servant, o· the eye of his maid,
27 tooth, o· his maidservant's tooth;
28 If an ox gore a man o· a woman,
29 he hath killed a man o· woman;
31 a son, o· have gored a daughter,
32 a manservant o· a maidservant;
33 o· if a man shall dig a pit, and not
33 it, and an ox o· an ass fall therein;
36 O· if it be known that the ox hath
22: 1 ox, o· a sheep, and kill it, o· sell it;
4 whether it be ox, o· ass, o· sheep;
5 a field o· vineyard to be eaten, and
6 o· the standing corn, o· the field, be
7 neighbour money o· stuff to keep,
9 o· for any manner of lost thing,
10 o· an ox, o· a sheep, o· any beast, to
10 o· be hurt, o· driven away, no man
14 it be hurt, o· die, the owner thereof
22 afflict any widow, o· fatherless child.
23: 4 enemy's ox o· his ass going astray,
28:43 o· when they come near unto the
29:34 the consecrations, o· of the bread,
30:20 o· when they come near to the altar
33 o· whosoever putteth any of it upon a
34:19 whether ox o· sheep, that is male.
Le 1:10 o· of the goats, for a burnt sacrifice;
14 of turtledoves, o· of young pigeons.
2: 4 o· unleavened wafers anointed with
3: 1 whether it be a male o· female, he
6 male o· female, he shall offer it
4:23 O· if his sin, wherein he hath
28 O· if his sin, which he hath sinned,
5: 1 whether he hath seen o· known of it;
2 O· if a soul touch any unclean thing,
2 o· a carcase of unclean cattle,
2 o· the carcase of unclean creeping
3 O· if he touch the uncleanness of
4 O· if a soul swear, pronouncing with
4 his lips to do evil, o· to do good,
6 lamb o· a kid of the goats, for a sin
7, 11 turtledoves, o· two young pigeons,
6: 2 him to keep, o· in fellowship,
2 o· in a thing taken away by violence,
2 o· hath deceived his neighbour;
3 O· have found that which was lost,
4 away, o· the thing which he hath
4 o· that which was delivered him to
4 o· the lost thing which he found,
5 O· all that about which he hath
7:16 be a vow, o· a voluntary offering, it
21 man, o· any unclean beast, o· any
23 of fat, of ox, o· of sheep, o· of goat.
26 whether it be of fowl o· of beast, in
11: 4 cud, o· of them that divide the hoof:
32 wood, o· raiment, o· skin, o· sack,
35 it be oven, o· ranges for pots, they
36 fountain o· pit, wherein there is plenty
42 o· whatsoever hath more feet
12: 6 fulfilled, for a son, o· for a daughter,
6 young pigeon, o· a turtledove, for a
7 that hath born a male o· a female.
8 two turtles, o· two young pigeons;
13: 2 a rising, a scab, o· bright spot, and
2 o· unto one of his sons the priests:
16 O· if the raw flesh turn again, and
19 white rising, o· a bright spot, white,
24 O· if there be any flesh, in the skin
24 spot, somewhat reddish, o· white;
29 If a man o· woman have a plague
29 plague upon the head o· the beard;
30 a leprosy upon the head o· beard.
38 o· also a woman have in the skin of
42 in the bald head, o· bald forehead,
42 his bald head, o· his bald forehead.
43 bald head, o· in his bald forehead,
47 garment, o· a linen garment;
48 warp, o· woof; of linen, o· of woollen;
48 skin, o· in any thing made of skin;
49 o· reddish in the garment, o·...skin,
49 o· in the woof, o· in any thing of skin;
51 warp, o· in the woof, o· in a skin,
51 o· in any work that is made of
52 o· woof, in woollen o· in linen, o· any
53 o· in the woof, o· in any thing of skin;
56 of the garment, o· out of the skin,
56 o· out of the warp, o· out of the woof:
57 o· in the woof, o· in any thing of
58 o· woof, o· whatsoever thing of skin
59 o· linen, either in the warp, o· woof,
59 o· any thing of skins, to pronounce
59 clean, o· to pronounce it unclean.
14:22 turtledoves, o· two young pigeons,
30 o· of the young pigeons, such as he
37 hollow strakes, greenish o· reddish,
15: 3 o· his flesh be stopped from his
14 turtledoves, o· two young pigeons,
23 o· on any thing whereon she sitteth,
25 o· if it run beyond the time of her
29 two turtles, o· two young pigeons,
16:29 o· a stranger that sojourneth among

Le 17: 3 an ox, o' lamb, o' goat, in the camp,
3 o' that killeth it out of the camp,
8 o' of the strangers which sojourn
8 a burnt offering o' sacrifice,
10, 13 o' of the strangers that sojourn
13 catcheth any beast o' fowl that may
15 o' that which was torn with beasts,
15 of your own country, o' a stranger,
18: 7 father, o' the nakedness of thy mother,
9 father, o' daughter of thy mother,
9 be born at home, o' born abroad,
10 o' of thy daughter's daughter, even
17 o' her daughter's daughter, to
19: 35 in meteyard, in weight, o' in measure.
20: 2 o' of the strangers that sojourn in
9 curseth his father o' his mother shall
9 cursed his father o' his mother;
17 o' his mother's daughter, and see
25 o' by fowl, o' by any manner of living
27 A man also o' woman that hath a
27 o' that is a wizard, shall surely be put
21: 7 a wife that is a whore, o' profane;
11 for his father, o' for his mother;
14 o' a divorced woman, o' profane,
14 o' an harlot, these shall he not take:
18 blind man, o' a lame, o' he that
18 flat nose, o' any thing superfluous,
19 O' a man that is brokenfooted,
19 is brokenfooted, o' brokenhanded,
20 O' crookbackt, o' a dwarf,
20 o' that hath a blemish in his eye,
20 a blemish in his eye, o' be scurvy,
20 o' scabbed, o' hath his stones
22: 4 is a leper, o' hath a running issue;
4 o' a man whose seed goeth from him;
5 O' whosoever toucheth any creeping
5 o' a man of whom he may take
8 dieth of itself, o' is torn with beasts,
10 of the priest, o' an hired servant,
13 daughter be a widow, o' divorced,
16 O' suffer them to bear the iniquity of
18 Israel, o' of the strangers in Israel,
19 beeves, of the sheep, o' of the goats.
21 o' a freewill offering in beeves
21 a freewill offering in beeves o' sheep,
22 o' broken, o' maimed, o' having a
22 o' scurvy, o' scabbed, ye shall not
23 bullock o' a lamb that hath any thing
23 superfluous o' lacking in his parts,
24 is bruised, o' crushed, o' broken, o' cut;
27 a bullock, o' a sheep, o' a goat, is
28 whether it be cow o' ewe, ye shall
25: 14 o' buyest ought of thy neighbour's
35 he be a stranger, o' a sojourner; that
36 thou no usury of him, o' increase: but
47 sojourner o' stranger wax rich by thee,
47 the stranger o' sojourner by thee,
49 o' his uncle's son, may redeem him,
49 o' any that is nigh of kin unto him
49 o' if he be able, he may redeem
26: 15 o' if your soul abhor my judgments,
27: 10 good for a bad, o' a bad for a good:
12 value it, whether it be good o' bad:
14 estimate it, whether it be good o' bad:
20 o' if he have sold the field to
26 whether it be ox o' sheep: it is the
27 o' if it be not redeemed, then it
28 possession, shall be sold o' redeemed:
30 o' of the fruit of the tree, is the Lord's:
32 the tithe of the herd, o' of the flock,
33 not search whether it be good o' bad,
Nu 5: 6 a man o' woman shall commit any
14 o' if the spirit of jealousy come upon
30 O' when the spirit of jealousy
6: 2 either man o' woman shall separate
3 of wine, o' vinegar of strong drink,
3 grapes, nor eat moist grapes, o' dried.
7 for his father, o' for his mother,
7 for his brother, o' for his sister, when
10 two turtles, o' two young pigeons,
9: 10 o' of your posterity shall be unclean
10 o' be in a journey afar off, yet he
21 o' by night that the cloud was taken
22 O' whether it were two days,
22 o' a month, o' a year, that the cloud
11: 8 it in mills, o' beat it in a mortar,
22 o' shall all the fish of the sea be
23 shall come to pass unto thee o' not.
13: 18 be strong o' weak, few o' many;
19 dwell in, whether it be good o' bad;
19 whether in tents, o' in strong holds;
20 whether it be fat o' lean, whether
20 there be wood therein o' not.
14: 2 o' would God we had died in this
15: 3 o' a sacrifice in performing a vow,
3 a vow, o' in a freewill offering,
3 o' in your solemn feasts, to make a
3 the Lord, of the herd, o' of the flock:
5 with the burnt offering o' sacrifice,
6 O' for a ram, thou shalt prepare for
8 o' for a sacrifice in performing a vow,
8 o' peace offering unto the Lord:
11 for one bullock, o' for one ram,
11 o' for a lamb, o' a kid.
14 o' whosoever be among you in your
30 he be born in the land, o' a stranger,
16: 14 o' given us inheritance of fields and
29 o' if they be visited after the
18: 15 whether it be of men o' beasts, shall
17 of a cow, o' the firstling of a sheep,
17 o' the firstling of a goat, thou shalt
19: 16 the open fields, o' a dead body,
16 o' a bone of a man,
16 o' a grave, shall be unclean seven
18 that touched a bone, o' one slain,
18 o' one dead, o' a grave:

Nu 20: 5 it is no place of seed, o' of figs,
5 o' of vines, o' of pomegranates;
17 the fields, o' through the vineyards,
21: 22 into the fields, o' into the vineyards;
22: 18 Lord my God, to do less o' more.
26 either to the right hand o' to the left.
23: 8 o' how shall I defy, whom the Lord
19 o' hath he spoken, and shall he not
24: 13 good o' bad of mine own mind;
30: 2 o' swear an oath to bind his soul
5 o' of her bonds wherewith she hath
6 o' uttered ought out of her lips,
10 o' bound her soul by a bond with an
13 it, o' her husband may make it void.
14 o' all her bonds, which are upon
32: 19 on yonder side Jordan, o' forward;
35: 18 O' if he smite him with an hand
20 o' hurl at him by laying of wait,
21 O' in enmity smite him with his
22 o' have cast upon him any thing
23 O' with any stone, wherewith a
De 3: 24 God is there in heaven o' in earth,
4: 16 the likeness of male o' female,
23, 25 image, o' the likeness of any thing,
32 is, o' hath been heard like it?
34 O' hath God assayed to go and take
5: 8 image, o' any likeness of any thing
8 above, o' that is in the earth beneath,
8 o' that is in the waters beneath the
21 o' his manservant, o' his maidservant,
21 ox, o' his ass, o' any thing that is thy
32 aside to the right hand o' to the left.
7: 14 be male o' female barren among you,
14 among you, o' among your cattle.
25 the silver o' gold that is on them,
8: 2 keep his commandments, o' no.
9: 5 o' for the uprightness of thine heart,
12: 17 thy corn, o' of thy wine, o' of thy oil,
17 o' the firstlings of thy herds,
17 o' of thy flock, nor any of thy vows
17 o' heave offering of thine hand:
13: 1 prophet, o' a dreamer of dreams,
1 and giveth thee a sign o' a wonder,
2 the sign o' the wonder come to pass,
3 prophet, o' that dreamer of dreams:
5 prophet, o' that dreamer of dreams,
6 mother, o' thy son, o' thy daughter,
6 daughter, o' the wife of thy bosom,
6 o' thy friend, which is as thine own
7 nigh unto thee, o' far off from thee,
14: 21 o' thou mayest sell it unto an alien:
24 o' if the place be too far from thee,
26 for oxen, o' for sheep, o' for wine,
26 o' for strong drink,
26 o' for whatsoever thy soul desireth:
15: 2 it of his neighbour, o' of his brother;
12 man, o' an Hebrew woman, be sold
21 therein, as if it be lame, o' blind,
21 o' have any ill blemish, thou shalt
17: 1 bullock, o' sheep, wherein is blemish,
1 o' any evilfavouredness: for that
2 man o' woman, that hath wrought
3 sun, o' moon, o' any of the host of
5 bring forth that man o' that woman,
5 gates, even that man o' that woman,
6 two witnesses, o' three witnesses,
12 the Lord thy God, o' unto the judge,
20 to the right hand, o' to the left:
18: 3 sacrifice, whether it be ox o' sheep;
10 son o' his daughter to pass through
10 o'...useth divinations, o' an observer
10 of times, o' an enchanter, o' a witch,
11 O' a charmer, o' a consulter with
11 spirits, o' a wizard, o' a necromancer.
20 o' that shall speak in the name of
19: 15 man for any iniquity, o' for any sin,
15 o' at the mouth of three witnesses,
21: 18 his father, o' the voice of his mother,
22: 1 brother's ox o' his sheep go astray,
2 o' if thou know him not, then thou
4 ass o' his ox fall down by the way,
6 way in any tree, o' on the ground,
6 whether they be young ones, o' eggs,
6 upon the young, o' upon the eggs,
23: 1 o' hath his privy member cut off,
3 An Ammonite o' Moabite shall not
18 o' the price of a dog, into the house of
24: 3 o' if the latter husband die, which
6 o' the upper millstone to pledge:
7 merchandise of him, o' selleth him;
14 o' of thy strangers that are in thy
27: 15 maketh any graven o' molten image,
16 light by his father o' his mother.
22 o' the daughter of his mother.
28: 14 day, to the right hand, o' to the left,
51 leave thee either corn, wine, o' oil,
51 o' the increase of thy kine,
51 o' flocks of thy sheep, until he have
29: 6 have ye drunk wine o' strong drink:
18 man, o' woman, o' family, o' tribe,
32: 36 and there is none shut up, o' left.
Jos 1: 7 it to the right hand o' to the left,
5: 13 thou for us, o' for our adversaries?
7: 3 two o' three thousand men go up
8: 17 was not a man left in Ai o' Beth-el,
20 power to flee this way o' that way:
22 let none of them remain o' escape.
10: 14 no day like that before it o' after it,
22: 22 in rebellion, o' if in transgression
23 o' if to offer thereon burnt offering
23 burnt offering o' meat offering,
23 o' if to offer peace offerings thereon,
28 so say to us o' to our generations in
29 for meat offerings, o' for sacrifices,
23: 6 to the right hand o' to the left;
24: 15 flood, o' the gods of the Amorites,

J'g 2: 22 as their fathers did keep it, o' not.
5: 8 a shield o' spear seen among forty
30 prey; to every man a damsel o' two;
9: 2 you, o' that one reign over you?
11: 25 o' did he ever fight against them,
13: 14 let her drink wine o' strong drink,
14: 3 brethren, o' among all my people,
6 he told not his father o' his mother
18: 19 o' that thou be a priest unto a
19: 13 all night, in Gibeah, o' in Ramah.
20: 28 my brother, o' shall I cease?
21: 22 fathers o' their brethren come
Ru 1: 16 o' to return from following after thee:
3: 10 young men, whether poor o' rich.
1Sa 2: 14 pan, o' kettle, o' caldron, o' pot;
6: 12 aside to the right hand o' to the left;
12: 3 I taken? o' whose ass have I taken?
3 I taken? o' whom have I defrauded?
3 o' of whose hand have I received any
13: 19 make them swords o' spears:
14: 6 Lord to save by many o' by few.
52 any strong man, o' any valiant man,
16: 7 o' on the height of his stature;
18: 18 life, o' my father's family in Israel,
20: 2 do nothing either great o' small,
10 o' what if thy father answer thee
12 to-morrow any time, o' the third day,
21: 3 mine hand, o' what there is present.
8 under thine hand spear o' sword?
22: 8 o' sheweth unto me that my son hath
15 nothing of all this, less o' more.
25: 31 o' that my lord hath avenged himself:
36 she told him nothing, less o' more,
26: 10 him; o' his day shall come to die;
10 o' he shall descend into battle, and
18 I done? o' what evil is in mine hand?
29: 3 with me these days, o' these years,
30: 2 slew not any, either great o' small,
2Sa 2: 21 to thy right hand o' to thy left,
3: 29 that hath an issue, o' that is a leper,
29 is a leper, o' that leaneth on a staff,
29 staff, o' that falleth on the sword,
29 on the sword, o' that lacketh bread.
35 if I taste bread, o' aught else, till
14: 19 turn to the right hand o' to the left
15: 4 man which hath any suit o' cause
21 whether in death o' life, even there
17: 9 in some pit, o' in some other place:
19: 35 taste what I eat o' what I drink?
42 cost? o' hath he given us any gift?
20: 20 that I should swallow up o' destroy.
24: 13 o' wilt thou flee three months before
13 o' that there be three days' pestilence
1Ki 3: 7 I know not how to go out o' come in.
8: 23 in heaven above, o' on earth beneath,
37 locust, o' if there be caterpiller;
38 any man, o' by all thy people Israel,
46 the land of the enemy, far o' near;
9: 6 from following me, ye o' your children,
15: 17 suffer any to go out o' come in to Asa
18: 10 there is no nation o' kingdom, whither
27 o' he is pursuing, o' he is in a journey,
27 a journey, o' peradventure he sleepeth,
20: 18 o' whether they be come out for war,
39 o' else thou shalt pay a talent of
21: 2 o', if it seem good to thee, I will give
6 o' else, if it please thee, I will give
22: 6 to battle, o' shall I forbear?
15 to battle, o' shall we forbear?
2Ki 2: 16 some mountain, o' into some valley.
21 thence any more death o' barren land.
4: 13 king, o' to the captain of the host?
6: 27 barnfloor, o' out of the winepress?
9: 32 to him out two o' three eunuchs.
12: 13 any vessels of gold, o' vessels of silver,
13: 19 have smitten five o' six times;
17: 34 statutes, o' after their ordinances,
34 o' after the law and commandment
20: 9 degrees, o' go back ten degrees?
22: 2 to the right hand o' to the left.
23: 10 son o' his daughter to pass through
1Ch 21: 12 o' three months to be destroyed
12 o' else three days the sword of the
2Ch 1: 11 not asked riches, wealth, o' honour,
6: 28 o' mildew, locust o' caterpillers;
28 sore o' whatsoever sickness there be;
29 what prayer o' what supplication
29 of any man, o' of all thy people Israel,
36 captives unto a land far off o' near;
7: 13 o' if I command the locusts to
13 o' if I send pestilence among my
8: 15 matter, o' concerning the treasures.
14: 11 o' with them that have no power:
15: 13 to death, whether small o' great,
13 great, whether man o' woman.
16: 1 let none go out o' come in to Asa king
18: 5, 14 to battle, o' shall I forbear?
30 Fight ye not with small o' great,
20: 9 judgment, o' pestilence, o' famine,
32: 15 for no god of any nation o' kingdom
36: 17 upon young man o' maiden,
17 old man, o' him that stooped for age:
Ezr 7: 24 o' ministers of this house of God,
24 to impose toll, tribute, o' custom,
26 be unto death, o' to banishment,
26 o' to confiscation of goods,
26 of goods, o' imprisonment.
9: 12 nor seek their peace o' their wealth
10: 13 is this a work of one day o' two:
Ne 2: 16 not whether I went, o' what I did;
5: 8 brethren? o' shall they be sold unto us?
10: 31 bring ware o' any victuals on the
31 on the sabbath, o' on the holy day:
13: 20 without Jerusalem once o' twice.
25 unto your sons, o' for yourselves.
Es 4: 11 whosoever, whether man o' woman,

Es 4:16 eat nor drink three days, night o' day:
8: 6 o' how can I endure to see the
9:12 o' what is thy request further? and it
Job 3:12 o' why the breasts that I should suck?
15 O' with princes that had gold, who
16 O' as an hidden untimely birth I had
4: 7 o' where were the righteous cut off?
6: 5 o' loweth the ox over his fodder?
6 o' is there any taste in the white of
12 of stones? o' is my flesh of brass?
22 o', Give a reward for me of your
23 O', Deliver me from the enemy's
23 o', Redeem me from the hand of the
7:12 Am I a sea, o' a whale, that thou
8: 3 o' doth the Almighty pervert justice?
10: 4 flesh? o' seest thou as man seeth?
11:10 off, and shut up, o' gather together,
12: 8 O' speak to the earth, and it shall
13: 9 o' as one man mocketh another, do
22 o' let me speak, and answer thou
15: 3 o' with speeches wherewith he can do
7 o' wast thou made before the hills?
16: 3 o' what emboldeneth thee that thou
22: 3 o' is it gain to him, that thou
11 O' darkness, that thou canst not
25: 4 o' how can he be clean that is born of
28:16 the precious onyx, o' the sapphire.
18 shall be made of coral, o' of pearls:
31: 5 o' if my foot hath hasted to deceit;
9 o' if I have laid wait at my neighbour's
13 my manservant o' of my maidservant,
16 o' have caused the eyes of the widow
17 O' have eaten my morsel myself
19 clothing, o' any poor without covering;
24 o' have said to the fine gold, Thou art
26 o' the moon walking in brightness;
27 o' my mouth hath kissed my hand:
29 o' lifted up myself when evil found
34 o' did the contempt of families terrify
38 o' that the furrows likewise thereof
39 o' have caused the owners thereof to
32:12 Job, o' that answered his words:
34:13 o' who hath disposed the whole world?
29 a nation, o' against a man only:
33 thou refuse, o' whether thou choose;
35: 6 o' if thy transgressions be multiplied,
7 o' what receiveth he of thine hand?
36:23 o' who can say, Thou hast wrought
29 clouds, o' the noise of his tabernacle?
37:13 correction, o' for his land, o' for mercy.
38: 5 o' who hath stretched the line upon
6 o' who laid the corner stone thereof;
8 O' who shut up the sea with doors,
16 o' hast thou walked in the search of
17 o' hast thou seen the doors of the
21 o' because the number of thy days is
22 o' hast thou seen the treasures of the
25 o' the way for the lightning of thunder;
28 o' who hath begotten the drops of
31 o' loose the bands of Orion?
32 o' canst thou guide Arcturus with his
36 o' who hath given understanding
37 o' who can stay the bottles of heaven,
39 o' fill the appetite of the young lions,
39: 1 o' canst thou mark when the hinds do
2 o' knowest thou the time when they
5 o' who hath loosed the bands of the
9 to serve thee, o' abide by thy crib?
10 o' will he harrow the valleys after
11 o' wilt thou leave thy labour to him?
13 o' wings and feathers unto the
15 o' that the wild beast may break them.
40: 9 o' canst thou thunder with a voice like
41: 1 o' his tongue with a cord which thou
2 o' bore his jaw through with a thorn?
5 o' wilt thou bind him for thy maidens?
7 irons? o' his head with fish spears?
13 o' who can come to him with his
20 as out of a seething pot o' caldron.
Ps 24: 3 o' who shall stand in his holy place?
32: 9 Be ye not as the horse, o' as the mule,
35:14 he had been my friend o' brother:
44:20 o' stretched out our hands to a strange
50: 8 thy sacrifices o' thy burnt offerings,
13 of bulls, o' drink the blood of goats?
16 o' that thou shouldest take my
66: *title* the chief Musician, A Song o' Psalm.
67: *title* on Neginoth, A Psalm o' Song.
68: *title* Musician, A Psalm o' Song of David.
69:31 than an ox o' bullock that hath horns
75: *title* A Psalm o' Song of Asaph.
76: *title* A Psalm o' Song of Asaph.
87: *title* A Psalm o' Song for the sons of
88: *title* A Song o' Psalm for the sons of
11 o' thy faithfulness in destruction?
89: 8 o' to thy faithfulness round about
90: 2 o' ever thou hadst formed the earth
92: *title* A Psalm o' Song for the sabbath day.
94:16 o' who will stand up for me against
108: *title* A Song o' Psalm of David.
120: 3 o' what shall be done unto thee, thou
131: 1 matters, o' in things too high for me.
132: 4 mine eyes, o' slumber to mine eyelids,
139: 7 o' whither shall I flee from thy
144: 3 o' the son of man, that thou makest
Pr 6: 7 having no guide, overseer, o' ruler,
7:22 o' as a fool to the correction of the
8: 8 nothing froward o' perverse in them.
23 the beginning, o' ever the earth was.
20:20 curseth his father o' his mother,
22:26 o' of them that are sureties for debts.
23:34 o' as he that lieth upon the top of a
28:24 robbeth his father o' his mother, and
29: 9 whether he rage o' laugh, there is no
30: 4 up into heaven, o' descended?
9 o' lest I be poor and steal, and take

Pr 30:32 o' if thou hast thought evil, lay
Ec 2:19 he shall be a wise man o' a fool?
25 o' who else can hasten here unto, more
5:12 whether he eat little o' much: but
9: 1 no man knoweth either love o' hatred
11: 3 o' toward the north, in the place
6 shall prosper, either this o' that,
6 o' whether they both shall be alike
12: 2 sun, o' the light, o' the moon, o' the
6 O' ever the silver cord be loosed,
6 o' the golden bowl be broken,
6 o' the pitcher be broken at the
6 o' the wheel broken at the cistern.
14 it be good, o' whether it be evil.
Ca 2: 9 is like a roe o' a young hart:
17 be thou like a roe o' a young hart
6:12 O' ever I was aware, my soul made me
8:14 thou like to a roe o' to a young hart
Isa 1:11 bullocks, o' of lambs, o' of he goats.
7:11 the depth, o' in the height above.
10:14 wing, o' opened the mouth, o' peeped.
15 o' shall the saw magnify itself
15 o' as if the staff should lift up itself,
17: 6 two o' three berries in the top of the
6 four o' five in the outmost fruitful
8 made, either the groves, o' the images.
19:15 head o' tail, branch o' rush, may do.
27: 5 O' let him take hold of my strength,
7 o' is he slain according to the
29: 8 o' as when a thirsty man dreameth,
16 o' shall the thing framed say of him
30:14 o' to take water withal out of the pit.
38:14 Like a crane o' a swallow, so did I
40:13 o' being his counseller hath taught
18 o' what likeness will ye compare unto
25 ye liken me, o' shall I be equal?
41:22 them; o' declare us things for to come.
23 do good, o' do evil, that we may be
42:19 o' deaf, as my messenger that I sent?
43: 9 o' let them hear, and say, It is truth.
44:10 a god, o' molten a graven image
45: 9 thou? o' thy work, He hath no hands?
10 o' to the woman, What hast thou
49:24 o' the lawful captive delivered?
50: 1 o' which of my creditors is it to
2 o' have I no power to deliver?
57:11 hast thou been afraid o' feared,
66: 8 o' shall a nation be born at once?
Jer 2:18 o' what hast thou to do in the way of
32 her ornaments, o' a bride her attire?
7:22 burnt offerings o' sacrifices:
11:14 neither lift up a cry o' prayer for them:
19 like a lamb o' an ox that is brought
13:23 his skin, o' the leopard his spots?
14:22 o' can the heavens give showers?
15: 5 o' who shall bemoan thee?
5 o' who shall go aside to ask how thou
16: 7 for their father o' for their mother.
10 against us? o' what is our iniquity?
10 o' what is our sin that we have
18:14 o' shall the cold flowing waters that
20:17 o' that my mother might have been
21:13 us? o' who shall enter into our
22:18 saying, Ah my brother! o', Ah sister!
18 him, saying, Ah lord! o', Ah his glory!
23:33 people, o' the prophet, o' a priest,
32:43 It is desolate without man o' beast;
34: 9 being an Hebrew o' an Hebrewess,
36:23 Jehudi had read three o' four leaves,
37:18 against thee, o' against thy servants,
18 thy servants, o' against this people,
40: 5 o' go wheresoever it seemeth
42: 6 it be good, o' whether it be evil, we
17 none of them shall remain o' escape
44:14 sojourn there, shall escape o' remain,
28 words shall stand, mine, o' theirs.
48:24 cities of the land of Moab, far o' near.
Eze 2: 5 hear, o' whether they will forbear,
7 hear, o' whether they will forbear:
3:11 hear o' whether they will forbear.
4:14 dieth of itself, o' is torn in pieces;
14: 7 o' of the stranger that sojourneth in
17 O' if I bring a sword upon that
19 O' if I send a pestilence into that
15: 2 o' than a branch which is among
3 o' will men take a pin of it to hang
17: 9 without great power o' many people
15 o' shall he break the covenant, and be
21:16 Go thee one way o' other, either on the
16 either on the right hand, o' on the left,
22:14 o' can thine hands be strong, in the
34: 6 and none did search o' seek after them.
44:22 o' a widow that had a priest before.
25 but for father, o' for mother,
25 o' for son, o' for daughter, for brother,
25 o' for sister that hath had no husband,
31 o' torn, whether it be fowl o' beast.
46:12 burnt offering o' peace offerings
Da 2:10 magician, o' astrologer, o' Chaldean.
4:19 dream, o' the interpretation thereof,
35 o' say unto him, What doest thou?
6: 4 there any error o' fault found in him.
7, 12 ask a petition of any God o' man
24 o' ever they came at the bottom of
11:29 not be as the former, o' as the latter.
Joe 1: 2 o' even in the days of your fathers?
Am 3:12 lion two legs, o' a piece of an ear;
4: 8 two o' three cities wandered unto one
5:19 o' went into the house, and leaned his
6: 2 o' their border greater than your
Mic 6: 7 o' with ten thousands of rivers of oil?
Hag 2:12 his skirt do touch bread, o' pottage,
12 o' wine, o' oil, o' any meat, shall it be
Zec 8:10 to him that went out o' came in
Mal 1: 8 with thee, o' accept thy person?
2:13 o' receiveth it with good will at your

Mal 2:17 o', Where is the God of judgment?
M't 5:17 destroy the law, o' the prophets:
18 one jot o' one tittle shall in no wise
36 not make one hair white o' black.
6:24 o' else he will hold to the one, and
25 ye shall eat, o' what ye shall drink;
31 we eat? o', What shall we drink?
31 o', Wherewithal shall we be clothed?
7: 4 O' how wilt thou say to thy brother,
9 O' what man is there of you, whom
10 O' if he ask a fish, will he give him
16 of thorns, o' figs of thistles?
9: 5 thee; o' to say, Arise, and walk?
10:11 And into whatsoever city o' town ye
14 ye depart out of that house o' city,
19 thought how o' what ye shall speak:
37 He that loveth father o' mother
37 he that loveth son o' daughter more
11: 3 come, o' do we look for another?
12: 5 O' have ye not read in the law, how
25 every city o' house divided against
29 O' else how can one enter into a
33 o' else make the tree corrupt, and
13:21 tribulation o' persecution ariseth
15: 4 He that curseth father o' mother,
5 say to his father o' his mother, It
6 honour not his father o' his mother,
16:14 Jeremias, o' one of the prophets.
26 soul? o' what shall a man give in
17:25 the earth take custom o' tribute?
25 their own children, o' of strangers?
18: 8 if thy hand o' thy foot offend thee,
8 to enter into life halt o' maimed,
8 than having two hands o' two feet
16 take with thee one o' two more,
16 the mouth of two o' three witnesses
20 For where two o' three are gathered
19:29 houses, o' brethren, o' sisters,
29 o' father, o' mother,
29 father,...mother, o' wife,
29 o' children, o' lands, for my name's
21:25 was it from heaven, o' of men?
22:17 to give tribute unto Cæsar, o' not?
23:17 o' the temple that sanctifieth the
19 o' the altar that sanctifieth the
24:23 you, Lo, here is Christ, o' there;
25:37 o' thirsty, and gave thee drink?
38 thee in? o' naked, and clothed thee?
39 O' when saw we thee sick,
39 o' in prison, and came unto thee?
44 hungred, o' athirst, o' a stranger,
44 o' naked, o' sick, o' in prison, and
27:17 o' Jesus which is called Christ?
M'r 2: 9 o' to say, Arise, and take up thy
3: 4 on the sabbath days, o' to do evil?
4 to save life, o' to kill? But they
33 Who is my mother, o' my brethren?
4:17 affliction o' persecution ariseth
21 under a bushel, o' under a bed?
30 o' with what comparison shall we
6:15 a prophet, o' as one of the prophets.
56 into villages, o' cities, o' country,
7:10 Whoso curseth father o' mother, let
11 shall say to his father o' mother, It
12 ought for his father o' his mother;
8:37 O' what shall a man give in
10:29 that hath left house, o' brethren,
29 o' sisters, o' father, o' mother,
29 father,...mother, o' wife,
29 o' children, o' lands, for my sake,
11:30 was it from heaven, o' of men?
12:14 to give tribute to Cæsar, o' not?
15 Shall we give, o' shall we not give?
13:21 Lo, here is Christ; o', lo, he is there;
35 cometh, at even, o' at midnight,
35 at midnight, o' at the cockcrowing,
35 the cockcrowing, o' in the morning:
Lu 2:24 turtledoves, o' two young pigeons.
3:15 whether he were the Christ, o' not;
5:23 o' to say, Rise up and walk?
6: 9 days to do good, o' to do evil?
9 evil? to save life, o' to destroy it?
7:19, 20 come? o' look we for another?
8:16 vessel, o' putteth it under a bed;
9:25 and lose himself, o' be cast away?
11:11 o' if ye ask a fish, will he for a fish
12 O' if he shall ask an egg, will
12:11 how o' what thing ye shall answer,
11 shall answer, o' what ye shall say:
14 me a judge o' a divider over you?
29 shall eat, o' what ye shall drink,
38 watch, o' come in the third watch,
41 this parable unto us, o' even to all?
13: 4 O' those eighteen, upon whom the
15 loose his ox o' his ass from the stall,
14: 5 have an ass o' an ox fallen into a pit,
12 thou makest a dinner o' a supper,
31 O' what king, going to make war
32 O' else, while the other is yet a
16:13 o' else he will hold to the one, and
17: 7 servant plowing o' feeding cattle,
21 shall they say, Lo here! o', lo there!
23 say to you, See here; o', see there:
18:11 o' even as this publican.
29 o' parents, o' brethren, o' wife,
29 o' children, for the kingdom of God's
20: 2 o' who is he that gave thee this
4 was it from heaven, o' of men?
22 to give tribute unto Cæsar, o' no?
22:27 sitteth at meat, o' he that serveth?
Joh 2: 6 two o' three firkins apiece.
4:27 o', Why talkest thou with her?
6:19 five and twenty o' thirty furlongs,
7:17 God, o' whether I speak of myself.
48 o' of the rulers o' of the Pharisees
9: 2 did sin, this man, o' his parents,

Joh 9:21 o' who hath opened his eyes, we
25 Whether he be a sinner o' no, I know
13:29 o', that he should give something
14:11 o' else believe me for the very
18:34 o' did others tell it thee of me?
Ac 1: 7 to know the times o' the seasons,
3:12 o' why look ye so earnestly on us,
12 by our own power o' holiness we
4: 7 By what power, o' by what name,
34 were possessors of lands o' houses
5:38 this counsel o' this work be of men,
7:49 o' what is the place of my rest?
8:34 of himself, o' of some other man?
9: 2 whether they were men o' women,
10:14 thing that is common o' unclean.
28 o' come unto one of another nation;
28 call any man common o' unclean.
11: 8 for nothing common o' unclean hath
17:21 to tell, o' to hear some new thing.)
29 like unto gold, o' silver, o' stone,
18:14 of wrong o' wicked lewdness,
19:12 the sick handkerchiefs o' aprons,
20:33 no man's silver, o' gold, o' apparel.
23: 9 a spirit o' an angel hath spoken to
15 o' ever he come near, are ready to
29 worthy of death o' of bonds.
24:20 O' else let these same here say, if
23 to minister o' come unto him.
25:11 o' have committed any thing
26:31 worthy of death o' of bonds.
28: 6 o' fallen down dead suddenly:
17 people, o' customs of our fathers,
21 shewed o' spake any harm of thee.
Ro 2: 4 O' despisest thou the riches of his
15 accusing o' else excusing one
3: 1 o' what profit is there of
4: 9 o' upon the uncircumcision also?
10 circumcision, o' in uncircumcision?
13 was not to Abraham, o' to his seed,
6:16 o' of obedience unto righteousness?
8:35 o' distress, o' persecution, o' famine,
35 o' nakedness, o' peril, o' sword?
9:11 having done any good o' evil, that
10: 7 O' Who shall descend into the deep?
11:34 o' who hath been his counsellor?
35 O' who hath first given to him, and
12: 7 O' ministry, let us wait on our
7 o' he that teacheth, on teaching;
8 O' he that exhorteth, on
14: 4 own master he standeth o' falleth.
8 whether we live therefore, o' die,
10 o' why dost thou set at nought
13 a stumblingblock o' an occasion
21 brother stumbleth, o' is offended,
21 is offended, o' is made weak.
1Co 1:13 o' were ye baptized in the name of
2: 1 excellency of speech o' of wisdom,
3:22 Paul, o' Apollos, o' Cephas,
22 o' the world, o' life, o' death,
22 o' things present, o' things to come;
4: 3 of you, o' of man's judgment:
21 come unto you with a rod, o' in love,
5:10 this world, o' with the covetous,
10 the covetous, o' extortioners,
10 the covetous, o' with idolaters;
11 be a fornicator, o' covetous,
11 o' an idolater, o' a railer,
11 o' a drunkard, o' an extortioner;
7:11 o' be reconciled to her husband:
15 A brother o' a sister is not under
16 o' how knowest thou, O man,
8: 5 whether in heaven o' in earth,
9: 6 O' I only and Barnabas, have not
7 o' who feedeth a flock, and eateth
8 o' saith not the law the same also?
10 O' saith he it altogether for our
10:19 o' that which is offered in sacrifice
31 eat, o' drink, o' whatsoever ye do,
11: 4 Every man praying o' prophesying,
5 woman that prayeth o' prophesieth
6 for a woman to be shorn o' shaven,
22 o' despise ye the church of God,
12:13 whether we be Jews o' Gentiles,
13 whether we be bond or free;
26 o' one member be honoured, all
13: 1 brass, o' a tinkling cymbal.
14: 6 by revelation, o' by knowledge,
6 o' by prophesying, o' by doctrine?
7 giving sound, whether pipe o' harp,
7 be known what is piped o' harped?
23 that are unlearned, o' unbelievers,
24 believeth not, o' one unlearned,
27 be by two, o' at the most by three,
29 the prophets speak two o' three,
36 from you, o' came it unto you only?
37 himself to be a prophet, o' spiritual,
15:11 whether it were I o' they, so we
37 of wheat, o' of some other grain:
2Co 1: 6 o' whether we be comforted, it is
13 than what ye read o' acknowledge;
17 o' the things that I purpose, do I
3: 1 o' need we, as some others,
1 o' letters of commendation from
5: 9 that, whether present o' absent,
10 done, whether it be good o' bad.
13 o' whether we be sober, it is for your
6:15 o' what part hath he that believeth
8:23 o' our brethren be enquired of,
9: 7 not grudgingly, o' of necessity:
10:12 o' compare ourselves with some
11: 4 o' if ye receive another spirit, which
4 o' another gospel, which ye have
12: 2 o' whether out of the body I cannot
3 in the body, o' out of the body,
6 me to be, o' that he heareth of me.
13: 1 the mouth of two o' three witnesses

Ga 1: 8 o' an angel from heaven, preach
10 do I now persuade men, o' God?
10 o' do I seek to please men? for if I
2: 2 I should run, o' had run, in vain.
3: 2, 5 the law, o' by the hearing of faith?
15 disannulleth, o' addeth thereto.
4: 9 God, o' rather are known of God,
Eph 3:20 above all that we ask o' think,
5: 3 all uncleanness, o' covetousness,
27 spot, o' wrinkle, o' any such thing;
6: 8 Lord, whether he be bond o' free.
Ph'p 1:18 whether in pretence, o' in truth,
20 whether it be by life, o' by death.
27 come and see you, o' else be absent,
2: 3 done through strife o' vainglory;
Col 1:16 they be thrones, o' dominions,
16 o' principalities, o' powers:
20 things in earth, o' things in heaven.
2:16 judge you in meat, o' in drink,
16 o' in respect of a holyday,
16 o' of the new moon, o'...the sabbath
3:17 ye do in word o' in deed, do all in
1Th 2:19 hope, o' joy, o' crown of rejoicing?
5:10 that, whether we wake o' sleep,
2Th 2: 2 shaken in mind, o' be troubled,
4 called God, o' that is worshipped;
15 whether by word, o' our epistle.
1Ti 2: 9 o' gold, o' pearls, o' costly array;
5: 4 widow have children o' nephews,
16 any man o' woman that believeth
19 but before two o' three witnesses.
Tit 1: 6 not accused of riot o' unruly.
3:12 Artemas unto thee, o' Tychicus,
Ph'm 18 wronged thee, o' oweth thee ought,
Heb 2: 6 o' the son of man, that thou visitest
10:28 under two o' three witnesses:
12:16 any fornicator, o' profane person,
20 o' thrust through with a dart:
Jas 2: 3 o' sit here under my footstool:
15 If a brother o' sister be naked, and
4:13 To day o' to morrow we will go into
15 we shall live, and do this, o' that.
1Pe 1:11 what, o' what manner of time the
2:14 O' unto governors, as unto them
3: 3 of gold, o' of putting on of apparel;
9 evil for evil, o' railing for railing:
4:15 o' as a thief, o' as an evildoer,
15 o' as a busybody in other men's
Re 2: 5, 16 o' else I will come unto thee
3:15 I would thou wert cold o' hot:)
13:16 right hand, o' in their foreheads:
17 that no man might buy o' sell, save
17 the mark, o' the name of the beast,
17 beast, o' the number of his name.
14: 9 mark in his forehead, o' in his hand,
20: 4 their foreheads, o' in their hands;
21:27 abomination, o' maketh a lie:

oracle See also ORACLES.
2Sa 16:23 had enquired at the o' of God:
1Ki 6: 5 both of the temple and of the o':
16 them for it within, even for the o',
19 And the o' he prepared in the house
20 the o' in the forepart was twenty
21 by the chains of gold before the o';
22 altar that was by the o' he overlaid
23 the o' he made two cherubims of
31 entering of the o' he made doors
7:49 and five on the left, before the o',
8: 6 his place, into the o' of the house,
8 out in the holy place before the o',
2Ch 3:16 he made chains, as in the o', and
4:20 after the manner before the o', of
5: 7 his place, to the o' of the house,
9 seen from the ark before the o';
Ps 28: 2 up my hands toward thy holy o'.

oracles
Ac 7:38 the lively o' to give unto us:
Ro 3: 2 were committed the o' of God.
Heb 5:12 the first principles of the o' of God;
1Pe 4:11 let him speak as the o' of God;

oration
Ac 12:21 throne, and made an o' unto them.

orator
Isa 3: 3 artificer, and the eloquent o'.
Ac 24: 1 with a certain o' named Tertullus,

orchard See also ORCHARDS.
Ca 4:13 plants are an o' of pomegranates,

orchards
Ec 2: 5 I made me gardens and o', and I

ordain See ORDAINED; ORDAINETH.
1Ch 9:22 the seer did o' in their set office.
17: 9 Also I will o' a place for my people
Isa 26:12 Lord, thou wilt o' peace for us:
1Co 7:17 walk. And so o' I in all churches.
Ti 1: 5 and o' elders in every city, as I

ordained
Nu 28: 6 was o' in mount Sinai for a sweet
1Ki 12:32 And Jeroboam o' a feast in the eighth
33 o' a feast unto the children of Israel:
2Ki 23: 5 had o' to burn incense in the
2Ch 11:15 And he o' him priests for the high
23:18 with singing, as it was o' by David.
29:27 the instruments o' by David king of
Es 9:27 The Jews o', and took upon them,
Ps 8: 2 thou o' strength because of thine
3 and the stars, which thou hast o';
81: 5 This he o' in Joseph for a
132:17 have o' a lamp for mine anointed.
Isa 30:33 Tophet is o' of old; yea, for the
Jer 1: 5 and I o' thee a prophet unto the
Da 2:24 Arioch, whom the king had o'
Hab 1:12 thou hast o' them for judgment;
M'r 3:14 o' twelve, that they should be with

Joh 15:16 I have chosen you, and o' you,
Ac 1:22 must one be o' to be a witness
10:42 was o' of God to be the Judge of
13:48 as were o' to eternal life believed.
14:23 when they had o' them elders in
16: 4 were o' of the apostles and elders
17:31 by that man whom he hath o';
Ro 7:10 which was o' to life, I found to be
13: 1 the powers that be are o' of God.
1Co 2: 7 God o' before the world unto our
9:14 Lord o' that they which preach
Ga 3:19 was o' by angels in the hand of a
Eph 2:10 o' that we should walk in them.
1Ti 2: 7 Whereunto I am o' a preacher,
2Ti *subscr.* o' the first bishop of the church
Tit *subscr.* o' the first bishop of the church
Heb 5: 1 o' for men in things pertaining to
8: 3 every high priest is o' to offer gifts
9: 6 when these things were thus o',
Jude 4 who were before of old o' to this

ordaineth
Ps 7:13 he o' his arrows against the

order^ See also ORDERED; ORDERETH; ORDERINGS.
Ex 26:17 set in o' one against another:
27:21 Aaron and his sons shall o' it from
39:37 even with the lamps to be set in o',
40: 4 the table, and set in o' the things
4 that are to be set in o' upon it;
23 And he set the bread in o' upon it
Le 1: 7 lay the wood in o' upon the fire:
8 and the fat, in o' upon the wood
12 and the priest shall lay them in o'
6:12 lay the burnt offering in o' upon it;
24: 3 shall Aaron o' it from the evening
4 shall o' the lamps upon the pure
8 every sabbath he shall set it in o'
Jos 2: 6 she had laid in o' upon the roof.
J'g 13:12 How shall we o' the child, and
2Sa 17:23 city, and put his household in o',
1Ki 18:33 And he put the wood in o', and cut
20:14 he said, Who shall o' the battle?
2Ki 20: 1 the Lord, Set thine house in o';
23: 4 and the priests of the second o',
1Ch 6:32 their office according to their o'.
15:13 we sought him not after the due o'.
23:31 according to the o' commanded
25: 2 according to the o' of the king.
6 according to the king's o' to Asaph,
2Ch 8:14 according to the o' of David his
13:11 shewbread also set they in o' upon
29:35 house of the Lord was set in o'.
Job 10:22 shadow of death, without any o',
23: 4 I would o' my cause before him,
33: 5 set thy words in o' before me,
37:19 o' our speech by reason of darkness.
Ps 40: 5 be reckoned up in o' unto thee:
50:21 and set them in o' before thine eyes.
110: 4 ever after the o' of Melchizedek.
119:133 O' my steps in thy word: and let
Ec 12: 9 out, and set in o' many proverbs.
Isa 9: 7 kingdom, to o' it, and to establish
38: 1 the Lord, Set thine house in o':
44: 7 declare it, and set it in o' for me,
Jer 46: 3 O' ye the buckler and shield, and
Eze 41: 6 over another, and thirty in o';
Lu 1: 1 in o' a declaration of those things
3 to write unto thee in o', most
8 before God in the o' of his course,
Ac 11: 4 and expounded it by o' unto them,
18:23 of Galatia and Phrygia in o',
1Co 11:34 rest will I set in o' when I come.
14:40 things be done decently and in o'.
15:23 every man in his own o': Christ
16: 1 as I have given o' to the churches
Col 2: 5 joying and beholding your o', and
Tit 1: 5 set in o' the things that are wanting,
Heb 5: 6 ever after the o' of Melchisedec.
10 priest after the o' of Melchisedec.
6:20 ever after the o' of Melchisedec.
7:11 rise after the o' of Melchisedec,
11 not be called after the o' of Aaron?
17 ever after the o' of Melchisedec.
21 ever after the o' of Melchisedec:)

ordered
J'g 6:26 top of this rock, in the o' place,
2Sa 23: 5 covenant, o' in all things, and
Job 13:18 I have o' my cause; I know that I
Ps 37:23 of a good man are o' by the Lord:

ordereth
Ps 50:23 to him that o' his conversation

orderings
1Ch 24:19 the o' of them in their service to

orderly See also DISORDERLY.
Ac 21:24 that thou thyself also walkest o',

ordinance See also ORDINANCES.
Ex 12:14 keep it a feast by an o' for ever.
17 your generations by an o' for ever.
24 observe this thing for an o' to thee
43 This is the o' of the passover:
13:10 therefore keep this o' in his season
15:25 for them a statute and an o', and
Le 18:30 Therefore shall ye keep mine o',
22: 9 They shall therefore keep mine o'.
Nu 9:14 according to the o' of the passover,
14 ye shall have one o', both for the
10: 8 shall be to you for an o' for ever
15:15 One o' shall be both for you of the
15 an o' for ever in your generations:
18: 8 and to thy sons, by an o' for ever.
19: 2 This is the o' of the law which the
31:21 This is the o' of the law which the
Jos 24:25 a statute and an o' in Shechem.
1Sa 30:25 it a statute and an o' for Israel
2Ch 2: 4 This is an o' for ever to Israel.

2Ch 35:13 with fire according to the *o'*: but
25 and made them an *o'* in Israel:
Ezr 3:10 after the *o'* of David king of Israel.
Ps 99: 7 and the *o'* that he gave them.
Isa 24: 5 the laws, changed the *o'*, broken
58: 2 forsook not the *o'* of their God:
Eze 45:14 Concerning the *o'* of oil, the bath
46:14 by a perpetual *o'* unto the Lord.
Mal 3:14 is it that we have kept his *o'*,
Ro 13: 2 the power, resisteth the *o'* of God:
1Pe 2:13 Submit...to every *o'* of man for

ordinances
Ex 18:20 thou shalt teach them *o'* and laws,
Le 18: 3 neither shall ye walk in their *o'*.
4 and keep mine *o'*, to walk therein:
Nu 9:12 all the *o'* of the passover they shall
2Ki 17:34 or after their *o'*, or after the law
37 And the statutes, and the *o'*, and
2Ch 33: 8 and the *o'* by the hand of Moses.
Ne 10:32 Also we made *o'* for us, to charge
Job 38:33 Knowest thou the *o'* of heaven?
Ps 119:91 this day according to thine *o'*:
Isa 58: 2 they ask of me the *o'* of justice;
Jer 31:35 the *o'* of the moon and of the stars
36 If those *o'* depart from before me,
33:25 not appointed the *o'* of heaven and
Eze 11:20 and keep mine *o'*, and do them:
43:11 all the *o'* thereof, and all the forms
11 and all the *o'* thereof, and do them.
18 These are the *o'* of the altar in the
44: 5 concerning all the *o'* of the house
Mal 3: 7 ye are gone away from mine *o'*,
Lu 1: 6 and *o'* of the Lord blameless.
1Co 11: 2 keep the *o'*, as I delivered them to
Eph 2:15 commandments contained in *o'*;
Col 2:14 Blotting out the handwriting of *o'*
20 in the world, are ye subject to *o'*,
Heb 9: 1 had also *o'* of divine service, and
10 divers washings, and carnal *o'*,

ordinary
Eze 16:27 and have diminished thine *o'* food,

Oreb (*o'-reb*)
J'g 7:25 of the Midianites, *O'* and Zeeb;
25 and they slew *O'* upon the rock *O'*,
25 brought the heads of *O'* and Zeeb to
8: 3 the princes of Midian, *O'* and Zeeb:
Ps 83:11 Make their nobles like *O'*, and like
Isa 10:26 slaughter of Midian at the rock of *O'*:

Oregim See JAARE-OREGIM.

Oren (*o'-ren*)
1Ch 2:25 and Bunah, and *O'*, and Ozem, and

organ See also ORGANS.
Ge 4:21 such as handle the harp and *o'*.
Job 21:12 and rejoice at the sound of the *o'*.
30:31 and my *o'* into the voice of them

organs
Ps 150: 4 with stringed instruments and *o'*.

Orion (*o-ri'-on*)
Job 9: 9 Arcturus, *O'*, and Pleiades, and
38:31 Pleiades, or loose the bands of *O'*?
Am 5: 8 that maketh the seven stars and *O'*,

ornament See also ORNAMENTS.
Pr 1: 9 be an *o'* of grace unto thy head,
4: 9 give to thine head an *o'* of grace:
25:12 of gold, and an *o'* of fine gold,
Isa 30:22 the *o'* of thy molten images of gold:
49:18 thee with them all, as with an *o'*,
Eze 7:20 As for the beauty of his *o'*, he set
1Pe 3: 4 the *o'* of a meek and quiet spirit,

ornaments
Ex 33: 4 and no man did put on him his *o'*.
5 now put off thy *o'* from thee, that
6 stripped themselves of their *o'* by
J'g 8:21 and took away the *o'* that were on
26 beside *o'*, and collars, and purple
2Sa 1:24 put on *o'* of gold upon your apparel.
Isa 3:18 their tinkling *o'* about their feet,
20 bonnets, and the *o'* of the legs,
61:10 decketh himself with *o'*,
Jer 2:32 Can a maid forget her *o'*, or a
4:30 thou deckest thee with *o'* of gold,
Eze 16: 7 and thou art come to excellent *o'*:
11 I decked thee also with *o'*, and I
23:40 eyes, and deckedst thyself with *o'*,

Ornan (*or'-nan*) See also ARAUNAH.
1Ch 21:15, 18 threshingfloor of *O'* the Jebusite.
20 *O'* turned back, and saw the angel;
20 Now *O'* was threshing wheat.
21 as David came to *O'*, *O'* looked and
22 Then David said to *O'*, Grant me the
23 *O'* said unto David, Take it to thee,
24 So David said to *O'*, Nay; but I will
25 So David gave to *O'* for the place six
28 threshingfloor of *O'* the Jebusite,
2Ch 3: 1 threshingfloor of *O'* the Jebusite.

Orpah (*or'-pah*)
Ru 1: 4 the name of the one was *O'*, and
14 and *O'* kissed her mother in law;

orphans
La 5: 3 We are *o'* and fatherless, our

Osee (*o'-see*) See also HOSEA; JOSHUA; OSHEA.
Ro 9:25 As he saith also in *O'*, I will call

Oshea (*o-she'-ah*) See also HOSHEA; OSEE.
Nu 13: 8 of Ephraim, *O'* the son of Nun.
16 called *O'* the son of Nun Jehoshua.

ospray
Le 11:13 and the ossifrage, and the *o'*,
De 14:12 and the ossifrage, and the *o'*,

ossifrage
Le 11:13 eagle, and the *o'*, and the ospray,
De 14:12 eagle, and the *o'*, and the ospray,

ostrich See also OSTRICHES.
Job 39:13 wings and feathers unto the *o'*?

ostriches
La 4: 3 cruel, like the *o'* in the wilderness.

other^ See also ANOTHER; OTHERS; OTHERWISE.
Ge 4:19 and the name of the *o'* Zillah.
8:10, 12 And he stayed yet *o'* seven days;
13:11 themselves the one from the *o'*.
28:17 is none *o'* but the house of God,
29:27 serve with me yet seven *o'* years.
30 served with him yet seven *o'* years.
31:50 if thou shalt take *o'* wives beside
32: 8 then the *o'* company which is left
41: 3 seven *o'* kine came up after them
3 stood by the *o'* kine upon the brink
19 seven *o'* kine came up after them,
43:14 he may send away your *o'* brother,
22 *o'* money have we brought down in
47:21 of Egypt even to the *o'* end thereof.
Ex 1:15 and the name of the *o'* Puah:
4: 7 it was turned again as his *o'* flesh.
14:20 one came not near the *o'* all the
17:12 one side, and the *o'* on the...side;
12 one side, and the...on the *o'* side;
18: 4 And the name of the *o'* was Eliezer;
7 asked each *o'* of their welfare;
20: 3 shalt have no *o'* gods before me.
23:13 no mention of the name of *o'* gods,
25:12 and two rings in the *o'* side of it.
19 one end, and the *o'* cherub on the
19 and the...cherub on the *o'* end:
32 the candlestick out of the *o'* side:
33 made like almonds in the *o'* branch,
26: 3 *o'* five curtains shall be coupled one to
13 and a cubit on the *o'* side of that
27 of the *o'* side of the tabernacle,
27:15 on the *o'* side shall be hangings
28:10 the *o'* six names of the rest on the
10 names of the rest on the *o'* stone,
25 the *o'* two ends of the two wreathen
27 two *o'* rings of gold thou shalt make,
27 against the *o'* coupling thereof,
29:19 And thou shalt take the *o'* ram;
39 the *o'* lamb thou shalt offer at even:
41 the *o'* lamb thou shalt offer at even,
30:32 neither shall ye make any *o'* like it,
32:15 and on the *o'* were they written.
34:14 For thou shalt worship no *o'* god:
36:10 and the *o'* five curtains he coupled
25 for the *o'* side of the tabernacle,
32 of the *o'* side of the tabernacle,
33 boards from the one end to the *o'*.
37: 3 and two rings upon the *o'* side of it.
8 cherub on the *o'* end of that side:
18 out of the *o'* side thereof:
38:15 for the *o'* side of the court gate,
39:20 And they made two *o'* golden rings,
20 over against the *o'* coupling thereof,
Le 5: 7 and the *o'* for a burnt offering,
6:11 put on *o'* garments, and carry forth
7:24 beasts, may be used in any *o'* use:
8:22 And he brought the *o'* ram, the
11:23 But all *o'* flying creeping things, which
12: 8 and the *o'* for a sin offering:
13:26 and it be no lower than the *o'* skin, but
14:22 offering, and the *o'* a burnt offering.
31 and the *o'* for a burnt offering,
42 they shall take *o'* stones, and put
42 and he shall take *o'* morter, and
15:15, 30 and the *o'* for a burnt offering;
16: 8 and the *o'* lot for the scapegoat.
18:18 beside the *o'* in her life time.
20:24 have separated you from *o'* people.
26 and have severed you from *o'* people,
25:53 the *o'* shall not rule with rigour over
Nu 6:11 and the *o'* for a burnt offering,
8:12 and the *o'* for a burnt offering,
10:21 and the *o'* did set up the tabernacle
11:26 and the name of the *o'* Medad:
31 were a day's journey on the *o'* side,
21:13 and pitched on the *o'* side of Arnon,
28: 4, 8 *o'* lamb shalt thou offer at even;
36: 3 to any of the sons of the *o'* tribes
De 4:32 the one side of heaven unto the *o'*,
5: 7 shalt have none *o'* gods before me.
6:14 Ye shall not go after *o'* gods, of the
7: 4 me, that they may serve *o'* gods:
8:19 walk after *o'* gods, and serve them,
11:16 and ye turn aside, and serve *o'* gods,
28 to go after *o'* gods, which ye have not
30 Are they not on the *o'* side Jordan,
13: 2 Let us go after *o'* gods, which thou
6 Let us go and serve *o'* gods, which
7 even unto the *o'* end of the earth;
13 Let us go and serve *o'* gods, which
17: 3 And hath gone and served *o'* gods,
18:20 shall speak in the name of *o'* gods,
28:14 to go after *o'* gods to serve them.
36 and there shalt thou serve *o'* gods,
64 the earth even unto the *o'*;
64 and there thou shalt serve *o'* gods,
29:26 For they went and served *o'* gods,
30:17 and worship *o'* gods, and serve them;
31:18 in that they are turned unto *o'* gods.
20 then will they turn unto *o'* gods,
Jos 2:10 Amorites,...on the *o'* side Jordan,
7: 7 and dwelt on the *o'* side Jordan!
8:22 the *o'* issued out of the city against
11:19 of Gibeon: all *o'* they took in battle.
12: 1 their land on the *o'* side Jordan
13:27 on the *o'* side Jordan eastward.
32 of Moab, on the *o'* side Jordan,
14: 3 an half tribe on the *o'* side Jordan:
17: 5 which were on the *o'* side Jordan;
20: 8 And on the *o'* side Jordan by Jericho

Jos 21:27 out of the *o'* half tribe of Manasseh
22: 4 Lord gave you on...*o'* side Jordan.
7 unto the *o'* half thereof gave Joshua
23:16 have gone and served *o'* gods, and
24: 2 dwelt on the *o'* side of the flood in
2 of Nachor: and they served *o'* gods.
3 from the *o'* side of the flood,
8 which dwelt on the *o'* side Jordan:
14 served on the *o'* side of the flood,
15 that were on the *o'* side of the flood,
16 forsake the Lord, to serve *o'* gods;
J'g 2:12 followed *o'* gods, of the gods of the
17 they went a whoring after *o'* gods,
19 in following *o'* gods to serve them,
7: 7 and let all the *o'* people go every man
25 to Gideon on the *o'* side Jordan.
9:44 and the two *o'* companies ran upon all
10: 8 that were on the *o'* side Jordan in
13 forsaken me, and served *o'* gods:
11:18 and pitched on the *o'* side of Arnon,
13:10 unto me, that came unto me the *o'* day.
16:17 become weak, and be like any *o'* man.
20 I will go out as at *o'* times before,
29 hand, and of the *o'* with his left.
20:30 array against Gibeah, as at *o'* times.
31 kill, as at *o'* times, in the highways,
31 and the *o'* to Gibeah in the field,
Ru 1: 4 and the name of the *o'* Ruth:
2:22 they meet thee not in any *o'* field.
1Sa 1: 2 and the name of the *o'* Peninnah:
3:10 and called as at *o'* times, Samuel,
8: 8 forsaken me, and served *o'* gods,
14: 1 garrison, that is on the *o'* side.
4 and a sharp rock on the *o'* side:
4 and the name of the *o'* Seneh.
5 *o'* southward over against Gibeah.
40 my son will be on the *o'* side.
17: 3 stood on a mountain on the *o'* side:
18:10 played with his hand, as at *o'* times:
19:21 he sent *o'* messengers, and they
20:25 king sat upon his seat, as at *o'* times,
21: 9 for there is no *o'* save that here.
26:13 Then David went over to the *o'* side,
19 the Lord, saying, Go, serve *o'* gods.
28: 8 himself, and put on *o'* raiment,
30:20 which they drave before those *o'* cattle,
31: 7 were on the *o'* side of the valley,
7 they that were on the *o'* side Jordan,
2Sa 1:24 clothed you in scarlet, with *o'* delights,
2:13 the *o'* on the...side of the pool.
13 the...on the *o'* side of the pool.
4: 2 and the name of the *o'* Rechab,
12: 1 city; the one rich, and the *o'* poor.
13:16 this evil is...greater than the *o'*
14: 6 but the one smote the *o'*, and slew
17: 9 now in some pit, or in some *o'* place:
24:22 and *o'* instruments of the oxen for
1Ki 3:22 the *o'* woman said, Nay; but the
23 the *o'* saith, Nay; but thy son is
25 half to the one, and half to the *o'*.
26 But the *o'* said, Let it be neither
6:24 cubits the *o'* wing of the cherub:
24 unto the uttermost part of the *o'*
25 And the *o'* cherub was ten cubits:
26 and so was it of the *o'* cherub.
27 of the *o'* cherub touched the *o'* wall;
34 the two leaves of the *o'* door were
7: 6 the *o'* pillars and the thick beam were
7 from one side of the floor to the *o'*.
16 height of the *o'* chapiter was five
17 and seven for the *o'* chapiter.
18 and so did he for the *o'* chapiter.
20 round about upon the *o'* chapiter.
23 cubits from the one brim to the *o'*:
9: 6 but go and serve *o'* gods, and
9 and have taken hold upon *o'* gods,
10:20 one side and on the *o'* upon the six
11: 4 turned away his heart after *o'* gods:
10 that he should not go after *o'* gods:
12:29 Beth-el, and the *o'* put he in Dan.
14: 9 hast gone and made thee *o'* gods,
18:23 I will dress the *o'* bullock, and lay
20:29 pitched one over against the *o'*
2Ki 3:22 saw the water on the *o'* side as red
5:17 offering nor sacrifice unto *o'* gods,
12: 7 Jehoiada the priest, and the *o'* priests,
17: 7 of Egypt, and had feared *o'* gods,
35 Ye shall not fear *o'* gods, nor bow
37 and ye shall not fear *o'* gods.
38 forget; neither shall ye fear *o'* gods.
22:17 have burned incense unto *o'* gods,
1Ch 6:78 on the *o'* side Jordan by Jericho,
9:32 And *o'* of their brethren, of the
12:37 And on the *o'* side of Jordan, of the
23:17 Eliezer had none *o'* sons; but the
2Ch 3:11 *o'* wing was likewise five cubits,
11 reaching to the wing of the *o'* cherub.
12 one wing of the *o'* cherub was five
12 the *o'* wing was five cubits also,
12 joining to the wing of the *o'* cherub.
17 right hand, and the *o'* on the left;
7:19 you, and shall go and serve *o'* gods,
22 laid hold on *o'* gods, and worshipped
9:19 and on the *o'* upon the six steps.
13: 9 the manner of the nations of *o'* lands?
20: 1 with them *o'* beside the Ammonites,
25:12 And *o'* ten thousand left alive did the
28:25 places to burn incense unto *o'* gods,
29:34 and until the *o'* priests had sanctified
30:23 took counsel to keep *o'* seven days:
23 they kept *o'* seven days with gladness.
32:13 done unto all the people of *o'* lands?
17 gods of the nations of *o'* lands have
22 from the hand of all *o'*, and guided
34:12 and *o'* of the Levites, all that could
25 have burned incense unto *o'* gods,

2Ch 35:13 the o· holy offerings sod they in pots,
Ezr 1:10 and ten, and o· vessels a thousand.
2:31 The children of the o· Elam, a
Ne 3:11 repaired the o· piece, and...tower
20 earnestly repaired the o· piece,
4:16 o· half of them held both the spears,
17 with the o· hand held a weapon.
5: 5 o· men have our lands...vineyards.
7:33 The men of the o· Nebo, fifty and
34 children of the o· Elam, a thousand
12:38 the o· company of them that gave
Es 9:16 the o· Jews that were in the king's
Job 8:12 down, it withereth before any o· herb.
24:24 they are taken out of the way as all o·,
Ps 73: 5 They are not in trouble as o· men;
5 neither are they plagued like o· men.
85:10 and peace have kissed each o·.
Ec 3:19 as the one dieth, so dieth the o·;
6: 5 this hath more rest than the o·.
7:14 set the one over against the o·,
Isa 26:13 o· lords beside thee have had dominion
49:20 shalt have, after thou hast lost the o·,
Jer 1:16 have burned incense unto o· gods,
7: 6 walk after o· gods to your hurt:
9 after o· gods whom ye know not;
18 out drink offerings unto o· gods.
11:10 went after o· gods to serve them:
13:10 walk after o· gods, to serve them,
16:11 have walked after o· gods, and have
13 shall ye serve o· gods day and night;
19: 4 burned incense in it unto o· gods,
13 out drink offerings unto o· gods.
22: 9 and worshipped o· gods, and served
24: 2 o· basket had very naughty figs,
25: 6 go not after o· gods to serve them,
33 even unto the o· end of the earth:
32:20 and in Israel, and among o· men; and
29 out drink offerings unto o· gods,
35:15 go not after o· gods to serve them,
36:16 they were afraid both one and o·,
44: 3 burn incense, and to serve o· gods,
5 to burn no incense unto o· gods.
8 burning incense unto o· gods in the
15 had burned incense unto o· gods,
Eze 1:23 straight, the one toward the o·:
16:34 from o· women in thy whoredoms,
21:16 Go thee one way or o·, either on the
40: 6 the o· threshold of the gate, which
40 on the o· side, which was at the
41: 1 and six cubits on the o· side, which
2 side, and five cubits on the o· side:
15 on the o· side, an hundred cubits,
19 toward the palm tree on the o· side:
21 the one as the appearance of the o·.
24 door, and two leaves for the o· door.
26 on the one side and on the o· side,
42:14 shall put on o· garments, and shall
44:19 and they shall put on o· garments;
45: 7 and on the o· side of the oblation
47: 7 trees on the one side and on the o·.
48: 8 in length as one of the o· parts, from
21 and on the o· of the holy oblation,
Da 2:11 there is none o· that can shew it
44 shall not be left to o· people, but
3:21 and their hats, and their o· garments,
29 is no o· God that can deliver after
7:20 and of the o· which came up, and
8: 3 but one was higher than the o·,
12: 5 behold, there stood o· two, the one
5 the o· on that side of the bank of
Ho 3: 1 who look to o· gods, and love
9: 1 not, O Israel, for joy, as o· people:
13:10 where is any o· that may save thee in
Ob 11 day...thou stoodest on the o· side,
Zec 4: 3 the o· upon the left side thereof.
11: 7 Beauty, and the o· I called Bands;
14 Then I cut asunder mine o· staff,
M't 4:21 he saw o· two brethren, James the
5:39 right cheek, turn to him the o· also.
6:24 will hate the one, and love the o·;
24 hold to the one, and despise the o·.
8:18 to depart unto the o· side.
28 when he was come to the o· side
12:13 it was restored whole, like as the o·.
45 with himself seven o· spirits
13: 8 But o· fell into good ground, and
14:22 to go before him unto the o· side,
16: 5 disciples were come to the o· side,
20:21 the o· on the left, in thy kingdom.
21:36 he sent o· servants more than the
41 his vineyard unto o· husbandmen,
22: 4 Again, he sent forth o· servants,
23:23 and not to leave the o· undone.
24:31 from one end of heaven to the o·.
40, 41 shall be taken, and the o· left.
25:11 Afterward came also the o· virgins,
16 and made them o· five talents.
17 received two, he also gained o· two.
20 came and brought o· five talents,
22 gained two o· talents beside them.
27:61 Mary Magdalene, and the o· Mary,
28: 1 Mary Magdalene and the o· Mary to
M'r 3: 5 hand was restored whole as the o·.
4: 8 o· fell on good ground, and did yield
19 the lusts of o· things entering in,
35 Let us pass over unto the o· side.
36 were also with him o· little ships.
5: 1 over unto the o· side of the sea,
21 again by ship unto the o· side,
6:45 to the o· side before unto Bethsaida,
7: 4 And many o· things there be, which
8 and many o· such like things ye do.
8:13 ship again departed to the o· side.
10:37 hand, and the o· on thy left hand,
12:31 is none o· commandment greater
32 God; and there is none o· but he:

M'r 15:27 right hand, and the o· on his left.
41 and many o· women which came up
Lu 3:18 many o· things in his exhortation
4:43 kingdom of God to o· cities also:
5: 7 partners, which were in the o· ship,
6:10 hand was restored whole as the o·.
29 on the one cheek offer also the o·;
7:41 hundred pence, and the o· fifty.
8: 8 And o· fell on good ground, and
22 over unto the o· side of the lake.
10: 1 Lord appointed o· seventy also,
31 saw him, he passed by on the o· side.
32 on him, and passed by on the o· side.
11:26 seven o· spirits more wicked than
42 and not to leave the o· undone.
14:32 while the o· is yet a great way off,
16:13 will hate the one, and love the o·;
13 hold to the one, and despise the o·.
17:24 unto the o· part under heaven; so
34 be taken, and the o· shall be left.
35 one shall be taken, and the o· left.
36 one shall be taken, and the o· left.
18:10 a Pharisee, and the o· a publican.
11 thee, that I am not as o· men are,
14 house justified rather than the o·:
22:65 many o· things blasphemously
23:32 And there were also two o·,
33 right hand, and the o· on the left.
40 But the o· answering rebuked him,
24:10 o· women that were with them,
Joh 4:38 o· men laboured, and ye are entered
6:22 stood on the o· side of the sea
22 that there was none o· boat there,
23 came o· boats from Tiberias nigh
25 him on the o· side of the sea,
10: 1 but climbeth up some o· way, the
16 o· sheep I have, which are not of
15:24 the works which none o· man did,
18:16 Then went out that o· disciple,
19:18 crucified him, and two o· with him,
32 the o· which was crucified with him.
20: 2 to the o· disciple, whom Jesus loved,
3 went forth, and that o· disciple, and
4 and the o· disciple did outrun Peter,
8 Then went in also that o· disciple,
12 at the head, and the o· at the feet,
25 o· disciples therefore said unto him,
30 And many o· signs truly did Jesus
21: 2 Zebedee, and two o· of his disciples.
8 the o· disciples came in a little ship;
25 also many o· things which Jesus did,
Ac 2: 4 began to speak with o· tongues,
40 with many o· words did he testify
4:12 Neither is there salvation in any o·:
12 none o· name under heaven given
5:29 Peter and the o· apostles answered
8:34 of himself, or of some o· man?
15: 2 Barnabas, and certain o· of them,
39 departed asunder one from the o·:
17: 9 security of Jason, and of the o·,
18 o· some, He seemeth to be a setter
19:39 any thing concerning o· matters,
23: 6 Sadducees, and the o· Pharisees,
26:22 saying none o· things than those
27: 1 Paul and certain o· prisoners unto
Ro 1:13 also, even as among o· Gentiles.
8:39 nor any o· creature, shall be able
13: 9 if there be any o· commandment,
1Co 1:16 know not whether I baptized any o·.
3:11 o· foundation can no man lay than
7: 5 Defraud ye not one the o·, except it
8: 4 that there is none o· God but one.
9: 5 as well as o· apostles, and as the
10:29 I say, not thine own, but of the o·:
11:21 one taketh before o· his own supper:
14:17 well, but the o· is not edified.
21 With men of o· tongues and...lips
21 With men of...tongues and o· lips
29 two or three, and let the o· judge.
15:37 of wheat, or of some o· grain:
2Co 1:13 we write none o· things unto you,
2:16 and to the o· the savour of life unto
8:13 I mean not that o· men be eased,
10:15 that is, of o· men's labours; but
11: 8 I robbed o· churches, taking wages
12:13 ye were inferior to o· churches,
13: 2 and to all o·, that, if I come again,
Ga 1: 8 any o· gospel unto you than that...we
9 any o· gospel unto you than that ye
19 But o· of the apostles saw I none,
2:13 the o· Jews dissembled likewise
4:22 bondmaid, the o· by a freewoman.
5:17 these are contrary the one to the o·:
Eph 3: 5 in o· ages was not made known
4:17 henceforth walk not as o· Gentiles
Ph'p 1:13 all the palace, and in all o· places;
17 But the o· of love, knowing that I am
2: 3 esteem o· better than themselves.
3: 4 any o· man thinketh that he hath
4: 3 and with o· my fellowlabourers,
2Th 1: 3 you all toward each o· aboundeth;
1Ti 1: 3 that they teach no o· doctrine,
10 be any o· thing that is contrary to
5:22 be partakers of o· men's sins:
Jas 5:12 the earth, neither by any o· oath:
1Pe 4:15 as a busybody in o· men's matters.
2Pe 3:16 as they do also the o· scriptures,
Re 2:24 will put upon you none o· burden.
8:13 by reason of the o· voices of the
17:10 one is, and the o· is not yet come;

others
Job 8:19 and out of the earth shall o· grow.
31:10 and let o· bow down upon her.
34:24 number, and set o· in their stead.
26 as wicked men in the open sight of o·;
Ps 49:10 perish, and leave their wealth to o·.

Pr 5: 9 Lest thou give thine honour unto o·,
Ec 7:22 thou thyself likewise hast cursed o·.
Isa 56: 8 Yet will I gather o· to him, beside
Jer 6:12 houses shall be turned unto o·, with
8:10 will I give their wives unto o·, and
Eze 9: 5 to the o· he said in mine hearing,
13: 6 and they have made o· to hope that
10 o· daubed it with untempered morter:
Da 7:19 which was diverse from all the o·,
11: 4 plucked up, even for o· beside those.
M't 5:47 only, what do ye more than o·?
15:30 dumb, maimed, and many o·, and
16:14 and o·, Jeremias, or one of the
20: 3 o· standing idle in the marketplace,
6 went out, and found o· standing idle,
21: 8 o· cut down branches from the trees,
26:67 o· smote him with the palms of
27:42 He saved o·; himself he cannot
M'r 6:15 O· said, That it is Elias.
15 And o· said, That it is a prophet, or
8:28 Elias; and o·, One of the prophets.
11: 8 o· cut down branches off the trees,
12: 5 and him they killed, and many o·;
9 and will give the vineyard unto o·.
15:31 He saved o·; himself he cannot save.
Lu 5:29 of publicans and of o· that sat down
8: 3 and many o·, which ministered
10 but to o· in parables; that seeing
9: 8 of o·, that one of the old prophets
19 o· say, that one of the old prophets
11:16 And o·, tempting him, sought of
18: 9 were righteous, and despised o·:
20:16 and shall give the vineyard to o·.
23:35 He saved o·; let him save himself,
24: 1 prepared, and certain o· with them.
Joh 7:12 He is a good man: o· said, Nay;
41 O· said, This is the Christ. But
9: 9 This is he: o· said, He is like him:
16 O· said, How can a man that is a
10:21 O· said, These are not the words of
12:29 o· said, An angel spake to him.
18:34 thyself, or did o· tell it thee of me?
Ac 2:13 O· mocking said, These men are
15:35 word of the Lord, with many o· also.
17:32 and o· said, We will hear thee again
34 named Damaris, and o· with them.
28: 9 o· also, which had diseases in the
1Co 9: 2 If I be not an apostle unto o·, yet
12 If o· be partakers of this power over
27 means, when I have preached to o·,
14:19 by my voice I might teach o· also,
2Co 3: 1 or need we, as some o·, epistles of
8: 8 occasion of the forwardness of o·,
Eph 2: 3 the children of wrath, even as o·.
Ph'p 2: 4 man also on the things of o·.
1Th 2: 6 glory, neither of you, nor yet of o·,
4:13 even as o· which have no hope.
5: 6 let us not sleep, as do o·; but let
1Ti 5:20 before all, that o· also may fear.
2Ti 2: 2 who shall be able to teach o· also.
Heb 9:25 place every year with blood of o·;
11:35 and o· were tortured, not accepting
36 o· had trial of cruel mockings and
Jude 23 And o· save with fear, pulling

otherwise^
2Sa 18:13 O· I should have wrought
1Ki 1:21 O· it shall come to pass, when my
2Ch 30:18 passover o· than it was written.
Ps 38:16 lest o· they should rejoice over me:
M't 6: 1 o· ye have no reward of your
Lu 5:36 if o·, then both the new maketh a
Ro 11: 6 works: o· grace is no more grace.
6 grace: o· work is no more work.
22 o· thou also shalt be cut off.
2Co 11:16 if o·, yet as a fool receive me, that
Ga 5:10 that ye will be none o· minded:
Ph'p 3:15 if in any thing ye be o· minded,
1Ti 5:25 and they that are o· cannot be hid.
6: 3 If any man teach o·, and consent
Heb 9:17 o· it is of no strength at all while

Othni *(oth'-ni)*
1Ch 26: 7 The sons of Shemaiah; O·, and

Othniel *(oth'-ne-el)*
Jos 15:17 O· the son of Kenaz, the brother
J'g 1:13 And O· the son of Kenaz, Caleb's
3: 9 even O· the son of Kenaz, Caleb's
11 and O· the son of Kenaz died.
1Ch 4:13 And the sons of Kenaz: O·, and
13 and the sons of O·; Hathath.
27:15 Heldai the Netophathite, of O·:

ouches
Ex 28:11 make them to be set in o· of gold.
13 And thou shalt make o· of gold;
14 fasten...wreathen chains to the o·.
25 thou shalt fasten in the two o·, and
39: 6 onyx stones inclosed in o· of gold.
13 they were inclosed in o· of gold in
16 they made two o· of gold, and two
18 chains they fastened in the two o·.

ought^ See also NOUGHT; OUGHTEST.
Ge 34: 7 which thing o· not to be done.
39: 6 he knew not o· he had, save
47:18 there is not o· left in the sight of my
Ex 5: 8 ye shall not diminish o· thereof:
11 yet not o· of your work shall be
19 shall not minish o· from your bricks
12:46 shalt not carry forth o· of the flesh
22:14 if a man borrow o· of his neighbour,
29:34 o· of the flesh of the consecrations,
Le 4: 2, 27 things which o· not to be done,
11:25 whosoever beareth o· of the carcase
19: 6 and if o· remain until the third day,
25:14 if thou sell o· unto thy neighbour,
14 or buyest o· of thy neighbour's hand,

Le 27:31 man will at all redeem o' of his tithes,
Nu 15:24 if o' be committed by ignorance
30 the soul that doeth o' presumptuously,
30: 6 vowed, or uttered o' out of her lips,
De 4: 2 neither shall ye diminish o' from it.
15: 2 that lendeth o' unto his neighbour
26:14 neither have I taken away o' thereof
14 nor given o' thereof for the dead:
Jos 21:45 failed not o' of any good thing
Ru 1:17 if o' but death part thee and me.
1Sa 12: 4 taken o' of any man's hand.
5 have not found o' in my hand.
25: 7 there o' missing unto them,
30:22 we will not give them o' of the spoil
2Sa 3:35 if I taste bread, or o' else,
13:12 no such thing o' to be done in Israel.
14:10 said, Whosoever saith o' unto thee,
19 o' that my lord the king hath spoken:
1Ch 12:32 times, to know what Israel o' to do;
15: 2 None o' to carry the ark of God but
2Ch 13: 5 O' ye not to know that the Lord God
Ne 5: 9 o' ye not to walk in the fear of God
Ps 76:11 presents unto him that o' to be feared.
M't 5:23 thy brother hath o' against thee;
21: 3 And if any man say o' unto you,
23:23 these o' ye to have done, and not
M'r 7:12 do o' for his father or his mother;
8:23 him, he asked him if he saw o'.
11:25 forgive, if ye have o' against any:
13:14 prophet, standing where it o' not,
Lu 11:42 these o' ye to have done, and not to
12:12 in the same hour what we o' to say.
13:14 six days in which men o' to work:
16 o' not this woman, being a daughter
18: 1 that men o' always to pray, and not
24:26 O' not Christ to have suffered
Joh 4:20 the place where men o' to worship.
33 any man brought him o' to eat?
13:14 also o' to wash one another's feet.
19: 7 a law, and by our law he o' to die,
Ac 4:32 o' of the things which he possessed
5:29 o' to obey God rather than men.
17:29 o' not to think that the Godhead
19:36 ye o' to be quiet, and to do nothing
20:35 labouring ye o' to support the weak,
21:21 o' not to circumcise their children,
24:19 Who o' to have been here before
19 object, if they had o' against me.
25:10 seat, where I o' to be judged:
24 that he o' not to live any longer.
26: 9 I o' to do many things contrary to
28:19 I had o' to accuse my nation of.
Ro 8:26 what we should pray for as we o':
12: 3 more highly than he o' to think;
15: 1 strong o' to bear the infirmities of
1Co 8: 2 nothing yet as he o' to know.
11: 7 indeed o' not to cover his head,
10 cause o' the woman to have power
2Co 2: 3 from them of whom I o' to rejoice:
7 ye o' rather to forgive him, and
12:11 for I o' to have been commended
14 o' not to lay up for the parents,
Eph 5:28 So o' men to love their wives as
6:20 may speak boldly, as I o' to speak.
Col 4: 4 make it manifest, as I o' to speak.
6 how ye o' to answer every man.
1Th 4: 1 how ye o' to walk and to please God,
2Th 3: 7 know how ye o' to follow us:
1Ti 5:13 speaking things which they o' not.
Tit 1:11 teaching things which they o' not,
Ph'm 18 wronged thee, or oweth thee o',
Heb 2: 1 o' to give the more earnest heed
5: 3 by reason hereof he o', as for the
12 for the time ye o' to be teachers,
Jas 3:10 these things o' not so to be.
4:15 For that ye o' to say, If the Lord will
2Pe 3:11 what manner of persons o' ye to be
1Jo 2: 6 o' himself also so to walk, even as
3:16 we o' to lay down our lives for the
4:11 us, we o' also to love one another.
3Jo 8 We therefore o' to receive such, that

oughtest
1Ki 2: 9 knowest what thou o' to do unto him;
M't 25:27 o' therefore to have put my money
Ac 10: 6 shall tell thee what thou o' to do.
1Ti 3:15 know how thou o' to behave thyself

ours See also OURSELVES.
Ge 26:20 herdmen, saying, The water is o':
31:16 hath taken from our father, that is o',
34:23 and every beast of theirs be o'?
Nu 32:32 on this side Jordan may be o'.
1Ki 22: 3 Know ye that Ramoth in Gilead is o',
Eze 36: 2 even the ancient high places are o' in
M'r 12: 7 and the inheritance shall be o'.
Lu 20:14 that the inheritance may be o'.
1Co 1: 2 Christ our Lord, both theirs and o':
2Co 1:14 as ye also are o' in the day of the
Tit 3:14 let o' also learn to maintain good
1Jo 2: 2 and not for o' only, but also for

ourselves
Ge 37:10 to bow down o' to thee to the earth?
44:16 we speak? or how shall we clear o'?
Nu 32:17 we o' will go ready armed before
De 2:35 we took cattle for a prey unto o',
3: 7 of the cities, we took for a prey to o'.
1Sa 14: 8 and we will discover o' unto them.
1Ch 19:13 and let us behave o' valiantly for our
Ezr 4: 3 but we o' together will build unto
8:21 we might afflict o' before our God,
Ne 10:32 to charge o' yearly with the third
Job 34: 4 let us know among o' what is good.
Ps 83:12 Let us take to o' the houses of God
Ps 100: 3 that hath made us, and not we o';
Pr 7:18 morning: let us solace o' with loves.
Isa 28:15 and under falsehood have we hid o':
56:12 and we will fill o' with strong drink;
Jer 50: 5 Come, and let us join o' to the Lord
Lu 22:71 we o' have heard of his own mouth.
Joh 4:42 for we have heard him o', and know
Ac 6: 4 will give o' continually to prayer,
23:14 have bound o' under a great curse,
Ro 8:23 but o' also, which have the first fruits
23 of the Spirit, even we o' groan
23 groan within o', waiting for the
15: 1 of the weak, and not to please o'.
1Co 11:31 For if we would judge o', we should
2Co 1: 4 we o' are comforted of God.
9 we had the sentence of death in o',
9 that we should not trust in o', but
3: 1 Do we begin again to commend o'?
5 that we are sufficient of o' to think
5 to think any thing as of o'; but our
4: 2 commending o' to every man's
5 For we preach not o', but Christ
5 o' your servants for Jesus' sake.
5:12 we commend not o' again unto you,
13 whether we be beside o', it is to God:
6: 4 approving o' as the ministers of
7: 1 let us cleanse o' from all filthiness
10:12 we dare not make o' of the number,
12 or compare o' with some that
14 stretch not o' beyond our measure,
12:19 think ye that we excuse o' unto you?
Ga 2:17 if...we o' also are found sinners, is
1Th 2:10 we behaved o' among you that believe:
2Th 1: 4 we o' glory in you in the churches
3: 7 behaved not o' disorderly among you;
9 to make o' an ensample unto you
Tit 3: 3 we o' also were sometimes foolish,
Heb 10:25 the assembling of o' together,
1Jo 1: 8 we deceive o', and the truth is not

outcast See also OUTCASTS.
Jer 30:17 they called thee an O', saying,

outcasts
Ps 147: 2 gathereth together the o' of Israel.
Isa 11:12 and shall assemble the o' of Israel,
16: 3 hide the o'; bewray not him that
4 Let mine o' dwell with thee, Moab;
27:13 and the o' in the land of Egypt,
56: 8 which gathereth the o' of Israel
Jer 49:36 the o' of Elam shall not come.

outer See also UTTER.
Eze 10: 5 was heard even to the o' court,
M't 8:12 shall be cast out into o' darkness:
22:13 and cast him into o' darkness;
25:30 servant into o' darkness: there

outgoings
Jos 17: 9 and the o' of it were at the sea:
18 and the o' of it shall be thine:
18:19 o' of the border were at the north
19:14 the o' thereof are in the valley of
22 o' of their border were at Jordan:
29 the o' thereof are at the sea from
33 and the o' thereof were at Jordan:
Ps 65: 8 the o' of the morning and evening

outlandish
Ne 13:26 him did o' women cause to sin.

outlived See also OVERLIVED.
J'g 2: 7 the elders that o' Joshua,

outmost See also UTMOST.
Ex 26:10 curtain that is o' in the coupling,
Nu 34: 3 o' coast of the salt sea eastward:
De 30: 4 out unto the o' parts of heaven,
Isa 17: 6 in the o' fruitful branches thereof,

outrageous
Pr 27: 4 Wrath is cruel, and anger is o';

outrun See also OVERRAN.
Joh 20: 4 the other disciple did o' Peter,

outside
J'g 7:11 unto the o' of the armed men
17 when I come to the o' of the camp,
19 came unto the o' of the camp in the
1Ki 7: 9 on the o' toward the great court.
Eze 40: 5 behold a wall on the o' of the house
M't 23:25 ye make clean the o' of the cup
26 the o' of them may be clean also.
Lu 11:39 make clean the o' of the cup and

outstretched
De 26: 8 a mighty hand, and with an o' arm,
Jer 21: 5 fight against you with an o' hand
27: 5 by my great power by my o' arm,

outward
Nu 35: 4 from the wall of the city and o'
1Sa 16: 7 man looketh on the o' appearance,
1Ch 26:29 for the o' business over Israel,
Ne 11:16 had the oversight of the o' business
Es 6: 4 Haman was come into the o' court
Eze 40:17 brought he me into the o' court,
20 the gate of the o' court that looked
34 arches...were toward the o' court;
44: 1 way of the gate of the o' sanctuary
M't 23:27 which indeed appear beautiful o',
Ro 2:28 which is o' in the flesh:
2Co 4:16 though our o' man perish, yet the
10: 7 on things after the o' appearance?
1Pe 3: 3 o' adorning of plaiting the hair,

outwardly
M't 23:28 so ye also o' appear righteous
Ro 2:28 is not a Jew, which is one o';

outwent
M'k 6:33 out of all cities, and o' them, and

oven See also OVENS.
Le 2: 4 of a meat offering baken in the o',
7: 9 offering that is baken in the o',
11:35 whether it be o', or ranges for pots,
26:26 shall bake your bread in one o',
Ps 21: 9 Thou shalt make them as a fiery o'
La 5:10 skin was black like an o' because
Ho 7: 4 as an o' heated by the baker, who
6 made ready their heart like an o',
7 They are all hot as an o', and have
Mal 4: 1 cometh, that shall burn as an o';
M't 6:30 and to morrow is cast into the o',
Lu 12:28 and to morrow is cast into the o';

ovens
Ex 8: 3 and into thine o', and into thy

over^ See also MOREOVER; OVERCHARGE; OVERCOME; OVERDRIVE; OVERFLOW; OVERLAY; OVERLIVED; OVERMUCH; OVERPASS; OVERPLUS; OVERRAN; OVERSEE; OVERSHADOW; OVERSIGHT; OVERSPREAD; OVERTAKE; OVERTHROW; OVERTURN; OVERWHELM; PASSOVER.
Ge 1:18 to rule o' the day and o' the night,
26 have dominion o' the fish of the sea,
26 o' the fowl of the air, and o' the cattle,
26 o' all the earth, and o' every creeping
28 o' the fish of the sea, and o' the fowl
28 and o' every living thing that moveth
3:16 thy husband, and he shall rule o' thee.
4: 7 his desire, and thou shalt rule o' him.
8: 1 made a wind to pass o' the earth,
9:14 when I bring a cloud o' the earth,
21:16 and sat her down o' against him
16 she sat o' against him, and lift up
24: 2 house, that ruled o' all that he had,
25:25 out red, all o' like an hairy garment;
27:29 be lord o' thy brethren, and let thy
31:21 he rose up, and passed o' the river,
52 I will not pass o' this heap to thee,
52 thou shalt not pass o' this heap and
32:10 my staff I passed o' this Jordan;
16 Pass o' before me, and put a space
21 So went the present o' before him:
22 and passed o' the ford Jabbok.
23 them o' the brook, and sent o' that
31 as he passed o' Penuel the sun rose
33: 3 And he passed o' before them, and
14 thee, pass o' before his servant:
36:31 any king o' the children of Israel.
37: 8 Shalt thou indeed reign o' us?
8 thou indeed have dominion o' us?
39: 4 made him overseer o' his house,
5 his house, and o' all that he had,
41:33 and set him o' the land of Egypt.
34 let him appoint officers o' the land,
40 Thou shalt be o' my house, and
41 set thee o' all the land of Egypt.
43 him ruler o' all the land of Egypt.
45 went out o' all the land of Egypt.
56 was o' all the face of the earth:
42: 6 Joseph was...governor o' the land,
47: 6 then make them rulers o' my cattle.
20 the famine prevailed o' them:
26 made it a law o' the land of Egypt
49:22 whose branches run o' the wall:
Ex 1: 8 there arose up a new king o' Egypt,
11 they did set o' them taskmasters
2:14 thee a prince and a judge o' us?
5:14 taskmasters had set o' them,
8: 5 hand with thy rod o' the streams,
5 o' the rivers, and o' the ponds, and
6 his hand o' the waters of Egypt;
9 said unto Pharaoh, Glory o' me:
10:12 out thine hand o' the land of Egypt
13 forth his rod o' the land of Egypt,
14 went up o' all the land of Egypt,
21 be darkness o' the land of Egypt,
12:13 I see the blood, I will pass o' you,
23 the Lord will pass o' the door, and
27 passed o' the houses of the children
14: 2 the sea, o' against Baal-zephon:
7 and captains o' every one of them.
16 stretch out thine hand o' the sea,
21 stretched out his hand o' the sea;
26 Stretch out thine hand o' the sea,
27 stretched forth his hand o' the sea,
15:16 till thy people pass o', O Lord,
16 till the people pass o', which thou
16:18 gathered much had nothing o',
23 that which remaineth o' lay up for
18:21 and place such o' them, to be
25 and made them heads o' the people,
25:27 O' against the border shall the
37 may give light o' against it.
26:12 o' the backside of the tabernacle.
13 hang o' the sides of the tabernacle
35 candlestick o' against the table on
28:27 o' against the other coupling
36:14 hair for the tent o' the tabernacle:
37: 9 their wings o' the mercy seat,
14 O' against the border were the rings,
39:20 o' against the other coupling
40:19 abroad the tent o' the tabernacle,
24 congregation, o' against the table,
36 taken up from o' the tabernacle,
Le 14: 5 an earthen vessel o' running water:
6 was killed o' the running water:
50 an earthen vessel o' running water:
16:21 confess o' him all the iniquities of
25:43 shalt not rule o' him with rigour;

Le 25:46 but o' your brethren the children of
46 not rule one o' another with rigour.
53 shall not rule with rigour o' him
26:16 I will even appoint o' you terror,
17 they that hate you shall reign o' you;
Nu 1:50 the Levites o' the tabernacle of
50 and o' all the vessels thereof, and
50 and o' all things that belong to it:
3:32 be chief o' the chief of the Levites,
49 of them that were o' and above
4: 6 shall spread o' it a cloth wholly of
5:30 him, and he be jealous o' his wife,
7: 2 were o' them that were numbered,
8: 2 o' against the candlestick.
3 o' against the candlestick,
10:10 trumpets o' your burnt offerings,
10 o' the sacrifices of your peace offerings;
14 o' his host was Nahshon the son of
15, 16 o' the host of the tribe of the
18 o' his host was Elizur the son of
19, 20 o' the host of the tribe of the
22 o' his host was Elishama the son of
23, 24 o' the host of the tribe of the
25 o' his host was Ahiezer the son of
26, 27 o' the host of the tribe of the
11:16 of the people, and officers o' them;
14:14 that thy cloud standeth o' them,
16:13 thyself altogether a prince o' us?
22: 5 earth, and they abide o' against me:
25:15 he was head o' a people, and of a
27:16 set a man o' the congregation,
31:14 with the captains o' thousands, and
14 and captains o' hundreds which came
48 which were o' thousands of the host,
32: 5 and bring us not o' Jordan.
7 from going o' into the land which
21 will go all of you armed o' Jordan
27 But thy servants will pass o', every
29 will pass with you o' Jordan, every
30 will not pass o' with you armed,
32 will pass o' armed before the Lord
33:51 When ye are passed o' Jordan into
35:10 ye be come o' Jordan into the land
De 1: 1 the plain o' against the Red sea,
13 and I will make them rulers o' you.
15 and made them heads o' you,
15 o' thousands,...captains o' hundreds,
15 captains o' fifties, and captains o' tens,
2:13 and get you o' the brook Zered.
13 And we went o' the brook Zered.
14 we were come o' the brook Zered,
18 Thou art to pass o' through Ar, the
19 o' against the children of Ammon,
24 and pass o' the river Arnon:
29 until I shall pass o' Jordan into the
3:18 pass o' armed before your brethren
25 let me go o', and see the good land
27 for thou shalt not go o' this Jordan.
28 he shall go o' before this people,
29 in the valley o' against Beth-peor.
4:14 land whither ye go o' to possess it.
21 that I should not go o' Jordan, and
22 this land, I must not go o' Jordan:
22 but ye shall go o', and possess that
26 ye go o' Jordan to possess it; ye
46 in the valley o' against Beth-peor,
9: 1 to pass o' Jordan this day, to go
3 God is he that goeth o' before thee;
11:30 the champaign o' against Gilgal,
31 ye shall pass o' Jordan to go in to
12:10 when ye go o' Jordan, and dwell
15: 6 and thou shalt reign o' many nations,
6 but they shall not reign o' thee.
17:14 I will set a king o' me, like as all
15 in any wise set him king o' thee,
15 shalt thou set king o' thee: thou
15 mayest not set a stranger o' thee,
21: 6 shall wash their hands o' the heifer
24:20 thou shalt not go o' the boughs again:
27: 2 day when ye shall pass o' Jordan
3 this law, when thou art passed o',
4 shall be when ye be gone o' Jordan,
12 when ye are come o' Jordan;
28:23 And thy heaven that is o' thy head
36 king which thou shalt set o' thee,
63 Lord rejoiced o' you to do you good,
63 will rejoice o' you to destroy you,
30: 9 the Lord will again rejoice o' thee
9 good, as he rejoiced o' thy fathers:
13 Who shall go o' the sea for us, and
18 passest o' Jordan...to possess it.
31: 2 Thou shalt not go o' this Jordan.
3 he will go o' before thee, and he
3 Joshua, he shall go o' before thee,
13 ye go o' Jordan to possess it.
15 stood o' the door of the tabernacle.
32:11 her nest, fluttereth o' her young,
47 ye go o' Jordan to possess it.
49 that is o' against Jericho;
34: 1 that is o' against Jericho.
4 but thou shalt not go o' thither.
6 of Moab, o' against Beth-peor:
Jos 1: 2 arise, go o' this Jordan, thou,
11 days ye shall pass o' this Jordan,
2:23 passed o', and came to Joshua the
3: 1 lodged there before they passed o'.
6 and pass o' before the people. And
11 all the earth passeth o' before you
14 from their tents, to pass o' Jordan,
16 passed o' right against Jericho.
17 Israelites passed o' on dry ground,
17 people were passed clean o' Jordan.
4: 1 people were clean passed o' Jordan,
3 ye shall carry them o' with you,
5 Pass o' before the ark of the Lord
7 when it passed o' Jordan, the

Jos 4: 8 and carried them o' with them unto
10 the people hasted and passed o'.
11 all the people were clean passed o',
11 that the ark of the Lord passed o',
12 tribe of Manasseh, passed o' armed
13 prepared for war passed o' before
18 flowed o' all his banks, as they did
22 came o' this Jordan on dry land.
23 before you, until ye were passed o',
23 before us, until we were gone o':
5: 1 of Israel, until we were passed o',
13 there stood a man o' against him
7: 7 all brought this people o' Jordan,
26 o' him a great heap of stones unto
8:31 o' which no man hath lift up any
33 of them o' against mount Gerizim,
33 them o' against mount Ebal;
9: 1 great sea o' against Lebanon,
18:13 went o' from thence toward Luz,
17 which is o' against the going up
18 toward the side o' against Arabah
22:11 o' against the land of Canaan,
19 pass ye o' unto the land of the
24:11 ye went o' Jordan, and came unto
J'g 3:28 and suffered not a man to pass o'.
5:13 dominion o' the nobles among
13 made me have dominion o' the mighty.
6:33 gathered together, and went o',
8: 4 came to Jordan, and passed o',
22 Rule thou o' us, both thou, and thy
23 said unto them, I will not rule o' you,
23 neither shall my son rule o' you:
23 the Lord shall rule o' you.
9: 2 and ten persons, reign o' you, or that
2 or that one reign o' you? remember
8 a time to anoint a king o' them;
8 the olive tree, Reign thou o' us.
9 and go to be promoted o' the trees?
10 fig tree, Come thou, and reign o' us.
11 and go to be promoted o' the trees?
12 vine, Come thou, and reign o' us.
13 and go to be promoted o' the trees?
14 Come thou, and reign o' us.
15 in truth ye anoint me king o' you,
18 king o' the men of Shechem:
22 had reigned three years o' Israel,
26 brethren, and went o' to Shechem:
10: 9 of Ammon passed o' Jordan to
18 head o' all the inhabitants of Gilead.
11: 8 head o' all the inhabitants of Gilead.
11 him head and captain o' them:
29 and he passed o' Gilead, and
29 and passed o' Mizpeh of Gilead,
29 o' unto the children of Ammon:
32 So Jephthah passed o' unto the
12: 1 passedst thou o' to fight against
3 passed o' against the children of
5 were escaped said, Let me go o';
14: 4 the Philistines had dominion o' Israel.
15:11 that the Philistines are rulers o' us?
19:10 and came o' against Jebus, which
12 Israel; we will pass o' to Gibeah.
20:43 down with ease o' against Gibeah
Ru 2: 5 servant that was set o' the reapers,
6 servant that was set o' the reapers
3: 9 thy skirt o' thine handmaid; for
1Sa 2: 1 mouth is enlarged o' mine enemies;
8: 1 that he made his sons judges o' Israel.
7 that I should not reign o' them.
9 the king that shall reign o' them.
11 of the king that shall reign o' you:
12 o' thousands, and captains o' fifties;
19 but we will have a king o' us;
9:16 to be captain o' my people Israel,
17 of this same shall reign o' my people.
10: 1 to be captain o' his inheritance?
19 unto him, Nay, but set a king o' us.
11:12 he that said, Shall Saul reign o' us?
12: 1 me, and have made a king o' you.
12 Nay; but a king shall reign o' us:
13 the Lord hath set a king o' you.
14 also the king that reigneth o' you
13: 1 he had reigned two years o' Israel,
7 of the Hebrews went o' Jordan to
14 him to be captain o' his people,
14: 1, 4 go o' to the Philistines' garrison.
5 northward o' against Michmash,
5 other southward o' against Gibeah.
6 and let us go o' unto the garrison
8 we will pass o' unto these men, and
23 battle passed o' unto Beth-aven.
47 Saul took the kingdom o' Israel,
15: 1 anoint thee to be king o' his people,
1 to anoint thee to be king...o' Israel;
7 that is o' against Egypt.
17 Lord anointed thee king o' Israel?
26 thee from being king o' Israel.
35 he had made Saul king o' Israel.
16: 1 him from reigning o' Israel? fill
17:50 David prevailed o' the Philistine
18: 5 Saul set him o' the men of war,
13 made him his captain o' a thousand;
19:20 standing as appointed o' them,
22: 2 he became a captain o' them: and
9 was set o' the servants of Saul,
23:17 and thou shalt be king o' Israel,
25:30 have appointed thee ruler o' Israel;
26:13 David went o' to the other side,
22 let one of the young men come o'
27: 2 passed o' with the six hundred men
30:10 could not go o' the brook Besor.
2Sa 1:17 lamentation o' Saul,...o' Jonathan
24 daughters of Israel, weep o' Saul,
2: 4 David king o' the house of Judah.
7 have anointed me king o' them.
8 and brought him o' to Mahanaim;

2Sa 2: 9 king o' Gilead, and o' the Ashurites,
9 and o' Jezreel, and o' Ephraim,
9 and o' Benjamin, and o' all Israel.
10 when he began to reign o' Israel,
11 in Hebron o' the house of Judah
15 arose and went o' by number
29 the plain, and passed o' Jordan,
3:10 of David o' Israel and o' Judah,
17 in times past to be king o' you:
21 reign o' all that thine heart desireth.
33 And the king lamented o' Abner,
34 all the people wept again o' him.
4:12 them up o' the pool in Hebron.
5: 2 when Saul was king o' us, thou
2 thou shalt be a captain o' Israel.
3 they anointed David king o' Israel.
5 he reigned o' Judah seven years
5 thirty and three years o' all Israel
12 had established him king o' Israel,
17 had anointed David king o' Israel,
23 o' against the mulberry trees.
6:21 me ruler o' the people of the Lord,
21 the people of the Lord, o' Israel:
7: 8 to be ruler o' my people, o' Israel:
11 judges to be o' my people Israel,
26 Lord of hosts is the God o' Israel:
8:15 And David reigned o' all Israel;
16 the son of Zeruiah was o' the host:
18 Benaiah...was o' both the Cherethites
10:17 together, and passed o' Jordan,
12: 7 I anointed thee king o' Israel,
15:22 David said to Ittai, Go and pass o'.
22 Ittai the Gittite passed o', and all
23 voice, and all the people passed o':
23 himself passed o' the brook Kidron,
23 all the people passed o', toward the
16: 9 let me go o', I pray thee, and take
13 on the hill's side o' against him,
17:16 wilderness, but speedily pass o';
19 a covering o' the well's mouth,
20 be gone o' the brook of water.
21 and pass quickly o' the water:
22 him, and they passed o' Jordan:
22 them that was not gone o' Jordan.
24 And Absalom passed o' Jordan,
18: 1 and captains of hundreds o' them.
8 o' the face of all the country:
24 went up to the roof o' the gate
33 up to the chamber o' the gate,
19:10 Absalom, whom we anointed o' us,
15 to conduct the king o' Jordan.
17 went o' Jordan before the king.
18 there went o' a ferry boat to carry
18 to carry o' the king's household,
18 the king, as he was come o' Jordan;
22 that I am this day king o' Israel?
31 and went o' Jordan with the king,
31 the king, to conduct him o' Jordan.
33 Come thou o' with me, and I will
36 will go a little way o' Jordan with
37 let him go o' with my lord the king;
38 Chimham shall go o' with me, and
39 And all the people went o' Jordan.
39 And when the king was come o', the
41 David's men with him, o' Jordan?
20:21 shall be thrown to thee o' the wall.
23 Joab was o' all the host of Israel:
23 Benaiah...was o' the Cherethites
23 Cherethites and o' the Pelethites:
24 And Adoram was o' the tribute:
22:30 by my God have I leaped o' a wall.
23: 3 He that ruleth o' men must be just,
23 And David set him o' his guard.
24: 5 And they passed o' Jordan, and
1Ki 1:34 anoint him there king o' Israel:
35 to be ruler o' Israel and o' Judah.
2:11 days that David reigned o' Israel
35 of Jehoiada in his room o' the host:
37 and passest o' the brook Kidron,
4: 1 Solomon was king o' all Israel.
4 the son of Jehoiada was o' the host:
5 son of Nathan was o' the officers:
6 And Ahishar was o' the household:
6 the son of Abda was o' the tribute.
7 had twelve officers o' all Israel,
21 And Solomon reigned o' all kingdoms
24 o' all the region on this side the river,
24 o' all the kings on this side the river:
5: 7 a wise son o' this great people.
14 and Adoniram was o' the levy.
16 officers which were o' the work,
16 which ruled o' the people that wrought
6: 1 year of Solomon's reign o' Israel,
7:20 o' against the belly which was by
39 eastward o' against the south.
8: 7 two wings o' the place of the ark,
16 David to be o' my people Israel.
9:23 officers that were o' Solomon's work,
23 bear rule o' the people that wrought
11:24 and became captain o' a band, when
25 Israel, and reigned o' Syria.
28 o' all the charge of the house of Joseph.
37 and shalt be king o' Israel.
42 reigned in Jerusalem o' all Israel
12:17 Judah, Rehoboam reigned o' them.
18 Adoram, who was o' the tribute;
20 and made him king o' all Israel:
13:30 mourned o' him, saying, Alas, my
14: 2 that I should be king o' this people.
7 thee prince o' my people Israel,
14 shall raise him up a king o' Israel,
15: 1 of Nebat reigned Abijam o' Judah.
9 king of Israel reigned Asa o' Judah.
25 Nadab...began to reign o' Israel
25 and reigned o' Israel two years.
33 to reign o' all Israel in Tirzah,

1Ki 16: 2 thee prince o' my people Israel;
8 Elah...to reign o' Israel in Tirzah,
16 king o' Israel that day in the camp.
18 and burnt the king's house o' him
23 Judah began Omri to reign o' Israel,
29 began Ahab...to reign o' Israel:
29 Ahab...reigned o' Israel in Samaria
19:15 anoint Hazael to be king o' Syria:
16 thou anoint to be king o' Israel:
20:29 pitched one o' against the other
22:31 captains that had rule o' his chariots,
41 of Asa began to reign o' Judah
51 began to reign o' Israel in Samaria
51 and reigned two years o' Israel.
2Ki 2: 8 they two went o' on dry ground.
9 to pass, when they were gone o',
14 and thither: and Elisha went o'.
3: 1 began to reign o' Israel in Samaria
5:11 and strike his hand o' the place,
8:13 that thou shalt be king o' Syria.
20 and made a king o' themselves.
21 So Joram went o' to Zair, and all
9: 3 have anointed thee king o' Israel.
6 anointed thee king o' the people
6 people of the Lord, even o' Israel.
12 I have anointed thee king o' Israel.
29 began Ahaziah to reign o' Judah.
10: 5 And he that was o' the house, and
5 he that was o' the city, the elders
22 unto him that was o' the vestry,
36 Jehu reigned o' Israel in Samaria
11: 3 And Athaliah did reign o' the land.
4 and fetched the rulers o' hundreds,
9 And the captains o' the hundreds did
10 to the captains o' hundreds did the
18 officers o' the house of the Lord.
19 And he took the rulers o' hundreds,
13: 1, 10 to reign o' Israel in Samaria
14 and wept o' his face, and said, O my
15: 5 the king's son was o' the house,
8 reign o' Israel in Samaria six
17 the son of Gadi to reign o' Israel,
23, 27 to reign o' Israel in Samaria,
17: 1 of Elah to reign in Samaria o' Israel
18:18, 37 which was o' the household,
19: 2 which was o' the household,
21:13 will stretch o' Jerusalem the line of
25:19 that was set o' the men of war,
22 o' them he made Gedaliah...ruler.
1Ch 1:43 king reigned o' the children of Israel;
5:11 of Gad dwelt o' against them.
6:31 David set o' the service of song
8:32 in Jerusalem, o' against them.
9:19 were o' the work of the service,
19 being o' the host of the Lord.
20 was the ruler o' them in time past,
26 o' the chambers and treasuries
31 o' the things that were made in the
32 were o' the shewbread, to prepare
38 o' against their brethren.
11: 2 shalt be ruler o' my people Israel.
3 they anointed David king o' Israel,
25 and David set him o' his guard.
12: 4 among the thirty, and o' the thirty;
14 one of the least was o' an hundred,
14 and the greatest o' a thousand.
15 are they that went o' Jordan in
38 to make David king o' all Israel:
14: 2 had confirmed him king o' Israel,
8 was anointed king o' all Israel,
14 o' against the mulberry trees.
15:25 and the captains o' thousands, went to
17: 7 be ruler o' my people Israel:
10 judges to be o' my people Israel.
18:14 So David reigned o' all Israel, and
15 the son of Zeruiah was o' the host;
17 was o' the Cherethites and the
19:17 all Israel, and passed o' Jordan,
21:16 hand stretched out o' Jerusalem.
22:10 of his kingdom o' Israel for ever.
23: 1 Solomon his son king o' Israel.
24:31 cast lots o' against their brethren
31 o' against their younger brethren.
26:20 Ahijah was o' the treasures of the
20 o' the treasures of the dedicated
22 which were o' the treasures of the
26 brethren were o' all the treasures
26 captains o' thousands and hundreds,
29 for the outward business o' Israel,
32 made rulers o' the Reubenites, the
27: 2 O' the first course for the first
4 o' the course of the second month
16 Furthermore o' the tribes of Israel:
25 And o' the king's treasures was
25 and o' the storehouses in the fields,
26 o' them that did the work of the
27 And o' the vineyards was Shimei
27 o' the increase of the vineyards for
28 o' the olive trees and the sycomore
28 and o' the cellars of oil was Joash:
29 o' the herds that fed in Sharon was
29 o' the herds that were in the valleys
30 O' the camels also was Obil the
30 and o' the asses was Jehdeiah the
31 And o' the flocks was Jaziz the
28: 1 and the captains o' the thousands,
1 and captains o' the hundreds, and
1 the stewards o' all the substance and
4 to be king o' Israel for ever:
4 me to make me king o' all Israel:
5 the kingdom of the Lord o' Israel.
29: 3 o' and above all that I have prepared
12 of thee, and thou reignest o' all:
26 son of Jesse reigned o' all Israel.
27 time that he reigned o' Israel was
30 and the times that went o' him,
1Ch 29:30 o' Israel, and o' all the kingdoms of
2Ch 1: 9 thou hast made me king o' a people
11 o' whom I have made thee king:
13 congregation, and reigned o' Israel.
2:11 he hath made thee king o' them.
4:10 the east end, o' against the south.
5: 8 their wings o' the place of the ark,
6: 5 to be a ruler o' my people Israel:
6 David to be o' my people Israel.
36 them o' before their enemies,
8:10 and fifty, that bare rule o' the people.
9: 8 made he thee king o' them, to do
26 And he reigned o' all the kings from
30 Jerusalem o' all Israel forty years.
10:17 Judah, Rehoboam reigned o' them.
18 Hadoram that was o' the tribute;
13: 1 began Abijah to reign o' Judah.
5 gave the kingdom o' Israel to David
19:11 chief priest is o' you in all matters
20: 6 rulest not thou o' all the kingdoms of
27 made them to rejoice o' their enemies.
31 Jehoshaphat reigned o' Judah: he
22:12 and Athaliah reigned o' the land.
23:14 of hundreds that were set o' the host,
25: 5 and made them captains o' thousands,
5 and captains o' hundreds, according
26:21 his son was o' the king's house,
31:12 o' which Cononiah the Levite was
14 was o' the freewill offerings of God,
32: 6 he set captains of war o' the people,
11 to give o' yourselves to die by famine
34:13 were o' the bearers of burdens,
36: 4 Eliakim his brother king o' Judah
10 his brother king o' Judah and
Ezr 4:10 and noble Asnapper brought o',
20 mighty kings also o' Jerusalem,
20 ruled o' all countries beyond the
9: 6 are increased o' our head, and
Ne 2: 7 convey me o' till I come...Judah;
3:10 even o' against the house. And
16 o' against the sepulchres of David,
19 piece o' against the going up to the
23 and Hashub o' against their house.
25 o' against the turning of the wall,
26 the place o' against the water gate
27 o' against the great tower that
28 every one o' against his house.
29 son of Immer o' against his house.
30 of Berechiah o' against his chamber.
31 o' against the gate of Miphkad, and
5:15 servants bare rule o' the people:
7: 2 of the palace, charge o' Jerusalem:
3 one to be o' against his house.
9:28 so that they had the dominion o' them:
37 the kings whom thou hast set o' us
37 they have dominion o' our bodies,
37 and o' our cattle, at their pleasure,
11: 9 of Senuah was second o' the city.
21 and Gispa were o' the Nethinims.
22 the singers were o' the business of
12: 8 which was o' the thanksgiving, he
9 o' against them in the watches.
24 their brethren o' against them,
24 man of God, ward o' against ward.
37 gate, which was o' against them,
38 gave thanks went o' against them,
44 o' the chambers for the treasures,
13:13 I made treasurers o' the treasuries,
26 God made him king o' all Israel:
Es 1: 1 o' an hundred and seven and twenty
8:12 that were o' every province, and
5: 1 house, o' against the king's house:
1 o' against the gate of the house.
8: 2 Mordecai o' the house of Haman.
9: 1 Jews hoped to have power o' them,
1 had rule o' them that hated them;)
Job 6: 5 or loweth the ox o' his fodder?
7:12 that thou settest a watch o' me?
14:16 dost thou not watch o' my sin?
16:11 me o' into the hands of the wicked.
26: 7 out the north o' the empty place,
34:13 hath given him a charge o' the earth?
41:34 king o' all the children of pride.
42:11 comforted him o' all the evil that
Ps 8: 6 dominion o' the works of thy hands;
12: 4 lips are our own: who is lord o' us?
13: 2 mine enemy be exalted o' me?
18:29 and by my God have I leaped o' a wall.
19:13 let them not have dominion o' me.
23: 5 my head with oil; my cup runneth o'.
25: 2 let not mine enemies triumph o' me.
27:12 not o' unto the will of mine enemies:
30: 1 hast not made my foes to rejoice o' me.
35:19 enemies wrongfully rejoice o' me:
24 and let them not rejoice o' me.
38: 4 iniquities are gone o' mine head:
16 otherwise they should rejoice o' me:
41:11 enemy doth not triumph o' me.
42: 7 and thy billows are gone o' me.
47: 2 he is a great King o' all the earth.
8 God reigneth o' the heathen: God
49:14 upright shall have dominion o' them
60: 8 o' Edom will I cast out my shoe:
65:13 valleys...are covered o' with corn;
66:12 hast caused men to ride o' our heads;
68:34 his excellency is o' Israel, and his
78:50 gave their life o' to the pestilence;
62 his people o' also unto the sword;
83:18 art the most high o' all the earth.
88:16 Thy fierce wrath goeth o' me; thy
91:11 shall give his angels charge o' thee,
103:16 For the wind passeth o' it, and it
19 heavens; and his kingdom ruleth o' all.
104: 9 bound that they may not pass o';
106:41 they that hated them ruled o' them.
108: 9 o' Edom will I cast out my shoe;
Ps 108: 9 o' Philistia will I triumph.
109: 6 Set thou a wicked man o' him: and
110: 6 wound the heads o' many countries.
118:18 hath not given me o' unto death.
119:133 any iniquity have dominion o' me.
124: 4 the stream had gone o' our soul:
5 proud waters had gone o' our soul.
145: 9 tender mercies are o' all his works.
Pr 17: 2 A wise servant shall have rule o' a son
19:10 for a servant to have rule o' princes.
11 glory to pass o' a transgression.
20:26 and bringeth the wheel o' them.
22: 7 The rich ruleth o' the poor, and the
24:31 lo, it was all grown o' with thorns,
25:28 that hath no rule o' his own spirit is
28:15 a wicked ruler o' the poor people.
Ec 1:12 I the Preacher was king o' Israel
2:19 yet shall he have rule o' all my labour
7:14 set the one o' against the other,
16 Be not righteous o' much; neither
16 neither make thyself o' wise: why
17 Be not o' much wicked, neither be
8: 8 power o' the spirit to retain the spirit;
9 one man ruleth o' another to his own
Ca 2: 4 and his banner o' me was love.
11 is past, the rain is o' and gone;
Isa 3: 4 princes, and babes shall rule o' them.
12 oppressors, and women rule o' them.
8: 7 shall come up o' all his channels,
7 channels, and go o' all his banks:
8 he shall overflow and go o', he
10:29 They are gone o' the passage: they
11:15 he shake his hand o' the river,
15 and make men go o' dryshod.
14: 2 and they shall rule o' their oppressors.
15: 2 shall howl o' Nebo, and o' Medeba:
16: 8 out, they are gone o' the sea.
19: 4 Egyptians will I give o' into the
4 and a fierce king shall rule o' them,
16 of hosts, which he shaketh o' it.
22:15 Shebna, which is o' the house, and
23: 2 of Zidon, that pass o' the sea,
6 Pass ye o' to Tarshish; howl, ye
11 stretched out his hand o' the sea,
12 of Zidon: arise, pass o' to Chittim;
25: 7 of the covering cast o' all people,
7 vail that is spread o' all nations.
26:13 beside thee have had dominion o' us:
28:19 by morning shall it pass o',
31: 5 it; and passing o' he will preserve
9 he shall pass o' to his strong hold
35: 8 the unclean shall not pass o' it;
36: 3 son, which was o' the house,
22 Hilkiah, that was o' the household,
37: 2 Eliakim, who was o' the household,
40:19 goldsmith spreadeth it o' with gold,
27 is passed o' from my God?
41: 2 him, and made him rule o' kings?
45:14 stature, shall come o' unto thee,
14 in chains they shall come o', and
47: 2 the thigh, pass o' the rivers.
51:10 a way for the ransomed to pass o'?
23 Bow down, that we may go o':
23 as the street, to them that went o'.
52: 5 that rule o' them make them to howl,
54: 9 should no more go o' the earth;
62: 5 bridegroom rejoiceth o' the bride,
5 so shall thy God rejoice o' thee.
63:19 thou never barest rule o' them; they
Jer 1:10 this day set thee o' the nations
10 and o' the kingdoms, to root out,
2:10 pass o' the isles of Chittim, and
5: 6 leopard shall watch o' their cities:
22 roar, yet can they not pass o' it?
6:17 Also I set watchmen o' you,
13:21 be captains, and as chief o' thee:
15: 3 I will appoint o' them four kinds,
23: 4 And I will set up shepherds o' them
31:28 that like as I have watched o' them,
28 so will I watch o' them, to build,
39 shall yet go forth o' against it
32:41 rejoice o' them to do them good,
33:26 to be rulers o' the seed of Abraham,
40: 5 made governor o' the cities of Judah,
11 that he had set o' them Gedaliah
41: 2 Babylon had made governor o' the land.
10 to go o' to the Ammonites.
43:10 spread his royal pavilion o' them.
44:27 I will watch o' them for evil,
48:32 thy plants are gone o' the sea,
40 shall spread his wings o' Moab.
49:19 man, that I may appoint o' her?
22 and spread his wings o' Bozrah:
50:44 man, that I may appoint o' her?
La 2:17 thine enemy to rejoice o' thee,
3:54 Waters flowed o' mine head; then I
5: 8 Servants have ruled o' us: there is
Eze 1:20, 21 were lifted up o' against them:
22 stretched forth o' their heads
25 firmament that was o' their heads,
26 firmament that was o' their heads
3:13 of the wheels o' against them,
9: 1 them that have charge o' the city to
10: 1 o' them as it were a sapphire
2 and scatter them o' the city.
4 stood o' the threshold of the house;
18 house, and stood o' the cherubims.
19 God of Israel was o' them above.
11:22 God of Israel was o' them above.
16: 8 and I spread my skirt o' thee, and
27 have stretched out my hand o' thee,
19: 8 and spread their net o' him: he
20:33 fury poured out, will I rule o' you:
27:32 for thee, and lament o' thee,
29:15 shall no more rule o' the nations.
32: 3 therefore spread out my net o' thee

Eze 32: 8 of heaven will I make dark o' thee,
31 be comforted o' all his multitude,
34: 23 I will set up one shepherd o' them,
37: 24 my servant, shall be king o' them;
40: 18 o' against the length of the gates
23 was o' against the gate toward the
41: 6 one o' another, and thirty in order;
15 o' against the separate place
16 three stories, o' against the door,
42: 1 was o' against the separate place,
3 O' against the twenty cubits which
3 o' against the pavement which was
7 without o' against the chambers,
10 o' against the separate place,
10 and o' against the building.
45: 6 o' against the oblation of the holy
7 be o' against one of the portions,
46: 9 but shall go forth o' against it.
47: 5 a river that I could not pass o':
5 a river that could not be passed o'.
20 a man come o' against Hamath.
48: 13 o' against the border of the
15 o' against the five and twenty
18, 18 o' against the oblation of the
21, 21 o' against the five and
21 o' against the portions for the
Da 1: 11 had set o' Daniel, Hananiah,
2: 38 and hath made thee ruler o' them all.
39 which shall bear rule o' all the earth.
48 o' the whole province of Babylon,
48 o' all the wise men of Babylon.
49 o' the affairs of the province of
3: 12 o' the affairs of the province of
4: 16 and let seven times pass o' him.
17 setteth up o' it the basest of men.
23 field, till seven times pass o' him;
25, 32 seven times shall pass o' thee,
5: 5 wrote o' against the candlestick
21 appointeth o' it whomsoever he
6: 1 to set o' the kingdom an hundred
1 should be o' the whole kingdom;
2 And o' these three presidents;
3 to set him o' the whole realm.
9: 1 o' the realm of the Chaldeans;
11: 39 he shall cause them to rule o' many,
40 and shall overflow and pass o'.
43 o' the treasures of gold and of silver,
43 o' all the precious things of Egypt:
Ho 10: 5 people thereof shall mourn o' it,
11 I passed o' upon her fair neck:
12: 4 he had power o' the angel, and
Joe 2: 17 that the heathen should rule o' them:
Ob 12 rejoiced o' the children of Judah
Jon 2: 3 and thy waves passed o' me.
4: 6 and made it to come up o' Jonah,
6 it might be a shadow o' his head,
Mic 3: 6 sun shall go down o' the prophets,
6 and the day shall be dark o' them.
4: 7 Lord shall reign o' them in mount
Na 3: 19 thee shall clap their hands o' thee:
Hab 1: 11 and he shall pass o', and offend,
14 things, that have no ruler o' them?
2: 19 it is laid o' with gold and silver,
Zep 3: 17 he will rejoice o' thee with joy;
17 he will joy o' thee with singing.
Hag 1: 10 heaven o' you is stayed from dew,
Zec 1: 21 up their horn o' the land of Judah
5: 3 o' the face of the whole earth:
9: 14 And the Lord shall be seen o' them,
14: 9 Lord shall be king o' all the earth:
M't 2: 9 o' where the young child was.
9: 1 passed o', and came into his own
10: 23 have gone o' the cities of Israel,
14: 34 And when they were gone o', they
20: 25 Gentiles exercise dominion o' them,
21: 2 Go into the village o' against you,
24: 45 hath made ruler o' his household,
47 make him ruler o' all his goods.
25: 21 hast been faithful o' a few things,
21 make thee ruler o' many things:
23 hast been faithful o' a few things,
23 make thee ruler o' many things:
27: 37 set up o' his head his accusation
45 there was darkness o' all the land
61 sitting o' against the sepulchre.
M'r 4: 35 Let us pass o' unto the other side.
5: 1 o' unto the other side of the sea,
21 Jesus was passed o' again by ship
6: 7 gave them power o' unclean spirits;
53 And when they had passed o', they
10: 42 are accounted to rule o' the Gentiles
42 Gentiles exercise lordship o' them;
11: 2 into the village o' against you:
12: 41 Jesus sat o' against the treasury,
13: 3 of Olives o' against the temple,
15: 26 of his accusation was written o',
33 was darkness o' the whole land
39 which stood o' against him,
Lu 1: 33 o' the house of Jacob for ever;
2: 8 watch o' their flock by night.
4: 10 give his angels charge o' thee,
39 he stood o' her, and rebuked the
6: 38 shaken together, and running o',
8: 22 o' unto the other side of the lake.
26 which is o' against Galilee.
9: 1 power and authority o' all devils,
10: 19 and o' all the power of the enemy:
11: 42 pass o' judgment and...love of God:
44 that walk o' them are not aware
12: 14 me a judge or a divider o' you?
42 shall make ruler o' his household,
44 make him ruler o' all that he hath.
15: 7 o' one sinner that repenteth,
7 more than o ninety and nine just
10 God o' one sinner that repenteth.
19: 14 not have this man to reign o' us.
Lu 19: 17 have thou authority o' ten cities.
19 to him, Be thou also o' five cities.
27 not that I should reign o' them,
30 ye into the village o' against you;
41 he beheld the city, and wept o' it,
22: 25 Gentiles exercise lordship o' them;
23: 38 written o' him in letters of Greek,
44 was a darkness o' all the earth
Joh 6: 1 Jesus went o' the sea of Galilee,
13 remained o' and above unto them
17 o' the sea toward Capernaum.
17: 2 thou hast given him power o' all flesh,
18: 1 his disciples o' the brook Cedron,
Ac 6: 3 we may appoint o' this business.
7: 10 made him governor o' Egypt and
11 there came a dearth o' all the land
16 were carried o' into Sychem, and
27 thee a ruler and a judge o' us?
8: 2 made great lamentation o' him.
16: 9 Come o' into Macedonia, and help
18: 23 went o' all the country of Galatia
19: 13 call o' them which had evil spirits
20: 2 when he had gone o' those parts,
15 the next day o' against Chios; and
28 o' the which the Holy Ghost hath
21: 2 a ship sailing o' unto Phenicia,
27: 5 we had sailed o' the sea of Cilicia
7 were come o' against Cnidus, the
7 under Crete, o' against Salmone;
Ro 1: 28 gave them o' to a reprobate mind,
5: 14 even o' them that had not sinned
6: 9 death hath no more dominion o' him.
14 sin shall not have dominion o' you:
7: 1 hath dominion o' a man as long as he
9: 5 who is o' all, God blessed for ever.
21 Hath not the potter power o' the clay,
10: 12 the same Lord o' all is rich unto all
15: 12 shall rise to reign o' the Gentiles;
1Co 7: 37 but hath power o' his own will,
9: 12 be partakers of this power o' you,
2Co 1: 24 that we have dominion o' your faith,
3: 13 Moses, which put a vail o' his face,
8: 15 had gathered much had nothing o';
11: 2 am jealous o' you with godly jealousy:
Eph 1: 22 him to be the head o' all things to
4: 19 themselves o' unto lasciviousness,
Col 2: 15 them openly, triumphing o' them in it.
1Th 3: 7 were comforted o' you in all our
5: 12 you, and are o' you in the Lord,
1Ti 2: 12 nor to usurp authority o' the man, but
Heb 2: 7 set him o' the works of thy hands:
3: 6 Christ as a son o' his own house;
9: 5 And o' it the cherubims of glory
10: 21 an high priest o' the house of God;
13: 7 them which have the rule o' you,
17 Obey them that have the rule o' you,
24 all them that have the rule o' you,
Jas 5: 14 let them pray o' him, anointing
1Pe 3: 12 of the Lord are o' the righteous,
5: 3 as being lords o' God's heritage,
Jude 7 giving themselves o' to fornication,
Re 2: 26 will I give power o' the nations:
6: 8 o' the fourth part of the earth,
9: 11 they had a king o' them, which is
11: 6 o' waters to turn them to blood,
10 the earth shall rejoice o' them,
13: 7 was given him o' all kindreds, and
14: 18 the altar, which had power o' fire;
15: 2 had gotten the victory o' the beast,
2 and o' his image, and o' his mark,
2 and o' the number of his name,
16: 9 which hath power o' these plagues:
17: 18 reigneth o' the kings of the earth.
18: 11 earth shall weep and mourn o' her;
20 Rejoice o' her, thou heaven, and ye

overcame
Ac 19: 16 o' them, and prevailed against
Re 3: 21 even as I also o', and am set down
12: 11 o' him by the blood of the Lamb,

overcharge See also OVERCHARGED.
2Co 2: 5 in part: that I may not o' you all.

overcharged
Lu 21: 34 your hearts be o' with surfeiting,

overcome See also OVERCAME; OVERCOMETH.
Ge 49: 19 Gad, a troop shall o' him:
19 but he shall o' at the last.
Ex 32: 18 of them that cry for being o': but
Nu 13: 30 it; for we are well able to o' it.
22: 11 I shall be able to o' them, and
2Ki 16: 5 Ahaz, but could not o' him.
Ca 6: 5 from me, for they have o' me:
Isa 28: 1 of them that are o' with wine!
Jer 23: 9 like a man whom wine hath o',
Lu 11: 22 shall come upon him, and o' him,
Joh 16: 33 of good cheer; I have o' the world.
Ro 3: 4 mightest o' when thou art judged.
12: 21 Be not o' of evil,
21 but o' evil with good.
2Pe 2: 19 for of whom a man is o', of the
20 again entangled therein, and o',
1Jo 2: 13 because ye have o' the wicked one.
14 and ye have o' the wicked one.
4: 4 little children, and have o' them:
Re 11: 7 and shall o' them, and kill them.
13: 7 with the saints, and to o' them:
17: 14 Lamb, and the Lamb shall o' them:

overcometh
1Jo 5: 4 is born of God o' the world: and
4 is the victory that o' the world,
5 Who is he that o' the world, but
Re 2: 7 To him that o' will I give to eat of
11 He that o' shall not be hurt of the
17 To him that o' will I give to eat of
Re 2: 26 he that o', and keepeth my works
3: 5 He that o', the same shall be
12 Him that o' will I make a pillar in
21 To him that o' will I grant to sit
21: 7 He that o' shall inherit all things;

overdrive
Ge 33: 13 if men should o' them one day,

overflow See also OVERFLOWED; OVERFLOWETH; OVERFLOWING; OVERFLOWN.
De 11: 4 water of the Red sea to o' them
Ps 69: 2 waters, where the floods o' me.
15 Let not the waterflood o' me,
Isa 8: 8 he shall o' and go over, he shall
10: 22 decreed shall o' with righteousness.
28: 17 waters shall o' the hiding place.
43: 2 the rivers, they shall not o' thee:
Jer 47: 2 shall o' the land, and all that is
Da 11: 10 one shall certainly come, and o',
26 destroy him, and his army shall o':
40 and shall o' and pass over.
Joe 2: 24 the fats shall o' with wine and oil.
3: 13 for the press is full, the fats o';

overflowed
Ps 78: 20 gushed out, and the streams o';
2Pe 3: 6 was, being o' with water, perished:

overfloweth
Jos 3: 15 Jordan o' all his banks all the

overflowing
Job 28: 11 He bindeth the floods from o';
38: 25 watercourse for the o' of waters,
Isa 28: 2 a flood of mighty waters o', shall
15, 18 when the o' scourge shall pass
30: 28 And his breath, as an o' stream,
Jer 47: 2 and shall be an o' flood, and shall
Eze 13: 11 there shall be an o' shower; and
13 be an o' shower in mine anger,
38: 22 an o' rain, and great hailstones,
Hab 3: 10 the o' of the water passed by: the

overflown
1Ch 12: 15 when it had o' all his banks; and
Job 22: 16 foundation was o' with a flood:
Da 11: 22 shall they be o' from before him,

overlaid
Ex 26: 32 of shittim wood o' with gold:
36: 34 he o' the boards with gold, and
34 the bars, and o' the bars with gold.
36 wood, and o' them with gold:
38 and he o' their chapiters and their
37: 2 And he o' it with pure gold within
4 wood, and o' them with gold.
11 he o' it with pure gold, and made
15 o' them with gold, to bear the table.
26 And he o' it with pure gold, both
28 wood, and o' them with gold.
38: 2 the same: and he o' it with brass.
6 wood, and o' them with brass.
28 o' their chapiters, and filleted them.
1Ki 3: 19 in the night; because she o' it.
6: 20 and he o' it with pure gold; and
21 Solomon o' the house within with
21 the oracle; and he o' it with gold.
22 the whole house he o' with gold,
22 altar...by the oracle he o' with gold.
28 And he o' the cherubims with gold.
30 floor of the house he o' with gold,
32 flowers, and o' them with gold,
10: 18 ivory, and o' it with the best gold.
2Ki 18: 16 Hezekiah king of Judah had o',
2Ch 3: 4 and he o' it within with pure gold.
5 which he o' with fine gold, and set
7 He o' also the house, the beams,
8 cubits: and he o' it with fine gold,
9 o' the upper chambers with gold.
10 work, and o' them with gold.
4: 9 and o' the doors of them with brass.
9: 17 of ivory, and o' it with pure gold.
Ca 5: 14 as bright ivory o' with sapphires.
Heb 9: 4 covenant o' round about with gold,

overlay See also OVERLAID.
Ex 25: 11 thou shalt o' it with pure gold,
11 within and without shalt thou o' it,
13 wood, and o' them with gold.
24 thou shalt o' it with pure gold, and
28 wood, and o' them with gold,
26: 29 thou shalt o' the boards with gold,
29 thou shalt o' the bars with gold.
37 o' them with gold, and their hooks
27: 2 and thou shalt o' it with brass.
6 wood, and o' them with brass.
30: 3 shalt o' it with pure gold, the top
5 wood, and o' them with gold.
1Ch 29: 4 to o' the walls of the houses

overlaying
Ex 38: 17 the o' of their chapiters of silver;
19 the o' of their chapiters and their

overlived See also OUTLIVED.
Jos 24: 31 the elders that o' Joshua,

overmuch
2Co 2: 7 be swallowed up with o' sorrow.

overpass See also OVERPAST.
Jer 5: 28 they o' the deeds of the wicked:

overpast
Ps 57: 1 until these calamities be o'.
Isa 26: 20 until the indignation be o'.

overplus
Le 25: 27 and restore the o' unto the man to

overran See also OUTRUN.
2Sa 18: 23 way of the plain, and o' Cushi.

overrunning
Na 1: 8 But with an o' flood he will make
oversee
1Ch 9:29 also were appointed to o' the vessels,
2Ch 2: 2 and six hundred to o' them.
overseer See also OVERSEERS.
Ge 39: 4 he made him o' over his house,
5 he had made him o' in his house,
Ne 11: 9 the son of Zichri was their o':
14 their o' was Zabdiel, the son of one
22 o' also of the Levites at Jerusalem
12:42 sang loud, with Jezrahiah their o'.
Pr 6: 7 having no guide, o', or ruler,
overseers
2Ch 2:18 o' to set the people a work.
31:13 o' under the hand of Cononiah
34:12 the o' of them were Jahath and
13 o' of all that wrought the work in
17 it into the hand of the o', and to
Ac 20:28 the Holy Ghost hath made you o',
overshadow See also OVERSHADOWED.
Lu 1:35 power of the Highest shall o' thee:
Ac 5:15 Peter passing by might o' some
overshadowed
M't 17: 5 behold, a bright cloud o' them:
M'r 9: 7 there was a cloud that o' them:
Lu 9:34 there came a cloud, and o' them:
oversight
Ge 43:12 hand; peradventure it was an o':
Nu 3:32 o' of them that keep the charge of
4:16 the o' of all the tabernacle, and of
2Ki 12:11 the o' of the house of the Lord:
22: 5 the o' of the house of the Lord:
9 the o' of the house of the Lord.
1Ch 9:23 had the o' of the gates of the house
2Ch 34:10 the o' of the house of the Lord,
Ne 11:16 had the o' of the outward business
13: 4 having the o' of the chamber of
1Pe 5: 2 among you, taking the o' thereof,
overspread See also OVERSPREADING.
Ge 9:19 of them was the whole earth o'.
overspreading
Da 9:27 and for the o' of abominations he
overtake See also OVERTAKE; OVERTAKETH.
Ge 44: 4 when thou dost o' them, say unto
Ex 15: 9 enemy said, I will pursue, I will o',
De 19: 6 while his heart is hot, and o' him,
28: 2 shall come on thee, and o' thee,
15 shall come upon thee, and o' thee:
45 and shall pursue thee, and o' thee,
Jos 2: 5 them quickly; for ye shall o' them.
1Sa 30: 8 after this troop? shall I o' them?
8 for thou shalt surely o' them, and
2Sa 15:14 lest he o' us suddenly, and bring
Isa 59: 9 from us, neither doth justice o' us:
Jer 42:16 sword, which ye feared, shall o' you
Ho 2: 7 lovers, but she shall not o' them;
10: 9 children of iniquity did not o' them.
Am 9:10 evil shall not o' nor prevent us.
13 the plowman shall o' the reaper,
1Th 5: 4 that day should o' you as a thief.
overtaken
Ps 18:37 mine enemies, and o' them:
Ga 6: 1 Brethren, if a man be o' in a fault,
overtaketh
1Ch 21:12 sword of thine enemies o' thee;
overthrew
Ge 19:25 And he o' those cities, and all the
29 he o' the cities in which Lot dwelt.
Ex 14:27 and the Lord o' the Egyptians in
De 29:23 which the Lord o' in his anger,
Ps 136:15 But o' Pharaoh and his host in the
Isa 13:19 God o' Sodom and Gomorrah,
Jer 20:16 be as the cities which the Lord o',
50:40 As God o' Sodom and Gomorrah
Am 4:11 as God o' Sodom and Gomorrah.
M't 21:12 o' the tables of...moneychangers,
M'r 11:15 o' the tables of the moneychangers,
Joh 2:15 changers' money, and o' the tables;
overthrow See also OVERTHREW; OVERTHROWETH; OVERTHROWN.
Ge 19:21 also, that I will not o' this city,
29 sent Lot out of the midst of the o',
Ex 23:24 but thou shalt utterly o' them,
De 12: 3 ye shall o' their altars, and break
29:23 therein, like the o' of Sodom, and
2Sa 10: 3 and to spy it out, and to o' it?
11:25 strong against the city, and o' it:
1Ch 19: 3 and to o', and to spy out the land?
Ps 106:26 to o' them in the wilderness:
27 To o' their seed also among the
140: 4 have purposed to o' my goings.
11 hunt the violent man to o' him.
Pr 18: 5 to o' the righteous in judgment.
Jer 49:18 in the o' of Sodom and Gomorrah
Hag 2:22 I will o' the throne of kingdoms,
22 I will o' the chariots, and those
Ac 5:39 if it be of God, ye cannot o' it;
2Ti 2:18 already; and o' the faith of some.
2Pe 2: 6 condemned them with an o',
overthroweth
Job 12:19 away spoiled, and o' the mighty.
Pr 13: 6 but wickedness o' the sinner.
21:12 but God o' the wicked for their
22:12 o' the words of the transgressor.
29: 4 but he that receiveth gifts o' it.
overthrown
Ex 15: 7 hast o' them that rose up against
J'g 9:40 and many were o' and wounded,
2Sa 17: 9 some of them be o' at the first,
2Ch 14:13 and the Ethiopians were o', that
Job 19: 6 Know now that God hath o' me,
Ps 141: 6 judges are o' in stony places,
Pr 11:11 it is o' by the mouth of the wicked.
12: 7 The wicked are o', and are not:
14:11 house of the wicked shall be o':
Isa 1: 7 it is desolate, as o' by strangers.
Jer 18:23 but let them be o' before thee;
La 4: 6 that was o' as in a moment, and
Da 11:41 and many countries shall be o':
Am 4:11 I have o' some of you, as God
Jon 3: 4 days, and Nineveh shall be o'.
1Co 10: 5 for they were o' in the wilderness.
overtook
Ge 31:23 they o' him in the mount Gilead.
25 Then Laban o' Jacob. Now
44: 6 And he o' them, and he spake unto
Ex 14: 9 and o' them encamping by the sea,
J'g 18:22 and o' the children of Dan.
20:42 but the battle o' them; and them
2Ki 25: 5 and o' him in the plains of Jericho:
Jer 39: 5 o' Zedekiah in the plains of Jericho:
52: 8 o' Zedekiah in the plains of Jericho;
La 1: 3 o' her between the straits.
overturn See also OVERTURNED; OVERTURNETH.
Job 12:15 them out, and they o' the earth.
Eze 21:27 I will o', o', o', it: and it shall be
overturned
J'g 7:13 and o' it, that the tent lay along.
overturneth
Job 9: 5 not: which o' them in his anger;
28: 9 he o' the mountains by the roots.
34:25 and he o' them in the night, so
overwhelm See also OVERWHELMED.
Job 6:27 Yea, ye o' the fatherless, and ye
overwhelmed
Ps 55: 5 upon me, and horror hath o' me.
61: 2 unto thee, when my heart is o':
77: 3 and my spirit was o'. Selah.
78:53 not: but the sea o' their enemies.
102: *title* of the afflicted, when he is o',
124: 4 Then the waters had o' us, the
142: 3 When my spirit was o' within me,
143: 4 is my spirit o' within me; my
owe See also OWED; OWEST; OWETH.
Ro 13: 8 O' no man any thing, but to love
owed
M't 18:24 o' him ten thousand talents.
28 which o' him an hundred pence:
Lu 7:41 the one o' five hundred pence, and
owest
M't 18:28 saying, Pay me that thou o'.
Lu 16: 5 How much o' thou unto my lord?
7 another, And how much o' thou?
Ph'm 19 o' unto me even thine own self
oweth
Ph'm 18 wronged thee, or o' thee ought,
owl See also OWLS.
Le 11:16 the o', and the night hawk,
17 the little o', and the cormorant,
17 the cormorant, and the great o',
De 14:15 the o', and the night hawk,
16 the little o', and the...swan,
16 and the great o', and the swan,
Ps 102: 6 I am like an o' of the desert.
Isa 34:11 the o' also and the raven shall
14 screech o' also shall rest there,
15 shall the great o' make her nest,
owls
Job 30:29 and a companion to o'.
Isa 13:21 and o' shall dwell there, and
34:13 dragons, and a court for o'.
43:20 me, the dragons and the o':
Jer 50:39 and the o' shall dwell therein:
Mic 1: 8 and mourning as the o'.
own^ See also OWNETH.
Ge 1:27 So God created man in his o' image,
30:25 that I may go unto mine o' place, and
30 shall I provide for mine o' house also?
40 and he put his o' flocks by themselves,
47:24 four parts shall be your o', for seed
Ex 5:16 but the fault is in thine o' people.
18:27 and he went his way into his o' land.
21:36 for ox; and the dead shall be his o'.
22: 5 man's field; of the best of his o' field,
5 and of the best of his o' vineyard,
32:13 to whom thou swarest by thine o' self,
Le 1: 3 shall offer it of his o' voluntary will
7:30 His o' hands...bring the offerings
14:15 into the palm of his o' left hand:
26 into the palm of his o' left hand:
16:29 it be one of your o' country, or a
17:15 whether it be one of your o' country,
18:10 for theirs is thine o' nakedness.
26 neither any of your o' nation, nor
19: 5 Lord, ye shall offer it at your o' will.
21:14 take a virgin of his o' people to wife.
22:19 offer at your o' will a male without
29 unto the Lord, offer it at your o' will.
24:22 as for one of your o' country: for I
25: 5 which groweth of its o' accord of thy
41 and shall return unto his o' family,
Nu 1:52 their tents, every man by his o' camp,
52 and every man by his o' standard,
2: 2 shall pitch by his o' standard, with
10:30 but I will depart to mine o' land, and
13:33 were in our o' sight as grasshoppers,
15:39 that ye seek not after your o' heart
39 and your o' eyes, after which ye use to
16:28 have not done them of mine o' mind.
38 of these sinners against their o' souls,
24:13 do either good or bad of mine o' mind;
Nu 27: 3 but died in his o' sin, and had no sons.
32:42 and called it Nobah, after his o' name.
36: 9 shall keep himself to his o' inheritance.
De 3:14 and called them after his o' name,
12: 8 man whatsoever is right in his o' eyes.
13: 6 or thy friend, which is as thine o' soul,
22: 2 shalt bring it unto thine o' house,
23:24 eat grapes thy fill at thine o' pleasure;
24:13 sleep in his o' raiment, and bless thee:
16 shall be put to death for his o' sin.
28:53 shalt eat the fruit of thine o' body,
33: 9 brethren, nor knew his o' children:
Jos 7:11 have put it even among their o' stuff.
20: 6 come unto his o' city, and unto his
6 and unto his o' house, unto the city
J'g 2:19 they ceased not from their o' doings,
7: 2 saying, Mine o' hand hath saved me.
8:29 Joash went and dwelt in his o' house.
17: 6 that which was right in his o' eyes.
21:25 that which was right in his o' eyes.
Ru 4: 6 lest I mar mine o' inheritance:
1Sa 2:20 And they went unto their o' home.
5:11 and let it go again to his o' place,
6: 9 way of his o' coast to Beth-shemesh,
13:14 sought him a man after his o' heart,
14:46 the Philistines went to their o' place.
15:17 thou wast little in thine o' sight,
18: 1 Jonathan loved him as his o' soul.
3 because he loved him as his o' soul.
20:17 for he loved him as he loved his o' soul.
30 the son of Jesse to thine o' confusion,
25:26 avenging thyself with thine o' hand,
33 avenging myself with mine o' hand.
39 wickedness of Nabal upon his o' head.
28: 3 buried him in Ramah,...in his o' city.
2Sa 4:11 a righteous person in his o' house
6:22 and will be base in mine o' sight:
7:10 they may dwell in a place of their o',
21 sake, and according to thine o' heart,
12: 3 it did eat of his o' meat, and drank of
3 drank of his o' cup, and lay in his
4 take of his o' flock and of his o' herd,
11 against thee out of thine o' house,
20 then he came to his o' house; and
14:24 said, Let him turn to his o' house,
24 So Absalom returned to his o' house,
18:13 wrought falsehood against mine o' life:
18 he called the pillar after his o' name:
19:28 them that did eat at thine o' table.
30 come again in peace unto his o' house.
37 that I may die in mine o' city, and be
39 him; and he returned unto his o' place.
23:21 hand, and slew him with his o' spear.
1Ki 1:12 that thou mayest save thine o' life, and
33 my son to ride upon mine o' mule,
2:23 spoken this word against his o' life.
26 thee to Anathoth, unto thine o' fields;
32 return his blood upon his o' head,
34 buried in his o' house in the wilderness.
37 thy blood shall be upon thine o' head.
44 thy wickedness upon thine o' head;
3: 1 made an end of building his o' house,
7: 1 Solomon was building his o' house
8:38 every man the plague of his o' heart,
9:15 house of the Lord, and his o' house,
10: 6 I heard in mine o' land of thy acts
11:19 him to wife the sister of his o' wife,
21 that I may go to mine o' country.
22 thou seekest to go to thine o' country?
12:16 now see to thine o' house, David.
33 which he had devised of his o' heart;
13:30 And he laid his carcase in his o' grave;
14:12 therefore, get thee to thine o' house:
17:19 abode, and laid him upon his o' bed.
22:36 city, and every man to his o' country.
2Ki 3:27 him, and returned to their o' land.
4:13 I dwell among mine o' people.
12:18 and his o' hallowed things, and all the
14: 6 man shall be put to death for his o' sin.
17:23 away out of their o' land to Assyria
29 every nation made gods of their o',
33 the Lord, and served their o' gods,
18:27 they may eat their o' dung, and drink
27 and drink their o' piss with you?
31 then eat ye every man of his o' vine,
32 you away to a land like your o' land,
19: 7 and shall return to his o' land; and
7 him to fall by the sword in his o' land.
34 this city, to save it, for mine o' sake,
20: 6 I will defend this city for mine o' sake,
21:18 buried in the garden of his o' house,
23 him, and slew the king in his o' house.
23:30 and buried him in his o' sepulchre.
1Ch 11:23 hand, and slew him with his o' spear.
17:19 according to thine o' heart, hast thou
21 went to redeem to be his o' people,
22 thou make thine o' people for ever;
29: 3 I have of mine o' proper good, of gold
14 and of thine o' have we given thee.
16 of thine hand, and is all thine o'.
2Ch 6:23 his way upon his o' head;
29 know his o' sore and his o' grief,
7:11 in his o' house, he prosperously
8: 1 house of the Lord, and his o' house,
9: 5 I heard in mine o' land of thine acts,
12 and went away to her o' land, she
10:16 and now, David, see to thine o' house.
16:14 they buried him in his o' sepulchres,
25: 4 but every man shall die for his o' sin.
15 their o' people out of thine hand?
31: 1 to his possession, into their o' cities.
32:21 with shame of face to his o' land.
21 they that came forth of his o' bowels
33:20 and they buried him in his o' house:
24 him, and slew him in his o' house.
Ezr 7:13 are minded of their o' freewill to

Ne 4: 4 their reproach upon their o' head,
6: 8 feignest them out of thine o' heart.
16 were much cast down in their o' eyes:
Es 1:22 man should bear rule in his o' house,
2: 7 were dead, took for his o' daughter.
9:25 Jews, should return upon his o' head,
Job 2:11 they came every one from his o' place;
5:13 taketh the wise in their o' craftiness:
9:20 mine o' mouth shall condemn me:
31 and mine o' clothes shall abhor me.
13:15 maintain mine o' ways before him.
15: 6 Thine o' mouth condemneth thee, and
6 yea, thine o' lips testify against thee.
18: 7 his o' counsel shall cast him down.
8 For he is cast into a net by his o' feet,
19:17 the children's sake of mine o' body.
20: 7 shall perish for ever like his o' dung:
32: 1 he was righteous in his o' eyes.
40:14 that thine o' right hand can save thee.
Ps 4: 4 commune with your o' heart upon
5:10 let them fall by their o' counsels;
7:16 mischief shall return upon his o' head,
16 shall come down upon his o' pate.
9:15 which they hid is their o' foot taken.
16 is snared in the work of his o' hands.
12: 4 our lips are our o': who is lord over
15: 4 He that sweareth to his o' hurt, and
20: 4 Grant thee according to thine o' heart,
21:13 exalted, Lord, in thine o' strength:
22:29 and none can keep alive his o' soul.
33:12 he hath chosen for his o' inheritance.
35:13 prayer returned into mine o' bosom.
36: 2 he flattereth himself in his o' eyes,
37:15 sword shall enter into their o' heart,
41: 9 mine o' familiar friend, in whom I
44: 3 land in possession by their o' sword,
3 neither did their o' arm save them:
45:10 forget also thine o' people, and thy
49:11 call their lands after their o' names.
50:20 thou slanderest thine o' mother's son.
64: 8 their o' tongue to fall upon themselves:
67: 6 God, even our o' God, shall bless us.
74:22 Arise, O God, plead thine o' cause:
77: 6 I commune with mine o' heart: and
78:29 for he gave them their o' desire;
52 his o' people to go forth like sheep,
81:12 gave them up unto their o' hearts' lust:
12 and they walked in their o' counsels.
94:23 bring upon them their o' iniquity,
23 cut them off in their o' wickedness;
106:39 were they defiled with their o' works,
39 a whoring with their o' inventions.
40 that he abhorred his o' inheritance.
109:29 their o' confusion as with a mantle.
138: 8 forsake not the works of thine o' hands.
140: 9 mischief of their o' lips cover them.
Pr 1:18 And they lay wait for their o' blood;
18 they lurk privily for their o' lives.
31 they eat of the fruit of their o' way,
31 and be filled with their o' devices.
3: 5 lean not unto thine o' understanding.
7 Be not wise in thine o' eyes: fear the
5:15 Drink waters out of thine o' cistern,
15 running waters out of thine o' well.
6:32 that doeth it destroyeth his o' soul.
8:36 that sinneth...wrongeth his o' soul:
11: 5 wicked shall fall by his o' wickedness.
6 shall be taken in their o' naughtiness.
17 merciful man doeth good to his o' soul:
19 evil pursueth it to his o' death.
29 He that troubleth his o' house shall
12:15 way of a fool is right in his o' eyes:
14:10 heart knoweth his o' bitterness;
14 in heart shall be filled with his o' ways:
20 poor is hated even of his o' neighbour:
15:27 greedy of gain troubleth his o' house;
32 instruction despiseth his o' soul:
16: 2 ways of a man are clean in his o' eyes;
18:11 as an high wall in his o' conceit.
17 is first in his o' cause seemeth just;
19: 8 that getteth wisdom loveth his o' soul:
16 commandment keepeth his o' soul;
20: 2 to anger sinneth against his o' soul.
6 proclaim every one his o' goodness:
24 a man then understand his o' way?
21: 2 way of a man is right in his o' eyes:
23: 4 be rich: cease from thine o' wisdom.
25:27 to search their o' glory is not glory.
28 he that hath no rule over his o' spirit
26: 5 lest he be wise in his o' conceit.
12 thou a man wise in his o' conceit?
16 sluggard is wiser in his o' conceit
27: 2 praise thee, and not thine o' mouth;
2 a stranger, and not thine o' lips.
28:10 he shall fall himself into his o' pit:
11 rich man is wise in his o' conceit;
26 that trusteth in his o' heart is a fool:
29:24 partner with a thief hateth his o' soul:
30:12 that are pure in their o' eyes, and yet
31:31 let her o' works praise her in the gates.
Ec 1:16 I communed with mine o' heart,
3:22 a man should rejoice in his o' works;
4: 5 hands together, and eateth his o' flesh.
7:22 thine o' heart knoweth that thou thyself
8: 9 ruleth over another to his o' hurt.
Ca 1: 6 but mine o' vineyard have I not kept.
Isa 2: 8 worship the work of their o' hands,
8 that which their o' fingers have made:
4: 1 saying, We will eat our o' bread,
1 and wear our o' apparel: only let us
5:21 them that are wise in their o' eyes,
21 eyes, and prudent in their o' sight!
9:20 eat every man the flesh of his o' arm:
13:14 shall every man turn to his o' people,
14 and flee every one into his o' land.
14: 1 Israel, and set them in their o' land:

Isa 23: 7 her o' feet shall carry her afar off to
31: 7 which your o' hands have made unto
36:12 they may eat their o' dung, and drink
12 dung, and drink their o' piss with you?
16 every one the waters of his o' cistern;
17 you away to a land like your o' land,
37: 7 a rumour, and return to his o' land;
7 to fall by the sword in his o' land.
35 this city to save it for mine o' sake,
43:25 thy transgressions for mine o' sake,
44: 9 they are their o' witnesses; they see
48:11 mine o' sake, even for mine o' sake,
49:26 that oppress thee with their o' flesh;
26 shall be drunken with their o' blood,
56:11 they all look to their o' way, every one
58: 7 hide not thyself from thine o' flesh?
13 honour him, not doing thine o' ways,
13 nor finding thine o' pleasure,
13 nor speaking thine o' words:
63: 5 mine o' arm brought salvation unto
65: 2 was not good; after their o' thoughts;
66: 3 Yea, they have chosen their o' ways,
Jer 2:19 Thine o' wickedness shall correct
30 o' sword hath devoured your prophets,
7:19 to the confusion of their o' faces?
9:14 after the imagination of their o' heart,
18:12 but we will walk after our o' devices,
23: 8 and they shall dwell in their o' land.
16 they speak a vision of their o' heart,
17 after the imagination of his o' heart,
26 prophets of the deceit of their o' heart;
25: 7 works of your hands to your o' hurt.
14 to the works of their o' hands.
27:11 will I let remain still in their o' land,
30:18 shall be builded upon her o' heap,
31:17 shall come again to their o' border.
30 every one shall die for his o' iniquity:
37: 7 return to Egypt into their o' land.
42:12 cause you to return to your o' land.
44: 9 their wives, and your o' wickedness,
17 thing goeth forth out of our o' mouth,
46:16 and let us go again to our o' people,
50:16 they shall flee every one to his o' land.
51: 9 let us go every one into his o' country:
52:27 away captive out of his o' land.
La 4:10 women have sodden their o' children:
Eze 11:21 their way upon their o' heads,
13: 2 that prophesy out of their o' hearts,
3 prophets, that follow their o' spirit,
17 which prophesy out of their o' heart;
14: 5 the house of Israel in their o' heart,
14 should deliver but their o' souls
20 shall but deliver their o' souls
16: 6 saw thee polluted in thine o' blood,
15 thou didst trust in thine o' beauty,
52 bear thine o' shame for thy sins that
54 thou mayest bear thine o' shame,
17:19 will I recompense upon his o' head.
20:26 And I polluted them in their o' gifts,
43 shall lothe yourselves in your o' sight
22:31 their o' way have I recompensed upon
23:34 thereof, and pluck off thine o' breasts:
29: 3 My river is mine o', and I have made
32:10 every man for his o' life, in the day
33: 4 his blood shall be upon his o' head.
13 if he trust to his o' righteousness,
34:13 and will bring them to their o' land,
36:17 house of Israel dwelt in their o' land,
17 they defiled it by their o' way and by
24 and will bring you into your o' land.
31 shall ye remember your o' evil ways,
31 shall lothe yourselves in your o' sight
32 and confounded for your o' ways,
37:14 and I shall place you in your o' land:
21 and bring them into their o' land:
39:28 have gathered them unto their o' land,
46:18 inheritance out of his o' possession:
Da 3:28 worship any god, except their o' God.
6:17 the king sealed it with his o' signet,
8:24 be mighty, but not by his o' power:
9:19 defer not, for thine o' sake, O my God:
11: 9 and shall return into his o' land.
16 shall do according to his o' will,
18 a prince for his o' behalf shall cause
18 without his o' reproach he shall cause
19 face toward the fort of his o' land:
28 do exploits, and return to his o' land.
Ho 7: 2 now their o' doings have beset them
10: 6 shall be ashamed of his o' counsel.
11: 6 them, because of their o' counsels.
12: 2 according to their o' understanding,
Joe 3: 4 your recompence upon your o' head;
7 your recompence upon your o' head:
Am 6:13 taken to us horns by our o' strength?
7:11 led away captive out of their o' land.
Ob 15 shall return upon thine o' head.
Jon 2: 8 lying vanities forsake their o' mercy.
Mic 7: 6 enemies are the men of his o' house.
Hag 1: 9 ye run every man unto his o' house.
Zec 5:11 and set there upon her o' base.
11: 5 and their o' shepherds pity them not.
12: 6 be inhabited again in her o' place,
Mal 3:17 a man spareth his o' son that serveth
M't 2:12 departed into their o' country another
7: 3 not the beam that is in thine o' eye?
4 and, behold, a beam is in thine o' eye?
5 cast out the beam out of thine o' eye;
9: 1 over, and came into his o' city.
10:36 foes shall be they of his o' household.
13:54 he was come into his o' country,
57 in his o' country, and in his o' house.
16:26 whole world, and lose his o' soul?
17:25 of their o' children, or of strangers?
20:15 to do what I will with mine o'?
25:14 who called his o' servants, and
27 have received mine o' with usury.

M't 27:31 and put his o' raiment on him, and
60 And laid it in his o' new tomb, which
M'r 6: 1 and came into his o' country;
4 but in his o' country and among
4 among his o' kin, and in his o' house.
7: 9 that ye may keep your o' tradition.
8: 3 away fasting to their o' houses,
36 whole world, and lose his o' soul?
15:20 and put his o' clothes on him,
Lu 1:23 he departed to his o' house.
56 and returned to her o' house.
2: 3 be taxed, every one into his o' city,
35 sword pierce through thy o' soul also
39 into Galilee, to their o' city Nazareth.
4:24 is accepted in his o' country.
5:25 lay, and departed to his o' house,
29 him a great feast in his o' house:
6:41 the beam that is in thine o' eye?
42 not the beam that is in thine o' eye?
42 out first the beam out of thine o' eye,
44 every tree is known by his o' fruit.
8:39 Return to thine o' house, and shew
9:26 when he shall come in his o' glory,
10:34 and set him on his o' beast, and
14:26 and his o' life also, he cannot be my
16:12 shall give you that which is your o'?
18: 7 shall not God avenge his o' elect,
19:22 Out of thine o' mouth will I judge thee,
23 have required mine o' with usury?
21:30 know of your o' selves that summer
22:71 ourselves have heard of his o'
Joh 1:11 He came unto his o', and his
11 and his o' received him not.
41 first findeth his o' brother Simon,
4:41 more believed because of his o' word;
44 hath no honour in his o' country.
5:30 I can of mine o' self do nothing:
30 I seek not mine o' will, but the
43 another shall come in his o' name,
6:38 not to do mine o' will, but the will
7:18 of himself seeketh his o' glory:
53 every man went unto his o' house.
8: 9 being convicted by their o' conscience,
44 a lie, he speaketh of his o':
50 I seek not mine o' glory: there is
10: 3 he calleth his o' sheep by name,
4 when he putteth forth his o' sheep,
12 whose o' the sheep are not,
13: 1 loved his o' which were in the world,
15:19 world, the world would love his o':
16:32 be scattered, every man to his o',
17: 5 glorify thou me with thine o' self
11 keep through thine o' name those
18:35 Thine o' nation and the chief priests
19:27 disciple took her unto his o' home.
20:10 away again unto their o' home.
Ac 1: 7 Father hath put in his o' power.
25 that he might go to his o' place.
2: 6 them speak in his o' language.
8 we every man in our o' tongue,
3:12 by our o' power or holiness we had
4:23 they went to their o' company,
32 which he possessed was his o';
5: 4 it remained, was it not thine o'?
4 sold, was it not in thine o' power?
7:21 and nourished him for her o' son.
41 In the works of their o' hands.
12:10 opened to them of his o' accord:
13:22 a man after mine o' heart, which
36 he had served his o' generation by
14:16 all nations to walk in their o' ways.
15:22 send chosen men of their o' company
17:28 also of your o' poets have said,
18: 6 Your blood be upon your o' heads;
20:28 hath purchased with his o' blood.
30 Also of your o' selves shall men arise,
21:11 and bound his o' hands and feet,
25:19 against him of their o' superstition,
26: 4 mine o' nation at Jerusalem,
27:19 day we cast out with our o' hands
28:30 years in his o' hired house, and
Ro 1:24 through the lusts of their o' hearts,
24 to dishonour their o' bodies between
4:19 he considered not his o' body now
8: 3 God sending his o' Son in the
32 that spared not his o' Son, but
10: 3 to establish their o' righteousness,
11:24 be graffed into their o' olive tree?
25 should be wise in your o' conceits;
12:16 Be not wise in your o' conceits.
14: 4 to his o' master he standeth or
5 be fully persuaded in his o' mind.
16: 4 my life laid down their o' necks:
18 our Jesus Christ, but their o' belly:
1Co 1:15 I had baptized in mine o' name.
3: 8 man shall receive his o' reward
8 reward according to his o' labour.
19 taketh the wise in their o' craftiness.
4: 3 yea, I judge not mine o' self.
12 labour, working with our o' hands:
6:14 also raise up us by his o' power.
18 sinneth against his o' body.
19 of God, and ye are not your o'?
7: 2 let every man have his o' wife, and
2 every woman have her o' husband.
4 wife hath not power of her o' body,
4 hath not power of his o' body, but
35 And this I speak for your o' profit;
37 but hath power over his o' will,
9: 7 warfare any time at his o' charges?
10:24 Let no man seek his o', but every
29 Conscience, I say, not thine o', but of
33 not seeking mine o' profit, but the
11:21 taketh before other his o' supper:
13: 5 seeketh not her o', is not easily
15:23 But every man in his o' order:

1Co 11: 38 him, and to every seed his *o'* body.
16: 21 of me Paul with mine *o'* hand.
2Co 6: 12 ye are straitened in your *o'* bowels.
8: 5 gave their *o'* selves to the Lord,
17 of his *o'* accord he went unto you.
11: 26 in perils by mine *o'* countrymen, in
13: 5 be in the faith, prove your *o'* selves.
5 Know ye not your *o'* selves, how that
Ga 1: 14 many my equals in mine *o'* nation,
4: 15 would have plucked out your *o'* eyes,
6: 4 let every man prove his *o'* work,
5 man shall bear his *o'* burden.
11 unto you with mine *o'* hand.
Eph 1: 11 after the counsel of his *o'* will:
20 set him at his *o'* right hand in the
5: 22 yourselves unto your *o'* husbands,
24 the wives be to their *o'* husbands
28 love their wives as their *o'* bodies.
29 no man ever yet hated his *o'* flesh;
Ph'p 2: 4 not every man on his *o'* things,
12 work out your *o'* salvation with fear
21 For all seek their *o'*, not the
3: 9 having mine *o'* righteousness,
Col 3: 18 yourselves unto your *o'* husbands,
1Th 2: 8 of God only, but also our *o'* souls,
14 like things of your *o'* countrymen,
15 Lord Jesus, and their *o'* prophets,
4: 11 be quiet, and to do your *o'* business,
11 and to work with your *o'* hands,
2Th 3: 12 they work, and eat their *o'* bread.
17 of Paul with mine *o'* hand, which
1Ti 1: 2 Timothy, my *o'* son in the faith:
3: 4 One that ruleth well his *o'* house,
5 know not how to rule his *o'* house,
12 children and their *o'* houses well.
5: 8 if any provide not for his *o'*, and
8 specially for those of his *o'* house,
6: 1 count their *o'* masters worthy of
2Ti 1: 9 according to his *o'* purpose and
3: 2 men shall be lovers of their *o'* selves,
4: 3 after their *o'* lusts shall they heap
Tit 1: 4 *o'* son after the common faith:
12 even a prophet of their *o'*, said,
2: 5 good, obedient to their *o'* husbands,
9 be obedient unto their *o'* masters,
Ph'm 12 him, that is, mine *o'* bowels:
19 have written it with mine *o'* hand,
19 unto me even thine *o'* self besides.
Heb 2: 4 Holy Ghost, according to his *o'* will?
3: 6 Christ as a son over his *o'* house;
4: 10 also hath ceased from his *o'* works,
7: 27 up sacrifice, first for his *o'* sins,
9: 12 but by his *o'* blood he entered in
12: 10 chastened...after their *o'* pleasure;
13: 12 the people with his *o'* blood,
Jas 1: 14 he is drawn away of his *o'* lust, and
18 Of his *o'* will begat he us with the
22 hearers only, deceiving your *o'* selves.
26 tongue, but deceiveth his *o'* heart,
1Pe 2: 24 Who his *o'* self bare our sins in his
24 our sins in his *o'* body on the tree,
3: 1 in subjection to your *o'* husbands;
5 subjection unto their *o'* husbands:
2Pe 2: 12 perish in their *o'* corruption;
13 themselves with their *o'* deceivings
22 dog is turned to his *o'* vomit again;
3: 3 scoffers, walking after their *o'* lusts,
16 scriptures, unto their *o'* destruction.
17 fall from your *o'* stedfastness.
1Jo 3: 12 Because his *o'* works were evil, and
Jude 6 but left their *o'* habitation, he
13 sea, foaming out their *o'* shame;
16 walking after their *o'* lusts; and
18 walk after their *o'* ungodly lusts.
Re 1: 5 us from our sins in his *o'* blood,

owner See also OWNERS.
Ex 21: 28 but the *o'* of the ox shall be quit.
29 and it hath been testified to his *o'*,
29 and his *o'* also shall be put to death.
34 The *o'* of the pit shall make it good,
34 give money unto the *o'* of them;
36 and his *o'* hath not kept him in; he
22: 11 and the *o'* of it shall accept thereof,
12 shall make restitution unto the *o'*
14 the *o'* thereof being not with it, he
15 the *o'* thereof be with it, he shall not
1Ki 16: 24 the name of Shemer, *o'* of the hill,
Isa 1: 3 The ox knoweth his *o'*, and the
Ac 27: 11 the master and the *o'* of the ship,

owners
Job 31: 39 the *o'* thereof to lose their life:
Pr 1: 19 taketh away the life of the *o'*
Ec 5: 11 good is there to the *o'* thereof,
13 riches kept for the *o'* thereof to
Lu 19: 33 the *o'* thereof said unto them,

owneth
Le 14: 35 And he that *o'* the house shall come
Ac 21: 11 bind the man that *o'* this girdle,

ox See also OXEN.
Ex 20: 17 nor his *o'*, nor his ass, nor any
21: 28 If an *o'* gore a man or a woman,
28 then the *o'* shall be surely stoned,
28 the owner of the *o'* shall be quit.
29 *o'* were wont to push with his horn
29 the *o'* shall be stoned, and his
32 If the *o'* shall push a manservant
32 silver, and the *o'* shall be stoned.
33 and an *o'* or an ass fall therein;
35 And if one man's *o'* hurt another's,
35 then they shall sell the live *o'*, and
35 the dead *o'* also they shall divide.
36 the *o'* hath used to push in time
36 in; he shall surely pay *o'* for *o'*;
22: 1 If a man shall steal an *o'*, or a
1 he shall restore five oxen for an *o'*,
4 whether it be *o'*, or ass, or sheep;
9 whether it be for *o'*, for ass, for
10 his neighbour an ass, or an *o'*, or
23: 4 meet thine enemy's *o'* or his ass
12 that thine *o'* and thine ass may
34: 19 thy cattle, whether *o'* or sheep,
Le 7: 23 shall eat no manner of fat, of *o'*,
17: 3 that killeth an *o'*, or lamb, or goat,
27: 26 whether it be *o'*, or sheep: it is the
Nu 7: 3 princes, and for each one an *o'*:
22: 4 as the *o'* licketh up the grass of the
De 5: 14 thine *o'*, nor thine ass, nor any of
21 his *o'*, or his ass, or any thing that
14: 4 ye shall eat: the *o'*, the sheep, and
5 and the wild *o'*, and the chamois.
18: 3 sacrifice, whether it be *o'* or sheep;
22: 1 brother's *o'* or his sheep go astray,
4 thy brother's ass or his *o'* fall down
10 not plow with an *o'* and an ass
25: 4 shalt not muzzle the *o'* when he
28: 31 Thine *o'* shall be slain before thine
Jos 6: 21 and *o'*, and sheep, and ass, with the
J'g 3: 31 hundred men with an *o'* goad:
6: 4 for Israel, neither sheep, nor *o'*,
1Sa 12: 3 whose *o'* have I taken? or whose ass
14: 34 Bring me hither every man his *o'*,
34 brought every man his *o'* with him
15: 3 infant and suckling, *o'* and sheep,
Ne 5: 18 was one *o'* and six choice sheep;
Job 6: 5 or loweth the *o'* over his fodder?
24: 3 take the widow's *o'* for a pledge.
40: 15 thee; he eateth grass as an *o'*.
Ps 69: 31 please the Lord better than an *o'*
106: 20 similitude of an *o'* that eateth grass.
Pr 7: 22 as an *o'* goeth to the slaughter, or
14: 4 increase is by the strength of the *o'*.
15: 17 a stalled *o'* and hatred therewith.
Isa 1: 3 The *o'* knoweth his owner, and the
11: 7 the lion shall eat straw like the *o'*.
32: 20 the feet of the *o'* and the ass.
66: 3 He that killeth an *o'* is as if he slew
Jer 11: 19 I was like a lamb or an *o'* that is
Eze 1: 10 they four had the face of an *o'* on
Lu 13: 15 the sabbath loose his *o'* or his ass
14: 5 an ass or an *o'* fallen into a pit,
1Co 9: 9 not muzzle the mouth of the *o'* that
1Ti 5: 18 not muzzle the *o'* that treadeth out

oxen
Ge 12: 16 and he had sheep, and *o'*, and he
20: 14 Abimelech took sheep, and *o'*, and
21: 27 And Abraham took sheep and *o'*,
32: 5 And I have *o'*, and asses, flocks,
34: 28 took their sheep, and their *o'*, and
Ex 9: 3 upon the *o'*, and upon the sheep:
20: 24 offerings, thy sheep, and thine *o'*:
22: 1 he shall restore five *o'* for an ox,
30 shalt thou do with thine *o'*, and
24: 5 peace offerings of *o'* unto the Lord.
Nu 7: 3 six covered wagons, and twelve *o'*;
6 Moses took the wagons and the *o'*,
7 Two wagons and four *o'* he gave
8 four wagons and eight *o'* he gave
Nu 7: 17, 23, 29, 35, 41, 47, 53, 59, 65, 71, 77,
83 two *o'*, five rams, five he goats,
87 All the *o'* for the burnt offering
88 all the *o'* for the sacrifice of the
22: 40 Balak offered *o'* and sheep, and sent
23: 1 and prepare me here seven *o'* and
De 14: 26 for *o'*, or for sheep, or for wine, or
Jos 7: 24 and his *o'*, and his asses, and his
1Sa 11: 7 he took a yoke of *o'*, and hewed
7 so shall it be done unto his *o'*.
14: 14 land, which a yoke of *o'* might plow.
32 took sheep, and *o'*, and calves, and
15: 9 the best of the sheep, and of the *o'*,
14 the lowing of the *o'* which I hear?
15 the best of the sheep and of the *o'*,
21 took of the spoil, sheep and *o'*, the
22: 19 *o'*, and asses, and sheep, with the
27: 9 took away the sheep, and the *o'*,
2Sa 6: 6 took hold of it; for the *o'* shook it.
13 paces, he sacrificed *o'* and fatlings.
24: 22 here be *o'* for burnt sacrifice, and
22 instruments of the *o'* for wood.
24 and the *o'* for fifty shekels of silver.
1Ki 1: 9 Adonijah slew sheep and *o'* and fat
19 And he hath slain *o'* and fat cattle
25 hath slain *o'* and fat cattle and sheep
4: 23 Ten fat *o'*, and twenty *o'* out of the
7: 25 It stood upon twelve *o'*, three
29 were lions, *o'*, and cherubims:
29 and beneath the lions and *o'* were
44 sea, and twelve *o'* under the sea;
8: 5 sacrificing sheep and *o'*, that could
63 two and twenty thousand *o'*, and an
19: 19 was plowing with twelve yoke of *o'*
20 And he left the *o'*, and ran after
21 took a yoke of *o'*, and slew them,
21 flesh with the instruments of the *o'*,
2Ki 5: 26 vineyards, and sheep, and *o'*, and
16: 17 the brasen *o'* that were under it,
1Ch 12: 40 and on mules, and on *o'*, and meat,
40 and wine, and oil, and *o'*, and sheep
13: 9 hold the ark; for the *o'* stumbled.
21: 23 thee the *o'* also for burnt offerings,
2Ch 4: 3 under it was the similitude of *o'*,
3 Two rows of *o'* were cast, when it
4 It stood upon twelve *o'*, three
15 One sea, and twelve *o'* under it.
5: 6 sacrificed sheep and *o'*, which could
7: 5 of twenty and two thousand *o'*,
15: 11 had brought, seven hundred *o'* and
18: 2 Ahab killed sheep and *o'* for him in
29: 33 six hundred *o'* and three thousand
31: 6 brought in the tithe of *o'* and sheep,
35: 8 small cattle, and three hundred *o'*.
9 small cattle, and five hundred *o'*.
12 Moses. And so did they with the *o'*.
Job 1: 3 camels, and five hundred yoke of *o'*,
14 The *o'* were plowing, and the asses
42: 12 camels, and a thousand yoke of *o'*,
Ps 8: 7 All sheep and *o'*, yea, and the beasts
144: 14 our *o'* may be strong to labour;
Pr 14: 4 Where no *o'* are, the crib is clean:
Isa 7: 25 shall be for the sending forth of *o'*,
22: 13 joy and gladness, slaying *o'*, and
30: 24 The *o'* likewise and the young asses
Jer 51: 23 the husbandman and his yoke of *o'*;
Da 4: 25, 32 make thee to eat grass as *o'*,
33 and did eat grass as *o'*, and his
5: 21 they fed him with grass like *o'*, and
Am 6: 12 rock? will one plow there with *o'*?
M't 22: 4 my *o'* and my fatlings are killed,
Lu 14: 19 I have bought five yoke of *o'*, and
Joh 2: 14 that sold *o'* and sheep and doves,
15 temple, and the sheep, and the *o'*;
Ac 14: 13 *o'* and garlands unto the gates,
1Co 9: 9 corn. Doth God take care for *o'*?

ox-goad See OX and GOAD.

Ozem (*o'-zem*)
1Ch 2: 15 *O'* the sixth, David the seventh:
25 and Oren, and *O'*, and Ahijah.

Ozias (*o-zi'-as*) See also UZZIAH.
M't 1: 8 begat Joram, and Joram begat *O'*;
9 And *O'* begat Joatham; and

Ozni (*oz'-ni*) See also OZNITES.
Nu 26: 16 Of *O'*, the family of the Oznites:

Oznites (*oz'-nites*)
Nu 26: 16 Of Ozni, the family of the *O'*: of

P.

Paaneah See ZAPH-NATH-PAANEAH.

Paarai (*pa'-ar-ahee*) See also NOARAI.
2Sa 23: 35 the Carmelite, *P'* the Arbite,

Pacatiana (*pa-ca-she-a'-nah*)
1Ti *subscr.* is the chiefest city of Phrygia *P'*.

paces See also APACE.
2Sa 6: 13 ark of the Lord had gone six *p'*,

pacified
Es 7: 10 Then was the king's wrath *p'*.
Eze 16: 63 when I am *p'* toward thee for all

pacifieth
Pr 21: 14 A gift in secret *p'* anger: and a
Ec 10: 4 for yielding *p'* great offences.

pacify See also PACIFIED; PACIFIETH.
Pr 16: 14 death: but a wise man will *p'* it.

Padan (*pa'-dan*) See also PADAN-ARAM.
Ge 48: 7 as for me, when I came from *P'*,

Padan-aram (*pa''-dan-a'-ram*)
Ge 25: 20 of Bethuel the Syrian of *P'*,
28: 2 go to *P'*, to the house of Bethuel
5 he went to *P'* unto Laban, son of
6 Jacob, and sent him away to *P'*,
7 his mother, and was gone to *P'*;
31: 18 which he had gotten in *P'*, for to go
33: 18 of Canaan, when he came from *P'*;
35: 9 again when he came out of *P'*, and
26 which were born to him in *P'*.
46: 15 which she bare unto Jacob in *P'*,

paddle
De 23: 13 shalt have a *p'* upon thy weapon;

Padon (*pa'-don*)
Ezr 2: 44 of Siaha, the children of *P'*,
Ne 7: 47 children of Sia, the children of *P'*.

Pagiel (*pa'-ghe-el*)
Nu 1: 13 Of Asher; *P'* the son of Ocran.
2: 27 Asher shall be *P'* the son of Ocran.
Nu 7: 72 eleventh day *P'* the son of Ocran,
77 the offering of *P'* the son of Ocran.
10: 26 of Asher was *P'* the son of Ocran.

Pahath-moab (*pa''-hath-mo'-ab*)
Ezr 2: 6 children of *P'*, of the children
8: 4 Of the sons of *P'*; Elihoenai the
10: 30 And of the sons of *P'*; Adna, and
Ne 3: 11 and Hashub the son of *P'*, repaired
7: 11 The children of *P'*, of the children
10: 14 The chief of the people; Parosh, *P'*,

Pai (*pa'-i*) See also PAU.
1Ch 1: 50 and the name of his city was *P'*;

paid See also PAYED.
Ezr 4: 20 and custom, was *p'* unto them.
Jon 1: 3 so he *p'* the fare thereof, and went
M't 5: 26 thou hast *p'* the uttermost farthing.
Lu 12: 59 till thou hast *p'* the very last mite.

pain See also PAINED; PAINFUL; PAINS.
Job 14: 22 his flesh upon him shall have *p'*,

Job 15:20 wicked man travaileth with p' all his
33:19 He is chastened also with p' upon
19 multitude of his bones with strong p':
Ps 25:18 upon mine affliction and my p';
48: 6 and p', as of a woman in travail.
Isa 13: 8 in p' as a woman that travaileth:
21: 3 are my loins filled with p': pangs
26:17 the time of her delivery, is in p',
18 been with child, we have been in p',
66: 7 before her p' came, she was
Jer 6:24 and p', as of a woman in travail.
12:13 they have put themselves to p',
15:18 Why is my p' perpetual, and my
22:23 the p' as of a woman in travail!
30:23 fall with p' upon the head of the
51: 8 take balm for her p', if so be she
Eze 30: 4 and great p' shall be in Ethiopia,
9 great p' shall come upon them,
16 Sin shall have great p', and No
Mic 4:10 Be in p', and labour to bring forth,
Na 2:10 and much p' is in all loins, and the
Ro 8:22 and travaileth in p' together until now.
Re 16:10 they gnawed their tongues for p',
21: 4 neither shall there be any more p':

pained
Ps 55: 4 My heart is sore p' within me: and
Isa 23: 5 be sorely p' at the report of Tyre.
Jer 4:19 bowels! I am p' at my very heart;
Joe 2: 6 face the people shall be much p':
Re 12: 2 in birth, and p' to be delivered.

painful
Ps 73:16 to know this, it was too p' for me;

painfulness
2Co 11:27 In weariness and p', in watchings

pains
1Sa 4:19 travailed; for her p' came upon her.
Ps 116: 3 the p' of hell gat hold upon me:
Ac 2:24 up, having loosed the p' of death:
Re 16:11 because of their p' and their sores,

painted See also PAINTEDST.
2Ki 9:30 she p' her face, and tired her
Jer 22:14 with cedar, and p' with vermilion.

paintedst
Eze 23:40 p' thy eyes, and deckedst thyself

painting
Jer 4:30 thou rentest thy face with p', in

pair See also REPAIR.
Am 2: 6 silver, and the poor for a p' of shoes;
8: 6 and the needy for a p' of shoes;
Lu 2:24 A p' of turtledoves, or two young
Re 6: 5 had a p' of balances in his hand.

palace See also PALACES.
1Ki 16:18 into the p' of the king's house,
21: 1 hard by the p' of Ahab king of
2Ki 15:25 in the p' of the king's house, with
20:18 in the p' of the king of Babylon.
1Ch 29: 1 p' is not for man, but for the Lord
19 these things, and to build the p',
2Ch 9:11 of the Lord, and to the king's p',
Ezr 4:14 maintenance from the king's p',
6: 2 p' that is in the province of the
Ne 1: 1 year, as I was in Shushan the p',
2: 8 make beams for the gates of the p'
7: 2 and Hananiah the ruler of the p',
Es 1: 2 which was in Shushan the p',
5 were present in Shushan the p',
5 of the garden of the king's p';
2: 3 young virgins unto Shushan the p',
5 Now in Shushan the p' there was a
8 together unto Shushan the p', to
3:15 decree was given in Shushan the p'.
7: 7 his wrath went into the p' garden:
8 king returned out of the p' garden
8:14 was given at Shushan the p'.
9: 6 in Shushan the p' the Jews slew
11 that were slain in Shushan the p'
12 hundred men in Shushan the p',
Ps 45:15 they shall enter into the king's p'.
144:12 after the similitude of a p':
Ca 8: 9 will build upon her a p' of silver:
Isa 25: 2 a p' of strangers to be no city; it
39: 7 in the p' of the king of Babylon.
Jer 30:18 p' shall remain after the manner
Da 1: 4 in them to stand in the king's p',
4: 4 house, and flourishing in my p':
29 he walked in the p' of the kingdom
5: 5 of the wall of the king's p': and
6:18 Then the king went to his p', and
8: 2 that I was at Shushan in the p',
11:45 shall plant the tabernacles of the p'
Am 4: 3 and ye shall cast them into the p',
Na 2: 6 and the p' shall be dissolved.
M't 26: 3 unto the p' of the high priest, who
58 afar off unto the high priest's p',
69 Now Peter sat without in the p':
M'r 14:54 even into the p' of the high priest:
66 And as Peter was beneath in the p',
Lu 11:21 strong man armed keepeth his p',
Joh 18:15 Jesus into the p' of the high priest.
Ph'p 1:13 in Christ are manifest in all the p',

palaces
2Ch 36:19 burnt all the p' thereof with fire,
Ps 45: 8 and cassia, out of the ivory p',
48: 3 is known in her p' for a refuge.
13 well her bulwarks, consider her p';
78:69 he built his sanctuary like high p',
122: 7 walls, and prosperity within thy p'.
Pr 30:28 with her hands, and is in kings' p'.
Isa 13:22 and dragons in their pleasant p':
23:13 they raised up the p' thereof; and
Isa 32:14 Because the p' shall be forsaken;
34:13 And thorns shall come up in her p',
Jer 6: 5 by night, and let us destroy her p'.
9:21 and is entered into our p', to cut off
17:27 it shall devour the p' of Jerusalem,
49:27 shall consume the p' of Ben-hadad.
La 2: 5 he hath swallowed up all her p':
7 of the enemy the walls of her p';
Eze 19: 7 he knew their desolate p', and he laid
25: 4 and they shall set their p' in thee,
Ho 8:14 and it shall devour the p' thereof.
Am 1: 4 shall devour the p' of Ben-hadad.
7 which shall devour the p' thereof:
10 which shall devour the p' thereof.
12 which shall devour the p' of Bozrah.
14 it shall devour the p' thereof, with
2: 2 and it shall devour the p' of Kirioth:
5 it shall devour the p' of Jerusalem.
3: 9 Publish in the p' at Ashdod, and
9 and in the p' in the land of Egypt,
10 up violence and robbery in their p'.
11 thee, and thy p' shall be spoiled.
6: 8 I abhor...Jacob, and hate his p':
Mic 5: 5 and when he shall tread in our p',

Palal *(pa'-lal)*
Ne 3:25 P' the son of Uzai, over against

pale
Isa 29:22 neither shall his face now wax p'.
Re 6: 8 I looked, and behold a p' horse:

paleness
Jer 30: 6 and all faces are turned into p'?

Palestina *(pal-es-ti'-nah)* See also PALESTINE; PHILISTIA.
Ex 15:14 hold on the inhabitants of P'.
Isa 14:29 Rejoice not thou, whole P', because
31 city; thou, whole P', art dissolved:

Palestine *(pal'-es-tine)* See also PALESTINA.
Joe 3: 4 Zidon, and all the coasts of P'?

Palet See BETH-PALET.

Pallu *(pal'-lu)* See also PALLUITES; PHALLU.
Ex 6:14 Hanoch, and P', Hezron, and
Nu 26: 5 of P', the family of the Palluites:
8 And the sons of P'; Eliab.
1Ch 5: 3 Hanoch, and P', Hezron, and

Palluites *(pal'-lu-ites)*
Nu 26: 5 of Pallu, the family of the P':

palm See also PALMS.
Ex 15:27 and threescore and ten p' trees:
Le 14:15, 26 into the p' of his own left hand:
23:40 branches of p' trees, goodly trees,
Nu 33: 9 and threescore and ten p' trees;
De 34: 3 Jericho, the city of p' trees, unto
J'g 1:16 went up out of the city of p' trees
3:13 and possessed the city of p' trees.
4: 5 under the p' tree of Deborah
1Ki 6:29, 32 cherubims and p' trees and open
32 cherubims, and upon the p' trees.
35 cherubims and p' trees and open
7:36 cherubims, lions, and p' trees,
2Ch 3: 5 and set thereon p' trees and chains.
28:15 to Jericho, the city of p' trees,
Ne 8:15 myrtle branches, and p' branches,
Ps 92:12 shall flourish like the p' tree:
Ca 7: 7 This thy stature is like to a p' tree,
8 I said, I will go up to the p' tree,
Jer 10: 5 They are upright as the p' tree,
Eze 40:16 and upon each post were p' trees.
22 and their arches, and their p' trees,
26 and it had p' trees, one on this side,
31, 34, 37 p' trees were upon the posts
41:18 made with cherubims and p' trees,
18 that a p' tree was between a cherub
19 toward the p' tree on the one side,
19 toward the p' tree on the other side:
20 were cherubims and p' trees made,
25 cherubims and p' trees, like as were
26 were narrow windows and p' trees
Joe 1:12 the p' tree also, and the apple tree,
Joh 12:13 Took branches of p' trees, and
18:22 struck Jesus with the p' of his

palm-branches See PALM and BRANCHES.

palmerworm
Joe 1: 4 That which the p' hath left hath
2:25 and the caterpiller, and the p',
Am 4: 9 increased, the p' devoured them:

palms
1Sa 5: 4 both the p' of his hands were cut
2Ki 9:35 the feet, and the p' of her hands.
Isa 49:16 graven...upon the p' of my hands;
Da 10:10 knees and upon the p' of my hands.
M't 26:67 smote him with...p' of their hands,
M'r 14:65 smote him with...p' of their hands.
Re 7: 9 robes, and p' in their hands;

palm-tree See PALM and TREE.

palsies
Ac 8: 7 and many taken with p', and that

palsy See also PALSIES.
M't 4:24 lunatick, and those that had...p';
8: 6 servant lieth at home sick of the p',
9: 2 brought to him a man sick of the p',
2 faith said unto the sick of the p';
6 (then saith he to the sick of the p',)
M'r 2: 3 him, bringing one sick of the p',
4 bed wherein the sick of the p' lay.
5 he said unto the sick of the p', Son,
9 easier to say to the sick of the p',
10 sins, (he saith to the sick of the p',)
Lu 5:18 a man which was taken with a p':
Lu 5:24 (he said unto the sick of the p',) I
Ac 9:33 eight years, and was sick of the p'.

Palti *(pal'-ti)*
Nu 13: 9 of Benjamin, P' the son of Raphu.

Paltiel *(pal'-te-el)* See also PHALTIEL.
Nu 34:26 of Issachar, P' the son of Azzan.

Paltite *(pal'-tite)* See also PELONITE.
2Sa 23:26 Helez the P', Ira the son of

Pamphylia *(pam-fil'-e-ah)*
Ac 2:10 Phrygia, and P', in Egypt, and
13:13 Paphos, they came to Perga in P':
14:24 Pisidia, they came to P'.
15:38 who departed from them from P',
27: 5 sailed over the sea of Cilicia and P',

pan See also PANS; FRYINGPANS.
Le 2: 5 be a meat offering baken in a p',
6:21 In a p' it shall be made with oil;
7: 9 and in the p', shall be the priest's
1Sa 2:14 he struck it into the p', or kettle,
2Sa 13: 9 she took a p', and poured them
1Ch 23:29 for that which is baked in the p',
Eze 4: 3 take thou unto thee an iron p',

pangs
Isa 13: 8 p' and sorrows shall take hold of
21: 3 p' have taken hold upon me, as
3 the p' of a woman that travaileth:
26:17 in pain, and crieth out in her p';
Jer 22:23 thou be when p' come upon thee,
48:41 as the heart of a woman in her p'.
49:22 as the heart of a woman in her p'.
50:43 and p' as of a woman in travail.
Mic 4: 9 p' have taken thee as a woman in

Pannag *(pan'-nag)*
Eze 27:17 market wheat of Minnith, and P',

pans See also FRYINGPANS.
Ex 27: 3 make his p' to receive his ashes,
Nu 11: 8 baked it in p', and made cakes of
1Ch 9:31 things that were made in the p'.
2Ch 35:13 in caldrons, and in p', and divided

pant See also PANTED; PANTETH.
Am 2: 7 That p' after the dust of the earth

panted
Ps 119:131 I opened my mouth, and p': for I
Isa 21: 4 My heart p', fearfulness

panteth
Ps 38:10 My heart p', my strength faileth
42: 1 the hart p' after the water brooks,
1 so p' my soul after thee, O God.

paper
Isa 19: 7 The p' reeds by the brooks, by the
2Jo 12 would not write with p' and ink:

paper-reeds See PAPER and REEDS.

Paphos *(pa'-fos)*
Ac 13: 6 had gone through the isle unto P',
13 and his company loosed from P',

paps
Eze 23:21 Egyptians for the p' of thy youth.
Lu 11:27 the p' which thou hast sucked
23:29 and the p' which never gave suck.
Re 1:13 about the p' with a golden girdle.

parable See also PARABLES.
Nu 23: 7 And he took up his p', and said,
18 he took up his p', and said, Rise up,
24: 3, 15 And he took up his p', and said,
20 he took up his p', and said, Amalek
21 took up his p', and said, Strong is
23 he took up his p', and said, Alas,
Job 27: 1 Moreover Job continued his p',
29: 1 Moreover Job continued his p',
Ps 49: 4 I will incline mine ear to a p': I will
78: 2 I will open my mouth in a p': I will
Pr 26: 7, 9 so is a p' in the mouth of fools.
Eze 17: 2 speak a p' unto the house of Israel;
24: 3 utter a p' unto the rebellious house,
Mic 2: 4 shall one take up a p' against you,
Hab 2: 6 all these take up a p' against him,
M't 13:18 ye therefore the p' of the sower.
24, 31 Another p' put he forth unto
33 Another p' spake he unto them;
34 without a p' spake he not unto them:
36 Declare unto us the p' of the tares
15:15 unto him, Declare unto us this p'.
21:33 Hear another p': There was a
24:32 Now learn a p' of the fig tree; When
M'r 4:10 with the twelve asked of him the p'.
13 unto them, Know ye not this p'?
34 without a p' spake he not unto them:
7:17 asked him concerning the p'.
12:12 he had spoken the p' against them:
13:28 Now learn a p' of the fig tree; When
Lu 5:36 And he spake also a p' unto them;
6:39 And he spake a p' unto them, Can
8: 4 out of every city, he spake by a p':
9 him, saying, What might this p' be?
11 Now the p' is this: The seed is the
12:16 he spake a p' unto them, saying,
41 Lord, speakest thou this p' unto us,
13: 6 He spake also this p'; A certain
14: 7 he put forth a p' to those which
15: 3 he spake this p' unto them, saying,
18: 1 he spake a p' unto them to this end,
9 And he spake this p' unto certain
19:11 he added and spake a p', because
20: 9 he to speak to the people this p';
19 had spoken this p' against them.
21:29 And he spake to them a p'; Behold
Joh 10: 6 This p' spake Jesus unto them:

parables
Eze 20: 49 say of me, Doth he not speak p·?
M't 13: 3 many things unto them in p·,
10 Why speakest thou unto them in p·?
13 Therefore speak I to them in p·:
34 Jesus unto the multitude in p·;
35 saying, I will open my mouth in p·;
53 when Jesus had finished these p·,
21: 45 and Pharisees had heard his p·,
22: 1 and spake unto them again by p·,
M'r 3: 23 and said unto them in p·, How can
4: 2 he taught them many things by p·,
11 all these things are done in p·:
13 and how then will ye know all p·?
33 many such p· spake he the word
12: 1 he began to speak unto them by p·.
Lu 8: 10 but to others in p·; that seeing they

paradise
Lu 23: 43 To day shalt thou be with me in p·.
2Co 12: 4 How that he was caught up into p·,
Re 2: 7 is in the midst of the p· of God.

Parah (pa'-rah)
Jos 18: 23 And Avim, and P·, and Ophrah,

paramours
Eze 23: 20 she doted upon their p·, whose

Paran (pa'-ran) See also EL-PARAN.
Ge 21: 21 he dwelt in the wilderness of P·:
Nu 10: 12 cloud rested in the wilderness of P·.
12: 16 and pitched in the wilderness of P·.
13: 3 them from the wilderness of P·:
26 unto the wilderness of P·, to
De 1: 1 Red sea, between P·, and Tophel,
33: 2 he shined forth from mount P·, and
1Sa 25: 1 went down to the wilderness of P·.
1Ki 11: 18 arose out of Midian, and came to P·:
18 they took men with them out of P·,
Hab 3: 3 and the Holy One from mount P·.

Parbar (par'-bar)
1Ch 26: 18 At P· westward, four at the
18 at the causeway, and two at P·.

parcel
Ge 33: 19 he bought a p· of a field, where he
Jos 24: 32 in a p· of ground which Jacob bought
Ru 4: 3 selleth a p· of land, which was our
1Ch 11: 13 was a p· of ground full of barley;
14 themselves in the midst of that p·,
Joh 4: 5 the p· of ground that Jacob gave

parched
Le 23: 14 eat neither bread, nor p· corn, nor
Jos 5: 11 and p· corn in the selfsame day.
Ru 2: 14 he reached her p· corn, and she
1Sa 17: 17 brethren an ephah of this p· corn,
25: 18 and five measures of p· corn, and an
2Sa 17: 28 and barley, and flour, and p· corn,
28 beans, and lentiles, and p· pulse,
Isa 35 7 p· ground shall become a pool,
Jer 17: 6 shall inhabit the p· places in the

parchments
2Ti 4: 13 the books, but especially the p·.

pardon See also PARDONED; PARDONETH.
Ex 23: 21 will not p· your transgressions:
34: 9 and p· our iniquity and our sin,
Nu 14: 19 P·, I beseech thee, the iniquity of
1Sa 15: 25 I pray thee, p· my sin, and turn
2Ki 5: 18 this thing the Lord p· thy servant,
18 Lord p· thy servant in this thing.
24: 4 blood; which the Lord would not p·.
2Ch 30: 18 The good Lord p· every one
Ne 9: 17 but thou art a God ready to p·,
Job 7: 21 dost thou not p· my transgression,
Ps 25: 11 O Lord, p· mine iniquity; for it is
Isa 55: 7 our God, for he will abundantly p·.
Jer 5: 1 seeketh the truth; and I will p· it.
7 How shall I p· thee for this? thy
33: 8 and I will p· all their iniquities,
50: 20 for I will p· them whom I reserve.

pardoned
Nu 14: 20 I have p· according to thy word:
Isa 40: 2 that her iniquity is p·: for she
La 3: 42 have rebelled: thou hast not p·.

pardoneth
Mic 7: 18 like unto thee, that p· iniquity,

pare
De 21: 12 shave her head, and p· her nails;

parents
M't 10: 21 shall rise up against their p·, and
M'r 13: 12 shall rise up against their p·, and
Lu 2: 27 the p· brought in the child Jesus,
41 his p· went to Jerusalem every year
8: 56 And her p· were astonished: but he
18: 29 hath left house, or p·, or brethren,
21: 16 ye shall be betrayed both by p·,
Joh 9: 2 who did sin, this man, or his p·,
3 hath this man sinned, nor his p·:
18 until they called the p· of him that
20 His p· answered them and said, We
22 These words spake his p·, because
23 Therefore said his p·, He is of age;
Ro 1: 30 of evil things, disobedient to p·,
2Co 12: 14 ought not to lay up for the p·, but
14 but the p· for the children.
Eph 6: 1 Children, obey your p· in the Lord:
Col 3: 20 obey your p· in all things: for
1Ti 5: 4 at home, and to requite their p·:
2Ti 3: 2 disobedient to p·, unthankful,
Heb 11: 23 was hid three months of his p·,

Parez See RIMMON-PAREZ.

parlour See also PARLOURS.
J'g 3: 20 and he was sitting in a summer p·,
23 shut the doors of the p· upon him,
24 the doors of the p· were locked,
25 he opened not the doors of the p·:
1Sa 9: 22 and brought them into the p·, and

parlours
1Ch 28: 11 and of the inner p· thereof, and of

Parmashta (par-mash'-tah)
Es 9: 9 And P·, and Arisai, and Aridai,

Parmenas (par'-me-nas)
Ac 6: 5 and Timon, and P·, and Nicolas a

Parnach (par'-nak)
Nu 34: 25 Zebulun, Elizaphan the son of P·.

Parosh (pa'-rosh) See also PHAROSH.
Ezr 2: 3 The children of P·, two thousand
10: 25 of the sons of P·; Ramiah, and
Ne 3: 25 After him Pedaiah the son of P·.
7: 8 The children of P·, two thousand
10: 14 The chief of the people; P·,

Parshandatha (par-shan'-da-thah)
Es 9: 7 P·, and Dalphon, and Aspatha,

part^A See also APART; DEPART; FOREPART; IMPART; PARTAKEST; PARTED; PARTETH; PARTING; PARTS.
Ge 41: 34 up the fifth p· of the land of Egypt
47: 24 shall give the fifth p· unto Pharaoh,
26 that Pharaoh should have the fifth p·;
Ex 16: 36 an omer is the tenth p· of an ephah.
19: 17 stood at the nether p· of the mount.
29: 26 the Lord: and it shall be thy p·.
40 the fourth p· of an hin of beaten oil;
40 and the fourth p· of an hin of wine for
Le 1: 16 cast it beside the altar on the east p·,
2: 6 Thou shalt p· it in pieces, and pour
16 of it, p· of the beaten corn thereof, and
16 and p· of the oil thereof, with all the
5: 11 his offering the tenth p· of an ephah
16 and shall add the fifth p· thereto, and
6: 5 shall add the fifth p· more thereto,
20 the tenth p· of an ephah of fine flour
7: 33 have the right shoulder for his p·.
8: 29 of consecration it was Moses' p·;
11: 35 whereupon any p· of their carcase
37 And if any p· of their carcase fall upon
38 any p· of their carcase fall thereon,
13: 41 from the p· of his head toward his face,
22: 14 he shall put the fifth p· thereof unto it,
23: 13 be of wine, the fourth p· of an hin.
27: 13 fifth p· thereof unto thy estimation.
15 he shall add the fifth p· of the money
16 unto the Lord some p· of a field of
19 he shall add the fifth p· of the money
27 and shall add a fifth p· of it thereto:
31 shall add thereto the fifth p· thereof.
Nu 5: 7 and add unto it the fifth p· thereof,
15 tenth p· of an ephah of barley meal;
15: 4 with the fourth p· of an hin of oil.
5 the fourth p· of an hin of wine for
6 with the third p· of an hin of oil.
7 offer the third p· of an hin of wine,
18: 20 thou have any p· among them:
20 I am thy p· and thine inheritance
26 the Lord, even a tenth p· of the tithe.
29 even the hallowed p· thereof out of it.
22: 41 might see the utmost p· of the people.
23: 10 the number of the fourth p· of Israel?
13 shalt see but the utmost p· of them,
28: 5 And a tenth p· of an ephah of flour
5 the fourth p· of an hin of beaten oil.
7 fourth p· of an hin for the one lamb:
14 and the third p· of an hin unto a ram,
14 the fourth p· of an hin unto a lamb:
De 10: 9 Levi hath no p· nor inheritance
12: 12 no p· nor inheritance with you.
14: 27 no p· nor inheritance with thee.
29 no p· nor inheritance with thee,)
18: 1 no p· nor inheritance with Israel:
33: 21 he provided the first p· for himself,
Jos 14: 4 they gave no p· unto the Levites
15: 1 the uttermost p· of the south coast.
5 the sea at the uttermost p· of Jordan:
13 a p· among the children of Judah,
18: 7 the Levites have no p· among you:
19: 9 for the p· of the children of Judah
22: 25 ye have no p· in the Lord: so shall
27 to come, Ye have no p· in the Lord.
Ru 1: 17 if ought but death p· thee and me.
2: 3 hap was to light on a p· of the field
3: 13 perform unto thee the p· of a kinsman,
13 well; let him do the kinsman's p·:
13 will not do the p· of a kinsman to thee,
13 will I do the p· of a kinsman to thee.
1Sa 9: 8 the fourth p· of a shekel of silver:
14: 2 tarried in the uttermost p· of Gibeah
23: 20 and our p· shall be to deliver him into
30: 24 as his p· is that goeth down to the
24 his p· be that tarrieth by the stuff:
24 by the stuff: they shall p· alike.
2Sa 14: 6 there was none to p· them, but
18: 2 sent forth a third p· of the people
2 and a third p· under the hand of Ittai
20: 1 We have no p· in David, neither
1Ki 6: 24 the uttermost p· of the one wing unto
24 the uttermost p· of the other were ten
31 side posts were a fifth p· of the wall.
33 of olive tree, a fourth p· of the wall.
2Ki 6: 25 the fourth p· of a cab of dove's dung
7: 5 come to the uttermost p· of the camp
8 came to the uttermost p· of the camp,
11: 5 A third p· of you that enter in on the
6 a third p· shall be at the gate of Sur;
2Ki 11: 6 and a third p· at the gate behind the
18: 23 be able on thy p· to set riders upon
1Ch 12: 29 the greatest p· of them had kept the
2Ch 23: 4 A third p·...entering on the sabbath,
5 And a third p· shall be at the king's
5 and a third p· at the gate of the
29: 16 went into the inner p· of the house
Ne 1: 9 unto the uttermost p· of the heaven,
3: 9 ruler of the half p· of Jerusalem.
12 ruler of the half p· of Jerusalem,
14 the ruler of p· of Beth-haccerem;
15 the ruler of p· of Mizpah; he
16 the ruler of the half p· of Beth-zur,
17 of the half p· of Keilah, in his p·.
18 the ruler of the half p· of Keilah.
5: 11 also the hundredth p· of the money,
9: 3 Lord their God one fourth p· of the day;
3 and another fourth p· they confessed,
10: 32 yearly with the third p· of a shekel
Job 32: 17 I said, I will answer also my p·,
41: 6 p· him among the merchants?
Ps 5: 9 their inward p· is very wickedness;
22: 18 p· my garments among them,
51: 6 hidden p· thou shalt make me to know
118: 7 The Lord taketh my p· with them
Pr 8: 26 highest p· of the dust of the world.
31 in the habitable p· of his earth;
17: 2 shall have p· of the inheritance
Isa 7: 18 uttermost p· of the rivers of Egypt,
24: 16 From the uttermost p· of the earth
36: 8 able on thy p· to set riders upon them.
44: 16 He burneth p· thereof in the fire;
16 with p· thereof he eateth flesh;
19 I have burned p· of it in the fire;
Eze 4: 11 by measure, the sixth p· of an hin:
5: 2 Thou shalt burn with fire a third p·
2 and thou shalt take a third p·, and
2 a third p· thou shalt scatter in the
12 A third p· of thee shall die with the
12 third p· shall fall by the sword round
12 scatter a third p· into all the winds,
39: 2 and leave but the sixth p· of thee,
45: 11 may contain the tenth p· of an homer,
11 the ophah the tenth p· of an homer:
13, 13 sixth p· of an ephah of an homer
14 offer the tenth p· of a bath out of the
17 prince's p· to give burnt offerings,
46: 14 morning, the sixth p· of an ephah,
14 and the third p· of an hin of oil, to
Da 1: 2 with p· of the vessels of the house
2: 33 his feet p· of iron and p· of clay.
41 p· of potters' clay, and p· of iron,
42 the toes of the feet were p· of iron,
42 p· of clay, so the kingdom shall be
5: 5 the king saw the p· of the hand
24 the p· of the hand sent from him;
Joe 2: 20 his hinder p· toward the utmost sea,
Am 7: 4 great deep, and did eat up a p·.
Zec 13: 9 bring the third p· through the fire,
M'r 4: 38 he was in the hinder p· of the ship,
9: 40 he that is not against us is on our p·.
13: 27 from the uttermost p· of the earth
27 to the uttermost p· of heaven.
Lu 10: 42 Mary hath chosen that good p·,
11: 36 be full of light, having no p· dark,
39 but your inward p· is full of ravening
17: 24 out of the one p· under heaven,
24 unto the other p· under heaven;
Joh 13: 8 thee not, thou hast no p· with me.
19: 23 four parts, to every soldier a p·;
Ac 1: 8 unto the uttermost p· of the earth.
17 had obtained p· of this ministry.
25 he may take p· of this ministry
5: 2 And kept back p· of the price, his wife
2 brought a certain p·, and laid it at
3 keep back p· of the price of the land?
8: 21 neither p· nor lot in this matter:
14: 4 and p· held with the Jews,
4 and p· with the apostles.
16: 12 chief city of that p· of Macedonia,
19: 32 more p· knew not wherefore they were
23: 6 that the one p· were Sadducees,
9 were of the Pharisees' p· arose,
27: 12 the more p· advised to depart thence
41 hinder p· was broken with the
Ro 11: 25 in p· is happened to Israel, until
1Co 12: 24 honour to that p· which lacked:
13: 9 know in p·, and we prophesy in p·.
10 which is in p· shall be done away.
12 now I know in p·; but then shall I
15: 6 the greater p· remain unto this
16: 17 lacking on your p· they have supplied.
2Co 1: 14 ye have acknowledged us in p·,
2: 5 he hath not grieved me, but in p·:
6: 15 or what p· hath he that believeth
Eph 4: 16 in the measure of every p·,
Tit 2: 8 is of the contrary p· may be ashamed,
Heb 2: 14 likewise took p· of the same;
7: 2 Abraham gave a tenth p· of all;
1Pe 4: 14 on their p· he is evil spoken of, but on
14 of, but on your p· he is glorified.
Re 6: 8 them over the fourth p· of the earth,
8: 8 the third p· of the sea became blood;
9 And the third p· of the creatures
9 and the third p· of the ships were
10 fell upon the third p· of the rivers,
11 the third p· of the waters became
12 the third p· of the sun was smitten,
12 smitten, and the third p· of the moon,
12 moon, and the third p· of the stars;
12 as the third p· of them was darkened,
12 the day shone not for a third p· of it,
9: 15 year, for to slay the third p· of men.
18 three was the third p· of men killed,
11: 13 and the tenth p· of the city fell, and in
12: 4 the third p· of the stars of heaven.

Re 20: 6 hath p' in the first resurrection:
21: 8 liars, shall have their p' in the lake
22: 19 away his p' out of the book of life,

partaker See also PARTAKERS.
Ps 50: 18 and hast been p' with adulterers.
1Co 9: 10 in hope should be p' of his hope.
23 I might be p' thereof with you.
10: 30 if I by grace be a p', why am I evil
1Ti 5: 22 neither be p' of other men's sins:
2Ti 1: 8 be thou p' of the afflictions of the
2: 6 must be first p' of the fruits.
1Pe 5: 1 a p' of the glory that shall be
2Jo 11 God speed is p' of his evil deeds.

partakers
M't 23: 30 we would not have been p' with
Ro 15: 27 made p' of their spiritual things,
1Co 9: 12 be p' of this power over you, are
13 at the altar are p' with the altar?
10: 17 for we are all p' of that one bread.
18 eat of the sacrifices p' of the altar?
21 ye cannot be p' of the Lord's table,
2Co 1: 7 that as ye are p' of the sufferings,
Eph 3: 6 p' of his promise in Christ by the
5: 7 Be not ye therefore p' with them.
Ph'p 1: 7 gospel, ye are all p' of my grace.
Col 1: 12 us meet to be p' of the inheritance
1Ti 6: 2 and beloved, p' of the benefit.
Heb 2: 14 as the children are p' of flesh and
3: 1 p' of the heavenly calling, consider
14 For we are made p' of Christ, if we
6: 4 were make p' of the Holy Ghost,
12: 8 whereof all are p', then are ye
10 we might be p' of his holiness.
1Pe 4: 13 ye are p' of Christ's sufferings;
2Pe 1: 4 might be p' of the divine nature,
Re 18: 4 that ye be not p' of her sins, and

partakest
Ro 11: 17 them p' of the root and fatness

parted See also DEPARTED; IMPARTED.
Ge 2: 10 and from thence it was p', and
2Ki 2: 11 of fire, and p' them both asunder;
14 waters, they p' hither and thither:
Job 38: 24 By what way is the light p', which
Joe 3: 2 among the nations, and p' my land.
M't 27: 35 and p' his garments, casting lots:
35 They p' my garments among them,
M'r 15: 24 they p' his garments, casting lots
Lu 23: 34 they p' his raiment, and cast lots.
24: 51 he was p' from them, and carried
Joh 19: 24 They p' my raiment among them,
Ac 2: 45 p' them to all men, as every man

parteth
Le 11: 3 Whatsoever p' the hoof, and is
De 14: 6 And every beast that p' the hoof,
Pr 18: 18 cease, and p' between the mighty.

Parthians (*par-the'-uns*)
Ac 2: 9 P', and Medes, and Elamites, and

partial
Mal 2: 9 but have been p' in the law,
Jas 2: 4 Are ye not then p' in yourselves,

partiality
1Ti 5: 21 another, doing nothing by p'.
Jas 3: 17 of mercy and good fruits, without p',

particular
1Co 12: 27 of Christ, and members in p'.
Eph 5: 33 every one of you in p' so love

particularly
Ac 21: 19 he declared p' what
Heb 9: 5 we cannot now speak p'.

parties
Ex 22: 9 cause of both p' shall come before the

parting See also DEPARTING.
Eze 21: 21 Babylon stood at the p' of the way,

partition
1Ki 6: 21 made a p' by the chains of gold.
Eph 2: 14 broken down the middle wall of p'

partly
Da 2: 42 shall be p' strong, and p' broken.
1Co 11: 18 you; and I p' believe it.
Heb10: 33 P', whilst ye were made a
33 p', whilst ye became companions

partner See also PARTNERS.
Pr 29: 24 Whoso is p' with a thief hateth his
2Co 8: 23 he is my p' and fellowhelper
Ph'm 17 If thou count me therefore a p',

partners
Lu 5: 7 And they beckoned unto their p',
10 Zebedee, which were p' with Simon.

partridge
1Sa 26: 20 as when one doth hunt a p' in the
Jer 17: 11 the p' sitteth on eggs, and hatcheth

parts^
Ge 47: 24 four p' shall be your own, for seed
Ex 33: 23 hand, and thou shalt see my back p':
Le 1: 8 Aaron's sons, shall lay the p', the
22: 23 thing superfluous or lacking in his p',
Nu 10: 5 lie on the east p' shall go forward.
11: 1 were in the uttermost p' of the camp.
31: 27 divide the prey into two p'; between
De 19: 3 giveth thee to inherit, into three p',
30: 4 out unto the outmost p' of heaven,
Jos 18: 5 they shall divide it into seven p':
6 describe the land into seven p',
9 it by cities into seven p' in a book,
1Sa 5: 9 they had emerods in their secret p'.
2Sa 19: 43 and said, We have ten p' in the king,
1Ki 6: 38 throughout all the p' thereof, and
7: 25 and all their hinder p' were inward.
16: 21 of Israel divided into two p':
2Ki 11: 7 two p' of all you that go forth on
2Ch 4: 4 and all their hinder p' were inward.
Ne 11: 1 nine p' to dwell in other cities.
Job 26: 14 these are p' of his ways: but how
38: 36 hath put wisdom in the inward p'?
41: 12 I will not conceal his p', nor his
Ps 2: 8 uttermost p' of the earth for thy
51: 6 thou desirest truth in the inward p':
63: 9 shall go into the lower p' of the earth.
65: 8 dwell in the uttermost p' are afraid
78: 66 he smote his enemies in the hinder p':
136: 13 which divided the Red sea into p':
139: 9 dwell in the uttermost p' of the sea;
15 wrought in the lowest p' of the earth.
Pr 18: 8 into the innermost p' of the belly.
20: 27 searching all the inward p' of the belly.
30 so do stripes the inward p' of the belly.
26: 22 into the innermost p' of the belly.
Isa 3: 17 the Lord will discover their secret p'.
16: 11 and mine inward p' for Kir-haresh.
44: 23 shout, ye lower p' of the earth:
Jer 31: 33 I will put my law in their inward p',
34: 18 and passed between the p' thereof,
19 passed between the p' of the calf;
Eze 26: 20 set thee in the low p' of the earth,
31: 14 death, to the nether p' of the earth,
16 comforted in the nether p' of the earth.
18 Eden unto the nether p' of the earth:
32: 18 unto the nether p' of the earth, with
24 into the nether p' of the earth, which
38: 15 from thy place out of the north p',
39: 2 thee to come up from the north p',
48: 8 in length as one of the other p',
Zec 13: 8 two p' therein shall be cut off and
M't 2: 22 he turned aside into the p' of Galilee:
12: 42 from the uttermost p' of the earth to
M'r 8: 10 came into the p' of Dalmanutha.
Lu 11: 31 came from the utmost p' of the earth
Joh 19: 23 his garments, and made four p',
Ac 2: 10 and in the p' of Libya about Cyrene,
20: 2 when he had gone over those p',
Ro 15: 23 having no more place in these p',
1Co 12: 23 our uncomely p' have more abundant
24 For our comely p' have no need: but
Eph 4: 9 first into the lower p' of the earth?
Re 16: 19 great city was divided into three p',

Paruah (*par'-u-ah*)
1Ki 4: 17 Jehoshaphat the son of P', in

Parvaim (*par-va'-im*)
2Ch 3: 6 and the gold was gold of P'.

Pas See PAS-DAMMIM.

Pasach (*pa'-sak*)
1Ch 7: 33 sons of Japhlet; P', and Bimhal,

Pas-dammim (*pas-dam'-mim*)
1Ch 11: 13 He was with David at P', and

Paseah (*pa-se'-ah*) See also PHASEAH.
1Ch 4: 12 Eshton begat Beth-rapha, and P',
Ezr 2: 49 children of Uzza, the children of P',
Ne 3: 6 repaired Jehoiada the son of P',

Pashur (*pash'-ur*)
1Ch 9: 12 the son of Jeroham, the son of P',
Ezr 2: 38 The children of P', a thousand two
10: 22 And of the sons of P'; Elioenai,
Ne 7: 41 The children of P', a thousand two
10: 3 P', Amariah, Malchijah,
11: 12 the son of P', the son of Malchiah,
Jer 20: 1 P' the son of Immer the priest,
2 P' smote Jeremiah the prophet,
3 P' brought forth Jeremiah out of
3 Lord hath not called thy name P',
6 P',...all that dwell in thine house
21: 1 king Zedekiah sent unto him P'
38: 1 and Gedaliah the son of P', and
1 and P' the son of Malchiah,

pass^ See also COMPASS; OVERPASS; PASSED; PASSEST; PASSETH; PASSING; PASSOVER; PAST; TRESPASS.
Ge 4: 14 it shall come to p', that every one
6: 1 it came to p', when men began to
7: 10 it came to p' after seven days, that
8: 1 made a wind to p' over the earth,
6 came to p' at the end of forty days,
13 it came to p' in the six hundredth
18: 3 p' not away, I pray thee, from thy
5 hearts; after that ye shall p' on:
24: 52 And it came to p', that, when
25: 11 to p' after the death of Abraham,
26: 8 came to p', when he had been there
27: 1 And it came to p', that when Isaac
30 it came to p', as soon as Isaac had
40 it shall come to p' when thou shalt
29: 10 came to p', when Jacob saw Rachel
13 it came to p', when Laban heard
23 it came to p' in the evening, that
25 it came to p' that in the morning,
30: 25 And it came to p', when Rachel had
32 will p' through all thy flock to day,
41 And it came to p', whensoever the
31: 10 it came to p' at the time that the
52 I will not p' over this heap to thee,
52 thou shalt not p' over this heap
32: 16 P' over before me, and put a space
33: 14 thee, p' over before his servant:
34: 25 And it came to p' on the third day,
35: 18 And it came to p', as her soul was
22 it came to p', when Israel dwelt in
37: 23 And it came to p', when Joseph was
38: 1 And it came to p' at that time, that
Ge 38: 9 and it came to p', when he went in
24 And it came to p' about three months
27 And it came to p' in the time of her
28 And it came to p', when she travailed,
29 it came to p', as he drew back his
39: 5 And it came to p' from the time that he
7 And it came to p' after these things,
10 And it came to p', as she spake to
11 And it came to p' about this time,
13 And it came to p', when she saw that
15 And it came to p', when he heard that
18 And it came to p', as I lifted up my
19 And it came to p', when his master
40: 1 And it came to p' after these things,
20 And it came to p' the third day, which
41: 1 And it came to p' at the end of two
8 And it came to p' in the morning
13 And it came to p', as he interpreted
32 and God will shortly bring it to p'.
42: 35 And it came to p' as they emptied
43: 2 it came to p', when they had eaten
21 it came to p', when we came to the
44: 24 And it came to p' when we came up
31 It shall come to p', when he seeth
46: 33 it shall come to p', when Pharaoh shall
47: 24 And it shall come to p' in the increase,
48: 1 And it came to p' after these things,
50: 20 to bring to p', as it is this day,
Ex 1: 10 and it come to p', that, when there
21 it came to p', because the midwives
2: 11 it came to p' in those days, when
23 And it came to p' in process of time,
3: 21 it shall come to p', that, when ye go,
4: 8, 9 come to p', if they will not believe
24 it came to p' by the way in the inn,
6: 28 it came to p' on the day when the
12: 12 For I will p' through the land of
13 I see the blood, I will p' over you,
23 the Lord will p' through to smite
23 the Lord will p' over the door, and
25 And it shall come to p', when ye be
26 And it shall come to p', when your
29 it came to p', that at midnight the
41 it came to p' at the end of the four
41 even the selfsame day it came to p',
51 And it came to p' the selfsame day,
13: 15 came to p', when Pharaoh would
17 it came to p', when Pharaoh had
14: 24 it came to p', that in the morning
15: 16 till thy people p' over, O Lord,
16 till the people p' over, which thou
16: 5 come to p', that on the sixth day
10 And it came to p', as Aaron spake
13 came to p', that at even the quails
22 it came to p', that on the sixth day
27 it came to p', that there went out
17: 11 And it came to p' when Moses held up
18: 13 And it came to p' on the morrow,
19: 16 it came to p' on the third day in the
22: 27 it shall come to p', when he crieth
32: 19 it came to p', as soon as he came
30 it came to p' on the morrow, that
33: 7 it came to p', that every one which
8 it came to p', when Moses went out
9 And it came to p', as Moses entered
19 make all my goodness p' before
22 come to p', while my glory passeth
22 thee with my hand while I p' by:
34: 29 it came to p', when Moses came
40: 17 it came to p' in the first month in
Le 9: 1 came to p' on the eighth day, that
18: 21 seed p' through the fire to Molech,
Nu 5: 27 come to p', that, if she be defiled,
7: 1 came to p' on the day that Moses
10: 35 And it came to p', when the ark set
11: 23 shall come to p' unto thee or not.
25 it came to p', that, when the spirit
16: 31 came to p', as he had made an end
42 came to p', when the congregation
17: 5 it shall come to p', that the man's rod,
8 it came to p', that on the morrow
20: 17 Let us p', I pray thee, through thy
17 we will not p' through the fields, or
18 Thou shalt not p' by me, lest I
21: 8 come to p', that every one that is
9 came to p', that if a serpent had
22 Let me p' through thy land: we
23 Israel to p' through his border:
22: 41 it came to p' on the morrow, that
26: 1 it came to p' after the plague, that
27: 7 of their father to p' unto them.
8 his inheritance to p' unto his
32: 27 But thy servants will p' over, every
29 will p' with you over Jordan, every
30 will not p' over with you armed,
32 We will p' over armed before the
33: 55 then it shall come to p', that those
56 come to p', that I shall do unto you,
34: 4 of Akrabbim, and p' on to Zin:
4 Hazar-addar, and p' on to Azmon:
De 1: 3 it came to p' in the fortieth year,
2: 4 Ye are to p' through the coast of
16 it came to p', when all the men of
18 Thou art to p' over through Ar,
24 and p' over the river Arnon:
27 Let me p' through thy land: I will
28 only I will p' through on my feet;
29 shall p' over Jordan into the land
30 Sihon...would not let us p' by him:
3: 18 ye shall p' over armed before your
5: 23 it came to p', when ye heard the
7: 12 it shall come to p', if ye hearken to
9: 1 Thou art to p' over Jordan this
11 it came to p' at the end of forty days
11: 13 And it shall come to p', if ye shall
29 it shall come to p', when the Lord

De 11:31 ye shall p' over Jordan to go in to
13: 2 the sign or the wonder come to p',
18:10 daughter to p' through the fire,
19 shall come to p', that whosoever
22 thing follow not, nor come to p',
24: 1 it come to p' that she find no favour
27: 2 day when ye shall p' over Jordan
28: 1 it shall come to p', if thou shalt
15 it shall come to p', if thou wilt not
63 it shall come to p', that as the Lord
29:19 it come to p', when he heareth the
30: 1 it shall come to p', when all these
31:21 shall come to p', when many evils
24 it came to p', when Moses made an
Jos 1: 1 it came to p', that the Lord spake
11 P' through the host, and command
11 ye shall p' over this Jordan, to go
14 but ye shall p' before your brethren
2: 5 it came to p' about the time of
3: 2 it came to p' after three days, that
6 and p' over before the people.
13 come to p', as soon as the soles of
14 it came to p', when the people
14 from their tents, to p' over Jordan,
4: 1 it came to p', when all the people
5 P' over before the ark of the
11 it came to p', when all the people
18 And it came to p', when the priests
5: 1 it came to p', when all the kings of
8 And it came to p', when they had
13 it came to p', when Joshua was by
6: 5 come to p', that when they make a
7 P' on, and compass the city, and
7 let him that is armed p' on before
8 it came to p', when Joshua had
15 And it came to p' on the seventh day,
16 And it came to p' at the seventh time,
20 came to p', when the people heard
8: 5 come to p', when they come out
14 it came to p', when the king of Ai
24 came to p', when Israel had made
9: 1 it came to p', when all the kings
16 came to p' at the end of three days
10: 1 it came to p', when Adoni-zedec
11 came to p', as they fled from before
20 And it came to p', when Joshua and
24 And it came to p', when they brought
27 And it came to p' at the time of the
11: 1 And it came to p', when Jabin king
15:18 it came to p', as she came unto him,
17:13 it came to p', when the children of
21:45 the house of Israel; all came to p'.
22:19 then p' ye over unto the land of
23: 1 it came to p' a long time after that
14 all are come to p' unto you, and
15 come to p', that as all good things
24:29 And it came to p' after these things,
J'g 1: 1 the death of Joshua it came to p',
14 And it came to p', when she came
28 And it came to p', when Israel was
2: 4 it came to p', when the angel of the
19 it came to p', when the judge was
3:27 And it came to p', when he was come,
28 and suffered not a man to p' over.
6: 7 it came to p', when the children of
25 And it came to p' the same night,
7: 9 And it came to p' the same night,
8:33 it came to p', as soon as Gideon was
9:42 it came to p' on the morrow, that
11: 4 And it came to p' in process of time,
17 Let me, I pray thee, p' through thy
19 Let us p', we pray thee, through
20 But Sihon trusted not Israel to p'
35 And it came to p', when he saw her,
39 it came to p' at the end of two months,
13:12 said, Now let thy words come to p'.
17 when thy sayings come to p' we may
20 it came to p', when the flame went
14:11 And it came to p', when they saw him,
15 And it came to p' on the seventh day,
15: 1 But it came to p' in a while after,
17 it came to p', when he had made an
16: 4 it came to p' afterward, that he loved
16 it came to p', when she pressed him
25 it came to p', when their hearts were
19: 1 And it came to p' in those days, when
5 And it came to p' on the fourth day,
12 Israel; we will p' over to Gibeah.
21: 3 why is this come to p' in Israel,
4 And it came to p' on the morrow, that
Ru 1: 1 Now it came to p' in the days when
19 it came to p', when they were come
3: 8 And it came to p' at midnight, that
1Sa 1:12 And it came to p', as she continued
20 it came to p', when the time was
2:36 it shall come to p', that every one
3: 2 it came to p' at that time, when Eli
4:18 And it came to p', when he made
5:10 And it came to p', as the ark of God
7: 2 And it came to p', while the ark abode
8: 1 it came to p', when Samuel was old,
9: 6 that he saith cometh surely to p':
26 it came to p' about the spring of
27 Bid the servant p' on before us,
10: 5 it shall come to p', when thou art
11 it came to p', when all that knew him
11:11 and it came to p', that they which
13:10 it came to p', that as soon as he had
22 So it came to p' in the day of battle,
14: 1 Now it came to p' upon a day, that
8 we will p' over unto these men,
19 And it came to p', while Saul talked
16: 6 And it came to p', when they were
8 and made him p' before Samuel.
9 Then Jesse made Shammah to p' by.
10 made seven of his sons to p' before

1Sa 16:16 shall come to p', when the evil spirit
23 it came to p', when the evil spirit
17:48 it came to p', when the Philistine
18: 1 it came to p', when he had made an
6 it came to p' as they came, when
10 And it came to p' on the morrow, that
19 came to p' at the time when Merab
30 it came to p', after they went forth,
20:27 And it came to p' on the morrow,
35 it came to p' in the morning, that
23: 6 And it came to p', when Abiathar
23 it shall come to p', if he be in the land,
24: 1 And it came to p', when Saul was
5 it came to p' afterward, that David's
16 And it came to p', when David had
25:30 it shall come to p', when the Lord
37 it came to p' in the morning, when
38 it came to p' about ten days after,
28: 1 And it came to p' in those days, that
30: 1 And it came to p', when David and his
31: 8 it came to p' on the morrow, when
2Sa 1: 1 it came to p' after the death of Saul,
2 It came even to p' on the third day,
2: 1 it came to p' after this, that David
23 it came to p', that as many as came
3: 6 And it came to p', while there was
4: 4 it came to p', as she made haste to
7: 1 it came to p', when the king sat in
4 And it came to p' that night, that
8: 1 it came to p', that David smote the
10: 1 came to p' after this, that the king
11: 1 And it came to p', after the year
2 came to p' in an eveningtide, that
14 it came to p' in the morning, that
16 it came to p', when Joab observed
12:18 it came to p' on the seventh day,
31 them p' through the brickkiln:
13: 1 And it came to p' after this, that
23 came to p' after two full years, that
30 came to p', while they were in the
36 came to p', as soon as he had made
15: 1 And it came to p' after this, that
22 David said to Ittai, Go and p' over.
32 came to p', that when David was
16:16 it came to p', when Hushai the
17: 9 will come to p', when some of them
16 speedily p' over; lest the king be
21 it came to p', after they were
21 and p' quickly over the water: for
27 came to p', when David was come
19:25 it came to p', when he was come
21:18 it came to p' after this, that there
1Ki 1:21 come to p', when my lord the king
2:39 came to p' at the end of three years,
3:18 came to p' the third day after that
5: 7 it came to p', when Hiram heard
6: 1 it came to p' in the four hundred
8:10 And it came to p', when the priests
9: 1 it came to p', when Solomon had
10 it came to p' at the end of twenty
11: 4 came to p', when Solomon was old,
15 it came to p', when David was in
29 it came to p' at that time when
12: 2 came to p', when Jeroboam the son
20 it came to p', when all Israel heard
13: 4 it came to p', when king Jeroboam
20 it came to p', as they sat at the table,
23 it came to p', after he had eaten
31 came to p', after he had buried him,
32 of Samaria, shall surely come to p'.
14:25 came to p' in the fifth year of king
15:21 it came to p', when Baasha heard
29 came to p', when he reigned, that
16:11 came to p', when he began to reign,
18 it came to p', when Zimri saw that
31 it came to p', as if it had been a
17: 7 it came to p' after a while, that the
17 came to p' after these things, that
18: 1 it came to p' after many days, that
6 between them to p' throughout it:
12 come to p', as soon as I am gone
17 came to p', when Ahab saw Elijah,
27 it came to p' at noon, that Elijah
29 came to p', when midday was past,
36 And it came to p' at the time of the
44 came to p' at the seventh time, that
45 came to p' in the mean while, that
19:17 come to p', that him that escapeth
20:12 came to p', when Benhadad heard
26 came to p' at the return of the year,
21: 1 it came to p' after these things,
15 it came to p', when Jezebel heard
16 came to p', when Ahab heard that
27 came to p', when Ahab heard those
22: 2 it came to p' in the third year, that
32, 33 came to p', when the captains of
2Ki 2: 1 And it came to p', when the Lord
9 it came to p', when they were gone
11 it came to p', as they still went on,
3: 5 came to p', when Ahab was dead,
15 it came to p', when the minstrel
20 it came to p' in the morning, when
4: 6 it came to p', when the vessels were
25 it came to p', when the man of God
40 came to p', as they were eating of
5: 7 came to p', when the king of Israel
6: 9 that thou p' not such a place; for
20 came to p', when they were come
24 And it came to p' after this, that
30 it came to p', when the king heard
7:18 came to p' as the man of God had
8: 3 came to p' at the seven years' end,
5 it came to p', as he was telling the
15 came to p' on the morrow, that he
9:22 came to p', when Joram saw Jehu,
10: 7 it came to p', when the letter came

2Ki 10: 9 it came to p' in the morning, that
25 came to p', as soon as he had made
13:21 came to p', as they were burying a
14: 5 came to p', as soon as the kingdom
15:12 generation. And so it came to p'.
16: 3 made his son to p' through...fire,
17:17 their daughters to p' through...fire,
18: 1 it came to p' in the third year of
9 it came to p' in the fourth year of
19: 1 it came to p', when king Hezekiah
25 now have I brought it to p', that
35 it came to p', that night, that the
37 came to p', as he was worshipping
20: 4 it came to p', afore Isaiah was gone
21: 6 made his son p' through the fire,
22: 3 came to p' in the eighteenth year
11 it came to p', when the king had
23:10 daughter to p' through the fire to
24:20 it came to p' in Jerusalem and
25: 1 it came to p' in the ninth year of
25 it came to p' in the seventh month,
27 it came to p' in the seventh and
1Ch 10: 8 it came to p' on the morrow, when
15:26 it came to p', when God helped the
29 And it came to p', as the ark of the
17: 1 it came to p', as David sat in his
3 it came to p' the same night, that
11 it shall come to p', when thy days
18: 1 after this it came to p', that David
19: 1 Now it came to p' after this, that
20: 1 it came to p', that after the year
4 it came to p' after this, that there
2Ch 5:11 And it came to p', when the priests
13 came even to p', as the trumpeters
8: 1 it came to p' at the end of twenty
10: 2 it came to p', when Jeroboam the
12: 1 it came to p', when Rehoboam had
2 it came to p', that in the fifth year
13:15 it came to p', that God smote
16: 5 came to p', when Baasha heard it,
18:31 it came to p', when the captains of
32 came to p', that, when the captains
20: 1 came to p' after this also, that the
21:19 came to p', that in process of time,
22: 8 came to p', that, when Jehu was
24: 4 it came to p' after this, that Joash
11 came to p', that at what time the
23 came to p' at the end of the year,
25: 3 came to p', when the kingdom was
14 came to p', after that Amaziah was
16 came to p', as he talked with him,
33: 6 his children to p' through the fire
34:19 it came to p', when the king had
Ne 1: 1 it came to p' in the month Chisleu,
4 it came to p', when I heard these
2: 1 it came to p' in the month Nisan,
14 beast that was under me to p'.
4: 1 came to p', that when Sanballat
7 it came to p', that when Sanballat,
12 it came to p', that when the Jews
15 it came to p', when our enemies
16 it came to p' from that time forth,
6: 1 Now it came to p', when Sanballat,
16 it came to p', that when all our
7: 1 it came to p', when the wall was
13: 3 it came to p', when they had heard
19 came to p', that when the gates of
Es 1: 1 came to p' in the days of Ahasuerus,
2: 8 came to p', when the king's...decree
3: 4 came to p', when they spake daily
5: 1 it came to p' on the third day, that
Job 6:15 the stream of brooks they p' away;
11:16 remember it as waters that p' away:
14: 5 his bounds that he cannot p';
19: 8 fenced up my way that I cannot p',
34:20 troubled at midnight, and p' away:
Ps 37: 5 him; and he shall bring it to p'.
7 who bringeth wicked devices to p'.
58: 8 let every one of them p' away:
78:13 and caused them to p' through;
80:12 which p' by the way do pluck her?
89:41 All that p' by the way spoil him: he
104: 9 a bound that they may not p' over;
136:14 made Israel to p' through the midst
148: 6 made a decree which shall not p'.
Pr 4:15 Avoid it, p' not by it, turn from it,
15 turn from it, and p' away.
8:29 should not p' his commandment:
16:30 his lips he bringeth evil to p'.
19:11 glory to p' over a transgression.
22: 3 but the simple p' on,...are punished.
27:12 but the simple p' on,...are punished.
Isa 2: 2 it shall come to p' in the last days,
3:24 come to p', that instead of sweet
4: 3 shall come to p', that he that is left
7: 1 it came to p' in the days of Ahaz the
7 stand, neither shall it come to p'.
18, 21 it shall come to p' in that day,
22 shall come to p', for the abundance
23 And it shall come to p' in that day,
8: 8 And he shall p' through Judah;
21 they shall p' through it, hardly
21 come to p', that when they shall
10:12 shall come to p', that when the Lord
20, 27 it shall come to p' in that day,
11:11 And it shall come to p' in that day,
14: 3 And it shall come to p' in the day
24 have thought, so shall it come to p';
16:12 it shall come to p', when it is seen
17: 4 And in that day it shall come to p',
21: 1 whirlwinds in...south p' through;
22: 7 shall come to p', that thy choicest
20 And it shall come to p' in that day,
23: 2 of Zidon, that p' over the sea,
6 P' ye over to Tarshish; howl, ye
10 P' through thy land as a river, O

Isa 23:12 arise, p' over to Chittim; there also
15 come to p' in that day, that Tyre
17 come to p' after the end of seventy
24:18 And it shall come to p' that he who
21 And it shall come to p' in that day,
27:12, 13 it shall come to p' in that day,
28:15, 18 the overflowing scourge shall p'
19 morning by morning shall it p' over,
21 bring to p' his act, his strange act.
30:32 where the grounded staff shall p',
31: 9 he shall p' over to his strong hold
33:21 neither...gallant ship p' thereby.
34:10 none shall p' through it for ever
35: 8 the unclean shall not p' over it;
36: 1 came to p' in the fourteenth year
37: 1 it came to p', when king Hezekiah
26 now have I brought it to p', that
38 came to p', as he was worshipping
42: 9 the former things are come to p',
46:11 spoken it, I will also bring it to p';
47: 2 the thigh, p' over the rivers.
48: 3 suddenly, and they came to p'.
5 it came to p' I shewed it thee: lest
51:10 a way for the ransomed to p' over?
65:24 come to p', that before they call,
66:23 it shall come to p', that from one
Jer 2:10 For p' over the isles of Chittim,
3: 9 it came to p' through the lightness
16 come to p', when ye be multiplied
4: 9 it shall come to p' at that day, saith
5:19 shall come to p', when ye shall say,
22 perpetual decree,...it cannot p' it:
22 they roar, yet can they not p' over it?
8:13 them shall p' away from them.
9:10 so that none can p' through them;
13: 6 it came to p' after many days, that
15: 2 it shall come to p', if they say unto
14 thee to p' with thine enemies into
16:10 shall come to p', when thou shalt
17:24 come to p', if ye diligently hearken
20: 3 it came to p' on the morrow, that
22: 8 many nations shall p' by this city,
25:12 come to p', when seventy years
26: 8 it came to p', when Jeremiah had
27: 8 it shall come to p', that the nation
28: 1 it came to p' the same year, in the
9 of the prophet shall come to p',
30: 8 shall come to p' in that day, saith
31:28 shall come to p', that like as I have
32:24 thou hast spoken is come to p';
35 daughters to p' through the fire
33:13 flocks p' again under the hands of
35:11 came to p', when Nebuchadrezzar
36: 1 it came to p' in the fourth year of
9 And it came to p' in the fifth year of
16 it came to p', when they had heard
23 it came to p', that when Jehudi had
37:11 came to p', that when the army of
39: 4 came to p', that when Zedekiah the
41: 1 it came to p' in the seventh month,
4 came to p' the second day after he
6 and it came to p', as he met them,
13 came to p', that when all the people
42: 4 come to p' that whatsoever thing
7 And it came to p' after ten days,
16 it shall come to p', that the sword,
43: 1 it came to p', that when Jeremiah
49:39 shall come to p' in the latter days,
51:43 neither doth any son of man p'
52: 3 came to p' in Jerusalem and Judah,
4 came to p' in the ninth year of his
31 came to p' in the seven and thirtieth
La 1:12 it nothing to you, all ye that p' by?
2:15 that p' by clap their hands at thee;
3:37 and it cometh to p', when the Lord
44 our prayer should not p' through.
4:21 cup also shall p' through unto thee:
Eze 1: 1 it came to p' in the thirtieth year,
3:16 came to p' at the end of seven days,
5: 1 and cause it to p' upon thine head
14 thee, in the sight of all that p' by.
17 and blood shall p' through thee;
8: 1 And it came to p' in the sixth year,
9: 8 came to p', while they were slaying
10: 6 And it came to p' that when he had
11:13 it came to p', when I prophesied,
12:25 I shall speak shall come to p';
14:15 noisome beasts to p' through the
15 no man may p' through because
16:21 to cause them to p' through the fire
23 And it came to p' after all thy
20:26 caused to p' through the fire all
31 your sons to p' through the fire,
37 will cause you to p' under the rod,
21: 7 cometh, and shall be brought to p',
23:37 to p' for them through the fire, to
24:14 it shall come to p', and I will do it;
26: 1 it came to p' in the eleventh year,
29:11 No foot of man shall p' through it,
11 nor foot of beast shall p' through it,
17 And it came to p' in the seven and
30:20 it came to p' in the eleventh year,
31: 1 it came to p' in the eleventh year,
32: 1 it came to p' in the twelfth year, in
17 came to p' also in the twelfth year,
19 Whom dost thou p' in beauty? go
33:21 it came to p' in the twelfth year of
28 desolate,...none shall p' through.
33 And when this cometh to p', (lo, it
37: 2 me to p' by them round about:
38:10 come to p', that at the same time
18 it shall come to p' at the same time
39:11 shall come to p' in that day, that
15 the passengers that p' through the
44:17 And it shall come to p', that when
46:21 and caused me to p' by the four
Eze 47: 5 was a river that I could not p' over:
9 it shall come to p', that every thing
10 it shall come to p', that the fishers
22 come to p', that ye shall divide it by
23 shall come to p', that in what tribe
Da 2:29 what should come to p' hereafter:
29 to thee what shall come to p'.
45 what shall come to p' hereafter:
4:16 and let seven times p' over him.
23 field, till seven times p' over him;
25, 32 and seven times shall p' over thee,
7:14 dominion, which shall not p' away,
8: 2 came to p', when I saw, that I was
15 came to p', when I, even I Daniel,
11:10 and overflow, and p' through:
40 and shall overflow and p' over.
Ho 1: 5 shall come to p' at that day, that
10 shall come to p', that in the place
2:21 come to p' in that day, I will hear,
Joe 2:28 it shall come to p' afterward, that
32 it shall come to p', that whosoever
3:17 shall no strangers p' through her
18 it shall come to p' in that day, that
Am 5: 5 Gilgal, and p' not to Beer-sheba:
17 for I will p' through thee, saith the
6: 2 P' ye unto Calneh, and see; and
9 come to p', if there remain ten
7: 2 it came to p', that when they had
8 not again p' by them any more:
8: 2 not again p' by them any more.
9 And it shall come to p' in that day,
Jon 4: 8 came to p', when the sun did arise,
Mic 1:11 P' ye away, thou inhabitant of
2: 8 the garment from them that p' by
13 and their king shall p' before them,
4: 1 in the last days it shall come to p',
5:10 And it shall come to p' in that day,
Nah 1:12 down, when he shall p' through.
15 wicked shall no more p' through
3: 7 come to p', that all they that look
Hab 1:11 mind change, and he shall p' over,
Zep 1: 8 shall come to p' in the day of the
10 And it shall come to p' in that day,
12 And it shall come to p' at that time,
2: 2 before the day p' as the chaff,
Zec 3: 4 caused thine iniquity to p' from
6:15 And this shall come to p', if ye will
7: 1 it came to p' in the fourth year of
13 it is come to p', that as he cried,
8:13 it shall come to p', that as ye were
20 yet come to p', that there shall come
23 shall come to p', that ten men shall
9: 8 and no oppressor shall p' through
10:11 p' through the sea with affliction,
12: 9 it shall come to p' in that day, that
13: 2 And it shall come to p' in that day,
2 the unclean spirit to p' out of the
3 it shall come to p', that when any
4 it shall come to p' in that day, that
8 it shall come to p', that in all the land,
14: 6, 13 it shall come to p' in that day, that
16 it shall come to p', that every one that
M't 5:18 Till heaven and earth p', one jot
18 one tittle shall in no wise p' from
7:28 came to p', when Jesus had ended
8:28 that no man might p' by that way.
9:10 came to p', as Jesus sat at meat in
11: 1 came to p', when Jesus had made
13:53 it came to p', that when Jesus had
19: 1 it came to p', that when Jesus had
24: 6 all these things must come to p',
34 This generation shall not p', till all
35 Heaven and earth shall p' away,
35 but my words shall not p' away.
26: 1 And it came to p', when Jesus had
39 possible, let this cup p' from me:
42 Father, if this cup may not p' away
M'r 1: 9 it came to p' in those days, that
2:15 it came to p', that, as Jesus sat at
23 it came to p', that he went through
4: 4 came to p', as he sowed, some fell
35 Let us p' over unto the other side.
11:23 which he saith shall come to p';
13:29 shall see these things come to p',
30 this generation shall not p', till all
31 Heaven and earth shall p' away:
31 but my words shall not p' away.
14:35 the hour might p' from him.
Lu 1: 8 came to p', that while he executed
23 came to p', that, as soon as the days
41 it came to p', that, when Elisabeth
59 came to p', that on the eighth day
2: 1 And it came to p' in those days, that
15 came to p', as the angels were gone
15 see this thing which is come to p',
46 it came to p', that after three days
3:21 it came to p', that Jesus also being
5: 1 it came to p', that, as the people
12 came to p', when he was in a certain
17 it came to p' on a certain day, as he
6: 1 it came to p' on the second sabbath
6 came to p' also on another sabbath,
12 it came to p' in those days, that he
7:11 it came to p' the day after, that he
8: 1 And it came to p' afterward, that
22 it came to p' on a certain day, that
40 it came to p', that, when Jesus was
9:18 came to p', as he was alone praying,
28 it came to p' about an eight days
33 came to p', as they departed from
37 it came to p', that on the next day,
51 came to p', when the time was come
57 came to p', that, as they went in the
10:38 it came to p', as they went, that he
11: 1 came to p', that, as he was praying
14 came to p', when the devil was gone
Lu 11:27 came to p', as he spake these things,
42 p' over judgment and the love of
12:55 will be heat; and it cometh to p'.
14: 1 it came to p', as he went into the
16:17 easier for heaven and earth to p',
22 it came to p', that the beggar died,
26 which would p' from hence to you
26 neither can they p' to us, that
17:11 And it came to p', as he went to
14 it came to p', that, as they went,
18:35 it came to p', that as he was come
36 And hearing the multitude p' by,
19: 4 see him: for he was to p' that way.
15 it came to p', that when he was
29 it came to p', when he was come
20: 1 it came to p', that on one of those
21: 7 when these things shall come to p'?
9 these things must first come to p';
28 these things begin to come to p',
31 when ye see these things come to p',
32 This generation shall not p' away,
33 Heaven and earth shall p' away:
33 but my words shall not p' away.
36 these things that shall come to p',
24: 4 it came to p', as they were much
12 himself at that which was come to p'.
15 And it came to p', that, while they
18 are come to p' there in these days?
30 it came to p', as he sat at meat with
51 it came to p', while he blessed them,
Joh 13:19 when it is come to p', ye may believe
14:29 I have told you before it come to p',
29 that, when it is come to p', ye might
15:25 But this cometh to p', that the word
Ac 2:17 it shall come to p' in the last days,
21 it shall come to p', that whosoever
3:23 it shall come to p', that every soul,
4: 5 it came to p' on the morrow, that
9:32 And it came to p', as Peter passed
37 it came to p' in those days, that
43 it came to p', that he tarried many
11:26 And it came to p', that a whole year
28 came to p' in the days of Claudius
14: 1 it came to p' in Iconium, that they
16:16 it came to p', as we went to prayer,
18:27 he was disposed to p' into Achaia,
19: 1 came to p', that, while Apollos was
21: 1 it came to p', that after we were
22: 6 it came to p', that, as I made my
17 it came to p', that, when I was come
27:44 so it came to p', that they escaped
28: 8 came to p', that the father of Publius
17 it came to p', that after three days
Ro 9:26 it shall come to p', that in the place
1Co 7:36 if she p' the flower of her age,
15:54 shall be brought to p' the saying
16: 5 I shall p' through Macedonia:
5 for I do p' through Macedonia.
2Co 1:16 And to p' by you into Macedonia,
1Th 3: 4 even as it came to p', and ye know.
Jas 1:10 of the grass he shall p' away.
1Pe 1:17 p' the time of your sojourning here
2Pe 3:10 the heavens shall p' away with a
Re 1: 1 which must shortly come to p';

passage See also PASSAGES.
Nu 20:21 Edom refused to give Israel p'
Jos 22:11 at the p' of the children of Israel.
1Sa 13:23 went out to the p' of Michmash.
Isa 10:29 They are gone over the p': they

passages
J'g 12: 5 Gileadites took the p' of Jordan
6 and slew him at the p' of Jordan:
1Sa 14: 4 between the p', by which Jonathan
Jer 22:20 cry from the p': for all thy lovers
51:32 And that the p' are stopped, and

passed See also COMPASSED; PASSEDST; PAST; TRESPASSED.
Ge 12: 6 And Abram p' through the land
15:17 a burning lamp that p' between
31:21 he rose up, and p' over the river,
32:10 with my staff I p' over this Jordan;
22 sons, and p' over the ford Jabbok.
31 as he p' over Penuel the sun rose
33: 3 he p' over before them, and bowed
37:28 p' by Midianites merchantmen;
Ex 12:27 p' over the houses of the children
34: 6 And the Lord p' by before him,
Nu 14: 7 which we p' through to search it
20:17 left, until we have p' thy borders.
33: 8 and p' through the midst of the sea
51 are p' over Jordan into the land of
De 2: 8 when we p' by from our brethren
8 and p' by the way of the wilderness
27: 3 of this law, when thou art p' over,
29:16 the nations through which ye p' by;
Jos 2:23 p' over, and came to Joshua the
3: 1 lodged there before they p' over.
4 ye have not p' this way heretofore.
16 people p' over...against Jericho.
17 the Israelites p' over on dry ground,
17 people were p' clean over Jordan.
4: 1 people were clean p' over Jordan,
7 when it p' over Jordan, the waters
10 and the people hasted and p' over.
11 all the people were clean p' over,
11 the ark of the Lord p' over, and the
12 tribe of Manasseh, p' over armed
13 thousand prepared for war p' over
23 until ye were p' over, as the Lord
5: 1 until we were p' over, that their
6: 8 priests...p' on before the Lord,
10:29 Then Joshua p' from Makkedah,
31 And Joshua p' from Libnah, and
34 Lachish Joshua p' unto Eglon,

Jos 15: 3 and *p* along to Zin, and ascended
3 and *p* along to Hezron, and went
4 From thence it *p* toward Azmon,
6 *p*...by the north of Beth-arabah;
7 the border *p* toward the waters of
10 and *p* along unto the side of mount
10 and *p* on to Timnah:
11 *p* along to mount Baalah, and went
16: 6 and *p* by it on the east to Janohah;
18: 9 men went and *p* through the land,
18 And *p* along toward the side over
19 And the border *p* along to the side
24:17 all the people through whom we *p*:
J'g 3:26 and *p* beyond the quarries, and
8: 4 Gideon came to Jordan, and *p* over,
10: 9 children of Ammon *p* over Jordan
11:29 he *p* over Gilead, and Manasseh,
29 and *p* over Mizpeh of Gilead, and
29 *p* over unto the children of Ammon.
32 Jephthah *p* over unto the children
12: 3 and *p* over against the children of
18:13 *p* thence unto mount Ephraim,
19:14 And they *p* on and went their way;
1Sa 9: 4 And he *p* through mount Ephraim,
4 and *p* through the land of Shalisha,
4 they *p* through the land of Shalim,
4 *p* through the land of...Benjamites,
27 pass on before us, (and he *p* on,)
14:23 the battle *p* over unto Beth-aven.
15:12 and *p* on, and gone down to Gilgal.
27: 2 *p* over with the six hundred men
29: 2 the Philistines *p* on by hundreds,
2 and his men *p* on in the rereward
2Sa 2:29 the plain, and *p* over Jordan, and
10:17 Israel together, and *p* over Jordan,
15:18 all his servants *p* on beside him;
18 from Gath, *p* on before the king.
22 And Ittai the Gittite *p* over, and all
23 voice, and all the people *p* over:
23 himself *p* over the brook Kidron,
23 Kidron, and all the people *p* over,
17:22 with him, and they *p* over Jordan:
24 And Absalom *p* over Jordan, he
24: 5 they *p* over Jordan, and pitched
1Ki 13:25 And, behold, men *p* by, and saw the
19:11 And, behold, the Lord *p* by, and a
19 and Elijah *p* by him, and cast his
20:39 as the king *p* by, he cried unto the
2Ki 4: 8 on a day, that Elisha *p* to Shunem,
8 that as oft as he *p* by, he turned
31 Gehazi *p* on before them, and laid
6:30 and he *p* by upon the wall, and the
14: 9 there *p* by a wild beast that was
1Ch 19:17 all Israel, and *p* over Jordan, and
2Ch 9:22 king Solomon *p* all the kings of
25:18 and there *p* by a wild beast that
30:10 So the posts *p* from city to city
Job 4:15 Then a spirit *p* before my face;
9:26 are *p* away as the swift ships:
15:19 and no stranger *p* among them.
28: 8 it, nor the fierce lion *p* by it.
Ps 18:12 was before him his thick clouds *p*,
37:36 Yet he *p* away, and, lo, he was
48: 4 assembled, they *p* by together.
90: 9 all our days are *p* away in thy
Ca 3: 4 but a little that I *p* from them,
Isa 10:28 come to Aiath, he is *p* to Migron;
40:27 judgment is *p* over from my God?
41: 3 He pursued them, and *p* safely;
Jer 2: 6 a land that no man *p* through, and
11:15 and the holy flesh is *p* from thee?
34:18 and *p* between the parts thereof,
19 *p* between the parts of the calf;
46:17 he hath *p* the time appointed.
Eze 16: 6 when I *p* by thee, and saw thee
8 Now when I *p* by thee, and looked
15 on every one that *p* by; his it
25 thy feet to every one that *p* by,
36:34 in the sight of all that *p* by.
47: 5 a river that could not be *p* over.
Da 3:27 the smell of fire had *p* on them.
6:18 to his palace, and *p* the night fasting:
Hos10:11 but I *p* over upon her fair neck: I
Jon 2: 3 billows and thy waves *p* over me.
Mic 2:13 up, and have *p* through the gate,
Na 3:19 not thy wickedness *p* continually?
Hab 3:10 the overflowing of the water *p* by:
Zec 7:14 no man *p* through nor returned:
M't 9: 1 entered into a ship, and *p* over,
9 And as Jesus *p* forth from thence,
20:30 when they heard that Jesus *p* by,
27:39 And they that *p* by reviled him,
M'r 2:14 as he *p* by, he saw Levi the son
5:21 Jesus was *p* over again by ship
6:35 place, and now the time is far *p*:
48 sea, and would have *p* by them.
53 And when they had *p* over, they
9:30 thence, and *p* through Galilee;
11:20 as they *p* by, they saw the fig tree
15:21 one Simon a Cyrenian, who *p* by,
29 And they that *p* by railed on him,
Lu 10:31 saw him, he *p* by on the other side.
32 him, and *p* by on the other side.
17:11 *p* through the midst of Samaria
19: 1 entered and *p* through Jericho.
Joh 5:24 but is *p* from death unto life.
8:59 the midst of them, and so *p* by.
9: 1 and as Jesus *p* by, he saw a man
Ac 9:32 Peter *p* throughout all quarters,
12:10 out, and *p* on through one street;
14:24 they had *p* throughout Pisidia,
15: 3 *p* through Phenice and Samaria,
17: 1 they had *p* through Amphipolis
23 For as I *p* by, and beheld your
19: 1 Paul having *p* through the upper
21 when he had *p* through Macedonia
Ro 5:12 so death *p* upon all men, for that
1Co 10: 1 cloud, and all *p* through the sea;
2Co 5:17 old things are *p* away; behold, all
Heb 4:14 priest, that is *p* into the heavens,
11:29 faith they *p* through the Red sea
1Jo 3:14 we have *p* from death unto life,
Re 21: 1 and the first earth were *p* away;
4 for the former things are *p* away.

passedst
J'g 12: 1 *p* thou over to fight against the

passengers
Pr 9:15 *p* who go right on their ways:
Eze 39:11 the valley of the *p* on the east of
11 and it shall stop the noses of the *p*:
14 land to bury with the *p* those that
15 the *p* that pass through the land,

passest See also COMPASSEST.
De 3:21 all the kingdoms whither thou *p*.
30:18 *p* over Jordan to go to possess it.
2Sa 15:33 If thou *p* on with me, then thou
1Ki 2:37 out, and *p* over the brook Kidron,
Isa 43: 2 When thou *p* through the waters,

passeth See also COMPASSETH.
Ex 30:13 them, every one that *p* among
14 Every one that *p* among them that
33:22 while my glory *p* by, that I will put
Le 27:32 whatsoever *p* under the rod, the
Jos 3:11 *p* over before you into Jordan.
16: 2 *p* along unto the borders of Archi
19:13 from thence *p* on along on the east
1Ki 9: 8 one that *p* by it shall be astonished,
2Ki 4: 9 of God, which *p* by us continually.
12: 4 of every one that *p* the account,
2Ch 7:21 to every one that *p* by it; so that
Job 9:11 he *p* on also, but I perceive him
14:20 for ever against him, and he *p*:
30:15 my welfare *p* away as a cloud.
37:21 the wind *p*, and cleanseth them.
Ps 8: 8 *p* through the paths of the seas.
78:39 a wind that *p* away, and cometh
103:16 For the wind *p* over it, and it is
144: 4 days are as a shadow that *p* away.
Pr 10:25 As the whirlwind *p*, so is the
26:17 He that *p* by, and meddleth with
Ec 1: 4 One generation *p* away, and
Isa 29: 5 shall be as chaff that *p* away:
Jer 9:12 wilderness, that none *p* through?
13:24 scatter them as the stubble that *p*
18:16 that *p* thereby shall be astonished,
19: 8 that *p* thereby shall be astonished
Eze 35: 7 and cut off from it him that *p* out
Ho 13: 3 and as the early dew that *p* away,
Mic 7:18 and *p* by the transgression of the
Zep 2:15 every one that *p* by her shall hiss,
3: 6 their streets waste, that none *p* by:
Zec 9: 8 army, because of him that *p* by,
Lu 18:37 that Jesus of Nazareth *p* by.
1Co 7:31 the fashion of this world *p* away.
Eph 3:19 love of Christ, which *p* knowledge,
Ph'p 4: 7 God, which *p* all understanding,
1Jo 2:17 the world *p* away, and the lust

passing See also COMPASSING; TRESPASSING.
J'g 19:18 We are *p* from Beth-lehem-judah
2Sa 1:26 was wonderful, *p* the love of women.
15:24 people had done *p* out of the city.
2Ki 6:26 king of Israel was *p* by upon the
Ps 84: 6 Who *p* through the valley of Baca
Pr 7: 8 *P* through the street near her
Isa 31: 5 and *p* over he will preserve it.
Eze 39:14 *p* through the land to bury with
Lu 4:30 he *p* through the midst of them
Ac 5:15 the shadow of Peter *p* by might
8:40 *p* through he preached in all the
16: 8 *p* by Mysia came down to Troas.
27: 8 hardly *p* it, came unto a place

passion See also PASSIONS; COMPASSION.
Ac 1: 3 shewed himself alive after his *p*

passions See also COMPASSIONS.
Ac 14:15 We also are men of like *p* with you,
Jas 5:17 a man subject to like *p* as we are,

passover See also PASSOVERS.
Ex 12:11 eat it in haste: it is the Lord's *p*.
21 to your families, and kill the *p*.
27 It is the sacrifice of the Lord's *p*,
43 This is the ordinance of the *p*:
48 and will keep the *p* to the Lord,
34:25 of the *p* be left unto the morning.
Le 23: 5 first month at even is the Lord's *p*.
Nu 9: 2 keep the *p* at his appointed season.
4 Israel, that they should keep the *p*.
5 kept the *p* on the fourteenth day
6 could not keep the *p* on that day:
10 he shall keep the *p* unto the Lord.
12 ordinances of the *p* they shall keep
13 and forbeareth to keep the *p*,
14 and will keep the *p* unto the Lord;
14 according to the ordinance of the *p*,
28:16 first month is the *p* of the Lord.
33: 3 morrow after the *p* the children
De 16: 1 keep the *p* unto the Lord thy God:
2 shalt therefore sacrifice the *p*
5 Thou mayest not sacrifice the *p*
6 thou shalt sacrifice the *p* at even,
Jos 5:10 kept the *p* on the fourteenth day
11 land on the morrow after the *p*,
2Ki 23:21 Keep the *p* unto the Lord your God,
22 there was not holden such a *p* from
23 this *p* was holden to the Lord in
2Ch 30: 1 to keep the *p* unto the Lord God
2 to keep the *p* in the second month.
2Ch 30: 5 to keep the *p* unto the Lord God
15 killed the *p* on the fourteenth day
18 yet did they eat the *p* otherwise
35: 1 Josiah kept a *p* unto the Lord in
1 killed the *p* on the fourteenth day
6 kill the *p*, and sanctify yourselves,
7 and kids, all for the *p* offerings,
8 unto the priests for the *p* offerings
9 unto the Levites for *p* offerings
11 they killed the *p*, and the priests
13 And they roasted the *p* with fire
16 to keep the *p*, and to offer burnt
17 that were present kept the *p* at that
18 was no *p* like to that kept in Israel
18 keep such a *p* as Josiah kept,
19 the reign of Josiah was this *p* kept.
Ezr 6:19 children of the captivity kept the *p*
20 killed the *p* for all the children of
Eze 45:21 of the month, ye shall have the *p*,
M't 26: 2 after two days is the feast of the *p*,
17 we prepare for thee to eat the *p*?
18 I will keep the *p* at thy house with
19 them; and they made ready the *p*.
M'r 14: 1 two days was the feast of the *p*,
12 when they killed the *p*, his disciples
12 prepare that thou mayest eat the *p*?
14 I shall eat the *p* with my disciples?
16 them: and they made ready the *p*.
Lu 2:41 every year at the feast of the *p*.
22: 1 drew nigh, which is called the *P*.
7 bread, when the *p* must be killed.
8 Go and prepare us the *p*, that we
11 I shall eat the *p* with my disciples?
13 them: and they made ready the *p*.
15 I have desired to eat this *p* with you
Joh 2:13 And the Jews' *p* was at hand, and
23 when he was in Jerusalem at the *p*,
6: 4 the *p*, a feast of the Jews, was nigh.
11:55 And the Jews' *p* was nigh at hand:
55 went...up to Jerusalem before the *p*,
12: 1 Jesus six days before the *p* came to
13: 1 Now before the feast of the *p*, when
18:28 but that they might eat the *p*.
39 release unto you one at the *p*:
19:14 And it was the preparation of the *p*,
1Co 5: 7 Christ our *p* is sacrificed for us:
Heb11:28 Through faith he kept the *p*, and

passovers
2Ch 30:17 the charge of the killing of the *p*

past See also OVERPASSED; PASSED.
Ge 50: 4 the days of his mourning were *p*,
Ex 21:29 to push with his horn in time *p*,
36 the ox hath used to push in time *p*,
Nu 21:22 way, until we be *p* thy borders.
De 2:10 Emims dwelt therein in times *p*,
4:32 ask now of the days that are *p*,
42 and hated him not in times *p*; and
19: 4 whom he hated not in time *p*;
6 as he hated him not in time *p*.
1Sa 15:32 Surely the bitterness of death is *p*.
19: 7 was in his presence, as in times *p*.
2Sa 3:17 for David in times *p* to be king
5: 2 in time *p*, when Saul was king over
11:27 And when the mourning was *p*,
16: 1 when David was a little *p* the top
1Ki 18:29 came to pass when midday was *p*,
1Ch 9:20 was the ruler over them in time *p*,
11: 2 time *p*, even when Saul was king,
Job 9:10 doeth great things *p* finding out;
14:13 me secret, until thy wrath be *p*,
17:11 My days are *p*, my purposes are
29: 2 Oh that I were as in months *p*,
Ps 90: 4 are but as yesterday when it is *p*,
Ec 3:15 God requireth that which is *p*.
Ca 2:11 the winter is *p*, the rain is over
Jer 8:20 harvest is *p*, the summer is ended,
M't 14:15 place, and the time is now *p*;
M'r 16: 1 when the sabbath was *p*, Mary
Lu 9:36 the voice was *p*, Jesus was found
Ac 12:10 *p* the first and the second ward,
14:16 in times *p* suffered all nations
27: 9 because the fast was...already *p*,
Ro 3:25 the remission of sins that are *p*,
11:30 in times *p* have not believed God,
33 and his ways *p* finding out!
Ga 1:13 heard of my conversation in time *p*
23 he which persecuted us in times *p*
5:21 as I have also told you in time *p*,
Eph 2: 2 Wherein in time *p* ye walked
3 all had our conversation in times *p*
11 that ye, being in time *p* Gentiles
4:19 Who being *p* feeling have given
2Ti 2:18 that the resurrection is *p* already;
Ph'm 11 in time *p* was to thee unprofitable,
Heb 1: 1 spake in time *p* unto the fathers
11:11 of a child when she was *p* age,
1Pe 2:10 Which in time *p* were not a people,
4: 3 the time *p* of our life may suffice
1Jo 2: 8 because the darkness is *p*, and
Re 9:12 One woe is *p*; and, behold, there
11:14 The second woe is *p*; and, behold,

pastor See also PASTORS.
Jer 17:16 have not hastened from being a *p*

pastors
Jer 2: 8 *p* also transgressed against me,
3:15 will give you *p* according to mine
10:21 *p* are become brutish, and have
12:10 Many *p*...destroyed my vineyard,
22:22 The wind shall eat up all thy *p*,
23: 1 Woe be unto the *p* that destroy
2 against the *p* that feed my people;
Eph 4:11 and some, *p* and teachers;

pasture See also PASTURES.
Ge 47: 4 servants have no *p*' for their flocks;
1Ch 4:39 valley, to seek *p*' for their flocks.
40 And they found fat *p*' and good, and
41 there was *p*' there for their flocks.
Job 39: 8 range of the mountains is his *p*'.
Ps 74: 1 smoke against the sheep of thy *p*'?
79:13 we, thy people and sheep of thy *p*'
95: 7 the people of his *p*', and the sheep
100: 3 his people, and the sheep of his *p*'.
Isa 32:14 a joy of wild asses, a *p*' of flocks;
Jer 23: 1 and scatter the sheep of my *p*'!
25:36 for the Lord hath spoiled their *p*'.
La 1: 6 become like harts that find no *p*',
Eze 34:14 I will feed them in a good *p*', and
14 and in a fat *p*' shall they feed upon
18 you to have eaten up the good *p*',
31 ye my flock, the flock of my *p*',
Ho 13: 6 According to their *p*', so were they
Joe 1:18 perplexed, because they have no *p*';
Joh 10: 9 shall go in and out, and find *p*'.

pastures
1Ki 4:23 and twenty oxen out of the *p*',
Ps 23: 2 maketh me to lie down in green *p*':
65:12 drop upon the *p*' of the wilderness:
13 The *p*' are clothed with flocks;
Isa 30:23 day shall thy cattle feed in large *p*'.
49: 9 their *p*' shall be in all high places.
Eze 34:18 your feet the residue of your *p*'?
45:15 hundred, out of the fat *p*' of Israel;
Joe 1:19 devoured the *p*' of the wilderness,
20 devoured the *p*' of the wilderness.
2:22 the *p*' of the wilderness do spring,

Patara (*pat'-a-rah*)
Ac 21: 1 Rhodes, and from thence unto *P*':

pate
Ps 7:16 shall come down upon his own *p*'.

path See also PATHS; PATHWAY.
Ge 49:17 an adder in the *p*', that biteth the
Nu 22:24 angel of the Lord stood in a *p*' of
Job 28: 7 is a *p*' which no fowl knoweth, and
30:13 They mar my *p*', they set forward
41:32 He maketh a *p*' to shine after him;
Ps 16:11 Thou wilt shew me the *p*' of life:
27:11 O Lord, and lead me in a plain *p*',
77:19 sea, and thy *p*' in the great waters,
119:35 Make me to go in the *p*' of thy
105 my feet, and a light unto my *p*'.
139: 3 Thou compassest my *p*' and my
142: 3 me, then thou knewest my *p*'.
Pr 1:15 them; refrain thy foot from their *p*':
2: 9 and equity; yea, every good *p*'.
4:14 Enter not into the *p*' of the wicked,
18 the *p*' of the just is as the shining
26 Ponder the *p*' of thy feet, and let
5: 6 shouldest ponder the *p*' of life,
Isa 26: 7 dost weigh the *p*' of the just.
30:11 of the way, turn aside out of the *p*',
40:14 taught him in the *p*' of judgment,
43:16 and a *p*' in the mighty waters;
Joe 2: 8 shall walk every one in his *p*':

Pathros (*path'-ros*) See also PATHRUSIM.
Isa 11:11 and from Egypt, and from *P*', and
Jer 44: 1 at Noph, and in the country of *P*',
15 dwelt in the land of Egypt, in *P*',
Eze 29:14 them to return into the land of *P*',
30:14 And I will make *P*' desolate, and

Pathrusim (*path-ru'-sim*)
Ge 10:14 And *P*', and Casluhim, (out of
1Ch 1:12 And *P*', and Casluhim, (of whom

paths
Job 6:18 *p*' of their way are turned aside;
8:13 So are the *p*' of all that forget God;
13:27 lookest narrowly unto all my *p*';
19: 8 and he hath set darkness in my *p*'.
24:13 thereof, nor abide in the *p*' thereof.
33:11 the stocks, he marketh all my *p*'.
38:20 know the *p*' to the house thereof?
Ps 8: 8 passeth through the *p*' of the seas.
17: 4 me from the *p*' of the destroyer.
5 Hold up my goings in thy *p*', that
23: 3 me in the *p*' of righteousness for
25: 4 thy ways, O Lord; teach me thy *p*'.
10 All the *p*' of the Lord are mercy
65:11 goodness; and thy *p*' drop fatness.
Pr 2: 8 He keepeth the *p*' of judgment, and
13 leave the *p*' of uprightness, to walk
15 and they froward in their *p*':
18 death, and her *p*' unto the dead.
19 take they hold of the *p*' of life.
20 and keep the *p*' of the righteous.
3: 6 him, and he shall direct thy *p*'.
17 and all her *p*' are peace.
4:11 wisdom; I have led thee in right *p*'.
7:25 her ways, go not astray in her *p*'.
8: 2 by the way in the places of the *p*'.
20 in the midst of the *p*' of judgment:
Isa 2: 3 his ways, and we will walk in his *p*':
3:12 err, and destroy the way of thy *p*'.
42:16 in *p*' that they have not known:
58:12 The restorer of *p*' to dwell in.
59: 7 and destruction are in their *p*'.
8 they have made them crooked *p*':
Jer 6:16 and ask for the old *p*', where is the
18:15 in their ways from the ancient *p*',
15 walk in *p*', in a way not cast up;
La 3: 9 stone, he hath made my *p*' crooked.
Ho 2: 6 wall, that she shall not find her *p*'.
Mic 4: 2 ways, and we will walk in his *p*':
M't 3: 3 of the Lord, make his *p*' straight.
M'r 1: 3 of the Lord, make his *p*' straight.
Lu 3: 4 of the Lord, make his *p*' straight.
Heb 12:13 made straight *p*' for your feet, lest

pathway
Pr 12:28 in the *p*' thereof...is no death.

patience
M't 18:26 Lord, have *p*' with me, and I will
29 Have *p*' with me, and I will pay
Lu 8:15 it, and bring forth fruit with *p*'.
21:19 In your *p*' possess ye your souls.
Ro 5: 3 that tribulation worketh *p*';
4 And *p*', experience; and experience,
8:25 not, then do we with *p*' wait for it.
15: 4 *p*' and comfort of the scriptures
5 Now the God of *p*' and consolation
2Co 6: 4 the ministers of God, in much *p*', in
12:12 were wrought among you in all *p*',
Col 1:11 unto all *p*' and longsuffering with
1Th 1: 3 and *p*' of hope in our Lord Jesus
2Th 1: 4 for your *p*' and faith in all your
1Ti 6:11 godliness, faith, love, *p*', meekness.
2Ti 3:10 faith, longsuffering, charity, *p*',
Tit 2: 2 sound in faith, in charity, in *p*'.
Heb 6:12 faith and *p*' inherit the promises.
10:36 For ye have need of *p*', that, after
12: 1 let us run with *p*' the race that is
Jas 1: 3 the trying of your faith worketh *p*'.
4 But let *p*' have her perfect work,
5: 7 and hath long *p*' for it, until he
10 of suffering affliction, and of *p*'.
11 Ye have heard of the *p*' of Job,
2Pe 1: 6 temperance *p*'; and to *p*' godliness;
Re 1: 9 the kingdom and *p*' of Jesus Christ,
2: 2 works, and thy labour, and thy *p*',
3 hast *p*', and for my name's sake
19 faith, and thy *p*', and thy works;
3:10 thou hast kept the word of my *p*',
13:10 it the *p*' and the faith of the saints.
14:12 Here is the *p*' of the saints: here

patient
Ec 7: 8 *p*' in spirit is better than the proud
Ro 2: 7 by *p*' continuance in well doing
12:12 in hope; *p*' in tribulation;
1Th 5:14 the weak, be *p*' toward all men.
2Th 3: 5 and into the *p*' waiting for Christ.
1Ti 3: 3 *p*', not a brawler, not covetous;
2Ti 2:24 gentle unto all men, apt to teach, *p*',
Jas 5: 7 Be *p*' therefore, brethren, unto the
8 Be ye also *p*'; stablish your hearts:

patiently
Ps 37: 7 in the Lord, and wait *p*' for him:
40: 1 I waited *p*' for the Lord; and he
Ac 26: 3 I beseech thee to hear me *p*'.
Heb 6:15 And so, after he had *p*' endured,
1Pe 2:20 for your faults, ye shall take it *p*'?
20 ye take it *p*', this as acceptable with

Patmos (*pat'-mos*)
Re 1: 9 was in the isle that is called *P*',

patriarch See also PATRIARCHS.
Ac 2:29 speak unto you of the *p*' David,
Heb 7: 4 the *p*' Abraham gave the tenth of

patriarchs
Ac 7: 8 and Jacob begat the twelve *p*'.
9 And the *p*', moved with envy, sold

patrimony
De 18: 8 which cometh of the sale of his *p*'.

Patrobas (*pat'-ro-bas*)
Ro 16:14 *P*', Hermes, and the brethren

pattern See also PATTERNS.
Ex 25: 9 after the *p*' of the tabernacle, and
9 the *p*' of all the instruments thereof,
40 *p*',...shewed thee in the mount.
Nu 8: 4 the *p*' which the Lord had shewed
Jos 22:28 the *p*' of the altar of the Lord,
2Ki 16:10 fashion of the altar, and the *p*' of it,
1Ch 28:11 *p*' of the porch, and of the houses
12 the *p*' of all that he had by the spirit,
18 and gold for the *p*' of the chariot of
19 me, even all the works of this *p*'.
Eze 43:10 and let them measure the *p*'.
1Ti 1:16 *p*' to them which should hereafter
Tit 2: 7 showing thyself a *p*' of good works:
Heb 8: 5 the *p*' shewed to thee in the mount.

patterns
Heb 9:23 *p*' of things in the heavens should

Pau (*pa'-u*) See also PAI.
Ge 36:39 and the name of his city was *P*':

Paul^ (*pawl*) See also PAUL'S; PAULUS; SAUL.
Ac 13: 9 Saul, (who also is called *P*',) filled
13 when *P*' and his company loosed
16 Then *P*' stood up, and beckoning
43 followed *P*' and Barnabas: who,
45 things which were spoken by *P*',
46 Then *P*' and Barnabas waxed bold,
50 raised persecution against *P*' and
14: 9 The same heard *P*' speak: who
11 the people saw what *P*' had done,
12 and *P*', Mercurius, because he was
14 when the apostles, Barnabas and *P*',
19 having stoned *P*', drew him out of
15: 2 *P*' and Barnabas had no small
2 determined that *P*' and Barnabas,
12 gave audience to Barnabas and *P*',
22 to Antioch with *P*' and Barnabas;
25 with our beloved Barnabas and *P*',
35 *P*' also and Barnabas continued in
36 *P*' said unto Barnabas, Let us go
38 *P*' thought not good to take him
40 And *P*' chose Silas, and departed,
16: 3 would *P*' have to go forth with him;
9 vision appeared to *P*' in the night;
14 the things which were spoken of *P*'.
17 The same followed *P*' and us, and
Ac 16:18 But *P*', being grieved, turned and
19 they caught *P*' and Silas, and drew
25 at midnight *P*' and Silas prayed,
28 *P*' cried with a loud voice, saying,
29 and fell down before *P*' and Silas,
36 this saying to *P*', The magistrates
37 But *P*' said unto them, They have
17: 2 And *P*', as his manner was, went in
4 and consorted with *P*' and Silas;
10 sent away *P*' and Silas by night
13 God was preached of *P*' at Berea,
14 sent away *P*' to go as it were to the
15 they that conducted *P*' brought him
16 while *P*' waited for them at Athens,
22 *P*' stood in the midst of Mars' hill,
33 So *P*' departed from among them.
18: 1 After these things *P*' departed from
5 *P*' was pressed in the spirit, and
9 spake the Lord to *P*' in the night by
12 with one accord against *P*', and
14 when *P*' was now about to open his
18 And *P*' after this tarried there yet a
19: 1 *P*' having passed through the upper
4 Then said *P*', John verily baptized
6 when *P*' had laid his hands upon
11 miracles by the hands of *P*':
13 you by Jesus whom *P*' preacheth.
15 Jesus I know, and *P*' I know; but
21 *P*' purposed in the spirit, when he
26 this *P*' hath persuaded and turned
30 And when *P*' would have entered in
20: 1 *P*' called unto him the disciples,
7 *P*' preached unto them, ready to
9 as *P*' was long preaching, he sunk
10 And *P*' went down, and fell on him,
13 there intending to take in *P*': for
16 *P*'...determined to sail by Ephesus,
21: 4 who said to *P*' through the Spirit,
13 Then *P*' answered, What mean ye
18 *P*' went in with us unto James;
26 *P*' took the men, and the next day
29 *P*' had brought into the temple.)
30 they took *P*', and drew him out of
32 the soldiers, they left beating of *P*'.
37 as *P*' was to be led into the castle,
39 But *P*' said, I am a man which am
40 *P*' stood on the stairs, and beckoned
22:25 *P*' said unto the centurion that
28 And *P*' said, But I was free born.
30 and brought *P*' down, and set him
23: 1 *P*', earnestly beholding the council,
3 Then said *P*' unto him, God shall
5 Then said *P*', I wist not, brethren,
6 *P*' perceived that the one part were
10 lest *P*' should have been pulled in
11 Be of good cheer, *P*': and said,
12 eat nor drink till they had killed *P*'.
14 eat nothing until we have slain *P*'.
16 entered into the castle, and told *P*'.
17 *P*' called one of the centurions unto
18 *P*' the prisoner called me unto him,
20 wouldest bring down *P*' to morrow
24 that they may set *P*' on, and bring
31 took *P*', and brought him by night
33 presented *P*' also before him.
24: 1 informed the governor against *P*'.
10 Then *P*', after that the governor
23 commanded a centurion to keep *P*',
24 he sent for *P*', and heard him
26 should have been given him of *P*',
27 the Jews a pleasure, left *P*' bound.
25: 2 the Jews informed him against *P*',
4 *P*' should be kept at Cæsarea, and
6 seat commanded *P*' to be brought.
7 grievous complaints against *P*',
9 answered *P*', and said, Wilt thou go
10 Then said *P*', I stand at Cæsar's
19 dead, whom *P*' affirmed to be alive.
21 *P*' had appealed to be reserved
23 morrow...*P*' was brought forth.
26: 1 Then Agrippa said unto *P*', Thou
1 *P*' stretched forth the hand, and
24 *P*', thou art beside thyself; much
28 Agrippa said unto *P*', Almost thou
29 *P*' said, I would to God, that not
27: 1 they delivered *P*' and certain other
3 Julius courteously entreated *P*',
9 already past, *P*' admonished them,
11 things which were spoken by *P*'.
21 *P*' stood forth in the midst of them,
24 Fear not, *P*'; thou must be brought
31 *P*' said to the centurion and to the
33 *P*' besought them all to take meat,
43 the centurion, willing to save *P*',
28: 3 *P*' had gathered a bundle of sticks,
8 to whom *P*' entered in, and prayed,
15 whom when *P*' saw, he thanked
16 *P*' was suffered to dwell by himself
17 days *P*' called the chief of the Jews
25 after that *P*' had spoken one word,
30 *P*' dwelt two whole years in his
Ro 1: 1 *P*', a servant of Jesus Christ, called
1Co 1: 1 *P*', called to be an apostle of Jesus
12 every one of you saith, I am of *P*';
13 was *P*' crucified for you? or were
13 were ye baptized in the name of *P*'?
3: 4 For while one saith, I am of *P*';
5 Who then is *P*', and who is Apollos,
22 Whether *P*', or Apollos, or Cephas,
16:21 of me *P*' with mine own hand.
2Co 1: 1 *P*', an apostle of Jesus Christ by the
10: 1 Now I *P*' myself beseech you by
Ga 1: 1 *P*', an apostle, (not of men, neither
5: 2 Behold, I *P*' say unto you, that if
Eph 1: 1 *P*', an apostle of Jesus Christ by
3: 1 For this cause I *P*', the prisoner of

Ph'p 1: 1 P' and Timotheus, the servants of
Col 1: 1 P', an apostle of Jesus Christ by
23 whereof I P' am made a minister:
4:18 salutation by the hand of me P'.
1Th 1: 1 P', and Silvanus, and Timotheus,
2:18 you, even I P', once and again;
2Th 1: 1 P', and Silvanus, and Timotheus,
3:17 The salutation of P' with mine own
1Ti 1: 1 P', an apostle of Jesus Christ by
2Ti 1: 1 P', an apostle of Jesus Christ by
subscr. P' was brought before Nero
Tit 1: 1 P', a servant of God, and an
Ph'm 1 P', a prisoner of Jesus Christ, and
9 being such an one as P' the aged,
19 I P' have written it with mine own
2Pe 3:15 even as our beloved brother P'

Paul's (*pawls*)
Ac 19:29 P' companions in travel, they
20:37 fell on P' neck, and kissed him,
21: 8 that were of P' company departed,
11 took P' girdle, and bound his own
23:16 And when P' sister's son heard of
25:14 declared P' cause unto the king,

Paulus See also PAUL.
Ac 13: 7 deputy of the country, Sergius P',

paved
Ex 24:10 were a p' work of a sapphire stone,
Ca 3:10 midst thereof being p' with love,

pavement
2Ki 16:17 it, and put it upon a p' of stones.
2Ch 7: 3 faces to the ground upon the p',
Es 1: 6 a p' of red, and blue, and white,
Eze 40:17 p' made for the court round about:
17 thirty chambers were upon the p'.
18 And the p' by the side of the gates
18 of the gates was the lower p'.
42: 3 p' which was for the utter court,
Joh 19:13 in a place that is called the P',

pavilion See also PAVILIONS.
Ps 18:11 his p' round about him were dark
27: 5 he shall hide me in his p': in the
31:20 shalt keep them secretly in a p'
Jer 43:10 shall spread his royal p' over them.

pavilions
2Sa 22:12 he made darkness p' round about
1Ki 20:12 drinking, he and the kings in the p',
16 drinking himself drunk in the p',

paw See also PAWETH; PAWS.
1Sa 17:37 delivered me out of...p' of the lion,
37 and out of the p' of the bear, he will

paweth
Job 39:21 He p' in the valley, and rejoiceth

paws
Le 11:27 And whatsoever goeth upon his p',

pay See also PAID; PAYED; PAYETH; REPAY.
Ex 21:19 he shall p' for the loss of his time,
22 he shall p' as the judges determine.
36 he shall surely p' ox for ox; and
22: 7 thief be found, let him p' double.
9 p' double unto his neighbour.
17 p' money according to the dowry
Nu 20:19 thy water, then I will p' for it;
De 23:21 thou shalt not slack to p' it: for
2Sa 15: 7 let me go and p' my vow, which I
1Ki 20:39 else thou shalt p' a talent of silver.
2Ki 4: 7 Go, sell the oil, and p' thy debt,
2Ch 8: 8 make to p' tribute until this day.
27: 5 children of Ammon p' unto him,
Ezr 4:13 will they not p' toll, tribute, and
Es 3: 9 will p' ten thousand talents of silver
4: 7 that Haman had promised to p' to
Job 22:27 thee, and thou shalt p' thy vows.
Ps 22:25 p' my vows before them that fear
50:14 and p' thy vows unto the most High:
66:13 offerings: I will p' thee my vows,
76:11 Vow, and p' unto the Lord your God:
116:14, 18, p' my vows unto the Lord now
Pr 19:17 he hath given will he p' him again.
22:27 If thou hast nothing to p', why
Ec 5: 4 a vow unto God, defer not to p' it;
4 p' that which thou hast vowed.
5 thou shouldest vow and not p'.
Jon 2: 9 I will p' that that I have vowed.
M't 17:24 Doth not your master p' tribute?
18:25 forasmuch as he had not to p', his
26 with me, and I will p' thee all.
28 saying, P' me that thou owest.
29 with me, and I will p' thee all.
30 prison, till he should p' the debt.
34 should p' all that was due unto him.
23:23 for ye p' tithe of mint and anise and
Lu 7:42 when they had nothing to p', he
Ro 13: 6 For this cause p' ye tribute also:

payed [*some eds.* PAID] See also PAID; REPAYED.
Pr 7:14 me; this day have I p' my vows.
Heb 7: 9 tithes, p' tithes in Abraham.

payeth See also REPAYETH.
Ps 37:21 borroweth, and p' not again:

payment
M't 18:25 that he had, and p' to be made.

Pazzez See BETH-PAZZEZ.

peace See also PEACEABLE; PEACEMAKERS.
Ge 15:15 thou shalt go to thy fathers in p';
24:21 man wondering at her held his p',
26:29 and have sent thee away in p':
31 and they departed from him in p'.
28:21 again to my father's house in p';
34: 5 Jacob held his p' until they were
41:16 give Pharaoh an answer of p'.
43:23 And he said, P' be to you, fear not:
44:17 get you up in p' unto your father.
Ex 4:18 And Jethro said to Moses, Go in p'.
14:14 you, and ye shall hold your p'.
18:23 shall also go to their place in p'.
20:24 offerings, and thy p' offerings,
24: 5 sacrificed p' offerings of oxen unto
29:28 of the sacrifice of their p' offerings,
32: 6 offerings, and brought p' offerings;
Le 3: 1 be a sacrifice of p' offering, if he
3 of the sacrifice of the p' offering
6 a sacrifice of p' offering unto the
9 of the sacrifice of the p' offering
4:10 of the sacrifice of p' offerings: and
26 fat of the sacrifice of p' offerings:
31 off the sacrifice of p' offerings: and
35 the sacrifice of the p' offerings;
6:12 thereon the fat of the p' offerings.
7:11 law of the sacrifice of p' offerings,
13 of thanksgiving of his p' offerings.
14 the blood of the p' offerings.
15, 18 of the sacrifice of his p' offerings
20, 21 of the sacrifice of p' offerings,
29 the sacrifice of his p' offerings unto
29 of the sacrifice of his p' offerings.
32 the sacrifices of your p' offerings.
33 the blood of the p' offerings, and
34 the sacrifices of their p' offerings,
37 of the sacrifice of the p' offerings;
9: 4 bullock and a ram for p' offerings,
18 ram for a sacrifice of p' offerings,
22 the burnt offering, and p' offerings.
10: 3 glorified. And Aaron held his p'.
14 out of the sacrifices of p' offerings
17: 5 them for p' offerings unto the Lord.
19: 5 ye offer a sacrifice of p' offerings
22:21 offereth a sacrifice of p' offerings
23:19 year for a sacrifice of p' offerings.
26: 6 I will give p' in the land, and ye
Nu 6:14 without blemish for p' offerings,
17 ram for a sacrifice of p' offerings
18 the sacrifice of the p' offerings.
26 upon thee, and give thee p'.
7:17, 23, 29, 35, 41, 47, 53, 59, 65, 71, 77, 83
sacrifice of p' offerings, two oxen,
88 for the sacrifice of the p' offerings
10:10 the sacrifices of your p' offerings;
15: 8 vow, or p' offerings unto the Lord:
25:12 give unto him my covenant of p':
29:39 offerings, and for your p' offerings.
30: 4 her father shall hold his p' at her;
7 held his p' at her in the day that
11 held his p' at her, and disallowed her
14 hold his p' at her from day to day;
14 he held his p' at her in the day
De 2:26 king of Heshbon with words of p',
20:10 against it, then proclaim p' unto it.
11 if it make thee answer of p', and
12 if it will make no p' with thee, but
23: 6 Thou shalt not seek their p' nor
27: 7 And thou shalt offer p' offerings,
29:19 I shall have p', though I walk in
Jos 8:31 Lord, and sacrificed p' offerings.
9:15 Joshua made p' with them, and
10: 1 Gibeon had made p' with Israel,
4 for it hath made p' with Joshua
21 to Joshua at Makkedah in p':
11:19 There was not a city that made p'
22:23 or if to offer p' offerings thereon,
27 sacrifices, and with our p' offerings;
J'g 4:17 was p' between Jabin the king of
6:23 him, P' be unto thee; fear not:
8: 9 When I come again in p', I will
11:31 I return in p' from the children of
18: 6 the priest said unto them, Go in p':
19 they said unto him, Hold thy p',
19:20 the old man said, P' be with thee;
20:26 and p' offerings before the Lord.
21: 4 burnt offerings and p' offerings.
1Sa 1:17 Eli answered and said, Go in p':
7:14 p' between Israel and the Amorites.
10: 8 sacrifice sacrifices of p' offerings:
27 no presents. But he held his p'.
11:15 sacrificed sacrifices of p' offerings
13: 9 offering to me, and p' offerings.
20: 7 is well; thy servant shall have p':
13 away, that thou mayest go in p':
21 for there is p' to thee, and no hurt;
42 Jonathan said to David, Go in p',
25: 6 in prosperity, P' be both to thee,
6 and p' be to thine house,
6 and p' be unto all that thou hast.
35 Go up in p' to thine house; see, I
29: 7 now return, and go in p', that thou
2Sa 3:21 Abner away; and he went in p'.
22 him away, and he was gone in p'.
23 him away, and he is gone in p'.
6:17 and p' offerings before the Lord.
18 burnt offerings and p' offerings,
10:19 made p' with Israel, and served
13:20 but hold now thy p', my sister: he
15: 9 the king said unto him, Go in p'.
27 return into the city in p', and your
17: 3 so all the people shall be in p'.
19:24 until the day he came again in p'.
30 again in p' unto his own house.
24:25 burnt offerings and p' offerings.
1Ki 2: 5 shed the blood of war in p',
6 head go down to the grave in p'.
33 there be p' for ever from the Lord.
3:15 offered p' offerings, and made a
4:24 and he had p' on all sides round
5:12 p' between Hiram and Solomon;
8:63 offered a sacrifice of p' offerings,
64 and the fat of the p' offerings:
1Ki 8:64 and the fat of the p' offerings.
9:25 p' offerings upon the altar which
20:18 Whether they be come out for p',
22:17 every man to his house in p'.
27 of affliction, until I come in p'.
28 If thou return at all in p', the Lord
44 Jehoshaphat made p' with the
2Ki 2: 3, 5 Yea, I know it; hold ye your p'.
5:19 And he said unto him, Go in p'.
7: 9 good tidings, and we hold our p':
9:17 them, and let him say, Is it p'?
18 said, Thus saith the king, Is it p'?
18 What hast thou to do with p'?
19 said, Thus saith the king, Is it p'?
19 What hast thou to do with p'?
22 Jehu, that he said, Is it p', Jehu?
22 And he answered, What p', so long
31 Had Zimri p', who slew his master?
16:13 the blood of his p' offerings,
18:36 But the people held their p', and
20:19 good, if p' and truth be in my days?
22:20 be gathered into thy grave in p';
1Ch 12:18 son of Jesse: p', p' be unto thee,
18 thee, and p' be to thine helpers;
16: 1 offered...p' offerings before God.
2 burnt offerings and the p' offerings,
19:19 made p' with David, and became
21:26 burnt offerings and p' offerings,
22: 9 give p' and quietness unto Israel
2Ch 7: 7 and the fat of p' offerings,
15: 5 was no p' to him that went out,
18:16 return...every man to his house in p'.
26 of affliction, until I return in p'.
27 If thou certainly return in p', then
19: 1 of Judah returned to his house in p'
29:35 with the fat of the p' offerings,
30:22 seven days, offering p' offerings,
31: 2 burnt offerings and for p' offerings,
33:16 p' offerings and thank offerings,
34:28 be gathered to thy grave in p',
Ezr 4:17 unto the rest beyond the river, P',
5: 7 thus; Unto Darius the king, all p'.
7:12 unto Ezra the priest,...perfect p',
9:12 nor seek their p' or their wealth
Ne 5: 8 Then held they their p', and found
8:11 Hold your p', for the day is holy;
Es 4:14 if thou altogether holdest thy p'
9:30 with words of p' and truth,
10: 3 and speaking p' to all his seed.
Job 5:23 of the field shall be at p' with thee.
24 that thy tabernacle shall be in p';
11: 3 thy lies make men hold their p'?
13: 5 ye would altogether hold your p'!
13 Hold your p', let me alone, that I
22:21 now thyself with him, and be at p':
25: 2 he maketh p' in his high places.
29:10 The nobles held their p', and their
33:31 me: hold thy p', and I will speak.
33 hold thy p', and I shall teach thee
Ps 4: 8 both lay me down in p', and sleep:
7: 4 unto him that was at p' with me;
28: 3 which speak p' to their neighbours,
29:11 Lord will bless his people with p'.
34:14 and do good; seek p', and pursue it.
35:20 For they speak not p': but they
37:11 themselves in the abundance of p'.
37 for the end of that man is p'.
39: 2 dumb with silence, I held my p',
12 hold not thy p' at my tears: for I
55:18 He hath delivered my soul in p'
20 against such as be at p' with him:
72: 3 mountains...bring p' to the people,
7 abundance of p' so long as the moon
83: 1 hold not thy p', and be not still,
85: 8 he will speak p' unto his people,
10 righteousness and p' have kissed
109: 1 Hold not thy p', O God of my
119:165 Great p' have they which love
120: 6 long dwelt with him that hateth p'.
7 I am for p': but when I speak, they
122: 6 Pray for the p' of Jerusalem: they
7 P' be within thy walls, and
8 I will now say, P' be within thee.
125: 5 iniquity: but p' shall be upon Israel.
128: 6 children, and p' upon Israel.
147:14 He maketh p' in thy borders, and
Pr 3: 2 long life, and p', shall they add to
17 and all her paths are p'.
7:14 I have p' offerings with me; this
11:12 of understanding holdeth his p'.
12:20 but to the counsellers of p' is joy.
16: 7 his enemies to be at p' with him.
17:28 Even a fool, when he holdeth his p',
Ec 3: 8 a time of war, and a time of p'.
Isa 9: 6 Father, The Prince of P'.
7 increase of his government and p'
26: 3 wilt keep him in perfect p', whose
12 Lord, thou wilt ordain p' for us:
27: 5 that he may make p' with me;
5 me; and he shall make p' with me.
32:17 work of righteousness shall be p';
33: 7 the ambassadors of p' shall weep
36:21 they held their p', and answered
38:17 for p' I had great bitterness: but
39: 8 shall be p' and truth in my days.
42:14 I have long time holden my p';
45: 7 I make p', and create evil: I the
48:18 then had thy p' been as a river, and
22 There is no p', saith the Lord, unto
52: 7 good tidings, that publisheth p';
53: 5 chastisement of our p' was upon
54:10 the covenant of my p' be removed,
13 great shall be the p' of thy children.
55:12 with joy, and be led forth with p':
57: 2 He shall enter into p': they shall
11 have not I held my p' even of old,

Isa 57:19 P', p' to him that is far off, and to
21 There is no p', saith my God, to the
59: 8 The way of p' they know not; and
8 goeth therein shall not know p'.
60:17 I will also make thy officers p', and
62: 1 Zion's sake will I not hold my p',
6 never hold their p' day nor night:
64:12 wilt thou hold thy p', and afflict us
66:12 I will extend p' to her like a river,
Jer 4:10 Ye shall have p'; whereas the sword
19 I cannot hold my p', because thou
6:14 saying, P', p'; when there is no p'.
8:11 saying, P', p'; when there is no p'.
15 We looked for p', but no good came;
12: 5 if in the land of p', wherein thou
12 of the land: no flesh shall have p'.
14:13 will give you assured p' in this place.
19 looked for p', and there is no good;
16: 5 taken away my p' from this people,
23:17 Lord hath said, Ye shall have p';
28: 9 prophet which prophesieth of p',
29: 7 seek the p' of the city whither I have
7 in the p' thereof shall ye have p'.
11 thoughts of p', and not of evil, to
30: 5 of trembling, of fear, and not of p'.
33: 6 the abundance of p' and truth.
34: 5 But thou shalt die in p': and with
43:12 he shall go forth from thence in p'.
La 3:17 removed my soul far off from p':
Eze 7:25 they shall seek p', and there shall
13:10 saying, P'; and there was no p';
16 which see visions of p' for her, and
16 there is no p', saith the Lord God.
34:25 make with them a covenant of p',
37:26 make a covenant of p' with them;
43:27 the altar, and your p' offerings;
45:15 burnt offering, and for p' offerings,
17 burnt offering, and the p' offerings,
46: 2 burnt offering and his p' offerings,
12 burnt offering or p' offerings
12 burnt offering and his p' offerings,
Da 4: 1 earth; P' be multiplied unto you.
6:25 earth; P' be multiplied unto you.
8:25 and by p' shall destroy many:
10:19 p' be unto thee, be strong, yea, be
Am 5:22 the p' offerings of your fat beasts.
Ob 7 men that were at p' with thee have
Mic 3: 5 bite with their teeth, and cry, P';
5: 5 this man shall be the p', when the
Na 1:15 good tidings, that publisheth p'!
Zep 1: 7 Hold thy p' at the presence of the
Hag 2: 9 in this place will I give p', saith
Zec 6:13 the counsel of p' shall be between
8:10 was there any p' to him that went
16 execute...judgment of truth and p'
19 therefore love the truth and p'.
9:10 he shall speak p' unto the heathen:
Mal 2: 5 covenant...with him of life and p';
6 he walked with me in p' and equity,
M't 10:13 worthy, let your p' come upon it:
13 worthy, let your p' return to you.
34 that I am come to send p' on earth:
34 I came not to send p', but a sword.
20:31 because they should hold their p':
26:63 But Jesus held his p'. And the high
M'r 1:25 Hold thy p', and come out of him.
3: 4 or to kill? But they held their p'.
4:39 and said unto the sea, P', be still.
5:34 go in p', and be whole of thy plague.
9:34 But they held their p': for by the
50 and have p' one with another.
10:48 him that he should hold his p':
14:61 held his p', and answered nothing.
Lu 1:79 to guide our feet into the way of p'.
2:14 on earth p', good will toward men.
29 lettest thou thy servant depart in p',
4:35 Hold thy p', and come out of him.
7:50 faith hath saved thee; go in p'.
8:48 hath made thee whole; go in p'.
10: 5 enter, first say, P' be to this house.
6 And if the son of p' be there, your
6 your p' shall rest upon it: if not, it
11:21 his palace, his goods are in p':
12:51 that I am come to give p' on earth?
14: 4 And they held their p'. And he
32 and desireth conditions of p'.
18:39 him, that he should hold his p':
19:38 p' in heaven,...glory in the highest.
40 if these should hold their p', the
42 things which belong unto thy p'!
20:26 at his answer, and held their p'.
24:36 saith unto them, P' be unto you.
Joh 14:27 P' I leave with you, my p' I give
16:33 you, that in me ye might have p'.
20:19 saith unto them, P' be unto you.
21 Jesus to them again, P' be unto you:
26 the midst, and said, P' be unto you.
Ac 10:36 preaching p' by Jesus Christ:
11:18 held their p', and glorified God,
12:17 with the hand to hold their p',
20 desired p'; because their country
15:13 after they had held their p', James
33 were let go in p' from the brethren
16:36 now therefore depart, and go in p'.
18: 9 but speak, and hold not thy p':
Ro 1: 7 Grace to you and p' from God our
2:10 But glory, honour, and p', to every
3:17 the way of p' have they not known:
5: 1 we have p' with God through our
8: 6 be spiritually minded is life and p'.
10:15 that preach the gospel of p', and
14:17 but righteousness, and p', and joy
19 after the things which make for p',
15:13 you with all joy and p' in believing,
33 Now the God of p' be with you all.
16:20 God of p' shall bruise Satan under
1Co 1: 3 Grace be unto you, and p', from God
7:15 cases: but God hath called us to p'.
14:30 sitteth by, let the first hold his p'.
33 the author of confusion, but of p',
16:11 but conduct him forth in p', that he
2Co 1: 2 to you and p' from God our Father,
13:11 comfort, be of one mind, live in p';
11 of love and p' shall be with you.
Ga 1: 3 Grace be to you and p' from God
5:22 the fruit of the Spirit is love, joy, p',
6:16 p' be on them, and mercy, and upon
Eph 1: 2 Grace be to you, and p', from God
2:14 For he is our p', who hath made
15 twain one new man, so making p';
17 preached p' to you which were afar
4: 3 unity of the Spirit in the bond of p'.
6:15 the preparation of the gospel of p';
23 P' be to the brethren, and love
Ph'p 1: 2 Grace be unto you, and p', from God
4: 7 the p' of God, which passeth all
9 and the God of p' shall be with you.
Col 1: 2 Grace be unto you, and p', from God
20 made p' through the blood of his
3:15 the p' of God rule in your hearts,
1Th 1: 1 Grace be unto you, and p', from God
5: 3 when they shall say, P' and safety;
13 And be at p' among yourselves.
23 And the very God of p' sanctify you
2Th 1: 2 Grace unto you, and p', from God
3:16 the Lord of p' himself give you p'
1Ti 1: 2 mercy, and p', from God our Father
2Ti 1: 2 mercy, and p', from God the Father
2:22 righteousness, faith, charity, p',
Tit 1: 4 mercy, and p', from God the Father
Ph'm 3 Grace to you, and p', from God our
Heb 7: 2 King of Salem, which is, King of p';
11:31 she had received the spies with p'.
12:14 Follow p' with all men, and
13:20 the God of p', that brought again
Jas 2:16 Depart in p', be ye warmed and
3:18 is sown in p' of them that make p'.
1Pe 1: 2 Christ: Grace unto you, and p', be
3:11 good; let him seek p', and ensue it.
5:14 P' be with you all that are in Christ
2Pe 1: 2 Grace and p' be multiplied unto
3:14 that ye may be found of him in p',
2Jo 3 Grace be with you, mercy, and p',
3Jo 14 P' be to thee. Our friends salute
Jude 2 you, and p', and love, be multiplied.
Re 1: 4 Grace be unto you, and p', from him
6: 4 thereon to take p' from the earth,

peaceable
Ge 34:21 These men are p' with us;
2Sa 20:19 that are p' and faithful in Israel:
1Ch 4:40 land was wide, and quiet, and p';
Isa 32:18 shall dwell in a p' habitation, and
Jer 25:37 the p' habitations are cut down
1Ti 2: 2 we may lead a quiet and p' life in
Heb12:11 the p' fruit of righteousness unto
Jas 3:17 first pure, then p', gentle, and easy

peaceably
Ge 37: 4 and could not speak p' unto him.
J'g 11:13 now...restore those lands again p'.
21:13 Rimmon, and to call p' unto them.
1Sa 16: 4 coming, and said, Comest thou p'?
5 And he said, P': I am come to
1Ki 2:13 And she said, Comest thou p'?
13 And he said, P'.
1Ch 12:17 If ye be come p' unto me to help me,
Jer 9: 8 one speaketh p' to his neighbour
Da 11:21 he shall come in p', and obtain
24 He shall enter p' even upon the
Ro 12:18 lieth in you, live p' with all men.

peacemakers
M't 5: 9 Blessed are the p': for they shall

peace-offering See PEACE and OFFERING.

peacocks
1Ki 10:22 and silver, ivory, and apes, and p'.
2Ch 9:21 and silver, ivory, and apes, and p'.
Job 39:13 thou the goodly wings unto the p'?

pearl See also PEARLS.
M't 13:46 he had found one p' of great price,
Re 21:21 every several gate was of one p':

pearls
Job 28:18 shall be made of coral, or of p':
M't 7: 6 cast ye your p' before swine,
13:45 a merchant man, seeking goodly p':
1Ti 2: 9 hair, or gold, or p', or costly array;
Re 17: 4 gold and precious stones and p',
18:12 and precious stones, and of p', and
16 gold, and precious stones, and p'!
21:21 the twelve gates were twelve p';

peculiar
Ex 19: 5 ye shall be a p' treasure unto me
De 14: 2 thee to be a p' people unto himself,
26:18 thee this day to be his p' people,
Ps 135: 4 and Israel for his p' treasure.
Ec 2: 8 and the p' treasure of kings and of
Tit 2:14 a p' people, zealous of good works.
1Pe 2: 9 an holy nation, a p' people;

Pedahel (*ped'-a-hel*)
Nu 34:28 Naphtali, P' the son of Ammihud.

Pedahzur (*pe-dah'-zur*)
Nu 1:10 Manasseh; Gamaliel the son of P'.
2:20 shall be Gamaliel the son of P'.
7:54 day offered Gamaliel the son of P'.
59 offering of Gamaliel the son of P'.
10:23 was Gamaliel the son of P'.

Pedaiah (*pe-dah'-yah*)
2Ki 23:36 the daughter of P' of Rumah.
1Ch 3:18 Malchiram also, and P', and
19 the sons of P' were, Zerubbabel,
27:20 of Manasseh, Joel the son of P':
Ne 3:25 After him P' the son of Parosh.
8: 4 on his left hand, P', and Mishael,
11: 7 the son of Joed, the son of P', the
13:13 the scribe, and of the Levites, P':

pedigrees
Nu 1:18 they declared their p' after their

peeled See also PILLED.
Isa 18: 2 to a nation scattered and p', to a
7 of a people scattered and p', and
Eze 29:18 bald, and every shoulder was p':

peep See also PEEPED.
Isa 8:19 and unto wizards that p', and that

peeped
Isa 10:14 wing, or opened the mouth, or p'.

Pekah (*pe'-kah*)
2Ki 15:25 But P' the son of Remaliah, a
27 P' the son of Remaliah began to
29 In the days of P' king of Israel
30 made a conspiracy against P' the
31 And the rest of the acts of P', and
32 In the second year of P' the son of
37 Syria, and P' the son of Remaliah.
16: 1 In the seventeenth year of P' the
5 P' son of Remaliah king of Israel
2Ch 28: 6 For P' the son of Remaliah slew in
Isa 7: 1 P' the son of Remaliah, king of

Pekahiah (*pe-ka-hi'-ah*)
2Ki 15:22 P' his son reigned in his stead.
23 P' the son of Menahem began to
26 And the rest of the acts of P', and

Pekod (*pe'-kod*)
Jer 50:21 and against the inhabitants of P':
Eze 23:23 all the Chaldeans, P', and Shoa,

Pelaiah (*pel-a-i'-ah*)
1Ch 3:24 and Eliashib, and P', and Akkub,
Ne 8: 7 P', and the Levites, caused the
10:10 Shebaniah, Hodijah, Kelita, P',

Pelaliah (*pel-a-li'-ah*)
Ne 11:12 the son of Jeroham, the son of P',

Pelatiah (*pel-a-ti'-ah*)
1Ch 3:21 the sons of Hananiah; P', and
4:42 having for their captains P', and
Ne 10:22 P', Hanan, Anaiah,
Eze 11: 1 and P' the son of Benaiah, princes
13 that P' the son of Benaiah died.

Peleg (*pe'-leg*) See also PHALEG.
Ge 10:25 two sons: the name of one was P';
11:16 four and thirty years, and begat P':
17 And Eber lived after he begat P'
18 P' lived thirty years, and begat
19 P' lived after he begat Reu two
1Ch 1:19 sons: the name of the one was P';
25 Eber, P', Reu,

Pelet (*pe'-let*) See also BETH-PALET.
1Ch 2:47 Gesham, and P', and Ephah, and
12: 3 and P', the sons of Azmaveth;

Peleth (*pe'-leth*)
Nu 16: 1 and On, the son of P', sons of
1Ch 2:33 the sons of Jonathan; P', and

Pelethites (*pel'-e-thites*)
2Sa 8:18 both the Cherethites and the P';
15:18 and all the P', and all the Gittites,
20: 7 the P', and all the mighty men:
23 the Cherethites and over the P':
1Ki 1:38 and the P', went down, and caused
44 the Cherethites, and the P', and
1Ch 18:17 over the Cherethites and the P';

pelican
Le 11:18 and the p', and the gier eagle,
De 14:17 And the p', and the gier eagle, and
Ps 102: 6 I am like a p' of the wilderness:

Pelonite (*pel'-o-nite*) See also PALLITE.
1Ch 11:27 the Harorite, Helez the P',
36 the Mecherathite, Ahijah the P',
27:10 seventh month was Helez the P',

pen See also PENKNIFE.
J'g 5:14 they that handle the p' of the
Job 19:24 they were graven with an iron p'
Ps 45: 1 tongue is the p' of a ready writer.
Isa 8: 1 roll, and write in it with a man's p'
Jer 8: 8 it; the p' of the scribes is in vain.
17: 1 Judah is written with a p' of iron,
3Jo 13 with ink and p' write unto thee:

pence
M't 18:28 which owed him an hundred p':
M'r 14: 5 for more than three hundred p',
Lu 7:41 the one owed five hundred p', and
10:35 he took out two p', and gave them
Joh 12: 5 ointment sold for three hundred p',

Peniel (*pe-ni'-el*) See also PENUEL.
Ge 32:30 called the name of the place P':

Peninnah (*pe-nin'-nah*)
1Sa 1: 2 and the name of the other P':
2 and P' had children, but Hannah
4 offered, he gave to P' his wife,

penknife
Jer 36:23 leaves, he cut it with the p', and

penny See also PENNYWORTH; PENCE.
M't 20: 2 with the labourers for a p' a day,
9 hour, they received every man a p'.
10 likewise received every man a p'.
13 not thou agree with me for a p'?

M't 22: 19 And they brought unto him a *p*'.
M'r 12: 15 bring me a *p*', that I may see it.
Lu 20: 24 Shew me a *p*'. Whose image and
Re 6: 6 A measure of wheat for a *p*', and
6 three measures of barley for a *p*';

pennyworth
M'r 6: 37 and buy two hundred *p*' of bread,
Joh 6: 7 Two hundred *p*' of bread is not

Pentecost (*pen'-te-cost*)
Ac 2: 1 the day of *P*' was fully come,
20: 16 to be at Jerusalem the day of *P*'.
1Co 16: 8 I will tarry at Ephesus until *P*'.

Penuel (*pe-nu'-el*) See also PENIEL.
Ge 32: 31 as he passed over *P*' the sun rose
J'g 8: 8 he went up thence to *P*', and spake
8 and the men of *P*' answered him
9 he spake also unto the men of *P*',
17 And he beat down the tower of *P*',
1Ki 12: 25 went out from thence, and built *P*'.
1Ch 4: 4 and *P*' the father of Gedor, and
8: 25 and *P*', the sons of Shashak;

penury
Pr 14: 23 talk of the lips tendeth only to *p*'.
Lu 21: 4 but she of her *p*' hath cast in all

people See also PEOPLE'S; PEOPLES.
Ge 11: 6 Lord said, Behold, the *p*' is one,
14: 16 and the women also, and the *p*'.
17: 14 soul shall be cut off from his *p*';
16 nations; kings of *p*' shall be of her.
19: 4 all the *p*' from every quarter:
23: 7 bowed himself to the *p*' of the land,
11 in the presence of the sons of my *p*'
12 bowed down himself before the *p*'
13 the audience of the *p*' of the land,
25: 8 years; and was gathered to his *p*'.
17 died; and was gathered unto his *p*'.
23 and two manner of *p*' shall be
23 the one *p*' shall be stronger than
23 be stronger than the other *p*'; and
26: 10 one of the *p*' might lightly have
11 And Abimelech charged all his *p*',
27: 29 Let *p*' serve thee, and nations bow
28: 3 thou mayest be a multitude of *p*';
29: 1 into the land of the *p*' of the east.
32: 7 divided the *p*' that was with him,
34: 16 you, and we will become one *p*'.
22 for to dwell with us, to be one *p*',
35: 6 and all the *p*' that were with him.
29 was gathered unto his *p*', being
41: 40 thy word shall all my *p*' be ruled:
55 the *p*' cried to Pharaoh for bread:
42: 6 and he it was that sold to all the *p*'
47: 21 as for the *p*', he removed them to
23 Then Joseph said unto the *p*',
48: 4 will make of thee a multitude of *p*';
19 know it: he also shall become a *p*',
49: 10 shall the gathering of the *p*' be.
16 Dan shall judge his *p*', as one of
29 I am to be gathered unto my *p*':
33 and was gathered unto his *p*'.
50: 20 is this day, to save much *p*' alive.
Ex 1: 9 And he said unto his *p*', Behold,
9 the *p*' of the children of Israel are
20 the *p*' multiplied, and waxed very
22 And Pharaoh charged all his *p*',
3: 7 surely seen the affliction of my *p*'
10 bring forth my *p*' the children of
12 thou hast brought forth the *p*' out
21 will give this *p*' favour in the sight
4: 16 be thy spokesman unto the *p*':
21 that he shall not let the *p*' go.
30 did the signs in the sight of the *p*'.
31 And the *p*' believed: and when they
5: 1 Let my *p*' go, that they may hold a
4 Aaron, let the *p*' from their works?
5 the *p*' of the land now are many,
6 same day the taskmasters of the *p*',
7 Ye shall no more give the *p*' straw
10 the taskmasters of the *p*' went out,
10 officers, and they spake to the *p*',
12 So the *p*' were scattered abroad
16 but the fault is in thine own *p*'.
22 hast thou so evil entreated this *p*'?
23 name, he hath done evil to this *p*';
23 hast thou delivered thy *p*' at all.
6: 7 I will take you to me for a *p*', and I
7: 4 and my *p*' the children of Israel,
14 he refuseth to let the *p*' go.
16 Let my *p*' go, that they may serve
8: 1 Let my *p*' go, that they may serve
3 of thy servants, and upon thy *p*',
4 up both on thee, and upon thy *p*',
8 the frogs from me, and from my *p*';
8 and I will let the *p*' go, that they
9 and for thy servants, and for thy *p*',
11 from thy servants, and from thy *p*';
20 Let my *p*' go, that they may serve
21 Else, if thou wilt not let my *p*' go,
21 upon thy servants, and upon thy *p*',
22 of Goshen, in which my *p*' dwell,
23 division between my *p*' and thy *p*':
29 from his servants, and from his *p*',
29 the *p*' go to sacrifice to the Lord.
31 from his servants, and from his *p*';
32 also, neither would he let the *p*' go.
9: 1 Let my *p*' go, that they may serve
7 and he did not let the *p*' go.
13 Let my *p*' go, that they may serve
14 upon thy servants, and upon thy *p*';
15 I may smite thee and thy *p*' with
17 exaltest thou thyself against my *p*',
27 and I and my *p*' are wicked.
Ex 10: 3 let my *p*' go, that they may serve
4 Else, if thou refuse to let my *p*' go,
11: 2 Speak now in the ears of the *p*', and
3 the Lord gave the *p*' favour in the
3 servants, and in the sight of the *p*'.
8 out, and all the *p*' that follow thee:
12: 27 *p*' bowed the head and worshipped.
31 get you forth from among my *p*',
33 Egyptians were urgent upon the *p*',
34 *p*' took their dough before it was
36 the Lord gave the *p*' favour in the
13: 3 Moses said unto the *p*', Remember
17 when Pharaoh had let the *p*' go,
17 Lest peradventure the *p*' repent
18 God led the *p*' about, through the
22 of fire by night, from before the *p*'.
14: 5 the king of Egypt that the *p*' fled:
5 servants was turned against the *p*',
6 chariot, and took his *p*' with him:
13 Moses said unto the *p*', Fear ye
31 the *p*' feared the Lord, and believed
15: 13 in thy mercy hast led forth the *p*'
14 *p*' shall hear, and be afraid: sorrow
16 still as a stone; till thy *p*' pass over,
16 O Lord, till the *p*' pass over, which
24 the *p*' murmured against Moses,
16: 4 and the *p*' shall go out and gather
27 there went out some of the *p*' on
30 So the *p*' rested on the seventh day.
17: 1 was no water for the *p*' to drink.
2 the *p*' did chide with Moses, and
3 the *p*' thirsted there for water; and
3 the *p*' murmured against Moses,
4 What shall I do unto this *p*'? they
5 Go on before the *p*', and take with
6 out of it, that the *p*' may drink.
13 discomfited Amalek and his *p*' with
18: 1 for Moses, and for Israel his *p*',
10 hath delivered the *p*' from under
13 that Moses sat to judge the *p*': and
13 and the *p*' stood by Moses from the
14 in law saw all that he did to the *p*',
14 thing that thou doest to the *p*'?
14 and all the *p*' stand by thee from
15 the *p*' come unto me to enquire of
18 thou, and this *p*' that is with thee:
19 Be thou for the *p*' to God-ward,
21 provide out of all the *p*' able men,
22 let them judge the *p*' at all seasons:
23 this *p*' shall also go to their place
25 and made them heads over the *p*',
26 they judged the *p*' at all seasons:
19: 5 treasure unto me above all *p*': for
7 and called for the elders of the *p*',
8 all the *p*' answered together, and
8 Moses returned the words of the *p*'
9 that the *p*' may hear when I speak
9 Moses told the words of the *p*' unto
10 Go unto the *p*', and sanctify them
11 come down in the sight of all the *p*'
12 set bounds unto the *p*' round about,
14 down from the mount unto the *p*',
14 sanctified the *p*'; and they washed
15 said unto the *p*', Be ready against
16 that all the *p*' that was in the camp
17 Moses brought forth the *p*' out of
21 Go down, charge the *p*', lest they
23 The *p*' cannot come up to mount
24 let not the priests and the *p*' break
25 Moses went down unto the *p*', and
20: 18 all the *p*' saw the thunderings, and
18 when the *p*' saw it, they removed,
20 Moses said unto the *p*', Fear not:
21 the *p*' stood afar off, and Moses
22: 25 If thou lend money to any of my *p*'
28 gods, now curse the ruler of thy *p*'.
23: 11 that the poor of thy *p*' may eat: and
27 will destroy all the *p*' to whom thou
24: 2 neither shall the *p*' go up with him.
3 Moses came and told the *p*' all the
3 and all the *p*' answered with one
7 and read in the audience of the *p*':
8 blood, and sprinkled it on the *p*',
30: 33 shall even be cut off from his *p*'.
38 shall even be cut off from his *p*'.
31: 14 shall be cut off from among his *p*'.
32: 1 when the *p*' saw that Moses delayed
1 *p*' gathered themselves together
3 the *p*' brake off the golden earrings
6 the *p*' sat down to eat and to drink,
7 for thy *p*', which thou broughtest
9 unto Moses, I have seen this *p*',
9 and, behold, it is a stiffnecked *p*':
11 thy wrath wax hot against thy *p*',
12 repent of this evil against thy *p*'.
14 which he thought to do unto his *p*'.
17 Joshua heard the noise of the *p*' as
21 Aaron, What did this *p*' unto thee,
22 thou knowest the *p*', that they are
25 Moses saw that the *p*' were naked;
28 there fell of the *p*' that day about
30 Moses said unto the *p*', Ye have
31 Oh, this *p*' have sinned a great sin,
34 lead the *p*' unto the place of which
35 the Lord plagued the *p*', because
33: 1 the *p*' which thou hast brought up
3 for thou art a stiffnecked *p*': lest I
4 when the *p*' heard these evil tidings,
5 of Israel, Ye are a stiffnecked *p*':
8 all the *p*' rose up, and stood every
10 And all the *p*' saw the cloudy pillar
10 all the *p*' rose up and worshipped,
12 sayest unto me, Bring up this *p*':
13 consider that this nation is thy *p*'.
16 that I and thy *p*' have found grace
16 shall we be separated, I and thy *p*',
Ex 33: 16 from all the *p*' that are upon the
34: 9 among us; for it is a stiffnecked *p*';
10 before all thy *p*' I will do marvels,
10 all the *p*' among which thou art
36: 5 *p*' bring much more than enough
6 *p*' were restrained from bringing.
Le 4: 3 sin according to the sin of the *p*';
27 if any one of the common *p*' sin
7: 20, 21 soul shall be cut off from his *p*'.
25 eateth it shall be cut off from his *p*'.
27 that soul shall be cut off from his *p*'.
9: 7 for thyself, and for the *p*': and
7 and offer the offering of the *p*', and
15 which was the sin offering for the *p*',
18 offerings, which was for the *p*': and
22 lifted up his hand toward the *p*',
23 and came out, and blessed the *p*':
23 of the Lord appeared unto all the *p*'.
24 when all the *p*' saw, they shouted,
10: 3 before all the *p*' I will be glorified.
6 lest wrath come upon all the *p*':
16: 15 the sin offering, that is for the *p*',
24 and the burnt offering of the *p*',
24 atonement for himself, and...the *p*'.
33 for all the *p*' of the congregation.
17: 4 shall be cut off from among his *p*':
9 shall be cut off from among his *p*'.
10 will cut him off from among his *p*'.
18: 29 shall be cut off from among their *p*'.
19: 8 shall be cut off from among his *p*'.
16 down as a talebearer among thy *p*':
18 against the children of thy *p*', but
20: 2 the *p*' of the land shall stone him
3 will cut him off from among his *p*';
4 the *p*' of the land do any ways hide
5 with Molech, from among their *p*'.
6 will cut him off from among his *p*'.
17 cut off in the sight of their *p*': 1121.
18 shall be cut off from among their *p*'.
24 have separated you from other *p*'.
26 severed you from other *p*', that ye
21: 1 defiled for the dead among his *p*':
4 being a chief man among his *p*', to
14 take a virgin of his own *p*' to wife.
15 he profane his seed among his *p*':
23: 29 shall be cut off from among his *p*'.
30 will I destroy from among his *p*'.
26: 12 be your God, and ye shall be my *p*'.
Nu 5: 21 a curse and an oath among thy *p*',
27 shall be a curse among her *p*'.
9: 13 shall be cut off from among his *p*':
11: 1 And when the *p*' complained, it
2 the *p*' cried unto Moses; and when
8 the *p*' went about, and gathered it,
10 Then Moses heard the *p*' weep
11 the burden of all this *p*' upon me?
12 Have I conceived all this *p*'? have I
13 I have flesh to give unto all this *p*'?
14 am not able to bear all this *p*' alone,
16 knowest to be the elders of the *p*',
17 bear the burden of the *p*' with thee,
18 And say thou unto the *p*', Sanctify
21 The *p*', among whom I am, are six
24 told the *p*' the words of the Lord,
24 seventy men of the elders of the *p*',
29 that all the Lord's *p*' were prophets,
32 the *p*' stood up all that day, and all
33 the Lord was kindled against the *p*',
33 Lord smote the *p*' with a very great
34 there they buried the *p*' that lusted.
35 the *p*' journeyed...unto Hazeroth;
12: 15 *p*' journeyed not till Miriam was
16 the *p*' removed from Hazeroth, and
13: 18 *p*' that dwelleth therein, whether
28 *p*' be strong that dwell in the land,
30 Caleb stilled the *p*' before Moses,
31 be not able to go up against the *p*';
32 the *p*' that we saw in it are men of a
14: 1 cried; and the *p*' wept that night.
9 neither fear ye the *p*' of the land;
11 How long will this *p*' provoke me?
13 broughtest up this *p*' in thy might
14 that thou Lord art among this *p*',
15 shalt kill all this *p*' as one man,
16 Lord was not able to bring this *p*'
19 the iniquity of this *p*' according
19 and as thou hast forgiven this *p*',
39 Israel: and the *p*' mourned greatly.
15: 26 seeing all the *p*' were in ignorance.
30 shall be cut off from among his *p*'.
16: 41 Ye have killed the *p*' of the Lord.
47 plague was begun among the *p*':
47 and made an atonement for the *p*'.
20: 1 and the *p*' abode in Kadesh; and
3 And the *p*' chode with Moses, and
20 came out against him with much *p*',
24 Aaron shall be gathered unto his *p*':
26 Aaron shall be gathered unto his *p*'.
21: 2 If thou wilt indeed deliver this *p*'
4 of the *p*' was much discouraged
5 And the *p*' spake against God, and
6 sent fiery serpents among the *p*',
6 and they bit the *p*'; and much
6 and much *p*' of Israel died.
7 Therefore the *p*' came to Moses,
7 us. And Moses prayed for the *p*'.
16 Gather the *p*' together, and I will
18 the nobles of the *p*' digged it, by the
23 Sihon gathered all his *p*' together,
29 thou art undone, O *p*' of Chemosh:
33 out against them, he, and all his *p*',
34 him into thy hand, and all his *p*',
35 him, and his sons, and all his *p*',
22: 3 And Moab was sore afraid of the *p*',
5 of the land of the children of his *p*',
5 there is a *p*' come out from Egypt

Nu 22: 6 I pray thee, curse me this p'; for
11 there is a p' come out of Egypt,
12 them; thou shalt not curse the p':
17 I pray thee, curse me this p'.
41 might see the utmost part of the p'.
23: 9 the p' shall dwell alone, and shall
24 the p' shall rise up as a great lion,
24:14 And now, behold, I go unto my p':
14 I will advertise thee what this p'
14 shall do to thy p' in the latter days.
25: 1 p' began to commit whoredom with
2 called the p' unto the sacrifices of
2 p' did eat, and bowed down to their
4 Take all the heads of the p', and
15 he was head over a p', and of a
26: 4 Take the sum of the p', from twenty
27:13 also shalt be gathered unto thy p',
31: 2 shalt thou be gathered unto thy p'.
3 Moses spake unto the p', saying,
32:15 and ye shall destroy all this p'.
33:14 was no water for the p' to drink.
De 1:28 The p' is greater and taller than we;
2: 4 And command thou the p', saying,
10 a p' great, and many, and tall, as
16 and dead from among the p',
21 A p' great, and many, and tall, as
32 out against us, he and all his p',
33 him, and his sons, and all his p'.
3: 1 out against us, he and all his p',
2 I will deliver him, and all his p',
3 the king of Bashan, and all his p':
28 for he shall go over before this p',
4: 6 is a wise and understanding p'.
10 Gather me the p' together, and I
20 to be unto him a p' of inheritance,
33 Did ever p' hear the voice of God
5:28 the voice of the words of this p',
6:14 the gods of the p' which are round
7: 6 thou art an holy p' unto the Lord
6 to be a special p' unto himself,
6 above all p' that are upon the face
7 were more in number than any p';
7 for ye were the fewest of all p':
14 Thou shalt be blessed above all p':
16 thou shalt consume all the p' which
19 all the p' of whom thou art afraid.
9: 2 A p' great and tall, the children of
6 for thou art a stiffnecked p'.
12 for thy p' which thou hast brought
13 I have seen this p', and, behold, it
13 and, behold, it is a stiffnecked p':
26 not thy p' and thine inheritance,
27 unto the stubbornness of this p',
29 are thy p' and thine inheritance,
10:11 take thy journey before the p', that
15 even you above all p', as it is this
13: 7 of the gods of the p' which are
9 afterwards the hand of all the p'.
14: 2 thou art an holy p' unto the Lord
2 hath chosen thee to be a peculiar p'
21 thou art an holy p' unto the Lord
16:18 judge the p' with just judgment.
17: 7 afterward the hands of all the p'.
13 And all the p' shall hear, and fear,
16 cause the p' to return to Egypt,
18: 3 be the priest's due from the p',
20: 1 a p' more than thou, be not afraid
2 approach and speak unto the p',
5 the officers shall speak unto the p',
8 shall speak further unto the p', and
9 an end of speaking unto the p',
9 captains of the armies to lead the p'.
11 that all the p' that is found therein
16 of the cities of these p', which the
21: 8 merciful, O Lord, unto thy p' Israel,
8 lay not innocent blood unto thy p' of
26:15 from heaven, and bless thy p' Israel,
18 thee this day to be his peculiar p',
19 mayest be an holy p' unto the Lord
27: 1 elders of Israel commanded the p',
9 thou art become the p' of the Lord
11 Moses charged the p' the same day,
12 upon mount Gerizim to bless the p',
15 the p' shall answer and say, Amen.
16, 17, 18, 19, 20, 21, 22, 23, 24, 25, 26
And all the p' shall say, Amen.
28: 9 thee an holy p' unto himself, as he
10 all p' of the earth shall see that
32 shall be given unto another p', and
64 shall scatter thee among all p',
29:13 thee to day for a p' unto himself,
31: 7 must go with this p' unto the land
12 Gather the p' together, men, and
16 and this p' will rise up, and go a
32: 6 the Lord, O foolish p' and unwise?
8 set the bounds of the p' according
9 For the Lord's portion is his p';
21 with those which are not a p';
36 Lord shall judge his p', and repent
43 Rejoice, O ye nations, with his p':
43 unto his land, and to his p'.
44 of this song in the ears of the p',
50 up, and be gathered unto thy p'; as
50 Hor, and was gathered unto his p':
33: 3 Yea, he loved the p'; all his saints
5 the heads of the p' and the tribes of
7 Judah, and bring him unto his p':
17 he shall push the p' together to
19 shall call the p' unto the mountain:
21 he came with the heads of the p',
29 O p' saved by the Lord, the shield
Jos 1: 2 thou, and all this p', unto the land
6 unto this p' shalt thou divide for an
10 commanded the officers of the p',
11 the host, and command the p',
3: 3 they commanded the p', saying,
Jos 3: 5 Joshua said unto the p', Sanctify
6 and pass over before the p'. And
6 covenant, and went before the p'.
14 the p' removed from their tents, to
14 ark of the covenant before the p';
16 and the p' passed over right against
17 p' were passed clean over Jordan.
4: 1 p' were clean passed over Jordan,
2 Take you twelve men out of the p',
10 Joshua to speak unto the p',
10 and the p' hasted and passed over.
11 all the p' were clean passed over,
11 priests, in the presence of the p'.
19 And the p' came up out of Jordan
24 all the p' of the earth might know
5: 4 All the p' that came out of Egypt,
5 p' that came out were circumcised:
5 p' that were born in the wilderness
6 all the p' that were men of war,
8 had done circumcising all the p',
6: 5 p' shall shout with a great shout;
5 the p' shall ascend up every man
7 And he said unto the p', Pass on,
8 Joshua had spoken unto the p',
10 And Joshua had commanded the p',
16 Joshua said unto the p', Shout; for
20 p' shouted when the priests blew
20 p' heard the sound of the trumpet,
20 the p' shouted with a great shout,
20 so that the p' went up into the city,
7: 3 unto him, Let not all the p' go up;
3 not all the p' to labour thither;
4 went up thither of the p' about
5 the hearts of the p' melted, and
7 at all brought this p' over Jordan,
13 sanctify the p', and say, Sanctify
8: 1 take all the p' of war with thee,
1 the king of Ai, and his p', and his
3 Joshua arose, and all the p' of war,
5 p' that are with me, will approach
9 lodged that night among the p'.
10 and numbered the p', and went up,
10 elders of Israel, before the p' to Ai.
11 And all the p',...went up, and drew
11 even the p' of war that were with
13 when they had set the p', even all
14 to battle, he and all his p', at a
16 the p' that were in Ai were called
20 the p' that fled to the wilderness
33 they should bless the p' of Israel.
10: 7 he, and all the p' of war with him,
13 stayed, until the p' had avenged
21 p' returned to the camp to Joshua
33 and Joshua smote him and his p',
11: 4 all their hosts with them, much p'
7 came, and all the p' of war with him,
14: 8 made the heart of the p' melt: but
17:14 I am a great p', forasmuch as the
15 If thou be a great p', then get thee
17 Thou art a great p', and hast great
24: 2 Joshua said unto all the p', Thus
16 p' answered and said, God forbid
17 the p' through whom we passed:
18 drave out from before us all the p',
19 Joshua said unto the p', Ye cannot
21 p' said unto Joshua, Nay; but we
22 And Joshua said unto the p', Ye are
24 p' said unto Joshua, The Lord our
25 made a covenant with the p' that
27 Joshua said unto all the p', Behold,
28 Joshua let the p' depart, every man
J'g 1:16 they went and dwelt among the p'.
2: 4 p' lifted up their voice, and wept.
6 when Joshua had let the p' go, the
7 the p' served the Lord all the days
12 the gods of the p' that were round
20 p' hath transgressed my covenant
3:18 away the p' that bare the present.
4:13 and all the p' that were with him,
5: 2 the p' willingly offered themselves.
9 themselves willingly among the p'.
11 the p' of the Lord go down to the
13 over the nobles among the p': the
14 thee, Benjamin, among thy p';
18 were a p' that jeoparded their lives
7: 1 the p' that were with him, rose up
2 The p' that are with thee are too
3 go to, proclaim in the ears of the p',
3 of the p' twenty and two thousand;
4 Gideon, The p' are yet too many;
5 down the p' unto the water: and
6 the rest of the p' bowed down upon
7 the other p' go every man unto his
8 the p' took victuals in their hand,
8: 5 of bread unto the p' that follow me;
9:29 to God this p' were under my hand!
32 thou and the p' that is with thee,
33 when he and the p' that is with him
34 the p' that were with him, by night,
35 up, and the p' that were with him,
36 And when Gaal saw the p', he said
36 there come p' down from the top of
37 come p' down by the middle of the
38 this the p' that thou hast despised?
42 that the p' went out into the field;
43 took the p', and divided them into
43 p' were come forth out of the city;
44 ran upon all the p'...in the fields,
45 he took the city, and slew the p'
48 and all the p' that were with him;
48 said unto the p' that were with him,
49 all the p' likewise cut down every
10:18 the p' and princes of Gilead said
11:11 the p' made him head and captain
20 Sihon gathered all his p' together,
21 and all his p' into the hand of Israel,
J'g 11:23 Amorites from before his p' Israel,
12: 2 I and my p' were at great strife with
14: 3 never a woman...among all my p',
16 a riddle unto the children of my p',
17 the riddle to the children of her p'.
16:24 when the p' saw him, they praised
30 upon the lords, and upon all the p'
18: 7 came to Laish, and saw the p'
10 ye shall come unto a p' secure, and
20 and went in the midst of the p'.
27 Laish, unto a p' that were at quiet
20: 2 the chief of all the p', even all the
2 in the assembly of the p' of God,
8 all the p' arose as one man, saying,
10 to fetch victual for the p', that they
16 Among all this p' there were seven
22 the p' the men of Israel encouraged
26 all the p', went up, and came unto
31 Benjamin went out against the p',
31 they began to smite of the p', and
21: 2 the p' came to the house of God, and
4 the morrow, that the p' rose early,
9 the p' were numbered, and, behold,
15 the p' repented them for Benjamin,
Ru 1: 6 the Lord had visited his p' in giving
10 we will return with thee unto thy p'.
15 sister in law is gone...unto her p',
16 thy p' shall be my p', and thy God
2:11 unto a p' which thou knewest not
3:11 all the city of my p' doth know that
4: 4 and before the elders of my p'. If
9 unto the elders, and unto all the p',
11 all the p' that were in the gate, and
1Sa 2:13 the priest's custom with the p' was,
23 of your evil dealings by all this p'.
24 ye make the Lord's p' to transgress.
29 of all the offerings of Israel my p'?
4: 3 the p' were come into the camp,
4 So the p' sent to Shiloh, that they
17 also a great slaughter among the p',
5:10 of Israel to us, to slay us and our p'.
11 that it slay us not, and our p': for
6: 6 did they not let the p' go, and they
19 he smote of the p' fifty thousand
19 the p' lamented, because the Lord
19 Lord had smitten many of the p'
8: 7 Hearken unto the voice of the p'
10 the words of the Lord unto the p'
19 the p' refused to obey the voice of
21 Samuel heard all the words of the p',
9: 2 he was higher than any of the p'.
12 there is a sacrifice of the p' to day
13 for the p' will not eat until he come,
16 him to be captain over my p' Israel,
16 save my p' out of the hand of the
16 I have looked upon my p', because
17 this same shall reign over my p'.
24 since I said, I have invited the p'.
10:11 the p' said one to another, What is
17 And Samuel called the p' together
23 when he stood among the p', he was
23 higher than any of the p' from his
24 Samuel said to all the p', See ye him
24 is none like him among all the p'?
24 the p' shouted, and said, God save
25 Samuel told the p' the manner of the
25 Samuel sent all the p' away, every
11: 4 the tidings in the ears of the p':
4 all the p' lifted up their voices, and
5 What aileth the p' that they weep?
7 the fear of the Lord fell on the p',
11 put the p' in three companies; and
12 the p' said unto Samuel, Who is he
14 said Samuel to the p', Come, and let
15 all the p' went to Gilgal; and there
12: 6 Samuel said unto the p', It is the
18 all the p' greatly feared the Lord
19 all the p' said unto Samuel, Pray
20 Samuel said unto the p', Fear not:
22 the Lord will not forsake his p' for
22 pleased the Lord to make you his p'.
13: 2 the rest of the p' he sent every man
4 p' were called together after Saul
5 p' as the sand which is on the sea
6 a strait, (for the p' were distressed,)
6 the p' did hide themselves in caves,
7 all the p' followed him trembling.
8 and the p' were scattered from him.
11 that the p' were scattered from me,
14 him to be captain over his p',
15 numbered the p' that were present
16 the p' that were present with them,
22 found in the hand of any of the p'
14: 2 the p' that were with him were
3 the p' knew not that Jonathan was
15 in the field, and among all the p':
17 said Saul unto the p' that were with
20 Saul and all the p' that were with
24 for Saul had adjured the p', saying,
24 so none of the p' tasted any food.
26 the p' were come into the wood,
26 mouth: for the p' feared the oath.
27 father charged the p' with the oath:
28 Then answered one of the p', and
28 and straitly charged the p' with an oath,
28 this day. And the p' were faint.
30 haply the p' had eaten freely to day
31 Aijalon: and the p' were very faint.
32 the p' flew upon the spoil, and took
32 the p' did eat them with the blood.
33 Behold, the p' sin against the Lord,
34 Disperse yourselves among the p',
34 all the p' brought every man his ox
38 near hither, all the chief of the p':
39 was not a man among all the p' that
40 p' said unto Saul, Do what seemeth

1Sa 14:41 were taken: but the p' escaped.
45 p' said unto Saul, Shall Jonathan
45 p' rescued Jonathan, that he died
15: 1 anoint thee to be king over his p',
4 Saul gathered the p' together, and
8 utterly destroyed all the p' with
9 Saul and the p' spared Agag, and
15 the p' spared the best of the sheep
21 the p' took of the spoil, sheep and
24 because I feared the p', and obeyed
30 thee, before the elders of my p',
17:27 p' answered him after this manner,
30 the p' answered him again after the
18: 5 accepted in the sight of all the p',
13 went out and came in before the p'.
23: 8 Saul called all the p' together to
26: 5 the p' pitched round about him.
7 Abishai came to the p' by night:
7 Abner and the p' lay...about him.
14 David cried to the p', and to Abner
15 came one of the p' in to destroy the
27:12 his p' Israel utterly to abhor him;
30: 4 David...the p' that were with him
6 for the p' spake of stoning him,
6 soul of all the p' was grieved, every
21 to meet the p' that were with him:
21 when David came near to the p', he
31: 9 of their idols, and among the p'.
2Sa 1: 4 that the p' are fled from the battle,
4 many of the p' also are fallen and
12 his son, and for the p' of the Lord,
2:26 bid the p' return from following
27 in the morning the p' had gone up,
28 a trumpet, and all the p' stood still,
30 he had gathered all the p' together,
3:18 I will save my p' Israel out of the
31 David said to Joab, and to all the p'
32 grave of Abner; and all the p' wept.
34 And all the p' wept again over him.
35 the p' came to cause David to eat
36 all the p' took notice of it, and it
36 the king did pleased all the p'.
37 all the p' and all Israel understood
5: 2 Thou shalt feed my p' Israel, and
12 kingdom for his p' Israel's sake.
6: 2 David arose,...went with all the p'
18 he blessed the p' in the name of the
19 And he dealt among all the p', even
19 p' departed every one to his house.
21 me ruler over the p' of the Lord,
7: 7 I commanded to feed my p' Israel,
8 to be ruler over my p', over Israel:
10 appoint a place for my p' Israel,
11 judges to be over my p' Israel, and
23 nation in the earth is like thy p',
23 whom God went to redeem for a p'
23 for thy land, before thy p', which
24 confirmed to thyself thy p' Israel
24 Israel to be a p' unto thee for ever:
8:15 judgment and justice unto all his p'.
10:10 the rest of the p' he delivered into
12 and let us play the men for our p',
13 and the p' that were with him,
11: 7 how Joab did, and how the p' did,
17 and there fell some of the p' of the
12:28 gather the rest of the p' together,
29 David gathered all the p' together,
31 he brought forth the p' that were
31 David and all the p' returned unto
13:34 there came much p' by the way of
14:13 such a thing against the p' of God?
15 because the p' have made me afraid:
15:12 for the p' increased continually
17 went forth, and all the p' after him,
23 and all the p' passed over: the king
23 all the p' passed over, toward the
24 until all the p' had done passing
30 all the p' that was with him covered
16: 6 all the p' and all the mighty men
14 and all the p' that were with him,
15 Absalom, and all the p' the men of
18 this p', and all the men of Israel,
17: 2 the p' that are with him shall flee;
3 will bring back all the p' unto thee:
3 so all the p' shall be in peace.
8 war, and will not lodge with the p'.
9 There is a slaughter among the p'
16 and all the p' that are with him.
22 and all the p' that were with him,
29 and for the p' that were with him,
29 The p' is hungry, and weary, and
18: 1 David numbered the p' that were
2 sent forth a third part of the p'
2 And the king said unto the p', I will
3 the p' answered, Thou shalt not go
4 all the p' came out by hundreds
5 all the p' heard when the king gave
6 p' went out into the field against
7 Where the p' of Israel were slain
8 wood devoured more p' that day
16 and the p' returned from pursuing
16 Israel: for Joab held back the p'.
19: 2 into mourning unto all the p':
2 p' heard say that day how the king
3 the p' gat them by stealth that day
3 p' being ashamed steal away when
8 they told unto all the p', saying,
8 And all the p' came before the king:
9 all the p' were at strife throughout
39 And all the p' went over Jordan.
40 the p' of Judah conducted the king,
40 king, and also half the p' of Israel.
20:12 man saw that all the p' stood still,
13 the p' went on after Joab, to pursue
15 p' that were with Joab battered
22 the woman went unto all the p' in

2Sa 22:28 And the afflicted p' thou wilt save:
44 from the strivings of my p', thou
44 p' which I knew not shall serve me
48 bringeth down the p' under me,
23:10 p' returned after him only to spoil.
11 and the p' fled from the Philistines.
24: 2 Beer-sheba, and number ye the p',
2 I may know the number of the p'.
3 the Lord thy God add unto the p',
4 king, to number the p' of Israel.
9 up the sum of the number of the p'
10 after that he had numbered the p'.
15 there died of the p' from Dan even
16 to the angel that destroyed the p',
17 he saw the angel that smote the p',
21 plague may be stayed from the p'.
1Ki 1:39 the p' said, God save king Solomon.
40 And all the p' came up after him,
40 the p' piped with pipes, and rejoiced
3: 2 the p' sacrificed in high places,
8 thy servant is in the midst of thy p'
8 which thou hast chosen, a great p',
9 understanding heart to judge thy p',
9 able to judge this thy so great a p'?
4:34 And there came of all p' to hear the
5: 7 David a wise son over this great p'.
16 ruled over the p' that wrought in
6:13 and will not forsake my p' Israel.
8:16 that I brought forth my p' Israel
16 chose David to be over my p' Israel.
30 thy servant, and of thy p' Israel,
33 When thy p' Israel be smitten down
34 and forgive the sin of thy p' Israel,
36 of thy servants, and of thy p' Israel,
36 land, which thou hast given to thy p'
38 by any man, or by all thy p' Israel,
41 stranger, that is not of thy p' Israel,
43 p' of the earth may know thy name,
43 to fear thee, as do thy p' Israel;
44 If thy p' go out to battle against
50 And forgive thy p' that have sinned
51 be thy p', and thine inheritance,
52 the supplication of thy p' Israel,
53 from among all the p' of the earth,
56 hath given rest unto his p' Israel,
59 cause of his p' Israel at all times,
60 all the p' of the earth may know,
66 the eighth day he sent the p' away:
66 his servant, and for Israel his p'.
9: 7 proverb and a byword among all p':
20 p' that were left of the Amorites,
23 bare rule over the p' that wrought
12: 5 again to me. And the p' departed.
6 advise that I may answer this p'?
7 thou wilt be a servant unto this p'
9 give ye that we may answer this p',
10 Thus shalt thou speak unto this p'
12 and all the p' came to Rehoboam
13 the king answered the p' roughly,
15 the king hearkened not unto the p';
16 the p' answered the king, saying,
23 to the remnant of the p', saying,
27 If this p' go up to do sacrifice in
27 then shall the heart of this p' turn
30 the p' went to worship before the
31 made priests of the lowest of the p',
13:33 made again of the lowest of the p'
14: 2 that I should be king over this p'.
7 I exalted thee from among the p',
7 made thee prince over my p' Israel,
16: 2 made thee prince over my p' Israel;
2 and hast made my p' Israel to sin,
15 And the p' were encamped against
16 p' that were encamped heard say,
21 p' of Israel divided into two parts:
21 half of the p' followed Tibni the son
22 the p' that followed Omri prevailed
22 against the p' that followed Tibni
18:21 Elijah came unto all the p', and
21 the p' answered him not a word.
22 Then said Elijah unto the p', I,
24 the p' answered and said, It is well
30 Elijah said unto all the p', Come
30 And all the p' came near unto him.
37 that this p' may know that thou art
39 when all the p' saw it, they fell on
19:21 gave unto the p', and they did eat.
20: 8 all the p' said unto him, Hearken
10 for all the p' that follow me.
15 after them he numbered all the p',
42 go for his life, and thy p' for his p'.
21: 9 set Naboth on high among the p':
12 set Naboth on high among the p'.
13 Naboth, in the presence of the p',
22: 4 I am as thou art, my p' as thy p',
28 Hearken, O p', every one of you.
43 for the p' offered and burnt incense
2Ki 3: 7 I am as thou art, my p' as thy p',
4:13 I dwell among mine own p'.
41 Pour out for the p', that they may
42 Give unto the p', that they may eat.
43 Give the p', that they may eat: for
6:18 Smite this p', I pray thee, with
30 the p' looked, and, behold, he had
7:16 the p' went out, and spoiled the
17, 20 p' trode upon him in the gate,
8:21 and the p' fled into their tents.
9: 6 have anointed thee king over the p'
10: 9 said to all the p', Ye be righteous:
18 Jehu gathered all the p' together,
11:13 the noise of the guard and of the p',
13 came to the p' into the temple of
14 and all the p' of the land rejoiced,
17 Lord and the king and the p', that
17 that they should be the Lord's p';
17 between the king also and the p'.

2Ki 11:18 all the p' of the land went into the
19 guard, and all the p' of the land;
20 And all the p' of the land rejoiced,
12: 3 p' still sacrificed and burnt incense
8 to receive no more money of the p',
13: 7 did he leave of the p' to Jehoahaz
14: 4 p' did sacrifice and burnt incense
21 all the p' of Judah took Azariah,
15: 4 the p' sacrificed and burnt incense
5 house, judging the p' of the land.
10 smote him before the p', and slew
35 p' sacrificed and burned incense
16: 9 and carried the p' of it captive to Kir,
15 offering of all the p' of the land,
18:26 ears of the p' that are on the wall.
36 But the p' held their peace, and
20: 5 tell Hezekiah the captain of my p',
21:24 the p' of the land slew all them that
24 p' of the land made Josiah his son
22: 4 keepers...have gathered of the p':
13 and for the p', and for all Judah,
23: 2 and all the p', both small and great:
3 And all the p' stood to the covenant.
6 the graves of the children of the p'.
21 And the king commanded all the p',
30 the p' of the land took Jehoahaz
35 and the gold of the p' of the land,
24:14 the poorest sort of the p' of the land.
25: 3 was no bread for the p' of the land.
11 Now the rest of the p' that were left
19 which mustered the p' of the land,
19 threescore men of the p' of the land
22 for the p' that remained in the land
26 And all the p', both small and great,
1Ch 5:25 after the gods of the p' of the land,
10: 9 unto their idols, and to the p'.
11: 2 Thou shalt feed my p' Israel, and
2 shalt be ruler over my p' Israel.
13 p' fled from before the Philistines.
13: 4 was right in the eyes of all the p'.
14: 2 up on high, because of his p' Israel.
16: 2 blessed the p' in the name of the
8 known his deeds among the p'.
20 from one kingdom to another p';
26 For all the gods of the p' are idols:
28 ye kindreds of the p', give unto the
36 p' said, Amen, and praised the Lord.
43 p' departed every man to his house:
17: 6 whom I commanded to feed my p',
7 shouldest be ruler over my p' Israel:
9 will ordain a place for my p' Israel,
10 commanded judges to be over my p'
21 in the earth is like thy p' Israel,
21 went to redeem to be his own p',
21 driving out nations...before thy p',
22 thy p' Israel didst thou make thine
22 thou make thine own p' for ever;
18:14 judgment and justice among...his p'.
19: 7 the king of Maachah and his p';
11 the rest of the p' he delivered unto
13 let us behave...valiantly for our p',
14 Joab and the p' that were with him
20: 3 brought out the p' that were in it,
3 all the p' returned to Jerusalem.
21: 2 to Joab and to the rulers of the p',
3 Lord make his p' an hundred times
5 gave the sum of the number of the p'
17 commanded the p' to be numbered?
17 but not on thy p', that they should
22 plague may be stayed from the p'.
22:18 before the Lord, and before his p'.
23:25 of Israel hath given rest unto his p',
28: 2 Hear me, my brethren, and my p':
21 princes and all the p' will be wholly
29: 9 Then the p' rejoiced, for that they
14 But who am I, and what is my p',
17 and now have I seen with joy thy p',
18 the thoughts of the heart of thy p',
2Ch 1: 9 king over a p' like the dust of the
10 go out and come in before this p':
10 who can judge this thy p', that is so
11 that thou mayest judge my p', over
2:11 Because the Lord hath loved his p',
18 overseers to set the p' a work.
6: 5 forth my p' out of the land of Egypt
5 man to be a ruler over my p' Israel:
6 have chosen David to be over my p'
21 of thy servant, and of thy p' Israel,
24 if thy p' Israel be put to the worse
25 and forgive the sin of thy p' Israel,
27 the sin of thy servants, and of thy p'
27 given unto thy p' for an inheritance.
29 of any man, or of all thy p' Israel,
32 which is not of thy p' Israel, but is
33 that all p' of the earth may know
33 and fear thee, as doth thy p' Israel,
34 If thy p' go out to war against their
39 forgive thy p' which have sinned
7: 4 Then the king and all the p' offered
5 the king and all the p' dedicated
10 he sent the p' away unto their tents,
10 and to Solomon, and to Israel his p'.
13 if I send pestilence among my p';
14 If my p', which are called by my
8: 7 the p' that were left of the Hittites,
10 and fifty, that bare rule over the p'.
10: 5 three days. And the p' departed.
6 ye me to return answer to this p'?
7 If thou be kind to this p', and please
9 we may return answer to this p',
10 Thus shalt thou answer the p' that
12 So Jeroboam and all the p' came to
15 the king hearkened not unto the p':
16 the p' answered the king, saying,
12: 3 p' were without number that came
13:17 And Abijah and his p' slew them

2Ch 14: 13 Asa and the p' that were with him
16: 10 And Asa oppressed some of the p'
17: 9 cities of Judah, and taught the p'.
18: 2 and for the p' that he had with him,
3 am as thou art, and my p' as thy p';
27 And he said, Hearken, all ye p'.
19: 4 he went out again through the p'
20: 7 of this land before thy p' Israel,
21 when he had consulted with the p',
25 Jehoshaphat and his p' came to take
33 the p' had not prepared their hearts
21: 14 plague will the Lord smite thy p',
19 And his p' made no burning for him,
23: 5 all the p' shall be in the courts of
6 the p' shall keep the watch of the
10 he set all the p', every man having
12 Athaliah heard the noise of the p'
12 she came to the p' into the house
13 and all the p' of the land rejoiced,
16 between him, and between all the p',
16 that they should be the Lord's p'.
17 all the p' went to the house of Baal,
20 nobles, and the governors of the p',
20 and all the p' of the land, and
21 And all the p' of the land rejoiced:
24: 10 the princes and all the p' rejoiced,
20 priest, which stood above the p',
23 destroyed all the princes of the p'
23 the princes...from among the p',
25: 11 And Amaziah...led forth his p', and
15 thou sought after the gods of the p',
15 which could not deliver their own p'
26: 1 all the p' of Judah took Uzziah,
21 house, judging the p' of the land.
27: 2 And the p' did yet corruptly.
29: 36 Hezekiah rejoiced, and all the p',
36 that God had prepared the p': for
30: 3 neither had the p' gathered
13 assembled at Jerusalem much p'
18 a multitude of the p', even many of
20 to Hezekiah, and healed the p'.
27 Levites arose and blessed the p':
31: 4 he commanded the p' that dwelt in
8 blessed the Lord, and his p' Israel.
10 the p' began to bring the offerings
10 for the Lord hath blessed his p';
32: 4 was gathered much p' together
6 he set captains of war over the p',
8 And the p' rested themselves upon
13 done unto all the p' of other lands?
14 that could deliver his p' out of mine
15 able to deliver his p' out of mine
17 not delivered their p' out of mine
17 the God of Hezekiah deliver his p'
18 unto the p' of Jerusalem that were
19 the gods of the p' of the earth,
33: 10 spake to Manasseh, and to his p':
17 the p' did sacrifice still in the high
25 the p' of the land slew all them that
25 p' of the land made Josiah his son
34: 30 and all the p', great and small:
35: 3 Lord your God, and his p' Israel,
5 families of your brethren the p',
7 And Josiah gave to the p', of
8 princes gave willingly unto the p',
12 of the families of the p', to
13 them speedily among all the p.
36: 1 the p' of the land took Jehoahaz the
14 priests, and the p', transgressed
15 because he had compassion on his p',
16 of the Lord arose against his p',
23 is there among you of all his p'?
Ezr 1: 3 is there among you of all his p'?
2: 2 of the men of the p' of Israel:
70 and the Levites, and some of the p',
3: 1 p' gathered themselves together
3 because of the p' of those countries:
11 the p' shouted with a great shout,
13 the p' could not discern the noise
13 the noise of the weeping of the p':
13 for the p' shouted with a loud shout,
4: 4 p' of the land weakened the hands
4 the hands of the p' of Judah, and
5: 12 carried the p' away into Babylon.
6: 12 dwell there destroy all kings and p',
7: 13 that all they of the p' of Israel, and
16 with the freewill offering of the p',
25 may judge all the p' that are beyond
8: 15 I viewed the p', and the priests,
36 they furthered the p', and the house
9: 1 The p' of Israel, and the priests,
1 separated...from...p' of the lands,
2 mingled with...p' of those lands:
11 the filthiness of the p' of the lands,
14 with the p' of these abominations?
10: 1 children: for the p' wept very sore.
2 strange wives of the p' of the land:
9 p' sat in the street of the house of
11 separate...from the p' of the land,
13 But the p' are many, and it is a time
Ne 1: 10 these are thy servants and thy p',
4: 6 for the p' had a mind to work.
13 I even set the p' after their families
14, 19 rulers, and to the rest of the p',
22 at the same time said I unto the p',
5: 1 And there was a great cry of the p'
13 the p' did according to this promise.
15 me were chargeable unto the p',
15 their servants bare rule over the p':
18 the bondage was heavy upon this p'.
19 to all that I have done for this p'.
7: 4 but the p' were few therein, and the
5 nobles, and the rulers, and the p',
7 number,...of...men of the p' of Israel
72 that which the rest of the p' gave
73 and the singers, and some of the p',

Ne 8: 1 p' gathered themselves together
3 ears of all the p' were attentive
5 the book in the sight of all the p';
5 (for he was above all the p';) when
5 he opened it, all the p' stood up:
6 And all the p' answered, Amen,
7 caused the p' to understand the law:
7 law: and the p' stood in their place.
9 and the Levites that taught the p',
9 said unto all the p', This day is holy
9 For all the p' wept, when they heard
11 So the Levites stilled all the p',
12 all the p' went their way to eat, and
13 the chief of the fathers of all the p',
16 So the p' went forth, and brought
9: 10 and on all the p' of his land:
24 their kings, and the p' of the land,
30 into the hand of the p' of the lands.
32 on our fathers, and on all thy p',
10: 14 The chief of the p'; Parosh,
28 And the rest of the p', the priests,
28 separated...from the p' of the lands
30 daughters unto the p' of the land,
31 And if the p' of the land bring ware
34 the priests, the Levites, and the p',
11: 1 rulers of the p' dwelt at Jerusalem:
1 the rest of the p' also cast lots, to
2 And the p' blessed all the men, that
24 in all matters concerning the p'.
12: 30 purified themselves, and...the p',
38 and the half of the p' upon the wall,
13: 1 of Moses in the audience of the p';
24 according to the language of each p'.
Es 1: 5 the king made a feast unto all the p'
11 shew...p' and...princes her beauty:
16 the p' that are in all the provinces
22 and to every p' after their language,
22 to the language of every p'.
2: 10 Esther had not shewed her p' nor
20 yet shewed her kindred nor her p';
3: 6 had shewed him the p' of Mordecai:
6 Ahasuerus, even the p' of Mordecai.
8 is a certain p' scattered abroad and
8 among the p' in all the provinces
8 their laws are diverse from all p';
11 silver is given to thee, the p' also,
12 to the rulers of every p' of every
12 to every p' after their language;
14 province was published unto all p',
4: 8 make request before him for her p'.
11 p' of the king's provinces, do know,
7: 3 petition, and my p' at my request:
4 For we are sold, I and my p', to be
8: 6 the evil that shall come unto my p'?
9 unto every p' after their language,
11 all the power of the p' and province
13 province was published unto all p'.
17 of the p' of the land became Jews;
9: 2 for the fear of them fell upon all p'.
10: 3 seeking the wealth of his p', and
Job 12: 2 No doubt but ye are the p', and
24 of the chief of the p' of the earth,
17: 6 made me also a byword of the p';
18: 19 have son nor nephew among his p',
34: 20 the p' shall be troubled at midnight,
30 reign not, lest the p' be ensnared.
36: 20 when p' are cut off in their place.
31 For by them judgeth he the p'; he
Ps 2: 1 and the p' imagine a vain thing?
3: 6 be afraid of ten thousands of p',
8 Lord: thy blessing is upon thy p'.
7: 7 congregation of the p' compass
8 The Lord shall judge the p':
9: 8 shall minister judgment to the p'
11 declare among the p' his doings.
14: 4 who eat up my p' as they eat bread,
7 back the captivity of his p', Jacob
18: 27 For thou wilt save the afflicted p';
43 me from the strivings of the p';
43 a p' whom I have not known shall
47 me, and subdueth the p' under me.
22: 6 of men, and despised of the p'.
31 righteousness unto a p' that shall
28: 9 Save thy p', and bless thine
29: 11 Lord will give strength unto his p';
11 Lord will bless his p' with peace.
33: 10 the devices of the p' of none effect.
12 p' whom he hath chosen for his own
35: 18 I will praise thee among much p'.
44: 2 thou didst afflict the p', and cast
12 Thou sellest thy p' for nought, and
14 shaking of the head among the p'.
45: 5 whereby the p' fall under thee.
10 forget also thine own p', and thy
12 the rich among the p' shall intreat
17 shall the p' praise thee for ever and
47: 1 O clap your hands, all ye p'; shout;
3 He shall subdue the p' under us,
9 The princes of the p' are gathered
9 even the p' of the God of Abraham:
49: 1 Hear this, all ye p'; give ear, all
50: 4 the earth, that he may judge his p'.
7 Hear, O my p', and I will speak;
53: 4 who eat up my p' as they eat bread:
6 back the captivity of his p', Jacob
56: 7 in thine anger cast down the p',
57: 9 praise thee, O Lord, among the p':
59: 11 Slay them not, lest my p' forget:
60: 3 hast shewed thy p' hard things:
62: 8 ye p', pour out your heart before
65: 7 waves, and the tumult of the p'.
66: 8 O bless our God, ye p', and make
67: 3 Let the p' praise thee, O God; let
3 O God; let all the p' praise thee.
4 thou shalt judge the p' righteously,
5 Let the p' praise thee, O God; let

Ps 67: 5 O God; let all the p' praise thee.
68: 7 thou wentest forth before thy p',
22 bring my p' again from the depths of
30 the bulls, with the calves of the p',
30 thou the p' that delight in war.
35 strength and power unto his p'.
72: 2 judge thy p' with righteousness,
3 shall bring peace to the p', and the
4 He shall judge the poor of the p',
73: 10 Therefore his p' return hither: and
74: 14 and gavest him to be meat to the p'
18 the foolish p' have blasphemed thy
77: 14 declared thy strength among the p'.
15 with thine arm redeemed thy p',
20 Thou leddest thy p' like a flock by
78: 1 Give ear, O my p', to my law:
20 also? can he provide flesh for his p'?
52 his own p' to go forth like sheep,
62 gave his p' over also unto the sword;
71 brought him to feed Jacob his p',
79: 13 we thy p' and sheep of thy pasture
80: 4 angry against the prayer of thy p'?
81: 8 O my p', and I will testify unto thee:
11 p' would not hearken to my voice;
13 Oh that my p' had hearkened unto
83: 3 taken crafty counsel against thy p',
85: 2 hast forgiven the iniquity of thy p',
6 that thy p' may rejoice in thee?
8 for he will speak peace unto his p',
87: 6 count when he writeth up the p',
89: 15 the p' that know the joyful sound:
19 exalted one chosen out of the p'.
50 the reproach of all the mighty p';
94: 5 They break in pieces thy p', O
8 ye brutish among the p': and ye
14 For the Lord will not cast off his p',
95: 7 we are the p' of his pasture, and
10 It is a p' that do err in their heart,
96: 3 heathen, his wonders among all p'.
7 O ye kindreds of the p', give unto
10 he shall judge the p' righteously.
13 and the p' with his truth.
97: 6 and all the p' see his glory.
98: 9 the world, and the p' with equity.
99: 1 Lord reigneth; let the p' tremble:
2 and he is high above all the p'.
100: 3 we are his p', and the sheep of his
102: 18 the p' which shall be created shall
22 When the p' are gathered together,
105: 1 known his deeds among the p'.
13 from one kingdom to another p';
20 even the ruler of the p', and let
24 he increased his p' greatly; and
25 He turned their heart to hate his p',
40 The p' asked, and he brought quails,
43 he brought forth his p' with joy,
44 they inherited the labour of the p';
106: 4 that thou bearest unto thy p':
40 of the Lord kindled against his p',
48 let all the p' say, Amen. Praise ye
107: 32 also in the congregation of the p',
108: 3 praise thee, O Lord, among the p':
110: 3 Thy p' shall be willing in the day
111: 6 He hath shewed his p' the power of
9 He sent redemption unto his p': he
113: 8 even with the princes of his p'.
114: 1 from a p' of strange language;
116: 14 now in the presence of all his p',
18 now in the presence of all his p',
117: 1 ye nations: praise him, all ye p'.
125: 2 so the Lord is round about his p'
135: 12 an heritage unto Israel his p'.
14 the Lord will judge his p', and he
136: 16 led his p' through the wilderness:
144: 2 who subdueth my p' under me.
15 Happy is that p', that is in such a
15 happy is that p', whose God is the
148: 11 Kings of the earth, and all p';
14 also exalteth the horn of his p',
14 of Israel, a p' near unto him.
149: 4 the Lord taketh pleasure in his p':
7 and punishments upon the p';
Pr 11: 14 Where no counsel is, the p' fall:
26 corn, the p' shall curse him: but
14: 28 of p' is the king's honour: but in
28 the want of p' is the destruction
34 but sin is a reproach to any p'.
24: 24 him shall the p' curse, nations
28: 15 is a wicked ruler over the poor p'.
29: 2 are in authority, the p' rejoice: but
2 wicked beareth rule, the p' mourn.
18 there is no vision, the p' perish:
30: 25 The ants are a p' not strong, yet
Ec 4: 16 There is no end of all the p', even
12: 9 he still taught the p' knowledge;
Isa 1: 3 not know, my p' doth not consider.
4 nation, a p' laden with iniquity,
10 law of our God, ye p' of Gomorrah.
2: 3 many p' shall go and say, Come
4 nations, and shall rebuke many p':
6 Therefore thou hast forsaken thy p'
3: 5 And the p' shall be oppressed, every
7 make me not a ruler of the p'.
12 As for my p', children are their
12 O my p', they which lead thee cause
13 plead, and standeth to judge the p'.
14 judgment with the ancients of his p',
15 What mean ye that ye beat my p'
5: 13 my p' are gone into captivity,
25 of the Lord kindled against his p',
6: 5 the midst of a p' of unclean lips:
9 Go, and tell this p', Hear ye indeed,
10 Make the heart of this p' fat, and
7: 2 heart of his p', as the trees of the
8 be broken, that it be not a p'.
17 bring upon thee, and upon thy p',

Isa 8: 6 p' refuseth the waters of Shiloah
9 Associate yourselves, O ye p', and
11 should not walk in the way of this p',
12 all them to whom this p' shall say,
19 should not a p' seek unto their God?
9: 2 The p' that walked in darkness have
9 the p' shall know, even Ephraim
13 the p' turneth not unto him that
16 the leaders of this p' cause them to
19 p' shall be as the fuel of the fire:
10: 2 the right from the poor of my p',
6 against the p' of my wrath will I
13 have removed the bounds of the p',
14 as a nest the riches of the p':
22 though thy p' Israel be as the sand
24 O my p' that dwellest in Zion, be
11: 10 shall stand for an ensign of the p';
11 to recover the remnant of his p',
16 highway for the remnant of his p',
12: 4 declare his doings among the p',
13: 4 The noise...like as of a great p';
14 shall every man turn to his own p',
14: 2 the p' shall take them, and bring
6 He who smote the p' in wrath with
20 destroyed thy land, and slain thy p':
32 the poor of his p' shall trust in it.
17: 12 Woe to the multitude of many p',
18: 2 to a p' terrible from their beginning
7 hosts of a p' scattered and peeled,
7 a p' terrible from their beginning
19: 25 saying, Blessed be Egypt my p',
22: 4 spoiling of the daughter of my p'.
23: 13 this p' was not, till the Assyrian
24: 2 as with the p', so with the priest;
4 haughty p' of the earth do languish.
13 the midst of the land among the p',
25: 3 shall the strong p' glorify thee, the
6 make unto...p' a feast of fat things,
7 of the covering cast over all p',
8 rebuke of his p' shall he take away
26: 11 be ashamed for their envy at the p';
20 p', enter thou into thy chambers,
27: 11 for it is a p' of no understanding:
28: 5 beauty, unto the residue of his p',
11 tongue will he speak to this p'.
14 rule this p' which is in Jerusalem.
29: 13 p' draw near me with their mouth,
14 a marvellous work among this p',
30: 5 all ashamed of a p' that could not
6 to a p' that shall not profit them.
9 That this is a rebellious p', lying
19 For the p' shall dwell in Zion at
26 bindeth up the breach of his p', and
28 bridle in the jaws of the p', causing
32: 13 Upon the land of my p' shall come
18 my p' shall dwell in a peaceable
33: 3 the noise of the tumult the p' fled;
12 p' shall be as the burnings of lime:
19 Thou shalt not see a fierce p',
19 a p' of a deeper speech than thou
24 the p' that dwell therein shall be
34: 1 hearken, ye p': let the earth hear,
5 and upon the p' of my curse, to
36: 11 ears of the p' that are on the wall.
40: 1 comfort ye my p', saith your God.
7 upon it: surely the p' is grass.
41: 1 let the p' renew their strength:
42: 5 he that giveth breath unto the p'
6 give thee for a covenant of the p',
22 But this is a p' robbed and spoiled;
43: 4 men for thee, and p' for thy life.
8 Bring...the blind p' that have eyes.
9 and let the p' be assembled: who
20 the desert, to give drink to my p',
21 This p' have I formed for myself;
44: 7 since I appointed the ancient p'?
47: 6 I was wroth with my p', I have
49: 1 hearken, ye p', from far; The Lord
8 give thee for a covenant of the p',
13 for the Lord hath comforted his p',
22 and set up my standard to the p':
51: 4 Hearken unto me, my p'; and give
4 to rest for a light of the p'.
5 and mine arms shall judge the p';
7 the p' in whose heart is my law;
16 and say unto Zion, Thou art my p'.
22 that pleadeth the cause of his p',
52: 4 My p' went down aforetime into
5 my p' is taken away for nought?
6 my p' shall know my name:
9 for the Lord hath comforted his p',
53: 8 for the transgression of my p' was
55: 4 given him for a witness to the p',
4 leader and commander to the p'.
56: 3 utterly separated me from his p':
7 called an house of prayer for all p'.
57: 14 block out of the way of my p'.
58: 1 shew my p' their transgression,
60: 2 earth, and gross darkness the p':
21 Thy p' also shall be all righteous:
61: 9 and their offspring among the p':
62: 10 gates; prepare ye the way of the p';
10 stones; lift up a standard for the p'.
12 they shall call them, The holy p',
63: 3 of the p' there was none with me:
6 tread down the p' in mine anger,
8 they are my p', children that will
11 the days of old, Moses, and his p',
14 so didst thou lead thy p', to make
18 p' of thy holiness have possessed
64: 9 we beseech thee, we are all thy p'.
65: 2 all the day unto a rebellious p',
3 A p' that provoketh me to anger
10 in, for my p' that have sought me.
18 a rejoicing, and her p' a joy.
19 in Jerusalem, and joy in my p':

Isa 65: 22 days of a tree are the days of my p',
Jer 1: 18 and against the p' of the land.
2: 11 my p' have changed their glory for
13 my p' have committed two evils;
31 wherefore say my p', We are lords;
32 yet my p' have forgotten me days
4: 10 thou hast greatly deceived this p'
11 it be said to this p' and to Jerusalem,
11 toward the daughter of my p', not
22 For my p' is foolish, they have not
5: 14 this p' wood, and it shall devour
21 Hear now this, O foolish p', and
23 But this p' hath a revolting and a
26 among my p' are found wicked men:
31 and my p' love to have it so: and
6: 14 of the daughter of my p' slightly,
19 I will bring evil upon this p', even
21 lay stumblingblocks before this p',
22 a p' cometh from the north country,
26 O daughter of my p', gird thee with
27 tower and a fortress among my p',
7: 12 for the wickedness of my p' Israel.
16 Therefore pray not thou for this p',
23 be your God, and ye shall be my p':
33 carcases of this p' shall be meat for
8: 5 is this p' of Jerusalem slidden back
7 but my p' know not the judgment of
11 of the daughter of my p' slightly,
19 of the cry of the daughter of my p'
21 the daughter of my p' am I hurt;
22 of the daughter of my p' recovered?
9: 1 the slain of the daughter of my p'!
2 I might leave my p', and go from
7 I do for the daughter of my p'?
15 I will feed them, even this p', with
10: 3 For the customs of the p' are vain:
11: 4 so shall ye be my p', and I will be
14 pray not thou for this p', neither
12: 14 have caused my p' Israel to inherit;
16 diligently learn the ways of my p',
16 they taught my p' to swear by Baal;
16 they be built in the midst of my p'.
13: 10 This evil p', which refuse to hear
11 they might be unto me for a p', and
14: 10 Thus saith the Lord unto his p',
11 Pray not for this p' for their good.
16 the p' to whom they prophesy shall
17 virgin daughter of my p' is broken
15: 1 mind could not be toward this p':
7 I will destroy my p', since they
20 unto this p' a fenced brazen wall.
16: 5 taken away my peace from this p',
10 shalt shew these p' all these words,
17: 19 in the gate of the children of the p',
18: 15 Because my p' hath forgotten me,
19: 1 and take of the ancients of the p',
11 so will I break this p' and this city,
14 Lord's house; and said to all the p',
21: 7 the p', and such as are left in this
8 unto this p' thou shalt say, Thus
22: 2 thy p' that enter in by these gates:
4 he, and his servants, and his p'.
23: 2 against the pastors that feed my p';
13 and caused my p' Israel to err.
22 had caused my p' to hear my words,
27 to cause my p' to forget my name
32 and cause my p' to err by their lies,
32 they shall not profit this p' at all,
33 when this p', or the prophet, or a
34 prophet, and the priest, and the p',
24: 7 they shall be my p', and I will be
25: 1 concerning all the p' of Judah in
2 spake unto all the p' of Judah, and
19 and his princes, and all his p';
20 And all the mingled p', and all the
24 mingled p' that dwell in the desert,
26: 7 the p' heard Jeremiah speaking
8 end of speaking...unto all the p',
8 prophets and all the p' took him,
9 p' were gathered against Jeremiah
11 unto the princes and to all the p',
12 unto all the princes and to all the p',
16 said the princes and all the p' unto
17 spake to all the assembly of the p',
18 and spake to all the p' of Judah,
23 into the graves of the common p'.
24 hand of the p' to put him to death.
27: 12 and serve him and his p', and live.
13 Why will ye die, thou and thy p', by
16 to the priests and to all this p',
28: 1 of the priests and of all the p',
5 and in the presence of all the p' that
7 ears, and in the ears of all the p';
11 spake in the presence of all the p',
15 thou makest this p' to trust in a lie.
29: 1 to all the p' whom Nebuchadnezzar
16 all the p' that dwelleth in this city,
25 all the p' that are at Jerusalem,
32 have a man to dwell among this p';
32 the good that I will do for my p',
30: 3 again the capitivity of my p' Israel
22 ye shall be my p', and I will be your
31: 1 of Israel, and they shall be my p'.
2 The p' which were left of the sword
7 Lord, save thy p', the remnant of
14 my p' shall be satisfied with my
33 their God, and they shall be my p'.
32: 21 brought forth thy p' Israel out of
38 And they shall be my p', and I will
42 all this great evil upon this p', so
33: 24 thou not what this p' have spoken,
24 they have despised my p', that they
34: 1 all the p', fought against Jerusalem,
8 had made a covenant with all the p'
10 when all the princes, and all the p',
19 priests, and all the p' of the land,

Jer 35: 16 this p' hath not hearkened unto me:
36: 6 words of the Lord in...ears of the p'
7 hath pronounced against this p'.
9 the Lord to all the p' in Jerusalem,
9 the p' that came from the cities of
10 house, in the ears of all the p'.
13 read the book in the ears of the p'.
14 thou hast read in the ears of the p',
37: 2 nor the p' of the land, did hearken
4 in and went out among the p':
12 thence in the midst of the p'.
18 thy servants, or against this p',
38: 1 had spoken unto all the p', saying,
4 the hands of all the p', in speaking
4 seeketh not the welfare of this p',
39: 8 and the houses of the p', with fire,
9 the remnant of the p' that remained
9 the rest of the p' that remained.
10 the guard left of the poor of the p',
14 home: so he dwelt among the p'.
40: 5 and dwell with him among the p':
6 among the p' that were left in the
41: 10 the residue of the p' that were in
10 all the p' that remained in Mizpah,
13 all the p' which were with Ishmael
14 p' that Ishmael had carried away
16 the remnant of the p' whom he had
42: 1 the p' from the least even unto the
8 all the p' from the least even to the
43: 1 end of speaking unto all the p' all
4 p', obeyed not the voice of the Lord,
44: 15 p' that dwelt in the land of Egypt,
20 Then Jeremiah said unto all the p',
20 all the p' which had given him that
21 princes, and the p' of the land, did
24 Jeremiah said unto all the p', and
46: 16 let us go again to our own p', and to
24 into the hand of the p' of the north.
48: 42 shall be destroyed from being a p',
46 the p' of Chemosh perisheth: for
49: 1 Gad, and his p' dwell in his cities?
50: 6 My p' hath been lost sheep: their
16 they shall turn every one to his p',
37 mingled p' that are in the midst of
41 a p' shall come from the north, and
51: 45 My p', go ye out of the midst of her,
58 the p' shall labour in vain, and the
52: 6 was no bread for the p' of the land.
15 captive certain of the poor of the p',
15 residue of the p' that remained in
25 who mustered the p' of the land;
25 men of the p' of the land, that were
28 p' whom Nebuchadrezzar carried
La 1: 1 city sit solitary, that was full of p'!
7 p' fell into the hand of the enemy,
11 All her p' sigh, they seek bread;
18 hear, I pray you, all p', and behold
2: 11 of the daughter of my p';
3: 14 I was a derision to all my p'; and
45 and refuse in the midst of the p'.
48 of the daughter of my p'.
4: 3 the daughter of my p' is become
6 daughter of my p' is greater than
10 of the daughter of my p'.
Eze 3: 5 not sent to a p' of a strange speech
6 to many p' of a strange speech and
11 unto the children of thy p', and
7: 27 the p' of the land shall be troubled:
11: 1 the son of Benaiah, princes of the p'.
17 will even gather you from the p',
20 they shall be my p', and I will be
12: 19 say unto the p' of the land, Thus
13: 9 not be in the assembly of my p',
10 because they have seduced my p',
17 against the daughters of thy p',
18 Will ye hunt the souls of my p', and
19 will ye pollute me among my p' for
19 lying to my p' that hear your lies?
21 and deliver my p' out of your hand,
23 deliver my p' out of your hand:
14: 8 him off from the midst of my p';
9 him from the midst of my p' Israel.
11 they may be my p', and I may be
17: 9 many p' to pluck it up by the roots
15 might give him horses and much p'.
18: 18 which is not good among his p', lo,
20: 34 I will bring you out from the p',
35 you into the wilderness of the p',
41 when I bring you out from the p',
21: 12 for it shall be upon my p', it shall
12 of the sword shall be upon my p':
22: 29 p' of the land have used oppression,
23: 24 and with an assembly of p', which
24: 18 spake unto the p' in the morning:
19 the p' said unto me, Wilt thou not
25: 7 I will cut thee off from the p', and
14 Edom by the hand of my p' Israel:
26: 2 broken that was the gates of the p';
7 and companies, and much p'.
11 he shall slay thy p' by the sword,
20 into the pit, with the p' of old time,
27: 3 merchant of the p' for many isles,
33 of the seas, thou filledst many p';
36 merchants among the p' shall hiss
28: 19 that know thee among the p' shall
25 p' among whom they are scattered,
29: 13 gather the Egyptians from the p':
30: 5 all the mingled p', and Chub, and
11 He and his p' with him, the
31: 12 the p' of the earth are gone down
32: 3 thee with a company of many p';
9 will also vex the hearts of many p',
10 will make many p' amazed at thee,
33: 2 speak to the children of thy p', and
2 p' of the land take a man of their
3 blow the trumpet, and warn the p';

Eze 33: 6 trumpet, and the *p*' be not warned;
12 say unto the children of thy *p*', The
17 Yet the children of thy *p*' say, The
30 children of thy *p*' still are talking
31 come unto thee as the *p*' cometh,
31 they sit before thee as my *p*', and
34:13 I will bring them out from the *p*',
30 even the house of Israel, are my *p*',
36: 3 talkers, and are an infamy of the *p*':
8 yield your fruit to my *p*' of Israel;
12 walk upon you, even my *p*' Israel;
15 the reproach of the *p*' any more,
20 These are the *p*' of the Lord, and
28 ye shall be my *p*', and I will be your
37:12 O my *p*', I will open your graves,
13 have opened your graves, O my *p*',
18 children of thy *p*' shall speak unto
23 so shall they be my *p*', and I will
27 their God, and they shall be my *p*'.
38: 6 his bands: and many *p*' with thee.
8 gathered out of many *p*', against
9 thy bands, and many *p*' with thee.
12 the *p*' that are gathered out of the
14 my *p*' of Israel dwelleth safely,
15 and many *p*' with thee, all of them
16 come up against my *p*' of Israel,
22 the many *p*' that are with him, an
39: 4 bands, and the *p*' that is with thee:
7 known in the midst of my *p*' Israel;
13 all the *p*' of the land shall bury
27 brought them again from the *p*',
42:14 those things which are for the *p*'.
44:11 sacrifice for the *p*', and they shall
19 even into the utter court to the *p*',
19 shall not sanctify the *p*' with their
23 shall teach my *p*' the difference
45: 8 shall no more oppress my *p*'; and
9 away your exactions from my *p*',
16 the *p*' of the land shall give this
22 prepare for himself and all the *p*'
46: 3 the *p*' of the land shall worship at
9 when the *p*' of the land shall come
18 my *p*' be not scattered every man
20 the utter court, to sanctify the *p*'.
24 shall boil the sacrifice of the *p*'.
Da 2:44 kingdom...not be left to other *p*',
3: 4 O *p*', nations, and languages,
7 all the *p*' heard the sound of the
7 all the *p*', the nations, and the
29 That every *p*', nation,...language,
4: 1 the king, unto all *p*', nations, and
5:19 him, all *p*', nations, and languages,
6:25 Darius wrote unto all *p*', nations,
7:14 that all *p*', nations, and languages,
27 be given to the *p*' of the saints of
8:24 destroy the mighty and the holy *p*'.
9: 6 fathers, and to all the *p*' of the land.
15 that hast brought thy *p*' forth out
16 Jerusalem and thy *p*' are become
19 and thy *p*' are called by thy name.
20 my sin and the sin of my *p*' Israel,
24 upon thy *p*' and upon thy holy
26 the *p*' of the prince that shall come
10:14 what shall befall thy *p*' in the
11:14 the robbers of thy *p*' shall exalt
15 neither his chosen *p*', neither shall
23 become strong with a small *p*'.
32 but the *p*' that do know their God
33 among the *p*' shall instruct many:
12: 1 standeth for the children of thy *p*':
1 that time thy *p*' shall be delivered,
7 to scatter the power of the holy *p*',
Ho 1: 9 for ye are not my *p*', and I will not
10 Ye are not my *p*', there it shall be
2:23 say to them which were not my *p*',
23 Thou art my *p*'; and they shall say,
4: 4 for thy *p*' are as they that strive
6 My *p*' are destroyed for lack of
8 They eat up the sin of my *p*', and
9 there shall be, like *p*', like priest:
12 My *p*' ask counsel at their stocks,
14 *p*' that doth not understand shall
6:11 I returned the captivity of my *p*'.
7: 8 hath mixed himself among the *p*';
9: 1 not, O Israel, for joy, as other *p*':
10: 5 the *p*' thereof shall mourn over it,
10 *p*' shall be gathered against them,
14 shall a tumult arise among thy *p*',
11: 7 my *p*' are bent to backsliding from
Joe 2: 2 a great *p*' and a strong; there hath
5 as a strong *p*' set in battle array.
6 face the *p*' shall be much pained:
16 Gather the *p*', sanctify the
17 Spare thy *p*', O Lord, and give not
17 should they say among the *p*',
18 jealous for his land, and pity his *p*'.
19 will answer and say unto his *p*',
26, 27 my *p*' shall never be ashamed.
3: 2 there for my *p*' and for my heritage
3 And they have cast lots for my *p*';
8 to the Sabeans, to a *p*' far off:
16 the Lord will be the hope of his *p*',
Am 1: 5 *p*' of Syria shall go into captivity
3: 6 the city, and the *p*' not be afraid?
7: 8 in the midst of my *p*' Israel:
15 Go, prophesy unto my *p*' Israel.
8: 2 end is come upon my *p*' of Israel;
9:10 All the sinners of my *p*' shall die
14 bring again the captivity of my *p*'
Ob 13 have entered into the gate of my *p*'
Jon 1: 8 country? and of what *p*' art thou?
3: 5 So the *p*' of Nineveh believed God,
Mic 1: 2 Hear, all ye *p*'; hearken, O earth,
9 he is come unto the gate of my *p*',
2: 4 hath changed the portion of my *p*':
8 Even of late my *p*' is risen up as an
Mic 2: 9 women of my *p*' have ye cast out
11 shall even be the prophet of this *p*'.
3: 3 Who also eat the flesh of my *p*', and
5 the prophets that make my *p*' err,
4: 1 the hills; and *p*' shall flow unto it.
3 he shall judge among many *p*',
5 *p*' will walk every one in the name
13 thou shalt beat in pieces many *p*':
5: 7 of many *p*' as a dew from the Lord,
8 in the midst of many *p*' as a lion
6: 2 hath a controversy with his *p*', and
3 O my *p*', what have I done unto
5 O my *p*', remember now what
16 shall bear the reproach of my *p*'.
7:14 Feed thy *p*' with thy rod, the flock
Na 3:13 *p*' in the midst of thee are women:
18 *p*' is scattered upon the mountains,
Hab 2: 5 and heapeth unto him all *p*':
8 remnant of the *p*' shall spoil thee;
10 thy house by cutting off many *p*',
13 the *p*' shall labour in the very fire,
13 and the *p*' shall weary themselves
3:13 forth for the salvation of thy *p*',
16 when he cometh up unto the *p*', he
Zep 1:11 all the merchant *p*' are cut down;
2: 8 they have reproached my *p*', and
9 residue of my *p*' shall spoil them,
9 remnant of my *p*' shall possess
10 magnified themselves against...*p*'
3: 9 I turn to the *p*' a pure language,
12 of thee an afflicted and poor *p*',
20 a praise among all *p*' of the earth,
Hag 1: 2 This *p*' say, The time is not come,
12 with the remnant of the *p*', obeyed
12 and the *p*' did fear before the Lord.
13 in the Lord's message unto the *p*',
14 spirit of all the remnant of the *p*';
2: 2 priest, and to the residue of the *p*',
4 and be strong, all ye *p*' of the land,
14 So is this *p*', and so is this nation
Zec 2:11 in that day, and shall be my *p*':
7: 5 Speak unto all the *p*' of the land,
8: 6 the remnant of this *p*' in these days,
7 I will save my *p*' from the east
8 shall be my *p*', and I will be their
11 not be unto the residue of this *p*' as
12 remnant of this *p*' to possess all
20 that there shall come *p*', and the
22 many *p*' and strong nations shall
9:16 in that day as the flock of his *p*':
10: 9 And I will sow them among the *p*':
11:10 which I had made with all the *p*'.
12: 2 unto all the *p*' round about, when
3 a burdensome stone for all *p*': all
3 though all the *p*' of the earth be
4 smite every horse of the *p*' with
6 shall devour all the *p*' round about,
13: 9 hear them: I will say, It is my *p*':
14: 2 residue of the *p*' shall not be cut off
12 Lord will smite all the *p*' that have
Mal 1: 4 The *p*' against whom the Lord hath
2: 9 base before all the *p*', according
M't 1:21 shall save his *p*' from their sins.
2: 4 and scribes of the *p*' together, he
6 Governor,...shall rule my *p*' Israel.
4:16 The *p*' which sat in darkness saw
23 all manner of disease among the *p*'.
24 they brought unto him all sick *p*'
25 great multitudes of *p*' from Galilee,
7:28 *p*' were astonished at his doctrine:
9:23 and the *p*' making a noise,
25 when the *p*' were put forth, he went
35 and every disease among the *p*'.
12:23 all the *p*' were amazed, and said,
46 While he yet talked to the *p*',
14:13 and when the *p*' had heard thereof,
15: 8 *p*' draweth nigh unto me with their
21:23 the elders of the *p*' came unto him
26 shall say, Of men; we fear the *p*';
26: 3 scribes, and the elders of the *p*',
5 there be an uproar among the *p*'.
47 chief priests and elders of the *p*'.
27: 1 and elders of the *p*' took counsel
15 to release unto the *p*' a prisoner,
25 Then answered all the *p*', and said,
64 him away, and say unto the *p*',
M'r 5:21 side, much *p*' gathered unto him:
24 and much *p*' followed him, and
6:33 And the *p*' saw them departing, and
34 saw much *p*', and was moved with
45 while he sent away the *p*'.
7: 6 *p*' honoureth me with their lips,
14 he had called all the *p*' unto him,
17 entered into the house from the *p*',
8: 6 commanded the *p*' to sit down on
6 and they did set them before the *p*'.
34 he had called the *p*' unto him with
9:15 And straightway all the *p*', when
25 Jesus saw that the *p*' came running
10: 1 and the *p*' resort unto him again;
46 disciples and a great number of *p*',
11:18 *p*' was astonished at his doctrine
32 say, Of men; they feared the *p*':
12:12 lay hold on him, but feared the *p*';
37 the common *p*' heard him gladly.
41 beheld how the *p*' cast money into
14: 2 lest there be an uproar of the *p*'.
15:11 But the chief priests moved the *p*',
15 so Pilate, willing to content the *p*',
Lu 1:10 multitude of the *p*' were praying
17 ready a *p*' prepared for the Lord.
21 And the *p*' waited for Zacharias,
68 hath visited and redeemed his *p*',
77 knowledge of salvation unto his *p*'
2:10 great joy, which shall be to all *p*'.
31 prepared before the face of all *p*';
Lu 2:32 and the glory of thy *p*' Israel.
3:10 And the *p*' asked him, saying,
15 And as the *p*' were in expectation,
18 preached he unto the *p*'.
21 Now when all the *p*' were baptized,
4:42 the *p*' sought him, and came unto
5: 1 *p*' pressed upon him to hear the
3 and taught the *p*' out of the ship.
6:17 multitude of *p*' out of all Judæa
7: 1 sayings in the audience of the *p*',
9 said unto the *p*' that followed
11 went with him, and much *p*'.
12 much *p*' of the city was with her.
16 and, That God hath visited his *p*'.
24 speak unto the *p*' concerning
29 And all the *p*' that heard him, and
8: 4 And when much *p*' were gathered
40 the *p*' gladly received him: for
42 as he went the *p*' thronged him.
47 declared unto him before all the *p*'
9:11 And the *p*', when they knew it,
13 go and buy meat for all this *p*'.
18 saying, Whom say the *p*' that I
37 from the hill, much *p*' met him.
11:14 dumb spake; and the *p*' wondered.
29 when the *p*' were gathered thick
12: 1 an innumerable multitude of *p*',
54 he said also to the *p*', When ye see
13:14 said unto the *p*', There are six days
17 the *p*' rejoiced for all the glorious
18:43 all the *p*', when they saw it, gave
19:47 chief of the *p*' sought to destroy
48 the *p*' were very attentive to hear
20: 1 as he taught the *p*' in the temple,
6 say, Of men; all the *p*' will stone us:
9 he to speak to the *p*' this parable;
19 and they feared the *p*': for they
26 take hold of his words before the *p*':
45 in the audience of all the *p*' he said
21:23 in the land, and wrath upon this *p*'.
38 all the *p*' came early in the morning
22: 2 kill him; for they feared the *p*'.
66 the elders of the *p*' and the chief
23: 4 to the chief priests and to the *p*',
5 He stirreth up the *p*', teaching
13 priests and the rulers and the *p*',
14 me, as one that perverteth the *p*':
27 followed him a great company of *p*',
35 And the *p*' stood beholding. And
48 And all the *p*' that came together
24:19 and word before God and all the *p*':
Joh 6:22 *p*' which stood on the other side
24 *p*' therefore saw that Jesus was
7:12 much murmuring among the *p*'
12 said, Nay; but he deceiveth the *p*':
20 *p*' answered and said, Thou hast a
31 many of the *p*' believed on him,
32 heard that the *p*' murmured such
40 Many of the *p*', therefore, when
43 was a division among the *p*'
49 this *p*' who knoweth not the law are
8: 2 all the *p*' came unto him; and he sat
11:42 because of the *p*' which stand by I
50 that one man should die for the *p*',
12: 9 Much *p*' of the Jews therefore knew
12 next day much *p*' that were come to
17 The *p*' therefore that was with him
18 For this cause the *p*' also met him,
29 The *p*' therefore, that stood by, and
34 *p*' answered him, We have heard
18:14 that one man should die for the *p*'.
Ac 2:47 and having favour with all the *p*'.
3: 9 the *p*' saw him walking and praising
11 all the *p*' ran together unto them in
12 he answered unto the *p*', Ye men of
23 be destroyed from among the *p*'.
4: 1 And as they spake unto the *p*', the
2 grieved that they taught the *p*', and
8 Ye rulers of the *p*', and elders of
10 you all, and to all the *p*' of Israel,
17 it spread no further among the *p*',
21 punish them, because of the *p*': for
25 and the *p*' imagine vain things?
27 *p*' of Israel, were gathered together,
5:12 and wonders wrought among the *p*';
13 them: but the *p*' magnified them.
20 and speak in the temple to the *p*'
25 in the temple, and teaching the *p*'.
26 they feared the *p*', lest they should
34 had in reputation among all the *p*',
37 and drew away much *p*' after him:
6: 8 wonders and miracles among the *p*'.
12 stirred up the *p*', and the elders,
7:17 the *p*' grew and multiplied in Egypt,
34 seen the affliction of my *p*'
8: 6 the *p*' with one accord gave heed
9 and bewitched the *p*' of Samaria,
10: 2 which gave much alms to the *p*',
41 Not to all the *p*', but unto witnesses
42 commanded us to preach unto the *p*',
11:24 much *p*' was added unto the Lord.
26 with the church, and taught much *p*'.
12: 4 Easter to bring him forth to the *p*'.
11 expectation of the *p*' of the Jews.
22 the *p*' gave a shout, saying, It is
13:15 any word of exhortation for the *p*',
17 God of this *p*' of Israel chose our
17 exalted the *p*' when they dwelt as
24 of repentance to all the *p*' of Israel.
31 who are his witnesses unto the *p*'.
14:11 the *p*' saw what Paul had done,
13 have done sacrifice with the *p*'.
14 and ran in among the *p*', crying out,
18 scarce restrained they the *p*', that,
19 who persuaded the *p*', and, having
15:14 take out of them a *p*' for his name.

Ac 17: 5 sought to bring them out to the p'.
8 And they troubled the p' and the
13 thither also, and stirred up the p'.
18: 10 thee: for I have much p' in this city.
19: 4 saying unto the p', that they should
26 and turned away much p', saying
30 would have entered in unto the p',
33 have made his defence unto the p'.
35 the townclerk had appeased the p',
21: 27 stirred up all the p', and laid hands
28 against the p', and the law, and
30 was moved, and the p' ran together:
35 soldiers for the violence of the p'.
36 For the multitude of the p' followed
39 thee, suffer me to speak unto the p'.
40 beckoned with the hand unto the p'.
23: 5 not speak evil of the ruler of thy p'.
24: 12 neither raising up the p', neither in
26: 17 Delivering thee from the p', and
23 should shew light unto the p', and
28: 2 barbarous p' shewed us no little
17 committed nothing against the p',
26 Go unto this p', and say, Hearing ye
27 the heart of this p' is waxed gross,
Ro 9: 25 also in Osee, I will call them my p',
25 which were not my p'; and her
26 said unto them, Ye are not my p';
10: 19 to jealousy by them that are no p',
21 a disobedient and gainsaying p'.
11: 1 then, Hath God cast away his p'?
2 God hath not cast away his p' which
15: 10 Rejoice, ye Gentiles, with his p'.
11 Gentiles; and laud him, all ye p'.
1Co 10: 7 The p' sat down to eat and drink,
14: 21 other lips will I speak unto this p';
2Co 6: 16 their God, and they shall be my p'.
Tit 2: 14 a peculiar p', zealous of good works.
Heb 2: 17 reconciliation for the sins of the p'.
4: 9 therefore a rest to the p' of God.
5: 3 as for the p', so also for himself, to
7: 5 to take tithes of the p' according
11 (for under it the p' received the law,)
8: 10 God, and they shall be to me a p':
9: 7 himself, and for the errors of the p':
19 spoken every precept to all the p'
19 sprinkled...the book, and all the p',
10: 30 again, The Lord shall judge his p'.
11: 25 suffer affliction with the p' of God,
13: 12 sanctify the p' with his own blood,
1Pe 2: 9 an holy nation, a peculiar p'; that
10 Which in time past were not a p',
10 but are now the p' of God: which
2Pe 2: 1 false prophets also among the p',
Jude 5 having saved the p' out of...Egypt,
Re 5: 9 and tongue, and p', and nation;
7: 9 and kindreds, and p', and tongues,
11: 9 And they of the p' and kindreds and
14: 6 and kindred, and tongue, and p',
18: 4 Come out of her, my p', that ye be
19: 1 a great voice of much p' in heaven,
21: 3 with them, and they shall be his p',

people's
Le 9: 15 And he brought the p' offering,
Eze 46: 18 shall not take of the p' inheritance
M't 13: 15 For this p' heart is waxed gross,
Heb 7: 27 his own sins, and then for the p':

peoples
Re 10: 11 prophesy again before many p',
17: 15 where the whore sitteth, are p', and

Peor (*pe'-or*) See also BAAL-PEOR; BETH-PEOR; PEOR'S.
Nu 23: 28 Balaam unto the top of P',
25: 18 beguiled you in the matter of P',
31: 16 against the Lord in the matter of P',
Jos 22: 17 Is the iniquity of P' too little for us,

Peor's
Nu 25: 18 the day of the plague for P' sake.

peradventure^
Ge 18: 24 P' there be fifty righteous within
28 P' there shall lack five of the fifty
29 P' there shall be forty found there.
30 P' there shall thirty be found there.
31 P' there shall be twenty found there.
32 P' ten shall be found there. And
31: 31 P' thou wouldest take by force
32: 20 his face; p' he will accept of me.
38: 11 Lest p' he die also, as his brethren
42: 4 said, Lest p' mischief befall him.
43: 12 your hand; p' it was an oversight:
44: 34 lest p' I see the evil that shall come
50: 15 Joseph will p' hate us, and will
Ex 13: 17 God said, Lest p' the people repent
32: 30 p' I shall make an atonement for
Nu 22: 6 p' I shall prevail, that we may smite
11 p' I shall be able to overcome them,
23: 3 p' the Lord will come to meet me:
27 p' it will please God that thou mayest
Jos 9: 7 P' ye dwell among us; and how
1Sa 6: 5 p' he will lighten his hand from off
9: 6 p' he can shew us our way that we
1Ki 18: 5 p' we may find grass to save the
27 p' he sleepeth, and must be awaked.
20: 31 of Israel: p' he will save thy life.
2Ki 2: 16 lest p' the Spirit of the Lord hath
Jer 20: 10 P' he will be enticed, and we shall
Ro 5: 7 yet p' for a good man some would
2Ti 2: 25 if God p' will give them repentance

Perazim (*per'-a-zim*) See also BAAL-PERAZIM.
Isa 28: 21 Lord shall rise up as in mount P',

perceive See also PERCEIVED; PERCEIVEST; PERCEIVETH; PERCEIVING.
De 29: 4 hath not given you an heart to p',
Jos 22: 31 day we p' that the Lord is among us,
1Sa 12: 17 p' and see that your wickedness is
2Sa 19: 6 for this day I p', that if Absalom
2Ki 4: 9 I p' that this is an holy man of God,
Job 9: 11 he passeth on also, but I p' him not.
23: 8 and backward, but I cannot p' him:
Pr 1: 2 to p' the words of understanding;
Ec 3: 22 I p' that there is nothing better,
Isa 6: 9 not; and see ye indeed, but p' not.
33: 19 deeper speech than thou canst p';
M't 13: 14 seeing ye shall see, and shall not p':
M'r 4: 12 seeing they may see, and not p';
7: 18 Do ye not p', that whatsoever thing
8: 17 p' ye not yet, neither understand?
Lu 8: 46 I p' that virtue is gone out of me.
Joh 4: 19 Sir, I p' that thou art a prophet.
12: 19 P' ye how ye prevail nothing?
Ac 8: 23 For I p' that thou art in the gall of
10: 34 I p' that God is no respecter of
17: 22 I p' that in all things ye are too
27: 10 I p'...this voyage will be with hurt
28: 26 and seeing ye shall see, and not p':
2Co 7: 8 p' that the same epistle hath made
1Jo 3: 16 Hereby p' we the love of God,

perceived
Ge 19: 33, 35 he p' not when she lay down,
J'g 6: 22 Gideon p' that he was an angel
1Sa 3: 8 And Eli p' that the Lord had called
28: 14 And Saul p' that it was Samuel,
2Sa 5: 12 David p'...the Lord had established
12: 19 David p' that the child was dead:
14: 1 p' that the king's heart was toward
1Ki 22: 33 p' that it was not the king of Israel
1Ch 14: 2 David p'...the Lord had confirmed
2Ch 18: 32 p'...it was not the king of Israel,
Ne 6: 12 I p' that God had not sent him;
16 p' that this work was wrought of
13: 10 p' that the portions of the Levites
Es 4: 1 Mordecai p' all that was done,
Job 38: 18 thou p' the breadth of the earth?
Ec 1: 17 I p' that this also is vexation of
2: 14 and I myself p' also that one event
Isa 64: 4 have not heard, nor p' by the ear,
Jer 23: 18 and hath p' and heard his word?
38: 27 him; for the matter was not p'.
M't 16: 8 Which when Jesus p', he said unto
21: 45 they p' that he spake of them.
22: 18 Jesus p' their wickedness, and said
M'r 2: 8 when Jesus p' in his spirit that
Lu 1: 22 they p' that he had seen a vision
5: 22 when Jesus p' their thoughts, he
9: 45 hid from them, that they p' it not:
20: 19 p' that he had spoken this parable
23 But he p' their craftiness, and said
Joh 6: 15 p'...they would come and take him
Ac 4: 13 p' that they were unlearned and
23: 6 p'...the one part were Sadducees,
29 I p' to be accused of questions of
Ga 2: 9 p' the grace that was given unto

perceivest
Pr 14: 7 p' not in him the lips of knowledge
Lu 6: 41 p' not the beam that is in thine

perceiveth
Job 14: 21 low, but he p' it not of them.
33: 14 once, yea twice, yet man p' it not.
Pr 31: 18 p' that her merchandise is good:

perceiving
M'r 12: 28 p' that he had answered them well,
Lu 9: 47 Jesus, p' the thought of their heart,
Ac 14: 9 p' that he had faith to be healed,

perdition
Joh 17: 12 of them is lost, but the son of p';
Ph'p 1: 28 is to them an evident token of p',
2Th 2: 3 of sin be revealed, the son of p';
1Ti 6: 9 drown men in destruction and p'.
Heb 10: 39 not of them who draw back unto p';
2Pe 3: 7 of judgment and p' of ungodly men.
Re 17: 8 of the bottomless pit, and go into p':
11 is of the seven, and goeth into p'.

Peres (*pe'-res*) See also UPHARSIN.
Da 5: 28 P'; Thy kingdom is divided, and

Peresh (*pe'-resh*)
1Ch 7: 16 a son, and she called his name P';

Perez (*pe'-rez*) See also PEREZ-UZZAH; PHARES.
1Ch 27: 3 Of the children of P' was the chief
Ne 11: 4 of Mahalaleel, of the children of P';
6 sons of P' that dwelt at Jerusalem

Perez-uzza (*pe''-rez-uz'-zah*) See also PEREZ-UZZAH.
1Ch 13: 11 that place is called P' to this day.

Perez-uzzah (*pe''-rez-uz'-zah*) See also PEREZ-UZZA.
2Sa 6: 8 name of the place P' to this day.

perfect See also PERFECTED; PERFECTING; UNPERFECT.
Ge 6: 9 Noah was a just man and p' in his
17: 1 walk before me, and be thou p'.
Le 22: 21 sheep, it shall be p' to be accepted;
De 18: 13 shalt be p' with the Lord thy God.
25: 15 shalt have a p' and just weight,
15 a p' and just measure shalt thou
32: 4 He is the Rock, his work is p':
1Sa 14: 41 Lord God of Israel, Give a p' lot.
2Sa 22: 31 As for God, his way is p'; the word
33 power: and he maketh my way p'.
1Ki 8: 61 Let your heart therefore be p'
11: 4 his heart was not p' with the Lord
15: 3 his heart was not p' with the Lord
14 nevertheless Asa's heart was p'
2Ki 20: 3 thee in truth and with a p' heart,
1Ch 12: 38 came with a p' heart to Hebron,
28: 9 serve him with a p' heart and with
29: 9 with p' heart they offered willingly
19 unto Solomon my son a p' heart,
2Ch 4: 21 made he of gold, and that p' gold;
15: 17 heart of Asa was p' all his days.
16: 9 them whose heart is p' toward him.
19: 9 faithfully, and with a p' heart.
25: 2 of the Lord, but not with a p' heart.
Ezr 7: 12 unto Ezra the priest,...p' peace,
Job 1: 1 and that man was p' and upright,
8 a p' and an upright man, one that
2: 3 a p' and an upright man, one that
8: 20 God will not cast away a p' man,
9: 20 if I say, I am p', it shall also prove
21 Though I were p', yet would I not
22 destroyeth the p' and the wicked
22: 3 that thou makest thy ways p'?
36: 4 he that is p' in knowledge is with
37: 16 of him which is p' in knowledge?
Ps 18: 30 As for God, his way is p': the
32 strength, and maketh my way p'.
19: 7 law of the Lord is p', converting
37: 37 Mark the p' man, and behold the
64: 4 they may shoot in secret at the p':
101: 2 behave myself wisely in a p' way.
2 within my house with a p' heart.
6 he that walketh in a p' way, he
138: 8 will p' that which concerneth me:
139: 22 I hate them with p' hatred: I
Pr 2: 21 land, and the p' shall remain in it.
4: 18 more and more unto the p' day.
11: 5 righteousness of the p' shall direct
Isa 18: 5 when the bud is p', and the sour
26: 3 Thou wilt keep him in p' peace, whose
38: 3 thee in truth and with a p' heart,
42: 19 who is blind as he that is p', and
Eze 16: 14 it was p' through my comeliness,
27: 3 thou hast said, I am of p' beauty.
11 they have made thy beauty p'.
28: 12 full of wisdom, and p' in beauty.
15 Thou wast p' in thy ways from the
M't 5: 48 Be ye therefore p', even as your
48 your Father which is in heaven is p'.
19: 21 If thou wilt be p', go and sell that
Lu 1: 3 having had p' understanding of all
6: 40 that is p' shall be as his master.
Joh 17: 23 that they may be made p' in one;
Ac 3: 16 hath given him this p' soundness
22: 3 p' manner of the law of the fathers.
24: 22 more p' knowledge of that way,
Ro 12: 2 and acceptable, and p', will of God.
1Co 2: 6 wisdom among them that are p':
13: 10 But when that which is p' is come,
2Co 12: 9 strength is made p' in weakness.
13: 11 Be p', be of good comfort, be of
Ga 3: 3 are ye now made p' by the flesh?
Eph 4: 13 unto a p' man, unto the measure
Ph'p 3: 12 attained, either were already p':
15 Let us therefore, as many as be p',
Col 1: 28 every man p' in Christ Jesus:
4: 12 that ye may stand p' and complete
1Th 3: 10 might p' that which is lacking
2Ti 3: 17 That the man of God may be p',
Heb 2: 10 the captain of their salvation p'
5: 9 And being made p', he became the
7: 19 For the law made nothing p', but
9: 9 make him that did the service p',
11 a greater and more p' tabernacle,
10: 1 make the comers thereunto p'.
11: 40 without us should not be made p'.
12: 23 to the spirits of just men made p'.
13: 21 Make you p' in every good work
Jas 1: 4 But let patience have her p' work,
4 be p' and entire, wanting nothing.
17 and every p' gift is from above,
25 looketh into the p' law of liberty,
2: 22 and by works was faith made p'?
3: 2 not in word, the same is a p' man,
1Pe 5: 10 suffered a while, make you p',
1Jo 4: 17 Herein is our love made p', that
18 but p' love casteth out fear:
18 that feareth is not made p' in love.
Re 3: 2 have not found thy works p'

perfected
2Ch 8: 16 So the house of the Lord was p'.
24: 13 and the work was p' by them,
Eze 27: 4 thy builders have p' thy beauty.
M't 21: 16 and sucklings thou hast p' praise?
Lu 13: 32 and the third day I shall be p'.
Heb 10: 14 by one offering he hath p' for ever
1Jo 2: 5 in him verily is the love of God p':
4: 12 in us, and his love is p' in us.

perfecting
2Co 7: 1 p' holiness in the fear of God.
Eph 4: 12 For the p' of the saints, for the

perfection See also PERFECTNESS.
Job 11: 7 find out the Almighty unto p'?
15: 29 shall he prolong the p' thereof
28: 3 darkness, and searcheth out all p':
Ps 50: 2 Out of Zion, the p' of beauty,
119: 96 I have seen an end of all p':
Isa 47: 9 shall come upon thee in their p'
La 2: 15 The p' of beauty, The joy of the
Lu 8: 14 this life, and bring no fruit to p'.
2Co 13: 9 this also we wish, even your p'.
Heb 6: 1 of Christ, let us go on unto p';
7: 11 p' were by the Levitical priesthood,

perfectly
Jer 23: 20 latter days ye shall consider it p'.
M't 14: 36 as touched were made p' whole.
Ac 18: 26 unto him the way of God more p'.
23: 15 would enquire something more p'

Ac 23:20 enquire somewhat of him more p'.
1Co 1:10 but that ye be p' joined together
1Th 5: 2 know p' that the day of the Lord

perfectness See also PERFECTION.
Col 3:14 on charity, which is the bond of p'.

perform See also PERFORMED; PERFORMETH; PERFORMING.
Ge 26: 3 I will p' the oath which I sware
Ex 18:18 art not able to p' it thyself alone.
Nu 4:23 all that enter in to p' the service,
De 4:13 which he commanded you to p',
9: 5 may p' the word which the Lord
23:23 of thy lips thou shalt keep and p';
25: 5 p' the duty of an husband's brother
7 p' the duty of my husband's brother.
Ru 3:13 p' unto thee the part of a kinsman,
1Sa 3:12 day I will p' against Eli all things
2Sa 14:15 p' the request of his handmaid.
1Ki 6:12 then will I p' my word with thee,
12:15 Lord, that he might p' his saying,
2Ki 23: 3 to p' the words of this covenant
24 he might p' the words of the law,
2Ch 10:15 that the Lord might p' his word,
34:31 to p' the words of the covenant
Es 5: 8 my petition, and to p' my request,
Job 5:12 their hands cannot p' their enterprise.
Ps 21:11 device, which they are not able to p'.
61: 8 ever, that I may daily p' my vows.
119:106 I have sworn, and I will p' it,
112 heart to p' thy statutes alway,
Isa 9: 7 zeal of the Lord of hosts will p' this.
19:21 vow a vow unto the Lord, and p' it.
44:28 and shall p' all my pleasure:
Jer 1:12 for I will hasten my word to p' it.
11: 5 p' the oath which I have sworn
28: 6 Lord p' thy words which thou hast
29:10 and p' my good word toward you,
33:14 will p' that good thing which I have
44:25 We will surely p' our vows that
25 your vows, and surely p' your vows.
Eze 12:25 will I say the word, and will p' it,
Mic 7:20 Thou wilt p' the truth to Jacob,
Na 1:15 thy solemn feasts, p' thy vows:
M't 5:33 shalt p' unto the Lord thine oaths:
Lu 1:72 p' the mercy promised to our
Ro 4:21 promised, he was able also to p'.
7:18 how to p' that which is good I find
2Co 8:11 Now therefore p' the doing of it;
Ph'p 1: 6 will p' it until the day of Jesus

performance
Lu 1:45 there shall be a p' of those things
2Co 8:11 so there may be a p' also out of

performed
1Sa 15:11 hath not p' my commandments.
13 p' the commandment of the Lord.
2Sa 21:14 p' all that the king commanded.
1Ki 8:20 And the Lord hath p' his word
2Ch 6:10 The Lord therefore hath p' his word
Ne 9: 8 and hast p' thy words; for thou art
Es 1:15 she hath not p' the commandment
5: 6 half of the kingdom it shall be p'.
7: 2 and it shall be p', even to the half
Ps 65: 1 and unto thee shall the vow be p'.
Isa 10:12 the Lord hath p' his whole work
Jer 23:20 have p' the thoughts of his heart:
30:24 he have p' the intents of his heart:
34:18 not p' the words of the covenant
35:14 The words of Jonadab...are p';
16 p' the commandment of their father,
51:29 purpose of the Lord shall be p'
Eze 37:14 the Lord have spoken it, and p' it,
Lu 1:20 day that these things shall be p',
2:39 p' all things according to the law
Ro 15:28 When therefore I have p' this,

performeth
Ne 5:13 that p' not this promise, even thus
Job 23:14 p' the thing that is appointed for
Ps 57: 2 unto God that p' all things for me.
Isa 44:26 p' the counsel of his messengers;

performing
Nu 15: 3 offering, or a sacrifice in p' a vow,
8 or for a sacrifice in p' a vow,

perfume See also PERFUMED; PERFUMES.
Ex 30:35 And thou shalt make it a p', a
37 for the p' which thou shalt make,
Pr 27: 9 Ointment and p' rejoice the heart:

perfumed
Pr 7:17 have p' my bed with myrrh, aloes,
Ca 3: 6 p' with myrrh and frankincense,

perfumes
Isa 57: 9 and didst increase thy p', and

Perga (*pur'-gah*)
Ac 13:13 they came to P' in Pamphylia:
14 when they departed from P', they
14:25 they had preached the word in P',

Pergamos (*pur'-ga-mos*)
Re 1:11 and unto P', and unto Thyatira,
2:12 angel of the church in P' write;

perhaps
Ac 8:22 if p' the thought of thine heart may
2Co 2: 7 lest p' such...should be swallowed
Ph'm 15 For p' he...departed for a season,

Perida (*per-i'-dah*) See also PERUDA.
Ne 7:57 of Sophereth, the children of P',

peril See also PERILS.
La 5: 9 gat our bread with the p' of our lives,
Ro 8:35 or nakedness, or p', or sword?

perilous
2Ti 3: 1 the last days p' times shall come.

perils
2Co 11:26 in p' of waters, in p' of robbers,
26 in p' by mine own countrymen,
26 p' by the heathen, in p' in the city,
26 in the city, in p' in the wilderness,
26 in the wilderness, in p' in the sea,
26 the sea, in p' among false brethren;

perish See also PERISHED; PERISHETH; PERISHING.
Ge 41:36 land p' not through the famine.
Ex 19:21 Lord to gaze, and many of them p'.
21:26 or the eye of his maid, that it p';
Le 26:38 And ye shall p' among the heathen,
Nu 17:12 Behold, we die, we p', we all p'.
24:20 latter end shall be that he p' for ever.
24 Eber, and he also shall p' for ever.
De 4:26 shall soon utterly p' from off the land
8:19 you this day that ye shall surely p'.
20 so shall ye p'; because ye would not
11:17 ye p' quickly from off the good land
26: 5 A Syrian ready to p' was my father,
28:20 destroyed, and until thou p' quickly;
22 they shall pursue thee until thou p'.
30:18 you this day, that ye shall surely p',
Jos 23:13 until ye p' from off this good land
16 shall p' quickly from off the good
J'g 5:31 So let all thine enemies p', O Lord:
1Sa 26:10 shall descend into battle, and p'.
27: 1 p' one day by the hand of Saul:
2Ki 9: 8 For the whole house of Ahab shall p':
Es 3:13 to kill, and to cause to p', all Jews,
4:16 according to the law: and if I p', I p'.
7: 4 to be destroyed, to be slain, and to p'.
8:11 to destroy, to slay, and to cause to p',
9:28 nor the memorial of them p' from
Job 3: 3 Let the day p' wherein I was born,
4: 9 By the blast of God they p', and by
20 p' for ever without any regarding it.
6:18 aside; they go to nothing, and p'.
8:13 and the hypocrite's hope shall p':
18:17 His remembrance shall p' from the
20: 7 he shall p' for ever like his own dung
29:13 blessing of him that was ready to p'
31:19 have seen any p' for want of clothing
34:15 All flesh shall p' together, and man
36:12 they shall p' by the sword, and
Ps 1: 6 but the way of the ungodly shall p'.
2:12 lest he be angry, and ye p' from the
9: 3 they shall fall and p' at thy presence.
18 expectation of the poor shall not p'
37:20 the wicked shall p', and the enemies
41: 5 When shall he die, and his name p'?
49:10 the fool and the brutish person p',
12 not: he is like the beasts that p'.
20 not, is like the beasts that p'.
68: 2 let the wicked p' at...presence of God.
73:27 they that are far from thee shall p':
80:16 p' at the rebuke of thy countenance.
83:17 let them be put to shame and p':
92: 9 Lord, for, lo, thine enemies shall p';
102:26 They shall p', but thou shalt endure:
112:10 the desire of the wicked shall p'.
146: 4 in that very day his thoughts p'.
Pr 10:28 expectation of the wicked shall p'.
11: 7 man dieth, his expectation shall p':
10 the wicked p', there is shouting.
19: 9 and he that speaketh lies shall p'.
21:28 A false witness shall p': but the man
28:28 when they p', the righteous increase.
29:18 there is no vision, the people p':
31: 6 drink unto him that is ready to p',
Ec 5:14 But those riches p' by evil travail:
Isa 26:14 and made all their memory to p'.
27:13 ready to p' in the land of Assyria,
29:14 wisdom of their wise men shall p',
41:11 they that strive with thee shall p'.
60:12 that will not serve thee shall p';
Jer 4: 9 that the heart of the king shall p',
6:21 neighbour and his friend shall p'.
10:11 they shall p' from the earth, and
15 time of their visitation they shall p'.
18:18 the law shall not p' from the priest,
27:10 drive you out, and ye should p'.
15 drive you out, and that ye might p',
40:15 and the remnant in Judah p'?
48: 8 the valley also shall p', and the plain
51:18 time of their visitation they shall p'.
Eze 7:26 but the law shall p' from the priest,
25: 7 cause thee to p' out of the countries:
Da 2:18 Daniel and his fellows should not p'
Am 1: 8 the remnant of the Philistines shall p',
2:14 the flight shall p' from the swift,
3:15 the houses of ivory shall p', and the
Jon 1: 6 will think upon us, that we p' not.
14 let us not p' for this man's life, and
3: 9 from his fierce anger, that we p' not?
Zec 9: 5 and the king shall p' from Gaza,
M't 5:29, 30 one of thy members should p',
8:25 him, saying, Lord, save us: we p'.
9:17 wine runneth out, and the bottles p':
18:14 one of these little ones should p'.
26:52 the sword shall p' with the sword.
M'r 4:38 Master, carest thou not that we p'?
Lu 5:37 be spilled, and the bottles shall p'.
8:24 saying, Master, master, we p'.
13: 3, 5 repent, ye shall all likewise p'.
33 that a prophet p' out of Jerusalem.
15:17 and to spare, and I p' with hunger!
21:18 shall not an hair of your head p'.
Joh 3:15 believeth in him should not p',
16 believeth in him should not p',
10:28 and they shall never p', neither
11:50 and that the whole nation p' not.
Ac 8:20 Thy money p' with thee,
13:41 ye despisers, and wonder, and p':
Ro 2:12 law shall also p' without law:
1Co 1:18 cross is to them that p' foolishness;
8:11 shall the weak brother p', for whom
2Co 2:15 that are saved, and in them that p':
4:16 but though our outward man p',
Col 2:22 Which all are to p' with the using;)
2Th 2:10 unrighteousness in them that p';
Heb 1:11 They shall p'; but thou remainest;
2Pe 2:12 utterly p' in their own corruption;
3: 9 not willing that any should p', but

perished
Nu 16:33 p' from among the congregation.
21:30 Heshbon is p' even unto Dibon,
Jos 22:20 man p' not alone in his iniquity.
2Sa 1:27 fallen, and the weapons of war p'!
Job 4: 7 thee, who ever p', being innocent?
30: 2 profit me, in whom old age was p'?
Ps 9: 6 their memorial is p' with them.
10:16 the heathen are p' out of his land.
83:10 Which p' at En-dor: they became
119:92 should then have p' in mine affliction.
Ec 9: 6 hatred, and their envy, is now p';
Jer 7:28 truth is p', and is cut off from their
48:36 riches that he hath gotten are p'.
49: 7 is counsel p' from the prudent?
La 3:18 and my hope is p' from the Lord:
Joe 1:11 because the harvest of the field is p'.
Jon 4:10 up in a night, and p' in a night:
Mic 4: 9 no king in thee? is thy counsellor p'?
7: 2 The good man is p' out of the earth:
M't 8:32 into the sea, and p' in the waters.
Lu 11:51 p' between the altar and the temple:
Ac 5:37 he also p'; and all, even as many
1Co 15:18 are fallen asleep in Christ are p'.
Heb 11:31 By faith the harlot Rahab p' not
2Pe 3: 6 being overflowed with water, p':
Jude 11 and p' in the gainsaying of Core.

perisheth
Job 4:11 The old lion p' for lack of prey, and
Pr 11: 7 and the hope of unjust men p'.
Ec 7:15 just man that p' in his righteousness,
Isa 57: 1 righteous p', and no man layeth
Jer 9:12 for what the land p' and is burned up
48:46 the people of Chemosh p': for thy
Joh 6:27 Labour not for the meat which p',
Jas 1:11 and the grace of the fashion of it p':
1Pe 1: 7 more precious than of gold that p',

perishing
Job 33:18 and his life from p' by the sword.

Perizzite (*per'-iz-zite*) See also PERIZZITES.
Ge 13: 7 the P' dwelled then in the land.
Ex 33: 2 and the Hittite, and the P',
34:11 and the Hittite, and the P',
Jos 9: 1 Amorite, the Canaanite, the P',
11: 3 P', and...Jebusite in the mountains,

Perizzites (*per'-iz-zites*)
Ge 15:20 Hittites, and the P', and the
34:30 among the Canaanites and the P':
Ex 3: 8 the P', and the Hivites, and the
17 the P', and the Hivites, and the
23:23 and the Hittites, and the P', and
De 7: 1 the P', and the Hivites, and the
20:17 and the P', the Hivites, and the
Jos 3:10 and the P', and the Girgashites,
12: 8 the P', the Hivites, and the
17:15 in the land of the P' and of the
24:11 the Amorites, and the P', and the
J'g 1: 4 Canaanites and the P' into their
5 slew the Canaanites and the P'.
3: 5 Hittites, and Amorites, and P',
1Ki 9:20 P', Hivites, and Jebusites, which
2Ch 8: 7 the P', and the Hivites, and the
Ezr 9: 1 the Canaanites, the Hittites, the P',
Ne 9: 8 Hittites, the Amorites, and the P',

perjured
1Ti 1:10 for liars, for p' persons, and if

permission
1Co 7: 6 But I speak this by p', and not of

permit See also PERMITTED.
1Co 16: 7 a while with you, if the Lord p'.
Heb 6: 3 And this will we do, if God p'.

permitted
Ac 26: 1 Thou art p' to speak for thyself.
1Co 14:34 it is not p' unto them to speak;

pernicious
2Pe 2: 2 many shall follow their p' ways;

perpetual
Ge 9:12 is with you, for p' generations:
Ex 29: 9 shall be theirs for a p' statute:
30: 8 a p' incense before the Lord
31:16 generations, for a p' covenant.
Le 3:17 a p' statute for your generations
6:20 fine flour for a meat offering p',
24: 9 Lord made by fire by a p' statute.
25:34 sold; for it is their p' possession.
Nu 19:21 it shall be a p' statute unto them,
Ps 9: 6 destructions are come to a p' end:
74: 3 thy feet unto the p' desolations;
78:66 he put them to a p' reproach.
Jer 5:22 bound of the sea by a p' decree,
8: 5 slidden back by a p' backsliding?
15:18 Why is my pain p', and my wound
18:16 land desolate, and a p' hissing;
23:40 and a p' shame, which shall not
25: 9 and an hissing, and p' desolations.
12 and will make it p' desolations.
49:13 the cities thereof shall be p' wastes.
50: 5 to the Lord in a p' covenant that

Jer 51: 39 and sleep a *p*' sleep, and not wake,
57 shall sleep a *p*' sleep, and not wake,
Eze 35: 5 Because thou hast had a *p*' hatred,
9 will make thee *p*' desolations, and
46: 14 by a *p*' ordinance unto the Lord.
Hab 3: 6 scattered, the *p*' hills did bow:
Zep 2: 9 and saltpits, and a *p*' desolation:

perpetually
1Ki 9: 3 mine heart shall be there *p*'.
2Ch 7: 16 mine heart shall be there *p*'.
Am 1: 11 all pity, and his anger did tear *p*',

perplexed
Es 3: 15 drink; but the city Shushan was *p*'.
Joe 1: 18 the herds of cattle are *p*', because
Lu 9: 7 And he was *p*', because that it was
24: 4 as they were much *p*' thereabout,
2Co 4: 8 we are *p*', but not in despair;

perplexity
Isa 22: 5 and of *p*' by the Lord God of hosts
Mic 7: 4 cometh; now shall be their *p*'.
Lu 21: 25 earth distress of nations, with *p*';

persecute See also PERSECUTED; PERSECUTEST; PERSECUTING.
Job 19: 22 Why do ye *p*' me as God, and are
28 Why *p*' we him, seeing the root of
Ps 7: 1 save me from all them that *p*' me,
5 Let the enemy *p*' my soul, and
10: 2 in his pride doth *p*' the poor:
31: 15 enemies,...from them that *p*' me.
35: 3 the way against them that *p*' me:
6 let the angel of the Lord *p*' them.
69: 26 they *p*' him who thou hast smitten;
71: 11 forsaken him: *p*' and take him;
83: 15 So *p*' them with thy tempest, and
119: 84 judgment on them that *p*' me?
86 they *p*' me wrongfully; help thou
Jer 17: 18 them be confounded that *p*' me,
29: 18 I will *p*' them with the sword,
La 3: 66 *P*' and destroy them in anger
M't 5: 11 men shall revile you, and *p*' you,
44 despitefully use you, and *p*' you;
10: 23 when they *p*' you in this city, flee
23: 34 and *p*' them from city to city:
Lu 11: 49 of them they shall slay and *p*':
21: 12 their hands on you, and *p*' you,
Joh 5: 16 therefore did the Jews *p*' Jesus,
15: 20 me, they will also *p*' you;
Ro 12: 14 Bless them which *p*' you: bless, and

persecuted
De 30: 7 that hate thee, which *p*' thee.
Ps 109: 16 but *p*' the poor and needy man,
119: 161 have *p*' me without a cause: but
143: 3 For the enemy hath *p*' my soul; he
Isa 14: 6 ruled the nations in anger, is *p*',
La 3: 43 covered with anger, and *p*' us:
M't 5: 10 are *p*' for righteousness' sake:
12 so *p*' they the prophets which were
Joh 15: 20 If they have *p*' me, they will also
Ac 7: 52 prophets have not your fathers *p*'?
22: 4 And I *p*' this way unto the death,
26: 11 I *p*' them even unto strange cities.
1Co 4: 12 we bless; being *p*', we suffer it:
15: 9 because I *p*' the church of God.
2Co 4: 9 *P*', but not forsaken; cast down,
Ga 1: 13 measure I *p*' the church of God,
23 he which *p*' us in times past now
4: 29 *p*' him that was born after the
1Th 2: 15 own prophets, and have *p*' us;
Re 12: 13 *p*' the woman which brought forth

persecutest
Ac 9: 4 him, Saul, Saul, why *p*' thou me?
5 said, I am Jesus whom thou *p*':
22: 7 me, Saul, Saul, why *p*' thou me?
8 Jesus of Nazareth, whom thou *p*'.
26: 14 Saul, Saul, why *p*' thou me? it is
15 he said, I am Jesus whom thou *p*'.

persecuting
Ph'p 3: 6 Concerning zeal, *p*' the church;

persecution See also PERSECUTIONS.
La 5: 5 Our necks are under *p*': we
M't 13: 21 or *p*' ariseth because of the word,
M'r 4: 17 or *p*' ariseth for the word's sake,
Ac 8: 1 was a great *p*' against the church
11: 19 the *p*' that arose about Stephen
13: 50 and raised *p*' against Paul and
Ro 8: 35 shall tribulation, or distress, or *p*',
Ga 5: 11 circumcision, why do I...suffer *p*'?
6: 12 suffer *p*' for the cross of Christ.
2Ti 3: 12 godly in Christ Jesus shall suffer *p*'.

persecutions
M'r 10: 30 and children, and lands, with *p*';
2Co 12: 10 *p*', in distresses for Christ's sake:
2Th 1: 4 faith in all your *p*' and tribulations
2Ti 3: 11 *P*', afflictions, which came unto me
11 at Lystra; what *p*' I endured:

persecutor See also PERSECUTORS.
1Ti 1: 13 before a blasphemer, and a *p*',

persecutors
Ne 9: 11 *p*' thou threwest into the deeps,
Ps 7: 13 his arrows against the *p*'.
119: 157 are my *p*' and mine enemies;
142: 6 very low: deliver me from my *p*';
Jer 15: 15 me, and revenge me of my *p*';
20: 11 therefore my *p*' shall stumble, and
La 1: 3 all her *p*' overtook her between
4: 19 Our *p*' are swifter than the eagles

perseverance
Eph 6: 18 with all *p*' and supplication for

Persia (*per'-she-ah*) See also ELAM; PERSIAN.
2Ch 36: 20 the reign of the kingdom of *P*':
22 the first year of Cyrus king of *P*',
22 up the spirit of Cyrus king of *P*',
23 Thus saith Cyrus king of *P*', All the
Ezr 1: 1 the first year of Cyrus king of *P*',
1 up the spirit of Cyrus king of *P*',
2 saith Cyrus king of *P*', The Lord
8 did Cyrus king of *P*' bring forth
3: 7 that they had of Cyrus king of *P*'.
4: 3 the king of *P*' hath commanded us.
5 all the days of Cyrus king of *P*',
5 the reign of Darius king of *P*'.
7 wrote...unto Artaxerxes king of *P*':
24 of the reign of Darius king of *P*'.
6: 14 Darius, and Artaxerxes king of *P*'.
7: 1 the reign of Artaxerxes king of *P*',
9: 9 us in the sight of the kings of *P*',
Es 1: 3 the power of *P*' and Media, the
14 the seven princes of *P*' and Media,
18 shall the ladies of *P*' and Media say
10: 2 of the kings of Media and *P*'?
Eze 27: 10 They of *P*' and of Lud and of Phut
38: 5 *P*', Ethiopia, and Libya with them;
Da 8: 20 are the kings of Media and *P*'.
10: 1 the third year of Cyrus king of *P*'
13 But the prince of the kingdom of *P*'
13 remained...with the kings of *P*'.
20 to fight with the prince of *P*':
11: 2 stand up yet three kings in *P*';

Persian (*per'-she-un*) See also PERSIANS.
Ne 12: 22 to the reign of Darius the *P*'.
Da 6: 28 and in the reign of Cyrus the *P*'.

Persians (*pur'-she-uns*) See also ELAMITES.
Es 1: 19 the laws of the *P*' and the Medes,
Da 5: 28 and given to the Medes and *P*'.
6: 8, 12 to the law of the Medes and *P*',
15 that the law of the Medes and *P*' is,

Persis (*pur'-sis*)
Ro 16: 12 Salute the beloved *P*', which

person A See also PERSONS.
Ge 39: 6 Joseph was a goodly *p*', and well
Ex 12: 48 no uncircumcised *p*' shall eat thereof.
Le 19: 15 not respect the *p*' of the poor,
15 nor honour the *p*' of the mighty:
Nu 5: 6 the Lord, and that *p*' be guilty;
19: 17 for an unclean *p*' they shall take of
18 And a clean *p*' shall take hyssop,
22 whatsoever the unclean *p*' toucheth
31: 19 whosoever hath killed any *p*', and
35: 11 which killeth any *p*' at unawares.
15 one that killeth any *p*' unawares
30 Whoso killeth any *p*', the murderer
30 shall not testify against any *p*' to
De 15: 22 and the clean *p*' shall eat it alike,
27: 25 reward to slay an innocent *p*'.
28: 50 shall not regard the *p*' of the old,
Jos 20: 3 that killeth any *p*' unawares and
9 that whosoever killeth any *p*' at
1Sa 9: 2 of Israel a goodlier *p*' than he:
16: 18 prudent in matters, and a comely *p*',
25: 35 voice, and have accepted thy *p*'.
2Sa 4: 11 men have slain a righteous *p*' in
14: 14 neither doth God respect any *p*':
17: 11 thou go to battle in thine own *p*'.
Job 13: 8 Will ye accept his *p*'? will ye
22: 29 up; and he shall save the humble *p*'.
32: 21 I pray you, accept any man's *p*';
Ps 15: 4 In whose eyes a vile *p*' is contemned;
49: 10 the fool and the brutish *p*' perish,
101: 4 from me: I will not know a wicked *p*'.
105: 37 not one feeble *p*' among their tribes.
Pr 6: 12 A naughty *p*', a wicked man,
18: 5 to accept the *p*' of the wicked,
24: 8 shall be called a mischievous *p*'.
28: 17 violence to the blood of any *p*'
Isa 32: 5 The vile *p*' shall be no more called
6 the vile *p*' will speak villany, and his
Jer 43: 6 every *p*' that Nebuzar-adan the
52: 25 them that were near the king's *p*',
Eze 16: 5 to the lothing of thy *p*', in the day
33: 6 and take any *p*' from among them,
44: 25 shall come at no dead *p*' to defile
Da 11: 21 in his estate shall stand up a vile *p*',
Mal 1: 8 or accept thy *p*'? saith the Lord
M't 22: 16 thou regardest not the *p*' of men.
27: 24 innocent of the blood of this just *p*':
M'r 12: 14 thou regardest not the *p*' of men,
Lu 20: 21 neither acceptest thou the *p*' of any,
1Co 5: 13 from among yourselves that wicked *p*'.
2Co 2: 10 forgave I it in the *p*' of Christ;
Ga 2: 6 to me: God accepteth no man's *p*':)
Heb 1: 3 and the express image of his *p*',
12: 16 any fornicator, or profane *p*', as Esau,
2Pe 2: 5 but saved Noah the eighth *p*', a

persons
Ge 14: 21 said unto Abram, Give me the *p*',
36: 6 and all the *p*' of his house, and his
Ex 16: 16 according to the number of your *p*';
Le 27: 2 the *p*' shall be for the Lord by thy
Nu 19: 18 and upon the *p*' that were there,
31: 28 soul of five hundred, both of the *p*',
30 take one portion of fifty, of the *p*', of
35 and two thousand *p*' in all,
40 the *p*' were sixteen thousand;
40 tribute was thirty and two *p*'.
46 And sixteen thousand *p*';)
De 1: 17 shall not respect *p*' in judgment;
10: 17 which regardeth not *p*', nor taketh
22 Egypt with threescore and ten *p*';
16: 19 thou shalt not respect *p*', neither
J'g 9: 2 which are threescore and ten *p*',
4 Abimelech hired vain and light *p*',
J'g 9: 5 being threescore and ten *p*', upon
18 threescore and ten *p*', upon one
20: 39 of the men of Israel about thirty *p*':
1Sa 9: 22 bidden, which were about thirty *p*'.
22: 18 five *p*' that did wear a linen ephod.
22 of all the *p*' of thy father's house.
2Ki 10: 6 the king's sons, being seventy *p*',
7 slew seventy *p*', and put their heads
2Ch 19: 7 nor respect of *p*', nor taking of
Job 13: 10 you, if ye do secretly accept *p*'.
34: 19 that accepteth not the *p*' of princes.
Ps 26: 4 I have not sat with vain *p*', neither
82: 2 and accept the *p*' of the wicked?
Pr 12: 11 he that followeth vain *p*' is void of
24: 23 not good to have respect of *p*' in
28: 19 after vain *p*' shall have poverty
21 To have respect of *p*' is not good:
Jer 52: 29 eight hundred thirty and two *p*':
30 seven hundred forty and five *p*':
30 the *p*' were four thousand and six
La 4: 16 respected not the *p*' of the priests,
Eze 17: 17 building forts, to cut off many *p*':
27: 13 traded the *p*' of men and vessels
Jon 4: 11 are more than sixscore thousand *p*'
Zep 3: 4 are light and treacherous *p*':
Mal 1: 9 means: will he regard your *p*'?
Lu 15: 7 than over ninety and nine just *p*',
Ac 10: 34 that God is no respecter of *p*':
17: 17 with the Jews, and with the devout *p*',
Ro 2: 11 there is no respect of *p*' with God.
2Co 1: 11 upon us by the means of many *p*'
Eph 6: 9 is there respect of *p*' with him.
Col 3: 25 done: and there is no respect of *p*'.
1Ti 1: 10 for liars, for perjured *p*', and if
Jas 2: 1 Lord of glory, with respect of *p*'.
9 if ye have respect to *p*', ye commit
1Pe 1: 17 who without respect of *p*' judgeth
2Pe 3: 11 what manner of *p*' ought ye to be in
Jude 16 having men's *p*' in admiration

persuade See also PERSUADED; PERSUADEST; PERSUADETH; PERSUADING.
1Ki 22: 20 Who shall *p*' Ahab, that he may
21 the Lord, and said, I will *p*' him.
22 Thou shalt *p*' him, and prevail
2Ch 32: 11 Doth not Hezekiah *p*' you to give
15 you, nor *p*' you on this manner,
Isa 36: 18 Beware lest Hezekiah *p*' you,
M't 28: 14 we will *p*' him, and secure you.
2Co 5: 11 the terror of the Lord, we *p*' men:
Ga 1: 10 For do I now *p*' men, or God? or

persuaded
2Ch 18: 2 and *p*' him to go up with him to
Pr 25: 15 By long forbearing is a prince *p*',
M't 27: 20 and elders *p*' the multitude that
Lu 16: 31 neither will they be *p*', though one
20: 6 they be *p*' that John was a prophet.
Ac 13: 43 *p*' them to continue in the grace of
14: 19 who *p*' the people, and, having
18: 4 and *p*' the Jews and the Greeks.
19: 26 *p*' and turned away much people,
21: 14 And when he would not be *p*', we
26: 26 I am *p*' that none of these things
Ro 4: 21 And being fully *p*' that, what he
8: 38 For I am *p*', that neither death,
14: 5 man be fully *p*' in his own mind.
14 and am *p*' by the Lord Jesus, that
15: 14 also am *p*' of you, my brethren,
2Ti 1: 5 and I am *p*' that in thee also.
12 and am *p*' that he is able to keep
Heb 6: 9 we are *p*' better things of you, and
11: 13 were *p*' of them, and embraced

persuadest
Ac 26: 28 thou *p*' me to be a Christian.

persuadeth
2Ki 18: 32 unto Hezekiah, when he *p*' you,
Ac 18: 13 This fellow *p*' men to worship God

persuading
Ac 19: 8 and *p*' the things concerning the
28: 23 *p*' them concerning Jesus, both out

persuasion
Ga 5: 8 *p*' cometh not of him that calleth

pertain See also APPERTAIN; PERTAINED; PERTAINETH; PERTAINING; PURTENANCE.
Le 7: 20 peace offerings, that *p*' unto the Lord,
21 offerings, which *p*' unto the Lord,
1Sa 25: 22 if I leave of all that *p*' to him by the
Ro 15: 17 in those things which *p*' to God.
1Co 6: 3 much more things that *p*' to this life?
2Pe 1: 3 unto us all things that *p*' unto life

pertained
Nu 31: 43 half that *p*' unto the congregation
Jos 24: 33 in a hill that *p*' to Phinehas his son,
J'g 6: 11 that *p*' unto Joash the Abi-ezrite:
1Sa 25: 21 was missed of all that *p*' unto him:
2Sa 2: 15 which *p*' to Ish-bosheth the son of
9: 9 *p*' to Saul and to all his house.
16: 4 are all that *p*' unto Mephibosheth.
1Ki 4: 10 to him *p*' Sochoh, and all the land of
12 to him *p*' Taanach and Megiddo, and
13 to him *p*' the towns of Jair the son of
13 to him also *p*' the region of Argob,
7: 48 all the vessels that *p*' unto the house
2Ki 24: 7 all that *p*' to the king of Egypt.
1Ch 9: 27 thereof every morning *p*' to them.
11: 31 that *p*' to the children of Benjamin,
2Ch 12: 4 the fenced cities which *p*' to Judah,
34: 33 that *p*' to the children of Israel,

pertaineth
Le 14: 32 get that which *p*' to his cleansing.
Nu 4: 16 the priest *p*' the oil for the light,
De 22: 5 wear that which *p*' unto a man,

1Sa 27: 6 Ziklag *p'* unto the kings of Judah
2Sa 6:12 Obed-edom, and all that *p'* unto him,
Ro 9: 4 to whom *p'* the adoption, and the
Heb 7:13 are spoken *p'* to another tribe,

pertaining
Jos 13:31 were *p'* unto the children of Machir
1Ch 26:32 every matter *p'* to God, and affairs
Ac 1: 3 things *p'* to the kingdom of God:
Ro 4: 1 as *p'* to the flesh, hath found?
1Co 6: 4 judgments of things *p'* to this life,
Heb 2:17 high priest in things *p'* to God,
5: 1 ordained for men in things *p'* to God,
9: 9 perfect, as *p'* to the conscience;

Peruda (*per'-u-dah*) See also PERIDA.
Ezr 2:55 of Sophereth, the children of *P'*,

perverse
Nu 22:32 because thy way is *p'* before me:
De 32: 5 are a *p'* and crooked generation.
1Sa 20:30 son of the *p'* rebellious woman,
Job 6:30 my taste discern *p'* things?
9:20 perfect, it shall also prove me *p'*.
Pr 4:24 and *p'* lips put far from thee.
8: 8 is nothing froward or *p'* in them.
12: 8 is of a *p'* heart shall be despised.
14: 2 is *p'* in his ways despiseth him.
17:20 a *p'* tongue falleth into mischief.
19: 1 he that is *p'* in his lips, and...a fool
23:33 thine heart shall utter *p'* things.
28: 6 he that is *p'* in his ways, though
18 *p'* in his ways shall fall at once.
Isa 19:14 The Lord hath mingled a *p'* spirit
M't 17:17 said, O faithless and *p'* generation,
Lu 9:41 said, O faithless and *p'* generation,
Ac 20:30 men arise, speaking *p'* things, to
Ph'p 2:15 midst of a crooked and *p'* nation,
1Ti 6: 5 *P'* disputings of men of corrupt

perversely
2Sa 19:19 that which thy servant did *p'* the
1Ki 8:47 We have sinned, and have done *p'*,
Ps 119:78 for they dealt *p'* with me without

perverseness
Nu 23:21 neither hath he seen *p'* in Israel:
Pr 11: 3 *p'* of transgressors shall destroy
15: 4 *p'* therein is a breach in the spirit.
Isa 30:12 trust in oppression and *p'*, and
59: 3 your tongue hath muttered *p'*.
Eze 9: 9 of blood, and the city full of *p'*:

pervert See also PERVERTED; PERVERTETH; PERVERTING.
De 16:19 and *p'* the words of the righteous.
24:17 *p'* the judgment of the stranger,
Job 8: 3 Doth God *p'* judgment?
3 or doth the Almighty *p'* justice?
34:12 will the Almighty *p'* judgment.
Pr 17:23 bosom to *p'* the ways of judgment.
31: 5 forget...law, and *p'* the judgment
Mic 3: 9 abhor judgment, and *p'* all equity.
Ac 13:10 to *p'* the right ways of the Lord?
Ga 1: 7 and would *p'* the gospel of Christ

perverted
1Sa 8: 3 and took bribes, and *p'* judgment.
Job 33:27 sinned, and *p'*...which was right,
Isa 47:10 thy knowledge, it hath *p'* thee;
Jer 3:21 they have *p'* their way, and they
23:36 *p'* the words of the living God,

perverteth
Ex 23: 8 and *p'* the words of the righteous.
De 27:19 cursed be he that *p'* the judgment
Pr 10: 9 that *p'* his ways shall be known.
19: 3 foolishness of man *p'* his way:
Lu 23:14 unto me, as one that *p'* the people;

perverting
Ec 5: 8 violent *p'* of judgment and justice
Lu 23: 2 We found this fellow *p'* the nation,

pestilence See also PESTILENCES.
Ex 5: 3 he fall upon us with *p'*, or with the
9:15 smite thee and thy people with *p'*;
Le 26:25 I will send the *p'* among you; and
Nu 14:12 I will smite them with the *p'*, and
De 28:21 shall make the *p'* cleave unto thee,
2Sa 24:13 there be three days' *p'* in thy land?
15 So the Lord sent a *p'* upon Israel
1Ki 8:37 be in the land famine, if there be *p'*,
1Ch 21:12 even the *p'*, in the land, and the
14 So the Lord sent *p'* upon Israel:
2Ch 6:28 if there be *p'*, if there be blasting,
7:13 or if I send *p'* among my people;
20: 9 sword, judgment, or *p'*, or famine,
Ps 78:50 but gave their life over to the *p'*;
91: 3 fowler, and from the noisome *p'*.
6 for the *p'* that walketh in darkness;
Jer 14:12 and by the famine, and by the *p'*.
21: 6 they shall die of a great *p'*.
7 as are left in this city from the *p'*,
9 and by the famine, and by the *p'*:
24:10 famine, and the *p'*, among them,
27: 8 with the famine, and with the *p'*,
13 sword, by the famine, and by the *p'*,
28: 8 of war, and of evil, and of *p'*.
29:17 the sword, the famine, and the *p'*,
18 the famine, and with the *p'*, and
32:24 famine, and of the *p'*: and what
36 and by the famine, and by the *p'*;
34:17 sword, to the *p'*, and to the famine;
38: 2 sword, by the famine, and by the *p'*:
42:17 sword, by the famine, and by the *p'*:
22 sword, by the famine, and by the *p'*,
44:13 sword, by the famine, and by the *p'*:
Eze 5:12 A third part...shall die with the *p'*,
17 *p'* and blood shall pass through
6:11 sword, by the famine, and by the *p'*.
12 He that is far off shall die of the *p'*;
7:15 and the *p'* and the famine within:
15 famine and *p'* shall devour him.
12:16 from the famine, and from the *p'*;
14:19 Or if I send a *p'* into that land, and
21 the noisome beast, and the *p'*, to
28:23 I will send into her *p'*, and blood
33:27 and in the caves shall die of the *p'*.
38:22 against him with *p'* and with blood;
Am 4:10 I have sent among you the *p'* after
Hab 3: 5 Before him went the *p'*, and

pestilences
M't 24: 7 *p'*, and earthquakes, in divers
Lu 21:11 divers places, and famines, and *p'*;

pestilent
Ac 24: 5 have found this man a *p'* fellow,

pestle
Pr 27:22 a mortar among wheat with a *p'*,

Peter (*pe'-tur*) See also CEPHAS; PETER'S; SIMON.
M't 4:18 And Simon called *P'*, and Andrew
10: 2 The first, Simon, who is called *P'*,
14:28 *P'* answered him and said, Lord,
29 when *P'* was come down out of the
15:15 Then answered *P'* and said unto
16:16 And Simon *P'* answered and said,
18 That thou art *P'*, and upon this
22 *P'* took him, and began to rebuke
23 said unto *P'*, Get thee behind me,
17: 1 Jesus taketh *P'*, James, and John
4 Then answered *P'*, and said unto
24 received tribute money came to *P'*,
26 *P'* saith unto him, Of strangers.
18:21 Then came *P'* to him, and said,
19:27 answered *P'* and said unto him,
26:33 *P'* answered and said unto him,
35 *P'* said unto him, Though I should
37 *P'* and the two sons of Zebedee,
40 saith unto *P'*, What, could ye not
58 *P'* followed him afar off unto the
69 Now *P'* sat without in the palace:
73 said to *P'*, Surely thou also art one
75 *P'* remembered the word of Jesus,
M'r 3:16 And Simon he surnamed *P'*;
5:37 to follow him, save *P'*, and James,
8:29 *P'* answereth and saith unto him,
32 *P'* took him, and began to rebuke
33 he rebuked *P'*, saying, Get thee
9: 2 Jesus taketh with him *P'*, and
5 *P'* answered and said to Jesus,
10:28 *P'* began to say unto him, Lo, we
11:21 *P'* calling to remembrance saith
13: 3 *P'* and James and John...Andrew
14:29 *P'* said unto him, Although all
33 he taketh with him *P'* and James
37 saith unto *P'*, Simon, sleepest thou?
54 *P'* followed him afar off, even into
66 *P'* was beneath in the palace, there
67 when she saw *P'* warming himself,
70 said again to *P'*, Surely thou art
72 *P'* called to mind the word that
16: 7 tell his disciples and *P'* that he
Lu 5: 8 When Simon *P'* saw it, he fell down
6:14 Simon, (whom he also named *P'*,)
8:45 *P'* and they that were with him
51 suffered no man to go in, save *P'*,
9:20 *P'* answering said, The Christ of
28 he took *P'* and John and James,
32 But *P'* and they that were with him
33 *P'* said unto Jesus, Master, it is
12:41 *P'* said unto him, Lord, speakest
18:28 Then *P'* said, Lo, we have left all,
22: 8 And he sent *P'* and John, saying,
34 I tell thee, *P'*, the cock shall not
54 house. And *P'* followed afar off.
55 together, *P'* sat down among them.
58 them. And *P'* said, Man, I am not.
60 *P'* said, Man, I know not what thou
61 Lord turned, and looked upon *P'*.
61 *P'* remembered the word of the
62 And *P'* went out, and wept bitterly.
24:12 Then arose *P'*, and ran unto the
Joh 1:44 Bethsaida,...city of Andrew and *P'*.
6:68 Simon *P'* answered him, Lord, to
13: 6 Then cometh he to Simon *P'*: and
6 *P'* saith unto him, Lord, dost thou
8 *P'* saith unto him, Thou shalt
9 Simon *P'* saith unto him, Lord, not
24 Simon *P'* therefore beckoned to
36 Simon *P'* said unto him, Lord,
37 *P'* said unto him, Lord, why cannot
18:10 Simon *P'* having a sword drew it,
11 said Jesus unto *P'*, Put up thy
15 And Simon *P'* followed Jesus, and
16 *P'* stood at the door without. Then
16 kept the door, and brought in *P'*.
17 damsel that kept the door unto *P'*,
18 *P'* stood with them, and warmed
25 And Simon *P'* stood and warmed
26 his kinsman whose ear *P'* cut off,
27 *P'* then denied again: and
20: 2 runneth, and cometh to Simon *P'*,
3 *P'* therefore went forth, and that
4 the other disciple did outrun *P'*,
6 cometh Simon *P'* following him,
21: 2 together Simon *P'*, and Thomas
3 Simon *P'* saith unto them, I go a
7 loved saith unto *P'*, It is the Lord.
7 *P'* heard that it was the Lord,
11 Simon *P'* went up, and drew the
15 Jesus saith to Simon *P'*, Simon,
17 *P'* was grieved because he said
20 *P'*, turning about, seeth the
Joh 21:21 *P'* seeing him saith to Jesus, Lord,
Ac 1:13 where abode both *P'*, and James,
15 *P'* stood up in the midst of the
2:14 *P'*, standing up with the eleven,
37 unto *P'* and to the rest of the
38 Then *P'* said unto them, Repent,
3: 1 *P'* and John went up together into
3 seeing *P'* and John about to go
4 *P'*, fastening his eyes upon him
6 *P'* said, Silver and gold have I
11 which was healed held *P'* and John,
12 when *P'* saw it he answered unto
4: 8 *P'*, filled with the Holy Ghost, said
13 saw the boldness of *P'* and John,
19 *P'* and John answered and said
5: 3 *P'* said, Ananias, why hath Satan
8 *P'* answered unto her, Tell me
9 *P'* said unto her, How is it that
15 the shadow of *P'* passing by might
29 *P'* and the other apostles answered
8:14 they sent unto them *P'* and John:
20 But *P'* said unto him, Thy money
9:32 *P'* passed throughout all quarters,
34 *P'* said unto him, Æneas, Jesus
38 disciples had heard that *P'* was
39 Then *P'* arose and went with them.
40 *P'* put them all forth, and kneeled
40 and when she saw *P'*, she sat up.
10: 5 one Simon, whose surname is *P'*:
9 *P'* went up upon the housetop to
13 voice to him, Rise, *P'*; kill and eat.
14 *P'* said, Not so, Lord; for I have
17 *P'* doubted in himself what this
18 which was surnamed *P'*, were
19 While *P'* thought on the vision, the
21 *P'* went down to the men which
23 morrow *P'* went away with them,
25 as *P'* was coming in, Cornelius met
26 *P'* took him up, saying, Stand up;
32 Simon, whose surname is *P'*;
34 *P'* opened his mouth, and said, Of
44 *P'* yet spake these words, the Holy
45 as many as came with *P'*,
46 magnify God. Then answered *P'*,
11: 2 *P'* was come up to Jerusalem,
4 *P'* rehearsed the matter from the
7 unto me, Arise, *P'*; slay and eat.
13 for Simon, whose surname is *P'*;
12: 3 proceeded further to take *P'* also.
5 *P'* therefore was kept in prison:
6 *P'*...sleeping between two soldiers,
7 he smote *P'* on the side, and raised
11 when *P'* was come to himself, he
13 as *P'* knocked at the door of the
14 told how *P'* stood before the gate.
16 But *P'* continued knocking: and
18 soldiers, what was become of *P'*.
15: 7 *P'* rose up, and said unto them,
Ga 1:18 I went up to Jerusalem to see *P'*,
2: 7 of the circumcision was unto *P'*;
8 he that wrought effectually in *P'*
11 But when *P'* was come to Antioch,
14 I said unto *P'* before them all,
1Pe 1: 1 *P'*, an apostle of Jesus Christ,
2Pe 1: 1 Simon *P'*, a servant and an apostle

Peter's (*pe'-turz*)
M't 8:14 Jesus was come into *P'* house,
Joh 1:40 him, was Andrew, Simon *P'* brother.
6: 8 Andrew, Simon *P'* brother, saith
Ac 12:14 And when she knew *P'* voice, she

Pethahiah (*peth-a-hi'-ah*)
1Ch 24:16 nineteenth to *P'*, the twentieth
Ezr 10:23 Kelaiah, (the same is Kelita,) *P'*,
Ne 9: 5 Hodijah, Shebaniah, and *P'*, said,
11:24 And *P'* the son of Meshezabeel, of

Pethor (*pe'-thor*)
Nu 22: 5 unto Balaam the son of Beor to *P'*,
De 23: 4 Balaam the son of Beor of *P'* of

Pethuel (*pe-thu'-el*)
Joe 1: 1 that came to Joel the son of *P'*.

petition See also PETITIONS.
1Sa 1:17 God of Israel grant thee thy *p'*
27 Lord hath given me my *p'* which I
1Ki 2:16 I ask one *p'* of thee, deny me not.
20 said, I desire one small *p'* of thee;
Es 5: 6 What is thy *p'*? and it shall be
7 and said, My *p'* and my request is;
8 if it please the king to grant my *p'*,
7: 2 What is thy *p'*, queen Esther? and
3 let my life be given me at my *p'*,
9:12 now what is thy *p'*? and it shall be
Da 6: 7 shall ask a *p'* of any God or man
12 that shall ask a *p'* of any God or man
13 maketh his *p'* three times a day.

petitions
Ps 20: 5 banners: the Lord fulfil all thy *p'*.
1Jo 5:15 have the *p'* that we desired of him.

Peulthai (*pe-ul'-thahee*)
1Ch 26: 5 the seventh, *P'* the eighth:

Phalec (*fa'-lek*) See also PELEG.
Lu 3:35 which was the son of *P'*, which

Phallu (*fal'-lu*) See also PALLU.
Ge 46: 9 sons of Reuben; Hanoch, and *P'*.

Phalti (*fal'-ti*) See also PHALTIEL.
1Sa 25:44 his daughter, David's wife, to *P'*

Phaltiel (*fal'-te-el*) See also PHALTI.
2Sa 3:15 even from *P'* the son of Laish.

Phanuel (*fan-u'-el*)
Lu 2:36 a prophetess, the daughter of *P'*,

Pharaoh (*fa'-ra-o*) See also PHARAOH'S; PHARAOH-HOPHRA; PHARAOH-NECHO.
Ge 12:15 The princes also of P· saw her,
15 and commended her before P·:
17 the Lord plagued P· and his house
18 P· called Abram, and said, What is
20 P· commanded his men concerning
39: 1 Potiphar, an officer of P·, captain
40: 2 P· was wroth against two of his
13 days shall P· lift up thine head,
14 and make mention of me unto P·,
17 of all manner of bakemeats for P·;
19 three days shall P· lift up thy head
41: 1 of full two years, that P· dreamed:
4 favoured and fat kine. So P· awoke.
7 and P· awoke, and, behold, it was a
8 and P· told them his dream; but
8 that could interpret them unto P·.
9 Then spake the chief butler unto P·,
10 P· was wroth with his servants,
14 Then P· sent and called Joseph,
14 his raiment, and came in unto P·.
15 And P· said unto Joseph, I have
16 Joseph answered P·, saying, It is
16 shall give P· an answer of peace.
17 P· said unto Joseph, In my dream,
25 And Joseph said unto P·,
25 The dream of P· is one: God hath
25 shewed P· what he is about to do.
28 thing which I have spoken unto P·:
28 is about to do he sheweth unto P·.
32 dream was doubled unto P· twice;
33 let P· look out a man discreet and
34 Let P· do this, and let him appoint
35 lay up corn under the hand of P·,
37 the thing was good in the eyes of P·,
38 P· said unto his servants, Can we
39 P· said unto Joseph, Forasmuch as
41 P· said unto Joseph, See, I have set
42 P· took off his ring from his hand,
44 And P· said unto Joseph, I am P·,
45 And P· called Joseph's name
46 years old when he stood before P·
46 went out from the presence of P·,
55 the people cried to P· for bread:
55 P· said unto all the Egyptians, Go
42:15 By the life of P· ye shall not go forth
16 by the life of P· surely ye are spies.
44:18 servant: for thou art even as P·.
45: 2 and the house of P· heard.
8 he hath made me a father to P·,
16 pleased P· well, and his servants.
17 P· said unto Joseph, Say unto thy
21 to the commandment of P·,
46: 5 which P· had sent to carry him.
31 I will go up, and shew P·, and say
33 to pass, when P· shall call you,
47: 1 Joseph came and told P·, and said,
2 men, and presented them unto P·.
3 P· said unto his brethren, What is
3 they said unto P·, Thy servants
4 They said moreover to P·, For to
5 P· spake unto Joseph, saying, Thy
7 before P·: and Jacob blessed P·.
8 P· said unto Jacob, How old art
9 Jacob said unto P·, The days of the
10 And Jacob blessed P·, and went
10 and went out from before P·.
11 of Rameses, as P· had commanded.
19 our land will be servants unto P·:
20 bought all the land of Egypt for P·;
22 had a portion assigned them of P·,
22 did eat their portion which P· gave
23 have bought you this day...for P·:
24 ye shall give the fifth part unto P·,
26 that P· should have the fifth part;
50: 4 Joseph spake unto the house of P·,
4 speak, I pray you, in the ears of P·,
6 P· said, Go up, and bury thy father,
7 him went up all the servants of P·,
Ex 1:11 they built for P· treasure cities,
19 the midwives said unto P·, Because
22 P· charged all his people, saying,
2: 5 daughter of P· came down to wash
15 Now when P· heard this thing, he
15 Moses fled from the face of P·, and
3:10 I will send thee unto P·, that thou
11 Who am I, that I should go unto P·,
4:21 thou do all those wonders before P·,
22 thou shalt say unto P·, Thus saith
5: 1 and Aaron went in, and told P·,
2 P· said, Who is the Lord, that I
5 P· said, Behold, the people of the
6 And P· commanded the same day
10 Thus saith P·, I will not give you
15 of Israel came and cried unto P·,
20 way, as they came forth from P·:
21 to be abhorred in the eyes of P·,
23 I came to P· to speak in thy name,
6: 1 shalt thou see what I will do to P·:
11 Go in, speak unto P· king of Egypt,
12 how then shall P· hear me, who am
13 Israel, and unto P· king of Egypt,
27 which spake to P· king of Egypt,
29 speak thou unto P· king of Egypt
30 and how shall P· hearken unto me?
7: 1 See, I have made thee a god to P·:
2 thy brother shall speak unto P·,
4 But P· shall not hearken unto you,
7 old, when they spake unto P·.
9 When P· shall speak unto you,
9 Take thy rod, and cast it before P·,
10 Moses and Aaron went in unto P·,
10 Aaron cast down his rod before P·,
11 Then P· also called the wise men
15 Get thee unto P· in the morning;
Ex 7:20 were in the river, in the sight of P·,
23 P· turned and went into his house,
8: 1 Go unto P·, and say unto him, Thus
8 P· called for Moses and Aaron,
9 Moses said unto P·, Glory over me:
12 and Aaron went out from P·:
12 which he had brought against P·.
15 when P· saw that there was respite,
19 Then the magicians said unto P·,
20 the morning, and stand before P·;
24 swarm of flies into the house of P·,
25 P· called for Moses and for Aaron,
28 P· said, I will let you go, that ye
29 swarms of flies may depart from P·,
29 let not P· deal deceitfully any more
30 And Moses went out from P·, and
31 the swarms of flies from P·,
32 P· hardened his heart at this time
9: 1 Go in unto P·, and tell him, Thus
7 P· sent, and, behold, there was not
7 And the heart of P· was hardened,
8 toward...heaven in the sight of P·.
10 of the furnace, and stood before P·;
12 the Lord hardened the heart of P·,
13 stand before P·, and say unto him,
20 the Lord among the servants of P·
27 P· sent, and called for Moses and
33 Moses went out of the city from P·,
34 when P· saw that the rain and the
35 heart of P· was hardened, neither
10: 1 said unto Moses, Go in unto P·:
3 Moses and Aaron came in unto P·,
6 himself, and went out from P·.
8 Aaron were brought again unto P·:
16 P· called for Moses and Aaron in
18 he went out from P·, and intreated
24 P· called unto Moses, and said, Go
28 P· said unto him, Get thee from
11: 1 I bring one plague more upon P·,
5 firstborn of P· that sitteth upon his
8 went out from P· in a great anger.
9 P· shall not hearken unto you;
10 did all these wonders before P·:
12:29 the firstborn of P· that sat on his
30 P· rose up in the night, he, and all
13:15 P· would hardly let us go, that the
17 when P· had let the people go, that
14: 3 P· will say of the children of Israel,
4 I will be honoured upon P·, and
5 heart of P· and of his servants was
8 The Lord hardened the heart of P·
9 all the horses and chariots of P·,
10 when P· drew nigh, the children of
17 and I will get me honour upon P·,
18 I have gotten me honour upon P·,
28 all the host of P· that came into the
15:19 the horse of P· went in with his
18: 4 delivered me from the sword of P·:
8 all that the Lord had done unto P·
10 and out of the hand of P·, who hath
De 6:22 and sore, upon Egypt, upon P·, and
7: 8 from the hand of P· king of Egypt.
18 what the Lord thy God did unto P·,
11: 3 did in the midst of Egypt unto P·
29: 2 eyes in the land of Egypt unto P·,
34:11 to do in the land of Egypt to P·, and
1Sa 6: 6 and P· hardened their hearts?
1Ki 3: 1 made affinity with P· king of Egypt,
9:16 P· king of Egypt had gone up, and
11: 1 together with the daughter of P·,
18 to Egypt, unto P· king of Egypt;
19 great favour in the sight of P·, so
20 household among the sons of P·.
21 Hadad said to P·, Let me depart,
22 Then P· said unto him, But what
2Ki 17: 7 under the hand of P· king of Egypt,
18:21 so is P· king of Egypt unto all that
23:35 gave the silver and the gold to P·;
35 to the commandment of P·:
1Ch 4:18 sons of Bithiah the daughter of P·,
2Ch 8:11 the daughter of P· out of the city of
Ne 9:10 signs and wonders upon P·, and
Ps 135: 9 the midst of thee, O Egypt, upon P·,
136:15 P· and his host in the Red sea:
Isa 19:11 wise counsellers of P· is become
11 how say ye unto P·, I am the son of
30: 2 themselves in the strength of P·,
3 the strength of P· be your shame,
36: 6 so is P· king of Egypt to all that
Jer 25:19 P· king of Egypt, and his servants,
46:17 P· king of Egypt is but a noise;
25 punish the multitude of No, and P·,
25 even P·, and all them that trust in
47: 1 before that P· smote Gaza.
Eze 17:17 shall P· with his mighty army and
29: 2 thy face against P· king of Egypt;
3 I am against thee, P· king of Egypt,
30:21 have broken the arm of P· king of
22 I am against P· king of Egypt,
25 and the arms of P· shall fall down;
31: 2 speak unto P· king of Egypt, and
18 This is P· and all his multitude,
32: 2 lamentation for P· king of Egypt,
31 P· shall see them, and shall be
31 even P· and all his army slain by the
32 even P· and all his multitude,
Ac 7:10 in the sight of P· king of Egypt;
13 kindred was made known unto P·.
Ro 9:17 For the scripture saith unto P·,

Pharaoh-hophra (*fa''-ra-o-hof'-rah*)
Jer 44:30 I will give P· king of Egypt into

Pharaoh-necho (*fa''-ra-o-ne'-ko*) See also PHARAOH-NECHOH.
Jer 46: 2 against the army of P· king of

Pharaoh-nechoh (*fa''-ra-o-ne'-ko*) See also PHARAOH-NECHO.
2Ki 23:29 P· king of Egypt went up against
33 P· put him in bands at Riblah in
34 P· made Eliakim the son of Josiah
35 to his taxation, to give it unto P·.

Pharaoh's (*fa'-ra-oze*)
Ge 12:15 woman was taken into P· house.
37:36 unto Potiphar, an officer of P·, and
40: 7 he asked P· officers that were with
11 P· cup was in my hand: and I took
11 and pressed them into P· cup,
11 and I gave the cup into P· hand.
13 shalt deliver P· cup into his hand,
20 third day, which was P· birthday,
21 and he gave the cup into P· hand:
45:16 fame thereof was heard in P· house,
47:14 brought the money into P· house.
20 over them: so the land became P·.
25 my lord, and we will be P· servants.
26 priests only, which became not P·.
Ex 2: 7 Then said his sister to P· daughter,
8 And P· daughter said unto her, Go.
9 P· daughter said unto her, Take
10 she brought him unto P· daughter,
5:14 P· taskmasters had set over them,
7: 3 And I will harden P· heart, and
13 And he hardened P· heart, that he
14 P· heart was hardened, he refuseth
22 P· heart was hardened, neither
8:19 and P· heart was hardened, and he
10: 7 P· servants said...How long
11 were driven out from P· presence.
20, 27 the Lord hardened P· heart,
11: 3 Egypt, in the sight of P· servants,
10 the Lord hardened P· heart, so that
14: 4 I will harden P· heart, that he shall
23 sea, even all P· horses, his chariots,
15: 4 P· chariots and...hosts hath he cast
De 6:21 We were P· bondmen in Egypt;
1Sa 2:27 they were in Egypt in P· house?
1Ki 3: 1 and took P· daughter, and brought
7: 8 made also an house for P· daughter,
9:24 P· daughter came up out of the city
11:20 Tahpenes weaned in P· house:
20 and Genubath was in P· household
Ca 1: 9 company of horses in P· chariots.
Jer 37: 5 P· army was come...out of Egypt:
7 P· army, which has come forth to
11 Jerusalem for fear of P· army, from
43: 9 which is at the entry of P· house
Eze 30:24 but I will break P· arms, and he
Ac 7:21 P· daughter took him up, and
Heb 11:24 be called the son of P· daughter;

Phares (*fa'-rez*) See also PHAREZ.
M't 1: 3 And Judas begat P· and Zara of
3 P· begat Esrom; and Esrom begat
Lu 3:33 Esrom, which was the son of P·,

Pharez (*fa'-rez*) See also PEREZ; PHARES; PHARZITES.
Ge 38:29 therefore his name was called P·.
46:12 and Shelah, and P·, and Zarah:
12 sons of P· were Hezron and Hamul.
Nu 26:20 of P·, the family of the Pharzites:
21 sons of P· were; of Hezron, the
Ru 4:12 thy house be like the house of P·,
18 the generations of P·: P· begat
1Ch 2: 4 his daughter in law bare him P·
5 sons of P·; Hezron, and Hamul.
4: 1 P·, Hezron, and Carmi, and Hur,
9: 4 children of P· the son of Judah.

Pharisee (*far'-i-see*) See also PHARISEE'S; PHARISEES.
M't 23:26 Thou blind P·, cleanse first that
Lu 7:39 the P· which had bidden him saw it,
11:37 P· besought him to dine with him:
38 when the P· saw it, he marveled
18:10 one a P·, and the other a publican.
11 The P· stood and prayed thus with
Ac 5:34 a P·, named Gamaliel, a doctor of
23: 6 Men and brethren, I am a P·,
6 the son of a P·: of the hope and
26: 5 sect of our religion I lived a P·.
Ph'p 3: 5 as touching the law, a P·;

Pharisee's (*far'-i-seze*)
Lu 7:36 he went into the P· house, and sat
37 Jesus sat at meat in the P· house,

Pharisees (*far'-i-seze*) See also PHARISEES'.
M't 3: 7 saw many of the P· and Sadducees
5:20 righteousness of the scribes and P·,
9:11 when the P· saw it, they said unto
14 Why do we and the P· fast oft, but
34 the P· said, He casteth out devils
12: 2 But when the P· saw it, they said,
14 the P· went out, and held a council
24 when the P· heard it, they said,
38 certain of the scribes and of the P·
15: 1 Then came to Jesus scribes and P·,
12 thou that the P· were offended,
16: 1 P· also with the Sadducees came,
6, 11 beware of the leaven of the P·
12 but of the doctrine of the P· and of
19: 3 P· also came unto him, tempting
21:45 and P· had heard his parables,
22:15 Then went the P·, and took counsel
34 the P· had heard that he had put
41 the P· were gathered together,
23: 2 scribes and the P· sit in Moses'
13, 14 [*], 15, 23, 25, 27, 29 P·, hypocrites!
27:62 chief priests and P· came together
M'r 2:16 the scribes and P· saw him eat with
18 of John and of the P· used to fast:
18 disciples of John and of the P· fast,
24 P· said unto him, Behold, why do

M'r 3: 6 the P· went forth, and straightway
7: 1 came together unto him the P·,
3 For the P·, and all the Jews, except
5 Then the P· and scribes asked him,
8:11 P· came...and began to question
15 beware of the leaven of the P·.
10: 2 the P· came to him, and asked him,
12:13 send unto him certain of the P·
Lu 5:17 were P· and doctors of the law
21 scribes and the P· began to reason,
30 their scribes and P· murmured
33 likewise the disciples of the P·;
6: 2 certain of the P· said unto them,
7 the scribes and P· watched him,
7:30 P· and lawyers rejected the counsel
36 one of the P· desired him that he
11:39 do ye P· make clean the outside of
42 woe unto you, P·! for ye tithe mint
43 Woe unto you, P·! for ye love the
44 Woe unto you, scribes and P·,
53 P· began to urge him vehemently,
12: 1 Beware ye of the leaven of the P·,
13:31 day there came certain of the P·,
14: 1 house of one of the chief P· to eat
3 spake unto the lawyers and P·,
15: 2 And the P· and scribes murmured,
16:14 P· also, who were covetous, heard
17:20 when he was demanded of the P·,
19:39 the P· from among the multitude
Joh 1:24 which were sent were of the P·.
3: 1 man of the P·, named Nicodemus,
4: 1 Lord knew how the P· had heard
7:32 P· heard that the people murmured
32 P· and...chief priests sent officers
45 officers to the chief priests and P·;
47 answered them the P·, Are ye also
48 rulers or of the P· believed on him?
8: 3 and P· brought unto him a woman
13 The P· therefore said unto him,
9:13 They brought to the P· him that
15 the P· also asked him how he had
16 said some of the P·, This man is not
40 some of the P· which were with him
11:46 went their ways to the P·, and told
47 gathered the chief priests and...P·
57 the P· had given a commandment,
12:19 The P· therefore said among
42 of the P· they did not confess him,
18: 3 officers from the...priests and P·,
Ac 15: 5 of the sect of the P· which believed,
23: 6 were Sadducees, and the other P·,
7 a dissension between the P· and
8 nor spirit: but the P· confess both.

Pharisees' (*far'-i-seez*)
Ac 23: 9 scribes that were of the P· part

Pharosh (*fa'-rosh*)
Ezr 8: 3 of Shechaniah, of the sons of P·;

Pharpar (*far'-par*)
2Ki 5:12 and P·, rivers of Damascus,

Pharzites (*far'-zites*)
Nu 26:20 of Pharez, the family of the P·: of

Phaseah (*fa-se'-ah*) See also PASEAH.
Ne 7:51 of Uzza, the children of P·,

Phebe (*fe'-be*)
Ro 16: 1 I commend unto you P· our sister,
subscr. sent by P· servant of the church at

Phelet See BETH-PHELET.

Phenice (*fe-ni'-se*) See also PHENICIA.
Ac 11:19 Stephen travelled as far as P·,
15: 3 passed through P· and Samaria,
27:12 means they might attain to P·,

Phenicia (*fe-nish'-e-ah*) See also PHENICE.
Ac 21: 2 finding a ship sailing...unto P·,

phial See VIAL.

Phichol (*fi'-kol*)
Ge 21:22 P· the chief captain of his host
32 P· the chief captain of his host,
26:26 P· the chief captain of his army.

Philadelphia (*fil-a-del'-fe-ah*)
Re 1:11 and unto Sardis, and unto P·, and
3: 7 angel of the church in P· write;

Philemon^ (*fi-le'-mon*)
Ph'm 1 unto P· our dearly beloved, and
subscr. Written from Rome to P·, by

Philetus (*fi-le'-tus*)
2Ti 2:17 of whom is Hymenæus and P·;

Philip (*fil'-ip*) See also PHILIP'S.
M't 10: 3 P·, and Bartholomew; Thomas,
M'r 3:18 Andrew, and P·, and Bartholomew,
Lu 3: 1 his brother P· tetrarch of Ituræa
6:14 and John, P· and Bartholomew,
Joh 1:43 findeth P·, and saith unto him,
44 Now P· was of Bethsaida, the city
45 P· findeth Nathanael, and saith
46 P· saith unto him, Come and see.
48 Before that P· called thee, when
6: 5 he saith unto P·, Whence shall we
7 P· answered him, Two hundred
12:21 same came therefore to P·, which
22 P· cometh and telleth Andrew: and
22 again Andrew and P· tell Jesus.
14: 8 P· saith unto him, Lord, shew us
9 yet hast thou not known me, P·?
Ac 1:13 P·, and Thomas, Bartholomew,
6: 5 P·, and Prochorus, and Nicanor,
8: 5 P· went down to...city of Samaria,
6 unto those things which P· spake,
12 when they believed P· preaching
13 baptized, he continued with P·.
26 angel of the Lord spake unto P·,
29 Then the Spirit said unto P·, Go
30 P· ran thither to him, and heard
31 he desired P· that he would come
34 And the eunuch answered P·, and
35 P· opened his mouth, and began
37 P· said, If thou believest with all
38 the water, both P· and the eunuch;
39 Spirit of the Lord caught away P·,
40 But P· was found at Azotus: and
21: 8 into the house of P· the evangelist,

Philippi (*fil-ip'-pi*) See also PHILIPPIANS.
M't 16:13 into the coasts of Cæsarea P·,
M'r 8:27 into the towns of Cæsarea P·:
Ac 16:12 And from thence to P·, which is
20: 6 And we sailed away from P· after
1Co *subscr.* Corinthians was written from P·
2Co *subscr.* Corinthians was written from P·,
Ph'p 1: 1 in Christ Jesus which are at P·,
1Th 2: 2 as ye know, at P·, we were bold in

Philippians^ (*fil-ip'-pe-uns*)
Ph'p 4:15 Now ye P· know also, that in the
subscr. It was written to the P· from Rome

Philip's (*fil'-ips*)
M't 14: 3 Herodias' sake, his brother P· wife.
M'r 6:17 Herodias' sake, his brother P· wife:
Lu 3:19 for Herodias his brother P· wife,

Philistia (*fil-is'-te-ah*) See also PALESTINE; PHILISTINE.
Ps 60: 8 P·, triumph thou because of me.
87: 4 behold P·, and Tyre, with Ethiopia;
108: 9 my shoe; over P· will I triumph.

Philistim (*fil-is'-tim*) See also PHILISTINES.
Ge 10:14 Casluhim, (out of whom came P·,)

Philistine (*fil-is'-tin*) See also PHILISTINES.
1Sa 17: 8 am not I a P·, and ye servants to
10 P· said, I defy the armies of Israel
11 Israel heard those words of the P·,
16 P· drew near morning and evening,
23 up the champion, the P· of Gath,
26 done to the man that killeth this P·,
26 for who is this uncircumcised P·,
32 will go and fight with this P·.
33 art not able to go against this P·
36 uncircumcised P· shall be as one
37 me out of the hand of this P·.
40 hand: and he drew near to the P·.
41 P· came on and drew near unto
42 P· looked about, and saw David,
43 the P· said unto David, Am I a dog,
43 the P· cursed David by his gods.
44 the P· said to David, Come to me,
45 said David to the P·, Thou comest
48 the P· arose, and came and drew
48 toward the army to meet the P·.
49 and smote the P· in his forehead,
50 prevailed over the P· with a sling,
50 and smote the P·, and slew him;
51 David ran, and stood upon the P·,
54 And David took the head of the P·,
55 saw David go forth against the P·,
57 from the slaughter of the P·,
57 before Saul with the head of the P·
18: 6 from the slaughter of the P·,
19: 5 life in his hand, and slew the P·,
21: 9 The sword of Goliath the P·, whom
22:10 him the sword of Goliath the P·.
2Sa 21:17 and smote the P·, and killed him.

Philistines (*fil-is'-tinz*) See also PHILISTIM; PHILISTINES'.
Ge 21:32 returned into the land of the P·.
26: 1 unto Abimelech king of the P·
8 Abimelech king of the P· looked
14 servants: and the P· envied him.
15 P· had stopped them, and filled
18 the P· had stopped them after the
Ex 13:17 the way of the land of the P·,
23:31 sea even unto the sea of the P·,
Jos 13: 2 all the borders of the P·, and all
3 five lords of the P·; the
J'g 3: 3 Namely, five lords of the P·, and
31 slew of the P· six hundred men
10: 6 the gods of the P·, and forsook the
7 sold them into the hands of the P·,
11 of Ammon, and from the P·?
13: 1 into the hand of the P· forty years.
5 Israel out of the hand of the P·.
14: 1 Timnath of the daughters of the P·.
2 Timnath of the daughters of the P·:
3 a wife of the uncircumcised P·?
4 sought an occasion against the P·:
4 the P· had dominion over Israel.
15: 3 I be more blameless than the P·,
5 go into the standing corn of the P·,
6 the P· said, Who hath done this?
6 the P· came up, and burnt her and
9 P· went up, and pitched in Judah,
11 not that the P· are rulers over us?
12 deliver thee into the hand of the P·.
14 Lehi, the P· shouted against him:
20 judged Israel in the days of the P·
16: 5 lords of the P· came up unto her,
8 lords of the P· brought up to her
9, 12, 14 The P· be upon thee, Samson.
18 and called for the lords of the P·,
18 lords of the P· came up unto her,
20 The P· be upon thee, Samson.
21 P· took him, and put out his eyes,
23 the lords of the P· gathered them
27 all the lords of the P· were there;
28 may be at once avenged of the P·
30 Samson said, Let me die with the P·.
1Sa 4: 1 went out against the P· to battle,
1 and the P· pitched in Aphek.
2 P· put themselves in array against
2 Israel was smitten before the P·:
3 smitten us to day before the P·?
6 when the P· heard the noise of the
7 the P· were afraid, for they said,
9 quit yourselves like men, O ye P·,
10 P· fought, and Israel was smitten,
17 and said, Israel is fled before the P·,
5: 1 And the P· took the ark of God, and
2 When the P· took the ark of God,
8 and gathered all the lords of the P·
11 together all the lords of the P·, and
6: 1 the country of the P· seven months.
2 the P· called for the priests and
4 the number of the lords of the P·:
12 the lords of the P· went after them
16 the five lords of the P· had seen it,
17 emerods which the P· returned for
18 the number of all the cities of the P·
21 P· have brought again the ark of
7: 3 deliver you out of the hand of the P·.
7 P· heard that the children of Israel
7 the lords of the P· went up against
7 heard it, they were afraid of the P·.
8 save us out of the hand of the P·.
10 the P· drew near to battle against
10 thunder on that day upon the P·,
11 pursued the P·, and smote them,
13 So the P· were subdued, and they
13 hand of the Lord was against the P·
14 which the P· had taken from Israel
14 deliver out of the hand of the P·.
9:16 my people out of the hand of the P·:
10: 5 where is the garrison of the P·:
12: 9 Hazor, and into the hand of the P·,
13: 3 smote the garrison of the P· that
3 was in Geba, and the P· heard of it.
4 had smitten a garrison of the P·,
4 had in abomination with the P·.
5, 11 the P· gathered themselves
12 P· will come down now upon me to
16 but the P· encamped in Michmash.
17 camp of the P· in three companies:
19 for the P· said, Lest the Hebrews
20 the Israelites went down to the P·,
23 the garrison of the P· went out to
14:11 unto the garrison of the P·: and
11 the P· said, Behold, the Hebrews
19 of the P· went on and increased:
21 Hebrews that were with the P·
22 when they heard that the P· fled,
30 greater slaughter among the P·?
31 they smote the P· that day from
36 us go down after the P· by night,
37 God, Shall I go down after the P·?
46 went up from following the P·:
46 and the P· went to their own place.
47 kings of Zobah, and against the P·:
52 war against the P· all the days of
17: 1 P· gathered together their armies
2 the battle in array against the P·.
3 P· stood on a mountain on the one
4 champion out of the camp of the P·,
19 valley of Elah, fighting with the P·.
21 the P· had put the battle in array,
23 name, out of the armies of the P·,
46 carcases of the hosts of the P· this
51 P· saw their champion was dead,
52 and shouted, and pursued the P·,
52 the wounded of the P· fell down by
53 returned from chasing after the P·,
18:17 let the hand of the P· be upon him.
21 hand of the P· may be against him.
25 but an hundred foreskins of the P·,
25 David fall by the hand of the P·.
27 slew of the P· two hundred men;
30 the princes of the P· went forth:
19: 8 fought with the P·, and slew them
23: 1 Behold, the P· fight against Keilah,
2 Shall I go and smite these P·?
2 Go, and smite the P·, and save
3 against the armies of the P·?
4 will deliver the P· into thine hand.
5 to Keilah, and fought with the P·,
27 for the P· have invaded the land.
28 David, and went against the P·:
24: 1 was returned from following the P·,
27: 1 escape into the land of the P·; and
7 David dwelt in the country of the P·
11 dwelleth in the country of the P·.
28: 1 P· gathered their armies together
4 P· gathered themselves together,
5 when Saul saw the host of the P·,
15 for the P· make war against me,
19 with thee into the hand of the P·:
19 of Israel into the hand of the P·.
29: 1 the P· gathered together all their
2 the lords of the P· passed on by
3 Then said the princes of the P·,
3 said unto the princes of the P·, Is
4 of the P· were wroth with him;
4 the princes of the P· said unto him,
7 displease not the lords of the P·.
9 the princes of the P· have said, He
11 to return into the land of the P·.
11 And the P· went up to Jezreel.
30:16 had taken out of the land of the P·,
31: 1 Now the P· fought against Israel:
1 of Israel fled from before the P·,
2 the P· followed hard upon Saul and
2 P· slew Jonathan, and Abinadab,
7 and the P· came and dwelt in them.
8 when the P· came to strip the slain,
9 into the land of the P· round about,

1Sa 31:11 that which the P' had done to Saul:
2Sa 1:20 lest the daughters of the P' rejoice,
3:14 for an hundred foreskins of the P'.
18 Israel out of the hand of the P', and
5:17 P' heard that they had anointed
17 all the P' came up to seek David;
18 The P' also came and spread
19 saying, Shall I go up to the P'?
19 deliver the P' into thine hand.
22 And the P' came up yet again, and
24 thee, to smite the host of the P'.
25 smote the P' from Geba until thou
8: 1 smote the P', and subdued them:
1 out of the hand of the P'.
12 children of Ammon, and of the P',
19: 9 us out of the hand of the P';
21:12 where the P' had hanged them,
12 the P' had slain Saul in Gilboa:
15 P' had yet war again with Israel;
15 him, and fought against the P':
18 again a battle with the P' at Gob:
19 again a battle in Gob with the P',
23: 9 with David, when they defied the P'
10 smote the P' until his hand was
11 P'...gathered together into a troop,
11 and the people fled from the P'.
12 and defended it, and slew the P':
13 of the P' pitched in the valley
14 of the P' was then in Beth-lehem.
16 brake through the host of the P',
1Ki 4:21 the river unto the land of the P',
15:27 which belonged to the P';
16:15 which belonged to the P'.
2Ki 8: 2 sojourned in the land of the P'
3 returned out of the land of the P':
18: 8 He smote the P', even unto Gaza,
1Ch 1:12 Casluhim, (of whom came the P',)
10: 1 Now the P' fought against Israel;
1 of Israel fled from before the P',
2 the P' followed hard after Saul,
2 P' slew Jonathan, and Abinadab,
7 and the P' came and dwelt in them.
8 the P' came to strip the slain,
9 and sent into the land of the P'.
11 all that the P' had done to Saul,
11:13 the P' were gathered together
13 the people fled from before the P'.
14 and delivered it, and slew the P';
15 host of the P' encamped in the
18 brake through the host of the P',
12:19 with the P' against Saul to battle:
19 lords of the P' upon advisement
14: 8 P' heard that David was anointed
8 all the P' went up to seek David.
9 the P' came and spread themselves
10 Shall I go up against the P'?
13 the P' yet again spread themselves
15 thee to smite the host of the P'.
16 smote the host of the P' from
18: 1 David smote the P', and subdued
1 towns out of the hand of the P'.
11 Ammon, and from the P', and from
20: 4 arose war at Gezer with the P':
5 there was war again with the P';
2Ch 9:26 river even unto the land of the P',
17:11 P' brought Jehoshaphat presents,
21:16 Jehoram the spirit of the P',
26: 6 warred against the P', and brake
6 about Ashdod, and among the P'.
7 God helped him against the P',
28:18 The P' also had invaded the cities
Ps 56: *title* when the P' took him in Gath.
83: 7 P' with the inhabitants of Tyre;
Isa 2: 6 and are soothsayers like the P',
9:12 Syrians before, and the P' behind;
11:14 shoulders of the P' toward the west;
Jer 25:20 all the kings of the land of the P',
47: 1 the prophet against the P',
4 day that cometh to spoil all the P',
4 the Lord will spoil the P', the
Eze 16:27 the daughters of the P', which are
57 the daughters of the P', which
25:15 the P' have dealt by revenge,
16 stretch out mine hand upon the P',
Am 1: 8 remnant of the P' shall perish,
6: 2 then go down to Gath of the P':
9: 7 P' from Caphtor, and the Syrians
Ob 19 and they of the plain the P': and
Zep 2: 5 O Canaan, the land of the P', I will
Zec 9: 6 I will cut off the pride of the P'.

Philistines' (*fil-is'-tinz*)
Ge 21:34 Abraham sojourned in...P' land
1Sa 14: 1 let us go over to the P' garrison,
4 to go over unto the P' garrison,
1Ch 11:16 P' garrison was then at Beth-lehem.

Philologus (*fil-ol'-o-gus*)
Ro 16:15 Salute P', and Julia, Nereus, and

philosophers
Ac 17:18 Then certain p' of the Epicureans,

philosophy
Col 2: 8 spoil you through p' and...deceit

Phinehas (*fin'-e-has*) See also PHINEHAS'.
Ex 6:25 she bare him P': these are the
Nu 25: 7 And when P', the son of Eleazar,
11 P', the son of Eleazar, the son of
31: 6 P' the son of Eleazar the priest,
Jos 22:13 P' the son of Eleazar the priest,
30 when P' the priest, and the princes
31 P' the son of Eleazar the priest
32 P' the son of Eleazar the priest,
24:33 a hill that pertained to P' his son,
J'g 20:28 P', the son of Eleazar, the son of
1Sa 1: 3 the two sons of Eli, Hophni and P',
1Sa 2:34 thy two sons, on Hophni and P';
4: 4 the two sons of Eli, Hophni and P',
11 of Eli, Hophni and P', were slain.
17 sons also, Hophni and P', are dead,
14: 3 Ichabod's brother, the son of P',
1Ch 6: 4 Eleazar begat P', P' begat Abishua,
50 Aaron; Eleazar his son, P' his son,
9:20 P' the son of Eleazar was the ruler
Ezr 7: 5 The son of Abishua, the son of P',
8: 2 Of the sons of P'; Gershom: of the
33 with him was Eleazar the son of P';
Ps 106:30 stood up P',...executed judgment:

Phinehas' (*fin'-e-has*)
1Sa 4:19 And his daughter in law, P' wife,

Phlegon (*fle'-gon*)
Ro 16:14 Salute Asyncritus, P', Hermas,

Phœbe See PHEBE.

Phœnice See PHENICE.

Phœnicia See PHENICIA.

Phœnician See PHENICIAN.

Phrygia (*frij'-e-ah*)
Ac 2:10 P', and Pamphylia, in Egypt, and
16: 6 when they had gone throughout P'
18:23 all the country of Galatia and P'
1Ti *subscr.* chiefest city of P' Pacatiana.

Phurah (*fu'-rah*)
J'g 7:10 go thou with P' thy servant down
11 went he down with P' his servant

Phut (*fut*) See also PUT.
Ge 10: 6 and Mizraim, and P', and Canaan.
Eze 27:10 of Persia and of Lud and of P'

Phuvah (*fu'-vah*) See also PUAH.
Ge 46:13 sons of Issachar; Tola, and P',

Phygellus (*fi-jel'-lus*)
2Ti 1:15 of whom are P' and Hermogenes.

phylacteries
M't 23: 5 they make broad their p', and

physician See also PHYSICIANS.
Jer 8:22 in Gilead; is there no p' there?
M't 9:12 They that be whole need not a p',
M'r 2:17 are whole have no need of the p',
Lu 4:23 me this proverb, P', heal thyself:
5:31 They that are whole need not a p';
Col 4:14 Luke, the beloved p', and Demas,

physicians
Ge 50: 2 commanded his servants the p'
2 and the p' embalmed Israel.
2Ch 16:12 sought not to the Lord, but to the p'.
Job 13: 4 of lies, ye are all p' of no value.
M'r 5:26 suffered many things of many p',
Lu 8:43 had spent all her living upon p',

Pi See PI-BESETH; PI-HAHIROTH.

Pi-beseth (*pi-be'-zeth*)
Eze 30:17 The young men of Aven and of P'

pick
Pr 30:17 ravens of the valley shall p' it out,

pictures
Nu 33:52 destroy all their p', and destroy
Pr 25:11 is like apples of gold in p' of silver.
Isa 2:16 Tarshish,...upon all pleasant p'.

piece See also APIECE; PIECES.
Ge 15:10 laid each p' one against another:
Ex 37: 7 of gold, beaten out of one p' made
Nu 10: 2 of a whole p' shalt thou make them:
J'g 9:53 woman cast a p' of a millstone
1Sa 2:36 crouch to him for a p' of silver and
36 that I may eat a p' of bread.
30:12 gave him a p' of a cake of figs,
2Sa 6:19 of bread, and a good p' of flesh,
11:21 a woman cast a p' of a millstone
23:11 a p' of ground full of lentiles:
2Ki 3:19 and mar every good p' of land with
25 on every good p' of land cast every
1Ch 16: 3 of bread, and a good p' of flesh,
Ne 3:11 repaired the other p', and the
19 another p' over against the going
20 earnestly repaired the other p',
21 Urijah the son of Koz another p',
24 the son of Henadad another p',
27 the Tekoites repaired another p',
30 the sixth son of Zalaph, another p'.
Job 41:24 as a p' of the nether millstone.
42:11 man also gave him a p' of money,
Pr 6:26 a man is brought to a p' of bread:
28:21 for a p' of bread that man will
Ca 4: 3 are like a p' of a pomegranate
6: 7 As a p' of a pomegranate are thy
Jer 37:21 give him daily a p' of bread out
Eze 24: 4 thereof into it, even every good p',
6 bring it out p' by p'; let no lot fall
Am 3:12 the lion two legs, or a p' of an ear;
4: 7 one p' was rained upon, and the
7 p' whereupon it rained not withered.
M't 9:16 putteth a p' of new cloth unto an
17:27 mouth, thou shalt find a p' of money:
M'r 2:21 seweth a p' of new cloth on an old
21 the new p' that filled it up taketh
Lu 5:36 putteth a p' of a new garment upon
36 the p' that was taken out of the
14:18 I have bought a p' of ground, and
15: 8 if she lose one p', doth not light a
9 have found the p' which I had lost.
24:42 gave him a p' of a broiled fish,

pieces See also SHOULDERPIECES.
Ge 15:17 that passed between those p'.
Ge 20:16 thy brother a thousand p' of silver:
33:19 father, for an hundred p' of money.
37:28 Ishmeelites for twenty p' of silver:
33 Joseph is without doubt rent in p'.
44:28 and I said, Surely he is torn in p';
45:22 he gave three hundred p' of silver,
Ex 15: 6 Lord, hath dashed in p' the enemy.
22:13 If it be torn in p', then let him bring
29:17 And thou shalt cut the ram in p',
17 put them unto his p', and unto his
Le 1: 6 burnt offering, and cut it into his p'.
12 he shall cut it into his p', with his
2: 6 Thou shalt part it in p', and pour
6:21 the baken p' of the meat offering
8:20 he cut the ram into p'; and Moses
20 the head, and the p', and the fat.
9:13 with the p' thereof, and the head:
Jos 24:32 Shechem for an hundred p' of silver:
J'g 9: 4 him threescore and ten p' of silver
16: 5 of us eleven hundred p' of silver.
19:29 with her bones, into twelve p',
20: 6 my concubine, and cut her in p',
1Sa 2:10 of the Lord shall be broken to p';
11: 7 yoke of oxen, and hewed them in p',
15:33 Samuel hewed Agag in p' before the
1Ki 11:30 on him, and rent it in twelve p':
31 to Jeroboam, Take thee ten p':
18:23 and cut it in p', and lay it on wood,
33 and cut the bullock in p', and laid
19:11 brake in p' the rocks before the Lord;
2Ki 2:12 clothes, and rent them in two p'.
5: 5 silver, and six thousand p' of gold,
6:25 was sold for fourscore p' of silver,
25 of dove's dung for five p' of silver.
11:18 and his images brake they in p'
18: 4 brake in p' the brasen serpent that
23:14 he brake in p' the images, and cut
24:13 cut in p' all the vessels of gold which
25:13 did the Chaldees break in p', and
2Ch 23:17 brake his altars and his images in p',
25:12 that they all were broken in p'.
28:24 cut in p' the vessels of the house of
31: 1 brake the images in p', and cut
34: 4 the molten images, he brake in p',
Job 16:12 me by my neck, and shaken me to p',
19: 2 soul, and brake me in p' with words?
34:24 brake in p' mighty men without
40:18 His bones are as strong p' of brass;
Ps 2: 9 dash them in p' like a potter's vessel.
7: 2 my soul like a lion, rending it in p',
50:22 that forget God, lest I tear you in p',
58: 7 his arrows, let them be as cut in p'.
68:30 submit himself with p' of silver:
72: 4 and shall break in p' the oppressor.
74:14 breakest the heads of leviathan in p',
89:10 Thou hast broken Rahab in p', as one
94: 5 They break in p' thy people, O Lord,
Ca 8:11 was to bring a thousand p' of silver.
Isa 3:15 mean ye that ye beat my people to p',
8: 9 ye shall be broken in p'; and give ear,
9 and ye shall be broken in p'; gird
9 yourselves,...ye shall be broken in p'.
13:16 children also shall be dashed to p'
18 also shall dash the young men to p';
30:14 potter's vessel that is broken in p';
45: 2 I will break in p' the gates of brass,
Jer 5: 6 goeth out thence shall be torn in p':
23:29 hammer that breaketh the rock in p'?
50: 2 Merodach is broken in p'; her idols
2 her images are broken in p'.
51:20 thee will I break in p' the nations,
21 break in p' the horse and his rider;
21 break in p' the chariot and his rider;
22 will I break in p' man and woman;
22 will I break in p' old and young;
22 break in p' the young man and the
23 break in p' with thee the shepherd and
23 will I break in p' the husbandman
23 I break in p' captains and rulers.
La 3:11 aside my ways, and pulled me in p':
Eze 4:14 that dieth of itself, or is torn in p';
13:19 of barley and for p' of bread,
24: 4 Gather the p' thereof into it, even
Da 2: 5 ye shall be cut in p', and your
34 of iron and clay, and brake them to p'.
35 and the gold, broken to p' together,
40 forasmuch as iron breaketh in p' and
40 these, shall it break in p' and bruise.
44 it shall break in p' and consume all
45 and that it break in p' the iron, the
3:29 and Abed-nego, shall be cut in p',
6:24 and brake all their bones in p' or
7: 7 it devoured and brake in p', and
19 which devoured, brake in p', and
23 shall tread it down, and break it in p'.
Ho 3: 2 her to me for fifteen p' of silver,
8: 6 of Samaria shall be broken in p'.
10:14 mother was dashed in p' upon her
13:16 their infants shall be dashed in p',
Mic 1: 7 images thereof shall be beaten to p',
3: 3 their bones, and chop them in p',
4:13 thou shalt beat in p' many people:
5: 8 treadeth down, and teareth in p',
Na 2: 1 He that dasheth in p' is come up
12 The lion did tear in p' enough for his
3:10 young children also were dashed in p'
Zec 11:12 for my price thirty p' of silver.
13 And I took the thirty p' of silver, and
16 the fat, and tear their claws in p'.
12: 3 themselves with it shall be cut in p',
M't 26:15 with him for thirty p' of silver.
27: 3 brought again the thirty p' of silver
5 cast down the p' of silver in the
6 the chief priests took the silver p',
9 And they took the thirty p' of silver.
M'r 5: 4 by him, and the fetters broken in p':

Lu 15: 8 what woman having ten p' of silver,
Ac 19:19 found it fifty thousand p' of silver.
23:10 should have been pulled in p' of
27:44 and some on broken p' of the ship.
pierce See also PIERCED; PIERCETH; PIERCING.
Nu 24: 8 p' them through with his arrows.
2Ki 18:21 it will go into his hand, and p' it:
Isa 36: 6 it will go into his hand, and p' it:
Lu 2:35 shall p' through thy own soul also,)
pierced
J'g 5:26 had p' and stricken through his
Job 30:17 My bones are p' in me in the night
Ps 22:16 me: they p' my hands and my feet.
Zec 12:10 look upon me whom they have p',
Joh 19:34 soldiers with a spear p' his side,
37 shall look on him whom they p'.
1Ti 6:10 p' themselves through with many
Re 1: 7 him, and they also which p' him:
pierceth
Job 40:24 eyes: his nose p' through snares.
piercing See also PIERCINGS.
Isa 27: 1 punish leviathan the p' serpent,
Heb 4:12 p' even to the dividing asunder of
piercings
Pr 12:18 speaketh like the p' of a sword:
piety
1Ti 5: 4 them learn first to show p' at
pigeon See also PIGEONS.
Ge 15: 9 and a turtledove, and a young p'.
Le 12: 6 and a young p', or a turtledove,
pigeons
Le 1:14 of turtledoves, or of young p'.
5: 7, 11 two turtledoves, or two young p',
12: 8 bring two turtles, or two young p';
14:22 two turtledoves, or two young p',
30 the turtledoves, or of the young p',
15:14 two turtledoves, or two young p',
29 her two turtles, or two young p',
Nu 6:10 bring two turtles, or two young p',
Lu 2:24 of turtledoves, or two young p'.
Pi-hahiroth (*pi-ha-hi'-roth*)
Ex 14: 2 they turn and encamp before P',
9 sea, beside P', before Baal-zephon.
Nu 33: 7 Etham, and turned again unto P',
8 And they departed from before P',
Pilate (*pi'-lut*)
M't 27: 2 him to Pontius P' the governor.
13 said P' unto him, Hearest thou not
17 P' said unto them, Whom will ye
22 P' saith unto them, What shall I do
24 When P' saw that he could prevail
58 went to P', and begged the body of
58 Then P' commanded the body to be
62 Pharisees came together unto P',
65 P' said unto them, Ye have a
M'r 15: 1 him away, and delivered him to P'.
2 P' asked him, Art thou the King of
4 And P' asked him again, saying,
5 nothing; so that P' marvelled.
9 P' answered them, saying, Will ye
12 P' answered and said again unto
14 P' said unto them, Why, what evil
15 And so P', willing to content the
43 went in boldly unto P', and craved
44 P' marvelled if he were already
Lu 3: 1 Pontius P' being governor of
13: 1 blood P' had mingled with their
23: 1 of them arose, and led him unto P'.
3 And P' asked him, saying, Art thou
4 said P' to the chief priests and to
6 When P' heard of Galilee, he asked
11 robe, and sent him again to P'.
12 P' and Herod were made friends
13 P', when he had called together
20 P' therefore, willing to release
24 P' gave sentence that it should be
52 This man went unto P', and begged
Joh 18:29 P' then went out unto them, and
31 Then said P' unto them, Take ye
33 P' entered into the judgment hall
35 P' answered, Am I a Jew? Thine
37 P' therefore said unto him, Art thou
38 P' saith unto him, What is truth?
19: 1 Then P' therefore took Jesus, and
4 P' therefore went forth again, and
5 P' saith unto them, Behold the man!
6 P' saith unto them, Take ye him,
8 P' therefore heard that saying,
10 Then saith P' unto him, Speakest
12 thenceforth P' sought to release
13 P' therefore heard that saying,
15 P' saith unto them, Shall I crucify
19 P' wrote a title, and put it on the
21 the chief priests of the Jews to P',
22 P' answered, What I have written
31 besought P' that their legs might
38 besought P' that he might take
38 of Jesus: and P' gave him leave.
Ac 3:13 denied him in the presence of P',
4:27 both Herod, and Pontius P', with
13:28 they P' that he should be slain.
1Ti 6:13 before Pontius P' witnessed a good
Pildash (*pil'-dash*)
Ge 22:22 and Hazo, and P', and Jidlaph,
pile
Isa 30:33 p' thereof is fire and much wood;
Eze 24: 9 will even make the p' for fire great.
Pileha (*pil'-e-hah*)
Ne 10:24 Hallohesh, P', Shobek,
Pileser See TIGLATH-PILESER.
pilgrim See PILGRIMS.
pilgrimage
Ge 47: 9 The days of the years of my p' are
9 my fathers in the days of their p'.
Ex 6: 4 land of Canaan, the land of their p',
Ps 119:54 my songs in the house of my p'.
pilgrims
Heb 11:13 strangers and p' on the earth.
1Pe 2:11 I beseech you as strangers and p',
pillar See also PILLARS.
Ge 19:26 him, and she became a p' of salt.
28:18 his pillows, and set it up for a p',
22 this stone, which I have set for a p',
31:13 where thou anointedst the p', and
45 took a stone, and set it up for a p'.
51 this heap, and behold this p', which
52 this p' be witness, that I will not
52 not pass over this heap and this p'
35:14 And Jacob set up a p' in the place
14 talked with him, even a p' of
20 And Jacob set a p' upon her grave:
20 that is the p' of Rachel's grave
Ex 13:21 them by day in a p' of a cloud, to
21 by night in a p' of fire, to give them
22 took not away the p' of the cloud
22 by day, nor the p' of fire by night,
14:19 the p' of the cloud went from before
24 through the p' of fire and of the
33: 9 the cloudy p' descended, and stood
10 the people saw the cloudy p' stand
Nu 12: 5 Lord came down in the p' of the
14:14 them, by day time in a p' of a cloud,
14 and in a p' of fire by night.
De 31:15 the tabernacle in a p' of a cloud:
15 p' of the cloud stood over the door
J'g 9: 6 of the p' that was in Shechem.
20:40 out of the city with a p' of smoke,
2Sa 18:18 and reared up for himself a p',
18 he called the p' after his own name:
1Ki 7:21 set up the right p', and called the
21 he set up the left p', and called
2Ki 11:14 the king stood by a p', as the
23: 3 the king stood by a p', and made a
25:17 the one p' was eighteen cubits,
17 the second p' with wreathen work.
2Ch 23:13 the king stood at his p' at the
Ne 9:12 them in the day by a cloudy p';
12 and in the night by a p' of fire,
19 p' of the cloud departed not from
19 neither the p' of fire by night, to
Ps 99: 7 spake unto them in the cloudy p':
Isa 19:19 a p' at the border thereof to the
Jer 1:18 defenced city, and an iron p', and
52:21 of one p' was eighteen cubits;
22 The second p' also and the
1Ti 3:15 the p' and ground of the truth.
Re 3:12 a p' in the temple of my God,
pillars
Ex 24: 4 p', according to the twelve tribes
26:32 it upon four p' of shittim wood
37 hanging five p' of shittim wood,
27:10 twenty p' thereof and their twenty
10 the hooks of the p', and their fillets
11 twenty p' and their twenty sockets
11 hooks of the p' and their fillets of
12 their p' ten, and their sockets ten.
14, 15 their p' three, and their sockets
16 p' shall be four, and their sockets
17 All the p' round about the court
35:11 his bars, his p', and his sockets,
17 his p', and their sockets, and the
36:36 thereunto four p' of shittim wood,
38 the five p' of it with their hooks:
38:10 Their p' were twenty, and their
10 the hooks of the p' and their fillets
11 their p' were twenty, and their
11 hooks of the p' and their fillets of
12 their p' ten, and their sockets ten;
12 hooks of the p' and their fillets of
14, 15 their p' three, and their sockets
17 the sockets for the p' were of brass;
17 hooks of the p' and their fillets of
17 all the p' of the court were filleted
19 their p' were four, and their sockets
28 shekels he made hooks for the p',
39:33 bars, and his p', and his sockets;
40 his p', and his sockets, and the
40:18 bars thereof, and reared up his p'.
Nu 3:36 and the p' thereof, and the sockets
37 the p' of the court round about,
4:31 bars thereof, and the p' thereof,
32 the p' of the court round about,
De 12: 3 break their p', burn their groves
J'g 16:25 and they set him between the p'.
26 Suffer me that I may feel the p'
29 took hold of the two middle p'
1Sa 2: 8 the p' of the earth are the Lord's,
1Ki 7: 2 upon four rows of cedar p',
2 with cedar beams upon the p'.
3 lay on forty five p', fifteen in a row.
6 And he made a porch of p'; the
6 the other p' and the thick beam
15 he cast two p' of brass, of eighteen
16 to set upon the tops of the p':
17 which were upon the top of the p';
18 And he made the p', and two rows
19 the top of the p' were of lily work
20 And the chapiters upon the two p'
21 the p' in the porch of the temple:
22 the top of the p' was lily work:
22 so was the work of the p' finished.
41 The two p', and the two bowls of
1Ki 7:41 that were on the top of the two p';
41 which were upon the top of the p';
42 the chapiters that were upon the p';
10:12 king made of the almug trees p'
2Ki 18:16 p' which Hezekiah king of Judah
25:13 p' of brass that were in the house
16 The two p', one sea, and the bases
1Ch 18: 8 made the brasen sea, and the p',
2Ch 3:15 he made before the house two p'
16 put them on the heads of the p';
17 reared up the p' before the temple,
4:12 the two p', and the pommels, and
12 were on the top of the two p',
12 which were on the top of the p';
13 chapiters which were upon the p'.
Es 1: 6 to silver rings and p' of marble:
Job 9: 6 place, and the p' thereof tremble.
26:11 The p' of heaven tremble and are
Ps 75: 3 are dissolved: I bear up the p' of it.
Pr 9: 1 she hath hewn out her seven p':
Ca 3: 6 of the wilderness like p' of smoke,
10 He made the p' thereof of silver,
5:15 His legs are as p' of marble, set
Jer 27:19 concerning the p', and concerning
52:17 p' of brass that were in the house
20 The two p', one sea, and twelve
21 concerning the p', the height of
Eze 40:49 and there were p' by the posts, one
42: 6 had not p' as the p' of the courts:
Joe 2:30 blood, and fire, and p' of smoke.
Ga 2: 9 and John, who seemed to be p',
Re 10: 1 the sun, and his feet as p' of fire:
pilled See also PEELED.
Ge 30:37 and p' white strakes in them, and
38 rods which he had p' before the
pillow See also PILLOWS.
1Sa 19:13 a p' of goats' hair for his bolster,
16 a p' of goats' hair for his bolster.
M'r 4:38 part of the ship, asleep on a p':
pillows
Ge 28:11 that place, and put them for his p',
18 the stone that he had put for his p',
Eze 13:18 women that sew p' in all armholes,
20 I am against your p', wherewith ye
Pilneser See TILGATH-PILNESER.
pilots
Eze 27: 8 that were in thee, were thy p'.
27 thy mariners, and thy p', thy
28 at the sound of the cry of thy p'.
29 all the p' of the sea, shall come
Piltai (*pil'-tahee*)
Ne 12:17 of Miniamin, of Moadiah, P';
pin See also PINS.
J'g 16:14 she fastened it with the p', and
14 went away with the p' of the beam,
Eze 15: 3 take a p' of it to hang any vessel
pine See also PINETH; PINING.
Le 26:39 that are left of you shall p' away
39 shall they p' away with them.
Ne 8:15 fetch olive branches, and p'
Isa 41:19 the desert the fir tree, and the p',
60:13 unto thee, the fir tree, the p' tree,
La 4: 9 these p' away, stricken through
Eze 24:23 shall p' away for your iniquities,
33:10 upon us, and we p' away in them,
pineth
M'r 9:18 with his teeth, and p' away:
pining
Isa 38:12 he will cut me off with p' sickness:
pinnacle
M't 4: 5 setteth him on a p' of the temple,
Lu 4: 9 and set him on a p' of the temple,
Pinon (*pi'-non*)
Ge 36:41 Aholibamah, duke Elah, duke P',
1Ch 1:52 Aholibamah, duke Elah, duke P',
pins
Ex 27:19 thereof, and all the p' thereof, and
19 the p' of the court shall be of brass.
35:18 The p' of the tabernacle, and the
18 the p' of the court, and their cords,
38:20 all the p' of the tabernacle, and of
31 and all the p' of the tabernacle,
31 all the p' of the court round about.
39:40 his cords, and his p', and all the
Nu 3:37 and their p', and their cords.
4:32 and their p', and their cords,
Isa 3:22 the wimples, and the crisping p',
pipe See also PIPED; PIPES.
1Sa 10: 5 with a tabret, and a p', and a harp,
Isa 5:12 viol, the tabret, and p', and wine,
30:29 one goeth with a p' to come into the
1Co 14: 7 giving sound, whether p' or harp,
piped
1Ki 1:40 and the people p' with pipes, and
M't 11:17 We have p' unto you, and ye have
Lu 7:32 We have p' unto you, and ye have
1Co 14: 7 it be known what is p' or harped?
pipers
Re 18:22 harpers, and musicians, and of p',
pipes
1Ki 1:40 and the people piped with p', and
Jer 48:36 heart shall sound for Moab like p',
36 mine heart shall sound like p' for
Eze 28:13 of thy tabrets and of thy p' was
Zec 4: 2 seven p' to the seven lamps, which
12 two golden p' empty the golden

Piram (*pi'-ram*)
Jos 10: 3 and unto *P*· king of Jarmuth, and

Pirathon (*pir'-a-thon*) See also PIRATHONITE.
J'g 12:15 was buried in *P*· in the land of

Pirathonite (*pir'-a-thon-ite*)
J'g 12:13 son of Hillel, a *P*·, judged Israel.
15 Abdon the son of Hillel the *P*· died,
2Sa 23:30 Benaiah the *P*·, Hiddai of the
1Ch 11:31 of Benjamin, Benaiah the *P*·,
27:14 month was Benaiah the *P*·, of the

Pisgah (*piz'-gah*) See also ASHDOTH-PISGAH; NEBO.
Nu 21:20 top of *P*·, which looketh toward
23:14 field of Zophim, to the top of *P*·,
De 3:27 Get thee up into the top of *P*·, and
4:49 the plain, under the springs of *P*·.
34: 1 the top of *P*·, that is over against

Pisidia (*pi-sid'-e-ah*)
Ac 13:14 they came to Antioch in *P*·, and
14:24 they had passed throughout *P*·

Pison (*pi'-son*)
Ge 2:11 The name of the first is *P*·: that

Pispah (*piz'-pah*)
1Ch 7:38 Jephunneh, and *P*·, and Ara.

piss See also PISSETH.
2Ki 18:27 and drink their own *p*· with you?
Isa 36:12 and drink their own *p*· with you?

pisseth
1Sa 25:22, 34 any that *p*· against the wall.
1Ki 14:10 him that *p*· against the wall, and
16:11 him not one that *p*· against a wall,
21:21 Ahab him that *p*· against the wall,
2Ki 9: 8 Ahab him that *p*· against the wall,

pit^ See also PITS.
Ge 37:20 him, and cast him into some *p*·,
22 but cast him into this *p*· that is in
24 took him, and cast him into a *p*·:
24 *p*· was empty, there was no water
28 and lifted up Joseph out of the *p*·,
29 And Reuben returned unto the *p*·;
29 behold, Joseph was not in the *p*·;
Ex 21:33 And if a man shall open a *p*·, or
33 if a man shall dig a *p*·, and not cover
34 owner of the *p*· shall make it good,
Le 11:36 Nevertheless a fountain or *p*·,
Nu 16:30 they go down quick into the *p*·;
33 went down alive into the *p*·, and
2Sa 17: 9 he is hid now in some *p*·, or in
18:17 cast him into a great *p*· in the wood,
23:20 and slew a lion in the midst of a *p*·
2Ki 10:14 slew them at the *p*· of the shearing
1Ch 11:22 slew a lion in a *p*· in a snowy day.
Job 17:16 go down to the bars of the *p*·.
33:18 keepeth back his soul from the *p*·,
24 him from going down to the *p*·:
28 his soul from going into the *p*·,
30 To bring back his soul from the *p*·,
Ps 7:15 He made a *p*·, and digged it, and
9:15 heathen are sunk down in the *p*·
28: 1 like them that go down into the *p*·.
30: 3 that I should not go down to the *p*·.
9 blood, when I go down to the *p*·?
35: 7 they hid for me their net in a *p*·,
40: 2 me up also out of an horrible *p*·,
55:23 down into the *p*· of destruction:
57: 6 they have digged a *p*· before me,
69:15 let not the *p*· shut her mouth upon
88: 4 with them that go down into the *p*·:
6 Thou hast laid me in the lowest *p*·,
94:13 the *p*· be digged for the wicked.
143: 7 unto them that go down into the *p*·.
Pr 1:12 as those that go down into the *p*·:
22:14 of strange women is a deep *p*·:
23:27 a strange woman is a narrow *p*·.
26:27 Whoso diggeth a *p*· shall fall
28:10 shall fall himself into his own *p*·:
17 doeth violence...shall flee to the *p*·;
Ec 10: 8 He that diggeth a *p*· shall fall into
Isa 14:15 down to hell, to the sides of the *p*·.
19 that go down to the stones of the *p*·;
24:17 Fear, and the *p*·, and the snare,
18 noise of...fear shall fall into the *p*·;
18 cometh up out of the midst of the *p*·
22 as prisoners are gathered in the *p*·,
30:14 to take water withal out of the *p*·.
38:17 it from the *p*· of corruption:
18 that go down into the *p*· cannot hope
51: 1 hole of the *p*· whence ye are digged.
14 that he should not die in the *p*·,
Jer 18:20 they have digged a *p*· for my soul.
22 have digged a *p*· to take me,
41: 7 cast them into the midst of the *p*·,
9 the *p*· wherein Ishmael had cast all
48:43 Fear, and the *p*·, and the snare,
44 from the fear shall fall into the *p*·;
44 and he that getteth up out of the *p*·
Eze 19: 4 he was taken in their *p*·, and
8 over him: he was taken in their *p*·.
26:20 with them that descend into the *p*·,
20 with them that go down to the *p*·,
28: 8 shall bring thee down to the *p*·,
31:14 with them that go down to the *p*·.
16 with them that descend into the *p*·:
32:18 with them that go down into the *p*·.
23 graves are set in the sides of the *p*·,
24 with them that go down to the *p*·.
25 with them that go down to the *p*·:
29, 30 with them that go down to the *p*·.
Zec 9:11 out of the *p*· wherein is no water.
M't 12:11 it fall into a *p*· on the sabbath day,
Lu 14: 5 an ass or an ox fallen into a *p*·,

Re 9: 1 given the key of the bottomless *p*·.
2 And he opened the bottomless *p*·;
2 there arose a smoke out of the *p*·,
2 by reason of the smoke of the *p*·.
11 is the angel of the bottomless *p*·,
11: 7 ascendeth out of the bottomless *p*·
17: 8 ascend out of the bottomless *p*·, and
20: 1 having the key of the bottomless *p*·
3 And cast him into the bottomless *p*·,

pitch See also PITCHED.
Ge 6:14 shalt *p*· it within and without
14 it within and without with *p*·.
Ex 2: 3 daubed it with slime and with *p*·,
Nu 1:52 of Israel shall *p*· their tents,
53 the Levites shall *p*· round about
2: 2 shall *p*· by his own standard,
2 of the congregation shall they *p*·.
3 Judah *p*· throughout their armies:
5 And those that do *p*· next unto him
12 And those which *p*· by him shall be
3:23 shall *p*· behind the tabernacle
29, 35 *p*· on the side of the tabernacle
De 1:33 you out a place to *p*· your tents in,
Jos 4:20 of Jordan, did Joshua *p*· in Gilgal.
Isa 13:20 neither shall the Arabian *p*· tent
34: 9 thereof shall be turned into *p*·,
9 thereof shall become burning *p*·.
Jer 6: 3 shall *p*· their tents against her

pitched
Ge 12: 8 east of Beth-el, and *p*· his tent,
13:12 and *p*· his tent toward Sodom.
26:17 *p*· his tent in the valley of Gerar,
25 an altar...and *p*· his tent there:
31:25 Jacob had *p*· his tent in the mount:
25 Laban...*p*· in the mount of Gilead.
33:18 and *p*· his tent before the city.
Ex 17: 1 *p*· in Rephidim: and there was no
19: 2 and had *p*· in the wilderness; and
33: 7 and *p*· it without the camp,
Nu 1:51 when the tabernacle is to be *p*·,
2:34 so they *p*· by their standards, and
9:17 children of Israel *p*· their tents.
18 commandment of the Lord they *p*·:
12:16 and *p*· in the wilderness of Paran.
21:10 Israel set forward, and *p*· in Oboth.
11 *p*· at Ije-abarim, in the wilderness
12 and *p*· in the valley of Zared.
13 and *p*· on the other side of Arnon,
22: 1 and *p*· in the plains of Moab on this
33: 5 from Rameses, and *p*· in Succoth.
6 from Succoth, and *p*· in Etham,
7 and they *p*· before Migdol.
8 of Etham, and *p*· in Marah.
9 ten palm trees; and they *p*· there.
15 and *p*· in the wilderness of Sinai.
16 Sinai, and *p*· in Kibroth-hattaavah.
18 from Hazeroth, and *p*· in Rithmah.
19 Rithmah, and *p*· in Rimmon-parez.
20 Rimmon-parez, and *p*· in Libnah.
21 from Libnah, and *p*· at Rissah.
22 from Rissah, and *p*· in Kehelathah.
23 and *p*· in mount Shapher.
25 Haradah, and *p*· in Makheloth.
27 from Tahath, and *p*· at Tarah.
28 from Tarah, and *p*· in Mithcah.
29 from Mithcah,...*p*· in Hashmonah.
31 Moseroth, and *p*· in Bene-jaakan.
33 Hor-hagidgad, and *p*· in Jotbathah.
36 and *p*· in the wilderness of Zin,
37 Kadesh, and *p*· in mount Hor;
41 mount Hor, and *p*· in Zalmonah.
42 from Zalmonah, and *p*· in Punon.
43 from Punon, and *p*· in Oboth.
44 from Oboth, and *p*· in Ije-abarim,
45 from Iim, and *p*· in Dibon-gad.
47 and *p*· in the mountains of Abarim,
48 *p*· in the plains of Moab by Jordan
49 *p*· by Jordan, from Beth-jesimoth
Jos 8:11 and *p*· on the north side of Ai:
11: 5 *p*· together at the waters of Merom,
J'g 4:11 and *p*· his tent unto the plain of
6:33 and *p*· in the valley of Jezreel.
7: 1 and *p*· beside the well of Harod:
11:18 and *p*· on the other side of Arnon,
20 and *p*· in Jahaz, and fought against
15: 9 the Philistines...*p*· in Judah,
18:12 and *p*· in Kirjath-jearim, in Judah:
1Sa 4: 1 battle, and *p*· beside Eben-ezer:
1 and the Philistines *p*· in Aphek.
13: 5 they came up, and *p*· in Michmash,
17: 1 *p*· between Shochoh and Azekah
2 *p*· by the valley of Elah, and set the
26: 3 And Saul *p*· in the hill of Hachilah,
5 to the place where Saul had *p*·:
5 and the people *p*· round about him.
28: 4 and came and *p*· in Shunem: and
4 together, and they *p*· in Gilboa.
29: 1 *p*· by a fountain which is in Jezreel.
2Sa 6:17 tabernacle that David had *p*· for it:
17:26 Absalom *p*· in the land of Gilead.
23:13 *p*· in the valley of Rephaim.
24: 5 passed over Jordan, and *p*· in Aroer,
1Ki 20:27 children of Israel *p*· before them
29 they *p*· one over against the other,
2Ki 25: 1 Jerusalem, and *p*· against it;
1Ch 15: 1 the ark of God, and *p*· it for a tent.
16: 1 of the tent that David had *p*· for it:
19: 7 who came and *p*· before Medeba.
2Ch 1: 4 had *p*· a tent for it at Jerusalem.
Jer 52: 4 Jerusalem, and *p*· against it,
Heb 8: 2 which the Lord *p*·, and not man.

pitcher See also PITCHERS.
Ge 24:14 Let down thy *p*·, I pray thee, that
15 with her *p*· upon her shoulder.

Ge 24:16 well, and filled her *p*·, and came up.
17 thee, drink a little water of thy *p*·.
18 and let down her *p*· upon her hand,
20 and emptied her *p*· into the trough,
43 a little water of thy *p*· to drink;
45 forth with her *p*· on her shoulder;
46 let down her *p*· from her shoulder,
Ec 12: 6 or the *p*· be broken at the fountain,
M'r 14:13 you a man bearing a *p*· of water:
Lu 22:10 meet you, bearing a *p*· of water;

pitchers
J'g 7:16 every man's hand, with empty *p*·,
16 and lamps within the *p*·.
19 and brake the *p*· that were in their
20 brake the *p*·, and held the lamps
La 4: 2 are they esteemed as earthen *p*·,

Pithom (*pi'-thom*)
Ex 1:11 treasure cities, *P*· and Raamses.

Pithon (*pi'-thon*)
1Ch 8:35 the sons of Micah were, *P*·, and
9:41 the sons of Micah were, *P*·, and

pitied
Ps 106:46 He made them also to be *p*· of all
La 2: 2 of Jacob, and hath not *p*·:
17 hath thrown down, and hath not *p*·:
21 anger; thou hast killed, and not *p*·.
3:43 thou hast slain, thou hast not *p*·.
Eze 16: 5 None eye *p*· thee, to do any of

pitieth
Ps 103:13 Like as a father *p*· his children,
13 so the Lord *p*· them that fear him.
Eze 24:21 eyes, and that which your soul *p*·;

pitiful
La 4:10 The hands of the *p*· women have
Jas 5:11 the Lord is very *p*·, and of tender
1Pe 3: 8 love as brethren, be *p*·, be

pits See also SALTPITS; SLIMEPITS.
1Sa 13: 6 rocks, and in high places, and in *p*·.
Ps 119:85 The proud have digged *p*· for me,
140:10 be cast into the fire; into deep *p*·,
Jer 2: 6 through a land of deserts and...*p*·,
14: 3 they came to the *p*·, and found no
La 4:20 the Lord, was taken in their *p*·,

pity See also PITIED; PITIETH; PITIFUL.
De 7:16 eye shall have no *p*· upon them:
13: 8 neither shall thine eye *p*· him,
19:13 Thine eye shall not *p*· him, but thou
21 thine eye shall not *p*·; but life shall
25:12 her hand, thine eye shall not *p*· her.
2Sa 12: 6 thing, and because he had no *p*·.
Job 6:14 is afflicted *p*· should be shewed
19:21 Have *p*· upon me, have *p*· upon me,
Ps 69:20 I looked for some to take *p*·, but
Pr 19:17 He that hath *p*· upon the poor
28: 8 it for him that will *p*· the poor.
Isa 13:18 no *p*· on the fruit of the womb;
63: 9 and in his *p*· he redeemed them;
Jer 13:14 I will not *p*·, nor spare, nor have
15: 5 For who shall have *p*· upon thee, O
21: 7 neither have *p*·, nor have mercy.
Eze 5:11 spare, neither will I have any *p*·.
7: 4 spare thee, neither will I have *p*·:
9 not spare, neither will I have *p*·:
8:18 not spare, neither will I have *p*·:
9: 5 your eye spare, neither have ye *p*·:
10 not spare, neither will I have *p*·,
36:21 But I had *p*· for mine holy name.
Joe 2:18 for his land, and *p*· his people.
Am 1:11 the sword, and did cast off all *p*·,
Jon 4:10 Thou hast had *p*· on the gourd,
Zec 11: 5 their own shepherds *p*· them not.
6 no more *p*· the inhabitants of the
M't 18:33 fellowservant,...I had *p*· on thee?

place^ See also BURYINGPLACE; COUCHINGPLACE; DWELLINGPLACE; FEEDINGPLACE; MARKETPLACE; PLACED; PLACES; THRESHINGPLACE.
Ge 1: 9 be gathered together unto one *p*·,
12: 6 the land unto the *p*· of Sichem,
13: 3 unto the *p*· where his tent had been
4 Unto the *p*· of the altar, which he
14 look from the *p*· where thou art
18:24 spare the *p*· for the fifty righteous
26 will spare all the *p*· for their sakes.
33 and Abraham returned unto his *p*·.
19:12 the city, bring them out of this *p*·:
13 we will destroy this *p*·, because the
14 and said, Up, get you out of this *p*·;
27 *p*· where he stood before the Lord:
20:11 the fear of God is not in this *p*·;
13 at every *p*· whither we shall come,
21:31 he called that *p*· Beer-sheba;
22: 3 the *p*· of which God had told him.
4 up his eyes, and saw the *p*· afar off.
9 the *p*· which God had told him of;
14 the name of that *p*· Jehovah-jireh:
26: 7 men of the *p*· asked him of his wife;
7 men of the *p*· should kill me for
28:11 he lighted upon a certain *p*·, and
11 he took of the stones of that *p*·, and
11 and lay down in that *p*· to sleep.
16 Surely the Lord is in this *p*·; and I
17 and said, How dreadful is this *p*·!
19 called the name of that *p*· Beth-el:
29: 3 upon the well's mouth in his *p*·.
22 together all the men of the *p*·, and
30:25 that I may go unto mine own *p*·,
31:55 departed, and returned unto his *p*·.
32: 2 the name of that *p*· Mahanaim.
30 called the name of the *p*· Peniel:
33:17 the name of the *p*· is called Succoth.
35: 7 altar, and called the *p*· El-beth-el:

Ge 35:13 in the p' where he talked with him.
14 in the p' where he talked with him,
15 the p' where God spake with him,
38:14 herself, and sat in an open p',
21 Then he asked the men of that p',
21 said, There was no harlot in this p'.
22 also the men of the p' said, that
22 that there was no harlot in this p'.
39:20 p' where the king's prisoners were
40: 3 the p' where Joseph was bound.
13 head, and restore thee unto thy p':
48: 9 whom God hath given me in this p'.
50:19 Fear not: for am I in the p' of God?
Ex 3: 5 p' whereon thou standest is holy
8 unto the p' of the Canaanites, and
10:23 rose any from his p' for three days:
13: 3 the Lord brought you out from this p':
15:17 the p', O Lord, which thou hast
16:29 abide ye every man in his p', let no
29 let no man go out of his p' on the
17: 7 called the name of the p' Massah,
18:21 p' such over them, to be rulers of
23 shall also go to their p' in peace.
21:13 thee a p' whither he shall flee.
23:20 into the p' which I have prepared.
26:33 between the holy p' and the most holy.
34 of the testimony in the most holy p'.
28:35 he goeth in unto the holy p' before the
43 the altar to minister in the holy p';
29:30 congregation to minister in the holy p'.
31 and seethe his flesh in the holy p'.
31:11 oil, and sweet incense for the holy p':
32:34 lead the people unto the p' of which
33:21 there is a p' by me, and thou shalt
35:19 to do service in the holy p', the holy
38:24 work in all the work of the holy p',
39: 1 to do service in the holy p', and made
41 to do service in the holy p', and the
Le 1:16 east part, by the p' of the ashes,
4:12 without the camp unto a clean p',
24 kill it in the p' where they kill the
29 in the p' of the burnt offering.
33 sin offering in the p' where they kill
6:11 without the camp unto a clean p'.
16 shall it be eaten in the holy p';
25 the p' where the burnt offering is
26 in the holy p' shall it be eaten, in
27 it was sprinkled in the holy p'.
30 to reconcile withal in the holy p',
7: 2 In the p' where they kill the burnt
6 it shall be eaten in the holy p': it
10:13 shall eat it in the holy p', because
14 shoulder shall ye eat in a clean p';
17 eaten the sin offering in the holy p'
18 not brought in within the holy p':
18 indeed have eaten it in the holy p',
13:19 p' of the boil...be a white rising,
23, 28 if the bright spot stay in his p',
14:13 the p' where he shall kill the sin
13 the burnt offering, in the holy p':
28 the p' of the blood of the trespass
40 shall cast them into an unclean p'
41 without the city into an unclean p':
42 put them in the p' of those stones;
45 out of the city into an unclean p'.
16: 2 times into the holy p' within the vail
3 shall Aaron come into the holy p':
16 make an atonement for the holy p',
17 make an atonement in the holy p',
20 an end of reconciling the holy p',
23 put on when he went into the holy p',
24 his flesh with water in the holy p',
27 make atonement in the holy p',
24: 9 they shall eat in the holy p':
Nu 2:17 man in his p' by their standards.
9:17 p' where the cloud abode, there
10:14 In the first p' went the standard of
29 journeying unto the p' of which
33 to search out a resting p' for them.
11: 3 the name of the p' Taberah:
34 of that p' Kibroth-hattaavah:
13:24 p' was called the brook Eschol,
14:40 p' which the Lord hath promised:
18:10 In the most holy p' shalt thou eat it;
31 ye shall eat it in every p', ye and
19: 9 without the camp in a clean p',
20: 5 to bring us in unto this evil p'?
5 it is no p' of seed, or of figs, or of
21: 3 called the name of the p' Hormah.
22:26 and stood in a narrow p', where
23: 3 thee. And he went to an high p'.
13 thee, with me unto another p',
27 I will bring thee unto another p';
24:11 Therefore now flee thou to thy p':
25 and went and returned to his p':
28: 7 holy p' shalt thou cause the strong
32: 1 behold, the p' was a p' for cattle;
17 have brought them unto their p':
33:54 be in the p' where his lot falleth;
De 1:31 went, until ye come into this p'.
33 you out a p' to pitch your tents
2:37 unto any p' of the river Jabbok,
9: 7 until ye came unto this p', ye
11: 5 until ye came into this p';
24 Every p' whereon the soles of your
12: 3 the names of them out of that p'.
5 p' which the Lord your God shall
11 a p' which the Lord your God shall
13 thy burnt offerings in every p' that
14 the p' which the Lord shall choose
18 p' which the Lord thy God shall
21 the p' which the Lord thy God hath
26 the p' which the Lord shall choose:
14:23 before the Lord thy God, in the p'
23 choose to p' his name there,
24 or if the p' be too far from thee,
De 14:25 unto the p' which the Lord thy God
15:20 by year in the p' which the Lord
16: 2 the p' which the Lord shall choose
2 shall choose to p' his name there.
6 at the p' which the Lord thy God
6 shall choose to p' his name in,
7 shalt roast and eat it in the p'
11 in the p' which the Lord thy God
11 hath chosen to p' his name there.
15 p' which the Lord shall choose:
16 in the p' which he shall choose;
17: 8 arise, and get thee up into the p'
10 they of that p' which the Lord
18: 6 the p' which the Lord shall choose;
21:19 city, and unto the gate of his p';
23:12 have a p' also without the camp,
16 p' which he shall choose in one of
26: 2 go unto the p' which the Lord
2 shall choose to p' his name there.
9 hath brought us into this p', and
27:15 and putteth it in a secret p'.
29: 7 And when ye came unto this p',
31:11 in the p' which he shall choose,
Jos 1: 3 Every p' that the sole of your foot
3: 3 then ye shall remove from your p',
4: 3 of the p' where the priests' feet stood
3 leave them in the lodging p', where ye
8 unto the p' where they lodged, and
9 p' where the feet of the priests which
18 of Jordan returned unto their p',
5: 9 the name of the p' is called Gilgal
15 p' whereon thou standest is holy.
7:26 p' was called, The valley of Achor,
8:19 arose quickly out of their p', and
9:27 in the p' which he should choose.
20: 4 give him a p', that he may dwell
J'g 2: 5 called the name of that p' Bochim:
6:26 top of this rock, in the ordered p',
7: 7 people go every man unto his p'.
21 stood every man in his p' round
9:55 departed every man unto his p'.
11:19 thee through thy land into my p'.
15:17 and called that p' Ramath-lehi.
19 an hollow p' that was in the jaw,
17: 8 to sojourn where he could find a p':
9 I go to sojourn where I may find a p'.
18: 3 and what makest thou in this p'?
10 p' where there is no want of any
12 called that p' Mahaneh-dan unto
19:16 men of the p' were Benjamites.
28 rose up, and gat him unto his p'.
20:22 p' where they put themselves in
33 of Israel rose up out of their p',
36 Israel gave p' to the Benjamites,
21:19 in a p' which is on the north side of
Ru 1: 7 forth out of the p' where she was,
3: 4 mark the p' where he shall lie,
4:10 and from the gate of his p': ye are
1Sa 3: 2 Eli was laid down in his p', and his
9 Samuel went and lay down in his p'.
5: 3 Dagon, and set him in his p' again.
11 let it go again to his own p', that it
6: 2 wherewith we shall send it to his p'.
9:12 of the people to day in the high p':
13 before he go up to the high p' to eat:
14 them, for to go up to the high p'.
19 go up before me unto the high p';
22 sit in the chiefest p' among them
25 down from the high p' into the city,
10: 5 coming down from the high p' with a
12 And one of the same p' answered and
13 prophesying, he came to the high p'.
12: 8 and made them dwell in this p'.
14: 9 we will stand still in our p', and
46 Philistines went to their own p'.
15:12 behold, he set him up a p', and is
19: 2 and abide in a secret p', and hide
20:19 p' where thou didst hide thyself
25 side, and David's p' was empty.
27 month, that David's p' was empty:
37 lad was come to the p' of the arrow
41 arose out of a p' toward the south,
21: 2 my servants to such and such a p'.
23:22 and see his p' where his haunt is,
28 called that p' Sela-hammahlekoth.
26: 5 to the p' where Saul had pitched:
5 David beheld the p' where Saul lay,
25 way, and Saul returned to his p'.
27: 5 them give me a p' in some town
29: 4 he may go again to his p' which
2Sa 2:16 p' was called Helkath-hazzurim,
23 there, and died in the same p':
23 came to the p' where Asahel fell
5:20 name of that p' Baal-perazim.
6: 8 the name of the p' Perez-uzzah
17 ark of the Lord, and set it in his p',
7:10 I will appoint a p' for my people
10 they may dwell in a p' of their own,
11:16 assigned Uriah unto a p' where
15:17 tarried in a p' that was far off.
19 return to thy p', and abide with
21 what p' my lord the king shall be,
17: 9 in some pit, or in some other p':
12 come upon him in some p' where he
18:18 called unto this day, Absalom's p'.
19:39 and he returned unto his own p'.
22:20 brought me forth also into a large p':
23: 7 burned with fire in the same p'.
1Ki 3: 4 for that was the great high p': a
4:12 unto the p' that is beyond Jokneam:
28 brought they unto the p' where
5: 9 the p' that thou shalt appoint me,
6:16 the oracle, even for the most holy p'.
7:50 of the inner house, the most holy p',
8: 6 covenant of the Lord unto his p',
6 to the most holy p', even under the
1Ki 8: 7 two wings over the p' of the ark,
8 out in the holy p' before the oracle,
10 priests were come out of the holy p',
13 a settled p' for thee to abide in for
21 I have set there a p' for the ark,
29 the p' of which thou hast said, My
29 servant shall make toward this p'.
30 when they shall pray toward this p':
30 hear thou in heaven thy dwelling p':
35 if they pray toward this p', and
39 thou in heaven thy dwelling p',
43 Hear thou in heaven thy dwelling p',
49 prayer...in heaven thy dwelling p',
10:19 on either side on the p' of the seat,
11: 7 build an high p' for Chemosh, the
13: 8 bread nor drunk water in this p':
16 drink water with thee in this p':
22 bread and drunk water in the p',
20:24 kings away, every man out of his p',
21:19 p' where dogs licked the blood of
22:10 in a void p' in the entrance of the
2Ki 5:11 and strike his hand over the p', and
6: 1 p' where we dwell with thee is too
2 let us make us a p' there, where we
6 fell it? And he shewed him the p'.
8 and such a p' shall be my camp.
9 Beware that thou pass not such a p';
10 king of Israel sent to the p' which
18:25 Lord against this p' to destroy it?
22:16 Behold, I will bring evil upon this p',
17 shall be kindled against this p', and
19 what I spake against this p', and
20 evil which I will bring upon this p'.
23:15 the high p' which Jeroboam the son of
15 altar and the high p' he brake down,
15 burned the high p', and stamped it
1Ch 6:32 the dwelling p' of the tabernacle of
49 for all the work of the p' most holy,
13:11 p' is called Perez-uzza to this day.
14:11 the name of that p' Baal-perazim.
15: 1 and prepared a p' for the ark of God,
3 up the ark of the Lord unto his p',
12 unto the p' that I have prepared for it.
16:27 and gladness are in his p'.
39 Lord in the high p' that was at Gibeon,
17: 9 ordain a p' for my people Israel,
9 and they shall dwell in their p', and
21:22 me the p' of this threshingfloor,
25 to Ornan for the p' six hundred
29 that season in the high p' at Gibeon.
23:32 and the charge of the holy p', and the
28:11 and of the p' of the mercy seat,
2Ch 1: 3 to the high p' that was at Gibeon;
4 p' which David had prepared for it:
13 to the high p' that was at Gibeon
3: 1 p' that David had prepared in the
4:22 doors thereof for the most holy p',
5: 7 covenant of the Lord unto his p',
7 into the most holy p', even under the
8 their wings over the p' of the ark,
11 priests were come out of the holy p':
6: 2 and a p' for thy dwelling for ever.
20 the p' whereof thou hast said that
20 thy servant prayeth toward this p'.
21 they shall make toward this p':
21 hear thou from thy dwelling p', even
26 yet if they pray toward this p', and
30 thou from heaven thy dwelling p',
33, 39 even from thy dwelling p', and
40 the prayer that is made in this p'.
41 arise, O Lord God, into thy resting p',
7:12 have chosen this p' to myself for
15 the prayer that is made in this p'.
9:18 stays on each side of the sitting p',
18: 9 they sat in a void p' at the entering in
20:26 name of the same p' was called,
24:11 it, and carried it to his p' again.
29: 5 forth the filthiness out of the holy p'.
7 in the holy p' unto the God of Israel.
30:16 they stood in their p' after their
27 came up to his holy dwelling p',
34:24 I will bring evil upon this p', and
25 shall be poured out upon this p',
27 heardest his words against this p',
28 evil that I will bring upon this p',
31 the king stood in his p', and made
35: 5 stand in the holy p' according to the
10 the priests stood in their p', and
15 the sons of Asaph were in their p',
36:15 on his people, and on his dwelling p':
Ezr 1: 4 whosoever remaineth in any p'
4 men of his p' help him with silver,
2:68 house of God to set it up in his p':
5:15 house of God be builded in his p'.
6: 3 the p' where they offered sacrifices,
5 at Jerusalem, every one to his p',
5 and p' them in the house of God'
7 build this house of God in his p'.
8:17 Iddo the chief at the p' Casiphia,
17 the Nethinims, at the p' Casiphia,
9: 8 and to give us a nail in his holy p',
Ne 1: 9 unto the p' that I have chosen to
2: 3 the p' of my fathers' sepulchres,
14 there was no p' for the beast that
3:16 p' over against the sepulchres of David,
26 p' over against the water gate toward
31 son unto the p' of the Nethinims,
4:20 In what p'...ye hear the sound of
8: 7 and the people stood in their p'.
9: 3 they stood up in their p', and read
13:11 together, and set them in their p'.
Es 2: 9 best p' of the house of the women.
4:14 arise to the Jews from another p';
7: 8 into the p' of the banquet of wine;
Job 2:11 came every one from his own p';
6:17 they are consumed out of their p'.

Job 7:10 shall his p· know him any more.
8:17 heap, and seeth the p· of stones.
18 If he destroy him from his p·, then
22 the dwelling p· of the wicked shall
9: 6 shaketh the earth out of her p·,
14:18 and the rock is removed out of his p·.
16:18 blood, and let my cry have no p·.
18: 4 the rock be removed out of his p·?
21 the p· of him that knoweth not God.
20: 9 shall his p· any more behold him.
26: 7 out the north over the empty p·,
27:21 a storm hurleth him out of his p·.
23 and shall hiss him out of his p·.
28: 1 and a p· for gold where they fine it.
6 stones of it are the p· of sapphires:
12, 20 is the p· of understanding?
23 and he knoweth the p· thereof.
36:16 thee out of the strait into a broad p·,
20 when people are cut off in their p·.
37: 1 my heart...is moved out of his p·.
38:10 And brake up for it my decreed p·,
12 the dayspring to know his p·;
19 darkness, where is the p· thereof,
39:28 the crag of the rock, and the strong p·.
40:12 tread down the wicked in their p·.
Ps 18:11 He made darkness his secret p·; his
19 me forth also into a large p·;
24: 3 or who shall stand in his holy p·?
26: 8 p· where thine honour dwelleth.
12 My foot standeth in an even p·: in
32: 7 Thou art my hiding p·; thou shalt
33:14 the p· of his habitation he looketh
37:10 shalt diligently consider his p·,
44:19 broken us in the p· of dragons,
46: 4 holy p· of the tabernacles of the most
52: 5 pluck thee out of thy dwelling p·,
66:12 broughtest us out into a wealthy p·.
68:17 them, as in Sinai, in the holy p·.
74: 7 the dwelling p· of thy name to the
76: 2 and his dwelling p· in Zion.
79: 7 and laid waste his dwelling p·.
81: 7 thee in the secret p· of thunder:
90: 1 Lord, thou hast been our dwelling p·
91: 1 He that dwelleth in the secret p· of
103:16 p· thereof shall know it no more.
104: 8 the p· which thou hast founded for
118: 5 me, and set me in a large p·.
119:114 Thou art my hiding p· and my
132: 5 until I find out a p· for the Lord,
Pr 1:21 She crieth in the chief p· of concourse,
14:26 his children shall have a p· of refuge.
15: 3 eyes of the Lord are in every p·,
24:15 righteous; spoil not his resting p·:
25: 6 stand not in the p· of great men:
27: 8 man that wandereth from his p·.
Ec 1: 5 hasteth to his p· where he arose.
7 p· from whence the rivers come,
3:16 under the sun the p· of judgment,
16 p· of righteousness, that iniquity
20 All go unto one p·; all are of the
6: 6 no good: do not all go to one p·?
8:10 and gone from the p· of the holy,
10: 4 up against thee, leave not thy p·;
6 dignity, and the rich sit in low p·.
11: 3 in the p· where the tree falleth,
Isa 4: 5 every dwelling p· of mount Zion,
6 and for a p· of refuge, and for a
5: 8 field to field, till there be no p·,
7:23 that every p· shall be, where there
13:13 earth shall remove out of her p·,
14: 2 them, and bring them to their p·:
16:12 that Moab is weary on the high p·,
18: 4 I will consider in my dwelling p·
7 the p· of the name of the Lord of
22:23 fasten him as a nail in a sure p·;
25 nail that is fastened in the sure p·
25: 5 strangers, as the heat in a dry p·;
26:21 cometh out of his p· to punish the
28: 8 so that there is no p· clean.
17 waters shall overflow the hiding p·.
25 barley and the rie in their p·?
30:32 p· where the grounded staff shall
32: 2 a man shall be as an hiding p· from
2 as rivers of water in a dry p·, as the
19 and the city shall be low in a low p·.
33:16 his p· of defence shall be the
21 will be unto us a p· of broad rivers
34:14 there, and find for herself a p· of rest.
35: 1 solitary p· shall be glad for them;
45:19 secret, in a dark p· of the earth:
46: 7 carry him, and set him in his p·,
7 from his p· shall he not remove:
13 and I will p· salvation in Zion for
49:20 ears, The p· is too straight for me:
20 give p· to me that I may dwell.
54: 2 Enlarge the p· of thy tent, and let
56: 5 p· and a name better than of sons
57:15 I dwell in the high and holy p·, with
60:13 beautify the p· of my sanctuary;
13 make the p· of my feet glorious.
65:10 valley of Achor a p· for the herds to
66: 1 and where is the p· of my rest?
Jer 4: 7 he is gone forth from his p· to
26 lo, the fruitful p· was a wilderness,
6: 3 they shall feed every one in his p·.
7: 3 will cause you to dwell in this p·.
6 shed not innocent blood in this p·,
7 will I cause you to dwell in this p·,
12 unto my p· which was in Shiloh,
14 unto the p· which I gave to you
20 shall be poured out upon this p·,
32 bury in Tophet, till there be no p·.
9: 2 lodging p· of wayfaring men; that I
13: 7 took the girdle from the p· where
14:13 give you assured peace in this p·.
16: 2 have sons or daughters in this p·

Jer 16: 3 daughters that are born in this p·,
9 will cause to cease out of this p·
17:12 is the p· of our sanctuary.
18:14 waters that come from another p· be
19: 3 I will bring evil upon this p·, the
4 me, and have estranged this p·,
4 this p· with the blood of innocents;
6 p· shall no more be called Tophet,
7 of Judah and Jerusalem in this p·;
11 Tophet, till there be no p· to bury.
12 Thus will I do unto this p·, saith
13 shall be defiled as the p· of Tophet,
22: 3 shed innocent blood in this p·.
11 which went forth out of this p·;
12 he shall die in the p· whither they
24: 5 whom I have sent out of this p· into
27:22 up, and restore them to this p·.
28: 3 will I bring again into this p· all
3 of Babylon took away from this p·,
4 will bring again to this p· Jeconiah
6 captive, from Babylon into this p·.
29:10 in causing you to return to this p·.
14 bring you again into the p· whence
32:37 will bring them again unto this p·,
33:10 there shall be heard in this p·,
12 Again in this p·, which is desolate
38: 9 like to die for hunger in the p·
40: 2 pronounced this evil upon this p·.
42:18 and ye shall see this p· no more.
22 in the p· whither ye desire to go
44:29 I will punish you in this p·, that ye
51:62 thou hast spoken against this p·,
Eze 3:12 the glory of the Lord from his p·.
6:13 the p· where they did offer sweet
7:22 they shall pollute my secret p·:
10:11 p· whither the head looked they
12: 3 from thy p· to another p· in their
16:24 also built unto thee an eminent p·,
24 made thee an high p· in every street.
25 thy high p· at every head of the way,
31 eminent p· in the head of every way,
31 makest thine high p· in every street;
39 shall throw down thine eminent p·,
17:16 the p· where the king dwelleth
20:29 is the high p· whereunto ye go?
21:19 choose thou a p·, choose it at the
30 I will judge thee in the p· where
26: 5 shall be a p· for the spreading of nets
14 shalt be a p· to spread nets upon;
37:14 I shall p· you in your own land:
26 I will p· them, and multiply them,
38:15 come from thy p· out of the north
39:11 give unto Gog a p· there of graves
41: 4 unto me, This is the most holy p·.
9 was the p· of the side chambers
11 were toward the p· that was left,
11 the breadth of the p· that was left
12 the separate p· at the end toward the
13 and the separate p·, and the building,
14 and of the separate p· toward the east,
15 the separate p· which was behind it,
42: 1 that was over against the separate p·,
10 over against the separate p·, and over
13 which are before the separate p·, they
13 trespass offering; for the p· is holy.
14 shall they not go out of the holy p·
20 the sanctuary and the profane p·.
43: 7 Son of man, the p· of my throne,
7 the p· of the soles of my feet, where
13 this shall be the higher p· of the altar.
21 he shall burn it in the appointed p· of
44:13 my holy things, in the most holy p·:
45: 3 the sanctuary and the most holy p·.
4 it shall be a p· for their houses,
4 and an holy p· for the sanctuary.
46:19 there was a p· on the two sides
20 the p· where the priests shall boil
47:10 they shall be a p· to spread forth nets;
48:15 shall be a profane p· for the city, for
Da 2:35 no p· was found for them: and the
8:11 p· of his sanctuary was cast down.
11:31 they shall p· the abomination that
Ho 1:10 p· where it was said unto them,
4:16 will feed them as a lamb in a large p·.
5:15 I will go and return to my p·, till
9:13 Tyrus, is planted in a pleasant p·:
11:11 and I will p· them in their houses,
13:13 p· of the breaking forth of children.
Joe 3: 7 I will raise them out of the p·
Am 8: 3 be many dead bodies in every p·;
Mic 1: 3 the Lord cometh forth out of his p·,
4 that are poured down a steep p·.
Na 1: 8 an utter end of the p· thereof,
3:17 p· is not known where they are.
Zep 1: 4 the remnant of Baal from this p·,
2:11 worship him every one from his p·,
15 a p· for beasts to lie down in! every
Hag 2: 9 and in this p· will I give peace,
Zec 6:12 and he shall grow up out of his p·,
10: 6 I will bring them again to p· them;
10 and p· shall not be found for them.
12: 6 be inhabited again in her own p·,
14:10 be lifted up, and inhabited in her p·,
10 gate unto the p· of the first gate,
Mal 1:11 in every p· incense shall be offered
M't 8:32 violently down a steep p· into the sea,
9:24 He said unto them, Give p·: for the
12: 6 in this p· is one...than the temple.
14:13 by ship into a desert p· apart:
15 This is a desert p·, and the time is
35 the men of that p· had knowledge
17:20 Remove hence to yonder p·; and it
24:15 the prophet, stand in the holy p·,
26:36 them unto a p· called Gethsemane,
52 Put up again thy sword into his p·:
27:33 come unto a p· called Golgotha,

M't 27:33 that is to say, a p· of a skull,
28: 6 Come see the p· where the Lord lay.
M'r 1:35 departed into a solitary p·, and
5:13 violently down a steep p· into the sea,
6:10 p· soever ye enter into an house,
10 abide till ye depart from that p·.
31 yourselves apart into a desert p·,
32 they departed into a desert p· by
35 This is a desert p·, and now the
11: 4 without in a p· where two ways met;
12: 1 and digged a p· for the winefat, and
14:32 to a p· which...named Gethsemane:
15:22 bring him unto the p· Golgotha,
22 being interpreted, The p· of a skull.
16: 6 behold the p· where they laid him.
Lu 4:17 found the p· where it was written,
37 went out into every p· of the country
42 departed and went into a desert p·;
8:33 violently down a steep p· into the
9:10 aside privately into a desert p·
12 for we are here in a desert p·.
10: 1 his face into every city and p·,
32 a Levite, when he was at the p·,
11: 1 as he was praying in a certain p·,
33 a candle, putteth it in a secret p·,
14: 9 and say to thee, Give this man p·;
16:28 also come into this p· of torment.
19: 5 And when Jesus came to the p·, he
22:40 when he was at the p·, he said unto
23: 5 beginning from Galilee to this p·
33 And when they were come to the p·,
Joh 4:20 in Jerusalem is the p· where men
5:13 away, a multitude being in that p·.
6:10 there was much grass in the p·.
23 unto the p· where they did eat
8:37 my word hath no p· in you.
10:40 p· where John at first baptized;
11: 6 still in the same p· where he was.
30 in that p· where Martha met him.
41 from the p· where the dead was laid.
48 take away both our p· and nation.
14: 2 you. I go to prepare a p· for you.
3 if I go and prepare a p· for you,
18: 2 which betrayed him, knew the p·:
19:13 in a p· that is called the Pavement,
17 his cross went forth into a p·
17 called the p· of a skull, which is
20 the p· where Jesus was crucified
41 the p· where he was crucified there
20: 7 wrapped together in a p· by itself.
Ac 1:25 fell, that he might go to his own p·.
2: 1 were all with one accord in one p·.
4:31 the p· was shaken where they
6:13 words against this holy p·, and the
14 of Nazareth shall destroy this p·,
7: 7 come forth, and serve me in this p·.
33 the p· where thou standest is holy
49 Lord: or what is the p· of my rest?
8:32 p· of the scripture which he read
12:17 departed, and went into another p·.
21:12 and they of that p·, besought him
28 people, and the law, and this p·:
28 and hath polluted this holy p·.
25:23 was entered into the p· of hearing,
27: 8 a p· which is called The fair havens;
41 into a p· where two seas met,
Ro 9:26 p· where it was said unto them,
12:19 but rather give p· unto wrath:
15:23 having no more p· in these parts,
1Co 1: 2 that in every p· call upon the name
11:20 come together therefore into one p·,
14:23 church be come together into one p·,
2Co 2:14 his knowledge by us in every p·.
Ga 2: 5 whom we gave p· by subjection,
Eph 4:27 Neither give p· to the devil.
1Th 1: 8 in every p· your faith to God-ward
Heb 2: 6 But one in a certain p· testified,
4: 4 spake in a certain p· of the seventh
5 And in this p· again, If they shall
5: 6 As he saith also in another p·, Thou
8: 7 no p· have been sought for the
9:12 he entered in once into the holy p·,
25 high priest entereth into the holy p·
11: 8 he was called to go out into a p·
12:17 for he found no p· of repentance,
Jas 2: 3 Sit thou here in a good p·; and
3:11 at the same p· sweet water and
2Pe 1:19 a light that shineth in a dark p·,
Re 2: 5 thy candlestick out of his p·,
12: 6 she hath a p· prepared of God,
8 was their p· found any more
14 into her p·, where she is nourished
16:16 a p· called in the Hebrew tongue
20:11 and there was found no p· for them.

placed
Ge 3:24 he p· at the east of the garden of
47:11 And Joseph p· his father and his
1Ki 12:32 and he p· in Beth-el the priests of
2Ki 17: 6 p· them in Halah and in Habor by
24 p· them in the cities of Samaria
26 p· in the cities of Samaria, know
2Ch 1:14 which he p· in the chariot cities,
4: 8 p· them in the temple, five on the
17: 2 he p· forces in all the fenced cities
Job 20: 4 old, since man was p· upon earth,
Ps 78:60 the tent which he p· among men;
Isa 5: 8 they may be p· alone in the midst
Jer 5:22 have p· the sand for the bound of
Eze 17: 5 he p· it by great waters, and set

places See also MARKETPLACES.
Ge 28:15 keep thee in all p· whither thou goest,
36:40 to their families after their p·,
Ex 20:24 p· where I record my name I will
25:27 be for p· of the staves to bear the
26:29 rings of gold for p· for the bars:

Ex 30: 4 they shall be for p' for the staves
36: 34 rings of gold to be p' for the bars,
37: 14 p' for the staves to bear the table.
27 p' for the staves to bear it withal.
38: 5 of brass, to be p' for the staves.
Le 26: 30 I will destroy your high p', and cut
Nu 21: 28 the lords of the high p' of Arnon.
22: 41 him up into the high p' of Baal,
33: 52 and quite pluck down all their high p':
De 1: 7 and unto all the p' nigh thereunto,
12: 2 Ye shall utterly destroy all the p',
32: 13 ride on the high p' of the earth,
33: 29 thou shalt tread upon their high p'.
Jos 5: 8 they abode in their p' in the camps
J'g 5: 11 of archers in the p' of drawing water,
18 the death in the high p' of the field
19: 13 one of these p' to lodge all night,
20: 33 Israel came forth out of their p',
1Sa 7: 16 and judged Israel in all those p'.
13: 6 in rocks, and in high p', and in pits.
23: 23 of all the lurking p' where he hideth
30: 31 to all the p' where David himself
2Sa 1: 19 of Israel is slain upon thy high p':
25 thou wast slain in thine high p'.
7: 7 In all the p' wherein I have walked
22: 34 feet: and setteth me upon my high p'.
46 shall be afraid out of their close p'.
1Ki 3: 2 Only the people sacrificed in high p',
3 only he...burnt incense in high p'.
12: 31 And he made an house of high p', and
32 priests of the high p' which he...made.
13: 2 he offer the priests of the high p'
32 against all the houses of the high p'
33 lowest...people, priests of the high p':
33 one of the priests of the high p'.
14: 23 For they also built them high p', and
15: 14 But the high p' were not removed:
22: 43 the high p' were not taken away;
43 and burnt incense yet in the high p'.
2Ki 12: 3 But the high p' were not taken away:
3 and burnt incense in the high p'.
14: 4 the high p' were not taken away:
4 and burnt incense on the high p'.
15: 4 that the high p' were not removed:
4 and burnt incense still on the high p'.
35 the high p' were not removed:
35 burned incense still in the high p'.
16: 4 burnt incense in the high p', and on
17: 9 built them high p' in all their cities,
11 they burnt incense in all the high p',
29 put them in the houses of the high p'
32 lowest of them priests of the high p',
32 for them in the houses of the high p'.
18: 4 He removed the high p', and brake the
22 whose high p' and...altars Hezekiah
19: 24 I dried up all the rivers of besieged p'.
21: 3 For he built up again the high p'
23: 5 in the high p' in the cities of Judah,
5 and in the p' round about Jerusalem;
8 defiled the high p' where the priests
8 brake down the high p' of the gates
9 the priests of the high p' came not up
13 high p' that were before Jerusalem,
14 filled their p' with...bones of men.
19 all the houses of the high p' that were
20 he slew all the priests of the high p'
1Ch 6: 54 dwelling p' throughout their castles
2Ch 8: 11 the p' are holy, whereunto the ark of
11: 15 ordained him priests for the high p',
14: 3 of the strange gods, and the high p',
5 away...the high p' and the images:
15: 17 But the high p' were not taken away
17: 6 he took away the high p' and groves
20: 33 the high p' were not taken away:
21: 11 he made high p' in the mountains
28: 4 burnt incense in the high p', and on
25 he made high p' to burn incense
31: 1 threw down the high p' and the altars
32: 12 taken away his high p' and his altars,
33: 3 For he built again the high p' which
17 people did sacrifice still in the high p',
19 and the p' wherein he built high
19 wherein he built high p', and set up
34: 3 purge...Jerusalem from the high p',
Ne 4: 12 From all p' whence ye shall return
13 set I in the lower p' behind the wall,
13 and on the higher p', I even set
12: 27 sought the Levites out of all...p',
Job 3: 14 built desolate p' for themselves;
20: 26 darkness shall be hid in his secret p':
21: 28 are the dwelling p' of the wicked?
25: 2 him, he maketh peace in his high p'.
37: 8 into dens, and remain in their p'.
Ps 10: 8 in the lurking p' of the villages:
8 in the secret p' doth he murder the
16: 6 lines are fallen unto me in pleasant p';
17: 12 were a young lion lurking in secret p'.
18: 33 feet, and setteth me upon my high p'.
45 and be afraid out of their close p'.
49: 11 their dwelling p' to all generations;
68: 35 thou art terrible out of thy holy p':
73: 18 thou didst set them in slippery p':
74: 20 the dark p' of the earth are full of the
78: 58 provoked him...with their high p',
95: 4 his hand are the deep p' of the earth:
103: 22 works in all p' of his dominion:
105: 41 they ran in the dry p' like a river.
109: 10 bread also out of their desolate p'.
110: 6 shall fill the p' with the dead bodies;
135: 6 in earth, in the seas, and all deep p'.
141: 6 judges are overthrown in stony p',
Pr 8: 2 She standeth in the top of high p',
2 by the way in the p' of the paths.
9: 3 crieth upon the highest p' of the city,
14 on a seat in the high p' of the city,
Ca 2: 14 the rock, in the secret p' of the stairs,

Isa 5: 17 and the waste p' of the fat ones shall
15: 2 to Bajith, and to Dibon, the high p',
32: 18 sure dwellings, and in quiet resting p';
36: 7 whose high p' and...altars Hezekiah
37: 25 up all the rivers of the besieged p'.
40: 4 made straight, and the rough p' plain:
41: 18 I will open rivers in high p', and
44: 26 I will raise up the decayed p' thereof:
45: 2 and make the crooked p' straight:
3 and hidden riches of secret p',
49: 9 their pastures shall be in all high p'.
19 For thy waste and thy desolate p',
51: 3 he will comfort all her waste p'; and
52: 9 together, ye waste p' of Jerusalem:
58: 12 be of thee shall build the old waste p':
14 to ride upon the high p' of the earth,
59: 10 we are in desolate p' as dead men.
Jer 3: 2 Lift up thine eyes unto the high p',
21 A voice was heard upon the high p',
4: 11 wind of the high p' in the wilderness
12 a full wind from those p' shall come
5: 1 and seek in the broad p' thereof, if
7: 29 and take up a lamentation on high p';
31 they have built the high p' of Tophet,
8: 3 in all the p' whither I have driven
12: 12 The spoilers are come upon all high p'
13: 17 my soul shall weep in secret p' for
14: 6 wild asses did stand in the high p',
17: 3 to the spoil, and thy high p' for sin,
6 but shall inhabit the parched p' in the
26 and from the p' about Jerusalem,
19: 5 have built also the high p' of Baal,
23: 10 the pleasant p' of the wilderness are
24 Can any hide himself in secret p' that
24: 9 all p' whither I shall drive them.
26: 18 of the house as the high p' of a forest.
29: 14 all the p' whither I have driven
32: 35 And they built the high p' of Baal,
44 and in the p' about Jerusalem, and in
33: 13 and in the p' about Jerusalem, and in
40: 12 all p' whither they were driven,
45: 5 for a prey in all p' whither thou
48: 35 him that offereth in the high p', and
49: 10 bare, I have uncovered his secret p',
La 2: 6 hath destroyed his p' of the assembly:
3: 6 He hath set me in dark p', as they that
10 in wait, and as a lion in secret p'.
Eze 6: 3 you, and I will destroy your high p'.
6 and the high p' shall be desolate;
7: 24 and their holy p' shall be defiled.
16: 16 and deckedst thy high p' with divers
39 and shall break down thy high p':
21: 2 and drop thy word toward the holy p',
26: 20 parts of the earth, in p' desolate of old,
34: 12 deliver them out of all p' where
13 in all the inhabited p' of the country.
26 the p' round about my hill a blessing;
36: 2 even the ancient high p' are ours in
36 that I the Lord build the ruined p',
38: 12 desolate p' that are now inhabited,
20 and the steep p' shall fall, and every
43: 7 of their kings in their high p'.
46: 23 was made with boiling p' under the
24 These are the p' of them that boil,
47: 11 But the miry p' thereof and the
Da 11: 24 upon the fattest p' of the province;
Ho 9: 6 the pleasant p' for their silver, nettles
10: 8 The high p' also of Aven, the sin of
Am 4: 6 and want of bread in all your p':
13 upon the high p' of the earth,
7: 9 the high p' of Isaac shall be desolate,
Mic 1: 3 tread upon the high p' of the earth.
5 and what are the high p' of Judah?
3: 12 the house as the high p' of the forest.
Hab 3: 19 make me to walk upon mine high p'.
Zec 3: 7 I will give thee p' to walk among
Mal 1: 4 will return and build the desolate p';
M't 12: 43 he walketh through dry p', seeking
13: 5 Some fell upon stony p', where they
20 that received the seed into stony p',
24: 7 and earthquakes, in divers p'.
M'r 1: 45 city, but was without in desert p':
13: 8 shall be earthquakes in divers p',
Lu 11: 24 he walketh through dry p', seeking
21: 11 earthquakes shall be in divers p',
Ac 24: 3 We accept it always, and in all p',
Eph 1: 3 blessings in heavenly p' in Christ:
20 his own right hand in the heavenly p',
2: 6 in heavenly p' in Christ Jesus:
3: 10 in heavenly p' might be known by
6: 12 spiritual wickedness in high p'.
Ph'p 1: 13 all the palace, and in all other p';
Heb 9: 24 into the holy p' made with hands,
Re 6: 14 island were moved out of their p'.

plague See also PLAGUED; PLAGUES.
Ex 11: 1 bring one p' more upon Pharaoh,
12: 13 p' shall not be upon you to destroy
30: 12 that there be no p' among them,
Le 13: 2 of his flesh like the p' of leprosy;
3 shall look on the p' in the skin of
3 the hair in the p' is turned white,
3 p' in sight be deeper than the skin
3 skin of his flesh, it is a p' of leprosy:
4 up him that hath the p' seven days:
5 if the p' in his sight be at a stay,
5 and the p' spread not in the skin;
6 behold, if the p' be somewhat dark,
6 p' spread not in the skin, the priest
9 When the p' of leprosy is in a man,
12 hath the p' from his head even to
13 pronounce him clean that hath...p':
17 if the p' be turned into white; then
17 pronounce him clean that hath...p':
20 p' of leprosy broken out of the boil.
22 pronounce him unclean: it is a p'.

Le 13: 25, 27 unclean: it is the p' of leprosy.
29 or woman have a p' upon the head
30 Then the priest shall see the p': and,
31 the priest look on the p' of the scall,
31 up him that hath the p' of the scall
32 day the priest shall look on the p':
44 unclean; his p' is in his head.
45 And the leper in whom the p' is, his
46 days wherein the p' shall be in him
47 garment...that the p' of leprosy is in,
49 if the p' be greenish or reddish in
49 it is a p' of leprosy, and shall be
50 the priest shall look upon the p',
50 up it that hath the p' seven days:
51 look on the p' on the seventh day:
51 if the p' be spread in the garment,
51 the p' is a fretting leprosy; it is
52 thing of skin, wherein the p' is:
53 the p' be not spread in the garment,
54 wash the thing wherein the p' is,
55 the priest shall look on the p', after
55 the p' have not changed his colour,
55 colour, and the p' be not spread;
56 the p' be somewhat dark after the
57 it is a spreading p': thou shalt burn
57 shalt burn that wherein the p' is
58 if the p' be departed from them,
59 This is the law of the p' of leprosy
14: 3 if the p' of leprosy be healed in the
32 him in whom is the p' of leprosy,
34 I put the p' of leprosy in a house of
35 there is as it were a p' in the house:
36 the priest go into it to see the p',
37 he shall look on the p', and, behold,
37 if the p' be in the walls of the house
39 p' be spread in the walls of the
40 away the stones in which the p' is,
43 if the p' come again, and break out
44 if the p' be spread in the house, it
48 the p' hath not spread in the house,
48 clean, because the p' is healed.
54 law for all manner of p' of leprosy,
Nu 8: 19 there be no p' among the children
11: 33 the people with a very great p'.
14: 37 died by the p' before the Lord.
16: 46 from the Lord; the p' is begun.
47 the p' was begun among the people:
48 the living; and the p' was stayed.
49 Now they that died in the p' were
50 congregation: and the p' was stayed.
25: 8 p' was stayed from the children of
9 and those that died in the p' were
18 slain in the day of the p' for Peor's
26: 1 it came to pass after the p', that the
31: 16 was a p' among the congregation
De 24: 8 Take heed in the p' of leprosy, that
28: 61 Also every sickness, and every p',
Jos 22: 17 was a p' in the congregation of the
1Sa 6: 4 for one p' was on you all, and on
2Sa 24: 21 p' may be stayed from the people.
25 and the p' was stayed from Israel.
1Ki 8: 37 of their cities; whatsoever p',
38 every man the p' of his own heart,
1Ch 21: 22 p' may be stayed from the people.
2Ch 21: 14 p' will the Lord smite thy people,
Ps 89: 23 face, and p' them that hate him.
91: 10 neither shall any p' come nigh thy
106: 29 and the p' brake in upon them.
30 judgment: and so the p' was stayed.
Zec 14: 12 this shall be the p' wherewith the
15 be the p' of the horse, of the mule,
15 shall be in these tents, as this p'.
18 there shall be the p', wherewith the
M'r 5: 29 that she was healed of that p'.
34 go in peace, and be whole of thy p'.
Re 16: 21 God because of the p' of the hail;
21 the p' thereof was exceeding great.

plagued
Ge 12: 17 Lord p' Pharaoh and his house
Ex 32: 35 the Lord p' the people, because
Jos 24: 5 I p' Egypt, according to that which
1Ch 21: 17 thy people, that they should be p'.
Ps 73: 5 neither are they p' like other men.
14 all the day long have I been p',

plagues
Ge 12: 17 plagued Pharaoh...with great p'
Ex 9: 14 at this time send all my p' upon
Le 26: 21 seven times more p' upon you
De 28: 59 Lord will make thy p' wonderful,
59 and the p' of thy seed, even great p',
29: 22 when they see the p' of that land,
1Sa 4: 8 smote the Egyptians with all the p'
Jer 19: 8 hiss because of all the p' thereof.
49: 17 and shall hiss at all the p' thereof.
50: 13 be astonished, and hiss at all her p'.
Ho 13: 14 O death, I will be thy p'; O grave,
M'r 3: 10 to touch him, as many as had p'.
Lu 7: 21 many of their infirmities and p',
Re 9: 20 which were not killed by these p'
11: 6 and to smite the earth with all p',
15: 1 angels having the seven last p';
6 of the temple, having the seven p',
8 seven p' of the seven angels were
16: 9 which hath power over these p':
18: 4 and that ye receive not of her p'.
8 shall her p' come in one day, death,
21: 9 seven vials full of the seven last p',
22: 18 God shall add unto him the p' that

plain See also PLAINS.
Ge 11: 2 found a p' in the land of Shinar;
12: 6 of Sichem, unto the p' of Moreh.
13: 10 and beheld all the p' of Jordan,
11 Lot chose him all the p' of Jordan;
12 Lot dwelled in the cities of the p',

Ge 13:18 came and dwelt in the p' of Mamre,
14:13 for he dwelt in the p' of Mamre the
19:17 neither stay thou in all the p';
25 those cities, and all the p', and all
28 and toward all the land of the p',
29 God destroyed the cities of the p',
25:27 Jacob was a p' man, dwelling in
De 1: 1 in the p' over against the Red sea,
7 places nigh thereunto, in the p',
2: 8 the way of the p' from Elath, and
3:10 the cities of the p', and all Gilead,
17 p' also, and Jordan, and the coast
17 even unto the sea of the p', even the
4:43 the wilderness, in the p' country,
49 p' on this side Jordan eastward,
49 even unto the sea of the p', under
34: 3 p' of the valley of Jericho, the city
Jos 3:16 down toward the sea of the p',
8:14 at a time appointed, before the p';
11:16 Goshen, and the valley, and the p',
12: 1 Hermon, and all the p' on the east:
3 the p' to the sea of Chinneroth on
3 and unto the sea of the p', even the
13: 9 all the p' of Medeba unto Dibon;
16 the river, and all the p' by Medeba;
17 and all her cities that are in the p';
21 all the cities of the p', and all the
20: 8 Bezer in the wilderness upon the p'
J'g 4:11 his tent unto the p' of Zaanaim,
9: 6 by the p' of the pillar that was in
37 come along by the p' of Meonenim.
11:33 and unto the p' of the vineyards,
1Sa 10: 3 thou shalt come to the p' of Tabor,
23:24 the p' on the south of Jeshimon.
2Sa 2:29 all that night through the p',
4: 7 them away through the p' all night
15:28 tarry in the p' of the wilderness,
18:23 Ahimaaz ran by the way of the p',
1Ki 7:46 In the p' of Jordan did the king
20:23 let us fight against them in the p',
25 we will fight against them in the p'.
2Ki 14:25 of Hamath unto the sea of the p',
25: 4 king went the way toward the p'.
2Ch 4:17 In the p' of Jordan did the king
Ne 3:22 the priests, the men of the p'.
6: 2 one of the villages in the p' of Ono.
12:28 p' country round about Jerusalem,
Ps 27:11 lead me in a p' path, because of
Pr 8: 9 all p' to him that understandeth,
15:19 way of the righteous is made p'.
Isa 28:25 he hath made p' the face thereof,
40: 4 straight, and the rough places p':
Jer 17:26 of Benjamin, and from the p',
21:13 of the valley, and rock of the p',
39: 4 and he went out the way of the p'.
48: 8 and the p' shall be destroyed, as
21 is come upon the p' country;
52: 7 they went by the way of the p'.
Eze 3:22 Arise, go forth into the p', and I
23 arose, and went forth into the p':
8: 4 to the vision that I saw in the p'.
Da 3: 1 he set it up in the p' of Dura, in the
Am 1: 5 the inhabitant from the p' of Aven,
Ob 19 and they of the p' the Philistines:
Hab 2: 2 vision, and make it p' upon tables,
Zec 4: 7 thou shalt become a p': and he
7: 7 inhabited the south and the p'?
14:10 All the land shall be turned as a p'
M'r 7:35 tongue was loosed, and he spake p'.
Lu 6:17 and stood in the p', and the

plainly
Ex 21: 5 if the servant shall p' say, I love
De 27: 8 all the words of this law very p'.
1Sa 2:27 p' appear unto the house of thy
10:16 He told us p' that the asses were
Ezr 4:18 sent unto us hath been p' read
Isa 32: 4 shall be ready to speak p'.
Joh 10:24 If thou be the Christ, tell us p'.
11:14 Then said Jesus unto them p',
16:25 I shall shew you p' of the Father.
29 him, Lo, now speakest thou p',
Heb 11:14 declare p' that they seek a country.

plainness
2Cor 3:12 hope, we use great p' of speech:

plains
Ge 18: 1 unto him in the p' of Mamre:
Nu 22: 1 and pitched in the p' of Moab on
26: 3 spake with them in the p' of Moab
63 children of Israel in the p' of Moab by
31:12 unto the camp at the p' of Moab,
33:48 and pitched in the p' of Moab by
49 unto Abel-shittim in the p' of Moab.
50 spake unto Moses in the p' of Moab
35: 1 spake unto Moses in the p' of Moab
36:13 children of Israel in the p' of Moab
De 11:30 Gilgal, beside the p' of Moreh?
34: 1 Moses went up from the p' of Moab
8 wept for Moses in the p' of Moab
Jos 4:13 unto battle, to the p' of Jericho.
5:10 month at even in the p' of Jericho.
11: 2 and of the p' south of Chinneroth,
12: 8 and in the p', and in the springs,
13:32 for inheritance in the p' of Moab,
2Sa 17:16 night in the p' of the wilderness,
2Ki 25: 5 overtook him in the p' of Jericho:
1Ch 27:28 trees that were in the low p' was
2Ch 9:27 trees that are in the low p' in
26:10 in the low country, and in the p':
Jer 39: 5 Zedekiah in the p' of Jericho:
52: 8 Zedekiah in the p' of Jericho;

plaister See also PLAISTERED.
Le 14:42 morter, and shall p' the house.
De 27: 2 great stones, and p' them with
De 27: 2 great stones, and...them with p':
4 Ebal, and thou shalt p' them with
4 Ebal, and thou shalt...them with p'.
Isa 38:21 and lay it for a p' upon the boil,
Da 5: 5 p' of the wall of the king's palace:

plaistered
Le 14:43 the house, and after it is p';
48 the house, after the house was p':

plaiting See also PLATTED.
1Pe 3: 3 outward adorning of p' the hair,

planes
Isa 44:13 he fitteth it with p', and he

planets
2Ki 23: 5 and to the p', and to all the hosts

planks
1Ki 6:15 floor of the house with p' of fir.
Eze 41:25 thick p' upon the face of...porch
26 of the house, and thick p'.

plant See also PLANTED; PLANTETH; PLANTING; PLANTS; SUPPLANT.
Ge 2: 5 every p' of the field before it was
Ex 15:17 shalt bring them in, and p' them
De 16:21 shalt not p' thee a grove of any
28:30 thou shalt p' a vineyard, and shalt
39 Thou shalt p' vineyards, and dress
2Sa 7:10 my people Israel, and will p' them,
2Ki 19:29 sow ye, and reap, and p' vineyards,
1Ch 17: 9 my people Israel, and will p' them,
Job 14: 9 and bring forth boughs like a p'.
Ps 107:37 sow the fields, and p' vineyards,
Ec 3: 2 a time to p', and a time to pluck up
Isa 5: 7 the men of Judah his pleasant p':
17:10 shalt thou p' pleasant plants, and
11 shalt thou make thy p' to grow,
37:30 ye, and reap, and p' vineyards,
41:19 will p' in the wilderness the cedar,
51:16 that I may p' the heavens, and lay
53: 2 grow up before him as a tender p',
65:21 they shall p' vineyards, and eat
22 they shall not p', and another eat:
Jer 1:10 to throw down, to build, and to p'.
2:21 art turned into the degenerate p' of
18: 9 a kingdom, to build and to p' it;
24: 6 and I will p' them, and not pluck
29: 5 p' gardens, and eat the fruit of them;
28 p' gardens, and eat the fruit of them.
31: 5 yet p' vines upon the mountains
5 the planters shall p', and shall eat
28 over them, to build, and to p', saith
32:41 I will p' them in this land assuredly
35: 7 nor sow seed, nor p' vineyard, nor
42:10 I will p' you, and not pluck you up:
Eze 17:22 p' it upon an high mountain and
23 of the height of Israel will I p' it:
28:26 build houses, and p' vineyards;
34:29 raise up for them a p' of renown,
36:36 and p' that that was desolate:
Da 11:45 p' the tabernacles of his palace
Am 9:14 and they shall p' vineyards, and
15 and I will p' them upon their land,
Zep 1:13 and they shall p' vineyards, but not
M't 15:13 p', which my heavenly Father

plantation
Eze 17: 7 water it by the furrows of her p'.

planted See also PLANTEDST; SUPPLANTED.
Ge 2: 8 Lord God p' a garden eastward
9:20 husbandman, and he p' a vineyard:
21:33 Abraham p' a grove in Beer-sheba,
Le 19:23 shall have p' all manner of trees
Nu 24: 6 lign aloes which the Lord hath p',
De 20: 6 man is he that hath p' a vineyard,
Jos 24:13 oliveyards which ye p' not do ye eat.
Ps 1: 3 shall be like a tree p' by the rivers
80: 8 cast out the heathen, and p' it.
15 which thy right hand hath p', and
92:13 that be p' in the house of the
94: 9 He that p' the ear, shall he not
104:16 of Lebanon, which he hath p';
Ec 2: 4 me houses; I p' me vineyards:
5 and I p' trees in them of all kinds of
3: 2 a time to pluck up that which is p';
Isa 5: 2 p' it with the choicest vine, and
40:24 they shall not be p'; yea, they shall
Jer 2:21 I had p' thee a noble vine, wholly
11:17 the Lord of hosts, that p' thee, hath
12: 2 Thou hast p' them, yea, they have
17: 8 shall be as a tree p' by the waters,
45: 4 which I have p' I will pluck up,
Eze 17: 5 of the land, and p' it in a fruitful field;
8 It was p' in a good soil by great
10 behold, being p', shall it prosper?
19:10 in thy blood, p' by the waters:
13 And now she is p' in the wilderness,
Ho 9:13 Tyrus, is p' in a pleasant place:
Am 5:11 ye have p' pleasant vineyards, but
M't 15:13 my heavenly Father hath not p',
21:33 which p' a vineyard, and hedged it
M'r 12: 1 A certain man p' a vineyard, and
Lu 13: 6 had a fig tree p' in his vineyard;
17: 6 the root, and be thou p' in the sea;
28 they sold, they p', they builded;
20: 9 A certain man p' a vineyard, and
Ro 6: 5 p' together in the likeness of his
1Co 3: 6 I have p', Apollos watered; but

plantedst
De 6:11 and olive trees, which thou p' not;
Ps 44: 2 with thy hand, and p' them; how

planters
Jer 31: 5 the p' shall plant, and shall eat

planteth
Pr 31:16 of her hands she p' a vineyard.
Isa 44:14 he p' an ash, and the rain doth
1Co 3: 7 neither is he that p' any thing,
8 Now he that p' and he that watereth
9: 7 who p' a vineyard, and eateth not

planting See also PLANTINGS.
Isa 60:21 the branch of my p', the work of
61: 3 the p' of the Lord, that he might

plantings
Mic 1: 6 the field, and as p' of a vineyard:

plants
1Ch 4:23 that dwelt among p' and hedges:
Ps 128: 3 children like olive p' round about
144:12 our sons may be as p' grown up
Ca 4:13 p' are...orchard of pomegranates,
Isa 16: 8 broken down the principal p'
17:10 shalt thou plant pleasant p', and
Jer 48:32 thy p' are gone over the sea, they
Eze 31: 4 rivers running round about...p',

plaster See PLAISTER.

plat See also PLAITING; PLATTER.
2Ki 9:26 I will requit thee in this p', saith
26 cast him into the p' of ground,

plate See also PLATES.
Ex 28:36 thou shalt make a p' of pure gold,
39:30 they made the p' of the holy crown
Le 8: 9 forefront, did he put the golden p',

plates
Ex 39: 3 they did beat the gold into thin p',
Nu 16:38 let them make them broad p' for
39 were made broad p' for a covering
1Ki 7:30 brasen wheels, and p' of brass:
36 For on the p' of the ledges thereof,
Jer 10: 9 Silver spread into p' is brought from

platted See also PLAITING.
M't 27:29 they had p' a crown of thorns,
M'r 15:17 p' a crown of thorns, and put it
Joh 19: 2 the soldiers p' a crown of thorns,

platter
M't 23:25 outside of the cup and of the p',
26 that which is within the cup and p',
Lu 11:39 the outside of the cup and the p';

play See also PLAYED; PLAYETH; PLAYING.
Ex 32: 6 and to drink, and rose up to p'.
De 22:21 to p' the whore in her father's house:
1Sa 16:16 he shall p' with his hand, and
17 me now a man that can p' well,
21:15 to p' the mad man in my presence?
2Sa 2:14 men now arise, and p' before us.
6:21 therefore will I p' before the Lord.
10:12 and let us p' the men for our people,
Job 40:20 where all the beasts of the field p'.
41: 5 thou p' with him as with a bird?
Ps 33: 3 p' skilfully with a loud noise.
104:26 thou hast made to p' therein.
Isa 11: 8 shall p' on the hole of the asp,
Eze 33:32 and can p' well on an instrument:
Ho 3: 3 thou shalt not p' the harlot, and thou
4:15 p' the harlot, yet let not Judah offend;
1Co 10: 7 eat and drink, and rose up to p'.

played See also DISPLAYED; PLAYEDST.
Ge 38:24 daughter in law hath p' the harlot;
J'g 19: 2 concubine p' the whore against him,
1Sa 16:23 an harp, and p' with his hand:
18: 7 answered one another as they p',
10 David p' with his hand, as at other
19: 9 and David p' with his hand.
26:21 I have p' the fool, and have erred
2Sa 6: 5 house of Israel p' before the Lord
2Ki 3:15 came to pass, when the minstrel p',
1Ch 13: 8 David and all Israel p' before God
Jer 3: 1 thou hast p' the harlot with many
6 tree, and there hath p' the harlot.
8 not, but went and p' the harlot also.
Eze 16:28 Thou hast p' the whore also with the
28 yea, thou hast p' the harlot with them,
23: 5 Aholah p' the harlot when she was
19 had p' the harlot in the land of Egypt.
Ho 2: 5 For their mother hath p' the harlot:

playedst
Eze 16:15 p' the harlot because of thy renown,
16 p' the harlot thereupon: the like

player See also PLAYERS.
1Sa 16:16 who is a cunning p' on a harp:

players
Ps 68:25 p' on instruments followed after;
87: 7 p' on instruments shall be there:

playeth
Eze 23:44 go in unto a woman that p' the harlot:

playing
Le 21: 9 she profane herself by p' the whore,
1Sa 16:18 Beth-lehemite that is cunning in p',
1Ch 15:29 saw king David dancing and p':
Ps 68:25 were the damsels p' with timbrels.
Jer 2:20 tree thou wanderest, p' the harlot.
Eze 16:41 cause thee to cease from p' the harlot,
Zec 8: 5 boys and girls p' in the streets

plea
De 17: 8 between p' and p', and between

plead See also IMPLEAD; PLEADED; PLEADETH; PLEADINGS.
J'g 6:31 Will ye p' for Baal? will ye save
31 he that will p' for him, let him be
31 let him p' for himself, because one

J'g 6:32 Let Baal p' against him, because
1Sa 24:15 and p' my cause, and deliver me
Job 9:19 who shall set me a time to p'?
13:19 Who is he that will p' with me?
16:21 one might p' for a man with God,
19: 5 and p' against me my reproach:
23: 6 Will he p' against me with his
Ps 35: 1 P' my cause, O Lord, with them
43: 1 Judge me, O God, and p' my cause
74:22 Arise, O God, p' thine own cause:
119:154 P' my cause, and deliver me:
Pr 22:23 the Lord will p' their cause, and
23:11 he shall p' their cause with thee.
31: 9 p' the cause of the poor and needy.
Isa 1:17 the fatherless, p' for the widow.
3:13 The Lord standeth up to p', and
43:26 remembrance: let us p' together:
66:16 will the Lord p' with all flesh:
Jer 2: 9 I will yet p' with you, saith the
9 your children's children will I p'.
29 Wherefore will ye p' with me? ye
35 I will p' with thee, because thou
12: 1 thou, O Lord, when I p' with thee:
25:31 he will p' with all flesh; he will
30:13 There none to p' thy cause, that
50:34 he shall thoroughly p' their cause,
51:36 Behold, I will p' thy cause, and take
Eze 17:20 and will p' with him there for his
20:35 will I p' with you face to face.
36 so will I p' with you, saith the Lord
38:22 will p' against him with pestilence
Ho 2: 2 P' with your mother, p': for she is
Joe 3: 2 p' with them there for my people
Mic 6: 2 people, and he will p' with Israel.
7: 9 until he p' my cause, and execute

pleaded
1Sa 25:39 the Lord that hath p' the cause
La 3:58 thou hast p' the causes of my soul;
Eze 20:36 Like as I p' with your fathers in

pleadeth
Job 16:21 as a man p' for his neighbour!
Isa 51:22 that p' the cause of his people,
59: 4 for justice, nor any p' for truth:

pleadings
Job 13: 6 and hearken to the p' of my lips.

pleasant
Ge 2: 9 every tree that is p' to the sight,
3: 6 it was p' to the eyes, and a tree
49:15 good, and the land that it was p';
2Sa 1:23 and Jonathan were lovely and p'
26 very p' hast thou been unto me:
1Ki 20: 6 whatsoever is p' in thine eyes,
2Ki 2:19 situation of this city is p', as my
2Ch 32:27 and for all manner of p' jewels;
Ps 16: 6 are fallen unto me in p' places;
81: 2 the p' harp with the psaltery.
106:24 they despised the p' land, they
133: 1 how p' it is for brethren to dwell
135: 3 praises unto his name; for it is p'.
147: 1 praises unto our God; for it is p':
Pr 2:10 and knowledge is p' to thy soul;
5:19 be as the loving hind and p' roe;
9:17 and bread eaten in secret is p'.
15:26 the words of the pure are p' words.
16:24 P' words are as an honeycomb,
22:18 p' thing if thou keep them within
24: 4 with all precious and p' riches.
Ec 11: 7 a p' thing it is for the eyes to
Ca 1:16 thou art fair, my beloved, yea, p':
4:13 of pomegranates, with p' fruits;
16 his garden, and eat his p' fruits.
7: 6 How fair and how p' art thou, O
13 gates are all manner of p' fruits,
Isa 2:16 Tarshish, and upon all p' pictures.
5: 7 the men of Judah his p' plant:
13:22 and dragons in their p' palaces:
17:10 shalt thou plant p' plants, and
32:12 for the teats, for the p' fields,
54:12 and all thy borders of p' stones.
64:11 all our p' things are laid waste.
Jer 3:19 and give thee a p' land, a goodly
12:10 p' portion a desolate wilderness.
23:10 p' places of the wilderness are
25:34 and ye shall fall like a p' vessel.
31:20 my dear son? is he a p' child?
La 1: 7 all her p' things that she had in
10 his hand upon all her p' things:
11 have given their p' things for meat
2: 4 slew all that were p' to the eye
Eze 26:12 walls, and destroy thy p' houses:
33:32 song of one that hath a p' voice,
Da 8: 9 the east, and toward the p' land.
10: 3 I ate no p' bread, neither came
11:38 precious stones, and p' things.
Ho 9: 6 p' places for their silver, nettles
13 Tyrus, is planted in a p' place:
13:15 the treasure of all p' vessels.
Joe 3: 5 temples my goodly p' things:
Am 5:11 ye have planted p' vineyards, but
Mic 2: 9 ye cast out from their p' houses;
Na 2: 9 glory out of all the p' furniture.
Zec 7:14 for they laid the p' land desolate.
Mal 3: 4 of Judah and Jerusalem be p'

pleasantness
Pr 3:17 Her ways are ways of p', and all

please See also DISPLEASE; PLEASED; PLEASETH; PLEASING.
Ex 21: 8 If she p' not her master, who
Nu 23:27 peradventure it will p' God
1Sa 20:13 if it p' my father to do thee evil,
2Sa 7:29 p' thee to bless the house of thy
1Ki 21: 6 else, if it p' thee, I will give thee
1Ch 17:27 p' thee to bless the house of thy
2Ch 10: 7 kind to this people, and p' them,
Ne 2: 5 If it p' the king, and if thy servant
7 If it p' the king, let letters be
Es 1:19 it p' the king, let there go a royal
3: 9 If it p' the king, let it be written
5: 8 if it p' the king to grant my petition,
7: 3 if it p' the king, let my life be given
8: 5 it p' the king, and if I have found
9:13 If it p' the king, let it be granted
Job 6: 9 it would p' God to destroy me;
20:10 children shall seek to p' the poor,
Ps 69:31 shall p' the Lord better than an ox
Pr 16: 7 When a man's ways p' the Lord,
Ca 2: 7 up, nor awake my love, till he p'.
3: 5 up, nor awake my love, till he p'.
8: 4 up, nor awake my love, until he p'.
Isa 2: 6 p' themselves in the children of
55:11 shall accomplish that which I p',
56: 4 and choose the things that p' me,
Joh 8:29 do always those things that p' him.
Ro 8: 8 that are in the flesh cannot p' God.
15: 1 the weak, and not to p' ourselves.
2 Let every one of us p' his neighbour
1Co 7:32 the Lord, how he may p' the Lord:
33 the world, how he may p' his wife.
34 world, how she may p' her husband.
10:33 Even as I p' all men in all things,
Ga 1:10 men, or God? or do I seek to p' men?
1Th 2:15 they p' not God, and are contrary
4: 1 how ye ought to walk and to p' God,
2Ti 2: 4 he may p' him who hath chosen him
Tit 2: 9 to p' them well in all things;
Heb11: 6 faith it is impossible to p' him:

pleased See also DISPLEASED.
Ge 28: 8 daughters of Canaan p' not
33:10 of God, and thou wast p' with me.
34:18 And their words p' Hamor,
45:16 and it p' Pharaoh well, and his
Nu 24: 1 Balaam saw that it p' the Lord
De 1:23 And the saying p' me well:
Jos 22:30 of Manasseh spake, it p' them.
33 thing p' the children of Israel;
J'g 13:23 If the Lord was p' to kill us, he
14: 7 and she p' Samson well.
1Sa 12:22 hath p' the Lord to make you his
18:20 Saul, and the thing p' him.
26 it p' David well to be the king's
2Sa 3:36 notice of it, and it p' them:
36 whatsoever the king did p' all
17: 4 the saying p' Absalom well,
19: 6 day, then it had p' thee well.
1Ki 3:10 the speech p' the Lord, that
9: 1 desire which he was p' to do,
12 him; and they p' him not.
2Ch 30: 4 the thing p' the king and all
Ne 2: 6 So it p' the king to send me; and I
Es 1:21 p' the king and the princes;
2: 4 And the thing p' the king;
9 And the maiden p' him, and
5:14 And the thing p' Haman; and he
Ps 40:13 Be p', O Lord, to deliver me: O
51:19 shalt thou be p' with the sacrifices
115: 3 hath done whatsoever he hath p'.
135: 6 Whatsoever the Lord p', that did
Isa 42:21 Lord is well p' for his righteousness'
53:10 Yet it p' the Lord to bruise him;
Da 6: 1 It p' Darius to set over the
Jon 1:14 O Lord, hast done as it p' thee.
Mic 6: 7 Lord be p' with thousands of rams,
Mal 1: 8 will he be p' with thee, or accept
M't 3:17 beloved Son, in whom I am well p'.
12:18 beloved, in whom my soul is well p':
14: 6 danced before them, and p' Herod.
17: 5 beloved Son, in whom I am well p';
M'r 1:11 beloved Son, in whom I am well p'.
6:22 came in, and danced, and p' Herod
Lu 3:22 beloved Son; in thee I am well p'.
Ac 6: 5 the saying p' the whole multitude:
12: 3 And because he saw it p' the Jews,
15:22 Then p' it the apostles and elders,
34 it p' Silas to abide there still.
Ro 15: 3 For even Christ p' not himself;
26 For it hath p' them of Macedonia
27 It hath p' them verily; and their
1Co 1:21 it p' God by the foolishness of
7:12 and she be p' to dwell with him,
13 if he be p' to dwell with her, let
10: 5 many of them God was not well p':
12:18 in the body, as it hath p' him.
15:38 giveth it a body as it hath p' him,
Ga 1:10 for if I yet p' men, I should not be
15 But when it p' God, who separated
Col 1:19 it p' the Father that in him should
Heb11: 5 had this testimony, that he p' God.
13:16 with such sacrifices God is well p'.
2Pe 1:17 beloved son, in whom I am well p'

pleasers See MENPLEASERS.

pleaseth
Ge 16: 6 hand; do to her as it p' thee.
20:15 thee: dwell where it p' thee.
J'g 14: 3 for me; for she p' me well.
Es 2: 4 the maiden which p' the king
Ec 7:26 whoso p' God shall escape
8: 3 for he doeth whatsoever p' him.

pleasing See also WELLPLEASING.
Es 8: 5 the king, and I be p' in his eyes,
Ho 9: 4 neither shall they be p' unto him:
Col 1:10 walk worthy of the Lord unto all p',
3:20 this is well p' unto the Lord.
1Th 2: 4 not as p' men, but God, which trieth
1Jo 3:22 those things that are p' in his sight.

pleasure See also DISPLEASURE; PLEASURES.
Ge 18:12 I am waxed old shall I have p',
De 23:24 eat grapes thy fill at thine own p';
1Ch 29:17 heart, and hast p' in uprightness.
Ezr 5:17 and let the king send his p' to us
10:11 God of your fathers, and do his p':
Ne 9:37 and over our cattle, at their p',
Es 1: 8 do according to every man's p'.
Job 21:21 For what p' hath he in his house
25 soul, and never eateth with p'.
22: 3 Is it any p' to the Almighty, that
Ps 5: 4 God that hath p' in wickedness:
35:27 p' in the prosperity of his servant.
51:18 Do good in thy good p' unto Zion:
102:14 thy servants take p' in her stones,
103:21 ye ministers of his, that do his p'.
105:22 To bind his princes at his p'; and
111: 2 of all them that have p' therein.
147:10 taketh not p' in the legs of a man.
11 Lord taketh p' in them that fear
149: 4 the Lord taketh p' in his people:
Pr 21:17 that loveth p' shall be a poor man;
Ec 2: 1 therefore enjoy p': and, behold,
5: 4 pay it: for he hath no p' in fools:
12: 1 thou shalt say, I have no p' in them;
Isa 21: 4 the night of my p' hath he turned
44:28 and shall perform all my p':
46:10 shall stand, and I will do all my p':
48:14 he will do his p' on Babylon, and
53:10 p' of the Lord shall prosper in his
58: 3 in the day of your fast ye find p',
13 from doing thy p' on my holy day;
13 own ways, nor finding thine own p',
Jer 2:24 snuffeth up the wind at her p';
22:28 is he a vessel wherein is no p'?
34:16 he had set at liberty at their p',
48:38 like a vessel wherein is no p'.
Eze 16:37 with whom thou hast taken p',
18:23 Have I any p' at all that the wicked
32 no p' in the death of him that dieth,
33:11 no p' in the death of the wicked;
Ho 8: 8 as a vessel wherein is no p'.
Hag 1: 8 I will take p' in it, and I will be
Mal 1:10 I have no p' in you, saith the Lord
Lu 12:32 your Father's good p' to give you
Ac 24:27 willing to shew the Jews a p',
25: 9 Festus, willing to do the Jews a p',
Ro 1:32 but have p' in them that do them.
2Co 12:10 Therefore I take p' in infirmities,
Eph 1: 5 according to the good p' of his will,
9 according to his good p' which he
Ph'p 2:13 both to will and to do of his good p'.
2Th 1:11 all the good p' of his goodness,
2:12 but had p' in unrighteousness.
1Ti 5: 6 But she that liveth in p' is dead
Heb10: 6 sacrifices...thou hast had no p'.
8 not, neither hadst p' therein;
38 my soul shall have no p' in him.
12:10 chastened...after their own p';
Jas 5: 5 Ye have lived in p' on the earth,
2Pe 2:13 count it p' to riot in the day time.
Re 4:11 and for thy p' they are and were

pleasures
Job 36:11 in prosperity, and their years in p'.
Ps 16:11 hand there are p' for evermore.
36: 8 them drink of the river of thy p'.
Isa 47: 8 thou that art given to p', that
Lu 8:14 cares and riches and p' of this life,
2Ti 3: 4 lovers of p' more than lovers of
Tit 3: 3 serving divers lusts and p', living
Heb11:25 to enjoy the p' of sin for a season;

pledge See also PLEDGES.
Ge 38:17 Wilt thou give me a p', till thou
18 he said, What p' shall I give thee?
20 his p' from the woman's hand:
Ex 22:26 thy neighbour's raiment to p',
De 24: 6 nether or the upper millstone to p':
6 for he taketh a man's life to p'.
10 go into his house to fetch his p'.
11 bring out the p' abroad unto thee.
12 thou shalt not sleep with his p':
13 shalt deliver him the p' again when
17 take the widow's raiment to p':
1Sa 17:18 brethren fare, and take their p'.
Job 22: 6 taken a p' from thy brother for
24: 3 they take the widow's ox for a p'.
9 breast, and take a p' of the poor.
Pr 20:16 a p' of him for a strange woman.
27:13 a p' of him for a strange woman.
Eze 18: 7 hath restored to the debtor his p',
12 hath not restored the p', and hath
16 hath not withholden the p', neither
33:15 If the wicked restore the p', give
Am 2: 8 clothes laid to p' by every altar,

pledges
2Ki 18:23 give p' to my lord...king of Assyria,
Isa 36: 8 give p', I pray thee, to my master

Pleiades (*ple'-ya-dez*)
Job 9: 9 maketh Arcturus, Orion, and P',
38:31 bind the sweet influences of P',

plenish See REPLENISH.

plenteous
Ge 41:34 of Egypt in the seven p' years.
47 And in the seven p' years the earth
De 28:11 Lord shall make thee p' in goods,
30: 9 make thee p' in every work of thine
2Ch 1:15 gold at Jerusalem as p' as stones,
Ps 86: 5 p' in mercy unto all them that call
15 and p' in mercy and truth.
103: 8 slow to anger, and p' in mercy.
130: 7 and with him is p' redemption.
Isa 30:23 earth, and it shall be fat and p':
Hab 1:16 portion is fat, and their meat p'.
M't 9:37 The harvest truly is p', but the

plenteousness
Ge 41:53 the seven years of *p*˙, that was in
Pr 21: 5 of the diligent tend only to *p*˙;

plentiful
Ps 68: 9 Thou, O God, didst send a *p*˙ rain,
Isa 16:10 away, and joy out of the *p*˙ field;
Jer 2: 7 I brought you into a *p*˙ country,
48:33 gladness is taken from the *p*˙ field,

plentifully
Job 26: 3 hast thou *p*˙ declared the thing
Ps 31:23 and *p*˙ rewardeth the proud doer.
Lu 12:16 certain rich man brought forth *p*˙:

plenty See also PLENTIFUL.
Ge 27:28 the earth, and *p*˙ of corn and wine:
41:29 come seven years of great *p*˙
30 the *p*˙ shall be forgotten in the land
31 *p*˙ shall not be known in the land
Le 11:36 pit, wherein there is *p*˙ of water,
1Ki 10:11 Ophir great *p*˙ of almug trees,
2Ch 31:10 enough to eat, and have left *p*˙:
Job 22:25 and thou shalt have *p*˙ of silver.
37:23 in judgment, and in *p*˙ of justice:
Pr 3:10 So shall thy barns be filled with *p*˙,
28:19 his land shall have *p*˙ of bread:
Jer 44:17 for then had we *p*˙ of victuals, and
Joe 2:26 And ye shall eat in *p*˙, and be

plot See PLAT

plotteth
Ps 37:12 The wicked *p*˙ against the just,

plough See also PLOW.
Lu 9:62 man, having put his hand to the *p*˙,

plow See also EAR; PLOUGH; PLOWED; PLOWETH; PLOWING; PLOWMAN; PLOWSHARES.
De 22:10 Thou shalt not *p*˙ with an ox and
1Sa 14:14 land, which a yoke of oxen might *p*˙
Job 4: 8 I have seen, they that *p*˙ iniquity,
Pr 20: 4 sluggard will not *p*˙ by reason of
Isa 28:24 the plowman *p*˙ all day to sow?
Ho 10:11 Judah shall *p*˙, and Jacob shall
Am 6:12 rock? will one *p*˙ there with oxen?
1Co 9:10 he that ploweth should *p*˙ in hope;

plowed
J'g 14:18 If ye had not *p*˙ with my heifer,
Ps 129: 3 The plowers *p*˙ upon my back:
Jer 26:18 Zion shall be *p*˙ like a field, and
Ho 10:13 Ye have *p*˙ wickedness, ye have
Mic 3:12 Zion for your sake be *p*˙ as a field,

plowers
Ps 129: 3 The *p*˙ plowed upon my back: they

ploweth
1Co 9:10 he that *p*˙ should plow in hope;

plowing
1Ki 19:19 was *p*˙ with twelve yoke of oxen
Job 1:14 The oxen were *p*˙, and the asses
Pr 21: 4 and the *p*˙ of the wicked, is sin.
Lu 17: 7 having a servant *p*˙ or feeding

plowman See also PLOWMEN.
Isa 28:24 Doth the *p*˙ plow all day to sow?
Am 9:13 the *p*˙ shall overtake the reaper,

plowmen
Isa 61: 5 sons of the alien shall be your *p*˙
Jer 14: 4 *p*˙ were ashamed, they covered their

plowshares
Isa 2: 4 shall beat their swords into *p*˙, and
Joe 3:10 Beat your *p*˙ into swords, and your
Mic 4: 3 shall beat their swords into *p*˙, and

pluck See also PLUCKED; PLUCKETH; PLUCKT.
Le 1:16 *p*˙ away his crop with his feathers,
Nu 33:52 *p*˙ down all their high places:
De 23:25 thou mayest *p*˙ the ears with thine
2Ch 7:20 will I *p*˙ them up by the roots out
Job 24: 9 *p*˙ the fatherless from the breast,
Ps 25:15 he shall *p*˙ my feet out of the net.
52: 5 *p*˙ thee out of thy dwelling place,
74:11 right hand? *p*˙ it out of thy bosom.
80:12 which pass by the way do *p*˙ her?
Ec 3: 2 time to *p*˙ up that which is planted;
Jer 12:14 I will *p*˙ them out of their land,
14 and *p*˙ out the house of Judah from
17 *p*˙ up and destroy that nation,
18: 7 to *p*˙ up, and to pull down, and to
22:24 hand, yet would I *p*˙ thee thence;
24: 6 plant them, and not *p*˙ them up.
31:28 to *p*˙ up, and to break down, and to
42:10 will plant you, and not *p*˙ you up:
45: 4 which I have planted I will *p*˙ up.
Eze 17: 9 to *p*˙ it up by the roots thereof.
23:34 *p*˙ off thine own breasts: and
Mic 3: 2 *p*˙ off their skin from off them,
5:14 And I will *p*˙ up thy groves out of
M't 5:29 right eye offend thee, *p*˙ it out,
12: 1 and began to *p*˙ the ears of corn,
18: 9 thine eye offend thee, *p*˙ it out,
M'r 2:23 they went, to *p*˙ the ears of corn.
9:47 if thine eye offend thee, *p*˙ it out:
Joh 10:28 any man *p*˙ them out of my hand.
29 to *p*˙ them out of my Father's hand.

plucked See also PLUCKT.
Ex 4: 7 *p*˙ it out of his bosom, and, behold,
De 28:63 ye shall be *p*˙ from off the land
Ru 4: 7 a man *p*˙ off his shoe, and gave it
2Sa 23:21 *p*˙ the spear out of the Egyptian's
1Ch 11:23 *p*˙ the spear out of the Egyptian's
Ezr 9: 3 *p*˙ off the hair of my head and of
Ne 13:25 *p*˙ off their hair, and made them
Job 29:17 and *p*˙ the spoil out of his teeth.
Isa 50: 6 cheeks to them that *p*˙ off the hair:
Jer 6:29 for the wicked are not *p*˙ away.
12:15 I have *p*˙ them out I will return,
31:40 it shall not be *p*˙ up, nor thrown
Eze 19:12 she was *p*˙ up in fury, she was cast
Da 7: 4 till the wings thereof were *p*˙,
8 the first horns *p*˙ up by the roots:
11: 4 for his kingdom shall be *p*˙ up,
Am 4:11 a firebrand *p*˙ out of the burning:
Zec 3: 2 not this a brand *p*˙ out of the fire?
M'r 5: 4 had been *p*˙ asunder by him, and
Lu 6: 1 his disciples *p*˙ the ears of corn,
17: 6 Be thou *p*˙ up by the root, and be
Ga 4:15 would have *p*˙ out your own eyes,
Jude 12 twice dead, *p*˙ up by the roots;

plucketh
Pr 14: 1 foolish *p*˙ it down with her hands.

pluckt See also PLUCKED.
Ge 8:11 her mouth was an olive leaf *p*˙ off:

plumbline
Am 7: 7 made by a *p*˙, with a *p*˙ in his hand.
8 what seest thou? And I said, A *p*˙.
8 I will set a *p*˙ in the midst of my

plummet
2Ki 21:13 and the *p*˙ of the house of Ahab:
Isa 28:17 line, and righteousness to the *p*˙:
Zec 4:10 shall see the *p*˙ in the hand of

plunge
Job 9:31 Yet shalt thou *p*˙ me in the ditch,

plus See OVERPLUS.

ply See REPLY; SUPPLY.

Pochereth (*po-ke'-reth*)
Ezr 2:57 the children of *P*˙ of Zebaim,
Ne 7:59 the children of *P*˙ of Zebaim,

poets
Ac 17:28 also of your own *p*˙ have said,

point See also APPOINT; POINTED; POINTS.
Ge 25:32 said, Behold, I am at the *p*˙ to die:
Nu 34: 7 ye shall *p*˙ out for you mount Hor:
8 mount Hor ye shall *p*˙ out your
10 ye shall *p*˙ out your east border
Jer 17: 1 and with the *p*˙ of a diamond:
Eze 21:15 have set the *p*˙ of the sword against
M'r 5:23 daughter lieth at the *p*˙ of death:
Joh 4:47 son: for he was at the *p*˙ of death.
Jas 2:10 yet offend in one *p*˙, he is guilty of all.

pointed See also APPOINTED.
Job 41:30 sharp *p*˙ things upon the mire.

points
Ec 5:16 in all *p*˙ as he came, so shall he
Heb 4:15 was in all *p*˙ tempted like as we are,

poison
De 32:24 with the *p*˙ of serpents of the dust.
33 Their wine is the *p*˙ of dragons, and
Job 6: 4 *p*˙ whereof drinketh up my spirit:
20:16 He shall suck the *p*˙ of asps: the
Ps 58: 4 Their *p*˙ is like the *p*˙ of a serpent:
140: 3 adders' *p*˙ is under their lips.
Ro 3:13 the *p*˙ of asps is under their lips:
Jas 3: 8 an unruly evil, full of deadly *p*˙.

pole
Nu 21: 8 fiery serpent, and set it upon a *p*˙:
9 of brass, and put it upon a *p*˙,

policy
Da 8:25 through his *p*˙...shall cause craft

polished
Ps 144:12 *p*˙ after the similitude of a palace:
Isa 49: 2 hid me, and made me a *p*˙ shaft;
Da 10: 6 his feet like in colour to *p*˙ brass,

polishing
La 4: 7 rubies, their *p*˙ was of sapphire:

poll See also POLLED; POLLS.
Nu 3:47 take five shekels apiece by the *p*˙,
Eze 44:20 they shall only *p*˙ their heads.
Mic 1:16 *p*˙ thee for thy delicate children;

polled
2Sa 14:26 And when he *p*˙ his head, (for it
26 at every year's end that he *p*˙ it;
26 heavy on him, therefore he *p*˙ it:)

polls
Nu 1: 2 names, every male by their *p*˙;
18 years old and upward, by their *p*˙.
20, 22 number of the names, by their *p*˙,
1Ch 23: 3 their number by their *p*˙, man by
24 by number of names by their *p*˙,

pollute See also POLLUTED; POLLUTING.
Nu 18:32 neither shall ye *p*˙ the holy things
35:33 So ye shall not *p*˙ the land wherein
Jer 7:30 is called by my name, to *p*˙ it.
Eze 7:21 for a spoil; and they shall *p*˙ it.
22 and they shall *p*˙ my secret place:
13:19 And will ye *p*˙ me among my people
20:31 ye *p*˙ yourselves with all your idols,
39 *p*˙ ye my holy name no more with
39: 7 I will not let them *p*˙ my holy name
44: 7 to *p*˙ it, even my house, when ye
Da 11:31 shall *p*˙ the sanctuary of strength,

polluted
Ex 20:25 thy tool upon it, thou hast *p*˙ it.
2Ki 23:16 burned...upon the altar, and *p*˙ it,
2Ch 36:14 *p*˙ the house of the Lord, which he
Ezr 2:62 as *p*˙, put from the priesthood.
Ne 7:64 as *p*˙, put from the priesthood.
Ps 106:38 and the land was *p*˙ with blood.
Isa 47: 6 I have *p*˙ mine inheritance, and
48:11 how should my name be *p*˙? and I
Jer 2:23 How canst thou say, I am not *p*˙, I
3: 1 shall not that land be greatly *p*˙?
2 and thou hast *p*˙ the land with thy
34:16 But ye turned and *p*˙ my name,
La 2: 2 he hath *p*˙ the kingdom and the
4:14 have *p*˙ themselves with blood, so
Eze 4:14 soul hath not been *p*˙; for, from
14:11 neither be *p*˙ any more with all
16: 6 saw thee *p*˙ in thine own blood,
22 naked and bare,...*p*˙ in thy blood.
20: 9 should not be *p*˙ before...heathen,
13 and my sabbaths they greatly *p*˙:
14 should not be *p*˙ before...heathen,
16 my statutes, but *p*˙ my sabbaths:
21 they *p*˙ my sabbaths: then I said,
22 be *p*˙ in the sight of the heathen,
24 had *p*˙ my sabbaths, and their eyes
26 I *p*˙ them in their own gifts, in
30 Are ye *p*˙ after the manner of your
23:17 she was *p*˙ with them, and her mind
30 because thou art *p*˙ with their idols.
36:18 idols wherewith they had *p*˙ it:
Ho 6: 8 iniquity, and is *p*˙ with blood.
9: 4 all that eat thereof shall be *p*˙:
Am 7:17 and thou shalt die in a *p*˙ land:
Mic 2:10 because it is *p*˙, it shall destroy
Zep 3: 1 Woe to her that is filthy and *p*˙, to
4 her priests have *p*˙ the sanctuary,
Mal 1: 7 Ye offer *p*˙ bread upon mine altar;
7 ye say, Wherein have we *p*˙ thee?
12 The table of the Lord is *p*˙; and the
Ac 21:28 temple,...hath *p*˙ this holy place.

polluting
Isa 56: 2, 6 keepeth the sabbath from *p*˙ it,

pollution See POLLUTIONS.
Eze 22:10 her that was set apart for *p*˙.

pollutions
Ac 15:20 that they abstain from *p*˙ of idols,
2Pe 2:20 have escaped the *p*˙ of the world

Pollux (*pol'-lux*)
Ac 28:11 whose sign was Castor and *P*˙.

pomegranate See POMEGRANATES.
Ex 28:34 bell and a *p*˙, a golden bell and a *p*˙,
39:26 A bell and a *p*˙, a bell and a *p*˙,
1Sa 14: 2 under a *p*˙ tree which is in Migron:
Ca 4: 3 thy temples are like a piece of a *p*˙
6: 7 As a piece of a *p*˙ are thy temples
8: 2 spiced wine of the juice of my *p*˙.
Joe 1:12 the *p*˙ tree, the palm tree also, and
Hag 2:19 the *p*˙, and the olive tree, hath not

pomegranate-tree See POMEGRANATE and TREE.

pomegranates
Ex 28:33 thou shalt make *p*˙ of blue, and of
39:24 upon the hems of the robe *p*˙ of blue,
25 and put the bells between the *p*˙
25 robe, round about between the *p*˙;
Nu 13:23 they brought of the *p*˙, and of the
20: 5 or of figs, or of vines, or of *p*˙;
De 8: 8 and vines, and fig trees, and *p*˙;
1Ki 7:18 that were upon the top, with *p*˙:
20 upon the two pillars had *p*˙ also above,
20 and the *p*˙ were two hundred in
42 And four hundred *p*˙ for the two
42 two rows of *p*˙ for one network,
2Ki 25:17 *p*˙ upon the chapiter round about,
2Ch 3:16 and made an hundred *p*˙, and put
4:13 hundred *p*˙ on the two wreaths;
13 two rows of *p*˙ on each wreath,
Ca 4:13 Thy plants are an orchard of *p*˙,
6:11 vine flourished, and the *p*˙ budded.
7:12 grape appear, and the *p*˙ bud forth:
Jer 52:22 *p*˙ upon the chapiters round about,
22 and the *p*˙ were like unto these.
23 were ninety and six *p*˙ on a side;
23 and all the *p*˙ upon the network

pommels
2Ch 4:12 and the *p*˙, and the chapiters
12, 13 cover the two *p*˙ of the chapiters

pomp
Isa 5:14 and their multitude, and their *p*˙,
14:11 Thy *p*˙ is brought down to the
Eze 7:24 make the *p*˙ of the strong to cease;
30:18 the *p*˙ of her strength shall cease
32:12 they shall spoil the *p*˙ of Egypt,
33:28 the *p*˙ of her strength shall cease;
Ac 25:23 come, and Bernice, with great *p*˙,

ponder See PONDERED; PONDERETH.
Pr 4:26 *P*˙ the path of thy feet, and let all
5: 6 thou shouldest *p*˙ the path of life,

pondered
Lu 2:19 things, and *p*˙ them in her heart.

pondereth
Pr 5:21 the Lord, and he *p*˙ all his goings.
21: 2 eyes: but the Lord *p*˙ the hearts.
24:12 not he that *p*˙ the heart consider it?

ponds
Ex 7:19 upon their rivers, and upon their *p*˙,
8: 5 over the rivers, and over the *p*˙,
Isa 19:10 all that make sluices and *p*˙ for fish.

Pontius (*pon'-she-us*)
M't 27: 2 him to *P*˙ Pilate the governor.
Lu 3: 1 *P*˙ Pilate being governor of Judæa,
Ac 4:27 both Herod, and *P*˙ Pilate, with the
1Ti 6:13 before *P*˙ Pilate witnessed a good

Pontus (*pon'-tus*)
Ac 2: 9 and Cappadocia, in P', and Asia,
18: 2 Jew named Aquila, born in P',
1Pe 1: 1 strangers scattered throughout P',

pool See also POOLS.
2Sa 2: 13 met together by the p' of Gibeon:
13 the one on the one side of the p',
13 other on the other side of the p'.
4: 12 them up over the p' in Hebron.
1Ki 22: 38 the chariot in the p' of Samaria;
2Ki 18: 17 by the conduit of the upper p',
20: 20 how he made a p', and a conduit,
Ne 2: 14 the fountain, and to the king's p':
3: 15 p' of Siloah by the king's garden,
16 and to the p' that was made, and
Isa 7: 3 end of the conduit of the upper p'
22: 9 together the waters of the lower p'.
11 two walls for the water of the old p':
35: 7 parched ground shall become a p',
36: 2 by the conduit of the upper p'.
41: 18 make the wilderness a p' of water,
Na 2: 8 Nineveh is...like a p' of water:
Joh 5: 2 there is...by the sheep market a p',
4 down at a certain season into the p',
7 is troubled, to put me into the p':
9: 7 him, Go, wash in the p' of Siloam,
11 Go to the p' of Siloam, and wash:

pools
Ex 7: 19 and upon all their p' of water,
Ps 84: 6 a well; the rain also filleth the p'.
Ec 2: 6 I made me p' of water, to water
Isa 14: 23 for the bittern, and p' of water:
42: 15 islands, and I will dry up the p'.

poor See also POORER; POOREST.
Ge 41: 19 kine...p' and very ill favoured and
Ex 22: 25 lend...to any of my people that is p'
23: 3 shalt thou countenance a p' man
6 not wrest the judgment of thy p'
11 that the p' of thy people may eat:
30: 15 more, and the p' shall not give less
Le 14: 21 if he be p', and cannot get so much;
19: 10 leave them for the p' and stranger:
15 not respect the person of the p',
23: 22 thou shalt leave them unto the p',
25: 25 If thy brother be waxen p', and
35 And if thy brother be waxen p', and
39 that dwelleth by thee be waxen p',
47 brother that dwelleth by him wax p',
De 15: 4 there shall be no p' among you;
7 If there be among you a p' man
7 shut thine hand from thy p' brother:
9 eye be evil against thy p' brother,
11 p' shall never cease out of the land:
11 to thy p', and to thy needy, in thy
24: 12 And if the man be p', thou shalt not
14 oppress an hired servant that is p'
15 he is p', and setteth his heart upon
J'g 6: 15 my family is p' in Manasseh, and
Ru 3: 10 not young men, whether p' or rich.
1Sa 2: 7 The Lord maketh p', and maketh
8 raiseth up the p' out of the dust,
18: 23 seeing that I am a p' man, and
2Sa 12: 1 city; the one rich, and the other p'.
3 But the p' man had nothing, save
4 took the p' man's lamb, and dressed
2Ki 25: 12 p' of the land to be vinedressers
Es 9: 22 one to another, and gifts to the p'.
Job 5: 15 he saveth the p' from the sword,
16 So the p' hath hope, and iniquity
20: 10 children shall seek to please the p',
19 oppressed and hath forsaken the p';
24: 4 p' of the earth hide themselves
9 breast, and take a pledge of the p'.
14 rising with the light killeth the p'
29: 12 I delivered the p' that cried, and
16 I was a father to the p': and the
30: 25 was not my soul grieved for the p'?
31: 16 withheld the p' from their desire,
19 clothing, or any p' without covering;
34: 19 the rich more than the p'?
28 the cry of the p' to come unto him,
36: 6 wicked: but giveth right to the p'.
15 delivereth the p' in his affliction,
Ps 9: 18 expectation of the p' shall not
10: 2 in his pride doth persecute the p':
8 eyes are privily set against the p'.
9 be lieth in wait to catch the p':
9 doth catch the p' when he draweth
10 the p' may fall by his strong ones.
14 p' committeth himself unto thee;
12: 5 For the oppression of the p',
14: 6 have shamed the counsel of the p',
34: 6 This p' man cried, and the Lord
35: 10 deliverest the p' from him that is too
10 the p' and the needy from him that
37: 14 bow, to cast down the p' and needy,
40: 17 I am p' and needy; yet the Lord
41: 1 is he that considereth the p':
49: 2 low and high, rich and p', together.
68: 10 prepared of thy goodness for the p'.
69: 29 But I am p' and sorrowful: let thy
33 For the Lord heareth the p', and
70: 5 I am p' and needy: make haste
72: 2 and thy p' with judgment.
4 He shall judge the p' of the people,
12 p' also, and him that hath no helper.
13 He shall spare the p' and needy,
74: 19 forget not...congregation of thy p'
21 the p' and needy praise thy name.
82: 3 Defend the p' and fatherless: do
4 Deliver the p' and needy: rid them
86: 1 hear me: for I am p' and needy.
107: 41 Yet setteth he the p' on high from
109: 16 persecuted the p' and needy man,
Ps 109: 22 For I am p' and needy, and my
31 stand at the right hand of the p',
112: 9 dispersed, he hath given to the p';
113: 7 raiseth up the p' out of the dust,
132: 15 I will satisfy her p' with bread.
140: 12 the afflicted, and the right of the p'.
Pr 10: 4 He becometh p' that dealeth with
15 the destruction of the p' is their
13: 7 there is that maketh himself p',
8 but the p' heareth not rebuke.
23 Much food is in the tillage of the p':
14: 20 The p' is hated even of his own
21 he that hath mercy on the p',
31 that oppresseth the p' reproacheth
31 him hath mercy on the p'.
17: 5 Whoso mocketh the p' reproacheth
18: 23 The p' useth intreaties; but the
19: 1 Better is the p' that walketh in his
4 p' is separated from his neighbour.
7 brethren of the p' do hate him:
17 that hath pity upon the p' lendeth
22 and a p' man is better than a liar.
21: 13 stoppeth his ears at...cry of the p',
17 loveth pleasure shall be a p' man:
22: 2 The rich and p' meet together:
7 The rich ruleth over the p', and the
9 he giveth of his bread to the p'.
16 that oppresseth the p' to increase
22 Rob not the p', because he is p':
28: 3 A p' man that oppresseth the
3 A...man that oppresseth the p'
6 Better is the p' that walketh in his
8 it for him that will pity the p'.
11 but the p' that hath understanding
15 a wicked ruler over the p' people.
27 that giveth unto the p' shall not
29: 7 considereth the cause of the p':
13 The p' and the deceitful man meet
14 king that faithfully judgeth the p',
30: 9 or lest I be p', and steal, and take
14 devour the p' from off the earth,
31: 9 plead the cause of the p' and needy.
20 She stretched out her hand to the p';
Ec 4: 13 Better is a p' and a wise child
14 born in his kingdom becometh p'.
5: 8 thou seest the oppression of the p',
6: 8 what hath the p', that knoweth to
9: 15 was found in it a p' wise man,
15 remembered that same p' man.
16 the p' man's wisdom is despised,
Isa 3: 14 spoil of the p' is in your houses.
15 pieces, and grind the faces of the p'?
10: 2 the right from the p' of my people,
30 be heard unto Laish, O p' Anathoth.
11: 4 righteousness shall he judge the p',
14: 30 the firstborn of the p' shall feed,
32 p' of his people shall trust in it.
25: 4 thou hast been a strength to the p',
26: 6 it down, even the feet of the p',
29: 19 the p' among men shall rejoice in
32: 7 to destroy the p' with lying
41: 17 When the p' and needy seek water,
58: 7 p' that are cast out to thy house?
66: 2 that is p' and of a contrite spirit,
Jer 2: 34 of the souls of the p' innocents:
5: 4 said, Surely these are p'; they are
20: 13 delivered the soul of the p' from the
22: 16 He judged the cause of the p' and
39: 10 guard left of the p' of the people,
40: 7 and of the p' of the land, of them
52: 15 certain of the p' of the people, and
16 the p' of the land for vinedressers
Eze 16: 49 the hand of the p' and needy.
18: 12 Hath oppressed the p' and needy,
17 hath taken off his hand from the p',
22: 29 and have vexed the p' and needy:
Da 4: 27 by shewing mercy to the p'; if it
Am 2: 6 silver, and the p' for a pair of shoes;
7 of the earth on the head of the p',
4: 1 which oppress the p', which crush
5: 11 as your treading is upon the p', and
12 turn aside the p' in the gate from
8: 4 the p' of the land to fail,
6 That we may buy the p' for silver,
Hab 3: 14 was as to devour the p' secretly.
Zep 3: 12 of thee an afflicted and p' people,
Zec 7: 10 widow,...the stranger, nor the p';
11: 7 even you, O p' of the flock.
11 p' of the flock that waited upon me
M't 5: 3 Blessed are the p' in spirit: for
11: 5 the p' have the gospel preached to
19: 21 that thou hast, and give to the p',
26: 9 sold for much, and given to the p'.
11 For ye have the p' always with you;
M'r 10: 21 thou hast, and give to the p', and
12: 42 there came a certain p' widow, and
43 this p' widow hath cast more in,
14: 5 and have been given to the p'.
7 ye have the p' with you always, and
Lu 4: 18 me to preach the gospel to the p';
6: 20 Blessed be ye p': for yours is the
7: 22 to the p' the gospel is preached.
14: 13 thou makest a feast, call the p', the
21 and bring in hither the p', and the
18: 22 hast, and distribute unto the p',
19: 8 half of my goods I give to the p';
21: 2 p' widow casting in thither two
3 p' widow hath cast in more than
Joh 12: 5 hundred pence, and given to the p'?
6 he said, not that he cared for the p';
8 the p' always ye have with you; but
13: 29 he should give something to the p'.
Ro 15: 26 p' saints which are at Jerusalem.
1Co 13: 3 I bestow all my goods to feed the p',
2Co 6: 10 as p', yet making many rich; as
8: 9 yet for your sakes he became p',
2Co 9: 9 abroad; he hath given to the p':
Ga 2: 10 that we should remember the p';
Jas 2: 2 in also a p' man in vile raiment;
3 say to the p', Stand thou there, or
5 not God chosen the p' of this world
6 But ye have despised the p'. Do
Re 3: 17 miserable, and p', and blind, and
13: 16 great, rich and p', free and bond,

poorer
Le 27: 8 if he be p' than thy estimation,

poorest
2Ki 24: 14 p' sort of the people of the land.

poplar See also POPLARS.
Ge 30: 37 Jacob took him rods of green p',

poplars
Ho 4: 13 hills, under oaks and p' and elms,

populous
De 26: 5 a nation, great, mighty, and p':
Na 3: 8 Art thou better than p' No, that

Poratha (*por'-a-thah*)
Es 9: 8 And P', and Adalia, and Aridatha,

porch See also PORCHES.
J'g 3: 23 Ehud went forth through the p',
1Ki 6: 3 p' before the temple of the house,
7: 6 he made a p' of pillars; the length
6 and the p' was before them: and the
7 Then he made a p' for the throne
7 judge, even the p' of judgment:
8 had another court within the p',
8 had taken to wife, like unto this p'.
12 Lord, and for the p' of the house.
19 pillars were of lily work in the p',
21 the pillars in the p' of the temple:
1Ch 28: 11 to Solomon...the pattern of the p',
2Ch 3: 4 p' that was in the front of the house,
8: 12 which he had built before the p',
15: 8 that was before the p' of the Lord.
29: 7 have shut up the doors of the p', and
17 came they to the p' of the Lord:
Eze 8: 16 between the p' and the altar, were
40: 7 p' of the gate within was one reed.
8 He measured also the p' of the gate
9 Then measured he the p' of the gate,
9 and the p' of the gate was inward.
15 the face of the p' of the inner gate
39 in the p' of the gate were two tables
40 which was at the p' of the gate,
48 brought me to the p' of the house,
48 measured each post of the p', five
49 length of the p' was twenty cubits,
41: 25 thick planks upon the face of the p'
26 the other side, on the sides of the p',
44: 3 he shall enter by the way of the p'
46: 2 shall enter by the way of the p' of
8 he shall go in by the way of the p'
Joe 2: 17 weep between the p' and the altar,
M't 26: 71 when he was gone out into the p',
M'r 14: 68 And he went out into the p'; and
Joh 10: 23 in the temple in Solomon's p'.
Ac 3: 11 in the p' that is called Solomon's,
5: 12 all with one accord in Solomon's p'.

porches
Eze 41: 15 temple, and the p' of the court;
Joh 5: 2 tongue Bethesda, having five P'.

Porcius (*por'-she-us*)
Ac 24: 27 after two years P' Festus came

port See also REPORT; SUPPORT.
Ne 2: 13 dragon well, and to the dung p',

porter See also PORTERS.
2Sa 18: 26 the watchman called unto the p',
2Ki 7: 10 and called unto the p' of the city:
1Ch 9: 21 was p' of the door of the tabernacle
2Ch 31: 14 the p' toward the east, was over the
M'r 13: 34 and commanded the p' to watch.
Joh 10: 3 To him the p' openeth; and the

porters
2Ki 7: 11 he called the p'; and they told it
1Ch 9: 17 the p' were, Shallum, and Akkub,
18 p' in the companies of the children
22 were chosen to be p' in the gates
24 In four quarters were the p',
26 these Levites, the four chief p',
15: 18 and Obed-edom, and Jeiel, the p'.
16: 38 of Jeduthun and Hosah to be p':
42 And the sons of Jeduthun were p'.
23: 5 Moreover four thousand were p';
26: 1 Concerning the divisions of the p':
12 these were the divisions of the p',
19 These are the divisions of the p'
2Ch 8: 14 p' also by their courses at every
23: 4 the Levites, shall be p' of the doors;
19 set the p' at the gates of the house
34: 13 were scribes, and officers, and p'.
35: 15 and the p' waited at every gate; they
Ezr 2: 42 children of the p': the children of
70 people, and the singers, and the p',
7: 7 Levites, and the singers, and the p',
24 priests and Levites, singers, p',
10: 24 and of the p'; Shallum, and
Ne 7: 1 p' and the singers and the Levites
45 The p': the children of Shallum,
73 priests, and the Levites, and the p',
10: 28 the priests, the Levites, the p', the
39 the priests that minister, and the p',
11: 19 Moreover the p', Akkub, Talmon,
12: 25 were p' keeping the ward at the
45 the p' kept the ward of their God,
47 portions of the singers and the p',
13: 5 Levites, and the singers, and the p';

portion See also PORTIONS.
Ge 14: 24 the p' of the men which went with
24 and Mamre; let them take their p'.
31: 14 yet any p' or inheritance for us in
47: 22 the priests had a p' assigned them
22 did eat their p' which Pharaoh gave
48: 22 to thee one p' above thy brethren,
Le 6: 17 given it unto them for their p' of
7: 35 This is the p' of the anointing of Aaron,
Nu 31: 30 thou shalt take one p' of fifty, of the
36 p' of them that went out to war,
47 Moses took one p' of fifty, both of
De 21: 17 a double p' of all that he hath:
32: 9 For the Lord's p' is his people;
33: 21 in a p' of the lawgiver, was he
Jos 17: 14 but one lot and one p' to inherit,
19: 9 of the p' of the children of Judah
1Sa 1: 5 unto Hannah he gave a worthy p';
9: 23 Bring the p' which I gave thee, of
1Ki 12: 16 What p' have we in David? neither
2Ki 2: 9 double p' of thy spirit be upon me.
9: 10 eat Jezebel in the p' of Jezreel,
21 met him in the p' of Naboth the
25 him in the p' of the field of Naboth
36 In the p' of Jezreel shall dogs eat
37 face of the field in the p' of Jezreel;
2Ch 10: 16 saying, What p' have we in David?
28: 21 For Ahaz took away a p' out of the
31: 3 also the king's p' of his substance
4 p' of the priests and the Levites,
16 his daily p' for their service in
Ezr 4: 16 have no p' on this side the river.
Ne 2: 20 but ye have no p', nor right, nor
11: 23 a certain p' should be for the singers,
12: 47 and the porters, every day his p':
Job 20: 29 the p' of a wicked man from God,
24: 18 their p' is cursed in the earth: he
26: 14 but how little a p' is heard of him?
27: 13 the p' of a wicked man with God,
31: 2 what p' of God is there from above?
Ps 11: 6 this shall be the p' of their cup.
16: 5 Lord is the p' of mine inheritance
17: 14 which have their p' in this life,
63: 10 sword: they shall be a p' for foxes.
73: 26 of my heart, and my p' for ever.
119: 57 Thou art my p', O Lord: I have
142: 5 and my p' in the land of the living.
Pr 31: 15 and a p' to her maidens.
Ec 2: 10 this was my p' of all my labour.
21 therein shall he leave it for his p'.
3: 22 in his own works; for that is his p':
5: 18 God giveth him: for it is his p'.
19 to eat thereof, and to take his p',
9: 6 neither have they any more a p'
9 for that is thy p' in this life, and in
11: 2 Give a p' to seven, and also to eight;
Isa 17: 14 This is the p' of them that spoil us,
53: 12 I divide him a p' with the great,
57: 6 stones of the stream is thy p';
61: 7 they shall rejoice in their p':
Jer 10: 16 p' of Jacob is not like them: for he
12: 10 have trodden my p' under foot,
10 pleasant p' a desolate wilderness.
13: 25 the p' of thy measures from me,
51: 19 The p' of Jacob is not like them;
52: 34 day a p' until the day of his death,
La 3: 24 The Lord is my p', saith my soul;
Eze 45: 1 unto the Lord, an holy p' of the land:
4 The holy p' of the land shall be for
6 against the oblation of the holy p':
7 And a p' shall be for the prince on the
7 other side of the oblation of the holy p',
7 before the oblation of the holy p', and
48: 1 are his sides east and west, a p' for Dan:
2 side unto the west side, a p' for Asher.
3 unto the west side, a p' for Naphtali.
4 unto the west side, a p' for Manasseh.
5 unto the west side, a p' for Ephraim.
6 unto the west side, a p' for Reuben.
7 unto the west side, a p' for Judah.
18 against the oblation of the holy p'
18 against the oblation of the holy p';
23 west side, Benjamin shall have a p'.
24 the west side, Simeon shall have a p'.
25 side unto the west side, Issachar a p'.
26 side unto the west side, Zebulun a p'.
27 east side unto the west side, Gad a p'.
Da 1: 8 with the p' of the king's meat, nor
13 eat of the p' of the king's meat:
15 did eat the p' of the king's meat.
16 took away the p' of their meat, and
4: 15 let his p' be with the beasts in the
23 let his p' be with the beasts of the
11: 26 they that feed of the p' of his meat
Mic 2: 4 hath changed the p' of my people:
Hab 1: 16 by them their p' is fat, and their
Zec 2: 12 Lord shall inherit Judah his p' in
M't 24: 51 him his p' with the hypocrites:
Lu 12: 42 their p' of meat in due season?
46 him his p' with the unbelievers.
15: 12 give me the p' of goods that falleth

portions
De 18: 8 shall have like p' to eat, besides
Jos 17: 5 fell ten p' to Manasseh, besides
1Sa 1: 4 her sons and her daughters, p':
2Ch 31: 19 give p' to all the males among the
Ne 8: 10 and send p' unto them for whom
12 and to send p', and to make great
12: 44 p' of the law for the priests and
47 gave the p' of the singers and the
13: 10 the p' of the Levites had not been
Es 9: 19 and of sending p' one to another.
22 and of sending p' one to another,
Eze 45: 7 shall be over against one of the p',
47: 13 Israel: Joseph shall have two p'.
48: 21 over against the p' for the prince:
29 these are their p', saith the Lord
Ho 5: 7 month devour them with their p'.

portray See POURTRAY.

possess See also DISPOSSESS; POSSESSED; POSSESSEST; POSSESSETH; POSSESSING.
Ge 22: 17 shall p' the gate of his enemies;
24: 60 let thy seed p' the gate of those
Le 20: 24 give it unto you to p' it, a land that
Nu 13: 30 Let us go up at once, and p' it;
14: 24 he went; and his seed shall p' it.
27: 11 of his family, and he shall p' it.
33: 53 I have given you the land to p' it.
De 1: 8 p' the land which the Lord sware
21 go up and p' it, as the Lord God of
39 will I give it, and they shall p' it.
2: 24 begin to p' it, and contend with
31 begin to p', that thou mayest
3: 18 hath given you this land to p' it:
20 until they also p' the land which
4: 1 go in and p' the land which the
5 in the land whither ye go to p' it.
14 the land whither ye go over to p' it.
22 shall go over, and p' that good land.
26 ye go over Jordan to p' it; ye shall
5: 31 the land which I give them to p' it.
33 days in the land which ye shall p'.
6: 1 in the land whither ye go to p' it:
18 mayest go in and p' the good land
7: 1 the land whither thou goest to p' it,
8: 1 and go in and p' the land which the
9: 1 p' nations greater and mightier
4 hath brought me in to p' this land:
5 heart, dost thou go to p' their land:
6 land to p' it for thy righteousness;
23 and p' the land which I have given
10: 11 they may go in and p' the land,
11: 8 be strong, and go in and p' the land,
8 the land, whither ye go to p' it;
10 whither thou goest in to p' it, is
11 the land, whither ye go to p' it, is a
23 p' greater nations and mightier
29 the land whither thou goest to p' it,
31 over Jordan to go in to p' the land
31 you, and ye shall p' it, and dwell
12: 1 of thy fathers giveth thee to p' it,
2 nations which ye shall p' served
29 whither thou goest to p' them, and
15: 4 thee for an inheritance to p' it:
17: 14 shalt p' it, and shalt dwell therein,
18: 14 these nations, which thou shalt p',
19: 2, 14 Lord thy God giveth thee to p' it.
21: 1 Lord thy God giveth thee to p' it,
23: 20 land whither thou goest to p' it.
25: 19 giveth thee an inheritance to p' it,
28: 21 land, whither thou goest to p' it.
63 land whither thou goest to p' it.
30: 5 possessed, and thou shalt p' it;
16 land whither thou goest to p' it.
18 passest over Jordan to go to p' it.
31: 3 before thee, and thou shalt p' them:
13 whither ye go over Jordan to p' it.
32: 47 whither ye go over Jordan to p' it.
33: 23 p' thou the west and the south.
Jos 1: 11 this Jordan, to go in to p' the land,
11 Lord your God giveth you to p' it.
18: 3 long are ye slack to go to p' the land,
23: 5 ye shall p' their land, as the Lord
24: 4 gave unto Esau mount Seir, to p' it;
8 hand, that ye might p' their land;
J'g 2: 6 unto his inheritance to p' the land.
11: 23 Israel, and shouldest thou p' it?
24 Wilt not thou p' that which
24 Chemosh thy god giveth thee to p'?
24 out from before us, them will we p'.
18: 9 to go, and to enter to p' the land.
1Ki 21: 18 whither he is gone down to p' it.
1Ch 28: 8 that ye may p' this good land, and
Ezr 9: 11 The land, unto which ye go to p' it,
Neh 9: 15 they should go in to p' the land
23 that they should go in to p' it.
Job 7: 3 I made to p' months of vanity,
13: 26 to p' the iniquities of my youth.
Isa 14: 2 house of Israel shall p' them in
21 do not rise, nor p' the land, nor
34: 11 and the bittern shall p' it; the owl
17 they shall p' it forever, from
57: 13 his trust in me shall p' the land,
61: 7 their land they shall p'...double:
Jer 30: 3 their fathers, and they shall p' it.
Eze 7: 24 and they shall p' their houses:
33: 25 blood: and shall ye p' the land?
26 wife: and shall ye p' the land?
35: 10 shall be mine, and we will p' it;
36: 12 and they shall p' thee, and thou
Da 7: 18 p' the kingdom for ever, even for
Ho 9: 6 their silver, nettles shall p' them:
Am 2: 10 to p' the land of the Amorite.
9: 12 they may p' the remnant of Edom,
Ob 17 of Jacob shall p' their possessions.
19 south shall p' the mount of Esau;
19 they shall p' the fields of Ephraim,
19 and Benjamin shall p' Gilead.
20 shall p' that of the Canaanites,
20 shall p' the cities of the south.
Hab 1: 6 p' the dwellingplaces that are not
Zep 2: 9 remnant of my people shall p'
Zec 8: 12 this people to p' all these things.
Lu 18: 12 I give tithes of all that I p'.
21: 19 In your patience p' ye your souls.
1Th 4: 4 p' his vessels in sanctification and

possessed See also DISPOSSESSED.
Nu 21: 24 and p' his land from Arnon unto
35 them alive: and they p' his land.
De 3: 12 this land which we p' at that time,
4: 47 they p' his land, and the land of Og
30: 5 the land which thy fathers p',
Jos 1: 15 they also have p' the land which
12: 1 p' their land on the other side
13: 1 yet very much land to be p'.
19: 47 the edge of the sword, and p' it,
21: 43 and they p' it, and dwelt therein.
22: 9 possession, whereof they were p',
J'g 3: 13 and p' the city of palm trees.
11: 21 p' all the land of the Amorites,
22 p' all the coasts of the Amorites,
2Ki 17: 24 p' Samaria, and dwelt in the cities
Neh 9: 22 so they p' the land of Sihon, and
24 children went in and p' the land,
25 p' houses full of all goods, wells
Ps 139: 13 For thou hast p' my reins: thou
Pr 8: 22 Lord p' me in the beginning of
Isa 63: 18 people of thy holiness have p' it
Jer 32: 15 shall be p' again in this land.
23 And they came in, and p' it; but
Da 7: 22 that the saints p' the kingdom.
M't 4: 24 those which were p' with devils,
8: 16 many that were p' with devils:
28 there met him two p' with devils,
33 befallen to the p' of the devils.
9: 32 him a dumb man p' with a devil.
12: 22 one p' with a devil, blind, and
M'r 1: 32 and them that were p' with devils.
5: 15 see him that was p' with the devil,
16 to him that was p' with the devil,
18 had been p' with the devil prayed
Lu 8: 36 was p' of the devils was healed.
Ac 4: 32 aught of the things which he p'
8: 7 of many that were p' with them:
16: 16 damsel p' with a spirit of divination
1Co 7: 30 that buy, as though they p' not;

possessest
De 26: 1 and p' it, and dwellest therein;

possesseth
Nu 36: 8 daughter, that p' an inheritance
Lu 12: 15 abundance of...things which he p'.

possessing
2Co 6: 10 nothing, and yet p' all things.

possession See also POSSESSIONS.
Ge 17: 8 Canaan, for an everlasting p';
23: 4 me a p' of a buryingplace with you,
9 p' of a buryingplace amongst you.
18 Unto Abraham for a p' in the
20 Abraham for a p' of a buryingplace
26: 14 had p' of flocks, and p' of herds,
36: 43 habitations in the land of their p':
47: 11 them a p' in the land of Egypt,
48: 4 seed after thee for an everlasting p'.
49: 30 Hittite for a p' of a buryingplace.
50: 13 the field for a p' of a buryingplace
Le 14: 34 Canaan, which I give to you for a p',
34 in a house of the land of your p';
25: 10 shall return every man unto his p',
13 shall return every man unto his p'.
24 all the land of your p' ye shall grant
25 and hath sold away some of his p',
27 it; that he may return unto his p'.
28 and he shall return unto his p'.
32 the houses of the cities of their p',
33 the city of his p', shall go out in the
33 p' among the children of Israel.
34 be sold; for it is their perpetual p'.
41 unto the p' of his fathers shall he
45 your land: and they shall be your p'.
46 after you, to inherit them for a p';
27: 16 some part of a field of his p', then
21 the p' thereof shall be the priest's.
22 which is not of the fields of his p';
24 whom the p' of the land did belong.
28 his p' shall be sold or redeemed:
Nu 24: 18 And Edom shall be a p', Seir also
18 Seir also shall be a p' for his
26: 56 According to the lot shall the p'
27: 4 Give unto us therefore a p' among
7 shalt surely give them a p' of an
32: 5 be given unto thy servants for a p',
22 shall be your p' before the Lord.
29 them the land of Gilead for a p':
32 p' of our inheritance on this side
35: 2 the inheritance of their p' cities to
8 of the p' of the children of Israel:
28 shall return into the land of his p'.
De 2: 5 mount Seir unto Esau for a p'.
9 not give thee of their land for a p';
9 unto the children of Lot for a p'.
12 land of his p', which the Lord gave
19 of the children of Ammon any p';
19 it unto the children of Lot for a p'.
3: 20 ye return every man unto his p',
11: 6 the substance that was in their p',
32: 49 unto the children of Israel for a p':
Jos 1: 15 return unto the land of your p',
12: 6 gave it for a p' unto the Reubenites,
7 for a p' according to their divisions;
13: 29 this was the p' of the half tribe of
21: 12 the son of Jephunneh for his p'.
41 the p' of the children of Israel were
22: 4 unto the land of your p', which
7 Moses had given p' in Bashan:
9 to the land of their p', whereof they
19 if the land of your p' be unclean,
19 unto the land of the p' of the Lord,
19 dwelleth, and take p' among us:
1Ki 21: 15 p' of the vineyard of Naboth the
16 the Jezreelite, to take p' of it.
19 Hast thou killed, and also taken p'?
1Ch 28: 1 p' of the king, and of his sons,

2Ch 11: 14 left their suburbs and their *p*.
20: 11 to come to cast us out of thy *p*.
31: 1 every man to his *p*, into their
Ne 11: 3 every one in his *p* in their cities,
Ps 2: 8 parts of the earth for thy *p*.
44: 3 got not the land in *p* by their own
69: 35 may dwell there, and have it in *p*.
83: 12 ourselves the houses of God in *p*.
Pr 28: 10 shall have good things in *p*.
Isa 14: 23 also make it a *p* for the bittern,
Eze 11: 15 unto us is this land given in *p*.
25: 4 to the men of the east for a *p*,
10 and will give them in *p*, that the
36: 2 ancient high places are ours in *p*:
3 might be a *p* unto the residue of
5 appointed my land into their *p*
44: 28 them no *p* in Israel: I am their *p*.
45: 5 for a *p* for twenty chambers.
6 ye shall appoint the *p* of the city
7 and of the *p* of the city, before the
7 before the *p* of the city, from the
8 In the land shall be his *p* in Israel:
46: 16 it shall be their *p* by inheritance.
18 to thrust them out of their *p*; but
18 sons inheritance out of his own *p*:
18 not scattered every man from his *p*.
48: 20 foursquare, with the *p* of the city.
21 and of the *p* of the city, over
22 Moreover, from the *p* of the Levites,
22 Levites, and from the *p* of the city,
Ac 5: 1 with Sapphira his wife, sold a *p*,
7: 5 he would give it to him for a *p*,
45 Jesus into the *p* of the Gentiles,
Eph 1: 14 redemption of the purchased *p*,

possessions
Ge 34: 10 therein, and get you *p* therein.
47: 27 and they had *p* therein, and grew,
Nu 32: 30 have *p* among you in the land
1Sa 25: 2 Maon, whose *p* were in Carmel;
1Ch 7: 28 And their *p* and habitations were,
9: 2 that dwelt in their *p* in their cities
2Ch 32: 29 cities, and *p* of flocks and herds in
Ec 2: 7 great *p* of great and small cattle
Ob 17 of Jacob shall possess their *p*.
M't 19: 22 sorrowful: for he had great *p*.
M'r 10: 22 grieved: for he had great *p*.
Ac 2: 45 And sold their *p* and goods, and
28: 7 quarters were *p* of the chief man

possessor See also POSSESSORS.
Ge 14: 19 high God, *p* of heaven and earth:
22 God, the *p* of heaven and earth,

possessors
Zec 11: 5 Whose *p* slay them, and hold
Ac 4: 34 *p* of lands or houses sold them,

possible See also IMPOSSIBLE.
M't 19: 26 but with God all things are *p*.
24: 24 if it were *p*, they shall deceive
26: 39 if it be *p*, let this cup pass from me:
M'r 9: 23 things are *p* to him that believeth.
10: 27 God: for with God all things are *p*.
13: 22 seduce, if it were *p*, even the elect.
14: 35 if it were *p*, the hour might pass
36 Father, all things are *p* unto thee;
Lu 18: 27 impossible with men are *p* with God.
Ac 2: 24 not *p* that he should be holden of it.
20: 16 it were *p* for him, to be at Jerusalem
27: 39 if it were *p*, to thrust in the ship.
Ro 12: 18 If it be *p*, as much as lieth in you,
Ga 4: 15 if it had been *p*, ye would have
Heb10: 4 it is not *p* that the blood of bulls

post See also POSTS.
Ex 12: 7 on the upper door *p* of the houses,
21: 6 to the door, or unto the door *p*;
1Sa 1: 9 upon a seat by a *p* of the temple
Job 9: 25 Now my days are swifter than a *p*:
Jer 51: 31 One *p* shall run to meet another,
Eze 40: 14 the *p* of the court round about the
16 and upon each *p* were palm trees.
48 and measured each *p* of the porch,
41: 3 and measured the *p* of the door, two
43: 8 their *p* by my posts, and the wall
46: 2 and shall stand by the *p* of the gate,

posterity
Ge 45: 7 to preserve you a *p* in the earth,
Nu 9: 10 you or of your *p* shall be unclean
1Ki 16: 3 I will take away the *p* of Baasha,
3 and the *p* of his house; and will
21: 21 will take away thy *p*, and will cut
Ps 49: 13 yet their *p* approve their sayings.
109: 13 Let his *p* be cut off; and in the
Da 11: 4 and not to his *p*, nor according to
Am 4: 2 hooks, and your *p* with fishhooks.

posts
Ex 12: 7 and strike it on the two side *p*
22 and the two side *p* with the blood
23 the lintel, and on the two side *p*,
De 6: 9 write them upon the *p* of thy house,
11: 20 write them upon the door *p* of
J'g 16: 3 gate of the city, and the two *p*,
1Ki 6: 31 lintel and side *p* were a fifth part
33 for the door of the temple *p* of olive
7: 5 all the doors and *p* were square,
2Ch 3: 7 beams, the *p*, and...walls thereof,
30: 6 *p* went with the letters from the
10 the *p* passed from city to city
Es 3: 13 the letters were sent by *p* into all
15 The *p* went out, being hastened by
8: 10 and sent letters by *p* on horseback,
14 So the *p* that rode upon mules and
Pr 8: 34 waiting at the *p* of my doors.
Isa 6: 4 the *p* of the door moved at the
57: 8 Behind the doors also and the *p*
Eze 40: 9 and the *p* thereof, two cubits; and
10 *p* had one measure on this side and
14 made also *p* of threescore cubits,
16 *p* within the gate round about,
21 the *p* thereof and the arches thereof
24 he measured the *p* thereof and the
26 on that side, upon the *p* thereof.
29 chambers thereof, and the *p* thereof,
31 palm trees were upon the *p* thereof:
33 chambers thereof, and the *p* thereof,
34 palm trees were upon the *p* thereof,
36 chambers thereof, the *p* thereof,
37 *p* thereof were toward the utter
37 palm trees were upon the *p* thereof,
38 thereof were by the *p* of the gates,
49 there were pillars by the *p*, one on
41: 1 measured the *p*, six cubits broad on
16 door *p*, and the narrow windows,
21 The *p* of the temple were squared,
43: 8 their post by my *p*, and the wall
45: 19 and put it upon the *p* of the house,
19 upon the *p* of the gate of the inner
Am 9: 1 the door, that the *p* may shake:

pot See also POTS; POTSHERD; WASHPOT; WATERPOT.
Ex 16: 33 Take a *p*, and put an omer full of
Le 6: 28 if it be sodden in a brasen *p*, it
J'g 6: 19 and he put the broth in a *p*, and
1Sa 2: 14 pan, or kettle, or caldron, or *p*;
2Ki 4: 2 thing in the house, save a *p* of oil.
38 his servant, Set on the great *p*,
39 shred them into the *p* of pottage:
40 man of God, there is death in the *p*.
41 meal. And he cast it into the *p*;
41 And there was no harm in the *p*.
Job 41: 20 as out of a seething *p* or caldron.
31 maketh the deep to boil like a *p*:
31 the sea like a *p* of ointment.
Pr 17: 3 The fining *p* is for silver, and the
27: 21 As the fining *p* for silver, and the
Ec 7: 6 the crackling of thorns under a *p*,
Jer 1: 13 I said, I see a seething *p*; and the
Eze 24: 3 Set on a *p*, set it on, and also
6 to the *p* whose scum is therein,
Mic 3: 3 chop them in pieces, as for the *p*,
Zec 14: 21 every *p* in Jerusalem and in Judah
Heb 9: 4 was the golden *p* that had manna,

potent See IMPOTENT.

potentate
1Ti 6: 15 who is the blessed and only *P*, the

Poti See POTI-PHERAH.

Potiphar (*pot'i-far*)
Ge 37: 36 sold him into Egypt unto *P*, an
39: 1 *P*, an officer of Pharaoh, captain

Poti-pherah (*po-tif'e-rah*)
Ge 41: 45 the daughter of *P* priest of On.
50 the daughter of *P* priest of On bare
46: 20 the daughter of *P* priest of On bare

pots See also WATERPOTS.
Ex 16: 3 when we sat by the flesh *p*, and
38: 3 *p*, and the shovels, and the basons,
Le 11: 35 whether it be oven, or ranges for *p*,
1Ki 7: 45 the *p*, and the shovels, and the
2Ki 25: 14 the *p*, and the shovels, and the
2Ch 4: 11 And Huram made the *p*, and the
16 The *p* also, and the shovels, and the
35: 13 other holy offerings sod they in *p*,
Ps 58: 9 Before your *p* can feel the thorns,
68: 13 Though ye have lien among the *p*,
81: 6 hands were delivered from the *p*.
Jer 35: 5 of the Rechabites *p* full of wine,
Zec 14: 20 *p* in the Lord's house shall be like
M'r 7: 4 *p*, brasen vessels, and of tables.
8 men, as the washing of *p* and cups:

potsherd See also POTSHERDS.
Job 2: 8 he took him a *p* to scrape himself
Ps 22: 15 My strength is dried up like a *p*;
Pr 26: 23 and a wicked heart are like a *p*
Isa 45: 9 Let the *p* strive with the potsherds

potsherds
Isa 45: 9 Let the potsherd strive with the *p*

pottage
Ge 25: 29 And Jacob sod *p*: and Esau came
25: 30 I pray thee, with that same red *p*;
34 gave Esau bread and *p* of lentiles;
2Ki 4: 38 and seethe *p* for the sons of the
39 and shred them into the pot of *p*:
40 pass, as they were eating of the *p*,
Hag 2: 12 with his skirt do touch bread, or *p*,

potter See also POTTER'S; POTTERS.
Isa 41: 25 morter, and as the *p* treadeth clay.
64: 8 we are the clay, and thou our *p*;
Jer 18: 4 was marred in the hand of the *p*:
4 as seemed good to the *p* to make it.
6 cannot I do with you as this *p*?
La 4: 2 the work of the hands of the *p*!
Zec 11: 13 said unto me, Cast it unto the *p*:
13 cast them to the *p* in the house of
Ro 9: 21 not the *p* power over the clay,
Re 2: 27 as the vessels of a *p* shall they be

potter's
Ps 2: 9 them in pieces like a *p* vessel.
Isa 29: 16 shall be esteemed as the *p* clay:
Jer 18: 2 Arise, and go down to the *p* house,
3 I went down to the *p* house, and,
6 Behold, as the clay is in the *p* hand,
19: 1 Go and get a *p* earthen bottle, and
11 city, as one breaketh a *p* vessel,
Da 2: 41 part of *p* clay, and part of iron,
M't 27: 7 bought with them the *p* field, to
10 And gave them for the *p* field, as

potters See also POTTERS'.
1Ch 4: 23 These were the *p*, and those that

potters'
Isa 30: 14 *p* vessel that is broken in pieces;

pound See also POUNDS.
1Ki 10: 17 three *p* of gold went to one shield:
Ezr 2: 69 five thousand *p* of silver, and one
Ne 7: 71 and two hundred *p* of silver.
72 gold, and two thousand *p* of silver,
Lu 19: 16 thy *p* hath gained ten pounds.
18 thy *p* hath gained five pounds.
20 here is thy *p*, which I have kept
24 Take from him the *p*, and give it to
Joh 12: 3 a *p* of ointment of spikenard,
19: 39 aloes, about a hundred *p* weight.

pounds
Lu 19: 13 servants, and delivered them ten *p*,
16 Lord, thy pound hath gained ten *p*.
18 Lord, thy pound hath gained five *p*.
24 and give it to him that hath ten *p*.
25 said unto him, Lord, he hath ten *p*.

pour See also POURED; POURETH; POURING.
Ex 4: 9 river, and *p* it upon the dry land:
29: 7 and *p* it upon his head, and anoint
12 *p* all the blood beside the bottom
30: 9 shall ye *p* drink offering thereon.
Le 2: 1 and he shall *p* oil upon it, and put
6 part it in pieces, and *p* oil thereon:
4: 7 shall *p* all the blood of the bullock
18 *p* out all the blood at the bottom
25 shall *p* out his blood at the bottom
30 *p* out all the blood thereof at the
34 shall *p* out all the blood thereof at
14: 15 *p* it into the palm of his own left
18 he shall *p* upon the head of him
26 priest shall *p* of the oil into the
41 they shall *p* out the dust that they
17: 13 shall even *p* out the blood thereof,
Nu 5: 15 he shall *p* no oil upon it, nor put
24: 7 he shall *p* the water out of his buckets,
De 12: 16 shall *p* it upon the earth as water.
24 shalt *p* it upon the earth as water.
15: 23 shalt *p* it upon the ground as water.
J'g 6: 20 this rock, and *p* out the broth.
1Ki 18: 33 and *p* it on the burnt sacrifice,
2Ki 4: 4 *p* out into all those vessels, and
41 *P* out for the people, that they may
9: 3 the box of oil, and *p* it on his head,
Job 36: 27 they *p* down rain according to the
Ps 42: 4 things, I *p* out my soul in me:
62: 8 *p* out your heart before him: God
69: 24 *P* out thine indignation upon them,
79: 6 *P* out thy wrath upon the heathen
Pr 1: 23 I will *p* out my spirit unto you, I
Isa 44: 3 *p* water upon him that is thirsty,
3 I will *p* my spirit upon thy seed,
45: 8 the skies *p* down righteousness:
Jer 6: 11 *p* it out upon the children abroad,
7: 18 to *p* out drink offerings unto other
10: 25 *P* out thy fury upon the heathen
14: 16 will *p* their wickedness upon them.
18: 21 *p* out their blood by the force of
44: 17, 18, 19, 25 *p* out drink offerings unto
La 2: 19 *p* out thine heart like water
Eze 7: 8 I shortly *p* out my fury upon thee,
14: 19 and *p* out my fury upon it in blood,
20: 8 I will *p* out my fury upon them,
13 *p* out my fury upon them in the
21 I would *p* out my fury upon them,
21: 31 *p* out mine indignation upon thee,
24: 3 set it on, and also *p* water into it:
30: 15 And I will *p* my fury upon Sin, the
Ho 5: 10 *p* out my wrath upon them like
Joe 2: 28 will *p* out my spirit upon all flesh;
29 those days will I *p* out my spirit.
Mic 1: 6 I will *p* down the stones thereof
Zep 3: 8 to *p* upon them mine indignation,
Zec 12: 10 I will *p* upon the house of David,
Mal 3: 10 heaven, and *p* you out a blessing,
Ac 2: 17 *p* out of my Spirit upon all flesh:
18 *p* out in those days of my Spirit;
Re 16: 1 *p* out the vials of the wrath of God

poured See also POUREDST.
Ge 28: 18 pillar, and *p* oil upon the top of it.
35: 14 and he *p* a drink offering thereon,
14 and he *p* oil thereon.
Ex 9: 33 the rain was not *p* upon the earth.
30: 32 Upon man's flesh shall it not be *p*,
Le 4: 12 place, where the ashes are *p* out,
12 where the ashes are *p* out shall he
8: 12 And he *p* of the anointing oil upon
15 *p* the blood at the bottom of the
9: 9 *p* out the blood at the bottom of
21: 10 whose head the anointing oil was *p*,
Nu 28: 7 cause the strong wine to be *p*
De 12: 27 *p* out upon the altar of the Lord
1Sa 1: 15 *p* out my soul before the Lord.
7: 6 water, and *p* it out before the Lord,
10: 1 vial of oil, and *p* it upon his head,
2Sa 13: 9 a pan, and *p* them out before him;
23: 16 thereof, but *p* it out unto the Lord.
1Ki 13: 3 that are upon it shall be *p* out.
5 and the ashes *p* out from the altar,
2Ki 3: 11 *p* water on the hands of Elijah.
4: 5 the vessels to her; and she *p* out.
40 So they *p* out for the men to eat.
9: 6 he *p* the oil on his head, and said
16: 13 *p* his drink offering, and sprinkled
1Ch 11: 18 drink of it, but *p* it out to the Lord,

2Ch 12: 7 my wrath shall not be p' out upon
34: 21 wrath of the Lord that is p' out upon
25 my wrath shall be p' out upon this
Job 3: 24 roarings are p' out like the waters.
10: 10 Hast thou not p' me out as milk,
29: 6 the rock p' me out rivers of oil;
30: 16 now my soul is p' out upon me;
Ps 22: 14 I am p' out like water, and all my
45: 2 grace is p' into thy lips: therefore
77: 17 The clouds p' out water: the skies
142: 2 p' out my complaint before him;
Ca 1: 3 thy name is as ointment p' forth,
Isa 26: 16 they p' out a prayer when thy
29: 10 hath p' out upon you the spirit
32: 15 spirit be p' upon us from on high,
42: 25 p' upon him the fury of his anger,
53: 12 hath p' out his soul unto death:
57: 6 hast thou p' a drink offering, thou
Jer 7: 20 my fury shall be p' out upon this
19: 13 p' out drink offerings unto other
32: 29 p' out drink offerings unto other
42: 18 and my fury hath been p' forth
18 so shall my fury be p' forth upon
44: 6 fury and mine anger was p' forth,
19 p' out drink offerings unto her,
La 2: 4 Zion: he p' out his fury like fire.
11 my liver is p' upon the earth, for
12 p' out into their mothers' bosom.
4: 1 p' out in the top of every street.
11 he hath p' out his fierce anger, and
Eze 16: 36 Because thy filthiness was p' out,
20: 28 p' out there their drink offerings.
33 with fury p' out, will I rule over
34 out arm, and with fury p' out.
22: 22 Lord have p' out my fury upon you.
31 I p' out mine indignation upon
23: 8 and p' their whoredom upon her.
24: 7 she p' it not upon the ground, to
36: 18 Wherefore I p' my fury upon them
39: 29 p' out my spirit upon the house
Da 9: 11 therefore the curse is p' upon us,
27 shall be p' upon the desolate.
Mic 1: 4 waters that are p' down a steep
Na 1: 6 his fury is p' out like fire, and the
Zep 1: 17 blood shall be p' out as dust, and
M't 26: 7 ointment, and p' it on his head,
12 hath p' this ointment on my body,
M'r 14: 3 the box, and p' it on his head.
Joh 2: 15 and p' out the changers' money,
Ac 10: 45 p' out the gift of the Holy Ghost.
Re 14: 10 p' out without mixture into the
16: 2 p' out his vial upon the earth;
3 angel p' out his vial upon the sea;
4 p' out his vial upon the rivers and
8 angel p' out his vial upon the sun;
10 angel p' out his vial upon the seat
12 p' out his vial upon the great river
17 angel p' out his vial into the air;

pouredst
Eze 16: 15 p' out thy fornications on every

poureth
Job 12: 21 He p' contempt upon princes, and
16: 13 p' out my gall upon the ground.
20 mine eye p' out tears unto God.
Ps 75: 8 p' out of the same: but the dregs
102: *title* p' out his complaint before the
107: 40 He p' contempt upon princes, and
Pr 15: 2 mouth of fools p' out foolishness.
28 of the wicked p' out evil things.
Am 5: 8 p' them out upon the face of the
9: 6 p' them out upon the face of the
Joh 13: 5 After that he p' water into a bason,

pouring
Eze 9: 8 p' out of thy fury upon Jerusalem?
Lu 10: 34 p' in oil and wine, and set him on his

pourtray See also POURTRAYED.
Eze 4: 1 and p' it upon the city, even

pourtrayed
Eze 8: 10 p' upon the wall round about.
23: 14 she saw men p' upon the wall,
14 the Chaldeans p' with vermilion,

poverty
Ge 45: 11 and all that thou hast, come to p'.
Pr 6: 11 thy p' come as one that travelleth,
10: 15 destruction of the poor is their p'.
11: 24 than is meet, but it tendeth to p'.
13: 18 P and shame shall be to him that
20: 13 not sleep, lest thou come to p';
23: 21 and the glutton shall come to p':
24: 34 thy p' come as one that travelleth;
28: 19 vain persons shall have p' enough.
22 not that p' shall come upon him.
30: 8 give me neither p' nor riches;
31: 7 Let him drink, and forget his p',
2Co 8: 2 deep p' abounded unto the riches
9 ye through his p' might be rich.
Re 2: 9 thy works, and tribulation, and p'.

powder See also POWDERS.
Ex 32: 20 it in the fire, and ground it to p',
De 28: 24 the rain of thy land p' and dust:
2Ki 23: 6 and stamped it small to p', and
6 the p' thereof upon the graves of
15 stamped it small to p', and burned
2Ch 34: 7 beaten the graven images into p',
M't 21: 44 shall fall, it will grind him to p'.
Lu 20: 18 shall fall, it will grind him to p'.

powders
Ca 3: 6 with all p' of the merchant?

power See also POWERFUL; POWERS.
Ge 31: 6 with all my p' I have served your
29 the p' of my hand to do you hurt:
32: 28 prince hast p' with God and with
49: 3 dignity, and the excellency of p':
Ex 9: 16 up, for to shew in thee my p';
15: 6 O Lord, is become glorious in p':
21: 8 strange nation he shall have no p',
32: 11 the land of Egypt with great p',
Le 26: 19 will break the pride of your p';
37 p' to stand before your enemies.
Nu 14: 17 let the p' of my lord be great,
22: 38 now any p' at all to say any thing?
De 4: 37 with his mighty p' out of Egypt;
8: 17 My p' and the might of mine hand
18 that giveth thee p' to get wealth,
9: 29 broughtest out by thy mighty p'
32: 36 he seeth that their p' is gone, and
Jos 8: 20 p' to flee this way or that way:
17: 17 a great people, and hast great p':
1Sa 9: 1 a Benjamite, a mighty man of p'.
30: 4 until they had no more p' to weep.
2Sa 22: 33 God is my strength and p': and
2Ki 17: 36 the land of Egypt with great p'
19: 26 their inhabitants were of small p',
1Ch 20: 1 Joab led forth the p' of the army,
29: 11 and the p', and the glory, and the
12 in thine hand is p' and might;
2Ch 14: 11 or with them that have no p':
20: 6 in thine hand is there not p' and
22: 9 no p' to keep still the kingdom.
25: 8 God hath p' to help, and to cast
26: 13 that made war with mighty p', to
32: 9 Lachish, and all his p' with him,)
Ezr 4: 23 them to cease by force and p'.
8: 22 his p' and his wrath is against all
Ne 1: 10 hast redeemed by thy great p',
5: 5 is it in our p' to redeem them;
Es 1: 3 p' of Persia and Media, the nobles
8: 11 p' of the people and province that
9: 1 Jews hoped to have p' over them,
10: 2 the acts of his p' and of his might,
Job 1: 12 all that he hath is in thy p'; only
5: 20 in war from the p' of the sword.
21: 7 old, yea, are mighty in p'?
23: 6 against me with his great p'?
24: 22 draweth also the mighty with his p':
26: 2 thou helped him that is without p'?
12 He divideth the sea with his p',
14 but the thunder of his p' who can
36: 22 Behold, God exalteth by his p':
37: 23 he is excellent in p', and in
41: 12 not conceal his parts, nor his p',
Ps 21: 13 so will we sing and praise thy p'.
22: 20 my darling from the p' of the dog.
37: 35 I have seen the wicked in great p',
49: 15 my soul from the p' of the grave:
59: 11 scatter them by thy p'; and bring
16 But I will sing of thy p'; yea, I
62: 11 this; that p' belongeth unto God.
63: 2 To see thy p' and thy glory, so as I
65: 6 mountains; being girded with p':
66: 3 through the greatness of thy p'
7 He ruleth by his p' for ever; his
68: 35 giveth strength and p' unto his
71: 18 thy p' to every one that is to come.
78: 26 by his p' he brought in the south
79: 11 according to the greatness of thy p'
90: 11 knoweth the p' of thine anger?
106: 8 make his mighty p' to be known.
110: 3 shall be willing in the day of thy p',
111: 6 his people the p' of his works,
145: 11 thy kingdom, and talk of thy p';
147: 5 Great is our Lord, and of great p':
150: 1 him in the firmament of his p'.
Pr 3: 27 it is in the p' of thine hand to do it.
18: 21 and life are in the p' of the tongue:
Ec 4: 1 of their oppressors there was p';
5: 19 hath given him p' to eat thereof,
6: 2 God giveth him not p' to eat thereof,
8: 4 the word of a king is, there is p':
8 no man that hath p' over the spirit
8 hath he p' in the day of death:
Isa 37: 27 their inhabitants were of small p',
40: 26 might, for that he is strong in p';
29 He giveth p' to the faint; and to
43: 17 and horse, the army and the p';
47: 14 deliver...from the p' of the flame:
50: 2 redeem? or have I no p' to deliver?
Jer 10: 12 He hath made the earth by his p',
27: 5 my great p' and by my outstretched
32: 17 by thy great p' and stretched out
51: 15 He hath made the earth by his p',
Eze 17: 9 without great p' or many people
22: 6 in thee to their p' to shed blood.
30: 6 pride of her p' shall come down:
Da 2: 37 given thee a kingdom, p', and
3: 27 whose bodies the fire had no p',
4: 30 kingdom by the might of my p',
6: 27 Daniel from the p' of the lions.
8: 6 ran unto him in the fury of his p'.
7 there was no p' in the ram to stand
22 out of the nation, but not in his p'.
24 And his p' shall be mighty, but not
24 be mighty, but not by his own p':
11: 6 shall not retain the p' of the arm;
25 shall stir up his p' and his courage
43 have p' over the treasures of gold
12: 7 to scatter the p' of the holy people,
Ho 12: 3 his strength he had p' with God:
4 Yea, he had p' over the angel, and
13: 14 ransom...from the p' of the grave;
Mic 2: 1 because it is in the p' of their hand.
3: 8 I am full of p' by the spirit of the
Na 1: 3 is slow to anger, and great in p',
2: 1 loins, strong, fortify thy p' mightily.
Hab 1: 11 imputing this his p' unto his god.
2: 9 be delivered from the p' of evil!
3: 4 and there was the hiding of his p'.
Zec 4: 6 Not by might, nor by p', but by my
9: 4 he will smite her p' in the sea;
M't 6: 13 kingdom, and the p', and the glory,
9: 6 Son of man hath p' on earth to
8 which had given such p' unto men.
10: 1 he gave them p' against unclean
22: 29 the scriptures, nor the p' of God.
24: 30 of heaven with p' and great glory.
26: 64 man sitting on the right hand of p',
28: 18 All p' is given unto me in heaven
M'r 2: 10 Son of man hath p' on earth to
3: 15 And to have p' to heal sicknesses,
6: 7 gave them p' over unclean spirits;
9: 1 the kingdom of God come with p'.
12: 24 scriptures, neither the p' of God?
13: 26 the clouds with great p' and glory.
14: 62 man sitting on the right hand of p',
Lu 1: 17 him in the spirit and p' of Elias, to
35 p' of the Highest shall overshadow
4: 6 All this p' will I give thee, and the
14 returned in the p' of the Spirit into
32 doctrine: for his word was with p'.
36 authority and p' he commandeth
5: 17 p' of the Lord was present to heal
24 Son of man hath p' upon earth to
9: 1 p' and authority over all devils,
43 amazed at the mighty p' of God.
10: 19 unto you p' to tread on serpents
19 and over all the p' of the enemy:
12: 5 hath killed hath p' to cast into hell;
20: 20 p' and authority of the governor.
21: 27 of man coming in a cloud with p'
22: 53 your hour, and the p' of darkness.
69 on the right hand of the p' of God.
24: 49 be endued with p' from on high.
Joh 1: 12 he p' to become the sons of God,
10: 18 I have p' to lay it down, and I
18 and I have p' to take it again.
17: 2 hast given him p' over all flesh,
19: 10 not that I have p' to crucify thee,
10 thee, and have p' to release thee?
11 have no p' at all against me,
Ac 1: 7 the Father hath put in his own p'.
8 But ye shall receive p', after that
3: 12 by our own p' or holiness we had
4: 7 By what p', or by what name, have
33 great p' gave the apostles witness
5: 4 sold, was it not in thine own p'?
6: 8 Stephen, full of faith and p', did
8: 10 This man is the great p' of God.
19 Saying, Give me also this p', that
10: 38 with the Holy Ghost and with p':
26: 18 and from the p' of Satan unto God,
Ro 1: 4 to be the Son of God with p',
16 it is the p' of God unto salvation
20 even his eternal p' and Godhead;
9: 17 that I might shew my p' in thee,
21 not the potter p' over the clay,
22 wrath, and to make his p' known,
13: 1 For there is no p' but of God: the
2 therefore resisteth the p',
3 thou then not be afraid of the p'?
15: 13 through the p' of the Holy Ghost.
19 by the p' of the Spirit of God; so
16: 25 to him that is of p' to stablish you
1Co 1: 18 which are saved it is the p' of God.
24 Christ the p' of God, and the
2: 4 demonstration of...Spirit and of p':
5 of men, but in the p' of God.
4: 19 which are puffed up, but the p'.
20 of God is not in word, but in p'.
5: 4 with the p' of our Lord Jesus Christ,
6: 12 not be brought under the p' of any.
14 will also raise up us by his own p'.
7: 4 wife hath not p' of her own body,
4 hath not p' of his own body, but
37 but hath p' over his own will, and
9: 4 Have we not p' to eat and to drink?
5 Have we not p' to lead...a sister,
6 have not we p' to forbear working?
12 be partakers of this p' over you,
12 we have not used this p'; but
18 I abuse not my p' in the gospel.
11: 10 the woman to have p' on her head
15: 24 all rule and all authority and p'.
43 in weakness; it is raised in p':
2Co 4: 7 excellency of the p' may be of God,
6: 7 the word of truth, by the p' of God,
8: 3 For to their p', I bear record, yea,
3 beyond their p' they were willing
12: 9 the p' of Christ may rest upon me.
13: 4 yet he liveth by the p' of God.
4 him by the p' of God toward you.
10 according to the p' which the Lord
Eph 1: 19 the exceeding greatness of his p'
19 to the working of his mighty p',
21 all principality, and p', and might,
2: 2 to the prince of the p' of the air,
3: 7 by the effectual working of his p'.
20 to the p' that worketh in us,
6: 10 Lord, and in the p' of his might.
Ph'p 3: 10 him, and the p' of his resurrection,
Col 1: 11 according to his glorious p', unto
13 us from the p' of darkness, and
2: 10 the head of all principality and p':
1Th 1: 5 but also in p', and in the Holy
2Th 1: 9 Lord, and from the glory of his p';
11 and the work of faith with p':
2: 9 all p' and signs and lying wonders,
3: 9 Not because we have not p', but to
1Ti 6: 16 be honour and p' everlasting.
2Ti 1: 7 of p', and of love, and of a sound
8 gospel according to the p' of God;
3: 5 but denying the p' thereof: from
Heb 1: 3 all things by the word of his p',
2: 14 him that had the p' of death, that

Heb 7:16 but after the *p*· of an endless life.
1Pe 1: 5 kept by the *p*· of God through faith
2Pe 1: 3 as his divine *p*· hath given unto us
16 you the *p*· and coming of our Lord
2:11 are greater in *p*· and might, bring
Jude 25 and majesty, dominion and *p*·,
Re 2:26 will I give *p*· over the nations:
4:11 to receive glory and honour and *p*·:
5:12 Lamb that was slain to receive *p*·,
13 and honour, and glory, and *p*·, be
6: 4 *p*· was given to him that sat thereon
8 *p*· was given unto them over the
7:12 *p*·, and might, be unto our God
9: 3 and unto them was given *p*·, as
3 the scorpions of the earth have *p*·.
10 *p*· was to hurt men five months.
19 their *p*· is in their mouth, and in
11: 3 I will give *p*· unto my two witnesses,
6 have *p*· to shut heaven, that it
6 have *p*· over waters to turn them to
17 hast taken to thee thy great *p*·,
12:10 our God, and the *p*· of his Christ:
13: 2 the dragon gave him his *p*·, and
4 which gave *p*· unto the beast: and
5 *p*· was given unto him to continue
7 and *p*· was given him over all
12 he exerciseth all the *p*· of the first
14 miracles which he had *p*· to do in
15 And he had *p*· to give life unto the
14:18 the altar, which had *p*· over fire;
15: 8 the glory of God, and from his *p*·;
16: 8 *p*· was given unto him to scorch men
9 which hath *p*· over these plagues:
17:12 receive *p*· as kings one hour with
13 *p*· and strength unto the beast.
18: 1 from heaven, having great *p*·;
19: 1 honour, and *p*·, unto the Lord our
20: 6 such the second death hath no *p*·,

powerful
Ps 29: 4 The voice of the Lord is *p*·; the
2Co 10:10 his letters,...are weighty and *p*·;
Heb 4:12 the word of God is quick, and *p*·,

powers
M't 24:29 *p*· of the heavens shall be shaken:
M'r 13:25 the *p*· that are in heaven shall be
Lu 12:11 unto magistrates, and *p*·, take ye
21:26 the *p*· of heaven shall be shaken.
Ro 8:38 angels, nor principalities, nor *p*·,
13: 1 soul be subject unto the higher *p*·.
1 the *p*· that be are ordained of God.
Eph 3:10 and *p*· in heavenly places might be
6:12 against principalities, against *p*·,
Col 1:16 dominions, or principalities, or *p*·:
2:15 having spoiled principalities and *p*·,
Tit 3: 1 be subject to principalities and *p*·,
Heb 6: 5 and the *p*· of the world to come,
1Pe 3:22 *p*· being made subject unto him.

practices
2Pe 2:14 they have exercised with covetous *p*·;

practise See also PRACTICES; PRACTISED.
Ps 141: 4 to *p*· wicked works with men that
Isa 32: 6 to *p*· hypocrisy, and to utter error
Da 8:24 and shall prosper, and *p*·, and shall
Mic 2: 1 when the morning is light, they *p*· it,

practised
1Sa 23: 9 Saul secretly *p*· mischief against
Da 8:12 ground; and it *p*·, and prospered.

Prætorium (*pre-to'-re-um*)
M'r 15:16 him away into the hall, called *P*·;

praise See also PRAISED; PRAISES; PRAISETH; PRAISING.
Ge 29:35 she said, Now will I *p*· the Lord:
49: 8 art he whom thy brethren shall *p*·:
Le 19:24 shall be holy to *p*· the Lord withal.
De 10:21 He is thy *p*·, and he is thy God,
26:19 in *p*·, and in name, and in honour;
J'g 5: 2 *P*· ye the Lord for the avenging
3 will sing *p*· to the Lord God of Israel.
1Ch 16: 4 and *p*· the Lord God of Israel:
35 thy holy name, and glory in thy *p*·.
23: 5 made, said David, to *p*· therewith.
30 morning to thank and *p*· the Lord,
25: 3 to give thanks and to *p*· the Lord.
29:13 thee, and *p*· thy glorious name.
2Ch 7: 6 the king had made to *p*· the Lord,
8:14 *p*· and minister before the priests,
20:19 stood up to *p*· the Lord God of
21 should *p*· the beauty of holiness,
21 the army, and to say, *P*· the Lord;
22 when they began to sing and to *p*·,
23:13 and such as taught to sing *p*·.
29:30 Levites to sing *p*· unto the Lord
31: 2 to *p*· in the gates of the tents of the
Ezr 3:10 *p*· the Lord, after the ordinance of
Ne 9: 5 exalted above all blessing and *p*·.
12:24 to *p*· and to give thanks, according
46 songs of *p*· and thanksgiving unto
Ps 7:17 I will *p*· the Lord according to his
17 sing *p*· to the name of the Lord
9: 1 I will *p*· thee, O Lord, with my
2 I will sing *p*· to thy name, O thou
14 I may shew forth all thy *p*· in the
21:13 so will we sing and *p*· thy power.
22:22 of the congregation will I *p*· thee.
23 Ye that fear the Lord, *p*· him; all
25 My *p*· shall be of thee in the great
26 shall *p*· the Lord that seek him:
28: 7 and with my song will I *p*· him.
30: 9 Shall the dust *p*· thee? shall it
12 that my glory may sing *p*· to thee,
33: 1 for *p*· is comely for the upright.
2 *P*· the Lord with harp: sing unto
34: 1 his *p*· shall continually be in my
Ps 35:18 I will *p*· thee among much people.
28 and of thy *p*· all the day long.
40: 3 my mouth, even *p*· unto our God:
42: 4 with the voice of joy and *p*·, with
5 shall yet *p*· him for the help of
11 for I shall yet *p*· him, who is the
43: 4 upon the harp will I *p*· thee, O God
5 for I shall yet *p*· him, who is the
44: 8 day long, and *p*· thy name for ever.
45:17 shall the people *p*· thee for ever
48:10 thy *p*· unto the ends of the earth:
49:18 and men will *p*· thee, when thou
50:23 Whoso offereth *p*· glorifieth me:
51:15 my mouth shall shew forth thy *p*·.
52: 9 I will *p*· thee for ever, because
54: 6 I will *p*· thy name, O Lord; for it is
56: 4 In God I will *p*· his word, in God I
10 In God will I *p*· his word: in the
10 in the Lord will I *p*· his word.
57: 7 is fixed: I will sing and give *p*·.
9 I will *p*· thee, O Lord, among the
61: 8 I sing *p*· unto thy name for ever,
63: 3 than life, my lips shall *p*· thee.
5 shall *p*· thee with joyful lips:
65: 1 *P*· waiteth for thee, O God, in
66: 2 of his name: make his *p*· glorious.
8 make the voice of his *p*· to be heard:
67: 3 Let the people *p*· thee, O God; let
3 O God; let all the people *p*· thee.
5 Let the people *p*· thee, O God; let
5 O God; let all the people *p*· thee.
69:30 *p*· the name of God with a song,
34 Let the heaven and earth *p*· him,
71: 6 my *p*· shall be continually of thee.
8 Let my mouth be filled with thy *p*
14 will yet *p*· thee more and more.
22 will also *p*· thee with the psaltery,
74:21 the poor and needy *p*· thy name.
76:10 the wrath of man shall *p*· thee:
79:13 forth thy *p*· to all generations.
86:12 I will *p*· thee, O Lord my God, with
88:10 shall the dead arise and *p*· thee?
89: 5 the heavens shall *p*· thy wonders,
98: 4 noise, and rejoice, and sing *p*·.
99: 3 *p*· thy great and terrible name;
100: *title* A Psalm of *p*·.
4 and into his courts with *p*·:
102:18 shall be created shall *p*· the Lord.
21 in Zion, and his *p*· in Jerusalem;
104:33 I will sing *p*· to my God while I
35 Lord, O my soul. *P*· ye the Lord.
105:45 and keep his laws. *P*· ye the Lord.
106: 1 *P*· ye the Lord. O give thanks
2 who can shew forth all his *p*·?
12 they his words; they sang his *p*·.
47 holy name, and to triumph in thy *p*·.
48 people say, Amen. *P*· ye the Lord.
107: 8, 15, 21, 31 Oh that men would *p*·
32 and *p*· him in the assembly of the
108: 1 I will sing and give *p*·, even with
3 I will *p*· thee, O Lord, among the
109: 1 not thy peace, O God of thy *p*·;
30 *p*· the Lord with my mouth;
30 will *p*· him among the multitude.
111: 1 *P*· ye the Lord, I will
1 *p*· the Lord with my whole heart,
10 his *p*· endureth for ever.
112: 1 *P*· ye the Lord. Blessed is the
113: 1 *P*· ye the Lord. *P*·, O ye servants
1 the Lord, *p*· the name of the Lord.
9 mother of children. *P*· ye the Lord.
115:17 The dead *p*· not the Lord, neither
18 forth...for evermore. *P*· the Lord.
116:19 thee, O Jerusalem. *P*· ye the Lord.
117: 1 O *p*· the Lord, all ye nations:
1 ye nations: *p*· him, all ye people.
2 endureth for ever. *P*· ye the Lord.
118:19 into them, and I will *p*· the Lord:
21 I will *p*· thee: for thou hast heard
28 Thou art my God, and I will *p*· thee:
119: 7 *p*· thee with uprightness of heart,
164 Seven times a day do I *p*· thee
171 My lips shall utter *p*·, when thou
175 my soul live, and it shall *p*· thee;
135: 1 *P*· ye the Lord. *P*· ye the name
1 *p*· him, O ye servants of the Lord.
3 *P*· the Lord; for the Lord is good:
21 at Jerusalem. *P*· ye the Lord.
138: 1 will *p*· thee with my whole heart:
1 the gods will I sing *p*· unto thee.
2 *p*· thy name for...lovingkindness
4 the kings of the earth shall *p*· thee,
139:14 I will *p*· thee; for I am fearfully
142: 7 of prison, that I may *p*· thy name:
145: *title* David's Psalm of *p*·.
2 I will *p*· thy name for ever and
4 generation shall *p*· thy works to
10 All thy works shall *p*· thee, O
21 shall speak the *p*· of the Lord:
146: 1 *P*· ye the Lord. *P*· the Lord, O
2 While I live I will *p*· the Lord: I will
10 all generations. *P*· ye the Lord.
147: 1 *P*· ye the Lord: for it is good to
1 it is pleasant; and *p*· is comely.
7 sing *p*· upon the harp unto our
12 *P*· the Lord, O Jerusalem;
12 Jerusalem; *p*· thy God, O Zion.
20 not known them. *P*· ye the Lord.
148: 1 *P*· ye the Lord. *P*· ye the Lord
1 the heavens: *p*· him in the heights.
2 *P*· ye him, all his angels:
2 his angels: *p*· ye him, all his hosts.
3 *P*· ye him, sun and moon:
3 moon: *p*· him, all ye stars of light:
4 *P*· him, ye heavens of heavens, and
5 Let them *p*· the name of the Lord:
Ps 148: 7 *P*· the Lord from the earth, ye
13 Let them *p*· the name of the Lord:
14 people, the *p*· of all his saints;
14 near unto him. *P*· ye the Lord.
149: 1 *P*· ye the Lord. Sing unto the Lord
1 and his *p*· in the congregation of
3 Let them *p*· his name in the
9 have all his saints. *P*· ye the Lord.
150: 1 *P*· ye the Lord.
1 *P*· God in his sanctuary:
1 *p*· him in the firmament of his
2 *P*· him for his mighty acts;
2 *p*· him according to his excellent
3 *P*· him with the sound of the
3 *p*· him with the psaltery and harp.
4 *P*· him with the timbrel and dance:
4 *p*· him with stringed instruments
5 *P*· him upon the loud cymbals:
5 *p*· him upon the high sounding
6 that hath breath *p*· the Lord.
6 the Lord. *P*· ye the Lord.
Pr 27: 2 Let another man *p*· thee, and not
21 for gold; so is a man to his *p*·.
28: 4 that forsake the law *p*· the wicked:
31:31 her own works *p*· her in the gates.
Isa 12: 1 O Lord, I will *p*· thee: though
4 *P*· the Lord, call upon his name,
25: 1 I will *p*· thy name; for thou hast
38:18 For the grave cannot *p*· thee, death
19 living, the living, he shall *p*· thee,
42: 8 neither my *p*· to graven images.
10 his *p*· from the end of the earth,
12 and declare his *p*· in the islands.
43:21 myself; they shall shew forth my *p*·.
48: 9 and for my *p*· will I refrain for thee,
60:18 walls Salvation, and thy gates *P*·.
61: 3 garment of *p*· for the spirit of
11 *p*· to spring forth before all the
62: 7 make Jerusalem a *p*· in the earth.
9 it shall eat it, and *p*· the Lord;
Jer 13:11 and for a *p*·, and for a glory:
17:14 I shall be saved: for thou art my *p*·.
26 sacrifices of *p*· unto the house of
20:13 *p*· ye the Lord: for he hath
31: 7 *p*· ye, and say, O Lord, save thy
33: 9 a *p*· and an honour before all the
11 *P*· the Lord of hosts: for the Lord
11 shall bring the sacrifice of *p*· into
48: 2 shall be no more *p*· of Moab:
49:25 is the city of *p*· not left, the city of
51:41 how is the *p*· of the whole earth
Da 2:23 I thank thee, and *p*· thee, O thou
4:37 Now I Nebuchadnezzar *p*· and extol
Joe 2:26 *p*· the name of the Lord your God,
Hab 3: 3 and the earth was full of his *p*·.
Zep 3:19 get them *p*· and fame in every land
20 and a *p*· among all people of the
M't 21:16 sucklings thou hast perfected *p*·?
Lu 18:43 when they saw it, gave *p*· unto God.
19:37 rejoice and *p*· God with a loud voice
Joh 9:24 said unto him, Give God the *p*·: we
12:43 For they loved the *p*· of men more
43 of men more than the *p*· of God.
Ro 2:29 whose *p*· is not of men, but of God.
13: 3 and thou shalt have *p*· of the same:
15:11 again, *P*· the Lord, all ye Gentiles;
1Co 4: 5 shall every man have *p*· of God.
11: 2 Now I *p*· you, brethren, that ye
17 I *p*· you, not that ye come together
22 shall I *p*· you in this? I *p*· you not.
2Co 8:18 brother, whose *p*· is in the gospel
Eph 1: 6 To the *p*· of the glory of his grace,
12 to the *p*· of his glory, who first
14 possession, unto the *p*· of his glory.
Ph'p 1:11 Christ, unto the glory and *p*· of God.
4: 8 if there be any *p*·, think on these
Heb 2:12 the church will I sing *p*· unto thee.
13:15 let us offer the sacrifice of *p*· to God
1Pe 1: 7 be found unto *p*· and honour and
2:14 and for the *p*· of them that do well.
4:11 whom be *p*· and dominion for ever
Re 19: 5 *P*· our God, all ye his servants,

praised
J'g 16:24 people saw him, they *p*· their god:
2Sa 14:25 none to be so much *p*· as Absalom
22: 4 on the Lord, who is worthy to be *p*·:
1Ch 16:25 is the Lord, and greatly to be *p*·:
36 people said, Amen, and *p*· the Lord.
23: 5 four thousand *p*· the Lord with the
2Ch 5:13 *p*· the Lord, saying, For he is good;
7: 3 and worshipped, and *p*· the Lord,
6 when David *p*· by their ministry;
30:21 Levites and the priests *p*· the Lord
Ezr 3:11 great shout, when they *p*· the Lord,
Ne 5:13 said, Amen, and *p*· the Lord.
Ps 18: 3 the Lord, who is worthy to be *p*·:
48: 1 greatly to be *p*· in the city of our
72:15 continually;...daily shall he be *p*·.
96: 4 Lord is great, and greatly to be *p*·:
113: 3 same the Lord's name is to be *p*·.
145: 3 is the Lord, and greatly to be *p*·;
Pr 31:30 feareth the Lord, she shall be *p*·.
Ec 4: 2 I *p*· the dead which are already
Ca 6: 9 the concubines, and they *p*· her.
Isa 64:11 house, where our fathers *p*· thee, is
Da 4:34 I *p*· and honoured him that liveth
5: 4 drank wine, and *p*· the gods of gold,
23 thou hast *p*· the gods of silver, and
Lu 1:64 loosed, and he spake, and *p*· God.

praises
Ex 15:11 fearful in *p*·, doing wonders?
2Sa 22:50 and I will sing *p*· unto thy name.
2Ch 29:30 And they sang *p*· with gladness,
Ps 9:11 Sing *p*· to the Lord, which
18:49 heathen,...sing *p*· unto thy name.

Ps 22: 3 that inhabitest the p' of Israel.
27: 6 yea, I will sing p' unto the Lord.
47: 6 Sing p' to God, sing p':
6 sing p' unto our King, sing p'.
7 sing ye p' with understanding.
56:12 O God: I will render p' unto thee.
68: 4 unto God, sing p' to his name:
32 the earth; O sing p' unto the Lord;
75: 9 I will sing p' to the God of Jacob.
78: 4 p' of the Lord, and his strength,
92: 1 to sing p' unto thy name, O most
108: 3 I will sing p' unto thee among the
135: 3 Lord is good: sing p' unto his name;
144: 9 ten strings will I sing p' unto thee.
146: 2 I will sing p' unto my God while I
147: 1 it is good to sing p' unto our God;
149: 3 sing p' unto him with the timbrel
6 the high p' of God be in their mouth,
Isa 60: 6 shew forth the p' of the Lord.
63: 7 and the p' of the Lord, according
Ac 16:25 prayed, and sang p' unto God:
1Pe 2: 9 shew forth the p' of him who hath

praiseth
Pr 31:28 her husband also, and he p' her.

praising
2Ch 5:13 heard in p' and thanking the Lord;
23:12 the people running and p' the king,
Ezr 3:11 p' and giving thanks unto the Lord;
Ps 84: 4 thy house: they will be still p' thee.
Lu 2:13 heavenly host, p' God, and saying,
20 glorifying and p' God for all the
24:53 in the temple, p' and blessing God.
Ac 2:47 P' God, and having favour with all
3: 8 walking, and leaping, and p' God.
9 people saw him walking and p' God:

pransing See also PRANSINGS.
Na 3: 2 the p' horses, and of the jumping

pransings
J'g 5:22 broken by the means of the p',
22 the p' of their mighty ones.

prating
Pr 10: 8 but a p' fool shall fall.
10 sorrow: but a p' fool shall fall.
3Jo 10 p' against us with malicious

pray^ See also PRAYED; PRAYETH; PRAYING.
Ge 12:13 Say, I p' thee, thou art my sister:
13: 8 Let there be no strife, I p' thee,
9 separate thyself, I p' thee, from me:
16: 2 I p' thee, go in unto my maid; it
18: 3 pass not away, I p' thee, from thy
4 a little water, I p' you, be fetched,
19: 2 now, my lords, turn in, I p' you,
7 said, I p' you, brethren, do not so
8 let me, I p' you, bring them out
20: 7 he shall p' for thee, and thou shalt
23:13 if thou wilt give it, I p' thee, hear
25:30 said to Jacob, Feed me, I p' thee,
27:19 I p' thee, sit and eat of my venison,
21 Come near, I p' thee, that I may
30:14 Give me, I p' thee, of thy son's
27 I p' thee, if I have found favour in
32:11 Deliver me, I p' thee, from the hand
29 said, Tell me, I p' thee, thy name.
33:10 Jacob said, Nay, I p' thee, if now I
11 Take, I p' thee, my blessing that is
14 Let my lord, I p' thee, pass over
34: 8 I p' you give her him to wife.
37: 6 Hear, I p' you, this dream which I
14 Go, I p' thee, see whether it be well
16 tell me, I p' thee, where they feed
38:16 Go to, I p' thee, let me come in unto
40: 8 to God? tell me them, I p' you.
14 shew kindness, I p' thee, unto me,
44:33 I p' thee, let thy servant abide
45: 4 brethren, Come near to me, I p' you.
47: 4 we p' thee, let thy servants dwell in
29 put, I p' thee, thy hand under my
29 bury me not, I p' thee, in Egypt:
50: 4 speak, I p' you, in the ears of
5 let me go up, I p' thee, and bury my
17 Forgive, I p' thee now, the trespass
17 we p' thee, forgive the trespass of
Ex 4:13 O my Lord, send, I p' thee, by
18 Let me go, I p' thee, and return
5: 3 let us go, we p' thee, three days'
10:17 forgive, I p' thee, my sin only this
32:32 blot me, I p' thee, out of thy book
33:13 therefore, I p' thee, if I have found
34: 9 let my Lord, I p' thee, go among us;
Nu 10:31 he said, Leave us not, I p' thee;
11:15 kill me, I p' thee, out of hand, if I
16: 8 Hear, I p' you, ye sons of Levi:
26 Depart, I p' you, from the tents of
20:17 Let us pass, I p' thee, through thy
21: 7 p' unto the Lord, that he take
22: 6 therefore, I p' thee, curse me this
16 Let nothing, I p' thee, hinder thee
17 therefore, I p' thee, curse me this
19 I p' you, tarry ye also here this
23:13 him, Come, I p' thee, with me unto
27 Come, I p' thee, I will bring thee
De 3:25 I p' thee, let me go over, and see the
Jos 2:12 I p' you, swear unto me by the Lord,
7:19 give, I p' thee, glory to the Lord
J'g 1:24 Shew us, we p' thee, the entrance
4:19 Give me, I p' thee, a little water to
6:18 Depart not hence, I p' thee, until I
39 let me prove, I p' thee, but this
8: 5 Give, I p' you, loaves of bread unto
9: 2 Speak, I p' you, in the ears of all the
38 go out, I p' now, and fight with
10:15 deliver us only, we p' thee, this day.
11:17 Let me, I p' thee, pass through thy
J'g 11:19 Let us pass, we p' thee, through thy
13: 4 beware, I p' thee, and drink not wine
15 I p' thee, let us detain thee, until
15: 2 take her, I p' thee, instead of her.
16: 6 Tell me, I p' thee, wherein thy great
10 now tell me, I p' thee, wherewith
28 Lord God, remember me, I p' thee,
28 strengthen me, I p' thee, only this
18: 5 Ask counsel, we p' thee, of God,
19: 6 Be content, I p' thee, and tarry all
8 said, Comfort thine heart, I p' thee.
9 evening, I p' you tarry all night:
11 Come, I p' thee, and let us turn in
23 nay, I p' you, do not so wickedly;
Ru 2: 7 I p' you, let me glean and gather
1Sa 2:36 Put me, I p' thee, into one of the
3:17 I p' thee hide it not from me: God
7: 5 I will p' for you unto the Lord.
9:18 Tell me, I p' thee, where the seer's
10:15 Tell me, I p' thee, what Samuel
12:19 P' for thy servants unto the Lord
23 the Lord in ceasing to p' for you:
14:29 see, I p' you, how mine eyes have
15:25 I p' thee, pardon my sin, and turn
30 honour me now, I p' thee, before
16:22 Let David, I p' thee, stand before
19: 2 now therefore, I p' thee, take heed
20:29 Let me go, I p' thee; for our family
29 let me get away, I p' thee, and see
22: 3 my mother, I p' thee, come forth,
23:22 Go, I p' you, prepare yet, and know
25: 8 give, I p' thee, whatsoever cometh
24 let thine handmaid, I p' thee, speak
25 Let not my lord, I p' thee, regard
26: 8 let me smite him, I p' thee, with the
11 I p' thee, take thou now the spear
19 I p' thee, let my lord the king hear
28: 8 said, I p' thee, divine unto me by the
22 I p' thee, hearken thou also unto
30: 7 I p' thee, bring me hither the ephod.
2Sa 1: 4 went the matter? I p' thee, tell me.
9 Stand, I p' thee, upon me, and slay
7:27 in his heart to p' this prayer unto
13: 5 him, I p' thee, let my sister Tamar
6 I p' thee, let Tamar my sister come,
13 I p' thee, speak unto the king; for
26 I p' thee, let my brother Amnon go
14: 2 I p' thee, feign thyself to be a
11 I p' thee, let the king remember the
12 Let thine handmaid, I p' thee,
18 Hide not from me, I p' thee, the
15: 7 I p' thee, let me go and pay my vow,
16: 9 go over, I p' thee, and take off his
18:22 let me, I p' thee, also run after
19:37 Let thy servant, I p' thee, turn back
20:16 say, I p' you, unto Joab, Come near
24:17 let thine hand, I p' thee, be against
1Ki 1:12 let me, I p' thee, give thee counsel,
2:17 I p' thee, unto Solomon the king,
20 of thee; I p' thee, say me not nay.
8:26 let thy word, I p' thee, be verified,
30 they shall p' toward this place:
33 confess thy name, and p', and make
35 if they p' toward this place, and
42 when he shall come and p' toward
44 and shall p' unto the Lord toward
48 p' unto thee toward their land, which
13: 6 p' for me, that my hand may be
14: 2 wife, Arise, I p' thee, and disguise
17:10 Fetch me, I p' thee, a little water in
11 Bring me, I p' thee, a morsel of
21 I p' thee, let this child's soul come
19:20 Let me, I p' thee, kiss my father
20: 7 I p' you, and see how this man
31 let us, I p' thee, put sackcloth on
32 Ben-hadad saith, I p' thee, let me
37 Smite me, I p' thee. And the man
22: 5 Enquire, I p' thee, at the word of
13 let thy word, I p' thee, be like the
2Ki 1:13 O man of God, I p' thee, let my life,
2: 2 unto Elisha, Tarry here, I p' thee;
4 him, Elisha, tarry here, I p' thee;
6 said unto him, Tarry, I p' thee,
9 And Elisha said, I p' thee, let a
19 said unto Elisha, Behold, I p' thee,
4:10 chamber, I p' thee, on the wall;
22 Send me, I p' thee, one of the young
26 Run now, I p' thee, to meet her, and
5: 7 wherefore consider, I p' you, and
15 I p' thee, take a blessing of thy
17 I p' thee, be given to thy servant
22 them, I p' thee, a talent of silver,
6: 2 Let us go, we p' thee, unto Jordan,
17 said, Lord, I p' thee, open his eyes,
18 Smite this people, I p' thee, with
7:13 Let some take, I p' thee, five of the
8: 4 Tell me, I p' thee, all the great
18:23 therefore, I p' thee, give pledges
1Ch 17:25 hath found in his heart to p'
21:17 let thine hand, I p' thee, O Lord
2Ch 6:24 p' and make supplication before
26 p' toward this place, and confess
32 if they come and p' in this house;
34 they p' unto thee toward this city
37 turn and p' unto thee in the land
38 p' toward their land, which thou
7:14 humble themselves, and p', and seek
18: 4 Enquire, I p' thee, at the word of
12 let thy word therefore, I p' thee, be
Ezr 6:10 p' for the life of the king, and of
Ne 1: 6 I p' before thee now, day and
11 prosper, I p' thee, thy servant this
5:10 I p' you, let us leave off this usury.
11 Restore, I p' you, to them, even this
Job 6:29 Return, I p' you, let it not be
8: 8 enquire, I p' thee, of the former age,
Job 21:15 should we have, if we p' unto him?
22:22 Receive, I p' thee, the law from his
32:21 Let me not, I p' you, accept any
33: 1 Job, I p' thee, hear my speeches, and
26 He shall p' unto God, and he will
42: 8 my servant Job shall p' for you:
Ps 5: 2 and my God: for unto thee will I p'.
32: 6 this shall every one that is godly p'
55:17 and morning, and at noon will I p'
122: 6 P' for the peace of Jerusalem: they
Isa 5: 3 of Judah, judge, I p' you, betwixt
16:12 shall come to his sanctuary to p';
29:11 Read this, I p' thee: and he saith,
36: 8 give pledges, I p' thee, to my master
11 Speak, I p' thee, unto thy servants
45:20 and p' unto a god that cannot save.
Jer 7:16 p' not thou for this people, neither
11:14 p' not thou for this people, neither
14:11 P' not for this people for their good.
21: 2 Enquire, I p' thee, of the Lord for
29: 7 and p' unto the Lord for it: for in
12 ye shall go and p' unto me, and I
32: 8 Buy my field, I p' thee, that is in
37: 3 P' now unto the Lord our God for
20 hear now, I p' thee, O my lord the
20 let my supplication, I p' thee, be
40:15 Let me go, I p' thee, and I will slay
42: 2 p' for us unto the Lord thy God,
4 I will p' unto the Lord your God
20 P' for us unto the Lord our God;
La 1:18 hear, I p' you, all people, and
Eze 33:30 Come, I p' you, and hear what is the
Jon 1: 8 Tell us, we p' thee, for whose cause
4: 2 said, I p' thee, O Lord, was not this
Mic 3: 1 Hear, I p' you, O heads of Jacob,
9 Hear this, I p' you, ye heads of the
Hag 2:15 now, I p' you, consider from this
Zec 7: 2 their men, to p' before the Lord,
8:21 us go speedily to p' before the Lord,
22 Jerusalem, and...p' before the Lord.
Mal 1: 9 now, I p' you, beseech God that
M't 5:44 p' for them which despitefully use
6: 5 to p' standing in the synagogues
6 p' to thy Father which is in secret;
7 when ye p', use not vain repetitions,
9 After this manner therefore p' ye:
9:38 P' ye therefore the Lord of the
14:23 up into a mountain apart to p':
19:13 put his hands on them and p':
24:20 p' ye that your flight be not in the
26:36 ye here, while I go and p' yonder.
41 Watch and p', that ye enter not into
53 that I cannot now p' to my Father,
M'r 5:17 they began to p' him to depart out
23 I p' thee, come and lay thy hands on
6:46 he departed into a mountain to p'.
11:24 things ye desire, when ye p', believe
13:18 p' ye that your flight be not in the
33 watch and p': for ye know not
14:32 disciples, Sit ye here, while I shall p'.
38 Watch ye and p', lest ye enter into
Lu 6:12 he went out into a mountain to p',
28 p' for them which despitefully use
9:28 and went up into a mountain to p'.
10: 2 p' ye therefore the Lord of the
11: 1 unto him, Lord, teach us to p',
2 When ye p', say, Our Father which
14:18 see it: I p' thee have me excused.
19 them: I p' thee have me excused.
16:27 I p' thee therefore, father, that thou
18: 1 men ought always to p', and not
10 went up into the temple to p';
21:36 ye therefore, and p' always, that
22:40 P' that ye enter not into
46 and p', lest ye enter into temptation.
Joh 14:16 I will p' the Father, and he shall
16:26 that I will p' the Father for you:
17: 9 I p' for them: I p' not for the
15 I p' not that thou shouldest take
20 Neither p' I for these alone, but
Ac 8:22 this thy wickedness, and p' God,
24 P' ye to the Lord for me, that
34 I p' thee, of whom speaketh the
10: 9 went up upon the housetop to p'
24: 4 I p' thee that thou wouldest hear
27:34 I p' you to take some meat: for
Ro 8:26 we should p' for as we ought:
1Co 11:13 comely that a woman p' unto God
14:13 tongue p' that he may interpret.
14 if I p' in an unknown tongue, my
15 it then? I will p' with the spirit,
15 will p' with the understanding also:
2Co 5:20 we p' you in Christ's stead, be ye
13: 7 Now p' to God that ye do no evil;
Ph'p 1: 9 And this I p', that your love may
Col 1: 9 do not cease to p' for you, and to
1Th 5:17 P' without ceasing.
23 I p' God your whole spirit and soul
25 Brethren, p' for us.
2Th 1:11 we p' always for you, that our God
3: 1 brethren, p' for us, that the word
1Ti 2: 8 therefore that men p' every where,
2Ti 4:16 I p' God that it may not be laid to
Heb13:18 P' for us: for we trust we have
Jas 5:13 among you afflicted? let him p'.
14 let them p' over him, anointing
16 p' one for another, that ye may
1Jo 5:16 I do not say that he shall p' for it.

prayed
Ge 20:17 So Abraham p' unto God: and
Nu 11: 2 when Moses p' unto the Lord,
21: 7 us. And Moses p' for the people.
De 9:20 I p' for Aaron also the same time.
26 I p' therefore unto the Lord, and
1Sa 1:10 p' unto the Lord, and wept sore.

1Sa 1:27 For this child I p'; and the Lord
2: 1 Hannah p', and said, My heart
8: 6 us. And Samuel p' unto the Lord.
2Ki 4:33 them twain, and p' unto the Lord.
6:17 Elisha p', and said, Lord, I pray
18 Elisha p' unto the Lord, and said,
19:15 Hezekiah p' before the Lord, and
20 That which thou hast p' to me
20: 2 to the wall, and p' unto the Lord,
2Ch 30:18 But Hezekiah p' for them, saying,
32:20 of Amoz, p' and cried to heaven.
24 the death, and p' unto the Lord:
33:13 p' unto him: and he was intreated
Ezr 10: 1 Now when Ezra had p', and when
Ne 1: 4 and p' before the God of heaven.
2: 4 So I p' to the God of heaven.
Job 42:10 Job, when he p' for his friends:
Isa 37:15 Hezekiah p' unto the Lord, saying,
21 Whereas thou hast p' to me
38: 2 the wall, and p' unto the Lord,
Jer 32:16 Neriah, I p' unto the Lord, saying,
Da 6:10 p', and gave thanks before his
9: 4 And I p' unto the Lord my God,
Jon 2: 1 Jonah p' unto the Lord his God
4: 2 And he p' unto the Lord, and said,
M't 26:39 fell on his face, and p', saying, O
42 away the second time, and p',
44 p' the third time, saying the same
M'r 1:35 a solitary place, and there p'.
5:18 p' him that he might be with him.
14:35 and p' that, if it were possible,
39 went away, and p', and spake the
Lu 5: 3 p' him that he would thrust out a
16 himself into the wilderness, and p'
9:29 And as he p', the fashion of his
18:11 stood and p' thus with himself,
22:32 p' for thee, that thy faith fail not:
41 cast, and kneeled down and p',
44 in an agony he p' more earnestly:
Joh 4:31 his disciples p' him, saying,
Ac 1:24 And they p', and said, Thou, Lord,
4:31 And when they had p', the place
6: 6 when they had p', they laid their
8:15 p' for them, that they might receive
9:40 forth, and kneeled down, and p';
10: 2 to the people, and p' to God alway
30 the ninth hour I p' in my house,
48 p' they him to tarry certain days.
13: 3 when they had fasted and p', and
14:23 p' with fasting, they commended
16: 9 man of Macedonia, and p' him,
25 Paul and Silas p', and sang
20:36 kneeled down, and p' with them all.
21: 5 kneeled down on the shore, and p'.
22:17 while I p' in the temple, I was in a
23:18 p' me to bring this young man
28: 8 Paul entered in, and p', and laid
Jas 5:17 he p' earnestly that it might not
18 he p' again, and the heaven gave

prayer See also PRAYERS.
2Sa 7:27 heart to pray this p' unto thee.
1Ki 8:28 thou respect unto the p' of thy
28 hearken unto the cry and to the p',
29 p' which thy servant shall make
38 p' and supplication soever be made
45 hear thou in heaven their p' and
49 Then hear thou their p' and their
54 made an end of praying all this p'
9: 3 him, I have heard thy p' and thy
2Ki 19: 4 lift up thy p' for the remnant that
20: 5 I have heard thy p', I have seen
2Ch 6:19 Have respect therefore to the p'
19 to the p' which thy servant prayeth
20 to hearken unto the p' which thy
29 p' or what supplication soever
35 hear thou from the heavens their p'
39 their p' and their supplications,
40 attent unto the p' that is made in
7:12 I have heard thy p', and have
15 unto the p' that is made in this
30:27 and their p' came up to his holy
33:18 Manasseh, and his p' unto his God,
19 His p' also, and how God was
Ne 1: 6 hear the p' of thy servant, which
11 attentive to the p' of thy servant,
11 and to the p' of thy servants, who
4: 9 Nevertheless we made our p' unto
11:17 begin the thanksgiving in p': and
Job 15: 4 and restrainest p' before God.
16:17 mine hands: also my p' is pure.
22:27 Thou shalt make thy p' unto him,
Ps 4: 1 mercy upon me, and hear my p'.
5: 3 will I direct my p' unto thee, and
6: 9 the Lord will receive my p'.
17: *title* A p' of David.
1 give ear unto my p', that goeth
35:13 p' returned into mine own bosom.
39:12 Hear my p', O Lord, and give ear
42: 8 p' unto the God of my life.
54: 2 Hear my p', O God; give ear to the
55: 1 Give ear to my p', O God; and hide
61: 1 my cry, O God; attend unto my p'.
64: 1 Hear my voice, O God, in my p':
65: 2 O thou that hearest p', unto thee
66:19 attended to the voice of my p'.
20 which hath not turned away my p',
69:13 for me, my p' is unto thee, O Lord,
72:15 p' also shall be made for him
80: 4 against the p' of thy people?
84: 8 O Lord God of hosts, hear my p':
86: *title* A p' of David.
6 Give ear, O Lord, unto my p';
88: 2 Let my p' come before thee: incline
13 morning shall my p' prevent thee.
90: *title* A p' of Moses the man of God.
Ps 102: *title* A p' of the afflicted, when he is
1 Hear my p', O Lord, and let my
17 will regard the p' of the destitute,
17 and not despise their p'.
109: 4 but I give myself unto p'.
7 and let his p' become sin.
141: 2 Let my p' be set forth before thee
5 yet my p' also shall be in their
142: *title* David; A P' when he was in
143: 1 Hear my p', O Lord, give ear to my
Pr 15: 8 the p' of the upright is his delight.
29 he heareth the p' of the righteous.
28: 9 his p' shall be an abomination.
Isa 26:16 poured out a p' when...chastening
37: 4 thy p' for the remnant that is left.
38: 5 I have heard thy p', I have seen
56: 7 them joyful in my house of p':
7 house shall be called an house of p'
Jer 7:16 neither lift up cry nor p' for them,
11:14 neither lift up a cry or p' for them:
La 3: 8 and shout, he shutteth out my p'.
44 that our p' should not pass through.
Da 9: 3 seek by p' and supplications, with
13 we not our p' before the Lord our
17 God, hear the p' of thy servant,
21 whiles I was speaking in p', even
Jon 2: 7 my p' came in unto thee, into thine
Hab 3: 1 A p' of Habakkuk the prophet
M't 17:21 not out but by p' and fasting.
21:13 shall be called the house of p'; but
22 whatsoever ye shall ask in p',
23:14 and for a pretence make long p':
M'r 9:29 by nothing, but by p' and fasting.
11:17 called of all nations the house of p'?
Lu 1:13 not, Zacharias: for thy p' is heard;
6:12 continued all night in p' to God.
19:46 My house is the house of p': but ye
22:45 when he rose up from p', and was
Ac 1:14 one accord in p' and supplication,
3: 1 the hour of p', being the ninth hour.
6: 4 will give ourselves continually to p',
10:31 And said, Cornelius, thy p' is heard,
12: 5 but p' was made without ceasing of
16:13 where p' was wont to be made;
16 as we went to p', a certain damsel
Ro 10: 1 desire and p' to God for Israel is,
12:12 continuing instant in p';
1Co 7: 5 give yourselves to fasting and p';
2Co 1:11 also helping together by p' for us,
9:14 by their p' for you, which long after
Eph 6:18 Praying always with all p' and
Ph'p 1: 4 Always in every p' of mine for you
19 to my salvation through your p',
4: 6 every thing by p' and supplication
Col 4: 2 Continue in p', and watch in the
1Ti 4: 5 sanctified by...word of God and p'.
Jas 5:15 the p' of faith shall save the sick,
16 fervent p' of a righteous man
1Pe 4: 7 therefore sober, and watch unto p'

prayers
Ps 72:20 p' of David the son of Jesse are
Isa 1:15 when ye make many p', I will not
M'r 12:40 and for a pretence make long p':
Lu 2:37 with fastings and p' night and day.
5:33 of John fast often, and make p',
20:47 and for a shew make long p':
Ac 2:42 and in breaking of bread, and in p'.
10: 4 Thy p' and thine alms are come up
Ro 1: 9 mention of you always in my p';
15:30 with me in your p' to God for me;
Eph 1:16 making mention of you in my p';
Col 4:12 labouring fervently for you in p',
1Th 1: 2 making mention of you in our p';
1Ti 2: 1 supplications, p', intercessions, and
5: 5 continueth in supplications and p'
2Ti 1: 3 have remembrance of thee in my p'
Ph'm 4 mention of thee always in my p',
22 through your p' I shall be given
Heb 5: 7 he had offered up p'...supplications
1Pe 3: 7 life; that your p' be not hindered.
12 and his ears are open unto their p':
Re 5: 8 odours, which are the p' of saints.
8: 3 offer it with the p' of all saints upon
4 came with the p' of the saints,

prayest
M't 6: 5 when thou p', thou shalt not be as
6 when thou p', enter into thy closet,

prayeth
1Ki 8:28 thy servant p' before thee to day:
2Ch 6:19 which thy servant p' before thee:
20 thy servant p' toward this place.
Isa 44:17 and worshippeth it, and p' unto it,
Ac 9:11 Saul, of Tarsus: for, behold, he p',
1Co 11: 5 every woman that p' or prophesieth
14:14 my spirit p', but my understanding

praying
1Sa 1:12 she continued p' before the Lord,
26 stood by thee here, p' unto the Lord.
1Ki 8:54 Solomon had made an end of p' all
2Ch 7: 1 Solomon had made an end of p',
Da 6:11 and found Daniel p' and making
9:20 And whiles I was speaking, and p',
M'r 11:25 And when ye stand p', forgive, if ye
Lu 1:10 people were p' without at the time
3:21 Jesus also being baptized, and p',
9:18 it came to pass, as he was alone p',
11: 1 as he was p' in a certain place,
Ac 11: 5 I was in the city of Joppa p': and in
12:12 many were gathered together p'.
1Co 11: 4 Every man p' or prophesying,
2Co 8: 4 P' us with much intreaty that we
Eph 6:18 P' always with all prayer and
Col 1: 3 Lord Jesus Christ, p' always for you,
Col 4: 3 p' also for us, that God would open
1Th 3:10 Night and day p' exceedingly that
Jude 20 holy faith, p' in the Holy Ghost,

preach See also PREACHED; PREACHEST; PREACHETH; PREACHING.
Ne 6: 7 prophets to p' of thee at Jerusalem,
Isa 61: 1 anointed me to p' good tidings
Jon 3: 2 p' unto it the preaching that I bid
M't 4:17 From that time Jesus began to p',
10: 7 as ye go, p', saying, The kingdom of
27 ear, that p' ye upon the housetops.
11: 1 to teach and to p' in their cities.
M'r 1: 4 p' the baptism of repentance for the
38 next towns, that I may p' there also:
3:14 that he might send them forth to p',
16:15 and p' the gospel to every creature.
Lu 4:18 me to p' the gospel to the poor;
18 to p' deliverance to the captives,
19 p' the acceptable year of the Lord.
43 I must p' the kingdom of God to
9: 2 he sent them to p' the kingdom of
60 thou and p' the kingdom of God.
Ac 5:42 not to teach and p' Jesus Christ.
10:42 he commanded us to p' unto the
14:15 and p' unto you that ye should turn
15:21 hath in every city them that p' him.
16: 6 Holy Ghost to p' the word in Asia,
10 us for to p' the gospel unto them.
17: 3 this Jesus, whom I p' unto you, is
Ro 1:15 I am ready to p' the gospel to you
10: 8 is, the word of faith, which we p';
15 shall they p', except they be sent?
15 of them that p' the gospel of peace,
15:20 so have I strived to p' the gospel,
1Co 1:17 not to baptize, but to p' the gospel:
23 But we p' Christ crucified, unto the
9:14 they which p' the gospel should
16 For though I p' the gospel, I have
16 woe is unto me, if I p' not the gospel!
18 when I p' the gospel, I may make
15:11 they, so we p', and so ye believed.
2Co 2:12 I came to Troas to p' Christ's gospel,
4: 5 For we p' not ourselves, but Christ
10:16 p' the gospel in the regions beyond
Ga 1: 8 p' any other gospel unto you than
9 man p' any other gospel unto you
16 I might p' him among the heathen;
2: 2 which I p' among the Gentiles,
5:11 if I yet p' circumcision, why do I
Eph 3: 8 I should p' among the Gentiles the
Ph'p 1:15 Some indeed p' Christ even of envy
16 The one p' Christ of contention,
Col 1:28 we p', warning every man, Whom
2Ti 4: 2 P' the word; be instant in season,
Re 14: 6 to p' unto them that dwell on the

preached
Ps 40: 9 have p' righteousness in the great
M't 11: 5 the poor have the gospel p' to them.
24:14 be p' in all the world for a witness
26:13 this gospel shall be p' in the whole
M'r 1: 7 And p', saying, There cometh one
39 And he p' in their synagogues
2: 2 and he p' the word unto them.
6:12 and p' that men should repent.
14: 9 this gospel shall be p' throughout
16:20 they went forth, and p' every where.
Lu 3:18 exhortation p' he unto the people.
4:44 And he p' in the synagogues of
7:22 raised, to the poor the gospel is p'.
16:16 that time the kingdom of God is p',
20: 1 in the temple, and p' the gospel,
24:47 should be p' in his name among all
Ac 3:20 which before was p' unto you:
4: 2 p' through Jesus the resurrection
8: 5 Samaria, and p' Christ unto them.
25 testified and p' the word of the
25 p' the gospel in many villages of
35 scripture, and p' unto him Jesus.
40 he p' in all the cities, till he came
9:20 he p' Christ in the synagogues,
27 how he had p' boldly at Damascus
10:37 after the baptism which John p';
13: 5 they p' the word of God in the
24 John had first p' before his coming
38 p' unto you the forgiveness of sins:
42 be p' to them the next sabbath.
14: 7 And there they p' the gospel.
21 they had p' the gospel to that city,
25 they had p' the word in Perga,
15:36 where we have p' the word of the
17:13 that the word of God was p' of Paul
18 because he p' unto them Jesus,
20: 7 Paul p' unto them, ready to depart
Ro 15:19 have fully p' the gospel of Christ.
1Co 9:27 when I have p' to others, I myself
15: 1 you the gospel which I p' unto you,
2 keep in memory what I p' unto you,
12 if Christ be p' that he rose from the
2Co 1:19 who was p' among you by us, even
11: 4 Jesus, whom we have not p',
7 I have p' to you the gospel of God
Ga 1: 8 that which we have p' unto you,
11 the gospel which was p' of me is not
3: 8 p' before the gospel unto Abraham,
4:13 I p' the gospel unto you at the
Eph 2:17 came and p' peace to you which
Ph'p 1:18 pretence, or in truth, Christ is p';
Col 1:23 which was p' to every creature
1Th 2: 9 we p' unto you the gospel of God.
1Ti 3:16 p' unto the Gentiles, believed on in
Heb 4: 2 For unto us was the gospel p', as
2 but the word p' did not profit them,
6 and they to whom it was first p'.
1Pe 1:12 them that have p' the gospel unto
25 which by the gospel is p' unto you.

1Pe 3:19 and p· unto the spirits in prison;
4: 6 for this cause was the gospel p·

preacher
Ec 1: 1 words of the P·, the son of David,
2 Vanity of vanities, saith the P·,
12 I the P· was king over Israel in
7:27 this have I found, saith the p·,
12: 8 Vanity of vanities, saith the p·; all
9 because the p· was wise, he still
10 p· sought to find out acceptable
Ro 10:14 how shall they hear without a p·?
1Ti 2: 7 I am ordained a p·, and an apostle,
2Ti 1:11 I am appointed a p·, and an apostle,
2Pe 2: 5 eighth person, a p· of righteousness,

preachest
Ro 2:21 that p· a man should not steal,

preacheth
Ac 19:13 you by Jesus whom Paul p·.
2Co 11: 4 if he that cometh p· another Jesus,
Ga 1:23 now p· the faith which once he

preaching
Jon 3: 2 unto it the p· that I bid thee.
M't 3: 1 p· in the wilderness of Judæa,
4:23 and p· the gospel of the kingdom,
9:35 and p· the gospel of the kingdom,
12:41 they repented at the p· of Jonas;
M'r 1:14 p· the gospel of the kingdom of
Lu 3: 3 p· the baptism of repentance for
8: 1 p· and shewing the glad tidings of
9: 6 p· the gospel, and healing every
11:32 they repented at the p· of Jonas;
Ac 8: 4 went every where p· the word.
12 believed Philip p· the things
10:36 Israel, p· peace by Jesus Christ:
11:19 p· the word to none but unto the
20 the Grecians, p· the Lord Jesus.
15:35 and p· the word of the Lord, with
20: 9 as Paul was long p·, he sunk down
25 have gone p· the kingdom of God,
28:31 P· the kingdom of God, and
Ro 16:25 gospel, and the p· of Jesus Christ,
1Co 1:18 For the p· of the cross is to them
21 by the foolishness of p· to save
2: 4 my p· was not with enticing words
15:14 be not risen, then is our p· vain,
2Co 10:14 to you also in p· the gospel of Christ:
2Ti 4:17 me the p· might be fully known,
Tit 1: 3 manifested his word through p·,

precept See also PRECEPTS.
Isa 28:10 p· must be upon p·, p· upon p·;
13 unto them p· upon p·, p· upon p·;
29:13 me is taught by the p· of men:
M'r 10: 5 your heart he wrote you this p·.
Heb 9:19 Moses had spoken every p· to all

precepts
Ne 9:14 and commandedst them p·,
Ps 119: 4 commanded us to keep thy p·
15 I will meditate in thy p·, and have
27 to understand the way of thy p·:
40 I have longed after thy p·: quicken
45 walk at liberty: for I seek thy p·.
56 This I had, because I kept thy p·.
63 thee, and of them that keep thy p·.
69 keep thy p· with my whole heart.
78 cause: but I will meditate in thy p·.
87 earth; but I forsook not thy p·.
93 I will never forget thy p·: for with
94 save me; for I have sought thy p·.
100 the ancients, because I keep thy p·.
104 thy p· I get understanding:
110 for me: yet I erred not from thy p·.
128 I esteem all thy p· concerning all
134 of man: so will I keep thy p·.
141 despised: yet do not I forget thy p·.
159 Consider how I love thy p·:
168 kept thy p· and thy testimonies:
173 help me; for I have chosen thy p·.
Jer 35:18 and kept all his p·, and done
Da 9: 5 even by departing from thy p· and

precious
Ge 24:53 and to her mother p· things.
De 33:13 for the p· things of heaven, for
14 p· fruits brought forth by the sun,
14 p· things put forth by the moon,
15 for the p· things of the lasting hills,
16 for the p· things of the earth and
1Sa 3: 1 of the Lord was p· in those days;
26:21 my soul was p· in thine eyes this
2Sa 12:30 a talent of gold with the p· stones:
1Ki 10: 2 and very much gold, and p· stones:
10 very great store, and p· stones:
11 plenty of almug trees, and p· stones.
2Ki 1:13 thy servants, be p· in thy sight.
14 let my life now be p· in thy sight.
20:13 all the house of his p· things,
13 the spices, and the p· ointment,
1Ch 20: 2 and there were p· stones in it;
29: 2 all manner of p· stones, and marble
8 they with whom p· stones were found
2Ch 3: 6 garnished the house with p· stones
9: 1 gold in abundance, and p· stones:
9 great abundance, and p· stones:
10 brought algum trees and p· stones.
20:25 the dead bodies, and p· jewels,
21: 3 and of gold, and of p· things, with
32:27 and for gold, and for p· stones,
Ezr 1: 6 with beasts, and with p· things,
8:27 vessels of fine copper, p· as gold.
Job 28:10 and his eyes seeth every p· thing.
16 gold of Ophir, with the p· onyx,
Ps 49: 8 the redemption of their soul is p·,
72:14 and p· shall their blood be in his
116:15 P· in the sight of the Lord is the
126: 6 and weepeth, bearing p· seed,
133: 2 It is like the p· ointment upon the
139:17 How p· also are thy thoughts
Pr 1:13 We shall find all p· substance, we
3:15 She is more p· than rubies: and all
6:26 adulteress will hunt for the p· life.
12:27 substance of a diligent man is p·.
17: 8 A gift is as a p· stone in the eyes
20:15 lips of knowledge are a p· jewel.
24: 4 with all p· and pleasant riches.
Ec 7: 1 name is better than p· ointment;
Isa 13:12 a man more p· than fine gold;
28:16 a tried stone, a p· corner stone,
39: 2 them the house of his p· things,
2 the spices, and the p· ointment,
43: 4 Since thou wast p· in my sight,
Jer 15:19 take forth the p· from the vile,
20: 5 and all the p· things thereof, and
La 4: 2 The p· sons of Zion, comparable to
Eze 22:25 taken the treasure and p· things;
27:20 Dedan...thy merchant in p· clothes
22 and with all p· stones, and gold.
28:13 every p· stone was thy covering,
Da 11: 8 p· vessels of silver and of gold;
38 and silver, and with p· stones,
43 over all the p· things of Egypt:
M't 26: 7 alabaster box of very p· ointment,
M'r 14: 3 of ointment of spikenard very p·;
1Co 3:12 silver, p· stones, wood, hay,
Jas 5: 7 waiteth for the p· fruit of the earth,
1Pe 1: 7 more p· than of gold that perisheth,
19 But with the p· blood of Christ, as
2: 4 of men, but chosen of God, and p·,
6 Sion a chief corner stone, elect, p·:
7 therefore which believe he is p·:
2Pe 1: 1 that have obtained like p· faith
4 exceeding great and p· promises:
Re 17: 4 decked with gold and p· stones and
18:12 silver, and p· stones, and of pearls,
12 all manner vessels of most p· wood,
16 decked with gold, and p· stones, and
21:11 light was like unto a stone most p·,
19 with all manner of p· stones.

predestinate See also PREDESTINATED.
Ro 8:29 also did p· to be conformed to the
30 whom he did p·, them he also

predestinated
Eph 1: 5 Having p· us unto the adoption
11 being p· according to the purpose

preeminence
Ec 3:19 a man hath no p· above a beast:
Col 1:18 all things he might have the p·.
3Jo 9 loveth to have the p· among them,

prefer See also PREFERRED; PREFERRING.
Ps 137: 6 If I p· not Jerusalem above my

preferred
Es 2: 9 he p· her and her maids unto the
Da 6: 3 this Daniel was p· above the
Joh 1:15 cometh after me is p· before me:
27 coming after me is p· before me,
30 a man which is p· before me:

preferring
Ro 12:10 love; in honour p· one another;
1Ti 5:21 without p· one before another,

premeditate
M'r 13:11 ye shall speak, neither do ye p·:

preparation See also PREPARATIONS.
1Ch 22: 5 will therefore now make p· for it.
Na 2: 3 flaming torches in the day of his p·,
M't 27:62 that followed the day of the p·,
M'r 15:42 was come, because it was the p·,
Lu 23:54 And that day was the p·, and the
Joh 19:14 And it was the p· of the passover,
31 because it was the p·, that the
42 because of the Jews' p· day;
Eph 6:15 with the p· of the gospel of peace;

preparations
Pr 16: 1 The p· of the heart in man, and

prepare See also PREPARED; PREPAREST; PREPARETH; PREPARING.
Ex 15: 2 God, and I will p· him an habitation:
16: 5 they shall p· that which they bring
Nu 15: 5 a drink offering shalt thou p· with
6 thou shalt p· for a meat offering
12 to the number that ye shall p·, so
23: 1 p· me here seven oxen and seven
29 and p· me here seven bullocks and
De 19: 3 Thou shalt p· thee a way, and
Jos 1:11 people, saying, P· you victuals;
22:26 Let us now p· to build us an altar,
1Sa 7: 3 p· your hearts unto the Lord, and
23:22 I pray you, p· ye, and know and
1Ki 18:44 Ahab, P· thy chariot, and get thee
1Ch 9:32 shewbread, to p· it every sabbath.
29:18 and p· their heart unto thee: and
2Ch 2: 9 to p· me timber in abundance:
31:11 to p· chambers in the house of the
35: 4 p· yourselves by the houses of your
6 yourselves, and p· your brethren,
Es 5: 8 banquet that I shall p· for them,
Job 8: 8 p· thyself to the search of their
11:13 If thou p· thine heart, and stretch
27:16 dust, and p· raiment as the clay;
17 He may p· it, but the just shall put
Ps 10:17 thou wilt p· their heart, thou wilt
59: 4 p· themselves without my fault:
61: 7 O p· mercy and truth, which may
107:36 they may p· a city for habitation;
Pr 24:27 P· thy work without, and make it
30:25 they p· their meat in the summer;
Isa 14:21 P· slaughter for his children for
21: 5 P· the table, watch in the
40: 3 P· ye the way of the Lord, make
20 to p· a graven image, that shall
57:14 ye up, p· the way, take up the
62:10 p· ye the way of the people; cast
65:11 that p· a table for that troop, and
Jer 6: 4 P· ye war against her; arise, and
12: 3 p· them for the day of slaughter.
22: 7 I will p· destroyers against thee,
46:14 Stand fast, and p· thee; for the
51:12 the watchmen, p· the ambushes:
27 p· the nations against her, call
28 P· against her the nations with the
Eze 4:15 thou shalt p· thy bread therewith.
12: 3 man, p· thee stuff for removing,
35: 6 I will p· thee unto blood, and blood
38: 7 and p· for thyself, thou, and all thy
43:25 thou p· every day a goat for a sin
25 they shall also p· a young bullock,
45:17 he shall p· the sin offering, and the
22 day shall the prince p· for himself
23 p· a burnt offering to the Lord,
24 shall p· a meat offering of an ephah
46: 2 priests shall p· his burnt offering
7 And he shall p· a meat offering, an
12 shall p· a voluntary burnt offering
12 he shall p· his burnt offering and
13 Thou shalt daily p· a burnt offering
13 thou shalt p· it every morning.
14 thou shalt p· a meat offering for it
15 Thus shall they p· the lamb, and
Joe 3: 9 P· war, wake up the mighty men,
Am 4:12 thee, p· to meet thy God, O Israel.
Mic 3: 5 they even p· war against him.
Mal 3: 1 and he shall p· the way before me:
M't 3: 3 P· ye the way of the Lord, make
11:10 which shall p· thy way before thee.
26:17 p· for thee to eat the passover?
M'r 1: 2 which shall p· thy way before thee.
3 P· ye the way of the Lord, make
14:12 Where wilt thou that we go and p·
Lu 1:76 face of the Lord to p· his ways;
3: 4 P· ye the way of the Lord, make
7:27 which shall p· thy way before thee.
22: 8 Go and p· us the passover, that we
9 him, Where wilt thou that we p·?
Joh 14: 2 told you. I go to p· a place for you.
3 And if I go and p· a place for you,
1Co 14: 8 who shall p· himself to the battle?
Ph'm 22 p· me also a lodging: for I trust

prepared See also PREPAREDST; UNPREPARED.
Ge 24:31 I have p· the house, and room for
27:17 and the bread, which she had p·,
Ex 12:39 neither had they p· for themselves
23:20 into the place which I have p·.
Nu 21:27 the city of Sihon be built and p·:
23: 4 unto him, I have p· seven altars,
Jos 4: 4 he had p· of the children of Israel,
13 forty thousand p· for war passed
2Sa 15: 1 Absalom p· him chariots and
1Ki 1: 5 he p· him chariots and horsemen,
5:18 so they p· timber and stones to
6:19 the oracle he p· in the house within,
2Ki 6:23 he p· great provision for them:
1Ch 12:39 for their brethren had p· for them.
15: 1 and p· a place for the ark of God,
3 his place, which he had p· for it.
12 unto the place that I have p· for it.
22: 3 And David p· iron in abundance for
5 So David p· abundantly before his
14 I have p· for the house of the Lord
14 timber also and stone have I p·;
29: 2 Now I have p· with all my might for
3 all that I have p· for the holy house,
16 we have p· to build thee an house
2Ch 1: 4 the place which David had p· for it:
3: 1 in the place that David had p· in
8:16 Now all the work of Solomon was p·
12:14 he p· not his heart to seek the Lord.
16:14 spices p· by the apothecaries' art:
17:18 thousand ready p· for the war.
19: 3 hast p· thine heart to seek God.
20:33 people had not p· their hearts unto
26:14 Uzziah p· for them throughout all
27: 6 p· his ways before the Lord his God.
29:19 his transgression, have we p· and
36 people, that God had p· the people:
31:11 of the Lord; and they p· them,
35:10 the service was p·, and the priests
14 the Levites p· for themselves,
15 brethren the Levites p· for them.
16 So all the service of the Lord was p·
20 this when Josiah had p· the temple,
Ezr 7:10 Ezra had p· his heart to seek...law
Ne 5:18 was p· for me daily was one ox
18 also the fowls were p· for me, and
8:10 unto them for whom nothing is p·:
13: 5 had p· for him a great chamber,
Es 5: 4 the banquet that I have p· for him.
5 to the banquet that Esther had p·.
12 banquet that she had p· but myself;
6: 4 the gallows that he had p· for him.
14 the banquet that Esther had p·.
7:10 the gallows that he had p· for
Job 28:27 it; he p· it, yea, and searched it out.
29: 7 city, when I p· my seat in the street!
Ps 7:13 also p· for him the instruments
9: 7 he hath p· his throne for judgment.
57: 6 They have p· a net for my steps;
68:10 God, hast p· thy goodness for
74:16 thou hast p· the light and the sun.
103:19 hath p· his throne in the heavens;
Pr 8:27 When he p· the heavens, I was

Pr 19:29 Judgments are p' for scorners, and
21:31 The horse is p' against the day of
Isa 30:33 of old; yea, for the king it is p';
64: 4 p' for him that waiteth for him.
Eze 23:41 bed, and a table p' before it,
28:13 thy pipes was p' in thee in the day
38: 7 Be thou p', and prepare for thyself,
Da 2: 9 have p' lying and corrupt words
Ho 2: 8 and gold, which they p' for Baal.
6: 3 going forth is p' as the morning;
Jon 1:17 p' a great fish to swallow up
4: 6 And the Lord God p' a gourd, and
7 God p' a worm when the morning
8 that God p' a vehement east wind;
Na 2: 5 and the defence shall be p'.
Zep 1: 7 the Lord hath p' a sacrifice, he hath
M't 20:23 for whom it is p' of my Father.
22: 4 Behold, I have p' my dinner: my
25:34 inherit the kingdom p' for you from
41 fire, p' for the devil and his angels:
M'r 10:40 be given to them for whom it is p'.
14:15 upper room furnished and p':
Lu 1:17 ready a people p' for the Lord.
2:31 p' before the face of all people;
12:47 his lord's will, and p' not himself,
23:56 and p' spices and ointments;
24: 1 the spices which they had p', and
Ro 9:23 which he had afore p' unto glory,
1Co 2: 9 hath p' for them that love him.
2Ti 2:21 use, and p' unto every good work.
Heb 10: 5 not, but a body hast thou p' me:
11: 7 p' an ark to the saving of his house;
16 God: for he hath p' for them a city.
Re 8: 6 trumpets p' themselves to sound.
9: 7 like unto horses p' unto battle;
15 which were p' for an hour, and a
12: 6 where she hath a place p' of God,
16:12 the kings of the east might be p'.
21: 2 p' as a bride adorned for her

preparedst
Ps 80: 9 Thou p' room before it, and didst

preparest
Nu 15: 8 thou p' a bullock for a burnt
Ps 23: 5 Thou p' a table before me in the
65: 9 thou p' them corn, when thou

prepareth
2Ch 30:19 That p' his heart to seek God, the
Job 15:35 vanity, and their belly p' deceit.
Ps 147: 8 who p' rain for the earth, who

preparing
Ne 13: 7 in p' him a chamber in the courts
1Pe 3:20 while the ark was a p', wherein

presbytery
1Ti 4:14 laying on of the hands of the p'.

prescribed
Isa 10: 1 grievousness which they have p';

prescribing
Ezr 7:22 and salt without p' how much.

presence^
Ge 3: 8 from the p' of the Lord God
4:16 Cain went out from the p' of the
16:12 dwell in the p' of all his brethren.
23:11 in the p' of the sons of my people
18 in the p' of the children of Heth,
25:18 died in the p' of all his brethren.
27:30 out from the p' of Isaac his father,
41:46 went out from the p' of Pharaoh,
45: 3 for they were troubled at his p'.
47:15 for why should we die in thy p'?
Ex 10:11 driven out from Pharaoh's p'.
33:14 My p' shall go with thee, and I
15 If thy p' go not with me, carry us
35:20 departed from the p' of Moses.
Le 22: 3 soul shall be cut off from my p':
Nu 20: 6 Moses and Aaron went from the p'
De 25: 9 unto him in the p' of the elders,
Jos 4:11 the priests, in the p' of the people.
8:32 in the p' of the children of Israel.
1Sa 18:11 David avoided out of his p' twice.
19: 7 he was in his p', as in times past.
10 he slipped away out of Saul's p',
21:15 to play the mad man in my p'?
2Sa 16:19 I not serve in the p' of his son?
19 as I have served in thy father's p',
19 so will I be in thy p'.
24: 4 went out from the p' of the king, to
1Ki 1:28 And she came into the king's p',
8:22 in the p' of all the congregation
12: 2 fled from the p' of king Solomon,
21:13 against Naboth in the p' of the
2Ki 3:14 that I regard the p' of Jehoshaphat
5:27 his p' a leper as white as snow.
13:23 cast he them from his p' as yet.
24:20 he had cast them out from his p',
25:19 of them that were in the king's p',
1Ch 16:27 Glory and honour are in his p';
33 wood sing out at the p' of the Lord,
24:31 Aaron in the p' of David the king,
2Ch 6:12 the p' of all the congregation of
9:23 earth sought the p' of Solomon,
10: 2 from the p' of Solomon the king,
20: 9 and in thy p', (for thy name is in
34: 4 down the altars of Baalim in his p';
Ne 2: 1 not been beforetime sad in his p'.
Es 1:10 in the p' of Ahasuerus the king.
8:15 went out from the p' of the king
Job 1:12 went forth from the p' of the Lord.
2: 7 Satan forth from the p' of the Lord.
23:15 Therefore am I troubled at his p':
Ps 9: 3 they shall fall and perish at thy p'.
Ps 16:11 of life: in thy p' is fulness of joy;
17: 2 sentence come forth from thy p';
23: 5 me in the p' of mine enemies:
31:20 hide them in the secret of thy p'
51:11 Cast me not away from thy p'; and
68: 2 the wicked perish at the p' of God.
8 also dropped at the p' of God:
8 itself was moved at the p' of God,
95: 2 before his p' with thanksgiving,
97: 5 like wax at the p' of the Lord,
5 p' of the Lord of the whole earth.
100: 2 come before his p' with singing.
114: 7 thou earth, at the p' of the Lord,
7 at the p' of the God of Jacob;
116:14 Lord now in the p' of all his people.
139: 7 whither shall I flee from thy p'?
140:13 the upright shall dwell in thy p'.
Pr 14: 7 Go from the p' of a foolish man,
17:18 surety in the p' of his friend.
25: 6 forth thyself in the p' of the king,
7 be put lower in the p' of the prince
Isa 1: 7 strangers devour it in your p', and
19: 1 of Egypt shall be moved at his p',
63: 9 and the angel of his p' saved them:
64: 1 mountains might flow...at thy p',
2 the nations may tremble at thy p'!
3 mountains flowed down at thy p'.
Jer 4:26 broken down at the p' of the Lord,
5:22 will ye not tremble at my p', which
23:39 fathers, and cast you out of my p':
28: 1 the p' of the priests and of all the
5 Hananiah in the p' of the priests,
5 and in the p' of all the people that
11 spake in the p' of all the people,
32:12 and in the p' of the witnesses that
52: 3 he had cast them out from his p',
Eze 38:20 of the earth, shall shake at my p',
Da 2:27 answered in the p' of the king,
Jon 1: 3 Tarshish from the p' of the Lord,
3 Tarshish from the p' of the Lord.
10 he fled from the p' of the Lord,
Na 1: 5 and the earth is burned at his p',
Zep 1: 7 thy peace at the p' of the Lord God:
Lu 1:19 that stand in the p' of God;
13:26 We have eaten and drunk in thy p',
14:10 in the p' of them that sit at meat
15:10 there is joy in the p' of the angels
Joh 20:30 did Jesus in the p' of his disciples,
Ac 3:13 and denied him in the p' of Pilate,
16 soundness in the p' of you all.
19 come from the p' of the Lord;
5:41 departed from the p' of the council,
27:35 thanks to God in the p' of them
1Co 1:29 That no flesh should glory in his p'.
2Co 10: 1 who in p' am base among you,
10 but his bodily p' is weak, and his
Ph'p 2:12 always obeyed, not as in my p' only,
1Th 2:17 from you for a short time in p',
19 in the p' of our Lord Jesus Christ
2Th 1: 9 from the p' of the Lord, and from
Heb 9:24 to appear in the p' of God for us:
Jude 24 faultless before the p' of his glory
Re 14:10 in the p' of the holy angels, and in
10 angels, and in the p' of the Lamb:

present^ See also PRESENTED; PRESENTING; PRESENTS.
Ge 32:13 came to his hand a p' for Esau
18 it is a p' sent unto my lord Esau:
20 I will appease him with the p' that
21 So went the p' over before him: and
33:10 then receive my p' at my hand: for
43:11 carry down the man a p', a little
15 the men took that p', and they took
25 made ready the p' against Joseph
26 brought him the p' which was in
Ex 34: 2 Sinai, and p' thyself there to me
Lev 14:11 p' the man that is to be made
16: 7 goats, and p' them before the Lord
27: 8 shall p' himself before the priest,
11 shall p' the beast before the priest:
Nu 3: 6 p' them before Aaron the priest,
De 31:14 p' yourselves in the tabernacle of
J'g 3:15 sent a p' unto Eglon the king of
17 he brought the p' unto Eglon king
18 he had made an end to offer the p',
18 away the people that bare the p'.
6:18 bring forth my p', and set it before
1Sa 9: 7 is not a p' to bring to the man of
10:19 p' yourselves before the Lord by
13:15 the people that were p' with him,
16 the people that were p' with them,
21: 3 in mine hand, or what there is p'.
30:26 a p' for you of the spoil of the
2Sa 20: 4 three days, and be thou here p'.
1Ki 9:16 a p' unto his daughter, Solomon's
10:25 they brought every man his p',
15:19 unto thee a p' of silver and gold;
20:27 were numbered, and were all p',
2Ki 8: 8 Take a p' in thine hand, and go,
9 took a p' with him, even of every
16: 8 it for a p' to the king of Assyria.
17: 4 no p' to the king of Assyria, as he
18:31 an agreement with me by a p',
20:12 letters and a p' unto Hezekiah:
1Ch 29:17 joy thy people, which are p' here,
2Ch 5:11 all the priests...p' were sanctified,
9:24 they brought every man his p',
29:29 all that were p' with him bowed
30:21 that were p' at Jerusalem kept the
31: 1 all Israel that were p' went out to
34:32 all that were p' in Jerusalem and
33 all that were p' in Israel to serve,
35: 7 for all that were p', to the number
17 that were p' kept the passover at
18 all Judah and Israel that were p',
Ezr 8:25 all Israel there p', had offered:
Es 1: 5 the people that were p' in Shushan
4:16 all the Jews that are p' in Shushan,
Job 1: 6 to p' themselves before the Lord,
2: 1 to p' themselves before the Lord,
1 them to p' himself before the Lord.
Ps 46: 1 strength, a very p' help in trouble.
Isa 18: 7 the p' be brought unto the Lord of
36:16 an agreement with me by a p',
39: 1 sent letters and a p' to Hezekiah:
Jer 36: 7 p' their supplication before the
42: 9 ye sent me to p' your supplication
Eze 27:15 for a p' horns of ivory and ebony.
Da 9:18 p' our supplications before thee
Ho 10: 6 Assyria for a p' to king Jareb:
Lu 2:22 Jerusalem, to p' him to the Lord;
5:17 of the Lord was p' to heal them.
13: 1 There were p' at that season some
Joh 14:25 unto you, being yet p' with you.
Ac 10:33 are we all here p' before God, to
21:18 James; and all the elders were p'.
25:24 all men which are here p' with us,
28: 2 because of the p' rain, and because
Ro 7:18 for to will is p' with me; but how
21 would do good, evil is p' with me.
8:18 sufferings of this p' time are not
38 nor things p', nor things to come,
11: 5 then at this p' time also there is a
12: 1 ye p' your bodies a living sacrifice,
1Co 3:22 or things p', or things to come;
4:11 unto this p' hour we both hunger,
5: 3 as absent in body, but p' in spirit,
3 have judged...as though I were p',
7:26 that this is good for the p' distress,
15: 6 greater part remain unto this p',
2Co 4:14 by Jesus, and shall p' us with you.
5: 8 body, and to be p' with the Lord.
9 that, whether p' or absent, we may
10: 2 when I am p' with that confidence,
11 we be also in deed when we are p'.
11: 2 I may p' you as a chaste virgin to
9 And when I was p' with you, and
13: 2 as if I were p', the second time;
10 being p' I should use sharpness,
Ga 1: 4 deliver us from this p' evil world,
4:18 not only when I am p' with you.
20 I desire to be p' with you now, and
Eph 5:27 p' it to himself a glorious church,
Col 1:22 p' you holy and unblameable and
28 may p' every man perfect in Christ
2Ti 4:10 me, having loved this p' world,
Tit 2:12 and godly, in this p' world;
Heb 9: 9 was a figure for the time then p',
12:11 no chastening for the p' seemeth
2Pe 1:12 and be established in the p' truth.
Jude 24 and to p' you faultless before the

presented
Ge 46:29 Goshen, and p' himself unto him;
47: 2 men, and p' them unto Pharaoh.
Le 2: 8 when it is p' unto the priest, he
7:35 p' them to minister unto the Lord
9:12 sons p' unto him the blood,
13 they p' the burnt offering unto him,
18 sons p' unto him the blood,
16:10 be the scapegoat, shall be p' alive
De 31:14 p' themselves in the tabernacle of
Jos 24: 1 and they p' themselves before God.
J'g 6:19 unto him under the oak, and p' it.
20: 2 p' themselves in the assembly of
1Sa 17:16 evening, and p' himself forty days.
Jer 38:26 I p' my supplication before the
Eze 20:28 they p' the provocation of their
M't 2:11 treasures, they p' unto him gifts;
Ac 9:41 saints and widows, p' her alive.
23:33 governor, p' Paul also before him.

presenting
Da 9:20 p' my supplication before the Lord

presently
1Sa 2:16 Let them not fail to burn the fat p',
Pr 12:16 A fool's wrath is p' known: but a
M't 21:19 And p' the fig tree withered away.
26:53 shall p' give me more than twelve
Ph'p 2:23 Him therefore I hope to send p',

presents
1Sa 10:27 him, and brought him no p'.
1Ki 4:21 brought p', and served Solomon
2Ki 17: 3 his servant, and gave him p'.
2Ch 17: 5 Judah brought to Jehoshaphat p';
11 brought Jehoshaphat p', and
32:23 and p' to Hezekiah king of Judah:
Ps 68:29 shall kings bring p' unto thee.
72:10 and of the isles shall bring p':
76:11 bring p' unto him that ought to be
Mic 1:14 thou give p' to Moresheth-gath:

preserve See also PRESERVED; PRESERVEST; PRESERVETH.
Ge 19:32, 34 we may p' seed of our father.
45: 5 did send me before you to p' life.
7 to p' you a posterity in the earth,
De 6:24 that he might p' us alive, as it is
Ps 12: 7 p' them from this generation for
16: 1 P' me, O God: for in thee do I put
25:21 integrity and uprightness p' me;
32: 7 thou shalt p' me from trouble;
40:11 and thy truth continually p' me.
41: 2 The Lord will p' him, and keep
61: 7 and truth, which may p' him.
64: 1 p' my life from fear of the enemy.
79:11 p' thou those that are appointed to
86: 2 P' my soul; for I am holy: O thou
121: 7 The Lord shall p' thee from all evil:
7 he shall p' thy soul.
8 Lord shall p' thy going out and thy
140: 1 man: p' me from the violent man;

Ps 140: 4 wicked; p· me from the violent man;
Pr 2:11 Discretion shall p· thee,
4: 6 her not, and she shall p· thee:
14: 3 the lips of the wise shall p· them.
20:28 Mercy and truth p· the king: and
22:12 The eyes of the Lord p· knowledge.
Isa 31: 5 it; and passing over he will p· it.
49: 8 and I will p· thee, and give thee
Jer 49:11 children, I will p· them alive;
Lu 17:33 shall lose his life shall p· it.
2Ti 4:18 p· me unto his heavenly kingdom:

preserved
Ge 32:30 God face to face, and my life is p·.
Jos 24:17 p· us in all the way wherein we
1Sa 30:23 who hath p· us, and delivered the
2Sa 8: 6, 14 p· David whithersoever he
1Ch 18: 6, 13 p· David whithersoever he went.
Job 10:12 thy visitation hath p· my spirit.
29: 2 as in the days when God p· me;
Ps 37:28 they are p· for ever: but the seed
Isa 49: 6 and to restore the p· of Israel:
Ho 12:13 Egypt, and by a prophet was he p·.
M't 9:17 into new bottles, and both are p·.
Lu 5:38 into new bottles; and both are p·.
1Th 5:23 be p· blameless unto the coming
Jude 1 and p· in Jesus Christ, and called:

preserver
Job 7:20 I do unto thee, O thou p· of men?

preservest
Ne 9: 6 is therein, and thou p· them all;
Ps 36: 6 O Lord, thou p· man and beast.

preserveth
Job 36: 6 He p· not the life of the wicked:
Ps 31:23 for the Lord p· the faithful, and
97:10 he p· the souls of his saints; he
116: 6 The Lord p· the simple: I was
145:20 The Lord p· all them that love him:
146: 9 The Lord p· the strangers; he
Pr 2: 8 and p· the way of his saints.
16:17 he that keepeth his way p· his soul.

presidents
Da 6: 2 And over these three p·; of whom
3 preferred above the p· and princes,
4 the p· and princes sought to find
6 these p· and princes assembled
7 All the p· of the kingdom, the

press See also PRESSED; PRESSES; PRESSETH; PRESSFAT; OPPRESS; WINEPRESS.
Joe 3:13 for the p· is full, the fats overflow;
Hag 2:16 draw out fifty vessels out of the p·,
M'r 2: 4 not come nigh unto him for the p·,
5:27 came in the p· behind, and touched
30 him, turned him about in the p·,
Lu 8:19 could not come at him for the p·.
45 multitude throng thee and p· thee,
19: 3 could not for the p·, because he
Ph'p 3:14 I p· toward the mark for the prize

pressed See also OPPRESSED.
Ge 19: 3 And he p· upon them greatly; and
9 they p· sore upon the man, even
40:11 and p· them into Pharaoh's cup,
J'g 16:16 she p· him daily with her words,
2Sa 13:25 he p· him: howbeit he would not
27 But Absalom p· him, that he let
Es 8:14 p· on by the king's commandment.
Eze 23: 3 there were their breasts p·, and
Am 2:13 Behold, I am p· under you, as a
13 as a cart is p· that is full of sheaves.
M'r 3:10 they p· upon him for to touch him,
Lu 5: 1 people p· upon him to hear the
6:38 good measure, p· down, and shaken
Ac 18: 5 Paul was p· in the spirit, and
2Co 1: 8 that we were p· out of measure,

presses See also WINEPRESSES.
Ne 13:15 treading wine p· on the sabbath,
Pr 3:10 p· shall burst out with new wine.
Isa 16:10 shall tread out no wine in their p·;

presseth See also OPPRESSETH.
Ps 38: 2 in me, and thy hand p· me sore.
Lu 16:16 preached, and every man p· into it.

pressfat
Hag 2:16 one came to the p· for to draw

presume See also PRESUMED.
De 18:20 shall p· to speak a word in my
Es 7: 5 that durst p· in his heart to do so?

presumed
Nu 14:44 they p· to go up unto the hill top:

presumptuous
Ps 19:13 thy servant also from p· sins;
2Pe 2:10 P· are they, selfwilled, they are

presumptuously
Ex 21:14 man come p· upon his neighbour,
Nu 15:30 But the soul that doeth ought p·,
De 1:43 and went p· up into the hill.
17:12 And the man that will do p·, and
13 and fear, and do no more p·.
18:22 the prophet hath spoken it p·:

pretence
M't 23:14 and for a p· make long prayer:
M'r 12:40 for a p· make long prayers: these
Ph'p 1:18 whether in p·, or in truth, Christ is

Pretorium See PRÆTORIUM.

prevail See also PREVAILED; PREVAILEST; PREVAILETH.
Ge 7:20 cubits upward did the waters p·;
Nu 22: 6 peradventure I shall p·, that we
J'g 16: 5 what means we may p· against him,
1Sa 2: 9 for by strength shall no man p·.
1Sa 17: 9 but if I p· against him, and kill him,
26:25 great things, and also shalt still p·.
1Ki 22:22 shalt persuade him, and p· also:
2Ch 14:11 God; let not man p· against thee.
18:21 entice him, and thou shalt also p·:
Es 6:13 thou shalt not p· against him, but
Job 15:24 they shall p· against him, as a king
18: 9 the robber shall p· against him.
Ps 9:19 Arise, O Lord; let not man p·: let
12: 4 With our tongue will we p·; our
65: 3 Iniquities p· against me: as for our
Ec 4:12 if one p· against him, two shall
Isa 7: 1 it, but could not p· against it.
16:12 to pray; but he shall not p·.
42:13 he shall p· against his enemies.
47:12 to profit, if so be thou mayest p·.
Jer 1:19 but they shall not p· against thee;
5:22 themselves, yet can they not p·;
15:20 they shall not p· against thee: for I
20:10 enticed, and we shall p· against him,
11 stumble, and they shall not p·:
Da 11: 7 deal against them, and shall p·:
M't 16:18 gates of hell shall not p· against it.
27:24 Pilate saw...he could p· nothing,
Joh 12:19 Perceive ye how ye p· nothing?

prevailed
Ge 7:18 the waters p·, and were increased
19 the waters p· exceedingly upon the
24 And the waters p· upon the earth
30: 8 with my sister, and I have p·:
32:25 he saw that he p· not against him,
28 with God and with men, and hast p·.
47:20 because the famine p· over them:
49:26 blessings of thy father have p·
Ex 17:11 held up his hand, that Israel p·:
11 he let down his hand, Amalek p·.
J'g 1:35 the hand of the house of Joseph p·,
3:10 p· against Chushan-rishathaim.
4:24 and p· against Jabin the king of
6: 2 hand of Midian p· against Israel:
1Sa 17:50 So David p· over the Philistine
2Sa 11:23 Surely the men p· against us,
24: 4 the king's word p· against Joab.
1Ki 16:22 the people that followed Omri p·
2Ki 25: 3 the famine p· in the city, and there
1Ch 5: 2 For Judah p· above his brethren,
21: 4 the king's word p· against Joab.
2Ch 8: 3 to Hamath-zobah, and p· against it.
13:18 children of Judah p·, because they
27: 5 Ammonites, and p· against them.
Ps 13: 4 enemy say, I have p· against him;
129: 2 yet they have not p· against me.
Jer 20: 7 art stronger than I, and hast p·:
38:22 thee on, and have p· against thee:
La 1:16 desolate, because the enemy p·.
Da 7:21 the saints, and p· against them;
Ho 12: 4 had power over the angel, and p·:
Ob 7 deceived thee, and p· against thee;
Lu 23:23 them and of the chief priests p·.
Ac 19:16 p· against them, so that they fled
20 grew the word of God, and p·.
Re 5: 5 David hath p· to open the book,
12: 8 p· not; neither was their place

prevailest
Job 14:20 Thou p· for ever against him,

prevaileth
La 1:13 my bones, and it p· against them:

prevent See also PREVENTED; PREVENTEST.
Job 3:12 Why did the knees p· me? or why
Ps 59:10 The God of my mercy shall p· me:
79: 8 thy tender mercies speedily p· us;
88:13 morning shall my prayer p· thee.
119:148 Mine eyes p· the night watches,
Am 9:10 evil shall not overtake nor p· us.
1Th 4:15 shall not p· them which are asleep.

prevented
2Sa 22: 6 about; the snares of death p· me;
19 p· me in the day of my calamity:
Job 30:27 not: the days of affliction p· me.
41:11 Who hath p· me, that I should
Ps 18: 5 about: the snares of death p· me.
18 They p· me in the day of my
119:147 I p· the dawning of the morning,
Isa 21:14 p· with their bread him that fled.
M't 17:25 come into the house, Jesus p· him,

preventest
Ps 21: 3 thou p· him with the blessings

prey
Ge 49: 9 from the p·, my son, thou art gone
27 morning he shall devour the p·,
Nu 14: 3 and our children should be a p·?
31 ones, which ye said should be a p·,
23:24 not lie down until he eat of the p·,
31:11 took all the spoil, and all the p·,
12 brought the captives, and the p·,
26 Take the sum of the p· that was
27 And divide the p· into two parts;
32 the p· which the men of war had
De 1:39 ones, which ye said should be a p·,
2:35 we took for a p· unto ourselves,
3: 7 cities, we took for a p· to ourselves,
Jos 8: 2 ye take for a p· unto yourselves:
27 Israel took for a p· unto themselves,
11:14 Israel took for a p· unto themselves;
J'g 5:30 have they not divided the p·; to
30 to Sisera a p· of divers colours,
30 p· of divers colours of needlework,
8:24, 25 every man the earrings of his p·.
2Ki 21:14 they shall become a p· and a spoil
Ne 4: 4 for a p· in the land of captivity:
Es 3:13 to take the spoil of them for a p·.
8:11 to take the spoil of them for a p·,
Es 9:15 on the p· they laid not their hand.
16 they laid not their hands on the p·.
Job 4:11 old lion perisheth for lack of p·,
9:26 as the eagle that hasteth to the p·.
24: 5 work; rising betimes for a p·:
38:39 Wilt thou hunt the p· for the lion?
39:29 thence she seeketh the p·, and her
Ps 17:12 as a lion that is greedy of his p·,
76: 4 excellent than the mountains of p·.
104:21 The young lions roar after their p·,
124: 6 not given us as a p· to their teeth.
Pr 23:28 She also lieth in wait as for a p·,
Isa 5:29 lay hold of the p·, and shall carry
10: 2 that widows may be their p·, and
6 to take the p·, and to tread them
31: 4 the young lion roaring on his p·,
33:23 is the p· of a great spoil divided;
23 spoil divided; the lame take the p·.
42:22 they are for a p·, and none
49:24 the p· be taken from the mighty,
25 p· of the terrible shall be delivered:
59:15 from evil maketh himself a p·:
Jer 21: 9 his life shall be unto him for a p·.
30:16 p· upon thee will I give for a p·.
38: 2 he shall have his life for a p·, and
39:18 thy life shall be for a p· unto thee:
45: 5 life will I give unto thee for a p· in
Eze 7:21 the hands of the strangers for a p·,
19: 3 and it learned to catch the p·;
6 lion, and learned to catch the p·,
22:25 like a roaring lion ravening the p·;
27 like wolves ravening the p·, to shed
26:12 and make a p· of thy merchandise:
29:19 and take her spoil, and take her p·;
34: 8 because my flock became a p·, and
22 and they shall no more be a p·;
28 shall no more be a p· to the heathen,
36: 4 became a p· and derision to the
5 minds, to cast it out for a p·.
38:12 To take a spoil, and to take a p·;
13 gathered thy company to take a p·?
Da 11:24 he shall scatter among them the p·,
Am 3: 4 in the forest, when he hath no p·?
Na 2:12 filled his holes with p·, and his dens
13 I will cut off thy p· from the earth,
3: 1 robbery; the p· departeth not;
Zep 3: 8 the day that I rise up to the p·:

price See also PRICES; PRISED.
Le 25:16 thou shalt increase the p· thereof,
16 thou shalt diminish the p· of it:
50 p· of his sale shall be according
51 give again the p· of his redemption
52 him again the p· of his redemption.
De 23:18 the p· of a dog, into the house of
2Sa 24:24 I will surely buy it of thee at a p·:
1Ki 10:28 received the linen yarn at a p·.
1Ch 21:22 shalt grant it me for the full p·:
24 I will verily buy it for the full p·:
2Ch 1:16 received the linen yarn at a p·.
Job 28:13 Man knoweth not the p· thereof;
15 be weighed for the p· thereof.
18 the p· of wisdom is above rubies.
Ps 44:12 increase thy wealth by their p·.
Pr 17:16 a p· in the hand of a fool to get
27:26 the goats are the p· of the field.
31:10 for her p· is far above rubies.
Isa 45:13 my captives, not for p· nor reward,
55: 1 without money and without p·.
Jer 15:13 will I give to the spoil without p·,
Zec 11:12 If you think good, give me my p·;
12 for my p· thirty pieces of silver.
13 a goodly p· that I was prised at of
M't 13:46 had found one pearl of great p·,
27: 6 because it is the p· of blood.
9 the p· of him that was valued,
Ac 5: 2 kept back part of the p·, his wife
3 keep back part of the p· of the land?
19:19 and they counted the p· of them,
1Co 6:20 For ye are bought with a p·:
7:23 Ye are bought with a p·; be not ye
1Pe 3: 4 is in the sight of God of great p·.

priced See PRISED.

prices
Ac 4:34 p· of the things that were sold,

pricked
Ps 73:21 grieved, and I was p· in my reins.
Ac 2:37 they were p· in their heart, and

pricking
Eze 28:24 shall be no more a p· brier unto

pricks
Nu 33:55 be p· in your eyes, and thorns
Ac 9: 5 for thee to kick against the p·.
26:14 for thee to kick against the p·.

pride
Le 26:19 I will break the p· of your power;
1Sa 17:28 I know thy p·, and the
2Ch 32:26 humbled himself for the p· of his
Job 33:17 purpose, and hide p· from man.
35:12 because of the p· of evil men.
41:15 His scales are his p·, shut up
34 a king over all the children of p·.
Ps 10: 2 wicked in his p· doth persecute
4 through the p· of his countenance
31:20 thy presence from the p· of man:
36:11 the foot of p· come against me,
59:12 them even be taken in their p·:
73: 6 p· compasseth them about as a
Pr 8:13 p·, and arrogancy, and the evil
11: 2 p· cometh, then cometh shame:
13:10 Only by p· cometh contention: but
14: 3 mouth of the foolish is a rod of p·:
16:18 P· goeth before destruction, and

Pr 29:23 man's *p'* shall bring him low: but
Isa 9: 9 in the *p'* and stoutness of heart,
16: 6 We have heard of the *p'* of Moab;
6 even of his haughtiness, and his *p'*,
23: 9 it, to stain the *p'* of all glory,
25:11 he shall bring down their *p'*
28: 1 Woe to the crown of *p'*, to the
3 The crown of *p'*, the drunkards of
Jer 13: 9 will I mar the *p'* of Judah,
9 and the great *p'* of Jerusalem.
17 weep in secret places for your *p'*;
48:29 We have heard the *p'* of Moab, (he
29 and his arrogancy, and his *p'*,
49:16 thee, and the *p'* of thine heart,
Eze 7:10 hath blossomed, *p'* hath budded.
16:49 Sodom, *p'*, fulness of bread, and
56 thy mouth in the day of thy *p'*,
30: 6 and the *p'* of her power shall come
Da 4:37 those that walk in *p'* he is able
5:20 his mind hardened in *p'*, he was
Ho 5: 5 the *p'* of Israel doth testify to his
7:10 the *p'* of Israel testifieth to his
Ob 3 *p'* of thine heart hath deceived
Zep 2:10 This shall they have for their *p'*,
3:11 them that rejoice in thy *p'*, and
Zec 9: 6 cut off the *p'* of the Philistines.
10:11 the *p'* of Assyria shall be brought
11: 3 for the *p'* of Jordan is spoiled.
M'r 7:22 eye, blasphemy, *p'*, foolishness:
1Ti 3: 6 being lifted up with *p'* he fall into
1Jo 2:16 lust of the eyes, and the *p'* of life,

priest See also PRIESTHOOD; PRIEST'S; PRIESTS.
Ge 14:18 was the *p'* of the most high God.
41:45 daughter of Poti-pherah *p'* of On.
50 of Poti-pherah *p'* of On bare unto
46:20 of Poti-pherah *p'* of On bare unto
Ex 2:16 *p'* of Midian had seven daughters:
3: 1 father in law, the *p'* of Midian:
18: 1 Jethro, the *p'* of Midian, Moses'
29:30 that son that is *p'* in his stead
31:10 holy garments for Aaron the *p'*,
35:19 holy garments for Aaron the *p'*,
38:21 Ithamar, son to Aaron the *p'*.
39:41 holy garments for Aaron the *p'*,
Le 1: 7 Aaron the *p'* shall put fire upon the
9 the *p'* shall burn all on the altar,
12 *p'* shall lay them in order on the
13 *p'* shall bring it all, and burn it
15 the *p'* shall bring it unto the altar,
17 the *p'* shall burn it upon the altar,
2: 2 *p'* shall burn the memorial of it
8 when it is presented unto the *p'*,
9 *p'* shall take from the meat offering
16 the *p'* shall burn the memorial of it,
3:11 the *p'* shall burn it upon the altar:
16 *p'* shall burn them upon the altar:
4: 3 *p'* that is anointed do sin according
5 *p'* that is anointed shall take of the
6 *p'* shall dip his finger in the blood,
7 *p'* shall put some of the blood upon
10 *p'* shall burn them upon the altar
16 *p'* that is anointed shall bring of
17 *p'* shall dip his finger in some of
20 the *p'* shall make an atonement for
25 the *p'* shall take of the blood of the
26 *p'* shall make an atonement for him
30 *p'* shall take of the blood thereof
31 *p'* shall make an atonement for him,
34 *p'* shall take of the blood of the sin
35 *p'* shall burn them upon the altar,
35 *p'* shall make an atonement for his
5: 6 *p'* shall make an atonement for him
8 shall bring them unto the *p'*, who
10 *p'* shall make an atonement for him
12 Then shall he bring it to the *p'*, and
12 the *p'* shall take his handful of it,
13 *p'* shall make an atonement for him
16 thereto, and give it unto the *p'*:
16 *p'* shall make an atonement for him
18 for a trespass offering, unto the *p'*:
18 *p'* shall make an atonement for him
6: 6 for a trespass offering, unto the *p'*:
7 *p'* shall make an atonement for him
10 *p'* shall put on his linen garment,
12 the *p'* shall burn wood on it every
22 the *p'* of his sons that is anointed
23 offering for the *p'* shall be wholly
26 The *p'* that offereth it for sin shall
7: 5 *p'* shall burn them upon the altar
7 the *p'* that maketh atonement
8 *p'* that offereth any man's burnt
8 *p'* shall have to himself the skin
31 *p'* shall burn the fat upon the altar:
32 ye give unto the *p'* for an heave
34 unto Aaron the *p'* and unto his sons
12: 6 of the congregation, unto the *p'*:
8 *p'* shall make an atonement for her,
13: 2 shall be brought unto Aaron the *p'*,
2 *p'* shall look on the plague in the
3 *p'* shall look on him, and pronounce
4 *p'* shall shut up him that hath the
5 *p'* shall look on him the seventh
5 *p'* shall shut him up seven days
6 the *p'* shall look on him again the
6 the *p'* shall pronounce him clean:
7 that he hath been seen of the *p'* for
7 he shall be seen of the *p'* again:
8 if the *p'* see that, behold, the scab
8 *p'* shall pronounce him unclean:
9 he shall be brought unto the *p'*;
10 And the *p'* shall see him: and,
11 *p'* shall pronounce him unclean,
12 foot wheresoever the *p'* looketh;
13 Then the *p'* shall consider: and
15 the *p'* shall see the raw flesh, and

Le 13:16 white, he shall come unto the *p'*;
17 And the *p'* shall see him: and,
17 the *p'* shall pronounce him clean
19 reddish, and it be shewed to the *p'*;
20 when the *p'* seeth it, behold, it be
20 *p'* shall pronounce him unclean:
21 if the *p'* look on it, and, behold,
21 *p'* shall shut him up seven days:
22 the *p'* shall pronounce him unclean:
23 the *p'* shall pronounce him clean.
25 the *p'* shall look upon it: and,
25 *p'* shall pronounce him unclean:
26 if the *p'* look on it, and, behold,
26 *p'* shall shut him up seven days:
27 *p'* shall look upon him the seventh
27 *p'* shall pronounce him unclean:
28 the *p'* shall pronounce him clean:
30 the *p'* shall see the plague: and,
30 *p'* shall pronounce him unclean:
31 *p'* look upon the plague of the scall,
31 *p'* shall shut up him that hath the
32 the *p'* shall look on the plague:
33 *p'* shall shut up him that hath the
34 day the *p'* shall look on the scall:
34 the *p'* shall pronounce him clean:
36 *p'* shall look on him: and, behold,
36 *p'* shall not seek for yellow hair;
37 the *p'* shall pronounce him clean.
39 Then the *p'* shall look: and, behold,
43 *p'* shall look upon it: and, behold,
44 the *p'* shall pronounce him utterly
49 and shall be shewed unto the *p'*:
50 the *p'* shall look upon the plague,
53 if the *p'* shall look, and, behold, the
54 *p'* shall command that they wash
55 And the *p'* shall look on the plague,
56 And if the *p'* look, and, behold, the
14: 2 He shall be brought unto the *p'*:
3 *p'* shall go forth out of the camp;
3 *p'* shall look, and, behold, if the
4 the *p'* command to take for him
5 *p'* shall command that one of the
11 the *p'* that maketh him clean shall
12 the *p'* shall take one he lamb, and
14 the *p'* shall take some of the blood
14 *p'* shall put it upon the tip of the
15 *p'* shall take some of the log of oil,
16 the *p'* shall dip his right finger in
17 the *p'* put upon the tip of the right
18 the *p'* shall make an atonement for
19 *p'* shall offer the sin offering, and
20 the *p'* shall offer the burnt offering
20 *p'* shall make an atonement for him,
23 day for his cleansing unto the *p'*,
24 the *p'* shall take the lamb of the
24 the *p'* shall wave them for a wave
25 the *p'* shall take some of the blood
26 *p'* shall pour of the oil into the palm
27 the *p'* shall sprinkle with his right
28 the *p'* shall put of the oil that is in
31 *p'* shall make an atonement for him
35 shall come and tell the *p'*, saying,
36 the *p'* shall command that they
36 before the *p'* go into it to see the
36 the *p'* shall go in to see the house:
38 the *p'* shall go out of the house to
39 the *p'* shall come again the seventh
40 the *p'* shall command that they
44 the *p'* shall come and look, and,
48 if the *p'* shall come in, and look
48 *p'* shall pronounce the house clean,
15:14 and give them unto the *p'*:
15 the *p'* shall offer them, the one for
15 *p'* shall make an atonement for him
29 pigeons, and bring them unto the *p'*,
30 the *p'* shall offer the one for a sin
30 the *p'* shall make an atonement
16:30 shall the *p'* make an atonement for
32 the *p'*, whom he shall anoint, and
17: 5 unto the *p'*, and offer them for
6 And the *p'* shall sprinkle the blood
19:22 *p'* shall make an atonement for him
21: 9 daughter of any *p'*, if she profane
10 the high *p'* among his brethren,
21 blemish of the seed of Aaron the *p'*
22:10 a sojourner of the *p'*, or an hired
11 if the *p'* buy any soul with his
14 it unto the *p'* with the holy thing.
23:10 first fruits of...harvest unto the *p'*:
11 the sabbath the *p'* shall wave it.
20 the *p'* shall wave them with the
20 shall be holy to the Lord for the *p'*.
27: 8 shall present himself before the *p'*,
8 the *p'* shall value him; according
8 that vowed shall the *p'* value him.
11 present the beast before the *p'*:
12 the *p'* shall value it, whether it be
12 who art the *p'*, so shall it be.
14 the *p'* shall estimate it, whether it
14 the *p'* shall estimate it, so shall it
18, 23 the *p'* shall reckon unto him the
Nu 3: 6 present them before Aaron the *p'*,
32 Eleazar the son of Aaron the *p'*
4:16 of Eleazar the son of Aaron the *p'*
28, 33 Ithamar the son of Aaron the *p'*.
5: 8 even to the *p'*; beside the ram of
9 which they bring unto the *p'*, shall
10 whatsoever any man giveth the *p'*,
15 the man bring his wife unto the *p'*,
16 the *p'* shall bring her near, and set
17 the *p'* shall take holy water in an
17 and of the dust...the *p'* shall take,
18 the *p'* shall set the woman before
18 *p'* shall have in his hand the bitter
19 the *p'* shall charge her by an oath,
21 *p'* shall charge the woman with an

Nu 5:21 the *p'* shall say unto the woman,
23 the *p'* shall write these curses in a
25 *p'* shall take the jealousy offering
26 the *p'* shall take an handful of the
30 *p'* shall execute upon her all this
6:10 or two young pigeons, to the *p'*, to
11 the *p'* shall offer the one for a sin
16 *p'* shall bring them before the Lord,
17 *p'* shall offer also his meat offering,
19 *p'* shall take the sodden shoulder
20 the *p'* shall wave them for a wave
20 this is holy for the *p'*, with the wave
7: 8 of Ithamar the son of Aaron the *p'*.
15:25 *p'* shall make an atonement for all
28 *p'* shall make an atonement for the
16:37 Eleazar the son of Aaron the *p'*,
39 Eleazar the *p'* took the brasen
18:28 heave offering to Aaron the *p'*.
19: 3 shall give her unto Eleazar the *p'*,
4 And Eleazar the *p'* shall take of her
6 the *p'* shall take cedar wood, and
7 Then the *p'* shall wash his clothes,
7 *p'* shall be unclean until the even.
25: 7 the son of Aaron the *p'*, saw it, he
11 son of Aaron the *p'*, hath turned
26: 1 Eleazar the son of Aaron the *p'*,
3 and Eleazar the *p'* spake with them
63 by Moses and Eleazar the *p'*, who
64 Moses and Aaron the *p'* numbered,
27: 2 Moses, and before Eleazar the *p'*,
19 And set him before Eleazar the *p'*,
21 he shall stand before Eleazar the *p'*
22 and set him before Eleazar the *p'*,
31: 6 Phinehas the son of Eleazar the *p'*,
12 unto Moses, and Eleazar the *p'*, and
13 Moses, and Eleazar the *p'*, and all
21 Eleazar the *p'* said unto the men of
26 and Eleazar the *p'*, and the chief
29 give it unto Eleazar the *p'*, for an
31 and Eleazar the *p'* did as the Lord
41 unto Eleazar the *p'*, as the Lord
51, 54 and Eleazar the *p'* took the gold
32: 2 unto Moses, and to Eleazar the *p'*,
28 Moses commanded Eleazar the *p'*,
33:38 the *p'* went up into mount Hor at
34:17 Eleazar the *p'*, and Joshua the son
35:25 in it unto the death of the high *p'*,
28 until the death of the high *p'*:
28 after the death of the high *p'* the
32 the land, until the death of the *p'*.
De 17:12 will not hearken unto the *p'* that
18: 3 shall give unto the *p'* the shoulder,
20: 2 *p'* shall approach and speak unto
26: 3 thou shalt go unto the *p'* that shall
4 *p'* shall take the basket out of thine
Jos 14: 1 which Eleazar the *p'*, and Joshua
17: 4 came near before Eleazar the *p'*,
19:51 which Eleazar the *p'*, and Joshua
20: 6 until the death of the high *p'* that
21: 1 the Levites unto Eleazar the *p'*,
4 the children of Aaron the *p'*, which
13 gave to the children of Aaron the *p'*
22:13 Phinehas the son of Eleazar the *p'*,
30 And when Phinehas the *p'*, and the
31 the son of Eleazar the *p'* said unto
32 Phinehas the son of Eleazar the *p'*,
J'g 17: 5 one of his sons, who became his *p'*.
10 and be unto me a father and a *p'*,
12 the young man became his *p'*, and
13 seeing I have a Levite to my *p'*.
18: 4 and hath hired me, and I am his *p'*.
6 *p'* said unto them, Go in peace:
17 *p'* stood in the entering of the gate
18 said the *p'* unto them, What do ye?
19 us, and be to us a father and a *p'*:
19 for thee to be a *p'* unto the house of
19 be a *p'* unto a tribe and a family in
24 my gods which I made, and the *p'*,
27 had made, and the *p'* which he had,
1Sa 1: 9 Now Eli the *p'* sat upon a seat by a
2:11 unto the Lord before Eli the *p'*.
14 the fleshhook brought up the *p'* took
15 Give flesh to roast for the *p'*; for
28 all the tribes of Israel to be my *p'*,
35 And I will raise me up a faithful *p'*,
14: 3 son of Eli, the Lord's *p'* in Shiloh,
19 while Saul talked unto the *p'*, that
19 Saul said unto the *p'*, Withdraw
36 Then said the *p'*, Let us draw near
21: 1 David to Nob to Ahimelech the *p'*:
2 David said unto Ahimelech the *p'*,
4 the *p'* answered David, and said,
5 David answered the *p'*, and said
6 So the *p'* gave him hallowed bread:
9 the *p'* said, The sword of Goliath
22:11 king sent to call Ahimelech the *p'*,
23: 9 he said to Abiathar the *p'*, Bring
30: 7 And David said to Abiathar the *p'*,
2Sa 15:27 king said also unto Zadok the *p'*,
1Ki 1: 7 and with Abiathar the *p'*: and
8 But Zadok the *p'*, and Benaiah the
19 of the king, and Abiathar the *p'*,
25 of the host, and Abiathar the *p'*;
26 me thy servant, and Zadok the *p'*,
32 David said, Call me Zadok the *p'*,
34 let Zadok the *p'* and Nathan the
38 So Zadok the *p'*, and Nathan the
39 Zadok the *p'* took an horn of oil out
42 the son of Abiathar the *p'* came:
44 with him Zadok the *p'*, and Nathan
45 And Zadok the *p'* and Nathan the
2:22 for him, and for Abiathar the *p'*,
26 unto Abiathar the *p'* said the king,
27 thrust out Abiathar from being *p'*
35 Zadok the *p'* did the king put in the
4: 2 Azariah the son of Zadok the *p'*,

2Ki 11: 9 that Jehoiada the p' commanded:
9 and came to Jehoiada the p'.
10 did the p' give king David's spears
15 Jehoiada the p' commanded the
15 p' had said, Let her not be slain in
18 slew Mattan the p' of Baal before
18 p' appointed officers over the house
12: 2 Jehoiada the p' instructed him.
7 Jehoash called for Jehoiada the p',
9 Jehoiada the p' took a chest, and
10 scribe and the high p' came up,
16: 10 the p' the fashion of the altar,
11 And Urijah the p' built an altar
11 Urijah the p' made it against king
15 Ahaz commanded Urijah the p',
16 Thus did Urijah the p', according
22: 4 Go up to Hilkiah the high p', that
8 And Hilkiah the high p' said unto
10 the p' hath delivered me a book.
12 king commanded Hilkiah the p',
14 So Hilkiah the p', and Ahikam, and
23: 4 commanded Hilkiah the high p',
24 the book that Hilkiah the p' found
25: 18 the guard took Seraiah the chief p',
18 Zephaniah the second p', and the
1Ch 16: 39 Zadok the p', and his brethren the
24: 6 the princes, and Zadok the p', and
27: 5 the son of Jehoiada, a chief p':
29: 22 chief governor, and Zadok to be p'.
2Ch 13: 9 be a p' of them that are no gods.
15: 3 without a teaching p', and without
19: 11 Amariah the chief p' is over you in
22: 11 the wife of Jehoiada the p', (for she
23: 8 Jehoiada the p' had commanded,
8 Jehoiada the p' dismissed not the
9 Jehoiada the p' delivered to the
14 Jehoiada the p' brought out the
14 For the p' said, Slay her not in the
17 slew Mattan the p' of Baal before
24: 2 all the days of Jehoiada the p'.
20 the son of Jehoiada the p', which
25 of the sons of Jehoiada the p',
26: 17 Azariah the p' went in after him,
20 And Azariah the chief p', and all
31: 10 Azariah the chief p' of the house of
34: 9 they came to Hilkiah the high p',
14 Hilkiah the p' found a book of the
18 the p' hath given me a book.
Ezr 2: 63 till there stood up a p' with Urim
7: 5 the son of Aaron the chief p':
11 Artaxerxes gave unto Ezra the p',
12 unto Ezra the p', a scribe of the
21 whatsoever Ezra the p', the scribe
8: 33 Meremoth the son of Uriah the p';
10: 10 Ezra the p' stood up, and said unto
16 Ezra the p', with certain chief of
Ne 3: 1 high p' rose up with his brethren
20 the house of Eliashib the high p'.
7: 65 till there stood up a p' with Urim
8: 2 Ezra the p' brought the law before
9 and Ezra the p' the scribe, and the
10: 38 p' the son of Aaron shall be with
12: 26 and of Ezra the p', the scribe.
13: 4 before this, Eliashib the p', having
13 the treasuries, Shelemiah the p',
28 the son of Eliashib the high p', was
Ps 110: 4 art a p' for ever after the order of
Isa 8: 2 witnesses to record, Uriah the p',
24: 2 as with the people, so with the p';
28: 7 the p' and the prophet have erred
Jer 6: 13 from the prophet even unto the p'
8: 10 from the prophet even unto the p'
14: 18 and the p' go about into a land
18: 18 the law shall not perish from the p',
20: 1 Pashur the son of Immer the p',
21: 1 the son of Maaseiah the p', saying,
23: 11 both prophet and p' are profane;
33 the prophet, or a p', shall ask thee,
34 the p', and the people, that shall
29: 25 son of Maaseiah the p', and to all
26 The Lord hath made thee p' in the
26 in the stead of Jehoiada the p',
29 Zephaniah the p' read this letter in
37: 3 the son of Maaseiah the p' to the
52: 24 the guard took Seraiah the chief p',
24 and Zephaniah the second p', and
La 2: 6 of his anger the king and the p'.
20 the p' and the prophet be slain in
Eze 1: 3 came expressly unto Ezekiel the p',
7: 26 the law shall perish from the p',
44: 13 to do the office of a p' unto me,
21 Neither shall any p' drink wine,
22 or a widow that had a p' before.
30 unto the p' the first of your dough,
45: 19 p' shall take of the blood of the sin
Hos 4: 4 are as they that strive with the p'.
6 that thou shalt be no p' to me:
9 there shall be, like people, like p':
Am 7: 10 the p' of Beth-el sent to Jeroboam
Hag 1: 1, 12, 14 son of Josedech, the high p',
2: 2 the son of Josedech, the high p',
4 son of Josedech, the high p';
Zec 3: 1 he shewed me Joshua the high p'
8 Hear now, O Joshua the high p',
6: 11 the son of Josedech, the high p';
13 he shall be a p' upon his throne:
M't 8: 4 shew thyself to the p', and offer
26: 3 unto the palace of the high p', who
57 him away to Caiaphas the high p',
62 And the high p' arose, and said unto
63 the high p' answered and said unto
65 Then the high p' rent his clothes,
M'r 1: 44 shew thyself to the p', and offer for
2: 26 in the days of Abiathar the high p',
14: 47 smote a servant of the high p', and
53 they led Jesus away to the high p':

M'r 14: 54 even into the palace of the high p':
60 the high p' stood up in the midst,
61 Again the high p' asked him, and
63 Then the high p' rent his clothes,
66 one of the maids of the high p':
Lu 1: 5 a certain p' named Zacharias, of
5: 14 and shew thyself to the p', and offer
10: 31 there came down a certain p' that
22: 50 smote the servant of the high p',
Joh 11: 49 being the high p' that same year,
51 but being high p' that year, he
18: 13 was the high p' that same year.
15 disciple was known unto the high p',
15 Jesus into the palace of the high p'.
16 which was known unto the high p',
19 The high p' then asked Jesus of his
22 Answerest thou the high p' so?
24 him bound unto Caiaphas the high p'.
26 One of the servants of the high p',
Ac 4: 6 Annas the high p', and Caiaphas,
6 were of the kindred of the high p',
5: 17 Then the high p' rose up, and all
21 But the high p' came, and they that
24 the high p' and the captain of the
27 council: and the high p' asked them,
7: 1 Then said the high p', Are these
9: 1 of the Lord, went unto the high p',
14: 13 Then the p' of Jupiter, Which was
22: 5 the high p' doth bear me witness,
23: 2 the high p' Ananias commanded
4 said, Revilest thou God's high p'?
5 brethren, that he was the high p':
24: 1 Ananias the high p' descended with
25: 2 high p' and the chief of the Jews
Heb 2: 17 a merciful and faithful high p' in
3: 1 and High P' of our profession,
4: 14 then that we have a great high p',
15 For we have not an high p' which
5: 1 every high p' taken from among
5 not himself to be made an high p';
6 Thou art a p' forever after the
10 of God an high p' after the order of
6: 20 made an high p' for ever after the
7: 1 p' of the most high God, who met
3 of God; abideth a p' continually.
11 p' should rise after the order of
15 of Melchisedec...ariseth another p',
17 Thou art a p' for ever after the
20 not without an oath he was made p':
21 Thou art a p' for ever after the
26 such an high p' became us, who is
8: 1 We have such an high p', who is set
3 For every high p' is ordained to
4 on earth, he should not be a p',
9: 7 went the high p' alone once every
11 But Christ being come an high p' of
25 high p' entereth into the holy place
10: 11 p' standeth daily ministering and
21 an high p' over the house of God;
13: 11 sanctuary by the high p' for sin,

priesthood
Ex 40: 15 shall surely be an everlasting p'
Nu 16: 10 with thee: and seek ye the p' also?
18: 1 shall bear the iniquity of your p'.
25: 13 the covenant of an everlasting p';
Jos 18: 7 p' of the Lord is their inheritance:
Ezr 2: 62 they, as polluted, put from the p'.
Ne 7: 64 they, as polluted, put from the p'.
13: 29 because they have defiled the p',
29 and the covenant of the p', and of
Heb 7: 5 who receive the office of the p',
11 perfection were by the Levitical p',
12 For the p' being changed, there is
14 Moses spake nothing concerning p'.
24 ever, hath an unchangeable p'.
1Pe 2: 5 up a spiritual house, an holy p',
9 a chosen generation, a royal p',

priest's
Ex 28: 1 minister unto me in the p' office,
3, 4 minister unto me in the p' office.
41 minister unto me in the p' office.
29: 1 minister unto me in the p' office:
9 the p' office shall be theirs for a
44 to minister to me in the p' office.
30: 30 minister unto me in the p' office.
31: 10 sons, to minister in the p' office,
35: 19 sons, to minister in the p' office.
39: 41 garments, to minister in the p' office.
40: 13 minister unto me in the p' office.
15 minister unto me in the p' office:
Le 5: 13 the remnant shall be the p', as a
7: 9 pan, shall be the p' that offereth it.
14 shall be the p' that sprinkleth the
35 unto the Lord in the p' office;
14: 13 for as the sin offering is the p', so
18, 29 oil that is in the p' hand he shall
16: 32 to minister in the p' office in his
22: 12 the p' daughter also be married
13 if the p' daughter be a widow, or
27: 21 possession thereof shall be the p'.
Nu 3: 3 to minister in the p' office.
4 Ithamar ministered in the p' office
10 they shall wait on their p' office:
18: 7 with thee shall keep your p' office
7 I have given your p' office unto you
De 10: 6 his son ministered in the p' office
18: 3 be the p' due from the people,
J'g 18: 20 And the p' heart was glad, and he
1Sa 2: 13 the p' custom with the people was
13 the p' servant came, while the flesh
15 p' servant came, and said to the
36 into one of the p' offices, that I
1Ch 6: 10 that executed the p' office in the
24: 2 and Ithamar executed the p' office.
2Ch 11: 14 from executing the p' office unto

2Ch 24: 11 and the high p' officer came and
Eze 44: 30 of your oblations, shall be the p':
Mal 2: 7 the p' lips should keep knowledge,
M't 26: 51 struck a servant of the high p',
58 him afar off unto the high p' palace,
Lu 1: 8 executed the p' office before God
9 to the custom of the p' office,
22: 54 brought him into the high p' house.
Joh 18: 10 it, and smote the high p' servant,

priests See also PRIESTS'.
Ge 47: 22 the land of the p' bought he not;
22 the p' had a portion assigned them
26 except the land of the p' only,
Ex 19: 6 shall be unto me a kingdom of p',
22 let the p' also, which come near
24 the p' and the people break through
Le 1: 5 the p', Aaron's sons, shall bring
8 And the p', Aaron's sons, shall lay
11 the p', Aaron's sons, shall sprinkle
2: 2 bring it to Aaron's sons the p':
3: 2 Aaron's sons the p' shall sprinkle
6: 29 the males among the p' shall eat
7: 6 Every male among the p' shall eat
13: 2 or unto one of his sons the p':
16: 33 shall make an atonement for the p',
21: 1 Speak unto the p' the sons of Aaron,
Nu 3: 3 Aaron, the p' which were anointed,
10: 8 sons of Aaron, the p', shall blow
De 17: 9 shalt come unto the p' the Levites,
18 which is before the p' the Levites:
18: 1 The p' the Levites, and all the
19: 17 before the p' and the judges, which
21: 5 p' the sons of Levi shall come near;
24: 8 the p' the Levites shall teach you:
27: 9 Moses and the p' the Levites spake
31: 9 it unto the p' the sons of Levi,
Jos 3: 3 and the p' the Levites bearing it,
6 Joshua spake unto the p', saying,
8 command the p' that bear the ark
13 feet of the p' that bear the ark of
14 p' bearing the ark of the covenant
15 feet of the p' that bare the ark were
17 p' that bare the ark of the covenant
4: 9 the feet of the p' which bare the ark
10 For the p' which bare the ark stood
11 of the Lord passed over, and the p',
16 Command the p' that bear the ark
17 Joshua therefore commanded the p',
18 p' that bare the ark of the covenant
6: 4 p' shall bear before the ark seven
4 the p' shall blow with the trumpets.
6 Joshua the son of Nun called the p',
6 let seven p' bear seven trumpets of
8 seven p' bearing the seven trumpets
9 the p' that blew with the trumpets,
9 p' going on, and blowing with the
12 the p' took up the ark of the Lord.
13 seven p' bearing seven trumpets
13 p' going on, and blowing with the
16 the p' blew with the trumpets,
20 shouted when the p' blew with the
8: 33 that side before the p' the Levites,
21: 19 of the children of Aaron, the p',
J'g 18: 30 his sons were p' to the tribe of Dan
1Sa 1: 3 the p' of the Lord, were there.
5: 5 neither the p' of Dagon, nor any
6: 2 Philistines called for the p' and the
22: 11 house, the p' that were in Nob:
17 Turn, and slay the p' of the Lord;
17 hand to fall upon the p' of the Lord
18 Turn thou, and fall upon the p'.
18 turned, and he fell upon the p',
19 Nob, the city of the p', smote he
21 that Saul had slain the Lord's p'.
2Sa 8: 17 the son of Abiathar, were the p';
15: 35 thee Zadok and Abiathar the p'?
35 it to Zadok and Abiathar the p'.
17: 15 unto Zadok and to Abiathar the p',
19: 11 to Zadok and to Abiathar the p',
20: 25 and Zadok and Abiathar were the p':
1Ki 4: 4 and Zadok and Abiathar were the p':
8: 3 came, and the p' took up the ark.
4 did the p' and the Levites bring up.
6 the p' brought in the ark of the
10 p' were come out of the holy place,
11 the p' could not stand to minister
12: 31 made p' of the lowest of the people,
32 in Beth-el the p' of the high places
13: 2 he offer the p' of the high places
33 lowest of the people p' of the high
33 one of the p' of the high places.
2Ki 10: 11 men, and his kinfolks, and his p',
19 Baal, all his servants, and all his p';
12: 4 And Jehoash said to the p', All the
5 Let the p' take it to them, every
6 p' had not repaired the breaches of
7 the priest, and the other p', and
8 p' consented to receive no more
9 p' that kept the door put therein
17: 27 Carry thither one of the p' whom
28 Then one of the p' whom they had
32 of them p' of the high places,
19: 2 the elders of the p', covered with
23: 2 the p', and the prophets, and all
4 p' of the second order, and the
5 put down the idolatrous p', whom
8 the p' out of the cities of Judah,
8 where the p' had burned incense,
9 p' of the high places came not up
20 And he slew all the p' of the high
1Ch 9: 2 p', Levites, and the Nethinims.
10 And of the p'; Jedaiah, and
30 sons of the p' made the ointment
13: 2 p' and Levites which are in their
15: 11 for Zadok and Abiathar the p',

1Ch 15:14 the p' and the Levites sanctified
24 the p', did blow with the trumpets
16: 6 and Jahaziel the p' with trumpets
39 the priest, and his brethren the p',
18:16 the son of Abiathar, were the p';
23: 2 Israel, with the p' and the Levites.
24: 6, 31 the chief of the fathers of the p'
28:13, 21 courses of the p' and the Levites,
2Ch 4: 6 the sea was for the p' to wash in.
9 he made the court of the p', and
5: 5 the p' and the Levites bring up.
7 the p' brought in the ark of the
11 p' were come out of the holy place:
11 p' that were present were sanctified,
12 them an hundred and twenty p'
14 p' could not stand to minister by
6:41 thy p', O Lord God, be clothed with
7: 2 p' could not enter into the house
6 the p' waited on their offices: the
6 p' sounded trumpets before them,
8:14 courses of the p' to their service,
14 and minister before the p', as
15 of the king unto the p' and Levites
11:13 the p' and the Levites that were
15 he ordained him p' for the high
13: 9 ye not cast out the p' of the Lord,
9 made you p' after the manner of
10 the p', which minister unto the
12 his p' with sounding trumpets to
14 and the p' sounded with the
17: 8 them Elishama and Jehoram, p'.
19: 8 set of the Levites, and of the p',
23: 4 of the p' and of the Levites, shall
6 save the p', and they that minister
18 by the hand of the p' the Levites,
24: 5 together the p' and the Levites,
26:17 fourscore p' of the Lord, that
18 to the p' the sons of Aaron, that
19 while he was wroth with the p',
19 before the p' in the house of the
20 all the p', looked upon him, and,
29: 4 brought in the p' and the Levites,
16 p' went into the inner part of the
21 the p' the sons of Aaron to offer
22 the p' received the blood, and
24 the p' killed them, and they made
26 and the p' with the trumpets.
34 the p' were too few, so that they
34 other p' had sanctified themselves:
34 to sanctify themselves than the p'.
30: 3 because the p' had not sanctified
15 p' and the Levites were ashamed,
16 the p' sprinkled the blood, which
21 the p' praised the Lord day by day,
24 a great number of p' sanctified
25 with the p' and the Levites, and all
27 p' the Levites arose and blessed
31: 2 appointed the courses of the p'
2 p' and Levites for burnt offerings
4 to give the portion of the p' and
9 Hezekiah questioned with the p'
15 in the cities of the p', in their set
17 the genealogy of the p' by the
19 the sons of Aaron the p', which
19 to all the males among the p', and to
34: 5 burnt the bones of the p' upon
30 the p', and the Levites, and all the
35: 2 he set the p' in their charges, and
8 willingly unto the people, to the p',
8 gave unto the p' for the passover
10 and the p' stood in their place,
11 p' sprinkled the blood from their
14 for themselves, and for the p':
14 the p' the sons of Aaron were
14 and for the p' the sons of Aaron.
18 the p', and the Levites, and all
36:14 the chief of the p', and the people,
Ezr 1: 5 and the p', and the Levites, with
2:36 The p': the children of Jedaiah,
61 And of the children of the p': the
70 So the p', and the Levites, and
3: 2 his brethren the p', and Zerubbabel
8 remnant of their brethren the p'
10 set the p' in their apparel with
12 many of the p' and Levites and
6: 9 to the appointment of the p' which
16 of Israel, the p', and the Levites,
18 they set the p' in their divisions,
20 p' and the Levites were purified
20 for their brethren the p', and for
7: 7 children of Israel, and of the p',
13 of his p' and Levites, in my realm,
16 of the p', offering willingly for the
24 touching any of the p' and Levites,
8:15 I viewed the people, and the p',
24 twelve of the chief of the p',
29 them before the chief of the p' and
30 So took the p' and the Levites the
9: 1 The people of Israel, and the p',
7 have we, our kings, and our p',
10: 5 arose Ezra, and made the chief p',
18 among the sons of the p' there were
Ne 2:16 told it to the Jews, nor to the p',
3: 1 rose up with his brethren the p',
22 after him repaired the p', the men
28 above the horse gate repaired the p',
5:12 Then I called the p', and took an
7:39 The p': the children of Jedaiah, of
63 And of the p': the children of
73 So the p', and the Levites, and the
8:13 the p', and the Levites, unto Ezra
9:32 on our princes, and on our p', and
34 our p', nor our fathers, kept thy
38 Levites, and p', seal unto it.
10: 8 Shemaiah: these were the p'.
28 the p', the Levites, the porters, the
Ne 10:34 we cast the lots among the p', the
36 p' that minister in the house of
37 unto the p', to the chambers of the
39 and the p' that minister, and the
11: 3 Israel, the p', and the Levites, and
10 Of the p': Jedaiah the son of
20 p', and the Levites, were in all the
12: 1 these are the p', and the Levites
7 These were the chief of the p' and
12 the days of Joiakim were p', the
22 also the p', to the reign of Darius
30 And the p' and the Levites purified
41 And the p'; Eliakim, Maaseiah,
44 of the law for the p' and Levites:
44 for Judah rejoiced for the p' and
13: 5 porters; and the offerings of the p'.
30 appointed the wards of the p' and
Ps 78:64 Their p' fell by the sword; and
99: 6 Moses and Aaron among his p', and
132: 9 p' be clothed with righteousness;
16 also clothe her p' with salvation:
Isa 37: 2 elders of the p' covered with
61: 6 shall be named the P' of the Lord:
66:21 take of them for p' and for Levites,
Jer 1: 1 of the p' that were in Anathoth in
18 against the p' thereof, and against
2: 8 The p' said not, Where is the Lord?
26 and their p', and their prophets,
4: 9 the p' shall be astonished, and the
5:31 the p' bear rule by their means;
8: 1 the bones of the p', and the bones
13:13 and the p', and the prophets, and
19: 1 and of the ancients of the p';
26: 7, 8 the p' and the prophets and all
11 Then spake the p' and the prophets
16 unto the p' and to the prophets;
27:16 I spake to the p' and to all this
28: 1 in the presence of the p' and of all
5 Hananiah in the presence of the p',
29: 1 to the p', and to the prophets, and
25 the priest, and to all the p', saying,
31:14 the soul of the p' with fatness,
32:32 their p', and their prophets, and
33:18 Neither shall the p' the Levites
21 and with the Levites the p', my
34:19 the eunuchs, and the p', and all
48: 7 forth into captivity with his p' and
49: 3 his p' and his princes together.
La 1: 4 p' sigh, her virgins are afflicted,
19 my p' and mine elders gave up the
4:13 the iniquities of her p', that have
16 respected not the persons of the p',
Eze 22:26 Her p' have violated my law, and
40:45 is for the p', the keepers of the
46 is toward the north is for the p',
42:13 the p' that approach unto the Lord
14 When the p' enter therein, then
43:19 shalt give to the p' the Levites
24 the p' shall cast salt upon them,
27 p' shall make your burnt offerings
44:15 But the p' the Levites, the sons of
31 p' shall not eat of any thing that is
45: 4 of the land shall be for the p' the
46: 2 p' shall prepare his burnt offering
19 into the holy chambers of the p',
20 p' shall boil the trespass offering
48:10 even for the p', shall be this holy
11 be for the p' that are sanctified of
13 over against the border of the p'
Ho 5: 1 Hear ye this, O p'; and hearken, ye
6: 9 so the company of p' murder in the
10: 5 the p' thereof that rejoiced on it,
Joe 1: 9 the p', the Lord's ministers, mourn.
13 yourselves, and lament, ye p':
2:17 Let the p', the ministers of the
Mic 3:11 p' thereof teach for hire, and the
Zep 1: 4 of the Chemarims with the p';
3: 4 her p' have polluted the sanctuary,
Hag 2:11 Ask now the p' concerning the law,
12 And the p' answered and said, No.
13 p' answered and said, It shall be
Zec 7: 3 unto the p' which were in the house
5 to the p', saying, When ye fasted
Mal 1: 6 you, O p', that despise my name.
2: 1 O ye p', this commandment is for
M't 2: 4 gathered all the chief p' and scribes
12: 4 were with him, but only for the p'?
5 the p' in the temple profane the
16:21 the elders and chief p' and scribes,
20:18 shall be betrayed unto the chief p'
21:15 when the chief p' and scribes saw
23 chief p' and the elders of the people
45 chief p' and Pharisees had heard
26: 3 assembled together the chief p',
14 Iscariot, went unto the chief p',
47 the chief p' and elders of the people.
59 Now the chief p', and elders, and
27: 1 the chief p' and elders of the people
3 of silver to the chief p' and elders,
6 the chief p' took the silver pieces,
12 accused of the chief p' and elders,
20 chief p' and elders persuaded the
41 also the chief p' mocking him, with
62 the chief p' and Pharisees came
28:11 and shewed unto the chief p' all the
M'r 2:26 is not lawful to eat but for the p',
8:31 of the chief p', and scribes, and be
10:33 shall be delivered unto the chief p',
11:18 the scribes and chief p' heard it,
27 there come to him the chief p', and
14: 1 the chief p' and the scribes sought
10 went unto the chief p' to betray
43 from the chief p' and the scribes
53 him were assembled all the chief p'
55 And the chief p' and all the council
15: 1 the chief p' held a consultation with
M'r 15: 3 the chief p' accused him of many
10 the chief p' had delivered him for
11 But the chief p' moved the people,
31 also the chief p' mocking said
Lu 3: 2 and Caiaphas being the high p', the
6: 4 lawful to eat but for the p' alone?
9:22 rejected of the elders and chief p'
17:14 Go shew yourselves unto the p'.
19:47 But the chief p' and the scribes
20: 1 the chief p' and the scribes came
19 the chief p' and the scribes the same
22: 2 the chief p' and scribes sought how
4 with the chief p' and captains, how
52 Then Jesus said unto the chief p',
66 the chief p' and the scribes came
23: 4 Then said Pilate to the chief p' and
10 the chief p' and scribes stood and
13 together the chief p' and the rulers
23 voices...of the chief p' prevailed.
24:20 chief p' and our rulers delivered
Joh 1:19 the Jews sent p' and Levites from
7:32 the Pharisees and the chief p' sent
45 came the officers to the chief p' and
11:47 Then gathered the chief p' and the
57 both the chief p' and the Pharisees
12:10 But the chief p' consulted that they
18: 3 from the chief p' and Pharisees,
35 Thine own nation and the chief p'
19: 6 the chief p' therefore and officers
15 The chief p' answered, We have no
21 the chief p' of the Jews to Pilate,
Ac 4: 1 spake unto the people, the p', and
23 the chief p' and elders had said
5:24 and the chief p' heard these things,
6: 7 the p' were obedient to the faith.
9:14 authority from the chief p' to bind
21 bring them bound unto the chief p'?
19:14 a Jew, and chief of the p', which did
22:30 and commanded the chief p' and all
23:14 they came to the chief p' and elders,
25:15 chief p' and the elders of the Jews
26:10 received authority from the chief p';
12 and commission from the chief p',
Heb 7:21 p' were made without an oath;
23 they truly were many p', because
27 needeth not daily, as those high p',
28 men high p' which have infirmity;
8: 4 that there are p' that offer gifts
9: 6 the p' went always into the first
Re 1: 6 made us kings and p' unto God
5:10 us unto our God kings and p': and
20: 6 they shall be p' of God and of

priests'

Jos 4: 3 place where the p' feet stood firm,
18 the soles of the p' feet were lifted
2Ki 12:16 house of the Lord: it was the p'.
Ezr 2:69 and one hundred p' garments.
Ne 7:70 hundred and thirty p' garments.
72 threescore and seven p' garments.
12:35 of the p' sons with trumpets:

prince See also PRINCE'S; PRINCES; PRINCESS.

Ge 23: 6 thou art a mighty p' among us:
32:28 as a p' hast thou power with God and
34: 2 p' of the country, saw her, he
Ex 2:14 thee a p' and a judge over us?
Nu 7:11 their offering, each p' on his day,
18 the son of Zuar, p' of Issachar,
24 p' of the children of Zebulun, did
30 p' of the children of Reuben, did
36 p' of the children of Simeon, did
42 p' of the children of Gad, offered:
48 p' of the children of Ephraim,
54 p' of the children of Manasseh:
60 p' of the children of Benjamin,
66 p' of the children of Dan, offered:
72 p' of the children of Asher, offered:
78 p' of the children of Naphtali,
16:13 thou make thyself altogether a p'
17: 6 him a rod apiece, for each p' one,
25:14 a p' of a chief house among the
18 the daughter of a p' of Midian,
34:18 ye shall take one p' of every tribe,
22 the p' of the tribe of the children of
23 the p' of the children of Joseph, for
24, 25, 26, 27, 28 the p' of the tribe of
Jos 22:14 of each chief house a p' throughout
2Sa 3:38 p' and a great man fallen this day
1Ki 11:34 make him p' all the days of his
14: 7 and made thee p' over my people
16: 2 and made thee p' over my people
1Ch 2:10 p' of the children of Judah;
5: 6 he was p' of the Reubenites.
Ezr 1: 8 unto Sheshbazzar, the p' of Judah.
Job 21:28 say, Where is the house of the p'?
31:37 as a p' would I go near unto him.
Pr 14:28 people is the destruction of the p'.
17: 7 fool: much less do lying lips a p'.
19: 6 will intreat the favour of the p':
25: 7 put lower in the presence of the p'
15 forbearing is a p' persuaded,
28:16 p' that wanteth understanding
Isa 9: 6 everlasting Father,...P' of Peace.
Jer 51:59 And this Seraiah was a quiet p'.
Eze 7:27 the p' shall be clothed with
12:10 This burden concerneth the p' in
12 p' that is among them shall bear
21:25 profane wicked p' of Israel, whose
28: 2 of man, say unto the p' of Tyrus,
30:13 no more a p' in the land of Egypt:
34:24 servant David a p' among them:
37:25 my servant David shall be their p'
38: 2 the chief p' of Meshech and Tubal,
3 the chief p' of Meshech and Tubal:
39: 1 chief p' of Meshech and Tubal:
44: 3 It is for the p'; the p', he shall sit

Eze 45: 7 a portion shall be for the *p'* on the
16 this oblation for the *p'* in Israel.
22 shall the *p'* prepare for himself and
46: 2 the *p'* shall enter by the way of the
4 offering that the *p'* shall offer unto
8 when the *p'* shall enter, he shall go
10 *p'* in the midst of them, when they
12 the *p'* shall prepare a voluntary
16 *p'* give a gift unto any of his sons,
17 after it shall return to the *p'*: but
18 the *p'* shalt not take of the people's
48: 21 And the residue shall be for the *p'*,
21 over against the portions for the *p'*:
22 of Benjamin, shall be for the *p'*.
Da 1: 7 the *p'* of the eunuchs gave names:
8 requested of the *p'* of the eunuchs
9 love with the *p'* of the eunuchs.
10 *p'* of the eunuchs said unto Daniel,
11 whom the *p'* of the eunuchs had set
18 *p'* of the eunuchs brought them in
8: 11 himself even to the *p'* of the host,
25 stand up against the *P'* of princes;
9: 25 unto the Messiah the *P'* shall be
26 people of the *p'* that shall come
10: 13 the *p'* of the kingdom of Persia
20 return to fight with the *p'* of Persia:
20 lo, the *p'* of Grecia shall come.
21 these things, but Michael your *p'*.
11: 18 a *p'* for his own behalf shall cause
22 yea, also the *p'* of the covenant.
12: 1 *p'* which standeth for the children
Ho 3: 4 without a king, and without a *p'*,
Mic 7: 3 *p'* asketh, and the judge asketh for
M't 9: 34 devils through the *p'* of the devils.
12: 24 by Beelzebub the *p'* of the devils.
M'r 3: 22 by the *p'* of the devils casteth he out
Joh 12: 31 shall the *p'* of this world be cast out.
14: 30 the *p'* of this world cometh, and hath
16: 11 the *p'* of this world is judged.
Ac 3: 15 killed the *P'* of life, whom God hath
5: 31 right hand to be a *P'* and a Saviour,
Eph 2: 2 to the *p'* of the power of the air,
Re 1: 5 and the *p'* of the kings of the earth.

prince's
Ca 7: 1 thy feet with shoes, O *p'* daughter!
Eze 45: 17 the *p'* part to give burnt offerings,
48: 22 in the midst of that which is the *p'*,

princes
Ge 12: 15 The *p'* also of Pharaoh saw her,
17: 20 twelve *p'* shall he beget, and I will
25: 16 twelve *p'* according to their nations.
Nu 1: 16 *p'* of the tribes of their fathers,
44 the *p'* of Israel, being twelve men:
7: 2 the *p'* of Israel, heads of the house
2 who were the *p'* of the tribes, and
3 a wagon for two of the *p'*, and for
10 the *p'* offered for dedicating of the
10 the *p'* offered their offering before
84 it was anointed, by the *p'* of Israel:
10: 4 then the *p'*, which are heads of the
16: 2 and fifty *p'* of the assembly, famous
17: 2 of all their *p'* according to the house
6 of their *p'* gave him a rod apiece,
21: 18 The *p'* digged the well, the nobles
22: 8 the *p'* of Moab abode with Balaam.
13 said unto the *p'* of Balak, Get you
14 *p'* of Moab rose up, and they went
15 Balak sent yet again *p'*, more, and
21 ass, and went with the *p'* of Moab.
35 Balaam went with the *p'* of Balak.
40 and to the *p'* that were with him.
23: 6 sacrifice, he, and all the *p'* of Moab.
17 and the *p'* of Moab with him.
27: 2 the *p'* and all the congregation,
31: 13 all the *p'* of the congregation, went
32: 2 unto the *p'* of the congregation,
36: 1 before Moses, and before the *p'*,
Jos 9: 15 *p'* of the congregation sware unto
18 *p'* of the congregation had sworn
18 murmured against their *p'*.
19 *p'* said unto all the congregation,
21 *p'* said unto them, Let them live;
21 as the *p'* had promised them.
13: 21 Moses smote with the *p'* of Midian,
17: 4 the son of Nun, and before the *p'*,
22: 14 And with him ten *p'*, of each chief
30 *p'* of the congregation and heads of
32 the *p'*, returned from the children
J'g 5: 3 O ye kings; give ear, O ye *p'*; I,
15 *p'* of Issachar were with Deborah;
7: 25 two *p'* of the Midianites, Oreb and
8: 3 into your hands the *p'* of Midian,
6 And the *p'* of Succoth said, Are the
14 unto him the *p'* of Succoth, and
10: 18 *p'* of Gilead said one to another,
1Sa 2: 8 to set them among *p'*, and to make
18: 30 Then the *p'* of the Philistines went
29: 3 Then said the *p'* of the Philistines,
3 said unto the *p'* of the Philistines,
4 the *p'* of the Philistines were wroth
4 *p'* of the Philistines said unto him,
9 the *p'* of the Philistines have said,
2Sa 10: 3 *p'* of the children of Ammon said
19: 6 regardest neither *p'* nor servants:
1Ki 4: 2 these were the *p'* which he had;
9: 22 his *p'*, and his captains, and rulers
20: 14 men of the *p'* of the provinces.
15 numbered the young men of the *p'*
17 *p'* of the provinces went out first;
19 *p'* of the provinces came out of the
2Ki 11: 14 *p'* and the trumpeters by the king,
24: 12 and his *p'*, and his officers: and the
14 all the *p'*, and all the mighty men
1Ch 4: 38 mentioned by their names were *p'*
7: 40 men of valour, chief of the *p'*.

1Ch 19: 3 *p'* of the children of Ammon said
22: 17 also commanded all the *p'* of Israel
23: 2 together all the *p'* of Israel, with
24: 6 them before the king, and the *p'*,
27: 22 were the *p'* of the tribes of Israel.
28: 1 David assembled all the *p'* of Israel,
1 *p'* of the tribes, and the captains of
21 also the *p'* and all the people will be
29: 6 *p'* of the tribes of Israel, and the
24 And all the *p'*, and the mighty men,
2Ch 12: 5 Rehoboam, and to the *p'* of Judah,
6 *p'* of Israel and the king humbled
17: 7 he sent to his *p'*, even to Ben-hail,
21: 4 and divers also of the *p'* of Israel.
9 Jehoram went forth with his *p'*,
22: 8 and found the *p'* of Judah, and the
23: 13 *p'* and the trumpets by the king:
24: 10 the *p'* and all the people rejoiced,
17 came the *p'* of Judah, and made
23 destroyed all the *p'* of the people
28: 14 and the spoil before the *p'* and all
21 the house of the king, and of the *p'*,
29: 30 *p'* commanded the Levites to sing
30: 2 king had taken counsel, and his *p'*,
6 and his *p'* throughout all Israel and
12 of the king and of the *p'*, by the
24 the *p'* gave to the congregation a
31: 8 when Hezekiah and the *p'* came and
32: 3 He took counsel with his *p'* and his
31 ambassadors of the *p'* of Babylon,
35: 8 *p'* gave willingly unto the people,
36: 18 treasures of the king, and of his *p'*;
Ezr 7: 28 and before all the king's mighty *p'*.
8: 20 David and the *p'* had appointed for
9: 1 things were done, the *p'* came to me,
2 the hand of the *p'* and rulers hath
10: 8 according to the counsel of the *p'*
Ne 9: 32 on our kings, on our *p'*, and on our
34 Neither have our kings, our *p'*, our
38 our *p'*, Levites, and priests, seal
12: 31 Then I brought up the *p'* of Judah
32 and half of the *p'* of Judah,
Es 1: 3 made a feast unto all his *p'* and his
3 the nobles and *p'* of the provinces,
11 the people and the *p'* her beauty:
14 the seven *p'* of Persia and Media,
16 before the king and the *p'*, Vashti
16 king only, but also to all the *p'*,
18 say this day unto all the king's *p'*,
21 saying pleased the king and the *p'*;
2: 18 made a great feast unto all his *p'*
3: 1 set his seat above all the *p'* that
5: 11 advanced him above the *p'* and
6: 9 of one of the king's most noble *p'*,
Job 3: 15 Or with *p'* that had gold, who filled
12: 19 He leadeth *p'* away spoiled, and
21 poureth contempt upon *p'*, and
29: 9 The *p'* refrained talking, and laid
34: 18 wicked? and to *p'*, Ye are ungodly?
19 accepteth not the persons of *p'*,
Ps 45: 16 mayest make *p'* in all the earth.
47: 9 The *p'* of the people are gathered
68: 27 the *p'* of Judah and their council,
27 the *p'* of Zebulun, and the *p'* of
31 *P'* shall come out of Egypt;
76: 12 He shall cut off the spirit of *p'*:
82: 7 men, and fall like one of the *p'*.
83: 11 yea, all their *p'* as Zebah, and as
105: 22 To bind his *p'* at his pleasure;
107: 40 He poureth contempt upon *p'*,
113: 8 That he may set him with *p'*,
8 even with the *p'* of his people.
118: 9 than to put confidence in *p'*.
119: 23 *P'* also did sit and speak against
161 *P'* have persecuted me without a
146: 3 Put not your trust in *p'*, nor in the
148: 11 *p'*, and all judges of the earth:
Pr 8: 15 kings reign, and *p'* decree justice.
16 By me *p'* rule, and nobles, even
17: 26 good, nor to strike *p'* for equity.
19: 10 for a servant to have rule over *p'*.
28: 2 of a land many are the *p'* thereof:
31: 4 wine; nor for *p'* strong drink:
Ec 10: 7 *p'* walking as servants upon the
16 and thy *p'* eat in the morning!
17 and thy *p'* eat in due season, for
Isa 1: 23 Thy *p'* are rebellious, and
3: 4 I will give children to be their *p'*,
14 of his people, and the *p'* thereof:
10: 8 Are not my *p'* altogether kings?
19: 11 *p'* of Zoan are fools, the counsel
13 The *p'* of Zoan are become fools,
13 *p'* of Noph are deceived; they have
21: 5 arise, ye *p'*, and anoint the shield.
23: 8 whose merchants are *p'*, whose
30: 4 For his *p'* were at Zoan, and his
31: 9 his *p'* shall be afraid of the ensign,
32: 1 and *p'* shall rule in judgment.
34: 12 and all her *p'* shall be nothing.
40: 23 bringeth the *p'* to nothing; he
41: 25 come upon *p'* as upon morter,
43: 28 profaned the *p'* of the sanctuary,
49: 7 *p'* also shall worship, because of
Jer 1: 18 against the *p'* thereof, against the
2: 26 they, their kings, their *p'*, and their
4: 9 perish, and the heart of the *p'*;
8: 1 the bones of his *p'*, and the bones
17: 25 *p'* sitting upon the throne of David,
25 and their *p'*, the men of Judah,
24: 1 the *p'* of Judah, with the carpenters
8 the king of Judah, and his *p'*,
25: 18 kings thereof, and the *p'* thereof,
19 and his servants, and his *p'*, and all
26: 10 the *p'* of Judah heard these things,
11 and the prophets unto the *p'* and to
12 spake Jeremiah unto all the *p'* and

Jer 26: 16 Then said the *p'* and all the people
21 men, and all the *p'*, heard his words,
29: 2 *p'* of Judah and Jerusalem, and the
32: 32 their kings, their *p'*, their priests,
34: 10 Now when all the *p'* and all the
19 The *p'* of Judah, and the *p'* of
21 king of Judah and his *p'* will I give
35: 4 was by the chamber of the *p'*, which
36: 12 all the *p'* sat there, even Elishama
12 son of Hananiah, and all the *p'*.
14 all the *p'* sent Jehudi the son of
19 Then said the *p'* unto Baruch, Go,
21 the *p'* which stood beside the king.
37: 14 and brought him to the *p'*.
15 the *p'* were wroth with Jeremiah,
38: 4 the *p'* said unto the king, We
17 unto the king of Babylon's *p'*,
18, 22 forth to the king of Babylon's *p'*,
22 forth to the king of Babylon's *p'*,
25 if the *p'* hear that I have talked
27 came all the *p'* unto Jeremiah, and
39: 3 *p'* of the king of Babylon came in,
3 residue of the *p'* of the king of
13 and all the king of Babylon's *p'*;
41: 1 the *p'* of the king, even ten men
44: 17 our fathers, our kings, and our *p'*,
21 fathers, your kings, and your *p'*,
48: 7 captivity with his priests and his *p'*
49: 3 and his priests and his *p'* together.
38 from thence the king and the *p'*,
50: 35 of Babylon, and upon her *p'*, and
51: 57 And I will make drunk her *p'*, and
52: 10 also all the *p'* of Judah in Riblah.
La 1: 6 her *p'* are become like harts that
2: 2 the kingdom and the *p'* thereof.
9 her *p'* are among the Gentiles: the
5: 12 *P'* are hanged up by their hand:
Eze 11: 1 son of Benaiah, *p'* of the people.
17: 12 the king thereof, and the *p'* thereof,
19: 1 a lamentation for the *p'* of Israel,
21: 12 shall be upon all the *p'* of Israel:
22: 6 Behold, the *p'* of Israel, every one
27 Her *p'* in the midst thereof are like
23: 15 heads, all of them *p'* to look to,
26: 16 all the *p'* of the sea shall come
27: 21 all the *p'* of Kedar, they occupied
32: 29 is Edom, her kings, and all her *p'*,
30 There be the *p'* of the north, all of
39: 18 the blood of the *p'* of the earth,
45: 8 my *p'* shall no more oppress my
9 Let it suffice you, O *p'* of Israel:
Da 1: 3 of the king's seed, and of the *p'*;
3: 2 king sent to gather together the *p'*,
3 Then the *p'*, the governors, and
27 the *p'*, governors, and captains,
5: 2 that the king, and his *p'*, his wives,
3 and the king, and his *p'*, his wives,
6: 1 an hundred and twenty *p'*, which
2 *p'* might give accounts unto them,
3 above the presidents and *p'*,
4 the presidents and *p'* sought to find
6 these presidents and *p'* assembled
7 the governors, and the *p'*, the
8: 25 stand up against the Prince of *p'*;
9: 6 our kings, our *p'*, and our fathers,
8 to our kings, to our *p'*, and to our
10: 13 Michael, one of the chief *p'*, came
11: 5 shall be strong, and one of his *p'*;
8 their *p'*, and with their precious
Ho 5: 10 *p'* of Judah were like them that
7: 3 and the *p'* with their lies.
5 the *p'* have made him sick with
16 their *p'* shall fall by the sword for
8: 4 have made *p'*, and I knew it not:
10 for the burden of the king of *p'*.
9: 15 no more: all their *p'* are revolters.
13: 10 thou saidst, Give me a king and *p'*?
Am 1: 15 captivity, he and his *p'* together,
2: 3 slay all the *p'* thereof with him,
Mic 3: 1 and ye *p'* of the house of Israel;
9 *p'* of the house...Israel, that abhor
Hab 1: 10 the *p'* shall be a scorn unto them:
Zep 1: 8 will punish the *p'*, and the king's
3: 3 *p'* within her are roaring lions;
M't 2: 6 not the least among the *p'* of Juda:
20: 25 that the *p'* of the Gentiles exercise
1Co 2: 6 nor of the *p'* of this world, that
8 none of the *p'* of this world knew:

princess See also PRINCESSES.
La 1: 1 and *p'* among the provinces, how

princesses
1Ki 11: 3 he had seven hundred wives, *p'*,

principal
Ex 30: 23 thou also unto thee *p'* spices,
Le 6: 5 restore it in the *p'*, and shall add
Nu 5: 7 his trespass with the *p'* thereof,
1Ki 4: 5 the son of Nathan was *p'* officer,
2Ki 25: 19 the *p'* scribe of the host, which
1Ch 24: 6 one *p'* household being taken for
31 the *p'* fathers over against their
Ne 11: 17 *p'* to begin the thanksgiving in
Pr 4: 7 Wisdom is the *p'* thing; therefore
Isa 16: 8 have broken down the *p'* plants
28: 25 and cast in the *p'* wheat and the
Jer 25: 34 in the ashes, ye *p'* of the flock:
35 nor the *p'* of the flock to escape.
36 an howling of the *p'* of the flock,
52: 25 and the *p'* scribe of the host who
Mic 5: 5 shepherds, and eight *p'* men.
Ac 25: 23 and *p'* men of the city,

principalities
Jer 13: 18 your *p'* shall come down, even
Ro 8: 38 nor *p'*, nor powers, nor things
Eph 3: 10 now unto the *p'* and powers in

Eph 6:12 but against *p*', against powers,
Col 1:16 or dominions, or *p*', or powers:
2:15 And having spoiled *p*' and powers,
Tit 3: 1 mind to be subject to *p*' and powers,

principality See also PRINCIPALITIES.
Eph 1:21 Far above all *p*', and power, and
Col 2:10 is the head of all *p*' and power:

principles
Heb 5:12 the first *p*' of the oracles of God;
6: 1 leaving the *p*' of the doctrine of

print See also PRINTED.
Le 19:28 dead, nor *p*' any marks upon you:
Job 13:27 a *p*' upon the heels of my feet.
Joh 20:25 in his hands the *p*' of the nails,
25 my finger into the *p*' of the nails,

printed
Job 19:23 oh that they were *p*' in a book!

Prisca (*pris'-cah*) See also PRISCILLA.
2Ti 4:19 Salute *P*' and Aquila, and the

Priscilla (*pris-sil'-lah*) See also PRISCA.
Ac 18: 2 come from Italy, with his wife *P*';
18 and with him *P*' and Aquila;
26 when Aquila and *P*' had heard,
Ro 16: 3 Greet *P*' and Aquila my helpers
1Co 16:19 Aquila and *P*' salute you much

prised
Zec 11:13 price that I was *p*' at of them.

prison See also IMPRISONED; PRISONS.
Ge 39:20 and put him into the *p*', a
20 and he was there in the *p*'.
21 sight of the keeper of the *p*'.
22 the keeper of the *p*' committed
22 prisoners that were in the *p*';
23 keeper of the *p*' looked not to
40: 3 into the *p*', the place where
5 which were bound in the *p*'.
42:16 ye shall be kept in *p*', that your
19 be bound in the house of your *p*':
J'g 16:21 and he did grind in the *p*' house.
25 for Samson out of the *p*' house;
1Ki 22:27 Put this fellow in the *p*', and
2Ki 17: 4 him up, and bound him in *p*'.
25:27 king of Judah out of *p*';
29 And changed his *p*' garments:
2Ch 16:10 seer, and put him in a *p*' house;
18:26 Put this fellow in the *p*', and
Ne 3:25 that was by the court of the *p*'
12:39 and they stood still in the *p*' gate.
Ps 142: 7 Bring my soul out of *p*', that I
Ec 4:14 out of *p*' he cometh to reign,
Isa 24:22 and shall be shut up in the *p*',
42: 7 bring out the prisoners from the *p*',
7 in darkness out of the *p*' house.
22 and they are hid in *p*' houses:
53: 8 He was taken from *p*' and from
61: 1 opening of the *p*' to them that are
Jer 29:26 thou shouldest put him in *p*' and
32: 2 was shut up in the court of the *p*',
8 came to me in the court of the *p*'
12 Jews that sat in the court of the *p*'.
33: 1 yet shut up in the court of the *p*',
37: 4 they had not put him into *p*'.
15 in *p*' in the house of Jonathan
15 for they had made that the *p*'.
18 that ye have put me in *p*'?
21 Jeremiah into the court of the *p*',
21 remained in the court of the *p*'.
38: 6 that was in the court of the *p*': and
13 remained in the court of the *p*'.
28 abode in the court of the *p*' until
39:14 Jeremiah out of the court of the *p*',
15 was shut up in the court of the *p*',
52:11 in *p*' till the day of his death.
31 brought him forth out of *p*',
33 And changed his *p*' garments:
M't 4:12 heard that John was cast into *p*',
5:25 officer, and thou be cast into *p*'.
11: 2 John had heard in the *p*' the works
14: 3 put him in *p*' for Herodias' sake,
10 sent, and beheaded John in the *p*'.
18:30 went and cast him into *p*', till he
25:36 I was in *p*', and ye came unto me.
39 when saw we thee sick, or in *p*',
43 sick, and in *p*', and ye visited me
44 or sick, or in *p*', and did not
M'r 1:14 after that John was put in *p*',
6:17 bound him in *p*' for Herodias' sake,
27 went and beheaded him in the *p*',
Lu 3:20 all, that he shut up John in *p*'.
12:58 and the officer cast thee into *p*'.
22:33 ready to go with thee, both into *p*',
23:19 and for murder, was cast into *p*'.)
25 and murder was cast into *p*',
Joh 3:24 For John was not yet cast into *p*'.
Ac 5:18 and put them in the common *p*'.
19 Lord by night opened the *p*' doors,
21 to the *p*' to have them brought.
22 and found them not in the *p*',
23 The *p*' truly found we shut with
25 the men whom ye put in *p*' are
8: 3 women committed them to *p*'.
12: 4 he put him in *p*', and delivered
5 Peter therefore was kept in *p*':
6 keepers before the door kept the *p*'.
7 and a light shined in the *p*': and he
17 had brought him out of the *p*'.
16:23 they cast them into *p*', charging
24 thrust them into the inner *p*', and
26 foundations...the *p*' were shaken:
27 keeper of the *p*' awaking out of
27 and seeing the *p*' doors open, he
36 keeper of the *p*' told this saying to
Ac 16:37 Romans, and have cast us into *p*';
40 And they went out of the *p*', and
26:10 of the saints did I shut up in *p*',
1Pe 3:19 preached unto the spirits in *p*';
Re 2:10 devil shall cast some of you into *p*',
20: 7 Satan shall be loosed out of his *p*',

prisoner See also FELLOWPRISONER; PRISONERS.
Ps 79:11 the sighing of the *p*' come before
102:20 To hear the groaning of the *p*';
M't 27:15 to release unto the people a *p*',
16 they had then a notable *p*', called
M'r 15: 6 he released unto them one *p*',
Ac 23:18 Paul the *p*' called me unto him, and
25:27 to me unreasonable to send a *p*',
28:17 was I delivered *p*' from Jerusalem
Eph 3: 1 Paul, the *p*' of Jesus Christ for you
4: 1 I therefore, the *p*' of the Lord,
2Ti 1: 8 of our Lord, nor of me his *p*':
Ph'm 1 Paul, a *p*' of Jesus Christ, and
9 and now also a *p*' of Jesus Christ.

prisoners See also FELLOWPRISONERS.
Ge 39:20 where the king's *p*' were bound:
22 all the *p*' that were in the prison;
Nu 21: 1 Israel, and took some of them *p*'.
Job 3:18 There the *p*' rest together; they
Ps 69:33 the poor, and despiseth not his *p*'.
146: 7 hungry. The Lord looseth the *p*':
Isa 10: 4 they shall bow down under the *p*',
14:17 that opened not the house of his *p*'?
20: 4 Assyria lead away...Egyptians *p*',
24:22 as *p*' are gathered in the pit, and
42: 7 to bring out the *p*' from the prison,
49: 9 That thou mayest say to the *p*', Go
La 3:34 his feet all the *p*' of the earth,
Zec 9:11 have sent forth thy *p*' out of the pit
12 to the strong hold, ye *p*' of hope:
Ac 16:25 unto God: and the *p*' heard them.
27 supposing that the *p*' had been fled.
27: 1 delivered Paul and certain other *p*'
42 soldiers' counsel was to kill the *p*',
28:16 delivered the *p*' to the captain of

prison-house See PRISON and HOUSE.

prisons
Lu 21:12 up to the synagogues, and into *p*',
Ac 22: 4 delivering into *p*' both men and
2Co 11:23 in *p*' more frequent, in deaths oft.

private See also PRIVY.
2Pe 1:20 is of any *p*' interpretation.

privately See also PRIVILY.
M't 24: 3 disciples came unto him *p*',
M'r 6:32 into a desert place by ship *p*'.
9:28 his disciples asked him *p*', Why
13: 3 John and Andrew asked him *p*',
Lu 9:10 aside *p*' into a desert place
10:23 and said *p*', Blessed are the eyes
Ac 23:19 and went with him aside *p*', and
Gal 2: 2 but *p*' to them which were of

privily See also PRIVATELY.
J'g 9:31 messengers unto Abimelech *p*',
1Sa 24: 4 cut off the skirt of Saul's robe *p*'.
Ps 10: 8 his eyes are *p*' set against the poor.
11: 2 *p*' shoot at the upright in heart.
31: 4 net that they have laid *p*' for me:
64: 5 they commune of laying snares *p*';
101: 5 Whoso *p*' slandereth his neighbour,
142: 3 have they *p*' laid a snare for me.
Pr 1:11 let us lurk *p*' for the innocent without
18 blood; they lurk *p*' for their own lives.
M't 1:19 was minded to put her away *p*'.
2: 7 when he had *p*' called the wise men,
Ac 16:37 and now do they thrust us out *p*'?
Gal 2: 4 came in *p*' to spy out our liberty
2Pe 2: 1 who *p*' shall bring in damnable

privy See also PRIVATE.
De 23: 1 or hath his *p*' member cut off,
1Ki 2:44 which thine heart is *p*' to, that
Eze 21:14 entereth into their *p*' chambers.
Ac 5: 2 price, his wife also being *p*' to it,

prize See also PRISED.
1Co 9:24 run all, but one receiveth the *p*'?
Ph'p 3:14 mark for the *p*' of the high calling

probate See REPROBATE.

proceed See also PROCEEDED; PROCEEDETH; PROCEEDING.
Ex 25:35 that *p*' out of the candlestick.
Jos 6:10 any word *p*' out of your mouth,
2Sa 7:12 which shall *p*' out of thy bowels,
Job 40: 5 yea, twice; but I will *p*' no further.
Isa 29:14 I will *p*' to do a marvellous work
51: 4 for a law shall *p*' from me, and I
Jer 9: 3 for they *p*' from evil to evil, and
30:19 out of them shall *p*' thanksgiving
21 shall *p*' from the midst of them;
Hab 1: 7 their dignity shall *p*' of themselves.
M't 15:18 things which *p*' out of the mouth
19 out of the heart *p*' evil thoughts,
M'r 7:21 the heart of men, *p*' evil thoughts,
Eph 4:29 communication *p*' out...your mouth,
3: 9 they shall *p*' no further: for their

proceeded
Nu 30:12 then whatsoever *p*' out of her lips
32:24 which hath *p*' out of your mouth.
J'g 11:36 which hath *p*' out of thy mouth;
Job 36: 1 Elihu also *p*', and said,
Lu 4:22 words which *p*' out of his mouth.
Joh 8:42 for I *p*' forth and came from God;
Ac 12: 3 he *p*' further to take Peter also.
Re 4: 5 out of the throne *p*' lightnings
19:21 which sword *p*' out of his mouth:

proceedeth
Ge 24:50 The thing *p*' from the Lord: we
Nu 30: 2 to all that *p*' out of his mouth.
De 8: 3 word that *p*' out of the mouth of
1Sa 24:13 Wickedness *p*' from the wicked:
Ec 10: 5 as an error which *p*' from the ruler:
La 3:38 most High *p*' not evil and good?
Hab 1: 4 therefore wrong judgment *p*'.
M't 4: 4 word that *p*' out of the mouth of
Joh 15:26 truth, which *p*' from the Father,
Jas 3:10 mouth *p*' blessing and cursing.
Re 11: 5 fire *p*' out of their mouth, and

proceeding
Re 22: 1 crystal, *p*' out of the throne of God

process
Ge 4: 3 And in *p*' of time it came to pass,
38:12 *p*' of time the daughter of Shuah
Ex 2:23 it came to pass in *p*' of time, that
J'g 11: 4 it came to pass in *p*' of time, that
2Ch 21:19 it came to pass, that in *p*' of time,

Prochorus (*prok'-o-rus*)
Ac 6: 5 Philip, and *P*', and Nicanor, and

proclaim See also PROCLAIMED; PROCLAIMETH; PROCLAIMING.
Ex 33:19 and I will *p*' the name of the Lord
Le 23: 2 ye shall *p*' to be holy convocations,
4 which ye shall *p*' in their seasons.
21 And ye shall *p*' on the selfsame day,
37 ye shall *p*' to be holy convocations,
25:10 *p*' liberty throughout all the land
De 20:10 against it, then *p*' peace unto it.
J'g 7: 3 *p*' in the ears of the people, saying,
1Ki 21: 9 *P*' a fast, and set Naboth on high
2Ki 10:20 *P*' a solemn assembly for Baal.
Ne 8:15 publish and *p*' in all their cities,
Es 6: 9 of the city, and *p*' before him,
Pr 20: 6 will *p*' every one his own goodness:
Isa 61: 1 to *p*' liberty to the captives, and
2 *p*' the acceptable year of the Lord,
Jer 3:12 Go and *p*' these words toward the
7: 2 *p*' there this word, and say, Hear
11: 6 *P*' all these words in the cities of
19: 2 *p*' there the words that I shall tell
34: 8 Jerusalem, to *p*' liberty unto them;
17 I *p*' a liberty for you, saith the Lord,
Joe 3: 9 *P*' ye this among the Gentiles;
Am 4: 5 *p*' and publish the free offerings:

proclaimed
Ex 34: 5 there, and *p*' the name of the Lord.
6 Lord passed by before him, and *p*',
36: 6 it to be *p*' throughout the camp,
1Ki 21:12 They *p*' a fast, and set Naboth on
2Ki 10:20 assembly for Baal. And they *p*' it.
23:16 man of God *p*', who *p*' these words.
17 *p*' these things that thou hast done
2Ch 20: 3 and *p*' a fast throughout all Judah.
Ezr 8:21 Then I *p*' a fast there, at the river
Es 6:11 *p*' before him, Thus shall it be done
Isa 62:11 the Lord hath *p*' unto the end of
Jer 36: 9 that they *p*' a fast before the Lord
Jon 3: 5 and *p*' a fast, and put on sackcloth,
7 he caused it to be *p*' and published
Lu 12: 3 shall be *p*' upon the housetops.

proclaimeth
Pr 12:23 the heart of fools *p*' foolishness.

proclaiming
Jer 34:15 in *p*' liberty every man to his
17 *p*' liberty, every one to his brother,
Re 5: 2 strong angel *p*' with a loud voice,

proclamation
Ex 32: 5 and Aaron made *p*', and said, To
1Ki 15:22 king Asa made a *p*' throughout
22:36 went a *p*' throughout the host
2Ch 24: 9 they made a *p*' through Judah
30: 5 make *p*' throughout all
36:22 he made a *p*' throughout all
Ezr 1: 1 he made a *p*' throughout all his
10: 7 they made *p*' throughout
Da 5:29 and made a *p*' concerning him,

procure See also PROCURED; PROCURETH.
Jer 26:19 we *p*' great evil against our souls.
33: 9 all the prosperity that I *p*' unto it.

procured
Jer 2:17 Hast thou not *p*' this unto thyself,
4:18 way and thy doings have *p*' these

procureth
Pr 11:27 diligently seeketh good *p*' favour:

produce
Isa 41:21 *P*' your cause, saith the Lord;

profane See also PROFANED; PROFANETH; PROFANING.
Le 18:21 shalt thou *p*' the name of thy God:
19:12 shalt thou *p*' the name of thy God:
20: 3 sanctuary, and to *p*' my holy name.
21: 4 among his people, to *p*' himself.
6 and not *p*' the name of their God:
7 take a wife that is a whore, or *p*';
9 *p*' herself by playing the whore,
12 nor *p*' the sanctuary of his God;
14 widow, or a divorced woman, or *p*',
15 he *p*' his seed among his people:
23 that he *p*' not my sanctuaries: for
22: 2 that they *p*' not my holy name in
9 it, and die therefore, if they *p*' it:
15 they shall not *p*' the holy things of
32 Neither shall ye *p*' my holy name;
Ne 13:17 that ye do, and *p*' the sabbath day?
Jer 23:11 both prophet and priest are *p*';
Eze 21:25 thou, *p*' wicked prince of Israel,

Eze 22:26 between the holy and p', neither
23:39 day into my sanctuary to p' it;
24:21 Behold, I will p' my sanctuary,
28:16 cast thee as p' out of the mountain
42:20 the sanctuary and the p' place.
44:23 difference between the holy and p',
48:15 shall be a p' place for the city, for
Am 2: 7 same maid, to p' my holy name:
M't 12: 5 priests in the temple p' the sabbath,
Ac 24: 6 hath gone about to p' the temple:
1Ti 1: 9 and for sinners, for unholy and p',
4: 7 But refuse p' and old wives' fables,
6:20 avoiding p' and vain babblings, and
2Ti 2:16 But shun p' and vain babblings:
Heb12:16 be any fornicator, or p' person,

profaned
Le 19: 8 hath p' the hallowed thing of the
Ps 89:39 thou hast p' his crown by casting
Isa 43:28 I have p' the princes of the
Eze 22: 8 things, and hast p' my sabbaths.
26 law, and have p' mine holy things:
26 sabbaths, and I am p' among them.
23:38 day, and have p' my sabbaths.
25: 3 my sanctuary, when it was p';
36:20 they went, they p' my holy name,
21 Israel had p' among the heathen,
22 ye have p' among the heathen,
23 which was p' among the heathen,
23 ye have p' in the midst of them;
Mal 1:12 But ye have p' it, in that ye say,
2:11 hath p' the holiness of the Lord

profaneness
Jer 23:15 the prophets of Jerusalem is p'

profaneth
Le 21: 9 the whore, she p' her father: she

profaning
Ne 13:18 upon Israel by p' the sabbath.
Mal 2:10 by p' the covenant of our fathers?

profess See also PROFESSED; PROFESSING.
De 26: 3 him, I p' this day unto the Lord
M't 7:23 then will I p' unto them, I never
Tit 1:16 They p' that they know God; but

professed
2Co 9:13 for your p' subjection unto the
1Ti 6:12 hast p' a good profession before

professing
Ro 1:22 P' themselves to be wise, they
1Ti 2:10 becometh women p' godliness)
6:21 some p' have erred concerning the

profession
1Ti 6:12 good p' before many witnesses.
Heb 3: 1 Apostle and High Priest of our p',
4:14 Son of God, let us hold fast our p'.
10:23 Let us hold fast the p' of our faith

profit See also PROFITABLE; PROFITED; PROFITETH; PROFITING.
Ge 25:32 what p' shall this birthright do to me?
37:26 What p' is it if we slay our brother,
1Sa 12:21 which cannot p' nor deliver; for
Es 3: 8 for the king's p' to suffer them.
Job 21:15 what p' should we have, if we
30: 2 the strength of their hands p' me,
35: 3 and, What p' shall I have, if I be
8 righteousness may p' the son of man.
Ps 30: 9 What p' is there in my blood, when
Pr 10: 2 of wickedness p' nothing: but
11: 4 Riches p' not in the day of wrath:
14:23 In all labour there is p': but the
Ec 1: 3 What p' hath a man of all his
2:11 and there was no p' under the sun.
3: 9 What p' hath he that worketh in
5: 9 the p' of the earth is for all: the
16 and what p' hath he that hath
7:11 is p' to them that see the sun.
Isa 30: 5 a people that could not p' them,
5 nor be an help nor p', but a shame,
6 to a people that shall not p' them.
44: 9 their delectable things shall not p';
47:12 if so be thou shalt be able to p', if
48:17 thy God which teacheth thee to p',
57:12 works; for they shall not p' thee.
Jer 2: 8 walked after things that do not p'.
11 glory for that which doth not p'.
7: 8 trust in lying words, that cannot p'.
12:13 themselves to pain, but shall not p':
16:19 and things wherein there is no p'.
23:32 they shall not p' this people at all,
Mal 3:14 what p' is it that we have kept his
M'r 8:36 For what shall it p' a man, if he
Ro 3: 1 what p' is there of circumcision?
1Co 7:35 And this I speak for your own p';
10:33 things, not seeking mine own p',
33 p' of many, that they may be saved.
12: 7 is given to every man to p' withal.
14: 6 what shall I p' you, except I shall
Ga 5: 2 Christ shall p' you nothing.
2Ti 2:14 strive not about words to no p',
Heb 4: 2 word preached did not p' them,
12:10 he for our p', that we might be
Jas 2:14 What doth it p', my brethren,
16 to the body; what doth it p'?

profitable See also UNPROFITABLE.
Job 22: 2 Can a man be p' unto God, as he
2 is wise may be p' unto himself?
Ec 10:10 but wisdom is p' to direct.
Isa 44:10 image that is p' for nothing?
Jer 13: 7 was marred, it was p' for nothing.
M't 5:29, 30 it is p' for thee that one of thy
Ac 20:20 back nothing that was p' unto you,
1Ti 4: 8 godliness is p' unto all things,
2Ti 3:16 and is p' for doctrine, for reproof,
4:11 for he is p' to me for the ministry.
Tit 3: 8 things are good and p' unto men.
Ph'm 11 but now p' to thee and to me:

profited
Job 33:27 which was right, and it p' me not;
M't 15: 5 thou mightest be p' by me;
16:26 For what is a man p', if he shall
M'r 7:11 thou mightest be p' by me; he
Ga 1:14 And p' in the Jews' religion above
Heb13: 9 p' them that have been occupied

profiteth
Job 34: 9 It p' a man nothing that he
Hab 2:18 What p' the graven image that the
Joh 6:63 the flesh p' nothing: the words
Ro 2:25 circumcision verily p', if thou keep
1Co 13: 3 have not charity, it p' me nothing.
1Ti 4: 8 For bodily exercise p' little:

profiting
1Ti 4:15 that thy p' may appear to all.

profound
Ho 5: 2 revolters are p' to make slaughter,

progenitors
Ge 49:26 blessings of my p' unto the utmost

prognosticators
Isa 47:13 stargazers, the monthly p', stand

prolong See also PROLONGED; PROLONGETH.
De 4:26 shall not p' your days upon it, but
40 mayest p' thy days upon the earth,
5:33 ye may p' your days in the land
11: 9 ye may p' your days in the land,
17:20 he may p' his days in his kingdom,
22: 7 and that thou mayest p' thy days.
30:18 shall not p' your days upon the land,
32:47 ye shall p' your days in the land,
Job 6:11 mine end, that I should p' my life?
15:29 neither shall he p' the perfection
Ps 61: 6 Thou wilt p' the king's life: and
Pr 28:16 covetousness shall p' his days.
Ec 8:13 neither shall he p' his days, which
Isa 53:10 seed, he shall p' his days, and the

prolonged
De 5:16 that thy days may be p', and that
6: 2 life; and that thy days may be p'.
Pr 28: 2 the state thereof shall be p'.
Ec 8:12 his days be p', yet surely I know
Isa 13:22 come, and her days shall not be p'.
Eze 12:22 The days are p', and every vision
25 it shall be no more p': for in your
28 shall none of my words be p' any
Da 7:12 lives were p' for a season and

prolongeth
Pr 10:27 The fear of the Lord p' days: but
Ec 7:15 a wicked man that p' his life in

promise See also PROMISED; PROMISES; PROMISING.
Nu 14:34 and ye shall know my breach of p'.
1Ki 8:56 failed one word of all his good p',
2Ch 1: 9 let thy p' unto David my father be
Ne 5:12 should do according to this p'.
13 performeth not this p', even thus
13 the people did according to this p'.
Ps 77: 8 doth his p' fail for evermore?
105:42 he remembered his holy p', and
Lu 24:49 the p' of my Father upon you:
Ac 1: 4 but wait for the p' of the Father,
2:33 Father, the p' of the Holy Ghost,
39 For the p' is unto you, and to your
7:17 when the time of the p' drew nigh,
13:23 according to his p', raised unto
32 p' which was made unto the fathers,
23:21 ready, looking for a p' from thee.
26: 6 for the hope of the p' made of God
7 Unto which p' our twelve tribes,
Ro 4:13 For the p', that he should be the
14 and the p' made of none effect:
16 the end the p' might be sure to all
20 He staggered not at the p' of God
9: 8 children of the p' are counted for
9 this is the word of p', At this time
Ga 3:14 the p' of the Spirit through faith.
17 should make the p' of none effect.
18 be of the law, it is no more of p':
18 but God gave it to Abraham by p'.
19 come to whom the p' was made;
22 that the p' by faith of Jesus Christ
29 and heirs according to the p'.
4:23 he of the freewoman was by p'.
28 as Isaac was, are the children of p'.
Eph 1:13 sealed with that holy Spirit of p',
2:12 from the covenants of p', having
3: 6 partakers of his p' in Christ by the
6: 2 is the first commandment with p';
1Ti 4: 8 having p' of the life that now is,
2Ti 1: 1 the p' of life which is in Christ
Heb 4: 1 a p' being left us of entering into
6:13 when God made p' to Abraham,
15 endured, he obtained the p'.
17 to shew unto the heirs of p' the
9:15 the p' of eternal inheritance.
10:36 of God, ye might receive the p'.
11: 9 faith he sojourned in the land of p',
9 the heirs with him of the same p':
39 through faith, received not the p':
2Pe 2:19 While they p' them liberty, they
3: 4 Where is the p' of his coming?
9 is not slack concerning his p',
13 according to his p', look for new
1Jo 2:25 the p' that he hath promised us,

promised See also PROMISEDST.
Ex 12:25 according as he hath p', that ye
Nu 14:40 place which the Lord hath p':
De 1:11 and bless you, as he hath p' you!)
6: 3 Lord God of thy fathers hath p'
9:28 into the land which he p' them,
10: 9 as the Lord thy God p' him.
12:20 thy border, as he hath p' thee, and
15: 6 God blesseth thee, as he p' thee:
19: 8 land which he p' to give unto thy
23:23 thou hast p' with thy mouth.
26:18 peculiar people, as he hath p' thee,
27: 3 God of thy fathers hath p' thee.
Jos 9:21 as the princes had p' them.
22: 4 unto your brethren, as he p' them:
23: 5 Lord your God hath p' unto you.
10 fighteth for you, as he hath p' you.
15 the Lord your God p' you; which
2Sa 7:28 p' this goodness unto thy servant:
1Ki 2:24 hath made me an house, as he p',
5:12 Solomon wisdom, as he p' him:
8:20 throne of Israel, as the Lord p',
56 Israel, according to all that he p':
56 which he p' by the hand of Moses
9: 5 as I p' to David thy father, saying,
2Ki 8:19 as he p' him to give him alway a
1Ch 17:26 p' this goodness unto thy servant:
2Ch 6:10 throne of Israel, as the Lord p',
15 that which thou hast p' him; and
16 which thou hast p' him, saying,
21: 7 as he p' to give a light to him and
Ne 9:23 which thou hadst p' to their fathers,
Es 4: 7 money that Haman had p' to pay
Jer 32:42 all the good that I have p' them.
33:14 that good thing which I have p'
M't 14: 7 he p' with an oath to give her
M'r 14:11 glad, and p' to give him money.
Lu 1:72 perform the mercy p' to our fathers,
22: 6 he p', and sought opportunity to
Ac 7: 5 yet he p' that he would give it...him
Ro 1: 2 he had p' afore by his prophets
4:21 what he had p', he was able also
Tit 1: 2 God, that cannot lie, p' before the
Heb10:23 wavering; (...he is faithful that p';)
11:11 judged him faithful who had p'.
12:26 now he hath p', saying, Yet once
Jas 1:12 Lord hath p' to them that love him.
2: 5 kingdom which he hath p' to them
1Jo 2:25 promise that he hath p' us, even

promisedst
1Ki 8:24 David my father that thou p' him:
25 David my father that thou p' him,
Ne 9:15 p' them that they should go in to

promises
Ro 9: 4 and the service of God, and the p';
15: 8 the p' made unto the fathers:
2Co 1:20 For all the p' of God in him are yea,
7: 1 Having therefore these p', dearly
Gal 3:16 and his seed were the p' made.
21 the law then against the p' of God?
Heb 6:12 faith and patience inherit the p'.
7: 6 and blessed him that had the p'.
8: 6 was established upon better p'.
11:13 faith, not having received the p',
17 he that had received the p' offered
33 obtained p', stopped the mouths of
2Pe 1: 4 exceeding great and precious p':

promising
Eze 13:22 his wicked way, by p' him life:

promote See also PROMOTED.
Nu 22:17 I will p' thee unto very great
37 able indeed to p' thee to honour?
24:11 to p' thee unto great honour; but
Es 3: 1 did king Ahasuerus p' Haman
Pr 4: 8 Exalt her, and she shall p' thee:

promoted
J'g 9: 9, 11, 13 go to be p' over the trees?
Es 5:11 wherein the king had p' him,
Da 3:30 Then the king p' Shadrach,

promotion
Ps 75: 6 p' cometh neither from the east,
Pr 3:35 but shame shall be the p' of fools.

pronounce See also PRONOUNCED; PRONOUNCING.
Le 5: 4 that a man shall p' with an oath,
13: 3 look on him, and p' him unclean.
6 the skin, the priest shall p' him clean:
8 then the priest shall p' him unclean:
11 and the priest shall p' him unclean,
13 he shall p' him clean that hath the
15 raw flesh, and p' him to be unclean:
17 then the priest shall p' him clean
20 the priest shall p' unclean: it is a
22 then the priest shall p' him unclean:
23 and the priest shall p' him clean.
25 the priest shall p' him unclean:
27 then the priest shall p' him unclean:
28 and the priest shall p' him clean; for
30 then the priest shall p' him unclean:
34 then the priest shall p' him clean:
37 and the priest shall p' him clean.
44 priest shall p' him utterly unclean;
59 to p' it clean, or to p' it unclean.
14: 7 and shall p' him clean, and shall let
48 the priest shall p' the house clean,
J'g 12: 6 he could not frame to p' it right.

pronounced
Ne 6:12 he p' this prophecy against me:
Jer 11:17 hath p' evil against thee, for the
16:10 p' all this great evil against us?
18: 8 nation, against whom I have p',
19:15 the evil that I have p' against it,
25:13 words which I have p' against it,
26:13 evil that he hath p' against you.
19 evil which he had p' against them?
34: 5 for I have p' the word, saith the

Jer 35:17 evil that I have p' against them:
36: 7 Lord hath p' against this people.
18 He p' all these words unto me
31 evil that I have p' against them;
40: 2 hath p' this evil upon this place.

pronouncing
Le 5: 4 swear, p' with his lips to do evil,

proof See also PROOFS; REPROOF.
2Co 2: 9 that I might know the p' of you,
8:24 p' of your love, and of our boasting
13: 3 a p' of Christ speaking in me,
Ph'p 2:22 But ye know the p' of him, that,
2Ti 4: 5 make full p' of thy ministry.

proofs See also REPROOFS.
Ac 1: 3 his passion by many infallible p',

proper
1Ch 29: 3 I have of mine own p' good, of
Ac 1:19 field is called in their p' tongue,
1Co 7: 7 every man hath his p' gift of God,
Heb11:23 they saw he was a p' child;

prophecies
1Co 13: 8 whether there be p', they shall
1Ti 1:18 the p' which went before on thee,

prophecy See also PROPHECIES.
2Ch 9:29 in the p' of Ahijah the Shilonite,
15: 8 and the p' of Oded the prophet,
Ne 6:12 he pronounced this p' against me:
Pr 30: 1 the son of Jakeh, even the p':
31: 1 the p' that his mother taught him.
Da 9:24 to seal up the vision and p', and
M't 13:14 them is fulfilled the p' of Esaias,
Ro 12: 6 that is given to us, whether p',
1Co 12:10 working of miracles; to another p';
13: 2 though I have the gift of p', and
1Ti 4:14 in thee, which was given thee by p',
2Pe 1:19 have also a more sure word of p';
20 that no p' of the scripture is of any
21 For the p' came not in old time by
Re 1: 3 they that hear the words of this p',
11: 6 it rain not in the days of their p':
19:10 testimony of Jesus is the spirit of p'.
22: 7 the sayings of the p' of this book.
10 the sayings of the p' of this book:
18 the words of the p' of this book,
19 the words of the book of this p',

prophesied
Nu 11:25 spirit rested upon them, they p',
26 tabernacle: and they p' in the camp.
1Sa 10:10 upon him, and he p' among them.
11 he p' among the prophets, that the
18:10 and he p' in the midst of the house:
19:20 of Saul, and they also p'.
21 messengers, and they p' likewise.
21 the third time, and they p' also.
23 he went on, and p', until he came
24 p' before Samuel in like manner,
1Ki 18:29 and they p' until the time of the
22:10 all the prophets p' before them.
12 all the prophets p' so, saying, Go
1Ch 25: 2 p' according to the order of the
3 also p' with a harp, to give thanks
2Ch 18: 7 for he never p' good unto me, but
9 all the prophets p' before them.
11 And all the prophets p' so, saying,
20:37 p' Eliezer...against Jehoshaphat,
Ezr 5: 1 p' unto the Jews that were in
Jer 2: 8 and the prophets p' by Baal, and
20: 1 that Jeremiah p' these things.
6 friends, to whom thou hast p' lies.
23:13 they p' in Baal, and caused my
21 not spoken to them, yet they p'.
25:13 hath p' against all the nations.
26: 9 thou p' in the name of the Lord,
11 for he hath p' against this city, as
18 Micah the Morasthite p' in the days
20 man that p' in the name of the Lord,
20 who p' against this city and against
28: 6 thy words which thou hast p',
8 old p' both against many countries,
29:31 that Shemaiah hath p' unto you,
37:19 your prophets which p' unto you,
Eze 11:13 to pass, when I p', that Pelatiah
37: 7 So I p' as I was commanded:
7 and as I p', there was a noise, and
10 So I p' as he commanded me, and
38:17 which p' in those days many years
Zec 13: 4 one of his vision, when he hath p';
M't 7:22 Lord, have we not p' in thy name?
11:13 prophets and the law p' until John.
M'r 7: 6 Well hath Esaias p' of you
Lu 1:67 the Holy Ghost, and p', saying,
Joh 11:51 he p' that Jesus should die for that
Ac 19: 6 and they spake with tongues, and p'.
1Co 14: 5 with tongues, but rather that ye p':
1Pe 1:10 who p' of the grace that should
Jude 14 Adam, p' of these, saying, Behold,

prophesieth
Jer 28: 9 The prophet which p' of peace,
Eze 12:27 he p' of the times that are far off.
Zec 13: 3 thrust him through when he p'.
1Co 11: 5 or p' with her head uncovered
14: 3 But he that p' speaketh unto men
4 but he that p' edifieth the church.
5 greater is he that p' than he that

prophesy See also PROPHESIED; PROPHESIETH; PROPHESYING.
Nu 11:27 and Medad do p' in the camp.
1Sa 10: 5 before them; and they shall p':
6 thou shalt p' with them, and shalt
1Ki 22: 8 he doth not p' good concerning me,
18 would p' no good concerning me,
1Ch 25: 1 who should p' with harps, with
2Ch 18:17 he would not p' good unto me, but
Isa 30:10 P' not unto us right things, speak
10 unto us smooth things, p' deceits:
Jer 5:31 The prophets p' falsely, and the
11:21 P' not in the name of the Lord,
14:14 The prophets p' lies in my name:
14 they p' unto you a false vision and
15 the prophets that p' in my name,
16 the people to whom they p' shall be
19:14 whither the Lord had sent him to p';
23:16 words of the prophets that p' unto
25 said, that p' lies in my name,
26 heart of the prophets that p' lies?
32 against them that p' false dreams,
25:30 p' thou against them all these
26:12 sent me to p' against this house
27:10 For they p' a lie unto you, to remove
14 Babylon: for they p' a lie unto you.
15 Lord, yet they p' a lie in my name;
15 and the prophets that p' unto you.
16 of your prophets that p' unto you,
16 Babylon: for they p' a lie unto you.
29: 9 p' falsely unto you in my name:
21 p' a lie unto you in my name;
32: 3 Wherefore dost thou p', and say,
Eze 4: 7 and thou shalt p' against it.
6: 2 of Israel, and p' against them,
11: 4 p' against them, p', O son of man.
13: 2 p' against the prophets of Israel
2 the prophets of Israel that p',
2 unto them that p' out of their own
16 the prophets of Israel which p'
17 daughters of thy people, which p'
17 heart; and p' thou against them,
20:46 p' against the forest of the south
21: 2 and p' against the land of Israel,
9 Son of man, p', and say, Thus saith
14 son of man, p', and smite thine
28 son of man, p' and say, Thus saith
25: 2 Ammonites, and p' against them;
28:21 against Zidon, and p' against it,
29: 2 king of Egypt, and p' against him,
30: 2 Son of man, p' and say, Thus saith
34: 2 p' against the shepherds of Israel,
2 p', and say unto them, Thus saith
35: 2 mount Seir, and p' against it,
36: 1 p' unto the mountains of Israel,
3 Therefore p' and say, Thus saith
6 P' therefore concerning the land of
37: 4 P' upon these bones, and say unto
9 P' unto the wind, p', son of man,
12 Therefore p' and say unto them,
38: 2 and Tubal, and p' against him,
14 son of man, p' and say unto Gog,
39: 1 thou son of man, p' against Gog,
Joe 2:28 sons and your daughters shall p',
Am 2:12 the prophets, saying, P' not.
3: 8 God hath spoken, who can but p'?
7:12 and there eat bread, and p' there:
13 p' not again any more at Beth-el:
15 me, Go, p' unto my people Israel.
16 Thou sayest, P' not against Israel,
Mic 2: 6 P' ye not, say they to them that
6 say they to them that p': they shall
6 they shall not p' to them, that they
11 I will p' unto thee of wine and of
Zec 13: 3 that when any shall yet p', then
M't 15: 7 well did Esaias p' of you, saying,
26:68 P' unto us, thou Christ, Who is he
M'r 14:65 him, and to say unto him, P':
Lu 22:64 P', who is it that smote thee?
Ac 2:17 sons and your daughters shall p',
18 of my Spirit; and they shall p':
21: 9 daughters, virgins, which did p'.
Ro 12: 6 let us p' according to the proportion
1Co 13: 9 we know in part, and we p' in part.
14: 1 gifts, but rather that ye may p'.
24 if all p', and there come in one that
31 For ye may all p' one by one, that
39 covet to p', and forbid not to speak
Re 10:11 Thou must p' again before many
11: 3 shall p' a thousand two hundred

prophesying See also PROPHESYINGS.
1Sa 10:13 when he had made an end of p',
19:20 the company of the prophets p',
Ezr 6:14 prospered through the p' of Haggai
1Co 11: 4 Every man praying or p', having
14: 6 or by knowledge, or by p', or by
22 but p' serveth not for them that

prophesyings
1Th 5:20 Despise not p'.

prophet See also PROPHETESS; PROPHET'S; PROPHETS.
Ge 20: 7 for he is a p', and he shall pray for
Ex 7: 1 Aaron thy brother shall be thy p'.
Nu 12: 6 If there be a p' among you, I the
De 13: 1 If there arise among you a p', or a
3 hearken unto the words of that p',
5 that p', or that dreamer of dreams,
18:15 thy God will raise up unto thee a P'
18 I will raise them up a P' from
20 But the p', which shall presume to
20 of other gods, even that p' shall die.
22 When a p' speaketh in the name of
22 p' hath spoken it presumptuously:
34:10 arose not a p' since in Israel like
J'g 6: 8 Lord sent a p' unto the children of
1Sa 3:20 established to be a p' of the Lord.
9: 9 a P' was before time called a Seer.)
22: 5 p' Gad said unto David, Abide not
2Sa 7: 2 the king said unto Nathan the p',
12:25 sent by the hand of Nathan the p':
24:11 of the Lord came unto the p' Gad,
1Ki 1: 8 Nathan the p', and Shimei, and Rei,
1Ki 1:10 Nathan the p', and Benaiah, and
22 the king, Nathan the p' also came
23 king, saying, Behold Nathan the p'.
32 the priest, and Nathan the p', and
34 Nathan the p' anoint him there
38, 44 and Nathan the p', and Benaiah
45 Nathan the p' have anointed him
11:29 p' Ahijah the Shilonite found him
13:11 there dwelt an old p' in Beth-el;
18 him, I am a p' also as thou art;
20 unto the p' that brought him back:
23 the p' whom he had brought back.
25 in the city where the old p' dwelt.
26 when the p' that brought him back
29 the p' took up the carcase of the
29 and the old p' came to the city, to
14: 2 there is Ahijah the p', which told
18 hand of his servant Ahijah the p'.
16: 7 by the hand of the p' Jehu the son
12 against Baasha by Jehu the p',
18:22 I only, remain a p' of the Lord;
36 Elijah the p' came near, and said,
19:16 thou anoint to be p' in thy room.
20:13 there came a p' unto Ahab king of
22 the p' came to the king of Israel,
38 So the p' departed, and waited for
22: 7 Is there not here a p' of the Lord
2Ki 3:11 Is there not here a p' of the Lord,
5: 3 were with the p' that is in Samaria!
8 know that there is a p' in Israel.
13 if the p' had bid thee do some great
6:12 but Elisha, the p' that is in Israel,
9: 1 the p' called one of the children of
4 even the young man the p', went to
14:25 Jonah the son of Amittai, the p',
19: 2 to Isaiah the p' the son of Amoz.
20: 1 the p' Isaiah the son of Amoz came
11 Isaiah the p' cried unto the Lord:
14 Then came Isaiah the p' unto king
23:18 of the p' that came out of Samaria.
1Ch 17: 1 David said to Nathan the p', Lo, I
29: 29 and in the book of Nathan the p',
2Ch 9:29 in the book of Nathan the p', and
12: 5 came Shemaiah the p' to Rehoboam,
15 in the book of Shemaiah the p', and
13:22 written in the story of the p' Iddo.
15: 8 and the prophecy of Oded the p',
18: 6 Is there not here a p' of the Lord
21:12 a writing to him from Elijah the p',
25:15 he sent unto him a p', which said
16 Then the p' forbare, and said, I
26:22 did Isaiah the p', the son of Amoz,
28: 9 a p' of the Lord was there, whose
29:25 the king's seer, and Nathan the p':
32:20 p' Isaiah the son of Amoz, prayed
32 written in the vision of Isaiah the p',
35:18 from the days of Samuel the p';
36:12 Jeremiah the p' speaking from the
Ezr 5: 1 Haggai the p', and Zechariah the
6:14 the prophesying of Haggai the p'
Ps 51: *title* Nathan the p' came unto him,
74: 9 there is no more any p': neither is
Isa 3: 2 man of war, the judge, and the p',
9:15 the p' that teacheth lies, he is the
28: 7 the priest and the p' have erred
37: 2 unto Isaiah the p' the son of Amoz.
38: 1 Isaiah the p' the son of Amoz came
39: 3 Isaiah the p' unto king Hezekiah,
Jer 1: 5 ordained thee a p' unto the nations.
6:13 from the p' even unto the priest
8:10 from the p' even unto the priest
14:18 both the p' and the priest go about
18:18 the wise, nor the word from the p'.
20: 2 Pashur smote Jeremiah the p', and
23:11 both p' and priest are profane; yea,
28 The p' that hath a dream, let him
33 or the p', or a priest shall ask thee,
34 And as for the p', and the priest,
37 Thus shalt thou say to the p', What
25: 2 Jeremiah the p' spake unto all the
28: 1 Hananiah the son of Azar the p',
5 p' Jeremiah said unto...p' Hananiah
6 Even the p' Jeremiah said, Amen:
9 The p' which prophesieth of peace,
9 the word of the p' shall come to
9 then shall the p' be known, that
10 Hananiah the p' took the yoke
10 from off the p' Jeremiah's neck,
11 And the p' Jeremiah went his way.
12 Lord came unto Jeremiah the p',
12 the p' had broken the yoke
12 off the neck of the p' Jeremiah,
15 p' Jeremiah unto Hananiah the p',
17 So Hananiah the p' died the same
29: 1 that Jeremiah the p' sent from
26 is mad, and maketh himself a p',
27 which maketh himself a p' to you?
29 in the ears of Jeremiah the p'.
32: 2 Jeremiah the p' was shut up in the
34: 6 Jeremiah the p' spake all these
36: 8 Jeremiah the p' commanded him,
26 the scribe and Jeremiah the p':
37: 2 which he spake by the p' Jeremiah.
3 the priest to the p' Jeremiah,
6 of the Lord unto the p' Jeremiah,
13 he took Jeremiah the p', saying,
38: 9 they have done to Jeremiah the p',
10 take up Jeremiah the p' out of the
14 took Jeremiah the p' unto him into
42: 2 And said unto Jeremiah the p', Let,
4 Jeremiah the p' said unto them, I
43: 6 and Jeremiah the p', and Baruch
45: 1 that Jeremiah the p' spake unto
46: 1 Lord which came to Jeremiah the p'
13 the Lord spake to Jeremiah the p',
47: 1 Lord that came to Jeremiah the p'

Jer 49:34 came to Jeremiah the p· against
50: 1 the Chaldeans by Jeremiah the p·.
51:59 which Jeremiah the p· commanded
La 2:20 the priest and the p· be slain in the
Eze 2: 5 there hath been a p· among them.
7:26 shall they seek a vision of the p·;
14: 4 his face, and cometh to the p·;
7 cometh to a p· to enquire of him
9 And if the p· be deceived when he
9 I the Lord have deceived that p·,
10 the punishment of the p· shall be
33:33 that a p· hath been among them.
Da 9: 2 the Lord came to Jeremiah the p·,
Ho 4: 5 p· also shall fall with thee in the
9: 7 the p· is a fool, the spiritual man
8 the p· is a snare of a fowler in all
12:13 by a p· the Lord brought Israel out
13 and by a p· was he preserved.
Am 7:14 I was no p·, neither was I a
Mic 2:11 shall even be the p· of this people.
Hab 1: 1 which Habakkuk the p· did see.
3: 1 A prayer of Habakkuk the p· upon
Hag 1: 1 word of the Lord by Haggai the p·
3 word of the Lord by Haggai the p·,
12 and the words of Haggai the p·,
2: 1 word of the Lord by the p· Haggai,
10 word of the Lord by Haggai the p·,
Zec 1: 1, 7 Berechiah, the son of Iddo the p·,
13: 5 shall say, I am no p·, I am an
Mal 4: 5 Behold, I will send you Elijah the p·
M't 1:22 was spoken of the Lord by the p·,
2: 5 for thus it is written by the p·,
15 was spoken of the Lord by the p·,
17 which was spoken by Jeremy the p·,
3: 3 that was spoken of by the p· Esaias,
4:14 spoken by Esaias the p·, saying,
8:17 which was spoken by Esaias the p·,
10:41 a p· in the name of a p· shall receive
11: 9 what went ye out for to see? A p·?
9 I say unto you, and more than a p·.
12:17 which was spoken by Esaias the p·,
39 to it, but the sign of the p· Jonas:
13:35 which was spoken by the p·,
57 A p· is not without honour, save in
14: 5 because they counted him as a p·.
16: 4 unto it, but the sign of the p· Jonas.
21: 4 which was spoken by the p·,
11 This is Jesus the p· of Nazareth of
26 people; for all hold John as a p·.
46 because they took him for a p·.
24:15 spoken of by Daniel the p·, stand in
27: 9 which was spoken by Jeremy the p·,
35 which was spoken by the p·, They
M'r 6: 4 A p· is not without honour, but in
15 others said, That it is a p·, or as one
11:32 John, that he was a p· indeed.
13:14 spoken of by Daniel the p·,
Lu 1:76 be called the p· of the Highest:
3: 4 book of the words of Esaias the p·,
4:17 unto him the book of the p· Esaias.
24 No p· is accepted in his own
27 Israel in the time of Eliseus the p·;
7:16 a great p· is risen up among us;
26 what went ye out for to see? A p·?
26 unto you, and much more than a p·.
28 a greater p· than John the Baptist:
39 This man, if he were a p·, would
11:29 it, but the sign of Jonas the p·.
13:33 that a p· perish out of Jerusalem.
20: 6 be persuaded that John was a p·.
24:19 which was a p· mighty in deed and
Joh 1:21 Art thou that p·? And he answered,
23 of the Lord, as said the p· Esaias.
25 Christ, nor Elias, neither that p·?
4:19 Sir, I perceive that thou art a p·.
44 that a p· hath no honour in his own
6:14 p· that should come into the world.
7:40 said, Of a truth this is the P·.
52 look: for out of Galilee ariseth no p·.
9:17 thine eyes? He said, He is a p·.
12:38 of Esaias the p· might be fulfilled,
Ac 2:16 which was spoken by the p· Joel;
30 being a p·, and knowing that God
3:22 A p· shall the Lord your God raise
23 soul, which will not hear that p·,
7:37 A p· shall the Lord your God raise
48 made with hands; as saith the p·,
8:28 in his chariot read Esaias the p·.
30 and heard him read the p· Esaias,
34 of whom speaketh the p· this? of
13: 6 sorcerer, a false p·, a Jew, whose
20 fifty years, until Samuel the p·.
21:10 Judæa a certain p·, named Agabus.
28:25 the Holy Ghost by Esaias the p·
1Co 14:37 If any man think himself to be a p·,
Tit 1:12 even a p· of their own, said, The
2Pe 2:16 voice forbad the madness of the p·.
Re 16:13 out of the mouth of the false p·.
19:20 the false p· that wrought miracles
20:10 where the beast and the false p· are,

prophetess
Ex 15:20 Miriam the p·, the sister of Aaron,
J'g 4: 4 Deborah, a p·, the wife of Lapidoth,
2Ki 22:14 went unto Huldah the p·, the wife
2Ch 34:22 appointed, went to Huldah the p·,
Ne 6:14 and on the p· Noadiah, and the rest
Isa 8: 3 And I went unto the p·; and she
Lu 2:36 was one Anna, a p·, the daughter
Re 2:20 Jezebel, which calleth herself a p·,

prophet's
Am 7:14 neither was I a p· son; but I was a
M't 10:41 prophet shall receive a p· reward;

prophets
Nu 11:29 that all the Lord's people were p·,
1Sa 10: 5 meet a company of p· coming down
10 behold, a company of p· met him;
11 he prophesied among the p·, then
11 Kish? Is Saul also among the p·?
12 proverb, Is Saul also among the p·?
19:20 they saw the company of the p·
24 they say, Is Saul also among the p·?
28: 6 by dreams, nor by Urim, nor by p·.
15 more, neither by p·, nor by dreams:
1Ki 18: 4 Jezebel cut off the p· of the Lord,
4 Obadiah took an hundred p·, and
13 Jezebel slew the p· of the Lord,
13 an hundred men of the Lord's p·
19 p· of Baal four hundred and fifty,
19 the p· of the groves four hundred,
20 gathered the p· together unto
22 Baal's p· are four hundred and fifty
25 said unto the p· of Baal, Choose
40 unto them, Take the p· of Baal; let
19: 1 how he had slain all the p· with the
10, 14 and slain thy p· with the sword;
20:35 man of the sons of the p· said unto
41 discerned him that he was of the p·.
22: 6 of Israel gathered the p· together,
10 all the p· prophesied before them.
12 all the p· prophesied so, saying, Go
13 the p· declare good unto the king
22 lying spirit in...mouth of all his p·.
23 in the mouth of all these thy p·,
2Ki 2: 3 sons of the p· that were at Beth-el
5 sons of the p· that were at Jericho
7 fifty men of the sons of the p· went,
15 And when the sons of the p· which
3:13 get thee to the p· of thy father,
13 to the p· of thy mother. And the
4: 1 of the wives of the sons of the p·
38 sons of the p· were sitting before
38 seethe pottage for the sons of the p·.
5:22 young men of the sons of the p·:
6: 1 the sons of the p· said unto Elisha,
9: 1 called one of the children of the p·,
7 the blood of my servants the p·,
10:19 call unto me all the p· of Baal, all
17:13 against Judah, by all the p·, and
13 I sent to you by my servants the p·.
23 had said by all his servants the p·.
21:10 Lord spake by his servants the p·,
23: 2 the priests, and the p·, and all the
24: 2 he spake by his servants the p·.
1Ch 16:22 anointed, and do my p· no harm.
2Ch 18: 5 together of p· four hundred men,
9 all the p· prophesied before them.
11 all the p· prophesied so, saying, Go
12 the p· declare good to the king
21 lying spirit in...mouth of all his p·.
22 spirit in the mouth of these thy p·,
20:20 believe his p·, so shall ye prosper.
24:19 Yet he sent p· to them, to bring
29:25 commandment of the Lord by...p·.
36:16 his words, and misused his p·,
Ezr 5: 1 Then the p·, Haggai the prophet,
2 were the p· of God helping them.
9:11 commanded by thy servants the p·,
Ne 6: 7 hast also appointed p· to preach
14 the rest of the p·, that would have
9:26 slew thy p· which testified against
30 against them by thy spirit in thy p·:
32 and on our priests, and on our p·,
Ps 105:15 anointed, and do my p· no harm.
Isa 29:10 the p· and your rulers, the seers
30:10 to the p·, Prophesy not unto us
Jer 2: 8 the p· prophesied by Baal, and
26 and their priests, and their p·,
30 own sword hath devoured your p·,
4: 9 astonished, and the p· shall wonder.
5:13 And the p· shall become wind, and
31 The p· prophesy falsely, and the
7:25 unto you all my servants the p·,
8: 1 the bones of the p·, and the bones
13:13 the priests, and the p·, and all the
14:13 the p· say unto them, Ye shall not
14 The p· prophesy lies in my name:
15 p· that prophesy in my name, and
15 famine shall those p· be consumed.
23: 9 me is broken because of the p·;
13 seen folly in the p· of Samaria;
14 seen also in the p· of Jerusalem
15 Lord of hosts concerning the p·;
15 the p· of Jerusalem is profaneness
16 not unto the words of the p· that
21 I have not sent these p·, yet they
25 I have heard what the p· said, that
26 this be in the heart of the p· that
26 p· of the deceit of their own heart;
30, 31 I am against the p·, saith the
25: 4 unto you all his servants the p·,
26: 5 the words of my servants the p·,
7, 8 So the priests and the p· and all
11 Then spake the priests and the p·
16 people unto the priests and to the p·;
27: 9 hearken not ye to your p·, nor to
14 not unto the words of the p· that
15 and the p· that prophesy unto you.
16 of your p· that prophesy unto you,
18 But if they be p·, and if the word
28: 8 The p· that have been before me
29: 1 and to the priests, and to the p·, and
8 Let not your p· and your diviners,
15 hath raised us up p· in Babylon;
19 unto them by my servants the p·,
32:32 and their p·, and the men of Judah,
35:15 unto you all my servants the p·,
37:19 Where are now your p· which
44: 4 unto you all my servants the p·,
La 2: 9 her p· also find no vision from the
14 Thy p· have seen vain and foolish
La 4:13 For the sins of her p·, and the
Eze 13: 2 prophesy against the p· of Israel
3 Woe unto the foolish p·, that follow
4 p· are like the foxes in the deserts.
9 be upon the p· that see vanity,
16 the p· of Israel which prophesy
22:25 conspiracy of her p· in the midst
28 her p· have daubed them with
38:17 time by my servants the p· of Israel,
Da 9: 6 hearkened unto thy servants the p·,
10 set before us by his servants the p·.
Ho 6: 5 have I hewed them by the p·;
12:10 I have also spoken by the p·, and I
10 by the ministry of the p·.
Am 2:11 And I raised up of your sons for p·,
12 And commanded the p·, saying,
3: 7 his secret unto his servants the p·.
Mic 3: 5 the p· that make my people err,
6 the sun shall go down over the p·,
11 the p· thereof divine for money:
Zep 3: 4 Her p· are light and treacherous
Zec 1: 4 whom the former p· have cried,
5 and the p·, do they live for ever?
6 I commanded my servants the p·,
7: 3 and to the p·, saying, Should I weep
7 Lord hath cried by the former p·,
12 sent in his spirit by the former p·:
8: 9 these words by the mouth of the p·,
13: 2 cause the p· and the unclean spirit
4 the p· shall be ashamed every one
M't 2:23 which was spoken by the p·,
5:12 so persecuted they the p· which
17 come to destroy the law, or the p·:
7:12 them: for this is the law and the p·.
15 Beware of false p·, which come to
11:13 For all the p· and the law
13:17 that many p· and righteous men
16:14 others, Jeremias, or one of the p·.
22:40 hang all the law and the p·.
23:29 ye build the tombs of the p·, and
30 with them in the blood of the p·.
31 children of them which killed the p·.
34 behold, I send unto you p·, and
37 thou that killest the p·, and stonest
24:11 And many false p· shall rise, and
24 and false p·, and shall shew great
26:56 of the p· might be fulfilled.
M'r 1: 2 As it is written in the p·, Behold,
6:15 it is a prophet, or as one of the p·.
8:28 Elias; and others, One of the p·.
13:22 false Christs and false p· shall rise,
Lu 1:70 spake by the mouth of his holy p·,
6:23 did their fathers unto the p·.
26 so did their fathers to the false p·.
9: 8 one of the old p· was risen again.
19 one of the old p· is risen again.
10:24 many p· and kings have desired
11:47 ye build the sepulchres of the p·,
49 I will send them p· and apostles,
50 That the blood of all the p·, which
13:28 all the p·, in the kingdom of God,
34 Jerusalem, which killeth the p·,
16:16 The law and the p· were until John:
29 him, They have Moses and the p·;
31 If they hear not Moses and the p·,
18:31 all things that are written by the p·
24:25 believe all that the p· have spoken:
27 beginning at Moses and all the p·,
44 in the law of Moses, and in the p·,
Joh 1:45 law, and the p·, did write, Jesus of
6:45 It is written in the p·, And they
8:52 Abraham is dead, and the p·; and
53 and the p· are dead: whom makest
Ac 3:18 shewed by the mouth of all his p·,
21 by the mouth of all his holy p·
24 and all the p· from Samuel and
25 Ye are the children of the p·, and of
7:42 it is written in the book of the p·,
52 Which of the p· have not your
10:43 To him give all the p· witness, that
11:27 days came p· from Jerusalem unto
13: 1 Antioch certain p· and teachers;
15 the reading of the law and the p·
27 nor yet the voices of the p· which
40 you, which is spoken of in the p·;
15:15 to this agree the words of the p·;
32 being p· also themselves, exhorted
24:14 written in the law and in the p·:
26:22 which the p· and Moses did say
27 Agrippa, believest thou the p·?
28:23 and out of the p·, from morning till
Ro 1: 2 by his p· in the holy scriptures,)
3:21 witnessed by the law and the p·;
11: 3 Lord, they have killed thy p·, and
16:26 the scriptures of the p·, according
1Co 12:28 apostles, secondarily p·, thirdly
29 are all p·? are all teachers? are all
14:29 Let the p· speak two or three, and
32 spirits of the p· are subject to the p·.
Eph 2:20 foundation of the apostles and p·,
3: 5 holy apostles and p· by the Spirit;
4:11 gave some, apostles; and some, p·;
1Th 2:15 the Lord Jesus, and their own p·,
Heb 1: 1 past unto the fathers by the p·,
11:32 also, and Samuel, and of the p·:
Jas 5:10 the p·, who have spoken in the
1Pe 1:10 salvation the p· have enquired
2Pe 2: 1 there were false p· also among
3: 2 were spoken before by the holy p·,
1Jo 4: 1 many false p· are gone out into
Re 10: 7 declared to his servants the p·.
11:10 these two p· tormented them that
18 reward unto thy servants the p·,
16: 6 shed the blood of saints and p·, and
18:20 heaven, and ye holy apostles and p·;
24 was found the blood of p·, and of

Re 22: 6 Lord God of the holy p', sent his
9 and of thy brethren the p', and

propitiation
Ro 3:25 a p' through faith in his blood,
1Jo 2: 2 he is the p' for our sins: and not
4:10 his Son to be the p' for our sins.

proportion
1Ki 7:36 according to the p' of every one,
Job 41:12 nor his power, nor his comely p'.
Ro 12: 6 according to the p' of faith;

proselyte See also PROSELYTES.
M't 23:15 sea and land to make one p', and
Ac 6: 5 and Nicolas a p' of Antioch:

proselytes
Ac 2:10 strangers of Rome, Jews and p',
13:43 and religious p' followed Paul and

prospect
Eze 40:44 and their p' was toward the south:
44 having the p' toward the north.
45 whose p' is toward the south,
46 whose p' is toward the north
42:15 gate whose p' is toward the east,
43: 4 gate whose p' is toward the east.

prosper See also PROSPERED; PROSPERETH.
Ge 24:40 angel with thee, and p' thy way;
42 if now thou do p' my way which I
39: 3 made all that he did to p' in his
23 he did, the Lord made it to p'.
Nu 14:41 of the Lord? but it shall not p'.
De 28:29 and thou shalt not p' in thy ways:
29: 9 that ye may p' in all that ye do.
Jos 1: 7 p' whithersoever thou goest.
1Ki 2: 3 mayest p' in all that thou doest,
22:12 Go up to Ramoth-gilead, and p':
15 Go, and p', for the Lord shall
1Ch 22:11 p' thou, and build the house of the
13 Then shalt thou p', if thou takest
2Ch 13:12 of your fathers; for ye shall not p'.
18:11 Go up to Ramoth-gilead, and p':
14 Go ye up, and p', and they shall be
20:20 believe his prophets, so shall ye p'.
24:20 that ye cannot p'? because ye have
26: 5 the Lord, God made him to p'.
Ne 1:11 and p', I pray thee, thy servant this
2:20 The God of heaven, he will p' us;
Job 12: 6 The tabernacles of robbers p', and
Ps 1: 3 and whatsoever he doeth shall p'.
73:12 the ungodly, who p' in the world;
122: 6 they shall p' that love thee.
Pr 28:13 covereth his sins shall not p':
Ec 11: 6 knowest not whether shall p',
Isa 53:10 of the Lord shall p' in his hand.
54:17 that is formed against thee shall p';
55:11 p' in the thing whereto I sent it.
Jer 2:37 and thou shalt not p' in them.
5:28 cause of the fatherless, yet they p';
10:21 therefore they shall not p', and all
12: 1 doth the way of the wicked p'?
20:11 for they shall not p': their
22:30 man that shall not p' in his days:
30 for no man of his seed shall p',
23: 5 a King shall reign and p', and
32: 5 the Chaldeans, ye shall not p'.
La 1: 5 are the chief, her enemies p';
Eze 16:13 and thou didst p' into a kingdom.
17: 9 Shall it p'? shall he not pull up
10 being planted, shall it p'? shall it
15 Shall he p'? shall he escape that
Da 8:24 shall p', and practise, and shall
25 shall cause craft to p' in his hand;
11:27 it shall not p': for yet the end shall
36 shall p' till the indignation be
3Jo 2 thou mayest p' and be in health,

prospered
Ge 24:56 seeing the Lord hath p' my way;
J'g 4:24 hand of the children of Israel p',
2Sa 11: 7 people did, and how the war p'.
2Ki 18: 7 and he p' whithersoever he went
1Ch 29:23 of David his father, and p':
2Ch 14: 7 every side. So they built and p'.
31:21 he did it with all his heart, and p'.
32:30 And Hezekiah p' in all his works.
Ezr 6:14 they p' through the prophesying
Job 9: 4 himself against him, and hath p'?
Da 6:28 Daniel p' in the reign of Darius,
8:12 ground; and it practised, and p'.
1Co 16: 2 him in store, as God hath p' him,

prospereth
Ezr 5: 8 fast on, and p' in their hands.
Ps 37: 7 because of him who p' in his way,
Pr 17: 8 whithersoever it turneth, it p'.
3Jo 2 be in health, even as thy soul p'.

prosperity
De 23: 6 not seek their peace nor their p'
1Sa 25: 6 shall ye say to him that liveth in p',
1Ki 10: 7 and p' exceedeth the fame which
Job 15:21 in p' the destroyer shall come
36:11 they shall spend their days in p',
Ps 30: 6 in my p' I said, I shall never be
35:27 pleasure in the p' of his servant.
73: 3 when I saw the p' of the wicked.
118:25 Lord, I beseech thee, send now p'.
122: 7 walls, and p' within thy palaces.
Pr 1:32 the p' of fools shall destroy them.
Ec 7:14 In the day of p' be joyful, but in
Jer 22:21 I spake unto thee in thy p'; but
33: 9 all the p' that I procure unto it.
La 3:17 far off from peace: I forgat p'.
Zec 1:17 My cities through p' shall yet be
7: 7 was inhabited and in p', and

prosperous
Ge 24:21 had made his journey p' or not.
39: 2 Joseph, and he was a p' man;
Jos 1: 8 then thou shalt make thy way p',
J'g 18: 5 our way which we go shall be p'.
Job 8: 6 habitation of thy righteousness p'.
Isa 48:15 him, and he shall make his way p'.
Zec 8:12 For the seed shall be p'; the vine
Ro 1:10 I might have a p' journey by the

prosperously
2Ch 7:11 in his own house, he p' effected.
Ps 45: 4 majesty ride p' because of truth

prostitute
Le 19:29 Do not p' thy daughter, to cause

protection
De 32:38 up and help you, and be your p'.

protest See also PROTESTED; PROTESTING.
Ge 43: 3 The man did solemnly p' unto us,
1Sa 8: 9 howbeit yet p' solemnly unto them,
1Co 15:31 I p' by your rejoicing which I have

protested
1Ki 2:42 by the Lord, and p' unto thee,
Jer 11: 7 I earnestly p' unto your fathers in
Zec 3: 6 angel of the Lord p' unto Joshua,

protesting
Jer 11: 7 rising early and p', saying, Obey

proud
Job 9:13 the p' helpers do stoop under him.
26:12 he smiteth through the p'.
38:11 here shall thy p' waves be stayed?
40:11 and behold every one that is p',
12 Look on every one that is p', and
Ps 12: 3 tongue that speaketh p' things:
31:23 plentifully rewarded the p' doer.
40: 4 respecteth not the p', nor such as
86:14 the p' are risen against me, and
94: 2 earth: render a reward to the p'.
101: 5 look and a p' heart will not I suffer.
119:21 rebuked the p' that are cursed,
51 p' have had me greatly in derision:
69 p' have forged a lie against me: but
78 Let the p' be ashamed; for they
85 The p' have digged pits for me,
122 good: let not the p' oppress me.
123: 4 and with the contempt of the p'.
124: 5 p' waters had gone over our soul.
138: 6 but the p' he knoweth afar off.
140: 5 p' have hid a snare for me, and
Pr 6:17 A p' look, a lying tongue, and
15:25 will destroy the house of the p':
16: 5 Every one that is p' in heart is an
19 to divide the spoil with the p'.
21: 4 high look, and a p' heart, and the
24 P' and haughty scorner is his
24 name, who dealeth in p' wrath.
28:25 He that is of a p' heart stirreth up
Ec 7: 8 is better than the p' in spirit.
Isa 2:12 upon every one that is p' and lofty,
13:11 the arrogancy of the p' to cease,
16: 6 the pride of Moab; he is very p':
Jer 13:15 hear me, and give ear; be not p':
43: 2 and all the p' men, saying unto
48:29 of Moab, (he is exceeding p')
50:29 hath been p' against the Lord,
31 am against thee, O thou most p',
32 the most p' shall stumble and fall.
Hab 2: 5 he is a p' man, neither keepeth
Mal 3:15 now we call the p' happy; yea,
4: 1 all the p', yea, and all that do
Lu 1:51 the p' in the imagination of their
Ro 1:30 of God, despiteful, p', boasters,
1Ti 6: 4 He is p', knowing nothing, but
2Ti 3: 2 p', blasphemers, disobedient to
Jas 4: 6 God resisteth the p', but giveth
1Pe 5: 5 God resisteth the p', and giveth

proudly
Ex 18:11 the thing wherein they dealt p'
1Sa 2: 3 Talk no more so exceeding p'; let
Ne 9:10 that they dealt p' against them.
16 But they and our fathers dealt p',
29 yet they dealt p', and hearkened
Ps 17:10 with their mouth they speak p'.
31:18 which speak grievous things p'
Isa 3: 5 the child shall behave himself p'
Ob 12 spoken p' in the day of distress.

prove See also PROVED; PROVETH; PROVING; APPROVE; REPROVE.
Ex 16: 4 that I may p' them, whether they
20:20 Fear not: for God is come to p' you,
De 8: 2 to humble thee, and to p' thee, to
16 thee, and that he might p' thee,
33: 8 whom thou didst p' at Massah,
J'g 2:22 through them I may p' Israel,
3: 1 to p' Israel by them, even as many
4 they were to p' Israel by them, to
6:39 let me p', I pray thee, but this once
1Ki 10: 1 came to p' him with hard questions.
2Ch 9: 1 to p' Solomon with hard questions
Job 9:20 perfect, it shall also p' me perverse.
Ps 26: 2 Examine me, O Lord, and p' me;
Ec 2: 1 Go to now, I will p' thee with mirth.
Da 1:12 P' thy servants, I beseech thee, ten
Mal 3:10 p' me now herewith, saith the Lord
Lu 14:19 yoke of oxen, and I go to p' them:
Joh 6: 6 And this he said to p' him: for he
Ac 24:13 Neither can they p' the things
25: 7 Paul, which they could not p'.
Ro 12: 2 that ye may p' what is that good,
2Co 8: 8 and to p' the sincerity of your love.
13: 5 be in the faith; p' your own selves.
Ga 6: 4 But let every man p' his own work,
1Th 5:21 P' all things; hold fast that which

proved See also APPROVED; REPROVED.
Ge 42:15 Hereby ye shall be p': By the life
16 prison, that your words may be p',
Ex 15:25 ordinance, and there he p' them,
1Sa 17:39 assayed to go; for he had not p' it.
39 with these: for I have not p' them.
Ps 17: 3 Thou hast p' mine heart; thou hast
66:10 thou, O God, hast p' us: thou hast
81: 7 I p' thee at the waters of Meribah.
95: 9 me, p' me, and saw my work.
Ec 7:23 All this have I p' by wisdom: I
Da 1:14 this matter, and p' them ten days.
Ro 3: 9 we have before p' both Jews and
2Co 8:22 p' diligent in many things, but
1Ti 3:10 let these also first be p'; then let
Heb 3: 9 your fathers tempted me, p' me,

provender
Ge 24:25 have both straw and p' enough,
32 gave straw and p' for the camels,
42:27 opened his sack to give his ass p' in
43:24 feet; and he gave their asses p'.
J'g 19:19 is both straw and p' for our asses;
21 house, and gave p' unto the asses:
Isa 30:24 ear the ground shall eat clean p',

proverb See also PROVERBS.
De 28:37 become an astonishment, a p',
1Sa 10:12 Therefore it became a p', Is Saul
24:13 As saith the p' of the ancients,
1Ki 9: 7 Israel shall be a p' and a byword
2Ch 7:20 to be a p' and a byword among all
Ps 69:11 and I became a p' to them.
Pr 1: 6 To understand a p', and the
Isa 14: 4 take up this p' against the king of
Jer 24: 9 to be a reproach and a p', a taunt
Eze 12:22 that p' that ye have in the land of
23 I will make this p' to cease, and they
23 no more use it as a p' in Israel;
14: 8 and will make him a sign and a p',
16:44 shall use this p' against thee,
18: 2 ye use this p' concerning the land
3 any more to use this p' in Israel.
Hab 2: 6 and a taunting p' against him,
Lu 4:23 Ye will surely say unto me this p',
Joh 16:29 thou plainly, and speakest no p'.
2Pe 2:22 unto them according to the true p',

proverbs^
Nu 21:27 Wherefore they that speak in p'
1Ki 4:32 And he spake three thousand p':
Pr 1: 1 The p' of Solomon the son of David,
10: 1 The p' of Solomon. A wise son
25: 1 These are also p' of Solomon, which
Ec 12: 9 out, and set in order many p'.
Eze 16:44 every one that useth p' shall use
Joh 16:25 have I spoken unto you in p':
25 shall no more speak unto you in p',

proveth See also APPROVETH; REPROVETH.
De 13: 3 for the Lord your God p' you, to

provide See also PROVIDED; PROVIDETH; PROVIDING.
Ge 22: 8 God will p' himself a lamb for a
30:30 shall I p' for mine own house also?
Ex 18:21 p' out of all the people able men,
1Sa 16:17 P' me now a man that can play
2Ch 2: 7 whom David my father did p'.
Ps 78:20 can he p' flesh for his people?
M't 10: 9 P' neither gold, nor silver, nor
Lu 12:33 p' yourselves bags which wax not
Ac 23:24 And p' them beasts, that they may
Ro 12:17 P' things honest in the sight of
1Ti 5: 8 But if any p' not for his own, and

provided
De 33:21 And he p' the first part for himself,
1Sa 16: 1 have p' me a king among his sons.
2Sa 19:32 he had p' the king of sustenance
1Ki 4: 7 which p' victuals for the king and his
27 p' victual for king Solomon, and
2Ch 32:29 he p' him cities, and possessions
Ps 65: 9 corn, when thou hast so p' for it.
Lu 12:20 things be, which thou hast p'?
Heb 11:40 God having p' some better thing

providence
Ac 24: 2 done unto this nation by thy p',

provideth
Job 38:41 Who p' for the raven his food?
Pr 6: 8 P' her meat in the summer, and

providing
2Co 8:21 P' for honest things, not only in

province See also PROVINCES.
Ezr 2: 1 the children of the p' that went up
5: 8 that we went into the p' of Judea,
6: 2 that is in the p' of the Medes,
7:16 canst find in all the p' of Babylon,
Ne 1: 3 The remnant that are left...in the p'
7: 6 These are the children of the p',
11: 3 are the chief of the p' that dwelt in
Es 1:22 into every p' according to the
3:12 governors that were over every p',
12 rulers of every people of every p'
14 commandment...given in every p'
4: 3 And in every p', whithersoever the
8: 9 unto every p' according to the
11 the power of the people and p' that
13 commandment...given in every p'
17 And in every p', and in every city,
9:28 family, every p', and every city;
Ec 5: 8 of judgment and justice in a p',
Da 2:48 ruler over the whole p' of Babylon,
49 over the affairs of the p' of Babylon:

Da 3: 1 plain of Dura, in the p' of Babylon.
12 over the affairs of the p' of Babylon,
30 Abed-nego, in the p' of Babylon.
8: 2 the palace, which is the p' of Elam;
11: 24 upon the fattest places of the p';
Ac 23: 34 letter, he asked of what p' he was.
25: 1 when Festus was come into the p',

provinces
1Ki 20: 14 young men of the princes of the p'.
15 young men of the princes of the p',
17 princes of the p' went out first;
19 of the princes of the p' came out
Ezr 4: 15 and hurtful unto kings and p',
Es 1: 1 hundred and seven and twenty p':)
3 the nobles and princes of the p',
16 in all the p' of the king Ahasuerus.
22 he sent letters into all the king's p',
2: 3 in all the p' of his kingdom, that
18 and he made a release to the p', and
3: 8 people in all the p' of thy kingdom;
13 sent by posts into all the king's p',
4: 11 the people of the king's p', do know,
8: 5 Jews which are in all the king's p':
9 and rulers of the p' which are from
9 hundred twenty and seven p', unto
12 day in all the p' of king Ahasuerus,
9: 2 all the p' of the king Ahasuerus,
3 And all the rulers of the p', and the
4 went out throughout all the p':
12 done in the rest of the king's p'?
16 Jews that were in the king's p'
20 in all the p' of the king Ahasuerus,
30 and seven p' of the kingdom of
Ec 2: 8 treasure of kings and of the p':
La 1: 1 nations, and princess among the p',
Eze 19: 8 him on every side from the p',
Da 3: 2 the rulers of the p', to come to the
3 and all the rulers of the p', were

proving See also APPROVING.
Ac 9: 22 p' that this is very Christ.
Eph 5: 10 P' what is acceptable unto...Lord.

provision
Ge 42: 25 and to give them p' for the way:
45: 21 and gave them p' for the way.
Jos 9: 5 of their p' was dry and mouldy.
12 our bread we took hot for our p'
1Ki 4: 7 man his month in a year made p'.
22 Solomon's p' for one day was
2Ki 6: 23 he prepared great p' for them:
1Ch 29: 19 for the which I have made p'.
Ps 132: 15 I will abundantly bless her p': I
Da 1: 5 them a daily p' of the king's meat,
Ro 13: 14 and make not p' for the flesh, to

provocation^ See also PROVOCATIONS.
1Ki 15: 30 Israel sin, by his p', wherewith he
21: 22 for the p' wherewith thou hast
Job 17: 2 not mine eye continue in their p'?
Ps 95: 8 not your heart, as in the p', and
Eze 20: 28 presented the p' of their offering:
Heb 3: 8 not your hearts, as in the p', in
15 harden not your hearts, as in the p',

provocations
2Ki 23: 26 of all the p' that Manasseh had
Ne 9: 18 Egypt, and had wrought great p';
26 to thee, and they wrought great p'.

provoke See also PROVOKED; PROVOKETH; PROVOKING.
Ex 23: 21 and obey his voice, p' him not;
Nu 14: 11 How long will this people p' me?
De 4: 25 Lord thy God, to p' him to anger:
9: 18 of the Lord, to p' him to anger.
31: 20 gods, and serve them, and p' me,
29 to p' him to anger through the
32: 21 I will p' them to anger with a
1Ki 14: 9 molten images, to p' me to anger,
16: 2 to p' me to anger with their sins;
26 sin, to p' the Lord God of Israel to anger
33 to p' the Lord God of Israel to anger
2Ki 17: 11 things to p' the Lord to anger:
17 of the Lord, to p' him to anger.
21: 6 of the Lord, to p' him to anger.
22: 17 they might p' me to anger with all
23: 19 had made to p' the Lord to anger,
2Ch 33: 6 of the Lord, to p' him to anger.
34: 25 that they might p' me to anger
Job 12: 6 and they that p' God are secure;
Ps 78: 40 did they p' him in the wilderness,
Isa 3: 8 Lord, to p' the eyes of his glory.
Jer 7: 18 that they may p' me to anger.
19 Do they p' me to anger? saith the
19 not p' themselves to the confusion of
11: 17 p' me to anger in offering incense
25: 6 p' me not to anger with the works
7 ye might p' me to anger with the
32: 29 unto other gods, to p' me to anger.
32 they have done to p' me to anger.
44: 3 have committed to p' me to anger,
8 p' me unto wrath with the works
Eze 8: 17 have returned to p' me to anger:
16: 26 thy whoredoms, to p' me to anger.
Lu 11: 53 to p' him to speak of many things:
Ro 10: 19 saith, I will p' you to jealousy by
11: 11 Gentiles, for to p' them to jealousy.
14 any means I may p' to emulation
1Co 10: 22 Do we p' the Lord to jealousy? are
Eph 6: 4 p' not your children to wrath:
Col 3: 21 p' not your children to anger,
Heb 3: 16 when they had heard, did p':
10: 24 to p' unto love and to good works:

provoked See also PROVOKEDST.
Nu 14: 23 any of them that p' me see it:
16: 30 that these men have p' the Lord.
De 9: 8 in Horeb ye p' the Lord to wrath,
22 ye p' the Lord to wrath.
32: 16 p' him to jealousy with strange
16 abominations p' they him to anger.
21 p' me to anger with their vanities:
J'g 2: 12 them, and p' the Lord to anger.
1Sa 1: 6 And her adversary also p' her sore,
7 so she p' her; therefore she wept;
1Ki 14: 22 they p' him to jealousy with their sins
15: 30 p' the Lord God of Israel to anger.
21: 22 thou hast p' me to anger,
22: 53 p' to anger the Lord God of Israel,
2Ki 21: 15 have p' me to anger, since the day
23: 26 that Manasseh had p' him withal.
1Ch 21: 1 and p' David to number Israel.
2Ch 28: 25 and p' to anger the Lord God of his
Ezr 5: 12 p' the God of heaven unto wrath,
Ne 4: 5 have p' thee to anger before the
Ps 78: 56 tempted and p' the most high
58 p' him to anger with their high
106: 7 but p' him at the sea, even at the
29 they p' him to anger with their
33 Because they p' his spirit, so that
43 but they p' him with their counsel,
Isa 1: 4 have p' the Holy One of Israel
Jer 8: 19 p' me to anger with their graven
32: 30 Israel have only p' me to anger
Ho 12: 14 Ephraim p' him to anger most
Zec 8: 14 when your fathers p' me to wrath,
1Co 13: 5 is not easily p', thinketh no evil;
2Co 9: 2 and your zeal hath p' very many.

provokedst
De 9: 7 thou p' the Lord thy God to wrath

provoketh
Pr 20: 2 whoso p' him to anger sinneth
Isa 65: 3 A people that p' me to anger
Eze 8: 3 of jealousy, which p' to jealousy.

provoking
De 32: 19 because of the p' of his sons, and
1Ki 14: 15 their groves, p' the Lord to anger.
16: 7 in p' him to anger with the work of
13 p' the Lord God of Israel to anger
Ps 78: 17 by p' the most High in the
Ga 5: 26 p' one another, envying one

prudence
2Ch 2: 12 a wise son, endued with p' and
Pr 8: 12 I wisdom dwell with p', and find
Eph 1: 8 toward us in all wisdom and p';

prudent
1Sa 16: 18 a man of war, and p' in matters,
Pr 12: 16 but a p' man covereth shame.
23 A p' man concealeth knowledge:
13: 16 p' man dealeth with knowledge:
14: 8 wisdom of the p' is to understand
15 but the p' man looketh well to his
18 the p' are crowned with knowledge.
15: 5 he that regardeth reproof is p'.
16: 21 wise in heart shall be called p':
18: 15 heart of the p' getteth knowledge;
19: 14 and a p' wife is from the Lord.
22: 3 A p' man foreseeth the evil, and
27: 12 A p' man foreseeth the evil, and
Isa 3: 2 and the p', and the ancient,
5: 21 eyes, and p' in their own sight!
10: 13 for I am p': and I have removed
29: 14 the understanding of their p' men
Jer 49: 7 is counsel perished from the p'? is
Ho 14: 9 p', and he shall know them? for the
Am 5: 13 p' shall keep silence in that time;
M't 11: 25 these things from the wise and p',
Lu 10: 21 these things from the wise and p',
Ac 13: 7 country, Sergius Paulus, a p' man;
1Co 1: 19 the understanding of the p'.

prudently
Isa 52: 13 my servant shall deal p', he shall

prune See also PRUNED; PRUNING.
Le 25: 3 years thou shalt p' thy vineyard,
4 sow thy field, nor p' thy vineyard.

pruned
Isa 5: 6 it shall not be p', nor digged;

pruning See also PRUNINGHOOKS.
Isa 18: 5 cut off the sprigs with p' hooks,

pruninghooks See also PRUNING and HOOKS.
Isa 2: 4 and their spears into p':
Joe 3: 10 swords, and your p' into spears:
Mic 4: 3 and their spears into p':

psalm See also PSALMS.
1Ch 16: 7 David delivered first this p' to thank
Ps 3: *title* A P' of David, when he fled from
4: *title* on Neginoth, A P' of David.
5: *title* upon Nehiloth, A P' of David.
6: *title* upon Sheminith, A P' of David.
8: *title* upon Gittith, A P' of David.
9: *title* upon Muth-labben, A P' of David.
11: *title* chief Musician, A P' of David.
12: *title* upon Sheminith, A P' of David.
13: *title* chief Musician, A P' of David.
14: *title* chief Musician, A P' of David.
15: *title* A P' of David.
18: *title* A P' of David, the servant of the
19: *title* chief Musician, A P' of David.
20: *title* chief Musician, A P' of David.
21: *title* chief Musician, A P' of David.
22: *title* Aijeleth Shahar, A P' of David.
23: *title* A P' of David.
24: *title* A P' of David.
25: *title* A P' of David.
26: *title* A P' of David.
27: *title* A P' of David.
28: *title* A P' of David.
Ps 29: *title* A P' of David.
30: *title* A P' and Song at the dedication
31: *title* the chief Musician, A P' of David.
32: *title* A P' of David, Maschil.
34: *title* A P' of David, when he changed
35: *title* A P' of David.
36: *title* A P' of David the servant of the
37: *title* A P' of David.
38: *title* A P' of David, to bring to
39: *title* even to Jeduthun, A P' of David.
40: *title* chief Musician, A P' of David.
41: *title* chief Musician, A P' of David.
47: *title* A P' for the sons of Korah.
48: *title* and P' for the sons of Korah.
49: *title* A P' for the sons of Korah.
50: *title* A P' of Asaph.
51: *title* A P' of David, when Nathan the
52: *title* A P' of David, when Doeg the
53: *title* Mahalath, Maschil, A P' of David.
54: *title* A P' of David, when the Ziphims
55: *title* Maschil, A P' of David.
61: *title* upon Neginah, A P' of David.
62: *title* to Jeduthun, A P' of David.
63: *title* A P' of David, when he was in
64: *title* chief Musician, A P' of David.
65: *title* A P' and Song of David.
66: *title* the chief Musician, A Song or P'.
67: *title* on Neginoth, A P' or Song.
68: *title* Musician, A P' or Song of David.
69: *title* Shoshannim, A P' of David.
70: *title* A P' of David, to bring to
72: *title* A P' for Solomon.
73: *title* A P' of Asaph.
75: *title* A P' or Song of Asaph.
76: *title* Neginoth, A P' or Song of Asaph.
77: *title* to Jeduthun, A P' of Asaph.
79: *title* A P' of Asaph.
80: *title* A P' of Asaph.
81: *title* upon Gittith, A P' of Asaph.
2 Take a P', and bring hither the
82: *title* A P' of Asaph.
83: *title* A Song or P' of Asaph.
84: *title* A P' for the sons of Korah.
85: *title* A P' for the sons of Korah.
87: *title* A P' or Song for the sons of
88: *title* A Song or P' for the sons of
92: *title* A P' or Song for the sabbath day.
98: *title* A P'.
5 the harp, and the voice of a p'.
100: *title* A P' of praise.
101: *title* A P' of David.
103: *title* A P' of David.
108: *title* A Song or P' of David.
109: *title* chief Musician, A P' of David.
110: *title* A P' of David.
138: *title* A P' of David.
139: *title* chief Musician, A P' of David.
140: *title* chief Musician, A P' of David.
141: *title* A P' of David.
143: *title* A P' of David.
144: *title* A P' of David.
145: *title* David's P' of praise.
Ac 13: 33 it is also written in the second p',
35 Wherefore he saith also in another p',
1Co 14: 26 every one of you hath a p', hath a

psalmist
2Sa 23: 1 Jacob, and the sweet p' of Israel,

psalms^
1Ch 16: 9 Sing unto him, sing p' unto him,
Ps 95: 2 a joyful noise unto him with p'.
105: 2 Sing unto him, sing p' unto him:
Lu 20: 42 himself saith in the book of P',
24: 44 and in the p', concerning me.
Ac 1: 20 it is written in the book of P', Let
Eph 5: 19 Speaking to yourselves in p' and
Col 3: 16 admonishing one another in p' and
Jas 5: 13 Is any merry? let him sing p'.

psalteries
2Sa 6: 5 even on harps, and on p', and on
1Ki 10: 12 harps also and p' for singers: there
1Ch 13: 8 and with harps, and with p', and
15: 16 musick, p' and harp and cymbals,
20 and Benaiah, with p' on Alamoth;
28 making a noise with p' and harps.
16: 5 and Jeiel with p' and with harps;
25: 1 prophesy with harps, with p',
6 with cymbals, p', and harps, for
2Ch 5: 12 having cymbals and p' and harps,
9: 11 and harps and p' for singers: and
20: 28 they came to Jerusalem with p' and
29: 25 with p', and with harps, according
Ne 12: 27 with cymbals, p', and with harps.

psaltery See also PSALTERIES.
1Sa 10: 5 from the high place with a p',
Ps 33: 2 sing unto him with the p' and an
57: 8 awake, p' and harp: I myself will
71: 22 also praise thee with the p', even
81: 2 the pleasant harp with the p'.
92: 3 of ten strings, and upon the p';
108: 2 Awake, p' and harp: I myself will
144: 9 upon a p' and an instrument of ten
150: 3 praise him with the p' and harp.
Da 3: 5 p', dulcimer, and all kinds of
7 p', and all kinds of musick,
10, 15 p', and dulcimer, and all kinds

Ptolemais (*tol-e-ma'-is*) See also ACCHO.
Ac 21: 7 from Tyre, we came to P', and

Pua (*pu'ah*) See also PUAH.
Nu 26: 23 of P', the family of the Punites:

Puah (*pu'-ah*) See also PHUVAH; PUA; PUNITES.
Ex 1: 15 and the name of the other P':
J'g 10: 1 Tola the son of P', the son of
1Ch 7: 1 sons of Issachar were, Tola, and P',

public See PUBLICK.

publican See also PUBLICANS.
M't 10: 3 Thomas, and Matthew the p';
18:17 thee as an heathen man and a p'.
Lu 5:27 and saw a p', named Levi, sitting
18:10 one a Pharisee, and the other a p'.
11 adulterers, or even as this p'.
13 And the p', standing afar off, would

publicans
M't 5:46 ye? do not even the p' the same?
47 others? do not even the p' so?
9:10 many p' and sinners came and sat
11 Why eateth your Master with p' and
11:19 a friend of p' and sinners.
21:31 That the p' and the harlots go into
32 the p' and the harlots believed him:
M'r 2:15 house, many p' and sinners sat also
16 saw him eat with p' and sinners,
16 and drinketh with p' and sinners?
Lu 3:12 Then came also p' to be baptized,
5:29 there was a great company of p'
30 eat and drink with p' and sinners?
7:29 the p', justified God, being baptized
34 a friend of p' and sinners!
15: 1 Then drew near unto him all the p'
19: 2 which was the chief among the p',

publick
M't 1:19 willing to make her a p' example,

publickly
Ac 18:28 convinced the Jews, and that p',
20:20 shewed you, and have taught you p',

publish See also PUBLISHED; PUBLISHETH.
De 32: 3 I will p' the name of the Lord:
1Sa 31: 9 to p' it in the house of their idols,
2Sa 1:20 p' it not in the streets of Askelon;
Ne 8:15 p' and proclaim in all their cities,
Ps 26: 7 That I may p' with the voice of
Jer 4: 5 and p' in Jerusalem; and say, Blow
16 behold, p' against Jerusalem, that
5:20 house of Jacob, and p' it in Judah,
31: 7 p' ye, praise ye, and say, O Lord,
46:14 Declare ye in Egypt,...p' in Migdol,
14 and p' in Noph and in Tahpanhes:
50: 2 ye among the nations, and p',
2 up a standard; p', and conceal not:
Am 3: 9 P' in the palaces at Ashdod, and in
4: 5 proclaim and p' the free offerings:
M'r 1:45 went out, and began to p' it much,
5:20 began to p' in Decapolis how great

published
Es 1:20 be p' throughout all his empire,
22 that it should be p' according to
3:14 province was p' unto all people,
8:13 province was p' unto all people,
Ps 68:11 the company of those that p' it.
Jon 3: 7 p' through Nineveh by the decree
M'r 7:36 the more a great deal they p' it;
13:10 must first be p' among all nations.
Lu 8:39 and p' throughout the whole city
Ac 10:37 which was p' throughout all Judæa.
13:49 And the word of the Lord was p'

publisheth
Isa 52: 7 good tidings, that p' peace;
7 tidings of good, that p' salvation;
Jer 4:15 p' affliction from mount Ephraim.
Na 1:15 good tidings, that p' peace!

Publius (*pub'-le-us*)
Ac 28: 7 of the island, whose name was P';
8 the father of P' lay sick of a fever

Pudens (*pu'-denz*)
2Ti 4:21 Eubulus greeteth thee, and P',

puffed
1Co 4: 6 that no one of you be p' up for one
18 Now some are p' up, as though I
19 the speech of them which are p' up,
5: 2 ye are p' up, and have not rather
13: 4 vaunteth not itself, is not p' up,
Col 2:18 vainly p' up by his fleshly mind,

puffeth
Ps 10: 5 for all his enemies, he p' at them.
12: 5 in safety from him that p' at him.
1Co 8: 1 Knowledge p' up, but charity

Puhites (*pu'-hites*)
1Ch 2:53 the Ithrites, and the P', and the

Pul (*pul*)
2Ki 15:19 And P' the king of Assyria came
19 gave P' a thousand talents of
1Ch 5:26 stirred up the spirit of P' king of
Isa 66:19 nations, to Tarshish, P', and Lud,

pull See also PULLED; PULLING.
1Ki 13: 4 he could not p' it in again to him.
Ps 31: 4 P' me out of the net that they
Isa 22:19 thy state shall he p' thee down.
Jer 1:10 to root out, and to p' down, and to
12: 3 p' them out like sheep for the
18: 7 and to p' down, and to destroy it;
24: 6 them, and not p' them down;
42:10 build you, and not p' you down,
Eze 17: 9 shall he not p' up the roots
Mic 2: 8 p' off the robe with the garment
M't 7: 4 p' out the mote out of thine eye;
Lu 6:42 p' out the mote that is in thine eye.
42 to p' out the mote that is in thy
12:18 I will p' down my barns, and build
14: 5 p' him out on the sabbath day?

pulled
Ge 8: 9 p' her in unto him into the ark.
19:10 and p' Lot into the house to them,
Ezr 6:11 timber be p' down from his house,
La 3:11 my ways, and p' me in pieces:
Am 9:15 no more be p' up out of their land
Zec 7:11 and p' away the shoulder, and
Ac 23:10 Paul should have been p' in pieces

pulling
2Co 10: 4 to the p' down of strong holds;)
Jude 23 with fear, p' them out of the fire;

pulpit
Ne 8: 4 the scribe stood upon a p' of wood,

pulse
2Sa 17:28 beans, and lentiles, and parched p',
Da 1:12 and let them give us p' to eat, and
16 should drink; and gave them p'.

punish See also PUNISHED.
Le 26:18 I will p' you seven times more for
24 p' you yet seven times for your
Pr 17:26 Also to p' the just is not good, nor
Isa 10:12 will p' the fruit of the stout heart
13:11 I will p' the world for their evil, and
24:21 shall p' the host of the high ones
26:21 to p' the inhabitants of the earth
27: 1 p' leviathan the piercing serpent,
Jer 9:25 that I will p' all them which are
11:22 of hosts, Behold, I will p' them:
13:21 thou say when he shall p' thee?
21:14 I will p' you according to the fruit
23:34 I will even p' that man and his
25:12 that I will p' the king of Babylon,
27: 8 that nation will I p', saith the Lord,
29:32 I will p' Shemaiah the Nehelamite,
30:20 and I will p' all that oppress them.
36:31 I will p' him and his seed and his
44:13 I will p' them that dwell in the land
29 I will p' you in this place, that ye
46:25 I will p' the multitude of No, and
50:18 I will p' the king of Babylon and
51:44 And I will p' Bel in Babylon, and
Ho 4: 9 I will p' them for their ways, and
14 I will not p' your daughters when
12: 2 will p' Jacob according to his ways;
Am 3: 2 I will p' you for all your iniquities.
Zep 1: 8 I will p' the princes, and the king's
9 day also will I p' all those that leap
12 p' the men that are settled on their
Zec 8:14 As I thought to p' you, when your
Ac 4:21 how they might p' them, because

punished See also UNPUNISHED.
Ex 21:20 his hand; he shall be surely p'.
21 a day or two, he shall not be p':
22 he shall be surely p', according as
Ezr 9:13 hast p' us less than our iniquities
Job 31:11 it is an iniquity to be p' by the judges.
28 were an iniquity to be p' by the judge:
Pr 21:11 When the scorner is p', the simple
22: 3 but the simple pass on, and are p'.
27:12 but the simple pass on, and are p'.
Jer 44:13 as I have p' Jerusalem, by the
50:18 as I have p' the king of Assyria.
Zep 3: 7 not be cut off, howsoever I p' them:
Zec 10: 3 the shepherds, and I p' the goats:
Ac 22: 5 unto Jerusalem, for to be p'.
26:11 I p' them oft in every synagogue,
2Th 1: 9 p'...everlasting destruction
2Pe 2: 9 unto the day of judgment to be p':

punishment See also PUNISHMENTS.
Ge 4:13 My p' is greater than I can bear.
Le 26:41, 43 accept of the p' of their iniquity:
1Sa 28:10 there shall no p' happen to thee for
Job 31: 3 strange p' to the workers of iniquity?
Pr 19:19 man of great wrath shall suffer p':
La 3:39 a man for the p' of his sins?
4: 6 p' of the iniquity of the daughter
6 than the p' of the sin of Sodom,
22 p' of thine iniquity...accomplished,
Eze 14:10 shall bear the p' of their iniquity:
10 the p' of the prophet shall be even
10 as the p' of him that seeketh unto
Am 1: 3, 6, 9, 11, 13 I will not turn away the p'
2: 1, 4, 6 will not turn away the p' thereof;
Zec 14:19 This shall be the p' of Egypt, and
19 the p' of all nations that come not
M't 25:46 shall go away into everlasting p':
2Co 2: 6 Sufficient to such a man is this p',
Heb 10:29 Of how much sorer p', suppose ye,
1Pe 2:14 sent by him for the p' of evildoers,

punishments
Job 19:29 bringeth the p' of the sword,
Ps 149: 7 upon the heathen, and p' upon the

Punites (*pu'-nites*)
Nu 26:23 of Pua, the family of the P':

Punon (*pu'-non*)
Nu 33:42 Zalmonah, and pitched in P'.
43 they departed from P', and pitched

Pur (*pur*) See also PURIM.
Es 3: 7 they cast P', that is, the lot,
9:24 and had cast P', that is, the lot, to
26 days Purim after the name of P'.

purchase See also PURCHASED.
Ge 49:32 The p' of the field and of the cave
Le 25:33 if a man p' of the Levites, then the
Jer 32:11 So I took the evidence of the p',
12 I gave the evidence of the p' unto
12 that subscribed the book of the p',
14 evidences, this evidence of the p',
16 the evidence of the p' unto Baruch
1Ti 3:13 p' to themselves a good degree,

purchased
Ge 25:10 Abraham p' of the sons of Heth:
Ex 15:16 pass over, which thou hast p'.
Ru 4:10 of Mahlon, have I p' to be my wife,
Ps 74: 2 which thou hast p' of old; the rod of
78:54 which his right hand had p'.
Ac 1:18 man p' a field with the reward of
8:20 gift of God may be p' with money.
20:28 he hath p' with his own blood.
Eph 1:14 redemption of the p' possession,

pure See also PURER.
Ex 25:11 thou shalt overlay it with p' gold,
17 shalt make a mercy seat of p' gold:
24 thou shalt overlay it with p' gold,
29 of p' gold shalt thou make them.
31 shalt make a candlestick of p' gold:
36 shall be one beaten work of p' gold.
38 thereof, shall be of p' gold.
39 a talent of p' gold shall he make it,
27:20 p' oil olive beaten for the light,
28:14 two chains of p' gold at the ends;
22 ends of wreathen work of p' gold.
36 thou shalt make a plate of p' gold,
30: 3 shalt overlay it with p' gold, the top
23 of p' myrrh five hundred shekels,
34 sweet spices with p' frankincense:
35 tempered together, p' and holy:
31: 8 and the p' candlestick with all his
37: 2 he overlaid it with p' gold within
6 he made the mercy seat of p' gold:
11 And he overlaid it with p' gold, and
16 covers to cover withal, of p' gold.
17 made the candlestick of p' gold: of
22 it was one beaten work of p' gold.
23 and his snuffdishes, of p' gold.
24 Of a talent of p' gold made he it,
26 he overlaid it with p' gold, both the
29 and the p' incense of sweet spices,
39:15 ends, of wreathen work of p' gold.
25 they made bells of p' gold, and put
30 plate of the holy crown of p' gold,
37 The p' candlestick, with the lamps
Le 24: 2 bring unto thee p' oil olive beaten
4 the lamps upon the p' candlestick
6 upon the p' table before the Lord.
7 p' frankincense upon each row,
De 32:14 drink the p' blood of the grape.
2Sa 22:27 the p' thou wilt shew thyself p';
1Ki 5:11 and twenty measures of p' oil:
6:20 he overlaid it with p' gold; and so
21 the house within with p' gold;
7:49 candlesticks of p' gold, five on the
50 spoons, and the censers of p' gold;
10:21 forest of Lebanon were of p' gold;
1Ch 28:17 Also p' gold for the fleshhooks,
2Ch 3: 4 he overlaid it within with p' gold.
4:20 before the oracle, of p' gold;
22 spoons, and the censers, of p' gold:
9:17 ivory, and overlaid it with p' gold.
20 forest of Lebanon were of p' gold:
13:11 they in order upon the p' table;
Ezr 6:20 all of them were p', and killed the
Job 4:17 a man be more p' than his Maker?
8: 6 If thou wert p' and upright; surely
11: 4 thou hast said, My doctrine is p',
16:17 in mine hands: also my prayer is p'.
25: 5 the stars are not p' in his sight.
28:19 shall it be valued with p' gold.
Ps 12: 6 words of the Lord are p' words:
18:26 the p' thou wilt shew thyself p';
19: 8 commandment of the Lord is p',
21: 3 settest a crown of p' gold on his
24: 4 hath clean hands, and a p' heart;
119:140 Thy word is very p': therefore
Pr 15:26 the words of the p' are pleasant
20: 9 heart clean, I am p' from my sin?
11 whether his work be p', and
21: 8 but as for the p', his work is right.
30: 5 Every word of God is p': he is a
12 a generation that are p' in their
Da 7: 9 hair of his head like the p' wool:
Mic 6:11 Shall I count them p' with the
Zep 3: 9 turn to the people a p' language,
Mal 1:11 unto my name, and a p' offering:
M't 5: 8 Blessed are the p' in heart: for
Ac 20:26 I am p' from the blood of all men.
Ro 14:20 All things indeed are p'; but it is
Ph'p 4: 8 are just, whatsoever things are p',
1Ti 1: 5 is charity out of a p' heart, and of
3: 9 of the faith in a p' conscience.
5:22 of other men's sins: keep thyself p'.
2Ti 1: 3 my forefathers with p' conscience,
2:22 call on the Lord out of a p' heart.
Tit 1:15 Unto the p' all things are p': but
15 and unbelieving is nothing p';
Heb 10:22 our bodies washed with p' water.
Jas 1:27 P' religion and undefiled before
3:17 wisdom that is from above is first p',
1Pe 1:22 love one another with a p' heart
2Pe 3: 1 I stir up your p' minds by way
1Jo 3: 3 purifieth himself, even as he is p'.
Re 15: 6 clothed in p' and white linen, and
21:18 and the city was p' gold, like unto
21 street of the city was p' gold, as it
22: 1 he shewed me a p' river of water

purely
Isa 1:25 and p' purge away the dross,

pureness
Job 22:30 delivered by the p' of thine hands.
Pr 22:11 He that loveth p' of heart, for the
2Co 6: 6 By p', by knowledge, by

purer
La 4: 7 Her Nazarites were p' than snow,
Hab 1:13 art of p' eyes than to behold evil,

purge See also PURGED; PURGETH; PURGING; PURIFY.
2Ch 34: 3 year he began to p' Judah and
Ps 51: 7 P' me with hyssop, and I shall be

Ps 65: 3 thou shalt p' them away.
79: 9 deliver us, and p' away our sins,
Isa 1:25 and purely p' away thy dross, and
Eze 20:38 p' out from among you the rebels.
43:20 thus shalt thou cleanse and p' it.
26 Seven days shall they p' the altar
Da 11:35 to p', and to make them white,
Mal 3: 3 and p' them as gold and silver,
M't 3:12 he will thoroughly p' his floor,
Lu 3:17 he will thoroughly p' his floor,
1Co 5: 7 P' out therefore the old leaven,
2Ti 2:21 If a man therefore p' himself from
Heb 9:14 p' your conscience from dead

purged
1Sa 3:14 shall not be p' with sacrifice nor
2Ch 34: 8 when he had p' the land, and the
Pr 16: 6 mercy and truth iniquity is p':
Isa 4: 4 have p' the blood of Jerusalem
6: 7 is taken away, and thy sin p'.
22:14 iniquity shall not be p' from you
27: 9 shall the iniquity of Jacob be p';
Eze 24:13 lewdness: because I have p' thee,
13 not p', thou shalt not be p' from
Heb 1: 3 had by himself p' our sins,
9:22 are by the law p' with blood;
10: 2 worshippers once p' should have
2Pe 1: 9 that he was p' from his old sins.

purgeth
Joh 15: 2 he p' it, that it may bring forth

purging
M'r 7:19 into the draught, p' all meats?

purification See also PURIFICATIONS.
Nu 19: 9 of separation: it is a p' for sin.
17 of the burnt heifer of p' for sin.
2Ch 30:19 to the p' of the sanctuary.
Ne 12:45 their God, and the ward of the p',
Es 2: 3 their things for p' be given them:
9 speedily gave her her things for p',
Lu 2:22 And when the days of her p'
Ac 21:26 accomplishment of the days of p',

purifications
Es 2:12 days of their p' accomplished,

purified
Le 8:15 with his finger, and p' the altar,
Nu 8:21 And the Levites were p', and they
31:23 nevertheless it shall be p' with the
2Sa 11: 4 she was p' from her uncleanness:
Ezr 6:20 priests and the Levites were p'
Ne 12:30 and the Levites p' themselves,
30 p' the people, and the gates, and
Ps 12: 6 furnace of earth, p' seven times.
Da 12:10 Many shall be p', and made
Ac 24:18 Asia found me p' in the temple,
Heb 9:23 heavens should be p' with these;
1Pe 1:22 ye have p' your souls in obeying

purifier
Mal 3: 3 sit as a refiner and p' of silver:

purifieth
Nu 19:13 and p' not himself, defileth the
1Jo 3: 3 hath this hope in him p' himself,

purify See also PURGE; PURIFIED; PURIFIETH; PURIFYING.
Nu 19:12 p' himself with it on the third day,
12 if he p' not himself the third day,
19 the seventh day he shall p' himself,
20 unclean, and shall not p' himself,
31:19 p' both yourselves and your
20 p' all your raiment, and all that is
Job 41:25 of breakings they p' themselves.
Isa 66:17 and p' themselves in the gardens
Eze 43:26 shall they purge the altar and p' it;
Mal 3: 3 and he shall p' the sons of Levi,
Joh 11:55 the passover, to p' themselves.
Ac 21:24 take, and p' thyself with them,
Tit 2:14 p' unto himself a peculiar people,
Jas 4: 8 p' your hearts, ye double minded.

purifying
Le 12: 4 blood of her p' three and thirty
4 the days of her p' be fulfilled.
5 blood of her p' three score and
6 the days of her p' are fulfilled,
Nu 8: 7 Sprinkle water of p' upon them,
1Ch 23:28 and in the p' of all holy things,
Es 2:12 things for the p' of the women;)
Joh 2: 6 manner of the p' of the Jews,
3:25 disciples and the Jews about p'.
Ac 15: 9 them, p' their hearts by faith.
21:26 the next day p' himself with them
Heb 9:13 sanctifieth to the p' of the flesh:

Purim (*pu'-rim*) See also PUR.
Es 9:26 called these days P' after the
28 these days of P' should not fail
29 confirm this second letter of P'.
31 To confirm these days of P' in
32 confirmed these matters of P';

purity
1Ti 4:12 charity, in spirit, in faith, in p'.
5: 2 the younger as sisters, with all p'.

purloining
Tit 2:10 Not p', but shewing all good

purple
Ex 25: 4 And blue, and p', and scarlet, and
26: 1 and blue, and p', and scarlet:
31 shalt make a vail of blue, and p',
36 door of the tent, of blue, and p',
27:16 of twenty cubits, of blue, and p',
28: 5 gold, and blue, and p', and scarlet,
6 ephod of gold, of blue, and of p',
Ex 28: 8 even of gold, of blue, and p', and
15 make it; of gold, of blue, and of p',
33 pomegranates of blue, and of p',
35: 6 And blue, and p', and scarlet, and
23 with whom was found blue, and p',
25 had spun, both of blue, and of p',
35 in blue, and in p', in scarlet, and
36: 8 twined linen, and blue, and p', and
35 he made a vail of blue, and p', and
37 tabernacle door of blue, and p', and
38:18 was needlework, of blue, and p',
23 an embroiderer in blue, and in p',
39: 1 of the blue, and p', and scarlet, and
2 and p', and scarlet, and fine twined
3 work it in the blue, and in the p',
5 of gold, blue, and p', and scarlet,
8 and p', and scarlet, and fine twined
24 robe pomegranates of blue, and p',
29 fine twined linen, and blue, and p',
Nu 4:13 and spread a p' cloth thereon:
J'g 8:26 p' raiment that was on the kings of
2Ch 2: 7 and in iron, and in p', and crimson,
14 in p', in blue, and in fine linen,
3:14 vail of blue, and p', and crimson,
Es 1: 6 with cords of fine linen and p' to
8:15 a garment of fine linen and p':
Pr 31:22 tapestry; her clothing is silk and p'.
Ca 3:10 the covering of it of p', the midst
7: 5 and the hair of thine head like p';
Jer 10: 9 blue and p' is their clothing: they
Eze 27: 7 blue and p' from the isles of Elishah
16 emeralds, p', and broidered work,
M'r 15:17 they clothed him with p', and
20 they took off the p' from him, and
Lu 16:19 was clothed in p' and fine linen,
Joh 19: 2 and they put on him a p' robe,
5 crown of thorns, and the p' robe.
Ac 16:14 Lydia, a seller of p', of the city of
Re 17: 4 arrayed in p' and scarlet colour,
18:12 and fine linen, and p', and silk,
16 was clothed in fine linen, and p',

purpose See also PURPOSED; PURPOSES; PURPOSETH; PURPOSING.
Ru 2:16 of the handfuls of p' for her, and
1Ki 5: 5 I p' to build an house unto the
2Ch 28:10 ye p' to keep under the children
Ezr 4: 5 against them, to frustrate their p'
Ne 8: 4 which they had made for the p';
Job 33:17 may withdraw man from his p',
Pr 20:18 p' is established by counsel: and
Ec 3: 1 to every p' under the heaven:
17 a time there for every p' and for
8: 6 Because to every p' there is time
Isa 1:11 To what p' is the multitude of your
14:26 is the p' that is purposed upon
30: 7 shall help in vain, and to no p':
Jer 6:20 To what p' cometh there to me incense
26: 3 which I p' to do unto them because
36: 3 evil which I p' to do unto them;
49:30 hath conceived a p' against you.
51:29 p' of the Lord shall be performed
Da 6:17 that the p' might not be changed
M't 26: 8 saying, To what p' is this waste?
Ac 11:23 with p' of heart they would cleave
26:16 I have appeared unto thee for this p',
27:13 that they had obtained their p',
43 Paul, kept them from their p';
Ro 8:28 are the called according to his p'.
9:11 the p' of God according to election
17 Even for this same p' have I raised
2Co 1:17 lightness? or the things that I p',
17 do I p' according to the flesh, that
Eph 1:11 p' of him who worketh all things
3:11 the eternal p' which he purposed
6:22 I have sent unto you for the same p',
Col 4: 8 I have sent unto you for the same p',
2Ti 1: 9 but according to his own p' and
3:10 doctrine, manner of life, p', faith,
1Jo 3: 8 For this p' the Son...was manifested,

purposed
2Ch 32: 2 that he was p' to fight against
Ps 17: 3 I am p' that my mouth shall not
140: 4 have p' to overthrow my goings.
Isa 14:24 as I have p', so shall it stand:
26 that is p' upon the whole earth:
27 For the Lord of hosts hath p', and
19:12 Lord of hosts hath p' upon Egypt.
23: 9 The Lord of hosts hath p' it, to
46:11 pass; I have p' it, I will also do it.
Jer 4:28 I have p' it, and will not repent,
49:20 hath p' against the inhabitants
50:45 that he hath p' against the land of
La 2: 8 The Lord hath p' to destroy the
Da 1: 8 Daniel p' in his heart that he
Ac 19:21 Paul p' in the spirit, when he had
20: 3 he p' to return through
Ro 1:13 oftentimes I p' to come unto you,
Eph 1: 9 which he hath p' in himself:
3:11 which he p' in Christ Jesus our

purposes
Job 17:11 my p' are broken off, even the
Pr 15:22 Without counsel p' are
Isa 19:10 shall be broken in the p' thereof,
Jer 49:20 and his p', that he hath purposed
50:45 and his p', that he hath purposed

purposeth
2Co 9: 7 according as he p' in his heart,

purposing
Ge 27:42 doth comfort himself, p' to kill thee.

purse See also PURSES.
Pr 1:14 among us; let us all have one p':
M'r 6: 8 no bread, no money in their p':
Lu 10: 4 Carry neither p', nor scrip, nor
Lu 22:35 I sent you without p', and scrip,
36 he that hath a p', let him take it,

purses
M't 10: 9 nor silver, nor brass in your p',

pursue See also ENSUE; PURSUED; PURSUETH; PURSUING.
Ge 35: 5 did not p' after the sons of Jacob.
Ex 15: 9 The enemy said, I will p', I will
De 19: 6 avenger of the blood p' the slayer,
28:22 they shall p' thee until thou perish.
45 shall p' thee, and overtake thee,
Jos 2: 5 p' after them quickly; for ye shall
8:16 called together to p' after them:
10:19 p' after your enemies, and smite
20: 5 the avenger of blood p' after him,
1Sa 24:14 after whom dost thou p'? after a
25:29 Yet a man is risen to p' thee, and
26:18 my lord thus p' after his servant?
30: 8 Shall I p' after this troop? shall I
8 P': for thou shalt surely overtake
2Sa 17: 1 I will arise and p' after David this
20: 6 lord's servants, and p' after him,
7, 13 p' after Sheba the son of Bichri.
24:13 thine enemies, while they p' thee?
Job 13:25 and wilt thou p' the dry stubble?
30:15 they p' my soul as the wind: and
Ps 34:14 and do good; seek peace, and p' it.
Isa 30:16 shall they that p' you be swift.
Jer 48: 2 Madmen; the sword shall p' thee.
Eze 35: 6 blood, and blood shall p' thee:
6 blood, even blood shall p' thee:
Ho 8: 3 is good: the enemy shall p' him.
Am 1:11 did p' his brother with the sword,
Na 1: 8 and darkness shall p' his enemies.

pursued
Ge 14:14 eighteen, and p' them unto Dan.
15 and p' them unto Hobah, which
31:23 p' after him seven days' journey;
36 thou hast so hotly p' after me?
Ex 14: 8 he p' after the children of Israel:
9 But the Egyptians p' after them,
23 And the Egyptians p', and went in
De 11: 4 overflow them as they p' after you,
Jos 2: 7 the men p' after them the way to
7 they which p' after them were gone
8:16 and they p' after Joshua, and were
17 the city open, and p' after Israel.
24: 6 the Egyptians p' after your fathers
J'g 1: 6 they p' after him, and caught him,
4:16 Barak p' after the chariots, and
22 as Barak p' Sisera, Jael came out
7:23 and p' after the Midianites.
25 and p' Midian, and brought the
8:12 he p' after them, and took the two
20:45 p' hard after them unto Gidom,
1Sa 7:11 and p' the Philistines, and smote
17:52 shouted, and p' the Philistines,
23:25 he p' after David in the wilderness
30:10 David p', he and four hundred
2Sa 2:19 And Asahel p' after Abner; and in
24 also and Abishai p' after Abner:
28 and p' after Israel no more, neither
20:10 Abishai his brother p' after Sheba
22:38 I have p' mine enemies, and
1Ki 20:20 Syrians fled; and Israel p' them:
2Ki 25: 5 of the Chaldees p' after the king,
2Ch 13:19 Abijah p' after Jeroboam, and took
14:13 were with him p' them unto Gerar:
Ps 18:37 I have p' mine enemies, and
Isa 41: 3 He p' them, and passed safely;
Jer 39: 5 the Chaldeans' army p' after them,
52: 8 the Chaldeans p' after the king,
La 4:19 they p' us upon the mountains,

pursuer See also PURSUERS.
La 1: 6 without strength before the p'.

pursuers
Jos 2:16 mountain, lest the p' meet you;
16 days, until the p' be returned:
22 days, until the p' were returned:
22 p' sought them throughout all the
8:20 turned back upon the p'.

pursueth
Le 26:17 ye shall flee when none p' you.
36 and they shall fall when none p'.
37 were before a sword, when none p':
Pr 11:19 tendeth to life: so he that p' evil
19 p' it to his own death.
13:21 Evil p' sinners: but to the
19: 7 he p' them with words, yet they
28: 1 The wicked flee when no man p':

pursuing
J'g 8: 4 were with him, faint, yet p' them.
5 I am p' after Zebah and Zalmunna,
1Sa 23:28 Saul returned from p' after David,
2Sa 3:22 David and Joab came from p' a troop,
18:16 returned from p' after Israel:
1Ki 18:27 he is talking, or he is p', or he is
22:33 that they turned back from p' him.
2Ch 18:32 turned back again from p' him.

purtenance See also PERTAIN.
Ex 12: 9 his legs, and with the p' thereof.

push See PUSHED; PUSHING.
Ex 21:29 ox were wont to p' with his horn
32 ox shall p' a manservant or a
36 ox hath used to p' in time past,
De 33:17 p' the people together to the ends
1Ki 22:11 these shalt thou p' the Syrians,
2Ch 18:10 p' Syria until they be consumed.
Job 30:12 they p' away my feet, and they
Ps 44: 5 thee will we p' down our enemies:
Da 11:40 the king of the south p' at him:

pushed
Eze 34: 21 p' all the diseased with your
pushing
Da 8: 4 I saw the ram p' westward, and
put^ See also PUTTEST; PUTTETH; PUTTING.
Ge 2: 8 there he p' the man whom he had
15 p' him into the garden of Eden to
3: 15 I will p' enmity between thee and
22 lest he p' forth his hand, and take
8: 9 he p' forth his hand, and took her,
19: 10 But the men p' forth their hand,
24: 2 P', I pray thee, thy hand under
9 the servant p' his hand under the
47 I p' the earring upon her face, and
26: 11 his wife shall surely be p' to death.
27: 15 p' them upon Jacob her younger
16 she p' the skins of the kids of the
28: 11 and p' them for his pillows, and
18 stone that he had p' for his pillows,
20 bread to eat, and raiment to p' on,
29: 3 p' the stone again upon the well's
30: 40 he p' his own flocks by themselves,
40 p' them not unto Laban's cattle.
42 were feeble, he p' them not in:
31: 34 p' them in the camel's furniture,
32: 16 p' a space betwixt drove and drove.
33: 2 And he p' the handmaids and their
35: 2 P' away the strange gods that are
37: 34 p' sackcloth upon his loins, and
38: 14 she p' her widow's garments off
19 and p' on the garments of her
28 that the one p' out his hand: and
39: 4 all that he had he p' into his hand.
20 him, and p' him into the prison,
40: 3 he p' them in ward in the house of
15 should p' me into the dungeon.
41: 10 p' me in ward in the captain of the
42 and p' it upon Joseph's hand, and
42 and p' a gold chain about his neck;
42: 17 he p' them altogether into ward
43: 22 who p' our money in our sacks.
44: 1 p' every man's money in his sack's
2 p' my cup, the silver cup, in the
46: 4 shall p' his hand upon thine eyes.
47: 29 p', I pray thee, thy hand under my
48: 18 p' thy right hand upon his head.
50: 26 and he was p' in a coffin in Egypt.
Ex 2: 3 pitch, and p' the child therein;
3: 5 p' off thy shoes from off thy feet,
22 ye shall p' them upon your sons,
4: 4 P' forth thine hand, and take it by
4 he p' forth his hand, and caught it,
6 P' now thine hand into thy bosom.
6 he p' his hand into his bosom: and
7 P' thine hand into thy bosom
7 p' his hand into his bosom again;
15 him, and p' words in his mouth:
21 which I have p' in thine hand:
5: 21 to p' a sword in their hand to slay
8: 23 p' a division between my people
11: 7 doth p' a difference between the
12: 15 shall p' away leaven out of your
15: 26 I will p' none of these diseases
16: 33 and p' an omer full of manna
17: 12 took a stone, and p' it under him,
14 utterly p' out the remembrance
19: 12 the mount shall be surely p' to death:
21: 12 that he die, shall be surely p' to death.
15 his mother, shall be surely p' to death.
16 hand, he shall surely be p' to death.
17 his mother, shall surely be p' to death.
29 and his owner also shall be p' to death.
22: 5 and shall p' in his beast, and shall
8 whether he have p' his hand unto
11 not p' his hand unto his neighbour's
19 a beast shall surely be p' to death.
23: 1 p' not thine hand with the wicked
24: 6 of the blood, and p' it in basons;
25: 12 and p' them in the four corners
14 shalt p' the staves into the rings
16 shalt p' into the ark the testimony
21 p' the mercy seat above upon the
21 the ark thou shalt p' the testimony
26 p' the rings in the four corners that
26: 11 and p' the taches into the loops,
34 p' the mercy seat upon the ark of
35 shalt p' the table on the north side.
27: 5 p' it under the compass of the altar
7 the staves shall be p' into the rings,
28: 12 shalt p' the two stones upon the
23 p' the two rings on the two ends
24 shalt p' the two wreathen chains
25 p' them on the shoulderpieces of the
26 shalt p' them upon the two ends
27 p' them on the two sides of the
30 p' in the breastplate of judgment
37 thou shalt p' it on a blue lace, that
41 p' them upon Aaron thy brother,
29: 3 shalt p' them into one basket,
5 p' upon Aaron the coat, and the
6 shalt p' the mitre upon his head,
6 p' the holy crown upon the mitre.
8 his sons, and p' coats upon them.
9 sons, and p' the bonnets on them:
10 p' their hands upon the head of
12 p' it upon the horns of the altar
15 p' their hands upon the head of
17 p' them unto his pieces, and unto
19 p' their hands upon the head of
20 p' it upon the tip of the right ear
24 shalt p' all in the hands of Aaron,
30 stead shall p' them on seven days,
30: 6 p' it before the vail that is by the
18 p' it between the tabernacle of the
18 and thou shalt p' water therein.
Ex 30: 36 p' of it before the testimony in the
31: 6 are wise hearted I have p' wisdom,
14 defileth it shall surely be p' to death:
15 day, he shall surely be p' to death.
32: 27 P' every man his sword by his
33: 4 man did p' on him his ornaments.
5 now p' off thy ornaments from
22 I will p' thee in a clift of the rock,
34: 33 with them, he p' a vail on his face.
35 and Moses p' the vail upon his face
35: 2 work therein shall be p' to death.
34 hath p' in his heart that he may
36: 1 in whom the Lord p' wisdom and
2 heart the Lord had p' wisdom,
37: 5 he p' the staves into the rings by
13 p' the rings upon the four corners
38: 7 he p' the staves into the rings on
39: 7 he p' them on the shoulders of the
16 p' the two rings in the two ends of
17 they p' the two wreathen chains of
18 p' them on the shoulderpieces of
19 p' them on the two ends of the
20 and p' them on the two sides of the
25 gold, and p' the bells between the
40: 3 p' therein the ark of the testimony,
5 p' the hanging of the door to the
7 altar, and shalt p' water therein.
13 p' upon Aaron the holy garments,
18 p' in the bars thereof, and reared
19 p' the covering of the tent above
20 and p' the testimony into the ark,
20 and p' the mercy seat above upon
22 he p' the table in the tent of the
24 he p' the candlestick in the tent of
26 p' the golden altar in the tent of the
29 he p' the altar of burnt offering by
30 p' water there, to wash withal.
Le 1: 4 he shall p' his hand upon the head
7 priest shall p' fire upon the altar,
2: 1 it, and p' frankincense thereon:
15 thou shalt p' oil upon it, and lay
4: 7, 18 p' some of the blood upon the
25, 30, 34 p' it upon the horns of the
5: 11 offering; he shall p' no oil upon it,
11 he p' any frankincense thereon:
6: 10 shall p' on his linen garment,
10 breeches shall he p' upon his
10 he shall p' them beside the altar.
11 And he shall p' off his garments,
11 and p' on other garments, and
12 in it; it shall not be p' out: and
8: 7 And he p' upon him the coat, and
7 and p' the ephod upon him, and he
8 he p' the breastplate upon him:
8 p' in the breastplate the Urim and
9 he p' the mitre upon his head;
9 forefront, did he p' the golden
13 sons, and p' coats upon them, and
13 girdles,...p' bonnets upon them;
15 p' it upon the horns of the altar
23 p' it upon the tip of Aaron's right
24 p' of the blood upon the tip of
26 one wafer, and p' them on the fat,
27 And he p' all upon Aaron's hands,
9: 9 p' it upon the horns of the altar,
20 p' the fat upon the beasts, and he
10: 1 his censer, and p' fire therein,
1 and p' incense thereon, and
10 p' difference between holy and
11: 32 it must be p' into water, and it
38 if any water be p' upon the seed,
13: 45 p' a covering upon his upper lip,
14: 14 p' it upon the tip of the right ear
17 p' upon the tip of the right ear
25 p' it upon the tip of the right ear
28 shall p' of the oil that is in his
29 shall p' upon the head of him that
34 p' the plague of leprosy in a house
42 p' them in the place of those stones;
15: 19 she shall be p' apart seven days:
16: 4 He shall p' on the holy linen coat,
4 flesh in water, and so p' them on.
13 shall p' the incense upon the fire
18 p' it upon the horns of the altar
23 shall p' off the linen garments,
23 which he p' on when he went into
24 and p' on his garments, and come
32 and shall p' on the linen clothes,
18: 19 is p' apart for her uncleanness.
19: 14 p' a stumblingblock before the
20 they shall not be p' to death,
20: 2 he shall surely be p' to death: the
9 shall be surely p' to death; he hath
10 adulteress shall surely be p' to death.
11 of them shall surely be p' to death;
12 of them shall surely be p' to death:
13 they shall surely be p' to death;
15 beast, he shall surely be p' to death:
16 they shall surely be p' to death; their
25 p' difference between clean beasts
27 is a wizard, shall surely be p' to death:
21: 7 woman p' away from her husband:
10 consecrated to p' on the garments,
22: 14 p' the fifth part thereof unto it,
24: 7 p' pure frankincense upon each
12 And they p' him in ward, that the
16 he shall surely be p' to death, and all
16 name of the Lord, shall be p' to death.
17 any man shall surely be p' to death.
21 killeth a man, he shall be p' to death.
26: 8 of you shall p' ten thousand to flight:
27: 29 redeemed; but shall surely be p' to
Nu 1: 51 that cometh nigh shall be p' to death.
3: 10, 38 cometh nigh shall be p' to death.
4: 6 shall p' thereon the covering of
6 and shall p' in the staves thereof.
Nu 4: 7 p' thereon the dishes, and the
8 and shall p' in the staves thereof.
10 they shall p' it, and all the vessels
10 skins, and shall p' it upon a bar.
11 and shall p' to the staves thereof:
12 p' them in a cloth of blue, and
12 skins, and shall p' them on a bar:
14 they shall p' upon it all the vessels
14 skins, and p' to the staves of it.
5: 2 p' out of the camp every leper,
3 male and female shall ye p' out,
3 without the camp shall ye p' them;
4 and p' them out without the camp:
15 it, nor p' frankincense thereon;
17 take, and p' it into the water:
18 p' the offering of memorial in her
6: 18 p' it in the fire which is under the
19 p' them upon the hands of the
27 they shall p' my name upon the
8: 10 p' their hands upon the Levites:
11: 17 thee, and will p' it upon them;
29 the Lord would p' his spirit upon
15: 34 they p' him in ward, because it
35 The man shall be surely p' to death:
38 p' upon the fringe of the borders
16: 7 And p' fire therein,
7 p' incense in them before the
14 thou p' out the eyes of these men?
17 his censer, and p' incense in them,
18 his censer, and p' fire in them,
46 Take a censer, and p' fire therein
46 off the altar, and p' on incense,
47 and he p' on incense, and made an
18: 7 that cometh nigh shall be p' to death.
19: 17 running water shall be p' thereto
20: 26, 28 and p' them upon Eleazar his
21: 9 of brass, and p' it upon a pole, and
23: 5 Lord p' a word in Balaam's mouth,
12 the Lord hath p' in my mouth?
16 and p' a word in his mouth, and
27: 20 shalt p' some of thine honour upon
35: 16, 17, 18 shall surely be p' to death.
21 smote him shall surely be p' to death;
30 shall be p' to death by the mouth of
31 but he shall be surely p' to death.
36: 3 shall be p' to the inheritance of
4 their inheritance be p' unto the
De 2: 25 I begin to p' the dread of thee
7: 15 will p' none of the evil diseases of
22 thy God will p' out those nations
10: 2 and thou shalt p' them in the ark.
5 p' the tables in the ark which I had
11: 29 shalt p' the blessing upon mount
12: 5 your tribes to p' his name there,
7 in all that ye p' your hand unto,
21 hath chosen to p' his name there
13: 5 of dreams shall be p' to death;
5 p' the evil away from the midst of
9 be first upon him to p' him to death,
16: 9 beginnest to p' the sickle to the corn.
17: 6 that is worthy of death be p' to death;
6 witness he shall not be p' to death,
7 be first upon him to p' him to death,
7 p' the evil away from among you.
12 shalt p' away the evil from Israel.
18: 18 will p' my words in his mouth;
19: 13 p' away the guilt of innocent
19 p' the evil away from among you.
21: 9 p' away the guilt of innocent blood
13 p' the raiment of her captivity
21 p' evil away from among you;
22 he be to be p' to death, and thou hang
22: 5 a man p' on a woman's garment:
19 may not p' her away all his days.
21 p' evil away from among you.
22 thou p' away evil from Israel.
24 shalt p' away evil from among you.
29 may not p' her away all his days.
23: 24 thou shalt not p' any in thy vessel.
24: 7 p' evil away from among you.
16 fathers shall not be p' to death for the
16 children be p' to death for the fathers:
16 shall be p' to death for his own sin.
25: 6 his name be not p' out of Israel.
26: 2 shalt p' it in a basket, and shalt
28: 14 p' a yoke of iron upon the neck
30: 7 thy God will p' all these curses
31: 19 p' it in their mouths, that this
26 law, and p' it in the side of the ark
32: 30 two p' ten thousand to flight, except
33: 10 they shall p' incense before thee,
14 precious things p' forth by the
Jos 1: 18 him, he shall be p' to death:
6: 24 they p' into the treasury of the
7: 6 and p' dust upon their heads.
11 p' it even among their own stuff.
10: 24 p' your feet upon the necks of
24 p' their feet upon the necks of
17: 13 they p' the Canaanites to tribute;
24: 7 he p' darkness between you and
14 and p' away the gods which your
23 p' away, said he, the strange gods
J'g 1: 28 they p' the Canaanites to tribute,
3: 21 And Ehud p' forth his left hand,
5: 26 She p' her hand to the nail, and her
6: 19 flour: the flesh he p' in a basket,
19 he p' the broth in a pot, and
21 angel of the Lord p' forth the end
31 be p' to death whilst it is yet morning:
37 p' a fleece of wool in the floor; and
7: 16 p' a trumpet in every man's hand,
8: 27 p' it in his city, even in Ophrah:
9: 15 and p' your trust in my shadow;
26 of Shechem p' their confidence in him.
49 and p' them to the hold, and set
10: 16 p' away the strange gods from

J'g 12: 3 I p' my life in my hands, and
14: 12 I will now p' forth a riddle unto
13 P' forth thy riddle, that we may
16 p' forth a riddle unto the children
15: 4 and p' a firebrand in the midst
15 and p' forth his hand, and took it,
16: 3 p' them upon his shoulders, and
21 took him, and p' out his eyes, and
18: 7 p' them to shame in any thing;
21 p' the little ones and the cattle
20: 13 Gibeah, that we may p' them to death,
13 and p' away evil from Israel.
20 Israel p' themselves in array to fight
22 p' themselves in array the first day.
30 p' themselves in array against Gibeah,
33 p' themselves in array at Baal-tamar:
21: 5 saying, He shall surely be p' to death.
Ru 3: 3 and p' thy raiment upon thee,
1Sa 1: 14 p' away thy wine from thee.
2: 36 P' me, I pray thee, into one of the
4: 2 Philistines p' themselves in array,
6: 8 p' the jewels of gold, which ye
15 and p' them on the great stone:
7: 3 then p' away the strange gods and
4 did p' away Baalim and Ashtaroth,
8: 16 asses, and p' them to his work.
11: 11 p' the people in three companies;
12 men, that we may p' them to death.
13 not a man be p' to death this day:
14: 26 no man p' his hand to his mouth:
27 he p' forth the end of the rod that
27 and p' his hand to his mouth; and
17: 21 Philistines had p' the battle in array,
38 p' an helmet of brass upon his
39 them. And David p' them off him.
40 p' them in a shepherd's bag which
49 And David p' his hand in his bag,
54 but he p' his armour in his tent.
19: 5 For he did p' his life in his hand,
13 p' a pillow of goat's hair for his
21: 6 to p' hot bread in the day when it
22: 17 king would not p' forth their hand
24: 10 will not p' forth mine hand against
28: 3 p' away those that had familiar
8 himself, and p' on other raiment,
21 I have p' my life in my hand, and
31: 10 they p' his armour in the house of
2Sa 1: 24 who p' on ornaments of gold upon
3: 34 bound, nor thy feet p' into fetters,
6: 6 Uzzah p' forth his hand to the ark
7: 15 Saul, whom I p' away before thee.
8: 2 two lines measured he to p' to death,
6 David p' garrisons in Syria of
14 And he p' garrisons in Edom;
14 all Edom p' he garrisons, and all
10: 8 p' the battle in array at the entering
9 p' them in array against the Syrians:
10 that he might p' them in array
12: 13 Lord also hath p' away thy sin;
31 therein, and p' them under saws,
13: 17 P' now this woman out from me,
19 Tamar p' ashes on her head, and
14: 2 and p' on now mourning apparel,
3 Joab p' the words in her mouth.
19 he p' all these words in the mouth
15: 5 he p' forth his hand, and took him,
17: 23 p' his household in order, and hanged
18: 12 would I not p' forth mine hand
19: 21 not Shimei be p' to death for this,
22 there any man be p' to death this day
20: 3 p' them in ward, and fed them,
21: 9 were p' to death in the days of harvest,
1Ki 2: 5 p' the blood of war upon his girdle
8 not p' thee to death with the sword.
24 Adonijah shall be p' to death this day.
26 will not at this time p' thee to death,
35 the king p' Benaiah the son of
35 priest did the king p' in the room of
5: 3 p' them under the soles of his feet.
7: 39 he p' five bases on the right side
51 p' among the treasures of the house
8: 9 which Moses p' there at Horeb,
9: 3 built, to p' my name there for ever;
10: 17 p' them in the house of the forest
24 which God had p' in his heart.
11: 36 chosen me to p' my name there.
12: 4 heavy yoke which he p' upon us,
9 thy father did p' upon us lighter?
29 Beth-el, and the other p' he in Dan.
13: 4 p' forth his hand from the altar,
4 hand, which he p' forth against
14: 21 of Israel, to p' his name there.
18: 23, 23 on wood, and p' no fire under:
25 of your gods, but p' no fire under.
33 And he p' the wood in order, and
42 and p' his face between his knees,
20: 6 they shall p' it in their hand, and
24 and p' captains in their rooms:
31 pray thee, p' sackcloth on our loins,
32 loins, and p' ropes on their heads,
21: 27 and p' sackcloth upon his flesh,
22: 10 throne, having p' on their robes,
23 hath p' a lying spirit in the mouth
27 P' this fellow in the prison, and
30 battle; but p' thou on thy robes.
2Ki 2: 20 a new cruse, and p' salt therein.
3: 2 he p' away the image of Baal that
21 all that were able to p' on armour,
4: 34 and p' his mouth upon his mouth,
6: 7 he p' out his hand, and took it.
9: 13 and p' it under him on the top of
10: 7 and p' their heads in baskets, and
11: 12 king's son, and p' the crown upon
12: 9 p' therein all the money that was
10 p' up in bags, and told the money
13: 16 P' thine hand upon the bow.

2Ki 13: 16 And he p' his hand upon it: and
16 Elisha p' his hands upon the king's
14: 6 not be p' to death for the children,
6 be p' to death for the fathers;
6 shall be p' to death for his own sin:
12 was p' to the worse before Israel;
16: 14 p' it on the north side of the altar.
17 p' it upon a pavement of stones.
17: 29 p' them in the houses of the high
18: 11 p' them in Halah and in Habor
24 p' thy trust on Egypt for chariots and
19: 28 I will p' my hook in thy nose, and
21: 4 In Jerusalem will I p' my name.
7 Israel, will I p' my name for ever:
23: 5 he p' down the idolatrous priests,
24 did Josiah p' away, that he might
33 p' him in bands at Riblah in the
33 p' the land to a tribute of an hundred
25: 7 p' out the eyes of Zedekiah, and
1Ch 5: 20 because they p' their trust in him.
10: 10 p' his armour in the house of their
12: 15 and they p' to flight all them of the
13: 9 Uzza p' forth his hand to hold the
10 because he p' his hand to the ark:
18: 6 p' garrisons in Syria-damascus;
13 And he p' garrisons in Edom; and
19: 9 and p' the battle in array before the
10 p' them in array against the Syrians.
16 they were p' to the worse before Israel,
17 when David had p' the battle in array
19 saw that they were p' to the worse
21: 27 and he p' up his sword again into
27: 24 was the number p' in the account
2Ch 1: 5 he p' before the tabernacle of the
2: 14 device which shall be p' to him,
3: 16 p' them on the heads of the pillars;
16 and p' them on the chains.
4: 6 and p' five on the right hand, and
5: 1 p' he among the treasures of the
10 two tables which Moses p' therein
6: 11 in it have I p' the ark, wherein is
20 thou wouldest p' thy name there;
24 thy people Israel be p' to the worse
9: 16 And the king p' them in the house
23 wisdom,...God had p' in his heart.
10: 4 his heavy yoke that he p' upon us,
9 yoke that thy father did p' upon us?
11 father p' a heavy yoke upon you,
11 you, I will p' more to your yoke:
11: 11 holds, and p' captains in them,
12 several city he p' shields and spears,
12: 13 of Israel, to p' his name there.
15: 8 p' away the abominable idols out
13 God of Israel should be p' to death,
16: 10 and p' him in a prison house; for
17: 19 whom the king p' in the fenced
18: 22 hath p' a lying spirit in the mouth
26 P' this fellow in the prison, and
29 battle; but p' thou on thy robes.
22: 11 and p' him and his nurse in a
23: 7 the house, he shall be p' to death:
11 son, and p' upon him the crown,
25: 22 was p' to the worse before Israel,
29: 7 and p' out the lamps, and have not
33: 7 Israel, will I p' my name for ever:
14 p' captains of war in all the fenced
34: 10 p' it in the hand of the workmen
35: 3 P' the holy ark in the house which
24 p' him in the second chariot that
36: 3 Egypt p' him down at Jerusalem,
7 p' them in his temple at Babylon.
22 his kingdom, and p' it also in writing,
Ezr 1: 1 his kingdom, and p' it also in writing,
7 p' them in the house of his gods;
2: 62 as polluted, p' from the priesthood.
6: 12 shall p' to their hand to alter and
7: 27 p' such a thing as this in the king's
10: 3 our God to p' away all the wives,
19 they would p' away their wives;
Ne 2: 12 p' in my heart to do at Jerusalem:
3: 5 p' not their necks to the work of
4: 23 me, none of us p' off our clothes,
23 every one p' them off for washing.
6: 14 that would have p' me in fear.
19 Tobiah sent letters to p' me in fear.
7: 5 And my God p' into mine heart to
64 as polluted, p' from the priesthood.
Es 4: 1 and p' on sackcloth with ashes,
11 is one law of his to p' him to death,
5: 1 Esther p' on her royal apparel,
8: 3 to p' away the mischief of Haman
9: 1 decree drew near to be p' in execution,
Job 1: 11 But p' forth thine hand now, and
12 himself p' not forth thine hand.
2: 5 But p' forth thine hand now, and
4: 18 Behold, he p' no trust in his servants;
11: 14 be in thine hand, p' it far away,
13: 14 and p' my life in mine hand?
17: 3 now, p' me in a surety with thee;
18: 5 light of the wicked shall be p' out,
6 his candle shall be p' out with him.
19: 13 hath p' my brethren far from me,
21: 17 is the candle of the wicked p' out!
22: 23 p' away iniquity far from thy
23: 6 but he would p' strength in me.
27: 17 but the just shall p' it on, and the
29: 14 I p' on righteousness, and it
38: 36 p' wisdom in the inward parts?
41: 2 thou p' an hook into his nose?
Ps 2: 12 are all they that p' their trust in him.
4: 5 and p' your trust in the Lord.
7 Thou hast p' gladness in my heart.
5: 11 that p' their trust in thee rejoice:
7: 1 Lord my God, in thee do I p' my trust:
8: 6 hast p' all things under his feet:
9: 5 thou hast p' out their name for

Ps 9: 10 thy name will p' their trust in thee:
20 P' them in fear, O Lord: that the
11: 1 In the Lord p' I my trust: how say ye
16: 1 O God: for in thee do I p' my trust.
17: 7 them which p' their trust in thee from
18: 22 not p' away his statutes from me.
25: 20 be ashamed; for I p' my trust in thee.
27: 9 p' not thy servant away in anger:
30: 11 thou hast p' off my sackcloth, and
31: 1 In thee, O Lord, do I p' my trust; let
18 Let the lying lips be p' to silence;
35: 4 and p' to shame that seek after my
36: 7 p' their trust under the shadow of thy
40: 3 hath p' a new song in my mouth,
14 and p' to shame that wish me evil.
44: 7 hast p' them to shame that hated us.
9 thou hast cast off, and p' us to shame;
53: 5 thou hast p' them to shame, because
55: 20 He hath p' forth his hands against
56: 4 his word, in God I have p' my trust;
8 p' thou my tears into thy bottle:
11 In God have I p' my trust: I will not
70: 2 backward, and p' to confusion,
71: 1 In thee, O Lord, do I p' my trust:
1 trust: let me never be p' to confusion.
73: 28 I have p' my trust in the Lord God,
78: 66 p' them to a perpetual reproach.
83: 17 yea, let them be p' to shame, and
88: 8 hast p' away mine acquaintance
18 and friend hast thou p' far from me,
118: 8 the Lord than to p' confidence in man.
9 Lord than to p' confidence in princes.
119: 31 O Lord, p' me not to shame.
125: 3 the righteous p' forth their hands
146: 3 P' not your trust in princes, nor in
Pr 4: 24 P' away from thee a froward
24 and perverse lips p' far from thee.
8: 1 understanding p' forth her voice?
13: 9 lamp of the wicked shall be p' out.
20: 20 shall be p' out in obscure darkness.
23: 2 And p' a knife to thy throat, if thou
24: 20 of the wicked shall be p' out.
25: 6 P' not forth thyself in the
7 shouldest be p' lower in the presence
8 thy neighbour hath p' thee to shame.
10 he that heareth it p' thee to shame,
30: 5 unto them that p' their trust in him.
Ec 3: 14 nothing can be p' to it, nor any
10: 10 then must he p' to more strength:
11: 10 and p' away evil from thy flesh:
Ca 5: 3 I have p' off my coat; how shall I
3 my coat; how shall I p' it on?
4 beloved p' in his hand by the hole
Isa 1: 16 p' away the evil of your doings
5: 20 p' darkness for light, and light for
20 that p' bitter for sweet, and sweet
10: 13 p' down the inhabitants like a
11: 8 p' his hand on the cockatrice' den.
20: 2 and p' off thy shoe from thy foot.
36: 9 p' thy trust on Egypt for chariots and
37: 29 will I p' my hook in thy nose, and
42: 1 I have p' my spirit upon him: he
43: 26 P' me in remembrance: let us plead
47: 11 thou shalt not be able to p' it off:
50: 1 divorcement, whom I have p' away?
1 transgressions is your mother p'
51: 9 p' on strength, O arm of the Lord;
16 I have p' my words in thy mouth,
23 p' it into the hand of them that
52: 1 awake; p' on thy strength, O Zion;
1 p' on thy beautiful garments, O
53: 10 he hath p' him to grief: when thou
54: 4 for thou shalt not be p' to shame:
59: 17 For he p' on righteousness as a
17 he p' on the garments of vengeance
21 which I have p' in thy mouth,
63: 11 that p' his holy Spirit within him?
Jer 1: 9 Then the Lord p' forth his hand,
9 I have p' my words in thy mouth.
3: 1 If a man p' away his wife, and she
8 I had p' her away, and given her
19 How shall I p' thee among the
4: 1 p' away thine abominations out of
7: 21 P' your burnt offerings unto your
8: 14 the Lord our God hath p' us to silence,
12: 13 they have p' themselves to pain, but
13: 1 girdle, and p' it upon thy loins,
1 thy loins, and p' it not in water.
2 of the Lord, and p' it on my loins.
18: 21 and let their men be p' to death;
20: 2 and p' him in the stocks that were
26: 15 that if ye p' me to death, ye shall
19 and all Judah p' him at all to death?
21 the king sought to p' him to death:
24 hand of the people to p' him to death.
27: 2 yokes, and p' them upon thy neck,
8 not p' their neck under the yoke of
28: 14 p' a yoke of iron upon the neck of
29: 26 thou shouldest p' him in prison,
31: 33 will p' my law in their inward parts,
32: 14 p' them in an earthen vessel, that
40 I will p' my fear in their hearts,
37: 4 for they had not p' him into prison.
15 p' him in prison in the house of
18 that ye have p' me in prison?
38: 4 thee, let this man be p' to death:
7 had p' Jeremiah in the dungeon;
12 P' now these old cast clouts and
15 wilt thou not surely p' me to death?
16 I will not p' thee to death, neither will
25 us, and we will not p' thee to death;
39: 7 Moreover he p' out Zedekiah's
18 because thou hast p' thy trust in me,
40: 10 and p' them in your vessels, and
43: 3 that they might p' us to death, and
46: 4 spears, and p' on the brigandines.

Jer 47: 6 p' up thyself into thy scabbard,
50:14 P' yourselves in array against
42 every one p' in array, like a man to
52:11 he p' out the eyes of Zedekiah;
11 p' him in prison till the day of his
27 p' them to death in Riblah in the land
Eze 3:25 they shall p' bands upon thee,
4: 9 and p' them in one vessel, and
8: 3 p' forth the form of an hand, and
17 they p' the branch to their nose.
10: 7 p' it into the hands of him that
11:19 I will p' a new spirit within you;
14: 3 and p' the stumblingblock of their
16:11 I p' bracelets upon thy hands, and
12 I p' a jewel on thy forehead, and
14 which I had p' upon thee,
17: 2 Son of man, p' forth a riddle, and
19: 9 they p' him in ward in chains, and
22:26 p' no difference between the holy and
23:42 p' bracelets upon their hands, and
24:17 p' on thy shoes upon thy feet, and
26:16 p' off their broidered garments:
29: 4 I will p' hooks in thy jaws, and I
30:13 will p' a fear in the land of Egypt.
21 to p' a roller to bind it, to make it
24 and p' my sword in his hand: but
25 p' my sword into the hand of the
32: 7 when I shall p' thee out, I will
25 p' in the midst of them that be
36:26 a new spirit will I p' within you:
27 I will p' my spirit within you, and
37: 6 p' breath in you, and ye shall live;
14 shall p' my spirit in you, and ye
19 and will p' them with him, even
38: 4 back, and p' hooks into thy jaws,
42:14 and shall p' on other garments,
43: 9 let them p' away their whoredom,
20 and p' it on the four horns of it,
44:19 they shall p' off their garments
19 they shall p' on other garments;
22 a widow, nor her that is p' away:
45:19 p' it upon the posts of the house,
Da 5:19 and whom he would he p' down.
29 and p' a chain of gold about his neck,
Ho 2: 2 therefore p' away her whoredoms
Joe 3:13 P' ye in the sickle, for the harvest
Am 6: 3 Ye that p' far away the evil day, and
Jon 3: 5 a fast, and p' on sackcloth, from
Mic 2:12 will p' them together as the sheep
7: 5 p' ye not confidence in a guide:
Zep 3:19 where they have been p' to shame.
Hag 1: 6 wages to p' it into a bag with holes.
M't 1:19 was minded to p' her away privily.
5:15 candle, and p' it under a bushel,
31 Whosoever shall p' away his wife,
32 whosoever shall p' away his wife,
6:25 for your body, what ye shall p' on.
8: 3 And Jesus p' forth his hand, and
9:16 that which is p' in to fill it up taketh
17 do men p' new wine into old bottles:
17 they p' new wine into new bottles,
25 when the people were p' forth, he
10:21 and cause them to be p' to death.
12:18 I will p' my spirit upon him, and
13:24, 31 parable p' he forth unto them,
14: 3 p' him in prison for Herodias' sake,
5 he would have p' him to death,
19: 3 for a man to p' away his wife for
6 together, let not man p' asunder.
7 divorcement, and to p' her away?
8 suffered you to p' away your wives:
9 Whosoever shall p' away his wife,
9 marrieth her which is p' away doth
13 he should p' his hands on them,
21: 7 and p' on them their clothes, and
22:34 had p' the Sadducees to silence,
25:27 p' my money to the exchangers,
26:52 P' up again thy sword into his
59 against Jesus, to p' him to death;
27: 1 against Jesus, to p' him to death:
6 for to p' them into the treasury,
28 him, and p' on him a scarlet robe.
29 thorns, they p' it upon his head,
31 and p' his own raiment on him,
48 p' it on a reed, and gave him to
M'r 1:14 after that John was p' in prison,
41 compassion, p' forth his hand,
2:22 wine must be p' into new bottles.
4:21 brought to be p' under a bushel,
5:40 But when he had p' them all out,
6: 9 sandals; and not p' on two coats.
7:32 beseech him to p' his hand upon
33 p' his fingers into his ears, and he
M'r 8:23 p' his hands upon him, he asked
25 p' his hands again upon his eyes,
10: 2 for a man to p' away his wife?
4 divorcement, and to p' her away.
9 together, let not man p' asunder.
11 shall p' away his wife, and marry
12 woman shall p' away her husband,
16 p' his hands upon them, and
13:12 shall cause them to be p' to death.
14: 1 him by craft, and p' him to death.
55 against Jesus to p' him to death;
15:17 thorns, and p' it about his head,
20 p' his own clothes on him, and led
36 full of vinegar, and p' it on a reed,
Lu 1:52 He hath p' down the mighty from
5:13 he p' forth his hand, and touched
38 new wine must be p' into new
8:54 p' them all out, and took her by
9:62 having p' his hand to the plough,
12:22 for the body, what ye shall p' on.
14: 7 And he p' forth a parable to those
15:22 the best robe, and p' it on him;
22 p' a ring on his hand, and shoes on
16: 4 I am p' out of the stewardship,
18 that is p' away from her husband
18:33 scourge him, and p' him to death:
21:16 shall they cause to be p' to death.
23:32 led with him to be p' to death.
Joh 5: 7 troubled, to p' me into the pool:
9:15 He p' clay upon mine eyes, and I
22 he should be p' out of the synagogue.
11:53 together for to p' him to death.
12: 6 bag, and bare what was p' therein.
10 might p' Lazarus also to death;
42 should be p' out of the synagogue:
13: 2 now p' into the heart of Judas
16: 2 shall p' you out of the synagogues:
18:11 P' up thy sword into the sheath:
31 for us to p' any man to death:
19: 2 of thorns, and p' it on his head,
2 and they p' on him a purple robe,
19 a title, and p' it on the cross.
29 vinegar, and p' it upon hyssop,
29 and p' it to his mouth.
20:25 p' my finger into the print of the
Ac 1: 7 Father hath p' in his own power.
4: 3 p' them in hold unto the next day:
5:18 and p' them in the common prison.
25 the men whom ye p' in prison are
34 p' the apostles forth a little space;
7:33 P' off thy shoes from thy feet:
9:40 But Peter p' them all forth, and
12: 4 him, he p' him in prison,
19 that they should be p' to death.
13:46 seeing ye p' it from you, and judge
15: 9 p' no difference between us and
10 to p' a yoke upon the neck of the
26:10 when they were p' to death, I gave
27: 6 into Italy; and he p' us therein.
Ro 13:12 let us p' on the armour of light.
14 But p' ye on the Lord Jesus Christ,
14:13 that no man p' a stumblingblock
1Co 5:13 p' away from among yourselves
7:11 not the husband p' away his wife.
12 with him, let him not p' her away.
13:11 a man, I p' away childish things.
15:24 he shall have p' down all rule and
25 hath p' all enemies under his feet.
27 hath p' all things under his feet.
27 saith all things are p' under him,
27 which did p' all things under him.
28 subject unto him that p' all things
53 corruptible must p'...incorruption,
53 this mortal must p' on immortality.
54 shall have p' on incorruption, and
54 mortal shall have p' on immortality,
2Co 3:13 which p' a vail over his face, that
8:16 which p' the same earnest care
Ga 3:27 into Christ have p' on Christ.
Eph 1:22 hath p' all things under his feet,
4:22 That ye p' off concerning the former
24 that ye p' on the new man, which
31 evil speaking, be p' away from you,
6:11 P' on the whole armour of God,
Col 3: 8 also p' off all these; anger, wrath,
9 p' off the old man with his deeds;
10 have p' on the new man, which is
12 P' on therefore, as the elect of God,
14 above all these things p' on charity,
1Th 2: 4 to be p' in trust with the gospel,
1Ti 1:19 having p' away concerning faith
4: 6 p' the brethren in remembrance
2Ti 1: 6 I p' thee in remembrance that
2Ti 2:14 things p' them in remembrance,
Tit 3: 1 P' them in mind to be subject to
Ph'm 18 ought, p' that on mine account;
Heb 2: 5 p' in subjection the world to come,
8 p' all things in subjection under his
8 he p' all in subjection under him,
8 nothing that is not p' under him.
8 not yet all things p' under him.
13 again, I will p' my trust in him.
6: 6 and p' him to an open shame.
8:10 I will p' my laws into their mind,
9:26 to p' away sin by the sacrifice of
10:16 I will p' my laws into their hearts,
Jas 3: 3 we p' bits in the horses' mouths,
1Pe 2:15 may p' to silence the ignorance of
3:18 being p' to death in the flesh, but
2Pe 1:12 to p' you always in remembrance
14 I must p' off this my tabernacle,
Jude 5 therefore p' you in remembrance,
Re 2:24 p' upon you none other burden:
11: 9 dead bodies to be p' in graves.
17:17 p' in their hearts to fulfil his will,

Put (*put*) See also PHUT.
1Ch 1: 8 sons of Ham; Cush,...Mizraim, P',
Na 3: 9 P' and Lubim were thy helpers.

Puteoli (*pu-te'-o-li*)
Ac 28:13 and we came the next day to P':

Putiel (*pu'-te-el*)
Ex 6:25 one of the daughters of P' to wife;

putrifying
Isa 1: 6 wounds, and bruises, and p' sores:

puttest
Nu 24:21 and thou p' thy nest in a rock.
De 12:18 all that thou p' thine hands unto.
15:10 in all that thou p' thine hand unto.
2Ki 18:14 which thou p' on me will I bear.
Job 13:27 Thou p' my feet also in the stocks,
Ps 119:119 Thou p' away all the wicked of
Hab 2:15 that p' thy bottle to him, and

putteth
Ex 30:33 p' any of it upon a stranger, shall
Nu 22:38 word that God p' in my mouth,
De 25:11 and p' forth her hand, and taketh
27:15 and p' it in a secret place.
1Ki 20:11 boast himself as he that p' it off.
Job 15:15 Behold, he p' no trust in his saints;
28: 9 p' forth his hand upon the rock;
33:11 He p' my feet in the stocks, he
Ps 15: 5 He that p' not out his money to
75: 7 he p' down one, and setteth up
Pr 28:25 he that p' his trust in the Lord shall be
29:25 whoso p' his trust in the Lord shall be
Ca 2:13 fig tree p' forth her green figs,
Isa 57:13 he that p' his trust in me shall
Jer 43:12 as a shepherd p' on his garment;
La 3:29 He p' his mouth in the dust; if so
Eze 14: 4, 7 p' the stumblingblock of his
Mic 3: 5 he that p' not into their mouths,
M't 9:16 p' a piece of new cloth unto an old
24:32 is yet tender, and p' forth leaves,
M'r 2:22 no man p' new wine into old bottles:
4:29 immediately he p' in the sickle,
13:28 is yet tender, and p' forth leaves,
Lu 5:36 p' a piece of a new garment upon
37 man p' new wine into old bottles;
8:16 with a vessel, or p' it under a bed;
11:33 a candle, p' it in a secret place,
16:18 Whosoever p' away his wife, and
Joh 10: 4 when he p' forth his own sheep,

putting
Ge 21:14 p' it on her shoulder, and the
Le 16:21 p' them...the head of the goat,
J'g 7: 6 lapped, p' their hand to their mouth,
Isa 58: 9 p' forth of the finger, and speaking
Mal 2:16 Israel, saith that he hateth p' away:
Ac 9:12 coming in,...p' his hand on him,
17 p' his hands on him said, Brother
19:33 the Jews p' him forward. And
Ro 15:15 as p' you in mind, because of the
Eph 4:25 Wherefore p' away lying, speak
Col 2:11 p' off the body of the sins of the
1Th 5: 8 p' on the breastplate of faith and
1Ti 1:12 faithful, p' me into the ministry;
2Ti 1: 6 in thee by the p' on of my hands.
1Pe 3: 3 of gold, or of p' on of apparel;
21 the p' away of the filth of the flesh,
2Pe 1:13 you up by p' you in remembrance;

pygarg
De 14: 5 the wild goat, and the p', and the

Q.

quails
Ex 16:13 pass, that at even the q' came up,
Nu 11:31 brought q' from the sea, and let
32 next day, and they gathered the q':
Ps 105:40 people asked, and he brought q',

quake See also EARTHQUAKE; QUAKED; QUAKING.
Joe 2:10 The earth shall q' before them;
Na 1: 5 The mountains q' at him, and the
M't 27:51 and the earth did q', and the rocks
Heb 12:21 said, I exceedingly fear and q':)

quaked
Ex 19:18 and the whole mount q' greatly.
1Sa 14:15 also trembled, and the earth q':

quaking
Eze 12:18 Son of man, eat thy bread with q',
Da 10: 7 but a great q' fell upon them, so

quantity
Isa 22:24 and the issue, all vessels of small q'.

quarrel
Le 26:25 avenge the q' of my covenant:
2Ki 5: 7 see how he seeketh a q' against me.
M'r 6:19 Herodias had a q' against him,
Col 3:13 if any man have a q' against any:

quarries
J'g 3:19 from the q' that were by Gilgal,
26 and passed beyond the q', and

quarter See also QUARTERS.
Ge 19: 4 all the people from every q':
Nu 34: 3 q' shall be from the wilderness
Jos 15: 5 north q' was from the bay of the sea
18:14 of Judah: this was the west q'.
15 the south q' was from the end of
Isa 47:15 shall wander every one to his q';
56:11 every one for his gain, from his q'
M'r 1:45 they came to him from every q'.

quarters
Ex 13: 7 leaven seen with thee in all thy q'.
De 22:12 upon the four q' of thy vesture,
1Ch 9:24 In four q' were the porters,
Jer 49:36 winds from the four q' of heaven,
Eze 38: 6 of Togarmah of the north q',
Ac 9:32 as Peter passed throughout all q',
16: 3 the Jews which were in those q':
28: 7 In the same q' were possessions
Re 20: 8 are in the four q' of the earth,

Quartus (*quar'-tus*)
Ro 16:23 saluteth you, and Q' a brother.

quaternions
Ac 12: 4 delivered him to four q' of soldiers

queen See also QUEENS.
1Ki 10: 1 the q' of Sheba heard of the fame
4 when the q' of Sheba had seen all
10 which the q' of Sheba gave to king
13 unto the q' of Sheba all her desire,
11:19 wife, the sister of Tahpenes the q'.
15:13 even her he removed from being q',
2Ki 10:13 the king and the children of the q'.
2Ch 9: 1 q' of Sheba heard of the fame of
3 q' of Sheba had seen the wisdom of
9 the q' of Sheba gave king Solomon.
12 Solomon gave to the q' of Sheba all
15:16 he removed her from being q',
Ne 2: 6 me, (the q' also sitting by him,)
Es 1: 9 Vashti the q' made a feast for the
11 bring Vashti the q' before the king
12 the q' Vashti refused to come at the
15 do unto the q' Vashti according to
16 Vashti the q' hath not done wrong
17 deed of the q' shall come abroad
17 Vashti the q' to be brought in
18 have heard of the deed of the q'.
2: 4 which pleaseth the king be q'
17 and made her q' instead of Vashti.
22 who told it unto Esther the q';
4: 4 was the q' exceedingly grieved;
5: 2 Esther the q' standing in the court,
3 her, What wilt thou, q' Esther?
12 the q' did let no man come in with
7: 1 came to banquet with Esther the q'.
2 What is thy petition, q' Esther?
3 Esther the q' answered and said,
5 said unto Esther the q', Who is he,
6 afraid before the king and the q'.
7 request for his life to Esther the q';
8 Will he force the q' also before me
8: 1 Jews' enemy unto Esther the q'.
7 Ahasuerus said unto Esther the q',
9:12 the king said unto Esther the q',
29 Then Esther the q', the daughter of
31 Esther the q' had enjoined them,
Ps 45: 9 right hand did stand the q' in gold
Jer 7:18 to make cakes to the q' of heaven,
13:18 Say unto the king and to the q',
29: 2 king, and the q', and the eunuchs,
44:17 incense unto the q' of heaven,
18 to burn incense to the q' of heaven,
19 burned incense to the q' of heaven,
25 to burn incense to the q' of heaven,
Da 5:10 the q' by reason of the words of
10 the q' spake and said, O king, live
M't 12:42 The q' of the south shall rise up in
Lu 11:31 The q' of the south shall rise up in
Ac 8:27 under Candace q' of the Ethiopians,
Re 18: 7 for she saith in her heart, I sit a q',

queens
Ca 6: 8 are threescore q', and fourscore
9 yea, the q' and the concubines, and
Isa 49:23 and their q' thy nursing mothers:

quench See also QUENCHED; UNQUENCHABLE.
2Sa 14: 7 they shall q' my coal which is left,
21:17 that thou q' not the light of Israel.
Ps 104:11 the wild asses q' their thirst.
Ca 8: 7 Many waters cannot q' love,
Isa 1:31 together, and none shall q' them.
42: 3 the smoking flax shall he not q':
Jer 4: 4 fire, and burn that none can q' it,
21:12 fire, and burn that none can q' it,
Am 5: 6 there be none to q' it in Beth-el.
M't 12:20 and smoking flax shall he not q',
Eph 6:16 q' all the fiery darts of the wicked.
1Th 5:19 Q' not the Spirit.

quenched
Nu 11: 2 unto the Lord, the fire was q'.
2Ki 22:17 this place, and shall not be q'.
2Ch 34:25 this place, and shall not be q'.
Ps 118:12 they are q' as the fire of thorns:
Isa 34:10 It shall not be q' night nor day;
43:17 they are extinct, they are q' as tow.
66:24 die, neither shall their fire be q';
Jer 7:20 it shall burn, and shall not be q'.
17:27 of Jerusalem, and it shall not be q'.
Eze 20:47 the flaming flame shall not be q',
48 have kindled it: it shall not be q'.
M'r 9:43 into the fire that never shall be q':
44 dieth not, and the fire is not q'.
45 into the fire that never shall be q':
46 dieth not, and the fire is not q'.
48 dieth not, and the fire is not q'.
Heb 11:34 Q' the violence of fire, escaped the

question See also QUESTIONED; QUESTIONING; QUESTIONS.
M't 22:35 which was a lawyer, asked him a q',
M'r 8:11 began to q' with him, seeking of
9:16 the scribes, What q' ye with them?
11:29 I will also ask of you one q', and
12:34 man after that durst ask him any q':
Lu 20:40 they durst not ask him any q' at all.
Joh 3:25 there arose a q' between some of
Ac 15: 2 apostles and elders about this q'.
18:15 if it be a q' of words and names,
19:40 we are in danger to be called in q'
23: 6 of the dead I am called in q'.
24:21 I am called in q' by you this day.
1Co 10:25 asking no q' for conscience sake:
27 asking no q' for conscience sake.

questioned
2Ch 31: 9 Hezekiah q' with the priests and
M'r 1:27 that they q' among themselves,
Lu 23: 9 he q' with him in many words;

questioning
M'r 9:10 q' one with another what the
14 them, and the scribes q' with them.

questions
1Ki 10: 1 came to prove him with hard q'.
3 And Solomon told her all her q':
2Ch 9: 1 to prove Solomon with hard q' at
2 And Solomon told her all her q':
M't 22:46 that day forth ask him any more q'.
Lu 2:46 hearing them, and asking them q'.
Ac 23:29 to be accused of q' of their law,
25:19 But had certain q' against him of
20 I doubted of such manner of q',
26: 3 to be expert in all customs and q'
1Ti 1: 4 genealogies, which minister q',
6: 4 about q' and strifes of words,
2Ti 2:23 But foolish and unlearned q' avoid,
Tit 3: 9 avoid foolish q', and genealogies,

quick See also ALIVE; LIVING; QUICKSANDS.
Le 13:10 there be q' raw flesh in the rising;
24 q' flesh that burneth have a white
Nu 16:30 and they go down q' into the pit;
Ps 55:15 and let them go down q' into hell:
124: 3 they had swallowed us up q', when
Isa 11: 3 shall make him of q' understanding
Ac 10:42 to be the Judge of q' and dead.
2Ti 4: 1 shall judge the q' and the dead at
Heb 4:12 the word of God is q', and powerful,
1Pe 4: 5 ready to judge the q' and the dead.

quicken See also QUICKENED; QUICKENETH; QUICKENING.
Ps 71:20 sore troubles, shalt q' me again,
80:18 q' us, and we will call upon thy
119:25 q' thou me according to thy word.
37 vanity; and q' thou me in thy way.
40 q' me in thy righteousness.
88 Q' me after thy lovingkindness; so
107 q' me, O Lord, according unto thy
149 q' me according to thy judgment.
154 me: q' me according to thy word.
156 q' me according to thy judgments.
159 Q' me, O Lord, according to thy
143:11 Q' me, O Lord, for thy name's sake:
Ro 8:11 also q' your mortal bodies by his

quickened
Ps 119:50 affliction: for thy word hath q' me.
93 for with them thou hast q' me.
1Co 15:36 that which thou sowest is not q',
Eph 2: 1 you hath he q', who were dead
5 hath q' us together with Christ,
Col 2:13 flesh, hath he q' together with him,
1Pe 3:18 in the flesh, but q' by the Spirit:

quickeneth
Joh 5:21 raiseth up the dead, and q' them;
21 even so the Son q' whom he will.
6:63 It is the spirit that q'; the flesh
Ro 4:17 even God, who q' the dead, and
1Ti 6:13 the sight of God, who q' all things,

quickening
1Co 15:45 last Adam was made a q' spirit.

quickly
Ge 18: 6 Make ready q' three measures of
27:20 is it that thou hast found it so q',
Ex 32: 8 turned aside q' out of the way
Nu 16:46 go q' unto the congregation, and
De 9: 3 them out, and destroy them q',
12 get thee down q' from hence;
12 they are q' turned aside out of the
16 had turned aside q' out of the way
11:17 lest ye perish q' from off the good
28:20 and until thou perish q'; because
Jos 2: 5 pursue after them q'; for ye shall
8:19 the ambush arose q' out of their
10: 6 come up to us q', and save us, and
23:16 ye shall perish q' from off the good
J'g 2:17 they turned q' out of the way
1Sa 20:19 then thou shalt go down q', and
2Sa 17:16 Now therefore send q', and tell
18 they went both of them away q',
21 Arise, and pass q' over the water:
2Ki 1:11 hath the king said, Come down q'.
2Ch 18: 8 Fetch q' Micaiah the son of Imla.
Ec 4:12 a threefold cord is not q' broken.
M't 5:25 Agree with thine adversary q',
28: 7 And go q', and tell his disciples
8 departed q' from the sepulchre
M'r 16: 8 they went out q', and fled from the
Lu 14:21 Go out q' into the streets and
16: 6 and sit down q', and write fifty.
Joh 11:29 she arose q', and came unto him.
13:27 unto him, That thou doest, do q'.
Ac 12: 7 him up, saying, Arise up q'.
22:18 get thee q' out of Jerusalem:
Re 2: 5 or else I will come unto thee q',
16 or else I will come unto thee q',
3:11 Behold, I come q': hold that fast
11:14 behold, the third woe cometh q'.
22: 7 Behold, I come q': blessed is he
12 I come q'; and my reward is with
20 saith, Surely I come q'. Amen.

quicksands
Ac 27:17 lest they should fall into the q',

quiet See also DISQUIET; QUIETED; QUIETETH.
J'g 16: 2 were q' all the night, saying, In
18: 7 of the Zidonians, q' and secure;
27 a people that were at q' and secure:
2Ki 11:20 rejoiced, and the city was in q':
1Ch 4:40 the land was wide, and q', and
2Ch 14: 1 his days the land was q' ten years.
5 the kingdom was q' before him.
20:30 the realm of Jehoshaphat was q':
23:21 the city was q', after that they had
Job 3:13 should I have lain still and been q',
26 had I rest, neither was I q':
21:23 being wholly at ease and q'.
Ps 35:20 them that are q' in the land.
107:30 are they glad because they be q';
Pr 1:33 and shall be q' from fear of evil.
Ec 9:17 of wise men are heard in q' more
Isa 7: 4 Take heed, and be q'; fear not,
14: 7 whole earth is at rest, and is q':
32:18 dwellings, and in q' resting places;
33:20 shall see Jerusalem a q' habitation,
Jer 30:10 shall be in rest, and be q', and
47: 6 how long will it be ere thou be q'?
7 How can it be q', seeing the Lord
49:23 sorrow on the sea; it cannot be q'.
51:59 And this Seraiah was a q' prince.
Eze 16:42 be q', and will be no more angry.
Na 1:12 Though they be q', and likewise
Ac 19:36 ye ought to be q', and to do
1Th 4:11 that ye study to be q', and to do
1Ti 2: 2 may lead a q' and peaceable life
1Pe 3: 4 ornament of a meek and q' spirit,

quieted
Ps 131: 2 I have behaved and q' myself,
Zec 6: 8 have q' my spirit in the north

quieteth
Job 37:17 he q' the earth by the south wind?

quietly
2Sa 3:27 in the gate to speak with him q',
La 3:26 q' wait for the salvation of the Lord.

quietness
J'g 8:28 the country was in q' forty years
1Ch 22: 9 will give peace and q' unto Israel
Job 20:20 he shall not feel q' in his belly,
34:29 When he giveth q', who then can
Pr 17: 1 is a dry morsel, and q' therewith,
Ec 4: 6 Better is an handful with q', than
Isa 30:15 in q' and in confidence shall be
32:17 q' and assurance for ever.
Ac 24: 2 that by thee we enjoy great q',
2Th 3:12 that with q' they work, and eat

quit See also ACQUIT.
Ex 21:19 shall he that smote him be q':
28 the owner of the ox shall be q'.
Jos 2:20 then we will be q' of thine oath
1Sa 4: 9 and q' yourselves like men,
9 q' yourselves like men, and fight.
1Co 16:13 faith, q' you like men, be strong.

quite
Ge 31:15 and hath q' devoured also our money.
Ex 23:24 and q' break down their images.
Nu 17:10 q' take away their murmurings
33:52 q' plucked down all their high places:
2Sa 3:24 hast sent him away, and he is q' gone?
Job 6:13 and is wisdom driven q' from me?
Hab 3: 9 Thy bow was made q' naked,

quiver See also QUIVERED.
Ge 27: 3 thy weapons, thy q' and thy bow,
Job 39:23 The q' rattleth against him, the
Ps 127: 5 Happy is the man that hath his q'
Isa 22: 6 Elam bare the q' with chariots of
49: 2 shaft; in his q' hath he hid me;
Jer 5:16 Their q' is as an open sepulchre,
La 3:13 of his q' to enter into my reins.

quivered
Hab 3:16 trembled; my lips q' at the voice:

R.

Raamah (*ra'-a-mah*)
Ge 10: 7 and Havilah, and Sabtah, and R',
7 the sons of R'; Sheba, and Dedan.
1Ch 1: 9 and Havilah, and Sabta, and R',
9 the sons of R'; Sheba, and Dedan.
Eze 27:22 The merchants of Sheba and R',

Raamiah (*ra-a-mi'-ah*)
Ne 7: 7 Azariah, R', Nahamani, Mordecai,

Raamses (*ra-am'-seze*) See also RAMESES.
Ex 1:11 treasure cities, Pithom, and R'.

Rab See RAB-MAG; RAB-SARIS; RAB-SHAKEH.

Rabbah (*rab'-bah*) See also RABBATH.
Jos 13:25 unto Aroer that is before R';
15:60 which is Kirjath-jearim, and R';
2Sa 11: 1 children of Ammon,...besieged R'.
12:26 And Joab fought against R' of the
27 I have fought against R', and have
29 went to R', and fought against it,
17:27 that Shobi the son of Nahash of R'
1Ch 20: 1 Ammon, and came and besieged R'.
1 Joab smote R', and destroyed it.
Jer 49: 2 an alarm of war to be heard in R'
3 cry, ye daughters of R', gird you
Eze 25: 5 I will make R' a stable for camels,
Am 1:14 will kindle a fire in the wall of R',

Rabbath (*rab'-bath*) See also RABBAH.
De 3:11 in R' of the children of Ammon?
Eze 21:20 that the sword may come to R'

Rabbi (*rab'-bi*) See also RABBONI.
M't 23: 7 and to be called of men, R', R'.
8 But be not ye called R': for one is
Joh 1:38 They said unto him, R', (which is
49 him, R', thou art the Son of God;
3: 2 R', we know...thou art a teacher

Joh 3:26 *R*, he that was with thee beyond
6:25 *R*, when camest thou hither?

Rabbim See BATH-RABBIM.

Rabbith (*rab'-bith*)
Jos 19:20 And *R*, and Kishion, and Abez,

Rabboni (*rab-bo'-ni*) See also RABBI.
Joh 20:16 herself, and saith unto him, *R*;

Rab-mag (*rab'-mag*)
Jer 39: 3 Rab-saris, Nergal-sharezer, *R*,
13 *R*, and all the king of Babylon's

Rab-saris (*rab'-sa-ris*)
2Ki 18:17 of Assyria sent Tartan and *R*
Jer 39: 3 *R*, Nergal-sharezer, Rab-mag,
13 *R*, and Nergal-sharezer, Rab-mag,

Rab-shakeh (*rab'-sha-keh*) See also RABSHAKEH.
2Ki 18:17 and *R* from Lachish to king
19 *R* said unto them, Speak ye now
26 unto *R*, Speak, I pray thee, to thy
27 *R* said unto them, Hath my master
28 Then *R* stood and cried with a loud
37 and told him the words of *R*.
19: 4 God will hear all the words of *R*,
8 So *R* returned, and found the king

Rabshakeh (*rab'-sha-keh*) See also RAB-SHAKEH.
Isa 36: 2 *R* from Lachish to Jerusalem
4 *R* said unto them, Say ye now to
11 *R*, Speak, I pray thee, unto thy
12 *R* said, Hath my master sent me
13 *R* stood, and cried with a loud
22 rent, and told him the words of *R*.
37: 4 thy God will hear the words of *R*,
8 So *R* returned, and found the king

Raca (*ra'-cah*)
M't 5:22 shall say to his brother, *R*, shall

race
Ps 19: 5 as a strong man to run a *r*.
Ec 9:11 the *r* is not to the swift, nor the
1Co 9:24 they which run in a *r* run all, but
Heb12: 1 patience the *r* that is set before us,

Rachab (*ra'-kab*) See also RAHAB.
M't 1: 5 Salmon begat Booz of *R*; and

Rachal (*ra'-kal*)
1Sa 30:29 And to them which were in *R*,

Rachel (*ra'-chel*) See also RACHEL'S; RAHEL.
Ge 29: 6 *R* his daughter cometh with the
9 *R* came with her father's sheep:
10 Jacob saw *R* the daughter of Laban
11 Jacob kissed *R*, and lifted up his
12 And Jacob told *R* that he was her
16 the name of the younger was *R*.
17 *R* was beautiful and well favoured.
18 And Jacob loved *R*; and said, I
18 will serve thee seven years for *R*
20 Jacob served seven years for *R*;
25 did I not serve with thee for *R*?
28 gave him *R* his daughter to wife
29 And Laban gave to *R* his daughter
30 he went in also unto *R*, and he
30 he loved also *R* more than Leah,
31 her womb: but *R* was barren.
30: 1 when *R* saw that she bare Jacob
1 *R* envied her sister; and said unto
2 Jacob's anger...kindled against *R*:
6 *R* said, God hath judged me, and
8 And *R* said, With great wrestlings
14 *R* said to Leah, Give me, I pray
15 And *R* said, Therefore he shall lie
22 And God remembered *R*, and God
25 pass, when *R* had borne Joseph,
31: 4 Jacob sent and called *R* and Leah
14 *R* and Leah answered and said
19 and *R* had stolen the images that
32 knew not that *R* had stolen them.
34 Now *R* had taken the images, and
33: 1 children unto Leah, and unto *R*,
2 and *R* and Joseph hindermost.
7 after came Joseph near and *R*,
35:16 and *R* travailed, and she had hard
19 *R* died, and was buried in the way
24 sons of *R*; Joseph, and Benjamin:
46:19 The sons of *R*, Jacob's wife;
22 These are the sons of *R*, which
25 Laban gave unto *R* his daughter,
48: 7 *R* died by me in the land of Canaan
Ru 4:11 thine house like *R* and like Leah,
M't 2:18 *R* weeping for her children, and

Rachel's (*ra'-chelz*)
Ge 30: 7 Bilhah *R* maid conceived again,
31:33 tent, and entered into *R* tent.
35:20 that is the pillar of *R* grave unto
25 the sons of Bilhah, *R* handmaid;
1Sa 10: 2 shalt find two men by *R* sepulchre

Raddai (*rad'-dahee*)
1Ch 2:14 Nethaneel the fourth, *R* the fifth,

rafters
Ca 1:17 house are cedar, and our *r* of fir.

rag See RAGGED; RAGS.

Ragau (*ra'-gaw*) See also REU.
Lu 3:35 Saruch, which was the son of *R*,

rage See also OUTRAGEOUS; RAGED; RAGETH; RAGING.
2Ki 5:12 he turned and went away in a *r*.
19:27 coming in, and thy *r* against me.
28 Because thy *r* against me and thy
2Ch 16:10 for he was in a *r* with him because
28: 9 slain them in a *r* that reacheth
Job 39:24 the ground with fierceness and *r*:
40:11 Cast abroad the *r* of thy wrath:
Ps 2: 1 Why do the heathen *r*, and the
Ps 7: 6 because of the *r* of mine enemies:
Pr 6:34 For jealousy is the *r* of a man:
29: 9 whether he *r* or laugh, there is
Isa 37:28 coming in, and thy *r* against me.
29 Because thy *r* against me, and thy
Jer 46: 9 ye horses; and *r*, ye chariots;
Da 3:13 Nebuchadnezzar in his *r* and
Ho 7:16 sword for the *r* of their tongue:
Na 2: 4 The chariots shall *r* in the streets,
Ac 4:25 Why did the heathen *r*, and the

raged
Ps 46: 6 The heathen *r*, the kingdoms

rageth
Pr 14:16 but the fool *r*, and is confident.

ragged
Isa 2:21 into the tops of the *r* rocks, for fear

raging
Ps 89: 9 Thou rulest the *r* of the sea:
Pr 20: 1 is a mocker, strong drink is *r*:
Jon 1:15 and the sea ceased from her *r*.
Lu 8:24 the wind and the *r* of the water:
Jude 13 *R* waves of the sea, foaming out

rags
Pr 23:21 shall clothe a man with *r*.
Isa 64: 6 righteousnesses are as filthy *r*;
Jer 38:11 old cast clouts and old rotten *r*,
12 and rotten *r* under thine armholes

Raguel (*ra-gu'-el*) See also REUEL.
Nu 10:29 unto Hobab, the son of *R* the

Rahab (*ra'-hab*) See also RACHAB.
Jos 2: 1 into an harlot's house, named *R*,
3 the king of Jericho sent unto *R*,
6:17 only *R* the harlot shall live, she
23 spies went in, and brought out *R*,
25 Joshua saved *R* the harlot alive,
Ps 87: 4 make mention of *R* and Babylon
89:10 Thou hast broken *R* in pieces, as
Isa 51: 9 Art thou not it that hath cut *R*,
Heb11:31 By faith the harlot *R* perished
Jas 2:25 was not *R* the harlot justified by

Raham (*ra'-ham*)
1Ch 2:44 And Shema begat *R*, the father of

Rahel (*ra'-hel*) See RACHEL.
Jer 31:15 *R* weeping for her children

rail See also RAILED; RAILING.
2Ch 32:17 also letters to *r* on the Lord God

railed
1Sa 25:14 our master; and he *r* on them.
M'r 15:29 And they that passed by *r* on him,
Lu 23:39 which were hanged *r* on him,

railer
1Co 5:11 idolater, or a *r*, or a drunkard,

railing See also RAILINGS.
1Pe 3: 9 rendering evil for evil, or *r* for *r*:
2Pe 2:11 bring not *r* accusation against
Jude 9 bring against him a *r* accusation,

railings
1Ti 6: 4 whereof cometh envy, strife, *r*, evil

raiment
Ge 24:53 of gold, and *r*, and gave them to
27:15 goodly *r* of her eldest son Esau,
27 and he smelled the smell of his *r*,
28:20 me bread to eat, and *r* to put on,
41:14 changed his *r*, and came in unto
45:22 he gave each man changes of *r*;
22 of silver, and five changes of *r*,
Ex 3:22 of silver, and jewels of gold, and *r*:
12:35 of silver, and jewels of gold, and *r*:
21:10 her food, her *r*, and her duty of
22: 9 for ass, for sheep, for *r*, or for any
26 take thy neighbour's *r* to pledge,
27 only, it is his *r* for his skin:
Le 11:32 it be any vessel of wood, or *r*, or
Nu 31:20 purify all your *r*, and all that is
De 8: 4 Thy *r* waxed not old upon thee,
10:18 stranger, in giving him food and *r*.
21:13 the *r* of her captivity from off her,
22: 3 and so shalt thou do with his *r*;
24:13 that he may sleep in his own *r*,
17 nor take a widow's *r* to pledge:
Jos 22: 8 with iron, and with very much *r*:
J'g 3:16 under his *r* upon his right thigh.
8:26 purple *r* that was on the kings of
Ru 3: 3 thee, and put thy *r* upon thee,
1Sa 28: 8 and put on other *r*, and he went,
2Ki 5: 5 pieces of gold, and ten changes of *r*.
7: 8 gold, and *r*, and went and hid it;
2Ch 9:24 vessels of gold, and *r*, harness,
Es 4: 4 and she sent *r* to clothe Mordecai,
Job 27:16 dust, and prepare *r* as the clay;
Ps 45:14 unto the king in *r* of needlework:
Isa 14:19 as the *r* of those that are slain,
63: 3 and I will stain all my *r*.
Eze 16:13 thy *r* was of fine linen, and silk,
Zec 3: 4 will clothe thee with change of *r*.
M't 3: 4 John had his *r* of camel's hair,
6:25 than meat, and the body than *r*?
28 And why take ye thought for *r*?
11: 8 for to see? A man clothed in soft *r*?
17: 2 and his *r* was white as the light.
27:31 put his own *r* on him, and led him
28: 3 and his *r* white as snow:
M'r 9: 3 his *r* became shining, exceeding
Lu 7:25 to see? A man clothed in soft *r*?
9:29 his *r* was white and glistering.
10:30 thieves, which stripped him of his *r*,
12:23 meat, and the body is more than *r*.
23:34 they parted his *r*, and cast lots.
Joh 19:24 They parted my *r* among them,
Ac 18: 6 he shook his *r*, and said unto them,
22:20 kept the *r* of them that slew him.
1Ti 6: 8 And having food and *r* let us be
Jas 2: 2 come in also a poor man in vile *r*;
Re 3: 5 same shall be clothed in white *r*;
18 and white *r*, that thou mayest be
4: 4 elders sitting, clothed in white *r*;

rain See also RAINBOW; RAINED.
Ge 2: 5 not caused it to *r* upon the earth,
7: 4 I will cause it to *r* upon the earth
12 the *r* was upon the earth forty
8: 2 the *r* from heaven was restrained;
Ex 9:18 cause it to *r* a very grievous hail,
33 *r* was not poured upon the earth.
34 when Pharaoh saw that the *r* and
16: 4 will *r* bread from heaven for you;
Le 26: 4 I will give you *r* in due season,
De 11:11 drinketh water of the *r* of heaven:
14 I will give you the *r* of your land
14 in his due season, the first *r* and
14 and the latter *r*, that thou mayest
17 up the heaven, that there be no *r*,
28:12 the *r* unto thy land in his season,
24 make the *r* of thy land powder and
32: 2 My doctrine shall drop as the *r*, my
2 the small *r* upon the tender herb,
1Sa 12:17 and he shall send thunder and *r*;
18 the Lord sent thunder and *r* that
2Sa 1:21 neither let there be *r*, upon you,
23: 4 the earth by clear shining after *r*.
1Ki 8:35 is shut up, and there is no *r*,
36 and give *r* upon thy land, which
17: 1 shall not be dew nor *r* these years,
7 there had been no *r* in the land.
14 the Lord sendeth *r* upon the earth.
18: 1 and I will send *r* upon the earth.
41 is a sound of abundance of *r*.
44 thee down, that the *r* stop thee not.
45 and wind, and there was a great *r*.
2Ki 3:17 see wind, neither shall ye see *r*;
2Ch 6:26 is shut up, and there is no *r*,
27 send *r* upon thy land, which thou
7:13 shut up heaven that there be no *r*,
Ezr 10: 9 of this matter, and for the great *r*.
13 it is a time of much *r*, and we are
Job 5:10 Who giveth *r* upon the earth, and
20:23 *r* it upon him while he is eating.
28:26 When he made a decree for the *r*,
29:23 they waited for me as for the *r*;
23 mouth wide as for the latter *r*.
36:27 they pour down *r* according to the
37: 6 to the small *r*, and to the great *r*
38:26 To cause it to *r* on the earth,
28 Hath the *r* a father? or who hath
Ps 11: 6 Upon the wicked he shall *r* snares,
68: 9 didst send a plentiful *r*, whereby
72: 6 come down like *r* upon the mown
84: 6 a well; the *r* also filleth the pools.
105:32 He gave them hail for *r*, and
135: 7 he maketh lightnings for the *r*;
147: 8 who prepareth *r* for the earth,
Pr 16:15 favour is as a cloud of the latter *r*.
25:14 is like clouds and wind without *r*.
23 The north wind driveth away *r*: so
26: 1 and as *r* in harvest, so honour is
28: 3 sweeping *r* which leaveth no food.
Ec 11: 3 If the clouds be full of *r*, they
12: 2 nor the clouds return after the *r*:
Ca 2:11 is past, the *r* is over and gone;
Isa 4: 6 a covert from storm and from *r*.
5: 6 the clouds that they *r* no
6 clouds that they...no *r* upon it.
30:23 shall he give the *r* of thy seed,
44:14 an ash, and the *r* doth nourish it.
55:10 For as the *r* cometh down, and the
Jer 3: 3 and there hath been no latter *r*;
5:24 the Lord our God, that giveth *r*,
10:13 he maketh lightnings with *r*, and
14: 4 for there was no *r* in the earth,
22 of the Gentiles that can cause *r*?
51:16 he maketh lightnings with *r*, and
Eze 1:28 is in the cloud in the day of *r*,
38:22 I will *r* upon him, and upon his
22 an overflowing *r*, and great
Ho 6: 3 and he shall come unto us as the *r*,
3 as the latter and former *r* unto the
10:12 and *r* righteousness upon you.
Joe 2:23 you the former *r* moderately,
23 cause to come down for you the *r*
23 down for you...the former *r*,
23 the latter *r* in the first month.
Am 4: 7 have withholden the *r* from you,
7 I caused it to *r* upon one city,
7 it not to *r* upon another city:
Zec 10: 1 Ask ye of the Lord *r* in the time of
1 of the latter *r*; so the Lord shall
1 and give them showers of *r*, to
14:17 even upon them shall be no *r*.
18 not up, and come not, that have no *r*.
M't 5:45 sendeth *r* on the just and on the
7:25, 27 And the *r* descended, and the
Ac 14:17 and gave us *r* from heaven, and
28: 2 because of the present *r*, and
Heb 6: 7 the earth which drinketh in the *r*
Jas 5: 7 he receive the early and latter *r*.
17 earnestly that it might not *r*:
18 again, and the heaven gave *r*,
Re 11: 6 it *r* not in the days of their

rainbow
Re 4: 3 was a *r* round about the throne,
10: 1 a *r* was upon his head, and his

rained
Ge 19:24 *r* upon Sodom and Gomorrah
Ex 9:23 *r* hail upon the land of Egypt.
Ps 78:24 *r* down manna upon them to eat,

Ps 78:27 He *r'* flesh also upon them as dust,
Eze 22:24 *r'* upon in the day of indignation.
Am 4: 7 one piece was *r'* upon, and the
7 whereupon it *r'* not withered.
Lu 17:29 *r'* fire and brimstone from heaven,
Jas 5:17 *r'* not on the earth for the space of

rainy
Pr 27:15 *r'* day and contentious woman are

raise See also RAISED; RAISETH; RAISING.
Ge 38: 8 her, and *r'* up seed to thy brother.
Ex 23: 1 Thou shalt not *r'* a false report:
De 18:15 God will *r'* up unto thee a Prophet
18 I will *r'* them up a Prophet from
25: 7 to *r'* up unto his brother a name
Jos 8:29 *r'* thereon a great heap of stones,
Ru 4: 5, 10 *r'* up the name of the dead upon
1Sa 2:35 will *r'* me up a faithful priest, that
2Sa 12:11 I will *r'* up evil against thee out of
17 him, to *r'* him up from the earth:
1Ki 14:14 Lord shall *r'* him up a king over
1Ch 17:11 that I will *r'* up thy seed after thee.
Job 3: 8 ready to *r'* up their mourning.
19:12 and *r'* up their way against me,
30:12 they *r'* up against me the ways of
Ps 41:10 merciful unto me, and *r'* me up,
Isa 15: 5 shall *r'* up a cry of destruction.
29: 3 and I will *r'* forts against thee.
44:26 and I will *r'* up the decayed places
49: 6 servant to *r'* up the tribes of Jacob,
58:12 thou shalt *r'* up the foundation
61: 4 shall *r'* up the former desolations,
Jer 23: 5 *r'* unto David a righteous Branch,
30: 9 king, whom I will *r'* up unto them.
50: 9 I will *r'* and cause to come up
32 fall, and none shall *r'* him up:
51: 1 I will *r'* up against Babylon, and
Eze 23:22 will *r'* up thy lovers against thee,
34:29 I will *r'* up for them a plant of
Ho 6: 2 in the third day he will *r'* us up, and
Joe 3: 7 I will *r'* them out of the place
Am 5: 2 land; there is none to *r'* her up.
6:14 I will *r'* up against you a nation,
9:11 day will I *r'* up the tabernacle of
11 I will *r'* up his ruins, and I will
Mic 5: 5 we *r'* against him seven shepherds,
Hab 1: 3 that *r'* up strife and contention.
6 lo, I *r'* up the Chaldeans, that
Zec 11:16 will *r'* up a shepherd in the land,
M't 3: 9 to *r'* up children unto Abraham.
10: 8 sick, cleanse the lepers, *r'* the dead,
22:24 and *r'* up seed unto his brother.
M'r 12:19 and *r'* up seed unto his brother.
Lu 3: 8 to *r'* up children unto Abraham.
20:28 and *r'* up seed unto his brother.
Joh 2:19 and in three days I will *r'* it up.
6:39 *r'* it up again at the last day.
40, 44, 54 will *r'* him up at the last day.
Ac 2:30 *r'* up Christ to sit on his throne;
3:22 shall the Lord your God *r'* up unto
7:37 shall the Lord your God *r'* up unto
26: 8 you, that God should *r'* the dead?
1Co 6:14 will also *r'* up us by his own power.
2Co 4:14 Jesus shall *r'* up us also by Jesus,
Heb 11:19 that God was able to *r'* him up,
Jas 5:15 sick, and the Lord shall *r'* him up;

raised
Ex 9:16 for this cause have I *r'* thee up,
Jos 5: 7 whom he *r'* up in their stead,
7:26 *r'* over him a great heap of stones
J'g 2:16 Nevertheless the Lord *r'* up judges,
18 when the Lord *r'* them up judges,
3: 9 *r'* up a deliverer to the children of
15 the Lord *r'* them up a deliverer,
2Sa 23: 1 the man who was *r'* up on high,
1Ki 5:13 Solomon *r'* a levy out of all Israel;
9:15 the levy which king Solomon *r'*;
2Ch 32: 5 and *r'* it up to the towers, and
33:14 and *r'* it up a very great height.
Ezr 1: 5 all them whose spirit God had *r'*,
Job 14:12 awake, nor be *r'* out of their sleep.
Ca 8: 5 I *r'* thee up under the apple tree:
Isa 14: 9 *r'* up from their thrones all the
23:13 they *r'* up the palaces thereof;
41: 2 Who *r'* up the righteous man from
25 have *r'* up one from the north, and
45:13 I have *r'* him up in righteousness,
Jer 6:22 a great nation shall be *r'* from the
25:32 a great whirlwind shall be *r'* from
29:15 The Lord hath *r'* us up prophets
50:41 many kings shall be *r'* up from
51:11 the Lord hath *r'* up the spirit of
Da 7: 5 and it *r'* up itself on one side,
Am 2:11 I *r'* up of your sons for prophets,
Zec 2:13 is *r'* up out of his holy habitation.
9:13 and *r'* up thy sons, O Zion, against
M't 1:24 Joseph being *r'* from sleep did as
11: 5 the deaf hear, the dead are *r'* up,
16:21 and be *r'* again the third day.
17:23 the third day he shall be *r'* again.
Lu 1:69 *r'* up an horn of salvation for us
7:22 the deaf hear, the dead are *r'*, to
9:22 be slain, and be *r'* the third day.
20:37 Now that the dead are *r'*, even
Joh 12: 1 dead, whom he *r'* from the dead.
9 whom he had *r'* from the dead.
17 *r'* him from the dead, bare record.
Ac 2:24 Whom God hath *r'* up, having
32 This Jesus hath God *r'* up, whereof
3:15 whom God hath *r'* from the dead;
26 God, having *r'* up his Son Jesus,
4:10 whom God *r'* from the dead, even
5:30 God of our fathers *r'* up Jesus,
10:40 Him God *r'* up the third day, and
12: 7 *r'* him up, saying, Arise up quickly.
13:22 he *r'* up unto them David to be
Ac 13:23 *r'* unto Israel a Saviour, Jesus:
30 But God *r'* him from the dead:
33 in that he hath *r'* up Jesus again;
34 that he *r'* him up from the dead,
37 he, whom God *r'* again, saw no
50 *r'* persecution against Paul and
17:31 that he hath *r'* him from the dead.
Ro 4:24 believe on him that *r'* up Jesus
25 was *r'* again for our justification.
6: 4 as Christ was *r'* up from the dead
9 Christ being *r'* from the dead dieth
7: 4 to him who is *r'* from the dead,
8:11 him that *r'* up Jesus from the dead
11 he that *r'* up Christ from the dead
9:17 same purpose have I *r'* thee up,
10: 9 God hath *r'* him from the dead,
1Co 6:14 God hath both *r'* up the Lord, and
15:15 of God that he *r'* up Christ:
15 whom he *r'* not up, if so be that the
16 dead rise not, then is not Christ *r'*:
17 Christ be not *r'*, your faith is vain;
35 will say, How are the dead *r'* up?
42 corruption, it is *r'* in incorruption:
43 sown in dishonour, it is *r'* in glory:
43 sown in weakness; it is *r'* in power:
44 body; it is *r'* a spiritual body.
52 dead shall be *r'* incorruptible, and
2Co 4:14 that he which *r'* up the Lord
Ga 1: 1 Father, who *r'* him from the dead;)
Eph 1:20 when he *r'* him from the dead, and
2: 6 hath *r'* us up together, and made
Col 2:12 who hath *r'* him from the dead.
1Th 1:10 whom he *r'* from the dead, even
2Ti 2: 8 seed of David was *r'* from the dead
Heb 11:35 received their dead *r'* to life again:
1Pe 1:21 God, that *r'* him up from the dead,

raiser
Da 11:20 up in his estate a *r'* of taxes

raiseth
1Sa 2: 8 He *r'* up the poor out of the dust,
Job 41:25 When he *r'* up himself, the
Ps 107:25 and *r'* the stormy wind, which
113: 7 *r'* up the poor out of the dust,
145:14 *r'* up all those that be bowed down.
146: 8 *r'* them that are bowed down:
Joh 5:21 For as the Father *r'* up the dead,
2Co 1: 9 but in God which *r'* the dead:

raising
Ho 7: 4 from *r'* after he hath kneaded
Ac 24:12 neither *r'* up the people,

raisins
1Sa 25:18 an hundred clusters of *r'*, and two
30:12 cake of figs, and two clusters of *r'*:
2Sa 16: 1 an hundred bunches of *r'*, and an
1Ch 12:40 cakes of figs, and bunches of *r'*, and

Rakem (*ra'-kem*)
1Ch 7:16 and his sons were Ulam and *R'*.

Rakkath (*rak'-kath*)
Jos 19:35 Hammath, *R'*, and Chinnereth,

Rakkon (*rak'-kon*)
Jos 19:46 And Me-jarkon, and *R'*, with the

ram See also RAM; RAM'S; RAMS.
Ge 15: 9 and a *r'* of three years old, and a
22:13 *r'* caught in a thicket by his horns:
13 Abraham went and took the *r'*, and
Ex 29:15 Thou shalt also take one *r'*; and
15 their hands upon the head of the *r'*.
16 And thou shalt slay the *r'*, and thou
17 thou shalt cut the *r'* in pieces, and
18 burn the whole *r'* upon the altar:
19 And thou shalt take the other *r'*;
19 their hands upon the head of the *r'*.
20 Then shalt thou kill the *r'*, and take
22 thou shalt take of the *r'* the fat and
22 for it is a *r'* of consecration:
26 of the *r'* of Aaron's consecration,
27 of the *r'* of the consecration, even of
31 shalt take the *r'* of the consecration,
32 his sons shall eat the flesh of the *r'*,
Le 5:15 unto the Lord a *r'* without blemish
16 with the *r'* of the trespass offering,
18 he shall bring a *r'* without blemish
6: 6 *r'* without blemish out of the flock,
8:18 the *r'* for the burnt offering:
18 their hands upon the head of the *r'*.
20 And he cut the *r'* into pieces; and
21 burnt the whole *r'* upon the altar:
22 the other *r'*, the *r'* of consecration:
22 their hands upon the head of the *r'*.
29 the *r'* of consecration it was Moses'
9: 2 a *r'* for a burnt offering, without
4 bullock and a *r'* for peace offerings,
18 bullock and the *r'* for a sacrifice of
19 the fat of the bullock and of the *r'*,
16: 3 and a *r'* for a burnt offering.
5 and one *r'* for a burnt offering.
19:21 even a *r'* for a trespass offering.
22 with the *r'* of the trespass offering
Nu 5: 8 the *r'* of the atonement, whereby an
6:14 one *r'* without blemish for peace
17 he shall offer the *r'* for a sacrifice of
19 take the sodden shoulder of the *r'*,
7:15, 21, 27, 33, 39, 45, 51, 57, 63, 69, 75, 81
One young bullock, one *r'*, one
15: 6 Or for a *r'*, thou shalt prepare for a
11 or for one *r'*, or for a lamb, or a kid.
23: 2 on every altar a bullock and a *r'*.
4 upon every altar a bullock and a *r'*.
14, 30 a bullock and a *r'* on every altar.
28:11 two young bullocks, and one *r'*,
12 mingled with oil, for one *r'*;
14 the third part of an hin unto a *r'*,
Nu 28:19 two young bullocks, and one *r'*, and
20 bullock, and two tenth deals for a *r'*;
27 two young bullocks, one *r'*, seven
28 bullock, two tenth deals unto one *r'*,
29: 2 one young bullock, one *r'*, and seven
3 bullock, and two tenth deals for a *r'*,
8 one young bullock, one *r'*, and seven
9 and two tenth deals to one *r'*,
14 two tenth deals to each *r'* of the two
36 one bullock, one *r'*, seven lambs of
37 offerings for the bullock, for the *r'*,
Ezr 10:19 a *r'* of the flock for their trespass.
Eze 43:23 a *r'* out of the flock without blemish,
25 and a *r'* out of the flock, without
45:24 and an ephah for a *r'*, and an hin of
46: 4 blemish, and a *r'* without blemish.
5 offering shall be an ephah for a *r'*,
6 blemish, and six lambs, and a *r'*:
7 an ephah for a *r'*, and for the lambs
11 an ephah to a *r'*, and to the lambs
Da 8: 3 the river a *r'* which had two horns:
4 I saw the *r'* pushing westward, and
6 came to the *r'* that had two horns,
7 I saw him come close unto the *r'*,
7 and smote the *r'*, and brake his two
7 and there was no power in the *r'* to
7 could deliver the *r'* out of his hand.
20 The *r'* which thou sawest having

Ram (*ram*)
Ru 4:19 Hezron begat *R'*, and *R'* begat
1Ch 2: 9 Jerahmeel, and *R'*, and Chelubai.
10 And *R'* begat Amminadab; and
25 of Hezron were, *R'* the firstborn,
27 And the sons of *R'* the firstborn
Job 32: 2 the Buzite, of the kindred of *R'*:

Rama (*ra'-mah*) See also RAMAH.
M't 2:18 In *R'* was there a voice heard,

Ramah (*ra'-mah*) See also RAMA; RAMATH.
Jos 18:25 Gibeon, and *R'*, and Beeroth,
19:29 And then the coast turneth to *R'*,
36 And Adamah, and *R'*, and Hazor,
J'g 4: 5 between *R'* and Beth-el in mount
19:13 lodge all night, in Gibeah, or in *R'*.
1Sa 1:19 and came to their house to *R'*: and
2:11 Elkanah went to *R'* to his house.
7:17 And his return was to *R'*; for there
8: 4 and came to Samuel unto *R'*,
15:34 Then Samuel went to *R'*; and Saul
16:13 So Samuel rose up, and went to *R'*.
19:18 came to Samuel to *R'*, and told him
19 Behold, David is at Naioth in *R'*.
22 Then went he also to *R'*, and came
22 Behold, they be at Naioth in *R'*.
23 he went thither to Naioth in *R'*: and
23 until he came to Naioth in *R'*.
20: 1 David fled from Naioth in *R'*, and
22: 6 abode in Gibeah under a tree in *R'*,
25: 1 and buried him in his house at *R'*.
28: 3 buried him in *R'*, even in his own
1Ki 15:17 up against Judah, and built *R'*,
21 that he left off building of *R'*, and
22 and they took away the stones of *R'*,
2Ki 8:29 the Syrians had given him at *R'*,
2Ch 16: 1 up against Judah, and built *R'*, to
5 he left off building of *R'*, and let his
6 they carried away the stones of *R'*,
22: 6 wounds which were given him at *R'*,
Ezr 2:26 The children of *R'* and Gaba, six
Ne 7:30 men of *R'* and Gaba, six hundred
11:33 Hazor, *R'*, Gittaim,
Isa 10:29 *R'* is afraid; Gibeah of Saul is fled.
Jer 31:15 the Lord; A voice was heard in *R'*,
40: 1 the guard had let him go from *R'*,
Ho 5: 8 in Gibeah, and the trumpet in *R'*:

Ramath (*ra'-math*) See also RAMAH; RAMATHAIM-ZOPHIM; RAMATHITE; RAMATH-LEHI; RAMATH-MIZPEH; RAMOTH-GILEAD.
Jos 19: 8 to Baalath-beer, *R'* of the south.

Ramathaim-zophim (*ram-a-tha''-im-zo'-fim*)
1Sa 1: 1 there was a certain man of *R'*, of

Ramathite (*ra'-math-ite*)
1Ch 27:27 the vineyards was Shimei the *R'*:

Ramath-lehi (*ra''-math-le'-hi*)
J'g 15:17 his hand, and called that place *R'*.

Ramath-mizpeh (*ra''-math-miz'-peh*)
Jos 13:26 And from Heshbon unto *R'*, and

Rameses (*ram'-e-seze*) See also RAAMSES.
Ge 47:11 best of the land, in the land of *R'*,
Ex 12:37 journeyed from *R'* to Succoth,
Nu 33: 3 And they departed from *R'* in the
5 children of Israel removed from *R'*,

Ramiah (*ra-mi'-ah*)
Ezr 10:25 sons of Parosh; *R'*, and Jeziah,

Ramoth (*ra'-moth*) See also JARMUTH; RAMAH; RAMOTH-GILEAD; REMETH.
De 4:43 and *R'* in Gilead, of the Gadites;
Jos 20: 8 *R'* in Gilead out of the tribe of Gad,
21:38 *R'* in Gilead with her suburbs, to be
1Sa 30:27 to them which were in south *R'*,
1Ki 22: 3 Know ye that *R'* in Gilead is ours,
1Ch 6:73 And *R'* with her suburbs, and Anem
80 *R'* in Gilead with her suburbs, and
Ezr 10:29 Adaiah, Jashub, and Sheal, and *R'*.

Ramoth-gilead (*ra''-moth-ghil'-e-ad*)
1Ki 4:13 The son of Geber, in *R'*; to him
22: 4 thou go with me to battle to *R'*?
6 Shall I go against *R'* to battle, or
12 saying, Go up to *R'*, and prosper:
15 shall we go against *R'* to battle, or
20 that he may go up and fall at *R'*?
29 the king of Judah went up to *R'*.

2Ki 8:28 against Hazael king of Syria in R·;
9: 1 of oil in thine hand, and go to R·:
4 young man the prophet, went to R·.
14 (Now Joram had kept R·, he and all
2Ch 18: 2 him to go up with him to R·.
3 Judah, Wilt thou go with me to R·?
5 Shall we go to R· to battle, or shall
11 saying, Go up to R·, and prosper:
14 shall we go to R· to battle, or shall
19 that he may go up and fall at R·?
28 the king of Judah went up to R·.
22: 5 against Hazael king of Syria at R·:

rampart
La 2: 8 the r· and the wall to lament;
Na 3: 8 whose r· was the sea, and her wall

ram's
Jos 6: 5 make a long blast with the r· horn,

rams See also RAMS'.
Ge 31:10 r· which leaped upon the cattle
12 r· which leap upon the cattle
38 and the r· of the flock have I not
32:14 two hundred ewes, and twenty r·,
Ex 29: 1 and two r· without blemish,
3 with the bullock, and the two r·.
35:23 red skins of r·, and badgers' skins,
Le 8: 2 for the sin offering, and two r·,
23:18 and one young bullock, and two r·:
Nu 7:17, 23, 29, 35, 41, 47, 53, 59, 65, 71, 77,
83 five r·, five he goats, five lambs of
87 were twelve bullocks, the r· twelve,
88 and four bullocks, the r· sixty,
23: 1 me here seven oxen and seven r·.
29 here seven bullocks and seven r·.
29:13 thirteen young bullocks, two r·, and
14 deals to each ram of the two r·,
17 offer twelve young bullocks, two r·,
18 offerings for the bullocks, for the r·,
20 third day eleven bullocks, two r·,
21 offerings for the bullocks, for the r·,
23 the fourth day ten bullocks, two r·,
24 offerings for the bullocks, for the r·,
26 the fifth day nine bullocks, two r·,
27 offerings for the bullocks, for the r·,
29 eight bullocks, two r·, and fourteen
30 offerings for the bullocks, for the r·,
32 seven bullocks, two r·, and fourteen
33 offerings for the bullocks, for the r·,
De 32:14 and r· of the breed of Bashan, and
1Sa 15:22 and to hearken than the fat of r·.
2Ki 3: 4 an hundred thousand r·, with the
1Ch 15:26 offered seven bullocks and seven r·.
29:21 a thousand bullocks, a thousand r·,
2Ch 13: 9 with a young bullock and seven r·,
17:11 thousand and seven hundred r·,
29:21 brought seven bullocks, and seven r·,
22 when they had killed the r·, they
32 an hundred r·, and two hundred
Ezr 6: 9 of, both young bullocks, and r·,
17 two hundred r·, four hundred
7:17 with this money bullocks, r·,
8:35 ninety and six r·, seventy and
Job 42: 8 now seven bullocks and seven r·,
Ps 66:15 of fatlings, with the incense of r·;
114: 4 The mountains skipped like r·, and
6 mountains, that ye skipped like r·;
Isa 1:11 am full of the burnt offerings of r·,
34: 6 with the fat of the kidneys of r·:
60: 7 the r· of Nebaioth shall minister
Jer 51:40 slaughter, like r· with he goats.
Eze 4: 2 set battering r· against it round
21:22 battering r· against the gates,
27:21 occupied with thee in lambs, and r·,
34:17 between the r· and the he goats.
39:18 of r·, of lambs, and of goats, of
45:23 and seven r· without blemish daily
Mic 6: 7 be pleased with thousands of r·,

rams'
Ex 25: 5 And r· skins dyed red, and badgers'
26:14 for the tent of r· skins dyed red,
35: 7 And r· skins dyed red, and badgers'
36:19 for the tent of r· skins dyed red,
39:34 the covering of r· skins dyed red,
Jos 6: 4 ark seven trumpets of r· horns:
6 bear seven trumpets of r· horns
8 the seven trumpets of r· horns
13 bearing seven trumpets of r· horns

ran^ See also OVERRAN.
Ge 18: 2 he r· to meet them from the tent
7 Abraham r· unto the herd, and
24:17 And the servants r· to meet her,
20 and r· again unto the well to draw
28 the damsel r·, and told them of her
29 Laban r· out unto the man, unto
29:12 son: and she r· and told her father.
13 son, that he r· to meet him, and
33: 4 Esau r· to meet him, and embraced
Ex 9:23 the fire r· along upon the ground;
Nu 11:27 there r· a young man, and told
16:47 and r· into the midst of the
Jos 7:22 and they r· unto the tent; and,
8:19 they r· as soon as he had stretched
J'g 7:21 and all the host r·, and cried, and
9:44 other companies r· upon all the
13:10 the woman made haste, and r·,
1Sa 3: 5 And he r· unto Eli, and said, Here
4:12 And there r· a man of Benjamin
10:23 they r· and fetched him thence: and
17:22 and r· into the army, and came and
48 and r· toward the army to meet the
51 Therefore David r·, and stood upon
20:36 And as the lad r·, he shot an arrow
2Sa 18:21 bowed himself unto Joab, and r·.
23 Ahimaaz r· by the way of the plain,
1Ki 2:39 of the servants of Shimei r· away
1Ki 18:35 the water r· round about the altar;
46 r· before Ahab to the entrance of
19:20 left the oxen, and r· after Elijah,
22:35 the blood r· out of the wound into
2Ch 32: 4 the brook that r· through the
Ps 77: 2 my sore r· in the night, and
105:41 r· in the dry places like a river.
133: 2 that r· down upon the beard, even
Jer 23:21 sent these prophets, yet they r·:
Eze 1:14 living creatures r· and returned
47: 2 r· out waters on the right side.
Da 8: 6 r· unto him in the fury of his
M't 8:32 swine r· violently down a steep
27:48 straightway one of them r·, and
M'r 5: 6 afar off, he r· and worshipped him,
13 r· violently down a steep place
6:33 r· afoot thither out of all cities,
55 And r· through that whole region
15:36 one r· and filled a spunge full of
Lu 8:33 herd r· violently down a steep
15:20 r·, and fell on his neck, and kissed
19: 4 he r· before, and climbed up into
24:12 Peter, and r· unto the sepulchre;
Joh 20: 4 So they r· both together: and the
Ac 3:11 people r· together unto them in
7:57 and r· upon him with one accord,
8:30 And Philip r· thither to him, and
12:14 the gate for gladness, but r· in,
14:14 r· in among the people, crying out,
21:30 and the people r· together: and
32 centurions, and r· down unto them:
27:41 they r· the ship aground; and the
Jude 11 and r· greedily after the error of

rang
1Sa 4: 5 shout, so that the earth r· again.
1Ki 1:45 rejoicing, so that the city r· again.

range See also RANGING; RANGES.
Job 39: 8 The r· of the mountains is his

ranges
Le 11:35 whether it be oven, or r· for pots,
2Ki 11: 8 he that cometh within the r·, let
15 Have her forth without the r·: and
2Ch 23:14 Have her forth of the r·: and

ranging
Pr 28:15 As a roaring lion, and a r· bear;

rank See also RANKS.
Ge 41: 5 up upon one stalk, r· and good.
7 devoured the seven r· and full ears.
Nu 2:16 they shall set forth in the second r·.
24 they shall go forward in the third r·
1Ch 12:33 thousand, which could keep r·:
38 men of war, that could keep r·,

ranks
1Ki 7: 4, 5 was against light in three r·.
Joe 2: 7 and they shall not break their r·:
M'r 6:40 And they sat down in r·, by

ransom See also RANSOMED.
Ex 21:30 the r· of his life whatsoever is
30:12 give every man a r· for his soul
Job 33:24 down to the pit: I have found a r·.
36:18 then a great r· cannot deliver thee.
Ps 49: 7 nor give to God a r· for him:
Pr 6:35 He will not regard any r·; neither
13: 8 The r· of a man's life are his riches:
21:18 The wicked shall be a r· for the
Isa 43: 3 I gave Egypt for thy r·, Ethiopia
Ho 13:14 I will r· them from the power of
M't 20:28 and to give his life a r· for many.
M'r 10:45 and to give his life a r· for many.
1Ti 2: 6 Who gave himself a r· for all, to be

ransomed
Isa 35:10 the r· of the Lord shall return,
51:10 sea a way for the r· to pass over?
Jer 31:11 r· him from the hand of him that

Rapha (*ra'-fah*) See also BETH-RAPHA; RE-PHAIAH.
1Ch 8: 2 Nohah the fourth, and R· the fifth.
37 R· was his son, Eleasah his son,

Raphu (*ra'-fu*)
Nu 13: 9 of Benjamin, Palti the son of R·.

rare
Da 2:11 a r· thing that the king requireth,

rase
Ps 137: 7 R· it, r· it, even to the foundation

rash
Ec 5: 2 Be not r· with thy mouth, and let
Isa 32: 4 r· shall understand knowledge,

rashly
Ac 19:36 to be quiet, and to do nothing r·.

rasor [*in most editions,* RAZOR]
Nu 6: 5 shall no r· come upon his head:
J'g 13: 5 and no r· shall come on his head:
16:17 hath not come a r· upon mine head;
1Sa 1:11 shall no r· come upon his head.
Ps 52: 2 like a sharp r·, working deceitfully.
Isa 7:20 Lord shave with a r· that is hired,
Eze 5: 1 take thee a barber's r·, and cause it

rate
Ex 16: 4 and gather a certain r· every day,
1Ki 10:25 horses, and mules, a r· year by year.
2Ki 25:30 of the king, a daily r· for every day,
2Ch 8:13 Even after a certain r· every day,
9:24 horses, and mules, a r· year by year.

rather^
Jos 22:24 have not r· done it for fear of this
2Sa 10: 3 hath not David r· sent his servants
2Ki 5:13 how much r· then, when he saith to
Job 7:15 strangling, and death r· than my life,
32: 2 he justified himself r· than God.
Job 36:21 hast thou chosen r· than affliction.
Ps 52: 3 lying r· than to speak righteousness.
84:10 I had r· be a doorkeeper in the
Pr 8:10 and knowledge r· than choice gold.
16:16 understanding r· to be chosen than
17:12 a man, r· than a fool in his folly.
22: 1 A good name is r· to be chosen than
1 loving favour r· than silver and gold.
M't 10: 6 But go r· to the lost sheep of the
28 r· fear him which is able to destroy
18: 8 r· than having two hands or two
9 r· than having two eyes to be cast
25: 9 go ye r· to them that sell, and buy
27:24 but that r· a tumult was made, he
M'r 5:26 nothing bettered, but r· grew worse,
15:11 should r· release Barabbas unto
Lu 10:20 but r· rejoice, because your names
11:28 Yea r·, blessed are they that hear
41 r· give alms of such things as ye
12:31 But r· seek ye the kingdom of God;
51 I tell you, Nay; but r· division:
17: 8 And will not r· say unto him, Make
18:14 to his house justified r· than the other:
Joh 3:19 men loved darkness r· than light,
Ac 5:29 We ought to obey God r· than men.
Ro 3: 8 And not r·, (as we be slanderously
8:34 died, yea r·, that is risen again,
11:11 r· through their fall salvation is come
12:19 but r· give place unto wrath: for
14:13 but judge this r·, that no man put
1Co 5: 2 puffed up, and have not r· mourned,
6: 7 Why do ye not r· take wrong? why
7 r· suffer yourselves to be defrauded?
7:21 thou mayest be made free, use it r·.
9:12 this power over you, are not we r·?
14: 1 gifts, but r· that ye may prophesy.
5 tongues, but r· that ye prophesied:
19 I had r· speak five words with my
2Co 2: 7 ye ought r· to forgive him, and
3: 8 of the spirit be r· glorious?
5: 8 r· to be absent from the body, and
12: 9 will I r· glory in my infirmities,
Ga 4: 9 known God, or r· are known of God,
Eph 4:28 but r· let him labour, working with
5: 4 convenient: but r· giving of thanks.
11 of darkness, but r· reprove them.
Ph'p 1:12 fallen out r· unto the furtherance of
1Ti 1: 4 r· than godly edifying which is in
4: 7 exercise thyself r· unto godliness.
6: 2 but r· do them service, because
Ph'm 9 Yet for love's sake I r· beseech thee,
Heb 11:25 Choosing r· to suffer affliction with
12: 9 r· be in subjection unto the Father
13 of the way; but let it r· be healed.
13:19 But I beseech you the r· to do this,
2Pe 1:10 Wherefore the r·, brethren, give

rattleth
Job 39:23 The quiver r· against him, the

rattling
Na 3: 2 the noise of the r· of the wheels,

raven See also RAVENING; RAVENS; RAVIN.
Ge 8: 7 And he sent forth a r·, which went
Le 11:15 Every r· after his kind;
De 14:14 And every r· after his kind,
Job 38:41 Who provideth for the r· his food?
Ca 5:11 locks are bushy, and black as a r·.
Isa 34:11 owl also and the r· shall dwell in it:

ravens
1Ki 17: 4 the r· to feed thee there.
6 the r· brought him bread and flesh
Ps 147: 9 food, and to the young r· which cry.
Pr 30:17 the r· of the valley shall pick it out,
Lu 12:24 Consider the r·: for they neither

ravening
Ps 22:13 mouths, as a r· and a roaring lion.
Eze 22:25 like a roaring lion r· the prey; they
27 are like wolves r· the prey, to shed
M't 7:15 but inwardly they are r· wolves.
Lu 11:39 part is full of r· and wickedness.

ravenous
Isa 35: 9 there, nor any r· beast shall go up
46:11 Calling a r· bird from the east, the
Eze 39: 4 give thee unto the r· birds of every

ravin See also RAVENING.
Ge 49:27 Benjamin shall r· as a wolf: in the
Na 2:12 with prey, and his dens with r·.

ravished
Pr 5:19 be thou r· always with her love.
20 son, be r· with a strange woman,
Ca 4: 9 Thou hast r· my heart, my sister,
9 thou hast r· my heart with one of
Isa 13:16 shall be spoiled, and their wives r·.
La 5:11 They r· the women in Zion, and
Zec 14: 2 houses rifled, and the women r·;

raw
Ex 12: 9 Eat not of it r·, nor sodden at all
Le 13:10 be quick r· flesh in the rising;
14 But when r· flesh appeareth in him,
15 the priest shall see the r· flesh, and
15 for the r· flesh is unclean: it is a
16 Or if the r· flesh turn again, and be
1Sa 2:15 have sodden flesh of thee, but r·.

raze See RASE.

razor See RASOR.

reach^ See also REACHED; REACHETH; REACHING.
Ge 11: 4 tower, whose top may r· unto heaven;
Ex 26:28 boards shall r· from end to end.
28:42 even unto the thighs shall they r·:
Le 26: 5 threshing shall r· unto the vintage,
5 vintage shall r· unto...sowing time:
Nu 34:11 shall r· unto the side of the sea of
35: 4 shall r· from the wall of the city and

Joh 20: 6 and his head r· unto the clouds;
Isa 8: 8 over, he shall r· even to the neck;
Jer 48: 32 they r· even to the sea of Jazer: the
Zec 14: 5 the mountains shall r· unto Azal:
Joh 20: 27 R· hither thy finger, and behold
27 r· hither thy hand, and thrust it
2Co 10: 13 us, a measure to r· even unto you.

reached
Ge 28: 12 and the top of it r· to heaven: and
Jos 19: 11 Maralah, and r· to Dabbasheth,
11 r· to the river...before Jokneam;
Ru 2: 14 and he r· her parched corn, and
Da 4: 11 the height thereof r· unto heaven,
20 whose height r· unto the heaven,
2Co 10: 14 as though we r· not unto you: for
Re 18: 5 For her sins have r· unto heaven,

reacheth
Nu 21: 30 unto Nophah, which r· unto Medeba.
Jos 19: 22 And the coast r· to Tabor, and
26 and r· to Carmel westward, and to
27 and r· to Zebulun, and to the valley
34 and r· to Zebulun on the south side,
34 and r· to Asher on the west side,
2Ch 28: 9 in a rage that r· up unto heaven.
Ps 36: 5 thy faithfulness r· unto the clouds.
108: 4 and thy truth r· unto the clouds.
Pr 31: 20 r· forth her hands to the needy.
Jer 4: 10 the sword r· unto the soul.
18 because it r· unto thine heart.
51: 9 for her judgment r· unto heaven,
Da 4: 22 is grown, and r· unto heaven,

reaching
2Ch 3: 11 cubits, r· to the wall of the house:
11 r· to the wing of the other cherub.
12 cubits, r· to the wall of the house:
Ph'p 3: 13 r· forth unto those things which

read See READEST; READETH; READING.
Ex 24: 7 r· in the audience of the people:
De 17: 19 r· therein all the days of his life:
31: 11 shalt r· this law before all Israel
Jos 8: 34 he r· all the words of the law,
35 which Joshua r· not before all the
2Ki 5: 7 the king of Israel had r· the letter,
19: 14 hand of the messengers, and r· it:
22: 8 the book to Shaphan, and he r· it.
10 And Shaphan r· it before the king.
16 which the king of Judah hath r·:
23: 2 he r· in their ears all the words of
2Ch 34: 18 And Shaphan r· it before the king.
24 have r· before the king of Judah:
30 he r· in their ears all the words of
Ezr 4: 18 hath been plainly r· before me.
23 Artaxerxes' letter was r· before
Ne 8: 3 And he r· therein before the street
8 they r· in the book in the law of God
18 he r· in the book of the law of God.
9: 3 r· in the book of the law of the Lord
13: 1 day they r· in the book of Moses
Es 6: 1 and they were r· before the king.
Isa 29: 11, 12 R· this, I pray thee: and he saith,
34: 16 out of the book of the Lord, and r·:
37: 14 hand of the messengers, and r· it:
Jer 29: 29 Zephaniah the priest r· this letter
36: 6 Therefore go thou, and r· in the roll,
6 shalt r· them in the ears of all Judah
10 r· Baruch in the book the words of
13 when Baruch r· the book in the ears
14 roll wherein thou hast r· in the ears
15 Sit down now, and r· it in our ears.
15 ears. So Baruch r· it in their ears.
21 Jehudi r· it in the ears of the king,
23 Jehudi had r· three or four leaves,
51: 61 see, and shalt r· all these words;
Da 5: 7 Whosoever shall r· this writing,
8 but they could not r· the writing,
15 that they should r· this writing,
16 now if thou canst r· the writing, and
17 I will r· the writing unto the king,
M't 12: 3 Have ye not r· what David did,
5 Or have ye not r· in the law, how
19: 4 Have ye not r·, that he which made
21: 16 have ye never r·, Out of the mouth
42 Did ye never r· in the scriptures,
22: 31 have ye not r· that which was spoken
M'r 2: 25 Have ye never r· what David did,
12: 10 And have ye not r· this scripture;
26 have ye not r· in the book of Moses,
Lu 4: 16 sabbath day, and stood up for to r·.
6: 3 Have ye not r· so much as this, what
Joh 19: 20 This title then r· many of the Jews:
Ac 8: 28 in his chariot r· Esaias the prophet.
30 heard him r· the prophet Esaias,
32 the scripture which he r· was this,
13: 27 prophets which are r· every sabbath
15: 21 being r· in the synagogues every
31 when they had r·, they rejoiced
23: 34 when the governor had r· the letter,
2Co 1: 13 than what ye r· or acknowledge;
3: 2 our hearts, known and r· of all men:
15 even unto this day, when Moses is r·,
Eph 3: 4 when ye r·, ye may understand my
Col 4: 16 when this epistle is r· among you,
16 that it be r· also in the church of the
16 r· the epistle from Laodicea.
1Th 5: 27 be r· unto all the holy brethren.
Re 5: 4 worthy to open and to r· the book,

readest
Lu 10: 26 is written in the law? how r· thou?
Ac 8: 30 Understandest thou what thou r·?

readeth
Hab 2: 2 tables, that he may run that r· it.
M't 24: 15 (whoso r·, let him understand:)
M'r 13: 14 (let him that r· understand,) then
Re 1: 3 Blessed is he that r·, and they that

readiness
Ac 17: 11 received the word with all r· of
2Co 8: 11 that as there was a r· to will, so
10: 6 a r· to revenge all disobedience,

reading
Ne 8: 8 caused them to understand the r·.
Jer 36: 8 r· in the book...words of the Lord
51: 63 hast made an end of r· this book,
Ac 13: 15 the r· of the law and the prophets
2Co 3: 14 away in the r· of the old testament;
1Ti 4: 13 Till I come, give attendance to r·,

ready See also ALREADY.
Ge 18: 6 Make r· quickly three measures
43: 16 men home, and slay, and make r·;
25 made r· the present against Joseph
46: 29 And Joseph made r· his chariot,
Ex 14: 6 he made r· his chariot, and took
17: 4 they be almost r· to stone me.
19: 11 And be r· against the third day:
15 people, Be r· against the third day:
34: 2 And be r· in the morning, and come
Nu 32: 17 But we ourselves will go r· armed
De 1: 41 ye were r· to go up into the hill.
26: 5 Syrian r· to perish was my father,
Jos 8: 4 far from the city, but be ye all r·:
J'g 6: 19 Gideon went in, and made r· a kid,
13: 15 we shall have made r· a kid for thee.
1Sa 25: 18 and five sheep r· dressed, and five
2Sa 15: 15 thy servants are r· to do whatsoever
18: 22 that thou hast no tidings r·?
1Ki 6: 7 was built of stone made r· before
2Ki 9: 21 And Joram said, Make r·.
21 And his chariot was made r·.
1Ch 12: 23 bands that were r· armed to the war,
24 eight hundred, r· armed to the war.
28: 2 and had made r· for the building:
2Ch 17: 18 thousand r· prepared for the war.
35: 14 they made r· for themselves,
Ezr 7: 6 a r· scribe in the law of Moses,
Ne 9: 17 but thou art a God r· to pardon,
Es 3: 14 they should be r· against that day.
8: 13 Jews should be r· against that day
Job 3: 8 are r· to raise up their mourning.
12: 5 He that is r· to slip with his feet
15: 23 day of darkness is r· at his hand.
24 him, as a king r· to the battle.
28 which are r· to become heaps.
17: 1 are extinct, the graves are r· for me.
18: 12 destruction shall be r· at his side.
29: 13 blessing of him that was r· to perish
32: 19 it is r· to burst like new bottles.
Ps 7: 12 hath bent his bow, and made it r·.
11: 2 make r· their arrow upon the string,
21: 12 thou shalt make r· thine arrows
38: 17 I am r· to halt, and my sorrow is
45: 1 tongue is the pen of a r· writer.
86: 5 Lord, art good, and r· to forgive;
88: 15 and r· to die from my youth up:
Pr 24: 11 and those that are r· to be slain;
31: 6 drink unto him that is r· to perish,
Ec 5: 1 be more r· to hear, than to give
Isa 27: 13 r· to perish in the land of Assyria,
30: 13 shall be to you as a breach r· to fall,
32: 4 shall be r· to speak plainly.
38: 20 The Lord was r· to save me: therefore
41: 7 saying, It is r· for the sodering:
51: 13 as if he were r· to destroy? and
Eze 7: 14 the trumpet, even to make all r·;
Da 3: 15 if ye be r· that at what time ye
Ho 7: 6 made r· their heart like an oven,
M't 22: 4 are killed, and all things are r·:
8 The wedding is r·, but they which
24: 44 Therefore be ye also r·: for in such
25: 10 they that were r· went in with him
26: 19 and they made r· the passover.
M'r 14: 15 prepared: there make r· for us.
16 and they made r· the passover.
38 The spirit truly is r·, but the flesh
Lu 1: 17 r· a people prepared for the Lord.
7: 2 unto him, was sick, and r· to die.
9: 52 Samaritans, to make r· for him.
12: 40 Be ye therefore r· also: for the
14: 17 Come; for all things are now r·.
17: 8 Make r· wherewith I may sup,
22: 12 room furnished: there make r·.
13 and they made r· the passover.
33 Lord, I am r· to go with thee, both
Joh 7: 6 come: but your time is alway r·.
Ac 10: 10 they made r·, he fell into a trance.
20: 7 r· to depart on the morrow; and
21: 13 I am r· not to be bound only, but
23: 15 he come near, are r· to kill him.
21 now are they r·, looking for a
23 Make r· two hundred soldiers to
Ro 1: 15 am r· to preach the gospel to you
2Co 8: 19 and declaration of your r· mind:
9: 2 Achaia was r· a year ago; and
3 that, as I said, ye may be r·:
5 that the same might be r·, as a
10: 16 line of things made r· to our hand.
12: 14 third time I am r· to come to you;
1Ti 6: 18 in good works, r· to distribute,
2Ti 4: 6 For I am now r· to be offered, and
Tit 3: 1 to be r· to every good work,
Heb 8: 13 waxeth old is r· to vanish away.
1Pe 1: 5 r· to be revealed in the last time.
3: 15 and be r· always to give an answer
4: 5 r· to judge the quick and the dead.
5: 2 for filthy lucre, but of a r· mind;
Re 3: 2 which remain, that are r· to die:
12: 4 the woman...r· to be delivered,
19: 7 and his wife hath made herself r·.

Reaia (*re-ah'-yah*) See also HAROEH; REAIAH.
1Ch 5: 5 Micah his son, R· his son, Baal his

Reaiah (*re-ah'-yah*) See also REAIA.
1Ch 4: 2 And R· the son of Shobal begat
Ezr 2: 47 of Gahar, the children of R·,
Ne 7: 50 The children of R·, the children of

realm
2Ch 20: 30 the r· of Jehoshaphat was quiet:
Ezr 7: 13 his priests and Levites, in my r·,
23 wrath against the r· of the king
Da 1: 20 astrologers that were in all his r·.
6: 3 to set him over the whole r·.
9: 1 king over the r· of the Chaldeans;
11: 2 stir up all against the r· of Grecia.

reap See also REAPED; REAPEST; REAPETH; REAPING.
Le 19: 9 ye r· the harvest of your land,
9 shalt not wholly r· the corners of
23: 10 and shall r· the harvest thereof,
22 ye r· the harvest of your land,
25: 5 of thy harvest thou shalt not r·,
11 neither r· that which groweth of
Ru 2: 9 eyes be on the field that they do r·,
1Sa 8: 12 his ground, and to r· his harvest,
2Ki 19: 29 in the third year sow ye, and r·,
Job 4: 8 and sow wickedness, r· the same.
24: 6 r· every one his corn in the field:
Ps 126: 5 that sow in tears shall r· in joy.
Pr 22: 8 soweth iniquity shall r· vanity:
Ec 11: 4 regardeth the clouds shall not r·.
Isa 37: 30 in the third year sow ye, and r·,
Jer 12: 13 sown wheat, but shall r· thorns:
Ho 8: 7 and they shall r· the whirlwind:
10: 12 in righteousness, r· in mercy;
Mic 6: 15 shalt sow, but thou shalt not r·;
M't 6: 26 neither do they r·, nor gather
25: 26 I r· where I sowed not, and gather
Lu 12: 24 ravens: for they neither sow nor r·;
Joh 4: 38 to r· that whereon ye bestowed no
1Co 9: 11 if we shall r· your carnal things?
2Co 9: 6 sparingly shall r· also sparingly;
6 bountifully shall r·...bountifully.
Ga 6: 7 man soweth, that shall he also r·.
8 shall of the flesh r· corruption;
8 of the Spirit r· life everlasting.
9 for in due season we shall r·, if we
Re 14: 15 Thrust in thy sickle, and r·: for
15 for the time is come for thee to r·;

reaped
Ho 10: 13 wickedness, ye have r· iniquity;
Jas 5: 4 who have r· down your fields,
4 the cries of them which have r·
Re 14: 16 the earth; and the earth was r·.

reaper See also REAPERS.
Am 9: 13 the plowman shall overtake the r·,

reapers
Ru 2: 3 gleaned in the field after the r·:
4 said unto the r·, The Lord be with
5 his servant that was set over the r·,
6 the servant that was set over the r·,
7 after the r· among the sheaves:
14 And she sat beside the r·: and he
2Ki 4: 18 he went out to his father to the r·.
M't 13: 30 I will say to the r·, Gather ye
39 world; and the r· are the angels.

reapest
Le 23: 22 corners of thy field when thou r·,
Lu 19: 21 and r· that thou didst not sow.

reapeth
Isa 17: 5 and r· the ears with his arm;
Joh 4: 36 he that r· receiveth wages, and
36 he that r· may rejoice together.
37 true, One soweth, and another r·.

reaping
1Sa 6: 13 were r· their wheat harvest in the
M't 25: 24 r· where thou hast not sown, and
Lu 19: 22 down, and r· that I do not sow:

rear See also REARED; REREWARD.
Ex 26: 30 thou shalt r· up the tabernacle
Le 26: 1 neither r· you up a standing image,
2Sa 24: 18 Go up, r· an altar unto the Lord in
Joh 2: 20 wilt thou r· it up in three days?

reared
Ex 40: 17 that the tabernacle was r· up.
18 Moses r· up the tabernacle, and
18 bars thereof, and r· up his pillars.
33 And he r· up the court round about
Nu 9: 15 day that the tabernacle was r· up
2Sa 18: 18 and r· up for himself a pillar,
1Ki 16: 32 And he r· up an altar for Baal in
2Ki 21: 3 and he r· up altars for Baal, and
2Ch 3: 17 And he r· up the pillars before the
33: 3 and he r· up altars for Baalim, and

rearward See REREWARD.

reason^ See also REASONABLE; REASONED; REASONING; REASONS.
Ge 41: 31 in the land by r· of that famine
47: 13 Canaan fainted by r· of the famine.
Ex 2: 23 Israel sighed by r· of the bondage,
23 up unto God by r· of the bondage,
3: 7 cry by r· of their taskmasters;
8: 24 corrupted by r· of the swarm of flies.
Nu 9: 10 shall be unclean by r· of a dead body,
18: 8 I given them by r· of the anointing,
32 And ye shall bear no sin by r· of
De 5: 5 for ye were afraid by r· of the fire,
23: 10 that is not clean by r· of uncleanness
Jos 9: 13 old by r· of the very long journey.
J'g 2: 18 by r· of them that oppressed them
1Sa 12: 7 may r· with you before the Lord
1Ki 9: 15 this is the r· of the levy which
2Ch 5: 14 stand to minister by r· of the
20: 15 by r· of this great multitude;
21: 15 fall out by r· of the sickness day
19 fell out by r· of his sickness:

Job 6:16 which are blackish by r· of the ice,
9:14 choose out my words to r· with him?
13: 3 and I desire to r· with God.
15: 3 Should he r· with unprofitable talk?
17: 7 Mine eye also is dim by r· of sorrow,
31:23 and by r· of his highness I could not
35: 9 By r· of the multitude of oppressions
9 cry out by r· of the arm of the mighty.
37:19 our speech by r· of darkness.
Ps 38: 8 have roared by r· of the disquietness
44:16 by r· of the enemy and avenger.
78:65 man that shouteth by r· of wine.
88: 9 eye mourneth by r· of affliction:
90:10 if by r· of strength they be fourscore
102: 5 By r· of the voice of my groaning my
Pr 20: 4 will not plow by r· of the cold;
26:16 seven men that can render a r·.
Ec 7:25 out wisdom, and the r· of things,
Isa 1:18 Come now, and let us r· together,
49:19 too narrow by r· of the inhabitants,
Eze 19:10 full of branches by r· of many waters.
21:12 terrors by r· of the sword shall be
26:10 By r· of the abundance of his horses
27:12, 16 thy merchant by r· of the multitude
28:17 wisdom by r· of thy brightness:
Da 4:36 time my r· returned unto me;
5:10 by r· of the words of the king and
8:12 daily sacrifice by r· of transgression,
Jon 2: 2 I cried by r· of mine affliction unto the
Mic 2:12 noise by r· of the multitude of men.
M't 16: 8 why r· ye among yourselves,
M'r 2: 8 Why r· ye these things in your
8:17 Why r· ye, because ye have no
Lu 5:21 and the Pharisees began to r·,
22 them, What r· ye in your hearts?
Joh 6:18 sea arose by r· of a great wind that
12:11 by r· of him many of the Jews
Ac 6: 2 It is not r· that we should leave the
18:14 r· would that I should bear with
Ro 8:20 by r· of him who hath subjected
2Co 3:10 by r· of the glory that excelleth.
Heb 5: 3 by r· hereof he ought, as for the
14 who by r· of use have their senses
7:23 suffered to continue by r· of death:
1Pe 3:15 a r· of the hope that is in you with
2Pe 2: 2 by r· of whom the way of truth
Re 8:13 earth by r· of the other voices of
9: 2 by r· of the smoke of the pit.
18:19 in the sea by r· of her costliness!

reasonable See also UNREASONABLE.
Ro 12: 1 unto God, which is your r· service.

reasoned
M't 16: 7 they r· among themselves, saying,
21:25 they r· among themselves, saying,
M'r 2: 8 that they so r· among themselves,
8:16 they r· among themselves, saying,
11:31 they r· with themselves, saying, If
Lu 20: 5 they r· with themselves, saying, If
14 they r· among themselves, saying,
24:15 they communed together and r·,
Ac 17: 2 r· with them out of the scriptures,
18: 4 r· in the synagogue every sabbath,
19 synagogue, and r· with the Jews.
24:25 And as he r· of righteousness,

reasoning
Job 13: 6 Hear now my r·, and hearken to
M'r 2: 6 sitting there, and r· in their hearts,
12:28 having heard them r· together,
Lu 9:46 Then there arose a r· among them,
Ac 28:29 had great r· among themselves.

reasons
Job 32:11 I gave ear to your r·, whilst ye
Isa 41:21 bring forth your strong r·, saith the

Reba (*Re'-bah*)
Nu 31: 8 Hur, and R·, five kings of Midian:
Jos 13:21 and R·, which were dukes of Sihon,

Rebecca (*re-bek'-kah*) See also REBEKAH.
Ro 9:10 R· also had conceived by one, even

Rebekah (*re-bek'-kah*) See also REBECCA; REBEKAH'S.
Ge 22:23 Bethuel begat R·: these eight
24:15 R· came out, who was born to
29 R· had a brother, and his name was
30 he heard the words of R· his sister,
45 R· came forth with her pitcher on
51 R· is before thee, take her, and go,
53 and raiment, and gave them to R·:
58 they called R·, and said unto her,
59 they sent away R· their sister, and
60 they blessed R·, and said unto her,
61 R· arose, and her damsels, and they
61 servant took R·, and went his way.
64 R· lifted up her eyes, and when she
67 took R·, and she became his wife;
25:20 years old when he took R· to wife,
21 of him, and R· his wife conceived.
28 of his venison: but R· loved Jacob.
26: 7 of the place should kill me for R·;
8 was sporting with R· his wife.
35 grief of mind unto Isaac and to R·.
27: 5 R· heard when Isaac spake to Esau
6 And R· spake unto Jacob her son,
11 Jacob said to R· his mother, Behold,
15 And R· took goodly raiment of her
42 Esau her elder son were told to R·:
46 R· said to Isaac, I am weary of my
28: 5 the Syrian, the brother of R·,
49:31 they buried Isaac and R· his wife;

Rebekah's (*re-bek'-kahz*)
Ge 29:12 brother, and that he was R· son:
35: 8 But Deborah R· nurse died, and

rebel See also REBELLED; REBELLEST; REBELS.
Nu 14: 9 Only r· not ye against the Lord,
Jos 1:18 doth r· against thy commandment,
22:16 r· this day against the Lord?
18 seeing ye r· to day against the Lord,
19 but r· not against the Lord, nor
19 against the Lord, nor r· against us,
29 God forbid that we should r· against
1Sa 12:14 not r· against the commandment
15 but r· against the commandment
Ne 2:19 ye do? will ye r· against the king?
6: 6 that thou and the Jews think to r·:
Job 24:13 of those that r· against the light;
Isa 1:20 But if ye refuse and r·, ye shall be
Ho 7:14 and wine, and they r· against me.

rebelled
Ge 14: 4 and in the thirteenth year they r·.
Nu 20:24 because ye r· against my word at
27:14 ye r· against my commandment in
De 1:26, 43 but r· against the commandment
9:23 ye r· against the commandment of
1Ki 12:19 So Israel r· against the house of
2Ki 1: 1 Then Moab r· against Israel after
3: 5 Moab r· against the king of Israel.
7 king of Moab hath r· against me:
18: 7 he r· against the king of Assyria,
24: 1 then he turned and r· against him.
20 Zedekiah r· against the king of
2Ch 10:19 And Israel r· against the house of
13: 6 up, and hath r· against his lord.
36:13 r· against king Nebuchadnezzar,
Ne 9:26 disobedient, and r· against thee,
Ps 5:10 for they have r· against thee.
105:28 and they r· not against his word.
107:11 they r· against the words of God,
Isa 1: 2 and they have r· against me.
63:10 they r·, and vexed his holy Spirit:
Jer 52: 3 Zedekiah r· against the king of
La 1:18 r· against his commandment:
20 for I have grievously r·: abroad
3:42 We have transgressed and have r·:
Eze 2: 3 nation that hath r· against me:
17:15 he r· against him in sending his
20: 8 they r· against me, and would not
13 r· against me in the wilderness:
21 the children r· against me: they
Da 9: 5 have r·, even by departing from
9 though we have r· against him;
Ho 13:16 for she hath r· against her God:

rebellest
2Ki 18:20 trust, that thou r· against me?
Isa 36: 5 trust, that thou r· against me?

rebellion
De 31:27 I know thy r·, and thy stiff neck:
Jos 22:22 if it be in r·, or if in transgression
1Sa 15:23 For r· is as the sin of witchcraft,
Ezr 4:19 r· and sedition have been made
Ne 9:17 in their r· appointed a captain to
Job 34:37 For he addeth r· unto his sin, he
Pr 17:11 An evil man seeketh only r·:
Jer 28:16 hast taught r· against the Lord.
29:32 he hath taught r· against the Lord.

rebellious
De 9: 7 ye have been r· against the Lord.
24 Ye have been r· against the Lord
21:18 a man have a stubborn and r· son,
20 This our son is stubborn and r·, he
31:27 ye have been r· against the Lord;
1Sa 20:30 son of the perverse r· woman, do
Ezr 4:12 building the r· and the bad city,
15 and know that this city is a r· city,
Ps 66: 7 let not the r· exalt themselves.
68: 6 but the r· dwell in a dry land.
18 yea, for the r· also, that the Lord
78: 8 a stubborn and r· generation; a
Isa 1:23 princes are r·, and companions of
30: 1 Woe to the r· children, saith the
9 this is a r· people, lying children,
50: 5 I was not r·, neither turned away
65: 2 hands all the day unto a r· people,
Jer 4:17 she hath been r· against me, saith
5:23 hath a revolting and a r· heart;
Eze 2: 3 to a r· nation that hath rebelled
5 (for they are a r· house,) yet shall
6 looks, though they be a r· house.
7 will forbear: for they are most r·.
8 Be not thou r· like that r· house:
3: 9 looks, though they be a r· house.
26 a reprover: for they are a r· house.
27 forbear: for they are a r· house.
12: 2 dwellest in the midst of a r· house,
2 hear not: for they are a r· house.
3 consider, though they be a r· house.
9 the house of Israel, the r· house,
25 O r· house, will I say the word, and
17:12 Say now to the r· house, Know ye
24: 3 utter a parable unto the r· house,
44: 6 thou shalt say to the r·, even to the

rebels
Nu 17:10 kept for a token against the r·;
20:10 Hear now, ye r·; must we fetch
Eze 20:38 purge out from among you the r·,

rebuke See also REBUKED; REBUKES; REBUKETH; REBUKING; UNREBUKABLE.
Le 19:17 in any wise r· thy neighbour, and
De 28:20 upon thee cursing, vexation and r·,
Ru 2:16 may glean them, and r· her not.
2Ki 19: 3 day is a day of trouble, and of r·,
1Ch 12:17 our fathers look thereon, and r· it.
Ps 6: 1 O Lord, r· me not in thine anger,
18:15 were discovered at thy r·, O Lord,
38: 1 O Lord, r· me not in thy wrath:
68:30 R· the company of spearmen, the
76: 6 At thy r·, O God of Jacob, both the
80:16 perish at the r· of thy countenance.
104: 7 At thy r· they fled; at the voice of
Pr 9: 8 r· a wise man, and he will love
13: 1 but a scorner heareth not r·.
8 riches: but the poor heareth not r·.
24:25 them that r· him shall be delight,
27: 5 Open r· is better than secret love.
Ec 7: 5 is better to hear the r· of the wise,
Isa 2: 4 and shall r· many people:
17:13 God shall r· them, and they shall
25: 8 r· of his people shall he take away
30:17 shall flee at the r· of one; at the
17 at the r· of five shall ye flee: till ye
37: 3 day is a day of trouble, and of r·,
50: 2 behold, at my r· I dry up the sea, I
51:20 fury of the Lord, the r· of thy God.
54: 9 be wroth with thee, nor r· thee.
66:15 fury, and his r· with flames of fire.
Jer 15:15 for thy sake I have suffered r·.
Ho 5: 9 shall be desolate in the day of r·:
Mic 4: 3 and r· strong nations afar off;
Zec 3: 2 The Lord r· thee, O Satan; even
2 hath chosen Jerusalem r· thee:
Mal 3:11 r· the devourer for your sakes, and
M't 16:22 took him, and began to r· him,
M'r 8:32 took him, and began to r· him.
Lu 17: 3 trespass against thee, r· him; and
19:39 unto him, Master, r· thy disciples.
Ph'p 2:15 the sons of God, without r·, in the
1Ti 5: 1 R· not an elder, but intreat him as
20 Them that sin r· before all, that
2Ti 4: 2 r·, exhort with all longsuffering
Tit 1:13 Wherefore r· them sharply, that
2:15 exhort, and r· with all authority.
Jude 9 but said, The Lord r· thee.
Re 3:19 many as I love, I r· and chasten:

rebuked
Ge 31:42 my hands, and r· thee yesternight.
37:10 and his father r· him, and said
Ne 5: 7 and I r· the nobles, and the rulers,
Ps 9: 5 Thou hast r· the heathen, thou
106: 9 He r· the Red sea also, and it was
119:21 hast r· the proud that are cursed,
M't 8:26 and r· the winds and the sea; and
17:18 And Jesus r· the devil; and he
19:13 pray: and the disciples r· them.
20:31 the multitude r· them, because they
M'r 1:25 And Jesus r· him, saying, Hold thy
4:39 he arose, and r· the wind, and said
8:33 he r· Peter, saying, Get thee behind
9:25 he r· the foul spirit, saying unto
10:13 his disciples r· those that brought
Lu 4:35 And Jesus r· him, saying, Hold thy
39 and r· the fever; and it left her:
8:24 he arose, and r· the wind and the
9:42 Jesus r· the unclean spirit, and
55 he turned, and r· them, and said,
18:15 his disciples saw it, they r· them.
39 they which went before r· him,
23:40 But the other answering r· him,
Heb 12: 5 nor faint when thou art r· of him:
2Pe 2:16 But was r· for his iniquity: the

rebuker
Ho 5: 2 I have been a r· of them all.

rebukes
Ps 39:11 When thou with r· dost correct
Eze 5:15 and in fury and in furious r·.
25:17 upon them with furious r·; and

rebuketh
Pr 9: 7 he that r· a wicked man getteth
28:23 He that r· a man afterwards shall
Am 5:10 They hate him that r· in the gate,
Na 1: 4 He r· the sea, and maketh it dry,

rebuking
2Sa 22:16 discovered, at the r· of the Lord,
Lu 4:41 he r· them suffered them not to

recall
La 3:21 This I r· to my mind, therefore

receipt
M't 9: 9 Matthew, sitting at r· of custom:
M'r 2:14 Alphæus sitting at the r· of custom,
Lu 5:27 Levi, sitting at the r· of custom:

receive See also RECEIVED; RECEIVETH; RECEIVING.
Ge 4:11 mouth to r· thy brother's blood
33:10 then r· my present at my hand:
38:20 to r· his pledge from the woman's
Ex 27: 3 make his pans to r· his ashes,
29:25 thou shalt r· them of their hands,
Nu 18:28 ye r· of the children of Israel;
De 9: 9 the mount to r· the tables of stone,
33: 3 every one shall r· of thy words.
1Sa 10: 4 which thou shalt r· of their hands.
2Sa 18:12 r· a thousand shekels of silver in
1Ki 5: 9 there, and thou shalt r· them:
8:64 too little to r· the burnt offerings,
2Ki 5:16 whom I stand, I will r· none.
26 to r· money, and to r· garments,
12: 7 r· no more money of your
8 to r· no more money of the people.
2Ch 7: 7 not able to r· the burnt offerings,
Job 2:10 we r· good at the hand of God,
10 of God, and shall we not r· evil?
22:22 R·, I pray thee, the law from his
27:13 they shall r· of the Almighty.
Ps 6: 9 the Lord will r· my prayer.
24: 5 r· the blessing from the Lord,
49:15 of the grave: for he shall r· me.
73:24 and afterward r· me to glory.
75: 2 When I shall r· the congregation I
Pr 1: 3 To r· the instruction of wisdom,
2: 1 My son, if thou wilt r· my words,

Pr 4:10 Hear, O my son, and r· my sayings;
8:10 R· my instruction, and not silver;
10: 8 The wise...will r· commandments:
19:20 Hear counsel, and r· instruction,
Isa 57: 6 Should I r· comfort in these?
Jer 5: 3 they have refused to r· correction:
9:20 your ear r· the word of his mouth,
17:23 might not hear, nor r· instruction.
32:33 have not hearkened to r· instruction.
35:13 Will ye not r· instruction to hearken
Eze 3:10 speak unto thee r· in thine heart,
16:61 when thou shalt r· thy sisters, thine
36:30 shall r· no more reproach of famine
Da 2: 6 ye shall r· of me gifts and rewards
Ho 10: 6 Ephraim shall r· shame, and
14: 2 all iniquity, and r· us graciously:
Mic 1:11 he shall r· of you his standing.
Zep 3: 7 fear me, thou wilt r· instruction;
Mal 3:10 shall not be room enough to r· it.
M't 10:14 whosoever shall not r· you, nor
41 shall r· a prophet's reward; and
41 shall r· a righteous man's reward.
11: 5 blind r· their sight, and the lame
14 if ye will r· it, this is Elias, which
18: 5 whoso shall r· one such little child
19:11 All men cannot r· this saying, save
12 that is able to r· it, let him r· it.
29 shall r· an hundredfold, and shall
20: 7 is right, that shall ye r·.
21:22 ask in prayer, believing, ye shall r·.
34 that they might r· the fruits of it.
23:14 ye shall r· the greater damnation.
M'r 2: 2 there was no room to r· them,
4:16 immediately r· it with gladness;
20 such as hear the word, and r· it,
6:11 whosoever shall not r· you, nor
9:37 shall r· one of such children in
37 whosoever shall r· me, receiveth not
10:15 shall not r· the kingdom of God as
30 he shall r· an hundredfold now in
51 Lord, that I might r· my sight.
11:24 ye pray, believe that ye r· them,
12: 2 he might r· from the husbandmen
40 these shall r· greater damnation.
Lu 6:34 to them of whom ye hope to r·,
34 lend to sinners, to r· as much again.
8:13 they hear, r· the word with joy;
9: 5 whosoever will not r· you, when ye
48 shall r· this child in my name
48 whosoever shall r· me receiveth
53 they did not r· him, because his
10: 8 city ye enter, and they r· you, eat
10 they r· you not, go your ways out
16: 4 they may r· me into their houses.
9 they may r· you into everlasting
18:17 shall not r· the kingdom of God as
30 not r· manifold more in this present
41 said, Lord, that I may r· my sight.
42 Jesus said unto him, R· thy sight:
19:12 to r· for himself a kingdom, and
20:47 same shall r· greater damnation.
23:41 for we r· the due reward of our
Joh 3:11 seen; and ye r· not our witness.
27 A man can r· nothing, except it be
5:34 But I r· not testimony from man:
41 I r· not honour from men.
43 Father's name, and ye r· me not:
43 in his own name, him ye will r·.
44 which r· honour one of another,
7:23 the sabbath day r· circumcision,
39 they that believe on him should r·:
14: 3 again, and r· you unto myself;
17 whom the world cannot r·, because
16:14 for he shall r· of mine, and shall
24 ask, and ye shall r·, that your joy
20:22 unto them, R· ye the Holy Ghost:
Ac 1: 8 But ye shall r· power, after that the
2:38 shall r· the gift of the Holy Ghost.
3: 5 expecting to r· something of them.
21 Whom the heaven must r· until
7:59 and saying, Lord Jesus, r· my spirit.
8:15 that they might r· the Holy Ghost:
19 hands, he may r· the Holy Ghost.
9:12 on him, that he might r· his sight.
17 that thou mightest r· thy sight, and
10:43 in him shall r· remission of sins.
16:21 which are not lawful for us to r·,
18:27 exhorting the disciples to r· him:
20:35 is more blessed to give than to r·.
22:13 unto me, Brother Saul, r· thy sight.
18 r· thy testimony concerning me.
26:18 they may r· forgiveness of sins,
Ro 5:17 they which r· abundance of grace
13: 2 shall r· to themselves damnation.
14: 1 that is weak in the faith r· ye,
15: 7 r· ye one another, as Christ also
16: 2 That ye r· her in the Lord, as
1Co 3: 8 man shall r· his own reward
14 thereupon, he shall r· a reward.
4: 7 hast thou that thou didst not r·?
7 thou didst r· it, why dost thou glory,
14: 5 that the church may r· edifying.
2Co 5:10 r· the things done in his body,
6: 1 ye r· not the grace of God in vain.
17 unclean thing; and I will r· you,
7: 2 R· us; we have wronged no man,
9 might r· damage by us in nothing.
8: 4 intreaty that we would r· the gift,
11: 4 or if ye r· another spirit, which ye
16 as a fool r· me, that I may boast
Ga 3:14 might r· the promise of the Spirit
4: 5 we might r· the adoption of sons.
Eph 6: 8 the same shall he r· of the Lord,
Ph'p 2:29 R· him therefore in the Lord with
Col 3:24 r· the reward of the inheritance:
25 r· for the wrong which he hath
Col 4:10 if he come unto you, r· him:)
1Ti 5:19 an elder r· not an accusation, but
Ph'm 12 thou therefore r· him, that is,
15 that thou shouldest r· him for ever;
17 a partner, r· him as myself.
Heb 7: 5 who r· the office of the priesthood,
8 And here men that die r· tithes;
9:15 might r· the promise of eternal
10:36 of God, ye might r· the promise.
11: 8 should after r· for an inheritance,
Jas 1: 7 he shall r· any thing of the Lord.
12 is tried, he shall r· the crown of life.
21 r· with meekness the engrafted
3: 1 shall r· the greater condemnation.
4: 3 Ye ask, and r· not, because ye ask
5: 7 until he r· the early and latter rain.
1Pe 5: 4 r· a crown of glory that fadeth not
2Pe 2:13 r· the reward of unrighteousness,
1Jo 3:22 whatsoever we ask, we r· of him,
5: 9 If we r· the witness of men, the
2Jo 8 but that we r· a full reward.
10 r· him not into your house, neither
3Jo 8 We therefore ought to r· such, that
10 doth he himself r· the brethren,
Re 4:11 to r· glory and honour and power:
5:12 Lamb that was slain to r· power,
13:16 to r· a mark in their right hand,
14: 9 r· his mark in his forehead, or in
17:12 but r· power as kings one hour with
18: 4 and that ye r· not of her plagues.

received See also RECEIVEDST.
Ge 26:12 land, and r· in the same year an
Ex 32: 4 And he r· them at their hand, and
36: 3 they r· of Moses all the offering,
Nu 12:14 after that let her be r· in again.
23:20 I have r· commandment to bless:
34:14 fathers, have r· their inheritance;
14 have r· their inheritance:
15 half tribe have r· their inheritance
36: 3, 4 the tribe whereunto they are r·:
Jos 13: 8 Gadites have r· their inheritance,
18: 2 had not yet r· their inheritance.
7 have r· their inheritance beyond
J'g 13:23 would not have r· a burnt offering
1Sa 12: 3 of whose hand have I r· any bribe
25:35 So David r· of her hand that which
1Ki 10:28 merchants r· the linen yarn at a
2Ki 19:14 Hezekiah r· the letter of the hand
1Ch 12:18 David r· them, and made them
2Ch 1:16 merchants r· the linen yarn at a
4: 5 r· and held three thousand baths.
29:22 and the priests r· the blood, and
30:16 they r· at the hand of the Levites.
Es 4: 4 from him: but he r· it not.
Job 4:12 and mine ear r· a little thereof.
Ps 68:18 thou hast r· gifts for men; yea, for
Pr 24:32 looked upon it, and r· instruction.
Isa 37:14 And Hezekiah r· the letter from the
40: 2 for she hath r· of the Lord's hand
Jer 2:30 children; they r· no correction:
Eze 18:17 hath not r· usury nor increase,
Zep 3: 2 she r· not correction; she trusted
M't 10: 8 freely ye have r·, freely give.
13:19 he which r· seed by the way side.
20 that r· the seed into stony places,
22 also that r· seed among the thorns
23 that r· seed into the good ground
17:24 they that r· tribute money came to
20: 9 hour, they r· every man a penny.
10 that they should have r· more;
10 they likewise r· every man a penny.
11 And when they had r· it, they
34 and immediately their eyes r· sight,
25:16 he that had r· the five talents went
17 And likewise he that had r· two,
18 But he that had r· one went and
20 so he that had r· five talents came
22 also that had r· two talents came
24 which had r· the one talent came
27 have r· mine own with usury.
M'r 7: 4 which they have r· to hold, as the
10:52 And immediately he r· his sight,
15:23 with myrrh: but he r· it not.
16:19 he was r· up into heaven, and sat on
Lu 6:24 for ye have r· your consolation.
8:40 returned, the people gladly r· him:
9:11 he r· them, and spake unto them
51 was come that he should be r· up,
10:38 Martha r· him into her house.
15:27 he hath r· him safe and sound.
18:43 And immediately he r· his sight,
19: 6 came down, and r· him joyfully.
15 returned, having r· the kingdom,
Joh 1:11 his own, and his own r· him not.
12 as many as r· him, to them gave
16 And of his fulness have all we r·,
3:33 He that hath r· his testimony hath
4:45 the Galilæans r· him, having seen
6:21 they willingly r· him into the ship:
9:11 I went and washed, and I r· sight.
15 asked him how he had r· his sight.
18 he had been blind, and r· his sight,
18 parents of him that had r· his sight.
10:18 This commandment have I r· of
13:30 He then having r· the sop went
17: 8 they have r· them, and have known
18: 3 then, having r· a band of men and
19:30 Jesus therefore had r· the vinegar,
Ac 1: 9 a cloud r· him out of their sight.
2:33 and having r· of the Father the
41 gladly r· his word were baptized:
3: 7 feet and ancle bones r· strength.
7:38 r· the lively oracles to give unto us:
53 r· the law by the disposition of
8:14 Samaria had r· the word of God,
17 them, and they r· the Holy Ghost.
Ac 9:18 he r· sight forthwith, and arose,
19 And when he had r· meat, he was
10:16 vessel was r· up again into heaven.
47 r· the Holy Ghost as well as we?
11: 1 Gentiles had also r· the word of
15: 4 they were r· of the church, and of
16:24 Who, having r· such a charge,
17: 7 Whom Jason hath r·: and these
11 they r· the word with all readiness
19: 2 Have ye r· the Holy Ghost since ye
20:24 which I have r· of the Lord Jesus,
21:17 the brethren r· us gladly.
22: 5 from whom also I r· letters unto
26:10 r· authority from the chief priests;
28: 2 fire, and r· us every one, because
7 who r· us, and lodged us three days
21 We neither r· letters out of Judæa
30 and r· all that came in unto him.
Ro 1: 5 we have r· grace and apostleship,
4:11 And he r· the sign of circumcision,
5:11 we have now r· the atonement.
8:15 ye have not r· the spirit of bondage
15 ye have r· the Spirit of adoption,
14: 3 that eateth: for God hath r· him.
15: 7 as Christ also r· us to the glory of
1Co 2:12 Now we have r·, not the spirit of
4: 7 glory, as if thou hadst not r· it?
11:23 I have r· of the Lord that which
15: 1 which also ye have r·, and wherein
3 you first of all that which I also r·,
2Co 4: 1 as we have r· mercy, we faint not;
7:15 with fear and trembling ye r· him.
11: 4 which ye have not r·, or another
24 times r· I forty stripes save one.
Ga 1: 9 unto you than that ye have r·,
12 For I neither r· it of man, neither
3: 2 R· ye the Spirit by the works of
4:14 but r· me as an angel of God, even
Ph'p 4: 9 ye have both learned, and r·, and
18 having r· of Epaphroditus the
Col 2: 6 ye have therefore r· Christ Jesus
4:10 whom ye r· commandments: if
17 which thou hast r· in the Lord,
1Th 1: 6 r· the word in much affliction,
2:13 when ye r· the word of God which
13 ye r· it not as the word of men,
4: 1 as ye have r· of us how ye ought
2Th 2:10 they r· not the love of the truth,
3: 6 the tradition which he r· of us.
1Ti 3:16 on in the world, r· up into glory.
4: 3 which God hath created to be r·
4 if it be r· with thanksgiving:
Heb 2: 2 r· a just recompense of reward;
7: 6 from them r· tithes of Abraham,
11 (for under it the people r· the law,)
10:26 r· the knowledge of the truth,
11:11 Sara herself r· strength to conceive
13 not having r· the promises, but
17 he that had r· the promises offered
19 whence also he r· him in a figure.
31 she had r· the spies with peace.
35 Women r· their dead raised to life
39 through faith, r· not the promise:
Jas 2:25 when she had r· the messengers,
1Pe 1:18 vain conversation r· by tradition
4:10 As every man hath r· the gift, even
2Pe 1:17 he r· from God the Father honour
1Jo 2:27 anointing which ye have r· of him
2Jo 4 we have r· a commandment from
Re 2:27 shivers: even as I r· of my Father.
3: 3 how thou hast r· and heard, and
17:12 which have r· no kingdom as yet;
19:20 that had r· the mark of the beast,
20: 4 r· his mark upon their foreheads,

receivedst
Lu 16:25 in thy lifetime r· thy good things,

receiver
Isa 33:18 is the scribe? where is the r·?

receiveth
J'g 19:18 is no man that r· me to house.
Job 35: 7 him? or what r· he of thine hand?
Pr 21:11 wise is instructed, he r· knowledge.
29: 4 but he that r· gifts overthroweth it.
Jer 7:28 Lord their God, nor r· correction:
Mal 2:13 or r· it with good will at your hand.
M't 7: 8 For every one that asketh r·; and
10:40 He that r· you r· me, and he
40 that r· me r· him that sent me.
41 He that r· a prophet in the name
41 he that r· a righteous man in the
13:20 the word, and anon with joy r· it;
18: 5 such little child in my name r· me.
M'r 9:37 little children in my name, r· me:
37 shall receive me, r· not me, but
Lu 9:48 receive this child in my name r· me:
48 receive me r· him that sent me:
11:10 every one that asketh r·; and he
15: 2 This man r· sinners, and eateth
Joh 3:32 and no man r· his testimony.
4:36 And he that reapeth r· wages, and
12:48 and r· not my words, hath one that
13:20 that r· whomsoever I send r· me;
20 he that r· me r· him that sent me.
1Co 2:14 the natural man r· not the things
9:24 race run all, but one r· the prize?
Heb 6: 7 it is dressed, r· blessing from God:
7: 8 but there he r· them, of whom it is
9 Levi also, who r· tithes, payed
12: 6 scourgeth every son whom he r·.
3Jo 9 among them, r· us not.
Re 2:17 man knoweth saving he that r· it.
14:11 whosoever r· the mark of his name.

receiving
2Ki 5:20 not r· at his hands that which he

Ac 17:15 r' a commandment unto Silas and
Ro 1:27 r' in themselves that recompence
11:15 what shall the r' of them be, but
Ph'p 4:15 me as concerning giving and r',
Heb12:28 Wherefore we r' a kingdom which
1Pe 1: 9 R' the end of your faith, even the
Rechab (*re'-kab*) See also RECHABITES.
2Sa 4: 2 and the name of the other R',
5 sons of Rimmon...R' and Baanah,
6 R' and Baanah his brother escaped.
9 R' and Baanah his brother, the
2Ki 10:15 the son of R' coming to meet him:
23 went, and Jehonadab the son of R',
1Ch 2:55 the father of the house of R'.
Ne 3:14 repaired Malchiah the son of R',
Jer 35: 6 of R' our father commanded us,
8 the voice of Jonadab the son of R'
14 words of Jonadab the son of R',
16 the son of R' have performed the
19 the son of R' shall not want a man
Rechabites (*rek'-ab-ites*)
Jer 35: 2 Go unto the house of the R', and
3 and the whole house of the R';
5 house of the R' pots full of wine,
18 said unto the house of the R',
Rechah (*re'-kah*)
1Ch 4:12 These are the men of R'.
Rechokim See JONATH-ELEM-RECHOKIM.
reckon See also RECKONED; RECKONING.
Le 25:50 he shall r' with him that bought
27:18, 23 the priest shall r' unto him the
Nu 4:32 name ye shall r' the instruments
Eze 44:26 they shall r' unto him seven days.
M't 18:24 And when he had begun to r', one
Ro 6:11 r' ye also yourselves to be dead
8:18 For I r' that the sufferings of this
reckoned
Nu 18:27 offering shall be r' unto you,
23: 9 shall not be r' among the nations.
2Sa 4: 2 Beeroth also was r' to Benjamin:
2Ki 12:15 they r' not with the men, into
1Ch 5: 1 and the genealogy is not to be r'
7 of their generations was r', were
17 All these were r' by genealogies in
7: 5 r' in all by their genealogies
7 and were r' by their genealogies
9: 1 all Israel were r' by genealogies;
22 These were r' by their genealogy in
2Ch 31:19 to all that were r' by genealogies
Ezr 2:62 those that were r' by genealogy,
8: 3 and with him were r' by genealogy
Ne 7: 5 that they might be r' by genealogy.
64 those that were r' by genealogy,
Ps 40: 5 cannot be r' up in order unto thee:
Isa 38:13 I r' till morning, that, as a lion,
Lu 22:37 was r' among the transgressors:
Ro 4: 4 is the reward not r' of grace, but
9 say that faith was r' to Abraham
10 How was it then r'? when he was
reckoneth
M't 25:19 cometh, and r' with them.
reckoning
2Ki 22: 7 there was no r' made with them
1Ch 23:11 they were in one r', according to
recommended
Ac 14:26 had been r' to the grace of God
15:40 being r' by the brethren unto the
recompence See also RECOMPENCES; RECOMPENSE.
De 32:35 me belongeth vengeance, and r';
Job 15:31 vanity: for vanity shall be his r'.
Pr 12:14 the r' of a man's hands shall be
Isa 35: 4 vengeance, even God with a r'; he
59:18 his adversaries, r' to his enemies;
18 to the islands he will repay r'.
66: 6 that rendereth r' to his enemies.
Jer 51: 6 he will render unto her a r'.
La 3:64 Render unto them a r', O Lord,
Hos 9: 7 the days of r' are come; Israel
Joe 3: 4 will ye render me a r'? and if ye
4, 7 return...r' upon your own head;
Lu 14:12 thee again, and a r' be made thee.
Ro 1:27 r' of their error which was meet.
11: 9 stumblingblock,...a r' unto them:
2Co 6:13 Now for a r' in the same, (I speak
Heb 2: 2 received a just r' of reward;
10:35 which hath great r' of reward.
11:26 respect unto the r' of the reward.
recompences
Isa 34: 8 year of r' for the controversy of
Jer 51:56 for the Lord God of r' shall surely
recompense See also RECOMPENCE; RECOMPENSED; RECOMPENSEST; RECOMPENSING.
Nu 5: 7 he shall r' his trespass with the
8 if the man have no kinsman to r'
Ru 2:12 The Lord r' thy work, and a full
2Sa 19:36 king r' it me with such a reward?
Job 34:33 he will r' it, whether thou refuse,
Pr 20:22 Say not thou, I will r' evil; but
Isa 65: 6 but will r', even r' into their bosom,
Jer 16:18 And first I will r' their iniquity
25:14 r' them according to their deeds,
50:29 r' her according to her work;
Eze 7: 3 and will r' upon thee all thine
4 I will r' thy ways upon thee, and
8 and will r' thee for all thine
9 I will r' thee according to thy ways
9:10 will r' their way upon their head.
11:21 r' their way upon their own heads,
16:43 will r' thy way upon thine head,
17:19 even it will I r' upon his own head.
23:49 they shall r' your lewdness upon
Ho 12: 2 to his doings will he r' him.
Joe 3: 4 if ye r' me, swiftly and speedily
Lu 14:14 they cannot r' thee: for thou shalt
Ro 12:17 R' to no man evil for evil. Provide
2Th 1: 6 with God to r' tribulation to them
Heb10:30 unto me, I will r', saith the Lord.
recompensed
Nu 5: 8 the trespass be r' unto the Lord,
2Sa 22:21 of my hands hath he r' me.
25 Lord hath r' me according to my
Ps 18:20 of my hands hath he r' me.
24 the Lord r' me according to my
Pr 11:31 righteous shall be r' in the earth:
Jer 18:20 Shall evil be r' for good? for they
Eze 22:31 way have I r' upon their heads,
Lu 14:14 thou shalt be r' at the resurrection
Ro 11:35 and it shall be r' unto him again?
recompensest
Jer 32:18 and r' the iniquity of the fathers
recompensing
2Ch 6:23 by r' his way upon his own head;
reconcile See also RECONCILED; RECONCILING.
Le 6:30 to r' withal in the holy place,
1Sa 29: 4 he r' himself unto his master?
Eze 45:20 simple: so shall ye r' the house.
Eph 2:16 r' both unto God in one body by the
Col 1:20 him to r' all things unto himself;
reconciled
M't 5:24 first be r' to thy brother, and then
Ro 5:10 r' to God by the death of his Son,
10 much more, being r', we shall be
1Co 7:11 unmarried, or be r' to her husband:
2Co 5:18 of God, who hath r' us to himself by
20 in Christ's stead, be ye r' to God.
Col 1:21 wicked works, yet now hath he r'
reconciliation
Le 8:15 sanctified it, to make r' upon it.
2Ch 29:24 made r' with their blood upon
Eze 45:15 offerings, to make r' for them,
17 to make r' for the house of Israel.
Da 9:24 and to make r' for iniquity, and to
2Co 5:18 hath given to us the ministry of r';
19 committed unto us the word of r'.
Heb 2:17 make r' for the sins of the people.
reconciling
Le 16:20 made an end of r' the holy place,
Ro 11:15 of them be the r' of the world,
2Co 5:19 Christ, r' the world unto himself,
record See also RECORDED; RECORDS.
Ex 20:24 where I r' my name I will come
De 30:19 heaven and earth to r' this day
31:28 heaven and earth to r' against
1Ch 16: 4 and to r', and to thank and praise
Ezr 6: 2 and therein was a r' thus written:
Job 16:19 in heaven, and my r' is on high.
Isa 8: 2 unto me faithful witnesses to r',
Joh 1:19 And this is the r' of John, when
32 John bare r', saying, I saw the
34 bare r' that this is the Son of God.
8:13 him, Thou bearest r' of thyself;
13 of thyself; thy r' is not true.
14 Though I bear r' of myself, yet
14 of myself, yet my r' is true: for
12:17 raised him from the dead, bare r'.
19:35 And he that saw it bare r', and
35 his r' is true: and he knoweth
Ac 20:26 I take you to r' this day, that I am
Ro 10: 2 bear them r' that they have a zeal
2Co 1:23 I call God for a r' upon my soul,
8: 3 I bear r', yea, and beyond their
Ga 4:15 for I bear you r', that, if it had
Ph'p 1: 8 For God is my r', how greatly I
Col 4:13 For I bear him r', that he hath a
1Jo 5: 7 are three that bear r' in heaven,
10 the r' that God gave of his Son.
11 this is the r', that God hath given
3Jo 12 itself: yea, and we also bear r';
12 and ye know that our r' is true.
Re 1: 2 Who bare r' of the word of God,
recorded
Ne 12:22 were r' chief of the fathers: also
recorder
2Sa 8:16 the son of Ahilud was r';
20:24 the son of Ahilud was r':
1Ki 4: 3 the son of Ahilud, the r'.
2Ki 18:18 and Joah the son of Asaph the r'.
37 and Joah the son of Asaph the r',
1Ch 18:15 Jehoshaphat the son of Ahilud, r'.
2Ch 34: 8 and Joah the son of Joahaz the r',
Isa 36: 3 and Joah, Asaph's son, the r'.
22 and Joah, the son of Asaph, the r',
records
Ezr 4:15 may be made in the book of the r'
15 thou find in the book of the r',
Es 6: 1 the book of r' of the chronicles;
recount
Na 2: 5 He shall r' his worthies: they
recover See also RECOVERED; RECOVERING.
J'g 11:26 did ye not r' them within that
1Sa 30: 8 them, and without fail r' all.
2Sa 8: 3 went to r' his border at the river
2Ki 1: 2 whether I shall r' of this disease.
5: 3 for he would r' him of his leprosy.
6 thou mayest r' him of his leprosy.
7 unto me to r' a man of his leprosy?
11 hand over the place, and r' the leper.
8: 8, 9 saying, Shall I r' of this disease?
10 him, Thou mayest certainly r':
14 me that thou shouldest surely r'.
2Ch 13:20 Neither did Jeroboam r' strength
14:13 that they could not r' themselves;
Ps 39:13 spare me, that I may r' strength,
Isa 11:11 to r' the remnant of his people,
38:16 so wilt thou r' me, and make me to
21 upon the boil, and he shall r'.
Ho 2: 9 will r' my wool and my flax given
M'r 16:18 on the sick, and they shall r'.
2Ti 2:26 may r' themselves out of the snare
recovered
1Sa 30:18 r' all that the Amalekites had
19 had taken to them: David r' all.
22 ought of the spoil that we have r',
2Ki 13:25 him, and r' the cities of Israel.
14:28 how he r' Damascus, and Hamath,
16: 6 time Rezin king of Syria r' Elath
20: 7 and laid it on the boil, and he r'.
Isa 38: 9 sick, and was r' of his sickness:
39: 1 that he had been sick, and was r'.
Jer 8:22 of the daughter of my people r'?
41:16 whom he had r' from Ishmael the
recovering
Lu 4:18 r' of sight to the blind, to set at
red See also RED; REDDISH.
Ge 25:25 And the first came out r', all over
30 thee, with that same r' pottage;
49:12 His eyes shall be r' with wine, and
Ex 25: 5 rams' skins dyed r', and badgers'
26:14 for the tent of rams' skins dyed r',
35: 7 rams' skins dyed r', and badgers'
23 r' skins of rams, and badgers' skins,
36:19 for the tent of rams' skins dyed r',
39:34 the covering of rams' skins dyed r',
Nu 19: 2 bring thee a r' heifer without spot,
2Ki 3:22 on the other side as r' as blood:
Es 1: 6 upon a pavement of r', and blue,
Ps 75: 8 there is a cup, and the wine is r';
Pr 23:31 thou upon the wine when it is r',
Isa 1:18 though they be r' like crimson,
27: 2 unto her, A vineyard of r' wine.
63: 2 art thou r' in thine apparel, and
Na 2: 3 of his mighty men is made r',
Zec 1: 8 behold a man riding upon a r' horse,
8 behind him were there r' horses,
6: 2 In the first chariot were r' horses;
M't 16: 2 be fair weather: for the sky is r'.
3 to day: for the sky is r' and lowring.
Re 6: 4 out another horse that was r':
12: 3 behold a great r' dragon, having
Red See also RED.
Ex 10:19 and cast them into the R' sea;
13:18 way the wilderness of the R' sea:
15: 4 also are drowned in the R' sea.
22 brought Israel from the R' sea,
23:31 will set thy bounds from the R' sea
Nu 14:25 wilderness by the way of the R' sea.
21: 4 mount Hor by the way of the R' sea,
14 What he did in the R' sea, and
33:10 Elim, and encamped by the R' sea.
11 And they removed from the R' sea,
De 1: 1 the plain over against the R' sea,
40 wilderness by...way of the R' sea.
2: 1 wilderness by the way of the R' sea,
11: 4 the water of the R' sea to overflow
Jos 2:10 dried up the water of the R' sea
4:23 Lord your God did to the R' sea,
24: 6 and horsemen unto the R' sea.
J'g 11:16 the wilderness unto the R' sea,
1Ki 9:26 on the shore of the R' sea, in the
Ne 9: 9 heardest their cry by the R' sea;
Ps 106: 7 him at the sea, even at the R' sea,
9 He rebuked the R' sea also, and it
22 and terrible things by the R' sea.
136:13 which divided the R' sea into parts:
15 Pharaoh and his host in the R' sea:
Jer 49:21 noise...was heard in the R' sea.
Ac 7:36 land of Egypt, and in the R' sea,
Heb11:29 passed through the R' sea as by dry
reddish See also RED.
Le 13:19 spot, white, and somewhat r',
24 bright spot, somewhat r', or white;
42 a white r' sore; it is a leprosy
43 if the rising of the sore be white r'
49 be greenish or r' in the garment,
14:37 with hollow strakes, greenish or r',
redeem See also REDEEMED; REDEEMETH; REDEEMING.
Ex 6: 6 r' you with a stretched out arm,
13:13 firstling of an ass thou shalt r'
13 if thou wilt not r' it, then thou shalt
13 firstborn of man...shalt thou r'.
15 all the firstborn of my children I r'.
34:20 firstling of an ass thou shalt r'
20 if thou r' him not, then shalt thou
20 firstborn of thy sons thou shalt r'.
Le 25:25 and if any of his kin come to r' it,
25 he r' that which his brother sold.
26 And if the man have none to r' it,
26 and himself be able to r' it;
29 he may r' it within a whole year
29 within a full year may he r' it.
32 may the Levites r' at any time.
48 one of his brethren may r' him:
49 or his uncle's son, may r' him,
49 unto him of his family may r' him;
49 or if he be able, he may r' himself.
27:13 But if he will at all r' it, then he
15 that sanctified it will r' his house,
19 that sanctified the field will...r' it,
20 And if he will not r' the field, or if
27 he shall r' it according to thine
31 will at all r' ought of his tithes,
Nu 18:15 firstborn of man shalt thou...r',
15 of unclean beasts shalt thou r'.
16 from a month old shalt thou r',
17 firstling of a goat, thou shalt not r';

Ru 4: 4 If thou wilt r· it, r· it: but
4 if thou wilt not r· it, then tell me,
4 there is none to r· it beside thee;
4 after thee. And he said, I will r· it.
6 I cannot r· it for myself, lest I mar
6 r· thou my right to thyself;
6 for I cannot r· it.
2Sa 7: 23 whom God went to r· for a people
1Ch 17: 21 God went to r· to be his own people,
Ne 5: 5 neither is it in our power to r· them;
Job 5: 20 famine he shall r· thee from death:
6: 23 R· me from the hand of the mighty?
Ps 25: 22 R· Israel, O God, out of all his
26: 11 r· me, and be merciful unto me.
44: 26 and r· us for thy mercies' sake.
49: 7 can by any means r· his brother,
15 God will r· my soul from the power
69: 18 Draw nigh unto my soul, and r· it:
72: 14 He shall r· their soul from deceit
130: 8 r· Israel from all his iniquities.
Isa 50: 2 shortened at all, that it cannot r·?
Jer 15: 21 I will r· thee out of the hand of
Ho 13: 14 grave; I will r· them from death:
Mic 4: 10 shall r· thee from the hand of thine
Ga 4: 5 To r· them that were under the
Tit 2: 14 he might r· us from all iniquity

redeemed See also REDEEMEDST.
Ge 48: 16 Angel which r· me from all evil,
Ex 15: 13 led forth the people...thou hast r·:
21: 8 then shall he let her be r·:
Le 19: 20 not at all r·, nor freedom given her;
25: 30 r· within the space of a full year,
31 they may be r·, and they shall go
48 After that he is sold he may be r·
54 And if he be not r· in these years,
27: 20 man, it shall not be r· any more.
27 if it be not r·, then it shall be sold
28 devoted thing,...shall be sold or r·:
29 None devoted,...shall be r·;
33 shall be holy; it shall not be r·.
Nu 3: 46 And for those that are to be r· of
48 the odd number of them is to be r·,
49 them that were r· by the Levites:
51 the money of them that were r·
18: 16 that are to be r· from a month old
De 7: 8 r· you out of the house of bondmen,
9: 26 thou hast r· through thy greatness,
13: 5 r· you out of the house of bondage,
15: 15 and the Lord thy God r· thee:
21: 8 people Israel, whom thou hast r·,
24: 18 the Lord thy God r· thee thence:
2Sa 4: 9 hath r· my soul out of all adversity,
1Ki 1: 29 hath r· my soul out of all distress,
1Ch 17: 21 whom thou hast r· out of Egypt?
Ne 1: 10 thou hast r· by thy great power,
5: 8 have r· our brethren the Jews,
Ps 31: 5 hast r· me, O Lord God of truth.
71: 23 and my soul, which thou hast r·.
74: 2 inheritance, which thou hast r·;
77: 15 hast with thine arm r· thy people,
106: 10 r· them from the hand of the enemy.
107: 2 Let the r· of the Lord say so, whom
2 hath r· from the hand of the enemy;
136: 24 And hath r· us from our enemies:
Isa 1: 27 Zion shall be r· with judgment,
29: 22 saith the Lord, who r· Abraham,
35: 9 there; but the r· shall walk there:
43: 1 Fear not: for I have r· thee, I have
44: 22 return unto me; for I have r· thee.
23 for the Lord hath r· Jacob, and
48: 20 The Lord hath r· his servant Jacob.
51: 11 the r· of the Lord shall return,
52: 3 and ye shall be r· without money.
9 his people, he hath r· Jerusalem.
62: 12 The holy people, The r· of the Lord:
63: 4 and the year of my r· is come.
9 his love and in his pity he r· them;
Jer 31: 11 For the Lord hath r· Jacob, and
La 3: 58 of my soul; thou hast r· my life.
Ho 7: 13 though I have r· them, yet they
Mic 6: 4 r· thee out of the house of servants;
Zec 10: 8 for I have r· them: and they shall
Lu 1: 68 hath visited and r· his people,
24: 21 he which should have r· Israel:
Ga 3: 13 Christ hath r· us from the curse
1Pe 1: 18 not r· with corruptible things,
Re 5: 9 and hast r· us to God by thy blood
14: 3 which were r· from the earth.
4 These were r· from among men,

redeemedst
2Sa 7: 23 which thou r· to thee from Egypt,

redeemer
Job 19: 25 I know that my r· liveth, and that
Ps 19: 14 O Lord, my strength, and my r·.
78: 35 rock, and the high God their r·.
Pr 23: 11 For their r· is mighty; he shall
Isa 41: 14 saith the Lord, and thy r·, the Holy
43: 14 Thus saith the Lord, your r·, the
44: 6 Israel, and his r· the Lord of hosts;
24 Thus saith the Lord, thy r·, and he
47: 4 As for our r·, the Lord of hosts is his
48: 17 Thus saith the Lord, thy R·, the
49: 7 the R· of Israel, and his Holy One,
26 Lord am thy Saviour and thy R·,
54: 5 and thy R· the Holy One of Israel;
8 on thee, saith the Lord thy R·.
59: 20 And the R· shall come to Zion, and
60: 16 Lord am thy Saviour and thy R·,
63: 16 thou, O Lord, art our father, our r·;
Jer 50: 34 Their R· is strong; The Lord of

redeemeth
Ps 34: 22 Lord r· the soul of his servants:
103: 4 Who r· thy life from destruction;

redeeming
Ru 4: 7 concerning r· and concerning
Eph 5: 16 R· the time, because the days are
Col 4: 5 them that are without, r· the time.

redemption
Le 25: 24 ye shall grant a r· for the land.
51 shall give again the price of his r·
52 give him again the price of his r·.
Nu 3: 49 Moses took the r· money of them
Ps 49: 8 (For the r· of their soul is precious,
111: 9 He sent r· unto his people: he
130: 7 mercy, and with him is plenteous r·.
Jer 32: 7 the right of r· is thine to buy it.
8 the r· is thine; buy it for thyself.
Lu 2: 38 that looked for r· in Jerusalem.
21: 28 heads; for your r· draweth nigh.
Ro 3: 24 through the r· that is in Christ Jesus:
8: 23 adoption, to wit, the r· of our body.
1Co 1: 30 and sanctification, and r·:
Eph 1: 7 whom we have r· through his blood,
14 the r· of the purchased possession,
4: 30 ye are sealed unto the day of r·.
Col 1: 14 whom we have r· through his blood,
Heb 9: 12 having obtained eternal r· for us.
15 for the r· of the transgressions that

redness
Pr 23: 29 cause? who hath r· of eyes?

redound
2Co 4: 15 of many r· to the glory of God.

Red-sea See RED and SEA.

reed See also REEDS.
1Ki 14: 15 as a r· is shaken in the water,
2Ki 18: 21 upon the staff of this bruised r·,
Job 40: 21 shady trees, in the covert of the r·,
Isa 36: 6 in the staff of this broken r·, on
42: 3 A bruised r· shall he not break, and
Eze 29: 6 a staff of r· to the house of Israel.
40: 3 in his hand, and a measuring r·;
5 a measuring r· of six cubits long
5 the breadth of the building, one r·;
5 and the height, one r·.
6 of the gate, which was one r· broad;
6 the gate, which was one r· broad.
7 was one r· long, and one r· broad;
7 porch of the gate within was one r·.
8 the porch of the gate within, one r·.
41: 8 were a full r· of six great cubits.
42: 16 east side with the measuring r·,
16, 17 the measuring r· round about,
18 reeds, with the measuring r·.
19 reeds with the measuring r·.
M't 11: 7 to see? A r· shaken with the wind?
12: 20 A bruised r· shall he not break, and
27: 29 head, and a r· in his right hand:
30 took the r·, and smote him on the
48 it with vinegar, and put it on a r·,
M'r 15: 19 smote him on the head with a r·,
36 full of vinegar, and put it on a r·,
Lu 7: 24 to see? A r· shaken with the wind?
Re 11: 1 was given me a r· like unto a rod:
21: 15 talked with me had a golden r· to
16 he measured the city with the r·,

reeds
Isa 19: 6 up: the r· and flags shall wither.
7 The paper r· by the brooks, by the
35: 7 shall be grass with r· and rushes.
Jer 51: 32 the r· they have burned with fire,
Eze 42: 16 measuring reed, five hundred r·,
17 the north side, five hundred r·,
18 the south side, five hundred r·,
19 side, and measured five hundred r·
20 round about, five hundred r· long,
45: 1 length of five and twenty thousand r·,
48: 8 five and twenty thousand r· in breadth,

reel
Ps 107: 27 They r· to and fro, and stagger
Isa 24: 20 earth shall r· to and fro like a

Reelaiah *(re-el-ah'-yah)*
Ezr 2: 2 Seraiah, R·, Mordecai, Bilshan,

refine See also REFINED.
Zec 13: 9 will r· them as silver is refined,

refined
1Ch 28: 18 for the altar of incense r· gold
29: 4 seven thousand talents of r· silver,
Isa 25: 6 of wines on the lees well r·.
48: 10 I have r· thee, but not with silver;
Zec 13: 9 and will refine them as silver is r·,

refiner See also REFINER'S.
Mal 3: 3 he shall sit as a r· and purifier of

refiner's
Mal 3: 2 for he is like a r· fire, and like

reformation
Heb 9: 10 on them until the time of r·.

reformed
Le 26: 23 if ye will not be r· by me by these

refrain See also REFRAINED; REFRAINETH.
Ge 45: 1 Joseph could not r· himself before
Job 7: 11 I will not r· my mouth; I will
Pr 1: 15 them; r· thy foot from their path:
Ec 3: 5 and a time to r· from embracing;
Isa 48: 9 for my praise will I r· for thee,
64: 12 Wilt thou r· thyself for these things,
Jer 31: 16 R· thy voice from weeping, and
Ac 5: 38 R· from these men, and let them
1Pe 3: 10 let him r· his tongue from evil,

refrained
Ge 43: 31 r· himself, and said, Set on bread.
Es 5: 10 Nevertheless Haman r· himself:
Job 29: 9 The princes r· talking, and laid
Ps 40: 9 I have not r· my lips, O Lord, thou
119: 101 r· my feet from every evil way,
Isa 42: 14 I have been still, and r· myself:
Jer 14: 10 they have not r· their feet,

refraineth
Pr 10: 19 sin: but he that r· his lips is wise.

refresh See also REFRESHED; REFRESHETH; REFRESHING.
1Ki 13: 7 home with me, and r· thyself,
Ac 27: 3 unto his friends to r· himself. *1958*
Ph'm 20 the Lord: r· my bowels in the Lord.

refreshed
Ex 23: 12 and the stranger, may be r·.
31: 17 seventh day he rested, and was r·.
1Sa 16: 23 so Saul was r·, and was well, and
2Sa 16: 14 weary, and r· themselves there.
Job 32: 20 I will speak, that I may be r·:
Ro 15: 32 of God, and may with you be r·.
1Co 16: 18 they have r· my spirit and yours:
2Co 7: 13 because his spirit was r· by you all.
2Ti 1: 16 he oft r· me, and was not ashamed
Ph'm 7 bowels of the saints are r· by thee,

refresheth
Pr 25: 13 for he r· the soul of his masters.

refreshing
Isa 28: 12 weary to rest; and this is the r·:
Ac 3: 19 the times of r· shall come from

refuge
Nu 35: 6 there shall be six cities for r·,
11 you cities to be cities of r· for you;
12 shall be unto you cities for r· from
13 give six cities shall ye have for r·.
14 Canaan, which shall be cities of r·.
15 These six cities shall be a r·, both
25 shall restore him to the city of his r·,
26 out the border of the city of his r·,
27 the borders of the city of his r·,
28 remained in the city of his r· until
32 him that is fled to the city of his r·,
De 33: 27 The eternal God is thy r·, and
Jos 20: 2 Appoint out for you cities of r·,
3 your r· from the avenger of blood.
21: 13, 21, 27, 32, 38 city of r· for the slayer:
2Sa 22: 3 my high tower, and my r·, my
1Ch 6: 57 Hebron, the city of r·, and Libnah
67 gave unto them, of the cities of r·,
Ps 9: 9 also will be a r· for the oppressed,
9 oppressed, a r· in times of trouble.
14: 6 poor, because the Lord is his r·.
46: 1 God is our r· and strength, a very
7, 11 us; the God of Jacob is our r·.
48: 3 is known in her palaces for a r·.
57: 1 of thy wings will I make my r·,
59: 16 and r· in the day of my trouble.
62: 7 my strength, and my r·, is in God.
8 before him: God is a r· for us.
71: 7 many; but thou art my strong r·.
91: 2 Lord, He is my r· and my fortress:
9 hast made the Lord, which is my r·,
94: 22 and my God is the rock of my r·.
104: 18 high hills are a r· for the wild goats;
142: 4 r· failed me; no man cared for
5 Thou art my r· and my portion in
Pr 14: 26 his children shall have a place of r·.
Isa 4: 6 for a place of r·, and for a covert
25: 4 a r· from the storm, a shadow from
28: 15 for we have made lies our r·,
17 hail shall sweep away the r· of lies,
Jer 16: 19 and my r· in the day of affliction,
Heb 6: 18 have fled for r· to lay hold upon the

refuse See also REFUSED; REFUSETH.
Ex 4: 23 if thou r· to let him go, behold, I
8: 2 if thou r· to let them go, behold, I
9: 2 if thou r· to let them go, and wilt
10: 3 long wilt thou r· to humble thyself
4 if thou r· to let my people go,
16: 28 r· ye to keep my commandments
22: 17 utterly r· to give her unto him,
1Sa 15: 9 every thing that was vile and r·,
Job 34: 33 whether thou r·, or whether thou
Pr 8: 33 and be wise, and r· it not.
21: 7 because they r· to do judgment.
25 him; for his hands r· to labour.
Isa 1: 20 But if ye r· and rebel, ye shall be
7: 15 that he may know to r· the evil,
16 the child shall know to r· the evil,
Jer 8: 5 hold fast deceit, they r· to return.
9: 6 through deceit they r· to know me,
13: 10 people, which r· to hear my words,
25: 28 r· to take the cup at thine hand to
38: 21 But if thou r· to go forth, this is
La 3: 45 and r· in the midst of the people.
Am 8: 6 yea, and sell the r· of the wheat?
Ac 25: 11 worthy of death, I r· not to die:
1Ti 4: 7 r· profane and old wives' fables,
5: 11 But the younger widows r·: for
Heb 12: 25 that ye r· not him that speaketh.

refused See also REFUSEDST.
Ge 37: 35 but he r· to be comforted; and he
39: 8 he r·, and said unto his master's
48: 19 his father r·, and said, I know it,
Nu 20: 21 Edom r· to give Israel passage
1Sa 8: 19 the people r· to obey the voice of
16: 7 stature; because I have r· him:
28: 23 But he r·, and said, I will not eat.
2Sa 2: 23 Howbeit he r· to turn aside:
13: 9 out before him; but he r· to eat.
1Ki 20: 35 thee. And the man r· to smite him.
21: 15 which he r· to give thee for money:
2Ki 5: 16 he urged him to take it; but he r·.
Ne 9: 17 r· to obey, neither were mindful of
Es 1: 12 Vashti r· to come at the king's
Job 6: 7 things that my soul r· to touch are

Ps 77: 2 not: my soul r' to be comforted.
78: 10 of God, and r' to walk in his law;
67 he r' the tabernacle of Joseph,
118: 22 The stone which the builders r' is
Pr 1: 24 Because I have called, and ye r';
Isa 54: 6 wife of youth, when thou wast r',
Jer 5: 3 they have r' to receive correction:
3 a rock; they have r' to return.
11: 10 which r' to hear my words; and
31: 15 r' to be comforted for her children,
50: 33 them fast; they r' to let them go.
Eze 5: 6 they have r' my judgments and
Ho 11: 5 king, because they r' to return.
Zec 7: 11 But they r' to hearken, and pulled
Ac 7: 35 Moses whom they r', saying, Who
1Ti 4: 4 God is good, and nothing to be r',
Heb 11: 24 r' to be called the son of Pharaoh's
12: 25 escaped not who r' him that spake

refusedst
Jer 3: 3 forehead, thou r' to be ashamed.

refuseth
Ex 7: 14 hardened, he r' to let the people go.
Nu 22: 13 the Lord r' to give me leave to go
14 said, Baalam r' to come with us.
De 25: 7 My husband's brother r' to raise up
Pr 10: 17 but he that r' reproof erreth.
13: 18 shall be to him that r' instruction:
15: 32 He that r' instruction despiseth
Isa 8: 6 people r' the waters of Shiloah
Jer 15: 18 incurable, which r' to be healed?

regard See also REGARDED; REGARDEST; REGARDETH; REGARDING.
Ge 45: 20 Also r' not your stuff;
Ex 5: 9 and let them not r' vain words.
Le 19: 31 R' not them that have familiar
De 28: 50 shall not r' the person of the old,
1Sa 4: 20 answered not, neither did she r' it.
25: 25 I pray thee, r' this man of Belial,
2Sa 13: 20 is thy brother; r' not this thing.
2Ki 3: 14 I r' the presence of Jehoshaphat
Job 3: 4 let not God r' it from above,
35: 13 neither will the Almighty r' it.
36: 21 Take heed, r' not iniquity: for
Ps 28: 5 they r' not the works of the Lord,
31: 6 hated them that r' lying vanities:
66: 18 If I r' iniquity in my heart, the
94: 7 neither shall the God of Jacob r' it.
102: 17 will r' the prayer of the destitute,
Pr 5: 2 That thou mayest r' discretion,
6: 35 He will not r' any ransom;
Ec 8: 2 that in r' of the oath of God.
Isa 5: 12 they r' not the work of the Lord,
13: 17 which shall not r' silver; and as
La 4: 16 he will no more r' them: they
Da 11: 37 shall he r' the God of his fathers,
37 desire of women, nor r' any god:
Am 5: 22 will I r' the peace offerings of
Hab 1: 5 and r', and wonder marvellously:
Mal 1: 9 means: will he r' your persons?
Lu 18: 4 I fear not God, nor r' man;
Ac 8: 11 to him they had r', because that
Ro 14: 6 day, to the Lord he doth not r' it.

regarded
Ex 9: 21 that r' not the word of the Lord
1Ki 18: 29 nor any to answer, nor any that r'.
1Ch 17: 17 r' me according to the estate of a
Ps 106: 44 Nevertheless he r' their affliction,
Pr 1: 24 out my hand, and no man r';
Da 3: 12 men, O king, have not r' thee:
Lu 1: 48 he hath r' the low estate of his
18: 2 feared not God, neither r' man:
Heb 8: 9 and I r' them not, saith the Lord.

regardest
2Sa 19: 6 thou r' neither princes nor servants:
Job 30: 20 I stand up, and thou r' me not.
M't 22: 16 for thou r' not the person of men.
M'r 12: 14 for thou r' not the person of men,

regardeth
De 10: 17 r' not persons, nor taketh reward:
Job 34: 19 nor r' the rich more than the poor?
39: 7 r' he the crying of the driver.
Pr 12: 10 man r' the life of his beast:
13: 18 that r' reproof shall be honoured.
15: 5 but he that r' reproof is prudent.
29: 7 but the wicked r' not to know it.
Ec 5: 8 that is higher than the highest r';
11: 4 that r' the clouds shall not reap.
Isa 33: 8 despised the cities, he r' no man.
Da 6: 13 of Judah, r' not thee, O king,
Mal 2: 13 he r' not the offering any more,
Ro 14: 6 r' the day, r' it unto the Lord;
6 he that r' not the day, to the Lord

regarding
Job 4: 20 perish for ever without any r' it.
Ph'p 2: 30 nigh unto death, not r' his life,

Regem (*re'-ghem*) See also REGEM-MELECH.
1Ch 2: 47 sons of Jahdai; R', and Jotham,

Regem-melech (*re''-ghem-me'-lek*)
Zec 7: 2 Sherezer and R', and their men,

regeneration
M't 19: 28 the r' when the Son of man shall
Tit 3: 5 he saved us, by the washing of r',

region See also REGIONS.
De 3: 4 all the r' of Argob, the kingdom of
13 the r' of Argob, with all Bashan,
1Ki 4: 11 of Abinadab, in all the r' of Dor;
13 r' of Argob, which is in Bashan,
24 over all the r' on this side the river,
M't 3: 5 and all the r' round about Jordan,
4: 16 sat in the r' and shadow of death
M'r 1: 28 all the r' round about Galilee.
6: 55 through that whole r' round about,
Lu 3: 1 and of the r' of Trachonitis, and
4: 14 through all the r' round about.
7: 17 throughout all the r' round about.
Ac 13: 49 published throughout all the r'.
14: 6 unto the r' that lieth round about:
16: 6 Phrygia and the r' of Galatia, and

regions
Ac 8: 1 throughout the r' of Judæa and
2Co 10: 16 preach the gospel in the r' beyond
11: 10 this boasting in the r' of Achaia.
Ga 1: 21 I came into the r' of Syria and

register
Ezr 2: 62 sought their r' among those that
Ne 7: 5 I found a r' of the genealogy of
64 sought their r' among those that

Rehabiah (*re-hab-i'-ah*)
1Ch 23: 17 sons of Eliezer were, R' the chief.
17 but the sons of R' were very many.
24: 21 Concerning R': of the sons of R',
26: 25 R' his son, and Jeshaiah his son,

rehearse See also REHEARSED.
Ex 17: 14 and r' it in the ears of Joshua:
J'g 5: 11 shall they r' the righteous acts of

rehearsed
1Sa 8: 21 he r' them in the ears of the Lord.
17: 31 spake, they r' them before Saul:
Ac 11: 4 But Peter r' the matter from the
14: 27 they r' all that God had done with

Rehob (*re'-hob*) See also BETH-REHOB.
Nu 13: 21 from the wilderness of Zin unto R',
Jos 19: 28 Hebron, and R', and Hammon, and
30 Ummah also, and Aphek, and R':
21: 31 suburbs, and R' with her suburbs;
J'g 1: 31 of Helbah, nor of Aphik, nor of R':
2Sa 8: 3 also Hadadezer, the son of R', king
12 spoil of Hadadezer, the son of R',
10: 8 Syrians of Zobah, and of R', and
1Ch 6: 75 suburbs, and R' with her suburbs:
Ne 10: 11 Micha, R', Hashabiah,

Rehoboam (*re-ho-bo'-am*) See also ROBOAM.
1Ki 11: 43 R' his son reigned in his stead.
12: 1 R' went to Shechem: for all Israel
3 of Israel came, and spake unto R',
6 king R' consulted with the old men,
12 the people came to R' the third day,
17 of Judah, R' reigned over them.
18 king R' sent Adoram, who was over
18 king R' made speed to get him up
21 when R' was come to Jerusalem,
21 to bring the kingdom again to R'
23 Speak unto R', the son of Solomon,
27 lord, even unto R' king of Judah,
27 and go again to R' king of Judah.
14: 21 R' the son of Solomon reigned in
21 R' was forty and one years old when
25 to pass in the fifth year of king R',
27 king R' made in their stead brasen
29 Now the rest of the acts of R', and
30 was war between R' and Jeroboam
31 And R' slept with his fathers, and
15: 6 was war between R' and Jeroboam
1Ch 3: 10 Solomon's son was R', Abia his son,
2Ch 9: 31 and R' his son reigned in his stead.
10: 1 And R' went to Shechem: for to
3 all Israel came and spake to R',
6 R' took counsel with the old men
12 and all the people came to R' on
13 R' forsook the counsel of the old
17 of Judah, R' reigned over them.
18 R' sent Hadoram that was over the
18 R' made speed to get him up to his
11: 1 when R' was come to Jerusalem,
1 bring the kingdom again to R'.
3 Speak unto R' the son of Solomon,
5 R' dwelt in Jerusalem, and built
17 made R' the son of Solomon strong,
18 R' took him Mahalath the daughter
21 R' loved Maachah the daughter of
22 R' made Abijah the son of Maachah
12: 1 R' had established the kingdom,
2 that in the fifth year of king R'
5 came Shemaiah the prophet to R',
10 king R' made shields of brass, and
13 So king R' strengthened himself in
13 for R' was one and forty years old
15 Now the acts of R', first and last,
15 wars between R' and Jeroboam
16 R' slept with his fathers, and was
13: 7 strengthened themselves against R'
7 R' was young and tenderhearted,

Rehoboth (*re'-ho-both*)
Ge 10: 11 Nineveh, and the city R', and
26: 22 and he called the name of it R';
36: 37 Saul of R' by the river reigned in
1Ch 1: 48 Shaul of R' by the river reigned in

Rehum (*re'-hum*) See also NEHUM.
Ezr 2: 2 Mizpar, Bigvai, R', Baanah.
4: 8 R' the chancellor and Shimshai
9 Then wrote R' the chancellor, and
17 an answer unto R' the chancellor,
23 letter was read before R', and
Ne 3: 17 the Levites, R' the son of Bani.
10: 25 R', Hashabnah, Maaseiah,
12: 3 Shechaniah, R', Meremoth,

Rei (*re'-i*)
1Ki 1: 8 the prophet, and Shimei, and R',

reign See also REIGNED; REIGNEST; REIGNETH; REIGNING.
Ge 37: 8 him, Shalt thou indeed r' over us?
Ex 15: 18 The Lord shall r' for ever and ever.
Le 26: 17 that hate you shall r' over you;
De 15: 6 thou shalt r' over many nations,
6 but they shall not r' over thee.
J'g 9: 2 threescore and ten persons, r' over
2 you, or that one r' over you?
8 the olive tree, R' thou over us.
10 fig tree, Come thou, and r' over us.
12 the vine, Come thou, and r' over us.
14 bramble, Come thou, and r' over us.
1Sa 8: 7 me, that I should not r' over them.
9 of the king that shall r' over them.
11 of the king that shall r' over you:
9: 17 this same shall r' over my people.
11: 12 that said, Shall Saul r' over us?
12: 12 Nay; but a king shall r' over us:
2Sa 2: 10 forty years old when he began to r'
3: 21 r' over all that thine heart desireth.
5: 4 thirty years old when he began to r',
1Ki 1: 11 not heard that Adonijah...doth r',
13 Solomon thy son shall r' after me,
13 throne? why then doth Adonijah r'?
17 Solomon thy son shall r' after me,
24 Adonijah shall r' after me, and he
30 Solomon thy son shall r' after me,
2: 15 their faces on me, that I should r':
6: 1 year of Solomon's r' over Israel,
11: 37 r' according to all that thy soul
14: 21 one years old when he began to r',
15: 25 And Nadab...began to r' over Israel
33 began Baasha...to r' over all Israel
16: 8 began Elah...to r' over Israel in
11 came to pass, when he began to r',
15 did Zimri r' seven days in Tirzah.
23 began Omri to r' over Israel, twelve
29 began Ahab...to r' over Israel:
22: 41 Jehoshaphat...to r' over Judah
42 five years old when he began to r';
51 Ahaziah...began to r' over Israel
2Ki 3: 1 Jehoram...began to r' over Israel
8: 16 Jehoram the son...began to r'.
17 old was he when he began to r';
25 did Ahaziah...begin to r'.
26 was Ahaziah when he began to r';
9: 29 began Ahaziah to r' over Judah.
11: 3 And Athaliah did r' over the land.
21 was Jehoash when he began to r'.
12: 1 year of Jehu Jehoash began to r';
13: 1 son of Jehu Jehoash began to r' over Israel
10 began Jehoash...to r' over Israel in
14: 2 five years old when he began to r',
23 Jeroboam...began to r' in Samaria,
15: 1 son of Amaziah king of Judah to r'.
2 old was he when he began to r',
8 did Zachariah...r' over Israel in
13 Shallum...son of Jabesh began to r'
17 the son of Gadi to r' over Israel,
23 Pekahiah...began to r' over Israel
27 Pekah...began to r' over Israel
32 son of Uzziah king of Judah to r'.
33 old was he when he began to r',
16: 1 Ahaz...son of Jotham...began to r'.
2 old was Ahaz when he began to r',
17: 1 began Hoshea...to r' in Samaria
18: 1 that Hezekiah...began to r'.
2 old was he when he began to r';
21: 1 twelve years old...he began to r',
19 two years old when he began to r',
22: 1 eight years old when he began to r',
23: 31 years old when he began to r';
33 that he might not r' in Jerusalem;
36 five years old when he began to r';
24: 8 years old when he began to r',
12 him in the eighth year of his r'.
18 one years old when he began to r',
25: 1 to pass in the ninth year of his r',
27 in the year that he began to r' did
1Ch 4: 31 their cities unto the r' of David.
26: 31 the fortieth year of the r' of David
29: 30 With all his r' and his might, and
2Ch 1: 8 hast made me to r' in his stead.
3: 2 month, in the fourth year of his r'.
12: 13 years old when he began to r',
13: 1 began Abijah to r' over Judah.
15: 10 the fifteenth year of the r' of Asa.
19 and thirtieth year of the r' of Asa.
16: 1 and thirtieth year of the r' of Asa
12 the thirty and ninth year of his r'
13 the one and fortieth year of his r'.
17: 7 third year of his r' he sent to his
20: 31 five years old when he began to r',
21: 5 two years old when he began to r',
20 old was he when he began to r',
22: 2 was Ahaziah when he began to r',
23: 3 Behold, the king's son shall r', as
24: 1 seven years old when he began to r',
25: 1 five years old when he began to r',
26: 3 was Uzziah when he began to r',
27: 1 five years old when he began to r',
8 years old when he began to r',
28: 1 years old when he began to r',
29: 1 Hezekiah began to r' when he was
3 He in the first year of his r', in the
19 king Ahaz in his r' did cast away
33: 1 years old when he began to r',
21 years old when he began to r',
34: 1 eight years old when he began to r',
3 in the eighth year of his r', while
8 the eighteenth year of his r', when
35: 19 eighteenth year of the r' of Josiah
36: 2 years old when he began to r',
5 five years old when he began to r',
9 eight years old when he began to r',
11 years old when he began to r',
20 the r' of the kingdom of Persia:
Ezr 4: 5 the r' of Darius king of Persia.

Ezr 4: 6 And in the r· of Ahasuerus, in the
6 in the beginning of his r·, wrote
24 the second year of the r· of Darius
6: 15 in the sixth year of the r· of Darius
7: 1 in the r· of Artaxerxes king of
8: 1 in the r· of Artaxerxes the king.
Ne 12: 22 to the r· of Darius the Persian.
Es 1: 3 In the third year of his r·, he made
2: 16 in the seventh year of his r·.
Job 34: 30 That the hypocrite r· not, lest the
Ps 146: 10 The Lord shall r· for ever, even thy
Pr 8: 15 By me kings r·, and princes decree
Ec 4: 14 For out of prison he cometh to r·;
Isa 24: 23 the Lord of hosts shall r· in mount
32: 1 a king shall r· in righteousness,
Jer 1: 2 in the thirteenth year of his r·.
22: 15 Shalt thou r·, because thou closest
23: 5 and a King shall r· and prosper,
26: 1 beginning of the r· of Jehoiakim
27: 1 beginning of the r· of Jehoiakim
28: 1 the beginning of the r· of Zedekiah
33: 21 have a son to r· upon his throne;
49: 34 the r· of Zedekiah king of Judah,
51: 59 in the fourth year of his r·.
52: 1 years old when he began to r·,
4 to pass in the ninth year of his r·,
31 in the first year of his r· lifted up
Da 1: 1 third year of the r· of Jehoiakim
2: 1 year of the r· of Nebuchadnezzar
6: 28 this Daniel prospered in the r· of
28 and in the r· of Cyrus the Persian.
8: 1 year of the r· of king Belshazzar
9: 2 In the first year of his r· I Daniel
Mic 4: 7 shall r· over them in mount Zion
M't 2: 22 that Archelaus did r· in Judæa in
Lu 1: 33 r· over the house of Jacob for ever;
3: 1 year of the r· of Tiberius Cæsar,
19: 14 not have this man to r· over us.
27 would not that I should r· over them,
Ro 5: 17 shall r· in life by one, Jesus Christ.)
21 grace r· through righteousness unto
6: 12 Let not sin...r· in your mortal body.
15: 12 shall rise to r· over the Gentiles;
1Co 4: 8 us: and I would to God ye did r·,
8 that we also might r· with you.
15: 25 For he must r·, till he hath put all
2Ti 2: 12 suffer, we shall also r· with him:
Re 5: 10 and we shall r· on the earth.
11: 15 and he shall r· for ever and ever.
20: 6 shall r· with him a thousand years.
22: 5 and they shall r· for ever and ever.

reigned
Ge 36: 31 kings that r· in the land of Edom,
31 before there r· any king over the
32 Bela the son of Beor r· in Edom:
33 and Jobab...r· in his stead.
34 and Husham...r· in his stead.
35 and Hadad...r· in his stead:
36 Samlah of Masrekah r· in his stead.
37 died, and Saul... r· in his stead.
38 the son of Achbor r· in his stead.
39 died, and Hadar r· in his stead:
Jos 12: 5 And r· in mount Hermon, and in
13: 10 Amorites, which r· in Heshbon,
12 which r· in Ashtaroth and in Edrei,
21 the Amorites, which r· in Heshbon,
J'g 4: 2 king of Canaan, that r· in Hazor;
9: 22 Abimelech had r· three years over
1Sa 13: 1 Saul r· one year; and when he had
1 he had r· two years over Israel,
2Sa 2: 10 reign over Israel, and r· two years.
5: 4 to reign, and he r· forty years.
5 he r· over Judah seven years and
5 he r· thirty and three years over
8: 15 And David r· over all Israel; and
10: 1 and Hanun his son r· in his stead.
16: 8 Saul, in whose stead thou hast r·;
1Ki 2: 11 that David r· over Israel were forty
11 seven years r· he in Hebron, and
11 and three years r· he in Jerusalem.
4: 21 And Solomon r· over all kingdoms
11: 24 dwelt therein, and r· in Damascus.
25 abhorred Israel, and r· over Syria.
42 Solomon r· in Jerusalem over all
43 Rehoboam his son r· in his stead.
12: 17 of Judah, Rehoboam r· over them.
14: 19 how he warred, and how he r·,
20 the days which Jeroboam r· were
20 and Nadab his son r· in his stead.
21 And Rehoboam...r· in Judah.
21 he r· seventeen years in Jerusalem,
31 And Abijam his son r· in his stead.
15: 1 son of Nebat r· Abijam over Judah.
2 Three years r· he in Jerusalem.
8 and Asa his son r· in his stead.
9 king of Israel r· Asa over Judah.
10 and one years r· he in Jerusalem.
24 Jehoshaphat his son r· in his stead.
25 Judah, and r· over Israel two years.
28 slay him, and r· in his stead.
29 it came to pass, when he r·, that he
16: 6 and Elah his son r· in his stead.
10 king of Judah, and r· in his stead.
22 so Tibni died, and Omri r·.
23 years: six years r· he in Tirzah.
28 and Ahab his son r· in his stead.
29 Ahab the son of Omri r· over Israel
22: 40 Ahaziah his son r· in his stead.
42 and he r· twenty and five years in
50 Jehoram his son r· in his stead.
51 Judah, and r· two years over Israel.
2Ki 1: 17 And Jehoram r· in his stead in the
3: 1 king of Judah, and r· twelve years.
27 that should have r· in his stead,
8: 15 he died: and Hazael r· in his stead.

2Ki 8: 17 and he r· eight years in Jerusalem.
24 and Ahaziah his son r· in his stead.
26 and he r· one year in Jerusalem.
10: 35 Jehoahaz his son r· in his stead.
36 the time that Jehu r· over Israel
12: 1 and forty years r· he in Jerusalem.
21 Amaziah his son r· in his stead.
13: 1 in Samaria, and r· seventeen years.
9 and Joash his son r· in his stead.
10 in Samaria, and r· sixteen years.
24 Ben-hadad his son r· in his stead.
14: 1 r· Amaziah the son of Joash king
2 and r· twenty and nine years in
16 Jeroboam his son r· in his stead.
23 Samaria, and r· forty and one years.
29 Zachariah his son r· in his stead.
15: 2 and he r· two and fifty years in
7 and Jotham his son r· in his stead.
10 and slew him, and r· in his stead.
13 and he r· a full month in Samaria.
14 and slew him, and r· in his stead.
17 Israel, and r· ten years in Samaria.
22 Pekahiah his son r· in his stead.
23 Israel in Samaria, and r· two years.
25 he killed him, and r· in his room.
27 in Samaria, and r· twenty years.
30 and slew him, and r· in his stead,
33 he r· sixteen years in Jerusalem.
38 and Ahaz his son r· in his stead.
16: 2 and r· sixteen years in Jerusalem,
20 Hezekiah his son r· in his stead.
18: 2 and he r· twenty and nine years in
19: 37 Esarhaddon his son r· in his stead.
20: 21 Manasseh his son r· in his stead.
21: 1 r· fifty and five years in Jerusalem.
18 and Amon his son r· in his stead.
19 and he r· two years in Jerusalem.
26 and Josiah his son r· in his stead.
22: 1 and he r· thirty and one years in
23: 31 he r· three months in Jerusalem.
36 he r· eleven years in Jerusalem.
24: 6 Jehoiachin his son r· in his stead.
8 he r· in Jerusalem three months.
18 he r· eleven years in Jerusalem.
1Ch 1: 43 kings that r· in the land of Edom
43 before any king r· over the children
44 Jobab the son...r· in his stead.
45 Husham...r· in his stead.
46 Hadad the son...r· in his stead.
47 Samlah of Masrekah r· in his stead.
48 Shaul of Rehoboth...r· in his stead.
49 the son of Achbor r· in his stead.
50 was dead, Hadad r· in his stead:
3: 4 he r· seven years and six months:
4 he r· thirty and three years.
18: 14 So David r· over all Israel, and
19: 1 died, and his son r· in his stead.
29: 26 David the son...r· over all Israel.
27 he r· over Israel was forty years;
27 seven years r· he in Hebron, and
27 and three years r· he in Jerusalem.
28 and Solomon his son r· in his stead.
2Ch 1: 13 congregation, and r· over Israel.
9: 26 And he r· over all the kings from
30 Solomon r· in Jerusalem over all
31 Rehoboam his son r· in his stead.
10: 17 of Judah, Rehoboam r· over them.
12: 13 himself in Jerusalem, and r·: for
13 he r· seventeen years in Jerusalem,
16 and Abijah his son r· in his stead.
13: 2 He r· three years in Jerusalem.
14: 1 and Asa his son r· in his stead.
17: 1 Jehoshaphat his son r· in his stead,
20: 31 And Jehoshaphat r· over Judah: he
31 he r· twenty and five years in
21: 1 Jehoram his son r· in his stead.
5 and he r· eight years in Jerusalem.
20 and he r· in Jerusalem eight years,
22: 1 son of Jehoram king of Judah r·.
2 and he r· one year in Jerusalem.
12 and Athaliah r· over the land.
24: 1 and he r· forty years in Jerusalem.
27 Amaziah his son r· in his stead.
25: 1 and he r· twenty and nine years in
26: 3 r· fifty and two years in Jerusalem.
23 and Jotham his son r· in his stead.
27: 1 he r· sixteen years in Jerusalem.
8 and r· sixteen years in Jerusalem.
9 and Ahaz his son r· in his stead.
28: 1 he r· sixteen years in Jerusalem:
27 Hezekiah his son r· in his stead.
29: 1 and he r· nine and twenty years in
32: 33 Manassah his son r· in his stead.
33: 1 and he r· fifty and five years in
20 and Amon his son r· in his stead.
21 and r· two years in Jerusalem.
34: 1 he r· in Jerusalem one and thirty
36: 2 he r· three months in Jerusalem.
5 he r· eleven years in Jerusalem:
8 Jehoiachin his son r· in his stead.
9 he r· three months and ten days in
11 and r· eleven years in Jerusalem.
Es 1: 1 (this is Ahasuerus which r·, from
Isa 37: 38 Esar-haddon his son r· in his stead.
Jer 22: 11 r· instead of Josiah his father,
37: 1 Zedekiah...r· instead of Coniah
52: 1 he r· eleven years in Jerusalem.
Ro 5: 14 death r· from Adam to Moses, even
17 one man's offence death r· by one;
21 as sin hath r· unto death, even so
1Co 4: 8 ye have r· as kings without us:
Re 11: 17 thee thy great power, and hast r·.
20: 4 and r· with Christ a thousand years.

reignest
1Ch 29: 12 come of thee, and thou r· over all;

reigneth
1Sa 12: 14 and also the king that r· over you
2Sa 15: 10 shall say, Absalom r· in Hebron.
1Ki 1: 18 now, behold, Adonijah r·; and now,
1Ch 16: 31 among the nations, The Lord r·.
Ps 47: 8 God r· over the heathen: God
93: 1 The Lord r·, he is clothed with
96: 10 the heathen that the Lord r·:
97: 1 The Lord r·; let the earth rejoice;
99: 1 The Lord r·; let the people
Pr 30: 22 For a servant when he r·; and a
Isa 52: 7 that saith unto Zion, Thy God r·!
Re 17: 18 which r· over the kings of the
19: 6 for the Lord God omnipotent r·.

reigning
1Sa 16: 1 rejected him from r· over Israel?

reins
Job 16: 13 he cleaveth my r· asunder, and
19: 27 my r· be consumed within me.
Ps 7: 9 God trieth the hearts and r·.
16: 7 my r· also instruct me in the night
26: 2 prove me; try my r· and my heart.
73: 21 grieved, and I was pricked in my r·.
139: 13 For thou hast possessed my r·:
Pr 23: 16 my r· shall rejoice, when thy lips
Isa 11: 5 faithfulness the girdle of his r·.
Jer 11: 20 that triest the r· and the heart,
12: 2 their mouth, and far from their r·.
17: 10 Lord search the heart, I try the r·,
20: 12 that seest the r· and the heart, let
La 3: 13 of his quiver to enter into my r·.
Re 2: 23 which searcheth the r· and hearts:

reject See also REJECTED; REJECTETH.
Ho 4: 6 I will also r· thee, and thou shalt
M'r 6: 26 sat with him, he would not r· her.
7: 9 well ye r· the commandment of God,
Tit 3: 10 first and second admonition r·;

rejected
1Sa 8: 7 they have not r· thee, but they
7 they have r· me, that I should not
10: 19 And ye have this day r· your God,
15: 23 thou hast r· the word of the Lord,
23 hath also r· thee from being king.
26 thou hast r· the word of the Lord,
26 Lord hath r· thee from being king
16: 1 r· him from reigning over Israel?
2Ki 17: 15 And they r· his statutes, and his
20 the Lord r· all the seed of Israel,
Isa 53: 3 He is despised and r· of men; a
Jer 2: 37 the Lord hath r· thy confidences,
6: 19 my words, nor to my law, but r· it.
30 because the Lord hath r· them.
7: 29 the Lord hath r· and forsaken the
8: 9 they have r· the word of the Lord;
14: 19 Hast thou utterly r· Judah? hath
La 5: 22 thou hast utterly r· us; thou art
Ho 4: 6 because thou hast r· knowledge, I
M't 21: 42 The stone which the builders r·,
M'r 8: 31 and be r· of the elders, and of the
12: 10 The stone which the builders r· is
Lu 7: 30 and lawyers r· the counsel of God
9: 22 be r· of the elders and chief priests
17: 25 things, and be r· of this generation.
20: 17 The stone which the builders r·,
Ga 4: 14 in my flesh ye despised not, nor r·;
Heb 6: 8 beareth thorns and briers is r·,
12: 17 inherited the blessing, he was r·:

rejecteth
Joh 12: 48 He that r· me, and receiveth not

rejoice See also REJOICED; REJOICEST; REJOICETH; REJOICING.
Le 23: 40 shall r· before the Lord your God
De 12: 7 shall r· in all that ye put your hand
12 shall r· before the Lord your God,
18 shalt r· before the Lord your God
14: 26 and thou shalt r·, thou, and thine
16: 11 shalt r· before the Lord thy God,
14 thou shalt r· in thy feast, thou, and
15 therefore thou shalt surely r·.
26: 11 thou shalt r· in every good thing
27: 7 and r· before the Lord thy God.
28: 63 Lord will r· over you to destroy
30: 9 will again r· over thee for good,
32: 43 R·, O ye nations, with his people:
33: 18 R·, Zebulun, in thy going out;
J'g 9: 19 this day, then r· ye in Abimelech,
19 and let him also r· in you:
16: 23 unto Dagon their god, and to r·:
1Sa 2: 1 because I r· in thy salvation.
19: 5 thou sawest it, and didst r·:
2Sa 1: 20 the daughters of the Philistines r·,
1Ch 16: 10 heart of them r· that seek the Lord.
31 be glad, and let the earth r·:
32 let the fields r·, and all that is
2Ch 6: 41 and let thy saints r· in goodness.
20: 27 made them to r· over their enemies.
Ne 12: 43 had made them r· with great joy:
Job 3: 22 Which r· exceedingly, and are glad,
20: 18 be, and he shall not r· therein.
21: 12 and r· at the sound of the organ.
Ps 2: 11 with fear, and r· with trembling.
5: 11 that put their trust in thee r·:
9: 2 I will be glad and r· in thee: I will
14 of Zion: I will r· in thy salvation.
13: 4 trouble me r· when I am moved.
5 my heart shall r· in thy salvation.
14: 7 Jacob shall r·, and Israel shall be
20: 5 We will r· in thy salvation, and in
21: 1 salvation how greatly shall he r·!
30: 1 not made my foes to r· over me.
31: 7 I will be glad and r· in thy mercy:
32: 11 Be glad in the Lord, and r·, ye

Ps 33: 1 R· in the Lord, O ye righteous:
21 For our heart shall r· in him.
35: 9 Lord: it shall r· in his salvation.
19 enemies wrongfully r· over me:
24 and let them not r· over me.
26 together that r· at mine hurt:
38: 16 otherwise they should r· over me:
40: 16 Let all those that seek thee r·
48: 11 Let mount Zion r·, let the
51: 8 bones...thou hast broken may r·.
53: 6 Jacob shall r·, and Israel shall be
58: 10 righteous shall r· when he seeth
60: 6 I will r·, I will divide Shechem,
63: 7 the shadow of thy wings will I r·.
11 But the king shall r· in God;
65: 8 outgoings of the morning...to r·.
12 the little hills r· on every side.
66: 6 on foot: there did we r· in him.
68: 3 be glad; let them r· before God:
3 yea, let them exceedingly r·.
4 name Jah, and r· before him.
70: 4 Let all those that seek thee r· and
71: 23 My lips shall greatly r· when I sing
85: 6 that thy people may r· in thee?
86: 4 R· the soul of thy servant: for unto
89: 12 and Hermon shall r· in thy name.
16 thy name shall they r· all the day:
42 hast made all his enemies to r·.
90: 14 we may r· and be glad all our days.
96: 11 Let the heavens r·, and let the
12 shall all the trees of the wood r·
97: 1 Lord reigneth; let the earth r·;
12 R· in the Lord, ye righteous; and
98: 4 make a loud noise, and r·, and
104: 31 the Lord shall r· in his works.
105: 3 heart of them r· that seek the Lord.
106: 5 may r· in the gladness of thy nation,
107: 42 The righteous shall see it, and r·:
108: 7 I will r·, I will divide Shechem,
109: 28 ashamed; but let thy servant r·.
118: 24 made; we will r· and be glad in it.
119: 162 I r· at thy word, as one that
149: 2 Israel r· in him that made him:
Pr 2: 14 Who r· to do evil, and delight
5: 18 and r· with the wife of thy youth.
23: 15 wise, my heart shall r·, even mine.
16 Yea, my reins shall r·, when thy
24 father of the righteous shall...r·:
25 and she that bare thee shall r·.
24: 17 R· not when thine enemy falleth,
27: 9 Ointment and perfume r· the heart:
28: 12 When righteous men do r·, there
29: 2 are in authority, the people r·:
6 but the righteous doth sing and r·.
31: 25 and she shall r· in time to come.
Ec 3: 12 but for a man to r·, and to do good
22 a man should r· in his own works;
4: 16 that come after shall not r· in him.
5: 19 his portion, and to r· in his labour;
11: 8 live many years, and r· in them all;
9 R·, O young man, in thy youth;
Ca 1: 4 we will be glad and r· in thee, we
Isa 8: 6 r· in Rezin and Remaliah's son;
9: 3 men r· when they divide the spoil.
13: 3 even them that r· in my highness.
14: 8 Yea, the fir trees r· at thee, and
29 R· not thou, whole Palestina,
23: 12 Thou shalt no more r·, O thou
24: 8 the noise of them that r· endeth,
25: 9 will be glad and r· in his salvation.
29: 19 poor among men shall r· in the
35: 1 and the desert shall r·, and blossom
2 and r· even with joy and singing:
41: 16 thou shalt r· in the Lord, and shalt
61: 7 they shall r· in their portion:
10 I will greatly r· in the Lord, my
62: 5 bride, so shall thy God r· over thee.
65: 13 my servants shall r·, but ye shall
18 But be ye glad and r· for ever in
19 And I will r· in Jerusalem, and joy
66: 10 R· ye with Jerusalem, and be glad
10 r· for joy with her, all ye that
14 your heart shall r·, and your bones
Jer 31: 13 shall the virgin r· in the dance,
13 make them r· from their sorrow.
32: 41 I will r· over them to do them good,
51: 39 them drunken, that they may r·,
La 2: 17 caused thine enemy to r· over thee,
4: 21 R· and be glad, O daughter of
Eze 7: 12 let not the buyer r·, nor the seller
35: 15 As thou didst r· at the inheritance
Ho 9: 1 R· not, O Israel, for joy, as other
Joe 2: 21 Fear not, O land; be glad and r·:
23 Zion, and r· in the Lord your God:
Am 6: 13 Ye which r· in a thing of nought,
Mic 7: 8 R· not against me, O mine enemy:
Hab 1: 15 therefore they r· and are glad.
3: 18 Yet I will r· in the Lord, I will joy
Zep 3: 11 of them that r· in thy pride,
14 be glad and r· with all the heart, O
17 save, he will r· over thee with joy;
Zec 2: 10 Sing and r·, O daughter of Zion:
4: 10 for they shall r·, and shall see the
9: 9 R· greatly, O daughter of Zion;
10: 7 heart shall r· as through wine:
7 their heart shall r· in the Lord.
M't 5: 12 R·, and be exceeding glad: for
Lu 1: 14 and many shall r· at his birth.
6: 23 R· ye in that day, and leap for joy:
10: 20 Notwithstanding in this r· not,
20 but rather r·, because your names
15: 6 R· with me; for I have found my
9 R· with me; for I have found the
19: 37 began to r· and praise God with a
Joh 4: 36 and he that reapeth may r· together.
5: 35 willing for a season to r· in his light.
14: 28 If ye loved me, ye would r·,
16: 20 and lament, but the world shall r·:
22 you again, and your heart shall r·,
Ac 2: 26 Therefore did my heart r·, and
Ro 5: 2 and r· in hope of the glory of God.
12: 15 R· with them that do r·, and weep
15: 10 R·, ye Gentiles, with his people.
1Co 7: 30 and they that r·, as though they
12: 26 all the members r· with it.
2Co 2: 3 from them of whom I ought to r·;
7: 9 I r·, not that ye were made sorry,
16 I r· therefore that I have confidence
Ga 4: 27 R·, thou barren that bearest not;
Ph'p 1: 18 I therein do r·, yea, and will r·.
2: 16 that I may r· in the day of Christ,
17 faith, I joy, and r· with you all.
18 cause also do ye joy, and r· with me.
28 when ye see him again, ye may r·,
3: 1 Finally, my brethren, r· in the Lord.
3 the spirit, and r· in Christ Jesus,
4: 4 R· in the Lord alway:
4 and again I say, R·.
Col 1: 24 Who now r· in my sufferings for
1Th 5: 16 R· evermore.
Jas 1: 9 Let the brother of low degree r·
4: 16 But now ye r· in your boastings:
1Pe 1: 6 Wherein ye greatly r·, though now
8 ye r· with joy unspeakable and full
4: 13 r·, inasmuch as ye are partakers
Re 11: 10 upon the earth shall r· over them,
12: 12 r·, ye heavens, and ye that dwell
18: 20 R· over her, thou heaven, and ye
19: 7 Let us be glad and r·, and give

rejoiced
Ex 18: 9 And Jethro r· for all the goodness
De 28: 63 Lord r· over you to do you good,
30: 9 for good, as he r· over thy fathers:
J'g 19: 3 saw him, he r· to meet him.
1Sa 6: 13 and saw the ark, and r· to see it.
11: 15 and all the men of Israel r· greatly.
1Ki 1: 40 with pipes, and r· with great joy,
5: 7 words of Solomon,...he r· greatly
2Ki 11: 14 and all the people of the land r·,
20 And all the people of the land r·,
1Ch 29: 9 the people r·, for that they offered
9 David...also r· with great joy.
2Ch 15: 15 And all Judah r· at the oath: for
23: 13 and all the people of the land r·,
21 And all the people of the land r·:
24: 10 the princes and all the people r·,
29: 36 And Hezekiah r·, and all the people,
30: 25 Israel, and that dwelt in Judah, r·.
Ne 12: 43 offered great sacrifices, and r·:
43 the wives also and the children r·:
44 for Judah r· for the priests and
Es 8: 15 city of Shushan r· and was glad.
Job 31: 25 If I r· because my wealth was great,
29 If I r· at the destruction of him
Ps 35: 15 But in mine adversity they r·, and
97: 8 and the daughters of Judah r·
119: 14 r· in the way of thy testimonies,
Ec 2: 10 for my heart r· in all my labour:
Jer 15: 17 assembly of the mockers, nor r·;
50: 11 Because ye were glad, because ye r·,
Eze 25: 6 r· in heart with all thy despite
Ho 10: 5 the priests thereof that r· on it,
Ob 12 thou have r· over the children of
M't 2: 10 they r· with exceeding great joy.
Lu 1: 47 my spirit hath r· in God my Saviour.
58 upon her; and they r· with her.
10: 21 In that hour Jesus r· in spirit,
13: 17 people r· for all the glorious things
Joh 8: 56 father Abraham r· to see my day:
Ac 7: 41 r· in the works of their own hands.
15: 31 read, they r· for the consolation.
16: 34 he set meat before them, and r·,
1Co 7: 30 that rejoice, as though they r· not;
2Co 7: 7 toward me; so that I r· the more.
Ph'p 4: 10 But I r· in the Lord greatly, that
2Jo 4 I r· greatly that I found of thy
3Jo 3 For I r· greatly, when the brethren

rejoicest
Jer 11: 15 when thou doest evil, then thou r·.

rejoiceth
1Sa 2: 1 and said, My heart r· in the Lord,
Job 39: 21 the valley, and r· in his strength:
Ps 16: 9 my heart is glad, and my glory r·:
19: 5 r· as a strong man to run a race.
28: 7 therefore my heart greatly r·;
Pr 11: 10 with the righteous, the city r·:
13: 9 The light of the righteous r·: but
15: 30 The light of the eyes r· the heart:
29: 3 Whoso loveth wisdom r· his father:
Isa 5: 14 he that r·, shall descend into it.
62: 5 the bridegroom r· over the bride,
64: 5 meetest him that r· and worketh
Eze 35: 14 When the whole earth r·, I will
M't 18: 13 he r· more of that sheep, than of
Joh 3: 29 r·...because of the bridegroom's
1Co 13: 6 R· not in iniquity,
6 but r· in the truth;
Jas 2: 13 and mercy r· against judgment.

rejoicing
1Ki 1: 45 they are come up from thence r·,
2Ch 23: 18 with r· and with singing, as it was
Job 8: 21 laughing, and thy lips with r·.
Ps 19: 8 of the Lord are right, r· the heart:
45: 15 and r· shall they be brought;
107: 22 and declare his works with r·.
118: 15 The voice of r· and salvation is in
119: 111 for they are the r· of my heart.
126: 6 doubtless come again with r·,
Pr 8: 30 his delight, r· always before him;
8: 31 R· in the habitable part of his
Isa 65: 18 I create Jerusalem a r·, and her
Jer 15: 16 me the joy and r· of mine heart:
Hab 3: 14 their r· was as to devour the poor
Zep 2: 15 is the r· city that dwelt carelessly,
Lu 15: 5 he layeth it on his shoulders, r·.
Ac 5: 41 r· that they were counted worthy to
8: 39 more: and he went on his way r·.
Ro 12: 12 R· in hope; patient in tribulation;
1Co 15: 31 by your r· which I have in Christ
2Co 1: 12 For our r· is this, the testimony of
14 that we are your r·, even as ye also
6: 10 As sorrowful, yet always r·; as
Ga 6: 4 shall he have r· in himself alone,
Ph'p 1: 26 your r· may be more abundant in
1Th 2: 19 is our hope, or joy, or crown of r·?
Heb 3: 6 r· of the hope firm unto the end.
Jas 4: 16 your boastings: all such r· is evil.

Rekem (*re'-kem*)
Nu 31: 8 were slain; namely, Evi, and R·,
Jos 13: 21 the princes of Midian, Evi, and R·,
18: 27 And R·, and Irpeel, and Taralah,
1Ch 2: 43 and Tappuah, and R·, and Shema.
44 Jorkoam: and R· begat Shemmai.

release See also RELEASED.
De 15: 1 seven years thou shalt make a r·.
2 And this is the manner of the r·:
2 unto his neighbour shall r· it;
2 because it is called the Lord's r·.
3 thy brother thine hand shall r·;
9 year, the year of r·, is at hand;
31: 10 in the solemnity of the year of r·,
Es 2: 18 and he made a r· to the provinces,
M't 27: 15 to r· unto the people a prisoner,
17 will ye that I r· unto you? Barabbas,
21 the twain will ye that I r· unto you?
M'r 15: 9 I r· unto you the King of the Jews?
11 rather r· Barabbas unto them.
Lu 23: 16 therefore chastise him, and r· him.
17 must r· one unto them at the feast.)
18 this man, and r· unto us Barabbas:
20 Pilate therefore, willing to r· Jesus,
Joh 18: 39 r· unto you one at the passover:
39 I r· unto you the King of the Jews?
19: 10 thee, and have power to r· thee?
12 thenceforth Pilate sought to r· him:

released
M't 27: 26 Then r· he Barabbas unto them:
M'r 15: 6 feast he r· unto them one prisoner,
15 the people, r· Barabbas unto them,
Lu 23: 25 And he r· unto them him that for

relied
2Ch 13: 18 they r· upon the Lord God of their
16: 7 thou hast r· on the king of Syria,
7 and not r· on the Lord thy God,

relief
Ac 11: 29 to send r· unto the brethren

relieve See also RELIEVED; RELIEVETH.
Le 25: 35 then thou shalt r· him: yea,
Isa 1: 17 seek judgment, r· the oppressed,
La 1: 11 things for meat to r· the soul:
16 comforter that should r· my soul is
19 sought their meat to r· their souls.
1Ti 5: 16 let them r· them, and let not the
16 that it may r· them that are widows

relieved
1Ti 5: 10 feet, if she have r· the afflicted,

relieveth
Ps 146: 9 he r· the fatherless and widow:

religion
Ac 26: 5 sect of our r· I lived a Pharisee.
Ga 1: 13 in time past in the Jews' r·, how
14 profited in the Jews' r· above many
Jas 1: 26 own heart, this man's r· is vain.
27 Pure r· and undefiled before God

religious
Ac 13: 43 many of the Jews and r· proselytes
Jas 1: 26 any man among you seem to be r·,

rely See also RELIED.
2Ch 16: 8 because thou didst r· on the Lord,

remain See also REMAINED; REMAINEST; REMAINETH; REMAINING.
Ge 38: 11 R· a widow at thy father's house,
Ex 8: 9 that they may r· in the river only?
11 they shall r· in the river only.
12: 10 nothing of it r· until the morning;
23: 18 shall the fat of my sacrifice r·
29: 34 of the bread, r· unto the morning,
Le 19: 6 ought r· until the third day, it shall
25: 28 r· in the hand of him that...bought
52 r· but few years unto the year of
27: 18 according to the years that r·,
Nu 33: 55 those which ye let r· of them shall
De 2: 34 of every city, we left none to r·:
16: 4 r· all night until the morning.
19: 20 which r· shall hear, and fear, and
21: 13 and shall r· in thine house, and
23 His body shall not r· all night
Jos 1: 14 shall r· in the land which Moses
2: 11 r· any more courage in any man,
8: 22 they let none of them r· or escape.
10: 27 mouth, which remain until this very day.
28 that were therein; he let none r·:
30 were therein; he let none r· in it;
23: 4 you by lot these nations that r·,
7 nations, these that r· among you;
12 even these that r· among you, and
J'g 5: 17 and why did Dan r· in ships?
21: 7, 16 do for wives for them that r·,
1Sa 20: 19 hand, and shalt r· by the stone Ezel.
1Ki 11: 16 (For six months did Joab r· there
18: 22 I only, r· a prophet of the Lord;

2Ki 7:13 thee, five of the horses that *r*,
Ezr 9:15 for we *r* yet escaped, as it is this
Job 21:32 grave, and shall *r* in the tomb.
27:15 that *r* of him shall be buried in
37: 8 go into dens, and *r* in their places.
Ps 55: 7 far off, and *r* in the wilderness.
Pr 2:21 land, and the perfect shall *r* in it.
21:16 *r* in the congregation of the dead.
Isa 10:32 yet shall he *r* at Nob that day: he
32:16 righteousness *r* in the fruitful
44:13 man; that it may *r* in the house.
65: 4 Which *r* among the graves, and
66:22 I will make, shall *r* before me,
22 shall your seed and your name *r*.
Jer 8: 3 residue...that *r* of this evil family,
3 *r* in all the places whither I have
17:25 and this city shall *r* for ever.
24: 8 of Jerusalem, that *r* in this land,
27:11 will I let *r* still in their own land,
19 of the vessels that *r* in this city,
21 the vessels that *r* in the house of
30:18 palace shall *r* after the manner
38: 4 the men of war that *r* in this city,
42:17 none of them shall *r* or escape
44: 7 Judah, to leave you none to *r*;
14 shall escape or *r*, that they should
51:62 that none shall *r* in it, neither
Eze 7:11 none of them shall *r*, nor of their
17:21 and they that *r* shall be scattered
31:13 all the fowls of the heaven *r*,
32: 4 all the fowls of the heaven to *r*
39:14 that *r* upon the face of the earth,
Am 6: 9 if there *r* ten men in one house,
Ob 14 that did *r* in the day of distress.
Zec 5: 4 shall *r* in the midst of his house,
12:14 All the families that *r*, every
Lu 10: 7 And in the same house *r*, eating
Joh 6:12 Gather up the fragments that *r*,
15:11 that my joy might *r* in you, and
16 fruit, and that your fruit should *r*:
19:31 bodies should not *r* upon the cross
1Co 7:11 if she depart, let her *r* unmarried,
15: 6 the greater part *r* unto this present,
1Th 4:15 and *r* unto the coming of the Lord
17 are alive and *r* shall be caught up
Heb12:27 which cannot be shaken may *r*.
1Jo 2:24 from the beginning shall *r* in you,
Re 3: 2 strengthen the things which *r*,

remainder
Ex 29:34 thou shalt burn the *r* with fire:
Le 6:16 the *r* thereof shall Aaron and his
7:16 also the *r* of it shall be eaten:
17 the *r* of the flesh of the sacrifice
2Sa 14: 7 name nor *r* upon the earth.
Ps 76:10 the *r* of wrath shalt thou restrain.

remained
Ge 7:23 Noah only *r* alive, and they that
14:10 they that *r* fled to the mountain.
Ex 8:31 from his people; there *r* not one.
10:15 there *r* not any green thing in
19 *r* not one locust in all the coasts
14:28 there *r* not so much as one of them.
Nu 11:26 *r* two of the men in the camp,
35:28 have *r* in the city of his refuge
36:12 their inheritance *r* in the tribe
De 3:11 only Og king of Bashan *r* of the
4:25 ye shall have *r* long in the land,
Jos 10:20 the rest which *r* of them entered
11:22 in Gath, and in Ashdod, there *r*.
13:12 who *r* of the remnant of the giants:
18: 2 *r* among the children of Israel
21:20 which *r* of the children of Kohath,
26 of the children of Kohath that *r*.
J'g 7: 3 and there *r* ten thousand.
1Sa 11:11 they which *r* were scattered, so that
23:14 *r* in a mountain in the wilderness
24: 3 his men *r* in the sides of the cave.
2Sa 13:20 Tamar *r* desolate in her brother
1Ki 22:46 which *r* in the days of his father
2Ki 10:11 Jehu slew all that *r* of the house of
17 he slew all that *r* unto Ahab in
13: 6 there *r* the grove also in Samaria.)
24:14 none *r*, save the poorest sort of
25:22 as for the people that *r* in the land
1Ch 13:14 ark of God *r* with the family of
Ec 2: 9 also my wisdom *r* with me.
Jer 34: 7 cities *r* of the cities of Judah.
37:10 there *r* but wounded men among
16 Jeremiah had *r* there many days;
21 Thus Jeremiah *r* in the court of the
38:13 and Jeremiah *r* in the court of the
39: 9 of the people that *r* in the city,
9 with the rest of the people that *r*.
41:10 all the people that *r* in Mizpah,
48:11 therefore his taste *r* in him, and
51:30 fight, they have *r* in their holds:
52:15 of the people that *r* in the city,
La 2:22 Lord's anger none escaped nor *r*:
Eze 3:15 *r* there astonished among them
Da 10: 8 and there *r* no strength in me:
13 I *r* there with the kings of Persia.
17 there *r* no strength in me,
M't 11:23 it would have *r* until this day.
14:20 fragments that *r* twelve baskets
Lu 1:22 unto them, and *r* speechless.
9:17 that *r* to them twelve baskets.
Joh 6:13 which *r* over and above unto them
Ac 5: 4 Whiles it *r*, was it not thine own?
27:41 stuck fast, and *r* unmovable, but

remainest
La 5:19 Thou, O Lord, *r* for ever; thy
Heb 1:11 They shall perish; but thou *r*;

remaineth
Ge 8:22 While the earth *r*, seedtime and
Ex 10: 5 which *r* unto you from the hail,
12:10 which *r* of it until the morning
16:23 that which *r* over lay up for you
26:12 the remnant that *r* of the curtains
12 the half curtain that *r*, shall hang
13 *r* in the length of the curtains of
Le 8:32 And that which *r* of the flesh and
10:12 Take the meat offering that *r* of
16:16 that *r* among them in the midst
Nu 24:19 shall destroy him that *r* of...city.
Jos 8:29 heap of stones, that *r* unto this day.
13: 1 there *r* yet very much land to be
2 This is the land that yet *r*: all the
J'g 5:13 made him that *r* have dominion
1Sa 6:18 which stone *r* unto this day in the
16:11 There *r* yet the youngest, and,
1Ch 17: 1 the covenant of the Lord *r* under
Ezr 1: 4 whosoever *r* in any place where
Job 19: 4 erred, mine error *r* with myself.
21:34 your answers there *r* falsehood?
41:22 In his neck *r* strength, and
Isa 4: 3 he that *r* in Jerusalem, shall be
Jer 38: 2 He that *r* in this city shall die
47: 4 and Zidon every helper that *r*:
Eze 6:12 he that *r* and is besieged shall die
Hag 2: 5 so my spirit *r* among you: fear ye
Zec 9: 7 he that *r*, even he, shall be for
Joh 9:41 say, We see; therefore your sin *r*.
1Co 7:29 it *r*, that both they that have
2Co 3:11 more that which *r* is glorious.
14 for until this day *r* the same vail
9: 9 poor: his righteousness *r* for ever.
Heb 4: 6 it *r* that some must enter therein,
9 *r* therefore a rest to the people of
10:26 there *r* no more sacrifice for sins,
1Jo 3: 9 his seed *r* in him: and he cannot

remaining
Nu 9:22 upon the tabernacle, *r* thereon,
De 3: 3 him until none was left to him *r*.
Jos 10:33 until he had left him none *r*.
37 he left none *r*, according to all that
39 he left none *r*: as he had done to
40 left none *r*, but utterly destroyed
11: 8 them, until they left them none *r*.
21:40 *r* of the families of the Levites,
2Sa 21: 5 *r* in any of the coasts of Israel,
2Ki 10:11 priests, until he left him none *r*.
1Ch 9:33 who *r* in the chambers were free:
Job 18:19 people, nor any *r* in his dwellings.
Ob 18 not be any *r* of the house of Esau;
Joh 1:33 Spirit descending, and *r* on him,

Remaliah (*rem-a-li'-ah*) See also REMALIAH'S.
2Ki 15:25 Pekah the son of *R*, a captain of
27 Pekah the son of *R* began to reign
30 against Pekah the son of *R*, and
32 Pekah the son of *R* king of Israel
37 of Syria, and Pekah the son of *R*.
16: 1 year of Pekah the son of *R*,
5 and Pekah son of *R* king of Israel
2Ch 28: 6 Pekah the son of *R* slew in Judah
Isa 7: 1 Pekah the son of *R*, king of Israel,
4 with Syria, and of the son of *R*.
5 Syria, Ephraim, and the son of *R*,

Remaliah's (*rem-a-li'-ahs*)
Isa 7: 9 and the head of Samaria is *R* son.
8: 6 and rejoice in Rezin and *R* son;

remedy
2Ch 36:16 his people, till there was no *r*.
Pr 6:15 shall he be broken without *r*.
29: 1 be destroyed, and that without *r*.

remember See also REMEMBERED; REMEMBEREST; REMEMBERETH; REMEMBERING.
Ge 9:15 And I will *r* my covenant, which
16 I may *r* the everlasting covenant
40:23 did not the chief butler *r* Joseph,
41: 9 saying, I do *r* my faults this day:
Ex 13: 3 *R* this day, in which ye came out
20: 8 *R* the sabbath day, to keep it holy.
32:13 *R* Abraham, Isaac, and Israel, thy
Le 26:42 will I *r* my covenant with Jacob,
42 covenant with Abraham will I *r*;
42 and I will *r* the land.
45 will for their sakes *r* the covenant
Nu 11: 5 We *r* the fish, which we did eat in
15:39 and *r* all the commandments of the
40 That ye may *r*, and do all my
De 5:15 And *r* that thou wast a servant in
7:18 but shalt well *r* what the Lord thy
8: 2 And thou shalt *r* all the way which
18 thou shalt *r* the Lord thy God: for
9: 7 *R*, and forget not, how thou
27 *R* thy servants, Abraham, Isaac,
15:15 shalt *r* that thou wast a bondman
16: 3 thou mayest *r* the day when thou
12 shalt *r* that thou wast a bondman
24: 9 *R* what the Lord thy God did unto
18, 22 shalt *r*...thou wast a bondman
25:17 *R* what Amalek did unto thee by
32: 7 *R* the days of old, consider the
Jos 1:13 *R* the word which Moses the
J'g 9: 2 *r* also that I am your bone and
16:28 *r* me, I pray thee, and strengthen
1Sa 1:11 and *r* me, and not forget thine
15: 2 I *r* that which Amalek did to
25:31 my lord, then *r* thine handmaid.
2Sa 14:11 let the king *r* the Lord thy God,
19:19 neither do thou *r* that which thy
2Ki 9:25 *r* how that, when I and thou rode
20: 3 *r* now how I have walked before
1Ch 16:12 *R* his marvellous works that he
2Ch 6:42 *r* the mercies of David thy servant.
Ne 1: 8 *R*, I beseech thee, the word that
4:14 *r* the Lord, which is great and
13:14 *R* me, O my God, concerning this,
13:22 *R* me, O my God, concerning this
29 *R* them, O my God, because they
31 *R* me, O my God, for good.
Job 4: 7 *R*, I pray thee, who ever perished,
7: 7 O *r* that my life is wind: mine eye
10: 9 *R*, I beseech thee, that thou hast
11:16 and *r* it as waters that pass away:
14:13 appoint me a set time, and *r* me!
21: 6 Even when I *r* I am afraid, and
36:24 *R* that thou magnify his work,
41: 8 upon him, *r* the battle, do no more.
Ps 20: 3 *R* all thy offerings, and accept thy
7 *r* the name of the Lord our God.
22:27 All the ends of the world shall *r*
25: 6 *R*, O Lord, thy tender mercies and
7 *R* not the sins of my youth, nor
7 *r* thou me for thy goodness' sake,
42: 4 When I *r* these things, I pour out
6 I *r* thee from the land of Jordan,
63: 6 When I *r* thee upon my bed, and
74: 2 *R* thy congregation, which thou
18 *R* this, that the enemy hath
22 *r* how the foolish man reproacheth
77:10 I will *r* the years of the right hand
11 I will *r* the works of the Lord:
11 surely I will *r* thy wonders of old.
79: 8 *r* not against us former iniquities:
89:47 *R* how short my time is: wherefore
50 *R*, Lord, the reproach of thy
103:18 to those that *r* his commandments
105: 5 *R* his marvellous works that he
106: 4 *R* me, O Lord, with the favour that
119:49 *R* the word unto thy servant, upon
132: 1 *r* David, and all his afflictions:
137: 6 If I do not *r* thee, let my tongue
7 *R*, O Lord, the children of Edom
143: 5 I *r* the days of old; I meditate on
Pr 31: 7 poverty, and *r* his misery no more.
Ec 5:20 not much *r* the days of his life;
11: 8 yet let him *r* the days of darkness;
12: 1 *R* now thy Creator in the days of
Ca 1: 4 we will *r* thy love more than wine:
Isa 38: 3 *R* now, O Lord, I beseech thee,
43:18 *R* ye not the former things, neither
25 own sake, and will not *r* thy sins.
44:21 *R* these, O Jacob and Israel; for
46: 8 *R* this, and shew yourselves men:
9 *R* the former things of old: for I
47: 7 neither didst *r* the latter end of it.
54: 4 and shalt not *r* the reproach of thy
64: 5 those that *r* thee in thy ways:
9 O Lord, neither *r* iniquity for ever:
Jer 2: 2 I *r* thee, the kindness of thy
3:16 to mind: neither shall they *r* it;
14:10 he will now *r* their iniquity, and
21 *r*, break not thy covenant with us.
15:15 *r* me, and visit me, and revenge
17: 2 Whilst their children *r* their altars
18:20 *R* that I stood before thee to speak
31:20 him, I do earnestly *r* him still:
34 and I will *r* their sin no more.
44:21 did not the Lord *r* them, and came
51:50 *r* the Lord afar off, and let
La 5: 1 *R*, O Lord, what is come upon us:
Eze 6: 9 you shall *r* me among the nations
16:60 Nevertheless I will *r* my covenant
61 shalt *r* thy ways, and be ashamed,
63 thou mayest *r*, and be confounded,
20:43 And there shall ye *r* your ways,
23:27 unto them, nor *r* Egypt any more.
36:31 Then shall ye *r* your own evil ways,
Ho 7: 2 that I *r* all their wickedness:
8:13 now will he *r* their iniquity, and
9: 9 therefore he will *r* their iniquity,
Mic 6: 5 *r* now what Balak king of Moab
Hab 3: 2 make known; in wrath *r* mercy.
Zec 10: 9 they shall *r* me in far countries;
Mal 4: 4 *R* ye the law of Moses my servant,
M't 16: 9 neither *r* the five loaves of the
27:63 Sir, we *r* that that deceiver said,
M'r 8:18 hear ye not? and do ye not *r*?
Lu 1:72 and to *r* his holy covenant;
16:25 Son, *r* that thou in thy lifetime
17:32 *R* Lot's wife.
23:42 *r* me when thou comest into thy
24: 6 *r* how he spake unto you when he
Joh 15:20 *R* the word that I said unto you,
16: 4 ye may *r* that I told you of them.
Ac 20:31 *r*, that by the space of three years
35 to *r* the words of the Lord Jesus,
1Co 11: 2 that ye *r* me in all things, and
Ga 2:10 would that we should *r* the poor;
Eph 2:11 Wherefore *r*, that ye being in time
Col 4:18 *R* my bonds. Grace be with you.
1Th 2: 9 For ye *r*, brethren, our labour and
2Th 2: 5 *R* ye not, that, when I was yet with
2Ti 2: 8 *R* that Jesus Christ of the seed of
Heb 8:12 their iniquities will I *r* no more.
10:17 sins and iniquities will I *r* no more.
13: 3 *R* them that are in bonds, as
7 *R* them which have the rule over
3Jo 10 will *r* his deeds which he doeth,
Jude 17 *r* ye the words which were spoken
Re 2: 5 *R* therefore from whence thou art
3: 3 *R* therefore how thou hast received

remembered
Ge 8: 1 And God *r* Noah, and every living
19:29 that God *r* Abraham, and sent Lot
30:22 And God *r* Rachel, and God
42: 9 And Joseph *r* the dreams which he
Ex 2:24 God *r* his covenant with Abraham,
6: 5 and I have *r* my covenant.
Nu 10: 9 shall be *r* before the Lord your God,
J'g 8:34 children of Israel *r* not the Lord
1Sa 1:19 Hannah his wife; and the Lord *r*
2Ch 24:22 Joash the king *r* not the kindness

Es 2: 1 r' Vashti, and what she had done,
9: 28 these days should be r' and kept
Job 24: 20 he shall be no more r'; and
Ps 45: 17 name to be r' in all generations:
77: 3 I r' God, and was troubled: I
78: 35 they r' that God was their rock,
39 For he r' that they were but flesh;
42 They r' not his hand, nor the day
98: 3 He hath r' his mercy and his truth
105: 8 He hath r' his covenant for ever,
42 For he r' his holy promise, and
106: 7 r' not the multitude of thy mercies;
45 And he r' for them his covenant,
109: 14 Let the iniquity of his fathers be r'
16 that he r' not to shew mercy, but
111: 4 made his wonderful works to be r':
119: 52 I r' thy judgments of old, O Lord;
55 I have r' thy name, O Lord, in the
136: 23 Who r' us in our low estate: for his
137: 1 yea, we wept, when we r' Zion.
Ec 9: 15 yet no man r' that same poor man.
Isa 23: 16 many songs, that thou mayest be r'.
57: 11 thou hast lied, and hast not r' me,
63: 11 Then he r' the days of old, Moses,
65: 17 and the former shall not be r', nor
Jer 11: 19 that his name may be no more r'.
La 1: 7 Jerusalem r' in the days of her
2: 1 r' not his footstool in the day of his
Eze 3: 20 which he hath done shall not be r';
16: 22, 43 hast not r' the days of thy youth,
21: 24 ye have made your iniquity to be r',
32 thou shalt be no more r': for I the
25: 10 that the Ammonites may not be r'
33: 13 his righteousnesses shall not be r';
Ho 2: 17 shall no more be r' by their name.
Am 1: 9 and r' not the brotherly covenant:
Jon 2: 7 soul fainted within me I r' the Lord:
Zec 13: 2 land, and they shall no more be r':
M't 26: 75 And Peter r' the word of Jesus,
Lu 22: 61 And Peter r' the word of the Lord,
24: 8 And they r' his words,
Joh 2: 17 his disciples r' that it was written,
22 his disciples r' that he had said this
12: 16 then r' they that these things were
Ac 11: 16 Then r' I the word of the Lord, how
Re 18: 5 and God hath r' her iniquities.

rememberest
Ps 88: 5 the grave, whom thou r' no more:
M't 5: 23 and there r' that thy brother hath

remembereth
Ps 9: 12 inquisition for blood, he r' them:
103: 14 our frame; he r' that we are dust.
La 1: 9 she r' not her last end; therefore
Joh 16: 21 child, she r' no more the anguish,
2Co 7: 15 he r' the obedience of you all, how

remembering
La 3: 19 R' mine affliction and my misery,
1Th 1: 3 R' without ceasing your work of

remembrance See also REMEMBRANCES.
Ex 17: 14 utterly put out the r' of Amalek
Nu 5: 15 memorial, bringing iniquity to r'.
De 25: 19 shalt blot out the r' of Amalek
32: 26 I would make the r' of them to cease
2Sa 18: 18 have no son to keep my name in r':
1Ki 17: 18 come unto me to call my sin to r',
Job 18: 17 His r' shall perish from the earth,
Ps 6: 5 For in death there is no r' of thee:
30: 4 thanks at the r' of his holiness.
34: 16 to cut off the r' of them from the
38: *title* A Psalm of David, to bring to r'
70: *title* A Psalm of David, to bring to r'.
77: 6 I call to r' my song in the night:
83: 4 name of Israel may be no more in r'.
97: 12 thanks at the r' of his holiness.
102: 12 and thy r' unto all generations.
112: 6 righteous shall be in everlasting r'.
Ec 1: 11 There is no r' of former things;
11 any r' of things that are to come
2: 16 there is no r' of the wise more than
Isa 26: 8 thy name, and to the r' of thee.
43: 26 Put me in r': let us plead together:
57: 8 the posts hast thou set up thy r':
La 3: 20 My soul hath them still in r',
Eze 21: 23 but he will call to r' the iniquity,
24 because,...that ye are come to r',
23: 19 calling to r' the days of her youth,
21 thou calledst to r' the lewdness of
29: 16 which bringeth their iniquity to r',
Mal 3: 16 a book of r' was written before
M'r 11: 21 Peter calling to r' saith unto him,
Lu 1: 54 servant Israel, in r' of his mercy;
22: 19 given for you: this do in r' of me.
Joh 14: 26 and bring all things to your r',
Ac 10: 31 and thine alms are had in r' in the
1Co 4: 17 shall bring you into r' of my ways
11: 24 broken for you: this do in r' of me.
25 do ye, as oft as ye drink it, in r' of me.
Ph'p 1: 3 thank...God upon every r' of you,
1Th 3: 6 that ye have good r' of us always,
1Ti 4: 6 the brethren in r' of these things,
2Ti 1: 3 I have r' of thee in my prayers
5 I call to r' the unfeigned faith
6 I put thee in r' that thou stir up
2: 14 Of these things put them in r',
Heb 10: 3 there is a r' again made of sins
32 But call to r' the former days, in
2Pe 1: 12 you always in r' of these things,
13 stir you up by putting you in r';
15 to have these things always in r'.
3: 1 up your pure minds by way of r':
Jude 5 I will therefore put you in r',
Re 16: 19 Babylon came in r' before God,

remembrances
Job 13: 12 Your r' are like unto ashes, your

Remeth (*re'-meth*) See also RAMOTH; JARMUTH.
Jos 19: 21 And R', and En-gannim, and

remission
M't 26: 28 is shed for many for the r' of sins.
M'r 1: 4 of repentance for the r' of sins.
Lu 1: 77 his people by the r' of their sins,
3: 3 of repentance for the r' of sins;
24: 47 and r' of sins should be preached
Ac 2: 38 of Jesus Christ for the r' of sins,
10: 43 in him shall receive r' of sins.
Ro 3: 25 for the r' of sins that are past,
Heb 9: 22 without shedding of blood is no r'.
10: 18 Now where r' of these is, there is no

remit See also REMITTED.
Joh 20: 23 Whose soever sins ye r', they are

remitted
Joh 20: 23 ye remit, they are r' unto them;

Remmon (*rem'-mon*) See also REMMON-METHOAR; RIMMON.
Jos 19: 7 R', and Ether, and Ashan; four

Remmon-methoar (*rem''-mon-meth'-o-ar*)
Jos 19: 13 and goeth out to R' to Neah;

remnant
Ex 26: 12 r' that remaineth of the curtains
Le 2: 3 r' of the meat offering shall be
5: 13 the r' shall be the priest's, as a meat
14: 18 r' of the oil that is in the priest's
De 3: 11 remained of the r' of giants;
28: 54 r' of his children which he shall
Jos 12: 4 which was of the r' of the giants,
13: 12 remained of the r' of the giants:
23: 12 cleave unto the r' of these nations,
2Sa 21: 2 but of the r' of the Amorites; and
1Ki 12: 23 to the r' of the people, saying,
14: 10 the r' of the house of Jeroboam,
22: 46 the r' of the sodomites, which
2Ki 19: 4 lift up thy prayer for the r' that
30 r' that is escaped of the house of
31 of Jerusalem shall go forth a r',
21: 14 forsake the r' of mine inheritance,
25: 11 with the r' of the multitude, did
1Ch 6: 70 of the r' of the sons of Kohath.
2Ch 30: 6 and he will return to the r' of you,
34: 9 and of all the r' of Israel, and of
Ezr 3: 8 r' of their brethren the priests
9: 8 our God, to leave us a r' to escape,
14 should be no r' nor escaping?
Ne 1: 3 r' that are left of the captivity
Job 22: 20 the r' of them the fire consumeth.
Isa 1: 9 had left unto us a very small r',
10: 20 in that day, that the r' of Israel,
21 The r' shall return, even the r' of
22 sea, yet a r' of them shall return:
11: 11 time to recover the r' of his people,
16 an highway for the r' of his people,
14: 22 the name, and r', and son, and
30 famine, and he shall slay thy r'.
15: 9 Moab, and upon the r' of the land.
16: 14 r' shall be very small and feeble.
17: 3 from Damascus, and the r' of Syria:
37: 4 lift up thy prayer for the r' that is
31 r' that is escaped of the house of
32 of Jerusalem shall go forth a r',
46: 3 and all the r' of the house of Israel,
Jer 6: 9 glean the r' of Israel as a vine:
11: 23 there shall be no r' of them: for
15: 11 Verily it shall be well with thy r';
23: 3 will gather the r' of my flock out
25: 20 and Ekron, and the r' of Ashdod,
31: 7 save thy people, the r' of Israel.
39: 9 captive...the r' of the people that
40: 11 of Babylon had left a r' of Judah,
15 and the r' in Judah perish?
41: 16 the r' of the people whom he had
42: 2 Lord thy God, even for all this r';
15 word of the Lord, ye r' of Judah;
19 concerning you, O ye r' of Judah;
43: 5 took all the r' of Judah, that were
44: 12 I will take the r' of Judah, that
14 none of the r' of Judah, which are
28 all the r' of Judah, that are gone
47: 4 the r' of the country of Caphtor.
5 cut off with the r' of their valley:
Eze 5: 10 whole r' of thee will I scatter into
6: 8 Yet will I leave a r', that ye may
11: 13 make a full end of the r' of Israel?
14: 22 therein shall be left a r' that shall
23: 25 thy r' shall fall by the sword: they
25: 16 and destroy the r' of the sea coast.
Joe 2: 32 in the r' whom the Lord shall call.
Am 1: 8 r' of the Philistines shall perish,
5: 15 be gracious unto the r' of Joseph.
9: 12 they may possess the r' of Edom,
Mic 2: 12 will surely gather the r' of Israel;
4: 7 I will make her that halted a r',
5: 3 r' of his brethren shall return
7 r' of Jacob shall be in the midst
8 the r' of Jacob shall be among the
7: 18 of the r' of his heritage?
Hab 2: 8 all the r' of the people shall spoil
Zep 1: 4 I will cut off the r' of Baal from
2: 7 for the r' of the house of Judah;
9 the r' of my people shall possess
3: 13 r' of Israel shall not do iniquity,
Hag 1: 12 with all the r' of the people, obeyed
14 spirit of all the r' of the people;
Zec 8: 6 in the eyes of the r' of this people
12 the r' of this people to possess all
M't 22: 6 And the r' took his servants, and
Ro 9: 27 of the sea, a r' shall be saved:
11: 5 is a r' according to the election of
Re 11: 13 the r' were affrighted, and gave
12: 17 make war with the r' of her seed,
19: 21 the r' were slain with the sword of

remove^ See also REMOVED; REMOVETH; REMOVING.
Ge 48: 17 to r' it from Ephraim's head unto
Nu 36: 7 of Israel r' from tribe to tribe:
9 the inheritance r' from one tribe
De 19: 14 not r' thy neighbour's landmark,
Jos 3: 3 then ye shall r' from your place,
J'g 9: 29 hand! then would I r' Abimelech.
2Sa 6: 10 So David would not r' the ark of
2Ki 23: 27 will r' Judah also out of my sight,
24: 3 to r' them out of his sight, for the
2Ch 33: 8 will I any more r' the foot of Israel
Job 24: 2 Some r' the landmarks; they
27: 5 not r' mine integrity from me.
Ps 36: 11 not the hand of the wicked r' me.
39: 10 R' thy stroke away from me: I
119: 22 R' from me reproach...contempt;
29 R' from me the way of lying: and
Pr 4: 27 nor to the left: r' thy foot from evil.
5: 8 R' thy way far from her, and come
22: 28 R' not the ancient landmark,
23: 10 R' not the old landmark; and
30: 8 R' far from me vanity and lies:
Ec 11: 10 r' sorrow from thy heart, and put
Isa 13: 13 the earth shall r' out of her place,
46: 7 from his place shall he not r':
Jer 4: 1 my sight, then shalt thou not r'.
27: 10 you, to r' you far from your land;
32: 31 should r' it from before my face,
50: 3 they shall r', they shall depart,
8 R' out of the midst of Babylon, and
Eze 12: 3 r' by day in their sight; and thou
3 r' from thy place to another place
21: 26 R' the diadem, and take off the
45: 9 r' violence and spoil, and execute
Ho 5: 10 were like them that r' the bound:
Joe 2: 20 r' far off from you the northern
3: 6 r' them far from their border.
Mic 2: 3 which ye shall not r' your necks;
Zec 3: 9 I will r' the iniquity of that land in
14: 4 mountain shall r' toward the north,
M't 17: 20 R' hence to yonder place; and it
20 to yonder place; and it shall r';
Lu 22: 42 be willing, r' this cup from me:
1Co 13: 2 faith, so that I could r' mountains,
Re 2: 5 r' thy candlestick out of his place,

removed
Ge 8: 13 Noah r' the covering of the ark,
12: 8 he r' from thence unto a mountain
13: 18 Then Abram r' his tent, and came
26: 22 he r' from thence, and digged
30: 35 he r' that day the he goats that
47: 21 he r' them to cities from one end
Ex 8: 31 and he r' the swarms of flies from
14: 19 angel r'...and went behind them;
20: 18 when the people saw it, they r',
Nu 12: 16 the people r' from Hazeroth, and
21: 12, 13 From thence they r', and pitched
33: 5 children of Israel r' from Rameses,
7 they r' from Etham, and turned
9 they r' from Marah, and came unto
10 they r' from Elim, and encamped
11 And they r' from the Red sea, and
14 they r' from Alush, and encamped
16 they r' from the desert of Sinai,
21 they r' from Libnah, and pitched
24 they r' from mount Shapher, and
25 they r' from Haradah, and pitched
26 And they r' from Makheloth, and
28 they r' from Tarah, and pitched in
32 And they r' from Bene-jaakan, and
34 And they r' from Jotbathah, and
36 And they r' from Ezion-gaber, and
37 they r' from Kadesh, and pitched
46 And they r' from Dibon-gad, and
47 they r' from Almon-diblathaim,
De 28: 25 be r' into all the kingdoms of the
Jos 3: 1 they r' from Shittim, and came to
14 when the people r' from their tents,
1Sa 6: 3 why his hand is not r' from you.
18: 13 Saul r' him from him, and made
2Sa 20: 12 he r' Amasa out of the highway
13 he was r' out of the highway,
1Ki 15: 12 r' all the idols that his fathers
13 even her he r' from being queen,
14 But the high places were not r':
2Ki 15: 4 Save that...high places were not r':
35 Howbeit...high places were not r':
16: 17 and r' the laver from off them;
17: 18 and r' them out of his sight: there
23 the Lord r' Israel out of his sight,
26 The nations which thou hast r',
18: 4 He r' the high places, and brake
23: 27 as I have r' Israel, and will cast off
1Ch 8: 6 and they r' them to Manahath:
7 and Ahiah, and Gera, he r' them,
2Ch 15: 16 king, he r' her from being queen,
35: 12 And they r' the burnt offerings,
Job 14: 18 and the rock is r' out of his place.
18: 4 shall the rock be r' out of his place?
19: 10 mine hope hath he r' like a tree.
36: 16 would he have r' thee out of the
Ps 46: 2 we fear, though the earth be r',
81: 6 I r' his shoulder from the burden:
103: 12 far hath he r' our transgressions
104: 5 that it should not be r' for ever.
125: 1 as mount Zion, which cannot be r',
Pr 10: 30 The righteous shall never be r':
Isa 6: 12 the Lord have r' men far away,
10: 13 I have r' the bounds of the people,
31 Madmenah is r'; the inhabitants
22: 25 fastened in the sure place be r',
24: 20 and shall be r' like a cottage; and
26: 15 r' it far unto all the ends of the
29: 13 but have r' their heart far from me,
30: 20 yet shall not thy teachers be r'

Isa 33:20 the stakes thereof shall ever be r'.
38:12 r' from me as a shepherd's tent:
54:10 shall depart, and the hills be r';
10 the covenant of my peace be r',
Jer 15: 4 them to be r' into all kingdoms of
24: 9 them to be r' into all the kingdoms
29:18 them to be r' to all the kingdoms
34:17 you to be r' into all the kingdoms
La 1: 8 sinned; therefore she is r':
3:17 hast r' my soul far off from peace:
Eze 7:19 streets, and their gold shall be r':
23:46 give them to be r' and spoiled.
36:17 the uncleanness of a r' woman.
Am 6: 7 stretched themselves shall be r'.
Mic 2: 4 how hath he r' it from me!
7:11 in that day shall the decree be far r'.
M't 21:21 Be thou r', and be thou cast into
M'r 11:23 Be thou r', and be thou cast into
Ac 7: 4 was dead, he r' him into this land,
13:22 when he had r' him, he raised up
Ga 1: 6 I marvel that ye are so soon r'

removeth
De 27:17 that r' his neighbour's landmark.
Job 9: 5 r' the mountains, and they know
12:20 r' away the speech of the trusty,
Ec 10: 9 Whoso r' stones shall be hurt
Da 2:21 he r' kings, and setteth up kings:

removing
Ge 30:32 r' from thence all the speckled
Isa 49:21 a captive, and r' to and fro? and
Eze 12: 3 of man, prepare thee stuff for r',
4 day in their sight, as stuff for r':
Heb12:27 r' of those things that are shaken,

Remphan (*rem'-fan*)
Ac 7:43 the star of your god R', figures

rend See also RENDING; RENT.
Ex 39:23 about the hole, that it should not r'.
Le 10: 6 neither r' your clothes; lest ye
13:56 he shall r' it out of the garment,
21:10 his head, nor r' his clothes;
2Sa 3:31 R' your clothes, and gird you with
1Ki 11:11 surely r' the kingdom from thee,
12 will r' it out of the hand of thy son.
13 I will not r' away all the kingdom;
31 r' the kingdom out of the hand of
2Ch 34:27 and didst r' thy clothes, and weep
Ec 3: 7 A time to r', and a time to sew; a
Isa 64: 1 that thou wouldest r' the heavens,
Eze 13:11 fall; and a stormy wind shall r' it.
13 r' it with a stormy wind in my fury;
29: 7 break, and r' all their shoulder:
Ho 13: 8 and will r' the caul of their heart,
Joe 2:13 And r' your heart, and not your
M't 7: 6 feet, and turn again and r' you.
Joh 19:24 Let us not r' it, but cast lots for it,

render See also RENDERED; RENDEREST; RENDERETH; RENDERING.
Nu 18: 9 which they shall r' unto me, shall
De 32:41 will r' vengeance to mine enemies,
43 r' vengeance to his adversaries,
J'g 9:57 did God r' upon their heads: and
1Sa 26:23 r' to every man his righteousness
2Ch 6:30 r' unto every man according unto
Job 33:26 r' unto man his righteousness.
34:11 work of a man shall he r' unto him,
Ps 28: 4 hands; r' to them their desert.
38:20 They also that r' evil for good are
56:12 God: I will r' praises unto thee.
79:12 r' unto our neighbours sevenfold
94: 2 earth: r' a reward to the proud.
116:12 What shall I r' unto the Lord for
Pr 24:12 not he r' to every man according to
29 r' to the man according to his work.
26:16 seven men that can r' a reason.
Isa 66:15 to r' his anger with fury, and his
Jer 51: 6 he will r' unto her a recompence.
24 I will r' unto Babylon and to all
La 3:64 R' unto them a recompence, O
Ho 14: 2 so will we r' the calves of our lips.
Joe 3: 4 will ye r' me a recompence? and if
Zec 9:12 that I will r' double unto thee;
M't 21:41 r' him the fruits in their seasons.
22:21 R' therefore unto Cæsar the things
M'r 12:17 R' to Cæsar the things that are
Lu 20:25 R' therefore unto Cæsar the things
Ro 2: 6 will r' to every man according to his
13: 7 R' therefore to all their dues:
1Co 7: 3 Let the husband r' unto the wife due
1Th 3: 9 what thanks can we r' to God again
5:15 that none r' evil for evil unto any

rendered
J'g 9:56 r' the wickedness of Abimelech,
2Ki 3: 4 and r' unto the king of Israel an
2Ch 32:25 Hezekiah r' not again according to
Pr 12:14 man's hands shall be r' unto him.

renderest
Ps 62:12 r' to every man according to his

rendereth
Isa 66: 6 that r' recompence to his enemies.

rendering
1Pe 3: 9 Not r' evil for evil, or railing for

rending
Ps 7: 2 my soul like a lion, r' it in pieces,

renew See also RENEWED; RENEWEST; RENEWING.
1Sa 11:14 Gilgal, and r' the kingdom there.
Ps 51:10 and r' a right spirit within me.
Isa 40:31 the Lord shall r' their strength;
41: 1 and let the people r' their strength:
La 5:21 be turned; r' our days as of old.
Heb 6: 6 to r' them again unto repentance;

renewed
2Ch15: 8 and r' the altar of the Lord, that
Job 29:20 and my bow was r' in my hand.
Ps 103: 5 thy youth is r' like the eagle's.
2Co 4:16 the inward man is r' day by day.
Eph 4:23 be r' in the spirit of your mind;
Col 3:10 which is r' in knowledge after the

renewest
Job 10:17 Thou r' thy witnesses against me,
Ps 104:30 and thou r' the face of the earth.

renewing
Ro 12: 2 transformed by the r' of your mind,
Tit 3: 5 regeneration,...r' of the Holy Ghost;

renounced
2Co 4: 2 But have r' the hidden things of

renown See also RENOWNED.
Ge 6: 4 men which were of old, men of r'.
Nu 16: 2 in the congregation, men of r':
Eze 16:14 thy r' went forth among...heathen
15 the harlot because of thy r', and
34:29 I will raise up for them a plant of r',
39:13 it shall be to them a r' the day that
Da 9:15 hast gotten thee r', as at this day;

renowned
Nu 1:16 were the r' of the congregation,
Isa 14:20 seed of evildoers shall never be r'.
Eze 23:23 and rulers great lords and r', all
26:17 the r' city, which wast strong in

rent See also RENTEST.
Ge 37:29 in the pit; and he r' his clothes.
33 is without doubt r' in pieces.
34 And Jacob r' his clothes, and put
44:13 they r' their clothes, and laded
Ex 28:32 of an habergeon, that it be not r'.
Le 13:45 his clothes shall be r', and his
Nu 14: 6 searched the land, r' their clothes:
Jos 7: 6 Joshua r' his clothes, and fell to the
9: 4 and wine bottles, old, and r', and
13 were new; and behold, they be r':
J'g 11:35 he saw her, that he r' his clothes,
14: 6 him, and he r' him as he would
6 as he would have r' a kid, and he
1Sa 4:12 the same day with his clothes r',
15:27 the skirt of his mantle, and it r'.
28 The Lord hath r' the kingdom of
28:17 Lord hath r' the kingdom out of
2Sa 1: 2 camp from Saul with his clothes r',
11 hold on his clothes, and r' them;
13:19 r' her garment of divers colours
31 stood by with their clothes r'.
15:32 came to meet him with his coat r',
1Ki 1:40 earth r' with the sound of them.
11:30 on him, and r' it in twelve pieces:
13: 3 the altar shall be r', and the ashes
5 the altar also was r', and the ashes
14: 8 And r' the kingdom away from the
19:11 and strong wind r' the mountains,
21:27 those words, that he r' his clothes,
2Ki 2:12 clothes, and r' them in two pieces.
5: 7 the letter, that he r' his clothes,
8 the king of Israel had r' his clothes,
8 Wherefore hast thou r' thy clothes?
6:30 the woman, that he r' his clothes;
11:14 Athaliah r' her clothes, and cried,
17:21 r' Israel from the house of David;
18:37 to Hezekiah with their clothes r',
19: 1 heard it, that he r' his clothes,
22:11 of the law, that he r' his clothes.
19 hast r' thy clothes, and wept before
2Ch 23:13 Then Athaliah r' her clothes, and
34:19 of the law, that he r' his clothes.
Ezr 9: 3 I r' my garment and my mantle,
5 and having r' my garment and my
Es 4: 1 Mordecai r' his clothes, and put on
Job 1:20 Then Job arose, and r' his mantle,
2:12 they r' every one his mantle, and
26: 8 the cloud is not r' under them.
Isa 3:24 and instead of a girdle a r'; and
36:22 to Hezekiah with their clothes r',
37: 1 heard it, that he r' his clothes,
Jer 36:24 not afraid, nor r' their garments,
41: 5 beards shaven, and their clothes r',
Eze 30:16 and No shall be r' asunder, and
M't 9:16 garment, and the r' is made worse.
26:65 Then the high priest r' his clothes,
27:51 veil of the temple was r' in twain
51 earth did quake, and the rocks r';
M'r 2:21 the old, and the r' is made worse.
9:26 the spirit cried, and r' him sore,
14:63 Then the high priest r' his clothes,
15:38 veil of the temple was r' in twain
Lu 5:36 then both the new maketh a r', and
23:45 the veil of the temple was r' in the
Ac 14:14 they r' their clothes, and ran in
16:22 the magistrates r' off their clothes,

rentest
Jer 4:30 thou r' thy face with painting,

repaid See REPAYED.

repair See also REPAIRED; REPAIRING.
2Ki 12: 5 them r' the breaches of the house,
7 Why r' ye not the breaches of the
8 to r' the breaches of the house.
12 hewed stone to r' the breaches of
12 was laid out for the house to r' it.
22: 5 to r' the breaches of the house,
6 and hewn stone to r' the house.
2Ch 24: 4 Joash was minded to r' the house
5 money to r' the house of your God
12 and carpenters to r' the house of
34: 8 to r' the house of the Lord his
10 Lord, to r' and amend the house:
Ezr 9: 9 and to r' the desolations thereof,
Isa 61: 4 and they shall r' the waste cities,

repaired
J'g 21:23 r' the cities, and dwelt in them.
1Ki 11:27 and r' the breaches of the city of
18:30 r' the altar of the Lord that was
2Ki 12: 6 not r' the breaches of the house.
14 r' therewith the house of the Lord.
1Ch 11: 8 and Joab r' the rest of the city.
2Ch 29: 3 house of the Lord, and r' them.
32: 5 r' Millo in the city of David, and
33:16 he r' the altar of the Lord, and
Ne 3: 4 next unto them r' Meremoth the
4 next unto them r' Meshullam the
4 next unto them r' Zadok the son of
5 next unto them the Tekoites r';
6 the old gate r' Jehoida the son of
7 them r' Melatiah the Gibeonite,
8 next unto him r' Uzziel the son of
8 Next unto him also r' Hananiah the
9 next unto them r' Rephaiah the son
10 next unto them r' Jedaiah the son
10 next unto him r' Hattush the son of
11 r' the other piece, and the tower of
12 next unto him r' Shallum the son
13 The valley gate r' Hanun, and the
14 the dung gate r' Malchiah the son
15 gate of the fountain r' Shallun the
16 After him r' Nehemiah the son of
17 after him r' the Levites, Rehum the
17 Next unto him r' Hashabiah, the
18 After him r' their brethren, Bavai
19 And next to him r' Ezer the son of
20 Zabbai earnestly r' the other piece,
21 After him r' Meremoth the son of
22 after him r' the priests, the men of
23 After him r' Benjamin and Hashub
23 After him r' Azariah the son of
24 After him r' Binnui the son of
27 them the Tekoites r' another piece,
28 above the horse gate r' the priests,
29 After them r' Zadok the son of
29 After him r' also Shemaiah the son
30 After him r' Hananiah the son of
30 After him r' Meshullam the son of
31 After him r' Malchiah the
32 the sheep gate r' the goldsmiths

repairer
Isa 58:12 The r' of the breach, The restorer

repairing
2Ch 24:27 and the r' of the house of God,

repay See also REPAYED; REPAYETH.
De 7:10 him, he will r' him to his face.
Job 21:31 shall r' him what he hath done?
41:11 prevented me, that I should r' him?
Isa 59:18 accordingly he will r', fury to his
18 the islands he will r' recompence.
Lu 10:35 when I come again, I will r' thee.
Ro 12:19 is mine; I will r', saith the Lord.
Ph'm 19 with mine own hand, I will r' it:

repayed [*some editions* REPAID]
Pr 13:21 to the righteous good shall be r'.

repayeth
De 7:10 r' them that hate him to their

repeateth
Pr 17: 9 he that r' a matter separateth

repent See also REPENTED; REPENTEST; REPENTETH; REPENTING.
Ex 13:17 the people r' when they see war,
32:12 r' of this evil against thy people.
Nu 23:19 the son of man, that he should r':
De 32:36 and r' himself for his servants,
1Sa 15:29 Strength of Israel will not lie nor r':
29 he is not a man, that he should r'.
1Ki 8:47 and r', and make supplication
Job 42: 6 myself, and r' in dust and ashes.
Ps 90:13 it r' thee concerning thy servants.
110: 4 Lord hath sworn, and will not r',
135:14 r' himself concerning his servants.
Jer 4:28 I have purposed it, and will not r',
18: 8 r' of the evil that I thought to do
10 my voice, then I will r' of the good,
26: 3 that I may r' me of the evil, which
13 and the Lord will r' him of the evil
42:10 I r' me of the evil that I have done
Eze 14: 6 R', and turn...from your idols;
18:30 R', and turn yourselves from all
24:14 will I spare, neither will I r';
Joe 2:14 knoweth if he will return and r',
Jon 3: 9 Who can tell if God will turn and r',
M't 3: 2 R' ye: for the kingdom of heaven
4:17 R': for the kingdom of heaven is at
M'r 1:15 hand: r' ye, and believe the gospel.
6:12 and preached that men should r'.
Lu 13: 3, 5 except ye r', ye shall all likewise
16:30 them from the dead, they will r'.
17: 3 him; and if he r', forgive him.
4 saying, I r'; thou shalt forgive him.
Ac 2:38 R', and be baptized every one of you
3:19 R' ye therefore, and be converted,
8:22 R' therefore of this thy wickedness,
17:30 all men every where to r':
26:20 that they should r' and turn to God,
2Co 7: 8 I do not r', though I did r': for I
Heb 7:21 The Lord sware and will not r',
Re 2: 5 whence thou art fallen, and r', and
5 out of his place, except thou r'.
16 R'; or else I will come unto thee
21 her space to r' of her fornication;
22 except they r' of their deeds.
3: 3 and heard, and hold fast, and r'.
19 be zealous therefore, and r'.

repentance
Ho 13:14 r' shall be hid from mine eyes.
M't 3: 8 Bring forth....fruits meet for r':

M't 3:11 baptize you with water unto r':
9:13 the righteous, but sinners to r'.
M'r 1: 4 and preach the baptism of r' for the
2:17 the righteous, but sinners to r'.
Lu 3: 3 preaching the baptism of r' for the
8 Bring forth...fruits worthy of r',
5:32 call the righteous, but sinners to r'.
15: 7 nine just persons, which need no r'.
24:47 And that r' and remission of sins
Ac 5:31 to give r' to Israel, and forgiveness
11:18 to the Gentiles granted r' unto life.
13:24 the baptism of r' to all the people
19: 4 baptized with the baptism of r',
20:21 r' toward God, and faith toward
26:20 to God, and do works meet for r'.
Ro 2: 4 goodness of God leadeth thee to r'?
11:29 and calling of God are without r'.
2Co 7: 9 sorry, but that ye sorrowed to r':
10 For godly sorrow worketh r' to
2Ti 2:25 God peradventure will give them r'
Heb 6: 1 laying again the foundation of r'
6 to renew them again unto r';
12:17 for he found no place of r', though
2Pe 3: 9 but that all should come to r'.

repented
Ge 6: 6 r' the Lord that he had made man
Ex 32:14 Lord r' of the evil which he thought
J'g 2:18 for it r' the Lord because of their
21: 6 children of Israel r'...for Benjamin
15 the people r' them for Benjamin,
1Sa 15:35 Lord r' that he had made Saul king
2Sa 24:16 the Lord r' him of the evil, and said
1Ch 21:15 beheld, and he r' him of the evil,
Ps 106:45 r' according to the multitude of his
Jer 8: 6 no man r' him of his wickedness,
20:16 the Lord overthrew, and r' not:
26:19 the Lord r' him of the evil which
31:19 Surely after that I was turned, I r';
Am 7: 3 Lord r' for this: It shall not be,
6 Lord r' for this: This also shall not
Jon 3:10 God r' of the evil, that he had said
Zec 8:14 saith the Lord of hosts, and I r' not:
M't 11:20 were done, because they r' not:
21 would have r' long ago in sackcloth
12:41 they r' at the preaching of Jonas;
21:29 not: but afterward he r', and went.
32 ye had seen it, r' not afterward,
27: 3 that he was condemned, r' himself,
Lu 10:13 they had a great while ago r',
11:32 they r' at the preaching of Jonas;
2Co 7:10 worketh repentance...not to be r' of:
12:21 and have not r' of the uncleanness
Re 2:21 of her fornication; and she r' not.
9:20 r' not of the works of their hands,
21 Neither r' they of their murders
16: 9 and they r' not to give him glory.
11 sores, and r' not of their deeds.

repentest
Jon 4: 2 kindness, and r' thee of the evil.

repenteth
Ge 6: 7 it r' me that I have made them.
1Sa 15:11 It r' me that I have set up Saul to
Joe 2:13 kindness, and r' him of the evil.
Lu 15: 7 in heaven over one sinner that r',
10 angels...over one sinner that r'.

repenting See also REPENTINGS.
Jer 15: 6 destroy thee; I am weary with r'.

repentings
Ho 11: 8 me, my r' are kindled together.

repetitions
M't 6: 7 But when ye pray, use not vain r',

Rephael (*re'-fa-el*)
1Ch 26: 7 sons of Shemaiah; Othni, and R',

Rephah (*re'-fah*)
1Ch 7:25 And R' was his son, also Resheph,

Rephaiah (*ref-a-i'-ah*) See also RAPHA; RHESA.
1Ch 3:21 the sons of R', the sons of Arnan,
4:42 and Neariah, and R', and Uzziel,
7: 2 sons of Tola; Uzzi, and R', and
9:43 Moza begat Binea; and R' his son,
Ne 3: 9 them repaired R' the son of Hur,

Rephaim (*re-fa'-im*) See also REPHAIMS.
2Sa 5:18, 22 themselves in the valley of R'.
23:13 pitched in the valley of R'.
1Ch 11:15 encamped in the valley of R'.
14: 9 themselves in the valley of R'.
Isa 17: 5 gathereth ears in the valley of R'.

Rephaims (*re-fa'-ims*) See also REPHAIM.
Ge 14: 5 and smote the R' in Ashteroth
15:20 and the Perizzites, and the R',

Rephidim (*ref'-i-dim*)
Ex 17: 1 of the Lord, and pitched in R':
8 and fought with Israel in R'.
19: 2 For they were departed from R',
Nu 33:14 and encamped at R', where was no
15 And they departed from R', and

replenish See also REPLENISHED.
Ge 1:28 and multiply, and r' the earth, and
9: 1 and multiply, and r' the earth.

replenished
Isa 2: 6 because they be r' from the east,
23: 2 that pass over the sea, have r'.
Jer 31:25 and I have r' every sorrowful soul.
Eze 26: 2 I shall be r', now she is laid waste:
27:25 wast r', and made very glorious

repliest
Ro 9:20 who art thou that r' against God?

report See also REPORTED.
Ge 37: 2 brought unto his father their evil r'.
Ex 23: 1 Thou shalt not raise a false r':
Nu 13:32 brought up an evil r' of the land
14:37 bring up the evil r' upon the land,
De 2:25 who shall hear r' of thee, and shall
1Sa 2:24 for it is no good r' that I hear:
1Ki 10: 6 was a true r' that I heard in mine
2Ch 9: 5 was a true r' which I heard in mine
Ne 6:13 might have matter for an evil r',
Pr 15:30 a good r' maketh the bones fat.
Isa 23: 5 As at the r' concerning Egypt,
5 be sorely pained at the r' of Tyre.
28:19 a vexation...to understand the r'.
53: 1 Who hath believed our r'? and to
Jer 20:10 R', say they, and we will r' it. All
50:43 king of Babylon hath heard the r'
Joh 12:38 Lord, who hath believed our r'?
Ac 6: 3 among you seven men of honest r',
10:22 and of good r' among all the nation
22:12 having a good r' of all the Jews
Ro 10:16 Lord, who hath believed our r'?
1Co 14:25 and r' that God is in you of a truth.
2Co 6: 8 By honour and dishonour, by evil r'
8 and good r': as deceivers, and yet
Ph'p 4: 8 whatsoever things are of good r';
1Ti 3: 7 he must have a good r' of them
Heb 11: 2 it the elders obtained a good r'.
39 obtained a good r' through faith,
3Jo 12 Demetrius hath good r' of all men,

reported
Ne 6: 6 It is r' among the heathen, and
7 and now shall it be r' to the king
19 they r' his good deeds before me,
Es 1:17 in their eyes, when it shall be r',
Eze 9:11 inkhorn by his side, r' the matter,
M't 28:15 commonly r' among the Jews is
Ac 4:23 and r' all that the chief priests and
16: 2 was well r' of by the brethren
Ro 3: 8 (as we be slanderously r', and as
1Co 5: 1 It is r' commonly that there is
1Ti 5:10 Well r' of for good works; if she
1Pe 1:12 which are now r' unto you by them

reproach See also REPROACHED; REPROACHES; REPROACHEST; REPROACHETH; REPROACHFULLY.
Ge 30:23 said, God hath taken away my r':
34:14 for that were a r' unto us:
Jos 5: 9 have I rolled away the r' of Egypt
Ru 2:15 among the sheaves, and r' her not:
1Sa 11: 2 and lay it for a r' upon all Israel.
17:26 and taketh away the r' from Israel?
25:39 hath pleaded the cause of my r'
2Ki 19: 4 hath sent to r' the living God;
16 hath sent him to r' the living God.
Ne 1: 3 are in great affliction and r':
2:17 Jerusalem, that we be no more a r'.
4: 4 turn their r' upon their own head,
5: 9 the r' of the heathen our enemies?
6:13 evil report, that they might r' me.
Job 19: 5 me, and plead against me my r':
20: 3 I have heard the check of my r',
27: 6 my heart shall not r' me so long
Ps 15: 3 up a r' against his neighbour.
22: 6 a r' of men, and despised of the
31:11 I was a r' among all mine enemies,
39: 8 make me not the r' of the foolish.
42:10 in my bones, mine enemies r' me;
44:13 makest us a r' to our neighbours,
57: 3 and save me from the r' of him
69: 7 for thy sake I have borne r';
10 soul with fasting, that was to my r'.
19 Thou hast known my r', and my
20 R' hath broken my heart; and I
71:13 be covered with r' and dishonour
74:10 how long shall the adversary r'?
78:66 he put them to a perpetual r'.
79: 4 are become a r' to our neighbours,
12 sevenfold into their bosom their r',
89:41 him: he is a r' to his neighbours.
50 Remember,...the r' of thy servants;
50 bosom the r' of all the mighty people;
102: 8 Mine enemies r' me all the day;
109:25 I became also a r' unto them:
119:22 Remove from me r' and contempt;
39 Turn away my r' which I fear: for
Pr 6:33 his r' shall not be wiped away.
14:34 but sin is a r' to any people.
18: 3 contempt, and with ignominy r'.
19:26 causeth shame, and bringeth r'.
22:10 yea, strife and r' shall cease.
Isa 4: 1 by thy name, to take away our r'.
30: 5 profit, but a shame, and also a r'.
37: 4 hath sent to r' the living God, and
17 hath sent to r' the living God.
51: 7 fear ye not the r' of men, neither
54: 4 remember the r' of thy widowhood
Jer 6:10 word of the Lord is unto them a r';
20: 8 the word of the Lord was made a r'
23:40 bring an everlasting r' upon you,
24: 9 be a r' and a proverb, a taunt and
29:18 an hissing, and a r', among all the
31:19 I did bear the r' of my youth.
42:18 astonishment, and a curse, and a r';
44: 8 a r' among all the nations of the
12 astonishment, and a curse, and a r'.
49:13 shall become a desolation, a r', a
51:51 because we have heard r': shame
La 3:30 smiteth him: he is filled full with r'.
61 Thou hast heard their r', O Lord,
5: 1 us: consider, and behold our r'.
Eze 5:14 a r' among the nations that are
15 So it shall be a r' and a taunt, an
16:57 of thy r' of the daughters of Syria,
21:28 Ammonites, and concerning their r';
22: 4 I made thee a r' unto the heathen,
36:15 bear the r' of the people any more,
30 shall receive no more r' of famine
Da 9:16 become a r' to all that are about us.
Da 11:18 cause the r' offered by him to cease;
18 without his own r' he shall cause it
Ho 12:14 his r' shall his Lord return unto
Joe 2:17 give not thine heritage to r', that
19 make you a r' among the heathen:
Mic 6:16 ye shall bear the r' of my people.
Zep 2: 8 I have heard the r' of Moab, and
3:18 to whom the r' of it was a burden.
Lu 1:25 to take away my r' among men.
6:22 and shall r' you, and cast out your
2Co 11:21 I speak as concerning r', as though
1Ti 3: 7 fall into r' and...snare of the devil.
4:10 we both labour and suffer r',
Heb 11:26 Esteeming the r' of Christ greater
13:13 without the camp, bearing his r'.

reproached
2Ki 19:22 hast thou r' and blasphemed?
23 messengers thou hast r' the Lord,
Job 19: 3 These ten times have ye r' me: ye
Ps 55:12 it was not an enemy that r' me;
69: 9 reproaches of them that r' thee are
74:18 this, that the enemy hath r', O Lord,
79:12 wherewith they have r' thee, O Lord.
89:51 Wherewith thine enemies have r',
51 they have r' the footsteps of thine
Isa 37:23 hast thou r' and blasphemed?
24 thy servants hast thou r' the Lord,
Zep 2: 8 whereby they have r' my people,
10 have r' and magnified themselves
Ro 15: 3 reproaches of them that r' thee
1Pe 4:14 If ye be r' for the name of Christ,

reproaches
Ps 69: 9 the r' of them that reproached thee
Isa 43:28 Jacob to the curse, and Israel to r'.
Ro 15: 3 The r' of them that reproached thee
2Co 12:10 take pleasure in infirmities, in r',
Heb 10:33 both by r' and afflictions; and

reproachest
Lu 11:45 Master, thus saying thou r' us also.

reproacheth
Nu 15:30 a stranger, the same r' the Lord;
Ps 44:16 For the voice of him that r' and
74:22 how the foolish man r' thee daily.
119:42 to answer him that r' me: for
Pr 14:31 oppresseth the poor r' his Maker:
17: 5 mocketh the poor r' his Maker:
27:11 that I may answer him that r' me.

reproachfully
Job 16:10 smitten me upon the cheek r';
1Ti 5:14 to the adversary to speak r'.

reprobate See also REPROBATES.
Jer 6:30 R' silver shall men call them,
Ro 1:28 God gave them over to a r' mind,
2Ti 3: 8 minds, r' concerning the faith.
Tit 1:16 and unto every good work r'.

reprobates
2Co 13: 5 Christ is in you, except ye be r'?
6 ye shall know that we are not r'.
7 which is honest, though we be as r'.

reproof See also REPROOFS.
Job 26:11 and are astonished at his r'.
Pr 1:23 Turn you at my r': behold, I will
25 counsel, and would none of my r':
30 my counsel: they despised all my r'.
5:12 and my heart despised r';
10:17 but he that refuseth r' erreth.
12: 1 but he that hateth r' is brutish.
13:18 that regardeth r' shall be honoured.
15: 5 but he that regardeth r' is prudent.
10 way: and he that hateth r' shall die.
31 The ear that heareth the r' of life
32 heareth r' getteth understanding.
17:10 A r' entereth more into a wise
29:15 The rod and r' give wisdom: but
2Ti 3:16 for doctrine, for r', for correction,

reproofs
Ps 38:14 and in whose mouth are no r'.
Pr 6:23 r' of instruction are the way of life:

reprove See also REPROVED; REPROVETH; UNREPROVABLE.
2Ki 19: 4 will r' the words which the Lord
Job 6:25 but what doth your arguing r'?
26 Do ye imagine to r' words, and the
13:10 He will surely r' you, if ye do
22: 4 Will he r' thee for fear of thee? will
Ps 50: 8 I will not r' thee for thy sacrifices
21 I will r' thee, and set them in order
141: 5 and let him r' me; it shall be an
Pr 9: 8 R' not a scorner, lest he hate thee:
19:25 and r' one that hath understanding,
30: 6 lest he r' thee, and thou be found a
Isa 11: 3 r' after the hearing of his ears:
4 r' with equity for the meek of the
37: 4 will r' the words which the Lord
Jer 2:19 and thy backslidings shall r' thee:
Ho 4: 4 let no man strive, nor r' another:
Joh 16: 8 is come, he will r' the world of sin,
Eph 5:11 of darkness, but rather r' them.
2Ti 4: 2 r', rebuke, exhort with all

reproved
Ge 20:16 with all other: thus she was r'.
21:25 Abraham r' Abimelech because
1Ch 16:21 yea, he r' kings for their sakes,
Ps 105:14 yea, he r' kings for their sakes;
Pr 29: 1 being often r' hardeneth his neck
Jer 29:27 why hast thou not r' Jeremiah
Hab 2: 1 what I shall answer when I am r'.
Lu 3:19 being r' by him for Herodias his
Joh 3:20 light, lest his deeds should be r'.
Eph 5:13 that are r' are made manifest by

reprover
Pr 25:12 is a wise r' upon an obedient ear.
Eze 3:26 dumb, and shalt not be to them a r':

reproveth
Job 40: 2 he that r' God, let him answer it.
Pr 9: 7 He that r' a scorner getteth to
15:12 scorner loveth not one that r' him:
Isa 29:21 a snare for him that r' in the gate,

reputation
Ec 10: 1 is in r' for wisdom and honour.
Ac 5:34 had in r' among all the people,
Ga 2: 2 privately to them which were of r',
Ph'p 2: 7 But made himself of no r', and
29 gladness; and hold such in r':

reputed
Job 18: 3 as beasts, and r' vile in your sight?
Da 4:35 of the earth are r' as nothing:

request See also REQUESTED; REQUESTS.
J'g 8:24 them, I would desire a r' of you,
2Sa 14:15 perform the r' of his handmaid.
22 hath fulfilled the r' of his servant.
Ezr 7: 6 the king granted him all his r',
Ne 2: 4 me, For what dost thou make r'?
Es 4: 8 make r' before him for her people.
5: 3 queen Esther? and what is thy r'?
6 and what is thy r'? even to the half
7 and said, My petition and my r' is;
8 my petition, and to perform my r',
7: 2 and what is thy r'? and it shall be
3 petition, and my people at my r':
7 Haman stood up to make r' for his
9:12 what is thy r' further? and it shall
Job 6: 8 Oh that I might have my r'; and
Ps 21: 2 not withholden the r' of his lips.
106:15 he gave them their r'; but sent
Ro 1:10 Making r', if by any means now at
Ph'p 1: 4 for you all making r' with joy,

requested
J'g 8:26 of the golden earrings that he r'
1Ki 19: 4 he r' for himself that he might die;
1Ch 4:10 God granted him that which he r'.
Da 1: 8 he r' the prince of the eunuchs
2:49 Then Daniel r' of the king, and he

requests
Ph'p 4: 6 let your r' be made known unto God.

require See also REQUIRED; REQUIREST; REQUIRETH; REQUIRING.
Ge 9: 5 your blood of your lives will I r';
5 the hand of every beast will I r' it,
5 brother will I r' the life of man.
31:39 of it; of my hand didst thou r' it,
43: 9 of my hand shalt thou r' him: if I
De 10:12 doth the Lord thy God r' of thee,
18:19 in my name, I will r' it of him.
23:21 thy God will surely r' it of thee;
Jos 22:23 thereon, let the Lord himself r' it;
1Sa 20:16 the Lord even r' it at the hand of
2Sa 3:13 but one thing I r' of thee, that is,
4:11 now r' his blood of your hand, and
19:38 whatsoever thou shalt r' of me,
1Ki 8:59 at all times, as the matter shall r':
1Ch 21: 3 then doth my lord r' this thing?
2Ch 24:22 The Lord look upon it, and r' it.
Ezr 7:21 the God of heaven, shall r' of you,
8:22 ashamed to r' of the king a band
Ne 5:12 them, and will r' nothing of them;
Ps 10:13 in his heart, Thou wilt not r' it.
Eze 3:18, 20 blood will I r' at thine hand.
20:40 there will I r' your offerings, and
33: 6 blood will I r' at the watchman's
8 his blood will I r' at thine hand.
34:10 I will r' my flock at their hand,
Mic 6: 8 and what doth the Lord r' of thee,
1Co 1:22 the Jews r' a sign, and the Greeks
7:36 and need so r', let him do what he

required
Ge 42:22 behold, also his blood is r'.
Ex 12:36 lent unto them such things as they r'.
1Sa 21: 8 the king's business r' haste.
2Sa 12:20 when he r', they set bread before
1Ch 16:37 continually, as every day's work r':
2Ch 8:14 priests, as the duty of every day r':
24: 6 hast thou not r' of the Levites to
Ezr 3: 4 as the duty of every day r';
Ne 5:18 r' not I the bread of the governor,
Es 2:15 she r' nothing but what Hegai the
Ps 40: 6 and sin offering hast thou not r'.
137: 3 us away captive r' of us a song;
3 they that wasted us r' of us mirth,
Pr 30: 7 Two things have I r' of thee; deny
Isa 1:12 who hath r' this at your hand, to
Lu 11:50 world, may be r' of this generation;
51 It shall be r' of this generation.
12:20 night thy soul shall be r' of thee:
48 is given, of him shall be much r':
19:23 have r' mine own with usury?
23:24 that it should be as they r'.
1Co 4: 2 Moreover it is r' in stewards, that

requirest
Ru 3:11 I will do to thee all that thou r':

requireth
Ec 3:15 and God r' that which is past.
Da 2:11 it is a rare thing that the king r',

requiring
Lu 23:23 voice, r' that he might be crucified.

requite See also REQUITED; REQUITING.
Ge 50:15 and will certainly r' us all the evil
De 32: 6 Do ye thus r' the Lord, O foolish
2Sa 2: 6 and I will also r' you this kindness,
16:12 the Lord will r' me good for his
2Ki 9:26 I will r' thee in this plat, saith the
Ps 10:14 and spite, to r' it with thy hand:
41:10 raise me up, that I may r' them.
Jer 51:56 God of recompences shall surely r'.
1Ti 5: 4 at home, and to r' their parents:

requited
J'g 1: 7 as I have done, so God hath r' me.
1Sa 25:21 and he hath r' me evil for good.

requiting
2Ch 6:23 by r' the wicked, by recompensing

rereward
Nu 10:25 which was the r' of all the camps
Jos 6: 9 and the r' came after the ark, the
13 but the r' came after the ark of the
1Sa 29: 2 passed on in the r' with Achish.
Isa 52:12 the God of Israel will be your r'.
58: 8 the glory of the Lord shall be thy r'.

rescue See also RESCUED; RESCUETH.
De 28:31 thou shalt have none to r' them.
Ps 35:17 look on? r' my soul from their
Ho 5:14 take away, and none shall r' him.

rescued
1Sa 14:45 So the people r' Jonathan, that he
30:18 away: and David r' his two wives.
Ac 23:27 came I with an army, and r' him,

rescueth
Da 6:27 He delivereth and r', and he

resemblance
Zec 5: 6 is there r' through all the earth.

resemble See also RESEMBLED.
Lu 13:18 like? and whereunto shall I r' it?

resembled
J'g 8:18 each one r' the children of a king.

Resen *(re'-zen)*
Ge 10:12 R' between Nineveh and Calah:

reserve See also RESERVED; RESERVETH.
Jer 3: 5 Will he r' his anger for ever? will
50:20 for I will pardon them whom I r'.
2Pe 2: 9 to r' the unjust unto the day of

reserved
Ge 27:36 thou not r' a blessing for me?
Nu 18: 9 most holy things, r' from the fire:
J'g 21:22 we r' not to each man his wife
Ru 2:18 gave to her that she had r' after
2Sa 8: 4 r' of them for an hundred chariots.
1Ch 18: 4 but r' of them an hundred chariots.
Job 21:30 is r' to the day of destruction?
38:23 Which I have r' against the time of
Ac 25:21 be r' unto the hearing of Augustus,
Ro 11: 4 I have r' to myself seven thousand
1Pe 1: 4 not away, r' in heaven for you,
2Pe 2: 4 darkness, to be r' unto judgment;
17 the mist of darkness is r' for ever.
3: 7 r' unto fire against the day of
Jude 6 hath r' in everlasting chains under
13 to whom is r' the blackness of

reserveth
Jer 5:24 r' unto us the appointed weeks of
Na 1: 2 and he r' wrath for his enemies.

Resheph *(re'-shef)*
1Ch 7:25 Rephah was his son, also R', and

residue
Ex 10: 5 eat the r' of that which is escaped,
1Ch 6:66 And the r' of the families of the sons
Ne 11:20 the r' of Israel, of the priests, and
Isa 21:17 the r' of the number of archers, the
28: 5 of beauty, unto the r' of his people,
38:10 am deprived of the r' of my years.
44:17 the r' thereof he maketh a god,
19 the r' thereof an abomination?
Jer 8: 3 r' of them that remain of this evil
15: 9 the r' of them will I deliver to the
24: 8 the r' of Jerusalem, that remain in
27:19 the r' of the vessels that remain in
29: 1 Jerusalem unto the r' of the elders
39: 3 the r' of the princes of the king of
41:10 all the r' of the people that were
52:15 r' of the people that remained in
Eze 9: 8 wilt thou destroy all the r' of Israel
23:25 thy r' shall be devoured by the fire.
34:18 your feet the r' of your pastures?
18 ye must foul the r' with your feet?
36: 3 unto the r' of the heathen,
4 derision to the r' of the heathen
5 against the r' of the heathen, and
48:18 And the r' in length over against
21 And the r' shall be for the prince,
Da 7: 7 stamped the r' with the feet of it:
19 and stamped the r' with his feet;
Zep 2: 9 r' of my people shall spoil them,
Hag 2: 2 and to the r' of the people, saying,
Zec 8:11 be unto the r' of this people as in
14: 2 r' of the people shall not be cut off
Mal 2:15 Yet had he the r' of the spirit.
M'r 16:13 they went and told it unto the r':
Ac 15:17 r' of the men might seek after the

resist See also RESISTED; RESISTETH.
Zec 3: 1 at his right hand to r' him.
M't 5:39 I say unto you, That ye r' not evil:
Lu 21:15 shall not be able to gainsay nor r'.
Ac 6:10 were not able to r' the wisdom and
7:51 ears, ye do always r' the Holy Ghost:
Ro 13: 2 and they that r' shall receive to
2Ti 3: 8 Moses, so do these also r' the truth:
Jas 4: 7 R' the devil, and he will flee from
5: 6 the just; and he doth not r' you.
1Pe 5: 9 Whom r' stedfast in the faith,

resisted
Ro 9:19 find fault? For who hath r' his will?
Heb 12: 4 Ye have not yet r' unto blood,

resisteth
Ro 13: 2 Whosoever therefore r' the power,
2 r' the ordinance of God: and they
Jas 4: 6 God r' the proud, but giveth grace
1Pe 5: 5 God r' the proud, and giveth grace

resolved
Lu 16: 4 I am r' what to do, that, when I

resort See also RESORTED.
Ne 4:20 trumpet, r' ye thither unto us:
Ps 71: 3 whereunto I may continually r':
M'r 10: 1 and the people r' unto him again;
Joh 18:20 whither the Jews always r';

resorted
2Ch 11:13 r' to him out of all their coasts.
M'r 2:13 and all the multitude r' unto him,
Joh 10:41 many r' unto him, and said, John
18: 2 Jesus ofttimes r' thither with his
Ac 16:13 unto the women which r' thither.

respect See also RESPECTED; RESPECTETH.
Ge 4: 4 And the Lord had r' unto Abel
5 and to his offering he had not r'.
Ex 2:25 Israel, and God had r' unto them.
Le 19:15 not r' the person of the poor,
26: 9 For I will have r' unto you, and
Nu 16:15 Lord, R' not thou their offering:
De 1:17 shall not r' persons in judgment;
16:19 thou shalt not r' persons, neither
2Sa 14:14 neither doth God r' any person:
1Ki 8:28 have thou r' unto the prayer of
2Ki 13:23 had r' unto them, because of his
2Ch 6:19 Have r' therefore to the prayer of
19: 7 Lord our God, nor r' of persons,
Ps 74:20 Have r' unto the covenant: for
119: 6 have r' unto all thy commandments.
15 precepts, and have r' unto thy ways.
117 r' unto thy statutes continually.
138: 6 yet hath he r' unto the lowly:
Pr 24:23 have r' of persons in judgment.
28:21 To have r' of persons is not good:
Isa 17: 7 have r' to the Holy One of Israel.
17: 8 r' that which his fingers have made,
22:11 r' unto him that fashioned it long
Ro 2:11 there is no r' of persons with God.
2Co 3:10 glorious had no glory in this r',
Eph 6: 9 is there r' of persons with him.
Ph'p 4:11 Not that I speak in r' of want: for
Col 2:16 or in r' of an holyday, or of the
3:25 and there is no r' of persons.
Heb 11:26 had r' unto the recompence of the
Jas 2: 1 Lord of glory, with r' of persons.
3 r' to him that weareth the gay
9 But if ye have r' to persons, ye
1Pe 1:17 who without r' of persons judgeth

respected
La 4:16 r' not the persons of the priests,

respecter
Ac 10:34 that God is no r' of persons:

respecteth
Job 37:24 r' not any that are wise of heart.
Ps 40: 4 and r' not the proud, nor such as

respite
Ex 8:15 Pharaoh saw that there was r',
1Sa 11: 3 Give us seven days' r', that we

rest See also RESTED; RESTETH; RESTING; RESTS.
Ge 8: 9 dove found no r' for the sole of her
18: 4 and r' yourselves under the tree.
30:36 Jacob fed the r' of Laban's flocks.
49:15 he saw that r' was good, and the
Ex 5: 5 make them r' from their burdens.
16:23 is the r' of the holy sabbath unto
23:11 thou shalt let it r' and lie still;
12 on the seventh day thou shalt r':
12 thine ox and thine ass may r', and
28:10 names of the r' on the other stone,
31:15 the seventh is the sabbath of r',
33:14 with thee, and I will give thee r'.
34:21 on the seventh day thou shalt r':
21 time and in harvest thou shalt r'.
35: 2 day, a sabbath of r' to the Lord:
Le 5: 9 r' of the blood shall be wrung out
14:17 r' of the oil that is in his hand
29 r' of the oil that is in the priest's
16:31 shall be a sabbath of r' unto you,
23: 3 seventh day is the sabbath of r',
32 shall be unto you a sabbath of r',
25: 4 be a sabbath of r' unto the land,
5 for it is a year of r' unto the land.
26:34 then shall the land r', and enjoy
35 long as it lieth desolate it shall r';
35 it did not r' in your sabbaths, when
Nu 31: 8 beside the r' of them that were slain;
32 r' of the prey which the men of
De 3:13 the r' of Gilead, and all Bashan,
20 have given r' unto your brethren,
5:14 maidservant may r' as well as thou.
12: 9 ye are not as yet come to the r'
10 he giveth you r' from all your
25:19 God hath given thee r' from all
28:65 shall the sole of thy foot have r':
Jos 1:13 Lord your God hath given you r',
15 Lord have given your brethren r',
3:13 shall r' in the waters of Jordan,
10:20 the r' which remained of them
13:27 the r' of the kingdom of Sihon
14:15 And the land had r' from war.
17: 2 the r' of the children of Manasseh
6 the r' of Manasseh's sons had the
21: 5 the r' of the children of Kohath
34 the r' of the Levites, out of the
44 Lord gave them r' round about,
22: 4 hath given r' unto your brethren,
23: 1 the Lord had given r' unto Israel

J'g 3:11 And the land had r' forty years.
30 the land had r' fourscore years.
5:31 And the land had r' forty years.
7: 6 the r' of the people bowed down
8 he sent all the r' of Israel every man
Ru 1: 9 grant you that ye may find r',
3: 1 shall I not seek r' for thee, that
18 the man will not be in r', until he
1Sa 13: 2 the r' of the people he sent every
15:15 the r' we have utterly destroyed.
2Sa 3:29 Let it r' on the head of Joab, and
7: 1 the Lord had given him r' round
11 thee to r' from all thine enemies.
10:10 the r' of the people he delivered
12:28 gather the r' of the people together,
21:10 the birds of the air to r' on them
1Ki 5: 4 the Lord my God hath given me r'
8:56 that hath given r' unto his people
11:41 the r' of the acts of Solomon, and
14:19 the r' of the acts of Jeroboam, how
29 the r' of the acts of Rehoboam, and
15: 7 Now the r' of the acts of Abijam,
23 The r' of all the acts of Asa, and
31 Now the r' of the acts of Nadab,
16: 5 Now the r' of the acts of Baasha,
14 Now the r' of the acts of Elah, and
20 Now the r' of the acts of Zimri,
27 Now the r' of the acts of Omri
20:30 But the r' fled to Aphek, into the
22:39 Now the r' of the acts of Ahab,
45 the r' of the acts of Jehoshaphat,
2Ki 1:18 Now the r' of the acts of Ahaziah
2:15 spirit of Elijah doth r' on Elisha.
4: 7 thou and thy children of the r'.
8:23 And the r' of the acts of Joram,
10:34 Now the r' of the acts of Jehu, and
12:19 And the r' of the acts of Joash, and
13: 8 Now the r' of the acts of Jehoahaz,
12 And the r' of the acts of Joash, and
14:15 the r' of the acts of Jehoash which
18 the r' of the acts of Amaziah, are
28 the r' of the acts of Jeroboam, and
15: 6 And the r' of the acts of Azariah,
11 And the r' of the acts of Zachariah,
15 the r' of the acts of Shallum, and
21 And the r' of the acts of Menahem,
26 And the r' of the acts of Pekahiah,
31 the r' of the acts of Pekah, and all
36 Now the r' of the acts of Jotham,
16:19 the r' of the acts of Ahaz which he
20:20 And the r' of the acts of Hezekiah,
21:17 the r' of the acts of Manasseh, and
25 the r' of the acts of Amon which he
23:28 the r' of the acts of Josiah, and all
24: 5 the r' of the acts of Jehoiakim, and
25:11 r' of the people that were left in
1Ch 4:43 smote the r' of the Amalekites
6:31 Lord, after that the ark had r'.
77 r' of the children of Merari were
11: 8 Joab repaired the r' of the city.
12:38 r' also of Israel were of one heart
16:41 and the r' that were chosen, who
19:11 r' of the people he delivered unto
22: 9 to thee, who shall be a man of r';
9 give him r' from all his enemies,
18 he not given you r' on every side?
23:25 hath given r' unto his people, that
24:20 r' of the sons of Levi were these:
28: 2 build an house of r' for the ark of
2Ch 9:29 Now the r' of the acts of Solomon,
13:22 And the r' of the acts of Abijah,
14: 6 for the land had r', and he had
6 because the Lord had given him r'
7 he hath given us r' on every side.
11 for we r' on thee, and in thy
15:15 Lord gave them r' round about.
20:30 his God gave him r' round about.
34 the r' of the acts of Jehoshaphat,
24:14 they brought the r' of the money
25:26 Now the r' of the acts of Amaziah,
26:22 the r' of the acts of Uzziah, first
27: 7 the r' of the acts of Jotham, and
28:26 r' of his acts and of all his ways,
32:32 the r' of the acts of Hezekiah,
33:18 the r' of the acts of Manasseh, and
35:26 the r' of the acts of Josiah, and
36: 8 the r' of the acts of Jehoiakim,
Ezr 4: 3 the r' of the chief of the fathers
7 and the r' of their companions,
9 and the r' of their companions;
10 r' of the nations whom the great
10 r' that are on this side the river,
17 r' of their companions that dwell
17 and unto the r' beyond the river,
6:16 r' of the children of the captivity,
7:18 the r' of the silver and the gold,
Ne 2:16 nor to the r' that did the work.
4:14, 19 to the r' of the people,
6: 1 and the r' of our enemies, heard
14 and the r' of the prophets, that
7:72 which the r' of the people gave
9:28 But after they had r', they did evil
10:28 the r' of the people, the priests,
11: 1 the r' of the people also cast lots, to
Es 9:12 in the r' of the king's provinces?
16 and had r' from their enemies,
Job 3:13 have slept: then had I been at r',
17 and there the weary be at r'.
18 There the prisoners r' together;
26 was not in safety, neither had I r',
11:18 thou shalt take thy r' in safety.
14: 6 Turn from him, that he may r',
17:16 when our r' together is in the dust.
30:17 season: and my sinews take no r'.
Ps 16: 9 my flesh also shall r' in hope.
17:14 leave the r' of their substance to

Ps 37: 7 R' in the Lord, and wait patiently
38: 3 neither is there any r' in my bones
55: 6 then would I fly away, and be at r'.
94:13 r' from the days of adversity,
95:11 they should not enter into my r'.
116: 7 Return unto thy r', O my soul; for
125: 3 the rod of the wicked shall not r'
132: 8 Arise, O Lord, into thy r'; thou,
14 This is my r' for ever: here will I
Pr 6:35 neither will he r' content, though thou
29: 9 he rage or laugh, there is no r'.
17 thy son, and he shall give thee r';
Ec 2:23 his heart taketh not r' in the night.
6: 5 this hath more r' than the other.
Ca 1: 7 makest thy flock to r' at noon:
Isa 7:19 shall r' all of them in the desolate
10:19 the r' of the trees of his forest
11: 2 spirit of the Lord shall r' upon
10 seek: and his r' shall be glorious.
14: 3 shall give thee r' from thy sorrow,
7 whole earth is at r', and is quiet:
18: 4 I will take my r', and I will
23:12 there also shalt thou have no r'.
25:10 shall the hand of the Lord r',
28:12 said, This is the r' wherewith
12 ye may cause the weary to r';
30:15 returning and r' shall ye be saved;
34:14 screech owl also shall r' there,
14 and find for herself a place of r'.
51: 4 my judgment to r' for a light of
57: 2 they shall r' in their beds, each
20 troubled sea, when it cannot r',
62: 1 for Jerusalem's sake I will not r',
7 give him no r', till he establish,
63:14 Spirit of the Lord caused him to r':
66: 1 and where is the place of my r'?
Jer 6:16 and ye shall find r' for your souls.
30:10 shall return, and shall be in r',
31: 2 when I went to cause him to r'.
39: 9 the r' of the people that remained.
45: 3 in my sighing, and I find no r'.
46:27 return, and be in r' and at ease,
47: 6 into thy scabbard, r', and be still.
50:34 that he may give r' to the land,
52:15 and the r' of the multitude.
La 1: 3 the heathen, she findeth no r':
2:18 day and night: give thyself no r';
5: 5 we labour, and have no r'.
Eze 5:13 cause my fury to r' upon them,
16:42 make my fury toward thee to r',
21:17 and I will cause my fury to r':
24:13 caused my fury to r' upon thee.
38:11 I will go to them that are at r',
44:30 the blessing to r' in thine house.
45: 8 r' of the land shall they give to the
48:23 As for the r' of the tribes, from the
Da 2:18 the r' of the wise men of Babylon.
4: 4 Nebuchadnezzar was at r' in mine
7:12 As concerning the r' of the beasts,
12:13 thou shalt r', and stand in thy lot
Mic 2:10 depart; for this is not your r':
Hab 3:16 I might r' in the day of trouble:
Zep 3:17 he will r' in his love, he will joy
Zec 1:11 the earth sitteth still, and is at r'.
9: 1 Damascus shall be the r' thereof:
11: 9 let the r' eat every one the flesh
M't 11:28 heavy laden, and I will give you r'.
29 and ye shall find r' unto your souls.
12:43 places, seeking r', and finding none.
26:45 Sleep on now, and take your r':
27:49 The r' said, Let be, let us see
M'r 6:31 into a desert place, and r' a while:
14:41 Sleep on now, and take your r':
Lu 10: 6 there, your peace shall r' upon it:
11:24 through dry places, seeking r';
12:26 why take ye thought for the r'?
24: 9 unto the eleven, and to all the r'.
Joh 11:13 had spoken of taking of r' in sleep.
Ac 2:26 also my flesh shall r' in hope:
37 Peter and to the r' of the apostles,
5:13 of the r' durst no man join himself
7:49 or what is the place of my r'?
9:31 had the churches r' throughout
27:44 And the r', some on boards, and
Ro 11: 7 obtained it, and the r' were blinded
1Co 7:12 But to the r' speak I, not the Lord:
11:34 r' will I set in order when I come.
2Co 2:13 I had no r' in my spirit, because I
7: 5 Macedonia, our flesh had no r',
12: 9 power of Christ may r' upon me.
2Th 1: 7 to you who are troubled r' with us,
Heb 3:11 They shall not enter into my r'.)
18 they should not enter into his r',
4: 1 being left us of entering into his r',
3 which have believed do enter into r',
3 if they shall enter into my r':
4 God did r' the seventh day from
5 If they shall enter into my r'.
8 For if Jesus had given them r',
9 therefore a r' to the people of God.
10 For he that is entered into his r',
11 labour therefore to enter into that r',
1Pe 4: 2 live the r' of his time in the flesh
Re 2:24 I say, and unto the r' in Thyatira,
4: 8 and they r' not day and night,
6:11 should r' yet for a little season,
9:20 r' of the men which were not killed
14:11 and they have no r' day nor night,
13 that they may r' from their labours;
20: 5 the r' of the dead lived not again

rested

Ge 2: 2 he r' on the seventh day from all
3 that in it he had r' from all his work
8: 4 the ark r' in the seventh month,
Ex 10:14 and r' in all the coasts of Egypt:
16:30 the people r' on the seventh day.

Ex 20:11 in them is, and r' the seventh day:
31:17 and on the seventh day he r', and
Nu 9:18 tabernacle they r' in their tents.
23 of the Lord they r' in the tents,
10:12 the cloud r' in the wilderness of
36 when it r', he said, Return, O Lord,
11:25 when the spirit r' upon them, they
26 Medad: and the spirit r' upon them;
Jos 11:23 tribes. And the land r' from war.
1Ki 6:10 they r' on the house with timber of
2Ch 32: 8 r' themselves upon the words of
Es 9:17 fourteenth day of the same r' they,
18 fifteenth day of the same they r',
22 the Jews r' from their enemies,
Job 30:27 My bowels boiled, and r' not: the
Lu 23:56 and r' the sabbath day according

restest

Ro 2:17 art called a Jew, and r' in the law,

resteth

Job 24:23 him to be in safety, whereon he r';
Pr 14:33 Wisdom r' in the heart of him that
Ec 7: 9 for anger r' in the bosom of fools.
1Pe 4:14 spirit of glory and of God r' upon

resting See also RESTINGPLACE.

Nu 10:33 to search out a r' place for them.
2Ch 6:41 O Lord God, into thy r' place, thou,
Pr 24:15 righteous; spoil not his r' place:
Isa 32:18 dwellings, and in quiet r' places;

restingplace See also RESTING and PLACE.

Jer 50: 6 hill, they have forgotten their r'.

restitution

Ex 22: 3 he should make full r'; if he have
5 his own vineyard, shall he make r'.
6 kindled...fire shall surely make r'.
12 he shall make r' unto the owner
Job 20:18 to his substance shall the r' be,
Ac 3:21 until the times of r' of all things,

restore See also RESTORED; RESTORETH.

Ge 20: 7 r' the man his wife; for he is a
7 if thou r' her not, know thou that
40:13 head, and r' thee unto thy place:
42:25 r' every man's money into his sack,
Ex 22: 1 he shall r' five oxen for an ox, and
4 ass, or sheep; he shall r' double.
Le 6: 4 r' that which he took violently
5 he shall even r' it in the principal,
24:21 that killeth a beast, he shall r' it:
25:27 r' the overplus unto the man to
28 But if he be not able to r' it to him,
Nu 35:25 r' him to the city of his refuge,
De 22: 2 and thou shalt r' it to him again.
J'g 11:13 r' those lands again peaceably.
17: 3 now therefore I will r' it unto thee.
1Sa 12: 3 eyes therewith? and I will r' it you.
2Sa 9: 7 will r' thee all the land of Saul thy
12: 6 And he shall r' the lamb fourfold,
16: 3 r' me the kingdom of my father.
1Ki 20:34 took from thy father, I will r';
2Ki 8: 6 R' all that was hers, and all the
Ne 5:11 R', I pray you, to them, even this
12 Then said they, We will r' them,
Job 20:10 and his hands shall r' their goods.
18 which he laboured for shall he r',
Ps 51:12 R' unto me the joy of thy
Pr 6:31 he be found, he shall r' sevenfold;
Isa 1:26 I will r' thy judges as at the first,
42:22 for a spoil, and none saith, R'.
49: 6 and to r' the preserved of Israel:
57:18 r' comforts unto him and to his
Jer 27:22 them up, and r' them to this place.
30:17 For I will r' health unto thee, and
Eze 33:15 If the wicked r' the pledge, give
Da 9:25 to r' and to build Jerusalem unto
Joe 2:25 I will r' to you the years that the
M't 17:11 shall first come, and r' all things.
Lu 19: 8 false accusation, I r' him fourfold.
Ac 1: 6 r' again the kingdom to Israel?
Ga 6: 1 r' such an one in the spirit of

restored

Ge 20:14 and r' him Sarah his wife.
40:21 And he r' the chief butler unto his
41:13 me he r' unto mine office, and him
42:28 My money is r'; and, lo, it is even
De 28:31 and shall not be r' to thee: thy
J'g 17: 3 had r' the eleven hundred shekels
4 he r' the money unto his mother;
1Sa 7:14 taken from Israel were r' to Israel,
1Ki 13: 6 that my hand may be r' me again.
6 the king's hand was r' him again,
2Ki 8: 1 whose son he had r' to life,
5 how he had r' a dead body to life,
5 woman, whose son he had r' to life,
5 is her son, whom Elisha r' to life.
14:22 He built Elath, and r' it to Judah,
25 He r' the coast of Israel from the
2Ch 8: 2 which Huram had r' to Solomon,
26: 2 He built Eloth, and r' it to Judah,
Ezr 6: 5 be r', and brought again unto the
Ps 69: 4 I r' that which I took not away.
Eze 18: 7 but hath r' to the debtor his pledge,
12 hath not r' the pledge, and hath
M't 12:13 it was r' whole, like as the other.
M'r 3: 5 his hand was r' whole as the other.
8:25 and he was r', and saw every man
Lu 6:10 his hand was r' whole as the other.
Heb 13:19 that I may be r' to you the sooner.

restorer

Ru 4:15 shall be unto thee a r' of thy life,
Isa 58:12 breach, The r' of paths to dwell in.

restoreth

Ps 23: 3 He r' my soul: he leadeth me in
M'r 9:12 cometh first, and r' all things;

restrain See also RESTRAINED; RESTRAINEST.
Job 15: 8 dost thou r· wisdom to thyself?
Ps 76:10 remainder of wrath shalt thou r·.
restrained
Ge 8: 2 and the rain from heaven was r·;
11: 6 now nothing will be r· from them,
16: 2 the Lord hath r· me from bearing:
Ex 36: 6 the people were r· from bringing.
1Sa 3:13 vile, and he r· them not.
Isa 63:15 mercies toward me? are they r·?
Eze 31:15 and I r· the floods thereof, and
Ac 14:18 sayings scarce r· they the people.
restrainest
Job 15: 4 off fear, and r· prayer before God.
restraint
1Sa 14: 6 there is no r· to the Lord to save
rests
1Ki 6: 6 he made narrowed r· round about,
resurrection
M't 22:23 which say that there is no r·, and
28 in the r· whose wife shall she be of
30 For in the r· they neither marry,
31 But as touching the r· of the dead,
27:53 came out the graves after his r·,
M'r 12:18 Sadducees, which say there is no r·;
23 In the r· therefore, when they shall
Lu 14:14 be recompensed at the r· of the just.
20:27 which deny that there is any r·;
33 in the r· whose wife of them is she?
35 that world, and the r· from the dead,
36 of God, being the children of the r·.
Joh 5:29 have done good, unto the r· of life;
29 done evil, unto the r· of damnation.
11:24 rise again in the r· at the last day.
25 unto her, I am the r·, and the life:
Ac 1:22 to be a witness with us of his r·.
2:31 this before spake of the r· of Christ,
4: 2 through Jesus the r· from the dead.
33 witness of the r· of the Lord Jesus:
17:18 preached unto them Jesus, and...r·.
32 when they heard of the r· of the dead,
23: 6 of the hope and r· of the dead I am
8 Sadducees say that there is no r·,
24:15 that there shall be a r· of the dead,
21 Touching the r· of the dead I am
Ro 1: 4 of holiness, by the r· from the dead:
6: 5 be also in the likeness of his r·:
1Co 15:12 you that there is no r· of the dead?
13 But if there be no r· of the dead, then
21 by man came also the r· of the dead.
42 So also is the r· of the dead. It is
Ph'p 3:10 know him, and the power of his r·,
11 attain unto the r· of the dead.
2Ti 2:18 saying that the r· is past already;
Heb 6: 2 of r· of the dead, and of eternal
11:35 that they might obtain a better r·:
1Pe 1: 3 lively hope by the r· of Jesus Christ
3:21 God,) by the r· of Jesus Christ:
Re 20: 5 were finished. This is the first r·.
6 is he that hath part in the first r·:
retain See also RETAINED; RETAINETH.
Job 2: 9 Dost thou still r· thine integrity?
Pr 4: 4 Let thine heart r· my words: keep
11:16 honour: and strong men r· riches.
Ec 8: 8 over the spirit to r· the spirit;
Da 11: 6 shall not r· the power of the arm;
Joh 20:23 whose soever sins ye r·, they are
Ro 1:28 like to r· God in their knowledge,
retained
J'g 7: 8 and r· those three hundred men:
19: 4 the damsel's father, r· him; and
Da 10: 8 corruption, and I r· no strength.
16 upon me, and I have r· no strength.
Joh 20:23 soever sins ye retain, they are r·.
Ph'm 13 Whom I would have r· with me,
retaineth
Pr 3:18 and happy is every one that r· her.
11:16 A gracious woman r· honour: and
Mic 7:18 he r· not his anger for ever,
retire See also RETIRED.
2Sa 11:15 and r· ye from him, that he may be
Jer 4: 6 r·, stay not: for I will bring
retired
J'g 20:39 the men of Israel r· in the battle,
2Sa 20:22 they r· from the city, every man
return See also RETURNED; RETURNETH; RETURNING.
Ge 3:19 bread, till thou r· unto the ground;
19 art, and unto dust shalt thou r·.
14:17 after his r· from the slaughter of
16: 9 R· to thy mistress, and submit
18:10 said, I will certainly r· unto thee
14 time appointed I will r· unto thee,
31: 3 R· unto the land of thy fathers, and
13 r· unto the land of thy kindred.
32: 9 R· unto thy country, and to thy
Ex 4:18 r· unto my brethren which are in
19 in Midian, Go, r· into Egypt:
21 When thou goest to r· into Egypt,
13:17 they see war, and they r· to Egypt:
Le 25:10 r· every man unto his possession,
10 shall r· every man unto his family.
13 r· every man unto his possession.
27 that he may r· unto his possession.
28 he shall r· unto his possession.
41 and shall r· unto his own family,
41 of his fathers shall he r·.
27:24 the field shall r· unto him of whom
Nu 10:36 said, R·, O Lord, unto the many
14: 3 not better for us to r· into Egypt?
4 captain, and let us r· into Egypt.
23: 5 R· unto Balak, and thus thou shalt
32:18 We will not r· unto our houses,
Nu 32:22 then afterward ye shall r·, and be
35:28 slayer shall r· into the land of his
De 3:20 r· every man unto his possession,
17:16 nor cause the people to r· to Egypt,
16 henceforth r· no more that way.
20: 5 let him go and r· to his house,
6 let him also go and r· unto his
7, 8 him go and r· unto his house,
30: 2 shalt r· unto the Lord thy God, and
3 will r· and gather thee from all the
8 thou shalt r· and obey the voice of
Jos 1:15 r· unto the land of your possession,
20: 6 then shall the slayer r·, and come
22: 4 therefore now r· ye, and get you
8 R· with much riches unto your
J'g 7: 3 let him r· and depart early from
11:31 I r· in peace from the children
Ru 1: 6 might r· from the country of Moab:
7 way to r· unto the land of Judah.
8 Go, r· each to her mother's house:
10 will r· with thee unto thy people.
15 gods: r· thou after thy sister in law.
16 or to r· from following after thee:
1Sa 6: 3 any wise r· him a trespass offering:
4 offering which we shall r· to him?
8 ye r· him for a trespass offering,
7: 3 If ye do r· unto the Lord with all
17 And his r· was to Ramah; for
9: 5 with him, Come, and let us r·;
15:26 unto Saul, I will not r· with thee:
26:21 r·, my son David: for I will no
29: 4 Make this fellow r·, that he may
7 Wherefore now r·, and go in peace,
11 to r· into the land of the Philistines.
2Sa 2:26 r· from following their brethren?
3:16 Then said Abner unto him, Go, r·.
10: 5 your beards be grown, and then r·.
12:23 him, but he shall not r· to me.
15:19 r· to thy place, and abide with the
20 r· thou, and take back thy brethren:
27 r· into the city in peace, and your
34 if thou r· to the city, and say unto
19:14 R· thou, and all thy servants.
24:13 I shall r· to him that sent me.
1Ki 2:32 r· his blood upon his own head,
33 blood...r· upon the head of Joab,
44 r· thy wickedness upon thine own
8:48 r· unto thee with all their heart,
12:24 r· every man to his house; for this
26 kingdom r· to the house of David:
13:16 I may not r· with thee, nor go in
19:15 r· on thy way to the wilderness of
20:22 r· of the year the king of Syria
26 came to pass at the r· of the year,
22:17 r· every man to his house in peace.
28 If thou r· at all in peace, the Lord
2Ki 18:14 I have offended; r· from me: that
19: 7 and shall r· to his own land: and I
33 he came, by the same shall he r·,
20:10 shadow r· backward ten degrees.
1Ch 19: 5 your beards be grown, and then r·.
2Ch 6:24 shall r· and confess thy name, and
38 they r· to thee with all their heart
10: 6 give ye me to r· answer to this
9 we may r· answer to this people,
11: 4 r· every man to his house: for this
18:16 let them r·...every man to his house
26 of affliction, until I r· in peace.
27 If thou certainly r· in peace, then
30: 6 he will r· to the remnant of you,
9 face from you, if ye r· unto him.
Ne 2: 6 be? and when wilt thou r·?
4:12 From all places whence ye shall r·
9:17 a captain to r· to their bondage:
Es 4:15 Esther bade them r· Mordecai this
9:25 Jews, should r· upon his own head,
Job 1:21 and naked shall I r· thither: the
6:29 R·, I pray you, let it not be iniquity;
29 yea, r· again, my righteousness is
7:10 He shall r· no more to his house,
10:21 Before I go whence I shall not r·,
15:22 believeth not that he shall r· out of
16:22 go the way whence I shall not r·.
17:10 for you all, do ye r·, and come now:
22:23 If thou r· to the Almighty, thou
33:25 shall r· to the days of his youth:
36:10 that they r· from iniquity.
39: 4 go forth, and r· not unto them.
Ps 6: 4 R·, O Lord, deliver my soul: oh
10 them r· and be ashamed suddenly.
7: 7 sakes therefore r· thou on high.
16 His mischief shall r· upon his own
59: 6 They r· at evening: they make a
14 And at evening let them r·; and
73:10 Therefore his people r· hither:
74:21 let not the oppressed r· ashamed:
80:14 R·, we beseech thee, O God of
90: 3 and sayest, R·, ye children of men.
13 R·, O Lord, how long? and let it
94:15 shall r· unto righteousness: and
104:29 they die, and r· to their dust.
116: 7 R· unto thy rest, O my soul; for
Pr 2:19 None that go unto her r· again,
26:27 rolleth a stone, it will r· upon him.
Ec 1: 7 rivers come, thither they r· again.
5:15 shall he r· to go as he came, and
12: 2 nor the clouds r· after the rain:
7 the dust r· to the earth as it was:
7 shall r· unto God who gave it.
Ca 6:13 R·, r·, O Shulamite;
13 r·, r·, that we may look upon thee.
Isa 6:13 it shall be a tenth, and it shall r·,
10:21 The remnant shall r·, even the
22 yet a remnant of them shall r·:
19:22 and they shall r· even to the Lord,
21:12 will enquire, enquire ye: r·, come.
Isa 35:10 the ransomed of the Lord shall r·,
37: 7 a rumour, and r· to his own land;
34 he came, by the same shall he r·,
44:22 r· unto me; for I have redeemed
45:23 in righteousness, and shall not r·,
51:11 the redeemed of the Lord shall r·,
55: 7 and let him r· unto the Lord, and
11 it shall not r· unto me void, but it
63:17 R· for thy servants' sake, the tribes
Jer 3: 1 man's, shall he r· unto her again?
1 r· again unto me, saith the Lord.
12 R·, thou backsliding Israel, saith
22 R·, ye backsliding children, and I
4: 1 If thou wilt r·, O Israel, saith the
1 Lord, r· unto me: and if thou wilt
5: 3 than a rock; they have refused to r·.
8: 4 shall he turn away, and not r·?
5 hold fast deceit, they refuse to r·.
12:15 I have plucked them out I will r·,
15: 7 since they r· not from their ways.
19 If thou r·, then will I bring thee
19 my mouth: let them r· unto thee;
19 but r· not thou unto them.
18:11 r· ye now every one from his evil
22:10 for he shall r· no more, nor see his
11 He shall not r· thither any more:
27 land whereunto they desire to r·,
27 thither shall they not r·.
23:14 none doth r· from his wickedness:
20 The anger of the Lord shall not r·,
24: 7 r· unto me with their whole heart.
29:10 in causing you to r· to this place.
30: 3 I will cause them to r· to the land
10 Jacob shall r·, and shall be in rest,
24 fierce anger of the Lord shall not r·,
31: 8 a great company shall r· thither.
32:44 for I will cause their captivity to r·,
33: 7 and the captivity of Israel to r·,
11 cause to r· the captivity of the land,
26 for I will cause their captivity to r·,
34:11 whom they had let go free, to r·,
16 set at liberty at their pleasure, to r·,
22 and cause them to r· to this city;
35:15 R· ye now every man from his evil
36: 3 may r· every man from his evil way;
7 will r· every one from his evil way,
37: 7 shall r· to Egypt into their own land.
20 not to r· to the house of Jonathan
38:26 cause me to r· to Jonathan's house,
42:12 cause you to r· to your own land.
44:14 should r· into the land of Judah,
14 have a desire to r· to dwell there:
14 shall r· but such as shall escape.
28 shall r· out of the land of Egypt
46:27 and Jacob shall r·, and be in rest
50: 9 expert man; none shall r· in vain.
Eze 7:13 the seller shall not r· to that which
13 multitude...which shall not r·;
13:22 should not r· from his wicked way,
16:55, 55 shall r· to their former estate,
55 shall r· to your former estate.
18:23 not that he should r· from his ways,
21: 5 sheath: it shall not r· any more.
30 Shall I cause it to r· into his sheath?
29:14 to r· into the land of Pathros,
35: 9 and thy cities shall not r·:
46: 9 shall not r· by the way of the gate
17 after it shall r· to the prince: but
47: 6 me to r· to the brink of the river.
Da 10:20 now will I r· to the fight with the
11: 9 and shall r· into his own land.
10 then shall he r·, and be stirred up,
13 For the king of the north shall r·,
28 r· into his land with great riches;
28 do exploits, and r· to his own land.
29 At the time appointed he shall r·,
30 he shall be grieved, and r·, and
30 shall even r·, and have intelligence
Ho 2: 7 I will go and r· to my first husband;
9 Therefore will I r·, and take away
3: 5 shall the children of Israel r·, and
5:15 I will go and r· to my place, till they
6: 1 Come, and let us r· unto the Lord:
7:10 do not r· to the Lord their God,
16 They r·, but not to the most High:
8:13 their sins: they shall r· to Egypt.
9: 3 but Ephraim shall r· to Egypt, and
11: 5 shall not r· into the land of Egypt,
5 his king, because they refused to r·.
9 I will not r· to destroy Ephraim:
12:14 reproach shall his Lord r· unto him.
14: 1 O Israel, r· unto the Lord thy God;
7 dwell under his shadow shall r·;
Joe 2:14 knoweth if he will r· and repent,
3: 4 speedily will I r· your recompence
7 and will r· your recompence upon
Ob 15 thy reward shall r· upon thine own
Mic 1: 7 they shall r· to the hire of an harlot.
5: 3 the remnant of his brethren shall r·
Mal 1: 4 r· and build the desolate places;
3: 7 R· unto me, and I will r· unto you,
7 But ye said, Wherein shall we r·?
18 Then shall ye r·, and discern
M't 2:12 that they should not r· to Herod,
10:13 not worthy, let your peace r· to you.
12:44 will r· into my house from whence
24:18 let him which is in the field r· back
Lu 8:39 R· to thine own house, and shew
11:24 r· unto my house whence I came
12:36 when he will r· from the wedding;
17:31 field, let him likewise not r· back.
19:12 to receive...a kingdom, and to r·.
Ac 13:34 now no more to r· to corruption,
15:16 After this I will r·, and will build
18:21 but I will r· again unto you, if God
20: 3 purposed to r· through Macedonia.

returned
Ge 8: 3 the waters *r* from off the earth
9 and she *r* unto him into the ark,
12 dove; which *r* not again unto him
14: 7 they *r*, and came to En-mishpat,
18: 33 and Abraham *r* unto his place.
21: 32 *r* into the land of the Philistines.
22: 19 So Abraham *r* unto his young men,
31: 55 departed, and *r* unto his place.
32: 6 the messengers *r* to Jacob, saying,
33: 16 So Esau *r* that day on his way unto
37: 29 And Reuben *r* unto the pit; and,
30 he *r* unto his brethren, and said,
38: 22 he *r* to Judah, and said, I cannot
42: 24 *r* to them again, and communed
43: 10 now we had *r* this second time.
18 the money that was *r* in our sacks
44: 13 every man his ass, and *r* to the city.
50: 14 And Joseph *r* into Egypt, he, and
Ex 4: 18 And Moses went and *r* to Jethro his
20 ass, and he *r* to the land of Egypt:
5: 22 And Moses *r* unto the Lord, and
14: 27 and the sea *r* to his strength when
28 And the waters *r*, and covered the
19: 8 Moses *r* the words of the people
32: 31 And Moses *r* unto the Lord, and
34: 31 all the rulers of the congregation *r*
Le 22: 13 and is *r* unto her father's house, as
Nu 13: 25 they *r* from searching of the land
14: 36 sent to search the land, who *r*,
16: 50 Aaron *r* unto Moses unto the door
23: 6 he *r* unto him, and, lo, he stood
24: 25 up, and went and *r* to his place:
De 1: 45 And ye *r* and wept before the Lord;
Jos 2: 16 three days, until the pursuers be *r*:
22 days, until the pursuers were *r*:
23 So the two men *r*, and descended
4: 18 waters of Jordan *r* unto their place
6: 14 the city once, and *r* into the camp:
7: 3 And they *r* to Joshua, and said
8: 24 that all the Israelites *r* unto Ai,
10: 15 And Joshua *r*, and all Israel with
21 And all the people *r* to the camp
38, 43 Joshua *r*, and all Israel with
22: 9 and the half tribe of Manasseh *r*,
32 *r* from the children of Reuben, and
J'g 2: 19 they *r*, and corrupted themselves
5: 29 her, yea, she *r* answer to herself,
7: 3 *r* of the people twenty and two
15 *r* into the host of Israel, and said,
8: 13 the son of Joash *r* from battle
11: 39 that she *r* unto her father, who did
14: 8 And after a time he *r* to take her,
21: 23 went and *r* unto their inheritance,
Ru 1: 22 So Naomi *r*,...Ruth the Moabitess,
22 *r* out of the country of Moab:
1Sa 1: 19 worshipped before the Lord, and *r*
6: 16 it, they *r* to Ekron the same day.
17 Philistines *r* for a trespass offering
17: 15 David went and *r* from Saul to feed
53 *r* from chasing after...Philistines,
57 *r* from the slaughter of...Philistine,
18: 6 *r* from the slaughter of...Philistine,
23: 28 Saul *r* from pursuing after David,
24: 1 *r* from following the Philistines,
25: 39 hath *r* the wickedness of Nabal
26: 25 on his way, and Saul *r* to his place.
27: 9 apparel, and *r*, and came to Achish.
2Sa 1: 1 David was *r* from the slaughter of
22 and the sword of Saul *r* not empty.
2: 30 And Joab *r* from following Abner:
3: 16 unto him, Go, return. And he *r*.
27 when Abner was *r* to Hebron, Joab
6: 20 David *r* to bless his household.
8: 13 he *r* from smiting of the Syrians
10: 14 So Joab *r* from the children of
11: 4 and she *r* unto her house.
12: 31 all the people *r* unto Jerusalem.
14: 24 So Absalom *r* to his own house,
16: 8 hath *r* upon thee all the blood of
17: 3 whom thou seekest is as if all *r*:
20 not find them, they *r* to Jerusalem.
18: 16 the people *r* from pursuing after
19: 15 So the king *r*, and came to Jordan.
39 him; and he *r* unto his own place.
20: 22 Joab *r* to Jerusalem unto the king.
23: 10 people *r* after him only to spoil.
1Ki 12: 24 *r* to depart, according to the word
13: 10 *r* not by the way that he came to
33 Jeroboam *r* not from his evil way,
19: 21 And he *r* back from him, and took
2Ki 2: 25 and from thence he *r* to Samaria.
3: 27 from him, and *r* to their own land.
4: 35 he *r*, and walked in the house
5: 15 And he *r* to the man of God, he and
7: 15 And the messengers *r*, and told the
8: 3 that the woman *r* out of the land
9: 15 king Joram was *r* to be healed in
14: 14 and hostages, and *r* to Samaria.
19: 8 Rab-shakeh *r*, and found the king
36 and went and *r*, and dwelt at
23: 20 upon them, and *r* to Jerusalem.
1Ch 16: 43 and David *r* to bless his house.
20: 3 and all the people *r* to Jerusalem.
2Ch 10: 2 it, that Jeroboam *r* out of Egypt.
11: 4 *r* from going against Jeroboam.
14: 15 in abundance, and *r* to Jerusalem.
19: 1 Jehoshaphat the king of Judah *r*
8 when they *r* to Jerusalem.
20: 27 Then they *r*, every man of Judah
22: 6 And he *r* to be healed in Jezreel
25: 10 and they *r* home in great anger.
24 hostages also, and *r* to Samaria.
28: 15 brethren: then they *r* to Samaria.
31: 1 Then all the children of Israel *r*,
32: 21 he *r* with shame of face to his own
2Ch 34: 7 land of Israel, he *r* to Jerusalem.
9 Benjamin;...they *r* to Jerusalem.
Ezr 5: 5 and then they *r* answer by letter
11 thus they *r* us answer, saying, We
Ne 2: 15 the gate of the valley, and so *r*.
4: 15 we *r* all of us to the wall, every one
9: 28 yet when they *r*, and cried unto
Es 2: 14 the morrow she *r* into the second
7: 8 the king *r* out of the palace garden
Ps 35: 13 my prayer *r* into mine own bosom.
60: *title* when Joab *r*, and smote of Edom
78: 34 *r* and enquired early after God.
Ec 4: 1 So I *r*, and considered all the
7 Then I *r*, and I saw vanity under
9: 11 I *r*, and saw under the sun, that
Isa 37: 8 So Rabshakeh *r*, and found the
37 went and *r*, and dwelt at Nineveh.
38: 8 So the sun *r* ten degrees, by which
Jer 3: 7 Turn thou unto me. But she *r* not.
14: 3 they *r* with their vessels empty;
40: 12 Even all the Jews *r* out of all places
41: 14 from Mizpah cast about and *r*,
43: 5 that were *r* from all nations,
Eze 1: 14 And the living creatures ran and *r*
8: 17 have *r* to provoke me to anger:
47: 7 Now when I had *r*, behold, at the
Da 4: 34 mine understanding *r* unto me,
36 same time my reason *r* unto me;
36 honour and brightness *r* unto me;
Ho 6: 11 I *r* the captivity of my people.
Am 4: 6, 8, 9, 10, 11 have ye not *r* unto me,
Zec 1: 6 and they *r* and said, Like as the
16 I am *r* to Jerusalem with mercies:
7: 14 that no man passed through nor *r*:
8: 3 I am *r* unto Zion, and will dwell in
M't 21: 18 as he *r* into the city, he hungered.
M'r 14: 40 when he *r*, he found them asleep
Lu 1: 56 months, and *r* to her own house.
2: 20 the shepherds *r*, glorifying and
39 they *r* into Galilee, to their own
43 as they *r*, the child Jesus tarried
4: 1 of the Holy Ghost *r* from Jordan,
14 Jesus *r* in the power of the Spirit
8: 37 up into the ship, and *r* back again.
40 to pass, that, when Jesus was *r*,
9: 10 the apostles, when they were *r*,
10: 17 And the seventy *r* again with joy,
17: 18 found that *r* to give glory to God,
19: 15 came to pass, that when he was *r*,
23: 48 done, smote their breasts, and *r*.
56 And they *r*, and prepared spices
24: 9 *r* from the sepulchre, and told all
33 the same hour, and *r* to Jerusalem,
52 and *r* to Jerusalem with great joy:
Ac 1: 12 Then *r* they unto Jerusalem from
5: 22 not in the prison, they *r*, and told,
8: 25 *r* to Jerusalem, and preached the
12: 25 and Saul *r* from Jerusalem, when
13: 13 John departing from them *r* to
14: 21 they *r* again to Lystra, and to
21: 6 took ship; and they *r* home again.
23: 32 to go with him, and *r* to the castle:
Ga 1: 17 and *r* again unto Damascus.
Heb 11: 15 have had opportunity to have *r*.
1Pe 2: 25 but are now *r* unto the Shepherd

returneth
Ps 146: 4 goeth forth, he *r* to his earth;
Pr 26: 11 As a dog *r* to his vomit,
11 so a fool *r* to his folly.
Ec 1: 6 the wind *r* again according to his
Isa 55: 10 from heaven, and *r* not thither,
Eze 35: 7 that passeth out and him that *r*.
Zec 9: 8 by, and because of him that *r*:

returning
Isa 30: 15 In *r* and rest shall ye be saved;
Lu 7: 10 *r* to the house, found the servant
Ac 8: 28 Was *r*, and sitting in his chariot
Heb 7: 1 *r* from the slaughter of the kings,

Reu (*re'-u*) See also RAGAU.
Ge 11: 18 lived thirty years, and begat *R*:
19 Peleg lived after he begat *R* two
20 And *R* lived two and thirty years,
21 *R* lived after he begat Serug two
1Ch 1: 25 Eber, Peleg, *R*,

Reuben (*ru'-ben*) See also REUBENITE.
Ge 29: 32 a son, and she called his name *R*:
30: 14 And *R* went in the days of wheat
35: 22 that *R* went and lay with Bilhah
23 sons of Leah; *R*, Jacob's firstborn,
37: 21 *R* heard it, and he delivered him
22 *R* said unto them, Shed no blood,
29 And *R* returned unto the pit; and,
42: 22 *R* answered them, saying, Spake I
37 *R* spake unto his father, saying,
46: 8 Jacob and his sons: *R*, Jacob's
9 the sons of *R*; Hanoch, and Phallu,
48: 5 as *R* and Simeon, they shall be
49: 3 *R*, thou art my firstborn, my
Ex 1: 2 *R*, Simeon, Levi, and Judah,
6: 14 sons of *R* the firstborn of Israel;
14 Carmi: these be the families of *R*.
Nu 1: 5 the tribe of *R*; Elizur the son of
20 the children of *R*, Israel's eldest
21 tribe of *R*, were forty and six
2: 10 be the standard of the camp of *R*
10 captain of the children of *R* shall
16 were numbered in the camp of *R*
7: 30 prince of the children of *R*, did
10: 18 the standard of the camp of *R* set
13: 4 tribe of *R*, Shammua the son of
16: 1 son of Peleth, sons of *R*, took men:
26: 5 *R*, the eldest son of Israel:
5 children of *R*; Hanoch, of whom
32: 1 Now the children of *R* and the
Nu 32: 2 the children of *R* came and spake
6 to the children of *R*, Shall your
25 children of *R* spake unto Moses,
29 children of *R* will pass with your
31 the children of *R* answered, saying,
33 of Gad and to the children of *R*,
37 the children of *R* built Heshbon,
34: 14 For the tribe of the children of *R*
De 11: 6 the sons of Eliab, the son of *R*:
27: 13 *R*, Gad, and Asher, and Zebulun,
33: 6 Let *R* live, and not die; and let not
Jos 4: 12 And the children of *R*, and the
13: 15 unto the tribe of the children of *R*
23 border of the children of *R* was
23 the inheritance of the children of *R*
15: 6 to the stone of Bohan the son of *R*:
18: 7 and Gad, and *R*, and half the tribe
17 to the stone of Bohan the son of *R*,
20: 8 upon the plain out of the tribe of *R*,
21: 7 families had out of the tribe of *R*,
36 out of the tribe of *R*, Bezer with
22: 9 children of *R* and the children
10, 11 children of *R* and the children
13 Israel sent unto the children of *R*,
15 they came unto the children of *R*,
21 Then the children of *R* and the
25 ye children of *R* and children of
30 the words that the children of *R*
31 priest said unto the children of *R*,
32 returned from the children of *R*,
33 the children of *R* and Gad dwelt.
34 the children of *R* and the children
J'g 5: 15, 16 divisions of *R* there were great
1Ch 2: 1 are the sons of Israel; *R*, Simeon,
5: 1 the sons of *R* the firstborn of Israel,
3 I say, of *R* the firstborn of Israel
18 The sons of *R*, and the Gadites,
6: 63 their families, out of the tribe of *R*,
78 given them out of the tribe of *R*,
Eze 48: 6 unto the west side, a portion for *R*.
7 And by the border of *R*, from the
31 one gate of *R*, one gate of Judah,
Re 7: 5 of *R* were sealed twelve thousand.

Reubenite (*ru'-ben-ite*) See also REUBENITES.
1Ch 11: 42 Adina the son of Shiza the *R*, a

Reubenites (*ru'-ben-ites*)
Nu 26: 7 These are the families of the *R*:
De 3: 12 cities thereof, gave I unto the *R*
16 unto the *R* and unto the Gadites
4: 43 in the plain country, of the *R*; and
29: 8 it for an inheritance unto the *R*,
Jos 1: 12 And to the *R*, and to the Gadites,
12: 6 it for a possession unto the *R*, and
13: 8 With whom the *R* and the Gadites
22: 1 Then Joshua called the *R*, and the
2Ki 10: 33 the Gadites, and the *R*, and the
1Ch 5: 6 captive: he was prince of the *R*.
26 he carried them away, even the *R*,
11: 42 a captain of the *R*, and thirty with
12: 37 the other side of Jordan, of the *R*,
26: 32 king David made rulers over the *R*,
27: 16 the ruler of the *R* was Eliezer the

Reuel (*re-u'-el*) See also DEUEL; JETHRO; RAGUEL.
Ge 36: 4 Eliphaz; and Bashemath bare *R*;
10 *R* the son of Bashemath the wife of
13 these are the sons of *R*; Nahath,
17 these are the sons of *R* Esau's son;
17 these are the dukes that came of *R*
Ex 2: 18 when they came to *R* their father,
Nu 2: 14 shall be Eliasaph the son of *R*.
1Ch 1: 35 The sons of Esau; Eliphaz, *R*, and
37 The sons of *R*; Nahath, Zerah,
9: 8 the son of *R*, the son of Ibnijah:

Reumah (*re-u'-mah*)
Ge 22: 24 his concubine, whose name was *R*,

reveal See also REVEALED; REVEALETH.
Job 20: 27 The heaven shall *r* his iniquity;
Jer 33: 6 will *r* unto them the abundance of
Da 2: 47 seeing thou couldest *r* this secret.
M't 11: 27 to whomsoever the Son will *r* him.
Lu 10: 22 and he to whom the Son will *r* him.
Ga 1: 16 To *r* his Son in me, that I might
Ph'p 3: 15 God shall *r* even this unto you.

revealed
De 29: 29 those things which are *r* belong
1Sa 3: 7 word of the Lord yet *r* unto him.
21 for the Lord *r* himself to Samuel
2Sa 7: 27 hast *r* to thy servant, saying, I will
Isa 22: 14 it was *r* in mine ears by the Lord
23: 1 the land of Chittim it is *r* to them.
40: 5 the glory of the Lord shall be *r*,
53: 1 to whom is the arm of the Lord *r*?
56: 1 and my righteousness to be *r*.
Jer 11: 20 for unto thee have I *r* my cause.
Da 2: 19 was the secret *r* unto Daniel in a
30 is not *r* to me for any wisdom
10: 1 Persia a thing was *r* unto Daniel,
M't 10: 26 covered, that shall not be *r*; and
11: 25 and hast *r* them unto babes.
16: 17 and blood hath not *r* it unto thee,
Lu 2: 26 *r* unto him by the Holy Ghost,
35 thoughts of many hearts may be *r*.
10: 21 and hast *r* them unto babes:
12: 2 nothing covered, that shall not be *r*;
17: 30 the day when the Son of man is *r*.
Joh 12: 38 hath the arm of the Lord been *r*?
Ro 1: 17 righteousness of God *r* from faith
18 the wrath of God is *r* from heaven
8: 18 the glory which shall be *r* in us.
1Co 2: 10 hath *r* them unto us by his Spirit:
3: 13 it, because it shall be *r* by fire;
14: 30 If any thing be *r* to another that
Ga 3: 23 faith which should afterwards be *r*.

Eph 3: 5 as it is now r' unto his holy apostles
2Th 1: 7 the Lord Jesus shall be r' from
2: 3 and that man of sin be r', the son
6 that he might be r' in his time.
8 then shall that Wicked be r', whom
1Pe 1: 5 ready to be r' in the last time.
12 Unto whom it was r', that not unto
4: 13 when his glory shall be r', ye may
5: 1 of the glory that shall be r':

revealer
Da 2: 47 and a r' of secrets, seeing thou

revealeth
Pr 11: 13 A talebearer r' secrets: but he
20: 19 about as a talebearer r' secrets:
Da 2: 22 He r' the deep and secret things:
28 is a God in heaven that r' secrets,
29 he that r' secrets maketh known to
Am 3: 7 he r' his secret unto his servants

revelation See also REVELATIONS.
Ro 2: 5 and r' of the righteous judgment of
16: 25 according to the r' of the mystery,
1Co 14: 6 I shall speak to you either by r', or
26 doctrine, hath a tongue, hath a r',
Ga 1: 12 it, but by the r' of Jesus Christ.
2: 2 And I went up by r', and
Eph 1: 17 unto you the spirit of wisdom and r'
3: 3 How that by r' he made known unto
1Pe 1: 13 unto you at the r' of Jesus Christ:
Re 1: 1 The R' of Jesus Christ, which God

revelations
2Co 12: 1 come to visions and r' of the Lord.
7 through the abundance of the r',

revellings
Ga 5: 21 drunkenness, r', and such like:
1Pe 4: 3 r', banquetings, and abominable

revenge See also REVENGED; REVENGES; REVENGETH; REVENGING.
Jer 15: 15 me, and r' me of my persecutors;
20: 10 and we shall take our r' on him.
Eze 25: 15 the Philistines hath dealt by r',
2Co 7: 11 desire, yea, what zeal, yea, what r'!
10: 6 readiness to r' all disobedience,

revenged
Eze 25: 12 and r' himself upon them;

revenger See also REVENGERS.
Nu 35: 19 The r' of blood himself shall slay
21 r' of blood shall slay the murderer,
24 between the slayer and...r' of blood
25 out of the hand of the r' of blood,
27 the r' of blood find him without
27 and the r' of blood kill the slayer;
Ro 13: 4 a r' to execute wrath upon him

revengers
2Sa 14: 11 suffer the r' of blood to destroy

revenges
De 32: 42 beginning of r' upon the enemy.

revengeth
Na 1: 2 God is jealous, and the Lord r';
2 the Lord r', and is furious; the

revenging
Ps 79: 10 r' of the blood of thy servants

revenue See also REVENUES.
Ezr 4: 13 shalt endamage the r' of the kings.
Pr 8: 19 gold; and my r' than choice silver.
Isa 23: 3 the harvest of the river, is her r';

revenues
Pr 15: 6 in the r' of the wicked is trouble.
16: 8 than great r' without right.
Jer 12: 13 shall be ashamed of your r' because

reverence See also REVERENCED.
Le 19: 30 sabbaths, and r' my sanctuary:
26: 2 my sabbaths, and r' my sanctuary:
2Sa 9: 6 he fell on his face, and did r'.
1Ki 1: 31 and did r' to the king, and said,
Es 3: 2 Mordecai bowed not, nor did him r'.
5 Mordecai bowed not, nor did him r',
Ps 89: 7 to be had in r' of all them that
M't 21: 37 son, saying, They will r' my son.
M'r 12: 6 them, saying, They will r' my son.
Lu 20: 13 they will r' him when they see him.
Eph 5: 33 wife see that she r' her husband.
Heb 12: 9 us, and we gave them r':
28 acceptably with r' and godly fear:

reverenced
Es 3: 2 king's gate, bowed, and r' Haman:

reverend
Ps 111: 9 ever: holy and r' is his name.

reverse
Nu 23: 20 hath blessed; and I cannot r' it.
Es 8: 5 to r' the letters devised by Haman
8 the king's ring, may no man r'.

revile See also REVILED; REVILEST; REVILINGS.
Ex 22: 28 Thou shalt not r' the gods, nor
M't 5: 11 are ye, when men shall r' you,

reviled
M't 27: 39 And they that passed by r' him,
M'r 15: 32 were crucified with him r' him.
Joh 9: 28 Then they r' him, and said, Thou
1Co 4: 12 being r', we bless; being
1Pe 2: 23 Who, when he was r',...not again;
23 Who when he was...r' not again;

revilers
1Co 6: 10 nor r', nor extortioners, shall

revilest
Ac 23: 4 said, R' thou God's high priest?

revilings
Isa 51: 7 neither be ye afraid of their r'.
Zep 2: 8 the r' of the children of Ammon,

revive See also REVIVED; REVIVING.
Ne 4: 2 r' the stones out of the heaps of
Ps 85: 6 Wilt thou not r' us again: that thy
138: 7 midst of trouble, thou wilt r' me:
Isa 57: 15 to r' the spirit of the humble, and
15 r' the heart of the contrite ones.
Ho 6: 2 after two days will he r' us: in the
14: 7 They shall r' as the corn, and grow
Hab 3: 2 r' thy work in the midst of the

revived
Ge 45: 27 the spirit of Jacob their father r':
J'g 15: 19 his spirit came again, and he r'.
1Ki 17: 22 came into him again, and he r'.
2Ki 13: 21 touched the bones of Elisha, he r',
Ro 7: 9 the commandment came, sin r',
14: 9 Christ both died, and rose, and r',

reviving
Ezr 9: 8 give us a little r' in our bondage.
9 to give us a r', to set up the house

revolt See also REVOLTED; REVOLTING.
2Ch 21: 10 did Libnah r' from under his hand;
Isa 1: 5 more? ye will r' more and more:
59: 13 God, speaking oppression and r',

revolted
2Ki 8: 20 Edom r' from under the hand of
22 Yet Edom r' from under the hand
22 Then Libnah r' at the same time.
2Ch 21: 8 In his days the Edomites r' from
10 So the Edomites r' from under the
Isa 31: 6 children of Israel have deeply r'.
Jer 5: 23 heart; they are r' and gone.

revolters
Jer 6: 28 They are all grievous r', walking
Ho 5: 2 the r' are profound to make a
9: 15 no more: all their princes are r'.

revolting
Jer 5: 23 hath a r' and a rebellious heart;

reward See also REWARDED; REWARDETH; REWARDS.
Ge 15: 1 shield, and thy exceeding great r'.
Nu 18: 31 r' for your service in the tabernacle
De 10: 17 not persons, nor taketh r':
27: 25 r' to slay an innocent person:
32: 41 and will r' them that hate me.
Ru 2: 12 a full r' be given thee of the Lord
1Sa 24: 19 Lord r' thee good for that thou
2Sa 3: 39 the Lord shall r' the doer of evil
4: 10 have given him a r' for his tidings:
19: 36 recompense it me with such a r'?
1Ki 13: 7 thyself, and I will give thee a r'.
2Ch 20: 11 Behold, I say, how they r' us, to
Job 6: 22 a r' for me of your substance?
7: 2 hireling looketh for the r' of his work:
Ps 15: 5 taketh r' against the innocent.
19: 11 keeping of them there is great r'.
40: 15 them be desolate for a r' of their
54: 5 shall r' evil unto mine enemies:
58: 11 there is a r' for the righteous:
70: 3 for a r' of their shame that say,
91: 8 and see the r' of the wicked.
94: 2 earth: render a r' to the proud.
109: 20 this be the r' of mine adversaries
127: 3 the fruit of the womb is his r'.
Pr 11: 18 righteousness shall be a sure r'.
21: 14 a r' in the bosom strong wrath.
24: 14 then there shall be a r', and thy
20 shall be no r' to the evil man;
25: 22 head, and the Lord shall r' thee.
Ec 4: 9 have a good r' for their labour.
9: 5 neither have they any more a r';
Isa 3: 11 r' of his hands shall be given him.
5: 23 Which justify the wicked for r',
40: 10 behold, his r' is with him, and his
45: 13 not for price nor r', saith the Lord
62: 11 his r' is with him, and his work
Jer 40: 5 guard gave him victuals and a r',
Eze 16: 34 and in that thou givest a r',
34 and no r' is given unto thee,
Ho 4: 9 ways, and r' them their doings.
9: 1 loved a r' upon every cornfloor.
Ob 15 thy r' shall return upon thine own
Mic 3: 11 heads thereof judge for r', and
7: 3 and the judge asketh for a r';
M't 5: 12 for great is your r' in heaven: for
46 which love you, what r' have ye?
6: 1 ye have no r' of your Father which
2 I say unto you, They have their r'.
4 secret himself shall r' thee openly.
5 say unto you, They have their r'.
6 seeth in secret shall r' thee openly.
16 I say unto you, They have their r'.
18 seeth in secret, shall r' thee openly.
10: 41 shall receive a prophet's r'; and
41 shall receive a righteous man's r'.
42 you, he shall in no wise lose his r'.
16: 27 he shall r' every man according
M'r 9: 41 unto you, he shall not lose his r'.
Lu 6: 23 behold, your r' is great in heaven:
35 your r' shall be great, and ye shall
23: 41 we receive the due r' of our deeds:
Ac 1: 18 a field with the r' of iniquity;
Ro 4: 4 worketh is the r' not reckoned of
1Co 3: 8 every man shall receive his own r'
14 thereupon, he shall receive a r'.
9: 17 do this thing willingly, I have a r':
18 What is my r' then? Verily that,
Col 2: 18 Let no man beguile you of your r'
3: 24 receive the r' of the inheritance:
1Ti 5: 18 The labourer is worthy of his r'.
2Ti 4: 14 the Lord r' him according to his
Heb 2: 2 received a just recompence of r';
10: 35 hath a great recompence of r'.
11: 26 unto the recompence of the r'.

2Pe 2: 13 receive the r' of unrighteousness,
2Jo 8 but that we receive a full r'.
Jude 11 after the error of Balaam for r',
Re 11: 18 shouldest give r' unto thy servants
18: 6 R' her even as she rewarded you,
22: 12 my r' is with me, to give every

rewarded
Ge 44: 4 Wherefore have ye r' evil for good?
1Sa 24: 17 thou hast r' me good, whereas
17 whereas I have r' thee evil.
2Sa 22: 21 The Lord r' me according to my
2Ch 15: 7 weak: for your work shall be r'.
Ps 7: 4 I have r' evil unto him that was
18: 20 The Lord r' me according to my
35: 12 They r' me evil for good to the
103: 10 r' us according to our iniquities.
109: 5 And they have r' me evil for good,
Pr 13: 13 the commandment shall be r'.
Isa 3: 9 they have r' evil unto themselves.
Jer 31: 16 for thy work shall be r', saith the
Re 18: 6 Reward her even as she r' you,

rewarder
Heb 11: 6 a r' of them that diligently seek

rewardeth
Job 21: 19 he r' him, and he shall know it.
Ps 31: 23 and plentifully r' the proud doer.
137: 8 r' thee as thou hast served us.
Pr 17: 13 Whoso r' evil for good, evil shall
26: 10 formed all things both r' the fool,
10 the fool, and r' transgressors.

rewards
Nu 22: 7 the r' of divination in their hand;
Isa 1: 23 gifts, and followeth after r':
Da 2: 6 ye shall receive of me gifts and r'
5: 17 thyself, and give thy r' to another;
Ho 2: 12 These are my r' that my lovers

Rezeph (*re'-zef*)
2Ki 19: 12 as Gozan, and Haran, and R', and
Isa 37: 12 as Gozan, and Haran, and R', and

Rezia (*re-zi'-ah*)
1Ch 7: 39 Ulla; Arah, and Haniel, and R'.

Rezin (*re'-zin*)
2Ki 15: 37 against Judah, R'...king of Syria.
16: 5 Then R' king of Syria and Pekah
6 At that time R' king of Syria
9 people...captive to Kir, and slew R'.
Ezr 2: 48 The children of R', the children of
Ne 7: 50 of Reaiah, the children of R', the
Isa 7: 1 that R' the king of Syria and Pekah
4 the fierce anger of R' with Syria,
8 and the head of Damascus is R';
8: 6 rejoice in R' and Remaliah's son;
9: 11 shall set up the adversaries of R'

Rezon (*re'-zon*)
1Ki 11: 23 adversary, R' the son of Eliadah,

Rhegium (*re'-je-um*)
Ac 28: 13 fetched a compass, and came to R':

Rhesa (*re'-sah*) See also REPHAIAH.
Lu 3: 27 which was the son of R', which

Rhoda (*ro'-dah*)
Ac 12: 13 damsel came to hearken, named R'.

Rhodes (*rodes*)
Ac 21: 1 and the day following unto R',

rib See also RIBBAND; RIBS.
Ge 2: 22 And the r',...made he a woman,
2Sa 2: 23 spear smote him under the fifth r',
3: 27 smote him there under the fifth r',
4: 6 they smote him under the fifth r':
20: 10 smote him therewith in the fifth r',

Ribai (*rib'-ahee*)
2Sa 23: 29 Ittai the son of R' out of Gibeah
1Ch 11: 31 Ithai the son of R' of Gibeah, that

ribband
Nu 15: 38 fringe of the borders a r' of blue:

ribbon See RIBBAND.

Riblah (*rib'-lah*)
Nu 34: 11 go down from Shepham to R',
2Ki 23: 33 put him in bands at R' in the land
25: 6 up to the king of Babylon to R';
20 them to the king of Babylon to R':
21 and slew them at R' in the land of
Jer 39: 5 to R' in the land of Hamath, where
6 slew the sons of Zedekiah in R'
52: 9 to R' in the land of Hamath;
10 slew...the princes of Judah in R'.
26 them to the king of Babylon to R'.
27 and put them to death in R' in the

ribs
Ge 2: 21 took one of his r', and closed up
Da 7: 5 it had three r' in the mouth of it

rich See also ENRICH; RICHER; RICHES.
Ge 13: 2 And Abram was very r' in cattle,
14: 23 shouldest say, I...made Abram r':
Ex 30: 15 The r' shall not give more, and
Le 25: 47 a sojourner or stranger wax r'
Ru 3: 10 young men, whether poor or r'.
1Sa 2: 7 Lord maketh poor, and maketh r':
2Sa 12: 1 the one r', and the other poor.
2 r' man had exceeding many flocks
4 came a traveller unto the r' man,
Job 15: 29 He shall not be r', neither shall
27: 19 The r' man shall lie down, but he
34: 19 nor regardeth the r' more than
Ps 45: 12 r' among the people shall intreat
49: 2 low and high, r' and poor, together.
16 thou afraid when one is made r',
Pr 10: 4 the hand of the diligent maketh r'.
15 r' man's wealth is his strong city:

Pr 10:22 blessing of the Lord, it maketh r·,
13: 7 There is that maketh himself r·,
14:20 but the r· hath many friends.
18:11 r· man's wealth is his strong city,
23 but the r· answereth roughly.
21:17 loveth wine and oil shall not be r·.
22: 2 The r· and poor meet together:
7 The r· ruleth over the poor, and
16 he that giveth to the r·, shall surely
23: 4 Labour not to be r·: cease from
28: 6 is perverse...though he be r·.
11 r· man is wise in his own conceit;
20 he that maketh haste to be r· shall
22 hasteth to be r· hath an evil eye,
Ec 5:12 abundance of the r· will not suffer
10: 6 dignity, and the r· sit in low place.
20 curse not the r· in thy bedchamber:
Isa 53: 9 wicked, and with the r· in his death;
Jer 5:27 are become great, and waxen r·.
9:23 not the r· man glory in his riches:
Eze 27:24 in chests of r· apparel, bound with
Ho 12: 8 Ephraim said, Yet I am become r·,
Mic 6:12 the r· men...are full of violence,
Zec 11: 5 Blessed be the Lord; for I am r·:
M't 19:23 a r· man shall hardly enter into
24 than for a r· man to enter into the
27:57 there came a r· man of Arimathæa,
M'r 10:25 than for a r· man to enter into the
12:41 many that were r· cast in much.
Lu 1:53 the r· he hath sent empty away.
6:24 But woe unto you that are r·!
12:16 The ground of a certain r· man
21 himself, and is not r· toward God.
14:12 kinsmen, nor thy r· neighbours;
16: 1, 19 There was a certain r· man,
21 which fell from the r· man's table:
22 r· man also died, and was buried;
18:23 very sorrowful: for he was very r·.
25 than for a r· man to enter into the
19: 2 among the publicans, and he was r·.
21: 1 saw the r· men casting their gifts
Ro 10:12 is r· unto all that call upon him.
1Co 4: 8 Now ye are full, now ye are r·, ye
2Co 6:10 as poor, yet making many r·;
8: 9 though he was r·, yet for your
9 through his poverty might be r·.
Eph 2: 4 God, who is r· in mercy, for his
1Ti 6: 9 that will be r· fall into temptation
17 Charge them that are r· in this
18 that they be r· in good works,
Jas 1:10 But the r·, in that he is made low:
11 So also shall the r· man fade away
2: 5 the poor of this world r· in faith,
6 Do not r· men oppress you, and
5: 1 Go to now, ye r· men, weep and
Re 2: 9 and poverty, (but thou art r·)
3:17 Because thou sayest, I am r·, and
18 in the fire, that thou mayest be r·;
6:15 the r· men, and the chief captains,
13:16 great, r· and poor, free and bond,
18: 3 merchants of the earth...waxed r·
15 things, which were made r· by her,
19 were made r· all that had ships

richer
Da 11: 2 fourth shall be far r· than they all:

riches
Ge 31:16 the r· which God hath taken from
36: 7 their r· were more than that they
Jos 22: 8 Return with much r· unto your
1Sa 17:25 king will enrich him with great r·,
1Ki 3:11 neither hast asked r· for thyself,
13 hast not asked, both r·, and honour:
10:23 exceeded...kings of the earth for r·
1Ch 29:12 Both r· and honour come of thee,
28 old age, full of days, r·, and honour:
2Ch 1:11 not asked r·, wealth, or honour,
12 I will give thee r·, and wealth, and
9:22 passed...the kings of the earth in r·
17: 5 he had r· and honour in abundance.
18: 1 Jehoshaphat had r· and honour in
20:25 both r· with the dead bodies, and
32:27 Hezekiah had exceeding much r·
Es 1: 4 the r· of his glorious kingdom and
5:11 told them of the glory of his r·, and
Job 20:15 He hath swallowed down r·, and
36:19 Will he esteem thy r·? no, not gold,
Ps 37:16 better than the r· of many wicked.
39: 6 he heapeth up r·, and knoweth not who
49: 6 boast...in the multitude of their r·;
52: 7 trusted in the abundance of his r·,
62:10 if r· increase, set not your heart
73:12 in the world; they increase in r·.
104:24 them all: the earth is full of thy r·.
112: 3 and r· shall be in his house:
119:14 testimonies, as much as in all r·.
Pr 3:16 in her left hand r· and honour.
8:18 R· and honour are with me; yea,
18 yea, durable r· and righteousness.
11: 4 R· profit not in the day of wrath:
16 honour: and strong men retain r·.
28 He that trusteth in his r· shall fall:
13: 7 himself poor, yet hath great r·.
8 ransom of a man's life are his r·:
14:24 The crown of the wise is their r·:
19:14 House and r· are the inheritance
22: 1 rather to be chosen than great r·,
4 and the fear of the Lord are r·, and
16 oppresseth the poor to increase his r·,
23: 5 r· certainly make themselves wings;
24: 4 with all precious and pleasant r·.
27:24 For r· are not for ever: and doth
30: 8 give me neither poverty nor r·;
Ec 4: 8 neither is his eye satisfied with r·;
5:13 r· kept for the owners thereof to
14 But those r· perish by evil travail:
Ec 5:19 whom God hath given r· and wealth,
6: 2 A man to whom God hath given r·,
9:11 nor yet r· to men of understanding,
Isa 8: 4 r· of Damascus and the spoil of
10:14 found as a nest the r· of the people:
30: 6 carry their r· upon the shoulders of
45: 3 and hidden r· of secret places,
61: 6 ye shall eat the r· of the Gentiles,
Jer 9:23 not the rich man glory in his r·:
17:11 he that getteth r·, and not by right,
48:36 r·...he hath gotten are perished.
Eze 26:12 they shall make a spoil of thy r·,
27:12 of the multitude of all kind of r·;
18 making, for the multitude of all r·;
27 r·, and thy fairs, thy merchandise,
33 earth with the multitude of thy r·
28: 4 thou hast gotten thee r·, and hast
5 traffick hast thou increased thy r·,
5 heart is lifted up because of thy r·:
Da 11: 2 through his r· he shall stir up all
13 a great army and with much r·.
24 them the prey, and spoil, and r·:
28 return into his land with great r·;
M't 13:22 world, and the deceitfulness of r·,
M'r 4:19 world, and the deceitfulness of r·,
10:23 they that have r· enter into the
24 that trust in r· to enter into the
Lu 8:14 are choked with cares and r· and
16:11 will commit to your trust the true r·?
18:24 they that have r· enter into the
Ro 2: 4 Or despisest thou the r· of his
9:23 make known the r· of his glory on
11:12 fall of them be the r· of the world,
12 diminishing of them the r· of the
33 depth of the r· both of the wisdom
2Co 8: 2 unto the r· of their liberality.
Eph 1: 7 according to the r· of his grace;
18 r· of the glory of his inheritance in
2: 7 shew the exceeding r· of his grace
3: 8 the unsearchable r· of Christ;
16 according to the r· of his glory, to
Ph'p 4:19 to his r· in glory by Christ Jesus.
Col 1:27 the r· of the glory of this mystery
2: 2 unto all r· of the full assurance of
1Ti 6:17 nor trust in uncertain r·, but in the
Heb 11:26 reproach of Christ greater r·
Jas 5: 2 Your r· are corrupted, and your
Re 5:12 was slain to receive power, and r·,
18:17 hour so great r· is come to nought.

richly
Col 3:16 the word of Christ dwell in you r·
1Ti 6:17 who giveth us r· all things to enjoy;

rid
Ge 37:22 he might r· him out of their hands,
Ex 6: 6 I will r· you out of their bondage,
Le 26: 6 will r· evil beasts out of the land,
Ps 82: 4 needy: r· them out of the hand of
144: 7 r· me, and deliver me out of great
11 R· me, and deliver me from the

riddance
Le 23:22 not make clean r· of the corners
Zep 1:18 for he shall make even a speedy r·

ridden
Nu 22:30 ass, upon which thou hast r· ever

riddle
J'g 14:12 I will now put forth a r· unto you:
13 Put forth thy r·, that we may hear
14 not in three days expound the r·.
15 that he may declare unto us the r·,
16 thou hast put forth a r· unto the
17 she told the r· to the children of her
18 heifer, ye had not found out my r·.
19 unto them which expounded the r·.
Eze 17: 2 Son of man, put forth a r·, and

ride See also RIDDEN; RIDETH; RIDING; RODE.
Ge 41:43 he made him to r· in the second
De 32:13 He made him r· on the high places
J'g 5:10 Speak, ye that r· on white asses, ye
2Sa 16: 2 be for the king's household to r· on;
19:26 me an ass, that I may r· thereon,
1Ki 1:33 cause Solomon my son to r· upon
38 Solomon to r· upon king David's
44 caused him to r· upon the king's
2Ki 10:16 So they made him r· in his chariot.
Job 30:22 thou causest me to r· upon it, and
Ps 45: 4 And in thy majesty r· prosperously
66:12 caused men to r· over our heads;
Isa 30:16 We will r· upon the swift; therefore
58:14 and I will cause thee to r· upon the
Jer 6:23 they r· upon horses, set in array
50:42 they shall r· upon horses, every one
Ho 10:11 I will make Ephraim to r·; Judah
14: 3 save us; we will not r· upon horses:
Hab 3: 8 thou didst r· upon thine horses and
Hag 2:22 chariots, and those that r· in them;

rider See also RIDERS.
Ge 49:17 so that this r· shall fall backward.
Ex 15: 1, 21 horse and his r· hath he thrown
Job 39:18 she scorneth the horse and his r·.
Jer 51:21 break in pieces the horse and his r·;
21 in pieces the chariot and his r·;
Zec 12: 4 and his r· with madness: and I

riders
2Ki 18:23 on thy part to set r· upon them.
Es 8:10 r· on mules, camels, and young
Isa 36: 8 on thy part to set r· upon them.
Hag 2:22 and their r· shall come down,
Zec 10: 5 r· on horses shall be confounded.

rideth
Le 15: 9 what saddle soever he r· upon that
De 33:26 who r· upon the heaven in thy help,
Es 6: 8 and the horse that the king r· upon,
Ps 68: 4 r· upon the heavens by his name
Ps 68:33 r· upon the heavens of heavens,
Isa 19: 1 the Lord r· upon a swift cloud, and
Am 2:15 he that r· the horse deliver himself.

ridges
Ps 65:10 Thou waterest the r· thereof

riding
Nu 22:22 Now he was r· upon his ass, and
2Ki 4:24 slack not thy r· for me, except I bid
Jer 17:25 r· in chariots and on horses, they,
22: 4 r· in chariots and on horses, he, and
Eze 23: 6 men, horsemen r· upon horses.
12 horsemen r· upon horses, all of them
23 all of them r· upon horses.
38:15 all of them r· upon horses, a great
Zec 1: 8 behold a man r· upon a red horse,
9: 9 lowly, and r· upon an ass, and

rie
Ex 9:32 wheat and the r· were not smitten:
Isa 28:25 barley and the r· in their place?

rifled
Zec 14: 2 shall be taken, and the houses r·,

right^ See also ARIGHT; UPRIGHT.
Ge 13: 9 left hand, then I will go to the r·;
9 if thou depart to the r· hand, then
18:25 the Judge of all the earth do r·?
24:48 which had led me in the r· way to
49 that I may turn to the r· hand, or
48:13 Ephraim in his r· hand toward
13 left hand toward Israel's r· hand,
14 Israel stretched out his r· hand,
17 r· hand upon the head of Ephraim,
18 put thy r· hand upon his head.
Ex 14:22, 29 wall unto them on their r· hand,
15: 6 Thy r· hand, O Lord, is become
6 thy r· hand, O Lord, hath dashed
12 Thou stretchedst out thy r· hand,
26 do that which is r· in his sight,
29:20 upon the tip of the r· ear of Aaron,
20 the tip of the r· ear of his sons,
20 upon the thumb of their r· hand,
20 upon the great toe of their r· foot,
22 is upon them, and the r· shoulder;
Le 7:32 r· shoulder shall ye give unto the
33 have the r· shoulder for his part.
8:23 it upon the tip of Aaron's r· ear,
23 upon the thumb of his r· hand,
23 upon the great toe of his r· foot.
24 blood upon the tip of their r· ear,
24 upon the thumbs of their r· hands,
24 upon the great toes of their r· feet:
25 and their fat, and the r· shoulder:
26 the fat, and upon the r· shoulder:
9:21 the r· shoulder Aaron waved for
14:14 put it upon the tip of the r· ear
14 and upon the thumb of his r· hand,
14 and upon the great toe of his r· foot:
16 dip his r· finger in the oil that is in
17 priest put upon the tip of the r· ear
17 and upon the thumb of his r· hand,
17 and upon the great toe of his r· foot,
25 it upon the tip of the r· ear of him
25 and upon the thumb of the r· hand,
25 and upon the great toe of his r· foot:
27 shall sprinkle with his r· finger
28 upon the tip of the r· ear of him
28 and upon the thumb of his r· hand,
28 and upon the great toe of his r· foot.
Nu 18:18 and as the r· shoulder are thine.
20:17 will not turn to the r· hand nor to
22:26 either to the r· hand or to the left.
27: 7 daughters of Zelophehad speak r·:
De 2:27 neither turn unto the r· hand nor
5:32 aside to the r· hand or to the left.
6:18 do that which is r· and good in the
12: 8 whatsoever is r· in his own eyes.
25 do that which is r· in the sight of
28 that which is good and r· in the
13:18 to do that which is r· in the eyes of
17:11 thee, to the r· hand, nor to the left.
20 to the r· hand, or to the left:
21: 9 which is r· in the sight of the Lord.
17 the r· of the firstborn is his.
28:14 day, to the r· hand, or to the left,
32: 4 without iniquity, just and r· is he.
33: 2 from his r· hand went a fiery law
Jos 1: 7 turn not from it to the r· hand or to
3:16 people passed over r· against Jericho.
9:25 seemeth good and r· unto thee to
17: 7 border went along on the r· hand
23: 6 not aside therefrom to the r· hand
J'g 3:16 under his raiment upon his r· thigh.
21 took the dagger from his r· thigh,
5:26 r· hand to the workmen's hammer;
7:20 trumpets in their r· hands to blow
12: 6 could not frame to pronounce it r·.
16:29 one with his r· hand, and of the
17: 6 every man did that which was r·
21:25 every man did that which was r· in
Ru 4: 6 redeem thou my r· to thyself; for I
1Sa 6:12 turned not aside to the r· hand or
11: 2 I may thrust out all your r· eyes,
12:23 teach you the good and the r· way:
2Sa 2:19 he turned not to the r· hand nor
21 Turn thee aside to thy r· hand or to
14:19 none can turn to the r· hand or to
15: 3 See, thy matters are good and r·;
16: 6 mighty men were on his r· hand
19:28 What r· therefore have I yet to cry
43 we have also more r· in David than ye:
20: 9 beard with the r· hand to kiss him.
24: 5 r· side of the city that lieth in the
1Ki 2:19 mother; and she sat on his r· hand.
6: 8 was in the r· side of the house:
7:21 he set up the r· pillar, and called

1Ki 7:39 bases on the r' side of the house.
39 the sea on the r' side of the house
49 five on the r' side, and five on the
11:33 do that which is r' in mine eyes,
38 and do that is r' in my sight, to
14: 8 to do that only which is r' in mine
15: 5 David did that which was r' in the
11 Asa did that which was r' in the
22:19 standing by him on his r' hand and
43 that which was r' in the eyes of
2Ki 10:15 Is thine heart r', as my heart is
30 executing that which is r' in mine
11:11 from the r' corner of the temple to
12: 2 Jehoash did that which was r' in
9 it beside the altar, on the r' side
14: 3 did that which was r' in the sight
15: 3, 34 that which was r' in the sight
16: 2 did not that which was r' in the
17: 9 things that were not r' against the
18: 3 did that which was r' in the sight
22: 2 And that which was r' in the sight
2 turned not aside to the r' hand or
23:13 were on the r' hand of the mount
1Ch 6:39 Asaph, who stood on his r' hand,
12: 2 could use both the r' hand and
13: 4 the thing was r' in the eyes of all
2Ch 3:17 one on the r' hand, and the other
17 of that on the r' hand Jachin,
4: 6 lavers, and put five on the r' hand,
7 five on the r' hand, and five on the
8 five on the r' side, and five on the
10 set the sea on the r' side of the
14: 2 did that which was good and r' in
18:18 of heaven standing on his r' hand
20:32 that which was r' in the sight of
23:10 from the r' side of the temple to
24: 2 Joash did that which was r' in the
25: 2 did that which was r' in the sight of
26: 4 did that which was r' in the sight of
27: 2 did that which was r' in the sight of
28: 1 he did not that which was r' in the
29: 2 did that which was r' in the sight of
31:20 that which was good and r' and
34: 2 did that which was r' in the sight of
2 declined neither to the r' hand,
Ezr 8:21 God, to seek of him a r' way for us,
Ne 2:20 but ye have no portion, nor r', nor
8: 4 and Maaseiah, on his r' hand;
9:13 and gavest them r' judgments,
33 for thou hast done r', but we have
12:31 one went on the r' hand upon the
Es 8: 5 the thing seem r' before the king,
Job 6:25 How forcible are r' words! but
23: 9 he hideth himself on the r' hand,
30:12 Upon my r' hand rise the youth;
33:27 and perverted that which was r',
34: 6 Should I lie against my r'? my
17 Shall even he that hateth r' govern?
23 will not lay upon man more than r';
35: 2 Thinkest thou this to be r', that
36: 6 wicked: but giveth r' to the poor.
40:14 thine own r' hand can save thee.
42: 7 spoken of me the thing that is r',
8 spoken of me the thing which is r',
Ps 9: 4 maintained my r' and my cause;
4 satest in the throne judging r'.
16: 8 he is at my r' hand, I shall not
11 at thy r' hand there are pleasures
17: 1 Hear the r', O Lord, attend unto
7 O thou that savest by thy r' hand
18:35 and thy r' hand hath holden me up,
19: 8 The statutes of the Lord are r',
20: 6 the saving strength of his r' hand.
21: 8 thy r' hand shall find out those that
26:10 and their r' hand is full of bribes.
33: 4 For the word of the Lord is r'; and
44: 3 but thy r' hand, and thine arm,
45: 4 thy r' hand shall teach thee terrible
6 of thy kingdom is a r' sceptre.
9 thy r' hand did stand the queen
46: 5 shall help her, and that r' early.
48:10 r' hand is full of righteousness.
51:10 and renew a r' spirit within me.
60: 5 save with thy r' hand, and hear
63: 8 thee: thy r' hand upholdeth me.
73:23 thou hast holden me by my r' hand.
74:11 thou thy hand, even thy r' hand?
77:10 of the r' hand of the most High.
78:37 their heart was not r' with him,
54 which his r' hand had purchased.
80:15 which thy r' hand hath planted,
17 be upon the man of thy r' hand,
89:13 thy hand, and high is thy r' hand.
25 sea, and his r' hand in the rivers.
42 up the r' hand of his adversaries;
91: 7 and ten thousand at thy r' hand;
98: 1 his r' hand, and his holy arm, hath
107: 7 he led them forth by the r' way,
108: 6 save with thy r' hand, and answer
109: 6 and let Satan stand at his r' hand.
31 stand at the r' hand of the poor,
110: 1 Sit thou at my r' hand, until I make
5 The Lord at thy r' hand shall strike
118:15 r' hand of the Lord doeth valiantly.
16 The r' hand of the Lord is exalted:
16 r' hand of the Lord doeth valiantly.
119:75 Lord, that thy judgments are r',
128 esteem all thy precepts...to be r';
121: 5 Lord is thy shade upon thy r' hand.
137: 5 let my r' hand forget her cunning.
138: 7 and thy r' hand shall save me.
139:10 and thy r' hand shall hold me.
140:12 the afflicted, and the r' of the poor.
142: 4 I looked on my r' hand, and beheld,
144: 8, 11 r' hand is a r' hand of falsehood.
Pr 3:16 Length of days is in her r' hand;
Pr 4:11 I have led thee in r' paths.
25 Let thine eyes look r' on, and let
27 Turn not to the r' hand nor to the
8: 6 opening of my lips...be r' things.
9 r' to them that find knowledge.
9:15 passengers...go r' on their ways:
12: 5 thoughts of the righteous are r':
15 way of a fool is r' in his own eyes:
14:12 There is a way which seemeth r'
16: 8 than great revenues without r'.
13 they love him that speaketh r'.
25 There is a way that seemeth r'
20:11 work be pure, and whether it be r'.
21: 2 Every way of a man is r' in his own
8 but as for the pure, his work is r'.
23:16 when thy lips speak r' things.
24:26 his lips that giveth a r' answer.
27:16 and the ointment of his r' hand,
Ec 4: 4 all travail, and every r' work,
10: 2 wise man's heart is at his r' hand;
Ca 2: 6 and his r' hand doth embrace me.
8: 3 and his r' hand should embrace me.
Isa 9:20 And he shall snatch on the r' hand,
10: 2 to take away the r' from the poor
30:10 Prophesy not unto us r' things,
21 when ye turn to the r' hand, and
32: 7 even when the needy speaketh r'.
41:10 the r' hand of my righteousness.
13 Lord thy God will hold thy r' hand,
44:20 Is there not a lie in my r' hand?
45: 1 Cyrus, whose r' hand I have holden,
19 I declare things that are r'.
48:13 r' hand...spanned the heavens:
54: 3 shalt break forth on the r' hand
62: 8 Lord hath sworn by his r' hand,
63:12 led them by the r' hand of Moses
Jer 2:21 thee a noble vine, wholly a r' seed:
5:28 r' of the needy do they not judge.
17:11 he that getteth riches, and not by r',
16 which came out of my lips was r'
22:24 were the signet upon my r' hand,
23:10 is evil, and their force is not r'.
32: 7 r' of redemption is thine to buy it.
8 for the r' of inheritance is thine,
34:15 and had done r' in my sight, in
49: 5 be driven out every man r' forth;
La 2: 3 he hath drawn back his r' hand
4 with his r' hand as an adversary,
3:35 To turn aside the r' of a man
Eze 1:10 the face of a lion, on the r' side:
4: 6 them, lie again on thy r' side,
10: 3 the cherubims stood on the r' side
16:46 sister, that dwelleth at thy r' hand,
18: 5 and do that which is lawful and r',
19 done that which is lawful and r',
21 and do that which is lawful and r',
27 doeth that which is lawful and r',
21:16 way or other, either on the r' hand,
22 At his r' hand was the divination
27 until he come whose r' it is;
33:14 and do that which is lawful and r';
16 done that which is lawful and r';
19 and do that which is lawful and r',
39: 3 arrows to fall out of thy r' hand.
47: 1 from the r' side of the house,
2 there ran out waters on the r' side.
Da 12: 7 held up his r' hand and his left
Ho 14: 9 for the ways of the Lord are r',
Am 3:10 they know not to do r', saith the
5:12 the poor in the gate from their r'.
Jon 4:11 discern between their r' hand and
Hab 2:16 cup of the Lord's r' hand shall be
Zec 3: 1 and Satan standing at his r' hand
4: 3 one upon the r' side of the bowl,
11 upon the r' side of the candlestick
11:17 upon his arm, and upon his r' eye:
17 his r' eye shall be utterly darkened.
12: 6 on the r' hand and on the left:
Mal 3: 5 turn aside the stranger from his r',
M't 5:29 if thy r' eye offend thee, pluck it
30 if thy r' hand offend thee, cut it off,
39 shall smite thee on thy r' cheek,
6: 3 hand know what thy r' hand doeth.
20: 4 whatsoever is r' I will give you.
7 and whatsoever is r', that shall ye
21 may sit, the one on thy r' hand,
23 but to sit on my r' hand, and on my
22:44 Sit thou on my r' hand, till I make
25:33 shall set the sheep on his r' hand,
34 King say unto them on his r' hand,
26:64 man sitting on the r' hand of power,
27:29 his head, and a reed in his r' hand:
38 one on the r' hand, and another on
M'r 5:15 and clothed, and in his r' mind:
10:37 we may sit, one on thy r' hand,
40 But to sit on my r' hand and on my
12:36 Sit thou on my r' hand, till I make
14:62 man sitting on the r' hand of power,
15:27 one on his r' hand, and the other
16: 5 a young man sitting on the r' side,
19 and sat on the r' hand of God.
Lu 1:11 standing on the r' side of the altar
6: 6 a man whose r' hand was withered.
8:35 Jesus, clothed, and in his r' mind:
10:28 unto him, Thou hast answered r':
12:57 yourselves judge ye not what is r'?
20:42 my Lord, Sit thou on my r' hand,
22:50 high priest, and cut off his r' ear.
69 on the r' hand of the power of God.
23:33 one on the r' hand, and the other
Joh 18:10 servant, and cut off his r' ear.
21: 6 the net on the r' side of the ship,
Ac 2:25 my face, for he is on my r' hand,
33 being by the r' hand of God exalted,
34 my Lord, Sit thou on my r' hand,
3: 7 And he took him by the r' hand,
Ac 4:19 Whether it be r' in the sight of
5:31 hath God exalted with his r' hand
7:55 standing on the r' hand of God,
56 standing on the r' hand of God.
8:21 thy heart is not r' in the sight of
13:10 to pervert the r' ways of the Lord?
Ro 8:34 who is even at the r' hand of God,
2Co 6: 7 righteousness on the r' hand and on
Ga 2: 9 gave...the r' hands of fellowship;
Eph 1:20 and set him at his own r' hand in
6: 1 parents in the Lord: for this is r'.
Col 3: 1 sitteth on the r' hand of God.
Heb 1: 3 the r' hand of the Majesty on high;
13 he at any time, Sit on my r' hand,
8: 1 is set on the r' hand of the throne of
10:12 sat down on the r' hand of God;
12: 2 at the r' hand of the throne of God.
13:10 whereof they have no r' to eat
1Pe 3:22 and is on the r' hand of God;
2Pe 2:15 Which have forsaken the r' way,
Re 1:16 he had in his r' hand seven stars:
17 And he laid his r' hand upon me,
20 which thou sawest in my r' hand,
2: 1 the seven stars in his r' hand,
5: 1 I saw in the r' hand of him that sat
7 took the book out of the r' hand of
10: 2 and he set his r' foot upon the sea,
13:16 to receive a mark in their r' hand,
22:14 they may have r' to the tree of life.

righteous See also UNRIGHTEOUS.
Ge 7: 1 thee have I seen r' before me in
18:23 Wilt thou also destroy the r' with
24 Peradventure there be fifty r'
24 place for the fifty r' that are therein?
25 to slay the r' with the wicked: and
25 that the r' should be as the wicked,
26 If I find in Sodom fifty r' within the
28 there shall lack five of the fifty r':
20: 4 Lord, wilt thou slay also a r' nation?
38:26 She hath been more r' than I;
Ex 9:27 Lord is r', and I and my people
23: 7 the innocent and r' slay thou not:
8 and perverteth the words of the r'.
Nu 23:10 Let me die the death of the r', and
De 4: 8 judgments so r' as all this law,
16:19 wise, and pervert the words of the r'
25: 1 then they shall justify the r', and
J'g 5:11 rehearse the r' acts of the Lord,
11 the r' acts toward the inhabitants
1Sa 12: 7 all the r' acts of the Lord, which he
24:17 to David, Thou art more r' than I:
2Sa 4:11 wicked men have slain a r' person
1Ki 2:32 who fell upon two men more r' and
8:32 and justifying the r', to give him
2Ki 10: 9 and said to all the people, Ye be r':
2Ch 6:23 and by justifying the r', by giving
12: 6 and they said, The Lord is r'.
Ezr 9:15 O Lord God of Israel, thou art r':
Ne 9: 8 performed thy words; for thou art r':
Job 4: 7 or where were the r' cut off?
9:15 though I were r', yet would I not
10:15 if I be r', yet will I not lift up my
15:14 of a woman, that he should be r'?
17: 9 The r' also shall hold on his way,
22: 3 to the Almighty, that thou art r'?
19 The r' see it, and are glad: and
23: 7 the r' might dispute with him;
32: 1 because he was r' in his own eyes.
34: 5 For Job hath said, I am r': and
35: 7 If thou be r', what givest thou him?
36: 7 withdraweth not...eyes from the r':
40: 8 me, that thou mayest be r'?
Ps 1: 5 in the congregation of the r'.
6 the Lord knoweth the way of the r':
5:12 For thou, Lord, wilt bless the r';
7: 9 for the r' God trieth the hearts and
11 God judgeth the r', and God is
11: 3 be destroyed, what can the r' do?
5 The Lord trieth the r': but the
7 the r' Lord loveth righteousness;
14: 5 God is in the generation of the r'.
19: 9 Lord are true and r' altogether.
31:18 and contemptuously against the r'.
32:11 glad in the Lord, and rejoice, ye r':
33: 1 Rejoice in the Lord, O ye r': for
34:15 eyes of the Lord are upon the r',
17 The r' cry, and the Lord heareth,
19 Many are the afflictions of the r':
21 that hate the r' shall be desolate.
35:27 be glad, that favour my r' cause:
37:16 little that a r' man hath is better
17 but the Lord upholdeth the r'.
21 the r' sheweth mercy, and giveth.
25 yet have I not seen the r' forsaken,
29 The r' shall inherit the land, and
30 mouth of the r' speaketh wisdom,
32 The wicked watcheth the r', and
39 But the salvation of the r' is of the
52: 6 The r' also shall see, and fear, and
55:22 never suffer the r' to be moved.
58:10 The r' shall rejoice when he seeth
11 Verily there is a reward for the r':
64:10 The r' shall be glad in the Lord,
68: 3 let the r' be glad; let them rejoice
69:28 and not be written with the r'.
72: 7 In his days shall the r' flourish;
75:10 horns of the r' shall be exalted.
92:12 The r' shall flourish like the palm
94:21 together against the soul of the r',
97:11 Light is sown for the r', and
12 Rejoice in the Lord, ye r'; and give
107:42 The r' shall see it, and rejoice:
112: 4 and full of compassion, and r'.
6 the r' shall be in everlasting
116: 5 Gracious is the Lord, and r'; yea,
118:15 is in the tabernacles of the r':

Ps 118: 20 Lord, into which the *r'* shall enter.
119: 7 have learned thy *r'* judgments.
62 thee because of thy *r'* judgments.
106 that I will keep thy *r'* judgments.
137 *R'* art thou, O Lord, and upright
138 that thou hast commanded are *r'*
160 thy *r'* judgments endureth for ever.
164 thee because of thy *r'* judgments.
125: 3 not rest upon the lot of the *r'*;
3 lest the *r'* put forth their hands
129: 4 Lord is *r'*: he hath cut asunder
140: 13 *r'* shall give thanks unto thy name:
141: 5 Let the *r'* smite me; it shall be a
142: 7 the *r'* shall compass me about; for
145: 17 The Lord is *r'* in all his ways, and
146: 8 bowed down: the Lord loveth the *r'*:
Pr 2: 7 layeth up sound wisdom for the *r'*:
20 men, and keep the paths of the *r'*.
3: 32 Lord: but his secret is with the *r'*.
10: 3 suffer the soul of the *r'* to famish:
11 mouth of a *r'* man is a well of life:
16 labour of the *r'* tendeth to life:
21 The lips of the *r'* feed many: but
24 the desire of the *r'* shall be granted.
25 the *r'* is an everlasting foundation.
28 hope of the *r'* shall be gladness:
30 The *r'* shall never be removed: but
32 The lips of the *r'* know what is
11: 8 The *r'* is delivered out of trouble,
10 When it goeth well with the *r'*, the
21 seed of the *r'* shall be delivered.
23 The desire of the *r'* is only good:
28 the *r'* shall flourish as a branch.
30 The fruit of the *r'* is a tree of life;
31 the *r'* shall be recompensed in the
12: 3 root of the *r'* shall not be moved.
5 The thoughts of the *r'* are right:
7 but the house of the *r'* shall stand.
10 A *r'* man regardeth the life of his
12 but the root of the *r'* yieldeth fruit.
26 The *r'* is more excellent than his
13: 5 A *r'* man hateth lying: but a
9 The light of the *r'* rejoiceth: but
21 but to the *r'* good shall be repayed.
25 The *r'* eateth to the satisfying of
14: 9 but among the *r'* there is favour.
19 the wicked at the gates of the *r'*.
32 but the *r'* hath hope in his death.
15: 6 house of the *r'* is much treasure:
19 the way of the *r'* is made plain.
28 heart of the *r'* studieth to answer:
29 but he heareth the prayer of the *r'*
16: 13 *R'* lips are the delight of kings;
18: 5 to overthrow the *r'* in judgment.
10 the *r'* runneth into it, and is safe.
21: 12 The *r'* man wisely considereth the
18 wicked shall be a ransom for the *r'*,
26 but the *r'* giveth and spareth not.
23: 24 The father of the *r'* shall greatly
24: 15 man, against the dwelling of the *r'*;
24 saith unto the wicked, Thou art *r'*;
25: 26 A *r'* man falling down before the
28: 1 but the *r'* are bold as a lion.
10 Whoso causeth the *r'* to go astray
12 When *r'* men do rejoice, there is
28 when they perish, the *r'* increase.
29: 2 When the *r'* are in authority, the
6 but the *r'* doth sing and rejoice.
7 *r'* considereth the cause of the poor:
16 but the *r'* shall see their fall.
Ec 3: 17 God shall judge the *r'* and the
7: 16 Be not *r'* over much; neither make
8: 14 according to the work of the *r'*:
9: 1 that the *r'*, and the wise, and their
2 there is one event to the *r'*, and to
Isa 3: 10 Say ye to the *r'*, that it shall be well
5: 23 away the righteousness of the *r'*
24: 16 we heard songs, even glory to the *r'*.
26: 2 *r'* nation which keepeth the truth
41: 2 Who raised up the *r'* man from
26 that we may say, He is *r'*? yea,
53: 11 shall my *r'* servant justify many;
57: 1 *r'* perisheth, and no man layeth
1 the *r'* is taken away from the evil
60: 21 Thy people also shall be all *r'*: they
Jer 12: 1 *R'* art thou, O Lord, when I plead
20: 12 O Lord of hosts, that triest the *r'*,
23: 5 will raise unto David a *r'* Branch,
La 1: 18 Lord is *r'*; for I have rebelled
Eze 3: 20 When a *r'* man doth turn from his
21 if thou warn the *r'* man, that the
21 that the *r'* sin not, and he doth not
13: 22 have made the heart of the *r'* sad,
16: 52 they are more *r'* than thou: yea,
18: 20 the righteousness of the *r'* shall be
24 when the *r'* turneth away from his
26 When a *r'* man turneth away from
21: 3 off from thee the *r'* and the wicked.
4 off from thee the *r'* and the wicked,
23: 45 the *r'* men, they shall judge them
33: 12 righteousness of the *r'* shall not
12 neither shall the *r'* be able to live
13 When I shall say to the *r'*, that he
18 *r'* turneth from his righteousness,
Da 9: 14 Lord our God is *r'* in all his works
Am 2: 6 because they sold the *r'* for silver,
Hab 1: 4 wicked doth compass about the *r'*;
13 the man that is more *r'* than he?
Mal 3: 18 between the *r'* and the wicked,
M't 9: 13 for I am not come to call the *r'*, but
10: 41 a *r'* man in the name of a *r'* man
41 shall receive a *r'* man's reward.
13: 17 *r'* men have desired to see those
43 shall the *r'* shine forth as the sun
23: 28 also outwardly appear *r'* unto men,
29 and garnish the sepulchres of the *r'*,
M't 23: 35 all the *r'* blood shed upon the earth,
35 blood of *r'* Abel unto the blood of
25: 37 Then shall the *r'* answer him,
46 but the *r'* into life eternal.
M'r 2: 17 I came not to call the *r'*, but sinners
Lu 1: 6 And they were both *r'* before God,
5: 32 I came not to call the *r'*, but sinners
18: 9 in themselves that they were *r'*,
23: 47 saying, Certainly this was a *r'* man.
Joh 7: 24 appearance, but judge *r'* judgment.
17: 25 O *r'* Father, the world hath not
Ro 2: 5 and revelation of the *r'* judgment of
3: 10 There is none *r'*, no, not one:
5: 7 scarcely for a *r'* man will one die:
19 of one shall many be made *r'*.
2Th 1: 5 token of the *r'* judgment of God,
6 Seeing it is a *r'* thing with God to
1Ti 1: 9 the law is not made for a *r'* man,
2Ti 4: 8 which the Lord, the *r'* judge, shall
Heb11: 4 he obtained witness that he was *r'*,
Jas 5: 16 prayer of a *r'* man availeth much.
1Pe 3: 12 the eyes of the Lord are over the *r'*,
4: 18 if the *r'* scarcely be saved, where
2Pe 2: 8 that *r'* man dwelleth among them,
8 vexed his *r'* soul from day to day
1Jo 2: 1 the Father, Jesus Christ the *r'*:
29 If ye know that he is *r'*, ye know
3: 7 righteousness is *r'*, even as he is *r'*.
12 were evil, and his brother's *r'*.
Re 16: 5 Thou art *r'*, O Lord, which art, and
7 true and *r'* are thy judgments.
19: 2 For true and *r'* are his judgments:
22: 11 be filthy still: and he that is *r'*,
11 let him be *r'* still: and he that is

righteously See also UNRIGHTEOUSLY.
De 1: 16 judge *r'* between every man and
Ps 67: 4 for thou shalt judge the people *r'*,
96: 10 he shall judge the people *r'*.
Pr 31: 9 Open thy mouth, judge *r'*, and
Isa 33: 15 He that walketh *r'*, and speaketh
Jer 11: 20 O Lord of hosts, that judgest *r'*,
Tit 2: 12 we should live soberly, *r'*, and
1Pe 2: 23 himself to him that judgeth *r'*:

righteousness See also RIGHTEOUSNESS'; RIGHTEOUSNESSES; UNRIGHTEOUSNESS.
Ge 15: 6 and he counted it to him for *r'*.
30: 33 shall my *r'* answer for me in time
Le 19: 15 but in *r'* shalt thou judge thy
De 6: 25 it shall be our *r'*, if we observe
9: 4 For my *r'* the Lord hath brought
5 Not for thy *r'*, or for the
6 good land to possess it for thy *r'*;
24: 13 it shall be *r'* unto thee before the
33: 19 they shall offer sacrifices of *r'*:
1Sa 26: 23 Lord render to every man his *r'*
2Sa 22: 21 rewarded me according to my *r'*:
25 recompensed me according to my *r'*;
1Ki 3: 6 before thee in truth, and in *r'*, and
8: 32 to give him according to his *r'*.
2Ch 6: 23 by giving him according to his *r'*.
Job 6: 29 yea, return again, my *r'* is in it.
8: 6 the habitation of thy *r'* prosperous.
27: 6 My *r'* I hold fast, and will not let it
29: 14 I put on *r'*, and it clothed me: my
33: 26 for he will render unto man his *r'*.
35: 2 saidst, My *r'* is more than God's?
8 thy *r'* may profit the son of man.
36: 3 and will ascribe *r'* to my Maker.
Ps 4: 1 me when I call, O God of my *r'*:
5 Offer the sacrifices of *r'*, and put
5: 8 Lead me, O Lord, in thy *r'* because
7: 8 me, O Lord, according to my *r'*,
17 praise the Lord according to his *r'*:
9: 8 And he shall judge the world in *r'*,
11: 7 For the righteous Lord loveth *r'*;
15: 2 walketh uprightly, and worketh *r'*,
17: 15 for me, I will behold thy face in *r'*:
18: 20 rewarded me according to my *r'*;
24 recompensed me according to my *r'*,
22: 31 shall declare his *r'* unto a people
23: 3 he leadeth me in the paths of *r'*
24: 5 *r'* from the God of his salvation.
31: 1 be ashamed: deliver me in thy *r'*.
33: 5 He loveth *r'* and judgment: the
35: 24 my God, according to thy *r'*;
28 my tongue shall speak of thy *r'*
36: 6 Thy *r'* is like the great mountains;
10 and thy *r'* to the upright in heart.
37: 6 bring forth thy *r'* as the light,
40: 9 I have preached *r'* in the great
10 not hid thy *r'* within my heart;
45: 4 of truth and meekness and *r'*;
7 lovest *r'*, and hatest wickedness:
48: 10 earth: thy right hand is full of *r'*.
50: 6 the heavens shall declare his *r'*:
51: 14 tongue shall sing aloud of thy *r'*.
19 pleased with the sacrifices of *r'*,
52: 3 and lying rather than to speak *r'*.
58: 1 Do ye...speak *r'*, O congregation?
65: 5 things in *r'* wilt thou answer us,
69: 27 and let them not come into thy *r'*.
71: 2 Deliver me in thy *r'*, and cause me
15 My mouth shall shew forth thy *r'*
16 I will make mention of thy *r'*, even
19 Thy *r'* also, O God, is very high,
24 My tongue also shall talk of thy *r'*
72: 1 and thy *r'* unto the king's son.
2 He shall judge thy people with *r'*,
3 people, and the little hills, by *r'*.
85: 10 *r'* and peace have kissed each
11 *r'* shall look down from heaven.
13 *R'* shall go before him; and shall
88: 12 thy *r'* in the land of forgetfulness?
89: 16 and in thy *r'* shall they be exalted.
Ps 94: 15 But judgment shall return unto *r'*:
96: 13 he shall judge the world with *r'*,
97: 2 *r'* and judgment are the habitation
6 The heavens declare his *r'*, and
98: 2 his *r'* hath he openly shewed in
9 with *r'* shall he judge the world,
99: 4 thou executest judgment and *r'* in
103: 6 Lord executeth *r'* and judgment
17 and his *r'* unto children's children;
106: 3 and he that doeth *r'* at all times.
31 counted unto him for *r'* unto all
111: 3 and his *r'* endureth for ever.
112: 3 house: and his *r'* endureth for ever.
9 the poor; his *r'* endureth for ever;
118: 19 Open to me the gates of *r'*: but
119: 40 precepts: quicken me in thy *r'*.
123 and for the word of thy *r'*.
142 Thy *r'* is an everlasting
142 is an everlasting *r'*, and thy law
144 *r'* of my testimonies is everlasting:
172 for all thy commandments are *r'*.
132: 9 let thy priests be clothed with *r'*;
143: 1 answer me, and in thy *r'*.
145: 7 goodness, and shall sing of thy *r'*.
Pr 2: 9 Then shalt thou understand *r'*,
8: 8 the words of my mouth are in *r'*;
18 me; yea, durable riches and *r'*.
20 I lead in the way of *r'*, in the
10: 2 but *r'* delivereth from death.
11: 4 but *r'* delivereth from death.
5 *r'* of the perfect shall direct his
6 *r'* of the upright shall deliver them:
18 to him that soweth *r'* shall be a
19 As *r'* tendeth to life: so he that
12: 17 speaketh truth sheweth forth *r'*:
28 In the way of *r'* is life; and in the
13: 6 *R'* keepeth him that is upright in
14: 34 *R'* exalteth a nation: but sin is a
15: 9 loveth him that followeth after *r'*.
16: 8 Better is a little with *r'* than great
12 for the throne is established by *r'*.
31 if it be found in the way of *r'*.
21: 21 that followeth after *r'* and mercy
21 mercy findeth life, *r'*, and honour.
25: 5 throne shall be established in *r'*.
Ec 3: 16 the place of *r'*, that iniquity was
7: 15 just man that perisheth in his *r'*,
Isa 1: 21 *r'* lodged in it; but now murderers.
26 The city of *r'*, the faithful city.
27 judgment,...her converts with *r'*.
5: 7 oppression; for *r'*, but behold a cry.
16 is holy shall be sanctified in *r'*.
23 take away the *r'* of the righteous
10: 22 decreed shall overflow with *r'*.
11: 4 with *r'* shall he judge the poor,
5 *r'* shall be the girdle of his loins,
16: 5 seeking judgment, and hasting *r'*.
26: 9 inhabitants of the world...learn *r'*.
10 wicked, yet will he not learn *r'*:
28: 17 to the line, and *r'* to the plummet:
32: 1 Behold, a king shall reign in *r'*,
16 and *r'* remain in the fruitful field.
17 And the work of *r'* shall be peace;
17 and the effect of *r'* quietness and
33: 5 filled Zion with judgment and *r'*.
41: 10 thee with the right hand of my *r'*.
42: 6 I the Lord have called thee in *r'*,
45: 8 and let the skies pour down *r'*:
8 and let *r'* spring up together;
13 I have raised him up in *r'*, and I
19 I the Lord speak *r'*, I declare
23 word...gone out of my mouth in *r'*,
24 in the Lord have I *r'* and strength:
46: 12 stouthearted, that are far from *r'*:
13 I bring near my *r'*; it shall not be
48: 1 Israel, but not in truth, nor in *r'*.
18 and thy *r'* as the waves of the sea:
51: 1 ye that follow after *r'*, ye that
5 My *r'* is near; my salvation is
6 and my *r'* shall not be abolished.
7 Hearken unto me, ye that know *r'*,
8 but my *r'* shall be for ever, and
54: 14 In *r'* shalt thou be established:
17 their *r'* is of me, saith the Lord.
56: 1 to come, and my *r'* to be revealed.
57: 12 I will declare thy *r'*, and thy works;
58: 2 my ways, as a nation that did *r'*,
8 and thy *r'* shall go before thee;
59: 16 him; and his *r'*, it sustained him.
17 For he put on *r'* as a breastplate,
60: 17 officers peace, and thine exactors *r'*.
61: 3 they might be called trees of *r'*,
10 covered me with the robe of *r'*,
11 so the Lord God will cause *r'* and
62: 1 *r'* thereof go forth as brightness,
2 And the Gentiles shall see thy *r'*,
63: 1 I that speak in *r'*, mighty to save.
64: 5 him that rejoiceth and worketh *r'*.
Jer 4: 2 in truth, in judgment, and in *r'*;
9: 24 lovingkindness, judgment, and *r'*,
22: 3 Execute ye judgment and *r'*, and
23: 6 he shall be called, The Lord Our *R'*.
33: 15 Branch of *r'* to grow up unto David;
15 execute judgment and *r'* in the
16 shall be called, The Lord our *r'*.
51: 10 Lord hath brought forth our *r'*:
Eze 3: 20 man doth turn from his *r'*, and
20 his *r'* which he hath done shall
14: 14 but their own souls by their *r'*,
20 deliver their own souls by their *r'*.
18: 20 the *r'* of the righteous shall be upon
22 in his *r'*...he hath done he shall live.
24 righteous turneth away from his *r'*,
24 All his *r'* that he hath done shall
26 righteous man turneth...from his *r'*,
33: 12 *r'* of the righteous shall not deliver

Eze 33:12 righteous be able to live for his r' in
13 if he trust to his own r', and
18 the righteous turneth from his r',
Da 4:27 and break off thy sins by r', and
9: 7 O Lord, r' belongeth unto thee,
16 O Lord, according to all thy r', I
24 to bring in everlasting r', and to
12: 3 that turn many to r' as the stars
Ho 2:19 I will betroth thee unto me in r',
10:12 Sow to yourselves in r', reap in
12 till he come and rain r' upon you.
Am 5: 7 and leave off r' in the earth,
24 waters, and r' as a mighty stream.
6:12 and the fruit of r' into hemlock:
Mic 6: 5 ye may know the r' of the Lord.
7: 9 the light, and I shall behold his r'.
Zep 2: 3 seek r', seek meekness: it may be
Zec 8: 8 be their God, in truth and in r'.
Mal 3: 3 offer unto the Lord an offering in r'.
4: 2 Sun of r' arise with healing in his
M't 3:15 thus it becometh us to fulfil all r'.
5: 6 which do hunger and thirst after r':
20 I say unto you, That except your r'
20 shall exceed the r' of the scribes
6:33 the kingdom of God, and his r';
21:32 John came unto you in the way of r',
Lu 1:75 In holiness and r' before him, all
Joh 16: 8 reprove the world of sin, and of r',
10 Of r', because I go to my Father,
Ac 10:35 he feareth him, and worketh r', is
13:10 of the devil, thou enemy of all r',
17:31 which he will judge the world in r'
24:25 as he reasoned of r', temperance,
Ro 1:17 therein is the r' of God revealed
2:26 keep the r' of the law, shall not
3: 5 commend the r' of God, what shall
21 But now r' of God without the law
22 Even the r' of God which is by faith
25 to declare his r' for the remission
26 To declare, I say, at this time his r':
4: 3 and it was counted unto him for r'.
5 ungodly, his faith is counted for r'.
6 man, unto whom God imputeth r'
9 was reckoned to Abraham for r'.
11 a seal of the r' of the faith which
11 that r' might be imputed unto them
13 the law, but through the r' of faith.
22 it was imputed to him for r'.
5:17 receive abundance...of the gift of r'
18 by the r' of one the free gift came
21 so might grace reign through r'
6:13 as instruments of r' unto God.
16 unto death, or of obedience unto r'?
18 sin, ye became the servants of r'.
19 yield your members servants to r'
20 servants of sin, ye were free from r'.
8: 4 the r' of the law might be fulfilled
10 but the Spirit is life because of r'.
9:28 the work, and cut it short in r':
30 followed not after r',...attained to r',
30 even the r' which is of faith.
31 which followed after the law of r',
31 hath not attained to the law of r'.
10: 3 For they being ignorant of God's r',
3 going about to establish her own r',
3 not submitted...unto the r' of God.
4 Christ is the end of the law for r'
5 describeth the r' which is of the law,
6 But the r' which is of faith speaketh
10 the heart man believeth unto r';
14:17 r', and peace, and joy in the Holy
1Co 1:30 is made unto us wisdom, and r',
15:34 Awake to r', and sin not; for
2Co 3: 9 ministration of r' exceed in glory.
5:21 might be made the r' of God in him.
6: 7 the armour of r' on the right hand
14 for what fellowship hath r' with
9: 9 the poor: his r' remaineth for ever.
10 and increase the fruits of your r';)
11:15 transformed as the ministers of r';
Ga 2:21 if r' come by the law, then Christ
3: 6 and it was accounted to him for r'.
21 r' should have been by the law.
5: 5 wait for the hope of r' by faith.
Eph 4:24 is created in r' and true holiness.
5: 9 is in all goodness and r' and truth;)
6:14 and having on the breastplate of r':
Ph'p 1:11 Being filled with the fruits of r',
3: 6 touching the r' which is in the law,
9 not having mine own r', which is of
9 the r' which is of God by faith:
1Ti 6:11 and follow after r', godliness, faith,
2Ti 2:22 but follow r', faith, charity, peace,
3:16 for correction, for instruction in r':
4: 8 there is laid up for me a crown of r',
Tit 3: 5 Not by works of r' which we have
Heb 1: 8 a sceptre of r' is the sceptre of thy
9 hast loved r', and hated iniquity;
5:13 milk is unskilful in the word of r':
7: 2 being by interpretation King of r',
11: 7 heir of the r' which is by faith.
33 wrought r', obtained promises,
12:11 it yieldeth the peaceable fruit of r'
Jas 1:20 of man worketh not the r' of God.
2:23 and it was imputed unto him for r':
3:18 And the fruit of r' is sown in peace
1Pe 2:24 dead to sins, should live unto r':
2Pe 1: 1 the r' of God and our Saviour Jesus
2: 5 the eighth person, a preacher of r',
21 not to have known the way of r',
3:13 a new earth, wherein dwelleth r'.
1Jo 2:29 every one that doeth r' is born of
3: 7 he that doeth r' is righteous, even
10 whosoever doeth not r' is not of God,
Re 19: 8 for the fine linen is the r' of saints.
11 in r' he doth judge and make war.

righteousness'
Ps 143:11 for thy r' sake bring my soul out
Isa 42:21 is well pleased for his r' sake;
M't 5:10 which are persecuted for r' sake:
1Pe 3:14 But and if ye suffer for r' sake,

righteousnesses
Isa 64: 6 and all our r' are as filthy rags;
Eze 33:13 all his r' shall not be remembered;
Da 9:18 supplications before thee for our r',

rightly See also UPRIGHTLY.
Ge 27:36 he said, Is not he r' named Jacob?
Lu 7:43 said unto him, Thou hast r' judged
20:21 that thou sayest and teachest r',
2Ti 2:15 ashamed, r' dividing the word of truth.

rigour
Ex 1:13 children of Israel to serve with r':
14 they made them serve, was with r'.
Le 25:43 Thou shalt not rule over him with r';
46 not rule one over another with r'.
53 other shall not rule with r' over him

Rimmon (*rim'-mon*) See also EN-RIMMON; GATH-RIMMON; RIMMON-PAREZ.
Jos 15:32 and Shilhim, and Ain, and R':
J'g 20:45 the wilderness unto the rock of R':
47 to the wilderness unto the rock R',
47 abode in the rock R' four months.
21:13 Benjamin that were in the rock R',
2Sa 4: 2 the sons of R' a Beerothite, of the
5, 9 the sons of R' the Beerothite,
2Ki 5:18 master goeth into the house of R'
18 I bow myself in the house of R':
18 bow down myself in the house of R',
1Ch 4:32 villages were, Etam, and Ain, R',
6:77 R' with her suburbs, Tabor with
Zec 14:10 Geba to R' south of Jerusalem:

Rimmon-parez (*rim"-mon-pa'-rez*)
Nu 33:19 from Rithmah, and pitched at R'.
20 And they departed from R', and

ring See also EARRING; RANG; RINGLEADER; RINGS; RINGSTRAKED.
Ge 41:42 Pharaoh took off his r' from his
Ex 26:24 above the head of it unto one r':
36:29 at the head thereof, to one r':
Es 3:10 the king took his r' from his hand,
12 and sealed with the king's r'.
8: 2 And the king took off his r', which
8 name, and seal it with the king's r':
8 name, and sealed with the king's r',
10 and sealed it with the king's r', and
Lu 15:22 put a r' on his hand, and shoes on
Jas 2: 2 assembly a man with a gold r',

ringleader
Ac 24: 5 a r' of the sect of the Nazarenes:

rings See also EARRINGS.
Ex 25:12 shalt cast four r' of gold for it,
12 two r' shall be in the one side of it,
12 and two r' in the other side of it.
14 thou shalt put the staves into the r'
15 staves shall be in the r' of the ark:
26 shalt make for it four r' of gold,
26 and put the r' in the four corners
27 against the border shall the r' be
26:29 make their r' of gold for places for
27: 4 four brasen r' in the four corners
7 the staves shall be put into the r',
28:23 upon the breastplate two r' of gold,
23 shalt put the two r' on the two ends
24 wreathen chains of gold in the two r'
26 And thou shalt make two r' of gold,
27 two other r' of gold thou shalt make,
28 shall bind the breastplate by the r'
28 unto the r' of the ephod with a lace
30: 4 two golden r' shalt thou make to it
35:22 bracelets, and earrings, and r', and
36:34 made their r' of gold to be places
37: 3 And he cast for it four r' of gold, to
3 even two r' upon the one side of it,
3 and two r' upon the other side of it.
5 he put the staves into the r' by the
13 And he cast for it four r' of gold,
13 put the r' upon the four corners
14 Over against the border were the r',
27 he made two r' of gold for it under
38: 5 he cast four r' for the four ends of
7 he put the staves into the r' on the
39:16 two ouches of gold, and two gold r';
16 and put the two r' in the two ends of
17 wreathen chains of gold in the two r'
19 they made two r' of gold, and put
20 And they made two other golden r',
21 did bind the breastplate by his r'
21 unto the r' of the ephod with a lace
Nu 31:50 chains, and bracelets, r', earrings,
Es 1: 6 to silver r' and pillars of marble:
Ca 5:14 His hands are as gold r' set with
Isa 3:21 The r', and nose jewels,
Eze 1:18 As for their r', they were so high
18 and their r' were full of eyes round

ringstraked
Ge 30:35 he goats that were r' and spotted,
39 brought forth cattle r', speckled,
40 the faces of the flocks toward the r',
31: 8 said thus, The r' shall be thy hire;
8 then bare all the cattle r'.
10 leaped upon the cattle were r',
12 which leap upon the cattle are r',

Rinnah (*rin'-nah*)
1Ch 4:20 of Shimon were, Amnon, and R',

rinsed
Le 6:28 be both scoured, and r' in water.
15:11 and hath not r' his hands in water,
12 vessel of wood shall be r' in water.

riot See also RIOTING.
Tit 1: 6 faithful children not accused of r'
1Pe 4: 4 with them to the same excess of r',
2Pe 2:13 count it pleasure to r' in the day

rioting
Ro 13:13 not in r' and drunkenness, not in

riotous
Pr 23:20 among r' eaters of flesh:
28: 7 is a companion of r' men shameth
Lu 15:13 wasted his substance with r' living.

rip See also RIPPED.
2Ki 8:12 and r' up their women with child.

ripe See also FIRSTRIPE; UNRIPE.
Ge 40:10 clusters...brought forth r' grapes:
Ex 22:29 delay to offer the first of thy r' fruits,
Jer 24: 2 figs, even like the figs that are first r':
Joe 3:13 in the sickle, for the harvest is r':
Re 14:15 for the harvest of the earth is r'.
18 earth; for her grapes are fully r'.

ripening
Isa 18: 5 the sour grape is r' in the flower,

Riphath (*ri'-fath*)
Ge 10: 3 sons of Gomer; Ashkenaz, and R',
1Ch 1: 6 sons of Gomer; Ashchenaz, and R',

ripped
2Ki 15:16 the women...with child he r' up.
Ho 13:16 women with child shall be r' up.
Am 1:13 have r' up the women with child of

rise See also ARISE; RISEN; RISEST; RISETH; RISING; ROSE.
Ge 19: 2 and ye shall r' up early, and go on
31:35 that I cannot r' up before thee;
Ex 8:20 R' up early in the morning, and
9:13 R' up early in the morning, and
12:31 R' up, and get you forth from
21:19 If he r' again, and walk abroad
Le 19:32 shalt r' up before the hoary head,
Nu 10:35 R' up, Lord, and let thine enemies
22:20 call thee, r' up, and go with them;
23:18 R' up, Balak, and hear; hearken
24 people shall r' up as a great lion,
24:17 a Sceptre shall r' out of Israel, and
De 2:13 Now r' up, said I, and get you over
24 R' ye up, take your journey, and
19:11 wait for him, and r' up against him,
15 One witness shall not r' up against
16 false witness r' up against any man
28: 7 thine enemies that r' up against
29:22 your children that shall r' up after
31:16 and this people will r' up, and go a
32:38 let them r' up and help you, and be
33:11 loins of them that r' against him,
11 hate him, that they r' not again.
Jos 8: 7 ye shall r' up from the ambush, and
18: 4 they shall r', and go through the
J'g 8:21 said, R' thou, and fall upon us:
9:33 r' early, and set upon the city:
20:38 make a great flame with smoke r'
1Sa 22:13 he should r' against me, to lie in
24: 7 suffered them not to r' against Saul.
29:10 r' up early in the morning with thy
2Sa 12:21 dead, thou didst r' and eat bread.
18:32 that r' against thee to do thee hurt,
2Ki 16: 7 of Israel, which r' up against me.
Ne 2:18 they said, Let us r' up and build.
Job 20:27 the earth shall r' up against him.
30:12 Upon my right hand r' the youth;
Ps 3: 1 many are they that r' up against me.
17: 7 from those that r' up against them.
18:38 them that they were not able to r':
48 above those that r' up against me:
27: 3 though war should r' against me,
35:11 False witnesses did r' up; they laid
36:12 down, and shall not be able to r'.
41: 8 that he lieth he shall r' up no more.
44: 5 them under that r' up against us.
59: 1 from them that r' up against me.
74:23 tumult of those that r' up against
92:11 of the wicked that r' up against me.
94:16 r' for me against the evildoers?
119:62 At midnight I will r' to give thanks
127: 2 It is vain for you to r' up early, to
139:21 not I grieved with those that r' up
140:10 pits, that they r' not up again.
Pr 24:22 their calamity shall r' suddenly;
28:12 but when the wicked r', a man is
28 When the wicked r', men hide
Ec 10: 4 spirit of the ruler r' up against
12: 4 shall r' up at the voice of the bird,
Ca 2:10 R' up, my love, my fair one, and
3: 2 I will r' now, and go about the city
Isa 5:11 Woe unto them that r' up early in
14:21 that they do not r', nor possess the
22 I will r' up against them, saith the
24:20 and it shall fall, and not r' again.
26:14 they are deceased, they shall not r':
28:21 the Lord shall r' up as in mount
32: 9 R' up, ye women that are at ease;
33:10 Now will I r', saith the Lord; now
43:17 lie down together, they shall not r':
54:17 tongue that shall r' against thee in
58:10 then shall thy light r' in obscurity,
Jer 25:27 and spue, and fall, and r' no more,
37:10 they r' up every man in his tent,
47: 2 waters r' up out of the north, and
49:14 against her, and r' up to the battle.
51: 1 of them that r' up against me,
64 shall not r' from the evil that I will
La 1:14 from whom I am not able to r' up.
Da 7:24 another shall r' after them; and
Am 5: 2 is fallen; she shall no more r': she
7: 9 r' against the house of Jeroboam

Am 8: 8 and it shall *r*· up wholly as a flood;
14 shall fall, and never *r*· up again.
9: 5 it shall *r*· up wholly like a flood;
Ob 1 let us *r*· up against her in battle.
Na 1: 9 affliction shall not *r*· up the second
Hab 2: 7 Shall they not *r*· up suddenly that
Zep 3: 8 the day that I *r*· up to the prey: for
Zec 14:13 shall *r*· up against the hand of his
M't 5:45 he maketh his sun to *r*· on the evil
10:21 and the children shall *r*· up against
12:41 men of Nineveh shall *r*· in judgment
42 south shall *r*· up in the judgment
20:19 and the third day he shall *r*· again.
24: 7 For nation shall *r*· against nation,
11 And many false prophets shall *r*·,
26:46 *R*·, let us be going: behold, he is at
27:63 After three days I will *r*· again.
M'r 3:26 And if Satan *r*· up against himself,
4:27 should sleep, and *r*· night and day,
8:31 and after three days *r*· again.
9:31 be killed, he shall *r*· the third day.
10:34 and the third day he shall *r*· again.
49 Be of good comfort, *r*·; he calleth
12:23 when they shall *r*·, whose wife
25 when they shall *r*· from the dead,
26 as touching the dead, that they *r*·:
13: 8 For nation shall *r*· against nation,
12 shall *r*· up against their parents,
22 Christs and false prophets shall *r*·,
14:42 *R*· up, let us go; lo, he that
Lu 5:23 thee; or to say, *R*· up and walk?
6: 8 *R*· up, and stand forth in the midst.
11: 7 in bed; I cannot *r*· and give thee.
8 Though he will not *r*· and give
8 he will *r*· and give him as many as
31 queen of the south shall *r*· up in
32 Nineve shall *r*· up in the judgment
12:54 ye see a cloud *r*· out of the west,
18:33 and the third day he shall *r*· again.
21:10 Nation shall *r*· against nation,
22:46 *r*· and pray, lest ye enter into
24: 7 crucified, and the third day *r*· again.
46 to *r*· from the dead the third day:
Joh 5: 8 unto him, *R*·, take up thy bed, and
11:23 her, Thy brother shall *r*· again.
24 I know that he shall *r*· again in the
20: 9 he must *r*· again from the dead.
Ac 3: 6 name of Jesus...of Nazareth *r*· up
10:13 to him, *R*·, Peter; kill, and eat.
26:16 *r*·, and stand upon thy feet: for I
23 first that should *r*· from the dead,
Ro 15:12 shall *r*· to reign over the Gentiles;
1Co 15:15 up, if so be that the dead *r*· not.
16 if the dead *r*· not,...is not Christ
29 the dead, if the dead *r*· not at all?
32 advantageth it me, if the dead *r*·
1Th 4:16 the dead in Christ shall *r*· first:
Heb 7:11 that another priest should *r*· after
Re 11: 1 *R*·, and measure the temple of
13: 1 saw a beast *r*· up out of the sea,

risen See also ARISEN.
Ge 19:23 The sun was *r*· upon the earth
Ex 22: 3 If the sun be *r*· upon him, there
Nu 32:14 ye are *r*· up in your fathers' stead,
J'g 9:18 ye are *r*· up against my father's
Ru 2:15 when she was *r*· up to glean, Boaz
1Sa 25:29 Yet a man is *r*· to pursue thee, and
2Sa 14: 7 the whole family is *r*· against thine
1Ki 8:20 I am *r*· up in the room of David my
2Ki 6:15 the servant...of God was *r*· early,
2Ch 6:10 am *r*· up in the room of David my
13: 6 Solomon the son of David, is *r*· up,
21: 4 Jehoram was *r*· up to the kingdom
Ps 20: 8 but we are *r*·, and stand upright.
27:12 witnesses are *r*· up against me,
54: 3 strangers are *r*· up against me,
86:14 the proud are *r*· against me, and
Isa 60: 1 glory of the Lord is *r*· upon thee.
Eze 7:11 Violence is *r*· up into a rod of
47: 5 for the waters were *r*·, waters to
Mic 2: 8 my people is *r*· up as an enemy:
M't 11:11 hath not *r*· a greater than John
14: 2 Baptist; he is *r*· from the dead;
17: 9 the Son of man be *r*· again from
26:32 But after I am *r*· again, I will go
27:64 the people, He is *r*· from the dead:
28: 6 He is not here: for he is *r*·, as he
7 his disciples that he is *r*· from the
M'r 6:14 John the Baptist was *r*· from the
16 beheaded: he is *r*· from the dead.
9: 9 Son of man were *r*· from the dead.
14:28 after that I am *r*·, I will go before
16: 6 he is *r*·; he is not here: behold the
9 Jesus was *r*· early the first day of
14 had seen him after he was *r*·.
Lu 7:16 a great prophet is *r*· up among us;
9: 7 that John was *r*· from the dead;
8 of the old prophets was *r*· again.
19 one of the old prophets is *r*· again.
13:25 the master of the house is *r*· up,
24: 6 He is not here, but is *r*·: remember
34 The Lord is *r*· indeed, and hath
Joh 2:22 therefore he was *r*· from the dead,
21:14 after that he was *r*· from the dead.
Ac 17: 3 suffered,...*r*· again from the dead;
Ro 8:34 died, yea rather, that is *r*· again,
1Co 15:13 of the dead, then is Christ not *r*·:
14 And if Christ be not *r*·, then is our
20 But now is Christ *r*· from the dead,
Col 2:12 *r*· with him through the faith of
3: 1 If ye then be *r*· with Christ, seek
Jas 1:11 sun is...*r*· with a burning heat,

risest
De 6: 7 liest down, and when thou *r*· up.
11:19 liest down, and when thou *r*· up.

riseth See also ARISETH.
De 22:26 a man *r*· against his neighbour,
Jos 6:26 *r*· up and buildeth this city Jericho:
2Sa 23: 4 when the sun *r*·, even a morning
Job 9: 7 commandeth the sun, and it *r*· not;
14:12 So man lieth down, and *r*· not:
24:22 he *r*· up, and no man is sure of life.
27: 7 he that *r*· up against me as the
31:14 then shall I do when God *r*· up?
Pr 24:16 falleth seven times, and *r*· up again:
31:15 She *r*· also while it is yet night, and
Isa 47:11 shalt not know from whence it *r*·:
Jer 46: 8 Egypt *r*· up like a flood, and his
Mic 7: 6 daughter *r*· up against her mother,
Joh 13: 4 He *r*· from supper, and laid aside

rising See also ARISING; SUNRISING; UPRISING.
Le 13: 2 have in the skin of his flesh a *r*·,
10 if the *r*· be white in the skin, and
10 there be quick raw flesh in the *r*·;
19 place of the boil there be a white *r*·,
28 it is a *r*· of the burning, and the
43 the *r*· of the sore be white reddish
14:56 for a *r*·, and for a scab, and for a
Nu 2: 3 east side toward the *r*· of the sun
Jos 12: 1 Jordan toward the *r*· of the sun,
2Ch 36:15 *r*· up betimes, and sending;
Ne 4:21 spears from the *r*· of the morning
Job 16: 8 my leanness *r*· up in me beareth
24: 5 their work; *r*· betimes for a prey:
14 murderer *r*· with the light killeth
Ps 50: 1 the earth from the *r*· of the sun
113: 3 From the *r*· of the sun unto the
Pr 27:14 *r*· early in the morning, it shall be
30:31 against whom there is no *r*· up.
Isa 41:25 from the *r*· of the sun shall he call
45: 6 may know from the *r*· of the sun,
59:19 and his glory from the *r*· of the sun.
60: 3 kings to the brightness of thy *r*·.
Jer 7:13 *r*· up early and speaking, but ye
25 *r*· up early and sending them:
11: 7 *r*· early and protesting, saying,
25: 3 unto you, *r*· early and speaking;
4 the prophets, *r*· early and sending
26: 5 both *r*· up early, and sending them,
29:19 *r*· up early and sending them;
32:33 *r*· up early and teaching them, yet
35:14 unto you, *r*· early and speaking;
15 *r*· up early and sending them,
44: 4 the prophets, *r*· early and sending
La 3:63 sitting down, and their *r*· up;
Mal 1:11 from the *r*· of the sun even unto
M'r 1:35 *r*· up a great while before day, he
9:10 the *r*· from the dead should mean.
16: 2 the sepulchre at the *r*· of the sun.
Lu 2:34 and *r*· again of many in Israel;

Rissah (*ris'-sah*)
Nu 33:21 from Libnah, and pitched at *R*·.
22 And they journeyed from *R*·, and

rites
Nu 9: 3 according to all the *r*· of it, and

Rithmah (*rith'-mah*)
Nu 33:18 Hazeroth, and pitched in *R*·.
19 And they departed from *R*·, and

river See also RIVER'S; RIVERS.
Ge 2:10 a *r*· went out of Eden to water the
13 the name of the second *r*· is Gihon:
14 name of the third *r*· is Hiddekel:
14 And the fourth *r*· is Euphrates.
15:18 I given this land, the *r*· of Egypt
18 unto the great *r*·, the *r*· Euphrates:
31:21 he rose up, and passed over the *r*·,
36:37 Saul of Rehoboth by the *r*· reigned
41: 1 and, behold, he stood by the *r*·.
2 came up out of the *r*· seven...kine
3 came up after them out of the *r*·,
3 other kine upon the brink of the *r*·.
17 I stood upon the bank of the *r*·:
18 came up out of the *r*· seven kine,
Ex 1:22 Every son...ye shall cast into the *r*·,
2: 5 came down to wash herself at the *r*·;
4: 9 shalt take of the water of the *r*·,
9 water...thou takest out of the *r*·
7:17 upon the waters which are in the *r*·,
18 the fish that is in the *r*· shall die,
18 and the *r*· shall stink; and the
18 lothe to drink of the water of the *r*·.
20 smote the waters that were in the *r*·,
20 all the waters that were in the *r*·,
21 And the fish that was in the *r*· died;
21 and the *r*· stank, and the Egyptians
21 could not drink...the water of the *r*·;
24 digged round about the *r*· for water
24 could not drink...the water of the *r*·.
25 that the Lord had smitten the *r*·.
8: 3 And the *r*· shall bring forth frogs
9 they may remain in the *r*· only?
11 they shall remain in the *r*· only.
17: 5 rod, wherewith thou smotest the *r*·,
23:31 and from the desert unto the *r*·:
Nu 22: 5 by the *r*· of the land of the children
34: 5 from Azmon unto the *r*· of Egypt,
De 1: 7 unto the great *r*·, the *r*· Euphrates.
2:24 and pass over the *r*· Arnon:
36 is by the brink of the *r*· of Arnon,
36 and from the city that is by the *r*·,
37 nor unto any place of the *r*· Jabbok,
3: 8 from the *r*· of Arnon unto mount
12 Aroer, which is by the *r*· Arnon,
16 from Gilead even unto the *r*· Arnon
16 the border even unto the *r*· Jabbok,
4:48 is by the bank of the *r*· Arnon,
11:24 from the *r*·, the *r*· Euphrates, even
Jos 1: 4 unto the great *r*·, the *r*· Euphrates,
12: 1 from the *r*· Arnon unto mount
Jos 12: 2 is upon the bank of the *r*· Arnon,
2 and from the middle of the *r*·, and
2 even unto the *r*· Jabbok, which is
13: 9 is upon the bank of the *r*· Arnon,
9 city that is in the midst of the *r*·,
16 that is on the bank of the *r*· Arnon,
16 city that is in the midst of the *r*·,
15: 4 and went out unto the *r*· of Egypt:
7 which is on the south side of the *r*·:
47 the *r*· of Egypt, and the great sea,
16: 8 westward unto the *r*· Kanah;
17: 9 the *r*· Kanah, southward of the *r*·:
9 was on the north side of the *r*·,
19:11 to the *r*· that is before Jokneam;
J'g 4: 7 will draw...to the *r*· Kishon Sisera,
13 Harosheth...unto the *r*· of Kishon.
5:21 The *r*· of Kishon swept them away,
21 that ancient *r*·, the *r*· Kishon.
2Sa 8: 3 his border at the *r*· Euphrates.
10:16 Syrians that were beyond the *r*·:
17:13 city, and...will draw it into the *r*·,
24: 5 lieth in the midst of the *r*· of Gad,
1Ki 4:21 from the *r*· unto the land of the
24 all the region on this side the *r*·,
24 over all the kings on this side the *r*·:
8:65 of Hamath unto the *r*· of Egypt,
14:15 shall scatter them beyond the *r*·,
2Ki 10:33 Aroer, which is by the *r*· Arnon,
17: 6 and in Habor by the *r*· of Gozan,
18:11 and in Habor by the *r*· of Gozan,
23:29 king of Assyria to the *r*· Euphrates:
24: 7 had taken from the *r*· of Egypt
7 unto the *r*· Euphrates all that
1Ch 1:48 Shaul of Rehoboth by the *r*·
5: 9 wilderness from the *r*· Euphrates:
26 and Hara, and to the *r*· Gozan,
18: 3 his dominion by the *r*· Euphrates.
19:16 Syrians that were beyond the *r*·:
2Ch 7: 8 of Hamath unto the *r*· of Egypt.
9:26 from the *r*· even unto the land of
Ezr 4:10 rest that are on this side the *r*·,
11 servants the men on this side the *r*·,
16 have no portion on this side the *r*·.
17 and unto the rest beyond the *r*·,
20 over all countries beyond the *r*·;
5: 3, 6 governor on this side the *r*·,
6 Apharsachites,...on this side the *r*·,
6: 6 Tatnai, governor beyond the *r*·,
6 Apharsachites,...beyond the *r*·,
8 even of the tribute beyond the *r*·,
13 Tatnai, governor on this side the *r*·,
7:21 treasurers which are beyond the *r*·,
25 the people that are beyond the *r*·,
8:15 to the *r*· that runneth to Ahava;
21 a fast there, at the *r*· of Ahava,
31 we departed from the *r*· of Ahava
36 to the governors on this side the *r*·:
Ne 2: 7, 9 to the governors beyond the *r*·,
3: 7 of the governor on this side the *r*·.
Job 40:23 drinketh up a *r*·, and hasteth not:
Ps 36: 8 drink of the *r*· of thy pleasures.
46: 4 There is a *r*·, the streams whereof
65: 9 enrichest it with the *r*· of God,
72: 8 and from the *r*· unto the ends of
80:11 sea, and her branches unto the *r*·.
105:41 they ran in the dry places like a *r*·.
Isa 7:20 namely, by them beyond the *r*·,
8: 7 up upon them the waters of the *r*·,
11:15 shall he shake his hand over the *r*·,
19: 5 the *r*· shall be wasted and dried up.
23: 3 seed of Sihor, the harvest of the *r*·,
10 Pass through thy land as a *r*·, O
27:12 channel of the *r*· unto the stream
48:18 then had thy peace been as a *r*·,
66:12 I will extend peace to her like a *r*·,
Jer 2:18 to drink the waters of the *r*?
17: 8 spreadeth out her roots by the *r*·,
46: 2 which was by the *r*· Euphrates in
6 the north by the *r*· Euphrates.
10 north country by the *r*· Euphrates.
La 2:18 let tears run down like a *r*· day
Eze 1: 1 the captives by the *r*· of Chebar,
3 of the Chaldeans by the *r*· Chebar;
3:15 that dwelt by the *r*· of Chebar, and
23 which I saw by the *r*· of Chebar:
10:15 that I saw by the *r*· of Chebar.
20 God of Israel by the *r*· of Chebar;
22 faces...I saw by the *r*· of Chebar,
29: 3 My *r*· is mine own, and I have
9 The *r*· is mine, and I have made it.
43: 3 vision...I saw by the *r*· Chebar;
47: 5 was a *r*· that I could not pass over:
5 a *r*· that could not be passed over.
6 me to return to the brink of the *r*·.
7 bank of the *r*· were very many trees
9 shall live whither the *r*· cometh.
12 by the *r*· upon the bank thereof, on
19 in Kadesh, the *r*· to the great sea.
48:28 and to the *r*· toward the great sea.
Da 8: 2 vision, and I was by the *r*· of Ulai.
3 there stood before the *r*· a ram
6 I had seen standing before the *r*·,
10: 4 as I was by the side of the great *r*·,
12: 5 on this side of the bank of the *r*·,
5 on that side of the bank of the *r*·.
6, 7 was upon the waters of the *r*·,
Am 6:14 unto the *r*· of the wilderness.
Mic 7:12 from the fortress even to the *r*·,
Zec 9:10 from the *r*· even to the ends of the
10:11 all the deeps of the *r*· shall dry up:
M'r 1: 5 baptized of him in the *r*· of Jordan,
Ac 16:13 we went out of the city by a *r*· side,
Re 9:14 bound in the great *r*· Euphrates.
16:12 vial upon the great *r*· Euphrates;
22: 1 shewed me a pure *r*· of water of life,
2 of it, and on either side of the *r*·.

river's
Ex 2: 3 laid it in the flags by the r' brink.
5 maidens walked...by the r' side;
7:15 thou shalt stand by the r' brink
Nu 24: 6 forth, as gardens by the r' side,

rivers
Ex 7:19 upon their streams, upon their r',
8: 5 over the r', and over the ponds,
Le 11: 9 waters, in the seas, and in the r',
10 scales in the seas, and in the r',
De 10: 7 to Jotbath, a land of r' of waters.
2Ki 5:12 and Pharpar, r' of Damascus,
19:24 up all the r' of besieged places.
Job 20:17 He shall not see the r', the floods,
28:10 cutteth out r' among the rocks;
29: 6 the rock poured me out r' of oil;
Ps 1: 3 a tree planted by the r' of water,
74:15 flood: thou driedst up mighty r'.
78:16 caused waters to run down like r'.
44 had turned their r' into blood;
89:25 sea, and his right hand in the r'.
107:33 He turneth r' into a wilderness,
119:136 R' of waters run down mine
137: 1 By the r' of Babylon, there we sat
Pr 5:16 and r' of waters in the streets.
21: 1 hand of the Lord, as the r' of water:
Ec 1: 7 All the r' run into the sea; yet the
7 the place from whence the r' come,
Ca 5:12 eyes of doves by the r' of waters,
Isa 7:18 uttermost part of the r' of Egypt,
18: 1 which is beyond the r' of Ethiopia:
2 whose land the r' have spoiled!
7 whose land the r' have spoiled, to
19: 6 And they shall turn the r' far away;
30:25 r' and streams of waters in the
32: 2 as rivers of water in a dry place,
33:21 a place of broad r' and streams;
37:25 all the r' of the besieged places.
41:18 I will open r' in high places, and
42:15 and I will make the r' islands, and
43: 2 and through the r', they shall not
19 the wilderness, and r' in the desert.
20 the wilderness, and r' in the desert,
44:27 Be dry, and I will dry up thy r':
47: 2 uncover the thigh, pass over the r'.
50: 2 the sea, I make the r' a wilderness:
Jer 31: 9 them to walk by the r' of waters
46: 7 whose waters are moved as the r'?
8 his waters are moved like the r';
La 3:48 runneth down with r' of water
Eze 6: 3 hills, to the r', and to the valleys;
29: 3 that lieth in the midst of his r',
4 will cause the fish of thy r' to stick
4 thee up out of the midst of thy r',
4 and all the fish of thy r' shall stick
5 thee and all the fish of thy r':
10 am against thee, and against thy r',
30:12 And I will make the r' dry, and sell
31: 4 r' running round about his plants,
4 little r' unto all the trees of the field.
12 are broken by all the r' of the land;
32: 2 and thou camest forth with thy r',
2 with thy feet, and fouledst their r'.
6 and the r' shall be full of thee.
14 and cause their r' to run like oil,
34:13 the mountains of Israel by the r',
35: 8 and in all thy r', shall they fall that
36: 4, 6 hills, to the r', and to the valleys,
47: 9 whithersoever the r' shall come,
Joe 1:20 for the r' of waters are dried up,
3:18 r' of Judah shall flow with waters,
Mic 6: 7 or with ten thousands of r' of oil?
Na 1: 4 it dry, and drieth up all the r':
2: 6 The gates of the r' shall be opened,
3: 8 No, that was situate among the r',
Hab 3: 8 the Lord displeased against the r'?
8 was thine anger against the r'? was
9 Thou didst cleave the earth with r'.
Zep 3:10 From beyond the r' of Ethiopia my
Joh 7:38 belly shall flow r' of living water.
Re 8:10 it fell upon the third part of the r',
16: 4 poured out his vial upon the r' and

Rizpah (*riz'-pah*)
2Sa 3: 7 a concubine, whose name was R',
21: 8 the king took the two sons of R'
10 And R' the daughter of Aiah took
11 told David what R'...had done.

road
1Sa 27:10 Whither have ye made a r' to day?

roar See also ROARED; ROARETH; ROARING; UP-ROAR.
1Ch 16:32 Let the sea r', and the fulness
Ps 46: 3 waters thereof r' and be troubled,
74: 4 Thine enemies r' in the midst of
96:11 let the sea r', and the fulness
98: 7 Let the sea r', and the fulness
104:21 The young lions r' after their prey,
Isa 5:29 lion, they shall r' like young lions:
29 yea, they shall r', and lay hold of
30 that day they shall r' against them
42:13 a man of war: he shall cry, yea, r';
59:11 We r' all like bears, and mourn
Jer 5:22 though they r', yet can they not
25:30 The Lord shall r' from on high,
30 mightily r' upon his habitation;
31:35 the sea when the waves thereof r';
50:42 their voice shall r' like the sea, and
51:38 They shall r' together like lions:
55 her waves do r' like great waters,
Ho 11:10 the Lord: he shall r' like a lion:
10 when he shall r', then the children
Joe 3:16 The Lord also shall r' out of Zion,
Am 1: 2 he said, The Lord will r' from Zion,
3: 4 Will a lion r' in the forest, when he

roared
J'g 14: 5 a young lion r' against him.
Ps 38: 8 r' by reason of the disquietness of
Isa 51:15 divided the sea, whose waves r':
Jer 2:15 The young lions r' upon him, and
Am 3: 8 The lion hath r', who will not fear?

roareth
Job 37: 4 After it a voice r': he thundereth
Jer 6:23 mercy; their voice r' like the sea;
Re 10: 3 a loud voice, as when a lion r':

roaring See also ROARINGS.
Job 4:10 The r' of the lion, and the voice of
Ps 22: 1 me, and from the words of my r'?
13 as a ravening and a r' lion.
32: 3 my bones waxed old through my r'
Pr 19:12 king's wrath is as the r' of a lion;
20: 2 fear of a king is as the r' of a lion:
28:15 As a r' lion, and a ranging bear;
Isa 5:29 Their r' shall be like a lion, they
30 shall roar...like the r' of the sea:
31: 4 and the young lion r' on his prey,
Eze 19: 7 thereof, by the noise of his r'.
22:25 like a r' lion ravening the prey;
Zep 3: 3 princes within her are r' lions;
Zec 11: 3 a voice of the r' of young lions;
Lu 21:25 the sea and the waves r';
1Pe 5: 8 devil, as a r' lion, walketh about,

roarings
Job 3:24 r' are poured out like the waters.

roast See also ROASTED; ROASTETH.
Ex 12: 8 the flesh in that night, r' with fire,
9 at all with water, but r' with fire;
De 16: 7 And thou shalt r' and eat it in the
1Sa 2:15 Give flesh to r' for the priest; for
Isa 44:16 He roasteth r', and is satisfied:

roasted
2Ch 35:13 And they r' the passover with fire
Isa 44:19 I have r' flesh, and eaten it: and
Jer 29:22 whom the king of Babylon r' in the

roasteth
Pr 12:27 slothful man r' not that which he
Isa 44:16 he r' roast, and is satisfied: yea,

rob See also ROBBED; ROBBETH.
Le 19:13 thy neighbour, neither r' him:
26:22 which shall r' you of your children,
1Sa 23: 1 and they r' the threshingfloors.
Pr 22:22 R' not the poor, because he is
Isa 10: 2 that they may r' the fatherless!
17:14 us, and the lot of them that r' us.
Eze 39:10 and r' those that robbed them, saith
Mal 3: 8 Will a man r' God? Yet ye have

robbed
J'g 9:25 they r' all that came along that
2Sa 17: 8 as a bear r' of her whelps in the
Ps 119:61 bands of the wicked have r' me:
Pr 17:12 Let a bear r' of her whelps meet a
Isa 10:13 and have r' their treasures, and I
42:22 But this is a people r' and spoiled;
Jer 50:37 her treasures; and they shall be r'.
Eze 33:15 pledge, give again that he had r',
39:10 rob those that r' them, saith the
Mal 3: 8 man rob God? Yet ye have r' me.
8 ye say, Wherein have we r' thee?
9 for ye have r' me, even this whole
2Co 11: 8 I r' other churches, taking wages

robber See also ROBBERS.
Job 5: 5 r' swalloweth up their substance.
18: 9 the r' shall prevail against him.
Eze 18:10 If he beget a son that is a r', a
Joh 10: 1 way, the same is a thief and a r'.
18:40 Barabbas. Now Barabbas was a r'.

robbers
Job 12: 6 The tabernacles of r' prosper, and
Isa 42:24 for a spoil, and Israel to the r'?
Jer 7:11 become a den of r' in your eyes?
Eze 7:22 for the r' shall enter into it, and
Da 11:14 the r' of thy people shall exalt
Ho 6: 9 And as troops of r' wait for a man,
7: 1 and the troop of r' spoileth without.
Ob 5 thieves came to thee, if r' by night,
Joh 10: 8 came before me are thieves and r':
Ac 19:37 which are neither r' of churches,
2Co 11:26 in perils of waters, in perils of r',

robbery
Ps 62:10 and become not vain in r': if
Pr 21: 7 The r' of the wicked shall destroy
Isa 61: 8 I hate r' for burnt offering; and
Eze 22:29 used oppression, and exercised r',
Am 3:10 violence and r' in their palaces.
Na 3: 1 city! it is all full of lies and r'; the
Ph'p 2: 6 it not r' to be equal with God:

robbeth
Pr 28:24 Whoso r' his father or his mother,

robe See also ROBES; WARDROBE.
Ex 28: 4 and a r', and a broidered coat,
31 make the r' of the ephod all of blue.
34 upon the hem of the r' round about.
29: 5 the coat, and the r' of the ephod,
39:22 the r' of the ephod of woven work,
23 was an hole in the midst of the r',
24 they made upon the hems of the r'
25 upon the hem of the r', round
26 round about the hem of the r' to
Le 8: 7 clothed him with the r', and put
1Sa 18: 4 Jonathan stripped himself of the r'
24: 4 cut off the skirt of Saul's r' privily.
11 see the skirt of thy r' in my hand:
11 in that I cut off the skirt of thy r',
1Ch 15:27 David was clothed with a r' of fine
Job 29:14 my judgment was as a r' and a

Isa 22:21 And I will clothe him with thy r',
61:10 me with the r' of righteousness,
Jon 3: 6 and he laid his r' from him, and
Mic 2: 8 ye pull off the r' with the garment
M't 27:28 him, and put on him a scarlet r'.
31 they took the r' off from him, and
Lu 15:22 Bring forth the best r', and put it
23:11 and arrayed him in a gorgeous r',
Joh 19: 2 and they put on him a purple r',
5 crown of thorns, and the purple r'.

robes
2Sa 13:18 for with such r' were the king's
1Ki 22:10 his throne, having put on their r',
30 the battle; but put thou on thy r'.
2Ch 18: 9 on his throne, clothed in their r',
29 the battle; but put thou on thy r'.
Eze 26:16 thrones, and lay away their r',
Lu 20:46 which desire to walk in long r',
Re 6:11 white r' were given unto every one
7: 9 clothed with white r', and palms in
13 these which are arrayed in white r'?
14 have washed their r', and made

Roboam (*ro-bo'-am*) See also REHOBOAM.
M't 1: 7 Solomon begat R'; and R' begat

rock See also ROCKS.
Ex 17: 6 thee there upon the r' in Horeb;
6 and thou shalt smite the r', and
33:21 me, and thou shalt stand upon a r':
22 I will put thee in a clift of a r', and
Nu 20: 8 ye unto the r' before their eyes;
8 forth to them water out of the r':
10 congregation together before the r',
10 we fetch you water out of this r'?
11 with his rod he smote the r' twice:
24:21 and thou puttest thy nest in a r'.
De 8:15 forth water out of the r' of flint;
32: 4 He is the R', his work is perfect:
13 him to suck honey out of the r',
13 and oil out of the flinty r';
15 esteemed the R' of his salvation.
18 Of the R' that begat thee thou art
30 except their R' had sold them, and
31 For their r' is not as our R', even
37 gods, their r' in whom they trusted,
J'g 1:36 from the r', and upward.
6:20 cakes, and lay them upon this r',
21 there rose up fire out of the r',
26 thy God upon the top of this r',
7:25 they slew Oreb upon the r' Oreb,
13:19 offered it upon a r' unto the Lord:
15: 8 dwelt in the top of the r' Etam.
11 went to the top of the r' Etam,
13 and brought him up from the r'.
20:45 wilderness unto the r' of Rimmon:
47 wilderness unto the r' Rimmon,
47 and abode in the r' Rimmon four
21:13 that were in the r' Rimmon, and
1Sa 2: 2 is there any r' like our God.
14: 4 was a sharp r' on the one side,
4 and a sharp r' on the other side:
23:25 wherefore he came down into a r',
2Sa 21:10 and spread it for her upon the r',
22: 2 said, The Lord is my r', and my
3 The God of my r'; in him will I
32 and who is a r', save our God?
47 Lord liveth; and blessed be my r';
47 the God of the r' of my salvation.
23: 3 said, the R' of Israel spake to me,
1Ch 11:15 went down to the r' to David, into
2Ch 25:12 them unto the top of the r', and
12 them down from the top of the r',
Ne 9:15 them out of the r' for their thirst,
Job 14:18 the r' is removed out of his place.
18: 4 the r' be removed out of his place?
19:24 iron pen and lead in the r' for ever!
24: 8 embrace the r' for want of a shelter.
28: 9 putteth forth his hand upon the r';
29: 6 the r' poured me out rivers of oil;
39: 1 wild goats of the r' bring forth?
28 dwelleth and abideth on the r',
28 upon the crag of the r', and the
Ps 18: 2 The Lord is my r', and my fortress,
31 Lord? or who is a r' save our God?
46 Lord liveth; and blessed be my r';
27: 5 me; he shall set me up upon a r'.
28: 1 Unto thee will I cry, O Lord my r';
31: 2 be thou my strong r', for an house
3 thou art my r' and my fortress;
40: 2 clay, and set my feet upon a r',
42: 9 I will say unto God my r', Why hast
61: 2 lead me to the r' that is higher
62: 2 He only is my r' and my salvation;
6 He only is my r' and my salvation:
7 the r' of my strength, and my
71: 3 thou art my r' and my fortress.
78:16 brought streams also out of the r',
20 he smote the r', that the waters
35 remembered that God was their r',
81:16 with honey out of the r' should I
89:26 God, and the r' of my salvation.
92:15 he is my r', and there is no
94:22 And my God is the r' of my refuge.
95: 1 noise to the r' of our salvation.
105:41 He opened the r', and the waters
114: 8 turned the r' into a standing water,
Pr 30:19 the way of a serpent upon a r';
Ca 2:14 that are in the clefts of the r', in
Isa 2:10 Enter into the r', and hide thee
8:14 stumbling and for a r' of offence
10:26 slaughter of Midian at...r' of Oreb:
17:10 mindful of the r' of thy strength,
22:16 an habitation for himself in a r'?
32: 2 shadow of a great r' in a weary land.
42:11 let the inhabitants of the r' sing,
48:21 the waters to flow out of the r' for

Isa 48:21 he clave the r' also, and the waters
51: 1 unto the r' whence ye are hewn,
Jer 5: 3 made their faces harder than a r';
13: 4 and hide it there in a hole of the r'.
18:14 snow...from the r' of the field?
21:13 of the valley, and r' of the plain,
23:29 hammer that breaketh the r' in
48:28 the cities, and dwell in the r', and
49:16 that dwellest in the clefts of the r',
Eze 24: 7 her: she set it upon the top of a r';
8 set her blood upon the top of a r',
26: 4 and make her like the top of a r'.
14 will make thee like the top of a r':
Am 6:12 Shall horses run upon the r'? will
Ob 3 that dwellest in the clefts of the r',
M't 7:24 which built his house upon a r':
25 not: for it was founded upon a r'.
16:18 upon this r' I will build my church;
27:60 which he had hewn out in the r':
M'r 15:46 sepulchre...was hewn out of a r':
Lu 6:48 and laid the foundation on a r':
48 it: for it was founded upon a r'.
8: 6 And some fell upon a r'; and as
13 They on the r' are they, which,
Ro 9:33 a stumblingstone and r' of offence:
1Co 10: 4 they drank of that spiritual R' that
4 them: and that R' was Christ.
1Pe 2: 8 a r' of offence, even to them which

rocks
Nu 23: 9 from the top of the r' I see him,
1Sa 13: 6 caves, and in thickets, and in r',
24: 2 men upon the r' of the wild goats.
1Ki 19:11 brake in pieces the r' before the
Job 28:10 cutteth out rivers among the r';
30: 6 caves of the earth, and in the r'.
Ps 78:15 He clave the r' in the wilderness,
104:18 goats; and the r' for the conies.
Pr 30:26 make they their houses in the r';
Isa 2:19 shall go into the holes of the r',
21 To go into the clefts of the r', and
21 and into the tops of the ragged r',
7:19 valleys, and in the holes of the r',
33:16 shall be the munitions of r':
57: 5 valleys under the clifts of the r'?
Jer 4:29 and climb up upon the r': every
16:16 hill, and out of the holes of the r'
51:25 and roll thee down from the r',
Na 1: 6 the r' are thrown down by him.
M't 27:51 earth did quake, and the r' rent;
Ac 27:29 we should have fallen upon r',
Re 6:15 and in the r' of the mountains;
16 And said to the mountains and r',

rod See also RODS.
Ex 4: 2 in thine hand? And he said, A r'.
4 it, and it became a r' in his hand:
17 shalt take this r' in thine hand,
20 and Moses took the r' of God in his
7: 9 Take thy r', and cast it before
10 and Aaron cast down his r' before
12 they cast down every man his r',
12 Aaron's r' swallowed up their rods.
15 r' which was turned to a serpent
17 smite with the r'...in mine hand
19 Say unto Aaron, Take thy r', and
20 he lifted up the r', and smote the
8: 5 Stretch forth thine hand with thy r'
16 Stretch out thy r', and smite the
17 stretched out his hand with his r',
9:23 stretched...his r' toward heaven:
10:13 stretched forth his r' over the land
14:16 but lift thou up thy r', and stretch
17: 5 and thy r', wherewith thou smotest
9 with the r' of God in mine hand.
21:20 his servant, or his maid, with a r',
Le 27:32 of whatsoever passeth under the r',
Nu 17: 2 and take of every one of them a r'
2 thou every man's name upon his r'.
3 Aaron's name upon the r' of Levi:
3 for one r' shall be for the head of
5 the man's r', whom I shall choose,
6 their princes gave him a r' apiece,
6 r' of Aaron was among their rods.
8 r' of Aaron for the house of Levi
9 looked, and took every man his r'.
10 Bring Aaron's r' again before the
20: 8 Take the r', and gather thou the
9 Moses took the r' from before the
11 with his r' he smote the rock twice:
1Sa 14:27 end of the r' that was in his hand,
43 end of the r' that was in mine hand,
2Sa 7:14 chasten him with the r' of men,
Job 9:34 Let him take his r' away from me,
21: 9 neither is the r' of God upon them.
Ps 2: 9 shalt break them with a r' of iron;
23: 4 r' and thy staff they comfort me.
74: 2 the r' of thine inheritance, which
89:32 their transgression with the r',
110: 2 the r' of thy strength out of Zion:
125: 3 the r' of the wicked shall not rest
Pr 10:13 a r' is for the back of him that is
13:24 that spareth his r' hateth his son:
14: 3 mouth of...foolish is a r' of pride:
22: 8 and the r' of his anger shall fail.
15 r' of correction shall drive it far
23:13 for if thou beatest him with the r',
14 Thou shalt beat him with the r',
26: 3 the ass, and a r' for the fool's back.
29:15 The r' and reproof give wisdom:
Isa 9: 4 shoulder, the r' of his oppressor,
10: 5 the r' of mine anger, and the staff
15 r' should shake itself against them
24 he shall smite thee with a r', and
26 and as his r' was upon the sea, so
11: 1 forth a r' out of the stem of Jesse,
4 smite the earth with the r' of his
Isa 14:29 r' of him that smote thee is broken:
28:27 a staff, and the cummin with a r'.
30:31 beaten down, which smote with a r'.
Jer 1:11 I said, I see a r' of an almond tree.
10:16 Israel is the r' of his inheritance:
48:17 staff broken, and the beautiful r'!
51:19 Israel is the r' of his inheritance:
La 3: 1 seen affliction by the r' of his wrath.
Eze 7:10 the r' hath blossomed, pride hath
11 is risen up into a r' of wickedness:
19:14 is gone out of a r' of her branches,
14 hath no strong r' to be a sceptre
20:37 cause you to pass under the r',
21:10 it contemneth the r' of my son, as
13 if the sword contemn even the r'?
Mic 5: 1 smite the judge of Israel with a r'
6: 9 hear ye the r', and who hath
7:14 Feed thy people with thy r', the
1Co 4:21 shall I come unto you with a r', or
Heb 9: 4 Aaron's r' that budded, and the
Re 2:27 shall rule them with a r' of iron;
11: 1 was given me a reed like unto a r':
12: 5 to rule all nations with a r' of iron:
19:15 he shall rule them with a r' of iron:

Rodanim See DODANIM.

rode
Ge 24:61 and they r' upon the camels, and
J'g 10: 4 had thirty sons that r' on thirty ass
12:14 that r' on threescore and ten ass
1Sa 25:20 And it was so, as she r' on the ass,
42 and arose, and r' upon an ass,
30:17 young men, which r' upon camels,
2Sa 18: 9 Absalom r' upon a mule, and the
22:11 he r' upon a cherub, and did fly:
1Ki 13:13 him the ass: and he r' thereon,
18:45 And Ahab r', and went to Jezreel.
2Ki 9:16 So Jehu r' in a chariot, and went to
25 I and thou r' together after Ahab
Ne 2:12 me, save the beast that I r' upon.
Es 8:14 the posts that r' upon mules and
Ps 18:10 he r' upon a cherub, and did fly:

rods
Ge 30:37 Jacob took him r' of green poplar,
37 white appear which was in the r'.
38 he set the r' which he had pilled
39 the flocks conceived before the r',
41 Jacob laid the r' before the eyes of
41 they might conceive among the r'.
Ex 7:12 Aaron's rod swallowed up their r'.
Nu 17: 2 house of their fathers, twelve r':
6 fathers' houses, even twelve r':
6 rod of Aaron was among their r'.
7 laid up the r' before the Lord in
9 Moses brought out all the r' from
Eze 19:11 strong r' for the sceptres of them
12 her strong r' were broken and
2Co 11:25 Thrice was I beaten with r', once

roe See also ROEBUCK; ROES.
2Sa 2:18 was as light of foot as a wild r'.
Pr 5:19 the loving hind and pleasant r';
6: 5 Deliver thyself as a r' from the
Ca 2: 9 beloved is like a r' or a young hart:
17 be thou like a r' or a young hart
8:14 thou like to a r' or to a young hart
Isa 13:14 And it shall be as the chased r',

roebuck See also ROEBUCKS.
De 12:15 as of the r', and as of the hart.
22 as the r' and the hart is eaten, so
14: 5 The hart, and the r', and the
15:22 it alike, as the r', and as the hart.

roebucks
1Ki 4:23 harts, and r', and fallowdeer,

roes
1Ch 12: 8 were as swift as the r' upon the
Ca 2: 7 by the r', and by the hinds of the
3: 5 by the r', and by the hinds of the
4: 5 like two young r' that are twins,
7: 3 like two young r' that are twins.

Rogel See EN-ROGEL.

Rogelim (ro'-ghel-im)
2Sa 17:27 and Barzillai the Gileadite of R',
19:31 the Gileadite came down from R',

Rohgah (ro'-gah)
1Ch 7:34 the sons of Shamer; Ahi, and R',

Roi See LAHAI-ROI.

roll See also ROLLED; ROLLETH; ROLLING; ROLLS.
Ge 29: 8 and till they r' the stone from the
Jos 10:18 R' great stones upon the mouth of
1Sa 14:33 r' a great stone unto me this day.
Ezr 6: 2 in the province of the Medes, a r',
Isa 8: 1 Take thee a great r', and write in
Jer 36: 2 Take thee a r' of a book, and write
4 unto him, upon a r' of a book,
6 and read in the r', which thou hast
14 Take in thine hand the r' wherein
14 Baruch...took the r' in his hand,
20 they laid up the r' in the chamber
21 king sent Jehudi to fetch the r':
23 until all the r' was consumed in
25 king that he would not burn the r':
27 that the king had burned the r',
28 Take thee again another r', and
28 words that were in the first r',
29 Thou hast burned this r', saying,
32 Then took Jeremiah another r',
51:25 and r' thee down from the rocks,
Eze 2: 9 and, lo, a r' of a book was therein;
3: 1 eat this r', and go speak unto the
2 and he caused me to eat that r'.
3 fill thy bowels with this r' that I
Mic 1:10 of Aphrah r' thyself in the dust.
Zec 5: 1 and looked, and behold a flying r'.
2 I see a flying r': the length thereof
M'r 16: 3 Who shall r' us away the stone

rolled
Ge 29: 3 they r' the stone from the well's
10 r' the stone from the well's mouth,
Jos 5: 9 I r' away the reproach of Egypt
Job 30:14 they r' themselves upon me.
Isa 9: 5 noise, and garments r' in blood;
34: 4 the heavens shall be r' together as
M't 27:60 and he r' a great stone to the door
28: 2 came and r' back the stone from
M'r 15:46 and r' a stone unto the door of the
16: 4 saw that the stone was r' away:
Lu 24: 2 stone r' away from the sepulchre.
Re 6:14 as a scroll when it is r' together;

roller
Eze 30:21 to put a r' to bind it, to make it

rolleth
Pr 26:27 he that r' a stone, it will return

rolling
Isa 17:13 a r' thing before the whirlwind.

rolls
Ezr 6: 1 was made in the house of the r',

Romamti-ezer (romam"-ti-e'-zur)
1Ch 25: 4 Giddalti, and R', Joshbekashah,
31 The four and twentieth to R', he,

Roman (ro'-mun) See also ROMANS.
Ac 22:25 you to scourge a man that is a R',
26 thou doest: for this man is a R'.
27 Tell me, art thou a R'? He said,
29 after he knew that he was a R', and
23:27 having understood that he was a R'.

Romans^ (ro'-muns)
Joh 11:48 R' shall come and take away both
Ac 16:21 neither to observe, being R'.
37 us openly uncondemned, being R',
38 when they heard that they were R'.
25:16 not the manner of the R' to deliver
28:17 Jerusalem into the hands of the R'.
Ro *subscr.* Written to the R' from

Rome (rome) See also ROMAN.
Ac 2:10 and strangers of R', Jews and
18: 2 all Jews to depart from R':) and
19:21 have been there, I must also see R'.
23:11 must thou bear witness also at R'.
28:14 days: and so we went toward R'.
16 And when we came to R', the
Ro 1: 7 To all that be in R', beloved of God,
15 gospel to you that are at R' also.
Ga *subscr.* the Galatians written from R'.
Eph *subscr.* from R' unto the Ephesians
Ph'p *subscr.* to the Philippians from R' by
Col *subscr.* Written from R' to the
2Ti 1:17 when he was in R', he sought me
subscr. was written from R', when
Ph'm *subscr.* Written from R' to Philemon,

roof See also ROOFS.
Ge 19: 8 they under the shadow of my r'.
De 22: 8 shalt make a battlement for thy r',
Jos 2: 6 them up to the r' of the house, and
6 she had laid in order upon the r'.
8 she came up unto them upon the r';
J'g 16:27 upon the r' about three thousand
2Sa 11: 2 upon the r' of the king's house:
2 and from the r' he saw a woman
18:24 the watchman went up to the r'
Ne 8:16 every one upon the r' of his house,
Job 29:10 cleaved to the r' of their mouth.
Ps 137: 6 cleave to the r' of my mouth; if I
Ca 7: 9 r' of thy mouth like the best wine
La 4: 4 cleaveth to the r' of his mouth for
Eze 3:26 cleave to the r' of thy mouth,
40:13 r' of one little chamber to the r' of
M't 8: 8 thou shouldest come under my r':
M'r 2: 4 uncovered the r' where he was:
Lu 7: 6 thou shouldest enter under my r':

roofs
Jer 19:13 upon whose r' they have burned
32:29 upon whose r' they have offered

room^ See also ROOMS.
Ge 24:23 is there r' in thy father's house
25 straw...enough, and r' to lodge in.
31 the house, and r' for the camels.
26:22 now the Lord hath made r' for us,
2Sa 19:13 me continually in the r' of Joab.
1Ki 2:35 of Jehoiada in his r' over the host:
35 the king put in the r' of Abiathar.
5: 1 him king in the r' of his father:
5 I will set upon thy throne in thy r',
8:20 I am risen up in the r' of David my
2Ki 15:25 he killed him, and reigned in his r'.
23:34 king in the r' of Josiah his father,
2Ch 26: 1 king in the r' of his father Amaziah.
Ps 31: 8 thou hast set my feet in a large r'.
80: 9 Thou preparedst r' before it, and
Pr 18:16 A man's gift maketh r' for him,
Mal 3:10 shall not be r' enough to receive it.
M't 2:22 Judæa in the r' of his father Herod,
M'r 2: 2 there was no r' to receive them.
14:15 shew you a large upper r' furnished
Lu 2: 7 there was no r' for them in the
12:17 have no r' where to bestow my fruits?
14: 8 sit not down in the highest r'; lest
9 with shame to take the lowest r'.
10 go sit down in the lowest r'; that
22 commanded, and yet there is r'.
22:12 shew you a large upper r' furnished:
Ac 1:13 in, they went up into an upper r',
24:27 Porcius Festus came into Felix' r':
1Co 14:16 occupieth the r' of the unlearned

rooms
Ge 6:14 *r*· shalt thou make in the ark, and
1Ki 20:24 place, and put captains in their *r*·:
1Ch 4:41 unto this day, and dwelt in their *r*·:
M't 23: 6 love the uppermost *r*· at feasts,
M'r 12:39 and the uppermost *r*· at feasts:
Lu 14: 7 how they chose out the chief *r*·;
20:46 synagogues,...the chief *r*· at feasts;

root See also ROOTED; ROOTS.
De 29:18 among you a *r*· that beareth gall
J'g 5:14 there a *r*· of them against Amalek;
1Ki 14:15 *r*· up Israel out of this good land,
2Ki 19:30 of Judah shall yet again take *r*·
Job 5: 3 I have seen the foolish taking *r*·:
14: 8 the *r*· thereof wax old in the earth,
19:28 the *r*· of the matter is found in me?
29:19 *r*· was spread out by the waters,
31:12 and would *r*· out all mine increase.
Ps 52: 5 and *r*· thee out of the land of the
80: 9 didst cause it to take deep *r*·, and it
Pr 12: 3 *r*· of the righteous shall not be
12 *r*· of the righteous yieldeth fruit.
Isa 5:24 so their *r*· shall be as rottenness,
11:10 that day there shall be a *r*· of Jesse,
14:29 out of the serpent's *r*· shall come
30 I will kill thy *r*· with famine, and he
27: 6 that come of Jacob to take *r*·:
37:31 house of Judah shall again take *r*·
40:24 their stock shall not take *r*· in the
53: 2 and as a *r*· out of a dry ground:
Jer 1:10 to *r*· out, and to pull down, and to
12: 2 yea, they have taken *r*·: they grow,
Eze 31: 7 for his *r*· was by great waters.
Ho 9:16 their *r*· is dried up, they shall bear
Mal 4: 1 leave them neither *r*· nor branch.
M't 3:10 ax is laid unto the *r*· of the trees:
13: 6 and because they had no *r*·, they
21 Yet hath he not *r*· in himself, but
29 ye *r*· up also the wheat with them.
M'r 4: 6 because it had no *r*·, it withered
17 And have no *r*· in themselves, and
Lu 3: 9 axe is laid unto the *r*· of the trees:
8:13 these have no *r*·, which for a while
17: 6 Be thou plucked up by the *r*·, and
Ro 11:16 and if the *r*· be holy, so are the
17 of the *r*· and fatness of the olive
18 bearest not the *r*·, but the *r*· thee.
15:12 There shall be a *r*· of Jesse, and he
1Ti 6:10 love of money is the *r*· of all evil:
Heb 12:15 lest any *r*· of bitterness springing
Re 5: 5 the tribe of Juda, the *R*· of David,
22:16 the *r*· and the offspring of David,

rooted
De 29:28 the Lord *r*· them out of their land
Job 18:14 His confidence shall be *r*· out of his
31: 8 eat; yea, let my offspring be *r*· out.
Pr 2:22 transgressors shall be *r*· out of it.
Zep 2: 4 day, and Ekron shall be *r*· up.
M't 15:13 hath not planted, shall be *r*· up.
Eph 3:17 ye, being *r*· and grounded in love,
Col 2: 7 *R*· and built up in him, and

roots
2Ch 7:20 will I pluck them up by the *r*· out
Job 8:17 His *r*· are wrapped about the heap,
18:16 His *r*· shall be dried up beneath,
28: 9 overturneth the mountains by the *r*·.
30: 4 and juniper *r*· for their meat.
Isa 11: 1 a Branch shall grow out of his *r*·:
Jer 17: 8 spreadeth out her *r*· by the river,
Eze 17: 6 and the *r*· thereof were under him:
7 vine did bend her *r*· toward him,
9 shall he not pull up the *r*· thereof,
9 to pluck it up by the *r*· thereof.
Da 4:15 the stump of his *r*· in the earth,
23 leave the stump of the *r*· thereof in
26 to leave the stump of the tree *r*·;
7: 8 first horns plucked up by the *r*·:
11: 7 out of a branch of her *r*· shall one
Ho 14: 5 and cast forth his *r*· as Lebanon.
Am 2: 9 from above, and his *r*· from beneath.
M'r 11:20 the fig tree dried up from the *r*·.
Jude 12 twice dead, plucked up by the *r*·;

rope See also ROPES.
Isa 5:18 and sin as it were with a cart *r*·:

ropes
J'g 16:11 If they bind me fast with new *r*·
12 Delilah therefore took new *r*·, and
2Sa 17:13 shall all Israel bring *r*· to that city,
1Ki 20:31 on our loins, and *r*· upon our heads,
32 loins, and put *r*· on their heads,
Ac 27:32 soldiers cut off the *r*· of the boat,

rose See also AROSE.
Ge 4: 8 *r*· up against Abel his brother,
18:16 And the men *r*· up from thence,
19: 1 Lot seeing them *r*· up to meet them;
20: 8 Abimelech *r*· early in the morning,
21:14 Abraham *r*· up early in the morning,
32 then Abimelech *r*· up, and Phichol
22: 3 And Abraham *r*· up early in the
3 and *r*· up, and went unto the place
19 they *r*· up and went together to
24:54 and they *r*· up in the morning, and
25:34 drink, and *r*· up, and went his way:
26:31 they *r*· up betimes in the morning,
28:18 Jacob *r*· up early in the morning,
31:17 Then Jacob *r*· up, and set his sons
21 he *r*· up, and passed over the river,
55 early in the morning Laban *r*· up,
32:22 he *r*· up that night, and took his
31 over Penuel the sun *r*· upon him,
37:35 daughters *r*· up to comfort him;
43:15 and *r*· up, and went down to Egypt,
46: 5 And Jacob *r*· up from Beer-sheba:
Ex 10:23 neither *r*· any from his place for
12:30 And Pharaoh *r*· up in the night, he,
15: 7 hast overthrown them that *r*· up
24: 4 and *r*· up early in the morning,
13 And Moses *r*· up, and his minister
32: 6 And they *r*· up early on the morrow,
6 eat and to drink, and *r*· up to play.
33: 8 that all the people *r*· up, and stood
10 the people *r*· up and worshipped,
34: 4 Moses *r*· up early in the morning,
Nu 14:40 And they *r*· up early in the morning,
16: 2 And they *r*· up before Moses, with
25 Moses *r*· up and went unto Dathan
22:13 And Balaam *r*· up in the morning,
14 And the princes of Moab *r*· up, and
21 And Balaam *r*· up in the morning,
24:25 And Balaam *r*· up, and went and
25: 7 *r*· up from among the congregation,
De 33: 2 and *r*· up from Seir unto them;
Jos 3: 1 Joshua *r*· early in the morning;
16 the waters...*r*· up upon an heap
6:12 Joshua *r*· early in the morning,
15 they *r*· early about the dawning of
7:16 Joshua *r*· up early in the morning,
8:10 Joshua *r*· up early in the morning,
14 that they hasted and *r*· up early,
J'g 6:21 and there *r*· up fire out of the rock,
38 for he *r*· up early on the morrow,
7: 1 Gideon,...*r*· up early, and pitched
9:34 And Abimelech *r*· up, and all the
35 and Abimelech *r*· up, and the people
43 he *r*· up against them, and smote
19: 5 morning, that he *r*· up to depart:
7, 9 when the man *r*· up to depart,
10 but he *r*· up and departed, and came
27 And her lord *r*· up in the morning,
28 the man *r*· up, and gat him unto his
20: 5 the men of Gibeah *r*· against me,
19 the children of Israel *r*· up in the
33 men of Israel *r*· up out of their place,
21: 4 the people *r*· early, and built there
Ru 3:14 she *r*· up before one could know
1Sa 1: 9 Hannah *r*· up after they had eaten
19 they *r*· up in the morning early,
15:12 when Samuel *r*· early to meet Saul
16:13 Samuel *r*· up, and went to Ramah.
17:20 David *r*· up early in the morning,
24: 7 But Saul *r*· up out of the cave, and
28:25 Then they *r*· up, and went away
29:11 So David...*r*· up early to depart
2Sa 15: 2 And Absalom *r*· up early, and stood
18:31 of all them that *r*· up against thee.
22:40 them that *r*· up...hast thou subdued
49 above them that *r*· up against me:
1Ki 1:49 and *r*· up, and went every man his
2:19 And the king *r*· up to meet her, and
3:21 I *r*· in the morning to give my child
21:16 *r*· up to go down to the vineyard
2Ki 3:22 they *r*· up early in the morning,
24 *r*· up and smote the Moabites, so
7: 5 And they *r*· up in the twilight, to
8:21 *r*· by night, and smote the Edomites
2Ch 20:20 And they *r*· early in the morning,
21: 9 *r*· up...and smote the Edomites
26:19 leprosy even *r*· up in his forehead
28:15 men...expressed by name *r*· up,
29:20 Then Hezekiah the king *r*· early,
Ezr 1: 5 Then *r*· up the chief of the fathers
5: 2 Then *r*· up Zerubbabel the son of
10: 6 Ezra *r*· up from before the house
Ne 3: 1 Then Eliashib the high priest *r*· up
4:14 And I looked, and *r*· up, and said
Job 1: 5 and *r*· up early in the morning,
Ps 18:39 subdued under me those that *r*· up
124: 2 our side, when men *r*· up against us:
Ca 2: 1 I am the *r*· of Sharon, and the lily
5: 5 I *r*· up to open to my beloved;
Isa 35: 1 rejoice, and blossom as the *r*·.
Jer 26:17 Then *r*· up certain of the elders
La 3:62 lips of those that *r*· up against me,
Da 8:24 was astonied, and *r*· up in haste,
8:27 I *r*· up, and did the king's business;
Jon 1: 3 Jonah *r*· up to flee unto Tarshish
4: 7 when the morning *r*· the next day,
Zep 3: 7 they *r*· early, and corrupted all
M'r 10:50 garment, *r*·, and came to Jesus.
Lu 4:29 *r*· up, and thrust him out of the city,
5:25 immediately he *r*· up before them,
28 he left all, *r*· up, and followed him.
16:31 though one *r*· from the dead.
22:45 And when he *r*· up from prayer, and
24:33 And they *r*· up the same hour, and
11:31 that she *r*· up hastily and went out,
Ac 5:17 Then the high priest *r*· up, and all
36 For before these days *r*· up Theudas,
37 After this man *r*· up Judas of
10:41 with him after he *r*· from the dead.
14:20 him, he *r*· up, and came into the city:
15: 5 *r*· up certain of the sect of the
7 Peter *r*· up, and said unto them,
16:22 *r*· up together against them: and
26:30 the king *r*· up, and the governor,
Ro 14: 9 this end Christ both died, and *r*·,
1Co 10: 7 to eat and drink, and *r*· up to play.
15: 4 and that he *r*· again the third day
12 preached that he *r*· from the dead,
2Co 5:15 which died for them, and *r*· again.
1Th 4:14 that Jesus died and *r*· again, even
Re 19: 3 her smoke *r*· up for ever and ever.

Rosh (*rosh*)
Ge 46:21 and *R*·, Muppim, and Huppim,

rot See also ROTTEN.
Nu 5:21 doth make thy thigh to *r*·, and thy
22 belly to swell, and thy thigh to *r*·:
27 shall swell, and her thigh shall *r*·:
Pr 10: 7 the name of the wicked shall *r*·.
Isa 40:20 chooseth a tree that will not *r*·; he

rotten
Job 13:28 he, as a *r*· thing, consumeth, as a
41:27 iron as straw,...brass as *r*· wood.
Jer 38:11 old cast clouts and old *r*· rags,
12 old cast clouts and *r*· rags under
Joe 1:17 The seed is *r*· under their clods,

rottenness
Pr 12: 4 ashamed is as *r*· in his bones.
14:30 flesh: but envy the *r*· of the bones.
Isa 5:24 so their root shall be as *r*·, and
Ho 5:12 and to the house of Judah as *r*·.
Hab 3:16 *r*· entered into my bones, and I

rough
De 21: 4 down the heifer unto a *r*· valley,
Isa 27: 8 he stayeth his *r*· wind in the day
40: 4 straight, and the *r*· places plain:
Jer 51:27 to come up as the *r*· caterpillers.
Da 8:21 the *r*· goat is the king of Grecia:
Zec 13: 4 wear a *r*· garment to deceive:
Lu 3: 5 the *r*· ways shall be made smooth;

roughly
Ge 42: 7 them, and spake *r*· unto them;
30 spake *r*· to us, and took us for spies
1Sa 20:10 what if thy father answer thee *r*·?
1Ki 12:13 the king answered the people *r*·,
2Ch 10:13 And the king answered them *r*·;
Pr 18:23 but the rich answereth *r*·.

round See also AROUND.
Ge 19: 4 compassed the house *r*·, both old
23:17 that were in all the borders *r*·
35: 5 the cities that were *r*· about them,
37: 7 your sheaves stood *r*· about, and
41:48 which was *r*· about every city,
Ex 7:24 Egyptians digged *r*· about the river
16:13 the dew lay *r*· about the host.
14 there lay a small *r*· thing, as
19:12 bounds unto the people *r*· about,
25:11 upon it a crown of gold *r*· about.
24 thereto a crown of gold *r*· about.
25 border of an hand breadth *r*· about,
25 crown to the border thereof *r*·
27:17 All the pillars *r*· about the court
28:32 woven work *r*· about the hole of it,
33 scarlet, *r*· about the hem thereof;
33 of gold between them *r*· about:
34 upon the hem of the robe *r*· about.
29:16 sprinkle it *r*· about upon the altar.
20 the blood upon the altar *r*· about.
30: 3 the sides thereof *r*· about, and the
3 unto it a crown of gold *r*· about.
37: 2 made a crown of gold to it *r*· about.
11 thereunto a crown of gold *r*· about.
12 border of an handbreadth *r*· about;
12 for the border thereof *r*· about.
26 the sides thereof *r*· about, and the
26 unto it a crown of gold *r*· about.
38:16 the hangings of the court *r*· about
20 and of the court *r*· about, were of
31 the sockets of the court *r*· about,
31 all the pins of the court *r*· about.
39:23 with a band *r*· about the hole, that
25 of the robe, *r*· about between the
26 *r*· about the hem of the robe to
40: 8 thou shalt set up the court *r*· about,
33 the court *r*· about the tabernacle
Le 1: 5 and sprinkle the blood *r*· about
11 shall sprinkle his blood *r*· about
8: 2 the blood upon the altar *r*· about.
8 the blood thereof *r*· about upon the
13 the blood thereof upon the altar *r*·
7: 2 he sprinkle *r*· about upon the altar.
8:15 upon the horns of the altar *r*· about
19, 24 the blood upon the altar *r*· about.
9:12 sprinkled *r*· about upon the altar.
18 sprinkled upon the altar *r*· about,
14:41 house to be scraped within *r*· about,
16:18 upon the horns of the altar *r*· about.
19:27 not *r*· the corners of your heads,
25:31 which have no wall *r*· about them
44 the heathen that are *r*· about you;
Nu 1:50 encamp *r*· about the tabernacle.
53 the Levites shall pitch *r*· about the
3:26 and by the altar *r*· about, and the
37 the pillars of the court *r*· about,
4:26 which is...by the altar *r*· about,
32 the pillars of the court *r*· about,
11:24 set them *r*· about the tabernacle.
31 the other side, *r*· about the camp,
32 for themselves *r*· about the camp.
16:34 all Israel that were *r*· about them
22: 4 lick up all that are *r*· about us, as
32:33 the cities of the country *r*· about.
34:12 with the coasts thereof *r*· about.
35: 2 suburbs for the cities *r*· about
4 a thousand cubits *r*· about.
De 6:14 the people which are *r*· about you;
12:10 from all your enemies *r*· about,
13: 7 the people which are *r*· about you,
21: 2 which are *r*· about him that is slain:
25:19 from all thine enemies *r*· about,
Jos 6: 3 war, and go *r*· about the city once.
7: 9 and shall environ us *r*·, and cut
15:12 of the children of Judah *r*· about
18:20 by the coasts thereof *r*· about,
19: 8 the villages...*r*· about these cities
21:11 with the suburbs thereof *r*· about it.
42 with their suburbs *r*· about them:
44 the Lord gave them rest *r*· about,
23: 1 from all their enemies *r*· about,
J'g 2:12 the people that were *r*· about them,
14 the hands of their enemies *r*· about,
7:21 man in his place *r*· about the camp:

J'g 19: 22 of Belial, beset the house r' about.
20: 5 beset the house r' about upon me
29 set liers in wait r' about Gibeah.
43 inclosed the Benjamites r' about,
1Sa 14: 21 camp from the country r' about,
23: 26 compassed David and his men r' about
26: 5 the people pitched r' about him.
7 and the people lay r' about him.
31: 9 the land of the Philistines r' about,
2Sa 5: 9 And David built r' about from Millo
7: 1 rest r' about from all his enemies;
22: 12 darkness pavilions r' about him,
1Ki 3: 1 and the wall of Jerusalem r' about.
4: 24 had peace on all sides r' about him.
31 fame was in all nations r' about.
6: 5 house he built chambers r' about,
5 the walls of the house r' about,
5 and he made chambers r' about:
6 he made narrowed rests r' about,
29 walls of the house r' about with
7: 12 the great court r' about was with
18 and two rows r' about upon the one
20 hundred in rows r' about upon the
23 it was r' all about, and his
23 thirty cubits did compass it r'
24 under the brim of it r' about there
24 cubit, compassing the sea r' about:
31 the mouth thereof was r' after the
31 their borders, foursquare, not r'.
35 a r' compass of half a cubit high:
36 every one, and additions r' about.
10: 19 top of the throne was r' behind:
18: 35 the water ran r' about the altar;
2Ki 6: 17 and chariots of fire r' about Elisha.
11: 8 ye shall compass the king r' about,
11 in his hand, r' about the king.
17: 15 heathen that were r' about them,
23: 5 in the places r' about Jerusalem;
25: 1 they built forts against it r' about.
4 were against the city r' about:) and
10 the walls of Jerusalem r' about.
17 upon the chapiter r' about, all of
1Ch 4: 33 their villages that were r' about
6: 55 and the suburbs thereof r' about it.
9: 27 lodged r' about the house of God,
10: 9 the land of the Philistines r' about,
11: 8 the city r' about, even from Millo r'
22: 9 rest from all his enemies r' about:
28: 12 of all the chambers r' about, of the
2Ch 4: 2 from brim to brim, r' in compass,
2 of thirty cubits did compass it r'
3 which did compass it r' about: ten
3 cubit, compassing the sea r' about.
14: 14 smote all the cities r' about Gerar;
15: 15 the Lord gave them rest r' about.
17: 10 lands that were r' about Judah,
20: 30 for his God gave him rest r' about.
23: 7 shall compass the king r' about,
10 the temple, by the king r' about.
34: 6 with their mattocks r' about.
Ne 12: 28 plain country r' about Jerusalem,
29 them villages r' about Jerusalem.
Job 10: 8 fashioned me together r' about;
16: 13 His archers compass me r' about,
19: 12 encamp r' about my tabernacle.
22: 10 snares are r' about thee, and
37: 12 turned r' about by his counsels:
41: 14 his teeth are terrible r' about.
Ps 3: 6 themselves against me r' about.
18: 11 his pavilion r' about him were
22: 12 bulls of Bashan have beset me r'.
27: 6 above mine enemies r' about me:
34: 7 encampeth r' about them that fear
44: 13 to them that are r' about us.
48: 12 about Zion, and go r' about her:
50: 3 be very tempestuous r' about him.
59: 6, 14 dog, and go r' about the city.
76: 11 be r' about him bring presents
78: 28 camp, r' about their habitations.
79: 3 like water r' about Jerusalem;
4 to them that are r' about us.
88: 17 r' about me daily like water;
89: 8 to thy faithfulness r' about thee?
97: 2 and darkness are r' about him:
3 burneth up his enemies r' about.
125: 2 mountains are r' about Jerusalem,
2 so the Lord is r' about his people
128: 3 like olive plants r' about thy table.
Ca 7: 2 navel is like a r' goblet, which
Isa 3: 18 and their r' tires like the moon,
15: 8 gone r' about the borders of Moab;
29: 3 I will camp against thee r' about,
42: 25 it hath set him on fire r' about,
49: 18 Lift up thine eyes r' about, and
60: 4 Lift up thine eyes r' about, and see:
Jer 1: 15 against all the walls thereof r' about,
4: 17 are they against her r' about;
6: 3 their tents against her r' about;
12: 9 the birds r' about are against her;
21: 14 shall devour all things r' about it.
25: 9 against all these nations r' about,
46: 5 for fear was r' about, saith the
14 sword shall devour r' about thee.
50: 14 in array against Babylon r' about:
15 Shout against her r' about: she
29 the bow, camp against it r' about;
32 it shall devour all r' about him.
51: 2 they shall be against her r' about.
52: 4 and built forts against it r' about.
7 Chaldeans were by the city r' about:)
14 all the walls of Jerusalem r' about.
22 upon the chapiters r' about, all
23 network were an hundred r' about.
La 1: 17 adversaries should be r' about him:
2: 3 fire, which devoureth r' about.
22 a solemn day my terrors r' about.

Eze 1: 18 full of eyes r' about them four.
27 the appearance of fire r' about
27 and it had brightness r' about.
28 of the brightness r' about.
4: 2 battering rams against it r' about.
5: 5 and countries that are r' about her.
6 the countries that are r' about her:
7 the nations that are r' about you,
7 the nations that are r' about you;
12 fall by the sword r' about thee;
14, 15 nations that are r' about thee,
6: 5 your bones r' about your altars.
13 their idols r' about their altars,
8: 10 pourtrayed upon the wall r' about.
10: 12 wheels, were full of eyes r' about,
11: 12 the heathen that are r' about you.
16: 37 gather them r' about against thee,
57 Syria, and all that are r' about her,
57 which despise thee r' about.
23: 24 and shield and helmet r' about:
27: 11 army were upon thy walls r' about,
11 shields upon thy walls r' about;
28: 24 thorn of all that are r' about them,
26 that despise them r' about them;
31: 4 rivers running r' about his plants,
32: 23 her company is r' about her grave:
24 her multitude r' about her grave,
25, 26 her graves are r' about him:
34: 26 and the places r' about my hill a
36: 4 the residue...that are r' about;
36 the heathen that are left r' about
37: 2 me to pass by them r' about: and,
40: 5 the outside of the house r' about,
14 post of the court r' about the gate.
16 posts within the gate r' about,
16 windows were r' about inward:
17 pavement...for the court r' about:
25 and in the arches thereof r' about,
29 and in the arches thereof r' about:
30 the arches r' about were five and
33 and in the arches thereof r' about:
36 and the windows to it r' about:
43 an hand broad, fastened r' about:
41: 5 r' about the house on every side.
6 for the side chambers r' about,
7 still upward r' about the house:
8 the height of the house r' about:
10 twenty cubits r' about the house
11 was left was five cubits r' about.
12 was five cubits thick r' about, and
16 galleries r' about on their three
16 door, cieled with wood r' about,
17 by all the wall r' about within and
19 through all the house r' about.
42: 15 the east, and measured it r' about.
16, 17 the measuring reed r' about.
20 it had a wall r' about, five hundred
43: 12 the whole limit thereof r' about
13 by the edge thereof r' about shall
20 and upon the border r' about:
45: 1 in all the borders thereof r' about.
2 in breadth, square r' about; and
2 and fifty cubits r' about for the
46: 23 a row of building r' about in them,
23 r' about them four, and it was
23 places under the rows r' about.
48: 35 It was r' about eighteen thousand
Joe 3: 11 gather yourselves together r' about:
12 to judge all the heathen r' about.
Am 3: 11 shall be even r' about the land;
Jon 2: 5 the depth closed me r' about, the
Na 3: 8 that had the waters r' about it,
Zec 2: 5 be unto her a wall of fire r' about,
7: 7 and the cities thereof r' about her,
12: 2 unto all the people r' about, when
6 shall devour all the people r' about,
14: 14 wealth of all the heathen r' about
M't 3: 5 all the region r' about Jordan,
14: 35 out into all that country r' about,
21: 33 vineyard, and hedged it r' about,
M'r 1: 28 all the region r' about Galilee.
3: 5 had looked r' about on them with
34 he looked r' about on them which
5: 32 he looked r' about to see her that
6: 6 And he went r' about the villages,
36 may go into the country r' about,
55 that whole region r' about, and
9: 8 when they had looked r' about,
10: 23 Jesus looked r' about, and saith
11: 11 looked r' about upon all things,
Lu 1: 65 on all that dwelt r' about them:
2: 9 glory of the Lord shone r' about
4: 14 through all the region r' about.
37 every place of the country r' about.
6: 10 looking r' about upon them all, he
7: 17 throughout all the region r' about.
8: 37 country of the Gadarenes r' about
9: 12 the towns and country r' about,
19: 43 compass thee r', and keep thee in
Joh 10: 24 Then came the Jews r' about him,
Ac 5: 16 the cities r' about unto Jerusalem,
9: 3 there shined r' about him a light
14: 6 the region that lieth r' about:
20 the disciples stood r' about him,
22: 6 heaven a great light r' about me.
25: 7 from Jerusalem stood r' about,
26: 13 of the sun, shining r' about me
Ro 15: 19 and r' about unto Illyricum, I
Heb 9: 4 overlaid r' about with gold,
Re 4: 3 was a rainbow r' about the throne,
4 r' about the throne were four and
6 and r' about the throne, were four
5: 11 many angels r' about the throne
7: 11 angels stood r' about the throne,

rouse
Ge 49: 9 an old lion; who shall r' him up?

rovers
1Ch 12: 21 David against the band of the r':

row See also ROWED; ROWING; ROWS.
Ex 28: 17 the first r' shall be a sardius, a
17 carbuncle: this shall be the first r'.
18 the second r' shall be an emerald,
19 the third r' a ligure, an agate, and
20 the fourth r' a beryl, and an onyx,
39: 10 the first r' was a sardius, a topaz,
10 a carbuncle: this was the first r'.
11 second r', an emerald, a sapphire,
12 the third r', a ligure, an agate, and
13 the fourth r', a beryl, an onyx, and
Le 24: 6 set them in two rows, six on a r',
7 put pure frankincense upon each r'
1Ki 6: 36 stone, and a r' of cedar beams.
7: 3 on forty five pillars, fifteen in a r'
12 stones, and a r' of cedar beams,
Ezr 6: 4 stones, and a r' of good timber:
Eze 46: 23 there was a r' of building round

rowed
Jon 1: 13 men r' hard to bring it to the land;
Joh 6: 19 they had r' about five and twenty

rowers
Eze 27: 26 Thy r' have brought thee into

rowing
M'r 6: 48 And he saw them toiling in r'; for

rows
Ex 28: 17 of stones, even four r' of stones:
39: 10 And they set in it four r' of stones:
Le 24: 6 And thou shalt set them in two r',
1Ki 6: 36 court with three r' of hewed stone,
7: 2 upon four r' of cedar pillars, with
4 And there were windows in three r',
12 was with three r' of hewed stones,
18 two r' round about upon the one
20 were two hundred in r' round about
24 the knops were cast in two r', when
42 r' of pomegranates for one network,
2Ch 4: 3 Two r' of oxen were cast, when it
13 r' of pomegranates on each wreath,
Ezr 6: 4 With three r' of great stones, and
Ca 1: 10 are comely with r' of jewels,
Eze 46: 23 with boiling places under the r'

royal
Ge 49: 20 fat, and he shall yield r' dainties.
Jos 10: 2 great city, as one of the r' cities,
1Sa 27: 5 thy servant dwell in the r' city with
2Sa 12: 26 of Ammon, and took the r' city.
1Ki 10: 13 Solomon gave her of his r' bounty.
2Ki 11: 1 arose and destroyed all the seed r'.
25: 25 the son of Elishama, the seed r',
1Ch 29: 25 such r' majesty as had not been
2Ch 22: 10 the seed r' of the house of Judah.
Es 1: 7 r' wine in abundance, according
9 feast for the women in the r' house
11 before the king with the crown r',
19 go a r' commandment from him,
19 king give her r' estate unto another
2: 16 king Ahasuerus into his house r'
17 he set the r' crown upon her head,
5: 1 Esther put on her r' apparel, and
1 upon his r' throne in the r' house,
6: 8 Let the r' apparel be brought
8 crown r' which is set upon his head:
8: 15 in r' apparel of blue and white,
Isa 62: 3 r' diadem in the hand of thy God.
Jer 41: 1 the son of Elishama, of the seed r',
43: 10 spread his r' pavilion over them.
Da 6: 7 together to establish a r' statute,
Ac 12: 21 Herod, arrayed in r' apparel, sat
Jas 2: 8 If ye fulfill the r' law according to
1Pe 2: 9 a r' priesthood, an holy nation, a

rubbing
Lu 6: 1 did eat, r' them in their hands.

rubbish
Ne 4: 2 heaps of the r' which are burned?
10 is decayed, and there is much r';

rubies
Job 28: 18 the price of wisdom is above r'.
Pr 3: 15 She is more precious than r': and
8: 11 For wisdom is better than r'; and
20: 15 There is gold, and a multitude of r':
31: 10 woman? for her price is far above r'.
La 4: 7 were more ruddy in body than r',

rudder
Ac 27: 40 the sea, and loosed the r' bands,

ruddy
1Sa 16: 12 Now he was r', and withal of a
17: 42 for he was but a youth, and r', and
Ca 5: 10 My beloved is white and r', the
La 4: 7 were more r' in body than rubies,

rude
2Co 11: 6 But though I be r' in speech, yet

rudiments
Col 2: 8 after the r' of the world, and not
20 be dead...from the r' of the world,

rue
Lu 11: 42 for ye tithe the mint and r' and all

Rufus (*ru'-fus*)
M'r 15: 21 the father of Alexander and R',
Ro 16: 13 Salute R' chosen in the Lord, and

Ruhamah (*ru-ha'-mah*) See also LO-RUHAMAH.
Ho 2: 1 Ammi; and to your sisters, R'.

ruin See also RUINED; RUINS.
Ps 89: 40 hast brought his strong holds to r'.
Pr 24: 22 who knoweth the r' of them both?
26: 28 and a flattering mouth worketh r'.
Isa 3: 6 and let this r' be under thy hand:

Isa 23: 13 thereof; and he brought it to *r*.
25: 2 city an heap; of a defenced city a *r*:
Eze 18: 30 so iniquity shall not be your *r*.
27: 27 midst of the seas in...day of thy *r*.
31: 13 Upon his *r* shall all the fowls of the
Lu 6: 49 and the *r* of that house was great.

ruined
Isa 3: 8 For Jerusalem is *r*, and Judah is
Eze 36: 35 and *r* cities are become fenced,
36 that I the Lord build the *r* places,

ruinous
2Ki 19: 25 waste fenced cities into *r* heaps.
Isa 17: 1 a city, and it shall be a *r* heap.
37: 26 waste defenced cities into *r* heaps.

ruins
Eze 21: 15 faint, and their *r* be multiplied:
Am 9: 11 and I will raise up his *r*, and I will
Ac 15: 16 I will build again the *r* thereof,

rule^ See also RULED; RULEST; RULETH; RULING; UNRULY.
Ge 1: 16 the greater light to *r* the day,
16 and the lesser light to *r* the night:
18 to *r* over the day and over the
3: 16 husband, and he shall *r* over thee.
4: 7 desire, and thou shalt *r* over him.
Le 25: 43 shalt not *r* over him with rigour;
46 *r* one over another with rigour.
53 shall not *r* with rigour over him in
J'g 8: 22 *R* thou over us, both thou, and
23 unto them, I will not *r* over you,
23 neither shall my son *r* over you:
23 you: the Lord shall *r* over you.
1Ki 9: 23 which bare *r* over the people that
22: 31 captains that had *r* over his chariots,
2Ch 8: 10 fifty, that bare *r* over the people.
Ne 5: 15 servants bare *r* over the people:
Es 1: 22 should bare *r* in his own house,
9: 1 Jews had *r* over them that hated
Ps 110: 2 *r* thou in the midst of thine
136: 8 The sun to *r* by day: for his
9 The moon and stars to *r* by night:
Pr 8: 16 By me princes *r*, and nobles,
12: 24 hand of the diligent shall bare *r*:
17: 2 servant shall have *r* over a son that
19: 10 a servant to have *r* over princes.
25: 28 hath no *r* over his own spirit is
29: 2 but when the wicked beareth *r*,
Ec 2: 19 he have *r* over all my labour
Isa 3: 4 and babes shall *r* over them.
12 oppressors,...women *r* over them.
14: 2 they shall *r* over their oppressors.
19: 4 a fierce king shall *r* over them,
28: 14 *r* this people which is in Jerusalem.
32: 1 and princes shall *r* in judgment.
40: 10 and his arm shall *r* for him:
41: 2 him, and made him *r* over kings?
52: 5 *r* over them make them to howl,
63: 19 thou never barest *r* over them;
Jer 5: 31 priests bare *r* by their means;
Eze 19: 11 the sceptres of them that bare *r*,
14 no strong rod to be a sceptre to *r*.
20: 33 poured out, will I *r* over you:
29: 15 shall no more *r* over the nations.
Da 2: 39 shall bare *r* over all the earth.
4: 26 known that the heavens do *r*.
11: 3 that shall *r* with great dominion,
39 shall cause them to *r* over many,
Joe 2: 17 the heathen should *r* over them:
Zec 6: 13 shall sit and *r* upon his throne;
M't 2: 6 that shall *r* my people Israel.
M'r 10: 42 accounted to *r* over the Gentiles
1Co 15: 24 he shall have put down all *r* and
2Co 10: 13 the *r* which God hath distributed
15 you according to our *r* abundantly,
Ga 6: 16 many as walk according to this *r*,
Ph'p 3: 16 let us walk by the same *r*, let us
Col 3: 15 the peace of God *r* in your hearts,
1Ti 3: 5 know not how to *r* his own house,
5: 17 the elders that *r* well be counted
Heb 13: 7 them which have the *r* over you,
17 Obey them that have...*r* over you,
24 Salute all...that have...*r* over you,
Re 2: 27 shall *r* them with a rod of iron;
12: 5 *r* all nations with a rod of iron:
19: 15 he shall *r* them with a rod of iron:

ruled
Ge 24: 2 house, that *r* over all that he had,
41: 40 word shall all my people be *r*:
Jos 12: 2 and *r* from Aroer, which is upon
Ru 1: 1 in the days when the judges *r*,
1Ki 5: 16 which *r* over the people that
1Ch 26: 6 that *r* throughout the house of
Ezr 4: 20 which have *r* over all countries
Ps 106: 41 that hated them *r* over them.
Isa 14: 6 he that *r* the nations in anger, is
La 5: 8 Servants have *r* over us: there is
Eze 34: 4 and with cruelty have ye *r* them.
Da 5: 21 God *r* in the kingdom of men,
11: 4 to his dominion which he *r*:

ruler See also RULER'S; RULERS.
Ge 41: 43 he made him *r* over all the land of
43: 16 he said to the *r* of his house,
45: 8 a *r* throughout all the land of
Ex 22: 28 nor curse the *r* of thy people.
Le 4: 22 When a *r* hath sinned, and done
Nu 13: 2 a man, every one a *r* among them.
J'g 9: 30 Zebul the *r* of the city heard the
1Sa 25: 30 appointed thee *r* over Israel;
2Sa 6: 21 me *r* over the people of the Lord,
7: 8 the sheep, to be *r* over my people,
20: 26 Jairite was a chief *r* about David.
1Ki 1: 35 appointed him to be *r* over Israel
11: 28 made him *r* over all the charge
2Ki 25: 22 them he made Gedaliah...*r*.
1Ch 5: 2 and of him came the chief *r*; but
9: 11 the *r* of the house of God;
20 Phinehas...was the *r* over them in
11: 2 shalt be *r* over my people Israel.
17: 7 be *r* over my people Israel:
26: 24 Shebuel...was *r* of the treasures.
27: 4 his course was Mikloth also the *r*:
16 *r* of the Reubenites was Eliezer the
28: 4 he hath chosen Judah to be the *r*;
2Ch 6: 5 to be a *r* over my people Israel:
7: 18 fail thee a man to be *r* in Israel.
11: 22 to be *r* among his brethren: for
19: 11 the *r* of the house of Judah, for
26: 11 the scribe and Maaseiah the *r*,
31: 12 which Cononiah the Levite was *r*,
13 Azariah the *r* of the house of God.
Ne 3: 9 *r* of the half part of Jerusalem.
12 *r* of the half part of Jerusalem, he
14 the *r* of part of Beth-haccerem;
15 Col-hozeh, the *r* of part of Mizpah;
16 the *r* of the half part of Beth-zur,
17 the *r* of the half part of Keilah,
18 the *r* of the half part of Keilah.
19 son of Jeshua, the *r* of Mizpah,
7: 2 and Hananiah the *r* of the palace,
11: 11 was the *r* of the house of God.
Ps 68: 27 is little Benjamin with their *r*,
105: 20 the *r* of the people, and let him
21 house, and *r* of all his substance:
Pr 6: 7 having no guide, overseer, or *r*,
23: 1 When thou sittest to eat with a *r*,
28: 15 is a wicked *r* over the poor people.
29: 12 If a *r* hearken to lies, all his
Ec 10: 4 the spirit of the *r* rise up against
5 which proceedeth from the *r*:
Isa 3: 6 be thou our *r*, and let this ruin
7 make me not a *r* of the people.
16: 1 Send ye the lamb to the *r* of the
Jer 51: 46 violence in the land, *r* against *r*.
Da 2: 10 there is no king, lord, nor *r*, that
38 hath made thee *r* over them all.
48 him *r* over the whole province of
5: 7, 16 be the third *r* in the kingdom.
29 be the third *r* in the kingdom.
Mic 5: 2 unto me that is to be *r* in Israel;
Hab 1: 14 things, that have no *r* over them?
M't 9: 18 came a certain *r*, and worshipped
24: 45 hath made *r* over his household,
47 make him *r* over all his goods.
25: 21, 23 make thee *r* over many things:
M'r 5: 35 from the *r* of the synagogue's
36 saith unto the *r* of the synagogue,
38 house of the *r* of the synagogue,
Lu 8: 41 and he was a *r* of the synagogue:
49 the *r* of the synagogue's house,
12: 42 shall make *r* over his household,
44 make him *r* over all that he hath.
13: 14 the *r* of the synagogue answered
18: 18 And a certain *r* asked him, saying,
Joh 2: 9 When the *r* of the feast had tasted
3: 1 named Nicodemus, a *r* of the Jews:
Ac 7: 27 made thee a *r* and a judge over us?
35 Who made thee a *r* and a judge?
35 God send to be a *r* and a deliverer
18: 8, 17 the chief *r* of the synagogue,
23: 5 speak evil of the *r* of thy people.

ruler's
Pr 29: 26 Many seek the *r* favour; but every
M't 9: 23 when Jesus came into the *r* house,

rulers^
Ge 47: 6 then make them *r* over my cattle.
Ex 16: 22 the *r* of the congregation came
18: 21 *r* of thousands, and *r* of hundreds,
21 *r* of fifties, and *r* of tens:
25 *r* of thousands, *r* of hundreds,
25 *r* of fifties, and *r* of tens.
34: 31 the *r* of the congregation returned
35: 27 And the *r* brought onyx stones,
De 1: 13 and I will make them *r* over you.
J'g 15: 11 that the Philistines are *r* over us?
2Sa 8: 18 and David's sons were chief *r*.
2Ki 10: 1 to Samaria, unto the *r* of Jezreel,
11: 4 and fetched the *r* over hundreds,
19 And he took the *r* over hundreds,
1Ch 21: 2 to Joab and to the *r* of the people,
26: 32 David made *r* over...Reubenites,
27: 31 these were the *r* of the substance
29: 6 with the *r* of the king's work,
2Ch 29: 20 and gathered the *r* of the city, and
35: 8 Jethiel, *r* of the house of God,
Ezr 9: 2 *r* hath been chief in this trespass
10: 14 *r* of all the congregation stand,
Ne 2: 16 the *r* knew not whither I went,
16 nor to the nobles, nor to the *r*, nor
4: 14 said unto the nobles, and to the *r*,
16 the *r* were behind all the house of
19 unto the nobles, and to the *r*, and
5: 7 I rebuked the nobles, and the *r*,
17 hundred and fifty of the Jews and *r*,
7: 5 together the nobles, and the *r*, and
11: 1 And the *r* of the people dwelt
12: 40 I, and the half of the *r* with me:
13: 11 Then contended I with the *r*, and
Es 3: 12 to the *r* of every people of every
8: 9 deputies and *r* of the provinces
9: 3 And all the *r* of the provinces, and
Ps 2: 2 and the *r* take counsel together,
Isa 1: 10 word of the Lord, ye *r* of Sodom;
14: 5 wicked, and the sceptre of the *r*.
22: 3 All thy *r* are fled together, they
29: 10 prophets and your *r*, the seers
49: 7 abhorreth, to a servant of *r*,
Jer 33: 26 to be *r* over the seed of Abraham,
51: 23 I break in pieces captains and *r*.
28 all the *r* thereof, and all the land
Jer 51: 57 and her *r*, and her mighty men:
Eze 23: 6 clothed with blue, captains and *r*,
12 and *r* clothed most gorgeously,
23 captains and *r*, great lords and
Da 3: 2 and all the *r* of the provinces, to
3 and all the *r* of the provinces, were
Ho 4: 18 her *r* with shame do love, Give ye.
M'r 5: 22 one of the *r* of the synagogue,
13: 9 before *r* and kings for my sake,
Lu 21: 12 kings and *r* for my name's sake.
23: 13 priests and the *r* and the people,
35 the *r* also with them derided him,
24: 20 chief priests and our *r* delivered
Joh 7: 26 Do the *r* know indeed that this is
48 of the *r* or of the Pharisees believed
12: 42 among the chief *r*...many believed
Ac 3: 17 ye did it, as did also your *r*.
4: 5 their *r*, and elders, and scribes,
8 Ye *r* of the people, and elders of
26 and the *r* were gathered together
13: 15 the *r* of the synagogue sent unto
27 dwell at Jerusalem, and their *r*,
14: 5 also of the Jews with their *r*, to use
16: 19 into the marketplace unto the *r*,
17: 6 brethren unto the *r* of the city,
8 the people and the *r* of the city,
Ro 13: 3 *r* are not a terror to good works,
Eph 6: 12 against the *r* of the darkness of

rulest
2Ch 20: 6 *r* not thou over all the kingdoms
Ps 89: 9 Thou *r* the raging of the sea: when

ruleth
2Sa 23: 3 He that *r* over men must be just,
Ps 59: 13 let them know that God *r* in Jacob
66: 7 He *r* by his power for ever; his
103: 19 and his kingdom *r* over all.
Pr 16: 32 he that *r* his spirit than he that
22: 7 The rich *r* over the poor, and the
Ec 8: 9 wherein one man *r* over another
9: 17 the cry of him that *r* among fools.
Da 4: 17, 25, 32 that the most High *r* in the
Ho 11: 12 but Judah yet *r* with God, and is
Ro 12: 8 he that *r*, with diligence; he that
1Ti 3: 4 One that *r* well his own house,

ruling
2Sa 23: 3 must be just, *r* in the fear of God.
Jer 22: 30 David, and *r* any more in Judah.
1Ti 3: 12 *r* their children and their own

Rumah (*ru'-mah*) See also ARUMAH.
2Ki 23: 36 the daughter of Padaiah of *R*.

rumbling
Jer 47: 3 at the *r* of his wheels, the fathers

rumour See also RUMOURS.
2Ki 19: 7 and he shall hear a *r*, and shall
Isa 37: 7 he shall hear a *r*, and return to
Jer 49: 14 I have heard a *r* from the Lord,
51: 46 fear for the *r* that shall be heard
46 a *r* shall both come one year, and
46 in another year shall come a *r*, and
Eze 7: 26 mischief, and *r* shall be upon *r*;
Ob 1 We have heard a *r* from the Lord,
Lu 7: 17 And this *r* of him went forth

rumours
M't 24: 6 shall hear of wars and *r* of wars:
M'r 13: 7 shall hear of wars and *r* of wars,

rump
Ex 29: 22 take of the ram the fat and the *r*,
Le 3: 9 the fat thereof, and the whole *r*, it
7: 3 the *r*, and the fat that covereth the
8: 25 And he took the fat, and the *r*, and
9: 19 the bullock and of the ram, the *r*,

run See also RAN; RUNNEST; RUNNETH; RUNNING; OUTRUN.
Ge 49: 22 whose branches *r* over the wall:
Le 15: 3 whether his flesh *r* with his issue,
25 or if it *r* beyond the time of her
J'g 18: 25 lest angry fellows *r* upon thee,
1Sa 8: 11 some shall *r* before his chariots.
17: 17 and *r* to the camp to thy brethren;
20: 6 that he might *r* to Beth-lehem his
36 *R*, find out now the arrows which
2Sa 15: 1 and fifty men to *r* before him.
18: 19 Let me now *r*, and bear the king
22 me, I pray thee, also *r* after Cushi.
22 Wherefore wilt thou *r*, my son,
23 But howsoever, said he, let me *r*.
23 And he said unto him, *R*. Then
22: 30 by thee I have *r* through a troop:
1Ki 1: 5 and fifty men to *r* before him.
2Ki 4: 22 that I may *r* to the man of God,
26 *R* now, I pray thee, to meet her,
5: 20 *r* after him, and take somewhat
2Ch 16: 9 the eyes of the Lord *r* to and fro
Ps 18: 29 by thee I have *r* through a troop;
19: 5 rejoiceth as a strong man to *r* a
58: 7 as waters which *r* continually:
59: 4 They *r* and prepare themselves
78: 16 waters to *r* down like rivers.
104: 10 valleys, which *r* among the hills.
119: 32 *r* the way of thy commandments,
136 of waters *r* down mine eyes,
Pr 1: 16 For their feet *r* to evil, and make
Ec 1: 7 All the rivers *r* into the sea; yet
Ca 1: 4 Draw me, we will *r* after thee:
Isa 33: 4 of locusts shall he *r* upon them.
40: 31 they shall *r*, and not be weary;
55: 5 that knew not thee shall *r* unto thee
59: 7 Their feet *r* to evil, and they make
Jer 5: 1 *R*...to and fro through the streets
9: 18 our eyes may *r* down with tears,
12: 5 If thou hast *r* with the footmen,
13: 17 weep sore, and *r* down with tears,

Jer 14:17 Let mine eyes r· down with tears
49: 3 and r· to and fro by the hedges;
19 I will suddenly make him r· away
50:44 I will make them suddenly r· away
51:31 One post shall r· to meet another,
La 2:18 let tears r· down like a river day
Eze 24:16 neither shall thy tears r· down.
32:14 and cause their rivers to r· like oil,
Da 12: 4 many shall r· to and fro, and
Joe 2: 4 and as horsemen, so shall they r·.
7 They shall r· like mighty men; they
9 They shall r· to and fro in the city;
9 they shall r· upon the wall, they
Am 5:24 let judgment r· down as waters,
6:12 Shall horses r· upon the rock?
8:12 shall r· to and fro to seek the word
Na 2: 4 they shall r· like the lightnings.
Hab 2: 2 that he may r· that readeth it.
Hag 1: 9 ye r· every man unto his own house.
Zec 2: 4 R·, speak to this young man, saying,
4:10 r· to and fro through the whole
M't 28: 8 did r· to bring his disciples word.
1Co 9:24 that they which r· in a race r· all,
24 prize? So r·, that ye may obtain.
26 therefore so r·, not as uncertainly;
Ga 2: 2 means I should r·, or had r·, in vain.
5: 7 Ye did r· well; who did hinder you
Ph'p 2:16 that I have not r· in vain, neither
Heb 12: 1 let us r· with patience the race that
1Pe 4: 4 strange that ye r· not with them to

runner See FORERUNNER.

runnest
Pr 4:12 and when thou r·, thou shalt not

runneth
Ezr 8:15 to the river that r· to Ahava;
Job 15:26 He r· upon him, even on his neck,
16:14 breach, he r· upon me like a giant.
Ps 23: 5 my head with oil; my cup r· over.
147:15 earth: his word r· very swiftly.
Pr 18:10 the righteous r· into it, and is safe.
La 1:16 eye, mine eye r· down with water,
3:48 Mine eye r· down with rivers of
M't 9:17 bottles break, and the wine r· out,
Joh 20: 2 Then she r·, and cometh to Simon
Ro 9:16 him that willeth, nor of him that r·,

running See also OVERRUNNING.
Le 14: 5 in an earthen vessel over r· water:
6 that was killed over the r· water:
50 in an earthen vessel over r· water:
51 the slain bird, and in the r· water,
52 of the bird, and with the r· water,
15: 2 hath a r· issue out of his flesh,
13 and bathe his flesh in r· water, and
22: 4 is a leper, or hath a r· issue;
Nu 19:17 r· water shall be put thereto in a
2Sa 18:24 looked, and behold a man r· alone.
26 the watchman saw another man r·:
26 said, Behold another man r· alone.
27 the r· of the foremost is like
27 the r· of Ahimaaz the son of Zadok.
2Ki 5:21 Naaman saw him r· after him, he
2Ch 23:12 noise of the people r· and praising
Pr 5:15 r· waters out of thine own well.
6:18 feet that be swift in r· to mischief,
Isa 33: 4 as the r· to and fro of locusts shall
Eze 31: 4 rivers r· round about his plants,
M'r 9:15 amazed, and r· to him saluted him.
25 that the people came r· together,
10:17 there came one r·, and kneeled to
Lu 6:38 and shaken together, and r· over,
Ac 27:16 And r· under a certain island
Re 9: 9 of many horses r· to battle.

rush See also BULRUSH; RUSHED; RUSHES; RUSHETH; RUSHING.
Job 8:11 Can the r· grow up without mire?
Isa 9:14 Israel head and tail, branch and r·,
17:13 nations shall r· like the rushing of
19:15 head or tail, branch or r·, may do.

rushed
J'g 9:44 Abimelech...r· forward, and stood
20:37 in wait hasted, and r· upon Gibeah;
Ac 19:29 they r· with one accord into the

rushes See also BULRUSHES.
Isa 35: 7 shall be grass with reeds and r·.

rusheth
Jer 8: 6 as the horse r· into the battle.

rushing
Isa 17:12 and to the r· of nations, that make
12 of nations, that make a r· like the
12 like the r· of mighty waters!
13 rush like the r· of many waters:
Jer 47: 3 at the r· of his chariots, and at the
Eze 3:12 behind me a voice of a great r·,
13 them, and a noise of a great r·.
Ac 2: 2 from heaven as of a r· mighty wind,

rust
M't 6:19 where moth and r· doth corrupt,
20 neither moth nor r· doth corrupt,
Jas 5: 3 the r· of them shall be a witness

Ruth (*rooth*)
Ru 1: 4 and the name of the other R·:
14 in law; but R· clave unto her.
16 R· said, Intreat me not to leave
22 returned, and R· the Moabitess,
2: 2 R· the Moabitess said unto Naomi,
8 Then said Boaz unto R·, Hearest
21 R· the Moabitess said, He said unto
22 Naomi said unto R· her daughter
3: 9 answered, I am R· thine handmaid:
4: 5 must buy it also of R· the Moabitess,
10 R· the Moabitess,...wife of Mahlon,
13 Boaz took R·, and she was his wife:
M't 1: 5 and Booz begat Obed of R·; and

rye See RIE.

S.

sabachthani (*sa-bak'-tha-ni*)
M't 27:46 loud voice, saying, Eli, Eli, lama s·?
M'r 15:34 voice, saying, Eloi, Eloi, lama s·?

Sabaoth (*sab'-a-oth*)
Ro 9:29 Except the Lord of S· had left us a
Jas 5: 4 into the ears of the Lord of s·.

Sabas See BARSABAS.

sabbath See also SABBATHS.
Ex 16:23 rest of the holy s· unto the Lord:
25 for to day is a s· unto the Lord:
26 on the seventh day, which is the s·,
29 that the Lord hath given you the s·,
20: 8 Remember the s· day, to keep it holy.
10 seventh day is the s· of the Lord thy
11 the Lord blessed the s· day, and
31:14 Ye shall keep the s· therefore; for it
15 but in the seventh is the s· of rest,
15 whosoever doeth any work in the s·
16 shall keep the s·, to observe the s·
35: 2 an holy day, a s· of rest to the Lord:
3 kindle no fire...upon the s· day.
Le 16:31 It shall be a s· of rest unto you, and
23: 3 but the seventh day is the s· of rest,
3 s· of the Lord in all your dwellings.
11 morrow after the s· the priest shall
15 you from the morrow after the s·,
16 unto the morrow after the seventh s·
24 shall ye have a s·, a memorial of
32 It shall be unto you a s· of rest,
32 unto even, shall ye celebrate your s·.
39 on the first day shall be a s·, and
39 on the eighth day shall be a s·.
24: 8 Every s· he shall set it in order
25: 2 then shall the land keep a s· unto
4 shall be a s· of rest unto the land,
4 a s· for the Lord: thou shalt neither
6 s· of the land shall be meat for you;
Nu 15:32 gathered sticks upon the s· day.
28: 9 And on the s· day two lambs of the
10 is the burnt offering of every s·,
De 5:12 Keep the s· day to sanctify it, as the
14 seventh day is the s· of the Lord
15 commanded thee to keep the s· day.
2Ki 4:23 it is neither new moon, nor s·.
11: 5 part of you that enter in on the s·
7 of all you that go forth on the s·,
9 men that were to come in on the s·,
9 them that should go out on the s·,
16:18 covert for the s· that they had built
1Ch 9:32 shewbread, to prepare it every s·.
2Ch 23: 4 third part of you entering on the s·,
8 men that were to come in on the s·,
8 them that were to go out on the s·:
36:21 as she lay desolate she kept s·,
Ne 9:14 And madest known...thy holy s·,
10:31 ware or any victuals on the s· day
31 would not buy it of them on the s·,
13:15 treading wine presses on the s·,
15 brought into Jerusalem on the s·
16 sold on the s· unto the children of
17 that ye do, and profane the s· day?
18 more wrath...by profaning the s·.
19 began to be dark before the s·,
19 not be opened till after the s·:
19 burden be brought in on the s· day.
21 forth came they no more on the s·.
22 keep the gates, to sanctify the s· day.
Ps 92: title A Psalm or Song for the s· day.
Isa 56: 2, 6 keepeth the s· from polluting it,
Isa 58:13 thou turn away thy foot from the s·,
13 and call the s· a delight, the holy of
66:23 another, and from one s· to another,
Jer 17:21 and bear no burden on the s· day,
22 burden out of your houses on the s·
22 hallow...the s· day, as I commanded
24 the gates of this city on the s· day,
24 but hallow the s· day, to do no work
27 hearken unto me to hallow the s·
27 gates of Jerusalem on the s· day;
Eze 46: 1 but on the s· it shall be opened, and
4 shall offer unto the Lord in the s·
12 offerings, as he did on the s· day:
Am 8: 5 and the s·, that we may set forth
M't 12: 1 Jesus went on the s· day through
2 is not lawful to do upon the s· day:
5 how that on the s· days the priests
5 in the temple profane the s·, and are
8 of man is Lord even of the s· day.
10 Is it lawful to heal on the s· days?
11 and if it fall into a pit on the s· day,
12 is lawful to do well on the s· days.
24:20 in the winter, neither on the s· day:
28: 1 In the end of the s·, as it began to
M'r 1:21 s· day he entered,..the synagogue,
2:23 through the corn fields on the s·
24 on the s·...that which is not lawful?
27 The s· was made for man, and not
27 for man, and not man for the s·:
28 Son of man is Lord also of the s·.
3: 2 he would heal him on the s· day;
4 it lawful to do good on the s· days,
6: 2 And when the s· day was come,
15:42 that is, the day before the s·,
16: 1 And when the s· was past, Mary
Lu 4:16 into the synagogue on the s· day,
31 and taught them on the s· days.
6: 1 pass on the second s· after the first,
2 is not lawful to do on the s· days?
5 Son of man is Lord also of the s·.
6 it came to pass also on another s·,
7 whether he would heal on the s·
9 lawful on the s· days to do good, or
13:10 in one of the synagogues on the s·.
14 that Jesus had healed on the s· day,
14 and be healed, and not on the s· day.
15 one of you on the s· loose his ox or
16 loosed from this bond on the s· day?
14: 1 Pharisees to eat bread on the s· day,
3 Is it lawful to heal on the s· day?
5 straightway pull him out on the s·
23:54 the preparation, and the s· drew on.
56 and rested the s· day according to
Joh 5: 9 and on the same day was the s·.
10 It is the s· day: it is not lawful for
16 had done these things on the s· day.
18 he not only had broken the s·, but
7:22 ye on the s· day circumcise a man.
23 on the s· day receive circumcision,
23 man every whit whole on the s· day?
9:14 s· day when Jesus made the clay,
16 because he keepeth not the s· day.
19:31 remain upon the cross on the s· day,
31 (for that s· day was an high day,)
Ac 1:12 from Jerusalem a s· day's journey.
13:14 into the synagogue on the s· day,
27 prophets which are read every s·
42 be preached to them the next s·.
44 next s· day came almost the whole
15:21 read in the synagogues every s· day.
Ac 16:13 on the s· we went out of the city by
17: 2 three s· days reasoned with them
18: 4 reasoned in the synagogue every s·,
Col 2:16 of the new moon, or of the s· days:

sabbath-day See SABBATH and DAY.

sabbaths
Ex 31:13 Verily my s· ye shall keep: for it
Le 19: 3 and his father, and keep my s·:
30 Ye shall keep my s·, and reverence
23:15 offering; seven s· shall be complete:
38 Beside the s· of the Lord, and beside
25: 8 thou shalt number seven s· of years
8 the space of the seven s· of years
26: 2 Ye shall keep my s·, and reverence
34 Then shall the land enjoy her s·,
34 shall the land rest, and enjoy her s·.
35 because it did not rest in your s·,
43 left of them, and shall enjoy her s·,
1Ch 23:31 sacrifices unto the Lord in the s·,
2Ch 2: 4 on the s·, and on the new moons,
8:13 on the s·, and on the new moons,
31: 3 and the burnt offerings for the s·,
36:21 until the land had enjoyed her s·:
Ne 10:33 of the s·, of the new moons, for the
Isa 1:13 the new moons and s·, the calling
56: 4 unto the eunuchs that keep my s·,
La 1: 7 saw her, and did mock at her s·.
2: 6 feasts and s· to be forgotten in
Eze 20:12 Moreover also I gave them my s·,
13 and my s· they greatly polluted:
16 in my statutes, but polluted my s·:
20 And hallow my s·; and they shall be
21 they polluted my s·: then I said,
24 statutes, and had polluted my s·,
22: 8 things, and hast profaned my s·.
26 and have hid their eyes from my s·,
23:38 same day, and have profaned my s·.
44:24 and they shall hallow my s·.
45:17 and in the new moons, and in the s·,
46: 3 in the s· and in the new moons.
Ho 2:11 her new moons, and her s·, and all

Sabeans (*sab-e'-uns*)
Job 1:15 And the S· fell upon them, and
Isa 45:14 and of the S·, men of stature,
Eze 23:42 brought S· from the wilderness,
Joe 3: 8 and they shall sell them to the S·,

Sabta (*sab'-tah*) See also SABTAH.
1Ch 1: 9 Seba, and Havilah, and S·, and

Sabtah (*sab'-tah*) See also SABTA.
Ge 10: 7 Seba, and Havilah, and S·, and

Sabtecha (*sab'-te-kah*) See also SABTECHAH.
1Ch 1: 9 Sabta, and Raamah, and S·,

Sabtechah (*sab'-te-kah*) See also SABTECHA.
Ge 10: 7 Sabtah, and Raamah, and S·:

Sacar (*sa'-kar*) See also SHARAR.
1Ch 11:35 Ahiam the son of S· the Hararite,
26: 4 Joah the third, and S· the fourth,

sack See also SACKBUT; SACKCLOTH; SACK'S; SACKS.
Ge 42:25 every man's money into his s·,
27 as one of them opened his s· to give
28 restored; and, lo, it is even in my s·:
35 bundle of money was in his s·:
43:21 money was in the mouth of his s·,
44:11 down every man his s· to the ground,
11 and opened every man his s·.

Ge 44:12 the cup was found in Benjamin's s'.
Le 11:32 of wood, or raiment, or skin, or s',

sackbut
Da 3: 5, 7, 10, 15 of the cornet, flute, harp, s',

sackcloth See also SACKCLOTHES.
Ge 37:34 clothes, put s' upon his loins, and
2Sa 3:31 your clothes, and gird you with s',
21:10 Rizpah the daughter of Aiah took s',
1Ki 20:31 us, I pray thee, put s' on our loins,
32 So they girded s' on their loins,
21:27 clothes, and put s' upon his flesh,
27 and fasted, and lay in s', and went
2Ki 6:30 he had s' within upon his flesh.
19: 1 clothes, and covered himself with s',
2 elders of the priests, covered with s',
1Ch 21:16 of Israel, who were clothed in s',
Es 4: 1 clothes, and put on s' with ashes,
2 into the king's gate clothed with s'.
3 and many lay in s' and ashes.
4 and to take away his s' from him:
Job 16:15 I have sewed s' upon my skin, and
Ps 30:11 thou hast put off my s', and girded
35:13 they were sick, my clothing was s':
69:11 I made s' also my garment; and I
Isa 3:24 of a stomacher a girding of s';
15: 3 they shall gird themselves with s':
20: 2 and loose the s' from off thy loins,
22:12 to baldness, and to girding with s':
32:11 you bare, and gird s' upon your loins.
37: 1 and covered himself with s', and
2 elders of the priests covered with s',
50: 3 and I make s' their covering.
58: 5 to spread s' and ashes under him?
Jer 4: 8 gird you with s', lament and howl:
6:26 gird thee with s', and wallow thyself
48:37 be cuttings, and upon the loins s'.
49: 3 of Rabbah, gird you with s'; lament,
La 2:10 they have girded themselves with s':
Eze 7:18 shall also gird themselves with s',
27:31 bald for thee, and gird them with s',
Da 9: 3 with fasting, and s', and ashes:
Joe 1: 8 Lament like a virgin girded with s'
13 come, lie all night in s', ye ministers
Am 8:10 and I will bring up s' upon all loins,
Jon 3: 5 proclaimed a fast, and put on s',
6 and covered him with s', and sat in
8 man and beast be covered with s',
M't 11:21 repented long ago in s' and ashes.
Lu 10:13 repented, sitting in s' and ashes.
Re 6:12 the sun became black as s' of hair,
11: 3 and threescore days, clothed in s'.

sackclothes
Ne 9: 1 with fasting, and with s', and

sack's
Ge 42:27 for, behold, it was in his s' mouth.
44: 1 every man's money in his s' mouth.
2 cup, in the s' mouth of the youngest,

sacks See also SACKS'.
Ge 42:25 Joseph commanded to fill their s'
35 to pass as they emptied their s',
43:12 the money...in the mouth of your s',
18 money that was returned in our s'
21 that we opened our s', and, behold,
22 tell who put our money in our s'.
23 hath given you treasure in your s':
44: 1 saying, Fill the men's s' with food,
Jos 9: 4 and took old s' upon their asses,

sacks'
Ge 44: 8 which we found in our s' mouths,

sacrifice See also SACRIFICED; SACRIFICES; SACRIFICETH; SACRIFICING.
Ge 31:54 Jacob offered s' upon the mount,
Ex 3:18 we may s' to the Lord our God.
5: 3 and s' unto the Lord our God; lest
8 Let us go and s' to our God.
17 Let us go and do s' to the Lord.
8: 8 go, they may do s' unto the Lord.
25 Go ye, s' to your God in the land.
26 we shall s' the abomination of the
26 shall we s' the abomination of the
27 and s' to the Lord our God, as he
28 ye may s' to the Lord your God in
29 the people go to s' to the Lord.
10:25 we may s' unto the Lord our God.
12:27 It is the s' of the Lord's passover,
13:15 I s' to the Lord all that openeth
20:24 s' thereon thy burnt offerings,
23:18 not offer the blood of my s' with
18 shall the fat of my s' remain
29:28 of the s' of their peace offerings,
30: 9 incense thereon, nor burnt s', nor
34:15 and do s' unto their gods, and
15 call thee, and thou eat of his s';
25 the blood of my s' with leaven;
25 the s' of the feast of the passover be
Le 1: 3 offering be a burnt s', of the herd,
9 to be a burnt s', an offering made
10 or of the goats, for a burnt s'; he
13 it is a burnt s', an offering made
14 if the burnt s' for his offering to
17 it is a burnt s', an offering made by
3: 1 oblation be a s' of peace offering,
3 offer of the s' of the peace offering
5 it on the altar upon the burnt s',
6 offering for a s' of peace offering
9 offer of the s' of the peace offering
4:10 bullock of the s' of peace offerings:
26 the fat of the s' of peace offerings:
31 from off the s' of peace offerings;
35 from the s' of the peace offerings;
7:11 law of the s' of peace offerings,
12 offer with the s' of thanksgiving
13 bread with the s' of thanksgiving
Le 7: 15 the flesh of the s' of his peace
16 if the s' of his offering be a vow,
16 same day that he offereth his s':
17 the remainder of the flesh of the s'
18 flesh of the s' of his peace offerings
20, 21 flesh of the s' of peace offerings,
29 offereth the s' of his peace offerings
29 of the s' of his peace offerings.
37 of the s' of the peace offerings;
8:21 a burnt s' for a sweet savour,
9: 4 offerings, to s' before the Lord;
17 beside the burnt s' of the morning.
18 the ram for a s' of peace offerings,
17: 8 offereth a burnt offering or s',
19: 5 if ye offer a s' of peace offerings
22:21 offereth a s' of peace offerings unto
29 ye will offer a s' of thanksgiving
23:19 ye shall s' one kid of the goats
19 year for a s' of peace offerings.
37 a meat offering, a s', and drink
27:11 they do not offer a s' unto the Lord,
Nu 6:17 the ram for a s' of peace offerings
18 it in the fire which is under the s'
7:17, 23, 29, 35, 41, 47, 53, 59, 65, 71, 77,
83 for a s' of peace offerings, two
88 all the oxen for the s' of the peace
15: 3 or a s' in performing a vow, or in
5 with the burnt offering or s', for
8 or for a s' in performing a vow, or
25 s' made by fire unto the Lord, and
23: 6 he stood by his burnt s', he, and
28: 6 a s' made by fire unto the Lord.
8 thou shalt offer it, a s' made by fire,
13 a s' made by fire unto the Lord.
19 ye shall offer a s' made by fire for a
24 the meat of the s' made by fire, of
29: 6 a s' made by fire unto the Lord.
13, 36 a s' made by fire, of a sweet
De 15:21 shalt not s' it unto the Lord thy
16: 2 shalt therefore s' the passover
5 Thou mayest not s' the passover
6 thou shalt s' the passover at even,
17: 1 shalt not s' unto the Lord thy God
18: 3 people, from them that offer a s',
33:10 whole burnt s' upon thine altar.
Jos 22:26 not for burnt offering, nor for s':
J'g 6:26 offer a burnt s' with the wood of
16:23 a great s' unto Dagon their god,
1Sa 1: 3 to s' unto the Lord of hosts in
21 offer unto the Lord the yearly s',
2:13 that, when any man offered s', the
19 her husband to offer the yearly s'.
29 Wherefore kick ye at my s' and at
3:14 shall not be purged with s' nor
9:12 s' of the people to day in the high
13 come, because he doth bless the s';
10: 8 to s' sacrifices of peace offerings:
15:15 oxen, to s' unto the Lord thy God;
21 s' unto the Lord thy God in Gilgal.
22 to obey is better than s', and to
16: 2 say, I am come to s' to the Lord.
3 call Jesse to the s', and I will
5 I am come to s' unto the Lord:
5 and come with me to the s'.
5 sons, and called them to the s'.
20: 6 there is a yearly s' there for all the
29 our family hath a s' in the city;
2Sa 24:22 here be oxen for burnt s', and
1Ki 3: 4 king went to Gibeon to s' there;
8:62 him, offered s' before the Lord.
63 And Solomon offered a s' of peace
12:27 this people go up to do s' in the
18:29 the offering of the evening s',
33 and pour it on the burnt s', and
36 of the offering of the evening s',
38 fell, and consumed the burnt s',
2Ki 5:17 neither burnt offering nor s' unto
10:19 I have a great s' to do to Baal;
14: 4 as yet the people did s' and burnt
16:15 offering, and the king's burnt s',
15 and all the blood of the s':
17:35 nor serve them, nor s' to them:
36 worship, and to him shall ye do s'.
2Ch 2: 6 save only to burn s' before him?
7: 5 And king Solomon offered a s' of
12 place to myself for an house of s'.
11:16 to s' unto the Lord God of their
28:23 will I s' to them, that they may
33:17 people did s'...in the high places,
Ezr 4: 2 we do s' unto him since the days of
9: 4 I sat astonied until...evening s'.
5 at the evening s' I arose up from
Ne 4: 2 will they s'? will they make an
Ps 20: 3 offerings, and accept thy burnt s';
40: 6 S' and offering thou didst not
50: 5 made a covenant with me by s'.
51:16 For thou desirest not s'; else
54: 6 I will freely s' unto thee: I will
107:22 And let them s' the sacrifices of
116:17 offer to thee...s' of thanksgiving,
118:27 bind the s' with cords, even unto
141: 2 up of my hands as the evening s'.
Pr 15: 8 s' of the wicked is an abomination
21: 3 acceptable to the Lord than s'.
27 s' of the wicked is abomination:
Ec 5: 1 hear, than to give the s' of fools:
Isa 19:21 day, and shall do s' and oblation;
34: 6 the Lord hath a s' in Bozrah, and
57: 7 thither wentest thou up to offer s'.
Jer 33:11 that shall bring the s' of praise
18 offerings, and to do s' continually.
46:10 the Lord God of hosts hath a s' in
Eze 39:17 yourselves on every side to my s'
17 that I do s' for you, even a great
17 s' upon the mountains of Israel,
19 s' which I have sacrificed for you.
Eze 40:42 slew the burnt offering and the s'.
44:11 offering and the s' for the people,
46:24 house shall boil the s' of the people.
Da 8:11 by him the daily s' was taken away,
12 daily s' by reason of transgression,
13 the vision concerning the daily s',
9:27 s' and the oblation to cease,
11:31 and shall take away the daily s',
12:11 the daily s' shall be taken away,
Ho 3: 4 and without a s', and without an
4:13 s' upon the tops of the mountains,
14 whores, and they s' with harlots:
6: 6 For I desired mercy, and not s';
8:13 They s' flesh for the sacrifices of
12:11 vanity: they s' bullocks in Gilgal;
13: 2 the men that s' kiss the calves.
Am 4: 5 a s' of thanksgiving with leaven,
Jon 1:16 and offered a s' unto the Lord,
2: 9 will s' unto thee with the voice of
Hab 1:16 Therefore they s' unto their net,
Zep 1: 7 for the Lord hath prepared a s',
8 pass in the day of the Lord's s',
Zec 14:21 they that s' shall come and take
Mal 1: 8 And if ye offer the blind for s', is it
M't 9:13 I will have mercy, and not s': for
12: 7 I will have mercy, and not s', ye
M'r 9:49 every s' shall be salted with salt.
Lu 2:24 And to offer a s' according to that
Ac 7:41 and offered s' unto the idol, and
14:13 and would have done s' with the
18 they had not done s' unto them.
Ro 12: 1 ye present your bodies a living s',
1Co 8: 4 that are offered in s' unto idols,
10:19 is offered in s' to idols is any thing?
20 the things which the Gentiles s',
20 they s' to devils, and not to God:
28 This is offered in s' unto idols, eat
Eph 5: 2 for us an offering and a s' to God
Ph'p 2:17 the s' and service of your faith,
4:18 s' acceptable, wellpleasing to God.
Heb 7:27 to offer up s', first for his own sins,
9:26 to put away sin by the s' of himself.
10: 5 S' and offering thou wouldest not,
8 S' and offering and burnt offerings
12 after he had offered one s' for sins
26 remaineth no more s' for sins,
11: 4 God a more excellent s' than Cain,
13:15 let us offer the s' of praise to God

sacrificed See also SACRIFICEDST.
Ex 24: 5 s' peace offerings of oxen unto the
32: 8 it, and have s' thereunto, and said,
De 32:17 They s' unto devils, not to God; to
Jos 8:31 the Lord, and s' peace offerings.
J'g 2: 5 and they s' there unto the Lord.
1Sa 2:15 said to the man that s', Give flesh
6:15 s' sacrifices the same day unto the
11:15 and there they s' sacrifices of peace
2Sa 6:13 six paces, he s' oxen and fatlings.
1Ki 3: 2 Only the people s' in high places,
3 only he s' and burnt incense in high
11: 8 incense and s' unto their gods.
2Ki 12: 3 the people still s' and burnt incense
15: 4 the people s' and burnt incense still
35 the people s' and burned incense
16: 4 he s' and burnt incense in the high
17:32 which s' for them in the houses of
1Ch 21:28 the Jebusite, then he s' there.
29:21 they s' sacrifices unto the Lord, and
2Ch 5: 6 s' sheep and oxen, which could not
28: 4 He s' also and burnt incense in the
23 he s' unto the gods of Damascus,
33:16 and s' thereon peace offerings and
22 Amon s' unto all the carved images
34: 4 graves of them that...s' unto them.
Ps 106:37 s' their sons and their daughters
38 they s' unto the idols of Canaan:
Eze 16:20 thou s' unto them to be devoured.
39:19 sacrifice which I have s' for you.
Ho 11: 2 they s' unto Baalim, and burned
1Co 5: 7 Christ our passover is s' for us:
Re 2:14 to eat things s' unto idols, and to
20 and to eat things s' unto idols.

sacrificedst
De 16: 4 which thou s' the first day at even,

sacrifices
Ge 46: 1 and offered s' unto the God of his
Ex 10:25 give us also s' and burnt offerings,
18:12 a burnt offering and s' for God:
Le 7:32 of the s' of your peace offerings.
34 off the s' of their peace offerings,
10:13 of the s' of the Lord made by fire:
14 out of the s' of peace offerings of
17: 5 children of Israel may bring their s',
7 no more offer their s' unto devils,
Nu 10:10 over the s' of your peace offerings;
25: 2 the people unto the s' of their gods:
28: 2 my bread for my s' made by fire,
De 12: 6 and your s', and your tithes, and
11 your burnt offerings, and your s',
27 the blood of thy s' shall be poured
32:38 Which did eat the fat of their s', and
33:19 they shall offer s' of righteousness:
Jos 13:14 s' of the Lord...of Israel made by fire
22:27 with our s', and with our peace
28 not for burnt offerings, nor for s';
29 for meat offerings, or for s', beside
1Sa 6:15 sacrificed s' the same day unto the
10: 8 to sacrifice s' of peace offerings:
11:15 they sacrificed s' of peace offerings
15:22 delight in burnt offerings and s', as
2Sa 15:12 even from Giloh, while he offered s'.
2Ki 10:24 they went in to offer s' and burnt
1Ch 16: 1 they offered burnt s' and peace
23:31 to offer all burnt s' unto the Lord
29:21 they sacrificed s' unto the Lord,

1Ch 29:21 and s' in abundance for all Israel:
2Ch 7: 1 the burnt offerings and the s'; and
4 people offered s' before the Lord.
13:11 every evening burnt s' and sweet
29:31 bring s' and thank offerings into
31 the congregation brought in s' and
Ezr 6: 3 the place where they offered s',
10 they may offer s' of sweet savours
Ne 12:43 that day they offered great s',
Ps 4: 5 Offer the s' of righteousness, and
27: 6 I offer in his tabernacle s' of joy;
50: 8 I will not reprove thee for thy s' or
51:17 The s' of God are a broken spirit:
19 with the s' of righteousness, with
66:15 unto thee burnt s' of fatlings, with
106:28 and ate the s' of the dead.
107:22 sacrifice the s' of thanksgiving, and
Pr 17: 1 than an house full of s' with strife.
Isa 1:11 the multitude of your s' unto me?
29: 1 ye year to year; let them kill s'.
43:23 hast thou honoured me with thy s'.
24 thou filled me with the fat of thy s':
56: 7 s' shall be accepted upon mine
Jer 6:20 nor your s' sweet unto me.
7:21 your burnt offerings unto your s',
22 concerning burnt offerings or s':
17:26 bringing burnt offerings, and s', and
26 incense, and bringing s' of praise,
Eze 20:28 and they offered there their s',
40:41 tables, whereupon they slew their s'.
Ho 4:19 be ashamed because of their s'.
8:13 flesh for the s' of mine offerings,
9: 4 their s' shall be unto them as the
Am 4: 4 and bring your s' every morning,
5:25 ye offered unto me s' and offerings
M'r 12:33 all whole burnt offerings and s'.
Lu 13: 1 Pilate had mingled with their s'.
Ac 7:42 offered to me slain beasts and s'
1Co 10:18 which eat of the s' partakers of the
Heb 5: 1 may offer both gifts and s' for sins:
8: 3 is ordained to offer gifts and s':
9: 9 were offered both gifts and s', that
23 with better s' than these.
10: 1 can never with those s' which they
3 in those s' there is a remembrance
6 In burnt offerings and s' for sin thou
11 offering oftentimes the same s',
13:16 with such s' God is well pleased.
1Pe 2: 5 to offer up spiritual s', acceptable

sacrificeth
Ex 22:20 He that s' unto any god, save unto
Ec 9: 2 him that s', and to him that s' not:
Isa 65: 3 s' in gardens, and burneth incense
66: 3 he that s' a lamb, as if he cut off a
Mal 1:14 s' unto the Lord a corrupt thing:

sacrificing
1Ki 8: 5 s' sheep and oxen, that could not
12:32 s' unto the calves that he had made:

sacrilege
Ro 2:22 idols, dost thou commit s'?

sad
Ge 40: 6 them, and, behold, they were s'.
1Sa 1:18 and her countenance was no more s'.
1Ki 21: 5 Why is thy spirit so s', that thou
Ne 2: 1 been beforetime s' in his presence.
2 Why is thy countenance s', seeing
3 should not my countenance be s',
Eze 13:22 made the heart of the righteous s',
22 whom I have made s'; and
M't 6:16 hypocrites, of a s' countenance:
M'r 10:22 he was s' at that saying, and went
Lu 24:17 to another, as ye walk, and are s'?

saddle See also SADDLED.
Le 15: 9 what s' soever he rideth upon that
2Sa 19:26 I will s' me an ass, that I may ride
1Ki 13:13 said unto his sons, S' me the ass.
27 to his sons, saying, S' me the ass.

saddled
Ge 22: 3 in the morning, and s' his ass,
Nu 22:21 in the morning, and s' his ass,
J'g 19:10 there were with him two asses s',
2Sa 16: 1 met him, with a couple of asses s',
17:23 he s' his ass, and arose, and gat him
1Ki 2:40 And Shimei arose, and s' his ass,
13:13 So they s' him the ass: and he rode
23 that he s' for him the ass, to wit,
27 Saddle me the ass. And they s' him.
2Ki 4:24 Then she s' an ass, and said to her

Sadducees (*sad'-du-sees*)
M't 3: 7 saw many of the Pharisees and S'
16: 1 Pharisees also with the S' came,
6 leaven of the Pharisees and...S'.
11 leaven of the Pharisees and...S'?
12 doctrine of the Pharisees and...S'.
22:23 The same day came to him the S',
34 that he had put the S' to silence,
M'r 12:18 Then come unto him the S', which
Lu 20:27 Then came to him certain of the S',
Ac 4: 1 captain of the temple, and the S',
5:17 (which is the sect of the S',) and
23: 6 perceived that the one part were S',
7 between the Pharisees and the S':
8 S' say that there is no resurrection,

sadly
Ge 40: 7 Wherefore look ye so s' to day?

sadness
Ec 7: 3 by the s' of the countenance the

Sadoc (*sa'-dok*)
M't 1:14 begat S'; and S' begat Achim;

safe See also SAFEGUARD.
1Sa 12:11 on every side, and ye dwelled s'.
2Sa 18:29, 32 Is the young man Absalom s'?
Job 21: 9 Their houses are s' from fear,
Ps 119:117 Hold...me up, and I shall be s':
Pr 18:10 runneth into it, and is safe.
29:25 his trust in the Lord shall be s'.
Isa 5:29 prey, and shall carry it away s',
Eze 34:27 and they shall be s' in their land,
Lu 15:27 he hath received him s' and sound.
Ac 23:24 and bring him s' unto Felix the
27:44 pass, that they escaped all s' to land.
Ph'p 3: 1 is not grievous, but for you it is s'.

safeguard
1Sa 22:23 but with me thou shalt be in s'.

safely
Le 26: 5 the full, and dwell in your land s'.
1Ki 4:25 And Judah and Israel dwelt s', every
Ps 78:53 he led them on s' so that they feared
Pr 1:33 hearkeneth unto me shall dwell s',
3:23 Then shalt thou walk in thy way s',
31:11 of her husband doth s' trust in her,
Isa 41: 3 He pursued them, and passed s';
Jer 23: 6 be saved, and Israel shall dwell s':
32:37 and I will cause them to dwell s':
33:16 saved, and Jerusalem shall dwell s':
Eze 28:26 And they shall dwell s' therein, and
34:25 they shall dwell s' in the wilderness,
28 they shall dwell s', and none shall
38: 8 and they shall dwell s' all of them.
11 them that are at rest, that dwell s',
14 my people of Israel dwelleth s',
39:26 when they dwelt s' in their land,
Ho 2:18 and will make them to lie down s'.
Zec 14:11 but Jerusalem shall be s' inhabited.
M'r 14:44 take him, and lead him away s':
Ac 16:23 charging the jailor to keep them s':

safety
Le 25:18 and ye shall dwell in the land in s'.
19 eat your fill, and dwell therein in s'.
De 12:10 round about, so that ye dwell in s';
33:12 beloved of the Lord shall dwell in s'
28 Israel then shall dwell in s' alone:
Job 3:26 I was not in s', neither had I rest,
5: 4 His children are far from s', and
11 which mourn may be exalted to s'.
11:18 and thou shalt take thy rest in s'.
24:23 Though it be given him to be in s',
Ps 4: 8 Lord, only makest me dwell in s'.
12: 5 set him in s' from him that puffeth
33:17 An horse is a vain thing for s':
Pr 11:14 multitude of counsellers there is s'.
21:31 day of battle: but s' is of the Lord.
24: 6 multitude of counsellers there is s'.
Isa 14:30 and the needy shall lie down in s':
Ac 5:23 prison...found we shut with all s',
1Th 5: 3 when they shall say, Peace and s';

saffron
Ca 4:14 Spikenard and s'; calamus and

said^ See also SAIDST.
Ge 1: 3 And God s', Let there be light: and
6 God s', Let there be a firmament in
9 God s', Let the waters under the
11 God s', Let the earth bring forth
14 God s', Let there be lights in the
20 God s', Let the waters bring forth
24 God s', Let the earth bring forth
26 And God s', Let us make man in our
28 God s' unto them, Be fruitful, and
29 God s', Behold, I have given you
2:18 God s', It is not good that the man
23 Adam s', This is now bone of my
3: 1 And he s' unto the woman, Yea,
1 hath God s', Ye shall not eat of every
2 And the woman s' unto the serpent,
3 God hath s', Ye shall not eat of it,
4 And the serpent s' unto the woman,
9 and s' unto him, Where art thou?
10 And he s', I heard thy voice in the
11 And he s', Who told thee that thou
12 And the man s', The woman whom
13 the Lord God s' unto the woman,
13 the woman s', The serpent beguiled
14 the Lord God s' unto the serpent,
16 Unto the woman he s', I will greatly
17 And unto Adam he s', Because thou
22 the Lord God s', Behold, the man
4: 1 and s', I have gotten a man from the
6 And the Lord s' unto Cain, Why art
9 And the Lord s' unto Cain, Where is
9 thy brother? And he s', I know not:
10 And he s', What hast thou done?
13 Cain s'...My punishment is greater
15 And the Lord s' unto him, Therefore
23 And Lamech s' unto his wives, Adah
25 For God, s' she, hath appointed me
6: 3 And the Lord s', My spirit shall not
7 And the Lord s', I will destroy man
13 And God s' unto Noah, The end of all
7: 1 the Lord s' unto Noah, Come thou
8:21 Lord s' in his heart, I will not again
9: 1 and s' unto them, Be fruitful, and
12 And God s', This is the token of the
17 God s' unto Noah, This is the token
25 he s', Cursed be Canaan; a servant
26 he s', Blessed be the...God of Shem,
10: 9 it is s', Even as Nimrod the mighty
11: 3 they s' one to another, Go to, let us
4 they s', Go to, let us build us a city,
6 Lord s', Behold, the people is one,
12: 1 Lord had s' unto Abram, Get thee
7 and s', Unto thy seed will I give this
11 that he s' unto Sarai his wife, Behold
18 Pharaoh called Abram, and s', What
13: 8 Abram s' unto Lot, Let there be no
14 Lord s' unto Abram, after that Lot
Ge 14:19 and s', Blessed be Abram of the
21 the king of Sodom s' unto Abram,
22 And Abram s' to the king of Sodom,
15: 2 Abram s', Lord God, What wilt thou
3 Abram s', Behold, to me thou hast
5 and s', Look now toward heaven, and
5 he s' unto him, So shall thy seed be.
7 he s' unto him, I am the Lord that
8 he s', Lord God, Whereby shall I
9 he s' unto him, Take me an heifer
13 he s' unto Abram, Know of a surety
16: 2 Sarai s' unto Abram, Behold now,
5 Sarai s' unto Abram, My wrong be
6 Abram s' unto Sarai, Behold, thy
8 he s', Hagar, Sarai's maid, whence
8 And she s', I flee from the face of my
9, 10, 11 angel of the Lord s' unto her,
13 for she s', Have I also here looked
17: 1 s' unto him, I am the Almighty God;
9 God s' unto Abraham, Thou shalt
15 God s' unto Abraham, As for Sarai
17 laughed, and s' in his heart, Shall a
18 And Abraham s' unto God, O that
19 And God s', Sarah thy wife shall bear
23 day, as God had s' unto him.
18: 3 And s', My Lord, if now I have found
5 And they s', So do, as thou hast s'.
6 into the tent unto Sarah, and s',
9 they s' unto him, Where is Sarah
9 And he s', Behold, in the tent.
10 And he s', I will certainly return
13 And the Lord s' unto Abraham,
15 he s', Nay; but thou didst laugh.
17 And the Lord s', Shall I hide from
20 And the Lord s', Because the cry of
23 Abraham drew near, and s', Wilt
26 the Lord s', If I find in Sodom fifty
27 Abraham answered and s', Behold
28 And he s', If I find there forty and
29 and s', Peradventure there shall be
29 And he s', I will not do it for forty's
30 he s' unto him, Oh let not the Lord
30 And he s', I will not do it, if I find
31 And he s', Behold now, I have taken
31 And he s', I wi l not destroy it for
32 he s', Oh let not the Lord be angry,
32 And he s', I will not destroy it for
19: 2 he s', Behold now, my lords, turn in,
2 they s', Nay; but we will abide in
5 called unto Lot, and s' unto him,
7 And s', I pray you, brethren, do not
9 s', Stand back. And they s' again,
12 And the men s' unto Lot, Hast thou
14 and s', Up, get you out of this place;
17 he s', Escape for thy life; look not
18 And Lot s' unto them, Oh, not so,
21 And he s' unto him, See, I have
31, 34 the firstborn s' unto the younger,
20: 2 Abraham s' of Sarah his wife, She is
3 a dream by night, and s' to him,
4 and he s', Lord, wilt thou slay also a
5 S' he not unto me, She is my sister?
5 even she herself s', He is my brother:
6 God s' unto him in a dream, Yea,
9 s' unto him, What hast thou done
10 Abimelech s' unto Abraham, What
11 And Abraham s', Because I thought,
13 I s' unto her, This is thy kindness
15 Abimelech s', Behold, my land is
16 And unto Sarah he s', Behold, I have
21: 1 the Lord visited Sarah as he had s',
6 And Sarah s', God hath made me to
7 she s', [559] Who would have s' unto
10 Wherefore she s' unto Abraham,
12 God s' unto Abraham, Let it not be
12 in all that Sarah hath s' unto thee,
16 for she s', Let me not see the death
17 and s' unto her, What aileth thee,
24 And Abraham s', I will swear.
26 Abimelech s', I wot not who hath
29 Abimelech s' unto Abraham, What
30 he s', For these seven ewe lambs
22: 1 tempt Abraham, and s' unto him,
1 and he s', Behold, here I am.
2 he s', Take now thy son, thine only
7 unto Abraham his father, and s', My
7 and he s', Here am I, my son,
7 he s', Behold the fire and the wood:
8 And Abraham s', My son, God will
11 s', Abraham,...and he s', Here am I.
12 he s', Lay not thine hand upon the
14 as it is s' to this day, In the mount
16 And s', By myself have I sworn,
24: 2 Abraham s' unto his eldest servant
5 servant s' unto him, Peradventure
6 Abraham s' unto him, Beware thou
12 And he s', O Lord God of my master
17 the servant ran to meet her, and s',
18 And she s', Drink, my lord: and she
19 she s', I will draw water for thy
23 And s', Whose daughter art thou?
24 she s' unto him, I am the daughter
25 She s' moreover unto him, We have
27 he s', Blessed be the Lord God of
31 he s', Come in, thou blessed of the
33 he s', I will not eat, until I have told
33 mine errand, And he s', Speak on.
34 And he s', I am Abraham's servant.
39 I s' unto my master, Peradventure
40 And he s' unto me, The Lord, before
42 and s', O Lord God of my master
45 and I s' unto her, Let me drink, I
46 and s', Drink, and I will give thy
47 and s', Whose daughter art thou?
47 she s', The daughter of Bethuel,
50 Laban and Bethuel answered and s',

Ge 24:54 and he s', Send me away unto my
55 her brother and her mother s', Let
56 he s' unto them, Hinder me not,
57 And they s', We will call the damsel,
58 s' unto her, Wilt thou go with this
58 And she s', I will go.
60 blessed Rebekah, and s' unto her,
65 she had s' unto the servant, What
65 the servant had s', It is my master:
25:22 she s', If it be so, why am I thus?
23 the Lord s' unto her, Two nations
30 Esau s' to Jacob, Feed me, I pray
31 And Jacob s', Sell me this day thy
32 Esau s', Behold, I am at the point
33 And Jacob s', Swear to me this day;
26: 2 Lord appeared unto him, and s', Go,
7 he s', She is my sister: for he feared
7 s' he, the men of the place should
9 And Abimelech called Isaac, and s',
9 And Isaac s' unto him, Because I s',
10 And Abimelech s', What is this thou
16 Abimelech s' unto Isaac, Go from
22 he s', For now the Lord hath made
24 and s', I am the God of Abraham
27 And Isaac s' unto them, Wherefore
28 And they s', We saw certainly that
28 and we s', Let there be now an oath
32 s' unto him, We have found water.
27: 1 eldest son, and s' unto him, My son:
1 he s' unto him, Behold, here am I
2 he s', Behold now, I am old, I know
11 And Jacob s' to Rebekah his mother,
13 his mother s' unto him, Upon me be
18 unto his father, and s', My father:
18 and he s', Here am I; who art thou,
19 And Jacob s' unto his father, I am
20 And Isaac s' unto his son, How is it
20 And he s', Because the Lord thy God
21 And Isaac s' unto Jacob, Come near,
22 s', The voice is Jacob's voice, but
24 he s', Art thou my very son Esau?
24 my very son Esau? And he s', I am.
25 he s', Bring it near to me, and I will
26 his father Isaac s' unto him, Come
27 s', See, the smell of my son is as the
31 and s' unto his father, Let my father
32 Isaac his father s' unto him, Who
32 he s', I am thy son, thy firstborn
33 trembled very exceedingly, and s',
34 s' unto his father, Bless me, even
35 And he s', Thy brother came with
36 And he s', Is not he rightly named
36 And he s', Hast thou not reserved a
37 Isaac answered and s' unto Esau,
38 Esau s' unto his father, Hast thou
39 Isaac his father answered and s'
41 Esau s' in his heart, The days of
42 and s' unto him, Behold, thy brother
46 Rebekah s' to Isaac, I am weary of
28: 1 s' unto him, Thou shalt not take a
13 s', I am the Lord God of Abraham
16 and he s', Surely the Lord is in this
17 and s', How dreadful is this place!
29: 4 Jacob s' unto them, My brethren,
4 And they s', Of Haran are we.
5 he s' unto them, Know ye Laban the
5 And they s', We know him.
6 And he s' unto them, Is he well?
6 And they s', He is well: and, behold,
7 he s', Lo, it is yet high day, neither
8 And they s', We cannot, until all the
14 Laban s' to him, Surely thou art my
15 Laban s' unto Jacob, Because thou
18 and s', I will serve thee seven years
19 Laban s', It is better that I give her
21 Jacob s' unto Laban, Give me my
25 he s' to Laban, What is this thou
26 Laban s', It must not be so done in
32 she s', Surely the Lord hath looked
33 and s', Because the Lord hath heard
34 s', Now this time will my husband
35 she s', Now will I praise the Lord:
30: 1 s' unto Jacob, Give me children, or
2 and he s', Am I in God's stead, who
3 she s', Behold my maid Bilhah, go
6 Rachel s', God hath judged me, and
8 Rachel s', With great wrestlings
11 Leah s', A troop cometh: and she
13 And Leah s', Happy am I, for the
14 Rachel s' to Leah, Give me, I pray
15 she s' unto her, Is it a small matter
15 And Rachel s', Therefore he shall lie
16 and s', Thou must come in unto me;
18 And Leah s', God hath given me my
20 Leah s', God hath endued me with a
23 and s', God hath taken away my
24 and s', The Lord shall add to me
25 that Jacob s' unto Laban, Send me
27 And Laban s' unto him, I pray thee,
28 And he s', Appoint me thy wages,
29 he s' unto him, Thou knowest how I
31 And he s', What shall I give thee?
31 Jacob s', Thou shalt not give me
34 Laban s', Behold, I would it might
31: 3 the Lord s' unto Jacob, Return unto
5 s' unto them, I see your father's
8 If he s' thus, The speckled shall be
8 if he s' thus, The ringstraked shall
11 saying, Jacob: And I s', Here am I.
12 And he s', Lift up now thine eyes,
14 s' unto him, Is there yet any portion
16 whatsoever God hath s' unto thee,
24 s' unto him, Take heed that thou
26 Laban s' to Jacob, What hast thou
31 Jacob answered and s' to Laban,
31 for I s', Peradventure thou wouldest

Ge 31:35 And she s' to her father, Let it not
36 and Jacob answered and s' to Laban,
43 Laban answered and s' unto Jacob,
46 Jacob s' unto his brethren, Gather
48 And Laban s', This heap is a witness
49 he s', The Lord watch between me
51 Laban s' to Jacob, Behold this heap,
32: 2 Jacob saw them, he s', This is God's
8 s', If Esau come to the one company,
9 And Jacob s', O God of my father
16 s' unto his servants, Pass over
20 he s', I will appease him with the
26 And he s', Let me go, for the day
26 he s', I will not let thee go, except
27 he s' unto him, What is thy name?
27 is thy name? And he s', Jacob.
28 he s', Thy name shall be called no
29 s', Tell me, I pray thee, thy name.
29 he s', Wherefore is it that thou dost
33: 5 and s', Who are those with thee?
5 he s', The children which God hath
8 he s', What meanest thou by all this
8 he s', These are to find grace in the
9 Esau s', I have enough, my brother;
10 And Jacob s', Nay, I pray thee, if now
12 And he s', Let us take our journey,
13 And he s' unto him, My lord knoweth
15 Esau s', Let me now leave with thee
15 And he s', What needeth it? let me
34:11 Shechem s' unto her father and unto
13 s', because he had defiled Dinah
14 And they s' unto them, We cannot
30 And Jacob s' to Simeon and Levi,
31 And they s', Should he deal with our
35: 1 And God s' unto Jacob, Arise, go up
2 Then Jacob s' unto his household,
10 God s' unto him, Thy name is Jacob:
11 And God s' unto him, I am God
17 the midwife s' unto her, Fear not;
37: 6 And he s' unto them, Hear, I pray
8 his brethren s' to him, Shalt thou
9 s', Behold, I have dreamed a dream
10 his father rebuked him, and s'
13 And Israel s' unto Joseph, Do not
13 them. And he s' to him, Here am I.
14 And he s' to him, Go, I pray thee,
16 he s', I seek my brethren: tell me, I
17 And the man s', They are departed
19 And they s' one to another, Behold,
21 hands; and s', Let us not kill him.
22 And Reuben s' unto them, Shed no
26 Judah s' unto his brethren, What
30 brethren, and s', The child is not;
32 father; and s', This have we found:
33 And he knew it, and s', It is my son's
35 and he s', For I will go down into the
38: 8 And Judah s' unto Onan, Go in unto
11 s' Judah to Tamar his daughter in
11 for he s', Lest peradventure he die
16 s', Go to, I pray thee, let me come in
16 And she s', What wilt thou give me,
17 he s', I will send thee a kid from the
17 she s', Wilt thou give me a pledge,
18 he s', What pledge shall I give thee?
18 And she s', Thy signet, and thy
21 And they s', There was no harlot
22 to Judah, and s', I cannot find her;
22 men of the place s', that there was
23 Judah s', Let her take it to her, lest
24 And Judah s', Bring her forth, and
25 she s', Discern, I pray thee, whose
26 Judah acknowledged them, and s',
29 and she s', How hast thou broken
39: 7 Joseph; and she s', Lie with me.
8 refused, and s' unto his master's wife,
40: 8 they s' unto him, We have dreamed
8 And Joseph s' unto them, Do not
9 and s' to him, In my dream, behold,
12 And Joseph s' unto him, This is the
16 he s' unto Joseph, I also was in my
18 Joseph answered and s', This is the
41:15 And Pharaoh s' unto Joseph, I have
17 Pharaoh s' unto Joseph, In my
25 Joseph s' unto Pharaoh, The dream
38 Pharaoh s' unto his servants, Can we
39 Pharaoh s' unto Joseph, Forasmuch
41 Pharaoh s' unto Joseph, See, I have
44 And Pharaoh s' unto Joseph, I am
51 God, s' he, hath made me forget all
54 come, according as Joseph had s':
55 Pharaoh s' unto all the Egyptians,
42: 1 Jacob s' unto his sons, Why do ye
2 And he s', Behold, I have heard that
4 for he s', Lest peradventure mischief
7 he s' unto them, Whence come ye?
7 they s', From the land of Canaan to
9 s' unto them, Ye are spies; to see
10 they s' unto him, Nay, my lord, but
12 he s' unto them, Nay, but to see the
13 And they s', Thy servants are twelve
14 Joseph s' unto them, That is it that
18 Joseph s' unto them the third day,
21 they s' one to another, We are verily,
28 he s' unto his brethren, My money is
31 we s' unto him, We are true men;
33 s' unto us, Hereby shall I know that
36 Jacob their father s' unto them, Me
38 he s', My son shall not go down with
43: 2 father s' unto them, Go again, buy
5 man s' unto us, Ye shall not see my
6 Israel s', Wherefore dealt ye so ill
7 they s', The man asked us straitly of
8 And Judah s' unto Israel his father,
11 father Israel s' unto them, If it must
16 he s' to the ruler of his house, Bring
18 they s', Because of the money that

Ge 43:20 And s', O sir, we came indeed down
23 And he s', Peace be to you, fear not:
27 welfare, and s', Is your father well,
29 and s', Is this your younger brother,
29 he s', God be gracious unto thee, my
31 and refrained himself, and s', Set on
44: 4 far off, Joseph s' unto his steward,
7 they s' unto him, Wherefore saith
10 he s', Now also let it be according
15 Joseph s' unto them, What deed is
16 Judah s', What shall we say unto my
17 he s', God forbid that I should do so:
18 and s', Oh my lord, let thy servant,
20 And we s' unto my lord, We have a
22 we s' unto my lord, The lad cannot
25 our father s', Go again, and buy us a
26 And we s', We cannot go down: if
27 my father s' unto us, Ye know that
28 and I s', Surely he is torn in pieces;
45: 3 Joseph s' unto his brethren, I am
4 Joseph s' unto his brethren, Come
4 And he s', I am Joseph your brother,
17 Pharaoh s' unto Joseph, Say unto
24 he s' unto them, See that ye fall not
27 words of Joseph, which he had s':
28 Israel s', It is enough; Joseph my
46: 2 s', Jacob, Jacob. And he s', Here am
3 And he s', I am God, the God of thy
30 Israel s' unto Joseph, Now let me
31 And Joseph s' unto his brethren, and
47: 1 and s', My father and my brethren,
3 Pharaoh s' unto his brethren, What
3 s' unto Pharaoh, Thy servants are
4 They s' moreover unto Pharaoh, For
8 Pharaoh s' unto Jacob, How old art
9 Jacob s' unto Pharaoh, The days of
15 unto Joseph, and s', Give us bread:
16 Joseph s', Give your cattle; and I
18 s' unto him, We will not hide it
23 Joseph s' unto the people, Behold,
25 they s', Thou hast saved our lives:
29 and s' unto him, If now I have found
30 in their buryingplace. And he s',
30 I will do as thou hast s'.
31 And he s', Swear unto me. And he
48: 2 one told Jacob, and s', Behold, thy
3 And Jacob s' unto Joseph, God
4 s' unto me, Behold, I will make thee
8 Joseph's sons, and s', Who are these?
9 Joseph s' unto his father, They are
9 he s', Bring them, I pray thee, unto
11 And Israel s' unto Joseph, I had not
15 blessed Joseph, and s', God, before
18 Joseph s' unto his father, Not so, my
19 his father refused, and s', I know it,
21 Israel s' unto Joseph, Behold, I die:
49: 1 s', Gather yourselves together, that
29 he charged them, and s' unto them,
50: 6 And Pharaoh s', Go up, and bury thy
11 s', This is a grievous mourning
15 they s', Joseph will peradventure
18 they s', Behold, we be thy servants.
19 And Joseph s' unto them, Fear not:
24 Joseph s' unto his brethren, I die:
Ex 1: 9 he s' unto his people, Behold, the
16 And he s', When ye do the office of
18 and s' unto them, Why have ye done
19 midwives s' unto Pharaoh, Because
2: 6 and s', This is one of the Hebrews'
7 s' his sister to Pharaoh's daughter,
8 Pharaoh's daughter s' to her, Go.
9 And Pharaoh's daughter s' unto her,
10 she s', Because I drew him out of the
13 and he s' to him that did the wrong,
14 he s', Who made thee a prince and
14 Moses feared, and s', Surely this
18 he s', How is it that ye are come so
19 they s', An Egyptian delivered us
20 he s' unto his daughters, And where
22 he s', I have been a stranger in a
3: 3 And Moses s', I will now turn aside,
4 and s', Moses, Moses. And he s',
5 And he s', Draw not nigh hither:
6 he s', I am the God of thy father,
7 And the Lord s', I have surely seen
11 And Moses s' unto God, Who am I,
12 And he s', Certainly I will be with
13 And Moses s' unto God, Behold,
14 And God s' unto Moses, I Am That I
14 and he s', Thus shalt thou say unto
15 God s' moreover unto Moses, Thus
17 And I have s', I will bring you up
4: 1 Moses answered and s', But, behold,
2 the Lord s' unto him, What is that
2 in thine hand? And he s', A rod.
3 And he s', Cast it on the ground.
4 Lord s' unto Moses, Put forth thine
6 Lord s' furthermore unto him, Put
7 he s', Put thine hand into thy bosom
10 Moses s' unto the Lord, O my Lord,
11 Lord s' unto him, Who hath made
13 And he s', O my Lord, send, I pray
14 and he s', Is not Aaron the Levite
18 and s' unto him, Let me go, I pray
18 And Jethro s' to Moses, Go in peace.
19 Lord s' unto Moses in Midian, Go,
21 Lord s' unto Moses, When thou goest
25 and s', Surely a bloody husband art
26 she s', A bloody husband thou art,
27 And the Lord s' to Aaron, Go into the
5: 2 And Pharaoh s', Who is the Lord,
3 And they s', The God of the Hebrews
4 And the king of Egypt s' unto them,
5 And Pharaoh s', Behold, the people
17 But he s', Ye are idle, ye are idle:
19 after it was s', Ye shall not minish

Ex 5: 21 they s' unto them, The Lord look
22 returned unto the Lord, and s', Lord,
6: 1 Lord s' unto Moses, Now shalt thou
2 and s' unto him, I am the Lord:
26 to whom the Lord s', Bring out the
30 Moses s' before the Lord, Behold, I
7: 1 Lord s' unto Moses, See, I have made
13 not unto them; as the Lord had s'.
14 the Lord s' unto Moses, Pharaoh's
22 not unto them; as the Lord had s'.
8: 8 and s', Intreat the Lord, that he
9 Moses s' unto Pharaoh, Glory over
10 And he s', To morrow.
10 he s', Be it according to thy word:
15 not unto them; as the Lord had s'.
16 the Lord s' unto Moses, Say unto
19 the magicians s' unto Pharaoh,
19 not unto them; as the Lord had s'.
20 the Lord s' unto Moses, Rise up
25 and s', Go ye, sacrifice to your God
26 And Moses s', It is not meet so to do;
28 And Pharaoh s', I will let you go,
29 And Moses s', Behold, I go out from
9: 1 the Lord s' unto Moses, Go in unto
8 Lord s' unto Moses and unto Aaron,
13 And the Lord s' unto Moses, Rise up
22 the Lord s' unto Moses, Stretch out
27 and said unto them, I have sinned
29 And Moses s' unto him, As soon as I
10: 1 the Lord s' unto Moses, Go in unto
3 and s' unto him, Thus saith the Lord
7 And Pharaoh's servants s' unto him,
8 he s' unto them, Go, serve the Lord
9 Moses s', We will go with our young
10 he s' unto them, Let the Lord be so
12 the Lord s' unto Moses, Stretch out
16 and he s', I have sinned against the
21 the Lord s' unto Moses, Stretch out
24 and s', Go ye, serve the Lord;
25 Moses s', Thou must give us also
28 Pharaoh s' unto him, Get thee from
29 Moses s', Thou hast spoken well,
11: 1 Lord s' unto Moses, Yet will I bring
4 And Moses s', Thus saith the Lord,
9 Lord s' unto Moses, Pharaoh shall
12: 21 and s' unto them, Draw out and take
31 and s', Rise up, and get you forth
31 go, serve the Lord, as ye have s'.
32 flocks and your herds, as ye have s',
33 for they s', We be all dead men.
43 the Lord s' unto Moses and Aaron,
13: 3 Moses s' unto the people, Remember
17 for God s', Lest peradventure the
14: 5 And they s', Why have we done this,
11 they s' unto Moses, Because there
13 And Moses s' unto the people, Fear
15 the Lord s' unto Moses, Wherefore
25 so that the Egyptians s', Let us flee
26 the Lord s' unto Moses, Stretch out
15: 9 The enemy s', I will pursue, I will
26 And s', If thou will diligently hearken
16: 3 the children of Israel s' unto them,
4 Then s' the Lord unto Moses, Behold,
6 And Moses and Aaron s' unto all the
8 And Moses s', This shall be, when
15 they s' one to another, It is manna:
15 And Moses s' unto them, This is the
19 And Moses s', Let no man leave of it
23 he s' unto them, This is that which
23 the Lord hath s', To morrow is
25 And Moses s', Eat that to day: for
28 the Lord s' unto Moses, How long
32 Moses s', This is the thing which
33 Moses s' unto Aaron, Take a pot,
17: 2 and s', Give us water that we may
2 And Moses s' unto them, Why chide
3 murmured against Moses, and s',
5 the Lord s' unto Moses, Go on before
9 Moses s' unto Joshua, Choose us
10 Joshua did as Moses had s' to him,
14 Lord s' unto Moses, Write this for a
16 he s', Because the Lord hath sworn
18: 3 for he s', I have been an alien in a
4 God of my father, s' he, was mine help,
6 s' unto Moses, I thy father in law
10 And Jethro s', Blessed be the Lord,
14 he s', What is this thing that thou
15 And Moses s' unto his father in law,
17 And Moses' father in law s' unto him,
24 in law, and did all that he had s'.
19: 8 people answered together, and s', All
9 the Lord s' unto Moses, Lo, I come
10 the Lord s' unto Moses, Go unto the
15 And he s' unto the people, Be ready
21 the Lord s' unto Moses, Go down,
23 Moses s' unto the Lord, The people
24 the Lord s' unto him, Away, get thee
20: 19 And they s' unto Moses, Speak thou
20 Moses s' unto the people, Fear not:
22 Lord s' unto Moses, Thus thou shalt
23: 13 in all things that I have s' unto you
24: 1 he s' unto Moses, Come up unto the
3 answered with one voice, and s', All
3 which the Lord hath s' will we do.
7 the people: and they s', All that the
7 that the Lord hath s' will we do,
8 and s', Behold the blood of the
12 Lord s' unto Moses, Come up to me
14 he s' unto the elders, Tarry ye here
30: 34 Lord s' unto Moses, Take unto thee
32: 1 and s' unto him, Up, make us gods,
2 And Aaron s' unto them, Break off
4 they s', These be thy gods, O Israel,
5 Aaron made proclamation, and s',
7 Lord s' unto Moses, Go, get thee
8 and s', These by thy gods, O Israel,
Ex 32: 9 the Lord s' unto Moses, I have seen
11 and s', Lord, why doth thy wrath
17 he s' unto Moses, There is a noise of
18 And he s', It is not the voice of them
21 And Moses s' unto Aaron, What did
22 And Aaron s', Let not the anger of
23 For they s' unto me, Make us gods,
24 I s' unto them, Whosoever hath any
26 and s', Who is on the Lord's side?
27 he s' unto them, Thus saith the Lord
29 Moses had s', Consecrate yourselves
30 Moses s' unto the people, Ye have
31 and s', Oh, this people have sinned
33 the Lord s' unto Moses, Whosoever
33: 1 the Lord s' unto Moses, Depart,
5 Lord had s' unto Moses, Say unto
12 Moses s' unto the Lord, See, thou
12 thou hast s', I know thee by name,
14 And he s', My presence shall go with
15 And he s' unto him, If thy presence
17 Lord s' unto Moses, I will do this
18 he s', I beseech thee, shew me thy
19 he s', I will make all my goodness
20 he s', Thou canst not see my face:
21 the Lord s', Behold, there is a place
34: 1 Lord s' unto Moses, Hew thee two
9 And he s', If now I have found grace
10 he s', Behold, I make a covenant:
27 Lord s' unto Moses, Write thou these
35: 1 s' unto them, These are the words
30 Moses s' unto the children of Israel,
Le 8: 5 Moses s' unto the congregation,
31 Moses s' unto Aaron, and to his sons,
9: 2 he s' unto Aaron, Take thee a young
6 And Moses s', This is the thing
7 And Moses s' unto Aaron, Go unto
10: 3 Then Moses s' unto Aaron, This is it
4 and s' unto them, Come near, carry
5 out of the camp; as Moses had s'.
6 And Moses s' unto Aaron, and unto
19 Aaron s' unto Moses, Behold, this
16: 2 Lord s' unto Moses, Speak unto
17: 12 I s' unto the children of Israel, No
14 I s' unto the children of Israel, Ye
20: 24 I have s' unto you, Ye shall inherit
21: 1 Lord s' unto Moses, Speak unto the
Nu 3: 40 Lord s' unto Moses, Number all the
7: 11 the Lord s' unto Moses, They shall
9: 7 men s' unto him, We are defiled by
8 Moses s' unto them, Stand still, and
10: 29 Moses s' unto Hobab, the son of
29 unto the place of which the Lord s',
30 he s' unto him, I will not go; but I
31 he s', Leave us not, I pray thee;
35 Moses s', Rise up, Lord, and let
36 when it rested, he s', Return, O Lord,
11: 4 and s', Who shall give us flesh to
11 Moses s' unto the Lord, Wherefore
16 Lord s' unto Moses, Gather unto me
21 Moses s', The people, among whom
21 thou hast s', I will give them flesh,
23 Lord s' unto Moses, Is the Lord's
27 s', Eldad and Medad do prophesy
28 and s', My lord Moses, forbid them.
29 Moses s' unto him, Enviest thou for
12: 2 And they s', Hath the Lord indeed
6 he s', Hear now my words: If there
11 Aaron s' unto Moses, Alas, my lord,
14 Lord s' unto Moses, If her father
13: 17 s' unto them, Get you up this way
27 s', We came unto the land whither
30 s', Let us go up at once, and possess
31 men that went up with him s', We be
14: 2 whole congregation s' unto them,
4 they s' one to another, Let us make
11 Lord s' unto Moses, How long will
13 Moses s' unto the Lord, Then the
20 Lord s', I have pardoned according
31 ones, which ye s' should be a prey,
35 I the Lord have s', I will surely do
41 Moses s', Wherefore now do ye
15: 35 Lord s' unto Moses, The man shall
16: 3 and against Aaron, and s' unto them,
8 Moses s' unto Korah, Hear, I pray
12 which s', We will not come up:
15 s' unto the Lord, Respect not thou
16 Moses s' unto Korah, Be thou and
22 fell upon their faces, and s', O God,
28 Moses s', Hereby ye shall know that
34 for they s', Lest the earth swallow
40 as the Lord s' to him by the hand
46 And Moses s' unto Aaron, Take a
17: 10 Lord s' unto Moses, Bring Aaron's
18: 1 Lord s' unto Aaron, Thou and thy
24 I have s' unto them, Among the
20: 10 s' unto them, Hear now, ye rebels;
18 Edom s' unto him, Thou shalt not
19 children of Israel s' unto him, We
20 he s', Thou shalt not go through.
21: 2 vowed a vow unto the Lord, and s',
7 people came to Moses, and s', We
8 Lord s' unto Moses, Make thee a
14 it is s' in the book of the wars of
34 Lord s' unto Moses, Fear him not:
22: 4 Moab s' unto the elders of Midian,
8 he s' unto them, Lodge here this
9 And God came unto Balaam, and s',
10 Balaam s' unto God, Balak the son
12 God s' unto Balaam, Thou shalt not
13 s' unto the princes of Balak, Get
14 went unto Balak, and s', Balaam
16 they came to Balaam, and s' to him,
18 answered and s' unto the servants
20 Balaam at night, and s' unto him,
28 she s' unto Balaam, What have I
29 Balaam s' unto the ass, Because
Nu 22: 30 the ass s' unto Balaam, Am not I
30 do so unto thee? And he s', Nay.
32 the angel of the Lord s' unto him,
34 Balaam s' unto the angel of the
35 angel of the Lord s' unto Balaam,
37 Balak s' unto Balaam, Did I not
38 And Balaam s' unto Balak, Lo, I am
23: 1 Balaam s' unto Balak, Build me
3 Balaam s' unto Balak, Stand by thy
4 and he s' unto him, I have prepared
5 s', Return unto Balak, and thus
7 And he took up his parable, and s',
11 Balak s' unto Balaam, What hast
12 And he answered and s', Must I not
13 Balak s' unto him, Come, I pray
15 he s' unto Balak, Stand here by my
16 s', Go again unto Balak, and say
17 Balak s' unto him, What hath the
18 and s', Rise up, Balak, and hear;
19 hath he s', and shall he not do it?
23 it shall be s' of Jacob and of Israel,
25 Balak s' unto Balaam, Neither curse
26 Balaam answered and s' unto Balak,
27 Balak s' unto Balaam, Come, I pray
29 Balaam s' unto Balak, Build me
30 Balak did as Balaam had s', and
24: 3 And he took up his parable and s',
3 Balaam the son of Beor hath s',
3 man whose eyes are open hath s':
4 He hath s', which heard the words
10 Balak s' unto Balaam, I called thee
12 Balaam s' unto Balak, Spake I not
15 he took up his parable, and s',
15 Balaam the son of Beor hath s',
15 man whose eyes are open hath s':
16 hath s', which heard the words of
20 and s', Amalek was the first of the
21 s', Strong is the dwellingplace, and
23 s', Alas, Who shall live when God
25: 4 And the Lord s' unto Moses, Take
5 Moses s' unto the judges of Israel,
26: 65 For the Lord had s' of them, They
27: 12 Lord s' unto Moses, Get thee up
18 the Lord s' unto Moses, Take thee
31: 15 Moses s' unto them, Have ye saved
21 the priest s' unto the men of war
49 they s' unto Moses, Thy servants
32: 5 s' they, if we have found grace in
6 Moses s' unto the children of Gad
16 s', We will build sheepfolds here
20 Moses s' unto them, If ye will do
29 Moses s' unto them, If the children
31 Lord hath s' unto thy servants, so
36: 2 they s', The Lord commanded my
5 the sons of Joseph hath s' well.
De 1: 14 ye answered me, and s', The thing
20 I s' unto you, Ye are come unto the
21 of thy fathers hath s' unto thee;
22 and s', We will send men before us,
25 s', It is a good land which the Lord
27 s', Because the Lord hated us, he
29 I s' unto you, Dread not, neither
39 ones, which ye s' should be a prey,
41 s' unto me, We have sinned against
42 Lord s' unto me, Say unto them, Go
2: 9 Lord s' unto me, Distress not the
13 rise up, s' I, and get you over the
31 Lord s' unto me, Behold, I have
3: 2 Lord s' unto me, Fear him not: for
26 Lord s' unto me, Let it suffice thee;
4: 10 when the Lord s' unto me, Gather
5: 1 s' unto them, Hear, O Israel, the
24 And ye s', Behold, the Lord our God
28 Lord s' unto me, I have heard the
28 have well s' all that they have spoken.
9: 3 as the Lord hath s' unto thee.
12 Lord s' unto me, Arise, get thee
25 Lord had s' he would destroy you.
26 and s', O Lord God, destroy not thy
10: 1 s' unto me, Hew the two tables of
11 Lord s' unto me, Arise, take thy
11: 25 tread upon, as he hath s' unto you.
17: 16 as the Lord hath s' unto you, Ye
18: 2 as he hath s' unto them.
17 Lord s' unto me, They have well
29: 2 s' unto them, Ye have seen all that
13 as he hath s' unto thee, and as he
31: 2 he s' unto them, I am an hundred
2 also the Lord hath s' unto me,
3 before thee, as the Lord hath s'.
7 s' unto him in the sight of all Israel,
14, 16 the Lord s' unto Moses, Behold,
23 the son of Nun a charge, and s', Be
32: 20 he s', I will hide my face from them,
26 I s', I would scatter them into
46 he s' unto them, Set your hearts
33: 2 he s', The Lord came from Sinai,
7 s', Hear, Lord, the voice of Judah,
8 And of Levi he s', Let thy Thummin
9 Who s' unto his father and to his
12 of Benjamin he s', The beloved of
13 of Joseph he s', Blessed of the Lord
18 of Zebulun he s', Rejoice, Zebulun,
20 And of Gad he s', Blessed be he that
22 of Dan he s', Dan is a lion's whelp:
23 And of Naphtali he s', O Naphtali,
24 of Asher he s', Let Asher be blessed
34: 4 Lord s' unto him, This is the land
Jos 1: 3 unto you, as I s' unto Moses.
2: 4 s' thus, There came men unto me,
9 she s' unto the men, I know that
16 she s' unto them, Get you to the
17 And the men s' unto her, We will be
21 she s', According unto your words,
24 they s' unto Joshua, Truly the Lord
3: 5 Joshua s' unto the people, Sanctify

Jos 3: 7 Lord s' unto Joshua, This day will
9 Joshua s' unto the children of Israel,
10 Joshua s', Hereby ye shall know
4: 5 Joshua s' unto them, Pass over
5: 2 that time the Lord s' unto Joshua,
9 Lord s' unto Joshua, This day have
13 s' unto him, Art thou for us, or for
14 he s', Nay; but as captain of the
14 did worship, and s' unto him, what
15 captain of the Lord's host s' unto
6: 2 Lord s' unto Joshua, See, I have
6 called the priests, and s' unto them,
7 he s' unto the people, Pass on, and
16 Joshua s' unto the people, Shout;
22 Joshua had s' unto the two men
7: 3 returned to Joshua, and s' unto him,
7 And Joshua s', Alas, O Lord God,
10 Lord s' unto Joshua, Get thee up;
19 Joshua s' unto Achan, My son, give,
20 s', Indeed I have sinned against
25 Joshua s', Why hast thou troubled
8: 1 the Lord s' unto Joshua, Fear not,
18 Lord s' unto Joshua, Stretch out
9: 6 And s' unto him, and to the men of
7 men of Israel s' unto the Hivites,
8 s' unto Joshua, We are thy servants.
8 Joshua s' unto them, Who art ye?
9 they s' unto him, From a very far
19 princes s' unto all the congregation,
21 the princes s' unto them, Let them
24 And they answered Joshua, and s',
10: 8 Lord s' unto Joshua, Fear them not:
12 s' in the sight of Israel, Sun, stand
18 Joshua s', Roll great stones upon
22 s' Joshua, Open the mouth of the
24 s' unto the captains of the men of
25 Joshua s' unto them, Fear not, nor
11: 6 Lord s' unto Joshua, Be not afraid
23 to all that the Lord s' unto Moses;
13: 1 the Lord s' unto him, Thou art old
14, 33 inheritance, as he s' unto them.
14: 6 Caleb...the Kenezite s' unto him,
6 thing that the Lord s' unto Moses
10 as he s', these forty and five years,
12 to drive them out, as the Lord s'.
15: 16 s', He that smiteth Kirjath-sepher,
18 Caleb s' unto her, What wouldest
17: 16 children of Joseph s', The hill is not
18: 3 Joshua s' unto the children of Israel,
22: 2 s' unto them, Ye have kept all that
21 s' unto the heads of the thousands
26 we s', Let us now prepare to build
28 s' we, that it shall be, when they
31 the priest s' unto the children of
23: 2 s' unto them, I am old and stricken
24: 2 Joshua s' unto all the people, Thus
16 people answered and s', God forbid
19 And Joshua s' unto the people, Ye
21 people s' unto Joshua, Nay; but we
22 Joshua s' unto the people, Ye are
22 And they s', We are witnesses.
23 put away, s' he, the strange gods
24 people s' unto Joshua, the Lord
27 And Joshua s' unto all the people,
J'g 1: 2 And the Lord s', Judah shall go up:
3 Judah s' unto Simeon his brother,
7 Adoni-bezek s', Threescore and ten
12 And Caleb s', He that smiteth
14 Caleb s' unto her, What wilt thou?
15 she s' unto him, Give me a blessing:
20 Hebron unto Caleb, as Moses s':
24 they s' unto him, Shew us, we pray
2: 1 s', I made you to go up out of Egypt,
1 I s', I will never break my covenant
3 Wherefore I also s', I will not drive
15 them for evil, as the Lord had s',
20 and he s', Because that this people
3: 19 s', I have a secret errand unto thee,
19 thee, O king: who s', Keep silence.
20 and Ehud s', I have a message from
24 they s', Surely he covereth his feet
28 he s' unto them, Follow after me:
4: 6 s' unto him, Hath not the Lord God
8 Barak s' unto her, If thou wilt go
9 she s', I will surely go with thee:
14 Deborah s' unto Barak, Up; for this
18 s' unto him, Turn in, my lord, turn
19 he s' unto her, Give me, I pray thee,
20 he s' unto her, Stand in the door of
22 s' unto him, Come, and I will shew
5: 23 ye Meroz, s' the angel of the Lord,
6: 8 which s' unto them, Thus saith the
10 I s' unto you, I am the Lord your
12 s' unto him, The Lord is with thee,
13 Gideon s' unto him, Oh my Lord, if
14 s', Go in this thy might, and thou
15 And he s' unto him, Oh my Lord,
16 the Lord s' unto him, Surely I will
17 he s' unto him, If now I have found
18 he s', I will tarry until thou come
20 the angel of God s' unto him, Take
22 Gideon s', Alas, O Lord God! for
23 the Lord s' unto him, Peace be unto
25 that the Lord s' unto him, Take thy
27 did as the Lord had s' unto him:
29 they s' one to another, Who hath
29 they s', Gideon the son of Joash
30 the men of the city s' unto Joash,
31 Joash s' unto all that stood against
36 Gideon s' unto God, If thou wilt
36 by mine hand, as thou hast s',
37 by mine hand, as thou hast s'.
39 Gideon s' unto God, Let not thine
7: 2, 4 Lord s' unto Gideon, The people
5 the Lord s' unto Gideon, Every one
7 the Lord s' unto Gideon, By the

J'g 7: 9 that the Lord s' unto him, Arise,
13 s', Behold, I dreamed a dream, and,
14 his fellow answered and s', This is
15 the host of Israel, and s', Arise;
17 he s' unto them, Look on me, and
8: 1 the men of Ephraim s' unto him,
2 he s' unto them, What have I done
3 toward him, when he had s' that.
5 he s' unto the men of Succoth,
6 princes of Succoth s', Are the hands
7 Gideon s', Therefore when the Lord
15 s', Behold Zebah and Zalmunna,
18 s' he unto Zebah and Zalmunna,
19 he s', They were my brethren, even
20 he s' unto Jether his firstborn, Up,
21 Zebah and Zalmunna s', Rise thou,
22 the men of Israel s' unto Gideon,
23 Gideon s' unto them, I will not rule
24 Gideon s' unto them, I would desire
9: 3 Abimelech; for they s', He is our
7 s' unto them, Hearken unto me, ye
8 s' unto the olive tree, Reign thou
9 olive tree s' unto them, Should I
10 trees s' to the fig tree, Come thou,
11 the fig tree s' unto them, Should I
12 s' the trees unto the vine, Come
13 vine s' unto them, Should I leave
14 s' all the trees unto the bramble,
15 And the bramble s' unto the trees,
28 Gaal the son of Ebed s', Who is
29 s' to Abimelech, Increase the army,
36 he s' to Zebul, Behold, there come
36 Zebul s' unto him, Thou seest the
37 Gaal spake again and s', See there
38 s' Zebul unto him, Where is now
48 s' unto the people that were with
54 s' unto him, Draw thy sword, and
10: 11 Lord s' unto the children of Israel,
15 children of Israel s' unto the Lord,
18 princes of Gilead s' one to another,
11: 2 s' unto him, Thou shalt not inherit
6 they s' unto Jephthah, Come, and be
7 And Jephthah s' unto the elders of
8 elders of Gilead s' unto Jephthah,
9 And Jephthah s' unto the elders of
10 elders of Gilead s' unto Jephthah,
15 s' unto him, Thus saith Jephthah,
19 Israel s' unto him, Let us pass, we
30 and s', If thou shalt without fail
35 clothes, and s', Alas, my daughter!
36 she s' unto him, My father, if thou
37 And she s' unto her father, Let this
38 And he s', Go. And he sent her away
12: 1 and s' unto Jephthah, Wherefore
2 Jephthah s' unto them, I and my
4 because they s', Ye Gileadites are
5 Ephraimites which were escaped s',
5 men of Gilead s' unto him, Art thou
5 thou an Ephraimite? If he s', Nay;
6 Then s' they unto him, Say now
6 he s' Sibboleth: for he could not
13: 3 s' unto her, Behold now, thou art
7 he s' unto me, Behold, thou shalt
8 s', O my Lord, let the man of God
10 s' unto him, Behold, the man hath
11 s' unto him, Art thou the man that
11 unto the woman, And he s', I am.
12 Manoah s', Now let thy words come
13 angel of the Lord s' unto Manoah,
13 I s' unto the woman let her beware.
15 Manoah s' unto the angel of the
16 angel of the Lord s' unto Manoah,
17 Manoah s' unto the angel of the
18 the angel of the Lord s' unto him,
22 Manoah s' unto his wife, We shall
23 his wife s' unto him, If the Lord
14: 2 and s', I have seen a woman in
3 father and his mother s' unto him,
3 Samson s' unto his father, Get her
12 Samson s' unto them, I will now
13 s' unto him, Put forth thy riddle,
14 he s' unto them, Out of the eater
15 s' unto Samson's wife, Entice thy
16 and s', Thou dost but hate me, and
16 And he s' unto her, Behold, I have
18 the men of the city s' unto him on
18 s' unto them, If ye had not plowed
15: 1 he s', I will go in to my wife into the
2 And her father s', I verily thought
3 Samson s' concerning them, Now
6 the Philistines s', Who hath done
7 Samson s' unto them, Though ye
10 the men of Judah s', Why are ye
11 and s' to Samson, Knowest thou not
11 he s' unto them, As they did unto
12 they s' unto him, We are come down
12 Samson s' unto them, Swear unto
16 Samson s', With the jawbone of an
18 called on the Lord, and s', Thou hast
16: 5 and s' unto her, Entice him, and see
6 And Delilah s' to Samson, Tell me, I
7 Samson s' unto her, If they bind
9 she s' unto him, The Philistines be
10 Delilah s' unto Samson, Behold,
11 he s' unto her, If they bind me fast
12 and s' unto him, The Philistines be
13 Delilah s' unto Samson, Hitherto
13 And he s' unto her, If thou weavest
14 s' unto him, The Philistines be upon
15 she s' unto him, How canst thou
17 her all his heart, and s' unto her,
20 she s', The Philistines be upon thee.
20 awoke out of his sleep, and s', I will
23, 24 they s', Our god hath delivered
25 that they s', Call for Samson, that he
26 Samson s' unto the lad that held

J'g 16: 28 and s', O Lord God, remember me,
30 And Samson s', Let me die with the
17: 2 he s' unto his mother, The eleven
2 his mother s', Blessed be thou of
3 his mother s', I had wholly
9 Micah s' unto him, Whence comest
9 he s' unto him, I am a Levite of
10 Micah s' unto him, Dwell with me,
13 Then s' Micah, Now know I that the
18: 2 s' unto them, Go, search the land:
3 and s' unto him, Who brought thee
4 he s' unto them, Thus and thus
5 they s' unto him, Ask counsel, we
6 priest s' unto them, Go in peace:
8 brethren s' unto them, What say
9 they s', Arise, that we may go up
14 s' unto their brethren, Do ye know
18 s' the priest unto them, What do
19 they s' unto him, Hold thy peace,
23 and s' unto Micah, What aileth thee,
24 he s', Ye have taken away my gods
25 children of Dan s' unto him, Let
19: 5 damsel's father s' said unto his son
6 the damsel's father had s' unto the
8 damsel's father s', Comfort thine
9 the damsel's father, s' unto him,
11 servant s' unto his master, Come, I
12 his master s' unto him, We will not
13 he s' unto his servant, Come, and let
17 the old man s', Whither goest thou?
18 And he s' unto him, We are passing
20 the old man s', Peace be with thee;
23 and s' unto them, Nay, my brethren,
28 he s' unto her, Up, and let us be
30 s', There was no such deed done
20: 3 Then s' the children of Israel, Tell
4 slain, answered and s', I came into
18 and s', Which of us shall go up first
18 the Lord s', Judah shall go up first.
23 And the Lord s', Go up against him.
28 Lord s', Go up; for to morrow I will
32 of Benjamin s', They are smitten
32 children of Israel s', Let us flee, and
39 s', Surely they are smitten down
21: 3 s', O Lord God of Israel, why is this
5 children of Israel s', Who is there
6 s', There is one tribe cut off from
8 And they s', What one is there of the
16 the elders of the congregation s',
17 s', There must be an inheritance
19 they s', Behold, there is a feast of
Ru 1: 8 Naomi s' unto her two daughters
10 s' unto her, Surely we will return
11 And Naomi s', Turn again, my
15 she s', Behold, thy sister in law is
16 Ruth s', Intreat me not to leave
19 them, and they s', Is this Naomi?
20 And she s' unto them, Call me not
2: 2 Ruth the Moabitess s' unto Naomi,
2 she s' unto her, Go, my daughter.
4 s' unto the reapers, The Lord be
5 Then s' Boaz unto his servant that
6 over the reapers answered and s',
7 she s', I pray you, let me glean and
8 s' Boaz unto Ruth, Hearest thou
10 and s' unto him, Why have I found
11 Boaz answered and s' unto her, It
13 she s', Let me find favour in thy
14 Boaz s' unto her, At mealtime come
19 And her mother in law s' unto her,
19 s', The man's name with whom I
20 Naomi s' unto her daughter in law,
20 And Naomi s' unto her, The man is
21 Ruth...s', He s' unto me also,
22 Naomi s' unto Ruth her daughter
3: 1 Then Naomi her mother in law s'
5 she s' unto her, All that thou sayest
9 And he s', Who art thou? And she
10 he s', Blessed be thou of the Lord,
14 he s', Let it not be known that a
15 he s', Bring the vail that thou hast
16 she s', Who art thou, my daughter?
17 she s', These six measure of barley
17 he s' to me, Go not empty unto thy
18 s' she, Sit still, my daughter, until
4: 1 unto whom he s', Ho, such a one!
2 the city, and s', Sit ye down here.
3 he s' unto the kinsman, Naomi, that
4 thee. And he s', I will redeem it.
5 Then s' Boaz, What day thou buyest
6 kinsman s', I cannot redeem it for
8 the kinsman s' unto Boaz, Buy it
9 Boaz s' unto the elders, and unto all
11 and the elders, s', We are witnesses.
14 woman s' unto Naomi, Blessed be
1Sa 1: 8 s' Elkanah her husband to her,
11 she vowed a vow, and s', O Lord of
14 Eli s' unto her, How long wilt thou
15 Hannah answered and s', No, my
17 Eli answered and s', Go in peace:
18 And she s', Let thine handmaid find
22 she s' unto her husband, I will not
23 Elkanah her husband s' unto her,
26 And she s', Oh my lord, as thy soul
2: 1 Hannah prayed, and s', My heart,
15 s' to the man that sacrificed, Give
16 if any man s' unto him, Let them
20 s', The Lord give thee seed of this
23 he s' unto them, Why do ye such
27 of God unto Eli, and s' unto him,
30 I s' indeed that thy house, and the
3: 5 he ran unto Eli, and s', Here am I;
5 he s', I called not; lie down again.
6, 8 went to Eli, and s', Here am I;
9 Therefore Eli s' unto Samuel, Go,
11 the Lord s' to Samuel, Behold, I

1Sa 3:16 called Samuel, and s', Samuel, my
17 he s', What is the thing that the
17 that the Lord hath s' unto thee?
17 all the things that he s' unto thee.
18 And he s', It is the Lord: let him
4: 3 the elders of Israel s', Wherefore
6 they s', What meaneth the noise of
7 they s', God is come into the camp.
7 And they s', Woe unto us! for there
14 he s', What meaneth the noise of
16 the man s' unto Eli, I am he that
16 he s', What is there done, my son?
17 the messenger answered and s',
20 that stood by her s' unto her,
22 she s', The glory is departed from
5: 7 they s', The ark of the God of Israel
8 and s', What shall we do with the
11 s', Send away the ark of the God of
6: 3 they s', If ye send away the ark of
4 s' they, What shall be the trespass
20 the men of Beth-shemesh s', Who is
7: 5 And Samuel s', Gather all Israel to
6 and s' there, We have sinned against
8 the children of Israel s' to Samuel,
8: 5 s' unto him, Behold, thou art old,
6 they s', Give us a king to judge us.
7 Lord s' unto Samuel, Hearken unto
11 he s', This will be the manner of the
19 they s', Nay; but we will have a king
22 the Lord s' to Samuel, Hearken unto
22 Samuel s' unto the men of Israel, Go
9: 3 Kish s' to Saul his son, Take now
5 s' to his servant that was with him,
6 s' unto him, Behold now, there is in
7 s' Saul to his servant, But, behold,
8 servant answered Saul again, and s',
10 s' [559] Saul to his servant, Well s';
11 and s' unto them, Is the seer here?
12 they answered them, and s', He is:
17 Lord s' unto him, Behold the man
18 s', Tell me, I pray thee, where the
19 Samuel answered Saul, and s', I am
21 and s', Am not I a Benjamite, of the
23 Samuel s' unto the cook, Bring the
23 of which I s' unto thee, Set it by thee.
24 Samuel s', Behold that which is left!
24 hath it been kept for thee since I s',
27 Samuel s' to Saul, Bid the servant
10: 1 and s', Is it not because the Lord
11 then the people s' one to another,
12 and s', But who is their father?
14 Saul's uncle s' unto him and to his
14 And he s', To seek the asses: and
15 And Saul's uncle s', Tell me, I pray
15 pray thee, what Samuel s' unto you.
16 Saul s' unto his uncle, He told us
18 s' unto the children of Israel, Thus
19 ye have s' unto him, Nay, but set a
24 Samuel s' to all the people, See ye
24 shouted, and s', God save the king.
27 children of Belial s', How shall this
11: 1 the men of Jabesh s' unto Nahash,
3 elders of Jabesh s' unto him, Give
5 and Saul s', What aileth the people
9 s' unto the messengers that came,
10 the men of Jabesh s', To morrow we
12 And the people s' unto Samuel, Who
12 Who is he that s', Shall Saul reign
13 And Saul s', There shall not a man
14 s' Samuel to the people, Come, and
12: 1 Samuel s' unto all Israel, Behold, I
1 your voice in all that ye s' unto me,
4 they s', Thou hast not defrauded
5 And he s' unto them, The Lord is
6 Samuel s' unto the people, It is the
10 the Lord, and s', We have sinned,
12 ye s' unto me, Nay; but a king shall
19 all the people s' unto Samuel, Pray
20 Samuel s' unto the people, Fear not:
13: 9 And Saul s', Bring hither a burnt
11 Samuel s', What hast thou done?
11 And Saul s', Because I saw that the
12 Therefore s' I, The Philistines will
13 Samuel s' to Saul, Thou hast done
19 Philistines s', Lest the Hebrews
14: 1 son of Saul s' unto the young man
6 And Jonathan s' to the young man
7 And his armourbearer s' unto him,
8 Then s' Jonathan, Behold, we will
11 Philistines s', Behold, the Hebrews
12 and s', Come up to us, and we will
12 Jonathan s' unto his armourbearer,
17 Then s' Saul unto the people that
18 Saul s' unto Ahiah, Bring hither the
19 Saul s' unto the priest, Withdraw
28 answered one of the people, and s',
29 Then s' Jonathan, My father hath
33 he s', Ye have transgressed: roll
34 Saul s', Disperse yourselves among
36 Saul s', Let us go down after the
36 they s', Do whatsoever seemeth good
36 Then s' the priest, Let us draw near
38 And Saul s', Draw ye near hither,
40 Then s' he unto all Israel, Be ye on
40 the people s' unto Saul, Do what
41 Therefore Saul s' unto the Lord God
42 And Saul s', Cast lots between me
43 Then Saul s' to Jonathan, Tell me
43 and s', I did but taste a little honey
45 And the people s' unto Saul, Shall
15: 1 Samuel also s' unto Saul, The Lord
6 And Saul s' unto the Kenites, Go,
13 Saul s' unto him, Blessed be thou of
14 Samuel s', What meaneth then this
15 Saul s', They have brought them
16 Then Samuel s' unto Saul, Stay, and

1Sa 15:16 the Lord hath s' to me this night.
16 And he s' unto him, Say on.
17 Samuel s', When thou wast little in
18 Lord sent thee on a journey, and s',
20 Saul s' unto Samuel, Yea, I have
22 Samuel s', Hath the Lord as great
24 Saul s' unto Samuel, I have sinned:
26 And Samuel s' unto Saul, I will not
28 And Samuel s' unto him, The Lord
30 he s', I have sinned: yet honour
32 Then s' Samuel, Bring ye hither to
32 And Agag s', Surely the bitterness of
33 Samuel s', As thy sword hath made
16: 1 And the Lord s' unto Samuel, How
2 Samuel s', How can I go? if Saul
2 And the Lord s', Take an heifer with
4 and s', Comest thou peaceably?
5 And he s', Peaceably: I am come to
6 and s', Surely the Lord's anointed is
7 But the Lord s' unto Samuel, Look
8, 9 s', Neither hath the Lord chosen
10 And Samuel s' unto Jesse, The Lord
11 Samuel s' unto Jesse, Are here all
11 And he s', There remaineth yet the
11 And Samuel s' unto Jesse, Send and
12 And the Lord s', Arise, anoint him:
15 And Saul's servants s' unto him,
17 Saul s' unto his servants, Provide
18 and s', Behold, I have seen a son of
19 s', Send me David thy son, which is
17: 8 and s' unto them, Why are ye come
10 the Philistine s', I defy the armies
17 Jesse s' unto David his son, Take
25 the men of Israel s', Have ye seen
28 and he s', Why camest thou down
29 David s', What have I now done?
32 And David s' to Saul, Let no man's
33 Saul s' to David, Thou art not able
34 David s' unto Saul, Thy servant kept
37 David s' moreover, The Lord that
37 And Saul s' unto David, Go, and the
39 David s' unto Saul, I cannot go with
43 the Philistine s' unto David, Am I a
44 Philistine s' to David, Come to me,
45 Then s' David to the Philistine,
55 he s' unto Abner, the captain of the
55 And Abner s', As thy soul liveth, O
56 the king s', Enquire thou whose
58 Saul s' to him, Whose son art thou,
18: 7 s', Saul hath slain his thousands,
8 and he s', They have ascribed unto
11 for he s', I will smite David even to
17 Saul s' to David, Behold my elder
17 Saul s', Let not mine hand be upon
18 And David s' unto Saul, Who am I?
21 Saul s', I will give him her, that she
21 Saul s' to David, Thou shalt this day
23 David s', Seemeth it to you a light
25 Saul s', Thus shall ye say to David,
19: 4 and s' unto him, Let not the king sin
14 to take David, she s', He is sick.
17 And Saul s' unto Michal, Why hast
17 answered Saul, He s' unto me, Let
22 s', Where are Samuel and David?
22 one s', Behold, they be at Naioth in
20: 1 and s' before Jonathan, What have I
2 And he s' unto him, God forbid;
3 David sware moreover, and s', Thy
4 s' Jonathan unto David, Whatsoever
5 s' unto Jonathan, Behold, to morrow
9 Jonathan s', Far be it from thee: for
10 s' David to Jonathan, Who shall tell
11 Jonathan s' unto David, Come, and
12 Jonathan s' unto David, O Lord God
18 Jonathan s' to David, To morrow is
27 and Saul s' unto Jonathan his son,
29 And he s', Let me go, I pray thee;
30 and he s' unto him, Thou son of the
32 Saul his father, and s' unto him,
36 he s' unto his lad, Run, find out now
37 Jonathan cried after the lad, and s',
40 s' unto him, Go, carry them to the
42 Jonathan s' to David, Go in peace,
21: 1 and s' unto him, Why art thou alone,
2 David s' unto Ahimelech the priest,
2 hath s' unto me, Let no man know
4 the priest answered David, and s',
5 David answered the priest, and s'
8 And David s' unto Ahimelech, And is
9 the priest s', The sword of Goliath
9 David s', There is none like that;
11 the servants of Achish s' unto him,
14 Then s' Achish unto his servants,
22: 3 he s' unto the king of Moab, Let my
5 And the prophet Gad s' unto David,
7 Then Saul s' unto his servants that
9 s', I saw the son of Jesse coming to
12 And Saul s', Hear now, thou son of
13 And Saul s' unto him, Why have ye
14 answered the king, and s', And who
16 the king s', Thou shalt surely die,
17 king s' unto the footmen that stood
18 the king s' to Doeg, Turn thou, and
22 David s' unto Abiathar, I knew it
23: 2 Lord s' unto David, Go, and smite
3 David's men s' unto him, Behold, we
4 Lord answered him and s', Arise, go
7 And Saul s', God hath delivered him
9 he s' to Abiathar the priest, Bring
10 s' David, O Lord God of Israel, thy
11 And the Lord s', He will come down.
12 s' David, Will the men of Keilah
12 Lord s', They will deliver thee up.
17 And he s' unto him, Fear not: for
21 Saul s', Blessed be ye of the Lord;
24: 4 And the men of David s' unto him,

1Sa 24: 4 day of which the Lord s' unto thee;
6 And he s' unto his men, The Lord
9 And David s' to Saul, Wherefore
10 I s', I will not put forth mine hand
16 Saul s', Is this thy voice, my son
17 And he s' to David, Thou art more
25: 5 and David s' unto the young men,
10 and s', Who is David? and who is the
13 David s' unto his men, Gird ye on
19 And she s' unto her servants, Go on
21 Now David had s', Surely in vain
24 fell at his feet, and s', Upon me, my
32 And David s' to Abigail, Blessed be
35 s' unto her, Go up in peace to thine
39 he s', Blessed be the Lord, that hath
41 on her face to the earth, and s',
26: 6 answered David and s' to Ahimelech
6 Abishai s', I will go down with thee.
8 Then s' Abishai to David, God hath
9 And David s' to Abishai, Destroy
10 David s' furthermore, As the Lord
14 Then Abner answered and s', Who
15 And David s' to Abner, Art not thou
17 s', Is this thy voice, my son David?
17 David s', It is my voice, my lord, O
18 he s', Wherefore doth my lord thus
21 Then s' Saul, I have sinned: return,
22 David answered and s', Behold the
25 Saul s' to David, Blessed be thou,
27: 1 And David s' in his heart, I shall
5 David s' unto Achish, If I have now
10 Achish s', Whither have ye made a
10 And David s', Against the south of
28: 1 And Achish s' unto David, Know thou
2 And David s' to Achish, Surely thou
2 And Achish s' to David, Therefore
7 Then s' Saul unto his servants, Seek
7 And his servants s' to him, Behold,
8 he s', I pray thee, divine unto me
9 And the woman s' unto him, Behold,
11 s' the woman, Whom shall I bring
11 And he s', Bring me up Samuel.
13 the king s' unto her, Be not afraid:
13 the woman s' unto Saul, I saw gods
14 he s' unto her, What form is he of?
14 And she s', an old man cometh up;
15 And Samuel s' to Saul, Why hast
16 Then s' Samuel, Wherefore then
21 s' unto him, Behold, thine handmaid
23 he refused, and s', I will not eat.
29: 3 s' the princes of the Philistines,
3 s' unto the princes of the Philistines,
4 princes of the Philistines s' unto
6 Achish called David, and s' unto
8 And David s' unto Achish, But what
9 Achish answered and s' to David, I
9 the princes of the Philistines have s',
30: 7 And David s' to Abiathar the priest,
13 And David s' unto him, To whom
13 he s', I am a young man of Egypt,
15 David s' to him, Canst thou bring
15 he s', Swear unto me by God, that
20 cattle, and s', This is David's spoil.
22 s', Because they went not with us,
23 Then s' David, Ye shall not do so,
31: 4 Then s' Saul unto his armourbearer,
2Sa 1: 3 And David s' unto him, From whence
3 he s' unto him, Out of the camp of
4 David s' unto him, How went the
5 David s' unto the young man that
6 And the young man that told him s',
8 And he s' unto me, Who art thou?
9 He s' unto me again, Stand, I pray
13 David s' unto the young man that
14 David s' unto him, How wast thou
15 and s', Go near, and fall upon him.
16 And David s' unto him, thy blood
2: 1 And the Lord s' unto him, Go up.
1 David s', Whither shall I go up?
1 And he s', Unto Hebron.
5 and said unto them, Blessed be ye
14 And Abner s' to Joab, Let the young
14 us. And Joab s', Let them arise.
20 him, and s', Art thou Asahel?
21 Abner s' to him, Turn thee aside
22 And Abner s' again to Asahel, Turn
26 s', Shall the sword devour for ever?
27 And Joab s', As God liveth, unless
3: 7 And Ish-bosheth s' to Abner,
8 and s', Am I a dog's head, which
13 he s', Well; I will make a league
16 Then s' Abner unto him, Go, return.
21 Abner s' unto David, I will arise
24 Joab came to the king, and s',
28 he s', I and my kingdom are
31 And David s' to Joab, and to all the
33 and s', Died Abner as a fool dieth?
38 And the king s' unto his servants,
4: 8 s' to the king, Behold the head of
9 and s' unto them, As the Lord liveth,
5: 2 and the Lord s' to thee, Thou shalt
8 David s' on that day, Whosoever
8 Wherefore they s', The blind and
19 And the Lord s' unto David, Go up:
20 and David smote them there, and s',
23 Lord, he s', Thou shalt not go up;
6: 9 s', How shall the ark of the Lord
20 and s', How glorious was the king
21 David s' unto Michal, It was before
7: 2 king s' unto Nathan the prophet,
3 Nathan s' to the king, Go, do all
18 and he s', Who am I, O Lord God?
25 it for ever, and do as thou hast s'.
9: 1 David s', Is there...any that is left
2 the king s' unto him, Art thou Ziba?
2 And he s', Thy servant is he.

2Sa 9: 3 king s', Is there not yet any of the
3 And Ziba s' unto the king, Jonathan
4 the king s' unto him, Where is he?
4 Ziba s' unto the king, Behold, he is
6 David s', Mephibosheth. And he
7 And David s' unto him, Fear not:
8 himself, and s', What is thy servant,
9 s' unto him, I have given unto thy
11 s' Ziba unto the king, According to
11 Mephibosheth, s' the king, he shall
10: 2 s' David, I will shew kindness unto
3 s' unto Hanun their lord, Thinkest
5 the king s', Tarry at Jericho until
11 he s', If the Syrians be too strong for
11: 3 And one s', Is not this Bath-sheba,
5 told David, and s', I am with child.
8 David s' to Uriah, Go down to thy
10 David s' unto Uriah, Camest thou
11 Uriah s' unto David, the ark, and
12 David s' to Uriah, Tarry here to-day
23 messenger s' unto David, Surely the
25 Then David s' unto the messenger,
12: 1 s' unto him, There were two men in
5 he s' to Nathan, As the Lord liveth,
7 Nathan s' to David, Thou art the
13 David s' unto Nathan, I have sinned
13 And Nathan s' unto David, The Lord
18 they s', Behold, while the child was
19 David s' unto his servants, Is the
19 child dead? And they s', He is dead.
21 Then s' his servants unto him, What
22 he s', While the child was yet alive,
22 for I s', Who can tell whether God
27 s', I have fought against Rabbah,
13: 4 he s' unto him, Why art thou, being
4 Amnon s' unto him, I love Tamar,
5 Jonadab s' unto him, Lay thee down
6 Amnon s' unto the king, I pray thee,
9 Amnon s', Have out all men from me.
10 Amnon s' unto Tamar, Bring the
11 s' unto her, Come lie with me, my
15 Amnon s' unto her, Arise, be gone.
16 she s' unto him, There is no cause:
17 s', Put now this woman out from me,
20 Absalom her brother s' unto her,
24 and s', Behold now, thy servant hath
25 king s' to Absalom, Nay, my son,
26 Then s' Absalom, If not, I pray thee,
26 the king s' unto him, Why should he
32 s', Let not my lord suppose that they
35 Jonadab s' unto the king, Behold,
35 come: as thy servant s', so it is.
14: 2 s' unto her, I pray thee, feign thyself
4 did obeisance, and s', Help, O king.
5 king s' unto her, What aileth thee?
7 they s', Deliver him that smote his
8 the king s' unto the woman, Go to
9 woman of Tekoah s' unto the king,
10 the king s', Whosoever saith ought
11 Then s' she, I pray thee, let the
11 he s', As the Lord liveth, there shall
12 the woman s', Let thine handmaid, I
12 my lord the king. And he s', Say on.
13 the woman s', Wherefore then hast
15 thy handmaid s', I will now speak
17 thine handmaid s', The word of my
18 the king answered and s' unto the
18 the woman s', Let my lord the king
19 the king s', Is not the hand of Joab
19 the woman answered and s', As thy
21 the king s' unto Joab, Behold now,
22 and Joab s', To day thy servant
24 the king s', Let him turn to his own
30 he s' unto his servants, See, Joab's
31 s' unto him, Wherefore have thy
15: 2 him, and s', Of what city art thou?
2 And he s', Thy servant is of one of
3 And Absalom s' unto him, See, thy
4 Absalom s' moreover, Oh that I were
7 Absalom s' unto the king, I pray
9 the king s' unto him, Go in peace.
14 And David s' unto all his servants
15 the king's servants s' unto the king,
19 Then s' the king to Ittai the Gittite,
21 And Ittai answered the king, and s',
22 David s' to Ittai, Go and pass over.
25 king s' unto Zadok, Carry back the
27 king s' also unto Zadok the priest,
31 David s', O Lord, I pray thee, turn
33 Unto whom David s', If thou passest
16: 2 the king s' unto Ziba, What meanest
2 Ziba s', The asses be for the king's
3 king s', And where is thy master's
3 Ziba s' unto the king, Behold, he
3 for he s', To day shall the house of
4 s' the king to Ziba, Behold, thine are
4 And Ziba s', I humbly beseech thee
7 And thus s' Shimei when he cursed,
9 Then s' Abishai the son of Zeruiah
10 king s', What have I to do with you,
10 Lord hath s' unto him, Curse David.
11 David s' to Abishai, and to all his
16 Hushai s' unto Absalom, God save
17 And Absalom s' to Hushai, Is this thy
18 Hushai s' unto Absalom, Nay; but
20 Then s' Absalom to Ahithophel, Give
21 Ahithophel s' unto Absalom, Go in
17: 1 Ahithophel s' unto Absalom, Let me
5 Then s' Absalom, Call now Hushai
7 And Hushai s' unto Absalom, The
8 s' Hushai, Thou knowest thy father
14 Absalom and all the men of Israel s',
15 s' Hushai unto Zadok and...Abiathar
20 they s', Where is Ahimaaz and
20 woman s' unto them, They be gone
21 and s' unto David, Arise, and pass

2Sa 17: 29 for they s', The people is hungry,
18: 2 king s' unto the people, I will surely
4 king s' unto them, What seemeth
10 and s',...I saw Absalom hanged in
11 And Joab s' unto the man that told
12 And the man s' unto Joab, Though I
14 Then s' Joab, I may not tarry thus
18 for he s', I have no son to keep my
19 Then s' Ahimaaz the son of Zadok,
20 And Joab s' unto him, Thou shalt not
21 s' Joab to Cushi, Go tell the king
22 Then s' Ahimaaz the son of Zadok yet
22 Joab s', Wherefore wilt thou run,
23 But howsoever, s' he, let me run.
23 And he s' unto him, Run. Then
25 the king s', If he be alone, there is
26 and s', Behold another man running
26 the king s', He also bringeth tidings.
27 And the watchman s', Me thinketh
27 the king s', He is a good man, and
28 and s' unto the king, All is well.
28 and s', Blessed be the Lord thy God,
29 king s', Is the young man Absalom
30 And the king s' unto him, Turn aside,
31 Cushi s', Tidings, my lord the king:
32 king s' unto Cushi, Is the young man
33 went, thus he s', O my son Absalom,
19: 5 to the king, and s', Thou hast shamed
19 And s' unto the king, Let not my lord
21 the son of Zeruiah answered and s',
22 David s', What have I to do with you,
23 Therefore the king s' unto Shimei,
25 king s' unto him, Wherefore wentest
26 for thy servant s', I will saddle me
29 the king s' unto him, Why speakest
29 I have s', Thou and Ziba divide the
30 And Mephibosheth s' unto the king,
33 And the king s' unto Barzillai, Come
34 Barzillai s' unto the king, How long
41 and s' unto the king, Why have our
43 and s', We have ten parts in the king,
20: 1 and s', We have no part in David,
4 s' the king to Amasa, Assemble me
6 David s' to Abishai, Now shall Sheba
9 Joab s' to Amasa, Art thou in health,
11 and s', He that favoureth Joab, and
17 her, the woman s', Art thou Joab?
17 she s' unto him, Hear the words of
20 And Joab answered and s', Far be it,
21 woman s' unto Joab, Behold his head
21: 2 the Gibeonites, and s' unto them;
3 David s' unto the Gibeonites, What
4 Gibeonites s' unto him, We will have
4 he s', What ye shall say, that will I
6 And the king s', I will give them.
22: 2 And he s', The Lord is my rock, and
23: 1 David the son of Jesse s', and the
1 and the sweet psalmist of Israel, s',
3 The God of Israel s', the Rock of
15 David longed, and s', Oh that one
17 And he s', Be it far from me, O Lord,
24: 2 For the king s' to Joab the captain of
3 Joab s' unto the king, Now the Lord
10 David s' unto the Lord, I have sinned
13 and s' unto him, Shall seven years of
14 David s' unto Gad, I am in a great
16 and s' to the angel that destroyed
17 and s', Lo, I have sinned, and I have
18 and s' unto him, Go up, rear an altar
21 Araunah s', Wherefore is my lord
21 David s', To buy the threshingfloor
22 Araunah s' unto David, Let my lord
23 Araunah s' unto the king, The Lord
24 And the king s' unto Araunah, Nay;
1Ki 1: 2 Wherefore his servants s' unto him,
16 the king s', What wouldest thou?
17 And she s' unto him, My lord, thou
24 And Nathan s', My lord, O king, hast
24 hast thou s', Adonijah shall reign
28 king David answered and s', Call me
29 the king sware, and s', As the Lord
31 and s', Let my lord king David live
32 king David s', Call me Zadok the
33 king also s' unto them, Take with
36 answered the king, and s', Amen:
39 people s', God save king Solomon.
41 he s', Wherefore is this noise of the
42 Adonijah s' unto him, Come in; for
43 Jonathan...s' to Adonijah, Verily our
48 thus s' the king, Blessed be the Lord
52 Solomon s', If he will shew himself a
53 and Solomon s' unto him, Go to thine
2: 4 there shall not fail thee (s' he) a man
13 and she s', Comest thou peaceably?
13 And he s', Peaceably.
14 He s' moreover, I have somewhat to
14 say unto thee. And she s', Say on.
15 he s', Thou knowest...the kingdom
16 not. And she s' unto him, Say on.
17 And he s', Speak, I pray thee, unto
18 Bath-sheba s', Well; I will speak for
20 she s', I desire one small petition
20 king s' unto her, Ask on, my mother:
21 she s', Let Abishag the Shunammite
22 answered and s' unto his mother,
26 unto Abiathar the priest s' the king,
30 and s' unto him, Thus saith the king,
30 And he s', Nay; but I will die here.
30 Thus s' Joab,...thus he answered
31 And the king s' unto him,
31 Do as he hath s', and fall upon him,
36 and s' unto him, Build thee an
38 Shimei s' unto the king, The saying
38 as my lord the king hath s', so will
42 and s' unto him, Did I not make thee
44 The king s' moreover to Shimei,

1Ki 3: 5 God s', Ask what I shall give thee.
6 Solomon s', Thou hast shewed unto
11 God s' unto him, Because thou hast
17 one woman s', O my lord, I and this
22 other woman s', Nay; but the living
22 this s', No; but the dead is thy son,
23 Then s' the king, The one saith,
24 And the king s', Bring me a sword.
25 the king s', Divide the living child
26 and she s', O my lord, give her the
26 But the other s', Let it be neither
27 king answered and s', Give her the
5: 7 and s', Blessed be the Lord this day,
8: 12 Lord s' that he would dwell in the
15 he s', Blessed be the Lord God of
18 the Lord s' unto David my father,
23 he s', Lord God of Israel, there is no
29 place of which thou hast s', My name
9: 3 the Lord s' unto him, I have heard
13 he s', What cities are these which
10: 6 And she s' to the king, It was a true
11: 2 Lord s' unto the children of Israel,
11 Wherefore the Lord s' unto Solomon,
21 Hadad s' to Pharaoh, Let me
22 Pharaoh s' unto him, But what hast
31 he s' to Jeroboam, Take thee ten
12: 5 And he s' unto them, Depart yet for
6 and s', How do ye advise that I may
9 And he s' unto them, What counsel
26 And Jeroboam s' in his heart, Now
28 And s' unto them, It is too much for
13: 2 and s', O altar, altar, thus saith the
6 and s' unto the man of God, Intreat
7 the king s' unto the man of God,
8 the man of God s' unto the king, If
12 their father s' unto them, What
13 And he s' unto his sons, Saddle me
14 he s' unto him, Art thou the man of
14 camest from Judah? And he s', I am.
15 Then he s' unto him, Come home
16 he s', I may not return with thee,
17 For it was s' to me by the word of
18 He s' unto him, I am a prophet also
26 he s', It is the man of God, who was
14: 2 And Jeroboam s' to his wife, Arise,
5 the Lord s' unto Ahijah, Behold, the
6 that he s', Come in, thou wife of
17: 1 s' unto Ahab, As the Lord God of
10 and s', Fetch me, I pray thee, a little
11 s', Bring me, I pray thee, a morsel of
12 she s', As the Lord thy God liveth,
13 And Elijah s' unto her, Fear not; go
13 go and do as thou hast s': but make
18 And she s' unto Elijah, What have I
19 And he s' unto her, Give me thy son.
20 And he cried unto the Lord, and s',
21 s', O Lord my God, I pray thee, let
23 and Elijah s', See, thy son liveth.
24 the woman s' to Elijah, Now by this
18: 5 And Ahab s' unto Obadiah, Go into
7 and s', Art thou that my lord Elijah?
9 And he s', What have I sinned, that
10 and when they s', He is not there; he
15 And Elijah s', As the Lord of hosts
17 Ahab s' unto him, Art thou he that
21 s', How long halt ye between two
22 Then s' Elijah unto the people, I,
24 all the people answered and s', It is
25 Elijah s' unto the prophets of Baal,
27 Elijah mocked them, and s', Cry
30 Elijah s' unto all the people, Come
33 and s', Fill four barrels with water,
34 And he s', Do it the second time.
34 And he s', Do it the third time. And
36 and s', Lord God of Abraham, Isaac,
39 they s', The Lord, he is the God; the
40 And Elijah s' unto them, Take the
41 Elijah s' unto Ahab, Get thee up, eat
43 s' to his servant, Go up now, look
43 and looked, and s', There is nothing.
43 And he s', Go again seven times.
44 he s', Behold, there ariseth a little
44 And he s', Go up, say unto Ahab,
19: 4 s', It is enough; now, O Lord, take
5 him, and s' unto him, Arise and eat.
7 touched him, and s', Arise and eat;
9 and he s' unto him, What doest thou
10 he s', I have been very jealous for
11 And he s', Go forth, and stand upon
13 and s', What doest thou here, Elijah?
14 he s', I have been very jealous for
15 Lord s' unto him, Go, return on thy
20 ran after Elijah, and s', Let me, I
20 And he s' unto him, Go back again:
20: 2 s' unto him, Thus saith Ben-hadad,
4 of Israel answered and s', My lord,
5 and s', Thus speaketh Ben-hadad,
7 s', Mark, I pray you, and see how
8 all the people s' unto him, Hearken
9 Wherefore he s' unto the messengers
10 and s', The gods do so unto me, and
11 of Israel answered and s', Tell him,
12 that he s' unto his servants, Set
14 And Ahab s', By whom? And he s',
14 he s', Who shall order the battle?
18 he s', Whether they be come out for
22 s' unto him, Go, strengthen thyself,
23 servants of the king of Syria s' unto
28 unto the king of Israel, and s', Thus
28 Syrians have s', The Lord is God of
31 servants s' unto him, Behold now,
32 s', Thy servant Ben-hadad saith,
32 And he s', Is he yet alive? he is my
33 and they s', Thy brother Ben-hadad.
33 Then he s', Go ye, bring him. Then
34 Ben-hadad s' unto him, The cities,

1Ki 20:34 Then s' Ahab, I will send thee away
35 the sons of the prophets s' unto his
36 s' he unto him, Because thou hast
37 man, and s', Smite me, I pray thee.
39 he s', Thy servant went out into the
39 me, and s', Keep this man: if by any
40 king of Israel s' unto him, So shall
42 he s' unto him, Thus saith the Lord,
21: 3 Naboth s' to Ahab, The Lord forbid
4 for he had s', I will not give thee the
5 s' unto him, Why is thy spirit so
6 he s' unto her, Because I spake
6 s' unto him, Give me thy vineyard
7 Jezebel his wife s' unto him, Dost
15 that Jezebel s' to Ahab, Arise, take
20 Ahab s' to Elijah, Hast thou found
22: 3 king of Israel s' unto his servants,
4 he s' unto Jehoshaphat, Wilt thou go
4 Jehoshaphat s' to the king of Israel,
5 And Jehoshaphat s' unto the king of
6 and s' unto them, Shall I go against
6 they s', Go up; for the Lord shall
7 Jehoshaphat s', Is there not here a
8 king of Israel s' unto Jehoshaphat,
8 Jehoshaphat s', Let not the king say
9 and s', Hasten hither Micaiah the
11 and he s', Thus saith the Lord, With
14 And Micaiah s', As the Lord liveth,
15 And the king s' unto him, Micaiah,
16 king s' unto him, How many times
17 And he s', I saw all Israel scattered
17 the Lord s', These have no master:
18 king of Israel s' unto Jehoshaphat,
19 he s', Hear thou therefore the word
20 Lord s', Who shall persuade Ahab,
20 one s' on this manner, and another
20 and another s' on that manner.
21 Lord, and s', I will persuade him.
22 the Lord s' unto him, Wherewith?
22 And he s', I will go forth, and I will
22 And he s', Thou shalt persuade him,
24 and s', Which way went the Spirit of
25 And Micaiah s', Behold, thou shalt
26 the king of Israel s', Take Micaiah,
28 And Micaiah s', If thou return at all
28 he s', Hearken, O people, every one
30 king of Israel s' unto Jehoshaphat,
32 that they s', Surely it is the king of
34 he s' unto the driver of his chariot,
49 Then s' Ahaziah the son of Ahab
2Ki 1: 2 and s' unto them, Go, enquire of
3 the angel of the Lord s' to Elijah
5 he s' unto them, Why are ye now
6 And they s' unto him, There came a
6 and s' unto us, Go, turn again unto
7 he s' unto them, What manner of
8 And he s', It is Elijah the Tishbite.
9 God, the king hath s', Come down.
10 And Elijah answered and s' to the
11 And he answered and s' unto him,
11 thus hath the king s', Come down
12 Elijah answered and s' unto them,
13 besought him, and s' unto him, O
15 the angel of the Lord s' unto Elijah,
16 And he s' unto him, Thus saith the
2: 2 Elijah s' unto Elisha, Tarry here, I
2 And Elisha s' unto him, As the Lord
3 and s' unto him, Knowest thou that
3 he s', Yea, I know it; hold ye your
4 Elijah s' unto him, Elisha, tarry
4 And he s', As the Lord liveth, and as
5 and s' unto him, Knowest thou that
6 And Elijah s' unto him, Tarry, I pray
6 he s', As the Lord liveth, and as thy
9 that Elijah s' unto Elisha, Ask what
9 Elisha s', I pray thee, let a double
10 And he s', Thou hast asked a hard
14 smote the waters, and s', Where is
15 they s', The spirit of Elijah doth rest
16 And they s' unto him, Behold now,
16 valley. And he s', Ye shall not send.
17 till he was ashamed, he s', Send.
18 he s' unto them, Did I not say unto
19 the men of the city s' unto Elisha,
20 And he s', Bring me a new cruse,
21 and s', Thus saith the Lord, I have
23 s' unto him, Go up, thou bald head;
3: 7 And he s', I will go up: I am as thou
8 he s', Which way shall we go up?
10 the king of Israel s', Alas! that the
11 Jehoshaphat s', Is there not here a
11 and s', Here is Elisha the son of
12 And Jehoshaphat s', The word of the
13 Elisha s' unto the king of Israel,
13 the king of Israel s' unto him, Nay:
14 And Elisha s', As the Lord of hosts
16 he s', Thus saith the Lord, Make
23 And they s', This is blood: the kings
4: 2 Elisha s' unto her, What shall I do
2 she s', Thine handmaid hath not
3 Then he s', Go, borrow thee vessels
6 she s' unto her son, Bring me yet a
6 he s' unto her, There is not a vessel
7 And he s', Go, sell the oil, and pay
9 she s' unto her husband, Behold
12 And he s' to Gehazi his servant, Call
13 he s' unto him, Say now unto her,
14 he s', What then is to be done for
15 he s', Call her. And when he had
16 he s', About this season, according
16 she s', Nay, my lord, thou man of
17 season that Elisha had s' unto her,
19 he s' unto his father, My head, my
19 And he s' to a lad, Carry him to his
22 s', Send me, I pray thee, one of the
23 he s', Wherefore wilt thou go to him

2Ki 4:23 And she s', It shall be well.
24 and s' to her servant, Drive, and go
25 he s' to Gehazi his servant, Behold,
27 the man of God s', Let her alone;
28 she s', Did I desire a son of my lord?
29 he s' to Gehazi, Gird up thy loins,
30 mother of the child s', As the Lord
36 Gehazi, and s', Call this Shunammite.
36 unto him, he s', Take up thy son.
38 he s' unto his servant, Set on the
40 and s', O thou man of God, there is
41 But he s', Then bring meal. And he
41 he s', Pour out for the people, that
42 he s', Give unto the people, that they
43 his servitor s', What, should I set
43 He s' again, Give the people, that
5: 3 she s' unto her mistress, Would God
4 thus s' the maid that is of the land
5 king of Syria s', Go to, go, and I
7 s', Am I God, to kill and to make
11 away, and s', Behold, I thought,
13 s', My father, if the prophet had bid
15 and he s', Behold, now I know that
16 But he s', As the Lord liveth, before
17 Naaman s', Shall there not then, I
19 And he s' unto him, Go in peace.
20 servant of Elisha, the man of God, s',
21 to meet him, and s', Is all well?
22 And he s', All is well. My master
23 Naaman s', Be content, take two
25 Elisha s' unto him, Whence comest
25 he s', Thy servant went no whither.
26 he s' unto him, Went not mine heart
6: 1 sons of the prophets s' unto Elisha,
3 And one s', Be content, I pray thee,
5 he cried, and s', Alas, master! for it
6 the man of God s', Where fell it?
7 Therefore s' he, Take it up to thee.
11 s' unto them, Will ye not shew me
12 one of his servants s', None, my lord,
13 he s', Go and spy where he is, that
15 his servant s' unto him, Alas, my
17 Elisha prayed, and s', Lord, I pray
18 s', Smite this people, I pray thee,
19 Elisha s' unto them, This is not the
20 that Elisha s', Lord, open the eyes
21 the king of Israel s' unto Elisha,
27 he s', If the Lord do not help thee,
28 king s' unto her, What aileth thee?
28 This woman s' unto me, Give thy
29 I s' unto her on the next day, Give
31 Then he s', God do so and more also
32 he s' to the elders, See ye how this
33 he s', Behold, this evil is of the Lord;
7: 1 Then Elisha s', Hear ye the word of
2 answered the man of God, and s',
2 he s', Behold, thou shalt see it with
3 they s' one to another, Why sit we
6 they s' one to another, Lo, the king
9 Then they s' one to another, We do
12 s' unto his servants, I will now shew
13 one of his servants answered and s',
17 he died, as the man of God had s',
19 answered the man of God, and s',
19 he s', Behold, thou shalt see it with
8: 5 Gehazi s', My lord, O king, this is
8 And the king s' unto Hazael, Take a
9 s', Thy son Ben-hadad king of Syria
10 And Elisha s' unto him, Go, say unto
12 Hazael s', Why weepeth my lord?
13 Hazael s', But what, is thy servant
14 who s' to him, What s' Elisha to
9: 1 and s' unto him, Gird up thy loins,
5 he s', I have an errand to thee,
5 And Jehu s', Unto which of all us?
5 And he s', To thee, O captain.
6 s' unto him, Thus saith the Lord
11 and one s' unto him, Is all well?
11 he s' unto them, Ye know the man,
12 And they s', It is false; tell us now.
12 he s', Thus and thus spake he to me,
15 Jehu s', If it be your minds, then let
17 as he came, and s', I see a company.
17 And Joram s', Take an horseman,
18 s', Thus saith the king, Is it peace?
18 Jehu s', What hast thou to do with
19 s', Thus saith the king, Is it peace?
21 Joram s', Make ready. And his
22 Jehu, that he s', Is it peace, Jehu?
23 s' to Ahaziah, There is treachery, O
25 s' Jehu to Bidkar his captain, Take
27 s', Smite him also in the chariot.
31 she s', Had Zimri peace, who slew
32 window, and s', Who is on my side?
33 he s', Throw her down. So they
34 s', Go, see now this cursed woman,
36 he s', This is the word of the Lord,
10: 4 and s', Behold, two kings stood not
8 he s', Lay ye them in two heaps at
9 s' to all the people, Ye be righteous:
13 king of Judah, and s', Who are ye?
14 he s', Take them alive. And they
15 s' to him, Is thine heart right, as
16 he s', Come with me, and see my
18 s' unto them, Ahab served Baal a
20 Jehu s', Proclaim a solemn assembly
22 s' unto him that was over the vestry,
23 s' unto the worshippers of Baal,
24 s', If any of the men whom I have
25 that Jehu s' to the guard and to the
30 Lord s' unto Jehu, Because thou
11:12 hands, and s', God save the king.
15 s' unto them, Have her forth without
15 priest had s', Let her not be slain
12: 4 Jehoash s' to the priests, All the
7 s' unto them, Why repair ye not the

2Ki 13:14 and s', O my father, my father! the
15 Elisha s' unto him, Take bow and
16 he s' to the king of Israel, Put thine
17 he s', Open the window eastward.
17 opened it. Then Elisha s', Shoot.
17 And he s', The arrow of the Lord's
18 he s', Take the arrows. And he took
18 he s' unto the king of Israel, Smite
19 and s', Thou shouldest have smitten
14:27 s' not that he would blot out the
17:12 the Lord had s' unto them, Ye shall
23 s'...all his servants the prophets.
18:19 Rab-shakeh s' unto them, Speak
22 hath s' to Judah and Jerusalem, Ye
25 The Lord s' to me, Go up against
26 Then s' Eliakim the son of Hilkiah,
27 Rab-shakeh s' unto them, Hath my
19: 3 And they s' unto him, Thus saith
6 And Isaiah s' unto them, Thus shall
15 and s', O Lord God of Israel, which
23 and hast s', With the multitude of
20: 1 s' unto him, Thus saith the Lord,
7 And Isaiah s', Take a lump of figs.
8 Hezekiah s' unto Isaiah, What shall
9 Isaiah s', This sign shalt thou have
14 s' unto him, What s' these men?
14 Hezekiah s', They are come from a
15 he s', What have they seen in thine
16 Isaiah s' unto Hezekiah, Hear the
19 Then s' Hezekiah unto Isaiah, Good
19 And he s', Is it not good, if peace
21: 4 of which the Lord s', In Jerusalem
7 of which the Lord s' to David, and
22: 8 the high priest s' unto Shaphan the
9 s', Thy servants have gathered the
15 And she s' unto them, Thus saith
23:17 he s', What title is that that I see?
18 he s', Let him alone; let no man
27 the Lord s', I will remove Judah
27 which, I s', My name shall be there.
24:13 of the Lord, as the Lord had s'.
25:24 s' unto them, Fear not to be the
1Ch 10: 4 Then s' Saul to his armourbearer,
11: 2 the Lord thy God s' unto thee, Thou
5 inhabitants of Jebus s' to David,
6 David s', Whosoever smiteth the
17 David longed, and s', Oh that one
19 s', My God forbid it me, that I should
12:17 answered and s' unto them, If ye be
18 and he s', Thine are we, David, and on
13: 2 David s' unto all the congregation
4 congregation s' that they would do
14:10 the Lord s' unto him, Go up; for I
11 Then David s', God hath broken in
14 God s' unto him, Go not up after
15: 2 Then David s', None ought to carry
12 s' unto them, Ye are the chief of the
16:36 all the people s', Amen, and praised
17: 1 that David s' to Nathan the prophet,
2 Then Nathan s' unto David, Do all
16 David...s', Who am I, O Lord God,
23 for ever, and do as thou hast s'.
19: 2 David s', I will shew kindness unto
3 the children of Ammon s' to Hanun,
5 the king s', Tarry at Jericho until
12 he s', If the Syrians be too strong
21: 2 David s' to Joab and to the rulers
8 David s' unto God, I have sinned
11 Gad came to David, and s' unto him,
13 David s' unto Gad, I am in a great
15 s' to the angel that destroyed, It is
17 David s' unto God, Is it not I that
22 David s' to Ornan, Grant me the
22 Ornan s' unto David, Take it to thee,
24 And king David s' to Ornan, Nay;
22: 1 David s', This is the house of the
5 David s', Solomon my son is young
7 David s' to Solomon, My son, as for
11 thy God, as he hath s' of thee.
23: 5 instruments which I made, s' David,
25 David s', The Lord God of Israel
27:23 Lord had s' he would increase Israel
28: 2 and s', Hear me, my brethren, and
3 God s' unto me, Thou shalt not build
6 he s' unto me, Solomon thy son, he
19 All this, s' David, the Lord made me
20 David s' to Solomon...Be strong
29: 1 David...s' unto all the congregation,
10 David s', Blessed be thou, Lord God
20 And David s' to all the congregation,
2Ch 1: 7 and s' unto him, Ask what I shall
8 Solomon s' unto God, Thou hast
11 God s' to Solomon, Because this was
2:12 Huram s' moreover, Blessed be the
6: 1 Then s' Solomon, The Lord hath
1 Lord hath s' that he would dwell
4 he s', Blessed be the Lord God of
8 But the Lord s' to David my father,
14 And s', O Lord God of Israel, there
20 hast s'...thou wouldest put thy name
7:12 and s' unto him, I have heard thy
8:11 for he s', My wife shall not dwell in
9: 5 And she s' to the king, It was a true
10: 5 he s' unto them, Come again unto
9 he s' unto them, What advice give
12: 5 and s' unto them, Thus saith the
6 and they s', The Lord is righteous.
13: 4 and s', Hear me, thou Jeroboam, and
14: 7 he s' unto Judah, Let us build these
11 and s', Lord, it is nothing with thee
15: 2 and s' unto him, Hear ye me, Asa,
16: 7 and s' unto him, Because thou hast
18: 3 And Ahab...s' unto Jehoshaphat
4 And Jehoshaphat s' unto the king of
5 and s' unto them, Shall we go to
5 they s', Go up; for God will deliver

2Ch 18: 6 Jehoshaphat s·, Is there not here a
7 king of Israel s· unto Jehoshaphat,
7 Jehoshaphat s·, Let not the king say
8 and s·, Fetch quickly Micaiah the
10 and s·, Thus saith the Lord, With
13 Micaiah s·, As the Lord liveth, even
14 king s· unto him, Micaiah, shall we
14 And he s·, Go ye up, and prosper,
15 king s· unto him, How many times
16 he s·, I did see all Israel scattered
16 the Lord s·, These have no master:
17 the king of Israel s· to Jehoshaphat,
18 Again he s·, Therefore hear the word
19 the Lord s·, Who shall entice Ahab
20 the Lord, and s·, I will entice him.
20 the Lord s· unto him, Wherewith?
21 he s·, I will go out, and be a lying
21 the Lord s·, Thou shalt entice him,
23 and s·, Which way went the Spirit
24 Micaiah s·, Behold, thou shalt see
25 king of Israel s·, Take ye Micaiah,
27 Micaiah s·, If thou certainly return
27 And he s·, Hearken, all ye people.
29 king of Israel s· unto Jehoshaphat,
31 that they s·, It is the king of Israel.
33 therefore he s· to his chariot man,
19: 2 s· to king Jehoshaphat, Shouldest
6 And s· to the judges, Take heed what
20: 6 And s·, O Lord God of our fathers,
15 he s·, Hearken ye, all Judah, and ye
20 Jehoshaphat stood and s·, Hear me,
22: 9 s· they, he is the son of Jehoshaphat,
23: 3 he s· unto them, Behold, the king's
3 Lord hath s· of the sons of David.
11 him, and s·, God save the king.
13 Athaliah rent her clothes, and s·,
14 and s· unto them, Have her forth of
14 priest s·, Slay her not in the house
24: 5 and s· to them, Go out unto the cities
6 and s· unto him, Why hast thou not
20 and s· unto them, Thus saith God,
22 died, he s·, The Lord look upon it,
25: 9 Amaziah s· to the man of God, But
15 a prophet, which s· unto him, Why
16 the king s· unto him, Art thou made
16 the prophet forbare, and s·, I know
26: 18 and s· unto him, It appertaineth not
23 for they s·, He is a leper: and
28: 9 and s· unto them, Behold, because
13 And s· unto them, Ye shall not bring
23 he s·, Because the gods of the kings
29: 5 s· unto them, Hear me, ye Levites,
18 and s·, We have cleansed all the
31 Hezekiah answered and s·, Now ye
33: 4 Lord had s·, In Jerusalem shall my
7 God had s· to David and to Solomon
34: 15 Hilkiah answered and s· to Shaphan
35: 3 And s· unto the Levites that taught
23 the king s· to his servants, Have me
Ezr 2: 63 Tirshatha s· unto them, that they
4: 2 and s· unto them, Let us build with
3 s· unto them, Ye have nothing to do
5: 3 and s· thus unto them, Who hath
4 s· we unto them after this manner,
9 s· unto them thus, Who commanded
15 And s· unto him, Take these vessels,
8: 28 I s· unto them, Ye are holy unto
9: 6 And s·, O my God, I am ashamed
10: 2 answered and s· unto Ezra, We have
5 s· unto them, Ye have transgressed
12 the congregation answered and s·
12 As thou hast s·, so must we do.
Ne 1: 3 they s· unto me, The remnant that
5 And s·, I beseech thee, O Lord God
2: 2 the king s· unto me, Why is thy
3 s· unto the king, Let the king live
4 king s· unto me, For what dost thou
5 I s· unto the king, If it please the
6 the king s· unto me, (the queen also
7 I s· unto the king, If it please the
17 s· I unto them, Ye see the distress
18 they s·, Let us rise up and build.
19 s·, What is this thing that ye do?
20 s· unto them, The God of heaven,
4: 2 and s·, What do these feeble Jews?
3 he s·, Even that which they build,
10 And Judah s·, The strength of the
11 adversaries s·, They shall not know,
12 they s· unto us ten times, From all
14, 19 s· unto the nobles, and to...rulers,
22 the same time s· I unto the people,
5: 2 For there were that s·, We, our sons,
3 were that s·, We have mortgaged
4 were also that s·, We have borrowed
7 and s· unto them, Ye exact usury,
8 I s· unto them, We after our ability
9 Also I s·, It is not good that ye do:
12 Then s· they, We will restore them,
13 I shook my lap, and s·, So God shake
13 And all the congregation s·, Amen,
6: 10 he s·, Let us meet together in the
11 I s·, Should such a man as I flee?
7: 3 I s· unto them, Let not the gates of
65 And the Tirshatha s· unto them,
8: 9 s· unto all the people, This day is
10 he s· unto them, Go your way, eat
9: 5 s·, Stand up and bless the Lord your
18 and s·, This is thy God that brought
13: 11 and s·, Why is the house of God
17 and s· unto them, What evil thing is
21 and s· unto them, Why lodge ye
Es 1: 13 Then the king s· to the wise men,
2: 2 Then s· the king's servants that
3: 3 s· unto Mordecai, Why transgressest
8 Haman s· unto king Ahasuerus,
11 king s· unto Haman, The silver is

Es 5: 3 s· the king unto her, What wilt thou,
5 king s·, Cause Haman to make haste,
5 that he may do as Esther hath s·.
6 king s· unto Esther at the banquet
7 answered Esther, and s·, My petition
8 do to morrow as the king hath s·.
12 Haman s· moreover, Yea, Esther
14 s· Zeresh his wife and all his friends
6: 3 king s·, What honour and dignity
3 s· the king's servants that ministered
4 And the king s·, Who is in the court?
5 king's servants s· unto him, Behold,
5 And the king s·, Let him come in.
6 king s· unto him, What shall be done
10 the king s· to Haman, Make haste,
10 as thou hast s·, and do even so to
13 s· his wise men and Zeresh his wife
7: 2 And the king s· again unto Esther
3 Esther the queen answered and s·,
5 king Ahasuerus answered and s·
6 And Esther s·, The adversary and
8 s· the king, Will he force the queen
9 chamberlains, s· before the king,
9 the king s·, Hang him thereon.
8: 5 And s·, If it please the king, and if
7 king Ahasuerus s· unto Esther the
9: 12 the king s· unto Esther the queen,
13 Then s· Esther, If it please the king,
Job 1: 5 Job s·, It may be that my sons have
7 Lord s· unto Satan, Whence comest
7 Satan answered the Lord, and s·,
8 the Lord s· unto Satan, Hast thou
9 s·, Doth Job fear God for nought?
12 the Lord s· unto Satan, Behold, all
14 and s·, The oxen were plowing, and
16 and s·, The fire of God is fallen from
17 s·, The Chaldeans made out three
18 and s·, Thy sons and thy daughters
21 s·, Naked came I out of my mother's
2: 2 Lord s· unto Satan, From whence
2 Satan answered the Lord, and s·,
3 the Lord s· unto Satan, Hast thou
4 the Lord, and s·, Skin for skin, yea,
6 And the Lord s· unto Satan, Behold,
9 s· his wife unto him, Dost thou still
10 But he s· unto her, Thou speakest
3: 2 And Job spake, and s·,
3 the night in which it was s·, There
4: 1 the Temanite answered and s·,
6: 1 But Job answered and s·,
8: 1 answered Bildad the Shuhite, and s·,
9: 1 Then Job answered and s·,
22 This is one thing, therefore I s· it,
11: 1 Zophar the Naamathite, and s·,
4 thou hast s·, My doctrine is pure,
12: 1 And Job answered and s·,
15: 1 Eliphaz the Temanite, and s·,
16: 1 Then Job answered and s·,
17: 14 I have s· to corruption, Thou art
18: 1 answered Bildad...Shuhite, and s·,
19: 1 Then Job answered and s·,
20: 1 Zophar the Naamathite, and s·,
21: 1 But Job answered and s·,
22: 1 the Temanite answered and s·,
17 Which s· unto God, Depart from us:
23: 1 Then Job answered and s·,
25: 1 answered Bildad the Shuhite, and s·,
26: 1 But Job answered and s·,
27: 1 Job continued his parable, and s·,
28: 28 unto man he s·, Behold, the fear of
29: 1 Job continued his parable, and s·,
18 Then I s·, I shall die in my nest, and
31: 24 or have s· to the fine gold, Thou art
31 If the men of my tabernacle s· not,
32: 6 the Buzite answered and s·, I am
7 I s·, Days should speak, and
10 I s·, Hearken to me; I also will shew
17 I s·, I will answer also my part, I
34: 1 Furthermore Elihu answered and s·,
5 For Job hath s·, I am righteous: and
9 For he hath s·, It profiteth a man
31 Surely it is meet to be s· unto God,
35: 1 Elihu spake moreover, and s·,
36: 1 Elihu also proceeded, and s·,
38: 1 Job out of the whirlwind, and s·,
11 s·, Hitherto shalt thou come, but no
40: 1 the Lord answered Job, and s·,
3 Then Job answered the Lord, and s·,
6 Job out of the whirlwind, and s·,
42: 1 Then Job answered the Lord, and s·,
7 Lord s· to Eliphaz the Temanite,
Ps 2: 7 Lord hath s· unto me, Thou art my
10: 6 s· in his heart, I shall not be moved:
11 s· in his heart, God hath forgotten:
13 hath s· in his heart, Thou wilt not
12: 4 s·, With our tongue will we prevail;
14: 1 The fool hath s· in his heart, There
16: 2 s· unto the Lord, Thou art my Lord:
18: *title* from the hand of Saul: And he s·,
27: 8 heart s· unto thee, Thy face, Lord,
30: 6 I s·, I shall never be moved.
31: 14 O Lord: I s·, Thou art my God.
22 I s· in my haste, I am cut off from
32: 5 I s·, I will confess my transgressions
35: 21 s·, Aha, aha, our eye hath seen it.
38: 16 I s·, Hear me, lest otherwise they
39: 1 I s·, I will take heed to my ways,
40: 7 Then s· I, Lo, I come: in the volume
41: 4 I s·, Lord, be merciful unto me: heal
52: *title* s· unto him, David is come to the
53: 1 The fool hath s· in his heart, There
54: *title* and s· to Saul, Doth not David hide
55: 6 And I s·, Oh that I had wings like a
68: 22 The Lord s·, I will bring again from
74: 8 s· in their hearts, Let us destroy
75: 4 I s· unto the fools, Deal not

Ps 77: 10 And I s·, This is my infirmity: but I
78: 19 they s·, Can God furnish a table in
82: 6 I have s·, Ye are gods; and all of
83: 4 They have s·, Come, and let us cut
12 Who s·, Let us take to ourselves the
87: 5 of Zion it shall be s·, This and that
89: 2 I have s·, Mercy shall be built up for
94: 18 When I s·, My foot slippeth; thy
95: 10 s·, It is a people that do err in their
102: 24 I s·, O my God, take me not away in
106: 23 he s· that he would destroy them,
110: 1 Lord s· unto my Lord, Sit thou at
116: 11 I s· in my haste, All men are liars.
119: 57 I have s· that I would keep thy
122: 1 I was glad when they s· unto me,
126: 2 then s· they among the heathen, The
137: 7 who s·, Rase it, rase it, even to the
140: 6 I s· unto the Lord, Thou art my God:
142: 5 I s·, Thou art my refuge and my
Pr 4: 4 taught me also, and s· unto me,
7: 13 with an impudent face s· unto him,
25: 7 better it is that it be s· unto thee,
Ec 1: 10 any thing whereof it may be s·,
2: 1 I s· in mine heart, Go to now, I will
2 I s· of laughter, It is mad: and of
15 s· I in my heart, As it happeneth
15 I s· in my heart, that this also is
3: 17 I s· in mine heart, God shall judge
18 I s· in mine heart concerning the
7: 23 I s·, I will be wise; but it was far
8: 14 I s· that this also is vanity.
9: 16 Then s· I, Wisdom is better than
Ca 2: 10 My beloved spake, and s· unto me,
3: 3 to whom I s·, Saw ye him whom my
7: 8 I s·, I will go up to the palm tree, I
Isa 5: 9 In mine ears s· the Lord of hosts, Of a
6: 3 s·, Holy, holy, holy, is the Lord of
5 s· I, Woe is me! for I am undone;
7 s·, Lo, this hath touched thy lips;
8 Then s· I, Here am I: send me.
9 And he s·, Go, and tell this people,
11 Then s· I, Lord, how long? And he
7: 3 s· the Lord unto Isaiah, Go forth now
12 But Ahaz s·, I will not ask, neither
13 And he s·, Hear ye now, O house of
8: 1 Moreover the Lord s· unto me, Take
3 s· the Lord to me, Call his name
14: 13 thou hast s· in thine heart, I will
18: 4 For so the Lord s· unto me, I will
20: 3 And the Lord s·, Like as my servant
21: 6 For thus hath the Lord s· unto me,
9 And he answered and s·, Babylon is
12 watchman s·, The morning cometh,
16 For thus hath the Lord s· unto me,
22: 4 s· I, Look away from me; I will weep
23: 12 he s·, Thou shalt no more rejoice, O
24: 16 But I s·, My leanness, my leanness,
25: 9 it shall be s· in that day, Lo, this
28: 12 To whom he s·, This is the rest
15 Because ye have s·, We have made
29: 13 Wherefore the Lord s·, Forasmuch
30: 16 But ye s·, No; for we will flee upon
32: 5 nor the churl s· to be bountiful.
36: 4 Rabshakeh s· unto them, Say ye now
7 and s· to Judah and to Jerusalem,
10 the Lord s· unto me, Go up against
11 Then s· Eliakim and Shebna and
12 But Rabshakeh s·, Hath my master
13 s·, Hear ye the words of the great
37: 3 And they s· unto him, Thus saith
6 Isaiah s· unto them, Thus shall ye
24 and hast s·, By the multitude of my
38: 1 s· unto him, Thus saith the Lord,
3 and s·, Remember now, O Lord, I
10 I s· in the cutting off of my days, I
11 I s·, I shall not see the Lord, even
21 Isaiah had s·, Let them take a lump
22 Hezekiah also had s·, What is the
39: 3 s· unto him, What s· these men?
3 Hezekiah s·, They had come from a
4 Then s· he, What have they seen in
5 Then s· Isaiah to Hezekiah, Hear
8 Then s· Hezekiah to Isaiah, Good is
8 He s· moreover, For there shall be
40: 6 The voice s·[*], Cry. And he s·, What
41: 6 every one s· to his brother, Be of
9 s· unto thee, Thou art my servant;
45: 19 I s· not unto the seed of Jacob, Seek
47: 10 thou hast s·, None seeth me. Thy
10 thou hast s· in thine heart, I am,
49: 3 s· unto me, Thou art my servant, O
4 Then I s·, I have laboured in vain, I
6 he s·, It is a light thing that thou
14 But Zion s·, The Lord hath forsaken
51: 23 which have s· to my soul, Bow down,
63: 8 he s·, Surely they are my people,
65: 1 I s·, Behold me, behold me, unto a
66: 5 sake, s·, Let the Lord be glorified:
Jer 1: 6 Then s· I, Ah, Lord God! behold, I
7 the Lord s· unto me, Say not, I am
9 the Lord s· unto me, Behold, I have
11 I s·, I see a rod of an almond tree.
12 s· the Lord unto me, Thou hast well
13 I s·, I see a seething pot; and the
14 Then the Lord s· to me, Out of the
2: 6 Neither s· they, Where is the Lord
8 priests s· not, Where is the Lord?
3: 6 Lord s· also unto me in the days of
7 I s· after she had done all these
11 Lord s· unto me, The backsliding
19 But I s·, How shall I put thee among
19 I s·, Thou shalt call me, My father;
4: 10 Then s· I, Ah, Lord God! surely
11 time shall it be s· to this people
27 Lord s·, The whole land shall be
5: 4 Therefore I s·, Surely these are

Jer 5:12 belied the Lord, and s', It is not he;
6: 6 the Lord of hosts s', Hew ye down
16 they s', We will not walk therein.
17 But they s', We will not hearken.
10:19 but I s', Truly this is a grief, and I
11: 5 answered I, and s', So be it, O Lord.
6 Lord s' unto me, Proclaim all these
9 the Lord s' unto me, A conspiracy
12: 4 they s', He shall not see our last
13: 6 the Lord s' unto me, Arise, go to
14:11 s' the Lord unto me, Pray not for
13 Then s' I, Ah, Lord God! behold,
14 the Lord s' unto me, The prophets
15: 1 s' the Lord unto me, Though Moses
11 Lord s', Verily it shall be well with
16:14 shall no more be s', The Lord liveth,
17:19 s' the Lord unto me, Go, and stand
18:10 wherewith I s' I would benefit them.
12 And they s', There is no hope: but
18 Then s' they, Come, and let us
19:14 house; and s' to all the people,
20: 3 s' Jeremiah unto him, The Lord
9 Then I s', I will not make mention
21: 3 s' Jeremiah unto them, Thus shall
23:17 Lord hath s', Ye shall have peace;
25 I have heard what the prophets s',
24: 3 s' the Lord unto me, What seest
3 And I s', Figs; the good figs, very
25: 5 They s', Turn ye again now every
26:16 Then s' the princes and all the people
28: 5 Then the prophet Jeremiah s' unto
6 Even the prophet Jeremiah s',
15 Then s' the prophet Jeremiah unto
29:15 ye have s', The Lord hath raised us
32: 6 Jeremiah s', The word of the Lord
8 s' unto me, Buy my field, I pray
25 thou hast s' unto me, O Lord God,
35: 5 and I s' unto them, Drink ye wine.
6 But they s', We will drink no wine:
11 that we s', Come, and let us go to
18 Jeremiah s' unto the house of the
36:15 And they s' unto him, Sit down now,
16 s' unto Baruch, We will surely tell
19 Then s' the princes unto Baruch,
37:14 Then s' Jeremiah, It is false; I fall
17 s', Is there any word from the Lord?
17 Lord? And Jeremiah s', There is:
17 for, s' he, thou shalt be delivered
18 Jeremiah s' unto king Zedekiah,
38: 4 the princes s' unto the king, We
5 Then Zedekiah the king s', Behold,
12 Ebed-melech...s' unto Jeremiah,
14 and the king s' unto Jeremiah, I
15 Then Jeremiah s' unto Zedekiah, If
17 Then s' Jeremiah unto Zedekiah,
19 Zedekiah the king s' unto Jeremiah,
20 But Jeremiah s', They shall not
24 Then s' Zedekiah unto Jeremiah,
25 what thou hast s' unto the king,
25 also what the king s' unto thee:
40: 2 took Jeremiah, and s' unto him,
3 and done according as he hath s':
5 he s', Go back also to Gedaliah the
14 s' unto him, Dost thou certainly
16 the son of Ahikam s' unto
41: 6 he s' unto them, Come to Gedaliah
8 among them that s' unto Ishmael,
42: 2 s' unto Jeremiah the prophet, Let,
4 Jeremiah the prophet s' unto them,
5 Then they s' to Jeremiah, The Lord
9 s' unto them, Thus saith the Lord,
19 The Lord hath s' concerning you,
44:20, 24 Jeremiah s' unto all the people,
46:16 they s', Arise, and let us go against
50: 7 their adversaries s', We offend not,
51:61 Jeremiah s' to Seraiah, When thou
La 3:18 And I s', My strength and my hope
54 mine head; then I s', I am cut off.
4:15 they s' among the heathen, They
20 of whom we s', Under his shadow
Eze 2: 1 he s' unto me, Son of man, stand
3 he s' unto me, Son of man, I send
3: 1 Moreover he s' unto me, Son of man,
3 s' unto me, Son of man, cause thy
4 And he s' unto me, Son of man, go,
10 Moreover he s' unto me, Son of man,
22 he s' unto me, Arise, go forth into
24 me, and s' unto me, Go, shut thyself
4:13 And the Lord s', Even thus shall the
14 Then s' I, Ah Lord God! behold, my
15 Then he s' unto me, Lo, I have
16 Moreover he s' unto me, Son of man,
6:10 I have not s' in vain that I would
8: 5 s' he unto me, Son of man, lift up
6 He s' furthermore unto me, Son of
8 Then s' he unto me, Son of man,
9 he s' unto me, Go in, and behold the
12 Then s' he unto me, Son of man,
13 He s' also unto me, Turn thee yet
15 s' he unto me, Hast thou seen this,
17 he s' unto me, Hast thou seen this,
9: 4 Lord s' unto him, Go through the
5 to the others he s' in mine hearing,
7 he s' unto them, Defile the house,
8 face, and cried, and s', Ah Lord God!
9 Then s' he unto me, The iniquity of
10: 2 and s', Go in between the wheels,
11: 2 Then s' he unto me, Son of man,
5 fell upon me, and s' unto me, Speak;
5 Thus have ye s', O house of Israel:
13 a loud voice, and s', Ah Lord God!
15 inhabitants of Jerusalem have s',
12: 9 the rebellious house, s' unto thee,
13:12 shall it not be s' unto you, Where
16: 6, 6 I s' unto thee when thou wast in
20: 7 s' I unto them, Cast ye away every

Eze 20: 8 then I s', I will pour out my fury
13 then I s', I would pour out my fury
18 But I s' unto their children in the
21 then I s', I would pour out my fury
29 Then I s' unto them, What is the
49 Then s' I, Ah Lord God! they say of
21:17 fury to rest: I the Lord have s' it.
23:36 Lord s' moreover unto me; Son of
43 Then s' I unto her that was old in
24:19 the people s' unto me, Wilt thou
26: 2 Tyrus hath s' against Jerusalem,
27: 3 thou hast s', I am of perfect beauty.
28: 2 thou hast s', I am a God, I sit in the
29: 3 hath s', My river is mine own, and
9 he hath s', The river is mine, and I
35:10 Because thou hast s', These two
36: 2 the enemy hath s' against you, Aha,
20 when they s' to them, These are the
37: 3 And he s' unto me, Son of man, can
4 Again he s' unto me, Prophesy upon
9 Then s' he unto me, Prophesy unto
11 Then he s' unto me, Son of man,
40: 4 the man s' unto me, Son of man,
45 he s' unto me, This chamber, whose
41: 4 and he s' unto me, This is the most
22 he s' unto me, This is the table
42:13 Then s' he unto me, The north
43: 7 And he s' unto me, Son of man, the
18 And he s' unto me, Son of man, thus
44: 2 Then s' the Lord unto me; This gate
5 the Lord s' unto me, Son of man,
46:20 Then s' he unto me, This is the place
24 s' he unto me, These are the places
47: 6 And he s' unto me, Son of man, hast
8 s' he unto me, These waters issue
Da 1:10 prince of the eunuchs s' unto Daniel,
11 Then s' Daniel to Melzar, whom the
18 king had s' he should bring them
2: 3 king s' unto them, I have dreamed
5 the king answered and s' to the
7 They answered again and s', Let
8 The king answered and s', I know
10 and s', There is not a man upon the
15 and s' to Arioch the king's captain,
20 Daniel answered and s', Blessed be
24 he went and s' thus unto him;
25 and s' thus unto him, I have found a
26 The king answered and s' to Daniel,
27 and s', The secret which the king
47 king answered unto Daniel, and s',
3: 9 and s' to the king, Nebuchadnezzar,
14 Nebuchadnezzar spake and s' unto
16 s' to the king, O Nebuchadnezzar,
24 spake, and s' unto his counsellors,
24 They answered and s' unto the king,
25 He answered and s', Lo, I see four
26 and s', Shadrach, Meshach, and
28 Nebuchadnezzar spake, and s',
4:14 cried aloud, and s' thus, Hew down
19 king spake, and s', Belteshazzar,
19 Belteshazzar answered and s', My
30 The king spake and s', Is not this
5: 7 and s' to the wise men of Babylon,
10 the queen spake and s', O king, live
13 king spake and s' unto Daniel, Art
17 Then Daniel answered and s' before
6: 5 Then s' these men, We shall not
6 and s' thus unto him, King Darius
12 The king answered and s', the
13 answered they and s' before the
15 and s' unto the king, Know, O king,
16 spake and s' unto Daniel, Thy God
20 spake and s' to Daniel, O Daniel,
21 Then s' Daniel unto the king, O
7: 2 Daniel spake and s', I saw in my
5 they s' thus unto it, Arise, devour
23 Thus he s', The fourth beast shall
8:13 saint s' unto that certain saint
14 he s' unto me, Unto two thousand
16 and s', Gabriel, make this man to
17 but he s' unto me, Understand, O
19 And he s', Behold, I will make thee
9: 4 s', O Lord, the great and dreadful
22 s', O Daniel, I am now come forth to
10:11 And he s' unto me, O Daniel, a man
12 s' he unto me, Fear not, Daniel: for
16 s' unto him that stood before me,
19 s', O man greatly beloved, fear not:
19 and s', Let my Lord speak; for
20 s' he, Knowest thou wherefore I
12: 6 one s' to the man clothed in linen,
8 then s' I, O my Lord, what shall be
9 And he s', Go thy way, Daniel: for
Ho 1: 2 Lord s' to Hosea, Go, take unto thee
4 the Lord s' unto him, Call his name
6 And God s' unto him, Call her name
9 s' God, Call his name Lo-ammi:
10 where it was s' unto them, Ye are
10 there it shall be s' unto them, Ye
2: 5 she s', I will go after my lovers, that
12 she hath s', These are my rewards
3: 1 Then s' the Lord unto me, Go yet,
3 And I s' unto her, Thou shalt abide
12: 8 Ephraim s', Yet I am become rich,
Joe 2:32 be deliverance, as the Lord hath s',
Am 1: 2 he s', The Lord will roar from Zion,
7: 2 then I s', O Lord God, forgive, I
5 Then s' I, O Lord God, cease, I
8 Lord s' unto me, Amos, what seest
8 seest thou? And I s', A plumbline.
8 Then s' the Lord, Behold, I will set
12 Also Amaziah s' unto Amos, O thou
14 and s' to Amaziah, I was no prophet,
15 the Lord s' unto me, Go, prophesy,
8: 2 And he s', Amos, what seest thou?
2 And I s', A basket of summer fruit.

Am 8: 2 s' the Lord unto me, The end is
9: 1 he s', Smite the lintel of the door,
Jon 1: 6 s' unto him, What meanest thou, O
7 And they s' every one to his fellow,
8 Then s' they unto him, Tell us, we
9 he s' unto them, I am an Hebrew;
10 s' unto him, Why hast thou done
11 Then s' they unto him, What shall
12 he s' unto them, Take me up, and
14 and s', We beseech thee, O Lord, we
2: 2 And s', I cried by reason of mine
4 Then I s', I am cast out of thy sight;
3: 4 and he cried, and s', Yet forty days,
10 he had s' that he would do unto
4: 2 and s', I pray thee, O Lord, was not
4 Then s' the Lord, Doest thou well to
8 and s', It is better for me to die than
9 God s' to Jonah, Doest thou well
9 he s', I do well to be angry, even
10 Then s' the Lord, Thou hast had
Mic 3: 1 And I s', Hear, I pray you, O heads
7:10 shall cover her which s' unto me,
Hab 2: 2 Lord answered me, and s', Write
Zep 2:15 that s' in her heart, I am, and there
3: 7 I s', Surely thou wilt fear me, thou
16 that day it shall be s' to Jerusalem,
Hag 2:12 And the priests answered and s', No.
13 Then s' Haggai, If one that is
13 priests answered and s', It shall be
14 Haggai, and s', So is this people,
Zec 1: 6 they returned and s', Like as the
9 Then s' I, O my lord, what are
9 angel that talked with me s' unto
10 the myrtle trees answered and s',
11 stood among the myrtle trees, and s',
12 angel of the Lord answered and s',
14 that communed with me s' unto me,
19 I s' unto the angel that talked with
21 Then s' I, What come these to do?
2: 2 Then s' I, Whither goest thou? And
2 And he s' unto me, To measure
4 And s' unto him, Run, speak to this
3: 2 And the Lord s' unto Satan, The
4 And unto him he s', Behold, I have
5 And I s', Let them set a fair mitre
4: 2 And s' unto me, What seest thou?
2 And I s', I have looked, and behold
5 with me answered and s' unto me,
5 these be? And I s', No, my lord.
11 Then answered I, and s' unto him,
12 I answered again, and s' unto him,
13 he answered me and s', Knowest
13 these be? And I s', No, my lord.
14 Then s' he, These are the two
5: 2 he s' unto me, What seest thou?
3 s' he unto me, This is the curse
5 s' unto me, Lift up now thine eyes,
6 And I s', What is it? And he s',
6 He s' moreover, This is their
8 And he s', This is wickedness. And
10 s' I to the angel that talked with
11 And he s' unto me, To build it an
6: 4 I answered and s' unto the angel
5 the angel answered and s' unto me,
7 and he s', Get you hence, walk to
11: 9 Then s' I, I will not feed you: that
12 And I s' unto them, if ye think good,
13 the Lord s' unto me, Cast it unto
15 And the Lord s' unto me, Take unto
Mal 1:13 Ye s' also, Behold, what a weariness
3: 7 But ye s', Wherein shall we return?
14 Ye have s', It is vain to serve God:
M't 2: 5 they s' unto him, In Bethlehem of
8 and s', Go and search diligently
3: 7 he s' unto them, O generation of
15 s' unto him, Suffer it to be so now:
4: 3 he s', If thou be the Son of God,
4 Jesus answered and s', It is written,
7 Jesus s' unto him, It is written
5:21, 27 it was s' by them of old time,
31 It hath been s', Whosoever shall put
33 it hath been s' by them of old time,
38 it hath been s', An eye for an eye,
43 it hath been s', Thou shalt love thy
8: 8 centurion answered and s', Lord, I
10 s' to them that followed, Verily I
13 Jesus s' unto the centurion, Go thy
19 s' unto him, Master, I will follow
21 another of his disciples s' unto him,
22 But Jesus s' unto him, Follow me;
32 And he s' unto them, Go. And when
9: 2 s' unto the sick of the palsy; Son,
3 of the scribes s' within themselves,
4 Jesus knowing their thoughts s',
11 s' unto his disciples, Why eateth
12 he s' unto them, They that be whole
15 Jesus s' unto them, Can the children
21 For she s' within herself, If I may
22 he s', Daughter, be of good comfort;
24 He s' unto them, Give place: for
28 this? They s' unto him, Yea, Lord.
34 Pharisees s', He casteth out devils
11: 3 And s' unto him, Art thou he that
4 s' unto them, Go and shew John
25 and s', I thank thee, O Father, Lord
12: 2 Pharisees saw it, they s' unto him,
3 he s' unto them, Have ye not read
11 he s' unto them, What man shall
23 and s', Is not this the son of David?
24 they s', This fellow doth not cast
25 and s' unto them, Every kingdom
39 answered and s' unto them, An evil
47 one s' unto him, Behold, thy mother
48 s' unto him that told him, Who is
49 and s', Behold my mother and my
13:10 and s' unto him, Why speakest thou

M't 13: 11 and s· unto them, Because it is given
27 s· unto him, Sir, didst not thou sow
28 He s· unto them, An enemy hath
28 The servants s· unto him, Wilt
29 But he s·, Nay; lest while ye gather
37 and s· unto them, He that soweth
52 s· he unto them, Therefore every
54 and s·, Whence hath this man this
57 s· unto them, A prophet is not
14: 2 s· unto his servants, This is John
4 John s· unto him, It is not lawful
8 s·, Give me here John Baptist's
16 Jesus s· unto them, They need not
18 He s·, Bring them hither to me.
28 Peter...s·, Lord, if it be thou, bid
29 And he s·, Come. And when Peter
31 and s· unto him, O thou of little
15: 3 and s· unto them, Why do ye also
10 s· unto them, Hear, and understand:
12 disciples, and s· unto him, Knowest
13 But he answered and s·, Every plant,
15 answered Peter and s· unto him,
16 Jesus s·, Are ye also yet without
24 answered and s·, I am not sent but
26 and s·, It is not meet to take the
27 she s·, Truth, Lord: yet the dogs
28 answered and s· unto her, O woman,
32 and s·, I have compassion on the
34 And they s·, Seven, and a few little
16: 2 and s· unto them, When it is evening,
6 Jesus s· unto them, Take heed and
8 he s· unto them, O ye of little faith,
14 they s·, Some say that thou art John
16 Peter answered and s·, Thou art
17 Jesus...s· unto him, Blessed art thou,
23 and s· unto Peter, Get thee behind
24 s· Jesus unto his disciples, If any
17: 4 and s· unto Jesus, Lord, it is good
5 a voice out of the cloud, which s·,
7 and s·, Arise, and be not afraid.
11 Jesus...s· unto them, Elias truly
17 Jesus answered and s·, O faithless
19 s·, Why could not we cast him out?
20 And Jesus s· unto them, Because
22 Jesus s· unto them, The Son of man
24 and s·, Doth not your master pay
18: 3 And s·, Verily I say unto you, Except
21 Peter to him, and s·, Lord, how oft
32 him, s· unto him, O thou wicked
19: 4 and s· unto them, Have ye not read,
5 And s·, For this cause shall a man
11 But he s· unto them, All men cannot
14 But Jesus s·, Suffer little children,
16 one came and s· unto him, Good
17 he s· unto him, Why callest thou me
18 Jesus s·, Thou shalt do no murder,
21 Jesus s· unto him, If thou wilt be
23 s· Jesus unto his disciples, Verily
26 and s· unto them, With men this is
27 answered Peter and s· unto him,
28 Jesus s· unto them, Verily I say
20: 4 And s· unto them; Go ye also into
13 and s·, Friend, I do thee no wrong:
17 apart in the way, and s· unto them,
21 And he s· unto her, What wilt thou?
22 Jesus answered and s·, Ye know not
25 Jesus called them unto him, and s·,
32 stood still, and called them, and s·,
21: 11 the multitude s·, This is Jesus the
13 And s· unto them, It is written, My
16 s· unto him, Hearest thou what
19 and s· unto it, Let no fruit grow on
21 Jesus answered and s· unto them,
23 and s·, By what authority doest
24 Jesus...s· unto them, I also will ask
27 Jesus, and s·, We cannot tell.
27 he s· unto them, Neither tell I you
28 and s·, Son, go work to day in my
29 He answered and s·, I will not: but
30 came to the second, and s· likewise.
30 And he answered and s·, I go, sir:
38 they s· among themselves, This is
22: 1 them again by parables, and s·,
13 s· the king to the servants, Bind
18 s·, Why tempt ye me, ye hypocrites?
24 Moses s·, If a man die, having no
29 Jesus...s· unto them, Ye do err,
37 Jesus s· unto him, Thou shalt love
44 Lord s· unto my Lord, Sit thou on
24: 2 Jesus s· unto them, See ye not all
4 Jesus...s· unto them, Take heed
25: 8 foolish s· unto the wise, Give us of
12 and s·, Verily I say unto you, I know
21 His lord s· unto him, Well done,
22 and s·, Lord, thou deliveredst unto
23 His lord s· unto him, Well done,
24 and s·, Lord, I knew thee that thou
26 His lord...s· unto him, Thou wicked
26: 1 sayings, he s· unto his disciples,
5 But they s·, Not on the feast day,
10 he s· unto them, Why trouble ye
15 s· unto them, What will ye give me,
18 he s·, Go into the city to such a man,
21 as they did eat, he s·, Verily I say
23 answered and s·, He that dippeth
25 Then Judas...answered and s·,
25 Master, is it I? He s· unto him,
25 unto him, Thou hast s·.
26 and s·, Take, eat; this is my body.
33 Peter...s· unto him, Though all men
34 Jesus s· unto him, Verily I say
35 Peter s· unto him, Though I...die
35 Likewise also s· all the disciples.
49 and s·, Hail, master; and kissed
50 And Jesus s· unto him, Friend,
52 s· Jesus unto him, Put up again
M't 26: 55 hour s· Jesus to the multitudes,
61 And s·, This fellow
61 This fellow s·, I am able to
62 and s· unto him, Answerest thou
63 high priest...s· unto him, I adjure
64 Jesus saith unto him, Thou hast s·:
66 and s·, He is guilty of death.
71 maid saw him, and s· unto them
73 and s· to Peter, Surely thou also
75 word of Jesus, which s· unto him,
27: 4 And they s·, What is that to us?
6 took the silver pieces, and s·, It is
11 Jesus s· unto him, Thou sayest.
13 s· Pilate unto him, Hearest thou
17 Pilate s· unto them, Whom will ye
21 governor...s· unto them, Whether
21 unto you? They s·, Barabbas.
23 the governor s·, Why, what evil
25 and s·, His blood be on us, and on
41 with the scribes and elders, s·,
43 for he s·, I am the Son of God.
47 s·, This man calleth for Elias.
49 The rest s·, Let be, let us see
63 we remember that that deceiver s·,
65 Pilate s· unto them, Ye have a
28: 5 angel...s· unto the women, Fear not
6 is not here: for he is risen, as he s·.
10 Then s· Jesus unto them, Be not
M'r 1: 17 Jesus s· unto them, Come ye after
37 they s· unto him, All men seek for
38 he s· unto them, Let us go into the
2: 5 he s· unto the sick of the palsy, Son,
8 he s· unto them, Why reason ye
14 and s· unto him, Follow me. And
16 they s· unto his disciples, How is it
19 And Jesus s·...Can the children
24 the Pharisees s· unto him, Behold,
25 he s· unto them, Have ye never read
27 s· unto them, The sabbath was made
3: 21 for they s·, He is beside himself.
22 scribes...s·, He hath Beelzebub,
23 and s· unto them in parables, How
30 Because they s·, He hath an unclean
32 s· unto him, Behold, thy mother
34 and s·, Behold my mother and my
4: 2 and s· unto them in his doctrine,
9 he s· unto them, He that hath ears
11 he s· unto them, Unto you it is given
13 he s· unto them, Know ye not this
21 he s· unto them, Is a candle brought
24 he s· unto them, Take heed what
26 And he s·, So is the kingdom of God,
30 And he s·, Whereunto shall we liken
39 and s· unto the sea, Peace, be still.
40 s· unto them, Why are ye so fearful?
41 s· one to another, What manner of
5: 7 and s·, What have I to do with
8 s· unto him, Come out of the man,
28 For she s·, If I may touch but his
30 and s·, Who touched my clothes?
31 disciples s· unto him, Thou seest
34 he s· unto her, Daughter, thy faith
35 certain which s·, Thy daughter is
41 and s· unto her, Talitha cumi;
6: 4 Jesus s· unto them, A prophet is not
10 s· unto them, In what place soever
14 s·, That John the Baptist was risen
15 Others s·, That it is Elias. And
15 And others s·, That it is a prophet,
16 he s·, It is John, whom I beheaded:
18 John had s· unto Herod, It is not
22 the daughter of the s· Herodias
22 king s· unto the damsel, Ask of me
24 and s· unto her mother, What shall I
24 she s·, The head of John the Baptist.
31 he s· unto them, Come ye yourselves
35 and s·, This is a desert place, and
37 and s· unto them, Give ye them to
7: 6 and s· unto them, Well hath Esaias
9 he s· unto them, Full well ye reject
10 For Moses s·, Honour thy father
14 he s· unto them, Hearken unto me
20 he s·, That which cometh out of the
27 Jesus s· unto her, Let the children
28 and s· unto him, Yes, Lord: yet the
29 s· unto her, For this saying go thy
8: 5 loaves have ye? And they s·, Seven.
20 took ye up? And they s·, Seven.
21 he s· unto them, How is it that ye
24 and s·, I see men as trees, walking.
34 he s· unto them, Whosoever will
9: 1 he s· unto them,...there be some
5 and s· to Jesus, Master, it is good
17 and s·, Master, I have brought
21 unto him? And he s·, Of a child.
23 Jesus s· unto him, If thou canst
24 and s· with tears, Lord, I believe;
26 insomuch that many s·, He is dead.
29 And he s· unto them, This kind
31 and s· unto them, The Son of man
36 him in his arms, he s· unto them,
39 But Jesus s·, Forbid him not: for
10: 3 and s· unto them, What did Moses
4 And they s·, Moses suffered to write
5 Jesus answered and s· unto them,
14 and s· unto them, Suffer the little
18 Jesus s· unto him, Why callest thou
20 and s· unto him, Master, all these
21 s· unto him, One thing thou lackest:
29 And Jesus answered and s·, Verily
36 And he s· unto them, What would
37 They s· unto him, Grant unto us
38 But Jesus s· unto them, Ye know
39 And they s· unto him, We can.
39 And Jesus s· unto them, Ye shall
51 Jesus answered and s· unto him,
M'r 10: 51 The blind man s· unto him, Lord,
52 And Jesus s· unto him, Go thy way;
11: 5 them that stood there s· unto them,
6 s· unto them even as Jesus had
14 Jesus answered and s· unto it, No
29 Jesus answered and s· unto them,
33 they answered and s· unto Jesus,
12: 7 husbandmen s· among themselves,
15 s· unto them, Why tempt ye me?
16 And they s· unto him, Cæsar's.
17, 24 Jesus answering s· unto them,
32 scribe s· unto him, Well, Master,
32 thou hast s· the truth: for there is
34 he s· unto him, Thou art not far
35 Jesus answered and s·, while he
36 David...s· by the Holy Ghost, The
36 The Lord s· to my Lord, Sit thou on
38 And he s· unto them in his doctrine,
13: 2 Jesus answering s· unto him, Seest
14: 2 But they s·, Not on the feast day,
4 and s·, Why was this waste of the
6 And Jesus s·, Let her alone; why
12 his disciples s· unto him, Where
16 and found as he had s· unto them:
18 Jesus s·, Verily I say unto you, One
19 one, Is it I? and another s·, Is it I?
20 he answered and s· unto them, It
22 gave to them, and s·, Take, eat:
24 he s· unto them, This is my blood
29 But Peter s· unto him, Although
31 wise. Likewise also s· they all.
36 And he s·, Abba, Father, all things
48 Jesus answered and s· unto them,
61 s· unto him, Art thou the Christ,
62 And Jesus s·, I am: and ye shall
67 and s·, And thou also wast with
70 they that stood by s· again to Peter,
72 the word that Jesus s· unto him,
15: 2 he answering s· unto him, Thou
12 s· again unto them, What will ye
14 Pilate s· unto them, Why, what evil
31 chief priests mocking s· among
35 heard it, s·, Behold, he calleth Elias.
39 he s·, Truly this man was the Son
16: 3 s· among themselves, Who shall
7 ye see him, as he s· unto you.
8 neither s· they any thing to any
15 he s· unto them, Go ye into all the
Lu 1: 13 the angel s· unto him, Fear not,
18 And Zacharias s· unto the angel,
19 angel...s· unto him, I am Gabriel,
28 angel came in unto her, and s·, Hail,
30 And the angel s· unto her, Fear not,
34 s· Mary unto the angel, How shall
35 angel...s· unto her, The Holy Ghost
38 Mary s·, Behold the handmaid of
42 s·, Blessed art thou among women,
46 Mary s·, My soul doth magnify the
60 his mother answered and s·, Not so;
61 they s· unto her, There is none of
2: 10 the angel s· unto them, Fear not:
15 shepherds s· one to another, Let us
24 which is s· in the law of the Lord,
28 his arms, and blessed God, and s·,
34 s· unto Mary his mother, Behold,
48 his mother s· unto him, Son, why
49 he s· unto them, How is it that ye
3: 7 Then s· he to the multitude that
12 s· unto him, Master, what shall we
13 he s· unto them, Exact no more
14 he s· unto them, Do violence to no
22 voice came from heaven, which s·,
4: 3 the devil s· unto him, If thou be the
6 the devil s· unto him, All this power
8 Jesus answered and s· unto him,
9 s· unto him, If thou be the Son of
12 Jesus answering s· unto him, It is
12 It is s·, Thou shalt not tempt the
22 they s·, Is not this Joseph's son?
23 he s· unto them, Ye will surely say
24 And he s·, Verily I say unto you,
43 he s· unto them, I must preach the
5: 4 he s· unto Simon, Launch out into
5 And Simon answering s· unto him,
10 And Jesus s· unto Simon, Fear not;
20 he s· unto him, Man, thy sins are
22 s· unto them, What reason ye in
24 (he s· unto the sick of the palsy,) I
27 and he s· unto him, Follow me.
31 And Jesus answering s· unto them,
33 s· unto him, Why do the disciples
34 he s· unto them, Can ye make the
6: 2 Pharisees s· unto them, Why do ye
3 Jesus answering them s·, Have ye
5 he s· unto them, That the Son of
8 and s· to the man which had the
9 s· Jesus unto them, I will ask you
10 he s· unto the man, Stretch forth
20 and s·, Blessed be ye poor: for
7: 9 s· unto the people that followed
13 on her, and s· unto her, Weep not.
14 he s·, Young man, I say unto thee,
20 they s·, John Baptist hath sent us
22 Jesus answering s· unto them, Go
31 the Lord s·, Whereunto then shall
40 And Jesus answering s· unto him,
43 Simon answered and s·, I suppose
43 he s· unto him, Thou hast rightly
44 and s· unto Simon, Seest thou this
48 s· unto her, Thy sins are forgiven.
50 he s· to the woman, Thy faith hath
8: 8 when he had s· these things, he
10 And he s·, Unto you it is given to
20 was told him by certain which s·,
21 and s· unto them, My mother and
22 and he s· unto them, Let us go over

Lu 8:25 s' unto them, Where is your faith?
28 and with a loud voice s',What have
30 And he s', Legion: because many
45 And Jesus s', Who touched me?
45 they that were with him s', Master,
46 Jesus s', Somebody hath touched
48 he s' unto her, Daughter, be of good
52 he s', Weep not; she is not dead,
9: 3 And he s' unto them, Take nothing
7 because that it was s' of some, that
9 Herod s', John have I beheaded:
12 came the twelve, and s' unto him,
13 But he s' unto them, Give ye them
13 And they s', We have no more but
14 he s' to his disciples, Make them
19 answering s', John the Baptist;
20 He s' unto them, But whom say ye
20 Peter answering s', The Christ of
23 And he s' to them all, If any man
33 Peter s' unto Jesus, Master, it is
33 for Elias: not knowing what he s'.
41 Jesus answering s', O faithless
43 Jesus did, he s' unto his disciples,
48 And s' unto them, Whosoever shall
49 John answered and s', Master, we
50 Jesus s' unto him, Forbid him not:
54 they s', Lord, wilt thou that we
55 s', Ye know not what manner of
57 a certain man s' unto him, Lord, I
58 And Jesus s' unto him, Foxes have
59 And he s' unto another, Follow me.
59 But he s', Lord, suffer me first to
60 Jesus s' unto him, Let the dead
61 another also s', Lord, I will follow
62 Jesus s' unto him, No man, having
10: 2 Therefore s' he unto them, The
18 he s' unto them, I beheld Satan
21 s', I thank thee, O Father, Lord of
23 s' privately, Blessed are the eyes
26 He s' unto him, What is written in
27 he answering s', Thou shalt love
28 And he s' unto him, Thou hast
29 to justify himself, s' unto Jesus,
30 Jesus answering s', A certain man
35 and s' unto him, Take care of him;
37 And he s', He that shewed mercy on
37 Then s' Jesus unto him, Go, and
40 came to him, and s', Lord, dost thou
41 And Jesus answered and s' unto her,
11: 1 one of his disciples s' unto him,
2 he s' unto them, When ye pray, say
5 And he s' unto them, Which of you
15 But some of them s', He casteth out
17 s' unto them, Every kingdom
27 s' unto him, Blessed is the womb
28 But he s', Yea rather, blessed are
39 And the Lord s' unto him, Now do
45 lawyers, and s' unto him, Master,
46 And he s', Woe unto you also, ye
49 also s' the wisdom of God, I will
53 as he s' these things unto them,
12:13 one of the company s' unto him,
14 he s' unto him, Man, who made me
15 And he s' unto them, Take heed,
18 And he s', This will I do: I will pull
20 God s' unto him, Thou fool, this
22 he s' unto his disciples, Therefore
41 Peter s' unto him, Lord, speakest
42 And the Lord s', Who then is that
54 he s' also to the people, When ye
13: 2 And Jesus answering s' unto them,
7 Then s' he unto the dresser of his
8 s' unto him, Lord, let it alone this
12 and s' unto her, Woman, thou art
14 s' unto the people, There are six
15 s', Thou hypocrite, doth not each
17 when he had s' these things, all
18 s' he, Unto what is the kingdom of
20 And again he s', Whereunto shall
23 s' one unto him, Lord, are there few
23 that be saved? And he s' unto them,
32 he s' unto them, Go ye, and tell that
14:12 s' he also to him that bade him,
15 he s' unto him, Blessed is he that
16 s' he unto him, A certain man made
18 s' unto him, I have bought a piece
19 another s', I have bought five yoke
20 another s', I have married a wife,
21 s' to his servant, Go out quickly
22 servant s', Lord, it is done as thou
23 lord s' unto the servant, Go out into
25 and he turned, and s' unto them,
15:11 he s', A certain man had two sons:
12 the younger of them s' to his father,
17 he s', How many hired servants of
21 the son s' unto him, Father, I have
22 the father s' to his servants, Bring
27 And he s' unto him, Thy brother is
29 s' to his father, Lo, these many
31 he s' unto him, Son, thou art ever
16: 1 s' also unto his disciples, There
2 s' unto him, How is it that I hear
3 steward s' within himself, What
5 s' unto the first, How much owest
6 he s', An hundred measures of oil.
6 And he s' unto him, Take thy bill,
7 Then s' he to another, And how
7 And he s', An hundred measures of
7 he s' unto him, Take thy bill, and
15 s' unto them, Ye are they which
24 he cried and s', Father Abraham,
25 But Abraham s', Son, remember
27 he s', I pray thee therefore, father,
30 And he s', Nay, father Abraham:
31 And he s' unto him, If they hear not
17: 1 Then s' he unto the disciples, It is

Lu 17: 5 apostles s' unto the Lord, Increase
6 Lord s', If ye had faith as a grain
13 s', Jesus, Master, have mercy on
14 s' unto them, Go shew yourselves
17 Jesus answering s', Were there not
19 he s' unto him, Arise, go thy way:
20 come, he answered them and s',
22 And he s' unto the disciples, The
37 they answered and s' unto him,
37 he s' unto them, Wheresoever the
18: 4 afterward he s' within himself,
6 the Lord s', Hear what the unjust
16 s', Suffer little children to come
19 Jesus s' unto him, Why callest thou
21 he s', All these have I kept from my
22 he s' unto him, yet lackest thou one
24 he s', How hardly shall they that
26 they that heard it s', Who then can
27 s', The things which are impossible
28 Then Peter s', Lo, we have left all,
29 And he s' unto them, Verily I say
31 s' unto them, Behold, we go up to
41 And he s', Lord, that I may receive
42 And Jesus s' unto him, Receive thy
19: 5 and s' unto him, Zacchæus, make
8 and s' unto the Lord; Behold, Lord,
9 and Jesus s' unto him, This day is
12 He s' therefore, A certain nobleman
13 s' unto them, Occupy till I come.
17 And he s' unto him, Well, thou good
19 he s' likewise to him, Be thou also
24 he s' unto them that stood by, Take
25 they s' unto him, Lord, he hath
32 found even as he had s' unto them.
33 the owners thereof s' unto them,
34 And they s', The Lord hath need of
39 the multitude s' unto him, Master,
40 he answered and s' unto them, I tell
20: 3 he answered and s' unto them, I will
8 Jesus s' unto them, Neither tell
13 Then s' the lord of the vineyard,
16 when they heard it, they s', God
17 s', What is this then that is written,
23 s' unto them, Why tempt ye me?
24 it? They answered and s', Cæsar's.
25 he s' unto them, Render therefore
34 Jesus answering s' unto them, The
39 certain of the scribes answering s',
39 Master, thou hast well s'.
41 And he s' unto them, How say they
42 The Lord s' unto my Lord, Sit thou
45 the people he s' unto his disciples,
21: 3 And he s', Of a truth I say unto you,
5 with goodly stones and gifts, he s',
8 And he s', Take heed that ye be not
10 Then s' he unto them, Nation
22: 9 And they s' unto him, Where wilt
10 And he s' unto them, Behold, when
13 and found as he had s' unto them:
15 And he s' unto them, With desire
17 the cup, and gave thanks, and s',
25 And he s' unto them, The kings of
31 And the Lord s', Simon, Simon,
33 he s' unto him, Lord, I am ready
34 And he s', I tell thee, Peter, the
35 And he s' unto them, When I sent
35 any thing? And they s', Nothing.
36 Then s' he unto them, But now, he
38 And they s', Lord, behold, here are
38 And he s' unto them, It is enough.
40 he s' unto them, Pray that ye enter
46 And s' unto them, Why sleep ye?
48 But Jesus s' unto him, Judas,
49 they s' unto him, Lord, shall we
51 Jesus answered and s', Suffer ye
52 Jesus s' unto the chief priests, and
56 s', This man was also with him.
58 and s', Thou art also of them.
58 And Peter s', Man, I am not.
60 And Peter s', Man, I know not what
61 how he had s' unto him, Before the
67 And he s' unto them, If I tell you,
70 s' they all, Art thou then the Son
70 he s' unto them, Ye say that I am.
71 they s', What need we any further
23: 3 he answered him and s', Thou
4 Then s' Pilate to the chief priests
14 S' unto them, Ye have brought this
22 And he s' unto them the third time,
28 s', Daughters of Jerusalem, weep
34 Then s' Jesus, Father, forgive
42 he s' unto Jesus, Lord, remember
43 Jesus s' unto him, Verily I say
46 had cried with a loud voice, he s',
46 having s' thus, he gave up the ghost.
24: 5 they s' unto them, Why seek ye the
17 he s' unto them, What manner of
18 Cleopas, answering s' unto him, Art
19 And he s' unto them, What things?
19 they s' unto him, concerning Jesus
23 angels, which s' that he was alive.
24 it even so as the women had s':
25 he s' unto them, O fools, and slow
32 they s' one to another, Did not our
38 s' unto them, Why are ye troubled?
41 he s' unto them, Have ye here any
44 he s' unto them, These are the
46 s' unto them, Thus it is written,
Joh 1:22 s' they unto him, Who art thou?
23 He s', I am the voice of one crying
23 the Lord, as s' the prophet Esaias.
25 s' unto him, Why baptizest thou
30 This is he of whom I s', After me
33 the same s' unto me, Upon whom
38 They s' unto him, Rabbi, (which is
42 he s', Thou art Simon the son of

Joh 1:46 Nathanael s' unto him, Can there
48, 50 Jesus answered and s' unto him
50 Because I s' unto thee, I saw thee
2:16 And s' unto them that sold doves,
18 answered the Jews and s' unto him,
19 Jesus answered and s' unto them,
20 Then s' the Jews, Forty and six
22 that he had s' this unto them;
22 and the word which Jesus had s'.
3: 2 s' unto him, Rabbi, we know that
3 Jesus answered and s' unto him,
7 s' unto thee, Ye must be born again.
9 Nicodemus answered and s' unto
10 Jesus answered and s' unto him,
26 came unto John, and s' unto him,
27 John answered and s', A man can
28 that I s', I am not the Christ, but
4:10, 13 Jesus answered and s' unto her,
17 The woman answered and s', I
17 Jesus s' unto her, Thou hast well
17 Thou hast well s', I have no
27 yet no man s', What seekest thou?
32 But he s' unto them, I have meat to
33 s' the disciples one to another,
42 s' unto the woman, Now we believe,
48 Then s' Jesus unto him, Except ye
52 they s' unto him, Yesterday at the
53 in the which Jesus s' unto him, Thy
5:10 The Jews therefore s' unto him
11 the same s' unto me, Take up thy
12 that which s' unto thee, Take up
14 s' unto him,...thou art made whole:
18 s' also that God was his Father,
19 answered Jesus and s' unto them,
6: 6 And this he s' to prove him: for he
10 Jesus s', Make the men sit down.
12 he s' unto his disciples, Gather up
14 s', This is of a truth that prophet
25 they s' unto him, Rabbi, when
26 Jesus answered them and s', Verily,
28 s' they unto him, What shall we do,
29 Jesus answered and s' unto them,
30 s' therefore unto him, What sign
32 Then Jesus s' unto them, Verily,
34 s' they unto him, Lord, evermore
35 Jesus s' unto them, I am the bread
36 But I s' unto you, That ye also have
41 because he s', I am the bread which
42 they s', Is not this Jesus, the son
43 s' unto them, Murmur not among
53 Jesus s' unto them, Verily, verily, I
59 These things s' he in the synagogue,
60 had heard this, s', This is an hard
61 s' unto them, Doth this offend you?
65 And he s',...that no man can come
65 Therefore s' I unto you, that no
67 s' Jesus unto the twelve, Will ye
7: 3 His brethren therefore s' unto him,
6 Then Jesus s' unto them, My time
9 he had s' these words unto them,
11 at the feast, and s', Where is he?
12 him: for some s', He is a good man:
12 others s', Nay; but he deceiveth the
16 and s', My doctrine is not mine, but
20 The people...s', Thou hast a devil:
21 s' unto them, I have done one work,
25 Then s' some of them of Jerusalem,
31 and s', When Christ cometh, will he
33 s' Jesus unto them, Yet a little
35 s' the Jews among themselves,
36 manner of saying is this that he s',
38 as the scripture hath s', out of his
40 s', Of a truth this is the Prophet.
41 Others s', This is the Christ. But
41 some s', Shall Christ come out of
42 scripture s', That Christ cometh
45 and they s' unto them, Why have ye
52 and s' unto him, Art thou also of
8: 6 This they s', tempting him, that
7 up himself, and s' unto them,
10 he s' unto her, Woman, where are
11 She s', No man, Lord. And
11 Jesus s',...Neither do I condemn
13 Pharisees therefore s' unto him,
14 s' unto them, Though I bear record
19 s' they unto him, Where is thy
21 s' Jesus again unto them, I go my
22 s' the Jews, Will he kill himself?
23 s' unto them, Ye are from beneath;
24 I s' therefore unto you, that ye
25 s' they unto him, Who art thou?
25 Even the same that I s' unto you
28 s' Jesus unto them, When ye have
31 Then s' Jesus to those Jews which
39 and s' unto him, Abraham is our
41 s' they to him, We be not born of
42 Jesus s' unto them, If God were
48 s' unto him, Say we not well that
52 s' the Jews unto him, Now we know
57 s' the Jews unto him, Thou art not
58 Jesus s' unto them, Verily, verily, I
9: 7 s' unto him, Go, wash in the pool of
8 s', Is not this he that sat and
9 Some s', This is he: others
9 others s', He is like him:
9 He is like him: but he s', I am he.
10 s' they unto him, How were thine
11 and s', A man that is called Jesus
11 and s' unto me, Go to the pool of
12 Then s' they unto him, Where is he?
12 Where is he? He s', I know not.
15 He s' unto them, He put clay upon
16 s' some of the Pharisees, This man
16 Others s', How can a man that is a
17 eyes? He s', He is a prophet.
20 s', We know that this is our son,

Joh 9:23 Therefore s' his parents, He is of
24 s' unto him, Give God the praise:
25 and s', Whether he be a sinner or
26 s' they to him again, What did he
28 him, and s', Thou art his disciple;
30 man answered and s' unto them,
34 They...s' unto him, Thou wast
35 s' unto him, Dost thou believe on
36 answered and s', Who is he, Lord,
37 Jesus s' unto him, Thou hast both
38 And he s', Lord, I believe. And he
39 Jesus s', For judgment I am come
40 and s' unto him, Are we blind also?
41 Jesus s' unto them, If ye were
10: 7 s' Jesus unto them again, Verily,
20 many of them s', He hath a devil,
21 Others s', These are not the words
24 s' unto him, How long dost thou
26 not of my sheep, as I s' unto you.
34 in your law, I s', Ye are gods?
36 because I s', I am the Son of God?
41 him, and s', John did no miracle:
11: 4 he s', This sickness is not unto
11 These things s' he: and after that
12 s' his disciples, Lord, if he sleep, he
14 s' Jesus unto them plainly, Lazarus
16 Then s' Thomas, which is called
21 s' Martha unto Jesus, Lord, if thou
25 s' unto her, I am the resurrection,
28 she had so s', she went her way,
34 And s', Where have ye laid him?
34 s' unto him, Lord, come and see.
36 s' the Jews, Behold how he loved
37 some of them s', Could not this
39 Jesus s', Take ye away the stone.
40 S' I not unto thee, that, if thou
41 s', Father, I thank thee that thou
42 of the people which stand by I s' it,
47 a council, and s', What do we? for
49 s' unto them, Ye know nothing at
12: 6 This he s', not that he cared for the
7 s' Jesus, Let her alone: against
19 Pharisees...s' among themselves,
29 and heard it, s' that it thundered:
29 others s', An angel spake to him.
30 Jesus...s', This voice came not
33 This he s', signifying what death
35 Jesus s' unto them, Yet a little
39 because that Esaias s' again,
41 These things s' Esaias, when he
44 Jesus cried and s', He that believeth
50 even as the Father s' unto me, so I
13: 7 Jesus...s' unto him, What I do
11 therefore s' he, Ye are not all clean.
12 s' unto them, Know ye what I have
21 When Jesus had thus s', he was
21 and testified, and s', Verily, verily,
27 s' Jesus unto him, That thou
29 Jesus had s' unto him, Buy those
31 Jesus s', Now is the Son of man
33 and as I s' unto the Jews, Whither
36 Simon Peter s' unto him, Lord,
37 Peter s' unto him, Lord, why
14:23 Jesus...s' unto him, If a man love
26 whatsoever I have s' unto you.
28 Ye have heard how I s' unto you, I
28 because I s', I go unto the Father:
15:20 the word that I s' unto you, The
16: 4 I s' not unto you at the beginning,
6 I have s' these things unto you,
15 therefore s' I, that he shall take of
17 s' some of his disciples among
18 They s' therefore, What is this
19 and s' unto them, Do ye enquire
19 that I s', A little while, and ye shall
29 His disciples s' unto him, Lo, now
17: 1 eyes to heaven, and s', Father, the
18: 4 and s' unto them, Whom seek ye?
6 then as he had s' unto them, I am
7 ye? And they s', Jesus of Nazareth.
11 s' Jesus unto Peter, Put up thy
20 and in secret have I s' nothing.
21 heard me, what I have s' unto
21 them: behold, they know what I s'.
25 They s' therefore unto him, Art not
25 He denied it, and s', I am not.
29 and s', What accusation bring ye
30 They...s' unto him, If he were not
31 s' Pilate unto them, Take ye him,
31 Jews...s' unto him, It is not lawful
33 s' unto him, Art thou the King of
37 s' unto him, Art thou a king then?
38 when he had s' this, he went out
19: 3 And s', Hail, King of the Jews!
21 s' the chief priests of the Jews to
21 that he s', I am king of the Jews.
24 s' therefore among themselves, Let
30 the vinegar, he s', It is finished:
20:14 she had thus s', she turned herself
20 he had so s', he shewed unto them
21 s' Jesus to them again, Peace be
22 he had s' this, he breathed on them
25 other disciples...s' unto him, We
25 he s' unto them, Except I shall see
26 midst, and s', Peace be unto you.
28 Thomas...s' unto him, My Lord
21: 6 And he s' unto them, Cast the net
17 s' unto him the third time, Lovest
17 he s' unto him, Lord, thou knowest
20 s', Lord, which is he that betrayeth
23 yet Jesus s' not unto him, He shall
Ac 1: 7 he s' unto them, It is not for you
11 Which also s', Ye men of Galilee,
15 in the midst of the disciples, and s',
24 and s', Thou, Lord, which knowest
2:13 Others mocking s', These men are
Ac 2:14 and s' unto them, Ye men of Judæa,
34 The Lord s' unto my Lord, Sit thou
37 s' unto Peter and to the rest of the
38 Peter s' unto them, Repent, and be
3: 4 him with John, s', Look on us.
6 Peter s', Silver and gold have I none;
22 Moses truly s' unto the fathers, A
4: 8 Peter,...s' unto them, Ye rulers of
19 s' unto them, Whether it be right
23 priests and elders had s' unto them.
24 s', Lord, thou art God, which hast
25 mouth of thy servant David hast s',
32 neither s' any of them that ought
5: 3 Peter s', Ananias, why hath Satan
8 And she s', Yea, for so much.
9 Peter s' unto her, How is it that ye
19 and brought them forth, and s',
29 and s', We ought to obey God rather
35 And s' unto them, Ye men of Israel,
6: 2 s', It is not reason that we should
11 men, which s', We have heard him
13 set up false witnesses, which s',
7: 1 Then s' the high priest, Are these
2 he s', Men, brethren, and fathers,
3 s' unto him, Get thee out of thy
7 be in bondage will I judge, s' God:
33 Then s' the Lord to him, Put off thy
37 which s' unto the children of Israel,
56 And s', Behold, I see the heavens
60 when he had s' this, he fell asleep.
8:20 But Peter s' unto him, Thy money
24 Simon, and s', Pray ye to the Lord
29 the Spirit s' unto Philip, Go near,
30 s', Understandest thou what thou
31 And he s', How can I, except some
34 s', I pray thee, of whom speaketh
36 the eunuch s', See, here is water;
37 Philip s', If thou believest with all
37 And he answered and s', I believe
9: 5 And he s', Who art thou, Lord?
5 the Lord s', I am Jesus whom thou
6 and astonished s', Lord, what wilt
6 the Lord s' unto him, Arise, and go
10 s' the Lord in a vision, Ananias.
10 And he s', Behold, I am here, Lord.
11 the Lord s' unto him, Arise, and go
15 the Lord s' unto him, Go thy way:
17 his hands on him s', Brother Saul,
21 heard him were amazed, and s';
34 Peter s' unto him, Æneas, Jesus
40 him to the body s', Tabitha, arise.
10: 4 was afraid, and s', What is it, Lord?
4 s' unto him, Thy prayers and thine
14 Peter s', Not so, Lord; for I have
19 Spirit s' unto him, Behold, three
21 s', Behold, I am he whom ye seek:
22 And they s', Cornelius the centurion,
28 he s' unto them, Ye know how that
30 Cornelius s', Four days ago I was
31 s', Cornelius, thy prayer is heard,
34 s', Of a truth I perceive that God
11: 8 But I s', Not so, Lord: for nothing
13 s' unto him, Send men to Joppa,
16 he s', John indeed baptized with
12: 8 the angel s' unto him, Gird thyself,
11 he s', Now I know of a surety, that
15 And they s' unto her, Thou art mad.
15 so. Then s' they, It is his angel.
17 he s', Go shew these things unto
13: 2 the Holy Ghost s', Separate me
10 And s', O full of all subtilty and all
16 beckoning with his hand s', Men of
22 and s', I have found David the son
25 he s', Whom think ye that I am?
34 s' on this wise, I will give you the
46 s', It was necessary that the word
14:10 S' with a loud voice, Stand upright
15: 1 and s', Except ye be circumcised after
7 Peter rose up, and s' unto them,
36 Paul s' unto Barnabas, Let us go
16:18 and s' to the spirit, I command thee
30 and s', Sirs, what must I do to be
31 they s', Believe on the Lord Jesus
37 But Paul s' unto them, They have
17:18 some s', What will this babbler say?
22 s', Ye men of Athens, I perceive
28 s', For we are also his offspring.
32 others s', We will hear thee again
18: 6 s' unto them, Your blood be upon
14 Gallio s' unto the Jews, If it were a
19: 2 He s' unto them, Have ye received
2 And they s' unto him, We have not
3 he s' unto them, Unto what then
3 And they s', Unto John's baptism.
4 s' Paul, John verily baptized with
15 evil spirit...s', Jesus I know, and
25 s', Sirs, ye know that by this craft
35 s', Ye men of Ephesus, what man
20:10 him s', Trouble not yourselves;
18 he s' unto them, Ye know, from the
35 words of the Lord Jesus, how he s',
21: 4 who s' to Paul through the Spirit,
11 s', Thus saith the Holy Ghost, So
20 s' unto him, Thou seest, brother,
37 he s' unto the chief captain, May I
37 Who s', Canst thou speak Greek?
39 Paul s', I am a man which am a
22: 8 And he s' unto me, I am Jesus of
10 And I s', What shall I do, Lord?
10 the Lord s' unto me, Arise, and go
13 s' unto me, Brother Saul, receive
14 he s', The God of our fathers hath
19 And I s', Lord, they know that I
21 he s' unto me, Depart: for I will
22 s', Away with such a fellow from
25 Paul s' unto the centurion that
Ac 22:27 captain came, and s' unto him,
27 art thou a Roman? He s', Yea.
28 And Paul s', But I was free born.
23: 1 earnestly beholding the council, s',
3 Then s' Paul unto him, God shall
4 s', Revilest thou God's high priest?
5 s' Paul, I wist not, brethren, that
7 when he had so s', there arose a
11 and s', Be of good cheer, Paul: for
14 and s', We have bound ourselves
17 s', Bring this young man unto the
18 and s', Paul the prisoner called me
20 And he s', The Jews have agreed
35 I will hear thee, s' he, when thine
24:22 s', When Lysias the chief captain
25: 5 Let them therefore, s' he, which
9 Paul, and s', Wilt thou go up to
10 Then s' Paul, I stand at Cæsar's
22 Agrippa s' unto Festus, I would
22 To morrow, s' he, thou shalt hear
24 And Festus s', King Agrippa, and
26: 1 Agrippa s' unto Paul, Thou art
15 And I s', Who art thou, Lord?
15 And he s', I am Jesus whom thou
24 Festus s' with a loud voice, Paul,
25 he s', I am not mad, most noble
28 Then Agrippa s' unto Paul, Almost
29 Paul s', I would to God, that not
32 s' Agrippa unto Festus, This man
27:10 s' unto them, Sirs, I perceive that
21 in the midst of them, and s', Sirs,
31 Paul s' to the centurion and to the
28: 4 s' among themselves, No doubt
6 minds, and s' that he was a god.
17 he s' unto them, Men and brethren,
21 And they s' unto him, We neither
29 he had s' these words, the Jews
Ro 7: 7 law had s', Thou shalt not covet.
9:12 s' unto her, The elder shall serve
26 s' unto them, Ye are not my people;
29 Esaias s' before, Except the Lord
1Co 11:24 he brake it, and s', Take, eat:
2Co 6:16 as God hath s', I will dwell in them.
7: 3 s' before, that ye are in our hearts
9: 3 that, as I s', ye may be ready:
12: 9 And he s' unto me, My grace is
Ga 1: 9 As we s' before, so say I now
2:14 I s' unto Peter before them all, If
Tit 1:12 s', The Cretians are alway liars,
Heb 1: 5 the angels s' he at any time, Thou
13 angels s' he at any time, Sit on my
3:10 and s', They do alway err in their
15 While it is s', To day if ye will hear
4: 3 as he s', As I have sworn in my
7 as it is s', To day if ye will hear his
5: 5 he that s' unto him, Thou art my
7:21 that s' unto him, The Lord sware
10: 7 Then s' I, Lo, I come (in the
8 Above when he s', Sacrifice and
9 Then s' he, Lo, I come to do thy
15 us: for after that he had s' before,
30 s', Vengeance belongeth unto me,
11:18 it was s', That in Isaac shall thy
12:21 Moses s', I exceedingly fear and
13: 5 he hath s', I will never leave thee,
Jas 2:11 that s', Do not commit adultery,
11 s' also, Do not kill. Now if thou
Jude 9 but s', The Lord rebuke thee.
Re 4: 1 which s', Come up hither, and I
5:14 And the four beasts s', Amen.
6:11 and it was s' unto them, that they
16 s' to the mountains and rocks,
7:14 I s' unto him, Sir, thou knowest.
14 he s' to me, These are they which
10: 8 s', Go and take the little book
9 and s' unto him, Give me the little
9 s' unto me, Take it, and eat it up;
11 s' unto me, Thou must prophesy
17: 7 angel s' unto me, Wherefore didst
19: 3 And again they s', Alleluia.
10 he s' unto me, See thou do it not:
21: 5 he that sat upon the throne s',
5 And he s' unto me, Write: for
6 And he s' unto me, It is done. I
22: 6 he s' unto me, These sayings are

saidst
Ge 12:19 Why s' thou, She is my sister? so
26: 9 and how s' thou, She is my sister?
32: 9 the Lord which s' unto me, Return
12 thou s', I will surely do thee good,
44:21 thou s' unto thy servants, Bring
23 thou s' unto thy servants, Except
Ex 32:13 s' unto them, I will multiply your
J'g 9:38 thy mouth, wherewith thou s',
1Ki 2:42 and thou s' unto me, The word that
Job 35: 2 that thou s', My righteousness is
3 For thou s', What advantage will
Ps 27: 8 When thou s', Seek ye my face; my
89:19 s', I have laid help upon one that is
Isa 47: 7 thou s', I shall be a lady for ever:
57:10 yet s' thou not, There is no hope:
Jer 2:20 thou s', I will not transgress; when
25 thou s', There is no hope: no; for I
22:21 but thou s', I will not hear.
La 3:57 called upon thee: thou s', Fear not.
Eze 25: 3 Because thou s', Aha, against my
Ho 13:10 whom thou s', Give me a king and
Joh 4:18 husband: in that s' thou truly.

sail See also MAINSAIL; SAILED; SAILING.
Isa 33:23 they could not spread the s':
Eze 27: 7 thou spreadest forth to be thy s';
Ac 20: 3 as he was about to s' into Syria,
16 For Paul had determined to s' by
27: 1 that we should s' into Italy, they
2 to s' by the coasts of Asia; one

Ac 27:17 strake s', and so were driven.
24 thee all them that s' with thee.
sailed
Lu 8:23 But as they s' he fell asleep: and
Ac 13: 4 and from thence they s' to Cyprus.
14:26 thence s' to Antioch, from whence
15:39 took Mark, and s' unto Cyprus;
18:18 brethren, and s' thence into Syria,
21 God will. And he s' from Ephesus.
20: 6 we s' away from Philippi after the
13 before to ship, and s' unto Assos,
15 we s' thence, and came the next
21: 3 on the left hand, and s' into Syria,
27: 4 we s' under Cyprus, because the
5 we had s' over the sea of Cilicia
7 when we had s' slowly many days,
7 we s' under Crete, over against
13 thence, they s' close by Crete.
sailing
Ac 21: 2 a ship s' over unto Phenicia, we
27: 6 a ship of Alexandria s' into Italy;
9 and when s' was now dangerous,
sailors
Re 18:17 s', and as many as trade by sea,
saint See also SAINTS.
Ps 106:16 and Aaron the s' of the Lord.
Da 8:13 Then I heard one s' speaking,
13 and another s' said unto that
13 said unto that certain s' which spake,
Ph'p 4:21 Salute every s' in Christ Jesus.
saints See also S.; SAINTS'.
De 33: 2 came with ten thousands of s':
3 all his s' are in thy hand: and
1Sa 2: 9 He will keep the feet of his s',
2Ch 6:41 and let thy s' rejoice in goodness.
Job 5: 1 to which of the s' wilt thou turn?
15:15 he putteth no trust in his s'; yea,
Ps 16: 3 But to the s' that are in the earth,
30: 4 Sing unto the Lord, O ye s' of his,
31:23 O love the Lord, all ye his s': for
34: 9 O fear the Lord, ye his s': for
37:28 and forsaketh not his s'; they are
50: 5 Gather my s' together unto me;
52: 9 name; for it is good before thy s'.
79: 2 the flesh of thy s' unto the beasts
85: 8 peace unto his people, and to his s':
89: 5 also in the congregation of the s'.
7 be feared in the assembly of the s
97:10 he preserveth the souls of his s';
116:15 of the Lord is the death of his s'.
132: 9 and let thy s' shout for joy.
16 and her s' shall shout aloud for joy.
145:10 Lord; and thy s' shall bless thee.
148:14 his people, the praise of all his s';
149: 1 praise in the congregation of s'.
5 Let the s' be joyful in glory: let
9 this honour have all his s'. Praise
Pr 2: 8 and preserveth the way of his s'.
Da 7:18 the s' of the most High shall take
21 same horn made war with the s',
22 judgment was given to the s' of the
22 that the s' possessed the kingdom.
25 wear out the s' of the most High,
27 people of the s' of the most High,
Ho 11:12 God, and is faithful with the s'.
Zec 14: 5 shall come, and all the s' with thee.
M't 27:52 bodies of the s' which slept arose,
Ac 9:13 much evil he hath done to thy s' at
32 also to the s' which dwelt at Lydda.
41 he had called the s' and widows,
26:10 many of the s' did I shut up in prison,
Ro 1: 7 Rome, beloved of God, called to be s':
8:27 he maketh intercession for the s'
12:13 Distributing to the necessity of s';
15:25 Jerusalem to minister unto the s'.
26 the poor s' which are at Jerusalem.
31 Jerusalem may be accepted of the s':
16: 2 her in the Lord, as becometh s',
15 and all the s' which are with them.
1Co 1: 2 in Christ Jesus, called to be s',
6: 1 the unjust, and not before the s'?
2 that the s' shall judge the world?
14:33 of peace, as in all churches of the s'.
16: 1 concerning the collection for the s',
15 addicted...to the ministry of the s',)
2Co 1: 1 all the s' which are in all Achaia:
8: 4 fellowship of...ministering to the s'.
9: 1 as touching the ministering to the s',
12 not only supplieth the want of the s',
13:13 All the s' salute you.
Eph 1: 1 to the s' which are at Ephesus, and
15 Lord Jesus, and love unto all the s',
18 the glory of his inheritance in the s',
2:19 fellowcitizens with the s', and of the
3: 8 who am less than the least of all s',
18 to comprehend with all s' what is the
4:12 For the perfecting of the s', for the
5: 3 named among you, as becometh s';
6:18 and supplication for all s';
Ph'p 1: 1 to all the s' in Christ Jesus which are
4:22 All the s' salute you, chiefly they
Col 1: 2 To the s' and faithful brethren in
4 the love which ye have to all the s',
12 of the inheritance of the s' in light:
26 but now is made manifest to his s':
1Th 3:13 the coming of...Christ with all his s'.
2Th 1:10 he shall come to be glorified in his s',
Ph'm 5 the Lord Jesus, and toward all s';
7 the bowels of the s' are refreshed by
Heb 6:10 in that ye have ministered to the s',
13:24 have the rule over you, and all the s'.
Jude 3 faith...once delivered unto the s'.
14 cometh with ten thousands of his s',
Re 5: 8 odours, which are the prayers of s'.
Re 8: 3 offer it with the prayers of all s'
4 came with the prayers of the s',
11:18 servants the prophets, and to the s',
13: 7 unto him to make war with the s',
10 the patience and the faith of the s'.
14:12 Here is the patience of the s': here
15: 3 true are thy ways, thou King of s'.
16: 6 shed the blood of s' and prophets,
17: 6 drunken with the blood of the s',
18:24 the blood of prophets, and of s', and
19: 8 fine linen is the righteousness of s'.
20: 9 and compassed the camp of the s'
saints'
1Ti 5:10 if she have washed the s' feet, if she
saith
Ge 22:16 myself have I sworn, s' the Lord,
32: 4 Thy servant Jacob s' thus, I have
41:55 unto Joseph; what he s' to you, do.
44: 7 Wherefore s' my lord these words?
45: 9 Thus s' thy son Joseph, God hath
Ex 4:22 Thus s' the Lord, Israel is my son,
5: 1 s' the Lord God of Israel, Let my
10 s' Pharaoh, I will not give you straw.
7:17 s' the Lord, In this thou shalt know
8: 1, 20 s' the Lord, Let my people go,
9: 1, 13 s' the Lord God of the Hebrews,
10: 3 s' the Lord God of the Hebrews,
11: 4 s' the Lord, About midnight will I
32:27 s' the Lord God of Israel, Put every
Nu 14:28 As truly as I live, s' the Lord, as ye
20:14 s' thy brother Israel, Thou knowest
22:16 Thus s' Balak the son of Zippor, Let
24:13 but what the Lord s', that will I
32:27 the Lord to battle, as my lord s'.
Jos 5:14 What s' my lord unto his servant?
7:13 s' the Lord God of Israel, There is
22:16 Thus s' the whole congregation of
24: 2 Thus s' the Lord God of Israel, Your
J'g 6: 8 s' the Lord God of Israel, I brought
11:15 s' Jephthah, Israel took not away
1Sa 2:27 s' the Lord, Did I plainly appear
30 Wherefore...Lord God of Israel s',
30 now the Lord s', Be it far from me:
9: 6 all that he s' cometh...to pass:
10:18 s' the Lord God of Israel, I brought
15: 2 s' the Lord of hosts, I remember
20: 3 he s', Let not Jonathan know this,
24:13 As s' the proverb of the ancients,
2Sa 7: 5 Thus s' the Lord, Shalt thou build
8 s' the Lord of hosts, I took thee
12: 7 Thus s' the Lord...I anointed thee
11 s' the Lord, Behold, I will raise up
14:10 Whosoever s' ought unto thee,
17: 5 and let us hear likewise what he s'.
24:12 Thus s' the Lord, I offer thee three
1Ki 2:30 him, Thus s' the king, Come forth.
3:23 one s', This is my son that liveth,
23 and the other s', Nay; but thy son is
11:31 thus s' the Lord, the God of Israel,
12:24 Thus the Lord, Ye shall not go up,
13: 2 said,O altar, altar, thus s' the Lord;
21 Thus s' the Lord, Forasmuch as
14: 7 Thus s' the Lord God of Israel,
17:14 For thus s' the Lord God of Israel.
20: 2 said unto him, Thus s' Ben-hadad,
13 Thus s' the Lord, Hast thou seen all
14 Thus s' the Lord, Even by the young
28 s' the Lord, Because the Syrians
32 Thy servant Ben-hadad s', I pray
42 s' the Lord, Because thou hast let go
21:19 Thus s' the Lord, Hast thou killed,
19 s' the Lord, In the place where dogs
22:11 s' the Lord, With these shalt thou
14 what the Lord s' unto me, that will
27 Thus s' the king, Put this fellow in
2Ki 1: 4 s' the Lord, Thou shalt not come
6 Thus s' the Lord, Is it not because
16 s' the Lord, Forasmuch as thou
2:21 s' the Lord, I have healed these
3:16 s' the Lord, Make this valley full of
17 s' the Lord, Ye shall not see wind,
4:43 for thus s' the Lord, They shall eat,
5:13 he s' to thee, Wash, and be clean?
7: 1 s' the Lord, To morrow about this
9: 3 s' the Lord, I have anointed thee
6 s' the Lord...I have anointed thee
12 s' the Lord, I have anointed thee
18, 19 Thus s' the king, Is it peace?
26 the blood of his sons, s' the Lord;
26 requite...in this plat, s' the Lord.
18:19 Thus s' the great king, the king of
29 Thus s' the king, Let not Hezekiah
31 thus s' the king of Assyria, Make an
19: 3 Thus s' Hezekiah, This day is a day
6 Thus s' the Lord, Be not afraid of
20 Thus s' the Lord God of Israel, That
32 s' the Lord concerning the king
33 come into this city, s' the Lord.
20: 1 Thus s' the Lord, Set thine house
5 Thus s' the Lord, the God of David
17 nothing shall be left, s' the Lord.
21:12 s' the Lord God of Israel, Behold,
22:15 s' the Lord God of Israel, Tell the
16 s' the Lord, Behold, I will bring evil
18 Thus s' the Lord God of Israel, As
19 also have heard thee, s' the Lord.
1Ch 17: 4 Thus s' the Lord, Thou shalt not
7 s' the Lord of hosts, I took thee
21:10 s' the Lord, I offer thee three things:
11 him, Thus s' the Lord, Choose thee
2Ch 11: 4 Thus s' the Lord, Ye shall not go up,
12: 5 s' the Lord, Ye have forsaken me,
18:10 s' the Lord, With these thou shalt
13 what my God s', that will I speak.
26 Thus s' the king, Put this fellow in
2Ch 20:15 s' the Lord unto you, Be not afraid
21:12 s' the Lord God of David thy father,
24:20 Thus s' God, Why transgress ye the
32:10 s' Sennacherib king of Assyria,
34:23 Thus s' the Lord God of Israel, Tell
24 Thus s' the Lord,...I will bring evil
26 Thus s' the Lord God of Israel
27 even heard thee also, s' the Lord.
36:23 Thus s' Cyrus king of Persia, All
Ezr 1: 2 Thus s' Cyrus king of Persia, The
Ne 6: 6 and Gashmu s' it, that thou and the
Job 28:14 The depth s', It is not in me: and
14 and the sea s', It is not in me.
33:24 and s', Deliver him from going
35:10 But none s', Where is God my maker,
37: 6 For he s' to the snow, Be thou on
39:25 He s' among the trumpets, Ha, ha;
Ps 12: 5 needy, now will I arise, s' the Lord;
36: 1 The transgression of the wicked s'
50:16 unto the wicked God s', What hast
Pr 9: 4, 16 understanding, she s' to him,
20:14 is naught, it is naught, s' the buyer:
22:13 The slothful man s', There is a lion
23: 7 Eat and drink, s' he to thee; but his
24:24 He that s' unto the wicked, Thou
26:13 The slothful man s', There is a lion
19 neighbour, and s', Am not I in sport?
28:24 and s', It is no transgression;
30:16 the fire that s' not, It is enough.
20 and s', I have done no wickedness.
Ec 1: 2 Vanity of vanities, s' the Preacher,
4: 8 neither s' he, For whom do I labour,
7:27 this have I found, s' the preacher,
10: 3 he s' to every one that he is a fool.
12: 8 Vanity of vanities, s' the preacher;
Isa 1:11 sacrifices unto me? s' the Lord:
18 let us reason together, s' the Lord:
24 s' the Lord, the Lord of hosts,
3:15 the poor? s' the Lord God of hosts.
16 Moreover the Lord s', Because the
7: 7 s' the Lord God, It shall not stand,
10: 8 For he s', Are not my princes
13 he s', By the strength of my hand,
24 thus s' the Lord God of hosts, O
14:22 against them, s' the Lord of hosts,
22 and son, and nephew, s' the Lord.
23 destruction, s' the Lord of hosts,
17: 3 the glory...of Israel, s' the Lord
6 thereof, s' the Lord God of Israel.
19: 4 shall rule over them, s' the Lord,
22:14 ye die, s' the Lord God of hosts,
15 s' the Lord God of hosts, Go, get
25 In that day, s' the Lord of hosts,
28:16 s' the Lord God,...I lay in Zion
29:11 and he s', I cannot; for it is sealed:
12 thee: and he s', I am not learned.
22 thus s' the Lord, who redeemed
30: 1 rebellious children, s' the Lord,
12 s' the Holy One of Israel, Because
15 s' the Lord God, the Holy One of
31: 9 afraid of the ensign, s' the Lord,
33:10 Now will I rise, s' the Lord; now
36: 4 Thus s' the great king, the king of
14 Thus s' the king, Let not Hezekiah
16 thus s' the king of Assyria, Make an
37: 3 Thus s' Hezekiah, This day is a day
6 Thus s' the Lord, Be not afraid of
21 s' the Lord God of Israel, Whereas
33 thus s' the Lord concerning the king
34 not come into this city, s' the Lord
38: 1 Thus s' the Lord, Set thine house in
5 say to Hezekiah, Thus s' the Lord,
39: 6 nothing shall be left, s' the Lord.
40: 1 comfort ye my people, s' your God.
25 or shall I be equal? s' the Holy One.
41:14 I will help thee, s' the Lord, and
21 Produce your cause, s' the Lord;
21 strong reasons, s' the King of Jacob
42: 5 s' God the Lord, he that created the
22 for a spoil, and none s', Restore.
43: 1 thus s' the Lord that created thee,
10 Ye are my witnesses, s' the Lord,
12 ye are my witnesses, s' the Lord,
14 Thus s' the Lord, your redeemer,
16 s' the Lord, which maketh a way in
44: 2 Thus s' the Lord that made thee,
6 Thus s' the Lord the king of Israel,
16 s', Aha, I am warm, I have seen the
17 s', Deliver me; for thou art my god.
24 Thus s' the Lord, thy redeemer,
26 that s' to Jerusalem, Thou shalt be
27 That s' to the deep, Be dry, and I
28 That s' of Cyrus, He is my shepherd,
45: 1 Thus s' the Lord to his anointed,
10 Woe...him that s' unto his father,
11 Thus s' the Lord, the Holy One of
13 nor reward, s' the Lord of hosts.
14 Thus s' the Lord, The labour of
18 thus s' the Lord that created the
48:17 Thus s' the Lord, thy Redeemer,
22 There is no peace, s' the Lord, unto
49: 5 s' the Lord that formed me from
7 Thus s' the Lord, the Redeemer of
8 Thus s' the Lord, In an acceptable
18 As I live, s' the Lord, thou shalt
22 Thus s' the Lord God, Behold, I
25 thus s' the Lord, Even the captives
50: 1 Thus s' the Lord, Where is the bill
51:22 Thus s' thy Lord the Lord, and thy
52: 3 For thus s' the Lord, Ye have sold
4 For thus s' the Lord God, My people
5 what have I here, s' the Lord,
5 make them to howl, s' the Lord;
7 that s' unto Zion, Thy God reigneth.
54: 1 of the married wife, s' the Lord.
6 when thou wast refused, s' thy God.

Isa 54: 8 on thee, s' the Lord thy Redeemer.
10 s' the Lord that hath mercy on thee.
17 righteousness is of me, s' the Lord.
55: 8 are your ways my ways, s' the Lord.
56: 1 s' the Lord, Keep ye judgment,
4 thus s' the Lord unto the eunuchs
8 gathereth the outcasts of Israel s',
57: 15 For thus s' the high and lofty One
19 to him that is near, s' the Lord;
21 no peace, s' my God, to the wicked.
59: 20 from transgression...s' the Lord.
21 covenant with them, s' the Lord;
21 mouth of thy seed's seed, s' the Lord,
65: 7 of your fathers together, s' the Lord,
8 Thus s' the Lord, As the new wine is
8 cluster, and one s', Destroy it not;
13 thus s' the Lord God, Behold, my
25 all my holy mountain, s' the Lord.
66: 1 Thus s' the Lord, The heaven is my
2 things have been, s' the Lord:
9 cause to bring forth? s' the Lord:
9 and shut the womb? s' thy God.
12 s' the Lord,...I will extend peace to
17 consumed together, s' the Lord.
20 mountain Jerusalem, s' the Lord,
21 priests and for Levites, s' the Lord.
22 remain before me, s' the Lord,
23 to worship before me, s' the Lord.
Jer 1: 8 thee to deliver thee, s' the Lord.
15 kingdoms of the north, s' the Lord;
19 thee, s' the Lord, to deliver thee.
2: 2 Thus s' the Lord; I remember thee,
3 shall come upon them, s' the Lord.
5 s' the Lord, What iniquity have
9 yet plead with you, s' the Lord,
12 be ye very desolate, s' the Lord.
19 my fear is not in thee, s' the Lord
22 marked before me, s' the Lord God.
29 all have transgressed...s' the Lord.
3: 1 yet return again to me, s' the Lord.
10 heart, but feignedly, s' the Lord.
12 thou backsliding Israel, s' the Lord;
12 for I am merciful, s' the Lord, and I
13 not obeyed my voice, s' the Lord.
14 backsliding children, s' the Lord;
16 s' the Lord, they shall say no more,
20 me, O house of Israel, s' the Lord.
4: 1 wilt return, O Israel, s' the Lord,
3 For thus s' the Lord to the men of
9 to pass at that day, s' the Lord,
17 rebellious against me, s' the Lord.
5: 9 visit for these things? s' the Lord:
11 dealt...treacherously...s' the Lord.
14 s' the Lord God of hosts, Because
15 far, O house of Israel, s' the Lord:
18 s' the Lord, I will not make a full
22 Fear ye not me? s' the Lord: will
29 visit for these things? s' the Lord:
6: 9 s' the Lord of hosts, They shall
12 inhabitants of the land, s' the Lord.
15 shall be cast down, s' the Lord.
16 Thus s' the Lord, Stand ye in the
21 thus s' the Lord, Behold, I will lay
22 Thus s' the Lord, Behold, a people
7: 3 Thus s' the Lord of hosts, the God
11 even I have seen it, s' the Lord.
13 done all these works, s' the Lord,
19 provoke me to anger? s' the Lord:
20 thus s' the Lord God; Behold, mine
21 s' the Lord of hosts, the God of
30 done evil in my sight, s' the Lord:
32 behold, the days come, s' the Lord,
8: 1 At that time, s' the Lord, they shall
3 I have driven them, s' the Lord of
4 Thus s' the Lord; Shall they fall,
12 they shall be cast down, s' the Lord.
13 surely consume them, s' the Lord:
17 and they shall bite you, s' the Lord.
9: 3 and they know not me, s' the Lord.
6 refuse to know me, s' the Lord.
7 thus s' the Lord of hosts, Behold,
9 them for these things? s' the Lord:
13 the Lord s', Because they have
15 thus s' the Lord of hosts, the God of
17 Thus s' the Lord of hosts, Consider
22 s' the Lord, Even the carcases
23 Thus s' the Lord, Let not the wise
24 these things I delight, s' the Lord.
25 the days come, s' the Lord, that I
10: 2 Thus s' the Lord, Learn not the
18 thus s' the Lord, Behold, I will sling
11: 3 s' the Lord God of Israel; Cursed be
11 s' the Lord, Behold, I will bring evil
21 s' the Lord of the men of Anathoth,
22 thus s' the Lord of hosts, Behold, I
12: 14 Thus s' the Lord against all mine
17 destroy that nation, s' the Lord.
13: 1 Thus s' the Lord unto me, Go and
9 s' the Lord, After this manner will
11 whole house of Judah, s' the Lord;
12 s' the Lord God of Israel, Every
13 s' the Lord, Behold, I will fill all the
14 and the sons together, s' the Lord:
25 thy measures from me, s' the Lord;
14: 10 Thus s' the Lord unto this people,
15 s' the Lord concerning the prophets
15: 2 s' the Lord; Such as are for death,
3 over them four kinds, s' the Lord:
6 Thou hast forsaken me, s' the Lord,
9 before their enemies, s' the Lord.
19 Therefore thus s' the Lord, If thou
20 and to deliver thee, s' the Lord.
16: 3 s' the Lord concerning the sons and
5 s' the Lord, Enter not into the house
5 from this people, s' the Lord,
9 thus s' the Lord of hosts, the God

Jer 16: 11 and have forsaken me, s' the Lord,
14 s' the Lord, that it shall no more
16 send for many fishers, s' the Lord,
17: 5 Thus s' the Lord; Cursed be the
21 Thus s' the Lord; Take heed to
24 hearken unto me, s' the Lord, to
18: 6 with you as this potter? s' the Lord.
11 s' the Lord; Behold, I frame evil
13 Therefore thus s' the Lord; Ask ye
19: 1 s' the Lord, Go and get a potter's
3 Thus s' the Lord of hosts, the God
6 days come, s' the Lord, that this
11 Thus s' the Lord of hosts; Even
12 I do unto this place, s' the Lord,
15 Thus s' the Lord of hosts, the God
20: 4 s' the Lord, Behold, I will make
21: 4 s' the Lord God of Israel; Behold, I
7 s' the Lord, I will deliver Zedekiah
8 s' the Lord; Behold, I set before
10 evil, and not for good, s' the Lord:
12 s' the Lord; Execute judgment in
13 and rock of the plain, s' the Lord;
14 fruit of your doings, s' the Lord:
22: 1 s' the Lord; Go down to the house
3 s' the Lord; Execute ye judgment
5 I swear by myself, s' the Lord,
6 thus s' the Lord unto the king's
11 thus s' the Lord touching Shallum
14 s', I will build me a wide house and
16 not this to know me? s' the Lord.
18 s' the Lord concerning Jehoiakim
24 s' the Lord, though Coniah the
30 Thus s' the Lord, Write ye this man
23: 1 sheep of my pasture! s' the Lord.
2 s' the Lord God of Israel against
2 evil of your doings, s' the Lord.
4 shall they be lacking, s' the Lord.
5 Behold, the days come, s' the Lord,
7 days come, s' the Lord, that they
11 their wickedness, s' the Lord.
12 year of their visitation, s' the Lord.
15 s' the Lord of hosts concerning the
16 Thus s' the Lord of hosts, Hearken
23 Am I a God at hand, s' the Lord,
24 I shall not see him? s' the Lord.
24 I fill heaven and earth? s' the Lord.
28 the chaff to the wheat? s' the Lord.
29 my word like as a fire? s' the Lord;
30, 31 against the prophets, s' the Lord,
31 use their tongues, and say, He s'.
32 prophesy false dreams, s' the Lord,
32 profit this people at all, s' the Lord.
33 I will even forsake you, s' the Lord.
38 thus s' the Lord; Because ye say
24: 5 Thus s' the Lord, the God of Israel;
8 surely thus s' the Lord, So will I
25: 7 hearkened unto me, s' the Lord;
8 thus s' the Lord of hosts; Because
9 families of the north, s' the Lord,
12 and that nation, s' the Lord, for
15 s' the Lord God of Israel unto me;
27 Thus s' the Lord of hosts, the God of
28 Thus s' the Lord of hosts; Ye shall
29 of the earth, s' the Lord of hosts.
31 wicked to the sword, s' the Lord.
32 s' the Lord of hosts, Behold, evil
26: 2 s' the Lord; Stand in the court of the
4 s' the Lord; If ye will not hearken
18 s' the Lord of hosts; Zion shall be
27: 2 s' the Lord to me; Make thee bonds
4 Thus s' the Lord of hosts, the God
8 nation will I punish, s' the Lord,
11 still in their own land, s' the Lord;
15 I have not sent them, s' the Lord,
16 Thus s' the Lord; Hearken not to
19 thus s' the Lord of hosts concerning
21 thus s' the Lord of hosts, the God of
22 day that I visit them, s' the Lord;
28: 4 that went into Babylon, s' the Lord:
11 s' the Lord; Even so will I break
13 Thus s' the Lord; Thou hast broken
14 thus s' the Lord of hosts, the God of
16 thus s' the Lord; Behold, I will cast
29: 4 Thus s' the Lord of hosts, the God of
8 thus s' the Lord of hosts, the God of
9 I have not sent them, s' the Lord.
10 For thus s' the Lord, That after
11 I think toward you, s' the Lord,
14 will be found of you, s' the Lord:
14 I have driven you, s' the Lord; and
16 that thus s' the Lord of the king
17 Thus s' the Lord of hosts; Behold,
19 to my words, s' the Lord, which
19 but ye would not hear, s' the Lord.
21 Thus s' the Lord of hosts, the God
23 and am a witness, s' the Lord.
31 s' the Lord concerning Shemaiah
32 thus s' the Lord; Behold, I will
32 will do for my people, s' the Lord;
30: 3 For, lo, the days come, s' the Lord,
3 Israel and Judah, s' the Lord:
5 thus s' the Lord; We have heard a
8 in that day, s' the Lord of hosts,
10 O my servant Jacob, s' the Lord;
11 I am with thee, s' the Lord, to save
12 For thus s' the Lord, Thy bruise is
17 heal thee of thy wounds, s' the Lord;
18 Thus s' the Lord; Behold, I will
21 approach unto me? s' the Lord.
31: 1 time, s' the Lord, will I be the God
2 Thus s' the Lord, the people which
7 For thus s' the Lord; Sing with
14 with my goodness, s' the Lord.
15 s' the Lord; A voice was heard in
16 s' the Lord; Refrain thy voice from
16 work...be rewarded, s' the Lord;

Jer 31: 17 is hope in thine end, s' the Lord,
20 have mercy upon him, s' the Lord.
23 s' the Lord of hosts, the God of
27 the days come, s' the Lord, that I
28 to build, and to plant, s' the Lord.
31 the days come, s' the Lord, that I
32 an husband unto them, s' the Lord:
33 s' the Lord, I will put my law in
34 the greatest of them, s' the Lord:
35 s' the Lord, which giveth the sun
36 depart from...me, s' the Lord,
37 s' the Lord; If heaven above can
37 that they have done, s' the Lord.
38 Behold, the days come, s' the Lord,
32: 3 s' the Lord,...I will give this city
5 be until I visit him, s' the Lord:
14, 15 s' the Lord of hosts, the God of
28 s' the Lord;...I will give this city
30 work of their hands, s' the Lord.
36 thus s' the Lord, the God of Israel,
42 thus s' the Lord; Like as I have
44 captivity to return, s' the Lord.
33: 2 s' the Lord the maker thereof, the
4 thus s' the Lord, the God of Israel,
10 Thus s' the Lord; Again there shall
11 the land, as at the first, s' the Lord.
12 Thus s' the Lord of hosts; Again in
13 him that telleth them, s' the Lord.
14 the days come, s' the Lord, that I
17 thus s' the Lord; David shall never
20 Thus s' the Lord; If ye can break
25 Thus s' the Lord; If my covenant
34: 2 Thus s' the Lord, the God of Israel;
2 s' the Lord;...I will give this city
4 Thus s' the Lord of thee, Thou shalt
5 pronounced the word, s' the Lord.
13 Thus s' the Lord, the God of Israel;
17 s' the Lord; Ye have not hearkened
17 a liberty for you, s' the Lord, to
22 I will command, s' the Lord, and
35: 13 Thus s' the Lord of hosts, the God
13 hearken to my words, s' the Lord.
17 thus s' the Lord God of hosts, the
18 Thus s' the Lord of hosts, the God
19 thus s' the Lord of hosts, the God
36: 29 Thus s' the Lord; Thou hast burned
30 thus s' the Lord of Jehoiakim king
37: 7 Thus s' the Lord, the God of Israel;
9 s' the Lord; Deceive not yourselves,
38: 2 Thus s' the Lord, He that remaineth
3 Thus s' the Lord, This city shall
17 Thus s' the Lord, the God of hosts,
39: 16 Thus s' the Lord of hosts, the God
17 deliver...in that day, s' the Lord:
18 put thy trust in me, s' the Lord.
42: 9 Thus s' the Lord, the God of Israel,
11 be not afraid of him, s' the Lord:
15, 18 s' the Lord of hosts, the God of
43: 10 s' the Lord of hosts, the God of
44: 2 s' the Lord of hosts, the God of
7 thus s' the Lord, the God of hosts,
11 thus s' the Lord of hosts, the God of
25 s' the Lord of hosts, the God of
26 sworn by my great name, s' the Lord,
29 be a sign unto you, s' the Lord,
30 s' the Lord; Behold, I will give
45: 2 Thus s' the Lord, the God of Israel,
4 The Lord s' thus; Behold, that
5 evil upon all flesh, s' the Lord:
46: 5 fear was round about, s' the Lord.
8 he s', I will go up, and will cover
18 As I live, s' the King, whose name
23 cut down her forest, s' the Lord,
25 the God of Israel, s'; Behold, I
26 as in the days of old, s' the Lord.
28 Fear not, O Jacob...s' the Lord:
47: 2 s' the Lord; Behold, waters rise
48: 1 Against Moab...s' the Lord of hosts,
12 the days come, s' the Lord, that
15 s' the King, whose name is the
25 and his arm is broken, s' the Lord.
30 I know his wrath, s' the Lord; but
35 cause to cease in Moab, s' the Lord,
38 wherein is no pleasure, s' the Lord.
40 For thus s' the Lord; Behold, he
43 inhabitant of Moab, s' the Lord.
44 year of their visitation, s' the Lord.
47 Moab in the latter days, s' the Lord.
49: 1 s' the Lord; Hath Israel no sons?
2 days come, s' the Lord, that I will
2 that were his heirs, s' the Lord.
5 thee, s' the Lord God of hosts,
6 children of Ammon, s' the Lord.
7 s' the Lord of hosts; Is wisdom no
12 s' the Lord; Behold, they whose
13 have sworn by myself, s' the Lord,
16 down from thence, s' the Lord.
18 s' the Lord, no man shall abide
26 cut off in that day, s' the Lord of
28 thus s' the Lord; Arise ye, go up
30 inhabitants of Hazor, s' the Lord;
31 dwelleth without care, s' the Lord,
32 from all sides thereof, s' the Lord.
35 Thus s' the Lord of hosts; Behold,
37 even my fierce anger, s' the Lord;
38 king and the princes, s' the Lord.
39 the captivity of Elam, s' the Lord.
50: 4 s' the Lord, the children of Israel
10 spoil her...be satisfied, s' the Lord.
18 thus s' the Lord of hosts, the God
20 s' the Lord, the iniquity of Israel
21 destroy after them, s' the Lord,
30 be cut off in that day, s' the Lord.
31 proud, s' the Lord God of hosts:
33 Thus s' the Lord of hosts; The
35 is upon the Chaldeans, s' the Lord,

Jer 50:40 neighbour cities...s' the Lord;
51: 1 s' the Lord; Behold, I will raise
24 in Zion in your sight, s' the Lord.
25 O destroying mountain, s' the Lord,
26 be desolate for ever, s' the Lord.
33 thus s' the Lord of hosts, the God
36 s' the Lord; Behold, I will plead
39 sleep, and not wake, s' the Lord.
48 unto her from the north, s' the Lord.
52 days come, s' the Lord, that I will
53 spoilers come unto her, s' the Lord.
57 not wake, s' the King, whose name
58 Thus s' the Lord of hosts; The
La 3:24 Lord is my portion, s' my soul;
37 Who is he that s', and it cometh to
Eze 2: 4 unto them, Thus s' the Lord God.
3:11 tell them, Thus s' the Lord God;
27 unto them, Thus s' the Lord God;
5: 5 s' the Lord God; This is Jerusalem:
7 thus s' the Lord God; Because ye
8 s' the Lord God; Behold, I, even I,
11 as I live, s' the Lord God; Surely,
6: 3 s' the Lord God to the mountains,
11 s' the Lord God; Smite with thine
7: 2 s' the Lord God unto the land of
5 s' the Lord God; An evil, an only
11: 5 s' the Lord; Thus have ye said, O
7 Therefore thus s' the Lord God;
8 sword upon you, s' the Lord God.
16, 17 say, Thus s' the Lord God;
21 upon their own heads, s' the Lord
12:10 Thus s' the Lord God; This burden
19 s' the Lord God of the inhabitants
23 s' the Lord God; I will make this
25 will perform it, s' the Lord God.
28 Thus s' the Lord God; There shall
28 shall be done, s' the Lord God.
13: 3 s' the Lord God; Woe unto the
6 divination, saying, The Lord s':
7 The Lord s' it; albeit I have not
8 s' the Lord God; Because ye have
8 am against you, s' the Lord God.
13 thus s' the Lord God; I will even
16 there is no peace, s' the Lord God.
18 And say, Thus s' the Lord God;
20 Wherefore thus s' the Lord God;
14: 4 unto them, Thus s' the Lord God;
6 s' the Lord God; Repent, and turn
11 may be their God, s' the Lord God.
14 righteousness, s' the Lord God.
16, 18, 20 as I live, s' the Lord God,
21 s' the Lord God; How much more
23 I have done in it, s' the Lord God.
15: 6 s' the Lord God; As the vine tree
8 committed a trespass, s' the Lord
16: 3 s' the Lord God unto Jerusalem;
8 a covenant with thee, s' the Lord
14 had put upon thee, s' the Lord God.
19 and thus it was, s' the Lord God.
23 woe unto thee! s' the Lord God;)
30 weak is thine heart, s' the Lord
36 Thus s' the Lord God; Because thy
43 way upon thine head, s' the Lord
48 s' the Lord God, Sodom thy sister
58 thine abominations, s' the Lord.
59 thus s' the Lord God; I will even
63 that thou hast done, s' the Lord
17: 3 s' the Lord God; A great eagle with
9 s' the Lord God; Shall it prosper?
16 As I live, s' the Lord God, Surely
19 thus s' the Lord God; As I live,
22 Thus s' the Lord God; I will also
18: 3 As I live, s' the Lord God, Ye shall
9 he shall surely live, s' the Lord God.
23 wicked should die? s' the Lord God:
29 Yet s' the house of Israel, The way
30 to his ways, s' the Lord God.
32 of him that dieth, s' the Lord God:
20: 3 Thus s' the Lord God; Are ye come
3 As I live, s' the Lord God, I will
5 Thus s' the Lord God; In the day
27 say unto them, Thus s' the Lord
30 s' the Lord God; Are ye polluted
31 As I live, s' the Lord God, I will
33 As I live, s' the Lord God, surely
36 I plead with you, s' the Lord God.
39 thus s' the Lord God; Go ye, serve
40 s' the Lord God, there shall all
44 ye house of Israel, s' the Lord God.
47 Thus s' the Lord God; Behold, I
21: 3 land of Israel, Thus s' the Lord;
7 brought to pass, s' the Lord God.
9 prophesy,...say, Thus s' the Lord;
13 shall be no more, s' the Lord God.
24 thus s' the Lord God; Because ye
26 Thus s' the Lord God; Remove the
28 Thus s' the Lord God concerning
22: 3 s' the Lord God, The city sheddeth
12 forgotten me, s' the Lord God.
19 thus s' the Lord God; Because ye
28 s' the Lord God, when the Lord
31 upon their heads, s' the Lord God.
23:22 Aholibah, thus s' the Lord God;
28 For thus s' the Lord God; Behold, I
32 Thus s' the Lord God; Thou shalt
34 I have spoken it, s' the Lord God.
35 thus s' the Lord God; Because thou
46 thus s' the Lord God; I will bring
24: 3 Thus s' the Lord God; Set on a pot,
6, 9 thus s' the Lord God; Woe to the
14 they judge thee, s' the Lord God.
21 Thus s' the Lord God; Behold, I
25: 3 Thus s' the Lord God; Because
6 For thus s' the Lord God; Because
8, 12 Thus s' the Lord God; Because
13 thus s' the Lord God; I will also

Eze 25:14 my vengeance, s' the Lord God.
15 Thus s' the Lord God; Because the
16 thus s' the Lord God; Behold, I will
26: 3 thus s' the Lord God; Behold, I am
5 I have spoken it, s' the Lord God:
7 thus s' the Lord God; Behold, I wil
14 have spoken it, s' the Lord God.
15 s' the Lord God to Tyrus; Shall not
19 thus s' the Lord God; When I shall
21 be found again, s' the Lord God.
27: 3 s' the Lord God; O Tyrus, thou
28: 2 s' the Lord God; Because thine heart
6 s' the Lord God; Because thou hast
10 I have spoken it, s' the Lord God.
12 s' the Lord God; Thou sealest up
22 say, Thus s' the Lord God; Behold,
25 s' the Lord God; When I shall have
29: 3 Thus s' the Lord God; Behold, I am
8 thus s' the Lord God; Behold, I will
13 thus s' the Lord God; At the end of
19 thus s' the Lord God; Behold, I will
20 wrought for me, s' the Lord God.
30: 2 s' the Lord God; Howl ye, Woe
6 s' the Lord; They also that uphold
6 it by the sword, s' the Lord God.
10, 13 s' the Lord God; I will also
22 thus s' the Lord God; Behold, I am
31:10 s' the Lord God; Because thou hast
15 s' the Lord God; In the day when
18 all his multitude, s' the Lord God.
32: 3 s' the Lord God; I will therefore
8 upon thy land, s' the Lord God.
11 s' the Lord God; The sword of the
14 to run like oil, s' the Lord God.
16 all her multitude, s' the Lord God.
31 slain by the sword, s' the Lord God.
32 all his multitude, s' the Lord God.
33:11 s' the Lord God, I have no pleasure
25 Thus s' the Lord God; Ye eat with
27 Thus s' the Lord God; As I live,
34: 2 s' the Lord God unto the shepherds;
8 s' the Lord God, surely because
10 Thus s' the Lord God; Behold, I am
11 s' the Lord God; Behold, I, even I,
15 them to lie down, s' the Lord God.
17 O my flock, thus s' the Lord God;
20 thus s' the Lord God unto them;
30 are my people, s' the Lord God.
31 I am your God, s' the Lord God.
35: 3 s' the Lord God; Behold, O mount
6 s' the Lord God, I will prepare
11 s' the Lord God, I will even do
14 Thus s' the Lord God; When the
36: 2 s' the Lord God; Because the enemy
3 Thus s' the Lord God; Because they
4 s' the Lord God to the mountains,
5 thus s' the Lord God; Surely in the
6 Thus s' the Lord God; Behold, I
7 thus s' the Lord God; I have lifted
13 s' the Lord God; Because they say
14 nations any more, s' the Lord God.
15 to fall any more, s' the Lord God.
22 Thus s' the Lord God; I do not this
23 I am the Lord, s' the Lord God,
32 s' the Lord God, be it known unto
33 Thus s' the Lord God; In the day
37 Thus s' the Lord God; I will yet for
37: 5 s' the Lord God unto these bones;
9 Thus s' the Lord God; Come from
12 Thus s' the Lord God; Behold, O my
14 it, and performed it, s' the Lord.
19, 21 Thus s' the Lord God; Behold, I
38: 3 Thus s' the Lord God; Behold, I am
10 Thus s' the Lord God; It shall also
14 Thus s' the Lord God; In that day
17 s' the Lord God; Art thou he of
18 the land of Israel, s' the Lord God,
21 my mountains, s' the Lord God:
39: 1 Thus s' the Lord God; Behold, I am
5 I have spoken it, s' the Lord God.
8 and it is done, s' the Lord God;
10 that robbed them, s' the Lord God.
13 I shall be glorified, s' the Lord God.
17 thus s' the Lord God; Speak unto
20 all men of war, s' the Lord God.
25 s' the Lord God; Now will I bring
29 house of Israel, s' the Lord God.
43:18 Son of man, thus s' the Lord God;
19 unto me, s' the Lord God, a young
27 I will accept you, s' the Lord God.
44: 6 Thus s' the Lord God; O ye house
9 Thus s' the Lord God; No stranger,
12 against them, s' the Lord God,
15 fat and the blood, s' the Lord God:
27 his sin offering, s' the Lord God.
45: 9 s' the Lord God; Let it suffice you,
9 from my people, s' the Lord God.
15 reconciliation for them, s' the Lord
18 Thus s' the Lord God; In the first
46: 1 s' the Lord God; The gate of the
16 s' the Lord God; If the prince give
47:13 s' the Lord God; This shall be the
23 his inheritance, s' the Lord God.
48:29 are their portions, s' the Lord God.
Ho 2:13 lovers, and forgat me, s' the Lord.
16 it shall be at that day, s' the Lord,
21 I will hear, s' the Lord, I will hear
11:11 them in their houses, s' the Lord.
Joe 2:12 Therefore also now, s' the Lord,
Am 1: 3 Thus s' the Lord; For three
5 into captivity unto Kir, s' the Lord.
6 Thus s' the Lord; For three
8 shall perish, s' the Lord God.
9, 11, 13 Thus s' the Lord; For three
15 his princes together, s' the Lord.
2: 1 Thus s' the Lord; For three

Am 2: 3 the princes...with him, s' the Lord.
4, 6 Thus s' the Lord; For three
11 ye children of Israel? s' the Lord.
16 away naked in that day, s' the Lord.
3:10 know not to do right, s' the Lord,
11 thus s' the Lord God; An adversary
12 s' the Lord; As the shepherd taketh
13 s' the Lord God, the God of hosts,
15 shall have an end, s' the Lord.
4: 3 them into the palace, s' the Lord.
5 ye children of Israel, s' the Lord
6, 8, 9, 10, 11 unto me, s' the Lord.
5: 3 For thus s' the Lord God; The city
4 thus s' the Lord unto the house of
16 the Lord, s' thus; Wailing shall be
17 will pass through thee, s' the Lord.
27 beyond Damascus, s' the Lord,
6: 8 s' the Lord the God of hosts, I
14 Israel, s' the Lord the God of hosts:
7: 3 this: It shall not be, s' the Lord.
6 also shall not be, s' the Lord God.
11 For thus Amos s', Jeroboam shall
17 thus s' the Lord; Thy wife shall be
8: 3 howlings in that day, s' the Lord
9 s' the Lord God, that I will cause
11 s' the Lord God, that I will send a
9: 7 O children of Israel? s' the Lord.
8 the house of Jacob, s' the Lord.
12 name, s' the Lord that doeth this.
13 come, s' the Lord, that the plowman
15 given them, s' the Lord thy God.
Ob 1 s' the Lord God concerning Edom;
3 that s' in his heart, Who shall bring
4 will I bring thee down, s' the Lord.
8 Shall I not in that day, s' the Lord,
Mic 2: 3 Therefore thus s' the Lord; Behold,
3: 5 Thus s' the Lord concerning the
4: 6 s' the Lord, will I assemble her
5:10 to pass in that day, s' the Lord,
6: 1 Hear ye now what the Lord s';
Na 1:12 s' the Lord; Though they be quiet,
2:13 against thee, s' the Lord of hosts,
3: 5 against thee, s' the Lord of hosts;
Hab 2:19 Woe unto him that s' to the wood,
Zep 1: 2 from off the land, s' the Lord.
3 man from off the land, s' the Lord.
10 to pass in that day, s' the Lord,
2: 9 as I live, s' the Lord of hosts, the
3: 8 wait ye upon me, s' the Lord, until
20 back your captivity...s' the Lord.
Hag 1: 5, 7 thus s' the Lord of hosts; Consider
8 it, and I will be glorified, s' the Lord.
9 Why? s' the Lord of hosts. Because
13 saying, I am with you, s' the Lord.
2: 4 strong, O Zerubbabel, s' the Lord;
4 ye people of the land, s' the Lord,
4 I am with you, s' the Lord of hosts:
6 thus s' the Lord of hosts; Yet once,
7 fill this house with glory, s' the Lord
8 gold is mine, s' the Lord of hosts.
9 of the former, s' the Lord of hosts:
9 I give peace, s' the Lord of hosts.
11 Thus s' the Lord of hosts; Ask now
14 this nation before me, s' the Lord;
17 yet ye turned not to me, s' the Lord.
23 day, s' the Lord of hosts, will I take
23 s' the Lord, and will make thee as
23 chosen thee, s' the Lord of hosts.
Zec 1: 3 Thus s' the Lord of hosts; Turn
3 ye unto me, s' the Lord of hosts,
3 unto you, s' the Lord of hosts.
4 Thus s' the Lord of hosts; Turn ye
4 nor hearken unto me, s' the Lord.
14 s' the Lord of hosts; I am jealous
16 thus s' the Lord; I am returned to
16 be built in it, s' the Lord of hosts,
17 Thus s' the Lord of hosts; My cities
2: 5 s' the Lord, will be unto her a wall
6 the land of the north, s' the Lord:
6 winds of the heaven, s' the Lord.
8 s' the Lord of hosts; After the glory
10 in the midst of thee, s' the Lord.
3: 7 s' the Lord of hosts; If thou wilt
9 the graving...s' the Lord of hosts,
10 s' the Lord of hosts, shall ye call
4: 6 by my spirit, s' the Lord of hosts.
5: 4 bring it forth, s' the Lord of hosts,
7:13 not hear, s' the Lord of hosts:
8: 2 s' the Lord of hosts; I was jealous
3 s' the Lord; I am returned unto
4 s' the Lord of hosts; There shall
6 Thus s' the Lord of hosts; If it be
6 mine eyes? s' the Lord of hosts.
7 s' the Lord of hosts; Behold, I will
9 Thus s' the Lord of hosts; Let your
11 former days, s' the Lord of hosts.
14 s' the Lord of hosts; As I thought
14 provoked me to wrath, s' the Lord
17 are things that I hate, s' the Lord.
19 Thus s' the Lord of hosts; The fast
20 Thus s' the Lord of hosts; It shall
23 s' the Lord of hosts; In those days
10:12 down in his name, s' the Lord.
11: 4 s' the Lord my God; Feed the flock
6 inhabitants of...land, s' the Lord:
12: 1 s' the Lord, which stretcheth forth
4 day, s' the Lord, I will smite every
13: 2 in that day, s' the Lord of hosts,
7 is my fellow, s' the Lord of hosts:
8 s' the Lord, two parts therein shall
Mal 1: 2 I have loved you, s' the Lord. Yet
2 Esau Jacob's brother? s' the Lord:
4 Edom s', We are impoverished, but
4 thus s' the Lord of hosts, They shall
6 s' the Lord of hosts unto you, O
8 thy person? s' the Lord of hosts.

Mal 1: 9 he regard your persons? *s'* the Lord
10 no pleasure in you, *s'* the Lord of
11 among the heathen, *s'* the Lord of
13 ye have snuffed at it, *s'* the Lord
13 this of your hand? *s'* the Lord.
14 a great King, *s'* the Lord of hosts,
2: 2 give glory unto my name, *s'* the Lord
4 might be with Levi, *s'* the Lord of
8 covenant of Levi, *s'* the Lord of
16 *s'* that he hateth putting away:
16 his garment, *s'* the Lord of hosts:
3: 1 he shall come, *s'* the Lord of hosts.
5 fear not me, *s'* the Lord of hosts.
7 I will return unto you, *s'* the Lord
10 prove me now herewith, *s'* the Lord
11 the time in the field, *s'* the Lord of
12 be a delightsome land, *s'* the Lord
13 been stout against me, *s'* the Lord.
17 shall be mine, *s'* the Lord of hosts,
4: 1 burn them up, *s'* the Lord of hosts,
3 I shall do this, *s'* the Lord of hosts.
M't 4: 6 *s'* unto him, If thou be the Son of
9 And *s'* unto him, All these things
10 *s'* Jesus unto him, Get thee hence,
19 And he *s'* unto them, Follow me,
7: 21 Not every one that *s'* unto me, Lord,
8: 4 Jesus *s'* unto him, See thou tell
7 Jesus *s'* unto him, I will come and
20 Jesus *s'* unto him, The foxes have
26 And he *s'* unto them, Why are ye
9: 6 (then *s'* he to the sick of the palsy,)
9 and he *s'* unto him, Follow me.
28 Jesus *s'* unto them, Believe ye that
37 Then *s'* he unto his disciples, The
12: 13 Then *s'* he to the man, Stretch forth
44 Then he *s'*, I will return into my
13: 14 which *s'*, By hearing ye shall hear,
51 Jesus *s'* unto them, Have ye
15: 34 And Jesus *s'* unto them, How many
16: 15 He *s'* unto them, But whom say ye
17: 25 He *s'*, Yes. And when he was come
26 Peter *s'* unto him, Of strangers.
26 Jesus *s'* unto him, Then are the
18: 22 Jesus *s'* unto him, I say not unto
19: 8 He *s'* unto them, Moses because of
18 He *s'* unto him, Which? Jesus said,
20 The young man *s'* unto him, All
20: 6 *s'* unto them, Why stand ye here
7 *s'* unto them, Go ye also into the
8 lord of the vineyard *s'* unto his
21 She *s'* unto him, Grant that these
23 he *s'* unto them, Ye shall drink
21: 16 Jesus *s'* unto them, Yea; have ye
31 Jesus *s'* unto them, Verily I say
42 Jesus *s'* unto them, Did ye never
22: 8 Then *s'* he to his servants, The
12 he *s'* unto him, Friend, how camest
20 he *s'* unto them, Whose is this
21 Then *s'* he unto them, Render
43 He *s'* unto them, How then doth
26: 18 The Master *s'*, My time is at hand;
31 *s'* Jesus unto them, All ye shall be
36 *s'* unto the disciples, Sit ye here,
38 Then *s'* he unto them, My soul is
40 *s'* unto Peter, What, could ye not
45 *s'* unto them, Sleep on now, and
64 Jesus *s'* unto him, Thou hast said:
27: 22 Pilate *s'* unto them, What shall I
M'r 1: 41 *s'* unto him, I will; be thou clean.
44 *s'* unto him, See thou say nothing
2: 10 (he *s'* to the sick of the palsy,)
17 Jesus heard it, he *s'* unto them,
3: 3 he *s'* unto the man which had the
4 he *s'* unto them, Is it lawful to do
5 *s'* unto the man, Stretch forth thine
4: 35 he *s'* unto them, Let us pass over
5: 19 *s'* unto him, Go home to thy friends,
36 *s'* unto the ruler of the synagogue,
39 he *s'* unto them, What make ye this
6: 38 He *s'* unto them, How many loaves
50 *s'* unto them, Be of good cheer: it
7: 18 And he *s'* unto them, Are ye so
34 *s'* unto him, Ephphatha, that is,
8: 1 his disciples unto him, and *s'* unto
12 *s'*, Why doth this generation seek
17 he *s'* unto them, Why reason ye,
29 he *s'* unto them, But whom say ye
29 Peter answereth and *s'* unto him,
9: 19 and *s'*, O faithless generation, how
35 called the twelve, and *s'* unto them,
10: 11 *s'* unto them, Whosoever shall put
23 *s'* unto his disciples, How hardly
24 answereth again, and *s'* unto them,
27 Jesus looking upon them *s'*, With
42 *s'* unto them, Ye know that they
11: 2 *s'* unto them, Go your way into the
21 *s'* unto him, Master, behold, the
22 *s'* unto them, Have faith in God.
23 things which he *s'* shall come to
23 he shall have whatsoever he *s'*.
33 And Jesus answering *s'* unto them,
12: 16 And he *s'* unto them, Whose is this
43 him his disciples, and *s'* unto them,
13: 1 one of his disciples *s'* unto him,
14: 13 *s'* unto them, Go ye into the city,
14 *s'*, Where is the guestchamber,
27 Jesus *s'* unto them, All ye shall be
30 And Jesus *s'* unto him, Verily I say
32 he *s'* to his disciples, Sit ye here,
34 *s'* unto them, My soul is exceeding
37 *s'* unto Peter, Simon, sleepest thou?
41 and *s'* unto them, Sleep on now,
45 and *s'*, Master, master: and kissed
63 and *s'*, What need we any further
15: 28 the scripture was fulfilled, which *s'*,
16: 6 he *s'* unto them, Be not affrighted:

Lu 3: 11 and *s'* unto them, He that hath two
5: 39 new: for he *s'*, This old is better.
7: 40 thee. And he *s'*, Master, say on.
11: 24 he *s'*, I will return unto my house
16: 29 Abraham *s'* unto him, They have
18: 6 Hear what the unjust judge *s'*.
19: 22 *s'* unto him, Out of thine own mouth
20: 42 And David himself *s'* in the book of
22: 11 The Master *s'* unto thee, Where is
24: 36 and *s'* unto them, Peace be unto
Joh 1: 21 Art thou Elias? And he *s'*, I am not.
29 *s'*, Behold the Lamb of God, which
36 he *s'*, Behold the Lamb of God!
38 and *s'* unto them, What seek ye?
39 He *s'* unto them, Come and see.
41 and *s'* unto him, We have found the
43 Philip, and *s'* unto him, Follow me.
45 and *s'* unto him, We have found him,
46 Philip *s'* unto him, Come and see.
47 and *s'* of him, Behold an Israelite
48 Nathanael *s'* unto him, Whence
49 Nathanael answered and *s'* unto
51 he *s'* unto him, Verily, verily, I say
2: 3 the mother of Jesus *s'* unto him,
4 Jesus *s'* unto her, Woman, what
5 His mother *s'* unto the servants,
5 Whatsoever he *s'* unto you, do it.
7 Jesus *s'* unto them, Fill the
8 he *s'* unto them, Draw out now, and
10 And *s'* unto him, Every man at the
3: 4 Nicodemus *s'* unto him, How can a
4: 7 Jesus *s'* unto her, Give me to drink.
9 *s'* the woman of Samaria unto him,
10 who it is that *s'* to thee, Give me to
11 The woman *s'* unto him, Sir, thou
15 woman *s'* unto him, Sir, give me
16 Jesus *s'* unto her, Go, call thy
19 woman *s'* unto him, Sir, I perceive
21 Jesus *s'* unto her, Woman, believe
25 woman *s'* unto him, I know that
26 Jesus *s'* unto her, I that speak unto
28 way into the city, and *s'* to the men,
34 Jesus *s'* unto them, My meat is to
49 nobleman *s'* unto him, Sir, come
50 Jesus *s'* unto him, Go thy way; thy
5: 6 he *s'* unto him, Wilt thou be made
8 Jesus *s'* unto him, Rise, take up thy
6: 5 he *s'* unto Philip, Whence shall we
8 Simon Peter's brother, *s'* unto him,
20 But he *s'* unto them, It is I; be not
42 then that he *s'*, I came down from
7: 50 Nicodemus *s'* unto them, (he that
8: 22 because he *s'*, Whither I go, ye
25 Jesus *s'* unto them, Even the same
39 Jesus *s'* unto them, If ye were
11: 7 after that *s'* he to his disciples, Let
11 and after that he *s'* unto them, Our
23 Jesus *s'* unto her, Thy brother
24 Martha *s'* unto him, I know that he
27 She *s'* unto him, Yea, Lord: I
39 *s'* unto him, Lord, by this time he
40 Jesus *s'* unto her, Said I not unto
44 Jesus *s'* unto them, Loose him, and
12: 4 Then *s'* one of his disciples, Judas
13: 6 Peter *s'* unto him, Lord, dost thou
8 Peter *s'* unto him, Thou shalt never
9 Simon Peter *s'* unto him, Lord, not
10 Jesus *s'* to him, He that is washed
25 breast *s'* unto him, Lord, who is it?
14: 5 Thomas *s'* unto him, Lord, we
6 Jesus *s'* unto him, I am the way,
8 Philip *s'* unto him, Lord, shew us
9 Jesus *s'* unto him, Have I been so
22 Judas *s'* unto him, not Iscariot,
16: 17 What is this that he *s'* unto us, A
18 What is this that he *s'*, A little
18 while? we cannot tell what he *s'*.
18: 5 Jesus *s'* unto them, I am he. And
17 *s'* the damsel that kept the door
17 man's disciples? He *s'*, I am not.
26 *s'*, Did not I see thee in the garden
38 Pilate *s'* unto him, What is truth?
38 *s'* unto them, I find in him no fault
19: 4 *s'* unto them, Behold, I bring him
5 Pilate *s'* unto them, Behold the man!
6 Pilate *s'* unto them, Take ye him,
9 *s'* unto Jesus, Whence art thou?
10 *s'* Pilate unto him, Speakest thou
14 he *s'* unto the Jews, Behold your
15 Pilate *s'* unto them, Shall I crucify
24 which *s'*, They parted my raiment
26 *s'* unto his mother, Woman, behold
27 *s'* he to the disciple, Behold thy
28 scripture might be fulfilled, *s'*, I
35 and he knoweth that he *s'* true, that
37 scripture *s'*, They shall look on him
20: 2 and *s'* unto them, They have taken
13 She *s'* unto them, Because they
15 *s'* unto her, Woman, why weepest
15 *s'* unto him, Sir, if thou have borne
16 Jesus *s'* unto her, Mary. She
16 and *s'* unto him, Rabboni; which is
17 Jesus *s'* unto her, Touch me not;
19 *s'* unto them, Peace be unto you.
22 *s'* unto them, Receive ye the Holy
27 *s'* he to Thomas, Reach hither thy
29 Jesus *s'* unto him, Thomas, because
21: 3 Simon Peter *s'* unto them, I go a
5 Jesus *s'* unto them, Children, have
7 loved *s'* unto Peter, It is the Lord.
10 Jesus *s'* unto them, Bring of the
12 Jesus *s'* unto them, Come and dine.
15 Jesus *s'* to Simon Peter, Simon, son
15 He *s'* unto him, Yea, Lord; thou
15 He *s'* unto him, Feed my lambs.
16 He *s'* to him again the second time,

Joh 21: 16 He *s'* unto him, Yea, Lord; thou
16 He *s'* unto him, Feed my sheep.
17 He *s'* unto him the third time,
17 Jesus *s'* unto him, Feed my sheep.
19 this, he *s'* unto him, Follow me.
21 *s'* to Jesus, Lord, and what shall
22 Jesus *s'* unto him, If I will that he
Ac 1: 4 which, *s'* he, ye have heard of me.
2: 17 to pass in the last days, *s'* God,
34 he *s'* himself, The Lord said unto
7: 48 with hands; as *s'* the prophet,
49 house will ye build me? *s'* the Lord:
12: 8 he *s'* unto him, Cast thy garment
13: 35 he *s'* also in another psalm, Thou
15: 17 *s'* the Lord, who doeth all these
21: 11 Thus *s'* the Holy Ghost, So shall
22: 2 kept the more silence: and he *s'*,)
Ro 3: 19 that what things soever the law *s'*,
19 *s'* to them who are under the law:
4: 3 what *s'* the Scripture? Abraham
9: 15 he *s'* to Moses, I will have mercy on
17 For the scripture *s'* unto Pharaoh,
25 he *s'* also in Osee, I will call them
10: 8 But what *s'* it? The word is nigh
11 For the scripture *s'*, Whosoever
16 Esaias *s'*, Lord, who hath believed
19 First Moses *s'*, I will provoke you to
20 Esaias is very bold, and *s'*, I was
21 to Israel he *s'*, All day long I have
11: 2 ye not what the scripture *s'* of Elias?
4 But what *s'* the answer of God unto
9 David *s'*, Let their table be made a
12: 19 is mine; I will repay, *s'* the Lord.
14: 11 As I live, *s'* the Lord, every knee
15: 10 again he *s'*, Rejoice, ye Gentiles,
12 Esaias *s'*, There shall be a root of
1Co 1: 12 every one of you *s'*, I am of Paul;
3: 4 For while one *s'*, I am of Paul; and
6: 16 for two, *s'* he, shall be one flesh.
9: 8 or *s'* not the law the same also?
10 Or *s'* he it altogether for our sakes?
14: 21 will they not hear me, *s'* the Lord.
34 under obedience, as also *s'* the law.
15: 27 But when he *s'* all things are put
2Co 6: 2 (For he *s'*, I have heard thee in a
17 and be ye separate, *s'* the Lord, and
18 daughters, *s'* the Lord Almighty.
Ga 3: 16 He *s'* not, And to seeds, as of many;
4: 30 Nevertheless what *s'* the scripture?
Eph 4: 8 Wherefore he *s'*, When he ascended
5: 14 Wherefore he *s'*, Awake thou that
1Ti 5: 18 For the scripture *s'*, Thou shalt not
Heb 1: 6 he *s'*, And let all the angels of God
7 of the angels he *s'*, Who maketh his
8 But unto the Son he *s'*, Thy throne, O
3: 7 (as the Holy Ghost *s'*, To day if ye
5: 6 *s'* also in another place, Thou art a
8: 5 for, See, *s'* he, that thou make all
8 For finding fault with them, he *s'*,
8 days come, *s'* the Lord, when I will
9 I regarded them not, *s'* the Lord.
10 Israel after those days, *s'* the Lord;
13 In that he *s'*, A new covenant, he
10: 5 he *s'*, Sacrifice and offering thou
16 *s'* the Lord, I will put my laws into
30 me, I will recompense, *s'* the Lord.
Jas 2: 23 the scripture was fulfilled which *s'*,
4: 5 the scripture *s'* in vain, The spirit
6 Wherefore he *s'*, God resisteth the
1Jo 2: 4 He that *s'*, I know him, and keepeth
6 He that *s'* he abideth in him ought
9 He that *s'* he is in the light, and
Re 1: 8 *s'* the Lord, which is, and which was,
2: 1 *s'* he that holdeth the seven stars in
7 him hear what the Spirit *s'* unto the
8 things *s'* the first and the last,
11 him hear what the Spirit *s'* unto the
12 These things *s'* he which hath the
17 him hear what the Spirit *s'* unto the
18 These things *s'* the Son of God, who
29 him hear what the Spirit *s'* unto the
3: 1 *s'* he that hath the seven Spirits
6 him hear what the Spirit *s'* unto the
7 These things *s'* he that is holy, he
13 him hear what the Spirit *s'* unto the
14 These things *s'* the Amen, the
22 him hear what the Spirit *s'* unto the
5: 5 of the elders *s'* unto me, Weep not:
14: 13 Yea, *s'* the Spirit, that they may rest
17: 15 he *s'* unto me, The waters which
18: 7 for she *s'* in her heart, I sit a queen,
19: 9 he *s'* unto me, Write, Blessed are
9 he *s'* unto me, These are the true
22: 9 *s'* he unto me, See thou do it not:
10 he *s'* unto me, Seal not the sayings
20 He which testifieth these things *s'*,

sake See also SAKES.
Ge 3: 17 cursed is the ground for thy *s'*;
8: 21 the ground any more for man's *s'*;
12: 13 it may be well with me for thy *s'*;
16 he entreated Abram well for her *s'*:
18: 29 he said, I will not do it for forty's *s'*.
31 I will not destroy it for twenty's *s'*.
32 I will not destroy it for ten's *s'*.
20: 11 they will slay me for my wife's *s'*.
26: 24 seed for my servant Abraham's *s'*.
30: 27 Lord hath blessed me for thy *s'*.
39: 5 Egyptian's house for Joseph's *s'*;
Ex 18: 8 and to the Egyptians for Israel's *s'*,
21: 26 let him go free for his eye's *s'*.
27 shall let him go free for his tooth's *s'*.
Nu 11: 29 said unto him, Enviest thou for my *s'*?
25: 11 zealous for my *s'* among them,
18 day of the plague for Peor's *s'*.
1Sa 12: 22 his people for his great name's *s'*:
23: 10 to destroy the city for my *s'*.

2Sa 5:12 kingdom for his people Israel's s'.
7:21 For thy word's s', and according to
9: 1 him kindness for Jonathan's s'?
7 for Jonathan thy father's s',
18: 5 gently for my s' with the young man,
1Ki 8:41 of a far country for thy name's s';
11:12 not do it for David thy father's s':
13 thy son for David my servant's s',
13 Jerusalem's s' which I have chosen.
32 one tribe for my servant David's s',
32 for Jerusalem's s', the city which I
34 of his life for David my servant's s',
15: 4 for David's s' did the Lord his God
2Ki 8:19 Judah for David his servant's s',
19:34 this city, to save it, for mine own s',
34 and for my servant David's s'.
20: 6 defend this city for mine own s',
6 and for my servant David's s'.
Ne 9:31 for thy great mercies' s' thou didst
Job 19:17 for the children's s' of my own body.
Ps 23: 3 of righteousness for his name's s'.
25: 7 me for thy goodness s', O Lord.
11 For thy name's s', O Lord, pardon
31: 3 for thy name's s' lead me, and
16 servant: save me for thy mercies' s'.
44:22 for thy s' are we killed all the day
26 redeem us for thy mercies' s'.
69: 6 God of hosts, be ashamed for my s:
6 seek thee be confounded for my s',
106: 8 he saved them for his name's s',
109:21 God the Lord, for thy name's s':
115: 1 for thy mercy, and for thy truth's s'.
132:10 servant David's s' turn not away
143:11 me, O Lord, for thy name's s':
11 righteousness' s' bring my soul out
Isa 37:35 this city to save it for mine own s',
35 and for my servant David's s'.
42:21 pleased for his righteousness' s';
43:14 For your s' I have sent to Babylon,
25 thy transgressions for mine own s',
48: 9 name's s' will I defer mine anger,
11 mine own s', even for mine own s',
62: 1 Zion's s' will I not hold my peace,
63:17 Return for thy servants' s', the
Jer 14: 7 us, do thou it for thy name's s':
21 Do not abhor us, for thy name's s',
15:15 for thy s' I have suffered rebuke.
Eze 20: 9, 14 I wrought for my name's s',
22 and wrought for my name's s', that
36:22 but for mine holy name's s', which
Da 9:17 that is desolate, for the Lord's s'.
19 not, for thine own s', O my God:
Jon 1:12 for my s' this great tempest is
Mic 3:12 shall Zion for your s' be plowed as
M't 5:10 persecuted for righteousness' s':
11 evil against you falsely, for my s'.
10:18 governors and kings for my s', for
22 hated of all men for my name's s':
39 that loseth his life for my s' shall
14: 3 put him in prison for Herodias' s',
9 nevertheless for the oath's s', and
16:25 will lose his life for my s' shall
19:12 for the kingdom of heaven's s'.
29 or lands, for my name's s', shall
24: 9 of all nations for my name's s'.
22 the elect's s' those days shall be
M'r 4:17 persecution ariseth for the word's s',
6:17 him in prison for Herodias' s',
26 yet for his oath's s', and for their
8:35 shall lose his life for my s' and
10:29 lands, for my s', and the gospel's,
13: 9 before rulers and kings for my s',
13 hated of all men for my name's s':
20 for the elect's s', whom he hath
Lu 6:22 as evil, for the Son of man's s'.
9:24 will lose his life for my s', the
18:29 for the kingdom of God's s'.
21:12 kings and rulers for my name's s'.
17 hated of all men for my name's s'.
Joh 12: 9 they came not for Jesus' s' only,
13:37 I will lay down my life for thy s'.
38 thou lay down thy life for my s'?
14:11 believe me for the very works' s'.
15:21 they do unto you for my name's s',
Ac 9:16 he must suffer for my name's s'.
26: 7 For which hope's s', king Agrippa,
Ro 4:23 was not written for his s' alone,
8:36 For thy s' we are killed all the day
13: 5 wrath, but also for conscience s'.
15:30 for the Lord Jesus Christ's s', and
1Co 4:10 We are fools for Christ's s', but ye
9:23 this I do for the gospel's s', that I
10:25, 27 no question for conscience s':
28 eat not for his s' that shewed it,
28 for conscience s': for the earth
2Co 4: 5 your servants for Jesus' s'.
11 delivered unto death for Jesus' s',
12:10 in distresses for Christ's s': for
Eph 4:32 for Christ's s' hath forgiven you.
Ph'p 1:29 him, but also to suffer for his s';
Col 1:24 Christ in my flesh for his body's s',
3: 6 For which things' s' the wrath of
1Th 1: 5 we were among you for your s'.
5:13 highly in love for their work's s'.
1Ti 5:23 a little wine for thy stomach's s',
Tit 1:11 they ought not, for filthy lucre's s'.
Ph'm 9 Yet for love's s' I rather beseech
1Pe 2:13 ordinance of man for the Lord's s':
3:14 if ye suffer for righteousness' s',
1Jo 2:12 are forgiven you for his name's s'.
2Jo 2 For the truth's s', which dwelleth
3Jo 7 for his name's s' they went forth,
Re 2: 3 and for my name's s' hast laboured,

sakes^
Ge 18:26 will spare all the place for their s'.
Le 26:45 for their s' remember the covenant
De 1:37 was angry with me for your s',
3:26 was wroth with me for your s',
4:21 was angry with me for your s',
J'g 21:22 Be favourable unto them for our s':
Ru 1:13 it grieveth me much for your s' that
1Ch 16:21 he reproved kings for their s',
Ps 7: 7 for their s' therefore return thou
105:14 yea, he reproved kings for their s',
122: 8 my brethren and companions' s',
Isa 65: 8 so will I do for my servants' s', that
Eze 36:22 I do not this for your s', O house of
32 Not for your s' do I this, saith the
Da 2:30 for their s' that shall make known
Mal 3:11 I will rebuke the devourer for your s',
M'r 6:26 and for their s' which sat with him,
Joh 11:15 glad for your s' that I was not there,
12:30 because of me, but for your s'.
17:19 And for their s' I sanctify myself,
Ro 11:28 they are enemies for your s':
28 are beloved for the fathers' s'.
1Co 4: 6 and to Apollos for your s';
9:10 saith he it altogether for our s'?
10 For our s', no doubt, this is
2Co 2:10 for your s' forgave I it in the
4:15 all things are for your s', that
8: 9 yet for your s' he became poor,
1Th 3: 9 joy for your s' before our God;
2Ti 2:10 endure all things for the elect's s',

Sala (*sa'-lah*) See also SALAH.
Lu 3:35 of Heber, which was the son of *S'*.

Salah (*sa'-lah*) See also SALA.
Ge 10:24 Arphaxad begat *S'*; and *S'* begat
11:12 five and thirty years, and begat *S'*
13 Arphaxad lived after he begat *S'*
14 *S'* lived thirty years, and begat
15 *S'* lived after he begat Eber four

Salamis (*sal'-a-mis*)
Ac 13: 5 And when they were at *S'*, they

Salathiel (*sa-la'-the-el*) See also SHEALTIEL.
1Ch 3:17 sons of Jeconiah; Assir, *S'* his
M't 1:12 to Babylon, Jechonias begat *S'*;
12 and *S'* begat Zorobabel;
Lu 3:27 which was the son of *S'*, which

Salcah (*sal'-kah*) See also SALCHAH.
Jos 12: 5 in mount Hermon, and in *S'*,
13:11 Hermon, and all Bashan unto *S'*;
1Ch 5:11 in the land of Bashan unto *S'*:

Salchah (*sal'-kah*) See also SALCAH.
De 3:10 all Bashan, unto *S'* and Edrei,

sale
Le 25:27 count the years of the s' thereof,
50 price of his s' shall be according
De 18: 8 cometh of the s' of his patrimony.

Salem (*sa'-lem*) See also JERUSALEM.
Ge 14:18 Melchizedek king of *S'* brought
Ps 76: 2 In *S'* also is his tabernacle, and his
Heb 7: 1 For this Melchisedec king of *S'*,
2 after that also King of *S'*, which is,

Salim (*sa'-lim*)
Joh 3:23 was baptizing in Ænon near to *S'*,

Sallai (*sal'-lahee*) See also SALLU.
Ne 11: 8 And after him Gabbai, *S'*, nine
12:20 Of *S'*, Kallai; of Amok, Eber;

Sallu (*sal'-lu*) See also SALLAI.
1Ch 9: 7 *S'* the son of Meshullam, the son
Ne 11: 7 *S'* the son of Meshullam, the son
12: 7 *S'*, Amok, Hilkiah, Jedaiah. These

Salma (*sal'-mah*) See also SALMON; ZALMA.
1Ch 2:11 begat *S'*, and *S'* begat Boaz,
51 *S'* the father of Beth-lehem,
54 The sons of *S'*; Beth-lehem, and

Salmon (*sal'-mon*) See also SALMA.
Ru 4:20 Nahshon, and Nahshon begat *S'*,
21 And *S'* begat Boaz, and Boaz
Ps 68:14 in it, it was white as snow in *S'*.
M't 1: 4 Naasson; and Naasson begat *S'*;
5 *S'* begat Booz of Rachab; and Booz
Lu 3:32 of Booz, which was the son of *S'*,

Salmone (*sal-mo'-ne*)
Ac 27: 7 under Crete, over against *S'*;

Salome (*sa-lo'-me*)
M'r 15:40 the less and of Joses, and *S'*;
16: 1 Mary the mother of James, and *S'*,

salt See also SALTED; SALTPITS.
Ge 14: 3 vale of Siddim, which is the s' sea.
19:26 him, and she became a pillar of s'.
Le 2:13 offering shalt thou season with s';
13 the s' of the covenant of thy God
13 thine offerings thou shalt offer s'.
Nu 18:19 it is a covenant of s' for ever before
34: 3 coast of the s' sea eastward:
12 out of it shall be at the s' sea:
De 3:17 the sea of the plain, even the s' sea,
29:23 land thereof is brimstone, and s',
Jos 3:16 the sea of the plain, even the s' sea,
12: 3 the sea of the plain, even the s' sea
15: 2 was from the shore of the s' sea,
5 And the east border was the s' sea,
62 and the city of *S'*, and En-gedi;
18:19 were at the north bay of the s' sea
J'g 9:45 down the city, and sowed it with s'.
2Sa 8:13 of the Syrians in the valley of s',
2Ki 2:20 Bring me a new cruse, and put s'
21 the waters, and cast the s' in there,
14: 7 He slew of Edom in the valley of s'
1Ch 18:12 slew...Edomites in the valley of s'
2Ch 13: 5 and to his sons by a covenant of s'?
25:11 went to the valley of s', and smote
Ezr 6: 9 wheat, s', wine, and oil, according
7:22 s' without prescribing how much.
Job 6: 6 is unsavoury be eaten without s'?
Ps 60: *title* smote of Edom in the valley of s'
Jer 17: 6 in a s' land and not inhabited.
Eze 43:24 priests shall cast s' upon them,
47:11 be healed; they shall be given to s.
M't 5:13 Ye are the s' of the earth: but if the
13 but if the s' have lost his savour,
M'r 9:49 sacrifice shall be salted with s'.
50 *S'* is good: but if the s' have lost
50 Have s' in yourselves, and have
Lu 14:34 *S'* is good: but if the s' have lost
Col 4: 6 alway with grace, seasoned with s',
Jas 3:12 both yield s' water and fresh.

salted
Eze 16: 4 not s' at all, nor swaddled at all.
M't 5:13 savour, wherewith shall it be s'?
M'r 9:49 For every one shall be s' with fire,
49 every sacrifice shall be s' with salt.

saltness
M'r 9:50 but if the salt have lost his s',

saltpits
Zep 2: 9 the breeding of nettles, and s', and

salt-sea See SALT and SEA.

Salu (*sa'-lu*)
Nu 25:14 was Zimri, the son of *S'*, a prince

salutation See also SALUTATIONS.
Lu 1:29 what manner of s' this should be.
41 when Elisabeth heard the s' of Mary,
44 voice of thy s' sounded in mine ears,
1Co 16:21 s' of me Paul with mine own hand.
Col 4:18 The s' by the hand of me Paul.
2Th 3:17 The s' of Paul with mine own hand,

salutations
M'r 12:38 and love s' in the marketplaces,

salute See also SALUTED; SALUTETH.
1Sa 10: 4 And they will s' thee, and give
13:10 to meet him, that he might s' him.
25:14 of the wilderness to s' our master;
2Sa 8:10 son unto king David, to s' him,
2Ki 4:29 if thou meet any man, s' him not;
29 and if any s' thee, answer him not
10:13 to s' the children of the king and
M't 5:47 And if ye s' your brethren only,
10:12 when ye come into an house, s' it.
M'r 15:18 began to s' him, Hail, King of the
Lu 10: 4 shoes: and s' no man by the way.
Ac 25:13 came unto Cæsarea to s' Festus.
Ro 16: 5 *S'* my wellbeloved Epænetus, who
7 *S'* Andronicus and Junia, my
9 *S'* Urbane, our helper in Christ,
10 *S'* Apelles approved in Christ.
10 *S'* them which are of Aristobulus'
11 *S'* Herodion my kinsman. Greet
12 *S'* Tryphena and Tryphosa, who
12 *S'* the beloved Persis, which
13 *S'* Rufus chosen in the Lord, and
14 *S'* Asyncritus, Phlegon, Hermas,
15 *S'* Philologus, and Julia, Nereus,
16 *S'* one another with an holy kiss.
16 The churches of Christ s' you.
21 and Sosipater, my kinsmen, s' you.
22 who wrote this epistle, s' you in the
1Co 16:19 The churches of Asia s' you.
19 Aquila and Priscilla s' you much in
2Co 13:13 All the saints s' you.
Ph'p 4:21 *S'* every saint in Christ Jesus.
22 All the saints s' you, chiefly they
Col 4:15 *S'* the brethren...in Laodicea,
2Ti 4:19 *S'* Prisca and Aquila, and the
Tit 3:15 All that are with me s' thee. Greet
Ph'm 23 There s' thee Epaphras, my
Heb 13:24 *S'* all them that have the rule over
24 all the saints. They of Italy s' you.
3Jo 14 Peace be to thee. Our friends s' thee.

saluted
J'g 18:15 house of Micah, and s' him.
1Sa 17:22 and came and s' his brethren.
30:21 near to the people, he s' them.
2Ki 10:15 he s' him, and said to him, Is thine
M'r 9:15 amazed, and running to him s' him.
Lu 1:40 house of Zacharias, and s' Elisabeth.
Ac 18:22 and gone up, and s' the church, he
21: 7 and s' the brethren, and abode with
19 when he had s' them, he declared

saluteth
Ro 16:23 and of the whole church, s' you.
23 the chamberlain of the city s' you,
Col 4:10 Aristarchus...s' you, and Marcus,
12 Epaphras, who is one of you,...s' you,
1Pe 5:13 church that is at Babylon, s'...you;

salvation
Ge 49:18 I have waited for thy s', O Lord.
Ex 14:13 still, and see the s' of the Lord,
15: 2 and song, and he is become my s':
De 32:15 lightly esteemed the Rock of his s'.
1Sa 2: 1 enemies; because I rejoice in thy s'.
11:13 Lord hath wrought s' in Israel.
14:45 wrought this great s' in Israel?
19: 5 Lord wrought a great s' for all
2Sa 22: 3 my shield, and the horn of my s',
36 also given me the shield of thy s':
47 be the God of the rock of my s'.
51 He is the tower of s' for his king:
23: 5 this is all my s', and all my desire,
1Ch 16:23 shew forth from day to day his s'.
35 Save us, O God of our s', and
2Ch 6:41 thy priests,...be clothed with s',
20:17 see the s' of the Lord with you,
Job 13:16 He also shall be my s': for an
Ps 3: 8 *S'* belongeth unto the Lord: thy

Ps 9:14 of Zion: I will rejoice in thy s'.
13: 5 my heart shall rejoice in thy s'.
14: 7 Oh that the s' of Israel were come
18: 2 buckler, and the horn of my s',
35 also given me the shield of thy s':
46 and let the God of my s' be exalted.
20: 5 We will rejoice in thy s', and in the
21: 1 and in thy s' how...shall he rejoice!
5 His glory is great in thy s': honour
24: 5 righteousness from...God of his s'.
25: 5 for thou art the God of my s';
27: 1 Lord is my light and my s'; whom
9 neither forsake me, O God of my s'.
35: 3 me: say unto my soul, I am thy s'.
9 the Lord: it shall rejoice in his s'.
37: 39 s' of the righteous is of the Lord:
38: 22 haste to help me, O Lord my s'.
40: 10 declared thy faithfulness and thy s':
16 let such as love...s' say continually,
50: 23 aright will I shew the s' of God.
51: 12 Restore unto me the joy of thy s';
14 O God, thou God of my s':
53: 6 Oh that the s' of Israel were come
62: 1 upon God: from him cometh my s'.
2, 6 He only is my rock and my s'; he
7 In God is my s' and my glory:
65: 5 thou answer us, O God of our s';
68: 19 benefits, even the God of our s'.
20 that is our God is the God of s';
69: 13 hear me, in the truth of thy s'.
29 let thy s', O God, set me up on high.
70: 4 let such as love...s' say continually.
71: 15 thy righteousness and thy s' all
74: 12 working s' in the midst of the
78: 22 in God, and trusted not in his s':
79: 9 Help us, O God of our s', for the
85: 4 Turn us, O God of our s', and cause
7 mercy, O Lord, and grant us thy s'.
9 his s' is nigh them that fear him;
88: 1 O Lord God of my s', I have cried
89: 26 my God, and the rock of my s'.
91: 16 I satisfy him, and shew him my s'.
95: 1 joyful noise to the rock of our s'.
96: 2 shew forth his s' from day to day.
98: 2 The Lord hath made known his s':
3 earth have seen the s' of our God.
106: 4 thy people: O visit me with thy s';
116: 13 I will take the cup of s', and call
118: 14 and song, and is become my s'.
15 The voice of rejoicing and s' is in
21 heard me, and art become my s'.
119: 41 O Lord, even thy s', according to
81 My soul fainteth for thy s': but I
123 Mine eyes fail for thy s', and for
155 S' is far from the wicked: for they
166 Lord, I have hoped for thy s', and
174 I have longed for thy s', O Lord;
132: 16 also clothe her priests with s':
140: 7 the Lord, the strength of my s',
144: 10 It is he that giveth s' unto kings:
149: 4 he will beautify the meek with s'.
Isa 12: 2 Behold, God is my s'; I will trust,
2 my song; he also is become my s'.
3 ye draw water out of the wells of s'.
17: 10 hast forgotten the God of thy s',
25: 9 will be glad and rejoice in his s'.
26: 1 s' will God appoint for walls and
33: 2 our s' also in the time of trouble.
6 of thy times, and strength of s':
45: 8 and let them bring forth s', and let
17 in the Lord with an everlasting s':
46: 13 be far off, and my s' shall not tarry:
13 I will place s' in Zion for Israel my
49: 6 my s' unto the end of the earth.
8 in a day of s' have I helped thee:
51: 5 my s' is gone forth, and mine arms
6 but my s' shall be for ever, and my
8 and my s' from generation to
52: 7 tidings of good, that publisheth s';
10 earth shall see the s' of our God.
56: 1 for my s' is near to come, and my
59: 11 for s', but it is far off from us.
16 his arm brought s' unto him; and
17 and an helmet of s' upon his head;
60: 18 but thou shalt call thy walls S', and
61: 10 me with the garments of s',
62: 1 s' thereof as a lamp that burneth.
11 of Zion, Behold, thy s' cometh;
63: 5 mine own arm brought s' unto me;
Jer 3: 23 Truly in vain is s' hoped for from the
23 Lord our God is the s' of Israel.
La 3: 26 quietly wait for the s' of the Lord.
Jon 2: 9 I have vowed. S' is of the Lord.
Mic 7: 7 I will wait for the God of my s':
Hab 3: 8 thine horses and thy chariots of s'?
13 forth for the s' of thy people,
13 even for s' with thine anointed;
18 Lord, I will joy in the God of my s'.
Zec 9: 9 he is just, and having s'; lowly,
Lu 1: 69 hath raised up an horn of s' for us
77 knowledge of s' unto his people by
2: 30 For mine eyes have seen thy s',
3: 6 And all flesh shall see the s' of God.
19: 9 This day is s' come to this house,
Joh 4: 22 we worship: for s' is of the Jews.
Ac 4: 12 Neither is there s' in any other: for
13: 26 to you is the word of this s' sent.
47 be for s' unto the ends of the earth.
16: 17 which shew unto us the way of s'.
28: 28 s' of God is sent unto the Gentiles,
Ro 1: 16 power of God unto s' to every one
10: 10 mouth confession is made unto s'.
11: 11 fall s' is come unto the Gentiles,
13: 11 s' nearer than when we believed.
2Co 1: 6 it is for your consolation and s',
6 it is for your consolation and s'.
2Co 6: 2 in the day of s' have I succoured
2 time; behold, now is the day of s'.)
7: 10 sorrow worketh repentance to s'
Eph 1: 13 of truth, the gospel of your s':
6: 17 And take the helmet of s', and the
Ph'p 1: 19 turn to my s' through your prayer,
28 but to you of s', and that of God.
2: 12 work out your own s' with fear and
1Th 5: 8 and for an helmet, the hope of s'.
9 but to obtain s' by our Lord Jesus
2Th 2: 13 you to s' through sanctification of
2Ti 2: 10 also obtain the s' which is in Christ
3: 15 are able to make thee wise unto s'
Tit 2: 11 the grace of God that bringeth s'
Heb 1: 14 for them who shall be heirs of s'?
2: 3 we escape, if we neglect so great s';
10 make the captain of their s' perfect
5: 9 author of eternal s' unto all them
6: 9 you, and things that accompany s',
9: 28 the second time without sin unto s'.
1Pe 1: 5 power of God through faith unto s'
9 your faith, even the s' of your souls.
10 Of which s' the prophets have
2Pe 3 15 the longsuffering of our Lord is s';
Jude 3 to write unto you of the common s',
Re 7: 10 S' to our God which sitteth upon
12: 10 Now is come s', and strength, and
19: 1 saying, Alleluia; S', and glory,

Samaria (*sa-ma'-re-ah*) See also SAMARITAN.
1Ki 13: 32 places which are in the cities of S',
16: 24 he bought the hill S' of Shemer for
24 of Shemer, owner of the hill, S'.
28 his fathers, and was buried in S':
29 Ahab...reigned over Israel in S'
32 of Baal, which he had built in S'.
18: 2 And there was a sore famine in S'.
20: 1 and he went up and besieged S',
10 if the dust of S' shall suffice for
17 There are men come out of S'.
34 Damascus, as my father made in S'.
43 and displeased, and came to S'.
21: 1 by the palace of Ahab king of S'.
18 Ahab king of Israel, which is in S':
22: 10 in the entrance of the gate of S';
37 king died, and was brought to S';
37 and they buried the king in S'.
38 washed the chariot in the pool of S';
51 began to reign over Israel in S' the
2Ki 1: 2 his upper chamber that was in S',
3 the messengers of the king of S',
2: 25 and from thence he returned to S'.
3: 1 began to reign over Israel in S' the
6 king Jehoram went out of S' the
5: 3 were with the prophet that is in S'!
6: 19 ye seek. But he led them to S'.
20 pass, when they were come into S'.
20 behold, they were in the midst of S'.
24 host, and went up, and besieged S'.
25 And there was a great famine in S':
7: 1 barley for a shekel, in the gate of S'.
18 about this time in the gate of S':
10: 1 And Ahab had seventy sons in S'.
1 Jehu wrote letters, and sent to S',
12 arose and departed, and came to S'.
17 And when he came to S', he slew
17 all that remained unto Ahab in S',
35 fathers: and they buried him in S'.
36 that Jehu reigned over Israel in S'
13: 1 began to reign over Israel in S',
6 there remained the grove also in S'.)
9 fathers; and they buried him in S':
10 Jehoahaz to reign over Israel in S',
13 Joash was buried in S' with the
14: 14 and hostages, and returned to S'.
16 was buried in S' with the kings of
23 king of Israel began to reign in S',
15: 8 of Jeroboam reign over Israel in S'
13 and he reigned a full month in S'.
14 up from Tirzah, and came to S',
14 Shallum the son of Jabesh in S',
17 Israel, and reigned ten years in S'.
23 began to reign over Israel in S',
25 smote him in S', in the palace
27 began to reign over Israel in S',
17: 1 the son of Elah to reign in S' over
5 and went up to S', and besieged it
6 the king of Assyria took S', and
24 and placed them in the cities of S'
24 and they possessed S', and dwelt in
26 and placed in the cities of S', know
28 whom they had carried...from S'
18: 9 king of Assyria came up against S',
10 king of Israel, S' was taken.
34 they delivered S' out of mine hand?
21: 13 over Jerusalem the line of S', and
23: 18 of the prophet that came out of S'.
19 places that were in the cities of S',
2Ch 18: 2 years he went down to Ahab to S'.
9 at the entering in of the gate of S';
22: 9 caught him, (for he was hid in S',)
25: 13 Judah, from S'...unto Beth-horon,
24 hostages also, and returned to S'.
28: 8 them, and brought the spoil to S'.
9 out before the host that came to S',
15 brethren: then they returned to S'.
Ezr 4: 10 and set in the cities of S', and the
17 their companions that dwell in S',
Ne 4: 2 his brethren and the army of S',
Isa 7: 9 And the head of Ephraim is S', and
9 the head of S' is Remaliah's son.
8: 4 the spoil of S' shall be taken away
9: 9 Ephraim and the inhabitant of S',
10: 9 as Arpad? is not S' as Damascus?
10 excel them of Jerusalem and of S';
11 I have done unto S' and her idols,
36: 19 they delivered S' out of my hand?
Jer 23: 13 seen folly in the prophets of S':
31: 5 vines upon the mountains of S':
41: 5 and from S', even fourscore men,
Eze 16: 46 thine elder sister is S', she and her
51 Neither hath S' committed half of
53 captivity of S' and her daughters,
55 S' and her daughters shall return
23: 4 S' is Aholah, and Jerusalem
33 with the cup of thy sister S'.
Ho 7: 1 and the wickedness of S': for they
8: 5 Thy calf, O S', hath cast thee off;
6 calf of S' shall be broken in pieces.
10: 5 inhabitants of S' shall fear because
7 As for S', her king is cut off as the
13: 16 S' shall become desolate; for she
Am 3: 9 upon the mountains of S', and
12 Israel be taken out that dwell in S'
4: 1 that are in the mountain of S',
6: 1 and trust in the mountain of S',
8: 14 that sware by the sin of S', and say,
Ob 19 of Ephraim, and the fields of S':
Mic 1: 1 saw concerning S' and Jerusalem.
5 transgression of Jacob? is it not S'?
6 will make S' as an heap of the field,
Lu 17: 11 he passed through the midst of S'
Joh 4: 4 And he must needs go through S'.
5 cometh he to a city of S', which
7 a woman of S' to draw water:
9 saith the woman of S' unto him,
9 of me, which am a woman of S'?
Ac 1: 8 and in S', and unto the uttermost
8: 1 the regions of Judæa and S', except
5 Philip went down to the city of S',
9 and bewitched the people of S',
14 S' had received the word of God,
9: 31 all Judæa and Galilee and S', and
15: 3 passed through Phenice and S',

Samaritan (*sa-mar'-i-tun*) See also SAMARITANS.
Lu 10: 33 But a certain S', as he journeyed,
17: 16 him thanks: and he was a S'.
Joh 8: 48 Say we not well that thou art a S',

Samaritans (*sa-mar'-i-tuns*)
2Ki 17: 29 places which the S' had made,
M't 10: 5 into any city of the S' enter...not:
Lu 9: 52 and entered into a village of the S',
Joh 4: 9 Jews have no dealings with the S'.)
39 many of the S' of that city believed
40 when the S' were come unto him,
Ac 8: 25 gospel in many villages of the S'.

same^ See also SELFSAME.
Ge 2: 13 the s' is it that compasseth the
5: 29 This s' shall comfort us concerning
6: 4 the s' became mighty men which
7: 11 the s' day were all the fountains
10: 12 and Calah: the s' is a great city.
14: 8 the king of Bela (the s' is Zoar;)
15: 18 s' day the Lord made a covenant
19: 37 the s' is the father of the Moabites
38 the s' is the father of the children
21: 8 feast the s' day...Isaac was weaned.
25: 30 thee, with that s' red pottage;
26: 12 and received in the s' year an
24 appeared unto him the s' night,
32: 13 And he lodged there that s' night;
41: 48 about every city, laid he up in the s'.
44: 6 he spake unto them these s' words.
48: 7 of Ephrath; the s' is Beth-lehem.
Ex 5: 6 Pharaoh commanded the s' day the
12: 6 fourteenth day of the s' month:
25: 31 and his flowers, shall be of the s'.
35, 35, 35 under two branches of the s',
36 and their branches shall be of the s':
28: 8 which is upon it, shall be of the s',
30: 2 the horns thereof shall be of the s'.
37: 17 knops, and his flowers, were of the s':
21, 21, 21 under two branches of the s',
22 and their branches were of the s':
25 of it; the horns thereof were of the s'.
38: 2 of it; the horns thereof were of the s':
39: 5 ephod, that was upon it, was of the s',
Le 7: 15 be eaten the s' day that it is offered;
16 be eaten the s' day that he offereth
19: 6 be eaten the s' day ye offer it, and on
22: 30 the s' day it shall be eaten up; ye
23: 6 fifteenth day of the s' month is the
28 ye shall do no work in that s' day:
29 shall not be afflicted in that s' day,
30 doeth any work in that s' day,
30 s' soul will I destroy from among
Nu 6: 11 shall hallow his head that s' day.
9: 13 s' soul shall be cut off from among
10: 32 do unto us, the s' will we do unto thee.
15: 30 the s' reproacheth the Lord; and
32: 10 anger was kindled the s' time, and
De 9: 20 I prayed for Aaron also the s' time.
14: 28 tithe of thine increase the s' year,
27: 11 Moses charged the people the s' day,
31: 22 Moses...wrote this song the s' day,
Jos 6: 15 the city after the s' manner seven
11: 16 of Israel, and the valley of the s';
15: 8 the Jebusite; the s' is Jerusalem:
J'g 6: 25 it came to pass the s' night, that the
7: 4 with thee, the s' shall go with thee;
4 not go with thee, the s' shall not go.
9 it came to pass the s' night, that
1Sa 4: 12 came to Shiloh the s' day with his
6: 15 sacrificed sacrifices the s' day unto
16 they returned to Ekron the s' day.
9: 17 this s' shall reign over my people.
10: 12 one of the s' place answered and said,
14: 35 the s' was the first altar that he built
17: 23 and spake according to the s' words:
30 and spake after the s' manner:
31: 6 all his men, that s' day together.

2Sa 2:23 there, and died in the s' place:
5: 7 of Zion: the s' is the city of David.
23: 7 burned with fire in the s' place.
8 the s' was Adino the Eznite: he
1Ki 7:35 and the borders thereof were of the s'.
8:64 The s' day did the king hallow the
13: 3 he gave a sign the s' day, saying,
9 again by the s' way that thou camest.
2Ki 3: 6 went out of Samaria the s' time,
8:22 Libnah revolted at the s' time.
19:29 year that which springeth of the s';
33 that he came, by the s' shall he return,
1Ch 1:27 Abram; the s' is Abraham.
4:33 that were round about the s' cities,
16:17 confirmed the s' to Jacob for a law,
17: 3 And it came to pass the s' night,
2Ch 7: 8 the s' time Solomon kept the feast
13: 9 s' may be a priest of them that are no
15:11 offered unto the Lord the s' time,
16:10 some of the people the s' time.
21:10 s' time also did Libnah revolt from
27: 5 of Ammon gave him the s' year an
32:12 Hath not the s' Hezekiah taken
30 This s' Hezekiah also stopped the
34:28 and upon the inhabitants of the s'.
35:16 service...was prepared the s' day,
Ezr 4:15 sedition within the s' of old time:
5: 3 At the s' time came to them Tatnai,
13 s' king Cyrus made a decree to build
16 Then came the s' Sheshbazzar,
6: 3 the s' Cyrus the king made a decree
10:23 and Kelaiah, (the s' is Kelita,)
Ne 4:22 the s' time said I unto the people,
6: 4 answered...after the s' manner.
10:37 that the s' Levites might have the
Es 9: 1 Adar, on the thirteenth day of the s',
17 fourteenth day of the s' rested they,
18 the fifteenth day of the s' they rested,
21 and the fifteenth day of the s', yearly,
Job 4: 8 and sow wickedness, reap the s'.
13: 2 What ye know, the s' do I know also:
Ps 68:23 the tongue of thy dogs in the s'.
75: 8 and he poureth out the s': but the
102:27 But thou art the s', and thy years
105:10 confirmed the s' unto Jacob for a law,
113: 3 the sun unto the going down of the s'
Pr 28:24 s' is the companion of a destroyer.
Ec 9:15 man remembered that s' poor man.
Isa 7:20 In the s' day shall the Lord shave
37:30 year that which springeth of the s':
34 he came, by the s' shall he return,
Jer 27: 8 will not serve the s' Nebuchadnezzar
28: 1 And it came to pass the s' year, in
17 the prophet died the s' year in the
31: 1 At the s' time, saith the Lord, will
39:10 vineyards and fields at the s' time.
Eze 3:18 the s' wicked man shall die in his
10:16 the s' wheels also turned not from
22 s' faces which I saw by the river of
21:26 the crown: this shall not be the s':
23:38 defiled my sanctuary in the s' day,
39 came the s' day into my sanctuary
24: 2 of the day, even of this s' day:
2 against Jerusalem this s' day.
38:10 at the s' time shall things come
18 the s' time when Gog shall come
44: 3 and shall go out by the way of the s'.
Da 3: 6 the s' hour be cast into the midst of
15 be cast the s' hour into the midst of
4:33 s' hour was the thing fulfilled upon
36 the s' time my reason returned unto
5: 5 s' hour came forth fingers of a man's
12 were found in the s' Daniel, whom
7:21 s' horn made war with the saints,
12: 1 was a nation even to that s' time:
Am 2: 7 his father will go in unto the s' maid,
Zep 1: 9 s' day also will I punish all those
Zec 6:10 and come thou the s' day, and go into
Mal 1:11 even unto the going down of the s'
M't 3: 4 s' John had his raiment of camel's
5:19 the s' shall be called great in the
46 do not even the publicans the s'?
10:19 that s' hour what ye shall speak.
12:50 the s' is my brother, and sister, and
13: 1 s' day went Jesus out of the house,
20 the s' is he that heareth the word,
15:22 woman...came out of the s' coasts,
18: 1 the s' time came the disciples unto
4 the s' is greatest in the kingdom
28 the s' servant went out, and found
21:42 s' is become the head of the corner:
22:23 s' day came to him the Sadducees,
24:13 unto the end, the s' shall be saved.
25:16 talents went and traded with the s',
26:23 in the dish, the s' shall betray me.
44 the third time, saying the s' words.
48 Whomsoever I...kiss, that s' is he:
55 In that s' hour said Jesus to the
27:44 with him, cast the s' in his teeth.
M'r 3:35 the s' is my brother, and my sister,
4:35 s' day, when the even was come,
8:35 the gospel's, the s' shall save it.
9:35 to be first, the s' shall be last of all,
10:10 asked him again of the s' matter.
13:13 unto the end, the s' shall be saved.
14:39 and prayed, and spake the s' words.
44 Whomsoever I...kiss, that s' is he;
Lu 2: 8 were in the s' country shepherds
25 the s' man was just and devout,
6:33 ye? for sinners also do even the s'.
38 s' measure that ye mete withal it
7:21 that s' hour he cured many of their
47 little is forgiven, the s' loveth little.
9:24 for my sake, the s' shall save it.
48 among you all, the s' shall be great.
10: 7 And in the s' house remain, eating

Lu 10:10 ways out into the streets of the s',
12:12 in the s' hour what ye ought to say.
13:31 The s' day there came certain of the
16: 1 s' was accused unto him that he
17:29 s' day that Lot went out of Sodom it
20:17 s' is become...head of the corner?
19 s' hour sought to lay hands on him:
47 s'...receive greater damnation.
23:40 thou art in the s' condemnation?
51 (The s' had not consented to the
24:13 went that s' day to a village called
33 And they rose up the s' hour, and
Joh 1: 2 s' was in the beginning with God.
7 The s' came for a witness, to bear
33 s' said unto me, Upon whom thou
33 s' is he which baptizeth with the
3: 2 The s' came to Jesus by night, and
26 the s' baptizeth, and all men come
4:53 knew that it was at the s' hour,
5: 9 and on the s' day was the sabbath.
11 s' said unto me, Take up thy bed,
36 s' works that I do, bear witness of
7:18 s' is true, and no unrighteousness
8:25 Even the s' that I said unto you,
10: 1 way, the s' is a thief and a robber.
11: 6 abode two days still in the s' place
49 being the high priest that s' year,
12:21 s' came therefore to Philip, which
48 s' shall judge him in the last day.
15: 5 the s' bringeth forth much fruit:
18:13 was the high priest that s' year.
20:19 s' day at evening, being the first
Ac 1:11 s' Jesus, which is taken up from
22 s' day that he was taken up from us,
2:36 that God hath made that s' Jesus,
41 s' day there were added unto them
7:19 s' dealt subtilly with our kindred,
35 s' did God send to be a ruler and a
8: 9 beforetime in the s' city used sorcery,
35 and began at the s' scripture, and
12: 6 the s' night Peter was sleeping
13:33 hath fulfilled the s' unto us their
14: 9 The s' heard Paul speak: who
15:27 also tell you the s' things by mouth.
16:17 s' followed Paul and us, and cried,
18 her. And he came out the s' hour.
33 took them the s' hour of the night,
18: 3 because he was of the s' craft, he
19:23 s' time there arose no small stir
21: 9 the s' man had four daughters,
22:13 the s' hour I looked up upon him.
24:20 Or else let these s' here say, if
28: 7 s' quarters were possessions of
Ro 1:32 not only do the s', but have pleasure
2: 1 that judgest doest the s' things.
3 and doest the s', that thou shalt
8:20 who hath subjected the s' in hope,
9:17 s' purpose have I raised thee up,
21 the s' lump to make one vessel unto
10:12 for the s' Lord over all is rich unto
12: 4 all members have not the s' office:
16 Be of the s' mind one toward another.
13: 3 and thou shalt have praise of the s':
1Co 1:10 that ye all speak the s' thing, and
10 the s' mind and in the s' judgment.
7:20 every man abide in the s' calling
8: 3 love God, the s' is known of him.
9: 8 or saith not the law the s' also?
10: 3 did all eat the s' spiritual meat;
4 did all drink the s' spiritual drink:
11:23 s' night in which he was betrayed
25 s' manner also he took the cup,
12: 4 diversities of gifts, but the s' Spirit.
5 of administrations, but the s' Lord.
6 it is the s' God which worketh all
8 word of knowledge by the s' Spirit;
9 To another faith by the s' Spirit; to
9 the gifts of healing by the s' Spirit;
25 have the s' care one for another.
15:39 All flesh is not the s' flesh: but
2Co 1: 6 in the enduring of the s' sufferings
2: 2 the s' which is made sorry by me?
3 And I wrote this s' unto you, lest,
3:14 day remaineth the s' vail untaken
18 are changed into the s' image from
4:13 We having the s' spirit of faith,
6:13 Now for a recompence in the s', (I
7: 8 the s' epistle hath made you sorry,
8: 6 also finish in you the s' grace also.
16 put the s' earnest care into the
19 by us to the glory of the s' Lord,
9: 4 in this s' confident boasting.
5 that the s' might be ready, as a
12:18 walked we not in the s' spirit?
18 walked we not in the s' steps?
Ga 2: 8 s' was mighty in me toward the
10 the s' which I also was forward
3: 7 the s' are the children of Abraham
Eph 3: 6 be fellowheirs, and of the s' body,
6: 8 the s' shall he receive of the Lord,
9 ye masters, do the s' things unto
22 sent unto you for the s' purpose,
Ph'p 1:30 Having the s' conflict which ye saw
2:18 For the s' cause also do ye joy, and
3: 1 To write the s' things to you, to me
16 let us walk by the s' rule, let us
16 rule, let us mind the s' thing.
4: 2 they be of the s' mind in the Lord.
Col 4: 2 watch in the s' with thanksgiving;
8 sent unto you for the s' purpose,
2Ti 2: 2 s' commit thou to faithful men,
Heb 1:12 but thou art the s', and thy years
2:14 himself likewise took part of the s';
4:11 fall after the s' example of unbelief.
6:11 one of you do shew the s' diligence
10:11 offering oftentimes the s' sacrifices,

Heb11: 9 the heirs with him of the s' promise:
13: 8 Jesus Christ the s' yesterday, and
Jas 3: 2 in word, the s' is a perfect man,
10 Out of the s' mouth proceedeth
11 the s' place sweet water and bitter?
1Pe 2: 7 s' is made the head of the corner,
4: 1 likewise with the s' mind: for he
4 with them to the s' excess of riot,
10 so minister the s' one to another,
5: 9 the s' afflictions are accomplished
2Pe 2:19 the s' is he brought in bondage.
3: 7 by the s' word are kept in store,
1Jo 2:23 Son, the s' hath not the Father:
27 as the s' anointing teacheth you
Re 3: 5 the s' shall be clothed in white
11:13 s' hour was...a great earthquake,
14:10 The s' shall drink of the wine of

Samgar-nebo *(sam″-gar-ne'-bo)*
Jer 39: 3 Nergal-sharezer, S', Sarsechim,

Samlah *(sam'-lah)*
Ge 36:36 S' of Masrekah reigned in his
37 S' died, and Saul of Rehoboth by
1Ch 1:47 S' of Masrekah reigned in his
48 S' was dead, Shaul of Rehoboth

Samos *(sa'-mos)*
Ac 20:15 and the next day we arrived at S'.

Samothracia *(sam-o-thra'-she-ah)*
Ac 16:11 came with a straight course to S',

Samson *(sam'-sun)* See also SAMSON'S.
J'g 13:24 a son, and called his name S':
14: 1 And S' went down to Timnath, and
3 S' said unto his father, Get her for
5 Then went S' down, and his father
7 woman; and she pleased S' well.
10 and S' made there a feast; for so
12 S' said unto them, I will now put
15: 1 that S' visited his wife with a kid;
3 And Samson s' concerning them,
4 S' went and caught three hundred
6 S', the son in law of the Timnite,
7 S' said unto them, Though ye have
10 To bind S' are we come up, to do
11 said to S', Knowest thou not that
12 S' said unto them, Sware unto me,
16 S' said, With the jawbone of an ass,
16: 1 Then went S' to Gaza, and saw
2 Gazites, saying, S' is come hither.
3 And S' lay till midnight, and arose
6 And Delilah said to S', Tell me, I
7 S' said unto her, If they bind me
9 The Philistines be upon thee, S'.
10 And Delilah said unto S', Behold,
12 The Philistines be upon thee, S'.
13 And Delilah said unto S', Hitherto
14,20 The Philistines be upon thee, S'.
23 delivered S' our enemy into our
25 Call for S', that he may make us
25 they called for S' out of the prison
26 S' said unto the lad that held him
27 that beheld while S' made sport.
28 S' called unto the Lord, and said,
29 And S' took hold of the two middle
30 And S' said, Let me die with the
Heb11:32 Barak, and of S', and of Jephthae;

Samson's *(sam'-suns)*
J'g 14:15 they said unto S' wife, Entice thy
16 S' wife wept before him, and said,
20 S' wife was given to his companion,

Samuel *(sam'-u-el)* See also SHEMUEL.
1Sa 1:20 a son, and called his name S',
2:18 But S' ministered before the Lord,
21 the child S' grew before the Lord.
26 the child S' grew on, and was in
3: 1 child S' ministered unto the Lord
3 was, and S' was laid down to sleep;
4 That the Lord called S': and he
6 And the Lord called yet again, S'.
6 S' arose and went to Eli, and said,
7 Now S' did not yet know the Lord,
8 the Lord called S' again the third
9 Eli said unto S', Go, lie down: and
9 S' went and lay down in his place.
10 and called as at other times, S', S'.
10 Then S' answered, Speak; for thy
11 the Lord said to S', Behold, I will
15 And S' lay until the morning, and
15 S' feared to show Eli the vision.
16 Eli called S', and said, S', my son.
18 S' told him every whit, and hid
19 S' grew, and the Lord was with
20 knew that S' was established to be
21 for the Lord revealed himself to S'
4: 1 the word of S' came to all Israel.
7: 3 S' spake unto all the house of
5 And S' said, Gather all Israel to
6 S' judged the children of Israel in
8 the children of Israel said to S',
9 And S' took a sucking lamb, and
9 S' cried unto the Lord for Israel;
10 as S' was offering up the burnt
12 Then S' took a stone, and set it
13 the Philistines all the days of S'.
15 S' judged Israel all the days of his
8: 1 when S' was old, that he made his
4 and came to S' unto Ramah,
6 But the thing displeased S', when
6 us. And S' prayed unto the Lord.
7 the Lord said unto S', Hearken
10 S' told all the words of the Lord
19 refused to obey the voice of S';
21 And S' heard all the words of the
22 the Lord said to S', Hearken unto
22 And S' said unto the men of Israel,

1Sa 9:14 behold, S· came out against them;
15 Now the Lord had told S· in his ear
17 when S· saw Saul, the Lord said
18 Saul drew near to S· in the gate,
19 S· answered Saul,...I am the seer:
22 And S· took Saul and his servant,
23 And S· said unto the cook, Bring
24 S· said, Behold that which is left!
24 So Saul did eat with S· that day.
25 S· communed with Saul upon the top
26 S· called Saul to the top of the
26 went out both of them, he and S·,
27 S· said to Saul, Bid the servant pass
10: 1 S· took a vial of oil, and poured it
9 had turned his back to go from S·,
14 they were no where, we came to S·.
15 Tell me,...what S· said unto you.
16 of the kingdom, whereof S· spake,
17 And S· called the people together
20 when S· had caused all the tribes of
24 S· said to all the people, See ye him
25 S· told the people the manner of
25 And S· sent all the people away,
11: 7 not forth after Saul and after S·,
12 the people said unto S·, Who is he
14 Then said S· to the people, Come,
12: 1 And S· said unto all Israel, Behold,
6 S· said unto...people, It is the Lord
11 Lord sent...Jephthah, and S·, and
18 So S· called unto the Lord; and the
18 greatly feared the Lord and S·.
19 people said unto S·, Pray for thy
20 S· said unto the people, Fear not:
13: 8 the set time that S· had appointed:
8 but S· came not to Gilgal; and the
10 S· came; and Saul went out to meet
11 And S· said, What hast thou done?
13 And S· said to Saul, Thou hast done
15 And S· arose, and gat him up from
15: 1 S·...said unto Saul, The Lord sent
10 came the word of the Lord unto S·,
11 And it grieved S·; and he cried unto
12 when S· rose early to meet Saul in
12 it was told S·, saying, Saul came
13 And S· came to Saul: and Saul said
14 S· said, What meaneth then this
16 S· said unto Saul, Stay, and I will
17 And S· said, When thou wast little
20 And Saul said unto S·, Yea, I have
22 And S· said, Hath the Lord as great
24 Saul said unto S·, I have sinned:
26 S· said unto Saul, I will not return
27 And as S· turned about to go away,
28 And S· said...The Lord hath rent
31 So S· turned again after Saul; and
32 Then said S·, Bring ye hither to me
33 S· said, As thy sword hath made
33 S· hewed Agag in pieces before the
34 Then S· went to Ramah; and Saul
35 S· came no more to see Saul until
35 nevertheless S· mourned for Saul:
16: 1 the Lord said unto S·, How long
2 And S· said, How can I go? if Saul
4 S· did that which the Lord spake,
7 Lord said unto S·, Look not on his
8 and made him pass before S·.
10 seven of his sons to pass before S·.
10 S· said unto Jesse, The Lord hath
11 S· said unto Jesse, Are here all thy
11 S· said unto Jesse, Send and fetch
13 Then S· took the horn of oil, and
13 So S· rose up, and went to Ramah.
19: 18 escaped, and came to S· to Ramah,
18 he and S· went and dwelt in Naioth.
20 S· standing as appointed over them,
22 and said, Where are S· and David?
24 and prophesied before S· in like
25: 1 And S· died; and all the Israelites
28: 3 Now S· was dead, and all Israel had
11 thee? And he said, Bring me up S·.
12 when the woman saw S·, she cried
14 And Saul perceived that it was S·,
15 And S· said to Saul, Why hast thou
16 Then said S·, Wherefore then dost
20 afraid, because of the words of S·:
1Ch 6:28 the sons of S·; the firstborn Vashni,
9:22 David and S· the seer did ordain
11: 3 to the word of the Lord by S·.
26:28 And all that S· the seer, and Saul
29:29 written in the book of S· the seer,
2Ch 35:18 from the days of S· the prophet;
Ps 99: 6 and S· among them that call upon
Jer 15: 1 Though Moses and S· stood before
Ac 3:24 Yea, and all the prophets from S·
13:20 and fifty years, until S· the prophet.
Heb11:32 of David also, and S·, and of the

Sanballat (*san-bal'-lat*)
Ne 2:10 When S· the Horonite, and Tobiah
19 when S· the Horonite, and Tobiah
4: 1 when S· heard that we builded the
7 to pass, that when S·, and Tobiah,
6: 1 came to pass, when S·, and Tobiah,
2 That S· and Geshem sent unto me,
5 Then sent S· his servant unto me
12 for Tobiah and S· had hired him.
14 God, think thou upon Tobiah and S·
13:28 was son in law to S· the Horonite:

sanctification
1Co 1:30 righteousness,...s·, and redemption:
1Th 4: 3 this is the will of God, even your s·,
4 possess his vessel in s· and honour;
2Th 2:13 to salvation through s· of the Spirit
1Pe 1: 2 Father, through s· of the Spirit, unto

sanctified
Ge 2: 3 blessed the seventh day, and s· it:
Ex 19:14 unto the people, and s· the people;
29:43 tabernacle shall be s· by my glory.
Le 8:10 all that was therein, and s· them.
15 at the bottom of the altar, and s· it,
30 and s· Aaron, and his garments,
10: 3 I will be s· in them that come nigh
27:15 if he that s· it will redeem his house,
19 if he that s· the field will in any wise
Nu 7: 1 and had anointed it, and s· it, and
1 had anointed them, and s· them;
8:17 land of Egypt I s· them for myself.
20:13 the Lord, and he was s· in them.
De 32:51 because ye s· me not in the midst
1Sa 7: 1 s· Eleazar his son to keep the ark
16: 5 And he s· Jesse and his sons, and
21: 5 it were s· this day in the vessel.
1Ch 15:14 priests and...Levites s· themselves
2Ch 5:11 priests that were present were s·,
7:16 have I chosen and s· this house,
20 house, which I have s· for my name,
29:15 their brethren, and s· themselves,
17 so they s· the house of the Lord in
19 vessels,...have we prepared and s·,
34 the other priests had s· themselves:
30: 3 had not s· themselves sufficiently,
8 sanctuary, which he hath s· for ever:
15 were ashamed, and s· themselves,
17 the congregation that were not s·:
24 number of priests s· themselves.
31:18 they s· themselves in holiness:
Ne 3: 1 they s· it, and set up the doors of it;
1 unto the tower of Meah they s· it,
12:47 they s· holy things unto the Levites;
47 s· them unto the children of Aaron.
Job 1: 5 about that Job sent and s· them, and
Isa 5:16 is holy shall be s· in righteousness.
13: 3 I have commanded my s· ones, I
Jer 1: 5 camest...out of the womb I s· thee,
Eze 20:41 will be s· in you before the heathen.
28:22 in her, and shall be s· in her.
25 be s·...in the sight of the heathen,
36:23 shall be s· in you before their eyes.
38:16 when I shall be s· in thee, O Gog,
39:27 am s· in them in the sight of many
48:11 the priests that are s· of the sons of
Joh 10:36 whom the Father hath s·, and sent
17:19 also might be s· through the truth.
Ac 20:32 among all them which are s·.
26:18 among them which are s· by faith
Ro 15:16 being s· by the Holy Ghost.
1Co 1: 2 to them that are s· in Christ Jesus,
6:11 but ye are washed, but ye are s·, but
7:14 unbelieving husband is s· by the wife,
14 unbelieving wife is s· by the husband:
1Ti 4: 5 For it is s· by the word of God and
2Ti 2:21 s·, and meet for the master's use, and
Heb 2:11 that sanctifieth and they who are s·
10:10 By the which will we are s· through
14 perfected for ever them that are s·.
29 of the covenant, wherewith he was s·,
Jude 1 them that are s· by God the Father,

sanctifieth
M't 23:17 gold, or the temple that s· the gold?
19 the gift, or the altar that s· the gift?
Heb 2:11 that s· and they who are sanctified
9:13 s· to the purifying of the flesh:

sanctify See also SANCTIFIED; SANCTIFIETH.
Ex 13: 2 S· unto me all the firstborn,
19:10 and s· them to day and to morrow,
22 let the priests...s· themselves,
23 bounds about the mount, and s· it.
28:41 and consecrate them, and s· them,
29:27 s· the breast of the wave offering,
33 made, to consecrate and to s· them:
36 it, and thou shalt anoint it, to s· it.
37 atonement for the altar, and s· it;
44 And I will s· the tabernacle of the
44 I will s· also both Aaron and his sons,
30:29 And thou shalt s· them, that they
31:13 that I am the Lord that doth s· you.
40:10 and all his vessels, and s· the altar:
11 shall anoint the laver...and s· it.
13 and anoint him, and s· him;
Le 8:11 the laver and his foot, to s· them.
12 head, and anointed him, to s· him.
11:44 ye shall therefore s· yourselves,
20: 7 S· yourselves therefore, and be ye
8 them: I am the Lord which s· you.
21: 8 Thou shalt s· him therefore; for he
8 I the Lord, which s· you, am holy.
15 his people: for I the Lord do s· him.
23 for I the Lord do s· them.
22: 9 profane it: I the Lord do s· them.
16 things: for I the Lord do s· them.
27:14 when a man shall s· his house to
16 a man shall s· unto the Lord some
17 If he s· his field from the year of
18 if he s· his field after the jubile,
22 if a man s· unto the Lord a field
26 Lord's firstling, no man shall s· it;
Nu 11:18 S· yourselves against to morrow,
20:12 s· me in the eyes of the children of
27:14 s· me at the water before their eyes:
De 5:12 Keep the sabbath day to s· it, as the
15:19 shalt s· unto the Lord thy God:
Jos 3: 5 said unto the people, S· yourselves:
7:13 Up, s· the people, and say,
13 S· yourselves against to morrow:
1Sa 16: 5 s· yourselves, and come with me to
1Ch 15:12 s· yourselves, both ye and your
23:13 he should s· the most holy things,
2Ch 29: 5 me, ye Levites, s· now yourselves,
5 and s· the house of the Lord God of
17 first day of the first month to s·,
34 upright in heart to s· themselves
30:17 not clean, to s· them unto the Lord
35: 6 kill the passover, and s· yourselves,
Ne 13:22 the gates, to s· the sabbath day.
Isa 8:13 S· the Lord of hosts himself; and
29:23 of him, they shall s· my name,
23 and s· the Holy One of Jacob, and
66:17 They that s· themselves, and purify
Eze 20:12 that I am the Lord that s· them.
36:23 And I will s· my great name, which
37:28 know that I the Lord do s· Israel,
38:23 I magnify myself, and s· myself;
44:19 shall not s· the people with their
46:20 the utter court, to s· the people.
Joe 1:14 S· ye a fast, call a solemn assembly,
2:15 s· a fast, call a solemn assembly:
16 s· the congregation, assemble the
Joh 17:17 S· them through thy truth: thy
19 for their sakes I s· myself, that they
Eph 5:26 he might s· and cleanse it with the
1Th 5:23 the very God of peace s· you wholly;
Heb13:12 he might s· the people with his own
1Pe 3:15 But s· the Lord God in your hearts:

sanctuaries
Le 21:23 that he profane not my s·: for I
26:31 and bring your s· unto desolation,
Jer 51:51 strangers are come into the s· of
Eze 28:18 Thou hast defiled thy s· by the
Am 7: 9 the s· of Israel shall be laid waste;

sanctuary See also SANCTUARIES.
Ex 15:17 S·, O Lord, which thy hands have
25: 8 let them make me a s·; that I may
30:13 shekel after the shekel of the s·:
24 after the shekel of the s·, and of
36: 1 of work for the service of the s·,
3 the work of the service of the s·,
4 that wrought all the work of the s·,
6 work for the offering of the s·.
38:24 shekels, after the shekel of the s·.
25 shekels, after the shekel of the s·:
26 shekel, after the shekel of the s·:
27 were cast the sockets of the s·, and
Le 4: 6 the Lord, before the vail of the s·.
5:15 of silver, after the shekel of the s·,
10: 4 from before the s· out of the camp.
12: 4 nor come into the s·, until the
16:33 make an atonement for the holy s·,
19:30 my sabbaths, and reverence my s·:
20: 3 to defile my s·, and to profane my
21:12 Neither shall he go out of the s·,
12 nor profane the s· of his God; for
26: 2 my sabbaths, and reverence my s·:
27: 3 silver, after the shekel of the s·.
25 according to the shekel of the s·:
Nu 3:28 keeping the charge of the s·.
31 vessels of the s· wherewith they
32 them that keep the charge of the s·.
38 keeping the charge of the s· for
47 shekel of the s· shalt thou take
50 shekels, after the shekel of the s·:
4:12 wherewith they minister in the s·,
15 made an end of covering the s·,
15 and all the vessels of the s·, as the
16 and of all that therein is, in the s·,
7: 9 the service of the s· belonging unto
13, 19, 25, 31, 37, 43, 49, 55, 61, 67, 73, 79,
85 shekels, after the shekel of the s·;
86 apiece, after the shekel of the s·;
8:19 of Israel come nigh unto the s·.
10:21 set forward, bearing the s·: and
18: 1 shall bear the iniquity of the s·:
3 not come nigh the vessels of the s·
5 ye shall keep the charge of the s·
16 shekels, after the shekel of the s·,
19:20 hath defiled the s· of the Lord:
Jos 24:26 oak, that was by the s· of the Lord.
1Ch 9:29 and all the instruments of the s·,
22:19 build ye the s· of the Lord God,
24: 5 for the governors of the s·, and
28:10 thee to build an house for the s·:
2Ch 20: 8 built thee a s· therein for thy name,
26:18 go out of the s·; for thou hast
29:21 kingdom, for the s·, and for Judah.
30: 8 unto the Lord, and enter into his s·,
19 to the purification of the s·.
36:17 the sword in the house of their s·,
Ne 10:39 where are the vessels of the s·, and
Ps 20: 2 Send thee help from the s·, and
63: 2 so as I have seen thee in the s·.
68:24 of my God, my King, in the s·.
73:17 Until I went into the s· of God;
74: 3 hath done wickedly in the s·.
7 They have cast fire into thy s·, they
77:13 Thy way, O God, is in the s·: who is
78:54 them to the border of his s·, even
69 built his s· like high palaces, like
96: 6 strength and beauty are in his s·.
102:19 down from the height of his s·;
114: 2 Judah was his s·, and Israel his
134: 2 Lift up your hands in the s·, and
150: 1 Praise God in his s·: praise him
Isa 8:14 he shall be for a s·; but for a stone
16:12 that he shall come to his s· to pray;
43:28 profaned the princes of the s·,
60:13 to beautify the place of my s·;
63:18 adversaries...trodden down thy s·.
Jer 17:12 beginning is the place of our s·.
La 1:10 the heathen entered into her s·,
2: 7 he hath abhorred his s·, he hath
20 prophet be slain in...s· of the Lord?
4: 1 stones of the s· are poured out in
Eze 5:11 because thou hast defiled my s·
8: 6 that I should go far off from my s·?
9: 6 is the mark; and begin at my s·.
11:16 yet will I be to them as a little s· in
23:38 have defiled my s· in the same day,

Eze 23: 39 same day into my s· to profane it;
24: 21 Behold, I will profane my s·, the
25: 3 thou saidst, Aha, against my s·,
37: 26 will set my s· in the midst of them
28 my s· shall be in the midst of them
41: 21 squared, and the face of the s·:
23 temple and the s· had two doors.
42: 20 make a separation between the s·
43: 21 place of the house, without the s·.
44: 1 the gate of the outward s· which
5 with every going forth of the s·.
7 have brought into my s· strangers,
7 to be in my s·, to pollute it, even
8 set keepers of my charge in my s·
9 in flesh, shall enter into my s·,
11 they shall be ministers in my s·,
15 kept the charge of my s· when the
16 They shall enter into my s·, and
27 the day that he goeth into the s·,
27 inner court, to minister in the s·,
45: 2 for the s· five hundred in length
3 the s· and the most holy place.
4 the priests the ministers of the s·,
4 houses, and an holy place for the s·.
18 without blemish, and cleanse the s·:
47: 12 waters they issued out of the s·:
48: 8 the s· shall be in the midst of it.
10 s· of the Lord shall be in the midst
21 s· of the house shall be in the midst
Da 8: 11 the place of his s· was cast down.
13 to give both the s· and the host to
14 days; then shall the s· be cleansed.
9: 17 cause thy face to shine upon thy s·
26 shall destroy the city and the s·;
11: 31 shall pollute the s· of strength, and
Zep 3: 4 her priests have polluted the s·,
Heb 8: 2 A minister of the s·, and of the true
9: 1 of divine service, and a worldly s·.
2 shewbread; which is called the s·.
13: 11 whose blood is brought into the s·

sand See also QUICKSANDS.
Ge 22: 17 s· which is upon the sea shore;
32: 12 make thy seed as the s· of the sea,
41: 49 gathered corn as the s· of the sea,
Ex 2: 12 the Egyptian, and hid him in the s·.
De 33: 19 seas, and of treasures hid in the s·.
Jos 11: 4 as the s· that is upon the sea shore
J'g 7: 12 the s· by the sea side for multitude.
1Sa 13: 5 as the s· which is on the sea shore
2Sa 17: 11 as the s· that is by the sea for
1Ki 4: 20 many, as the s· which is by the sea
29 as the s· that is on the sea shore.
Job 6: 3 be heavier than the s· of the sea:
29: 18 I shall multiply my days as the s·.
Ps 78: 27 fowls like as the s· of the sea:
139: 18 are more in number than the s·:
Pr 27: 3 stone is heavy, and the s· weighty;
Isa 10: 22 people Israel be as the s· of the sea,
48: 19 Thy seed also had been as the s·,
Jer 5: 22 have placed the s· for the bound of
15: 8 to me above the s· of the seas:
33: 22 neither the s· of the sea measured:
Ho 1: 10 Israel shall be as the s· of the sea,
Hab 1: 9 shall gather the captivity as the s·.
M't 7: 26 which built his house upon the s·:
Ro 9: 27 of Israel be as the s· of the sea,
Heb11: 12 as the s· which is by the sea shore
Re 13: 1 And I stood upon the s· of the sea,
20: 8 the number...is as the s· of the sea.

sandals
M'r 6: 9 But be shod with s·; and not put
Ac 12: 8 Gird thyself, and bind on thy s·.

sang
Ex 15: 1 Then s· Moses and the children of
Nu 21: 17 Then Israel s· this song, Spring up,
J'g 5: 1 Then s· Deborah and Barak the
1Sa 29: 5 Is not this David, of whom they s·
2Ch 29: 28 the singers s·, and the trumpeters
30 they s· praises with gladness, and
Ezr 3: 11 And they s· together by course in
Ne 12: 42 the singers s· loud, with Jezrahiah
Job 38: 7 the morning stars s· together, and
Ps 7: *title* David, which he s· unto the Lord,
106: 12 they his words; they s· his praise.
Ac 16: 25 prayed, and s· praises unto God:

sank
Ex 15: 5 they s· into the bottom as a stone.
10 s· as lead in the mighty waters.

Sansannah (*san-san'-nah*) See also KIRJATH-SANNAH.
Jos 15: 31 Ziklag, and Madmannah, and S·,

sap
Ps 104: 16 The trees of the Lord are full of s·;

Saph (*saf*) See also SIPHAI.
2Sa 21: 18 Sibbechai the Hushathite slew S·.

Saphir (*sa'-fur*)
Mic 1: 11 ye away, thou inhabitant of S·,

Sapphira (*saf-fi'-rah*)
Ac 5: 1 named Ananias, with S· his wife,

sapphire See also SAPPHIRES.
Ex 24: 10 were a paved work of a s· stone,
28: 18 row shall be an emerald, a s·, and
39: 11 the second row, an emerald, a s·,
Job 28: 16 with the precious onyx, or the s·.
La 4: 7 rubies, their polishing was of s·:
Eze 1: 26 as the appearance of a s· stone:
10: 1 over them as it were a s· stone, as
28: 13 and the jasper, the s·, the emerald,
Re 21: 19 was jasper; the second, s·; the

sapphires
Job 28: 6 stones of it are the place of s·: and
Ca 5: 14 is as bright ivory overlaid with s·.
Isa 54: 11 and lay thy foundations with s·.

Sara (*sa'-rah*) See also SARAH.
Heb11: 11 S· herself received strength to
1Pe 3: 6 as S· obeyed Abraham, calling him

Sarah (*sa'-rah*) See also SARA; SARAH'S; SARAI; SERAH.
Ge 17: 15 Sarai, but S· shall her name be.
17 shall S·, that is ninety years old,
19 S· thy wife shall bare thee a son
21 which S· shall bare unto thee at
18: 6 hastened into the tent unto S·, and
9 unto him, Where is S· thy wife?
10 lo, S· thy wife shall have a son.
10 S· heard it in the tent door, which
11 Abraham and S· were old and well
11 with S· after the manner of women.
12 S· laughed within herself, saying,
13 Wherefore did S· laugh, saying,
14 of life, and S· shall have a son.
15 S· denied, saying, I laughed not;
20: 2 Abraham said of S· his wife, She is
2 king of Gerar sent, and took S·.
14 and restored him S· his wife.
16 And unto S· he said, Behold, I have
18 because of S· Abraham's wife.
21: 1 the Lord visited S· as he had said,
1 Lord did unto S· as he had spoken.
2 S· conceived, and bare Abraham a
3 him, whom S· bare to him, Isaac.
6 And S· said, God hath made me to
7 S· should have given children suck?
9 And S· saw the son of Hagar the
12 in all that S· hath said unto thee,
23: 1 S· was an hundred and seven and
1 were the years of the life of S·.
2 S· died in Kirjath-arba; the same
2 and Abraham came to mourn for S·,
19 Abraham buried S· his wife in the
24: 36 S· my master's wife bare a son to
25: 10 Abraham buried, and S· his wife.
49: 31 buried Abraham and S· his wife;
Nu 26: 46 of the daughter of Asher was S·.
Isa 51: 2 father, and unto S· that bare you:
Ro 9: 9 I come, and S· shall have a son.

Sarah's (*sa'-rahs*)
Ge 24: 67 her into his mother S· tent, and
25: 12 S· handmaid, bare unto Abraham:
Ro 4: 19 yet the deadness of S· womb:

Sarai (*sa'-rahee*) See also SARAH; SARAI'S.
Ge 11: 29 the name of Abram's wife was S·;
30 S· was barren; she had no child.
31 and S· his daughter in law, his son
12: 5 Abram took S· his wife, and Lot
11 he said unto S· his wife, Behold
17 with great plagues because of S·
16: 1 Now S· Abram's wife bare him no
2 S· said unto Abram, Behold now,
2 Abram hearkened to the voice of S·.
3 S· Abram's wife took Hagar her
5 S· said unto Abram, My wrong be
6 Abram said unto S·, Behold, thy
6 when S· dealt hardly with her, she
8 from the face of my mistress S·.
17: 15 As for S· thy wife, thou shalt not
15 thou shalt not call her name S·, but

Sarai's (*sa'-rahees*)
Ge 16: 8 he said, Hagar, S· maid, whence

Saraph (*sa'-raf*)
1Ch 4: 22 S·, who had the dominion in Moab,

sardine
Re 4: 3 upon like a jasper and a s· stone:

Sardis (*sar'-dis*)
Re 1: 11 and unto Thyatira, and unto S·,
3: 1 the angel of the church in S· write;
4 Thou hast a few names even in S·

Sardites (*sar'-dites*)
Nu 26: 26 of Sered, the family of the S·: of

sardius (*sar'-de-us*)
Ex 28: 17 the first row shall be a s·, a topaz,
39: 10 the first row was a s·, a topaz, and
Eze 28: 13 thy covering, the s·, and the diamond,
Re 21: 20 The fifth, sardonyx; the sixth, s·;

sardonyx (*sar'-do-nix*)
Re 21: 20 The fifth, s·; the sixth, sardius;

Sarepta (*sa-rep'-tah*) See also ZAREPHATH.
Lu 4: 26 save unto S·, a city of Sidon, unto

Sargon (*sar'-gon*)
Isa 20: 1 S· the king of Assyria sent him,)

Sarid (*sa'-rid*)
Jos 19: 10 of their inheritance was unto S·:
12 And turned from S· eastward

Saron (*sa'-ron*) See also SHARON.
Ac 9: 35 all that dwelt at Lydda and S· saw

Sarsechim (*sar'-se-kim*)
Jer 39: 3 Nergal-sharezer, Samgar-nebo, S·,

Saruch (*sa'-ruk*) See also SERUG.
Lu 3: 35 Which was the son of S·, which

sat See also SATEST.
Ge 18: 1 he s· in the tent door in the heat
19: 1 and Lot s· in the gate of Sodom:
21: 16 and s· her down over against him a
16 And she s· over against him, and
31: 34 the images,...and s· upon them.
37: 25 And they s· down to eat bread: and
38: 14 and s· in an open place, which is by
43: 33 they s· before him, the firstborn
48: 2 himself, and s· upon the bed.
Ex 2: 15 Midian: and he s· down by a well.
12: 29 of Pharaoh that s· on his throne
16: 3 when we s· by the flesh pots, and
17: 12 put it under him, and he s· thereon
18: 13 that Moses s· to judge the people:
32: 6 people s· down to eat and to drink,
Le 15: 6 whereon he s· that hath the issue
22 toucheth any thing that she s· upon
De 33: 3 and they s· down at thy feet;
J'g 6: 11 and s· under an oak which was in
13: 9 the woman as she s· in the field:
19: 6 And they s· down, and did eat and
15 s· him down in a street of the city:
20: 26 wept, and s· there before the Lord,
Ru 2: 14 And she s· beside the reapers: and
4: 1 to the gate, and s· him down there:
1 And he turned aside, and s· down.
2 ye down here. And they s· down.
1Sa 1: 9 Eli the priest s· upon a seat by a
4: 13 Eli s· upon a seat by the wayside
19: 9 as he s· in his house with his javelin
20: 24 the king s· him down to eat meat.
25 king s· upon his seat, as at other
25 Abner s· by Saul's side, and David's
28: 23 from the earth, and s· upon the bed.
2Sa 2: 13 they s· down, the one on the one side
7: 1 pass, when the king s· in his house,
18 David in, and s· before the Lord,
18: 24 And David s· between the two gates:
19: 8 the king arose, and s· in the gate.
23: 8 The Tachmonite that s· in the seat,
1Ki 2: 12 s· Solomon upon the throne of David
19 and s· down on his throne, and
19 and she s· on his right hand.
13: 20 came to pass, as they s· at the table,
16: 11 reign, as soon as he s· on his throne,
19: 4 and s· down under a juniper tree:
21: 13 children of Belial, and s· before him:
22: 10 king of Judah s· each on his throne,
2Ki 1: 9 behold, he s· on the top of an hill.
4: 20 mother, he s· on her knees till noon,
6: 32 But Elisha s· in his house, and the
32 house, and the elders s· with him;
11: 19 he s· on the throne of the kings.
13: 13 and Jeroboam s· upon his throne:
1Ch 17: 1 to pass, as David s· in his house,
16 king came and s· before the Lord,
29: 23 Solomon s· on the throne of the Lord
2Ch 18: 9 s· either of them on his throne,
9 and they s· in a void place at the
Ezr 9: 3 of my beard, and s· down astonied.
4 and I s· astonied until the evening
10: 9 s· in the street of the house of God,
16 s· down in the first day of the tenth
Ne 1: 4 I s· down and wept, and mourned
8: 17 booths, and s· under the booths:
Es 1: 2 king Ahasuerus s· on the throne
14 which s· the first in the kingdom;)
2: 19 then Mordecai s· in the king's gate.
21 while Mordecai s· in the king's gate,
3: 15 king and Haman s· down to drink;
5: 1 the king s· upon his royal throne
Job 2: 8 and he s· down among the ashes.
13 s· down with him upon the ground
29: 25 I chose out their way, and s· chief,
Ps 26: 4 I have not s· with vain persons,
137: 1 rivers of Babylon, there we s· down,
Ca 2: 3 I s· down under his shadow with
Jer 3: 2 In the ways hast thou s· for them,
15: 17 I s· not in the assembly of the
17 I s· alone because of thy hand: for
26: 10 s· down in the entry of the new gate
32: 12 that s· in the court of the prison.
36: 12 and, lo, all the princes s· there,
22 Now the king s· in the winterhouse
39: 3 came in, and s· in the middle gate,
Eze 3: 15 of Chebar, and I s· where they s·,
8: 1 of the month, as I s· in mine house,
1 the elders of Judah s· before me,
14 s· women weeping for Tammuz.
14: 1 elders...unto me, and s· before me.
20: 1 elders of Israel...and s· before me.
Da 2: 49 but Daniel s· in the gate of the king.
Jon 3: 6 with sackcloth, and s· in ashes.
4: 5 and s· on the east side of the city,
5 booth, and s· under it in the shadow,
M't 4: 16 The people which s· in darkness
16 which s· in the region and shadow
9: 10 as Jesus s· at meat in the house,
10 and s· down with him and his
13: 1 the house, and s· by the sea side.
2 that he went into a ship, and s·;
48 they drew to shore, and s· down,
14: 9 them which s· with him at meat,
15: 29 a mountain, and s· down there.
24: 3 as he s· upon the mount of Olives,
26: 7 it on his head, as he s· at meat.
20 come, he s· down with the twelve.
55 I s· daily with you teaching in the
58 went in, and s· with the servants,
69 Now Peter s· without in the palace:
28: 2 stone from the door, and s· upon it
M'r 2: 15 as Jesus s· at meat in his house,
15 sinners s· also together with Jesus
3: 32 And the multitude s· about him,
34 looked...on them which s· about him,
4: 1 into a ship, and s· in the sea;
6: 22 Herod and them that s· with him,
26 for their sakes which s· with him,
40 they s· down in ranks, by hundreds,
9: 35 he s· down, and called the twelve,
10: 46 s· by the highway side begging.
11: 2 colt tied, whereon never man s·;
7 on him; and he s· upon him.

M'r 12: 41 Jesus s· over against the treasury,
13: 3 as he s· upon the mount of Olives
14: 3 as he s· at meat,...came a woman
18 as they s· and did eat, Jesus said,
54 and he s· with the servants, and
16: 14 unto the eleven as they s· at meat,
19 and s· on the right hand of God.
Lu 4: 20 again to the minister, and s· down.
5: 3 s· down, and taught the people out
29 of others that s· down with them.
7: 15 he that was dead s· up, and began
36 house, and s· down to meat.
37 knew that Jesus s· at meat in the
49 And they that s· at meat with him
10: 39 Mary which also s· at Jesus' feet,
11: 37 he went in, and s· down to meat.
14: 15 one of them that s· at meat with
18: 35 blind man s· by the way side
19: 30 tied, whereon never yet man s·:
22: 14 the hour was come, he s· down, and
55 Peter s· down among them.
56 maid beheld him as he s· by the
24: 30 as he s· at meat with them, he took
Joh 4: 6 his journey, s· thus on the well:
6: 3 and there he s· with his disciples.
10 So the men s· down, in number
8: 2 and he s· down, and taught them.
9: 8 Is not this he that s· and begged?
11: 20 him: but Mary s· still in the house.
12: 2 them that s· at the table with him.
14 had found a young ass, s· thereon;
19: 13 s· down in the judgment seat in a
Ac 2: 3 of fire, and it s· upon each of them.
3: 10 it was he which s· for alms at the
6: 15 all that s· in the council, looking
9: 40 and when she saw Peter, she s· up.
12: 21 s· upon his throne, and made an
13: 14 on the sabbath day, and s· down.
14: 8 there s· a certain man at Lystra,
16: 13 and we s· down, and spake unto
20: 9 And there s· in a window a certain
25: 17 I s· on the judgment seat, and
26: 30 Bernice,...they that s· with them:
1Co 10: 7 people s· down to eat and drink,
Heb 1: 3 s· down on the right hand of the
10: 12 s· down on the right hand of God;
Re 4: 2 heaven, and one s· on the throne.
3 he that s· was to look upon like a
9 thanks to him that s· on the throne,
10 before him that s· on the throne,
5: 1 hand of him that s· on the throne
7 hand of him that s· upon the throne.
6: 2 he that s· on him had a bow; and a
4 was given to him that s· thereon to
5 s· on him had a pair of balances
8 his name that s· on him was Death,
9: 17 and them that s· on them, having
11: 16 which s· before God on their seats,
14: 14 one s· like unto the Son of man,
15 voice to him that s· on the cloud,
16 s· on the cloud thrust in his sickle
19: 4 God that s· on the throne, saying,
11 s· upon him was called Faithful
19 against him that s· on the horse,
21 sword of him that s· upon the horse,
20: 4 thrones, and they s· upon them,
11 white throne, and him that s· on
21: 5 he that s· upon the throne said,

Satan (*sa'-tun*) See also SATAN'S.
1Ch 21: 1 S· stood up against Israel, and
Job 1: 6 and S· came also among them.
7 Lord said unto S·, Whence comest
7 S· answered the Lord, and said,
8 the Lord said unto S·, Hast thou
9 S· answered the Lord, and said,
12 Lord said unto S·, Behold, all that
12 S· went forth from the presence of
2: 1 and S· came also among them to
2 Lord said unto S·, From whence
2 S· answered the Lord, and said,
3 the Lord said unto S·, Hast thou
4 S· answered the Lord, and said,
6 Lord said unto S·, Behold, he is in
7 went S· forth from the presence of
Ps 109: 6 and let S· stand at his right hand.
Zec 3: 1 S· standing at his right hand to
2 the Lord said unto S·, The Lord
2 Lord rebuke thee, O S·; even the
M't 4: 10 unto him, Get thee hence, S·:
12: 26 And if S· cast out S·, he is divided
16: 23 Get thee behind me, S·: thou art
M'r 1: 13 forty days, tempted of S·; and was
3: 23 parables, How can S· cast out S·?
26 S· rise up against himself, and be
4: 15 S· cometh immediately, and taketh
8: 33 saying, Get thee behind me, S·:
Lu 4: 8 unto him, Get thee behind me, S·:
10: 18 I beheld S· as lightning fall from
11: 18 S· also be divided against himself,
13: 16 of Abraham, whom S· hath bound,
22: 3 Then entered S· into Judas
31 S· hath desired to have you, that
Joh 13: 27 after the sop S· entered into him.
Ac 5: 3 why hath S· filled thine heart to lie
26: 18 from the power of S· unto God, that
Ro 16: 20 bruise S· under your feet shortly.
1Co 5: 5 To deliver such an one unto S·
7: 5 that S· tempt you not for your
2Co 2: 11 S· should get an advantage of us:
11: 14 S· himself is transformed into an
12: 7 the messenger of S· to buffet me,
1Th 2: 18 and again; but S· hindered us.
2Th 2: 9 is after the working of S· with all
1Ti 1: 20 whom I have delivered unto S·,
5: 15 are already turned aside after S·.
Re 2: 9 not, but are the synagogue of S·.
2: 13 slain among you, where S· dwelleth.
24 have not known the depths of S·,
3: 9 make them of the synagogue of S·,
12: 9 serpent, called the Devil, and S·,
20: 2 serpent, which is the Devil, and S·,
7 S· shall be loosed out of his prison,

Satan's (*sa'-tuns*)
Re 2: 13 dwellest, even where S· seat is:

satest
Ps 9: 4 s· in the throne judging right.
Eze 23: 41 s· upon a stately bed, and a table

satiate See also SATIATED; UNSATIABLE.
Jer 31: 14 And I will s· the soul of the priests
46: 10 and it shall be s· and made drunk

satiated
Jer 31: 25 I have s· the weary soul, and I

satisfaction
Nu 35: 31 no s· for the life of a murderer,
32 no s· for him that is fled to the city

satisfied
Ex 15: 9 my lust shall be s· upon them; I
Le 26: 26 and ye shall eat, and not be s·.
De 14: 29 shall come, and shall eat and be s·;
33: 23 O Naphtali, s· with favour, and
Job 19: 22 God, and are not s· with my flesh?
27: 14 offspring shall not be s· with bread.
31: 31 had of his flesh! we cannot be s·.
Ps 17: 15 I shall be s·, when I awake, with
22: 26 The meek shall eat and be s·: they
36: 8 They shall be abundantly s· with
37: 19 days of famine they shall be s·.
59: 15 meat, and grudge if they be not s·.
63: 5 My soul shall be s· as with marrow
65: 4 we shall be s· with the goodness of
81: 16 of the rock should I have s· thee.
104: 13 earth is s· with the fruit of thy
105: 40 s· them with the bread of heaven.
Pr 12: 11 He that tilleth his land shall be s·
14 A man shall be s· with good by the
14: 14 a good man shall be s· from himself.
18: 20 A man's belly shall be s· with the
19: 23 he that hath it shall abide s·; he
20: 13 and thou shalt be s· with bread.
27: 20 so the eyes of man are never s·.
30: 15 are three things that are never s·,
Ec 1: 8 the eye is not s· with seeing, nor
4: 8 neither is his eye s· with riches;
5: 10 He that loveth silver shall not be s·
Isa 9: 20 left hand, and they shall not be s·:
44: 16 flesh; he roasteth roast, and is s·:
53: 11 travail of his soul, and shall be s·:
66: 11 suck, and be s· with the breasts
Jer 31: 14 and my people shall be s· with my
50: 10 all that spoil her shall be s·, saith
19 and his soul shall be s· upon mount
La 5: 6 the Assyrians, to be s· with bread.
Eze 16: 28 them, and yet couldest not be s·.
29 and yet thou wast not s· herewith.
Joe 2: 19 oil, and ye shall be s· therewith:
26 ye shall eat in plenty, and be s·,
Am 4: 8 drink water; but they were not s·:
Mic 6: 14 Thou shalt eat, but not be s·; and
Hab 2: 5 and is as death, and cannot be s·,

satisfiest
Ps 145: 16 s· the desire of every living thing.

satisfieth
Ps 103: 5 s· thy mouth with good things;
107: 9 he s· the longing soul, and filleth
Isa 55: 2 your labour for that which s· not?

satisfy See also SATISFIED; SATISFIEST; SATISFIETH; SATISFYING.
Job 38: 27 s· the desolate and waste ground;
Ps 90: 14 O s· us early with thy mercy; that
91: 16 With long life will I s· him, and
132: 15 I will s· her poor with bread.
Pr 5: 19 let her breasts s· thee at all times;
6: 30 if he steal to s· his soul when he
Isa 58: 10 hungry, and s· the afflicted soul;
11 s· thy soul in drought, and make
Eze 7: 19 they shall not s· their souls,
M'r 8: 4 can a man s· these men with bread

satisfying
Pr 13: 25 eateth to the s· of his soul: but
Col 2: 23 any honour to the s· of the flesh.

satyr (*sa'-tur*) See also SATYRS.
Isa 34: 14 and the s· shall cry to his fellow;

satyrs (*sa'-turs*)
Isa 13: 21 there, and s· shall dance there.

Saul (*sawl*) See also PAUL; SAUL'S; SHAUL.
Ge 36: 37 and S· of Rehoboth by the river
38 And S· died, and Baal-hanan the
1Sa 9: 2 he had a son, whose name was S·,
3 Kish said to S· his son, Take now
5 S· said to his servant that was with
7 said S· to his servant, But, behold,
8 the servant answered S· again, and
10 said S· to his servant, Well said;
15 told Samuel...a day before S· came,
17 when Samuel saw S·, the Lord said
18 S· drew near to Samuel in the gate,
19 Samuel answered S·, and said, I am
21 S· answered and said, Am not I a
22 Samuel took S· and his servant,
24 was upon it, and set it before S·.
24 So S· did eat with Samuel that day.
25 communed with S· upon the top of
26 Samuel called S· to the top of the
26 S· arose, and they went out both of
27 Samuel said to S·, Bid the servant
10: 11, 12 Is S· also among the prophets?
16 S· said unto his uncle, He told us
21 and S· the son of Kish was taken:
26 S· also went home to Gibeah; and
11: 4 the messengers to Gibeah of S·,
5 S· came after the herd out of the
5 S· said, What aileth the people that
6 And the Spirit of God came upon S·
7 cometh not forth after S· and after
11 that S· put the people in three
12 he that said, Shall S· reign over us?
13 S· said, There shalt not a man be
15 made S· king before the Lord in
15 there S· and all the men of Israel
13: 1 S· reigned one year; and when he
2 S· chose him three thousand men
2 two thousand were with S· in
3 S· blew the trumpet throughout all
4 S· had smitten a garrison of the
4 called together after S· to Gilgal.
7 As for S·, he was yet in Gilgal, and
9 And S· said, Bring hither a burnt
10 and S· went out to meet him, that
11 And S· said, Because I saw that the
13 Samuel said to S·, Thou hast done
15 S· numbered the people that were
16 S·, and Jonathan his son, and the
22 of the people that were with S· and
22 with S· and with Jonathan his son
14: 1 that Jonathan the son of S· said
2 S· tarried in the uttermost part of
16 the watchmen of S· in Gibeah of
17 said S· unto the people that were
18 S· said unto Ahiah, Bring hither
19 while S· talked unto the priest, that
19 S· said unto the priest, Withdraw
20 And S· and all the people that were
21 Israelites that were with S· and
24 S· had adjured the people, saying,
33 Then they told S·, saying, Behold,
34 S· said, Disperse yourselves among
35 S· built an altar unto the Lord: the
36 S· said, Let us go down after the
37 S· asked counsel of God, Shall I go
38 S· said, Draw ye near hither, all the
40 the people said unto S·, Do what
41 S· said unto the Lord God of Israel,
41 S· and Jonathan were taken: but
42 And S· said, Cast lots between me
43 S· said to Jonathan, Tell me what
44 S· answered, God do so and more
45 people said unto S·, Shall Jonathan
46 Then S· went up from following
47 S· took the kingdom over Israel,
49 the sons of S· were Jonathan, and
51 And Kish was the father of S·; and
52 the Philistines all the days of S·:
52 when S· saw any strong man, or any
15: 1 Samuel also said unto S·, The Lord
4 S· gathered the people together,
5 S· came to a city of Amalek, and
6 And S· said unto the Kenites, Go,
7 And S· smote the Amalekites from
9 S· and the people spared Agag, and
11 repenteth me that I have set up S·
12 Samuel rose early to meet S· in
12 Samuel, saying, S· came to Carmel,
13 Samuel came to S·: and S· said
15 S· said, They have brought them
16 Samuel said unto S·, Stay, and I
20 S· said unto Samuel, Yea, I have
24 S· said unto Samuel, I have sinned:
26 And Samuel said unto S·, I will not
31 So Samuel turned again after S·;
31 and S· worshipped the Lord.
34 and S· went up to his house
34 up to his house to Gibeah of S·.
35 And Samuel came no more to see S·
35 Samuel mourned for S·: and the
35 repented that he had made S· king
16: 1 How long wilt thou mourn for S·,
2 I go? if S· hear it, he will kill me.
14 Spirit of the Lord departed from S·,
17 S· said unto his servants, Provide
19 S· sent messengers unto Jesse, and
20 sent them by David his son unto S·.
21 And David came to S·, and stood
22 S· sent to Jesse, saying, Let David,
23 evil spirit from God was upon S·,
23 so S· was refreshed, and was well,
17: 2 And S· and the men of Israel were
8 a Philistine, and ye servants to S·?
11 When S· and all Israel heard those
12 for an old man in the days of S·,
13 sons of Jesse went and followed S·
14 and the three eldest followed S·.
15 David went and returned from S·
19 S·, and they, and all the men of
31 they rehearsed them before S·:
32 And David said to S·, Let no man's
33 S· said to David, Thou art not able
34 David said unto S·, Thy servant
37 S· said unto David, Go, and the
38 S· armed David with his armour,
39 And David said unto S·, I cannot go
55 S· saw David go forth against the
57 S· with the head of the Philistine
58 S· said unto him, Whose son art
18: 1 made an end of speaking unto S·,
2 S· took him that day, and would let
5 David went...whithersoever S· sent
5 S· set him over the men of war,
6 singing...dancing, to meet king S·,
7 said, S· has slain his thousands,
8 S· was very wroth, and the saying
9 S· eyed David from that day and
10 evil spirit from God came upon S·,

1Sa 18:11 *S·* cast the javelin; for he said, I
12 *S·* was afraid of David, because the
12 him, and was departed from *S·*.
13 *S·* removed him from him, and
15 *S·* saw that he behaved himself very
17 *S·* said to David, Behold my elder
17 *S·* said, Let not my hand be upon
18 And David said unto *S·*, Who am I?
20 they told *S·*, and the thing pleased
21 *S·* said, I will give him her, that she
21 *S·* said to David, Thou shalt this
22 And *S·* commanded his servants,
24 the servants of *S·* told him, saying,
25 *S·* said, Thus shall ye say to David,
25 *S·* thought to make David fall by
27 *S·* gave him Michal his daughter to
28 *S·* saw and knew that the Lord was
29 *S·* was yet the more afraid of David;
29 and *S·* became David's enemy
30 wisely than all the servants of *S·*;
19: 1 *S·* spake to Jonathan his son, and
2 *S·* my father seeketh to kill thee:
4 spake good of David unto *S·* his
6 *S·* hearkened unto the voice of
6 *S·* sware, As the Lord liveth, he
7 Jonathan brought David to *S·*, and
9 spirit from the Lord was upon *S·*,
10 *S·* sought to smite David even to
11 *S·*...sent messengers unto David's
14 *S·* sent messengers to take David,
15 *S·* sent the messengers again to
17 *S·* said unto Michal, Why hast thou
17 Michal answered *S·*, He said unto
18 and told him all that *S·* had done to
19 And it was told *S·*, saying, Behold,
20 *S·* sent messengers to take David:
20 was upon the messengers of *S·*,
21 told *S·*, he sent other messengers,
21 *S·* sent messengers...the third
24 Is *S·* also among the prophets?
20:26 *S·* spake not any thing that day:
27 and *S·* said unto Jonathan his son,
28 And Jonathan answered *S·*, David
32 Jonathan answered *S·* his father,
33 *S·* cast a javelin at him to smite
21: 7 a certain man of the servants of *S·*
7 of the herdmen that belonged to *S·*.
10 and fled that day for fear of *S·*, and
11 *S*. hath slain his thousands, and
22: 6 *S·* heard that David was discovered,
6 *S·* abode in Gibeah under a tree in
7 *S·* said unto his servants that stood
9 was set over the servants of *S·*, and
12 And *S·* said, Hear now, thou son of
13 And *S·* said unto him, Why have ye
21 that *S·* had slain the Lord's priests.
22 there, that he would surely tell *S·*:
23: 7 told *S·* that David was come to
7 *S·* said, God hath delivered him
8 *S·* called all the people...to war,
9 that *S·* secretly practised mischief
10 that *S·* seeketh to come to Keilah,
11 will *S·* come down, as thy servant
12 and my men into the hand of *S·*?
13 told *S·* that David was escaped
14 *S·* sought him every day, but God
15 that *S·* was come...to seek his life:
17 hand of *S·* my father shall not find
17 that also *S·* my father knoweth.
19 Then came up the Ziphites to *S·* to
21 *S·* said, Blessed be ye of the Lord;
24 arose, and went to Ziph before *S·*:
25 *S·*...and his men went to seek him.
25 when *S·* heard that, he pursued
26 And *S·* went on this side of the
26 haste to get away for fear of *S·*;
26 *S·* and his men compassed David
27 there came a messenger unto *S·*,
28 *S·* returned from pursuing after
24: 1 *S·* was returned from following the
2 *S·* took three thousand chosen men
3 and *S·* went in to cover his feet:
7 suffered them not to rise against *S·*.
7 But *S·* rose up out of the cave, and
8 cried after *S·*, saying, My lord the
8 when *S·* looked behind him, David
9 And David said to *S·*, Wherefore
16 of speaking these words unto *S·*,
16 *S·* said, Is this thy voice, my son
16 *S·* lifted up his voice, and wept.
22 sware unto *S·*. And *S·* went home;
25:44 *S·* had given Michal his daughter,
26: 1 Ziphites came unto *S·* to Gibeah,
2 *S·* arose, and went down to the
3 *S·* pitched in the hill of Hachilah,
3 saw that *S·* came after him in the
4 understood that *S·* was come in
5 to the place where *S·* had pitched:
5 and David beheld...where *S·* lay,
5 *S·* lay in the trench, and the people
6 go down with me to *S·* to the camp?
7 *S·* lay sleeping within the trench,
17 *S·* knew David's voice, and said, Is
21 Then said *S·*, I have sinned:
25 *S·* said to David, Blessed be thou,
25 way, and *S·* returned to his place.
27: 1 perish one day by the hand of *S·*:
1 *S·* shall despair of me, to seek me
4 was told *S·* that David was fled to
28: 3 And *S·* had put away those that had
4 and *S·* gathered all Israel together,
5 *S·* saw the host of the Philistines,
6 *S·* enquired of the Lord, the Lord
7 Then said *S·* unto his servants,
8 *S·* disguised himself, and put on
9 thou knowest what *S·* hath done,

1Sa 28:10 *S·* sware to her by the Lord, saying,
12 the woman spake to *S·*, saying,
12 thou deceived me? for thou art *S·*.
13 woman said unto *S·*, I saw gods
14 *S·* perceived that it was Samuel,
15 Samuel said to *S·*, Why hast thou
15 *S·* answered, I am sore distressed;
20 *S·* fell straightway all along on the
21 the woman came unto *S·*, and saw
25 And she brought it before *S·*, and
29: 3 Is not this David, the servant of *S·*
5 *S·* slew his thousands, and David
31: 2 Philistines followed hard upon *S·*
3 the battle went sore against *S·*,
4 said *S·* unto his armourbearer,
4 *S·* took a sword, and fell upon it.
5 armourbearer saw...*S·* was dead,
6 So *S·* died, and his three sons, and
7 and that *S·* and his sons were dead,
8 found *S·* and his three sons fallen
11 the Philistines had done to *S·*;
12 took the body of *S·* and the bodies
2Sa 1: 1 came to pass after the death of *S·*,
2 a man came out of the camp from *S·*
4 *S·* and Jonathan his son are dead
5 *S·* and Jonathan his son be dead?
6 behold, *S·* leaned upon his spear;
12 fasted until even, for *S·*, and for
17 with this lamentation over *S·* and
21 is vilely cast away, the shield of *S·*,
22 sword of *S·* returned not empty.
23 *S·* and Jonathan were lovely and
24 daughters of Israel, weep over *S·*,
2: 4 were they that buried *S·*.
5 shewed this kindness...unto *S·*,
7 for your master *S·* is dead, and also
8 took Ish-bosheth the son of *S·*,
12 servants of Ish-bosheth...son of *S·*,
15 pertained to Ish-bosheth...son of *S·*,
3: 1 long war between the house of *S·*
1 the house of *S·* waxed weaker and
6 was war between the house of *S·*
6 himself strong for the house of *S·*.
7 *S·* had a concubine, whose name
8 kindness...unto the house of *S·*
10 the kingdom from the house of *S·*,
4: 4 tidings came of *S·* and Jonathan
8 head of Ish-bosheth the son of *S·*
8 avenged my lord...this day of *S·*,
10 told me, saying, Behold, *S·* is dead,
5: 2 past, when *S·* was king over us,
6:20 the daughter of *S·* came out to meet
23 the daughter of *S·* had no child
7:15 as I took it from *S·*, whom I put
9: 1 any that is left of the house of *S·*,
2 was of the house of *S·* a servant
3 there not yet any of the house of *S·*,
6 the son of Jonathan, the son of *S·*,
7 restore thee all the land of *S·* thy
9 master's son all that pertained to *S·*
12: 7 delivered thee out of the hand of *S·*;
16: 5 man of the family of the house of *S·*,
8 all the blood of the house of *S·*,
19:17 Ziba the servant of the house of *S·*,
24 Mephibosheth son of *S·* came
21: 1 It is for *S·*, and for his bloody house
2 *S·* sought to slay them in his zeal
4 will have no silver nor gold of *S·*,
6 will hang them up in Gibeah of *S·*,
7 the son of Jonathan the son of *S·*,
7 David and Jonathan the son of *S·*.
8 two sons...whom she bare unto *S·*,
8 sons of Michal the daughter of *S·*,
11 what Rizpah...the concubine of *S·*,
12 David went and took the bones of *S·*
12 Philistines had slain *S·* in Gilboa:
13 up from thence the bones of *S·* and
14 bones of *S·* and Jonathan his son
22: 1 enemies, and out of the hand of *S·*:
1Ch 5:10 in the days of *S·* they made war
8:33 Ner begat Kish, and Kish begat *S·*,
33 and *S·* begat Jonathan, and
9:39 Ner begat Kish; and Kish begat *S·*;
39 and *S·* begat Jonathan, and
10: 2 Philistines followed hard after *S·*,
2 and Malchi-shua, the sons of *S·*.
3 And the battle went sore against *S·*,
4 Then said *S·* to his armourbearer,
4 So *S·* took a sword, and fell upon it.
5 his armourbearer saw that *S·* was
6 So *S·* died, and his three sons, and
7 and that *S·* and his sons were dead,
8 they found *S·* and his sons fallen
11 that the Philistines had done to *S·*,
12 men, and took away the body of *S·*,
13 So *S·* died for his transgression
11: 2 time past, even when *S·* was king,
12: 1 kept himself close because of *S·*
19 came with the Philistines against *S·*
19 He will fall to his master *S·* to the
23 to turn the kingdom of *S·* to him,
29 of Benjamin, the kindred of *S·*,
29 kept the ward of the house of *S·*.
13: 3 enquired not at it in the days of *S·*.
15:29 Michal the daughter of *S·* looking
26:28 the seer, and *S·* the son of Kish,
Ps 18:*title* enemies, and from the hand of *S·*:
52:*title* the Edomite came and told *S·*,
54:*title* the Ziphims came and said to *S·*,
57:*title* when he fled from *S·* in the cave.
59:*title* when *S·* sent, and they watched
Isa 10:29 is afraid; Gibeah of *S·* is fled.
Ac 7:58 man's feet, whose name was *S·*.
8: 1 *S·* was consenting unto his death.
3 As for *S·*, he made havock of the
9: 1 *S·*, yet breathing out threatenings

Ac 9: 4 *S·*, *S·*, why persecutest thou me?
8 And *S·* arose from the earth; and
11 house of Judas for one called *S·*,
17 Brother *S·*, the Lord, even Jesus,
19 *S·* certain days with the disciples
22 *S·* increased the more in strength,
24 their laying await was known of *S·*.
26 when *S·* was come to Jerusalem,
11:25 Barnabas to Tarsus, for to seek *S·*:
30 by the hands of Barnabas and *S·*.
12:25 and *S·* returned from Jerusalem,
13: 1 up with Herod the tetrarch, and *S·*.
2 Separate me Barnabas and *S·* for
7 who called for Barnabas and *S·*,
9 Then *S·*, (who also is called Paul,)
21 gave unto them *S·* the son of Cis,
22: 7 *S·*, *S·*, why persecutest thou me?
13 me, Brother *S·*, receive thy sight.
26:14 *S·*, *S·*, why persecutest thou me?

Saul's (*sawls*)
1Sa 9: 3 asses of Kish *S·* father were lost.
10:14 *S·* uncle said unto him and to his
15 *S·* uncle said, Tell me, I pray thee,
14:50 the name of *S·* wife was Ahinoam,
50 was Abner, the son of Ner, *S·* uncle.
16:15 *S·* servants said unto him, Behold
18: 5 and also in the sight of *S·* servants.
10 and there was a javelin in *S·* hand.
19 *S·* daughter should have been given
20 Michal *S·* daughter loved David:
23 *S·* servants spake those words in
28 that Michal *S·* daughter loved him.
19: 2 Jonathan *S·* son delighted much in
10 he slipped away out of *S·* presence,
20:25 and Abner sat by *S·* side, and
30 Then *S·* anger was kindled against
23:16 Jonathan *S·* son arose, and went to
24: 4 and cut off the skirt of *S·* robe
5 because he had cut off *S·* skirt.
26:12 the cruse of water from *S·* bolster;
31: 2 and Melchi-shua, *S·* sons.
2Sa 2: 8 But Abner...captain of *S·* host,
10 Ish-bosheth *S·* son was forty years
3:13 thou first bring Michal *S·* daughter,
14 messengers to Ish-bosheth *S·* son,
4: 1 *S·* son heard that Abner was dead
2 And *S·* son had two men that were
4 Jonathan, *S·* son, had a son...lame
6:16 Michal *S·* daughter looked through
9: 9 the king called to Ziba, *S·* servant,
1Ch 12: 2 even of *S·* brethren of Benjamin.

save^ See also SAVED; SAVEST; SAVETH; SAVING.
Ge 12:12 kill me, but they will *s·* thee alive.
14:24 *S·* only that which the young men
39: 6 *s·* the bread which he did eat.
45: 7 and to *s·* your lives by a great
50:20 is this day, to *s·* much people alive.
Ex 1:22 and every daughter ye shall *s·* alive.
12:16 *s·* that which every man must eat,
22:20 any god, *s·* unto the Lord only,
Nu 14:30 *s·* Caleb the son of Jephunneh,
26:65 *s·* Caleb the son of Jephunneh.
32:12 *S·* Caleb the son of Jephunneh
De 1:36 *S·* Caleb the son of Jephunneh;
15: 4 *S·* when there shall be no poor
20: 4 against your enemies, to *s·* you.
16 *s·* alive nothing that breatheth:
22:27 cried, and there was none to *s·* her.
28:29 evermore, and no man shall *s·* thee.
Jos 2:13 that ye will *s·* alive my father,
10: 6 come up to us quickly, and *s·* us,
11:13 burned none of them, *s·* Hazor
19 *s·* the Hivites the inhabitants of
14: 4 in the land, *s·* cities to dwell in,
22:22 the Lord, (*s·* us not this day,)
J'g 6:14 shalt *s·* Israel from the hand of the
15 Lord, wherewith shall I *s·* Israel?
31 ye plead for Baal? will ye *s·* him?
36, 37 thou wilt *s·* Israel by mine hand,
7: 7 men that lapped will I *s·* you, and
14 else *s·* the sword of Gideon
1Sa 4: 3 it may *s·* us out of the hand of our
7: 8 that he will *s·* us out of the hand of
9:16 he may *s·* my people out of the hand
10:24 shouted, and said, God *s·* the king
27 said, How shall this man *s·* us?
11: 3 and then, if there be no man to *s·* us,
14: 6 is no restraint to the Lord to *s·* by
19:11 If thou *s·* not thy life to night,
21: 9 for there is no other *s·* that here.
23: 2 smite...Philistines, and *s·* Keilah.
30:17 *s·* four hundred young men,
22 *s·* to every man his wife and his
2Sa 3:18 servant David I will *s·* my people
12: 3 nothing, *s·* one little ewe lamb,
16:16 God *s·* the king, God *s·* the king.
22:28 the afflicted people thou wilt *s·*:
32 For who is God, *s·* the Lord? and
32 and who is a rock, *s·* our God?
42 looked, but there was none to *s·*;
1Ki 1:12 thou mayest *s·* thine own life, and
25 and say, God *s·* king Adonijah.
34 and say, God *s·* king Solomon.
39 people said, God *s·* king Solomon.
3:18 the house, *s·* we two in the house.
8: 9 the ark *s·* the two tables of stone,
15: 5 *s·* only in the matter of Uriah the
18: 5 to *s·* the horses and mules alive,
20:31 peradventure he will *s·* thy life.
22:31 *s·* only with the king of Israel.
2Ki 7: 4 if they *s·* us alive, we shall live;
11:12 hands, and said, God *s·* the king.
15: 4 *S·* that the high places were not
16: 7 *s·* me out of the hand of the king
19:19 *s·* thou us out of his hand, that all

2Ki 19:34 I will defend this city, to s· it, for
24:14 s· the poorest sort of the people of
1Ch 16:35 ye, S· us, O God of our salvation,
2Ch 2: 6 s· only to burn sacrifice before him?
5:10 nothing in the ark s· the two tables
18:30 s· only with the king of Israel.
23: 6 house of the Lord, s· the priests,
11 him, and said, God s· the king.
Ne 2:12 s· the beast that I rode upon.
6:11 go into the temple to s· his life?
Job 2: 6 he is in thine hand; but s· his life.
20:20 not s· of that which he desired.
22:29 and he shall s· the humble person.
40:14 thine own right hand can s· thee.
Ps 3: 7 s· me, O my God: for thou hast
6: 4 soul: oh s· me for thy mercies' sake.
7: 1 s· me from all them that persecute
18:27 thou wilt s· the afflicted people; but
31 For who is God s· the Lord?
31 or who is a rock s· our God?
41 but there was none to s· them:
20: 9 S·, Lord: let the king hear us when
22:21 S· me from the lion's mouth: for
28: 9 S· thy people, and bless thine
31: 2 for an house of defence to s· me.
16 s· me for thy mercies' sake.
37:40 them from the wicked, and s· them,
44: 3 neither did their own arm s· them:
6 bow, neither shall my sword s· me.
54: 1 S· me, O God, by thy name, and
55:16 upon God; and the Lord shall s· me.
57: 3 and s· me from the reproach of him
59: 2 and s· me from bloody men.
60: 5 s· with thy right hand, and hear
69: 1 S· me, O God; for the waters are
35 For God will s· Zion, and will build
71: 2 thine ear unto me, and s· me.
3 hast given commandment to s· me;
72: 4 he shall s· the children of the needy,
13 and shall s· the souls of the needy.
76: 9 to s· all the meek of the earth.
80: 2 thy strength, and come and s· us.
86: 2 s· thy servant that trusteth in
16 and s· the son of thine handmaid.
106:47 S· us, O Lord our God, and gather
108: 6 s· with thy right hand, and answer
109:26 O s· me according to thy mercy:
31 to s· him from those that condemn
118:25 S· now, I beseech thee, O Lord:
119:94 I am thine, s· me; for I have
146 cried unto thee; s· me, and I shall
138: 7 and thy right hand shall s· me.
145:19 hear their cry, and will s· them.
Pr 20:22 on the Lord, and he shall s· thee.
Isa 25: 9 waited for him, and he will s· us:
33:22 the Lord is our king; he will s· us.
35: 4 your God...will come and s· you.
37:20 Lord our God, s· us from his hand,
35 For I will defend this city to s· it
38:20 The Lord was ready to s· me:
45:20 and pray unto a god that cannot s·.
46: 7 nor s· him out of his trouble.
47:13 s· thee from these things that shall
15 to his quarter; none shall s· thee.
49:25 with thee, and I will s· thy children.
59: 1 is not shortened, that it cannot s·;
63: 1 in righteousness, mighty to s·.
Jer 2:27 they will say, Arise, and s· us.
28 s· thee in the time of thy trouble:
11:12 shall not s· them at all in the time
14: 9 as a mighty man that cannot s·?
15:20 for I am with thee to s· thee and to
17:14 s· me, and I shall be saved: for thou
30:10 for, lo, I will s· thee from afar, and
11 with thee, saith the Lord, to s· thee:
31: 7 s· thy people, the remnant of Israel.
42:11 for I am with you to s· you, and to
46:27 I will s· thee from afar off, and thy
48: 6 Flee, s· your lives, and be like the
La 4:17 for a nation that could not s· us.
Eze 3:18 from his wicked way, to s· his life;
13:18 will ye s· the souls alive that come
19 to s· the souls alive that should not
18:27 and right, he shall s· his soul alive.
34:22 Therefore will I s· my flock, and
36:29 I will also s· you from all your
37:23 but I will s· them out of all their
Da 6: 7 s· of thee, O king, he shall be cast
12 s· of thee, O king, shall be cast
Ho 1: 7 will s· them by the Lord their God,
7 and will not s· them by bow, nor by
13:10 that may s· thee in all thy cities?
14: 3 Asshur shall not s· us; we will not
Hab 1: 2 of violence, and thou wilt not s·!
Zep 3:17 he will s·, he will rejoice over thee
19 and I will s· her that halteth, and
Zec 8: 7 I will s· my people from the east
13 so will I s· you, and ye shall be a
9:16 the Lord their God shall s· them in
10: 6 I will s· the house of Joseph, and I
12: 7 Lord also shall s· the tents of Judah
M't 1:21 shall s· his people from their sins.
8:25 him, saying, Lord, s· us: we perish.
11:27 any man the Father, s· the Son,
13:57 honour, s· in his own country, and
14:30 sink, he cried, saying, Lord, s· me.
16:25 whosoever will s· his life shall lose
17: 8 they saw no man, s· Jesus only.
18:11 is come to s· that which was lost.
19:11 saying, s· they to whom it is given.
27:40 buildest it in three days, s· thyself.
42 saved others; himself he cannot s·.
49 whether Elias will come to s· him.
M'r 3: 4 or to do evil? to s· life, or to kill?
5:37 no man to follow him, s· Peter, and
6: 5 s· that he laid his hands upon a few
M'r 6: 8 for their journey, s· a staff only;
8:35 whosoever will s· his life shall lose
35 the gospel's, the same shall s· it.
9: 8 saw no man any more, s· Jesus only
15:30 S· thyself, and come down from
31 saved others; himself he cannot s·.
Lu 4:26 s· unto Sarepta, a city of Sidon,
6: 9 do evil? to s· life, or to destroy it?
8:51 suffered no man to go in, s· Peter,
9:24 whosoever will s· his life shall lose
24 for my sake, the same shall s· it.
56 destroy men's lives, but to s· them.
17:18 give glory to God, s· this stranger.
33 shall seek to s· his life shall lose it;
18:19 none is good, s· one, that is, God.
19:10 seek and to s· that which was lost.
23:35 let him s· himself, if he be Christ,
37 be the king of the Jews, s· thyself.
39 If thou be Christ, s· thyself and us.
Joh 6:22 s· that one whereinto his disciples
46 s· he which is of God, he hath seen
12:27 Father, s· me from this hour: but
47 judge the world, but to s· the world.
13:10 needeth not s· to wash his feet, but
Ac 2:40 S· yourselves from this untoward
20:23 S· that the Holy Ghost witnesseth
21:25 s· only that they keep themselves
27:43 the centurion, willing to s· Paul,
Ro 11:14 flesh, and might s· some of them.
1Co 1:21 preaching to s· them that believe.
2: 2 s· Jesus Christ, and him crucified.
11 s· the spirit of man which is in him?
7:16 whether thou shalt s· thy husband?
16 whether thou shalt s· thy wife?
9:22 that I might by all means s· some.
2Co 11:24 received I forty stripes s· one.
Ga 1:19 none, s· James the Lord's brother.
6:14 s· in the cross of our Lord Jesus
1Ti 1:15 came into the world to s· sinners;
4:16 thou shalt both s· thyself, and them
Heb 5: 7 that was able to s· him from death,
7:25 also to s· them to the uttermost
Jas 1:21 word, which is able to s· your souls.
2:14 have not works? can faith s· him?
4:12 who is able to s· and to destroy: who
5:15 the prayer of faith shall s· the sick,
20 his way shall s· a soul from death,
1Pe 3:21 even baptism doth also now s· us
Jude 23 others s· with fear, pulling them
Re 13:17 or sell, s· he that had the mark,

saved
Ge 47:25 Thou hast s· our lives: let us find
Ex 1:17 but s· the men children alive.
18 and have s· the men children alive?
14:30 the Lord s· Israel that day out of
Nu 10: 9 ye shall be s· from your enemies.
22:33 I had slain thee, and s· her alive.
31:15 Have ye s· all the women alive?
De 33:29 O people s· by the Lord, the shield
Jos 6:25 Joshua s· Rahab the harlot alive,
J'g 7: 2 saying, Mine own hand hath s· me.
8:19 if ye had s· them alive, I would not
21:14 them wives which they had s· alive
1Sa 10:19 s· you out of all your adversities
14:23 So the Lord s· Israel that day: and
23: 5 David s· the inhabitants of Keilah.
27:11 David s· neither man nor woman
2Sa 19: 5 which this day have s· thy life,
9 king s· us out of the hand of our
22: 4 shall I be s· from mine enemies.
2Ki 6:10 and s· himself there, not once nor
14:27 s· them by the hand of Jeroboam
1Ch 11:14 s· them by a great deliverance.
2Ch 32:22 Thus the Lord s· Hezekiah and the
Ne 9:27 who s· them out of the hand of their
Ps 18: 3 shall I be s· from mine enemies.
33:16 is no king s· by the multitude of
34: 6 and s· him out of all his troubles.
44: 7 thou hast s· us from our enemies,
80: 3 face to shine; and we shall be s·.
7, 19 to shine; and we shall be s·.
106: 8 he s· them for his name's sake,
10 he s· them from the hand of him
107:13 he s· them out of their distresses.
Pr 28:18 walketh uprightly shall be s·: but
Isa 30:15 returning and rest shall ye be s·;
43:12 I have declared, and have s·, and
45:17 But Israel shall be s· in the Lord
22 Look unto me, and be ye s·, all the
63: 9 the angel of his presence s· them:
64: 5 is continuance, and we shall be s·.
Jer 4:14 wickedness, that thou mayest be s·.
8:20 summer is ended, and we are not s·.
17:14 save me, and I shall be s·: for thou
23: 6 In his days Judah shall be s·, and
30: 7 trouble; but he shall be s· out of it.
33:16 In those days shall Judah be s·,
M't 10:22 endureth to the end shall be s·.
19:25 amazed, saying, Who then can be s·?
24:13 unto the end, the same shall be s·.
22 there should no flesh be s·: but for
27:42 He s· others; himself he cannot
M'r 10:26 themselves, Who then can be s·?
13:13 unto the end, the same shall be s·.
20 those days, no flesh should be s·:
15:31 He s· others; himself he cannot
16:16 believeth and is baptized shall be s·;
Lu 1:71 we should be s· from our enemies,
7:50 Thy faith hath s· thee; go in peace.
8:12 lest they should believe and be s·.
13:23 him, Lord, are there few that be s·?
18:26 heard it said, Who then can be s·?
42 thy sight: thy faith hath s· thee.
23:35 He s· others; let him save himself,
Joh 3:17 the world through him might be s·.
5:34 things I say, that ye might be s·.
Joh 10: 9 if any man enter in, he shall be s·,
Ac 2:21 on the name of the Lord shall be s·.
47 church daily such as should be s·.
4:12 among men, whereby we must be s·.
11:14 thou and all thy house shall be s·.
15: 1 manner of Moses, ye cannot be s·.
11 the grace of...Christ we shall be s·,
16:30 said, Sirs, what must I do to be s·?
31 thou shalt be s·, and thy house.
27:20 all hope that we should be s· was
31 abide in the ship, ye cannot be s·.
Ro 5: 9 shall be s· from wrath through him.
10 reconciled, we shall be s· by his life.
8:24 For we are s· by hope: but hope
9:27 of the sea, a remnant shall be s·:
10: 1 Israel is, that they might be s·.
9 from the dead, thou shalt be s·.
13 the name of the Lord shall be s·.
11:26 And so all Israel shall be s·: as it
1Co 1:18 unto us which are s· it is the power
3:15 but he himself shall be s·; yet so
5: 5 the spirit may be s· in the day of
10:33 profit of many, that they may be s·.
15: 2 By which also ye are s·, if ye keep
2Co 2:15 in them that are s·, and in them
Eph 2: 5 with Christ, (by grace ye are s·;)
8 by grace are ye s· through faith;
1Th 2:16 the Gentiles that they might be s·,
2Th 2:10 of the truth, that they might be s·.
1Ti 2: 4 Who will have all men to be s·, and
15 she shall be s· in childbearing, if
2Ti 1: 9 Who hath s· us, and called us with
Tit 3: 5 but according to his mercy he s· us,
1Pe 3:20 is, eight souls were s· by water.
4:18 And if the righteous scarcely be s·,
2Pe 2: 5 but s· Noah the eighth person, a
Jude 5 s· the people out of the land of
Re 21:24 which are s· shall walk in the light

savest
2Sa 22: 3 saviour; thou s· me from violence.
Job 26: 2 how s· thou the arm that hath no
Ps 17: 7 O thou that s· by thy right hand

saveth
1Sa 14:39 the Lord liveth, which s· Israel,
17:47 Lord s· not with sword and spear:
Job 5:15 he s· the poor from the sword, from
Ps 7:10 God, which s· the upright in heart.
20: 6 I that the Lord s· his anointed;
34:18 s· such as be of a contrite spirit.
107:19 he s· them out of their distresses.

saving
Ge 19:19 hast shewed unto me in s· my life;
Ne 4:23 s· that every one put them off for
Ps 20: 6 the s· strength of his right hand.
28: 8 the s· strength of his anointed.
67: 2 the s· health among all nations.
Ec 5:11 s· the beholding of them with their
Am 9: 8 s· that I will not utterly destroy
M't 5:32 s· for the cause of fornication,
Lu 4:27 cleansed, s· Naaman the Syrian.
Heb 10:39 that believe to the s· of the soul.
11: 7 an ark to the s· of his house; by
Re 2:17 knoweth s· he that receiveth it.

saviour See also SAVIOURS.
2Sa 22: 3 tower, and my refuge, my s·;
2Ki 13: 5 (And the Lord gave Israel a s·, so
Ps 106:21 They forgat God their s·, which had
Isa 19:20 he shall send them a s·, and a great
43: 3 God, the Holy One of Israel, thy S·:
11 Lord; and beside me there is no s·.
45:15 thyself, O God of Israel, the S·.
21 a just God and a S·; there is none
49:26 know that I the Lord am thy S· and
60:16 know that I the Lord am thy S· and
63: 8 that will not lie: so he was their S·.
Jer 14: 8 the s· thereof in time of trouble,
Ho 13: 4 me: for there is no s· beside me.
Lu 1:47 spirit hath rejoiced in God my S·.
2:11 this day in the city of David a S·,
Joh 4:42 the Christ, the S· of the world.
Ac 5:31 right hand to be a Prince and a S·,
13:23 his promise raised unto Israel a S·,
Eph 5:23 church: and he is the s· of the body.
Ph'p 3:20 we look for the S·, the Lord Jesus
1Ti 1: 1 the commandment of God our S·,
2: 3 acceptable in the sight of...our S·;
4:10 God, who is the S· of all men,
2Ti 1:10 appearing of our S· Jesus Christ,
Tit 1: 3 the commandment of God our S·;
4 and the Lord Jesus Christ our S·.
2:10 the doctrine of God our S· in all
13 great God and our S· Jesus Christ,
3: 4 and love of God our S· toward man
6 through Jesus Christ our S·;
2Pe 1: 1 righteousness of God and our S·
11 kingdom of our Lord and S· Jesus
2:20 the knowledge of the Lord and S·
3: 2 us the apostles of the Lord and S·:
18 the knowledge of our Lord and S·
1Jo 4:14 Father sent the Son to be the S· of
Jude 25 To the only wise God our S·, be

saviours
Ne 9:27 mercies thou gavest them s·, who
Ob 21 s· shall come up on mount Zion to

savour See also SAVOUREST; SAVOURS.
Ge 8:21 And the Lord smelled a sweet s·;
Ex 5:21 ye have made our s· to be abhorred
29:18 it is a sweet s·, an offering made by
25 for a sweet s· before the Lord:
41 for a sweet s·, an offering made by
Le 1: 9, 13, 17 of a sweet s· unto the Lord.
2: 2 by fire, of a sweet s· unto the Lord:
9 by fire, of a sweet s· unto the Lord.

Le 2:12 be burnt on the altar for a sweet s'.
3: 5 by fire, of a sweet s' unto the Lord.
16 offering made by fire for a sweet s':
4:31 altar for a sweet s' unto the Lord;
6:15 burn it upon the altar for a sweet s',
21 offer for a sweet s' unto the Lord.
8:21 was a burnt sacrifice for a sweet s',
28 were consecrations for a sweet s':
17: 6 the fat for a sweet s' unto the Lord.
23:13 by fire unto the Lord for a sweet s':
18 by fire, of sweet s' unto the Lord.
26:31 smell the s' of your sweet odours.
Nu 15: 3 to make a sweet s' unto the Lord,
7 wine, for a sweet s' unto the Lord.
10, 13 fire, of a sweet s' unto the Lord.
14 by fire, of a sweet s' unto the Lord;
24 for a sweet s' unto the Lord, with
18:17 by fire, for a sweet s' unto the Lord.
28: 2 made by fire, for a sweet s' unto me,
6 in mount Sinai for a sweet s',
8 by fire, of a sweet s' unto the Lord,
13 for a burnt offering of a sweet s', a
24 by fire, of a sweet s' unto the Lord:
27 offering for a sweet s' unto the Lord;
29: 2 offering for a sweet s' unto the Lord;
6 for a sweet s', a sacrifice made by
8 offering unto the Lord for a sweet s':
13 by fire, of a sweet s' unto the Lord;
36 by fire, of a sweet s' unto the Lord:
Ec 10: 1 apothecary to send...a stinking s':
Ca 1: 3 of the s' of thy good ointments
Eze 6:13 did offer sweet s' to all their idols.
16:19 set it before them for a sweet s':
20:28 there also they made their sweet s',
41 I will accept you with your sweet s',
Joe 2:20 and his ill s' shall come up,
M't 5:13 but if the salt have lost his s',
Lu 14:34 but if the salt have lost his s',
2Co 2:14 manifest the s' of his knowledge
15 are unto God a sweet s' of Christ,
16 we are the s' of death unto death;
16 to the other the s' of life unto life.
Eph 5: 2 to God for a sweetsmelling s'.

savourest
M't 16:23 s' not the things that be of God,
M'r 8:33 s' not the things that be of God,

savours
Ezr 6:10 sweet s' unto the God of heaven,

savoury See also UNSAVOURY.
Ge 27: 4 make me s' meat, such as I love,
7 me venison, and make me s' meat,
9 I will make...s' meat for thy father,
14 his mother made s' meat, such as
17 she gave the s' meat and the bread,
31 And he also had made s' meat, and

saw See also FORESAW; SAWED; SAWEST; SAWN; SAWS.
Ge 1: 4 God s' the light, that it was good:
10, 12, 18, 21, 25 God s' that it was good.
31 God s' every thing that he had made,
3: 6 woman s' that the tree was good
6: 2 the sons of God s' the daughters of
5 God s' that the wickedness of man
9:22 s' the nakedness of his father,
23 they s' not their father's nakedness.
12:15 The princes also of Pharaoh s' her,
16: 4, 5 she s' that she had conceived,
18: 2 and when he s' them, he ran to meet
21: 9 And Sarah s' the son of Hagar the
19 her eyes, and she s' a well of water;
22: 4 up his eyes, and s' the place afar off.
24:30 when he s' the earring and bracelets
63 and he lifted up his eyes, and s',
64 when she s' Isaac, she lighted off
26: 8 looked out at a window, and s', and
28 We s' certainly...the Lord was with
28: 6 When Esau s' that Isaac had blessed
29:10 when Jacob s' Rachel the daughter
31 the Lord s' that Leah was hated,
30: 1 Rachel s' that she bare Jacob no
9 Leah s' that she had left bearing,
31:10 up mine eyes, and s' in a dream,
32: 2 And when Jacob s' them, he said,
25 he s' that he prevailed not against
33: 5 and s' the women and the children;
34: 2 Shechem...s' her, he took her, and
37: 4 s' that their father loved him more
18 And when they s' him afar off, even
38: 2 Judah s'...a daughter of a certain
14 for she s' that Shelah was grown,
15 When Judah s' her, he thought her
39: 3 his master s' that the Lord was with
13 she s' that he had left his garment
40:16 chief baker s' that the interpretation
41:19 as I never s' in all the land of Egypt
22 And I s' in my dream, and, behold,
42: 1 when Jacob s' that there was corn
7 And Joseph s' his brethren, and he
21 in that we s' the anguish of his soul,
35 their father s' the bundles of money,
43:16 when Joseph s' Benjamin with them,
29 eyes, and s' his brother Benjamin,
44:28 in pieces; and I s' him not since:
45:27 he s' the wagons which Joseph had
48:17 when Joseph s' that his father laid
49:15 And he s' that rest was good, and
50:11 s' the mourning in the floor of Atad,
15 s' that their father was dead, they
23 And Joseph s' Ephraim's children
Ex 2: 2 when she s' him that he was a goodly
5 when she s' the ark among the flags,
6 she had opened it, she s' the child:
12 when he s' that there was no man,
3: 4 Lord s' that he turned aside to see,

Ex 8:15 Pharaoh s' that there was respite,
9:34 when Pharaoh s' that the rain and
10:23 They s' not one another, neither
14:30 and Israel s' the Egyptians dead
31 And Israel s' that great work which
16:15 when the children of Israel s' it,
18:14 And when Moses' father in law s' all
20:18 all the people s' the thunderings,
18 when the people s' it, they removed,
24:10 And they s' the God of Israel: and
11 they s' God, and did eat and
32: 1 the people s' that Moses delayed
5 when Aaron s' it, he built an altar
19 that he s' the calf, and the dancing:
25 Moses s' that the people were naked;
33:10 all the people s' the cloudy pillar
34:30 all the children of Israel s' Moses,
35 children of Israel s'...face of Moses,
Le 9:24 when all the people s', they shouted,
Nu 13:28 we s' the children of Anak there.
32 people that we s' in it are men of a
33 we s' the giants, the sons of Anak,
20:29 congregation s'...Aaron was dead,
22: 2 Balak...s' all that Israel had done
23 And the ass s' the angel of the Lord
25, 27 the ass s' the angel of the Lord,
31 and he s' the angel of the Lord
33 And the ass s' me, and turned from
24: 1 Balaam s' that it pleased the Lord
2 and he s' Israel abiding in his tents
4, 16 s' the vision of the Almighty,
25: 7 the son of Aaron the priest, s' it,
32: 1 and when they s' the land of Jazer,
9 valley of Eshcol, and s' the land,
De 1:19 terrible wilderness, which ye s' by
4:12 of the words, but s' no similitude;
15 for ye s' no manner of similitude on
7:19 temptations which thine eyes s',
32:19 when the Lord s' it, he abhorred
Jos 7:21 I s' among the spoils a goodly
8:14 when the king of Ai s' it, that they
20 they s', and, behold, the smoke of
21 Israel s' that the ambush had taken
J'g 1:24 the spies s' a man come forth out of
3:24 when they s' that, behold, the doors
9:36 when Gaal s' the people, he said to
55 the men of Israel s' that Abimelech
11:35 when he s' her, that he rent his
12: 3 when I s' that ye delivered me not,
14: 1 and s' a woman in Timnath of the
11 when they s' him, that they brought
16: 1 to Gaza, and s' there an harlot, and
18 when Delilah s' that he had told all
24 And when the people s' him, they
18: 7 s' the people that were therein, how
26 Micah s' that they were too strong
19: 3 the father of the damsel s' him, he
17 he s' a wayfaring man in the street
30 all that s' it said, There was no
20:36 of Benjamin s'...they were smitten:
41 s' that evil was come upon them.
Ru 1:18 s' that she was stedfastly minded
2:18 mother in law s' what she...gleaned:
1Sa 5: 7 the men of Ashdod s' that it was so,
6:13 lifted up their eyes, and s' the ark,
9:17 And when Samuel s' Saul, the Lord
10:11 that knew him beforetime s' that,
14 when we s' that they were no where,
12:12 when ye s' that Nahash the king of
13: 6 men of Israel s' that they were in a
11 I s' that the people were scattered
14:52 and when Saul s' any strong man,
17:24 when they s' the man, fled from
42 Philistine looked about,...s' David,
51 Philistines s' their champion was
55 Saul s' David go forth against the
18:15 Saul s' that he behaved himself
28 Saul s' and knew that the Lord was
19:20 they s' the company of the prophets
22: 9 s' the son of Jesse coming to Nob,
23:15 David s' that Saul was come out to
25:23 when Abigail s' David, she hasted,
25 I thine handmaid s' not the young
26: 3 he s' that Saul came after him into
12 no man s' it, or knew it, neither
28: 5 Saul s' the host of the Philistines,
12 when the woman s' Samuel, she
13 I s' gods ascending out of the
21 and s' that he was sore troubled,
31: 5 armourbearer s'...Saul was dead,
7 s' that the men of Israel fled, and
2Sa 1: 7 he looked behind him, he s' me,
6:16 s' king David leaping and dancing
10: 6 s' that they stank before David,
9 Joab s' that the front of the battle
14 Ammon s'...the Syrians were fled,
15 Syrians s' that they were smitten
19 servants to Hadarezer s' that they
11: 2 he s' a woman washing herself;
12:19 when David s' that his servants
14:24, 28 and s' not the king's face.
17:18 Nevertheless a lad s' them, and told
23 s' that his counsel was not followed,
18:10 a certain man s' it, and told Joab,
10 I s' Absalom hanged in an oak.
26 watchman s' another man running:
29 I s' a great tumult, but I knew not
20:12 when the man s' that all the people
12 s' that every one that came by him
24:17 s' the angel that smote the people,
20 s' the king and his servants coming
1Ki 3:28 s' that the wisdom of God was in
12:16 Israel s' that the king hearkened
13:25 and s' the carcase cast in the way,
16:18 Zimri s' that the city was taken,
18:17 when Ahab s' Elijah, that Ahab

1Ki 18:39 when all the people s' it, they fell
19: 3 when he s' that, he arose, and went
22:17 I s' all Israel scattered upon the
19 I s' the Lord sitting on his throne,
32 the captains of the chariots s'
2Ki 2:12 And Elisha s' it, and he cried, My
12 he s' him no more: and he took
15 were to view at Jericho s' him,
3:22 s' the water on the other side as red
26 of Moab s' that the battle was too
4:25 when the man of God s' her afar off,
5:21 Naaman s' him running after him,
6:17 eyes of the young man; and he s':
20 Lord opened their eyes, and they s';
21 said unto Elisha, when he s' them,
9:22 when Joram s' Jehu, that he said,
27 Ahaziah the king of Judah s' this,
11: 1 s' that her son was dead, she arose
12:10 they s' that there was much money
13: 4 for he s' the oppression of Israel,
14:26 the Lord s' the affliction of Israel,
16:10 s' an altar that was at Damascus:
12 Damascus, the king s' the altar:
1Ch 10: 5 armourbearer s'...Saul was dead,
7 were in the valley s' that they fled,
15:29 window s' king David dancing and
19: 6 the children of Ammon s' that they
10 Now when Joab s' that the battle
15 Ammon s'...the Syrians were fled,
16 Syrians s' that they were put to the
19 servants of Hadarezer s' that they
21:16 and s' the angel of the Lord stand
20 Ornan turned back, and s' the angel;
21 Ornan, Ornan looked and s' David,
28 when David s' that the Lord had
2Ch 7: 3 children of Israel s' how the fire
10:16 s' that the king would not hearken
12: 7 the Lord s' that they humbled
15: 9 s' that the Lord his God was with
18:18 s' the Lord sitting upon his throne,
31 of the chariots s' Jehoshaphat,
22:10 Ahaziah s' that her son was dead,
24:11 they s' that there was much money,
25:21 they s' one another in the face,
31: 8 the princes came and s' the heaps,
32: 2 Hezekiah s' that Sennacherib was
Ne 6:16 heathen that were about us s' these
13:15 days s' I in Judah some treading
23 s' I Jews that had married wives of
Es 1:14 s' the king's face, and which sat
3: 5 Haman s' that Mordecai bowed not
5: 2 when the king s' Esther the queen
9 Haman s' Mordecai in the king's
7: 7 s' that there was evil determined
Job 2:13 s' that his grief was very great.
3:16 as infants which never s' light.
20: 9 eye...which s' him shall see him
29: 8 The young men s' me, and hid
11 when the eye s' me, it gave witness
31:21 when I s' my help in the gate:
32: 5 Elihu s' that there was no answer
42:16 s' his sons, and his sons' sons, even
Ps 48: 5 They s' it, and so they marvelled;
73: 3 I s' the prosperity of the wicked.
77:16 s' thee, O God, the waters s' thee;
95: 9 me, proved me, and s' my work.
97: 4 world: the earth s', and trembled.
114: 3 The sea s' it, and fled: Jordan was
Pr 24:32 Then I s', and considered it well:
Ec 2:13 I s' that wisdom excelleth folly, as
24 This also I s', that it was from the
3:16 I s' under the sun the place of
4: 7 and I s' vanity under the sun.
8:10 And so I s' the wicked buried, who
9:11 I returned, and s' under the sun,
Ca 3: 3 S' ye him whom my soul loveth?
6: 9 daughters s' her, and blessed her;
Isa 1: 1 which he s' concerning Judah and
2: 1 son of Amoz s' concerning Judah
6: 1 I s' also the Lord sitting upon a
10:15 the s' magnify itself against him
21: 7 he s' a chariot with a couple of
41: 5 The isles s' it, and feared; the ends
59:15 the Lord s' it, and it displeased him
16 And he s' that there was no man,
Jer 3: 7 her treacherous sister Judah s' it.
8 And I s', when for all the causes
39: 4 Zedekiah the king of Judah s' them,
41:13 people...with Ishmael s' Johanan
44:17 and were well, and s' no evil.
La 1: 7 adversaries s' her, and did mock at
Eze 1: 1 opened, and I s' visions of God.
27 And I s' as the colour of amber, as
27 s' as it were the appearance of fire,
28 when I s' it, I fell upon my face, and
3:23 which I s' by the river of Chebar:
8: 4 to the vision that I s' in the plain.
10 I went in and s'; and behold every
10:15 that I s' by the river of Chebar.
20 creature that I s' under the God of
22 which I s' by the river of Chebar,
11: 1 I s' Jaazaniah the son of Azur, and
16: 6 s' thee polluted in thine own blood,
50 I took them away as I s' good.
19: 5 when she s' that she had waited, and
20:28 then they s' every high hill, and all
23:11 when her sister Aholibah s' this,
13 Then I s' that she was defiled, that
14 when she s' men pourtrayed upon
16 as soon as she s' them with her eyes,
41: 8 I s' also the height of the house
43: 3 appearance of the vision which I s',
3 even according to the vision that I s'
3 like the vision that I s' by the river
Da 3:27 s' these men, upon whose bodies
4: 5 I s' a dream which made me afraid,

Da 4:10 I s', and behold a tree in the midst
13 I s' in the visions of my head upon
23 whereas the king s' a watcher and
5: 5 s' the part of the hand that wrote.
7: 2 and said, I s' in my vision by night,
7 After this I s' in the night visions,
13 I s' in the night visions, and,
8: 2 And I s' in a vision; and it came to
2 when I s', that I was at Shushan
2 and I s' in a vision, and I was by
3 Then I lifted up mine eyes, and s',
4 I s' the ram pushing westward, and
7 I s' him come close unto the ram,
10: 7 And I Daniel alone s' the vision:
7 men...with me s' not the vision;
8 left alone, and s' this great vision,
Ho 5:13 When Ephraim s' his sickness, and
13 and Judah s' his wound, then went
9:10 I s' your fathers as the firstripe in
13 Ephraim, as I s' Tyrus, is planted
Am 1: 1 which he s' concerning Israel in
9: 1 I s' the Lord standing upon the
Jon 3:10 And God s' their works, that they
Mic 1: 1 which he s' concerning Samaria
Hab 3: 7 I s'...tents of Cushan in affliction:
10 The mountains s' thee, and they
Hag 2: 3 that s' this house in her first glory?
Zec 1: 8 I s' by night, and behold a man
18 Then lifted I up mine eyes, and s',
M't 2: 9 the star, which they s' in the east,
10 When they s' the star, they rejoiced
11 s' the young child with Mary his
16 when he s' that he was mocked of
3: 7 when he s' many of the Pharisees
16 he s' the Spirit of God descending
4:16 which sat in darkness s' great light;
18 s' two brethren, Simon called Peter,
21 thence, he s' other two brethren,
8:14 he s' his wife's mother laid, and
18 Now when Jesus s' great multitudes
34 when they s' him, they besought
9: 8 But when the multitudes s' it, they
9 he s' a man, named Matthew,
11 when the Pharisees s' it, they said
22 when he s' her, he said, Daughter,
23 and s' the minstrels and the people
36 But when he s' the multitudes, he
12: 2 But when the Pharisees s' it, they
22 blind and dumb both spake and s'.
14:14 forth, and s' a great multitude,
26 disciples s' him walking on the sea,
30 when he s' the wind boisterous, he
15:31 when they s' the dumb to speak,
17: 8 they s' no man, save Jesus only.
18:31 fellowservants s' what was done,
20: 3 and s' others standing idle in the
21:15 scribes s' the wonderful things that
19 when he s' a fig tree in the way, he
20 the disciples s' it, they marvelled,
38 when the husbandmen s' the son,
22:11 s' there a man which had not on a
25:37 Lord, when s' we thee an hungred,
38 When s' we thee a stranger, and
39 when s' we thee sick, or in prison,
44 Lord, when s' we thee an hungred,
26: 8 But when his disciples s' it, they
71 another maid s' him, and said unto
27: 3 when he s' that he was condemned,
24 When Pilate s' that he could prevail
54 s' the earthquake, and those
28:17 when they s' him, they worshipped
M'r 1:10 he s' the heavens opened, and the
16 he s' Simon and Andrew his brother
19 he s' James the son of Zebedee, and
2: 5 When Jesus s' their faith, he said
12 We never s' it on this fashion.
14 he s' Levi the son of Alphæus
16 Pharisees s' him eat with publicans
3:11 unclean spirits, when they s' him,
5: 6 when he s' Jesus afar off, he ran
16 And they that s' it told them how it
22 when he s' him, he fell at his feet,
6:33 And the people s' them departing,
34 when he came out, s' much people,
48 And he s' them toiling in rowing;
49 they s' him walking upon the sea,
50 they all s' him, and were troubled.
7: 2 they s' some of his disciples eat
8:23 him, he asked him if he s' ought.
25 restored, and s' every man clearly.
9: 8 s' no man any more, save Jesus
14 he s' a great multitude about them,
20 when he s' him, straightway the
25 When Jesus s' that the people came
38 we s' one casting out devils in thy
10:14 But when Jesus s' it, he was much
11:20 they s' the fig tree dried up from the
12:34 s' that he answered discreetly, he
14:67 when she s' Peter warming himself,
69 a maid s' him again, and began to
15:39 s' that he so cried out, and gave up
16: 4 s' that the stone was rolled away:
5 s' a young man sitting on the right
Lu 1:12 And when Zacharias s' him, he was
29 when she s' him, she was troubled
2:48 And when they s' him, they were
5: 2 s' two ships standing by the lake:
8 When Simon Peter s' it, he fell down
20 when he s' their faith, he said unto
27 s' a publican, named Levi, sitting
7:13 And when the Lord s' her, he had
39 Pharisee which had bidden him s' it,
8:28 When he s' Jesus, he cried out, and
34 When they that fed them s' what
36 They also which s' it told them by
47 the woman s' that she was not hid,
Lu 9:32 they were awake, they s' his glory,
49 we s' one casting out devils in thy
54 disciples James and John s' this,
10:31 when he s' him, he passed by on the
33 when he s' him, he had compassion
11:38 And when the Pharisee s' it, he
13:12 when Jesus s' her, he called her to
15:20 father s' him, and had compassion,
17:14 And when he s' them, he said unto
15 when he s' that he was healed,
18:15 but when his disciples s' it, they
24 Jesus s'...he was very sorrowful,
43 all the people, when they s' it, gave
19: 5 he looked up, and s' him, and said
7 when they s' it, they all murmured,
20:14 when the husbandmen s' him, they
21: 1 s' the rich men casting their gifts
2 s' also a certain poor widow casting
22:49 they which were about him s' what
58 after a little while another s' him,
23: 8 And when Herod s' Jesus, he was
47 the centurion s' what was done,
24:24 had said: but him they s' not.
Joh 1:32 I s' the Spirit descending from
34 I s', and bare record that this is
38 turned, and s' them following, and
39 They came and s' where he dwelt,
47 Jesus s' Nathanael coming to him,
48 wast under the fig tree, I s' thee.
50 thee, I s' thee under the fig tree,
2:23 they s' the miracles which he did.
5: 6 When Jesus s' him lie, and knew
6: 2 they s' his miracles which he did
5 s' a great company come unto him,
22 s' that there was none other boat
24 people...s' that Jesus was not there,
26 me, not because ye s' the miracles,
8:10 and s' none but the woman, he
56 my day: and he s' it, and was glad.
9: 1 s' a man which was blind from his
11:31 when they s' Mary, that she rose up,
32 come where Jesus was, and s' him,
33 Jesus therefore s' her weeping,
12:41 said Esaias, when he s' his glory,
19: 6 chief priests...and officers s' him,
26 When Jesus therefore s' his mother,
33 and s' that he was dead already,
35 And he that s' it bare record, and
20: 5 in, s' the linen clothes lying, yet
8 sepulchre, and he s', and believed.
14 s' Jesus standing, and knew not
20 glad, when they s' the Lord.
21: 9 land, they s' a fire of coals there,
Ac 3: 9 all the people s' him walking and
12 when Peter s' it, he answered unto
4:13 s' the boldness of Peter and John,
6:15 s' his face as it had been the face
7:31 When Moses s' it, he wondered at
55 and s' the glory of God, and Jesus
8:18 Simon s' that through laying on of
39 that the eunuch s' him no more:
9: 8 eyes were opened, he s' no man:
35 dwelt at Lydda and Saron s' him,
40 and when she s' Peter, she sat up.
10: 3 He s' in a vision evidently about
11 s' heaven opened, and a certain
11: 5 in a trance I s' a vision, A certain
6 s' fourfooted beasts of the earth,
12: 3 because he s' it pleased the Jews,
9 angel; but thought he s' a vision.
16 had opened the door, and s' him,
13:12 deputy, when he s' what was done,
36 unto his fathers, and s' corruption:
37 God raised again, s' no corruption.
45 when the Jews s' the multitudes,
14:11 the people s' what Paul had done,
16:19 her masters s' that the hope of their
17:16 when he s' the city wholly given
21:27 when they s' him in the temple,
32 when they s' the chief captain and
22: 9 were with me s' indeed the light,
18 And s' him saying unto me, Make
26:13 I s' in the way a light from heaven,
28: 4 barbarians s' the venomous beast
6 and s' no harm come to him, they
15 whom when Paul s', he thanked
Ga 1:19 other of the apostles s' I none, save
2: 7 when they s' that the gospel of the
14 I s' that they walked not uprightly
Ph'p 1:30 the same conflict which ye s' in me,
Heb 3: 9 me, and s' my works forty years.
11:23 they s' he was a proper child; and
Re 1: 2 Christ, and of all things that he s'.
12 I s' seven golden candlesticks;
17 when I s' him, I fell at his feet as
4: 4 I s' four and twenty elders sitting,
5: 1 s' in the right hand of him that sat
2 s' a strong angel proclaiming with
6: 1 I s' when the Lamb opened one of
2 And I s', and behold a white horse:
9 s' under the altar the souls of them
7: 1 s' four angels standing on the four
2 I s' another angel ascending from
8: 2 I s' the seven angels which stood
9: 1 I s' a star fall from heaven unto the
17 thus I s' the horses in the vision,
10: 1 s' another mighty angel come down
5 angel which I s' stand upon the sea
11:11 fear fell upon them which s' them.
12:13 dragon s' that he was cast unto
13: 1 and s' a beast rise up out of the sea,
2 which I s' was like unto a leopard,
3 And I s' one of his heads as it were
14: 6 s' another angel fly in the midst of
15: 1 I s' another sign in heaven, great
2 s' as it were a sea of glass mingled
Re 16:13 I s' three unclean spirits like frogs
17: 3 and I s' a woman sit upon a scarlet
6 I s' the woman drunken with the
6 and when I s' her, I wondered with
18: 1 these things I s' another angel come
18 they s' the smoke of her burning,
19:11 I s' heaven opened, and behold a
17 I s' an angel standing in the sun;
19 I s' the beast, and the kings of the
20: 1 And I s' an angel come down from
4 s' thrones, and they sat upon them,
4 and I s' the souls of them that were
11 I s' a great white throne, and him
12 And I s' the dead, small and great,
21: 1 I s' a new heaven and a new earth:
2 And I John s' the holy city, new
22 I s' no temple therein: for the Lord
22: 8 I John s' these things, and heard

sawed
1Ki 7: 9 s' with saws, within and without,

sawest
Ge 20:10 What s' thou, that thou hast done
1Sa 19: 5 Israel: thou s' it, and didst rejoice:
28:13 Be not afraid: for what s' thou?
2Sa 18:11 behold, thou s' him, and why didst
Ps 50:18 When thou s' a thief, then thou
Isa 57: 8 lovedst their bed where thou s' it.
Da 2:31 king, s', and behold a great image.
34 Thou s' till that a stone was cut out
41 whereas thou s' the feet and toes,
41 as thou s' the iron mixed with miry
43 thou s' iron mixed with miry clay,
45 thou s' that the stone was cut of the
4:20 The tree that thou s', which grew,
8:20 The ram which thou s' having two
Re 1:20 of the seven stars which thou s' in
20 candlesticks which thou s' are the
17: 8 The beast that thou s' was, and is
12 the ten horns which thou s' are ten
15 The waters which thou s', where
16 the ten horns which thou s' upon
18 woman which thou s' is that great

sawn
Heb11:37 were stoned, they were s' asunder,

saws
2Sa 12:31 and put them under s', and under
1Ki 7: 9 sawed with s', within and without,
1Ch 20: 3 cut them with s', and with harrows

say^ See also GAINSAY; SAID; SAITH; SAYING.
Ge 12:12 that they shall s', This is his wife:
13 S', I pray thee, thou art my sister:
14:23 thou...s', I have made Abram rich:
20:13 come, s' of me, He is my brother.
24:14 damsel to whom I shall s', Let down
14 she shall s', Drink, and I will give
43 and I s' to her, Give me, I pray thee,
44 And she s' to me, Both drink thou,
26: 7 for he feared to s', She is my wife;
32:18 Then thou shalt s', They be thy
20 s' ye...Behold, thy servant Jacob
34:11 what ye shall s' unto me I will give.
12 according as ye shall s' unto me;
37:17 I heard them s', Let us go to Dothan.
20 and we will s', Some evil beast hath
41:15 I have heard s' of thee, that thou
43: 7 he would s', Bring your brother down?
44: 4 s' unto them, Wherefore have ye
16 said, What shall we s' unto my lord?
45: 9 and s' unto him, Thus saith thy son
17 S' unto thy brethren, This do ye;
46:31 and shew Pharaoh, and s' unto him,
33 shall s', What is your occupation?
34 That ye shall s', Thy servants' trade
50:17 So shall ye s' unto Joseph, Forgive,
Ex 3:13 and shall s' unto them, The God of
13 and they shall s' to me, What is his
13 name? what shall I s' unto them?
14, 15 thou s' unto the children of Israel,
16 s' unto them, The Lord God of your
18 ye shall s' unto him, The Lord God
4: 1 for they will s', The Lord hath not
12 and teach thee what thou shalt s'.
22 thou shalt s' unto Pharaoh, Thus
23 I s' unto thee, Let my son go, that
5:16 and they s' to us, Make brick: and,
17 ye s', Let us go and do sacrifice to
6: 6 s' unto the children of Israel, I am
29 of Egypt all that I s' unto thee.
7: 9 then thou shalt s' unto Aaron, Take
16 thou shalt s' unto him, The Lord
19 S' unto Aaron, Take thy rod, and
8: 1 Go unto Pharaoh, and s' unto him,
5 S' unto Aaron, Stretch forth thine
16 S' unto Aaron, Stretch out thy rod,
20 s' unto him, Thus saith the Lord,
9:13 before Pharaoh, and s' unto him,
12:26 your children shall s' unto you,
27 ye shall s', It is the sacrifice of the
13:14 thou shalt s' unto him, By strength
14: 3 Pharaoh will s' of the children of
16: 9 S' unto all the congregation of the
19: 3 shalt thou s' to the house of Jacob,
20:22 shalt s' unto the children of Israel,
21: 5 if the servant shall plainly s', I love
32:12 and s', For mischief did he bring
33: 5 S' unto the children of Israel, Ye are
Le 1: 2 and s' unto them, If any man of you
15: 2 and s' unto them, When any man
17: 2 and s' unto them; This is the thing
8 shalt s' unto them, Whatsoever man
18: 2 and s' unto them, I am the Lord your
19: 2 and s' unto them, Ye shall be holy:
20: 2 thou shalt s' to the children of Israel,
21: 1 and s' unto them, There shall none

Le 22: 3 S' unto them, Whosoever he be of
18 and s' unto them, Whatsoever he be
23: 2 and s'...Concerning the feasts of
10 and s' unto them, When ye be come
25: 2 and s' unto them, When ye come into
20 And if ye shall s', What shall we eat
27: 2 and s'...When a man shall make a
Nu 5:12 s' unto them, If any man's wife go
19 and s' unto the woman, If no man
21 the priest shall say unto the woman,
22 the woman shall s', Amen, amen.
6: 2 and s' unto them, When either man
8: 2 and s' unto him, When thou lightest
11:12 shouldest s' unto me, Carry them
18 s' thou unto the people, Sanctify
14:28 S' unto them, As truly as I live,
15: 2 and s' unto them, When ye be come
18 and s' unto them, When ye come into
18:26 and s' unto them, When ye take of
30 s' unto them, When ye have heaved
21:27 that speak in proverbs s', Come into
22:19 the Lord will s' unto me more.
20 word which I shall s' unto thee,
38 any power at all to s' any thing?
23:16 Go again unto Balak, and s' thus.
25:12 Wherefore s', Behold, I give unto
28: 2 and s' unto them, My offering, and
3 s' unto them, This is the offering
33:51 s' unto them, When ye are passed
34: 2 and s' unto them, When ye come into
35:10 s' unto them, When ye be come over
De 1:42 S' unto them, Go not up, neither
4: 6 and s', Surely this great nation is a
5:27 all that the Lord our God shall s':
30 Go s' to them, Get you into your tents
6:21 thou shalt s' unto thy son, We were
7:17 shalt s' in thine heart, These nations
8:17 And thou s' in thine heart, My power
9: 2 and of whom thou hast heard s', Who
28 s', Because the Lord was not able
12:20 and thou shalt s', I will eat flesh,
13:12 thou shalt hear s' in one of thy cities,
15:16 if he s' unto thee, I will not go
17:14 shalt s', I will set a king over me,
18:21 s' in thine heart, How shall we know
20: 3 shall s' unto them, Hear, O Israel,
8 and they shall s', What man is there
21: 7 and s', Our hands have not shed this
20 shall s' unto the elders of his city,
22:14 and s', I took this woman, and when
16 father shall s' unto the elders, I gave
25: 7 s', My husband's brother refuseth to
8 to it, and s', I like not to take her:
9 answer and s', So shall it be done
26: 3 and s' unto him, I profess this day
5 s' before the Lord thy God, A Syrian
13 shalt s' before the Lord thy God,
27:14 and s' unto all the men of Israel with
15 people shall answer and s', Amen.
16, 17, 18, 19, 20, 21, 22, 23, 24, 25, 26
And all the people shall s', Amen.
28:67 morning thou shalt s', Would God
67 and at even thou shalt s', Would God
29:22 shall s', when they see the plagues
24 Even all nations shall s', Wherefore
25 shall s', Because they have forsaken
30:12, 13 thou shouldest s', Who shall go
31:17 s' in that day, Are not these evils
32:27 lest they should s', Our hand is high,
37 he shall s', Where are their gods,
40 hand to heaven, and s', I live for ever
33:27 thee; and shall s', Destroy them.
Jos 7: 8 O Lord, what shall I s', when Israel
13 and s', Sanctify yourselves against
8: 6 for they will s', They flee before us,
9:11 s' unto them, We are your servants:
22:11 And the children of Israel heard s',
27 children may not s' to our children
28 when they should so s' to us or to
28 we may s' again, Behold the pattern
J'g 4:20 enquire of thee, and s', Is there any
20 man here? that thou shalt s', No.
7: 4 of whom I s' unto thee, This shall go
4 of whomsoever I s'...This shall not
11 And thou shalt hear what they s';
18 and s', The sword of the Lord, and
9:54 that men s' not of me, A woman slew
12: 6 they unto him, S' now Shibboleth:
16:15 How canst thou s', I love thee, when
18: 8 brethren said unto them, What s' ye?
24 and what is this that ye s' unto me,
21:22 we will s' unto them, Be favourable
Ru 1:12 If I should s', I have hope, if I
1Sa 2:36 and shall s', Put me, I pray thee, into
3: 9 that thou shalt s', Speak, Lord; for
8: 7 people in all that they s' unto thee:
10: 2 and they will s' unto thee, The asses
11: 9 s' unto the men of Jabesh-gilead,
13: 4 Israel heard s' that Saul had smitten
14: 9 If they s' thus unto us, Tarry until
10 if they s' thus, Come up unto us;
34 and s' unto them, Bring me hither
15:16 And he said unto him, S' on.
16: 2 and s', I am come to sacrifice to the
18:22 and s', Behold, the king hath delight
25 Thus shall ye s' to David, The king
19:24 Wherefore they s', Is Saul also among
20: 6 then s', David earnestly asked leave
7 If he s' thus, It is well; thy servant
21 If I expressly s' unto the lad, Behold,
22 But if I s' thus unto the young man,
25: 6 s' to him that liveth in prosperity,
2Sa 7: 8 thou s' unto my servant David,
20 And what can David s' more unto
11:20 and he s' unto thee, Wherefore
21 then s' thou, Thy servant Uriah the
2Sa 11:25 thou s' unto Joab, Let not this thing
13: 5 s' unto him, I pray thee, let my sister
28 when I s' unto you, Smite Amnon;
14:12 lord the king. And he said, S' on.
32 to s', Wherefore am I come from
15:10 then ye shall s', Absalom reigneth
26 But if he thus s', I have no delight
34 and s' unto Absalom, I will be thy
16:10 Who shall then s', Wherefore hast
17: 9 whosoever heareth it will s', There
19: 2 the people heard s' that day how the
13 And s' ye to Amasa, Art thou not of
20:16 s', I pray you, unto Joab, Come near
21: 4 What ye shall s', that will I do for
24: 1 moved David against them to s', Go,
12 Go and s' unto David, Thus saith
1Ki 1:13 s' unto him, Didst not thou, my lord,
25 him, and s', God save king Adonijah.
34 and s', God save king Solomon.
36 God of my lord the king s' so too.
2:14 I have somewhat to s' unto thee.
14 unto thee. And she said, S' on.
16 not. And she said unto him, S' on.
17 king, (for he will not s' thee nay,)
20 thee; I pray thee, s' me not nay.
20 mother: for I will not s' thee nay.
9: 8 they shall s', Why hath the Lord
12:10 thus shalt thou s' unto them, My
13:22 of the which the Lord did s' to thee,
14: 5 thus shalt thou s' unto her: for it
16:16 people that were encamped heard s',
18:44 Go up, s' unto Ahab, Prepare thy
22: 8 said, Let not the king s' so.
27 And s', Thus saith the king, Put this
2Ki 1: 3 s' unto them, Is it not because
6 s' unto him, Thus saith the Lord,
2:18 them, Did I not s' unto you, Go not?
4:13 S' now unto her, Behold, thou hast
26 and s' unto her, Is it well with thee?
28 did I not s', Do not deceive me?
7: 4 If we s', We will enter into the city,
13 behold, I s', they are even as all the
8:10 him, Go, s' unto him, Thou mayest
9: 3 and s', Thus saith the Lord, I have
17 them, and let him s', Is it peace?
37 they shall not s', This is Jezebel.
18:22 But if ye s' unto me, We trust in the
19: 6 Thus shall ye s' to your master, Thus
9 when he heard s' of Tirhakah king
22:18 thus shall ye s' to him, Thus saith
1Ch 5: 3 sons, I s', of Reuben the firstborn of
16:31 and let men s' among the nations,
35 And s' ye, Save us, O God of our
17: 7 shalt thou s' unto my servant David,
21:18 Lord commanded Gad to s' to David,
2Ch 7:21 that he shall s', Why hath the Lord
10:10 thus shalt thou s' unto them, My
18: 7 said, Let not the king s' so.
15 thou s' nothing but the truth to me
26 And s', Thus saith the king, Put this
20:11 Behold, I s', how they reward us, to
21 and to s', Praise the Lord; for his
34:26 so shall ye s' unto him, Thus saith
Ezr 8:17 what they should s' unto Iddo,
9:10 God, what shall we s' after this?
Ne 7: 7 I s', of the men of the people of Israel
8 to give it, I s', to his seed, and hast
Es 1:18 s' this day unto all the king's
Job 6:22 Did I s', Bring unto me? or, Give a
7: 4 I lie down, I s', When shall I arise,
13 I s', My bed shall comfort me, my
9:12 will s' unto him, What doest thou?
20 if I s', I am perfect, it shall also prove
27 If I s', I will forget my complaint,
10: 2 s' unto God, Do not condemn me;
19:28 ye should s', Why persecute we him,
20: 7 they which have seen him shall s',
21:14 they s' unto God, Depart from us;
28 For ye s', Where is the house of the
22:29 thou shalt s', There is lifting up;
23: 5 understand what he would s' unto
28:22 Destruction and death s', We have
32:11 whilst ye searched out what to s'.
13 Lest ye should s', We have found
33:27 men, and if any s', I have sinned,
32 If thou hast anything to s', answer
34:18 Is it fit to s' to a king, Thou art
36:23 or who can s', Thou hast wrought
37:19 Teach us what we shall s' unto him;
38:35 go, and s' unto thee, Here we are?
Ps 3: 2 Many there be which s' of my soul,
4: 6 There be many that s', Who will
11: 1 how s' ye to my soul, Flee as a bird to
13: 4 Lest mine enemy s', I have prevailed
27:14 thine heart: wait, I s', on the Lord.
35: 3 s' unto my soul, I am thy salvation.
10 All my bones shall s', Lord, who is
25 Let them not s' in their hearts, Ah,
25 let them not s', We have swallowed
27 yea, let them s' continually, Let the
40:15 shame that s' unto me, Aha, aha.
16 as love thy salvation s' continually,
41: 8 An evil disease, s' they, cleaveth fast
42: 3 they continually s' unto me, Where
9 I will s' unto God my rock, Why hast
10 while they s' daily unto me, Where
58:11 So that a man shall s', Verily there
59: 7 their lips: for who, s' they, doth hear?
64: 5 they s', Who shall see them?
66: 3 S' unto God, How terrible art thou
70: 3 a reward of their shame that s', Aha,
4 as love thy salvation s' continually,
73:11 And they s', How doth God know?
15 If I s', I will speak thus; behold, I
79:10 Wherefore should the heathen s',
91: 2 I will s' of the Lord, He is my refuge
Ps 94: 7 Yet they s', The Lord shall not see.
96:10 S' among the heathen that the Lord
106:48 and let all the people s', Amen.
107: 2 Let the redeemed of the Lord s' so,
115: 2 Wherefore should the heathen s',
118: 2 Let Israel now s', that his mercy
3 Let the house of Aaron now s', that
4 Let them now that fear the Lord s',
122: 8 I will now s', Peace be within thee.
124: 1 was on our side, now may Israel s';
129: 1 from my youth, may Israel now s':
8 Neither do they which go by s', The
130: 6 I s', more than they that watch for the
139:11 If I s', Surely the darkness shall
Pr 1:11 If they s', Come with us, let us lay
3:28 S' not unto thy neighbour, Go, and
5:12 s', How have I hated instruction,
7: 4 S' unto wisdom, Thou art my sister;
20: 9 Who can s', I have made my heart
22 S' not thou, I will recompense evil:
24:29 S' not, I will do so to him as he hath
30: 9 deny thee, and s', Who is the Lord?
15 yea, four things s' not, It is enough:
Ec 5: 6 neither s' thou before the angel,
6: 3 I s', that an untimely birth is better
7:10 S' not thou, What is the cause that
8: 4 who may s' unto him, What doest
12: 1 nigh, when thou shalt s', I have no
Isa 2: 3 many people shall go and s', Come
3:10 S' ye to the righteous, that it shall
5:19 That s', Let him make speed, and
7: 4 And s' unto him, Take heed, and be
8:12 S' ye not, A confederacy, to all them
12 them to whom this people shall s', A
19 when they shall s' unto you, Seek
9: 9 that s' in the pride and stoutness of
12: 1 in that day thou shalt s', O Lord,
4 that day shall ye s', Praise the Lord,
14: 4 s', How hath the oppressor ceased!
10 they shall speak and s' unto thee,
19:11 how s' ye unto Pharaoh, I am the son
20: 6 of this isle shall s' in that day,
22:15 which is over the house, and s',
29:15 dark, and they s', Who seeth us?
16 the work s' of him that made it,
16 thing framed s' of him that framed
30:10 Which s' to the seers, See not; and
22 thou shalt s' unto it, Get thee hence.
33:24 inhabitant shall not s', I am sick:
35: 4 S' to them that are of a fearful
36: 4 S' ye now to Hezekiah, Thus saith
5 I s', sayest thou,...I have counsel
7 thou s' to me, We trust in the Lord
37: 6 Thus shall ye s' unto your master,
9 heard s' concerning Tirhakah king
38: 5 Go, and s' to Hezekiah, Thus saith
15 What shall I s'? he hath both
40: 9 s' unto the cities of Judah, Behold
41:26 that we may s', He is righteous?
27 The first shall s' to Zion, Behold,
42:17 s' to the molten images, Ye are our
43: 6 I will s' to the north, Give up; and
9 or let them hear, and s', It is truth.
44: 5 One shall s', I am the Lord's; and
19 knowledge nor understanding to s',
20 nor s', Is there not a lie in my right
45: 9 the clay s' to him that fashioneth it,
24 shall one s', in the Lord have I
48: 5 shouldest s', Mine idol hath done
7 thou...s', Behold, I knew them.
20 s' ye, The Lord hath redeemed his
49: 9 thou mayest s' to the prisoners, Go
20 s' again in thine ears, The place is
21 Then shalt thou s' in thine heart,
51:16 s' unto Zion, Thou art my people.
56: 3 eunuch s', Behold, I am a dry tree.
12 Come ye, s' they, I will fetch wine,
57:14 And shall s', Cast ye up, cast ye up,
58: 3 we fasted, s' they, and thou seest not?
9 cry, and he shall s', Here I am.
62:11 world, S' ye to the daughter of Zion,
65: 5 Which s', Stand by thyself, come not
Jer 1: 7 said unto me, s' not, I am a child:
2:23 canst thou s', I am not polluted, I
27 time of their trouble they will s',
31 wherefore s' my people, We are
3: 1 They s', If a man put away his wife,
12 and s', Return, thou backsliding
16 s' no more, The ark of the covenant
4: 5 s', Blow ye the trumpet in the land:
5 and s', Assemble yourselves, and let
5: 2 though they s', The Lord liveth;
15 understandest what they s'.
19 shall come to pass, when ye shall s',
24 Neither s' they in their heart, Let us
7: 2 s', Hear the word of the Lord, all ye
10 s', We are delivered to do all these
28 shalt s' unto them, This is a nation
8: 4 Moreover thou shalt s' unto them,
8 How do ye s', We are wise, and the
10:11 Thus shall ye s' unto them, The
11: 3 And s' thou unto them, Thus saith
13:12 they shall s' unto thee, Do we not
13 Then shalt thou s' unto them, Thus
18 S' unto the king and to the queen,
21 thou s' when he shall punish thee?
22 if thou s' in thine heart, Wherefore
14:13 the prophets s' unto them, Ye shall
15 yet they s', Sword and famine shall
17 thou shalt s' this word unto them;
15: 2 if they s' unto thee, Whither shall
16:10 they shall s' unto thee, Wherefore
11 shalt thou s' unto them, Because
19 and shall s', Surely our fathers have
17:15 they s' unto me, Where is the word
20 s' unto them, Hear ye the word of

Jer 19: 3 And s', Hear ye the word of the Lord,
11 shalt s' unto them, Thus saith the
20: 10 Report, s' they, and we will report it.
21: 3 them, Thus shall ye s' to Zedekiah:
8 And unto this people thou shalt s',
11 s', Hear ye the word of the Lord;
13 which s', Who shall come down
22: 2 And s', Hear the word of the Lord, O
8 shall s' every man to his neighbour,
23: 7 shall no more s', The Lord liveth,
17 s' still unto them that despise me,
17 s'...No evil shall come upon you.
31 use their tongues, and s', He saith.
33 then s' unto them, What burden?
34 shall s', The burden of the Lord,
35 ye s' every one to his neighbour,
37 Thus shalt thou s' to the prophet,
38 since ye s', The burden of the Lord;
38 Because ye s' this word, The burden
38 shall not s', The burden of the Lord;
25: 27 Therefore thou shalt s' unto them,
28 then shalt thou s' unto them, Thus
30 s' unto them, The Lord shall roar
26: 4 And thou shalt s' unto them, Thus
27: 4 them to s' unto their masters, Thus
4 Thus shall ye s' unto your masters;
31: 7 ye, and s', O Lord, save thy people,
10 and s', He that scattered Israel will
29 In those days they shall s' no more,
32: 3 and s', Thus saith the Lord, Behold,
36 concerning this city, whereof ye s',
43 whereof ye s', It is desolate without
33: 10 which ye s' shall be desolate without
11 voice of them that shall s', Praise
36: 29 shalt s' to Jehoiakim king of Judah,
37: 7 shall ye s' to the king of Judah,
38: 22 those women shall s', Thy friends
25 s' unto thee, Declare unto us now
26 thou shalt s' unto them, I presented
39: 12 him even as he shall s' unto thee.
42: 13 But if ye s', We will not dwell in
20 all that the Lord our God shall s',
43: 2 not sent thee to s', Go not into Egypt
10 s' unto them, Thus saith the Lord
45: 3 Thou didst s', Woe is me now! for
4 Thus shalt thou s' unto him, The
46: 14 s' ye, Stand fast, and prepare thee;
48: 14 How s' ye, We are mighty and strong
17 s', How is the strong staff broken,
19 that escapeth, and s', What is done?
50: 2 conceal not: s', Babylon is taken,
51: 35 shall the inhabitant of Zion s'; and
35 of Chaldea, shall Jerusalem s'.
62 Then shalt thou s', O Lord, thou
64 thou shalt s', Thus shall Babylon
La 2: 12 They s' to their mothers, Where is
16 they s', We have swallowed her up:
Eze 2: 4 thou shalt s' unto them, Thus saith
8 of man, hear what I s' unto thee;
3: 18 When I s' unto the wicked, Thou
27 thou shalt s' unto them, Thus saith
6: 3 s', Ye mountains of Israel, hear the
11 s', Alas for all the evil abominations
8: 12 for they s', The Lord seeth us not;
9: 9 they s', The Lord hath forsaken the
11: 3 Which s', It is not near; let us build
16, 17 Therefore s', Thus saith the Lord
12: 10 S' thou unto them, Thus saith the
11 S', I am your sign: like as I have
19 s' unto the people of the land, Thus
23 but s' unto them, The days are at
25 I s' the word, and will perform it,
27 house of Israel s', The vision that
28 Therefore s' unto them, Thus saith
13: 2 and s' thou unto them that prophesy
7 whereas ye s', The Lord saith it;
11 S' unto them which daub it with
15 s' unto you, The wall is no more,
18 s', Thus saith the Lord God; Woe to
14: 4 s' unto them, Thus saith the Lord
6 s' unto the house of Israel, Thus
17 and s', Sword, go through the land;
16: 3 s', Thus saith the Lord God unto
17: 3 And s', Thus saith the Lord God; A
9 S' thou, Thus saith the Lord God;
12 S' now to the rebellious house, Know
18: 19 Yet s' ye, Why? doth not the son
25 Yet ye s', The way of the Lord is not
19: 2 s', What is thy mother? A lioness:
20: 3 the elders of Israel, and s' unto them,
5, 27 s' unto them, Thus saith the Lord
30 s' unto the house of Israel, Thus
32 ye s', We will be as the heathen, as
47 s' to the forest of the south, Hear the
49 they s' of me, Doth he not speak
21: 3 s' to the land of Israel, Thus saith
7 when they s' unto thee, Wherefore
9 and s', Thus saith the Lord;
9 S', A sword, a sword is sharpened,
24 I s', that ye are come to remembrance,
28 and s', Thus saith the Lord God
28 even s' thou, The sword, the sword
22: 3 s' thou, Thus saith the Lord God,
24 s' unto her, Thou art the land that
24: 3 s' unto them, Thus saith the Lord
25: 3 s' unto the Ammonites, Hear the
8 Because that Moab and Seir do s',
26: 17 s' to thee, How art thou destroyed,
27: 3 And s' unto Tyrus, O thou that art
28: 2 s' unto the prince of Tyrus, Thus
9 yet s' before him that slayeth thee,
12 the king of Tyrus, and s' unto him,
22 and s', Thus saith the Lord God,
29: 3 and s', Thus saith the Lord God;
30: 2 and s', Thus saith the Lord God;
32: 2 s' unto him, Thou art like a young

Eze 33: 2 and s' unto them, When I bring the
8 When I s' unto the wicked, O wicked
11 S' unto them, As I live, saith the
12 s' unto the children of thy people,
13 When I shall s' to the righteous,
14 I s' unto the wicked, Thou shalt
17 Yet the children of thy people s', The
20 Yet ye s', The way of the Lord is not
25 Wherefore s' unto them, Thus saith
27 S' thou thus unto them, Thus saith
34: 2 s' unto them, Thus saith the Lord
35: 3 s' unto it, Thus saith the Lord God;
36: 1 s', Ye mountains of Israel, hear the
3 prophesy and s', Thus saith the
6 s' unto the mountains, and to the
13 s' unto you, Thou land devourest up
22 s' unto the house of Israel, Thus
35 And they shall s', This land that was
37: 4 s' unto them, O ye dry bones, hear
9 and s' to the wind, Thus saith the
11 they s', Our bones are dried, and our
12 s' unto them, Thus saith the Lord
19 S' unto them, Thus saith the Lord
21 s' unto them, Thus saith the Lord
38: 3 And s', Thus saith the Lord God;
11 And thou shalt s', I will go up to the
13 s' unto thee, Art thou come to take
14 prophesy and s' unto Gog, Thus
39: 1 prophesy against Gog, and s', Thus
44: 5 all that I s' unto thee concerning
6 thou shalt s' to the rebellious, even
Da 4: 35 or s' unto him, What doest thou?
5: 11 king, I s', thy father made master of
Ho 2: 1 S' ye unto your brethren, Ammi;
7 shall she s', I will go and return to
23 I will s' to them which were not my
23 and they shall s', Thou art my God.
10: 3 now they shall s', We have no king,
8 shall s' to the mountains, Cover us;
13: 2 they s' of them, Let the men that
14: 2 s' unto him, Take away all iniquity,
3 will we s' any more to the work of
8 Ephraim shall s', What have I to do
Joe 2: 17 and let them s', Spare thy people, O
17 should they s' among the people,
19 Lord will answer and s' unto his
3: 10 spears: let the weak s', I am strong.
Am 3: 9 s', Assemble yourselves upon the
4: 1 s' to their masters, Bring, and let us
5: 16 s' in all the highways, Alas! alas!
6: 10 s' unto him that is by the sides of
10 any with thee? and he shall s', No.
10 Then shall he s', Hold thy tongue:
13 which s', Have we not taken to us
8: 14 and s', Thy god, O Dan, liveth; and,
9: 10 which s', The evil shall not overtake
Mic 2: 4 and s', We be utterly spoiled: he
6 ye not, s' they to them that prophesy:
3: 11 and s', Is not the Lord among us?
4: 2 s', Come, and let us go up to the
11 thee, that s', Let her be defiled, and
Na 3: 7 thee, and s', Nineveh is laid waste:
Hab 2: 1 to see what he will s' unto me,
6 against him, and s', Woe to him
Zep 1: 12 s' in their heart, The Lord will not
Hag 1: 2 This people s', The time is not come,
Zec 1: 3 s' thou unto them, Thus saith the
11: 5 they that sell them s', Blessed be the
12: 5 governors of Judah shall s' in their
13: 3 s' unto him, Thou shalt not live;
5 he shall s', I am no prophet, I am an
6 s' unto him, What are these wounds
9 hear them: I will s', It is my people:
9 they shall s', The Lord is my God.
Mal 1: 2 Yet ye s', Wherein hast thou loved
5 and ye shall s', The Lord will be
6 ye s', Wherein have we despised thy
7 and ye s', Wherein have we polluted
7 In that ye s', The table of the Lord
12 But ye have profaned it, in that ye s',
2: 14 Yet ye s', Wherefore? Because the
17 Yet ye s', Wherein have we wearied
17 When ye s', Every one that doeth
3: 8 But ye s', Wherein have we robbed
13 ye s', What have we spoken so much
M't 3: 9 think not to s' within yourselves,
9 I s' unto you, that God is able of
4: 17 and to s', Repent: for the kingdom
5: 11 s' all manner of evil against you
18 I s' unto you, Till heaven and earth
20 For I s' unto you, That except your
22 But I s' unto you, That whosoever
22 whosoever shall s' to his brother,
22 but whosoever shall s', Thou fool,
26 I s' unto thee, Thou shalt by no
28, 32 I s' unto you, That whosoever
34 But I s' unto you, Swear not at all;
39 But I s' unto you, That ye resist not
44 I s' unto you, Love your enemies,
6: 2, 5, 16 I s' unto you, They have their
25 I s' unto you, Take no thought for
29 I s' unto you, That even Solomon
7: 4 Or how wilt thou s' to thy brother,
22 Many will s' to me in that day, Lord,
8: 9 I s' to this man, Go, and he goeth;
10 I s' unto you, I have not found so
11 I s' unto you, That many shall come
9: 5 easier, to s', Thy sins be forgiven
5 thee; or to s', Arise, and walk?
10: 15 I s'...It shall be more tolerable
23 I s' unto you, Ye shall not have gone
42 I s' unto you, he shall in no wise lose
11: 7 to s' unto the multitudes concerning
9 yea, I s' unto you, and more than a
11 I s' unto you, Among them that are
18 and they s', He hath a devil.

M't 11: 19 they s', Behold a man gluttonous,
22 But I s'...It shall be more tolerable
24 But I s'...it shall be more tolerable
12: 6 But I s' unto you, That in this place
31 I s' unto you, All manner of sin and
36 I s' unto you, That every idle word
13: 17 I s' unto you, That many prophets
30 I will s' to the reapers, Gather
51 They s' unto him, Yea, Lord.
14: 17 s' unto him, We have...five loaves,
15: 5 But ye s', Whosoever shall
5 s' to his father or his mother, It is
33 his disciples s' unto him, Whence
16: 2 it is evening, ye s', It will be fair
13 men s' that I the Son of man am?
14 Some s' that thou art John the
15 them, But whom s' ye that I am?
18 And I s' also...That thou art Peter,
28 Verily I s'...There be some standing
17: 10 Why then s' the scribes that Elias
12 I s' unto you, That Elias is come
20 verily I s' unto you, If ye have faith
20 ye shall s' unto this mountain,
18: 3 Verily I s'...Except ye be converted,
10 for I s' unto you, That in heaven
13 I s' unto you, he rejoiceth more
18 I s'...Whatsoever ye shall bind on
19 I s' unto you, That if two of you
22 I s' not unto thee, Until seven times:
19: 7 They s' unto him, Why did Moses
9 I s' unto you, Whosoever shall put
10 His disciples s' unto him, If the case
23 Verily I s' unto you, That a rich man
24 again I s'...It is easier for a camel
28 I s'...That ye which have followed
20: 7 They s' unto him, Because no man
22 They s' unto him, We are able.
33 s' unto him, Lord, that our eyes
21: 3 And if any man s' ought unto you,
3 ye shall s', The Lord hath need of
16 him, Hearest thou what these s'?
21 I s' unto you, If ye have faith, and
21 if ye shall s' unto this mountain,
25 If we shall s', From heaven;
25 he will s' unto us, Why did ye not
26 But if we shall s', Of men; we fear
31 They s' unto him, The first. Jesus
31 I s' unto you, That the publicans
41 They s' unto him, He will miserably
43 s' I unto you, The kingdom of God
22: 21 They s' unto him, Cæsar's. Then
23 which s'...there is no resurrection,
42 They s' unto him, The son of David.
23: 3 their works: for they s', and do not.
16 ye blind guides, which s', Whosoever
30 And s', If we had been in the days
36 Verily I s' unto you, All these things
39 I s' unto you, Ye shall not see me
39 till ye shall s', Blessed is he that
24: 2 I s'...There shall not be left one
23 if any man shall s'...Lo, here is
26 shall s'...Behold, he is in the desert;
34 I s' unto you, This generation
47 I s'...That he shall make him ruler
48 evil servant shall s' in his heart,
25: 12 I s' unto you, I know you not.
34 King s' unto them on his right
40 King shall answer and s' unto them,
40 Verily I s' unto you, Inasmuch as
41 he s' also unto them on the left
45 Verily I s' unto you, Inasmuch as
26: 13 Verily I s' unto you, Wheresoever
18 and s' unto him, The Master saith,
21 Verily I s' unto you, that one of you
22 them to s' unto him, Lord, is it I?
29 But I s' unto you, I will not drink
34 I s' unto thee, That this night,
64 I s' unto you, Hereafter shall ye
27: 22 They all s'...Let him be crucified.
33 that is to s', a place of a skull,
46 that is to s', My God, my God, why
64 and s' unto the people, He is risen
28: 13 S' ye, His disciples came by night,
M'r 1: 44 See thou s' nothing to any man:
2: 9 s' to the sick of the palsy, Thy sins
9 or to s', Arise, and take up thy bed,
11 I s' unto thee, Arise, and take up
18 come and s'...Why do the disciples
3: 28 Verily I s' unto you, All sins shall
4: 38 and s' unto him, Master, carest thou
5: 41 Damsel, I s' unto thee, arise.
6: 11 I s'...It shall be more tolerable
37 And they s'...Shall we go and buy
38 knew, they s', Five, and two fishes.
7: 2 that is to s', with unwashen, hands,
11 But ye s', If a man shall
11 shall s' to his father or mother,
11 It is Corban, that is to s', a gift, by
8: 12 I s' unto you, There shall no sign
19 ye up? They s' unto him, Twelve.
27 them, Whom do men s' that I am?
28 John the Baptist: but some s', Elias;
29 them, But whom s' ye that I am?
9: 1 I s' unto you, That there be some
6 For he wist not what to s'; for
11 Why s' the scribes that Elias must
13 I s' unto you, That Elias is indeed
41 I s' unto you, he shall not lose his
10: 15 I s' unto you, Whosoever shall not
28 Peter began to s'...Lo, we have left
29 Verily I s' unto you, There is no man
47 and s', Jesus, thou son of David,
11: 3 man s' unto you, Why do ye this?
3 s' ye that the Lord hath need of
23 I s' unto you, That whosoever
23 shall s' unto this mountain, Be thou

M'r 11:24 I s' unto you, What things soever
28 And s' unto him, By what authority
31 If we shall s', From heaven:
31 he will s', Why...did ye not believe
32 But if we shall s', Of men; they
12:14 they s' unto him, Master, we know
18 which s' there is no resurrection;
35 How s' the scribes that Christ is the
13: 5 began to s', Take heed that no man
21 if any man shall s' to you, Lo, here
30 Verily I s'...that this generation
37 And what I s' unto you I s' unto all,
14: 9 Verily I s' unto you, Wheresoever
14 s' ye to the goodman of the house,
18 Verily I s' unto you, One of you
19 to s' unto him one by one, Is it I?
25 I s' unto you, I will drink no more
30 Verily I s' unto thee, That this day,
58 We heard him s', I will destroy this
65 him, and to s' unto him, Prophesy:
69 began to s'...This is one of them.
Lu 3: 8 begin not to s' within yourselves,
8 for I s' unto you, That God is able
4:21 he began to s' unto them, This day
23 surely s' unto me this proverb,
24 Verily I s' unto you, No prophet is
5:23 easier, to s', Thy sins be forgiven
23 thee; or to s', Rise up and walk?
24 I s' unto thee, Arise, and take up
6:27 But I s' unto you which hear, Love
42 how canst thou s' to thy brother,
46 and do not the things which I s'?
7: 7 but s' in a word, and my servant
8 I s' unto one, Go, and he goeth;
9 I s' unto you, I have not found so
14 Young man, I s' unto thee, Arise.
26 Yea, I s' unto you, and much more
28 I s' unto you, Among those that are
33 wine; and ye s', He hath a devil.
34 and ye s', Behold a gluttonous man,
40 I have somewhat to s' unto thee.
40 thee. And he saith, Master, s' on.
47 I s' unto thee, Her sins, which are
49 s' within themselves, Who is this
9:18 Whom s' the people that I am?
19 John the Baptist;...some s', Elias;
19 others s',...one of the old prophets
20 But whom s' ye that I am? Peter
10: 5 first s', Peace be to this house.
9 s' unto them, The kingdom of God
10 into the streets of the same, and s',
12 I s'...that it shall be more tolerable
11: 2 When ye pray, s', Our Father which
5 s' unto him, Friend, lend me three
7 answer and s', Trouble me not:
8 I s' unto you, Though he will not
9 I s' unto you, Ask, and it shall be
18 because ye s' that I cast out devils
29 to s', This is an evil generation:
51 I s' unto you, It shall be required
12: 1 he began to s' unto his disciples
4 I s' unto you my friends, Be not
5 hell; yea, I s' unto you, Fear him.
8 Also I s'...Whosoever shall confess
11 shall answer, or what ye shall s':
12 the same hour what ye ought to s'.
19 And I will s' to my soul, Soul, thou
22 I s' unto you, Take no thought
27 I s' unto you, that Solomon in all
37 I s' unto you, that he shall gird
44 I s'...that he will make him ruler
45 and if that servant s' in his heart,
54 ye s', There cometh a shower;
55 wind blow, ye s', There will be heat;
13:24 for many, I s'...will seek to enter
25 and s' unto you, I know you not
26 shall ye begin to s', We have eaten
27 shall s', I tell you, I know you not
35 I s' unto you, Ye shall not see me,
35 when ye shall s', Blessed is he
14: 9 s' to thee, Give this man place;
10 he may s' unto thee, Friend, go
17 to s' to them that were bidden,
24 I s' unto you, That none of those
15: 7 I s' unto you, that likewise joy
10 I s' unto you, there is joy in the
18 will s' unto him, Father, I have
16: 9 I s' unto you, Make to yourselves
17: 6 ye might s' unto this sycamine
7 will s' unto him by and by, when
8 will not rather s' unto him, Make
10 s', We are unprofitable servants:
21 Neither shall they s', Lo here! or,
23 they shall s' to you, See here; or,
18:17 Verily I s' unto you, Whosoever
29 Verily I s' unto you, There is no
19:26 I s' unto you, That unto every one
31 thus shall ye s' unto him, Because
20: 5 If we shall s', From heaven;
5 he will s', Why then believed ye
6 if we s', Of men; all the people
41 How s' they that Christ is David's
21: 3 Of a truth I s' unto you, that this
32 Verily I s' unto you, This generation
22:11 ye shall s' unto the goodman of
16 For I s' unto you, I will not any
18 For I s' unto you, I will not drink
37 For I s' unto you, that this that is
70 said unto them, Ye s' that I am.
23:29 in the which they shall s', Blessed
30 they begin to s' to the mountains,
43 Verily I s' unto thee, To day shalt
Joh 1:38 (which is to s', being interpreted,
51 I s' unto you, Hereafter ye shall
3: 3, 5 verily, I s' unto thee, Except a
11 Verily, verily, I s' unto thee, We

Joh 4:20 and ye s', that in Jerusalem is the
35 S' not ye, There are yet four months,
35 behold, I s' unto you, Lift up your
5:19 verily, I s' unto you, The Son can
24 I s' unto you, He that heareth my
25 I s' unto you, The hour is coming,
34 these things I s', that ye might be
6:26 verily, I s' unto you, Ye seek me,
32 I s' unto you, Moses gave you not
47 I s' unto you, He that believeth on
53 I s' unto you, Except ye eat the
7:26 and they s' nothing unto him. Do
8: 4 s' unto him, Master, this woman
26 things to s' and to judge of you:
34 verily, I s' unto you, Whosoever
46 And if I s' the truth, why do ye not
48 S' we not well that thou art a
51 I s' unto you, If a man keep my
54 of whom ye s', that he is your God:
55 and if I should s', I know him not,
58 I s' unto you, Before Abraham was,
9:17 They s' unto the blind man again,
19 your son, who ye s' was born blind?
41 but now ye s', We see; therefore
10: 1 Verily, verily, I s' unto you, He that
7 I s' unto you, I am the door of the
36 S' ye of him, whom the Father
11: 8 His disciples s' unto him, Master,
12:24 verily, I s' unto you, Except a corn
27 what shall I s'? Father, save me
49 should s', and what I should speak.
13:13 Master and Lord: and ye s' well;
16 I s' unto you, The servant is not
20 I s' unto you, He that receiveth
21 I s' unto you, that one of you shall
33 ye cannot come; so now I s' to you.
38 I s' unto thee, The cock shall not
14:12 I s' unto you, He that believeth on
16:12 yet many things to s' unto you, but
20 I s' unto you, That ye shall weep
23 verily, I s' unto you, Whatsoever ye
26 I s' not unto you, that I will pray
20:13 s' unto her, Woman, why weepest
16 Rabboni; which is to s', Master.
17 s' unto them, I ascend unto my
21: 3 They s' unto him, We also go with
18 I s' unto thee, When thou wast
Ac 1:19 Aceldama, that is to s', The field of
3:22 whatsoever he shall s' unto you.
4:14 they could s' nothing against it.
5:38 now I s' unto you, Refrain from
6:14 For we have heard him s', that
10:37 That word, I s', ye know which was
13:15 exhortation for the people, s' on.
17:18 said, What will this babbler s'?
21:23 therefore this that we s' to thee:
23: 8 s' that there is no resurrection,
18 hath something to s' unto thee.
30 to s' before thee what they had
24:20 else let these same here s', if they
26:22 which...Moses did s' should come:
28:26 and s', Hearing ye shall hear,
Ro 3: 5 of God, what shall we s'? Is God
8 as some affirm that we s',) Let us
26 I s', at this time his righteousness:
4: 1 s' then that Abraham our father,
9 we s' that faith was reckoned to
6: 1 What shall we s' then? Shall we
7: 7 What shall we s' then? Is the law
8:31 shall we then s' to these things?
9: 1 I s' the truth in Christ, I lie not,
14 What shall we s' then? Is there
19 Thou wilt s' then unto me, Why
20 Shall the thing formed s' to him
30 What shall we s' then? That the
10: 6 S' not in thine heart, Who shall
18 I s', Have they not heard? Yes
19 But I s', Did not Israel know? Yes
11: 1 I s' then, Hath God cast away his
11 I s' then, Have they stumbled that
19 Thou wilt s' then, The branches
12: 3 For I s', through the grace given
15: 8 s' that Jesus Christ was a minister
1Co 1:12 Now this I s', that every one of you
15 s' that I had baptized in mine
7: 8 I s' therefore to the unmarried
26 I s', that it is good for a man so to be.
29 I s', brethren, the time is short:
9: 8 S' I these things as a man? or
10:15 to wise men; judge ye what I s'.
19 What s' I then? that the idol is any
20 But I s', that the things which the
28 But if any man s' unto you, This
29 Conscience, I s', not thine own,
11:22 What shall I s' to you? shall I
12: 3 no man can s'...Jesus is the Lord,
15 If the foot shall s', Because I am
16 if the ear shall s', Because I am
21 the eye cannot s' unto the hand, I
14:16 s' Amen at thy giving of thanks,
23 will they not s' that ye are mad?
15:12 how s' some among you that there
35 But some man will s', How are the
50 Now this I s', brethren, that flesh
2Co 5: 8 We are confident, I s', and willing
9: 4 we (that we s' not, ye) should be
6 thus I s', He which soweth sparingly,
10:10 For his letters, s' they, are weighty
11:16 I s' again, Let no man think me a
12: 6 for I will s' the truth: but now I
Ga 1: 9 so s' I...again, If any man preach
3:17 this I s', that the covenant that
4: 1 Now I s', That the heir, as long as
5: 2 I Paul s' unto you, that if ye be
16 I s' then, Walk in the Spirit, and ye
Eph 4:17 This I s'...and testify in the Lord,

Ph'p 4: 4 alway: and again I s', Rejoice.
Col 1:20 by him, I s', whether they be things
2: 4 And this I s', lest any man should
4:17 s' to Archippus, Take heed to the
1Th 4:15 this we s' unto you by the word
5: 3 For when they shall s', Peace and
1Ti 1: 7 understanding neither what they s',
2Ti 2: 7 Consider what I s'; and the Lord
Tit 2: 8 having no evil thing to s' of you.
Ph'm 19 I do not s' to thee how thou owest
21 thou wilt also do more than I s'.
Heb 5:11 whom we have many things to s',
7: 9 And as I may so s', Levi also,
9:11 that is to s', not of this building;
10:20 through the veil, that is to s', his flesh;
11:14 they that s' such things declare
32 what shall I more s'? for the time
13: 6 So that we may boldly s', The Lord
Jas 1:13 Let no man s' when he is tempted,
2: 3 and s' unto him, Sit thou here in a
3 s' to the poor, Stand thou there, or
14 though a man s' he hath faith, and
16 one of you s' unto them, Depart
18 a man may s', Thou hast faith,
4:13 Go to now, ye that s', To day or
15 that ye ought to s', If the Lord will,
1Jo 1: 6 If we s' that we have fellowship
8 If we s' that we have no sin, we
10 If we s' that we have not sinned,
4:20 If a man s', I love God, and hateth
5:16 do not s' that he shall pray for it.
Re 2: 2 them which s' they are apostles,
9 of them which s' they are Jews,
24 unto you I s', and unto the rest
3: 9 which s' they are Jews, and are
6: 3 the second beast s', Come and see.
5 the third beast s', Come and see.
6 in the midst of the four beasts s',
7 the fourth beast s', Come and see.
16: 5 heard the angel of the waters s',
7 heard another out of the altar s',
22:17 the Spirit and the bride s', Come.
17 And let him that heareth s', Come.

sayers See GAINSAYERS; SOOTHSAYERS.

sayest
Ex 33:12 s' unto me, Bring up this people:
Nu 22:17 I will do whatsoever thou s' unto
Ru 3: 5 All that thou s' unto me I will do.
1Ki 18:11, 14 And now thou s', Go, tell thy lord,
2Ki 18:20 Thou s',...I have counsel and
2Ch 25:19 Thou s', Lo, thou hast smitten the
Ne 5:12 of them; so will we do as thou s'.
6: 8 are no such things done as thou s',
Job 22:13 And thou s', How doth God know?
35:14 thou s' thou shalt not see him, yet
Ps 90: 3 and s', Return, ye children of men.
Pr 24:12 If thou s', Behold, we knew it not;
Isa 36: 5 I say, s' thou, (but they are but vain
40:27 Why s' thou, O Jacob,...speakest,
47: 8 that s' in thine heart, I am, and none
Jer 2:35 Yet thou s', Because I am innocent,
35 because thou s', I have not sinned.
Am 7:16 Thou s', Prophesy not against Israel,
M't 26:70 saying, I know not what thou s'.
27:11 And Jesus said unto him, Thou s'.
M'r 5:31 thee, and s' thou, Who touched me?
14:68 neither understand I what thou s'.
15: 2 answering said unto him, Thou s' it.
Lu 8:45 and s' thou, Who touched me?
20:21 that thou s' and teachest rightly,
22:60 said, Man, I know not what thou s'.
23: 3 answered him and said, Thou s' it.
Joh 1:22 sent us. What s' thou of thyself?
8: 5 should be stoned: but what s' thou?
33 how s' thou, Ye shall be made free?
52 thou s', If a man keep my saying,
9:17 What s' thou of him, that he hath
12:34 how s' thou, The Son of man must
14: 9 and how s' thou then, Shew us the
18:34 S' thou this thing of thyself, or did
37 answered, Thou s' that I am a king.
Ro 2:22 that s' a man should not commit
1Co 14:16 he understandeth not what thou s'?
Re 3:17 thou s', I am rich, and increased

saying See also GAINSAYING; SAYINGS; SOOTHSAYING.
Ge 1:22 God blessed them, s', Be fruitful,
2:16 s', Of every tree of the garden thou
3:17 s', Thou shalt not eat of it: cursed
5:29 called his name Noah, s', This same
8:15 And God spake unto Noah, s',
9: 8 Noah, and to his sons with him, s',
15: 1 s', Fear not, Abram: I am thy shield,
4 him, s', This shall not be thine heir;
18 s', Unto thy seed have I given this
17: 3 face: and God talked with him, s',
18:12 Sarah laughed within herself, s',
13 Wherefore did Sarah laugh, s', Shall
15 Sarah denied, s', I laughed not; for
19:15 Lot, s', Arise, take thy wife, and thy
21:22 spake unto Abraham, s', God is with
22:20 that it was told Abraham, s', Behold,
23: 3 and spake unto the sons of Heth, s',
5 answered Abraham, s' unto him,
8 he communed with them, s', If it be
10 went in at the gate of his city, s',
13 s', But if thou wilt give it, I pray
14 answered Abraham, s' unto him,
24: 7 and that sware unto me, s', Unto thy
30 the words of Rebekah his sister, s',
37 my master made me swear, s', Thou
26:11 Abimelech charged all his people, s',
20 herdmen, s', The water is ours: and
27: 6 spake unto Jacob her son, s', Behold,
6 speak unto Esau thy brother, s',

Ge 28: 6 s', Thou shalt not take a wife of the
20 Jacob vowed a vow, s', If God will be
31: 1 heard the words of Laban's sons, s',
11 spake unto me in a dream, s', Jacob:
29 spake unto me yesternight, s', Take
32: 4 he commanded them, s', Thus shall
6 the messengers returned to Jacob, s',
17 commanded the foremost, s', When
17 and asketh thee, s', Whose art thou?
19 s', On this manner shall ye speak
34: 4 s', Get me this damsel to wife.
8 with them, s', The soul of my son
20 with the men of their city, s',
37: 11 but his father observed the s'.
15 asked him, s', What seekest thou?
38: 13 Tamar, s', Behold thy father in law
21 s', Where is the harlot, that was
24 s', Tamar thy daughter in law hath
25 s', By the man, whose these are, am
28 thread, s', This came out first.
39: 12 him by his garment, s', Lie with me:
14 and spake unto them, s', See, he hath
17 s', The Hebrew servant, which thou
19 unto him, s', After this manner did
40: 7 s', Wherefore look ye so sadly to day?
41: 9 s', I do remember my faults this day:
16 Pharaoh, s', It is not in me: God
42: 14 I spake unto you, s', Ye are spies:
22 them, s', Spake I not unto you, s', Do
28 s' one to another, What is this that
29 told him all that befell unto them; s',
37 Reuben spake unto his father, s',
43: 3 Judah spake unto him, s', The man
3 protest unto us, s', Ye shall not see
7 kindred, s', Is your father yet alive?
44: 1 s', Fill the men's sacks with food, as
19 My lord asked his servants, s', Have
32 unto my father, s', If I bring him not
45: 16 s', Joseph's brethren are come: and
26 told him, s', Joseph is yet alive, and
47: 5 unto Joseph, s', Thy father and thy
48: 20 day, s', In thee shall Israel bless,
20 s', God make thee as Ephraim and as
50: 4 s', If now I have found grace in
4 pray you, in the ears of Pharaoh, s',
5 My father made me swear, s', Lo, I
16 sent a messenger unto Joseph, s',
16 did command before he died, s',
25 s', God will surely visit you, and ye
Ex 1: 22 his people, s', Every son that is born
3: 16 unto me, s', I have surely visited you,
5: 6 of the people, and their officers, s',
8 s', Let us go and sacrifice to our God.
10 s', Thus saith Pharaoh, I will not
13 taskmasters hasted them, s', Fulfil
15 cried unto Pharaoh, s', Wherefore
6: 10 And the Lord spake unto Moses, s',
12 And Moses spake before the Lord, s',
29 spake unto Moses, s', I am the Lord:
7: 8 unto Moses and unto Aaron, s',
9 unto you, s', Shew a miracle for you:
16 s', Let my people go, that they may
9: 5 s', To morrow the Lord shall do this
11: 8 themselves unto me, s', Get thee out,
12: 1 and Aaron in the land of Egypt, s',
3 s', In the tenth day of this month
13: 1 And the Lord spake unto Moses, s',
8 shew thy son in that day, s', This is
14 in time to come, s', What is this?
19 Israel, s', God will surely visit you;
14: 1 And the Lord spake unto Moses, s',
12 we did tell thee in Egypt, s', Let us
15: 1 and spake, s', I will sing unto the
24 Moses, s', What shall we drink?
16: 11 And the Lord spake unto Moses, s',
12 them, s', At even ye shall eat flesh,
17: 4 Moses cried unto the Lord, s', What
7 s', Is the Lord among us, or not?
19: 3 s', Thus shalt thou say to the house
12 s', Take heed to yourselves, that ye
23 s', Set bounds about the mount, and
20: 1 And God spake all these words, s',
25: 1 And the Lord spake unto Moses, s',
30: 11, 17, 22 the Lord spake unto Moses, s',
31 speak unto the children of Israel, s',
31: 1, 12 the Lord spake unto Moses, s',
13 s', Verily my sabbaths ye shall keep:
33: 1 Jacob, s', Unto thy seed will I give it:
35: 4 of Israel, s', This is the thing which
4 thing which the Lord commanded, s',
36: 5 spake unto Moses, s', The people
6 s', Let neither man nor woman make
40: 1 And the Lord spake unto Moses, s',
Le 1: 1 tabernacle of the congregation, s',
4: 1 And the Lord spake unto Moses, s',
2 Israel, s', If a soul shall sin through
5: 14 And the Lord spake unto Moses, s',
6: 1, 8 the Lord spake unto Moses, s',
9 Command Aaron and his sons, s',
19, 24 the Lord spake unto Moses, s',
25 s', This is the law of the sin offering:
7: 22 And the Lord spake unto Moses, s',
23 s', Ye shall eat no manner of fat, of
28 And the Lord spake unto Moses, s',
29 of Israel, s', He that offereth the
8: 1 And the Lord spake unto Moses, s',
31 s', Aaron and his sons shall eat it.
9: 3 s', Take ye a kid of the goats for a
10: 3 s', I will be sanctified in them that
8 And the Lord spake unto Aaron, s',
16 of Aaron which were left alive, s',
11: 1 Moses and to Aaron, s' unto them,
2 s', These are the beasts which ye
12: 1 And the Lord spake unto Moses, s',
2 s', If a woman have conceived seed,
13: 1 Lord spake unto Moses and Aaron, s',
Le 14: 1 And the Lord spake unto Moses, s',
33 spake unto Moses and unto Aaron, s',
35 tell the priest, s', It seemeth to me
15: 1 spake unto Moses and to Aaron, s',
17: 1 And the Lord spake unto Moses, s',
2 which the Lord hath commanded, s',
18: 1 And the Lord spake unto Moses, s',
19: 1 And the Lord spake unto Moses, s',
20: 1 And the Lord spake unto Moses, s',
21: 16 And the Lord spake unto Moses, s',
17 Speak unto Aaron, s', Whosoever he
22: 1, 17, 26 the Lord spake unto Moses, s',
23: 1, 9, 23 the Lord spake unto Moses, s',
24 s', In the seventh month, in the first
26, 33 the Lord spake unto Moses, s',
34 s', The fifteenth day of this seventh
24: 1, 13 the Lord spake unto Moses, s',
15 s', Whosoever curseth his God shall
25: 1 spake unto Moses in mount Sinai, s',
27: 1 And the Lord spake unto Moses, s',
Nu 1: 1 come out of the land of Egypt, s',
48 the Lord had spoken unto Moses, s',
2: 1 spake unto Moses and unto Aaron, s',
3: 5, 11 the Lord spake unto Moses, s',
14 Moses in the wilderness of Sinai, s',
44 And the Lord spake unto Moses, s',
4: 1, 17 unto Moses and unto Aaron, s',
21 And the Lord spake unto Moses, s',
5: 1, 5, 11 the Lord spake unto Moses, s',
6: 1, 22 the Lord spake unto Moses, s',
23 s', On this wise ye shall bless
23 ye shall bless...Israel, s' unto them
7: 4 And the Lord spake unto Moses, s',
8: 1, 5, 23 the Lord spake unto Moses, s',
9: 1 come out of the land of Egypt, s',
9 And the Lord spake unto Moses, s',
10 s', If any man of you or of your
10: 1 And the Lord spake unto Moses, s',
11: 13 s', Give us flesh, that we may eat.
18 s', Who shall give us flesh to eat?
20 s', Why came we forth out of Egypt?
12: 13 s', Heal her now, O God, I beseech
13: 1 And the Lord spake unto Moses, s',
32 s', The land, through which we have
14: 7 s', The land, which we passed
15 heard the fame of thee will speak, s',
17 according as thou hast spoken, s',
26 spake unto Moses and unto Aaron, s',
40 s', Lo, we be here, and will go up
15: 1, 17, 37 Lord spake unto Moses, s',
16: 5 s', Even to morrow the Lord will
20 spake unto Moses and unto Aaron, s',
23 And the Lord spake unto Moses, s',
24 s', Get you up from about the
26 s', Depart, I pray you, from the tents
36 And the Lord spake unto Moses, s',
41 s', Ye have killed the people of the
44 And the Lord spake unto Moses, s',
17: 1 And the Lord spake unto Moses, s',
12 Moses, s', Behold, we die, we perish,
18: 25 And the Lord spake unto Moses, s',
19: 1 spake unto Moses and unto Aaron, s',
2 s', Speak unto the children of Israel,
20: 3 s', Would God that we had died when
7 And the Lord spake unto Moses, s',
23 by the coast of the land of Edom, s',
21: 21 unto Sihon king of the Amorites, s',
22: 5 s', Behold, there is a people come
10 king of Moab, hath sent unto me, s',
23: 7 s', Come, curse me Jacob, and come,
26 s', All that the Lord speaketh, that
24: 12 which thou sentest unto me, s',
25: 10, 16 the Lord spake unto Moses, s',
26: 1 and unto Eleazar...the priest, s',
3 of Moab by Jordan near Jericho, s',
52 And the Lord spake unto Moses, s',
27: 2 tabernacle of the congregation, s',
6 And the Lord spake unto Moses, s',
8 s', If a man die, and have no son,
15 And Moses spake unto the Lord, s',
28: 1 And the Lord spake unto Moses, s',
30: 1 s', This is the thing which the
31: 1 And the Lord spake unto Moses, s',
3 s', Arm some of yourselves unto the
25 And the Lord spake unto Moses, s',
32: 2 the princes of the congregation, s',
10 the same time, and he sware, s',
25 of Reuben spake unto Moses, s', Thy
31 children of Reuben answered, s', As
33: 50 of Moab by Jordan near Jericho, s',
34: 1 And the Lord spake unto Moses, s',
13 children of Israel, s', This is the
16 And the Lord spake unto Moses, s',
35: 1 of Moab by Jordan near Jericho, s',
9 And the Lord spake unto Moses, s',
36: 5 word of the Lord, s', The tribe of
6 s', Let them marry to whom they
De 1: 5 began Moses to declare this law, s',
6 s', Ye have dwelt long enough in this
9 s', I am not able to bear you myself
16 s', Hear the causes between your
23 the s' pleased me well: and I took
28 s', The people is greater and taller
34 words, and was wroth, and sware, s',
37 s', Thou also shalt not go in thither.
2: 2 And the Lord spake unto me, s',
4 s', Ye are to pass through the coast
17 That the Lord spake unto me, s',
26 of Heshbon with words of peace, s',
3: 18 s', The Lord your God hath given
21 s', Thine eyes have seen all that
23 I besought the Lord at that time, s',
5: 5 and went not up into the mount;) s',
6: 20 s', What mean the testimonies, and
9: 4 s', For my righteousness the Lord
13 me, s', I have seen this people, and.
De 9: 23 s', Go up and possess the land which
12: 30 s', How did these nations serve their
13: 2 s', Let us go after other gods, which
6 s', Let us go and serve other gods,
12 hath given thee to dwell there, s',
13 s', Let us go and serve other gods,
15: 9 s', The seventh year, the year of
11 s', Thou shalt open thine hand wide
18: 16 s', Let me not hear again the voice
19: 7 s', Thou shalt separate three cities
20: 5 s', What man...hath built a new
22: 17 s', I found not thy daughter a maid;
27: 1 s', Keep all the commandments
9 s', Take heed, and hearken, O Israel;
11 charged the people the same day, s',
29: 19 s', I shall have peace, though I walk
31: 10 s', At the end of every seven years,
25 ark of the covenant of the Lord, s',
32: 48 unto Moses that selfsame day, s',
34: 4 s', I will give it unto thy seed: I have
Jos 1: 1 the son of Nun, Moses' minister, s',
10 Joshua commanded the officers...s',
11 s', Prepare you victuals; for within
12 tribe of Manasseh, spake Joshua, s',
13 s', The Lord your God hath given
16 s', All that thou commandest us we
2: 1 s', Go view the land, even Jericho.
2 s', Behold, there came men in hither
3 s', Bring forth the men that are come
3: 3 s', When ye see the ark of the
6 s', Take up the ark of the covenant,
8 s', When ye are come to the brink of
4: 1 that the Lord spake unto Joshua, s',
3 s', Take you hence out of the midst
6 s', What mean ye by these stones?
15 And the Lord spake unto Joshua, s',
17 priests, s', Come ye up out of Jordan.
21 s', When your children shall ask
21 come, s', What mean these stones?
22 s', Israel came over this Jordan on
6: 10 s', Ye shall not shout, nor make any
26 s', Cursed be the man before the
7: 2 them, s', Go up and view the country.
8: 4 them, s', Behold, ye shall lie in wait
9: 11 s', Take victuals with you for the
22 s', Wherefore have ye beguiled us,
22 s', We are very far from you; when
10: 3 and unto Debir king of Eglon, s',
6 s', Slack not thy hand from thy
17 s', The five kings are found hid in a
14: 9 s', Surely the land whereon thy feet
17: 4 s', The Lord commanded Moses to
14 s', Why hast thou given me but one
17 s', Thou art a great people, and hast
18: 8 s', Go and walk through the land,
20: 1 The Lord also spake unto Joshua, s',
2 s', Appoint out for you cities of
21: 2 s', The Lord commanded by the hand
22: 8 s', Return with much riches unto
15 Gilead, and they spake with them, s',
24 s', In time to come your children
24 s', What have ye to do with the
J'g 1: 1 s', Who shall go up for us against
4: 6 s', Go and draw toward mount Tabor,
5: 1 the son of Abinoam on that day, s',
6: 13 s', Did not the Lord bring us up from
32 s', Let Baal plead against him,
7: 2 s', Mine own hand hath saved me.
3 s', Whosoever is fearful and afraid,
24 s', Come down against...Midianites,
8: 9 s', When I come again in peace, I will
15 s', Are the hands of Zebah and
9: 1 the house of his mother's father, s',
31 s', Behold, Gaal the son of Ebed and
10: 10 s', We have sinned against thee, both
11: 12 s', What hast thou to do with me,
17 s', Let me, I pray thee, pass through
13: 6 s', A man of God came unto me, and
15: 13 s', No; but we will bind thee fast,
16: 2 Gazites, s', Samson is come hither.
2 s', In the morning, when it is day,
18 s', Come up this once, for he hath
19: 22 s', Bring forth the man that came
20: 8 s', We will not any of us go to his
12 s', What wickedness is this that is
23 s', Shall I go up again to battle
28 s', Shall I yet again go out to battle
21: 1 s', There shall not any of us give his
5 s', He shall surely be put to death.
10 s', Go and smite the inhabitants
18 s', Cursed be he that giveth a wife to
20 s', Go...lie in wait in the vineyards;
Ru 2: 15 s', Let her glean even among the
4: 4 s', Buy it before the inhabitants, and
17 s', There is a son born to Naomi; and
1Sa 1: 20 s', Because I have asked him of the
4: 21 s', The glory is departed from
5: 10 s', They have brought about the ark
6: 2 s', What shall we do to the ark of the
21 s', The Philistines have brought
7: 3 s', If ye do return unto the Lord
12 s', Hitherto hath the Lord helped us.
9: 15 Lord had told Samuel in his ear...s',
26 s', Up, that I may send thee away.
10: 2 you, s', What shall I do for my son?
11: 7 s', Whosoever cometh not forth after
13: 3 the land, s', Let the Hebrews hear.
14: 24, 28 s', Cursed be the man that
33 told Saul, s', Behold, the people sin
15: 10 word of the Lord unto Samuel, s',
12 Samuel, s', Saul came to Carmel,
16: 22 s', Let David,...stand before me;
17: 26 s', What shall be done to the man
27 s', So shall it be done to the man
18: 8 wroth, and the s' displeased him;
22 s', Commune with David secretly,

1Sa 18:24 s', On this manner spake David.
19: 2 s', Saul my father seeketh to kill
11 s', If thou save not thy life to night,
15 s', Bring him up to me in the bed,
19 s',...David is at Naioth in Ramah.
20:16 s', Let the Lord even require it at
21 send a lad, s', Go, find out the arrows.
42 s', The Lord be between me and
21:11 s', Saul hath slain his thousands,
23: 1 s',...the Philistines fight against
2 David enquired of the Lord, s', Shall
19 s', Doth not David hide himself with
27 unto Saul, s', Haste thee, and come;
24: 1 s', Behold, David is in the wilderness
8 cried after Saul, s', My lord the king.
9 s', Behold, David seeketh thy hurt?
25:14 Nabal's wife, s', Behold, David sent
40 unto her, s', David sent us unto thee,
26: 1 s', Doth not David hide himself in
6 s', Who will go down with me to
14 Ner, s', Answerest thou not, Abner?
19 the Lord, s', Go, serve other gods.
27:11 Gath, s', Lest they should tell on us,
11 s', So did David, and so will be his
12 s', He hath made his people Israel
28:10 s', As the Lord liveth, there shall no
12 s', Why hast thou deceived me? for
29: 5 s', Saul slew his thousands, and
30: 8 s', Shall I pursue after this troop?
26 s', Behold a present for you of the
2Sa 1:16 s', I have slain the Lord's anointed.
2: 1 enquired of the Lord, s', Shall I go
4 s', That the men of Jabesh-gilead
3:12 on his behalf, s', Whose is the land?
12 s' also, Make thy league with me,
14 Saul's son, s', Deliver me my wife
17 s', Ye sought for David in times
18 s', By the hand of my servant David
23 told Joab, s', Abner the son of Ner
35 David sware, s', So do God to me,
4:10 told me, s', Behold, Saul is dead,
5: 1 s',...we are thy bone and thy flesh.
6 s', Except thou take away the blind
19 s', Shall I go up to the Philistines?
6:12 s', The Lord hath blessed the house
7: 4 of the Lord came unto Nathan, s',
7 s', Why build ye not me an house of
26 s', The Lord of hosts is the God
27 s', I will build thee an house:
11: 6 Joab, s', Send me Uriah the Hittite.
10 s', Uriah went not down unto his
15 s', Set ye Uriah in the forefront
19 s', When thou hast made an end of
13: 7 s', Go not to thy brother Amnon's
28 s', Mark ye now when Amnon's
30 s', Absalom hath slain all the king's
14:32 I sent unto thee, s', Come hither,
15: 8 s', If the Lord shall bring me again
10 s', As soon as ye hear the sound of
13 s', The hearts of the men of Israel
31 David, s', Ahithophel is among the
17: 4 the s' pleased Absalom well, and
6 s', Ahithophel hath spoken after
6 shall we do after his s'? if not;
16 s', Lodge not this night in the
18: 5 s', Deal gently for my sake with the
12 s', Beware that none touch the
19: 8 s',...the king doth sit in the gate.
9 s', The king saved us out of the
11 s', Speak unto the elders of Judah,
11 s', Why are ye the last to bring the
20:18 s', They were wont to speak in old
18 s', They shall surely ask counsel at
21:17 s', Thou shalt go no more out with
24:11 the prophet Gad, David's seer, s',
19 David, according to the s' of Gad,
1Ki 1: 5 exalted himself, s', I will be king:
6 time in s', Why hast thou done so?
11 s', Hast thou not heard that
13 s', Assuredly Solomon thy son shall
17 s', Assuredly Solomon thy son shall
23 s', Behold Nathan the prophet.
30 s', Assuredly Solomon thy son shall
47 s', God make the name of Solomon
51 s',...Adonijah feareth king Solomon:
51 s', Let king Solomon swear unto me
2: 1 and he charged Solomon his son, s',
4 s', If thy children take heed to their
8 s', I will not put thee to death
23 king Solomon sware by the Lord, s',
29 of Jehoiada, s', Go, fall upon him.
30 s', Thus said Joab, and thus he
38 said unto the king, The s' is good:
39 s', Behold, thy servants be in Gath.
42 s', Know for a certain, on the day
5: 2 And Solomon sent to Hiram, s',
5 s', Thy son, whom I will set upon
8 s', I have considered the things
6:11 of the Lord came to Solomon, s',
8:15 hath with his hand fulfilled it, s',
25 s', There shall not fail thee a man
47 s', We have sinned, and have done
55 of Israel with a loud voice, s',
9: 5 s', There shall not fail thee a man
12: 3 came, and spake unto Rehoboam, s',
7 s', If thou wilt be a servant unto
9 s', Make the yoke which thy father
10 s', Thus shalt thou speak unto this
10 s', Thy father made our yoke heavy,
12 s', Come to me again the third day.
14 s', My father made your yoke heavy,
15 that he might perform his s',
16 s', What portion have we in David?
22 unto Shemaiah the man of God, s',
23 and to the remnant of the people, s',
13: 3 s', This is the sign which the Lord

1Ki 13: 4 Jeroboam heard the s' of the man
4 from the altar, s', Lay hold on him.
9 s', Eat no bread, nor drink water,
18 s', Bring him back with thee into
21 Judah, s', Thus saith the Lord,
27 to his sons, s', Saddle me the ass.
30 over him, s', Alas, my brother.
31 s', When I am dead, then bury me
32 the s' which he cried by the word
15:18 Syria, that dwelt at Damascus, s',
29 according unto the s' of the Lord,
16: 1 son of Hanani against Baasha, s',
17: 2, 8 of the Lord came unto him, s',
15 did according to the s' of Elijah:
18: 1 s', Go, shew thyself unto Ahab;
26 until noon, s', O Baal, hear us.
31 came, s', Israel shall be thy name:
19: 2 s', So let the gods do to me, and
20: 4 according to thy s', I am thine,
5 s', Although I have sent unto thee,
5 s', Thou shalt deliver me thy
13 s', Thus saith the Lord, Hast thou
17 s', There are men come out of
21: 2 s', Give me thy vineyard, that I may
9 s', Proclaim a fast, and set Naboth
10 s', Thou didst blaspheme God and
14 sent to Jezebel, s', Naboth is stoned,
17 Lord came to Elijah the Tishbite, s',
19 s', Thus saith the Lord, Hast
19 s', Thus saith the Lord, In the
23 s', The dogs shall eat Jezebel by
28 Lord came to Elijah the Tishbite, s',
22:12 s', Go up to Ramoth-gilead, and
13 s', Behold now, the words of the
31 s', Fight neither with small nor
36 s', Every man to his city, and every
2Ki 2:22 according to the s' of Elisha
3: 7 s', The king of Moab hath rebelled
4: 1 s', Thy servant my husband is dead;
31 told him, s', The child is not awaked.
5: 4 s', Thus and thus said the maid
6 s', Now when this letter is come
8 s', Wherefore hast thou rent thy
10 s', Go and wash in Jordan seven
14 to the s' of the man of God: and
22 s',...even now there be come to
6: 8 s', In such and such a place shall be
9 s', Beware that thou pass not
13 told him, s', Behold he is in Dothan.
26 unto him, s', Help, my lord, O king.
7:10 s', We came to the camp of the
12 s', When they come out of the city,
14 host of the Syrians, s', Go and see.
18 s', Two measures of barley for a
8: 1 s', Arise, and go thou and thine
2 after the s' of the man of God:
4 s', Tell me, I pray thee, all the
6 s', Restore all that was hers, and all
7 s', The man of God is come hither.
8, 9 s', Shall I recover of this disease?
9:12 s', Thus saith the Lord, I have
13 blew with trumpets, s', Jehu is king.
18 s', The messenger came to them,
20 s', He came even unto them, and
36 s', In the portion of Jezreel shall
10: 1 that brought up Ahab's children, s',
5 sent to Jehu, s', We are thy servants,
6 s', If ye be mine, and if ye will
8 s', They have brought the heads of
17 according to the s' of the Lord,
11: 5 s', This is the thing that ye shall
14: 6 s', The fathers shall not be put to
8 s', Come, let us look one another in
9 Judah, s', The thistle that was in
9 s', Give thy daughter to my son to
15:12 s', Thy sons shall sit on the throne of
16: 7 s', I am thy servant and thy son:
15 s', Upon the great altar burn
17:13 s', Turn ye from your evil ways,
26 s', The nations which thou hast
27 s', Carry thither one of the priests
35 s', Ye shall not fear other gods, nor
18:14 s', I have offended: return from me
28 s', Hear the word of the great king,
30 s', The Lord will surely deliver us,
32 you, s', The Lord will deliver us.
36 commandment...s', Answer him not.
19: 9 messengers again unto Hezekiah, s',
10 s', Let not thy God in whom thou
10 s', Jerusalem shall not be delivered
20 s', Thus saith the Lord God of Israel,
20: 2 wall, and prayed unto the Lord, s',
4 word of the Lord came to him, s',
21:10 by his servants the prophets, s',
22: 3 scribe, to the house of the Lord, s',
10 s', Hilkiah the priest hath delivered
12 Asahiah a servant of the king's, s',
23:21 s', Keep the passover unto the Lord
1Ch 4: 9 s', Because I bare him with sorrow.
10 Jabez called on the God of Israel, s',
11: 1 s', Behold, we are thy bone and thy
12:19 s', He will fall to his master Saul to
13:12 s', How shall I bring the ark of God
14:10 David enquired of God, s', Shall I go
16:18 S', Unto thee will I give the land of
22 S', Touch not mine anointed, and do
17: 3 the word of God came to Nathan, s',
6 s', Why have ye not built me an
24 s', The Lord of hosts is the God of
21: 9 spake unto Gad, David's seer, s',
10 Go and tell David, s', Thus saith the
19 David went up at the s' of Gad,
22: 8 s',Thou hast shed blood abundantly,
17 of Israel to help Solomon his son, s',
2Ch 2: 3 s', As thou didst deal with David my
5:13 praised the Lord, s', For he is good:

2Ch 6: 4 his mouth to my father David, s',
16 s', There shall not fail thee a man
37 s', We have sinned, we have done
7: 3 praised the Lord, s', For he is good:
18 s', There shall not fail thee a man
10: 3 came and spake to Rehoboam, s',
6 s', What counsel give ye me to return
7 s', If thou be kind to this people,
9 s', Ease somewhat the yoke that thy
10 s', Thus shalt thou answer the people
10 s', Thy father made our yoke heavy,
12 s', Come again to me on the third
14 s', My father made your yoke heavy,
16 s', What portion have we in David?
11: 2 to Shemaiah the man of God, s',
3 all Israel in Judah and Benjamin, s',
12: 7 s', They have humbled themselves;
16: 2 of Syria, that dwelt at Damascus, s',
18:11 s', Go up to Ramoth-gilead, and
12 s', Behold, the words of the prophets
19 And one spake s' after this manner,
19 and another s' after that manner.
30 s', Fight ye not with small or great,
19: 9 s', Thus shall ye do in the fear of the
20: 2 s', There cometh a great multitude
8 a sanctuary therein for thy name, s',
37 s', Because thou hast joined thyself
21:12 s', Thus saith the Lord God of David
25: 4 s', The fathers shall not die for the
7 s', O king, let not the army of Israel
17 s', Come, let us see one another in
18 s', The thistle that was in Lebanon
18 s', Give thy daughter to my son to
30: 6 s', Ye children of Israel, turn again
18 s', The good Lord pardon every one
32: 4 s', Why should the kings of Assyria
6 and spake comfortably to them, s',
9 all Judah that were at Jerusalem, s',
11 s', The Lord our God shall deliver
12 s', Ye shall worship before one altar,
17 s', As the gods of the nations of other
34:16 s', All that was committed to thy
18 s', Hilkiah the priest hath given me
20 Asaiah a servant of the king's, s',
35:21 s', What have I to do with thee, thou
36:22 and put it also in writing, s',
Ezr 1: 1 and put it also in writing, s',
5:11 s', We are the servants of the God
8:22 s', The hand of our God is upon all
9: 1 s', The people of Israel, and the
11 s', The land, unto which ye go to
Ne 1: 8 s', If ye transgress, I will scatter you
6: 2 s', Come, let us meet together in
3 s', I am doing a great work, so that
7 s', There is a king in Judah: and
8 s', There are no such things done
9 s', Their hands shall be weakened
8:11 s', Hold your peace, for the day is
15 s', Go forth unto the mount, and
13:25 s', Ye shall not give your daughters
Es 1:21 the s' pleased the king and the
Job 4:16 was silence, and I heard a voice, s',
8:18 deny him, s', I have not seen thee.
15:23 abroad for bread, s', Where is it?
24:15 twilight, s', No eye shall see me:
33: 8 I have heard the voice of thy words, s',
Ps 2: 2 the Lord, and against his anointed, s',
22: 7 out the lip, they shake the head, s',
49: 4 open my dark s' upon the harp.
71:11 S', God hath forsaken him:
105:11 S', Unto thee will I give the land of
15 S', Touch not mine anointed, and do
119:82 s', When wilt thou comfort me?
137: 3 s', Sing us one of the songs of Zion.
Pr 1:21 in the city she uttereth her words, s',
Ec 1:16 s', Lo, I am come to great estate,
Ca 5: 2 s', Open to me, my sister, my love,
Isa 3: 6 s', Thou hast clothing, be thou our
7 swear, s', I will not be an healer;
4: 1 s', We will eat our own bread, and
6: 8 s', Whom shall I send, and who will
7: 2 s', Syria is confederate with
5 taken evil counsel against thee, s',
10 the Lord spake again unto Ahaz, s',
8: 5 Lord spake also unto me again, s',
11 not walk in the way of this people, s',
14: 8 s', Since thou art laid down, no feller
16 s', Is this the man that made the earth
24 s', Surely as I have thought, so
16:14 s', Within three years, as the years
18: 2 s', Go, ye swift messengers, to a nation
19:25 s', Blessed be Egypt my people,
20: 2 s', Go and loose the sackcloth from
23: 4 s', I travail not, nor bring forth
29:11, 12 learned, s', Read this, I pray thee:
30:21 s', This is the way, walk ye in it,
36:15 s', The Lord will surely deliver us:
18 you, s', The Lord will deliver us.
21 commandment...s', Answer him not.
37: 9 he sent messengers to Hezekiah, s',
10 s', Let not thy God in whom thou
10 s', Jerusalem shall not be given into
15 Hezekiah prayed unto the Lord, s',
21 s', Thus saith the Lord God of
38: 4 the word of the Lord to Isaiah, s',
41: 7 s', It is ready for the sodering: and
13 s' unto thee, Fear not; I will help
44:28 even s' to Jerusalem, Thou shalt be
45:14 s', Surely God is in thee; and there
46:10 s', My counsel shall stand, and I
56: 3 s', The Lord hath utterly separated
63:11 s', Where is he that brought them up
Jer 1: 4 word of the Lord came unto me, s',
11 me, s', Jeremiah, what seest thou?
13 second time, s', What seest thou?
2: 1 the word of the Lord came to me, s',

Jer 2: 2 s', Thus saith the Lord: I remember
27 S' to a stock, Thou art my father;
4: 10 s', Ye shall have peace; whereas the
31 s', Woe is me now! for my soul is
5: 20 Jacob, and publish it in Judah, s',
6: 14 s', Peace, peace; when there is no
17 s', Hearken to the sound of the
7: 1 came to Jeremiah from the Lord, s',
4 s', The temple of the Lord, The
23 s', Obey my voice, and I will be your
8: 6 wickedness, s', What have I done?
11 s', Peace, peace; when there is no
11: 1 came to Jeremiah from the Lord, s',
4 s', Obey my voice, and do them,
6 s', Hear ye...words of this covenant,
7 and protesting, s', Obey my voice,
19 s', Let us destroy the tree with the
21 s', Prophesy not in the name of the
13: 3 came unto me the second time, s',
8 word of the Lord came unto me, s',
16: 1 of the Lord came also unto me, s',
18: 1 came to Jeremiah from the Lord, s',
5 word of the Lord came to me, s',
11 Jerusalem, s', Thus saith the Lord;
20: 10 s', Peradventure he will be enticed,
15 s', A man child is born unto thee;
21: 1 the son of Maaseiah the priest, s',
22: 18 s', Ah my brother! or, Ah sister!
18 s', Ah lord! or, Ah his glory!
23: 25 s', I have dreamed, I have dreamed.
33 s', What is the burden of the Lord?
38 s', Ye shall not say, The burden of
24: 4 word of the Lord came unto me, s',
25: 2 all the inhabitants of Jerusalem, s',
26: 1 came this word from the Lord, s',
8 took him, s', Thou shalt surely die.
9 s', This house shall be like Shiloh,
11 s', This man is worthy to die; for
12 s', The Lord sent me to prophesy
17 to all the assembly of the people, s',
18 s', Thus saith the Lord of hosts;
27: 1 unto Jeremiah from the Lord, s',
9 s', Ye shall not serve the king of
12 s', Bring your necks under the yoke
14 s', Ye shall not serve the king of
16 people, s', Thus saith the Lord;
16 you, s',...the vessels of the Lord's
28: 1 the priests and of all the people, s',
2 s', I have broken the yoke of the
11 the people, s', Thus saith the Lord;
12 the neck of the prophet Jeremiah, s',
13 Go and tell Hananiah, s', Thus
29: 3 Nebuchadnezzar king of Babylon,) s',
22 s',...Lord make thee like Zedekiah
24 to Shemaiah the Nehelamite, s',
25 s', Because thou hast sent letters
25 priest, and to all the priests, s',
28 Babylon, s', This captivity is long:
30 word of the Lord unto Jeremiah, s',
31 s', Thus saith the Lord concerning
30: 1 came to Jeremiah from the Lord, s',
2 s', Write thee all the words that I
17 Outcast, s', This is Zion, whom no man
31: 3 me, s', Yea, I have loved thee with an
34 his brother, s', Know the Lord:
32: 3 s', Wherefore dost thou prophesy,
6 word of the Lord came unto me, s',
7 s', Buy thee my field that is in
13 I charged Baruch before them, s',
16 Neriah, I prayed unto the Lord, s',
26 word of the Lord unto Jeremiah, s',
33: 1 shut up in the court of the prison, s',
19 of the Lord came unto Jeremiah, s',
23 of the Lord came to Jeremiah, s',
24 s', The two families which the Lord
34: 1 and against all the cities thereof, s',
5 s', Ah lord! for I have pronounced
12 to Jeremiah from the Lord, s',
13 out of the house of bondmen, s',
35: 1 the son of Josiah king of Judah, s',
6 s', Ye shall drink no wine, neither
12 word of the Lord unto Jeremiah, s',
15 s', Return ye now every man from
36: 1 unto Jeremiah from the Lord, s',
5 s', I am shut up; I cannot go into
14 s', Take in thine hand the roll
17 they asked Baruch, s', Tell us now,
27 wrote at the mouth of Jeremiah, s',
29 s', Why hast thou written therein,
29 s', The king of Babylon shall
37: 3 s', Pray now unto the Lord our
6 Lord unto the prophet Jeremiah, s',
9 s', The Chaldeans shall surely
13 prophet, s', Thou fallest away to the
19 s', The king of Babylon shall not
38: 1 had spoken unto all the people, s',
8 house, and spake to the king, s',
10 s', Take from hence thirty men with
16 s', As the Lord liveth, that made
39: 11 the captain of the guard, s',
15 shut up in the court of the prison, s',
16 s', Thus saith the Lord of hosts,
40: 9 s', Fear not to serve the Chaldeans:
15 s', Let me go, I pray thee, and I
42: 14 S', No; but we will go into the land
20 s', Pray for us unto the Lord our
43: 2 s' unto Jeremiah, Thou speakest
8 unto Jeremiah in Tahpanhes, s',
44: 1 and in the country of Pathros, s',
4 s', Oh, do not this abominable thing
15 in Pathros, answered Jeremiah, s',
20 which had given him that answer, s',
25 s'; Ye and your wives have both
25 s', We will surely perform our vows
26 of Egypt, s', The Lord God liveth.
45: 1 the son of Josiah king of Judah, s',

Jer 48: 39 shall howl, s', How is it broken down!
49: 4 s', Who shall come unto me?
14 s', Gather ye together, and come
34 of Zedekiah king of Judah, s',
50: 5 s', Come, and let us join ourselves
51: 14 s', Surely I will fill thee with men, as
La 2: 15 s', Is this the city that men call The
Eze 3: 12 s', Blessed be the glory of the Lord
16 word of the Lord came unto me, s',
6: 1 word of the Lord came unto me, s',
7: 1 word of the Lord came unto me, s',
9: 1 s', Cause them that have charge
11 s', I have done as thou...commanded
10: 6 s', Take fire from between the
11: 14 word of the Lord came unto me, s',
12: 1 of the Lord also came unto me, s',
8 the word of the Lord unto me, s',
17 the word of the Lord came to me, s',
21 word of the Lord came unto me, s',
22 s', The days are prolonged, and
26 the word of the Lord came to me, s',
13: 1 word of the Lord came unto me, s',
6 lying divination, s', The Lord saith:
10 have seduced my people, s', Peace;
14: 2 word of the Lord came unto me, s',
12 of the Lord came again to me, s',
15: 1 word of the Lord came unto me, s',
16: 1 word of the Lord came unto me, s',
44 s', As...the mother, so...her daughter.
17: 1, 11 of the Lord came unto me, s',
18: 1 of the Lord came unto me again, s',
2 s', The fathers have eaten sour
20: 2 the word of the Lord unto me, s',
5 them, s', I am the Lord your God;
45 word of the Lord came unto me, s',
21: 1, 8 word of the Lord came unto me, s',
18 of the Lord came unto me again, s',
22: 1, 17, 23 of the Lord came unto me, s',
28 s', Thus saith the Lord God, when
23: 1 the Lord came again unto me, s',
24: 1, 15, 20 of the Lord came unto me, s',
25: 1 of the Lord came again unto me, s',
26: 1 word of the Lord came unto me, s',
27: 1 of the Lord came again unto me, s',
32 s', What city is like Tyrus, like the
28: 1 of the Lord came again unto me, s',
11, 20 of the Lord came unto me, s',
29: 1, 17 of the Lord came unto me, s',
30: 1 the Lord came again unto me, s',
20 word of the Lord came unto me, s',
31: 1 word of the Lord came unto me, s',
32: 1, 17 of the Lord came unto me, s',
33: 1 word of the Lord came unto me, s',
10 s', If our transgressions and our
21 unto me, s', The city is smitten.
23 word of the Lord came unto me, s',
24 speak, s', Abraham was one, and he
30 s', Come, I pray you, and hear what
34: 1 word of the Lord came unto me, s',
35: 1 word of the Lord came unto me, s',
12 s', They are laid desolate, they are
36: 16 word of the Lord came unto me, s',
37: 15 of the Lord came again unto me, s',
18 s', Wilt thou not shew us what thou
38: 1 word of the Lord came unto me, s',
Da 4: 8 and before him I told the dream, s',
23 s', Hew the tree down, and destroy
31 s', O king Nebuchadnezzar, to thee
Am 2: 12 the prophets, s', Prophesy not.
3: 1 up from the land of Egypt, s',
7: 10 s', Amos hath conspired against the
8: 5 S', When will the new moon be gone,
Jon 1: 1 unto Jonah the son of Amittai, s',
3: 1 unto Jonah the second time, s',
7 s', Let neither man nor beast, herd
4: 2 was not this my s', when I was
Mic 2: 11 s', I will prophesy unto thee of wine
Hag 1: 1 son of Josedech, the high priest, s',
2 s', This people say, The time is not
3 the Lord by Haggai the prophet, s',
13 s', I am with you, saith the Lord.
2: 1 the Lord by the prophet Haggai, s',
2 and to the residue of the people, s',
10 the Lord by Haggai the prophet, s',
11 the priests concerning the law, s',
20 and twentieth day of the month, s',
21 s', I will shake the heavens and the
Zec 1: 1 the son of Iddo the prophet, s', The
4 s', Thus saith the Lord of hosts;
7 the son of Iddo the prophet, s',
14 Cry thou, s', Thus saith the Lord of
17 Cry yet, s', Thus saith the Lord of
21 s', These are the horns which have
2: 4 s', Jerusalem shall be inhabited as
3: 4 s', Take away the filthy garments
6 the Lord protested unto Joshua, s',
4: 4 me, s', What are these, my lord?
6 s', This is the word of the Lord unto
6 s', Not by might, nor by power, but
8 word of the Lord came unto me, s',
6: 8 s',...these that go toward the north
9 word of the Lord came unto me, s',
12 s', Thus speaketh the Lord of hosts,
12 s', Behold the man whose name is
7: 3 s', Should I weep in the fifth month,
4 of the Lord of hosts unto me, s',
5 s', When ye fasted and mourned in
8 of the Lord came unto Zechariah, s',
9 s', Execute true judgment, and shew
8: 1 the Lord of hosts came to me, s',
18 the Lord of hosts came unto me, s',
21 s', Let us go speedily to pray before
23 s', We will go with you: for we have
M't 1: 20 s', Joseph, thou son of David, fear
22 of the Lord by the prophet, s',
2: 2 S', Where is he that is born King

M't 2: 13 s', Arise, and take the young child
15 s', Out of Egypt have I called my
17 spoken by Jeremy the prophet, s',
20 S', Arise, and take the young child
3: 2 And s', Repent ye: for the kingdom
3 s', The voice of one crying in the
14 s', I have need to be baptized of
17 s', This is my beloved Son, in whom
4: 14 spoken by Esaias the prophet, s',
5: 2 his mouth, and taught them, s',
6: 31 no thought, s', What shall we eat?
8: 2 s', Lord, if thou wilt, thou canst
3 him, s', I will; be thou clean.
6 s', Lord, my servant lieth at home
17 s', Himself took our infirmities, and
25 him, s', Lord, save us: we perish.
27 s', What manner of man is this, that
29 s', What have we to do with thee,
31 s', If thou cast us out, suffer us to
9: 14 s', Why do we and the Pharisees
18 s', My daughter is even now dead:
27 s', Thou son of David, have mercy
29 s', According to your faith be it unto
30 them, s', See that no man know it.
33 s', It was never so seen in Israel.
10: 5 s', Go not into the way of...Gentiles,
11: 17 s', We have piped unto you, and ye
12: 10 s', Is it lawful to heal on...sabbath
17 spoken by Esaias the prophet, s',
38 s', Master, we would see a sign from
13: 3 s', Behold, a sower went forth to
24 them s', The kingdom of heaven is
31 s', The kingdom of heaven is like to
35 s', I open my mouth in parables;
36 s', Declare unto us the parable of
14: 15 s', This is a desert place, and the
26 s', It is a spirit; and they cried out
27 s', Be of good cheer; it is I; be not
30 to sink, he cried, s', Lord, save me.
33 s', Of a truth thou art the Son of
15: 1 and Pharisees,...of Jerusalem, s',
4 s', Honour thy father and mother:
7 well did Esaias prophesy of you, s',
12 offended, after they heard this s'?
22 s', Have mercy on me, O Lord,
23 s', Send her away; for she crieth
25 worshipped him, s', Lord, help me.
16: 7 s', It is because we have taken no
13 s', Whom do men say that I the Son
22 him, s', Be it far from thee, Lord:
17: 9 s', Tell the vision to no man, until
10 s', Why then say the scribes that
14 man, kneeling down to him, and s',
25 him, s', What thinkest thou, Simon?
18: 1 Jesus, s', Who is the greatest in the
26 s', Lord, have patience with me,
28 throat, s', Pay me that thou owest.
29 s', Have patience with me, and I
19: 3 tempting him, and s' unto him, Is
11 All men cannot receive this s',
22 when the young man heard that s',
25 s', Who then can be saved?
20: 12 S', These last have wrought but
30, 31 s', Have mercy on us, O Lord,
21: 2 S' unto them, Go into the village
4 was spoken by the prophet, s',
9 s', Hosanna to the son of David:
10 the city was moved, s', Who is this?
15 s', Hosanna to the son of David;
20 s', How soon is the fig tree
25 s', If we shall say, From heaven; he
37 son, s', They will reverence my son.
22: 4 s', Tell them which are bidden,
16 s', Master, we know that thou art
24 S', Master, Moses said, If a man
31 was spoken unto you by God, s',
35 a question, tempting him, and s',
42 S', What think ye of Christ? whose
43 David in spirit call him Lord, s',
23: 2 S', The scribes and the Pharisees
24: 3 s', Tell us, when shall these things
5 come in my name, s', I am Christ;
25: 9 s', Not so; lest there be not enough
11 virgins, s', Lord, Lord, open to us.
20 and brought other five talents, s',
37, 44 s', Lord, when saw we thee an
45 s', Verily I say unto you, Inasmuch
26: 8 s', To what purpose is this waste?
17 s' unto him, Where wilt thou that
27 it to them, s', Drink ye all of it;
39 s', O my Father, if it be possible, let
42 prayed, s', O my Father, if this cup
44 the third time, s' the same words.
48 s', Whomsoever I shall kiss, that
65 s', He hath spoken blasphemy;
68 S', Prophesy unto us, thou Christ,
69 s', Thou also wast with Jesus of
70 s', I know not what thou sayest.
74 and to swear, s', I know not the man.
27: 4 S', I have sinned in that I have
9 s', And they took the thirty pieces
11 s', Art thou the King of the Jews?
19 s', Have thou nothing to do with
23 the more, s', Let him be crucified.
24 s', I am innocent of the blood of
29 him, s', Hail, King of the Jews!
40 And s', Thou that destroyest the
46 voice, s', Eli, Eli, lama sabachthani?
54 s', Truly this was the Son of God.
63 S', Sir, we remember that that
28: 9 behold, Jesus met them, s', All hail.
13 S', Say ye, His disciples came by
15 and this s' is commonly reported
18 s', All power is given unto me in
M'r 1: 7 s', There cometh one mightier than
11 heaven, s', Thou art my beloved Son,

M'r 1:15 s', The time is fulfilled, and the
24 S', Let us alone; what have we to
25 s', Hold thy peace, and come out of
27 themselves, s', What thing is this?
40 and s' unto him, If thou wilt, thou
2:12 s', We never saw it on this fashion.
3:11 cried, s', Thou art the Son of God.
33 them, s', Who is my mother, or my
5: 9 answered, s', My name is Legion:
12 s', Send us into the swine, that we
23 s', My little daughter lieth at the
6: 2 s', From whence hath this man
25 s', I will that thou give me by and
7:29 unto her, For this s' go thy way;
37 s', He hath done all things well:
8:15 he charged them, s', Take heed,
16 s', It is because we have no bread.
26 s', Neither go into the town, nor
27 s' unto them, Whom do men say
32 And he spake that s' openly. And
33 s', Get thee behind me, Satan:
9: 7 s', This is my beloved Son: hear
10 they kept that s' with themselves,
11 s', Why say the scribes that Elias
25 s' unto him, Thou dumb and deaf
32 But they understood not that s',
38 s', Master, we saw one casting out
10:22 he was sad at that s', and went
26 s' among themselves, Who then
33 S', Behold, we go up to Jerusalem;
35 s', Master, we would that thou
49 s' unto him, Be of good comfort,
11: 9 s', Hosanna; Blessed is he that
17 s' unto them, Is it not written, My
31 s', If we shall say, From heaven;
12: 6 s', They will reverence my son.
18 and they asked him, s',
26 s', I am the God of Abraham, and
13: 6 s', I am Christ; and shall deceive
14:44 s', Whomsoever I shall kiss, that
57 bare false witness against him, s',
60 s', Answerest thou nothing? what
68 he denied, s', I know not, neither
71 s', I know not this man of whom ye
15: 4 again, s', Answerest thou nothing?
9 s', Will ye that I release unto you
29 and s', Ah, thou that destroyest the
34 s', Eloi, Eloi, lama sabachthani?
36 gave him to drink, s', Let alone;
Lu 1:24 and hid herself five months, s',
29 him, she was troubled at his s',
63 and wrote, s', His name is John.
66 s', What manner of child shall this
67 the Holy Ghost, and prophesied, s',
2:13 heavenly host praising God, and s',
17 abroad the s' which was told
50 the s' which he spake unto them.
3: 4 s', The voice of one crying in the
10 him, s', What shall we do then?
14 him, s', And what shall we do?
16 John answered, s' unto them all,
4: 4 s', It is written, That man shall
34 S', Let us alone; what have we to
35 rebuked him, s', Hold thy peace,
36 themselves, s', What a word is this!
41 s', Thou art Christ the Son of God.
5: 8 s', Depart from me; for I am a
12 s', Lord, if thou wilt, thou canst
13 him, s', I will: be thou clean.
21 s', Who is this which speaketh
26 s', We have seen strange things to
30 s', Why do ye eat and drink, with
7: 4 s', That he was worthy for whom
6 s' unto him, Lord, trouble not
16 s', That a great prophet is risen up
19, 20 s', Art thou he that should
32 s', We have piped unto you, and
39 s', This man, if he were a prophet,
8: 9 s',What might this parable be?
24 him, s', Master, master, we perish.
25 s' one to another, What manner of
30 s', What is thy name? And he
38 him: but Jesus sent him away, s',
49 s' to him, Thy daughter is dead;
50 s', Fear not: believe only, and*
54 hand, and called, s', Maid, arise.
9:18 s', Whom say the people that I am?
22 S', The Son of man must suffer
35 s', This is my beloved Son: hear
38 s', Master, I beseech thee, look
45 But they understood not this s',
45 they feared to ask him of that s'.
10:17 s', Lord, even the devils are subject
25 s',...what shall I do to inherit
11:45 thus s' thou reproachest us also.
12:16 s', The ground of a certain rich man
17 And he thought within himself, s',
13:25 s', Lord, Lord, open unto us; and
31 s' unto him, Get thee out, and
14: 3 s', Is it lawful to heal on the
5 s', Which of you shall have an ass
7 the chief rooms; s' unto them,
30 S', This man began to build, and
15: 2 s', This man receiveth sinners, and
3 spake this parable unto them, s',
6 s' unto them, Rejoice with me; for
9 s', Rejoice with me; for I have
17: 4 s', I repent; thou shalt forgive him.
18: 2 S', There was in a city a judge,
3 s', Avenge me of mine adversary.
13 s', God be merciful to me a sinner.
18 s', Good Master, what shall I do to
34 this s' was hid from them, neither
38 cried, s', Jesus, thou son of David,
41 S', What wilt thou that I shall do
19: 7 s', That he was gone to be guest

Lu 19:14 s', We will not have this man to
16, 18 s', Lord, thy pound hath gained
20 s', Lord, behold, here is thy pound,
30 S', Go ye into the village over
38 S', Blessed be the King that
42 S', If thou hadst known, even thou,
46 S' unto them, It is written, My
20: 2 s', Tell us, by what authority doest
5 s', If we shall say, From heaven;
14 s', This is the heir: come, let us
21 s', Master, we know...thou sayest
28 S', Master, Moses wrote unto us,
21: 7 s', Master,...when shall these things
8 s', I am Christ; and the time
22: 8 s', Go and prepare us the passover,
19 s', This is my body which is given
20 s', This cup is the new testament
42 S', Father, if thou be willing,
57 him, s', Woman, I know him not.
59 s', Of a truth this fellow also was
64 s', Prophesy, who is it that smote
66 and led him into their council, s',
23: 2 s', We found this fellow perverting
2 s' that he himself is Christ a King.
3 s', Art thou the King of the Jews?
5 fierce, s', He stirreth up the people,
18 s', Away with this man, and release
21 cried, s', Crucify him, crucify him.
35 s', He saved others; let him save
37 s', If thou be the king of the Jews,
39 s', If thou be Christ, save thyself
40 s', Dost not thou fear God, seeing
47 s', Certainly this was a righteous
24: 7 S', The Son of man must be
23 s', that they had also seen a vision
29 constrained him, s', Abide with us:
34 S', The Lord is risen indeed, and
Joh 1:15 s', This was he of whom I spake,
26 s', I baptize with water: but there
32 s', I saw the Spirit descending
4:31 prayed him, s', Master, eat.
37 herein is that s' true, One soweth,
39 on him for the s' of the woman,
42 we believe, not because of thy s':
51 and told him, s', Thy son liveth.
6:52 s', How can this man give us his
60 This is an hard s'; who can hear it?
7:15 s', How knoweth this man letters,
28 s', Ye both know me, and ye know
36 manner of s' is this that he said,
37 s', if any man thirst, let him come
40 when they heard this s', said, Of a
8:12 s', I am the light of the world: he
51, 52 If a man keep my s', he shall
55 but I know him, and keep his s'.
9: 2 s', Master, who did sin, this man,
19 s', Is this your son, who ye say was
10:33 s', For a good work we stone thee
11: 3 s', Lord,...he whom thou lovest is
28 s', The Master is come, and calleth
31 s', She goeth unto the grave to
32 s' unto him, Lord, if thou hadst
12:21 him, s', Sir, we would see Jesus.
23 s', The hour is come, that the Son
28 s', I have both glorified it, and will
12:38 That the s' of Esaias the prophet
15:20 if they have kept my s', they will
18: 9 That the s' might be fulfilled,
22 s', Answerest thou the high priest
32 s' of Jesus might be fulfilled,
40 s', Not this man, but Barabbas.
19: 6 out, s', Crucify him, crucify him.
8 Pilate therefore heard that s', he
12 s', If thou let this man go, thou
13 Pilate therefore heard that s', he
21:23 this s' abroad among the brethren,
Ac 1: 6 s', Lord, wilt thou at this time
2: 7 s' one to another, Behold, are not
12 s' one to another, What meaneth
40 s', Save yourselves from this
3:25 s' unto Abraham, And in thy seed
4:16 S', What shall we do to these men?
5:23 S', The prison truly found we shut
25 s', Behold, the men whom ye put
28 S', Did not we straitly command
6: 5 s' pleased the whole multitude:
7:26 s', Sirs, ye are brethren; why do
27 s', Who made thee a ruler and a
29 Then fled Moses at this s', and
32 S', I am the God of thy fathers, the
35 s', Who made thee a ruler and a
40 S' unto Aaron, Make us gods to go
59 s', Lord Jesus, receive my spirit.
8:10 s', This man is the great power of
19 S', Give me also this power, that on
26 s', Arise and go toward the south
9: 4 a voice s' unto him, Saul, Saul, why
10: 3 him, and s' unto him, Cornelius.
26 Peter took him up, s', Stand up;
11: 3 S', Thou wentest in to men
4 expounded it by order unto them, s',
7 I heard a voice s' unto me, Arise,
18 s', Then hath God also to the
12: 7 raised him up, s', Rise up quickly.
22 s', It is the voice of a god, and not
13:15 s', Ye men and brethren, if ye have
47 s', I have set thee to be a light of the
14:11 s' in the speech of Lycaonia, The
15 s', Sirs, why do ye these things?
15: 5 s',...it was needful to circumcise
13 s', Men and brethren, hearken unto
24 s', Ye must be circumcised, and
16: 9 s', Come over into Macedonia, and
15 s', If ye have judged me to be
17 s', These men are the servants of
20 s', These men, being Jews, do

Ac 16:28 s', Do thyself no harm: for we
35 serjeants, s', Let those men go.
36 of the prison told this s' to Paul,
17: 7 s' that there is another king, one
19 s', May we know what this new
18:13 S', This fellow persuadeth men to
21 s', I must by all means keep this
19: 4 s' unto the people, that they should
13 s', We adjure you by Jesus whom
21 s', After I have been there, I must
26 s' that they be no gods, which are
28 s', Great is Diana of the Ephesians.
20:23 s' that the bonds and afflictions
21:14 s', The will of the Lord be done.
21 s'...they ought not to circumcise
40 unto them in the Hebrew tongue, s',
22: 7 heard a voice s' unto me, Saul, Saul,
18 saw him s' unto me, Make haste,
26 s', Take heed what thou doest:
23: 9 s', We find no evil in this man:
12 s' that they would neither eat nor
23 s', Make ready two hundred
24: 2 s', Seeing that by thee we enjoy
9 s' that these things were so.
25:14 s', There is a certain man left in
26:14 s' in the Hebrew tongue, Saul, Saul,
22 s' none other things than those
31 s', This man doeth nothing worthy
27:24 S', Fear not, Paul; thou must be
33 s', This day is the fourteenth day
28:26 S', Go unto this people, and say,
Ro 4: 7 S', Blessed are they whose iniquities
11: 2 intercession...against Israel, s',
13: 9 is briefly comprehended in this s',
1Co 11:25 s', This cup is the new testament
15:54 then shall be brought to pass the s'
Ga 3: 8 s', in thee shall all nations be blessed.
1Ti 1:15 This is a faithful s', and worthy of
3: 1 This is a true s', If a man desire the
4: 9 This is a faithful s' and worthy of
2Ti 2:11 It is a faithful s': For if we be dead
18 s' that the resurrection is past
Tit 3: 8 This is a faithful s', and these
Heb 2: 6 s', What is man, that thou art
12 S', I will declare thy name unto my
4: 7 s' in David, To day, after so long a
6:14 S', Surely blessing I will bless thee
8:11 man his brother, s', Know the Lord:
9:20 S',This is the blood of the testament
12:26 s',...I shake not the earth only,
2Pe 3: 4 And s', Where is the promise of his
Jude 14 s', Behold, the Lord cometh with
Re 1:11 S', I am Alpha and Omega, the first
17 hand upon me, s' unto me, Fear not;
4: 8 day and night, s', Holy, holy, holy,
10 their crowns before the throne, s',
5: 9 a new song, s', Thou art worthy
12 S' with a loud voice, Worthy is the
13 heard I s', Blessing, and honour,
6: 1 of the four beasts s', Come and see.
10 s', How long, O Lord, holy and true,
7: 3 S', Hurt not the earth, neither the
10 s', Salvation to our God which
12 S', Amen: Blessing, and glory, and
13 s' unto me, What are these which
8:13 s' with a loud voice, Woe, woe, woe,
9:14 S' to the sixth angel which had the
10: 4 voice from heaven s' unto me, Seal
11: 1 s', Rise, and measure the temple of
12 s' unto them, Come up hither.
15 s', The kingdoms of this world are
17 S', We give thee thanks, O Lord God
12:10 s' in heaven, Now is come salvation,
13: 4 s', Who is like unto the beast? who
14 s' to them that dwell on the earth,
14: 7 S' with a loud voice, Fear God, and
8 s', Babylon is fallen, is fallen, that
9 s' with a loud voice, If any man
13 s' unto me, Write, Blessed are the
18 s', Thrust in thy sharp sickle, and
15: 3 s', Great and marvellous are thy
16: 1 s' to the seven angels, Go your ways,
17 from the throne, s', It is done.
17: 1 with me, s' unto me, Come hither;
18: 2 s', Babylon the great is fallen, is
4 s', Come out of her, my people, that
10 s', Alas, alas that great city Babylon,
16 And s', Alas, alas that great city,
18 s', What city is like unto this great
19 s', Alas, alas that great city,
21 s', Thus...shall that great city be
19: 1 much people in heaven, s', Alleluia;
4 on the throne, s', Amen; Alleluia.
5 throne, s', Praise our God, all ye his
6 of mighty thunderings, s', Alleluia:
17 s' to all the fowls that fly in the
21: 3 s', Behold, the tabernacle of God is
9 s', Come hither, I will shew thee the

sayings
Nu 14:39 Moses told these s' unto all the
J'g 13:17 that when thy s' come to pass we
1Sa 25:12 and came and told him all those s'.
2Ch 13:22 Abijah, and his ways, and his s',
33:19 written among the s' of the seers.
Ps 49:13 their posterity approve their s'.
78: 2 parable: I will utter dark s' of old:
Pr 1: 6 words of the wise, and their dark s'.
4:10 Hear, O my son, and receive my s';
20 words; incline thine ear unto my s'.
M't 7:24 whosoever heareth these s' of
26 one that heareth these s' of mine,
28 when Jesus had ended these s', the
19: 1 when Jesus had finished these s',
26: 1 when Jesus...finished all these s',
Lu 1:65 all these s' were noised abroad
2:51 but his mother kept all these s' in

Lu 6:47 heareth my s', and doeth them,
7: 1 ended all his s' in the audience of
9:28 about an eight days after these s',
44 Let these s' sink...into your ears:
Joh 10:19 again among the Jews for these s'.
14:24 loveth me not keepeth not my s':
Ac 14:18 with these s' scarce restrained
19:28 when they heard these s', they were
Ro 3: 4 mightest be justified in thy s',
Re 19: 9 me, These are the true s' of God.
22: 6 me, These s' are faithful and true:
7 that keepeth the s' of the prophecy
9 them which keep the s' of this book:
10 Seal not the s' of the prophecy of

scab See also SCABBED.
Le 13: 2 a rising, a s', or bright spot, and it
6 pronounce him clean: it is but a s':
7 s' spread much abroad in the skin,
8 behold, the s' spreadeth in the skin,
14:56 and for a s', and for a bright spot:
De 28:27 and with the s', and with the itch,
Isa 3:17 will smite with a s' the crown of

scabbard
Jer 47: 6 put up thyself into thy s', rest, and

scabbed
Le 21:20 or s', or hath his stones broken;
22:22 scurvy, or s', ye shall not offer these

scaffold
2Ch 6:13 Solomon had made a brasen s', of

scales
Le 11: 9 whatsoever hath fins and s' in the
10 that have not fins and s' in the seas,
12 Whatsoever hath no fins nor s' in
De 14: 9 all that have fins and s' shall ye eat:
10 hath not fins and s' ye may not eat:
Job 41:15 His s' are his pride, shut up
Isa 40:12 and weighed the mountains in s',
Eze 29: 4 cause the fish...to stick unto thy s',
4 all the fish...shall stick unto thy s'.
Ac 9:18 fell from his eyes as it had been s':

scaleth
Pr 21:22 wise man s' the city of the mighty,

scall
Le 13:30 it is a dry s', even a leprosy upon
31 priest look on the plague of the s',
31 shall shut up him that hath...the s'
32 and behold, if the s' spread not,
32 the s' be not in sight deeper than
33 but the s' shall he not shave;
33 shall shut up him that hath the s'
34 day the priest shall look on the s':
34 if the s' be not spread in the skin,
35 if the s' spread much in the skin
36 if the s' be spread in the skin,
37 But if the s' be in his sight at a stay,
37 the s' is healed, he is clean: and
14:54 manner of plague of leprosy, and s',

scalp
Ps 68:21 hairy s' of such an one as goeth

scant
Mic 6:10 the s' measure that is abominable?

scapegoat
Le 16: 8 Lord, and the other lot for the s'.
10 on which the lot fell to be the s',
10 him go for a s' into the wilderness.
26 goat for the s' shall wash his

scarce See also SCARCELY.
Ge 27:30 Jacob was yet s' gone out from the
Ac 14:18 s' restrained they the people,
27: 7 s' were come over against Cnidus,

scarcely See also SCARCE.
Ro 5: 7 s' for a righteous man will one die:
1Pe 4:18 if the righteous s' be saved, where

scarceness
De 8: 9 thou shalt eat bread without s',

scarest
Job 7:14 Then thou s' me with dreams,

scarlet
Ge 38:28 bound upon his hand a s' thread,
30 had the s' thread upon his hand:
Ex 25: 4 purple, and s', and fine linen,
26: 1 and blue, and purple, and s':
31 vail of blue, and purple, and s',
36 of blue, and purple, and s', and
27:16 of blue, and purple, and s', and
28: 5 purple, and s', and fine linen.
6 of blue, and of purple, of s', and
8 gold, of blue, and purple, and s',
15, 33 blue, and of purple, and of s',
35: 6 And blue, and purple, and s',
23 found blue, and purple, and s',
25 of blue, and of purple, and of s',
35 in blue, and in purple, in s', and
36: 8 and blue, and purple, and s':
35 vail of blue, and purple, and s',
37 door of blue, and purple, and s',
38:18 of blue, and purple, and s', and
23 purple, and in s', and fine linen.
39: 1 of the blue, and purple, and s',
2 gold, blue, and purple, and s',
3 in the purple, and in the s',
5, 8 gold, blue, and purple, and s',
24 of blue, and purple, and s', and
29 purple, and s', of needlework;
Le 14: 4 cedar wood, and s', and hyssop:
6 and the cedar wood, and the s',
49 cedar wood, and s', and hyssop:
51 and the hyssop, and the s', and
52 with the hyssop, and with the s':
Nu 4: 8 spread upon them a cloth of s',
Nu 19: 6 cedar wood, and hyssop, and s',
Jos 2:18 shalt bind this line of s' thread in
21 bound the s' line in the window.
2Sa 1:24 over Saul, who clothed you in s',
Pr 31:21 household are clothed with s'.
Ca 4: 3 Thy lips are like a thread of s',
Isa 1:18 though your sins be as s', they
La 4: 5 they that were brought up in s'
Da 5: 7 shall be clothed with s', and have
16 thou shalt be clothed with s', and
29 they clothed Daniel with s', and put
Na 2: 3 red, the valiant men are in s':
M't 27:28 him, and put on him a s' robe.
Heb 9:19 water, and s' wool, and hyssop,
Re 17: 3 woman sit upon a s' coloured beast,
4 arrayed in purple and s' colour,
18:12 and purple, and silk, and s', and all
16 in fine linen, and purple, and s',

scarlet-coloured See SCARLET and COLOURED.

scatter See also SCATTERED; SCATTERETH; SCATTERING.
Ge 11: 9 did the Lord s' them abroad upon
49: 7 in Jacob, and s' them in Israel.
Le 26:33 I will s' you among the heathen,
Nu 16:37 and s' thou the fire yonder; for
De 4:27 shall s' you among the nations,
28:64 Lord shall s' thee among all people,
32:26 said, I would s' them into corners,
1Ki 14:15 and shall s' them beyond the river,
Ne 1: 8 s' you abroad among the nations:
Ps 59:11 s' them by thy power; and bring
68:30 s' thou the people that delight in
106:27 and to s' them in the lands.
144: 6 Cast forth lightning, and s' them:
Isa 28:25 the fitches, and s' the cummin,
41:16 and the whirlwind shall s' them:
Jer 9:16 s' them also among the heathen,
13:24 will I s' them as the stubble that
18:17 I will s' them as with an east wind
23: 1 that destroy and s' the sheep of my
49:32 I will s' into all winds them that
36 will s' them toward all those winds;
Eze 5: 2 third part thou shalt s' in the wind;
10 remnant...will I s' into all the winds.
12 and I will s' a third part into all the
6: 5 s' your bones...about your altars.
10: 2 coals...and s' them over the city.
12:14 I will s' toward every wind all that
15 shall s' them among the nations,
20:23 would s' them among the heathen,
22:15 I will s' thee among the heathen,
29:12 I will s' the Egyptians among the
30:23, 26 will s' the Egyptians among the
Da 4:14 off his leaves, and s' his fruit:
11:24 he shall s' among them the prey,
12: 7 to s' the power of the holy people,
Hab 3:14 came out as a whirlwind to s' me:
Zec 1:21 over the land of Judah to s' it.

scattered
Ge 11: 4 we be s' abroad upon the face of
8 So the Lord s' them abroad from
Ex 5:12 people were s' abroad throughout
Nu 10:35 Lord, and let thine enemies be s';
De 30: 3 the Lord thy God hath s' thee.
1Sa 11:11 that they which remained were s',
13: 8 and the people were s' from him.
11 that the people were s' from me,
2Sa 18: 8 the battle was there s' over the
22:15 he sent out arrows, and s' them;
1Ki 22:17 I saw all Israel s' upon the hills, as
2Ki 25: 5 and all his army were s' from him.
2Ch 18:16 all Israel s' upon the mountains,
Es 3: 8 is a certain people s' abroad and
Job 4:11 stout lion's whelps are s' abroad.
18:15 brimstone shall be s' upon his
Ps 18:14 sent out his arrows, and s' them;
44:11 and hast s' us among the heathen.
53: 5 God hath s' the bones of him that
60: 1 hast cast us off, thou hast s' us,
68: 1 God arise, let his enemies be s':
14 When the Almighty s' kings in it,
89:10 thou hast s' thine enemies with
92: 9 the workers of iniquity shall be s'.
141: 7 Our bones are s' at the grave's
Isa 18: 2 to a nation s' and peeled, to a
7 present...of a people s' and peeled,
33: 3 up of thyself the nations were s'.
Jer 3:13 hast s' thy ways to the strangers
10:21 and all their flocks shall be s'.
23: 2 Ye have s' my flock, and driven
30:11 all nations whither I have s' thee,
31:10 He that s' Israel will gather him,
40:15 gathered unto thee should be s',
50:17 Israel is a s' sheep; the lions have
52: 8 and all his army was s' from him.
Eze 6: 8 shall be s' through the countries.
11:16 have s' them among the countries,
17 the countries where ye have been s',
17:21 shall be s' toward all winds:
20:34 of the countries wherein ye are s',
41 countries wherein ye have been s';
28:25 the people among whom they are s',
29:13 the people whither they were s':
34: 5 And they were s', because there is
5 of the field, when they were s'.
6 was s' upon all the face of the earth,
12 he is among his sheep that are s';
12 all places where they have been s'
21 horns, till ye have s' them abroad;
36:19 And I s' them among the heathen,
46:18 s' every man from his possession.
Joe 3: 2 they have s' among the nations,
Na 3:18 people is s' upon the mountains,
Hab 3: 6 the everlasting mountains were s',
Zec 1:19, 21 the horns which have s' Judah,
Zec 7:14 I s' them with a whirlwind among
13: 7 and the sheep shall be s': and I
M't 9:36 were s' abroad, as sheep having
26:31 of the flock shall be s' abroad.
M'r 14:27 shepherd, and the sheep shall be s'.
Lu 1:51 s' the proud in the imagination of
Joh 11:52 children of God that were s' abroad.
16:32 is now come, that ye shall be s',
Ac 5:36 were s', and brought to nought.
8: 1 they were all s' abroad throughout
4 they that were s' abroad went
11:19 they which were s' abroad upon the
Jas 1: 1 twelve tribes which are s' abroad,
1Pe 1: 1 strangers s' throughout Pontus,

scattereth
Job 37:11 cloud: he s' his bright cloud:
38:24 s' the east wind upon the earth?
Ps 147:16 he s' the hoarfrost like ashes.
Pr 11:24 There is that s', and yet increaseth;
20: 8 s' away all evil with his eyes.
26 A wise king s' the wicked, and
Isa 24: 1 s' abroad the inhabitants thereof.
M't 12:30 gathereth not with me s' abroad.
Lu 11:23 he that gathereth not with me s'.
Joh 10:12 catcheth them, and s' the sheep.

scattering
Isa 30:30 s', and tempest, and hailstones.

scent
Job 14: 9 through the s' of water it will bud,
Jer 48:11 in him, and his s' is not changed.
Ho 14: 7 s' thereof shall be as the wine of

sceptre See also SCEPTRES.
Ge 49:10 s' shall not depart from Judah,
Nu 24:17 and a S' shall rise out of Israel,
Es 4:11 king shall hold out the golden s',
5: 2 held out to Esther the golden s'.
2 near, and touched the top of the s'.
8: 4 out the golden s' toward Esther.
Ps 45: 6 and ever: the s' of thy kingdom
6 of thy kingdom is a right s'.
Isa 14: 5 the wicked, and the s' of the rulers.
Eze 19:14 she hath no strong rod to be a s' to
Am 1: 5 him that holdeth the s' from the
8 him that holdeth the s' from Ashkelon,
Zec 10:11 the s' of Egypt shall depart away.
Heb 1: 8 a s' of righteousness is the s' of

sceptres
Eze 19:11 she had strong rods for the s' of

Sceva (*see'-vah*)
Ac 19:14 there were seven sons of one S',

schism
1Co 12:25 there should be no s' in the body;

scholar
1Ch 25: 8 the great, the teacher as the s'.
Mal 2:12 the master and the s', out of the

school See also SCHOOLMASTER.
Ac 19: 9 daily in the s' of one Tyrannus.

schoolmaster
Ga 3:24 law was our s' to bring us unto
25 we are no longer under a s'.

science
Da 1: 4 knowledge, and understanding s',
1Ti 6:20 oppositions of s' falsely so called:

scoff
Hab 1:10 And they shall s' at the kings,

scoffers
2Pe 3: 3 shall come in the last days s',

scorch See also SCORCHED.
Re 16: 8 unto him to s' men with fire.

scorched
M't 13: 6 the sun was up, they were s';
M'r 4: 6 when the sun was up, it was s';
Re 16: 9 And men were s' with great heat,

score See FOURSCORE; SIXSCORE; THREESCORE.

scorn See also SCORNEST; SCORNETH; SCORNFUL; SCORNING.
2Ki 19:21 thee, and laughed thee to s';
2Ch 30:10 but they laughed them to s', and
Ne 2:19 heard it, they laughed us to s',
Es 3: 6 s' to lay hands on Mordecai alone;
Job 12: 4 the just upright man is laughed to s'.
16:20 My friends s' me: but mine eye
22:19 and the innocent laugh them to s'.
Ps 22: 7 they that see me laugh me to s':
44:13 a s' and a derision to them that
79: 4 a s' and derision to them that are
Isa 37:22 thee, and laughed thee to s';
Eze 23:32 thou shalt be laughed to s' and
Hab 1:10 princes shall be a s' unto them:
M't 9:24 sleepeth...they laughed him to s'.
M'r 5:40 And they laughed him to s'. But
Lu 8:53 they laughed him to s', knowing

scorner See also SCORNERS.
Pr 9: 7 He that reproveth a s' getteth to
8 Reprove not a s', lest he hate thee:
13: 1 but a s' heareth not rebuke.
14: 6 A s' seeketh wisdom, and findeth
15:12 A s' loveth not one that reproveth
19:25 Smite a s', and the simple will
21:11 When the s' is punished, the simple
24 Proud and haughty s' is his name,
22:10 Cast out the s', and contention
24: 9 the s' is an abomination to men.
Isa 29:20 the s' is consumed, and all that

scorners
Pr 1:22 the s' delight in their scorning,
3:34 Surely he scorneth the s': but he
19:29 Judgments are prepared for s',
Ho 7: 5 he stretched out his hand with s'.

scornest
Pr 9:12 if thou s', thou alone shalt bear
Eze 16:31 as an harlot, in that thou s' hire;

scorneth
Job 39: 7 He s' the multitude of the city,
18 high, she s' the horse and his rider.
Pr 3:34 Surely he s' the scorners: but he
19:28 An ungodly witness s' judgment:

scornful
Ps 1: 1 nor sitteth in the seat of the s'.
Pr 29: 8 S' men bring a city into a snare:
Isa 28:14 the word of the Lord, ye s' men,

scorning
Job 34: 7 who drinketh up s' like water?
Ps 123: 4 the s' of those that are at ease,
Pr 1:22 the scorners delight in their s',

scorpion See also SCORPIONS.
Lu 11:12 ask an egg, will he offer him a s'?
Re 9: 5 torment was as the torment of a s',

scorpions
De 8:15 were fiery serpents, and s', and
1Ki 12:11, 14 but I will chastise you with s'.
2Ch 10:11, 14 but I will chastise you with s'.
Eze 2: 6 thee, and thou dost dwell among s':
Lu 10:19 power to tread on serpents and s',
Re 9: 3 as the s' of the earth have power.
10 And they had tails like unto s', and

scoured
Le 6:28 pot, it shall be both s', and rinsed

scourge See also SCOURGED; SCOURGES; SCOURGETH; SCOURGING.
Job 5:21 be hid from the s' of the tongue:
9:23 If the s' slay suddenly, he will
Isa 10:26 the Lord of hosts shall stir up a s'
28:15 overflowing s' shall pass through,
18 overflowing s' shall pass through,
M't 10:17 will s' you in their synagogues;
20:19 to mock, and to s', and to crucify
23:34 some of them shall ye s' in your
M'r 10:34 shall s' him, and shall spit upon
Lu 18:33 they shall s' him, and put him to
Joh 2:15 he had made a s' of small cords,
Ac 22:25 Is it lawful for you to s' a man

scourged
Le 19:20 she shall be s'; they shall not be
M't 27:26 and when he had s' Jesus, he
M'r 15:15 when he had s' him, to be crucified.
Joh 19: 1 therefore took Jesus, and s' him.

scourges
Jos 23:13 s' in your sides, and thorns in your

scourgeth
Heb 12: 6 s' every son whom he receiveth.

scourging See also SCOURGINGS.
Ac 22:24 that he should be examined by s';

scourgings
Heb 11:36 trial of cruel mockings and s',

scouring See OFFSCOURING.

scrabbled
1Sa 21:13 and s' on the doors of the gate,

scrape See also SCRAPED.
Le 14:41 the dust that they s' off without
Job 2: 8 a potsherd to s' himself withal;
Eze 26: 4 I will also s' her dust from her,

scraped
Le 14:41 cause the house to be s' within
43 and after he hath s' the house,

screech
Isa 34:14 the s' owl also shall rest there,

scribe See also ASCRIBE; DESCRIBE; PRESCRIBED; SCRIBE'S; SCRIBES.
2Sa 8:17 priests; and Seraiah was the s';
20:25 And Sheva was s': and Zadok and
2Ki 12:10 the king's s' and the high priest
18:18, 37 Shebna the s', and Joah the son
19: 2 Shebna the s', and the elder of the
22: 3 the son of Meshullam, the s', to the
8 priest said unto Shaphan the s',
9 Shaphan the s' came to the king,
10 Shaphan the s' shewed the king,
12 And Shaphan the s', and Asahiah a
25:19 and the principal s' of the host,
1Ch 18:16 the priests; and Shavsha was s';
24: 6 Shemaiah...son of Nethaneel the s',
27:32 a counseller, a wise man, and a s':
2Ch 24:11 king's s' and...high priest's officer
26:11 Jeiel the s' and Maaseiah the ruler,
34:15 Hilkiah...said to Shaphan the s',
18 Then Shaphan the s' told the king,
20 and Shaphan the s', and Asaiah a
Ezr 4: 8 and Shimshai the s' wrote a letter
9 the chancellor, and Shimshai the s',
17 chancellor, and to Shimshai the s',
23 before Rehum, and Shimshai the s',
7: 6 a ready s' in the law of Moses,
11 gave unto Ezra the priest, the s',
11 even a s' of the...commandments
12, 21 s' of the law of...God of heaven,
Ne 8: 1 and they spake unto Ezra the s'
4 And Ezra the s' stood upon a pulpit
9 and Ezra the priest the s', and the
13 were gathered...unto Ezra the s',
12:26 and of Ezra the priest, the s'.
36 of God, and Ezra the s' before them.
13:13 Shelemiah...and Zadok the s',
Isa 33:18 Where is the s'? where is the
36: 3 Shebna the s', and Joah, Asaph's
22 Shebna the s', and Joah, the son of
37: 2 and Shebna the s', and the elders of
Jer 36:10 Gemariah...son of Shaphan the s',
12 sat there, even Elishama the s', and
20 in the chamber of Elishama the s',
26 to take Baruch the s' and Jeremiah
32 roll, and gave it to Baruch the s',
37:15 in the house of Jonathan the s':
20 to the house of Jonathan the s',
52:25 and the principal s' of the host, who
M't 8:19 And a certain s' came, and said
13:52 every s' which is instructed unto
M'r 12:32 the s' said unto him, Well, Master,
1Co 1:20 Where is the wise? where is the s'?

scribe's
Jer 36:12 king's house, into the s' chamber:
21 it out of Elishama the s' chamber.

scribes
1Ki 4: 3 and Ahiah, the sons of Shisha, s';
1Ch 2:55 the families of the s' which dwelt at
2Ch 34:13 and of the Levites there were s',
Es 3:12 Then were the king's s' called on
8: 9 Then were the king's s' called at
Jer 8: 8 he it; the pen of the s' is in vain.
M't 2: 4 chief priests and s' of the people
5:20 exceed the righteousness of the s'
7:29 having authority, and not as the s'.
9: 3 behold, certain of the s' said within
12:38 certain of the s' and of the Pharisees
15: 1 came to Jesus s' and Pharisees,
16:21 the elders and chief priests and s',
17:10 Why then say the s' that Elias must
20:18 the chief priests and unto the s',
21:15 when the chief priests and s' saw
23: 2 s' and the Pharisees sit in Moses'
13 But woe unto you, s' and Pharisees,
14 Woe unto you, s' and Pharisees,
15, 23, 25, 27, 29 Woe unto you, s' and
34 prophets, and wise men, and s':
26: 3 the chief priests, and the s', and the
57 s' and the elders were assembled.
27:41 mocking him, with the s' and elders,
M'r 1:22 had authority, and not as the s'.
2: 6 were certain of the s' sitting there,
16 the s' and Pharisees saw him eat
3:22 s' which came down from Jerusalem
7: 1 Pharisees, and certain of the s',
5 the Pharisees and s' asked him,
8:31 and of the chief priests, and s',
9:11 Why say the s' that Elias must first
14 and the s' questioning with them.
16 he asked the s', What question ye
10:33 the chief priests, and unto the s';
11:18 And the s' and chief priests heard it,
27 the chief priests, and the s', and the
12:28 And one of the s' came, and having
35 How say the s' that Christ is the son
38 Beware of the s', which love to go
14: 1 chief priests and the s' sought how
43 from the chief priests and the s' and
53 priests and the elders and the s'.
15: 1 consultation with the elders and s'
31 said among themselves with the s',
Lu 5:21 s' and...Pharisees began to reason,
30 their s' and Pharisees murmured
6: 7 the s' and Pharisees watched him,
9:22 the elders and chief priests and s',
11:44 Woe unto you, s' and Pharisees,
53 s' and the Pharisees began to urge
15: 2 Pharisees and s' murmured, saying,
19:47 the chief priests and the s' and the
20: 1 priests and the s' came upon him
19 chief priests and...s' the same hour
39 certain of the s' answering said,
46 Beware of the s', which desire to
22: 2 the chief priests and s' sought how
66 priests and the s' came together,
23:10 And the chief priests and s' stood
Joh 8: 3 s' and Pharisees brought unto him
Ac 4: 5 that their rulers, and elders, and s',
6:12 the people, and the elders, and the s',
23: 9 s' that were of the Pharisees' part

scrip
1Sa 17:40 bag which he had, even in a s';
M't 10:10 Nor s' for your journey, neither
M'r 6: 8 no s', no bread, no money in their
Lu 9: 3 neither staves, nor s', neither
10: 4 Carry neither purse, nor s', nor
22:35 sent you without purse, and s', and
36 let him take it, and likewise his s':

scripture See also SCRIPTURES.
Da 10:21 which is noted in the s' of truth:
M'r 12:10 have ye not read this s': The stone
15:28 the s' was fulfilled, which saith,
Lu 4:21 This day is this s' fulfilled in your
Joh 2:22 they believed the s', and the word
7:38 as the s' hath said, out of his belly
42 Hath not the s' said, That Christ
10:35 came, and the s' cannot be broken;
13:18 that the s' may be fulfilled, He that
17:12 that the s' might be fulfilled.
19:24 that the s' might be fulfilled, which
28 that the s' might be fulfilled, saith,
36 s' should be fulfilled, A bone of him
37 again another s' saith, They shall
20: 9 For as yet they knew not the s',
Ac 1:16 s' must needs have been fulfilled,
8:32 The place of the s' which he read
35 began at the same s', and preached
Ro 4: 3 For what saith the s'? Abraham
9:17 the s' saith unto Pharaoh, Even for
10:11 the s' saith, Whosoever believeth
11: 2 Wot ye not what the s' saith of Elias?
Ga 3: 8 the s', forseeing that God would
22 the s' hath concluded all under sin,
4:30 Nevertheless what saith the s'?
1Ti 5:18 the s' saith, Thou shalt not muzzle
2Ti 3:16 All s' is given by inspiration of God,
Jas 2: 8 the royal law according to the s',
23 And the s' was fulfilled which saith,
4: 5 ye think that the s' saith in vain,
1Pe 2: 6 Wherefore...it is contained in the s',
2Pe 1:20 no prophecy of the s' is of...private

scriptures
M't 21:42 Did ye never read in the s', The
22:29 Ye do err, not knowing the s', nor
26:54 how then shall the s' be fulfilled,
56 s' of the prophets might be fulfilled,
M'r 12:24 err, because ye know not the s',
14:49 me not: but the s' must be fulfilled.
Lu 24:27 expounded unto them in all the s'
32 and while he opened to us the s'?
45 that they might understand the s',
Joh 5:39 Search the s'; for in them ye think
Ac 17: 2 reasoned with them out of the s',
11 and searched the s' daily, whether
18:24 eloquent man, and mighty in the s',
28 shewing by the s' that Jesus was
Ro 1: 2 afore by his prophets in the holy s',)
15: 4 patience and comfort of the s' we
16:26 by the s' of the prophets, according
1Co 15: 3 died for our sins according to the s';
4 the third day according to the s':
2Ti 3:15 child thou hast known the holy s',
2Pe 3:16 wrest, as they do also the other s',

scroll
Isa 34: 4 shall be rolled together as a s':
Re 6:14 And the heaven departed as a s'

scull See SKULL.

scum
Eze 24: 6 to the pot whose s' is therein,
6 and whose s' is not gone out of it!
11 that the s' of it may be consumed.
12 great s' went not forth out of her:
12 her s' shall be in the fire.

scurvy
Le 21:20 hath a blemish in his eye, or be s',
22:22 or maimed, or having a wen, or s'

Scythian (*sith'-e-un*)
Col 3:11 Barbarian, S', bond nor free:

sea See also SEAFARING; SEAS.
Ge 1:26, 28 dominion over the fish of the s',
9: 2 and upon all the fishes of the s';
14: 3 vale of Siddim, which is the salt s'.
22:17 sand which is upon the s' shore;
32:12 make thy seed as the sand of the s',
41:49 gathered corn as the sand of the s',
49:13 shall dwell at the haven of the s';
Ex 10:19 and cast them into the Red s';
13:18 way of the wilderness of the Red s':
14: 2 between Migdol and the s', over
2 before it shall ye encamp by the s'.
9 overtook them encamping by the s',
16 stretch out thine hand over the s',
16 ground through the midst of the s'.
21 stretched out his hand over the s';
21 s' to go back by a strong east wind
21 and made the s' dry land, and the
22 midst of the s' upon the dry ground:
23 in after them to the midst of the s',
26 Stretch out thine hand over the s',
27 stretched forth his hand over the s',
27 and the s' returned to his strength
27 Egyptians in the midst of the s'.
28 that came into the s' after them;
29 upon dry land in the midst of the s';
30 Egyptians dead upon the s' shore.
15: 1 rider hath he thrown into the s'.
4 his host hath he cast into the s':
4 also are drowned in the Red s'.
8 congealed in the heart of the s'.
10 with thy wind, the s' covered them:
19 and with his horsemen into the s',
19 the waters of the s' upon them;
19 on dry land in the midst of the s'.
21 rider hath he thrown into the s'.
22 brought Israel from the Red s',
20:11 the s', and all that in them is, and
23:31 will set thy bounds from the Red s'
31 even unto the s' of the Philistines,
Nu 11:22 fish of the s' be gathered together
31 and brought quails from the s', and
13:29 and the Canaanites dwell by the s',
14:25 wilderness by the way of the Red s':
21: 4 Hor by the way of the Red s',
14 What he did in the Red s', and in the
33: 8 midst of the s' into the wilderness,
10 Elim, and encamped by the Red s'.
11 And they removed from the Red s',
34: 3 coast of the salt s' eastward:
5 goings out of it shall be at the s'.
6 even have the great s' for a border:
7 great s' ye shall point out for you
11 the side of the s' of Chinnereth
12 out of it shall be at the salt s':
De 1: 1 in the plain over against the Red s',
7 in the south, and by the s' side,
40 wilderness by the way of the Red s'.
2: 1 wilderness by the way of the Red s',
3:17 the s' of the plain, even the salt s',
4:49 even unto the s' of the plain, under
11: 4 the Red s' to overflow them as they
24 uttermost s' shall your coast be.
30:13 Neither is it beyond the s', that
13 Who shall go over the s' for us, and
34: 2 land of Judah, unto the utmost s',
Jos 1: 4 unto the great s' toward the going
2:10 up the water of the Red s' for you,
3:16 the s' of the plain, even the salt s',
4:23 Lord your God did to the Red s',

Jos 5: 1 Canaanites, which were by the s',
9: 1 all the coasts of the great s' over
11: 4 the sand that is upon the s' shore
12: 3 the plain to the s' of Chinneroth on
3 east, and unto the s' of the plain,
3 plain, even the salt s' on the east,
13: 27 the edge of the s' of Chinnereth on
15: 2 was from the shore of the salt s',
4 out of that coast were at the s':
5 And the east border was the salt s',
5 s' at the uttermost part of Jordan:
11 out of the border were at the s'.
12 the west border was to the great s',
46 From Ekron even unto the s', all
47 great s', and the border thereof:
16: 3 the goings out thereof are at the s'.
6 toward the s' to Michmethah on
8 goings out thereof were at the s'.
17: 9 the outgoings of it were at the s':
10 Manasseh's,...the s' is his border;
18: 14 and compassed the corner of the s'
19 were at the north bay of the salt s'
19: 11 their border went up toward the s',
29 at the s' from the coast to Achzib:
23: 4 even unto the great s' westward.
24: 6 of Egypt: and ye came unto the s';
6 and horsemen unto the Red s'.
7 and brought the s' upon them, and
J'g 5: 17 Asher continued on the s' shore,
7: 12 sand by the s' side for multitude.
11: 16 the wilderness unto the Red s',
1Sa 13: 5 as the sand which is on the s' shore
2Sa 17: 11 as the sand that is by the s' for
22: 16 the channels of the s' appeared, the
1Ki 4: 20 as the sand which is by the s' in
29 as the sand that is on the s' shore.
5: 9 down from Lebanon unto the s':
9 I will convey them by s' in floats
7: 23 And he made a molten s', ten cubits
24 compassing the s' round about:
25 the s' was set above upon them,
39 he set the s' on the right side of
44 s', and twelve oxen under the s';
9: 26 Eloth, on the shore of the Red s',
27 that had knowledge of the s', with
10: 22 king had at s' a navy of Tharshish
18: 43 Go up now, look toward the s'. And
44 ariseth a little cloud out of the s',
2Ki 14: 25 Hamath unto the s' of the plain,
16: 17 down the s' from off the brasen
25: 13 the brasen s' that was in the house
16 The two pillars, one s', and the
1Ch 16: 32 Let the s' roar, and the fulness
18: 8 Solomon made the brasen s', and
2Ch 2: 16 it to thee in floats by s' to Joppa;
4: 2 he made a molten s' of ten cubits
3 compassing the s' round about.
4 and the s' was set above upon them,
6 s' was for the priests to wash in.
10 he set the s' on the right side of the
15 One s', and twelve oxen under it.
8: 17 at the s' side in the land of Edom.
18 that had knowledge of the s'; and
20: 2 beyond the s' on this side Syria;
Ezr 3: 7 from Lebanon to the s' of Joppa,
Ne 9: 9 heardest their cry by the Red s';
11 And thou didst divide the s' before
11 through the midst of the s' on...dry
Es 10: 1 land, and upon the isles of the s'.
Job 6: 3 be heavier than the sand of the s':
7: 12 Am I a s', or a whale, that thou
9: 8 treadeth upon the waves of the s'.
11: 9 the earth, and broader than the s'.
12: 8 the fishes of the s' shall declare
14: 11 As the waters fail from the s', and
26: 12 He divideth the s' with his power,
28: 14 and the s' saith, It is not with me.
36: 30 and covereth the bottom of the s'.
38: 8 Or who shut up the s' with doors,
16 entered into the springs of the s'?
41: 31 he maketh the s' like a pot of
Ps 8: 8 the fish of the s', and whatsoever
33: 7 He gathereth the waters of the s'
46: 2 be carried into the midst of the s';
65: 5 them that are afar off upon the s':
66: 6 He turned the s' into dry land: they
68: 22 again from the depths of the s':
72: 8 have dominion also from s' to s',
74: 13 didst divide the s' by the strength:
77: 19 Thy way is in the s', and thy path
78: 13 He divided the s', and caused them
27 fowls like as the sand of the s':
53 the s' overwhelmed their enemies.
80: 11 sent out her boughs unto the s',
89: 9 Thou rulest the raging of the s':
25 I will set his hand also in the s',
93: 4 than the mighty waves of the s'.
95: 5 The s' is his, and he made it: and
96: 11 let the s' roar, and the fulness
98: 7 Let the s' roar, and the fulness
104: 25 So is this great and wide s', wherein
106: 7 him at the s', even at the Red s'.
9 He rebuked the Red s' also, and it
22 and terrible things by the Red s'.
107: 23 that go down to the s' in ships, that
114: 3 The s' saw it, and fled: Jordan was
5 What ailed thee, O thou s', that
136: 13 which divided the Red s' into parts:
15 Pharaoh and his host in the Red s':
139: 9 in the uttermost parts of the s';
146: 6 the s', and all that therein is:
Pr 8: 29 When he gave to the s' his decree,
23: 34 lieth down in the midst of the s',
30: 19 way of a ship in the midst of the s';
Ec 1: 7 into the s'; yet the s' is not full;
Isa 5: 30 them like the roaring of the s':
Isa 9: 1 afflict her by the way of the s',
10: 22 Israel be as the sand of the s',
26 as his rod was upon the s', so shall
11: 9 the Lord, as the waters cover the s'.
11 and from the islands of the s'.
15 the tongue of the Egyptian s';
16: 8 out, they are gone over the s'.
18: 2 sendeth ambassadors by the s',
19: 5 the waters shall fail from the s',
21: 1 The burden of the desert of the s'.
23: 2 of Zidon, that pass over the s', have
4 for the s' hath spoken, even the
4 even the strength of the s', saying,
11 stretched out his hand over the s',
24: 14 they shall cry aloud from the s'.
15 God of Israel in the isles of the s'.
27: 1 slay the dragon that is in the s'.
42: 10 ye that go down to the s', and all
43: 16 which maketh a way in the s', and
48: 18 righteousness as the waves of the s'.
50: 2 at my rebuke I dry up the s', I
51: 10 not it which hath dried the s', the
10 made the depths of the s' a way for
15 Lord thy God that divided the s',
57: 20 the wicked are like the troubled s',
60: 5 the abundance of the s' shall be
63: 11 that brought them up out of the s'
Jer 5: 22 the sand for the bound of the s'
6: 23 their voice roareth like the s'; and
25: 22 the isles which are beyond the s',
27: 19 concerning the s', and concerning
31: 35 which divideth the s' when the
33: 22 the sand of the s' measured: so
46: 18 and as Carmel by the s', so shall he
47: 7 Ashkelon, and against the s' shore?
48: 32 thy plants are gone over the s', they
32 they reach even to the s' of Jazer:
49: 21 thereof was heard in the Red s'.
23 there is sorrow on the s'; it cannot
50: 42 their voice shall roar like the s',
51: 36 I will dry up her s', and make her
42 The s' is come up upon Babylon:
52: 17 the brasen s' that was in the house
20 The two pillars, one s', and twelve
La 2: 13 for thy breach is great like the s':
4: 3 Even the s' monsters draw out
Eze 25: 16 destroy...remnant of the s' coast.
26: 3 s' causeth his waves to come up.
5 of nets in the midst of the s': for
16 all the princes of the s' shall come
17 which wast strong in the s', she and
18 that are in the s' shall be troubled
27: 3 art situate at the entry of the s',
9 ships of the s' with their mariners
29 all the pilots of the s', shall come
32 the destroyed in the midst of the s'?
38: 20 So that the fishes of the s', and the
39: 11 the passengers on the east of the s':
47: 8 into the desert, and go into the s':
8 being brought forth into the s',
10 as the fish of the great s', exceeding
15 the north side from the great s',
17 And the border from the s' shall be
18 from the border unto the east s'.
19 in Kadesh, the river to the great s'.
20 west side also shall be the great s'
48: 28 and to the river toward the great s'.
Da 7: 2 heaven strove upon the great s'.
3 great beasts came up from the s',
Ho 1: 10 Israel shall be as...sand of the s',
4: 3 fishes of the s' also shall be taken
Joe 2: 20 with his face toward the east s', and
20 hinder part toward the utmost s',
Am 5: 8 that calleth for the waters of the s',
8: 12 And they shall wander from s' to s',
9: 3 my sight in the bottom of the s',
6 that calleth for the waters of the s',
Jon 1: 4 sent out a great wind into the s',
4 was a mighty tempest in the s', so
5 that were in the ship into the s',
9 which hath made the s' and the dry
11 that the s' may be calm unto us?
11 unto us? for the s' wrought, and was
12 up, and cast me forth into the s';
12 so shall the s' be calm unto
13 s' wrought, and was tempestuous.
15 Jonah, and cast him forth into the s':
15 and the s' ceased from her raging.
Mic 7: 12 from s' to s', and from mountain
19 their sins into the depths of the s'.
Na 1: 4 He rebuketh the s', and maketh it
3: 8 about it, whose rampart was the s',
8 and her wall was from the s'?
Hab 1: 14 makest men as the fishes of the s',
2: 14 the Lord, as the waters cover the s'.
3: 8 was thy wrath against the s', that
15 walk through the s' with thine
Zep 1: 3 the heaven, and the fishes of the s',
2: 5 unto the inhabitants of the s' coast,
6 the s' coast shall be dwellings and
Hag 2: 6 heavens, and the earth, and the s',
Zec 9: 4 he will smite her power in the s';
10 dominion shall be from s' even to s',
10: 11 pass through the s' with affliction,
11 and shall smite the waves in the s',
14: 8 half of them toward the former s',
8 half of them toward the hinder s':
M't 4: 13 which is upon the s' coast, in the
15 by the way of the s', beyond Jordan,
18 Jesus, walking by the s' of Galilee,
18 brother, casting a net into the s':
8: 24 arose a great tempest in the s',
26 and rebuked the winds and the s';
27 even the winds and the s' obey him!
32 down a steep place into the s', and
13: 1 of the house, and sat by the s' side.
M't 13: 47 unto a net, that was cast into the s',
14: 24 ship was now in the midst of the s',
25 went unto them, walking on the s'.
26 disciples saw him walking on the s',
15: 29 came nigh unto the s' of Galilee;
17: 27 go thou to the s', and cast an hook,
18: 6 were drowned in the depth of the s'.
21: 21 and be thou cast into the s';
23: 15 ye compass s' and land to make one
M'r 1: 16 as he walked by the s' of Galilee, he
16 brother casting a net into the s':
2: 13 he went forth again by the s' side;
3: 7 himself with his disciples to the s':
4: 1 began again to teach by the s' side:
1 entered into a ship, and sat in the s';
1 whole multitude was by the s' on
39 and said unto the s', Peace, be still.
41 even the wind and the s' obey him?
5: 1 over unto the other side of the s',
13 down a steep place into the s',
13 thousand;) and...choked in the s'.
21 him: and he was nigh unto the s'.
6: 47 the ship was in the midst of the s',
48 unto them, walking upon the s',
49 they saw him walking upon the s',
7: 31 he came unto the s' of Galilee,
9: 42 neck, and he were cast into the s'.
11: 23 and be thou cast into the s';
Lu 6: 17 from the s' coast of Tyre and Sidon,
17: 2 his neck, and he cast into the s',
6 root, and be thou planted in the s';
21: 25 the s' and the waves roaring;
Joh 6: 1 Jesus went over the s' of Galilee,
1 Galilee, which is the s' of Tiberias.
16 his disciples went down unto the s',
17 went over the s' toward Capernaum.
18 s' arose by reason of a great wind
19 they see Jesus walking on the s',
22 stood on the other side of the s' saw
25 him on the other side of the s',
21: 1 the disciples at the s' of Tiberias;
7 and did cast himself into the s'.
Ac 4: 24 made heaven, and earth, and the s',
7: 36 in the Red s', and in the wilderness
10: 6 whose house is by the s' side:
32 one Simon a tanner by the s' side:
14: 15 made heaven, and earth, and the s',
17: 14 away Paul to go as it were to the s':
27: 5 we had sailed over the s' of Cilicia
30 had let down the boat into the s',
38 and cast out the wheat into the s',
40 committed themselves unto the s',
43 should cast themselves first into the s',
28: 4 though he hath escaped the s', yet
Ro 9: 27 of Israel be as the sand of the s',
1Co 10: 1 cloud, and all passed through the s';
2 Moses in the cloud and in the s';
2Co 11: 26 in perils in the s', in perils among
Heb 11: 12 is by the s' shore innumerable.
29 passed through the Red s' as by dry
Jas 1: 6 that wavereth is like a wave of the s'
3: 7 and of things in the s', is tamed,
Jude 13 Raging waves of the s', foaming
Re 4: 6 was a s' of glass like unto crystal:
5: 13 such as are in the s', and all that
7: 1 not blow on the earth, nor on the s',
2 given to hurt the earth and the s',
3 Hurt not the earth, neither the s',
8: 8 with fire was cast into the s': and
8 third part of the s' became blood;
9 the creatures which were in the s',
10: 2 and he set his right foot upon the s',
5 angel which I saw stand upon the s'
6 s', and the things which are therein,
8 the angel which standeth upon the s'
12: 12 inhabiters of the earth and of the s'!
13: 1 And I stood upon the sand of the s',
1 and saw a beast rise up out of the s',
14: 7 the s', and the fountains of waters.
15: 2 were a s' of glass mingled with fire:
2 stand on the s' of glass, having the
16: 3 poured out his vial upon the s'; and
3 and every living soul died in the s'.
18: 17 sailors, and as many as trade by s',
19 made rich all that had ships in the s'
21 millstone, and cast it into the s',
20: 8 of whom is as the sand of the s'.
13 s' gave up the dead which were in it;
21: 1 away; and there was no more s'.

seafaring
Eze 26: 17 that wast inhabited of s' men, the

seal See also SEALED; SEALEST; SEALETH; SEALING; SEALS.
1Ki 21: 8 name, and sealed them with his s',
Ne 9: 38 Levites, and priests, s' unto it.
Es 8: 8 name, and s' it with the king's ring:
Job 38: 14 It is turned as clay to the s'; and
41: 15 shut up together as with a close s'.
Ca 8: 6 Set me as a s' upon thine heart,
6 as a s' upon thine arm: for love is
Isa 8: 16 s' the law among my disciples.
Jer 32: 44 subscribe evidences, and s' them,
Da 9: 24 to s' up the vision and prophecy,
12: 4 shut up the words, and s' the book,
Joh 3: 33 hath set to his s' that God is true.
Ro 4: 11 s' of the righteousness of the faith
1Co 9: 2 s' of mine apostleship are ye in the
2Ti 2: 19 of God standeth sure, having this s',
Re 6: 3 when he had opened the second s',
5 when he had opened the third s',
7 when he had opened the fourth s',
9 And when he had opened the fifth s',
12 when he had opened the sixth s',
7: 2 east, having the s' of the living God:
8: 1 when he had opened the seventh s',

Re 9: 4 not the s' of God in their foreheads.
10: 4 *S'* up those things which the seven
20: 3 shut him up, and set a s' upon him,
22: 10 *S'* not the sayings of the prophecy

sealed
De 32: 34 and s' up among my treasures?
1Ki 21: 8 name, and s' them with his seal,
Ne 10: 1 Now those that s' were, Nehemiah,
Es 3: 12 written, and s' with the king's ring.
8: 8 name, and s' with the king's ring,
10 s' it with the king's ring, and sent
Job 14: 17 My transgression is s' up in a bag,
Ca 4: 12 a spring shut up, a fountain s'.
Isa 29: 11 as the words of a book that is s',
11 and he saith, I cannot; for it is s':
Jer 32: 10 subscribed the evidence, and s' it,
11 which was s' according to the law
14 both which is s', and this evidence
Da 6: 17 the king s' it with his own signet,
12: 9 up and s' till the time of the end.
Joh 6: 27 for him hath God the Father s'.
Ro 15: 28 this, and have s' to them this fruit,
2Co 1: 22 Who hath also s' us, and given the
Eph 1: 13 s' with that holy Spirit of promise,
4: 30 are s' unto the day of redemption.
Re 5: 1 the backside, s' with seven seals.
7: 3 we have s' the servants of our God
4 the number of them which were s':
4 there were s' an hundred and forty
5 of Juda were s' twelve thousand.
5 Reuben were s' twelve thousand.
5 of Gad were s' twelve thousand.
6 of Aser were s' twelve thousand.
6 Nepthalim were s' twelve thousand.
6 Manasses were s' twelve thousand.
7 of Simeon were s' twelve thousand.
7 of Levi were s' twelve thousand.
7 Issachar were s' twelve thousand.
8 Zabulon were s' twelve thousand.
8 Joseph were s' twelve thousand.
8 Benjamin were s' twelve thousand.

sealest
Eze 28: 12 Thou s' up the sum, full of

sealeth
Job 9: 7 riseth not; and s' up the stars.
33: 16 of men, and s' their instruction,
37: 7 He s' up the hand of every man;

sealing
M't 27: 66 s' the stone, and setting a watch.

seals
Re 5: 1 the backside, sealed with seven s'.
2 book, and to loose the s' thereof?
5 and to loose the seven s' thereof.
9 the book, and to open the s' thereof:
6: 1 when the Lamb opened one of the s',

seam
Joh 19: 23 now the coat was without s', woven

sea-monster See SEA and MONSTER.

search See also SEARCHED; SEARCHEST; SEARCHETH; SEARCHING; UNSEARCHABLE.
Le 27: 33 He shall not s' whether it be good
Nu 10: 33 to s' out a resting place for them.
13: 2 men, that they may s' the land of
32 through which we have gone to s'
14: 7 which we passed through to s' it,
36 which Moses sent to s' the land,
38 the men that went to s' the land,
De 1: 22 and they shall s' us out the land,
33 to s' you out a place to pitch your
13: 14 shalt thou enquire, and make s',
Jos 2: 2 of Israel to s' out the country.
3 be come to s' out all the country.
J'g 18: 2 to spy out the land, and to s' it;
2 said unto them, Go, s' the land:
1Sa 23: 23 that I will s' him out throughout
2Sa 10: 3 to s' the city, and to spy it out,
1Ki 20: 6 and they shall s' thine house, and
2Ki 10: 23 *S'*, and look that there be here
1Ch 19: 3 servants come unto thee for to s',
Ezr 4: 15 s' may be made in the book of the
19 and s' hath been made, and it is
5: 17 be s' made in the king's treasure
6: 1 s' was made in the house of the
Job 8: 8 thyself to the s' of their fathers:
13: 9 Is it good that he should s' you
38: 16 walked in the s' of the depth?
Ps 44: 21 Shall not God s' this out? for he
64: 6 They s' out iniquities; they
6 they accomplish a diligent s':
77: 6 and my spirit made diligent s'.
139: 23 *S'* me,...and know my heart:
Pr 25: 2 of kings is to s' out a matter.
27 to s' their own glory is not glory.
Ec 1: 13 to seek and s' out by wisdom
7: 25 and to s', and to seek out wisdom,
Jer 2: 34 I have not found it by secret s',
17: 10 I the Lord s' the heart, I try the
29: 13 shall s' for me with all your heart.
La 3: 40 Let us s' and try our ways, and
Eze 34: 6 none did s' or seek after them.
8 did my shepherds s' for my flock,
11 I, will both s' my sheep, and seek
39: 14 end of seven months shall they s'.
Am 9: 3 will s' and take them out thence;
Zep 1: 12 I will s' Jerusalem with candles,
M't 2: 8 s' diligently for the young child;
Joh 5: 39 *S'* the scriptures; for in them ye
7: 52 *S'*, and look: for out of Galilee

searched
Ge 31: 34 Laban s' all the tent, but found
35 he s', but found not the images.
37 whereas thou hast s' all my stuff,
44: 12 he s', and began at the eldest,
Nu 13: 21 s' the land from the wilderness
32 of the land which they had s' unto
14: 6 were of them that s' the land, rent
34 of the days in which ye s' the land,
De 1: 24 the valley of Eshcol, and s' it out.
Job 5: 27 Lo this, we have s' it, so it is;
28: 27 it; he prepared it, yea, and s' it out.
29: 16 the cause which I knew not I s' out.
32: 11 whilst ye s' out what to say.
36: 26 the number of his years be s' out.
Ps 139: 1 O Lord, thou hast s' me, and
Jer 31: 37 the foundations of the earth s' out
46: 23 though it cannot be s'; because
Ob 6 How are the things of Esau s' out!
Ac 17: 11 s' the scriptures daily, whether
1Pe 1: 10 have enquired and s' diligently,

searchest
Job 10: 6 mine iniquity, and s' after my sin?
Pr 2: 4 and s' for her as for hid treasures;

searcheth
1Ch 28: 9 for the Lord s' all hearts, and
Job 28: 3 and s' out all perfection: the
39: 8 and he s' after every green thing.
Pr 18: 17 his neighbour cometh and s' him.
28: 11 hath understanding s' him out.
Ro 8: 27 And he that s' the hearts knoweth
1Co 2: 10 for the Spirit s' all things, yea, the
Re 2: 23 he which s' the reins and hearts:

searching See also SEARCHINGS.
Nu 13: 25 they returned from s' of the land
Job 11: 7 Canst thou by s' find out God?
Pr 20: 27 s' all the inward parts of the belly.
Isa 40: 28 is no s' of his understanding.
1Pe 1: 11 *S'* what, or what manner of time

searchings
J'g 5: 16 there were great s' of heart.

seared
1Ti 4: 2 conscience s' with a hot iron;

seas
Ge 1: 10 of the waters called he *S'*: and
22 and fill the waters in the s', and
Le 11: 9 and scales in the waters, in the s',
10 have not fins and scales in the s',
De 33: 19 suck of the abundance of the s',
Ne 9: 6 the s', and all that is therein, and
Ps 8: 8 passeth through the paths of the s'.
24: 2 For he hath founded it upon the s',
65: 7 Which stilleth the noise of the s',
69: 34 the s', and every thing that moveth
135: 6 earth, in the s', and all deep places.
Isa 17: 12 a noise like the noise of the s';
Jer 15: 8 to me above the sand of the s':
Eze 27: 4 borders are in the midst of the s',
25 very glorious in the midst of the s'.
26 broken thee in the midst of the s'.
27 shall fall into the midst of the s' in
33 thy wares went forth out of the s',
34 thou shalt be broken by the s' in
28: 2 seat of God, in the midst of the s';
8 that are slain in the midst of the s'.
32: 2 and thou art as a whale in the s':
Da 11: 45 of his palace between the s' in the
Jon 2: 3 the deep, in the midst of the s';
Ac 27: 41 into a place where two s' met,

sea-shore See SEA and SHORE.

sea-side See SEA and SIDE.

season See also SEASONED; SEASONS.
Ge 40: 4 and they continued a s' in ward.
Ex 13: 10 keep this ordinance in his s' from
Le 2: 13 offering shalt thou s' with salt;
26: 4 I will give you rain in due s', and
Nu 9: 2 the passover at his appointed s'.
3 ye shall keep it in his appointed s':
7 of the Lord in his appointed s'
13 of the Lord in his appointed s',
28: 2 to offer unto me in their due s'.
De 11: 14 the rain of your land in his due s',
16: 6 the s' that thou camest forth out
28: 12 the rain unto thy land in his s',
Jos 24: 7 dwelt in the wilderness a long s'.
2Ki 4: 16 About this s', according to the
17 bare a son at that s' that Elisha had
2Ch 15: 3 a long s' Israel hath been without
Job 5: 26 shock of corn cometh in in his s'.
30: 17 are pierced in me in the night s':
38: 32 bring forth Mazzaroth in his s'?
Ps 1: 3 bringeth forth his fruit in his s';
22: 2 in the night s', and am not silent.
104: 27 give them their meat in due s'.
145: 15 givest them their meat in due s'.
Pr 15: 23 a word spoken in due s', how good
Ec 3: 1 To every thing there is a s', and a
10: 17 and thy princes eat in due s', for
Isa 50: 4 know how to speak a word in s' to
Jer 5: 24 the former and the latter, in his s':
33: 20 not be day and night in their s';
Eze 34: 26 the shower to come down in his s';
Da 7: 12 their lives were prolonged for a s'
Ho 2: 9 and my wine in the s' thereof, and
M't 24: 45 to give them meat in due s'?
M'r 9: 50 saltness, wherewith will ye s' it?
12: 2 the s' he sent to the husbandmen
Lu 1: 20 which shall be fulfilled in their s'.
4: 13 he departed from him for a s'.
12: 42 them their portion of meat in due s'?
13: 1 were present at that s' some that
20: 10 at the s' he sent a servant to the
23: 8 he was desirous to see him of a long s',
Joh 5: 4 down at a certain s' into the pool,
35 ye were willing for a s' to rejoice
Ac 13: 11 blind, not seeing the sun for a s'.
19: 22 he himself stayed in Asia for a s'.
24: 25 when I have a convenient s', I will
2Co 7: 8 sorry, though it were but for a s'.
Ga 6: 9 for in due s' we shall reap, if we
2Ti 4: 2 Preach the word; be instant in s',
2 be instant...out of s'; reprove,
Ph'm 15 he therefore departed for a s', that
Heb 11: 25 enjoy the pleasures of sin for a s';
1Pe 1: 6 rejoice, though now for a s', if
Re 6: 11 they should rest yet for a little s',
20: 3 that he must be loosed a little s'.

seasoned
Lu 14: 34 his savour, wherewith shall it be s'?
Col 4: 6 be alway with grace, s' with salt,

seasons
Ge 1: 14 let them be for signs, and for s',
Ex 18: 22 them judge the people at all s':
26 they judged the people at all s':
Le 23: 4 which ye shall proclaim in their s'.
Ps 16: 7 reins also instruct me in the night s'.
104: 19 He appointed the moon for s':
Da 2: 21 he changeth the times and the s':
M't 21: 41 render him the fruits in their s'.
Ac 1: 7 for you to know the times or the s',
14: 17 us rain from heaven, and fruitful s',
20: 18 I have been with you at all s',
1Th 5: 1 of the times and the s', brethren,

seat See also MERCYSEAT; SEATED; SEATS; SEATWARD.
Ex 25: 17 shalt make a mercy s' of pure gold:
18 in the two ends of the mercy s'.
19 even of the mercy s' shall ye make the
20 the mercy s' with their wings, and
20 toward the mercy s' shall the faces
21 put the mercy s' above upon the ark;
22 with thee from above the mercy s',
26: 34 put the mercy s' upon the ark of the
30: 6 before the mercy s' that is over the
31: 7 and the mercy s' that is thereupon,
35: 12 staves thereof, with the mercy s',
37: 6 he made the mercy s' of pure gold:
7 on the two ends of the mercy s';
8 out of the mercy s' made he the
9 with their wings over the mercy s',
39: 35 the staves thereof, and the mercy s',
40: 20 and put the mercy s' above upon the
Le 16: 2 within the vail before the mercy s',
2 in the cloud upon the mercy s'.
13 the incense may cover the mercy s'
14 finger upon the mercy s' eastward;
14 and before the mercy s' shall he
15 and sprinkle it upon the mercy s',
15 and before the mercy s':
Nu 7: 89 unto him from off the mercy s' that
J'g 3: 20 thee. And he arose out of his s'.
1Sa 1: 9 Eli the priest sat upon a s' by a post
4: 13 lo, Eli sat upon a s' by the wayside
18 he fell from off the s' backward by
20: 18 because thy s' will be empty.
25 And the king sat upon his s', as at
25 times, even upon a s' by the wall:
2Sa 23: 8 The Tachmonite that sat in the s',
1Ki 2: 19 s' to be set for the king's mother;
10: 19 either side on the place of the s',
1Ch 28: 11 and of the place of the mercy s',
Es 3: 1 and set his s' above all the princes
Job 23: 3 that I might come even to his s'!
29: 7 I prepared my s' in the street!
Ps 1: 1 nor sitteth in the s' of the scornful.
Pr 9: 14 on a s' in the high places of the
Eze 8: 3 the s' of the image of jealousy,
28: 2 I am a God, I sit in the s' of God,
Am 6: 3 cause the s' of violence to come
M't 23: 2 and the Pharisees sit in Moses' s':
27: 19 he was set down on the judgment s',
Joh 19: 13 and sat down in the judgment s' in a
Ac 18: 12 and brought him to the judgment s',
16 he drave them from the judgment s'.
17 and beat him before the judgment s'.
25: 6 next day sitting on the judgment s'
10 Paul, I stand at Cæsar's judgment s',
17 the morrow I sat on the judgment s',
Ro 14: 10 before the judgment s' of Christ.
2Co 5: 10 before the judgment s' of Christ;
Re 2: 13 dwellest, even where Satan's s' is:
13: 2 and his s', and great authority.
16: 10 out his vial upon the s' of the beast;

seated See also SET.
De 33: 21 portion of the lawgiver, was he s';

seats
M't 21: 12 and the s' of them that sold doves,
23: 6 and the chief s' in the synagogues,
M'r 11: 15 and the s' of them that sold doves;
12: 39 the chief s' in the synagogues, and
Lu 1: 52 put down the mighty from their s',
11: 43 uppermost s' in the synagogues,
20: 46 the highest s' in the synagogues,
Jas 2: 6 draw you before the judgment s'?
Re 4: 4 throne were four and twenty s':
4 upon the s' I saw four and twenty
11: 16 which sat before God on their s',

seatward
Ex 37: 9 to the mercy s' were the faces of the

Seba (*se'-bah*) See also SABEANS; SHEBA.
Ge 10: 7 *S'*, and Havilah, and Sabtah, and
1Ch 1: 9 *S'*, and Havilah, and Sabta, and
Ps 72: 10 of Sheba and *S'* shall offer gifts.
Isa 43: 3 ransom, Ethiopia and *S'* for thee.

Sebat (*se'-bat*)
Zec 1: 7 month, which is the month *S'*.

Secacah (*se-ca'-cah*)
Jos 15: 61 Beth-arabah, Middin, and *S'*.

Sechu (*se'-ku*)
1Sa 19:22 came to a great well that is in *S'*:
second^
Ge 1: 8 and the morning were the s' day.
2:13 the name of the s' river is Gihon:
6:16 with lower, s', and third stories
7:11 in the s' month, the seventeenth
8:14 in the s' month, on the seven and
22:15 Abraham out of heaven the s' time,
30: 7 again, and bare Jacob a s' son.
12 Leah's maid bare Jacob a s' son.
32:19 And so commanded he the s', and
41: 5 he slept and dreamed the s' time:
43 made him to ride in the s' chariot
52 name of the s' called he Ephraim:
43:10 now we had returned this s' time.
47:18 they came unto him the s' year,
Ex 2:13 And when he went out the s' day,
16: 1 on the fifteenth day of the s' month
26: 4 curtain, in the coupling of the s'.
5 that is in the coupling of the s';
10 the curtain which coupleth the s'.
20 And for the s' side of the tabernacle
28:18 And the s' row shall be an emerald,
36:11 curtain, in the coupling of the s'.
12 which was in the coupling of the s':
17 the curtain which coupleth the s'.
39:11 the s' row, an emerald, a sapphire,
40:17 in the first month in the s' year,
Le 5:10 offer the s' for a burnt offering,
13:58 then it shall be washed the s' time,
Nu 1: 1 on the first day of the s' month,
1 s' year after they were come out of
18 on the first day of the s' month,
2:16 they shall set forth in the s' rank.
7:18 s' day Nethaneel the son of Zuar,
9: 1 in the first month of the s' year
11 fourteenth day of the s' month at
10: 6 When ye blow an alarm the s' time,
11 twentieth day of the s' month, in
11 the s' year,...the cloud was taken
29:17 on the s' day ye shall offer twelve
Jos 5: 2 circumcise...of Israel the s' time.
6:14 s' day they compassed the city once,
10:32 took it on the s' day, and smote it
19: 1 And the s' lot came forth to Simeon,
J'g 6:25 the s' bullock of seven years old,
26 and take the s' bullock, and offer a
28 the s' bullock was offered upon the
20:24 children of Benjamin the s' day.
25 them out of Gibeah the s' day, and
1Sa 8: 2 and the name of his s', Abiah:
20:27 which was the s' day of the month,
34 eat no meat the s' day of the month:
26: 8 I will not smite him the s' time.
2Sa 3: 3 And his s', Chileab, of Abigail the
14:29 when he sent again the s' time,
1Ki 6: 1 month Zif, which is the s' month,
9: 2 appeared to Solomon the s' time,
15:25 the s' year of Asa king of Judah,
18:34 And he said, Do it the s' time.
34 And they did it the s' time.
19: 7 angel...came again the s' time,
2Ki 1:17 in the s' year of Jehoram the son
9:19 Then he sent out a s' on horseback,
10: 6 Then he wrote a letter the s' time
14: 1 s' year of Joash son of Jehoahaz
15:32 In the s' year of Pekah the son of
19:29 in the s' year that which springeth
23: 4 the priests of the s' order, and the
25:17 like unto these had the s' pillar
18 and Zephaniah the s' priest, and
1Ch 2:13 Abinadab the s', and Shimma the
3: 1 the s', Daniel, of Abigail the
15 s' Jehoiakim, the third Zedekiah,
7:15 the name of the s' was Zelophehad:
8: 1 Ashbel the s', and Aharah the third,
39 Jehush the s', and Eliphelet the
12: 9 Ezer the first, Obadiah the s', Eliab
15:18 their brethren of the s' degree,
23:11 was the chief, and Zizah the s':
19 Amariah the s', Jahaziel the third,
20 Micah the first, and Jesiah the s'.
24: 7 forth to Jehoiarib, the s' to Jedaiah,
23 Jeriah the first, Amariah the s',
25: 9 the s' to Gedaliah, who with his
26: 2 Jediael the s', Zebadiah the third,
4 Jehozabad the s', Joah the third,
11 Hilkiah the s', Tebaliah the third,
27: 4 And over the course of the s' month
29:22 made Solomon...king the s' time,
2Ch 3: 2 build in the s' day of the s' month,
27: 5 him, both the s' year, and the third.
30: 2 keep the passover in the s' month.
13 unleavened bread in the s' month,
15 the fourteenth day of the s' month:
35:24 and put him in the s' chariot that
Ezr 1:10 silver basons of a s' sort four
3: 8 Now in the s' year of their coming
8 in the s' month, began Zerubbabel
4:24 the s' year of the reign of Darius
Ne 8:13 the s' day were gathered together
11: 9 son of Senuah was s' over the city.
17 and Bakbukiah the s' among his
Es 2:14 she returned into the s' house of
19 were gathered together the s' time,
7: 2 said again unto Esther on the s' day
9:29 to confirm this s' letter of Purim.
Job 42:14 and the name of the s', Kezia;
Ec 4: 8 is one alone, and there is not a s';
15 with the s' child that shall stand
Isa 11:11 shall set his hand again the s' time
37:30 the s' year that which springeth of
Jer 1:13 the Lord came unto me the s' time,
13: 3 the Lord came unto me the s' time,
33: 1 came unto Jeremiah the s' time,
Jer 41: 4 s' day after he had slain Gedaliah,
52:22 s' pillar also and the pomegranates
24 and Zephaniah the s' priest, and
Eze 10:14 the s' face was the face of a man,
43:22 on the s' day thou shalt offer a kid
Da 2: 1 in the s' year of...Nebuchadnezzar
7: 5 another beast, a s', like to a bear,
Jon 3: 1 Lord came unto Jonah the s' time,
Na 1: 9 affliction shall not rise up the s' time.
Zep 1:10 and an howling from the s', and
Hag 1: 1 In the s' year of Darius the king,
15 in the s' year of Darius the king.
2:10 month, in the s' year of Darius,
Zec 1: 1 month, in the s' year of Darius,
7 Sebat, in the s' year of Darius,
6: 2 and in the s' chariot black horses;
M't 21:30 came to the s', and said likewise.
22:26 Likewise the s' also, and the third,
39 s' is like unto it, Thou shalt love
26:42 He went away again the s' time,
M'r 12:21 the s' took her, and died, neither
31 the s' is like,...Thou shalt love
14:72 And the s' time the cock crew.
Lu 6: 1 it came to pass on the s' sabbath
12:38 if he shall come in the s' watch, or
19:18 s' came, saying, Lord, thy pound
20:30 the s' took her to wife, and he died
Joh 3: 4 the s' time into his mother's womb,
4:54 again the s' miracle that Jesus did,
21:16 He saith to him again the s' time,
Ac 7:13 the s' time Joseph was made known
10:15 spake unto him again the s' time,
12:10 were past the first and the s' ward,
13:33 as it is also written in the s' psalm,
1Co 15:47 the s' man is the Lord from heaven.
2Co 1:15 that ye might have a s' benefit;
13: 2 as if I were present, the s' time;
subscr. The s' epistle to the Corinthians
2Th *subscr.* The s' epistle to...Thessalonians
2Ti *subscr.* The s' epistle unto Timotheus,
subscr. brought before Nero the s' time.
Tit 3:10 after the first and s' admonition
Heb 8: 7 no place have been sought for the s'.
9: 3 And after the s' veil, the tabernacle
7 into the s' went the high priest
28 he appear the s' time without sin
10: 9 first, that he may establish the s'.
2Pe 3: 1 This s' epistle, beloved, I now write
Re 2:11 shall not be hurt of the s' death.
4: 7 a lion, and the s' beast like a calf,
6: 3 and when he had opened the s' seal,
3 I heard the s' beast say, Come and
8: 8 And the s' angel sounded, and as it
11:14 The s' woe is past; and, behold, the
16: 3 And the s' angel poured out his vial
20: 6 on such the s' death hath no power,
14 lake of fire. This is the s' death.
21: 8 brimstone: which is the s' death.
19 was jasper; the s', sapphire; the

secondarily
1Co 12:28 first apostles, s' prophets, thirdly

secret See also SECRETS.
Ge 49: 6 soul, come not thou into their s';
De 27:15 and putteth it in a s' place.
29:29 s' things belong unto the Lord
J'g 3:19 I have a s' errand unto thee, O
13:18 after my name, seeing it is s'?
1Sa 5: 9 had emerods in their s' parts.
19: 2 and abide in a s' place, and hide
Job 14:13 that thou wouldest keep me s',
15: 8 Hast thou heard the s' of God?
11 is there any s' thing with thee?
20:26 darkness...be hid in his s' places:
29: 4 s' of God was upon my tabernacle:
40:13 and bind their faces in s'.
Ps 10: 8 in the s' places doth he murder
17:12 a young lion lurking in s' places.
18:11 He made darkness his s' place;
19:12 cleanse thou me from s' faults.
25:14 The s' of the Lord is with them
27: 5 in the s' of his tabernacle shall he
31:20 hide them in the s' of thy presence
64: 2 Hide me from the s' counsel of the
4 may shoot in s' at the perfect:
81: 7 thee in the s' place of thunder:
90: 8 thee, our s' sins in the light of thy
91: 1 dwelleth in the s' place of the most
139:15 from thee, when I was made in s',
Pr 3:32 but his s' is with the righteous.
9:17 and bread eaten in s' is pleasant.
21:14 A gift in s' pacifieth anger: and a
25: 9 and discover not a s' to another:
27: 5 rebuke is better than s' love.
Ec 12:14 judgment, with every s' thing,
Ca 2:14 in the s' places of the stairs, let
Isa 3:17 Lord will discover their s' parts.
45: 3 hidden riches of s' places, that
19 I have not spoken in s', in a dark
48:16 I have not spoken in s' from the
Jer 2:34 I have not found it by s' search, but
13:17 weep in s' places for your pride;
23:24 Can any hide himself in s' places
49:10 I have uncovered his s' places, and
La 3:10 in wait, and as a lion in s' places.
Eze 7:22 and they shall pollute my s' place:
28: 3 is no s' that they can hide from
Da 2:18 God of heaven concerning this s';
19 s' revealed unto Daniel in a night
22 revealeth the deep and s' things:
27 s' which the king hath demanded
30 this s' is not revealed to me for
47 seeing thou couldest reveal this s'.
4: 9 and no s' troubleth me, tell me the
Am 3: 7 revealeth his s' unto his servants
M't 6: 4 That thine alms may be in s': and
M't 6: 4 and thy Father which seeth in s'
6 pray to thy Father which is in s';
6 thy Father which seeth in s' shall
18 but unto thy Father which is in s':
18 thy Father, which seeth in s', shall
13:35 things which have been kept s'
24:26 behold, he is in the s' chambers;
M'r 4:22 neither was any thing kept s', but
Lu 8:17 For nothing is s', that shall not
11:33 a candle, putteth it in a s' place,
Joh 7: 4 no man that doeth any thing in s',
10 not openly, but as it were in s'.
18:20 and in s' have I said nothing.
Ro 16:25 was kept s' since the world began,
Eph 5:12 which are done of them in s'.

secretly
Ge 31:27 didst thou flee away s', and steal
De 13: 6 entice thee s', saying, Let us go
27:24 he that smiteth his neighbour s'.
28:57 eat them for want of all things s' in
Jos 2: 1 out of Shittim two men to spy s',
1Sa 18:22 Commune with David s', and say.
23: 9 Saul s' practised mischief against
2Sa 12:12 For thou didst it s': but I will do
2Ki 17: 9 the children of Israel did s' those
Job 4:12 a thing was s' brought to me,
13:10 you, if ye do s' accept persons.
31:27 my heart hath been s' enticed, or
Ps 10: 9 He lieth in wait s' as a lion in his
31:20 shalt keep them s' in a pavilion
Jer 37:17 king asked him s' in his house,
38:16 the king sware s' unto Jeremiah,
40:15 spake to Gedaliah in Mizpah s',
Hab 3:14 was as to devour the poor s'.
Joh 11:28 way, and called Mary her sister s',
19:38 Jesus, but s' for fear of the Jews,

secrets
De 25:11 hand, and taketh him by the s':
Job 11: 6 shew thee the s' of wisdom, that
Ps 44:21 for he knoweth the s' of the heart.
Pr 11:13 A talebearer revealeth s': but he
20:19 about as a talebearer revealeth s':
Da 2:28 a God in heaven that revealeth s',
29 and he that revealeth s' maketh
47 lord of kings, and a revealer of s',
Ro 2:16 God shall judge the s' of men
1Co 14:25 the s' of his heart made manifest:

sect
Ac 5:17 (which is the s' of the Sadducees,)
15: 5 up certain of the s' of the Pharisees
24: 5 ringleader of the s' of the Nazarenes;
26: 5 the most straitest s' of our religion
28:22 for as concerning this s', we know

Secundus (*se-cun'-dus*)
Ac 20: 4 Aristarchus and *S'*; and Gaius

secure
J'g 8:11 the host: for the host was s'.
18: 7 of the Zidonians, quiet and s';
10 ye shall come unto a people s', and
27 a people that were at quiet and s':
Job 11:18 thou shalt be s', because there is
12: 6 and they that provoke God are s';
M't 28:14 will persuade him, and s' you.

securely
Pr 3:29 seeing he dwelleth s' by thee.
Mic 2: 8 pass by s' as men averse from war.

security
Ac 17: 9 when they had taken s' of Jason,

sedition See also SEDITIONS.
Ezr 4:15 that they have moved s' within
19 rebellion and s' have been made
Lu 23:19 for a certain s' made in the city,
25 for s' and murder was cast into
Ac 24: 5 a mover of s' among all the Jews

seditions
Ga 5:20 emulations, wrath, strife, s',

seduce See also SEDUCED; SEDUCETH; SEDUCING.
M'r 13:22 to s', if it were possible, even the
1Jo 2:26 you, concerning them that s' you.
Re 2:20 to teach and to s' my servants to

seduced
2Ki 21: 9 Manasseh s' them to do more evil
Isa 19:13 they have also s' Egypt, even they
Eze 13:10 they have s' my people, saying,

seducers
2Ti 3:13 and s' shall wax worse and worse,

seduceth
Pr 12:26 the way of the wicked s' them.

seducing
1Ti 4: 1 giving heed to s' spirits, and

see^ See also OVERSEE; SAW; SEEING; SEEN; SEEST; SEETH.
Ge 2:19 to s' what he would call them:
8: 8 to s' if the waters were abated
11: 5 Lord came down to s' the city and
12:12 when the Egyptians shall s' thee,
18:21 and s' whether they have done
19:21 unto him, *S'*, I have accepted thee
21:16 me not s' the death of the child.
27: 1 were dim, so that he could not s',
27 *S'*, the smell of my son is as the
31: 5 I s' your father's countenance, that
12 s', all the rams which leap upon the
50 s', God is witness betwixt me and
32:20 me, and afterward I will s' his face;
34: 1 out to s' the daughters of the land,
37:14 s' whether it be well with thy
20 s' what will become of his dreams.
39:14 *S'*, he hath brought in an Hebrew
41:41 *S'*, I have set thee over all the land

Ge 42: 9, 12 to s' the nakedness of the land
43: 3, 5 Ye shall not s' my face, except
44: 23 you, ye shall s' my face no more.
26 for we may not s' the man's face,
34 lest peradventure I s' the evil that
45: 12 behold, your eyes s', and the eyes
24 S' that ye fall not out by the way.
28 I will go and s' him before I die.
48: 10 dim for age, so that he could not s'.
11 I had not thought to s' thy face:
Ex 1: 16 women, and s' them upon the stools;
3: 3 turn aside, and s' this great sight,
4 Lord saw that he turned aside to s',
4: 18 and s' whether they be yet alive.
21 s' that thou do all those wonders
5: 19 did s' that they were in evil case,
6: 1 thou s' what I will do to Pharaoh:
7: 1 S', I have made thee a god to
10: 5 one cannot be able to s' the earth:
28 heed to thyself, s' my face no more;
29 I will s' thy face again no more.
12: 13 when I s' the blood, I will pass over
13: 17 the people repent when they s' war,
14: 13 and s' the salvation of the Lord,
13 s' them again no more for ever.
16: 7 ye shall s' the glory of the Lord; for
29 S', for that the Lord hath given you
32 they may s' the bread wherewith I
22: 8 to s' whether he have put his hand
23: 5 s' the ass of him that hateth thee
31: 2 S', I have called by name Bezaleel
33: 12 S', thou sayest unto me, Bring up
20 he said, Thou canst not s' my face:
20 there shall no man s' me, and live.
23 and thou shalt s' my back parts:
34: 10 art shall s' the work of the Lord:
35: 30 S', the Lord hath called by name
Le 13: 8 the priest s' that, behold, the scab
10 And the priest shall s' him: and,
15 And the priest shall s' the raw flesh,
17 And the priest shall s' him: and,
30 Then the priest shall s' the plague:
14: 36 priest go into it to s' the plague,
36 priest shall go in to s' the house:
20: 17 and s' her nakedness, and she s' his
Nu 4: 20 not go in to s' when the holy things
11: 15 and let me not s' my wretchedness.
23 thou shalt s' now whether my word
13: 18 And s' the land, what it is; and the
14: 23 they shall not s' the land which I
23 any of them that provoked me s' it:
22: 41 that thence he might s' the utmost
23: 9 from the top of the rocks I s' him,
13 from whence thou mayest s' them:
13 thou shalt s' but the utmost part of
13 of them, and shalt not s' them all:
24: 17 I shall s' him, but not now: I shall
27: 12 and s' the land which I have given
32: 8 from Kadesh-barnea to s' the land.
11 shall s' the land which I swear unto
De 1: 35 evil generation s' that good land,
36 son of Jephunneh; he shall s' it, and
3: 25 and s' the good land that is beyond
28 inherit the land...thou shalt s'.
4: 28 which neither s', nor hear, nor eat,
18: 16 neither let me s' this great fire any
22: 1 Thou shalt not s' thy brother's ox
4 Thou shalt not s' thy brother's ass
23: 14 that he s' no unclean thing in thee,
28: 10 s' that thou art called by the name
34, 67 thine eyes which thou shalt s'.
68 Thou shalt s' it no more again: and
29: 4 eyes to s', and ears to hear, unto
22 they s' the plagues of that land,
30: 15 S', I have set before thee this day
32: 20 I will s' what their end shall be: for
39 S' now that I, even I, am he, and
52 thou shalt s' the land before thee;
34: 4 caused thee to s' it with thine eyes,
Jos 3: 3 ye s' the ark of the covenant of the
6: 2 S', I have given into thine hand
8: 1 s', I have given into thine hand the
8 ye do. S', I have commanded you.
22: 10 by Jordan, a great altar to s' to.
J'g 9: 37 said, S' there come people down
14: 8 aside to s' the carcase of the lion:
16: 5 s' wherein his great strength lieth,
21: 21 s', and, behold, if the daughters of
1Sa 2: 32 s' an enemy in my habitation, in
3: 2 to wax dim, that he could not s';
4: 15 eyes were dim, that he could not s'.
6: 9 s', if it goeth up by the way of his
13 saw the ark, and rejoiced to s' it.
10: 24 S' ye him whom the Lord hath
12: 16 stand and s' this great thing, which
17 and s' that your wickedness is great,
14: 17 now, and s' who is gone from us.
29 s', I pray you, how mine eyes have
38 s' wherein this sin hath been this
15: 35 Samuel came no more to s' Saul
17: 28 that thou mightest s' the battle.
19: 3 and what I s', that I will tell thee.
15 the messengers again to s' David,
20: 29 I pray thee, and s' my brethren.
21: 14 servants, Lo, ye s' the man is mad:
23: 22 and s' his place where his haunt is,
23 S' therefore, and take knowledge of
24: 11 s', yea, s' the skirt of thy robe in my
11 and s' that their is neither evil nor
15 s', and plead my cause, and deliver
25: 35 s', I have hearkened to thy voice,
26: 16 s' where the king's spear is, and the
2Sa 3: 13 Thou shalt not s' my face, except
13 when thou comest to s' my face.
7: 2 S' now, I dwell in an house of
13: 5 when thy father cometh to s' thee,

2Sa 13: 5 I may s' it, and eat it at her hand.
6 when the king was come to s' him,
14: 24 house, and let him not s' my face.
30 S', Joab's field is near mine, and he
32 let me s' the king's face: and if
15: 3 S', thy matters are good and right;
28 S', I will tarry in the plain of the
24: 3 eyes of my lord the king may s' it:
13 s' what answer I shall return to him
1Ki 9: 12 came out from Tyre to s' the cities
12: 16 now s' to thine own house, David.
14: 4 Ahijah could not s'; for his eyes
17: 23 and Elijah said, S', thy son liveth.
20: 7 s' how this man seeketh mischief:
22 and mark, and s' what thou doest:
22: 25 Behold, thou shalt s' in that day,
2Ki 2: 10 s' me when I am taken from thee,
3: 14 not look toward thee, nor s' thee.
17 not s' wind, neither shall ye s' rain;
6: 17 thee, open his eyes, that he may s'.
20 eyes of these men, that they may s'.
32 S' ye how this son of a murderer
7: 2 thou shalt s' it with thine eyes, but
13 consumed:) and let us send and s'.
14 of the Syrians, saying, Go and s'.
19 shalt s' it with thine eyes, but shalt
8: 29 Ahaziah...went down to s' Joram
9: 16 Judah was come down to s' Joram.
17 he came, and said, I s' a company.
34 Go, s' now this cursed woman, and
10: 16 me, and s' my zeal for the Lord.
19: 16 open, Lord, thine eyes, and s': and
22: 20 thine eyes shall not s' all the evil
23: 17 he said, What title is that that I s'?
2Ch 10: 16 now, David, s' to thine own house.
18: 16 did s' all Israel scattered upon the
24 Behold, thou shalt s' on that day
20: 17 and s' the salvation of the Lord with
22: 6 Ahaziah...went down to s' Jehoram
24: 5 and s' that ye hasten the matter.
25: 17 let us s' one another in the face.
29: 8 to hissing, as ye s' with your eyes.
30: 7 gave them up to desolation, as ye s'.
34: 28 thine eyes s' all the evil that I will
Ezr 4: 14 for us to s' the king's dishonour,
Ne 2: 17 Ye s' the distress that we are in,
4: 11 They shall not know, neither s', till
9: 9 didst s' the affliction of our fathers
Es 3: 4 to s' whether Mordecai's matters
5: 13 as I s' Mordecai the Jew sitting at
8: 6 For how can I endure to s' the evil
6 to s' the destruction of my kindred?
Job 3: 9 let it s' the dawning of the day:
6: 21 ye s' my casting down, and are
7: 7 mine eye shall no more s' good.
8 seen me shall s' me no more:
9: 11 he goeth by me, and I s' him not:
25 they flee away, they s' no good.
10: 15 therefore s' thou mine affliction;
17: 15 as for my hope, who shall s' it?
19: 26 body, yet in my flesh shall I s' God:
27 Whom I shall s' for myself, and
20: 9 which saw him shall s' him no more:
17 He shall not s' the rivers, the
21: 20 His eyes shall s' his destruction,
22: 11 Or darkness, that thou canst not s';
19 The righteous s' it, and are glad:
23: 9 the right hand, that I cannot s' him:
24: 1 that know him not s' his days?
15 saying, No eye shall s' me:
28: 27 Then did he s' it, and declare it;
31: 4 Doth not he s' my ways, and count
33: 26 and he shall s' his face with joy:
28 pit, and his life shall s' the light.
34: 32 That which I s' not teach thou me:
35: 5 Look unto the heavens, and s';
14 thou sayest thou shalt not s' him,
36: 25 Every man may s' it; man may
37: 21 now men s' not the bright light
Ps 10: 11 hideth his face; he will never s' it.
14: 2 to s' if...any that did understand,
16: 10 thine Holy One to s' corruption.
22: 7 they that s' me laugh me to scorn:
27: 13 to s' the goodness of the Lord in the
31: 11 that did s' me without fled from me.
34: 8 taste and s' that the Lord is good:
12 many days, that he may s' good?
36: 9 life: in thy light shall we s' light.
37: 34 wicked are cut off, thou shalt s' it.
40: 3 many shall s' it, and fear, and shall
41: 6 if he come to s' me, he speaketh
49: 9 live for ever, and not s' corruption.
19 fathers; they shall never s' light.
52: 6 The righteous also shall s', and fear,
53: 2 to s' if...any that did understand,
58: 8 that they may not s' the sun.
59: 10 God shall let me s' my desire upon
63: 2 To s' thy power and thy glory, so as
64: 5 they say, Who shall s' them?
8 all that s' them shall flee away.
66: 5 Come and s' the works of God: he
69: 23 eyes be darkened, that they s' not;
32 humble shall s' this, and be glad:
74: 9 We s' not our signs: there is no
86: 17 that they which hate me may s' it,
89: 48 that liveth, and shall not s' death?
91: 8 and s' the reward of the wicked.
92: 11 s' my desire on mine enemies,
94: 7 The Lord shall not s', neither shall
9 formed the eye, shall he not s'?
97: 6 and all the people s' his glory.
106: 5 That I may s' the good of thy chosen,
107: 24 These s' the works of the Lord, and
42 righteous shall s' it, and rejoice:
112: 8 he s' his desire upon his enemies.
10 wicked shall s' it, and be grieved:

Ps 115: 5 eyes have they, but they s' not:
118: 7 I s' my desire upon them that hate
119: 74 thee will be glad when they s' me;
128: 5 thou shalt s' the good of Jerusalem
6 thou shalt s' thy children's children,
135: 16 eyes have they, but they s' not;
139: 16 Thine eyes did s' my substance,
24 s' if there be any wicked way in me,
Pr 24: 18 Lest the Lord s' it, and it displease
29: 16 but the righteous shall s' their fall.
Ec 1: 10 it may be said, S', this is new?
2: 3 till I might s' what was that good
3: 18 s' that they themselves are beasts.
22 him to s' what shall be after him?
7: 11 is profit to them that s' the sun.
8: 16 and to s' the business that is done
Ca 2: 14 let me s' thy countenance, let me
6: 11 of nuts to s' the fruits of the valley,
11 to s' whether the vine flourished,
13 What will ye s' in the Shulamite?
7: 12 let us s' if the vine flourish,
Isa 5: 19 hasten his work, that we may s' it:
6: 9 and s' ye indeed, but perceive not.
10 lest they s' with their eyes, and hear
13: 1 Isaiah the son of Amoz did s'.
14: 16 that s' thee shall narrowly look
18: 3 s' ye, when he lifteth up an ensign
26: 11 hand is lifted up, they will not s':
11 but they shall s', and be ashamed
29: 18 the blind shall s' out of obscurity,
30: 10 Which say to the seers, S' not;
20 but thine eyes shall s' thy teachers:
32: 3 eyes of them that s' shall not be dim,
33: 17 eyes shall s' the king in his beauty:
19 Thou shalt not s' a fierce people,
20 s' Jerusalem a quiet habitation,
35: 2 they shall s' the glory of the Lord,
37: 17 open thine eyes, O Lord, and s':
38: 11 I said, I shall not s' the Lord, even
40: 5 and all flesh shall s' it together:
41: 20 That they may s', and know, and
42: 18 and look, ye blind, that ye may s'.
44: 9 they s' not, nor know; that they
18 shut their eyes, that they cannot s':
48: 6 Thou hast heard, s' all this; and
49: 7 Kings shall s' and arise, princes
52: 8 for they shall s' eye to eye, when
10 shall s' the salvation of our God.
15 had not been told them shall they s';
53: 2 when we...s' him, there is no beauty
10 he shall s' his seed, he shall prolong
11 He shall s' of the travail of his soul,
60: 4 up thine eyes round about, and s':
5 Then thou shalt s', and flow
61: 9 all that s' them shall acknowledge
62: 2 Gentiles shall s' thy righteousness,
64: 9 s', we beseech thee, we are all thy
66: 14 when ye s' this, your heart shall
18 they shall come, and s' my glory.
Jer 1: 10 S', I have this day set thee over the
11 I said, I s' a rod of an almond tree.
13 And I said, I s' a seething pot; and
2: 10 over the isles of Chittim, and s';
10 and s' if there be such a thing.
19 s' that it is an evil thing and bitter,
23 s' thy way in the valley, know what
31 O generation, s' ye the word of the
3: 2 and s' where thou hast not been lien
4: 21 How long shall I s' the standard,
5: 1 s' now, and know, and seek in the
12 shall we s' sword nor famine:
21 which have eyes, and s' not; which
6: 16 Stand ye in the ways, and s', and
7: 12 s' what I did to it for the wickedness
11: 20 let me s' thy vengeance on them:
12: 4 said, He shall not s' our last end.
14: 13 Ye shall not s' the sword, neither
17: 6 and shall not s' when good cometh;
8 and shall not s' when heat cometh,
20: 12 let me s' thy vengeance on them:
18 the womb to s' labour and sorrow,
22: 10 no more, nor s' his native country.
12 and shall s' this land no more.
23: 24 secret places that I shall not s' him?
30: 6 and s' whether a man doth travail
6 do I s' every man with his hands
42: 14 Egypt, where we shall s' no war,
18 and ye shall s' this place no more.
51: 61 and shalt s', and shalt read all these
La 1: 11 s', O Lord, and consider; for I am
12 s' if there be any sorrow like unto
Eze 8: 6 thou shalt s' greater abominations.
13, 15 shalt s' greater abominations
12: 2 which have eyes to s', and s' not;
6 face, that thou s' not the ground:
12 he s' not the ground with his eyes.
13 shall he not s' it, though he...die
13: 9 upon the prophets that s' vanity,
16 which s' visions of peace for her,
23 ye shall s' no more vanity, nor
14: 22 s' their way and their doings:
23 ye s' their ways and their doings:
16: 37 they may s' all thy nakedness.
20: 48 flesh shall s' that I the Lord have
21: 29 Whiles they s' vanity unto thee,
32: 31 Pharaoh shall s' them, and shall
33: 6 the watchman s' the sword come,
39: 21 heathen shall s' my judgment that
Da 1: 10 should he s' your faces worse liking
2: 8 ye s' the thing is gone from me.
3: 25 Lo, I s' four men loose, walking in
5: 23 which s' not, nor hear, nor know:
Joe 2: 28 your young men shall s' visions:
Am 6: 2 Pass ye unto Calneh, and s'; and
Jon 4: 5 s' what would become of the city.
Mic 6: 9 man of wisdom shall s' thy name:

Mic 7:10 she that is mine enemy shall s' it,
16 nations shall s' and be confounded
Hab 1: 1 Habakkuk the prophet did s'.
2: 1 to s' what he will say unto me,
Zep 3:15 thou shalt not s' evil any more.
Hag 2: 3 how do ye s' it now? is it not in
Zec 2: 2 s' what is the breadth thereof, and
4:10 shall s' the plummet in the hand of
5: 2 And I answered, I s' a flying roll;
5 s' what is this that goeth forth.
9: 5 Askelon shall s' it, and fear;
5 Gaza also shall s' it, and be very
10: 7 yea, their children shall s' it, and
Mal 1: 5 your eyes shall s', and ye shall say,
M't 5: 8 in heart: for they shall s' God.
16 that they may s' your good works,
7: 5 then shalt thou s' clearly to cast
8: 4 unto him, S' thou tell no man;
9:30 saying, S' that no man know it.
11: 4 things which ye do hear and s':
7 ye out into the wilderness to s'?
8, 9 But what went ye out for to s'?
12:38 we would s' a sign from thee.
13:13 because they seeing s' not; and
14 and seeing ye shall s', and shall not
15 they should s' with their eyes,
16 blessed are your eyes, for they s':
17 have desired to s' those things
17 those things which ye s', and have
15:31 lame to walk, and the blind to s':
16:28 till they s' the Son of man coming
22:11 the king came in to s' the guests,
23:39 Ye shall not s' me henceforth, till
24: 2 them, S' ye not all these things?
6 s' that ye be not troubled: for all
15 s' the abomination of desolation,
30 shall s' the Son of man coming in
33 when ye shall s' all these things,
26:58 sat with the servants, to s' the end.
64 s' the Son of man sitting on the
27: 4 What is that to us? s' thou to that.
24 blood of this just person: s' ye to it.
49 s' whether Elias will come to save
28: 1 the other Mary to s' the sepulchre.
6 s' the place where the Lord lay.
7 there shall ye s' him: lo, I have
10 Galilee, and there shall they s' me.
M'r 1:44 S' thou say nothing to any man:
4:12 That seeing they may s', and not
5:14 to s' what it was that was done.
15 s' him that was possessed with
32 to s' her that had done this thing.
6:38 many loaves have ye? go and s'.
8:18 Having eyes, s' ye not? and having
24 and said, I s' men as trees, walking.
12:15 bring me a penny, that I may s' it.
13: 1 s' what manner of stones and
14 s' the abomination of desolation,
26 shall they s'...Son of man coming
29 shall s' these things come to pass,
14:62 s' the Son of man sitting on the
15:32 cross, that we may s' and believe.
36 s' whether Elias will come to take
16: 7 there shall ye s' him, as he said
Lu 2:15 and s' this thing which is come to
26 that he should not s' death, before
3: 6 flesh shall s' the salvation of God.
6:42 thou s' clearly to pull out the mote
7:22 that the blind s', the lame walk,
24 out into the wilderness for to s'?
25, 26 But what went ye out to s'?
8:10 that seeing they might not s', and
16 they which enter in may s' the light.
20 stand without, desiring to s' thee.
35 they went out to s' what was done;
9: 9 things? And he desired to s' him.
27 till they s' the kingdom of God.
10:23 eyes which s' the things that ye s':
24 have desired to s' those things
24 those things which ye s', and have
11:33 they which come in may s' the light.
12:54 ye s' a cloud rise out of the west,
55 when ye s' the south wind blow, ye
13:28 ye shall s' Abraham, and Isaac,
35 Ye shall not s' me, until the time
14:18 and I must needs go and s' it:
17:22 desire to s' one of the days of the
22 Son of man, and ye shall not s' it.
23 they shall say to you, S' here; or,
23 s' there: go not after them, nor
19: 3 he sought to s' Jesus who he was;
4 up into a sycomore tree to s' him:
20:13 reverence him when they s' him.
21:20 shall s' Jerusalem compassed with
27 shall they s'...Son of man coming
30 ye s' and know of your own selves
31 ye s' these things come to pass,
23: 8 desirous to s' him of a long season,
24:39 it is I myself: handle me, and s';
39 flesh and bones, as ye s' me have.
Joh 1:33 thou shalt s' the Spirit descending,
39 He saith unto them, Come and s'.
46 Philip saith unto him, Come and s'.
50 shalt s' greater things than these.
51 Hereafter ye shall s' heaven open,
3: 3 he cannot s' the kingdom of God.
36 not the Son shall not s' life; but
4:29 s' a man, which told me all things
48 Except ye s' signs and wonders, ye
6:19 they s' Jesus walking on the sea,
30 that we may s', and believe thee?
62 ye shall s' the Son of man ascend
7: 3 thy disciples also may s' the works
8:51 my saying, he shall never s' death.
56 Abraham rejoiced to s' my day:
9:15 mine eyes, and I washed, and do s'
Joh 9:19 blind? how then doth he now s'?
25 that, whereas I was blind, now I s'.
39 that they which s' not might s'; and
39 they which s' might be made blind.
41 but now ye say, We s'; therefore
11:34 said unto him, Lord, come and s'.
40 thou shouldest s' the glory of God?
12: 9 that they might s' Lazarus also,
21 him, saying, Sir, we would s' Jesus.
40 they should not s' with their eyes,
14:19 seeth me no more: but ye s' me:
16:10 my Father, and ye s' me no more;
16 little while, and ye shall not s' me:
16 a little while, and ye shall s' me,
17 while, and ye shall not s' me: and
17 a little while, and ye shall s' me:
19 while, and ye shall not s' me: and
19 a little while, and ye shall s' me?
22 but I will s' you again, and your
18:26 Did not I s' thee in the garden with
20:25 I shall s' in his hands the print of
Ac 2:17 your young men shall s' visions,
27 thine Holy One to s' corruption.
31 neither his flesh did s' corruption.
33 this, which ye now s' and hear.
3:16 strong, whom ye s' and know:
7:56 I s' the heavens opened, and the
8:36 eunuch said, S', here is water;
13:35 thine Holy One to s' corruption.
15:36 word of the Lord, and s' how they do.
19:21 been there, I must also s' Rome.
26 Moreover ye s' and hear, that not
20:25 of God, shall s' my face no more.
38 they should s' his face no more.
22:11 I could not s' for the glory of that
14 his will, and s' that Just One,
23:22 S' thou tell no man that thou hast
25:24 ye s' this man, about whom all the
28:20 have I called for you, to s' you, and
26 and seeing ye shall s', and not
27 lest they should s' with their eyes,
Ro 1:11 I long to s' you, that I may impart
7:23 I s' another law in my members,
8:25 But if we hope for that we s' not,
11: 8 eyes that they should not s', and ears
10 be darkened, that they may not s',
15:21 he was not spoken of, they shall s':
24 for I trust to s' you in my journey,
1Co 1:26 For ye s' your calling, brethren,
8:10 For if any man s' thee which hast
13:12 now we s' through a glass, darkly;
16: 7 I will not s' you now by the way;
10 s' that he may be...without fear:
2Co 8: 7 s' that ye abound in this grace also.
Ga 1:18 went up to Jerusalem to s' Peter,
6:11 Ye s' how large a letter I have
Eph 3: 9 all men s' what is the fellowship
5:15 S' then that ye walk circumspectly,
Ph'p 1:27 whether I come and s' you, or else
2:23 as I shall s' how it will go with me.
28 that, when ye s' him again, ye may
1Th 2:17 more abundantly to s' your face
3: 6 always, desiring greatly to s' us,
6 us, as we also to s' you:
10 praying...that we might s' your face,
5:15 S' that none render evil for evil
1Ti 6:16 whom no man hath seen, nor can s':
2Ti 1: 4 Greatly desiring to s' thee, being
Heb 2: 8 s' not yet all things put under him.
9 we s' Jesus, who was made a little
3:19 So we s' that they could not enter in
8: 5 S', saith he, that thou make all
10:25 more, as ye s' the day approaching.
11: 5 that he should not s' death;
12:14 which no man shall s' the Lord:
25 S'...ye refuse not him that speaketh.
13:23 if he come shortly, I will s' you.
Jas 2:24 Ye s' then how that by works a
1Pe 1: 8 in whom, though now ye s' him not,
22 s' that ye love one another with a
3:10 that will love life, and s' good days.
2Pe 1: 9 is blind, and cannot s' afar off,
1Jo 3: 2 him; for we shall s' him as he is.
5:16 If any man s' his brother sin a sin
3Jo 14 But I trust I shall shortly s' thee,
Re 1: 7 and every eye shall s' him, and
12 to s' the voice that spake with me.
3:18 with eyesalve, that thou mayest s'.
6: 1 the four beasts saying, Come and s'.
3 the second beast say, Come and s'.
5 the third beast say, Come and s'.
6 s' thou hurt not the oil and the wine.
7 the fourth beast say, Come and s'.
9:20 which neither can s', nor hear, nor
11: 9 shall s' their dead bodies three days
16:15 walk naked, and they s' his shame.
18: 7 no widow, and shall s' no sorrow.
9 shall s' the smoke of her burning,
19:10 he said unto me, S' thou do it not:
22: 4 And they shall s' his face; and his
9 saith he unto me, S' thou do it not:
seed See also SEED'S; SEEDS; SEEDTIME.
Ge 1:11 the herb yielding s', and the fruit
11 after his kind, whose s' is in itself,
12 and herb yielding s' after his kind,
12 yielding fruit, whose s' was in itself,
29 given you every herb bearing s',
29 is the fruit of a tree yielding s';
3:15 and between thy s' and her s';
4:25 appointed me another s' instead of
7: 3 to keep s' alive upon the face of all
9: 9 with you, and with your s' after you;
12: 7 Unto thy s' will I give this land:
13:15 will I give it, and to thy s' for ever.
16 I will make thy s' as the dust of the
16 then shall thy s' also be numbered.
Ge 15: 3 Behold, to me thou hast given no s':
5 said unto him, So shall thy s' be.
13 thy s' shall be a stranger in a land
18 Unto thy s' have I given this land,
16:10 I will multiply thy s' exceedingly,
17: 7 between me and thee and thy s'
7 unto thee, and to thy s' after thee.
8 unto thee, and to thy s' after thee,
9 thou, and thy s' after thee in their
10 between me and you and thy s'
12 any stranger, which is not of thy s'.
19 covenant, and with his s' after him.
19:32, 34 may preserve s' of our father.
21:12 for in Isaac shall thy s' be called.
13 make a nation, because he is thy s'.
22:17 I will multiply thy s' as the stars of
17 thy s' shall possess the gate of his
18 And in thy s' shall all the nations of
24: 7 Unto thy s' will I give this land;
60 let thy s' possess the gate of those
26: 3 for unto thee, and unto thy s', I will
4 make thy s' to multiply as the stars
4 give unto thy s' all these countries;
4 and in thy s' shall all the nations of
24 and multiply thy s' for my servant
28: 4 to thee, and to thy s' with thee;
13 to thee will I give it, and to thy s';
14 And thy s' shall be as the dust of
14 and in thy s' shall all the families
32:12 make thy s' as the sand of the sea,
35:12 to thy s' after thee will I give the
38: 8 her, and raise up s' to thy brother.
9 knew that the s' should not be his;
9 that he should give s' to his brother.
46: 6 Jacob, and all his s' with him:
7 all his s' brought he with him into
47:19 give us s', that we may live, and not
23 here is s' for you, and ye shall sow
24 for s' of the field, and for your food,
48: 4 and will give this land to thy s' after
11 lo, God hath shewed me also thy s'.
19 his s' shall become a multitude of
Ex 16:31 and it was like coriander s', white;
28:43 statute for ever unto him and his s'
30:21 to him and to his s' throughout
32:13 I will multiply your s' as the stars
13 spoken of will I give unto your s',
33: 1 saying, Unto thy s' will I give it:
Le 11:37 carcase fall upon any sowing s'
38 But if any water be put upon the s',
12: 2 If a woman have conceived s', and
15:16 any man's s' of copulation go out
17 whereon is the s' of copulation,
18 man shall lie with s' of copulation,
32 him whose s' goeth from him,
18:21 any of thy s' pass through the fire
19:19 not sow thy field with mingled s':
20: 2 giveth any of his s' unto Molech;
3 he hath given of his s' unto Molech,
4 he giveth of his s' unto Molech,
21:15 Neither shall he profane his s'
17 saying, Whosoever he be of thy s'
21 hath a blemish of the s' of Aaron
22: 3 Whosoever he be of all your s'
4 What man soever of the s' of Aaron
4 man whose s' goeth from him;
26:16 and ye shall sow your s' in vain, for
27:16 estimation...be according to the s'
16 homer of barley s' shall be valued
30 whether of the s' of the land, or of
Nu 5:28 shall be free, and shall conceive s'.
11: 7 And the manna was as coriander s',
14:24 he went; and his s' shall possess it.
16:40 which is not of the s' of Aaron,
18:19 unto thee and to thy s' with thee.
20: 5 it is no place of s', or of figs, or of
24: 7 and his s' shall be in many waters,
25:13 shall have it, and his s' after him,
De 1: 8 unto them and to their s' after them.
4:37 he chose their s' after them, and
10:15 and he chose their s' after them,
11: 9 to give unto them and to their s', a
10 where thou sowedst thy s', and
14:22 truly tithe all the increase of thy s',
22: 9 fruit of thy s' which thou hast sown,
28:38 carry much s' out into the field,
46 a wonder, and upon thy s' for ever.
59 the plagues of thy s', even great
30: 6 thine heart, and the heart of thy s',
19 that both thou and thy s' may live:
31:21 out of the mouths of their s':
34: 4 saying, I will give it unto thy s':
Jos 24: 3 of Canaan, and multiplied his s',
Ru 4:12 s' which the Lord shall give thee
1Sa 2:20 The Lord give thee s' of this woman
8:15 he will take the tenth of your s',
20:42 between my s' and thy s' for ever.
24:21 thou wilt not cut off my s' after me,
2Sa 4: 8 king this day of Saul, and of his s',
7:12 I will set up thy s' after thee, which
22:51 David, and to his s' for evermore.
1Ki 2:33 and upon the head of his s' for ever:
33 but upon David, and upon his s',
11:14 he was of the king's s' in Edom.
39 I will for this afflict the s' of David,
18:32 would contain two measures of s'.
2Ki 5:27 unto thee, and unto thy s' for ever.
11: 1 arose and destroyed all the s' royal.
17:20 the Lord rejected all the s' of Israel,
25:25 the son of Elishama, of the s' royal,
1Ch 16:13 O ye s' of Israel his servant, ye
17:11 that I will raise up thy s' after thee,
2Ch 20: 7 gavest it to the s' of Abraham thy
22:10 arose and destroyed all the s' royal
Ezr 2:59 their father's house, and their s',
9: 2 holy s' have mingled themselves

Ne 7:61 their father's house, nor their s'
9: 2 s' of Israel separated themselves
8 to give it, I say, to his s', and hast
Es 6:13 If Mordecai be of the s' of the Jews,
9:27 took upon them, and upon their s',
28 memorial...perish from their s'.
31 for themselves and for their s',
10: 3 and speaking peace to all his s'.
Job 5:25 know also that thy s' shall be great,
21: 8 Their s' is established in their sight
39:12 that he will bring home thy s', and
Ps 18:50 David, and to his s' for evermore.
21:10 s' from among the children of men.
22:23 all ye the s' of Jacob, glorify him;
23 and fear him, all ye the s' of Israel.
30 A s' shall serve him; it shall be
25:13 and his s' shall inherit the earth.
37:25 forsaken, nor his s' begging bread.
26 and lendeth; and his s' is blessed.
28 the s' of the wicked shall be cut off.
69:36 s' also of his servants shall inherit
89: 4 Thy s' will I establish for ever, and
29 His s' also will I make to endure for
36 His s' shall endure for ever, and his
102:28 their s' shall be established before
105: 6 O ye s' of Abraham his servant, ye
106:27 overthrow their s' also among the
112: 2 His s' shall be mighty upon earth;
126: 6 and weepeth, bearing precious s',
Pr 11:21 but the s' of the righteous shall be
Ec 11: 6 In the morning sow thy s', and in
Isa 1: 4 a s' of evildoers, children that are
5:10 s' of an homer shall yield an ephah.
6:13 so the holy s' shall be the substance
14:20 the s' of evildoers shall never be
17:11 shalt thou make thy s' to flourish:
23: 3 by great waters the s' of Sihor, the
30:23 shall he give the rain of thy s', that
41: 8 the s' of Abraham my friend.
43: 5 I will bring thy s' from the east,
44: 3 I will pour my spirit upon thy s',
45:19 I said not unto the s' of Jacob, Seek
25 If the Lord shall all the s' of Israel
48:19 Thy s' also had been as the sand,
53:10 he shall see his s', he shall prolong
54: 3 thy s' shall inherit the Gentiles,
55:10 that it may give s' to the sower,
57: 3 s' of the adulterer and the whore.
4 of transgression, a s' of falsehood,
59:21 nor out of the mouth of thy s',
21 nor of the mouth of thy seed's s',
61: 9 their s' shall be known among the
9 the s' which the Lord hath blessed.
65: 9 I will bring forth a s' out of Jacob,
23 are the s' of the blessed of the Lord,
66:22 your s' and your name remain.
Jer 2:21 thee a noble vine, wholly a right s':
7:15 even the whole s' of Ephraim.
22:28 are they cast out, he and his s', and
30 for no man of his s' shall prosper,
23: 8 led the s' of the house of Israel out
29:32 Shemaiah the Nehelamite,...his s':
30:10 s' from the land of their captivity;
31:27 s' of man, and with the s' of beast.
36 s' of Israel also shall cease from
37 cast off all the s' of Israel for all
33:22 will I multiply the s' of David my
26 will I cast away the s' of Jacob,
26 I will not take any of his s' to be
26 to be rulers over the s' of Abraham,
35: 7 nor sow s', nor plant vineyard,
9 have we vineyard, nor field, nor s':
36:31 I will punish him and his s' and his
41: 1 the son of Elishama, of the s' royal,
46:27 s' from the land of their captivity;
49:10 his s' is spoiled, and his brethren,
Eze 17: 5 He took also of the s' of the land,
13 And hath taken of the king's s', and
20: 5 unto the s' of the house of Jacob,
43:19 Levites that be of the s' of Zadok,
44:22 of the s' of the house of Israel,
Da 1: 3 of the king's s', and of the princes;
2:43 themselves with the s' of men:
9: 1 Ahasuerus, of the s' of the Medes,
Joe 1:17 The s' is rotten under their clods,
Am 9:13 of grapes him that soweth s';
Hag 2:19 Is the s' yet in the barn? yea, as
Zec 8:12 For the s' shall be prosperous; the
Mal 2: 3 I will corrupt your s', and spread
15 one? That he might seek a godly s'.
M't 13:19 which received s' by the way side.
20 received the s' into stony places,
22 that received s' among the thorns
23 received s' into the good ground
24 which sowed good s' in his field:
27 not thou sow good s' in thy field?
31 heaven is like to a grain of mustard s',
37 the good s' is the Son of man;
38 the good s' are the children of the
17:20 ye have faith as a grain of mustard s',
22:24 and raise up s' unto his brother.
M'r 4:26 should cast s' into the ground;
27 the s' should spring and grow up,
31 It is like a grain of mustard s',
12:19 and raise up s' unto his brother.
20 took a wife, and dying left no s'.
21 her, and died, neither left he any s':
22 the seven had her, and left no s':
Lu 1:55 to Abraham, and to his s' for ever.
8: 5 A sower went out to sow his s':
11 is this: The s' is the word of God.
13:19 It is like a grain of mustard s', which
17: 6 ye had faith as a grain of mustard s',
20:28 and raise up s' unto his brother.
Joh 7:42 Christ cometh of the s' of David,
8:33 We be Abraham's s', and were

Joh 8:37 I know that ye are Abraham's s';
Ac 3:25 in thy s' shall all the kindreds of
7: 5 possession, and to his s' after him,
6 his s' should sojourn in a strange
13:23 Of this man's s' hath God according
Ro 1: 3 which was made of the s' of David
4:13 was not to Abraham, or to his s',
16 promise might be sure to all the s';
18 was spoken, So shall thy s' be.
9: 7 because they are the s' of Abraham,
7 but, In Isaac shall thy s' be called.
8 the promise are counted for the s'.
29 the Lord of Sabaoth had left us a s',
11: 1 an Israelite, of the s' of Abraham,
1Co 15:38 him, and to every s' his own body.
2Co 9:10 he that ministereth s' to the sower
10 food, and multiply your s' sown,
11:22 Are they the s' of Abraham? so am
Ga 3:16 and his s' were the promises made.
16 one, And to thy s', which is Christ.
19 till the s' should come to whom the
29 Christ's, then are ye Abraham's s',
2Ti 2: 8 Jesus Christ of the s' of David was
Heb 2:16 he took on him the s' of Abraham.
11:11 received strength to conceive s',
18 That in Isaac shall thy s' be called:
1Pe 1:23 born again, not of corruptible s',
1Jo 3: 9 for his s' remaineth in him: and
Re 12:17 war with the remnant of her s',

seed's
Isa 59:21 out of the mouth of thy s' seed,

seeds
De 22: 9 not sow thy vineyard with divers s':
M't 13: 4 some s' fell by the way side, and the
32 which indeed is the least of all s':
M'r 4:31 is less than all the s' that be in the
Ga 3:16 He saith not, And to s', as of many;

seedtime
Ge 8:22 s' and harvest, and cold and heat,

seeing^ See also FORESEEING.
Ge 15: 2 wilt thou give me, s' I go childless,
18:18 s' that Abraham shall surely become a
19: 1 Lot s' them rose up to meet them;
24:56 s' the Lord hath prospered my way;
28: 8 And Esau s' that the daughters of
44:30 s' that his life is bound up in the lad's
Ex 4:11 the dumb, or the deaf, or the s',
21: 8 s' he hath dealt deceitfully with her.
22:10 hurt, or driven away, no man s' it:
23: 9 s' ye were strangers in the land of
Le 10:17 in the holy place, s' it is most holy,
Nu 15:26 s' all the people were in ignorance.
16: 3 you, s' all the congregation are holy,
35:23 s' him not, and cast it upon him,
Jos 17:14 to inherit, s' I am a great people,
22:18 s' ye rebel to day against the Lord,
J'g 13:18 thus after my name, s' it is secret?
17:13 s' I have a Levite to my priest.
19:23 s' that this man is come into mine
21: 7 s' we have sworn by the Lord that
16 s' the women are destroyed out of
Ru 1:21 s' the Lord hath testified against me,
2:10 knowledge of me, s' I am a stranger?
1Sa 16: 1 s' I have rejected him from reigning
17:36 s' he hath defied the armies of the
18:23 s' that I am a poor man, and lightly
24: 6 him, s' he is the anointed of the Lord.
25:26 s' the Lord hath withholden thee from
28:16 s' the Lord is departed from thee, and
2Sa 13:39 concerning Amnon, s' he was dead.
15:20 s' I go whither I may, return thou,
18:22 s' that thou hast no tidings ready?
19:11 s' the speech of all Israel is come to
1Ki 1:48 this day, mine eyes even s' it.
11:28 Solomon s' the young man that
2Ki 10: 2 s' your master's sons are with you,
1Ch 12:17 s' there is no wrong in my hands, the
2Ch 2: 6 s' the heaven and heaven of heavens
Ezr 9:13 s' that thou our God hast punished
Ne 2: 2 countenance sad, s' thou art not sick?
Job 14: 5 S' his days are determined, the
19:28 s' the root of the matter is found in
21:22 s' he judgeth those that are high.
34 s' in your answers there remaineth
28:21 S' it is hid from the eyes of all living,
Ps 22: 8 deliver him, s' he delighted in him.
50:17 S' thou hatest instruction, and castest
Pr 17:16 get wisdom, s' he hath no heart to it?
20:12 The hearing ear, and the s' eye,
Ec 1: 8 the eye is not satisfied with s', nor
2:16 s' that which now is in the days to
6:11 S' there be many things that
Isa 21: 3 it; I was dismayed at the s' of it.
33:15 and shutteth his eyes from s' evil;
42:20 S' many things, but thou observest
49:21 S' I have lost my children, and am
Jer 11:15 s' she hath wrought lewdness with
47: 7 s' the Lord hath given it a charge
Eze 16:30 s' thou doest all these things, the
17:18 S' he despised the oath by breaking
21: 4 S' then that I will cut off from
22:28 s' vanity, and divining lies unto
Da 2:47 s' thou couldest reveal this secret.
Ho 4: 6 s' thou hast forgotten the law of thy
M't 5: 1 s' the multitudes, he went up into
9: 2 Jesus s' their faith said unto the
13:13 parables: because they s' see not;
14 s' ye shall see, and shall not perceive:
M'r 4:12 s' they may see, and not perceive;
11:13 s' a fig tree afar off having leaves,
Lu 1:34 shall this be, s' I know not a man?
5:12 who s' Jesus fell on his face, and
8:10 s' they might not see, and hearing
23:40 s' thou art in the...condemnation?

Joh 2:18 us, s' that thou doest these things?
9: 7 therefore, and washed, and came s'.
21:21 Peter s' him saith to Jesus, Lord,
Ac 2:15 s' it is but the third hour of the day.
31 He s' this before spake of the
3: 3 Who s' Peter and John about to go
7:24 And s' one of them suffer wrong, he
8: 6 and s' the miracles which he did.
9: 7 hearing a voice, but s' no man.
13:11 blind, not s' the sun for a season.
46 but s' ye put it from you, and judge
16:27 s' the prison doors open, he drew
17:24 s' that he is Lord of heaven and
25 s' he giveth to all life, and breath,
19:36 S' then that these things cannot be
24: 2 S' that by thee we enjoy great
28:26 and s' ye shall see, and not perceive:
Ro 3:30 S' it is one God, which shall justify
1Co 14:16 s' he understandeth not what thou
2Co 3:12 S' then that we have such hope, we
4: 1 s' we have this ministry, as we have
11:18 S' that many glory after the flesh,
19 gladly, s' ye yourselves are wise.
Col 3: 9 s' that ye have put off the old man
2Th 1: 6 S' it is a righteous thing with God
Heb 4: 6 S' therefore it remaineth that some
14 S' then that we have a great high
5:11 uttered, s' ye are dull of hearing.
6: 6 s' they crucify to themselves the Son
7:25 s' he ever liveth to make intercession
8: 4 s' that there are priests that offer
11:27 endured, as s' him who is invisible.
12: 1 s' we also are compassed about
1Pe 1:22 S' ye have purified your souls in
2Pe 2: 8 among them, in s' and hearing,
3:11 S' then that all these things shall be
14 s' that ye look for such things, be
17 s' ye know these things before,

seek See also SEEKEST; SEEKETH; SEEKING; SOUGHT.
Ge 37:16 I s' my brethren: tell me, I pray
43:18 that he may s' occasion against us,
Le 13:36 priest shall not s' for yellow hair;
19:31 neither s' after wizards, to be
Nu 15:39 ye s' not after your own heart and
16:10 thee: and s' ye the priesthood also?
24: 1 times, to s' for enchantments,
De 4:29 thou shalt s' the Lord thy God,
29 if thou s' him with all thy heart
12: 5 even unto his habitation shall ye s',
22: 2 thee until thy brother s' after it,
23: 6 Thou shalt not s' their peace nor
Ru 3: 1 shall I not s' rest for thee, that it
1Sa 9: 3 with thee, and arise, go s' the asses.
10: 2 which thou wentest to s' are found:
14 And he said, To s' the asses: and
16:16 to s' out a man, who is a cunning
23:15 Saul was come out to s' his life:
25 Saul...and his men went to s' him.
24: 2 went to s' David and his men upon
25:26 they that s' evil to my lord, be as
29 to pursue thee, and to s' thy soul:
26: 2 s' David in the wilderness of Ziph.
20 of Israel is come out to s' a flea, as
27: 1 to s' me any more in any coast of
28: 7 S' me a woman that hath a
2Sa 5:17 the Philistines came up to s' David;
1Ki 2:40 Gath to Achish to s' his servants:
18:10 my lord hath not sent to s' thee:
19:10, 14 they s' my life, to take it away.
2Ki 2:16 go, we pray thee, and s' thy master:
6:19 bring you to the man whom ye s'.
1Ch 4:39 valley, to s' pasture for their flocks.
14: 8 the Philistines went up to s' David.
16:10 of them rejoice that s' the Lord.
11 S' the Lord and his strength,
11 strength, s' his face continually.
22:19 your soul to s' the Lord your God;
28: 8 s' for all the commandments of the
9 if thou s' him, he will be found of
2Ch 7:14 s' my face, and turn from their
11:16 set their hearts to s' the Lord God
12:14 prepared not his heart to s' the
14: 4 commanded Judah to s' the Lord
15: 2 if ye s' him, he will be found of you;
12 into a covenant to s' the Lord God
13 whosoever would not s' the Lord
19: 3 hast prepared thine heart to s' God.
20: 3 and set himself to s' the Lord, and
4 of Judah they came to s' the Lord.
30:19 prepareth his heart to s' God, the
31:21 the commandments, to s' his God,
34: 3 began to s' after the God of David
Ezr 4: 2 for we s' your God, as ye do; and we
6:21 land, to s' the Lord God of Israel,
7:10 his heart to s' the law of the Lord,
8:21 to s' of him a right way for us, and
22 upon all them for good that s' him:
9:12 nor s' their peace or their wealth
Ne 2:10 to s' the welfare of the children of
Job 5: 8 I would s' unto God, and unto God
7:21 thou shalt s' me in the morning,
8: 5 If thou wouldest s' unto God
20:10 children shall s' to please the poor,
Ps 4: 2 love vanity, and s' after leasing?
9:10 not forsaken them that s' thee.
10: 4 countenance, will not s' after God:
15 s' out his wickedness till thou find
14: 2 that did understand, and s' God.
22:26 shall praise the Lord that s' him:
24: 6 the generation of them that s' him,
6 him, that s' thy face, O Jacob.
27: 4 of the Lord, that will I s' after;
8 When thou saidst, S' ye my face;
8 unto thee, Thy face, Lord, will I s'.
34:10 that s' the Lord shall not want

Ps 34:14 do good; s· peace, and pursue it.
35: 4 put to shame that s· after my soul:
38:12 s· after my life lay snares for me:
12 that s· my hurt speak mischievous
40:14 that s· after my soul to destroy it;
16 Let all those that s· thee rejoice
53: 2 did understand, that did s· God.
54: 3 and oppressors s· after my soul:
63: 1 art my God; early will I s· thee:
9 those that s· my soul, to destroy
69: 6 those that s· thee be confounded
32 your heart shall live that s· God.
70: 2 confounded that s· after my soul:
4 all those that s· thee rejoice and be
71:13 and dishonour that s· my hurt.
24 unto shame, that s· my hurt.
83:16 that they may s· thy name, O Lord.
104:21 prey, and s· their meat from God.
105: 3 of them rejoice that s· the Lord.
4 S· the Lord, and his strength:
4 strength: s· his face evermore.
109:10 let them s· their bread also out of
119: 2 that s· him with the whole heart.
45 at liberty: for I s· thy precepts.
155 wicked: for they s· not thy statutes.
176 s· thy servant; for I do not forget
122: 9 the Lord our God I will s· thy good.
Pr 1:28 they shall s· me early, but they
7:15 diligently to s· thy face, and I have
8:17 those that s· me early shall find me.
21: 6 to and fro of them that s· death.
23:30 they that go to s· mixed wine.
35 shall I awake? I will s· it yet again.
28: 5 they that s· the Lord understand
29:10 the upright: but the just s· his soul.
26 Many s· the ruler's favour; but
Ec 1:13 my heart to s· and search out by
7:25 to search, and to s· out wisdom,
8:17 though a man labour to s· it out,
Ca 3: 2 will s· him whom my soul loveth:
6: 1 that we may s· him with thee.
Isa 1:17 s· judgment, relieve the oppressed,
8:19 S· unto them that have familiar
19 not a people s· unto their God? for
9:13 them, neither do they s· the Lord
11:10 to it shall the Gentiles s·: and his
19: 3 and they shall s· to the idols, and to
26: 9 within me will I s· thee early:
29:15 Woe unto them that s· deep to hide
31: 1 of Israel, neither s· the Lord!
34:16 S· ye out of the book of the Lord,
41:12 Thou shalt s· them, and shalt not
17 When the poor and needy s· water,
45:19 the seed of Jacob, S· ye me in vain:
51: 1 righteousness, ye that s· the Lord:
55: 6 S· ye the Lord while he may be
58: 2 Yet they s· me daily, and delight
Jer 2:24 all they that s· her will not weary
33 trimmest thou thy way to s· love?
4:30 despise thee, they will s· thy life.
5: 1 and s· in the broad places thereof,
11:21 that s· thy life, saying, Prophesy
19: 7 hands of them that s· their lives:
9 and they that s· their lives, shall
21: 7 the hand of those that s· their life:
22:25 the hand of them that s· thy life,
29: 7 s· the peace of the city whither I
13 ye shall s· me, and find me, when
30:14 forgotten thee; they s· thee not;
34:20 the hand of them that s· their life:
21 the hand of them that s· their life,
38:16 hand of these men that s· thy life.
44:30 the hand of them that s· his life;
45: 5 things for thyself? s· them not:
46:26 hand of those that s· their lives,
49:37 and before them that s· their life:
50: 4 shall go, and s· the Lord their God.
La 1:11 All her people sigh, they s· bread;
Eze 7:25 they shall s· peace, and there shall
26 shall they s· a vision of the prophet;
34: 6 none did search or s· after them.
11 search my sheep, and s· them out.
12 so will I s· out my sheep, and will
16 I will s· that which was lost, and
Da 9: 3 to s· by prayer and supplications,
Ho 2: 7 she shall s· them, but shall not
3: 5 s· the Lord their God, and David
5: 6 and with their herds to s· the Lord;
15 their offence, and s· my face: in
15 affliction they will s· me early.
7:10 their God, nor s· him for all this.
10:12 for it is time to s· the Lord, till he
Am 5: 4 Israel, S· ye me, and ye shall live:
5 But s· not Beth-el, nor enter into
6 S· the Lord, and ye shall live; lest
8 S· him that maketh the seven stars
14 S· good, and not evil, that ye may
8:12 and fro to s· the word of the Lord,
Na 3: 7 shall I s· comforters for thee?
11 s· strength because of the enemy.
Zep 2: 3 S· ye the Lord, all ye meek of the
3 s· righteousness, s· meekness: it
Zec 8:21 Lord, and to s· the Lord of hosts:
22 shall come to s· the Lord of hosts
11:16 neither shall s· the young one, nor
12: 9 I will s· to destroy all the nations
Mal 2: 7 should s· the law at his mouth:
15 That he might s· a godly seed.
3: 1 and the Lord, whom ye s·, shall
M't 2:13 s· the young child to destroy him.
6:32 all these things do the Gentiles s·:)
33 But s· ye first the kingdom of God,
7: 7 s·, and ye shall find; knock, and it
28: 5 ye s· Jesus, which was crucified.
M'r 1:37 said unto him, All men s· for thee.
3:32 thy brethren without s· for thee.
M'r 8:12 this generation s· after a sign?
16: 6 Ye s· Jesus of Nazareth, which was
Lu 11: 9 s·, and ye shall find; knock, and it
29 they s· a sign; and there shall no
12:29 And s· not ye what ye shall eat, or
30 the nations of the world s· after:
31 rather s· ye the kingdom of God;
13:24 for many,...will s· to enter in, and
15: 8 and s· diligently till she find it?
17:33 shall s· to save his life shall lose it;
19:10 s· and to save that which was lost.
24: 5 s· ye the living among the dead?
Joh 1:38 and saith unto them, What s· ye?
5:30 because I s· not mine own will, but
44 s· not the honour that cometh
6:26 Ye s· me, not because ye saw the
7:25 not this he, whom they s· to kill?
34, 36 Ye shall s· me, and shall not
8:21 ye shall s· me, and shall die in your
37 ye s· to kill me, because my word
40 But now ye s· to kill me, a man
50 And I s· not mine own glory: there
13:33 Ye shall s· me: and as I said unto
18: 4 and said unto them, Whom s· ye?
7 asked he them again, Whom s· ye?
8 if therefore ye s· me, let these go
Ac 10:19 him, Behold, three men s· thee.
21 said, Behold, I am he whom ye s·:
11:25 Barnabas to Tarsus, for to s· Saul:
15:17 of men might s· after the Lord,
17:27 That they should s· the Lord, if
Ro 2: 7 in well doing s· for glory and
11: 3 am left alone, and they s· my life.
1Co 1:22 and the Greeks s· after wisdom:
7:27 unto a wife? s· not to be loosed.
27 loosed from a wife? s· not a wife.
10:24 Let no man s· his own, but every
14:12 s· that ye may excel to the edifying
2Co 12:14 for I s· not yours, but you: for the
13: 3 ye s· a proof of Christ speaking in
Ga 1:10 or do I s· to please men? for if I
2:17 while we s· to be justified by Christ,
Ph'p 2:21 For all s· their own, not the things
Col 3: 1 s· those things which are above,
Heb11: 6 of them that diligently s· him.
14 plainly that they s· a country.
13:14 city, but we s· one to come.
1Pe 3:11 let him s· peace, and ensue it.
Re 9: 6 in those days shall men s· death,

seekest
Ge 37:15 asked him, saying, What s· thou?
J'g 4:22 shew thee the man whom thou s·.
2Sa 17: 3 the man whom thou s· is as if all
20:19 thou s· to destroy a city and a
1Ki 11:22 that thou s· to go to thine own country?
Pr 2: 4 If thou s· her as silver, and
Jer 45: 5 s· thou great things for thyself?
Joh 4:27 yet no man said, What s· thou?
20:15 why weepest thou? whom s· thou?

seeketh
1Sa 19: 2 Saul my father s· to kill thee: now
20: 1 thy father, that he s· my life?
22:23 for he that s· my life s· thy life:
23:10 that Saul s· to come to Keilah, to
24: 9 saying, Behold, David s· thy hurt?
2Sa 16:11 forth of my bowels, s· my life:
1Ki 20: 7 and see how this man s· mischief:
2Ki 5: 7 see how he s· a quarrel against me.
Job 39:29 From thence she s· the prey, and
Ps 37:32 the righteous, and s· to slay him.
Pr 11:27 s· good procureth favour: but
27 he that s· mischief, it shall come
14: 6 A scorner s· wisdom, and findeth
15:14 hath understanding s· knowledge:
17: 9 covereth a transgression s· love;
11 an evil man s· only rebellion:
19 exalteth his gate s· destruction.
18: 1 s· and intermeddleth with all
15 the ear of the wise s· knowledge.
31:13 She s· wool, and flax, and
Ec 7:28 Which yet my soul s·, but I find
Isa 40:20 s· unto him a cunning workman
Jer 5: 1 executeth judgment,...s· the truth;
30:17 is Zion, whom no man s· after.
38: 4 s· not the welfare of this people,
La 3:25 wait for him, to the soul that s· him.
Eze 14:10 punishment of him that s· unto
34:12 As a shepherd s· out his flock in
M't 7: 8 receiveth; and he that s· findeth;
12:39 evil...generation s· after a sign;
16: 4 wicked...generation s· after a sign;
18:12 and s· that which is gone astray?
Lu 11:10 receiveth; and he that s· findeth;
Joh 4:23 the Father s· such to worship him.
7: 4 he himself s· to be known openly.
18 speaketh of himself s· his own glory:
18 he that s· his glory that sent him,
8:50 there is one that s· and judgeth.
Ro 3:11 there is none that s· after God.
11: 7 not obtained that which he s· for;
1Co 13: 5 itself unseemly, s· not her own,

seeking
Es 10: 3 s· the wealth of his people, and
Isa 16: 5 judging, and s· judgment, and
M't 12:43 places, s· rest, and findeth none.
13:45 a merchant man, s· goodly pearls:
M'r 8:11 him, s· of him a sign from heaven,
Lu 2:45 back again to Jerusalem, s· him.
11:24 walketh through dry places, s· rest;
54 and s· to catch something out of his
13: 7 three years I come s· fruit on this
Joh 6:24 came to Capernaum, s· for Jesus.
Ac 13: 8 s· to turn away the deputy from the
11 s· some to lead him by the hand.
1Co 10:33 not s· mine own profit, but the
1Pe 5: 8 about, s· whom he may devour:

seem See also SEEMED; SEEMETH.
Ge 27:12 shall s· to him as a deceiver;
De 15:18 It shall not s· hard unto thee,
25: 3 brother should s· vile unto thee.
Jos 24:15 s· evil unto you to serve the
1Sa 24: 4 as it shall s· good unto thee.
2Sa 19:37 what shall s· good unto thee.
38 which shall s· good unto thee:
1Ki 21: 2 if it s· good to thee, I will give
1Ch 13: 2 If it s· good unto you, and that it
Ezr 5:17 if it s· good to the king, let there be
7:18 whatsoever shall s· good to thee,
Ne 9:32 let not all the trouble s· little
Es 5: 4 If it s· good unto the king, let the
8: 5 the thing s· right before the king,
Jer 40: 4 If it s· good unto thee to come
4 but if it s· ill unto thee to come
Na 2: 4 they shall s· like torches, they
1Co 11:16 if any man s· to be contentious,
12:22 body, which s· to be more feeble,
2Co 10: 9 I may not s· as if I would terrify
Heb 4: 1 of you should s· to come short of it.
Jas 1:26 man among you s· to be religious,

seemed
Ge 19:14 he s· as one that mocked unto
29:20 s· unto him but a few days,
2Sa 3:19 all that s· good to Israel, and
19 that s· good to the whole house of
Ec 9:13 the sun, and it s· great unto me:
Jer 18: 4 as s· good to the potter to make it.
27: 5 have given it unto whom it s· meet
M't 11:26 for so it s· good in thy sight.
Lu 1: 3 It s· good to me also, having had
10:21 for so it s· good in thy sight.
24:11 words s· to them as idle tales, and
Ac 15:25 s· good unto us, being assembled
28 For it s· good to the Holy Ghost,
Ga 2: 6 But of these who s· to be somewhat,
6 s· to be somewhat in conference
9 and John, who s· to be pillars

seemeth
Le 14:35 It s· to me there is as it were a
Nu 16: 9 S· it but a small thing unto you,
Jos 9:25 as it s· good and right unto thee
J'g 10:15 us whatsoever s· good unto thee;
19:24 unto them what s· good unto you:
1Sa 1:23 Do what s· thee good; tarry until
3:18 let him do what s· him good.
11:10 with us all that s· good unto you.
14:36 Do whatsoever s· good unto thee.
40 Do what s· good unto thee.
18:23 S· it to you a light thing to be a
2Sa 10:12 Lord do that which s· him good.
15:26 him do to me as s· good unto him.
18: 4 What s· you best I will do.
24:22 offer up what s· good unto him:
Es 3:11 with them as it s· good to thee.
Pr 14:12 a way which s· right unto a man,
16:25 is a way that s· right unto a man,
18:17 that is first in his own cause s· just;
Jer 26:14 do with me as s· good and meet
40: 4 it s· good and convenient for thee
5 wheresoever it s· convenient unto
Eze 34:18 S· it a small thing unto you to have
Lu 8:18 even that which he s· to have.
Ac 17:18 He s· to be a setter forth of strange
25:27 it s· to me unreasonable to send a
1Co 3:18 you s· to be wise in this world,
Heb12:11 for the present s· to be joyous, but

seemly See also UNSEEMLY.
Pr 19:10 Delight is not s· for a fool; much
26: 1 so honour is not s· for a fool.

seen
Ge 7: 1 thee have I s· righteous before me
8: 5 were the tops of the mountains s·.
9:14 the bow shall be s· in the cloud:
22:14 the mount of the Lord it shall be s·.
31:12 I have s· all that Laban doeth unto
42 God hath s· mine affliction and the
32:30 I have s· God face to face, and my
33:10 for therefore I have s· thy face,
10 as though I had s· the face of God,
45:13 Egypt, and of all that ye have s·;
46:30 let me die, since I have s· thy face,
Ex 3: 7 I have surely s· the affliction of my
9 and I have also s· the oppression
16 s· that which is done to you in Egypt:
10: 6 nor thy fathers' fathers have s·,
13: 7 no leavened bread be s· with thee,
7 shall there be leaven s· with thee
14:13 for the Egyptians whom ye have s·
19: 4 Ye have s· what I did unto the
20:22 Ye have s· that I have talked with
32: 9 unto Moses, I have s· this people,
33:23 parts: but my face shall not be s·.
34: 3 any man be s· throughout all the
Le 5: 1 whether he hath s· or known of it;
13: 7 that he hath been s· of the priest
7 he shall be s· of the priest again:
Nu 14:14 that thou Lord art s· face to face,
22 those men which have s· my glory,
23:21 neither hath he s· perverseness in
27:13 And when thou hast s· it, thou also
De 1:28 we have s· the sons of the Anakims
31 s· how that the Lord thy God bare
3:21 eyes have s· all that the Lord your
4: 3 Your eyes have s· what the Lord did
9 the things which thine eyes have s·,
5:24 s· this day that God doth talk with
9:13 I have s· this people, and, behold,
10:21 things, which thine eyes have s·.
11: 2 have not s· the chastisement of the

De 11: 7 your eyes have s' all the great acts
16: 4 shall be no leavened bread s' with
21: 7 blood, neither have our eyes s' it.
29: 2 Ye have s' all that the Lord did
3 temptations...thine eyes have s',
17 And ye have s' their abominations,
33: 9 and to his mother, I have not s' him;
Jos 23: 3 have s' all that the Lord your God
24: 7 your eyes have s' what I have done
J'g 2: 7 who had s' all the great works of
5: 8 was there a shield or spear s' among
6: 22 I have s' an angel of the Lord face
9: 48 What ye have s' me do, make haste,
13: 22 surely die, because we have s' God.
14: 2 I have s' a woman in Timnath of the
18: 9 we have s' the land, and, behold,
19: 30 was no such deed done nor s' from
1Sa 6: 16 lords of the Philistines had s' it,
16: 18 Behold, I have s' a son of Jesse the
17: 25 Have ye s' this man that is come
23: 22 haunt is, and who hath s' him there:
24: 10 eyes have s' how that the Lord had
2Sa 17: 17 not be s' to come into the city:
18: 21 Go tell the king what thou hast s'.
22: 11 was s' upon the wings of the wind.
1Ki 6: 18 was cedar; there was no stone s'.
8: 8 that the ends of the staves were s'
8 and they were not s' without: and
10: 4 when the queen of Sheba had s' all
7 I came, and mine eyes had s' it:
12 trees, nor were s' unto this day.
13: 12 s' what way the man of God went,
20: 13 thou s' all this great multitude?
2Ki 9: 26 s' yesterday the blood of Naboth,
20: 5 thy prayer, I have s' thy tears:
15 What have they s' in thine house?
15 that are in mine house have they s':
23: 29 at Megiddo, when he had s' him.
1Ch 29: 17 now have I s' with joy thy people,
2Ch 5: 9 ends of...staves were s' from the ark
9 but they were not s' without.
9: 3 queen of Sheba had s' the wisdom
6 I came, and mine eyes had s' it:
11 none such s' before in the land of
Ezr 3: 12 men, that had s' the first house,
Es 9: 26 they had s' concerning this matter,
Job 4: 8 as I have s', they that plow iniquity,
5: 3 I have s' the foolish taking root:
7: 8 The eye of him that hath s' me
8: 18 him, saying, I have not s' thee.
10: 18 up the ghost, and no eye had s' me!
13: 1 mine eye hath s' all this, mine ear
15: 17 that which I have s' I will declare;
20: 7 they which have s' him shall say,
27: 12 all ye yourselves have s' it; why
28: 7 which the vulture's eye hath not s':
31: 19 If I have s' any perish for want of
33: 21 consumed...that it cannot be s';
21 bones that were not s' stick out.
38: 17 s' the doors of the shadow of death?
22 hast thou s' the treasures of the hail,
Ps 10: 14 Thou hast s' it; for thou beholdest
18: 15 the channels of waters were s',
35: 21 said, Aha, aha, our eye hath s' it.
22 This thou hast s', O Lord: keep not
37: 25 have I not s' the righteous forsaken,
35 I have s' the wicked in great power,
48: 8 s' in the city of the Lord of hosts,
54: 7 mine eye hath s' his desire upon
55: 9 s' violence and strife in the city.
63: 2 as I have s' thee in the sanctuary.
68: 24 They have s' thy goings, O God;
90: 15 the years wherein we have s' evil.
98: 3 have s' the salvation of our God.
119: 96 I have s' an end of all perfection:
Pr 25: 7 the prince whom thine eyes have s'.
Ec 1: 14 I have s' all the works that are done
3: 10 I have s' the travail, which God hath
4: 3 who hath not s' the evil work that
5: 13 evil which I have s' under the sun,
18 Behold that which I have s': it is
6: 1 evil which I have s' under the sun,
5 Moreover he hath not s' the sun,
6 twice told, yet hath he s' no good:
7: 15 have I s' in the days of my vanity:
8: 9 All this have I s', and applied my
9: 13 This wisdom have I s' also under
10: 5 evil which I have s' under the sun,
7 I have s' servants upon horses, and
Isa 6: 5 for mine eyes have s' the King, the
9: 2 in darkness have s' a great light:
16: 12 when it is s' that Moab is weary
22: 9 s' also the breaches of the city
38: 5 heard thy prayer, I have s' thy tears:
39: 4 What have they s' in thine house?
4 that is in mine house have they s':
44: 16 Aha, I am warm, I have s' the fire:
47: 3 uncovered,...thy shame shall be s':
57: 18 I have s' his ways, and will heal him:
60: 2 and his glory shall be s' upon thee.
64: 4 by the ear, neither hath the eye s',
66: 8 a thing? who hath s' such things?
19 my fame, neither have s' my glory;
Jer 1: 12 Thou hast well s': for I will hasten
3: 6 s' that which backsliding Israel
7: 11 even I have s' it, saith the Lord.
12: 3 hast s' me, and tried mine heart
13: 27 I have s' thine adulteries, and thy
23: 13 s' folly in the prophets of Samaria,
14 s' also in the prophets of Jerusalem
44: 2 Ye have s' all the evil that I have
46: 5 Wherefore have I s' them dismayed
La 1: 8 they have s' her nakedness:
10 hath s' that the heathen entered
2: 14 have s' vain and foolish things
14 but have s' for thee false burdens
La 2: 16 for; we have found, we have s' it.
3: 1 I am the man that hath s' affliction
59 O Lord, thou hath s' my wrong:
60 Thou hast s' all their vengeance
Eze 8: 12 hast thou s' what the ancients of
15, 17 Hast thou s' this, O son of man?
11: 24 So the vision that I had s' went up
13: 3 own spirit, and have s' nothing!
6 s' vanity and lying divination,
7 Have ye not s' a vain vision, and
8 ye have spoken vanity, and s' lies,
47: 6 me, Son of man, hast thou s' this?
Da 2: 26 me the dream which I have s',
4: 9 visions of my dream that I have s',
18 I king Nebuchadnezzar have s'.
8: 6 I had s' standing before the river,
15 I, even I Daniel, had s' the vision,
9: 21 Gabriel, whom I had s' in the vision
Ho 6: 10 I have s' an horrible thing in the
Zec 9: 8 for now have I s' with mine eyes.
14 And the Lord shall be s' over them.
10: 2 and the diviners have s' a lie, and
M't 2: 2 for we have s' his star in the east,
6: 1 alms before men, to be s' of them:
5 that they may be s' of men.
9: 33 saying, It was never so s' in Israel.
13: 17 ye see, and have not s' them;
21: 32 ye, when ye had s' it, repented not
23: 5 works they do for to be s' of men:
M'r 9: 1 they have s' the kingdom of God
9 no man what things they had s',
16: 11 was alive, and had been s' of her,
14 believed not them which had s' him
Lu 1: 22 perceived that he had s' a vision in
2: 17 they had s' it, they made known
20 things that they had heard and s',
26 before he had s' the Lord's Christ.
30 For mine eyes have s' thy salvation,
5: 26 We have s' strange things to day.
7: 22 tell John what things ye have s' and
9: 36 of those things which they had s'.
10: 24 ye see, and have not s' them;
19: 37 the mighty works that they had s';
23: 8 he hoped to have s' some miracle
24: 23 they had also s' a vision of angels,
37 supposed that they had s' a spirit.
Joh 1: 18 No man hath s' God at any time;
3: 11 know, and testify that we have s';
32 what he hath s' and heard, that he
4: 45 having s' all the things that he did
5: 37 voice at any time, nor s' his shape.
6: 14 had s' the miracle that Jesus did,
36 ye also have s' me, and believe
46 that any man hath s' the Father,
46 is of God, he hath s' the Father.
8: 38 which I have s' with my Father:
38 which ye have s' with your father.
57 old, and hast thou s' Abraham?
9: 8 had s' him that he was blind,
37 Thou hast both s' him, and it is he
11: 45 had s' the things which Jesus did,
14: 7 ye know him, and have s' him.
9 that hath s' me hath s' the Father;
15: 24 now have they both s' and hated me
20: 18 disciples that she had s' the Lord,
25 said unto him, We have s' the Lord.
29 because thou hast s' me, thou hast
29 blessed are they that have not s'
Ac 1: 3 being s' of them forty days, and
11 as ye have s' him go into heaven.
4: 20 which we have s' and heard.
7: 34 I have s',...the affliction of my
34 I have s' the affliction of my people,
44 to the fashion that he had s'.
9: 12 hath s' in a vision a man named
27 how he had s' the Lord in the way,
10: 17 vision which he had s' should mean,
11: 13 how he had s' an angel in his house,
23 came, and had s' the grace of God,
13: 31 And he was s' many days of them
16: 10 And after he had s' the vision,
40 and when they had s' the brethren,
21: 29 (For they had s' before with him
22: 15 of what thou hast s' and heard.
26: 16 of these things which thou hast s',
Ro 1: 20 creation of the world are clearly s',
8: 24 but hope that is s' is not hope: for
1Co 2: 9 Eye hath not s', nor ear heard,
9: 1 have I not s' Jesus Christ our
15: 5 And that he was s' of Cephas,
6 he was s' of above five hundred
7 After that, he was s' of James;
8 And last of all he was s' of me also,
2Co 4: 18 look not at the things which are s',
18 but at the things which are not s':
18 things which are s' are temporal;
18 things which are not s' are eternal.
Ph'p 4: 9 and heard, and s' in me, do;
Col 2: 1 as have not s' my face in the flesh;
18 those things which he hath not s',
1Ti 3: 16 justified in the Spirit, s' of angels,
6: 16 whom no man hath s', nor can see:
Heb 11: 1 for, the evidence of things not s'.
3 things which are s' were not made
7 warned of God of things not s' as yet,
13 but having s' them afar off, and
Jas 5: 11 and have s' the end of the Lord;
1Pe 1: 8 Whom having not s', ye love; in
1Jo 1: 1 which we have s' with our eyes,
2 and we have s' it, and bear witness,
3 That which we have s' and heard
3: 6 whosoever sinneth hath not s' him,
4: 12 No man hath s' God at any time.
14 And we have s' and do testify that
20 not his brother whom he hath s',
20 he love God whom he hath not s'?
3Jo 11 he that doeth evil hath not s' God.
Re 1: 19 Write the things...thou hast s',
11: 19 there was s' in his temple the ark
22: 8 And when I had heard and s', I fell

seer See also OVERSEER; SEER'S; SEERS.
1Sa 9: 9 Come, and let us go to the s': for
9 Prophet was beforetime called a S'.)
11 and said unto them, Is the s' here?
19 answered Saul, and said, I am the s':
2Sa 15: 27 Zadok the priest, Art not thou a s'?
24: 11 unto the prophet Gad, David's s',
1Ch 9: 22 David and Samuel the s' did ordain
21: 9 Lord spake unto Gad, David's s',
25: 5 the sons of Heman the king's s' in
26: 28 all that Samuel the s', and Saul
29: 29 in the book of Samuel the s',
29 and in the book of Gad the s',
2Ch 9: 29 and in the visions Iddo the s'
12: 15 Iddo the s' concerning genealogies?
16: 7 Hanani the s' came to Asa king
10 Then Asa was wroth with the s',
19: 2 of Hanani the s' went out to meet
29: 25 of David, and of Gad the king's s',
30 of David, and of Asaph the s'.
35: 15 Heman, and Jeduthun the king's s';
Am 7: 12 O thou s', go, flee thee away into

seer's
1Sa 9: 18 Tell me,...where the s' house is.

seers See also OVERSEERS.
2Ki 17: 13 all the prophets, and by all the s',
2Ch 33: 18 words of the s' that spake to him
19 written among the sayings of the s'.
Isa 29: 10 your rulers, the s' hath he covered.
30: 10 Which say to the s', See not; and
Mic 3: 7 Then shall the s' be ashamed, and:

seest
Ge 13: 15 For all the land which thou s', to
16: 13 spake unto her, Thou God s' me;
31: 43 and all that thou s' is mine: and
Ex 10: 28 day thou s' my face thou shalt die,
De 4: 19 and when thou s' the sun, and the
12: 13 offerings in every place...thou s':
20: 1 and s' horses, and chariots, and a
21: 11 s' among the captives a beautiful
J'g 9: 36 s' the shadow of the mountains as
1Ki 21: 29 S' thou how Ahab humbleth
Job 10: 4 of flesh? or s' thou as man seeth?
Pr 22: 29 S' thou a man diligent in his
26: 12 S' thou a man wise in his own
29: 20 S' thou a man that is hasty in his
Ec 5: 8 thou s' the oppression of the poor,
Isa 58: 3 fasted, say they, and thou s' not?
7 when thou s' the naked, that thou
Jer 1: 11 saying, Jeremiah, what s' thou?
13 second time, saying, What s' thou?
7: 17 S' thou not what they do in the
20: 12 and s' the reins and the heart, let
24: 3 unto me, What s' thou, Jeremiah?
32: 24 to pass; and, behold, thou s' it.
Eze 8: 6 Son of man, s' thou what they do?
40: 4 declare all that thou s' to the house
Da 1: 13 as thou s', deal with thy servants
Am 7: 8 said unto me, Amos, what s' thou?
8: 2 And he said, Amos, what s' thou?
Zec 4: 2 And said unto me, What s' thou?
5: 2 he said unto me, What s' thou?
M'r 5: 31 s' the multitude thronging thee,
13: 2 him, S' thou these great buildings?
Lu 7: 44 unto Simon, S' thou this woman?
Ac 21: 20 him, Thou s', brother, how many
Jas 2: 22 S' thou how faith wrought with his
Re 1: 11 What thou s', write in a book, and

seeth See also FORSEETH.
Ge 16: 13 here looked after him that s' me?
44: 31 when he s' that the lad is not with
Ex 4: 14 when he s' thee, he will be glad in
12: 23 he s' the blood upon the lintel, and
Le 13: 20 when the priest s' it, behold, it be
De 32: 36 he s' that their power is gone, and
1Sa 16: 7 him: for the Lord s' not as man
7 not as man s'; for man looketh
2Ki 2: 19 this city is pleasant, as my lord s':
Job 8: 17 heap, and s' the place of stones.
10: 4 of flesh? or seest thou as man s'?
11: 11 he s' wickedness also; will he not
22: 14 a covering to him, that he s' not;
28: 10 his eye s' every precious thing.
24 and s' under the whole heaven;
34: 21 of man, and he s' all his goings.
42: 5 the ear: but now mine eye s' thee.
Ps 37: 13 for he s' that his day is coming.
49: 10 he s' that wise men die, likewise
58: 10 rejoice when he s' the vengeance:
Ec 8: 16 neither day nor night s' sleep with
Isa 21: 6 let him declare what he s'.
28: 4 he that looketh upon it s', while it
29: 15 the dark, and they say, Who s' us?
23 when he s' his children, the work
47: 10 thou hast said, None s' me. Thy
Eze 8: 12 The Lord s' us not; the Lord hath
9: 9 the earth, and the Lord s' not.
12: 27 vision that he s' is for many days
18: 14 s' all his father's sins which he
33: 3 s' the sword come upon the land,
39: 15 when any s' a man's bone, then
M't 6: 4 and thy Father which s' in secret
6 thy Father which s' in secret shall
18 which s' in secret, shall reward thee
M'r 5: 38 s' the tumult, and them that wept
Lu 16: 23 s' Abraham afar off, and Lazarus
Joh 1: 29 John s' Jesus coming unto him,
5: 19 but what he s' the Father do: for
6: 40 that every one which s' the Son,
9: 21 means he now s', we know not; or

Joh 10: 12 s· the wolf coming, and leaveth
11: 9 he s· the light of this world.
12: 45 that s· me s· him that sent me.
14: 17 it s· him not, neither knoweth him:
19 and the world s· me no more; but
20: 1 s· the stone taken away from the
6 sepulchre, and s· the linen clothes
12 s· two angels in white sitting, the
21: 20 s· the disciple whom Jesus loved
Ro 8: 24 for what a man s·, why doth he
2Co 12: 6 me above that which he s· me to be,
1Jo 3: 17 and s· his brother have need.

seethe See also SEETHING; SOD.
Ex 16: 23 to day, and s· that ye will s·;
23: 19 not s· a kid in his mother's milk.
29: 31 and s· his flesh in the holy place.
34: 26 not s· a kid in his mother's milk.
De 14: 21 not s· a kid in his mother's milk.
2Ki 4: 38 and s· pottage for the sons of the
Eze 24: 5 let them s· the bones of it therein.
Zec 14: 21 and take of them, and s· therein:

seethed See SOD.

seething
1Sa 2: 13 came while the flesh was in s·,
Job 41: 20 as out of a s· pot or caldron.
Jer 1: 13 I see a s· pot; and the face thereof

Segub (*se'-gub*)
1Ki 16: 34 thereof in his youngest son S·.
1Ch 2: 21 years old; and she bare him S·.
22 And S· begat Jair, who had three

Seir (*se'-ur*)
Ge 14: 6 And the Horites in their mount S·,
32: 3 his brother unto the land of S·, the
33: 14 until I come unto my lord unto S·.
16 that day on his way unto S·.
36: 8 Thus dwelt Esau in mount S·: Esau
9 father of the Edomites in mount S·:
20 These are the sons of S· the Horite,
21 children of S· in the land of Edom.
30 among their dukes in the land of S·.
Nu 24: 18 S· also shall be a possession for his
De 1: 2 from Horeb by the way of mount S·
44 as bees do, and destroyed you in S·,
2: 1 we compassed mount S· many days.
4 children of Esau, which dwell in S·;
5 I have given mount S· unto Esau
8 children of Esau, which dwelt in S·,
12 Horims also dwelt in S· beforetime;
22 children of Esau, which dwelt in S·,
29 children of Esau which dwelt in S·,
33: 2 and rose up from S· unto them;
Jos 11: 17 mount Halak, that goeth up to S·,
12: 7 mount Halak, that goeth up to S·;
15: 10 Baalah westward unto mount S·,
24: 4 and I gave unto Esau mount S·, to
J'g 5: 4 Lord, when thou wentest out of S·,
1Ch 1: 38 the sons of S·; Lotan, and Shobal,
4: 42 five hundred men, went to mount S·,
2Ch 20: 10 of Ammon and Moab and mount S·,
22 of Ammon, Moab, and mount S·,
23 the inhabitants of mount S·,
23 an end of the inhabitants of S·,
25: 11 of the children of S· ten thousand.
14 the gods of the children of S·,
Isa 21: 11 Dumah. He calleth to me out of S·,
Eze 25: 8 Because that Moab and S· do say,
35: 2 set thy face against mount S·, and
3 Behold, O mount S·, I am against
7 I make mount S· most desolate,
15 thou shalt be desolate, O mount S·,

Seirath (*se'-ur-ath*)
J'g 3: 26 the quarries, and escaped unto S·.

seize See also SEIZED.
Jos 8: 7 the ambush, and s· upon the city:
Job 3: 6 that night, let darkness s· upon it:
Ps 55: 15 Let death s· upon them, and let
M't 21: 38 and let us s· on his inheritance.

seized
Jer 49: 24 to flee, and fear hath s· on her:

Sela (*se'-lah*) See also SELAH; SELA-HAMMAH-LEKOTH.
Isa 16: 1 the land from S· to the wilderness,

Selah (*se'-lah*) See also JOKTHEEL; SELA.
2Ki 14: 7 and took S· by war, and called the
Ps 3: 2 is no help for him in God. S·.
4 heard me out of his holy hill. S·.
8 blessing is upon thy people. S·.
4: 2 vanity, and seek after leasing? S·.
4 upon your bed, and be still. S·.
7: 5 lay mine honour in the dust. S·.
9: 16 of his own hands. Higgaion. S·.
20 know themselves to be but men. S·.
20: 3 and accept thy burnt sacrifice; S·.
21: 2 the request of his lips. S·.
24: 6 that seek thy face, O Jacob. S·.
10 hosts, he is the King of glory. S·.
32: 4 into the drought of summer. S·.
5 forgavest the iniquity of my sin. S·.
7 with songs of deliverance. S·.
39: 5 best state is altogether vanity. S·.
11 surely every man is vanity. S·.
44: 8 and praise thy name for ever. S·.
46: 3 shake with the swelling thereof. S·.
7, 11 God of Jacob is our refuge. S·.
47: 4 of Jacob whom he loved. S·.
48: 8 God will establish it for ever. S·.
49: 13 approve their sayings. S·.
15 grave: for he shall receive me. S·.
50: 6 for God is judge himself. S·.
52: 3 than to speak righteousness. S·.
5 out of the land of the living. S·.
54: 3 have not set God before them. S·.
Ps 55: 7 and remain in the wilderness. S·.
19 even he that abideth of old. S·.
57: 3 him that would swallow me up. S·.
6 they are fallen themselves. S·.
59: 5 to any wicked transgressors. S·.
13 unto the ends of the earth. S·.
60: 4 displayed because of the truth. S·.
61: 4 trust in the covert of thy wings. S·.
62: 4 mouth, but they curse inwardly. S·.
8 him: God is a refuge for us. S·.
66: 4 they shall sing to thy name. S·.
7 the rebellious exalt themselves. S·.
15 I will offer bullocks with goats. S·.
67: 1 cause his face to shine upon us; S·.
4 govern the nations upon earth. S·.
68: 7 march through the wilderness; S·:
19 even the God of our salvation. S·.
32 O sing praises unto the Lord; S·:
75: 3 I bear up the pillars of it. S·.
76: 3 and the sword, and the battle. S·.
9 save all the meek of the earth. S·.
77: 3 my spirit was overwhelmed. S·.
9 shut up his tender mercies? S·.
15 the sons of Jacob and Joseph. S·.
81: 7 thee at the waters of Meribah. S·.
82: 2 the persons of the wicked? S·.
83: 8 holpen the children of Lot. S·.
84: 4 they will be still praising thee. S·.
8 give ear, O God of Jacob. S·.
85: 2 thou hast covered all their sin. S·.
87: 3 spoken of thee, O city of God. S·.
6 that this man was born there. S·.
88: 7 afflicted me with all thy waves. S·.
10 the dead arise and praise thee? S·.
89: 4 thy throne to all generations. S·.
37 as a faithful witness in heaven. S·.
45 hast covered him with shame. S·.
48 from the hand of the grave? S·.
140: 3 poison is under their lips. S·.
5 they have set gins for me. S·.
8 lest they exalt themselves. S·.
143: 6 after thee, as a thirsty land. S·.
Hab 3: 3 Holy One from mount Paran. S·.
9 of the tribes, even thy word. S·.
13 the foundation unto the neck. S·.

Sela-hammahlekoth (*se''-lah-ham-mah'-le-koth*)
1Sa 23: 28 therefore they called that place S·.

Seled (*se'-led*)
1Ch 2: 30 sons of Nadab; S·, and Appaim:
30 but S· died without children.

Seleucia (*sel-u-si'-ah*)
Ac 13: 4 the Holy Ghost, departed unto S·;

self See also HERSELF; HIMSELF; ITSELF; MYSELF; SELFSAME; SELFWILL; SELVEDGE; SELVES; THYSELF.
Ex 32: 13 to whom thou swarest by thine own s·,
Joh 5: 30 I can of mine own s· do nothing:
17: 5 glorify thou me with thine own s·
1Co 4: 3 yea, I judge not mine own s·.
Ph'm 19 owest unto me even thine own s·
1Pe 2: 24 Who his own s· bare our sins in his

selfsame
Ge 7: 13 In the s· day entered Noah,
17: 23 of their foreskin in the s· day,
26 in the s· day was Abraham
Ex 12: 17 this s· day have I brought your
41 even the s· day it came to pass,
51 And it came to pass the s· day,
Le 23: 14 s· day that ye have brought
21 ye shall proclaim on the s· day,
De 32: 48 spake unto Moses that s· day,
Jos 5: 11 and parched corn in the s· day.
Eze 40: 1 the s· day the hand of the Lord
M't 8: 13 servant was healed in the s· hour.
1Co 12: 11 worketh that one and the s· Spirit,
2Co 5: 5 wrought us for the s· thing is
7: 11 For behold this s· thing, that ye

selfwill See also SELFWILLED.
Ge 49: 6 their s· they digged down a wall.

selfwilled
Tit 1: 7 not s·, not soon angry, not given to
2Pe 2: 10 Presumptuous are they, s·, they

sell See also SELLEST; SELLETH; SOLD.
Ge 25: 31 said, S· me this day thy birthright.
37: 27 and let us s· him to the Ishmeelites,
Ex 21: 7 s· his daughter to be a maidservant,
8 to s· her unto a strange nation he
35 then they shall s· the live ox, and
22: 1 ox, or a sheep, and kill it, or s· it;
Le 25: 14 thou s· ought unto thy neighbour,
15 of the fruits he shall s· unto thee:
16 of the fruits doth he s· unto thee.
29 s· a dwelling house in a walled city,
47 and s· himself unto the stranger or
De 2: 28 Thou shalt s· me meat for money,
14: 21 thou mayest s· it unto an alien:
21: 14 shalt not s· her at all for money,
J'g 4: 9 the Lord shall s· Sisera into the
1Ki 21: 25 did s· himself to work wickedness
2Ki 4: 7 Go, s· the oil, and pay thy debt, and
Ne 5: 8 and will ye even s· your brethren?
10: 31 victuals on the sabbath day to s·,
Pr 23: 23 Buy the truth, and s· it not; also
Eze 30: 12 s· the land into the hand of the
48: 14 And they shall not s· of it, neither
Joe 3: 8 And I will s· your sons and your
8 they shall s· them to the Sabeans,
Am 8: 5 be gone, that we may s· corn?
6 yea, and s· the refuse of the wheat?
Zec 11: 5 they that s· them say, Blessed be
M't 19: 21 go and s· that thou hast, and give
25: 9 go ye rather to them that s·, and
M'r 10: 21 s· whatsoever thou hast, and give
Lu 12: 33 S· that ye have, and give alms;
18: 22 s· all that thou hast, and distribute
22: 36 no sword, let him s· his garment,
Jas 4: 13 and buy and s·, and get gain:
Re 13: 17 that no man might buy or s·, save

seller See also SELLERS.
Isa 24: 2 as with the buyer, so with the s·;
Eze 7: 12 buyer rejoice, nor the s· mourn:
13 For the s· shall not return to that
Ac 16: 14 named Lydia, a s· of purple,

sellers
Ne 13: 20 merchants and s· of all kinds of

sellest
Ps 44: 12 Thou s· thy people for nought,

selleth
Ex 21: 16 that stealeth a man, and s· him,
De 24: 7 merchandise of him, or s· him;
Ru 4: 3 s· a parcel of land, which was our
Pr 11: 26 upon the head of him that s· it.
31: 24 She maketh fine linen, and s· it;
Na 3: 4 s· nations through her whoredoms,
M't 13: 44 goeth and s· all that he hath, and

selvedge
Ex 26: 4 from the s· in the coupling; and
36: 11 from the s· in the coupling:

selves^ See also OURSELVES; THEMSELVES; YOURSELVES.
Lu 21: 30 own s· that summer is now nigh
Ac 20: 30 Also of your own s· shall men arise,
2Co 8: 5 first gave their own s· to the Lord,
13: 5 be in the faith; prove your own s·.
5 Know ye not your own s·, how that
2Ti 3: 2 men shall be lovers of their own s·,
Jas 1: 22 hearers only, deceiving...own s·.

Sem (*sem*) See also SHEM.
Lu 3: 36 which was the son of S·, which

Semachiah (*sem-a-ki'-ah*)
1Ch 26: 7 were strong men, Elihu, and S·.

semblance See RESEMBLANCE.

Semei (*sem'-e-i*) See also SHEMAIAH.
Lu 3: 26 which was the son of S·, which

Senaah (*sen'-a-ah*) See also HASSENAAH.
Ezr 2: 35 The children of S·, three thousand
Ne 7: 38 The children of S·, three thousand

senate
Ac 5: 21 all the s· of the children of Israel,

senators
Ps 105: 22 pleasure; and teach his s· wisdom.

send See also SENDEST; SENDETH; SENDING; SENT.
Ge 24: 7 he shall s· his angel before thee,
12 thee, s· me good speed this day,
40 will s· his angel with thee, and
54 said, S· me away unto my master.
56 s· me away that I may go to my
27: 45 then I will s·, and fetch thee from
30: 25 s· me away, that I may go unto
37: 13 come, and I will s· thee unto them.
38: 17 I will s· thee a kid from the flock.
17 thou give me a pledge, till thou s· it?
42: 16 S· one of you, and let him fetch
43: 4 If thou wilt s· our brother with us,
5 But if thou wilt not s· him, we will
8 S· the lad with me, and we will
14 he may s· away your other brother,
45: 5 For God did s· me before you to
Ex 3: 10 I will s· thee unto Pharaoh, that
4: 13 he said, O my Lord, s·, I pray thee,
13 the hand of him whom thou wilt s·.
7: 2 that he s· the children of Israel out
8: 21 I will s· swarms of flies upon thee,
9: 14 will at this time s· all my plagues
19 S· therefore now, and gather thy
12: 33 they might s· them out of the land
23: 20 I s· an Angel before thee, to keep
27 I will s· my fear before thee, and
28 And I will s· hornets before thee,
33: 2 And I will s· an angel before thee;
12 know whom thou wilt s· with me.
Le 16: 21 shall s· him away by the hand of a
26: 22 will also s· wild beasts among you,
25 I will s· the pestilence among you;
36 I will s· a faintness into their
Nu 13: 2 S· thou men, that may search the
2 of their fathers shall ye s· a man,
22: 37 earnestly s· unto thee to call thee?
31: 4 of Israel, shall ye s· to the war.
De 1: 22 We will s· men before us, and they
7: 20 the Lord thy God will s· the hornet
11: 15 I will s· grass in thy fields for thy
19: 12 elders...shall s· and fetch him
24: 1 hand, and s· her out of his house,
28: 20 The Lord shall s· upon the cursing,
48 which the Lord shall s· against thee,
32: 24 s· the teeth of beasts upon them,
Jos 18: 4 I will s· them, and they shall rise,
J'g 13: 8 thou didst s· come again unto us,
1Sa 5: 11 S· away the ark of the God of Israel,
6: 2 wherewith we shall s· it to his place.
3 s· away the ark of the God of Israel,
3 s· it not empty; but in any wise
8 and s· it away, that it may go.
9: 16 And I will s· thee a man out of the land
26 saying, Up, that I may s· thee away.
11: 3 we may s· messengers unto all the
12: 17 and he shall s· thunder and rain;
16: 1 s· thee to Jesse the Beth-lehemite:
11 said unto Jesse, S· and fetch him:
19 S· me David thy son, which is with
20: 12 I then s· not unto thee, and shew

1Sa 20:13 will shew it thee, and s· thee away,
21 I will s· a lad, saying, Go, find out
31 now s· and fetch him unto me, for
21: 2 the business whereabout I s· thee,
25:25 men of my lord, whom thou didst s·.
2Sa 11: 6 saying, S· me Uriah the Hittite.
14:32 that I may s· thee to the king, to
15:36 by them ye shall s· unto me every
17:16 Now therefore s· quickly, and tell
1Ki 8:44 whithersoever thou shalt s· them,
18: 1 and I will s· rain upon the earth.
19 s·, and gather to me all Israel unto
20: 6 Yet I will s· my servants unto thee
9 that thou didst s· for to thy servant
34 s· thee away with this covenant.
2Ki 2:16 valley. And he said, Ye shall not s·.
17 till he was ashamed, he said, S·.
4:22 S· me, I pray thee, one of the young
5: 5 s· a letter unto the king of Israel.
7 doth s· unto me to recover a man
6:13 he is, that I may s· and fetch him.
7:13 consumed:) and let us s· and see.
9:17 an horseman, and s· to meet them,
15:37 the Lord began to s· against Judah
19: 7 I will s· a blast upon him, and he
1Ch 13: 2 let us s· abroad unto our brethren
2Ch 2: 3 and didst s· him cedars to build him
7 S· me now therefore a man cunning
8 S· me also cedar trees, fir trees,
15 of, let him s· unto his servants:
6:27 s· rain upon thy land, which thou
34 the way that thou shalt s· them,
7:13 if I s· pestilence among my people;
28:16 Ahaz s· unto the kings of Assyria
32: 9 king of Assyria s· his servants to
Ezr 5:17 let the king s· his pleasure to us
Ne 2: 5 thou wouldest s· me unto Judah,
6 So it pleased the king to s· me;
8:10 s· portions unto them for whom
12 and to drink, and to s· portions,
Job 21:11 They s· forth their little ones like
38:35 Canst thou s· lightnings, that they
Ps 20: 2 S· thee help from the sanctuary,
43: 3 O s· out thy light and thy truth:
57: 3 He shall s· from heaven, and save
3 God shall s· forth his mercy and his
68: 9 O God, didst s· a plentiful rain,
33 lo, he doth s· out his voice, and
110: 2 shall s· the rod of thy strength
118:25 I beseech thee, s· now prosperity.
144: 7 S· thine hand from above; rid me,
Pr 10:26 is the sluggard to them that s· him.
22:21 of truth to them that s· unto thee?
25:13 messenger to them that s· him:
Ec 10: 1 to s· forth a stinking savour:
Isa 6: 8 Whom shall I s·, and who will go
8 Then said I, Here am I; s· me.
10: 6 I will s· him against an hypocritical
16 s· among his fat ones leanness;
16: 1 S· ye the lamb to the ruler of the
19:20 and he shall s· them a saviour, and
32:20 s· forth thither the feet of the ox
37: 7 I will s· a blast upon him, and he
57: 9 and didst s· thy messengers far off,
66:19 I will s· those that escape of them
Jer 1: 7 shalt go to all that I shall s· thee,
2:10 and s· unto Kedar, and consider
8:17 I will s· serpents, cockatrices,
9:16 and I will s· a sword after them, till
17 and s· for cunning women, that they
16:16 I will s· for many fishers, saith the
16 and after will I s· for many hunters,
24:10 I will s· the sword, the famine, and
25: 9 I will s· and take all the families of
15 all the nations, to whom I s· thee,
16 sword that I will s· among them.
27 sword which I will s· among you.
27: 3 And s· them to the king of Edom,
29:17 I will s· upon them the sword, the
31 S· to all them of the captivity,
42: 5 the Lord thy God shall s· thee to us.
6 Lord our God, to whom we s· thee;
43:10 I will s· and take Nebuchadrezzar
48:12 that I will s· unto him wanderers,
49:37 and I will s· the sword after them,
51: 2 And will s· unto Babylon fanners,
Eze 2: 3 I s· thee to the children of Israel,
4 I do s· thee unto them; and thou
5:16 shall s· upon them the evil arrows
16 and which I will s· to destroy you:
17 So will I s· upon you famine and
7: 3 and I will s· mine anger upon thee,
14:13 and will s· famine upon it, and will
19 Or if I s· a pestilence into that land,
21 When I s· my four sore judgments
28:23 For I will s· into her pestilence, and
39: 6 And I will s· a fire on Magog, and
Ho 8:14 but I will s· a fire upon his cities,
Joe 2:19 I will s· you corn, and wine, and oil,
Am 1: 4 s· a fire into the house of Hazael,
7 I will s· a fire on the wall of Gaza,
10 I will s· a fire on the wall of Tyrus,
12 But I will s· a fire upon Teman,
2: 2 But I will s· a fire upon Moab, and
5 But I will s· a fire upon Judah, and
8:11 that I will s· a famine in the land,
Mal 2: 2 I will even s· a curse upon you, and
3: 1 Behold, I will s· my messenger,
4: 5 I will s· you Elijah the prophet
M't 9:38 s· forth labourers into his harvest.
10:16 I s· you forth as sheep in the midst
34 I am come to s· peace on earth:
34 I come not to s· peace, but a sword.
11:10 I s· my messenger before thy face,
12:20 he s· forth judgment unto victory.
13:41 Son of man shall s· forth his angels,

M't 14:15 s· the multitude away, that they
15:23 S· her away; for she crieth after us.
32 I will not s· them away fasting, lest
21: 3 and straightway he will s· them.
23:34 behold, I s· unto you prophets, and
24:31 he shall s· his angels with a great
M'r 1: 2 I s· my messenger before thy face,
3:14 he might s· them forth to preach,
5:10 that he would not s· them away out
12 S· us into the swine, that we may
6: 7 to s· them forth by two and two;
36 S· them away, that they may go
8: 3 if I s· them away fasting to their
11: 3 straightway he will s· him hither.
12:13 s· unto him certain of the Pharisees
13:27 then shall he s· his angels, and shall
Lu 7:27 I s· my messenger before thy face,
9:12 S· the multitude away, that they
10: 2 s· forth labourers into his harvest.
3 s· you forth as lambs among wolves.
11:49 I will s· them prophets and apostles,
12:49 I am come to s· fire on the earth;
16:24 s· Lazarus, that he may dip the tip
27 s· him to my father's house:
20:13 I will s· my beloved son: it may be
24:49 I s· the promise of my Father upon
Joh 13:20 whomsoever I s· receiveth me;
14:26 whom the Father will s· in my name,
15:26 I will s· unto you from the Father,
16: 7 but if I depart, I will s· him unto you.
17: 8 have believed that thou didst s· me.
20:21 hath sent me, even so s· I you.
Ac 3:20 And he shall s· Jesus Christ, which
7:34 now come, I will s· thee into Egypt.
35 the same did God s· to be a ruler
10: 5 s· men to Joppa, and call for one
22 angel to s· for thee into his house,
32 S· therefore to Joppa, and call
11:13 S· men to Joppa, and call for Simon,
29 s· relief unto the brethren which
15:22 s· chosen men of their own company
23 and elders and brethren s· greeting
25 to s· chosen men unto you with our
22:21 for I will s· thee far hence unto the
25: 3 he would s· for him to Jerusalem,
21 be kept till I might s· him to Cæsar.
25 Augustus, I...determined to s· him.
27 to me unreasonable to s· a prisoner,
26:17 Gentiles, unto whom now I s· thee,
1Co 16: 3 will I s· to bring your liberality
Ph'p 2:19 to s· Timotheus shortly unto you,
23 Him...I hope to s· presently, so
25 necessary to s· to you Epaphroditus,
2Th 2:11 God shall s· them strong delusion,
Tit 3:12 When I shall s· Artemas unto thee,
Jas 3:11 fountain s· forth at the same time
Re 1:11 s· it unto the seven churches
11:10 and shall s· gifts one to another;

sendest
De 15:13 thou s· him out free from thee,
18 thou s· him away free from thee;
Jos 1:16 whithersoever thou s· us, we will
2Ki 1: 6 thou s· to enquire of Baal-zebub
Job 14:20 his continuance, and s· him away.
Ps 104:30 Thou s· forth thy spirit, they are

sendeth
De 24: 3 hand, and s· her out of his house;
1Ki 17:14 until the day that the Lord s· rain
Job 5:10 and s· waters upon the fields:
12:15 he s· them out, and they overturn
Ps 104:10 He s· the springs into the valleys,
147:15 He s· forth his commandment upon
18 He s· out his word, and melteth
Pr 26: 6 s· a message by the hand of a fool
Ca 1:12 my spikenard s· forth the smell
Isa 18: 2 That s· ambassadors by the sea,
M't 5:45 and s· rain on the just and on the
M'r 11: 1 he s· forth two of his disciples,
14:13 And he s· forth two of his disciples,
Lu 14:32 he s· an ambassage, and desireth
Ac 23:26 excellent governor Felix s· greeting.

sending
2Sa 13:16 this evil in s· me away is greater
2Ch 36:15 rising up betimes, and s·; because
Es 9:19 and of s· portions one to another.
22 and of s· portions one to another,
Ps 78:49 by s· evil angels among them.
Isa 7:25 it shall be for the s· forth of oxen,
Jer 7:25 daily rising up early and s· them:
25: 4 prophets, rising early and s· them;
26: 5 both rising up early, and s· them,
29:19 rising up early and s· them;
35:15 rising up early and s· them,
44: 4 prophets, rising early and s· them,
Eze 17:15 in s· his ambassadors into Egypt,
Ro 8: 3 God s· his own Son in the likeness

Seneh (*se'-neh*)
1Sa 14: 4 and the name of the other S·.

Senir (*se'-nur*) See also SHENIR.
1Ch 5:23 Bashan unto Baal-hermon and S·,
Eze 27: 5 thy ship boards of fir trees of S·:

Sennacherib (*sen-nak'-er-ib*)
2Ki 18:13 did S· king of Assyria come up
19:16 and hear the words of S·, which
20 thou hast prayed to me against S·
36 So S· king of Assyria departed,
2Ch 32: 1 S· king of Assyria came, and
2 Hezekiah saw that S· was come,
9 this did S· king of Assyria send his
10 Thus saith S· king of Assyria,
22 the hand of S· the king of Assyria,
Isa 36: 1 that S· king of Assyria came up

Isa 37:17 and hear all the words of S·, which
21 thou hast prayed to me against S·
37 So S· king of Assyria departed,

sense See also SENSES.
Ne 8: 8 of God distinctly, and gave the s·,

senses
Heb 5:14 have their s· exercised to discern

sensual
Jas 3:15 above, but is earthly, s·, devilish.
Jude 19 s·, having not the Spirit.

sent See also ASSENT; CONSENT; PRESENT; SENTEST.
Ge 3:23 the Lord God s· him forth from
8: 7 And he s· forth a raven, which went
8 And he s· forth a dove from him, to
10 again he s· forth the dove out of the
12 s· forth the dove; which returned
12:20 and they s· him away, and his wife,
19:13 the Lord hath s· us to destroy it.
29 and s· Lot out of the midst of the
20: 2 and Abimelech king of Gerar s·, and
21:14 the child, and s· her away: and she
24:59 they s· away Rebekah their sister,
25: 6 s· them away from Isaac his son,
26:27 me, and have s· me away from you?
29 and have s· thee away in peace:
31 and Isaac s· them away, and they
27:42 she s· and called Jacob her younger
28: 5 And Isaac s· away Jacob: and he
6 and s· him away to Padan-aram,
31: 4 And Jacob s· and called Rachel and
27 might have s· thee away with mirth,
42 thou hadst s· me away now empty.
32: 3 Jacob s· messengers before him to
5 and I have s· to tell my lord, that I
18 is a present s· unto my lord Esau:
23 he took them, and s· them over
23 brook, and s· over all that he had.
37:14 s· him out of the vale of Hebron,
32 they s· the coat of many colours,
38:20 Judah s· the kid by the hand of his
23 I s· this kid, and thou hast not found
25 she s· to her father in law, saying,
41: 8 s· and called for all the magicians
14 then Pharaoh s· and called Joseph,
42: 4 Jacob s· not with his brethren;
43:34 he took and s· messes unto them
44: 3 was light, the men were s· away,
45: 7 God s· me before you to preserve
8 it was not you that s· me hither,
23 And to his father he s· after this
24 So he s· his brethren away, and
27 the wagons which Joseph had s· to
46: 5 the wagons which Pharaoh had s·
28 s· Judah before him unto Joseph,
50:16 they s· a messenger unto Joseph,
Ex 2: 5 flags, she s· her maid to fetch it.
3:12 token unto thee, that I have s· thee:
13 God of your fathers hath s· me
14 of Israel, I Am hath s· me unto you.
15 God of Jacob, hath s· me unto you:
4:28 words of the Lord who had s· him,
5:22 why is it that thou hast s· me?
7:16 Lord God of the Hebrews hath s· me
9: 7 And Pharaoh s·, and, behold, there
23 and the Lord s· thunder and hail,
27 Pharaoh s·, and called for Moses
18: 2 wife, after he had s· her back,
24: 5 he s· young men of the children of
Nu 13: 3 s· them from the wilderness of
16 which Moses s· to spy out the land.
17 Moses s· them to spy out the land
14:36 which Moses s· to search the land,
16:12 And Moses s· to call Dathan and
28 shall know that the Lord hath s· me
29 men; then the Lord hath not s· me.
20:14 Moses s· messengers from Kadesh
16 he heard our voice, and s· an angel,
21: 6 Lord s· fiery serpents among the
21 Israel s· messengers unto Sihon
32 And Moses s· to spy out Jaazer,
22: 5 He s· messengers...unto Balaam
10 king of Moab, hath s· unto me,
15 And Balak s· yet again princes,
40 oxen and sheep, and s· to Balaam,
31: 6 And Moses s· them to the war, a
32: 8 s· them from Kadesh-barnea to see
De 2:26 s· messengers out of the wilderness
9:23 Lord s· you from Kadesh-barnea,
24: 4 former husband, which s· her away,
34:11 which the Lord s· him to do in the
Jos 2: 1 s· out of Shittim two men to spy
3 the king of Jericho s· unto Rahab,
21 And she s· them away, and they
6:17 she hid the messengers that we s·.
25 which Joshua s· to spy out Jericho.
7: 2 Joshua s· men from Jericho to Ai,
22 So Joshua s· messengers, and they
8: 3 valour, and s· them away by night.
9 Joshua therefore s· them forth:
10: 3 king of Jerusalem s· unto Hoham
6 the men of Gibeon s· unto Joshua
11: 1 that he s· to Jobab king of Madon,
14: 7 s· me from Kadesh-barnea to espy
11 I was in the day that Moses s· me:
22: 6 blessed them, and s· them away:
7 And when Joshua s· them away also
13 s· unto the children of Reuben,
24: 5 I s· Moses also and Aaron, and I
9 and s· and called Balaam the son
12 And I s· the hornet before you,
J'g 1:23 of Joseph s· to descry Beth-el.
3:15 Israel s· a present unto Eglon
18 he s· away the people that bare the

J'g 4: 6 she s' and called Barak the son of
5:15 he was s' on foot into the valley.
6: 8 Lord s' a prophet unto the children
14 the Midianites: have not I s' thee?
35 he s' messengers throughout all
35 he s' messengers unto Asher, and
7: 8 he s' all the rest of Israel every
24 Gideon s' messengers throughout
9:23 Then God s' an evil spirit between
31 he s' messengers unto Abimelech
11:12 Jephthah s' messengers unto the
14 Jephthah s' messengers again unto
17 Israel s' messengers unto the king
17 they s' unto the king of Moab: but
19 Israel s' messengers unto Sihon
28 words of Jephthah which he s' him.
38 And he s' her away for two months:
12: 9 daughters, whom he s' abroad,
16:18 she s' and called for the lords of
18: 2 children of Dan s' of their family
19:29 s' her into all the coast of Israel.
20: 6 s' her throughout all the country
12 tribes of Israel s' men through all
21:10 the congregation s' thither twelve
13 congregation s' some to speak to
1Sa 4: 4 So the people s' to Shiloh, that
5: 8 s' therefore and gathered all the
10 they s' the ark of God to Ekron.
11 s' and gathered together all...lords
6:21 s' messengers to the inhabitants
10:25 And Samuel s' all the people away,
11: 7 s' them throughout all the coasts of
12: 8 then the Lord s' Moses and Aaron,
11 the Lord s' Jerubbaal, and Bedan,
18 Lord s' thunder and rain that day:
13: 2 people he s' every man to his tent.
15: 1 The Lord s' me to anoint thee to be
18 the Lord s' thee on a journey, and
20 gone the way which the Lord s' me,
16:12 he s', and brought him in. Now he
19 Saul s' messengers unto Jesse, and
20 s' them by David his son unto Saul.
22 Saul s' to Jesse, saying, Let David,
17:31 before Saul: and he s' for him.
18: 5 out whithersoever Saul s' him,
19:11 s' messengers unto David's house,
14 Saul s' messengers to take David,
15 Saul s' the messengers again to
17 s' away mine enemy, that he is
20 Saul s' messengers to take David:
21 told Saul, he s' other messengers,
21 Saul s' messengers again the third
20:22 for the Lord hath s' thee away.
22:11 the king s' to call Ahimelech the
25: 5 And David s' out ten young men,
14 David s' messengers out of the
32 which s' thee this day to meet me:
39 And David s' and communed with
40 David s' us unto thee, to take thee
26: 4 David therefore s' out spies, and
30:26 he s' of the spoil unto the elders of
31: 9 s' into the land of the Philistines
2Sa 2: 5 David s' messengers unto the men
3:12 Abner s' messengers to David on
14 David s' messengers to Ish-bosheth
15 Ish-bosheth s', and took her from
21 David s' Abner away; and he went
22 for he had s' him away, and he was
23 to the king, and he hath s' him away,
24 is it that thou hast s' him away,
26 he s' messengers after Abner,
5:11 Hiram king of Tyre s' messengers
8:10 Toi s' Joram...unto king David,
9: 5 Then king David s', and fetched
10: 2 And David s' to comfort him by the
3 he hath s' comforters unto thee?
3 not David rather s' his servants
4 to their buttocks, and s' them away.
5 he s' to meet them, because the
6 children of Ammon s' and hired
7 when David heard of it, he s' Joab.
16 Hadarezer s', and brought out the
11: 1 that David s' Joab, and his servants
3 And David s' and enquired after the
4 David s' messengers, and took her;
5 s' and told David, and said, I am
6 David s' to Joab, saying, Send me
6 And Joab s' Uriah to David.
14 and s' it by the hand of Uriah.
18 Then Joab s' and told David all the
22 David all that Joab had s' him for.
27 David s' and fetched her to his
12: 1 the Lord s' Nathan unto David.
25 he s' by the hand of Nathan the
27 And Joab s' messengers to David,
13: 7 David s' home to Tamar, saying,
14: 2 And Joab s' to Tekoah, and fetched
29 Absalom s' for Joab, to have s' him
29 when he s' again the second time,
32 I s' unto thee, saying, Come hither,
15:10 Absalom s' spies throughout all
12 And Absalom s' for Ahithophel the
18: 2 David s' forth a third part of the
29 When Joab s' the king's servant,
19:11 And king David s' to Zadok and to
14 they s' this word unto the king,
22:15 he s' out arrows, and scattered
17 He s' from above, he took me; he
24:13 I shall return to him that s' me.
15 So the Lord s' a pestilence upon
1Ki 1:44 the king hath s' with him Zadok
53 So king Solomon s', and they
2:25 Solomon s' by the hand of Benaiah
29 Then Solomon s' Benaiah the son of
36, 42 king s' and called for Shimei,
5: 1 Hiram king of Tyre s' his servants

1Ki 5: 2 And Solomon s' to Hiram, saying,
8 Hiram s' to Solomon, saying, I have
14 And he s' them to Lebanon, ten
7:13 And king Solomon s' and fetched
8:66 eighth day he s' the people away:
9:14 And Hiram s' to the king sixscore
27 Hiram s' in the navy his servants,
12: 3 That they s' and called him. And
18 Then king Rehoboam s' Adoram,
20 they s' and called him unto the
14: 6 am s' to thee with heavy tidings.
15:18 king Asa s' them to Ben-hadad, the
19 have s' unto thee a present of silver
20 s' the captains of the hosts which
18:10 my lord hath not s' to seek thee:
20 Ahab s' unto all the children of
19: 2 Jezebel s' a messenger unto Elijah,
20: 2 he s' messengers to Ahab king of
5 Although I have s' unto thee,
7 for he s' unto me for my wives, and
10 Ben-hadad s' unto him, and said,
17 Ben-hadad s' out, and they told
34 with him, and s' him away.
21: 8 s' the letters unto the elders and to
11 did as Jezebel had s' unto them,
11 letters which she had s' unto them.
14 Then they s' to Jezebel, saying,
2Ki 1: 2 he s' messengers, and said unto
6 again unto the king that s' you,
9 the king s' unto him a captain of
11 he s' unto him another captain of
13 he s' again a captain of the third
16 thou has s' messengers to enquire
2: 2 for the Lord hath s' me to Beth-el.
4 for the Lord hath s' me to Jericho.
6 for the Lord hath s' me to Jordan.
17 They s' therefore fifty men; and
3: 7 he went and s' to Jehoshaphat the
5: 6 therewith s' Naaman my servant
8 his clothes, that he s' to the king,
10 Elisha s' a messenger unto him,
22 My master hath s' me, saying,
6: 9 the man of God s' unto the king of
10 the king of Israel s' to the place
14 Therefore s' he thither horses, and
23 eaten and drunk, he s' them away,
32 the king s' a man from before him:
32 how this son of a murderer hath s'
7:14 king s' after the host of the Syrians,
8: 9 king of Syria hath s' me to thee,
9:19 he s' out a second on horseback,
10: 1 wrote letters, and s' to Samaria,
5 elders also,...s' to Jehu, saying,
7 baskets, and s' him them to Jezreel.
21 Jehu s' through all Israel: and all
11: 4 Jehoiada s' and fetched the rulers
12:18 and s' it to Hazael king of Syria:
14: 8 Amaziah s' messengers to Jehoash,
9 the king of Israel s' to Amaziah
9 s' to the cedar that was in Lebanon,
19 but they s' after him to Lachish,
16: 7 So Ahaz s' messengers to
8 and s' it for a present to the king of
10 king Ahaz s' to Urijah the priest
11 king Ahaz had s' from Damascus:
17: 4 he had s' messengers to So king of
13 which I s' to you by my servants
25 Lord s' lions among them, which
26 he hath s' lions among them, and,
18:14 king of Judah s' to the king of
17 the king of Assyria s' Tartan and
27 my master s' me to thy master, and
27 hath he not s' me to the men which
19: 2 he s' Eliakim, which was over the
4 hath s' to reproach the living God;
9 s' messengers again unto Hezekiah,
16 s' him to reproach the living God.
20 the son of Amoz s' to Hezekiah,
20:12 Babylon, s' letters and a present
22: 3 that the king s' Shaphan the son of
15 Tell the man that s' you to me,
18 which s' you to enquire of the Lord,
23: 1 And the king s', and they gathered
16 and s', and took the bones out of
24: 2 Lord s' against him bands of the
2 s' them against Judah to destroy it,
1Ch 8: 8 Moab, after he had s' them away;
10: 9 s' into the land of the Philistines
12:19 upon advisement s' him away,
14: 1 Hiram king of Tyre s' messengers
18:10 s' Hadoram his son to king David,
19: 2 David s' messengers to comfort him
3 he hath s' comforters unto thee?
4 their buttocks, and s' them away.
5 he s' to meet them: for the men
6 s' a thousand talents of silver to
8 when David heard of it, he s' Joab,
16 they s' messengers, and drew forth
21:12 shall bring again to him that s' me.
14 Lord s' pestilence upon Israel:
15 God s' an angel unto Jerusalem to
2Ch 2: 3 Solomon s' to Huram the king of
11 in writing, which he s' to Solomon,
13 And now I have s' a cunning man,
7:10 s' the people away into their tents,
8:18 Huram s' him by the hands of his
10: 3 And they s' and called him. So
18 Then king Rehoboam s' Hadoram
16: 2 and s' to Ben-hadad king of Syria,
3 I have s' thee silver and gold; go,
4 s' the captains of his armies against
17: 7 year of his reign he s' to his princes,
8 And with them he s' Levites, even
24:19 he s' prophets to them, to bring
23 and s' all the spoil of them unto the
25:13 the army which Amaziah s' back,

2Ch 25:15 he s' unto him a prophet, which
17 s' to Joash, the son of Jehoahaz,
18 Joash king of Israel s' to Amaziah
18 s' to the cedar that was in Lebanon,
27 but they s' to Lachish after him,
30: 1 And Hezekiah s' to all Israel and
32:21 the Lord s' an angel, which cut off
31 who s' unto him to enquire of the
34: 8 he s' Shaphan the son of Azaliah,
23 Tell ye the man that s' you to me,
26 who s' you to enquire of the Lord,
29 the king s' and gathered together
35:21 he s' ambassadors to him, saying,
36:10 Nebuchadnezzar s', and brought
15 God of their fathers s' to them by
Ezr 4:11 copy of the letter that they s' unto
14 have we s' and certified the king;
17 s' the king an answer unto Rehum
18 The letter which ye s' unto us hath
5: 6 the river, s' unto Darius the king:
7 They s' a letter unto him, wherein
6:13 that which Darius the king had s',
7:14 as thou art s' of the king, and of
8:16 Then s' I for Eliezer, for Ariel, for
17 I s' them with commandment unto
Ne 2: 9 Now the king had s' captains of
6: 2 Sanballat and Geshem s' unto me,
3 I s' messengers unto them, saying,
4 they s' unto me four times after
5 Then s' Sanballat his servant unto
8 Then I s' unto him, saying, There
12 I perceived that God had not s' him;
17 nobles of Judah s' many letters
19 And Tobiah s' letters to put me in
Es 1:22 For he s' letters into all the king's
3:13 letters were s' by posts into all the
4: 4 she s' raiment to clothe Mordecai,
5:10 he s' and called for his friends, and
8:10 and s' letters by posts on horseback,
9:20 and s' letters unto all the Jews that
30 he s' the letters unto all the Jews,
Job 1: 4 s' and called for their three sisters
5 that Job s' and sanctified them,
22: 9 Thou hast s' widows away empty,
39: 5 Who hath s' out the wild ass free?
Ps 18:14 Yea, he s' out his arrows, and
16 He s' from above, he took me, he
59: *title* when Saul s', and they watched
77:17 the skies s' out a sound: thine
78:25 food: he s' them meat to the full.
45 s' divers sorts of flies among them,
80:11 She s' out her boughs unto the sea,
105:17 He s' a man before them, even
20 The king s' and loosed him; even
26 He s' Moses his servant; and Aaron
28 He s' darkness, and made it dark;
106:15 but s' leanness into their soul.
107:20 He s' his word, and healed them,
111: 9 He s' redemption unto his people:
135: 9 Who s' tokens and wonders into the
Pr 9: 3 She hath s' forth her maidens: she
17:11 messenger shall be s' against him.
Isa 9: 8 The Lord s' a word into Jacob, and
20: 1 Sargon the king of Assyria s' him,)
36: 2 king of Assyria s' Rabshakeh from
12 my master s' me to thy master
12 hath he not s' me to the men that
37: 2 And he s' Eliakim, who was over
4 hath s' to reproach the living God,
9 it, he s' messengers to Hezekiah,
17 hath s' to reproach the living God.
21 the son of Amoz s' unto Hezekiah,
39: 1 s' letters and a present to Hezekiah:
42:19 or deaf, as my messenger that I s'?
43:14 For your sake I have s' to Babylon,
48:16 God, and his Spirit, hath s' me.
55:11 prosper in the thing whereto I s' it.
61: 1 s' me to bind up the brokenhearted,
Jer 7:25 even s' unto you all my servants the
14: 3 their nobles have s' their little ones
14 I s' them not, neither have I
15 I s' them not, yet they say, Sword
19:14 the Lord had s' him to prophesy;
21: 1 king Zedekiah s' unto him Pashur
23:21 I have not s' these prophets, yet
32 yet I s' them not, nor commanded
38 I have s' unto you, saying, Ye shall
24: 5 whom I have s' out of this place
25: 4 hath s' unto you all his servants the
17 unto whom the Lord had s' me:
26: 5 the prophets, whom I s' unto you,
12 The Lord s' me to prophesy against
15 Lord hath s' me unto you to speak
22 king s' men into Egypt, namely,
27:15 I have not s' them, saith the Lord,
28: 9 that the Lord hath truly s' him.
15 The Lord hath not s' thee; but thou
29: 1 the prophet s' from Jerusalem unto
3 king of Judah s' unto Babylon to
9 I have not s' them, saith the Lord.
19 I s' unto them by my servants the
20 whom I have s' from Jerusalem to
25 Because thou hast s' letters in thy
28 therefore he s' unto us in Babylon,
31 I s' him not, and he caused you to
35:15 s' also unto you all my servants the
36:14 all the princes s' Jehudi the son
21 the king s' Jehudi to fetch the roll:
37: 3 Zedekiah the king s' Jehucal the
7 s' you unto me to enquire of me;
17 Zedekiah the king s', and took him
38:14 Then Zedekiah the king s', and took
39:13 the captain of the guard s', and
14 Even they s', and took Jeremiah
40:14 s' Ishmael the son of Nethaniah to
42: 9 s' me to present your supplication

Jer 42:20 ye s' me unto the Lord your God,
21 the which he hath s' me unto you.
43: 1 Lord their God had s' him to them,
2 Lord our God hath not s' thee to
44: 4 I s' unto you all my servants the
49:14 ambassador is s' unto the heathen,
La 1:13 From above hath he s' fire into my
Eze 2: 9 behold, an hand was s' unto me;
3: 5 For thou art not s' to a people of a
6 Surely, had I s' thee to them, they
13: 6 and the Lord hath not s' them: and
23:16 and s' messengers unto them into
40 that ye have s' for men to come
40 unto whom a messenger was s';
31: 4 s' out her little rivers unto all the
Da 3: 2 the king s' to gather together the
28 the God...who hath s' his angel,
5:24 the part of the hand s' from him;
6:22 My God hath s' his angel, and hath
10:11 upright: for unto thee am I now s'.
Ho 5:13 the Assyrian, and s' to king Jareb:
Joe 2:25 great army which I s' among you.
Am 4:10 I have s' among you the pestilence
7:10 priest of Beth-el s' to Jeroboam
Ob 1 and an ambassador is s' among the
Jon 1: 4 the Lord s' out a great wind into
Mic 6: 4 I s' before thee Moses, Aaron, and
Hag 1:12 as the Lord their God had s' him,
Zec 1:10 the Lord hath s' to walk to and fro
2: 8 he s' me unto the nations which
9 that the Lord of hosts hath s' me.
11 Lord of hosts hath s' me unto thee.
4: 9 Lord of hosts hath s' me unto you.
6:15 Lord of hosts hath s' me unto you.
7: 2 they had s' unto the house of God
12 Lord of hosts hath s' in his spirit
9:11 I have s' forth thy prisoners out of
Mal 2: 4 that I have s' this commandment
M't 2: 8 And he s' them to Bethlehem, and
16 s' forth, and slew all the children
10: 5 These twelve Jesus s' forth, and
40 receive me receiveth him that s' me.
11: 2 of Christ, he s' two of his disciples,
13:36 Then Jesus s' the multitude away,
14:10 he s', and beheaded John in the
22 while he s' the multitudes away.
23 when he had s' the multitudes away,
35 they s' out into all that country
15:24 I am not s' but unto the lost sheep
39 he s' away the multitude, and took
20: 2 a day, he s' them into his vineyard.
21: 1 of Olives, then s' Jesus two disciples,
34 s' his servants to the husbandmen,
36 he s' other servants more than the
37 last of all he s' unto them his son,
22: 3 s' forth his servants to call them
4 he s' forth other servants, saying,
7 s' forth his armies, and destroyed
16 they s' out unto him their disciples
23:37 stonest them which are s' unto thee,
27:19 his wife s' unto him, saying, Have
M'r 1:43 him, and forthwith s' him away;
3:31 standing without, s' unto him,
4:36 they had s' away the multitude,
6:17 s' forth and laid hold upon John,
27 the king s' an executioner, and
45 while he s' away the people.
46 And when he had s' them away, he
8: 9 thousand: and he s' them away.
26 he s' him away to his house, saying,
9:37 receiveth not me, but him that s' me.
12: 2 he s' to the husbandmen a servant,
3 beat him, and s' him away empty.
4 he s' unto them another servant;
4 s' him away shamefully handled.
5 again he s' another; and him they
6 he s' him also last unto them,
Lu 1:19 am s' to speak unto thee, and to
26 the angel Gabriel was s' from God
53 the rich he hath s' empty away.
4:18 s' me to heal the brokenhearted, to
26 But unto none of them was Elias s',
43 cities also: for therefore am I s'.
7: 3 s' unto him the elders of the Jews,
6 the centurion s' friends to him,
10 they that were s', returning to the
19 of his disciples, s' them to Jesus,
20 John Baptist hath s' us unto thee,
8:38 with him: but Jesus s' him away,
9: 2 he s' them to preach the kingdom
48 receive me receiveth him that s' me:
52 And s' messengers before his face:
10: 1 s' them two and two before his face
16 me, despiseth him that s' me.
13:34 stonest them that are s' unto thee;
14:17 s' his servant at supper time to say
15:15 s' him into his fields to feed swine.
19:14 and s' a message after him, saying,
29 of Olives, he s' two of his disciples,
32 they that were s' went their way,
20:10 he s' a servant to the husbandmen.
10 beat him, and s' him away empty.
11 And again he s' another servant:
11 shamefully,...s' him away empty.
12 And again he s' a third: and they
20 s' forth spies, which should feign
22: 8 he s' Peter and John, saying, Go and
35 When I s' you without purse, and
23: 7 he s' him to Herod, who himself
11 robe, and s' him again to Pilate.
15 nor yet Herod: for I s' you to him;
Joh 1: 6 There was a man s' from God,
8 was s' to bear witness of that Light.
19 Jews s' priests and Levites from
22 give an answer to them that s' us.
24 which were s' were of the Pharisees.
Joh 1:33 that s' me to baptize with water,
3:17 God s' not his Son into the world to
28 Christ, but that I am s' before him.
34 God hath s' speaketh the words of
4:34 is to do the will of him that s' me,
38 I s' you to reap that whereon ye
5:23 not the Father which hath s' him.
24 believeth on him that s' me, hath
30 will of the Father which hath s' me.
33 Ye s' unto John, and he bare
36 of me, that the Father hath s' me.
37 Father himself, which hath s' me,
38 for whom he hath s', him ye believe
6:29 ye believe on him whom he hath s'.
38 will, but the will of him that s' me.
39 the Father's will which hath s' me
40 this is the will of him that s' me,
44 Father which hath s' me draw him:
57 As the living Father hath s' me,
7:16 is mine, but his that s' me.
18 that seeketh his glory that s' him,
28 he that s' me is true, whom ye know
29 am from him, and he hath s' me.
32 chief priests s' officers to take him.
33 and then I go unto him that s' me.
8:16 but I and the Father that s' me.
18 Father that s' me beareth witness of
26 he that s' me is true; and I speak
29 he that s' me is with me: the Father
42 came I of myself, but he s' me.
9: 4 work the works of him that s' me,
7 (which is by interpretation, *S'*.)
10:36 sanctified, and s' into the world,
11: 3 Therefore his sisters s' unto him,
42 may believe that thou hast s' me.
12:44 not on me, but on him that s' me.
45 that seeth me seeth him that s' me.
49 but the Father which s' me, he gave
13:16 is s' greater than he that s' him.
20 me receiveth him that s' me.
14:24 mine, but the Father's which s' me.
15:21 they know not him that s' me.
16: 5 now I go my way to him that s' me;
17: 3 Jesus Christ, whom thou hast s'.
8 As thou hast s' me into the world,
18 have I also s' them into the world.
21 may believe that thou hast s' me.
23 may know that thou hast s' me,
25 have known that thou hast s' me.
18:24 had s' him bound unto Caiaphas
20:21 as my Father hath s' me, even so
Ac 3:26 his Son Jesus, s' him to bless you,
5:21 and s' to the prison to have them
7:12 Egypt, he s' out our fathers first.
14 Then s' Joseph,...called his father
8:14 they s' unto them Peter and John:
9:17 hath s' me, that thou mightest
30 and s' him forth to Tarsus.
38 they s' unto him two men, desiring
10: 8 unto them, he s' them to Joppa.
17 the men which were s' from
20 doubting nothing:...I have s' them.
21 to the men which were s' unto him
29 gainsaying, as soon as I was s' for:
29 for what intent ye have s' for me?
33 Immediately therefore I s' to thee;
36 God s' unto the children of Israel,
11:11 I was, s' from Cæsarea unto me.
22 and they s' forth Barnabas, that he
30 s' it to the elders by the hands of
12:11 that the Lord hath s' his angel,
13: 3 hands on them, they s' them away.
4 being s' forth by the Holy Ghost,
15 of the synagogue s' unto them,
26 you is the word of this salvation s'.
15:27 s' therefore Judas and Silas, who
16:35 magistrates s' the serjeants, saying,
36 magistrates have s' to let you go:
17:10 s' away Paul and Silas by night
14 the brethren s' away Paul to go as
19:22 he s' into Macedonia two of them
31 s' unto him, desiring him that he
20:17 s' to Ephesus, and called the elders
23:30 I s' straightway to thee, and gave
24:24 he s' for Paul, and heard him
26 wherefore he s' for him the oftener,
28:28 salvation...is s' unto the Gentiles,
Ro 10:15 shall they preach, except they be s'?
subscr. s' by Phebe servant of the church
1Co 1:17 For Christ s' me not to baptize, but
4:17 cause have I s' unto you Timotheus,
2Co 8:18 we have s' with him the brother,
22 we have s' with them our brother,
9: 3 Yet have I s' the brethren, lest our
12:17 any of them whom I s' unto you?
18 Titus, and with him I s' a brother.
Gal 4: 4 God s' forth his Son, made of a
6 God hath s' forth the Spirit of his
Eph 6:22 Whom I have s' unto you for the
Ph'p 2:28 s' him therefore the more carefully,
4:16 ye s' once and again unto my
18 the things which were s' from you,
Col 4: 8 Whom I have s' unto you for the
1Th 3: 2 And s' Timotheus, our brother, and
5 I s' to know your faith, lest by some
2Ti 4:12 And Tychicus have I s' to Ephesus.
Ph'm 12 Whom I have s' again: thou
Heb 1:14 s' forth to minister for them who
Jas 2:25 and had s' them out another way?
1Pe 1:12 Holy Ghost s' down from heaven;
2:14 unto them that are s' by him for
1Jo 4: 9 God s' his only begotten Son into
10 and s' his Son to be the propitiation
14 Father s' the Son to be the Saviour
Re 1: 1 he s' and signified it by his angel
5: 6 of God s' forth into all the earth.
Re 22: 6 God of the holy prophets s' his angel
16 Jesus have s' mine angel to testify

sentence See also SENTENCES.
De 17: 9 shall shew thee the s' of judgment:
10 thou shalt do according to the s',
11 According to the s' of the law
11 from the s' which they shall shew
Ps 17: 2 Let my s' come forth from thy
Pr 16:10 divine s' is in the lips of the king:
Ec 8:11 s' against an evil work is not
Jer 4:12 also will I give s' against them.
Lu 23:24 Pilate gave s' that it should be
Ac 15:19 my s' is, that we trouble not them,
2Co 1: 9 we had the s' of death in ourselves,

sentences
Da 5:12 shewing of hard s', and dissolving
8:23 understanding dark s', shall stand

sentest
Ex 15: 7 thou s' forth thy wrath, which
Nu 13:27 unto the land whither thou s' us,
24:12 messengers which thou s' unto me,
1Ki 5: 8 the things which thou s' to me for:

Senuah (*sen'-u-ah*) See also HASSENUAH.
Ne 11: 9 son of *S'* was second over the city.

Seorim (*se-o'-rim*)
1Ch 24: 8 third to Harim, the fourth to *S'*,

separate See also SEPARATED; SEPARATETH; SEPARATING.
Ge 13: 9 s' thyself, I pray thee, from me:
30:40 And Jacob did s' the lambs, and
49:26 him that was s' from his brethren.
Le 15:31 shall ye s' the children of Israel
22: 2 s' themselves from the holy things
Nu 6: 2 s' themselves to vow a vow of a
2 to s' themselves unto the Lord:
3 He shall s' himself from wine and
8:14 thou s' the Levites from among the
16:21 *S'* yourselves from among this
De 19: 2 Thou shalt s' three cities for thee
7 Thou shalt s' three cities for thee.
29:21 s' him unto evil out of all the tribes
Jos 16: 9 the s' cities for the children of
1Ki 8:53 s' them from among all the people
Ezr 10:11 s' yourselves from the people of the
Jer 37:12 to s' himself thence in the midst
Eze 41:12 was before the s' place at the end
13 the s' place, and the building, with
14 and of the s' place toward the east,
15 the s' place which was behind it,
42: 1 that was over against the s' place,
10 the east, over against the s' place,
13 which are before the s' place, they
M't 25:32 he shall s' them one from another,
Lu 6:22 shall s' you from their company,
Ac 13: 2 *S'* me Barnabas and Saul for the
Ro 8:35 shall s' us from the love of Christ?
39 able to s' us from the love of God,
2Co 6:17 them, and be ye s', saith the Lord,
Heb 7:26 undefiled, s' from sinners, and

separated
Ge 13:11 they s' themselves the one from
14 after that Lot was s' from him,
25:23 two manner of people shall be s'
Ex 33:16 so shall we be s', I and thy people,
Le 20:24 have s' you from other people.
25 I have s' from you as unclean.
Nu 16: 9 God of Israel hath s' you from the
De 10: 8 time the Lord s' the tribe of Levi,
32: 8 when he s' the sons of Adam, he
33:16 him that was s' from his brethren.
1Ch 12: 8 there s' themselves unto David into
23:13 and Aaron was s', that he should
25: 1 s' to the service of the sons of Asaph,
2Ch 25:10 Then Amaziah s' them, to wit, the
Ezr 6:21 s' themselves unto them from the
8:24 Then I s' twelve of the chief of the
9: 1 not s' themselves from the people of
10: 8 himself s' from the congregation of
16 all of them by their names, were s',
Ne 4:19 we are s' upon the wall, one far
9: 2 seed of Israel s' themselves from
10:28 all they that had s' themselves from
13: 3 they s' from Israel all the mixed
Pr 18: 1 desire a man, having s' himself,
19: 4 the poor is s' from his neighbour.
Isa 56: 3 Lord hath utterly s' me from his
59: 2 your iniquities have s' between you
Hos 4:14 themselves are s' with whores,
9:10 s' themselves unto that shame;
Ac 19: 9 from them, and s' the disciples,
Ro 1: 1 apostle, s' unto the gospel of God,
Ga 1:15 who s' me from my mother's womb,
2:12 he withdrew and s' himself, fearing

separateth
Nu 6: 5 which he s' himself unto the Lord,
6 that he s' himself unto the Lord
Pr 16:28 and a whisperer s' chief friends.
17: 9 repeateth a matter s' very friends.
Eze 14: 7 which s' himself from me, and

separating
Zec 7: 3 s' myself, as I have done these so

separation
Le 12: 2 according to the days of the s' for
5 be unclean two weeks, as in her s':
15:20 she lieth upon in her s' shall be
25 many days out of the time of her s',
25 if it run beyond the time of her s';
25 shall be as the days of her s': she
26 be unto her as the bed of her s':
26 as the uncleanness of her s'.
Nu 6: 4 All the days of his s' shall he eat
5 days of the vow of his s' there shall

Nu 6: 8 the days of his s· he is holy unto
12 unto the Lord the days of his s·,
12 be lost, because his s· was defiled.
13 when the days of his s· are fulfilled:
18 shave the head of his s· at the door
18 take the hair of the head of his s·,
19 after the hair of his s· is shaven:
21 his offering unto the Lord for his s·,
21 he must do after the law of his s·.
19: 9 children of Israel for a water of s·:
13 the water of s· was not sprinkled
20 water of s· hath not been sprinkled
21 he that sprinkleth the water of s·
21 he that toucheth water of s·
31: 23 be purified with the water of s·:
Eze 42: 20 to make a s· between the sanctuary

Sephar (*se'-far*)
Ge 10: 30 as thou goest unto *S*· a mount of

Sepharad (*sef'-a-rad*)
Ob 20 the captivity...which is in *S*·.

Sepharvaim (*sef-ar-va'-im*) See also SEPHARVITES.
2Ki 17: 24 and from Hamath, and from *S*·,
31 and Anammelech, the gods of *S*·.
18: 34 where are the gods of *S*·, Hena,
19: 13 the king of the city of *S*·, of Hena,
Isa 36: 19 Arphad? where are the gods of *S*·?
37: 13 and the king of the city of *S*·, Hena,

Sepharvites (*sef'-ar-vites*)
2Ki 17: 31 the *S*· burnt their children in fire

sepulchre See also SEPULCHRES.
Ge 23: 6 shall withhold from thee his s·,
De 34: 6 but no man knoweth of his s·
J'g 8: 32 and was buried in the s· of Joash
1Sa 10: 2 shalt find two men by Rachel's s·
2Sa 2: 32 buried him in the s· of his father,
4: 12 and buried it in the s· of Abner in
17: 23 was buried in the s· of his father.
21: 14 Zelah, in the s· of Kish his father:
1Ki 13: 22 not come unto the s· of thy fathers.
31 s· wherein the man of God is buried;
2Ki 9: 28 him in his s· with his fathers
13: 21 cast the man into the s· of Elisha:
21: 26 in his s· in the garden of Uzza:
23: 17 It is the s· of the man of God,
30 and buried him in his own s·.
Ps 5: 9 their throat is an open s·; they
Isa 22: 16 thou hast hewed thee out a s· here,
16 that heweth him out a s· on high,
Jer 5: 16 Their quiver is as an open s·, they
M't 27: 60 a great stone to the door of the s·,
61 Mary, sitting over against the s·.
64 s· be made sure until the third day,
66 So they went, and made the s· sure,
28: 1 and the other Mary to see the s·.
8 they departed quickly from the s·
M'r 15: 46 laid him in a s· which was hewn
46 a stone unto the door of the s·.
16: 2 they came unto the s· at the rising
3 the stone from the door of the s·?
5 And entering into the s·, they saw
8 out quickly, and fled from the s·;
Lu 23: 53 and laid it in a s· that was hewn
55 beheld the s·, and how his body
24: 1 morning, they came unto the s·,
2 the stone rolled away from the s·.
9 returned from the s·, and told all
12 arose Peter, and ran unto the s·;
22 which were early at the s·;
24 which were with us went to the s·,
Joh 19: 41 in the garden a new s·, wherein
42 day; for the s· was nigh at hand.
20: 1 when it was yet dark, unto the s·,
1 the stone taken away from the s·.
2 taken away the Lord out of the s·,
3 other disciple, and came to the s·.
4 outrun Peter, and came...to the s·.
6 and went into the s·, and seeth the
8 disciple, which came first to the s·,
11 But Mary stood without at the s·
11 stooped down, and looked in the s·,
Ac 2: 29 his s· is with us unto this day.
7: 16 and laid in the s· that Abraham
13: 29 from the tree, and laid him in a s·.
Ro 3: 13 Their throat is an open s·; with

sepulchres
Ge 23: 6 in the choice of our s· bury thy
2Ki 23: 16 he spied the s· that were there in
16 and took the bones out of the s·, and
2Ch 16: 14 And they buried him in his own s·,
21: 20 David, but not in the s· of the kings.
24: 25 buried him not in the s· of the kings.
28: 27 him not into the s· of the kings of
32: 33 in the chiefest of the s· of the sons
35: 24 buried in one of the s· of his fathers.
Ne 2: 3 the city, the place of my fathers' s·,
5 unto the city of my fathers' s·, that
3: 16 place over against the s· of David,
M't 23: 27 ye are like unto whited s·, which
29 garnish the s· of the righteous,
Lu 11: 47 for ye build the s· of the prophets,
48 killed them, and ye build their s·.

Serah (*se'-rah*) See also SARAH; TIMNATH-SERAH.
Ge 46: 17 and Beriah, and *S*· their sister:
1Ch 7: 30 and Beriah, and *S*· their sister.

Seraiah (*se-ra-i'-ah*) See also SHAVSHA.
2Sa 8: 17 priests; and *S*· was the scribe;
2Ki 25: 18 the guard took *S*· the chief priest,
23 and *S*· the son of Tanhumeth the
1Ch 4: 13 the sons of Kenaz; Othniel, and *S*·:
14 and *S*· begat Joab, the father of
35 the son of Josibiah, the son of *S*·,
6: 14 begat *S*·, and *S*· begat Jehozadak,
Ezr 2: 2 Jeshua, Nehemiah, *S*·, Reelaiah,
7: 1 Ezra the son of *S*·, the son of
Ne 10: 2 *S*·, Azariah, Jeremiah,
11: 11 *S*· the son of Hilkiah, the son of
12: 1 and Jeshua: *S*·, Jeremiah, Ezra,
12 chief of the fathers: of *S*·, Meraiah;
Jer 36: 26 *S*· the son of Azriel, and Shelemiah
40: 8 and *S*· the son of Tanhumeth, and
51: 59 commanded *S*· the son of Neriah,
59 And this *S*· was a quiet prince.
61 Jeremiah said to *S*·, When thou
52: 24 the guard took *S*· the chief priest,

seraphims (*ser'-a-fims*)
Isa 6: 2 Above it stood the s·: each one
6 Then flew one of the s· unto me,

Sered (*se'-red*) See also SARDITES.
Ge 46: 14 sons of Zebulun; *S*·, and Elon,
Nu 26: 26 of *S*·, the family of the Sardites:

Sergius (*sur'-je-us*)
Ac 13: 7 *S*· Paulus, a prudent man; who

serjeants
Ac 16: 35 the magistrates sent the s·, saying,
38 the s· told these words unto the

serpent See also SERPENT'S; SERPENTS.
Ge 3: 1 s· was more subtil than any beast
2 woman said unto the s·, We may eat
4 s· said unto the woman, Ye shall not
13 The s· beguiled me, and I did eat.
14 Lord God said unto the s·, Because
49: 17 Dan shall be a s· by the way, an
Ex 4: 3 on the ground, and it became a s·;
7: 9 Pharaoh, and it shall become a s·.
10 his servants, and it became a s·.
15 the rod which was turned to a s·
Nu 21: 8 Make thee a fiery s·, and set it
9 Moses made a s· of brass, and put
9 that if a s· had bitten any man,
9 when he beheld the s· of brass, he
2Ki 18: 4 the brasen s· that Moses had made:
Job 26: 13 hand hath formed the crooked s·.
Ps 58: 4 poison is like the poison of a s·:
140: 3 sharpened their tongues like a s·;
Pr 23: 32 At the last it biteth like a s·, and
30: 19 the way of a s· upon a rock; the way
Ec 10: 8 breaketh an hedge, a s· shall bite
11 s· will bite without enchantment;
Isa 14: 29 his fruit shall be a fiery flying s·.
27: 1 punish leviathan the piercing s·,
1 even leviathan that crooked s·; and
30: 6 lion, the viper and fiery flying s·,
Jer 46: 22 voice thereof shall go like a s·;
Am 5: 19 hand on the wall, and a s· bit him.
9: 3 sea, thence will I command the s·,
Mic 7: 17 They shall lick the dust like a s·,
M't 7: 10 ask a fish, will he give him a s·?
Lu 11: 11 fish, will he for a fish give him a s·?
Joh 3: 14 And as Moses lifted up the s· in the
2Co 11: 3 as the s· beguiled Eve through his
Re 12: 9 old s·, called the Devil, and Satan,
14 half a time, from the face of the s·.
15 the s· cast out of his mouth water
20: 2 old s·, which is the Devil, and Satan,

serpent's
Isa 14: 29 out of the s· root shall come forth
65: 25 and dust shall be the s· meat.

serpents
Ex 7: 12 man his rod, and they became s·:
Nu 21: 6 the Lord sent fiery s· among the
7 that he take away the s· from us.
De 8: 15 wilderness, wherein were fiery s·,
32: 24 with the poison of s· of the dust.
Jer 8: 17 I will send s·, cockatrices, among
M't 10: 16 be ye therefore wise as s·, and
23: 33 Ye s·, ye generation of vipers, how
M'r 16: 18 They shall take up s·; and if they
Lu 10: 19 power to tread on s· and scorpions,
1Co 10: 9 tempted, and were destroyed of s·.
Jas 3: 7 of s·, and of things in the sea, is
Re 9: 19 for their tails were like unto s·,

Serug (*se'-rug*) See also SARUCH.
Ge 11: 20 and thirty years, and begat *S*·:
21 Reu lived after he begat *S*· two
22 *S*· lived thirty years, and begat
23 *S*· lived after he begat Nahor two
1Ch 1: 26 *S*·, Nahor, Terah,

servant See also BONDSERVANT; MAIDSERVANT; SERVANT'S; SERVANTS; SERVITOR.
Ge 9: 25 a s· of servants shall he be unto
26, 27 Shem;...Canaan shall be his s·.
18: 3 not away, I pray thee, from thy s·:
5 therefore are ye come to your s·.
19: 19 thy s· hath found grace in thy sight,
24: 2 Abraham said unto his eldest s·
5 s· said unto him, Peradventure
9 the s· put his hand under the thigh
10 And the s· took ten camels of the
14 that thou hast appointed for thy s·
17 the s· ran to meet her, and said,
34 And he said, I am Abraham's s·.
52 Abraham's s· heard their words,
53 And the s· brought forth jewels of
59 and Abraham's s·, and his men.
61 the s· took Rebekah, and went his
65 she had said unto the s·, What man
65 the s· had said, It is my master:
66 the s· told Isaac all things that
26: 24 thy seed for my s· Abraham's sake.
32: 4 Thy s· Jacob saith thus, I have
10 thou hast shewed unto thy s·; for
18 shalt say, They be thy s· Jacob's;
Ge 32: 20 Behold, thy s· Jacob is behind us.
33: 5 God hath graciously given thy s·.
14 I pray thee, pass over before his s·:
39: 17 Hebrew s·, which thou hast brought
19 After this manner did thy s· to me;
41: 12 s· to the captain of the guard; and
43: 28 Thy s· our father is in good health,
44: 10 whom it is found shall be my s·;
17 the cup is found, he shall be my s·;
18 let thy s·, I pray thee, speak a word
18 not thine anger burn against thy s·:
24 we came up unto thy s· my father,
27 thy s· my father said unto us, Ye
30 when I come to thy s· my father,
31 bring down the gray hairs of thy s·
32 thy s· became surety for the lad
33 let thy s· abide instead of the lad a
49: 15 and became a s· unto tribute.
Ex 4: 10 thou hast spoken unto thy s·: but
12: 44 every man's s· that is bought for
45 an hired s· shall not eat thereof.
14: 31 the Lord, and his s· Moses.
21: 2 If thou buy an Hebrew s·, six years
5 If the s· shall plainly say, I love my
20 if a man smite his s·, or his maid,
26 And if a man smite the eye of his s·,
33: 11 but his s· Joshua, the son of Nun,
Le 22: 10 hired s·, shall not eat of the holy
25: 6 and for thy s·, and for thy maid,
6 and for thy hired s·, and for thy
40 as an hired s·, and as a sojourner,
50 according to the time of an hired s·
53 a yearly hired s· shall he be with
Nu 11: 11 hast thou afflicted thy s·? and
28 the son of Nun, the s· of Moses,
12: 7 My s· Moses is not so, who is
8 to speak against my s· Moses?
14: 24 But my s· Caleb, because he had
De 3: 24 begun to shew thy s· thy greatness,
5: 15 thou wast a s· in the land of Egypt,
15: 17 door, and he shall be thy s· for ever.
18 hath been worth a double hired s·
23: 15 not deliver unto his master the s·
24: 14 shalt not oppress an hired s· that
34: 5 So Moses the s· of the Lord died
Jos 1: 1 death of Moses the s· of the Lord
2 Moses my s· is dead; now therefore
7 Moses my s· commanded thee:
13 which Moses the s· of the Lord
15 which Moses the Lord's s· gave you
5: 14 What saith my lord unto his s·?
8: 31 As Moses the s· of the Lord
33 As Moses the s· of the Lord had
9: 24 commanded his s· Moses to give
11: 12 them, as Moses the s· of the Lord
15 the Lord commanded Moses his s·,
12: 6 Them did Moses the s· of the Lord
6 Moses the s· of the Lord gave it
13: 8 Moses the s· of the Lord gave them;
14: 7 Moses the s· of the Lord sent me
18: 7 Moses the s· of the Lord gave them.
22: 2 Moses...s· of the Lord commanded
4 Moses the s· of the Lord gave you
5 Moses the s· of the Lord charged
24: 29 the son of Nun, the s· of the Lord,
J'g 2: 8 the son of Nun, the s· of the Lord,
7: 10 with Phurah thy s· down to the
11 went he down with Phurah his s·
15: 18 deliverance into the hand of thy s·:
19: 3 having his s· with him, and a
9 he, and his concubine, and his s·,
11 the s· said unto his master, Come,
13 he said unto his s·, Come, and let
Ru 2: 5 Boaz unto his s· that was set over
6 the s· that was set over the reapers
1Sa 2: 13 the priest's s· came, while the flesh
15 the priest's s· came, and said to the
3: 9 Speak, Lord; for thy s· heareth.
10 answered, Speak; for thy s· heareth.
9: 5 Saul said to his s· that was with
7 said Saul to his s·, But, behold, if
8 And the s· answered Saul again,
10 Then said Saul to his s·, Well said;
22 And Samuel took Saul and his s·,
27 Saul, Bid the s· pass on before us,
10: 14 uncle said unto him and to his s·,
17: 32 thy s· will go and fight with this
34 Thy s· kept his father's sheep, and
36 Thy s· slew both the lion and the
58 I am the son of thy s· Jesse the
19: 4 Let not the king sin against his s·,
20: 7 It is well; thy s· shall have peace:
8 thou shalt deal kindly with thy s·;
8 hast brought thy s· into a covenant
22: 8 hath stirred up my s· against me,
15 king impute any thing unto his s·,
15 for thy s· knew nothing of all this,
23: 10 s· hath certainly heard that Saul
11 come down, as thy s· hath heard?
11 of Israel I beseech thee, tell thy s·.
25: 39 and hath kept his s· from evil: for
41 handmaid be a s· to wash the feet
26: 18 my lord thus pursue after his s·?
19 the king hear the words of his s·.
27: 5 why should thy s· dwell in the royal
12 therefore he shall be my s· for ever.
28: 2 thou shalt know what thy s· can do.
29: 3 Is not this David, the s· of Saul the
8 what hast thou found in thy s· so
30: 13 man of Egypt, s· to an Amalekite;
2Sa 3: 18 By the hand of my s· David I will
7: 5 Go and tell my s· David, Thus saith
8 so shalt thou say unto my s· David,
20 for thou, Lord God, knowest thy s·.
21 things, to make thy s· know them.
25 thou hast spoken concerning thy s·,

2Sa 7:26 and let the house of thy s' David be
27 of Israel, hast revealed to thy s',
27 hath thy s' found in his heart to
28 promised this goodness unto thy s':
29 thee to bless the house of thy s',
29 let the house of thy s' be blessed
9: 2 there was of the house of Saul a s'
2 Ziba? And he said, Thy s' is he.
6 and he answered, Behold thy s'!
8 What is thy s', that thou shouldest
9 the king called to Ziba, Saul's s',
11 commanded his s', so shall thy s'
11:21 Thy s' Uriah the Hittite is dead.
24 and thy s' Uriah the Hittite is dead
13:17 called his s' that ministered unto
18 Then his s' brought her out, and
24 now, thy s' hath sheepshearers;
24 and his servants go with thy s'.
35 sons come: as thy s' said, so it is.
14:19 thy s' Jacob, he bade me, and he
20 hath thy s' Joab done this thing:
22 To day thy s' knoweth that I have
22 hath fulfilled the request of his s'.
15: 2 Thy s' is of one of the tribes of
8 thy s' vowed a vow while I abode
21 life, even there also will thy s' be.
34 Absalom, I will be thy s', O king;
34 have been thy father's s' hitherto,
34 so will I now also be thy s': then
16: 1 Ziba the s' of Mephibosheth met
18:29 sent the king's s', and me thy s',
19:17 Ziba the s' of the house of Saul,
19 remember that which thy s' did
20 thy s' doth know...I have sinned:
26 My lord, O king, my s' deceived me:
26 for thy s' said, I will saddle me an
26 to the king; because thy s' is lame.
27 he hath slandered thy s' unto my
28 didst thou set thy s' among them
35 can thy s' taste what I eat or what
35 then should thy s' be yet a burden
36 Thy s' will go a little way over
37 Let thy s', I pray thee, turn back
37 But behold thy s' Chimham; let
24:10 take away the iniquity of thy s';
21 is my lord the king come to his s'?
1Ki 1:19 Solomon thy s' hath he not called.
26 But me, even me thy s', and Zadok
26 thy s' Solomon, hath he not called.
27 thou hast not shewed it unto thy s',
51 to day that he will not slay his s'
2:38 the king hath said, so will thy s' do.
3: 6 shewed unto thy s' David my father
7 made thy s' king instead of David
8 thy s' is in the midst of thy people
9 Give...thy s' an understanding
8:24 Who hast kept with thy s' David
25 keep with thy s' David my father
26 thou spakest unto thy s' David my
28 respect unto the prayer of thy s',
28 which thy s' prayeth before thee
29 the prayer which thy s' shall make
30 thou to the supplication of thy s',
52 unto the supplication of thy s',
53 spakest by the hand of Moses thy s',
56 promised by...hand of Moses his s'.
59 that he maintain the cause of his s',
66 the Lord had done for David his s',
11:11 from thee, and will give it to thy s'.
26 Ephrathite of Zereda, Solomon's s',
32 one tribe for my s' David's sake,
36 that David my s' may have a light
38 commandments, as David my s' did;
12: 7 If thou wilt be a s' unto this people
14: 8 thou hast not been as my s' David,
18 spake by the hand of his s' Ahijah
15:29 which he spake by his s' Ahijah the
16: 9 And his s' Zimri, captain of half his
18: 9 deliver thy s' into the hand of Ahab,
12 but I thy s' fear the Lord from my
36 that I am thy s', and that I have
43 And said to his s', Go up now,
19: 3 to Judah, and left his s' there.
20: 9 that thou didst send for to thy s'
32 Thy s' Ben-hadad saith, I pray thee,
39 Thy s' went out into the midst of
40 as thy s' was busy here and there,
2Ki 4: 1 saying, Thy s' my husband is dead;
1 that thy s' did fear the Lord: and
12 he said to Gehazi his s', Call this
24 and said to her s', Drive, and go
25 he said to Gehazi his s', Behold,
38 he said unto his s', Set on the great
5: 6 sent Naaman my s' to thee, that
15 pray thee, take a blessing of thy s'.
17 given to thy s' two mules' burden
17 thy s' will henceforth offer neither
18 this thing the Lord pardon thy s',
18 the Lord pardon thy s' in this thing.
20 the s' of Elisha the man of God,
25 he said, Thy s' went no whither.
6:15 the s' of the man of God was risen
15 And his s' said unto him, Alas, my
8: 4 Gehazi the s' of the man of God,
13 said, But what, is thy s' a dog,
9:36 spake by his s' Elijah the Tishbite.
10:10 which he spake by his s' Elijah.
14:25 spake by the hand of his s' Jonah,
16: 7 saying, I am thy s' and thy son:
17: 3 and Hoshea became his s', and gave
18:12 Moses...s' of the Lord commanded,
19:34 sake, and for my s' David's sake.
20: 6 sake, and for my s' David's sake.
21: 8 my s' Moses commanded them.
22:12 and Asahiah a s' of the king's,
24: 1 and Jehoiakim became his s' three
2Ki 25: 8 guard, a s' of the king of Babylon,
1Ch 2:34 And Sheshan had a s', an Egyptian,
35 his daughter to Jarha his s' to wife;
6:49 all that Moses the s' of God had
16:13 O ye seed of Israel his s', ye children
17: 4 Go and tell David my s', Thus saith
7 shalt thou say unto my s' David,
18 to thee for the honour of thy s'?
18 for thou knowest thy s'.
23 concerning thy s' and concerning
24 house of David thy s' be established
25 s' that thou wilt build him...house:
25 s' hath found in his heart to pray
26 promised this goodness unto thy s':
27 thee to bless the house of thy s',
21: 8 thee, do away the iniquity of thy s';
2Ch 1: 3 Moses the s' of the Lord had made
6:15 which hast kept with thy s' David
16 keep with thy s' David my father
17 thou hast spoken unto thy s' David.
19 therefore to the prayer of thy s',
19 which thy s' prayeth before thee:
20 thy s' prayeth toward this place.
21 unto the supplications of thy s',
42 the mercies of David thy s'.
13: 6 the s' of Solomon the son of David,
24: 6 of Moses the s' of the Lord, and of
9 that Moses the s' of God laid upon
32:16 God, and against his s' Hezekiah.
34:20 scribe, and Asaiah a s' of the king's,
Ne 1: 6 mayest hear the prayer of thy s',
7 thou commandedst thy s' Moses.
8 thou commandedst thy s' Moses,
11 be attentive to the prayer of thy s',
11 prosper, I pray thee, thy s' this day,
2: 5 and if thy s' have found favour in
10 and Tobiah the s', the Ammonite,
19 Tobiah the s', the Ammonite, and
4:22 with his s' lodge within Jerusalem,
6: 5 sent Sanballat his s' unto me in
9:14 laws, by the hand of Moses thy s':
10:29 was given by Moses the s' of God,
Job 1: 8 Hast thou considered my s' Job,
2: 3 Hast thou considered my s' Job,
3:19 and the s' is free from his master.
7: 2 a s' earnestly desireth the shadow,
19:16 I called my s', and he gave me no
41: 4 wilt thou take him for a s' for ever?
42: 7 that is right, as my s' Job hath.
8 and go to my s' Job, and offer up
8 and my s' Job shall pray for you:
8 thing which is right, like my s' Job.
Ps 18: *title* of David, the s' of the Lord, who
19:11 by them is thy s' warned: and in
13 thy s' also from presumptuous
27: 9 me; put not thy s' away in anger:
31:16 Make thy face to shine upon thy s':
35:27 pleasure in the prosperity of his s'.
36: *title* of David the s' of the Lord.
69:17 And hide not thy face from thy s';
78:70 He chose David also his s', and took
86: 2 save thy s' that trusteth in thee.
4 Rejoice the soul of thy s': for unto
16 give thy strength unto thy s', and
89: 3 I have sworn unto David my s',
20 I have found David my s'; with my
39 made void the covenant of thy s':
105: 6 O ye seed of Abraham his s', ye
17 even Joseph, who was sold for a s':
26 He sent Moses his s'; and Aaron
42 holy promise, and Abraham his s'.
109:28 be ashamed; but let thy s' rejoice.
116:16 O Lord, truly I am thy s';
16 I am thy s', and the son of thine
119:17 Deal bountifully with thy s', that I
23 thy s' did meditate in thy statutes.
38 Stablish thy word unto thy s', who
49 Remember the word unto thy s',
65 Thou hast dealt well with thy s', O
76 according to thy word unto thy s'.
84 How many are the days of thy s'?
122 Be surety for thy s' for good: let not
124 thy s' according unto thy mercy,
125 am thy s'; give me understanding,
135 Make thy face to shine upon thy s';
140 very pure: therefore thy s' loveth it.
176 astray like a lost sheep; seek thy s';
132:10 thy s' David's sake turn not away
136:22 Even an heritage unto Israel his s':
143: 2 enter not into judgment with thy s':
12 that afflict my soul: for I am thy s'.
144:10 who delivereth David his s' from the
Pr 11:29 and the fool shall be s' to the wise
12: 9 He that is despised, and hath a s',
14:35 king's favour is toward a wise s':
17: 2 A wise s' shall have rule over a son
19:10 much less for a s' to have rule over
22: 7 and the borrower is s' to the lender.
29:19 A s' will not be corrected by words:
21 He that delicately bringeth up his s'
30:10 Accuse not a s' unto his master,
22 For a s' when he reigneth; and a
Ec 7:21 lest thou hear thy s' curse thee:
Isa 20: 3 Like as my s' Isaiah hath walked
22:20 I will call my s' Eliakim the son of
24: 2 as with the s', so with his master;
37:35 sake, and for my s' David's sake.
41: 8 But thou, Israel, art my s', Jacob
9 and said unto thee, Thou art my s';
42: 1 Behold my s', whom I uphold; mine
19 Who is blind, but my s'? or deaf, as
19 perfect, and blind as the Lord's s'?
43:10 and my s' whom I have chosen:
44: 1 Yet now hear, O Jacob my s'; and
2 Fear not, O Jacob, my s'; and thou,
21 for thou art my s': I have formed
Isa 44:21 thou art my s': O Israel, thou shalt
26 That confirmeth the word of his s',
48:20 Lord hath redeemed his s' Jacob.
49: 3 Thou art my s', O Israel, in whom
5 me from the womb to be his s',
6 thing that thou shouldest be my s'
7 nation abhorreth, to a s' of rulers,
50:10 that obeyeth the voice of his s', that
52:13 Behold, my s' shall deal prudently,
53:11 shall my righteous s' justify many;
Jer 2:14 Is Israel a s'? is he a homeborn
25: 9 and...the king of Babylon, my s',
27: 6 hand of...the king of Babylon, my s';
30:10 fear thou not, O my s' Jacob, saith
33:21 covenant be broken with David my s',
22 I multiply the seed of David my s',
26 the seed of Jacob, and David my s',
34:16 and caused every man his s', and
43:10 and take...the king of Babylon, my s',
46:27 But fear not thou, O my s' Jacob,
28 Fear thou not, O Jacob my s', saith
Eze 28:25 land...I have given to my s' Jacob.
34:23 shall feed them, even my s' David;
24 my s' David a prince among them;
37:24 David my s' shall be king over them;
25 that I have given unto Jacob my s',
25 my s' David shall be their prince
Da 6:20 O Daniel, s' of the living God, is
9:11 in the law of Moses the s' of God,
17 O our God, hear the prayer of thy s',
10:17 how can the s' of this my lord talk
Hag 2:23 I take thee, O Zerubbabel, my s',
Zec 3: 8 I will bring forth my s' the Branch.
Mal 1: 6 son...his father, and a s' his master:
4: 4 Remember ye the law of Moses my s',
M't 8: 6 s' lieth at home sick of the palsy,
8 only, and my s' shall be healed.
9 to my s', Do this, and he doeth it.
13 his s' was healed in the selfsame
10:24 master, nor the s' above his lord
25 as his master, and the s' as his lord.
12:18 Behold my s', whom I have chosen;
18:26 The s' therefore fell down, and
27 the lord of that s' was moved with
28 But the same s' went out, and found
32 O thou wicked s', I forgave thee all
20:27 chief among you, let him be your s':
23:11 greatest among you shall be your s'.
24:45 Who then is a faithful and wise s',
46 Blessed is that s', whom his lord
48 if that evil s' shall say in his heart,
50 lord of that s' shall come in a day
25:21 Well done, thou good and faithful s':
23 Well done, good and faithful s';
26 Thou wicked and slothful s', thou
30 unprofitable s' into outer darkness:
26:51 and struck a s' of the high priest's,
M'r 9:35 shall be last of all, and s' of all.
10:44 be the chiefest, shall be s' of all.
12: 2 he sent to the husbandmen a s',
4 again he sent unto them another s';
14:47 and smote a s' of the high priest,
Lu 1:54 He hath holpen his s' Israel, in
69 for us in the house of his s' David;
2:29 lettest thou thy s' depart in peace,
7: 2 a certain centurion's s', who was
3 that he would come and heal his s'.
7 a word, and my s' shall be healed.
8 to my s', Do this, and he doeth it.
10 the s' whole that had been sick.
12:43 Blessed is that s', whom his lord
45 But and if that s' say in his heart,
46 lord of that s' will come in a day
47 that s', which knew his lord's will,
14:17 And sent his s' at supper time to say
21 So that s' came, and shewed his lord
21 angry said to his s', Go out quickly
22 the s' said, Lord, it is done as thou
23 lord said unto his s', Go out into
16:13 No s' can serve two masters: for
17: 7 having a s' plowing or feeding
9 Doth he thank that s' because he
19:17 said unto him, Well, thou good s':
22 will I judge thee, thou wicked s'.
20:10 he sent a s' to the husbandmen,
11 And again he sent another s': and
22:50 them smote the s' of the high priest,
Joh 8:34 committeth sin is the s' of sin.
35 the s' abideth not in the house for
12:26 I am, there shall also my s' be:
13:16 The s' is not greater than his lord;
15:15 s' knoweth not what his lord doeth:
20 The s' is not greater than his lord.
18:10 and smote the high priest's s', and
Ac 4:25 Who by the mouth of thy s' David
Ro 1: 1 Paul, a s' of Jesus Christ, called
14: 4 that judgest another man's s'?
16: 1 sister, which is a s' of the church
subscr. sent by Phebe s' of the church
1Co 7:21 Art thou called being a s'? care
22 being a s', is the Lord's freeman:
22 is called, being free, is Christ's s'.
9:19 yet have I made myself s' unto all,
Ga 1:10 I should not be the s' of Christ.
4: 1 a child, differeth nothing from a s',
7 Wherefore thou art no more a s',
Ph'p 2: 7 and took upon him the form of a s',
Col 4:12 who is one of you, a s' of Christ,
2Ti 2:24 the s' of the Lord must not strive;
Tit 1: 1 Paul, a s' of God, and an apostle of
Ph'm 16 Not now as a s', but above a s',
subscr. Philemon, by Onesimus a s'.
Heb 3: 5 faithful in all his house, as a s',
Jas 1: 1 James, a s' of God and of the Lord
2Pe 1: 1 Simon Peter, a s' and an apostle of
Jude 1 Jude, the s' of Jesus Christ, and

Re 1: 1 it by his angel unto his s· John:
15: 3 sing the song of Moses the s· of God,
servant's
Ge 19: 2 in, I pray you, into your s· house,
2Sa 7:19 hast spoken also of thy s· house
1Ki 11:13 to thy son for David my s· sake,
34 days of his life for David my s· sake,
2Ki 8:19 destroy Judah for David his s· sake,
1Ch 17:17 hast also spoken of thy s· house
19 Lord, for thy s· sake, and according
Isa 45: 4 For Jacob my s· sake, and Israel
Joh 18:10 ear. The s· name was Malchus.
servants See also SERVANTS'; MAIDSERVANTS; MENSERVANTS; WOMENSERVANTS.
Ge 9:25 a servant of s· shall he be unto his
14:14 he armed his trained s·, born in his
15 he and his s·, by night, and smote
20: 8 Abimelech...called all his s·, and told
21:25 Abimelech's s· had violently taken
26:14 of herds, and great store of s·:
15 which his father's s· had digged
19 And Isaac's s· digged in the valley,
25 and there Isaac's s· digged a well.
32 that Isaac's s· came, and told him
27:37 brethren have I given to him for s·;
32:16 delivered...into the hand of his s·,
16 said unto his s·, Pass over before
40:20 that he made a feast unto all his s·:
20 and of the chief baker among his s·.
41:10 Pharaoh was wroth with his s·, and
37 Pharaoh, and in the eyes of all his s·.
38 Pharaoh said unto his s·, Can we
42:10 but to buy food are thy s· come.
11 we are true men, thy s· are no spies.
13 Thy s· are twelve brethren, the sons
44: 7 God forbid that thy s· should do
9 whomsoever of thy s· it be found,
16 found out the iniquity of thy s·:
16 behold, we are my lord's s·, both
19 My lord asked his s·, saying, Have
21 thou saidst unto thy s·, Bring him
23 And thou saidst unto thy s·, Except
31 and thy s· shall bring down the gray
45:16 it pleased Pharaoh well, and his s·.
47: 3 Thy s· are shepherds, both we, and
4 thy s· have no pasture for their
4 thy s· dwell in the land of Goshen.
19 and we and our land will be s· unto
25 lord, and we will be Pharaoh's s·.
50: 2 commanded his s· the physicians
7 him went up all the s· of Pharaoh,
17 trespass of the s· of the God of thy
18 and they said, Behold, we be thy s·.
Ex 5:15 dealest thou thus with thy s·?
16 There is no straw given unto thy s·,
16 and, behold, thy s· are beaten; but
21 Pharaoh, and in the eyes of his s·,
7:10 before Pharaoh, and before his s·,
20 Pharaoh, and in the sight of his s·;
8: 3 bed, and into the house of thy s·,
4 thy people, and upon all thy s·.
9 I intreat for thee, and for thy s·,
11 from thy houses, and from thy s·,
21 of flies upon thee, and upon thy s·,
29, 31 from Pharaoh, from his s·, and
9:14 upon thine heart, and upon thy s·,
20 feared...among the s· of Pharaoh
20 made his s· and his cattle flee into
21 left his s· and his cattle in the field.
30 But as for thee and thy s·, I know
34 hardened his heart, he and his s·.
10: 1 his heart, and the heart of his s·,
6 houses, and the houses of all thy s·,
7 And Pharaoh's s· said unto him,
11: 3 in the sight of Pharaoh's s·, and in
8 all these thy s· shall come down
12:30 up in the night, he, and all his s·,
14: 5 the heart of Pharaoh and of his s·
32:13 Abraham, Isaac, and Israel, thy s·,
Le 25:42 For they are my s·, which I brought
55 unto me the children of Israel are s·;
55 they are my s· whom I brought
Nu 22:18 and said unto the s· of Balak,
22 ass, and his two s· were with him.
31:49 Thy s· have taken the sum of the
32: 4 for cattle, and thy s· have cattle:
5 let this land be given unto thy s·
25 s· will do as my lord commandeth.
27 But thy s· will pass over, every man
31 As the Lord hath said unto thy s·,
De 9:27 Remember thy s·, Abraham, Isaac,
29: 2 unto Pharaoh, and unto all his s·,
32:36 and repent himself for his s·, when
43 he will avenge the blood of his s·,
34:11 to Pharaoh, and to all his s·, and to
Jos 9: 8 said unto Joshua, We are thy s·.
9 a very far country thy s· are come
11 and say unto them, We are your s·:
24 Because it was certainly told thy s·,
10: 6 Slack not thy hand from thy s·;
J'g 3:24 When he was gone out, his s· came;
6:27 Then Gideon took ten men of his s·,
19:19 the young man which is with thy s·:
1Sa 4: 9 ye be not s· unto the Hebrews, as
8:14 of them, and give them to his s·.
15 and give to his officers, and to his s·.
17 your sheep: and ye shall be his s·.
9: 3 Take now one of the s· with thee,
12:19 Pray for thy s· unto the Lord thy
16:15 And Saul's s· said unto him, Behold
16 Let our lord now command thy s·,
17 And Saul said unto his s·, Provide
18 Then answered one of the s·, and
17: 8 I a Philistine, and ye s· to Saul?
9 to kill me, then will we be your s·:

1Sa 17: 9 kill him, then shall ye be our s·,
18: 5 and also in the sight of Saul's s·.
22 And Saul commanded his s·, saying,
22 in thee, and all his s· love thee:
23 And Saul's s· spake those words in
24 And the s· of Saul told him, saying,
26 And when his s· told David these
30 more wisely than all the s· of Saul;
19: 1 Jonathan his son, and to all his s·,
21: 2 I have appointed my s· to such
7 man of the s· of Saul was there
11 the s· of Achish said unto him, Is
14 Then said Achish unto his s·, Lo, ye
22: 6 all his s· were standing about him;)
7 Saul said unto his s· that stood
9 which was set over the s· of Saul,
14 faithful among all thy s· as David,
17 But the s· of the king would not put
24: 7 So David stayed his s· with these
25: 8 cometh to thine hand unto thy s·,
10 Nabal answered David's s·, and
10 be many s· now a days that break
19 she said unto her s·, Go on before
40 when the s· of David were come to
41 wash the feet of the s· of my lord.
28: 7 Then said Saul unto his s·, Seek
7 his s· said to him, Behold, there is
23 his s·, together with the woman,
25 it before Saul, and before his s·;
29:10 in the morning with thy master's s·
2Sa 2:12 and the s· of Ish-bosheth the son of
13 the s· of David, went out, and met
15 Saul, and twelve of the s· of David.
17 men of Israel, before the s· of David.
30 there lacked of David's s· nineteen
31 But the s· of David had smitten of
3:22 the s· of David and Joab came from
38 king said unto his s·, Know ye not
6:20 the eyes of the handmaids of his s·,
8: 2 so the Moabites became David's s·,
6 the Syrians became s· to David,
7 shields of gold that were on the s·
14 they of Edom became David's s·.
9:10 thy sons, and thy s·, shall till the
10 Ziba had fifteen sons and twenty s·.
12 Ziba were s· unto Mephibosheth.
10: 2 comfort him by the hand of his s·
2 David's s· came into the land of the
3 David rather sent his s· unto thee,
4 Hanun took David's s·, and shaved
19 the kings that were s· to Hadarezer
11: 1 sent Joab, and his s· with him, and
9 house with all the s· of his lord,
11 my lord Joab, and the s· of my lord,
13 to lie on his bed with the s· of his
17 of the people of the s· of David;
24 shot from off the wall upon thy s·;
24 and some of the king's s· be dead,
12:18 s· of David feared to tell him that
19 David saw that his s· whispered,
19 David said unto his s·, Is the child
21 Then said his s· unto him, What
13:24 thee, and his s· go with thy servant.
28 Absalom had commanded his s·,
29 s· of Absalom did unto Amnon as
31 s· stood by with their clothes rent.
36 also and all his s· wept very sore.
14:30 Therefore he said unto his s·, See,
30 Absalom's s· set the field on fire.
31 have thy s· set my field on fire?
15:14 David said unto all his s· that were
15 the king's s· said unto the king,
15 thy s· are ready to do whatsoever
18 And all his s· passed on beside him;
16: 6 and at all the s· of King David: and
11 said to Abishai, and to all his s·,
17:20 Absalom's s· came to the woman to
18: 7 were slain before the s· of David,
9 And Absalom met the s· of David.
19: 5 this day the face of all thy s·,
6 regardest neither princes nor s·:
7 and speak comfortably unto thy s·:
14 king, Return thou, and all thy s·.
17 sons and his twenty s· with him;
20: 6 take thou thy lord's s·, and pursue
21:15 went down, and his s· with him,
22 of David, and by the hand of his s·.
24:20 and his s· coming on toward him:
1Ki 1: 2 Wherefore his s· said unto him, Let
9 all the men of Judah the king's s·:
33 Take with you the s· of your lord,
47 the king's s· came to bless our lord
2:39 s· of Shimei ran away unto Achish
39 saying, Behold, thy s· be in Gath.
40 to Gath to Achish to seek his s·:
40 went, and brought his s· from Gath.
3:15 and made a feast to all his s·.
5: 1 Hiram...sent his s· unto Solomon;
6 my s· shall be with thy s·: and unto
6 will I give hire for thy s· according
9 My s· shall bring them down from
8:23 covenant and mercy with thy s·
32 heaven, and do, and judge thy s·,
36 forgive the sin of thy s·, and of thy
9:22 they were men of war, and his s·,
27 And Hiram sent in the navy his s·,
27 of the sea, with the s· of Solomon.
10: 5 his table, and the sitting of his s·,
8 happy are these thy s·, which stand
13 to her own country, she and her s·.
11:17 certain Edomites of his father's s·
12: 7 then they will be thy s· for ever.
15:18 them into the hand of his s·: and
20: 6 Yet I will send my s· unto thee to
6 house, and the houses of thy s·;
12 he said unto his s·, Set yourselves

1Ki 20:23 the s· of the king of Syria said unto
31 his s· said unto him, Behold now,
22: 3 the king of Israel said unto his s·,
49 Let my s· go with thy s· in the
2Ki 1:13 and the life of these fifty thy s·, be
2:16 be with thy s· fifty strong men;
3:11 of the king of Israel's s· answered
5:13 his s· came near, and spake unto
23 and laid them upon two of his s·;
6: 3 I pray thee, and go with thy s·.
8 took counsel with his s·, saying,
11 and he called his s·, and said unto
12 one of his s· said, None, my lord,
7:12 in the night, and said unto his s·,
13 one of his s· answered and said,
9: 7 I may avenge the blood of my s·
7 the blood of all the s· of the Lord,
11 came forth to the s· of his lord: and
28 And his s· carried him in a chariot
10: 5 sent to Jehu, saying, We are thy s·,
19 Baal, all his s·, and all his priests;
23 with you none of the s· of the Lord,
12:20 his s· arose, and made a conspiracy,
21 his s·, smote him, and he died;
14: 5 slew his s· which had slain the king
17:13 I sent to you by my s· the prophets.
23 had said by all his s· the prophets.
18:24 of the least of my master's s·, and
26 Speak,...to thy s· in the Syrian
19: 5 So the s· of king Hezekiah came to
6 the s· of the king of Assyria have
21:10 Lord spake by his s· the prophets,
23 the s· of Amon conspired against
22: 9 Thy s· have gathered the money
23:30 his s· carried him in a chariot dead
24: 2 he spake by his s· the prophets.
10 the s· of Nebuchadnezzar king of
11 the city, and his s· did besiege it.
12 he, and his mother, and his s·, and
25:24 Fear not to be the s· of the Chaldees:
1Ch 18: 2 the Moabites became David's s·,
6 and the Syrians became David's s·,
7 shields of gold that were on the s·
13 all the Edomites became David's s·.
19: 2 the s· of David came into the land
3 are not his s· come unto thee for to
4 Wherefore Hanun took David's s·,
19 the s· of Hadarezer saw that they
19 with David, and became his s·:
20: 8 David, and by the hand of his s·.
21: 3 king, are they not all my lord's s·?
2Ch 2: 8 that thy s· can skill to cut timber
8 behold, my s· shall be with thy s·,
10 I will give to thy s·, the hewers
15 spoken of, let him send unto his s·:
6:14 and shewest mercy unto thy s·, that
23 and judge thy s·, by requiting the
27 forgive the sin of thy s·, and of thy
8: 9 Solomon make no s· for his work;
18 sent him by the hands of his s·
18 s· that had knowledge of the sea;
18 they went with the s· of Solomon
9: 4 his table, and the sitting of his s·,
7 happy are these thy s·, which stand
10 And the s· also of Huram, and the
10 s· of Solomon, which brought gold
12 to her own land, she and her s·.
21 to Tarshish with the s· of Huram:
10: 7 to them, they will be thy s· for ever.
12: 8 Nevertheless they shall be his s·;
24:25 his own s· conspired against him
25: 3 slew his s· that had killed the king
32: 9 of Assyria send his s· to Jerusalem,
16 his s· spake yet more against the
33:24 And his s· conspired against him,
34:16 that was committed to thy s·, they
35:23 king said to his s·, Have me away;
24 His s· therefore took him out of the
36:20 where they were s· to him and his
Ezr 2:55 The children of Solomon's s·: the
58 and the children of Solomon's s·,
65 Beside their s· and their maids, of
4:11 Thy s· the men on this side the
5:11 We are the s· of the God of heaven
9:11 commanded by thy s· the prophets,
Ne 1: 6 for the children of Israel thy s·, and
10 these are thy s· and thy people,
11 to the prayer of thy s·, who desire
2:20 we his s· will arise and build: but
4:16 half of my s· wrought in the work,
23 I, nor my brethren, nor my s·, nor
5: 5 sons and our daughters to be s·,
10 my s·, might exact of them money
15 their s· bare rule over the people:
16 my s· were gathered thither unto
7:57 The children of Solomon's s·: the
60 and the children of Solomon's s·,
9:10 upon Pharaoh, and on all his s·, and
36 Behold, we are s· this day, and for
36 good thereof, behold, we are s· in it:
11: 3 and the children of Solomon's s·.
13:19 some of my s· set I at the gates,
Es 1: 3 unto all his princes and his s·;
2: 2 Then said the king's s· that
18 unto all his princes and his s·,
3: 2 all the king's s·, that were in the
3 Then the king's s·, which were in
4:11 All the king's s·, and the people of
5:11 above the princes and s· of the king.
6: 3 Then said the king's s· that
5 the king's s· said unto him, Behold,
Job 1:15 have slain the s· with the edge of the
16 burned up the sheep, and the s·, and
17 and slain the s· with the edge of the
4:18 Behold, he put no trust in his s·;
Ps 34:22 Lord redeemeth the soul of his s·;

Ps 69:36 The seed also of his s' shall inherit
79: 2 The dead bodies of thy s' have they
10 the revenging of the blood of thy s'
89:50 Remember,...the reproach of thy s';
90:13 let it repent thee concerning thy s'.
16 Let thy work appear unto thy s',
102:14 thy s' take pleasure in her stones,
28 children of thy s' shall continue,
105:25 people, to deal subtilly with his s'.
113: 1 Praise, O ye s' of the Lord, praise
119:91 thine ordinances: for all are thy s'.
123: 2 as the eyes of s' look unto the hand
134: 1 ye the Lord, all ye s' of the Lord,
135: 1 praise him, O ye s' of the Lord.
9 upon Pharaoh, and upon all his s'.
14 repent himself concerning his s'.
Pr 29:12 to lies, all his s' are wicked.
Ec 2: 7 I got me s' and maidens, and had
7 and had s' born in my house; also
10: 7 I have seen s' upon horses, and
7 and princes walking as s' upon the
Isa 14: 2 of the Lord for s' and handmaids:
36: 9 of the least of my master's s',
11 Speak,...unto thy s' in the Syrian
37: 5 s' of king Hezekiah came to Isaiah.
6 the s' of the king of Assyria have
24 By thy s'...reproached the Lord,
54:17 the heritage of the s' of the Lord,
56: 6 the name of the Lord, to be his s',
65: 9 it, and my s' shall dwell there.
13 s' shall eat, but ye shall be hungry:
13 my s' shall drink, but ye shall be
13 my s' shall rejoice, but ye shall be
14 my s' shall sing for joy of heart, but
15 and call his s' by another name:
66:14 Lord shall be known toward his s',
Jer 7:25 even sent unto you all my s' the
21: 7 Zedekiah king of Judah, and his s',
22: 2 throne of David, thou, and thy s',
4 and on horses, he, and his s', and
25: 4 hath sent unto you all his s' the
19 king of Egypt, and his s', and his
26: 5 hearken to the words of my s' the
29:19 unto them by my s' the prophets,
34:11 caused the s' and the handmaids,
11 them into subjection for s' and for
16 unto you for s' and for handmaids.
35:15 I have sent also unto you all my s'
36:24 nor any of his s' that heard all these
31 punish him and his seed and his s'
37: 2 But neither he, nor his s', nor the
18 against thee, or against thy s', or
44: 4 Howbeit I sent unto you all my s'
46:26 and into the hands of his s': and
La 5: 8 S' have ruled over us: there is none
Eze 38:17 I have spoken in old time by my s'
46:17 of his inheritance to one of his s',
Da 1:12 Prove thy s', I beseech thee, ten
13 and as thou seest, deal with thy s'.
2: 4 tell thy s' the dream, and we will
7 Let the king tell his s' the dream,
3:26 ye s' of the most high God, come
28 delivered his s' that trusted in him,
9: 6 have we hearkened unto thy s' the
10 which he set before us by his s' the
Joe 2:29 And also upon the s' and upon the
Am 3: 7 revealeth his secret unto his s' the
Mic 6: 4 redeemed thee out of...house of s';
Zec 1: 6 I commanded my s' the prophets,
2: 9 they shall be a spoil to their s':
M't 13:27 the s' of the householder came and
28 s' said unto him, Wilt thou then
14: 2 And said unto his s', This is John
18:23 which would take account of his s'.
21:34 he sent his s' to the husbandmen,
35 husbandmen took his s', and beat
36 he sent other s' more than the first:
22: 3 sent forth his s' to call them that
4 he sent forth other s', saying, Tell
6 And the remnant took his s', and
8 saith he to his s', The wedding is
10 s' went out into the highways, and
13 said the king to the s', Bind him
25:14 who called his own s', and delivered
19 time the lord of those s' cometh,
26:58 and sat with the s', to see the end.
M'r 1:20 in the ship with the hired s',
13:34 and gave authority to his s', and to
14:54 he sat with the s', and warmed
65 s' did strike him with the palms of
Lu 12:37 Blessed are those s', whom the
38 find them so, blessed are those s'.
15:17 many hired s' of my father's have
19 son: make me as one of thy hired s'.
22 But the father said to his s', Bring
26 he called one of the s', and asked
17:10 say, We are unprofitable s': we
19:13 he called his ten s', and delivered
15 he commanded these s' to be called
Joh 2: 5 His mother saith unto the s',
9 the s' which drew the water knew;)
4:51 going down, his s' met him, and
15:15 Henceforth I call you not s';
18:18 the s' and officers stood there, who
26 One of the s' of the high priest,
36 this world, then would my s' fight,
Ac 2:18 on my s' and on my handmaidens
4:29 and grant unto thy s', that with all
10: 7 he called two of his household s' and
16:17 are the s' of the most high God,
Ro 6:16 whom ye yield yourselves s' to obey,
16 his s' ye are to whom ye obey;
17 thanked, that ye were the s' of sin,
18 ye became the s' of righteousness.
19 your members s' to uncleanness
19 your members s' to righteousness

Ro 6:20 when ye were the s' of sin, ye were
22 and become s' to God, ye have your
1Co 7:23 a price; be not ye the s' of men.
2Co 4: 5 ourselves your s' for Jesus' sake.
Eph 6: 5 S', be obedient to them that are
6 but as the s' of Christ, doing the
Ph'p 1: 1 s' of Jesus Christ, to all the saints
Col 3:22 S', obey in all things your masters
4: 1 give unto your s' that which is just
1Ti 6: 1 as many s' as are under the yoke
Tit 2: 9 Exhort s' to be obedient unto their
1Pe 2:16 maliciousness, but as the s' of God.
18 S', be subject to your masters
2Pe 2:19 they...are the s' of corruption:
Re 1: 1 to shew unto his s' things which
2:20 to teach and to seduce my s' to
7: 3 we have sealed the s' of our God in
10: 7 hath declared to his s' the prophets.
11:18 reward unto thy s' the prophets,
19: 2 hath avenged the blood of his s' at
5 Praise our God, all ye his s', and ye
22: 3 in it; and his s' shall serve him:
6 sent his angel to shew unto his s'

servants'
Ge 46:34 s' trade hath been about cattle
Ex 8:24 of Pharaoh, and into his s' houses,
Isa 63:17 Return, for thy s' sake, the tribes of
65: 8 so will I do for my s' sake, that I

serve See also OBSERVE; PRESERVE; RESERVE; SERVED; SERVEST; SERVETH; SERVING.
Ge 15:13 is not theirs, and shall s' them;
14 that nation, whom they shall s' also,
25:23 and the elder shall s' the younger.
27:29 Let people s' thee, and nations bow
40 thou live, and shalt s' thy brother;
29:15 thou therefore s' me for nought?
18 I will s' thee seven years for Rachel
25 did not I s' with thee for Rachel?
27 s' with me yet seven other years.
Ex 1:13 children of Israel to s' with rigour:
14 they made them s', was with rigour.
3:12 ye shall s' God upon this mountain.
4:23 Let my son go, that he may s' me:
7:16 they may s' me in the wilderness:
8: 1, 20 people go, that they may s' me.
9: 1 my people go, that they may s' me.
10: 3 my people go, that they may s' me.
8 them, Go, s' the Lord your God:
11 ye that are men, and s' the Lord;
24 Moses, and said, Go ye, s' the Lord;
26 we take to s' the Lord our God;
26 not with what we must s' the Lord,
12:31 and go, s' the Lord, as ye have said.
14:12 that we may s' the Egyptians?
12 better for us to s' the Egyptians,
20: 5 down thyself to them, nor s' them:
21: 2 servant, six years he shall s': and
6 aul; and he shall s' him for ever.
23:24 down to their gods, nor s' them,
25 And ye shall s' the Lord your God,
33 if thou s' their gods, it will surely
Le 25:39 compel him to s' as a bondservant:
40 and shall s' thee unto the year of
Nu 4:24 families of the Gershonites, to s',
26 is made for them: so shall they s'.
8:25 thereof, and shall s' no more:
18: 7 and within the vail; and ye shall s':
21 for their service which they s', even
De 4:19 to worship them, and s' them, for
28 there ye shall s' gods, the work of
5: 9 thyself unto them, nor s' them:
6:13 fear the Lord thy God, and s' him,
7: 4 me, that they may s' other gods:
16 neither shalt thou s' their gods;
8:19 walk after other gods, and s' them,
10:12 to s' the Lord thy God with all thy
20 him shalt thou s', and to him shalt
11:13 and to s' him with all your heart
16 ye turn aside, and s' other gods,
12:30 How did these nations s' their gods?
13: 2 hast not known, and let us s' them;
4 and ye shall s' him, and cleave unto
6, 13 Let us go and s' other gods,
15:12 unto thee, and s' thee six years;
20:11 unto thee, and they shall s' thee.
28:14 to go after other gods to s' them.
36 and there shalt thou s' other gods,
48 shalt thou s' thine enemies which
64 and there thou shalt s' other gods,
29:18 and s' the gods of these nations;
30:17 worship other gods, and s' them;
31:20 turn unto other gods, and s' them,
Jos 16:10 unto this day, and s' under tribute.
22: 5 and to s' him with all your heart
23: 7 neither s' them, nor bow yourselves
24:14 and s' him in sincerity and in truth:
14 and in Egypt; and s' ye the Lord.
15 it seem evil unto you to s' the Lord,
15 choose you this day whom ye will s';
15 and my house, we will s' the Lord.
16 forsake the Lord, to s' other gods;
18 therefore will we also s' the Lord;
19 Ye cannot s' the Lord: for he is an
20 the Lord, and s' strange gods, then
21 Nay; but we will s' the Lord.
22 have chosen you the Lord, to s' him.
24 The Lord our God will we s', and
J'g 2:19 in following other gods to s' them,
9:28 is Shechem, that we should s' him?
28 s' the men of Hamor the father of
28 Shechem: for why should we s' him?
38 Abimelech, that we should s' him?
1Sa 7: 3 unto the Lord, and s' him only:
10: 7 that thou do as occasion s' thee;
11: 1 covenant with us,...we will s' thee.

1Sa 12:10 of our enemies, and we will s' thee.
14 If ye will fear the Lord, and s' him,
20 but s' the Lord with all your heart;
24 s' him in truth with all your heart:
17: 9 shall ye be our servants, and s' us.
26:19 the Lord, saying, Go, s' other gods.
2Sa 15: 8 Jerusalem, then I will s' the Lord.
16:19 And again, whom should I s'?
19 should I not s' in the presence of
22:44 which I knew not shall s' me.
1Ki 9: 6 go and s' other gods, and worship
12: 4 upon us, lighter,...we will s' thee.
7 and wilt s' them, and answer them,
2Ki 10:18 little; but Jehu shall s' him much.
17:35 nor s' them, nor sacrifice to them:
25:24 land, and s' the king of Babylon;
1Ch 28: 9 s' him with a perfect heart and with
2Ch 7:19 and shall go and s' other gods, and
10: 4 he put upon us, and we will s' thee.
29:11 to stand before him, to s' him,
30: 8 and s' the Lord your God, that the
33:16 commanded Judah to s' the Lord
34:33 all that were present in Israel to s',
33 even to s' the Lord their God. And
35: 3 s' now the Lord your God, and his
Job 21:15 Almighty, that we should s' him?
36:11 If they obey and s' him, they shall
39: 9 the unicorn be willing to s' thee,
Ps 2:11 S' the Lord with fear, and rejoice
18:43 whom I have not known shall s' me.
22:30 A seed shall s' him; it shall be
72:11 before him: all nations shall s' him.
97: 7 be all they that s' graven images,
100: 2 S' the Lord with gladness: come
101: 6 in a perfect way, he shall s' me.
102:22 and the kingdoms, to s' the Lord.
Isa 14: 3 wherein thou wast made to s',
19:23 and the Egyptians shall s' with the
43:23 caused thee to s' with an offering,
24 hast made me to s' with thy sins,
56: 6 themselves to the Lord, to s' him,
60:12 that will not s' thee shall perish;
Jer 5:19 so shall ye s' strangers in a land
11:10 went after other gods to s' them:
13:10 walk after other gods, to s' them,
16:13 ye s' other gods day and night;
17: 4 will cause thee to s' thine enemies
25: 6 go not after other gods to s' them,
11 nations shall s' the king of Babylon
14 kings shall s' themselves of them
27: 6 have I given him also to s' him.
7 And all nations shall s' him, and
7 kings shall s' themselves of him.
8 not s' the same Nebuchadnezzar
9 Ye shall not s' the king of Babylon:
11 of the king of Babylon, and s' him,
12 and s' him and his people, and live.
13 that will not s' the king of Babylon?
14 Ye shall not s' the king of Babylon:
17 s' the king of Babylon, and live:
28:14 that they may s' Nebuchadnezzar
14 and they shall s' him: and I have
30: 8 shall no more s' themselves of him:
9 they shall s' the Lord their God,
34: 9 none should s' himself of them, to
10 none should s' themselves of them
35:15 go not after other gods to s' them,
40: 9 Fear not to s' the Chaldeans: dwell
9 land, and s' the king of Babylon,
10 s' the Chaldeans, which will *5975.
44: 3 to s' other gods, whom they knew
Eze 20:32 countries, to s' wood and stone.
39 Go ye, s' ye every one his idols,
40 all of them in the land, s' me:
29:18 caused his army to s' a great service
48:18 for food unto them that s' the city.
19 And they that s' the city shall s'
19 s' it out of all the tribes of Israel.
Da 3:12 they s' not thy gods, nor worship
14 do not ye s' my gods, nor worship
17 God whom we s' is able to deliver
18 we will not s' thy gods, nor worship
28 might not s' nor worship any god,
7:14 and languages, should s' him:
27 dominions shall s' and obey him.
Zep 3: 9 Lord, to s' him with one consent.
Mal 3:14 Ye have said, It is vain to s' God:
M't 4:10 God, and him only shalt thou s'.
6:24 No man can s' two masters: for
24 Ye cannot s' God and mammon.
Lu 1:74 might s' him without fear,
4: 8 thy God, and him only shalt thou s'.
10:40 my sister hath left me to s' alone?
12:37 and will come forth and s' them.
15:29 Lo, these many years do I s' thee,
16:13 No servant can s' two masters: for
13 Ye cannot s' God and mammon.
17: 8 sup, and gird thyself, and s' me.
22:26 he that is chief, as he that doth s'.
Joh 12:26 If any man s' me, let him follow
26 if any man s' me, him will my
Ac 6: 2 leave the word of God, and s' tables.
7: 7 come forth, and s' me in this place.
27:23 of God, whose I am, and whom I s',
Ro 1: 9 whom I s' with my spirit in the
6: 6 henceforth we should not s' sin.
7: 6 we should s' in newness of spirit,
25 mind I myself s' the law of God;
9:12 her, The elder shall s' the younger.
16:18 such s' not our Lord Jesus Christ,
Ga 5:13 flesh, but by love s' one another.
Col 3:24 for ye s' the Lord Christ.
1Th 1: 9 idols to s' the living and true God;
2Ti 1: 3 whom I s' from my forefathers
Heb 8: 5 Who s' unto the example and
9:14 dead works to s' the living God?

Heb12:28 we may s' God acceptably with
13:10 right to eat which s' the tabernacle.
Re 7:15 s' him day and night in his temple:
3 it; and his servants shall s' him:

served^ See also OBSERVED; PRESERVED; RESERVED; SERVEDST.
Ge 14: 4 years they s' Chedorlaomer, and
29:20 Jacob s' seven years for Rachel;
30 s' with him yet seven other years.
30:26 children, for whom I have s' thee,
29 Thou knowest how I have s' thee,
31: 6 all my power have I s' your father.
41 I s' thee fourteen years for thy two
39: 4 grace in his sight, and he s' him:
40: 4 Joseph with them, and he s' them:
De 12: 2 ye shall possess s' their gods,
17: 3 And hath gone and s' other gods,
29:26 For they went and s' other gods,
Jos 23:16 and have gone and s' other gods,
24: 2 of Nachor: and they s' other gods.
14, 15 the gods which your fathers s'
31 Israel s' the Lord all the days of
J'g 2: 7 people s' the Lord all the days of
11 sight of the Lord, and s' Baalim:
13 Lord, and s' Baal and Ashtaroth.
3: 6 to their sons, and s' their gods.
7 God, and s' Baalim and the groves.
8 Israel s' Cushan-rishathaim eight
14 Israel s' Eglon the king of Moab
8: 1 him, Why hast thou s' us thus,
10: 6 and s' Baalim, and Ashtaroth, and
6 forsook the Lord, and s' not him.
10 forsaken our God, and...s' Baalim.
13 forsaken me, and s' other gods:
16 from among them, and s' the Lord:
1Sa 7: 4 and Ashtaroth, and s' the Lord only.
8: 8 forsaken me, and s' other gods,
12:10 and have s' Baalim and Ashtaroth:
2Sa 10:19 made peace with Israel, and s' them.
16:19 as I have s' in thy father's presence,
1Ki 4:21 s' Solomon all the days of his life.
9: 9 have worshipped them, and s' them:
16:31 went and s' Baal, and worshipped
22:53 For he s' Baal, and worshipped him,
2Ki 10:18 unto them, Ahab s' Baal a little;
17:12 For they s' idols, whereof the Lord
16 all the host of heaven, and s' Baal.
33 the Lord, and s' their own gods,
41 Lord, and s' their graven images,
18: 7 the king of Assyria, and s' him not.
21: 3 all the host of heaven, and s' them.
21 and s' the idols that his father s',
1Ch 27: 1 and their officers that s' the king
2Ch 7:22 worshipped them, and s' them:
24:18 fathers, and s' groves and idols:
33: 3 all the host of heaven, and s' them.
22 his father had made, and s' them;
Ne 9:35 have not s' thee in their kingdom,
Es 1:10 s' in the presence of Ahasuerus
Ps 106:36 And they s' their idols: which
137: 8 rewardeth thee as thou hast s' us.
Ec 5: 9 the king himself is s' by the field.
Jer 5:19 and s' strange gods in your land, so
8: 2 have loved, and whom they have s',
16:11 after other gods, and have s' them,
22: 9 worshipped other gods, and s' them.
34:14 and when he hath s' thee six years,
52:12 which s' the king of Babylon,
Eze 29:18 service that he had s' against it:
20 labour wherewith he s' against it,
34:27 of those that s' themselves of them.
Ho 12:12 Israel s' for a wife, and for a wife
Lu 2:37 s' God with fastings and prayers
Joh 12: 2 made him a supper; and Martha s':
Ac 13:36 after he had s' his own generation
Ro 1:25 and s' the creature more than the
Ph'p 2:22 he hath s' with me in the gospel.

servedst
De 28:47 s' not the Lord...with joyfulness,

servest See also PRESERVEST.
Da 6:16 Thy God whom thou s' continually,
20 thy God, whom thou s' continually,

serveth See also PRESERVETH.
Nu 3:36 thereof, and all that s' thereto,
Mal 3:17 spareth his own son that s' him.
18 that s' God and him that s' him not.
Lu 22:27 that sitteth at meat, or he that s'?
27 but I am among you as he that s'.
Ro 14:18 he that in these things s' Christ is
1Co 14:22 but prophesying s', not for them that
Ga 3:19 Wherefore then s' the law? It was

service See also BONDSERVICE; EYESERVICE.
Ge 29:27 for the s' which thou shalt serve
30:26 knowest my s' which I have done
Ex 1:14 and in all manner of s' in the field:
14 all their s',...was with rigour.
12:25 promised, that ye shall keep this s'.
26 unto you, What mean ye by this s'?
13: 5 thou shalt keep this s' in this month.
27:19 the tabernacle in all the s' thereof,
30:16 it for the s' of the tabernacle of the
31:10 And the cloths of s', and the holy
35:19 The cloths of s', to do
19 to do s' in the holy place,
21 and for all his s', and for the holy
24 shittim wood for any work of the s',
36: 1 of work for the s' of the sanctuary,
3 the work of the s' of the sanctuary,
5 than enough for the s' of the work,
38:21 for the s' of the Levites, by the hand
39: 1 scarlet, they made cloths of s',
1 do s' in the holy place, and made
40 vessels of the s' of the tabernacle,
41 The cloths of s' to do
Ex 39:41 to do s' in the holy place,
Nu 3: 7, 8 to do the s' of the tabernacle.
26 the cords of it for all the s' thereof.
31 the hanging, and all the s' thereof.
4: 4 shall be the s' of the sons of Kohath
19 and appoint them every one to his s'
23 all that enter in to perform the s',
24 s' of the families of the Gershonites,
26 and all the instruments of their s',
27 s' of the sons of the Gershonites,
27 their burdens, and in all their s':
28 is the s' of the families...of Gershon
30 every one that entereth into the s',
31 according to all their s' in the
32 instruments, and with all their s':
33 s' of the families...of Merari,
33 according to all their s', in the
35 every one that entereth into the s',
37 that might do s' in the tabernacle
39 every one that entereth into the s',
41 that might do s' in the tabernacle
43 every one that entereth into the s',
47 came to do the s' of the ministry,
47 s' of the burden in the tabernacle
49 every one according to his s', and
7: 5 may be to do the s' of the tabernacle
5 to every man according to his s'.
7 of Gershon, according to their s':
8 of Merari, according unto their s',
9 s' of the sanctuary belonging unto
8:11 they may execute the s' of the Lord.
15 go in to do the s' of the tabernacle
19 do the s' of the children of Israel
22 went the Levites in to do their s'
24 wait upon the s' of the tabernacle
25 cease waiting upon the s' thereof,
26 keep the charge, and shall do no s'.
16: 9 to do the s' of the tabernacle of the
18: 4 for all the s' of the tabernacle:
6 to do the s' of the tabernacle of the
7 priest's office unto you as a s' of gift:
21 for their s' which they serve,
21 even the s' of the tabernacle of the
23 shall do the s' of the tabernacle of
31 reward for your s' in the tabernacle
Jos 22:27 that we might do the s' of the Lord
1Ki 12: 4 thou the grievous s' of thy father,
1Ch 6:31 whom David set over the s' of song
48 all manner of s' of the tabernacle
9:13 work of the s' of the house of God.
19 were over the work of the s', keepers
23:24 work for the s' of the house of the
26 any vessels of it for the s' thereof.
28 for the s' of the house of the Lord,
28 work of the s' of the house of God;
32 in the s' of the house of the Lord.
24: 3 according to their offices in their s'.
19 the orderings of them in their s'
25: 1 separated to the s' of the sons of
1 workmen according to their s' was:
6 harps, for the s' of the house of God,
26: 8 able men for strength for the s',
30 the Lord, and in the s' of the king.
28:13 work of the s' of the house of the
13 the vessels of s' in the house of the
14 all instruments of all manner of s';
14 all instruments of every kind of s':
20 finished all the work for the s' of the
21 for all the s' of the house of God:
21 skilful man, for any manner of s':
29: 5 is willing to consecrate his s'
7 gave for the s' of the house of God
2Ch 8:14 the courses of the priests to their s',
12: 8 that they may know my s', and
8 s' of the kingdoms of the countries.
24:12 to such as did the work of the s' of
29:35 So the s' of the house of the Lord
31: 2 every man according to his s', the
16 daily portion for their s' in their
21 began in the s' of the house of God,
34:13 the work in any manner of s':
35: 2 and encouraged them to the s' of the
10 So the s' was prepared, and the
15 they might not depart from their s';
16 all the s' of the Lord was prepared
Ezr 6:18 their courses, for the s' of God,
7:19 given thee for the s' of the house
8:20 had appointed for the s' of the
Ne 10:32 the third part of a shekel for the s'
Ps 104:14 cattle, and herb for the s' of man:
Jer 22:13 useth his neighbour's s' without
Eze 29:18 caused his army to serve a great s'
18 the s' that he had served against it:
44:14 of the house, for all the s' thereof,
Joh 16: 2 will think that he doeth God s'.
Ro 9: 4 and the s' of God, and the promises;
12: 1 God, which is your reasonable s'.
15:31 s' which I have for Jerusalem may
2Co 9:12 administration of this s' not only
11: 8 taking wages of them, to do you s'.
Ga 4: 8 did s' unto them which by nature
Eph 6: 7 With good will doing s', as to the
Ph'p 2:17 the sacrifice and s' of your faith,
30 to supply your lack of s' toward me
1Ti 6: 2 but rather do them s', because
Heb 9: 1 had also ordinances of divine s',
6 accomplishing the s' of God.
9 make him that did the s' perfect,
Re 2:19 thy works, and charity, and s',

servile
Le 23: 7, 8 ye shall do no s' work therein.
21 ye shall do no s' work therein: it
25 Ye shall do no s' work therein: but
35, 36 ye shall do no s' work therein.
Nu 28:18 do no manner of s' work therein:
25 convocation; ye shall do no s' work.
Nu 28:26 convocation; ye shall do no s' work:
29: 1 convocation; ye shall do no s' work:
12 convocation ye shall do no s' work,
35 ye shall do no s' work therein:

serving
Ex 14: 5 we have let Israel go from s' us?
De 15:18 to thee, in s' thee six years:
Lu 10:40 was cumbered about much s', and
Ac 20:19 S' the Lord with all humility of
26: 7 instantly s' God day and night,
Ro 12:11 fervent in spirit; s' the Lord;
Tit 3: 3 s' divers lusts and pleasures, living

servitor
2Ki 4:43 And his s' said, What, should I

servitude
2Ch 10: 4 thou somewhat the grievous s' of
La 1: 3 affliction, and because of great s':

set^ See also BESET; SEATED; SETTEST; SETTETH; SETTING.
Ge 1:17 God s' them in the firmament of
4:15 And the Lord s' a mark upon Cain,
6:16 of the ark shalt thou s' in the side
9:13 I do s' my bow in the cloud, and it
17:21 shall bear unto thee at this s' time
18: 8 had dressed, and s' it before them;
19:16 forth, and s' him without the city.
21: 2 s' time of which God had spoken
28 Abraham s' seven ewe lambs of
29 which thou hast s' by themselves?
24:33 And there was s' meat before him
28:11 all night, because the sun was s';
12 behold a ladder s' up on the earth,
18 pillows, and s' it up for a pillar,
22 stone, which I have s' for a pillar,
30:36 he s' three days' journey betwixt
38 he s' the rods which he had pilled
40 s' the faces of the flocks toward
31:17 and s' his sons and his wives upon
21 and s' his face toward the mount
37 s' it here before my brethren and
45 Jacob took a stone, and s' it up for
35:14 Jacob s' up a pillar in the place
20 Jacob s' a pillar upon her grave:
41:33 and s' him over the land of Egypt.
41 s' thee over all the land of Egypt.
43: 9 unto thee, and s' him before thee,
31 himself, and said, S' on bread.
32 And they s' on for him by himself,
44:21 that I may s' mine eyes upon him.
47: 7 father, and s' him before Pharaoh:
48:20 he s' Ephraim before Manasseh.
Ex 1:11 they did s' over them taskmasters
4:20 his sons, and s' them upon an ass,
5:14 taskmasters had s' over them,
7:23 did he s' his heart to this also.
9: 5 And the Lord appointed a s' time,
13:12 thou shalt s' apart unto the Lord all
19:12 thou shalt s' bounds unto the people
23 S' bounds about the mount, and
21: 1 which thou shalt s' before them.
23:31 s' thy bounds from the Red sea
25: 7 and stones to be s' in the ephod,
30 shalt s' upon the table shewbread
26:17 s' in order one against another:
35 shalt s' the table without the vail,
28:11 them to be s' in ouches of gold.
17 shalt s' in it settings of stones,
20 be s' in gold in their inclosings.
31: 5 in cutting of stones, to s' them,
32:22 people, that they are s' on mischief.
35: 9 and stones to be s' for the ephod,
27 and stones to be s', for the ephod,
33 the cutting of stones, to s' them,
37: 3 to be s' by the four corners of it;
39:10 they s' in it four rows of stones:
37 even with the lamps to be s' in order,
40: 2 first month shalt thou s' up the
4 table, and s' in order the things
4 that are to be s' in order upon it;
5 And thou shalt s' the altar of gold
6 thou shalt s' the altar of the burnt
7 And thou shalt s' the laver between
8 thou shalt s' up the court round
18 s' up the boards thereof, and put in
20 and s' the staves on the ark, and put
21 and s' up the vail of the covering,
23 he s' the bread in order upon it
28 he s' up the hanging at the door
30 he s' the laver between the tent of
33 s' up the hanging of the court gate.
Le 17:10 even s' my face against that soul
20: 3 I will s' my face against that man,
5 I will s' my face against that man,
6 even s' my face against that soul,
24: 6 thou shalt s' them in two rows,
8 he shall s' it in order before the
26: 1 neither shall ye s' up any image
11 I will s' my tabernacle among you:
17 And I will s' my face against you,
Nu 1:51 pitched, the Levites shall s' it up:
2: 9 armies. These shall first s' forth.
16 shall s' forth in the second rank.
17 congregation shall s' forward with
17 encamp, so shall they s' forward,
34 so they s' forward, every one after
4:15 as the camp is to s' forward; after
5:16 near, and s' her before the Lord:
18, 30 s' the woman before the Lord,
7: 1 had fully s' up the tabernacle,
8:13 thou shalt s' the Levites before
10:17 and the sons of Merari s' forward,
18 of the camp of Reuben s' forward
21 And the Kohathites s' forward,
21 the other did s' up the tabernacle

Nu 10:22 children of Ephraim *s·* forward
25 of the children of Dan *s·* forward,
28 their armies, when they *s·* forward.
35 to pass, when the ark *s·* forward,
11:24 and *s·* them round about the
21: 8 fiery serpent, and *s·* it upon a pole:
10 the children of Israel *s·* forward,
22: 1 the children of Israel *s·* forward,
24: 1 *s·* his face toward the wilderness.
27:16 *s·* a man over the congregation,
19, 22 *s·* him before Eleazar the
29:39 do unto the Lord in your *s·* feasts,
De 1: 8 I have *s·* the land before you: go
21 God hath *s·* the land before thee:
4: 8 law, which I *s·* before you this day?
44 law...Moses *s·* before the children
7: 7 Lord did not *s·* his love upon you,
11:26 I *s·* before you this day a blessing
32 which I *s·* before you this day.
14:24 God shall choose to *s·* his name
16:22 shalt thou *s·* thee up any image;
17:14 I will *s·* a king over me, like as all
15 in any wise *s·* him king over thee,
15 brethren shalt thou *s·* king over
15 mayest not *s·* a stranger over thee,
19:14 time have *s·* in thine inheritance,
26: 4 *s·* it down before the altar of the
10 shalt *s·* it before the Lord thy God,
27: 2 thou shalt *s·* thee up great stones,
4 ye shall *s·* up these stones, which I
28: 1 God will *s·* thee on high above all
36 king which thou shalt *s·* over thee,
56 to *s·* the sole of her foot upon the
30: 1 curse, which I have *s·* before thee,
15 I have *s·* before thee this day life
19 I have *s·* before you life and death,
32: 8 he *s·* the bounds of the people
22 *s·* on fire the foundations of the
46 *S·* your hearts unto all the words
Jos 4: 9 Joshua *s·* up twelve stones in the
6:26 son shall he *s·* up the gates of it.
8: 8 that ye shall *s·* the city on fire:
12 *s·* them to lie in ambush between
13 when they had *s·* the people, even
19 and hasted and *s·* the city on fire.
10:18 and *s·* men by it for to keep them:
18: 1 and *s·* up the tabernacle of the
24:25 *s·* them a statute and an ordinance
26 and *s·* it up there under an oak,
J'g 1: 8 the sword, and *s·* the city on fire.
6:18 my present, and *s·* it before thee.
7: 5 him shalt thou *s·* by himself;
19 they had but newly *s·* the watch:
22 Lord *s·* every man's sword against
9:25 men of Shechem *s·* liers in wait for
33 rise early, and *s·* upon the city:
49 and *s·* the hold on fire upon them;
15: 5 when he had *s·* the brands on fire,
16:25 they *s·* him between the pillars.
18:30 children of Dan *s·* up the graven
31 *s·* them up Micah's graven image,
20:22 *s·* their battle again in array in
29 And Israel *s·* liers in wait round
36 which they had *s·* beside Gibeah.
48 *s·* on fire all the cities that they
Ru 2: 5, 6 his servant that was *s·* over the
1Sa 2: 8 to *s·* them among princes, and to
8 he hath *s·* the world upon them.
5: 2 of Dagon, and *s·* it by Dagon.
3 and *s·* him in his place again.
6:18 they *s·* down the ark of the Lord:
7:12 *s·* it between Mizpeh and Shen,
9:20 days ago, *s·* not thy mind on them;
23 I said unto thee, *S·* it by thee.
24 was upon it, and *s·* it before Saul.
24 is left! *s·* it before thee, and eat:
10:19 him, Nay, but *s·* a king over us.
12:13 the Lord hath *s·* a king over you.
13: 8 *s·* time that Samuel had appointed:
15:11 that I have *s·* up Saul to be king:
12 he *s·* him up a place, and is gone
17: 2 *s·* the battle in array against the
8 come out to *s·* your battle in array?
18: 5 Saul *s·* him over the men of war,
30 so that his name was much *s·* by.
22: 9 was *s·* over the servants of Saul,
26:24 thy life was much *s·* by this day
24 much *s·* by in the eyes of the Lord,
28:22 *s·* a morsel of bread before thee;
2Sa 3:10 to *s·* up the throne of David over
6: 3 *s·* the ark of God upon a new cart,
17 of the Lord, and *s·* it in his place,
7:12 I will *s·* up thy seed after thee,
10:17 the Syrians *s·* themselves in array
11:15 *S·* ye Uriah in the forefront of the
12:20 they *s·* bread before him, and he
30 stones: and it was *s·* on David's head.
14:30 barley there; go and *s·* it on fire.
30 servants *s·* the field on fire.
31 thy servants *s·* my field on fire?
15:24 and they *s·* down the ark of God;
18: 1 and *s·* captains of thousands and
13 wouldest have *s·* thyself against
19:28 thou *s·* thy servant among them
20: 5 he tarried longer than the *s·* time
23:23 And David *s·* him over his guard.
1Ki 2:15 that all Israel *s·* their faces on me,
19 seat to be *s·* for the king's mother;
24 *s·* me on the throne of David my
5: 5 whom I will *s·* upon thy throne in
6:19 to *s·* there the ark of the covenant
27 And he *s·* the cherubims within the
7:16 to *s·* upon the tops of the pillars:
21 he *s·* up the pillars in the porch of
21 and he *s·* up the right pillar, and
21 he *s·* up the left pillar, and called
1Ki 7:25 and the sea was *s·* above upon them,
39 he *s·* the sea on the right side of
8:21 I have *s·* there a place for the ark,
9: 6 my statutes which I have *s·* before
10: 9 to *s·* thee on the throne of Israel:
12:29 And he *s·* the one in Beth-el, and
14: 4 eyes were *s·* by reason of his age.
15: 4 to *s·* up his son after him, and to
16:34 and *s·* up the gates thereof in his
20:12 servants, *S·* yourselves in array.
12 they *s·* themselves in array against
21: 9 and *s·* Naboth on high among the
10 *s·* two men, sons of Belial, before
12 and *s·* Naboth on high among the
2Ki 4: 4 shalt *s·* aside that which is full.
10 and let us *s·* for him there a bed,
38 *S·* on the great pot, and seethe
43 should I *s·* this before an hundred
44 So he *s·* it before them, and they
6:22 *s·* bread and water before them.
8:12 strong holds wilt thou *s·* on fire,
10: 3 and *s·* him on his father's throne,
12: 4 money that every man is *s·* at,
9 *s·* it beside the altar, on the right
17 and Hazael *s·* his face to go up to
17:10 *s·* them up images and groves in
18:23 on thy part to *s·* riders upon them.
20: 1 *S·* thine house in order; for thou
21: 7 he *s·* a graven image of the grove
25:19 an officer that was *s·* over the men
28 *s·* his throne above the throne of
1Ch 6:31 David *s·* over the service of song
9:22 seer did ordain in their *s·* office.
26 chief porters, were in their *s·* office,
31 *s·* office over the things that were
11:14 *s·* themselves in the midst of that
25 and David *s·* him over his guard.
16: 1 *s·* it in the midst of the tent that
19:10 that the battle was *s·* against him
11 and they *s·* themselves in array
17 *s·* the battle in array against them.
21:18 *s·* up an altar unto the Lord in
22: 2 *s·* masons to hew wrought stones
19 *s·* your heart and your soul to seek
23: 4 *s·* forward the work of the house
31 new moons, and on the *s·* feasts,
29: 2 onyx stones, and stones to be *s·*,
3 I have *s·* my affection to the house of
2Ch 2:18 he *s·* threescore and ten thousand
18 overseers to *s·* the people a work.
3: 5 *s·* thereon palm trees and chains.
4: 7 and *s·* them in the temple, five on
10 he *s·* the sea on the right side of the
19 tables whereon the shewbread was *s·*;
6:10 and am *s·* on the throne of Israel,
13 had *s·* it in the midst of the court:
7:19 statutes...which I have *s·* before you,
9: 8 in thee to *s·* thee on his throne,
11:16 as *s·* their hearts to seek the Lord
13: 3 And Abijah *s·* the battle in array
3 Jeroboam also *s·* the battle in array
11 the shewbread also *s·* they in order
14:10 *s·* the battle in array in the valley
17: 2 *s·* garrisons in the land of Judah,
19: 5 he *s·* judges in the land throughout
8 did Jehoshaphat *s·* of the Levites,
20: 3 and *s·* himself to seek the Lord,
17 *s·* yourselves, stand ye still, and
22 the Lord *s·* ambushments against
23:10 And he *s·* all the people, every man
14 that were *s·* over the host,
19 And he *s·* the porters at the gates
20 and *s·* the king upon the throne of
24: 8 and *s·* it without at the gate of the
13 *s·* the house of God in his state,
25:14 Seir, and *s·* them up to be his gods,
29:25 he *s·* the Levites in the house of the
35 house of the Lord was *s·* in order.
31: 3 new moons, and for the *s·* feasts,
15 of the priests, in their *s·* office, to
18 for in their *s·* office they sanctified
32: 6 *s·* captains of war over the people,
33: 7 And he *s·* a carved image, the idol
19 *s·* up groves and graven images,
34:12 of the Kohathites, to *s·* it forward;
35: 2 he *s·* the priests in their charges,
Ezr 2:68 house of God to *s·* it up in his place:
3: 3 they *s·* the altar upon his bases;
5 and of all the *s·* feasts of the Lord
8 *s·* forward the work of the house
9 to *s·* forward the workmen in the
10 they *s·* the priests in their apparel
4:10 and *s·* in the cities of Samaria,
12 and have *s·* up the walls thereof,
13 be builded, the walls *s·* up again,
16 again, and the walls thereof *s·* up,
5:11 king of Israel builded and *s·* up.
6:11 being *s·* up, let him be hanged
18 *s·* the priests in their divisions,
7:25 *s·* magistrates and judges, which
9: 9 to *s·* up the house of our God, and
Ne 1: 9 I have chosen to *s·* my name there.
2: 6 to send me; and I *s·* him a time.
3: 1 sanctified it, and *s·* up the doors of
3, 6, 13, 14, 15 *s·* up the doors thereof,
4: 9 *s·* a watch against them day and
13 Therefore *s·* I in the lower places
13 *s·* the people after their families
5: 7 *s·* a great assembly against them.
6: 1 *s·* up the doors upon the gates;)
7: 1 was built, and I had *s·* up the doors.
9:37 kings whom thou hast *s·* over us
10:33 the new moons, for the *s·* feasts,
13:11 together,...*s·* them in their place.
19 some of my servants *s·* I at the gates,
Es 2:17 *s·* the royal crown upon her head,
Es 3: 1 and *s·* his seat above all the princes
6: 8 royal which is *s·* upon his head:
8: 2 Esther *s·* Mordecai over the house
Job 5:11 To *s·* up on high those that be low;
6: 4 terrors of God do *s·* themselves in
7:17 shouldest *s·* thine heart upon him?
20 thou *s·* me as a mark against thee,
9:19 who shall *s·* me a time to plead?
14:13 wouldest appoint me a *s·* time,
16:12 pieces, and *s·* me up for his mark.
19: 8 he hath *s·* darkness in my paths.
30: 1 have *s·* with the dogs of my flock.
13 path, they *s·* forward my calamity,
33: 5 *s·* thy words in order before me,
34:14 If he *s·* his heart upon man, if he
24 and *s·* others in their stead.
36:16 that which should be *s·* on thy table
38:10 place, and *s·* bars and doors,
33 *s·* the dominion...in the earth?
Ps 2: 2 kings of the earth *s·* themselves,
6 Yet have I *s·* my king upon my
3: 6 have *s·* themselves against him
4: 3 the Lord hath *s·* apart him that is
8: 1 *s·* thy glory above the heavens.
10: 8 are privily *s·* against the poor.
12: 5 I will *s·* him in safety from him
16: 8 have *s·* the Lord always before me:
17:11 *s·* their eyes bowing down to the
19: 4 hath he *s·* a tabernacle for the sun,
20: 5 of our God we will *s·* up our banners:
27: 5 he shall *s·* me up upon a rock.
31: 8 hast *s·* my feet in a large room.
40: 2 clay, and *s·* my feet upon a rock,
50:21 *s·* them in order before thine eyes.
54: 3 they have not *s·* God before them.
57: 4 even among them that are *s·* on fire,
62:10 *s·* not your heart upon them.
69:29 salvation, O God, *s·* me up on high.
73: 9 They *s·* their mouth against the
18 didst *s·* them in slippery places:
74: 4 they *s·* up their ensigns for signs.
17 hast *s·* all the borders of the earth:
78: 7 they might *s·* their hope in God,
8 that *s·* not their heart aright, and
85:13 shall *s·* us in the way of his steps.
86:14 and have not *s·* thee before them.
89:25 I will *s·* his hand also in the sea,
42 hast *s·* up the right hand of his
90: 8 Thou hast *s·* our iniquities before
91:14 Because he hath *s·* his love upon me,
14 I will *s·* him on high, because he hath
101: 3 I will *s·* no wicked thing before
102:13 to favour her, yea, the *s·* time, is come.
104: 9 Thou hast *s·* a bound that they
109: 6 *S·* thou a wicked man over him:
113: 8 That he may *s·* him with princes,
118: 5 me, and *s·* me in a large place.
122: 5 there are *s·* thrones of judgment,
132:11 thy body will I *s·* upon thy throne.
140: 5 wayside; they have *s·* gins for me.
141: 2 be *s·* forth before thee as incense;
3 *S·* a watch, O Lord, before my
Pr 1:25 have *s·* at nought all my counsel,
8:23 I was *s·* up from everlasting, from
27 he *s·* a compass upon the face of
22:28 landmark,...thy fathers have *s·*.
23: 5 Wilt thou *s·* thine eyes upon that
Ec 3:11 he hath *s·* the world in their heart,
7:14 God also hath *s·* the one over
8:11 of men is fully *s·* in them to do evil.
10: 6 Folly is *s·* in great dignity, and
12: 9 and *s·* in order many proverbs.
Ca 5:12 washed with milk, and fitly *s·*.
14 are as gold rings *s·* with the beryl:
15 *s·* upon sockets of fine gold: his
7: 2 heap of wheat *s·* about with lilies.
8: 6 *S·* me as a seal upon thine heart,
Isa 3:24 and instead of well *s·* hair baldness;
7: 6 and *s·* a king in the midst of it, even
9:11 Lord shall *s·* up the adversaries
11:11 the Lord shall *s·* his hand again the
12 *s·* up an ensign for the nations,
14: 1 and *s·* them in their own land: and
17:10 and shalt *s·* it with strange slips:
19: 2 I will *s·* the Egyptians against
21: 6 Go, *s·* a watchman, let him declare
8 I am *s·* in my ward whole nights:
22: 7 horsemen shall *s·* themselves in
23:13 they *s·* up the towers thereof, they
27: 4 *s·* the briers and thorns against
11 women come, and *s·* them on fire:
36: 8 thy part to *s·* riders upon them.
38: 1 *S·* thine house in order: for thou
41:19 I will *s·* in the desert the fir tree,
42: 4 he have *s·* judgment in the earth:
25 it hath *s·* him on fire round about,
44: 7 declare it,...*s·* it in order for me,
45:20 that *s·* up the wood of their graven
46: 7 him, and *s·* him in his place, and
49:22 *s·* up my standard to the people:
50: 7 have I *s·* my face like a flint, and
57: 7 mountain hast thou *s·* thy bed:
8 hast thou *s·* up thy remembrance:
62: 6 *s·* watchmen upon thy walls, O
66:19 I will *s·* a sign among them, and I
Jer 1:10 this day *s·* thee over the nations
15 they shall *s·* every one his throne
4: 6 *S·* up the standard toward Zion:
5:26 they *s·* a trap, they catch men.
6: 1 Tekoa, and *s·* up a sign of fire in
17 Also I *s·* watchmen over you,
23 *s·* in array as men for war against
27 I have *s·* thee for a tower and a
7:12 where I *s·* my name at the first,
30 they have *s·* their abominations in
9:13 my law which I *s·* before them,

Jer 10:20 more, and to s· up my curtains.
11:13 ye s· up altars to that shameful
21: 8 I s· before you the way of life, and
10 I have s· my face against this city
23: 4 I will s· up shepherds over them
24: 1 of figs were s· before the temple
6 s· mine eyes upon them for good,
26: 4 law, which I have s· before you,
31:21 *S·* thee up waymarks, make thee
21 s· thine heart toward the highway,
29 the children's teeth are s· on edge.
30 grape, his teeth shall be s· on edge.
32:20 s· signs and wonders in the land
29 shall come and s· fire on this city,
34 they s· their abominations in the
34:16 had s· at liberty at their pleasure,
35: 5 I s· before the sons of the house
38:22 Thy friends have s· thee on, and
40:11 s· over them Gedaliah the son of
42:15 s· your faces to enter into Egypt,
17 that s· their faces to go into Egypt
43:10 will s· his throne upon these stones
44:10 I s· before you and before your
11 I will s· my face against you for
12 s· their faces to go into the land of
49:38 And I will s· my throne in Elam,
50: 2 and publish, and s· up a standard;
9 s· themselves in array against her;
51:12 *S·* up the standard upon the walls
12 s· up the watchmen, prepare the
27 *S·* ye up a standard in the land,
52:32 s· his throne above the throne of
La 2:17 he hath s· up the horn of thine
3: 6 He hath s· me in dark places, as
12 and s· me as a mark for the arrow.
Eze 2: 2 s· me upon my feet, that I heard
3:24 s· me upon my feet, and speak with
4: 2 it; s· the camp also against it, and
2 s· battering rams against it round
3 and s· it for a wall of iron between
3 s· thy face against it, and it shall
7 shalt s· thy face toward the siege of
5: 5 s· it in the midst of the nations
6: 2 s· thy face toward the mountains
7:20 his ornament, he s· it in majesty:
20 have I s· it far from them.
9: 4 s· a mark upon the foreheads of
12: 6 I have s· thee for a sign unto the
13:17 s· thy face against the daughters
14: 3 men have s· up their idols in their
8 will s· my face against that man,
15: 7 And I will s· my face against them;
7 when I s· my face against them.
16:18 hast s· mine oil and mine incense
19 even s· it before them for a sweet
17: 4 he s· it in a city of merchants.
5 waters, and s· it as a willow tree.
22 of the high cedar, and will s· it;
18: 2 the children's teeth are s· on edge?
19: 8 nations s· against him on every
20:46 s· thy face toward the south, and
21: 2 s· thy face toward Jerusalem, and
15 I have s· the point of the sword
16 left, whithersoever thy face is s·.
22: 7 they s· light by father and mother:
10 her that was s· apart for pollution.
23:24 s· against thee buckler and shield
24 I will s· judgment before them,
25 I will s· my jealousy against thee,
41 hast s· mine incense and mine oil.
24: 2 king of Babylon s· himself against
3 *S·* on a pot, s· it on, and also pour
7 she s· it upon the top of a rock;
8 I have s· her blood upon the top of
11 s· it empty upon the coals thereof,
25 whereupon they s· their minds,
25: 2 Son of man, s· thy face against
4 they shall s· their palaces in thee,
26: 9 shall s· engines of war against thy
20 s· thee in the low parts of the
20 s· glory in the land of the living;
27:10 thee; they s· forth thy comeliness.
28: 2, 6 s· thine heart as the heart of
14 I have s· thee so: thou wast upon
21 of man, s· thy face against Zidon,
29: 2 s· thy face against Pharaoh king
30: 8 when I have s· a fire in Egypt, and
14 and will s· fire in Zoan, and will
16 And I will s· fire in Egypt: Sin shall
31: 4 the deep s· him up on high with
32: 8 and s· darkness upon thy land,
23 graves are s· in the sides of the pit,
25 They have s· her a bed in the midst
33: 2 and s· for him their watchman:
7 I have s· thee a watchman unto the
34:23 And I will s· up one shepherd over
35: 2 s· thy face against mount Seir, and
37: 1 and s· me down in the midst of the
26 will s· my sanctuary in the midst
38: 2 s· thy face against Gog, the land of
39: 9 and shall s· on fire and burn the
15 then shall he s· up a sign by it,
21 s· my glory among the heathen,
40: 2 s· me upon a very high mountain,
4 s· thine heart upon all that I shall
44: 8 ye have s· keepers of my charge in
Da 1:11 the eunuchs had s· over Daniel,
2:44 God of heaven s· up a kingdom,
49 and he s· Shadrach, Meshach, and
3: 1 he s· it up in the plain of Dura, in
2 Nebuchadnezzar the king had s· up.
3 Nebuchadnezzar the king had s· up;
3 that Nebuchadnezzar had s· up.
5 Nebuchadnezzar the king hath s· up:
7 Nebuchadnezzar the king had s· up.
12 whom thou hast s· over the affairs

Da 3:12 image which thou hast s· up.
14 golden image which I have s· up?
18 golden image which thou hast s· up.
5:19 and whom he would he s· up; and
6: 1 It pleased Darius to s· over the
3 to s· him over the whole realm.
14 s· his heart on Daniel to deliver
7:10 judgment was s·, and the books
8:18 he touched me, and s· me upright.
9: 3 I s· my face unto the Lord God, to
10 he s· before us by his servants the
10:10 which s· me upon my knees and
12 didst s· thine heart to understand,
15 I s· my face toward the ground,
11:11 shall s· forth a great multitude;
13 shall s· forth a multitude greater
17 He shall also s· his face to enter
12:11 that maketh desolate s· up, there
Ho 2: 3 s· her as in the day that she was
3 s· her like a dry land, and slay
4: 8 s· their heart on their iniquity.
6:11 he hath s· an harvest for thee,
8: 1 *S·* the trumpet to thy mouth. He
4 They have s· up kings, but not by
11: 8 how shall I s· thee as Zeboim?
Joe 2: 5 a strong people s· in battle array.
Am 7: 8 s· a plumbline in the midst of my
8: 5 we may s· forth wheat, making the
9: 4 s· mine eyes upon them for evil,
Ob 4 thou s· thy nest among the stars,
Na 3: 6 and will s· thee as a gazingstock.
13 gates of thy land shall be s· wide
Hab 2: 1 and s· me upon the tower, and
9 that he may s· his nest on high,
Zec 3: 5 them s· a fair mitre upon his head.
5 they s· a fair mitre upon his head,
5:11 and s· there upon her own base.
6:11 s· them upon the head of Joshua
8:10 I s· all men every one against his
Mal 3:15 that work wickedness are s· up;
M't 5: 1 and when he was s·, his disciples
14 that is s· on an hill cannot be hid.
10:35 to s· a man at variance against his
18: 2 and s· him in the midst of them,
21: 7 clothes, and they s· him thereon.
25:33 s· the sheep on his right hand, but
27:19 was s· down on the judgment seat,
37 s· up over his head his accusation
M'r 1:32 at even, when the sun did s·, they
4:21 and not to be s· on a candlestick?
6:41 to his disciples to s· before them;
8: 6 to his disciples to s· before them;
6 they did s· them before the people.
7 to s· them also before them.
9:12 many things, and be s· at nought.
36 and s· him in the midst of them:
12: 1 s· an hedge about it, and digged a
Lu 1: 1 to s· forth in order a declaration of
2:34 child is s· for the fall and rising
4: 9 s· him on a pinnacle of the temple,
18 s· at liberty them that are bruised,
7: 8 also am a man s· under authority,
9:16 disciples to s· before the multitude.
47 took a child, and s· him by him,
51 s· his face to go to Jerusalem,
10: 8 such things as are s· before you:
34 wine, and s· him on his own beast,
11: 6 I have nothing to s· before him?
19:35 the colt, and they s· Jesus thereon.
22:55 and were s· down together, Peter
23:11 his men of war s· him at nought,
Joh 2: 6 there were s· there six waterpots
10 beginning doth s· forth good wine;
3:33 hath s· to his seal that God is true.
6:11 disciples to them that were s· down;
8: 3 when they had s· her in the midst,
13:12 garments, and was s· down again,
19:29 was s· a vessel full of vinegar:
Ac 4: 7 when they had s· them in the midst,
11 the stone which was s· at nought
5:27 they s· them before the council:
6: 6 Whom they s· before the apostles:
13 And s· up false witnesses, which
7: 5 not so much as to s· his foot on:
26 would have s· them at one again,
12:21 upon a s· day Herod, arrayed in
13: 9 the Holy Ghost, s· his eyes on him,
47 I have s· thee to be a light of the
15:16 ruins thereof, and I will s· it up:
16:34 his house, he s· meat before them,
17: 5 and s· all the city on an uproar,
18:10 and no man shall s· on thee to hurt
19:27 is in danger to be s· at nought;
21: 2 we went abroad, and s· forth.
22:30 down, and s· him before them.
23:24 beasts, that they may s· Paul on,
26:32 man might have been s· at liberty,
Ro 3:25 hath s· forth to be a propitiation
14:10 dost thou s· at nought thy brother?
1Co 4: 9 God hath s· forth us the apostles
6: 4 s· them to judge who are least
10:27 whatsoever is s· before you, eat,
11:34 rest will I s· in order when I come.
12:18 But now hath God s· the members
28 And God hath s· some in the church,
Ga 3: 1 Christ hath been evidently s· forth,
Eph 1:20 s· him at his own right hand in
Ph'p 1:17 s· for the defence of the gospel.
Col 3: 2 *S·* your affection on things above,
Tit 1: 5 shouldest s· in order the things
Heb 2: 7 didst s· him over the works of thy
6:18 hold upon the hope s· before us:
8: 1 who is s· on the right hand of the
12: 1 the race that is s· before us,
2 for the joy that was s· before him
2 is s· down at the right hand of the

Heb 13:23 our brother Timothy is s· at liberty;
Jas 3: 6 nature; and it is s· on fire of hell.
Jude 7 flesh, are s· forth for an example,
Re 3: 8 I have s· before thee an open door,
21 am s· down with my Father in his
4: 2 behold, a throne was s· in heaven,
10: 2 he s· his right foot upon the sea,
20: 3 him up, and s· a seal upon him,

Seth (*seth*) See also SHETH.
Ge 4:25 a son, and called his name *S·*:
26 to *S·*, to him also there was born a
5: 3 his image; and called his name *S·*:
4 of Adam after he had begotten *S·*
6 *S·* lived an hundred and five years,
7 *S·* lived after he begat Enos eight
8 And all the days of *S·* were nine
Lu 3:38 Enos, which was the son of *S·*,

Sethur (*se'-thur*)
Nu 13:13 of Asher, *S·* the son of Michael.

setter See also UNDERSETTERS.
Ac 17:18 to be a s· forth of strange gods:

settest
De 23:20 in all that thou s· thine hand to
28: 8 in all that thou s· thine hand unto;
20 in all that thou s· thine hand unto
Job 7:12 that thou s· a watch over me?
13:27 s· a print upon the heels of my feet.
Ps 21: 3 thou s· a crown of pure gold on
41:12 and s· me before thy face for ever.

setteth
Nu 1:51 when the tabernacle s· forward,
4: 5 And when the camp s· forward,
De 24:15 is poor, and s· his heart upon it:
27:16 that s· light by his father or his
2Sa 22:34 and s· me upon my high places.
Job 28: 3 He s· an end to darkness, and
Ps 18:33 and s· me upon my high places.
36: 4 he s· himself in a way that is not
65: 6 his strength s· fast the mountains;
68: 6 God s· the solitary in families: he
75: 7 down one, and s· up another.
83:14 flame s· the mountains on fire;
107:41 s· he the poor on high from affliction,
Jer 5:26 they lay wait, as he that s· snares;
43: 3 of Neriah s· thee on against us,
Eze 14: 4 that s· up his idols in his heart,
7 and s· up his idols in his heart,
Da 2:21 removeth kings, and s· up kings:
4:17 and s· up over it the basest of men.
M't 4: 5 and s· him on the pinnacle of the
Lu 8:16 s· it on a candlestick, that they
Jas 3: 6 s· on fire the course of nature;

setting See also SETTINGS.
Eze 43: 8 In their s· of their threshold by
M't 27:66 sealing the stone, and s· a watch.
Lu 4:40 Now when the sun was s·, all they

settings
Ex 28:17 thou shalt set in it s· of stones,

settle See also SETTLED; SETTLEST.
1Ch 17:14 I will s· him in mine house and
Eze 36:11 will s· you after your old estates,
43:14 the lower s· shall be two cubits,
14 the lesser s· even to the greater
14 greater s· shall be four cubits,
17 the s· shall be fourteen cubits long
20 and on the four corners of the s·,
45:19 upon the four corners of the s· of
Lu 21:14 *S·* it therefore in your hearts, not
1Pe 5:10 stablish, strengthen, s· you.

settled
1Ki 8:13 a s· place for thee to abide in for
2Ki 8:11 he s· his countenance stedfastly,
Ps 119:89 O Lord, thy word is s· in heaven.
Pr 8:25 Before the mountains were s·,
Jer 48:11 he hath s· on his lees, and hath
Zep 1:12 the men that are s· on their lees:
Col 1:23 in the faith grounded and s·, and

settlest
Ps 65:10 thou s· the furrows thereof: thou

seven See also SEVENFOLD; SEVENS; SEVENTEEN.
Ge 5: 7 Enos eight hundred and s· years,
25 an hundred eighty and s· years,
26 Lamech s· hundred eighty and
31 days of Lamech were s· hundred
31 seventy and s· years: and he died.
7: 4 s· days, and I will cause it to rain
10 it came to pass after s· days, that
8:10, 12 And he stayed yet other s· days;
12 he stayed yet other s· days, and
14 s· and twentieth day of the month,
11:21 Serug two hundred and s· years,
21:28 Abraham set s· ewe lambs of the
29 What mean these s· ewe lambs
30 these s· ewe lambs shalt thou take
23: 1 Sarah was an hundred and s· and
25:17 hundred and thirty and s· years:
29:18 will serve thee s· years for Rachel
20 Jacob served s· years for Rachel
27 serve with me yet s· other years.
30 served with him yet s· other years.
31:23 pursued after him s· days' journey;
33: 3 himself to the ground s· times,
41: 2 of the river s· well favoured kine
3 s· other kine came up after them
4 eat up the s· well favoured and fat
5 s· ears of corn came up upon one
6 s· thin ears and blasted with the
7 And the s· thin ears devoured the
7 devoured the s· rank and full ears.
18 came up out of the river s· kine,

Ge 41:19 s' other kine came up after them.
20 kine did eat up the first s' fat kine:
22 s' ears came up in one stalk, full
23 s' ears, withered, thin, and blasted
24 ears devoured the s' good ears:
26 The s' good kine are s' years; and
26 and the s' good ears are s' years:
27 the s' thin and ill favoured kine
27 came up after them are s' years;
27 the s' empty ears blasted with the
27 east wind shall be s' years of famine.
29 there come s' years of great plenty
30 arise after them s' years of famine;
34 of Egypt in the s' plenteous years.
36 land against the s' years of famine,
47 in the s' plenteous years the earth
48 up all the food of the s' years,
53 the s' years of plenteousness, that
54 s' years of dearth began to come,
46:25 unto Jacob: all the souls were s'.
47:28 was an hundred forty and s' years.
50:10 a mourning for his father s' days.
Ex 2:16 priest of Midian had s' daughters:
6:16 an hundred thirty and s' years.
20 hundred and thirty and s' years.
7:25 s' days were fulfilled, after that
12:15 S' days shall ye eat unleavened
19 S' days shall there be no leaven
13: 6 S' days thou shalt eat unleavened
7 bread shall be eaten s' days; and
22:30 s' days it shall be with his dam; on
23:15 shalt eat unleavened bread s' days,
25:37 shalt make the s' lamps thereof:
29:30 his stead shall put them on s' days,
35 s' days shalt thou consecrate them.
37 S' days thou shalt make an
34:18 S' days thou shalt eat unleavened
37:23 And he made his s' lamps, and his
38:24 and s' hundred and thirty shekels,
25 thousand s' hundred and threescore
28 thousand s' hundred seventy and
Le 4: 6 and sprinkle of the blood s' times
17 sprinkle it s' times before the Lord,
8:11 thereof upon the altar s' times,
33 of the congregation in s' days,
33 for s' days shall he consecrate you.
35 congregation day and night s' days,
12: 2 then she shall be unclean s' days;
13: 4 him that hath the plague s' days:
5 shall shut him up s' days more:
21, 26 priest shall shut him up s' days:
31 hath the plague of the scall s' days:
33 that hath the scall s' days more:
50 up it that hath the plague s' days:
54 he shall shut it up s' days more:
14: 7 cleansed from the leprosy s' times,
8 tarry abroad out of his tent s' days.
16 of the oil with his fingers s' times
27 is in his left hand s' times before
38 and shut up the house s' days:
51 and sprinkle the house s' times:
15:13 he shall number to himself s' days
19 she shall be put apart s' days: and
24 him, he shall be unclean s' days;
28 she shall number to herself s' days,
16:14 of the blood with his finger s' times.
19 upon it with his finger s' times,
22:27 it shall be s' days under the dam;
23: 6 s' days ye must eat unleavened
8 made by fire unto the Lord s' days:
15 s' sabbaths shall be complete:
18 s' lambs without blemish of the
34 feast of tabernacles for s' days unto
36 S' days ye shall offer an offering
39 keep a feast unto the Lord s' days:
40 before the Lord your God s' days.
41 keep a feast unto the Lord s' days
42 Ye shall dwell in booths s' days; all
25: 8 shalt number s' sabbaths of years
8 years unto thee, s' times s' years;
8 space of the s' sabbaths of years
26:18 I will punish you s' times more
21 I will bring s' times more plagues
24 and will punish you yet s' times
28 chastise you s' times for your sins.
Nu 1:31 were fifty and s' thousand and four
39 and two thousand and s' hundred.
2: 8 were fifty and s' thousand and four
26 and two thousand and s' hundred.
31 thousand and fifty and s' thousand
3:22 numbered of them were s' thousand
4:36 were two thousand s' hundred and
8: 2 the s' lamps shall give light over
12:14 should she not be ashamed s' days?
14 be shut out from the camp s' days,
15 was shut out from the camp s' days:
13:22 Hebron was built s' years before
16:49 fourteen thousand and s' hundred,
19: 4 of the congregation s' times:
11 any man shall be unclean s' days.
14 the tent, shall be unclean s' days.
16 or a grave, shall be unclean s' days.
23: 1 unto Balak, Build me here s' altars,
1 me here s' oxen and s' rams.
4 I have prepared s' altars, and I
14 built s' altars, and offered a bullock
29 unto Balak, Build me here s' altars,
29 me here s' bullocks and s' rams.
26: 7 and three thousand and s' hundred
34 and two thousand and s' hundred.
51 a thousand s' hundred and thirty.
28:11 s' lambs of the first year without
17 s' days shall unleavened bread be
19 ram, and s' lambs of the first year:
21 lamb, throughout the s' lambs:
24 offer daily, throughout the s' days,

Nu 28:27 one ram, s' lambs of the first year;
29 one lamb, throughout the s' lambs;
29: 2 s' lambs of the first year without
4 one lamb, throughout the s' lambs:
8 ram, and s' lambs of the first year;
10 one lamb, throughout the s' lambs:
12 keep a feast unto the Lord s' days:
32 on the seventh day s' bullocks, two
36 s' lambs of the first year without
31:19 ye abide without the camp s' days:
36 three hundred thousand and s' and
43 thirty thousand and s' thousand
52 sixteen thousand s' hundred and
De 7: 1 s' nations greater and mightier
15: 1 s' years thou shalt make a release.
16: 3 s' days shalt thou eat unleavened
4 with thee in all thy coast s' days:
9 S' weeks shalt thou number unto
9 begin to number the s' weeks from
13 the feast of tabernacles s' days,
15 S' days shalt thou keep a solemn
28: 7 way, and flee before thee s' ways.
25 them, and flee s' ways before them:
31:10 At the end of every s' years, in the
Jos 6: 4 s' priests shall bear before the ark
4 ye shall compass the city s' times,
4 s' trumpets of rams' horns: and
6 let s' priests bear s' trumpets of
8 s' priests bearing the s' trumpets
13 And s' priests bearing s' trumpets
15 after the same manner s' times:
15 they compassed the city s' times.
18: 2 the children of Israel s' tribes,
5 they shall divide it into s' parts:
6 describe the land into s' parts, and
9 described it by cities into s' parts
J'g 6: 1 into the hand of Midian s' years.
25 the second bullock of s' years old,
8:26 a thousand and s' hundred shekels
12: 9 And he judged Israel s' years.
14:12 me within the s' days of the feast,
17 she wept before him the s' days,
16: 7 If they bind me with s' green withs
8 brought up to her s' green withs
13 weavest the s' locks of my head
19 to shave off the s' locks of his head;
20:15 numbered s' hundred chosen men.
16 s' hundred chosen men lefthanded;
Ru 4:15 which is better to thee than s' sons,
1Sa 2: 5 so that the barren hath born s';
6: 1 country of the Philistines s' months.
10: 8 s' days shalt thou tarry, till I come
11: 3 Give us s' days' respite, that we
13: 8 And he tarried s' days, according to
16:10 Jesse made s' of his sons to pass
31:13 a tree at Jabesh, and fasted s' days.
2Sa 2:11 the house of Judah was s' years
5: 5 over Judah s' years and six months:
8: 4 chariots, and s' hundred horsemen,
10:18 slew the men of s' hundred chariots
21: 6 s' men of his sons be delivered unto
9 they fell all s' together, and were
23:39 the Hittite: thirty and s' in all.
24:13 s' years of famine come unto thee
1Ki 2:11 s' years reigned he in Hebron, and
6: 6 and the third was s' cubits broad:
38 it. So was he s' years in building it.
7:17 s' for the one chapiter, and s' for the
8:65 s' days and s' days, even fourteen
11: 3 he had s' hundred wives, princesses,
16:15 did Zimri reign s' days in Tirzah.
18:43 And he said, Go again s' times.
19:18 I have left me s' thousand in Israel,
20:15 children of Israel, being s' thousand.
29 one over against the other s' days.
30 fell upon twenty and s' thousand of
2Ki 3: 9 a compass of s' days' journey:
26 took with him s' hundred men that
4:35 the child sneezed s' times, and the
5:10 Go and wash in Jordan s' times,
14 dipped himself s' times in Jordan,
8: 1 also come upon the land s' years.
2 the land of the Philistines s' years.
3 it came to pass at the s' years' end,
11:21 S' years old was Jehoash when he
24:16 the men of might, even s' thousand,
25:27 pass in the s' and thirtieth year of
27 on the s' and twentieth day of the
1Ch 3: 4 he reigned s' years and six months:
24 and Dalaiah, and Anani, s'.
5:13 and Jachan, and Zia, and Heber, s'.
18 four and forty thousand s' hundred
7: 5 fourscore and s' thousand.
9:13 and s' hundred and threescore;
25 to come after s' days from time to
10:12 oak in Jabesh, and fasted s' days.
12:25 war, s' thousand and one hundred.
27 three thousand and s' hundred;
34 and spear thirty and s' thousand.
15:26 they offered s' bullocks and s' rams.
18: 4 s' thousand horsemen, and twenty
19:18 slew of the Syrians s' thousand men
26:30 a thousand and s' hundred, were
32 and s' hundred chief fathers, whom
29: 4 s' thousand talents of refined silver,
27 s' years reigned he in Hebron, and
2Ch 7: 8 Solomon kept the feast s' days,
9 the dedication of the altar s' days,
9 and the feast s' days.
13: 9 with a young bullock and s' rams,
15:11 s' hundred oxen and s' thousand
17:11 s' thousand and s' hundred rams,
11 and s' thousand and s' hundred
24: 1 Joash was s' years old when he
26:13 and s' thousand and five hundred,
29:21 brought s' bullocks, and s' rams,

2Ch 29:21 and s' lambs, and s' he goats, for a
30:21 feast of unleavened bread s' days
22 eat throughout the feast s' days,
23 took counsel to keep other s' days:
23 kept other s' days with gladness.
24 bullocks and s' thousand sheep;
35:17 feast of unleavened bread s' days.
Ezr 2: 5 Arah, s' hundred seventy and five.
9 Zaccai, s' hundred and threescore.
25 s' hundred and forty and three.
33 Ono, s' hundred twenty and five.
38 thousand two hundred forty and s'.
65 there were s' thousand three
65 three hundred thirty and s'
66 Their horses were s' hundred thirty
67 thousand s' hundred and twenty.
6:22 unleavened bread s' days with joy:
7:14 king, and of his s' counsellors,
8:35 seventy and s' lambs, twelve he
Ne 7:14 Zaccai, s' hundred and threescore.
18 six hundred threescore and s'.
19 two thousand threescore and s'.
29 Beeroth, s' hundred forty and three.
37 Ono, s' hundred twenty and one.
41 thousand two hundred forty and s'.
67 maidservants, of whom there were s'
67 three hundred thirty and s': and
68 horses, s' hundred thirty and six:
69 s' hundred and twenty asses.
72 threescore and s' priests' garments.
8:18 they kept the feast s' days; and on
Es 1: 1 over an hundred and s' and twenty
5 both unto great and small, s' days,
10 s' chamberlains that served in the
14 the s' princes of Persia and Media,
2: 9 s' maidens, which were meet to be
8: 9 hundred twenty and s' provinces,
9:30 hundred twenty and s' provinces
Job 1: 2 there were born unto him s' sons
3 also was s' thousand sheep, and
2:13 the ground s' days and s' nights,
5:19 in s' there shall no evil touch thee.
42: 8 you now s' bullocks and s' rams,
13 also s' sons and three daughters.
Ps 12: 6 furnace of earth, purified s' times.
119:164 S' times a day do I praise thee
Pr 6:16 s' are an abomination unto him:
9: 1 she hath hewn out her s' pillars:
24:16 For a just man falleth s' times, and
26:16 s' men that can render a reason.
25 are s' abominations in his heart.
Ec 11: 2 Give a portion to s', and also to
Isa 4: 1 s' women shall take hold of one
11:15 shall smite it in the s' streams,
30:26 sevenfold, as the light of s' days,
Jer 15: 9 that hath borne s' languisheth:
34:14 end of s' years let ye go every man
52:25 s' men of them that were near the
30 captive of the Jews s' hundred
31 s' and thirtieth year of the captivity
Eze 3:15 astonished among them s' days.
16 came to pass at the end of s' days,
29:17 pass in the s' and twentieth year,
39: 9 shall burn them with fire s' years:
12 s' months shall the house of Israel
14 end of s' months shall they search.
40:22 they went up into it by s' steps;
26 there were s' steps to go up to it,
41: 3 the breadth of the door, s' cubits.
43:25 S' days shalt thou prepare every
26 S' days shall they purge the altar
44:26 they shall reckon unto him s' days.
45:21 the passover, a feast of s' days;
23 s' days of the feast he shall prepare
23 s' bullocks and s' rams without
23 without blemish daily the s' days;
25 the like in the feast of the s' days,
Da 3:19 the furnace one s' times more
4:16 and let s' times pass over him.
23 field, till s' times pass over him;
25, 32 and s' times shall pass over thee,
9:25 the Prince shall be s' weeks, and
Am 5: 8 Seek him that maketh the s' stars
Mic 5: 5 we raise against him s' shepherds,
Zec 3: 9 upon one stone shall be s' eyes:
4: 2 top of it, and his s' lamps thereon,
2 and s' pipes to the...lamps, which
2 pipes to the s' lamps, which are
10 hand of Zerubbabel with those s';
M't 12:45 s' other spirits more wicked than
15:34 they said, S', and a few little fishes.
36 And he took the s' loaves and the
37 meat that was left s' baskets full.
16:10 Neither the s' loaves of the four
18:21 and I forgive him? till s' times?
22 say not unto thee, Until s' times:
22 but, Until seventy times s'.
22:25 Now there were with us s' brethren:
28 whose wife shall she be of the s'?
M'r 8: 5 loaves have ye? And they said, S'.
6 and he took the s' loaves, and gave
8 meat that was left s' baskets.
20 when the s' among four thousand,
20 took ye up? And they said, S'.
12:20 Now there were s' brethren: and
22 And the s' had her, and left no seed
23 them? for the s' had her to wife.
16: 9 out of whom he had cast s' devils.
Lu 2:36 had lived with an husband s' years
8: 2 out of whom went s' devils,
11:26 him s' other spirits more wicked
17: 4 against thee s' times in a day,
4 and s' times in a day turn again to
20:29 There were therefore s' brethren:
31 and in like manner the s' also: and
33 them is she? for s' had her to wife.

Ac 6: 3 among you s· men of honest report,
13: 19 destroyed s· nations in the land of
19: 14 there were s· sons of one Sceva, a
20: 6 five days; where we abode s· days.
21: 4 disciples, we tarried there s· days:
8 which was one of the s·; and abode
27 And when the s· days were almost
28: 14 desired to tarry with them s· days:
Ro 11: 4 to myself s· thousand men, who
Heb 11: 30 were compassed about s· days.
Re 1: 4 John to the s· churches which are
4 and from the s· Spirits which are
11 the s· churches which are in Asia;
12 I saw s· golden candlesticks;
13 in the midst of the s· candlesticks
16 he had in his right hand s· stars:
20 The mystery of the s· stars which
20 and the s· golden candlesticks.
20 The s· stars are the angels of the s·
20 and the s· candlesticks which thou
20 thou sawest are the s· churches.
2: 1 he that holdeth the s· stars in his
1 midst of the s· golden candlesticks;
3: 1 s· Spirits of God, and the s· stars;
4: 5 there were s· lamps of fire burning
5 which are the s· Spirits of God.
5: 1 the backside, sealed with s· seals.
5 and to loose the s· seals thereof.
6 slain, having s· horns and s· eyes,
6 which are the s· Spirits of God
8: 2 And I saw the s· angels which stood
2 to them were given s· trumpets.
6 s· angels which had the s· trumpets
10: 3 s· thunders uttered their voices.
4 s· thunders had uttered their voices,
4 which the s· thunders uttered, and
11: 13 were slain of men s· thousand: and
12: 3 having s· heads and ten horns, and
3 and s· crowns upon his heads.
13: 1 having s· heads and ten horns, and
15: 1 s· angels having the s· last plagues;
6 s· angels came out of the temple,
6 having the s· plagues, clothed in
7 unto the s· angels s· golden vials
8 the s· plagues of the s· angels were
16: 1 saying to the s· angels, Go your
17: 1 the s· angels which had the s· vials,
3 having s· heads and ten horns.
7 hath the s· heads and ten horns.
9 The s· heads are s· mountains, on
10 there are s· kings: five are fallen,
11 and is of the s·, and goeth into
21: 9 came unto me one of the s· angels
9 s· vials full of the s· last plagues,

sevenfold
Ge 4: 15 vengeance...be taken on him s·.
24 If Cain shall be avenged s·, truly
24 truly Lamech seventy and s·.
Ps 79: 12 render unto our neighbours s· into
Pr 6: 31 if he be found, he shall restore s·;
Isa 30: 26 and the light of the sun shall be s·.

seven-hundred See SEVEN and HUNDRED.

sevens
Ge 7: 2 beast thou shalt take to thee by s·,
3 Of fowls also of the air by s·, the

seventeen
Ge 37: 2 Joseph, being s· years old,
47: 28 in the land of Egypt s· years:
J'g 8: 14 even threescore and s· men.
1Ki 14: 21 reigned s· years in Jerusalem.
2Ki 13: 1 Samaria, and reigned s· years.
1Ch 7: 11 s· thousand and two hundred
2Ch 12: 13 he reigned s· years in Jerusalem.
Ezr 2: 39 of Harim, a thousand and s·.
Ne 7: 42 of Harim, a thousand and s·.
Jer 32: 9 the money, even s· shekels of

seventeenth
Ge 7: 11 month, the s· day of the month,
8: 4 on the s· day of the month,
1Ki 22: 51 Israel in Samaria the s· year
2Ki 16: 1 the s· year of Pekah the son of
1Ch 24: 15 The s· to Hezir, the eighteenth
25: 24 The s· to Joshbekashah, he,

seventh
Ge 2: 2 s· day God ended his work which
2 rested on the s· day from all his
3 And God blessed the s· day, and
8: 4 the ark rested in the s· month, on
Ex 12: 15 from the first day until the s· day,
16 in the s· day there shall be an holy
13: 6 s· day shall be a feast to the Lord.
16: 26 but on the s· day, which is the
27 people on the s· day for to gather,
29 go out of his place on the s· day.
30 So the people rested on the s· day.
20: 10 s· day is the sabbath of the Lord
11 in them is, and rested the s· day:
21: 2 and in the s· he shall go out free
23: 11 s· year thou shalt let it rest and lie
12 and on the s· day thou shalt rest:
24: 16 s· day he called unto Moses out of
31: 15 in the s· is the sabbath of rest, holy
17 on the s· day he rested, and was
34: 21 but on the s· day thou shalt rest:
35: 2 s· day there shall be to you an holy
Le 13: 5 priest shall look on him the s· day:
6 shall look on him again the s· day:
27 shall look upon him the s· day:
32, 34 s· day the priest shall look on
51 look on the plague on the s· day:
14: 9 But it shall be on the s· day, that
39 priest shall come again the s· day,
16: 29 that in the s· month, on the tenth
23: 3 the s· day is the sabbath of rest, a
Le 23: 8 the s· day is an holy convocation:
16 s· sabbath shall ye number fifty
24 the s· month, in the first day of the
27 on the tenth day of this s· month
34 The fifteenth day of this s· month
39 in the fifteenth day of the s· month,
41 ye shall celebrate it in the s· month.
25: 4 But in the s· year shall be a sabbath
9 on the tenth day of the s· month,
20 say, What shall we eat the s· year?
Nu 6: 9 on the s· day shall he shave it.
7: 48 On the s· day Elishama the son of
19: 12 and on the s· day he shall be clean:
12 the s· day he shall not be clean.
19 on the third day, and on the s· day:
19 and on the s· day he shall purify
28: 25 on the s· day ye shall have an holy
29: 1 in the s· month, on the first day of
7 on the tenth day of this s· month
12 on the fifteenth day of the s· month
32 And on the s· day seven bullocks,
31: 19 on the third day, and on the s· day.
24 wash your clothes on the s· day,
De 5: 14 But the s· day is the sabbath of the
15: 9 The s· year, the year of release, is
12 s· year thou shalt let him go free
16: 8 s· day shall be a solemn assembly
Jos 6: 4 the s· day ye shall compass the city
15 And it came to pass on the s· day,
16 And it came to pass at the s· time,
19: 40 the s· lot came out for the tribe of
J'g 14: 15 And it came to pass on the s· day,
17 on the s· day, that he told her,
18 s· day before the sun went down,
2Sa 12: 18 on the s· day, that the child died.
1Ki 8: 2 Ethanim, which is the s· month.
16: 10, 15 in the twenty and s· year of Asa
18: 44 And it came to pass at the s· time,
20: 29 in the s· day the battle was joined:
2Ki 11: 4 s· year Jehoiada sent and fetched
12: 1 the s· year of Jehu Jehoash began
13: 10 In the thirty and s· year of Joash
15: 1 the twenty and s· year of Jeroboam
18: 9 which was the s· year of Hoshea
25: 8 month, on the s· day of the month,
25 in the s· month, that Ishmael
1Ch 2: 15 Ozem the sixth, David the s·:
12: 11 Attai the sixth, Eliel the s·,
24: 10 s· to Hakkoz, the eighth to Abijah,
25: 14 The s· to Jesharelah, he, his sons,
26: 3 Jehohanan the sixth, Elioenai the s·.
5 Ammiel the sixth, Issachar the s·,
27: 10 The s· captain for the s· month was
2Ch 5: 3 feast which was in the s· month.
7: 10 and twentieth day of the s· month
23: 1 in the s· year Jehoiada strengthened
31: 7 and finished them in the s· month.
Ezr 3: 1 And when the s· month was come,
6 From the first day of the s· month
7: 7 the s· year of Artaxerxes the king.
8 was in the s· year of the king.
Ne 7: 73 and when the s· month came, the
8: 2 upon the first day of the s· month.
14 booths in the feast of the s· month:
10: 31 and that we would leave the s· year,
Es 1: 10 s· day, when the heart of the king
2: 16 Tebeth, in the s· year of his reign.
Jer 28: 17 died the same year in the s· month.
41: 1 in the s· month, that Ishmael
52: 28 in the s· year three thousand Jews
Eze 20: 1 And it came to pass in the s· year,
30: 20 month, in the s· day of the month,
45: 20 shalt do the s· day of the month
25 In the s· month, in the fifteenth day
Hag 2: 1 In the s· month, in the one and
Zec 7: 5 mourned in the fifth and s· month,
8: 19 the fast of the s·, and the fast of the
M't 22: 26 also, and the third, unto the s·.
Joh 4: 52 at the s· hour the fever left him.
Heb 4: 4 spake...of the s· day on this wise,
4 rest the s· day from all his works.
Jude 14 And Enoch also, the s· from Adam,
Re 8: 1 when he had opened the s· seal,
10: 7 the days of the voice of the s· angel,
11: 15 And the s· angel sounded; and
16: 17 And the s· angel poured out his vial
21: 20 the s·, chrysolite; the eighth, beryl;

seven-thousand See SEVEN and THOUSAND.

seventy
Ge 4: 24 truly Lamech s· and sevenfold.
5: 12 And Cainan lived s· years, and begat
31 seven hundred s· and seven years:
11: 26 And Terah lived s· years, and begat
12: 4 and Abram was s· and five years old
Ex 1: 5 of the loins of Jacob were s· souls:
24: 1 Abihu, and s· of the elders of Israel;
9 Abihu, and s· of the elders of Israel:
38: 28 seven hundred s· and five shekels
29 brass of the offering was s· talents,
Nu 7: 13, 19, 25, 31, 37 bowl of s· shekels,
43 a silver bowl of s· shekels, after
49, 55, 61, 67, 73, 79 bowl of s· shekels,
85 and thirty shekels, each bowl s·:
11: 16 me s· men of the elders of Israel,
24 s· men of the elders of the people,
25 him, and gave it unto the s· elders:
31: 32 and s· thousand and five thousand
J'g 9: 56 father, in slaying his s· brethren:
2Sa 24: 15 to Beer-sheba s· thousand men.
2Ki 10: 1 And Ahab had s· sons in Samaria.
6 the king's sons, being s· persons,
7 the king's sons, and slew s· persons,
1Ch 21: 14 there fell of Israel s· thousand men.
Ezr 2: 3 thousand an hundred s· and two.
4 three hundred s· and two.
Ezr 2: 5 of Arah, seven hundred s· and five.
36 Jeshua, nine hundred s· and three.
40 children of Hodaviah, s· and four.
8: 7 of Athaliah, and with him s· males.
14 Zabbud, and with them s· males.
35 s· and seven lambs, twelve he goats
Ne 7: 8 thousand an hundred s· and two.
9 three hundred s· and two.
39 Jeshua, nine hundred s· and three.
43 children of Hodevah, s· and four.
11: 19 gates, were an hundred s· and two.
Es 9: 16 of their foes s· and five thousand,
Isa 23: 15 Tyre shall be forgotten s· years,
15 end of s· years shall Tyre sing as an
17 to pass after the end of s· years,
Jer 25: 11 serve the king of Babylon s· years.
12 when s· years are accomplished,
29: 10 after s· years be accomplished at
Eze 8: 11 before them s· men of the ancients
41: 12 toward the west was s· cubits broad;
Da 9: 2 that he would accomplish s· years
24 S· weeks are determined upon thy
Zec 7: 5 even those s· years, did ye at all fast
M't 18: 22 times: but, Until s· times seven.
Lu 10: 1 the Lord appointed other s· also,
17 And the s· returned again with joy,

seventy-thousand See SEVENTY and THOUSAND.

sever See also SEVERED.
Ex 8: 22 s· in that day the land of Goshen,
9: 4 shall s· between the cattle of Israel
Eze 39: 14 they shall s· out men of continual
M't 13: 49 s· the wicked from among the just,

several
Nu 28: 13 a s· tenth deal of flour mingled with
21 A s· tenth deal shalt thou offer for
29 A s· tenth deal unto one lamb,
29: 10 A s· tenth deal for one lamb,
15 And a s· tenth deal to each lamb of the
2Ki 15: 5 death, and dwelt in a s· house.
2Ch 11: 12 And in every s· city he put shields and
26: 21 death, and dwelt in a s· house,
28: 25 in every s· city of Judah he made high
31: 19 suburbs of their cities, in every s· city,
M't 25: 15 man according to his s· ability;
Re 21: 21 every s· gate was of one pearl:

severally
1Co 12: 11 dividing to every man s· as he will.

severed
Le 20: 26 and have s· you from other people,
De 4: 41 s· three cities on this side Jordan
J'g 4: 11 had s· himself from the Kenites,

severity
Ro 11: 22 Behold...the goodness and s· of God:
22 on them which fell, s·; but toward

sew See also SEWED; SEWEST; SEWETH.
Ec 3: 7 A time to rend, and a time to s·;
Eze 13: 18 Woe to the women that s· pillows

sewed
Ge 3: 7 they s· fig leaves together, and
Job 16: 15 I have s· sackcloth upon my skin,

sewest
Job 14: 17 and thou s· up mine iniquity.

seweth
M'r 2: 21 No man...s· a piece of new cloth

Shaalabbin (*sha-al-ab'-bin*) See also SHAALBIM.
Jos 19: 42 And S·, and Ajalon, and Jethlah,

Shaalbim (*sha-al'-bim*) See also SHAALABBIN; SHAALBONITE.
J'g 1: 35 mount Heres in Aijalon, and in S·:
1Ki 4: 9 son of Dekar, in Makaz, and in S·,

Shaalbonite (*sha-al'-bo-nite*)
2Sa 23: 32 Eliahba the S·, of the sons of
1Ch 11: 33 the Baharumite, Eliahba the S·,

Shaaph (*sha'-af*)
1Ch 2: 47 and Pelet, and Ephah, and S·.
49 She bare also S· the father of

Shaaraim (*sha-a-ra'-im*) See also SHARAIM; SHARUHEN.
1Sa 17: 52 fell down by the way to S·, even
1Ch 4: 31 and at Beth-birei, and at S·.

Shaashgaz (*sha-ash'-gaz*)
Es 2: 14 to the custody of S·, the king's

Shabbethai (*shab'-be-thahee*)
Ezr 10: 15 and S· the Levite helped them.
Ne 8: 7 S·, Hodijah, Maaseiah, Kelita,
11: 16 And S· and Jozabad, of the chief of

Shachia (*sha-ki'-ah*)
1Ch 8: 10 And Jeuz, and S·, and Mirma.

shade See also SHADOW.
Ps 121: 5 Lord is thy s· upon thy right hand.

shadow See also OVERSHADOW; SHADE; SHADOWING; SHADOWS.
Ge 19: 8 come they under the s· of my roof.
J'g 9: 15 come and put your trust in my s·:
36 Thou seest the s· of the mountains
2Ki 20: 9 shall the s· go forward ten degrees,
10 for the s· to go down ten degrees:
10 the s· return backward ten degrees.
11 the s· ten degrees backward, by
1Ch 29: 15 our days on the earth are as a s·,
Job 3: 5 and the s· of death stain it; let a
7: 2 servant earnestly desireth the s·,
8: 9 our days upon earth are a s·:)
10: 21 of darkness and the s· of death;
22 and of the s· of death, without any
12: 22 bringeth out to light the s· of death.
14: 2 is cut down: he fleeth also as a s·,
16: 16 on my eyelids is the s· of death;

Job 17: 7 and all my members are as a s·.
24:17 is to them even as the s· of death:
17 are in the terrors of the s· of death.
28: 3 of darkness, and the s· of death.
34:22 is no darkness, nor s· of death.
38:17 seen the doors of the s· of death?
40:22 trees cover him with their s·; the
Ps 17: 8 hide me under the s· of thy wings,
23: 4 the valley of the s· of death,
36: 7 trust under the s· of thy wings.
44:19 and covered us with the s· of death.
57: 1 in the s· of thy wings will I make
63: 7 in the s· of thy wings will I rejoice.
80:10 hills were covered with the s· of it,
91: 1 abide under the s· of the Almighty.
102:11 days are like a s· that declineth;
107:10 in darkness and in the s· of death,
14 out of darkness and the s· of death.
109:23 I am gone like the s· when it
144: 4 days are as a s· that passeth away.
Ec 6:12 vain life which he spendeth as a s·?
8:13 prolong his days, which are as a s·;
Ca 2: 3 I sat down under his s· with great
Isa 4: 6 tabernacle for a s· in the daytime
9: 2 dwell in the land of the s· of death,
16: 3 make thy s· as the night in the
25: 4 a s· from the heat, when the blast
5 even the heat with the s· of a cloud:
30: 2 and to trust in the s· of Egypt!
3 the trust in the s· of Egypt your
32: 2 s· of a great rock in a weary land.
34:15 and hatch, and gather under her s·:
38: 8 bring again the s· of the degrees,
49: 2 in the s· of his hand hath he hid me,
51:16 thee in the s· of mine hand,
Jer 2: 6 of drought, and of the s· of death,
13:16 light, he turn it into the s· of death,
48:45 fled stood under the s· of Heshbon
La 4:20 Under his s· we shall live among
Eze 17:23 the s· of the branches thereof shall
31: 6 under his s· dwelt all great nations.
12 the earth are gone down from his s·,
17 dwelt under his s· in the midst of
Da 4:12 beasts of the field had s· under it,
Ho 4:13 because the s· thereof is good:
14: 7 dwell under his s· shall return;
Am 5: 8 the s· of death into the morning,
Jon 4: 5 sat under it in the s·, till he might
6 that it might be a s· over his head,
M't 4:16 sat in the region and s· of death
M'r 4:32 the air may lodge under the s· of it.
Lu 1:79 in darkness and in the s· of death,
Ac 5:15 the s· of Peter passing by might
Col 2:17 Which are a s· of things to come;
Heb 8: 5 example and s· of heavenly things,
10: 1 the law having a s· of good things
Jas 1:17 variableness, neither s· of turning.

shadowing
Isa 18: 1 Woe to the land s· with wings,
Eze 31: 3 with a s· shroud, and of an high
Heb 9: 5 of glory s· the mercyseat;

shadows
Ca 2:17 day break, and the s· flee away,
4: 6 the day break, and the s· flee away,
Jer 6: 4 s· of the evening are stretched out.

Shadrach (*sha'-drak*) See also HANANIAH.
Da 1: 7 and to Hananiah, of S·; and to
2:49 set S·, Meshach, and Abed-nego,
3:12 of the province of Babylon, S·,
13 and fury commanded to bring S·,
14 them, Is it true, O S·, Meshach, and
16 S·, Meshach, and Abed-nego,
19 his visage was changed against S·,
20 that were in his army to bind S·,
22 slew those men that took up S·,
23 S·, Meshach, Abed-nego, fell down
26 said, S·, Meshach, and Abed-nego,
26 Then S·, Meshach, and Abed-nego,
28 Blessed be the God of S·, Meshach,
29 thing amiss against the God of S·,
30 the king promoted S·, Meshach, and

shady
Job 40:21 He lieth under the s· trees, in the
22 The s· trees cover him with their

shaft
Ex 25:31 his s·, and his branches, his bowls,
37:17 his s·, and his branch, his bowls,
Nu 8: 4 beaten gold, unto the s· thereof,
Isa 49: 2 me, and made me a polished s·;

Shage (*sha'-ghe*)
1Ch 11:34 the son of S· the Hararite,

Shahar (*sha'-har*) See also ZARETH-SHAHAR.
Ps 22: *title* chief Musician upon Aijeleth S·,

Shaharaim (*sha-ha-ra'-im*)
1Ch 8: 8 S· begat children in the country

Shahazimah (*sha-haz'-i-mah*)
Jos 19:22 coast reacheth to Tabor, and S·,

shake See also SHAKED; SHAKEN; SHAKETH; SHAKING; SHOOK.
J'g 16:20 times before, and s· myself.
Ne 5:13 So God s· out every man from his
Job 4:14 which made all my bones to s·,
15:33 s· off his unripe grape as the vine,
16: 4 you, and s· mine head at you.
Ps 22: 7 shoot out the lip, they s· the head,
46: 3 mountains s· with the swelling
69:23 make their loins continually to s·.
72:16 fruit thereof shall s· like Lebanon:
Isa 2:19, 21 ariseth to s· terribly the earth.
10:15 if the rod should s· itself against
32 he shall s· his hand against the
11:15 shall he s· his hand over the river,
Isa 13: 2 s· the hand, that they may go into
13 I will s· the heavens, and the
14:16 to tremble, that did s· kingdoms;
24:18 the foundations of the earth do s·.
33: 9 and Carmel s· off their fruits.
52: 2 S· thyself from the dust; arise, and
Jer 23: 9 all my bones s·; I am like a
Eze 26:10 thy walls shall s· at the noise of
15 the isles s· at the sound of thy fall,
27:28 suburbs shall s· at the sound of the
31:16 nations to s· at the sound of his fall,
38:20 of the earth, shall s· at my presence,
Da 4:14 s· off his leaves, and scatter his
Joe 3:16 the heavens and the earth shall s·:
Am 9: 1 of the door, that the posts may s·:
Hag 2: 6 while, and I will s· the heavens,
7 I will s· all nations, and the desire
21 I will s· the heavens and the earth;
Zec 2: 9 I will s· mine hand upon them, and
M't 10:14 or city, s· off the dust of your feet.
28: 4 for fear of him the keepers did s·,
M'r 6:11 s· off the dust under your feet for
Lu 6:48 that house, and could not s· it: for
9: 5 s· off the very dust from your feet
Heb 12:26 once more I s· not the earth only,

shaked See also SHAKEN; SHOOK.
Ps 109:25 upon me they s· their heads.

Shakeh See RAB-SHAKEH.

shaken See also SHAKED.
Le 26:36 the sound of a s· leaf chase them;
1Ki 14:15 Israel, as a reed is s· in the water,
2Ki 19:21 of Jerusalem hath s· her head at
Ne 5:13 even thus be he s· out, and
Job 16:12 by my neck, and s· me to pieces,
38:13 the wicked might be s· out of it?
Ps 18: 7 of the hills moved and were s·,
Isa 37:22 of Jerusalem hath s· her head at
Na 2: 3 the fir trees shall be terribly s·.
3:12 if they be s·, they shall even fall
M't 11: 7 to see? A reed s· with the wind?
24:29 powers of the heavens shall be s·:
M'r 13:25 that are in heaven shall be s·.
Lu 6:38 measure, pressed down, s· together,
7:24 to see? A reed s· with the wind?
21:26 the powers of heaven shall be s·.
Ac 4:31 the place was s· where they were
16:26 foundations of the prison were s·:
2Th 2: 2 That ye be not soon s· in mind, or
Heb 12:27 removing of those things that are s·,
27 which cannot be s· may remain.
Re 6:13 when she is s· of a mighty wind.

shaketh
Job 9: 6 s· the earth out of her place, and
Ps 29: 8 of the Lord s· the wilderness;
8 Lord s· the wilderness of Kadesh.
60: 2 the breaches thereof; for it s·.
Isa 10:15 itself against him that s· it? as
19:16 Lord of hosts, which he s· over it.
33:15 that s· his hands from holding of

shaking
Job 41:29 he laugheth at the s· of a spear.
Ps 44:14 a s· of the head among the people.
Isa 17: 6 left in it, as the s· of an olive tree,
19:16 the s· of the hand of the Lord of
24:13 shall be as the s· of an olive tree,
30:32 battles of s· will he fight with it.
Eze 37: 7 was a noise, and behold a s·, and
38:19 be a great s· in the land of Israel;

Shalal See MAHER-SHALAL-HASH-BAZ.

Shalem (*sha'-lem*)
Ge 33:18 And Jacob came to S·, a city of

Shalim (*sha'-lim*)
1Sa 9: 4 passed through the land of S·,

Shalisha (*shal'-i-shah*) See also BAAL-SHALISHA.
1Sa 9: 4 passed through the land of S·,

SHOULD.

Shallecheth (*shal'-le-keth*)
1Ch 26:16 westward, with the gate S·, by the

Shallum (*shal'-lum*) See also JEHOAHAZ; MESHELEMIAH; SHILLEM.
2Ki 15:10 S· the son of Jabesh conspired
13 S· the son of Jabesh began to
14 and smote S· the son of Jabesh in
15 And the rest of the acts of S·, and
22:14 the wife of S· the son of Tikvah,
1Ch 2:40 Sisamai, and Sisamai begat S·,
41 S· begat Jekamiah, and Jekamiah
3:15 the third Zedekiah, the fourth S·.
4:25 S· his son, Mibsam his son,
6:12 begat Zadok, and Zadok begat S·,
13 S· begat Hilkiah, and Hilkiah
7:13 Jezer, and S·, the sons of Bilhah.
9:17 the porters were, S·, and Akkub,
17 their brethren: S· was the chief;
19 And S· the son of Kore, the son of
31 the firstborn of S· the Korahite,
2Ch 28:12 Jehizkiah the son of S·, and Amasa
34:22 the wife of S· the son of Tikvath,
Ezr 2:42 the children of S·, the children of
7: 2 The son of S·, the son of Zadok,
10:24 porters; S·, and Telem, and Uri.
42 S·, Amariah, and Joseph.
Ne 3:12 repaired S· the son of Halohesh,
7:45 The porters: the children of S·,
Jer 22:11 saith the Lord touching S· the son
32: 7 Hanameel the son of S· thine uncle
35: 4 chamber of Maaseiah the son of S·,

Shallun (*shal'-lun*)
Ne 3:15 gate of the fountain repaired S·

Shalmai (*shal'-mahee*)
Ezr 2:46 the children of S·, the children of
Ne 7:48 of Hagaba, the children of S·,

Shalman (*shal'-man*) See also SHALMANESER.
Ho 10:14 as S· spoiled Beth-arbel in the day

Shalmaneser (*shal-man-e'-zer*) See also SHALMAN.
2Ki 17: 3 him came up S· king of Assyria;
18: 9 that S· king of Assyria came up

Shalom See JEHOVAH-SHALOM.

Shama (*sha'-mah*)
1Ch 11:44 S· and Jehiel the sons of Hothan

Shamariah (*sham-a-ri'-ah*) See also SHEMARIAH.
2Ch 11:19 Jeush, and S·, and Zaham.

shambles
1Co 10:25 Whatsoever is sold in the s·, that

shame See also ASHAMED; SHAMED; SHAMEFACEDNESS; SHAMEFUL; SHAMELESSLY; SHAMETH.
Ex 32:25 made them naked unto their s·
J'g 18: 7 that might put them to s· in any
1Sa 20:34 because his father had done him s·
2Sa 13:13 whither shall I cause my s· to go?
2Ch 32:21 with s· of face to his own land.
Job 8:22 hate thee shall be clothed with s·;
Ps 4: 2 long will ye turn my glory into s·?
35: 4 put to s· that seek after my soul:
26 let them be clothed with s· and
40:14 and put to s· that wish me evil.
15 for a reward of their s· that say
44: 7 hast put them to s· that hated us.
9 hast cast off, and put us to s·;
15 the s· of my face hath covered me,
53: 5 thou hast put them to s·, because
69: 7 reproach; s· hath covered my face.
19 known my reproach, and my s·,
70: 3 for a reward of their s· that say,
71:24 for they are brought unto s·, that
83:16 Fill their faces with s·; that they
17 let them be put to s·, and perish:
89:45 thou hast covered him with s·.
109:29 adversaries be clothed with s·,
119:31 O Lord, put me not to s·.
132:18 His enemies will I clothe with s·:
Pr 3:35 s· shall be the promotion of fools.
9: 7 a scorner getteth to himself s·:
10: 5 in harvest is a son that causeth s·.
11: 2 pride cometh, then cometh s·: but
12:16 but a prudent man covereth s·.
13: 5 is loathsome, and cometh to s·.
18 Poverty and s· shall be to him
14:35 is against him that causeth s·.
17: 2 have rule over a son that causeth s·.
18:13 it, it is folly and s· unto him.
19:26 mother, is a son that causeth s·.
25: 8 thy neighbour hath put thee to s·.
10 he that heareth it put thee to s·,
29:15 himself bringeth his mother to s·.
Isa 20: 4 uncovered, to the s· of Egypt.
22:18 shall be the s· of thy lord's house.
30: 3 strength of Pharaoh be your s·,
5 profit, but a s·, and also a reproach.
47: 3 yea, thy s· shall be seen:
50: 6 not my face from s· and spitting.
54: 4 for thou shalt not be put to s·:
4 shalt forget the s· of thy youth,
61: 7 For your s· ye shall have double;
Jer 3:24 s· hath devoured the labour of our
25 We lie down in our s·, and our
13:26 thy face, that thy s· may appear.
20:18 days should be consumed with s·?
23:40 a perpetual s·, which shall not be
46:12 The nations have heard of thy s·,
48:39 hath Moab turned the back with s·!
51:51 s· hath covered our faces: for
Eze 7:18 and s· shall be upon all faces, and
16:52 bear thine own s· for thy sins that
52 confounded also, and bear thy s·,
54 That thou mayest bear thine own s·,
63 mouth any more because of thy s·,
32:24, 25 yet have they borne their s·
30 and bear their s· with them that go
34:29 neither bear the s· of the heathen
36: 6 yet have borne the s· of the heathen:
7 about you, they shall bear their s·.
15 bear in thee the s· of the heathen
39:26 After that they have borne their s·,
44:13 but they shall bear their s·, and
Da 12: 2 to s· and everlasting contempt.
Ho 4: 7 will I change their glory into s·.
18 her rulers with s· do love, Give ye.
9:10 separated themselves...that s·;
10: 6 Ephraim shall receive s·, and
Ob 10 brother Jacob s· shall cover thee,
Mic 1:11 of Saphir, having thy s· naked:
2: 6 them, that they shall not take s·.
7:10 s· shall cover her which said unto
Na 3: 5 and the kingdoms thy s·.
Hab 2:10 hast consulted s· to thy house by
16 Thou art filled with s· for glory:
Zep 3: 5 but the unjust knoweth no s·.
19 land where they have been put to s·.
Lu 14: 9 begin with s· to take the lowest
Ac 5:41 worthy to suffer s· for his name.
1Co 4:14 I write not these things to s· you,
6: 5 I speak to your s·. Is it so, that
11: 6 it be a s· for a woman to be shorn
14 have long hair, it is a s· unto him?
22 of God, and s· them who have not?
14:35 s· for women to speak in...church.
15:34 of God: I speak this to your s·.
Eph 5:12 a s· even to speak of those things
Ph'p 3:19 and whose glory is in their s·, who
Heb 6: 6 afresh, and put him to an open s·.

Heb12: 2 endured the cross, despising the s',
Jude 13 the sea, foaming out their own s';
Re 3: 18 s' of thy nakedness do not appear;
16: 15 he walk naked, and they see his s'.

shamed See also ASHAMED.
Ge 38: 23 Let her take it to her, lest we be s':
2Sa 19: 5 hast s' this day the faces of all thy
Ps 14: 6 Ye have s' the counsel of the poor,

Shamed (*sha'-med*)
1Ch 8: 12 and S' who built Ono, and Lod,

shamefacedness
1Ti 2: 9 apparel, with s' and sobriety;

shameful
Jer 11: 13 have ye...altars to that s' thing,
Hab 2: 16 s' spewing shall be on thy glory.

shamefully
Ho 2: 5 that conceived them hath done s':
M'r 12: 4 head, and sent him away s' handled.
Lu 20: 11 beat him also, and entreated him s',
1Th 2: 2 and were s' entreated, as ye know,

shamelessly
2Sa 6: 20 vain fellows s' uncovereth himself!

Shamer (*sha'-mur*) See also SHOMER.
1Ch 6: 46 the son of Bani, the son of S',
7: 34 the sons of S'; Ahi, and Rohgah,

shameth
Pr 28: 7 of riotous men s' his father.

Shamgar (*sham'-gar*)
J'g 3: 31 him was S' the son of Anath,
5: 6 In the days of S' the son of Anath,

Shamhuth (*sham'-huth*) See also SHAMMOTH.
1Ch 27: 8 fifth month was S' the Izrahite:

Shamir (*sha'-mur*)
Jos 15: 48 And in the mountains, S', and
J'g 10: 1 he dwelt in S' in mount Ephraim.
2 and died, and was buried in S'.
1Ch 24: 24 Michah: of the sons of Michah; S'.

Shamma (*sham'-mah*) See also SHAMMAH.
1Ch 7: 37 and Hod, and S', and Shilshah,

Shammah (*sham'-mah*) See also SHAMMA; SHAMMOTH; SHIMEA; SHIMMA.
Ge 36: 13 and Zerah, S', and Mizzah:
17 duke Zerah, duke S', duke Mizzah:
1Sa 16: 9 Then Jesse made S' to pass by.
17: 13 him Abinadab, and the third S'.
2Sa 23: 11 after him was S' the son of Agee
25 S' the Harodite, Elika the Harodite,
33 S' the Hararite, Ahiam the son of
1Ch 1: 37 Nahath, Zerah, S', and Mizzah.

Shammai (*sham'-mahee*)
1Ch 2: 28 sons of Onam were, S', and Jada.
28 And the sons of S'; Nadab, and
32 the sons of Jada the brother of S':
44 Jorkoam: and Rekem begat S'.
45 And the son of S' was Maon: and
4: 17 and she bare Miriam, and S', and

Shammoth (*sham'-moth*) See also SHAMMAH: SHAMHUTH.
1Ch 11: 27 S' the Harorite, Helez the

Shammua (*sham-mu'-ah*) See also SHAMMUAH; SHEMAIAH; SHIMEA.
Nu 13: 4 of Reuben, S' the son of Zaccur.
1Ch 14: 4 S', and Shobab, Nathan, and
Ne 11: 17 and Abda the son of S', the son of
12: 18 Of Bilgah, S'; of Shemaiah,

Shammuah (*sham-mu'-ah*) See also SHAMMUA.
2Sa 5: 14 S', and Shobab, and Nathan, and

Shamsherai (*sham'-she-rahee*)
1Ch 8: 26 S', and Sheariah, and Athaliah,

Shan See BETH-SHAN.

shape See also SHAPEN; SHAPES.
Lu 3: 22 a bodily s' like a dove upon him,
Joh 5: 37 voice at any time, nor seen his s'.

shapen
Ps 51: 5 I was s' in iniquity; and in sin

shapes
Re 9: 7 s' of the locusts were like unto

Shapham (*sha'-fam*)
1Ch 5: 12 Joel the chief, and S' the next,

Shaphan (*sha'-fan*)
2Ki 22: 3 the king sent S' the son of Azaliah,
8 high priest said unto S' the scribe,
8 And Hilkiah gave the book to S',
9 And S' the scribe came to the king,
10 And S' the scribe shewed the king,
10 And S' read it before the king.
12 Ahikam the son of S', and Achbor
12 and S' the scribe, and Asahiah a
14 S', and Asahiah, went unto Huldah
25: 22 son of Ahikam, the son of S', ruler.
2Ch 34: 8 he sent S' the son of Azaliah, and
15 answered and said to S' the scribe,
15 Hilkiah delivered the book to S'.
16 And S' carried the book to the king,
18 Then S' the scribe told the king,
18 And S' read it before the king.
20 Hilkiah, and Ahikam the son of S',
20 the son of Micah, and S' the scribe,
Jer 26: 24 the hand of Ahikam the son of S',
29: 3 By the hand of Elasah the son of S',
36: 10 Gemariah the son of S' the scribe,
11 the son of Gemariah, the son of S'
12 and Gemariah the son of S', and
39: 14 the son of Ahikam the son of S',
40: 5 the son of Ahikam the son of S',
9 son of Ahikam the son of S' sware

Jer 40: 11 the son of Ahikam the son of S';
41: 2 son of Ahikam the son of S' with
43: 6 the son of Ahikam the son of S',
Eze 8: 11 stood Jaazaniah the son of S', with

Shaphat (*sha'-fat*)
Nu 13: 5 of Simeon, S' the son of Hori.
1Ki 19: 16 son of S' of Abel-meholah shalt
19 found Elisha the son of S', who was
2Ki 3: 11 Here is Elisha the son of S', which
6: 31 if the head of Elisha the son of S'
1Ch 3: 22 Bariah, and Neariah, and S', six.
5: 12 next, and Jaanai, and S' in Bashan.
27: 29 in the valleys was S' the son of

Shapher (*sha'-fur*)
Nu 33: 23 and pitched in mount S'.
24 And they removed from mount S',

Sharai (*sha'-rahee*)
Ezr 10: 40 Machnadebai, Shashai, S',

Sharaim (*sha-ra'-im*) See also SHAARAIM.
Jos 15: 36 S', and Adithaim, and Gederah,

Sharar (*sha'-rar*) See also SARAR.
2Sa 23: 33 Ahiam the son of S' the Hararite,

share See also PLOWSHARES.
1Sa 13: 20 to sharpen every man his s', and

Sharezer (*sha-re'-zur*) See also SHEREZER.
2Ki 19: 37 and S' his son smote him with the
Isa 37: 38 and S' his son smote him with the

Sharon (*sha'-run*) See also SARON; SHARONITE.
1Ch 5: 16 and in all the suburbs of S', upon
27: 29 over the herds that fed in S' was
Ca 2: 1 I am the rose of S', and the lily of
Isa 33: 9 S' is like a wilderness; and Bashan
35: 2 the excellency of Carmel and S',
65: 10 And S' shall be a fold of flocks, and

Sharonite (*sha'-run-ite*)
1Ch 27: 29 fed in Sharon was Shitrai the S':

sharp See also SHARPER.
Ex 4: 25 Then Zipporah took a s' stone,
Jos 5: 2 unto Joshua, Make thee s' knives,
3 Joshua made him s' knives, and
1Sa 14: 4 was a s' rock on the one side,
4 and a s' rock on the other side:
Job 41: 30 S' stones are under him: he
30 s' pointed things upon the mire.
Ps 45: 5 Thine arrows are s' in the heart
52: 2 mischiefs; like a s' rasor, working
57: 4 and their tongue a s' sword.
120: 4 S' arrows of the mighty, with
Pr 5: 4 s' as a twoedged sword.
25: 18 maul, and a sword, and a s' arrow.
Isa 5: 28 Whose arrows are s', and all their
41: 15 a new s' threshing instrument
49: 2 made my mouth like a s' sword;
Eze 5: 1 take thee a s' knife, take thee a
Ac 15: 39 contention was so s' between them,
Re 1: 16 mouth went a s' twoedged sword:
2: 12 hath the s' sword with two edges;
14: 14 crown, and in his hand a s' sickle.
17 heaven, he also having a s' sickle.
18 cry to him that had the s' sickle,
18 Thrust in thy s' sickle, and gather
19: 15 out of his mouth goeth a s' sword,

sharpen See also SHARPENED; SHARPENETH.
1Sa 13: 20 to s' every man his share, and his
21 for the axes, and to s' the goads.

sharpened
Ps 140: 3 They have s' their tongues like a
Eze 21: 9 A sword, a sword is s', and also
10 It is s' to make a sore slaughter;
11 this sword is s', and it is furbished,

sharpeneth
Job 16: 9 mine enemy s' his eyes upon me.
Pr 27: 17 Iron s' iron; so a man s' the

sharper
Mic 7: 4 the most upright is s' than a thorn
Heb 4: 12 and s' than any twoedged sword,

sharply
J'g 8: 1 And they did chide with him s'.
Tit 1: 13 Wherefore rebuke them s', that

sharpness
2Co 13: 10 lest being present I should use s'.

Sharuhen (*sha-ru'-hen*) See also SHAARAIM; SHILHIM.
Jos 19: 6 And Beth-lebaoth, and S';

Shashai (*sha'-shahee*)
Ezr 10: 40 Machnadebai, S', Sharai,

Shashak (*sha'-shak*)
1Ch 8: 14 And Ahio, S', and Jeremoth,
25 and Penuel, the sons of S';

Shaul (*sha'-ul*) See also SAUL; SHAULITES.
Ge 46: 10 and S' the son of a Canaanitish
Ex 6: 15 S' the son of a Canaanitish woman:
Nu 26: 13 of S', the family of the Shaulites.
1Ch 1: 48 S' of Rehoboth by the river reigned
49 when S' was dead, Baal-hanan the
4: 24 and Jamin, Jarib, Zerah, and S':
6: 24 son, Uzziah his son, and S' his son.

Shaulites (*sha'-ul-ites*)
Nu 26: 13 of Shaul, the family of the S'.

shave See also SHAVED; SHAVEN.
Le 13: 33 but the scall shall he not s';
14: 8 s' off all his hair, and wash himself
9 s' all his hair off his head and his
9 even all his hair he shall s' off: and
21: 5 they s' off the corner of their beard,
Nu 6: 9 shall s' his head in the day of his

Nu 6: 9 on the seventh day shall he s' it.
18 shall s' the head of his separation
8: 7 let them s' all their flesh, and
De 21: 12 she shall s' her head, and pare
J'g 16: 19 to s' off the seven locks of his head;
Isa 7: 20 Lord s' with a rasor that is hired,
Eze 44: 20 Neither shall they s' their heads,
Ac 21: 24 them, that they may s' their heads:

shaved See also SHAVEN.
Ge 41: 14 and he s' himself, and changed his
2Sa 10: 4 s' off the one half of their beards,
1Ch 19: 4 s' them, and cut off their garments
Job 1: 20 s' his head, and fell down upon

Shaveh (*sha'-veh*)
Ge 14: 5 and the Emims in S' Kiriathaim,
17 at the valley of S', which is the

Shaveh-kiriathaim See SHAVEH and KIRIATHAIM.

shaven See also SHAVED.
Le 13: 33 He shall be s', but the scall shall
Nu 6: 19 the hair of his separation is s':
J'g 16: 17 if I be s', then my strength will go
22 hair...grow again after he was s'.
Jer 41: 5 men, having their beards s', and
1Co 11: 5 is even all one as if she were s'.
6 for a woman to be shorn or s', let

Shavsha (*shav'-shah*) See also SERAIAH; SHEVA; SHISHA.
1Ch 18: 16 the priests; and S' was scribe:

sheaf See also SHEAVES.
Ge 37: 7 and, lo, my s' arose, and also stood
7 about, and made obeisance to my s'.
Le 23: 10 shall bring a s' of the firstfruits
11 shall wave the s' before the Lord,
12 ye wave the s' an he lamb without
15 brought the s' of the wave offering;
De 24: 19 and hast forgot a s' in the field,
Job 24: 10 take away the s' from the hungry,
Zec 12: 6 and like a torch of fire in a s';

Sheal (*she'-al*)
Ezr 10: 29 Jashub, and S', and Ramoth.

Shealtiel (*she-al'-te-el*) See also SALATHIEL.
Ezr 3: 2 and Zerubbabel the son of S', and
8 began Zerubbabel the son of S',
5: 2 rose up Zerubbabel the son of S',
Ne 12: 1 up with Zerubbabel the son of S',
Hag 1: 1 unto Zerubbabel the son of S',
12 Then Zerubbabel the son of S', and
14 spirit of Zerubbabel the son of S',
2: 2 now to Zerubbabel the son of S',
23 my servant, the son of S', saith

Shean See BETH-SHEAN.

shear See also SHEARER; SHEARING; SHORN.
Ge 31: 19 And Laban went to s' his sheep:
38: 13 up to Timnath to s' his sheep.
De 15: 19 nor s' the firstling of thy sheep.
1Sa 25: 4 that Nabal did s' his sheep.

Shear See SHEAR-JASHUB.

shearer See also SHEARERS.
Ac 8: 32 like a lamb dumb before his s',

shearers See also SHEEPSHEARERS.
1Sa 25: 7 I have heard that thou hast s':
11 flesh that I have killed for my s',
Isa 53: 7 as a sheep before her s' is dumb, so

Sheariah (*she-a-ri'-ah*)
1Ch 8: 38 Ishmael, and S', and Obadiah,
9: 44 Ishmael, and S', and Obadiah,

shearing
1Sa 25: 2 he was s' his sheep in Carmel.
2Ki 10: 12 at the s' house in the way,
14 at the pit of the s' house, even

shearing-house See SHEARING and HOUSE.

Shear-jashub (*she''-ar-ja'-shub*)
Isa 7: 3 meet Ahaz, thou, and S' thy son,

sheath
1Sa 17: 51 and drew it out of his s' thereof,
2Sa 20: 8 upon his loins in the s' thereof;
1Ch 21: 27 put his sword again into the s'
Eze 21: 3 forth my sword out of his s',
4 my sword go forth out of his s'
5 drew forth my sword out of his s':
30 cause it to return into his s'? I will
Joh 18: 11 Put up thy sword into the s':

sheaves
Ge 37: 7 we were binding s' in the fields,
7 behold, your s' stood round about,
Ru 2: 7 after the reapers among the s':
15 Let her glean even among the s',
Ne 13: 15 bringing in s', and lading asses;
Ps 126: 6 rejoicing, bringing his s' with him.
129: 7 nor he that bindeth s' his bosom.
Am 2: 13 a cart is pressed that is full of s'.
Mic 4: 12 gather them as the s' into the floor.

Sheba (*she'-bah*) See also BATH-SHEBA; BEER-SHEBA; SHEBAH.
Ge 10: 7 sons of Raamah; S', and Dedan.
28 And Obal, and Abimael, and S',
25: 3 And Jokshan begat S', and Dedan.
Jos 19: 2 inheritance Beer-sheba, and S',
2Sa 20: 1 man of Belial, whose name was S',
2 and followed S' the son of Bichri:
6 S' the son of Bichri do us more
7 pursue after S' the son of Bichri,
10 pursued after S' the son of Bichri.
13 pursue after S' the son of Bichri.
21 S' the son of Bichri by name,
22 the head of S' the son of Bichri,

1Ki 10: 1 queen of S· heard of the fame of
4 queen of S· had seen all Solomon's
10 queen of S· gave to king Solomon.
13 unto the queen of S· all her desire,
1Ch 1: 9 sons of Raamah; S·, and Dedan.
22 And Ebal, and Abimael, and S·,
32 sons of Jokshan; S·, and Dedan.
5:13 Meshullam; and S·, and Jorai,
2Ch 9: 1 queen of S· heard of the fame of
3 queen of S· had seen the wisdom
9 spice as the queen of S· gave king
12 to the queen of S· all her desire,
Job 6:19 companies of S· waited for them.
Ps 72:10 kings of S· and Seba shall offer
15 shall be given of the gold of S·:
Isa 60: 6 all they from S· shall come: they
Jer 6:20 there to me incense from S·, and
Eze 27:22 The merchants of S· and Raamah,
23 the merchants of S·, Asshur, and
38:13 S·, and Dedan, and the merchants

Shebah (*she'-bah*) See also SHEBA.
Ge 26:33 And he called it S·: therefore the

Shebam (*she'-bam*) See also SHIBMAH.
Nu 32: 3 Elealeh, and S·, and Nebo, and

Shebaniah (*sheb-a-ni'-ah*) See also SHECHANIAH.
1Ch 15:24 And S·, and Jehoshaphat, and
Ne 9: 4 Kadmiel, S·, Bunni, Sherebiah,
5 Hodijah, S·, and Pethahiah, said,
10: 4 Hattush, S·, Malluch,
10 their brethren, S·, Hodijah, Kelita,
12 Zaccur, Sherebiah, S·,
12:14 Melicu, Jonathan; of S·, Joseph;

Shebarim (*sheb'-a-rim*)
Jos 7: 5 from before the gate even unto S·,

Sheber (*she'-bur*)
1Ch 2:48 Caleb's concubine, bare S·, and

Shebna (*sheb'-nah*)
2Ki 18:18 S· the scribe, and Joah the son of
26 S·, and Joah, unto Rab-shakeh,
37 S· the scribe, and Joah the son of
19: 2 the household, and S· the scribe,
Isa 22:15 unto this treasurer, even unto S·,
36: 3 over the house, and S· the scribe,
11 Then said Eliakim and S· and
22 S· the scribe, and Joah, the son of
37: 2 S· the scribe, and the elders of the

Shebuel (*she-bu'-el*) See also SHUBAEL.
1Ch 23:16 of Gershom, S· was the chief.
25: 4 Uzziel, S·, and Jerimoth,
26:24 And S· the son of Gershom, the son

Shecaniah (*shek-a-ni'-ah*) See also SHEBANIAH; SHECHANIAH.
1Ch 24:11 ninth to Jeshuah, the tenth to S·,
2Ch 31:15 and Shemaiah, Amariah, and S·,

Shechaniah (*shek-a-ni'-ah*) See also SHEBANIAH; SHECANIAH.
1Ch 3:21 sons of Obadiah, the sons of S·.
22 the sons of S·; Shemaiah: and the
Ezr 8: 3 Of the sons of S·, of the sons of
5 Of the sons of S·; the son of
10: 2 And S· the son of Jehiel, one of
Ne 3:29 also Shemaiah the son of S·, the
6:18 son in law of S· the son of Arah;
12: 3 S·, Rehum, Meremoth,

Shechem (*she'-kem*) See also SHECHEMITES; SHECHEM'S; SICHEM; SYCHEM.
Ge 33:18 came to Shalem, a city of S·,
34: 2 S· the son of Hamor the Hivite,
4 S· spake unto his father Hamor,
6 father of S· went out unto Jacob
8 son S· longeth for your daughter:
11 S· said unto her father and unto
13 And the sons of Jacob answered S·
18 their words pleased Hamor, and S·
20 Hamor and S· his son came unto
24 unto S· his son hearkened all that
26 they slew Hamor and S· his son
35: 4 under the oak which was by S·.
37:12 to feed their father's flock in S·.
13 thy brethren feed the flock in S·?
14 vale of Hebron, and he came to S·.
Nu 26:31 S·, the family of the Shechemites:
Jos 17: 2 and for the children of S·, and for
7 Michmethah, that lieth before S·;
20: 7 and S· in mount Ephraim, and
21:21 gave them S· with her suburbs in
24: 1 all the tribes of Israel to S·, and
25 a statute and an ordinance in S·.
32 up out of Egypt, buried they in S·,
32 the father of S· for an hundred
J'g 8:31 And his concubine that was in S·,
9: 1 son of Jerubbaal went to S· unto
2 in the ears of all the men of S·,
3 in the ears of all the men of S· all
6 the men of S· gathered together,
6 plain of the pillar that was in S·.
7 Hearken unto me, ye men of S·,
18 king over the men of S·, because
20 and devour the men of S·, and the
20 fire come out from the men of S·,
23 Abimelech and the men of S·; and
23 the men of S· dealt treacherously
24 upon the men of S·, which aided
25 And the men of S· set liers in wait
26 his brethren, and went over to S·:
26 men of S· put their confidence in
28 Who is Abimelech, and who is S·,
28 the men of Hamor the father of S·:
31 and his brethren be come to S·;
34 they laid wait against S· in four
39 went out before the men of S·, and
J'g 9:41 that they should not dwell in S·.
46 men of the tower of S· heard that,
47 the men of the tower of S· were
49 men of the tower of S· died also,
57 And all the evil of the men of S·
21:19 that goeth up from Beth-el to S·,
1Ki 12: 1 And Rehoboam went to S·: for all
1 were come to S· to make him king.
25 Then Jeroboam built S· in mount
1Ch 6:67 S· in mount Ephraim with her
7:19 of Shemidah were, Ahain, and S·,
28 S· also and the towns thereof,
2Ch 10: 1 And Rehoboam went to S·: for to
1 S· were all Israel come to make
Ps 60: 6 I will divide S·, and mete out the
108: 7 I will rejoice, I will divide S·, and
Jer 41: 5 That there came certain from S·,

Shechemites (*she'-kem-ites*)
Nu 26:31 of Shechem, the family of the S·:

Shechem's (*she'-kems*)
Ge 33:19 the children of Hamor, S· father,
34:26 and took Dinah out of S· house,

shed See also SHEDDETH; SHEDDING.
Ge 9: 6 by man shall his blood be s·: for
37:22 S· no blood, but cast him into
Ex 22: 2 die, there shall no blood be s· for him.
3 him, there shall be blood s· for him;
Le 17: 4 he hath s· blood; and that man
Nu 35:33 be cleansed of the blood that is s·
33 but by the blood of him that s· it.
De 19:10 That innocent blood be not s· in
21: 7 Our hands have not s· this blood,
1Sa 25:26 thee from coming to s· blood,
31 thou hast s· blood causeless, or
33 me this day from coming to s· blood,
2Sa 20:10 s· out his bowels to the ground,
1Ki 2: 5 and s· the blood of war in peace,
31 the innocent blood, which Joab s·,
2Ki 21:16 Manasseh s· innocent blood very
24: 4 for the innocent blood that he s·:
1Ch 22: 8 Thou hast s· blood abundantly, and
8 thou hast s· much blood upon the
28: 3 a man of war, and hast s· blood.
Ps 79: 3 Their blood have they s· like water
10 blood of thy servants which is s·.
106:38 s· innocent blood, even the blood
Pr 1:16 to evil, and make haste to s· blood.
6:17 and hands that s· innocent blood,
Isa 59: 7 make haste to s· innocent blood:
Jer 7: 6 s· not innocent blood in this place,
22: 3 s· innocent blood in this place.
17 and for to s· innocent blood, and
La 4:13 s· the blood of the just in the midst
Eze 16:38 wedlock and s· blood are judged;
22: 4 in thy blood that thou hast s·: and
6 in thee to their power to s· blood.
9 are men that carry tales to s· blood:
12 have they taken gifts to s· blood;
27 ravening the prey, to s· blood, and
23:45 manner of women that s· blood;
33:25 toward your idols, and s· blood:
35: 5 hast s· the blood of the children
36:18 that they had s· upon the land,
Joe 3:19 s· innocent blood in their land.
M't 23:35 righteous blood s· upon the earth,
26:28 s· for many for the remission of sins.
M'r 14:24 testament, which is s· for many.
Lu 11:50 which was s· from the foundation
22:20 in my blood, which is s· for you.
Ac 2:33 he hath s· forth this, which ye now
22:20 blood of thy martyr Stephen was s·,
Ro 3:15 Their feet are swift to s· blood:
5: 5 the love of God is s· abroad in our
Tit 3: 6 s· on us abundantly through Jesus
Re 16: 6 For they have s· the blood of saints

shedder
Eze 18:10 son that is a robber, a s· of blood,

sheddeth
Ge 9: 6 Whoso s· man's blood, by man
Eze 22: 3 The city s· blood in the midst of it,

shedding
Heb 9:22 and without s· of blood is no

Shedeur (*shed'-e-ur*)
Nu 1: 5 of Reuben; Elizur the son of S·.
2:10 Reuben shall be Elizur the son of S·.
7:30 the fourth day Elizur the son of S·,
35 the offering of Elizur the son of S·.
10:18 his host was Elizur the son of S·.

sheep See also SHEEPCOTE; SHEEPFOLD; SHEEPMASTER; SHEEP'S; SHEEPSHEARERS; SHEEPSKINS; SHEPHERD.
Ge 4: 2 Abel was a keeper of s·, but Cain
12:16 he had s·, and oxen, and he asses,
20:14 And Abimelech took s·, and oxen,
21:27 And Abraham took s· and oxen, and
29: 2 were three flocks of s· lying by it;
3 watered the s·, and put the stone
6 his daughter cometh with the s·.
7 water ye the s·, and go and feed
8 well's mouth; then we water the s·.
9 Rachel came with her father's s·:
10 s· of Laban his mother's brother,
30:32 all the brown cattle among the s·,
33 the goats, and brown among the s·,
35 and all the brown among the s·,
31:19 And Laban went to shear his s·:
38:13 goeth up to Timnath to shear his s·.
Ex 9: 3 upon the oxen, and upon the s·:
12: 5 ye shall take it out from the s·, or
20:24 offerings, thy s·, and thine oxen:
22: 1 If a man shall steal an ox, or a s·,
Ex 22: 1 oxen for an ox, and four s· for a
1 for an ox, and four...for a s·.
4 whether it be ox, or ass, or s·; he
9 whether it be for ox, for ass, for s·,
10 an ass, or an ox, or a s·, or any
30 with thine oxen, and with thy s·:
34:19 whether ox or s·, that is male.
Le 1:10 of the s·, or of the goats, for a
7:23 of fat, of ox, or of s·, or of goat.
22:19 the beeves, of the s·, or of the goats.
21 a freewill offering in beeves or s·,
27 When a bullock, or a s·, or a goat,
27:26 whether it be ox, or s·: it is the
Nu 18:17 the firstling of a s·, or the firstling
22:40 And Balak offered oxen and s·, and
27:17 not as s· which have no shepherd.
31:28 and of the asses, and of the s·:
32 thousand and five thousand s·,
36 thousand and five hundred s·:
37 And the Lord's tribute of the s· was
43 seven thousand and five hundred s·,
32:24 little ones, and folds for your s·;
36 fenced cities: and folds for s·.
De 7:13 and the flocks of thy s·, in the land
14: 4 eat: the ox, the s·, and the goat,
26 for oxen, or for s·, or for wine, or
15:19 nor shear the firstling of thy s·.
17: 1 bullock, or s·, wherein is blemish,
18: 3 sacrifice, whether it be ox or s·;
4 and the first of the fleece of thy s·,
22: 1 brother's ox or his s· go astray,
28: 4, 18 kine, and the flocks of thy s·.
31 s· shall be given unto thine enemies,
51 of thy kine, or flocks of thy s·,
32:14 Butter of kine, and milk of s·, with
Jos 6:21 and s·, and ass, with the edge of
7:24 his asses, and his s·, and his tent,
J'g 6: 4 Israel, neither s·, nor ox, nor ass.
1Sa 8:17 He will take the tenth of your s·:
14:32 and took s·, and oxen, and calves,
34 every man his s·, and slay them
15: 3 infant and suckling, ox and s·,
9 the best of the s·, and of the oxen,
14 meaneth then this bleating of the s·
15 the people spared the best of the s·
21 people took of the spoil, s· and oxen,
16:11 and, behold, he keepeth the s·.
19 David thy son, which is with the s·.
17:15 from Saul to feed his father's s· at
20 left the s· with a keeper, and took,
28 whom hast thou left those few s·
34 Thy servant kept his father's s·,
22:19 and s·, with the edge of the sword.
25: 2 he had three thousand s·, and a
2 he was shearing his s· in Carmel.
4 that Nabal did shear his s·.
16 we were with them keeping the s·.
18 of wine, and five s· ready dressed.
27: 9 took away the s·, and the oxen, and
2Sa 7: 8 sheepcote, from following the s·,
17:29 And honey, and butter, and s·, and
24:17 but these s·, what have they done?
1Ki 1: 9 Adonijah slew s· and oxen and fat
19 hath slain oxen and fat cattle and s·
25 and fat cattle and s· in abundance,
4:23 an hundred s·, beside harts, and
8: 5 sacrificing s· and oxen, that could
63 hundred and twenty thousand s·.
22:17 as s· that have not a shepherd:
2Ki 5:26 and vineyards, and s·, and oxen,
1Ch 5:21 s· two hundred and fifty thousand,
12:40 oil, and oxen, and s· abundantly:
17: 7 even from following the s·, that thou
21:17 for these s·, what have they done?
2Ch 5: 6 sacrificed s· and oxen, which could
7: 5 hundred and twenty thousand s·:
14:15 away s· and camels in abundance,
15:11 oxen and seven thousand s·.
18: 2 Ahab killed s· and oxen for him in
16 as s· that have no shepherd: and
29:33 oxen and three thousand s·.
30:24 bullocks and seven thousand s·;
24 bullocks and ten thousand s·: and
31: 6 brought in the tithe of oxen and s·,
Ne 3: 1 priests, and they builded the s· gate;
32 corner unto the s· gate repaired
5:18 daily was one ox and six choice s·;
12:39 tower of Meah, even unto the s· gate:
Job 1: 3 substance...was seven thousand s·,
16 hath burned up the s·, and the
31:20 warmed with the fleece of my s·;
42:12 for he had fourteen thousand s·,
Ps 8: 7 All s· and oxen, yea, and the
44:11 us like s· appointed for meat;
22 are counted as s· for the slaughter.
49:14 Like s· they are laid in the grave;
74: 1 smoke against the s· of thy pasture?
78:52 his own people to go forth like s·,
79:13 we thy people and s· of thy pasture
95: 7 his pasture, and the s· of his hand.
100: 3 his people, and the s· of his pasture.
119:176 I have gone astray like a lost s·;
144:13 our s· may bring forth thousands
Ca 4: 2 Thy teeth are like a flock of s· that
6: 6 Thy teeth are as a flock of s· which
Isa 7:21 nourish a young cow, and two s·;
13:14 and as a s· that no man taketh up:
22:13 slaying oxen, and killing s·, eating
53: 6 All we like s· have gone astray; we
7 and as a s· before her shearers is
Jer 12: 3 them out like s· for the slaughter,
23: 1 and scatter the s· of my pasture!
50: 6 My people hath been lost s·: their
17 Israel is a scattered s·; the lions
Eze 34: 6 My s· wandered through all the
11 even I, will both search my s·, and

Eze 34:12 in the day that he is among his s'
12 so will I seek out my s', and will
Ho 12:12 for a wife, and for a wife he kept s'.
Joe 1:18 the flocks of s' are made desolate.
Mic 2:12 them together as the s' of Bozrah,
5: 8 a young lion among the flocks of s':
Zec 13: 7 and the s' shall be scattered: and I
M't 9:36 abroad, as s' having no shepherd.
10: 6 go rather to the lost s' of the house
16 I send you forth as s' in the midst
12:11 that shall have one s', and if it fall
12 then is a man better than a s'?
15:24 but unto the lost s' of the house of
18:12 if a man have an hundred s', and
13 he rejoiceth more of that s', than of
25:32 divideth his s' from the goats:
33 he shall set the s' on his right hand,
26:31 the s' of the flock shall be scattered
M'r 6:34 were as s' not having a shepherd:
14:27 and the s' shall be scattered.
Lu 15: 4 man of you, having an hundred s',
6 I have found my s' which was lost.
Joh 2:14 that sold oxen and s' and doves,
15 temple, and the s', and the oxen;
5: 2 Jerusalem by the s' market a pool,
10: 2 the door is the shepherd of the s'.
3 openeth; and the s' hear his voice:
3 and he calleth his own s' by name,
4 when he putteth forth his own s',
4 before them, and the s' follow him:
7 unto you, I am the door of the s'.
8 but the s' did not hear them.
11 shepherd giveth his life for the s'.
12 shepherd, whose own the s' are not,
12 and leaveth the s', and fleeth: and
12 them, and scattereth the s'.
13 hireling, and careth not for the s'.
14 know my s', and am known of mine.
15 and I lay down my life for the s'.
16 And other s' I have, which are not
26 ye are not of my s', as I said unto
27 My s' hear my voice, and I know
21:16 He saith unto him, Feed my s'.
17 Jesus saith unto him, Feed my s'.
Ac 8:32 He was led as a s' to the slaughter;
Ro 8:36 accounted as s' for the slaughter.
Heb13:20 Jesus, that great shepherd of the s',
1Pe 2:25 For ye were as s' going astray; but
Re 18:13 and beasts, and s', and horses, and

sheepcote See also SHEEPCOTES.
2Sa 7: 8 I took thee from the s', from
1Ch 17: 7 I took thee from the s', even from

sheepcotes
1Sa 24: 3 he came to the s' by the way,

sheepfold See also SHEEPFOLDS.
Joh 10: 1 not by the door into the s', but

sheepfolds
Nu 32:16 build s' here for our cattle,
J'g 5:16 Why abodest thou among the s'.
Ps 78:70 and took him from the s':

sheep-gate See SHEEP and GATE.

sheep-market See SHEEP and MARKET.

sheepmaster
2Ki 3: 4 And Mesha king of Moab was a s',

sheep's
M't 7:15 which come to you in s' clothing,

sheepshearers
Ge 38:12 went...unto his s' to Timnath,
2Sa 13:23 Absalom had s' in Baal-hazor,
24 Behold now, thy servant hath s';

sheepskins
Heb11:37 they wandered about in s' and

sheet See also SHEETS.
Ac 10:11 great s' knit at the four corners,
11: 5 as it had been a great s', let down

sheets
J'g 14:12 will give you thirty s' and thirty
13 then shall ye give me thirty s' and

Shehariah (*she-ha-ri'-ah*)
1Ch 8:26 Shamsherai, and S', and Athaliah,

shekel (*she'-kul*) See also SHEKELS.
Ge 24:22 golden earring of half a s' weight,
Ex 30:13 half a s' after the s' of the
13 sanctuary: (a s' is twenty gerahs:)
13 an half s' shall be the offering of
15 shall not give less than half a s',
24 after the s' of the sanctuary,
38:24 after the s' of the sanctuary.
25 after the s' of the sanctuary:
26 for every man, that is, half a s',
26 after the s' of the sanctuary,
Le 5:15 after the s' of the sanctuary,
27: 3 silver, after the s' of the sanctuary.
25 according to the s' of the sanctuary:
25 twenty gerahs shall be the s'.
Nu 3:47 after the s' of the sanctuary shalt
47 (the s' is twenty gerahs:)
50 after the s' of the sanctuary:
7:13, 19, 25, 31, 37, 43, 49, 55, 61, 67, 73,
79 after the s' of the sanctuary;
85 after the s' of the sanctuary:
86 apiece, after the s' of the sanctuary:
18:16 after the s' of the sanctuary,
1Sa 9: 8 the fourth part of a s' of silver:
2Ki 7: 1 of fine flour be sold for a s', and
1 and two measures of barley for a s',
16 of fine flour was sold for a s', and
16 and two measures of barley for a s',
18 Two measures of barley for a s',
18 and a measure of fine flour for a s',
Ne 10:32 the third part of a s' for the service
Eze 45:12 And the s' shall be twenty gerahs:
Am 8: 5 the ephah small, and the s' great,

shekels
Ge 23:15 worth four hundred s' of silver;
16 four hundred s' of silver, current
Ex 21:32 unto their master thirty s' of silver,
30:23 spices, of pure myrrh five hundred s',
23 much, even two hundred and fifty s',
23 calamus two hundred and fifty s',
24 And of cassia five hundred s',
38:24 and seven hundred and thirty s',
25 and threescore and fifteen s',
28 seven hundred seventy and five s'
29 two thousand and four hundred s'.
Le 5:15 with thy estimation by s' of silver,
27: 3 estimation shall be fifty s' of silver,
4 thy estimation shall be thirty s'
5 shall be of the male twenty s',
5 and for the female ten s'.
6 be of the male five s' of silver,
6 estimation shall be three s' of silver.
7 thy estimation shall be fifteen s',
7 and for the female ten s'.
16 shall be valued at fifty s' of silver.
Nu 3:47 even take five s' apiece by the poll,
50 hundred and threescore and five s',
7:13 was an hundred and thirty s',
13 one silver bowl of seventy s', after
14 One spoon of ten s' of gold, full of
19 was an hundred and thirty s',
19 one silver bowl of seventy s', after
20 One spoon of gold of ten s', full of
25 was an hundred and thirty s',
25 one silver bowl of seventy s', after
26 One golden spoon of ten s', full of
31 of an hundred and thirty s',
31 one silver bowl of seventy s', after
32 One golden spoon of ten s', full of
37 was an hundred and thirty s',
37 one silver bowl of seventy s', after
38 One golden spoon of ten s', full of
43 of an hundred and thirty s',
43 a silver bowl of seventy s', after
44 One golden spoon of ten s', full of
49 was an hundred and thirty s',
49 one silver bowl of seventy s', after
50 One golden spoon of ten s', full of
55 of an hundred and thirty s',
55 one silver bowl of seventy s', after
56 One golden spoon of ten s', full of
61 was an hundred and thirty s',
61 one silver bowl of seventy s', after
62 One golden spoon of ten s', full of
67 was an hundred and thirty s',
67 one silver bowl of seventy s', after
68 One golden spoon of ten s', full of
73 was an hundred and thirty s',
73 one silver bowl of seventy s', after
74 One golden spoon of ten s', full of
79 was an hundred and thirty s',
79 one silver bowl of seventy s', after
80 One golden spoon of ten s', full of
85 weighing an hundred and thirty s',
85 two thousand and four hundred s',
86 full of incense, weighing ten s' apiece,
86 spoons was an hundred and twenty s'.
18:16 estimation, for the money of five s',
31:52 thousand seven hundred and fifty s'.
De 22:19 amerce him in an hundred s' of silver,
29 the damsel's father fifty s' of silver,
Jos 7:21 and two hundred s' of silver, and
21 a wedge of gold of fifty s' weight,
J'g 8:26 thousand and seven hundred s' of gold;
17: 2 The eleven hundred s' of silver that
3 had restored the eleven hundred s' of
4 mother took two hundred s' of silver,
10 and I will give thee ten s' of silver by
1Sa 17: 5 coat was five thousand s' of brass.
7 weighed six hundred s' of iron:
2Sa 14:26 hair of his head two hundred s'
18:11 would have given thee ten s' of silver,
12 a thousand s' of silver in mine hand,
21:16 weighed three hundred s' of brass in
24:24 and the oxen for fifty s' of silver.
1Ki 10:16 hundred s' of gold went to one target.
29 of Egypt for six hundred s' of silver,
2Ki 15:20 of each man fifty s' of silver, to
1Ch 21:25 for the place six hundred s' of gold
2Ch 1:17 a chariot for six hundred s' of silver,
3: 9 of the nails was fifty s' of gold.
9:15 hundred s' of beaten gold went to one
16 hundred s' of gold went to one shield.
Ne 5:15 and wine, beside forty s' of silver;
Jer 32: 9 money, even seventeen s' of silver.
Eze 4:10 shall be by weight, twenty s' a day:
45:12 twenty s', five and twenty s',
12 fifteen s', shall be your maneh.

Shelah (*she'-lah*) See also SALAH; SHELANITES.
Ge 38: 5 a son; and called his name S':
11 house, till S' my son be grown:
14 for she saw that S' was grown,
26 that I gave her not to S' my son.
46:12 of Judah; Er, and Onan, and S',
Nu 26:20 of S', the family of the Shelanites:
1Ch 1:18 Arphaxad begat S', and S' begat
24 Shem, Arphaxad, S',
2: 3 of Judah; Er, and Onan, and S':
4:21 The sons of S' the son of Judah

Shelanites (*she'-lan-ites*)
Nu 26:20 S', the family of the Shelanites:

Shelemiah (*shel-e-mi'-ah*) See also MESHELEMIAH; SHALLUM.
1Ch 26:14 And the lot eastward fell to S'.
Ezr 10:39 And S', and Nathan, and Adaiah,
41 Azareel, and S', Shemariah,
Ne 3:30 repaired Hananiah the son of S',
13:13 over the treasuries, S' the priest,
Jer 36:14 the son of S', the son of Cushi,
26 Azriel, and S' the son of Abdeel, to
37: 3 the king sent Jehucal the son of S'
13 name was Irijah, the son of S',
38: 1 and Jucal the son of S', and Pashur

Sheleph (*she'-lef*)
Ge 10:26 Joktan begat Almodad, and S',
1Ch 1:20 Joktan begat Almodad, and S',

Shelesh (*she'-lesh*)
1Ch 7:35 and Imna, and S', and Amal.

Shelomi (*shel'-o-mi*)
Nu 34:27 of Asher, Ahihud the son of S'.

Shelomith (*shel'-o-mith*) See also SHELOMOTH.
Le 24:11 his mother's name was S', the
1Ch 3:19 and Hananiah, and S' their sister:
23: 9 S', and Haziel, and Haran, three.
18 Of the sons of Izhar; S' their chief.
26:25 and Zichri his son, and S' his son.
26 Which S' and his brethren were
28 thing, it was under the hand of S',
2Ch 11:20 Abijah, and Attai, and Ziza, and S'.
Ezr 8:10 And of the sons of S'; the son of

Shelomoth (*shel'-o-moth*) See also SHELOMITH.
1Ch 24:22 S': of the sons of S'; Jahath.

shelter
Job 24: 8 embrace the rock for want of a s'.
Ps 61: 3 thou hast been a s' for me, and a

Shelumiel (*she-lu'-me-el*)
Nu 1: 6 S' the son of Zurishaddai.
2:12 shall be S' the son of Zurishaddai.
7:36 fifth day S' the son of Zurishaddai,
41 of S' the son of Zurishaddai.
10:19 was S' the son of Zurishaddai.

Shem (*shem*) See also SEM.
Ge 5:32 Noah begat S', Ham, and Japheth.
6:10 Noah begat three sons, S', Ham,
7:13 same day entered Noah, and S',
9:18 that went forth of the ark, were S',
23 S' and Japheth took a garment,
26 Blessed be the Lord God of S';
27 he shall dwell in the tents of S';
10: 1 the sons of Noah; S', Ham, and
21 Unto S' also, the father of all the
22 children of S'; Elam, and Asshur,
31 the sons of S', after their families,
11:10 These are the generations of S':
10 S' was an hundred years old, and
11 S' lived after he begat Arphaxad
1Ch 1: 4 Noah, S', Ham, and Japheth.
17 The sons of S'; Elam, and Asshur,
24 S', Arphaxad, Shelah,

Shema (*she'-mah*) See also SHEMAIAH; SHIMHI.
Jos 15:26 Amam, and S', and Moladah,
1Ch 2:43 and Tappuah, and Rekem, and S'.
44 And S' begat Raham, the father of
5: 8 Bela the son of Azaz, the son of S',
8:13 Beriah also, and S', who were
Ne 8: 4 him stood Mattithiah, and S', and

Shemaah (*shem'-a-ah*)
1Ch 12: 3 the sons of S' the Gebeathite;

Shemaiah (*shem-a-i'-ah*) See also SHAMMUA; SHEMA; SHIMEI; SIMEI.
1Ki 12:22 word of God came unto S' the
1Ch 3:22 And the sons of Shechaniah; S':
22 and the sons of S'; Hattush, and
4:37 the son of Shimri, the son of S';
5: 4 S' his son, Gog his son, Shimei his
9:14 S' the son of Hasshub, the son of
16 And Obadiah the son of S', the son
15: 8 S' the chief, and his brethren two
11 S', and Eliel, and Amminadab,
24: 6 And S' the son of Nethaneel the
26: 4 S' the firstborn, Jehozabad the
6 Also unto S' his son were sons
7 The sons of S'; Othni, and Rephael,
2Ch 11: 2 the word of the Lord came to S'
12: 5 came S' the prophet to Rehoboam,
7 the word of the Lord came to S',
15 they not written in the book of S'
17: 8 with them he sent Levites, even S',
29:14 sons of Jeduthun; S', and Uzziel.
31:15 and S', Amariah, and Shecaniah,
35: 9 also, and S' and Nethaneel, his
Ezr 8:13 are these, Eliphelet, Jeiel, and S',
16 sent I for Eliezer, for Ariel, for S',
10:21 and Elijah, and S', and Jehiel, and
31 Ishijah, Malchiah, S', Shimeon,
Ne 3:29 After him repaired also S' the son
6:10 I came unto the house of S' the
10: 8 Bilgai, S'; these were the priests.
11:15 the Levites: S' the son of Hashub,
12: 6 S', and Joiarib, Jedaiah,
18 Shammua; of S', Jehonathan;
34 Benjamin, and S', and Jeremiah,
35 the son of S', the son of Mattaniah,
36 And his brethren, S', and Azarael,
42 And Maaseiah, and S', and Eleazar,
Jer 26:20 the son of S' of Kirjath-jearim,
29:24 Thus shalt thou also speak to S'
31 Thus saith the Lord concerning S'
31 that S' hath prophesied unto you,
32 I will punish S' the Nehelamite,
36:12 and Delaiah the son of S', and

Shemariah (*shem-a-ri'-ah*) See also SHAMARIAH.
1Ch 12: 5 Bealiah, and S', and Shephatiah

Ezr 10: 32 Benjamin, Malluch, and *S*.
41 Azareel, and Shelemiah, *S*.
Shemeber (*shem-e'-bur*)
Ge 14: 2 *S* king of Zeboiim, and the king
Shemer (*she'-mur*)
1Ki 16: 24 bought the hill Samaria of *S* for
24 after the name of *S*, owner of the
Shemesh See BETH-SHEMESH; EN-SHEMESH; IR-SHEMESH.
Shemida (*shem-i'-dah*) See also SHEMIDAH.
Nu 26: 32 *S*, the family of the Shemidaites:
Jos 17: 2 Hepher, and for the children of *S*:
Shemidah (*shem-i'-dah*) See also SHEMIDA; SHEMIDAITES.
1Ch 7: 19 And the sons of *S* were, Ahian,
Shemidaites (*shem'-i-dah-ites*)
Nu 26: 32 of Shemida, the family of the *S*:
Sheminith (*shem'-i-nith*)
1Ch 15: 21 with harps on the *S* to excel.
Ps 6: *title* Musician on Neginoth upon *S*,
12: *title* To the chief Musician upon *S*,
Shemiramoth (*she-mir'-a-moth*)
1Ch 15: 18 and Jaaziel, and *S*, and Jehiel,
20 and Aziel, and *S*, and Jehiel, and
16: 5 to him Zachariah, Jeiel, and *S*,
2Ch 17: 8 Asahel, and *S*, and Jehonathan,
Shemite See BETH-SHEMITE.
Shemuel (*shem-u'-el*) See also SAMUEL.
Nu 34: 20 Simeon, *S* the son of Ammihud.
1Ch 6: 33 the son of Joel, the son of *S*,
7: 2 *S*, heads of their father's house,
Shen (*shen*)
1Sa 7: 12 and set it between Mizpeh and *S*,
Shenazar (*she-na'-zar*)
1Ch 3: 18 also, and Pedaiah, and *S*,
Shenir (*she'-nur*) See also SENIR; SION.
De 3: 9 and the Amorites call it *S*;)
Ca 4: 8 from the top of *S* and Hermon,
Shepham (*she'-fam*) See also SHIPHMITE.
Nu 34: 10 border from Hazar-enan to *S*:
11 shall go down from *S* to Riblah,
Shephathiah (*shef-a-thi'-ah*) See also SHEPHATIAH.
1Ch 9: 8 and Meshullam, the son of *S*, the
Shephatiah (*shef-a-ti'-ah*) See also SHEPHATHIAH.
2Sa 3: 4 and the fifth, *S* the son of Abital;
1Ch 3: 3 The fifth, *S* of Abital: the sixth,
12: 5 Shemariah, and *S* the Haruphite,
27: 16 Simeonites, *S* the son of Maachah:
2Ch 21: 2 and Azariah, and Michael, and *S*:
Ezr 2: 4 The children of *S*, three hundred
57 The children of *S*, the children of
8: 8 And of the sons of *S*; Zebadiah the
Ne 7: 9 The children of *S*, three hundred
59 The children of *S*, the children of
11: 4 the son of *S*, the son of Mahalaleel,
Jer 38: 1 Then *S* the son of Mattan, and
shepherd See also SHEPHERD'S; SHEPHERDS.
Ge 46: 34 every *s* is an abomination
49: 24 (from thence is the *s*, the stone of
Nu 27: 17 be not as sheep which have no *s*.
1Ki 22: 17 hills, as sheep that have not a *s*:
2Ch 18: 16 as sheep that have no *s*: and the
Ps 23: 1 The Lord is my *s*; I shall not want.
80: 1 Give ear, O *S* of Israel, thou that
Ec 12: 11 which are given from one *s*.
Isa 40: 11 He shall feed his flock like a *s*: he
44: 28 That saith of Cyrus, He is my *s*,
63: 11 of the sea with the *s* of his flock?
Jer 31: 10 and keep him, as a *s* doth his flock.
43: 12 as a *s* putteth on his garment;
49: 19 and who is that *s* that will stand
50: 44 and who is that *s* that will stand
51: 23 in pieces...the *s* and his flock;
Eze 34: 5 scattered, because there is no *s*:
8 because there was no *s*, neither did
12 As a *s* seeketh out his flock in the
23 And I will set up one *s* over them,
23 feed them, and he shall be their *s*.
37: 24 and they all shall have one *s*: they
Am 3: 12 As the *s* taketh out of the mouth of
Zec 10: 2 troubled, because there was no *s*.
11: 15 yet the instruments of a foolish *s*.
16 lo, I will raise up a *s* in the land,
17 Woe to the idol *s* that leaveth the
13: 7 Awake, O sword, against my *s*,
7 smite the *s*, and the sheep shall be
M't 9: 36 abroad, as sheep having no *s*.
25: 32 as a *s* divideth his sheep from the
26: 31 I will smite the *s*, and the sheep of
M'r 6: 34 they were as sheep not having a *s*:
14: 27 I will smite the *s*, and the sheep
Joh 10: 2 in by the door is the *s* of the sheep.
11 I am the good *s*: the good *s* giveth
12 that is an hireling, and not the *s*,
14 I am the good *s*, and know my
16 there shall be one fold, and one *s*.
Heb 13: 20 Jesus, that great *s* of the sheep,
1Pe 2: 25 returned unto the *S* and Bishop of
5: 4 And when the chief *S* shall appear,
shepherd's
1Sa 17: 40 put them in a *s* bag which he had,
Isa 38: 12 is removed from me as a *s* tent:
shepherds See also SHEPHERDS'.
Ge 46: 32 the men are *s*, for their trade
47: 3 Thy servants are *s*, both we,
Ex 2: 17 And the *s* came and drove them
19 us out of the hand of the *s*, and
1Sa 25: 7 now thy *s* which were with us, we
Isa 13: 20 neither shall the *s* make their fold
31: 4 when a multitude of *s* is called forth
Isa 56: 11 they are *s* that cannot understand:
Jer 6: 3 The *s* with their flocks shall come
23: 4 And I will set up *s* over them which
25: 34 Howl, ye *s*, and cry; and wallow
35 And the *s* shall have no way to flee,
36 A voice of the cry of the *s*, and an
33: 12 an habitation of *s* causing their
50: 6 their *s* have caused them to go
Eze 34: 2 prophesy against the *s* of Israel,
2 saith the Lord God unto the *s*; Woe
2 Woe be to the *s* of Israel that do
2 should not the *s* feed the flocks?
7 ye *s*, hear the word of the Lord;
8 did my *s* search for my flock,
8 but the *s* fed themselves, and fed
9 O ye *s*, hear the word of the Lord;
10 Behold, I am against the *s*; and I
10 neither shall the *s* feed themselves
Am 1: 2 habitations of the *s* shall mourn,
Mic 5: 5 shall we raise against him seven *s*,
Na 3: 18 Thy *s* slumber, O king of Assyria:
Zep 2: 6 be dwellings and cottages for *s*, and
Zec 10: 3 anger was kindled against the *s*,
11: 3 is a voice of the howling of the *s*;
5 and their own *s* pity them not.
8 Three *s* also I cut off in one month;
Lu 2: 8 country *s* abiding in the field,
15 the *s* said one to another, Let us
18 which were told them by the *s*.
20 And the *s* returned, glorifying and
shepherds'
Ca 1: 8 feed thy kids beside the *s* tents.
Shephi (*she'-fi*) See also SHEPHO.
1Ch 1: 40 and Ebal, *S*, and Onam.
Shepho (*she'-fo*) See also SHEPHI.
Ge 36: 23 and Ebal, *S*, and Onam.
Shephuphan (*shef'-u-fan*) See also SHUPHAM; SHUPPIM.
1Ch 8: 5 And Gera, and *S*, and Huram.
Sherah (*she'-rah*) See also UZZEN-SHERAH.
1Ch 7: 24 his daughter was *S*, who built
sherd See also POTSHERD; SHERDS; SHRED.
Isa 30: 14 be found in the bursting of it a *s*
sherds See also POTSHERDS.
Eze 23: 34 thou shalt break the *s* thereof,
Sherebiah (*sher-e-bi'-ah*)
Ezr 8: 18 and *S*, with his sons and his
24 *S*, Hashabiah, and ten of their
Ne 8: 7 and Bani, and *S*, Jamin, Akkub,
9: 4 Bunni, *S*, Bani, and Chenani, and
5 Bani, Hashabniah, *S*, Hodijah,
10: 12 Zaccur, *S*, Shebaniah,
12: 8 Binnui, Kadmiel, *S*, Judah, and
24 Hashabiah, *S*, and Jeshua the son
Sheresh (*she'-resh*)
1Ch 7: 16 the name of his brother was *S*;
Sherezer (*she-re'-zur*) See also SHAREZER.
Zec 7: 2 *S* and Regem-melech, and their
sheriffs
Da 3: 2, 3 the *s*, and all the rulers of the
Sheshach (*she'-shak*) See also BABYLON.
Jer 25: 26 king of *S* shall drink after them.
51: 41 How is *S* taken! and how is the
Sheshai (*she'-shahee*)
Nu 13: 22 *S*, and Talmai, the children of
Jos 15: 14 sons of Anak, *S*, and Ahiman, and
J'g 1: 10 and they slew *S*, and Ahiman, and
Sheshan (*she'-shan*)
1Ch 2: 31 And the sons of Ishi; *S*.
31 And the children of *S*; Ahlai.
34 *S* had no sons, but daughters,
34 And *S* had a servant, an Egyptian,
35 *S* gave his daughter to Jarha his
Sheshbazzar (*shesh-baz'-zur*) See also ZERUBBABEL.
Ezr 1: 8 and numbered them unto *S*, the
11 All these did *S* bring up with them
5: 14 unto one, whose name was *S*, whom
16 Then came the same *S*, and laid
Sheth (*sheth*) See also SETH.
Nu 24: 17 and destroy all the children of *S*.
1Ch 1: 1 Adam, *S*, Enosh,
Shethar (*she'-thar*) See also SHETHAR-BOZNAI.
Es 1: 14 Carshena, *S*, Admatha, Tarshish,
Shethar-boznai (*she'-thar-boz'-nahee*)
Ezr 5: 3 and *S*, and their companions, and
6 and *S*, and his companions the
6: 6 *S*, and your companions the
13 *S*,...their companions, according
Sheva (*she'-vah*) See also SHAVSHA.
2Sa 20: 25 And *S* was scribe: and Zadok and
1Ch 2: 49 *S* the father of Machbenah, and
shew See also SHEWBREAD; SHEWED; SHEWEST; SHEWETH; SHEWING.
Ge 12: 1 unto a land that I will *s* thee:
20: 13 thy kindness which thou shalt *s*
24: 12 and *s* kindness unto my master
40: 14 *s* kindness, I pray thee, unto me,
46: 31 I will go up, and *s* Pharaoh, and
Ex 7: 9 you, saying, *S* a miracle for you:
9: 16 up, for to *s* in thee my power;
10: 1 that I might *s* these my signs
13: 8 thou shalt *s* thy son in that day,
14: 13 which he will *s* to you to day: for
18: 20 shalt *s* them the way wherein
25: 9 According to all that I *s* thee,
33: 13 *s* me now thy way, that I may
Ex 33: 18 I beseech thee, *s* me thy glory.
19 will *s* mercy on whom I will *s* mercy.
Nu 16: 5 the Lord will *s* who are his, and
De 1: 33 to *s* you by what way ye should go,
3: 24 to *s* thy servants thy greatness,
5: 5 to *s* you the word of the Lord:
7: 2 with them, nor *s* mercy unto them:
13: 17 of his anger, and *s* thee mercy,
17: 9 they shall *s* thee the sentence of
10 the Lord shall choose shall *s* thee;
11 sentence which they shall *s* thee,
28: 50 of the old, nor *s* favour to the young:
32: 7 ask thy father, and he will *s* thee;
Jos 2: 12 ye will also *s* kindness unto my
5: 6 he would not *s* them the land,
J'g 1: 24 *S* us, we pray thee, the entrance
24 the city, and we will *s* thee mercy.
4: 22 will *s* thee the man...thou seekest.
6: 17 *s* me a sign that thou talkest with
1Sa 3: 15 Samuel feared to *s* Eli the vision.
8: 9 and *s* them the manner of the king
9: 6 peradventure he can *s* us our way
27 I may *s* thee the word of God.
10: 8 and *s* thee what thou shalt do.
14: 12 up to us, and we will *s* you a thing.
16: 3 I will *s* thee what thou shalt do:
20: 2 or small, but that he will *s* it me:
12 send not unto thee, and *s* it thee;
13 then I will *s* it thee, and send thee
14 *s* me the kindness of the Lord,
22: 17 he fled, and did not *s* it to me.
25: 8 young men, and they will *s* thee.
2Sa 2: 6 *s* kindness and truth unto you:
3: 8 *s* kindness this day unto the house
9: 1 may *s* him kindness for Jonathan's
3 that I may *s* the kindness of God
7 surely *s* thee kindness for Jonathan
10: 2 I will *s* kindness unto Hanun the
15: 25 *s* me both it, and his habitation:
22: 26 merciful thou wilt *s* thyself merciful,
26 man thou wilt *s* thyself upright.
27 the pure thou wilt *s* thyself pure;
27 froward thou wilt *s* thyself unsavoury.
1Ki 1: 52 If he will *s* himself a worthy man,
2: 2 therefore, and *s* thyself a man;
7 *s* kindness unto...sons of Barzillai
18: 1 saying, Go, *s* thyself unto Ahab;
2 Elijah went to *s* himself unto Ahab.
15 I will surely *s* myself unto him
2Ki 6: 11 *s* me which of us is for the king
7: 12 *s* you what the Syrians have done
1Ch 16: 23 *s*...from day to day his salvation.
19: 2 I will *s* kindness unto Hanun the
2Ch 16: 9 to *s* himself strong in the behalf of
Ezr 2: 59 could not *s* their father's house,
Ne 7: 61 could not *s* their father's house,
9: 19 of fire by night, to *s* them light,
Es 1: 11 to *s* the people...her beauty:
2: 10 charged her...she should not *s* it.
4: 8 to *s* it unto Esther, and to declare
Job 10: 2 *s* me wherefore thou contendest
11: 6 *s* thee the secrets of wisdom,
15: 17 I will *s* thee, hear me; and that
32: 6 and durst not *s* you mine opinion.
10 to me; I also will *s* mine opinion.
17 my part, I also will *s* mine opinion.
33: 23 to *s* unto man his uprightness:
36: 2 Suffer me a little, and I will *s*
Ps 4: 6 that say, Who will *s* us any good?
9: 1 *s* forth all thy marvellous works.
14 That I may *s* forth all thy praise
16: 11 Thou wilt *s* me the path of life:
17: 7 *S* thy marvellous lovingkindness,
18: 25 merciful thou wilt *s* thyself merciful;
25 man thou wilt *s* thyself upright;
26 the pure thou wilt *s* thyself pure;
26 froward thou wilt *s* thyself froward.
25: 4 *S* me thy ways, O Lord; teach me
14 and he will *s* them his covenant.
39: 6 every man walketh in a vain *s*:
50: 23 will I *s* the salvation of God.
51: 15 my mouth shall *s* forth thy praise.
71: 15 shall *s* forth thy righteousness
79: 13 *s* forth thy praise to all generations.
85: 7 *S* us thy mercy, O Lord, and
86: 17 *S* me a token for good; that they
88: 10 Wilt thou *s* wonders to the dead?
91: 16 him, and *s* him my salvation.
92: 2 To *s* forth thy lovingkindness in
15 To *s* that the Lord is upright: he
94: 1 vengeance belongeth, *s* thyself.
96: 2 *s*...his salvation from day to day.
106: 2 who can *s* forth all his praise?
109: 16 he remembered not to *s* mercy,
Pr 18: 24 hath friends must *s* himself friendly:
Isa 3: 9 The *s* of their countenance doth
27: 11 formed them will *s* them no favour.
30: 30 *s* the lighting down of his arm,
41: 22 and *s* us what shall happen:
22 let them *s* the former things, what
23 *S* the things that are to come
43: 9 this, and *s* us former things?
21 they shall *s* forth my praise.
44: 7 shall come, let them *s* unto them.
46: 8 Remember this, and *s* yourselves men:
47: 6 thou didst *s* them no mercy;
49: 9 are in darkness, *S* yourselves.
58: 1 *s* my people their transgression,
60: 6 *s* forth the praises of the Lord.
Jer 16: 10 shalt *s* this people all these words,
13 where I will not *s* you favour.
18: 17 I will *s* them the back, and not
33: 3 *s* thee great and mighty things,
42: 3 the Lord thy God may *s* us the way
12 And I will *s* mercies unto you,
50: 42 they are cruel, and will not *s* mercy:

Jer 51: 31 to s· the king of Babylon...his city
Eze 22: 2 shalt s· her all her abominations.
33: 31 their mouth they s· much love.
37: 18 thou not s· us what thou meanest
40: 4 heart upon all that I shall s· thee;
4 that I might s· them unto thee art
43: 10 s· the house to the house of Israel.
11 s· them the form of the house,
Da 2: 2 for to s· the king his dreams.
4 and we will s· the interpretation.
6 But if ye s· the dream, and the
6 therefore s· me the dream, and the
7 we will s· the interpretation of it.
9 that ye can s· me the interpretation
10 earth that can s· the king's matter:
11 there is none other that can s· it
16 s· the king the interpretation.
24 s· unto the king the interpretation.
27 the soothsayers, s· unto the king;
4: 2 I thought it good to s· the signs
5: 7 s· me the interpretation thereof,
12 and he will s· the interpretation.
15 they could not s· the interpretation
9: 23 forth, and I am come to s· thee;
10: 21 I will s· thee that which is noted
11: 2 And now will I s· thee the truth.
Joe 2: 30 I will s· wonders in the heavens
Mic 7: 15 I s· unto him marvellous things.
Na 3: 5 I will s· the nations thy nakedness,
Hab 1: 3 Why dost thou s· me iniquity, and
Zec 1: 9 unto me, I will s· thee what these be.
7: 9 and s· mercy and compassions
M't 8: 4 thy way, s· thyself to the priest,
11: 4 Go and s· John again those things
12: 18 shall s· judgment to the Gentiles.
14: 2 mighty works do s·...themselves
16: 1 would s· them a sign from heaven.
21 began Jesus to s· unto his disciples,
22: 19 S· me the tribute money. And
24: 1 s· him the buildings of the temple.
24 shall s· great signs and wonders;
M'r 1: 44 thy way, s· thyself to the priest,
6: 14 mighty works do s·...themselves
13: 22 and shall s· signs and wonders, to
14: 15 he will s· you a large upper room
Lu 1: 19 and to s· thee these glad tidings.
5: 14 but go, and s· thyself to the priest,
6: 47 I will s· you to whom he is like:
8: 39 s· how great things God hath done
17: 14 Go s· yourselves unto the priests.
20: 24 S· me a penny. Whose image and
47 and for a s· make long prayers:
22: 12 he shall s· you a large upper room
Joh 5: 20 s· him greater works than these,
7: 4 things, s· thyself to the world.
11: 57 knew where he was, he should s· it,
14: 8 s· us the Father, and it sufficeth
9 sayest thou then, S· us the Father?
16: 13 and he will s· you things to come.
14, 15 of mine, and shall s· it unto you.
25 I shall s· you plainly of the Father.
Ac 1: 24 s· whether of these two thou hast
2: 19 I will s· wonders in heaven above,
7: 3 into the land which I shall s· thee.
9: 16 For I will s· him how great things
12: 17 Go s· these things unto James, and
16: 17 s· unto us the way of salvation.
24: 27 willing to s· the Jews a pleasure,
26: 23 should s· light unto the people,
Ro 2: 15 s· the work of the law written in
9: 17 that I might s· my power in thee,
22 What if God, willing to s· his wrath,
1Co 11: 26 ye do s· the Lord's death till he
12: 31 s· I unto you a more excellent way.
15: 51 I s· you a mystery; We shall not
2Co 8: 24 Wherefore s· ye to them, and before
Ga 6: 12 desire to make a fair s· in the flesh,
Eph 2: 7 he might s· the exceeding riches
Col 2: 15 he made a s· of them openly,
23 things have indeed a s· of wisdom
1Th 1: 9 s· of us what manner of entering
1Ti 1: 16 might s· forth all longsuffering,
5: 4 learn first to s· piety at home, and
6: 15 Which in his times he shall s·,
2Ti 2: 15 Study to s· thyself approved unto
Heb 6: 11 one of you do s· the same diligence
17 to s· unto the heirs of promise the
Jas 2: 18 s· me thy faith without thy works,
18 I will s· thee my faith by my works.
3 : 13 let him s· out of a good conversation
1Pe 2: 9 should s· forth the praises of him
1Jo 1: 2 and s· unto you that eternal life,
Re 1: 1 to s· unto his servants things which
4: 1 I will s· thee things which must be
17: 1 I will s· unto thee the judgment of
21: 9 I will s· thee the bride, the Lamb's
22: 6 to s· unto his servants the things

shewbread
Ex 25: 30 shalt set upon the table s·
35: 13 and all his vessels, and the s·,
39: 36 the vessels thereof, and the s·;
Nu 4: 7 upon the table of s· they shall spread
1Sa 21: 6 was no bread there but the s·,
1Ki 7: 48 of gold, whereupon the s· was,
1Ch 9: 32 were over the s·, to prepare it
23: 29 Both for the s·, and for the fine
28: 16 he gave gold for the tables of s·,
2Ch 2: 4 incense, and for the continual s·,
4: 19 tables whereon the s· was set;
13: 11 the s· also set they in order
29: 18 and the s· table, with all the vessels
Ne 10: 33 For the s·, and...the continual
M't 12: 4 eat the s·, which was not lawful
M'r 2: 26 eat the s·, which is not lawful
Lu 6: 4 and did take and eat the s·, and
Heb 9: 2 and the table, and the s·;

shewed See also SHEWEDST.
Ge 19: 19 thou hast s· unto me in saving my
24: 14 hast s· kindness unto my master.
32: 10 which thou hast s· unto thy servant;
39: 21 with Joseph, and s· him mercy,
41: 25 God hath s· Pharaoh what he is
39 Forasmuch as God hath s· thee all
48: 11 lo, God hath s· me also thy seed.
Ex 15: 25 and the Lord s· him a tree, which
25: 40 which was s· thee in the mount.
26: 30 which was s· thee in the mount.
27: 8 as it was s· thee in the mount, so
Le 13: 19 reddish, and it be s· to the priest;
49 and shall be s· unto the priest:
24: 12 mind of the Lord might be s· them.
Nu 8: 4 pattern...the Lord had s· Moses,
13: 26 and s· them the fruit of the land.
14: 11 signs...I have s· among them?
De 4: 35 Unto thee it was s·, that thou
36 upon earth he s· thee his great fire;
5: 24 Lord our God hath s· us his glory
6: 22 the Lord s· signs and wonders,
34: 1 Lord s· him all the land of Gilead,
12 terror which Moses s· in the sight
Jos 2: 12 since I have s· you kindness, that
J'g 1: 25 when he s· them the entrance into
4: 12 And they s· Sisera that Barak
8: 35 s· they kindness to the house of
35 to all the goodness which he had s·
13: 10 and ran, and s· her husband, and
23 neither would he have s· us all
16: 18 for he hath s· me all his heart.
Ru 2: 11 It hath fully been s· me, all that thou
19 she s· her mother in law with whom
3: 10 s· more kindness in the latter
1Sa 11: 9 messengers...s· it to the men of
15: 6 s· kindness to all the children of
19: 7 Jonathan s· him all those things.
22: 21 Abiathar s· David...Saul had slain
24: 18 s· this day how...thou hast dealt
2Sa 2: 5 s· this kindness unto your lord,
10: 2 as his father s· kindness unto me.
11: 22 s· David all that Joab had sent him
1Ki 1: 27 hast not s· it unto thy servant,
3: 6 hast s· unto thy servant David my
16: 27 he did, and his might that he s·,
22: 45 and his might that he s·, and how
2Ki 6: 6 fell it? And he s· him the place.
8: 10 Lord hath s· me that he shall...die.
13 Lord hath s· me thou shalt be king
11: 4 Lord, and s· them the king's son.
20: 13 s· them...the house of his precious
13 nothing...that Hezekiah s· them not.
15 treasures that I have not s· them.
22: 10 Shaphan the scribe s· the king,
1Ch 19: 2 his father s· kindness to me.
2Ch 1: 8 hast s· great mercy unto David my
7: 10 the Lord had s· unto David, and to
Ezr 9: 8 grace hath been s· from the Lord
Es 1: 4 he s· the riches of his glorious
2: 10 Esther had not s· her people nor
20 Esther had not yet s· her kindred
3: 6 had s· him the people of Mordecai:
Job 6: 14 pity should be s· from his friend;
Ps 31: 21 he hath s· me his marvellous kindness
60: 3 Thou hast s· thy people hard things:
71: 18 I have s· thy strength unto this
20 hast s· me great and sore troubles,
78: 11 his wonders that he had s· them.
98: 2 righteousness hath he openly s· in
105: 27 They s· his signs among them, and
111: 6 hath s· his people the power of his
118: 27 is the Lord, which hath s· us light:
142: 2 him; I s· before him my trouble.
Pr 26: 26 wickedness shall be s· before the
Ec 2: 19 I have s· myself wise under the sun.
Isa 26: 10 Let favour be s· to the wicked, yet
39: 2 s· them the house of his precious
2 dominion, that Hezekiah s· them not,
4 treasures that I have not s· them.
40: 14 s·...him the way of understanding?
43: 12 have saved, and I have s·, when
48: 3 out of my mouth, and I s· them;
5 before it came to pass I s· it thee:
6 s· thee new things from this time,
Jer 24: 1 The Lord s· me, and, behold, two
38: 21 the word that the Lord hath s· me:
Eze 11: 25 the things that the Lord had s· me.
20: 11 and s· them my judgments, which
22: 26 neither have they s· difference
Am 7: 1 hath the Lord God s· unto me;
4 Thus hath the Lord God s· unto me:
7 Thus he s· me: and, behold, the
8: 1 Thus hath the Lord God s· unto me:
Mic 6: 8 He hath s· thee, O man, what is
Zec 1: 20 the Lord s· me four carpenters.
3: 1 And he s· me Joshua the high priest
M't 28: 11 and s· unto the chief priests all the
Lu 1: 51 He hath s· strength with his arm;
58 Lord had s· great mercy upon her;
4: 5 s· unto him all the kingdoms of the
7: 18 of John s· him of all these things.
10: 37 he said, He that s· mercy on him.
14: 21 came, and s· his lord these things.
20: 37 even Moses s· at the bush, when
24: 40 he s· them his hands and his
Joh 10: 32 good works have I s· you from my
20: 20 he s· unto them his hands and his
21: 1 Jesus s· himself again to the
1 and on this wise s· he himself.
14 third time that Jesus s· himself to
Ac 1: 3 To whom also he s· himself alive
3: 18 s· by...mouth of all his prophets,
4: 22 this miracle of healing was s·.
7: 26 he s· himself unto them as they
36 s· wonders and signs in the land

Ac 7: 52 slain them which s· before of the
10: 28 God hath s· me that I should not
40 day, and s· him openly;
11: 13 he s· us how he had seen an angel
19: 18 and confessed, and s· their deeds.
20: 20 but have s· you, and have taught
35 I have s· you all things, how that
23: 22 thou hast s· these things to me.
26: 20 s· first unto them of Damascus, and
28: 2 people s· us no little kindness:
21 came s· or spake any harm of thee.
Ro 1: 19 for God hath s· it unto them.
1Co 10: 28 eat not for his sake that s· it, and
Heb 6: 10 which ye have s· toward his name,
8: 5 the pattern s· to thee in the mount.
Jas 2: 13 mercy, that hath s· no mercy;
2Pe 1: 14 our Lord Jesus Christ hath s· me.
Re 21: 10 and s· me that great city, the holy
22: 1 he s· me a pure river of water of
8 the angel which s· me these things.

shewedst
Ne 9: 10 And s· signs and wonders upon
Jer 11: 18 it: then thou s· me their doings.

shewest
2Ch 6: 14 s· mercy unto thy servants, that walk
Job 10: 16 thou s· thyself marvellous upon me.
Jer 32: 18 Thou s· lovingkindness unto
Joh 2: 18 What sign s· thou unto us, seeing
6: 30 What sign s· thou then, that we

sheweth
Ge 41: 28 about to do he s· unto Pharaoh.
Nu 23: 3 and whatsoever he s· me I will tell
1Sa 22: 8 is none that s· me that my son
8 or s· unto me that my son hath
2Sa 22: 51 and s· mercy to his anointed, unto
Job 36: 9 Then he s· them their work, and
33 The noise thereof s· concerning it,
Ps 18: 50 and s· mercy to his anointed, to
19: 1 the firmament s· his handywork.
2 night unto night s· knowledge.
37: 21 righteous s· mercy, and giveth.
112: 5 A good man s· favour, and lendeth:
147: 19 He s· his word unto Jacob, his
Pr 12: 17 He that speaketh truth s· forth
27: 25 tender grass s· itself, and herbs
Isa 41: 26 there is none that s·, yea, there is
M't 4: 8 and s· him all the kingdoms of the
Joh 5: 20 s· him all things that himself doeth:
Ro 9: 16 runneth, but of God that s· mercy.
12: 8 he that s· mercy, with cheerfulness.

shewing
Ex 20: 6 s· mercy unto thousands of them
De 5: 10 s· mercy unto thousands of them
Ps 78: 4 s· to the generation to come the
Ca 2: 9 s· himself through the lattice.
Da 4: 27 iniquities by s· mercy to the poor;
5: 12 s· of hard sentences, and dissolving
Lu 1: 80 till the day of his s· unto Israel.
8: 1 preaching and s· the glad tidings
Ac 9: 39 s· the coats and garments which
18: 28 s· by the scriptures that Jesus was
2Th 2: 4 of God, s· himself that he is God.
Tit 2: 7 s· thyself a pattern of good works:
7 in doctrine s· uncorruptness, gravity,
10 but s· all good fidelity; that
3: 2 gentle, s· all meekness unto all men.

Shibboleth (*shib'-bo-leth*) See also SIBBOLETH.
J'g 12: 6 said they unto him, Say now *S*·:

Shibmah (*shib'-mah*) See also SHEBAM; SIBMAH.
Nu 32: 38 names being changed,) and *S*·:

Shicron (*shi'-cron*)
Jos 15: 11 and the border was drawn to *S*·,

shield See also SHIELDS.
Ge 15: 1 Fear not, Abram: I am thy s·, and
De 33: 29 by the Lord, the s· of thy help,
J'g 5: 8 was there a s· or spear seen among
1Sa 17: 7 one bearing a s· went before him.
41 man that bare the s· went before
45 and with a spear, and with a s·:
2Sa 1: 21 s· of the mighty is vilely cast away,
21 the s· of Saul, as though he had not
22: 3 he is my s·, and the horn of my
36 given me the s· of thy salvation:
1Ki 10: 17 three pound of gold went to one s·:
2Ki 19: 32 nor come before it with s·, nor cast
1Ch 12: 8 that could handle s· and buckler,
24 The children of Judah that bare s·
34 with s· and spear thirty and seven
2Ch 9: 16 shekels of gold went to one s·.
17: 17 him armed men with bow and s·
25: 5 that could handle spear and s·.
Job 39: 23 the glittering spear and the s·.
Ps 3: 3 But thou, O Lord, art a s· for me;
5: 12 thou compass him as with a s·.
18: 35 given me the s· of thy salvation:
28: 7 The Lord is my strength and my s·;
33: 20 the Lord: he is our help and our s·.
35: 2 Take hold of s· and buckler, and
59: 11 bring them down, O Lord our s·.
76: 3 he the arrows of the bow, the s·,
84: 9 Behold, O God our s·, and look
11 For the Lord God is a sun and s·:
91: 4 his truth shall be thy s· and
115: 9, 10, 11 he is their help and their s·.
119: 114 art my hiding place and my s·:
144: 2 my s·, and he in whom I trust;
Pr 30: 5 he is a s· unto them that put their
Isa 21: 5 arise, ye princes, and anoint the s·.
22: 6 and Kir uncovered the s·.
Jer 46: 3 Order ye the buckler and s·, and
9 the Libyans, that handle the s·;
Eze 23: 24 buckler and s· and helmet round
27: 10 hanged the s· and helmet in thee;

Eze 38: 5 all of them with s' and helmet:
Na 2: 3 s' of his mighty men is made red,
Eph 6: 16 taking the s' of faith, wherewith

shields
2Sa 8: 7 David took the s' of gold that were
1Ki 10: 17 three hundred s' of beaten gold;
14: 26 took away all the s' of gold which
27 made in their stead brasen s', and
2Ki 11: 10 give king David's spears and s',
1Ch 18: 7 David took the s' of gold that were
2Ch 9: 16 three hundred s' made of beaten
11: 12 every several city he puts s' and
12: 9 he carried away also the s' of gold
10 king Rehoboam made s' of brass,
14: 8 that bare s' and drew bows, two
23: 9 spears, and bucklers, and s', that
26: 14 them throughout all the host s',
32: 5 and darts and s' in abundance.
27 and for s', and for all manner of
Ne 4: 16 the spears, the s', and the bows,
Ps 47: 9 the s' of the earth belong unto God:
Ca 4: 4 bucklers, all s' of mighty men.
Isa 37: 33 nor come before it with s', nor
Jer 51: 11 bright the arrows; gather the s':
Eze 27: 11 hanged their s' upon thy walls
38: 4 company with bucklers and s',
39: 9 both the s' and the bucklers, the

Shiggaion (*shig-gah'-yon*) See also SHIGIONOTH.
Ps 7: *title* S' of David, which he sang unto

Shigionoth (*shig-i'-o-noth*) See also SHIGGAION.
Hab 3: 1 Habakkuk the prophet upon S'.

Shihon (*shi'-hon*)
Jos 19: 19 And Haphraim, and S', and

Shihor (*shi'-hor*) See also SHIHOR-LIBNATH; SIHOR.
1Ch 13: 5 from S' of Egypt even unto the

Shihor-libnath (*shi''-hor-lib'-nath*)
Jos 19: 26 to Carmel westward, and to S';

Shilhi (*shil'-hi*)
1Ki 22: 42 was Azubah the daughter of S'.
2Ch 20: 31 was Azubah the daughter of S'.

Shilhim (*shil'-him*) See also SHAARAIM; SHARUHEN.
Jos 15: 32 Lebaoth, and S', and Ain, and

Shillem (*shil'-lem*) See also SHALLUM; SHILLEMITES.
Ge 46: 24 and Guni, and Jezer, and S'.
Nu 26: 49 of S', the family of the Shillemites.

Shillemites (*shil'-lem-ites*)
Nu 26: 49 of Shillem, the family of the S'.

Shiloah (*shi-lo'-ah*) See also SILOAH; SILOAM.
Isa 8: 6 people refuseth the waters of S'

Shiloh (*shi'-loh*) See also SHILONITE; TAANATH-SHILOH.
Ge 49: 10 between his feet, unto S' come;
Jos 18: 1 of Israel assembled together at S',
8 lots for you before the Lord in S'.
9 again to Joshua to the host at S'.
10 Joshua cast lots for them in S'
19: 51 an inheritance by lot in S' before
21: 2 spake unto them at S' in the land
22: 9 the children of Israel out of S',
12 together at S', to go up to war
J'g 18: 31 that the house of God was in S'.
21: 12 brought them unto the camp to S',
19 is a feast of the Lord in S' yearly
21 daughters of S' come out to dance
21 his wife of the daughters of S',
1Sa 1: 3 sacrifice unto the Lord...in S'.
9 rose up after they had eaten in S',
24 unto the house of the Lord in S':
2: 14 they did in S' unto all the Israelites
3: 21 the Lord appeared again in S':
21 revealed himself to Samuel in S'
4: 3 the covenant of the Lord out of S',
4 So the people sent to S', that they
12 came to S' the same day with his
14: 3 the Lord's priest in S', wearing an
1Ki 2: 27 concerning the house of Eli in S'.
14: 2 and get thee to S': behold, there is
4 did so, and arose, and went to S',
Ps 78: 60 he forsook the tabernacle of S',
Jer 7: 12 unto my place which was in S',
14 your fathers, as I have done to S'.
26: 6 will I make this house like S', and
9 This house shall be like S', and
41: 5 certain from Shechem, from S',

Shiloni (*shi-lo'-ni*) See also SHILONITE.
Ne 11: 5 son of Zechariah, the son of S'.

Shilonite (*shi'-lon-ite*) See also SHILONI; SHILONITES.
1Ki 11: 29 the S' found him in the way;
12: 15 the Lord spake by Ahijah the S'
15: 29 spake by his servant Ahijah the S':
2Ch 9: 29 in the prophecy of Ahijah the S',
10: 15 spake by the hand of Ahijah the S'

Shilonites (*shi'-lon-ites*)
1Ch 9: 5 And of the S'; Asaiah the firstborn,

Shilshah (*shil'-shah*)
1Ch 7: 37 Shamma, and S', and Ithran, and

Shimea (*shim'-e-ah*) See also SHAMMAH; SHAMMUA; SHAMMUAH; SHIMEAH; SHIMEATHITES; SHIMMA.
1Ch 3: 5 S', and Shobab, and Nathan, and
6: 30 S' his son, Haggiah his son, Asaiah
39 son of Berachiah, the son of S',
20: 7 Jonathan the son of S' David's

Shimeah (*shim'-e-ah*) See also SHIMEA; SHIMEAM.
2Sa 13: 3 the son of S' David's brother:
32 the son of S' David's brother,
21: 21 Jonathan the son of S' the
1Ch 8: 32 And Mikloth begat S'. And these

Shimeam (*shim'-e-am*) See also SHIMEA.
1Ch 9: 38 And Mikloth begat S'. And they

Shimeath (*shim'-e-ath*)
2Ki 12: 21 For Jozachar the son of S', and
2Ch 24: 26 the son of S' an Ammonitess, and

Shimeathites (*shim'-e-ath-ites*)
1Ch 2: 55 the Tirathites, the S', and

Shimei (*shim'-e-i*) See also SHEMAIAH; SHIMHI; SHIMI; SHIMITES.
Nu 3: 18 by their families; Libni, and S'.
2Sa 16: 5 whose name was S', the son of
7 And thus said S' when he cursed,
13 S' went along on the hill's side over
19: 16 S' the son of Gera, a Benjamite,
18 S' the son of Gera fell down before
21 Shall not S' be put to death for this,
23 the king said unto S', Thou shalt
1Ki 1: 8 Nathan the prophet, and S', and
2: 8 hast with thee S' the son of Gera,
36 And the king sent and called for S',
38 S' said unto the king, The saying
38 S' dwelt in Jerusalem many days.
39 two of the servants of S' ran away
39 And they told S', saying, Behold,
40 And S' arose, and saddled his ass,
40 S' went, and brought his servants
41 was told Solomon that S' had gone
42 And the king sent and called for S',
44 The king said moreover to S', Thou
4: 18 S' the son of Elah, in Benjamin:
1Ch 3: 19 Pedaiah were, Zerubbabel, and S':
4: 26 son, Zacchur his son, S' his son.
27 And S' had sixteen sons and six
5: 4 his son, Gog his son, S' his son,
6: 17 sons of Gershom; Libni, and S'.
29 Libni his son, S' his son, Uzza his
42 the son of Zimmah, the son of S',
23: 7 Gershonites were, Laadan, and S'.
9 The sons of S'; Shelomith, and
10 And the sons of S' were, Jahath,
10 These four were the sons of S'.
25: 17 The tenth to S', he, his sons, and
27: 27 over the vineyards was S' the
2Ch 29: 14 the sons of Heman; Jehiel, and S':
31: 12 and S' his brother was the next.
13 the hand of Cononiah and S' his
Ezr 10: 23 of the Levites; Jozabad, and S',
33 Jeremai, Manasseh, and S'.
38 And Bani, and Binnui, S',
Es 2: 5 the son of Jair, the son of S', the
Zec 12: 13 the family of S' a part, and their

Shimeon (*shim'-e-on*) See also SIMEON.
Ezr 10: 31 Ishijah, Malchiah, Shemaiah, S',

Shimhi (*shim'-hi*) See also SHEMA; SHIMEI.
1Ch 8: 21 and Shimrath, the sons of S';

Shimi (*shi'-mi*) See also SHIMEI; SHIMITES.
Ex 6: 17 S', according to their families.

Shimites (*shi'-mites*)
Nu 3: 21 Libnites, and the family of the S':

Shimma (*shim'-mah*) See also SHAMMAH.
1Ch 2: 13 the second, and S' the third,

Shimon (*shi'-mon*)
1Ch 4: 20 the sons of S' were, Amnon, and

Shimrath (*shim'-rath*)
1Ch 8: 21 and S', the sons of Shimhi;

Shimri (*shim'-ri*) See also SIMRI.
1Ch 4: 37 the son of Jedaiah, the son of S',
11: 45 Jediael the son of S', and Joha his
2Ch 29: 13 sons of Elizaphan; S', and Jeiel:

Shimrith (*shim'-rith*) See also SHOMER.
2Ch 24: 26 and Jehozabad the son of S' a

Shimrom (*shim'-rom*) See also SHIMRON.
1Ch 7: 1 and Puah, Jashub, and S', four.

Shimron (*shim'-ron*) See also SHIMROM; SHIMRONITES; SHIMRON-MERON.
Ge 46: 13 and Phuvah, and Job, and S'.
Nu 26: 24 of S', the family of the Shimronites.
Jos 11: 1 and to the king of S', and to the
19: 15 Kattath, and Nahallal, and S', and

Shimronites (*shim'-ron-ites*)
Nu 26: 24 of Shimron, the family of the S'.

Shimron-meron (*shim''-ron-me'-ron*) See also SHIMRON.
Jos 12: 20 The king of S', one; the king of

Shimshai (*shim'-shahee*)
Ezr 4: 8 S' the scribe wrote a letter
9 and S' the scribe, and the rest
17 to S' the scribe, and to the rest of
23 S' the scribe, and their companions,

Shinab (*shi'-nab*)
Ge 14: 2 S' king of Admah, and Shemeber

Shinar (*shi'-nar*)
Ge 10: 10 and Calneh, in the land of S'.
11: 2 found a plain in the land of S';
14: 1 in the days of Amraphel king of S',
9 Amraphel king of S', and Arioch
Isa 11: 11 and from S', and from Hamath,
Da 1: 2 land of S' to the house of his god;
Zec 5: 11 build it an house in the land of S':

shine See also SHINED; SHINETH; SHINING; SHONE.
Nu 6: 25 Lord make his face s' upon thee,
Job 3: 4 neither let the light s' upon it.
10: 3 s' upon the counsel of the wicked?
11: 17 thou shalt s' forth, thou shalt be
18: 5 the spark of his fire shall not s'.
22: 28 the light shall s' upon thy ways.
36: 32 commandeth it not to s' by the cloud
37: 15 caused the light of his cloud to s'?
41: 18 By his neesings a light doth s',
32 He maketh a path to s' after him;
Ps 31: 16 thy face to s' upon thy servant:
67: 1 and cause his face to s' upon us.
80: 1 between the cherubims, s' forth.
3 and cause thy face to s'; and we
7, 19 cause thy face to s'; and we
104: 15 oil to make his face to s', and
119: 135 thy face to s' upon thy servant;
Ec 8: 1 man's wisdom maketh his face to s'.
Isa 13: 10 shall not cause her light to s'.
60: 1 Arise, s'; for thy light is come,
Jer 5: 28 They are waxen fat, they s': yea,
Da 9: 17 thy face to s' upon thy sanctuary
12: 3 they that be wise shall s' as the
M't 5: 16 Let your light so s' before men,
13: 43 Then shall the righteous s' forth
17: 2 his face did s' as the sun, and his
2Co 4: 4 image of God, should s' unto them.
6 who commanded the light to s'
Ph'p 2: 15 among whom ye s' as lights in
Re 18: 23 light of a candle shall s' no more
21: 23 neither of the moon, to s' in it:

shined See also SHONE.
De 33: 2 he s' forth from mount Paran, and
Job 29: 3 When his candle s' upon my head,
31: 26 If I beheld the sun when it s', or
Ps 50: 2 perfection of beauty, God hath s'.
Isa 9: 2 upon them hath the light s'.
Eze 43: 2 and the earth s' with his glory.
Ac 9: 3 s' round about him a light from
12: 7 him, and a light s' in the prison:
2Co 4: 6 of darkness, hath s' in our hearts,

shineth
Job 25: 5 even to the moon, and it s' not;
Ps 139: 12 but the night s' as the day: the
Pr 4: 18 s' more and more unto the perfect
M't 24: 27 east, and s' even unto the west;
Lu 17: 24 s' unto the other part under
Joh 1: 5 And the light s' in darkness; and
2Pe 1: 19 unto a light that s' in a dark place,
1Jo 2: 8 is past, and the true light now s'.
Re 1: 16 was as the sun s' in his strength.

shining
2Sa 23: 4 of the earth by clear s' after rain.
Pr 4: 18 path of the just is as the s' light,
Isa 4: 5 the s' of a flaming fire by night:
Joe 2: 10 the stars shall withdraw their s':
3: 15 the stars shall withdraw their s'.
Hab 3: 11 at the s' of thy glittering spear.
M'r 9: 3 And his raiment became s',
Lu 11: 36 bright s' of a candle doth give thee
24: 4 men stood by them in s' garments:
Joh 5: 35 He was a burning and a s' light:
Ac 26: 13 s' round about me and them

ship See also FORESHIP; SHIPMASTER; SHIPMEN; SHIPPING; SHIPS; SHIPWRECK.
Pr 30: 19 way of a s' in the midst of the sea;
Isa 33: 21 oars, neither shall gallant s' pass
Eze 27: 5 made all thy s' boards of fir trees
Jon 1: 3 he found a s' going to Tarshish:
4 that the s' was like to be broken.
5 the wares that were in the s' into
5 gone down into the sides of the s';
M't 4: 21 in a s' with Zebedee their father,
22 they immediately left the s' and
8: 23 when he was entered into a s', his
24 the s' was covered with the waves:
9: 1 he entered into a s', and passed
13: 2 so that he went into a s', and sat;
14: 13 he departed thence by s' into a
22 his disciples to get into a s', and
24 s' was now in the midst of the sea,
29 Peter was come down out of the s',
32 when they were come into the s',
33 they that were in the s' came and
15: 39 took s', and came into the coasts
M'r 1: 19 were in the s' mending their nets.
20 left their father Zebedee in the s'
3: 9 that a small s' should wait on him
4: 1 so that he entered into a s', and
36 took him even as he was in the s'.
37 and the waves beat into the s', so
38 he was in the hinder part of the s'.
5: 2 when he was come out of the s',
18 And when he was come into the s',
21 again by s' unto the other side,
6: 32 into a desert place by s' privately.
45 his disciples to get into the s',
47 the s' was in the midst of the sea,
51 he went up unto them into the s';
54 when they were come out of the s',
8: 10 straightway he entered into a s'
13 and entering into the s' again
14 had they in the s' with them more
Lu 5: 3 and taught the people out of the s',
7 which were in the other s', that
8: 22 that he went into a s' with his
37 and he went up into the s', and
Joh 6: 17 entered into a s', and went over the
19 sea, and drawing nigh unto the s':
21 willingly received him into the s':
21 and immediately the s' was at the
21: 3 and entered into a s' immediately;

Joh 21: 6 the net on the right side of the *s*˙,
8 other disciples came in a little *s*˙;
Ac 20: 13 we went before to *s*˙, and sailed
38 they accompanied him unto the *s*˙.
21: 2 And finding a *s*˙ sailing over unto
3 the *s*˙ was to unlade her burden.
6 leave one of another, we took *s*˙;
27: 2 entering into a *s*˙ of Adramyttium,
6 centurion found a *s*˙ of Alexandria
10 not only of the lading and *s*˙, but
11 the master and the owner of the *s*˙,
15 And when the *s*˙ was caught, and
17 used helps, undergirding the *s*˙;
18 the next day they lightened the *s*˙;
19 own hands the tackling of the *s*˙.
22 man's life among you, but of the *s*˙.
30 were about to flee out of the *s*˙,
31 Except these abide in the *s*˙, ye
37 were in all in the *s*˙ two hundred
38 they lightened the *s*˙, and cast out
39 it were possible, to thrust in the *s*˙.
41 seas met, they ran the *s*˙ aground;
44 some on broken pieces of the *s*˙.
28: 11 we departed in a *s*˙ of Alexandria,

Shiphi (*shi'-fi*)
1Ch 4: 37 And Ziza the son of *S*˙, the son of

Shiphmite (*shif'-mite*)
1Ch 27: 27 wine cellars was Zabdi the *S*˙:

Shiphrah (*shif'-rah*)
Ex 1: 15 which the name of the one was *S*˙,

Shiphtan (*shif'-tan*)
Nu 34: 24 Ephraim, Kemuel the son of *S*˙.

shipmaster
Jon 1: 6 So the *s*˙ came to him, and
Re 18: 17 every *s*˙, and all the company in

shipmen
1Ki 9: 27 *s*˙ that had knowledge of the
Ac 27: 27 *s*˙ deemed that they drew near to
30 the *s*˙ were about to flee out of the

shipping
Joh 6: 24 they also took *s*˙, and came to

ships
Ge 49: 13 and he shall be for an haven of *s*˙;
Nu 24: 24 *s*˙ shall come from the coast of
De 28: 68 bring thee into Egypt again with *s*˙,
J'g 5: 17 and why did Dan remain in *s*˙?
1Ki 9: 26 made a navy of *s*˙ in Ezion-geber,
22: 48 Jehoshaphat made *s*˙ of Tharshish
48 the *s*˙ were broken at Ezion-geber.
49 go with thy servants in the *s*˙.
2Ch 8: 18 him by the hands of his servants *s*˙,
9: 21 the king's *s*˙ went to Tarshish with
21 the *s*˙ of Tarshish bringing gold,
20: 36 him to make *s*˙ to go to Tarshish:
36 they made the *s*˙ in Ezion-gaber.
37 the *s*˙ were broken, that they were
Job 9: 26 are passed away as the swift *s*˙:
Ps 48: 7 Thou breakest the *s*˙ of Tarshish
104: 26 There go the *s*˙: there is that
107: 23 They that go down to the sea in *s*˙,
Pr 31: 14 She is like the merchants' *s*˙; she
Isa 2: 16 And upon all the *s*˙ of Tarshish,
23: 1 Howl, ye *s*˙ of Tarshish; for it is
14 Howl, ye *s*˙ of Tarshish: for your
43: 14 Chaldeans, whose cry is in the *s*˙.
60: 9 for me, and the *s*˙ of Tarshish first,
Eze 27: 9 *s*˙ of the sea with their mariners
25 The *s*˙ of Tarshish did sing of thee
29 shall come down from their *s*˙,
30: 9 messengers go forth from me in *s*˙
Da 11: 30 *s*˙ of Chittim shall come against
40 with horsemen, and with many *s*˙;
M'r 4: 36 were also with him other little *s*˙.
Lu 5: 2 saw two *s*˙ standing by the lake:
3 And he entered into one of the *s*˙,
7 they came, and filled both the *s*˙,
11 they had brought their *s*˙ to land,
Jas 3: 4 Behold also the *s*˙, which though
Re 8: 9 third part of the *s*˙ were destroyed.
18: 17 all the company in *s*˙, and sailors,
19 made rich all that had *s*˙ in the sea

shipwreck
2Co 11: 25 thrice I suffered *s*˙, a night and a
1Ti 1: 19 concerning faith have made *s*˙:

Shisha (*shi'-shah*) See also SHAVSHA.
1Ki 4: 3 and Ahiah, the sons of *S*˙, scribes;

Shishak (*shi'-shak*)
1Ki 11: 40 into Egypt, unto *S*˙ king of Egypt,
14: 25 *S*˙ king of Egypt came up against
2Ch 12: 2 *S*˙ king of Egypt came up against
5 together to Jerusalem because of *S*˙.
5 I also left you in the hand of *S*˙.
7 upon Jerusalem by the hand of *S*˙.
9 *S*˙ king of Egypt came up against

Shitrai (*shit'-ra-i*)
1Ch 27: 29 in Sharon was *S*˙ the Sharonite:

shittah (*shit'-tah*) See also BETH-SHITTAH; SHITTIM.
Isa 41: 19 cedar, the *s*˙ tree, and the myrtle,

shittah-tree See SHITTAH and TREE.

shittim See also SHITTAH; SHITTIM.
Ex 25: 5 and badgers' skins, and *s*˙ wood,
10 they shall make an ark of *s*˙ wood:
13 thou shalt make staves of *s*˙ wood,
23 shalt also make a table of *s*˙ wood:
28 shalt make the staves of *s*˙ wood,
26: 15 boards for the tabernacle of *s*˙ wood
26 thou shalt make bars of *s*˙ wood;
32 hang it upon four pillars of *s*˙ wood
Ex 26: 37 the hanging five pillars of *s*˙ wood,
27: 1 thou shalt make an altar of *s*˙ wood,
6 for the altar, staves of *s*˙ wood, and
30: 1 of *s*˙ wood shalt thou make it.
5 shalt make the staves of *s*˙ wood,
35: 7 and badgers' skins, and *s*˙ wood,
24 with whom was found *s*˙ wood for
36: 20 for the tabernacle of *s*˙ wood,
31 And he made bars of *s*˙ wood; five
36 thereunto four pillars of *s*˙ wood,
37: 1 Bezaleel made the ark of *s*˙ wood:
4 and he made staves of *s*˙ wood, and
10 And he made the table of *s*˙ wood:
15 And he made the staves of *s*˙ wood,
25 made the incense altar of *s*˙ wood:
28 And he made the staves of *s*˙ wood,
38: 1 altar of burnt offering of *s*˙ wood:
6 And he made the staves of *s*˙ wood,
De 10: 3 And I made an ark of *s*˙ wood, and

Shittim (*shit'-tim*) See also ABEL-SHITTIM.
Nu 25: 1 And Israel abode in *S*˙, and the
Jos 2: 1 son of Nun sent out of *S*˙ two men
3: 1 they removed from *S*˙, and came
Joe 3: 18 and shall water the valley of *S*˙.
Mic 6: 5 answered him from *S*˙ unto Gilgal;

shittim-wood See SHITTIM and WOOD.

shivers
Re 2: 27 potter shall they be broken to *s*˙:

Shiza (*shi'-zah*)
1Ch 11: 42 Adina the son of *S*˙ the Reubenite,

Shoa (*sho'-ah*)
Eze 23: 23 all the Chaldeans, Pekod, and *S*˙,

Shobab (*sho'-bab*)
2Sa 5: 14 Shammuah, and *S*˙, and Nathan,
1Ch 2: 18 sons are these; Jesher, and *S*˙,
3: 5 Shimea, and *S*˙, and Nathan, and
14: 4 and *S*˙, Nathan, and Solomon,

Shobach (*sho'-bak*) See also SHOPHACH.
2Sa 10: 16 and *S*˙ the captain of the host of
18 smote *S*˙ the captain of their host,

Shobai (*sho'-bahee*)
Ezr 2: 42 the children of *S*˙, in all an
Ne 7: 45 of Hatita, the children of *S*˙, an

Shobal (*sho'-bal*)
Ge 36: 20 Lotan, and *S*˙, and Zibeon, and
23 And the children of *S*˙ were these;
29 duke Lotan, duke *S*˙, duke Zibeon,
1Ch 1: 38 the sons of Seir, and Lotan, and *S*˙,
40 The sons of *S*˙; Alion, and
2: 50, 52 *S*˙ the father of Kirjath-jearim,
4: 1 and Carmi, and Hur, and *S*˙.
2 And Reaiah the son of *S*˙ begat

Shobek (*sho'-bek*)
Ne 10: 24 Hallohesh, Pileha, *S*˙,

Shobi (*sho'-bi*)
2Sa 17: 27 *S*˙ the son of Nahash of Rabbah of

Shocho (*sho'-ko*) See also SHOCHOH.
2Ch 28: 18 and *S*˙ with the villages thereof,

Shochoh (*sho'-ko*) See also SHOCHO; SHOCO; SOCHOH; SOCO; SOCOH.
1Sa 17: 1 and were gathered together at *S*˙,
1 pitched between *S*˙ and Azekah,

shock See also SHOCKS.
Job 5: 26 *s*˙ of corn cometh in in his season.

shocks
J'g 15: 5 and burnt up both the *s*˙, and also

Shoco (*sho'-co*) See also SHOCHOH.
2Ch 11: 7 Beth-zur, and *S*˙, and Adullam,

shod See also DRYSHOD; UNSHOD.
2Ch 28: 15 arrayed them, and *s*˙ them, and
Eze 16: 10 and *s*˙ thee with badgers' skin, and
M'r 6: 9 But be *s*˙ with sandals; and not
Eph 6: 15 your feet *s*˙ with the preparation

shoe See also SHOD; SHOELATCHET; SHOE'S; SHOES.
De 25: 9 and loose his *s*˙ from off his foot,
10 of him that hath his *s*˙ loosed.
29: 5 *s*˙ is not waxen old upon thy foot.
Jos 5: 15 Loose thy *s*˙ from off thy foot; for
Ru 4: 7 a man plucked off his *s*˙, and gave
8 it for thee. So he drew off his *s*˙.
Ps 60: 8 over Edom will I cast out my *s*˙:
108: 9 over Edom will I cast out my *s*˙;
Isa 20: 2 and put off thy *s*˙ from thy foot.

shoelatchet
Ge 14: 23 from a thread even to a *s*˙,

shoe's
Joh 1: 27 *s*˙ latchet I am not worthy to

shoes
Ex 3: 5 put off thy *s*˙ from off thy feet,
12: 11 your *s*˙ on your feet, and your staff
De 33: 25 Thy *s*˙ shall be iron and brass;
Jos 9: 5 old *s*˙ and clouted upon their feet,
13 our *s*˙ are become old by reason of
1Ki 2: 5 and in his *s*˙ that were on his feet.
Ca 7: 1 How beautiful are thy feet with *s*˙,
Isa 5: 27 the latchet of their *s*˙ be broken:
Eze 24: 17 and put on thy *s*˙ upon thy feet,
23 heads, and your *s*˙ upon your feet:
Am 2: 6 and the poor for a pair of *s*˙;
8: 6 and the needy for a pair of *s*˙;
M't 3: 11 whose *s*˙ I am not worthy to bear:
10: 10 neither two coats, neither *s*˙, nor
M'r 1: 7 the latchet of whose *s*˙ I am not
Lu 3: 16 the latchet of whose *s*˙ I am not
10: 4 neither purse, nor scrip, nor *s*˙:
15: 22 on his hand, and *s*˙ on his feet:
Lu 22: 35 without purse, and scrip, and *s*˙,
Ac 7: 33 Put off thy *s*˙ from thy feet: for the
13: 25 *s*˙ of his feet I am not worthy to

Shoham (*sho'-ham*)
1Ch 24: 27 Beno, and *S*˙, and Zaccur, and

Shomer (*sho'-mur*) See also SHAMER; SHIMRITH.
2Ki 12: 21 and Jehozabad the son of *S*˙, his
1Ch 7: 32 And Heber begat Japhlet, and *S*˙,

shone See also SHINED.
Ex 34: 29 wist not that the skin of his face *s*˙
30 behold, the skin of his face *s*˙; and
35 that the skin of Moses' face *s*˙: and
2Ki 3: 22 and the sun *s*˙ upon the water, and
Lu 2: 9 and the glory of the Lord *s*˙ round
Ac 22: 6 *s*˙ from heaven a great light round
Re 8: 12 the day *s*˙ not for a third part of it,

shook See also SHAKED.
2Sa 6: 6 took hold of it; for the oxen *s*˙ it.
22: 8 Then the earth *s*˙ and trembled:
8 foundations of heaven moved and *s*˙.
Ne 5: 13 Also I *s*˙ my lap, and said, So God
Ps 18: 7 Then the earth *s*˙ and trembled;
68: 8 The earth *s*˙, the heavens also
77: 18 world: the earth trembled and *s*˙.
Isa 23: 11 over the sea, he *s*˙ the kingdoms:
Ac 13: 51 *s*˙ off the dust of their feet against
18: 6 he *s*˙ his raiment, and said unto
28: 5 he *s*˙ off the beast into the fire, and
Heb 12: 26 Whose voice then *s*˙ the earth: but

shoot See also SHOOTETH; SHOOTING; SHOT.
Ex 36: 33 the middle bar to *s*˙ through the
1Sa 20: 20 *s*˙ three arrows on the side thereof,
36 find out now the arrows which I *s*˙.
2Sa 11: 20 that they would *s*˙ from the wall?
2Ki 13: 17 Then Elisha said, *S*˙. And he shot.
19: 32 into this city, nor *s*˙ an arrow there,
1Ch 5: 18 and sword, and to *s*˙ with bow,
2Ch 26: 15 *s*˙ arrows and great stones withal.
Ps 11: 2 privily *s*˙ at the upright in heart.
22: 7 they *s*˙ out the lip, they shake the
58: 7 he bendeth his bow to *s*˙ his arrows,
64: 3 bend their bows to *s*˙ their arrows,
4 may *s*˙ in secret at the perfect:
4 suddenly do they *s*˙ at him, and
7 God shall *s*˙ at them with an arrow;
144: 6 *s*˙ out thine arrows, and destroy
Isa 37: 33 into this city, nor *s*˙ an arrow there,
Jer 50: 14 bow, *s*˙ at her, spare no arrows:
Eze 31: 14 *s*˙ up their top among the thick
36: 8 ye shall *s*˙ forth your branches, and
Lu 21: 30 When they now *s*˙ forth, ye see

shooters
2Sa 11: 24 *s*˙ shot from off the wall upon thy

shooteth
Job 8: 16 his branch *s*˙ forth in his garden.
Isa 27: 8 In measure, when it *s*˙ forth, thou
M'r 4: 32 *s*˙ out great branches; so that

shooting
1Ch 12: 2 the left in hurling stones and *s*˙ arrows
Am 7: 1 of the *s*˙ up of the latter growth;

Shophach (*sho'-fak*) See also SHOBACH.
1Ch 19: 16 and *S*˙ the captain of the host of
18 Killed *S*˙ the captain of the host.

Shophan (*sho'-fan*) See also ZAPHON.
Nu 32: 35 *S*˙, and Jaazer, and Jogbehah,

shore
Ge 22: 17 the sand which is upon the sea *s*˙;
Ex 14: 30 the Egyptians dead upon the sea *s*˙.
Jos 11: 4 that is upon the sea *s*˙ in multitude,
15: 2 was from the *s*˙ of the salt sea,
J'g 5: 17 Asher continued on the sea *s*˙,
1Sa 13: 5 as the sand which is on the sea *s*˙
1Ki 4: 29 as the sand that is on the sea *s*˙.
9: 26 on the *s*˙ of the Red sea, in the
Jer 47: 7 Ashkelon, and against the sea *s*˙?
M't 13: 2 whole multitude stood on the *s*˙.
48 when it was full, they drew to *s*˙,
M'r 6: 53 of Gennesaret, and drew to the *s*˙.
Joh 21: 4 now come, Jesus stood on the *s*˙:
Ac 21: 5 and we kneeled down on the *s*˙, and
27: 39 discovered a certain creek with a *s*˙,
40 to the wind, and made toward *s*˙.
Heb 11: 12 as the sand which is by the sea *s*˙

shorn
Ca 4: 2 a flock of sheep that are even *s*˙,
Ac 18: 18 having *s*˙ his head in Cenchrea:
1Co 11: 6 be not covered, let her also be *s*˙:
6 it be a shame for a woman to be *s*˙

short See also SHORTER.
Nu 11: 23 Is the Lord's hand waxed *s*˙?
2Ki 10: 32 days the Lord began to cut Israel *s*˙:
Job 17: 12 the light is *s*˙ because of darkness.
20: 5 the triumphing of the wicked is *s*˙,
Ps 89: 47 Remember how *s*˙ my time is:
Ro 3: 23 and come *s*˙ of the glory of God;
9: 28 and cut it *s*˙ in righteousness:
28 a *s*˙ work will the Lord make upon
1Co 7: 29 this I say, brethren, the time is *s*˙:
1Th 2: 17 being taken from you for a *s*˙ time
Heb 4: 1 of you should seem to come *s*˙ of it.
Re 12: 12 knoweth that he hath but a *s*˙ time.
17: 10 he must continue a *s*˙ space.

shortened
Ps 89: 45 The days of his youth hast thou *s*˙:
102: 23 strength in the way; he *s*˙ my days.
Pr 10: 27 the years of the wicked shall be *s*˙.
Isa 50: 2 Is my hand *s*˙ at all, that it cannot
59: 1 Behold, the Lord's hand is not *s*˙,
M't 24: 22 except those days should be *s*˙,

M't 24:22 elect's sake those days shall be s'.
M'r 13:20 that the Lord had s' those days,
20 he hath chosen, he hath s' the days.

shorter
Isa 28:20 the bed is s' than that a man can
Eze 42: 5 Now the upper chambers were s':

shortly
Ge 41:32 and God will s' bring it to pass.
Jer 27:16 s' be brought again from Babylon:
Eze 7: 8 I s' pour out my fury upon thee,
Ac 25: 4 himself...depart s' thither.
Ro 16:20 bruise Satan under your feet s'.
1Co 4:19 I will come to you s', if the Lord
Ph'p 2:19 to send Timotheus s' unto you,
24 that I also myself shall come s'.
1Ti 3:14 thee, hoping to come unto thee s':
2Ti 4: 9 thy diligence to come s' unto me:
Heb 13:23 with whom, if he come s', I will see
2Pe 1:14 that s' I must put off this my
3Jo 14 But I trust I shall s' see thee, and
Re 1: 1 which must s' come to pass;
22: 6 things which must s' be done.

Shoshannim (*sho-shan'-nim*) See also SHOSHANNIM-EDUTH.
Ps 45: *title* To the chief Musician upon *S'*.
69: *title* To the chief Musician upon *S'*.

Shoshannim-Eduth (*sho-shan''-nim-e'-duth*)
Ps 80: *title* To the chief Musician upon *S'*.

shot See also BOWSHOT.
Ge 40:10 budded, and her blossoms s' forth;
49:23 and s' at him, and hated him:
Ex 19:13 surely be stoned, or s' through;
Nu 21:30 We have s' at them; Heshbon is
1Sa 20:20 thereof, as though I s' at a mark.
36 ran, he s' an arrow beyond him.
37 the arrow which Jonathan had s',
2Sa 11:24 And the shooters s' from off the wall
2Ki 13:17 Then Elisha said, Shoot. And he s'.
2Ch 35:23 And the archers s' at king Josiah;
Ps 18:14 and he s' out lightnings, and
Jer 9: 8 tongue is as an arrow s' out; it
Eze 17: 6 forth branches, and s' forth sprigs.
7 s' forth her branches toward him,
31: 5 multitude of waters,...he s' forth.
10 he hath s' up his top among the

should See also SHOULDEST.
Ge 2:18 is not good that the man s' be alone;
4:15 Cain, lest any finding him s' kill him.
18:25 that the righteous s' be as the wicked,
21: 7 that Sarah s' have given children suck!
23: 8 it be your mind that I s' bury my dead
26: 7 men of the place s' kill me for Rebekah;
27:45 why s' I be deprived also of you both
29: 7 is it time that the cattle s' be gathered
19 than that I s' give her to another man:
30:38 s' conceive when they came to drink.
33:13 and if men s' overdrive them one day,
34:31 *S'* he deal with our sister as with an
38: 9 Onan knew that the seed s' not be his;
9 that he s' give seed to his brother.
40:15 that they s' put me into the dungeon.
43:25 heard that they s' eat bread there.
44: 7 God forbid that thy servants s' do
8 how then s' we steal out of thy lord's
17 he said, God forbid that I s' do so:
22 for if he s' leave his father, his father
47:15 for why s' we die in thy presence? for
26 that Pharaoh s' have the fifth part;
Ex 3:11 Who am I, that I s' go unto Pharaoh,
11 and that I s' bring forth the children
5: 2 I s' obey his voice to let Israel go?
14:12 than that we s' die in the wilderness?
22: 3 him; for he s' make full restitution;
32:12 Wherefore s' the Egyptians speak,
35: 1 hath commanded, that ye s' do them.
39: 7 that they s' be stones for a memorial
23 about the hole, that it s' not rend.
Le 4:13, 22 things which s' not be done,
9: 6 the Lord commanded that ye s' do:
10:18 ye s' indeed have eaten it in the holy
19 s' it have been accepted in the sight
20:26 from other people, that ye s' be mine.
24:23 s' bring forth him that had cursed
26:13 that ye s' not be their bondmen;
27:26 beasts, which s' be the Lord's firstling,
Nu 7: 9 that they s' bear upon their shoulders.
9: 4 Israel, that they s' keep the passover.
11:13 Whence s' I have flesh to give unto all
12:14 s' she not be ashamed seven days?
14: 3 wives and our children s' be a prey?
31 little ones, which ye said s' be a prey,
15:34 not declared what s' be done to him.
20: 4 that we and our cattle s' die there?
23:19 God is not a man, that he s' lie; neither
19 the son of man, that he s' repent:
27: 4 Why s' the name of our father be done
32: 9 that they s' not go into the land which
35:28 Because he s' have remained in the city
32 he s' come again to dwell in the land,
De 1:18 that time all the things which ye s' do.
33 to shew you by what way ye s' go, and
39 little ones, which ye said s' be a prey,
4: 5 that ye s' do so in the land whither ye
21 and sware that I s' not go over Jordan,
21 that I s' not go in unto that good land,
42 which s' kill his neighbour unawares,
5:25 Now therefore why s' we die? for this
17:16 to the end that he s' multiply horses:
20:18 so s' ye sin against the Lord your God.
25: 3 if he s' exceed, and beat him above
3 then thy brother s' seem vile unto thee.
29:18 Lest there s' be among you a man, or
18 lest there s' be among you a root that

De 32:27 adversaries s' behave themselves
27 and lest they s' say, Our hand is high,
30 How s' one chase a thousand, and two
Jos 8:29 that they s' take his carcase down
33 that they s' bless the people of Israel.
9:27 day, in the place which he s' choose.
11:20 they s' come against Israel in battle,
22:28 s' so say to us or to our generations
29 that we s' rebel against the Lord,
24:16 God forbid that we s' forsake the Lord,
J'g 8: 6 that we s' give bread unto thine army?
15 that we s' give bread unto thy men
9: 9 *S'* I leave my fatness, wherewith by
11 *S'* I forsake my sweetness, and my
13 *S'* I leave my wine, which cheereth
28 who is Shechem, that we s' serve him?
28 of Shechem: for why s' we serve him?
38 is Abimelech, that we s' serve him?
41 that they s' not dwell in Shechem.
20:38 they s' make a great flame with smoke
21: 3 s' be to day one tribe lacking in Israel?
22 them at this time, that ye s' be guilty.
Ru 1:12 If I s' say, I have hope,
12 if I s' have an husband also to night,
12 also to night, and s' also bear sons;
1Sa 2:30 thy father, s' walk before me for ever:
8: 7 me, that I s' not reign over them.
9: 6 he can shew us our way that we s' go.
10:22 further, if the man s' yet come thither.
12:21 for then s' ye go after vain things,
23 forbid that I s' sin against the Lord
15:21 which s' have been utterly destroyed,
29 for he is not a man, that he s' repent.
17:26 he s' defy the armies of the living God?
18:18 that I s' be son in law to the king?
19 daughter s' have been given to David,
19: 1 his servants, that they s' kill David.
17 me, Let me go; why s' I kill thee?
20: 2 s' my father hide this thing from me?
5 s' not fail to sit with the king at meat:
22:13 that he s' rise against me, to lie in
24: 6 The Lord forbid that I s' do this thing
26:11 forbid that I s' stretch forth mine hand
27: 1 that I s' speedily escape into the land
5 s' thy servant dwell in the royal city
11 Lest they s' tell on us, saying, So did
29: 4 for wherewith s' he reconcile himself
4 s' it not be with the heads of these men?
2Sa 2:22 s' I smite thee to the ground?
22 how then s' I hold up my face to Joab
12:23 now he is dead, wherefore s' I fast?
13:26 unto him, Why s' he go with thee?
15:20 s' I this day make thee go up and down
16: 9 Why s' this dead dog curse my lord
19 And again, whom s' I serve?
19 s' I not serve in...presence of his son?
18:12 Though I s' receive a thousand shekels
13 I s' have wrought falsehood against
19:19 that the king s' take it to his heart.
22 ye s' this day be adversaries unto me?
34 that I s' go up with the king unto
35 s' thy servant be yet a burden unto
36 why s' the king recompense it me
43 advice s' not be first had in bringing
20:20 me, that I s' swallow up or destroy.
21: 5 we s' be destroyed from remaining in
23:17 far from me, O Lord, that I s' do this:
1Ki 1:27 who s' sit on the throne of my lord
2: 1 of David drew nigh that he s' die;
15 set their faces on me, that I s' reign:
6: 6 beams s' not be fastened in the walls
8:36 the good way wherein they s' walk,
11:10 that he s' not go after other gods:
14: 2 me that I s' be king over this people.
21: 3 I s' give the inheritance of my fathers
2Ki 3:27 son that s' have reigned in his stead,
4:43 s' I set this before an hundred men?
6:33 what s' I wait for the Lord any longer?
7:19 the Lord s' make windows in heaven,
8:13 a dog, that he s' do this great thing?
11: 9 them that s' go out on the sabbath,
17 that they s' be the Lord's people;
17:15 them, that they s' not do like them.
28 taught them how they s' fear the Lord.
18:35 s' deliver Jerusalem out of mine hand?
22:19 s' become a desolation and a curse,
1Ch 9:28 they s' bring them in and out by tale.
11:19 forbid it me, that I s' do this thing:
16:42 for those that s' make a sound,
21:17 on thy people, that they s' be plagued.
18 David s' go up, and set up an altar
23:13 he s' sanctify the most holy things,
32 s' keep the charge of the tabernacle
25: 1 who s' prophesy with harps, with
29:14 that we s' be able to offer so willingly
2Ch 2: 6 am I then, that I s' build him an house,
4:20 they s' burn after the manner before
6:27 the good way, wherein they s' walk;
15:13 Lord God of Israel s' be put to death,
20:21 that s' praise the beauty of holiness,
23:16 king, that they s' be the Lord's people.
19 was unclean in any thing s' enter in.
25:13 that they s' not go with him to battle,
29:11 that ye s' minister unto him, and burn
24 sin offering s' be made for all Israel.
30: 1 they s' come to the house of the Lord
5 that they s' come to keep the passover
32: 4 Why s' the kings of Assyria come, and
14 your God s' be able to deliver you
Ezr 2:63 they s' not eat of the most holy things,
4:22 why s' damage grow to the hurt of the
7:23 s' there be wrath against the realm
8:17 told them what they s' say unto Iddo,
17 that s' bring unto us ministers
9:14 *S'* we...break thy commandments,
14 there s' be no remnant nor escaping?

Ezr 10: 5 that they s' do according to this word.
7 they s' gather themselves together
8 all his substance s' be forfeited, and
Ne 2: 3 why s' not my countenance be sad,
5:12 they s' do according to this promise.
6: 3 why s' the work cease, whilst I leave
11 And I said, *S'* such a man as I flee?
13 that I s' be afraid, and do so, and sin,
7:65 they s' not eat of the most holy things,
8:14 children of Israel s' dwell in booths
15 s' publish and proclaim in all their
9:12 light in the way wherein they s' go.
15 that they s' go in to possess the land.
19 light, and the way wherein they s' go.
23 fathers, that they s' go in to possess it.
10:37 s' bring the firstfruits of our dough,
11:23 a certain portion s' be for the singers,
13: 1 s' not come into the congregation of
2 Balaam against them, that he s' curse
19 I commanded that the gates s' be shut,
19 s' not be opened till after the sabbath:
19 there s' no burden be brought in on
22 that they s' cleanse themselves, and
22 that they s' come and keep the gates,
Es 1: 8 they s' do...to every man's pleasure.
22 that every man s' bear rule in his own
22 that it s' be published according to
2:10 charged her that she s' not shew it.
11 Esther did, and what s' become of her.
3:14 that they s' be ready against that day.
4: 8 her that she s' go in unto the king,
8:13 the Jews s' be ready against that day
9:21 they s' keep the fourteenth day of the
22 they s' make them days of feasting
25 s' return upon his own head, and that
25 his sons s' be hanged on the gallows.
27 so as it s' not fail, that they would keep
28 these days s' be remembered and kept
28 days of Purim s' not fail from among
Job 3:12 me? or why the breasts that I s' suck?
13 now s' I have lain still and been quiet,
13 still and been quiet, I s' have slept:
6:10 Then s' I yet have comfort; yea, I
11 What is my strength, that I s' hope?
11 is mine end, that I s' prolong my life?
14 pity s' be shewed from his friend;
8: 7 yet thy latter end s' greatly increase.
9: 2 but how s' man be just with God?
32 a man, as I am, that I s' answer him,
32 we s' come together in judgment.
10:19 I s' have been as though I had not
19 I s' have been carried from the womb
11: 2 *S'* not the multitude of words be
2 and s' a man full of talk be justified?
3 *S'* thy lies make men hold their peace?
13: 5 your peace! and it s' be your wisdom.
9 Is it good that he s' search you out?
15: 2 *S'* a wise man utter vain knowledge,
3 *S'* he reason with unprofitable talk?
14 What is man, that he s' be clean? and
14 of a woman, that he s' be righteous?
16: 5 of my lips s' asswage your grief.
19:28 But ye s' say, Why persecute we him,
21: 4 so, why s' not my spirit be troubled?
15 is the Almighty, that we s' serve him?
15 what profit s' we have, if we pray unto
23: 7 so s' I be delivered for ever from my
27: 5 God forbid that I s' justify you: till I
31: 1 why then s' I think upon a maid?
28 I s' have denied the God that is above.
32: 7 I said, Days s' speak, and
7 multitude of years s' teach wisdom.
13 Lest ye s' say, We have found out
34: 6 *S'* I lie against my right? my wound
9 that he s' delight himself with God.
10 it from God that he s' do wickedness;
10 Almighty, that he s' commit iniquity.
23 he s' enter into judgment with God.
33 *S'* it be according to thy mind? he will
36:16 and that which s' be set on thy table
16 be set on thy table s' be full of fatness.
41:11 prevented me, that I s' repay him?
Ps 27: 3 Though an host s' encamp against me,
3 though war s' rise against me, in this
30: 3 alive, that I s' not go down to the pit.
38:16 lest otherwise they s' rejoice over me:
49: 5 Wherefore s' I fear in the days of evil,
9 That he s' still live for ever, and not
69:22 which s' have been for their welfare,
73:15 I s' offend against the generation of
78: 5 s' make them known to their children:
6 even the children which s' be born;
6 who s' arise and declare them to their
79:10 Wherefore s' the heathen say, Where
81:14 I s' soon have subdued their enemies,
15 haters of the Lord s' have submitted
15 their time s' have endured for ever.
16 s' have fed them also with the finest
16 of the rock s' I have satisfied thee.
95:11 that they s' not enter into my rest.
104: 5 that it s' not be removed for ever.
106:23 his wrath, lest he s' destroy them.
115: 2 Wherefore s' the heathen say, Where
119:92 I s'...have perished in mine affliction.
139:18 If I s' count them, they are more in
143: 8 to know the way wherein I s' walk;
Pr 8:29 waters s' not pass his commandment:
22: 6 Train up a child in the way he s' go:
27 s' he take away thy bed from under
Ec 2: 3 which they s' do under the heaven all
18 I s' leave it unto the man that shall
24 a man, than that he s' eat and drink,
24 that he s' make his soul enjoy good
3:13 also that every man s' eat and drink,
14 doeth it, that men s' fear before him.
22 a man s' rejoice in his own works,

Ec 5: 6 wherefore s· God be angry at thy voice,
7:14 that man s· find nothing after him.
Ca 1: 7 why s· I be as one that turneth aside
8: 1 when I s· find thee without, I would
1 kiss thee; yea, I s· not be despised.
3 His left hand s· be under my head,
3 and his right hand s· embrace me.
Isa 1: 5 Why s· ye be stricken any more? ye
9 remnant, we s· have been as Sodom,
9 we s· have been like unto Gomorrah.
5: 2 he looked that it s· bring forth grapes,
4 I looked that it s· bring forth grapes,
8:11 I s· not walk in the way of this people,
19 s· not a people seek unto their God?
10:15 if the rod s· shake itself against them
15 or as if the staff s· lift up itself, as if it
36:20 Lord s· deliver Jerusalem out of my
41: 7 it with nails, that it s· not be moved.
48:11 for how s· my name be polluted? and I
19 his name s· not have been cut off nor
49:15 she s· not have compassion on the son
50: 4 that I s· know how to speak a word in
51:14 and that he s· not die in the pit, nor
14 in the pit, nor that his bread s· fail.
53: 2 is no beauty that we s· desire him.
54: 9 waters of Noah s· no more go over the
57: 6 offering. *S·* I receive comfort in these?
16 for the spirit s· fail before me, and the
63:13 wilderness, that they s· not stumble?
Jer 5:17 thy sons and thy daughters s· eat:
20:18 my days s· be consumed with shame?
23:22 s· have turned them from their evil
25:29 name, and s· ye be utterly unpunished?
26:24 that they s· not give him into the hand
27:10 I s· drive you out, and ye s· perish.
17 wherefore s· this city be laid waste?
29:26 that ye s· be officers in the house of
32:31 I s· remove it from before my face,
35 they s· do this abomination, to cause
33:20 and that there s· not be day and night
21 that he s· not have a son to reign upon
24 they s· be no more a nation before
34: 9 That every man s· let his manservant,
9 that none s· serve himself of them,
10 that every one s· let his manservant,
10 that none s· serve themselves of them
37:10 yet s· they rise up every man in his
21 s· commit Jeremiah into the court
21 they s· give him daily a piece of bread
39:14 Shaphan, that he s· carry him home:
40:15 wherefore s· he slay thee, that all the
15 are gathered unto thee s· be scattered,
44:14 they s· return into the land of Judah,
46:13 king of Babylon s· come and smite the
51:53 Babylon s· mount up to heaven,
53 and though she s· fortify the height
60 all the evil that s· come upon Babylon,
La 1:10 they s· not enter thy congregation.
16 comforter that s· relieve my soul is far
17 his adversaries s· be round about him:
3:26 It is good that a man s· both hope and
44 that our prayer s· not pass through.
4:12 enemy s· have entered into the gates
Eze 8: 6 that I s· go far off from my sanctuary?
13:19 bread, to slay the souls that s· not die,
19 to save the souls alive that s· not live,
22 he s· not return from his wicked way,
14: 3 s· I be enquired of at all by them?
14 they s· deliver but their own souls by
18:23 any pleasure...that the wicked s· die?
23 not that he s· return from his ways,
19: 9 his voice s· no more be heard upon the
20: 9, 14 that it s· not be polluted before the
22 it s· not be polluted in the sight of the
25 judgments whereby they s· not live;
21:10 s· we then make mirth? it contemneth
22:30 s· make up the hedge, and stand in
30 for the land, that I s· not destroy it:
24: 8 top of a rock, that it s· not be covered.
33:10 away in them, how s· we then live?
34: 2 s· not the shepherds feed the flocks?
Da 1: 3 he s· bring certain of the children of
10 why s· he see your faces worse liking
16 meat, and the wine that they s· drink;
18 the king had said he s· bring them in,
2:13 forth that the wise men s· be slain;
18 Daniel and his fellows s· not perish
29 bed, what s· come to pass hereafter:
46 they s· offer an oblation and sweet
3:11 s· be cast into the midst of a burning
19 they s· heat the furnace one seven
5:15 that they s· read this writing, and
29 s· be the third ruler in the kingdom.
6: 1 which s· be over the whole kingdom.
2 and the king s· have no damage.
23 they s· take Daniel up out of the den.
7:14 nations, and languages, s· serve him:
Ho 10: 3 Lord; what then s· a king do to us?
10 in my desire that I s· chastise them;
13:13 he s· not stay long in the place of the
Joe 2:17 that the heathen s· rule over them:
17 s· they say among the people, Where
Jon 4:11 s· not I spare Nineveh, that great city,
Mic 6:16 that I s· make thee a desolation, and
Zep 3: 7 so their dwelling s· not be cut off,
Hag 1: 2 time that the Lord's house s· be built.
Zec 7: 3 saying, *S·* I weep in the fifth month,
7 *S·* ye not hear the words which the
11 their ears, that they s· not hear.
12 lest they s· hear the law, and the
8: 6 s· it also be marvellous in mine eyes?
Mal 1:13 s· I accept this of your hand? saith the
2: 7 the priest's lips s· keep knowledge,
7 and they s· seek the law at his mouth:
M't 2: 4 of them where Christ s· be born.
12 that they s· not return to Herod,

M't 5:29 that one of thy members s· perish,
29 thy whole body s· be cast into hell.
30 that one of thy members s· perish,
30 thy whole body s· be cast into hell.
7:12 ye would that men s· do to you,
11: 3 Art thou he that s· come, or do we
12:16 that they s· not make him known:
13:15 any time they s· see with their eyes,
15 and s· understand with their heart,
15 s· be converted, and I s· heal them.
15:33 Whence s· we have so much bread in
16:11 that ye s· beware of the leaven of the
20 s· tell no man that he was Jesus the
17:27 lest we s· offend them, go thou to the
18:14 that one of these little ones s· perish.
30 into prison, till he s· pay the debt.
34 he s· pay all that was due unto him.
19:13 he s· put his hands on them, and pray:
20:10 that they s· have received more;
31 because they s· hold their peace:
24:22 except those days s· be shortened,
22 there s· no flesh be saved: but for the
25:27 coming I s· have received mine own
26:35 Though I s· die with thee, yet will
27:20 multitude that they s· ask Barabbas,
M'r 3: 9 a small ship s· wait on him because of
9 multitude, lest they s· throng him.
12 that they s· not make him known.
14 twelve, that they s· be with him,
4:12 at any time they s· be converted,
12 and their sins s· be forgiven them.
22 secret, but that it s· come abroad.
26 a man s· cast seed into the ground;
27 And s· sleep, and rise night and day,
27 and the seed s· spring and grow up,
5:43 them straitly that no man s· know it;
43 that something s· be given her to eat.
6: 8 they s· take nothing for their journey,
12 and preached that men s· repent.
7:36 them that they s· tell no man:
8:30 them that they s· tell no man of him.
9: 9 s· tell no man what things they had
10 the rising from the dead s· mean.
18 disciples that they s· cast him out;
30 would not that any man s· know it.
34 themselves, who s· be the greatest.
10:13 to him, that he s· touch them: and
32 what things s· happen unto him,
36 What would ye that I s· do for you?
48 him that he s· hold his peace:
51 What wilt thou that I s· do unto thee?
11:16 that any man s· carry any vessel
12:19 that his brother s· take his wife, and
13:20 those days, no flesh s· be saved:
14:31 If I s· die with thee, I will not
15:11 that he s· rather release Barabbas
24 upon them, what every man s· take.
Lu 1:29 what manner of salutation this s· be.
43 mother of my Lord s· come to me?
57 time came that she s· be delivered;
71 we s· be saved from our enemies, and
2: 1 that all the world s· be taxed.
6 accomplished that she s· be delivered.
26 that he s· not see death, before he had
4:42 him, that he s· not depart from them.
5: 7 that they s· come and help them.
6:31 as ye would that men s· do to you,
7: 4 was worthy for whom he s· do this:
19, 20 Art thou he that s· come? or look
8:12 lest they s· believe and be saved.
56 they s· tell no man what was done.
9:13 except we s· go and buy meat for all
31 he s· accomplish at Jerusalem.
46 them, which of them s· be greatest.
51 was come that he s· be received up,
15:32 It was meet that we s· make merry,
17: 2 he s· offend one of these little ones.
6 planted in the sea; and it s· obey
20 when the kingdom of God s· come,
18:39 him, that he s· hold his peace: but he
19:11 of God s· immediately appear.
27 would not that I s· reign over them,
40 if these s· hold their peace, the stones
20:10 s· give him of the fruit of the vineyard:
20 which s· feign themselves just men,
28 his brother s· take his wife, and raise
22:23 them it was that s· do this thing.
24 of them s· be accounted the greatest.
23:24 that it s· be as they required.
24:16 holden that they s· not know him.
21 he which s· have redeemed Israel:
47 remission of sins s· be preached in his
Joh 1:31 that he s· be made manifest to Israel,
2:25 needed not that any s· testify of man:
3:15 believeth in him s· not perish,
16 believeth in him s· not perish,
20 light, lest his deeds s· be reproved.
5:23 That all men s· honour the Son, even
6:14 prophet that s· come into the world.
39 he hath given me I s· lose nothing,
39 s· raise it up again at the last day.
64 believed not, and who s· betray him.
71 for he it was that s· betray him.
7:23 the law of Moses s· not be broken;
39 that believe on him s· receive:
8: 5 us, that such s· be stoned:
19 ye s· have known my Father also.
55 and if I s· say, I know him not, I
9: 3 of God s· be made manifest in him.
22 he s· be put out of the synagogue.
41 If ye were blind, ye s· have no sin:
11:27 of God, which s· come into the world.
37 even this man s· not have died?
50 that one man s· die for the people,
51 that Jesus s· die for that nation;
52 he s· gather together in one the

Joh 11:57 he s· shew it, that they might take
12: 4 Simon's son, which s· betray him,
23 that the Son of man s· be glorified.
33 signifying what death he s· die.
40 that they s· not see with their eyes,
40 and be converted, and I s· heal them.
42 they s· be put out of the synagogue:
46 on me s· not abide in darkness.
49 what I s· say, and what I s· speak.
13: 1 hour was come that he s· depart out
11 For he knew who s· betray him;
15 that ye s· do as I have done to you.
24 that he s· ask who it s· be of whom
29 that he s· give something to the poor.
14: 7 me, ye s· have known my Father also:
15:16 that ye s· go and bring forth fruit,
16 fruit, and that your fruit s· remain;
16: 1 unto you, that ye s· not be offended.
30 needest not that any man s· ask thee:
17: 2 s· give eternal life to as many as thou
18: 4 all things that s· come upon him,
14 that one man s· die for the people.
28 judgment hall, lest they s· be defiled;
32 signifying what death he s· die.
36 I s· not be delivered to the Jews:
37 that I s· bear witness unto the truth.
39 that I s· release unto you one at the
19:31 bodies s· not remain upon the cross on
36 done, that the scripture s· be fulfilled,
21:19 by what death he s· glorify God.
23 brethren, that that disciple s· not die:
25 which, if they s· be written every one,
25 contain the books that s· be written.
Ac 1: 4 they s· not depart from Jerusalem,
2:24 not possible that he s· be holden of
25 right hand, that I s· not be moved:
47 the church daily such as s· be saved.
3:18 his prophets, that Christ s· suffer,
5:26 people, lest they s· have been stoned.
28 you that ye s· not teach in this name?
40 they s· not speak in...name of Jesus,
6: 2 that we s· leave the word of God, and
7: 6 his seed s· sojourn in a strange land;
6 that they s· bring them into bondage,
44 he s· make it according to the fashion
8:31 can I, except some man s· guide me?
10:17 vision which he hath seen s· mean,
28 that I s· not call any man common
47 water, that these s· not be baptized,
11:22 that he s· go as far as Antioch.
28 s· be great dearth throughout all
12:19 commanded...they s· be put to death.
13:28 desired they Pilate that he s· be slain.
46 word of God s· first have been spoken
14:15 that ye s· turn from these vanities
15: 2 s· go up to Jerusalem unto the apostles
7 Gentiles by my mouth s· hear the word
17:27 That they s· seek the Lord, if haply
18:14 reason would that I s· bear with you:
19: 4 people, that they s· believe on him
4 on him which s· come after him, that
27 great goddess Diana s· be despised,
27 her magnificence s· be destroyed,
20:38 that they s· see his face no more.
21: 4 that he s· not go up to Jerusalem.
16 an old disciple, with whom we s· lodge.
26 an offering s· be offered for every one
22:22 earth: for it is not fit that he s· live.
24 that he s· be examined by scourging;
29 him which s· have examined him:
23:10 Paul s· have been pulled in pieces of
27 and s· have been killed of them:
24:23 he s· forbid none of his acquaintance
26 that money s· have been given him of
25: 4 that Paul s· be kept at Cæsarea, and
26: 8 s· it be thought a thing incredible
8 with you, that God s· raise the dead?
20 that they s· repent and turn to God,
22 prophets and Moses...say s· come:
23 That Christ s· suffer, and that he
23 suffer, and that he s· be the first that
23 be the first that s· rise from the dead,
23 s· shew light unto the people, and
27: 1 determined that we s· sail into Italy,
17 lest they s· fall into the quicksands,
20 all hope that we s· be saved was then
21 ye s· have hearkened unto me, and
29 lest we s· have fallen upon rocks,
42 lest any of them s· swim out, and
43 s· cast themselves first into the sea,
28: 6 looked when he s· have swollen,
27 lest they s· see with their eyes, and
27 with their heart, and s· be converted,
27 be converted, and I s· heal them.
Ro 2:21 that preachest a man s· not steal,
22 sayest a man s· not commit adultery,
4:13 that he s· be the heir of the world,
6: 4 so we also s· walk in newness of life.
6 that henceforth we s· not serve sin.
12 that ye s· obey it in the lusts thereof.
7: 4 that ye s· be married to another,
4 that we s· bring forth fruit unto God.
6 that we s· serve in newness of spirit,
8:26 know not what we s· pray for as we
11: 8 eyes that they s· not see, and ears
8 and ears that they s· not hear;) unto
11 Have they stumbled that they s· fall?
25 that ye s· be ignorant of this mystery,
25 ye s· be wise in your own conceits;
15:16 I s· be the minister of Jesus Christ to
20 lest I s· build upon another man's
1Co 1:15 s· say that I had baptized in mine own
17 the cross of Christ s· be made of none
29 That no flesh s· glory in his presence.
2: 5 your faith s· not stand in the wisdom
4: 3 small thing that I s· be judged of you,

1Co 5: 1 that one s' have his father's wife.
9:10 he that ploweth s' plow in hope;
10 in hope s' be partaker of his hope.
12 lest we s' hinder the gospel of Christ.
14 preach the gospel s' live of the gospel.
15 things, that it s' be so done unto me:
15 any man s' make my glorying void.
27 to others, I myself s' be a castaway.
10: 1 I would not that ye s' be ignorant,
6 intent we s' not lust after evil things,
20 that ye s' have fellowship with devils.
11:31 judge ourselves, we s' not be judged.
32 s' not be condemned with the world.
12:25 there s' be no schism in the body;
25 s' have the same care one for another.
2Co 1: 9 that we s' not trust in ourselves, but
17 that with me there s' be yea yea, and
2: 3 I s' have sorrow from them of whom I
4 not that ye s' be grieved, but that ye
7 such a one s' be swallowed up with
11 Lest Satan s' get an advantage of us:
4: 4 the image of God, s' shine unto them.
5:15 s' not henceforth live unto themselves,
8:20 no man s' blame us in this abundance
9: 3 lest our boasting of you s' be in vain
4 s' be ashamed in this same confident
10: 8 though I s' boast somewhat more of
8 destruction, I s' not be ashamed:
11: 3 so your minds s' be corrupted from
12: 6 lest any man s' think of me above
7 lest I s' be exalted above measure
7 me, lest I s' be exalted above measure.
13: 7 evil; not that we s' appear approved,
7 that ye s' do that which is honest,
10 lest being present I s' use sharpness,
Ga 1:10 men, I s' not be the servant of Christ.
2: 2 lest by any means I s' run, or had run,
9 that we s' go unto the heathen, and
10 would that we s' remember the poor;
3: 1 that ye s' not obey the truth, before
17 it s' make the promise of none effect.
19 the seed s' come to whom the promise
21 verily righteousness s' have been by
23 the faith which s' afterwards be
5: 7 you that ye s' not obey the truth?
6:12 s' suffer persecution for the cross of
14 God forbid that I s' glory, save in the
Eph 1: 4 s' be holy and without blame before
12 s' be to the praise of his glory, who
2: 9 Not of works, lest any man s' boast.
10 ordained that we s' walk in them.
3: 6 That the Gentiles s' be fellowheirs,
8 I s' preach among the Gentiles the
5:27 it s' be holy and without blemish.
Ph'p 1:12 But I would ye s' understand,
2:10 the name of Jesus every knee s' bow,
11 every tongue s' confess that Jesus
27 lest I s' have sorrow upon sorrow.
Col 1:19 that in him s' all fulness dwell;
2: 4 lest any man s' beguile you with
1Th 3: 3 That no man s' be moved by these
4 that we s' suffer tribulation;
4: 3 that ye s' abstain from fornication:
4 one of you s' know how to possess his
5: 4 that day s' overtake you as a thief.
10 or sleep, we s' live together with him.
2Th 2:11 delusion, that they s' believe a lie;
3:10 any would not work, neither s' he eat.
1Ti 1:16 them which s' hereafter believe
Tit 2:12 we s' live soberly, righteously, and
3: 7 we s' be made heirs according to the
Ph'm 14 that thy benefit s' not be as it were
Heb 2: 1 lest at any time we s' let them slip.
9 he by the grace of God s' taste death
3:18 whom sware he that they s' not enter
4: 1 any of you s' seem to come short of it.
7:11 was there that another priest s' rise
8: 4 were on earth, he s' not be a priest,
7 then s' no place have been sought for
9:23 of things in the heaven s' be purified
25 Nor yet that he s' offer himself often,
10: 2 purged s' have no more conscience
4 of bulls and of goats s' take away sins.
11: 5 translated that he s' not see death;
8 a place which he s' after receive
28 destroyed the firstborn s' touch them.
40 without us s' not be made perfect.
12:19 that the word s' not be spoken to them
Jas 1:18 that we s' be a kind of firstfruits of his
1Pe 1:10 of the grace that s' come unto you:
11 Christ, and the glory that s' follow.
2: 9 that ye s' shew forth the praises of
21 example, that ye s' follow his steps:
24 to sins, s' live unto righteousness:
3: 9 called, that ye s' inherit the blessing.
4: 2 That he no longer s' live the rest of
2Pe 2: 6 those that after s' live ungodly;
3: 9 not willing that any s' perish, but
9 but that all s' come to repentance.
1Jo 3: 1 that we s' be called the sons of God:
11 beginning, that we s' love one another.
23 we s' believe on the name of his Son
4: 3 ye have heard that it s' come; and
2Jo 6 from the beginning, ye s' walk in it.
Jude 3 ye s' earnestly contend for the faith
18 they told you there s' be mockers
18 s' walk after their own ungodly lusts.
Re 6: 4 earth, and that they s' kill one another:
11 they s' rest yet for a little season,
11 that s' be killed as they were,
11 be killed as they were, s' be fulfilled.
7: 1 the wind s' not blow on the earth, nor
8: 3 that he s' offer it with the prayers of
9: 4 that they s' not hurt the grass of the
5 it was given that they s' not kill them,
5 that they s' be tormented five months:
Re 9:20 that they s' not worship devils, and
10: 6 that there s' be time no longer:
7 the mystery of God s' be finished, as
11:18 that they s' be judged, and that thou
12: 6 they s' feed her there a thousand two
13:14 they s' make an image to the beast,
15 the image of the beast s' both speak,
15 the image of the beast s' be killed,
19: 8 that she s' be arrayed in fine linen,
15 that with it he s' smite the nations:
20: 3 that he s' deceive the nations no more,
3 till the thousand years s' be fulfilled:

shoulder^ See also SHOULDERPIECES; SHOULDERS.
Ge 21:14 unto Hagar, putting it on her s',
24:15 brother, with her pitcher upon her s'.
45 forth with her pitcher on her s';
49:15 bowed his s' to bear, and became
Ex 29:22 is upon them, and the right s';
27 the s' of the heave offering, which
Le 7:32 the right s' shall ye give unto the
33 shall have the right s' for his part.
34 and the heave s' have I taken of
8:25 and their fat, and the right s':
26 on the fat, and upon the right s':
9:21 and the right s' Aaron waved
10:14 and heave s' shall ye eat in a clean
15 heave s' and the wave breast shall
Nu 6:19 take the sodden s' of the ram,
20 with the wave breast and heave s':
18:18 breast and as the right s' are thine.
De 18: 3 shall give unto the priest the s',
Jos 4: 5 man of you a stone upon his s',
J'g 9:48 and took it, and laid it on his s',
1Sa 9:24 And the cook took up the s', and
Ne 9:29 withdrew the s', and hardened
Job 31:22 mine arm fall from my s' blade,
36 Surely I would take it upon my s',
Ps 81: 6 I removed his s' from the burden:
Isa 9: 4 and the staff of his s', the rod of his
6 government shall be upon his s':
10:27 shall be taken away from off thy s',
22:22 house of David will I lay upon his s';
46: 7 They bear him upon the s', they
Eze 12: 7 I bear it upon my s' in their sight,
12 bear upon his s' in the twilight,
24: 4 good piece, the thigh, and the s';
29: 7 didst break, and rend all their s':
18 bald, and every s' was peeled:
34:21 have thrust with side and with s',
Zec 7:11 to hearken, and pulled away the s',

shoulder-blade See SHOULDER and BLADE.

shoulderpieces
Ex 28: 7 It shall have the two s' thereof
25 on the s' of the ephod before it.
39: 4 They made s' for it, to couple it
18 and put them on the s' of the ephod,

shoulders
Ge 9:23 and laid it upon both their s', and
Ex 12:34 up in their clothes upon their s'.
28:12 stones upon the s' of the ephod
12 upon his two s' for a memorial.
39: 7 he put them on the s' of the ephod,
Nu 7: 9 that they should bear upon their s'.
De 33:12 and he shall dwell between his s'.
J'g 16: 3 put them upon his s', and carried
1Sa 9: 2 from his s' and upward he was
10:23 the people from his s' and upward.
17: 6 a target of brass between his s'.
1Ch 15:15 bare the ark of God upon their s'
2Ch 35: 3 shall not be a burden upon your s':
Isa 11:14 fly upon the s' of the Philistines
14:25 burden depart from off their s'.
30: 6 riches upon the s' of young asses,
49:22 shall be carried upon their s'.
Eze 12: 6 sight shalt thou bear it upon thy s',
M't 23: 4 borne, and lay them on men's s';
Lu 15: 5 hath found it, he layeth it on his s',

shouldest
Ge 3:11 commanded thee that thou s' not eat?
14:23 lest thou s' say, I have made Abram
26:10 thou s' have brought guiltiness upon
29:15 s' thou therefore serve me for nought?
Nu 11:12 that thou s' say unto me, Carry them
De 4:19 s' be driven to worship them, and
26:18 thou s' keep all his commandments;
29:12 That thou s' enter into covenant
30:12 It is not in heaven, that thou s' say,
13 is it beyond the sea, that thou s' say,
J'g 11:23 people Israel, and s' thou possess it?
Ru 2:10 that thou s' take knowledge of me,
1Sa 20: 8 why s' thou bring me to thy father?
2Sa 9: 8 thou s' look upon such a dead dog
1Ki 1:20 that thou s' tell them who shall sit
2Ki 8:14 told me that thou s' surely recover.
13:19 Thou s' have smitten five or six
14:10 for why s' thou meddle to thy hurt,
10 that thou s' fall, even thou, and
19:25 thou s' be to lay waste fenced cities
1Ch 17: 7 s' be ruler over my people Israel:
2Ch 19: 2 S' thou help the ungodly, and love
25:16 forbear; why s' thou be smitten?
19 why s' thou meddle to thine hurt,
18 that thou s' fall, even thou, and
Job 7:17 is man, that thou s' magnify him?
17 thou s' set thine heart upon him?
18 that thou s' visit him every morning,
10: 3 it good unto thee that thou s' oppress,
3 thou s' despise the work of thine
38:20 thou s' take it to the bound thereof,
20 thou s' know the paths to the house
Ps 50:16 s' take my covenant in thy mouth?
130: 3 If thou, Lord, s' mark iniquities, O
Pr 5: 6 Lest thou s' ponder the path of life,
Pr 25: 7 than that thou s' be put lower in the
27:22 thou s' bray a fool in a mortar among
Ec 5: 5 Better is it that thou s' not vow,
5 than that thou s' vow and not pay.
7:16 wise: why s' thou destroy thyself?
17 why s' thou die before thy time?
18 is good that thou s' take hold of this;
Isa 37:26 that thou s' be to lay waste defenced
48: 5 lest thou s' say, Mine idol hath done
7 lest thou s' say, Behold, I knew them.
17 thee by the way that thou s' go.
49: 6 light thing that thou s' be my servant
51:12 s' be afraid of a man that shall die,
Jer 14: 8 why s' thou be as a stranger in the
9 Why s' thou be as a man astonied,
29:26 that thou s' put him in prison, and in
49:16 s' make thy nest as high as the eagle,
Ob 12 thou s' not have looked on the day of
12 neither s' thou have rejoiced over
12 neither s' thou have spoken proudly
13 Thou s' not have entered into the
13 thou s' not have looked on their
14 s' thou have stood in the crossway,
14 neither s' thou have delivered up
M't 8: 8 that thou s' come under my roof:
18:33 S' not thou also have had compassion
M'r 10:35 thou s' do for us whatsoever we shall
Lu 7: 6 that thou s' enter under my roof:
Joh 11:40 believe, thou s' see the glory of God?
17:15 thou s' take them out of the world,
15 that thou s' keep them from the evil.
Ac 13:47 that thou s' be for salvation unto the
22:14 that thou s' know his will, and see
14 and s' hear the voice of his mouth.
Tit 1: 5 that thou s' set in order the things
Ph'm 15 that thou s' receive him for ever;
Re 11:18 thou s' give reward unto thy servants
18 s' destroy them which destroy the

shout See also SHOUTED; SHOUTETH; SHOUTING.
Ex 32:18 voice of them that s' for mastery,
Nu 23:21 the s' of a king is among them.
Jos 6: 5 the trumpet, all the people shall s'
5 with a great s'; and the wall of
10 shall not s', nor make any noise
10 day I bid you s'; then shall ye s'.
16 Joshua said unto the people, S'; for
20 the people shouted with a great s',
1Sa 4: 5 all Israel shouted with a great s',
6 Philistines heard the noise of the s',
6 noise of this great s' in the camp
2Ch 13:15 Then the men of Judah gave a s':
Ezr 3:11 the people shouted with a great s',
13 not discern the noise of the s' of joy
13 the people shouted with a loud s',
Ps 5:11 let them ever s' for joy, because
32:11 s' for joy, all ye that are upright in
35:27 Let them s' for joy, and be glad,
47: 1 s' unto God with the voice of
5 God is gone up with a s', the Lord
65:13 they s' for joy, they also sing.
132: 9 and let thy saints s' for joy.
16 her saints shall s' aloud for joy.
Isa 12: 6 Cry out and s', thou inhabitant of
42:11 s' from the top of the mountains.
44:23 s', ye lower parts of the earth:
Jer 25:30 he shall give a s', as they that
31: 7 s' among the chief of the nations:
50:15 S' against her round about: she
51:14 they shall lift up a s' against thee.
La 3: 8 when I cry and s', he shutteth out
Zep 3:14 s', O Israel; be glad and rejoice
Zec 9: 9 Zion; s', O daughter of Jerusalem:
Ac 12:22 And the people gave a s', saying,
1Th 4:16 descend from heaven with a s',

shouted
Ex 32:17 the noise of the people as they s',
Le 9:24 when all the people saw, they s',
Jos 6:20 people s' when the priests blew
20 the people s' with a great shout,
J'g 15:14 Lehi, the Philistines s' against him:
1Sa 4: 5 all Israel s' with a great shout, so
10:24 the people s', and said, God save the
17:20 to the fight, and s' for the battle.
52 of Israel and of Judah arose, and s',
2Ch 13:15 as the men of Judah s', it came to
Ezr 3:11 all the people s' with a great shout,
12 voice; and many s' aloud for joy:
13 for the people s' with a loud shout,
Job 38: 7 and all the sons of God s' for joy?

shouteth
Ps 78:65 man that s' by reason of wine.

shouting See also SHOUTINGS.
2Sa 6:15 up the ark of the Lord with s',
1Ch 15:28 up the ark...of the Lord with s',
2Ch 15:14 with a loud voice, and with s', and
Job 39:25 thunder of the captains, and the s'.
Pr 11:10 when the wicked perish, there is s'.
Isa 16: 9 for the s' for thy summer fruits
10 singing, neither shall there be s':
10 made their vintage s' to cease.
Jer 20:16 morning, and the s' at noontide;
48:33 none shall tread with s';
33 their s' shall be no s'.
Eze 21:22 to lift up the voice with s',
Am 1:14 thereof, with s' in the day of battle,
2: 2 Moab shall die with tumult, with s',

shoutings
Zec 4: 7 the headstone thereof with s',

shovel See also SHOVELS.
Isa 30:24 hath been winnowed with the s'

shovels
Ex 27: 3 and his s', and his basons, and his
38: 3 pots, and the s', and the basons,

Nu 4:14 the fleshhooks, and the s', and the
1Ki 7:40 Hiram made the lavers, and the s',
45 pots, and the s', and the basons:
2Ki 25:14 pots, and the s', and the snuffers,
2Ch 4:11 Huram made the pots, and the s',
16 The pots also, and the s', and the
Jer 52:18 The caldrons also, and the s', and

show See SHEW.

shower See also SHOWERS.
Eze 13:11 there shall be an overflowing s';
13 and there shall be an overflowing s'
34:26 I will cause the s' to come down in
Lu 12:54 ye say, There cometh a s'; and so

showers
De 32: 2 and as the s' upon the grass:
Job 24: 8 wet with the s' of the mountains,
Ps 65:10 thou makest it soft with s': thou
72: 6 grass: as s' that water the earth.
Jer 3: 3 the s' have been withholden, and
14:22 rain? or can the heavens give s'?
Eze 34:26 there shall be s' of blessing.
Mic 5: 7 the Lord, as the s' upon the grass,
Zec 10: 1 clouds, and give them s' of rain,

shrank
Ge 32:32 eat not of the sinew which s',
32 Jacob's thigh in the sinew that s'.

shred See also SHERD.
2Ki 4:39 s' them into the pot of pottage:

shrines
Ac 19:24 which made silver s' for Diana,

shrink See SHRANK.

shroud
Eze 31: 3 and with a shadowing s', and of an

shrubs
Ge 21:15 cast the child under one of the s'.

Shua (*shu'-ah*) See also BATH-SHUA; SHUAH.
1Ch 2: 3 daughter of S' the Canaanitess.
7:32 and Hotham, and S' their sister.

Shuah (*shu'-ah*) See also SHUA; SHUHITE.
Ge 25: 2 and Midian, and Ishbak, and S'.
38: 2 Canaanite, whose name was S';
12 daughter of S' Judah's wife died;
1Ch 1:32 and Midian, and Ishbak, and S'.
4:11 the brother of S' begat Mehir,

Shual (*shu'-al*) See also HAZAR-SHUAL.
1Sa 13:17 to Ophrah, unto the land of S':
1Ch 7:36 and Harnepher, and S', and Beri,

Shubael^ (*shu'-ba-el*) See also SHEBUEL.
1Ch 24:20 Of the sons of Amram; S': of the
25:20 thirteenth to S', he, his sons, and

Shuham (*shu'-ham*) See also HUSHIM; SHUHAMITES.
Nu 26:42 S', the family of the Shuhamites.

Shuhamites (*shu'-ham-ites*)
Nu 26:42 of Shuham, the family of the S'.
43 the families of the S', according

Shuhite (*shu'-hite*)
Job 2:11 the Temanites, and Bildad the S',
8: 1 Then answered Bildad the S', and
18: 1 Then answered Bildad the S', and
25: 1 Then answered Bildad the S', and
42: 9 the Temanite and Bildad the S'

Shulamite (*shu'-lam-ite*)
Ca 6:13 Return, return, O S'; return,
13 What will ye see in the S'? As it

Shumathites (*shu'-math-ites*)
1Ch 2:53 the Puhites, and the S', and the

shun See also SHUNNED.
2Ti 2:16 But s' profane and vain babblings:

Shunammite (*shu'-nam-mite*)
1Ki 1: 3 and found Abishag a S', and
15 Abishag the S' ministered unto
2:17 he give me Abishag the S' to wife.
21 Abishag the S' be given to Adonijah
22 ask Abishag the S' for Adonijah?
2Ki 4:12 to Gehazi his servant, Call this S'.
25 servant; Behold, yonder is that S':
36 called Gehazi, and said, Call this S'.

Shunem (*shu'-nem*) See also SHUNAMMITE.
Jos 19:18 Jezreel, and Chesulloth, and S',
1Sa 28: 4 and came and pitched in S':
2Ki 4: 8 on a day, that Elisha passed to S',

Shuni (*shu'-ni*) See also SHUNITES.
Ge 46:16 and Haggi, S', and Ezbon, Eri,
Nu 26:15 of S', the family of the Shunites:

Shunites (*shu'-nites*)
Nu 26:15 of Shuni, the family of the S':

shunned
Ac 20:27 I have not s' to declare unto you

Shupham (*shu'-fam*) See also SHEPHUPHAN; SHUPHAMITES.
Nu 26:39 S', the family of the Shuphamites:

Shuphamites (*shu'-fam-ites*)
Nu 26:39 Of Shupham, the family of the S':

Shuppim (*shup'-pim*) See also MUPPIM; SHEPHUPHAN.
1Ch 7:12 S' also, and Huppim, the children
15 to wife the sister of Huppim and S',
26:16 To S' and Hosah the lot came forth

Shur (*shur*)
Ge 16: 7 by the fountain in the way to S'.
20: 1 dwelled between Kadesh and S',
25:18 they dwelt from Havilah unto S',
Ex 15:22 went out into the wilderness of S';
1Sa 15: 7 Havilah until thou comest to S',
27: 8 as thou goest to S', even unto the

Shushan (*shu'-shan*) See also SHOSHANNIM; SHUSHAN-EDUTH.
Ne 1: 1 year, as I was in S' the palace,
Es 1: 2 throne...which was in S' the palace,
5 the people that were present in S'
2: 3 all the fair young virgins unto S'
5 in S' the palace...was a certain Jew,
8 were gathered together unto S'
3:15 decree was given in S' the palace.
15 but the city S' was perplexed.
4: 8 of the decree that was given at S'
16 all the Jews that are present in S',
8:14 decree was given at S' the palace.
15 the city of S' rejoiced and was glad.
9: 6 in S' the palace the Jews slew and
11 the number of those...slain in S'
12 destroyed five hundred men in S'
13 granted to the Jews which are in S'
14 and the decree was given at S';
15 the Jews that were in S' gathered
15 and slew three hundred men at S';
18 the Jews that were at S' assembled
Da 8: 2 saw, that I was at S' in the palace,

Shushan-eduth (*shu''-shan-e'-duth*)
Ps 60: *title* To the chief Musician upon S',

shut See also SHUTTETH; SHUTTING.
Ge 7:16 him: and the Lord s' him in.
19: 6 unto them, and s' the door after him,
10 house to them, and s' to the door.
Ex 14: 3 the wilderness hath s' them in.
Le 13: 4 priest shall s' up him that hath the
5 priest shall s' him up seven days
11 unclean, and shall not s' him up:
21, 26 priest shall s' him up seven days:
31, 33 priest shall s' up him that hath
50 s' up it that hath the plague seven
54 he shall s' it up seven days more:
14:38 and s' up the house seven days:
46 into the house...while that it is s'
Nu 12:14 let her be s' out from the camp
15 Miriam was s' out from the camp
De 11:17 s' up the heaven, that there be no
15: 7 nor s' thine hand from thy poor
32:30 and the Lord had s' them up?
36 and there is none s' up, or left.
Jos 2: 7 were gone out, they s' the gate.
6: 1 Jericho was straitly s' up because
J'g 3:23 and s' the doors of the parlour upon
9:51 they of the city, and s' it to them,
1Sa 1: 5 but the Lord had s' up her womb.
6 the Lord had s' up her womb.
6:10 and s' up their calves at home:
23: 7 for he is s' in, by entering into a
2Sa 20: 3 s' up unto the day of their death,
1Ki 8:35 When heaven is s' up, and there is
14:10 him that is s' up and left in Israel,
21:21 him that is s' up and left in Israel,
2Ki 4: 4 thou shalt s' the door upon thee
5 and s' the door upon her and upon
21 s' the door upon him, and went out.
33 and s' the door upon them twain,
6:32 s' the door, and hold him fast at the
9: 8 him that is s' up and left in Israel.
14:26 for there was not any s' up, nor any
17: 4 the king of Assyria s' him up, and
2Ch 6:26 When the heaven is s' up, and there
7:13 I s' up heaven that there be no rain,
28:24 s' up the doors of the house of the
29: 7 have s' up the doors of the porch,
Ne 6:10 son of Mehetabeel, who was s' up;
10 let us s' the doors of the temple:
7: 3 let them s' the doors, and bar them:
13:19 that the gates should be s', and
Job 3:10 s' not up the doors of my mother's
11:10 If he cut off, and s' up, or gather
38: 8 Or who s' up the sea with doors,
41:15 s' up together as with a close seal.
Ps 31: 8 s' me up into the hand of the enemy;
69:15 not the pit s' her mouth upon me.
77: 9 in anger s' up his tender mercies?
88: 8 I am s' up, and I cannot come
Ec 12: 4 the doors shall be s' in the streets,
Ca 4:12 a spring s' up, a fountain sealed.
Isa 6:10 their ears heavy, and s' their eyes;
22:22 he shall open, and none shall s';
22 and he shall s', and none shall open.
24:10 every house is s' up, that no man
22 and shall be s' up in the prison,
26:20 and s' thy doors about thee:
44:18 for he hath s' their eyes, that they
45: 1 and the gates shall not be s';
52:15 kings shall s' their mouths at him:
60:11 they shall not be s' day nor night;
66: 9 to bring forth, and s' the womb?
Jer 13:19 cities of the south shall be s' up,
20: 9 a burning fire s' up in my bones,
32: 2 Jeremiah...was s' up in the court
3 For Zedekiah...had s' him up,
33: 1 while he was yet s' up in the court
36: 5 saying, I am s' up; I cannot go
39:15 while he was s' up in the court of
Eze 3:24 Go, s' thyself within thine house.
44: 1 toward the east; and it was s'.
2 This gate shall be s', it shall not be
2 entered in...therefore it shall be s'.
46: 1 shall be s' the six working days;
2 gate shall not be s' until...evening.
12 going forth one shall s' the gate.
Da 6:22 and hath s' the lions' mouths, that
8:26 wherefore s' thou up the vision;
12: 4 But thou, O Daniel, s' up the words,
Mal 1:10 would s' the doors for nought?
M't 6: 6 and when thou hast s' thy door,
M't 23:13 for ye s' up the kingdom of heaven
25:10 the marriage: and the door was s'.
Lu 3:20 all, that he s' up John in prison.
4:25 heaven was s' up three years and
11: 7 the door is now s', and my children
13:25 is risen up, and hath s' to the door,
Joh 20:19 doors were s' where the disciples
26 then came Jesus, the doors being s',
Ac 5:23 The prison truly found we s' with
21:30 and forthwith the doors were s'.
26:10 of the saints did I s' up in prison,
Ga 3:23 s' up unto the faith which should
Re 3: 8 open door, and no man can s' it:
11: 6 These have power to s' heaven, that
20: 3 the bottomless pit, and s' him up,
21:25 the gates of it shall not be s' at all

Shuthalhites (*shu'-thal-hites*)
Nu 26:35 Shuthelah, the family of the S':

Shuthelah (*shu'-the-lah*) See also SHUTHALHITES.
Nu 26:35 of S' the family of...Shuthalhites:
36 And these are the sons of S':
1Ch 7:20 sons of Ephraim; S', and Bered
21 And Zabad his son, and S' his son,

shutteth
Job 12:14 he s' up a man, and there can be
Pr 16:30 He s' his eyes to devise froward
17:28 that s' his lips is esteemed a man
Isa 33:15 and s' his eyes from seeing evil;
La 3: 8 and shout, he s' out my prayer.
1Jo 3:17 s' up his bowels of compassion
Re 3: 7 he that openeth, and no man s';
7 and s', and no man openeth;

shutting
Jos 2: 5 about the time of s' of the gate,

shuttle
Job 7: 6 days are swifter than a weaver's s',

Sia (*si'-ah*) See also SIAHA.
Ne 7:47 children of S', the children of

Siaha (*si'-a-hah*) See also SIA.
Ezr 2:44 children of S', the children of

Sibbecai (*sib'-be-cahee*) See also SIBBECHAI.
1Ch 11:29 S' the Hushathite, Ilai the Ahohite,
27:11 was S' the Hushathite, of the sons

Sibbechai (*sib'-be-kahee*) See also SIBBECAI.
2Sa 21:18 S' the Hushathite slew Saph,
1Ch 20: 4 S' the Hushathite slew Sippai,

Sibboleth (*sib'-bo-leth*) See also SHIBBOLETH.
J'g 12: 6 and he said S': for he could not

Sibmah (*sib'-mah*)
Jos 13:19 S', and Zareth-shahar in the
Isa 16: 8 languish, and the vine of S': the
9 weeping of Jazer the vine of S':
Jer 48:32 O vine of S', I will weep for thee

Sibraim (*sib'-ra-im*)
Eze 47:16 S', which is between the border of

Sichem (*si'-kem*) See also SHECHEM; SYCHEM.
Ge 12: 6 the land unto the place of S',

sick
Ge 48: 1 Joseph, Behold, thy father is s':
Le 15:33 of her that is s' of her flowers, and
1Sa 19:14 to take David, she s', He is s'.
30:13 because three days agone I fell s'.
2Sa 12:15 bare unto David, and it was very s'.
13: 2 that he fell s' for his sister Tamar;
5 on thy bed, and make thyself s':
6 lay down, and made himself s':
1Ki 14: 1 Abijah the son of Jeroboam fell s'.
5 of thee for her son; for he is s':
17:17 the mistress of the house, fell s';
2Ki 1: 2 that was in Samaria, and was s':
8: 7 the king of Syria was s'; and it
29 Ahab in Jezreel, because he was s'.
13:14 Elisha was fallen s' of his sickness
20: 1 days was Hezekiah s' unto death.
12 heard that Hezekiah had been s'.
2Ch 22: 6 Ahab at Jezreel, because he was s'.
32:24 days Hezekiah was s' to the death,
Ne 2: 2 sad, seeing thou art not s'? this
Ps 35:13 when they were s', my clothing
Pr 13:12 Hope deferred maketh the heart s':
23:35 shalt thou say, and I was not s':
Ca 2: 5 me with apples: for I am s' of love.
5: 8 that ye tell him, I am s' of love.
Isa 1: 5 the whole head is s', and the whole
33:24 inhabitant shall not say, I am s':
38: 1 days was Hezekiah s' unto death.
9 king of Judah, when he had been s',
39: 1 he had heard that he had been s',
Jer 14:18 them that are s' with famine!
Eze 34: 4 have ye healed that which was s',
16 will strengthen that which was s':
Da 8:27 fainted, and was s' certain days;
Ho 7: 5 king the princes have made him s'
Mic 6:13 will I make thee s' in smiting thee,
Mal 1: 8 if ye offer the lame and s', is it not
13 was torn, and the lame, and the s';
M't 4:24 brought unto him all s' people
8: 6 servant...at home s' of the palsy,
14 wife's mother laid,...s' of a fever.
16 and healed all that were s':
9: 2 brought...a man s' of the palsy,
2 faith said unto the s' of the palsy;
6 (then saith he to the s' of the palsy,)
12 physician, but they that are s'.
10: 8 Heal the s', cleanse the lepers,
14:14 toward them, and he healed their s'.
25:36 I was s', and ye visited me: I was
39 when saw we thee s', or in prison,
43 s', and in prison, and ye visited me
44 naked, or s', or in prison, and did

M'r 1:30 Simon's wife's mother lay s' of a
34 he healed many that were s'
2: 3 him, bringing one s' of the palsy,
4 bed wherein the s' of the palsy lay.
5 he said unto the s' of the palsy, Son,
9 it easier to say to the s' of the palsy,
10 sins, (he saith to the s' of the palsy,)
17 physician, but they that are s':
6: 5 laid his hands upon a few s' folks,
13 anointed with oil many that were s',
55 in beds those that were s',
56 they laid the s' in the streets, and
16:18 they shall lay hands on the s', and
Lu 4:40 all they that had any s' with divers
5:24 (he said unto the s' of the palsy,)
31 physician; but they that are s'.
7: 2 him, was s', and ready to die.
10 the servant whole that had been s'.
9: 2 kingdom of God, and to heal the s'.
10: 9 And heal the s' that are therein,
Joh 4:46 whose son was s' at Capernaum.
11: 1 Now a certain man was s', named
2 hair, whose brother Lazarus was s'.)
3 behold, he whom thou lovest is s'.
6 had heard therefore that he was s',
Ac 5:15 they brought forth the s' into the
16 bringing s' folks, and them which
9:33 years, and was s' of the palsy.
37 days, that she was s', and died:
19:12 brought unto the s' handkerchiefs
28: 8 father of Publius lay s' of a fever and
Ph'p 2:26 ye had heard that he had been s'.
27 indeed he was s' nigh unto death:
2Ti 4:20 Trophimus have I left at Miletum s'.
Jas 5:14 Is any s' among you? let him call
15 prayer of faith shall save the s',

sickle
De 16: 9 beginnest to put the s' to the corn.
23:25 not move a s' unto thy neighbour's
Jer 50:16 that handleth the s' in the time of
Joe 3:13 Put ye in the s', for the harvest is
M'r 4:29 immediately he putteth in the s',
Re 14:14 crown, and in his hand a sharp s'.
15 cloud, Thrust in thy s', and reap:
16 cloud thrust in his s' on the earth;
17 heaven, he also having a sharp s'.
18 cry to him that had the sharp s',
18 Thrust in thy sharp s', and gather
19 angel thrust in his s' into the earth,

sickly
1Co 11:30 many are weak and s' among you,

sickness See also SICKNESSES.
Ex 23:25 I will take s' away from the midst
Le 20:18 lie with a woman having her s',
De 7:15 will take away from thee all s',
28:61 Also every s', and every plague,
1Ki 8:37 plague, whatsoever s' there be;
17:17 his s' was so sore, that there was
2Ki 13:14 Now Elisha was fallen sick of his s'
2Ch 6:28 sore or whatsoever s' there be:
21:15 shalt have great s' by disease of
15 bowels fall out by reason of the s'
19 bowels fell out by reason of his s':
Ps 41: 3 wilt make all his bed in his s'.
Ec 5:17 sorrow and wrath with his s'.
Isa 38: 9 sick, and was recovered of his s':
12 he will cut me off with pining s',
Ho 5:13 When Ephraim saw his s', and
M't 4:23 healing all manner of s' and all
9:35 healing every s' and every disease
10: 1 to heal all manner of s' and all
Joh 11: 4 This s' is not unto death, but for

sicknesses
De 28:59 sore s', and of long continuance.
29:22 s' which the Lord hath laid upon
M't 8:17 our infirmities, and bare our s'.
M'r 3:15 to have power to heal s', and to

Siddim (*sid'-dim*)
Ge 14: 3 joined together in the vale of *S'*,
8 battle with them in the vale of *S'*;
10 the vale of *S'* was full of slimepits;

side^ See also ASIDE; BACKSIDE; BESIDE; INSIDE; OUTSIDE; SIDES; UPSIDE.
Ge 6:16 ark shalt thou set in the s' thereof;
38:21 harlot, that was openly by the way s'?
Ex 2: 5 walked along by the river's s'; and
12: 7 strike it on the two s' posts and on
22 strike the lintel and the two s' posts
23 upon the lintel, and on the two s' posts,
17:12 one s', and the other on the other s';
25:12 rings shall be in the one s' of it,
12 and two rings in the other s' of it.
32 of the candlestick out of the one s',
32 the candlestick out of the other s':
26:13 a cubit on the one s', and a cubit on
13 the other s' of that which remaineth
13 on this s' and on that s', to cover
18 boards on the south s' southward.
20 the second s' of the tabernacle on
20 the north s' there shall be twenty
26 of the one s' of the tabernacle,
27 of the other s' of the tabernacle, and
27 boards of the s' of the tabernacle,
35 the s' of the tabernacle toward the
35 shalt put the table on the north s'.
27: 9 for the south s' southward there
9 an hundred cubits long for one s':
11 likewise for the north s' in length
12 the west s' shall be hangings of fifty
13 breadth of the court on the east s'
14 The hangings of one s' of the gate
15 on the other s' shall be hangings
28:26 is in the s' of the ephod inward.
32:15 on the one s' and on the other were
Ex 32:26 said, Who is on the Lord's s'? let him
27 Put every man his sword by his s',
36:11 uttermost s' of another curtain,
23 boards for the south s' southward:
25 for the other s' of the tabernacle,
31 of the one s' of the tabernacle,
32 of the other s' of the tabernacle,
37: 3 even two rings upon the one s' of it,
3 and two rings upon the other s' of it.
8 One cherub on the end on this s',
8 cherub on the other end on that s':
18 out of the one s' thereof, and
18 out of the other s' thereof:
38: 9 south s' southward the hangings
11 for the north s' the hangings were
12 for the west s' were hangings of
13 for the east s' eastward fifty cubits.
14 hangings of the one s' of the gate
15 for the other s' of the court gate,
39:19 was on the s' of the ephod inward.
40:22 the s' of the tabernacle northward,
24 the s' of the tabernacle southward.
Le 1:11 shall kill it on the s' of the altar
15 be wrung out at the s' of the altar:
5: 9 sin offering upon the s' of the altar;
Nu 2: 3 the east s' toward the rising of the
10 On the south s' shall be the standard
18 On the west s' shall be the standard
25 camp of Dan shall be on the north s'
3:29 the s' of the tabernacle southward.
35 the s' of the tabernacle northward.
10: 6 the camps that lie on the south s'
11:31 it were a day's journey on this s',
31 a day's journey on the other s',
16:27 Dathan, and Abiram, on every s':
21:13 pitched on the other s' of Arnon,
22: 1 Moab on this s' Jordan by Jericho.
24 being on this s', and a wall on that s'.
24: 6 as gardens by the river's s', as the
32:19 not inherit...on yonder s' Jordan,
19 is fallen to us on this s' Jordan
32 inheritance on this s' Jordan may
34:11 to Riblah, on the east s' of Ain;
11 unto the s' of the sea of Chinnereth
15 their inheritance on this s' Jordan
35: 5 on the east s' two thousand cubits,
5 on the south s' two thousand cubits,
5 on the west s' two thousand cubits,
5 on the north s' two thousand cubits;
14 give three cities on this s' Jordan,
De 1: 1 unto all Israel on this s' Jordan in
5 On this s' Jordan, in the land of
7 in the south, and by the sea s',
3: 8 land that was on this s' Jordan,
4:32 one s' of heaven unto the other,
41 cities on this s' Jordan toward the
46 On this s' Jordan, in the valley over
47 were on this s' Jordan toward the
49 plain on this s' Jordan eastward,
11:30 Are they not on the other s' Jordan,
31:26 in the s' of the ark of the covenant
Jos 1:14 Moses gave you on this s' Jordan;
15 gave you on this s' Jordan toward
2:10 that were on the other s' Jordan,
5: 1 were on the s' of Jordan westward,
7: 2 Beth-aven, on the east s' of Beth-el,
7 and dwelt on the other s' Jordan!
8: 9 Beth-el and Ai, on the west s' of Ai:
11 and pitched on the north s' of Ai:
12 and Ai, on the west s' of the city.
22 in the midst of Israel, some on this s',
22 and some on that s': and they smote
33 their judges, stood on this s' the ark
33 that s' before the priests the Levites,
9: 1 which were on this s' Jordan, in
12: 1 other s' Jordan toward the rising
7 Israel smote on this s' Jordan on
13:27 on the other s' Jordan eastward.
32 of Moab, on the other s' Jordan, by
14: 3 half tribe on the other s' Jordan:
15: 3 to the south s' to Maaleh-acrabbim,
3 on the south s' unto Kadesh-barnea,
7 which is on the s' side of the river:
8 along unto the south s' of the Jebusite;
10 along unto the s' of mount Jearim,
10 which is Chesalon, on the north s',
11 unto the s' of Ekron northward:
16: 5 inheritance on the east s' was
6 to Michmethah on the north s';
17: 5 which were on the other s' Jordan;
9 was on the north s' of the river,
18:12 border on the north s' was from
12 border went up to the s' of Jericho
12 of Jericho on the north s', and went
13 to the s' of Luz, which is Beth-el,
13 the south s' of the nether Beth-horon.
16 to the s' of Jebusi on the south,
18 toward the s' over against Arabah
19 the s' of Beth-hoglah northward:
20 was the border of it on the east s'.
19:14 it on the north s' to Hannathon:
27 toward the north s' of Beth-emek,
34 reacheth to Zebulun on the south s',
34 and reacheth to Asher on the west s',
20: 8 on the other s' Jordan by Jericho
22: 4 gave you on the other s' Jordan.
7 their brethren on this s' Jordan
24: 2 Your fathers dwelt on the other s'
3 from the other s' of the flood, and
8 which dwelt on the other s' Jordan;
14 fathers served on the other s' of
15 were on the other s' of the flood,
30 the north s' of the hill of Gaash.
J'g 2: 9 on the north s' of the hill Gaash.
7: 1 Midianites were on the north s'
12 sand by the sea s' for multitude.
J'g 7:18 also on every s' of all the camp,
25 to Gideon on the other s' Jordan.
8:34 of all their enemies on every s':
10: 8 that were on the other s' Jordan
11:18 by the east s' of the land of Moab,
18 pitched on the other s' of Arnon,
19: 1 on the s' of mount Ephraim, who
18 toward the s' of mount Ephraim;
21:19 which is on the north s' of Beth-el,
19 on the east s' of the highway that
1Sa 4:18 backward by the s' of the gate,
6: 8 in a coffer by the s' thereof; and
12:11 hand of your enemies on every s',
14: 1 garrison, that is on the other s'.
4 was a sharp rock on the one s',
4 and a sharp rock on the other s':
40 he unto all Israel, Be ye on one s',
40 my son will be on the other s'.
47 against all his enemies on every s',
17: 3 stood on a mountain on the one s',
3 stood on a mountain on the other s':
20:20 I will shoot three arrows on the s'
21 the arrows are on this s' of thee,
25 and Abner sat by Saul's s', and
23:26 went on this s' of the mountain,
26 his men on that s' of the mountain:
26:13 David went over to the other s',
31: 7 Israel that were on the other s' of
7 that were on the other s' Jordan,
2Sa 2:13 the one on the one s' of the pool,
13 the other on the other s' of the pool.
16 thrust his sword in his fellow's s';
13:34 by the way of the hill s' behind
16:13 Shimei went along on the hill's s'
18: 4 And the king stood by the gate s',
24: 5 on the right s' of the city that lieth
1Ki 4:24 all the region on this s' the river,
24 all the kings on this s' the river:
5: 3 which were about him on every s',
4 hath given me rest on every s',
6: 8 was in the right s' of the house:
31 lintel and s' posts were a fifth part
7: 7 cedar from one s' of the floor to the
30 molten, at the s' of every addition.
39 bases on the right s' of the house,
39 and five on the left s' of the house:
39 the sea on the right s' of the house
49 of pure gold, five on the right s', and
10:19 were stays on either s' on the place of
20 twelve lions stood there on the one s'
2Ki 3:22 the water on the other s' as red
12: 9 it beside the altar, on the right s'
16:14 put it on the north s' of the altar.
1Ch 4:39 even unto the east s' of the valley,
6:78 on the other s' Jordan by Jericho,
78 on the east s' of Jordan, were
12:18 Thine are we, David, and on thy s',
37 on the other s' of Jordan, of the
22:18 he not given you rest on every s'?
26:30 them of Israel on this s' Jordan
2Ch 4: 8 five on the right s', and five on the
10 he set the sea on the right s' of the
8:17 at the sea s' in the land of Edom.
9:18 stays on each s' of the sitting place,
19 lions stood there on the one s', and
14: 7 he hath given us rest on every s'.
20: 2 beyond the sea on this s' Syria;
23:10 from the right s' of the temple to
10 to the left s' of the temple, along by
32:22 and guided them on every s'.
30 to the west s' of the city of David.
33:14 on the west s' of Gihon, in the valley,
Ezr 4:10 rest that are on this s' the river,
11 the men on this s' the river, and at
16 have no portion on this s' the river.
5: 3, 6 Tatnai, governor on this s' the
6 which were on this s' the river,
6:13 Tatnai, governor on this s' the river,
8:36 the governors on this s' the river:
Ne 3: 7 of the governor on this s' the river.
4:18 had his sword girded by his s',
Job 1:10 about all that he hath on every s'?
18:11 shall make him afraid on every s',
12 destruction...be ready at his s'.
19:10 He hath destroyed me on every s',
Ps 12: 8 The wicked walk on every s', when
31:13 fear was on every s': while they
65:12 the little hills rejoice on every s'.
71:21 and comfort me on every s'.
91: 7 A thousand shall fall at thy s', and
118: 6 Lord is on my s'; I will not fear:
124: 1, 2 been the Lord who was on our s',
Ec 4: 1 s' of their oppressors there was
Isa 60: 4 daughters...be nursed at thy s'.
Jer 6:25 the enemy and fear is on every s'.
20:10 defaming of many, fear on every s'.
49:29 cry unto them, Fear is on every s'.
52:23 and six pomegranates on a s';
Eze 1:10 the face of a lion, on the right s':
10 had the face of an ox on the left s';
23 had two, which covered on this s',
23 had two, which covered on that s',
4: 4 Lie thou also upon thy left s', and
6 lie again on thy right s', and thou
8 turn thee from one s' to another,
9 days that thou shalt lie upon thy s',
9: 2 with a writer's inkhorn by his s':
3 had the writer's inkhorn by his s';
11 which had the inkhorn by his s',
10: 3 cherubims stood on the right s' of
11:23 mountain which is on the east s' of
16:33 come unto thee on every s' for thy
19: 8 nations set against him on every s':
23:22 bring them against thee on every s';
25: 9 I will open the s' of Moab from the
28:23 by the sword upon her on every s';

Eze 34: 21 thrust with s· and with shoulder,
36: 3 and swallowed you up on every s·,
37: 21 and will gather them on every s·,
39: 17 gather yourselves on every s· to my
40: 10 on this s·, and three on that s·:
10 measure on this s· and on that s·.
12 chambers was one cubit on this s·,
12 the space was one cubit on that s·:
12 on this s·, and six cubits on that s·.
18 pavement by the s· of the gates
21 three on this s· and three on that s·;
26 on this s·, and another on that s·,
34, 37 thereof, on this s·, and on that s·:
39 on this s·, and two tables on that s·,
40 at the s· without, as one goeth up
40 and on the other s·, which was at
41 on this s·, and four tables on that s·,
41 by the s· of the gate; eight tables,
44 was at the s· of the north gate;
44 one at the s· of the east gate having
48 on this s·, and five cubits on that s·:
48 on this s·, and three cubits on that s·.
49 one on this s·, and another on that s·.
41: 1 six cubits broad on the one s·,
1 six cubits broad on the other s·,
2 were five cubits on the one s·,
2 and five cubits on the other s·:
5 the breadth of every s· chamber,
5 round about the house on every s·.
6 And the s· chambers were three,
6 of the house for the s· chambers
7 still upward to the s· chambers:
8 the foundations of the s· chambers
9 was for the s· chamber without,
9 was the place of the s· chambers
10 about the house on every s·.
11 the doors of the s· chambers were
15 galleries thereof on the one s· and
15 on the other s·, an hundred cubits,
19 toward the palm tree on the one s·,
19 toward the palm tree on the other s·:
26 palm trees on the one s· and on
26 and on the other s·, on the sides of
26 upon the s· chambers of the house,
42: 9 was the entry on the east s·, as
16 east s· with the measuring reed,
17 the north s·, five hundred reeds,
18 the south s·, five hundred reeds,
19 He turned about to the west s·, and
45: 7 shall be for the prince on the one s·
7 other s· of the oblation of the holy
7 city, from the west s· westward,
7 and from the east s· eastward:
46: 19 which was at the s· of the gate,
47: 1 from the right s· of the house,
1 house, at the south s· of the altar.
2 there ran out waters on...right s·.
7 many trees on the one s· and on the
12 upon the bank thereof, on this s· and
12 on that s·, shall grow all trees for
15 of the land toward the north s·,
17 Hamath. And this is the north s·.
18 the east s· ye shall measure from
18 east sea. And this is the east s·.
19 And the south s· southward, from
19 And this is the south s· southward.
20 The west s· also shall be the great
20 Hamath. This is the west s·.
48: 2 the border of Dan, from the east s·
2 the west s·, a portion for Asher.
3 the east s· even unto the west s·,
4, 5 from the east s· unto the west s·,
6 the east s· even unto the west s·,
7, 8 from the east s· unto the west s·,
8 from the east s· unto the west s·:
16 the north s· four thousand and five
16 the south s· four thousand and five
16 the east s· four thousand and five
16 the west s· four thousand and five
21 on the one s· and on the other of the
23, 24, 25, 26, 27 east s· unto the west s·,
28 of Gad, at the south s· southward,
30 out of the city on the north s·,
32 at the east s· four thousand and
33 the south s· four thousand and five
34 the west s· four thousand and five
Da 7: 5 and it raised up itself on one s·,
10: 4 I was by the s· of the great river,
11: 17 but she shall not stand on his s·,
12: 5 on this s· of the bank of the river,
5 the other on that s· of the bank of
Ob 11 that thou stoodest on the other s·,
Jon 4: 5 and sat on the east s· of the city,
Zec 4: 3 one upon the right s· of the bowl,
3 and the other upon the left s· thereof.
11 upon the right s· of the candlestick
11 and upon the left s· thereof?
5: 3 shall be cut off as on this s· according
3 shall be cut off as on that s· according
M't 8: 18 to depart unto the other s·.
28 when he was come to the other s·
13: 1 of the house, and sat by the sea s·.
4 some seeds fell by the way s', and
19 which received seed by the way s·.
14: 22 to go before him unto the other s',
16: 5 disciples were come to the other s·,
20: 30 blind men sitting by the way s·,
M'r 2: 13 he went forth again by the sea s·;
4: 1 began again to teach by the sea s·:
4 as he sowed, some fell by the way s·,
15 And these are they by the way s·,
35 Let us pass over unto the other s·.
5: 1 over unto the other s· of the sea,
21 again by ship unto the other s·,
6: 45 the other s· before unto Bethsaida,
8: 13 ship again departed to the other s·.
M'r 10: 1 Judæa by the farther s· of Jordan:
46 sat by the highway s· begging.
16: 5 young man sitting on the right s·,
Lu 1: 11 standing on the right s· of the altar
8: 5 he sowed, some fell by the way s·;
12 Those by the way s· are they that
22 over unto the other s· of the lake.
10: 31 him, he passed by on the other s·.
32 him, and passed by on the other s·.
18: 35 man sat by the way s· begging:
19: 43 round, and keep thee in on every s·,
Joh 6: 22 stood on the other s· of the sea
25 found him on the other s· of the
19: 18 other with him, on either s· one,
34 with a spear pierced his s·, and
20: 20 unto them his hands and his s·.
25 and thrust my hand into his s·, I
27 thy hand, and thrust it into my s·:
21: 6 Cast the net on the right s· of the
Ac 10: 6 he whose house is by the sea s·:
32 one Simon a tanner by the sea s·:
12: 7 smote Peter on the s·, and raised
16: 13 went out of the city by a river s·,
2Co 4: 8 We are troubled on every s·, yet not
7: 5 but we were troubled on every s·;
Re 22: 2 on either s· of the river, was there

side-chamber See SIDE and CHAMBER.

side-posts See SIDE and POSTS.

sides
Ex 25: 14 into the rings by the s· of the ark,
32 shall come out of the s· of it;
26: 13 hang over the s· of the tabernacle
22 the s· of the tabernacle westward
23 of the tabernacle in the two s·.
27 tabernacle, for the two s· westward.
27: 7 be upon the two s· of the altar,
28: 27 two s· of the ephod underneath,
30: 3 and the s· thereof round about,
4 the two s· of it shalt thou make it;
32: 15 were written on both their s·;
36: 27 the s· of the tabernacle westward
28 of the tabernacle in the two s·.
32 the tabernacle for the s· westward.
37: 5 into the rings by the s· of the ark,
18 going out of the s· thereof;
26 and the s· thereof round about,
27 upon the two s· thereof, to be
38: 7 the rings on the s· of the altar,
39: 20 two s· of the ephod underneath,
Nu 33: 55 your eyes, and thorns in your s·,
Jos 23: 13 and scourges in your s·, and thorns
J'g 2: 3 they shall be as thorns in your s·,
5: 30 colours of needlework on both s·,
1Sa 24: 3 remained in the s· of the cave.
1Ki 4: 24 and he had peace on all s· round
6: 16 cubits on the s· of the house,
2Ki 19: 23 mountains, to the s· of Lebanon,
Ps 48: 2 mount Zion, on the s· of the north,
128: 3 vine by the s· of thine house:
Isa 14: 13 congregation, in the s· of the north:
15 down to hell, to the s· of the pit.
37: 24 mountains, to the s· of Lebanon;
66: 12 ye shall be borne upon her s·, and
Jer 6: 22 be raised from the s· of the earth.
48: 28 nest in the s· of the hole's mouth.
49: 32 their calamity from all s· thereof,
Eze 1: 8 under their wings on their four s·;
17 went, they went upon their four s·:
10: 11 went, they went upon their four s·;
32: 23 graves are set in the s· of the pit,
41: 2 the s· of the door were five cubits
26 on the s· of the porch, and upon
42: 20 He measured it by the four s·: it
46: 19 a place on the two s· westward.
48: 1 for these are his s· east and west;
Am 6: 10 him that is by the s· of the house,
Jon 1: 5 gone down into the s· of the ship;

Sidon (*si'-don*) See also SIDONIANS; ZIDON.
Ge 10: 15 And Canaan begat *S*· his firstborn,
19 of the Canaanites was from *S*·,
M't 11: 21 had been done in Tyre and *S*·,
22 be more tolerable for Tyre and *S*·
15: 21 into the coasts of Tyre and *S*·.
M'r 3: 8 and they about Tyre and *S*·, a great
7: 24 into the borders of Tyre and *S*·,
31 from the coasts of Tyre and *S*·,
Lu 4: 26 save unto Sarepta, a city of *S*·, unto
6: 17 from the sea coast of Tyre and *S*·,
10: 13 had been done in Tyre and *S*·,
14 be more tolerable for Tyre and *S*·
Ac 12: 20 displeased with them of Tyre and *S*·:
27: 3 And the next day we touched at *S*·.

Sidonians (*si-do'-ne-uns*) See also ZIDONIANS.
De 3: 9 Which Hermon the *S*· call Sirion;
Jos 13: 4 and Mearah that is beside the *S*·,
6 and all the *S*·, them will I drive out
J'g 3: 3 and all the Canaanites, and the *S*·,
1Ki 5: 6 skill to hew timber like unto the *S*·.

siege See also BESIEGE.
De 20: 19 down...to employ them in the s·:
28: 53 in the s·, and in the straitness,
55 he hath nothing left in the s·, and
57 secretly in the s· and straitness,
1Ki 15: 27 and all Israel laid s· to Gibbethon.
2Ch 32: 9 but he himself laid s· against Lachish,
10 ye abide in the s· in Jerusalem?
Isa 29: 3 and will lay s· against thee with a
Jer 19: 9 eat the flesh of his friend in the s·
Eze 4: 2 And lay s· against it, and build a
3 and thou shalt lay s· against it.
7 face toward the s· of Jerusalem,
8 thou hast ended the days of thy s·.
5: 2 when the days of the s· are fulfilled:
Mic 5: 1 troops: he hath laid s· against us:
Na 3: 14 Draw thee waters for the s·, fortify
Zec 12: 2 shall be in the s· both against Judah

sieve
Isa 30: 28 the nations with the s· of vanity:
Am 9: 9 nations, like as corn is sifted in a s·,

sift See also SIFTED.
Isa 30: 28 to s· the nations with the sieve of
Am 9: 9 I will s· the house of Israel among
Lu 22: 31 you, that he may s· you as wheat:

sifted
Am 9: 9 nations, like as corn is s· in a sieve,

sigh See also SIGHED; SIGHEST; SIGHETH; SIGHING; SIGHS.
Isa 24: 7 all the merryhearted do s·.
La 1: 4 priests s·, her virgins are afflicted,
11 All her people s·, they seek bread;
21 They have heard that I s·: there is
Eze 9: 4 upon the foreheads of the men that s·
21: 6 *S*· therefore, thou son of man, with
6 with bitterness s· before their eyes.

sighed
Ex 2: 23 children of Israel s· by reason of
M'r 7: 34 And looking up to heaven, he s·,
8: 12 he s· deeply in his spirit, and saith,

sighest
Eze 21: 7 say unto thee, Wherefore s· thou?

sigheth
La 1: 8 yea, she s·, and turneth backward.

sighing
Job 3: 24 For my s· cometh before I eat, and
Ps 12: 5 of the poor, for the s· of the needy,
31: 10 with grief, and my years with s·:
79: 11 the s· of the prisoner come before
Isa 21: 2 the s· thereof have I made to cease.
35: 10 and sorrow and s· shall flee away.
Jer 45: 3 fainted in my s·, and I find no rest.

sighs
La 1: 22 for my s· are many, and my heart is

sight See also OVERSIGHT; SIGHTS.
Ge 2: 9 every tree that is pleasant to the s·,
18: 3 now I have found favour in thy s·,
19: 19 servant hath found grace in thy s·,
21: 11 was very grievous in Abraham's s·
12 Let it not be grievous in thy s·
23: 4 may bury my dead out of my s·.
8 should bury my dead out of my s·;
32: 5 lord,...I may find grace in thy s·.
33: 8 to find grace in the s· of my lord.
10 if now I have found grace in thy s·,
15 me find grace in the s· of my lord.
38: 7 was wicked in the s· of the Lord;
39: 4 And Joseph found grace in his s·,
21 him favour in the s· of the keeper
47: 18 not ought left in the s· of my lord,
25 us find grace in the s· of my lord,
29 If now I have found grace in thy s·,
Ex 3: 3 turn aside, and see this great s·,
21 favour in the s· of the Egyptians:
4: 30 did the signs in the s· of the people.
7: 20 in the river, in the s· of Pharaoh,
20 and in the s· of his servants; and
9: 8 the heaven in the s· of Pharaoh.
11: 3 favour in the s· of the Egyptians.
3 in the s· of Pharaoh's servants, and
3 and in the s· of the people.
12: 36 favour in the s· of the Egyptians,
15: 26 wilt do that which is right in his s·,
17: 6 Moses did so in the s· of the elders
19: 11 down in the s· of all the people upon
24: 17 the s· of the glory of the Lord
33: 12 hast also found grace in my s·.
13 if I have found grace in thy s·,
13 that I may find grace in thy s·: and
16 people have found grace in thy s·?
17 for thou hast found grace in my s·,
34: 9 If now I have found grace in thy s·,
40: 38 in the s· of all the house of Israel,
Le 10: 19 been accepted in the s· of the Lord?
13: 3 the plague in s· be deeper than the
4 in s· be not deeper than the skin,
5 if the plague in his s· be at a stay,
20 it be in s· lower than the skin,
25, 30 it be in s· deeper than the skin;
31 it be not in s· deeper than the skin,
32 be not in s· deeper than the skin;
34 nor be in s· deeper than the skin;
37 if the scall be in his s· at a stay,
14: 37 which in s· are lower than the
20: 17 be cut off in the s· of their people:
25: 53 rule with rigour over him in thy s·.
26: 45 of Egypt in the s· of the heathen,
Nu 3: 4 in the s· of Aaron their father.
11: 11 have I not found favour in thy s·,
15 If I have found favour in thy s·;
13: 33 were in our own s· as grasshoppers,
33 and so we were in their s·.
19: 5 one shall burn the heifer in his s·;
20: 27 Hor in the s· of all the congregation.
25: 6 woman in the s· of Moses, and in
6 the s· of all the congregation of the
27: 19 and give him a charge in their s·.
32: 5 if we have found grace in thy s·, let
13 had done evil in the s· of the Lord,
33: 3 hand in the s· of all the Egyptians.
De 4: 6 wisdom...in the s· of the nations,
25 shall do evil in the s· of the Lord
37 brought thee out in his s· with his
6: 18 and good in the s· of the Lord:
9: 18 wickedly in the s· of the Lord, to
12: 25 which is right in the s· of the Lord.
28 good and right in the s· of the Lord

De 17: 2 wickedness in the s' of the Lord
21: 9 which is right in the s' of the Lord.
28: 34 mad for the s' of thine eyes which
67 for the s' of thine eyes which thou
31: 7 unto him in the s' of all Israel,
29 ye will do evil in the s' of the Lord,
34: 12 Moses shewed in the s' of all Israel.
Jos 3: 7 magnify thee in the s' of all Israel,
4: 14 Joshua in the s' of all Israel; and
10: 12 and he said in the s' of Israel, Sun,
23: 5 and drive them from out of your s';
24: 17 did those great signs in our s', and
J'g 2: 11 Israel did evil in the s' of the Lord,
3: 7 Israel did evil in the s' of the Lord,
12 did evil again in the s' of the Lord:
12 had done evil in the s' of the Lord.
4: 1 again did evil in the s' of the Lord,
6: 1 Israel did evil in the s' of the Lord:
17 If now I have found grace in thy s',
21 of the Lord departed out of his s'.
10: 6 did evil again in the s' of the Lord,
13: 1 did evil again in the s' of the Lord;
Ru 2: 2 him in whose s' I shall find grace.
13 Let me find favour in thy s', my
1Sa 1: 18 handmaid find grace in thy s'.
12: 17 ye have done in the s' of the Lord,
15: 17 thou wast little in thine own s',
19 and didst evil in the s' of the Lord?
16: 22 for he hath found favour in my s'.
18: 5 was accepted in the s' of all the
5 also in the s' of Saul's servants.
29: 6 me in the host is good in my s':
9 know that thou art good in my s',
2Sa 6: 22 and will be base in mine own s':
7: 9 off all thine enemies out of thy s',
19 was yet a small thing in thy s',
12: 9 of the Lord, to do evil in his s'?
11 with thy wives in the s' of this sun.
13: 5 dress the meat in my s', that I
6 make me a couple of cakes in my s',
8 made cakes in his s', and did bake
14: 22 that I have found grace in thy s',
16: 4 thee that I may find grace in thy s',
22 concubines in the s' of all Israel.
22: 25 to my cleanness in his eye s'.
1Ki 8: 25 shall not fail thee a man in my s'
9: 7 my name, will I cast out of my s';
11: 6 did evil in the s' of the Lord, and
19 great favour in the s' of Pharaoh,
38 do that is right in my s', to keep
14: 22 Judah did evil in the s' of the Lord,
15: 26, 34 he did evil in the s' of the Lord,
16: 7 evil...he did in the s' of the Lord,
19 in doing evil in the s' of the Lord,
30 Omri did evil in the s' of the Lord
21: 20 to work evil in the s' of the Lord.
25 wickedness in the s' of the Lord,
22: 52 he did evil in the s' of the Lord, and
2Ki 1: 13 thy servants, be precious in thy s'.
14 my life now be precious in thy s'.
3: 2 wrought evil in the s' of the Lord;
18 a light thing in the s' of the Lord:
8: 18 and he did evil in the s' of the Lord.
27 and did evil in the s' of the Lord,
12: 2 was right in the s' of the Lord all
13: 2 which was evil in the s' of the Lord,
11 which was evil in the s' of the Lord;
14: 3 was right in the s' of the Lord,
24 which was evil in the s' of the Lord:
15: 3 was right in the s' of the Lord,
9 which was evil in the s' of the Lord,
18, 24, 28 was evil in the s' of the Lord:
34 was right in the s' of the Lord: he
16: 2 was right in the s' of the Lord his
17: 2 which was evil in the s' of the Lord,
17 to do evil in the s' of the Lord, to
18 and removed them out of his s':
20 until he had cast them out of his s'.
23 Lord removed Israel out of his s',
18: 3 was right in the s' of the Lord,
20: 3 done that which was good in thy s'.
21: 2 which was evil in the s' of the Lord,
6 wickedness in the s' of the Lord,
15 done that which was evil in my s',
16 which was evil in the s' of the Lord.
20 which was evil in the s' of the Lord,
22: 2 was right in the s' of the Lord,
23: 27 remove Judah also out of my s',
32, 37 was evil in the s' of the Lord,
24: 3 to remove them out of his s', for
9, 19 was evil in the s' of the Lord,
1Ch 2: 3 was evil in the s' of the Lord; and
19: 13 do that which is good in his s'.
22: 8 blood upon the earth in my s'.
28: 8 therefore in the s' of all Israel the
29: 25 exceedingly in the s' of all Israel,
2Ch 6: 16 shall not fail thee a man in my s'
7: 20 will I cast out of my s', and will
20: 32 was right in the s' of the Lord.
22: 4 he did evil in the s' of the Lord like
24: 2 was right in the s' of the Lord all
25: 2 was right in the s' of the Lord,
26: 4 was right in the s' of the Lord,
27: 2 was right in the s' of the Lord,
28: 1 was right in the s' of the Lord,
29: 2 was right in the s' of the Lord,
32: 23 magnified in the s' of all nations
33: 2 which was evil in the s' of the Lord,
6 much evil in the s' of the Lord,
22 which was evil in the s' of the Lord,
34: 2 was right in the s' of the Lord,
36: 5 evil in the s' of the Lord his God.
9 which was evil in the s' of the Lord.
12 evil in the s' of the Lord his God.
Ezr 9: 9 us in the s' of the kings of Persia,
Ne 1: 11 him mercy in the s' of this man.

Ne 2: 5 servant have found favour in thy s',
8: 5 book in the s' of all the people;
Es 2: 15 in the s' of all them that looked
17 obtained grace and favour in his s'
5: 2 that she obtained favour in his s':
8 found favour in the s' of the king,
7: 3 have found favour in thy s', O king,
8: 5 and if I have found favour in his s',
Job 15: 15 the heavens are not clean in his s'.
18: 3 beasts, and reputed vile in your s'?
19: 15 stranger: I am an alien in their s'.
21: 8 established in their s' with them,
25: 5 the stars are not pure in his s'.
34: 26 wicked men in...open s' of others;
41: 9 be cast down even at the s' of him?
Ps 5: 5 foolish shall not stand in thy s':
9: 19 the heathen be judged in thy s'.
10: 5 are far above out of his s': as for
19: 14 be acceptable in thy s', O Lord,
51: 4 sinned and done this evil in thy s':
72: 14 precious...their blood be in his s'.
76: 7 who may stand in thy s' when once
78: 12 did he in the s' of their fathers,
79: 10 known among the heathen in our s'
90: 4 For a thousand years in thy s' are
98: 2 shewed in the s' of the heathen.
101: 7 telleth lies shall not tarry in my s'.
116: 15 Precious in the s' of the Lord is the
143: 2 in thy s' shall no man living be
Pr 1: 17 net is spread in the s' of any bird.
3: 4 understanding in the s' of God and
4: 3 beloved in the s' of my mother.
Ec 2: 26 man that is good in his s' wisdom,
6: 9 Better is the s' of the eyes than
8: 3 Be not hasty to go out of his s':
11: 9 heart, and in the s' of thine eyes:
Isa 5: 21 eyes, and prudent in their own s'!
11: 3 not judge after the s' of his eyes,
26: 17 so have we been in thy s', O Lord.
38: 3 done that which is good in thy s'.
43: 4 Since thou wast precious in my s',
Jer 4: 1 thine abominations out of my s',
7: 15 And I will cast you out of my s', as
30 of Judah have done evil in my s',
15: 1 cast them out of my s', and let
18: 10 If it do evil in my s', that it obey not
23 neither blot...their sin from thy s',
19: 10 break the bottle in...s' of the men
32: 12 in the s' of Hanameel mine uncle's
34: 15 and had done right in my s',
43: 9 in the s' of the men of Judah;
51: 24 they have done in Zion in your s',
Eze 4: 12 that cometh out of man, in their s'.
5: 8 of thee in the s' of the nations.
14 thee, in the s' of all that pass by.
10: 2 the city. And he went in in my s'.
19 mounted up from the earth in my s':
12: 3 and remove by day in their s';
3 place to another place in their s':
4 forth thy stuff by day in their s',
4 shalt go forth at even in their s',
5 Dig...through the wall in their s',
6 In their s' shalt thou bear it upon
7 bare it upon my shoulder in their s'.
16: 41 upon thee in the s' of many women:
20: 9 in whose s' I made myself known
14 in whose s' I brought them out.
22 be polluted in the s' of the heathen,
22 in whose s' I brought them forth.
43 lothe yourselves in your own s'
21: 23 as a false divination in their s',
22: 16 in thyself in the s' of the heathen,
28: 18 the s' of all them that behold thee.
25 in them in the s' of the heathen,
36: 31 lothe yourselves in your own s'
34 in the s' of all that passed by.
39: 27 in them in the s' of many nations;
43: 11 and write it in their s', that they
Da 4: 11 and the s' thereof to the end of all
20 and the s' thereof to all the earth;
Ho 2: 2 her whoredoms out of her s',
10 lewdness in the s' of her lovers,
6: 2 us up, and we shall live in his s'.
Am 9: 3 though they be hid from my s' in
Jon 2: 4 Then I said, I am cast out of thy s';
Mal 2: 17 evil is good in the s' of the Lord,
M't 11: 5 The blind receive their s', and the
26 for so it seemed good in thy s'.
20: 34 immediately their eyes received s',
M'r 10: 51 Lord, that I might receive my s'.
52 And immediately he received his s',
Lu 1: 15 shall be great in the s' of the Lord,
4: 18 and recovering of s' to the blind,
7: 21 many that were blind he gave s'.
10: 21 for so it seemed good in thy s'.
15: 21 against heaven, and in thy s',
16: 15 is abomination in the s' of God.
18: 41 Lord, that I may receive my s'.
42 Jesus said unto him, Receive thy s':
43 And immediately he received his s',
23: 48 that came together to that s',
24: 31 him; and he vanished out of their s'.
Joh 9: 11 went and washed, and I received s'.
15 him how he had received his s'.
18 had been blind, and received his s',
18 parents of him that...received his s'.
Ac 1: 9 cloud received him out of their s'.
4: 19 Whether it be right in...s' of God
7: 10 and wisdom in the s' of Pharaoh
31 saw it, he wondered at the s':
8: 21 heart is not right in the s' of God.
9: 9 And he was three days without s',
12 him, that he might receive his s'.
17 that thou mightest receive thy s',
18 he received s' forthwith, and arose,
10: 31 in remembrance in the s' of God.

Ac 22: 13 me, Brother Saul, receive thy s'.
Ro 3: 20 shall no flesh be justified in his s':
12: 17 things honest in the s' of all men.
2Co 2: 17 the s' of God speak we in Christ.
4: 2 man's conscience in the s' of God.
5: 7 (For we walk by faith, not by s':)
7: 12 care for you in the s' of God might
8: 21 not only in the s' of the Lord, but
21 Lord, but also in the s' of men.
Ga 3: 11 by the law in the s' of God, it is
Col 1: 22 and unreproveable in his s':
1Th 1: 3 in the s' of God and our Father;
1Ti 2: 3 in the s' of God our Saviour;
6: 13 I give thee charge in the s' of God,
Heb 4: 13 that is not manifest in his s':
12: 21 And so terrible was the s', that
13: 21 that which is wellpleasing in his s',
Jas 4: 10 yourselves in the s' of the Lord,
1Pe 3: 4 is in the s' of God of great price.
1Jo 3: 22 things that are pleasing in his s'.
Re 4: 3 throne, in s' like unto an emerald.
13: 13 on the earth in the s' of men,
14 power to do in the s' of the beast;

sights
Lu 21: 11 fearful s' and great signs shall

sign See also ENSIGN; SIGNED; SIGNS.
Ex 4: 8 hearken to the voice of the first s',
8 will believe the voice of the latter s'.
8: 23 people: to morrow shall this s' be.
13: 9 for a s' unto thee upon thine hand,
31: 13 for it is a s' between me and you
17 a s' between me and the children of
Nu 16: 38 they shall be a s' unto the children
26: 10 fifty men: and they became a s'.
De 6: 8 bind them for a s' upon thine hand,
11: 18 bind them for a s' upon your hand,
13: 1 and giveth thee a s' or a wonder,
2 the s' or the wonder come to pass,
28: 46 they shall be upon thee for a s' and
Jos 4: 6 That this may be a s' among you,
J'g 6: 17 me a s' that thou talkest with me.
20: 38 there was an appointed s' between
1Sa 2: 34 this shall be a s' unto thee, that
14: 10 hand: and this shall be a s' unto us.
1Ki 13: 3 he gave a s' the same day, saying,
3 the s' which the Lord hath spoken;
5 according to the s' which the man of
2Ki 19: 29 And this shall be a s' unto thee, Ye
20: 8 What shall be the s' that the Lord
9 This s' shalt thou have of the Lord,
2Ch 32: 24 unto him, and he gave him a s'.
Isa 7: 11 Ask thee a s' of the Lord thy God;
14 the Lord himself shall give you a s';
19: 20 it shall be for a s' and for a witness
20: 3 s' and wonder upon Egypt and upon
37: 30 this shall be a s' unto thee, Ye shall
38: 7 this shall be a s' unto thee from the
22 What is the s' that I shall go up to
55: 13 for an everlasting s' that shall not be
66: 19 I will set a s' among them, and I
Jer 6: 1 up a s' of fire in Beth-haccerem:
44: 29 And this shall be a s' unto you,
Eze 4: 3 shall be a s' to the house of Israel.
12: 6 for a s' unto the house of Israel.
11 Say, I am your s': like as I have
14: 8 will make him a s' and a proverb,
20: 12 to be a s' between me and them,
20 shall be a s' between me and you,
24: 24 Thus Ezekiel is unto you a s':
27 and thou shalt be a s' unto them;
39: 15 then shall he set up a s' by it, till
Da 6: 8 and s' the writing, that it be not
M't 12: 38 we would see a s' from thee.
39 generation seeketh after a s';
39 and there shall no s' be given to it,
39 but the s' of the prophet Jonas:
16: 1 would shew them a s' from heaven.
4 generation seeketh after a s';
4 and there...no s' be given unto it,
4 but the s' of the prophet Jonas.
24: 3 what shall be the s' of thy coming,
30 appear the s' of the Son of man in
26: 48 that betrayed him gave them a s',
M'r 8: 11 seeking of him a s' from heaven,
12 doth this generation seek after a s'?
12 no s' be given unto this generation.
13: 4 what shall be the s' when all these
Lu 2: 12 And this shall be a s' unto you; Ye
34 and for a s' which shall be spoken
11: 16 sought of him a s' from heaven.
29 an evil generation: they seek a s';
29 and there shall no s' be given it,
29 but the s' of Jonas the prophet.
30 Jonas was a s' unto the Ninevites,
21: 7 what s' will there be when these
Joh 2: 18 him, What s' shewest thou unto us,
6: 30 What s' shewest thou then, that we
Ac 28: 11 whose s' was Castor and Pollux.
Ro 4: 11 he received the s' of circumcision,
1Co 1: 22 For the Jews require a s', and the
14: 22 Wherefore tongues are for a s',
Re 15: 1 I saw another s' in heaven, great

signed See also ASSIGNED.
Da 6: 9 king Darius s' the writing and the
10 Daniel knew that the writing was s',
12 Hast thou not s' a decree, that
13 nor the decree that thou hast s', but

signet See also SIGNETS.
Ge 38: 18 Thy s', and thy bracelets, and thy
25 the s', and bracelets, and staff.
Ex 28: 11 stone, like the engravings of a s',
21 names, like the engravings of a s';
36 upon it, like the engravings of a s',
39: 14 names, like the engravings of a s',
30 like to the engravings of a s',

Jer 22:24 were the s' upon my right hand,
Da 6:17 the king sealed it with his own s',
17 and with the s' of his lords; that the
Hag 2:23 Lord, and will make thee as a s':

signets
Ex 39: 6 of gold, graven, as s' are graven,

signification
1Co 14:10 and none of them is without s'.

signified
Ac 11:28 s' by the spirit that there should be
Re 1: 1 s' it by his angel unto his servant

signifieth
Heb 12:27 s' the removing of those things

signify See also SIGNIFIED; SIGNIFIETH; SIGNIFYING.
Ac 21:26 to s' the accomplishment of the
23:15 to the council s' to the chief captain
25:27 to s' the crimes laid against him.
1Pe 1:11 of Christ which was in them did s',

signifying
Joh 12:33 said, s' what death he should die.
18:32 spake, s' what death he should die.
21:19 s' by what death he should glorify
Heb 9: 8 The Holy Ghost this s', that the

signs See also ENSIGNS.
Ge 1:14 let them be for s', and for seasons,
Ex 4: 9 will not believe also these two s',
17 hand, wherewith thou shalt do s'.
28 all the s' which he had commanded
30 did the s' in the sight of the people.
7: 3 my s' and my wonders in the land of
10: 1 might shew these my s' before him:
2 and my s' which I have done among
Nu 14:11 for all the s' which I have shewed
De 4:34 by s', and by wonders, and by war,
6:22 the Lord shewed s' and wonders,
7:19 and the s', and the wonders, and the
26: 8 and with s', and with wonders:
29: 3 the s', and those great miracles:
34:11 In all the s' and the wonders, which
Jos 24:17 which did those great s' in our sight,
1Sa 10: 7 when these s' are come unto thee,
9 all those s' came to pass that day.
Ne 9:10 s' and wonders upon Pharaoh, and
Ps 74: 4 they set up their ensigns for s'.
9 We see not our s': there is no more
78:43 How he had wrought his s' in Egypt,
105:27 shewed his s' among them,
Isa 8:18 are for s' and for wonders in Israel
Jer 10: 2 not dismayed at the s' of heaven;
32:20 hast set s' and wonders in the land
21 out of the land of Egypt with s', and
Da 4: 2 I thought it good to shew the s' and
3 How great are his s'! and how
6:27 and he worketh s' and wonders in
M't 16: 3 ye not discern the s' of the times?
24:24 shall shew great s' and wonders;
M'r 13:22 and shall shew s' and wonders, to
16:17 And these s' shall follow them that
20 and confirming the word with s'
Lu 1:62 they made s' to his father, how he
21:11 s' shall there be from heaven.
25 And there shall be s' in the sun,
Joh 4:48 Except ye see s' and wonders, ye
20:30 many other s' truly did Jesus in the
Ac 2:19 above, and s' in the earth beneath;
22 by miracles and wonders and s',
43 wonders and s' were done by the
4:30 that s' and wonders may be done by
5:12 were many s' and wonders wrought
7:36 shewed wonders and s' in the land
8:13 miracles and s' which were done.
14: 3 granted s' and wonders to be done
Ro 15:19 Through mighty s' and wonders, by
2Co 12:12 Truly the s' of an apostle were
12 in s', and wonders, and mighty
2Th 2: 9 of Satan with all power and s' and
Heb 2: 4 witness, both with s' and wonders,

Sihon (*si'-hon*)
Nu 21:21 Israel sent messengers unto S',
23 S' would not suffer Israel to pass
23 but S' gathered all his people
26 For Heshbon was the city of S' the
27 city of S' be built and prepared:
28 a flame from the city of S': it hath
29 into captivity unto S' king of the
34 him as thou didst unto S' king of
32:33 kingdom of S' king of the Amorites,
De 1: 4 After he had slain S' the king of
2:24 into thine hand S' the Amorite,
26 wilderness of Kedemoth unto S'
30 S' king of Heshbon would not let us
31 have begun to give S' and his land
32 Then S' came out against us, he
3: 2 as thou didst unto S' king of the
6 as we did unto S' king of Heshbon,
4:46 land of S' king of the Amorites,
29: 7 this place, S' the king of Heshbon,
31: 4 shall do unto them as he did to S'
Jos 2:10 the other side Jordan, S' and Og,
9:10 to S' king of Heshbon, and to Og
12: 2 S' king of the Amorites, who dwelt
5 the border of S' king of Heshbon.
13:10 cities of S' king of the Amorites,
21 all the kingdom of S' king of the
21 which were dukes of S', dwelling
27 kingdom of S' king of Heshbon,
J'g 11:19 Israel sent messengers unto S'
20 But S' trusted not Israel to pass
20 S' gathered all his people together,
21 Lord God of Israel delivered S' and
1Ki 4:19 country of S' king of the Amorites,

Ne 9:22 So they possessed the land of S',
Ps 135:11 S' king of the Amorites, and Og
136:19 S' king of the Amorites: for his
Jer 48:45 and a flame from the midst of S',

Sihor (*si'-hor*) See also SHIHOR.
Jos 13: 3 From S', which is before Egypt,
Isa 23: 3 And by great waters the seed of S',
Jer 2:18 Egypt, to drink the waters of S'?

Silas (*si'-las*) See also SILVANUS.
Ac 15:22 Barsabas,...S', chief men among
27 have sent therefore Judas and S',
32 Judas and S', being prophets also
34 it pleased S' to abide there still.
40 And Paul chose S', and departed,
16:19 they caught Paul and S', and drew
25 at midnight Paul and S' prayed,
29 and fell down before Paul and S',
17: 4 and consorted with Paul and S';
10 sent away Paul and S' by night
14 but S' and Timotheus abode there
15 receiving a commandment unto S'
18: 5 when S' and Timotheus were come

silence
J'g 3:19 thee, O king: who said, Keep s'.
Job 4:16 there was s', and I heard a voice,
29:21 waited, and kept s' at my counsel.
31:34 that I kept s', and went not out of
Ps 31:18 Let the lying lips be put to s';
32: 3 When I kept s', my bones waxed
35:22 keep not s': O Lord, be not far
39: 2 I was dumb with s', I held my
50: 3 shall come, and shall not keep s':
21 hast thou done, and I kept s';
83: 1 Keep not thou s', O God: hold not
94:17 my soul had almost dwelt in s'.
115:17 neither any that go down into s'.
Ec 3: 7 a time to keep s', and a time to
Isa 15: 1 is laid waste, and brought to s';
41: 1 Keep s' before me, O islands; and
62: 6 mention of the Lord, keep not s',
65: 6 I will not keep s', but will
Jer 8:14 the Lord our God hath put us to s',
La 2:10 sit upon the ground, and keep s':
3:28 He sitteth alone and keepeth s',
Am 5:13 Therefore the prudent shall keep s'
8: 3 shall cast them forth with s'.
Hab 2:20 temple: let all the earth keep s'
M't 22:34 he had put the Sadducees to s',
Ac 15:12 Then all the multitude kept s',
21:40 when there was made a great s',
22: 2 to them, they kept the more s':
1Co 14:28 let him keep s' in the church; and
34 Let your women keep s' in the
1Ti 2:11 Let the woman learn in s' with all
12 over the man, but to be in s'.
1Pe 2:15 put to s' the ignorance of foolish
Re 8: 1 there was s' in heaven about the

silent
1Sa 2: 9 the wicked shall be s' in darkness;
Ps 22: 2 in the night season, and am not s'.
28: 1 O Lord my rock; be not s' to me:
1 lest, if thou be s' to me, I become
30:12 sing praise to thee, and not be s'.
31:17 and let them be s' in the grave.
Isa 47: 5 Sit thou s', and get thee into
Jer 8:14 cities, and let us be s' there: for
Zec 2:13 Be s', O all flesh, before the Lord:

silk
Pr 31:22 her clothing is s' and purple.
Eze 16:10 linen, and I covered thee with s'.
13 raiment was of fine linen, and s',
Re 18:12 and purple, and s', and scarlet,

Silla (*sil'-lah*)
2Ki 12:20 Millo, which goeth down to S'.

silly
Job 5: 2 man, and envy slayeth the s' one.
Ho 7:11 Ephraim also is like a s' dove
2Ti 3: 6 lead captive s' women laden with

Siloah (*si-lo'-ah*) See also SHILOAH; SILOAM.
Ne 3:15 the wall of the pool of S' by the

Siloam (*si-lo'-am*) See also SILOAH.
Lu 13: 4 upon whom the tower in S' fell,
Joh 9: 7 him, Go, wash in the pool of S',
11 said unto me, Go to the pool of S',

Silvanus (*sil-va'-nus*) See also SILAS.
2Co 1:19 even by me and S' and Timotheus,
1Th 1: 1 Paul, and S', and Timotheus, unto
2Th 1: 1 Paul, and S', and Timotheus, unto
1Pe 5:12 By S', a faithful brother unto you,

silver See also SILVERLINGS; SILVERSMITH.
Ge 13: 2 was very rich in cattle, in s', and
20:16 thy brother a thousand pieces of s':
23:15 worth four hundred shekels of s';
16 Abraham weighed to Ephron the s',
16 four hundred shekels of s', current
24:35 given him flocks, and herds, and s',
53 servants brought forth jewels of s',
37:28 Ishmeelites for twenty pieces of s':
44: 2 the s' cup, in the sack's mouth of
8 we steal out of thy lord's house s' or
45:22 he gave three hundred pieces of s',
Ex 3:22 in her house, jewels of s', and
11: 2 of her neighbour, jewels of s', and
12:35 of the Egyptians jewels of s', and
20:23 shall not make with me gods of s',
21:32 their master thirty shekels of s',
25: 3 of them; gold, and s', and brass,
26:19 forty sockets of s' under the twenty
21 And their forty sockets of s'; two
25 boards, and their sockets of s',
32 gold, upon the four sockets of s'.

Ex 27:10 pillars and their fillets shall be of s'.
11 the pillars and their fillets of s'.
17 the court shall be filleted with s';
17 their hooks shall be of s', and their
31: 4 to work in gold, and in s', and in
35: 5 the Lord; gold, and s', and brass,
24 offer an offering of s' and brass
32 to work in gold, and in s', and in
36:24 forty sockets of s' he made under
26 And their forty sockets of s'; two
30 sockets were sixteen sockets of s',
36 he cast for them four sockets of s'.
38:10 pillars and their fillets were of s'.
11, 12 pillars and their fillets of s'.
17 the pillars and their fillets of s';
17 overlaying of their chapiters of s';
17 of the court were filleted with s'.
19 their hooks of s', and the overlaying
19 their chapiters and their fillets of s'.
25 the s' of them that were numbered
27 the hundred talents of s' were cast
Le 5:15 with thy estimation by shekels of s',
27: 3 estimation shall be fifty shekels of s',
6 be of the male five shekels of s',
6 for the female...three shekels of s'.
16 be valued at fifty shekels of s'.
Nu 7:13 And his offering was one s' charger,
13 one s' bowl of seventy shekels,
19 for his offering one s' charger,
19 one s' bowl of seventy shekels,
25 His offering was one s' charger,
25 one s' bowl of seventy shekels,
31 His offering was one s' charger of
31 one s' bowl of seventy shekels,
37 His offering was one s' charger,
37 one s' bowl of seventy shekels,
43 His offering was one s' charger of
43 a s' bowl of seventy shekels, after
49 His offering was one s' charger
49 one s' bowl of seventy shekels,
55 His offering was one s' charger of
55 one s' bowl of seventy shekels,
61 His offering was one s' charger,
61 one s' bowl of seventy shekels,
67 His offering was one s' charger,
67 one s' bowl of seventy shekels,
73 His offering was one s' charger,
73 one s' bowl of seventy shekels,
79 His offering was one s' charger,
79 one s' bowl of seventy shekels,
84 chargers of s', twelve s' bowls,
85 Each charger of s' weighing an
85 s' vessels weighed two thousand
10: 2 Make thee two trumpets of s'; of a
22:18 give me his house full of s' and gold,
24:13 give me his house full of s' and gold,
31:22 Only the gold, and the s', the brass,
De 7:25 thou shalt not desire the s' or gold
8:13 thy s' and thy gold is multiplied,
17:17 multiply to himself s' and gold.
22:19 him in an hundred shekels of s',
29 damsel's father fifty shekels of s',
29:17 idols, wood and stone, s' and gold,
Jos 6:19 But all the s', and gold, and vessels
24 only the s', and the gold, and the
7:21 and two hundred shekels of s', and
21 midst of my tent, and the s' under it.
22 hid in his tent, and the s' under it.
24 and the s', and the garment, and the
22: 8 with s', and with gold, and with
24:32 for an hundred pieces of s':
J'g 9: 4 him threescore and ten pieces of s'
16: 5 of us eleven hundred pieces of s'.
17: 2 The eleven hundred shekels of s'
2 mine ears, behold, the s' is with me;
3 the eleven hundred shekels of s'
3 dedicated the s' unto the Lord
4 took two hundred shekels of s',
10 and I will give thee ten shekels of s'
1Sa 2:36 and crouch to him for a piece of s'
9: 8 the fourth part of a shekel of s':
2Sa 8:10 brought with him vessels of s',
11 s' and gold that he had dedicated
18:11 have given thee ten shekels of s',
12 receive a thousand shekels of s' in
21: 4 We will have no s' nor gold of Saul,
24:24 and the oxen for fifty shekels of s'.
1Ki 7:51 even the s', and the gold, and the
10:21 were of pure gold; none were of s':
22 bringing gold, and s', ivory, and
25 vessels of s', and vessels of gold,
27 s' to be in Jerusalem as stones,
29 for six hundred shekels of s', and
15:15 into the house of the Lord, s', and
18 Asa took all the s' and the gold
19 unto thee a present of s' and gold;
16:24 of Shemer for the two talents of s',
20: 3 Thy s' and thy gold is mine; thy
5 Thou shalt deliver me thy s', and
7 and for my s', and for my gold;
39 or else thou shalt pay a talent of s'.
2Ki 5: 5 and took with him ten talents of s',
22 give them, I pray thee, a talent of s',
23 bound two talents of s' in two bags,
6:25 was sold for fourscore pieces of s',
25 of dove's dung for five pieces of s'.
7: 8 and carried thence s', and gold, and
12:13 the house of the Lord bowls of s',
13 any vessels of gold, or vessels of s',
14:14 And he took all the gold and s', and
15:19 gave Pul a thousand talents of s',
20 of each man fifty shekels of s', to
16: 8 Ahaz took the s' and gold that was
18:14 Judah three hundred talents of s'
15 Hezekiah gave him all the s' that
20:13 the s', and the gold, and the spices,

2Ki 22: 4 may sum the s' which is brought
23: 33 tribute of an hundred talents of s',
35 Jehoiakim gave the s' and the gold
35 he exacted the s' and the gold of the
25: 15 were of gold, in gold, and of s', in s',
1Ch 18: 10 all manner of vessels of gold and s'
11 s' and the gold that he brought
19: 6 sent a thousand talents of s' to hire
22: 14 a thousand thousand talents of s';
16 Of the gold, the s', and the brass,
28: 14 of all manner of service; s' also
14 for all instruments of s' by weight
15 for the candlesticks of s' by weight,
16 and likewise s' for the tables of s':
17 for every bason; and likewise s'
17 by weight for every bason of s':
29: 2 of gold, and the s' for things of s',
3 own proper good, of gold and s',
4 seven thousand talents of refined s',
5 of gold, and the s' for things of s',
7 and of s' ten thousand talents, and
2Ch 1: 15 made s' and gold...as plenteous
17 for six hundred shekels of s', and
2: 7 cunning to work in gold, and in s',
14 skilful to work in gold, and in s',
5: 1 and the s', and the gold, and all the
9: 14 brought gold and s' to Solomon.
20 were of pure gold: none were of s';
21 bringing gold, and s', ivory, and
24 vessels of s', and vessels of gold,
27 made s' in Jerusalem as stones,
15: 18 dedicated, s', and gold, and vessels.
16: 2 Asa brought out s' and gold out of
3 behold, I have sent thee s' and gold;
17: 11 brought...presents, and tribute s';
21: 3 father gave them great gifts of s',
24: 14 spoons, and vessels of gold and s'.
25: 6 Israel for an hundred talents of s'.
24 And he took all the gold and the s',
27: 5 same year an hundred talents of s',
32: 27 he made himself treasuries for s',
36: 3 the land in an hundred talents of s'
Ezr 1: 4 men of his place help him with s'
6 hands with vessels of s', with gold,
9 of gold, a thousand chargers of s',
10 s' basons of a second sort four
11 All the vessels of gold and of s'
2: 69 and five thousand pound of s',
5: 14 And the vessels also of gold and s'
6: 5 also let the golden and s' vessels
7: 15 And to carry the s' and gold, which
16 all the s' and gold that thou canst
18 with the rest of the s' and the gold,
22 Unto an hundred talents of s', and
8: 25 And weighed unto them the s',
26 six hundred and fifty talents of s',
26 and s' vessels an hundred talents,
28 the s' and the gold are a freewill
30 the weight of the s', and the gold,
33 was the s' and the gold...weighed
Ne 5: 15 and wine, beside forty shekels of s';
7: 71 and two hundred pound of s'.
72 gold, and two thousand pound of s',
Es 1: 6 to s' rings and pillars of marble:
6 the beds were of gold and s', upon
3: 9 I will pay ten thousand talents of s'
11 s' is given to thee, the people also,
Job 3: 15 who filled their houses with s':
22: 25 and thou shalt have plenty of s'.
27: 16 Though he heap up s' as the dust,
17 and the innocent shall divide the s'.
28: 1 Surely there is a vein for the s',
15 s' be weighed for the price thereof.
Ps 12: 6 as s' tried in a furnace of earth,
66: 10 thou hast tried us, as s' is tried.
68: 13 the wings of a dove covered with s',
30 submit himself with pieces of s':
105: 37 He brought them forth also with s'
115: 4 Their idols are s' and gold, the work
119: 72 me than thousands of gold and s'.
135: 15 idols of the heathen are s' and gold,
Pr 2: 4 If thou seekest her as s', and
3: 14 is better than the merchandise of s',
8: 10 Receive my instruction, and not s';
19 and my revenue than choice s'.
10: 20 tongue of the just is as choice s':
16: 16 rather to be chosen than s'!
17: 3 fining pot is for s', and the furnace
22: 1 and loving favour rather than s' and
25: 4 Take away the dross from the s',
11 like apples of gold in pictures of s'.
26: 23 a potsherd covered with s' dross.
27: 21 fining pot for s', and the furnace
Ec 2: 8 I gathered me also s' and gold, and
5: 10 He that loveth s' shall not be
10 shall not be satisfied with s';
12: 6 Or ever the s' cord be loosed, or the
Ca 1: 11 borders of gold with studs of s'.
3: 10 He made the pillars thereof of s',
8: 9 will build upon her a palace of s':
11 was to bring a thousand pieces of s'.
Isa 1: 22 Thy s' is become dross, thy wine
2: 7 Their land also is full of s' and gold,
20 day a man shall cast his idols of s',
13: 17 Medes...which shall not regard s';
30: 22 covering of thy graven images of s',
31: 7 man shall cast away his idols of s',
39: 2 the s', and the gold, and the spices,
40: 19 with gold, and casteth s' chains.
46: 6 and weigh s' in the balance, and
48: 10 I have refined thee, but not with s';
60: 9 their s' and their gold with them,
17 and for iron I will bring s', and for
Jer 6: 30 Reprobate s' shall men call them,
10: 4 They deck it with s' and with gold;
9 S' spread into plates is brought

Jer 32: 9 even seventeen shekels of s'.
52: 19 gold, and that which was of s' in s',
Eze 7: 19 shall cast their s' in the streets,
19 their s' and their gold shall not be
16: 13 wast thou decked with gold and s';
17 fair jewels of my gold and of my s',
22: 18 they are even the dross of s'.
20 they gather s', and brass, and iron,
22 As s' is melted in the midst of the
27: 12 with s', iron, tin, and lead, they
28: 4 gold and s' into thy treasures:
38: 13 to carry away s' and gold, to take
Da 2: 32 gold, his breast and his arms of s',
35 clay, the brass, the s', and the gold,
45 brass, the clay, the s', and the gold;
5: 2 to bring the golden and s' vessels
4 praised the gods of gold, and of s',
23 thou hast praised the gods of s',
11: 8 with their precious vessels of s'
38 shall he honour with gold, and s',
43 the treasures of gold and of s', and
Ho 2: 8 and multiplied her s' and gold,
3: 2 her to me for fifteen pieces of s',
8: 4 of their s' and their gold have they
9: 6 pleasant places for their s', nettles
13: 2 them molten images of their s', and
Joe 3: 5 ye have taken my s' and my gold,
Am 2: 6 they sold the righteous for s', and
8: 6 That we may buy the poor for s',
Na 2: 9 Take ye the spoil of s', take the
Hab 2: 19 it is laid over with gold and s', and
Zep 1: 11 all they that bear s' are cut off:
18 Neither their s' nor their gold shall
Hag 2: 8 s' is mine, and the gold is mine,
Zec 6: 11 Then take s' and gold, and make
9: 3 heaped up s' as the dust, and fine
11: 12 for my price thirty pieces of s'.
13 I took the thirty pieces of s', and
13: 9 and will refine them as s' is refined,
14: 14 together, gold, and s', and apparel,
Mal 3: 3 sit as a refiner and purifier of s':
3 and purge them as gold and s',
M't 10: 9 neither gold, nor s', nor brass in
26: 15 with him for thirty pieces of s'.
27: 3 the thirty pieces of s' to the chief
5 he cast down the pieces of s' in the
6 the chief priests took the s' pieces,
9 took the thirty pieces of s', the price
Lu 15: 8 what woman having ten pieces...s',
Ac 3: 6 said, S' and gold have I none; but
17: 29 the Godhead is like unto gold, or s',
19: 19 found it fifty thousand pieces of s'.
24 which make s' shrines for Diana,
20: 33 I have coveted no man's s', or gold,
1Co 3: 12 this foundation gold, s', precious
2Ti 2: 20 not only vessels of gold and of s',
Jas 5: 3 Your gold and s' is cankered; and
1Pe 1: 18 corruptible things, as s' and gold,
Re 9: 20 devils, and idols of gold, and s', and
18: 12 The merchandise of gold, and s',

silverlings
Isa 7: 23 a thousand vines at a thousand s',

silversmith
Ac 19: 24 certain man named Demetrius, a s',

Simeon (*sim'-e-un*) See also SHIMEON; SIMEONITES; SIMON.
Ge 29: 33 also: and she called his name S'.
34: 25 of the sons of Jacob, S' and Levi,
30 And Jacob said to S' and Levi, Ye
35: 23 and S', and Levi, and Judah, and
42: 24 and took from them S', and bound
36 Joseph is not, and S' is not, and ye
43: 23 And he brought S' out unto them.
46: 10 And the sons of S'; Jemuel, and
48: 5 as Reuben and S', they shall be
49: 5 S' and Levi are brethren;
Ex 1: 2 Reuben, S', Levi, and Judah,
6: 15 And the sons of S'; Jemuel, and
15 woman: these are the families of S'.
Nu 1: 6 Of S'; Shelumiel the son of
22 Of the children of S', by their
23 even of the tribe of S', were fifty
2: 12 by him shall be the tribe of S':
12 captain of the children of S' shall
7: 36 prince of the children of S', did
10: 19 of the tribe of the children of S'
13: 5 Of the tribe of S', Shaphat the son
26: 12 The sons of S' after their families:
34: 20 of the tribe of the children of S',
De 27: 12 S', and Levi, and Judah, and
Jos 19: 1 the second lot came forth to S',
1, 8 children of S' according to their
9 inheritance of the children of S':
9 children of S' had their inheritance
21: 4 and out of the tribe of S', and out
9 of the tribe of the children of S',
J'g 1: 3 Judah said unto S' his brother,
3 into thy lot. So S' went with him.
17 Judah went with S' his brother,
1Ch 2: 1 Reuben, S', Levi, and Judah,
4: 24 The sons of S' were, Nemuel, and
42 even of the sons of S', five hundred
6: 65 of the tribe of the children of S',
12: 25 Of the children of S', mighty men
2Ch 15: 9 Ephraim and Manasseh,...out of S':
34: 6 and S', even unto Naphtali, with
Eze 48: 24 west side, S' shall have a portion.
25 by the border of S', from the east
33 one gate of S', one gate of
Lu 2: 25 Jerusalem, whose name was S';
34 And S' blessed them, and said unto
3: 30 Which was the son of S', which was
Ac 13: 1 and S' that was called Niger, and
15: 14 S' hath declared how God at the
Re 7: 7 the tribe of S' were sealed twelve

Simeonites (*sim'-e-un-ites*)
Nu 25: 14 of a chief house among the S'.
26: 14 These are the families of the S',
1Ch 27: 16 of the S', Shephatiah the son of

similitude See also SIMILITUDES.
Nu 12: 8 the s' of the Lord shall he behold:
De 4: 12 voice of the words, but saw no s';
15 ye saw no manner of s' on the day
16 the s' of any figure, the likeness of
2Ch 4: 3 under it was the s' of oxen, which
Ps 106: 20 their glory into the s' of an ox
144: 12 polished after the s' of a palace:
Da 10: 16 s' of the sons of men touched my
Ro 5: 14 the s' of Adam's transgression,
Heb 7: 15 the s' of Melchisedec there ariseth
Jas 3: 9 are made after the s' of God.

similitudes
Ho 12: 10 and used s', by the ministry of the

Simon (*si'-mun*) See also BAR-JONA; NIGER; PETER; SIMEON; SIMON'S; ZELOTES.
M't 4: 18 S' called Peter, and Andrew his
10: 2 The first, S', who is called Peter,
4 S' the Canaanite, and Judas
13: 55 and Joses, and S', and Judas?
16: 16 S' Peter answered and said, Thou
17 Blessed art thou, S' Bar-jona: for
17: 25 What thinkest thou, S'? of whom
26: 6 in the house of S' the leper,
27: 32 a man of Cyrene, S' by name: him
M'r 1: 16 he saw S' and Andrew his brother
29 entered into the house of S' and
36 S' and they that were with him
3: 16 And S' he surnamed Peter;
18 Thaddæus, and S' the Canaanite,
6: 3 and Joses, and of Juda, and S'?
14: 3 in the house of S' the leper, as he
37 saith unto Peter, S', sleepest thou?
15: 21 they compel one S' a Cyrenian, who
Lu 5: 4 he said unto S', Launch out into
5 And S' answering said unto him,
8 When S' Peter saw it, he fell down
10 which were partners with S'.
10 Jesus said unto S', Fear not; from
6: 14 S', (whom he also named Peter,)
15 of Alphæus, and S' called Zelotes,
7: 40 S', I have somewhat to say unto
43 S' answered and said, I suppose
44 unto S', Seest thou this woman?
22: 31 S', S', behold, Satan hath desired
23: 26 away, they laid hold upon one S',
24: 34 indeed, and hath appeared to S'.
Joh 1: 40 was Andrew, S' Peter's brother.
41 He first findeth his own brother S',
42 Thou art S' the son of Jona: thou
6: 8 Andrew, S' Peter's brother, saith
68 Then S' Peter answered him, Lord,
71 of Judas Iscariot the son of S': for
13: 6 Then cometh he to S' Peter: and
9 S' Peter saith unto him, Lord, not
24 S' Peter therefore beckoned to him,
26 it to Judas Iscariot, the son of S'.
36 S' Peter said unto him, Lord,
18: 10 S' Peter having a sword drew it,
15 S' Peter followed Jesus, and so did
25 S' Peter stood and warmed himself.
20: 2 runneth, and cometh to S' Peter,
6 cometh S' Peter following him, and
21: 2 There were together S' Peter, and
3 S' Peter saith unto them, I go a
7 when S' Peter heard that it was
11 S' Peter went up, and drew the net
15 Jesus saith to S' Peter, S', son of
16, 17 S', son of Jonas, lovest thou me?
Ac 1: 13 S' Zelotes, and Judas the brother
8: 9 there was a certain man, called S',
13 Then S' himself believed also: and
18 when S' saw that through laying
24 Then answered S', and said, Pray
9: 43 days in Joppa with one S' a tanner.
10: 5 for one S', whose surname is Peter:
6 He lodgeth with one S' a tanner,
18 S', which was surnamed Peter,
32 call hither S', whose surname is
32 in the house of one S' a tanner by
11: 13 call for S', whose surname is Peter;
2Pe 1: 1 S' Peter, a servant and an apostle

Simon's (*si'-muns*)
M'r 1: 30 But S' wife's mother lay sick of a
Lu 4: 38 and entered into S' house. And
38 S' wife's mother was taken with a
5: 3 into one of the ships, which was S',
Joh 12: 4 disciples, Judas Iscariot, S' son,
13: 2 the heart of Judas Iscariot, S' son,
Ac 10: 17 had made enquiry for S' house,

simple
Ps 19: 7 Lord is sure, making wise the s'.
116: 6 The Lord preserveth the s': I was
119: 130 giveth understanding unto the s'.
Pr 1: 4 To give subtilty to the s', to the
22 How long, ye s' ones, will ye love
32 the turning away of the s' shall
7: 7 And beheld among the s' ones, I
8: 5 O ye s', understand wisdom: and,
9: 4 Whoso is s', let him turn in hither:
13 she is s', and knoweth nothing.
16 Whoso is s', let him turn in hither:
14: 15 The s' believeth every word: but
18 s' inherit folly: but the prudent
19: 25 a scorner, and the s' will beware:
21: 11 is punished, the s' is made wise:
22: 3 the s' pass on, and are punished.
27: 12 the s' pass on, and are punished.
Eze 45: 20 that erreth, and for him that is s':

Ro 16:18 deceive the hearts of the s'.
19 is good, and s' concerning evil.

simplicity
2Sa 15:11 and they went in their s', and they
Pr 1:22 ye simple ones, will ye love s'?
Ro 12: 8 that giveth, let him do it with s';
2Co 1:12 that in s' and godly sincerity, not
11: 3 from the s' that is in Christ.

Simri (*sim'-ri*) See also SHIMRI.
1Ch 26:10 Hosah,...had sons; S' the chief,

sin See also SINFUL; SINNED; SINNEST; SINNETH; SINNING; SINS.
Ge 4: 7 doest not well, s' lieth at the door.
18:20 because their s' is very grievous;
20: 9 me and on my kingdom a great s'?
31:36 what is my s', that thou hast so
39: 9 wickedness, and s' against God?
42:22 saying, Do not s' against the child;
50:17 of thy brethren, and their s';
Ex 10:17 forgive,...my s' only this once,
20:20 before your faces, that ye s' not.
23:33 lest they make thee s' against me:
29:14 the camp: it is a s' offering.
36 every day a bullock for a s' offering
30:10 of the s' offering of atonements:
32:21 brought so great a s' upon them?
30 people, Ye have sinned a great s':
30 make an atonement for your s'.
31 this people have sinned a great s',
32 now, if thou wilt forgive their s'—;
34 visit I will visit their s' upon them.
34: 7 iniquity and transgression and s',
9 pardon our iniquity and our s',
Le 4: 2 a soul shall s' through ignorance
3 If the priest that is anointed do s'
3 according to the s' of the people;
3 then let him bring for his s',
3 unto the Lord for a s' offering.
8 fat of the bullock for the s' offering;
13 of Israel s' through ignorance,
14 When the s', which they have
14 offer a young bullock for the s',
20 with the bullock for a s' offering,
21 a s' offering for the congregation.
23 if his s', wherein he hath sinned,
24 before the Lord: it is a s' offering.
25 take of the blood of the s' offering
26 for him as concerning his s',
27 any one of the common people s'
28 Or if his s', which he hath sinned,
28 for his s' which he hath sinned.
29 upon the head of the s' offering,
29 slay the s' offering in the place of
32 if he bring a lamb for a s' offering,
33 upon the head of the s' offering,
33 slay it for a s' offering in the place
34 take of the blood of the s' offering
35 make an atonement for his s' that
5: 1 if a soul s', and hear the voice of
6 for his s' which he hath sinned,
6 a kid of the goats, for a s' offering;
6 for him concerning his s'.
7 one for a s' offering, and the other
8 which is for the s' offering first,
9 the blood of the s' offering upon the
9 of the altar: it is a s' offering.
10 him for his s' which he hath sinned,
11 ephah of fine flour for a s' offering;
11 thereon: for it is a s' offering.
12 unto the Lord: it is a s' offering.
13 touching his s' that he hath sinned
15 s' through ignorance, in the holy
17 And if a soul s', and commit any of
6: 2 If a soul s', and commit a trespass
17 is most holy, as is the s' offering.
25 This is the law of the s' offering:
25 shall the s' offering be killed before
26 that offereth it for s' shall eat it:
30 no s' offering, whereof any of the
7: 7 As the s' offering is, so is the
37 and of the s' offering, and of the
8: 2 and a bullock for the s' offering,
14 the bullock for the s' offering:
14 of the bullock for the s' offering.
9: 2 thee a young calf for a s' offering,
3 a kid of the goats for a s' offering;
7 the altar, and offer thy s' offering,
8 and slew the calf of the s' offering,
10 above the liver of the s' offering,
15 was the s' offering for the people,
15 slew it, and offered it for s', as the
22 from offering of the s' offering,
10:16 sought the goat of the s' offering,
17 have ye not eaten the s' offering in
19 have they offered their s' offering
19 I had eaten the s' offering to day,
12: 6 or a turtledove, for a s' offering,
8 and the other for a s' offering:
14:13 where he shall kill the s' offering
13 as the s' offering is the priest's, so
19 the priest shall offer the s' offering,
22 and the one shall be a s' offering,
31 able to get, the one for a s' offering,
15:15 the one for a s' offering, and the
30 shall offer the one for a s' offering,
16: 3 a young bullock for a s' offering,
5 kids of the goats for a s' offering,
6 offer his bullock of the s' offering,
9 fell, and offer him for a s' offering.
11 bring the bullock of the s' offering,
11 kill the bullock of the s' offering,
15 he kill the goat of the s' offering,
25 fat of the s' offering shall he burn
27 And the bullock for the s' offering,

Le 16:27 and the goat for the s' offering,
19:17 and not suffer s' upon him.
22 for his s' which he hath done:
22 the s' which he hath done shall be
20:20 they shall bear their s': they shall
22: 9 lest they bear s' for it, and die
23:19 kid of the goats for a s' offering,
24:15 curseth his God shall bear his s'.
Nu 5: 6 commit any s' that men commit,
7 Then they shall confess their s'
6:11 offer the one for a s' offering, and
14 without blemish for a s' offering,
16 shall offer his s' offering, and his
7:16, 22, 28, 34, 40, 46, 52, 58, 64, 70,
76, 82 of the goats for a s' offering:
87 the kids of the goats for s' offering
8: 8 shalt thou take for a s' offering.
12 shalt offer the one for a s' offering,
9:13 that man shall bear his s'.
12:11 lay not the s' upon us, wherein
15:24 kid of the goats for a s' offering.
25 their s' offering before the Lord,
27 if any soul s' through ignorance,
27 of the first year for a s' offering.
16:22 shall one man s', and wilt thou be
18: 9 and every s' offering of theirs, and
22 lest they bear s', and die.
32 ye shall bear no s' by reason of it,
19: 9 separation: it is a purification for s'.
17 burnt heifer of purification for s',
27: 3 but died in his own s', and had no
28:15 kid of the goats for a s' offering
22 one goat for a s' offering, to make
29: 5 kid of the goats for a s' offering,
11 kid of the goats for a s' offering;
11 beside the s' offering of atonement,
16, 19 kid of the goats for a s' offering;
22 one goat for a s' offering; beside
25 kid of the goats for a s' offering;
28, 31, 34, 38 one goat for a s' offering;
32:23 be sure your s' will find you out.
De 9:21 I took your s', the calf which ye had
27 to their wickedness, nor to their s':
15: 9 thee, and it be s' unto thee.
19:15 for any iniquity, or for any s',
15 in any s' that he sinneth: at the
20:18 so should ye s' against the Lord
21:22 And if a man have committed a s'
22:26 the damsel no s' worthy of death:
23:21 thee; and it would be s' in thee.
22 to vow, it shall be no s' in thee.
24: 4 thou shalt not cause the land to s',
15 the Lord, and it be s' unto thee.
16 shall be put to death for his own s'.
1Sa 2:17 the s' of the young men was very
25 If one man s' against another, the
25 but if a man s' against the Lord,
12:23 God forbid that I should s' against
14:33 people s' against the Lord, in that
34 s' not against the Lord in eating
38 see wherein this s' hath been this
15:23 rebellion is as the s' of witchcraft,
25 I pray thee, pardon my s', and turn
19: 4 Let not the king s' against his
5 wilt thou s' against innocent blood,
20: 1 what is my s' before thy father,
2Sa 12:13 Lord also hath put away thy s';
1Ki 8:34 forgive the s' of thy people Israel,
35 thy name, and turn from their s',
36 and forgive the s' of thy servants,
46 If they s' against thee, (for there
12:30 And this thing became a s': for
13:34 became s' unto...house of Jeroboam,
14:16 the sins of Jeroboam, who did s',
16 and who made Israel to s'.
15:26 way of his father, and in his s',
26 wherewith he made Israel to s'.
30 sinned, and which he made Israel s',
34 the way of Jeroboam, and in his s'
34 wherewith he made Israel to s'.
16: 2 hast made my people Israel to s',
13 by which they made Israel to s',
19 the way of Jeroboam, and in his s'
19 which he did, to make Israel to s'.
26 way of Jeroboam...and in his s'
26 wherewith he made Israel to s',
17:18 me to call my s' to remembrance,
21:22 me to anger, and made Israel to s'.
22:52 Jeroboam...who made Israel to s':
2Ki 3: 3 Jeroboam...which made Israel to s';
10:29 Jeroboam...who made Israel to s',
31 Jeroboam, which made Israel to s'.
12:16 s' money was not brought into the
13: 2 of Nebat, which made Israel to s';
6 of Jeroboam, who made Israel s',
11 Jeroboam...who made Israel s':
14: 6 shall be put to death for his own s'.
24 Jeroboam...who made Israel to s'.
15: 9, 18, 24, 28 who made Israel to s'.
17:21 and made them s' [2398] a great s'.
21:11 and hath made Judah also to s'
16 beside his s' wherewith he made
16 wherewith he made Judah to s',
17 he did, and his s' that he sinned,
23:15 Jeroboam...who made Israel to s',
2Ch 6:22 If a man s' against his neighbour,
25 forgive the s' of thy people Israel,
26 thy name, and turn from their s',
27 and forgive the s' of thy servants,
36 If they s' against thee, (for there
7:14 heaven, and will forgive their s',
25: 4 every man shall die for his own s'.
29:21 for a s' offering for the kingdom,
23 for the s' offering before the king
24 s' offering should be made for all
Ezr 6:17 and for a s' offering for all Israel,

Ezr 8:35 twelve he goats for a s' offering:
Ne 4: 5 and let not their s' be blotted out
6:13 should be afraid, and do so, and s',
10:33 s' offerings to make an atonement
13:26 Did not Solomon king of Israel s'
26 did outlandish women cause to s'.
Job 2:10 all this did not Job s' with his lips.
5:24 thy habitation, and shalt not s'.
10: 6 and searchest after my s'?
14 If I s', then thou markest me, and
13:23 know my transgression and my s'.
14:16 dost thou not watch over my s'?
20:11 bones are full of the s' of his youth,
31:30 have I suffered my mouth to s'
34:37 he addeth rebellion unto his s',
35: 3 I have, if I be cleansed from my s'?
Ps 4: 4 Stand in awe, and s' not: commune
32: 1 is forgiven, whose s' is covered.
5 I acknowledged my s' unto thee,
5 thou forgavest the iniquity of my s'.
38: 3 rest in my bones because of my s'.
18 iniquity; I will be sorry for my s'.
39: 1 ways, that I s' not with my tongue:
40: 6 s' offering hast thou not required.
51: 2 and cleanse me from my s'.
3 and my s' is ever before me.
5 in s' did my mother conceive me.
59: 3 my transgression, nor for my s',
12 the s' of their mouth and the words
85: 2 thou hast covered all their s'.
109: 7 and let his prayer become s'.
14 and let not the s' of his mother be
119:11 that I might not s' against thee.
Pr 10:16 to life: the fruit of the wicked to s'.
19 of words there wanteth not s':
14: 9 Fools make a mock at s': but
34 but s' is a reproach to any people.
20: 9 heart clean, I am pure from my s'?
21: 4 and the plowing of the wicked, is s'.
24: 9 The thought of foolishness is s':
Ec 5: 6 thy mouth to cause thy flesh to s';
Isa 3: 9 they declare their s' as Sodom,
5:18 and s' as it were with a cart rope:
6: 7 is taken away, and thy s' purged.
27: 9 is all the fruit to take away his s';
30: 1 spirit, that they may add s' to s':
31: 7 hands have made unto you for a s'.
53:10 make his soul an offering for s',
12 he bare the s' of many, and made
Jer 16:10 or what is our s' that we have
18 their iniquity and their s' double;
17: 1 s' of Judah is written with a pen of
3 spoil, and thy high places for s',
18:23 neither blot out their s' from thy
31:34 I will remember their s' no more.
32:35 abomination, to cause Judah to s'.
36: 3 forgive their iniquity and their s'.
51: 5 was filled with s' against the Holy
La 4: 6 the punishment of the s' of Sodom,
Eze 3:20 warning, he shall die in his s',
21 man, that the righteous s' not,
21 and he doth not s', he shall surely
18:24 and in his s' that he hath sinned,
33:14 if he turn from his s', and do that
40:39 burnt offering and the s' offering
42:13 meat offering, and the s' offering,
43:19 a young bullock for a s' offering,
21 the bullock also of the s' offering,
22 without blemish for a s' offering;
25 every day a goat for a s' offering:
44:27 he shall offer his s' offering, saith
29 meat offering, and the s' offering,
45:17 he shall prepare the s' offering, and
19 take of the blood of the s' offering,
22 the land a bullock for a s' offering.
23 of the goats daily for a s' offering.
25 days, according to the s' offering,
46:20 trespass offering and the s' offering
Da 9:20 my s' and the s' of my people Israel
Ho 4: 8 They eat up the s' of my people,
8:11 hath made many altars to s',
11 altars shall be unto him to s'.
10: 8 places also of Aven, the s' of Israel,
12: 8 none iniquity in me that were s'.
13: 2 And now they s' more and more,
12 Ephraim is bound up; his s' is hid.
Am 8:14 that swear by the s' of Samaria,
Mic 1:13 she is the beginning of the s' to
3: 8 transgression, and to Israel his s'.
6: 7 of my body for the s' of my soul?
Zec 13: 1 fountain...for s' and...uncleanness.
M't 12:31 All manner of s' and blasphemy
18:21 oft shall my brother s' against me,
Joh 1:29 taketh away the s' of the world.
5:14 s' no more, lest a worse thing
8: 7 He that is without s' among you,
11 condemn thee: go, and s' no more.
34 committeth s' is the servant of s'.
46 Which of you convinceth me of s'?
9: 2 Master, who did s', this man, or his
41 ye were blind, ye should have no s':
41 We see; therefore your s' remaineth.
15:22 unto them, they had not had s': but
22 now they have no cloke for their s'.
24 other man did, they had not had s':
16: 8 he will reprove the world of s', and
9 Of s', because they believe not on me;
19:11 delivered me...hath the greater s'.
Ac 7:60 Lord, lay not this s' to their charge.
Ro 3: 9 Gentiles, that they are all under s';
20 for by the law is the knowledge of s'.
4: 8 whom the Lord will not impute s'.
5:12 by one man s' entered into the world,
12 into the world, and death by s';
13 until the law s' was in the world:
13 s' is not imputed when there is no

Ro 5:20 But where s· abounded, grace did
21 That as s· hath reigned unto death,
6: 1 Shall we continue in s·, that grace
2 How shall we that are dead to s·, live
6 the body of s· might be destroyed,
6 henceforth we should not serve s·.
7 For he that is dead is freed from s·.
10 in that he died, he died unto s· once:
11 ye also...to be dead indeed unto s·,
12 Let not s· therefore reign in your
13 of unrighteousness unto s·:
14 s· shall not have dominion over you:
15 shall we s·, because we are not under
16 whether of s· unto death, or of
17 that ye were the servants of s·, but
18 Being then made free from s·, ye
20 For when ye were the servants of s·,
22 But now being made free from s·,
23 For the wages of s· is death: but the
7: 7 Is the law s·? God forbid. Nay,
7 I had not known s·, but by the law:
8 But s·, taking occasion by the
8 For without the law s· was dead.
9 the commandment came, s· revived,
11 For s·, taking occasion by the
13 But s·, that it might appear s·,
13 that s· by the commandment might
14 but I am carnal, sold under s·.
17, 20 it, but s· that dwelleth in me.
23 me into captivity to the law of s·
25 God; but with the flesh the law of s·.
8: 2 me free from the law of s· and death.
3 likeness for sinful flesh, and for s·,
3 condemned s· in the flesh:
10 you, the body is dead because of s·;
14:23 for whatsoever is not of faith is s·.
1Co 6:18 Every s· that a man doeth is without
8:12 when ye s· so against the brethren,
12 weak conscience, ye s· against Christ.
15:34 Awake to righteousness, and s· not;
56 The sting of death is s·; and the
56 and the strength of s· is the law.
2Co 5:21 him to be s· for us, who knew no s·;
Ga 2:17 is therefore Christ the minister of s·?
3:22 hath concluded all under s·, that
Eph 4:26 Be ye angry, and s· not: let not the
2Th 2: 3 that man of s· be revealed, the son
1Ti 5:20 Them that s· rebuke before all,
Heb 3:13 through the deceitfulness of s·.
4:15 like as we are, yet without s·.
9:26 hath he appeared to put away s·
28 appear...without s· unto salvation.
10: 6 burnt offerings and sacrifices for s·
8 burnt offerings and offering for s·
18 is, there is no more offering for s·.
26 if we s· wilfully after that we have
11:25 than to enjoy the pleasures of s· for
12: 1 s· which doth so easily beset us,
4 unto blood, striving against s·.
13:11 sanctuary by the high priest for s·,
Jas 1:15 it bringeth forth s·: and s·, when it
2: 9 respect of persons, ye commit s·,
4:17 and doeth it not, to him it is s·.
1Pe 2:22 Who did no s·, neither was guile
4: 1 in the flesh hath ceased from s·;
2Pe 2:14 and that cannot cease from s·;
1Jo 1: 7 his Son cleanseth us from all s·.
8 If we say that we have no s·, we
2: 1 write I unto you, that ye s· not.
1 if any man s·, we have an advocate
3: 4 committeth s· transgresseth also
4 for s· is the transgression of the law.
5 away our sins; and in him is no s·.
8 He that committeth s· is of the devil;
9 is born of God doth not commit s·;
9 he cannot s·, because he is born of
5:16 If any man see his brother s·
16 a s· which is not unto death, he
16 for them that s· not unto death.
16 There is a s· unto death: I do not
17 All unrighteousness is s·: and there
17 and there is a s· not unto death.

Sin (*sin*)
Ex 16: 1 came unto the wilderness of S·,
17: 1 journeyed from the wilderness of S·,
Nu 33:11 encamped in the wilderness of S·.
12 journey out of the wilderness of S·,
Eze 30:15 And I will pour my fury upon S·,
16 S· shall have great pain, and No

Sina (*si'-nah*) See also SINAI.
Ac 7:30 him in the wilderness of mount S·
38 which spake to him in the mount S·,

Sinai (*si'-nahee*) See also HOREB; SINA.
Ex 16: 1 which is between Elim and S·, on
19: 1 came they into the wilderness of S·.
2 were come to the desert of S·, and
11 of all the people upon mount S·.
18 And mount S· was altogether on a
20 Lord came down upon mount S·,
23 cannot come up to mount S·: for
24:16 of the Lord abode upon mount S·,
31:18 him upon mount S·, two tables
34: 2 up in the morning unto mount S·,
4 and went up unto mount S·, as the
29 Moses came down from mount S·
32 had spoken with him in mount S·.
Le 7:38 commanded Moses in mount S·, in
38 the Lord, in the wilderness of S·.
25: 1 spake unto Moses in mount S·,
26:46 children of Israel in mount S· by
27:34 the children of Israel in mount S·.
Nu 1: 1 unto Moses in the wilderness of S·,
19 them in the wilderness of S·.
3: 1 spake with Moses in mount S·.
4 the Lord, in the wilderness of S·,
Nu 3:14 unto Moses in the wilderness of S·,
9: 1 unto Moses in the wilderness of S·,
5 at even in the wilderness of S·:
10:12 journeys out of...wilderness of S·;
26:64 of Israel in the wilderness of S·.
28: 6 which was ordained in mount S·
33:15 and pitched in the wilderness of S·.
16 removed from the desert of S·,
De 33: 2 The Lord came from S·, and rose
J'g 5: 5 even that S· from before the Lord
Ne 9:13 camest down also upon mount S·,
Ps 68: 8 even S· itself was moved at the
17 the Lord is among them, as in S·,
Ga 4:24 the one from the mount S·, which
25 this Agar is mount S· in Arabia,

since ^ See also SITH.
Ge 30:30 Lord hath blessed thee s· my coming:
44:28 in pieces; and I saw him not s·:
46:30 let me die, s· I have seen thy face,
Ex 4:10 nor s· thou hast spoken unto thy
5:23 s· I came to Pharaoh to speak in
9:18 in Egypt s· the foundation thereof
10: 6 s· the day that they were upon the
Nu 22:30 hast ridden ever s· I was thine
De 4:32 s· the day that God created man
34:10 a prophet s· in Israel like unto
Jos 2:12 s· I have shewed you kindness,
14:10 s· the Lord spake this word unto
Ru 2:11 law s· the death of thine husband:
1Sa 8: 8 works which they have done s· the
9:24 hath it been kept for thee s· I said,
21: 5 about these three days, s· I came out,
29: 3 him s· he fell unto me unto this day?
6 s· the day of thy coming unto me unto
2Sa 7: 6 s· the time that I brought up the
11 as s· the time that I commanded
1Ki 8:16 S· the day that I brought forth my
2Ki 8: 6 field s· the day that she left the land,
21:15 s· the day their fathers came forth
1Ch 17: 5 s· the day that I brought up Israel
10 s· the time that I commanded judges
2Ch 6: 5 S· the day that I brought forth my
30:26 s· the time of Solomon the son of
31:10 S· the people began to bring the
Ezr 4: 2 unto him s· the days of Esar-haddon
5:16 s· that time even until now hath
9: 7 s· the days of our fathers have we been
Ne 8:17 s· the days of Jeshua the son of Nun
9:32 s· the time of the kings of Assyria
Job 20: 4 s· man was placed upon earth,
38:12 commanded the morning s· thy days;
Isa 14: 8 S· thou art laid down, no feller is
16:13 spoken concerning Moab s· that time.
43: 4 S· thou wast precious in my sight,
44: 7 me, s· I appointed the ancient people?
64: 4 s· the beginning of the world men
Jer 7:25 S· the day that your fathers came
15: 7 s· they return not from their ways.
20: 8 For s· I spake, I cried out, I cried
23:38 s· ye say, The burden of the Lord;
31:20 for s· I spake against him, I do
44:18 s· we left off to burn incense
48:27 for s· thou spakest of him, thou
Da 12: 1 as never was s· there was a nation
Hag 2:16 S· those days were, when one came
M't 24:21 not s· the beginning of the world to
M'r 9:21 How long is it ago s· this came
Lu 1:70 have been s· the world began:
7:45 but this woman s· the time I came in
16:16 s· that time the kingdom of God is
24:21 third day s· these things were done.
Joh 9:32 S· the world began was it not
Ac 3:21 holy prophets s· the world began.
19: 2 the Holy Ghost s· ye believed?
24:11 but twelve days s· I went up to
Ro 16:25 was kept secret s· the world began,
1Co 15:21 For s· by man came death, by man
2Co 13: 3 S· ye seek a proof of Christ
Col 1: 4 S· we heard of your faith in Christ
6 also in you, s· the day ye heard of it,
9 s· the day we heard it, do not cease
Heb 7:28 of the oath, which was s· the law,
9:26 s· the foundation of the world:
2Pe 3: 4 s· the fathers fell asleep, all
Re 16:18 such as was not s· men were

sincere
Ph'p 1:10 ye may be s· and without offence
1Pe 2: 2 desire the s· milk of the word, that

sincerely
J'g 9:16 if ye have done truly and s·, in
19 If ye then have dealt truly and s·
Ph'p 1:16 preach Christ of contention, not s·,

sincerity
Jos 24:14 and serve him in s· and in truth:
1Co 5: 8 with the unleavened bread of s· and
2Co 1:12 that in simplicity and godly s·, not
2:17 but as of s·, but as of God, in the
8: 8 and to prove the s· of your love.
Eph 6:24 love our Lord Jesus Christ in s·.
Tit 2: 7 shewing uncorruptness, gravity, s·,

sinew See also SINEWS.
Ge 32:32 eat not of the s· which shrank,
32 Jacob's thigh in the s· that shrank.
Isa 48: 4 and thy neck is an iron s·, and thy

sinews
Job 10:11 hast fenced me with bones and s·.
30:17 season: and my s· take no rest.
40:17 the s· of his stones are wrapped
Eze 37: 6 And I will lay s· upon you, and will
8 s· and the flesh came up upon them,

sinful
Nu 32:14 an increase of s· men, to augment
Isa 1: 4 Ah s· nation, a people laden with
Am 9: 8 Lord God are upon the s· kingdom,
M'r 8:38 this adulterous and s· generation;
Lu 5: 8 from me; for I am a s· man, O Lord.
24: 7 delivered into the hands of s· men,
Ro 7:13 sin...might become exceeding s·.
8: 3 own Son in the likeness of s· flesh,

sing ^ See also SANG; SINGETH; SINGING; SUNG.
Ex 15: 1 I will s· unto the Lord, for he hath
21 S· ye to the Lord, for he hath
32:18 the noise of them that s· do I hear.
Nu 21:17 Spring up, O well; s· ye unto it:
J'g 5: 3 I, even I, will s· unto the Lord;
3 will s· praise to the Lord of Israel.
1Sa 21:11 s· one to another of him in dances,
2Sa 22:50 I will s· praises unto thy name.
1Ch 16: 9 S· unto him,...talk ye of all his
9 s· psalms unto him, talk ye of all
23 S· unto the Lord, all the earth;
33 shall the trees of the wood s· out
2Ch 20:22 they began to s· and to praise,
23:13 and such as taught to s· praise.
29:30 to s· praise unto the Lord with the
Job 29:13 the widow's heart to s· for joy.
Ps 7:17 will s· praise to the name of the Lord
9: 2 I will s· praise to thy name, O thou
11 S· praises to the Lord, which
13: 6 I will s· unto the Lord, because he
18:49 and s· praises unto thy name.
21:13 so will we s· and praise thy power.
27: 6 sacrifice of joy; I will s·, yea,
6 I will s· praises unto the Lord.
30: 4 S· unto the Lord, O ye saints of his,
12 that my glory may s· praise to thee.
33: 2 s· unto him with the psaltery and
3 S· unto him a new song; play
47: 6 S· praises to God, s· praises:
6 s· praises unto our King, s· praises.
7 s· ye praises with understanding.
51:14 shall s· aloud of thy righteousness.
57: 7 is fixed: I will s· and give praise.
9 s· unto thee among the nations.
59:16 But I will s· of thy power; yea, I
16 I will s· aloud of thy mercy in the
17 Unto thee, O my strength, will I s·:
61: 8 So will I s· praise unto thy name for
65:13 they shout for joy, they also s·.
66: 2 S· forth the honour of his name:
4 worship thee, and...s· unto thee;
4 they shall s· to thy name. Selah.
67: 4 the nations be glad and s· for joy:
68: 4 S· unto God,...extol him that rideth
4 s· praises to his name: extol him
32 S· unto God, ye kingdoms of the
32 O s· praises unto the Lord; Selah:
71:22 unto thee will I s· with the harp,
23 greatly rejoice when I s· unto thee;
75: 9 I will s· praises to the God of Jacob.
81: 1 S· aloud unto God our strength:
89: 1 I will s· of the mercies of the Lord
92: 1 and to s· praises unto thy name, O
95: 1 O come, let us s· unto the Lord:
96: 1 O s· unto the Lord a new song:
1 s· unto the Lord, all the earth.
2 S· unto the Lord, bless his name;
98: 1 O s· unto the Lord a new song; for
4 noise, and rejoice, and s· praise.
5 S· unto the Lord with the harp;
101: 1 I will s· of mercy and judgment:
1 unto thee, O Lord, will I s·.
104:12 which s· among the branches.
33 s· unto the Lord as long as I live:
33 s· praise to my God while I have
105: 2 S· unto him,...talk ye of all his
2 s· psalms unto him: talk ye of
108: 1 I will s· and give praise, even with
3 I will s· praises unto thee among
135: 3 s· praises unto his name; for it is
137: 3 S· us one of the songs of Zion.
4 s· the Lord's song in a strange
138: 1 the gods will I s· praise unto thee.
5 shall s· in the ways of the Lord:
144: 9 I will s· a new song unto thee, O
9 ten strings will I s· praises unto
145: 7 and shall s· of thy righteousness.
146: 2 I will s· praises unto...God while I
147: 1 is good to s· praises unto our God;
7 S· unto...Lord with thanksgiving;
7 s· praise upon the harp unto our
149: 1 S· unto the Lord a new song, and
3 s· praises unto him with...timbrel
5 let them s· aloud upon their beds.
Pr 29: 6 the righteous doth s· and rejoice.
Isa 5: 1 will I s· to my wellbeloved a song
12: 5 S· unto the Lord; for he hath
23:15 years shall Tyre s· as an harlot.
16 make sweet melody, s· many songs,
24:14 shall s· for the majesty of the
26:19 Awake and s·, ye that dwell in
27: 2 In that day s· ye unto her, A
35: 6 and the tongue of the dumb s·:
42:10 S· unto the Lord a new song, and
11 let the inhabitants of the rock s·,
44:23 S·, O ye heavens; for the Lord
49:13 S·, O heavens; and be joyful, O
52: 8 the voice together shall they s·:
9 joy, s· together, ye waste places of
54: 1 S·, O barren, thou that didst not
65:14 servants shall s· for joy of heart,
Jer 20:13 S· unto the Lord, praise ye the
31: 7 S· with gladness for Jacob, and
12 come and s· in the height of Zion,
51:48 that is therein, shall s· for Babylon:
Eze 27:25 ships of Tarshish did s· of thee in
Ho 2:15 she shall s· there, as in the days
Zep 2:14 voice shall s· in the windows;
3:14 S·, O daughter of Zion; shout, O
Zec 2:10 S· and rejoice, O daughter of Zion:

Ro 15: 9 Gentiles, and s· unto thy name.
1Co 14: 15 also: I will s· with the spirit, and
15 will s· with the understanding also.
Heb 2: 12 the church will I s· praise unto thee.
Jas 5: 13 is any merry? let him s· psalms.
Re 15: 3 And they s· the song of Moses the

singed
Da 3: 27 nor was an hair of their head s·,

singer See also SINGERS.
1Ch 6: 33 Heman a s·, the son of Joel, the
Hab 3: 19 To the chief s· on my stringed

singers
1Ki 10: 12 harps also and psalteries for s·:
1Ch 9: 33 these are the s·, chief of the fathers
15: 16 the s· with instruments of musick,
19 So the s·, Heman, Asaph, and
27 that bare the ark and the s·, and
27 the master of the song with the s·:
2Ch 5: 12 the Levites which were the s·, all of
13 the trumpeters and s· were as one,
9: 11 and harps and psalteries for s·:
20: 21 he appointed s· unto the Lord, and
23: 13 the s· with instruments of musick,
29: 28 and the s· sang, and the trumpets
35: 15 And the s· the sons of Asaph were
Ezr 2: 41 The s·: the children of Asaph, an
70 people, and the s·, and the porters,
7: 7 priests, and the Levites, and the s·,
24 Levites, s·, porters, Nethinims,
10: 24 Of the s· also; Eliashib: and of
Ne 7: 1 and the s· and the Levites were
44 The s·: the children of Asaph, an
73 Levites, and the porters, and the s·,
10: 28 the Levites, the porters, the s·, the
39 minister,...the porters, and the s·:
11: 22 the s· were over the business of the
23 certain portion should be for the s·,
12: 28 And the sons of the s· gathered
29 s· had builded them villages round
42 the s· sang loud, with Jezrahiah
45 both the s· and the porters kept
46 of old there were chief of the s·,
47 gave the portions of the s· and the
13: 5 be given to the Levites, and the s·,
10 the Levites, and the s·, that did the
Ps 68: 25 The s· went before, the players on
87: 7 As well the s· as the players on
Ec 2: 8 I gat me men s· and women s·, and
Eze 40: 44 the chambers of the s· in the inner

singeth
Pr 25: 20 so is he that s· songs to an heavy

singing
1Sa 18: 6 cities of Israel, s· and dancing,
2Sa 19: 35 the voice of s· men and s· women?
1Ch 6: 32 of the congregation with s·, until
13: 8 with s·, and with harps, and with
2Ch 23: 18 Moses, with rejoicing and with s·,
30: 21 s· with loud instruments unto the
35: 25 all the s· men and the s· women
Ezr 2: 65 two hundred s· men and s· women.
Ne 7: 67 and five s· men and s· women.
12: 27 with thanksgivings, and with s·,
Ps 100: 2 come before his presence with s·.
126: 2 laughter, and our tongue with s·:
Ca 2: 12 time of the s· of birds is come,
Isa 14: 7 is quiet: they break forth into s·.
16: 10 the vineyards there shall be no s·:
35: 2 and rejoice even with joy and s·:
44: 23 break forth into s·, ye mountains,
48: 20 with a voice of s· declare ye, tell
49: 13 break forth into s·, O mountains;
51: 11 return, and come with s· unto Zion;
54: 1 break forth into s·, and cry aloud,
55: 12 shall break forth before you into s·,
Zep 3: 17 love, he will joy over thee with s·.
Eph 5: 19 s· and making melody in your
Col 3: 16 s· with grace in your hearts to the

single
M't 6: 22 if therefore thine eye be s·, thy
Lu 11: 34 therefore when thine eye is s·, thy

singleness
Ac 2: 46 with gladness and s· of heart,
Eph 6: 5 in s· of your heart, as unto Christ;
Col 3: 22 but in s· of heart, fearing God:

singular
Le 27: 2 when a man shall make a s· vow,

Sinim (*si'-nim*)
Isa 49: 12 and these from the land of *S*·.

Sinite (*si'-nite*)
Ge 10: 17 Hivite, and the Arkite, and the *S*·,
1Ch 1: 15 Hivite, and the Arkite, and the *S*·,

sink See also SANK; SUNK.
Ps 69: 2 I s· in deep mire, where there is
14 out of the mire, and let me not s·:
Jer 51: 64 Thus shall Babylon s·, and shall
M't 14: 30 beginning to s·, he cried, saying,
Lu 5: 7 the ships, so that they began to s·.
9: 44 sayings s· down into your ears:

sinned
Ex 9: 27 unto them, I have s· this time:
34 he s· yet more, and hardened his
10: 16 I have s· against the Lord your God,
32: 30 the people, Ye have s· a great sin:
31 Oh, this people have s· a great sin,
33 Whosoever hath s· against me, him
Le 4: 3 bring for his sin, which he hath s·,
14 sin, which they have s· against it, is
22 When a ruler hath s·, and done
23 if his sin, wherein he hath s·, come
28 if his sin, which he hath s·, come to
Le 4: 28 for his sin which he hath s·.
5: 5 that he shall confess that he hath s·
6 Lord for his sin which he hath s·,
10 for him for his sin which he hath s·,
11 that s· shall bring for his offering
13 as touching his sin that he hath s·
6: 4 because he hath s·, and is guilty,
Nu 6: 11 for him, for that he s· by the dead,
12: 11 foolishly, and wherein we have s·.
14: 40 Lord hath promised: for we have s·.
21: 7 We have s·, for we have spoken
22: 34 I have s·; for I knew not that thou
32: 23 behold, ye have s· against the Lord:
De 1: 41 We have s· against the Lord, we
9: 16 ye had s· against the Lord your God,
18 because of all your sins which ye s·,
Jos 7: 11 Israel hath s·, and they have also
20 Indeed I have s· against the Lord
J'g 10: 10 saying, We have s· against thee,
15 We have s·: do thou unto us
11: 27 I have not s· against thee, but thou
1Sa 7: 6 We have s· against the Lord.
12: 10 unto the Lord, and said, We have s·,
15: 24 Saul said unto Samuel, I have s·:
30 Then he said, I have s·: yet honour
19: 4 because he hath not s· against thee,
24: 11 and I have not s· against thee;
26: 21 Then said Saul, I have s·: return,
2Sa 12: 13 Nathan, I have s· against the Lord.
19: 20 servant doth know that I have s·:
24: 10 I have s· greatly in that I have done:
17 Lo, I have s·, and I have done
1Ki 8: 33 because they have s· against thee,
35 because they have s· against thee;
47 saying, We have s·, and have done
50 And forgive thy people that have s·
15: 30 the sins of Jeroboam which he s·,
16: 13 of Elah his son, by which they s·,
19 his sins which he s· in doing evil
18: 9 What have I s·, that thou wouldest
2Ki 17: 7 Israel had s· against the Lord their
21: 17 that he did, and his sin that he s·,
1Ch 21: 8 said unto God, I have s· greatly,
17 even I it is that have s· and done
2Ch 6: 24, 26 because they have s· against
37 We have s·, we have done amiss,
39 forgive thy people which have s·
Ne 1: 6 which we have s· against thee:
6 I and my father's house have s·.
9: 29 but s· against thy judgments,
Job 1: 5 It may be that my sons have s·,
22 In all this Job s· not, nor charged
7: 20 I have s·; what shall I do unto thee,
8: 4 If thy children have s· against him,
24: 19 doth the grave those which have s·.
33: 27 if any say, I have s·, and perverted
Ps 41: 4 my soul; for I have s· against thee.
51: 4 Against thee, thee only, have I s·,
78: 17 And they s· yet more against him
32 For all this they s· still, and believed
106: 6 We have s· with our fathers, we
Isa 42: 24 Lord, he against whom we have s·?
43: 27 Thy first father hath s·, and thy
64: 5 thou art wroth; for we have s·:
Jer 2: 35 because thou sayest, I have not s·.
3: 25 for we have s· against the Lord our
8: 14 because we have s· against the Lord.
14: 7 are many; we have s· against thee.
20 fathers: for we have s· against thee.
33: 8 whereby they have s· against me;
8 iniquities, whereby they have s·,
40: 3 because ye have s· against the Lord,
44: 23 because ye have s· against the Lord,
50: 7 they have s· against the Lord,
14 for she hath s· against the Lord.
La 1: 8 Jerusalem hath grievously s·;
5: 7 Our fathers have s·, and are not;
16 head: woe unto us, that we have s·!
Eze 18: 24 and in his sin that he hath s·, in
28: 16 thee with violence, and thou hast s·:
37: 23 dwellingplaces, wherein they...s·,
Da 9: 5 We have s·, and have committed
8 because we have s· against thee.
11 because we have s· against him.
15 we have s·, we have done wickedly.
Ho 4: 7 increased, so they s· against me:
10: 9 thou hast s· from the days of Gibeah:
Mic 7: 9 Lord, because I have s· against him,
Hab 2: 10 people, and hath s· against thy soul.
Zep 1: 17 they have s· against the Lord:
M't 27: 4 I have s· in that I have betrayed
Lu 15: 18, 21 Father, I have s· against heaven,
Joh 9: 3 Neither hath this man s·, nor his
Ro 2: 12 For as many as have s· without law
12 and as many as have s· in the law
3: 23 For all have s·, and come short of
5: 12 upon all men, for that all have s·:
14 that had not s· after the similitude
16 And not as it was by one that s·, so
1Co 7: 28 and if thou marry, thou hast not s·;
28 if a virgin marry, she hath not s·.
2Co 12: 21 many which have s· already,
13: 2 to them which heretofore have s·,
Heb 3: 17 was it not with them that had s·,
2 Pe 2: 4 God spared not the angels that s·,
1Jo 1: 10 If we say that we have not s·, we

sinner See also SINNERS.
Pr 11: 31 much more the wicked and the s·.
13: 6 wickedness overthroweth the s·.
22 the wealth of the s· is laid up for
Ec 2: 26 but to the s· he giveth travail, to
7: 26 but the s· shall be taken by her.
8: 12 Though a s· do evil an hundred
9: 2 as is the good, so is the s·; and he
18 but one s· destroyeth much good.
Isa 65: 20 the s· being an hundred years old
Lu 7: 37 woman in the city, which was a s·,
39 that toucheth him: for she is a s·.
15: 7 heaven over one s· that repenteth,
10 of God over one s· that repenteth.
18: 13 saying, God be merciful to me a s·.
19: 7 to be guest with a man that is a s·.
Joh 9: 16 man that is a s· do such miracles?
24 we know that this man is a s·.
25 Whether he be a s· or no, I know not:
Ro 3: 7 why yet am I also judged as a s·?
Jas 5: 20 converteth the s· from the error of
1Pe 4: 18 shall the ungodly and the s· appear?

sinners
Ge 13: 13 men of Sodom were wicked and s·
Nu 16: 38 The censers of these s· against
1Sa 15: 18 destroy the s· the Amalekites,
Ps 1: 1 nor standeth in the way of s·, nor
5 nor s· in the congregation of the
25: 8 therefore will he teach s· in the way.
26: 9 Gather not my soul with s·, nor my
51: 13 s· shall be converted unto thee.
104: 35 s· be consumed out of the earth,
Pr 1: 10 if s· entice thee, consent thou not.
13: 21 Evil pursueth s·: but to the
23: 17 Let not thine heart envy s·: but be
Isa 1: 28 of the transgressors and of the s·
13: 9 and he shall destroy the s· thereof
33: 14 The s· in Zion are afraid; fearfulness
Am 9: 10 All the s· of my people shall die by
M't 9: 10 many publicans and s· came and
11 your Master with publicans and s·?
13 the righteous, but s· to repentance.
11: 19 a friend of publicans and s·.
26: 45 is betrayed into the hands of s·.
M'r 2: 15 publicans and s· sat also together
16 saw him eat with publicans and s·,
16 and drinketh with publicans and s·?
17 the righteous, but s· to repentance.
14: 41 is betrayed into the hands of s·.
Lu 5: 30 eat and drink with publicans and s·?
32 the righteous, but s· to repentance.
6: 32 for s· also love those that love them.
33 ye? for s· also do even the same.
34 s· also lend to s·, to receive as much
7: 34 a friend of publicans and s·!
13: 2 were s· above all the Galilæans,
4 were s· above all men that dwelt
15: 1 publicans and s· for to hear him.
2 This man receiveth s·, and eateth
Joh 9: 31 we know that God heareth not s·:
Ro 5: 8 while we were yet s·, Christ died for
19 disobedience many were made s·,
Ga 2: 15 by nature, and not s· of the Gentiles,
17 we ourselves also are found s·, is
1Ti 1: 9 for the ungodly and for s·, for unholy
15 Jesus came into the world to save s·;
Heb 7: 26 undefiled, separate from s·, and
12: 3 contradiction of s· against himself,
Jas 4: 8 Cleanse your hands, ye s·; and
Jude 15 ungodly s· have spoken against him.

sinnest
Job 35: 6 If thou s·, what doest thou against

sinneth
Nu 15: 28 for the soul that s· ignorantly,
28 s· by ignorance before the Lord,
29 for him that s· through ignorance,
De 19: 15 for any sin, in any sin that he s·:
1Ki 8: 46 (for there is no man that s· not,)
2Ch 6: 36 (for there is no man which s· not,)
Pr 8: 36 s· against me wrongeth his own
14: 21 He that despiseth his neighbour s·:
19: 2 and he that hasteth with his feet s·.
20: 2 whoso provoketh him to anger s·
Ec 7: 20 earth, that doeth good, and s· not.
Eze 14: 13 when the land s· against me by
18: 4 mine: the soul that s·, it shall die.
20 The soul that s·, it shall die. The
33: 12 righteousness in the day that he s·.
1Co 6: 18 fornication s· against his own body.
7: 36 let him do what he will, he s· not:
Tit 3: 11 he that is such is subverted, and s·,
1Jo 3: 6 Whosoever abideth in him s· not:
6 whosoever s· hath not seen him,
8 for the devil s· from the beginning.
5: 18 whosoever is born of God s· not;

sinning
Ge 20: 6 for I also withheld thee from s·
Le 6: 3 these that a man doeth, s· therein:

sin-offering See SIN and OFFERING.

sins
Le 16: 16 their transgressions in all their s·:
21 their transgressions in all their s·,
30 from all your s· before the Lord.
34 of Israel for all their s· once a year.
26: 18 you seven times more for your s·.
21 upon you according to your s·.
24 you yet seven times for your s·.
28 chastise you seven times for your s·.
Nu 16: 26 lest ye be consumed in all their s·.
De 9: 18 because of all your s· which ye
Jos 24: 19 your transgressions nor your s·.
1Sa 12: 19 added unto all our s· this evil,
1Ki 14: 16 up because of the s· of Jeroboam,
22 their s· which they had committed,
15: 3 he walked in all the s· of his father,
30 the s· of Jeroboam which he sinned,
16: 2 provoke me to anger with their s·;
13 For all the s· of Baasha, and the s·
13 and the s· of Elah his son, by which
19 his s· which he sinned in doing evil
31 him to walk in the s· of Jeroboam
2Ki 3: 3 he cleaved unto the s· of Jeroboam
10: 29 s· of Jeroboam the son of Nebat,

2Ki 10: 31 not from the s' of Jeroboam,
13: 2 and followed the s' of Jeroboam
6 the s' of the house of Jeroboam,
11 from all the s' of Jeroboam the son
14: 24 from all the s' of Jeroboam the son
15: 9, 18, 24, 28 s' of Jeroboam the son of
17: 22 walked in all the s' of Jeroboam
24: 3 for the s' of Manasseh, according to
2Ch 28: 10 you, s' against the Lord your God?
13 ye intend to add more to our s'
33: 19 and all his s', and his trespass, and
Ne 1: 6 and confess the s' of the children of
9: 2 and stood and confessed their s',
37 hast set over us because of our s':
Job 13: 23 many are mine iniquities and s'?
Ps 19: 13 servant also from presumptuous s';
25: 7 Remember not the s' of my youth,
18 and my pain; and forgive all my s'.
51: 9 Hide thy face from my s', and blot
69: 5 and my s' are not hid from thee.
79: 9 deliver us, and purge away our s',
90: 8 our secret s' in the light of thy
103: 10 hath not dealt with us after our s';
Pr 5: 22 be holden with the cords of his s'.
10: 12 up strifes: but love covereth all s'.
28: 13 covereth his s' shall not prosper:
Isa 1: 18 though your s' be as scarlet, they
38: 17 hast cast all my s' behind thy back.
40: 2 Lord's hand double for all her s'.
43: 24 hast made me to serve with thy s',
25 sake, and will not remember thy s'.
44: 22 as a cloud, thy s': return unto me;
58: 1 and the house of Jacob their s'.
59: 2 your s' have hid his face from you,
12 thee, and our s' testify against us:
Jer 5: 25 and your s' have withholden good
14: 10 their iniquity, and visit their s'.
15: 13 and that for all thy s', even in all
30: 14 because thy s' were increased.
15 because thy s' were increased, I
50: 20 the s' of Judah, and they shall not
La 3: 39 man for the punishment of his s'?
4: 13 For the s' of her prophets, and the
22 of Edom; he will discover thy s'.
Eze 16: 51 Samaria committed half of thy s';
52 for thy s' that thou hast committed
18: 14 that seeth all his father's s' which
21 all his s' that he hath committed,
*21: 24 all your doings your s' do appear;
23: 49 ye shall bear the s' of your idols:
33: 10 If our transgressions and our s' be
16 of his s' that he hath committed
Da 4: 27 break off thy s' by righteousness,
9: 16 for our s', and for the iniquities
24 to make an end of s', and to make
Ho 8: 13 their iniquity, and visit their s':
9: 9 their iniquity, he will visit their s'.
Am 5: 12 transgressions and your mighty s':
Mic 1: 5 and for the s' of the house of Israel.
6: 13 thee desolate because of thy s'.
7: 19 their s' into the depths of the sea.
M't 1: 21 shall save his people from their s'.
3: 6 of him in Jordan, confessing their s'.
9: 2 good cheer; thy s' be forgiven thee.
5 to say, Thy s' be forgiven thee; or
6 hath power on earth to forgive s',
26: 28 shed for many for the remission of s'.
M'r 1: 4 of repentance for the remission of s'.
5 river of Jordan, confessing their s'.
2: 5 palsy, Son, thy s' be forgiven thee.
7 who can forgive s' but God only?
9 the palsy, Thy s' be forgiven thee;
10 hath power on earth to forgive s',
3: 28 s' shall be forgiven unto the sons of
4: 12 their s' should be forgiven them.
Lu 1: 77 people by the remission of their s',
3: 3 repentance for the remission of s';
5: 20 him, Man, thy s' are forgiven thee.
21 Who can forgive s', but God alone?
23 to say, Thy s' be forgiven thee; or to
24 hath power upon earth to forgive s',
7: 47 Her s', which are many, are forgiven;
48 he said unto her, Thy s' are forgiven.
49 Who is this that forgiveth s' also?
11: 4 forgive us our s'; for we also forgive
24: 47 remission of s' should be preached
Joh 8: 21 seek me, and shall die in your s':
24 unto you, that ye shall die in your s':
24 that I am he, ye shall die in your s'.
9: 34 Thou wast altogether born in s',
20: 23 Whose soever s' ye remit, they are
23 whose soever s' ye retain, they are
Ac 2: 38 Jesus Christ for the remission of s',
3: 19 that your s' may be blotted out,
5: 31 to Israel, and forgiveness of s'.
10: 43 in him receive shall remission of s'.
13: 38 unto you the forgiveness of s':
22: 16 be baptized, and wash away thy s',
26: 18 they may receive forgiveness of s',
Ro 3: 25 for the remission of s' that are past,
4: 7 forgiven, and whose s' are covered.
7: 5 the motions of s', which were by the
11: 27 when I shall take away their s'.
1Co 15: 3 how that Christ died for our s'
17 faith is vain; ye are yet in your s'.
Ga 1: 4 Who gave himself for our s', that he
Eph 1: 7 the forgiveness of s', according to
2: 1 who were dead in trespasses and s';
5 Even when we were dead in s',
Col 1: 14 blood, even the forgiveness of s':
2: 11 off the body of the s' of the flesh by
13 And you, being dead in your s'
1Th 2: 16 be saved, to fill up their s' alway:
1Ti 5: 22 be partaker of other men's s':
24 Some men's s' are open beforehand,
2Ti 3: 6 captive silly women laden with s',
Heb 1: 3 he had by himself purged our s', sat
2: 17 reconciliation for the s' of the people.
5: 1 offer both gifts and sacrifices for s':
3 so also for himself, to offer for s'.
7: 27 first for his own s', and then for the
8: 12 and their s' and their iniquities will I
9: 28 once offered to bear the s' of many;
10: 2 have had no more conscience of s'.
3 is a remembrance again made of s'
4 and of goats should take away s'.
11 which can never take away s':
12 he had offered one sacrifice for s'
17 s' and iniquities will I remember
26 remaineth no more sacrifice for s',
Jas 5: 15 if he have committed s', they shall
20 and shall hide a multitude of s'.
1Pe 2: 24 own self bare our s' in his own body
24 that we, being dead to s', should live
3: 18 Christ also hath once suffered for s',
4: 8 shall cover the multitude of s'.
2Pe 1: 9 that he was purged from his old s'.
1Jo 1: 9 If we confess our s', he is faithful and
9 faithful and just to forgive us our s',
2: 2 And he is the propitiation for our s':
2 but also for the s' of the whole world.
12 because your s' are forgiven you for
3: 5 was manifested to take away our s';
4: 10 Son to be the propitiation for our s'.
Re 1: 5 and washed us from our s' in his own
18: 4 that ye be not partakers of her s',
5 her s' have reached unto heaven,

Sion (*si'-on*) See also SHENIR; SIRION; ZION.
De 4: 48 unto mount *S'*, which is Hermon.
Ps 65: 1 waiteth for thee, O God, in *S'*:
M't 21: 5 Tell ye the daughter of *S'*, Behold,
Joh 12: 15 Fear not, daughter of *S'*: behold,
Ro 9: 33 I lay in *S'* a stumblingstone and
11: 26 shall come out of *S'* the Deliverer.
Heb 12: 22 But ye are come unto mount *S'*,
1Pe 2: 6 I lay in *S'* a chief corner stone,
Re 14: 1 lo, a Lamb stood on the mount *S'*,

Siphmoth (*sif'-moth*)
1Sa 30: 28 and to them which were in *S'*,

Sippai (*sip'-pahee*) See also SAPH.
1Ch 20: 4 Sibbechai the Hushathite slew *S'*,

sir See also SIRS.
Ge 43: 20 O s', we came indeed down at the
M't 13: 27 *S'*, didst not thou sow good seed in
21: 30 and said, I go, s'; and went not.
27: 63 *S'*, we remember that that deceiver
Joh 4: 11 *S'*, thou hast nothing to draw with,
15 *S'*, give me this water, that I thirst
19 *S'*, I perceive...thou art a prophet.
49 *S'*, come down ere my child die.
5: 7 *S'*, I have no man, when the water
12: 21 saying, *S'*, we would see Jesus.
20: 15 *S'*, if thou have borne him hence,
Re 7: 14 I said unto him, *S'*, thou knowest.

Sirah (*si'-rah*)
2Sa 3: 26 him again from the well of *S'*:

Sirion (*sir'-e-on*) See also HERMON.
De 3: 9 Hermon the Sidonians call *S'*;
Ps 29: 6 Lebanon and *S'* like a...unicorn

sirs
Ac 7: 26 *S'*, ye are brethren; why do ye
14: 15 saying, *S'*, why do ye these things?
16: 30 *S'*, what must I do to be saved?
19: 25 *S'*, ye know that by this craft we
27: 10 *S'*, I perceive that this voyage will
21 *S'*, ye should have hearkened unto
25 Wherefore, s', be of good cheer: for

Sisamai (*sis'-a-mahee*)
1Ch 2: 40 Eleasah begat *S'*, and *S'* begat

Sisera (*sis'-e-rah*)
J'g 4: 2 the captain of whose host was *S'*,
7 *S'* the captain of Jabin's army, with
9 the Lord shall sell *S'* into the hand
12 And they shewed *S'* that Barak the
13 And *S'* gathered together all his
14 Lord hath delivered *S'* into thine
15 And the Lord discomfited *S'*, and
15 that *S'* lighted down off his chariot,
16 host of *S'* fell upon the edge of the
17 *S'* fled away on his feet to the tent
18 And Jael went out to meet *S'*, and
22 as Barak pursued *S'*, Jael came out
22 *S'* lay dead, and the nail was in his
5: 20 in their courses fought against *S'*.
26 and with the hammer she smote *S'*,
28 The mother of *S'* looked out at a
30 to *S'* a prey of divers colours, a
1Sa 12: 9 he sold them into the hand of *S'*,
Ezr 2: 53 the children of *S'*, the children of
Ne 7: 55 the children of *S'*, the children of
Ps 83: 9 as to *S'*, as to Jabin, at the brook

sister See also SISTER'S; SISTERS.
Ge 4: 22 the s' of Tubal-cain was Naamah.
12: 13 Say, I pray thee, thou art my s':
19 Why saidst thou, She is my s'? so I
20: 2 said of Sarah his wife, She is my s':
5 Said he not unto me, She is my s'?
12 And yet indeed she is my s'; she is
24: 30 heard the words of Rebekah his s',
59 they sent away Rebekah their s',
60 and said unto her, Thou art our s',
25: 20 the s' to Laban the Syrian.
26: 7 said, She is my s': for he feared
9 and how saidst thou, She is my s'?
28: 9 the s' of Nebajoth, to be his wife.
30: 1 no children, Rachel envied her s';
8 have I wrestled with my s', and I
Ge 34: 13 he had defiled Dinah their s':
14 our s' to one that is uncircumcised;
27 because they had defiled their s'.
31 deal with our s' as with an harlot?
36: 3 Ishmael's daughter, s' of Nebajoth.
22 Heman; and Lotan's s' was Timna.
46: 17 Isui, and Beriah, and Serah their s':
Ex 2: 4 And his s' stood afar off, to wit what
7 said his s' to Pharaoh's daughter,
6: 20 Jochebed his father's s' to wife;
23 Amminadab s' of Naashon, to wife;
15: 20 the prophetess, the s' of Aaron,
Le 18: 9 nakedness of thy s' the daughter
11 begotten of thy father, she is thy s',
12 the nakedness of thy father's s':
13 the nakedness of thy mother's s':
18 shalt thou take a wife to her s',
20: 17 And if a man shall take his s', his
19 the nakedness of thy mother's s', nor
19 of thy father's s': for he uncovereth
21: 3 And for his s' a virgin, that is nigh
Nu 6: 7 mother, for his brother, or for his s',
25: 18 of a prince of Midian, their s',
26: 59 and Moses, and Miriam their s'.
De 27: 22 Cursed be he that lieth with his s',
J'g 15: 2 not her younger s' fairer than she?
Ru 1: 15 thy s' in law is gone back unto her
15 gods: return thou after thy s' in law.
2Sa 13: 1 the son of David had a fair s',
2 that he fell sick for his s' Tamar;
4 Tamar, my brother Absalom's s'.
5 let my s' Tamar come, and give me
6 let Tamar my s' come, and make me
11 unto her, Come lie with me, my s'.
20 thee? but hold now thy peace, my s':
22 because he had forced his s' Tamar.
32 the day that he forced his s' Tamar.
17: 25 Nahash, s' to Zeruiah Joab's mother.
1Ki 11: 19 him to wife the s' of his own wife,
19 wife, the s' of Tahpenes the queen.
20 s' of Tahpenes bare him Genubath
2Ki 11: 2 But Jehosheba,...s' of Ahaziah,
1Ch 1: 39 Homam: and Timna was Lotan's s'.
3: 9 the concubines, and Tamar their s'.
19 Hananiah, and Shelomith their s':
4: 3 name of their s' was Hazelelponi:
19 of his wife Hodiah the s' of Naham,
7: 15 took to wife the s' of Huppim and
18 And his s' Hammoleketh bare Ishod,
30 and Beriah, and Serah their s'.
32 and Hotham, and Shua their s'.
2Ch 22: 11 (for she was the s' of Ahaziah,) hid
Job 17: 14 Thou art my mother, and my s'.
Pr 7: 4 Say unto wisdom, Thou art my s';
Ca 4: 9 Thou hast ravished my heart, my s',
10 How fair is thy love, my s', my
12 A garden inclosed is my s', my
5: 1 I am come into my garden, my s', my
2 knocketh, saying, Open to me, my s',
8: 8 We have a little s', and she hath no
8 what shall we do for our s' in the day
Jer 3: 7 her treacherous s' Judah saw it.
8 her treacherous s' Judah feared not,
10 her treacherous s' Judah hath not
22: 18 Ah my brother! or, Ah s'! they shall
Eze 16: 45 and thou art the s' of thy sisters,
46 And thine elder s' is Samaria, she
46 thy younger s', that dwelleth at thy
48 Sodom thy s' hath not done, she nor
49 was the iniquity of thy s' Sodom,
56 For thy s' Sodom was not mentioned
22: 11 another in thee hath humbled his s',
23: 4 the elder, and Aholibah her s':
11 when her s' Aholibah saw this, she
11 more than her s' in her whoredoms.
18 my mind was alienated from her s'.
31 hast walked in the way of thy s';
33 with the cup of thy s' Samaria.
44: 25 or for s' that hath had no husband,
M't 12: 50 the same is my brother, and s', and
M'r 3: 35 the same is my brother, and my s',
Lu 10: 39 And she had a s' called Mary, which
40 not care that my s' hath left me to
Joh 11: 1 the town of Mary and her s' Martha.
5 Now Jesus loved Martha, and her s',
28 called Mary her s' secretly, saying,
39 Martha, the s' of him that was dead,
19: 25 his mother, and his mother's s',
Ro 16: 1 I commend unto you Phebe our s',
15 and Julia, Nereus, and his s', and
1Co 7: 15 A brother or a s' is not under
9: 5 we not power to lead about a s', a
Jas 2: 15 If a brother or s' be naked, and
2Jo 13 The children of thy elect s' greet

sister-in-law See SISTER and LAW.

sister's
Ge 24: 30 and bracelets upon his s' hands,
29: 13 heard the tidings of Jacob his s' son,
Le 20: 17 he hath uncovered his s' nakedness;
1Ch 7: 15 whose s' name was Maachah;) and
Eze 23: 32 shalt drink of thy s' cup deep and
Ac 23: 16 when Paul's s' son heard of their
Col 4: 10 and Marcus, s' son to Barnabas,

sisters
Jos 2: 13 and my brethren, and my s', and all
1Ch 2: 16 Whose s' were Zeruiah, and Abigail.
Job 1: 4 called for their three s' to eat and to
42: 11 him all his brethren, and all his s',
Eze 16: 45 thou art the sister of thy s', which
51 hast justified thy s' in all thine
52 Thou also, which hast judged thy s',
52 in that thou hast justified thy s'.
55 thy s', Sodom and her daughters,
61 when thou shalt receive thy s', thine
Ho 2: 1 Ammi; and to your s', Ruhamah.

M't 13:56 And his s', are they not all with us?
19:29 forsaken houses, or brethren, or s',
M'r 6: 3 and are not his s' here with us?
10:29 hath left house, or brethren, or s',
30 houses, and brethren, and s', and
Lu 14:26 and children, and brethren, and s',
Joh 11: 3 Therefore his s' sent unto him,
1Ti 5: 2 the younger as s', with all purity.
sit See also SAT; SITTEST; SITTETH; SITTING.
Ge 27:19 s' and eat of my venison, that thy
Nu 32: 6 go to war, and shall ye s' here?
J'g 5:10 ye that s' in judgment, and walk by
Ru 3:18 S' still, my daughter, until thou
4: 1 a one! turn aside, s' down here.
2 the city, and said, S' ye down here.
1Sa 9:22 made them s' in the chiefest place
16:11 for we will not s' down till he come
20: 5 fail to s' with the king at meat:
2Sa 19: 8 Behold, the king doth s' in the gate.
1Ki 1:13 and he shall s' upon my throne?
17 and he shall s' upon my throne,
20 shall s' on the throne of my lord
24 and he shall s' upon my throne?
27 should s' on the throne of my lord
30 he shall s' upon my throne in my
35 may come and s' upon my throne;
48 hath given one to s' on my throne
3: 6 him a son to s' on his throne, as it
8:20 s' on the throne of Israel, as the
25 sight to s' on the throne of Israel;
2Ki 7: 3 Why s' we here until we die?
4 and if we s' still here, we die also.
10:30 shall s' on the throne of Israel.
15:12 Thy sons shall s' on the throne of
18:27 me to the men which s' on the wall,
1Ch 28: 5 Solomon...to s' upon the throne of
2Ch 6:16 to s' upon the throne of Israel;
Ps 26: 5 and will not s' with the wicked.
69:12 They that s' in the gate speak
107:10 Such as s' in darkness and in the
110: 1 S' thou at my right hand, until I
119:23 Princes also did s' and speak
127: 2 you to rise up early, to s' up late,
132:12 shall also s' upon thy throne for
Ec 10: 6 dignity, and the rich s' in low place.
Isa 3:26 desolate shall s' upon the ground.
14:13 I will s' also upon the mount of the
16: 5 he shall s' upon it in truth in the
30: 7 this, Their strength is to s' still.
36:12 to the men that s' upon the wall,
42: 7 s' in darkness out of the prison
47: 1 Come down, and s' in the dust, O
1 of Babylon, s' on the ground:
5 S' thou silent, and get thee into
8 I shall not s' as a widow, neither
14 to warm at, nor fire to s' before it.
52: 2 arise, and s' down; O Jerusalem:
Jer 8:14 Why do we s' still? assemble
13:13 kings that s' upon David's throne,
18 queen, humble yourselves, s' down:
16: 8 to s' with them to eat and to drink.
33:17 want a man to s' upon the throne of
36:15 S' down now, and read it in our
30 have none to s' upon the throne of
48:18 from thy glory, and s' in thirst; for
La 1: 1 How doth the city s' solitary, that
2:10 the daughter of Zion s' upon the
Eze 26:16 they shall s' upon the ground, and
28: 2 I s' in the seat of God, in the midst
33:31 they s' before thee as my people,
44: 3 he shall s' in it to eat bread before
Da 7: 9 the Ancient of days did s', whose
26 But the judgment shall s', and they
Joe 3:12 will I s' to judge all the heathen
Mic 4: 4 shall s' every man under his vine
7: 8 when I s' in darkness, the Lord
Zec 3: 8 and thy fellows that s' before thee:
6:13 shall s' and rule upon his throne;
Mal 3: 3 he shall s' as a refiner and purifier
M't 8:11 shall s' down with Abraham, and
14:19 multitude to s' down on the grass,
15:35 multitude to s' down on the ground.
19:28 Son of man shall s' in the throne
28 ye also shall s' upon twelve thrones,
20:21 that these my two sons may s', the
23 to s' on my right hand, and on my
22:44 S' thou on my right hand, till I
23: 2 the Pharisees s' at Moses' seat:
25:31 then shall he s' upon the throne of
26:36 S' ye here, while I go and pray
M'r 6:39 to make all s' down by companies
8: 6 people to s' down on the ground:
10:37 Grant unto us that we may s', one
40 But to s' on my right hand and on
12:36 S' thou on my right hand, till I
14:32 S' ye here, while I shall pray.
Lu 1:79 light to them that s' in darkness
9:14 Make them s' down by fifties in a
15 did so, and made them all s' down.
12:37 and make them to s' down to meat,
13:29 s' down in the kingdom of God.
14: 8 s' not down in the highest room;
10 go and s' down in the lowest room;
10 of them that s' at meat with thee.
16: 6 s' down quickly, and write fifty.
17: 7 the field, Go and s' down to meat?
20:42 Lord, S' thou on my right hand,
22:30 s' on thrones judging the twelve
69 Son of man s' on the right hand
Joh 6:10 Jesus said, Make the men s' down.
Ac 2:30 raise up Christ to s' on his throne;
34 Lord, S' thou on my right hand,
8:31 he would come up and s' with him.
1Co 8:10 s' at meat in the idol's temple,
Eph 2: 6 made us s' together in heavenly
Heb 1:13 S' on my right hand, until I make
Jas 2: 3 him, S' thou here in a good place;
3 or s' here under my footstool:
Re 3:21 grant to s' with me in my throne,
17: 3 woman s' upon a scarlet coloured
18: 7 I s' a queen, and am no widow, and
19:18 of them that s' on them, and the
sith See also SINCE.
Eze 35: 6 s' thou hast not hated blood, even
Sitnah *(sit'-nah)*
Ge 26:21 and he called the name of it S'.
sittest
Ex 18:14 why s' thou thyself alone, and all
De 6: 7 them when thou s' in thine house,
11:19 them when thou s' in thine house,
Ps 50:20 Thou s' and speakest against thy
Pr 23: 1 When thou s' to eat with a ruler,
Jer 22: 2 that s' upon the throne of David,
Ac 23: 3 s' thou to judge me after the law,
sitteth
Ex 11: 5 Pharaoh that s' upon his throne,
Le 15: 4 every thing, whereon he s', shall be
6 he that s' on any thing whereon he
20 every thing also that she s' upon
23 bed, or on any thing whereon she s',
26 and whatsoever she s' upon shall be
De 17:18 when he s' upon the throne of his
1Ki 1:46 Solomon s' on the throne of the
Es 6:10 the Jew, that s' at the king's gate:
Ps 1: 1 nor s' in the seat of the scornful.
2: 4 that s' in the heavens shall laugh:
10: 8 He s' in the lurking places of the
29:10 The Lord s' upon the flood;
10 yea, the Lord s' King for ever.
47: 8 s' upon the throne of his holiness.
99: 1 he s' between the cherubims; let
Pr 9:14 For she s' at the door of her house,
20: 8 that s' in the throne of judgment
31:23 when he s' among the elders of the
Ca 1:12 While the king s' at his table, my
Isa 28: 6 to him that s' in judgment,
40:22 that s' upon the circle of the earth,
Jer 17:11 As the partridge s' on eggs, and
29:16 that s' upon the throne of David,
La 3:28 He s' alone and keepeth silence,
Zec 1:11 all the earth s' still, and is at rest.
5: 7 that s' in the midst of the ephah.
M't 23:22 of God, and by him that s' thereon.
Lu 14:28 s' not down first, and counteth
31 s' not down first, and consulteth
22:27 is greater, he that s' at meat, or he
27 is not he that s' at meat? but I am
1Co 14:30 be revealed to another that s' by,
Col 3: 1 Christ s' on the right hand of God.
2Th 2: 4 he as God s' in the temple of God,
Re 5:13 unto him that s' upon the throne,
6:16 face of him that s' on the throne,
7:10 our God which s' upon the throne,
15 he that s' on the throne shall dwell
17: 1 whore that s' upon many waters:
9 mountains, on which the woman s'
15 where the whore s', are peoples,
sitting See also DOWNSITTING.
De 22: 6 and the dam s' upon the young, or
J'g 3:20 and he was s' in a summer parlour,
1Ki 10: 5 table, and the s' of his servants,
13:14 and found him s' under an oak:
22:19 I saw the Lord s' on his throne, and
2Ki 4:38 of the prophets were s' before him:
9: 5 the captains of the host were s';
2Ch 9: 4 table, and the s' of his servants,
18 stays on each side of the s' place,
18:18 I saw the Lord s' upon his throne,
Ne 2: 6 unto me, (the queen also s' by him,
Es 5:13 Mordecai...s' at the king's gate.
Isa 6: 1 I saw also the Lord s' upon a throne,
Jer 17:25 princes s' upon the throne of David,
22: 4 kings s' upon the throne of David,
30 s' upon the throne of David, and
38: 7 then s' in the gate of Benjamin;
La 3:63 Behold their s' down, and their
M't 9: 9 s' at the receipt of custom:
11:16 unto children s' in the markets,
20:30 two blind men s' by the way side,
21: 5 thee, meek, and s' upon an ass,
26:64 Son of man s' on the right hand
27:36 s' down they watched him there;
61 Mary, s' over against the sepulchre.
M'r 2: 6 were certain of the scribes s' there,
14 Alphæus s' at the receipt of custom,
5:15 had the legion, s', and clothed, and
14:62 Son of man s' on the right hand of
16: 5 a young man s' on the right side,
Lu 2:46 s' in the midst of the doctors, both
5:17 and doctors of the law s' by, which
27 Levi, s' at the receipt of custom:
7:32 unto children s' in the marketplace,
8:35 s' at the feet of Jesus, clothed, and
10:13 repented, s' in sackcloth and ashes.
Joh 2:14 and the changers of money s':
12:15 King cometh, s' on an ass's colt.
20:12 And seeth two angels in white s',
Ac 2: 2 all the house where they were s'.
8:28 s' in his chariot read Esaias the
25: 6 next day s' on the judgment seat
Re 4: 4 I saw four and twenty elders s',
sitting-place See SITTING and PLACE.
situate
1Sa 14: 5 one was s' northward over against
Eze 27: 3 that art s' at the entry of the sea,
Na 3: 8 No, that was s' among the rivers,
situation
2Ki 2:19 the s' of this city is pleasant, as
Ps 48: 2 Beautiful for s', the joy of the
Sivan *(si'-van)*
Es 8: 9 third month, that is, the month S'
six See also SIXSCORE; SIXTEEN.
Ge 7: 6 Noah was s' hundred years old
11 the s' hundredth year of Noah's life,
8:13 in the s' hundredth and first year,
16:16 Abram was fourscore and s' years
30:20 because I have born him s' sons:
31:41 and s' years for thy cattle:
46:26 the souls were threescore and s';
Ex 12:37 s' hundred thousand on foot that
14: 7 he took s' hundred chosen chariots,
16:26 S' days ye shall gather it; but on
20: 9 S' days shalt thou labour, and do
11 s' days the Lord made heaven and
21: 2 servant, s' years he shall serve:
23:10 s' years thou shalt sow thy land,
12 S' days thou shalt do thy work, and
24:16 and the cloud covered it s' days:
25:32 s' branches shall come out of the
33 the s' branches that come out of the
35 the s' branches that proceed out of
26: 9 and s' curtains by themselves, and
22 westward thou shalt make s' boards.
28:10 S' of their names on one stone, and
10 s' names of the rest on the other
31:15 S' days may work be done; but in
17 s' days the Lord made heaven and
34:21 S' days thou shalt work, but on the
35: 2 S' days shall work be done, but on
36:16 and s' curtains by themselves.
27 westward he made s' boards.
37:18 s' branches going out of the sides
19 the s' branches going out of the
21 to the s' branches going out of it.
38:26 for s' hundred thousand and three
Le 12: 5 purifying threescore and s' days.
23: 3 S' days shall work be done: but
24: 6 set them in two rows, s' on a row,
25: 3 S' years thou shalt sow thy field,
3 and s' years thou shalt prune thy
Nu 1:21 and s' thousand and five hundred.
25 five thousand s' hundred and fifty.
27 fourteen thousand and s' hundred.
46 s' hundred thousand and three
2: 4 fourteen thousand and s' hundred.
9 and s' thousand and four hundred.
11 and s' thousand and five hundred.
15 thousand and s' hundred and fifty
31 seven thousand and s' hundred.
32 s' hundred thousand and three
3:28 eight thousand and s' hundred,
34 were s' thousand and two hundred.
4:40 two thousand and s' hundred and
7: 3 s' covered wagons, and twelve oxen;
11:21 are s' hundred thousand footmen;
26:41 and five thousand and s' hundred.
51 of Israel, s' hundred thousand and
31:32 s' hundred thousand and seventy
37 was s' hundred and threescore and
38 beeves were thirty and s' thousand;
44 And thirty and s' thousand beeves,
35: 6 there shall be s' cities for refuge,
13 s' cities shall ye have for refuge.
15 These s' cities shall be a refuge,
De 5:13 S' days thou shalt labour, and do
15:12 unto thee, and serve thee s' years;
18 to thee, in serving thee s' years:
16: 8 S' days thou shalt eat unleavened
Jos 6: 3 once. Thus shalt thou do s' days.
14 into the camp: so they did s' days.
7: 5 smote...about thirty and s' men:
15:59, 62 s' cities with their villages.
J'g 3:31 slew of the Philistines s' hundred
12: 7 Jephthah judged Israel s' years.
18:11, 16 s' hundred men appointed with
17 s' hundred men that were appointed
20:15 cities twenty and s' thousand men
47 s' hundred men turned and fled to
Ru 3:15 he measured s' measures of barley,
17 s' measures of barley gave he me;
1Sa 13: 5 chariots, and s' thousand horsemen,
15 with him, about s' hundred men.
14: 2 him were about s' hundred men;
17: 4 height was s' cubits and a span.
7 spear's head weighed s' hundred
23:13 men, which were about s' hundred,
27: 2 passed over with the s' hundred men
30: 9 s' hundred men that were with
2Sa 2:11 was seven years and s' months.
5: 5 Judah seven years and s' months:
6:13 ark of the Lord had gone s' paces,
15:18 s' hundred men which came after
21:20 that had on every hand s' fingers,
20 and on every foot s' toes, four and
1Ki 6: 6 and the middle was s' cubits broad,
10:14 Solomon in one year was s' hundred
14 threescore and s' talents of gold,
16 s' hundred shekels of gold went to
19 The throne had s' steps, and the
20 and on the other upon the s' steps:
29 for s' hundred shekels of silver,
11:16 s' months did Joab remain there
16:23 s' years reigned he in Tirzah.
2Ki 5: 5 and s' thousand pieces of gold, and
11: 3 in the house of the Lord s' years.
13:19 have smitten five or s' times;
15: 8 over Israel in Samaria s' months.
1Ch 3: 4 s' were born unto him in Hebron;
4 reigned seven years and s' months:
22 and Neariah, and Shaphat, s'.
4:27 had sixteen sons and s' daughters;
7: 2 twenty thousand and s' hundred.
4 for war, s' and thirty thousand men:
40 was twenty and s' thousand men.
8:38 And Azel had s' sons, whose names

1Ch 9: 6 brethren, s· hundred and ninety.
9 nine hundred and fifty and s·.
44 And Azel had s· sons, whose names
12: 24 s· thousand and eight hundred,
26 Levi four thousand and s· hundred.
35 and eight thousand and s· hundred.
20: 6 s· on each hand, and s· on each foot:
21: 25 s· hundred shekels of gold by
23: 4 and s· thousand were officers and
25: 3 Hashabiah, and Mattithiah, s·,
26: 17 Eastward were s· Levites,
2Ch 1: 17 a chariot for s· hundred shekels of
2: 2 and s· hundred to oversee them.
17 three thousand and s· hundred.
18 thousand and s· hundred overseers
3: 8 amounting to s· hundred talents.
9: 13 Solomon in one year was s· hundred
13 threescore and s· talents of gold;
15 s· hundred shekels of beaten gold
18 there were s· steps to the throne,
19 and on the other upon the s· steps.
16: 1 s· and thirtieth year of the reign
22: 12 hid in the house of God s· years:
26: 12 were two thousand and s· hundred.
29: 33 were s· hundred oxen and three
35: 8 and s· hundred small cattle, and
Ezr 2: 10 of Bani, s· hundred forty and two.
11 of Bebai, s· hundred twenty and
13 Adonikam, s· hundred sixty and s·.
14 Bigvai, two thousand fifty and s·.
22 The men of Netophah, fifty and s·.
26 Gaba, s· hundred twenty and one.
30 Magbish, an hundred fifty and s·.
35 three thousand and s· hundred
60 Nekoda, s· hundred fifty and two.
66 were seven hundred thirty and s·;
67 s· thousand seven hundred and
8: 26 s· hundred and fifty talents of
35 for all Israel, ninety and s· rams,
Ne 5: 18 was one ox and s· choice sheep;
7: 10 of Arah, s· hundred fifty and two.
15 Binnui, s· hundred forty and eight.
16 of Bebai, s· hundred twenty and
18 Adonikam, s· hundred threescore
20 of Adin, s· hundred fifty and five.
30 Gaba, s· hundred twenty and one.
62 Nekoda, s· hundred forty and two.
68 horses, seven hundred thirty and s·:
69 s· thousand seven hundred and
Es 2: 12 to wit, s· months with oil of myrrh,
12 and s· months with sweet odours,
Job 5: 19 He shall deliver thee in s· troubles:
42: 12 s· thousand camels, and a thousand
Pr 6: 16 These s· things doth the Lord hate:
Isa 6: 2 seraphims: each one had s· wings;
Jer 34: 14 when he hath served thee s· years,
52: 23 were ninety and s· pomegranates
30 were four thousand and s· hundred.
Eze 9: 2 s· men came from the way of the
40: 5 a measuring reed of s· cubits long
12 s· cubits on this side, and s· cubits
41: 1 s· cubits broad on the one side, and
1 s· cubits broad on the other side,
3 two cubits; and the door, s· cubits;
5 the wall of the house, s· cubits;
8 were a full reed of s· great cubits.
46: 1 shall be shut the s· working days;
4 shall be s· lambs without blemish,
6 blemish, and s· lambs, and a ram:
Da 3: 1 and the breadth thereof s· cubits:
M't 17: 1 after s· days Jesus taketh Peter,
M'r 9: 2 after s· days Jesus taketh with him
Lu 4: 25 shut up three years and s· months,
13: 14 are s· days in which men ought to
Joh 2: 6 were set there s· waterpots of stone,
20 Forty and s· years was this temple
12: 1 s· days before the passover came to
Ac 11: 12 these s· brethren accompanied me,
18: 11 there a year and s· months,
Jas 5: 17 space of three years and s· months.
Re 4: 8 each of them s· wings about him;
13: 18 is S· hundred threescore and s·.
14: 20 thousand and s· hundred furlongs.

six-hundred See SIX and HUNDRED.

sixscore
1Ki 9: 14 to the king s· talents of gold.
Jon 4: 11 more than s· thousand

sixteen
Ge 46: 18 she bare unto Jacob, even s·
Ex 26: 25 sockets of silver, s· sockets;
36: 30 their sockets were s· sockets of
Nu 26: 22 s· thousand and five hundred.
31: 40 the persons were s· thousand;
46 And s· thousand persons;)
52 s· thousand seven hundred and
Jos 15: 41 s· cities with their villages.
19: 22 s· cities with their villages.
2Ki 13: 10 Samaria, and reigned s· years.
14: 21 which was s· years old, and
15: 2 S· years old was he when he
33 reigned s· years in Jerusalem.
16: 2 reigned s· years in Jerusalem,
1Ch 4: 27 Shimei had s· sons and six
24: 4 of Eleazar there were s· chief
2Ch 13: 21 two sons, and s· daughters.
26: 1 Uzziah, who was s· years old,
3 S· years old was Uzziah when
27: 1 reigned s· years in Jerusalem.
8 reigned s· years in Jerusalem.
28: 1 reigned s· years in Jerusalem:
Ac 27: 37 threescore and s· souls.

sixteenth
1Ch 24: 14 to Bilgah, the s· to Immer,
25: 23 The s· to Hananiah, he, his
2Ch 29: 17 in the s· day of the first month

sixth
Ge 1: 31 and the morning were the s· day.
30: 19 again, and bare Jacob the s· son.
Ex 16: 5 on the s· day they shall prepare
22 on the s· day they gathered twice
29 on the s· day the bread of two days;
26: 9 shalt double the s· curtain in the
Le 25: 21 blessing upon you in the s· year,
Nu 7: 42 On the s· day Eliasaph the son of
29: 29 on the s· day eight bullocks, two
Jos 19: 32 The s· lot came out to the children
2Sa 3: 5 the s·, Ithream, by Eglah David's
1Ki 16: 8 In the twenty and s· year of Asa
2Ki 18: 10 even in the s· year of Hezekiah,
1Ch 2: 15 Ozem the s·, David the seventh:
3: 3 s·, Ithream by Eglah his wife.
12: 11 Attai the s·, Eliel the seventh,
24: 9 to Malchijah, the s· to Mijamin,
25: 13 The s· to Bukkiah, he, his sons, and
26: 3 Elam the fifth, Jehohanan the s·,
5 Ammiel the s·, Issachar the
27: 9 The s· captain for the s· month was
Ezr 6: 15 was in the s· year of the reign of
Ne 3: 30 and Hanun the s· son of Zalaph,
Eze 4: 11 by measure, the s· part of an hin:
8: 1 pass in the s· year, in the s· month,
39: 2 and leave but the s· part of thee,
45: 13 offer; the s· part of an ephah of an
13 give the s· part of an ephah of an
46: 14 the s· part of an ephah, and the
Hag 1: 1 of Darius the king, in the s· month,
15 and twentieth day of the s· month,
M't 20: 5 out about the s· and ninth hour,
27: 45 the s· hour there was darkness
M'r 15: 33 when the s· hour was come, there
Lu 1: 26 the s· month the angel Gabriel was
36 this is the s· month with her, who
23: 44 it was about the s· hour, and there
Joh 4: 6 well: and it was about the s· hour.
19: 14 passover, and about the s· hour:
Ac 10: 9 housetop to pray about the s· hour:
Re 6: 12 when he had opened the s· seal,
9: 13 the s· angel sounded, and I heard a
14 Saying to the s· angel which had
16: 12 And the s· angel poured out his vial
21: 20 The fifth, sardonyx; the s·, sardius;

six-thousand See SIX and THOUSAND.

sixty See also SIXTYFOLD.
Ge 5: 15 Mahalaleel lived s· and five years,
18 Jared lived an hundred s· and two
20 Jared were nine hundred s· and two
21 And Enoch lived s· and five years,
23 of Enoch were three hundred s· and
27 Methuselah were nine hundred s·
Le 27: 3 from twenty years old even unto s·
7 if it be from s· years old and above;
Nu 7: 88 the rams s·, the he goats s·,
88 the lambs of the first year s·. This
Ezr 2: 13 Adonikam, six hundred s· and six.
M't 13: 23 some an hundredfold, some s·,
M'r 4: 8 some thirty, and some s·, and some
20 some thirtyfold, some s·, and some

sixtyfold
M't 13: 8 some s·, some thirtyfold.

size
Ex 36: 9 the curtains were all of one s·.
15 the eleven curtains were of one s·.
1Ki 6: 25 were of one measure and one s·.
7: 37 casting, one measure, and one s·.
1Ch 23: 29 for all manner of measure and s·;

skies
2Sa 22: 12 waters, and thick clouds of the s·.
Ps 18: 11 waters and thick clouds of the s·.
77: 17 out water: the s· sent out a sound:
Isa 45: 8 let the s· pour down righteousness:
Jer 51: 9 and is lifted up even to the s·.

skilful See also UNSKILFUL.
1Ch 5: 18 and s· in war, were four and forty
15: 22 about the song, because he was s·.
28: 21 every willing s· man, for any
2Ch 2: 14 s· to work in gold, and in silver, in
Eze 21: 31 of brutish men, and s· to destroy.
Da 1: 4 favoured, and s· in all wisdom,
Am 5: 16 such as are s· of lamentation to

skilfully
Ps 33: 3 song; play s· with a loud noise.

skilfulness
Ps 78: 72 them by the s· of his hands.

skill See also SKILFUL.
1Ki 5: 6 can s· to hew timber like unto the
2Ch 2: 7 s· to grave with the cunning men
8 thy servants can s· to cut timber
34: 12 could s· of instruments of musick.
Ec 9: 11 nor yet favour to men of s·; but
Da 1: 17 and s· in all learning and wisdom:
9: 22 to give thee s· and understanding.

skin See also FORESKIN; SKINS.
Ex 22: 27 only, it is his raiment for his s·:
29: 14 the flesh of the bullock, and his s·,
34: 29 wist not that the s· of his face shone
30 behold, the s· of his face shone;
35 that the s· of Moses' face shone:
Le 4: 11 And the s· of the bullock, and all
7: 8 himself the s· of the burnt offering
11: 32 vessel of wood, or raiment, or s·, or
13: 2 have in the s· of his flesh a rising,
2 it be in the s· of his flesh like the
3 on the plague in the s· of the flesh:
3 be deeper than the s· of his flesh,
4 spot be white in the s· of his flesh,
4 in sight be not deeper than the s·,
5 and the plague spread not in the s·;
Le 13: 6 the plague spread not in the s·, the
7 scab spread much abroad in the s·,
8 the scab spreadeth in the s·, then
10 if the rising be white in the s·, and
11 an old leprosy in the s· of his flesh,
12 leprosy break out abroad in the s·,
12 leprosy cover all the s· of him that
18 in the s· thereof, was a boil, and is
20 it be in sight lower than the s·. and
21 and if it be not lower than the s·,
22 if it spread much abroad in the s·,
24 s· whereof there is a hot burning,
25 it be in sight deeper than the s·;
26 it be no lower than the other s·,
27 it be spread much abroad in the s·,
28 his place, and spread not in the s·,
30 if it be in sight deeper than the s·;
31 it be not in sight deeper than the s·,
32 be not in s· deeper then the s·;
34 if the scall be not spread in the s·,
34 nor be in sight deeper than the s·;
35 if the scall spread much in the s·
36 if the scall be spread in the s·, the
38 in the s· of their flesh bright spots,
39 bright spots in the s· of their flesh
39 spot that groweth in the s·; he is
43 appeareth in the s· of the flesh;
48 in a s·, or in any thing made of s·;
49 reddish in the garment, or in the s·,
49 in the woof, or in any thing of s·;
51 the warp, or in the woof, or in a s·,
51 or in any work that is made of s·;
52 or any thing of s·, wherein the
53 or in the woof, or in any thing of s·;
56 out of the garment, or out of the s·,
57 or in the woof, or in any thing of s·;
58 or whatsoever thing of s· it be,
15: 17 And every garment, and every s·,
Nu 19: 5 burn the heifer in his sight; her s·,
Job 2: 4 S· for s·, yea, all that a man
7: 5 my s· is broken, and become
10: 11 hast clothed me with s· and flesh,
16: 15 have sewed sackcloth upon my s·,
18: 13 shall devour the strength of his s·:
19: 20 My bone cleaveth to my s· and to
20 and I am escaped with the s· of my
26 though after my s· worms destroy
30: 30 My s· is black upon me, and my
41: 7 thou fill his s· with barbed irons?
Ps 102: 5 my bones cleave to my s·.
Jer 13: 23 Can the Ethiopian change his s·,
La 3: 4 flesh and my s· hath he made old;
4: 8 their s· cleaveth to their bones; it
5: 10 Our s· was black like an oven
Eze 16: 10 and shod thee with badgers' s·, and
37: 6 upon you, and cover you with s·,
8 and the s· covered them above: but
Mic 3: 2 pluck off their s· from off them,
3 and flay their s· from off them; and
M'r 1: 6 a girdle of a s· about his loins;

skins See also FORESKINS; GOATSKINS; SHEEPSKINS.
Ge 3: 21 did the Lord God make coats of s·,
27: 16 she put the s· of the kids of the
Ex 25: 5 rams' s· dyed red, and badgers' s·,
26: 14 for the tent of rams' s· dyed red,
14 and a covering above of badgers' s·.
35: 7 rams' s· dyed red, and badgers' s·,
23 and red s· of rams, and badgers' s·,
36: 19 for the tent of rams' s· dyed red,
19 and a covering of badgers' s· above
39: 34 the covering of rams' s· dyed red,
34 the covering of badgers' s·, and the
Le 13: 59 warp, or woof, or any thing of s·,
16: 27 they shall burn in the fire their s·,
Nu 4: 6 thereon the covering of badgers' s·,
8 same with a covering of badgers' s·,
10 within a covering of badgers' s·,
11 it with a covering of badgers' s·,
12 them with a covering of badgers' s·,
14 upon it a covering of badgers' s·,
25 covering of the badgers' s· that is
31: 20 all that is made of s·, and all work

skip See also SKIPPED; SKIPPING.
Ps 29: 6 them also to s· like a calf;

skipped See also SKIPPEDST.
Ps 114: 4 The mountains s· like rams, and
6 mountains, that ye s· like rams;

skippedst
Jer 48: 27 spakest of him, thou s· for joy.

skipping
Ca 2: 8 the mountains, s· upon the hills.

skirt See also SKIRTS.
De 22: 30 wife, nor discover his father's s·.
27: 20 he uncovereth his father's s·.
Ru 3: 9 spread therefore thy s· over thine
1Sa 15: 27 laid hold upon the s· of his mantle,
24: 4 cut off the s· of Saul's robe privily.
5 because he had cut off Saul's s·.
11 see the s· of thy robe in my hand:
11 in that I cut off the s· of thy robe,
Eze 16: 8 and I spread my s· over thee, and
Hag 2: 12 holy flesh in the s· of his garment,
12 and with his s· do touch bread, or
Zec 8: 23 hold of the s· of him that is a Jew,

skirts
Ps 133: 2 down to the s· of his garments;
Jer 2: 34 Also in thy s· is found the blood of
13: 22 iniquity are thy s· discovered, and
26 I discover thy s· upon thy face,
La 1: 9 Her filthiness is in her s·; she
Eze 5: 3 number, and bind them in thy s·.
Na 3: 5 will discover thy s· upon thy face,

skull
J'g 9:53 head, and all to brake his s'.
2Ki 9:35 found no more of her than the s',
M't 27:33 that is to say, a place of a s',
M'r 15:22 being interpreted, The place of a s'
Joh 19:17 into a place called the place of a s',
sky See also SKIES.
De 33:26 and in his excellency on the s',
Job 37:18 thou with him spread out the s',
M't 16: 2 be fair weather: for the s' is red.
3 day: for the s' is red and lowering.
3 ye can discern the face of the s';
Lu 12:56 ye can discern the face of the s'
Heb11:12 so many as the stars of the s' in
slack See also SLACKED.
De 7:10 not be s' to him that hateth him,
23:21 thy God, thou shalt not s' to pay it:
Jos 10: 6 S' not thy hand from thy servants;
18: 3 How long are ye s' to go to possess
2Ki 4:24 s' not thy riding for me, except I
Pr 10: 4 poor that dealeth with a s' hand:
Zep 3:16 Zion, Let not thine hands be s'.
2Pe 3: 9 The Lord is not s' concerning his
slacked
Hab 1: 4 the law is s', and judgment doth
slackness
2Pe 3: 9 promise, as some men count s';
slain
Ge 4:23 I have s' a man to my wounding,
34:27 sons of Jacob came upon the s',
Le 14:51 them in the blood of the s' bird,
26:17 shall be s' before your enemies:
Nu 11:22 flocks of the herds be s' for
14:16 hath s' them in the wilderness.
19:16 one that is s' with a sword in
18 a bone, or one s', or one dead, or a
22:33 surely now also I had s' thee, and
23:24 and drink the blood of the s'.
25:14 name of the Israelite that was s',
14 was s' with the Midianitish woman,
15 Midianitish woman that was s' was
18 was s' in the day of the plague for
31: 8 the rest of them that were s';
19 and whosoever hath touched any s
De 1: 4 he had s' Sihon the king of the
21: 1 be found s' in the land which the
1 it be not known who hath s' him:
2 are round about him that is s':
3 city which is next unto the s' man,
6 that are next unto the s' man, shall
28:31 Thine ox shall be s' before thine
32:42 with the blood of the s' and of the
Jos 11: 6 deliver them up all s' before Israel
13:22 among them that were s' by them.
J'g 9:18 and have s' his sons, threescore
15:16 an ass have I s' a thousand men.
20: 4 husband of the woman that was s',
5 night, and thought to have s' me:
1Sa 4:11 Hophni and Phinehas, were s'.
18: 7 Saul hath s' his thousands, and
19: 6 the Lord liveth, he shall not be s
11 to morrow thou shalt be s'.
20:32 Wherefore shall he be s'? what
21:11 Saul hath s' his thousands, and
22:21 Saul had s' the Lord's priests.
31: 1 and fell down s' in mount Gilboa.
8 the Philistines came to strip the s',
2Sa 1:16 I have s' the Lord's anointed.
19 The beauty of Israel is s' upon thy
22 From the blood of the s', from the
25 thou wast s' in thine high places.
3:30 he had s' their brother Asahel at
4:11 men have s' a righteous person in
12: 9 and hast s' him with the sword of
13:30 Absalom hath s' all the king's
32 s' all the young men the king's
18: 7 people of Israel were s' before the
21:12 Philistines had s' Saul in Gilboa:
16 sword, thought to have s' David.
1Ki 1:19, 25 s' oxen and fat cattle and sheep
9:16 s' the Canaanites that dwelt in the
11:15 host was gone up to bury the s',
13:26 which hath torn him, and s' him,
16:16 and hath also s' the king:
19: 1 how he had s' all the prophets
10, 14 s' thy prophets with the sword;
2Ki 3:23 the kings are surely s', and they
11: 2 the king's sons which were s';
2 from Athaliah, so that he was not s'.
8 within the ranges, let him be s':
15 Let her not be s' in the house of the
16 king's house: and there was she s'
14: 5 his servants which had s' the king
1Ch 5:22 there fell down many s', because
10: 1 and fell down s' in mount Gilboa.
8 the Philistines came to strip the s',
11:11 hundred s' by him at one time.
2Ch 13:17 fell down s' of Israel five hundred
21:13 also hast s' thy brethren of thy
22: 1 to the camp had s' all the eldest.
9 and when they had s' him, they
11 among the king's sons that were s',
23:14 her, let him be s' with the sword.
21 they had s' Athaliah with the sword.
28: 9 and ye have s' them in a rage that
Es 7: 4 my people, to be destroyed, to be s',
9:11 of those that were s' in Shushan
12 The Jews have s' and destroyed
Job 1:15, 17 s' the servants with the edge of
39:30 and where the s' are, there is she.
Ps 62: 3 ye shall be s' all of you: as a
88: 5 like the s' that lie in the grave,
89:10 Rahab in pieces, as one that is s';
Pr 7:26 strong men have been s' by her.
Pr 22:13 without, I shall be s' in the streets.
24:11 and those that are ready to be s';
Isa 10: 4 and they shall fall under the s'.
14:19 as the raiment of those that are s',
20 thy land, and s' thy people:
22: 2 s' men are not s' with the sword,
26:21 and shall no more cover her s'.
27: 7 he s' according to the slaughter of
7 of them that are s' by him?
34: 3 Their s' also shall be cast out, and
66:16 the s' of the Lord shall be many.
Jer 9: 1 the s' of the daughter of my people
14:18 then behold the s' with the sword
18:21 young men be s' by the sword in
25:33 s' of the Lord shall be at that day
33: 5 whom I have s' in mine anger
41: 4 day after he had s' Gedaliah,
9 he had s' because of Gedaliah,
9 filled it with them that were s'.
16 s' Gedaliah the son of Ahikam,
18 son of Nethaniah had s' Gedaliah
51: 4 the s' shall fall in the land of the
47 her s' shall fall in the midst of her.
49 hath caused the s' of Israel to fall,
49 shall fall the s' of all the earth.
La 2:20 the priest and the prophet be s' in
21 s' them in the day of thine anger;
3:43 thou hast s', thou hast not pitied.
4: 9 They that be s' with the sword are
9 than they that be s' with hunger:
Eze 6: 4 down your s' men before your idols.
7 the s' shall fall in the midst of you,
13 when their s' men shall be among
9: 7 house, and fill the courts with the s'
11: 6 have multiplied your s' in this city,
6 filled the streets thereof with the s'
7 Your s' whom ye have laid in the
16:21 That thou hast s' my children, and
21:14 the third time, the sword of the s':
14 sword of the great men that are s',
29 upon the necks of them that are s',
23:39 when they had s' their children to
26: 6 the field shall be s' by the sword;
28: 8 are s' in the midst of the seas.
30: 4 when the s' shall fall in Egypt, and
11 Egypt, and fill the land with the s'.
31:17 them that be s' with the sword;
18 with them that be s' by the sword.
32:20 of them that are s' by the sword:
21 lie uncircumcised, s' by the sword.
22 all of them s', fallen by the sword:
23, 24 all of them s', fallen by the sword,
25 set her a bed in the midst of the s'
25 uncircumcised, s' by the sword:
25 put in the midst of them that be s'.
26 uncircumcised, s' by the sword,
28 them that are s' with the sword.
29 by them that were s' by the sword:
30 which are gone down with the s';
30 with them that be s' by the sword,
31 Pharaoh and all his army s' by the
32 them that are s' with the sword,
35: 8 fill his mountains with his s' men:
8 they fall that are s' with the sword.
37: 9 breathe upon these s', that they
Da 2:13 that the wise men should be s';
13 Daniel and his fellows to be s'.
5:30 was...the king of the Chaldeans s'.
7:11 I beheld even till the beast was s',
11:26 and many shall fall down s'.
Ho 6: 5 s' them by the words of my mouth:
Am 4:10 young men have I s' with the sword,
Na 3: 3 and there is a multitude of s', and
Zep 2:12 also, ye shall be s' by my sword.
Lu 9:22 be s', and be raised the third day.
Ac 2:23 wicked hands have crucified and s':
5:36 who was s'; and all, as many as
7:42 have ye offered to me s' beasts and
52 they have s' them which shewed
13:28 they Pilate that he should be s'.
23:14 eat nothing until we have s' Paul.
Eph 2:16 cross, having s' the enmity thereby:
Heb11:37 were s' with the sword:
Re 2:13 martyr, who was s' among you,
5: 6 stood a Lamb as it had been s',
9 thou wast s', and hast redeemed
12 Worthy is the Lamb that was s' to
6: 9 that were s' for the word of God,
11:13 were s' of men seven thousand:
13: 8 the Lamb s' from the foundation
18:24 of all that were s' upon the earth.
19:21 remnant were s' with the sword of
slander See also SLANDERED; SLANDEREST; SLANDERETH; SLANDERS.
Nu 14:36 by bringing up a s' upon the land,
Ps 31:13 For I have heard the s' of many:
Pr 10:18 and he that uttereth a s', is a fool.
slandered
2Sa 19:27 hath s' thy servant unto my lord
slanderest
Ps 50:20 s' thine own mother's son.
slandereth
Ps 101: 5 Whoso privily s' his neighbour,
slanderously
Ro 3: 8 (as we be s' reported, and as some
slanders
Jer 6:28 revolters, walking with s':
9: 4 every neighbour will walk with s'.
slanderers
1Ti 3:11 must their wives be grave, not s',
slang
1Sa 17:49 and took thence a stone, and s' it,
slaughter
Ge 14:17 from the s' of Chedorlaomer,
Jos 10:10 and slew them with a great s' at
20 slaying them with a very great s',
J'g 11:33 the vineyards, with a very great s'.
15: 8 them hip and thigh with a great s':
1Sa 4:10 and there was a very great s'; for
17 there hath been also a great s'
6:19 many of the people with a great s'
14:14 And that first s', which Jonathan
30 not been now a much greater s'
17:57 David returned from the s' of the
18: 6 David was returned from the s' of
19: 8 and slew them with a great s';
23: 5 and smote them with a great s'.
2Sa 1: 1 David was returned from the s' of
17: 9 s' among the people that follow
18: 7 there was there a great s' that day
1Ki 20:21 slew the Syrians with a great s'.
2Ch 13:17 people slew them with a great s':
25:14 come from the s' of the Edomites,
28: 5 who smote him with a great s'.
Es 9: 5 the sword, and s', and destruction,
Ps 44:22 we are counted as sheep for the s'.
Pr 7:22 as an ox goeth to the s', or as a
Isa 10:26 according to the s' of Midian at
14:21 Prepare s' for his children for the
27: 7 according to the s' of them that
30:25 of waters in the day of the great s',
34: 2 he hath delivered them to the s'.
6 a great s' in the land of Idumea.
53: 7 he is brought as a lamb to the s',
65:12 and ye shall all bow down to the s':
Jer 7:32 of Hinnom, but the valley of s':
11:19 or an ox that is brought to the s';
12: 3 pull them out like sheep for the s',
3 and prepare them for the day of s'.
19: 6 of Hinnom, but The valley of s'.
25:34 for the days of your s' and of your
48:15 young men are gone...to the s',
50:27 let them go down to the s': woe
51:40 them down like lambs to the s',
Eze 9: 2 every man a s' weapon in his hand;
21:10 It is sharpened to make a sore s';
15 bright, it is wrapped up for the s'.
22 to open the mouth in the s', to lift
28 is drawn: for the s' it is furbished,
26:15 when the s' is made in the midst
Ho 5: 2 revolters are profound to make s',
Ob 9 mount of Esau may be cut off by s'
Zec 11: 4 my God; Feed the flock of the s';
7 And I will feed the flock of s', even
Ac 8:32 He was led as a sheep to the s';
9: 1 s' against the disciples of the Lord,
Ro 8:36 are accounted as sheep for the s'.
Heb 7: 1 returning from the s' of the kings,
Jas 5: 5 your hearts, as in a day of s'.
slave See also SLAVES.
Jer 2:14 Israel a servant? is he a homeborn s'?
slaves
Re 18:13 chariots, and s', and souls of men.
slay See also SLAIN; SLAYETH; SLAYING; SLEW.
Ge 4:14 one that findeth me shall s' me.
18:25 s' the righteous with the wicked:
20: 4 thou s' also a righteous nation?
11 they will s' me for my wife's sake.
22:10 and took the knife to s' his son.
27:41 then will I s' my brother Jacob.
34:30 together against me, and s' me;
37:18 conspired against him to s' him.
20 let us s' him, and cast him into
26 What profit is it if we s' our brother,
42:37 S' my two sons, if I bring him not
43:16 Bring these men home, and s',
Ex 2:15 this thing, he sought to s' Moses.
4:23 I will s' thy son, even thy firstborn.
5:21 put a sword in their hand to s' us.
21:14 his neighbour, to s' him with guile;
23: 7 innocent and righteous s' thou not:
29:16 And thou shalt s' the ram, and
32:12 out, to s' them in the mountains,
27 s' every man his brother, and every
Le 4:29 s' the sin offering in the place of
33 s' it for a sin offering in the place
14:13 he shall s' the lamb in the place
20:15 death: and ye shall s' the beast.
Nu 19: 3 one shall s' her before his face:
25: 5 S' ye every one his men that were
35:19 himself shall s' the murderer:
19 he meeteth him, he shall s' him.
21 of blood shall s' the murderer,
De 9:28 out to s' them in the wilderness.
19: 6 the way is long, and s' him;
27:25 reward to s' an innocent person:
Jos 13:22 children of Israel s' with the sword
J'g 8:19 saved them alive, I would not s' you.
20 his firstborn, Up, and s' them.
9:54 Draw thy sword, and s' me, that
1Sa 2:25 because the Lord would s' them.
5:10 ark...to us, to s' us and our people.
11 that it s' us not, and our people:
14:34 sheep, and s' them here, and eat;
15: 3 but s' both man and woman,
19: 5 blood, to s' David without a cause?
11 him, and to s' him in the morning:
15 to me in the bed, that I may s' him.
20: 8 be in me iniquity, s' me thyself;
33 determined of his father to s' David.
22:17 Turn, and s' the priests of the Lord;
2Sa 1: 9 Stand...upon me, and s' me: for
3:37 it was not of the king to s' Abner
21: 2 Saul sought to s' them in his zeal
1Ki 1:51 not s' his servant with the sword.
3:26 the living child, and in no wise s' it.
27 the living child, and in no wise s' it:

1Ki 15:28 did Baasha s' him, and reigned in
17:18 to remembrance, and to s' my son?
18: 9 into the hand of Ahab, to s' me?
12 he cannot find thee, he shall s' me:
14 Elijah is here: and he shall s' me.
19:17 the sword of Hazael shall Jehu s':
17 the sword of Jehu shall Elisha s'.
20:36 from me, a lion shall s' thee.
2Ki 8:12 young men wilt thou s' with the
10:25 the captains, Go in, and s' them;
17:26 s' them, because they know not
2Ch 20:23 utterly to s' and destroy them:
23:14 S' her not in the house of the Lord,
Ne 4:11 and s' them, and cause the work to
6:10 for they will come to s' thee;
10 the night will they come to s' thee.
Es 8:11 to s', and to cause to perish, all the
Job 9:23 If the scourge s' suddenly, he will
13:15 Though he s' me, yet will I trust
20:16 the viper's tongue shall s' him.
Ps 34:21 Evil shall s' the wicked: and they
37:14 and to s' such as be of upright
32 righteous, and seeketh to s' him.
59:11 S' them not, lest my people forget:
94: 6 s' the widow and the stranger, and
109:16 might even s' the broken in heart.
139:19 Surely thou wilt s' the wicked,
Pr 1:32 away of the simple shall s' them,
Isa 11: 4 of his lips shall he s' the wicked.
14:30 and he shall s' thy remnant.
27: 1 he shall s' the dragon that is in the
65:15 for the Lord God shall s' thee, and
Jer 5: 6 lion out of the forest shall s' them,
15: 3 sword to s', and the dogs to tear,
18:23 their counsel against me to s' me:
20: 4 and shall s' them with the sword.
29:21 he shall s' them before your eyes;
40:14 son of Nethaniah to s' thee?
15 and I will s' Ishmael the son of
15 wherefore should he s' thee, that
41: 8 that said unto Ishmael, S' us not:
50:27 S' all her bullocks; let them go
Eze 9: 6 S' utterly old and young, both
13:19 to s' the souls that should not die,
23:47 they shall s' their sons and their
26: 8 s' with the sword thy daughters in
11 he shall s' thy people by the sword,
40:39 to s' thereon the burnt offering
44:11 they shall s' the burnt offering and
Da 2:14 was gone forth to s' the wise men
Ho 2: 3 a dry land, and s' her with thirst.
9:16 I s' even the beloved fruit of their
Am 2: 3 will s' all the princes thereof with
9: 1 s' the last of them with the sword:
4 the sword, and it shall s' them:
Hab 1:17 spare continually to s' the nations?
Zec 11: 5 Whose possessors s' them, and hold
Lu 11:49 and some of them they shall s' and
19:27 hither, and s' them before me.
Joh 5:16 Jesus, and sought to s' him,
Ac 5:33 heart, and took counsel to s' them.
9:29 but they went about to s' him.
11: 7 unto me, Arise, Peter; s' and eat.
Re 9:15 year, for to s' the third part of men.

slayer See also MANSLAYER.
Nu 35:11 that the s' may flee thither, which
24 between the s' and the revenger
25 congregation shall deliver the s'
26 But if the s' shall at any time come
27 the revenger of blood kill the s';
28 s' shall return into the land of his
De 4:42 That the s' might flee thither,
19: 3 that every s' may flee thither.
4 this is the case of the s', which
6 avenger of the blood pursue the s',
Jos 20: 3 That the s' that killeth any person
5 they shall not deliver the s' up into
6 then shall the s' return, and come
21:13, 21, 27, 32, 38 city of refuge for...s';
Eze 21:11 to give it into the hand of the s'.

slayeth
Ge 4:15 him, Therefore whosoever s' Cain,
De 22:26 his neighbour, and s' him,
Job 5: 2 man, and envy s' the silly one.
Eze 28: 9 before him that s' thee, I am God?
9 in the hand of him that s' thee.

slaying
Jos 8:24 end of s' all the inhabitants of Ai
10:20 had made an end of s' them with
J'g 9:56 father, in s' his seventy brethren:
1Ki 17:20 whom I sojourn, by s' her son?
Isa 22:13 s' oxen, and killing sheep, eating
57: 5 s' the children in the valleys
Eze 9: 8 to pass, while they were s' them,

sleep See also ASLEEP; SLEEPEST; SLEEPETH; SLEEPING; SLEPT.
Ge 2:21 a deep s' to fall upon Adam, and
15:12 down, a deep s' fell upon Abram;
28:11 and lay down in that place to s'.
16 And Jacob awaked out of his s',
31:40 and my s' departed from mine eyes.
Ex 22:27 for his skin: wherein shall he s'?
De 24:12 poor, shall not s' with his pledge:
13 that he may s' in his own raiment,
31:16 thou shalt s' with thy fathers; and
J'g 16:14 And he awaked out of s', and went
19 she made him s' upon her knees;
20 he awoke out of his s', and said,
1Sa 3: 3 was, and Samuel was laid down to s';
26:12 a deep s' from the Lord was fallen
2Sa 7:12 and thou shalt s' with thy fathers,
1Ki 1:21 the king shall s' with his fathers,
Es 6: 1 that night could not the king s',
Job 4:13 when deep s' falleth on men,
Job 7:21 for now shall I s' in the dust; and
14:12 awake, nor be raised out of their s'.
33:15 when deep s' falleth upon men, in
Ps 4: 8 both lay me down in peace, and s':
13: 3 God: lighten mine eyes, lest I s'
3 lest I...the s' of death;
76: 5 spoiled, they have slept their s':
6 and horse is cast into a dead s'.
78:65 the Lord awaked as one out of s',
90: 5 as with a flood; they are as a s':
121: 4 Israel shall neither slumber nor s'.
127: 2 for so he giveth his beloved s'.
132: 4 I will not give s' to mine eyes, or
Pr 3:24 down, and thy s' shall be sweet,
4:16 For they s' not, except they have
16 and their s' is taken away, unless
6: 4 Give not s' to thine eyes, nor
9 How long wilt thou s', O sluggard?
9 when wilt thou arise out of thy s'?
10 Yet a little s', a little slumber, a
10 a little folding of the hands to s':
19:15 Slothfulness casteth into a deep s';
20:13 Love not s', lest thou come to
24:33 Yet a little s', a little slumber, a
33 a little folding of the hands to s':
Ec 5:12 s' of a labouring man is sweet,
12 of the rich will not suffer him to s'.
8:16 nor night seeth s' with his eyes:)
Ca 5: 2 I s', but my heart waketh: it is the
Isa 5:27 none shall slumber nor s'; neither
29:10 out upon you the spirit of deep s',
Jer 31:26 and my s' was sweet unto me.
51:39 that they may rejoice, and s'
39 a perpetual s', and not wake,
57 mighty men: and they shall s'
57 a perpetual s', and not wake
Eze 34:25 wilderness, and s' in the woods.
Da 2: 1 and his s' brake from him.
6:18 him: and his s' went from him.
8:18 I was in a deep s' on my face
10: 9 then was I in a deep s' on my face,
12: 2 many of them that s' in the dust
Zec 4: 1 man that is wakened out of his s',
M't 1:24 Joseph being raised from s' did as
26:45 S' on now, and take your rest:
M'r 4:27 And should s', and rise night and
14:41 S' on now, and take your rest:
Lu 9:32 were with him were heavy with s':
22:46 Why s' ye? rise and pray, lest ye
Joh 11:11 that I may awake him out of s'.
12 Lord, if he s', he shall do well.
13 had spoken of taking of rest in s'.
Ac 13:36 fell on s', and was laid unto his
16:27 of the prison awaking out of his s',
20: 9 being fallen into a deep s':
9 he sunk down with s', and fell
Ro 13:11 it is high time to awake out of s':
1Co 11:30 sickly among you, and many s'.
15:51 We shall not all s', but we shall all
1Th 4:14 so them also which s' in Jesus
5: 6 let us not s', as do others; but let
7 For they that s' s' in the night;
10 for us, that, whether we wake or s',

sleeper
Jon 1: 6 What meanest thou, O s'? arise,

sleepest
Ps 44:23 why s' thou, O Lord? arise, cast
Pr 6:22 when thou s', it shall keep thee;
M'r 14:37 saith unto Peter, Simon, s' thou?
Eph 5:14 Awake thou that s', and arise from

sleepeth
1Ki 18:27 peradventure he s', and must be
Pr 10: 5 s' in harvest is a son that causeth
Ho 7: 6 wait: their baker s' all the night;
M't 9:24 for the maid is not dead, but s'.
M'r 5:39 the damsel is not dead, but s'.
Lu 8:52 Weep not; she is not dead, but s'.
Joh 11:11 unto them, Our friend Lazarus s';

sleeping
1Sa 26: 7 Saul lay s' within the trench, and
Isa 56:10 s', lying down, loving to slumber.
M'r 13:36 coming suddenly he find you s'.
14:37 he cometh, and findeth them s',
Lu 22:45 he found them s' for sorrow,
Ac 12: 6 Peter was s' between two soldiers,

sleight
Eph 4:14 by the s' of men, and cunning

slept
Ge 2:21 to fall upon Adam, and he s': and
41: 5 And he s' and dreamed the second
2Sa 11: 9 Uriah s' at the door of the king's
1Ki 2:10 David s' with his fathers, and was
3:20 while thine handmaid s', and laid
11:21 that David s' with his fathers, and
43 And Solomon s' with his fathers,
14:20 he s' with his fathers, and Nadab
31 And Rehoboam s' with his fathers,
15: 8 And Abijam s' with his fathers; and
24 Asa s' with his fathers, and was
16: 6 So Baasha s' with his fathers, and
28 So Omri s' with his fathers, and
19: 5 he lay and s' under a juniper tree,
22:40 So Ahab s' with his fathers; and
50 Jehoshaphat s' with his fathers,
2Ki 8:24 And Joram s' with his fathers, and
10:35 And Jehu s' with his fathers: and
13: 9 And Jehoahaz s' with his fathers;
13 And Joash s' with his fathers; and
14:16 And Jehoash s' with his fathers,
22 that the king s' with his fathers,
29 And Jeroboam s' with his fathers,
15: 7 So Azariah s' with his fathers; and
22 And Menahem s' with his fathers;
38 Jotham s' with his fathers, and was
2Ki 16:20 Ahaz s' with his fathers, and was
20:21 And Hezekiah s' with his fathers:
21:18 And Manasseh s' with his fathers,
24: 6 So Jehoiakim s' with his fathers:
2Ch 9:31 Solomon s' with his fathers, and he
12:16 And Rehoboam s' with his fathers,
14: 1 So Abijah s' with his fathers, and
16:13 Asa s' with his fathers, and died in
21: 1 Jehoshaphat s' with his fathers,
26: 2 that the king s' with his fathers.
23 So Uzziah s' with his fathers, and
27: 9 Jotham s' with his fathers, and they
28:27 And Ahaz s' with his fathers, and
32:33 And Hezekiah s' with his fathers,
33:20 So Manasseh s' with his fathers, and
Job 3:13 and been quiet, I should have s':
Ps 3: 5 I laid me down and s'; I awaked;
76: 5 spoiled, they have s' their sleep:
M't 13:25 But while men s', his enemy came
25: 5 tarried, they all slumbered and s'.
27:52 bodies of the saints which s' arose,
28:13 and stole him away while we s'.
1Co 15:20 the firstfruits of them that s'.

slew See also SLEWEST.
Ge 4: 8 Abel his brother, and s' him.
25 seed instead of Abel, whom Cain s'.
34:25 the city boldly, and s' all the males.
26 they s' Hamor and Shechem his son
38: 7 of the Lord; and the Lord s' him.
10 the Lord: wherefore he s' him also.
49: 6 for in their anger they s' a man,
Ex 2:12 he s' the Egyptian, and hid him in
13:15 the Lord s' all the firstborn in the
Le 8:15 And he s' it; and Moses took the
23 And he s' it; and Moses took of the
9: 8 s' the calf of the sin offering, which
12 And he s' the burnt offering; and
15 s' it, and offered it for sin, as the
18 He s' also the bullock and the ram
Nu 31: 7 Moses; and they s' all the males.
8 they s' the kings of Midian, beside
8 son of Beor they s' with the sword.
Jos 8:21 again, and s' the men of Ai.
9:26 of Israel, that they s' them not.
10:10 s' them with a great slaughter at
11 children of Israel s' with...sword.
26 Joshua smote them, and s' them,
11:17 took, and smote them, and s' them.
J'g 1: 4 s' of them in Bezek ten thousand
5 and they s' the Canaanites and the
10 and they s' Sheshai, and Ahiman,
17 s' the Canaanites that inhabited
3:29 they s' of Moab at that time about
31 s' of the Philistines six hundred
7:25 they s' Oreb upon the rock Oreb,
25 and Zeeb they s' at the winepress of
8:17 Penuel, and s' the men of the city.
18 were they whom ye s' at Tabor?
21 arose, and s' Zebah and Zalmunna,
9: 5 s' his brethren...sons of Jerubbaal,
24 their brother, which s' them; and
44 were in the fields, and s' them.
45 s' the people that was therein,
54 say not of me, A woman s' him.
12: 6 s' him at the passages of Jordan:
14:19 s' thirty men of them, and took
15:15 and s' a thousand men therewith.
16:24 our country, which s' many of us.
30 the dead which he s' at his death
30 than they which he s' in his life.
20:45 and s' two thousand men of them.
1Sa 1:25 they s' a bullock, and brought the
4: 2 and they s' of the army in the field
11:11 s' the Ammonites until the heat of
14:13 and his armourbearer s' after him.
32 calves, and s' them on the ground:
34 him that night, and s' them there.
17:35 beard, and smote him, and s' him.
36 Thy servant s' both the lion and
50 smote the Philistine, and s' him;
51 and s' him, and cut off his head
18:27 s' of the Philistines two hundred
19: 5 in his hand, and s' the Philistine,
8 and s' them with a great slaughter;
22:18 s' on that day fourscore and five
29: 5 Saul s' his thousands, and David
30: 2 they s' not any, either great or
31: 2 and the Philistines s' Jonathan,
2Sa 1:10 So I stood upon him, and s' him,
3:30 and Abishai his brother s' Abner,
4: 7 and they smote him, and s' him,
10 hold of him, and s' him in Ziklag,
12 and they s' them, and cut off their
8: 5 David s' of the Syrians two and
10:18 David s' the men of seven hundred
14: 6 one smote the other, and s' him.
7 the life of his brother whom he s';
18:15 and smote Absalom, and s' him.
21: 1 house, because he s' the Gibeonites,
18 Sibbechai the Hushathite s' Saph,
19 s' the brother of Goliath the Gittite,
21 the brother of David s' him.
23: 8 hundred, whom he s' at one time.
12 defended it, and s' the Philistines:
18 three hundred, and s' them, and
20 he s' two lionlike men of Moab:
20 and s' a lion in the midst of a pit
21 And he s' an Egyptian, a goodly
21 and s' him with his own spear.
1Ki 1: 9 Adonijah s' sheep and oxen and
2: 5 and unto Amasa...whom he s',
32 than he, and s' them with the sword,
34 up, and fell upon him, and s' him:
11:24 when David s' them of Zobah:
13:24 met him by the way, and s' him:
16:11 that he s' all the house of Baasha:

1Ki 18:13 I did when Jezebel s· the prophets
40 brook Kishon, and s· them there.
19:21 took a yoke of oxen, and s· them,
20:20 And they s· every one his man:
21 and s· the Syrians with a great
29 Israel s· of the Syrians an hundred
36 him, a lion found him, and s· him.
2Ki 9:31 Zimri peace, who s· his master?
10: 7 king's sons, and s· seventy persons,
9 against my master, and s· him:
9 but who s· all these?
11 So Jehu s· all that remained of the
14 s· them at the pit of the shearing
17 he s· all that remained unto Ahab
11:18 and s· Mattan the priest of Baal
20 they s· Athaliah with the sword
12:20 and s· Joash in the house of Millo,
14: 5 s· his servants which had slain the
6 children of...murderers he s· not:
7 s· of Edom in the valley of salt ten
19 him to Lachish, and s· him there.
15:10, 14 s· him, and reigned in his stead,
30 s· him, and reigned in his stead,
16: 9 of it captive to Kir, and s· Rezin.
17:25 them, which s· some of them.
21:23 and s· the king in his own house.
24 s· all them that had conspired
23:20 he s· all the priests of the high
29 he s· him at Megiddo, when he had
25: 7 And they s· the sons of Zedekiah
21 s· them at Riblah in the land
1Ch 2: 3 sight of the Lord; and he s· him.
7:21 that were born in that land s·,
10: 2 and the Philistines s· Jonathan,
14 s· him, and turned the kingdom
11:14 delivered it, and s· the Philistines;
20 against three hundred, he s· them,
22 he s· two lionlike men of Moab:
22 s· a lion in a pit in a snowy day.
23 he s· an Egyptian, a man of great
23 and s· him with his own spear.
18: 5 David s· of the Syrians two and
12 s· of the Edomites in the valley of
19:18 and David s· of the Syrians seven
20: 4 Sibbechai the Hushathite s· Sippai,
5 Elhanan the son of Jair s· Lahmi
7 of Shimea David's brother s· him.
2Ch 13:17 And Abijah and his people s· them
21: 4 s· all his brethren with the sword,
22: 8 ministered to Ahaziah, he s· them.
11 Athaliah, so that she s· him not.
23:15 the king's house, they s· her there.
17 and s· Mattan the priest of Baal
24:22 not the kindness...but s· his son.
25 and s· him on his bed, and he died:
25: 3 he s· his servants that had killed
4 But he s· not their children, but
27 to Lachish after him, and s· him
28: 6 s· in Judah an hundred and
7 s· Maaseiah the king's son, and
32:21 s· him there with the sword.
33:24 and s· him in his own house.
25 s· all them that had conspired
36:17 who s· their young men with the
Ne 9:26 and s· thy prophets which testified
Es 9: 6 Jews s· and destroyed five hundred
10 the enemy of the Jews, s· they;
15 s· three hundred men at Shushan;
16 and s· of their foes seventy and five
Ps 78:31 s· the fattest of them, and smote
34 When he s· them, then they sought
105:29 waters into blood, and s· their fish.
135:10 great nations, and s· mighty kings;
136:18 And s· famous kings: for his mercy
Isa 66: 3 killeth an ox as if he s· a man;
Jer 20:17 he s· me not from the womb; or
26:23 king; who s· him with the sword,
39: 6 Babylon s· the sons of Zedekiah
6 Babylon s· all the nobles of Judah.
41: 2 s· him, whom the king of Babylon
3 Ishmael also s· all the Jews that
7 the son of Nethaniah s· them, and
8 s· them not among their brethren.
52:10 Babylon s· the sons of Zedekiah
10 he s· also all the princes of Judah
La 2: 4 s· all that were pleasant to the eye
Eze 9: 7 they went forth, and s· in the city.
23:10 daughters, and s· her with the sword:
40:41 whereupon they s·...sacrifices.
42 they s· the burnt offering and the
Da 3:22 the flame of the fire s· those men
5:19 whom he would he s·; and whom he
M't 2:16 s· all the children...in Bethlehem,
21:39 out of the vineyard, and s· him.
22: 6 them spitefully, and s· them.
23:35 s· between the temple and...altar.
Lu 13: 4 tower in Siloam fell, and s· them,
Ac 5:30 raised up Jesus, whom ye s· and
10:39 whom they s· and hanged on a tree:
22:20 kept the raiment of them that s· him.
Ro 7:11 deceived me, and by it s· me.
1Jo 3:12 wicked one, and s· his brother.
12 And wherefore s· he him? Because

slewest
1Sa 21: 9 whom thou s· in the valley of Elah,

slidden
Jer 8: 5 this people of Jerusalem s· back

slide See also BACKSLIDING; SLIDDEN; SLIDETH.
De 32:35 their foot shall s· in due time:
Ps 26: 1 the Lord; therefore I shall not s·.
37:31 his heart; none of his steps shall s·.

slideth
Ho 4:16 s· back as a backsliding heifer:

slight See SLEIGHT.

slightly
Jer 6:14 of the daughter of my people s·,
8:11 of the daughter of my people s·,

slime See also SLIMEPITS.
Ge 11: 3 stone, and s· had they for morter.
Ex 2: 3 daubed it with s· and with pitch,

slimepits
Ge 14:10 the vale of Siddim was full of s·;

sling See also SLANG; SLINGS; SLINGSTONES.
J'g 20:16 could s· stones at an hair breadth,
1Sa 17:40 and his s· was in his hand: and he
50 with a s· and with a stone,
25:29 enemies, them shall he s· out, as
29 as out of the middle of a s·.
Pr 26: 8 As he that bindeth a stone in a s·,
Jer 10:18 s· out the inhabitants of the land
Zec 9:15 devour, and subdue with s· stones;

slingers
2Ki 3:25 the s· went about it, and smote it.

slings
2Ch 26:14 and bows, and s· to cast stones.

slingstones See also SLING and STONES.
Job 41:28 s· are turned with him into

slip See also SLIPPED; SLIPPETH; SLIPS.
2Sa 22:37 me; so that my feet did not s·.
Job 12: 5 He that is ready to s· with his feet
Ps 17: 5 thy paths, that my footsteps s· not.
18:36 under me, that my feet did not s·.
Heb 2: 1 at any time we should let them s·.

slipped
1Sa 19:10 he s· away out of Saul's presence,
Ps 73: 2 gone; my steps had well nigh s·.

slippery
Ps 35: 6 Let their way be dark and s: and
73:18 thou didst set them in s· places:
Jer 23:12 way shall be unto them as s· ways

slippeth
De 19: 5 and the head s· from the helve,
Ps 38:16 when my foot s·, they magnify
94:18 When I said, My foot s·; thy mercy,

slips
Isa 17:10 and shalt set it with strange s·:

slothful
J'g 18: 9 be not s· to go, and to enter to
Pr 12:24 but the s· shall be under tribute.
27 The s· man roasteth not that which
15:19 way of the s· man is as an hedge
18: 9 He also that is s· in his work is
19:24 A s· man hideth his hand in his
21:25 The desire of the s· killeth him;
22:13 The s· man saith, There is a lion
24:30 I went by the field of the s·, and by
26:13 The s· man saith, There is a lion in
14 hinges, so doth the s· upon his bed.
15 s· hideth his hand in his bosom;
M't 25:26 Thou wicked and s· servant, thou
Ro 12:11 Not s· in business; fervent in spirit;
Heb 6:12 That ye be not s·, but followers of

slothfulness
Pr 19:15 S· casteth into a deep sleep; and
Ec 10:18 By much s· the building decayeth;

slow
Ex 4:10 s· of speech, and of a s· tongue.
Ne 9:17 s· to anger, and of great kindness,
Ps 103: 8 s· to anger, and plenteous in mercy,
145: 8 s· to anger, and of great mercy.
Pr 14:29 He that is s· to wrath is of great
15:18 that is s· to anger appeaseth strife.
16:32 He that is s· to anger is better than
Joe 2:13 s· to anger, and of great kindness,
Jon 4: 2 s· to anger, and of great kindness,
Na 1: 3 The Lord is s· to anger, and great in
Lu 24:25 O fools, and s· of heart to believe
Tit 1:12 alway liars, evil beasts, s· bellies.
Jas 1:19 to hear, s· to speak, s· to wrath:

slowly
Ac 27: 7 when we had sailed s· many days,

sluggard
Pr 6: 6 Go to the ant, thou s·; consider
9 How long wilt thou sleep, O s·?
10:26 so is the s· to them that send him.
13: 4 The soul of the s· desireth, and
20: 4 The s· will not plow by reason of
26:16 The s· is wiser in his own conceit

sluices
Isa 19:10 that make s· and ponds for fish.

slumber See also SLUMBERED; SLUMBERETH; SLUMBERING.
Ps 121: 3 he that keepeth thee will not s·.
4 Israel shall neither s· nor sleep.
132: 4 to my eyes, or s· to mine eyelids,
Pr 6: 4 thine eyes, nor s· to thine eyelids.
10 Yet a little sleep, a little s·, a little
24:33 Yet a little sleep, a little s·, a little
Isa 5:27 none shall s· nor sleep; neither
56:10 sleeping, lying down, loving to s·.
Na 3:18 Thy shepherds s·, O king of
Ro 11: 8 hath given them the spirit of s·,

slumbered
M't 25: 5 tarried, they all s· and slept.

slumbereth
2Pe 2: 3 not, and their damnation s· not.

slumberings
Job 33:15 upon men, in s· upon the bed;

small See also SMALLEST.
Ge 19:11 with blindness, both s· and great:
30:15 a s· matter that thou hast taken
Ex 9: 9 shall become s· dust in all the land
16:14 wilderness...lay a s· round thing,
14 as s· as the hoar frost on the ground.
18:22 every s· matter they shall judge:
26 s· matter they judged themselves.
30:36 thou shalt beat some of it very s·,
Le 16:12 full of sweet incense beaten s·,
Nu 16: 9 it but a s· thing unto you, that
13 s· thing that thou hast brought us
32:41 and took the s· towns thereof,
De 1:17 hear the s· as well as the great;
9:21 stamped it, and ground it very s·,
21 even until it was as s· as dust:
25:13 divers weights, a great and a s·.
14 divers measures, a great and a s·.
32: 2 as the s· rain upon the tender herb,
1Sa 5: 9 men of the city, both s· and great,
20: 2 will do nothing either great or s·,
30: 2 slew not any, either great or s·,
19 to them, neither s· nor great,
2Sa 7:19 this was yet a s· thing in thy sight,
17:13 be not one s· stone found there.
22:43 I beat them as s· as the dust of the
1Ki 2:20 I desire one s· petition of thee;
19:12 and after the fire a still s· voice.
22:31 Fight neither with s· nor great,
2Ki 19:26 their inhabitants were of s· power,
23: 2 all the people, both s· and great:
6, 15 and stamped it s· to powder,
25:26 all the people, both s· and great,
1Ch 17:17 this was a s· thing in thine eyes,
25: 8 ward, as well the s· as the great,
26:13 lots, as well the s· as the great,
2Ch 15:13 put to death, whether s· or great,
18:30 Fight ye not with s· or great, save
24:24 came with a s· company of men,
31:15 as well to the great as to the s·:
34:30 and all the people, great and s·:
35: 8 thousand and six hundred s· cattle,
9 offerings five thousand s· cattle.
36:18 of the house of God, great and s·,
Es 1: 5 both unto great and s·, seven days,
20 honour, both to great and s·.
Job 3:19 The s· and great are there; and the
8: 7 Though thy beginning was s·, yet
15:11 consolations of God s· with thee?
36:27 he maketh s· the drops of water:
37: 6 likewise to the s· rain, and to the
Ps 18:42 did I beat them s· as the dust before
104:25 both s· and great beasts.
115:13 fear the Lord, both s· and great.
119:141 I am s· and despised: yet do not
Pr 24:10 day of adversity, thy strength is s·.
Ec 2: 7 possessions of great and s· cattle
Isa 1: 9 left unto us a very s· remnant,
7:13 Is it a s· thing for you to weary men,
16:14 the remnant shall be very s· and
22:24 all vessels of s· quantity, from the
29: 5 thy strangers shall be like s· dust,
37:27 their inhabitants were of s· power,
40:15 counted as the s· dust of the balance.
41:15 the mountains, and beat them s·,
43:23 me the s· cattle of thy burnt offerings:
54: 7 For a s· moment have I forsaken
60:22 and a s· one a strong nation:
Jer 16: 6 Both the great and the s· shall die
30: 19 them, and they shall not be s·.
44:28 Yet a s· number that escape the
49:15 I will make thee s· among the
Eze 16:20 of thy whoredoms a s· matter,
34:18 Seemeth it a s· thing unto you to
Da 11:23 become strong with a s· people.
Am 7: 2, 5 shall Jacob arise? for he is s·.
8: 5 forth wheat, making the ephah s·,
Ob 2 made thee s· among the heathen:
Zec 4:10 hath despised the day of s· things?
M'r 3: 9 that a s· ship should wait on him
8: 7 And they had a few s· fishes: and
Joh 2:15 he had made a scourge of s· cords,
6: 9 five barley loaves,...two s· fishes:
Ac 12:18 was no s· stir among the soldiers,
15: 2 no s· dissension and disputation
19:23 arose no s· stir about that way.
24 no s· gain unto the craftsman;
26:22 witnessing both to s· and great,
27:20 and no s· tempest lay on us, all
1Co 4: 3 with me it is a very s· thing that
Jas 3: 4 turned about with a very s· helm,
Re 11:18 that fear thy name, s· and great;
13:16 both s· and great, rich and poor,
19: 5 that fear him, both s· and great.
18 free and bond, both s· and great.
20:12 And I saw the dead, s· and great,

smallest
1Sa 9:21 of the s· of the tribes of Israel?
1Co 6: 2 unworthy to judge the s· matters?

smart
Pr 11:15 for a stranger shall s· for it:

smell See also SMELLED; SMELLETH; SMELLING.
Ge 27:27 he smelled the s· of his raiment,
27 s· of my son is as the s· of a field
Ex 30:38 make like unto that, to s· thereto,
Le 26:31 will not s· the savour of your sweet
De 4:28 see, nor hear, nor eat, nor s·.
Ps 45: 8 All thy garments s· of myrrh, and
115: 6 noses have they, but they s· not:
Ca 1:12 my spikenard sendeth forth the s·
2:13 the tender grape give a good s·,
4:10 and the s· of thine ointments than
11 the s· of thy garments is like the
11 garments is like the s· of Lebanon.
7: 8 and the s· of thy nose like apples;
13 The mandrakes give a s·, and at
Isa 3:24 instead of sweet s· there shall be
Da 3:27 nor the s· of fire had passed on

Hos 14: 6 olive tree, and his s' as Lebanon.
Am 5:21 not s' in your solemn assemblies.
Ph'p 4:18 an odour of a sweet s', a sacrifice

smelled
Ge 8:21 And the Lord s' a sweet savour;
27:27 and he s' the smell of his raiment,

smelleth
Job 39:25 and he s' the battle afar off, the

smelling See also SWEETSMELLING.
Ca 5: 5 my fingers with sweet s' myrrh,
13 lilies, dropping sweet s' myrrh.
1Co 12:17 were hearing, where were the s'?

smite See also SMITEST; SMITETH; SMITING; SMITTEN; SMOTE.
Ge 8:21 neither will I again s' any more
32: 8 come to the one company, and s' it,
11 him, lest he will come and s' me,
Ex 3:20 s' Egypt with all my wonders which
7:17 I will s' with the rod that is in mine
8: 2 I will s' all thy borders with frogs:
16 and s' the dust of the land, that it
9:15 I may s' thee and thy people with
12:12 will s' all the firstborn in the land of
13 you, when I s' the land of Egypt.
23 pass through to s' the Egyptians;
23 come in unto your houses to s' you.
17: 6 thou shalt s' the rock, and there
21:18 and one s' another with a stone, or
20 And if a man s' his servant, or his
26 if a man s' the eye of his servant,
27 he s' out his manservant's tooth,
Nu 14:12 I will s' them with the pestilence,
22: 6 that we may s' them, and that I may
24:17 and shall s' the corners of Moab,
25:17 Vex the Midianites, and s' them:
35:16 if he s' him with an instrument of
17 if he s' him with throwing a stone,
18 if he s' him with an hand weapon
21 Or in enmity s' him with his hand,
De 7: 2 thou shalt s' them, and utterly
13:15 Thou shalt surely s' the inhabitants
19:11 and s' him mortally that he die, and
20:13 thou shalt s' every male thereof
28:22 shall s' thee with a consumption,
27 s' thee with the botch of Egypt,
28 Lord shall s' thee with madness,
35 The Lord shall s' thee in the knees,
33:11 s' through the loins of them that
Jos 7: 3 thousand men go up and s' Ai;
10: 4 help me, that we may s' Gibeon:
19 and s' the hindmost of them;
12: 6 Lord and the children of Israel s':
13:12 these did Moses s', and cast them
J'g 6:16 shalt s' the Midianites as one man.
20:31 and they began to s' of the people,
39 Benjamin began to s' and kill of the
21:10 saying, Go and s' the inhabitants of
1Sa 15: 3 Now go and s' Amalek, and utterly
17:46 I will s' thee, and take thine head
18:11 I will s' David even to the wall with
19:10 Saul sought to s' David even to the
20:33 Saul cast a javelin at him to s' him:
23: 2 Shall I go and s' these Philistines?
2 Go, and s' the Philistines, and save
26: 8 therefore let me s' him, I pray thee,
8 and I will not s' him the second time.
10 Lord liveth, the Lord shall s' him;
2Sa 2:22 should I s' thee to the ground?
5:24 to s' the host of the Philistines.
13:28 when I say unto you, S' Amnon;
15:14 and s' the city with the edge of the
17: 2 flee; and I will s' the king only:
18:11 thou not s' him there to the ground?
1Ki 14:15 the Lord shall s' Israel, as a reed
20:35 word of the Lord, S' me, I pray thee.
35 And the man refused to s' him.
37 man, and said, S' me, I pray thee.
2Ki 3:19 And ye shall s' every fenced city,
6:18 S' this people, I pray thee, with
21 shall I s' them? shall I s' them?
22 answered, Thou shalt not s' them:
22 thou s' those whom thou hast taken
9: 7 thou shalt s' the house of Ahab thy
27 and said, S' him also in the chariot.
13:17 thou shalt s' the Syrians in Aphek,
18 king of Israel, S' upon the ground.
19 now thou shalt s' Syria but thrice.
1Ch 14:15 to s' the host of the Philistines.
2Ch 21:14 plague will the Lord s' thy people,
Ps 121: 6 The sun shall not s' thee by day,
141: 5 Let the righteous s' me; it shall be
Pr 19:25 S' a scorner, and the simple will
Isa 3:17 Lord will s' with a scab the crown
10:24 he shall s' thee with a rod, and
11: 4 he shall s' the earth with the rod of
15 and shall s' it in the seven streams,
19:22 And the Lord shall s' Egypt: he
22 he shall s' and heal it: and they
49:10 shall the heat nor sun s' them:
58: 4 and to s' with the fist of wickedness:
Jer 18:18 and let us s' him with the tongue,
21: 6 And I will s' the inhabitants of this
7 he shall s' them with the edge of the
43:11 he shall s' the land of Egypt, and
46:13 come and s' the land of Egypt.
49:28 which Nebuchadrezzar...shall s',
Eze 5: 2 part, and s' about it with a knife:
6:11 S' with thine hand, and stamp with
9: 5 after him through the city, and s':
21:12 s' therefore upon thy thigh.
14 and s' thine hands together, and
17 I will also s' mine hands together,
32:15 when I shall s' all them that dwell
39: 3 And I will s' thy bow out of thy left
Am 3:15 I will s' the winter house with the
6:11 and he will s' the great house with
9: 1 S' the lintel of the door, that the
Mic 5: 1 s' the judge of Israel with a rod
Na 2:10 the knees s' together, and much
Zec 9: 4 and he will s' her power in the sea;
10:11 and shall s' the waves in the sea,
11: 6 they shall s' the land, and out of
12: 4 s' every horse with astonishment,
4 s' every horse of the people with
13: 7 s' the shepherd, and the sheep shall
14:12 the Lord will s' all the people that
18 the Lord will s' the heathen that
Mal 4: 6 come and s' the earth with a curse.
M't 5:39 shall s' thee on thy right cheek,
24:49 begin to s' his fellowservants,
26:31 I will s' the shepherd, and the
M'r 14:27 I will s' the shepherd, and the
Lu 22:49 Lord, shall we s' with the sword?
Ac 23: 2 by him to s' him on the mouth.
3 God shall s' thee, thou whited wall:
2Co 11:20 if a man s' you on the face.
Re 11: 6 to s' the earth with all plagues,
19:15 with it he should s' the nations:

smiters
Isa 50: 6 I gave my back to the s', and my

smitest
Ex 2:13 Wherefore s' thou thy fellow?
Joh 18:23 evil: but if well, why s' thou me?

smiteth
Ex 21:12 He that s' a man, so that he die,
15 he that s' his father, or his mother,
De 25:11 out of the hand of him that s' him,
27:24 he that s' his neighbour secretly.
Jos 15:16 He that s' Kirjath-sepher, and
J'g 1:12 He that s' Kirjath-sepher, and
2Sa 5: 8 and s' the Jebusites, and the lame
1Ch 11: 6 Whosoever s' the Jebusites first
Job 26:12 he s' through the proud.
Isa 9:13 turneth not unto him that s' them,
La 3:30 giveth his cheek to him that s' him:
Eze 7: 9 know that I am the Lord that s'.
Lu 6:29 him that s' thee on the one cheek

smith See also COPPERSMITH; SMITHS.
1Sa 13:19 no s' found throughout all the
Isa 44:12 The s' with the tongs both
54:16 created the s' that bloweth the

smiths
2Ki 24:14 and all the craftsmen and s':
16 craftsmen and s' a thousand, all
Jer 24: 1 with the carpenters and s', from
29: 2 and the carpenters, and the s', were

smiting
Ex 2:11 he spied an Egyptian s' an Hebrew,
2Sa 8:13 he returned from s' of the Syrians
1Ki 20:37 him, so that in s' he wounded him.
2Ki 3:24 they went forward s' the Moabites,
Mic 6:13 will I make thee sick in s' thee,

smitten
Ex 7:25 that the Lord had s' the river.
9:31 And the flax and the barley was s':
32 the wheat and the rie were not s':
22: 2 breaking up, and be s' that he die,
Nu 14:42 ye be not s' before your enemies.
22:28 thou hast s' me these three times?
32 thou s' thine ass these three times?
33: 4 which the Lord had s' among them:
De 1:42 lest ye be s' before your enemies.
28: 7 thee to be s' before thy face: they
25 thee to be s' before thine enemies:
J'g 1: 8 s' it with the edge of the sword,
20:32 They are s' down before us, as at
36 of Benjamin saw that they were s':
39 Surely they are s' down before us,
1Sa 4: 2 Israel was s' before the Philistines:
3 Wherefore hath the Lord s' us to
10 Philistines fought, and Israel was s',
5:12 died not were s' with the emerods:
6:19 the Lord had s' many of the people
7:10 and they were s' before Israel.
13: 4 that Saul had s' a garrison of the
30: 1 s' Ziklag, and burned it with fire;
2Sa 2:31 servants of David...s' of Benjamin,
8: 9 that David had s' all the host of
10 against Hadadezer, and s' him:
10:15, 19 that they were s' before Israel,
11:15 ye from him, that he may be s',
1Ki 8:33 When thy people Israel be s' down
11:15 he had s' every male in Edom;
2Ki 2:14 when he also had s' the waters,
3:23 and they have s' one another: now
13:19 shouldest have s' five or six times;
19 s' Syria till thou hadst consumed it:
14:10 Thou hast indeed s' Edom, and
1Ch 18: 9 how David had s' all the host of
10 against Hadarezer, and s' him;
2Ch 20:22 against Judah; and they were s'.
25:16 forbear; why shouldest thou be s'?
19 Lo, thou hast s' the Edomites;
26:20 out, because the Lord had s' him.
28:17 Edomites had come and s' Judah,
Job 16:10 they have s' me upon the cheek
Ps 3: 7 s' all mine enemies upon the cheek
69:26 persecute him whom thou hast s';
102: 4 My heart is s', and withered like
143: 3 he hath s' my life down to the
Isa 5:25 against them, and hath s' them:
24:12 and the gate is s' with destruction.
27: 7 Hath he s' him, as he smote those
53: 4 stricken, s' of God, and afflicted.
Jer 2:30 In vain have I s' your children;
14:19 why hast thou s' us, and there is no
37:10 ye had s' the whole army of the
Eze 22:13 have s' mine hand at thy dishonest
33:21 unto me, saying, The city is s'.
40: 1 year after that the city was s', in
Ho 6: 1 he hath s', and he will bind us up.
9:16 Ephraim is s', their root is dried
Am 4: 9 I have s' you with blasting and
Ac 23: 3 me to be s' contrary to the law?
Re 8:12 the third part of the sun was s',

smoke See also SMOKING.
Ge 19:28 the s' of the country went up as
28 went up as the s' of a furnace.
Ex 19:18 Sinai was altogether on a s',
18 fire: and the s' thereof ascended
18 ascended as the s' of a furnace,
De 29:20 jealousy shall s' against that man,
Jos 8:20 the s' of the city ascended up to
21 and that the s' of the city ascended,
J'g 20:38 great flame with s' rise up out of
40 up out of the city with a pillar of s',
2Sa 22: 9 went up a s' out of his nostrils, and
Job 41:20 Out of his nostrils goeth s', as out
Ps 18: 8 went up a s' out of his nostrils, and
37:20 into s' shall they consume away.
68: 2 As s' is driven away, so drive them
74: 1 thine anger s' against the sheep
102: 3 my days are consumed like s', and
104:32 toucheth the hills, and they s'.
119:83 am become like a bottle in the s';
144: 5 the mountains, and they shall s'.
Pr 10:26 to the teeth, and as s' to the eyes,
Ca 3: 6 of the wilderness like pillars of s',
Isa 4: 5 assemblies, a cloud and s' by day,
6: 4 and the house was filled with s'.
9:18 mount up like the lifting up of s'.
14:31 there shall come from the north a s',
34:10 the s' thereof shall go up for ever:
51: 6 heavens shall vanish away like s',
65: 5 These are a s' in my nose, a fire that
Hos 13: 3 and as the s' out of the chimney.
Joe 2:30 blood, and fire, and pillars of s'.
Na 2:13 I will burn her chariots in the s',
Ac 2:19 blood, and fire, and vapour of s':
Re 8: 4 And the s' of the incense, which
9: 2 and there arose a s' out of the pit,
2 as the s' of a great furnace; and the
2 was darkened by reason of the s'
3 there came out of the s' locusts
17 issued fire and s' and brimstone.
18 killed, by the fire, and by the s',
14:11 the s' of their torment ascendeth
15: 8 filled with s' from the glory of God,
18: 9 they shall see the s' of her burning,
18 when they saw the s' of her burning,
19: 3 And her s' rose up for ever and ever.

smoking
Ge 15:17 behold a s' furnace, and a burning
Ex 20:18 the trumpet, and the mountain s':
Isa 7: 4 the two tails of these s' firebrands,
42: 3 the s' flax shall he not quench:
M't 12:20 and s' flax shall he not quench,

smooth See also SMOOTHER; SMOOTHETH.
Ge 27:11 a hairy man, and I am a s' man:
16 hands, and upon the s' of his neck:
1Sa 17:40 chose him five s' stones out of the
Isa 30:10 speak unto us s' things, prophesy
57: 6 Among the s' stones of the stream
Lu 3: 5 the rough ways shall be made s';

smoother
Ps 55:21 of his mouth were s' than butter,
Pr 5: 3 and her mouth is s' than oil:

smootheth
Isa 41: 7 and he that s' with the hammer

smote See also SMOTEST.
Ge 14: 5 and s' the Rephaims in Ashteroth
7 s' all the country of the Amalekites,
15 by night, and s' them, and pursued
19:11 s' the men that were at the door of
36:35 who s' Midian in the field of Moab,
Ex 7:20 s' the waters that were in the river,
8:17 his rod, and s' the dust of the earth,
9:25 the hail s' throughout the land of
25 the hail s' every herb of the field,
12:27 Egypt, when he s' the Egyptians,
29 the Lord s' all the firstborn in the
21:19 then shall he that s' him be quit:
Nu 3:13 that I s' all the firstborn in the land
8:17 that I s' every firstborn in the land
11:33 Lord s' the people with a very great
14:45 and s' them, and discomfited them,
20:11 with his rod he s' the rock twice:
21:24 Israel s' him with the edge of the
35 So they s' him, and his sons, and
22:23 Balaam s' the ass, to turn her into
25 the wall: and he s' her again.
27 and he s' the ass with a staff.
24:10 and he s' his hands together:
32: 4 the country which the Lord s'
35:21 he that s' him shall surely be put to
De 2:33 we s' him, and his sons, and all his
3: 3 we s' him until none was left to him
4:46 Moses and the children of Israel s',
25:18 the way, and s' the hindmost of thee,
29: 7 us unto battle, and we s' them:
Jos 7: 5 men of Ai s' of them about thirty
5 and s' them in the going down:
8:22 they s' them, so that they let none
24 unto Ai, and s' it with the edge of
9:18 the children of Israel s' them not,
10:10 and s' them to Azekah, and unto
26 afterward Joshua s' them, and slew
28 and s' it with the edge of the sword,
30 he s' it with the edge of the sword,
32 and s' it with the edge of the sword,
33 and Joshua s' him and his people.

Jos 10: 35, 37 s· it with the edge of the sword,
39 s· them with the edge of the sword,
40 Joshua s·...the country of the hills,
41 s· them from Kadesh-barnea even
11: 8 who s· them, and chased them unto
8 s· them, until they left them none
10 s· the king thereof with the sword:
11 s· all the souls that were therein
12 s· them with the edge of the sword,
14 every man they s· with the edge of
17 their kings he took, and s· them.
12: 1 land, which the children of Israel s·,
7 Joshua and the children of Israel s·
13: 21 whom Moses s· with the princes of
19: 47 and s· it with the edge of the sword,
20: 5 he s· his neighbour unwittingly,
J'g 1: 25 they s· the city with the edge of the
3: 13 and Amalek, and went and s· Israel,
4: 21 and s· the nail into his temples,
5: 26 with the hammer she s· Sisera,
26 she s· off his head, when she had
7: 13 unto a tent, and s· it that it fell,
8: 11 Gideon went up...and s· the host:
9: 43 rose up against them, and s· them.
11: 21 hand of Israel, and they s· them:
33 And he s· them from Aroer, even
12: 4 and the men of Gilead s· Ephraim,
15: 8 s· them hip and thigh with a great
18: 27 s· them with the edge of the sword,
20: 35 Lord s· Benjamin before Israel:
37 s· all the city with the edge of the
48 s· them with the edge of the sword,
1Sa 4: 8 are the Gods that s· the Egyptians
5: 6 s· them with emerods, even Ashdod
9 s· the men of the city, both small
6: 9 that it is not his hand that s· us;
19 he s· the men of Beth-shemesh,
7: 11 pursued the Philistines, and s· them,
13: 3 s· the garrison of the Philistines
14: 31 And they s· the Philistines that day
48 an host, and s· the Amalekites, and
15: 7 And Saul s· the Amalekites from
17: 35 I went out after him, and s· him,
35 caught him by his beard, and s· him,
49 and s· the Philistine in his forehead,
50 with a stone, and s· the Philistine,
19: 10 and he s· the javelin into the wall:
22: 19 s· he with the edge of the sword,
23: 5 and s· them with a great slaughter.
24: 5 afterward, that David's heart s· him,
25: 38 the Lord s· Nabal, that he died.
27: 9 David s· the land, and left neither
30: 17 David s· them from the twilight
2Sa 1: 15 him. And he s· him that he died.
2: 23 spear s· him under the fifth rib,
3: 27 and s· him there under the fifth rib,
4: 6 and they s· him under the fifth rib:
7 and they s· him, and slew him, and
5: 20 and David s· them there, and said,
25 s· the Philistines from Geba until
6: 7 and God s· him there for his error;
8: 1 that David s· the Philistines, and
2 he s· Moab, and measured them
3 David s· also Hadadezer, the son of
10: 18 s· Shobach...captain of their host,
11: 21 Who s· Abimelech the son of
14: 6 the one s· the other, and slew him.
7 Deliver him that s· his brother, that
18: 15 and s· Absalom, and slew him.
20: 10 he s· him therewith in the fifth rib,
21: 17 and s· the Philistine, and killed him.
23: 10 s· the Philistines until his hand was
24: 10 David's heart s· him after that he
17 he saw the angel that s· the people,
1Ki 15: 20 the cities of Israel, and s· Ijon, and
27 and Baasha s· him at Gibbethon,
29 he s· all the house of Jeroboam;
16: 10 Zimri went in and s· him, and killed
20: 21 s· the horses and chariots, and slew
37 the man s· him, so that in smiting
22: 24 near, and s· Micaiah on the cheek,
34 s· the king of Israel between the
2Ki 2: 8 his mantle,...and s· the waters,
14 the mantle... and s· the waters,
3: 24 rose up and s· the Moabites,
25 the slingers went about it, and s· it.
6: 18 s· them with blindness according
8: 21 rose by night, and s· the Edomites
9: 24 and s· Jehoram between his arms,
10: 25 s· them with the edge of the sword;
32 Hazael s· them in all the coasts of
12: 21 his servants, s· him, and he died;
13: 18 And he s· thrice, and stayed.
15: 5 And the Lord s· the king, so that he
10 s· him before the people, and slew
14 and s· Shallum the son of Jabesh in
16 Then Menahem s· Tiphsah, and all
16 not to him, therefore he s· it;
25 against him, and s· him in Samaria,
30 s· him, and slew him, and reigned
18: 8 s· the Philistines, even unto Gaza,
19: 35 s· in the camp of the Assyrians an
37 his sons s· him with the sword:
25: 21 And the king of Babylon s· them,
25 ten men with him, and s· Gedaliah,
1Ch 1: 46 which s· Midian in the field of Moab,
4: 41 s· their tents, and the habitations,
43 they s· the rest of the Amalekites
13: 10 kindled against Uzza, and he s· him,
14: 11 and David s· them there.
16 s· the hosts of the Philistines from
18: 1 that David s· the Philistines, and
2 And he s· Moab; and the Moabites
3 David s· Hadarezer king of Zobah
20: 1 Joab s· Rabbah, and destroyed it.
21: 7 this thing; therefore he s· Israel.
2Ch 13: 15 God s· Jeroboam and all Israel
14: 12 Lord s· the Ethiopians before Asa,
14 they s· all the cities round about
15 They s· also the tents of cattle, and
16: 4 and they s· Ijon, and Dan, and
18: 23 and s· Micaiah upon the cheek, and
33 s· the king of Israel between the
21: 9 up by night, and s· the Edomites
18 the Lord s· him in his bowels with
22: 5 and the Syrians s· Joram.
25: 11 and s· of the children of Seir ten
13 and s· three thousand of them, and
28: 5 and they s· him, and carried away
5 who s· him with a great slaughter.
23 gods of Damascus, which s· him:
Ne 13: 25 s· certain of them, and plucked off
Es 9: 5 the Jews s· all their enemies with
Job 1: 19 s· the four corners of the house,
2: 7 s· Job with sore boils from the
Ps 60: *title* and s· of Edom in the valley of
78: 20 he s· the rock, that the waters
31 s· down the chosen men of Israel.
51 And s· all the firstborn in Egypt;
66 And he s· his enemies in the hinder
105: 33 He s· their vines also and their fig
36 He s· also all the firstborn in their
135: 8 Who s· the firstborn of Egypt, both
10 Who s· great nations, and slew
136: 10 him that s· Egypt in their firstborn:
17 To him which s· great kings: for
Ca 5: 7 me, they s· me, they wounded me;
Isa 10: 20 again stay upon him that s· them;
14: 6 He who s· the people in wrath with
29 rod of him that s· thee is broken:
27: 7 Hath he smitten him, as he s·
7 those that s· him? or is he slain
30: 31 beaten down, which s· with a rod.
37: 36 and s· in the camp of the Assyrians
38 his sons s· him with the sword;
41: 7 the hammer him that s· the anvil,
57: 17 was I wroth, and s· him: I hid me,
60: 10 for in my wrath I s· thee, but in my
Jer 20: 2 Pashur s· Jeremiah the prophet,
31: 19 was instructed, I s· upon my thigh:
37: 15 wroth with Jeremiah, and s· him,
41: 2 s· Gedaliah the son of Ahikam the
46: 2 Nebuchadrezzar king of Babylon s·
47: 1 before that Pharaoh s· Gaza.
52: 27 And the king of Babylon s· them,
Da 2: 34 s· the image upon his feet that were
35 the stone that s· the image became
5: 6 his knees s· one against another.
8: 7 and s· the ram, and brake his two
Jon 4: 7 and it s· the gourd that it withered.
Hag 2: 17 I s· you with blasting and with
M't 26: 51 the high priest's, and s· off his ear.
67 others s· him with the palms of
68 thou Christ, Who is he that s· thee?
27: 30 the reed, and s· him on the head.
M'r 14: 47 and s· a servant of the high priest,
15: 19 s· him on the head with a reed,
Lu 18: 13 s· upon his breast, saying, God be
22: 50 s· the servant of the high priest,
63 held Jesus mocked him,...s· him.
64 Prophesy, who is it that s· thee?
23: 48 s· their breasts, and returned.
Joh 18: 10 and s· the high priest's servant,
19: 3 they s· him with their hands.
Ac 7: 24 oppressed, and s· the Egyptian:
12: 7 he s· Peter on the side, and raised
23 angel of the Lord s· him, because

smotest
Ex 17: 5 rod, wherewith thou s· the river,

Smyrna (*smir'-na*)
Re 1: 11 unto *S*·, and unto Pergamos, and
2: 8 unto the angel of the church in *S*·

snail
Le 11: 30 and the lizard, and the s·, and the
Ps 58: 8 As a s· which melteth, let every

snare See also SNARED; SNARES.
Ex 10: 7 shall this man be a s· unto us?
23: 33 it will surely be a s· unto thee.
34: 12 it be for a s· in the midst of thee:
De 7: 16 for that will be a s· unto thee.
J'g 2: 3 their gods shall be a s· unto you.
8: 27 thing became a s· unto Gideon,
1Sa 18: 21 that she may be a s· to him, and
28: 9 then layest thou a s· for my life,
Job 18: 8 feet, and he walketh upon a s·.
10 s· is laid for him in the ground,
Ps 69: 22 Let their table become a s· before
91: 3 thee from the s· of the fowler, and
106: 36 idols: which were a s· unto them.
119: 110 The wicked have laid a s· for me:
124: 7 bird out of the s· of the fowlers:
7 s· is broken, and we are escaped.
140: 5 The proud have hid a s· for me, and
142: 3 have they privily laid a s· for me.
Pr 7: 23 as a bird hasteth to the s·, and
18: 7 and his lips are the s· of his soul.
20: 25 It is a s· to the man who devoureth
22: 25 his ways, and get a s· to thy soul.
29: 6 of an evil man there is a s·: but the
8 Scornful men bring a city into a s·:
25 The fear of man bringeth a s·:
Ec 9: 12 birds that are caught in the s·;
Isa 8: 14 and for a s· to the inhabitants of
24: 17 the pit, and the s·, are upon thee,
18 of the pit shall be taken in the s·:
29: 21 lay a s· for him that reproveth in
Jer 48: 43 the pit, and the s·, shall be upon
44 of the pit shall be taken in the s·:
50: 24 I have laid a s· for thee, and thou
La 3: 47 Fear and a s· is come upon us,
Eze 12: 13 and he shall be taken in my s·:
17: 20 him, and he shall be taken in my s·,
Ho 5: 1 ye have been a s· on Mizpah, and
9: 8 the prophet is a s· of a fowler in all
Am 3: 5 a bird fall in a s· upon the earth,
5 shall one take up a s· from the
Lu 21: 35 as a s· shall it come on all them
Ro 11: 9 Let their table be made a s·, and a
1Co 7: 35 not that I may cast a s· upon you,
1Ti 3: 7 reproach and the s· of the devil.
6: 9 rich fall into temptation and a s·,
2Ti 2: 26 themselves out of the s· of the devil,

snared See also ENSNARED.
De 7: 25 unto thee, lest thou be s· therein:
12: 30 thou be not s· by following them,
Ps 9: 16 wicked is s· in the work of his own
Pr 6: 2 s· with the words of thy mouth,
12: 13 wicked is s· by the transgression
Ec 9: 12 the sons of men s· in an evil time,
Isa 8: 15 be broken, and be s·, and be taken.
28: 13 and be broken, and s·, and taken.
42: 22 they are all of them s· in holes,

snares
Jos 23: 13 shall be s· and traps unto you,
2Sa 22: 6 the s· of death prevented me;
Job 22: 10 Therefore s· are round about thee,
40: 24 eyes: his nose pierceth through s·.
Ps 11: 6 Upon the wicked he shall rain s·,
18: 5 the s· of death prevented me.
38: 12 seek after my life lay s· for me:
64: 5 they commune of laying s· privily;
141: 9 me from the s· which they have
Pr 13: 14 life, to depart from the s· of death.
14: 27 life, to depart from the s· of death.
22: 5 Thorns and s· are in the way of
Ec 7: 26 whose heart is s· and nets, and
Jer 5: 26 lay wait, as he that setteth s·;
18: 22 to take me, and hid s· for my feet.

snatch
Isa 9: 20 And he shall s· on the right hand,

sneezed
2Ki 4: 35 and the child s· seven times, and

sneezings See NEESINGS.

snorting
Jer 8: 16 The s· of his horses was heard

snout
Pr 11: 22 As a jewel of gold in a swine's s·,

snow
Ex 4: 6 behold, his hand was leprous as s·.
Nu 12: 10 became leprous, white as s·: and
2Sa 23: 20 in the midst of a pit in time of s·:
2Ki 5: 27 his presence a leper as white as s·.
Job 6: 16 the ice, and wherein the s· is hid:
9: 30 If I wash myself with s· water, and
24: 19 and heat consume the s· waters:
37: 6 For he saith to the s·, Be thou on
38: 22 entered into the treasures of the s·?
Ps 51: 7 me, and I shall be whiter than s·.
68: 14 in it, it was white as s· in Salmon.
147: 16 He giveth s· like wool: he
148: 8 Fire, and hail; s·, and vapours;
Pr 25: 13 As the cold of s· in the time of
26: 1 As s· in summer, and as rain in
31: 21 She is not afraid of the s· for her
Isa 1: 18 scarlet, they shall be as white as s·;
55: 10 down, and the s· from heaven, and
Jer 18: 14 Will a man leave the s· of Lebanon
La 4: 7 Her Nazarites were purer than s·,
Da 7: 9 whose garment was white as s·,
M't 28: 3 and his raiment white as s·:
M'r 9: 3 shining, exceeding white as s·;
Re 1: 14 were white like wool, as white as s·;

snowy
1Ch 11: 22 slew a lion in a pit in a s· day.

snuff See SNUFFDISHES; SNUFFED; SNUFFETH.

snuffdishes
Ex 25: 38 the s· thereof, shall be of pure
37: 23 his snuffers, and his s·, of pure gold.
Nu 4: 9 lamps, and his tongs, and his s·,

snuffed
Jer 14: 6 they s· up the winds like dragons;
Mal 1: 13 ye have s· at it, saith the Lord of

snuffers
Ex 37: 23 made his seven lamps, and his s·,
1Ki 7: 50 the bowls, and the s·, and the
2Ki 12: 13 of the Lord bowls of silver, s·,
25: 14 pots, and the shovels, and the s·,
2Ch 4: 22 And the s·, and the basons, and the
Jer 52: 18 and the s·, and the bowls, and the

snuffeth
Jer 2: 24 s· up the wind at her pleasure;

so^ See also ALSO; INSOMUCH; SOEVER.
Ge 1: 7 the firmament: and it was s·.
9 the dry land appear: and it was s·.
11 itself, upon the earth: and it was s·.
15 light upon the earth: and it was s·.
24 earth after his kind: and it was s·.
27 *S*· God created man in his own image,
30 green herb for meat: and it was s·.
3: 24 *S*· he drove out the man; and he
6: 22 God commanded him, s· did he.
11: 8 *S*· the Lord scattered them abroad
12: 4 *S*· Abram departed, as the Lord had
19 s· I might have taken her to me to
13: 6 s· that they could not dwell together.
16 s· that if a man can number the
15: 5 unto him, *S*· shall thy seed be.
18: 5 they said, *S*· do, as thou hast said.
19: 7 pray you, brethren, do not s· wickedly.
11 s· that they wearied themselves to find

Ge 19:18 said unto them, Oh, not s', my Lord:
20:17 S' Abraham prayed unto God: and
21: 6 s' that all that hear will laugh with me.
25:22 she said, If it be s', why am I thus?
27:20 is it that thou hast found it s' quickly,
23 Esau's hands: s' he blessed him.
28:21 S' that I come again to my father's
29:26 not be s' done in our country,
28 And Jacob did s', and fulfilled her
30:33 S' shall my righteousness answer for
42 s' the feebler were Laban's, and the
31:21 S' he fled with all that he had; and he
28 hast now done foolishly in s' doing.
36 thou hast s' hotly pursued after me?
32:19 s' commanded he the second, and
21 S' went the present over before him:
33:16 S' Esau returned that day on his way
34:12 Ask me never s' much dowry and gift,
35: 6 S' Jacob came to Luz, which is in the
37:14 S' he sent him out of the vale of
40: 7 Wherefore look ye s' sadly to day?
41: 4 and fat kine. S' Pharaoh awoke.
13 as he interpreted to us, s' it was;
21 as at the beginning. S' I awoke.
39 there is none s' discreet and wise as
57 the famine was s' sore in all lands.
42:20 s' shall your words be verified,
20 ye shall not die. And they did s'.
34 s' will I deliver you your brother, and
43: 6 Wherefore dealt ye s' ill with me, as to
11 If it must be s' now, do this; take
34 mess was five times s' much as
44: 5 ye have done evil in s' doing.
17 God forbid that I should do s':
45: 8 S' now it was not you that sent me
21 And the children of Israel did s':
24 S' he sent his brethren away, and
47:13 s' that the land of Egypt and all the
20 them: s' the land became Pharaoh's.
28 s' the whole age of Jacob was an
48:10 dim for age, s' that he could not see.
18 Not s', my father: for this is the
49:17 s' that his rider shall fall backward.
50: 3 for s' are fulfilled the days of
17 S' shall ye say unto Joseph,
26 S' Joseph died, being an hundred and
Ex 1:10 us, and s' get them up out of the land.
2:18 that ye are come s' soon to day?
4:26 S' he let him go: then she said, A
5:12 S' the people were scattered abroad
22 thou s' evil entreated this people?
6: 9 Moses spake s' unto the children
7: 6 Lord commanded them, s' did they.
10 did s' as the Lord had commanded:
20 And Moses and Aaron did s', as the
22 did s' with their enchantments:
8:24 the Lord did s'; and there came a
9:24 S' there was hail, and fire mingled
10:10 Let the Lord be s' with you, as I
11 Not s': go now ye that are men,
15 earth, s' that the land was darkened;
20 s' that he would not let the children
11:10 s' that he would not let the children
12:28 Moses and Aaron, s' did they.
36 s' that they lent unto them such
50 Moses and Aaron, s' did they.
14: 4 I am the Lord. And they did s'.
20 s' that the one came not near the
25 s' that the Egyptians said, Let us flee
28 remained not s' much as one of
15:22 S' Moses brought Israel from the
16:30 S' the people rested on the seventh
34 Moses, s' Aaron laid it up before the
17: 6 And Moses did s' in the sight of
10 S' Joshua did as Moses had said to
18:22 s' shall it be easier for thyself, and
23 God commanded thee s', then thou
24 S' Moses hearkened to the voice of
19:16 s' that all the people that was in the
25 S' Moses went down unto the people,
21:12 that smiteth a man, s' that he die,
22 s' that her fruit depart from her, and
22: 6 s' that the stacks of corn, or the
25: 9 thereof, even s' shall ye make it.
33 s' in the six branches that come
27: 8 in the mount, s' shall they make it.
28: 7 and s' it shall be joined together.
30:21 S' they shall wash their hands and
23 of sweet cinnamon half s' much, even
32:21 hast brought s' great a sin upon
24 S' they gave it me: then I cast it into
33:16 s' shall we be separated, I and thy
36:13 taches: s' it became one tabernacle.
37:19 s' throughout the six branches
39:32 commanded Moses, s' did they.
42 s' the children of Israel made all
43 even s' had they done it: and Moses
40:16 Lord commanded him, s' did he.
33 gate. S' Moses finished the work.
Le 4:20 offering, s' shall he do with this:
7: 7 offering is, s' is the trespass offering:
8:34 s' the Lord hath commanded to do, to
35 die not: for s' I am commanded:
36 S' Aaron and his sons did all things
10: 5 S' they went near, and carried them
13 made by fire: for s' I commanded.
11:32 until the even; s' it shall be cleansed.
14:13 the priest's, s' is the trespass offering:
21 if he be poor, and cannot get s' much;
16: 4 flesh in water, and s' put them on.
16 s' shall he do for the tabernacle of
24:19 done, s' shall it be done to him;
20 s' shall it be done to him again.
26:15 s' that ye will not do all my
27:12 it, who art the priest, s' shall it be.
14 shall estimate it, s' shall it stand.
Nu 1:19 commanded Moses, s' he numbered
45 S' were all those that were numbered
54 commanded Moses, s' did they.
2:17 s' shall they set forward, every man
34 s' they pitched by their standards,
34 s' they set forward, every one after
4:26 made for them: s' shall they serve.
5: 4 the children of Israel did s', and
4 Moses, s' did the children of Israel.
6:21 s' he must do after the law of his
8: 4 Moses, s' he made the candlestick.
7 clothes, and s' make themselves clean.
20 s' did the children of Israel unto
22 the Levites, s' did they unto them.
9: 5 Moses, s' did the children of Israel.
14 the manner thereof, s' shall he do:
16 S' it was alway: the cloud covered
20 s' it was, when the cloud was a few
21 s' it was, when the cloud abode from
12: 7 My servant Moses is not s', who is
13:21 S' they went up, and searched the
33 and s' we were in their sight.
14:28 in mine ears, s' will I do to you:
15:12 prepare, s' shall ye do to every one
14 the Lord; as ye do, s' he shall do.
15 s' shall the stranger be before the
20 threshingfloor, s' shall ye heave it.
16:27 S' they gat up from the tabernacle
17:11 And Moses did s': as the Lord
11 Lord commanded him, s' did he.
20: 8 s' thou shalt give the congregation
21:35 S' they smote him, and his sons, and
22:35 S' Balaam went with the princes of
25: 8 S' the plague was stayed from the
31: 5 S' there were delivered out of the
32:23 if ye will not do s', behold, ye have
28 S' concerning them Moses
31 unto thy servants, s' will we do.
35: 7 S' all the cities which ye shall give
16 an instrument of iron, s' that he die,
33 S' ye shall not pollute the land
36: 3 s' shall it be taken from the lot of our
4 s' shall their inheritance be taken
7 S' shall not the inheritance of the
10 Moses, s' did the daughters of
De 1:11 you a thousand times s' many more
15 S' I took the chief of your tribes, wise
43 S' I spake unto you; and ye would
46 S' ye abode in Kadesh many days,
2: 5 no, not s' much as a foot breadth;
16 S' it came to pass, when all the men
3: 3 S' the Lord our God delivered into
21 s' shall the Lord do unto all the
29 S' we abode in the valley over against
4: 5 that ye should do s' in the land
7 For what nation is there s' great,
7 who hath God s' nigh unto them, as
8 And what nation is there s' great, that
8 and judgments s' righteous as all this
7: 4 s' will the anger of the Lord be
19 s' shall the Lord thy God do unto
8: 5 s' the Lord thy God chasteneth thee.
20 before your face, s' shall ye perish;
9: 3 s' shalt thou drive them out, and
8 s' that the Lord was angry with you
15 S' I turned and came down from the
12: 4 shall not do s' unto the Lord your
10 round about, s' that ye dwell in safety;
22 is eaten, s' thou shalt eat them:
30 gods? even s' will I do likewise.
31 shalt not do s' unto the Lord thy
13: 5 S' shalt thou put the evil away from
14:24 s' that thou art not able to carry
17: 7 S' thou shalt put the evil away from
18:14 hath not suffered thee s' to do.
19:10 inheritance, and s' blood be upon thee.
19 s' shalt thou put the evil away from
20:18 s' should ye sin against the Lord your
21: 9 S' shalt thou put away the guilt of
21 s' shalt thou put evil away from
22: 3 s' shalt thou do with his raiment;
5 all that do s' are abomination unto
21 s' shalt thou put evil away from
22 s' shalt thou put away evil from Israel.
24 s' thou shalt put away evil from
26 slayeth him, even s' is this matter:
24: 8 them, s' ye shall observe to do.
25: 9 S' shall it be done unto that man
28:34 S' that thou shalt be mad for the
54 S' that the man that is tender among
55 S' that he will not give to any of them
63 s' the Lord will rejoice over you
29:22 S' that the generation to come of
30:17 turn away, s' that thou wilt not hear,
31:17 s' that they will say in that day, Are
33:25 as thy days, s' shall thy strength be.
34: 5 S' Moses the servant of the Lord died
8 s' the days of weeping and mourning
Jos 1: 5 was with Moses, s' I will be with thee:
17 s' will we hearken unto thee:
2:21 According unto your words, s' be it.
23 S' the two men returned, and
3: 7 was with Moses, s' I will be with thee.
4: 8 did s' as Joshua commanded,
5:15 standest is holy. And Joshua did s'.
6:11 S' the ark of the Lord compassed the
14 the camp: s' they did six days.
20 S' the people shouted when the
20 s' that the people went up into the
27 S' the Lord was with Joshua; and his
7: 4 S' there went up thither of the people
16 S' Joshua rose up early in the morning,
22 S' Joshua sent messengers, and they
26 S' the Lord turned from...fierceness
8: 3 S' Joshua arose, and all the people of
22 s' they were in the midst of Israel,
Jos 8:22 s' that they let none of them
25 s' it was, that all that fell that day,
9:26 s' did he unto them, and delivered
10: 1 s' he had done to Ai and her king;
7 S' Joshua ascended from Gilgal, he,
23 And they did s', and brought forth
39 s' he did to Debir, and to the king
40 S' Joshua smote all the country of the
11: 7 S' Joshua came, and all the people of
15 s' did Moses command Joshua,
15 command Joshua,...s' did Joshua;
16 S' Joshua took all that land, the hills,
23 S' Joshua took the whole land,
14: 5 s' the children of Israel did, and
11 even s' is my strength now, for war,
12 if s' be the Lord will be with me,
15: 7 s' northward, looking toward Gilgal,
16: 4 S' the childern of Joseph, Manasseh
19:51 S' they made an end of dividing the
21:40 S' all the cities for the children of
22: 6 S' Joshua blessed them, and sent
25 s' shall your children make our
28 they should s' say to us or to our
23:15 s' shall the Lord bring upon you
24:10 still: s' I delivered you out of his hand.
25 S' Joshua made a covenant with the
28 S' Joshua let the people depart, every
J'g 1: 3 thy lot. S' Simeon went with him.
7 done, s' God hath requited me.
35 prevailed, s'...they became tributaries.
2:14 s' that they could not any longer
17 of the Lord; but they did not s'.
3:14 S' the children of Israel served Eglon
22 s'...he could not draw the dagger
30 S' Moab subdued that day under the
4:14 S' Barak went down from mount
15 s' that Sisera lighted down off his
21 fast asleep and weary. S' he died.
23 S' God subdued on that day Jabin the
5:28 Why is his chariot s' long in coming?
31 S' let all thine enemies perish, O
6: 3 And s' it was, when Israel had sown,
20 pour out the broth. And he did s'.
27 s' it was, because he feared his father's
38 it was s': for he rose up early on
40 God did s' that night: for it was
7: 1 s'...the host of the Midianites were
5 S' he brought down the people unto
8 S' the people took victuals in their
15 it was s', when Gideon heard the
17 be that, as I do, s' shall ye do.
19 S' Gideon, and the hundred men that
8:18 As thou art, s' were they; each
21 for as the man is, s' is his strength.
28 s' that they lifted up their heads no
9:49 s' that all the men of the tower of
10: 9 s' that Israel was sore distressed.
11: 5 And it was s', that when the children
10 if we do not s' according to thy
21 s' Israel possessed all the land of the
23 S' now the Lord God of Israel hath
24 S' whomsoever the Lord our God
32 S' Jephthah passed over unto the
12: 5 and it was s', that when those
13:19 S' Manoah took a kid with a meat
14:10 S' his father went down unto the
10 for s' used the young men to do.
15 us to take that we have? is it not s'?
15:11 me, s' have I done unto them.
16: 9 fire. S' his strength was not known.
16 s' that his soul was vexed unto death;
30 S' the dead which he slew at his
17:10 thy victuals. S' the Levite went in.
18:21 S' they turned and departed, and put
19: 4 s' they did eat and drink, and lodged
21 S' he brought him into his house, and
23 nay, I pray you, do not s' wickedly;
24 this man do not s' vile a thing.
25 s' the man took his concubine, and
30 And it was s', that all that saw it said,
20:11 S' all the men of Israel were gathered
36 S' the children of Benjamin saw that
46 S' that all which fell that day of
21:14 and yet s' they sufficed them not.
23 And the children of Benjamin did s',
Ru 1:17 Lord do s' to me, and more also, if
19 S' they two went out until they
22 S' Naomi returned, and Ruth the
2: 7 s' she came, and hath continued even
17 S' she gleaned in the field until even,
23 S' she kept fast by the maidens of
4: 8 it for thee. S' he drew off his shoe.
13 S' Boaz took Ruth, and she was his
1Sa 1: 7 as he did s' year by year, when she
7 s' she provoked her; therefore she
9 S' Hannah rose up after they had
18 S' the woman went her way, and did
23 S' the woman abode, and gave her son
2: 3 Talk no more s' exceeding proudly;
5 s' that the barren hath born seven;
14 S' they did in Shiloh unto all the
21 visited Hannah, s' that she conceived,
3: 9 S' Samuel went and lay down in his
17 God do s' to thee, and more also, if
4: 4 S' the people sent to Shiloh, that they
5 shout, s' that the earth rang again.
5: 7 men of Ashdod saw that it was s',
9 it was s', that, after they had carried
11 S' they sent and gathered together
6:10 And the men did s'; and took two
7:13 S' the Philistines were subdued, and
8: 8 gods, s' do they also unto thee.
9:10 S' they went unto the city where the
21 then speakest thou s' to me?
24 S' Saul did eat with Samuel that day.
10: 9 it was s', that, when he had turned his

1Sa 11: 7 s' shall it be done unto his oxen.
11 it was s' on the morrow, that Saul
11 s' that two of them were not left
12: 18 S' Samuel called unto the Lord; and
13: 22 S' it came to pass in the day of
14: 15 s' it was a very great trembling.
23 S' the Lord saved Israel that day: and
24 S' none of the people tasted any food.
44 God do s' and more also: for thou
45 S' the people rescued Jonathan, that
47 S' Saul took the kingdom over Israel,
15: 6 S' the Kenites departed from among
31 S' Samuel turned again after Saul;
33 s' shall thy mother be childless
16: 13 S' Samuel rose up, and went to
23 s' Saul was refreshed, and was well,
17: 27 S' shall it be done to the man that
50 S' David prevailed over the Philistine
18: 30 s' that his name was much set by.
19: 12 S' Michal let David down through a
17 Why hast thou deceived me s', and
18 S' David fled, and escaped, and came
20: 2 this thing from me? it is not s'.
13 The Lord do s' and much more to
16 S' Jonathan made a covenant with the
24 S' David hid himself in the field: and
34 S' Jonathan arose from the table in
21: 6 S' the priest gave him hallowed bread:
22: 14 And who is s' faithful among all thy
23: 5 S' David and his men went to Keilah,
5 S' David saved the inhabitants of
24: 7 S' David stayed his servants with
25: 12 S' David's young men turned their
20 it was s', as she rode on the ass, that
21 s' that nothing was missed of all that
22 S' and more also do God unto the
25 for as his name is, s' is he; Nabal
35 S' David received of her hand that
26: 7 S' David and Abishai came to the
12 S' David took the spear and the cruse
24 s' let my life be much set by in the
25 S' David went on his way, and Saul
27: 1 s' shall I escape out of his hand.
11 S' did David, and s' will be his
28: 23 S' he arose from the earth, and sat
29: 8 thy servant s' long as I have been with
11 S' David and his men rose up early to
30: 3 S' David and his men came to the
9 S' David went, he and the six hundred
10 were s' faint that they could not go
21 were s' faint that they could not follow
23 Ye shall not do s', my brethren,
24 s' shall his part be that tarrieth by the
25 And it was s' from that day forward,
31: 6 S' Saul died, and his three sons, and
2Sa 1: 2 and s' it was, when he came to David,
10 S' I stood upon him, and slew him,
2: 2 S' David went up thither, and his two
16 side; s' they fell down together:
28 S' Joab blew a trumpet, and all the
31 s' that three hundred and threescore
3: 9 S' do God to Abner, and more also,
9 to David, even s' I do to him;
20 S' Abner came to David to Hebron,
30 S' Joab and Abishai his brother slew
34 before wicked men, s' fellest thou.
35 S' do God to me, and more also, if
5: 3 S' all the elders of Israel came to the
9 S' David dwelt in the fort, and called
25 And David did s', as the Lord had
6: 10 S' David would not remove the ark of
12 S' David went and brought up the ark
13 it was s', that when they that bare the
15 S' David and all the house of Israel
19 S' all the people departed every one to
7: 8 s' shalt thou say unto my servant
17 s' did Nathan speak unto David.
8: 2 And s' the Moabites became David's
9: 11 his servant, s' shall thy servant do.
13 S' Mephibosheth dwelt in Jerusalem:
10: 14 S' Joab returned from the children of
19 S' the Syrians feared to help the
11: 12 S' Uriah abode in Jerusalem that day,
20 if s' be that the king's wrath arise,
20 approached ye s' nigh unto the city
22 S' the messenger went, and came and
12: 31 S' David and all the people returned
13: 2 And Amnon was s' vexed, that he fell
6 S' Amnon lay down, and made
8 S' Tamar went to her brother
15 s' that the hatred wherewith he hated
20 S' Tamar remained desolate in her
35 come: as thy servant said, s' it is.
38 S' Absalom fled, and went to Geshur,
14: 3 S' Joab put the words in her mouth.
7 s' they shall quench my coal which is
17 s' is my lord the king to discern
23 S' Joab arose and went to Geshur,
24 S' Absalom returned to his own house,
25 be s' much praised as Absalom for
28 S' Absalom dwelt two full years in
33 S' Joab came to the king, and told
15: 2 it was s', that when any man that had
5 it was s', that when any man came
6 s' Absalom stole the hearts of the men
9 S' he arose, and went to Hebron.
34 s' will I now also be thy servant:
37 S' Hushai David's friend came into
16: 10 s' let him curse, because the
10 say, Wherefore hast thou done s'?
19 presence, s' will I be in thy presence.
22 S' they spread Absalom a tent upon
23 s' was...the counsel of Ahithophel
17: 3 s' all the people shall be in peace.
12 S' shall we come upon him in some
12 shall not be left s' much as one.
2Sa 17: 26 S' Israel and Absalom pitched in the
18: 6 S' the people went out into the field
19: 13 God do s' to me, and more also, if
14 s' that they sent this word unto the
15 S' the king returned, and came to
20: 2 S' every man of Israel went up from
3 S' they were shut up unto the day of
5 S' Amasa went to assemble the men
10 s' he smote him therewith in the fifth
10 S' Joab and Abishai his brother
18 and s' they ended the matter.
21 The matter is not s': but a man of
22: 4 s' shall I be saved from mine enemies.
35 s' that a bow of steel is broken by
37 under me; s' that my feet did not slip.
23: 5 my house be not s' with God; yet
24: 8 S' when they had gone through all
13 S' Gad came to David, and told him,
15 S' the Lord sent a pestilence upon
24 S' David bought the threshingfloor
25 S' the Lord was intreated for the
1Ki 1: 3 S' they sought for a fair damsel
6 in saying, Why hast thou done s'?
30 even s' will I certainly do this day.
36 God of my lord the king say s' too.
37 king, even s' be he with Solomon,
38 S' Zadok the priest, and Nathan the
40 s' that the earth rent with the sound
45 rejoicing, s' that the city rang again.
53 S' king Solomon sent, and they
2: 7 for s' they came to me when I fled
10 S' David slept with his fathers, and
27 S' Solomon thrust out Abiathar from
34 S' Benaiah the son of Jehoiada went
38 hath said, s' will thy servant do.
46 S' the king commanded Benaiah the
3: 9 judge this thy s' great a people?
12 s' that there was none like thee before
13 s' that there shall not be any among
4: 1 S' king Solomon was king over all
5: 4 s' that there is neither adversary nor
10 S' Hiram gave Solomon cedar trees
18 s' they prepared timber and stones to
6: 7 s' that there was neither hammer nor
9 S' he built the house, and finished it;
14 S' Solomon built the house, and
20 and s' covered the altar which was of
21 S' Solomon overlaid the house within
26 and s' was it of the other cherub.
27 s' that the wing of the one touched the
33 S' also made he for the door of the
38 S' was he seven years in building it.
7: 9 s' on the outside toward the great
18 and s' did he for the other chapiter.
22 s' was the work of the pillars finished.
40 S' Hiram made an end of doing all
51 S' was ended all the work that king
8: 11 S' that the priests could not stand to
25 s' that thy children take heed
46 s' that they carry them away captives
48 And s' return unto thee with all their
54 And it was s', that when Solomon had
63 S' the king and all the children of
9: 25 the Lord. S' he finished the house.
10: 13 S' she turned and went to her own
23 S' king Solomon exceeded all the
29 and s' for all the kings of the Hittites,
11: 19 s' that he gave him to wife the sister
12: 12 S' Jeroboam and all the people came
16 S' when all Israel saw that the king
16 S' Israel departed unto their tents.
19 S' Israel rebelled against the house
32 S' did he in Beth-el, sacrificing
33 S' he offered upon the altar which he
13: 4 s' that he could not pull it in again to
9 s' was it charged me by the word
10 S' he went another way, and returned
13 S' they saddled him the ass: and he
19 S' he went back with him, and did
14: 4 Jeroboam's wife did s', and arose,
6 And it was s', when Ahijah heard the
28 And it was s', when the king went into
15: 20 S' Ben-hadad hearkened unto...Asa,
16: 6 S' Baasha slept with his fathers, and
22 s' Tibni died, and Omri reigned.
28 S' Omri slept with his fathers, and
17: 5 S' he went and did according unto the
10 S' he arose and went to Zarephath.
17 and his sickness was s' sore, that
18: 4 For it was s', when Jezebel cut off the
6 S' they divided the land between them
12 s' when I come and tell Ahab, and he
16 S' Obadiah went to meet Ahab, and
20 S' Ahab sent unto all the children of
42 S' Ahab went up to eat and to drink.
19: 2 S' let the gods do to me, and more
13 And it was s', when Elijah heard it,
19 S' he departed thence, and found
20: 10 The gods do s' unto me, and more
19 S' these young men of the princes of
25 unto their voice, and did s'.
29 And s' it was, that in the seventh day
32 S' they girded sackcloth on their
34 S' he made a covenant with him, and
37 s' that in smiting he wounded him.
38 S' the prophet departed, and waited
40 him, S' shall thy judgment be;
21: 8 S' she wrote letters in Ahab's name,
22: 8 said, Let not the king say s'.
15 S' he came to the king. And the king
22 prevail also: go forth, and do s'.
29 S' the king of Israel and Jehoshaphat
37 S' the king died, and was brought to
40 S' Ahab slept with his fathers; and
2Ki 1: 17 S' he died according to the word of
2: 2 thee. S' they went down to Beth-el.
2Ki 2: 4 leave thee. S' they came to Jericho.
8 s' that they two went over on dry
10 from thee, it shall be s' unto thee;
10 but if not, it shall not be s'.
22 S' the waters were healed unto this
3: 9 S' the king of Israel went, and the
12 S' the king of Israel and Jehoshaphat
24 s' that they fled before them: but
4: 5 S' she went from him, and shut the
8 s' it was, that as oft as he passed by,
25 S' she went and came unto the man of
40 S' they poured out for the men to eat.
44 S' he set it before them, and they did
5: 8 And it was s', when Elisha the man of
9 S' Naaman came with his horses and
12 S' he turned and went away in a rage.
19 S' he departed from him a little way.
21 S' Gehazi followed after Naaman.
6: 4 S' he went with them. And when
23 S' the bands of Syria came no more
29 S' we boiled my son, and did eat him:
31 God do s' and more also to me, if
7: 10 S' they came and called unto the
16 S' a measure of fine flour was sold for
20 And s' it fell out unto him: for the
8: 6 S' the king appointed unto her a
9 S' Hazael went to meet him, and took
14 S' he departed from Elisha, and came
15 spread it on his face, s' that he died:
21 S' Joram went over to Zair, and all the
9: 4 S' the young man, even the young
14 S' Jehu the son of Jehoshaphat the
16 S' Jehu rode in a chariot, and went to
18 S' there went one on horseback to
22 s' long as the whoredoms of thy
22 and her witchcrafts are s' many?
27 And they did s' at the going up to Gur,
33 S' they threw her down: and some of
37 s' that they shall not say, This is
10: 11 S' Jehu slew all that remained of the
16 S' they made him ride in his chariot.
21 s' that there was not a man left that
11: 2 Athaliah, s' that he was not slain.
6 s' shall ye keep the watch of the
12: 6 But it was s', that in the three and
10 And it was s', when they saw that
13: 24 S' Hazael king of Syria died; and
15: 5 s' that he was a leper unto the day of
7 S' Azariah slept with his fathers;
12 And s' it came to pass.
20 S' the king of Assyria turned back,
16: 7 S' Ahaz sent messengers to
11 s' Urijah the priest made it
17: 7 For s' it was, that the children of
23 S' was Israel carried away out of
25 And s' it was at the beginning of their
32 S' they feared the Lord, and made
41 S' these nations feared the Lord, and
41 their fathers, s' do they unto this day.
18: 5 s' that after him was none like him
21 s' is Pharaoh king of Egypt unto
19: 5 S' the servants of king Hezekiah
8 S' Rab-shakeh returned, and found
36 S' Sennacherib king of Assyria
22: 14 S' Hilkiah the priest, and Ahikam,
23: 18 S' they let his bones alone, with the
24: 6 S' Jehoiakim slept with his fathers:
25: 6 S' they took the king, and brought
21 S' Judah was carried away out of
1Ch 9: 1 S' all Israel were reckoned by
23 S' they and their children had the
10: 4 S' Saul took a sword, and fell upon it.
6 S' Saul died, and his three sons, and
13 S' Saul died for his transgression
11: 6 S' Joab the son of Zeruiah went first
9 S' David waxed greater and greater:
13: 4 said that they would do s': for
5 S' David gathered all Israel together,
13 S' David brought not the ark home to
14: 11 S' they came up to Baal-perazim; and
15: 14 S' the priests and...Levites sanctified
17 S' the Levites appointed Heman the
19 S' the singers, Heman, Asaph, and
25 S' David, and the elders of Israel, and
16: 1 S' they brought the ark of God, and
37 S' he left there before the ark of the
18: 14 S' David reigned over all Israel, and
19: 2 S' the servants of David came into the
7 S' they hired thirty and two thousand
14 S' Joab and the people that were with
17 S' when David had put the battle in
20: 3 s' dealt David with all the cities
21: 3 an hundred times s' many more
11 S' Gad came to David, and said unto
14 S' the Lord sent pestilence upon
25 S' David gave to Ornan for the place
22: 5 S' David prepared abundantly before
23: 1 S' when David was old and full of
25: 7 S' the number of them, with their
29: 14 able to offer s' willingly after this sort?
2Ch 1: 3 S' Solomon, and all the congregation
10 judge this thy people, that is s' great?
17 s' brought they out horses for all the
2: 3 dwell therein, even s' deal with me.
5: 14 S' that the priests could not stand to
6: 16 yet s' that thy children take heed to
31 s' long as they live in the land
7: 5 s' the king and all the people dedicated
21 s' that he shall say, Why hath the
8: 14 for s' had David the man of God
16 S' the house of the Lord was
9: 12 S' she turned, and went away to her
10: 3 S' Jeroboam and all Israel came and
12 S' Jeroboam and all the people came
15 S' the king hearkened not unto the
16 S' all Israel went to their tents.

2Ch 11: 17 S· they strengthened the kingdom of
12: 9 S· Shishak king of Egypt came up
13 S· king Rehoboam strengthened
13: 9 s·...whosoever cometh to consecrate
13 s· they were before Judah, and the
17 s· there fell down slain of Israel five
14: 1 S· Abijah slept with his fathers, and
7 side. S· they built and prospered.
12 S· the Lord smote the Ethiopians
15: 10 S· they gathered themselves together
17: 10 s· that they made no war against
18: 7 said, Let not the king say s·.
11 And all the prophets prophesied s·,
21 also prevail: go out, and do even s·.
28 S· the king of Israel and Jehoshaphat
29 S· the king of Israel disguised
19: 10 s· wrath come upon you, and upon
20: 6 s· that none is able to withstand thee?
20 your God, s· shall ye be established;
20 his prophets, s· shall ye prosper.
25 gathering of the spoil, it was s· much.
30 S· the realm of Jehoshaphat was
21: 10 S· the Edomites revolted from under
17 s· that there was never a son left him,
19 sickness: s· he died of sore diseases.
22: 1 S· Ahaziah the son of Jehoram king
9 S· the house of Ahaziah had no power
11 S· Jehoshabeath, the daughter of the
11 Athaliah, s· that she slew him not.
23: 8 S· the Levites and all Judah did
15 S· they laid hands on her; and when
24: 13 S· the workmen wrought, and the
24 S· they executed judgment against
25: 21 S· Joash the king of Israel went up;
26: 23 S· Uzziah slept with his fathers, and
27: 5 S· much did the children of
6 S· Jotham became mighty, because
28: 14 S· the armed men left the captives
29: 17 s· they sanctified the house of the
22 S· they killed the bullocks, and the
25 s· was the commandment of the Lord
34 s· that they could not flay all the
35 S· the service of the house of the
30: 5 S· they established a decree to make
6 S· the posts went with the letters
9 s· that they should come again into
10 S· the posts passed from city to city
26 S· there was great joy in Jerusalem:
32: 4 S· there was gathered much people
17 s· shall not the God of Hezekiah
21 S· he returned with shame of face to
23 s· that he was magnified in the sight
26 s· that the wrath of the Lord came not
33: 8 s· that they will take heed to do all
9 S· Manasseh made Judah and the
20 S· Manasseh slept with his fathers,
34: 6 s· did he in the cities of Manasseh,
26 s· shall ye say unto him, Thus saith
28 S· they brought the king word again.
35: 6 S· kill the passover, and sanctify *
10 S· the service was prepared, and the
12 And s· did they with the oxen.
16 S· all the service of the Lord was
Ezr 2: 70 S· the priests, and the Levites, and
3: 13 S· that the people could not discern
4: 15 s· shalt thou find in the book of the
24 S· it ceased unto the second year of
5: 17 whether it be s·, that a decree was
6: 13 king had sent, s· they did speedily.
8: 23 S· we fasted and besought our God
30 S· took the priests and the Levites the
9: 2 s· that the holy seed have mingled
14 s· that there should be no remnant
10: 12 As thou hast said, s· must we do.
16 the children of the captivity did s·.
Ne 2: 4 S· I prayed to the God of heaven.
6 S· it pleased the king to send me; and
11 S· I came to Jerusalem, and was there
15 the gate of the valley, and s· returned.
18 S· they strengthened their hands for
4: 6 S· built we the wall; and all the wall
10 s· that we are not able to build the
18 girded by his side, and s· builded.
21 S· we laboured in the work: and half
23 S· neither I, nor my brethren, nor my
5: 12 them; s· will we do as thou sayest.
13 S· God shake out every man from
15 s· did not I, because of the fear of
6: 3 work, s· that I cannot come down:
13 be afraid, and do s·, and sin, and
15 S· the wall was finished in the twenty
7: 73 S· the priests, and the Levites, and the
8: 8 S· they read in the book in the law of
11 S· the Levites stilled all the people,
16 S· the people went forth, and brought
17 not the children of Israel done s·.
9: 10 S· didst thou get thee a name, as it
11 s· that they went through the midst of
21 wilderness, s·...they lacked nothing;
22 s· they possessed the land of Sihon,
24 S· the children went in and possessed
25 s· they did eat, and were filled, and
28 s· that they had the dominion over
12: 40 S· stood the two companies of them
43 s· that the joy of Jerusalem was heard
13: 20 S· the merchants and sellers of all
21 if ye do s· again, I will lay hands on
Es 1: 8 for s· the king had appointed to all
13 (for s· was the king's manner
17 s·...they shall despise their husbands
2: 4 pleased the king; and he did s·.
8 S· it came to pass, when the king's
12 (for s· were the days of their
16 S· Esther was taken unto king
17 s· that he set the royal crown upon her
3: 2 for the king had s· commanded

Es 4: 4 S· Esther's maids and her
6 S· Hatach went forth to Mordecai
16 s· will I go in unto the king, which
17 S· Mordecai went his way, and did
5: 2 it was s·, when the king saw Esther
2 S· Esther drew near, and touched the
5 S· the king and Haman came to the
13 s· long as I see Mordecai the Jew
6: 6 S· Haman came in. And the king
10 do even s· to Mordecai the Jew,
7: 1 S· the king and Haman came to
5 presume in his heart to do s·?
10 S· they hanged Haman on the gallows
8: 4 S· Esther arose, and stood before the
14 S· the posts that rode upon mules and
9: 14 king commanded it s· to be done:
27 s· as it should not fail, that they would
Job 1: 3 s· that this man was the greatest of
5 And it was s·, when the days of their
12 S· Satan went forth from the presence
2: 7 S· went Satan forth from the presence
13 S· they sat down with him upon the
5: 12 s· that their hands cannot perform
16 S· the poor hath hope, and iniquity
27 Lo this, we have searched it, s· it is;
7: 3 S· am I made to possess months of
9 s· he that goeth down to the grave
15 S· that my soul chooseth strangling,
20 thee, s· that I am a burden to myself?
8: 13 S· are the paths of all that forget
9: 2 I know it is s· of a truth: but how
30 and make my hands never s· clean;
35 fear him; but it is not s· with me.
13: 9 mocketh another, do ye s· mock him?
14: 12 S· man lieth down, and riseth not:
23: 7 s· should I be delivered for ever from
24: 19 s· doth the grave those which have
25 And if it be not s· now, who will make
27: 6 reproach me s· long as I live.
32: 1 S· these three men ceased to answer
22 in s· doing my maker would soon take
33: 20 S· that his life abhorreth bread, and
34: 25 the night, s· that they are destroyed.
28 S· that they cause the cry of the poor
35: 15 because it was not s·, he hath visited
36: 16 Even s· would he have removed thee
41: 10 None is s· fierce that dare stir him up:
16 One is s· near to another, that no air
42: 7 And it was s·, that after the Lord had
9 S· Eliphaz the Temanite and Bildad
12 S· the Lord blessed the latter end of
15 were no women found s· fair as the
17 S· Job died, being old and full of days.
Ps 1: 4 The ungodly are not s·: but are
7: 7 S· shall the congregation of the people
18: 3 s· shall I be saved from mine enemies.
34 s· that a bow of steel is broken by
21: 13 s· will we sing and praise thy power.
22: 1 why art thou s· far from helping me,
26: 6 s· will I compass thine altar, O Lord:
35: 25 their hearts, Ah, s· would we have it:
37: 3 s· shalt thou dwell in the land, and
40: 12 me, s· that I am not able to look up;
42: 1 s· panteth my soul after thee, O
45: 11 S· shall the king greatly desire thy
48: 5 They saw it, and s· they marvelled;
8 s· have we seen in the city of the
10 s· is thy praise unto the ends of the
58: 5 charmers, charming never s· wisely.
11 S· that a man shall say, Verily there
61: 8 S· will I sing praise unto thy name
63: 2 s· as I have seen thee in the
64: 8 S· they shall make their own tongue
65: 9 when thou hast s· provided for it.
68: 2 s· let the wicked perish at the presence
72: 7 s· long as the moon endureth.
73: 20 s·, O Lord, when thou awakest, thou
22 S· foolish was I, and ignorant: I was
77: 4 I am s· troubled that I cannot speak.
13 who is s· great a God as our God?
78: 21 s· a fire was kindled against Jacob,
29 S· they did eat, and were well filled:
53 them on safely s· that they feared not:
60 S· that he forsook the tabernacle of
72 S· he fed them according to the
79: 13 S· we thy people and sheep of thy
80: 12 s· that all they which pass by the way
18 S· will not we go back from thee:
81: 12 S· I gave them up unto their own
83: 15 S· persecute them with thy
90: 11 according to thy fear, s· is thy wrath.
12 S· teach us to number our days,
102: 4 grass; s· that I forget to eat my bread.
15 S· the heathen shall fear the name of
103: 5 s· that thy youth is renewed like the
11 s· great is his mercy toward them that
12 s· far hath he removed our
13 s· the Lord pitieth them that fear him.
104: 25 S· is this great and wide sea, wherein
106: 9 s· he led them through the depths, as
30 and s· the plague was stayed.
32 s· that it went ill with Moses for their
33 s· that he spake unadvisedly with his
107: 2 Let the redeemed of the Lord say s·,
29 s· that the waves thereof are still.
30 s· he bringeth them unto their desired
38 s· that they are multiplied greatly;
109: 17 loved cursing, s· let it come unto him:
17 in blessing, s· let it be far from him.
18 s· let it come into his bowels like
115: 8 s· is every one that trusteth in them.
119: 27 s· shall I talk of thy wondrous works.
42 S· shall I have wherewith to answer
44 S· shall I keep thy law continually
88 s· shall I keep the testimony of thy
123: 2 s· our eyes wait upon the Lord

Ps 125: 2 s· the Lord is round about his people
127: 2 for s· he giveth his beloved sleep.
4 man; s· are children of the youth.
135: 18 s· is every one that trusteth in them.
147: 20 hath not dealt s· with any nation:
Pr 1: 19 S· are the ways of every one that is
2: 2 S· that thou incline thine ear unto
3: 4 S· shalt thou find favour and good
10 S· thy barns be filled with plenty,
22 S· shall they be life unto thy soul, and
6: 11 S· shall thy poverty come as one that
29 S· he that goeth in to his
7: 13 S· she caught him, and kissed him,
10: 25 passeth, s· is the wicked no more:
26 s· is the sluggard to them that send
11: 19 s· he that pursueth evil pursueth it to
22 s· is a fair woman which is without
15: 7 heart of the foolish doeth not s·.
19: 24 not s· much as bring it to his mouth
20: 30 s· do stripes the inward parts of the
23: 7 he thinketh in his heart, s· is he:
24: 14 S· shall the knowledge of wisdom
29 I will do s· to him as he hath done
34 S· shall thy poverty come as one that
25: 12 s· is a wise reprover upon an obedient
13 s· is a faithful messenger to them that
16 eat s· much as is sufficient for thee,
17 he be weary of thee, and s· hate thee.
20 s· is he that singeth songs to an heavy
23 s· doth an angry countenance a
25 s· is good news from a far country.
27 s· for men to search their own glory is
26: 1 s· honour is not seemly for a fool.
2 s· the curse causeless shall not
7 s· is a parable in the mouth of fools.
8 s· is he that giveth honour to a
9 s· is a parable in the mouth of fools.
11 vomit, s· a fool returneth to his folly.
14 s· doth the slothful upon his bed.
19 S· is the man that deceiveth his
20 s· where there is no talebearer, the
21 s· is a contentious man to kindle
27: 8 s· is a man that wandereth from
9 s· doth the sweetness of a man's
17 s· a man sharpeneth the countenance
18 s· he that waiteth on his master shall
19 face, s· the heart of man to man.
20 s· the eyes of man are never satisfied.
21 for gold; s· is a man to his praise.
28: 15 s· is a wicked ruler over the poor
30: 33 s· the forcing of wrath bringeth forth
31: 11 s· that he shall have no need of spoil.
Ec 2: 9 S· I was great, and increased more
15 the fool, s· it happeneth even to me;
3: 11 s· that no man can find out the
19 the one dieth, s· dieth the other;
19 s· that a man hath no preeminence
4: 1 S· I returned, and considered all the
5: 16 points as he came, s· shall he go:
6: 2 s· that he wanteth nothing for his soul
3 s· that the days of his years be many,
7: 6 pot, s· is the laughter of the fool:
8: 10 And s· I saw the wicked buried,
10 in the city where they had s· done:
9: 2 as is the good, s· is the sinner; and he
12 s· are the sons of men snared in
10: 1 s· doth a little folly him that is in
Ca 2: 2 s· is my love among the daughters.
3 s· is my beloved among the sons.
5: 9 that thou dost s· charge us?
Isa 6: 13 s· the holy seed shall be the substance
10: 7 Howbeit he meaneth not s·,
7 neither doth his heart think s·; but
11 s· do to Jerusalem and her idols?
26 s· shall he lift it up after the manner
14: 24 I have purposed, s· shall it stand:
16: 2 s· the daughters of Moab shall be at
6 wrath: but his lies shall not be s·.
18: 4 For s· the Lord said unto me, I will
20: 2 And he did s·, walking naked and
4 S· shall the king of Assyria lead
21: 1 s· it cometh from the desert, from a
22: 22 s· he shall open, and none shall shut;
23: 1 s· that there is no house, no entering
5 s· shall they be sorely pained at the
24: 2 with the people, s· with the priest;
2 with the servant, s· with his master;
2 with the maid, s· with her mistress;
2 as with the buyer, s· with the seller;
2 with the lender, s· with the borrower;
2 s· with the giver of usury to him.
26: 17 s· have we been in thy sight, O
28: 8 s· that there is no place clean.
30: 14 s· that there shall not be found in the
31: 4 s· shall the Lord of hosts come
36: 6 s· is Pharaoh king of Egypt to all
37: 5 S· the servants of king Hezekiah
8 S· Rabshakeh returned, and found the
37 S· Sennacherib king of Assyria
38: 8 S· the sun returned ten degrees, by
13 s· will he break all my bones:
14 crane or a swallow, s· did I chatter:
16 s· wilt thou recover me, and make me
40: 20 He that is s· impoverished that he
41: 7 S· the carpenter encouraged the
47: 7 s· that thou didst not lay these
12 if s· be thou shalt be able to profit,
12 if s· be thou mayest prevail.
52: 15 S· shall he sprinkle many nations;
53: 7 dumb, s· he openeth not his mouth.
54: 9 s· have I sworn that I would not be
55: 9 s· are my ways higher than your
11 S· shall my word be that goeth
59: 19 S· shall they fear the name of the
60: 15 s· that no man went through thee,
61: 11 s· the Lord God will cause

Isa 62: 5 a virgin, s' shall thy sons marry thee:
5 s' shall thy God rejoice over thee.
63: 8 will not lie: s' he was their Saviour.
14 s' didst thou lead thy people, to
65: 8 s' will I do for my servants' sakes,
66: 13 comforteth, s' will I comfort you;
22 s' shall your seed and your name
Jer 2: 26 s' is the house of Israel ashamed;
36 Why gaddest thou about s' much
3: 20 s' have ye dealt treacherously with
5: 19 s' shall ye serve strangers in a land
27 s' are their houses full of deceit:
31 and my people love to have it s':
6: 7 s' she casteth out her wickedness:
9: 10 s' that none can pass through
10: 18 them, that they may find it s'.
11: 4 s' shall ye be my people, and I will be
5 and said, S' be it, O Lord.
13: 2 S' I got a girdle according to the
5 S' I went, and hid it by Euphrates,
11 s' have I caused to cleave unto me
17: 11 s' he that getteth riches, and not by
18: 4 s' he made it again another vessel,
6 s' are ye in mine hand, O house of
19: 11 Even s' will I break this people
21: 2 if s' be that the Lord will deal with us
24: 2 not be eaten, they were s' bad.
3 cannot be eaten, they are s' evil.
5 s' will I acknowledge them that
8 cannot be eaten, they are s' evil;
8 S' will I give Zedekiah the king of
26: 3 If s' be they will hearken, and turn
7 S' the priests and the prophets and
28: 6 Amen: the Lord do s': the Lord
11 Even s' will I break the yoke of
17 S' Hananiah the prophet died the
29: 17 cannot be eaten, they are s' evil.
30: 7 day is great, s' that none is like it:
31: 28 s' will I watch over them, to build,
32: 8 S' Hanameel mine uncle's son came
11 S' I took the evidence of the
42 s' will I bring upon them all the
33: 22 s' will I multiply the seed of David
26 s' that I will not take any of his seed
34: 5 s' shall they burn odours for thee;
36: 14 S' Baruch the son of Neriah took the
15 ears. S' Baruch read it in their ears.
21 S' the king sent Jehudi to fetch the
37: 14 s' Irijah took Jeremiah, and brought
38: 6 mire: s' Jeremiah sunk in the mire.
11 S' Ebed-melech took the men with
12 the cords. And Jeremiah did s'.
13 S' they drew up Jeremiah with cords,
16 S' Zedekiah the king sware secretly
20 s' it shall be well unto thee, and thy
23 S' they shall bring out all thy wives
27 S' they left off speaking with him;
28 S' Jeremiah abode in the court of the
39: 13 S' Nebuzar-adan the captain of the
14 home: s' he dwelt among the people.
40: 5 S' the captain of the guard gave him
41: 7 it was s', when they came into the
8 S' he forbare, and slew them not
14 S' all the people that Ishmael had
42: 17 S' shall it be with all the men that set
18 s' shall my fury be poured forth
20 s' declare unto us, and we will do it.
43: 4 S' Johanan the son of Kareah, and all
7 S' they came into the land of Egypt:
44: 14 S' that none of the remnant of Judah,
22 S' that the Lord could no longer bear,
46: 18 Carmel by the sea, s' shall he come.
48: 30 the Lord; but it shall not be s';
30 his lies shall not s' effect it.
50: 40 s' shall no man abide there, neither
51: 8 her pain, if s' be she may be healed.
49 s' at Babylon shall fall the slain of all
60 S' Jeremiah wrote in a book all the
52: 5 S' the city was besieged unto the
6 s' that there was no bread for the
26 S' Nebuzar-adan the captain of the
La 2: 22 s' that in the day of the Lord's anger
3: 29 the dust; if s' be there may be hope.
4: 14 s' that men could not touch their
5: 20 for ever, and forsake us s' long time?
Eze 1: 18 were s' high that they were dreadful;
28 s' was the appearance of the
3: 2 S' I opened my mouth, and he caused
4: 5 s' shalt thou bear the iniquity of the
5: 15 S' it shall be a reproach and a taunt,
17 S' will I send upon you famine and
6: 14 S' will I stretch out my hand upon
8: 5 S' I lifted up mine eyes the way
10 S' I went in and saw; and behold
11: 24 S' the vision that I had seen went up
12: 7 And I did s' as I was commanded:
11 done, s' shall it be done unto them:
13: 14 S' will I break down the wall that ye
14 s' that the foundation thereof shall
14: 15 s' that it be desolate, that no man
17 s' that I cut off man and beast from it:
15: 6 s' will I give the inhabitants of
16: 16 shall not come, neither shall it be s'.
42 S' will I make my fury toward thee
44 As is the mother, s' is her daughter.
17: 6 s' it became a vine, and brought forth
18: 4 s' also the soul of the son is mine:
30 s' iniquity shall not be your ruin.
20: 36 s' will I plead with you, saith the
22: 20 s' will I gather you in mine anger
22 s' shall ye be melted in the midst
23: 18 S' she discovered her whoredoms,
27 s' that thou shalt not lift up thine
44 s' went they in unto Aholah and
24: 18 S' I spake unto the people in the
19 things are to us, that thou doest s'?
Eze 28: 14 and I have set thee s': thou wast upon
31: 9 s' that all the trees of Eden, that
33: 7 S' thou, O son of man, I have set thee
34: 12 s' will I seek out my sheep, and
35: 15 desolate, s' will I do unto thee:
36: 38 s' shall the waste cities be filled
37: 7 S' I prophesied as I was commanded:
10 S' I prophesied as he commanded me,
23 s' shall they be my people, and I will
38: 20 S' that the fishes of the sea, and the
39: 7 S' will I make my holy name known
10 S' that they shall take no wood out of
22 S' the house of Israel shall know that
23 enemies; s' fell they all by the sword.
40: 5 s' he measured the breadth of the
47 S' he measured the court, an hundred
41: 4 S' he measured the length thereof,
7 s' increased from the lowest chamber
13 S' he measured the house, an hundred
18 s' that a palm tree was between a
19 S' that the face of a man was toward
43: 5 S' the spirit took me up, and brought
15 S' the altar shall be four cubits; and
27 and s' forward, the priests shall make
45: 20 s' thou shalt do the seventh day
20 simple: s' shall ye reconcile the house.
47: 21 S' shall ye divide this land unto you
Da 1: 5 s' nourishing them three years, that
14 S' he consented to them in this
2: 2 S' they came and stood before the
15 is the decree s' hasty from the king?
42 s' the kingdom shall be partly strong,
3: 17 If it be s', our God whom we serve is
5: 6 s' that the joints of his loins were
6: 23 S' Daniel was taken up out of the den,
28 S' this Daniel prospered in the reign
8: 4 s' that no beasts might stand before
17 S' he came near where I stood: and
10: 7 s' that they fled to hide themselves.
11: 9 S' the king of the south shall come
15 S' the king of the north shall come,
30 s' shall he do; he shall even return,
Ho 1: 3 S' he went and took Gomer the
3: 2 S' I bought her to me for fifteen pieces
3 man: s' will I also be for thee.
4: 7 s' they sinned against me:
6: 9 s' the company of priests murder in
8: 7 if s' be it yield, the strangers shall
10: 15 S' shall Beth-el do unto you
11: 2 them, s' they went from them:
14: 2 s' will we render the calves of our
Joe 2: 4 as horsemen, s' shall they run.
3: 17 S' shall ye know that I am the Lord
Am 3: 12 s' shall the children of Israel be
4: 8 S' two or three cities wandered unto
5: 9 s' that the spoiled shall come against
14 and s' the Lord, the God of hosts,
Ob 16 s' shall all the heathen drink
Jon 1: 3 s' he paid the fare thereof, and went
4 s' that the ship was like to be broken.
6 S' the shipmaster came to him, and
7 S' they cast lots, and the lot fell upon
12 s' shall the sea be calm unto you: for
15 S' they took up Jonah, and cast him
3: 3 S' Jonah arose, and went unto
5 S' the people of Nineveh believed God,
4: 5 S' Jonah went out of the city, and sat
6 S' Jonah was exceeding glad of the
Mic 2: 2 s' they oppress a man and his house,
5: 14 of thee: s' will I destroy thy cities.
7: 3 mischievous desire: s' they wrap it up.
Zep 3: 6 s' that there is no man, that there
7 s' their dwelling should not be cut off,
Hag 2: 5 s' my spirit remaineth among you:
14 S' is this people, and s' is this
14 s' is every work of their hands;
Zec 1: 6 doings, s' hath he dealt with us.
14 S' the angel that communed with me
21 s' that no man did lift up his head:
3: 5 S' they set a fair mitre upon his head,
6: 7 S' they walked to and fro through the
7: 3 as I have done these s' many years?
13 s' they cried, and I would not hear;
8: 15 S' again have I thought in these
10: 1 s' the Lord shall make bright clouds,
11: 11 s' the poor of the flock that waited
12 S' they weighed for my price thirty
14: 15 And s' shall be the plague of the
Mal 3: 13 have we spoken s' much against thee?
M't 1: 17 S' all the generations from
3: 15 said unto him, Suffer it to be s' now:
5: 12 s' persecuted they the prophets
16 Let your light s' shine before men,
19 and shall teach men s', he shall be
47 do not even the publicans s'?
6: 30 if God s' clothe the grass of the
7: 12 do to you, do ye even s' to them:
17 Even s' every good tree bringeth
8: 10 I have not found s' great faith, no,
13 hast believed, s' be it done unto thee.
28 s' that no man might pass by that
31 S' the devils besought him, saying,
9: 19 followed him, and s' did his disciples.
33 It was never s' seen in Israel.
11: 26 Even s', Father: for...it seemed
26 for s' it seemed good in thy sight.
12: 40 s' shall the Son of man be three
45 Even s' shall it be also unto this
13: 2 s' that he went into a ship, and
27 S' the servants of the householder
32 s' that the birds of the air come
40 s' shall it be in the end of this
49 S' shall it be at the end of the
15: 33 s' much bread in the wilderness,
33 as to fill s' great a multitude?
18: 13 if s' be that he find it, verily I say
M't 18: 14 Even s' it is not the will of your
31 S' when his fellowservants saw
35 S' likewise shall my heavenly
19: 8 from the beginning it was not s'.
10 of the man be s' with his wife,
12 s' born from their mother's womb:
20: 8 S' when even was come, the lord
16 S' the last shall be first, and the
26 But it shall not be s' among you:
34 S' Jesus had compassion on them,
22: 10 S' those servants went out into
23: 28 Even s' ye also outwardly appear
24: 27 s' shall also the coming of the
33 S' likewise ye, when ye shall see
37, 39 s' shall also the coming of the
46 when he cometh shall find s' doing.
25: 9 Not s'; lest there be not enough for
20 s' he that had received five talents
27: 64 s' the last error shall be worse
28: 15 S' they took the money, and did as
M'r 2: 2 not s' much as about the door:
8 s' reasoned within themselves,
3: 20 again, s' that they could not
20 could not s' much as eat bread.
4: 1 s' that he entered into a ship, and
17 and s' endured but for a time:
26 said, S' is the kingdom of God,
32 s' that the fowls of the air may
37 the ship, s' that it was now full.
40 unto them, Why are ye s' fearful?
6: 31 they had no leisure s' much as to
7: 18 Are ye s' without understanding
36 s' much the more a great deal
8: 8 S' they did eat, and were filled:
9: 3 s' as no fuller on earth can white
10: 8 s' then they are no more twain,
43 But s' shall it not be among you:
13: 29 S' ye in like manner, when ye shall
14: 59 neither s' did their witness agree
15: 5 nothing; s' that Pilate marvelled.
15 s' Pilate, willing to content the people,
39 saw that he s' cried out, and gave
16: 19 S' then after the Lord had
Lu 1: 21 that he tarried s' long in the temple.
60 Not s'; but he shall be called John.
2: 6 s' it was, that, while they were there,
21 which was s' named of the angel
5: 7 ships, s' that they began to sink.
10 And s' was also James and John,
15 s' much the more went there a
6: 3 Have ye not read s' much as this,
10 And he did s': and his hand was
26 s' did their fathers to the false
7: 9 I have not found s' great faith,
9: 15 they did s', and made them all sit
10: 21 them unto babes: even s', Father;
21 for s' it seemed good in thy sight.
11: 2 be done, as in heaven, s' in earth.
30 s' shall also the Son of man be to
12: 21 S' is he that layeth up treasure for
28 If then God s' clothe the grass,
38 and find them s', blessed are those
43 when he cometh shall find s' doing.
54 There cometh a shower; and s' it is.
14: 21 S' that servant came, and shewed
33 S' likewise, whosoever he be of
16: 5 S' he called every one of his lord's
26 s' that they which would pass
17: 10 S' likewise ye, when ye shall have
24 s' shall also the Son of man be in
26 s' shall it be also in the days of the
18: 13 would not lift up s' much as his eyes
39 cried s' much the more, Thou son
20: 15 S'...cast him out of the vineyard,
20 that s' they might deliver him unto
21: 31 S' likewise ye, when ye see these
34 s' that day come upon you unawares.
22: 26 But ye shall not be s': but he that
24: 24 found it even s' as the women had
Joh 3: 8 s' is every one that is born of the
14 s' must the Son of man be lifted up:
16 For God s' loved the world, that
4: 40 S' when the Samaritans were
46 S' Jesus came again into Cana of
53 S' the father knew that it was at
5: 21 even s' the Son quickeneth whom
26 s' hath he given to the Son to have
6: 9 but what are they among s' many?
10 S' the men sat down, in number
19 S' when they had rowed about five
57 s' he that eateth me, even he shall
7: 43 S' there was a division among the
8: 7 S' when they continued asking
59 midst of them, and s' passed by.
10: 15 me, even s' know I the Father:
11: 28 And when she had s' said, she
12: 37 done s' many miracles before them,
50 Father said unto me, s' I speak.
13: 12 S' after he had washed their feet,
13 Lord: and ye say well; for s' I am.
33 ye cannot come; s' now I say to you.
14: 2 if it were not s', I would have told you.
9 Have I been s' long time with you,
31 gave me commandment, even s' I
15: 8 fruit; s' shall ye be my disciples.
9 loved me, s' have I loved you:
17: 18 even s' have I also sent them into the
18: 15 Jesus, and s' did another disciple:
22 Answereth thou the high priest s'?
20: 4 S' they ran both together: and the
20 when he had s' said, he shewed
21 hath sent me, even s' send I you.
21: 11 and for all there were s' many, yet
15 S' when they had dined, Jesus
Ac 1: 11 shall s' come in like manner as ye
3: 12 or why look ye s' earnestly on us, as

Ac 3:18 should suffer, he hath s· fulfilled.
4:21 S· when they...further threatened
5: 8 ye sold the land for s· much?
8 And she said, Yea, for s· much.
32 s· is also the Holy Ghost, whom God
7: 1 high priest, Are these things s·?
5 no, not s· much as to set his foot on:
8 and s· Abraham begat Isaac, and
15 S· Jacob went down into Egypt,
19 s· that they cast out their young
51 as your fathers did, s· do ye.
8:32 s· opened he not his mouth:
10:14 Peter said, Not s·, Lord; for I have
11: 8 But I said, Not s·, Lord: for nothing
12: 8 bind on thy sandals. And s· he did.
15 constantly affirmed...it was even s·.
13: 4 S· they, being sent forth by the
8 s· is his name by interpretation)
47 s· hath the Lord commanded us,
14: 1 and s· spake, that a great multitude
15:30 S· when they were dismissed, they
39 contention was s· sharp between
39 s· Barnabas took Mark, and sailed
16: 5 s· were the churches established in
26 s· that the foundations of the
17:11 whether those things were s·.
33 S· Paul departed from among
19: 2 have not s· much as heard whether
10 s· that all they which dwelt in Asia
12 S· that from his body were brought
14 chief of the priests, which did s·.
16 s· that they fled out of that house
20 S· mightily grew the word of God
22 S· he sent into Macedonia two of them
27 S· that not only this our craft is in
20:11 till break of day, s· he departed.
13 for s· had he appointed, minding
24 s· that I might finish my course
35 s· labouring ye ought to support
21:11 S· shall the Jews at Jerusalem bind
35 s· it was, that he was borne of the
22:24 wherefore they cried s· against
23: 7 And when he had s· said, there
11 s· must thou bear witness also at
18 S· he took him, and brought him
22 S· the chief captain then let the
24: 9 saying that these things were s·.
14 s· worship I the God of my fathers,
27:17 strake sail, and s· were driven.
44 s· it came to pass, that they escaped
28: 9 S· when this was done, others
14 and s· we went toward Rome.
Ro 1:15 S·, as much as in me is, I am ready
20 s· that they are without excuse:
4:18 was spoken, S· shall thy seed be.
5: 3 And not only s·, but we glory in
11 And not only s·, but we also joy in God
12 s· death passed upon all men, for
15 the offence, s· also is the free gift.
16 was by one that sinned, s· is the gift:
18 even s· by the righteousness of one
19 s· by the obedience of one shall
21 even s· might grace reign through
6: 3 s· many of us as were baptized
4 s· we also should walk in newness
19 even s· now yield your members
7: 2 to her husband s· long as he liveth;
3 S· then if, while her husband
3 s· that she is no adulteress, though
25 S· then with the mind I myself
8: 8 S· then they that are in the flesh
9 if s· be that the Spirit of God dwell in
17 if s· be that we suffer with him, that
9:16 S· then it is not of him that willeth,
10:17 S· then faith cometh by hearing,
11: 5 Even s· then at this present time
16 root be holy, s· are the branches.
26 And s· all Israel shall be saved: as it
31 s· have these also now not believed,
12: 5 S· we, being many, are one body
20 in s· doing thou shalt heap coals
14:12 S· then every one of us shall give
15:19 s· that from Jerusalem, and
20 Yea, s· have I strived to preach the
1Co 1: 7 S· that ye come behind in no gift;
2:11 even s· the things of God knoweth
3: 7 S· then neither is he that planteth
15 shall be saved; yet s· as by fire.
4: 1 Let a man s· account of us, as of
5: 1 not s· much as named among the
3 him that hath s· done this deed,
6: 5 Is it s·, that there is not a wise man
7:17 called every one, s· let him walk.
17 And s· ordain I in all churches.
26 that it is good for a man s· to be.
36 need s· require, let him do what he
37 hath s· decreed in his heart that
38 S· then he that giveth her in
40 But she is happier if she s· abide,
8:12 when ye sin s· against the brethren,
9:14 Even s· hath the Lord ordained
15 that it should be s· done unto me:
24 prize? S· run, that ye may obtain.
26 therefore s· run, not as uncertainly;
26 s· fight I, not as one that beateth
11:12 s· is the man also by the woman;
28 and s· let him eat of that bread,
12:12 are one body: s· also is Christ.
13: 2 s· that I could remove mountains,
14: 9 S· likewise ye, except ye utter by
10 s· many kinds of voices in the
12 Even s· ye, forasmuch as ye are
25 s· falling down on his face he will
15:11 s· we preach, and s· ye believed.
15 up, if s· be that the dead rise not.
22 s· in Christ shall be all made alive.

1Co 15:42 S· also is the resurrection of the
45 s· it is written, The first man Adam
54 S· when this corruptible shall
16: 1 churches of Galatia, even s· do ye.
2Co 1: 5 s· our consolation also aboundeth
7 s· shall ye be also of the consolation.
10 delivered us from s· great a death,
2: 7 S· that contrariwise ye ought
3: 7 s· that the children of Israel could
4:12 S· then death worketh in us, but
5: 3 If s· be that being clothed we shall
7: 7 me; s· that I rejoiced the more.
14 even s· our boasting, which I made
8: 6 s· he would also finish in you the
11 s· there may be a performance also
9: 7 purposeth in his heart, s· let him give;
10: 7 is Christ's, even s· are we Christ's.
11: 3 s· your minds should be corrupted
9 unto you, and s· will I keep myself.
22 Are they Hebrews? s· am I.
22 Are they Israelites? s· am I.
22 they the seed of Abraham? s· am I.
12:16 But be it s·, I did not burden you:
Ga 1: 6 that ye are s· soon removed from
9 we said before, s· say I now again,
3: 3 Are ye s· foolish? having begun in
4 suffered s· many things in vain?
9 S· then they which be of faith are
4: 3 Even s· we, when we were children,
29 after the Spirit, even s· it is now.
31 S· then, brethren, we are not
5:17 s· that ye cannot do the things
6: 2 and s· fulfil the law of Christ.
Eph 2:15 twain one new man, s· making peace;
4:20 But ye have not s· learned Christ;
21 If s· be that ye have heard him, and
5:24 s· let the wives be to their own
28 S· ought men to love their wives as
33 s· love his wife even as himself;
Ph'p 1:13 S· that my bonds in Christ are
20 s· now also Christ shall be magnified
2:23 s· soon as I shall see how it will go
3:17 s· as ye have us for an ensample.
4: 1 s· stand fast in the Lord, my dearly
Col 2: 6 Jesus the Lord, s· walk ye in him:
3:13 Christ forgave you, s· also do ye.
1Th 1: 7 S· that ye were ensamples to all
8 s· that we need not to speak any
2: 4 with the gospel, even s· we speak;
8 S· being affectionately desirous of
4: 1 s· ye would abound more and more.
14 even s· them also which sleep in
17 s· shall we ever be with the Lord.
5: 2 s· cometh as a thief in the night.
2Th 1: 4 S· that we ourselves glory in you
2: 4 s· that he as God sitteth in the
3:17 token in every epistle: s· I write.
1Ti 1: 4 godly edifying which is in faith: s· do.
3:11 Even s· must their wives be grave,
6:20 oppositions of science falsely s· called:
2Ti 3: 8 s· do these also resist the truth:
Heb 1: 4 s· much better than the angels,
2: 3 if we neglect s· great salvation;
3:11 S· I sware in my wrath, They
19 S· we see that they could not enter
4: 7 To day, after s· long a time; as it
5: 3 s· also for himself, to offer for sins.
5 S· also Christ glorified not himself
6:15 And s·, after he had patiently
7: 9 And as I may s· say, Levi also, who
22 By s· much was Jesus made a
9:28 S· Christ was once offered to bear
10:25 s· much the more, as ye see the
33 of them that were s· used.
11: 3 s· that things which are seen were
12 s· many as the stars of the sky in
12: 1 with s· great a cloud of witnesses,
1 the sin which doth s· easily beset us,
20 And if s· much as a beast touch the
21 And s· terrible was the sight, that
13: 6 S· that we may boldly say, The
Jas 1:11 s· also shall the rich man fade
2:12 S· speak ye, and s· do, as they that
17 Even s· faith, if it hath not works,
26 s· faith without works is dead also.
3: 4 which though they be s· great,
5 s· the tongue is a little member,
6 s· is the tongue among our
10 these things ought not s· to be.
12 s· can no fountain both yield salt
1Pe 1:15 s· be ye holy in all manner of
2: 3 If s· be ye have tasted that the Lord
15 For s· is the will of God, that with
3:17 if the will of God be s·, that ye suffer
4:10 s· minister the same one to another,
2Pe 1:11 s· an entrance shall be ministered
1Jo 2: 6 him ought himself also s· to walk,
4:11 Beloved, if God s· loved us, we ought
17 as he is, s· are we in this world.
Re 1: 7 because of him. Even s·, Amen.
2:15 S· hast thou also them that hold
3:16 S· then because thou art lukewarm,
8:12 s· as the third part of them was
13:13 s· that he maketh fire come down
16: 7 Even s·, Lord God Almighty, true
18 the earth, s· mighty an earthquake,
18 an earthquake, and s· great.
18: 7 s· much torment and sorrow give
17 s· great riches is come to nought.
22:20 Amen. Even s·, come, Lord Jesus.

So (*so*)
2Ki 17: 4 messengers to S· king of Egypt,

soaked
Isa 34: 7 their land shall be s· with blood,

soap See SOPE.

so-be-it See so.

sober
2Co 5:13 or whether we be s·, it is for your
1Th 5: 6 others; but let us watch and be s·.
8 But let us, who are of the day, be s·,
1Ti 3: 2 husband of one wife, vigilant, s·,
11 wives be grave, not slanderers, s·,
Tit 1: 8 a lover of good men, s·, just,
2: 2 That the aged men be s·, grave,
4 teach the young women to be s·,
6 likewise exhort to be s· minded.
1Pe 1:13 be s·, and hope to the end for the
4: 7 be ye therefore s·, and watch unto
5: 8 Be s·, be vigilant; because your

soberly
Ro 12: 3 but to think s·, according as
Tit 2:12 we should live s·, righteously, and

sober-minded See SOBER and MINDED.

soberness
Ac 26:25 forth the words of truth and s·.

sobriety
1Ti 2: 9 with shamefacedness and s·; not
15 and charity and holiness with s·.

Socho (*so'-ko*) See also SOCHOH.
1Ch 4:18 and Heber the father of S·, and

Sochoh (*so'-ko*) See also SHOCHOH; SOCHO; SOCOH.
1Ki 4:10 to him pertained S·, and all the

socket See also SOCKETS.
Ex 38:27 hundred talents, a talent for a s·.

sockets
Ex 26:19 forty s· of silver under the twenty
19 two s· under one board for his two
19 and two s· under another board for
21 And their forty s· of silver;
21 two s· under one board,
21 and two s· under another board.
25 and their s· of silver, sixteen s·;
25 two s· under one board,
25 and two s· under another board.
32 be of gold, upon the four s· of silver.
37 shalt cast five s· of brass for them.
27:10 their twenty s· shall be of brass;
11 pillars and their twenty s· of brass;
12 their pillars ten, and their s· ten.
14, 15 pillars three, and their s· three.
16 shall be four, and their s· four.
17 be of silver, and their s· of brass.
18 twined linen, and their s· of brass.
35:11 his bars, his pillars, and his s·,
17 his pillars, and their s·, and the
36:24 forty s· of silver he made under the
24 two s· under one board for his two
24 two s· under another board for his
26 And their forty s· of silver;
26 two s· under one board,
26 and two s· under another board.
30 and their s· were sixteen s· of silver,
30 under every board two s·.
36 he cast for them four s· of silver.
38 but their five s· were of brass.
38:10 twenty, and their brasen s· twenty;
11 and their s· of brass twenty;
12 their pillars ten, and their s· ten;
14 pillars three, and their s· three.
15 pillars three, and their s· three.
17 the s· for the pillars were of brass;
19 were four, and their s· of brass four;
27 were cast the s· of the sanctuary,
27 sanctuary, and the s· of the vail;
27 hundred s· of the hundred talents,
30 s· to the door of the tabernacle
31 And the s· of the court round about,
31 and the s· of the court gate, and all
39:33 his bars, and his pillars, and his s·,
40 of the court, his pillars, and his s·,
40:18 fastened his s·, and set up the boards
Nu 3:36 the pillars thereof, and the s· thereof,
37 their s·, and their pins, and their
4:31 the pillars thereof, and s· thereof,
32 their s·, and their pins, and their
Ca 5:15 of marble, set upon s· of fine gold:

Socoh (*so'-ko*) See also SOCHOH.
Jos 15:35 and Adullam, S·, and Azekah,
48 Shamir, and Jattir, and S·,

sod See also SEETHE; SODDEN.
Ge 25:29 And Jacob s· pottage: and Esau
2Ch 35:13 other holy offerings s· they in pots,

sodden
Ex 12: 9 it raw, nor s· at all with water,
Le 6:28 the earthen vessel wherein it is s·
28 and if it be s· in a brasen pot, it
Nu 6:19 priest shall take the s· shoulder
1Sa 2:15 he will not have s· flesh of thee,
La 4:10 women have s· their own children:

sodering
Isa 41: 7 saying, It is ready for the s·:

Sodi (*so'-di*)
Nu 13:10 Zebulun, Gaddiel the son of S·.

Sodom (*sod'-om*) See also SODOMA; SODOMITE.
Ge 10:19 goest, unto S·, and Gomorrah,
13:10 before the Lord destroyed S· and
12 and pitched his tent toward S·.
13 men of S· were wicked and sinners
14: 2 made war with Bera king of S·,
8 there went out the king of S·, and
10 kings of S· and Gomorrah fled,
11 they took all the goods of S· and
12 brother's son, who dwelt in S·, and

Ge 14:17 the king of *S'* went out to meet
21 And the king of *S'* said unto Abram,
22 And Abram said to the king of *S'*, I
18:16 from thence, and looked toward *S'*:
20 cry of *S'* and Gomorrah is great,
22 from thence, and went toward *S'*:
26 said, If I find in *S'* fifty righteous
19: 1 And there came two angels to *S'* at
1 even; and Lot sat in the gate of *S'*:
4 the men of *S'*, compassed the house
24 rained upon *S'* and upon Gomorrah
28 he looked toward *S'* and Gomorrah,
De 29:23 like the overthrow of *S'*, and
32:32 For their vine is of the vine of *S'*,
Isa 1: 9 we should have been as *S'*, and we
10 word of the Lord, ye rulers of *S'*;
3: 9 and they declare their sin as *S'*,
13:19 as when God overthrew *S'* and
Jer 23:14 they are all of them unto me as *S'*,
49:18 the overthrow of *S'* and Gomorrah
50:40 As God overthrew *S'* and Gomorrah
La 4: 6 the punishment of the sin of *S'*,
Eze16:46 right hand, is *S'* and her daughters.
48 *S'* thy sister hath not done, she nor
49 this was the iniquity of thy sister *S'*,
53 captivity of *S'* and her daughters,
55 thy sisters, *S'* and her daughters,
56 thy sister *S'* was not mentioned by
Am 4:11 God overthrew *S'* and Gomorrah,
Zep 2: 9 Surely Moab shall be as *S'*, and the
M't 10:15 more tolerable for the land of *S'*
11:23 done in thee, had been done in *S'*,
24 more tolerable for the land of *S'*
M'r 6:11 shall be more tolerable for *S'* and
Lu 10:12 more tolerable in that day for *S'*,
17:29 same day that Lot went out of *S'*
2Pe 2: 6 And turning the cities of *S'* and
Jude 7 Even as *S'* and Gomorrha, and the
Re 11: 8 city, which spiritually is called *S'*

Sodoma (*sod'-o-mah*) See also SODOM.
Ro 9:29 we had been as *S'*, and been made

sodomite (*sod'-om-ite*) See also SODOMITES.
De 23:17 nor a *s'* of the sons of Israel.

sodomites (*sod'-om-ites*)
1Ki 14:24 there were also *s'* in the land:
15:12 took away the *s'* out of the land,
22:46 And the remnant of the *s'*, which
2Ki 23: 7 he brake down the houses of the *s'*,

soever See also WHATSOEVER; WHENSOEVER; WHERESOEVER; WHITHERSOEVER; WHOMSOEVER; WHOSESOEVER; WHOSOEVER.
Le 15: 9 what saddle *s'* he rideth upon that
17: 3 man *s'* there be of the house of Israel,
22: 4 What man *s'* of the seed of Aaron is a
De 12:32 What thing *s'* I command you,
2Sa 15:35 that what thing *s'* thou shalt hear out
24: 3 unto the people, how many *s'* they be,
1Ki 8:38 What prayer and supplication *s'*
2Ch 6:29 what prayer or what supplication *s'*
19:10 And what cause *s'* shall come to you
M'r 3:28 blasphemies wherewith *s'* they
6:10 what place *s'* ye enter into an
11:24 What things *s'* ye desire, when
Joh 5:19 for what things *s'* he doeth, these
20:23 Whose *s'* sins ye remit, they are
23 and whose *s'* sins ye retain, they are
Ro 3:19 that what things *s'* the law saith,

soft See also SOFTER.
Job 23:16 For God maketh my heart *s'*, and
41: 3 will he speak *s'* words unto thee?
Ps 65:10 thou makest it *s'* with showers:
Pr 15: 1 A *s'* answer turneth away wrath:
25:15 and a *s'* tongue breaketh the bone.
M't 11: 8 A man clothed in *s'* raiment?
8 behold, they that wear *s'* clothing
Lu 7:25 A man clothed in *s'* raiment?

softer
Ps 55:21 his words were *s'* than oil, yet

softly
Ge 33:14 I will lead on *s'*, according as the
J'g 4:21 and went *s'* unto him, and smote
Ru 3: 7 came *s'* and uncovered his feet,
1Ki 21:27 and lay in sackcloth, and went *s'*.
Isa 8: 6 the waters of Shiloah that go *s'*,
38:15 I shall go *s'* all my years in the
Ac 27:13 And when the south wind blew *s'*,

soil
Eze17: 8 It was planted in a good *s'* by

sojourn See also SOJOURNED; SOJOURNER; SOJOURNETH; SOJOURNING.
Ge 12:10 went down into Egypt to *s'* there;
19: 9 This one fellow came in to *s'*, and
26: 3 *S'* in this land, and I will be with
47: 4 For to *s'* in the land are we come;
Ex 12:48 when a stranger shall *s'* with thee,
Le 17: 8 the strangers which *s'* among you,
10, 13 the strangers that *s'* among you,
19:33 And if a stranger *s'* with thee in
20: 2 or of the strangers that *s'* in Israel,
25:45 the strangers that do *s'* among you,
Nu 9:14 if a stranger shall *s'* among you,
15:14 And if a stranger *s'* with you, or
J'g 17: 8 to *s'* where he could find a place:
9 I go to *s'* where I may find a place.
Ru 1: 1 went to *s'* in the country of Moab,
1Ki 17:20 evil upon the widow with whom I *s'*,
2Ki 8: 1 and *s'* wheresoever thou canst *s'*:
Ps 120: 5 Woe is me, that I *s'* in Mesech, that
Isa 23: 7 feet shall carry her afar off to *s'*.
52: 4 aforetime into Egypt to *s'* there;
Jer 42:15 enter into Egypt, and go to *s'* there;
17 faces to go into Egypt to *s'* there;
Jer 42:22 whither ye desire to go and to *s'*.
43: 2 say, Go not into Egypt to *s'* there:
44:12, 14, 28 the land of Egypt to *s'* there,
La 4:15 They shall no more *s'* there.
Eze 20:38 out of the country where they *s'*,
47:22 to the strangers that *s'* among you,
Ac 7: 6 should *s'* in a strange land;

sojourned
Ge 20: 1 Kadesh and Shur, and *s'* in Gerar.
21:23 to the land wherein thou hast *s'*.
34 And Abraham *s'* in the Philistines'
32: 4 I have *s'* with Laban, and stayed
35:27 where Abraham and Isaac *s'*.
De 18: 6 gates out of all Israel, where he *s'*,
26: 5 Egypt, and *s'* there with a few,
J'g 17: 7 who was a Levite, and he *s'* there.
19:16 and he *s'* in Gibeah: but the men
2Ki 8: 2 and *s'* in the land of the Philistines
Ps 105:23 and Jacob *s'* in the land of Ham.
Heb11: 9 faith he *s'* in the land of promise,

sojourner See also SOJOURNERS.
Ge 23: 4 I am a stranger and a *s'* with you:
Le 22:10 a *s'* of the priest, or an hired
25:35 though he be a stranger, or a *s'*;
40 But as an hired servant, and as a *s'*,
47 a *s'* or stranger wax rich by thee,
47 sell himself unto the stranger or *s'*
Nu 35:15 and for the *s'* among them: that
Ps 39:12 and a *s'*, as all my fathers were.

sojourners
Le 25:23 ye are strangers and *s'* with me.
2Sa 4: 3 and were *s'* there until this day.)
1Ch 29:15 are strangers before thee, and *s'*,

sojourneth
Ex 3:22 of her that *s'* in her house, jewels
12:49 unto the stranger that *s'* among
Le 16:29 or a stranger that *s'* among you:
17:12 any stranger that *s'* among you eat
18:26 nor any stranger that *s'* among you:
25: 6 for thy stranger that *s'* with thee,
Nu 15:15 for the stranger that *s'* with you,
16 for the stranger that *s'* with you.
26 the stranger that *s'* among them;
29 the stranger that *s'* among them.
19:10 the stranger that *s'* among them,
Jos 20: 9 the stranger that *s'* among them,
Ezr 1: 4 remaineth in any place where he *s'*,
Eze14: 7 or of the stranger that *s'* in Israel,
47:23 that in what tribe the stranger *s'*,

sojourning
Ex 12:40 the *s'* of the children of Israel,
J'g 19: 1 a certain Levite *s'* on the side of
1Pe 1:17 the time of your *s'* here in fear:

solace
Pr 7:18 let us *s'* ourselves with loves.

sold
Ge 25:33 he *s'* his birthright unto Jacob.
31:15 for he hath *s'* us, and hath quite
37:28 and *s'* Joseph to the Ishmeelites for
36 Midianites *s'* him into Egypt unto
41:56 and *s'* unto the Egyptians; and
42: 6 he it was that *s'* to all the people
45: 4 brother, whom ye *s'* into Egypt.
5 yourselves, that ye *s'* me hither:
47:20 Egyptians *s'* every man his field,
22 wherefore they *s'* not their lands.
Ex 22: 3 then he shall be *s'* for his theft.
Le 25:23 The land shall not be *s'* for ever:
25 hath *s'* away...of his possession,
25 redeem that which his brother *s'*.
27 unto the man to whom he *s'* it;
28 that which is *s'* shall remain in
29 within a whole year after it is *s'*;
33 then the house that was *s'*, and the
34 of their cities may not be *s'*;
39 waxen poor, and be *s'* unto thee;
42 they shall not be *s'* as bondmen.
48 After...he is *s'* he may be redeemed
50 from the year that he was *s'* to him
27:20 he have *s'* the field to another man,
27 be *s'* according to thy estimation.
28 possession, shall be *s'* or redeemed:
De 15:12 Hebrew woman, be *s'* unto thee,
28:68 ye shall be *s'* unto your enemies
32:30 except their Rock had *s'* them, and
J'g 2:14 he *s'* them into the hands of their
3: 8 and he *s'* them into the hand of
4: 2 Lord *s'* them into the hand of Jabin
10: 7 and he *s'* them into the hands of the
1Sa 12: 9 he *s'* them into the hand of Sisera,
1Ki 21:20 hast *s'* thyself to work evil in the
2Ki 6:25 ass's head was *s'* for fourscore pieces
7: 1 of fine flour be *s'* for a shekel,
16 of fine flour was *s'* for a shekel,
17:17 and *s'* themselves to do evil in the
Ne 5: 8 which were *s'* unto the heathen;
8 or shall they be *s'* unto us?
13:15 in the day wherein they *s'* victuals.
16 *s'* on the sabbath unto the children
Es 7: 4 For we are *s'*, I and my people, to
4 if we had been *s'* for bondmen and
Ps 105:17 Joseph, who was *s'* for a servant:
Isa 50: 1 creditors is it to whom I have *s'* you?
1 iniquities have ye *s'* yourselves,
52: 3 Ye have *s'* yourselves for nought;
Jer 34:14 which hath been *s'* unto thee;
La 5: 4 money; our wood is *s'* unto us.
Eze 7:13 shall not return to that which is *s'*,
Joe 3: 3 *s'* a girl for wine, that they might
6 have ye *s'* unto the Grecians,
7 the place whither ye have *s'* them,
Am 2: 6 they *s'* the righteous for silver, and
M't 10:29 not two sparrows *s'* for a farthing?
M't 13:46 went and *s'* all that he had, and
18:25 his lord commanded him to be *s'*,
21:12 that *s'* and bought in the temple,
12 the seats of them that *s'* doves,
26: 9 ointment might have been *s'* for
M'r 11:15 that *s'* and bought in the temple,
15 and the seats of them that *s'* doves;
14: 5 *s'* for more than three hundred
Lu 12: 6 five sparrows *s'* for two farthings,
17:28 they bought, they *s'*, they planted,
19:45 to cast out them that *s'* therein, and
Joh 2:14 in the temple those that *s'* oxen and
16 said unto them that *s'* doves, Take
12: 5 this ointment *s'* for three hundred
Ac 2:45 And *s'* their possessions and goods,
4:34 of lands or houses *s'* them, and
34 prices of the things that were *s'*,
37 Having land, *s'* it, and brought the
5: 1 Sapphira his wife, *s'* a possession,
4 and after it was *s'*, was it not in
8 whether ye *s'* the land for so much?
7: 9 with envy, *s'* Joseph into Egypt:
Ro 7:14 but I am carnal, *s'* under sin.
1Co 10:25 Whatsoever is *s'* in the shambles,
Heb12:16 morsel of meat *s'* his birthright.

soldering See SODERING.

soldier See also SOLDIERS.
Joh 19:23 made four parts, to every *s'* a part;
Ac 10: 7 a devout *s'* of them that waited on
28:16 by himself with a *s'* that kept him.
2Ti 2: 3 as a good *s'* of Jesus Christ.
4 who hath chosen him to be a *s'*.

soldiers See also FELLOWSOLDIERS; SOLDIERS'.
1Ch 7: 4 fathers, were bands of *s'* for war,
11 thousand and two hundred *s'*,
2Ch 25:13 the *s'* of the army which Amaziah
Ezr 8:22 to require of the king a band of *s'*
Isa 15: 4 the armed *s'* of Moab...cry out;
M't 8: 9 authority, having *s'* under me:
27:27 the *s'* of the governor took Jesus
27 unto him the whole band of *s'*.
28:12 they gave large money unto the *s'*,
M'r 15:16 the *s'* led him away into the hall,
Lu 3:14 the *s'* likewise demanded of him,
7: 8 authority, having under me *s'*,
23:36 the *s'* also mocked him, coming to
Joh 19: 2 the *s'* platted a crown of thorns,
23 *s'*, when they had crucified Jesus,
24 These things therefore the *s'* did.
32 Then came the *s'*, and brake the
34 one of the *s'* with a spear pierced
Ac 12: 4 him to four quaternions of *s'* to
6 Peter was sleeping between two *s'*,
18 was no small stir among the *s'*,
21:32 Who immediately took *s'* and
32 saw the chief captain and the *s'*,
35 that he was borne of the *s'* for the
23:10 commanded the *s'* to go down, and
23 Make ready two hundred *s'* to go to
31 the *s'*, as it was commanded them,
27:31 said to the centurion and to the *s'*,
32 Then the *s'* cut off the ropes of the

soldiers'
Ac 27:42 And the *s'* counsel was to kill the

sole See also SOLES.
Ge 8: 9 no rest for the *s'* of her foot,
De 28:35 from the *s'* of thy foot unto the top
56 to set the *s'* of her foot upon the
65 shall the *s'* of thy foot have rest:
Jos 1: 3 the *s'* of your foot shall tread upon,
2Sa 14:25 from the *s'* of his foot even to the
2Ki 19:24 with the *s'* of my feet have I dried
Job 2: 7 the *s'* of his foot unto his crown.
Isa 1: 6 *s'* of the foot even unto the head
37:25 with the *s'* of my feet have I dried
Eze 1: 7 *s'* of their feet was like the *s'* of a

solemn
Le 23:36 it is a *s'* assembly; and ye shall
Nu 10:10 gladness, and in your *s'* days,
15: 3 in your *s'* feasts, to make a sweet
29:35 day ye shall have a *s'* assembly:
De 16: 8 seventh day shall be a *s'* assembly
15 thou keep a *s'* feast unto the Lord
2Ki 10:20 Proclaim a *s'* assembly for Baal.
2Ch 2: 4 on the *s'* feasts of the Lord your
7: 9 day they made a *s'* assembly:
8:13 new moons, and on the *s'* feasts,
Ne 8:18 the eighth day was a *s'* assembly,
Ps 81: 3 appointed, on our *s'* feast day.
92: 3 upon the harp with a *s'* sound.
Isa 1:13 it is iniquity, even the *s'* meeting.
La 1: 4 because none come to the *s'* feasts:
2: 6 Lord hath caused the *s'* feasts and
7 Lord, as in the day of a *s'* feast.
22 called as in a *s'* day my terrors
Eze 36:38 of Jerusalem in her *s'* feasts; so
46: 9 before the Lord in the *s'* feasts,
Ho 2:11 her sabbaths, and all her *s'* feasts.
9: 5 What will ye do in the *s'* day, and
12: 9 as in the days of the *s'* feast.
Joe 1:14 ye a fast, call a *s'* assembly,
2:15 sanctify a fast, call a *s'* assembly:
Am 5:21 not smell in your *s'* assemblies.
Na 1:15 keep thy *s'* feasts, perform thy
Zep 3:18 are sorrowful for the *s'* assembly,
Mal 2: 3 even the dung of your *s'* feasts;

solemnities
Isa 33:20 Look upon Zion, the city of our *s'*:
Eze 45:17 in all *s'* of the house of Israel:
46:11 in the *s'* the meat offering shall be

solemnity See also SOLEMNITIES.
De 31:10 in the *s'* of the year of release,
Isa 30:29 the night when a holy *s'* is kept;

solemnly
Ge 43: 3 The man did s· protest unto us,
1Sa 8: 9 howbeit yet protest s· unto them,

soles
De 11:24 s· of your feet shall tread shall be
Jos 3:13 the s· of the feet of the priests that
4:18 s· of the priests' feet were lifted
1Ki 5: 3 put them under the s· of his feet.
Isa 60:14 down at the s· of thy feet; and
Eze 43: 7 and the place of the s· of my feet,
Mal 4: 3 be ashes under the s· of your feet

solitarily
Mic 7:14 which dwell s· in the wood, in the

solitary
Job 3: 7 Lo, let that night be s·, let no
30: 3 For want and famine they were s·;
Ps 68: 6 God setteth the s· in families: he
107: 4 in the wilderness in a s· way;
Isa 35: 1 s· place shall be glad for them;
La 1: 1 How doth the city sit s·, that was
M'r 1:35 out, and departed into a s· place,

Solomon^ (*sol'-o-mun*) See also JEDIDIAH; SOLOMON'S.
2Sa 5:14 Shobab, and Nathan, and S·,
12:24 a son, and he called his name S·:
1Ki 1:10 and S· his brother, he called not.
11 unto Bath-sheba the mother of S·,
12 own life, and the life of thy son S·.
13, 17 S· thy son shall reign after me,
19 S· thy servant hath he not called.
21 I and my son S· shall be counted
26 thy servant S·, hath he not called.
30 S· thy son shall reign after me,
33 S· my son to ride upon mine own
34 and say, God save king S·.
37 even so be he with S·, and make
38 and caused S· to ride upon king
39 of the tabernacle, and anointed S·.
39 the people said, God save king S·.
43 king David hath made S· king.
46 also S· sitteth on the throne of the
47 name of S· better than thy name,
50 And Adonijah feared because of S·,
51 And it was told S·, saying, Behold,
51 Adonijah feareth king S·: for, lo,
51 Let king S· swear unto me to day
52 S· said, If he will shew himself a
53 So king S· sent, and they brought
53 and bowed himself to king S·:
53 and S· said unto him, Go to thine
2: 1 and he charged S· his son, saying,
12 sat S· upon the throne of David
13 to Bath-sheba the mother of S·.
17 Speak, I pray thee, unto S· the king,
19 Bath-sheba...went unto king S·,
22 king S· answered and said unto his
23 Then king S· sware by the Lord,
25 And king S· sent by the hand of
27 S· thrust out Abiathar from being
29 it was told king S· that Joab was
29 Then S· sent Benaiah the son of
41 And it was told S· that Shimei had
45 king S· shall be blessed, and the
46 was established in the hand of S·.
3: 1 And S· made affinity with Pharaoh
3 S· loved the Lord, walking in the
4 burnt offerings, did S· offer upon
5 Lord appeared to S· in a dream by
6 S· said, Thou hast shewed unto
10 Lord, that S· had asked this thing.
15 And S· awoke, and behold, it was a
4: 1 king S· was king over all Israel.
7 And S· had twelve officers over all
11 had Taphath the daughter of S· to
15 Basmath the daughter of S· to
21 S· reigned over all kingdoms from
21 served S· all the days of his life.
25 to Beer-sheba, all the days of S·.
26 S· had forty thousand stalls of
27 provided victual for king S·, and
29 S· wisdom and understanding
34 all people to hear the wisdom of S·,
5: 1 of Tyre sent his servants unto S·;
2 And S· sent to Hiram, saying,
7 when Hiram heard the words of S·,
8 Hiram sent to S·, saying, I have
10 So Hiram gave S· cedar trees and
11 S· gave Hiram twenty thousand
11 gave S· to Hiram year by year.
12 the Lord gave S· wisdom, as he
12 was peace between Hiram and S·;
13 S· raised a levy out of all Israel;
15 And S· had threescore and ten
6: 2 house which king S· built for the
11 the word of the Lord came to S·,
14 So S· built the house, and finished
21 S· overlaid the house within with
7: 1 But S· was building his own house
8 S· made also an house for Pharaoh's
13 king S· sent and fetched Hiram out
14 he came to king S·, and wrought all
40 work that he made king S· for the
45 which Hiram made to king S· for
47 S· left all the vessels unweighed,
48 And S· made all the vessels that
51 all the work that king S· made for
51 And S· brought in the things which
8: 1 S· assembled the elders of Israel,
1 Israel, unto king S· in Jerusalem,
2 assembled themselves unto king S·
5 king S·, and all the congregation of
12 Then spake S·, The Lord said that
22 S· stood before the altar of the Lord
54 S· had made an end of praying all
1Ki 8:63 And S· offered a sacrifice of peace
65 at that time S· held a feast, and all
9: 1 when S· had finished the building
2 appeared to S· the second time,
10 when S· had built the two houses,
11 king of Tyre had furnished S· with
11 king S· gave Hiram twenty cities
12 the cities which S· had given him;
15 of the levy which king S· raised;
17 S· built Gezer, and Beth-horon the
19 all the cities of store that S· had,
19 and that which S· desired to build
21 upon those did S· levy a tribute of
22 of Israel did S· make no bondmen:
24 house which S· had built for her:
25 a year did S· offer burnt offerings
26 king S· made a navy of ships in
27 of the sea, with the servants of S·,
28 talents, and brought it to king S·.
10: 1 of Sheba heard of the fame of S·
2 and when she was come to S·, she
3 S· told her all her questions: there
10 the queen of Sheba gave to king S·.
13 S· gave unto the queen of Sheba all
13 S· gave her of his royal bounty.
14 of gold that came to S· in one year
16 king S· made two hundred targets
21 accounted of in the days of S·.
23 So king S· exceeded all the kings
24 all the earth sought to S·, to hear
26 S· gathered together chariots and
28 S· had horses brought out of Egypt,
11: 1 king S· loved many strange women,
2 gods: S· clave unto these in love.
4 when S· was old, that his wives
5 S· went after Ashtoreth the goddess
6 S· did evil in the sight of the Lord,
7 S· build an high place for Chemosh,
9 Lord was angry with S·, because
11 the Lord said unto S·, Forasmuch
14 stirred up an adversary unto S·,
25 to Israel all the days of S·,
27 S· built Millo, and repaired the
28 S· seeing the young man that he
31 the kingdom out of the hand of S·,
40 S· sought...to kill Jeroboam. And
40 was in Egypt until the death of S·.
41 And the rest of the acts of S·, and
41 in the book of the acts of S·?
42 time that S· reigned in Jerusalem
43 S· slept with his fathers, and was
12: 2 fled from the presence of king S·,
6 men, that stood before S· his father
21 again to Rehoboam the son of S·.
23 unto Rehoboam, the son of S·,
14:21 Rehoboam the son of S· reigned in
26 shields of gold which S· had made.
2Ki 21: 7 said to David, and to S· his son,
23:13 S· the king of Israel had builded
24:13 the vessels of gold which S· king of
25:16 bases which S· had made for the
1Ch 3: 5 Shobab, and Nathan, and S·, four,
6:10 temple that S· built in Jerusalem.)
32 S· had built the house of the Lord
14: 4 and Shobab, Nathan, and S·,
18: 8 wherewith S· made the brasen sea,
22: 5 S· my son is young and tender, and
6 Then he called for S· his son, and
7 David said to S·, My son, as for me,
9 for his name shall be S·, and I will
17 princes of Israel to help S· his son,
23: 1 made S· his son king over Israel.
28: 5 chosen S· my son to sit upon the
6 S· thy son, he shall build my house
9 S· my son, know thou the God of
11 Then David gave to S· his son the
20 David said to S· his son, Be strong
29: 1 S· my son, whom alone God hath
19 give unto S· my son a perfect heart,
22 they made S· the son of David king
23 S· sat on the throne of the Lord as
24 submitted themselves unto S· the
25 the Lord magnified S· exceedingly
28 and S· his son reigned in his stead.
2Ch 1: 1 And S·...was strengthened in his
2 Then S· spake unto all Israel, to the
3 So S·, and all the congregation
5 and S· and the congregation sought
6 S· went up thither to the brasen
7 that night did God appear unto S·,
8 And S· said unto God, Thou hast
11 And God said to S·, Because this
13 Then S· came from his journey to
14 And S· gathered chariots and
16 S· had horses brought out of Egypt,
2: 1 S· determined to build an house for
2 And S· told out threescore and ten
3 S· sent to Huram the king of Tyre,
11 in writing, which he sent to S·,
17 S· numbered all the strangers that
3: 1 S· began to build the house of the
3 things wherein S· was instructed
4:11 that he was to make for king S· for
16 Huram his father make to king S·
18 S· made all these vessels in great
19 S· made all the vessels that were
5: 1 all the work that S· made for the
1 and S· brought in all the things that
2 S· assembled the elders of Israel,
6 king S·, and all the congregation
6: 1 Then said S·, The Lord hath said
13 For S· had made a brasen scaffold,
7: 1 S· had made an end of praying,
5 S· offered a sacrifice of twenty and
7 Moreover S· hallowed the middle of
7 the brasen altar which S· had made
2Ch 7: 8 time S· kept the feast seven days
10 had shewed unto David, and to S·,
11 S· finished the house of the Lord,
12 the Lord appeared to S· by night,
8: 1 wherein S· had built the house of
2 which Huram had restored to S·,
2 S· built them, and caused the
3 And S· went to Hamath-zobah, and
6 and all the store cities that S· had,
6 and all that S· desired to build in
8 them did S· make to pay tribute
9 of Israel did S· make no servants
11 And S· brought up the daughter of
12 S· offered burnt offerings unto the
16 work of S· was prepared unto the
17 Then went S· to Ezion-geber, and
18 with the servants of S· to Ophir,
18 gold, and brought them to king S·.
9: 1 of Sheba heard of the fame of S·,
1 she came to prove S· with hard
1 and when she was come to S·, she
2 And S· told her all her questions:
2 nothing hid from S· which he told
3 of Sheba had seen the wisdom of S·,
9 as the queen of Sheba gave king S·.
10 servants of S·, which brought gold
12 S· gave to the queen of Sheba all
13 weight of gold that came to S· in
14 brought gold and silver to S·.
15 king S· made two hundred targets
20 drinking vessels of king S· were
20 accounted of in the days of S·.
22 S· passed all the kings of the earth
23 kings...sought the presence of S·,
25 And S· had four thousand stalls for
28 they brought unto S· horses out of
29 Now the rest of the acts of S·, first
30 S· reigned in Jerusalem over all
31 And S· slept with his fathers, and
10: 2 he had fled from the presence of S·
6 stood before S· his father while he
11: 3 unto Rehoboam the son of S·, king
17 Rehoboam the son of S· strong,
17 walked in the way of David and S·.
12: 9 shields of gold which S· had made.
13: 6 the servant of S· the son of David,
7 against Rehoboam the son of S·,
30:26 for since the time of S· the son of
33: 7 had said to David and to S· his son,
35: 3 house which S· the son of David
4 to the writing of S· his son.
Ne 12:45 commandment of David, and of S·
13:26 Did not S· king of Israel sin by
Ps 72: *title* A Psalm for S·.
127: *title* A Song of degrees for S·.
Pr 1: 1 The proverbs of S· the son of David,
10: 1 proverbs of S·. A wise son maketh
25: 1 These are also proverbs of S·, which
Ca 1: 5 of Kedar, as the curtains of S·.
3: 9 King S· made himself a chariot of
11 and behold king S· with the crown
8:11 S· had a vineyard at Baal-hamon;
12 thou, O S·, must have a thousand,
Jer 52:20 king S· had made in the house of
M't 1: 6 and David the king begat S· of her/
7 S· begat Roboam; and Roboam
6:29 S· in all his glory was not arrayed
12:42 the earth to hear the wisdom of S·;
42 behold, a greater than S· is here.
Lu 11:31 the earth to hear the wisdom of S·;
31 behold, a greater than S· is here.
12:27 S· in all his glory was not arrayed
Ac 7:47 But S· built him an house.

Solomon's (*sol'-o-muns*)
1Ki 4:22 And S· provision for one day was
27 all that came unto king S· table,
30 S· wisdom excelled the wisdom of
5:16 Beside the chief of S· officers which
18 S· builders, and Hiram's builders
6: 1 fourth year of S· reign over Israel,
9: 1 S· desire which he was pleased to
16 present unto his daughter, S· wife.
23 the officers that were over S· work,
10: 4 of Sheba had seen all S· wisdom,
21 all king S· drinking vessels were of
11:26 S· servant, whose mother's name
1Ch 3:10 S· son was Rehoboam, Abia his son,
2Ch 7:11 all that came into S· heart to make
8:10 were the chief of king S· officers,
Ezr 2:55 The children of S· servants: the
58 and the children of S· servants,
Ne 7:57 The children of S· servants: the
60 and the children of S· servants,
11: 3 and the children of S· servants.
Ca 1: 1 The song of songs, which is S·.
3: 7 Behold his bed, which is S·;
Joh 10:23 walked in the temple in S· porch.
Ac 3:11 them in the porch that is called S·,
5:12 all with one accord in S· porch.

solve See DISSOLVE; RESOLVED.

some^ See also BURDENSOME; DELIGHTSOME; LOATHSOME; NOISOME; SOMEBODY; SOMETHING; SOMETIME; SOMEWHAT; WEARISOME; WHOLESOME.
Ge 19:19 lest s· evil take me, and I die:
30:35 and every one that had s· white in it,
37:20 slay him, and cast him into s· pit,
20 S· evil beast hath devoured him:
47: 2 he took s· of his brethren, even
Ex 16:17 did so, and gathered, s· more, s· less.
20 but s· of them left of it until the
27 went out s· of the people on the
30:36 thou shalt beat s· of it very small,
Le 4: 7 the priest shall put s· of the blood
17 shall dip his finger in s· of the blood,

Le 4:18 put s' of the blood upon the horns
14:14 take s' of the blood of the trespass
15 the priest shall take s' of the log of oil,
27 with his right finger s' of the oil that
25:25 hath sold away s' of his possession,
27:16 s' part of a field of his possession.
Nu 5:20 s' man have lain with thee beside
21: 1 Israel, and took s' of them prisoners.
27:20 shalt put s' of thine honour upon him,
31: 3 Arm s' of yourselves unto the war,
De 24: 1 hath found s' uncleanness in her:
Jos 8:22 s' on this side, and s' on that side:
J'g 21:13 whole congregation sent s' to speak
Ru 2:16 let fall also s' of the handfuls of
1Sa 8:11 and s' shall run before his chariots.
13: 7 s' of the Hebrews went over Jordan to
24:10 and s' bade me kill thee: but mine eye
27: 5 let them give me a place in s' town
2Sa 11:17 and there fell s' of the people of the
24 and s' of the king's servants be dead,
17: 9 he is hid now in s' pit, or in s' other
9 s' of them be overthrown at the first,
12 shall we come upon him in s' place
1Ki 14:13 in him there is found s' good thing
2Ki 2:16 and cast him upon s' mountain,
16 mountain, or unto s' valley.
5:13 had bid thee do s' great thing,
7: 9 light, s' mischief will come upon us:
13 Let s' take, I pray thee, five of the
9:33 s' of her blood was sprinkled on the
17:25 among them, which slew s' of them.
1Ch 4:42 s' of them, even of the sons of Simeon,
9:29 *S'* of them also were appointed to
30 And s' of the sons of the priests made
12:19 And there fell s' of Manasseh to David,
2Ch 12: 7 I will grant them s' deliverance;
16:10 And Asa oppressed s' of the people
17:11 Also s' of the Philistines brought
20: 2 there came s' that told Jehoshaphat,
Ezr 2:68 And s' of the chief of the fathers, when
70 s' of the people, and the singers, and
7: 7 there went up s' of the children of
10:44 s' of them had wives by whom they
Ne 2:12 night, I and s' few men with me;
5: 3 *S'* also there were that said, We have
5 s' of our daughters are brought unto
6: 2 in s' one of the villages in the plain of
7:70 s' of the chief of the fathers gave
71 s' of the chief of the fathers gave to
73 and the singers and s' of the people,
11:25 s' of the children of Judah dwelt at
12:44 s' appointed over the chambers for
13:15 in Judah s' treading wine presses on
19 s' of my servants set I at the gates,
Job 24: 2 *S'* remove the landmarks; they
Ps 20: 7 *S'* trust in chariots, and s' in
69:20 and I looked for s' to take pity, but
Pr 4:16 away, unless they cause s' to fall.
Jer 49: 9 they not leave s' gleaning grapes?
Eze 6: 8 have s' that shall escape the sword
Da 8:10 it cast down s' of the host and of the
11:35 s' of them of understanding shall fall,
12: 2 shall awake, s' to everlasting life,
2 s' to shame...everlasting contempt.
Am 4:11 I have overthrown s' of you, as God
Ob 5 thee, would they not leave s' grapes?
M't 13: 4 s' seeds fell by the way side,
5 *S'* fell...stony places, where
7 s' fell among thorns; and the
8 forth fruit, s' an hundredfold,
8 s' sixtyfold, s' thirtyfold.
23 bringeth forth, s'...hundredfold,
24 hundredfold, s' sixty, s' thirty.
16:14 *S'* say...thou art John the Baptist:
14 s', Elias; and others, Jeremias,"
28 There be s' standing here, which
19:12 For there are s' eunuchs, which were
12 and there are s' eunuchs, which were
23:34 s' of them ye shall kill and crucify;
34 s' of them shall ye scourge in your
27:47 *S'* of them that stood there, when
28:11 s' of the watch came into the city,
17 worshipped him: but s' doubted.
M'r 2: 1 entered into Capernaum after s' days;
4: 4 he sowed, s' fell by...way side,
5 s' fell on stony ground, where it
7 and s' fell among thorns, and the
8 and brought forth, s' thirty,
8 and s' sixty, and s' an hundred.
20 and bring forth fruit, s' thirtyfold,
20 s' sixty, and s' an hundred.
7: 2 saw s' of his disciples eat bread
8:28 s' say, Elias; and others, One of
9: 1 be s' of them that stand here,
12: 5 many others; beating s', and
5 others; beating...and killing s'
14: 4 were s' that had indignation
65 And s' began to spit on him, and to
15:35 And s' of them that stood by, when
Lu 8: 5 sowed, s' fell by the way side;
6 s' fell upon a rock; and as soon as
7 And s' fell among thorns; and the
9: 7 because that it was said of s', that
8 And of s', that Elias had appeared;
19 but s' say, Elias; and others say,
27 there be s' standing here, which
11:15 But s' of them said, He casteth out
49 and s' of them they shall slay and
13: 1 s' that told him of the Galilæans,
19:39 s' of the Pharisees from among the
21: 5 And as s' spake of the temple, how
16 s' of you shall they cause to be put to
23: 8 have seen s' miracle done by him.
Joh 3:25 between s' of John's disciples and
6:64 are s' of you that believe not.
7:12 for s' said, He is a good man:

Joh 7:25 Then said s' of them of Jerusalem,
41 s' said, Shall Christ come out of
44 s' of them would have taken him;
9: 9 *S'* said, This is he: others said, He
16 said s' of the Pharisees, This man
40 s' of the Pharisees which were with
10: 1 but climbeth up s' other way, the
11:37 s' of them said, Could not this
46 s' of them went their ways to the
13:29 s' of them thought, because Judas
16:17 Then said s' of his disciples among
Ac 5:15 by might overshadow s' of them.
8: 9 out that himself was s' great one:
31 I, except s' man should guide me?
34 this? of himself, or of s' other man?
11:20 s' of them were men of Cyprus and
13:11 seeking s' to lead him by the hand.
15:36 And s' days after Paul said unto
17: 4 s' of them believed, and consorted
18 s' said, What will this babbler say?
18 s', He seemeth to be a setter forth
21 to tell, or to hear s' new thing.)
32 the resurrection...s' mocked:
18:23 after he had spent s' time there,
19:32 *S'*...cried one thing, and s' another:
21:34 And s' cried one thing, s' another,
27:27 that they drew near to s' country;
34 I pray you to take s' meat: for this is
36 good cheer, and they also took s' meat.
44 And the rest, s' on boards,
44 on boards, and s' on broken pieces
28:24 s' believed the things which
24 were spoken, and s' believed not.
Ro 1:11 impart unto you s' spiritual gift,
13 I might have s' fruit among you
3: 3 For what if s' did not believe? shall
8 and as s' affirm that we say,) Let
5: 7 good man s' would even dare to die.
11:14 flesh, and might save s' of them.
17 if s' of the branches be broken off,
15:15 more boldly unto you in s' sort,
1Co 4:18 Now s' are puffed up, as though I
6:11 And such were s' of you: but ye are
8: 7 for s' with conscience of the idol
9:22 that I might by all means save s'.
10: 7 be ye idolaters, as were s' of them;
8 fornication,...s' of them committed,
9 Christ, as s' of them also tempted,
10 ye, as s' of them also murmured,
12:28 God hath set s' in the church,
15: 6 present, but s' are fallen asleep.
12 say s' among you that there is no
34 s' have not the knowledge of God:
35 s' man will say, How are the dead
37 of wheat, or of s' other grain:
2Co 3: 1 or need we, as s' others, epistles of
10: 2 bold against s', which think of us
12 or compare ourselves with s' that
Ga 1: 7 but there be s' that trouble you,
Eph 4:11 And he gave s', apostles;
11 apostles; and s', prophets; and
11 and s', evangelists; and s', pastors
Ph'p 1:15 *S'* indeed preach Christ even of
15 and strife; and s' also of good will:
Col 3: 7 the which ye also walked s' time,
1Th 3: 5 lest by s' means the tempter have
2Th 3:11 are s' which walk among you
1Ti 1: 3 s' that they teach no other doctrine,
6 s' having swerved have turned
19 s' having put away concerning faith
4: 1 times s' shall depart from the faith,
5:15 s' are already turned aside after
24 *S'* men's sins are open beforehand,
24 and s' men they follow after.
25 also the good works of s' are manifest
6:10 which while s' coveted after, they
21 s' professing have erred concerning
2Ti 2:18 and overthrow the faith of s'.
20 and of earth; s' to honour,
20 to honour, and s' to dishonour.
Heb 3: 4 For every house is builded by s'
16 For s', when they had heard, did
4: 6 it remaineth that s' must enter
10:25 together, as the manner of s' is;
11:40 provided s' better thing for us,
13: 2 thereby s' have entertained angels
1Pe 4:12 though s' strange thing happened
2Pe 3: 9 as s' men count slackness; but
16 s' things hard to be understood,
Jude 22 s' have compassion, making

somebody
Lu 8:46 Jesus said, *S'* hath touched me:
Ac 5:36 Theudas, boasting himself to be s';

something
1Sa 20:26 *S'* hath befallen him, he is not
M'r 5:43 that s' should be given her to eat.
Lu 11:54 to catch s' out of his mouth, that
Joh 13:29 that he should give s' to the poor.
Ac 3: 5 expecting to receive s' of them.
23:15 s' more perfectly concerning him:
18 thee, who hath s' to say unto thee.
Ga 6: 3 a man think himself to be s', when

sometime See also SOME and TIME; SOMETIMES.
Col 1:21 you, that were s' alienated and
1Pe 3:20 Which s' were disobedient, when

sometimes See also SOMETIME.
Eph 2:13 ye who s' were far off are made
5: 8 For ye were s' darkness, but now
Tit 3: 3 we ourselves also were s' foolish,

somewhat
Le 4:13 they have done s' against any of the
22 done s' through ignorance against
27 while he doeth s' against any of the
13: 6 behold, if the plague be s' dark,

Le 13:19 bright spot, white, and s' reddish,
21 than the skin, but be s' dark;
24 bright spot, s' reddish, or white;
26 the other skin, but be s' dark;
28 not in the skin, but it be s' dark;
56 be s' dark after the washing of it;
1Ki 2:14 I have s' to say unto thee. And
2Ki 5:20 run after him, and take s' of him.
2Ch 10: 4 ease thou s' the grievous servitude
9 Ease s' the yoke that thy father did
10 but make thou it s' lighter for us;
Lu 7:40 Simon, I have s' to say unto thee.
Ac 23:20 enquire s' of him more perfectly.
25:26 had, I might have s' to write.
Ro 15:24 I be s' filled with your company.
2Co 5:12 that ye may have s' to answer them
10: 8 boast s' more of our authority,
Ga 2: 6 But of these who seemed to be s',
6 who seemed to be s' in conference
Heb 8: 3 that this man have s' also to offer.
Re 2: 4 Nevertheless I have s' against thee.

son See also SON'S; SONS.
Ge 4:17 after the name of his s', Enoch.
25 she bare a s', and called his name
26 to him also there was born a s';
5: 3 begat a s' in his own likeness, after
28 and two years, and begat a s':
9:24 his younger s' had done unto him.
11:31 Terah took Abram his s', and Lot
31 Lot the s' of Haran his son's s', and
31 daughter in law, his s' Abram's wife;
12: 5 and Lot his brother's s', and all
14:12 took Lot, Abram's brother's s', who
16:11 art with child, and shalt bear a s',
15 Hagar bare Abram a s': and Abram
17:16 her, and give thee a s' also of her:
19 thy wife shall bear thee a s' indeed;
23 And Abraham took Ishmael his s',
25 Ishmael his s' was thirteen years
26 circumcised, and Ishmael his s'.
18:10 lo, Sarah thy wife shall have a s'.
14 of life, and Sarah shall have a s'.
19:12 s' in law, and thy sons, and thy
37 the firstborn bare a s', and called
38 she also bare a s', and called his
21: 2 bare Abraham a s' in his old age.
3 Abraham called the name of his s'
4 Abraham circumcised his s' Isaac
5 his s' Isaac was born unto him.
7 I have born him a s' in his old age.
9 And Sarah saw the s' of Hagar the
10 out this bondwoman and her s':
10 for the s' of this bondwoman shall
10 shall not be heir with my s', even
11 Abraham's sight because of his s'.
13 s' of the bondwoman will I make a
23 with my s', nor with my son's s':
22: 2 And he said, Take now thy s',
2 thine only s' Isaac, whom thou
3 men with him, and Isaac his s',
6 and laid it upon Isaac his s'; and
7 and he said, Here am I, my s'.
8 My s', God will provide himself a
9 and bound Isaac his s', and laid
10 and took the knife to slay his s'.
12 seeing thou hast not withheld thy s',
12 withheld...thine only s' from me.
13 burnt offering in the stead of his s'.
16 thing, and hast not withheld thy s',
16 withheld...thine only s':
23: 8 for me to Ephron the s' of Zohar,
24: 3 shalt not take a wife unto my s' of
4 and take a wife unto my s' Isaac.
5 must I needs bring thy s' again
6 that thou bring not my s' thither
7 thou shalt take a wife unto my s'
8 only bring not my s' thither again.
15 was born to Bethuel, s' of Milcah,
24 daughter of Bethuel the s' of Milcah,
36 master's wife bare a s' to my master
37 shalt not take a wife to my s' of the
38 kindred, and take a wife unto my s'.
40 take a wife for my s' of my kindred,
44 appointed out for my master's s'.
47 daughter of Bethuel, Nahor's s',
48 brother's daughter unto his s'.
25: 6 sent them away from Isaac his s',
9 the field of Ephron the s' of Zohar
11 that God blessed his s' Isaac;
12 of Ishmael, Abraham's s',
19 generations of Isaac, Abraham's s':
27: 1 he called Esau his eldest s', and
1 and said unto him, My s': and he
5 when Isaac spake to Esau his s'.
6 Rebekah spake unto Jacob her s',
8 therefore, my s', obey my voice
13 Upon me be thy curse, my s': only
15 raiment of her eldest s' Esau,
15 them upon Jacob her youngest s':
17 into the hand of her s' Jacob.
18 Here am I; who art thou, my s'?
20 Isaac said unto his s', How is it
20 thou hast found it so quickly, my s'?
21 that I may feel thee, my s', whether
21 thou be my very s' Esau or not.
24 he said, Art thou my very s' Esau?
26 Come near now, and kiss me, my s'.
27 the smell of my s' is as the smell of
32 I am thy s', thy firstborn Esau.
37 shall I do now unto thee, my s'?
42 these words of Esau her elder s'
42 and called Jacob her younger s',
43 therefore, my s', obey my voice;
28: 5 Laban, s' of Bethuel the Syrian,
9 daughter of Ishmael Abraham's s',
29: 5 Know ye Laban the s' of Nahor?

Ge 29:12 and that he was Rebekah's s':
13 the tidings of Jacob his sister's s',
32 And Leah conceived, and bare a s',
33 she conceived again, and bare a s';
33 hath therefore given me this s' also:
34 she conceived again, and bare a s';
35 she conceived again, and bare a s':
30: 5 conceived, and bare Jacob a s'.
6 my voice, and hath given me a s':
7 again, and bare Jacob a second s'.
10 Zilpah Leah's maid bare Jacob a s'.
12 Leah's maid bare Jacob a second s'.
17 and bare Jacob the fifth s'.
19 again, and bare Jacob the sixth s'.
23 And she conceived, and bare a s';
24 Lord shall add to me another s'.
34: 2 And when Shechem the s' of Hamor
8 soul of my s' Shechem longeth for
18 Hamor, and Shechem Hamor's s'.
20 Hamor and Shechem his s' came
24 Hamor and unto Shechem his s'
26 slew Hamor and Shechem his s'
35:17 not; thou shalt have this s' also.
36:10 Eliphaz the s' of Adah the wife of
10 Reuel the s' of Bashemath the wife
12 concubine to Eliphaz Esau's s';
15 of Eliphaz the firstborn s' of Esau;
17 are the sons of Reuel Esau's s';
32 Bela the s' of Beor reigned in Edom:
33 Jobab the s' of Zerah of Bozrah
35 Hadad the s' of Bedad, who smote
38 Baal-hanan the s' of Achbor reigned
39 Baal-hanan the s' of Achbor died,
37: 3 because he was the s' of his old age:
34 and mourned for his s' many days.
35 go down into the grave unto my s'
38: 3 And she conceived, and bare a s';
4 she conceived again, and bare a s';
5 yet again conceived, and bare a s';
11 house, till Shelah my s' be grown:
26 that I gave her not to Shelah my s'.
42:38 My s' shall not go down with you;
43:29 brother Benjamin, his mother's s',
29 God be gracious unto thee, my s'.
45: 9 Thus saith thy s' Joseph, God hath
28 enough; Joseph my s' is yet alive:
46:10 and Shaul the s' of a Canaanitish
47:29 die: and he called his s' Joseph, and
48: 2 Behold, thy s' Joseph cometh unto
19 said, I know it, my s', I know it:
49: 9 the prey, my s', thou art gone up:
50:23 also of Machir the s' of Manasseh
Ex 1:16 if it be a s', then ye shall kill him:
22 Every s' that is born ye shall cast
2: 2 woman conceived, and bare a s':
10 daughter, and he became her s'.
22 she bare him a s', and he called
4:22 Thus saith the Lord, Israel is my s',
23 Let my s' go, that he may serve me:
23 behold, I will slay thy s', even thy
25 and cut off the foreskin of her s',
6:15 and Shaul the s' of a Canaanitish
25 Eleazar Aaron's s' took him one of
10: 2 ears of thy s', and of thy son's s',
13: 8 thou shalt shew thy s' in that day,
14 be when thy s' asketh thee in time
20:10 not do any work, thou, nor thy s',
21: 9 if he have betrothed her unto his s',
31 Whether he have gored a s', or have
23:12 and the s' of thy handmaid, and the
29:30 that s' that is priest in his stead
31: 2 Bezaleel the s' of Uri, the s' of Hur,
6 Aholiab, the s' of Ahisamach, of the
32:29 every man upon his s', and upon
33:11 Joshua, the s' of Nun, a young man,
35:30 Bezaleel the s' of Uri, the s' of Hur,
34 Aholiab, the s' of Ahisamach, of the
38:21 of Ithamar, s' to Aaron the priest.
22 Bezaleel the s' of Uri, the s' of Hur,
23 him was Aholiab, s' of Ahisamach,
Le 12: 6 her purifying are fulfilled, for a s',
21: 2 and for his s', and for his daughter,
24:10 the s' of an Israelitish woman,
10 this s' of the Israelitish woman
11 Israelitish woman's s' blasphemed
25:49 Either his uncle, or his uncle's s',
Nu 1: 5 Reuben; Elizur the s' of Shedeur.
6 Shelumiel the s' of Zurishaddai.
7 Nahshon the s' of Amminadab.
8 Issachar; Nethaneel the s' of Zuar.
9 Of Zebulun; Eliab the s' of Helon.
10 Elishama the s' of Ammihud:
10 Gamaliel the s' of Pedahzur.
11 Benjamin; Abidan the s' of Gideoni.
12 Ahiezer the s' of Ammishaddai.
13 Of Asher; Pagiel the s' of Ocran.
14 Of Gad; Eliasaph the s' of Deuel.
15 Of Naphtali; Ahira the s' of Enan.
20 children of Reuben, Israel's eldest s',
2: 3 Nahshon the s' of Amminadab
5 Nethaneel the s' of Zuar shall be
7 and Eliab the s' of Helon shall be
10 shall be Elizur the s' of Shedeur.
12 be Shelumiel the s' of Zurishaddai.
14 shall be Eliasaph the s' of Reuel.
18 be Elishama the s' of Ammihud.
20 be Gamaliel the s' of Pedahzur.
22 shall be Abidan the s' of Gideoni.
25 be Ahiezer the s' of Ammishaddai.
27 shall be Pagiel the s' of Ocran.
29 shall be Ahira the s' of Enan.
3:24 shall be Eliasaph the s' of Lael.
30 shall be Elizaphan the s' of Uzziel.
32 Eleazar the s' of Aaron the priest
35 was Zuriel the s' of Abihail:
4:16 Eleazar the s' of Aaron the priest

Nu 4:28, 33 Ithamar...s' of Aaron the priest.
7: 8 Ithamar the s' of Aaron the priest.
12 was Nahshon the s' of Amminadab,
17 of Nahshon the s' of Amminadab.
18 Nethaneel the s' of Zuar, prince of
23 offering of Nethaneel the s' of Zuar.
24 Eliab the s' of Helon, prince of the
29 the offering of Eliab the s' of Helon.
30 Elizur the s' of Shedeur, prince of
35 offering of Elizur the s' of Shedeur.
36 Shelumiel the s' of Zurishaddai,
41 of Shelumiel the s' of Zurishaddai.
42 Eliasaph the s' of Deuel, prince of
47 offering of Eliasaph the s' of Deuel.
48 day Elishama the s' of Ammihud,
53 of Elishama the s' of Ammihud.
54 offered Gamaliel the s' of Pedahzur,
59 of Gamaliel the s' of Pedahzur.
60 Abidan the s' of Gideoni, prince of
65 offering of Abidan the s' of Gideoni.
66 day Ahiezer the s' of Ammishaddai,
71 of Ahiezer the s' of Ammishaddai.
72 Pagiel the s' of Ocran, prince of the
77 offering of Pagiel the s' of Ocran.
78 Ahira the s' of Enan, prince of
83 the offering of Ahira the s' of Enan.
10:14 was Nahshon the s' of Amminadab.
15 was Nethaneel the s' of Zuar.
16 Zebulun was Eliab the s' of Helon.
18 host was Elizur the s' of Shedeur.
19 Shelumiel the s' of Zurishaddai.
20 of Gad was Eliasaph the s' of Deuel.
22 was Elishama the s' of Ammihud.
23 was Gamaliel the s' of Pedahzur.
24 was Abidan the s' of Gideoni.
25 was Ahiezer the s' of Ammishaddai.
26 of Asher was Pagiel the s' of Ocran.
27 Naphtali was Ahira the s' of Enan.
29 said unto Hobab, the s' of Raguel
11:28 Joshua the s' of Nun, the servant of
13: 4 Reuben, Shammua the s' of Zaccur.
5 of Simeon, Shaphat the s' of Hori.
6 Judah, Caleb the s' of Jephunneh.
7 of Issachar, Igal the s' of Joseph.
8 of Ephraim, Oshea the s' of Nun.
9 of Benjamin, Palti the s' of Raphu.
10 of Zebulun, Gaddiel the s' of Sodi.
11 of Manasseh, Gaddi the s' of Susi.
12 of Dan, Ammiel the s' of Gemalli.
13 of Asher, Sethur the s' of Michael.
14 of Naphtali, Nahbi the s' of Vophsi.
15 tribe of Gad, Geuel the s' of Machi.
16 called Oshea...s' of Nun Jehoshua.
14: 6 And Joshua the s' of Nun, and
6 and Caleb the s' of Jephunneh,
30 save Caleb the s' of Jephunneh,
30 and Joshua the s' of Nun.
38 But Joshua the s' of Nun, and Caleb
38 and Caleb the s' of Jephunneh,
16: 1 Now Korah, the s' of Izhar,
1 the s' of Kohath, the s' of Levi, and
1 of Eliab, and On, the s' of Peleth,
37 Eleazar the s' of Aaron the priest,
20:25 Take Aaron and Eleazar his s', and
26 and put them upon Eleazar his s':
28 and put them upon Eleazar his s';
22: 2 Balak the s' of Zippor saw all that
4 Balak the s' of Zippor was king of
5 Balaam the s' of Beor to Pethor,
10 Balak...s' of Zippor, king of Moab,
16 Thus saith Balak the s' of Zippor,
23:18 hearken unto me, thou s' of Zippor:
19 s' of man, that he should repent:
24: 3, 15 Balaam the s' of Beor hath said,
25: 7 when Phinehas, the s' of Eleazar,
7 the s' of Aaron the priest, saw it, he
11 Phinehas, the s' of Eleazar, the
11 the s' of Aaron the priest, hath
14 Zimri, the s' of Salu, a prince of a
26: 1 Eleazar the s' of Aaron the priest,
5 Reuben, the eldest s' of Israel: the
33 Zelophehad the s' of Hepher had
65 save Caleb the s' of Jephunneh,
65 and Joshua the s' of Nun.
27: 1 of Zelophehad, the s' of Hepher,
1 the s' of Gilead, the s' of Machir,
1 the s' of Manasseh, of the families
1 of Manasseh the s' of Joseph:
4 his family, because he hath no s'?
8 If a man die, and have no s', then
18 Take thee Joshua the s' of Nun, a
31: 6 Phinehas...s' of Eleazar the priest,
8 Balaam also the s' of Beor they slew
32:12 Save Caleb the s' of Jephunneh the
12 and Joshua the s' of Nun: for they
28 Joshua the s' of Nun, and the chief
33 tribe of Manasseh the s' of Joseph,
39 children of Machir...s' of Manasseh
40 unto Machir the s' of Manasseh;
41 Jair the s' of Manasseh went and
34:17 the priest, and Joshua the s' of Nun.
19 Judah, Caleb the s' of Jephunneh.
20 Shemuel the s' of Ammihud.
21 Benjamin, Elidad the s' of Chislon.
22 of Dan, Bukki the s' of Jogli.
23 Manasseh, Hanniel the s' of Ephod.
24 Kemuel the s' of Shiphtan.
25 Elizaphan the s' of Parnach.
26 of Issachar, Paltiel the s' of Azzan.
27 of Asher, Ahihud the s' of Shelomi.
28 Pedahel the s' of Ammihud.
36: 1 the s' of Machir, the s' of Manasseh,
12 sons of Manasseh the s' of Joseph,
De 1:31 bare thee, as a man doth bear his s',
36 Save Caleb the s' of Jephunneh; he
38 But Joshua the s' of Nun, which

De 3:14 Jair the s' of Manasseh took all the
5:14 not do any work, thou, nor thy s',
6: 2 thou, and thy s', and thy son's s',
20 when thy s' asketh thee in time to
21 Then thou shalt say unto thy s', We
7: 3 thou shalt not give unto his s',
3 nor his daughter...unto thy s'.
4 turn away thy s' from following me,
8: 5 as a man chasteneth his s', so the
10: 6 Eleazar his s' ministered in the
11: 6 the sons of Eliab, the s' of Reuben:
12:18 thou, and thy s', and thy daughter,
13: 6 the s' of thy mother, or thy s', or thy
16:11, 14 and thy s', and thy daughter,
18:10 maketh his s' or...daughter to pass
21:15 if the firstborn s' be hers that was
16 may not make the s' of the beloved
16 firstborn before the s' of the hated,
17 acknowledge the s' of the hated for
18 have a stubborn and rebellious s',
20 our s' is stubborn and rebellious,
23: 4 Balaam the s' of Beor of Pethor of
28:56 and toward her s', and toward her
31:23 gave Joshua the s' of Nun a charge,
32:44 he, and Hoshea the s' of Nun.
34: 9 Joshua the s' of Nun was full of
Jos 1: 1 spake unto Joshua the s' of Nun,
2: 1 And Joshua the s' of Nun sent out of
23 and came to Joshua the s' of Nun,
6: 6 And Joshua the s' of Nun called the
26 in his youngest s' shall he set up the
7: 1 for Achan, the s' of Carmi,
1 the s' of Zabdi, the s' of Zerah, of
18 man; and Achan, the s' of Carmi,
18 the s' of Zabdi, the s' of Zerah, of the
19 And Joshua said unto Achan, My s',
24 took Achan the s' of Zerah, and the
13:22 Balaam also the s' of Beor, the
31 of Machir the s' of Manasseh,
14: 1 the priest, and Joshua the s' of Nun,
6, 13, 14 Caleb the s' of Jephunneh
15: 6 the stone of Bohan the s' of Reuben:
8 by the valley of the s' of Hinnom
13 unto Caleb the s' of Jephunneh he
17 Othniel the s' of Kenaz, the brother
17: 2 of Manasseh the s' of Joseph by
3 But Zelophehad, the s' of Hepher,
3 the s' of Gilead, the s' of Machir,
3 the s' of Manasseh, had no sons, but
4 and before Joshua the s' of Nun,
18:16 the valley of the s' of Hinnom,
17 the stone of Bohan the s' of Reuben,
19:49 Joshua the s' of Nun among them:
51 the priest, and Joshua the s' of Nun,
21: 1 and unto Joshua the s' of Nun, and
12 they to Caleb the s' of Jephunneh
22:13 Phinehas...s' of Eleazar the priest,
20 not Achan the s' of Zerah commit
31 Phinehas the s' of Eleazar the priest
32 Phinehas...s' of Eleazar the priest,
24: 9 Then Balak the s' of Zippor, king
9 and called Balaam the s' of Beor
29 Joshua the s' of Nun, the servant
33 And Eleazar the s' of Aaron died;
33 that pertained to Phinehas his s',
J'g 1:13 Othniel the s' of Kenaz, Caleb's
2: 8 Joshua the s' of Nun, the servant
3: 9 Othniel the s' of Kenaz, Caleb's
11 and Othniel the s' of Kenaz died.
15 Ehud the s' of Gera, a Benjamite,
31 him was Shamgar the s' of Anath,
4: 6 called Barak the s' of Abinoam out
12 Barak the s' of Abinoam was gone
5: 1 Barak the s' of Abinoam on that
6 days of Shamgar the s' of Anath,
12 captive, thou s' of Abinoam.
6:11 his s' Gideon threshed wheat by
29 Gideon the s' of Joash hath done
30 Joash, Bring out thy s', that he
7:14 sword of Gideon the s' of Joash,
8:13 Gideon the s' of Joash returned
22 and thy s', and thy son's s' also:
23 neither shall my s' rule over you:
29 Jerubbaal the s' of Joash went and
31 she also bare him a s', whose name
32 Gideon the s' of Joash died in a
9: 1 Abimelech the s' of Jerubbaal went
5 Jotham...youngest s' of Jerubbaal
18 Abimelech,...s' of his maidservant,
26 Gaal the s' of Ebed came with his
28 Gaal the s' of Ebed said, Who is
28 is not he the s' of Jerubbaal? and
30 the words of Gaal the s' of Ebed,
31 Behold, Gaal the s' of Ebed and his
35 And Gaal the s' of Ebed went out,
57 curse of Jotham...s' of Jerubbaal.
10: 1 Tola the s' of Puah, the s' of Dodo,
11: 1 and he was the s' of an harlot: and
2 thou art the s' of a strange woman.
25 better than Balak the s' of Zippor,
34 her he had neither s' nor daughter.
12:13 after him Abdon the s' of Hillel, a
15 And Abdon the s' of Hillel, the
13: 3 thou shalt conceive, and bear a s'.
5, 7 shalt conceive, and bear a s';
24 the woman bare a s', and called
15: 6 Samson,...s' in law of the Timnite,
17: 2 be thou of the Lord, my s'.
3 the Lord from my hand for my s',
18:30 Jonathan, the s' of Gershom,
30 the s' of Manasseh, he and his
19: 5 father said unto his s' in law,
20:28 And Phinehas, the s' of Eleazar,
28 the s' of Aaron, stood before it
Ru 4:13 her conception, and she bare a s'.
17 There is a s' born to Naomi; and

1Sa 1: 1 was Elkanah, the s' of Jeroham,
1 the s' of Elihu, the s' of Tohu,
1 the s' of Zuph, an Ephrathite:
20 that she bare a s', and called his
23 gave her s' suck until she weaned
3: 6 I called not, my s'; lie down again.
16 Samuel, and said, Samuel, my s'.
4: 16 said, What is there done, my s'?
20 Fear not; for thou hast born a s'.
7: 1 Eleazar his s' to keep the ark of
9: 1 Kish, the s' of Abiel, the s' of Zeror,
1 s' of Bechorath, the s' of Aphiah,
2 he had a s', whose name was Saul,
3 Kish said to Saul his s', Take now
10: 2 saying, What shall I do for my s'?
11 that is come unto the s' of Kish?
21 and Saul the s' of Kish was taken:
13: 16 Saul, and Jonathan his s', and the
22 Saul and with Jonathan his s' was
14: 1 that Jonathan the s' of Saul said
3 Ahiah, the s' of Ahitub, I-chabod's
3 brother, the s' of Phinehas, the
3 the s' of Eli, the Lord's priest
39 though it be in Jonathan my s', he
40 I and Jonathan my s' will be on
42 between me and Jonathan my s'.
50 Abner, the s' of Ner, Saul's uncle.
51 father of Abner was the s' of Abiel.
16: 18 a s' of Jesse the Beth-lehemite,
19 Send me David thy s', which is
20 them by David his s' unto Saul.
17: 12 David was the s' of that Ephrathite
17 Jesse said unto David his s', Take
55 Abner, whose s' is this youth? And
56 thou whose s' the stripling is.
58 Whose s' art thou, thou young man?
58 I am the s' of thy servant Jesse the
18: 18 I should be s' in law to the king?
21 shalt this day be my s' in law in
22 therefore be the king's s' in law.
23 light thing to be a king's s' in law,
26 well to be the king's s' in law:
27 he might be the king's s' in law.
19: 1 Saul spake to Jonathan his s',
2 Jonathan Saul's s' delighted much
20: 27 and Saul said unto Jonathan his s'
27 cometh not the s' of Jesse to meat,
30 Thou s' of the perverse rebellious
30 thou hast chosen the s' of Jesse
31 For as long as the s' of Jesse liveth
22: 7 the s' of Jesse give every one of you
8 sheweth me that my s' hath made
8 a league with the s' of Jesse,
8 my s' hath stirred up my servant
9 I saw the s' of Jesse coming to Nob
9 Nob, to Ahimelech the s' of Ahitub.
11 call Ahimelech...the s' of Ahitub,
12 said, Hear now, thou s' of Ahitub.
13 me, thou and the s' of Jesse,
14 as David,...the king's s' in law,
20 of Ahimelech the s' of Ahitub,
23: 6 Abiathar the s' of Ahimelech fled
16 Jonathan Saul's s' arose, and went
24: 16 said, Is this thy voice, my s' David?
25: 8 thy servants, and to thy s' David.
10 David? and who is the s' of Jesse?
17 for he is such a s' of Belial, that a
44 to Phalti the s' of Laish, which was
26: 5 Abner the s' of Ner, the captain of
6 and to Abishai the s' of Zeruiah,
14 and to Abner the s' of Ner, saying,
17 said, Is this thy voice, my s' David?
21 I have sinned: return, my s' David:
25 Blessed be thou, my s' David:
27: 2 unto Achish, the s' of Maoch, king
30: 7 Abiathar the priest, Ahimelech's s',
2Sa 1: 4 Saul and Jonathan his s' are dead
5 Saul and Jonathan his s' be dead?
12 for Saul, and for Jonathan his s',
13 I am the s' of a stranger, an
17 over Saul and over Jonathan his s'
2: 8 But Abner the s' of Ner, captain of
8 took Ish-bosheth, the s' of Saul,
10 Ish-bosheth Saul's s' was forty
12 Abner...s' of Ner, and the servants
12 of Ish-bosheth the s' of Saul, went
13 And Joab the s' of Zeruiah, and the
15 to Ish-bosheth the s' of Saul, and
3: 3 Absalom the s' of Maacah the
4 fourth, Adonijah the s' of Haggith;
4 fifth, Shephatiah the s' of Abital;
14 to Ish-bosheth Saul's s', saying,
15 even from Phaltiel the s' of Laish.
23 Abner the s' of Ner came to the
25 Thou knowest Abner the s' of Ner,
28 the blood of Abner the s' of Ner:
37 king to slay Abner the s' of Ner.
4: 1 Saul's s' heard that Abner was
2 Saul's s' had two men that were
4 Saul's s', had a s' that was lame
8 head of Ish-bosheth the s' of Saul
7: 14 his father, and he shall be my s'.
8: 3 also Hadadezer, the s' of Rehob,
10 Toi sent Joram his s' unto king
12 spoil of Hadadezer, s' of Rehob,
16 Joab the s' of Zeruiah was over the
16 Jehoshaphat the s' of Ahilud was
17 And Zadok the s' of Ahitub, and
17 and Ahimelech, the s' of Abiathar,
18 Benaiah the s' of Jehoiada was
9: 3 Jonathan hath yet a s', which is
4, 5 in Machir, the s' of Ammiel,
6 Mephibosheth, the s' of Jonathan,
6 the s' of Saul, was come unto David,
9 I have given unto thy master's s'
10 master's s' may have food to eat:

2Sa 9: 10 thy master's s' shall eat bread
12 And Mephibosheth had a young s'.
10: 1 Hanun his s' reigned in his stead.
2 unto Hanun the s' of Nahash, as
11: 21 Abimelech the s' of Jerubbesheth?
27 became his wife, and bare him a s'.
12: 24 and she bare a s', and he called his
13: 1 Absalom the s' of David had a fair
1 Amnon the s' of David loved her.
3 Jonadab, the s' of Shimeah David's
4 art thou, being the king's s', lean
25 Nay, my s', let us not all now go,
32 Jonadab, the s' of Shimeah David's
37 went to Talmai, the s' of Ammihud,
37 David mourned for his s' every day.
14: 1 Joab the s' of Zeruiah perceived
11 any more, lest they destroy my s'.
11 there shall not one hair of thy s' fall
16 destroy me and my s' together
15: 27 two sons with you, Ahimaaz thy s',
27 and Jonathan the s' of [illegible]thar.
36 their two sons, Ahimaa[illegible]adok's s'.
36 and Jonathan Abiathar's s';
16: 3 said, And where is thy master's s'?
5 name was Shimei, the s' of Gera:
8 into the hand of Absalom thy s':
9 Then said Abishai the s' of Zeruiah
11 Behold, my s', which came forth of
19 I not serve in the presence of his s'?
17: 25 Amasa was a man's s', whose name
27 Shobi the s' of Nahash of Rabbah,
27 and Machir the s' of Ammiel of
18: 2 hand of Abishai the s' of Zeruiah,
12 mine hand against the king's s':
18 said, I have no s' to keep my name
19 Then said Ahimaaz the s' of Zadok,
20 because the king's s' is dead.
22 Then said Ahimaaz the s' of Zadok
22 Wherefore wilt thou run, my s',
27 running of Ahimaaz the s' of Zadok
33 said, O my s' Absalom, my s', my s'
33 for thee, O Absalom, my s', my s'!
19: 2 how the king was grieved for his s'.
4 with a loud voice, O my s' Absalom,
4 Absalom, O Absalom, my s', my s'!
16 Shimei the s' of Gera, a Benjamite,
18 Shimei the s' of Gera fell down
21 Abishai the s' of Zeruiah answered
24 Mephibosheth the s' of Saul came
20: 1 name was Sheba, the s' of Bichri,
1 we inheritance in the s' of Jesse:
2 and followed Sheba the s' of Bichri:
6 Sheba the s' of Bichri do us more
7 pursue after Sheba the s' of Bichri.
10 pursued after Sheba the s' of Bichri.
13 pursue after Sheba the s' of Bichri.
21 Sheba the s' of Bichri by name,
22 the head of Sheba the s' of Bichri,
23 Benaiah the s' of Jehoiada was over
24 Jehoshaphat the s' of Ahilud was
21: 7 Mephibosheth, the s' of Jonathan
7 of Jonathan the s' of Saul,
7 David and Jonathan the s' of Saul.
8 up for Adriel the s' of Barzillai the
12 and the bones of Jonathan his s'
13 and the bones of Jonathan his s';
14 bones of Saul and Jonathan his s'
17 Abishai the s' of Zeruiah succoured
19 Elhanan the s' of Jaare-oregim,
21 Jonathan the s' of Shimeah the
23: 1 David the s' of Jesse said, and the
9 Eleazar the s' of Dodo the Ahohite,
11 was Shammah the s' of Agee the
18 And Abishai,...the s' of Zeruiah,
20 And Benaiah the s' of Jehoiada, the
20 the s' of a valiant man, of Kabzeel,
22 did Benaiah the s' of Jehoiada,
24 Elhanan the s' of Dodo of
26 Ira the s' of Ikkesh the Tekoite,
29 Heleb the s' of Baanah, a
29 Ittai the s' of Ribai out of Gibeah
33 Ahiam the s' of Sharar the Hararite
34 Eliphelet the s' of Ahasbai,
34 the s' of the Maachathite,
34 Eliam the s' of Ahithophel the
36 Igal the s' of Nathan of Zobah,
37 to Joab the s' of Zeruiah, and
1Ki 1: 5 Adonijah the s' of Haggith exalted
7 with Joab the s' of Zeruiah, and
8 and Benaiah the s' of Jehoiada,
11 Adonijah the s' of Haggith doth
12 life, and the life of thy s' Solomon.
13, 17 Solomon thy s' shall reign after
21 I and my s' Solomon...be counted
26 and Benaiah the s' of Jehoiada,
30 Solomon thy s' shall reign after me,
32 and Benaiah the s' of Jehoiada.
33 cause Solomon my s' to ride upon
36 Benaiah the s' of Jehoiada answered
38 and Benaiah the s' of Jehoiada,
42 Jonathan...s' of Abiathar the priest
44 and Benaiah the s' of Jehoiada,
2: 1 he charged Solomon his s', saying,
5 what Joab the s' of Zeruiah did to
5 Israel, unto Abner the s' of Ner,
5 and unto Amasa the s' of Jether,
8 with thee Shimei the s' of Gera,
13 Adonijah the s' of Haggith came to
22 and for Joab the s' of Zeruiah.
25 hand of Benaiah the s' of Jehoiada;
29 sent Benaiah the s' of Jehoiada,
32 Abner the s' of Ner, captain of the
32 Amasa the s' of Jether, captain of
34 Benaiah the s' of Jehoiada went up,
35 king put Benaiah the s' of Jehoiada
39 Achish s' of Maachah king of Gath.

1Ki 2: 46 Benaiah the s' of Jehoiada;
3: 6 given him a s' to sit on his throne,
20 and took my s' from beside me,
21 it was not my s', which I did bear.
22 living is my s',...the dead is thy s'.
22 dead is thy s',...the living is my s'.
23 my s'...liveth, and thy s' is the dead:
23 thy s' is dead, and my s' is...living.
26 for her bowels yearned upon her s',
4: 2 Azariah the s' of Zadok the priest,
3 Jehoshaphat the s' of Ahilud, the
4 Benaiah the s' of Jehoiada was over
5 Azariah the s' of Nathan was over
5 Zabud...s' of Nathan was principal
6 Adoniram the s' of Abda was over
8 The s' of Hur, in mount Ephraim:
9 The s' of Dekar, in Makaz, and in
10 The s' of Hesed, in Aruboth; to
11 The s' of Abinadab, in all the
12 Baana the s' of Ahilud; to him
13 The s' of Geber, in Ramoth-gilead;
13 towns of Jair the s' of Manasseh,
14 Ahinadab the s' of Iddo had
16 Baanah the s' of Hushai was in
17 Jehoshaphat the s' of Paruah, in
18 Shimei the s' of Elah, in Benjamin:
19 Geber the s' of Uri was in the
5: 5 Thy s', whom I will set upon thy
7 hath given unto David a wise s'
7: 14 He was a widow's s' of the tribe of
8: 19 thy s' that shall come forth out of
11: 12 rend it out of the hand of thy s'.
13 but will give one tribe to thy s' for
20 bare him Genubath his s', whom
23 adversary, Rezon the s' of Eliadah,
26 And Jeroboam the s' of Nebat, an
36 And unto his s' will I give one tribe,
43 and Rehoboam his s' reigned in his
12: 2 when Jeroboam the s' of Nebat,
15 unto Jeroboam the s' of Nebat.
16 we inheritance in the s' of Jesse:
21 to Rehoboam the s' of Solomon.
23 unto Rehoboam, the s' of Solomon,
14: 1 Abijah the s' of Jeroboam fell sick.
5 to ask a thing of thee for her s';
20 Nadab his s' reigned in his stead.
21 Rehoboam...s' of Solomon reigned
31 Abijam his s' reigned in his stead.
15: 1 of king Jeroboam the s' of Nebat
4 to set up his s' after him, and to
8 and Asa his s' reigned in his stead.
18 Ben-hadad, the s' of Tabrimon,
18 the s' of Hezion, king of Syria,
24 Jehoshaphat his s' reigned in his
25 Nadab the s' of Jeroboam began to
27 And Baasha the s' of Ahijah, of the
33 began Baasha the s' of Ahijah to
16: 1 came to Jehu the s' of Hanani
3 house of Jeroboam the s' of Nebat.
6 Elah his s' reigned in his stead.
7 the prophet Jehu the s' of Hanani
8 began Elah the s' of Baasha to reign
13 Baasha, and the sins of Elah his s',
21 followed Tibni the s' of Ginath,
22 that followed Tibni the s' of Ginath:
26 way of Jeroboam the s' of Nebat,
28 Ahab his s' reigned in his stead.
29 began Ahab the s' of Omri to reign
29 Ahab the s' of Omri reigned over
30 Ahab the s' of Omri did evil in the
31 sins of Jeroboam the s' of Nebat,
34 thereof in his youngest s' Segub,
34 he spake by Joshua the s' of Nun.
17: 12 go in and dress it for me and my s',
13 after make for thee and for thy s'.
17 the s' of the woman, the mistress of
18 to remembrance, and to slay my s'?
19 he said unto her, Give me thy s'.
20 whom I sojourn, by slaying her s'?
23 and Elijah said, See, thy s' liveth.
19: 16 Jehu the s' of Nimshi shalt thou
16 and Elisha the s' of Shaphat of
19 found Elisha the s' of Shaphat, who
21: 22 house of Jeroboam the s' of Nebat,
22 house of Baasha the s' of Ahijah,
22: 8 one man, Micaiah the s' of Imlah,
9 hither Micaiah the s' of Imlah.
11 And Zedekiah the s' of Chenaanah
24 Zedekiah the s' of Chenaanah went
26 the city, and to Joash the king's s';
40 Ahaziah his s' reigned in his stead.
41 Jehoshaphat the s' of Asa began to
49 said Ahaziah the s' of Ahab unto
50 Jehoram his s' reigned in his stead.
51 Ahaziah...s' of Ahab began to reign
52 way of Jeroboam the s' of Nebat,
2Ki 1: 17 of Jehoram the s' of Jehoshaphat
17 of Judah; because he had no s'.
3: 1 Now Jehoram the s' of Ahab began
3 sins of Jeroboam the s' of Nebat,
11 Here is Elisha the s' of Shaphat,
27 took his eldest s' that should have
4: 6 that she said unto her s', Bring me
16 time of life, thou shalt embrace a s'
17 and bare a s' at that season that
28 said, Did I desire a s' of my lord?
36 unto him, he said, Take up thy s'.
37 and took up her s', and went out.
6: 28 Give thy s', that we may eat him
28 and we will eat my s' to morrow.
29 So we boiled my s', and did eat him:
29 Give thy s', that we may eat him:
29 eat him: and she hath hid her s'.
31 head of Elisha the s' of Shaphat
32 See ye how this s' of a murderer
8: 1, 5 whose s' he had restored to life,

2Ki 8: 5 and this is her s', whom Elisha
9 Thy s' Ben-hadad king of Syria
16 Joram the s' of Ahab king of Israel,
16 Jehoram the s' of Jehoshaphat king
24 Ahaziah his s' reigned in his stead.
25 Joram the s' of Ahab king of Israel
25 Ahaziah the s' of Jehoram king of
27 the s' in law of the house of Ahab.
28 he went with Joram the s' of Ahab
29 Ahaziah the s' of Jehoram king of
29 down to see Joram the s' of Ahab
9: 2 look out there Jehu the s' of
2 Jehoshaphat the s' of Nimshi,
9 house of Jeroboam the s' of Nebat,
9 house of Baasha the s' of Ahijah:
14 So Jehu the s' of Jehoshaphat the
14 the s' of Nimshi conspired
20 driving of Jehu the s' of Nimshi;
29 of Joram the s' of Ahab began
10: 15 on Jehonadab the s' of Rechab
23 and Jehonadab the s' of Rechab,
29 sins of Jeroboam the s' of Nebat,
35 And Jehoahaz his s' reigned in his
11: 1 Athaliah...saw that her s' was dead,
2 took Joash the s' of Ahaziah, and
4 and shewed them the king's s'.
12 And he brought forth the king's s',
12: 21 For Jozachar the s' of Shimeath,
21 and Jehozabad the s' of Shomer,
21 Amaziah his s' reigned in his stead.
13: 1 of Joash the s' of Ahaziah king of
1 Jehoahaz the s' of Jehu began to
2 sins of Jeroboam the s' of Nebat,
3 hand of Ben-hadad the s' of Hazael,
9 Joash his s' reigned in his stead.
10 Jehoash the s' of Jehoahaz to reign
11 sins of Jeroboam the s' of Nebat,
24 and Ben-hadad his s' reigned in his
25 Jehoash the s' of Jehoahaz took
25 hand of Ben-hadad the s' of Hazael
14: 1 year of Joash s' of Jehoahaz king
1 Amaziah the s' of Joash king of
8 to Jehoash, the s' of Jehoahaz
8 s' of Jehu, king of Israel, saying,
9 Give thy daughter to my s' to wife:
13 the s' of Jehoash the s' of Ahaziah,
16 Jeroboam his s' reigned in his stead.
17 Amaziah the s' of Joash king of
17 the death of Jehoash s' of Jehoahaz
23 Amaziah the s' of Joash king of
23 Jeroboam the s' of Joash king of
24 sins of Jeroboam the s' of Nebat,
25 servant Jonah, the s' of Amittai,
27 hand of Jeroboam the s' of Joash.
29 Zachariah his s' reigned in his
15: 1 began Azariah s' of Amaziah king
5 Jotham the king's s' was over the
7 Jotham his s' reigned in his stead.
8 did Zachariah the s' of Jeroboam
9 sins of Jeroboam the s' of Nebat,
10 Shallum the s' of Jabesh conspired
13 Shallum the s' of Jabesh began to
14 Menahem the s' of Gadi went up
14 smote Shallum the s' of Jabesh
17 Menahem the s' of Gadi to reign
18 sins of Jeroboam the s' of Nebat,
22 Pekahiah his s' reigned in his
23 Pekahiah the s' of Menahem began
24 sins of Jeroboam the s' of Nebat,
25 But Pekah the s' of Remaliah, a
27 Pekah the s' of Remaliah began to
28 sins of Jeroboam the s' of Nebat,
30 Hoshea the s' of Elah made a
30 against Pekah the s' of Remaliah,
30 year of Jotham the s' of Uzziah.
32 Pekah the s' of Remaliah king of
32 Jotham the s' of Uzziah king of
37 and Pekah the s' of Remaliah.
38 and Ahaz his s' reigned in his stead.
16: 1 year of Pekah the s' of Remaliah
1 Ahaz the s' of Jotham king of Judah
3 made his s' to pass through the fire,
5 Pekah s' of Remaliah king of Israel
7 I am thy servant and thy s': come
20 Hezekiah his s' reigned in his stead.
17: 1 began Hoshea the s' of Elah to reign
21 Jeroboam the s' of Nebat king:
18: 1 of Hoshea s' of Elah king of Israel,
1 that Hezekiah the s' of Ahaz king
9 of Hoshea s' of Elah king of Israel,
18 to them Eliakim the s' of Hilkiah,
18 Joah the s' of Asaph the recorder.
26 Then said Eliakim the s' of Hilkiah,
37 came Eliakim the s' of Hilkiah,
37 Joah the s' of Asaph the recorder,
19: 2 to Isaiah the prophet the s' of Amoz.
20 Isaiah the s' of Amoz sent to
37 Esarhaddon his s' reigned in his
20: 1 prophet Isaiah the s' of Amoz came
12 Berodach-baladan,...s' of Baladan,
21 Manasseh his s' reigned in his stead.
21: 6 made his s' pass through the fire,
7 said to David, and to Solomon his s',
18 Amon his s' reigned in his stead.
24 made Josiah his s' king in his stead.
26 Josiah his s' reigned in his stead.
22: 3 sent Shaphan the s' of Azaliah,
3 the s' of Meshullam, the scribe, to
12 and Ahikam the s' of Shaphan,
12 and Achbor the s' of Michaiah, and
14 the wife of Shallum the s' of Tikvah,
14 the s' of Harhas, keeper of the
23: 10 make his s' or his daughter to pass
15 which Jeroboam the s' of Nebat,
30 took Jehoahaz the s' of Josiah,
34 made Eliakim the s' of Josiah king

2Ki 24: 6 Jehoiachin his s' reigned in his
25: 22 made Gedaliah the s' of Ahikam,
22 the s' of Shaphan, ruler.
23 even Ishmael the s' of Nethaniah,
23 and Johanan the s' of Careah, and
23 Seraiah the s' of Tanhumeth the
23 Jaazaniah the s' of a Maachathite,
25 that Ishmael the s' of Nethaniah,
25 the s' of Elishama, of the seed royal,
1Ch 1: 43 of Israel; Bela the s' of Beor:
44 Jobab the s' of Zerah of Bozrah
46 Hadad the s' of Bedad, which
49 Baal-hanan the s' of Achbor reigned
2: 18 And Caleb the s' of Hezron begat
45 And the s' of Shammai was Maon:
50 the sons of Caleb the s' of Hur,
3: 2 Absalom the s' of Maachah the
2 fourth, Adonijah the s' of Haggith:
10 And Solomon's s' was Rehoboam,
10 Abia his s', Asa his s',
10 Jehoshaphat his s',
11 Joram his s', Ahaziah his s',
11 Joash his s',
12 Amaziah his s',
12 Azariah his s', Jotham his s',
13 Ahaz his s', Hezekiah his s',
13 Manasseh his s',
14 Amon his s', Josiah his s'.
16 Jeconiah his s', Zedekiah his s'.
17 of Jeconiah; Assir, Salathiel his s',
4: 2 And Reaiah the s' of Shobal begat
8 of Aharhel the s' of Harum.
15 sons of Caleb the s' of Jephunneh;
21 The sons of Shelah the s' of Judah
25 Shallum his s',
25 Mibsam his s', Mishma his s'.
26 Hamuel his s', Zacchur his s',
26 Shimei his s'.
34 and Joshah the s' of Amaziah,
35 Joel, and Jehu the s' of Josibiah,
35 the s' of Seraiah, the s' of Asiel,
37 Ziza the s' of Shiphi, the s' of Allon,
37 the s' of Jedaiah, the s' of Shimri,
37 the s' of Shemaiah;
5: 1 the sons of Joseph the s' of Israel:
4 sons of Joel; Shemaiah his s',
4 Gog his s', Shimei his s',
5 Micah his s',
5 Reaia his s', Baal his s',
6 Beerah his s', whom
8 And Bela the s' of Azaz,
8 the s' of Shema, the s' of Joel, who
14 children of Abihail the s' of Huri,
14 the s' of Jaroah, the s' of Gilead,
14 s' of Michael, the s' of Jeshishai,
14 the s' of Jahdo, the s' of Buz;
15 Ahi the s' of Abdiel, the s' of Guni,
6: 20 Of Gershom; Libni his s',
20 Jahath his s', Zimmah his s',
21 Joah his s', Iddo his s',
21 Zerah his s', Jeaterai his s'.
22 sons of Kohath; Amminadab his s',
22 Korah his s', Assir his s',
23 Elkanah his s', and Ebiasaph
23 Ebiasaph his s', and Assir his s',
24 Tahath his s', Uriel his s',
24 Uzziah his s', and Shaul his s'.
26 Zophai his s', and Nahath his s'.
27 Eliab his s', Jeroham his s',
27 Elkanah his s'.
29 sons of Merari; Mahli, Libni his s',
29 Shimei his s', Uzza his s',
30 Shimea his s', Haggiah his s',
30 Asaiah his s'.
33 Heman a singer, the s' of Joel,
33 the s' of Shemuel,
34 s' of Elkanah, the s' of Jeroham,
34 the s' of Eliel, the s' of Toah,
35 The s' of Zuph, the s' of Elkanah,
35 the s' of Mahath, the s' of Amasai,
36 The s' of Elkanah, the s' of Joel,
36 s' of Azariah, the s' of Zephaniah,
37 The s' of Tahath, the s' of Assir,
37 the s' of Ebiasaph, the s' of Korah,
38 The s' of Izhar, the s' of Kohath,
38 the s' of Levi, the s' of Israel.
39 even Asaph the s' of Berachiah,
39 the s' of Shimea,
40 s' of Michael, the s' of Baaseiah,
40 of Baaseiah, the s' of Malchiah,
41 The s' of Ethni, the s' of Zerah,
41 of Zerah, the s' of Adaiah,
42 The s' of Ethan, the s' of Zimmah,
42 of Zimmah, the s' of Shimei,
43 The s' of Jahath, the s' of Gershom,
43 of Gershom, the s' of Levi.
44 left hand: Ethan the s' of Kishi,
44 the s' of Abdi, the s' of Malluch,
45 of Hashabiah, the s' of Amaziah,
45 of Amaziah, the s' of Hilkiah,
46 The s' of Amzi, the s' of Bani, the
46 of Bani, the s' of Shamer,
47 The s' of Mahli, the s' of Mushi,
47 the s' of Merari, the s' of Levi.
50 the sons of Aaron; Eleazar his s',
50 Phinehas his s', Abishua his s',
51 Bukki his s', Uzzi his s',
51 Zerahiah his s',
52 Meraioth his s',
52 Amariah his s', Ahitub his s',
53 Zadok his s', Ahimaaz his s'.
56 gave to Caleb the s' of Jephunneh.
7: 16 the wife of Machir bare a s', and
17 sons of Gilead, the s' of Machir,
17 the s' of Manasseh.
20 Shuthelah, and Bered his s', and

1Ch 7: 20 and Tahath his s',
20 Eladah his s', and Tahath his s',
21 Zabad his s', and Shuthelah his s',
23 she conceived, and bare a s', and he
25 Rephah was his s', also Resheph,
25 and Telah his s', and Tahan his s',
26 Laadan his s', Ammihud his s',
26 Elishama his s',
27 Non his s', Jehoshuah his s'.
29 children of Joseph the s' of Israel.
8: 30 his firstborn s' Abdon, and Zur, and
34 the s' of Jonathan was Merib-baal;
37 begat Binea: Rapha was his s',
37 Eleasah his s', Azel his s':
9: 4 Uthai the s' of Ammihud,
4 the s' of Omri, the s' of Imri,
4 s' of Bani, of the children of Pharez
4 children of Pharez the s' of Judah.
7 Sallu the s' of Meshullam,
7 s' of Hodaviah, the s' of Hasenuah,
8 And Ibneiah the s' of Jeroham,
8 Elah the s' of Uzzi, the s' of Michri,
8 Meshullam the s' of Shephathiah,
8 the s' of Reuel, the s' of Ibnijah;
11 And Azariah the s' of Hilkiah,
11 the s' of Meshullam,
11 the s' of Zadok, the s' of Meraioth,
11 s' of Ahitub, the ruler of the house
12 And Adaiah the s' of Jeroham,
12 s' of Pashur, the s' of Malchijah,
12 and Maasiai the s' of Adiel,
12 s' of Jahzerah, the s' of Meshullam,
12 s' of Meshillemith, the s' of Immer;
14 Shemaiah the s' of Hasshub, the
14 the s' of Azrikam,
14 the s' of Hashabiah, of the sons of
15 and Mattaniah the s' of Micah,
15 the s' of Zichri, the s' of Asaph;
16 And Obadiah the s' of Shemaiah,
16 the s' of Galal, the s' of Jeduthun,
16 and Berechiah the s' of Asa,
16 the s' of Elkanah, that dwelt in
19 And Shallum the s' of Kore,
19 the s' of Ebiasaph, the s' of Korah,
20 Phinehas the s' of Eleazar was the
21 Zechariah the s' of Meshelemiah
36 And his firstborn s' Abdon, then
40 the s' of Jonathan was Merib-baal:
43 begat Binea; and Rephaiah his s',
43 Eleasah his s', Azel his s'.
10: 14 kingdom unto David the s' of Jesse.
11: 6 So Joab the s' of Zeruiah went first
12 him was Eleazar the s' of Dodo,
22 Benaiah the s' of Jehoiada, the
22 the s' of a valiant man of Kabzeel,
24 did Benaiah the s' of Jehoiada,
26 of Joab, Elhanan the s' of Dodo of
28 Ira the s' of Ikkesh the Tekoite,
30 Heled the s' of Baanah the
31 Ithai the s' of Ribai of Gibeah, that
34 Jonathan the s' of Shage the
35 Ahiam the s' of Sacar the Hararite,
35 the Hararite, Eliphal the s' of Ur,
37 Carmelite, Naarai the s' of Ezbai,
38 Nathan, Mibhar the s' of Haggeri,
39 of Joab the s' of Zeruiah,
41 the Hittite, Zabad the s' of Ahlai,
42 Adina the s' of Shiza the
43 Hanan the s' of Maachah, and
45 Jediael the s' of Shimri, and Joha
12: 1 close because of Saul the s' of Kish:
18 and on thy side, thou s' of Jesse:
15: 17 appointed Heman the s' of Joel;
17 brethren, Asaph the s' of Berechiah;
17 Ethan the s' of Kushaiah;
16: 38 Obed-edom also the s' of Jeduthun
17: 13 his father, and he shall be my s':
18: 10 sent Hadoram his s' to king David,
12 Abishai the s' of Zeruiah slew of
15 Joab the s' of Zeruiah was over the
15 and Jehoshaphat the s' of Ahilud,
16 And Zadok the s' of Ahitub, and
16 Abimelech the s' of Abiathar, were
17 Benaiah the s' of Jehoiada was
19: 1 and his s' reigned in his stead.
2 unto Hanun the s' of Nahash.
20: 5 Elhanan the s' of Jair slew Lahmi
6 he also was the s' of the giant.
7 Jonathan the s' of Shimea David's
22: 5 said, Solomon my s' is younger and
6 Then he called for Solomon his s',
7 David said to Solomon, My s', as
9 a s' shall be born to thee, who shall
10 he shall be my s', and I will be his
11 Now, my s', the Lord be with thee;
17 of Israel to help Solomon his s',
23: 1 he made Solomon his s' king over
24: 6 Shemaiah the s' of Nethaneel the
6 and Ahimelech the s' of Abiathar,
29 Kish: the s' of Kish was Jerahmeel.
26: 1 was Meshelemiah the s' of Kore, of
6 Shemaiah his s' were sons born,
14 Then for Zechariah his s', a wise
24 And Shebuel the s' of Gershom,
24 the s' of Moses, was ruler over
25 by Eliezer; Rehabiah his s', and
25 Jeshaiah his s', and Joram his s',
25 Zichri his s', and Shelomith his s'.
28 the seer, and Saul the s' of Kish,
28 and Abner the s' of Ner,
28 and Joab the s' of Zeruiah, had
27: 2 was Jashobeam the s' of Zabdiel:
5 was Benaiah the s' of Jehoiada,
6 his course was Ammizabad his s'.
7 and Zebadiah his s' after him:
9 Ira the s' of Ikkesh the Tekoite:

1Ch 27: 16 was Eliezer the s' of Zichri:
16 Shephatiah the s' of Maachah:
17 Hashabiah the s' of Kemuel:
18 Issachar, Omri the s' of Michael:
19 Zebulun, Ishmaiah the s' of Obadiah:
19 Naphtali, Jerimoth the s' of Azriel:
20 Hoshea the s' of Azaziah:
20 Manasseh, Joel the s' of Pedaiah:
21 in Gilead, Iddo the s' of Zechariah:
21 Benjamin, Jaasiel the s' of Abner:
22 Of Dan, Azareel the s' of Jeroham.
24 Joab the s' of Zeruiah began to
25 was Azmaveth the s' of Adiel:
25 was Jehonathan the s' of Uzziah:
26 ground was Ezri the s' of Chelub:
29 was Shaphat the s' of Adlai:
32 Jehiel the s' of Hachmoni was with
34 was Jehoiada the s' of Benaiah,
28: 5 chosen Solomon my s' to sit upon
6 Solomon thy s', he shall build
6 for I have chosen him to be my s',
9 Solomon my s', know thou the God
11 gave to Solomon his s' the pattern
20 And David said to Solomon his s',
29: 1 Solomon my s', whom alone God
19 unto Solomon my s' a perfect heart,
22 made Solomon the s' of David king
26 David the s' of Jesse reigned over
28 Solomon his s' reigned in his stead.
2Ch 1: 1 And Solomon the s' of David was
5 Bezaleel the s' of Uri, the s' of Hur,
2: 12 given to David the king a wise s',
14 The s' of a woman of the daughters
6: 9 thy s' which shall come forth out of
9: 29 against Jeroboam the s' of Nebat?
31 and Rehoboam his s' reigned in his
10: 2 when Jeroboam the s' of Nebat,
15 to Jeroboam the s' of Nebat.
16 none inheritance in the s' of Jesse:
11: 3 unto Rehoboam the s' of Solomon,
17 Rehoboam the s' of Solomon strong,
18 of Jerimoth the s' of David to wife,
18 daughter of Eliab the s' of Jesse;
22 Abijah the s' of Maachah the chief,
12: 16 Abijah his s' reigned in his stead.
13: 6 Yet Jeroboam the s' of Nebat, the
6 servant of Solomon the s' of David,
7 against Rehoboam...s' of Solomon,
14: 1 and Asa his s' reigned in his stead.
15: 1 came upon Azariah the s' of Oded:
17: 1 Jehoshaphat his s' reigned in his
16 him was Amasiah the s' of Zichri,
18: 7 the same is Micaiah the s' of Imla.
8 Fetch quickly Micaiah the s' of Imla.
10 And Zedekiah the s' of Chenaanah
23 Zedekiah the s' of Chenaanah came
25 the city, and to Joash the king's s';
19: 2 Jehu the s' of Hanani the seer went
11 and Zebadiah the s' of Ishmael, the
20: 14 upon Jahaziel the s' of Zechariah,
14 the s' of Benaiah, the s' of Jeiel, the
14 the s' of Mattaniah, a Levite of the
34 in the book of Jehu the s' of Hanani,
37 Then Eliezer the s' of Dodavah of
21: 1 Jehoram his s' reigned in his stead.
17 there was never a s' left him, save
22: 1 made Ahaziah his youngest s' king
1 So Ahaziah the s' of Jehoram king
5 went with Jehoram the s' of Ahab
6 And Azariah the s' of Jehoram king
6 down to see Jehoram the s' of Ahab
7 against Jehu the s' of Nimshi,
9 they, he is the s' of Jehoshaphat,
10 Athaliah...saw that her s' was dead,
11 took Joash the s' of Ahaziah, and
23: 1 Azariah the s' of Jeroham, and
1 and Ishmael the s' of Jehohanan,
1 and Azariah the s' of Obed, and
1 and Maaseiah the s' of Adaiah, and
1 and Elishaphat the s' of Zichri,
3 Behold, the king's s' shall reign,
11 they brought out the king's s', and
24: 20 Zechariah...s' of Jehoiada the priest,
22 had done to him, but slew his s'.
26 Zabad the s' of Shimeath an
26 Jehozabad the s' of Shimrith a
27 Amaziah his s' reigned in his stead.
25: 17 sent to Joash, the s' of Jehoahaz,
17 the s' of Jehu, king of Israel,
18 Give thy daughter to my s' to wife:
23 took Amaziah...the s' of Joash,
23 of Joash, the s' of Jehoahaz,
25 And Amaziah the s' of Joash king of
25 death of Joash s' of Jehoahaz king
26: 21 Jotham his s' was over the king's
22 Isaiah the prophet, the s' of Amoz,
23 Jotham his s' reigned in his stead.
27: 9 Ahaz his s' reigned in his stead.
28: 3 in the valley of the s' of Hinnom,
6 Pekah the s' of Remaliah slew in
7 slew Maaseiah the king's s', and
12 Azariah the s' of Johanan,
12 Berechiah the s' of Meshillemoth,
12 and Jehizkiah the s' of Shallum,
12 and Amasa the s' of Hadlai, stood
27 and Hezekiah his s' reigned in his
29: 12 arose, Mahath the s' of Amasai,
12 and Joel the s' of Azariah, of the
12 sons of Merari, Kish the s' of Abdi,
12 and Azariah the s' of Jehalelel:
12 Joah the s' of Zimmah,
12 and Eden the s' of Joah:
30: 26 time of Solomon the s' of David
31: 14 Kore the s' of Imnah the Levite, the
32: 20 the prophet Isaiah the s' of Amoz,
32 Isaiah the prophet, the s' of Amoz,

2Ch 32: 33 And Manasseh his s' reigned in his
33: 6 in the valley of the s' of Hinnom:
7 said to David and to Solomon his s',
20 Amon his s' reigned in his stead.
25 made Josiah his s' king in his stead.
34: 8 he sent Shaphan the s' of Azaliah,
8 Joah the s' of Joahaz the recorder,
20 and Ahikam the s' of Shaphan,
20 and Abdon the s' of Micah, and
22 wife of Shallum the s' of Tikvath,
22 Tikvath, the s' of Hasrah, keeper of
35: 3 which Solomon the s' of David king
4 to the writing of Solomon his s'.
36: 1 land took Jehoahaz the s' of Josiah,
8 and Jehoiachin his s' reigned in his
Ezr 3: 2 stood up Jeshua the s' of Jozadak,
2, 8 Zerubbabel the s' of Shealtiel,
8 and Jeshua the s' of Jozadak, and
5: 1 and Zechariah the s' of Iddo,
2 up Zerubbabel the s' of Shealtiel,
2 and Jeshua the s' of Jozadak, and
6: 14 and Zechariah the s' of Iddo.
7: 1 of Persia, Ezra the s' of Seraiah,
1 the s' of Azariah, the s' of Hilkiah,
2 The s' of Shallum, the s' of Zadok,
2 of Zadok, the s' of Ahitub,
3 s' of Amariah, the s' of Azariah,
3 of Azariah, the s' of Meraioth,
4 The s' of Zerahiah, the s' of Uzzi,
4 of Uzzi, the s' of Bukki,
5 s' of Abishua, the s' of Phinehas,
5 the s' of Eleazar, s' of Aaron the
8: 4 Elihoenai the s' of Zerahiah, and
5 the s' of Jahaziel, and with him
6 Ebed the s' of Jonathan, and with
7 Jeshaiah the s' of Athaliah, and
8 Zebadiah the s' of Michael, and
9 Obadiah the s' of Jehiel, and with
10 the s' of Josiphiah, and with him
11 Zechariah the s' of Bebai, and with
12 Johanan the s' of Hakkatan, and
18 Mahli,...s' of Levi, the s' of Israel;
33 hand of Meremoth the s' of Uriah
33 was Eleazar the s' of Phinehas;
33 was Jozabad the s' of Jeshua, and
33 Noadiah the s' of Binnui, Levites;
10: 2 And Shechaniah the s' of Jehiel,
6 of Johanan the s' of Eliashib:
15 Only Jonathan the s' of Asahel and
15 Jahaziah the s' of Tikvah were
18 sons of Jeshua the s' of Jozadak,
Ne 1: 1 of Nehemiah the s' of Hachaliah.
3: 2 them builded Zaccur the s' of Imri.
4 Meremoth...s' of Urijah,...s' of Koz.
4 Meshullam the s' of Berechiah,
4 Berechiah, the s' of Meshezabeel.
4 repaired Zadok the s' of Baana.
6 repaired Jehoiada the s' of Paseah
6 and Meshullam the s' of Besodeiah
8 repaired Uzziel the s' of Harhaiah,
8 the s' of one of the apothecaries,
9 repaired Rephaiah the s' of Hur,
10 Jedaiah the s' of Harumaph, even
10 Hattush the s' of Hashabniah.
11 Malchijah the s' of Harim, and
11 Hashub the s' of Pahath-moab,
12 repaired Shallum the s' of Halohesh,
14 repaired Malchiah the s' of Rechab,
15 repaired Shallun the s' of Col-hozeh,
16 repaired Nehemiah the s' of Azbuk,
17 repaired...Rehum the s' of Bani.
18 brethren, Bavai the s' of Henadad,
19 him repaired Ezer the s' of Jeshua,
20 Baruch the s' of Zabbai earnestly
21 Meremoth...s' of Urijah...s' of Koz
23 Azariah the s' of Maaseiah
23 the s' of Ananiah by his house.
24 repaired Binnui the s' of Henadad
25 Palal the s' of Uzai, over against
25 After him Pedaiah the s' of Parosh.
29 repaired Zadok the s' of Immer
29 Shemaiah the s' of Shechaniah,
30 Hananiah the s' of Shelemiah,
30 and Hanun the sixth s' of Zalaph,
30 Meshullam the s' of Berechiah
31 Malchiah the goldsmith's s'
6: 10 house of Shemaiah the s' of Delaiah
10 the s' of Mehetabeel, who was shut
18 he was the s' in law of Shechaniah
18 of Shechaniah the s' of Arah;
18 and his s' Johanan had taken the
18 of Meshullam the s' of Berechiah.
8: 17 days of Jeshua the s' of Nun unto
10: 1 Nehemiah,...the s' of Hachaliah,
9 both Jeshua the s' of Azaniah,
38 priest the s' of Aaron shall be with
11: 4 Judah; Athaiah the s' of Uzziah,
4 s' of Zechariah, the s' of Amariah,
4 the s' of Shephatiah,
4 the s' of Mahalaleel,
5 And Maaseiah the s' of Baruch,
5 the s' of Col-hozeh,
5 s' of Hazaiah, the s' of Adaiah,
5 s' of Joiarib, the s' of Zechariah,
5 of Zechariah, the s' of Shiloni.
7 Sallu the s' of Meshullam,
7 the s' of Joed, the s' of Pedaiah,
7 s' of Kolaiah, the s' of Maaseiah,
7 the s' of Ithiel, the s' of Jesaiah.
9 And Joel the s' of Zichri was their
9 Judah the s' of Senuah was second
10 Jedaiah the s' of Joiarib, Jachin.
11 Seraiah the s' of Hilkiah,
11 the s' of Meshullam,
11 the s' of Zadok, the s' of Meraioth,
11 the s' of Ahitub, was the ruler of

Ne 11: 12 and Adaiah the s' of Jeroham,
12 the s' of Pelaliah,
12 the s' of Amzi, the s' of Zechariah,
12 the s' of Pashur, the s' of Malchiah,
13 and Amashai the s' of Azareel,
13 s' of Ahasai, the s' of Meshillemoth,
13 the s' of Immer,
14 Zabdiel, the s' of one of the great
15 Shemaiah the s' of Hashub,
15 the s' of Azrikam,
15 s' of Hashabiah, the s' of Bunni;
17 And Mattaniah the s' of Micha,
17 the s' of Zabdi, the s' of Asaph, was
17 and Abda the s' of Shammua,
17 the s' of Galal, the s' of Jeduthun.
22 was Uzzi the s' of Bani, the
22 the s' of Hashabiah,
22 the s' of Mattaniah, the s' of Micha.
24 Pethahiah the s' of Meshezabeel, of
24 children of Zerah the s' of Judah,
12: 1 Zerubbabel the s' of Shealtiel, and
23 days of Johanan the s' of Eliashib.
24 Jeshua the s' of Kadmiel, with their
26 days of Joiakim the s' of Jeshua,
26 the s' of Jozadak, and in the days
35 Zechariah the s' of Jonathan,
35 the s' of Shemaiah,
35 s' of Mattaniah, the s' of Michaiah,
35 the s' of Zaccur, the s' of Asaph:
45 of David, and of Solomon his s'.
13: 13 them was Hanan the s' of Zaccur,
13 the s' of Mattaniah: for they were
28 Joiada, the s' of Eliashib the high
28 was s' in law to Sanballat the
Es 2: 5 name was Mordecai, the s' of Jair,
5 the s' of Shimei, the s' of Kish, a
3: 1, 10 Haman the s' of Hammedatha
8: 5 by Haman the s' of Hammedatha
9: 10, 24 Haman the s' of Hammedatha,
Job 18: 19 shall neither have s' nor nephew
25: 6 the s' of man, which is a worm?
32: 2 wrath of Elihu the s' of Barachel
6 Elihu the s' of Barachel the Buzite
35: 8 may profit the s' of man.
Ps 2: 7 hath said unto me, Thou art my *S'*:
12 Kiss the *S'*, lest he be angry, and
3: *title* when he fled from Absalom his s'.
8: 4 s' of man, that thou visitest him?
50: 20 slanderest thine own mother's s'.
72: 1 righteousness unto the king's s'.
20 prayers of David the s' of Jesse are
80: 17 upon the s' of man whom thou
86: 16 and save the s' of thine handmaid.
89: 22 nor the s' of wickedness afflict him.
116: 16 and the s' of thine handmaid:
144: 3 or the s' of man, that thou makest
146: 3 nor in the s' of man, in whom there
Pr 1: 1 of Solomon the s' of David, king
8 My s', hear the instruction of thy
10 My s', if sinners entice thee,
15 My s', walk not thou in the way
2: 1 My s', if thou wilt receive my
3: 1 My s', forget not my law; but let
11 My s', despise not the chastening
12 even as a father the s' in whom he
21 My s', let not them depart from
4: 3 For I was my father's s', tender
10 Hear, O my s', and receive my
20 My s', attend to my words; incline
5: 1 My s', attend unto my wisdom, and
20 why wilt thou, my s', be ravished
6: 1 My s', if thou be surety for thy
3 Do this now, my s', and deliver
20 My s', keep thy father's
7: 1 My s', keep my words, and lay up
10: 1 A wise s' maketh a glad father:
1 but a foolish s' is the heaviness of
5 gathereth in summer is a wise s':
5 harvest is a s' that causeth shame.
13: 1 A wise s' heareth his father's
24 that spareth his rod hateth his s':
15: 20 A wise s' maketh a glad father: but
17: 2 servant shall have rule over a s'
25 A foolish s' is a grief to his father,
19: 13 A foolish s' is the calamity of his
18 Chasten thy s' while there is hope,
26 is a s' that causeth shame, and
27 Cease, my s', to hear the
23: 15 My s', if thine heart be wise, my
19 Hear thou, my s', and be wise, and
26 My s', give me thine heart, and let
24: 13 My s', eat thou honey, because it is
21 My s', fear thou the Lord and the
27: 11 My s', be wise, and make my heart
28: 7 Whoso keepeth the law is a wise s':
29: 17 Correct thy s', and he shall give
21 shall have him become his s' at
30: 1 The words of Agur the s' of Jakeh,
31: 2 my s'?...what, the s' of my womb?
2 and what, the s' of my vows?
Ec 1: 1 of the Preacher, the s' of David,
5: 14 and he begetteth a s', and there is
10: 17 when thy king is the s' of nobles,
12: 12 And further, by these, my s', be
Isa 1: 1 The vision of Isaiah the s' of Amoz,
2: 1 word that Isaiah the s' of Amoz
7: 1 the days of Ahaz the s' of Jotham,
1 the s' of Uzziah, the king of Judah,
1 and Pekah the s' of Remaliah, king
3 thou, and Shear-jashub thy s', at
4 Syria, and of the s' of Remaliah,
5 Ephraim, and of the s' of Remaliah,
6 midst of it, even the s' of Tabeal:
9 head of Samaria is Remaliah's s'.
14 virgin shall conceive, and bare a s',
8: 2 Zechariah the s' of Jeberechiah.

Isa 8: 3 and she conceived, and bare a s'.
6 rejoice in Rezin and Remaliah's s';
9: 6 child is born, unto us a s' is given:
13: 1 Isaiah the s' of Amoz did see.
14:12 O Lucifer, s' of the morning! how
22 and remnant, and s', and nephew,
19:11 Pharaoh, I am the s' of the wise,
11 the s' of ancient kings?
20: 2 the Lord by Isaiah the s' of Amoz,
22:20 servant Eliakim the s' of Hilkiah:
36: 3 unto him Eliakim, Hilkiah's s',
3 and Joah, Asaph's s', the recorder.
22 came Eliakim, the s' of Hilkiah,
22 Joah, the s' of Asaph, the recorder,
37: 2 Isaiah the prophet the s' of Amoz.
21 Isaiah the s' of Amoz sent unto
38 Esar-haddon his s' reigned in his
38: 1 Isaiah the prophet the s' of Amoz
39: 1 Merodach-baladan,...s' of Baladan,
49:15 compassion on the s' of her womb?
51:12 and of the s' of man which shall be
56: 2 and the s' of man that layeth hold
3 Neither let the s' of the stranger,
Jer 1: 1 of Jeremiah the s' of Hilkiah,
2 days of Josiah the s' of Amon king
3 days of Jehoiakim the s' of Josiah
3 year of Zedekiah the s' of Josiah
6:26 thee mourning, as for an only s',
7:31 in the valley of the s' of Hinnom,
32 nor the valley of the s' of Hinnom,
15: 4 of Manasseh the s' of Hezekiah
19: 2 unto the valley of the s' of Hinnom,
6 nor The valley of the s' of Hinnom,
20: 1 Pashur the s' of Immer the priest,
21: 1 unto him Pashur the s' of Melchiah,
1 and Zephaniah the s' of Maaseiah
22:11 touching Shallum the s' of Josiah
18 Jehoiakim the s' of Josiah king of
24 Coniah the s' of Jehoiakim king of
24: 1 Jeconiah the s' of Jehoiakim king
25: 1 year of Jehoiakim the s' of Josiah
3 year of Josiah the s' of Amon king
26: 1 reign of Jehoiakim the s' of Josiah
20 Urijah the s' of Shemaiah of
22 Elnathan the s' of Achbor, and
24 hand of Ahikam the s' of Shaphan
27: 1 reign of Jehoiakim the s' of Josiah
7 him, and his s', and his son's s',
20 Jeconiah the s' of Jehoiakim king
28: 1 that Hananiah the s' of Azur the
4 Jeconiah the s' of Jehoiakim king
29: 3 hand of Elasah the s' of Shaphan,
3 and Gemariah the s' of Hilkiah,
21 of Israel, of Ahab the s' of Kolaiah,
21 of Zedekiah the s' of Maaseiah,
25 Zephaniah the s' of Maaseiah the
31:20 Is Ephraim my dear s'? is he a
32: 7 Hanameel the s' of Shallum thine
8 So Hanameel mine uncle's s' came
9 the field of Hanameel my uncle's s',
12 unto Baruch the s' of Neriah,
12 the s' of Maaseiah,
12 sight of Hanameel mine uncle's s',
16 unto Baruch the s' of Neriah,
35 in the valley of the s' of Hinnom,
33:21 should not have a s' to reign upon
35: 1 of Jehoiakim the s' of Josiah king
3 took Jaazaniah the s' of Jeremiah,
3 the s' of Habaziniah, and his
4 Hanan, the s' of Igdaliah, a man of
4 of Maaseiah the s' of Shallum, the
6 for Jonadab the s' of Rechab our
8 voice of Jonadab the s' of Rechab
14 words of Jonadab the s' of Rechab,
16 sons of Jonadab the s' of Rechab
19 Jonadab the s' of Rechab shall not
36: 1 Jehoiakim the s' of Josiah king of
4 called Baruch the s' of Neriah: and
8 And Baruch the s' of Neriah did
9 Jehoiakim the s' of Josiah king of
10 of Gemariah the s' of Shaphan the
11 When Michaiah the s' of Gemariah,
11 s' of Shaphan, had heard out of the
12 and Delaiah the s' of Shemaiah,
12 and Elnathan the s' of Achbor,
12 and Gemariah the s' of Shaphan,
12 and Zedekiah the s' of Hananiah,
14 sent Jehudi the s' of Nethaniah,
14 the s' of Shelemiah, the s' of Cushi,
14 Baruch the s' of Neriah took the roll
26 Jerahmeel the s' of Hammelech,
26 and Seraiah the s' of Azriel, and
26 and Shelemiah the s' of Abdeel,
32 Baruch the scribe, the s' of Neriah;
37: 1 Zedekiah the s' of Josiah reigned
1 instead of Coniah...s' of Jehoiakim,
3 sent Jehucal the s' of Selemiah
3 and Zephaniah the s' of Maaseiah
13 was Irijah, the s' of Shelemiah, the
13 the s' of Hananiah; and he took
38: 1 Then Shephatiah the s' of Mattan,
1 and Gedaliah the s' of Pashur,
1 and Jucal the s' of Shelemiah,
1 and Pashur the s' of Malchiah,
6 of Malchiah the s' of Hammelech,
39:14 unto Gedaliah the s' of Ahikam
14 the s' of Shaphan, that he should
40: 5 also to Gedaliah the s' of Ahikam
5 the s' of Shaphan, whom the king
6 unto Gedaliah the s' of Ahikam to
7 made Gedaliah the s' of Ahikam
8 even Ishmael the s' of Nethaniah,
8 and Seraiah the s' of Tanhumeth,
8 Jezaniah the s' of a Maachathite,
9 And Gedaliah the s' of Ahikam
9 the s' of Shaphan sware unto them
Jer 40:11 them Gedaliah the s' of Ahikam
11 the s' of Shaphan;
13 Johanan the s' of Kareah, and all
14 sent Ishmael the s' of Nethaniah
14 Gedaliah the s' of Ahikam believed
15 Johanan the s' of Kareah spake to
15 slay Ishmael the s' of Nethaniah,
16 Gedaliah the s' of Ahikam said unto
16 said unto Johanan the s' of Kareah,
41: 1 that Ishmael the s' of Nethaniah
1 s' of Elishama, of the seed royal,
1 unto Gedaliah the s' of Ahikam to
2 arose Ishmael the s' of Nethaniah,
2 smote Gedaliah the s' of Ahikam
2 the s' of Shaphan with the sword,
6 Ishmael the s' of Nethaniah went
6 Come to Gedaliah the s' of Ahikam.
7 Ishmael the s' of Nethaniah slew
9 Ishmael the s' of Nethaniah filled
10 to Gedaliah the s' of Ahikam:
10 and Ishmael the s' of Nethaniah
11 when Johanan the s' of Kareah, and
11 that Ishmael the s' of Nethaniah
12 with Ishmael the s' of Nethaniah,
13 saw Johanan the s' of Kareah, and
14 went unto Johanan the s' of Kareah.
15 But Ishmael the s' of Nethaniah
16 took Johanan the s' of Kareah, and
16 from Ishmael the s' of Nethaniah,
16 had slain Gedaliah the s' of Ahikam,
18 Ishmael the s' of Nethaniah had
18 slain Gedaliah the s' of Ahikam,
42: 1 and Johanan the s' of Kareah,
1 and Jezaniah the s' of Hoshaiah,
8 called he Johanan the s' of Kareah,
43: 2 spake Azariah the s' of Hoshaiah,
2 and Johanan the s' of Kareah, and
3 Baruch the s' of Neriah setteth the
4 So Johanan the s' of Kareah, and
5 But Johanan the s' of Kareah, and
6 with Gedaliah the s' of Ahikam the
6 the s' of Shaphan, and Jeremiah
6 and Baruch the s' of Neriah.
45: 1 spake unto Baruch the s' of Neriah,
1 Jehoiakim the s' of Josiah king of
46: 2 Jehoiakim the s' of Josiah king of
49:18 neither shall a s' of man dwell in it.
33 there, nor any s' of man dwell in it.
50:40 shall any s' of man dwell therein.
51:43 doth any s' of man pass thereby.
59 Seraiah the s' of Neriah,
59 the s' of Maaseiah, when he went
Eze 1: 3 Ezekiel the priest, the s' of Buzi,
2: 1 S' of man, stand upon thy feet, and
3 S' of man, I send thee to the
6 s' of man, be not afraid of them,
8 s' of man, hear what I say unto
3: 1 S' of man, eat that thou findest;
3 S' of man, cause thy belly to eat,
4 S' of man, go, get thee unto the
10 S' of man, all my words that I shall
17 S' of man, I have made thee a
25 O s' of man, behold, they shall put
4: 1 s' of man, take thee a tile, and lay
16 S' of man, behold, I will break the
5: 1 s' of man, take thee a sharp knife,
6: 2 S' of man, set thy face toward the
7: 2 thou s' of man, thus saith the Lord
8: 5 S' of man, lift up thine eyes now
6 S' of man, seest thou what they do?
8 S' of man, dig now in the wall: and
11 stood Jaazaniah the s' of Shaphan,
12 S' of man, hast thou seen what the
15, 17 Hast thou seen this,O s' of man?
11: 1 I saw Jaazaniah the s' of Azur,
1 and Pelatiah the s' of Benaiah,
2 S' of man, these are the men that
4 them, prophesy, O s' of man.
13 that Pelatiah the s' of Benaiah died.
15 S' of man, thy brethren, even thy
12: 2 S' of man, thou dwellest in the
3 thou s' of man, prepare thee stuff
9 S' of man, hath not the house of
18 S' of man, eat thy bread with
22 S' of man, what is that proverb that
27 S' of man, behold, they of the house
13: 2 S' of man, prophesy against the
17 thou s' of man, set thy face against
14: 3 S' of man, these men have set up
13 S' of man, when the land sinneth
20 deliver neither s' nor daughter;
15: 2 S' of man, What is the vine tree
16: 2 S' of man, cause Jerusalem to know
17: 2 S' of man, put forth a riddle, and
18: 4 so also the soul of the s' is mine:
10 If he beget a s' that is a robber, a
14 Now, lo, if he beget a s', that seeth
19 the s' bear the iniquity of the father?
19 s' hath done that which is lawful
20 s' shall not bear the iniquity of the
20 father bear the iniquity of the s':
20: 3 S' of man, speak unto the elders of
4 s' of man, wilt thou judge them?
27 s' of man, speak unto the house of
46 S' of man, set thy face toward the
21: 2 S' of man, set thy face toward
6 Sigh therefore, thou s' of man, with
9 S' of man, prophesy, and say, Thus
10 it contemneth the rod of my s', as
12 Cry and howl, s' of man: for it shall
14 s' of man, prophesy, and smite
19 s' of man, appoint thee two ways,
28 thou, s' of man, prophesy and say,
22: 2 Now, thou s' of man, wilt thou judge,
18 s' of man, the house of Israel is to
24 S' of man, say unto her, Thou art
Eze 23: 2 S' of man, there were two women,
36 S' of man, wilt thou judge Aholah
24: 2 S' of man, write thee the name of
16 S' of man, behold, I take away
25 s' of man, shall it not be in the day
25: 2 S' of man, set thy face against the
26: 2 S' of man, because that Tyrus hath
27: 2 s' of man, take up a lamentation
28: 2 S' of man, say unto the prince of
12 S' of man, take up a lamentation
21 S' of man, set thy face against
29: 2 S' of man, set thy face against
18 S' of man, Nebuchadrezzar king of
30: 2 S' of man, prophesy and say, Thus
21 S' of man, I have broken the arm
31: 2 S' of man, speak unto Pharaoh
32: 2 S' of man, take up a lamentation
18 S' of man, wail for the multitude
33: 2 S' of man, speak to the children of
7 So thou, O s' of man, I have set thee
10 s' of man, speak unto the house of
12 s' of man, say unto the children of
24 S' of man, they that inhabit those
30 thou s' of man, the children of thy
34: 2 S' of man, prophesy against the
35: 2 S' of man, set thy face against
36: 1 Also, thou s' of man, prophesy unto
17 S' of man, when the house of Israel
37: 3 me, S' of man, can these bones live?
9 prophesy, s' of man, and say to the
11 S' of man, these bones are the
16 thou s' of man, take thee one stick,
38: 2 S' of man, set thy face against Gog,
14 s' of man, prophesy and say unto
39: 1 s' of man, prophesy against Gog,
17 s' of man, thus saith the Lord God;
40: 4 S' of man, behold with thine eyes,
43: 7 S' of man, the place of my throne,
10 Thou s' of man, shew the house to
18 S' of man, thus saith the Lord
44: 5 S' of man, mark well, and behold
25 mother, or for s', or for daughter,
47: 6 me, S' of man, hast thou seen this?
Da 3:25 of the fourth is like the S' of God.
5:22 And thou his s', O Belshazzar, hast
7:13 one like the S' of man came with
8:17 unto me, Understand, O s' of man:
9: 1 year of Darius the s' of Ahasuerus,
Ho 1: 1 came unto Hosea, the s' of Beeri,
1 days of Jeroboam the s' of Joash,
3 which conceived, and bare him a s'.
8 she conceived, and bare a s'.
11: 1 him, and called my s' out of Egypt.
13:13 he is an unwise s'; for he should
Joe 1: 1 that came to Joel the s' of Pethuel.
Am 1: 1 days of Jeroboam the s' of Joash
7:14 neither was I a prophet's s';
8:10 make it as the mourning of an only s'.
Jon 1: 1 came unto Jonah the s' of Amittai,
Mic 6: 5 Balaam the s' of Beor answered
7: 6 For the s' dishonoureth the father,
Zep 1: 1 unto Zephaniah the s' of Cushi,
1 s' of Gedaliah, the s' of Amariah,
1 of Amariah, the s' of Hizkiah, in
1 the days of Josiah the s' of Amon,
Hag 1: 1 unto Zerubbabel the s' of Shealtiel,
1 and to Joshua the s' of Josedech,
12 Then Zerubbabel the s' of Shealtiel,
12 and Joshua the s' of Josedech, the
14 of Zerubbabel the s' of Shealtiel,
14 spirit of Joshua the s' of Josedech,
2: 2 to Zerubbabel the s' of Shealtiel,
2 and to Joshua the s' of Josedech,
4 be strong, O Joshua, s' of Josedech,
23 my servant, the s' of Shealtiel,
Zec 1: 1 unto Zechariah, s' of Berechiah,
1 the s' of Iddo the prophet,
7 Zechariah, the s' of Berechiah,
7 the s' of Iddo the prophet,
6:10 house of Josiah the s' of Zephaniah;
11 head of Joshua the s' of Josedech,
14 and to Hen the s' of Zephaniah, for
12:10 as one mourneth for his only s',
Mal 1: 6 A s' honoureth his father, and a
3:17 as a man spareth his own s' that
M't 1: 1 of Jesus Christ, the s' of David,
1 of David, the s' of Abraham.
20 Joseph, thou s' of David, fear not to
21 she shall bring forth a s', and thou
23 child, and shall bring forth a s',
25 had brought forth her firstborn s':
2:15 Out of Egypt have I called my s'.
3:17 This is my beloved S', in whom I
4: 3 If thou be the S' of God, command
6 If thou be the S' of God, cast
21 James the s' of Zebedee, and John his
7: 9 if his s' ask bread, will he give him
8:20 S' of man hath not where to lay his
29 do with thee, Jesus, thou S' of God?
9: 2 S', be of good cheer; thy sins be
6 S' of man hath power on earth to
27 Thou s' of David, have mercy on us.
10: 2 James the s' of Zebedee, and John his
3 James the s' of Alphæus, and
23 Israel, till the S' of man be come.
37 loveth s' or daughter more than me
11:19 The S' of man came eating and
27 and no man knoweth the S', but the
27 any man the Father, save the S',
27 whomsoever the S' will reveal him.
12: 8 S' of man is Lord...of the sabbath
23 and said, Is not this the s' of David?
32 a word against the S' of man,
40 shall the S' of man be three days
13:37 the good seed is the S' of man;
41 The S' of man shall send forth his

M't 13:55 Is not this the carpenter's s'? is not
14:33 Of a truth thou art the S' of God.
15:22 on me, O Lord, thou s' of David;
16:13 men say that I the S' of man am?
16 the Christ, the S' of the living God.
27 S' of man shall come in the glory
28 till they see the S' of man coming
17: 5 This is my beloved S', in whom I
9 until the S' of man be risen again
12 shall...the S' of man suffer of them.
15 Lord, have mercy on my s': for he
22 S' of man shall be betrayed into
18:11 For the S' of man is come to save
19:28 S' of man shall sit in the throne of
20:18 S' of man shall be betrayed unto
28 S' of man came not to be ministered
30, 31 on us, O Lord, thou s' of David.
21: 9 saying, Hosanna to the s' of David:
15 saying, Hosanna to the s' of David;
28 S', go work to day in my vineyard.
37 last of all he sent unto them his s',
37 saying, They will reverence my s'.
38 when the husbandmen saw the s',
22: 2 which made a marriage for his s',
42 think ye of Christ? whose s' is he?
42 They say unto him, The s' of David.
45 call him Lord, how is he his s'?
23:35 blood of Zacharias s' of Barachias,
24:27 also the coming of the S' of man be.
30 sign of the S' of man in heaven:
30 the S' of man coming in the clouds
37, 39 the coming of the S' of man be.
44 ye think not the S' of man cometh.
25:13 wherein the S' of man cometh.
31 S' of man shall come in his glory,
26: 2 and the S' of man is betrayed to be
24 the S' of man goeth as it is written
24 by whom the S' of man is betrayed!
45 S' of man is betrayed into the hands
63 thou be the Christ, the S' of God.
64 the S' of man sitting on the right
27:40 If thou be the S' of God, come down
43 for he said, I am the S' of God.
54 Truly this was the S' of God.
28:19 name of the Father, and of the S',
M'r 1: 1 of Jesus Christ, the S' of God;
11 Thou art my beloved S', in whom I
19 he saw James the s' of Zebedee, and
2: 5 S', thy sins be forgiven thee.
10 the S' of man hath power on earth
14 he saw Levi the s' of Alphæus sitting
28 S' of man is Lord...of the sabbath.
3:11 saying, Thou art the S' of God.
17 And James the s' of Zebedee, and
18 and James the s' of Alphæus, and
5: 7 thou S' of the most high God?
6: 3 this the carpenter, the s' of Mary,
8:31 S' of man must suffer many things,
38 shall the S' of man be ashamed,
9: 7 This is my beloved S': hear him.
9 S' of man were risen from the dead
12 how it is written of the S' of man,
17 I have brought unto thee my s',
31 The S' of man is delivered into the
10:33 S' of man shall be delivered unto
45 For...the S' of man came not to be
46 blind Bartimæus, the s' of Timæus,
47 Jesus, thou s' of David, have mercy
48 Thou s' of David, have mercy on me.
12: 6 Having yet therefore one s', his
6 saying, They will reverence my s'.
35 that Christ is the s' of David?
37 Lord; and whence is he then his s'?
13:12 to death, and the father the s';
26 see the S' of man coming in the
32 neither the S', but the Father.
34 For the S' of man is as a man taking
14:21 S' of man indeed goeth, as it is
21 by whom the S' of man is betrayed!
41 S' of man is betrayed into the hands
61 the Christ, the S' of the Blessed?
62 S' of man sitting on the right hand
15:39 Truly this man was the S' of God.
Lu 1:13 wife Elisabeth shall bear thee a s',
31 bring forth a s', and shalt call his
32 shall be called the S' of the Highest:
35 thee shall be called the S' of God.
36 also conceived a s' in her old age:
57 and she brought forth a s'.
2: 7 she brought forth her firstborn s',
48 S', why hast thou thus dealt with
3: 2 came unto John the s' of Zacharias
22 Thou art my beloved S'; in thee
23 (as was supposed) the s' of Joseph,
23 which was the s' of Heli,
24 Which was the s' of Matthat,
24 which was the s' of Levi,
24 which was the s' of Melchi,
24 which was the s' of Janna,
24 which was the s' of Joseph,
25 Which was the s' of Mattathias,
25 which was the s' of Amos,
25 which was the s' of Naum,
25 which was the s' of Esli,
25 which was the s' of Nagge,
26 Which was the s' of Maath,
26 which was the s' of Mattathias,
26 which was the s' of Semei,
26 which was the s' of Joseph,
26 which was the s' of Juda,
27 Which was the s' of Joanna,
27 which was the s' of Rhesa,
27 which was the s' of Zorobabel,
27 which was the s' of Salathiel,
27 which was the s' of Neri,
28 Which was the s' of Melchi,
Lu 3:28 which was the s' of Addi,
28 which was the s' of Cosam,
28 which was the s' of Elmodam,
28 which was the s' of Er,
29 Which was the s' of Jose,
29 which was the s' of Eliezer,
29 which was the s' of Jorim,
29 which was the s' of Matthat,
29 which was the s' of Levi,
30 Which was the s' of Simeon,
30 which was the s' of Juda,
30 which was the s' of Joseph,
30 which was the s' of Jonan,
30 which was the s' of Eliakim,
31 Which was the s' of Melea,
31 which was the s' of Menan,
31 which was the s' of Mattatha,
31 which was the s' of Nathan,
31 which was the s' of David,
32 Which was the s' of Jesse,
32 which was the s' of Obed,
32 which was the s' of Booz,
32 which was the s' of Salmon,
32 which was the s' of Naasson,
33 Which was the s' of Aminadab,
33 which was the s' of Aram,
33 which was the s' of Esrom,
33 which was the s' of Phares,
33 which was the s' of Juda,
34 Which was the s' of Jacob,
34 which was the s' of Isaac,
34 which was the s' of Abraham,
34 which was the s' of Thara,
34 which was the s' of Nachor,
35 Which was the s' of Saruch,
35 which was the s' of Ragau,
35 which was the s' of Phalec,
35 which was the s' of Heber,
35 which was the s' of Sala,
36 Which was the s' of Cainan,
36 which was the s' of Arphaxad,
36 which was the s' of Sem,
36 which was the s' of Noe,
36 which was the s' of Lamech,
37 Which was the s' of Mathusala,
37 which was the s' of Enoch,
37 which was the s' of Jared,
37 which was the s' of Maleleel,
37 which was the s' of Cainan,
38 Which was the s' of Enos,
38 which was the s' of Seth,
38 which was the s' of Adam,
38 which was the s' of God.
4: 3 If thou be the S' of God, command
9 If thou be the S' of God, cast
22 they said, Is not this Joseph's s'?
41 Thou art Christ the S' of God.
5:24 S' of man hath power upon earth
6: 5 S' of man is Lord...of the sabbath.
15 James the s' of Alphæus, and Simon
22 as evil, for the S' of man's sake.
7:12 the only s' of his mother, and she
34 The S' of man is come eating and
8:28 Jesus, thou S' of God most high?
9:22 S' of man must suffer many things,
26 shall the S' of man be ashamed,
35 This is my beloved S': hear him.
38 I beseech thee, look upon my s':
41 suffer you? Bring thy s' hither.
44 S' of man shall be delivered into
56 S' of man is not come to destroy
58 the S' of man hath not where to lay
10: 6 and if the s' of peace be there, your
22 no man knoweth who the S' is, but
22 and who the Father is, but the S',
22 and he to whom the S' will reveal
11:11 If a s' shall ask bread of any of you
30 the S' of man be to this generation.
12: 8 shall the S' of man also confess
10 speak a word against the S' of man,
40 S' of man cometh at an hour when
53 shall be divided against the s',
53 and the s' against the father; the
15:13 younger s' gathered all together,
19 no more worthy to be called thy s':
21 And the s' said unto him, Father, I
21 no more worthy to be called thy s'.
24 For this my s' was dead, and is
25 Now his elder s' was in the field:
30 But as soon as this thy s' was come,
31 S', thou art ever with me, and all
16:25 S', remember that thou in thy
17:22 one of the days of the S' of man,
24 also the S' of man be in his day.
26 be also in the days of the S' of man.
30 day when the S' of man is revealed.
18: 8 when the S' of man cometh, shall he
31 prophets concerning the S' of man
38, 39 s' of David, have mercy on me.
19: 9 as he also is a s' of Abraham.
10 For the S' of man is come to seek
20:13 I will send my beloved s': it may be
41 say they that Christ is David's s'?
44 him Lord, how is he then his s'?
21:27 see the S' of man coming in a cloud
36 and to stand before the S' of man.
22:22 And truly the S' of man goeth, as it
48 betrayest thou the S' of man with a
69 the S' of man sit on the right hand
70 all, Art thou then the S' of God?
24: 7 S' of man must be delivered into
Joh 1:18 the only begotten S', which is in
34 record that this is the S' of God.
42 Thou art Simon the s' of Jona:
45 Jesus of Nazareth, the s' of Joseph.
49 Rabbi, thou art the S' of God;
Joh 1:51 descending upon the S' of man.
3:13 the S' of man which is in heaven.
14 so must the S' of man be lifted up:
16 that he gave his only begotten S',
17 God sent not his S' into the world
18 name of the only begotten S' of God.
35 The Father loveth the S', and hath
36 He that believeth on the S' hath
36 and he that believeth not the S'
4: 5 that Jacob gave to his s' Joseph.
46 whose s' was sick at Capernaum.
47 would come down, and heal his s':
50 unto him, Go thy way; thy s' liveth.
51 told him, saying, Thy s' liveth.
53 Jesus said unto him, Thy s' liveth:
5:19 The S' can do nothing of himself,
19 these also doeth the S' likewise.
20 For the Father loveth the S', and
21 so the S' quickeneth whom he will.
22 committed all judgment unto the S':
23 That all men should honour the S',
23 He that honoureth not the S'
25 shall hear the voice of the S' of God:
26 hath he given to the S' to have life
27 also, because he is the S' of man.
6:27 which the S' of man shall give unto
40 that every one which seeth the S',
42 Is not this Jesus, the s' of Joseph,
53 ye eat the flesh of the S' of man,
62 shall see the S' of man ascend up
69 art that Christ, the S' of the living
71 of Judas Iscariot the s' of Simon:
8:28 ye have lifted up the S' of man,
35 for ever: but the S' abideth ever.
36 S' therefore shall make you free, ye
9:19 Is this your s', who ye say was born
20 We know that this is our s', and
35 Dost thou believe on the S' of God?
10:36 because I said, I am the S' of God?
11: 4 the S' of God might be glorified
27 thou art the Christ, the S' of God,
12: 4 Simon's s', which should betray him,
23 the S' of man should be glorified.
34 The S' of man must be lifted up?
34 lifted up? who is this S' of man?
13: 2 Iscariot, Simon's s', to betray him;
26 it to Judas Iscariot, the s' of Simon.
31 Now is the S' of man glorified,
14:13 Father may be glorified in the S'.
17: 1 the hour is come; glorify thy S',
1 that thy S' also may glorify thee:
12 them is lost, but the s' of perdition;
19: 7 he made himself the S' of God.
26 his mother, Woman, behold thy s'!
20:31 Jesus is the Christ, the S' of God;
21:15 s' of Jonas, lovest thou me more than
16, 17 Simon, s' of Jonas, lovest thou me?
Ac 1:13 James the s' of Alphæus, and Simon
3:13 fathers,...glorified his S' Jesus;
26 having raised up his S' Jesus, sent
4:36 interpreted, The s' of consolation,)
7:21 and nourished him for her own s'.
56 the S' of man standing on the right
8:37 that Jesus Christ is the S' of God.
9:20 that he is the S' of God.
13:21 gave unto them Saul the s' of Cis,
22 I have found David the s' of Jesse,
33 Thou art my S', this day have I
16: 1 Timotheus,...s' of a certain woman,
23: 6 am a Pharisee, the s' of a Pharisee:
16 And when Paul's sister's s' heard of
Ro 1: 3 his S' Jesus Christ our Lord,
4 declared to be the S' of God with
9 my spirit in the gospel of his S',
5:10 reconciled...by the death of his S',
8: 3 sending his own S' in the likeness
29 be conformed to the image of his S',
32 He that spared not his own S', but
9: 9 I come, and Sarah shall have a s'.
1Co 1: 9 of his S' Jesus Christ our Lord.
4:17 Timotheus, who is my beloved s',
15:28 the S' also himself be subject unto
2Co 1:19 For the S' of God, Jesus Christ,
Ga 1:16 To reveal his S' in me, that I might
2:20 I live by the faith of the S' of God,
4: 4 God sent forth his S', made of a
6 the Spirit of his S' into your hearts,
7 art no more a servant, but a s';
7 if a s', then an heir of God through
30 Cast out the bondwoman and her s':
30 s' of the bondwoman shall not be
30 heir with the s' of the freewoman.
Eph 4:13 of the knowledge of the S' of God,
Ph'p 2:22 him, that, as a s' with the father,
Col 1:13 into the kingdom of his dear S':
4:10 Marcus, sister's s' to Barnabas,
1Th 1:10 to wait for his S' from heaven,
2Th 2: 3 be revealed, the s' of perdition;
1Ti 1: 2 Timothy, my own s' in the faith:
18 I commit unto thee, s' Timothy,
2Ti 1: 2 To Timothy, my dearly beloved s':
2: 1 my s', be strong in the grace that
Tit 1: 4 To Titus, mine own s' after the
Ph'm 10 I beseech thee for my s' Onesimus,
Heb 1: 2 last days spoken unto us by his S',
5 Thou art my S', this day have I
5 Father, and he shall be to me a S'?
8 unto the S' he saith, Thy throne,
2: 6 the s' of man, that thou visitest him?
3: 6 Christ as a s' over his own house;
4:14 the heavens, Jesus the S' of God,
5: 5 him, Thou art my S', to day have I
8 Though he were a S', yet learned he
6: 6 they crucify...the S' of God afresh,
7: 3 but made like unto the S' of God;
28 maketh the S', who is consecrated

Heb10: 29 trodden under foot the S' of God,
11: 17 offered up his only begotten s',
24 the s' of Pharaoh's daughter;
12: 5 My s', despise not...the chastening
6 and scourgeth every s' whom he
7 s' is he whom the father chasteneth
Jas 2: 21 offered Isaac his s' upon the altar?
1Pe 5: 13 you; and so doth Marcus my s'.
2Pe 1: 17 This is my beloved S', in whom I am
2: 15 the way of Balaam the s' of Bosor,
1Jo 1: 3 and with his S' Jesus Christ.
7 the blood of Jesus Christ his S'
2: 22 that denieth the Father and the S'.
23 Whosoever denieth the S', the same
23 he that acknowledgeth the S' hath
24 ye also shall continue in the S',
3: 8 For this purpose the S' of God was
23 believe on the name of his S' Jesus
4: 9 God sent his only begotten S' into
10 his S' to be the propitiation for our
14 S' to be the Saviour of the world.
15 confess that Jesus is the S' of God,
5: 5 believeth that Jesus is the S' of God?
9 which he hath testified of his S'.
10 He that believeth on the S' of God
10 the record that God gave of his S'.
11 life, and this life is in his S'.
12 He that hath the S' hath life; and
12 hath not the S' of God hath not life.
13 on the name of the S' of God;
13 on the name of the S' of God.
20 we know that the S' of God is come,
20 is true, even in his S' Jesus Christ.
2Jo 3 Jesus Christ, the S' of the Father,
9 he hath both the Father and the S'.
Re 1: 13 one like unto the S' of man,
2: 18 These things saith the S' of God,
14: 14 one sat like unto the S' of man,
21: 7 be his God, and he shall be my s'.

song^ See also SONGS.
Ex 15: 1 of Israel this s' unto the Lord,
2 The Lord is my strength and s',
Nu 21: 17 Israel sang this s', Spring up, O
De 31: 19 therefore write ye this s' for you,
19 that this s' may be a witness for me
21 this s' shall testify against them as
22 Moses therefore wrote this s' the
30 of Israel the words of this s',
32: 44 and spake all the words of this s' in
J'g 5: 12 Deborah: awake, awake, utter a s':
2Sa 22: 1 unto the Lord the words of this s'
1Ch 6: 31 David set over the service of s'
15: 22 chief of the Levites, was for s':
22 he instructed about the s', because
27 Chenaniah the master of the s' with
25: 6 the hands of their father for s' in
2Ch 29: 27 s' of the Lord began also with the
Job 30: 9 And now am I their s', yea, I am
Ps 18: *title* unto the Lord...words of this s'
28: 7 and with my s' will I praise him.
30: *title* A Psalm and S' at the dedication
33: 3 Sing unto him a new s'; play
40: 3 he hath put a new s' in my mouth,
42: 8 in the night his s' shall be with me,
45: *title* of Korah, Maschil, A S' of loves.
46: *title* of Korah, A S' upon Alamoth.
48: *title* A S' and Psalm for the sons of
65: *title* A Psalm and S' of David.
66: *title* the chief Musician, A S' or Psalm.
67: *title* on Neginoth, A Psalm or S'.
68: *title* Musician, A Psalm or S' of David.
69: 12 and I was the s' of the drunkards.
30 praise the name of God with a s',
75: *title* A Psalm or S' of Asaph.
76: *title* A Psalm or S' of Asaph.
77: 6 I call to remembrance my s' in the
83: *title* A S' or Psalm of Asaph.
87: *title* Psalm or S' for the sons of Korah.
88: *title* S' or Psalm for the sons of Korah,
92: *title* A Psalm or S' for the sabbath day.
96: 1 O sing unto the Lord a new s':
98: 1 O sing unto the Lord a new s'; for
108: *title* A S' or Psalm of David.
118: 14 The Lord is my strength and s',
120: *title* A S' of degrees.
121: *title* A S' of degrees.
122: *title* A S' of degrees of David.
123: *title* A S' of degrees.
124: *title* A S' of degrees of David.
125: *title* A S' of degrees.
126: *title* A S' of degrees.
127: *title* A S' of degrees for Solomon.
128: *title* A S' of degrees.
129: *title* A S' of degrees.
130: *title* A S' of degrees.
131: *title* A S' of degrees of David.
132: *title* A S' of degrees.
133: *title* A S' of degrees of David.
134: *title* A S' of degrees.
137: 3 captive required of us a s';
4 How shall we sing the Lord's s' in a
144: 9 I will sing a new s' unto thee, O
149: 1 Sing unto the Lord a new s', and
Ec 7: 5 for a man to hear the s' of fools.
Ca 1: 1 The s' of songs, which is Solomon's.
Isa 5: 1 will sing to my wellbeloved a s'
12: 2 Jehovah is my strength and my s';
24: 9 shall not drink wine with a s';
26: 1 this s' be sung in the land of Judah;
30: 29 Ye shall have a s', as in the night
42: 10 Sing unto the Lord a new s', and
La 3: 14 my people; and their s' all the day.
Eze 33: 32 art unto them as a very lovely s'
Re 5: 9 And they sung a new s', saying,
14: 3 And they sung as it were a new s'
3 no man could learn that s' but the
Re 15: 3 And they sing the s' of Moses the
3 and the s' of the Lamb, saying,

songs
Ge 31: 27 thee away with mirth, and with s',
1Ki 4: 32 and his s' were a thousand and five.
1Ch 25: 7 instructed in the s' of the Lord,
Ne 12: 46 s' of praise and thanksgiving unto
Job 35: 10 maker, who giveth s' in the night;
Ps 32: 7 me about with s' of deliverance.
119: 54 Thy statutes have been my s' in
137: 3 Sing us one of the s' of Zion.
Pr 25: 20 he that singeth s' to an heavy heart.
Ca 1: 1 The song of s', which is Solomon's.
Isa 23: 16 make sweet melody, sing many s',
24: 16 part of the earth have we heard s',
35: 10 to Zion with s' and everlasting
38: 20 we will sing my s' to the stringed
Eze 26: 13 cause the noise of thy s' to cease;
Am 5: 23 away from me the noise of thy s';
8: 3 And the s' of the temple shall be
10 and all your s' into lamentation;
Eph 5: 19 psalms and hymns and spiritual s',
Col 3: 16 psalms and hymns and spiritual s',

son-in-law See SON and LAW.

son's
Ge 11: 31 Lot the son of Haran his s' son,
16: 15 Abram called his s' name, which
21: 23 with my son, nor with my s' son:
24: 51 let her be thy master's s' wife, as
27: 25 me, and I will eat of my s' venison,
31 arise, and eat of his s' venison,
30: 14 Give me,...of thy s' mandrakes.
15 take away my s' mandrakes also?
15 thee to night for thy s' mandrakes.
16 hired thee with my s' mandrakes.
37: 32 now whether it be thy s' coat or no.
33 knew it, and said, It is my s' coat;
Ex 10: 2 ears of thy son, and of thy s' son,
Le 18: 10 The nakedness of thy s' daughter,
15 she is thy s' wife; thou shalt not
17 shalt thou take her s' daughter,
De 6: 2 thou, and thy son, and thy s' son,
J'g 8: 22 and thy son, and thy s' son also:
1Ki 11: 35 the kingdom out of his s' hand,
21: 29 in his s' days will I bring the evil
Pr 30: 4 his name, and what is his s' name,
Jer 27: 7 him, and his son, and his s' son,

sons^ See also SONS'.
Ge 5: 4, 7, 10, 13, 16, 19, 22, 26, 30 begat s' and
6: 2 the s' of God saw the daughters of
4 the s' of God came in unto the
10 Noah begat three s', Shem, Ham,
18 come into the ark, thou, and thy s',
7: 7 Noah went in, and his s', and his
13 Ham, and Japheth, the s' of Noah,
13 three wives of his s' with them,
8: 16 ark, thou, and thy wife, and thy s',
18 Noah went forth, and his s', and his
9: 1 God blessed Noah and his s', and
8 unto Noah, and to his s' with him,
18 the s' of Noah, that went forth of
19 These are the three s' of Noah: and
10: 1 the generations of the s' of Noah;
1 unto them were s' born after the
2 The s' of Japheth; Gomer, and
3 the s' of Gomer; Ashkenaz, and
4 And the s' of Javan; Elishah, and
6 the s' of Ham; Cush, and Mizraim,
7 the s' of Cush; Seba, and Havilah,
7 and the s' of Raamah; Sheba, and
20 These are the s' of Ham, after their
25 unto Eber were born two s': the
29 all these were the s' of Joktan.
31 These are the s' of Shem, after
32 are the families of the s' of Noah,
11: 11, 13, 15, 17, 19, 21, 23, 25 begat s' and
19: 12 son in law, and thy s', and thy
14 out, and spake unto his s' in law,
14 one that mocked unto his s' in law.
23: 3 and spake unto the s' of Heth,
11 the presence of the s' of my people
16 in the audience of the s' of Heth,
20 of a buryingplace by the s' of Heth.
25: 3 the s' of Dedan were Asshurim, and
4 And the s' of Midian; Ephah, and
6 But unto the s' of the concubines,
9 his s' Isaac and Ishmael buried
10 purchased of the s' of Heth: there
13 are the names of the s' of Ishmael,
16 These are the s' of Ishmael, and
27: 29 thy mother's s' bow down to thee:
29: 34 because I have born him three s':
30: 20 me, because I have born him six s':
35 gave them into the hand of his s'.
31: 1 he heard the word's of Laban's s',
17 his s' and his wives upon camels;
28 not suffered me to kiss my s' and
55 kissed his s' and his daughters,
32: 22 womenservants, and his eleven s',
34: 5 now his s' were with his cattle in
7 s' of Jacob came out of the field
13 s' of Jacob answered Shechem and
25 two of the s' of Jacob, Simeon and
27 s' of Jacob came upon the slain,
35: 5 did not pursue after the s' of Jacob.
22 Now the s' of Jacob were twelve:
23 The s' of Leah; Reuben, Jacob's
24 And the s' of Rachel; Joseph and
25 s' of Bilhah, Rachel's handmaid;
26 the s' of Zilpah, Leah's handmaid,
26 these are the s' of Jacob, which
29 his s' Esau and Jacob buried him.
36: 5 these are the s' of Esau, which were
6 Esau took his wives, and his s', and
Ge 36: 10 These are the names of Esau's s';
11 s' of Eliphaz were Teman, Omar,
12 were the s' of Adah Esau's wife.
13 are the s' of Reuel; Nahath, and
13 the s' of Bashemath Esau's wife.
14 the s' of Aholibamah, the daughter
15 These were dukes of the s' of Esau:
15 s' of Eliphaz the firstborn son of
16 Edom; these were the s' of Adah.
17 are the s' of Reuel Esau's son;
17 the s' of Bashemath Esau's wife.
18 the s' of Aholibamah Esau's wife;
19 the s' of Esau, who is Edom, and
20 These are the s' of Seir the Horite,
37: 2 the lad was with the s' of Bilhah,
2 with the s' of Zilpah, his father's
35 his s' and all his daughters rose up
41: 50 And unto Joseph were born two s'
42: 1 Jacob said unto his s', Why do ye
5 the s' of Israel came to buy corn
11 We are all one man's s'; we are
13 the s' of one man in the land of
32 twelve brethren, s' of our father:
37 Slay my two s', if I bring him not
44: 27 know that my wife bare me two s':
46: 5 s' of Israel carried Jacob their
7 His s', and his sons' s' with him,
8 came into Egypt, Jacob and his s':
9 s' of Reuben; Hanoch, and Phallu,
10 s' of Simeon; Jemuel, and Jamin,
11 the s' of Levi; Gershon, Kohath,
12 the s' of Judah; Er, and Onan,
12 the s' of Pharez were Hezron and
13 And the s' of Issachar; Tolah, and
14 the s' of Zebulun; Sered, and Elon,
15 These be the s' of Leah, which she
15 the souls of his s' and his daughters
16 the s' of Gad; Ziphion, and Haggi,
17 And the s' of Asher; Jimnah, and
17 and the s' of Beriah; Heber, and
18 These are the s' of Zilpah, whom
19 The s' of Rachel Jacob's wife;
21 And the s' of Benjamin were Belah,
22 These are the s' of Rachel, which
23 And the s' of Dan; Hushim.
24 s' of Naphtali; Jahzeel, and Guni,
25 These are the s' of Bilhah, which
27 the s' of Joseph, which were born
48: 1 and he took with him his two s',
5 thy two s', Ephraim and Manasseh,
8 Israel beheld Joseph's s', and said,
9 They are my s', whom God hath
49: 1 Jacob called unto his s', and said,
2 together, and hear, ye s' of Jacob;
33 made an end of commanding his s',
50: 12 his s' did unto him according as he
13 his s' carried him into the land of
Ex 3: 22 and ye shall put them upon your s',
4: 20 And Moses took his wife and his s',
6: 14 The s' of Reuben the firstborn of
15 And the s' of Simeon; Jemuel, and
16 are the names of the s' of Levi
17 s' of Gershon; Libni, and Shimi,
18 And the s' of Kohath; Amram, and
19 And the s' of Merari; Mahali, and
21 And the s' of Izhar; Korah, and
22 And the s' of Uzziel; Mishael, and
24 And the s' of Korah; Assir, and
10: 9 with our s' and with our daughters,
12: 24 to thee and to thy s' for ever.
18: 3 her two s'; of which the name of
5 came with his s' and his wife unto
6 thy wife, and her two s' with her.
21: 4 she have born him s' or daughters;
22: 29 firstborn of thy s' shalt thou give
27: 21 Aaron and his s' shall order it
28: 1 thy brother, and his s' with him,
1 Eleazar and Ithamar, Aaron's s'.
4 for Aaron thy brother, and his s',
40 Aaron's s' thou shalt make coats,
41 thy brother, and his s' with him;
43 be upon Aaron, and upon his s',
29: 4 Aaron and his s' thou shalt bring
8 shalt bring his s', and put coats
9 with girdles, Aaron and his s', and
9 shalt consecrate Aaron and his s',
10, 15, 19 Aaron and his s' shall put
20 the tip of the right ear of his s',
21 upon his garments, and upon his s',
21 upon the garments of his s' with
21 and his garments and his s', and
24 Aaron, and in the hands of his s';
27 and of that which is for his s':
32 Aaron and his s' shall eat the flesh
35 thou do unto Aaron, and to his s',
44 sanctify also both Aaron and his s',
30: 19 Aaron and his s' shall wash their
30 thou shalt anoint Aaron and his s',
31: 10 the garments of his s', to minister
32: 2 the ears of your wives, of your s',
26 the s' of Levi gathered themselves
34: 16 take of their daughters unto thy s',
16 and make thy s' go a whoring after
20 All the firstborn of thy s' thou
35: 19 the garments of his s', to minister
39: 27 work for Aaron, and for his s',
40: 12 thou shalt bring Aaron and his s'
14 thou shalt bring his s', and clothe
31 Moses and Aaron and his s' washed
Le 1: 5 Aaron's s', shall bring the blood,
7 s' of Aaron the priest shall put fire
8 Aaron's s', shall lay the parts, the
11 Aaron's s', shall sprinkle his blood
2: 2 And he shall bring it to Aaron's s'
3: 2 Aaron's s' the priests shall sprinkle
5 And Aaron's s' shall burn it on the

Le 3: 8 Aaron's s' shall sprinkle the blood
13 and the s' of Aaron shall sprinkle
6: 9 Command Aaron and his s', saying,
14 the s' of Aaron shall offer it before
16 thereof shall Aaron and his s' eat:
20 the offering of Aaron and of his s',
22 priest of his s' that is anointed in
25 Speak unto Aaron and to his s',
7: 10 shall all the s' of Aaron have, one
33 He among the s' of Aaron, that
34 Aaron the priest and unto his s' by
35 of the anointing of his s', out of
8: 2 Take Aaron and his s' with him,
6 Moses brought Aaron and his s',
13 Moses brought Aaron's s', and put
14, 18, 22 Aaron and his s' laid their
24 he brought Aaron's s', and Moses
30 his garments, and upon his s', and
30 and his s', and his sons' garments
31 said unto Aaron and to his s',
31 saying, Aaron and his s' shall eat it.
36 So Aaron and his s' did all things
9: 1 that Moses called Aaron and his s',
9 the s' of Aaron brought the blood
12, 18 Aaron's s' presented unto him
10: 1 Nadab and Abihu, the s' of Aaron,
4 the s' of Uzziel the uncle of Aaron,
6 Eleazar and unto Ithamar, his s',
9 drink,thou, nor thy s' with thee,
12 unto Ithamar, his s' that were left,
14 thy s', and thy daughters with thee:
16 the s' of Aaron which were left
18: 2 or unto one of his s' the priests:
16: 1 the death of the two s' of Aaron,
17: 2 Speak unto Aaron, and unto his s',
21: 1 unto the priests the s' of Aaron,
24 told it unto Aaron, and to his s',
22: 2 Speak unto Aaron, and to his s',
18 Speak unto Aaron, and to his s',
26: 29 And ye shall eat the flesh of your s',
Nu 2: 14 and the captain of the s' of Gad
18 the captain of the s' of Ephraim
22 the captain of the s' of Benjamin
3: 2 are the names of the s' of Aaron;
3 are the names of the s' of Aaron,
9 the Levites unto Aaron and to his s':
10 thou shalt appoint Aaron and his s',
17 were the s' of Levi by their names;
18 are the names of the s' of Gershon
19 the s' of Kohath by their families;
20 the s' of Merari by their families;
25 the charge of the s' of Gershon in
29 The families of the s' of Kohath
36 charge of the s' of Merari shall be
38 and Aaron and his s', keeping the
48 redeemed, unto Aaron and to his s'.
51 redeemed unto Aaron and to his s',
4: 2 Take the sum of the s' of Kohath
2 from among the s' of Levi, after
4 be the service of the s' of Kohath
5 Aaron shall come, and his s', and
15 when Aaron and his s' have made
15 s' of Kohath shall come to bear it:
15 are the burden of the s' of Kohath
19 Aaron and his s' shall go in, and
22 also the sum of the s' of Gershon,
27 appointment of Aaron and his s'
27 service of the s' of the Gershonites,
28 the families of the s' of Gershon
29 As for the s' of Merari, thou shalt
33 of the families of the s' of Merari,
34 numbered the s' of the Kohathites
38 numbered of the s' of Gershon,
41 the families of the s' of Gershon,
42, 45 the families of the s' of Merari,
6: 23 Speak unto Aaron and unto his s',
7: 7 he gave unto the s' of Gershon,
8 oxen he gave unto the s' of Merari,
9 unto the s' of Kohath he gave none:
8: 13 before Aaron, and before his s',
19 as a gift to Aaron and to his s'
22 before Aaron, and before his s': as
10: 8 And the s' of Aaron, the priests,
17 s' of Gershon and the s' of Merari
13: 33 we saw the giants, the s' of Anak,
16: 1 and Abiram, the s' of Eliab,
1 of Peleth, s' of Reuben, took men:
7 too much upon you, ye s' of Levi.
8 Hear, I pray you, ye s' of Levi:
10 all thy brethren the s' of Levi with
12 and Abiram, the s' of Eliab: which
27 wives, and their s', and their little
18: 1 Thou and thy s' and thy father's
1 s' with thee shall bear the iniquity
2 and thy s' with thee shall minister
7 thy s' with thee shall keep your
8 to thy s', by an ordinance for ever.
9 most holy for thee and for thy s'.
11 to thy s' and to thy daughters with
19 thy s' and thy daughters with thee,
21: 29 he hath given his s' that escaped,
35 So they smote him, and his s', and
26: 8 And the s' of Pallu; Eliab.
9 the s' of Eliab; Nemuel and Dathan,
12 s' of Simeon after their families:
19 The s' of Judah were Er and Onan:
20 the s' of Judah after their families
21 the s' of Pharez were; of Hezron,
23 s' of Issachar after their families:
26 s' of Zebulun after their families:
28 The s' of Joseph after their families
29 Of the s' of Manasseh: of Machir,
30 These are the s' of Gilead: of
33 the son of Hepher had no s', but
35 s' of Ephraim after their families:
36 And these are the s' of Shuthelah:
Nu 26: 37 the families of the s' of Ephraim
37 the s' of Joseph after their families.
38 s' of Benjamin after their families:
40 s' of Bela were Ard and Naaman:
41 s' of Benjamin after their families:
42 the s' of Dan after their families:
45 Of the s' of Beriah: of Heber, the
47 are the families of the s' of Asher
48 s' of Naphtali after their families:
27: 3 died in his own sin, and had no s'.
36: 1 of the families of the s' of Joseph,
3 to any of the s' of the other tribes
5 tribe of the s' of Joseph hath said
11 unto their father's brothers' s':
12 the families of the s' of Manasseh
De 1: 28 we have seen the s' of the Anakims
2: 33 we smote him, and his s', and all
4: 9 teach them thy s', and thy sons' s';
11: 6 Dathan and Abiram, the s' of Eliab,
12: 12 ye, and your s', and your daughters,
31 even their s' and their daughters
18: 5 of the Lord, him and his s' for ever.
21: 5 the priests the s' of Levi shall come
16 maketh his s' to inherit that which
23: 17 nor a sodomite of the s' of Israel.
28: 32 s' and thy daughters shall be given
53 flesh of thy s' and of thy daughters,
31: 9 it unto the priests the s' of Levi,
32: 8 when he separated the s' of Adam,
19 because of the provoking of his s',
Jos 7: 24 wedge of gold, and his s', and his
15: 14 drove thence the three s' of Anak,
17: 3 the son of Manasseh, had no s', but
6 had an inheritance among his s':
6 rest of Manasseh's s' had the land
24: 32 Jacob bought of the s' of Hamor
J'g 1: 20 expelled thence...three s' of Anak.
3: 6 gave their daughters to their s',
8: 19 brethren, even the s' of my mother:
30 Gideon had threescore and ten s'
9: 2 either that all the s' of Jerubbaal,
5 his brethren the s' of Jerubbaal,
18 have slain his s', threescore and ten
24 threescore and ten s' of Jerubbaal
10: 4 he had thirty s' that rode on thirty
11: 2 Gilead's wife bare him s'; and his
2 wife's s' grew up, and they thrust
12: 9 had thirty s', and thirty daughters,
9 daughters from abroad for his s'.
14 he had forty s' and thirty nephews,
17: 5 and consecrated one of his s', who
11 man was unto him as one of his s'.
18: 30 he and his s' were priests to the
19: 22 certain s' of Belial, beset the house
Ru 1: 1 Moab,he,and his wife, and his two s'.
2 the name of his two s' Mahlon and
3 and she was left, and her two s'.
5 left of her two s' and her husband.
11 there yet any more s' in my womb,
12 to night, and should also bear s';
4: 15 which is better to thee than seven s'.
1Sa 1: 3 two s' of Eli, Hophni and Phinehas,
4 her s' and her daughters, portions:
8 am not I better to thee than ten s'?
2: 12 Now the s' of Eli were s' of Belial;
21 she conceived, and bare three s' and
22 all that his s' did unto all Israel;
24 Nay, my s'; for it is no good report
29 and honourest thy s' above me, to
34 thy two s', Hophni and Phinehas,
3: 13 because his s' made themselves vile,
4: 4, 11 s' of Eli, Hophni and Phinehas,
17 two s' also, Hophni and Phinehas,
8: 1 he made his s' judges over Israel.
3 his s' walked not in his ways, but
5 and thy s' walk not in thy ways:
11 He will take your s', and appoint
12: 2 and, behold, my s' are with you:
14: 49 s' of Saul were Jonathan, and Ishui,
16: 1 provided me a king among his s'.
5 And he sanctified Jesse and his s',
10 Jesse made seven of his s' to pass
17: 12 was Jesse; and he had eight s':
13 eldest s' of Jesse...followed Saul
13 names of his three s' that went to
22: 20 one of the s' of Ahimelech the son
28: 19 shalt thou and thy s' be with me:
30: 3 and their s' and their daughters,
6 every man for his s' and for his
19 nor great, neither s' nor daughters,
31: 2 hard upon Saul and upon his s';
2 and Melchi-shua, Saul's s'.
6 So Saul died, and his three s', and
7 and that Saul and his s' were dead,
8 found Saul and his three s' fallen in
12 body of Saul and the bodies of his s'
2Sa 2: 18 there were three s' of Zeruiah there
3: 2 unto David were s' born in Hebron:
39 s' of Zeruiah be too hard for me:
4: 2 the s' of Rimmon a Beerothite,
5, 9 the s' of Rimmon the Beerothite,
5: 13 yet s' and daughters born to David.
6: 3 Uzzah and Ahio, the s' of Abinadab,
8: 18 and David's s' were chief rulers.
9: 10 Thou...and thy s', and thy servants,
10 had fifteen s' and twenty servants.
11 at my table, as one of the king's s'.
13: 23 Absalom invited all the king's s'.
27 and all the king's s' go with him.
29 Then all the king's s' arose, and
30 Absalom hath slain all the king's s',
32 slain...the young men the king's s';
33 think that all the king's s' are dead:
35 king, Behold, the king's s' come:
36 the king's s' came, and lifted up
14: 6 thy handmaid had two s', and they
2Sa 14: 27 Absalom there were born three s',
15: 27 in peace, and your two s' with you,
36 have there with them their two s',
16: 10 I to do with you, ye s' of Zeruiah?
19: 5 lives of thy s' and of thy daughters,
17 fifteen s' and his twenty servants
22 I to do with you, ye s' of Zeruiah,
21: 6 Let seven men of his s' be delivered
8 the king took the two s' of Rizpah
8 five s' of Michal...daughter of Saul,
16 which was of the s' of the giant,
18 which was of the s' of the giant.
23: 6 the s' of Belial shall be all of them as
32 of the s' of Jashen, Jonathan,
1Ki 1: 9 called all his brethren the king's s',
19 and hath called all the s' of the king,
25 and hath called all the king's s',
2: 7 kindness unto the s' of Barzillai
4: 3 Ahiah, the s' of Shisha, scribes;
31 and Darda, the s' of Mahol: and
11: 20 household among the s' of Pharaoh.
12: 31 which were not of the s' of Levi.
13: 11 and his s' came and told him all
12 his s' had seen what way the man
13 And he said unto his s', saddle me
27 he spake to his s', saying, Saddle
31 he spake to his s', saying, When I
18: 31 of the tribes of the s' of Jacob,
20: 35 man of the s' of the prophets said
21: 10 set two men, s' of Belial, before
2Ki 2: 3, 5 the s' of the prophets that were
7 men of the s' of the prophets went,
15 when the s' of the prophets which
4: 1 wives of the s' of the prophets unto
1 come to take unto him my two s'
4 door upon thee and upon thy s',
5 the door upon her and upon her s',
38 the s' of the prophets were sitting
38 pottage for the s' of the prophets.
5: 22 men of the s' of the prophets: give
6: 1 s' of the prophets said unto Elisha,
9: 26 of Naboth, and the blood of his s',
10: 1 Ahab had seventy s' in Samaria.
2 seeing your master's s' are with
3 and meetest of your master's s',
6 heads of the men your master's s',
6 Now the king's s', being seventy
7 that they took the king's s', and
8 brought the heads of the king's s'.
11: 2 and stole from among the king's s'
15: 12 Thy s' shall sit on the throne of
17: 17 caused their s' and their daughters
19: 37 and Sharezer his s' smote him with
20: 18 of thy s' that shall issue from thee,
25: 7 they slew the s' of Zedekiah before
1Ch 1: 5 s' of Japheth; Gomer, and Magog,
6 the s' of Gomer; Ashchenaz, and
7 s' of Javan; Elishah, and Tarshish,
8 The s' of Ham; Cush, and Mizraim,
9 s' of Cush; Seba, and Havilah, and
9 And the s' of Raamah; Sheba, and
17 s' of Shem; Elam, and Asshur, and
19 And unto Eber were born two s':
23 All these were the s' of Joktan.
28 The s' of Abraham; Isaac, and
31 These are the s' of Ishmael.
32 Now the s' of Keturah, Abraham's
32 s' of Jokshan; Sheba, and Dedan.
33 s' of Midian; Ephah, and Epher,
33 All these are the s' of Keturah.
34 The s' of Isaac; Esau and Israel.
35 The s' of Esau; Eliphaz, Reuel, and
36 s' of Eliphaz; Teman, and Omar,
37 The s' of Reuel; Nahath, Zerah,
38 s' of Seir; Lotan, and Shobal, and
39 the s' of Lotan; Hori, and Homam:
40 s' of Shobal; Alian, and Manahath,
40 the s' of Zibeon; Aiah, and Anah.
41 The s' of Anah; Dishon. And the
41 s' of Dishon; Amram, and Eshban,
42 The s' of Ezer; Bilhan, and Zavan,
42 The s' of Dishan; Uz, and Aran.
2: 1 These are the s' of Israel; Reuben,
3 The s' of Judah; Er, and Onan,
4 Zerah. All the s' of Judah were five.
5 s' of Pharez; Hezron, and Hamul.
6 the s' of Zerah; Timri, and Ethan;
7 s' of Carmi; Achar, the troubler of
8 And the s' of Ethan; Azariah.
9 s' also of Hezron, that were born
16 s' of Zeruiah; Abishai, and Joab,
18 her s' are these; Jesher, and
23 these belonged to the s' of Machir
25 the s' of Jerahmeel the firstborn of
27 And the s' of Ram the firstborn of
28 s' of Onam were, Shammai, and
28 the s' of Shammai; Nadab, and
30 s' of Nadab; Seled, and Appaim:
31 And the s' of Appaim; Ishi.
31 the s' of Ishi; Sheshan. And the
32 s' of Jada the brother of Shammai;
33 s' of Jonathan; Peleth, and Zaza.
33 These were the s' of Jerahmeel.
34 Sheshan had no s', but daughters.
42 Now the s' of Caleb the brother of
42 the s' of Mareshah the father of
43 s' of Hebron; Korah, and Tappuah,
47 s' of Jahdai; Regem, and Jotham,
50 These were the s' of Caleb the son
52 the father of Kirjath-jearim had s':
54 The s' of Salma; Beth-lehem, and
3: 1 Now these were the s' of David,
9 These were all the s' of David,
9 beside the s' of the concubines, and
15 the s' of Josiah were, the firstborn
16 s' of Jehoiakim; Jeconiah his son,

1Ch 3:17 s' of Jeconiah; Assir, Salathiel his
19 the s' of Pedaiah were, Zerubbabel,
19 s' of Zerubbabel; Meshullam, and
21 the s' of Hananiah; Pelatiah, and
21 the s' of Rephaiah, the s' of Arnan,
21 s' of Obadiah, the s' of Shechaniah.
22 the s' of Shechaniah; Shemaiah:
22 s' of Shemaiah; Hattush, and Igeal,
23 the s' of Neariah: Elioenai, and
24 s' of Elioenai were, Hodaiah, and
4: 1 s' of Judah; Pharez, Hezron, and
4 are the s' of Hur, the firstborn
6 These were the s' of Naarah.
7 And the s' of Helah were, Zereth,
13 s' of Kenaz; Othniel, and Seraiah:
13 and the s' of Othniel; Hathath.
15 s' of Caleb the son of Jephunneh;
15 and the s' of Elah, even Kenaz.
16 s' of Jehaleleel; Ziph, and Ziphah,
17 And the s' of Ezra were, Jether, and
18 And these are the s' of Bithiah the
19 And the s' of his wife Hodiah the
20 And the s' of Shimon were, Amnon,
20 And the s' of Ishi were, Zoheth, and
21 s' of Shelah the son of Judah were,
24 The s' of Simeon were, Nemuel, and
26 the s' of Mishma; Hamuel his son,
27 And Shimei had sixteen s' and six
42 of them, even of the s' of Simeon,
42 Rephaiah, and Uzziel, the s' of Ishi.
5: 1 s' of Reuben the firstborn of Israel,
1 the s' of Joseph the son of Israel:
3 The s',...of Reuben the firstborn
4 The s' of Joel; Shemaiah his son,
18 The s' of Reuben, and the Gadites,
6: 1 s' of Levi; Gershon, Kohath, and
2 s' of Kohath; Amram, Izhar, and
3 s' also of Aaron; Nadab and Abihu,
16 s' of Levi; Gershom, Kohath, and
17 be the names of the s' of Gershom;
18 the s' of Kohath were, Amram, and
19 The s' of Merari; Mahli, and Mushi.
22 s' of Kohath; Amminadab his son,
25 And the s' of Elkanah; Amasai, and
26 the s' of Elkanah; Zophai his son,
28 s' of Samuel; the firstborn Vashni,
29 s' of Merari; Mahli, Libni his son,
33 Of the s' of the Kohathites: Heman
44 And their brethren the s' of Merari
49 But Aaron and his s' offered upon
50 And these are the s' of Aaron;
54 in their coasts, of the s' of Aaron,
57 to the s' of Aaron they gave the
61 And unto the s' of Kohath, which
62 to the s' of Gershom throughout
63 Unto the s' of Merari were given by
66 of the families of the s' of Kohath
70 of the remnant of the s' of Kohath.
71 Unto the s' of Gershom were given
7: 1 Now the s' of Issachar were, Tola,
2 the s' of Tola; Uzzi, and Rephaiah,
3 And the s' of Uzzi; Izrahiah: and
3 the s' of Izrahiah; Michael, and
4 for they had many wives and s'.
6 s' of Benjamin; Bela, and Becher, and
7 And the s' of Bela; Ezbon, and
8 And the s' of Becher; Zemira, and
8 All these are the s' of Becher.
10 The s' also of Jediael; Bilhan: and
10 s' of Bilhan; Jeush, and Benjamin,
11 All these are the s' of Jediael, by
12 of Ir, and Hushim, the s' of Aher.
13 s' of Naphtali; Jahziel, and Guni,
13 and Shallum, the s' of Bilhah.
14 s' of Manasseh; Ashriel, whom she
16 and his s' were Ulam and Rakem.
17 And the s' of Ulam; Bedan. These
17 the s' of Gilead, the son of Machir,
19 the s' of Shemidah were, Ahian,
20 the s' of Ephraim; Shuthelah, and
30 The s' of Asher; Imnah, and Isuah,
31 And the s' of Beriah; Heber, and
33 And the s' of Japhlet; Pasach, and
34 And the s' of Shamer; Ahi, and
35 And the s' of his brother Helem;
36 The s' of Zophah; Suah, and
38 And the s' of Jether; Jephunneh,
39 the s' of Ulla; Arah, and Haniel,
8: 3 And the s' of Bela were, Addar, and
6 And these are the s' of Ehud: these
10 These were his s', heads of the
12 s' of Elpaal; Eber, and Misham,
16 Ispah, and Joha, the s' of Beriah;
18 and Jobab, the s' of Elpaal;
21 and Shimrath, the s' of Shimhi;
25 and Penuel, the s' of Shashak;
27 and Zichri, the s' of Jeroham.
35 And the s' of Micah were, Pithon,
38 And Azel had six s', whose names
38 All these were the s' of Azel.
39 the s' of Eshek his brother were,
40 the s' of Ulam were mighty men of
40 and had many s', and sons' s', an
40 All these are of the s' of Benjamin.
9: 5 Asaiah the firstborn, and his s'.
6 of the s' of Zerah; Jeuel, and their
7 of the s' of Benjamin; Sallu the
30 of the s' of the priests made the
32 the s' of the Kohathites, were over
41 And the s' of Micah were, Pithon,
44 Azel had six s', whose names are
44 Hanan: these were the s' of Azel.
10: 2 hard after Saul, and after his s';
2 and Malchi-shua, the s' of Saul.
6 So Saul died, and his three s', and
7 and that Saul and his s' were dead,

1Ch 10: 8 they found Saul and his s' fallen in
12 of Saul, and the bodies of his s',
11: 34 The s' of Hashem the Gizonite,
44 Shama and Jehiel the s' of Hothan
46 and Joshaviah the s' of Elnaam,
12: 3 the s' of Shemaah the Gibeathite;
3 and Pelet, the s' of Azmaveth;
7 the s' of Jeroham of Gedor.
14 These were of the s' of Gad,
14: 3 David begat more s' and daughters.
15: 5 Of the s' of Kohath; Uriel the chief,
6 the s' of Merari; Asaiah the chief,
7 the s' of Gershom; Joel the chief,
8 Of the s' of Elizaphan; Shemaiah
9 Of the s' of Hebron; Eliel the chief,
10 Of the s' of Uzziel; Amminadab the
17 of the s' of Merari their brethren,
16: 42 the s' of Jeduthun were porters.
17: 11 after thee, which shall be of thy s';
18: 17 s' of David were chief about the
21: 20 four s' with him hid themselves.
23: 6 into courses among the s' of Levi,
8 s' of Laadan; the chief was Jehiel,
9 s' of Shimei; Shelomith, and Haziel,
10 s' of Shimei were, Jahath, Zina, and
10 These four were the s' of Shimei.
11 Jeush and Beriah had not many s';
12 The s' of Kohath; Amram, Izhar,
13 The s' of Amram; Aaron and Moses:
13 holy things, he and his s' for ever,
14 s' were named of the tribe of Levi
15 The s' of Moses were, Gershom, and
16 Of the s' of Gershom, Shebuel was
17 the s' of Eliezer were, Rehabiah the
17 And Eliezer had none other s'; but
17 the s' of Rehabiah were very many.
18 the s' of Izhar; Shelomith the chief.
19 the s' of Hebron; Jeriah the first,
20 Of the s' of Uzziel; Micah the first,
21 The s' of Merari; Mahli, and Mushi.
21 The s' of Mahli; Eleazar, and Kish.
22 Eleazar died, and had no s', but
22 brethren the s' of Kish took them.
23 The s' of Mushi; Mahli, and Eder,
24 These were the s' of Levi after the
28 to wait on the s' of Aaron for the
32 the charge of the s' of Aaron their
24: 1 are the divisions of the s' of Aaron.
1 The s' of Aaron; Nadab, and Abihu,
3 both Zadok of the s' of Eleazar, and
3 and Ahimelech of the s' of Ithamar,
4 men found of the s' of Eleazar
4 than of the s' of Ithamar; and thus
4 Among the s' of Eleazar there were
4 and eight among the s' of Ithamar
5 of God, were of the s' of Eleazar,
5 and of the s' of Ithamar.
20 And the rest of the s' of Levi were
20 Of the s' of Amram; Shubael: of
20 of the s' of Shubael; Jehdeiah.
21 of the s' of Rehabiah, the first was
22 of the s' of Shelomoth; Jahath.
23 the s' of Hebron; Jeriah the first,
24 Of the s' of Uzziel; Michah:
24 of the s' of Michah; Shamir.
25 of the s' of Isshiah; Zechariah.
26 s' of Merari were Mahli and Mushi:
26 Mushi: the s' of Jaaziah; Beno.
27 The s' of Merari by Jaaziah; Beno,
28 Mahli came Eleazar, who had no s'.
30 s' also of Mushi; Mahli, and Eder,
30 were the s' of the Levites after the
31 their brethren the s' of Aaron
25: 1 of the s' of Asaph, and of Heman,
2 the s' of Asaph; Zaccur, and Joseph,
2 the s' of Asaph under the hands of
3 the s' of Jeduthun; Gedaliah, and
4 s' of Heman; Bukkiah, Mattaniah,
5 All these were the s' of Heman the
5 God gave to Heman fourteen s' and
9 who with his brethren and s' were
10 Zaccur, he, his s', and his brethren,
11 to Izri, he, his s', and his brethren,
12 to Nethaniah, he, his s', and his
13 to Bukkiah, he, his s', and his
14 to Jesharelah, he, his s', and his
15 to Jeshaiah, he, his s', and his
16 to Mattaniah, he, his s', and his
17 Shimei, he, his s', and his brethren,
18 Azareel, he, his s', and his brethren,
19 to Hashabiah, he, his s', and his
20 Shubael, he, his s', and his brethren,
21 to Mattithiah, he, his s', and his
22 to Jeremoth, he, his s', and his
23 to Hananiah, he, his s', and his
24 Joshbekashah, he, his s', and his
25 Hanani, he, his s', and his brethren,
26 to Mallothi, he, his s', and his
27 to Eliathah, he, his s', and his
28 Hothir, he, his s', and his brethren,
29 to Giddalti, he, his s', and his
30 to Mahazioth, he, his s', and his
31 Romamti-ezer, he, his s', and his
26: 1 the son of Kore, of the s' of Asaph.
2 And the s' of Meshelemiah were,
4 Moreover the s' of Obed-edom were,
6 unto Shemaiah his son were s' born,
7 The s' of Shemaiah; Othni, and
8 All these of the s' of Obed-edom:
8 they and their s' and their brethren,
9 Meshelemiah had s' and brethren,
10 of the children of Merari, had s';
11 all the s' and brethren of Hosah
15 and to his s' the house of Asuppim.
19 of the porters among the s' of Kore,
19 and among the s' of Merari.

1Ch 26: 21 As concerning the s' of Laadan;
21 the s' of the Gershonite Laadan,
22 The s' of Jehieli; Zetham, and Joel
29 Chenaniah and his s' were for the
27: 32 Hachmoni was with the king's s':
28: 1 possession of the king, and of his s',
4 among the s' of my father he liked
5 And of all my s', (for the Lord hath
5 hath given me many s',) he hath
29: 24 and all the s' likewise of king David,
2Ch 5: 12 with their s' and their brethren,
11: 14 Jeroboam and his s' had cast them
21 and begat twenty and eight s', and
13: 5 to him and to his s' by a covenant
8 Lord in the hand of the s' of David;
9 the s' of Aaron, and the Levites,
10 unto the Lord, are the s' of Aaron,
21 and begat twenty and two s', and
20: 14 a Levite of the s' of Asaph,
21: 2 had brethren the s' of Jehoshaphat,
2 these were the s' of Jehoshaphat
7 a light to him and to his s' for ever.
17 in the king's house, and his s' also,
17 Jehoahaz, the youngest of his s'.
22: 8 the s' of the brethren of Ahaziah,
11 among the king's s' that were slain,
23: 3 Lord hath said of the s' of David.
11 Jehoiada and his s' anointed him,
24: 3 and he begat s' and daughters.
7 For the s' of Athaliah, that wicked
25 for the blood of the s' of Jehoiada
27 Now concerning his s', and the
26: 18 but to the priests the s' of Aaron,
28: 8 women, s', and daughters, and took
29: 9 our s' and our daughters and our
11 My s', be not now negligent: for the
12 Azariah, of the s' of the Kohathites:
12 of the s' of Merari, Kish the son of
13 And of the s' of Elizaphan; Shimri,
13 and of the s' of Asaph; Zechariah,
14 And of the s' of Heman; Jehiel, and
14 of the s' of Jeduthun; Shemaiah,
21 the s' of Aaron to offer them on the
31: 18 their wives, and their s', and their
19 Also of the s' of Aaron the priests,
32: 33 of the sepulchres of the s' of David:
34: 12 the Levites, of the s' of Merari;
12 of the s' of the Kohathites,
35: 14 priests the s' of Aaron were busied
14 and for the priests the s' of Aaron.
15 the singers the s' of Asaph were in
36: 20 servants to him and his s' until
Ezr 3: 9 stood Jeshua with his s' and his
9 Kadmiel and his s', the s' of Judah,
9 the s' of Henadad, with their s' and
10 and the Levites the s' of Asaph with
6: 10 the life of the king, and of his s'.
7: 23 the realm of the king and his s'?
8: 2 Of the s' of Phinehas; Gershom:
2 of the s' of Ithamar; Daniel: of the
2 Daniel: of the s' of David; Hattush.
3 Of the s' of Shechaniah, of the
3 of the s' of Pharosh; Zachariah:
4 s' of Pahath-moab; Elihoenai
5 Of the s' of Shechaniah; the son of
6 Of the s' also of Adin; Ebed the son
7 And of the s' of Elam; Jeshaiah the
8 of the s' of Shephatiah; Zebadiah
9 Of the s' of Joab; Obadiah the son
10 And of the s' of Shelomith; the son
11 And of the s' of Bebai; Zechariah
12 And of the s' of Azgad; Johanan the
13 of the last s' of Adonikam, whose
14 Of the s' also of Bigvai; Uthai, and
15 found there none of the s' of Levi.
18 of the s' of Mahli, the son of Levi,
18 his s' and his brethren, eighteen;
19 him Jeshaiah of the s' of Merari,
19 his brethren and their s', twenty;
9: 2 for themselves, and for their s':
12 not your daughters unto their s',
12 take their daughters unto your s',
10: 2 one of the s' of Elam, answered and
18 among the s' of the priests there
18 of the s' of Jeshua the son of
20 of the s' of Immer; Hanani, and
21 of the s' of Harim; Maaseiah, and
22 And of the s' of Pashur; Elioenai,
25 of the s' of Parosh; Ramiah, and
26 And of the s' of Elam; Mattaniah,
27 And of the s' of Zattu; Elioenai,
28 Of the s' also of Bebai; Jehohanan,
29 And of the s' of Bani; Meshullam,
30 of the s' of Pahath-moab; Adna,
31 And of the s' of Harim; Eliezer,
33 Of the s' of Hashum; Mattenai,
34 Of the s' of Bani; Maadai, Amram,
43 Of the s' of Nebo; Jeiel, Mattithiah,
Ne 3: 3 gate did the s' of Hassenaah build,
4: 14 and fight for your brethren, your s',
5: 2 We, our s', and our daughters, are
5 we bring into bondage our s' and
10: 9 Binnui of the s' of Henadad,
28 their s', and their daughters, every
30 nor take their daughters for our s':
36 Also the firstborn of our s', and of
11: 6 All the s' of Perez that dwelt at
7 these are the s' of Benjamin; Sallu
22 Of the s' of Asaph, the singers were
12: 23 The s' of Levi, the chief of the
28 And the s' of the singers gathered
35 of the priests' s' with trumpets;
13: 25 give your daughters unto their s',
25 take their daughters unto your s',
28 one of the s' of Joiada, the son of
10 The ten s' of Haman the son of

Es 9:12 palace, and the ten *s*· of Haman;
13 let Haman's ten *s*· be hanged upon
14 and they hanged Haman's ten *s*·.
25 he and his *s*· should be hanged on
Job 1: 2 him seven *s*· and three daughters.
4 his *s*· went and feasted in their
5 It may be that my *s*· have sinned,
6 when the *s*· of God came to present
13 when his *s*· and his daughters were
18 Thy *s*· and thy daughters were
2: 1 when the *s*· of God came to present
14:21 His *s*· came to honour, and he
38: 7 all the *s*· of God shouted for joy?
32 thou guide Arcturus with his *s*·?
42:13 also seven *s*· and three daughters.
16 saw his *s*·, and his sons' *s*·, even
Ps 4: 2 O ye *s*· of men, how long will ye
31:19 trust in thee before the *s*· of men!
33:13 he beholdeth all the *s*· of men.
42: *title* Maschil, for the *s*· of Korah.
44: *title* Musician for the *s*· of Korah.
45: *title* Shoshannim, for the *s*· of Korah.
46: *title* chief Musician for the *s*· of Korah
47: *title* A Psalm for the *s*· of Korah.
48: *title* and Psalm for the *s*· of Korah.
49: *title* A Psalm for the *s*· of Korah.
57: 4 even the *s*· of men, whose teeth are
58: 1 judge uprightly, O ye *s*· of men?
77:15 people, the *s*· of Jacob and Joseph.
84: *title* A Psalm for the *s*· of Korah.
85: *title* A Psalm for the *s*· of Korah.
87: *title* Psalm or Song for the *s*· of Korah.
88: *title* Psalm for the *s*· of Korah, to the
89: 6 who among the *s*· of the mighty can
106:37 they sacrificed their *s*· and their
38 even the blood of their *s*· and of
144:12 That our *s*· may be as plants grown
145:12 To make known to the *s*· of men
Pr 8: 4 and my voice is to the *s*· of man.
31 delights were with the *s*· of men.
Ec 1:13 hath God given to the *s*· of man to
2: 3 was that good for the *s*· of men,
8 and the delights of the *s*· of men,
3:10 God hath given to the *s*· of men
18 concerning...estate of the *s*· of men,
19 that which befalleth the *s*· of men
8:11 heart of the *s*· of men is fully set in
9: 3 heart of the *s*· of men is full of evil,
12 so are the *s*· of men snared in an
Ca 2: 3 so is my beloved among the *s*·.
Isa 37:38 Adrammelech and Sharezer his *s*·
39: 7 thy *s*· that shall issue from thee,
43: 6 bring my *s*· from far, and my
45:11 things to come concerning my *s*·,
49:22 shall bring thy *s*· in their arms,
51:18 none to guide her among all the *s*·
18 taketh her by the hand of all the *s*·
20 Thy *s*· have fainted, they lie at the
52:14 his form more than the *s*· of men:
56: 5 and a name better than of *s*· and
6 Also the *s*· of the stranger, that
57: 3 ye *s*· of the sorceress, the seed of
60: 4 thy *s*· shall come from far, and thy
9 to bring thy *s*· from far, their silver
10 the *s*· of strangers shall build up
14 *s*· also of them that afflicted thee
61: 5 the *s*· of the alien shall be your
62: 5 virgin, so shall thy *s*· marry thee:
8 *s*· of the stranger shall not drink
Jer 3:24 herds, their *s*· and their daughters.
5:17 *s*· and thy daughters should eat:
6:21 fathers and...*s*· together shall fall
7:31 burn their *s*· and their daughters in
11:22 *s*· and their daughters shall die by
13:14 the fathers and the *s*· together,
14:16 nor their *s*·, nor their daughters:
16: 2 shalt thou have *s*· or daughters in
3 saith the Lord concerning the *s*·
19: 5 to burn their *s*· with fire for burnt
9 them to eat the flesh of their *s*· and
29: 6 wives, and beget *s*· and daughters;
6 and take wives for your *s*·, and give
6 they may bear *s*· and daughters;
32:19 upon all the ways of the *s*· of men:
35 their *s*· and their daughters to pass
35: 3 his brethren, and all his *s*·, and the
4 the chamber of the *s*· of Hanan, the
5 I set before the *s*· of the house of
6 neither ye, nor your *s*· for ever:
8 wives, our *s*·, nor our daughters;
14 commanded his *s*· not to drink wine,
16 Because the *s*· of Jonadab the son
39: 6 of Babylon slew the *s*· of Zedekiah
40: 8 and Jonathan the *s*· of Kareah,
8 the *s*· of Ephai the Netophathite,
48:46 for thy *s*· are taken captives, and
49: 1 Hath Israel no *s*·? hath he no heir?
52:10 of Babylon slew the *s*· of Zedekiah
La 4: 2 precious *s*· of Zion, comparable to
Eze 5:10 the fathers shall eat the *s*· in the
10 and the *s*· shall eat their fathers;
14:16 deliver neither *s*· nor daughters;
18 deliver neither *s*· nor daughters,
22 forth, both *s*· and daughters:
16:20 thou hast taken thy *s*· and thy
20:31 your *s*· to pass through the fire,
23: 4 and they bare *s*· and daughters.
10 they took her *s*· and her daughters,
25 shall take thy *s*· and thy daughters;
37 have also caused their *s*·, whom
47 they shall slay their *s*· and their
24:21 your *s*· and your daughters whom
25 minds, their *s*· and their daughters,
40:46 altar: these are the *s*· of Zadok
46 among the *s*· of Levi, which come
44:15 priests the Levites, the *s*· of Zadok,
Eze 46:16 prince give a gift unto any of his *s*·,
18 he shall give his *s*· inheritance out
48:11 are sanctified of the *s*· of Zadok;
Da 5:21 he was driven from the *s*· of men;
10:16 like the similitude of the *s*· of men
11:10 But his *s*· shall be stirred up, and
Ho 1:10 Ye are the *s*· of the living God.
Joe 1:12 withered away from the *s*· of men.
2:28 your *s*· and your daughters shall
3: 8 will sell your *s*· and your daughters
Am 2:11 I raised up of your *s*· for prophets,
7:17 thy *s*· and thy daughters shall fall
Mic 5: 7 man, nor waiteth for the *s*· of men.
Zec 9:13 and raised up thy *s*·, O Zion,
13 against thy *s*·, O Greece, and made
Mal 3: 3 and he shall purify the *s*· of Levi,
6 ye *s*· of Jacob are not consumed.
M't 20:20 of Zebedee's children with her *s*·,
21 Grant that these my two *s*· may sit,
21:28 A certain man had two *s*·; and he
26:37 Peter and the two *s*· of Zebedee,
M'r 3:17 which is, The *s*· of thunder:
28 shall be forgiven unto the *s*· of men
10:35 James and John, the *s*· of Zebedee,
Lu 5:10 James, and John, the *s*· of Zebedee,
11:19 by whom do your *s*· cast them out?
15:11 he said, A certain man had two *s*·:
Joh 1:12 he power to become the *s*· of God,
21: 2 the *s*· of Zebedee, and two other
Ac 2:17 your *s*· and your daughters shall
7:16 sum of money of the *s*· of Emmor
29 of Madian, where he begat two *s*·.
19:14 there were seven *s*· of one Sceva,
Ro 8:14 Spirit of God, they are the *s*· of God.
19 the manifestation of the *s*· of God.
1 Co 4:14 but as my beloved *s*· I warn you.
2 Co 6:18 ye shall be my *s*· and daughters,
Ga 4: 5 might receive the adoption of *s*·.
6 because ye are *s*·, God hath sent
22 Abraham had two *s*·, the one by a
Eph 3: 5 not made known unto the *s*· of men,
Ph'p 2:15 the *s*· of God, without rebuke,
Heb 2:10 in bringing many *s*· unto glory,
7: 5 they that are of the *s*· of Levi, who
11:21 blessed both the *s*· of Joseph; and
12: 7 God dealeth with you as with *s*·;
8 then are ye bastards, and not *s*·.
1 Jo 3: 1 we should be called the *s*· of God:
2 Beloved, now are we the *s*· of God,

sons'
Ge 6:18 wife, and thy *s*· wives with thee.
7: 7 his wife, and his *s*· wives with him,
8:16 sons, and thy *s*· wives with thee.
18 his wife, and his *s*· wives with him:
46: 7 His sons, and his *s*· sons with him,
7 his daughters, and his *s*· daughters,
26 besides Jacob's *s*· wives, all the
Ex 29:21 sons, and his *s*· garments with him.
28 it shall be Aaron's and his *s*· by a
29 of Aaron shall be his *s*· after him,
39:41 and his *s*· garments, to minister in
Le 2: 3, 10 shall be Aaron's and his *s*·:
7:31 breast shall be Aaron's and his *s*·.
8:27 hands, and upon his *s*· hands,
30 and upon his *s*· garments with him,
30 sons, and his *s*· garments with him.
10:13 it is thy due, and thy *s*· due, of the
14 for they be thy due, and thy *s*· due,
15 shall be thine, and thy *s*· with thee,
24: 9 And it shall be Aaron's and his *s*·
De 4: 9 them thy sons, and thy *s*· sons;
1Ch 8:40 and *s*· sons, an hundred and fifty.
Job 42:16 his *s*· sons, even four generations.
Eze 46:16 inheritance thereof shall be his *s*·:
17 but his inheritance shall be his *s*·

soon see also SOONER.
Ge 18:33 as *s*· as he had left communing
27:30 as *s*· as Isaac had made an end of
44: 3 As *s*· as the morning was light, the
Ex 2:18 How is it that ye are come so *s*·
9:29 As *s*· as I am gone out of the city, I
32:19 as *s*· as he came nigh unto the camp,
De 4:26 ye shall *s*· utterly perish from off
Jos 2: 7 as *s*· as they which pursued after
11 And as *s*· as we had heard these
3:13 as *s*· as the soles of the feet of the
8:19 as *s*· as he had stretched out his hand
29 and as *s*· as the sun was down, Joshua
J'g 8:33 to pass, as *s*· as Gideon was dead,
9:33 as *s*· as the sun is up, thou shalt rise
1Sa 9:13 As *s*· as ye be come into the city, ye
13:10 that as *s*· as he had made an end of
20:41 And as *s*· as the lad was gone, David
29:10 and as *s*· as ye be up early in the
2Sa 6:18 And as *s*· as David had made an end
13:36 as *s*· as he had made an end of
15:10 As *s*· as ye hear the sound of the
22:45 as *s*· as they hear, they shall be
1Ki 16:11 as *s*· as he sat on his throne, that he
18:12 pass, as *s*· as I am gone up from thee,
20:36 as *s*· as thou art departed from me,
36 as *s*· as he was departed from him,
2Ki 10: 2 Now as *s*· as this letter cometh to you,
25 as *s*· as he had made an end of offering
14: 5 as *s*· as the kingdom was confirmed
2Ch 31: 5 as *s*· as the commandment came
Job 32:22 my maker would *s*· take me away.
Ps 18:44 *s*· as they hear of me, they shall obey
37: 2 shall *s*· be cut down like the grass,
58: 3 go astray as *s*· as they be born,
68:31 Ethiopia shall *s*· stretch out her
81:14 *s*· have subdued their enemies,
90:10 for it is *s*· cut off, and we fly away.
106:13 They *s*· forgat his works; they
Pr 14:17 that is *s*· angry dealeth foolishly:
Isa 66: 8 *s*· as Zion travailed, she brought
Eze 23:16 *s*· as she saw them with her eyes,
M't 21:20 How *s*· is the fig tree withered
M'r 1:42 And as *s*· as he had spoken,
5:36 As *s*· as Jesus heard the word that
11: 2 and as *s*· as ye be entered into it, ye
14:45 And as *s*· as he was come, he goeth
Lu 1:23 *s*· as the days of his ministration
44 as *s*· as the voice of thy salutation
8: 6 *s*· as it was sprung up, it withered
15:30 as *s*· as this thy son was come,
22:66 And as *s*· as it was day, the elders
23: 7 And as *s*· as he knew that he belonged
Joh 11:20 as *s*· as she heard that Jesus was
29 As *s*· as she heard that, she arose
16:21 but as *s*· as she is delivered of the
18: 6 As *s*· then as he had said unto
21: 9 As *s*· then as they were come to
Ac 10:29 gainsaying, as *s*· as I was sent for:
12:18 as *s*· as it was day, there was no
Ga 1: 6 ye are so *s*· removed from him
Ph'p 2:23 so *s*· as I shall see how it will go
2Th 2: 2 That ye be not *s*· shaken in mind,
Tit 1: 7 not *s*· angry, not given to wine, no
Re 10:10 as *s*· as I had eaten it, my belly
12: 4 for to devour her child as *s*· as it

sooner^
Heb 13:19 I may be restored to you the *s*·.

sooth See FORSOOTH; SOOTHSAYER.

soothsayer See also SOOTHSAYERS.
Jos 13:22 Balaam also the son of Beor, the *s*·,

soothsayers
Isa 2: 6 and are *s*· like the Philistines, and
Da 2:27 the *s*·, shew unto the king;
4: 7 the Chaldeans, and the *s*·: and I
5: 7 the Chaldeans, and the *s*·.
11 astrologers, Chaldeans, and *s*·;
Mic 5:12 and thou shalt have no more *s*·:

soothsaying
Ac 16:16 her masters much gain by *s*·:

sop
Joh 13:26 He it is, to whom I shall give a *s*·,
26 when he had dipped the *s*·, he gave
27 after the *s*· Satan entered into him.
30 He then having received the *s*·

Sopater (*so'-pa-tur*) See also SOSIPATER.
Ac 20: 4 accompanied him into Asia *S*· of

sope
Jer 2:22 and take thee much *s*·, yet thine
Mal 3: 2 refiner's fire, and like fullers' *s*·:

Sophereth (*so-fe'-reth*)
Ezr 2:55 of Sotai, the children of *S*·, the
Ne 7:57 of Sotai, the children of *S*·, the

sorcerer See also SORCERERS; SORCERESS.
Ac 13: 6 they found a certain *s*·, a false
8 But Elymas the *s*· (for so is his

sorcerers
Ex 7:11 called the wise men and the *s*·:
Jer 27: 9 nor to your *s*·, which speak unto
Da 2: 2 and the *s*·, and the Chaldeans, for
Mal 3: 5 be a swift witness against the *s*·,
Re 21: 8 and whoremongers, and *s*·, and
22:15 For without are dogs, and *s*·, and

sorceress
Isa 57: 3 near hither, ye sons of the *s*·,

sorceries
Isa 47: 9 for the multitude of thy *s*·, and
12 and with the multitude of thy *s*·,
Ac 8:11 he had bewitched them with *s*·.
Re 9:21 of their murders, nor of their *s*·,
18:23 by thy *s*· were all nations deceived.

sorcery See also SORCERIES.
Ac 8: 9 beforetime in the same city used *s*·,

sore See also SORER; SORES.
Ge 19: 9 And they pressed *s*· upon the man,
20: 8 ears: and the men were *s*· afraid.
31:30 thou *s*· longedst after thy father's
34:25 when they were *s*·, that two of
41:56 the famine waxed *s*· in the land of
57 the famine was so *s*· in all lands.
43: 1 And the famine was *s*· in the land.
47: 4 famine is *s*· in the land of Canaan:
13 the famine was very *s*·, so that the
50:10 a great and very *s*· lamentation:
Ex 14:10 them; and they were *s*· afraid:
Le 13:42 bald forehead, a white reddish *s*·;
43 rising of the *s*· be white reddish
Nu 22: 3 Moab was *s*· afraid of the people,
De 6:22 signs and wonders, great and *s*·,
28:35 a *s*· botch that cannot be healed,
59 and *s*· sicknesses, and of long
Jos 9:24 we were *s*· afraid of our lives
J'g 10: 9 so that Israel was *s*· distressed.
14:17 her, because she lay *s*· upon him:
15:18 And he was *s*· athirst, and called
20:34 all Israel, and the battle was *s*·:
21: 2 up their voices, and wept *s*·;
1Sa 1: 6 adversary also provoked her *s*·,
10 prayed unto the Lord, and wept *s*·.
5: 7 his hand is *s*· upon us, and upon
14:52 was *s*· war against the Philistines
17:24 fled from him, and were *s*· afraid.
21:12 was *s*· afraid of Achish the king of
28:15 Saul answered, I am *s*· distressed;
20 on the earth, and was *s*· afraid,
21 and saw that he was *s*· troubled,
31: 3 the battle went *s*· against Saul,
3 he was *s*· wounded of the archers.
4 would not; for he was *s*· afraid.

2Sa 2:17 there was a very s' battle that day;
13:36 and all his servants wept very s'.
1Ki 17:17 and his sickness was so s', that
18: 2 there was a s' famine in Samaria.
2Ki 3:26 that the battle was too s' for him,
6:11 king of Syria was s' troubled for this
20: 3 thy sight. And Hezekiah wept s'.
1Ch 10: 3 the battle went s' against Saul,
4 would not; for he was s' afraid.
2Ch 6:28 whatsoever s' or whatsoever
29 one shall know his own s' and his
21:19 so he died of s' diseases. And his
28:19 and transgressed s' against the Lord.
35:23 me away; for I am s' wounded.
Ezr 10: 1 for the people wept very s'.
Ne 2: 2 of heart. Then I was very s' afraid,
13: 8 it grieved me s': therefore I cast
Job 2: 7 smote Job with s' boils from the
5:18 For he maketh s', and bindeth up:
Ps 2: 5 and vex them in his s' displeasure.
6: 3 My soul is also s' vexed: but thou,
10 enemies be ashamed and s' vexed:
38: 2 in me, and thy hand presseth me s'.
8 I am feeble and s' broken: I
11 friends stand aloof from my s';
44:19 s' broken us in the place of dragons,
55: 4 My heart is s' pained within me: and
71:20 shewed me great and s' troubles,
77: 2 my s' ran in the night, and ceased
118:13 Thou hast thrust s' at me that I might
18 The Lord hath chastened me s': but
Ec 1:13 this s' travail hath God given to
4: 8 is also vanity, yea, it is a s' travail.
5:13 a s' evil which I have seen under
16 this also is a s' evil, that in all
Isa 27: 1 his s' and great and strong sword
38: 3 sight. And Hezekiah wept s'.
59:11 like bears, and mourn s' like doves:
64: 9 Be not wroth very s', O Lord,
12 thy peace, and afflict us very s'?
Jer 13:17 and mine eye shall weep s', and run
22:10 but weep s' for him that goeth away:
50:12 mother shall be s' confounded;
52: 6 the famine was s' in the city, so
La 1: 2 She weepeth s' in the night, and her
3:52 Mine enemies chased me s', like a
Eze 14:21 I send my four s' judgments upon
21:10 sharpened to make a s' slaughter;
27:35 and their kings shall be s' afraid,
Da 6:14 was s' displeased with himself,
Mic 2:10 you, even with a s' destruction.
Zec 1: 2 s' displeased with your fathers.
15 very s' displeased with the heathen
M't 17: 6 on their face, and were s' afraid.
15 for he is lunatick, and s' vexed:
21:15 of David; they were s' displeased,
M'r 6:51 were s' amazed in themselves
9: 6 to say; for they were s' afraid.
26 the spirit cried, and rent him s',
14:33 began to be s' amazed, and to be
Lu 2: 9 them: and they were s' afraid.
Ac 20:37 they all wept s', and fell on Paul's
Re 16: 2 fell a noisome and grievous s' upon

Sorek (*so'-rek*)
J'g 16: 4 loved a woman in the valley of *S*',

sorely
Ge 49:23 The archers have s' grieved him,
Isa 23: 5 they be s' pained at the report of Tyre.

sorer
Heb 10:29 Of how much s' punishment,

sores
Isa 1: 6 and bruises, and putrifying s':
Lu 16:20 was laid at his gate, full of s',
21 the dogs came and licked his s'.
Re 16:11 because of their pains and their s',

sorrow See also SORROWED; SORROWETH; SORROWFUL; SORROWING; SORROWS.
Ge 3:16 said, I will greatly multiply thy s'
16 in s' shalt thou bring forth
17 in s' shalt thou eat of it all the
42:38 my gray hairs with s' to the grave.
44:29 my gray hairs with s' to the grave.
31 our father with s' to the grave.
Ex 15:14 s'...take hold on the inhabitants
Le 26:16 the eyes, and cause s' of heart:
De 28:65 failing of eyes, and s' of mind:
1Ch 4: 9 Because I bare him with s'.
Ne 2: 2 this is nothing else but s' of heart.
Es 9:22 turned unto them from s' to joy,
Job 3:10 womb, nor hid s' from mine eyes.
6:10 yea, I would harden myself in s':
17: 7 eye also is dim by reason of s',
41:22 s' is turned into joy before him.
Ps 13: 2 soul, having s' in my heart daily?
38:17 my s' is continually before me.
39: 2 from good; and my s' was stirred.
55:10 mischief...and s' are in the midst
90:10 yet is their strength labour and s';
107:39 oppression, affliction, and s'.
116: 3 upon me: I found trouble and s'.
Pr 10:10 winketh with the eye causeth s':
22 rich, and he addeth no s' with it.
15:13 but by s' of the heart the spirit is
17:21 begetteth a fool doeth it to his s':
23:29 Who hath woe? who hath s'? who
Ec 1:18 knowledge increaseth s'.
5:17 s' and wrath with his sickness.
7: 3 *S*' is better than laughter: for by
11:10 Therefore remove s' from thy heart,
Isa 5:30 the land, behold darkness and s',
14: 3 shall give thee rest from thy s',
17:11 day of grief and of desperate s'.
29: 2 there shall be heaviness and s':
Isa 35:10 and s' and sighing shall flee away.
50:11 mine hand; ye shall lie down in s'.
51:11 s' and mourning shall flee away.
65:14 but ye shall cry for s' of heart, and
Jer 8:18 I would comfort myself against s',
20:18 of the womb to see labour and s',
30:15 s' is incurable for the multitude
31:12 they shall not s' any more at all.
13 make them rejoice from their s'.
45: 3 Lord hath added grief to my s';
49:23 there is s' on the sea; it cannot be
51:29 And the land shall tremble and s':
La 1:12 if there be any s' like unto my s',
18 you, all people, and behold my s':
3:65 Give them s' of heart, thy curse
Eze 23:33 be filled with drunkenness and s',
Ho 8:10 they shall s' a little for the burden
Lu 22:45 he found them sleeping for s',
Joh 16: 6 unto you, s' hath filled your heart.
20 but your s' shall be turned into joy.
21 when she is in travail hath s',
22 And ye now therefore have s': but I
Ro 9: 2 and continual s' in my heart.
2Co 2: 3 s' from them of whom I ought to
7 be swallowed up with overmuch s'.
7:10 For godly s' worketh repentance to
10 the s' of the world worketh death.
Ph'p 2:27 also, lest I should have s' upon s'.
1Th 4:13 that ye s' not, even as others which
Re 18: 7 so much torment and s' give her:
7 am no widow, and shall see no s'.
21: 4 neither s', nor crying, neither shall

sorrowed
2Co 7: 9 sorry, but that ye s' to repentance:
11 thing, that ye s' after a godly sort,

sorroweth
1Sa 10: 2 s' for you, saying, What shall I

sorrowful
1Sa 1:15 lord, I am a woman of a s' spirit:
Job 6: 7 refused to touch are as my s' meat.
Ps 69:29 But I am poor and s': let thy
Pr 14:13 Even in laughter the heart is s';
Jer 31:25 I have replenished every s' soul.
Zep 3:18 are s' for the solemn assembly,
Zec 9: 5 also shall see it, and be very s',
M't 19:22 that saying, he went away s': for
26:22 they were exceeding s', and began
37 and began to be s' and very heavy.
38 My soul is exceeding s', even unto
M'r 14:19 And they began to be s', and to say
34 My soul is exceeding s' unto death:
Lu 18:23 when he heard this, he was very s':
24 when Jesus saw that he was very s',
Joh 16:20 and ye shall be s', but your sorrow
2Co 6:10 As s', yet alway rejoicing; as poor,
Ph'p 2:28 and that I may be the less s'.

sorrowing
Lu 2:48 father and I have sought thee s'.
Ac 20:38 *S*' most of all for the words which

sorrows
Ex 3: 7 taskmasters; for I know their s';
2Sa 22: 6 s' of hell compassed me about;
Job 9:28 I am afraid of all my s', I know
21:17 God distributeth s' in his anger.
39: 3 young ones, they cast out their s'.
Ps 16: 4 Their s' shall be multiplied that
18: 4 The s' of death compassed me,
5 s' of hell compassed me about:
32:10 Many s' shall be to the wicked: but
116: 3 The s' of death compassed me,
127: 2 sit up late, to eat the bread of s':
Ec 2:23 all his days are s', and his travail
Isa 13: 8 and s' shall take hold of them;
53: 3 a man of s', and acquainted with
4 our griefs, and carried our s':
Jer 13:21 shall not s' take thee, as a woman
49:24 anguish and s' have taken her, as a
Da 10:16 vision my s' are turned upon me,
Ho 13:13 The s' of a travailing woman shall
M't 24: 8 All these are the beginning of s'.
M'r 13: 8 these are the beginnings of s'.
1Ti 6:10 themselves through with many s'.

sorry
1Sa 22: 8 is none of you that is s' for me,
Ne 8:10 neither be ye s'; for the joy of the
Ps 38:18 iniquity; I will be s' for my sin.
Isa 51:19 thee; who shall be s' for thee?
M't 14: 9 And the king was s': nevertheless
17:23 again. And they were exceeding s'.
18:31 what was done, they were very s',
M'r 6:26 And the king was exceeding s';
2Co 2: 2 For if I make you s', who is he
2 the same which is made s' by me?
7: 8 though I made you s' with a letter,
8 the same epistle hath made you s',
9 rejoice, not that ye were made s',
9 were made s' after a godly manner,

sort^ See also CONSORTED; RESORT; SORTS.
Ge 6:19 two of every s' shalt thou bring into
20 two of every s' shall come unto thee,
7:14 his kind, every bird of every s'.
2Ki 24:14 save the poorest s' of the people
1Ch 24: 5 were divided by lot, one s' with another;
29:14 able to offer so willingly after this s'?
2Ch 30: 5 long time in such s' as it was written.
Ezr 1:10 silver basons of a second s' four
4: 8 to Artaxerxes the king in this s':
Ne 6: 4 unto me four times after this s';
Eze 39: 4 unto the ravenous birds of every s',
44:30 of every s' of your oblations, shall be
Da 1:10 children which are of your s'?
3:29 God that can deliver after this s'.
Ac 17: 5 certain lewd fellows of the baser s',
Ro 15:15 more boldly unto you in some s',
1Co 3:13 every man's work of what s' it is.
2Co 7:11 that ye sorrowed after a godly s', what
2Ti 3: 6 For of this s' are they which creep into
3Jo 6 on their journey after a godly s',

sorts
De 22:11 shalt not wear a garment of divers s',
Ne 5:18 in ten days store of all s' of wine:
Ps 78:45 He sent divers s' of flies among them,
105:31 spake, and there came divers s' of flies,
Ec 2: 8 musical instruments, and that of all s'.
Eze 27:24 thy merchants in all s' of things,
38: 4 clothed with all s' of armour,

Sosipater (*so-sip'-a-tur*) See also SOPATER.
Ro 16:21 and *S*', my kinsmen, salute you.

Sosthenes (*sos'-the-neze*)
Ac 18:17 Greeks took *S*', the chief ruler
1Co 1: 1 will of God, and *S*' our brother,

Sotai (*so'-tahee*)
Ezr 2:55 the children of *S*', the children of
Ne 7:57 the children of *S*', the children of

sottish
Jer 4:22 they are s' children, and they

sought See also BESOUGHT.
Ge 43:30 and he s' where to weep; and he
Ex 2:15 this thing, he s' to slay Moses.
4:19 the men are dead which s' thy life.
24 Lord met him, and s' to kill him.
33: 7 every one which s' the Lord went
Le 10:16 Moses diligently s' the goat of the
Nu 35:23 his enemy, neither s' his harm:
De 13:10 he hath s' to thrust thee away from
Jos 2:22 the pursuers s' them throughout
J'g 14: 4 that he s' an occasion against the
18: 1 the Danites s' them an inheritance
1Sa 10:21 when they s' him, he could not be
13:14 Lord hath s' him a man after his
14: 4 by which Jonathan s' to go over
19:10 Saul s' to smite David even to the
23:14 And Saul s' him every day, but God
27: 4 and he s' no more again for him.
2Sa 3:17 Ye s' for David in times past to be
4: 8 Saul thine enemy, which s' thy life;
17:20 they had s' and could not find them,
21: 2 and Saul s' to slay them in his zeal
1Ki 1: 2 Let there be s' for my lord the king
3 So they s' for a fair damsel
10:24 And all the earth s' to Solomon,
11:40 Solomon s'...to kill Jeroboam.
2Ki 2:17 s' three days, but found him not.
1Ch 15:13 we s' him not after the due order.
26:31 the reign of David they were s' for,
2Ch 1: 5 and the congregation s' unto it.
9:23 earth s' the presence of Solomon,
14: 7 we have s' the Lord our God,
7 we have s' him, and he hath given
15: 4 and s' him, he was found of them.
15 and s' him with their whole desire;
16:12 his disease he s' not to the Lord,
17: 3 David, and s' not unto Baalim;
4 s' to the Lord God of his father,
22: 9 he s' Ahaziah: and they caught
9 who s' the Lord with all his heart.
25:15 s' after the gods of the people,
20 they s' after the gods of Edom.
26: 5 he s' God in the days of Zechariah,
5 as long as he s' the Lord, God made
Ezr 2:62 These s' their register among
Ne 7:64 These s' their register among those
12:27 they s' the Levites out of all their
Es 2: 2 fair young virgins s' for the king:
21 s' to lay hand on...king Ahasuerus.
3: 6 Haman s' to destroy all the Jews
6: 2 s' to lay hand on...king Ahasuerus.
9: 2 lay hand on such as s' their hurt:
Ps 34: 4 I s' the Lord, and he heard me,
37:36 I s' him, but he could not be found.
77: 2 day of my trouble I s' the Lord:
78:34 he slew them, then they s' him:
86:14 violent men have s' after my soul;
111: 2 s' out of all...that have pleasure
119:10 my whole heart have I s' thee:
94 save me; for I have s' thy precepts.
Ec 2: 3 I s' in mine heart to give myself
7:29 they have s' out many inventions.
12: 9 and s' out, and set in order many
10 s' to find out acceptable words:
Ca 3: 1 bed I s' him whom my soul loveth:
1, 2 I s' him, but I found him not.
5: 6 I s' him, but I could not find him;
Isa 62:12 called, *S*' out, A city not forsaken.
65: 1 I am s' of them that asked not for
1 am found of them that s' me not:
10 in, for my people that have s' me.
Jer 8: 2 whom they have s', and whom they
10:21 brutish, and have not s' the Lord:
26:21 the king s' to put him to death:
44:30 his enemy, and that s' his life.
50:20 iniquity of Israel shall be s' for,
La 1:19 while they s' their meat to relieve
Eze 22:30 And I s' for a man among them,
26:21 though thou be s' for, yet shalt
34: 4 neither have ye s' that which was
Da 2:13 they s' Daniel and his fellows to
4:36 and my lords s' unto me; and I was
6: 4 s' to find occasion against Daniel
8:15 the vision, and s' for the meaning,
Ob 6 how are his hidden things s' up!
Zep 1: 6 those that have not s' the Lord,
Zec 6: 7 and s' to go that they might walk
M't 2:20 which s' the young child's life.
21:46 when they s' to lay hands on him,
26:16 he s' opportunity to betray him.

M't 26:59 s' false witness against Jesus, to
M'r 11:18 and s' how they might destroy him
12:12 And they s' to lay hold on him, but
14: 1 scribes s' how they might take him
11 he s' how he might conveniently
55 council s' for witness against Jesus
Lu 2:44 they s' him among their kinsfolk
48 and I have s' thee sorrowing.
49 unto them, How is it that ye s' me?
4:42 the people s' him, and came unto
5:18 and they s' means to bring him in,
6:19 whole multitude s' to touch him:
11:16 him, s' of him a sign from heaven.
13: 6 and he came and s' fruit thereon,
19: 3 And he s' to see Jesus who he was;
47 of the people s' to destroy him,
20:19 same hour s' to lay hands on him;
22: 2 scribes s' how they might kill him;
6 s' opportunity to betray him unto
Joh 5:16 persecute Jesus, and s' to slay him,
18 the Jews s' the more to kill him,
7: 1 because the Jews s' to kill him.
11 Then the Jews s' him at the feast,
30 Then they s' to take him: but no
10:39 they s' again to take him: but he
11: 8 the Jews of late s' to stone thee;
56 Then s' they for Jesus, and spake
19:12 thenceforth Pilate s' to release him:
Ac 12:19 And when Herod had s' for him,
17: 5 s' to bring them out to the people.
Ro 9:32 Because they s' it not by faith, but
10:20 I was found of them that s' me not;
1Th 2: 6 Nor of men s' we glory, neither of
2Ti 1:17 he s' me out very diligently, and
Heb 8: 7 then should no place have been s'
12:17 though he s' it carefully with tears.
soul See also SOUL'S; SOULS.
Ge 2: 7 life; and man became a living s'.
12:13 and my s' shall live because of thee.
17:14 that s' shall be cut off from his
19:20 a little one?) and my s' shall live.
27: 4 my s' may bless thee before I die.
19 venison, that thy s' may bless me.
25 venison, that my s' may bless thee.
31 venison, that thy s' may bless me.
34: 3 And his s' clave unto Dinah the
8 The s' of my son Shechem longeth
35:18 as her s' was in departing, (for she
42:21 that we saw the anguish of his s',
49: 6 O my s', come not thou into their
Ex 12:15 that s' shall be cut off from Israel.
19 even that s' shall be cut off from the
30:12 give every man a ransom for his s'
31:14 that s' shall be cut off from among
Le 4: 2 If a s' shall sin through ignorance
5: 1 And if a s' sin, and hear the voice
2 Or if a s' touch any unclean thing,
4 Or if a s' swear, pronouncing with
15 If a s' commit a trespass, and sin
17 And if a s' sin, and commit any of
6: 2 If a s' sin, and commit a trespass
7:18 the s' that eateth of it shall bear his
20 the s' that eateth of the flesh of the
20 even that s' shall be cut off from
21 the s' that shall touch any unclean
21 even that s' shall be cut off from his
25 the s' that eateth it shall be cut off
27 Whatsoever s' it be that eateth any
27 even that s' shall be cut off from his
17:10 will even set my face against that s'
11 maketh an atonement for the s'.
12 No s' of you shall eat blood, neither
15 every s' that eateth that which died
19: 8 that s' shall be cut off from among
20: 6 the s' that turneth after such as
6 even set my face against that s',
22: 3 that s' shall be cut off from my
6 The s' which hath touched any such
11 But if the priest buy any s' with his
23:29 whatsoever s' it be that shall not be
30 whatsoever s' it be that doeth any
30 same s' will I destroy from among
26:11 and my s' shall not abhor you.
15 or if your s' abhor my judgments,
30 idols, and my s' shall abhor you.
43 their s' abhorred my statutes.
Nu 9:13 same s' shall be cut off from among
11: 6 But now our s' is dried away: there
15:27 if any s' sin through ignorance,
28 make an atonement for the s' that
30 But the s' that doeth ought
30 that s' shall be cut off from among
31 that s' shall utterly be cut off;
19:13 that s' shall be cut off from Israel:
20 that s' shall be cut off from among
22 s' that toucheth it shall be unclean
21: 4 and the s' of the people was much
5 and our s' loatheth this light bread.
30: 2 an oath to bind his s' with a bond;
4 wherewith she hath bound her s',
4 wherewith she hath bound her s',
5 wherewith she hath bound her s',
6 lips, wherewith she bound her s';
7 bonds wherewith she bound her s'
8 lips, wherewith she bound her s',
10 bound her s' by a bond with an oath;
11 bond wherewith she bound her s'
12 or concerning the bond of her s',
13 every binding oath to afflict the s',
31:28 one s' of five hundred, both of the
De 4: 9 and keep thy s' diligently, lest thou
29 with all thy heart and with all thy s'.
6: 5 all thine heart, and with all thy s',
10:12 with all thy heart and with all thy s',
11:13 all your heart and with all your s',
18 words in your heart and in your s',
De 12:15 whatsoever thy s' lusteth after,
20 because thy s' longeth to eat flesh;
20, 21 whatsoever thy s' lusteth after.
13: 3 all your heart and with all your s'.
6 friend, which is as thine own s',
14:26 for whatsoever thy s' lusteth after,
26 or for whatsoever thy s' desireth:
26:16 all thine heart, and with all thy s'.
30: 2 all thine heart, and with all thy s';
6 all thine heart, and with all thy s',
10 all thine heart, and with all thy s'.
Jos 22: 5 all your heart and with all your s'.
J'g 5:21 O my s', thou hast trodden down
10:16 his s' was grieved for the misery of
16:16 so that his s' was vexed unto death;
1Sa 1:10 And she was in bitterness of s', and
15 poured out my s' before the Lord.
26 as thy s' liveth, my lord, I am the
2:16 take as much as thy s' desireth;
17:55 As thy s' liveth, O king, I cannot
18: 1 that the s' of Jonathan was knit
1 was knit with the s' of David,
1 Jonathan loved him as his own s'.
3 because he loved him as his own s'.
20: 3 as thy s' liveth, there is but a step
4 Whatsoever thy s' desireth, I will
17 he loved him as he loved his own s'.
23:20 according to all the desire of thy s'
24:11 yet thou huntest my s' to take it.
25:26 and as thy s' liveth, seeing the Lord
29 to pursue thee, and to seek thy s':
29 s' of my lord shall be bound in the
26:21 my s' was precious in thine eyes
30: 6 the s' of all the people was grieved,
2Sa 4: 9 who hath redeemed my s' out of all
5: 8 blind, that are hated of David's s',
11:11 as thy s' liveth, I will not do this
13:39 the s' of king David longed to go forth
14:19 As thy s' liveth, my lord the king,
1Ki 1:29 redeemed my s' out of all distress,
2: 4 all their heart and with all their s',
8:48 all their heart, and with all their s',
11:37 according to all that thy s' desireth,
17:21 let this child's s' come into him
22 the s' of the child came into him,
2Ki 2: 2, 4, 6 Lord liveth, and as thy s' liveth,
4:27 for her s' is vexed within her:
30 Lord liveth, and as thy s' liveth,
23: 3 with all their heart and all their s',
25 all his heart, and with all his s',
1Ch 22:19 set your heart and your s' to seek
2Ch 6:38 all their heart and with all their s'
15:12 all their heart and with all their s';
34:31 all his heart, and with all his s',
Job 3:20 and life unto the bitter in s';
6: 7 things that my s' refused to touch
7:11 complain in the bitterness of my s'.
15 So that my s' chooseth strangling,
9:21 yet would I not know my s':
10: 1 My s' is weary of my life; I will
1 speak in the bitterness of my s'.
12:10 hand is the s' of every living thing,
14:22 and his s' within him shall mourn.
16: 4 if your s' were in my soul's stead, I
19: 2 How long will ye vex my s', and
21:25 dieth in the bitterness of his s', and
23:13 and what his s' desireth, even that
24:12 the s' of the wounded crieth out:
27: 2 Almighty, who hath vexed my s';
8 when God taketh away his s'?
30:15 they pursue my s' as the wind:
16 now my s' is poured out upon me;
25 was not my s' grieved for the poor?
31:30 to sin by wishing a curse to his s'.
33:18 keepeth back his s' from the pit,
20 bread, and his s' dainty meat.
22 his s' draweth near unto the grave,
28 He will deliver his s' from going
30 To bring back his s' from the pit,
Ps 3: 2 Many there be which say of my s',
6: 3 My s' is also sore vexed: but thou,
4 Return, O Lord, deliver my s': O
7: 2 Lest he tear my s' like a lion,
5 Let the enemy persecute my s',
11: 1 how say ye to my s', Flee as a bird
5 that loveth violence his s' hateth.
13: 2 long shall I take counsel in my s',
16: 2 O my s', thou hast said unto the Lord
10 thou wilt not leave my s' in hell;
17:13 deliver my s' from the wicked,
19: 7 Lord is perfect, converting the s':
22:20 Deliver my s' from the sword; my
29 and none can keep alive his own s'
23: 3 He restoreth my s': he leadeth me
24: 4 not lifted up his s' unto vanity,
25: 1 thee, O Lord, do I lift up my s'.
13 His s' shall dwell at ease; and his
20 O keep my s', and deliver me: let
26: 9 Gather not my s' with sinners, nor
30: 3 brought up my s' from the grave:
31: 7 hast known my s' in adversities;
9 with grief, yea, my s' and my belly.
33:19 To deliver their s' from death, and
20 Our s' waiteth for the Lord: he is
34: 2 My s' shall make her boast in the
22 The Lord redeemeth the s' of his
35: 3 say unto my s', I am thy salvation.
4 put to shame that seek after my s':
7 cause they have digged for my s'.
9 my s' shall be joyful in the Lord:
12 evil for good to the spoiling of my s'.
13 I humbled my s' with fasting; and
17 rescue my s' from...destructions,
40:14 that seek after my s' to destroy it;
41: 4 heal my s'; for I have sinned
42: 1 so panteth my s' after thee, O God.
Ps 42: 2 My s' thirsteth for God, for the
4 things, I pour out my s' in me:
5 Why art thou cast down, O my s'?
6 God, my s' is cast down within me:
11 Why art thou cast down, O my s'?
43: 5 Why art thou cast down, O my s'?
44:25 For our s' is bowed down to the
49: 8 redemption of their s' is precious,
15 But God will redeem my s' from the
18 while he lived he blessed his s':
54: 3 and oppressors seek after my s':
4 is with them that uphold my s'.
55:18 He hath delivered my s' in peace
56: 6 my steps, when they wait for my s'.
13 hast delivered my s' from death:
57: 1 for my s' trusteth in thee: yea, in
4 My s' is among lions: and I lie even
6 for my steps; my s' is bowed down:
59: 3 For, lo, they lie in wait for my s':
62: 1 Truly my s' waiteth upon God:
5 My s', wait thou only upon God;
63: 1 my s' thirsteth for thee, my flesh
5 My s' shall be satisfied as with
8 My s' followeth hard after thee:
9 those that seek my s', to destroy
66: 9 Which holdeth our s' in life, and
16 declare what he hath done for my s'.
69: 1 the waters are come in unto my s'.
10 and chastened my s' with fasting,
18 Draw nigh unto my s', and redeem
70: 2 confounded that seek after my s':
71:10 they that lay wait for my s' take
13 that are adversaries to my s';
23 my s', which thou hast redeemed.
72:14 shall redeem their s' from deceit
74:19 deliver not the s' of thy turtledove
77: 2 my s' refused to be comforted.
78:50 he spared not their s' from death,
84: 2 My s' longeth, yea, even fainteth
86: 2 Preserve my s'; for I am holy: O
4 Rejoice the s' of thy servant: for
4 unto thee, O Lord, do I lift up my s'.
13 delivered my s' from the lowest
14 violent men...sought after my s'; and
88: 3 For my s' is full of troubles: and
14 Lord, why castest thou off my s'?
89:48 shall he deliver his s' from the hand
94:17 my s' had almost dwelt in silence.
19 thy comforts delight my s'.
21 against the s' of the righteous,
103: 1 Bless the Lord, O my s': and all
2 Bless the Lord, O my s', and forget
22 dominion: bless the Lord, O my s'.
104: 1 Bless the Lord, O my s'. O Lord
35 Bless thou the Lord, O my s'.
106:15 but sent leanness into their s'.
107: 5 and thirsty, their s' fainted in them.
9 For he satisfieth the longing s', and
9 filleth the hungry s' with goodness.
18 s' abhorreth all manner of meat;
26 their s' is melted because of trouble.
109:20 them that speak evil against my s'.
31 him from those that condemn his s'.
116: 4 Lord, I beseech thee, deliver my s'.
7 Return unto thy rest, O my s'; for
8 hast delivered my s' from death,
119:20 My s' breaketh for the longing that
25 My s' cleaveth unto the dust:
28 My s' melteth for heaviness:
81 My s' fainteth for thy salvation:
109 My s' is continually in my hand:
129 therefore doth my s' keep them.
167 My s' hath kept thy testimonies;
175 Let my s' live, and it shall praise
120: 2 Deliver my s', O Lord, from lying
6 My s' hath long dwelt with him
121: 7 all evil: he shall preserve thy s'.
123: 4 Our s' is exceedingly filled with the
124: 4 us, the stream had gone over our s':
5 proud waters had gone over our s'.
7 Our s' is escaped as a bird out of
130: 5 I wait for the Lord, my s' doth wait,
6 My s' waiteth for the Lord more
131: 2 my s' is even as a weaned child.
138: 3 me with strength in my s'.
139:14 and that my s' knoweth right well.
141: 8 my trust; leave not my s' destitute.
142: 4 failed me; no man cared for my s'.
7 Bring my s' out of prison, that I
143: 3 the enemy hath persecuted my s';
6 my s' thirsteth after thee, as a
8 walk; for I lift up my s' unto thee.
11 sake bring my s' out of trouble.
12 destroy all them that afflict my s':
146: 1 Lord. Praise the Lord, O my s'.
Pr 2:10 knowledge is pleasant unto thy s';
3:22 So shall they be life unto thy s',
6:30 a thief, if he steal to satisfy his s'
32 that doeth it destroyeth his own s'.
8:36 against me wrongeth his own s':
10: 3 not suffer the s' of the righteous to
11:17 man doeth good to his own s':
25 The liberal s' shall be made fat:
13: 2 the s' of the transgressors shall eat
4 The s' of the sluggard desireth, and
4 s' of the diligent shall be made fat.
19 accomplished is sweet to the s':
25 eateth to the satisfying of his s':
15:32 instruction despiseth his own s':
16:17 keepeth his way preserveth his s'.
24 as an honeycomb, sweet to the s',
18: 7 and his lips are the snare of his s'.
19: 2 that the s' be without knowledge,
8 getteth wisdom loveth his own s':
15 and an idle s' shall suffer hunger.
16 commandment keepeth his own s';

Pr 19:18 let not thy s' spare for his crying.
20: 2 anger sinneth against his own s'.
21:10 The s' of the wicked desireth evil:
23 tongue keepeth his s' from troubles.
22: 5 he that doth keep his s' shall be far
23 spoil the s' of those that spoiled
25 his ways, and get a snare to thy s'.
23:14 and shalt deliver his s' from hell.
24:12 he that keepeth thy s', doth not he
14 knowledge of wisdom be unto thy s':
25:13 he refresheth the s' of his masters.
25 As cold waters to a thirsty s', so is
27: 7 The full s' loatheth an honeycomb;
7 to the hungry s' every bitter thing
29:10 upright: but the just seek his s'.
17 he shall give delight unto thy s'.
24 with a thief hateth his own s':
Ec 2:24 he should make his s' enjoy good
4: 8 labour, and bereave my s' of good?
6: 2 he wanteth nothing for his s' of all
3 and his s' be not filled with good,
7:28 Which yet my s' seeketh, but I find
Ca 1: 7 Tell me, O thou whom my s' loveth,
3: 1 I sought him whom my s' loveth:
2 I will seek him whom my s' loveth:
3 Saw ye him whom my s' loveth?
4 I found him whom my s' loveth:
5: 6 gone: my s' failed when he spake:
6:12 my s' made me like the chariots of
Isa 1:14 your appointed feasts my s' hateth:
3: 9 Woe unto their s'! for they have
10:18 his fruitful field, both s' and body:
26: 8 the desire of our s' is to thy name,
9 With my s' have I desired thee in
29: 8 he awaketh, and his s' is empty:
8 he is faint, and his s' hath appetite:
32: 6 to make empty the s' of the hungry,
38:15 my years in the bitterness of my s'.
17 thou hast in love to my s' delivered
42: 1 elect, in whom my s' delighteth;
44:20 aside, that he cannot deliver his s',
51:23 which have said to thy s', Bow down,
53:10 thou shalt make his s' an offering
11 He shall see of the travail of his s',
12 hath poured out his s' unto death:
55: 2 let your s' delight itself in fatness.
3 me: hear, and your s' shall live;
58: 3 wherefore have we afflicted our s',
5 a day for a man to afflict his s'? is it
10 thou draw out thy s' to the hungry,
10 hungry, and satisfy the afflicted s';
11 and satisfy thy s' in drought, and
61:10 my s' shall be joyful in my God;
66: 3 s' delighteth in their abominations.
Jer 4:10 the sword reacheth unto the s'.
19 O my s', the sound of the trumpet,
31 s' is wearied because of murderers.
5: 9, 29 s' be avenged on such a nation
6: 8 lest my s' depart from thee; lest
9: 9 shall not my s' be avenged on such
12: 7 the dearly beloved of my s' into the
13:17 my s' shall weep in secret places
14:19 Judah? hath thy s' lothed Zion?
18:20 for they have digged a pit for my s'.
20:13 he hath delivered the s' of the poor
31:12 and their s' shall be as a watered
14 I will satiate the s' of the priests
25 I have satiated the weary s', and I
25 replenished every sorrowful s'.
32:41 whole heart and with my whole s'.
38:16 Lord liveth, that made us this s',
17 then thy s' shall live, and this city
20 well unto thee, and thy s' shall live.
50:19 his s' shall be satisfied upon mount
51: 6 and deliver every man his s': be
45 deliver ye every man his s' from
La 1:11 things for meat to relieve the s':
16 comforter that should relieve my s'
2:12 when their s' was poured out into
3:17 thou hast removed my s' far off
20 My s' hath them...in remembrance,
24 Lord is my portion, saith my s';
25 for him, to the s' that seeketh him,
58 hast pleaded the causes of my s';
Eze 3:19 but thou hast delivered thy s'.
21 also thou hast delivered thy s'.
4:14 my s' hath not been polluted:
18: 4 are mine; as the s' of thine father,
4 so also the s' of the son is mine:
4 the s' that sinneth, it shall die.
20 The s' that sinneth, it shall die.
27 and right, he shall save his s' alive.
24:21 and that which your s' pitieth;
33: 5 taketh warning shall deliver his s'.
9 but thou hast delivered thy s'.
Ho 9: 4 bread for their s' shall not come
Jon 2: 5 me about, even to the s': the
7 When my s' fainted within me I
Mic 6: 7 of my body for the sin of my s'?
7: 1 my s' desired the firstripe fruit.
Hab 2: 4 his s' which is lifted up is not
10 and hast sinned against thy s'.
Zec 11: 8 one month; and my s' lothed them,
8 and their s' also abhorred me.
M't 10:28 but are not able to kill the s':
28 to destroy both s' and body in hell.
12:18 in whom my s' is well pleased:
16:26 whole world, and lose his own s'?
26 a man give in exchange for his s'?
22:37 all thy heart, and with all thy s',
26:38 My s' is exceeding sorrowful, even
M'r 8:36 whole world, and lose his own s'?
37 a man give in exchange for his s'?
12:30 all thy heart, and with all thy s',
33 understanding, and with all the s',
14:34 My s' is exceeding sorrowful unto

Lu 1:46 said, My s' doth magnify the Lord,
2:35 shall pierce through thy own s'.
10:27 all thy heart, and with all thy s',
12:19 say to my s', S', thou hast much
20 this night thy s' shall be required
Joh 12:27 Now is my s' troubled; and what
Ac 2:27 thou wilt not leave my s' in hell,
31 that his s' was not left in hell,
43 And fear came upon every s': and
3:23 every s', which will not hear that
4:32 were of one heart and of one s':
Ro 2: 9 every s' of man that doeth evil;
13: 1 Let every s' be subject unto the
1Co 15:45 man Adam was made a living s';
2Co 1:23 call God for a record upon my s',
1Th 5:23 your whole spirit and s' and body
Heb 4:12 dividing asunder of s' and spirit,
6:19 we have as an anchor of the s',
10:38 my s' shall have no pleasure in
39 that believe to the saving of the s'.
Jas 5:20 his way shall save a s' from death,
1Pe 2:11 lusts, which war against the s';
2Pe 2: 8 vexed his righteous s' from day to
3Jo 2 in health, even as thy s' prospereth.
Re 16: 3 and every living s' died in the sea.
18:14 fruits that thy s' lusted after are

soul's
Job 16: 4 if your soul were in my s' stead,

souls
Ge 12: 5 and the s' that they had gotten in
46:15 the s' of his sons and his daughters
18 bare unto Jacob, even sixteen s'.
22 to Jacob: all the s' were fourteen.
25 unto Jacob: all the s' were seven.
26 All the s' that came with Jacob
26 all the s' were threescore and six;
27 born him in Egypt, were two s':
27 all the s' of the house of Jacob,
Ex 1: 5 all the s' that came out of the loins
5 the loins of Jacob were seventy s':
12: 4 according to the number of the s';
30:15, 16 make an atonement for your s'.
Le 16:29 ye shall afflict your s', and do no
31 ye shall afflict your s', by a statute
17:11 to make an atonement for your s':
18:29 the s' that commit them shall be
20:25 make your s' abominable by beast,
23:27 ye shall afflict your s', and offer an
32 of rest, and ye shall afflict your s':
Nu 16:38 these sinners against their own s',
29: 7 ye shall afflict your s': ye shall not
30: 9 they have bound their s', shall
31:50 to make an atonement for our s'
Jos 10:28, 30 and all the s' that were therein;
32 and all the s' that were therein,
35 and all the s' that were therein he
37 and all the s' that were therein;
37 and all the s' that were therein.
39 all the s' that were therein; he left
11:11 smote all the s' that were therein
23:14 all your hearts and in all your s',
1Sa 25:29 the s' of thine enemies, them shall
Ps 72:13 and shall save the s' of the needy.
97:10 preserveth the s' of his saints; he
Pr 11:30 life; and he that winneth s' is wise.
14:25 A true witness delivereth s': but a
Isa 57:16 and the s' which I have made.
Jer 2:34 the blood of the s' of the poor
6:16 and ye shall find rest for your s'.
26:19 procure great evil against our s'.
44: 7 ye this great evil against your s',
La 1:19 sought their meat to relieve their s'.
Eze 7:19 they shall not satisfy their s',
13:18 the head of every stature to hunt s'!
18 Will ye hunt the s' of my people,
18 will ye save the s' alive that come
19 to slay the s' that should not die,
19 to save the s' alive that should not
20 there hunt the s' to make them fly,
20 your arms, and will let the s' go,
20 s' that ye hunt to make them fly.
14:14 they should deliver but their own s'
20 they shall but deliver their own s'
18: 4 Behold, all s' are mine; as the soul
22:25 they have devoured s'; they have
27 to shed blood, and to destroy s', to
M't 11:29 and ye shall find rest unto your s'.
Lu 21:19 your patience possess ye your s'.
Ac 2:41 unto them about three thousand s'.
7:14 kindred, threescore and fifteen s'.
14:22 Confirming the s' of the disciples,
15:24 with words, subverting your s',
27:37 hundred threescore and sixteen s'.
1Th 2: 8 of God only, but also our own s',
Heb 13:17 for they watch for your s', as they
Jas 1:21 word, which is able to save your s'.
1Pe 1: 9 faith, even the salvation of your s'.
22 have purified your s' in obeying the
2:25 Shepherd and Bishop of your s'.
3:20 is, eight s' were saved by water.
4:19 commit the keeping of their s' to
2Pe 2:14 from sin; beguiling unstable s':
Re 6: 9 under the altar the s' of them that
18:13 chariots, and slaves, and s' of men.
20: 4 the s' of them that were beheaded

sound See also SOUNDED; SOUNDETH; SOUNDING; SOUNDS.
Ex 28:35 and his s' shall be heard when he
Le 25: 9 trumpet of the jubile to s' on the
9 the trumpet s' throughout all your
26:36 the s' of a shaken leaf shall chase
Nu 10: 7 blow, but ye shall not s' an alarm.
Jos 6: 5 when ye hear the s' of the trumpet,
20 people heard the s' of the trumpet,
2Sa 5:24 the s' of a going in the tops of the

2Sa 6:15 and with the s' of the trumpet.
15:10 as ye hear the s' of the trumpet,
1Ki 1:40 the earth rent with the s' of them.
41 Joab heard the s' of the trumpet,
14: 6 when Ahijah heard the s' of her feet,
18:41 there is a s' of abundance of rain.
2Ki 6:32 s' of his master's feet behind him?
1Ch 14:15 hear a s' of going in the tops of the
15:19 to s' with cymbals of brass;
28 and with s' of the cornet, and with
16: 5 but Asaph made a s' with cymbals;
42 for those that should make a s',
2Ch 5:13 one s' to be heard in praising and
Ne 4:20 ye hear the s' of the trumpet,
Job 15:21 A dreadful s' is in his ears: in
21:12 and rejoice at the s' of the organ.
37: 2 the s' that goeth out of his mouth.
39:24 he that it is the s' of the trumpet.
Ps 47: 5 the Lord with the s' of a trumpet.
77:17 out water: the skies sent out a s':
89:15 the people that know the joyful s':
92: 3 upon the harp with a solemn s'.
98: 6 With trumpets and s' of cornet
119:80 Let my heart be s' in thy statutes;
150: 3 him with the s' of the trumpet:
Pr 2: 7 He layeth up s' wisdom for the
3:21 keep s' wisdom and discretion:
8:14 Counsel is mine, and s' wisdom: I
14:30 A s' heart is the life of the flesh:
Ec 12: 4 when the s' of the grinding is low,
Isa 16:11 my bowels shall s' like an harp for
Jer 4:19 the s' of the trumpet, the alarm of
21 and hear the s' of the trumpet?
6:17 Hearken to the s' of the trumpet.
8:16 trembled at the s' of the neighing
25:10 s' of the millstones, and the light
42:14 nor hear the s' of the trumpet,
48:36 mine heart shall s' for Moab like
36 mine heart shall s' like pipes for
50:22 A s' of battle is in the land, and of
51:54 A s' of a cry cometh from Babylon,
Eze 10: 5 the s' of the cherubims' wings was
26:13 the s' of thy harps shall be no more
15 the isles shake at the s' of thy fall,
27:28 shake at the s' of the cry of thy
31:16 nations to shake at the s' of his fall,
33: 4 whosoever heareth the s' of the
5 He heard the s' of the trumpet, and
Da 3: 5 ye hear the s' of the cornet, flute,
7 people heard the s' of the cornet,
10 that shall hear the s' of the cornet,
15 ye hear the s' of the cornet, flute,
Joe 2: 1 s' an alarm in my holy mountain:
Am 2: 2 and with the s' of the trumpet:
6: 5 That chant to the s' of the viol, and
M't 6: 2 do not s' a trumpet before thee, as
24:31 angels with a great s' of a trumpet,
Lu 15:27 he hath received him safe and s'.
Joh 3: 8 thou hearest the s' thereof, but
Ac 2: 2 there came a s' from heaven as of
Ro 10:18 their s' went into all the earth,
1Co 14: 7 even things without life giving s',
8 if the trumpet give an uncertain s',
15:52 the trumpet shall s', and the dead
1Ti 1:10 that is contrary to s' doctrine;
2Ti 1: 7 and of love, and of a s' mind.
13 Hold fast the form of s' words,
4: 3 they will not endure s' doctrine;
Tit 1: 9 he may be able by s' doctrine both
13 that they may be s' in the faith;
2: 1 things which become s' doctrine:
2 s' in faith, in charity, in patience.
8 S' speech, that cannot be
Heb 12:19 And the s' of a trumpet, and the
Re 1:15 his voice as the s' of many waters.
8: 6 angels...prepared themselves to s'.
13 the three angels, which are yet to s'!
9: 9 and the s' of their wings was as the
9 as the s' of chariots of many horses
10: 7 angel, when he shall begin to s',
18:22 s' of a millstone shall be heard no

sounded^
1Sa 20:12 when I have s' my father about
2Ch 7: 6 priests s' trumpets before them,
13:14 the priests s' with the trumpets.
23:13 rejoiced, and s' with trumpets,
29:28 sang, and the trumpeters s':
Ne 4:18 he that s' the trumpet was by me.
Lu 1:44 of thy salutation s' in mine ears,
Ac 27:28 s', and found it twenty fathoms:
28 they s' again, and found it fifteen
1Th 1: 8 you s' out the word of the Lord
Re 8: 7 The first angel s', and there
8 the second angel s', and as it were
10 the third angel s', and there fell a
12 the fourth angel s', and the third
9: 1 the fifth angel s', and I saw a star
13 the sixth angel s', and I heard a
11:15 And the seventh angel s'; and there

soundeth
Ex 19:13 when the trumpet s' long, they shall

sounding
1Ch 15:16 harps and cymbals, s', by lifting
2Ch 5:12 twenty priests s' with trumpets:)
13:12 with s' trumpets to cry alarm
Ps 150: 5 him upon the high s' cymbals.
Isa 63:15 the s' of thy bowels and of thy
Eze 7: 7 not the s' again of the mountains.
1Co 13: 1 I am become as s' brass, or a

soundness
Ps 38: 3 no s' in my flesh because of thine
7 and there is no s' in my flesh.
Isa 1: 6 unto the head there is no s' in it;
Ac 3:16 him hath given him this perfect s'

sounds
1Co 14: 7 they give a distinction in the *s*'.

sour
Isa 18: 5 and the *s*' grape is ripening in the
Jer 31:29 The fathers have eaten a *s*' grape,
30 every man that eateth the *s*' grape,
Eze 18: 2 The fathers have eaten *s*' grapes,
Ho 4:18 Their drink is *s*': they have

south See also SOUTHWARD.
Ge 12: 9 going on still toward the *s*'.
13: 1 had, and Lot with him, into the *s*'.
3 journey from the *s*'...to Beth-el,
20: 1 from thence toward the *s*' country,
24:62 for he dwelt in the *s*' country.
28:14 east, and to the north, and to the *s*':
Ex 26:18 boards on the *s*' side southward.
35 of the tabernacle toward the *s*':
27: 9 *s*' side southward there shall be
36:23 boards for the *s*' side southward:
38: 9 *s*' side southward the hangings of
Nu 2:10 the *s*' side shall be the standard
10: 6 camps that lie on the *s*' side shall
13:22 And they ascended by the *s*', and
29 Amalekites dwell in...the *s*':
21: 1 Canaanite, which dwelt in the *s*',
33:40 which dwelt in the *s*' in the land of
34: 3 your *s*' quarter shall be from the
3 your *s*' border shall be the outmost
4 turn from the *s*' to the ascent of
4 be from the *s*' to Kadesh-barnea,
35: 5 on the *s*' side two thousand cubits,
De 1: 7 in the vale, and in the *s*', and by the
33:23 possess thou the west and the *s*'.
34: 3 the *s*', and the plain of the valley of
Jos 10:40 country of the hills, and of the *s*',
11: 2 and of the plains *s*' of Chinneroth,
16 all the *s*' country, and all the land
12: 3 the *s*', under Ashdoth-pisgah:
8 wilderness, and in the *s*' country;
13: 4 From the *s*', all the land of the
15: 1 the uttermost part of the *s*' coast.
2 their *s*' border was from the shore
3 to the *s*' side to Maaleh-acrabbim,
3 on the *s*' side unto Kadesh-barnea,
4 the sea: this shall be your *s*' coast.
7 which is on the *s*' side of the river:
8 unto the *s*' side of the Jebusite;
19 for thou hast given me a *s*' land;
18: 5 shall abide in their coast on the *s*',
13 hill that lieth on the *s*' side of the
15 the *s*' quarter was from the end of
16 to the side of Jebusi on the *s*', and
19 the salt sea at the *s*' end of Jordan:
19 of Jordan: this was the *s*' coast.
19: 8 to Baalath-beer, Ramath of the *s*'.
34 reacheth to Zebulun on the *s*' side,
J'g 1: 9 in the mountain, and in the *s*', and
15 for thou hast given me a *s*' land;
16 which lieth in the *s*' of Arad;
21:19 Shechem, and on the *s*' of Lebonah.
1Sa 20:41 arose out of a place toward the *s*',
23:19 which is on the *s*' of Jeshimon?
24 in the plain on the *s*' of Jeshimon.
27:10 said, Against the *s*' of Judah, and
10 against the *s*' of the Jerahmeelites,
10 and against the *s*' of the Kenites.
30: 1 the Amalekites had invaded the *s*',
14 upon the *s*' of the Cherethites,
14 to Judah, and upon the *s*' of Caleb;
27 to them which were in *s*' Ramoth,
2Sa 24: 7 they went out to the *s*' of Judah,
1Ki 7:25 and three looking toward the *s*',
39 house eastward over against the *s*'.
1Ch 9:24 toward the east, west, north, and *s*'.
2Ch 4: 4 and three looking toward the *s*',
10 of the east end, over against the *s*'.
28:18 low country, and of the *s*' of Judah,
Job 9: 9 and the chambers of the *s*'.
37: 9 Out of the *s*' cometh...whirlwind:
17 quieteth the earth by the *s*' wind?
39:26 stretch her wings toward the *s*'?
Ps 75: 6 from the west, nor from the *s*'.
78:26 power he brought in the *s*' wind.
89:12 north and the *s*' thou hast created
107: 3 from the north, and from the *s*'.
126: 4 O Lord, as the streams in the *s*'.
Ec 1: 6 The wind goeth toward the *s*',
11: 3 and if the tree fall toward the *s*',
Ca 4:16 O north wind; and come, thou *s*';
Isa 21: 1 As whirlwinds in the *s*' pass
30: 6 The burden of the beasts of the *s*':
43: 6 up; and to the *s*', Keep not back:
Jer 13:19 The cities of the *s*' shall be shut
17:26 the mountains, and from the *s*',
32:44 valley, and in the cities of the *s*':
33:13 the vale, and in the cities of the *s*',
Eze 20:46 man, set thy face toward the *s*',
46 and drop thy word toward the *s*',
46 against the forest of the *s*' field;
47 say to the forest of the *s*', Hear the
47 all faces from the *s*' to the north
21: 4 all flesh from the *s*' to the north:
40: 2 was as the frame of a city on the *s*'.
24 that he brought me toward the *s*',
24 and behold a gate toward the *s*':
27 in the inner court toward the *s*':
27 from gate to gate toward the *s*'
28 to the inner court by the *s*' gate:
28 he measured the *s*' gate according
44 their prospect was toward the *s*':
45 whose prospect is toward the *s*',
41:11 and another door toward the *s*':
42:12 chambers that were toward the *s*'
13 chambers and the *s*' chambers,
18 measured the *s*' side, five hundred
Eze 46: 9 go out by the way of the *s*' gate;
9 entereth by the way of the *s*' gate
47: 1 the house, at the *s*' side of the altar.
19 And the *s*' side southward, from
19 And this is the *s*' side southward.
48:10 and toward the *s*' five and twenty
16 the *s*' side four thousand and five
17 and toward the *s*' two hundred and
28 of Gad, at the *s*' side southward,
33 at the *s*' side four thousand and
Da 8: 9 toward the *s*', and toward the east,
11: 5 the king of the *s*' shall be strong,
6 for the king's daughter of the *s*'
9 So the king of the *s*' shall come
11 the king of the *s*' shall be moved
14 stand up against the king of the *s*':
15 arms of the *s*' shall not withstand,
25 courage against the king of the *s*'
25 king of the *s*' shall be stirred up to
29 return, and come toward the *s*';
40 shall the king of the *s*' push at
Ob 19 And they of the *s*' shall possess the
20 shall possess the cities of the *s*'.
Zec 6: 6 go forth toward the *s*' country.
7: 7 inhabited the *s*' and the plain?
9:14 shall go with whirlwinds of the *s*'.
14: 4 north, and half of it toward the *s*'.
10 Geba to Rimmon *s*' of Jerusalem:
M't 12:42 queen of the *s*' shall rise up in the
Lu 11:31 queen of the *s*' shall rise up in the
12:55 And when ye see the *s*' wind blow,
13:29 and from the *s*', and shall sit down
Ac 8:26 Arise, and go toward the *s*' unto
27:12 toward the *s*' west and north west.
13 And when the *s*' wind blew softly,
28:13 and after one day the *s*' wind blew,
Re 21:13 three gates; on the *s*' three gates;

south-country See SOUTH and COUNTRY.

south-quarter See SOUTH and QUARTER.

south-side See SOUTH and SIDE.

southward
Ge 13:14 *s*', and eastward, and westward:
Ex 26:18 twenty boards on the south side *s*'.
27: 9 south side *s*' there shall be hangings
36:23 twenty boards for the south side *s*':
38: 9 on the south side *s*' the hangings
40:24 the south side of the tabernacle *s*'.
Nu 3:29 on the side of the tabernacle *s*'.
13:17 Get you up this way *s*', and go up
De 3:27 northward, and *s*', and eastward,
Jos 15: 1 the wilderness of Zin *s*' was the
2 sea, from the bay that looketh *s*':
21 Judah toward the coast of Edom *s*'
17: 9 unto the river Kanah, *s*' of the river:
10 *S*' it was Ephraim's, and northward
18:13 side of Luz, which is Beth-el, *s*';
14 compassed the corner of the sea *s*',
14 hill that lieth before Beth-horon *s*':
1Sa 14: 5 the other *s*' over against Gibeah.
1Ch 26:15 To Obed-edom *s*'; and to his sons
17 northward four a day, *s*' four a day,
Eze 47:19 And the south side *s*', from Tamar
19 sea. And this is the south side *s*'.
48:28 border of Gad, at the south side *s*',
Da 8: 4 westward, and northward, and *s*';

south-west See SOUTH and WEST.

south-wind See SOUTH and WIND.

sow See also SOWED; SOWEST; SOWETH; SOWING; SOWN.
Ge 47:23 for you, and ye shall *s*' the land.
Ex 23:10 six years thou shalt *s*' thy land,
Le 19:19 shalt not *s*' thy field with mingled
25: 3 Six years thou shalt *s*' thy field,
4 thou shalt neither *s*' thy field, nor
11 ye shall not *s*', neither reap that
20 we shall not *s*', nor gather in our
22 And ye shall *s*' the eight year, and
26:16 and ye shall *s*' your seed in vain,
De 22: 9 shalt not *s*' thy vineyard with divers
2Ki 19:29 in the third year *s*' ye, and reap,
Job 4: 8 plow iniquity, and *s*' wickedness,
31: 8 Then let me *s*', and let another eat;
Ps 107:37 *s*' the fields, and plant vineyards,
126: 5 that *s*' in tears shall reap in joy.
Ec 11: 4 observeth the wind shall not *s*';
6 In the morning *s*' thy seed, and in
Isa 28:24 the plowman plow all day to *s*'?
30:23 seed, that thou shalt *s*' the ground
32:20 Blessed are ye that *s*' beside all
37:30 in the third year *s*' ye, and reap,
Jer 4: 3 ground, and *s*' not among thorns.
31:27 that I will *s*' the house of Israel and
35: 7 shall ye build house, nor *s*' seed,
Ho 2:23 I will *s*' her unto me in the earth;
10:12 *S*' to yourselves in righteousness,
Mic 6:15 Thou shalt *s*', but thou shalt not
Zec 10: 9 I will *s*' them among the people:
M't 6:26 the fowls of the air: for they *s*' not,
13: 3 Behold, a sower went forth to *s*';
27 Sir, didst thou not *s*' good seed in
M'r 4: 3 there went out a sower to *s*':
Lu 8: 5 A sower went out to *s*' his seed:
12:24 for they neither *s*' nor reap; which
19:21 and reapest that thou didst not *s*'.
22 down, and reaping that I did not *s*':
2Pe 2:22 and the *s*' that was washed to her

sowed See also SOWEDST.
Ge 26:12 Then Isaac *s*' in that land, and
J'g 9:45 down the city, and *s*' it with salt.
M't 13: 4 when he *s*', some seeds fell by the
24 unto a man which *s*' good seed in
25 came and *s*' tares among the wheat,
31 which a man took, and *s*' in his field:
M't 13:39 The enemy that *s*' them is the devil;
25:26 knewest that I reap where I *s*' not,
M'r 4: 4 as he *s*', some fell by the way side,
Lu 8: 5 as he *s*', some fell by the way side;

sowedst
De 11:10 where thou *s*' thy seed, and

sower
Isa 55:10 that it may give seed to the *s*',
Jer 50:16 Cut off the *s*' from Babylon, and
M't 13: 3 Behold, a *s*' went forth to sow;
18 Hear ye...the parable of the *s*'.
M'r 4: 3 Behold, there went out a *s*' to sow:
14 The *s*' soweth the word.
Lu 8: 5 A *s*' went out to sow his seed: and
2Co 9:10 he that ministereth seed to the *s*'

sowest
1Co 15:36 which thou *s*' is not quickened,
37 And that which thou *s*',
37 thou *s*' not that body that shall be

soweth
Pr 6:14 continually; he *s*' discord.
19 that *s*' discord among brethren.
11:18 but to him that *s*' righteousness
16:28 A froward man *s*' strife: and a
22: 8 He that *s*' iniquity shall reap
Am 9:13 treader of grapes him that *s*' seed:
M't 13:37 He that *s*' the good seed is the Son
M'r 4:14 The sower *s*' the word.
Joh 4:36 that both he that *s*' and he that
37 true, One *s*', and another reapeth.
2Co 9: 6 He which *s*' sparingly shall reap
6 he which *s*' bountifully shall reap
Ga 6: 7 whatsoever a man *s*', that shall he
8 For he that *s*' to his flesh shall of
8 but he that *s*' to the Spirit shall of

sowing
Le 11:37 their carcase fall upon any *s*' seed
26: 5 shall reach unto the *s*' time:

sowing-time See SOWING and TIME.

sown
Ex 23:16 which thou hast *s*' in the field:
Le 11:37 any sowing seed which is to be *s*',
De 21: 4 which is neither eared nor *s*',
22: 9 fruit of thy seed which thou hast *s*',
29:23 and burning, that it is not *s*', nor
J'g 6: 3 And so it was when Israel had *s*',
Ps 97:11 Light is *s*' for the righteous, and
Isa 19: 7 every thing *s*' by the brooks, shall
40:24 yea, they shall not be *s*': yea,
61:11 things that are *s*' in it to spring
Jer 2: 2 in a land that was not *s*'.
12:13 They have *s*' wheat, but shall reap
Eze 36: 9 you, and ye shall be tilled and *s*':
Ho 8: 7 For they have *s*' the wind, and they
Na 1:14 that no more of thy name be *s*':
Hag 1: 6 Ye have *s*' much, and bring in
M't 13:19 that which was *s*' in his heart.
25:24 reaping where thou hast not *s*',
M'r 4:15 the way side, where the word is *s*';
15 the word that was *s*' in their hearts.
16 which are *s*' on stony ground; who,
18 they which are *s*' among thorns;
20 they which are *s*' on good ground;
31 when it is *s*' in the earth, is less
32 But when it is *s*', it groweth up, and
1Co 9:11 have *s*' unto you spiritual things,
15:42 It is *s*' in corruption; it is raised in
43 It is *s*' in dishonour; it is raised in
43 it is *s*' in wickedness; it is raised in
44 It is *s*' a natural body; it is raised
2Co 9:10 multiply your seed *s*', and increase
Jas 3:18 fruit of righteousness is *s*' in peace

space^
Ge 29:14 abode with him the *s*' of a month.
32:16 put a *s*' betwixt drove and drove.
Le 25: 8 the *s*' of the seven sabbaths of
30 within the *s*' of a full year, then
De 2:14 And the *s*' in which we came from
Jos 3: 4 shall be a *s*' between you and it,
1Sa 26:13 a great *s*' being between them:
Ezr 9: 8 a little *s*' grace hath been shewed
Jer 28:11 within the *s*' of two full years.
Eze 40:12 *s*' also before the little chambers
12 the *s*' was one cubit on that side:
Lu 22:59 And about the *s*' of one hour after
Ac 5: 7 it was about the *s*' of three hours
34 to put the apostles forth a little *s*';
13:20 the *s*' of four hundred and fifty years.
21 of Benjamin, but the *s*' of forty years.
15:33 after they had tarried there a *s*',
19: 8 boldly for the *s*' of three months,
10 continued by the *s*' of two years;
34 about the *s*' of two hours cried out,
20:31 the *s*' of three years I ceased not
Jas 5:17 the *s*' of three years and six months.
Re 2:21 And I gave her *s*' to repent of her
8: 1 in heaven about the *s*' of half an hour.
14:20 *s*' of a thousand and six hundred
17:10 cometh, he must continue a short *s*'.

Spain (*spane*)
Ro 15:24 I take my journey into *S*', I will
28 fruit, I will come by you into *S*'.

spake^ See also SPAKEST.
Ge 8:15 And God *s*' unto Noah, saying,
9: 8 And God *s*' unto Noah, and to his
16:13 name of the Lord that *s*' unto her,
18:29 And he *s*' unto him yet again, and
19:14 out, and *s*' unto his sons in law,
21:22 chief captain...*s*' unto Abraham,
22: 7 Isaac *s*' unto Abraham his father,
23: 3 *s*' unto the sons of Heth, saying,
13 he *s*' unto Ephron in the audience

Ge 24: 7 which s' unto me, and that sware
30 Thus s' the man unto me: that he
27: 5 when Isaac s' to Esau his son.
6 Rebekah s' unto Jacob her son,
29: 9 And while he yet s' with them,
31: 11 angel of God s' unto me in a dream
29 the God of your father s' unto me
34: 3 and s' kindly unto the damsel.
4 And Shechem s' unto his father
35: 15 the place where God s' with him,
39: 10 as she s' to Joseph day by day,
14 house, and s' unto them, saying,
17 And she s' unto him according to
19 of his wife, which she s' unto him,
41: 9 s' the chief butler unto Pharaoh,
42: 7 them, and s' roughly unto them;
14 That is it that I s' unto you, saying,
22 S' I not unto you, saying, Do not
23 he s' unto them by an interpreter.
30 lord of the land, s' roughly to us,
37 Reuben s' unto his father, saying,
43: 3 And Judah s' unto him, saying, The
27 well, the old man of whom ye s'?
29 brother, of whom ye s' unto me?
44: 6 and he s' unto them these same
46: 2 God s' unto Israel in the visions of
47: 5 Pharaoh s' unto Joseph, saying, Thy
49: 28 it that their fathers s' unto them,
50: 4 were past, Joseph s' unto the house
17 And Joseph wept when they s' unto
21 them, and s' kindly unto them.
Ex 1: 15 s' to the Hebrew midwives,
4: 30 Aaron s' all the words which the
5: 10 and they s' to the people, saying,
6: 2 And God s' unto Moses, and said
9 And Moses s' so unto the children
10 And the Lord s' unto Moses, saying,
12 And Moses s' before the Lord,
13 Lord s' unto Moses and unto Aaron,
27 These are they which s' to Pharaoh
28 day when the Lord s' unto Moses
29 That the Lord s' unto Moses, saying,
7: 7 old, when they s' unto Pharaoh.
8 Lord s' unto Moses and unto Aaron,
19 Lord s' unto Moses, Say unto Aaron,
8: 1 And the Lord s' unto Moses, Go unto
5 Lord s' unto Moses, Say unto Aaron,
12: 1 the Lord s' unto Moses and Aaron
13: 1 the Lord s' unto Moses, saying,
14: 1 And the Lord s' unto Moses, saying,
15: 1 this song unto the Lord, and s',
16: 9 Moses s' unto Aaron, Say unto all
10 Aaron s' unto the...congregation
11 And the Lord s' unto Moses, saying,
19: 19 Moses s', and God answered him by
25 unto the people, and s' unto them.
20: 1 And God s' all these words, saying,
25: 1 And the Lord s' unto Moses, saying,
30: 11, 17 the Lord s' unto Moses, saying,
22 Moreover the Lord s' unto Moses,
31: 1 And the Lord s' unto Moses, saying,
12 And the Lord s' unto Moses, saying,
33: 11 Lord s' unto Moses face to face,
34: 34 and s' unto the children of Israel
35: 4 Moses s' unto all the congregation
36: 5 And they s' unto Moses, saying, The
40: 1 the Lord s' unto Moses, saying,
Le 1: 1 s' unto him out of the tabernacle of
4: 1 And the Lord s' unto Moses, saying,
5: 14 And the Lord s' unto Moses, saying,
6: 1, 8, 19, 24 Lord s' unto Moses, saying,
7: 22, 28 the Lord s' unto Moses, saying,
8: 1 And the Lord s' unto Moses, saying,
10: 3 This is it that the Lord s', saying, I
8 And the Lord s' unto Aaron, saying,
12 And Moses s' unto Aaron, and unto
11: 1 Lord s' unto Moses and to Aaron,
12: 1 And the Lord s' unto Moses, saying,
13: 1 the Lord s' unto Moses and Aaron,
14: 1 And the Lord s' unto Moses, saying,
33 Lord s' unto Moses and untoAaron,
15: 1 Lord s' unto Moses and to Aaron,
16: 1 Lord s' unto Moses after the death
17: 1 And the Lord s' unto Moses, saying,
18: 1 And the Lord s' unto Moses, saying,
19: 1 And the Lord s' unto Moses, saying,
20: 1 And the Lord s' unto Moses, saying,
21: 16 And the Lord s' unto Moses, saying,
22: 1, 17, 26 Lord s' unto Moses, saying,
23: 1, 9, 23, 26, 33 Lord s' unto Moses,
24: 1, 13 the Lord s' unto Moses, saying,
23 Moses s' to the children of Israel,
25: 1 Lord s' unto Moses in mount Sinai,
27: 1 And the Lord s' unto Moses, saying,
Nu 1: 1 And the Lord s' unto Moses in the
2: 1 Lord s' unto Moses and unto Aaron,
3: 1 Lord s' with Moses in mount Sinai.
5, 11 the Lord s' unto Moses, saying,
14 And the Lord s' unto Moses in the
44 And the Lord s' unto Moses, saying,
4: 1, 17 Lord s' unto Moses and...Aaron,
21 And the Lord s' unto Moses, saying,
5: 1 And the Lord s' unto Moses, saying,
4 as the Lord s' unto Moses, so did
5, 11 the Lord s' unto Moses, saying,
6: 1, 22 the Lord s' unto Moses, saying,
7: 4 And the Lord s' unto Moses, saying,
89 cherubims: and he s' unto him.
8: 1, 5, 23 Lord s' unto Moses, saying,
9: 1 And the Lord s' unto Moses in the
4 And Moses s' unto the children of
9 And the Lord s' unto Moses, saying,
10: 1 And the Lord s' unto Moses, saying,
11: 25 down in a cloud, and s' unto him,
12: 1 Miriam and Aaron s' against Moses
4 the Lord s' suddenly unto Moses,

Nu 13: 1 the Lord s' unto Moses, saying,
14: 7 they s' unto all the company of the
26 Lord s' unto Moses and...Aaron,
15: 1, 17 And the Lord s' unto Moses,
37 And the Lord s' unto Moses, saying,
16: 5 he s' unto Korah and unto all his
20 Lord s' unto Moses and unto Aaron,
23 And the Lord s' unto Moses, saying,
26 And he s' unto the congregation,
36, 44 the Lord s' unto Moses, saying,
17: 1 And the Lord s' unto Moses, saying,
6 And Moses s' unto the children of
12 children of Israel s' unto Moses,
18: 8 And the Lord s' unto Aaron,
20 And the Lord s' unto Aaron,
25 the Lord s' unto Moses, saying,
19: 1 Lord s' unto Moses and unto Aaron,
20: 3 people chode with Moses, and s',
7 the Lord s' unto Moses, saying,
12 Lord s' unto Moses and Aaron,
23 the Lord s' unto Moses and Aaron
21: 5 And the people s' against God,
22: 7 and s' unto him the words of Balak.
24: 12 S' I not also to thy messengers
25: 10, 16 the Lord s' unto Moses, saying,
26: 1 Lord s' unto Moses and...Eleazar
3 Moses and Eleazar the priest s'
52 And the Lord s' unto Moses, saying,
27: 6 And the Lord s' unto Moses, saying,
15 Moses s' unto the Lord, saying,
28: 1 And the Lord s' unto Moses, saying,
30: 1 And Moses s' unto the heads of the
31: 1 And the Lord s' unto Moses, saying,
3 And Moses s' unto the people,
25 And the Lord s' unto Moses, saying,
32: 2 Reuben came and s' unto Moses,
25 children of Reuben s' unto Moses,
33: 50 Lord s' unto Moses in the plains
34: 1, 16 the Lord s' unto Moses, saying,
35: 1 Lord s' unto Moses in the plains
9 And the Lord s' unto Moses, saying,
36: 1 came near, and s' before Moses,
De 1: 1 which Moses s' unto all Israel
3 Moses s' unto the children of Israel,
6 Lord our God s' unto us in Horeb,
9 I s' unto you at that time, saying, I
43 So I s' unto you; and ye would not
2: 1 Red sea, as the Lord s' unto me:
2 And the Lord s' unto me, saying,
17 That the Lord s' unto me, saying,
4: 12 Lord s' unto you out of the midst
15 that the Lord s' unto you in Horeb
45 Moses s' unto the children of Israel,
5: 22 the Lord s' unto all your assembly
28 of your words, when ye s' unto me;
9: 10 the Lord s' with you in the mount
13 Furthermore the Lord s' unto me,
10: 4 the Lord s' unto you in the mount
13: 2 to pass, whereof he s' unto thee,
27: 9 the Levites s' unto all Israel, saying,
28: 68 by the way whereof I s' unto thee,
31: 1 Moses went and s' these words
30 And Moses s' in the ears of all the
32: 44 and s' all the words of this song
48 Lord s' unto Moses that selfsame
Jos 1: 1 the Lord s' unto Joshua the son of
12 the tribe of Manasseh, s' Joshua,
3: 6 Joshua s' unto the priests, saying,
4: 1 that the Lord s' unto Joshua, saying,
8 as the Lord s' unto Joshua,
12 of Israel, as Moses s' unto them:
15 the Lord s' unto Joshua, saying,
21 And he s' unto the children of Israel,
7: 2 and s' unto them, saying, Go up and
9: 11 inhabitants of our country s' to us,
22 them, and he s' unto them, saying,
10: 12 Then s' Joshua to the Lord in the
14: 10 the Lord s' this word unto Moses,
12 whereof the Lord s' in that day;
17: 14 children of Joseph s' unto Joshua,
17 Joshua s' unto the house of Joseph,
20: 1 Lord also s' unto Joshua, saying,
2 I s' unto you by the hand of Moses:
21: 2 they s' unto them at Shiloh in the
22: 8 he s' unto them, saying, Return
15 and they s' with them, saying,
30 and the children of Manasseh s',
23: 14 things which the Lord your God s'
24: 27 the words of the Lord which he s'
J'g 2: 4 the angel of the Lord s' these words
8: 8 Penuel, and s' unto them likewise:
9 he s' also unto the men of Penuel,
9: 3 his mother's brethren s' of him in
37 Gaal s' again and said, See there
15: 13 And they s' unto him, saying, No;
19: 22 and s' to the master of the house,
Ru 4: 1 kinsman of whom Boaz s' came
1Sa 1: 13 Now Hannah, she s' in her heart;
7: 3 And Samuel s' unto all the house of
9: 9 went to enquire of God, thus he s',
17 the man whom I s' to thee of! this
10: 16 the kingdom, whereof Samuel s', he
16: 4 Samuel did that which the Lord s',
17: 23 s' according to the same words:
26 David s' to the men that stood by
28 heard when he s' unto the men;
30 and s' after the same manner:
31 words were heard which David s',
18: 23 Saul's servants s' those words in the
24 saying, On this manner s' David.
19: 1 And Saul s' to Jonathan his son, and
4 And Jonathan s' good of David unto
20: 26 Saul s' not any thing that day: for
25: 9 s' to Nabal according to all those
40 they s' unto her, saying, David sent
28: 12 and the woman s' to Saul, saying,

1Sa 28: 17 hath done to him, as he s' by me:
30: 6 for the people s' of stoning him,
2Sa 3: 19 And Abner also s' in the ears of
5: 1 s', saying, Behold, we are thy bone
6 which s' unto David, saying, Except
7: 7 s' I a word with any of the tribes
12: 18 child was yet alive, we s' unto him,
13: 22 And Absalom s' unto his brother
14: 4 the woman of Tekoah s' to the king,
17: 6 Absalom s' unto him, saying,
20: 18 Then she s', saying, They were wont
22: 1 David s' unto the Lord the words
23: 2 The Spirit of the Lord s' by me, and
3 the Rock of Israel s' to me, He that
24: 17 David s' unto the Lord when he saw
1Ki 1: 11 Nathan s' unto Bath-sheba the
42 while he yet s', behold, Jonathan
2: 4 word which he s' concerning me,
27 he s' concerning the house of Eli in
3: 22 son. Thus they s' before the king.
26 Then s' the woman whose the living
4: 32 he s' three thousand proverbs:
33 he s' of trees, from the cedar tree
33 he s' also of beasts, and of fowl, and
5: 5 the Lord s' unto David my father,
6: 12 which I s' unto David thy father:
8: 12 Then s' Solomon, The Lord said
15 s' with his mouth unto David
20 hath performed his word that he s',
12: 3 Israel came, and s' unto Rehoboam,
7 they s' unto him, saying, If thou
10 grown up with him s' unto him,
10 unto this people that s' unto thee,
14 s' to them after the counsel of the
15 which the Lord s' by Ahijah the
13: 18 an angel s' unto me by the word of
26 of the Lord, which he s' unto him.
27 he s' to his sons, saying, Saddle me
31 him, that he s' to his sons, saying,
14: 18 he s' by the hand of his servant
15: 29 which he s' by his servant Ahijah
16: 12 which he s' against Baasha by Jehu
34 which he s' by Joshua the son of
17: 16 of the Lord, which he s' by Elijah.
20: 28 God, and s' unto the king of Israel,
21: 2 Ahab s' unto Naboth, saying, Give
6 I s' unto Naboth the Jezreelite, and
23 of Jezebel also s' the Lord, saying,
22: 13 gone to call Micaiah s' unto him,
38 the word of the Lord which he s'.
2Ki 1: 9 he s' unto him, Thou man of God,
2: 22 to the saying of Elisha which he s'.
5: 13 s' unto him, and said, My father, if
7: 17 who s' when the king came down
8: 1 Then s' Elisha unto the woman,
9: 12 Thus and thus s' he to me, saying,
36 which he s' by his servant Elijah
10: 10 the Lord s' concerning the house of
10 which he s' by his servant Elijah.
17 of the Lord, which he s' to Elijah.
14: 25 he s' by the hand of his servant
15: 12 of the Lord which he s' unto Jehu,
17: 26 they s' to the king of Assyria,
18: 28 in the Jews' language, and s',
21: 10 And the Lord s' by his servants the
22: 19 heardest what I s' against this place,
24: 2 he s' by his servants the prophets.
25: 28 And he s' kindly to him, and set his
1Ch 15: 16 David s' to the chief of the Levites
17: 6 s' I a word to any of the judges of
21: 9 And the Lord s' unto Gad, David's
19 which he s' in the name of the Lord.
2Ch 1: 2 Then Solomon s' unto all Israel, to
6: 4 that which he s' with his mouth
10: 3 all Israel came and s' to Rehoboam,
7 they s' unto him, saying, If thou be
10 brought up with him s' unto him,
10 answer the people that s' unto thee,
15 which he s' by the hand of Ahijah
18: 12 that went to call Micaiah s' to him,
19 one s' saying after this manner,
30: 22 Hezekiah s' comfortably unto all
32: 6 s' comfortably to them, saying,
16 his servants s' yet more against the
19 s' against the God of Jerusalem,
24 he s' unto him, and he gave him a
33: 10 And the Lord s' to Manasseh, and
18 words of the seers that s' to him in
34: 22 and they s' to her to that effect.
35: 25 the singing women s' of Josiah in
Ne 4: 2 he s' before his brethren and the
8: 1 and they s' unto Ezra the scribe to
13: 24 their children s' half in the speech
Es 3: 4 pass, when they s' daily unto him,
4: 10 Again Esther s' unto Hatach, and
8: 3 And Esther s' yet again before the
Job 2: 13 and none s' a word unto him: for
3: 2 And Job s', and said,
19: 18 I arose, and they s' against me.
29: 22 After my words they s' not again: and
32: 16 (for they s' not, but stood still, and
35: 1 Elihu s' moreover, and said,
Ps 18: *title* who s' unto the Lord the words
33: 9 For he s', and it was done; he
39: 3 burned: then s' I with my tongue,
78: 19 Yea, they s' against God; they said,
99: 7 He s' unto them in the cloudy pillar:
105: 31 He s', and there came divers sorts
34 He s', and the locusts came, and
106: 33 so that he s' unadvisedly with his
Pr 30: 1 the man s' unto Ithiel, even unto
Ca 2: 10 My beloved s', and said unto me,
5: 6 gone: my soul failed when he s':
Isa 7: 10 Lord s' again unto Ahaz, saying,
8: 5 The Lord s' also unto me again,
11 For the Lord s' thus to me with a

Isa 20: 2 At the same time s· the Lord by
65: 12 when I s·, ye did not hear; but did
66: 4 when I s·, they did not hear: but
Jer 7: 13 I s· unto you, rising up early and
22 For I s· not unto your fathers, nor
8: 6 and heard, but they s· not aright:
14: 14 them, neither s· unto them:
19: 5 which I commanded not, nor s· it.
20: 8 For since I s·, I cried out, I cried
22: 21 I s· unto thee in thy prosperity; but
25: 2 the prophet s· unto all the people of
26: 11 s· the priests and the prophets unto
12 s· Jeremiah unto all the princes
17 s· to all the assembly of the people,
18 s· to all the people of Judah, saying,
27: 12 I s· also to Zedekiah king of Judah
16 Also I s· to the priests and to all
28: 1 s· unto me in the house of the Lord,
11 And Hananiah s· in the presence of
30: 4 that the Lord s· concerning Israel
31: 20 for since I s· against him, I do
34: 6 Jeremiah the prophet s· all these
36: 2 nations, from the day I s· unto thee,
37: 2 he s· by the prophet Jeremiah.
38: 8 the king's house, and s· to the king,
40: 15 the son of Kareah s· to Gedaliah in
43: 2 s· Azariah the son of Hoshaiah, and
45: 1 that Jeremiah the prophet s· unto
46: 13 word that the Lord s· to Jeremiah
50: 1 that the Lord s· against Babylon
51: 12 done that which he s· against the
52: 32 And s· kindly unto him, and set his
Eze 1: 28 and I heard a voice of one that s·.
2: 2 spirit entered into me when he s·.
2 that I heard him that s· unto me.
3: 24 me upon my feet, and s· with me,
10: 2 he s· unto the man clothed with
11: 25 I s· unto them of the captivity
24: 18 So I s· unto the people in the
Da 1: 3 And the king s· unto Ashpenaz the
2: 4 Then s· the Chaldeans to the king
3: 9 They s· and said to the king
14 Nebuchadnezzar s· and said unto
19 therefore he s·, and commanded
24 rose up in haste, and s·, and said
26 s·, and said, Shadrach, Meshach,
28 Then Nebuchadnezzar s·, and said,
4: 19 The king s·, and said, Belteshazzar,
30 The king s·, and said, Is not this
5: 7 king s·, and said to the wise men
10 and the queen s· and said, O king,
13 the king s· and said unto Daniel,
6: 12 and s· before the king concerning
16 the king s· and said unto Daniel,
20 and the king s· and said to Daniel,
7: 2 Daniel s· and said, I saw in my
11 the great words which the horn s·:
20 a mouth that s· very great things,
8: 13 unto that certain saint which s·,
9: 6 which s· in thy name to our kings,
12 which he s· against us, and against
10: 16 then I opened my mouth, and s·,
Ho 12: 4 in Beth-el, and there he s· with us;
13: 1 When Ephraim s· trembling, he
Jon 2: 10 And the Lord s· unto the fish, and
Hag 1: 13 s· Haggai the Lord's messenger
Zec 1: 21 he s·, saying, These are the horns
3: 4 And he answered and s· unto those
4: 4 So I answered and s· to the angel
6 Then he answered and s· unto me,
6: 8 he upon me, and s· unto me,
Mal 3: 16 the Lord s· often one to another:
M't 9: 18 While he s· these things unto them,
33 the devil was cast out, the dumb s·
12: 22 blind and dumb both s· and saw.
13: 3 he s· many things...in parables,
33 Another parable s· he unto them;
34 these things s· Jesus...in parables;
34 and without a parable s· he not
14: 27 straightway Jesus s· unto them,
16: 11 I s· it not to you concerning bread,
17: 5 While he yet s·, behold, a bright
13 s· unto them of John the Baptist.
21: 45 they perceived that he s· of them.
22: 1 s· unto them again by parables,
23: 1 Then s· Jesus to the multitude,
26: 47 And while he yet s·, lo, Judas, one
28: 18 And Jesus came and s· unto them,
M'r 3: 9 he s· to his disciples, that a small
4: 33 many such parables s· he the word
34 But without a parable s· he not
5: 35 While he yet s·, there came from
7: 35 tongue was loosed, and he s· plain.
8: 32 And he s· that saying openly. And
9: 18 and I s· to thy disciples that they
12: 26 how in the bush God s· unto him,
14: 31 But he s· the more vehemently,
39 prayed, and s· the same words.
43 while he yet s·, cometh Judas, one
Lu 1: 42 And she s· out with a loud voice,
55 As he s· to our fathers, to Abraham,
64 and his tongue loosed, and he s·,
70 As he s· by the mouth of his holy
2: 38 s· of him to all them that looked
50 the saying which he s· unto them.
4: 36 amazed, and s· among themselves,
5: 36 he s· also a parable unto them;
6: 39 And he s· a parable unto them,
7: 39 he s· within himself, saying, This
8: 4 out of every city, he s· by a parable:
49 While he yet s·, there cometh one
9: 11 and s· unto them of the kingdom
31 s· of his decease which he should
34 While he thus s·, there came a
11: 14 devil was gone out, the dumb s·;
27 as he s· these things, a certain
Lu 11: 37 And as he s·, a certain Pharisee
12: 16 he s· a parable unto them, saying,
13: 6 He s· also this parable; A certain
14: 3 s· unto the lawyers and Pharisees,
15: 3 And he s· this parable unto them,
18: 1 he s· a parable unto them to this
9 he s· this parable unto certain
19: 11 he added and s· a parable, because
20: 2 And s· unto him, saying, Tell us,
21: 5 And as some s· of the temple, how
29 he s· to them a parable; Behold
22: 47 And while he yet s·, behold a
60 while he yet s·, the cock crew.
65 blasphemously s· they against him.
23: 20 to release Jesus, s· again to them.
24: 6 remember how he s· unto you
36 And as they thus s·, Jesus himself
44 are the words which I s· unto you,
Joh 1: 15 This was he of whom I s·, He that
2: 21 he s· of the temple of his body.
6: 71 He s· of Judas Iscariot the son of
7: 13 Howbeit no man s· openly of him
39 (But this s· he of the Spirit, which
46 Never man s· like this man.
8: 12 Then s· Jesus again unto them,
20 words s· Jesus in the treasury,
27 that he s· to them of the Father.
30 As he s· these words, many
9: 22 These words s· his parents,
29 We know that God s· unto Moses:
10: 6 This parable s· Jesus unto them:
6 what things they were which he s·
41 things that John s· of this man
11: 13 Howbeit Jesus s· of his death:
51 And this s· he not of himself:
56 and s· among themselves, as they
12: 29 others said, An angel s· to him.
36 These things s· Jesus, and
38 might be fulfilled, which he s·,
41 he saw his glory, and s· of him.
13: 22 another, doubting of whom he s·.
24 who it should be of whom he s·.
28 knew for what intent he s· this
17: 1 These words s· Jesus, and lifted
18: 9 might be fulfilled, which he s·,
16 and s· unto her that kept the door,
20 I s· openly to the world; I ever
32 he s·, signifying what death he
21: 19 s· he, signifying by what death he
Ac 1: 16 David s· before concerning Judas,
2: 31 s· of the resurrection of Christ,
4: 1 And as they s· unto the people,
31 s· the word of God with boldness.
6: 10 wisdom and...spirit by which he s·.
7: 6 And God s· on this wise, That his
38 angel which s· to him in the mount
8: 6 unto those things which Philip s·,
26 angel of the Lord s· unto Philip,
9: 29 s· boldly in the name of the Lord
10: 7 the angel which s· unto Cornelius
15 voice s· unto him again the second
44 While Peter yet s· these words,
11: 20 s· unto the Grecians, preaching the
13: 45 s· against those things which were
14: 1 and so s·, that a great multitude
16: 13 s· unto the women which resorted
32 s· unto him the word of the Lord,
18: 9 s· the Lord to Paul in the night by
25 s· and taught diligently the things
19: 6 and s· with tongues, and prophesied.
8 s· boldly for the space of three
9 but s· evil of that way before the
20: 38 of all for the words which he s·,
21: 40 he s· unto them in the Hebrew
22: 2 he s· in the Hebrew tongue to them,
9 heard not the voice of him that s·
26: 24 And as he thus s· for himself,
28: 19 But when the Jews s· against it,
21 shewed or s· any harm of thee.
25 Well s· the Holy Ghost by Esaias
1Co 13: 11 When I was a child, I s· as a child,
14: 5 I would that ye all s· with tongues,
2Co 7: 14 as we s· all things to you in truth,
Ga 4: 15 Where is then the blessedness ye s· of?
Heb 1: 1 s· in time past unto the fathers
4: 4 For he s· in a certain place of the
7: 14 of which tribe Moses s· nothing
12: 25 refused him that s· on earth, who
2Pe 1: 21 men of God s· as they were moved
Re 1: 12 And I turned to see the voice that s
10: 8 from heaven s· unto me again,
13: 11 like a lamb, and he s· as a dragon.

spakest
J'g 13: 11 the man that s· unto the woman?
17: 2 cursedst, and s· of also in mine ears,
1Sa 28: 21 thy words which thou s· unto me.
1Ki 8: 24 thou s· also with thy mouth, and
26 thou s· unto thy servant David my
53 as thou s· by the hand of Moses thy
2Ch 6: 15 s· with thy mouth, and hast fulfilled
Ne 9: 13 and s· with them from heaven, and
Ps 89: 19 Then thou s· in vision to thy holy
Jer 48: 27 for since thou s· of him, thou

span. See also SPANNED.
Ex 28: 16 a s· shall be the length thereof,
16 a s· shall be the breadth thereof.
39: 9 a s· was the length thereof, and a
9 and a s· the breadth thereof, being
1Sa 17: 4 whose height was six cubits and a s·.
Isa 40: 12 and meted out heaven with the s·,
La 2: 20 fruit, and children of a s· long?
Eze 43: 13 thereof round about shall be a s·:

spanned
Isa 48: 13 right hand hath s· the heavens:

spare See also SPARED; SPARETH; SPARING.
Ge 18: 24 also destroy and not s· the place
26 will s· all the place for their sakes.
De 13: 8 eye pity him, neither shalt thou s·,
29: 20 The Lord will not s· him, but then
1Sa 15: 3 that they have, and s· them not;
Ne 13: 22 s· me according to the greatness
Job 6: 10 let him not s·; for I have not
16: 13 my reins asunder, and doth not s·;
20: 13 Though he s· it, and forsake it not;
27: 22 shall cast upon him, and not s·:
30: 10 me, and s· not to spit in my face.
Ps 39: 13 O s· me, that I may recover
72: 13 He shall s· the poor and needy,
Pr 6: 34 will not s· in the day of vengeance.
19: 18 let not thy soul s· for his crying.
Isa 9: 19 fire: no man shall s· his brother.
13: 18 their eye shall not s· children.
30: 14 broken in pieces; he shall not s·:
54: 2 s· not, lengthen thy cords, and
58: 1 Cry aloud, s· not, lift up thy voice
Jer 13: 14 I will not pity, nor s·, nor have
21: 7 he shall not s· them, neither have
50: 14 bow, shoot at her, s· no arrows:
51: 3 s· ye not her young men; destroy
Eze 5: 11 neither shall mine eye s·, neither
7: 4 mine eye shall not s· thee, neither
9 And mine eye shall not s·, neither
8: 18 mine eye shall not s·, neither will I
9: 5 let not your eye s·, neither have ye
10 mine eye shall not s·, neither will I
24: 14 I will not go back, neither will I s·,
Joe 2: 17 S· thy people, O Lord, and give not
Jon 4: 11 should not I s· Nineveh, that great
Hab 1: 17 and not s· continually to slay the
Mal 3: 17 I will s· them, as a man spareth
Lu 15: 17 have bread enough and to s·,
Ro 11: 21 take heed lest he also s· not thee.
1Co 7: 28 trouble in the flesh: but I s· you.
2Co 1: 23 to s· you I came not as yet unto
13: 2 that, if I come again, I will not s·:

spared
1Sa 15: 9 But Saul and the people s· Agag,
15 people s· the best of the sheep and
24: 10 but mine eye s· thee; and I said,
2Sa 12: 4 he s· to take of his own flock and
21: 7 But the king s· Mephibosheth, the
2Ki 5: 20 my master hath s· Naaman this
Ps 78: 50 he s· not their soul from death,
Eze 20: 17 mine eye s· them from destroying
Ro 8: 32 He that s· not his own Son, but
11: 21 if God s· not the natural branches,
2Pe 2: 4 if God s· not the angels that sinned,
5 And s· not the old world, but saved

spareth
Pr 13: 24 He that s· his rod hateth his son:
17: 27 that hath knowledge s· his words:
21: 26 but the righteous giveth and s· not.
Mal 3: 17 man s· his own son that serveth

sparing
Ac 20: 29 wolves enter...not s· the flock.

sparingly
2Co 9: 6 which soweth s· shall reap also s·;

spark See also SPARKS.
Job 18: 5 the s· of his fire shall not shine.
Isa 1: 31 as tow, and the maker of it as a s·,

sparkled
Eze 1: 7 s· like the colour of burnished

sparks
Job 5: 7 trouble, as the s· fly upward.
41: 19 lamps, and s· of fire leap out.
Isa 50: 11 compass yourselves about with s·:
11 and in the s· that ye have kindled.

sparrow See also SPARROWS.
Ps 84: 3 Yea, the s· hath found an house,
102: 7 am as a s· alone upon the house

sparrows
M't 10: 29 Are not two s· sold for a farthing?
31 ye are of more value than many s·.
Lu 12: 6 not five s· sold for two farthings,
7 ye are of more value than many s·.

spat See also SPITTED.
Joh 9: 6 he s· on the ground, and made

speak See also SPAKE; SPEAKEST; SPEAKETH; SPEAKING; SPOKEN; UNSPEAKABLE.
Ge 18: 27 taken upon me to s· unto the Lord,
30 not the Lord be angry, and I will s·:
31 taken upon me to s· unto the Lord:
32 and I will s· yet but this once:
24: 33 mine errand. And he said, S· on.
50 we cannot s· unto thee bad or good.
27: 6 I heard thy father s· unto Esau thy
31: 24 Take heed that thou s· not to Jacob
29 thou heed that thou s· not to Jacob
32: 4 Thus shall ye s· unto my lord Esau;
19 this manner shall ye s· unto Esau,
37: 4 could not s· peaceably unto him.
44: 16 say unto my lord? what shall we s·?
18 thee, s· a word in my lord's ears,
50: 4 s·,...in the ears of Pharaoh, saying,
Ex 4: 14 brother? I know that he can s· well.
15 And thou shalt s· unto him, and put
5: 23 came to Pharaoh to s· in thy name,
6: 11 s· unto Pharaoh king of Egypt, that
29 s· thou unto Pharaoh king of Egypt
7: 2 shalt s· all that I command thee:
2 thy brother shall s· unto Pharaoh,
9 When Pharaoh shall s· unto you,
11: 2 S· now in the ears of the people,
12: 3 S· ye unto all the congregation of

Ex 14: 2 *S·* unto the children of Israel, that
15 *s·* unto the children of Israel, that
16: 12 *s·* unto them, saying, At even ye
19: 6 shalt *s·* unto the children of Israel.
9 may hear when I *s·* with thee, and
20: 19 said unto Moses, *S·* thou with us,
19 let not God *s·* with us, lest we die.
23: 2 neither shalt thou *s·* in a cause to
22 obey his voice, and do all that I *s·*;
25: 2 *S·* unto the children of Israel, that
28: 3 *s·* unto all that are wise hearted,
29: 42 will meet you, to *s·* there unto thee.
30: 31 shalt *s·* unto the children of Israel,
31: 13 *S·* thou...unto the children of Israel,
32: 12 Wherefore should the Egyptians *s·*.
34: 34 in before the Lord to *s·* with him,
35 until he went in to *s·* with him.
Le 1: 2 *S·* unto the children of Israel, and
4: 2 *S·* unto the children of Israel,
6: 25 *S·* unto Aaron and to his sons,
7: 23, 29 *S·* unto the children of Israel,
9: 3 the children of Israel thou shalt *s·*,
11: 2 *S·* unto the children of Israel,
12: 2 *S·* unto the children of Israel,
15: 2 *S·* unto the children of Israel, and
16: 2 *S·* unto Aaron thy brother, that he
17: 2 *S·* unto Aaron, and unto his sons,
18: 2 *S·* unto the children of Israel, and
19: 2 *S·* unto all the congregation of the
21: 1 *S·* unto the priests the sons of
17 *S·* unto Aaron, saying, Whosoever
22: 2 *S·* unto Aaron and to his sons, that
18 *S·* unto Aaron, and to his sons, and
23: 2, 10, 24, 34 *S·* unto...children of Israel.
24: 15 shalt *s·* unto the children of Israel,
25: 2 *S·* unto the children of Israel, and
27: 2 *S·* unto the children of Israel, and
Nu 5: 6, 12 *S·* unto the children of Israel,
6: 2 *S·* unto the children of Israel, and
23 *S·* unto Aaron and unto his sons,
7: 89 Moses was gone...to *s·* with him,
8: 2 *S·* unto Aaron, and say unto him,
9: 10 *S·* unto the children of Israel,
12: 6 and will *s·* unto him in a dream.
8 With him will I *s·* mouth to mouth,
8 afraid to *s·* against my servant
14: 15 have heard the fame of thee will *s·*,
15: 2, 18, 38 *S·* unto...children of Israel,
16: 24 *S·* unto the congregation, saying,
37 *S·* unto Eleazar the son of Aaron
17: 2 *S·* unto the children of Israel, and
18: 26 Thus *s·* unto the Levites, and say
19: 2 *S·* unto the children of Israel, that
20: 8 *s·* ye unto the rock before their eyes;
21: 27 they that *s·* in proverbs say, Come
22: 8 as the Lord shall *s·* unto me:
35 I...*s·* unto thee, that thou shalt *s·*.
38 putteth in my mouth, that shall I *s·*.
23: 5 unto Balak, and thus thou shalt *s·*.
12 to *s·* that which the Lord hath put
24: 13 what the Lord saith, that will I *s·*?
27: 7 daughters of Zelophehad *s·* right:
8 shalt *s·* unto the children of Israel,
33: 51 *S·* unto the children of Israel, and
35: 10 *S·* unto the children of Israel, and
De 3: 26 *s·* no more unto me of this matter.
5: 1 judgments which I *s·* in your ears
27 *s·* thou unto us all that the Lord
27 the Lord our God shall *s·* unto thee;
31 *s·* unto thee all the commandments,
9: 4 *S·* not thou in thine heart, after
11: 2 for I *s·* not with your children which
18: 18 *s·* unto them all that I...command
19 words which he shall *s·* in my name,
20 presume to *s·* a word in my name,
20 I have not commanded him to *s·*,
20 shall *s·* in the name of other gods,
20: 2 approach and *s·* unto the people,
5 the officers shall *s·* unto the people,
8 the officers shall *s·* further unto the
25: 8 city shall call him, and *s·* unto him:
26: 5 shalt *s·* and say before the Lord
27: 14 And the Levites shall *s·*, and say
31: 28 I may *s·* these words in their ears,
32: 1 Give ear, O ye heavens, and I will *s·*;
Jos 4: 10 Lord commanded Joshua to *s·* unto
20: 2 *S·* to the children of Israel, saying,
22: 24 children might *s·* unto our children,
J'g 5: 10 *S·*, ye that ride on white asses,
6: 39 me, and I will *s·* but this once:
9: 2 *S·*, I pray you, in the ears of all the
19: 3 to *s·* friendly unto her, and to bring
30 it, take advice, and *s·* your minds.
21: 13 to *s·* to the children of Benjamin
1Sa 3: 9 *S·*, Lord; for thy servant heareth.
10 *S·*; for thy servant heareth.
25: 17 Belial, that a man cannot *s·* to him.
24 handmaid,...*s·* in thine audience,
2Sa 3: 19 went also to *s·* in the ears of David
27 in the gate to *s·* with him quietly,
7: 17 vision, so did Nathan *s·* unto David.
13: 13 Now...I pray thee, *s·* unto the king;
14: 3 and *s·* on this manner unto him.
12 *s·* one word unto my lord the king.
13 the king doth *s·* this thing as one
15 to *s·* of this thing unto my lord the
15 said, I will now *s·* unto the king;
18 said, Let my lord the king now *s·*.
17: 6 do after his saying? if not; *s·* thou.
19: 7 *s·* comfortably unto thy servants:
10 why *s·* ye not a word of bringing
11 *S·* unto the elders of Judah,
20: 16 Come near...that I may *s·* with thee.
18 They were wont to *s·* in old time,
1Ki 2: 17 said, *S·*, I pray thee, unto Solomon
18 I will *s·* for thee unto the king.
1Ki 2: 19 to *s·* unto him for Adonijah.
12: 7 and *s·* good words to them, then
10 Thus shalt thou *s·* unto this people.
23 *S·* unto Rehoboam, the son of
21: 19, 19 And thou shalt *s·* unto him,
22: 13 of them, and *s·* that which is good.
14 Lord saith unto me, that will I *s·*.
24 Spirit...from me to *s·* unto thee?
2Ki 18: 19 *S·* ye now to Hezekiah, Thus saith
26 *S·*,...to thy servants in the Syrian
27 and to thee, to *s·* these words?
19: 10 Thus shall ye *s·* to Hezekiah king
1Ch 17: 15 so did Nathan *s·* unto David.
18 What can David *s·* more to thee for the
2Ch 10: 7 them, and *s·* good words to them,
11: 3 *S·* unto Rehoboam the son of
18: 12 one of theirs, and *s·* thou good.
13 what my God saith, that will I *s·*.
23 Spirit...from me to *s·* unto thee?
32: 17 God of Israel, and to *s·* against him
Ne 13: 24 could not *s·* in the Jews' language,
Es 5: 14 to morrow *s·* thou unto the king
6: 4 to *s·* unto the king to hang Mordecai
Job 7: 11 will *s·* in the anguish of my spirit;
8: 2 How long wilt thou *s·* these
9: 19 If I *s·* of strength, lo, he is strong: and
35 Then would I *s·*, and not fear him;
10: 1 I will *s·* in the bitterness of my soul.
11: 5 But oh that God would *s·*, and open
12: 8 *s·* to the earth, and it shall teach
13: 3 Surely I would *s·* to the Almighty,
7 Will ye *s·* wickedly for God? and
13 peace, let me alone, that I may *s·*,
22 or let me *s·*, and answer thou me.
16: 4 I also could *s·* as ye do: if your soul
6 Though I *s·*, my grief is not
18: 2 mark, and afterwards we will *s·*.
21: 3 Suffer me that I may *s·*; and after
27: 4 My lips shall not *s·* wickedness, nor
32: 7 Days should *s·*, and multitude of
20 I will *s·*, that I may be refreshed:
33: 31 me: hold thy peace, and I will *s·*.
32 me: *s·*, for I desire to justify thee.
34: 33 I: therefore *s·* what thou knowest.
36: 2 I have yet to *s·* on God's behalf.
37: 20 Shall it be told him that I *s·*?
20 if a man *s·*,...he shall be swallowed
41: 3 will he *s·* soft words unto thee?
42: 4 Hear, I beseech thee, and I will *s·*:
Ps 2: 5 shall he *s·* unto them in his wrath,
5: 6 shalt destroy them that *s·* leasing:
12: 2 They *s·* vanity every one with his
2 and with a double heart do they *s·*.
17: 10 with their mouth they *s·* proudly.
28: 3 which *s·* peace to their neighbours,
29: 9 doth every one *s·* of his glory.
31: 18 which *s·* grievous things proudly
35: 20 For they *s·* not peace: but they
28 shall *s·* of thy righteousness and
38: 12 that seek my hurt *s·* mischievous
40: 5 if I would declare and *s·* of them,
41: 5 Mine enemies *s·* evil of me, When
45: 1 I *s·* of the things which I have made
49: 3 My mouth shall *s·* of wisdom; and
50: 7 Hear, O my people, and I will *s·*; O
52: 3 rather than to *s·* righteousness.
58: 1 Do ye indeed *s·* righteousness, O
59: 12 cursing and lying which they *s·*.
63: 11 mouth of them that *s·* lies shall be
69: 12 that sit in the gate *s·* against me;
71: 10 For mine enemies *s·* against me;
73: 8 They are corrupt, and *s·* wickedly
8 oppression: they *s·* loftily.
15 If I say, I will *s·* thus; behold, I
75: 5 on high: *s·* not with a stiff neck.
77: 4 I am so troubled that I cannot *s·*.
85: 8 will hear what God the Lord will *s·*:
8 he will *s·* peace unto his people,
94: 4 shall they utter and *s·* hard things?
109: 20 them that *s·* evil against my soul.
115: 5 They have mouths, but they *s·* not:
7 *s·* they through their throat.
119: 23 Princes...did sit and *s·* against me:
46 I will *s·* of thy testimonies also
172 My tongue shall *s·* of thy word:
120: 7 but when I *s·*, they are for war.
127: 5 but they shall *s·* with the enemies
135: 16 They have mouths, but they *s·* not;
139: 20 For they *s·* against thee wickedly,
145: 5 I will *s·* of the glorious honour of
6 men shall *s·* of the might of thy
11 They shall *s·* of the glory of thy
21 My mouth shall *s·* the praise of the
Pr 8: 6 for I will *s·* of excellent things;
7 For my mouth shall *s·* truth; and
23: 9 *S·* not in the ears of a fool: for he
16 when thy lips *s·* right things.
Ec 3: 7 to keep silence, and a time to *s·*;
Ca 7: 9 lips of those that are asleep to *s·*.
Isa 8: 10 *s·* the word, and it shall not stand:
20 they *s·* not according to this word,
14: 10 they shall *s·* and say unto thee,
19: 18 Egypt *s·* the language of Canaan,
28: 11 another tongue will he *s·* to this
29: 4 and shalt *s·* out of the ground, and
30: 10 *s·* unto us smooth things, prophesy
32: 4 the stammerers shall be ready to *s·*
6 the vile person will *s·* villany, and
36: 11 *S·*, I pray thee, unto thy servants
11 *s·* not to us in the Jews' language,
12 and to thee to *s·* these words?
37: 10 Thus shall ye *s·* to Hezekiah king
40: 2 *S·* ye comfortably to Jerusalem,
41: 1 them come near; then let them *s·*:
45: 19 I the Lord *s·* righteousness, I
50: 4 know how to *s·* a word in season
Isa 52: 6 that day that I am he that doth *s·*:
56: 3 hath joined himself to the Lord, *s·*,
59: 4 they trust in vanity, and *s·* lies;
63: 1 I that *s·* in righteousness, mighty
Jer 1: 6 Ah, Lord God! behold, I cannot *s·*:
7 I command thee thou shalt *s·*.
17 *s·* unto them all that I command
5: 5 great men, and will *s·* unto them;
14 Because ye *s·* this word, behold, I
6: 10 To whom shall I *s·*, and give
7: 27 shalt *s·* all these words unto them;
9: 5 neighbour, and will not *s·* the truth:
5 have taught their tongue to *s·* lies,
22 *S·*, Thus saith the Lord, Even the
10: 5 as the palm tree, but *s·* not: they
11: 2 and *s·* unto the men of Judah, and
12: 6 though they *s·* fair words unto thee.
13: 12 thou shalt *s·* unto them this word;
18: 7, 9 I shall *s·* concerning a nation,
11 go to, *s·* to the men of Judah, and
20 before thee to *s·* good for them,
20: 9 him, nor *s·* any more in his name.
22: 1 of Judah, and *s·* there this word,
23: 16 they *s·* a vision of their own heart,
28 word, let him *s·* my word faithfully.
26: 2 and *s·* unto all the cities of Judah,
2 I command thee to *s·* unto them;
8 commanded him to *s·* unto all the
15 *s·* all these words in your ears.
27: 9 your sorcerers, which *s·* unto you,
14 of the prophets that *s·* unto you,
28: 7 this word that I *s·* in thine ears,
29: 24 shalt thou also *s·* to Shemaiah the
32: 4 shall *s·* with him mouth to mouth,
34: 2 Go and *s·* to Zedekiah king of
3 he shall *s·* with thee mouth to
35: 2 the Rechabites, and *s·* unto them,
38: 20 of the Lord, which I *s·* unto thee:
39: 16 Go and *s·* to Ebed-melech the
Eze 2: 1 thy feet, and I will *s·* unto thee.
7 thou shalt *s·* my words unto them,
3: 1 and go *s·* unto the house of Israel.
4 and *s·* with my words unto them.
10 all my words that I shall *s·* unto
11 and *s·* unto them, and tell them,
27 when I *s·* with thee, I will open thy
11: 5 upon me, and said unto me, *S·*;
12: 25 For I am the Lord: I will *s·*, and
25 word that I shall *s·* shall come to
14: 4 Therefore *s·* unto them, and say
17: 2 and *s·* a parable unto the house of
20: 3 man, *s·* unto the elders of Israel,
27 man, *s·* unto the house of Israel,
49 of me, Doth he not *s·* parables?
24: 21 *S·* unto the house of Israel, Thus
27 and thou shalt *s·*, and be no more
29: 3 *S·*, and say, Thus saith the Lord
31: 2 *s·* unto Pharaoh king of Egypt,
32: 21 strong among the mighty shall *s·*
33: 2 *s·* to the children of thy people, and
8 dost not *s·* to warn the wicked from
10 man, *s·* unto the house of Israel;
10 ye *s·*, saying, If our transgressions
24 those wastes of the land of Israel *s·*,
30 *s·* one to another, every one to his
37: 18 of thy people shall *s·* unto thee,
39: 17 *S·* unto every feathered fowl, and
Da 2: 9 and corrupt words to *s·* before me,
3: 29 which *s·* any thing amiss against
7: 25 he shall *s·* great words against
10: 11 understand the words that I *s·*
19 said, Let my lord *s·*; for thou hast
11: 27 and they shall *s·* lies at one table;
36 shall *s·* marvellous things against
Ho 2: 14 and *s·* comfortably unto her.
Hab 2: 3 but at the end it shall *s·*, and not
Zep 3: 13 shall not do iniquity, nor *s·* lies;
Hag 2: 2 *S·* now to Zerubbabel the son of
21 *S·* to Zerubbabel, governor of
Zec 2: 4 Run, *s·* to this young man, saying,
6: 12 And *s·* unto him, saying, Thus
7: 3 to *s·* unto the priests which were
5 *S·* unto all the people of the land,
8: 16 *S·* ye every man the truth to his
9: 10 he shall *s·* peace unto the heathen:
M't 8: 8 *s·* the word only, and my servant
10: 19 thought how or what ye shall *s·*:
19 in that same hour what ye shall *s·*.
20 For it is not ye that *s·*, but the
27 in darkness, that *s·* ye in light:
12: 34 can ye, being evil, *s·* good things?
36 every idle word that men shall *s·*,
46 without, desiring to *s·* with him.
47 without, desiring to *s·* with thee.
13: 13 Therefore *s·* I to them in parables:
15: 31 when they saw the dumb to *s·*, the
M'r 1: 34 and suffered not the devils to *s·*,
2: 7 doth this man thus *s·* blasphemies?
7: 37 the deaf to hear, and the dumb to *s·*.
9: 39 name, that can lightly *s·* evil of me.
12: 1 began to *s·* unto them by parables.
13: 11 beforehand what ye shall *s·*,
11 given you in that hour, that *s·* ye:
11 for it is not ye that *s·*, but the Holy
14: 71 know not this man of whom ye *s·*.
16: 17 they shall *s·* with new tongues;
Lu 1: 19 and am sent to *s·* unto thee, and to
20 shalt be dumb, and not able to *s·*,
22 out, he could not *s·* unto them:
4: 41 them suffered them not to *s·*:
6: 26 when all men shall *s·* well of you!
7: 15 was dead sat up, and began to *s·*.
24 *s·* unto...people concerning John,
11: 53 provoke him to *s·* of many things:
12: 10 *s·* a word against the Son of man,
13 Master, *s·* to my brother, that he

Lu 20: 9 he to s' to the people this parable:
Joh 1: 37 the two disciples heard him s', and
40 One of the two which heard John s'.
3: 11 We s' that we do know, and testify
4: 26 unto her, I that s' unto thee am he.
6: 63 the words that I s' unto you, they
7: 17 be of God, or whether I s' of myself.
8: 26 and I s' to the world those things
28 hath taught me, I s' these things.
38 I s' that which I have seen with my
9: 21 ask him: he shall s' for himself.
12: 49 I should say, and what I should s'.
50 whatsoever I s' therefore, even as
50 as the Father said unto me, so I s'.
13: 18 I s' not of you all: I know whom I
14: 10 the words that I s' unto you
10 I s' not of myself: but the Father
16: 13 for he shall not s' of himself; but
13 he shall hear, that shall he s':
25 no more s' unto you in proverbs,
17: 13 these things I s' in the world, that
Ac 2: 4 they began to s' with other tongues,
6 heard them s' in his own language.
7 are not all these which s' Galilæans?
11 we do hear them s' in our tongues
29 let me freely s'...of the patriarch
4: 17 they s' henceforth to no man in
18 commanded them not to s' at all
20 s' the things which we have seen
29 all boldness they may s' thy word,
5: 20 Go, stand and s' in the temple to the
40 should not s' in the name of Jesus,
6: 11 heard him s' blasphemous words
13 man ceaseth not to s' blasphemous
10: 32 when he cometh, shall s' unto thee.
46 they heard them s' with tongues,
11: 15 as I began to s', the Holy Ghost fell
14: 9 The same heard Paul s': who
18: 9 Be not afraid, but s', and hold not
26 began to s' boldly in the synagogue:
21: 37 chief captain, May I s' unto thee?
37 Who said, Canst thou s' Greek?
39 suffer me to s' unto the people.
23: 5 shalt not s' evil of the ruler of thy
24: 10 had beckoned unto him to s',
26: 1 Thou art permitted to s' for thyself.
25 but s' forth the words of truth and
26 things, before whom...I s' freely:
28: 20 you, to see you, and to s' with you:
Ro 3: 5 taketh vengeance? (I s' as a man)
6: 19 I s' after the manner of men
7: 1 (for I s' to them that know the law,)
11: 13 For I s' to you Gentiles, inasmuch
15: 18 I will not dare to s' of any of those
1Co 1: 10 that ye all s' the same thing, and
2: 6 we s' wisdom among them that
7 But we s' the wisdom of God in a
13 Which things also we s', not in the
3: 1 not s' unto you as unto spiritual,
6: 5 I s' to your shame. Is it so, that
7: 6 I s' this by permission, and not of
12 But to the rest s' I, not the Lord:
35 And this I s' for your own profit;
10: 15 I s' as to wise men; judge ye what I
12: 30 do all s' with tongues? do all
13: 1 I s' with the tongues of men and of
14: 6 except I shall s' to you either by
9 spoken? for ye shall s' into the air.
18 I s' with tongues more than ye all:
19 I had rather s' five words with my
21 other lips will I s' unto this people;
23 one place, and all s' with tongues,
27 any man s' in an unknown tongue,
28 let him s' to himself, and to God.
29 Let the prophets s' two or three,
34 it is not permitted unto them to s';
35 is a shame for women to s' in the
39 and forbid not to s' with tongues.
15: 34 of God: I s' this to your shame.
2Co 2: 17 in the sight of God s' we in Christ.
4: 13 we also believe, and therefore s';
6: 13 (I s' as unto my children,) be ye also
7: 3 I s' not this to condemn you: for I
8: 8 I s' not by commandment, but by
11: 17 That which I s', I s' it not after the
21 I s' as concerning reproach, as
21 bold, (I s' foolishly,) I am bold also.
23 Christ? (I s' as a fool) I am more;
12: 19 we s' before God in Christ: but we
Ga 3: 15 I s' after the manner of men;
Eph 4: 25 s' every man truth with his
5: 12 a shame even to s' of those things
32 but I s' concerning Christ and the
6: 20 that therein I may s' boldly, as I ought
20 boldly, as I ought to s'.
Ph'p 1: 14 are much more bold to s' the word
4: 11 Not that I s' in respect of want:
Col 4: 3 to s' the mystery of Christ, for
4 make it manifest, as I ought to s'.
1Th 1: 8 so that we need not to s' any thing.
2: 2 bold in our God to s' unto you the
4 trust with the gospel, even so we s';
16 Forbidding us to s' to the Gentiles
1Ti 2: 7 s' the truth in Christ, and lie not;)
5: 14 to the adversary to s' reproachfully.
Tit 2: 1 s' thou the things which become
15 These things s', and exhort, and
3: 2 To s' evil of no man, to be no
Heb 2: 5 the world to come, whereof we s'.
6: 9 salvation, though we thus s'.
9: 5 we cannot now s' particularly.
Jas 1: 19 to hear, slow to s', slow to wrath:
2: 12 So s' ye, and so do, as they that
4: 11 S' not evil one of another,
1Pe 2: 12 they s' against you as evildoers,
3: 10 and his lips that they s' no guile:
1Pe 3: 16 whereas they s' evil of you, as of
4: 11 If any man s', let him
11 him s' as the oracles of God;
2Pe 2: 10 are not afraid to s' evil of dignities.
12 s' evil of the things that they
18 when they s' great swelling words
1Jo 4: 5 therefore s' they of the world, and
2Jo 12 s' face to face, that our joy may be
3Jo 14 thee, and we shall s' face to face.
Jude 8 dominion, and s' evil of dignities.
10 these s' evil of those things which
Re 2: 24 the depths of Satan, as they s';
13: 15 image of the beast should both s',

speaker
Ps 140: 11 not an evil s' be established
Ac 14: 12 because he was the chief s'.

speakest
1Sa 9: 21 wherefore then s' thou so to me?
2Sa 19: 29 him, Why s' thou any more of thy
2Ki 6: 12 words...thou s' in thy bedchamber.
Job 2: 10 Thou s' as one of the foolish women
Ps 50: 20 sittest and s' against thy brother;
51: 4 mightest be justified when thou s',
Isa 40: 27 Why sayest thou, O Jacob, and s', O
Jer 40: 16 for thou s' falsely of Ishmael.
43: 2 unto Jeremiah, Thou s' falsely:
Eze 3: 18 nor s' to warn the wicked from his
Zec 13: 3 thou s' lies in the name of the Lord:
M't 13: 10 Why s'...unto them in parables?
Lu 12: 41 Lord, s' thou this parable unto us,
Joh 16: 29 unto him, Lo, now s' thou plainly,
29 thou plainly, and s' no proverb.
19: 10 unto him, S' thou not unto me?
Ac 17: 19 new doctrine, whereof thou s', is?

speaketh
Ge 45: 12 it is my mouth that s' unto you.
Ex 33: 11 to face, as a man s' unto his friend.
Nu 23: 26 All that the Lord s', that I must do?
De 18: 22 When a prophet s' in the name of
1Ki 20: 5 said, Thus s' Ben-hadad, saying,
Job 2: 10 as one of the foolish women s'.
17: 5 He that s' flattery to his friends,
33: 14 God s' once, yea twice, yet man
Ps 12: 3 the tongue that s' proud things:
15: 2 and s' the truth in his heart.
37: 30 mouth of the righteous s' wisdom,
41: 6 if he come to see me, he s' vanity:
144: 8 Whose mouth s' vanity, and their
11 children, whose mouth s' vanity,
Pr 2: 12 the man that s' froward things;
6: 13 he s' with his feet, he teacheth
19 A false witness that s' lies, and he
10: 32 mouth of the wicked s' frowardness.
12: 17 He that s' truth showeth forth
18 s' like the piercings of a sword:
14: 25 but a deceitful witness s' lies.
16: 13 and they love him that s' right.
19: 5 he that s' lies shall not escape.
9 and he that s' lies shall perish.
21: 28 man that heareth s' constantly.
26: 25 When he s' fair, believe him not:
Isa 9: 17 and every mouth s' folly.
32: 7 words, even when the needy s' right.
33: 15 righteously, and s' uprightly;
Jer 9: 8 as an arrow shot out; it s' deceit:
8 one s' peaceably to his neighbour
10: 1 word which the Lord s' unto you,
28: 2 Thus s' the Lord of hosts, the God
29: 25 Thus s' the Lord of hosts, the God
30: 2 Thus s' the Lord God of Israel,
Eze 10: 5 of the Almighty God when he s'.
Am 5: 10 they abhor him that s' uprightly.
Hag 1: 2 Thus s' the Lord of hosts, saying,
Zec 6: 12 Thus s' the Lord of hosts, saying,
7: 9 Thus s' the Lord of hosts, saying,
M't 10: 20 of your Father which s' in you.
12: 32 whosoever s' a word against the
32 whosoever s' against the Holy
34 out...of the heart the mouth s'.
Lu 5: 21 Who is this which s' blasphemies?
6: 45 of the heart his mouth s'.
Joh 3: 31 earth is earthly, and s' of the earth:
34 God hath sent s' the words of God:
7: 18 He that s' of himself seeketh his
26 But, lo, he s' boldly, and they say
8: 44 When he s' a lie, he s' of his own:
19: 12 himself a king s' against Cæsar.
Ac 2: 25 For David s' concerning him, I
8: 34 thee, of whom s' the prophet this?
Ro 10: 6 which is of faith s' on this wise,
1Co 14: 2 he that s' in an unknown tongue
2 s' not unto men, but unto God: for
2 in the spirit he s' mysteries.
3 he that prophesieth s' unto men
4 s' in an unknown tongue edifieth
5 than he that s' with tongues,
11 be unto him that s' a barbarian,
11 and he that s' shall be a barbarian
13 let him that s' in an unknown
1Ti 4: 1 the Spirit s' expressly, that in the
Heb 11: 4 and by it he being dead yet s'.
12: 5 which s' unto you as unto children,
24 that s' better things than that of
25 See that ye refuse not him that s'.
25 away from him that s' from heaven:
Jas 4: 11 He that s' evil of his brother, and
11 s' evil of the law, and judgeth the
Jude 16 mouth s' great swelling words,

speaking See also SPEAKINGS.
Ge 24: 15 to pass, before he had done s',
45 before I had done s' in mine heart,
Ex 34: 33 till Moses had done s' with them,
Nu 7: 89 heard the voice of one s' unto him
Nu 16: 31 made an end of s' all these words,
De 4: 33 God s' out of the midst of the fire,
5: 26 God s' out of the midst of the fire,
11: 19 s' of them when thou sittest in
20: 9 made an end of s' unto the people,
32: 45 Moses made an end of s' all these
J'g 15: 17 when he had made an end of s',
Ru 1: 18 with her, then she left s' unto her.
1Sa 18: 1 had made an end of s' unto Saul,
24: 16 an end of s' these words unto Saul,
2Sa 13: 36 soon as he had made an end of s',
2Ch 36: 12 the prophet s' from the mouth of the
Es 10: 3 people, and s' peace to all his seed.
Job 1: 16, 17, 18 While he was yet s', there
4: 2 who can withhold himself from s'?
32: 15 answered no more: they left off s'.
Ps 34: 13 evil, and thy lips from s' guile.
58: 3 as soon as they be born, s' lies.
Isa 58: 9 forth of the finger, and s' vanity;
13 pleasure, nor s' thine own words:
59: 13 s' oppression and revolt, conceiving
65: 24 while they are yet s', I will hear.
Jer 7: 13 rising up early and s', but ye heard
25: 3 rising early and s'; but ye have
26: 7 heard Jeremiah s' these words in
8 Jeremiah had made an end of s' all
35: 14 unto you, rising early and s'; but
38: 4 people, in s' such words unto them:
27 So they left off s' with him; for the
43: 1 had made an end of s' unto all the
Eze 43: 6 I heard him s' unto me out of the
Da 7: 8 man, and a mouth s' great things.
8: 13 Then I heard one saint s', and
18 Now as he was s' with me, I was in
9: 20 And whiles I was s', and praying,
21 whiles I was s' in prayer, even the
M't 6: 7 shall be heard for their much s'.
Lu 5: 4 Now when he had left s', he said
Ac 1: 3 s' of the things pertaining to the
7: 44 s' unto Moses, that he should
13: 43 who, s' to them, persuaded them
14: 3 abode they s' boldly in the Lord,
20: 30 s' perverse things, to draw away
26: 14 I heard a voice s' unto me, and
1Co 12: 3 that no man s' by the Spirit of God
14: 6 I come unto you s' with tongues,
2Co 13: 3 ye seek a proof of Christ s' in me,
Eph 4: 15 s' the truth in love, may grow up
31 and evil s', be put away from you,
5: 19 S' to yourselves in psalms and
1Ti 4: 2 S' lies in hypocrisy; having their
5: 13 s' things which they ought not.
1Pe 4: 4 same excess of riot, s' evil of you:
2Pe 2: 16 the dumb ass s' with man's voice
3: 16 epistles, s' in them of these things;
Re 13: 5 him a mouth s' great things and

speakings
1Pe 2: 1 and envies, and all evil s',

spear See also SPEARMEN; SPEAR'S; SPEARS.
Jos 8: 18 Stretch out the s' that is in thy
18 Joshua stretched out the s' that
26 wherewith he stretched out the s',
J'g 5: 8 a shield or s' seen among forty
1Sa 13: 22 neither sword nor s' found in the
17: 7 staff of his s' was like a weaver's
45 to me with a sword, and with a s',
47 Lord saveth not with sword and s':
21: 8 here under thine hand s' or sword?
22: 6 having his s' in his hand, and all
26: 7 his s' stuck in the ground at his
8 with the s' even to the earth at
11 now the s' that is at his bolster,
12 So David took the s' and the cruse
16 now see where the king's s' is, and
22 and said, Behold the king's s'! and
2Sa 1: 6 behold, Saul leaned upon his s';
2: 23 end of the s' smote him under the
23 that the s' came out behind him;
21: 16 s' weighed three hundred shekels
19 of whose s' was like a weaver's
23: 7 with iron and the staff of a s'; and
8 lift up his s' against eight hundred,
18 up his s' against three hundred,
21 the Egyptian had a s' in his hand;
21 the s' out of the Egyptian's hand,
21 hand, and slew him with his own s'.
1Ch 11: 11 up his s' against three hundred
20 up his s' against three hundred,
23 was a s' like a weaver's beam; and
23 the s' out of the Egyptian's hand,
23 hand, and slew him with his own s'.
12: 24 of Judah that bare shield and s'
34 them with shield and s' thirty and
20: 5 whose s' staff was like a weaver's
2Ch 25: 5 that could handle s' and shield.
Job 39: 23 the glittering s' and the shield.
41: 26 the s', the dart, nor the habergeon.
29 he laugheth at the shaking of a s'.
Ps 35: 3 Draw out also the s', and stop the
46: 9 bow, and cutteth the s' in sunder;
Jer 6: 23 They shall lay hold on bow and s';
Na 3: 3 bright sword and the glittering s':
Hab 3: 11 at the shining of thy glittering s'.
Joh 19: 34 soldiers with a s' pierced his side,

spearmen
Ps 68: 30 Rebuke the company of s', the
Ac 23: 23 s' two hundred, at the third hour

spear's
1Sa 17: 7 his s' head weighed six hundred

spears
1Sa 13: 19 Hebrews make them swords or s':
2Ki 11: 10 give king David's s' and shields,
2Ch 11: 12 several city he put shields and s',

2Ch 14: 8 of men that bare targets and s',
23: 9 to the captains of hundreds s',
26: 14 all the host shields, and s', and
Ne 4: 13 their swords, their s', and their
16 half of them held both the s', and
21 half of them held the s' from the
Job 41: 7 irons? or his head with fish s'?
Ps 57: 4 whose teeth are s' and arrows,
Isa 2: 4 and their s' into pruninghooks:
Jer 46: 4 furbish the s', and put on the
Eze 39: 9 and the handstaves, and the s', and
Joe 3: 10 and your pruninghooks into s':
Mic 4: 3 and their s' into pruninghooks:

special
De 7: 6 to be a s' people unto himself,
Ac 19: 11 God wrought s' miracles

specially See also ESPECIALLY.
De 4: 10 S' the day that thou stoodest before
Ac 25: 26 and s' before thee, O king Agrippa,
1Ti 4: 10 of all men, s' of those that believe.
5: 8 and s' for those of his own house,
Tit 1: 10 s' they of the circumcision:
Ph'm 16 servant, a brother beloved, s' to me,

speckled
Ge 30: 32 thence all the s' and spotted cattle,
32 the spotted and s' among the goats:
33 not s' and spotted among the goats,
35 she goats that were s' and spotted,
39 cattle ringstraked, s', and spotted.
31: 8 said thus, The s' shall be thy wages;
8 wages; then all the cattle bare s':
10 were ringstraked, s', and grisled.
12 are ringstraked, s', and grisled:
Jer 12: 9 heritage is unto me as a s' bird,
Zec 1: 8 there red horses, s', and white.

spectacle
1Co 4: 9 we are made a s' unto the world,

sped
J'g 5: 30 Have they not s'? have they not

speech See also SPEECHES; SPEECHLESS.
Ge 4: 23 of Lamech, hearken unto my s':
11: 1 was of one language, and of one s'.
7 not understand one another's s'.
Ex 4: 10 but I am slow of s', and of a slow
De 22: 14 give occasions of s' against her,
17 given occasions of s' against her,
32: 2 my s' shall distil as the dew, as the
2Sa 14: 20 To fetch about this form of s' hath
19: 11 s' of all Israel is come to the king,
1Ki 3: 10 s' pleased the Lord, that Solomon
2Ch 32: 18 with a loud voice in the Jews' s',
Ne 13: 24 spake half in the s' of Ashdod, and
Job 12: 20 removeth away the s' of the trusty,
13: 17 Hear diligently my s', and my
21: 2 Hear diligently my s', and let this be
24: 25 and make my s' nothing worth?
29: 22 and my s' dropped upon them.
37: 19 we cannot order our s' by reason of
Ps 17: 6 thine ear to me, and hear my s'.
19: 2 Day unto day uttereth s', and night
3 There is no s' nor language, where
Pr 7: 21 With her much fair s' she caused
17: 7 Excellent s' becometh not a fool:
Ca 4: 3 of scarlet, and thy s' is comely:
Isa 28: 23 my voice; hearken, and hear my s'.
29: 4 thy s' shall be low out of the dust,
4 thy s' shall whisper out of the dust.
32: 9 daughters; give ear unto my s'.
33: 19 a people of a deeper s' than thou
Jer 31: 23 use this s' in the land of Judah,
Eze 1: 24 the voice of s', as the noise of an
3: 5 not sent to a people of a strange s'
6 to many a people of a strange s' and
Hab 3: 2 O Lord, I have heard thy s', and
M't 26: 73 them; for thy s' bewrayeth thee.
M'r 7: 32 and had an impediment in his s';
14: 70 and thy s' agreeth thereto.
Joh 8: 43 Why do ye not understand my s'?
Ac 14: 11 saying in the s' of Lycaonia,
20: 7 continued his s' until midnight.
1Co 2: 1 with excellency of s' or of wisdom,
4 my s' and my preaching was not
4: 19 not the s' of them which are puffed
2Co 3: 12 hope, we use great plainness of s':
7: 4 Great is my boldness of s' toward
10: 10 is weak, and his s' contemptible.
11: 6 But though I be rude in s', yet not
Col 4: 6 Let your s' be alway with grace,
Tit 2: 8 Sound s', that cannot be condemned;

speeches
Nu 12: 8 apparently, and not in dark s';
Job 6: 26 and the s' of one that is desperate,
15: 3 s' wherewith he can do no good?
32: 14 will I answer him with your s'.
33: 1 Job, I pray thee, hear my s', and
Ro 16: 18 fair s' deceive the hearts of the
Jude 15 hard s' which ungodly sinners have

speechless
M't 22: 12 wedding garment? And he was s'.
Lu 1: 22 unto them, and remained s'.
Ac 9: 7 which journeyed with him stood s',

speed See also SPED.
Ge 24: 12 send me good s' this day, and shew
1Sa 20: 38 the lad, Make s', haste, stay not.
2Sa 15: 14 make s' to depart, lest he overtake
1Ki 12: 18 Rehoboam made s' to get him up to
2Ch 10: 18 Rehoboam made s' to get him up to
Ezr 6: 12 a decree; let it be done with s'.
Isa 5: 19 Let him make s', and hasten his
26 they shall come with s' swiftly:
Ac 17: 15 for to come to him with all s',

2Jo 10 house, neither bid him God s':
11 For he that biddeth him God s' is

speedily
Ge 44: 11 they s' took down every man his
1Sa 27: 1 I should s' escape into the land of
2Sa 17: 16 the wilderness, but s' pass over;
2Ch 35: 13 divided them s' among all the people.
Ezr 6: 13 the king had sent, so they did s'.
7: 17 thou mayest buy s' with this money
21 shall require of you, it be done s',
26 judgment be executed s' upon him,
Es 2: 9 and he s' gave her her things for
Ps 31: 2 thine ear to me; deliver me s':
69: 17 for I am in trouble: hear me s'.
79: 8 thy tender mercies s' prevent us:
102: 2 in the day when I call answer me s'.
143: 7 Hear me s', O Lord: my spirit
Ec 8: 11 an evil work is not executed s',
Isa 58: 8 thine health shall spring forth s':
Joe 3: 4 s' will I return your recompence
Zec 8: 21 us go s' to pray before the Lord,
Lu 18: 8 that he will avenge them s'.

speedy
Zep 1: 18 a s' riddance of all them that dwell

spend See also SPENDEST; SPENDETH; SPENT.
De 32: 23 I will s' mine arrows upon them.
Job 21: 13 They s' their days in wealth, 1086
36: 11 shall s' their days in prosperity,
Ps 90: 9 we s' our years as a tale that is told.
Isa 55: 2 do ye s' money for that which is
Ac 20: 16 he would not s' the time in Asia:
2Co 12: 15 I will very gladly s' and be spent

spendest
Lu 10: 35 whatsoever thou s' more, when I

spendeth
Pr 21: 20 wise; but a foolish man s' it up.
29: 3 with harlots s' his substance.
Ec 6: 12 vain life which he s' as a shadow?

spent
Ge 21: 15 And the water was s' in the bottle,
47: 18 my lord, how that our money is s';
Le 26: 20 your strength shall be s' in vain:
J'g 19: 11 were by Jebus, the day was far s';
1Sa 9: 7 for the bread is s' in our vessels,
Job 7: 6 shuttle, and are s' without hope.
Ps 31: 10 For my life is s' with grief, and
Isa 49: 4 I have s' my strength for nought,
Jer 37: 21 all the bread in the city were s'.
M'r 5: 26 had s' all that she had, and was
6: 35 when the day was now far s', his
Lu 8: 43 which had s' all her living upon
15: 14 when he had s' all, there arose a
24: 29 evening, and the day is far s'.
Ac 17: 21 there s' their time in nothing else,
18: 23 after he had s' some time there,
27: 9 Now when much time was s', and
Ro 13: 12 The night is far s', the day is at
2Co 12: 15 gladly spend and be s' for you;

spewing See also SPUE.
Hab 2: 16 shameful s' shall be on thy glory.

spice See also SPICED; SPICES.
Ex 35: 28 s', and oil for the light, and for
1Ki 10: 15 of the traffick of the s' merchants,
2Ch 9: 9 there any such s' as the queen of
Ca 5: 1 gathered my myrrh with my s';
Eze 24: 10 consume the flesh, and s' it well,

spiced
Ca 8: 2 cause thee to drink of s' wine of

spice-merchants See SPICE and MERCHANTS.

spicery
Ge 37: 25 bearing s' and balm and myrrh,

spices
Ge 43: 11 s', and myrrh, nuts, and almonds:
Ex 25: 6 s' for anointing oil, and for sweet
30: 23 also unto thee principal s', of pure
34 Take unto thee sweet s', stacte,
34 sweet s' with pure frankincense:
35: 8 s' for anointing oil, and for the
37: 29 and the pure incense of sweet s',
1Ki 10: 2 with camels that bare s', and very
10 of gold, and of s' very great store,
10 no more such abundance of s' as
25 garments, and armour, and s', and
2Ki 20: 13 gold, and the s', and the precious
1Ch 9: 29 and the frankincense, and the s'.
30 priests made the ointment of the s'.
2Ch 9: 1 and camels that bare s', and gold in
9 of gold, and of s' great abundance,
24 raiment, harness, and s', horses,
16: 14 sweet odours and divers kinds of s'
32: 27 precious stones, and for s', and
Ca 4: 10 smell of thine ointments than all s'!
14 and aloes, with all the chief s':
16 that the s' thereof may flow out.
5: 13 His cheeks are as a bed of s', as
6: 2 into his garden, to the beds of s',
8: 14 hart upon the mountains of s'.
Isa 39: 2 and the gold, and the s', and the
Eze 27: 22 in thy fairs with chief of all s',
M'r 16: 1 and Salome, had bought sweet s',
Lu 23: 56 and prepared s' and ointments;
24: 1 bringing the s' which they had
Joh 19: 40 wound it in linen clothes with the s',

spider See also SPIDER'S.
Pr 30: 28 The s' taketh hold with her hands,

spider's
Job 8: 14 and whose trust shall be a s' web.
Isa 59: 5 eggs, and weave the s' web:

spied See also ESPIED.
Ex 2: 11 And he s' an Egyptian smiting an
Jos 6: 22 men that had s' out the country,
2Ki 9: 17 he s' the company of Jehu as he
13: 21 that, behold, they s' a band of men;
23: 16 he s' the sepulchres that were there
24 abominations that were s' in the

spies
Ge 42: 9 and said unto them, Ye are s';
11 true men, thy servants are no s'.
14 spake unto you, saying, Ye are s':
16 the life of Pharaoh surely ye are s'.
30 and took us for s' of the country.
31 We are true men; we are no s':
34 I know that ye are no s', but that
Nu 21: 1 Israel came by the way of the s';
Jos 6: 23 young men that were s' went in,
J'g 1: 24 the s' saw a man come forth out
1Sa 26: 4 David therefore sent out s', and
2Sa 15: 10 Absalom sent s' throughout all the
Lu 20: 20 watched him, and sent forth s',
Heb 11: 31 when she had received the s' with

spikenard
Ca 1: 12 my s' sendeth forth the smell
4: 13 pleasant fruits; camphire, with s',
14 S' and saffron; calamus and
M'r 14: 3 box of ointment of s' very
Joh 12: 3 Mary a pound of ointment of s

spilled See also SPILT.
Ge 38: 9 that he s' it on the ground, lest
M'r 2: 22 the bottles, and the wine is s',
Lu 5: 37 will burst the bottles, and be s',

spilt See also SPILLED.
2Sa 14: 14 and are as water s' on the ground,

spin See also SPUN.
Ex 35: 25 that were wise hearted did s'
M't 6: 28 they toil not, neither do they s':
Lu 12: 27 grow: they toil not, they s' not;

spindle
Pr 31: 19 She layeth her hands to the s',

spirit (or Spirit) See also SPIRITS.
Ge 1: 2 S' of God moved upon the face of
6: 3 My s' shall not always strive with
41: 8 morning that his s' was troubled;
38 is, a man in whom the S' of God is?
45: 27 the s' of Jacob their father revived:
Ex 6: 9 not unto Moses for anguish of s',
28: 3 I have filled with the s' of wisdom,
31: 3 I have filled him with the s' of God,
35: 21 one whom his s' made willing,
31 hath filled him with the s' of God,
Le 20: 27 or woman that hath a familiar s',
Nu 5: 14, 14 s' of jealousy came upon him,
30 the s' of jealousy cometh upon him,
11: 17 take of the s' which is upon thee,
25 took of the s' that was upon him,
25 when the s' rested upon them, they
26 and the s' rested upon them; and
29 Lord would put his s' upon them!
14: 24 he had another s' with him, and
24: 2 and the s' of God came upon him.
27: 18 of Nun, a man in whom is the s',
De 2: 30 the Lord thy God hardened his s',
34: 9 of Nun was full of the s' of wisdom;
Jos 5: 1 was there s' in them any more,
J'g 3: 10 the S' of the Lord came upon him,
6: 34 S' of the Lord came upon Gibeon,
9: 23 Then God sent an evil s' between
11: 29 Then the S' of the Lord came upon
13: 25 S' of the Lord began to move him
14: 6 S' of the Lord came mightily upon
19 the S' of the Lord came upon him,
15: 14 S' of the Lord came mightily upon
19 his s' came again, and he revived:
1Sa 1: 15 I am a woman of a sorrowful s':
10: 6 S' of the Lord will come upon thee,
10 and the S' of God came upon him,
11: 6 And the S' of God came upon Saul
16: 13 S' of the Lord came upon David
14 S' of the Lord departed from Saul,
14 evil s' from the Lord troubled him.
15 an evil s' from God troubleth thee.
16 the evil s' from God is upon thee,
23 the evil s' from God was upon Saul,
23 and the evil s' departed from him.
18: 10 evil s' from God came upon Saul,
19: 9 evil s' from the Lord was upon Saul,
20 S' of God was upon the messengers
23 the S' of God was upon him also,
28: 7 a woman that hath a familiar s',
7 is a woman that hath a familiar s',
8 divine unto me by the familiar s',
30: 12 eaten, his s' came again to him:
2Sa 23: 2 The S' of the Lord spake by me,
1Ki 10: 5 Lord; there was no more s' in her.
18: 12 the S' of the Lord shall carry thee
21: 5 Why is thy s' so sad, that thou
22: 21 And there came forth a s', and stood
22 I will be a lying s' in the mouth of
23 hath put a lying s' in the mouth of
24 Which way went the S' of the Lord
2Ki 2: 9 double portion of thy s' be upon me.
15 The s' of Elijah doth rest on Elisha.
16 S' of the Lord hath taken him up,
1Ch 5: 26 up the s' of Pul king of Assyria,
26 and the s' of Tilgath-pilneser king
10: 13 of one that had a familiar s',
12: 18 Then the s' came upon Amasai,
28: 12 pattern of all that he had by the s',
2Ch 9: 4 Lord; there was no more s' in her.
15: 1 the S' of God came upon Azariah
18: 20 Then there came out a s', and stood

2Ch 18:21 be a lying s' in the mouth of all his
22 hath put a lying s' in the mouth of
23 Which way went the S' of the Lord
20:14 came the S' of the Lord in the midst
21:16 Jehoram the s' of the Philistines,
24:20 the S' of God came upon Zechariah
33: 6 and dealt with a familiar s', and
36:22 up the s' of Cyrus king of Persia,
Ezr 1: 1 up the s' of Cyrus king of Persia,
5 all them whose s' God had raised,
Ne 9:20 gavest also thy good s' to instruct
30 testifiedst against them by thy s' in
Job 4:15 Then a s' passed before my face;
6: 4 poison whereof drinketh up my s':
7:11 I will speak in the anguish of my s';
10:12 visitation hath preserved my s'.
15:13 that turnest thy s' against God,
20: 3 and the s' of my understanding
21: 4 why should not my s' be troubled?
26: 4 and whose s' came from thee?
13 By his s' he hath garnished the
27: 3 and the s' of God is in my nostrils;
32: 8 But there is a s' in man: and the
18 the s' within me constraineth me.
33: 4 The S' of God hath made me, and
34:14 if he gather unto himself his s' and
Ps 31: 5 Into thine hand I commit my s':
32: 2 and in whose s' there is no guile.
34:18 saveth such as be of a contrite s'.
51:10 and renew a right s' within me.
11 and take not thy holy s' from me.
12 and uphold me with thy free s'.
17 sacrifices of God are a broken s':
76:12 He shall cut off the s' of princes:
77: 3 and my s' was overwhelmed.
6 and my s' made diligent search.
78: 8 whose s' was not stedfast with God.
104:30 Thou sendest forth thy s', they are
106:33 Because they provoked his s', so
139: 7 Whither shall I go from thy s'? or
142: 3 When my s' was overwhelmed
143: 4 is my s' overwhelmed within me;
7 speedily, O Lord: my s' faileth:
10 thou art my God: thy s' is good;
Pr 1:23 I will pour out my s' unto you, I
11:13 he that is of a faithful s' concealeth
14:29 he that is hasty of s' exalteth folly.
15: 4 perverseness...is a breach in the s'.
13 sorrow of the heart the s' is broken.
16:18 and an haughty s' before a fall.
19 be of an humble s' with the lowly,
32 and he that ruleth his s' than he
17:22 but a broken s' drieth the bones.
27 understanding is of an excellent s'.
18:14 The s' of a man will sustain his
14 but a wounded s' who can bear?
20:27 The s' of man is the candle of the
25:28 that hath no rule over his own s'
29:23 shall uphold the humble in s'.
Ec 1:14 all is vanity and vexation of s'.
17 that this also is vexation of s'.
2:11 all was vanity and vexation of s',
17 all is vanity and vexation of s'.
26 also is vanity and vexation of s'.
3:21 the s' of man that goeth upward,
21 s' of the beast that goeth downward
4: 4 is also vanity and vexation of s'.
6 full with travail and vexation of s'.
16 also is vanity and vexation of s'.
6: 9 is also vanity and vexation of s'.
7: 8 and the patient in s' is better
8 is better than the proud in s'.
9 Be not hasty in thy s' to be angry:
8: 8 power over the s' to retain the s';
10: 4 If the s' of the ruler rise up against
11: 5 knowest not...the way of the s',
12: 7 and the s' shall return unto God
Isa 4: 4 midst thereof by the s' of judgment,
4 judgment, and by the s' of burning.
11: 2 s' of the Lord shall rest upon him,
2 the s' of wisdom and understanding,
2 the s' of counsel and might,
2 the s' of knowledge and of the fear
19: 3 s' of Egypt shall fail in the midst
14 Lord hath mingled a perverse s'
26: 9 with my s' within me will I seek
28: 6 a s' of judgment to him that sitteth
29: 4 be, as of one that hath a familiar s',
10 out upon you the s' of deep sleep,
24 They also that erred in s' shall
30: 1 with a covering, but not of my s',
31: 3 and their horses flesh, and not s'.
32:15 Until the s' be poured upon us from
34:16 and his s' it hath gathered them.
38:16 all these things is the life of my s':
40: 7 the s' of the Lord bloweth upon it:
13 hath directed the S' of the Lord,
42: 1 I have put my s' upon him: he shall
5 and s' to them that walk therein:
44: 3 I will pour my s' upon thy seed,
48:16 Lord God, and his S', hath sent me.
54: 6 a woman forsaken and grieved in s',
57:15 that is of a contrite and humble s',
15 to revive the s' of the humble and
16 for the s' should fail before me, and
59:19 S' of the Lord...lift up a standard
21 My s' that is upon thee, and my
61: 1 The S' of the Lord God is upon me;
3 of praise for the s' of heaviness;
63:10 rebelled, and vexed his holy S':
11 he that put his holy S' within him?
14 S' of the Lord caused him to rest:
65:14 and shall howl for vexation of s'.
66: 2 him that is poor and of a contrite s',
Jer 51:11 up the s' of the kings of the Medes:
Eze 1:12 whither the s' was to go, they went;

Eze 1:20 Whithersoever the s' was to go
20 went, thither was their s' to go;
20, 21 s' of the living creature was in
2: 2 s' entered into me when he spake
3:12 Then the s' took me up, and I heard
14 So the s' lifted me up, and took me
14 in bitterness, in the heat of my s';
24 Then the s' entered into me, and
8: 3 s' lifted me up between the earth
10:17 the s' of the living creature was in
11: 1 Moreover the s' lifted me up, and
5 the S' of the Lord fell upon me,
19 and I will put a new s' within you;
24 Afterwards the s' took me up, and
24 brought me...by the S' of God into
13: 3 prophets, that follow their own s',
18:31 make you a new heart and a new s':
21: 7 be feeble, and every s' shall faint,
36:26 and a new s' will I put within you:
27 And I will put my s' within you,
37: 1 carried me out in the s' of the Lord,
14 And shall put my s' in you, and ye
39:29 poured out my s' upon the house of
43: 5 So the s' took me up, and brought
Da 2: 1 wherewith his s' was troubled,
3 s' was troubled to know the dream.
4: 8 in whom is the s' of the holy gods:
9 the s' of the holy gods is in thee,
18 for the s' of the holy gods is in thee.
5:11 in whom is the s' of the holy gods;
12 Forasmuch as an excellent s', and
14 that the s' of the gods is in thee,
6: 3 because an excellent s' was in him;
7:15 I Daniel was grieved in my s' in the
Ho 4:12 s' of whoredoms hath caused them
5: 4 s' of whoredoms is in the midst of
Joe 2:28 I will pour out my s' upon all flesh;
29 in those days will I pour out my s'.
Mic 2: 7 is the s' of the Lord straitened?
11 If a man walking in the s' and
3: 8 full of power by the s' of the Lord,
Hag 1:14 stirred up the s' of Zerubbabel the
14 s' of Joshua the son of Josedech,
14 s' of all the remnant of the people;
2: 5 so my s' remaineth among you:
Zec 4: 6 might, nor by power, but by my s',
6: 8 quieted my s' in the north country.
7:12 the Lord of hosts hath sent in his s'
12: 1 formeth the s' of man within him.
10 the s' of grace and of supplications:
13: 2 prophets and the unclean s' to pass
Mal 2:15 Yet had he the residue of the s'.
15 Therefore take heed to your s'.
16 therefore take heed to your s',
M't 3:16 he saw the S' of God descending
4: 1 led up of the s' into the wilderness
5: 3 Blessed are the poor in s': for
10:20 S' of your Father which speaketh
12:18 I will put my s' upon him, and he
28 I cast out devils by the S' of God,
43 When the unclean s' is gone out of
14:26 were troubled, saying, It is a s';
22:43 doth David in s' call him Lord,
26:41 the s' indeed is willing, but the
M'r 1:10 and the S' like a dove descending
12 immediately the s' driveth him
23 a man with an unclean s'; and he
26 when the unclean s' had torn him,
2: 8 Jesus perceived in his s' that they
3:30 they said, He hath an unclean s'.
5: 2 tombs a man with an unclean s',
8 out of the man, thou unclean s'.
6:49 they supposed it had been a s',
7:25 daughter had an unclean s',
8:12 And he sighed deeply in his s', and
9:17 thee my son, which hath a dumb s';
20 him, straightway the s' tare him;
25 he rebuked the foul s', saying unto
25 Thou dumb and deaf s', I charge
26 And the s' cried, and rent him sore,
14:38 The s' truly is ready, but the flesh
Lu 1:17 him in the s' and power of Elias,
47 And my s' hath rejoiced in God my
80 child grew, and waxed strong in s',
2:27 came by the S' into the temple:
40 child grew, and waxed strong in s',
4: 1 led by the S' into the wilderness,
14 in the power of the S' into Galilee:
18 The S' of the Lord is upon me,
33 which had a s' of an unclean devil,
8:29 unclean s' to come out of the man.
55 her s' came again, and she arose
9:39 And, lo, a s' taketh him, and he
42 And Jesus rebuked the unclean s',
55 not what manner of s' ye are of.
10:21 In that hour Jesus rejoiced in s',
11:13 Father give the Holy S' to them
24 When the unclean S' is gone out of
13:11 woman which had a s' of infirmity
23:46 into thy hands I commend my s':
24:37 supposed that they had seen a s'.
39 for a s' hath not flesh and bones, as
Joh 1:32 I saw the S' descending from
33 thou shalt see the S' descending,
3: 5 be born of water and of the S',
6 that which is born of the S' is s'.
8 is every one that is born of the S'.
34 God giveth not the S' by measure
4:23 shall worship the Father in s' and
24 God is a S': and they that worship
24 him must worship him in s' and in
6:63 It is the s' that quickeneth; the
63 you, they are s', and they are life.
7:39 (But this spake he of the S', which
11:33 her, he groaned in the s', and was
13:21 thus said, he was troubled in s',

Joh 14:17 Even the S' of truth; whom the
15:26 the S' of truth, which proceedeth
16:13 when he, the S' of truth, is come,
Ac 2: 4 as the S' gave them utterance.
17 God, I will pour out of my S' upon
18 pour out in those days of my S';
5: 9 to tempt the S' of the Lord?
6:10 the wisdom and the s' by which he
7:59 saying, Lord Jesus, receive my s'.
8:29 Then the S' said unto Philip, Go
39 S' of the Lord caught away Philip,
10:19 S' said unto him, Behold, three
11:12 And the s' bade me go with them,
28 and signified by the s' that there
16: 7 but the S' suffered them not.
16 with a s' of divination met us,
18 grieved, turned and said to the s',
17:16 his s' was stirred in him, when he
18: 5 Paul was pressed in the s', and
25 being fervent in the s', he spake
19:15 And the evil s' answered and said,
16 the man in whom the evil s' was
21 Paul purposed in the s', when he
20:22 go bound in the s' unto Jerusalem,
21: 4 who said to Paul through the S',
23: 8 resurrection, neither angel, nor s':
9 but if a s' or an angel hath spoken
Ro 1: 4 according to the s' of holiness, by
9 I serve with my s' in the gospel of
2:29 in the s', and not in the letter;
7: 6 we should serve in newness of s',
8: 1 not after the flesh, but after the S'.
2 the law of the S' of life in Christ
4 not after the flesh, but after the S'.
5 after the S' the things of the S'.
9 are not in the flesh, but in the S',
9 be that the S' of God dwell in you.
9 any man have not the S' of Christ,
10 S' is life because of righteousness.
11 the S' of him that raised up Jesus
11 by his S' that dwelleth in you.
13 if ye through the S' do mortify the
14 many as are led by the S' of God,
15 have not received the s' of bondage
15 have received the S' of adoption,
16 S' itself beareth witness with our
16 beareth witness with our s', that
23 which have the firstfruits of the S',
26 Likewise the S' also helpeth our
26 S' itself maketh intercession for us
27 knoweth what is the mind of the S',
11: 8 hath given them the s' of slumber,
12:11 fervent in s'; serving the Lord;
15:19 by the power of the S' of God;
30 and for the love of the S', that ye
1Co 2: 4 but in demonstration of the S' and
10 revealed them unto us by his S':
10 for the S' searcheth all things, yea,
11 save the s' of man which is in him?
11 knoweth no man, but the S' of God.
12 received, not the s' of the world,
12 world, but the s' which is of God;
14 not the things of the S' of God:
3:16 that the S' of God dwelleth in you?
4:21 in love, and in the s' of meekness?
5: 3 absent in body, but present in s',
4 my s', with the power of our Lord
5 that the s' may be saved in the day
6:11 Jesus, and by the S' of our God.
17 is joined unto the Lord is one s'.
20 and in your s', which are God's.
7:34 may be holy both in body and in s':
40 also that I have the S' of God.
12: 3 no man speaking by the S' of God
4 diversities of gifts, but the same S'.
7 of the S' is given to every man to
8 one is given by the S' the word of
8 word of knowledge by the same S';
9 To another faith by the same S';
9 the gifts of healing by the same S';
11 that one and the selfsame S',
13 by one S' are we all baptized into
13 been all made to drink into one S'.
14: 2 in the s' he speaketh mysteries.
14 an unknown tongue, my s' prayeth,
15 I will pray with the s', and I will
15 I will sing with the s', and I will
16 when thou shalt bless with the S',
15:45 Adam was made a quickening s'.
16:18 For they have refreshed my s' and
2Co 1:22 and given the earnest of the S' in
2:13 I had no rest in my s', because I
3: 3 but with the S' of the living God;
6 not of the letter, but of the s': for
6 letter killeth, but the s' giveth life.
8 the ministration of the s' be rather
17 Now the Lord is that S': and where
17 where the S' of the Lord is, there is
18 glory, even as by the S' of the Lord.
4:13 We having the same s' of faith,
5: 5 given unto us the earnest of the S'.
7: 1 all filthiness of the flesh and s',
13 because his s' was refreshed by you
11: 4 or if ye receive another s', which ye
12:18 walked we not in the same s'?
Ga 3: 2 Received ye the S' by the works of
3 having begun in the S', are ye now
5 that ministereth to you the S', and
14 might receive the promise of the S'
4: 6 sent forth the S' of his Son into
29 him that was born after the S',
5: 5 we through the S' wait for the hope
16 Walk in the S', and ye shall not
17 For the flesh lusteth against the S',
17 and the S' against the flesh: and
18 But if ye be led of the S', ye are not

Ga 5:22 fruit of the S· is love, joy, peace,
25 If we live in the S·, let us also walk
25 let us also walk in the S·.
6: 1 such an one in the s· of meekness;
8 soweth to the S· shall of the S· reap
18 Lord Jesus Christ be with your s·.
Eph 1:13 sealed with that holy S· of promise,
17 may give unto you the s· of wisdom
2: 2 the s· that now worketh in the
18 access by one S· unto the Father.
22 habitation of God through the S·.
3: 5 apostles and prophets by the S·;
16 strengthened with might by his S·
4: 3 to keep the unity of the S· in the
4 There is one body, and one S·,
23 be renewed in the s· of your mind;
30 And grieve not the holy S· of God,
5: 9 (For the fruit of the S· is in all
18 excess; but be filled with the S·;
6:17 the sword of the S·, which is the
18 prayer and supplication in the S·,
Ph'p 1:19 supply of the S· of Jesus Christ,
27 that ye stand fast in one s·, with
2: 1 of love, if any fellowship of the S·,
3: 3 which worship God in the s·, and
Col 1: 8 unto us your love in the S·.
2: 5 yet am I with you in the s·, joying
1Th 4: 8 hath also given unto us his holy S·.
5:19 Quench not the S·.
23 your whole s· and soul and body be
2Th 2: 2 neither by s·, nor by word, nor by
8 consume with the s· of his mouth,
13 through sanctification of the S·
1Ti 3:16 justified in the S·, seen of angels,
4: 1 Now the S· speaketh expressly,
12 in charity, in s·, in faith, in purity.
2Ti 1: 7 hath not given us the s· of fear;
4:22 Lord Jesus Christ be with thy s·.
Ph'm 25 Lord Jesus Christ be with your s·.
Heb 4:12 the dividing asunder of soul and s·,
9:14 who through the eternal s· offered
10:29 done despite unto the S· of grace?
Jas 2:26 as the body without the s· is dead,
4: 5 The s· that dwelleth in us lusteth
1Pe 1: 2 through sanctification of the S·,
11 S· of Christ which was in them did
22 obeying the truth through the S·
3: 4 ornament of a meek and quiet s·,
18 the flesh, but quickened by the S·:
4: 6 but live according to God in the s·.
14 s· of glory and of God resteth upon
1Jo 3:24 by the S· which he hath given us.
4: 1 Beloved, believe not every s·, but
2 Hereby know ye the S· of God:
2 Every s· that confesseth that Jesus
3 every s· that confesseth not that
3 this is that s· of antichrist, whereof
6 the s· of truth, and the s· of error.
13 because he hath given us of his S·.
5: 6 it is the S· that beareth witness,
6 witness, because the S· is truth.
8 s·, and the water, and the blood:
Jude 19 sensual, having not the S·.
Re 1:10 I was in the S· on the Lord's day,
2: 7, 11, 17 S· saith unto the churches;
29 the S· saith unto the churches.
3: 6, 13, 22 S· saith unto the churches.
4: 2 And immediately I was in the s·:
11:11 the S· of life from God entered into
14:13 Yea, saith the S·, that they may
17: 3 So he carried me away in the s·
18: 2 devils, and the hold of every foul s·,
19:10 of Jesus is the s· of prophecy.
21:10 And he carried me away in the s· to
22:17 the S· and the bride say, Come.

spirits
Le 19:31 Regard not...that have familiar s·,
20: 6 turneth after such as have familiar s·,
Nu 16:22 God, the God of the s· of all flesh,
27:16 Lord, the God of the s· of all flesh,
De 18:11 or a consulter with familiar s·, or
1Sa 28: 3 put away those that had familiar s·,
9 cut off those that have familiar s·,
2Ki 21: 6 dealt with familiar s· and wizards:
23:24 Moreover...workers with familiar s·,
Ps 104: 4 Who maketh his angels s·; his
Pr 16: 2 eyes; but the Lord weigheth the s·.
Isa 8:19 Seek...them that have familiar s·,
19: 3 and to them that have familiar s·,
Zec 6: 5 are the four s· of the heavens,
M't 8:16 he cast out the s· with his word,
10: 1 gave them power against unclean s·,
12:45 seven other s· more wicked than
M'r 1:27 commandeth he even the unclean s·,
3:11 unclean s·, when they saw him, fell
5:13 And the unclean s· went out, and
6: 7 gave them power over unclean s·;
Lu 4:36 he commandeth the unclean s·,
6:18 that were vexed with unclean s·:
7:21 and plagues, and of evil s·; and
8: 2 which had been healed of evil s·
10:20 that the s· are subject unto you;
11:26 seven other s· more wicked than
Ac 5:16 which were vexed with unclean s·:
8: 7 unclean s·, crying with loud voice,
19:12 and the evil s· went out of them.
13 call over them which had evil s·
1Co 12:10 to another discerning of s·; to
14:32 s· of the prophets are subject to the
1Ti 4: 1 giving heed to seducing s·, and
Heb 1: 7 Who maketh his angels s·, and his
14 Are they not all ministering s·, sent
12: 9 in subjection unto the Father of s·,
23 to the s· of just men made perfect,
1Pe 3:19 and preached unto the s· in prison;
1Jo 4: 1 try the s· whether they are of God:
Re 1: 4 the seven S· which are before his
3: 1 he that hath the seven S· of God,
4: 5 which are the seven S· of God.
5: 6 which are the seven S· of God sent
16:13 three unclean s· like frogs come out
14 they are the s· of devils, working

spiritual
Ho 9: 7 is a fool, the s· man is mad,
Ro 1:11 may impart unto you some s· gift,
7:14 For we know that the law is s·: but
15:27 made partakers of their s· things,
1Co 2:13 comparing s· things with s·.
15 But he that is s· judgeth all things,
3: 1 not speak unto you as unto s·,
9:11 If we have sown unto you s· things,
10: 3 And did all eat the same s· meat;
4 And did all drink the same s· drink:
4 drank of that s· Rock that followed
12: 1 Now concerning s· gifts, brethren, I
14: 1 after charity, and desire s· gifts,
12 as ye are zealous of s· gifts, seek
37 himself to be a prophet, or s·,
15:44 natural body; it is raised a s· body.
44 natural body, and there is a s· body.
46 that was not first which is s·, but
46 and afterward that which is s·.
Ga 6: 1 ye which are s·, restore such an one
Eph 1: 3 blessed us with all s· blessings in
5:19 in psalms and hymns and s· songs,
6:12 against s· wickedness in high
Col 1: 9 all wisdom and s· understanding;
3:16 in psalms and hymns and s· songs,
1Pe 2: 5 stones, are built up a s· house,
5 priesthood, to offer up s· sacrifices,

spiritually
Ro 8: 6 but to be s· minded is life and
1Co 2:14 because they are s· discerned.
Re 11: 8 which s· is called Sodom and Egypt,

spit See also SPAT; SPITTED; SPITTING.
Le 15: 8 he that hath the issue s· upon him
Nu 12:14 her father had but s· in her face,
De 25: 9 and s· in his face, and shall answer
Job 30:10 me, and spare not to s· in my face.
M't 26:67 Then did they s· in his face, and
27:30 And they s· upon him, and took the
M'r 7:33 and he s·, and touched his tongue;
8:23 when he had s· on his eyes, and put
10:34 and shall s· upon him, and shall
14:65 And some began to s· on him, and to
15:19 did s· upon him, and bowing their

spite See also DESPITE; SPITEFULLY.
Ps 10:14 thou beholdest mischief and s·, to

spitefully
M't 22: 6 servants, and entreated them s·,
Lu 18:32 shall be mocked, and s· entreated,

spitted See also SPAT.
Lu 18:32 spitefully entreated, and s· on:

spitting
Isa 50: 6 hid not my face from shame and s·.

spittle
1Sa 21:13 let his s· fall down upon his beard.
Job 7:19 alone till I swallow down my s·?
Joh 9: 6 ground, and made clay of the s·,

spoil See also SPOILED; SPOILEST; SPOILETH; SPOILING; SPOILS.
Ge 49:27 and at night he shall divide the s·.
Ex 3:22 and ye shall s· the Egyptians.
15: 9 will overtake, I will divide the s·;
Nu 31: 9 and took the s· of all their cattle,
11 And they took all the s·, and all the
12 and the s·, unto Moses, and Eleazer
53 (For the men of war had taken s·,
De 2:35 the s· of the cities which we took.
3: 7 the cattle, and the s· of the cities,
13:16 thou shalt gather all the s· of it into
16 and all the s· thereof every whit,
20:14 all the s· thereof, shalt thou take
14 shalt eat the s· of thine enemies,
Jos 8: 2 only the s· thereof, and the cattle
27 s· of that city Israel took for a prey
11:14 the s· of these cities, and the cattle,
22: 8 divide the s· of your enemies with
J'g 5:30 the necks of them that take the s·?
14:19 men of them, and took their s·,
1Sa 14:30 had eaten freely to day of the s· of
32 And the people flew upon the s·,
36 and s· them until the morning light
15:19 but didst fly upon the s·, and didst
21 But the people took of the s·, sheep
30:16 because of all the great s· that they
19 neither s·, nor any thing that they
20 cattle, and said, This is David's s·.
22 will not give them ought of the s·
26 of the s· unto the elders of Judah,
26 a present for you of the s· of the
2Sa 3:22 and brought in a great s· with them:
8:12 and of the s· of Hadadezer, son of
12:30 he brought forth the s· of the city
23:10 returned after him only to s·.
2Ki 3:23 now therefore, Moab, to the s·.
21:14 prey and a s· to all their enemies;
1Ch 20: 2 he brought also exceeding much s·
2Ch 14:13 they carried away very much s·.
14 was exceeding much s· in them.
15:11 of the s· which they had brought,
20:25 came to take away the s· of them,
25 three days in gathering of the s·,
24:23 sent all the s· of them unto the king
25:13 thousand of them, and took much s·.
2Ch 28: 8 took also away much s· from them,
8 and brought the s· to Samaria.
14 the s· before the princes and all the
15 with the s· clothed all that were
Ezr 9: 7 to a s·, and to confusion of face, as
Es 3:13 to take the s· of them for a prey.
8:11 to take the s· of them for a prey,
9:10 on the s· laid they not their hand.
Job 29:17 and plucked the s· out of his teeth.
Ps 44:10 which hate us s· for themselves.
68:12 that tarried at home divided the s·.
89:41 All that pass by the way s· him:
109:11 and let the strangers s· his labour.
119:162 word, as one that findeth great s·.
Pr 1:13 we shall fill our houses with s·:
16:19 than to divide the s· with the proud.
22:23 and s· the soul of those that spoiled
24:15 righteous; s· not his resting place:
31:11 so that he shall have no need of s·.
Ca 2:15 the little foxes, that s· the vines:
Isa 3:14 the s· of the poor is in your houses.
8: 4 the s· of Samaria shall be taken
9: 3 men rejoice when they divide the s·.
10: 6 to take the s·, and to take the prey,
11:14 they shall s· them of the east
17:14 is the portion of them that s· us,
33: 1 when thou shalt cease to s·, thou
4 your s· shall be gathered like the
23 is the prey of a great s· divided;
42:22 for a s·, and none saith, Restore.
24 Who gave Jacob for a s·, and
53:12 divide the s· with the strong;
Jer 5: 6 wolf of the evenings shall s· them,
6: 7 violence and s· is heard in her;
15:13 thy treasures will I give to the s·
17: 3 and all thy treasures to the s·, and
20: 5 which shall s· them, and take them,
8 cried out, I cried violence and s·;
30:16 and they that s· thee shall be a
16 shall be a s·, and all that prey
47: 4 cometh to s· all the Philistines,
4 for the Lord will s· the Philistines,
49:28 to Kedar, and s· the men of the east.
32 the multitude of their cattle a s·:
50:10 And Chaldea shall be a s·: all that
10 all that s· her shall be satisfied,
Eze 7:21 to the wicked of the earth for a s·;
14:15 they s· it, so that it be desolate,
25: 7 will deliver thee for a s· to the
26: 5 it shall become a s· to the nations.
12 they shall make a s· of thy riches,
29:19 and take her s·, and take her prey;
32:12 they shall s· the pomp of Egypt,
38:12 To take a s·, and to take a prey;
13 thee, Art thou come to take a s·?
13 cattle and goods, to take a great s·?
39:10 and they shall s· those that spoiled
45: 9 remove violence and s·, and
Da 11:24 among them the prey, and s·, and
33 by captivity, and by s·, many days.
Ho 10: 2 altars, he shall s· their images.
13:15 he shall s· the treasure of all
Na 2: 9 the s· of silver, take the s· of gold:
Hab 2: 8 of the people shall s· thee;
17 and the s· of beasts, which made
Zep 2: 9 residue of my people shall s· them,
Zec 2: 9 shall be a s· to their servants:
14: 1 thy s· shall be divided in the midst
M't 12:29 man's house, and s· his goods,
29 man? and then he will s· his house.
M'r 3:27 man's house, and s· his goods,
27 man; and then he will s· his house.
Col 2: 8 Beware lest any man s· you

spoiled
Ge 34:27 came upon the slain, and s· the city,
29 s· even all that was in the house.
Ex 12:36 And they s· the Egyptians.
De 28:29 be only oppressed and s· evermore,
J'g 2:14 the hands of spoilers that s· them,
16 of the hand of those that s· them.
1Sa 14:48 of the hands of them that s· them.
17:53 Philistines, and they s· their tents.
2Ki 7:16 out, and s· the tents of the Syrians.
2Ch 14:14 and they s· all the cities; for there
Job 12:17 He leadeth counsellers away s·,
19 He leadeth princes away s·, and
Ps 76: 5 The stouthearted are s·, they have
Pr 22:23 the soul of those that s· them.
Isa 13:16 their houses shall be s·, and their
18: 2 whose land the rivers have s·!
7 whose land the rivers have s·, to the
24: 3 be utterly emptied, and utterly s·:
33: 1 that spoilest, and thou wast not s·;
1 cease to spoil, thou shalt be s·;
42:22 But this is a people robbed and s·;
Jer 2:14 he a homeborn slave? why is he s·?
4:13 Woe unto us! for we are s·.
20 is cried; for the whole land is s·:
20 suddenly are my tents s·, and my
30 when thou art s·, what wilt thou do?
9:19 heard out of Zion, How are we s·!
10:20 My tabernacle is s·, and all my
21:12 deliver him that is s· out of the
22: 3 deliver the s· out of the hand of the
25:36 for the Lord hath s· their pasture.
48: 1 Woe unto Nebo! for it is s·:
15 Moab is s·, and gone up out of her
20 tell ye it in Arnon, that Moab is s·,
49: 3 Howl, O Heshbon, for Ai is s·: cry,
10 his seed is s·, and his brethren, and
51:55 Because the Lord hath s· Babylon,
Eze 18: 7 hath s· none by violence, hath
12 16 hath s· by violence,
18 s· his brother by violence, and did
23:46 give them to be removed and s·.

Eze 39:10 they shall spoil those that s· them.
Ho 10:14 and all thy fortresses shall be s·,
14 as Shalman s· Beth-arbel in the
Am 3:11 thee, and thy palaces shall be s·.
5: 9 strengtheneth the s· against the
9 that the s· shall come against the
Mic 2: 4 and say, We be utterly s·: he hath
Hab 2: 8 thou hast s· many nations, all the
Zec 2: 8 me unto the nations which s· you:
11: 2 fallen; because the mighty are s·:
3 for their glory is s·: a voice of the
3 lions; for the pride of Jordan is s·
Col 2:15 having s· principalities...powers,

spoiler See also SPOILERS.
Isa 16: 4 to them from the face of the s·:
4 the s· ceaseth, the oppressors are
21: 2 treacherously, and the s· spoileth.
Jer 6:26 the s· shall suddenly come upon us.
15: 8 of the young men a s· at noonday:
48: 8 the s· shall come upon every city,
18 s· of Moab shall come upon thee,
32 s· is fallen upon thy summer fruits
51:56 Because the s· is come upon her,

spoilers
J'g 2:14 the hands of s· that spoiled them,
1Sa 13:17 the s· came out of the camp of the
14:15 and the s·, they also trembled, and
2Ki 17:20 them into the hand of s·, until
Jer 12:12 s· are come upon all high places
51:48 the s· shall come unto her from the
53 yet from me shall s· come unto her,

spoilest
Isa 33: 1 Woe to thee that s·, and thou wast

spoileth
Ps 35:10 the needy from him that s· him?
Isa 21: 2 treacherously, and the spoiler s·.
Ho 7: 1 the troop of robbers s· without.
Na 3:16 the cankerworm s·, and fleeth away.

spoiling
Ps 35:12 evil for good to the s· of my soul.
Isa 22: 4 because of the s· of the daughter
Jer 48: 3 s· and great destruction.
Hab 1: 3 for s· and violence are before me:
Heb10: 34 took joyfully the s· of your goods,

spoils
Jos 7:21 among the s· a goodly Babylonish
1Ch 26:27 Out of the s· won in battles did
Isa 25:11 together with the s· of their hands.
Lu 11:22 he trusted, and divideth his s·.
Heb 7: 4 Abraham gave the tenth of the s·.

spoke See SPAKE; SPOKEN; SPOKES; SPOKESMAN.

spoken
Ge 12: 4 as the Lord had s· unto him;
18:19 that which he had s· of him.
19:21 this city, for the which thou hast s·.
21: 1 Lord did unto Sarah as he had s·.
2 time of which God had s· to him.
24:51 son's wife, as the Lord hath s·.
28:15 done that which I have s· to thee of.
41:28 thing...I have s· unto Pharaoh:
44: 2 to the word that Joseph had s·.
Ex 4:10 nor since thou hast s· unto thy
30 which the Lord had s· unto Moses,
9:12 as the Lord had s· unto Moses.
35 go; as the Lord had s· by Moses.
10:29 Thou hast s· well, I will see thy
19: 8 All that the Lord hath s· we will do.
32:13 all this land that I have s· of will I
34 place of which I have s· unto thee:
33:17 do this thing also that thou hast s·:
34:32 all that the Lord had s· with him in
Le 10:11 which the Lord hath s· unto them
Nu 1:48 the Lord had s· unto Moses, saying,
10:29 the Lord hath s· good concerning
12: 2 the Lord indeed s· only by Moses?
2 hath he not s· also by us? And the
14:17 be great, according as thou hast s·,
28 as ye have s· in mine ears, so will I
15:22 which the Lord hath s· unto Moses,
21: 7 for we have s· against the Lord,
23: 2 And Balak did as Balaam had s·;
17 unto him, What hath the Lord s·?
19 or hath he s·, and shall he not make
De 1:14 thing which thou hast s· is good for
5:28 which they have s· unto thee:
28 have well said all that they have s·.
6:19 before thee, as the Lord hath s·.
13: 5 he hath s· to turn you away from
18:17 Lord said unto me, They have well s·
17 that which they have s·.
21 word which the Lord hath not s·?
22 thing which the Lord hath not s·,
22 prophet hath s· it presumptuously:
26:19 the Lord thy God, as he hath s·.
Jos 6: 8 when Joshua had s· unto the people,
21:45 the Lord had s· unto the house of
Ru 2:13 for thou hast s· friendly unto thine
1Sa 1:16 and grief have I s· hitherto.
3:12 things which I have s· concerning
20:23 matter which thou and I have s· of,
25:30 the good that he hath s· concerning
2Sa 2:27 unless thou hadst s·, surely then in
3:18 the Lord hath s· of David, saying,
6:22 maidservants which thou hast s· of,
7:19 hast s· also of thy servant's house
25 word that thou hast s· concerning
29 for thou, O Lord God, hast s· it:
14:19 ought that my lord the king hath s·:
17: 6 Ahithophel hath s· after this
1Ki 2:23 if Adonijah have not s· this word
12: 9 this people, who have s· to me,
1Ki 13: 3 is the sign which the Lord hath s·;
11 words which he had s· unto the king,
14:11 the air eat: for the Lord hath s· it.
18:24 answered and said, It is well s·.
21: 4 the Jezreelite had s· to him: for
22:23 Lord hath s· evil concerning thee.
28 peace, the Lord hath not s· by me.
2Ki 1:17 of the Lord which Elijah had s·.
4:13 wouldest thou be s· for to the king,
7:18 the man of God had s· to the king,
19:21 the Lord hath s· concerning him;
20: 9 will do the thing that he hath s·:
19 word of the Lord which thou hast s·.
1Ch 17:17 hast also s· of thy servant's house
23 thou hast s· concerning thy servant
2Ch 2:15 the wine, which my lord hath s· of,
6:10 his word that he hath s·:
17 thou hast s· unto thy servant David.
10: 9 people, which have s· to me, saying,
18:22 the Lord hath s· evil against thee.
27 then hath not the Lord s· by me.
36:22 word...s· by the mouth of Jeremiah
Ezr 8:22 we had s· unto the king, saying,
Ne 2:18 king's words that he had s· unto me.
Es 6:10 nothing fail of all...thou hast s·.
7: 9 who had s· good for the king,
Job 21: 3 and after that I have s·, mock on.
32: 4 Elihu had waited till Job had s·.
33: 2 my tongue hath s· in my mouth.
8 Surely thou hast s· in mine hearing,
34:35 Job hath s· without knowledge,
40: 5 Once have I s·; but I will not
42: 7 Lord had s· these words unto Job,
7 for ye have not s· of me the thing
8 that ye have not s· of me the thing
Ps 50: 1 God, even the Lord, hath s·, and
60: 6 God hath s· in his holiness; I will
62:11 God hath s· once; twice have I
66:14 and my mouth hath s·, when I was
87: 3 Glorious things are s· of thee, O
108: 7 God hath s· in his holiness; I will
109: 2 s· against me with a lying tongue.
116:10 believed, therefore have I s·: I was
Pr 15:23 a word s· in due season, how good
25:11 word fitly s· is like apples of gold
Ec 7:21 no heed unto all words that are s·;
Ca 8: 8 the day when she shall be s· for?
Isa 1: 2 ear, O earth: for the Lord hath s·,
20 for the mouth of the Lord hath s· it.
16:13 the word that the Lord hath s·
14 But now the Lord hath s·, saying,
21:17 the Lord God of Israel hath s· it.
22:25 be cut off: for the Lord hath s· it.
23: 4 O Zidon: for the sea hath s·, even
24: 3 for the Lord hath s· this word.
25: 8 the earth: for the Lord hath s· it.
31: 4 For thus hath the Lord s· unto me,
37:22 the word which the Lord hath s·
38: 7 will do this thing that he hath s·;
15 hath both s· unto me, and himself
39: 8 is the word...which thou hast s·.
40: 5 for the mouth of the Lord hath s· it.
45:19 I have not s· in secret, in a dark
46:11 I have s· it, I will also bring it to
48:15 I, even I, have s·; yea, I have
16 I have not s· in secret from the
58:14 for the mouth of the Lord hath s· it.
59: 3 your lips have s· lies, your tongue
Jer 3: 5 thou hast s· and done evil things as
4:28 because I have s· it, I have purposed
9:12 the mouth of the Lord hath s·.
13:15 be not proud: for the Lord hath s·.
23:21 I have not s· to them, yet they
35, 37 and, What hath the Lord s·?
25: 3 and I have s· unto you, rising early
26:16 he hath s· to us in the name of the
27:13 the Lord hath s· against the nation
29:23 have s· lying words in my name,
30: 2 Write...all the words that I have s·
32:24 what thou hast s· is come to pass;
33:24 not what this people have s·, saying,
35:14 I have s· unto you, rising early
17 because I have s· unto them, but
36: 2 write...all the words that I have s·
4 which he had s· unto him, upon a
38: 1 words that Jeremiah had s· unto
44:16 the word that thou hast s· unto us
25 your wives have both s· with your
48: 8 be destroyed, as the Lord hath s·.
51:62 thou hast s· against this place, to
Eze 5:13 I the Lord have s· it in my zeal,
15 rebukes. I the Lord have s· it.
17 upon thee. I the Lord have s· it.
12:28 word which I have s· shall be done,
13: 7 have ye not s· a lying divination,
7 Lord saith it; albeit I have not s·?
8 Because ye have s· vanity, and
14: 9 deceived when he hath s· a thing,
17:21 know that I the Lord have s· it.
24 I the Lord have s· and have done it.
21:32 for I the Lord have s· it.
22:14 I the Lord have s· it, and will do it.
28 God, when the Lord hath not s·.
23:34 I have s· it, saith the Lord God.
24:14 I the Lord have s· it: it shall come
26: 5 for I have s· it, saith the Lord God:
14 for I the Lord have s· it, saith the
28:10 for I have s· it, saith the Lord God.
30:12 of strangers: I the Lord have s· it.
34:24 among them; I the Lord have s· it.
35:12 thy blasphemies which thou hast s·
36: 5 in the fire of my jealousy have I s·
6 I have s· in my jealousy and in my
36 I the Lord have s· it, and I will do it.
37:14 ye know that I the Lord have s· it,
38:17 he of whom I have s· in old time
Eze 38:19 and in the fire of my wrath have I s·,
39: 5 for I have s· it, saith the Lord God.
8 this is the day whereof I have s·.
Da 4:31 Nebuchadnezzar, to thee it is s·;
10:11 when he had s· this word unto me,
15 when he had s· such words unto
19 And when he had s· unto me, I was
Ho 7:13 yet they have s· lies against me.
10: 4 They have s· words, swearing
12:10 I have also s· by the prophets, and
Joe 3: 8 far off: for the Lord hath s· it.
Am 3: 1 word that the Lord hath s· against
8 the Lord hath s·, who can but
5:14 shall be with you, as ye have s·.
Ob 12 shouldest thou have s· proudly in
18 of Esau; for the Lord hath s· it.
Mic 4: 4 mouth of the Lord of hosts hath s·
6:12 the inhabitants thereof have s· lies,
Zec 10: 2 For the idols have s· vanity, and the
Mal 3:13 What have we s· so much against
M't 1:22 which was s· of the Lord by the
2:15 which was s· of the Lord by the
17 which was s· by Jeremy the prophet,
23 which was s· by the prophets,
3: 3 that was s· of by the prophet Esaias,
4:14 which was s· by Esaias the prophet,
8:17 which was s· by Esaias the prophet,
12:17 which was s· by Esaias the prophet,
13:35 which was s· by the prophet,
21: 4 which was s· by the prophet,
22:31 that which was s· unto you by God,
24:15 s· of by Daniel the prophet, stand
26:65 saying, He hath s· blasphemy;
27: 9 was s· by Jeremy the prophet,
35 which was s· by the prophet,
M'r 1:42 And as soon as he had s·,
5:36 Jesus heard the word that was s·,
12:12 had s· the parable against them:
13:14 s· of by Daniel the prophet,
14: 9 be s· of for a memorial of her.
16:19 after the Lord had s· unto them,
Lu 2:33 those things which were s· of him.
34 for a sign which shall be s· against;
12: 3 whatsoever ye have s· in darkness
3 ye have s· in the ear in closets
18:34 they the things which were s·.
19:28 And when he had thus s·, he went
20:19 had s· this parable against them.
24:25 all that the prophets have s·:
40 when he had thus s·, he shewed
Joh 4:50 word that Jesus had s· unto him,
9: 6 When he had thus s·, he spat on the
11:13 had s· of taking of rest in sleep.
43 And when he thus had s·, he cried
12:48 the word that I have s·, the same
49 For I have not s· of myself; but
14:25 These things have I s· unto you,
15: 3 the word which I have s· unto you.
11 These things have I s· unto you,
22 if I had not come and s· unto them,
16: 1 These things have I s· unto you,
25 have I s· unto you in proverbs:
33 These things I have s· unto you,
18: 1 When Jesus had s· these words,
22 when he had thus s·, one of the
23 If I have s· evil, bear witness of
20:18 he had s· these things unto her.
21:19 And when he had s· this, he saith
Ac 1: 9 when he had s· these things, while
2:16 which was s· by the prophet Joel;
3:21 God hath s· by the mouth of all
24 as many as have s·, have likewise
8:24 none of these things...ye have s·
9:27 way, and that he had s· to him,
13:40 you, which is s· of in the prophets;
45 things which were s· by Paul,
46 should first have been s· to you.
16:14 the things which were s· of Paul.
19:36 these things cannot be s· against,
41 when he had thus s·, he dismissed
20:36 when he had thus s·, he kneeled
23: 9 a spirit or an angel hath s· to him,
26:30 And when he had thus s·, the king
27:11 things which were s· by Paul.
35 he had thus s·, he took bread,
28:22 that every where it is s· against.
24 believed the things which were s·,
25 after that Paul had s· one word,
Ro 1: 8 that your faith is s· of throughout
4:18 according to that which was s·, So
14:16 Let not then your good be evil s· of:
15:21 To whom he was not s· of, they
1Co 10:30 why am I evil s· of for that for
14: 9 how shall it be known what is s·?
2Co 4:13 believed, and therefore have I s·;
Heb 1: 2 last days s· unto us by his Son,
2: 2 word s· by angels was stedfast,
3 the first began to be s· by the Lord,
3: 5 things which were to be s· after;
4: 8 afterward have s· of another day.
7:13 he of whom these things are s·
8: 1 things...we have s· this is the sum.
9:19 when Moses had s· every precept
12:19 should not be s· to them any more:
13: 7 who have s· unto you the word of
Jas 5:10 who have s· in the name of the
1Pe 4:14 on their part he is evil s· of, but on
2Pe 2: 2 the way of truth shall be evil s· of.
3: 2 s· before by the holy prophets,
Jude 15 which ungodly sinners have s·
17 were s· before of the apostles

spokes
1Ki 7:33 their felloes, and their s·, were all

spokesman
Ex 4:16 he shall be thy s· unto the people:

sponge See SPUNGE.

spoon See also SPOONS.
Nu 7:14 One s' of ten shekels of gold, full
20 One s' of gold of ten shekels, full of
26, 32, 38, 44, 50, 56, 62, 68, 74, 80 One
golden s' of ten shekels, full of

spoons
Ex 25:29 the dishes thereof, and s' thereof,
37:16 the table, his dishes, and his s',
Nu 4: 7 thereon the dishes, and the s', and
7:84 silver bowls, twelve s' of gold:
86 The golden s' were twelve, full of
86 the gold of the s' was an hundred
1Ki 7:50 and the s', and the censers of pure
2Ki 25:14 the snuffers, and the s', and all the
2Ch 4:22 and the s', and the censers, of pure
24:14 s', and vessels of gold and silver.
Jer 52:18 the bowls, and the s', and all the
19 the candlesticks, and the s', and

sport See also SPORTING.
J'g 16:25 Samson, that he may make us s'.
25 house: and he made them s':
27 that beheld while Samson made s'.
Pr 10:23 It is as s' to a fool to do mischief:
26:19 neighbour, and saith, Am...I in s'?
Isa 57: 4 Against whom do ye s' yourselves?

sporting
Ge 26: 8 behold, Isaac was s' with Rebekah
2Pe 2:13 s' themselves with their own

spot See also SPOTS; SPOTTED.
Le 13: 2 flesh a rising, a scab, or bright s',
4 If the bright s' be white in the skin
19 be a white rising, or a bright s',
23 But if the bright s' stay in his place,
24 that burneth have a white bright s',
25 the hair in the bright s' be turned
26 be no white hair in the bright s',
28 And if the bright s' stay in his place,
39 it is a freckled s' that groweth in
14:56 and for a scab, and for a bright s':
Nu 19: 2 bring thee a red heifer without s',
28: 3 lambs of the first year without s',
9 lambs of the first year without s',
11 lambs of the first year without s';
29:17, 26 of the first year without s':
De 32: 5 their s' is not...of his children:
5 is not the s' of his children: they
Job 11:15 thou lift up thy face without s';
Ca 4: 7 fair, my love; there is no s' in thee.
Eph 5:27 not having s', or wrinkle, or any
1Ti 6:14 keep this commandment without s',
Heb 9:14 offered himself without s' to God,
1Pe 1:19 without blemish and without s':
2Pe 3:14 found of him in peace, without s',

spots
Le 13:38 bright s', even white bright s';
39 if the bright s' in the skin of their
Jer 13:23 his skin, or the leopard his s'?
2Pe 2:13 *S'* they are and blemishes,
Jude 12 These are s' in your feasts of

spotted See also UNSPOTTED.
Ge 30:32 all the speckled and s' cattle, and
32 s' and speckled among the goats:
33 is not speckled and s' among the
35 goats that were ringstraked and s',
35 goats that were speckled and s',
39 ringstraked, speckled, and s'.
Jude 23 even the garment s' by the flesh.

spouse See also ESPOUSED; SPOUSES.
Ca 4: 8 with me from Lebanon, my s',
9 my heart, my sister, my s'; thou
10 fair is thy love, my sister, my s'!
11 Thy lips, O my s', drop as the
12 garden inclosed is my sister, my s';
5: 1 into my garden, my sister, my s':

spouses
Ho 4:13 and your s' shall commit adultery.
14 your s' when they commit adultery:

spouts See WATERSPOUTS.

sprang See also SPRUNG.
M'r 4: 5 and immediately it s' up, because
8 yield fruit that s' up and increased,
Lu 8: 7 and the thorns s' up with it, and
8 fell on good ground, and s' up,
Ac 16:29 he called for a light, and s' in, and
Heb 7:14 that our Lord s' out of Juda; of
11:12 Therefore s' there even of one, and

spread^ See also OVERSPREAD; SPREADEST; SPREADETH; SPREADING.
Ge 10:18 of the Canaanites s' abroad.
28:14 thou shalt s' abroad to the west,
33:19 a field, where he had s' his tent,
35:21 and s' his tent beyond the tower of
Ex 9:29 I will s' abroad my hands unto the
33 and s' abroad his hands unto the
37: 9 the cherubims s' out their wings on
40:19 And he s' abroad the tent over the
Le 13: 5 and the plague s' not in the skin;
6 and the plague s' not in the skin,
7 if the scab s' much abroad in the
22 if it s' much abroad in the skin,
23 spot stay in his place, and s' not,
27 if it be s' much abroad in the skin,
28 his place, and s' not in the skin,
32 if the scall s' not, and there be in it
34 if the scall be not s' in the skin,
35 But if the scall s' much in the skin
36 behold, if the scall be s' in the skin,
51 if the plague be s' in the garment,
53 the plague be not s' in the garment,
Le 13:55 colour, and the plague be not s';
14:39 if the plague be s' in the walls of
44 if the plague be s' in the house, it
48 the plague hath not s' in the house,
Nu 4: 6 shall s' over it a cloth wholly of
7 they shall s' a cloth of blue, and
8 shall s' upon them a cloth of scarlet,
11 altar they shall s' a cloth of blue,
13 altar, and s' a purple cloth thereon:
14 they shall s' upon it a covering of
11:32 and they s' them all abroad for
24: 6 As the valleys are they s' forth, as
De 22:17 shall s' the cloth before the elders
J'g 8:25 And they s' a garment, and did cast
15: 9 Judah, and s' themselves in Lehi.
Ru 3: 9 s' therefore thy skirt over thine
1Sa 30:16 were s' abroad upon all the earth,
2Sa 5:18, 22 and s' themselves in the valley
16:22 So they s' Absalom a tent upon
17:19 s' a covering over the well's mouth,
19 and s' ground corn thereon; and
21:10 and s' it for her upon the rock,
22:43 the street, and did s' them abroad.
1Ki 6:32 and s' gold upon the cherubims,
8: 7 the cherubims s' forth their two
22 s' forth his hands toward heaven:
38 and s' forth his hands toward this
54 with his hands s' up to heaven.
2Ki 8:15 and s' it on his face, so...he died:
19:14 the Lord, and s' it before the Lord.
1Ch 14: 9 Philistines came ...s' themselves
13 Philistines yet again s' themselves
28:18 cherubims, that s' out their wings,
2Ch 3:13 wings of...cherubims s' themselves
5: 8 the cherubims s' forth their wings
6:12 of Israel, and s' forth his hands:
13 s' forth his hands toward heaven,
29 s' forth his hands in this house:
26: 8 and his name s' abroad even to the
15 And his name s' far abroad; for he
Ezr 9: 5 s' out my hands unto the Lord my
Job 29:19 My root was s' out by the waters,
37:18 thou with him s' out the sky,
Ps 105:39 He s' a cloud for a covering; and
140: 5 they have s' a net by the wayside;
Pr 1:17 Surely in vain the net is s' in the
Isa 1:15 And when ye s' forth your hands,
14:11 the worm is s' under thee, and the
19: 8 they that s' nets upon the waters
25: 7 the vail that is s' over all nations.
11 And he shall s' forth his hands in
33:23 mast, they could not s' the sail:
37:14 the Lord, and s' it before the Lord.
42: 5 he that s' forth the earth, and that
58: 5 to s' sackcloth and ashes under
65: 2 I have s' out my hands all the day
Jer 8: 2 they shall s' them before the sun,
10: 9 Silver s' into plates is brought
43:10 he shall s' his royal pavilion over
48:40 and shall s' his wings over Moab.
49:22 and s' his wings over Bozrah: and
La 1:10 The adversary hath s' out his hand
13 he hath s' a net for my feet, he hath
Eze 2:10 And he s' it before me; and it was
12:13 My net also will I s' upon him, and
16: 8 I s' my skirt over thee, and covered
17:20 And I will s' my net upon him, and
19: 8 and s' their net over him:
26:14 shalt be a place to s' nets upon;
32: 3 I will therefore s' out my net over
47:10 shall be a place to s' forth nets;
Ho 5: 1 Mizpah, and a net s' upon Tabor.
7:12 go, I will s' my net upon them;
14: 6 His branches shall s', and his
Joe 2: 2 morning s' upon the mountains:
Hab 1: 8 horsemen shall s' themselves,
Zec 1:17 prosperity shall yet be s' abroad;
2: 6 s' you abroad as the four winds
Mal 2: 3 seed, and s' dung upon your faces,
M't 9:31 s' abroad his fame in all that
21: 8 s' their garments in the way;
M'r 1:28 immediately his fame s' abroad
11: 8 many s' their garments in the way:
Lu 19:36 they s' their clothes in the way.
Ac 4:17 it s' no further among the people,
1Th 1: 8 faith to God-ward is s' abroad;

spreadest
Eze 27: 7 which thou s' forth to be thy sail;

spreadeth
Le 13: 8 the scab s' in the skin, then the
De 32:11 As an eagle...s' abroad her wings,
Job 9: 8 Which alone s' out the heavens,
26: 9 throne, and s' his cloud upon it.
36:30 Behold, he s' his light upon it,
41:30 he s' sharp pointed things upon
Pr 29: 5 his neighbour s' a net for his feet.
Isa 25:11 that swimmeth s' forth his hands
40:19 the goldsmith s' it over with gold,
22 s' them out as a tent to dwell in:
44:24 s' abroad the earth by myself;
Jer 4:31 that s' her hands, saying, Woe is
17: 8 that s' out her roots by the river,
La 1:17 Zion s' forth her hands, and there

spreading See also OVERSPREADING; SPREADINGS.
Le 13:57 thing of skin; it is a s' plague:
Ps 37:35 s' himself like a green bay tree.
Eze 17: 6 became a s' vine of low stature,
26: 5 be a place for the s' of nets in the

spreadings
Job 36:29 understand the s' of the clouds,

sprigs
Isa 18: 5 cut off the s' with pruning hooks,
Eze 17: 6 forth branches, and shot forth s'.

spring See also DAYSPRING; OFFSPRING; SPRANG; SPRINGETH; SPRINGING; SPRINGS; SPRUNG.
Nu 21:17 sang this song, *S'* up, O well;
De 8: 7 and depths that s' out of valleys
J'g 19:25 when the day began to s', they let
1Sa 9:26 to pass about the s' of the day,
2Ki 2:21 forth unto the s' of the waters,
Job 5: 6 neither doth trouble s' out of the
38:27 bud of the tender herb to s' forth?
Ps 85:11 Truth shall s' out of the earth; and
92: 7 When the wicked s' as the grass,
Pr 25:26 fountain, and a corrupt s'.
Ca 4:12 a s' shut up, a fountain sealed.
Isa 42: 9 before they s' forth I tell you of
43:19 now it shall s' forth; shall ye not
44: 4 they shall s' up as among the grass,
45: 8 let righteousness s' up together;
58: 8 thine health shall s' forth speedily:
11 like a s' of water, whose waters
61:11 that are sown in it to s' forth;
11 and praise to s' forth before all the
Eze 17: 9 wither in all the leaves of her s',
Ho 13:15 and his s' shall become dry, and
Joe 2:22 pastures of the wilderness do s',
M'r 4:27 and the seed should s' and grow up,

springeth
1Ki 4:33 the hyssop that s' out of the wall:
2Ki 19:29 year that which s' of the same;
Isa 37:30 year that which s' of the same:
Ho 10: 4 thus judgment s' up as hemlock

springing
Ge 26:19 and found there a well of s' water.
2Sa 23: 4 as the tender grass s' out of the earth
Ps 65:10 thou blessest the s' thereof.
Joh 4:14 of water s' up into everlasting life.
Heb 12:15 lest any root of bitterness s' up

springs
De 4:49 the plain, under the s' of Pisgah.
Jos 10:40 of the s', and all their kings;
12: 8 and in the s', and in the wilderness,
15:19 land; give me also s' of water.
19 her the upper s', and the nether s'.
J'g 1:15 land; give me also s' of water.
15 her the upper s' and the nether s'.
Job 38:16 entered into the s' of the sea?
Ps 87: 7 be there: all my s' are in thee.
104:10 He sendeth the s' into the valleys,
Isa 35: 7 and the thirsty land s' of water:
41:18 and the dry land s' of water.
49:10 s' of water shall he guide them.
Jer 51:36 up her sea, and make her s' dry.

sprinkle See also SPRINKLED; SPRINKLETH; SPRINKLING.
Ex 9: 8 let Moses s' it toward the heaven
29:16 and s' it round about the altar.
20 s' the blood upon the altar round
21 s' it upon Aaron, and upon his
Le 1: 5 s' the blood round about upon the
11 s' his blood round about upon the
3: 2 shall s' the blood upon the altar
8 s' the blood thereof round about
13 s' the blood thereof upon the altar
4: 6 s' of the blood seven times before
17 s' it seven times before the Lord,
5: 9 s' of the blood of the sin offering
7: 2 he s' round about upon the altar.
14: 7 s' upon him that is to be cleansed
16 shall s' of the oil with his finger
27 shall s' with his right finger some
51 water, and s' the house seven times:
16:14 and s' it with his finger upon the
14 he s' of the blood with his finger
15 and s' it upon the mercy seat, and
19 he shall s' of the blood upon it with
17: 6 priest shall s' the blood upon the
Nu 8: 7 *S'* water of purifying upon them,
18:17 shalt s' their blood upon the altar,
19: 4 s' of her blood directly before the
18 s' it upon the tent, and upon all the
19 the clean person shall s' upon the
2Ki 16:15 and s' upon it all the blood of the
Isa 52:15 So shall he s' many nations; the
Eze 36:25 will I s' clean water upon you, and
43:18 thereon, and to s' blood thereon.

sprinkled
Ex 9:10 Moses s' it up toward heaven;
24: 6 half of the blood he s' on the altar.
8 the blood, and s' it on the people,
Le 6:27 when there is s' of the blood
27 whereon it was s' in the holy place.
8:11 he s'...upon the altar seven times,
19, 24 and Moses s' the blood upon
30 s' it upon Aaron, and upon his
9:12 he s' round about upon the altar.
18 which he s' upon the altar round
Nu 19:13 water of separation was not s' upon
20 water...hath not been s' upon him:
2Ki 9:33 of her blood was s' on the wall,
16:13 s' the blood of his peace offerings,
2Ch 29:22 the blood, and s' it on the altar:
22 they s' the blood upon the altar:
22 they s' the blood upon the altar.
30:16 the priests s' the blood, which they
35:11 the priests s' the blood from their
Job 2:12 s' dust upon their heads toward
Isa 63: 3 blood...be s' upon my garments,
Heb 9:19 and s' both the book, and all the
21 s' with blood both the tabernacle,
10:22 hearts s' from an evil conscience.

sprinkleth
Le 7:14 be the priest's that s' the blood
Nu 19:21 he that s' the water of separation

sprinkling
Heb 9:13 ashes of an heifer s· the unclean,
11:28 the passover, and the s· of blood,
12:24 to the blood of s·, that speaketh
1Pe 1: 2 and s· of the blood of Jesus Christ:
sprout
Job 14: 7 be cut down, that it will s· again,
sprung See also SPRANG.
Ge 41: 6 the east wind s· up after them.
23 the east wind, s· up after them:
Le 13:42 a leprosy s· up in his bald head,
M't 4:16 and shadow of death light is s· up.
13: 5 and forthwith they s· up, because
7 the thorns s· up, and choked them:
26 But when the blade was s· up, and
Lu 8: 6 soon as it was s· up, it withered
spue See also SPEWING; SPUED.
Le 18:28 That the land s· not you out also,
20:22 to dwell therein, s· you not out.
Jer 25:27 be drunken, and s·, and fall, and
Re 3:16 I will s· thee out of my mouth.
spued
Le 18:28 as it s· out the nations that were
spun
Ex 35:25 brought that which they had s·,
26 them up in wisdom s· goats' hair.
spunge
M't 27:48 a s·, and filled it with vinegar,
M'r 15:36 ran and filled a s· full of vinegar.
Joh 19:29 and they filled a s· with vinegar,
spy See also ESPY; SPIED; SPIES.
Nu 13:16 Moses sent to s· out the land.
17 Moses sent them to s· out the land
21:32 And Moses sent to s· out Jaazer,
Jos 2: 1 of Shittim two men to s· secretly,
6:25 Joshua sent to s· out Jericho.
J'g 18: 2 to s· out the land, and to search it;
14 went to s· out the country of Laish,
17 men that went to s· out the land
2Sa 10: 3 to search the city, and to s· it out,
2Ki 6:13 Go and s· where he is, that I may
1Ch 19: 3 overthrow, and to s· out the land?
Ga 2: 4 came in privily to s· out our liberty
square See also FOURSQUARE; SQUARED; SQUARES; STONESQUARERS.
1Ki 7: 5 all the doors and posts were s·,
Eze 43:16 s· in the four squares thereof.
45: 2 hundred in breadth, s· round about;
squared
Eze 41:21 The posts of the temple were s·,
squares
Eze 43:16 square in the four s· thereof.
17 and fourteen broad in the four s·
stability
Isa 33: 6 shall be the s· of thy times,
stable See also UNSTABLE.
1Ch 16:30 the world also shall be s·, that it
Eze 25: 5 will make Rabbah a s· for camels,
stablish See also ESTABLISH; STABLISHED; STABLISHETH.
2Sa 7:13 I will s· the throne of his kingdom
1Ch 17:12 and I will s· his throne for ever.
18: 3 to s· his dominion by the river
2Ch 7:18 Then will I s· the throne of thy
Es 9:21 To s· this among them, that they
Ps 119:38 S· thy word unto thy servant, who
Ro 16:25 to s· you according to my gospel,
1Th 3:13 To the end he may s· your hearts
2Th 2:17 and s· you in every good word and
3: 3 who shall s· you, and keep you
Jas 5: 8 Be ye also patient; s· your hearts:
1Pe 5:10 make you perfect, s·, strengthen,
stablished See also ESTABLISHED.
2Ch 17: 5 the Lord s· the kingdom in his
Ps 93: 1 the world also is s·, that it cannot
148: 6 He hath also s· them for ever and
Col 2: 7 and s· in the faith, as ye have been
stablisheth See also ESTABLISHETH.
Hab 2:12 blood, and s· a city by iniquity!
2Co 1:21 he which s· us with you in Christ,
Stachys (*sta'-kis*)
Ro 16: 9 in Christ, and S· my beloved.
stacks
Ex 22: 6 in thorns, so that the s· of corn,
stacte (*stac'-te*)
Ex 30:34 Take unto thee sweet spices, s·,
staff See also STAVES.
Ge 32:10 for with my s· I passed over this
38:18 and thy s· that is in thine hand.
25 the signet, and bracelets, and s·.
Ex 12:11 feet, and your s· in your hand;
21:19 and walk abroad upon his s·, then
Le 26:26 have broken the s· of your bread,
Nu 13:23 bare it between two upon a s·;
22:27 and he smote the ass with a s·.
J'g 6:21 put forth the end of the s· that was
1Sa 17: 7 And the s· of his spear was like a
40 And he took his s· in his hand, and
2Sa 3:29 is a leper, or that leaneth on a s·,
21:19 the s· of whose spear was like a
23: 7 with iron and the s· of a spear;
21 but he went down to him with a s·,
2Ki 4:29 and take my s· in thine hand, and
29 lay my s· upon the face of the child.
31 and laid the s· upon the face of the
18:21 thou trustest upon the s· of this
1Ch 11:23 he went down to him with a s·,
20: 5 spear s· was like a weaver's beam.
Ps 23: 4 rod and thy s· they comfort me.
105:16 he brake the whole s· of bread.
Isa 3: 1 from Judah the stay and the s·,
9: 4 the s· of his shoulder, the rod of
10: 5 and the s· in their hand is mine
15 or as if the s· should lift up itself,
24 and shall lift up his s· against thee,
14: 5 hath broken the s· of the wicked,
28:27 the fitches are beaten out with a s·,
30:32 where the grounded s· shall pass,
36: 6 Lo, thou trustest in the s· of this
Jer 48:17 How is the strong s· broken, and
Eze 4:16 I will break the s· of bread in
5:16 and will break your s· of bread:
14:13 and will break the s· of the bread
29: 6 they have been a s· of reed to the
Ho 4:12 and their s· declareth unto them:
Zec 8: 4 every man with his s· in his hand
11:10 And I took my s·, even Beauty,
14 Then I cut asunder mine other s·,
M'r 6: 8 for their journey, save a s· only;
Heb 11:21 leaning upon the top of his s·.
stagger See also STAGGERED; STAGGERETH.
Job 12:25 them to s· like a drunken man.
Ps 107:27 fro, and s· like a drunken man,
Isa 29: 9 they s·, but not with strong drink.
staggered
Ro 4:20 He s· not at the promise of God
staggereth
Isa 19:14 as a drunken man s· in his vomit.
staid See STAYED.
stain
Job 3: 5 and the shadow of death s· it;
Isa 23: 9 to s· the pride of all glory, and to
63: 3 and I will s· all my raiment.
stairs
1Ki 6: 8 with winding s· into the middle
2Ki 9:13 it under him on the top of the s·,
Ne 3:15 the s· that go down from the city
9: 4 up upon the s·, of the Levites,
12:37 up by the s· of the city of David,
Ca 2:14 rock, in the secret places of the s·,
Eze 40: 6 east, and went up the s· thereof,
43:17 his s· shall look toward the east.
Ac 21:35 And when he came upon the s·, so
40 Paul stood on the s·, and beckoned
stakes
Isa 33:20 not one of the s· thereof shall ever
54: 2 thy cords, and strengthen thy s·;
stalk See also STALKS.
Ge 41: 5 ears of corn came up upon one s·,
22 seven ears came up in one s·, full
Ho 8: 7 reap the whirlwind: it hath no s·:
stalks
Jos 2: 6 and hid them with the s· of flax,
stall See also STALLED; STALLS.
Am 6: 4 calves out of the midst of the s·;
Mal 4: 2 and grow up as calves of the s·.
Lu 13:15 loose his ox or his ass from the s·,
stalled
Pr 15:17 than a s· ox and hatred therewith.
stalls
1Ki 4:26 had forty thousand s· of horses
2Ch 9:25 had four thousand s· for horses
32:28 and s· for all manner of beasts, and
Hab 3:17 there shall be no herd in the s·:
stammerers
Isa 32: 4 s· shall be ready to speak plainly.
stammering
Isa 28:11 with s· lips and another tongue
33:19 of a s· tongue, that thou canst not
stamp See also STAMPED; STAMPING.
2Sa 22:43 I did s· them as the mire of the
Eze 6:11 thine hand, and s· with thy foot,
stamped
De 9:21 and burnt it with fire, and s· it,
2Ki 23: 6 s· it small to powder, and cast the
15 s· it small to powder, and burned
2Ch 15:16 Asa cut down her idol, and s· it,
Eze 25: 6 and s· with the feet, and rejoiced
Da 7: 7 s· the residue with the feet of it:
19 and s· the residue with his feet;
8: 7 to the ground, and s· upon him:
10 to the ground, and s· upon them.
stamping
Jer 47: 3 noise of the s· of the hoofs of his
stanched
Lu 8:44 immediately her issue of blood s·.
stand See also STANDEST; STANDETH; STANDING; STOOD; WITHSTAND.
Ge 19: 9 And they said, S· back. And they
24:13 I s· here by the well of water; and
43 Behold, I s· by the well of water;
Ex 7:15 thou shalt s· by the river's brink
8:20 morning, and s· before Pharaoh;
9:11 the magicians could not s· before
13 morning, and s· before Pharaoh,
14:13 Fear ye not, s· still, and see the
17: 6 I will s· before thee there upon the
9 I will s· on the top of the hill with
18:14 and all the people s· by thee from
33:10 cloudy pillar s· at the tabernacle
21 me, and thou shalt s· upon a rock:
Le 18:23 shall any woman s· before a beast
19:16 shalt thou s· against the blood of
Le 26:37 power to s· before your enemies.
27:14 shall estimate it, so shall it s·.
17 to thy estimation it shall s·.
Nu 1: 5 of the men that shall s· with you:
9: 8 S· still, and I will hear what the
11:16 that they may s· there with thee.
16: 9 and to s· before the congregation
23: 3 S· by thy burnt offering, and I
15 S· here by thy burnt offering, while
27:21 shall s· before Eleazar the priest,
30: 4 then all her vows shall s·, and
4 she hath bound her soul shall s·.
5 she hath bound her soul, shall s·:
7 then her vows shall s·, and her
7 she bound her soul, shall s·.
9 have bound their souls, shall s·
11 then all her vows shall s·, and every
11 wherewith...bound her soul shall s·.
12 the bond of her soul, shall not s·:
35:12 until he s· before the congregation
De 5:31 But as for thee, s· thou here by me,
7:24 no man be able to s· before thee,
9: 2 can s· before the children of Anak!
10: 8 to s· before the Lord to minister
11:25 no man be able to s· before you:
18: 5 to s· to minister in the name of
7 do, which s· there before the Lord.
19:17 shall s· before the Lord, before the
24:11 Thou shalt s· abroad, and the man
25: 8 if he s· to it, and say, I like not to
27:12 These shall s· upon mount Gerizim
13 shall s· upon mount Ebal to curse;
29:10 Ye s· this day all of you before the
Jos 1: 5 not any man be able to s· before
3: 8 Jordan, ye shall s· still in Jordan.
13 and they shall s· upon an heap.
7:12 could not s· before their enemies,
13 canst not s· before thine enemies,
10: 8 not a man of them s· before thee.
12 Sun, s· thou still upon Gibeon;
20: 4 shall s· at the entering of the gate
6 until he s· before the congregation
23: 9 man hath been able to s· before you
J'g 2:14 could not...s· before their enemies.
4:20 S· in the door of the tent, and it
1Sa 6:20 Who is able to s· before this holy
9:27 but s· thou still a while, that I may
12: 7 Now therefore s· still, that I may
16 Now...s· and see this great thing,
14: 9 then we will s· still in our place,
16:22 Let David, I pray thee, s· before me;
19: 3 And I will go out and s· beside my
2Sa 1: 9 S·, I pray thee, upon me, and slay
18:30 unto him, Turn aside, and s· here.
1Ki 1: 2 and let her s· before the king, and
8:11 the priests could not s· to minister
10: 8 thy servants, which s· continually
17: 1 of Israel liveth, before whom I s·,
18:15 of hosts liveth, before whom I s·,
19:11 s· upon the mount before the Lord.
2Ki 3:14 Lord...liveth, before whom I s·,
5:11 will surely come out to me, and s·,
16 the Lord liveth, before whom I s·, I
6:31 if the head of Elisha...s· on him
10: 4 before him: how then shall we s·?
1Ch 21:16 angel of the Lord s· between the
23:30 to s· every morning to thank and
2Ch 5:14 the priests could not s· to minister
9: 7 which s· continually before thee,
20: 9 we s· before this house, and in thy
17 s· ye still, and see the salvation of
29:11 Lord hath chosen you to s· before
34:32 Jerusalem and Benjamin to s· to it.
35: 5 s· in the holy place according to the
Ezr 9:15 we cannot s· before thee because of
10:13 and we are not able to s· without,
14 our rulers of all the congregation s·,
Ne 7: 3 while they s· by, let them shut the
9: 5 S· up and bless the Lord your God
Es 3: 4 Mordecai's matters would s·:
8:11 and to s· for their life, to destroy,
Job 8:15 upon his house, but it shall not s·:
19:25 he shall s· at the latter day upon
30:20 I s· up, and thou regardest me
33: 5 thy words in order before me, s· up.
37:14 Hearken unto this, O Job: s· still,
38:14 the seal; and they s· as a garment.
41:10 who then is able to s· before me?
Ps 1: 5 the ungodly shall not s· in the
4: 4 S· in awe, and sin not: commune
5: 5 foolish shall not s· in thy sight:
20: 8 but we are risen, and s· upright.
24: 3 or who shall s· in his holy place?
30: 7 made my mountain to s· strong:
33: 8 inhabitants of the world s· in awe
35: 2 buckler, and s· up for mine help.
38:11 My lovers and my friends s· aloof
11 my sore; and my kinsmen s· afar off.
45: 9 thy right hand did s· the queen in
73: 7 Their eyes s· out with fatness:
76: 7 and who may s· in thy sight when
78:13 made the waters to s· as an heap.
89:28 my covenant shall s· fast with him.
43 not made him to s· in the battle.
94:16 who will s· up for me against the
109: 6 and let Satan s· at his right hand.
31 he shall s· at the right hand of the
111: 8 They s· fast for ever and ever, and
122: 2 Our feet shall s· within thy gates,
130: 3 iniquities, O Lord, who shall s·?
134: 1 which by night s· in the house of the
135: 2 Ye that s· in the house of the Lord,
147:17 morsels: who can s· before his cold?
Pr 12: 7 the house of the righteous shall s·.
19:21 counsel of the Lord, that shall s·.
22:29 business? he shall s· before kings;

Pr 22:29 he shall not s· before mean men.
25: 6 s· not in the place of great men:
27: 4 but who is able to s· before envy?
Ec 4:15 second child that shall s· up in his
8: 3 of his sight: s· not in an evil thing;
Isa 7: 7 It shall not s·, neither shall it
8:10 speak the word, and it shall not s·:
11:10 s· for an ensign of the people;
14:24 as I have purposed, so shall it s·:
21: 8 I s·...upon the watchtower
27: 9 groves and images shall not s· up.
28:18 agreement with hell shall not s·;
32: 8 and by liberal things shall he s·.
40: 8 word of our God shall s· for ever.
44:11 gathered together, let them s· up;
46:10 My counsel shall s·, and I will do
47:12 S· now with thine enchantments,
13 the monthly prognosticators, s· up,
48:13 call unto them, they s· up together.
50: 8 let us s· together: who is mine
51:17 awake, s· up, O Jerusalem, which
61: 5 strangers shall s· and feed your
65: 5 Which say, S· by thyself, come not
Jer 6:16 S· ye in the ways, and see, and
7: 2 S· in the gate of the Lord's house,
10 come and s· before me in this house,
14: 6 wild asses did s· in the high places,
15:19 again, and thou shalt s· before me:
17:19 Go and s· in the gate of the children
26: 2 S· in the court of the Lord's house,
35:19 want a man to s· before me for ever.
44:28 shall know whose words shall s·,
29 words shall surely s· against you
46: 4 and s· forth with your helmets;
14 S· fast, and prepare thee; for the
21 they did not s·, because the day of
48:19 inhabitant of Aroer, s· by the way,
49:19 who is that shepherd that will s·
50:44 who is that shepherd that will s·
51:50 the sword, go away, s· not still:
Eze 2: 1 Son of man, s· upon thy feet, and I
13: 5 to s· in the battle in the day of the
17:14 keeping of his covenant it might s·.
22:30 s· in the gap before me for the land,
27:29 ships, they shall s· upon the land;
29: 7 madest all their loins to be at a s·
31:14 their trees s· up in their height,
33:26 Ye s· upon your sword, ye work
44:11 shall s· before them to minister unto
15 and they shall s· before me to offer
24 they shall s· in judgment; and
46: 2 and shall s· by the post of the gate,
47:10 that the fishers shall s· upon it from
Da 1: 4 in them to s· in the king's palace,
5 they might s· before the king.
2:44 kingdoms, and it shall s· for ever.
7: 4 and made s· upon the feet as a man,
8: 4 that no beasts might s· before him,
7 there was no power in the ram to s·
22 four kingdoms shall s· up out of the
23 dark sentences, shall s· up.
25 shall also s· up against the Prince
10:11 I speak unto thee, and s· upright:
11: 2 there shall s· up yet three kings in
3 And a mighty king shall s· up, that
4 when he shall s· up, his kingdom
6 neither shall he s·, nor his arm:
7 branch of her roots shall one s· up
14 many s· up against the king of the
16 will, and none shall s· before him:
16 and he shall s· in the glorious land,
17 she shall not s· on his side, neither
20 s· up in his estate a raiser of taxes
21 his estate shall s· up a vile person,
25 mighty army; but he shall not s·:
31 And arms shall s· on his part, and
12: 1 And at that time shall Michael s· up,
13 s· in thy lot at the end of the days.
Am 2:15 shall he s· that handleth the bow;
Mic 5: 4 he shall s· and feed in the strength
Na 1: 6 Who can s· before his indignation?
2: 8 S·, s·, shall they cry; but none shall
Hab 2: 1 I will s· upon my watch, and set me
Zec 3: 7 to walk among these that s· by.
4:14 s· by the Lord of the whole earth.
14: 4 his feet shall s· in that day upon
12 away while they s· upon their feet,
Mal 3: 2 who shall s· when he appeareth?
M't 12:25 divided against itself shall not s·:
26 how shall then his kingdom s·?
47 mother and thy brethren s· without,
20: 6 them, Why s· ye here all the day idle?
24:15 the prophet, s· in the holy place,
M'r 3: 3 had the withered hand, S· forth.
24 itself, that kingdom cannot s·.
25 against itself, that house cannot s·.
26 and be divided, he cannot s·, but
9: 1 there be some of them that s· here,
11:25 And when ye s· praying, forgive,
Lu 1:19 that s· in the presence of God;
6: 8 Rise up, and s· forth in the midst.
8:20 mother and thy brethren s· without,
11:18 himself, how shall his kingdom s·?
13:25 and ye begin to s· without, and to
21:36 and to s· before the Son of man.
Joh 11:42 of the people which s· by I said it,
Ac 1:11 why s· ye gazing up into heaven?
4:10 this man s· here before you whole.
5:20 Go, s· and speak in the temple to
8:38 commanded the chariot to s· still:
10:26 S· up; I myself also am a man.
14:10 loud voice, S· upright on thy feet.
25:10 I s· at Cæsar's judgment seat,
26: 6 I s· and am judged for the hope of
16 But rise, and s· upon thy feet: for
Ro 5: 2 faith into this grace wherein we s·,
9:11 God according to election might s·,
14: 4 up: for God is able to make him s·.
10 we shall all s· before the judgment
1Co 2: 5 should not s· in the wisdom of men,
15: 1 have received, and wherein ye s·;
30 why s· we in jeopardy every hour?
16:13 s· fast in the faith, quit you like
2Co 1:24 of your joy: for by faith ye s·.
Ga 4:20 my voice; for I s· in doubt of you.
5: 1 S· fast therefore in the liberty
Eph 6:11 may be able to s· against the wiles
13 evil day, and having done all, to s·.
14 S· therefore, having your loins girt
Ph'p 1:27 that ye s· fast in one spirit, with
4: 1 so s· fast in the Lord, my dearly
Col 4:12 ye may s· perfect and complete in
1Th 3: 8 we live, if ye s· fast in the Lord.
2Th 2:15 s· fast, and hold the traditions
Jas 2: 3 S· thou there, or sit here under
1Pe 5:12 the true grace of God wherein ye s·.
Re 3:20 Behold, I s· at the door, and knock:
6:17 come; and who shall be able to s·?
10: 5 angel which I saw s· upon the sea
15: 2 s· on the sea of glass, having the
18:15 shall s· afar off for the fear of her
20:12 I saw the dead,...s· before God;

standard See also STANDARDBEARER; STANDARDS.
Nu 1:52 and every man by his own s·,
2: 2 of Israel shall pitch by his own s·,
3 they of the s· of the camp of Judah
10 be the s· of the camp of Reuben
18 be the s· of the camp of Ephraim
25 The s· of the camp of Dan shall be
10:14 went the s· of the camp...of Judah
18 And the s· of the camp of Reuben
22 the s· of the camp...of Ephraim
25 And the s· of the camp...of Dan
Isa 49:22 and set up my s· to the people:
59:19 Spirit of the Lord shall lift up a s·
62:10 stones; lift up a s· for the people.
Jer 4: 6 Set up the s· toward Zion: retire,
21 How long shall I see the s·, and
50: 2 and publish, and set up a s·;
51:12 Set...s· upon the walls of Babylon,
27 Set ye up a s· in the land, blow the

standardbearer
Isa 10:18 shall be as when a s· fainteth.

standards
Nu 2:17 every man in his place by their s·.
31 shall go hindmost with their s·.
34 so they pitched by their s·, and so

standest See also UNDERSTANDEST.
Ge 24:31 wherefore s· thou without? for I
Ex 3: 5 the place whereon thou s· is holy
Jos 5:15 the place whereon thou s· is holy.
Ps 10: 1 Why s· thou afar off, O Lord? why
Ac 7:33 for the place where thou s· is holy
Ro 11:20 broken off, and thou s· by faith.

standeth See also UNDERSTANDETH.
Nu 14:14 and that thy cloud s· over them,
De 1:38 son of Nun, which s· before thee,
17:12 that s· to minister there before the
29:15 him that s· here with us this day
J'g 16:26 pillars whereupon the house s·,
Es 6: 5 Behold, Haman s· in the court.
7: 9 gallows...s· in the house of Haman.
Ps 1: 1 nor s· in the way of sinners, nor
26:12 My foot s· in an even place: in the
33:11 The counsel of the Lord s· for ever,
82: 1 God s· in the congregation of the
119:161 but my heart s· in awe of thy word.
Pr 8: 2 She s· in the top of high places, by
Ca 2: 9 he s· behind our wall, he looketh
Isa 3:13 The Lord s· up to plead,
13 and s· to judge the people.
46: 7 and set him in his place, and he s·;
59:14 backward, and justice s· afar off:
Da 12: 1 prince which s· for the children of
Zec 11:16 broken, nor feed that that s· still:
Joh 1:26 but there s· one among you, whom
3:29 which s· and heareth him,
Ro 14: 4 to his own master he s· or falleth.
1Co 7:37 he that s· stedfast in his heart,
8:13 I will eat no flesh while the world s·,
10:12 let him that thinketh he s· take
2Ti 2:19 the foundation of God s· sure,
Heb 10:11 every priest s· daily ministering
Jas 5: 9 behold, the judge s· before the door.
Re 10: 8 the angel which s· upon the sea and

standing See also UNDERSTANDING.
Ex 22: 6 stacks of corn, or the s· corn,
26:15 tabernacle of shittim wood s· up.
36:20 tabernacle of shittim wood, s· up.
Le 26: 1 neither rear you up a s· image,
Nu 22:23, 31 angel of the Lord s· in the way,
De 23:25 When thou comest into the s· corn
25 sickle unto thy neighbour's s· corn.
J'g 15: 5 into the s· corn of the Philistines,
5 the shocks, and also the s· corn,
1Sa 19:20 Samuel s· as appointed over them,
22: 6 his servants were s· about him;)
1Ki 13:25 and the lion s· by the carcase:
28 ass and the lion s· by the carcase:
22:19 and all the host of heaven s· by him
2Ch 9:18 place, and two lions s· by the stays:
18:18 the host of heaven s· on his right
Es 5: 2 Esther the queen s· in the court,
Ps 69: 2 deep mire, where there is no s·:
107:35 the wilderness into a s· water,
114: 8 turned the rock into a s· water,
Da 8: 6 I had seen s· before the river,
Am 9: 1 I saw the Lord s· upon the altar:
Mic 1:11 he shall receive of you his s·.
Mic 5:13 thy s· images out of the midst of
Zec 3: 1 the high priest s· before the angel
1 Satan s· at his right hand to resist
6: 5 from s· before the Lord of all the
M't 6: 5 to pray s· in the synagogues
16:28 There be some s· here, which shall
20: 3 others s· idle in the marketplace,
6 went out, and found others s· idle,
M'r 3:31 and, s· without, sent unto him,
13:14 desolation,...s· where it ought not,
Lu 1:11 s· on the right side of the altar of
5: 2 And saw two ships s· by the lake:
9:27 there be some s· here, which shall
18:13 publican, s· afar off, would not lift
Joh 8: 9 and the woman s· in the midst.
19:26 disciple s· by, whom he loved,
20:14 herself back, and saw Jesus s·,
Ac 2:14 Peter, s· up with the eleven, lifted
4:14 the man which was healed s· with
5:23 keepers s· without before the doors:
25 put in prison are s· in the temple,
7:55 Jesus s· on the right hand of God,
56 Son of man s· on the right hand of
22:20 I also was s· by, and consenting
24:21 voice, that I cried s· among them,
Heb 9: 8 the first tabernacle was yet s·:2192.
2Pe 3: 5 earth s· out of the water and in
Re 7: 1 four angels s· on the four corners
11: 4 two candlesticks s· before the God
18:10 S· afar off for...fear of her torment,
19:17 And I saw an angel s· in the sun;

stank
Ex 7:21 and the river s·, and the Egyptians
8:14 upon heaps: and the land s·.
16:20 morning, and it bred worms, and s·:
2Sa 10: 6 saw that they s· before David, the

star See also STARGAZERS; STARS.
Nu 24:17 shall come a S· out of Jacob, and
Am 5:26 your images, the s· of your god,
M't 2: 2 for we have seen his s· in the east,
7 what time the s· appeared.
9 the s·, which they saw in the east,
10 When they saw the s·, they rejoiced
Ac 7:43 and the s· of your god Remphan,
1Co 15:41 for one s· differeth from another
41 differeth from another s· in glory.
2Pe 1:19 the day s· arise in your hearts:
Re 2:28 And I will give him the morning s·.
8:10 there fell a great s· from heaven,
11 name of the s· is called Wormwood:
9: 1 I saw a s· fall from heaven unto the
22:16 and the bright and morning s·.

stare
Ps 22:17 bones: they look and s· upon me.

stargazers
Isa 47:13 now the astrologers, the s·,

stars
Ge 1:16 the night: he made the s· also.
15: 5 now toward heaven, and tell the s·,
22:17 thy seed as the s· of the heaven,
26: 4 seed to multiply as the s· of heaven,
37: 9 eleven s· made obeisance to me.
Ex 32:13 your seed as the s· of heaven, and
De 1:10 as the s· of heaven for multitude.
4:19 the sun, and the moon, and the s·,
10:22 made thee as the s· of heaven for
28:62 ye were as the s· of heaven for
J'g 5:20 the s· in their courses fought
1Ch 27:23 Israel like to the s· of the heavens.
Ne 4:21 the morning till the s· appeared.
9:23 thou as the s· of heaven, and
Job 3: 9 Let the s· of the twilight...be dark;
9: 7 it riseth not; and sealeth up the s·.
22:12 and behold the height of the s·, how
25: 5 yea, the s· are not pure in his sight,
38: 7 When the morning s· sang together,
Ps 8: 3 the moon and the s·, which thou
136: 9 The moon and s· to rule by night:
147: 4 He telleth the number of the s·;
148: 3 moon: praise him, all ye s· of light.
Ec 12: 2 moon, or the s·, be not darkened,
Isa 13:10 For the s· of heaven and the
14:13 will exalt my throne above the s·
Jer 31:35 and of the s· for a light by night,
Eze 32: 7 and make the s· thereof dark;
Da 8:10 host and of the s· to the ground,
12: 3 as the s· for ever and ever.
Joe 2:10 the s· shall withdraw their shining:
3:15 the s· shall withdraw their shining.
Am 5: 8 Seek him that maketh the seven s·
Ob 4 thou set thy nest among the s·,
Na 3:16 merchants above the s· of heaven:
M't 24:29 and the s· shall fall from heaven,
M'r 13:25 And the s· of heaven shall fall, and
Lu 21:25 sun, and in the moon, and in the s·;
Ac 27:20 sun nor s· in many days appeared,
1Co 15:41 moon, and another glory of the s·:
Heb 11:12 as the s· of the sky in multitude,
Jude 13 wandering s·, to whom is reserved
Re 1:16 he had in his right hand seven s·:
20 The mystery of the seven s· which
20 seven s· are the angels of the seven
2: 1 he that holdeth the seven s· in his
3: 1 Spirits of God, and the seven s·;
6:13 the s· of heaven fell unto the earth,
8:12 moon, and the third part of the s·;
12: 1 upon her head a crown of twelve s·:
4 the third part of the s· of heaven,

state See also ESTATE.
Ge 43: 7 The man asked us straitly of our s·,
2Ch 24:13 they set the house of God in his s·,
Es 1: 7 according to the s· of the king.
2:18 according to the s· of the king.
Ps 39: 5 at his best s· is altogether vanity.

Pr 27:23 to know the s· of thy flocks, and
28: 2 the s· thereof shall be prolonged.
Isa 22:19 and from thy s· shall he pull thee
M't 12:45 the last s· of that man is worse than
Lu 11:26 the last s· of that man is worse than
Ph'p 2:19 comfort, when I know your s·.
20 will naturally care for your s·.
4:11 in whatsoever s· I am, therewith to
Col 4: 7 my s· shall Tychicus declare

stately
Eze 23:41 satest upon a s· bed, and a table

station
Isa 22:19 And I will drive thee from thy s·.

stature
Nu 13:32 we saw in it are men of a great s·.
1Sa 16: 7 or on the height of his s·; because
2Sa 21:20 where was a man of great s·, that
1Ch 11:23 an Egyptian, a man of great s·,
20: 6 Gath, where was a man of great s·,
Ca 7: 7 This thy s· is like to a palm tree,
Isa 10:33 high ones of s· shall be hewn down,
45:14 and of the Sabeans, men of s·,
Eze 13:18 the head of every s· to hunt souls!
17: 6 became a spreading vine of low s·,
19:11 her s· was exalted among the thick
31: 3 shadowing shroud,...of an high s·;
M't 6:27 can add one cubit unto his s·?
Lu 2:52 Jesus increased in wisdom and s·,
12:25 thought can add to his s· one cubit?
19: 3 press, because he was little of s·.
Eph 4:13 unto the measure of the s· of the

statute See also STATUTES.
Ex 15:25 there he made for them a s· and
27:21 it shall be a s· for ever unto their
28:43 it shall be a s· for ever unto him
29: 9 shall be theirs for a perpetual s·:
28 and his sons' by a s· for ever
30:21 and it shall be a s· for ever to them,
Le 3:17 It shall be a perpetual s· for your
6:18 It shall be a s· for ever in your
22 it is a s· for ever unto the Lord; it
7:34 and unto his sons by a s· for ever
36 by a s· for ever throughout their
10: 9 be a s· for ever throughout your
15 sons' with thee, by a s· for ever;
16:29 this shall be a s· for ever unto you:
31 afflict your souls, by a s· for ever.
34 shall be an everlasting s· unto you,
17: 7 This shall be a s· for ever unto
23:14 be a s· for ever throughout your
21 it shall be a s· for ever in all your
31 be a s· for ever throughout your
41 It shall be a s· for ever in your
24: 3 it shall be a s· for ever in your
9 made by fire by a perpetual s·.
Nu 18:11, 19 with thee, by a s· for ever:
23 be a s· for ever throughout your
19:10 among them, for a s· for ever.
21 it shall be a perpetual s· unto them,
27:11 children of Israel a s· of judgment,
35:29 things shall be for a s· of judgment
Jos 24:25 set them a s· and an ordinance in
1Sa 30:25 he made it a s· and an ordinance
Ps 81: 4 For this was a s· for Israel, and a
Da 6: 7 together to establish a royal s·,
15 no decree nor s· which the king

statutes
Ge 26: 5 my commandments, my s·, and my
Ex 15:26 commandments, and keep...his s·,
18:16 do make them know the s· of God,
Le 10:11 all the s· which the Lord hath
18: 5 Ye shall therefore keep my s·, and
26 Ye shall therefore keep my s· and
19:19 Ye shall keep my s·. Thou shalt
37 Therefore shall ye observe all my s·,
20: 8 ye shall keep my s·, and do them:
22 Ye shall therefore keep all my s·,
25:18 Wherefore ye shall do my s·, and
26: 3 If ye walk in my s·, and keep my
15 And if ye shall despise my s·, or if
43 because their soul abhorred my s·.
46 These are the s· and judgments and
Nu 30:16 These are the s·, which the Lord
De 4: 1 unto the s· and unto the judgments,
5 I have taught you s· and judgments,
6 which shall hear all these s·, and
8 that hath s· and judgments so
14 me at that time to teach you s· and
40 Thou shalt keep therefore his s·,
45 are the testimonies, and the s·, and
5: 1 the s· and judgments which I speak
31 all the commandments, and the s·,
6: 1 are the commandments, the s·, and
2 all his s· and his commandments,
17 his s·, which he hath commanded
20 mean the testimonies, and the s·,
24 commanded us to do all these s·,
7:11 keep the commandments, and the s·,
8:11 his s·, which I command thee this
10:13 his s·, which I command thee this
11: 1 and keep his charge, and his s·,
32 ye shall observe to do all the s·
12: 1 These are the s· and judgments,
16:12 thou shalt observe and do these s·.
17:19 the words of this law and these s·,
26:16 hath commanded thee to do these s·
17 to keep his s·, and...commandments,
27:10 do his commandments and his s·,
28:15 his s· which I command thee this
45 keep his commandments and his s·
30:10, 16 his commandments and his s·
2Sa 22:23 as for his s·, I did not depart from
1Ki 2: 3 to walk in his ways, to keep his s·,
3: 3 walking in the s· of David his

1Ki 3:14 keep my s· and...commandments,
6:12 if thou wilt walk in my s·, and
8:58 his commandments, and his s·,
61 to walk in his s·, and to keep his
9: 4 wilt keep my s· and my judgments:
6 keep my commandments and...s·
11:11 not kept my covenant and my s·,
33 to keep my s· and my judgments,
34 kept my commandments and my s·:
38 keep my s· and my commandments,
2Ki 17: 8 And walked in the s· of the heathen,
13 keep my commandments and my s·,
15 And they rejected his s·, and his
19 walked in the s· of Israel which
34 neither do they after their s·, or
37 And the s·, and the ordinances,
23: 3 his testimonies and his s· with all
1Ch 22:13 heed to fulfil the s· and judgments
29:19 thy testimonies, and thy s·, and to
2Ch 7:17 observe my s· and my judgments;
19 if ye turn away, and forsake my s·
19:10 s· and judgments, ye shall even
33: 8 to the whole law and the s· and
34:31 his testimonies, and his s·, with all
Ezr 7:10 to teach in Israel s· and judgments.
11 of the Lord, and of his s· to Israel.
Ne 1: 7 kept the commandments, nor the s·,
9:13 laws, good s· and commandments:
14 s·, and laws, by the hand of Moses
10:29 Lord, and his judgments and his s·;
Ps 18:22 I did not put away his s· from me.
19: 8 The s· of the Lord are right,
50:16 hast thou to do to declare my s·,
89:31 If they break my s·, and keep not
105:45 That they might observe his s·,
119: 5 ways were directed to keep thy s·!
8 I will keep thy s·: O forsake me not
12 art thou, O Lord: teach me thy s·.
16 I will delight myself in thy s·: I
23 thy servant did meditate in thy s·.
26 thou heardest me: teach me thy s·.
33 me, O Lord, the way of thy s·; and
48 loved; and I will meditate in thy s·.
54 Thy s· have been my songs in the
64 full of thy mercy: teach me thy s·.
68 and doest good; teach me thy s·.
71 afflicted; that I might learn thy s·.
80 Let my heart be sound in thy s·;
83 smoke; yet do I not forget thy s·.
112 mine heart to perform thy s· alway,
117 and I will have respect unto thy s·
118 down all them that err from thy s·:
124 unto thy mercy, and teach me thy s·.
135 thy servant; and teach me thy s·.
145 hear me, O Lord: I will keep thy s·.
155 wicked: for they seek not thy s·.
171 when thou hast taught me thy s·.
147:19 his s· and...judgments unto Israel.
Jer 44:10 nor in my s·, that I set before you
23 nor in his s·, nor in his testimonies;
Eze 5: 6 my s· more than the countries that
6 refused my judgments and my s·,
7 have not walked in my s·, neither
11:12 for ye have not walked in my s·,
20 That they may walk in my s·, and
18: 9 Hath walked in my s·, and hath
17 judgments, hath walked in my s·;
19 hath kept all my s·, and hath done
21 keep all my s·, and do that which is
20:11 And I gave them my s·, and shewed
13 they walked not in my s·, and they
16 walked not in my s·, but polluted
18 Walk...not in the s· of your fathers,
19 Lord your God; walk in my s·,
21 they walked not in my s·, neither
24 but had despised my s·, and had
25 gave them...s· that were not good,
33:15 walk in the s· of life, without
36:27 cause you to walk in my s·, and ye
37:24 and observe my s·, and do them.
44:24 they shall keep my laws and my s·
Mic 6:16 For the s· of Omri are kept, and all
Zec 1: 6 But my words and my s·, which I
Mal 4: 4 Israel, with the s· and judgments.

staunched See STANCHED.

staves See also HANDSTAVES.
Ex 25:13 thou shalt make s· of shittim wood,
14 thou shalt put the s· into the rings
15 The s· shall be in the rings of the
27 shall the rings be for places of the s·
28 shalt make the s· of shittim wood,
27: 6 And thou shalt make s· for the altar,
6 s· of shittim wood, and overlay them
7 the s· shall be put into the rings,
7 the s· shall be upon the two sides of
30: 4 for places for the s· to bear it withal.
5 shalt make the s· of shittim wood,
35:12 The ark, and the s· thereof, with the
13 The table, and his s·, and all his
15 And the incense altar, and his s·,
16 grate, his s·, and all his vessels, the
37: 4 And he made s· of shittim wood, and
5 he put the s· into the rings by the
14 places for the s· to bear the table.
15 And he made the s· of shittim wood,
27 to be places for the s· to bear it
28 And he made the s· of shittim wood,
38: 5 grate of brass, to be places for the s·.
6 And he made the s· of shittim wood,
7 he put the s· into the rings on the
39:35 of the testimony, and the s· thereof,
39 grate...his s·, and all his vessels,
40:20 the ark, and set the s· on the ark,
Nu 4: 6 blue, and shall put in the s· thereof.
8 and shall put in the s· thereof.

Nu 4:11 and shall put to the s· thereof:
14 badgers' skins, and put to the s· of it.
21:18 of the lawgiver, with their s·.
1Sa 17:43 that thou comest to me with s·?
1Ki 8: 7 covered the ark and the s· thereof
8 they drew out the s·, that the ends
8 s· were seen out in the holy place
1Ch 15:15 upon their shoulders with the s·
2Ch 5: 8 covered the ark and the s· thereof
9 And they drew out the s· of the ark,
9 ends of the s· were seen from the ark
Hab 3:14 didst strike through with his s·
Zec 11: 7 I took unto me two s·; the one I
M't 10:10 coats, neither shoes, nor yet s·:
26:47 great multitude with swords and s·,
55 against a thief with swords and s·
M'r 14:43 great multitude with swords and s·,
48 with swords and with s· to take me?
Lu 9: 3 your journey, neither s·, nor scrip,
22:52 against a thief, with swords and s·?

stay See also STAYED; STAYETH; STAYS.
Ge 19:17 neither s· thou in all the plain;
Ex 9:28 let you go, and ye shall s· no longer.
Le 13: 5 the plague in his sight be at a s·,
23, 28 if the bright spot s· in his place,
37 if the scall be in his sight at a s·,
Jos 10:19 And s· ye not, but pursue after your
Ru 1:13 would ye s· for them from having
1Sa 15:16 S·, and I will tell thee what the
20:38 the lad, Make speed, haste, s· not.
2Sa 22:19 calamity: but the Lord was my s·.
24:16 It is enough: s· now thine hand.
1Ch 21:15 It is enough, s· now thine hand.
Job 37: 4 will not s· them when his voice
38:37 who can s· the bottles of heaven,
Ps 18:18 calamity: but the Lord was my s·.
Pr 28:17 flee to the pit; let no man s· him.
Ca 2: 5 S· me with flagons, comfort me
Isa 3: 1 from Judah the s· and the staff,
1 the staff, the whole s· of bread,
1 bread, and the whole s· of water,
10:20 no more...s· upon him that smote
20 shall s· upon the Lord, the Holy
19:13 are the s· of the tribes thereof.
29: 9 S· yourselves, and wonder; cry
30:12 and perverseness, and s· thereon:
31: 1 s· on horses, and trust in chariots,
48: 2 and s·...upon the God of Israel;
50:10 of the Lord, and s· upon his God.
Jer 4: 6 toward Zion: retire, s· not:
20: 9 with forbearing, and I could not s·.
Da 4:35 none can s· his hand, or say unto
Ho 13:13 he should not s· long in the place

stayed
Ge 8:10 And he s· yet other seven days;
12 And he s· yet other seven days;
32: 4 with Laban, and s· there until now:
Ex 10:24 your flocks and your herds be s·:
17:12 Aaron and Hur s· up his hands,
Nu 16:48, 50 and the plague was s·.
25: 8 plague was s· from the children of
De 10:10 I s· in the mount, according to the
Jos 10:13 the sun stood still, and the moon s·,
1Sa 20:19 And when thou hast s· three days,
24: 7 David s· his servants with these
30: 9 those that were left behind s·.
2Sa 17:17 and Ahimaaz s· by En-rogel; for
24:21 plague may be s· from the people.
25 and the plague was s· from Israel.
1Ki 22:35 the king was s· up in his chariot
2Ki 4: 6 not a vessel more. And the oil s·.
13:18 And he smote thrice, and s·.
15:20 back, and s· not there in the land.
1Ch 21:22 plague may be s· from the people.
2Ch 18:34 king...s· himself up in his chariot
Job 38:11 here shall thy proud waves be s·?
Ps 106:30 and so the plague was s·.
Isa 26: 3 peace, whose mind is s· on thee:
La 4: 6 moment, and no hands s· on her.
Eze 31:15 and the great waters were s·:
Hag 1:10 the heaven over you is s· from dew,
10 and the earth is s· from her fruit.
Lu 4:42 s· him, that he should not depart
Ac 19:22 he himself s· in Asia for a season.

stayeth
Isa 27: 8 he s· his rough wind in the day of

stays
1Ki 10:19 there were s· on either side on
19 and two lions stood beside the s·.
2Ch 9:18 s· on each side of the sitting place,
18 and two lions standing by the s·:

stead^ See also BESTEAD; INSTEAD; STEADS; STEDFAST.
Ge 22:13 burnt offering in the s· of his son.
30: 2 Am I in God's s·, who hath withheld
36:33 died, and Jobab...reigned in his s·.
34 and Husham...reigned in his s·.
35 died, and Hadad...reigned in his s·.
36 and Samlah...reigned in his s·.
37 died, and Saul...reigned in his s·.
38 Baal-hanan...reigned in his s·.
39 died, and Hadar reigned in his s·:
Ex 29:30 And that son that is priest in his s·
Le 6:22 his sons that is anointed in his s·
16:32 the priest's office in his father's s·.
Nu 32:14 ye are risen up in your fathers' s·,
De 2:12 before them, and dwelt in their s·;
22 and dwelt in their s· even unto this
23 them, and dwelt in their s·.
10: 6 in the priest's office in his s·
Jos 5: 7 whom he raised up in their s·,
2Sa 10: 1 Hanun his son reigned in his s·.
16: 8 Saul, in whose s· thou hast reigned;
1Ki 1:30 shall sit upon my throne in my s·;

1Ki 1:35 for he shall be king in my s':
11:43 Rehoboam his son reigned in his s'.
14:27 Rehoboam made in their s' brasen
31 Abijam his son reigned in his s'.
15: 8 and Asa his son reigned in his s'.
24 Jehoshaphat...reigned in his s'.
28 Baasha...reigned in his s'.
16: 6 and Elah his son reigned in his s'.
10 And Zimri...and reigned in his s'.
22:40 Ahaziah his son reigned in his s'.
50 Jehoram his son reigned in his s'.
2Ki 1:17 And Jehoram reigned in his s' in
3:27 that should have reigned in his s',
8:15 died: and Hazael reigned in his s'.
24 Ahaziah his son reigned in his s'.
10:35 Jehoahaz his son reigned in his s'.
12:21 Amaziah his son reigned in his s'.
13: 9 and Joash his son reigned in his s'.
24 Ben-hadad his son reigned in his s'.
14:16 Jeroboam his son reigned in his s'.
29 Zachariah his son reigned in his s'.
15: 7 Jotham his son reigned in his s'.
10 And Shallum...reigned in his s'.
14 Menahem...reigned in his s'.
22 Pekahiah his son reigned in his s'.
30 And Hoshea...reigned in his s'.
38 and Ahaz his son reigned in his s'.
16:20 Hezekiah his son reigned in his s'.
19:37 Esarhaddon...reigned in his s'.
20:21 Manasseh his son reigned in his s'.
21:18 and Amon his son reigned in his s'.
24 made Josiah his son king in his s'.
26 Josiah his son reigned in his s'.
23:30 made him king in his father's s'.
24: 6 Jehoiachin his son reigned in his s'.
17 his father's brother king in his s'.
1Ch 1:44 dead, Jobab...reigned in his s'.
45 dead, Husham...reigned in his s'.
46 dead, Hadad...reigned in his s':
47 dead, Samlah...reigned in his s'.
48 dead, Shaul...reigned in his s'.
49 Baal-hanan...reigned in his s'.
50 was dead, Hadad reigned in his s'.
19: 1 died, and his son reigned in his s'.
2Ch 1: 8 and hast made me to reign in his s'.
12:16 and Abijah his son reigned in his s'.
14: 1 and Asa his son reigned in his s'.
17: 1 Jehoshaphat...reigned in his s',
21: 1 Jehoram his son reigned in his s'.
22: 1 made Ahaziah...king in his s':
24:27 Amaziah his son reigned in his s'.
27: 9 And Ahaz his son reigned in his s'.
28:27 Hezekiah his son reigned in his s'.
32:33 Manasseh his son reigned in his s'.
33:20 and Amon his son reigned in his s'.
25 made Josiah his son king in his s'.
36: 1 Jehoahaz...king in his father's s'.
8 Jehoiachin his son reigned in his s'.
Job 16: 4 if your soul were in my soul's s', I
33: 6 according to thy wish in God's s':
34:24 number, and set others in their s'.
Pr 11: 8 and the wicked cometh in his s'.
Isa 37:38 Esar-haddon...reigned in his s'.
Jer 29:26 thee priest in the s' of Jehoiada
2Co 5:20 we pray you in Christ's s', be ye
Ph'm 13 in thy s' he might have ministered

steadfast See STEDFAST.

steads
1Ch 5:22 dwelt in their s' until the captivity.

steady
Ex 17:12 his hands were s' until the going

steal See also STEALETH; STEALING; STOLE; STOLEN.
Ge 31:27 secretly, and s' away from me;
44: 8 should we s' out of thy lord's house
Ex 20:15 Thou shalt not s'.
22: 1 If a man shall s' an ox, or a sheep,
Le 19:11 Ye shall not s', neither deal falsely,
De 5:19 Neither shalt thou s'.
2Sa 19: 3 as people being ashamed s' away
Pr 6:30 if he s' to satisfy his soul when he
30: 9 or lest I be poor, and s', and take
Jer 7: 9 Will ye s', murder, and commit
23:30 that s' my words every one from his
M't 6:19 thieves break through and s':
20 thieves do not break through nor s':
19:18 Thou shalt not s', Thou shalt not
27:64 come by night, and s' him away,
M'r 10:19 Do not kill, Do not s', Do not bear
Lu 18:20 Do not kill, Do not s', Do not bear
Joh 10:10 The thief cometh not, but for to s',
Ro 2:21 a man should not s', dost thou s'?
13: 9 shalt not kill, Thou shalt not s',
Eph 4:28 Let him that stole s' no more: but

stealers See MENSTEALERS.

stealeth
Ex 21:16 he that s' a man, and selleth him,
Job 27:20 tempest s' him away in the night.
Zec 5: 3 for every one that s' shall be cut off

stealing
De 24: 7 If a man be found s' any of his
Ho 4: 2 and lying, and killing, and s', and

stealth
2Sa 19: 3 them by s' that day into the city,

stedfast
Job 11:15 yea, thou shalt be s', and shalt not
Ps 78: 8 whose spirit was not s' with God.
37 neither were they s' in his covenant.
Da 6:26 is the living God, and s' for ever,
1Co 7:37 he that standeth s' in his heart,
15:58 my beloved brethren, be ye s',
2Co 1: 7 And our hope of you is s', knowing,
Heb 2: 2 if the word spoken by angels was s',
3:14 of our confidence s' unto the end;
6:19 anchor of the soul, both sure and s',
1Pe 5: 9 Whom resist s' in the faith,

stedfastly
Ru 1:18 she was s' minded to go with her,
2Ki 8:11 he settled his countenance s',
Lu 9:51 s' set his face to go to Jerusalem,
Ac 1:10 they looked s' toward heaven as
2:42 they continued s' in the apostles'
6:15 looking s' on him, saw his face as
7:55 looked up s' into heaven, and saw
14: 9 Paul speak: who s' beholding him,
2Co 3: 7 could not s' behold the face of
13 could not s' look to the end of that

stedfastness
Col 2: 5 and the s' of your faith in Christ.
2Pe 3:17 the wicked, fall from your own s'.

steel
2Sa 22:35 bow of s' is broken by mine arms.
Job 20:24 and the bow of s' shall strike him
Ps 18:34 bow of s' is broken by mine arms.
Jer 15:12 the northern iron and the s'?

steep
Eze 38:20 s' places shall fall, and every wall
Mic 1: 4 that are poured down a s' place.
M't 8:32 ran violently down a s' place into
M'r 5:13 herd ran violently down a s' place
Lu 8:33 herd ran violently down a s' place

stem
Isa 11: 1 forth a rod out of the s' of Jesse,

step See also STEPPED; STEPPETH; STEPS.
1Sa 20: 3 is but a s' between me and death.
Job 31: 7 If my s' hath turned out of the way,

Stephanas (*stef'-a-nas*)
1Co 1:16 baptized also the household of S':
16:15 brethren, (ye know the house of S',
17 I am glad of the coming of S' and
subscr. was written from Philippi by S'.

Stephen (*ste'-ven*)
Ac 6: 5 they chose S', a man full of faith
8 And S', full of faith and power, did
9 and of Asia, disputing with S'.
7:59 they stoned S', calling upon God,
8: 2 devout men carried S' to his burial,
11:19 the persecution that arose about S'
22:20 blood of thy martyr S' was shed,

stepped
Joh 5: 4 the troubling of the water s' in

steppeth
Joh 5: 7 coming, another s' down before

steps See also FOOTSTEPS.
Ex 20:26 thou go up by s' unto mine altar,
2Sa 22:37 hast enlarged my s' under me;
1Ki 10:19 The throne had six s', and the top
20 and on the other upon the six s':
2Ch 9:18 And there were six s' to the throne,
19 and on the other upon the six s'.
Job 14:16 For now thou numberest my s':
18: 7 s' of his strength shall be straitened,
23:11 My foot hath held his s', his way
29: 6 When I washed my s' with butter,
31: 4 see my ways, and count all my s'?
37 unto him the number of my s';
Ps 17:11 have now compassed us in our s':
18:36 hast enlarged my s' under me,
37:23 The s' of a good man are ordered
31 his heart; none of his s' shall slide.
44:18 have our s' declined from thy way;
56: 6 they mark my s', when they wait
57: 6 have prepared a net for my s';
73: 2 gone; my s' had well nigh slipped.
85:13 shall set us in the way of his s'.
119:133 Order my s' in thy word: and let
Pr 4:12 thy s' shall not be straitened;
5: 5 to death; her s' take hold on hell.
16: 9 way: but the Lord directeth his s'.
Isa 26: 6 the poor, and the s' of the needy.
Jer 10:23 man that walketh to direct his s'.
La 4:18 They hunt our s', that we cannot
Eze 40:22 they went up unto it by seven s';
26 there were seven s' to go up to it,
31, 34, 37 going up to it had eight s'.
49 he brought me by the s' whereby
Da 11:43 the Ethiopians shall be at his s'.
Ro 4:12 walk in the s' of that faith of our
2Co 12:18 spirit? walked we not in the same s'?
1Pe 2:21 that ye should follow his s':

stern
Ac 27:29 cast four anchors out of the s',

steward See also STEWARDS.
Ge 15: 2 the s' of my house is this
43:19 to the s' of Joseph's house,
44: 1 commanded the s' of his house,
4 far off, Joseph said unto his s',
1Ki 16: 9 Arza s' of his house in Tirzah.
M't 20: 8 of the vineyard saith unto his s',
Lu 8: 3 the wife of Chuza Herod's s', and
12:42 then is that faithful and wise s',
16: 1 a certain rich man, which had a s';
2 for thou mayest be no longer s'.
3 Then the s' said within himself,
8 the lord commended the unjust s',
Tit 1: 7 must be blameless, as the s' of God;

stewards
1Ch 28: 1 the s' over all the substance and
1Co 4: 1 and s' of the mysteries of God.
2 Moreover it is required in s', that a
1Pe 4:10 s' of the manifold grace of God.

stewardship
Lu 16: 2 give an account of thy s'; for thou
3 lord taketh away from me the s':
4 when I am put out of the s', they

stick See also CANDLESTICK; STICKETH; STICKS STUCK.
2Ki 6: 6 And he cut down a s', and cast it
Job 33:21 bones that were not seen s' out.
41:17 they s' together, that they cannot
Ps 38: 2 For thine arrows s' fast in me, and
La 4: 8 is withered, it is become like a s'.
Eze 29: 4 the fish of thy rivers to s' unto thy
4 the fish of thy rivers shall s' unto
37:16 thou son of man, take thee one s',
16 then take another s', and write upon
16 For Joseph, the s' of Ephraim, and
17 them one to another into one s';
19 Behold, I will take the s' of Joseph,
19 with him, even with the s' of Judah,
19 and make them one s', and they

sticketh
Pr 18:24 is a friend that s' closer than a

sticks
Nu 15:32 they found a man that gathered s'
33 they that found him gathering s'
1Ki 17:10 woman was there gathering of s':
12 behold, I am gathering two s', that
Eze 37:20 the s' whereon thou writest shall
Ac 28: 3 Paul had gathered a bundle of s',

stiff See also STIFFHEARTED; STIFFNECKED.
De 31:27 thy rebellion, and thy s' neck:
Ps 75: 5 on high: speak not with a s' neck.
Jer 17:23 but made their neck s', that they

stiffened
2Ch 36:13 but he s' his neck, and hardened

stiffhearted
Eze 2: 4 are impudent children and s'.

stiffnecked
Ex 32: 9 and, behold, it is a s' people:
33: 3 thee; for thou art a s' people:
5 Ye are a s' people: I will come
34: 9 among us; for it is a s' people;
De 9: 6 for thou art a s' people.
13 and, behold, it is a s' people:
10:16 your heart, and be no more s'.
2Ch 30: 8 be ye not s', as your fathers
Ac 7:51 Ye s' and uncircumcised in heart

still^ See also STILLED; STILLEST; STILLETH.
Ge 12: 9 going on s' toward the south.
41:21 but they were s' ill favoured, as at the
Ex 14:13 not stand s', and see the salvation of
15:16 arm they shall be as s' as a stone;
23:11 thou shalt let it rest and lie s';
Le 13:57 And if it appear s' in the garment,
Nu 9: 8 them, Stand s', and I will hear what
14:38 that went to search the land, lived s'.
Jos 3: 8 Jordan, ye shall stand s' in Jordan.
10:12 Sun, stand thou s' upon Gibeon;
13 And the sun stood s', and the moon
13 So the sun stood s' in the midst of
11:13 cities that stood s' in their strength,
24:10 Balaam; therefore he blessed you s':
J'g 18: 9 it is very good: and are ye s'?
1Sa 9:27 but stand thou s' a while, that I may
12: 7 Now therefore stand s', that I may
25 But if ye shall s' do wickedly, ye shall
14: 9 then we will stand s' in our place,
26:25 great things, and also shalt s' prevail.
2Sa 2:23 Asahel fell down and died stood s'.
28 and all the people stood s', and
11: 1 But David tarried s' at Jerusalem.
16: 5 came forth, and cursed s' as he came.
18:30 And he turned aside, and stood s'.
20:12 saw that all the people stood s',
12 every one that came by him stood s'.
1Ki 19:12 and after the fire a s' small voice.
22: 3 Gilead is ours, and we be s', and
2Ki 2:11 And it came to pass, as they s' went on,
7: 4 and if we sit s' here, we die also.
12: 3 the people s' sacrificed and burnt
15: 4 burnt incense s' on the high places.
35 and burned incense s' in the high
2Ch 20:17 stand ye s', and see the salvation of
22: 9 no power to keep s' the kingdom.
33:17 did sacrifice s' in the high places,
Ne 12:39 they stood s' in the prison gate.
Job 2: 3 s' he holdeth fast his integrity,
9 Dost thou s' retain thine integrity?
3:13 For now should I have lain s' and
4:16 It stood s', but I could not discern
20:13 but keep it s' within his mouth:
32:16 they spake not, but stood s', and
37:14 stand s', and consider the wondrous
Ps 4: 4 heart upon your bed, and be s'.
8: 2 thou mightest s' the enemy and
23: 2 leadeth me beside the s' waters.
46:10 Be s', and know that I am God: I
49: 9 That he should s' live for ever, and
68:21 one as goeth on s' in his trespasses.
76: 8 the earth feared, and was s',
78:32 For all this they sinned s', and
83: 1 thy peace, and be not s', O God.
84: 4 they will be s' praising thee.
92:14 They shall s' bring forth fruit in old
107:29 so that the waves thereof are s'.
139:18 when I awake, I am s' with thee.
Ec 12: 9 he s' taught the people knowledge;
Isa 5:25 but his hand is stretched out s'.
9:17, 21 but his hand is stretched out s'.
10: 4 but his hand is stretched out s'.
23: 2 Be s', ye inhabitants of the isle;
30: 7 this, Their strength is to sit s'.

Isa 42:14 I have been *s'*, and refrained
Jer 8:14 Why do we sit *s'*? assemble
23:17 They say *s'* unto them that despise me,
27:11 I let remain *s'* in their own land,
31:20 I do earnestly remember him *s'*:
42:10 If ye will *s'* abide in this land, then
47: 6 into thy scabbard, rest, and be *s'*.
51:50 the sword, go away, stand not *s'*:
La 3:20 soul hath them *s'* in remembrance,
Eze 33:30 thy people *s'* are talking against thee
41: 7 a winding about *s'* upward to the side
7 about the house went *s'* upward
7 breadth of the house was *s'* upward,
Hab 3:11 The sun and moon stood *s'* in
Zec 1:11 all the earth sitteth *s'*, and is at
11:16 nor feed that that standeth *s'*:
M't 20:32 Jesus stood *s'*, and called them,
M'r 4:39 said unto the sea, Peace, be *s'*.
10:49 Jesus stood *s'*, and commanded
Lu 7:14 and they that bare him stood *s'*.
Joh 7: 9 unto them, he abode *s'* in Galilee.
11: 6 abode two days *s'* in the same place
20 him: but Mary sat *s'* in the house.
Ac 8:38 commanded the chariot to stand *s'*:
15:34 it pleased Silas to abide there *s'*.
17:14 Silas and Timotheus abode there *s'*.
Ro 11:23 also, if they abide not *s'* in unbelief,
1Ti 1: 3 thee to abide *s'* at Ephesus, when
Re 22:11 is unjust, let him be unjust *s'*:
11 which is filthy, let him be filthy *s'*:
11 righteous, let him be righteous *s'*:
11 he that is holy, let him be holy *s'*.

stilled
Nu 13:30 Caleb *s'* the people before Moses,
Ne 8:11 So the Levites *s'* all the people,

stillest
Ps 89: 9 waves thereof arise, thou *s'* them.

stilleth
Ps 65: 7 Which *s'* the noise of the seas,

sting See also STINGETH; STINGS.
1Co 15:55 O death, where is thy *s'*? O grave,
56 The *s'* of death is sin; and the

stingeth
Pr 23:32 a serpent, and *s'* like an adder.

stings
Re 9:10 and there were *s'* in their tails:

stink See STANK; STINKETH.
Ge 34:30 have troubled me to make me to *s'*
Ex 7:18 shall die, and the river shall *s'*;
16:24 it did not *s'*, neither was there any
Ps 38: 5 My wounds *s'* and are corrupt
Isa 3:24 of sweet smell there shall be *s'*;
34: 3 their *s'* shall come up out of their
Joe 2:20 his *s'* shall come up, and his ill
Am 4:10 made the *s'* of your camps to come

stinketh
Isa 50: 2 their fish *s'*, because there is no
Joh 11:39 him, Lord, by this time he *s'*:

stinking
Ec 10: 1 to send forth a *s'* savour: so

stir See also BESTIR; STIRRED; STIRRETH; STIRS.
Nu 24: 9 a great lion: who shall *s'* him up?
Job 17: 8 the innocent shall *s'* up himself
41:10 is so fierce that dare *s'* him up:
Ps 35:23 *S'* up thyself, and awake to my
78:38 and did not *s'* up all his wrath.
80: 2 and Manasseh *s'* up thy strength,
Pr 15: 1 but grievous words *s'* up anger.
Ca 2: 7 ye *s'* not up, nor awake my love,
3: 5 ye *s'* not up, nor awake my love,
8: 4 ye *s'* not up, nor awake my love,
Isa 10:26 Lord of hosts shall *s'* up a scourge
13:17 I will *s'* up the Medes against them,
42:13 he shall *s'* up jealousy like a man
Da 11: 2 shall *s'* up all against the realm of
25 And he shall *s'* up his power and
Ac 12:18 no small *s'* among the soldiers,
19:23 there arose no small *s'* about that
2Ti 1: 6 that thou *s'* up the gift of God,
2Pe 1:13 to *s'* you up by putting you in
3: 1 I *s'* up your pure minds by way of

stirred
Ex 35:21 every one whose heart *s'* him up,
26 women whose heart *s'* them up in
36: 2 one whose heart *s'* him up to come
1Sa 22: 8 son hath *s'* up my servant against
26:19 Lord have *s'* thee up against me,
1Ki 11:14 the Lord *s'* up an adversary unto
23 God *s'* him up another adversary,
21:25 whom Jezebel his wife *s'* up.
1Ch 5:26 the God of Israel *s'* up the spirit
2Ch 21:16 the Lord *s'* up against Jehoram the
36:22 Lord *s'* up the spirit of Cyrus king
Ezr 1: 1 Lord *s'* up the spirit of Cyrus king
Ps 39: 2 good; and my sorrow was *s'*.
Da 11:10 But his sons shall be *s'* up, and
10 then shall he return, and be *s'* up,
25 king of the south shall be *s'* up to
Hag 1:14 And the Lord *s'* up the spirit of
Ac 6:12 And they *s'* up the people, and the
13:50 the Jews *s'* up the devout and
14: 2 Jews *s'* up the Gentiles, and
17:13 thither also, and *s'* up the people.
16 his spirit was *s'* in him, when
21:27 *s'* up all the people, and laid

stirreth
De 32:11 As an eagle *s'* up her nest,
Pr 10:12 Hatred *s'* up strifes: but love
15:18 A wrathful man *s'* up strife: but
28:25 is of a proud heart *s'* up strife:
Pr 29:22 An angry man *s'* up strife, and a
Isa 14: 9 it *s'* up the dead for thee, even all
64: 7 that *s'* up himself to take hold of
Lu 23: 5 He *s'* up the people, teaching

stirs
Isa 22: 2 Thou that art full of *s'*, a

stock See also GAZINGSTOCK; STOCKS.
Le 25:47 to the *s'* of the stranger's family:
Job 14: 8 the *s'* thereof die in the ground;
Isa 40:24 their *s'* shall not take root in the
44:19 shall I fall down to the *s'* of a tree?
Jer 2:27 Saying to a *s'*, Thou art my father;
10: 8 the *s'* is a doctrine of vanities.
Ac 13:26 children of the *s'* of Abraham, and
Ph'p 3: 5 the eighth day, of the *s'* of Israel,

stocks
Job 13:27 puttest my feet also in the *s'*, and
33:11 He putteth my feet in the *s'*, he
Pr 7:22 a fool to the correction of the *s'*;
Jer 3: 9 adultery with stones and with *s'*.
20: 2 put him in the *s'* that were in the
3 forth Jeremiah out of the *s'*.
29:26 put him in prison, and in the *s'*.
Ho 4:12 My people ask counsel at their *s'*,
Ac 16:24 and made their feet fast in the *s'*.

Stoicks (*sto'-ics*)
Ac 17:18 and of the *S'*, encountered him.

stole See also STOLEN.
Ge 31:20 Jacob *s'* away unawares to Laban
2Sa 15: 6 Absalom *s'* the hearts of the men
2Ki 11: 2 *s'* him from among the king's sons
2Ch 22:11 *s'* him from among the king's sons
M't 28:13 and *s'* him away while we slept.
Eph 4:28 Let him that *s'* steal no more: but

stolen
Ge 30:33 that shall be counted *s'* with me.
31:19 Rachel had *s'* the images that were
26 thou hast *s'* away unawares to me,
30 wherefore hast thou *s'* my gods?
32 knew not that Rachel had *s'* them.
39 whether *s'* by day, or *s'* by night.
40:15 I was *s'* away out of the land of the
Ex 22: 7 and it be *s'* out of the man's house;
12 if it be *s'* from him, he shall make
Jos 7:11 have also *s'*, and dissembled also,
2Sa 19:41 the men of Judah *s'* thee away,
21:12 had *s'* them from the street of
Pr 9:17 *S'* waters are sweet, and bread
Ob 5 not have *s'* till they have enough?

stomacher
Isa 3:24 of a *s'* a girding of sackcloth;

stomach's
1Ti 5:23 a little wine for thy *s'* sake and

stone See also BRIMSTONE; HEADSTONE; MILLSTONE; STONED; STONE'S; STONES; STONESQUARERS; STONEST; STONING; STUMBLINGSTONE.
Ge 2:12 there is bdellium and the onyx *s'*.
11: 3 And they had brick for *s'*, and slime
28:18 the *s'* that he had put for his pillows,
22 this *s'*, which I have set for a pillar,
29: 2 a great *s'* was upon the well's mouth.
3 rolled the *s'* from the well's mouth,
3 put the *s'* again upon the well's
8 roll the *s'* from the well's mouth;
10 rolled the *s'* from the well's mouth,
31:45 And Jacob took a *s'*, and set it up for
35:14 talked with him, even a pillar of *s'*:
49:24 is the shepherd, the *s'* of Israel:)
Ex 4:25 Zipporah took a sharp *s'*, and cut
7:19 vessels of wood, and in vessels of *s'*.
8:26 their eyes, and will they not *s'* us?
15: 5 they sank into the bottom as a *s'*.
16 arm they shall be as still as a *s'*;
17: 4 they be almost ready to *s'* me.
12 they took a *s'*, and put it under him,
20:25 if thou wilt make me an altar of *s'*,
25 thou shalt not build it of hewn *s'*:
21:18 and one smite another with a *s'*,
24:10 it were a paved work of a sapphire *s'*,
12 and I will give thee tables of *s'*, and
28:10 Six of their names on one *s'*, and the
10 six names of the rest on the other *s'*,
11 With the work of an engraver in *s'*,
31:18 two tables of testimony, tables of *s'*,
34: 1 Hew thee two tables of *s'* like unto
4 he hewed two tables of *s'* like unto
4 took in his hand the two tables of *s'*.
Le 20: 2 of the land shall *s'* him with stones.
27 they shall *s'* them with stones:
24:14 and let all the congregation *s'* him.
16 congregation shall certainly *s'* him:
23 the camp, and *s'* him with stones.
26: 1 neither shall ye set up any image of *s'*
Nu 14:10 all the congregation bade *s'* them
15:35 congregation...*s'* him with stones
35:17 if he smite him with throwing a *s'*,
23 Or with any *s'*, wherewith a man
De 4:13 he wrote them upon two tables of *s'*.
28 work of men's hands, wood and *s'*,
5:22 he wrote them in two tables of *s'*,
9: 9 the mount to receive the tables of *s'*,
10 delivered unto me two tables of *s'*
11 Lord gave me the two tables of *s'*,
10: 1 Hew thee two tables of *s'* like unto
3 and hewed two tables of *s'* like unto
13:10 thou shalt *s'* him with stones, that
17: 5 and shalt *s'* them with stones, till
21:21 all the men of his city shall *s'* him
22:21 the men of her city shall *s'* her with
24 ye shall *s'* them with stones that
28:36 thou serve other gods, wood and *s'*.
De 28:64 have known, even wood and *s'*.
29:17 and their idols, wood and *s'*, silver
Jos 4: 5 take ye up every man of you a *s'*
15: 6 border went up to the *s'* of Bohan
18:17 descended to the *s'* of Bohan the son
24:26 took a great *s'*, and set it up there
27 this *s'* shall be a witness unto us;
J'g 9: 5 and ten persons, upon one *s'*:
18 and ten persons, upon one *s'*, and
1Sa 6:14 there, where there was a great *s'*:
15 were, and put them on the great *s'*:
18 even unto the great *s'* of Abel, whereon
18 which *s'* remaineth unto this day in
7:12 Then Samuel took a *s'*, and set it
14:33 roll a great *s'* unto me this day.
17:49 and took thence a *s'*, and slang it,
49 that the *s'* sunk into his forehead;
50 Philistine with a sling and with a *s'*,
20:19 and shalt remain by the *s'* Ezel.
25:37 within him, and he became as a *s'*.
2Sa 17:13 be not one small *s'* found there.
20: 8 at the great *s'* which is in Gibeon,
1Ki 1: 9 and fat cattle by the *s'* of Zoheleth,
6: 7 built of *s'* made ready before it was
18 all was cedar; there was no *s'* seen.
36 court with three rows of hewed *s'*,
8: 9 in the ark save the two tables of *s'*,
21:10 carry him out, and *s'* him, that he
2Ki 3:25 piece of land cast every man his *s'*,
12:12 And to masons, and hewers of *s'*,
12 buy timber and hewed *s'* to repair
19:18 work of men's hands, wood and *s'*:
22: 6 to buy timber and hewn *s'* to repair
1Ch 22:14 timber also and *s'* have I prepared;
15 hewers and workers of *s'* and
2Ch 2:14 brass, in iron, in *s'*, and in timber,
34:11 to buy hewn *s'*, and timber for
Ne 4: 3 shall even break down their *s'* wall.
9:11 as a *s'* into the mighty waters.
Job 28: 2 and brass is molten out of the *s'*.
38: 6 or who laid the corner *s'* thereof;
30 The waters are hid as with a *s'*, and
41:24 His heart is as firm as a *s'*; yea, as
Ps 91:12 lest thou dash thy foot against a *s'*.
118:22 The *s'* which the builders refused
22 is become the head *s'* of the corner.
Pr 17: 8 A gift is as a precious *s'* in the eyes
24:31 the *s'* wall thereof was broken down.
26: 8 As he that bindeth a *s'* in a sling,
27 and he that rolleth a *s'*, it will return
27: 3 A *s'* is heavy, and the sand weighty;
Isa 8:14 but for a *s'* of stumbling and for a
28:16 Zion for a foundation a *s'*, a tried *s'*,
16 a precious corner *s'*, a sure
37:19 work of men's hands, wood and *s'*:
Jer 2:27 and to a *s'*, Thou hast brought me
51:26 not take of thee a *s'* for a corner,
26 nor a *s'* for foundations; but thou
63 that thou shalt bind a *s'* to it, and
La 3: 9 inclosed my ways with hewn *s'*,
53 the dungeon, and cast a *s'* upon me.
Eze 1:26 as the appearance of a sapphire *s'*:
10: 1 over them as it were a sapphire *s'*,
9 was as the colour of a beryl *s'*.
16:40 and they shall *s'* thee with stones,
20:32 the countries, to serve wood and *s'*.
23:47 company shall *s'* them with stones,
28:13 every precious *s'* was thy covering,
40:42 four tables were of hewn *s'* for the
Da 2:34 that a *s'* was cut out without hands,
35 the *s'* that smote the image became
45 the *s'* was cut out of the mountain
5: 4 of brass, of iron, of wood, and of *s'*.
23 of brass, iron, wood, and *s'*, which
6:17 And a *s'* was brought, and laid upon
Am 5:11 ye have built houses of hewn *s'*,
Hab 2:11 For the *s'* shall cry out of the wall,
19 to the dumb *s'*, Arise, it shall teach!
Hag 2:15 a *s'* was laid upon a *s'* in the temple
Zec 3: 9 behold the *s'* that I have laid before
9 upon one *s'* shall be seven eyes:
7:12 their hearts as an adamant *s'*,
12: 3 make Jerusalem a burdensome *s'*
M't 4: 6 thou dash thy foot against a *s'*.
7: 9 ask bread, will he give him a *s'*?
21:42 The *s'* which the builders rejected,
44 shall fall on this *s'* shall be broken:
24: 2 not be left here one *s'* upon another,
27:60 rolled a great *s'* to the door of the
66 sealing the *s'*, and setting a watch.
28: 2 came and rolled back the *s'* from
M'r 12:10 The *s'* which the builders rejected
13: 2 not be left one *s'* upon another,
15:46 and rolled a *s'* unto the door of the
16: 3 roll us away the *s'* from the door
4 they saw that the *s'* was rolled
Lu 4: 3 command this *s'* that it be made
11 thou dash thy foot against a *s'*.
11:11 is a father, will he give him a *s'*?
19:44 leave in thee one *s'* upon another;
20: 6 all the people will *s'* us: for they
17 The *s'* which the builders rejected,
18 shall fall upon that *s'* be broken;
21: 6 not be left one *s'* upon another,
23:53 in a sepulchre that was hewn in *s'*,
24: 2 they found the *s'* rolled away from
Joh 1:42 which is by interpretation, A *s'*.
2: 6 were set there six waterpots of *s'*,
8: 7 you, let him first cast a *s'* at her.
10:31 Jews took...stones again to *s'* him.
32 which of those works do ye *s'* me?
33 For a good work we *s'* thee not;
11: 8 the Jews of late sought to *s'* thee;
38 It was a cave, and a *s'* lay upon it.
39 Jesus said, Take ye away the *s'*.
41 they took away the *s'* from the

Joh 20: 1 seeth the s' taken away from the
Ac 4: 11 This is the s' which was set at
14: 5 them despitefully, and to s' them,
17: 29 is like unto gold, or silver, or s'.
2Co 3: 3 not in tables of s', but in fleshy
Eph 2: 20 himself being the chief corner s';
1Pe 2: 4 whom coming, as unto a living s',
6 I lay in Sion a chief corner s', elect,
7 s' which the builders disallowed,
8 And a s' of stumbling, and a rock of
Re 2: 17 and will give him a white s',
17 and in the s' a new name written,
4: 3 like a jasper and a sardine s':
9: 20 gold, and silver, and brass, and s',
16: 21 every s' about the weight of a talent:
18: 21 mighty angel took up a s' like a
21: 11 was like unto a s' most precious,
11 like a jasper s', clear as crystal;

stoned
Ex 19: 13 but he shall surely be s', or shot
21: 28 then the ox shall be surely s', and
29 the ox shall be s', and his owner
32 of silver, and the ox shall be s'.
Nu 15: 36 s' him with stones, and he died;
Jos 7: 25 And all Israel s' him with stones,
25 after they had s' them with stones.
1Ki 12: 18 and all Israel s' him with stones,
21: 13 s' him with stones, that he died.
14 saying, Naboth is s', and is dead.
15 Jezebel heard that Naboth was s',
2Ch 10: 18 children of Israel s' him with
24: 21 and s' him with stones at the
M't 21: 35 and killed another, and s' another.
Joh 8: 5 commanded us, that such...be s':
Ac 5: 26 lest they should have been s'.
7: 58 him out of the city, and s' him:
59 they s' Stephen, calling upon God,
14: 19 having s' Paul, drew him out of
2Co 11: 25 once was I s', thrice I suffered
Heb 11: 37 They were s', they were sawn
12: 20 it shall be s', or thrust through

stone's
Lu 22: 41 from them about a s' cast,

stones See also CHALKSTONES; HAILSTONES; MILLSTONES; SLINGSTONES.
Ge 28: 11 and he took of the s' of that place,
31: 46 said unto his brethren, Gather s';
46 and they took s', and made an heap:
Ex 25: 7 Onyx s', and s' to be set in the ephod,
28: 9 And thou shalt take two onyx s', and
11 shalt thou engrave the two s' with
12 put the two s' upon the shoulders of
12 for s' of memorial unto the children
17 And thou shalt set in it settings of s',
17 even four rows of s': the first row
21 the s' shall be with the names of the
31: 5 And in cutting of s', to set them, and
35: 9 onyx s', and s' to be set for the ephod,
27 And the rulers brought onyx s', and
27 and s' to be set, for the ephod, and
33 And in the cutting of s', to set them,
39: 6 wrought onyx s' inclosed in ouches
7 be s' for a memorial to the children
10 And they set in it four rows of s': the
14 the s' were according to the names
Le 14: 40 take away the s' in which the plague
42 And they shall take other s', and put
42 and put them in the place of those s';
43 after that he hath taken away the s',
45 break down the house, the s' of it,
20: 2 of the land shall stone him with s'.
27 death: they shall stone them with s':
21: 20 or scabbed, or hath his s' broken;
24: 23 of the camp, and stone him with s'.
Nu 14: 10 bade stone them with s'.
15: 35 congregation shall stone him with s'
36 and stoned him with s', and he died;
De 8: 9 a land whose s' are iron, and out of
13: 10 thou shalt stone him with s', that he
17: 5 shalt stone them with s', till they die.
21: 21 of his city shall stone him with s',
22: 21 shall stone her with s' that she die:
24 ye shall stone them with s' that they
23: 1 He that is wounded in the s', or hath
27: 2 that thou shalt set thee up great s',
4 that ye shall set up these s', which I
5 unto the Lord thy God, an altar of s':
6 altar of the Lord thy God of whole s':
8 write upon the s' all the words of
Jos 4: 3 the priests' feet stood firm, twelve s',
6 saying, What mean ye by these s'?
7 these s' shall be for a memorial unto
8 took up twelve s' out of the midst of
9 Joshua set up twelve s' in the midst
20 those twelve s', which they took out
21 come, saying, What mean these s'?
7: 25 And all Israel stoned him with s',
25 after they had stoned them with s'.
26 raised over him a great heap of s'
8: 29 and raise thereon a great heap of s',
31 an altar of whole s', over which no
32 he wrote there upon the s' a copy of
10: 11 Lord cast down great s' from heaven
18 Roll great s' upon the mouth of the
27 and laid great s' in the cave's mouth,
J'g 20: 16 could sling s' at an hair breadth,
1Sa 17: 40 chose him five smooth s' out of the
2Sa 12: 30 a talent of gold with the precious s':
16: 6 And he cast s' at David, and at all
13 and threw s' at him, and cast dust.
18: 17 and laid a very great heap of s' upon
1Ki 5: 17 and they brought great s', costly s',
17 hewed s', to lay the foundation of
18 prepared timber and s' to build the
7: 9 All these were of costly s', according
10 was of costly s', even great s',
10 s' of ten cubits, and s' of eight cubits.
11 And above were costly s', after the
11 after the measures of hewed s',
12 was with three rows of hewed s',
10: 2 and very much gold, and precious s':
10 very great store, and precious s':
11 of almug trees, and precious s'.
27 made silver to be in Jerusalem as s',
12: 18 all Israel stoned him with s', that he
15: 22 and they took away the s' of Ramah,
18: 31 Elijah took twelve s', according to
32 with the s' he built an altar in the
38 the wood, and the s', and the dust,
21: 13 and stoned him with s', that he died.
2Ki 3: 19 mar every good piece of land with s'.
25 Kir-haraseth left they the s' thereof;
16: 17 and put it upon a pavement of s'.
1Ch 12: 2 right hand and the left in hurling s'
20: 2 and there were precious s' in it; and
22: 2 he set masons to hew wrought s' to
29: 2 wood for things of wood; onyx s',
2 and s' to be set, glistering
2 glistering s', and of divers colours,
2 manner of precious s', and marble s'
8 with whom precious s' were found
2Ch 1: 15 gold at Jerusalem as plenteous as s',
3: 6 garnished the house with precious s'
9: 1 gold in abundance, and precious s':
9 great abundance, and precious s':
10 brought algum trees and precious s'.
27 king made silver in Jerusalem as s',
10: 18 children of Israel stoned him with s',
16: 6 they carried away the s' of Ramah,
24: 21 stoned him with s' at...commandment
26: 14 and bows, and slings to cast s'.
15 to shoot arrows and great s' withal.
32: 27 and for gold, and for precious s',
Ezr 5: 8 which is builded with great s', and
6: 4 With three rows of great s', and a
Ne 4: 2 they revive the s' out of the heaps
Job 5: 23 be in league with the s' of the field:
6: 12 Is my strength the strength of s'? or
8: 17 the heap, and seeth the place of s'.
14: 19 waters wear the s': thou washest
22: 24 the gold of Ophir as the s' of the
28: 3 the s' of darkness, and the shadow of
6 s' of it are the place of sapphires:
40: 17 the sinews of his s' are wrapped
41: 30 Sharp s' are under him: he
Ps 18: 12 clouds passed, hail s' and coals of fire.
13 gave his voice; hail s' and coals of fire.
102: 14 thy servants take pleasure in her s',
137: 9 thy little ones against the s'.
144: 12 our daughters may be as corner s',
Ec 3: 5 A time to cast away s', and a time to
5 a time to gather s' together; a time
10: 9 Whoso removeth s' shall be hurt
Isa 5: 2 it, and gathered out the s' thereof,
9: 10 but we will build with hewn s':
14: 19 that go down to the s' of the pit;
27: 9 when he maketh all the s' of the altar
34: 11 of confusion, and the s' of emptiness.
54: 11 I will lay thy s' with fair colours, and
12 and all thy borders of pleasant s'.
57: 6 Among the smooth s' of the stream is
60: 17 and for wood brass, and for s' iron:
62: 10 up the highway; gather out the s';
Jer 3: 9 committed adultery with s' and with
43: 9 Take great s' in thine hand, and hide
10 set his throne upon these s' that I
La 3: 16 broken my teeth with gravel s',
4: 1 s' of the sanctuary are poured out in
Eze 16: 40 and they shall stone thee with s',
23: 47 company shall stone them with s',
26: 12 they shall lay thy s' and thy timber
27: 22 and with all precious s', and gold.
28: 14 down in the midst of the s' of fire.
16 from the midst of the s' of fire.
Da 11: 38 and with precious s', and pleasant
Mic 1: 6 I will pour down the s' thereof into
Zec 5: 4 the timber thereof and the s' thereof.
9: 15 devour, and subdue with sling s';
16 for they shall be as the s' of a crown,
M't 3: 9 able of these s' to raise up children
4: 3 that these s' be made bread.
M'r 5: 5 crying, and cutting himself with s'.
12: 4 and at him they cast s', and
13: 1 see what manner of s' and what
Lu 3: 8 able of these s' to raise up children
19: 40 the s' would immediately cry out.
21: 5 adorned with goodly s' and gifts,
Joh 8: 59 Then took they up s' to cast at him:
10: 31 the Jews took up s' again to stone
1Co 3: 12 gold, silver, precious s', wood, hay,
2Co 3: 7 death, written and engraven in s',
1Pe 2: 5 Ye also, as lively s', are built up a
Re 17: 4 decked with gold and precious s'
18: 12 gold, and silver, and precious s',
16 decked with gold, and precious s',
21: 19 with all manner of precious s'.

stonesquarers
1Ki 5: 18 builders did hew them, and the s':

stonest
M't 23: 37 s' them which are sent unto thee,
Lu 13: 34 s' them that are sent unto thee;

stoning
1Sa 30: 6 for the people spake of s' him,

stony
Ps 141: 6 are overthrown in s' places,
Eze 11: 19 take the s' heart out of their flesh,
36: 26 away the s' heart out of your flesh,
M't 13: 5 Some fell upon s' places, where
20 received the seed into s' places,
M'r 4: 5 And some fell on s' ground, where
16 which are sown on s' ground;

stood See also STOODEST; UNDERSTOOD; WITHSTOOD.
Ge 18: 2 and, lo, three men s' by him:
8 and he s' by them under the tree,
22 Abraham s' yet before the Lord.
19: 27 place where he s' before the Lord:
23: 3 Abraham s' up...before his dead,
7 And Abraham s' up, and bowed
24: 30 he s' by the camels at the well.
28: 13 And, behold, the Lord s' above it,
37: 7 my sheaf arose, and also s' upright;
7 your sheaves s' round about, and
41: 1 and, behold, he s' by the river.
3 s' by the other kine upon the brink
17 I s' upon the bank of the river:
46 years old when he s' before Pharaoh
43: 15 to Egypt, and s' before Joseph.
45: 1 before all them that s' by him;
1 And there s' no man with him,
Ex 2: 4 his sister s' afar off, to wit what
17 but Moses s' up and helped them,
5: 20 met Moses...who s' in the way,
9: 10 furnace, and s' before Pharaoh;
14: 19 their face, and s' behind them:
15: 8 the floods s' upright as an heap,
18: 13 and the people s' by Moses from
19: 17 and they s' at the nether part of
20: 18 it, they removed, and s' afar off.
21 And the people s' afar off, and
32: 26 Moses s' in the gate of the camp,
33: 8 and s' every man at his tent door,
9 s' at the door of the tabernacle,
34: 5 the cloud, and s' with him there,
Le 9: 5 drew near and s' before the Lord.
Nu 11: 32 And the people s' up all that day,
12: 5 s' in the door of the tabernacle,
16: 18 and s' in the door of the tabernacle
27 and s' in the door of their tents,
48 s' between the dead and the living;
22: 22 angel of the Lord s' in the way
24 angel of the Lord s' in a path of
26 further, and s' in a narrow place,
23: 6 lo, he s' by his burnt sacrifice, he,
17 behold, he s' by his burnt offering,
27: 2 And they s' before Moses, and
De 4: 11 near and s' under the mountain;
5: 5 (I s' between the Lord and you at
31: 15 pillar of the cloud s' over the door
Jos 3: 16 waters which came...from above s'
17 priests...s' firm on dry ground
4: 3 where the priests' feet s' firm,
9 bare the ark of the covenant s':
10 which bare the ark s' in the midst
5: 13 these s' a man over against him with
8: 33 s' on this side the ark and on that
10: 13 And the sun s' still, and the moon
13 So the sun s' still in the midst of
11: 13 cities that s' still in their strength,
20: 9 until he s' before the congregation.
21: 44 s' not a man of all their enemies
J'g 3: 19 all that s' by him went out from
6: 31 Joash said unto all that s' against
7: 21 And they s' every man in his place
9: 7 he went and s' in the top of mount
35, 44 s' in the entering of the gate of
16: 29 pillars upon which the house s',
18: 16 Dan, s' by the entering of the gate.
17 priest s' in the entering of the gate
20: 28 Aaron, s' before it in those days,)
1Sa 1: 26 I am the woman that s' by thee
3: 10 the Lord came, and s', and called
4: 20 women that s' by her said unto her,
6: 14 s' there, where there was a great
10: 23 and when he s' among the people,
16: 21 came to Saul, and s' before him:
17: 3 the Philistines s' on a mountain
3 Israel s' on a mountain on the other
8 he s' and cried unto the armies of
26 David spake to the men that s' by
51 David...s' upon the Philistine, and
22: 7 his servants that s' about him,
17 unto the footmen that s' about him,
26: 13 and s' on the top of an hill afar off;
2Sa 1: 10 So I s' upon him, and slew him,
2: 23 where Asahel fell down...s' still,
25 troop, and s' on the top of an hill.
28 trumpet, and all the people s' still,
13: 31 s' by with their clothes rent.
15: 2 and s' beside the way of the gate:
18: 4 And the king s' by the gate side,
30 And he turned aside, and s' still.
20: 11 And one of Joab's men s' by him,
12 man saw that all the people s' still,
12 every one that came by him s' still.
15 the city, and it s' in the trench:
23: 12 he s' in the midst of the ground,
1Ki 1: 28 presence, and s' before the king.
3: 15 s' before the ark of the covenant of
16 unto the king, and s' before him.
7: 25 It s' upon twelve oxen, three looking
8: 14 all the congregation of Israel s';)
22 Solomon s' before the altar of the
55 And he s', and blessed all the
10: 19 and two lions s' beside the stays.
20 twelve lions s' there on the one side
12: 6 that s' before Solomon his father
8 with him, and which s' before him:
13: 1 Jeroboam s' by the altar to burn
24 cast in the way, and the ass s' by it,
24 the lion also s' by the carcase.
19: 13 and s' in the entering in of the cave.
22: 21 a spirit, and s' before the Lord,
2Ki 2: 7 went, and s' to view afar off:

2Ki 2: 7 afar off: and they two s· by Jordan.
13 back, and s· by the bank of Jordan;
3: 21 and upward, and s· in the border.
4: 12 had called her, she s· before him.
15 had called her, she s· in the door.
5: 9 s· at the door of the house of Elisha.
15 and came, and s· before him:
25 went in, and s· before his master.
8: 9 and came and s· before him, and
9: 17 there s· a watchman on the tower
10: 4 Behold, two kings s· not before him:
9 went out, and s·, and said to all the
11: 11 And the guard s·, every man with
14 behold, the king s· by a pillar, as
13: 21 he revived, and s· up on his feet.
18: 17 and s· by the conduit of the upper
28 Then Rab-shakeh s· and cried with
23: 3 the king s· by a pillar, and made a
3 all the people s· to the covenant.
1Ch 6: 39 Asaph, who s· on his right hand,
44 the sons of Merari s· on the left hand:
21: 1 And Satan s· up against Israel,
15 angel...s· by the threshingfloor
28: 2 David the king s· up upon his feet,
2Ch 3: 13 and they s· on their feet, and their
4: 4 It s· upon twelve oxen, three looking
5: 12 harps, s· at the east end of the altar,
6: 3 all the congregation of Israel s·.
12 he s· before the altar of the Lord
13 upon it he s·, and kneeled down
7: 6 before them, and all Israel s·.
9: 19 twelve lions s· there on the one side
10: 6 old men that had s· before Solomon
8 young men...that s· before him.
13: 4 And Abijah s· up upon mount
18: 20 a spirit, and s· before the Lord,
20: 5 Jehoshaphat s· in the congregation
13 And all Judah s· before the Lord,
19 s· up to praise the Lord God of
20 Jehoshaphat s· and said, Hear me,
23 Moab s· up against the inhabitants
23: 13 king s· at his pillar at the entering
24: 20 priest, which s· above the people,
28: 12 s· up against them that came from
29: 26 Levites s· with the instruments of
30: 16 they s· in their place after their
34: 31 the king s· in his place, and made
35: 10 and the priests s· in their place,
Ezr 2: 63 till there s· up a priest with Urim
3: 2 s· up Jeshua the son of Jozadak,
9 Then s· Jeshua with his sons and
10: 10 Ezra the priest s· up, and said unto
Ne 7: 65 till there s· up a priest with Urim
8: 4 Ezra the scribe s· upon a pulpit of
4 and beside him s· Mattithiah, and
5 he opened it, all the people s· up:
7 law: and the people s· in their place.
9: 2 and s· and confessed their sins,
3 they s· up in their place, and read
4 Then s· up upon the stairs, of the
12: 39 and they s· still in the prison gate.
40 So s· the two companies of them
Es 5: 1 s· in the inner court of the king's
9 the king's gate, that he s· not up,
7: 7 Haman s· up to make request for
8: 4 Esther arose, and s· before the king,
9: 16 together, and s· for their lives,
Job 4: 15 face; the hair of my flesh s· up:
16 It s· still, but I could not discern
29: 8 and the aged arose, and s· up.
30: 28 the sun: I s· up, and I cried in the
32: 16 (for they spake not, but s· still,
Ps 33: 9 done; he commanded, and it s· fast.
104: 6 the waters s· above the mountains.
106: 23 not Moses his chosen s· before him
30 Then s· up Phinehas, and executed
Isa 6: 2 Above it s· the seraphims: each one
36: 2 he s· by the conduit of the upper
13 Then Rabshakeh s·, and cried with
Jer 15: 1 Moses and Samuel s· before me, yet
18: 20 I s· before thee to speak good for
19: 14 and he s· in the court of the Lord's
23: 18 hath s· in the counsel of the Lord,
22 But if they had s· in my counsel,
28: 5 all the people that s· in the house of
36: 21 princes which s· beside the king.
44: 15 all the women that s· by, a great
46: 15 they s· not, because the Lord did
48: 45 They that fled s· under the shadow
La 2: 4 he s· with his right hand as an
Eze 1: 21 and when those s·, these s·; and
24 when they s·, they let down their
25 when they s·, and had let down
3: 23 the glory of the Lord s· there, as
8: 11 there s· before them seventy men
11 in the midst of them s· Jaazaniah
9: 2 in, and s· beside the brasen altar.
10: 3 the cherubims s· on the right side
4 and s· over the threshold of the house;
6 went in, and s· beside the wheels.
17 When they stood, these s·; and
18 house, and s· over the cherubims.
19 every one s· at the door of the east
11: 23 s· upon the mountain which is on
21: 21 king of Babylon s· at the parting
37: 10 lived, and s· up upon their feet,
40: 3 reed; and he s· in the gate.
43: 6 the house; and the man s· by me.
47: 1 of the house s· toward the east,
Da 1: 19 therefore s· they before the king.
2: 2 they came and s· before the king.
31 was excellent, s· before thee;
3: 3 and they s· before the image that
7: 10 times ten thousand s· before him:
16 near unto one of them that s· by,
8: 3 there s· before the river a ram
Da 8: 15 s· before me as the appearance of
17 So he came near where I s·: and
22 whereas four s· up for it, four
10: 11 this word unto me, I s· trembling.
16 said unto him that s· before me,
11: 1 s· to confirm and to strengthen
12: 5 behold, there s· other two, the one
Ho 10: 9 there they s·: the battle in Gibeah
Am 7: 7 the Lord s· upon a wall made by a
Ob 14 thou have s· in the crossway, to
Hab 3: 6 He s·, and measured the earth: he
11 The sun and moon s· still in their
Zec 1: 8 he s· among the myrtle trees that
10 man that s· among the myrtle trees
11 angel...s· among the myrtle trees,
3: 3 garments, and s· before the angel.
4 unto those that s· before him,
5 And the angel of the Lord s· by.
M't 2: 9 s· over where the young child was.
12: 46 mother and his brethren s· without,
13: 2 the whole multitude s· on the shore.
20: 32 And Jesus s· still, and called them,
26: 73 while came unto him they that s· by,
27: 11 And Jesus s· before the governor:
47 Some of them that s· there, when
M'r 10: 49 Jesus s· still, and commanded him
11: 5 certain of them that s· there said
14: 47 of them that s· by drew a sword,
60 the high priest s· up in the midst,
69 began to say to them that s· by,
70 they that s· by said again to Peter,
15: 35 And some of them that s· by, when
39 centurion, which s· over against
Lu 4: 16 sabbath day, and s· up for to read.
39 And he s· over her, and rebuked
5: 1 he s· by the lake of Gennesaret,
6: 8 midst. And he arose and s· forth.
17 down with them, and s· in the plain,
7: 14 and they that bare him s· still.
38 s· at his feet behind him weeping,
9: 32 and the two men that s· with him.
10: 25 behold, a certain lawyer s· up, and
17: 12 that were lepers, which s· afar off:
18: 11 Pharisee s· and prayed thus with
40 And Jesus s·, and commanded him
19: 8 And Zacchæus s·, and said unto the
24 And he said unto them that s· by,
23: 10 scribes s· and vehemently accused
35 And the people s· beholding. And
49 s· afar off, beholding these things.
24: 4 two men s· by them in shining
36 Jesus...s· in the midst of them,
Joh 1: 35 Again the next day after John s·,
6: 22 people which s· on the other side of
7: 37 Jesus s· and cried, saying, If any
11: 56 themselves, as they s· in the temple,
12: 29 The people therefore, that s· by,
18: 5 which betrayed him, s· with them.
16 But Peter s· at the door without.
18 the servants and officers s· there,
18 Peter s· with them, and warmed
22 officers which s· by struck Jesus
25 Peter s· and warmed himself.
19: 25 s· by the cross of Jesus his mother.
20: 11 Mary s· without at the sepulchre
19 came Jesus and s· in the midst, and
26 s· in the midst, and said, Peace be
21: 4 now come, Jesus s· on the shore:
Ac 1: 10 men s· by them in white apparel;
15 days Peter s· up in the midst of the
3: 8 And he leaping up s·, and walked,
4: 26 The kings of the earth s· up, and
5: 34 Then s· there up one in the council,
9: 7 journeyed with him s· speechless,
39 all the widows s· by him weeping,
10: 17 house, and s· before the gate,
30 s· before me in bright clothing,
11: 13 which s· and said unto him, Send
28 And there s· up one of them named
12: 14 told how Peter s· before the gate.
13: 16 Then Paul s· up, and beckoning
14: 20 the disciples s· round about him,
16: 9 There s· a man of Macedonia, and
17: 22 Paul s· in the midst of Mars' hill,
21: 40 Paul s· on the stairs, and beckoned
22: 13 Came unto me, and s·, and said
25 said unto the centurion that s· by,
23: 2 them that s· by him to smite him
4 And they that s· by said, Revilest
11 night following the Lord s· by him,
24: 20 in me, while I s· before the council,
25: 7 Jews...from Jerusalem s· round
18 whom when the accusers s· up, they
27: 21 Paul s· forth in the midst of them,
23 For there s· by me this night the
2Ti 4: 16 first answer no man s· with me,
17 Lord s· with me, and strengthened
Heb 9: 10 Which s· only in meats and drinks,
Re 5: 6 s· a Lamb as it had been slain,
7: 9 s· before the throne, and before the
11 angels s· round about the throne,
8: 2 seven angels which s· before God;
3 angel came and s· at the altar,
11: 1 and the angel s·, saying, Rise, and
11 them, and they s· upon their feet;
12: 4 and the dragon s· before the woman
13: 1 And I s· upon the sand of the sea,
14: 1 lo, a Lamb s· on the mount Sion,
18: 17 as many as trade by sea, s· afar off,

stoodest
Nu 22: 34 I knew not that thou s· in the way
De 4: 10 day that thou s· before the Lord
Ob 11 day that thou s· on the other side,

stool See also FOOTSTOOL; STOOLS.
2Ki 4: 10 there a bed, and a table, and a s·,

stools
Ex 1: 16 women, and see them upon the s·;

stoop See also STOOPED; STOOPETH; STOOPING.
Job 9: 13 proud helpers do s· under him.
Pr 12: 25 in the heart of man maketh it s·:
Isa 46: 2 They s·, they bow down together;
M'r 1: 7 I am not worthy to s· down and

stooped
Ge 49: 9 he s· down, he couched as a lion,
1Sa 24: 8 David s· with his face to the earth,
28: 14 he s· with his face to the ground,
2Ch 36: 17 old man, or him that s· for age:
Joh 8: 6 But Jesus s· down, and with his
8 again he s· down, and wrote on the
20: 11 she s· down, and looked into the

stoopeth
Isa 46: 1 Bel boweth down, Nebo s·, their

stooping
Lu 24: 12 and s· down, he beheld the linen
Joh 20: 5 And he s· down, and looking in, saw

stop See also STOPPED; STOPPETH.
1Ki 18: 44 down, that the rain s· thee not.
2Ki 3: 19 s· all wells of water, and mar every
2Ch 32: 3 to s· the waters of the fountains
Ps 35: 3 and s· the way against them that
107: 42 and all iniquity shall s· her mouth.
Eze 39: 11 and it shall s· the noses of the
2Co 11: 10 no man shall s· me of this boasting

stopped See also UNSTOPPED.
Ge 8: 2 the windows of heaven were s·,
26: 15 the Philistines had s· them, and
18 for the Philistines had s· them after
Le 15: 3 or his flesh be s· from his issue, it
2Ki 3: 25 and they s· all the wells of water,
2Ch 32: 4 who s· all the fountains, and the
30 s· the upper watercourse of Gihon,
Ne 4: 7 that the breaches began to be s·,
Ps 63: 11 of them that speak lies shall be s·.
Jer 51: 32 that the passages are s·, and the
Zec 7: 11 s· their ears, that they should not
Ac 7: 57 s· their ears, and ran upon him
Ro 3: 19 that every mouth may be s·, and all
Tit 1: 11 Whose mouths must be s·, who
Heb 11: 33 promises, s· the mouths of lions,

stoppeth
Job 5: 16 hope, and iniquity s· her mouth.
Ps 58: 4 like the deaf adder that s· her ear;
Pr 21: 13 Whoso s· his ears at the cry of the
Isa 33: 15 that s· his ears from hearing of blood,

store See also RESTORE; STOREHOUSE.
Ge 26: 14 of herds, and great s· of servants:
41: 36 that food shall be for s· to the land
Le 25: 22 fruits come in ye shall eat of the old s·.
26: 10 And ye shall eat old s·, and bring
De 28: 5, 17 shall be thy basket and thy s·.
32: 34 Is not this laid up in s· with me, and
1Ki 9: 19 the cities of s· that Solomon had,
10: 10 and of spices very great s·, and
2Ki 20: 17 which thy fathers have laid up in s·
1Ch 29: 16 all this s· that we have prepared
2Ch 8: 4 all the s· cities, which he built in
6 all the s· cities that Solomon had,
11: 11 s· of victual, and of oil and wine.
16: 4 and all the s· cities of Naphtali.
17: 12 in Judah castles, and cities of s·.
31: 10 that which is left is this great s·.
Ne 5: 18 in ten days s· of all sorts of wine:
Ps 144: 13 be full, affording all manner of s·:
Isa 39: 6 which thy fathers have laid up in s·
Am 3: 10 who s· up violence and robbery in
Na 2: 9 for there is none end of the s· and
1Co 16: 2 every one of you lay by him in s·,
1Ti 6: 19 Laying up in s· for themselves a
2Pe 3: 7 by the same word are kept in s·,

store-cities See STORE and CITIES.

storehouse See also STOREHOUSES.
Mal 3: 10 Bring ye all the tithes into the s·,
Lu 12: 24 which neither have s· nor barn;

storehouses
Ge 41: 56 And Joseph opened all the s·, and
De 28: 8 the blessing upon thee in thy s·,
1Ch 27: 25 and over the s· in the fields, in the
2Ch 32: 28 S· also for the increase of corn,
Ps 33: 7 heap: he layeth up the depth in s·.
Jer 50: 26 the utmost border, open her s·:

stories^
Ge 6: 16 second, and third s· shalt thou make it.
Eze 42: 3 was gallery against gallery in three s·.
6 For they were in three s·, but had not
Am 9: 6 that buildeth his s· in the heaven,

stork
Le 11: 19 the s·, the heron after her kind,
De 14: 18 And the s·, and the heron after her
Ps 104: 17 as for the s·, the fir trees are her
Jer 8: 7 the s· in the heaven knoweth her
Zec 5: 9 had wings like the wings of a s·:

storm
Job 21: 18 chaff that the s· carrieth away.
27: 21 as a s· hurleth him out of his place.
Ps 55: 8 my escape from the windy s· and
83: 15 and make them afraid with thy s·.
107: 29 He maketh the s· a calm, so that
Isa 4: 6 for a covert from s· and from rain,
25: 4 a refuge from the s·, a shadow from
4 blast...is as a s· against the wall.
28: 2 tempest of hail and a destroying s·,
29: 6 great noise, with s· and tempest,
Eze 38: 9 shalt ascend and come like a s·,

Na 1: 3 in the whirlwind and in the s',
M'r 4:37 there arose a great s' of wind, and
Lu 8:23 there came down a s' of wind on

stormy
Ps 107:25 raiseth the s' wind, which lifteth
148: 8 vapours; s' wind fulfilling his word:
Eze 13:11 fall; and a s' wind shall rend it.
13 even rend it with a s' wind in my

story See also STORIES.
2Ch 13:22 in the s' of the prophet of Iddo.
24:27 in the s' of the book of the kings.

stout See also STOUTHEARTED.
Job 4:11 the s' lion's whelps are scattered
Isa 10:12 punish the fruit of the s' heart of
Da 7:20 look was more s' than his fellows.
Mal 3:13 words have been s' against me,

stouthearted
Ps 76: 5 The s' are spoiled, they have
Isa 46:12 Hearken unto me, ye s', that

stoutness
Isa 9: 9 say in the pride and s' of heart,

straight See also STRAIGHTWAY; STRAIT.
Jos 6: 5 ascend up every man s' before him.
20 the city, every man s' before him,
1Sa 6:12 the kine took the s' way to the
2Ch 32:30 brought it s' down to the west side
Ps 5: 8 make thy way s' before my face.
Pr 4:25 let thine eyelids look s' before thee.
Ec 1:15 is crooked cannot be made s':
7:13 for who can make that s', which he
Isa 40: 3 make s' in the desert a highway
4 the crooked shall be made s', and
42:16 before them, and crooked things s'.
45: 2 and make the crooked places s':
Jer 31: 9 by the river of waters in a s' way,
Eze 1: 7 their feet were s' feet; and the sole
9 they went every one s' forward.
12 they went every one s' forward:
23 the firmament were their wings s',
10:22 they went every one s' forward.
M't 3: 3 of the Lord, make his paths s'.
M'r 1: 3 way of the Lord, make his paths s'.
Lu 3: 4 way of the Lord, make his paths s'.
5 and the crooked shall be made s',
13:13 and immediately she was made s',
Joh 1:23 Make s' the way of the Lord, as
Ac 9:11 into the street which is called S',
16:11 with a s' course to Samothracia,
21: 1 came with a s' course unto Coos,
Heb 12:13 And make s' paths for your feet,

straightly See STRAITLY.

straightway
1Sa 9:13 into the city, ye shall s' find him,
28:20 Saul fell s' all along on the earth,
Pr 7:22 He goeth after her s', as an ox
Da 10:17 s' there remained no strength in
M't 3:16 went up s' out of the water: and,
4:20 they s' left their nets, and followed
14:22 s' Jesus constrained his disciples
27 But s' Jesus spake unto them,
21: 2 s' ye shall find an ass tied, and a
3 of them; and s' he will send them.
25:15 ability; and s' took his journey.
27:48 And s' one of them ran, and took a
M'r 1:10 And s' coming up out of the water,
18 And s' they forsook their nets, and
20 And s' he called them: and they
21 s' on the sabbath day he entered
2: 2 s' many were gathered together,
3: 6 s' took counsel with the Herodians
5:29 s' the fountain of her blood was
42 s' the damsel arose, and walked;
6:25 And she came in s' with haste unto
45 And s' he constrained his disciples
54 out of the ship, s' they knew him,
7:35 And s' his ears were opened, and
8:10 s' he entered into a ship with his
9:15 s' all the people, when they beheld
20 he saw him, s' the spirit tare him;
24 s' the father of the child cried out,
11: 3 and s' he will send him hither.
14:45 he was come, he goeth s' to him,
15: 1 s' in the morning the chief priests
Lu 5:39 drunk old wine s' desireth new:
8:55 came again, and she arose s':
12:54 s' ye say, There cometh a shower;
14: 5 not s' pull him out on the sabbath
Joh 13:32 himself, and shall s' glorify him.
Ac 5:10 Then fell she down s' at his feet,
9:20 And s' he preached Christ in the
16:33 was baptized, he and all his, s'.
22:29 Then s' they departed from him
23:30 man, I sent s' to thee, and gave
Jas 1:24 s' forgetteth what manner of man

strain See also RESTRAIN.
M't 23:24 blind guides, which s' at a gnat,

strait See also STRAIGHT; STRAITEST; STRAITS.
1Sa 13: 6 Israel saw that they were in a s',
2Sa 24:14 said unto Gad, I am in a great s':
2Ki 6: 1 dwell with thee is too s' for us.
1Ch 21:13 said unto Gad, I am in a great s':
Job 36:16 remove thee out of the s' into a
Isa 49:20 ears, The place is too s' for me:
M't 7:13 Enter ye in at the s' gate: for wide
14 s' is the gate, and narrow is the
Lu 13:24 Strive to enter in at the s' gate:
Ph'p 1:23 For I am in a s' betwixt two,

straiten See also STRAITENED; STRAITENETH.
Jer 19: 9 that seek their lives, shall s' them.

straitened
Job 18: 7 steps of his strength shall be s',
37:10 the breadth of the waters is s'.
Pr 4:12 goest, thy steps shall not be s';
Eze 42: 6 the building was s' more than the
Mic 2: 7 Jacob, is the spirit of the Lord s'?
Lu 12:50 am I s' till it be accomplished!
2Co 6:12 Ye are not s' in us, but ye are
12 but ye are s' in your own bowels.

straiteneth
Job 12:23 the nations, and s' them again.

straitest
Ac 26: 5 that after the most s' sect of our

straitly
Ge 43: 7 The man asked us s' of our state,
Ex 13:19 had s' sworn the children of Israel,
Jos 6: 1 Jericho was s' shut up because
1Sa 14:28 Thy father s' charged the people
M't 9:30 Jesus s' charged them, saying, See
M'r 1:43 he s' charged him, and forthwith sent
3:12 And he s' charged them that they
5:43 he charged them s' that no man
Lu 9:21 he s' charged them, and commanded
Ac 4:17 let us s' threaten them, that they
5:28 Did not we s' command you that ye

straitness
De 28:53, 55 in the siege, and in the s',
57 things secretly in the siege and s',
Job 36:16 broad place, where there is no s';
Jer 19: 9 of his friend in the siege and s',

straits
Job 20:22 of his sufficiency he shall be in s':
La 1: 3 overtook her between the s'.

strake See also STRAKES; STRUCK.
Ac 27:17 s' sail, and so were driven.

strakes
Ge 30:37 and pilled white s' in them, and
Le 14:37 walls of the house with hollow s',

strange See also ESTRANGED; STRANGER.
Ge 35: 2 Put away the s' gods...among you,
4 gave unto Jacob all the s' gods
42: 7 but made himself s' unto them,
Ex 2:22 I have been a stranger in a s' land.
18: 3 I have been an alien in a s' land:
21: 8 to sell her unto a s' nation he shall
30: 9 Ye shall offer no s' incense
Le 10: 1 and offered s' fire before the Lord,
Nu 3: 4 they offered s' fire before the Lord,
26:61 they offered s' fire before the Lord.
De 32:12 and there was no s' god with him.
16 him to jealousy with s' gods,
Jos 24:20 the Lord, and serve s' gods, then
23 the s' gods which are among you,
J'g 10:16 put away the s' gods from among
11: 2 thou art the son of a s' woman.
1Sa 7: 3 then put away the s' gods and
1Ki 11: 1 Solomon loved many s' women,
8 likewise did he for all his s' wives,
2Ki 19:24 have digged and drunk s' waters,
2Ch 14: 3 away the altars of the s' gods,
33:15 he took away the s' gods, and the
Ezr 10: 2 have taken s' wives of the people
10 and have taken s' wives, to increase
11 of the land, and from the s' wives.
14 all them which have taken s' wives
17 all the men that had taken s' wives
18 found that had taken s' wives:
44 All these had taken s' wives: and
Ne 13:27 transgress...in marrying s' wives?
Job 19: 3 that ye make yourselves s' to me.
17 My breath is s' to my wife,
31: 3 a s' punishment to the workers
Ps 44:20 stretched out...hands to a s' god;
81: 9 There shall no s' god be in thee;
9 shalt thou worship any s' god.
114: 1 Jacob from a people of s' language;
137: 4 sing the Lord's song in a s' land?
144: 7 from the hand of s' children;
Pr 2:16 deliver thee from the s' woman,
5: 3 the lips of a s' woman drop as an
20 son, be ravished with a s' woman,
6:24 of the tongue of a s' woman.
7: 5 keep thee from the s' woman,
20:16 a pledge of him for a s' woman.
21: 8 way of man is froward and s':
22:14 mouth of s' women is a deep pit:
23:27 and a s' woman is a narrow pit.
33 Thine eyes shall behold s' women,
27:13 a pledge of him for a s' woman.
Isa 17:10 and shalt set it with s' slips:
28:21 he may do his work, his s' work;
21 bring to pass his act, his s' act.
43:12 there was no s' god among you:
Jer 2:21 the degenerate plant of a s' vine
5:19 and served s' gods in your land,
8:19 images, and with s' vanities?
Eze 3: 5 not sent to a people of a s' speech
6 Not to many people of a s' speech
Da 11:39 most strong holds with a s' god,
Ho 5: 7 they have begotten s' children:
8:12 they were counted as a s' thing.
Zep 1: 8 as are clothed with s' apparel.
Mal 2:11 married the daughter of a s' god.
Lu 5:26 We have seen s' things to day.
Ac 7: 6 seed should sojourn in a s' land;
17:18 to be a setter forth of s' gods:
20 certain s' things to our ears:
26:11 I persecuted them...unto s' cities.
Heb 11: 9 land of promise, as in a s' country,
13: 9 about with divers and s' doctrines.
1Pe 4: 4 think it s'...ye run not with them
12 think it not s' concerning the fiery
1Pe 4:12 some s' thing happened unto you:
Jude 7 and going after s' flesh, are set

strangely
De 32:27 should behave themselves s',

stranger See also STRANGER'S; STRANGERS.
Ge 15:13 be a s' in a land that is not theirs,
17: 8 the land wherein thou art a s',
12 bought with money of any s',
27 bought with money of the s',
23: 4 I am a s' and a sojourner with you:
28: 4 the land wherein thou art a s',
37: 1 land wherein his father was a s',
Ex 2:22 I have been a s' in a strange land.
12:19 whether he be a s', or born in the
43 There shall no s' eat thereof:
48 when a s' shall sojourn with thee,
49 the s' that sojourneth among you.
20:10 nor thy s' that is within thy gates:
22:21 Thou shalt neither vex a s', nor
23: 9 Also thou shalt not oppress a s':
9 for ye know the heart of a s', seeing
12 son of thy handmaid, and the s',
29:33 but a s' shall not eat thereof,
30:33 putteth any of it upon a s',
Le 16:29 a s' that sojourneth among you:
17:12 any s' that sojourneth among you
15 be one of your own country, or a s',
18:26 any s' that sojourneth among you:
19:10 shalt leave them for the poor and s':
33 if a s' sojourn with thee in your land,
34 But the s' that dwelleth with you
22:10 There shall no s' eat of the holy
12 daughter...married unto a s',
13 but there shall no s' eat thereof.
23:22 them unto the poor, and the s':
24:16 as well the s', as he that is born in
22 as well for the s', as for one of your
25: 6 thy s' that sojourneth with thee,
35 though he be a s', or a sojourner;
47 sojourner or s' wax rich by thee,
47 and sell himself unto the s' or
Nu 1:51 s' that cometh nigh shall be put
3:10, 38 s' that cometh nigh shall be put
9:14 if a s' shall sojourn among you,
14 for the s', and for him that was born
15:14 And if a s' sojourn with you, or
15 for the s' that sojourneth with you,
15 so shall the s' be before the Lord.
16 for the s' that sojourneth with you.
26 the s' that sojourneth among them;
29 the s' that sojourneth among them.
30 he be born in the land, or a s',
16:40 no s', which is not of the seed
18: 4 a s' shall not come nigh unto you.
7 the s' that cometh nigh shall be put
19:10 s' that sojourneth among them,
35:15 children of Israel, and for the s',
De 1:16 brother, and the s' that is with him.
5:14 nor thy s' that is within thy gates;
10:18 and loveth the s', in giving him food
19 Love ye therefore the s': for ye
14:21 shalt give it unto the s' that is in thy
29 and the s', and the fatherless, and
16:11, 14 the s', and the fatherless, and
17:15 mayest not set a s' over thee,
23: 7 because thou wast a s' in his land.
20 Unto a s' thou mayest lend upon
24:17 not pervert the judgment of the s',
19, 20, 21 it shall be for the s', for the
25: 5 not marry without unto a s':
26:11 and the s' that is among you.
12 s', the fatherless, and the widow,
13 unto the s', to the fatherless, and to
27:19 perverteth the judgment of the s',
28:43 The s' that is within thee shall get
29:11 and thy s' that is in thy camp,
22 the s' that shall come from a far
31:12 and thy s' that is within thy gates,
Jos 8:33 as well the s', as he that was born
20: 9 for the s' that sojourneth among
J'g 19:12 aside hither into the city of a s',
Ru 2:10 knowledge of me, seeing I am a s'?
2Sa 1:13 answered, I am the son of a s',
15:19 thou art a s', and also an exile.
1Ki 3:18 was no s' with us in the house,
8:41 Moreover concerning a s', that is
43 all that the s' calleth to thee for:
2Ch 6:32 Moreover concerning the s', which
33 to all that the s' calleth to thee for;
Job 15:19 and no s' passed among them.
19:15 and my maids, count me for a s':
31:32 The s' did not lodge in the street:
Ps 39:12 I am a s' with thee, and a sojourner
69: 8 I am...a s' unto my brethren,
94: 6 They slay the widow and the s',
119:19 I am a s' in the earth: hide not thy
Pr 2:16 from the s' which flattereth with
5:10 thy labours be in the house of a s';
20 and embrace the bosom of a s'?
6: 1 hast stricken thy hand with a s',
7: 5 from the s' which flattereth with
11:15 that is surety for a s' shall smart
14:10 a s' doth not intermeddle with his
20:16 his garment that is surety for a s':
27: 2 a s', and not thine own lips.
13 his garment that is surety for a s'.
Ec 6: 2 eat thereof, but a s' eateth it:
Isa 56: 3 Neither let the son of the s', that
6 Also the sons of the s', that join
62: 8 the sons of the s' shall not drink
Jer 7: 6 If ye oppress not the s', the
14: 8 thou be as a s' in the land, and
22: 3 no wrong, do no violence to the s'.
Eze 14: 7 the s' that sojourneth in Israel,

Eze 22: 7 dealt by oppression with the s':
29 have oppressed the s' wrongfully.
44: 9 s', uncircumcised in heart,
9 of any s' that is among the
47: 23 in what tribe the s' sojourneth,
Ob 12 in the day that he became a s';
Zec 7: 10 widow, nor the fatherless, the s',
Mal 3: 5 turn aside the s' from his right,
M't 25: 35 I was a s', and ye took me in:
38 When saw we thee a s', and took
43 I was a s', and ye took me not in:
44 or a s', or naked, or sick, or in
Lu 17: 18 to give glory to God, save this s'.
24: 18 Art thou only a s' in Jerusalem,
Joh 10: 5 And a s' will they not follow, but
Ac 7: 29 was a s' in the land of Madian,

stranger's
Le 22: 25 Neither from a s' hand shall
25: 47 or to the stock of the s' family:

strangers See also STRANGERS'.
Ge 31: 15 Are we not counted of him s'? for
36: 7 and the land wherein they were s'
Ex 6: 4 pilgrimage, wherein they were s'.
22: 21 for ye were s' in the land of Egypt.
23: 9 ye were s' in the land of Egypt.
Le 17: 8, 10, 13 s' which sojourn among you,
19: 34 for ye were s' in the land of Egypt:
20: 2 of the s' that sojourn in Israel, that
22: 18 house of Israel, or of the s' in Israel,
25: 23 ye are s' and sojourners with me.
45 the s' that do sojourn among you,
De 10: 19 ye were s' in the land of Egypt.
24: 14 thy s' that are in thy land within
31: 16 after the gods of the s' of the land,
Jos 8: 35 s' that were conversant among
2Sa 22: 45 S' shall submit themselves
46 S' shall fade away, and they
1Ch 16: 19 but few, even a few, and s' in it.
22: 2 to gather together the s' that
29: 15 For we are s' before thee, and
2Ch 2: 17 Solomon numbered all the s'
15: 9 the s' with them out of Ephraim
30: 25 the s' that came out of the land of
Ne 9: 2 Israel separated...from all s',
13: 30 Thus cleansed I them from all s',
Ps 18: 44 s' shall submit themselves
45 The s' shall fade away, and be
54: 3 For s' are risen up against me,
105: 12 yea, very few, and s' in it.
109: 11 and let the s' spoil his labour.
146: 9 The Lord preserveth the s'; he
Pr 5: 10 Lest s' be filled with thy wealth;
Isa 1: 7 land, s' devour it in your presence,
7 it is desolate, as overthrown by s'.
2: 6 themselves in the children of s'.
5: 17 places of the fat ones shall s' eat.
14: 1 the s' shall be joined with them,
25: 2 a palace of s' to be no city; it
5 shalt bring down the noise of s', as
29: 5 multitude of thy s'...be like...dust,
60: 10 sons of s' shall build up thy walls,
61: 5 s' shall stand and feed your flocks,
Jer 2: 25 for I have loved s', and after them
3: 13 hast scattered thy ways to the s'
5: 19 so shall ye serve s' in a land that
30: 8 s' shall no more serve themselves
35: 7 days in the land where ye be s'.
51: 51 s' are come into the sanctuaries
La 5: 2 Our inheritance is turned to s', our
Eze 7: 21 into the hands of the s' for a prey,
11: 9 and deliver you into the hands of s',
16: 32 taketh s' instead of her husband!
28: 7 therefore I will bring s' upon thee,
10 uncircumcised by the hand of s':
30: 12 that is therein, by the hand of s':
31: 12 And s', the terrible of the nations,
44: 7 brought into my sanctuary s',
47: 22 to the s' that sojourn among you,
Hos 7: 9 S' have devoured his strength,
8: 7 it yield, the s' shall swallow it up.
Joe 3: 17 shall no s' pass through her any
Ob 11 s' carried away captive his forces,
M't 17: 25 of their own children, or of s'?
26 Peter saith unto him, Of s'. Jesus
27: 7 the potter's field, to bury s' in.
Joh 10: 5 for they know not the voice of s'
Ac 2: 10 s' of Rome, Jews and proselytes,
13: 17 dwelt as s' in...land of Egypt,
17: 21 s' which were there spent their
Eph 2: 12 s' from the covenants of promise,
19 ye are no more s' and foreigners,
1Ti 5: 10 up children, if she have lodged s',
Heb 11: 13 confessed that they were s' and
13: 2 Be not forgetful to entertain s':
1Pe 1: 1 to the s' scattered throughout
2: 11 I beseech you as s' and pilgrims,
3Jo 5 doest to the brethren, and to s';

strangers'
Pr 5: 17 thine own, and not s' with thee.

strangled
Na 2: 12 whelps, and s' for his lionesses,
Ac 15: 20 fornication, and from things s',
29 and from blood, and from things s',
21: 25 and from s', and from fornication.

strangling
Job 7: 15 So that my soul chooseth s', and

straw See also STRAWED.
Ge 24: 25 We have both s' and provender
32 s' and provender for the camels,
Ex 5: 7 give the people s' to make brick,
7 go and gather s' for themselves.
10 Pharaoh, I will not give you s'.
Ex 5: 11 get you s' where ye can find it: yet
12 to gather stubble instead of s'.
13 daily tasks, as when there was s'.
16 is no s' given unto thy servants,
18 for there shall no s' be given you,
J'g 19: 19 Yet there is both s' and provender
1Ki 4: 28 Barley also and s' for the horses
Job 41: 27 He esteemeth iron as s', and brass
Isa 11: 7 and the lion shall eat s' like the ox.
25: 10 even as s' is trodden down for the
65: 25 lion shall eat s' like the bullock:

strawed See also STROWED.
Ex 32: 20 powder, and s' it upon the water,
M't 21: 8 the trees, and s' them in the way.
25: 24 gathering where thou hast not s':
26 and gather where I have not s':
M'r 11: 8 the trees, and s' them in the way.

stray See ASTRAY.

streaked See STRAKED.

streaks See STRAKES.

stream See also STREAMS.
Nu 21: 15 at the s' of the brooks that goeth
Job 6: 15 as the s' of brooks they pass away;
Ps 124: 4 us, the s' had gone over our soul:
Isa 27: 12 of the river unto the s' of Egypt,
30: 28 his breath, as an overflowing s',
33 like a s' of brimstone, doth kindle
57: 6 Among the smooth stones of the s'
66: 12 of the Gentiles like a flowing s':
Da 7: 10 A fiery s' issued and came forth
Am 5: 24 and righteousness as a mighty s'.
Lu 6: 48 the s' beat vehemently upon that
49 against which the s' did beat

streams
Ex 7: 19 the waters of Egypt, upon their s',
8: 5 thine hand with thy rod over the s',
Ps 46: 4 the s' whereof shall make glad the
78: 16 He brought s' also out of the rock,
20 gushed out, and the s' overflowed;
126: 4 O Lord, as the s' in the south.
Ca 4: 15 waters, and s' from Lebanon.
Isa 11: 15 and shall smite it in the seven s',
30: 25 rivers and s' of waters in the day
33: 21 us a place of broad rivers and s';
34: 9 the s' thereof shall be turned into
35: 6 break out, and s' in the desert.

street See also STREETS.
Ge 19: 2 we will abide in the s' all night.
De 13: 16 of it into the midst of the s' thereof,
Jos 2: 19 the doors of thy house into the s',
J'g 19: 15 he sat him down in a s' of the city:
17 wayfaring man in the s' of the city:
20 upon me; only lodge not in the s'.
2Sa 21: 12 them from the s' of Beth-shan,
22: 43 stamp them as the mire of the s',
2Ch 29: 4 them together into the east s',
32: 6 him in the s' of the gate of the city,
Ezr 10: 9 sat in the s' of the house of God,
Ne 8: 1 s' that was before the water gate;
3 s' that was before the water gate
16 and in the s' of the water gate, and
16 in the s' of the gate of Ephraim.
Es 4: 6 to Mordecai unto the s' of the city,
6: 9, 11 horseback through the s' of the
Job 18: 17 shall have no name in the s'.
29: 7 when I prepared my seat in the s'!
31: 32 stranger did not lodge in the s':
Pr 7: 8 through the s' near her corner;
Isa 42: 2 his voice to be heard in the s'.
51: 23 as the s', to them that went over.
59: 14 truth is fallen in the s', and equity
Jer 37: 21 piece of bread out of the bakers' s',
La 2: 19 for hunger in the top of every s'.
4: 1 poured out in the top of every s'.
Eze 16: 24 thee an high place in every s'.
31 makest thine high place in every s';
Da 9: 25 the s' shall be built again, and the
Ac 9: 11 the s' which is called Straight,
12: 10 out, and passed on through one s';
Re 11: 8 dead bodies shall lie in the s' of
21: 21 the s' of the city was pure gold, as it
22: 2 In the midst of the s' of it, and on

streets
2Sa 1: 20 publish it not in the s' of Askelon;
1Ki 20: 34 shalt make s' for thee in Damascus,
Ps 18: 42 cast them out as the dirt in the s'.
55: 11 and guile depart not from her s'.
144: 13 and ten thousands in our s':
14 there be no complaining in our s'.
Pr 1: 20 she uttereth her voice in the s':
5: 16 abroad, and rivers of waters in the s'.
7: 12 Now is she without, now in the s',
22: 13 without, I shall be slain in the s'.
26: 13 a lion in the way; a lion is in the s'.
Ec 12: 4 the doors shall be shut in the s',
5 and the mourners go about the s':
Ca 3: 2 now, and go about the city in the s',
Isa 5: 25 were torn in the midst of the s'.
10: 6 them down like the mire of the s'.
15: 3 In their s' they shall gird themselves
3 in their s', every one shall howl,
24: 11 is a crying for wine in the s'; all
51: 20 they lie at the head of all the s', as
Jer 5: 1 and fro through the s' of Jerusalem,
7: 17 of Judah and in the s' of Jerusalem?
34 from the s' of Jerusalem, the voice
9: 21 and the young men from the s'.
11: 6 Judah, and in the s' of Jerusalem,
13 the number of the s' of Jerusalem
14: 16 be cast out in the s' of Jerusalem
33: 10 Judah, and in the s' of Jerusalem,
44: 6 of Judah and in the s' of Jerusalem;
9 Judah, and in the s' of Jerusalem?
Jer 44: 17 Judah, and in the s' of Jerusalem:
21 Judah, and in the s' of Jerusalem,
48: 38 of Moab, and in the s' thereof:
49: 26 her young men shall fall in her s',
50: 30 shall her young men fall in the s',
51: 4 that are thrust through in her s'.
La 2: 11 and the sucklings swoon in the s'
12 swooned as the wounded in the s'
21 the old lie on the ground in the s':
4: 5 delicately are desolate in the s':
8 they are not known in the s':
14 wandered as blind men in the s',
18 steps, that we cannot go in our s':
Eze 7: 19 shall cast their silver in the s',
11: 6 filled the s' thereof with the slain.
26: 11 shall he tread down all thy s':
28: 23 pestilence, and blood into her s';
Am 5: 16 Wailing shall be in all the s';
Mic 7: 10 trodden down as the mire of the s'.
Na 2: 4 The chariots shall rage in the s',
3: 10 dashed in pieces at...top of...the s':
Zep 3: 6 I made their s' waste, that none
Zec 8: 4 and old women dwell in the s' of
5 s' of the city shall be full of boys
5 and girls playing in the s' thereof.
9: 3 and fine gold as the mire of the s'.
10: 5 in the mire of the s' in the battle:
M't 6: 2 in the synagogues and in the s',
5 and in the corners of the s',
12: 19 any man hear his voice in the s'.
M'r 6: 56 they laid the sick in the s', and
Lu 10: 10 go your ways out into the s' of
13: 26 and thou hast taught in our s'.
14: 21 Go out quickly into the s' and lanes
Ac 5: 15 brought forth the sick into the s',

strength
Ge 4: 12 shall not...yield unto thee her s';
49: 3 might, and the beginning of my s',
24 But his bow abode in s', and the
Ex 13: 3 by s' of hand the Lord brought you
14 By s' of hand the Lord brought us
16 by s' of hand the Lord brought us
14: 27 sea returned to his s' when the
15: 2 The Lord is my s' and song, and
13 thou hast guided them in thy s'
Le 26: 20 And your s' shall be spent in vain:
Nu 23: 22 hath as it were the s' of an unicorn.
24: 8 hath as it were the s' of an unicorn:
De 21: 17 for he is the beginning of his s';
33: 25 and as thy days, so shall thy s' be.
Jos 11: 13 cities that stood still in their s',
14: 11 s' was then, even so is my s' now,
J'g 5: 21 soul, thou hast trodden down s'.
8: 21 for as the man is, so is his s'.
16: 5 and see wherein his great s' lieth,
6 Tell me,...wherein thy great s' lieth,
9 the fire. So his s' was not known.
15 told me wherein thy great s' lieth.
17 shaven, then my s' will go from me,
19 him, and his s' went from him.
1Sa 2: 4 that stumbled are girded with s'.
9 for by s' shall no man prevail.
10 and he shall give s' unto his king,
15: 29 the S' of Israel will not lie nor
28: 20 and there was no s' in him; for he
22 and eat, that thou mayest have s',
2Sa 22: 33 God is my s' and power: and he
40 hast girded me with s' to battle:
1Ki 19: 8 and went in the s' of that meat
2Ki 9: 24 Jehu drew a bow with his full s',
18: 20 I have counsel and s' for the war.
19: 3 and there is not s' to bring forth.
1Ch 16: 11 Seek the Lord and his s', seek his
27 s' and gladness are in his place.
28 give unto the Lord glory and s'.
26: 8 able men for s' for the service,
29: 12 make great, and to give s' unto all.
2Ch 6: 41 place, thou, and the ark of thy s':
13: 20 Neither did Jeroboam recover s'
Ne 4: 10 The s' of the bearers of burdens
8: 10 for the joy of the Lord is your s'.
Job 6: 11 What is my s', that I should hope?
12 Is my s' the s' of stones? or is my
9: 4 is wise in heart, and mighty in s':
19 If I speak of s', lo, he is strong:
12: 13 With him is wisdom and s', he
16 With him is s' and wisdom: the
21 weakeneth the s' of the mighty.
18: 7 steps of his s' shall be straitened,
12 His s' shall be hungerbitten, and
13 It shall devour the s' of his skin:
13 firstborn of death shall devour his s'.
21: 23 One dieth in his full s', being
23: 6 power? No; but he would put s' in me.
26: 2 savest...the arm that hath no s'?
30: 2 the s' of their hands profit me,
36: 5 he is mighty in s' and wisdom.
19 no, not gold, nor all the forces of s'.
37: 6 and to the great rain of his s'.
39: 11 trust him, because his s' is great?
19 Hast thou given the horse s'?
21 the valley, and rejoiceth in his s':
40: 16 his s' is in his loins, and his force
41: 22 In his neck remaineth s', and
Ps 8: 2 sucklings hast thou ordained s'
18: 1 I will love thee, O Lord, my s'.
2 my God, my s', in whom I will
32 It is God that girded me with s',
39 For thou hast girded me with s',
19: 14 O Lord, my s', and my redeemer.
20: 6 with...saving s' of his right hand.
21: 1 king shall joy in thy s', O Lord;
13 Be...exalted, Lord, in thine own s':
22: 15 My s' is dried up like a potsherd;
19 O my s', haste thee to help me.

Ps 27: 1 Lord is the s' of my life; of whom
28: 7 The Lord is my s' and my shield;
8 The Lord is their s', and he is the
8 is the saving s' of his anointed.
29: 1 give unto the Lord glory and s'.
11 Lord will give s' unto his people;
31: 4 privily for me: for thou art my s'.
10 my s' faileth because of mine
33: 16 man is not delivered by much s'.
17 he deliver any by his great s'.
37: 39 is their s' in the time of trouble.
38: 10 heart panteth, my s' faileth me:
39: 13 O spare me, that I may recover s',
43: 2 For thou art the God of my s':
46: 1 God is our refuge and s', a very
52: 7 the man that made not God his s':
54: 1 thy name, and judge me by thy s'.
59: 9 Because of his s' will I wait upon
17 Unto thee, O my s', will I sing: for
60: 7 Ephraim...is the s' of mine head;
62: 7 the rock of my s', and my refuge,
65: 6 by...s' setteth fast the mountains;
68: 28 Thy God hath commanded thy s':
34 Ascribe ye s' unto God: his
34 Israel, and his s' is in the clouds.
35 that giveth s'...unto his people.
71: 9 forsake me not when my s' faileth.
16 I will go in the s' of the Lord God:
18 I have shewed thy s' unto this
73: 4 in their death: but their s' is firm.
26 but God is the s' of my heart, and
74: 13 Thou didst divide the sea by thy s':
77: 14 declared thy s' among the people.
78: 4 the praises of the Lord, and his s',
51 chief of their s' in the tabernacles
61 And delivered his s' into captivity.
80: 2 and Manasseh stir up my s',
81: 1 Sing aloud unto God our s': make
84: 5 is the man whose s' is in thee;
7 They go from s' to s', every one of
86: 16 give thy s' unto thy servant, and
88: 4 pit: I am as a man that hath no s':
89: 17 For thou art the glory of their s':
90: 10 by reason of s' they be fourscore
10 yet is their s' labour and sorrow;
93: 1 the Lord is clothed with s',
95: 4 the s' of the hills is his also.
96: 6 s' and beauty are in his sanctuary.
7 give unto the Lord glory and s'.
99: 4 The king's s' also loveth judgment;
102: 23 He weakened my s' in the way; he
103: 20 ye his angels, that excel in s', that
105: 4 Seek the Lord, and his s': seek his
36 their land, the chief of all their s'.
108: 8 Ephraim...is the s' of mine head;
110: 2 send the rod of thy s' out of Zion:
118: 14 The Lord is my s' and song, and is
132: 8 thy rest; thou, and the ark of thy s'.
138: 3 strengthenedst...with s' in my soul.
140: 7 the Lord, the s' of my salvation,
144: 1 Blessed be the Lord my s', which
147: 10 delighteth not in...s' of the horse:
Pr 8: 14 I am understanding; I have s'.
10: 29 The way of the Lord is s' to the
14: 4 increase is by the s' of the ox.
20: 29 glory of young men is their s':
21: 22 and casteth down the s' of the
24: 5 a man of knowledge increaseth s'.
10 day of adversity, thy s' is small.
31: 3 Give not thy s' unto women, nor
17 She girdeth her loins with s', and
25 S' and honour are her clothing;
Ec 9: 16 said I, Wisdom is better than s':
10: 10 edge, then must he put to more s':
17 princes eat in due season, for s',
Isa 5: 22 men of s' to mingle strong drink:
10: 13 By the s' of my hand I have done
12: 2 Jehovah is my s' and my song;
17: 10 been mindful of the rock of thy s',
23: 4 hath spoken, even the s' of the sea,
10 of Tarshish: there is no more s'.
14 Tarshish: for your s' is laid waste.
25: 4 For thou hast been a s' to the poor,
4 a s' to the needy in his distress,
26: 4 Lord Jehovah is everlasting s':
27: 5 Or let him take hold of my s',
28: 6 for s' to them that turn the battle
30: 2 themselves in the s' of Pharaoh,
3 the s' of Pharaoh be your shame,
7 I cried...Their s' is to sit still.
15 and in confidence shall be your s':
33: 6 of thy times, and s' of salvation:
36: 5 I have counsel and s' for war:
37: 3 and there is not s' to bring forth.
40: 9 tidings, lift up thy voice with s';
29 have no might he increaseth s'.
31 the Lord shall renew their s';
41: 1 and let the people renew their s':
42: 25 of his anger, and the s' of battle:
44: 12 worketh it with the s' of his arms:
12 yea, he is hungry, and his s' faileth:
45: 24 Lord have I righteousness and s':
49: 4 I have spent my s' for nought, and
5 Lord, and my God shall be my s'.
51: 9 awake, put on s', O arm of the Lord,
52: 1 awake; put on thy s', O Zion;
62: 8 hand, and by the arm of his s',
63: 1 travelling in...greatness of his s'?
6 bring down their s' to the earth.
15 where is thy zeal and thy s', the
Jer 16: 19 O Lord, my s', and my fortress,
20: 5 I will deliver all the s' of this city,
51: 53 should fortify the height of her s',
La 1: 6 they are gone without s' before
14 he hath made my s' to fall, the
3: 18 My s' and my hope is perished

Eze 24: 21 excellency of your s', the desire
25 when I take from them their s',
30: 15 my fury upon Sin, the s' of Egypt;
18 pomp of her s' shall cease in her:
33: 28 and the pomp of her s' shall cease;
Da 2: 37 thee a kingdom, power, and s',
41 shall be in it of the s' of the iron,
10: 8 and there remained no s' in me:
8 corruption, and I retained no s'.
16 upon me, and I have retained no s'.
17 there remained no s' in me, neither
11: 2 by his s' through his riches he
15 neither shall there be any s' to
17 to enter with the s' of his whole
31 shall pollute the sanctuary of s',
Ho 7: 9 Strangers have devoured his s',
12: 3 by his s' he had power with God:
Joe 2: 22 tree and the vine do yield their s'.
3: 16 the s' of the children of Israel.
Am 3: 11 shall bring down thy s' from thee,
6: 13 taken to us horns by our own s'?
Mic 5: 4 and feed in the s' of the Lord,
Na 3: 9 Ethiopia and Egypt were her s',
11 seek s' because of the enemy.
Hab 3: 19 The Lord God is my s', and he will
Hag 2: 22 destroy the s' of the kingdoms of
Zec 12: 5 shall be my s' in the Lord of hosts
M'r 12: 30 all thy mind, and with all thy s':
33 all the soul, and with all the s',
Lu 1: 51 He hath shewed s' with his arm;
10: 27 all thy soul, and with all thy s',
Ac 3: 7 feet and ancle bones received s'.
9: 22 But Saul increased the more in s',
Ro 5: 6 For when we were yet without s',
1Co 15: 56 is sin; and the s' of sin is the law.
2Co 1: 8 pressed out of measure, above s',
12: 9 s' is made perfect in weakness.
Heb 9: 17 of no s' at all while the testator
11: 11 Sara...received s' to conceive seed,
Re 1: 16 was as the sun shineth in his s'.
3: 8 thou hast a little s', and hast kept
5: 12 and riches, and wisdom, and s',
12: 10 Now is come salvation, and s', and
17: 13 their power and s' unto the beast.

strengthen See also STRENGTHENED; STRENGTHENETH; STRENGTHENING.
De 3: 28 and encourage him, and s' him:
J'g 16: 28 s' me, I pray thee, only this once,
1Ki 20: 22 Go, s' thyself, and mark, and see
Ezr 6: 22 to s' their hands in the work of the
Ne 6: 9 therefore, O God, s' my hands.
Job 16: 5 I would s' you with my mouth, and
Ps 20: 2 sanctuary, and s' thee out of Zion;
27: 14 and he shall s' thine heart:
31: 24 courage, and he shall s' your heart.
41: 3 Lord will s' him upon the bed of
68: 28 s', O God, that which thou hast
89: 21 mine arm also shall s' him.
119: 28 s'...me according unto thy word.
Isa 22: 21 robe, and s' him with thy girdle,
30: 2 to s'...in the strength of Pharaoh,
33: 23 they could not well s' their mast,
35: 3 S' ye the weak hands, and confirm
41: 10 I will s' thee; yea, I will help thee;
54: 2 thy cords, and s' thy stakes;
Jer 23: 14 they s' also the hands of evildoers,
Eze 7: 13 s' himself in the iniquity of his life.
16: 49 s' the hand of the poor and needy.
30: 24 s' the arms of the king of Babylon,
25 s' the arms of the king of Babylon,
34: 16 and will s' that which was sick:
Da 11: 1 I, stood to confirm and to s' him.
Am 2: 14 and the strong shall not s' his force,
Zec 10: 6 And I will s' the house of Judah,
12 And I will s' them in the Lord;
Lu 22: 32 art converted, s' thy brethren.
1Pe 5: 10 perfect, stablish, s', settle you.
Re 3: 2 and s' the things which remain,

strengthened See also STRENGTHENEDST.
Ge 48: 2 Israel s' himself, and sat upon
J'g 3: 12 Lord s' Eglon the king of Moab
7: 11 shall thine hands be s' to go down
1Sa 23: 16 the wood, and s' his hand in God.
2Sa 2: 7 Therefore now let your hands be s',
1Ch 11: 10 s' themselves...in his kingdom,
2Ch 1: 1 Solomon...was s' in his kingdom,
11: 17 So they s' the kingdom of Judah,
12: 1 the kingdom, and had s' himself,
13 So king Rehoboam s' himself in
13: 7 s' themselves against Rehoboam
17: 1 and s' himself against Israel.
21: 4 s' himself, and slew all his brethren
23: 1 seventh year Jehoiada s' himself,
24: 13 house of God in his state, and s' it.
25: 11 Amaziah s' himself, and led forth
26: 8 for he s' himself exceedingly.
28: 20 and distressed him, but s' him not.
32: 5 Also he s' himself, and built up all
Ezr 1: 6 s' their hands with vessels of silver,
7: 28 I was s' as the hand of the Lord my
Ne 2: 18 s' their hands for this good work.
Job 4: 3 and thou hast s' the weak hands.
4 and thou hast s' the feeble knees.
Ps 52: 7 and s' himself in his wickedness.
147: 13 he hath s' the bars of thy gates;
Pr 8: 28 he s' the fountains of the deep:
Eze 13: 22 and s' the hands of the wicked,
34: 4 The diseased have ye not s', neither
Da 10: 18 appearance of a man, and he s' me,
19 he had spoken unto me, I was s',
19 my lord speak; for thou hast s' me.
11: 6 and he that s' her in these times.
12 but he shall not be s' by it.
Ho 7: 15 I have bound and s' their arms,
Ac 9: 19 he had received meat, he was s'.

Eph 3: 16 to be s' with might by his Spirit
Col 1: 11 S' with all might, according to his
2Ti 4: 17 Lord stood with me, and s' me;

strengthenedst
Ps 138: 3 s' me with strength in my soul.

strengtheneth
Job 15: 25 s' himself against the Almighty.
Ps 104: 15 and bread which s' man's heart.
Pr 31: 17 with strength, and s' her arms.
Ec 7: 19 Wisdom s' the wise more than ten
Isa 44: 14 the oak, which he s' for himself
Am 5: 9 s' the spoiled against the strong,
Ph'p 4: 13 things through Christ which s' me.

strengthening
Lu 22: 43 an angel...from heaven, s' him.
Ac 18: 23 in order, s' all the disciples.

stress See DISTRESS.

stretch See also STRETCHED; STRETCHEST; STRETCHETH; STRETCHING.
Ex 3: 20 s' out my hand, and smite Egypt
7: 5 I s' forth mine hand upon Egypt,
19 s' out thine hand upon the waters
8: 5 S' forth thine hand with thy rod
16 S' out thy rod, and smite the dust
9: 15 For now I will s' out my hand, that
22 S'...thine hand toward heaven,
10: 12 S' out thine hand over...Egypt
21 S' out thine hand toward heaven,
14: 16 and s' out thine hand over the sea,
26 S' out thine hand over the sea, that
25: 20 cherubims...s' forth their wings
Jos 8: 18 S' out the spear that is in thy
1Sa 24: 6 to s' forth mine hand against him,
26: 9 s' forth his hand against the Lord's
11, 23 s'...mine hand against the Lord's
2Sa 1: 14 not afraid to s' forth thine hand
2Ki 21: 13 I will s' over Jerusalem the line
Job 11: 13 s' out thine hands toward him;
30: 24 not s' out his hand to the grave,
39: 26 s' her wings toward the south?
Ps 68: 31 Ethiopia shall soon s' out her
138: 7 s'...thine hand against the wrath
143: 6 I s' forth my hands unto thee:
Isa 28: 20 than that a man can s' himself
31: 3 the Lord shall s' out his hand,
34: 11 s' out upon it the line of confusion,
54: 2 and let them s' forth the curtains
Jer 6: 12 s'...my hand upon the inhabitants
10: 20 none to s' forth my tent any more,
15: 6 will I s' out my hand against thee,
51: 25 I will s' out mine hand upon thee,
Eze 6: 14 So will I s' out my hand upon them,
14: 9 and I will s' out my hand upon him,
13 then will I s' out mine hand upon it,
25: 7 I will s' out mine hand upon thee,
13 also s' out mine hand upon Edom,
16 s'...mine hand upon the Philistines,
30: 25 s' it out upon the land of Egypt.
35: 3 I will s' out mine hand against thee,
Da 11: 42 He shall s' forth his hand also
Am 6: 4 s' themselves upon their couches,
Zep 1: 4 also s' out mine hand upon Judah,
2: 13 s' out his hand against the north,
M't 12: 13 he to the man, S' forth thine hand.
M'r 3: 5 unto the man, S' forth thine hand.
Lu 6: 10 unto the man, S' forth thy hand.
Joh 21: 18 old, thou shalt s' forth thy hands,
2Co 10: 14 we s' not ourselves beyond our

stretched See also OUTSTRETCHED; STRETCHEDST.
Ge 22: 10 And Abraham s' forth his hand,
48: 14 And Israel s' out his right hand,
Ex 6: 6 will redeem you with a s' out arm,
8: 6 Aaron s'...his hand over the waters
17 Aaron s' out his hand with his rod,
9: 23 Moses s'...his rod toward heaven:
10: 13 Moses s' forth his rod over...Egypt,
22 Moses s'...his hand toward heaven;
14: 21 Moses s' out his hand over the sea;
27 Moses s' forth his hand over the sea,
De 4: 34 a mighty hand, and by a s' out arm,
5: 15 a mighty hand and by a s' out arm:
7: 19 mighty hand, and the s' out arm,
9: 29 mighty power and by thy s' out arm.
11: 2 mighty hand, and his s' out arm,
Jos 8: 18 Joshua s' out the spear that he had
19 as soon as he had s' out his hand:
26 back, wherewith he s' out the spear,
2Sa 24: 16 when the angel s' out his hand
1Ki 6: 27 s'...the wings of the cherubims,
8: 42 hand, and of thy s' out arm;)
17: 21 he s' himself upon the child three
2Ki 4: 34 and he s' himself upon the child;
35 went up, and s' himself upon him:
17: 36 with great power and a s' out arm,
1Ch 21: 16 sword...s' out over Jerusalem.
2Ch 6: 32 mighty hand, and thy s' out arm;
Job 38: 5 or who hath s' the line upon it?
Ps 44: 20 s'...our hands to a strange god;
88: 9 I have s' out my hands unto thee.
136: 6 To him that s' out the earth above
12 strong hand, and...a s' out arm:
Pr 1: 24 I have s' out my hand, and no man
Isa 3: 16 and walk with s' forth necks and
5: 25 s' forth his hand against them,
25 away, but his hand is s' out still.
9: 12, 17, 21 but his hand is s' out still.
10: 4 away, but his hand is s' out still.
14: 26 hand...s' out upon all the nations.
27 his hand is s' out, and who shall
16: 8 her branches are s' out, they are
23: 11 He s' out his hand over the sea, he
42: 5 the heavens, and s' them out;

Isa 45:12 my hands, have s' out the heavens,
51:13 that hath s' forth the heavens, and
Jer 6: 4 shadows of the evening are s' out.
10:12 s' out the heavens by his discretion.
32:17 by thy great power and s' out arm,
21 strong hand, and with a s' out arm,
51:15 and hath s' out the heaven by his
La 2: 8 he hath s' out a line, he hath not
Eze 1:11 and their wings were s' upward;
22 s' forth over their heads above.
10: 7 And one cherub s' forth his hand
16:27 I have s' out my hand over thee,
20:33 and with a s' out arm, and with fury
34 mighty hand, and with a s' out arm,
Ho 7: 5 he s' out his hand with scorners.
Am 6: 7 and the banquet of them that s'
Zec 1:16 shall be s' forth upon Jerusalem.
M't 12:13 he s' it forth; and it was restored
49 And he s' forth his hand toward his
14:31 Jesus s' forth his hand, and caught
26:51 s' out his hand, and drew his sword,
M'r 3: 5 And he s' it out: and his hand was
Lu 22:53 ye s' forth no hands against me:
Ac 12: 1 Herod the king s' forth his hands
26: 1 Then Paul s' forth the hand, and
Ro 10:21 I have s' forth my hands unto a

stretchedst
Ex 15:12 Thou s' out thy right hand, the

stretchest
Ps 104: 2 s' out the heavens like a curtain:

stretcheth
Job 15:25 he s' out his hand against God,
26: 7 He s' out the north over the empty
Pr 31:20 She s' out her hand to the poor;
Isa 40:22 s' out the heavens as a curtain,
44:13 The carpenter s' out his rule; he
24 that s' forth the heavens alone;
Zec 12: 1 Lord, which s' forth the heavens,

stretching
Isa 8: 8 the s' out of his wings shall fill the
Ac 4:30 By s' forth thine hand to heal; and

strewed See STRAWED.

stricken See also STRUCK.
Ge 18:11 Sarah were old and well s' in age;
24: 1 Abraham was old, and well s' in age:
Jos 13: 1 Now Joshua was old and s' in years,
1 Thou art old and s' in years, and
23: 1 that Joshua waxed old and s' in age.
2 unto them, I am old and s' in age:
J'g 5:26 and s' through his temples.
1Ki 1: 1 king David was old and s' in years;
Pr 6: 1 hast s' thy hand with a stranger,
23:35 They have s' me, shalt thou say,
Isa 1: 5 Why should ye be s' any more?
16: 7 shall ye mourn; surely they are s'.
53: 4 yet we did esteem him s', smitten
8 transgression of my people...he s'.
Jer 5: 3 thou hast s' them, but they have
La 4: 9 s' through for want of the fruits of
Lu 1: 7 both were now well s' in years.
18 man, and my wife well s' in years.

strife See also STRIFES.
Ge 13: 7 was a s' between the herdmen of
8 said unto Lot, Let there be no s',
Nu 27:14 of Zin, in the s' of the congregation,
De 1:12 and your burden, and your s'?
J'g 12: 2 I and my people were at great s'
2Sa 19: 9 the people were at s' throughout
Ps 31:20 a pavilion from the s' of tongues.
55: 9 have seen violence and s' in the city.
80: 6 us a s' unto our neighbours:
106:32 angered him...at the waters of s'.
Pr 15:18 A wrathful man stirreth up s':
18 that is slow to anger appeaseth s'.
16:28 A froward man soweth s': and a
17: 1 an house full of sacrifices with s'.
14 The beginning of s' is as when one
19 loveth transgression that loveth s':
20: 3 honour for a man to cease from s':
22:10 yea, s' and reproach shall cease.
26:17 meddleth with s' belonging not
20 is no talebearer, the s' ceaseth.
21 is a contentious man to kindle s'.
28:25 is of a proud heart stirreth up s':
29:22 An angry man stirreth up s', and a
30:33 forcing of wrath bringeth forth s'.
Isa 58: 4 Behold, ye fast for s' and debate,
Jer 15:10 a man of s' and a man of contention
Eze 47:19 even to the waters of s' in Kadesh,
48:28 unto the waters of s' in Kadesh,
Hab 1: 3 and there are that raise up s' and
Lu 22:24 there was also a s' among them,
Ro 13:13 wantonness, not in s' and envying.
1Co 3: 3 you envying, and s', and divisions,
Ga 5:20 emulations, wrath, s', seditions,
Ph'p 1:15 preach Christ even of envy and s';
2: 3 Let nothing be done through s' or
1Ti 6: 4 whereof cometh envy, s', railings,
Heb 6:16 oath...is to them an end of all s'.
Jas 3:14 envying and s' in your hearts,
16 For where envying and s' is, there

strifes
Pr 10:12 Hatred stirreth up s': but love
2Co 12:20 envyings, wraths, s', backbitings,
1Ti 6: 4 about questions and s' of words,
2Ti 2:23 knowing that they do gender s'.

strike See also STRAKE; STRICKEN; STRIKETH; STRUCK.
Ex 12: 7 and s' it on the two side posts
22 s' the lintel and the two side posts
De 21: 4 and shall s' off the heifer's neck
2Ki 5:11 and s' his hand over the place,
Job 17: 3 is he that will s' hands with me?
20:24 bow of steel shall s' him through.
Ps 110: 5 The Lord...shall s' through kings
Pr 7:23 Till a dart s' through his liver; as
17:26 good, nor to s' princes for equity.
22:26 Be not...one of them that s' hands,
Hab 3:14 didst s' through with his staves
M'r 14:65 did s' him with the palms of their

striker
1Ti 3: 3 Not given to wine, no s', not greedy
Tit 1: 7 not given to wine, no s', not given to

striketh
Job 34:26 He s' them as wicked men in the
Pr 17:18 void of understanding s' hands,
Re 9: 5 a scorpion, when he s' a man.

string See also STRINGED; STRINGS.
Ps 11: 2 ready their arrow upon the s',
M'r 7:35 the s' of his tongue was loosed,

stringed
Ps 150: 4 praise him with s' instruments
Isa 38:20 my songs to the s' instrument
Hab 3:19 chief singer on my s' instruments.

strings
Ps 21:12 arrows upon thy s' against the
33: 2 and an instrument of ten s'.
92: 3 Upon an instrument of ten s', and
144: 9 and an instrument of ten s' will I

strip See also STRIPPED.
Nu 20:26 s' Aaron of his garments, and put
1Sa 31: 8 the Philistines came to s' the slain,
1Ch 10: 8 the Philistines came to s' the slain,
Isa 32:11 s' you, and make you bare, and
Eze 16:39 shall s' thee also of thy clothes,
23:26 shall also s' thee out of thy clothes,
Ho 2: 3 Lest I s' her naked, and set her as

stripe See also STRIPES.
Ex 21:25 wound for wound, s' for s'.

stripes
De 25: 3 Forty s' he may give him, and
3 him above these with many s',
2Sa 7:14 with the s' of the children of men:
Ps 89:32 rod, and their iniquity with s'.
Pr 17:10 than an hundred s' into a fool.
19:29 and s' for the back of fools.
20:30 so do s' the inward parts of the
Isa 53: 5 and with his s' we are healed.
Lu 12:47 will, shall be beaten with many s'.
48 commit things worthy of s', shall
48 shall be beaten with few s'. For
Ac 16:23 they had laid many s' upon them,
33 of the night, and washed their s';
2Co 6: 5 In s', in imprisonments, in tumults,
11:23 in s' above measure, in prisons
24 times received I forty s' save one.
1Pe 2:24 by whose s' ye were healed.

stripling
1Sa 17:56 Enquire...whose son this s' is.

stripped See also STRIPT.
Ex 33: 6 children of Israel s' themselves
Nu 20:28 Moses s' Aaron of his garments,
1Sa 18: 4 Jonathan s' himself of the robe
19:24 And he s' off his clothes also, and
31: 9 off his head, and s' off his armour,
1Ch 10: 9 when they had s' him, they took
2Ch 20:25 which they s' off for themselves,
Job 19: 9 He hath s' me of my glory, and
22: 6 and s' the naked of their clothing.
Mic 1: 8 and howl, I will go s' and naked:
M't 27:28 And they s' him, and put on him a
Lu 10:30 which s' him of his raiment, and

stript See also STRIPPED.
Ge 37:23 they s' Joseph out of his coat, his

strive See also STRIVED; STRIVETH; STRIVING.
Ge 6: 3 My spirit shall not...s' with man,
26:20 did s' with Isaac's herdmen,
Ex 21:18 if men s' together, and one smite
22 If men s', and hurt a woman with
De 25:11 men s' together one with another,
33: 8 whom thou didst s' at the waters
J'g 11:25 did he ever s' against Israel, or did
Job 33:13 Why dost thou s' against him? for
Ps 35: 1 Lord, with them that s' with me:
Pr 3:30 S' not with a man without cause,
25: 8 Go not forth hastily to s', lest thou
Isa 41:11 they that s' with thee shall perish.
45: 9 the potsherd s' with the potsherds
Ho 4: 4 no man s', nor reprove another:
4 are as they that s' with the priest.
M't 12:19 He shall not s', nor cry; neither
Lu 13:24 S' to enter in at the strait gate:
Ro 15:30 ye s' together with me in your
2Ti 2: 5 if a man also s' for masteries, yet
5 not crowned, except he s' lawfully.
14 s' not about words to no profit,
24 servant of the Lord must not s';

strived See also STRIVEN; STROVE.
Ro 15:20 so have I s' to preach the gospel,

striven See also STRIVED.
Jer 50:24 thou hast s' against the Lord.

striveth
Isa 45: 9 unto him that s' with his Maker!
1Co 9:25 every man that s' for the mastery

striving See also STRIVINGS.
Ph'p 1:27 one mind s' together for the faith
Col 1:29 s' according to his working, which
Heb 12: 4 resisted unto blood, s' against sin.

strivings
2Sa 22:44 delivered me from the s' of my
Ps 18:43 delivered me from the s' of the
Tit 3: 9 contentions, and s' about the law;

stroke See also STROKES.
De 17: 8 between s' and s', being matters
19: 5 his hand fetcheth a s' with the axe
21: 5 controversy and every s' be tried:
Es 9: 5 enemies with the s' of the sword,
Job 23: 2 s' is heavier than my groaning.
36:18 he take thee away with his s':
Ps 39:10 Remove thy s' away from me: I
Isa 14: 6 the people...with a continual s',
30:26 and healeth the s' of their wound.
Eze 24:16 the desire of thine eyes with a s':

strokes
Pr 18: 6 and his mouth calleth for s'.

strong See also STRONGER; STRONGEST.
Ge 49:14 Issachar is a s' ass couching
24 were made s' by the hands of the
Ex 6: 1 a s' hand shall he let them go,
1 a s' hand shall he drive them out
10:19 Lord turned a mighty s' west wind,
13: 9 for with a s' hand hath the Lord
14:21 sea to go back by a s' east wind
Le 10: 9 Do not drink wine nor s' drink, thou,
Nu 6: 3 himself from wine and s' drink, and
3 or vinegar of s' drink, neither shall he
13:18 whether they be s' or weak, few
19 whether in tents, or in s' holds;
28 people be s' that dwell in the land,
20:20 much people, and with a s' hand.
21:24 the children of Ammon was s'.
24:21 S' is thy dwellingplace, and thou
28: 7 thou cause the s' wine to be poured
De 2:36 was not one city too s' for us:
11: 8 that ye may be s', and go in and
14:26 for sheep, or for wine, or for s' drink,
29: 6 have ye drunk wine or s' drink:
31: 6 Be s' and of a good courage, fear
7, 23 Be s' and of a good courage, for
Jos 1: 6 Be s' and of a good courage: for
7 be thou s' and very courageous,
9 Be s' and of a good courage; be
18 only be s' and of a good courage.
10:25 be s' and of good courage: for
14:11 As yet I am as s' this day as I was
17:13 children of Israel were waxen s',
18 chariots, and though they be s'.
19:29 to Ramah, and to the s' city Tyre;
23: 9 before you great nations and s':
J'g 1:28 came to pass, when Israel was s',
6: 2 mountains,...caves, and s' holds.
9:51 was a s' tower within the city,
13: 4 and drink not wine nor s' drink, and
7 and now drink no wine nor s' drink,
14 neither let her drink wine or s' drink,
14:14 out of the s' came forth sweetness.
18:26 Micah saw that they were too s'
1Sa 1:15 have drunk neither wine nor s' drink,
4: 9 Be s', and quit yourselves like
14:52 when Saul saw any s' man, or any
23:14 abode in the wilderness in s' holds,
19 not David hide...with us in s' holds
29 and dwelt in s' holds at En-gedi.
2Sa 3: 6 Abner made himself s' for the
5: 7 David took the s' hold of Zion:
10:11 If the Syrians be too s' for me,
11 if the children of Ammon be too s'
11:25 thy battle more s' against the city,
15:12 And the conspiracy was s'; for the
16:21 the hands of all...with thee be s'.
22:18 delivered me from my s' enemy,
18 me: for they were too s' for me.
24: 7 And came to the s' hold of Tyre,
1Ki 2: 2 be thou s' therefore, and shew
8:42 great name, and of thy s' hand,
19:11 and s' wind rent the mountains,
2Ki 2:16 be with thy servants fifty s' men;
8:12 their s' holds wilt thou set on fire,
24:16 all that were s' and apt for war,
1Ch 19:12 If the Syrians be too s' for me,
12 children of Ammon be too s' for
22:13 be s', and of good courage; dread
26: 7 whose brethren were s' men,
9 had sons and brethren, s' men,
28:10 the sanctuary: be s', and do it.
20 his son, be s' and of good courage,
2Ch 11:11 he fortified the s' holds, and put
12 and made them exceeding s',
17 Rehoboam the son of Solomon s',
15: 7 Be ye s' therefore, and let not your
16: 9 shew himself s' in...behalf of them
25: 8 wilt go, do it, be s' for the battle:
26:15 marvellously helped, till he was s'.
16 But when he was s', his heart was
32: 7 Be s' and courageous, be not
Ezr 9:12 that ye may be s', and eat the good
Ne 1:10 great power, and by thy s' hand.
9:25 they took s' cities, and a fat land,
Job 8: 2 of thy mouth be like a s' wind?
9:19 If I speak of strength, lo, he is s':
30:21 with thy s' hand thou opposest
33:19 multitude of his bones with s' pain:
37:18 spread out the sky, which is s',
39:28 crag of the rock, and the s' place.
40:18 His bones are as s' pieces of brass;
Ps 10:10 the poor may fall by his s' ones.
18:17 delivered me from my s' enemy,
17 me: for they were too s' for me.
19: 5 and rejoiceth as a s' man to run a
22:12 s' bulls of Bashan have beset me
24: 8 The Lord s' and mighty, the Lord
30: 7 made my mountain to stand s':

Ps 31: 2 be thou my s· rock, for an house
21 marvellous kindness in a s· city.
35:10 the poor from him that is too s·
38:19 are lively, and they are s·: and
60: 9 Who will bring me into the s· city?
61: 3 and a s· tower from the enemy.
71: 3 Be thou my s· habitation,
7 many; but thou art my s· refuge.
80:15 that thou madest s· for thyself.
17 whom thou madest s· for thyself.
89: 8 who is a s· Lord like unto thee?
10 thine enemies with thy s· arm.
13 s· is thy hand, and high is thy
40 hast brought his s· holds to ruin.
108:10 Who will bring me into the s· city?
136:12 With a s· hand, and with a
144:14 That our oxen may be s· to labour;
Pr 7:26 many s· men have been slain by
10:15 rich man's wealth is his s· city:
11:16 honour: and s· men retain riches.
14:26 fear of the Lord is s· confidence:
18:10 The name of the Lord is a s· tower:
11 The rich man's wealth is his s· city,
19 is harder to be won than a s· city:
20: 1 Wine is a mocker, s· drink is raging:
21:14 a reward in the bosom s· wrath.
24: 5 A wise man is s·; yea, a man of
30:25 The ants are a people not s·, yet
31: 4 to drink wine; nor for princes s· drink:
6 Give s· drink unto him that is ready to
Ec 9:11 nor the battle to the s·, neither yet
12: 3 the s· men shall bow themselves,
Ca 8: 6 for love is s· as death; jealousy is
Isa 1:31 And the s· shall be as tow, and the
5:11 that they may follow s· drink; that
22 men of strength to mingle s· drink:
8: 7 waters of the river, s· and many,
11 spake thus to me with a s· hand,
17: 9 shall his s· cities be as a forsaken
23:11 city, to destroy the s· holds thereof.
24: 9 s· drink shall be bitter to them that
25: 3 shall the s· people glorify thee,
26: 1 We have a s· city; salvation will
27: 1 great and s· sword shall punish
28: 2 the Lord hath a mighty and s· one,
7 through s· drink are out of the way;
7 prophet have erred through s· drink,
7 are out of the way through s· drink;
22 lest your bands be made s·: for I
29: 9 they stagger, but not with s· drink.
31: 1 in horsemen,...they are very s·;
9 and shall pass over to his s· hold
35: 4 of a fearful heart, be s·, fear not:
40:10 Lord God will come with s· hand,
26 might, for that he is s· in power;
41:21 bring forth your s· reasons, saith
53:12 shall divide the spoil with the s·;
56:12 we will fill ourselves with s· drink;
60:22 and a small one a s· nation:
Jer 8:16 sound of the neighing of his s· ones;
21: 5 outstretched hand and...a s· arm,
32:21 with wonders, and with a s· hand,
47: 3 of the hoofs of his s· horses, at the
48:14 mighty and s· men for the war?
17 How is the s· staff broken, and the
18 and he shall destroy thy s· holds.
41 the s· holds are surprised, and the
49:19 against the habitation of the s·:
50:34 Their Redeemer is s·; the Lord of
44 Jordan unto the habitation of the s·:
51:12 make the watch s·, set up the
La 2: 2 s· holds of the daughter of Judah;
5 he hath destroyed his s· holds, and
Eze 3: 8 thy face s· against their faces,
8 forehead s· against their foreheads.
14 hand of the Lord was s· upon me.
7:24 make the pomp of the s· to cease:
19:11 she had s· rods for the sceptres of
12 s· rods were broken and withered;
14 she hath no s· rod to be a sceptre
22:14 endure, or can thine hands be s·,
26:11 s· garrisons shall go down to the
17 city, which wast s· in the sea,
30:21 to make it s· to hold the sword.
22 the s·, and that which was broken;
32:21 s· among the mighty shall speak
34:16 I will destroy the fat and the s·;
Da 2:40 fourth kingdom shall be s· as iron:
42 the kingdom shall be partly s·, and
4:11 The tree grew, and was s·, and the
20 The tree...which grew, and was s·,
22 king, that art grown and become s·:
7: 7 and terrible, and s· exceedingly;
8: 8 when he was s·, the great horn
10:19 be unto thee, be s·, yea, be s·.
11: 5 the king of the south shall be s·,
5 and he shall be s· above him, and
23 become s· with a small people.
24 his devices against the s· holds,
32 that do know their God shall be s·.
39 shall he do in the most s· holds
Joe 1: 6 is come up upon my land, s·,
2: 2 a great people and a s·; there hath
5 as a s· people set in battle array.
11 for he is s· that executeth his word:
3:10 spears: let the weak say, I am s·.
Am 2: 9 cedars, and he was s· as the oaks;
14 s· shall not strengthen his force,
5: 9 the spoiled against the s·,
Mic 2:11 unto thee of wine and of s· drink;
4: 3 and rebuke s· nations afar off;
7 her that was cast far off a s· nation:
8 s· hold of the daughter of Zion,
5:11 and throw down all thy s· holds:
6: 2 and ye s· foundations of the earth:
Na 1: 7 a s· hold in the day of trouble;
Na 2: 1 make thy loins s·, fortify thy power
3:12 s· holds shall be like fig trees with
14 for the siege, fortify thy s· holds:
14 the morter, make s· the brickkiln.
Hab 1:10 they shall deride every s· hold;
Hag 2: 4 Yet now be s·, O Zerubbabel, saith
4 be s·, O Joshua, son of Josedech,
4 and be s·, all ye people of the land,
Zec 8: 9 Let your hands be s·, ye that hear
13 fear not, but let your hands be s·.
22 s· nations shall come to seek the
9: 3 Tyrus did build herself a s· hold,
12 Turn you to the s· hold, ye
M't 12:29 one enter into a s· man's house,
29 except he first bind the s· man?
M'r 3:27 can enter into a s· man's house,
27 except he will first bind the s· man;
Lu 1:15 drink neither wine nor s· drink;
80 child grew, and waxed s· in spirit,
2:40 child grew, and waxed s· in spirit,
11:21 s· man armed keepeth his palace,
Ac 3:16 his name hath made this man s·,
Ro 4:20 was s· in faith, giving glory to God;
15: 1 We...that are s· ought to bear the
1Co 4:10 we are weak, but ye are s·;
16:13 the faith, quit you like men, be s·.
2Co 10: 4 to the pulling down of s· holds;)
12:10 for when I am weak, then am I s·.
13: 9 when we are weak, and ye are s·:
Eph 6:10 my brethren, be s· in the Lord,
2Th 2:11 God shall send them s· delusion,
2Ti 2: 1 my son, be s· in the grace that is
Heb 5: 7 with s· crying and tears unto him
12 need of milk, and not of s· meat.
14 But s· meat belongeth to them that
6:18 we might have a s· consolation,
11:34 out of weakness were made s·,
1Jo 2:14 young men, because ye are s·, and
Re 5: 2 I saw a s· angel proclaiming with
18: 2 he cried mightily with a s· voice,
8 s· is the Lord God who judgeth

strong-drink See STRONG and DRINK.

stronger
Ge 25:23 shall be s· than the other people;
30:41 the s· cattle did conceive,
42 were Laban's, and the s· Jacob's.
Nu 13:31 people; for they are s· than we.
J'g 14:18 honey? and what is s· than a lion?
2Sa 1:23 eagles, they were s· than lions.
3: 1 but David waxed s·...and the
1 but David waxed...s·, and the
13:14 but, being s· than she, forced her,
1Ki 20:23 therefore they were s· than we;
23, 25 surely we shall be s· than they.
Job 17: 9 that hath clean hands shall be s·
9 that hath clean hands shall be...s·,
Ps 105:24 made them s· than their enemies.
142: 6 persecutors; for they are s· than I.
Jer 20: 7 thou art s· than I, and hast
31:11 hand of him that was s· than he.
Lu 11:22 when a s· than he shall come upon
1Co 1:25 the weakness of God is s· than men.
10:22 to jealousy? are we s· than he?

strongest
Pr 30:30 A lion which is s· among beasts,

strong-hold See STRONG and HOLD.

strongly
Ezr 6: 3 the foundations thereof be s· laid;

strove See also STRIVED.
Ge 26:20 Esek; because they s· with him.
21 another well, and s· for that also:
22 another well;...for that they s· not:
Ex 2:13 men of the Hebrews s· together:
Le 24:10 of Israel s· together in the camp;
Nu 20:13 children of Israel s· with the Lord,
26: 9 who s· against Moses and against
9 when they s· against the Lord:
2Sa 14: 6 they two s· together in the field,
Ps 60: *title* when he s· with Aram-naharaim
Da 7: 2 four winds of the heaven s· upon
Joh 6:52 Jews...s· among themselves,
Ac 7:26 he shewed himself...as they s·,
23: 9 the Pharisees' part arose, and s·,

strowed See also STRAWED.
2Ch 34: 4 s· it upon the graves of them that

struck See also STRAKE; STRICKEN.
1Sa 2:14 And he s· it into the pan, or kettle,
2Sa 12:15 the Lord s· the child that Uriah's
20:10 the ground, and s· him not again:
2Ch 13:20 and the Lord s· him, and he died.
M't 26:51 s· a servant of the high priest's,
Lu 22:64 him, they s· him on the face,
Joh 18:22 s· Jesus with the palm of his

struggled
Ge 25:22 children s· together within her;

stubble
Ex 5:12 to gather s· instead of straw.
15: 7 wrath, which consumed them as s·.
Job 13:25 and wilt thou pursue the dry s·?
21:18 They are as s· before the wind,
41:28 slingstones are turned...into s·.
29 Darts are counted as s·: he
Ps 83:13 wheel; as the s· before the wind.
Isa 5:24 as the fire devoureth the s·, and
33:11 chaff, ye shall bring forth s·:
40:24 shall take them away as s·.
41: 2 sword, and as driven s· to his bow.
47:14 Behold, they shall be as s·; the fire
Jer 13:24 scatter them as the s· that passeth
Joe 2: 5 flame of fire that devoureth the s·,
Ob 18 flame, and the house of Esau for s·,
Na 1:10 they shall be devoured as s·
Mal 4: 1 all that do wickedly, shall be s·:
1Co 3:12 precious stones, wood, hay, s·;

stubborn
De 21:18 man have a s· and rebellious son,
20 This our son is s· and rebellious,
J'g 2:19 doings, nor from their s· way.
Ps 78: 8 a s· and rebellious generation;
Pr 7:11 (She is loud and s·; her feet abide

stubbornness
De 9:27 look not unto the s· of this people,
1Sa 15:23 and s· is as iniquity and idolatry.

stuck
1Sa 26: 7 his spear s· in the ground at his
Ps 119:31 I have s· unto thy testimonies:
Ac 27:41 the forepart s· fast, and remained

studs
Ca 1:11 borders of gold with s· of silver.

studieth
Pr 15:28 of the righteous s· to answer:
24: 2 For their heart s· destruction, and

study See also STUDIETH.
Ec 12:12 much s· is a weariness of the flesh.
1Th 4:11 that ye s· to be quiet, and to do
2Ti 2:15 *S*· to shew thyself approved unto

stuff
Ge 31:37 thou hast searched all my s·,
37 thou found of all thy household s·?
45:20 Also regard not your s·; for the
Ex 22: 7 his neighbour money or s· to keep,
36: 7 s· they had was sufficient for all
Jos 7:11 put it even among their own s·.
1Sa 10:22 he hath hid himself among the s·.
25:13 and two hundred abode by the s·.
30:24 his part be that tarrieth by the s·:
Ne 13: 8 forth all the household s· of Tobiah
Eze 12: 3 prepare thee s· for removing,
4 shalt thou bring forth thy s· by day
4 in their sight, as s· for removing:
7 I brought forth my s· by day,
7 as s· for captivity, and in the even
Lu 17:31 housetop, and his s· in the house,

stumble See also STUMBLED; STUMBLETH; STUMBLING.
Pr 3:23 safely, and thy foot shall not s·.
4:12 thou runnest, thou shalt not s·.
19 they know not at what they s·.
Isa 5:27 shall be weary nor s· among them;
8:15 And many among them shall s·,
28: 7 err in vision, they s· in judgment.
59:10 we s· at noon day as in the night;
63:13 wilderness, that they should not s·?
Jer 13:16 feet s· upon the dark mountains,
18:15 caused them to s· in their ways
20:11 therefore my persecutors shall s·,
31: 9 way, wherein they shall not s·:
46: 6 shall s·, and fall toward the north
50:32 the most proud shall s· and fall,
Da 11:19 shall s· and fall, and not be found
Na 2: 5 they shall s· in their walk; they
3: 3 corpses; they s· upon their corpses:
Mal 2: 8 have caused many to s· at the law;
1Pe 2: 8 even to them which s· at the word,

stumbled
1Sa 2: 4 that s· are girded with strength.
1Ch 13: 9 to hold the ark; for the oxen s·.
Ps 27: 2 eat up my flesh, they s· and fell.
Jer 46:12 man hath s· against the mighty,
Ro 9:32 they s· at that stumblingstone;
11:11 Have they s· that they should fall?

stumbleth
Pr 24:17 thine heart be glad when he s·:
Joh 11: 9 man walk in the day, he s· not,
10 if a man walk in the night, he s·,
Ro 14:21 any thing whereby thy brother s·,

stumbling See also STUMBLINGBLOCK; STUMBLINGSTONE.
Isa 8:14 for a stone of s· and for a rock of
57:14 take up the s· block out of the way
1Pe 2: 8 And a stone of s·, and a rock of
1Jo 2:10 there is none occasion of s· in him.

stumblingblock See also STUMBLINGBLOCKS.
Le 19:14 deaf, nor put a s· before the blind,
Isa 57:14 [*in some editions*] s· out of the way
Eze 3:20 iniquity, and I lay a s· before him,
7:19 because it is the s· of their iniquity.
14: 3 put the s· of their iniquity before
4, 7 and putteth the s· of his iniquity
Ro 11: 9 made a snare, and a trap, and a s·,
14:13 no man put a s· or an occasion to
1Co 1:23 unto the Jews a s·, and unto the
8: 9 become a s· to them that are weak.
Re 2:14 to cast a s· before the children of

stumblingblocks
Jer 6:21 I will lay s· before this people,
Zep 1: 3 sea, and the s· with the wicked;

stumblingstone
Ro 9:32 For they stumbled at that s·;
33 I lay in Zion a s· and rock of

stump
1Sa 5: 4 only the s· of Dagon was left to him.
Da 4:15 leave the s· of his roots in the
23 yet leave the s· of the roots thereof
26 to leave the s· of the tree roots;

Suah (*su'-ah*)
1Ch 7:36 *S*·, and Harnepher, and Shual,

subdue See also SUBDUED; SUBDUETH.
Ge 1:28 and replenish the earth, and s· it:
1Ch 17:10 Moreover I will s·...thine enemies.
Ps 47: 3 He shall s· the people under us,
Isa 45: 1 holden, to s· nations before him;
Da 7:24 first, and he shall s· three kings.
Mic 7:19 he will s· our iniquities; and thou
Zec 9:15 devour, and s· with sling stones;
Ph'p 3:21 to s· all things unto himself.

subdued See also SUBDUEDST.
Nu 32:22 the land be s· before the Lord:
29 and the land shall be s· before you;
De 20:20 war with thee, until it be s·.
Jos 18: 1 And the land was s· before them.
J'g 3:30 So Moab was s· that day under the
4:23 So God s· on that day Jabin the
8:28 was Midian s· before the children
11:33 the children of Ammon were s·
1Sa 7:13 So the Philistines were s·, and they
2Sa 8: 1 smote the Philistines, and s· them:
11 of all nations which he s·;
22:40 against me hast thou s· under me.
1Ch 18: 1 smote the Philistines, and s· them,
20: 4 of the giant: and they were s·.
22:18 and the land is s· before the Lord,
Ps 18:39 thou hast s· under me those that
81:14 should soon have s· their enemies,
1Co 15:28 all things shall be s· unto him,
Heb 11:33 Who through faith s· kingdoms,

subduedst
Ne 9:24 and thou s· before them the

subdueth
Ps 18:47 me, and s· the people under me.
144: 2 trust; who s· my people under me.
Da 2:40 in pieces and s· all things: and as

subject See also SUBJECTED.
Lu 2:51 Nazareth, and was s· unto them:
10:17 devils are s· unto us through thy
20 not, that the spirits are s· unto you;
Ro 8: 7 for it is not s· to the law of God,
20 the creature was made s· to vanity,
13: 1 every soul be s· unto the higher
5 Wherefore ye must needs be s·, not
1Co 14:32 the prophets are s· to the prophets.
15:28 the Son also himself be s· unto him
Eph 5:24 as the church is s· unto Christ,
Col 2:20 the world, are ye s· to ordinances,
Tit 3: 1 in mind to be s· to principalities
Heb 2:15 all their lifetime s· to bondage.
Jas 5:17 Elias...a man s· to like passions
1Pe 2:18 Servants, be s· to your masters
3:22 powers being made s· unto him.
5: 5 all of you be s· one to another, and

subjected
Ro 8:20 who hath s· the same in hope,

subjection
Ps 106:42 brought into s· under their hand.
Jer 34:11 brought them into s· for servants
16 to return, and brought them into s·,
1Co 9:27 my body, and bring it into s·:
2Co 9:13 your professed s· unto the gospel
Ga 2: 5 To whom we gave place by s·, no,
1Ti 2:11 woman learn in silence with all s·.
3: 4 his children in s· with all gravity;
Heb 2: 5 not put in s· the world to come,
8 Thou hast put all things in s· under
8 in that he put all in s· under him,
12: 9 rather be in s· unto the Father of
1Pe 3: 1 be in s· to your own husbands;
5 in s· unto their own husbands:

submit See also SUBMITTED; SUBMITTING.
Ge 16: 9 and s· thyself under her hands.
2Sa 22:45 Strangers shall s· themselves unto
Ps 18:44 strangers shall s· themselves unto
66: 3 shall thine enemies s· themselves
68:30 s· himself with pieces of silver:
1Co 16:16 That ye s· yourselves unto such,
Eph 5:22 Wives, s· yourselves unto your own
Col 3:18 Wives, s· yourselves unto your own
Heb 13:17 rule over you, and s· yourselves:
Jas 4: 7 S· yourselves therefore to God.
1Pe 2:13 S· yourselves to every ordinance
5: 5 s· yourselves unto the elder.

submitted
1Ch 29:24 s· themselves unto Solomon
Ps 81:15 should have s· themselves unto
Ro 10: 3 have not s· themselves unto the

submitting
Eph 5:21 S· yourselves one to another in

suborned
Ac 6:11 Then they s· men, which said,

subscribe See also SUBSCRIBED.
Isa 44: 5 s· with his hand unto the Lord,
Jer 32:44 and s· evidences, and seal them,

subscribed
Jer 32:10 I s· the evidence, and sealed it,
12 witnesses that s· the book of the

substance
Ge 7: 4 living s· that I have made will I
23 And every living s· was destroyed
12: 5 all their s· that they had gathered,
13: 6 for their s· was great, so that they
15:14 shall they come out with great s·.
34:23 shall not their cattle and their s·
36: 6 all his s·, which he had got in the
De 11: 6 s· that was in their possession,
33:11 Bless, Lord, his s·, and accept the
Jos 14: 4 for their cattle and for their s·.
1Ch 27:31 rulers of the s· which was king
28: 1 the stewards over all the s· and
2Ch 21:17 away all the s· that was found in
31: 3 portion of his s· for the burnt
32:29 God had given him s· very much.
35: 7 these were of the king's s·.
Ezr 8:21 for our little ones, and for all our s·.
10: 8 elders, all his s· should be forfeited,
Job 1: 3 His s· also was seven thousand
10 and his s· is increased in the land.
5: 5 the robber swalloweth up their s·.
6:22 Give a reward for me of your s·?
15:29 rich, neither shall his s· continue,
20:18 according to his s· shall the
22:20 Whereas our s· is not cut down,
30:22 upon it, and dissolvest my s·.
Ps 17:14 leave the rest of their s· to their babes.
105:21 his house, and ruler of all his s·:
139:15 My s· was not hid from thee,
16 Thine eyes did see my s·, yet
Pr 1:13 We shall find all precious s·, we
3: 9 Honour the Lord with thy s·, and
6:31 he shall give all the s· of his house.
8:21 those that love me to inherit s·;
10: 3 casteth away the s· of the wicked.
12:27 the s· of a diligent man is precious.
28: 8 and unjust gain increaseth his s·,
29: 3 with harlots spendeth his s·.
Ca 8: 7 give all the s· of his house for love,
Isa 6:13 as an oak, whose s· is in them,
13 the holy seed shall be the s· thereof.
Jer 15:13 Thy s· and thy treasures will I
17: 3 I will give thy s· and all thy
Hos 12: 8 rich, I have found me out s·:
Ob 13 laid hands on their s· in the day of
Mic 4:13 their s· unto the Lord of the whole
Lu 8: 3 ministered unto him of their s·.
15:13 wasted his s· with riotous living.
Heb 10:34 a better and an enduring s·.
11: 1 faith is the s· of things hoped for,

subtil
Ge 3: 1 the serpent was more s· than any
2Sa 13: 3 and Jonadab was a very s· man.
Pr 7:10 attire of an harlot, and s· of heart.

subtilly
1Sa 23:22 told me that he dealeth very s·.
Ps 105:25 to deal s· with his servants.
Ac 7:19 The same dealt s· with our kindred,

subtilty
Ge 27:35 The brother came with s·, and
2Ki 10:19 But Jehu did it in s·, to the intent
Pr 1: 4 To give s· to the simple, to the
M't 26: 4 that they might take Jesus by s·,
Ac 13:10 O full of all s· and all mischief,
2Co 11: 3 beguiled Eve through his s·,

subtle See SUBTIL.

suburbs
Le 25:34 field of the s· of their cities may
Nu 35: 2 unto the Levites s· for the cities
3 and the s· of them shall be for their
4 the s· of the cities, which ye shall
5 shall be to them the s· of the cities.
7 them shall ye give with their s·.
Jos 14: 4 their s· for their cattle and for their
21: 2 with the s· thereof for our cattle.
3 the Lord, these cities and their s·.
8 Levites these cities with their s·,
11 with the s· thereof round about it.
13 the priest Hebron with her s·,
13 the slayer; and Libnah with her s·,
14 And Jattir with her s·,
14 and Eshtemoa with her s·,
15 And Holon with her s·,
15 and Debir with her s·,
16 And Ain with her s·,
16 and Juttah with her s·,
16 and Beth-shemesh with her s·;
17 of Benjamin, Gibeon with her s·,
17 Geba with her s·,
18 Anathoth with her s·,
18 and Almon with her s·; four cities.
19 were thirteen cities with their s·.
21 gave them Shechem with her s· in
21 the slayer; and Gezer with her s·,
22 And Kibzaim with her s·,
22 and Beth-horon with her s·;
23 tribe of Dan, Eltekeh with her s·,
23 Gibbethon with her s·,
24 Aijalon with her s·,
24 Gath-rimmon with her s·;
25 of Manasseh, Tanach with her s·,
25 and Gath-rimmon with her s·;
26 All the cities were ten with their s·
27 gave Golan in Bashan with her s·,
27 and Beesh-terah with her s·;
28 of Issachar, Kishon with her s·,
28 Dabareh with her s·,
29 Jarmuth with her s·,
29 En-gannim with her s·; four cities.
30 tribe of Asher, Mishal with her s·,
30 Abdon with her s·,
31 Helkath with her s·,
31 and Rehob with her s·; four cities.
32 Kedesh in Galilee with her s·,
32 and Hammoth-dor with her s·,
32 and Kartan with her s·;
33 were thirteen cities with their s·.
34 of Zebulun, Jokneam with her s·,
34 and Kartah with her s·,
35 Dimnah with her s·,
35 Nahalal with her s·; four cities.
36 tribe of Reuben, Bezer with her s·,
36 and Jahazah with her s·,
37 Kedemoth with her s·,
37 and Mephaath with her s·;
38 Ramoth in Gilead with her s·,
Jos 21:38 slayer; and Mahanaim with her s·,
39 Heshbon with her s·,
39 Jazer with her s·; four cities in all.
41 forty and eight cities with their s·.
42 cities were every one with their s·
2Ki 23:11 chamberlain, which was in the s·,
1Ch 5:16 towns, and in all the s· of Sharon,
6:55 and the s· thereof round about it.
57 Hebron,...and Libnah with her s·,
57 Jattir, and Eshtemoa, with their s·,
58 And Hilen with her s·,
58 Debir with her s·,
59 And Ashan with her s·,
59 and Beth-shemesh with her s·:
60 of Benjamin; Geba with her s·,
60 and Alemeth with her s·,
60 and Anathoth with her s·.
64 Levites these cities with their s·.
67 Shechem...with her s·;
67 they gave also Gezer with her s·,
68 And Jokmeam with her s·,
68 and Beth-horon with her s·,
69 And Aijalon with her s·,
69 and Gath-rimmon with her s·:
70 of Manasseh; Aner with her s·,
70 and Bileam with her s·,
71 Golan in Bashan with her s·,
71 and Ashtaroth with her s·:
72 of Issachar; Kedesh with her s·,
72 Daberath with her s·,
73 And Ramoth with her s·,
73 and Anem with her s·:
74 tribe of Asher; Mashal with her s·,
74 and Abdon with her s·,
75 And Hukok with her s·,
75 and Rehob with her s·:
76 Kedesh in Galilee with her s·,
76 and Hammon with her s·,
76 and Kirjathaim with her s·.
77 of Zebulun, Rimmon with her s·,
77 Tabor with her s·:
78 Bezer in the wilderness with her s·,
78 and Jahzah with her s·,
79 Kedemoth also with her s·,
79 and Mephaath with her s·:
80 Ramoth in Gilead with her s·,
80 and Mahanaim with her s·,
81 And Heshbon with her s·,
81 and Jazer with her s·.
13: 2 which are in their cities and s·,
2Ch 11:14 left their s· and their possession,
31:19 in the fields of the s· of their cities,
Eze 27:28 The s· shall shake at the sound of
45: 2 round about for the s· thereof.
48:15 for the city, for dwelling, and for s·:
17 the s· of the city shall be toward

subvert See also SUBVERTED; SUBVERTING.
La 3:36 To s· a man in his cause, the Lord
Tit 1:11 who s· whole houses, teaching

subverted
Tit 3:11 Knowing that he that is such is s·,

subverting
Ac 15:24 you with words, s· your souls,
2Ti 2:14 profit, but to the s· of the hearers.

succeed See also SUCCEEDED; SUCCEEDEST.
De 25: 6 shall s· in the name of his brother

succeeded
De 2:12 but the children of Esau s· them,
21, 22 they s· them, and dwelt in their

succeedest
De 12:29 and thou s· them, and dwellest in
19: 1 and thou s· them, and dwellest in

success
Jos 1: 8 and then thou shalt have good s·.

succor See SUCCOUR.

Succoth (*suc'-coth*) See also SUCCOTH-BENOTH.
Ge 33:17 Jacob journeyed to S·, and built
17 the name of the place is called S·.
Ex 12:37 journeyed from Rameses to S·,
13:20 they took their journey from S·,
Nu 33: 5 from Rameses, and pitched in S·.
6 they departed from S·, and pitched
Jos 13:27 Beth-nimrah, and S·, and Zaphon,
J'g 8: 5 men of S·, Give, I pray you, loaves
6 And the princes of S· said, Are the
8 as the men of S· had answered him.
14 a young man of the men of S·,
14 he described...the princes of S·,
15 And he came unto the men of S·,
16 with them he taught the men of S·.
1Ki 7:46 ground between S· and Zarthan.
2Ch 4:17 ground between S· and Zeredathah.
Ps 60: 6 and mete out the valley of S·.
108: 7 and mete out the valley of S·.

Succoth-benoth (*suc''-coth-be'-noth*)
2Ki 17:30 And the men of Babylon made S·

succour See also SUCCOURED.
2Sa 8: 5 Syrians of Damascus came to s·
18: 3 that thou s· us out of the city.
Heb 2:18 is able to s· them that are tempted.

succoured
2Sa 21:17 Abishai the son of Zeruiah s· him,
2Co 6: 2 the day of salvation have I s· thee:

succourer
Ro 16: 2 for she hath been a s· of many,

such^
Ge 4:20 was the father of s· as dwell in tents,
20 and of s· as have cattle.
21 the father of all s· as handle the harp
27: 4 make me savoury meat, s· as I love,

Ge 27:46 the daughters of Heth, s· as these
30:32 the goats: and of s· shall be my hire.
41:19 s· as I never saw in all the land of
38 Can we find s· a one as this is, a
44:15 wot ye not that s· a man as I can
Ex 10:14 there were no s· locusts as they,
14 neither after them shall be s·.
12:36 they lent unto them s· things as they
18:21 s· as fear God, men of truth, hating
21 and place s· over them, to be rulers of
34:10 s· as have not been done in all the
Le 10:19 and s· things have befallen me:
11:34 that on which s· water cometh shall
34 be drunk in every s· vessel shall be
14:22 young pigeons, s· as he is able to get;
30 young pigeons, s· as he can get;
31 Even s· as he is able to get, the one
20:6 that turneth after s· as have familiar
22:6 touched any s· shall be unclean until
27:9 man giveth of s· unto the Lord shall
Nu 8:16 instead of s· as open every womb,
De 4:32 hath been any s· thing as this great
5:29 O that there were s· an heart in
13:11 shall do no more any s· wickedness
14 s· abomination is wrought among
16:9 from s· time as thou beginnest to put
17:4 that s· abomination is wrought in
19:20 commit no more any s· evil among
25:16 For all that do s· things, and all
J'g 3:2 s· as before knew nothing thereof;
13:23 have told us s· things as these.
18:23 that thou comest with s· a company?
19:30 was no s· deed done nor seen from
Ru 4:1 Ho, s· a one! turn aside, sit down
1Sa 2:23 unto them, Why do ye s· things?
4:7 not been s· a thing heretofore.
21:2 servants to s· [6423] and s· a place.
25:17 for he is s· a son of Belial, that a man
2Sa 9:8 look upon s· a dead dog as I am?
12:8 given unto thee s· and s· things.
13:12 no s· thing ought to be done in
18 for with s· robes were the king's
14:13 then hast thou thought s· a thing
16:2 that s· as be faint in the wilderness
19:36 recompense...with s· a reward?
1Ki 10:10 no more s· abundance of spices
12 there came no s· almug trees, nor
2Ki 6:8 In s·... a place shall be my camp.
8 and s· a place shall be my camp.
9 Beware...thou pass not s· a place;
7:19 in heaven, might s· a thing be?
19:29 year s· things as grow of themselves,
21:12 I am bringing s· evil upon Jerusalem
23:22 there was not holden s· a passover
25:15 bowls, and s· things as were of gold,
1Ch 12:33, 36 s· as went forth to battle, expert in
29:25 bestowed upon him s· royal majesty
2Ch 1:12 s· as none of the kings have had
4:6 s· things as they offered for the burnt
9:9 s· spice as the queen of Sheba gave
11 there were none s· seen before in
11:16 s· as set their hearts to seek the Lord
23:13 and s· as taught to sing praise.
24:12 Jehoiada gave it to s· as did the work
12 and also s· as wrought iron and brass
30:5 long time in s· sort as it was written.
35:18 keep s· a passover as Josiah kept,
Ezr 4:10, 11 side the river, and at s· a time.
17 the river, Peace, and at s· a time.
6:21 all s· as had separated themselves
7:12 perfect peace, and at s· a time.
25 all s· as know the laws of thy God;
27 put s· a thing as this in the king's
8:31 and of s· as lay in wait by the way.
9:13 hast given us s· deliverance as this;
10:3 the wives, and s· as are born of them,
Ne 6:8 are no s· things done as thou sayest,
11 I said, Should s· a man as I flee?
Es 2:9 with s· things as belonged to her, and
4:11 s· to whom the king shall hold out
14 the kingdom for s· a time as this?
9:2 lay hand on s· as sought their hurt:
27 upon all s· as joined themselves unto
Job 12:3 knoweth not s· things as these?
14:3 open thine eyes upon s· an one,
15:13 lettest s· words go out of thy mouth?
16:2 I have heard many s· things:
18:21 s· are the dwellings of the wicked,
23:14 and many s· things are with him.
Ps 25:10 and truth unto s· as keep his covenant
27:12 me, and s· as breathe out cruelty.
34:18 saveth s· as be of a contrite spirit.
37:14 slay s· as be of upright conversation.
22 s· as be blessed of him shall inherit
40:4 proud, nor s· as turn aside to lies.
16 let s· as love thy salvation say
50:21 I was altogether s· an one as thyself:
55:20 against s· as be at peace with him:
68:21 scalp of s· an one as goeth on still
70:4 let s· as love thy salvation say
73:1 even to s· as are of a clean heart.
103:18 To s· as keep his covenant, and to
107:10 S· as sit in darkness and in the
125:5 for s· as turn aside unto their crooked
139:6 S· knowledge is too wonderful for me;
144:15 is that people, that is in s· a case:
Pr 11:20 s· as are upright in their way are his
28:4 s· as keep the law contend with them.
30:20 S· is the way of an adulterous
31:8 all s· as are appointed to destruction.
Ec 4:1 the tears of s· as were oppressed,
Isa 9:1 dimness shall not be s· as was in her
10:20 s· as are escaped of the house of
20:6 Behold, s· is our expectation,
37:30 eat this year s· as groweth of itself;
58:5 Is it s· a fast that I have chosen?
Isa 66:8 Who hath heard s· a thing?
8 who hath seen s· things?
Jer 2:10 and see if there be s· a thing.
5:9, 29 avenged on s· a nation as this?
9:9 soul be avenged on s· a nation as
15:2 Lord; S· as are for death, to death;
2 and s· as for the sword, to the sword;
2 and s· as are for the famine, to the
2 and s· as are for the captivity, to the
18:13 heathen, who hath heard s· things:
21:7 and s· as are left in this city from the
38:4 in speaking s· words unto them:
43:11 deliver s· as are for death to death;
11 and s· as are for captivity to captivity;
11 s· as are for the sword to the sword.
44:14 shall return but s· as shall escape.
Eze 17:15 he escape that doeth s· things?
18:14 considereth, and doeth not s· like,
Da 1:4 s· as had ability in them to stand in
2:10 asked s· things at any magician,
10:15 he had spoken s· words unto me,
11:32 And s· as do wickedly against the
12:1 trouble, s· as never was since there
Am 5:16 and s· as are skilful of lamentation to
Mic 5:15 heathen, s· as they have not heard.
Zep 1:8 and all s· as are clothed with strange
M't 9:8 had given s· power unto men.
18:5 shall receive one s· little child in my
19:14 for of s· is the kingdom of heaven.
24:21 s· as was not since the beginning
44 in s· an hour as ye think not the Son
26:18 Go into the city to s· a man, and
M'r 4:18 thorns; s· as hear the word,
20 s· as hear the word, and receive it,
33 with many s· parables spake he
6:2 even s· mighty works are wrought
7:8 many other s· like things ye do.
13 and many s· like things do ye.
9:37 receive one of s· children in my
10:14 not; for of s· is the kingdom of God.
13:7 for s· things must needs be; but the
19 s· as was not from the beginning
Lu 9:9 is this, of whom I hear s· things?
10:7 and drinking s· things as they give:
8 eat s· things as are set before you:
11:41 give alms of s· things as ye have;
13:2 because they suffered s· things?
18:13 not: for of s· is the kingdom of God.
Joh 4:23 Father seeketh s· to worship him.
7:32 the people murmured s· things
8:5 us, that s· should be stoned:
9:16 man that is a sinner do s· miracles?
Ac 2:47 church daily s· as should be saved.
3:6 I none; but s· as I have give I thee:
15:24 whom we gave no s· commandment:
16:24 Who, having received s· a charge,
18:15 I will be no judge of s· matters.
21:25 that they observe no s· thing,
22:22 with s· a fellow from the earth:
25:18 accusation of s· things as I supposed:
20 I doubted of s· manner of questions,
26:29 and altogether s· as I am, except
28:10 they laded us with s· things as were
Ro 1:32 s· things are worthy of death,
2:2 them which commit s· things.
3 judgest them which do s· things,
16:18 they that are s· serve not our Lord
1Co 5:1 s· fornication as is not so much as
5 To deliver s· an one unto Satan for
11 with s· an one no not to eat.
6:11 And s· were some of you: but ye
7:15 is not under bondage in s· cases:
28 s· shall have trouble in the flesh:
10:13 taken you but s· as is common to man:
11:16 we have no s· custom, neither the
15:48 s· are they also that are earthy:
48 s· are they also that are heavenly.
16:16 that ye submit yourselves unto s·,
18 acknowledge ye them that are s·.
2Co 2:6 Sufficient to s· a man is this
7 s· a one should be swallowed up
3:4 s· trust have we through Christ
12 Seeing then that we have s· hope,
10:11 Let s· an one think this, that,
11 s· as we are in word by letters
11 s· will we be also in deed when we
11:13 For s· are false apostles, deceitful
12:2 s· an one caught up to the third
3 And I knew s· a man, (whether in
5 Of s· an one will I glory: yet of
20 I shall not find you s· as I would,
20 found unto you s· as ye would not:
Ga 5:21 revellings, and s· like:
21 which do s· things shall not inherit
23 against s· there is no law.
6:1 restore s· an one in the spirit of
Eph 5:27 spot, or wrinkle, or any s· thing;
Ph'p 2:29 gladness; and hold s· in reputation:
1Th 4:6 the Lord is the avenger of all s·,
2Th 3:12 them that are s· we command and
1Ti 6:5 godliness: from s· withdraw thyself.
2Ti 3:5 power thereof: from s· turn away.
Tit 3:11 that he that is s· is subverted, and
Ph'm 9 being s· an one as Paul the aged,
Heb 5:12 are become s· as have need of milk,
7:26 s· an high priest became us, who
8:1 We have s· an high priest, who is
11:14 For they that say s· things declare
12:3 him that endured s· contradiction
13:5 content with s· things as ye have:
16 s· sacrifices God is well pleased.
Jas 4:13 to morrow we will go into s· a city,
16 boastings: all s· rejoicing is evil.
2Pe 1:17 there came s· a voice to him from
3:14 seeing that ye look for s· things,
3Jo 8 We therefore ought to receive s·,
Re 5:13 and s· as are in the sea, and all that
16:18 s· as was not since men were upon
20:6 on s· the second death hath no

Suchathites (*soo'-kath-ites*)
1Ch 2:55 the Shimeathites, and S·

suck See also SUCKED; SUCKING.
Ge 21:7 should have given children s·?
De 32:13 him to s· honey out of the rock,
33:19 s· of the abundance of the seas,
1Sa 1:23 gave her son s· until she weaned
1Ki 3:21 in the morning to give my child s·,
Job 3:12 why the breasts that I should s·?
20:16 He shall s· the poison of asps:
39:30 Her young ones also s· up blood:
Isa 60:16 also s· the milk of the Gentiles,
16 and shalt s· the breast of kings:
66:11 That ye may s·, and be satisfied
12 then shall ye s·, ye shall be borne
La 4:3 they give s· to their young ones:
Eze 23:34 shalt even drink it and s· it out,
Joe 2:16 and those that s· the breasts:
M't 24:19 and to them that give s· in those
M'r 13:17 to them that give s· in those days!
Lu 21:23 to them that give s· in those days!
23:29 and the paps which never gave s·.

sucked
Ca 8:1 that s· the breasts of my mother!
Lu 11:27 and the paps which thou hast s·.

sucking
Nu 11:12 nursing father beareth the s· child,
1Sa 7:9 Samuel took a s· lamb, and offered
Isa 11:8 the s· child shall play on the hole
49:15 Can a woman forget her s· child,
La 4:4 The tongue of the s· child cleaveth

suckling See also SUCKLINGS.
De 32:25 the s· also with the man of gray
1Sa 15:3 infant and s·, ox and sheep, camel
Jer 44:7 you man and woman, child and s·,

sucklings
1Sa 22:19 men and women, children and s·,
Ps 8:2 Out of the mouth of babes and s·
La 2:11 and the s· swoon in the streets
M't 21:16 Out of the mouth of babes and s·

sudden
Job 22:10 thee, and s· fear troubleth thee;
Pr 3:25 Be not afraid of s· fear, neither of
1Th 5:3 then s· destruction cometh upon

suddenly
Nu 6:9 if any man die very s· by him,
12:4 And the Lord spake s· unto Moses,
35:22 if he thrust him s· without enmity,
De 7:4 against you, and destroy thee s·.
Jos 10:9 therefore came unto them s·, and
11:7 them by the waters of Merom s·;
2Sa 15:14 lest he overtake us s·, and bring
2Ch 29:36 people: for the thing was done s·.
Job 5:3 root: but s· I cursed his habitation.
9:23 If the scourge slay s·, he will laugh
Ps 6:10 them return and be ashamed s·.
64:4 s· do they shoot at him, and fear
7 arrow; s· shall they be wounded.
Pr 6:15 shall his calamity come s·;
15 s· shall he be broken without
24:22 For their calamity shall rise s·;
29:1 shall s· be destroyed, and that
Ec 9:12 time, when it falleth s· upon them.
Isa 29:5 yea, it shall be at an instant s·.
30:13 breaking cometh s· at an instant.
47:11 desolation shall come upon thee s·,
48:3 them; I did them s·, and they came
Jer 4:20 s· are my tents spoiled, and my
6:26 the spoiler shall s· come upon us.
15:8 I have caused him to fall upon it s·,
18:22 shalt bring a troop s· upon them:
49:19 s· make him run away from her:
50:44 make them s· run away from her:
51:8 Babylon is s· fallen and destroyed:
Hab 2:7 Shall they not rise up s· that shall
Mal 3:1 seek, shall s· come to his temple,
M'r 9:8 s·, when they had looked round
13:36 coming s· he find you sleeping.
Lu 2:13 And s· there was with the angel a
9:39 taketh him, and he s· crieth out;
Ac 2:2 s· there came a sound from heaven
9:3 s· there shined round about him a
16:26 s· there was a great earthquake,
22:6 s· there shone from heaven a great
28:6 swollen, or fallen down dead s·:
1Ti 5:22 Lay hands s· on no man, neither

sue
M't 5:40 If any man will s· thee at the law,

suffer See also SUFFERED; SUFFEREST; SUFFERETH; SUFFERING.
Ex 12:23 will not s· the destroyer to come
22:18 Thou shalt not s· a witch to live.
Le 2:13 shalt thou s· the salt...to be lacking
19:17 neighbour,...not s· sin upon him.
22:16 Or s· them to bear the iniquity of
Nu 21:23 Sihon would not s· Israel to pass
Jos 10:19 s· them not to enter into their cities:
J'g 1:34 would not s· them to come down to
15:1 father would not s· him to go in.
16:26 S· me that I may feel the pillars
2Sa 14:11 not s· the revengers of blood to
1Ki 15:17 that he might not s· any to go out
Es 3:8 not for the king's profit to s· them.
Job 9:18 will not s· me to take my breath,
21:3 S· me that I may speak; and after
24:11 tread their winepresses, and s· thirst.
36:2 S· me a little, and I will shew thee
Ps 9:13 consider my trouble which I s· of them
16:10 wilt thou s· thine Holy One to see

Ps 34:10 young lions do lack, and s· hunger:
55:22 he shall never s· the righteous to
88:15 I s· thy terrors I am distracted.
89:33 from him, nor s· my faithfulness to fail.
101: 5 and a proud heart will not I s·.
121: 3 will not s· thy foot to be moved:
Pr 10: 3 will not s· the...righteous to famish:
19:15 sleep; and an idle soul shall s· hunger.
19 great wrath shall s· punishment:
Ec 5: 6 S· not thy mouth to cause thy flesh
12 the rich will not s· him to sleep.
Eze 44:20 heads, nor s· their locks to grow long;
M't 3:15 said unto him, S· it to be so now:
8:21 s· me first to go and bury my
31 s· us to go away into the herd of
16:21 s· many things of the elders and
17:12 also the Son of man s· of them.
17 with you? how long shall I s· you?
19:14 S· little children, and forbid them
23:13 neither s· ye them that are entering
M'r 7:12 ye s· him no more to do ought for
8:31 Son of man must s· many things,
9:12 man, that he must s· many things,
19 with you? how long shall I s· you?
10:14 S· the little children to come unto
11:16 would not s· that any man should
Lu 8:32 would s· them to enter into them.
9:22 Son of man must s· many things,
41 shall I be with you, and s· you?
59 Lord, s· me first to go and bury my
17:25 But first must he s· many things,
18:16 S· little children to come unto me,
22:15 this passover with you before I s·:
51 answered and said, S· ye thus far.
24:46 and thus it behoved Christ to s·,
Ac 2:27 wilt thou s· thine Holy One to see
3:18 prophets, that Christ should s·,
5:41 counted worthy to s· shame for his
7:24 seeing one of them s· wrong, he
9:16 him how great things he must s·
13:35 shalt not s· thine Holy One to see
21:39 s· me to speak unto the people.
26:23 That Christ should s·, and that he
Ro 8:17 If so be that we s· with him, that
1Co 3:15 shall be burned, he shall s· loss:
4:12 bless; being persecuted, we s· it:
6: 7 rather s· yourselves to be defrauded?
9:12 but s· all things, lest we should
10:13 will not s· you to be tempted above
12:26 whether one member s·, all the
26 all the members s· with it; or one
2Co 1: 6 same sufferings which we also s·:
11:19 For ye s· fools gladly, seeing ye
20 For ye s·, if a man bring you into
Ga 5:11 why do I yet s· persecution? then
6:12 should s· persecution for the cross
Ph'p 1:29 on him, but also to s· for his sake;
4:12 both to abound and to s· need.
1Th 3: 4 before that we should s· tribulation;
2Th 1: 5 kingdom of God, for which ye also s·:
1Ti 2:12 I s· not a woman to teach, nor to
4:10 we both labour and s· reproach,
2Ti 1:12 which cause I also s· these things:
2: 9 Wherein I s· trouble, as an evil doer,
12 If we s·, we shall also reign with
3:12 Christ Jesus shall s· persecution.
Heb 11:25 Choosing rather to s· affliction
13: 3 and them which s· adversity, as
22 s· the word of exhortation: for
1Pe 2:20 when ye do well, and s· for it, ye
3:14 if ye s· for righteousness' sake,
17 that ye s· for well doing, than for
4:15 let none of you s· as a murderer, or
16 if any man s· as a Christian, let him
19 let them that s· according to the
Re 2:10 of those things which thou shalt s·:
11: 9 not s· their dead bodies to be put in

suffered
Ge 20: 6 s· I thee not to touch her.
31: 7 but God s· him not to hurt me.
28 not s· me to kiss my sons and my
De 8: 3 and s· thee to hunger, and fed thee
18:14 thy God hath not s· thee so to do.
J'g 3:28 Moab, and s· not a man to pass over.
1Sa 24: 7 and s· them not to rise against Saul.
2Sa 21:10 and s· neither the birds of the air
1Ch 16:21 He s· no man to do them wrong:
Job 31:30 Neither have I s· my mouth to sin
Ps 105:14 He s· no man to do them wrong:
Jer 15:15 that for thy sake I have s· rebuke.
M't 3:15 all righteousness. Then he s· him.
19: 8 s· you to put away your wives:
24:43 have s· his house to be broken up.
27:19 for I have s· many things this day
M'r 1:34 and s· not the devils to speak,
5:19 Howbeit Jesus s· him not, but saith
26 s· many things of many physicians,
37 And he s· no man to follow him,
10: 4 s· to write a bill of divorcement,
Lu 4:41 rebuking...s· them not to speak:
8:32 enter into them. And he s· them.
51 he s· no man to go in, save Peter,
12:39 s· his house to be broken through.
13: 2 because they s· such things?
24:26 not Christ to have s· these things,
Ac 13:18 s· he their manners in the
14:16 s· all nations to walk in their own
16: 7 but the Spirit s· them not.
17: 3 that Christ must needs have s·,
19:30 people, the disciples s· him not.
28:16 Paul was s· to dwell by himself
2Co 7:12 nor for his cause that s· wrong, but
11:25 was I stoned, thrice I s· shipwreck,
Ga 3: 4 Have ye s· so many things in vain?
Ph'p 3: 8 I have s· the loss of all things,
1Th 2: 2 even after that we had s· before,
2:14 s· like things of your...countrymen,
Heb 2:18 he himself hath s· being tempted,
5: 8 he obedience by the things...he s·:
7:23 were not s· to continue by reason
9:26 For then must he often have s·
13:12 his own blood, s· without the gate.
1Pe 2:21 because Christ also s· for us,
23 when he s·, he threatened not; but
3:18 Christ also hath once s· for sins,
4: 1 as Christ hath s· for us in the flesh
1 for he that hath s· in the flesh hath
5:10 after that ye have s· a while, make

sufferest
Re 2:20 thou s· that woman Jezebel,

suffereth
Ps 66: 9 and s· not our feet to be moved.
107:38 and s· not their cattle to decrease.
M't 11:12 the kingdom of heaven s· violence,
Ac 28: 4 sea, yet vengeance s· not to live.
1Co 13: 4 Charity s· long, and is kind;

suffering See also LONGSUFFERING; SUFFERINGS.
Ac 27: 7 the wind not s· us, we sailed under
Heb 2: 9 than the angels for the s· of death,
Jas 5:10 for an example of s· affliction,
1Pe 2:19 God endure grief, s· wrongfully.
Jude 7 s· the vengeance of eternal fire.

sufferings
Ro 8:18 I reckon that the s· of this present
2Co 1: 5 as the s· of Christ abound in us,
6 enduring of the same s· which we
7 that as ye are partakers of the s·,
Ph'p 3:10 and the fellowship of his s·,
Col 1:24 Who now rejoice in my s· for you,
Heb 2:10 their salvation perfect through s·.
1Pe 1:11 testified beforehand the s· of Christ,
4:13 as ye are partakers of Christ's s·;
5: 1 and a witness of the s· of Christ,

suffice See also SUFFICED; SUFFICETH.
Nu 11:22 herds be slain for them, to s· them?
22 gathered...for them, to s· them?
De 3:26 Lord said unto me, Let it s· thee;
1Ki 20:10 dust of Samaria...s· for handfuls
Eze 44: 6 it s· you of all your abominations,
45: 9 Let it s· you, O princes of Israel:
1Pe 4: 3 the time past of our life may s· us

sufficed
J'g 21:14 and yet so they s· them not.
Ru 2:14 corn, and she did eat, and was s·,
18 she had reserved after she was s·.

sufficeth
Joh 14: 8 shew us the Father, and it s· us.

sufficiency
Job 20:22 In the fulness of his s· he shall be
2Co 3: 5 of ourselves; but our s· is of God;
9: 8 always having all s· in all things,

sufficient
Ex 36: 7 stuff they had was s· for all the
De 15: 8 surely lend him s· for his need,
33: 7 let his hands be s· for him; and
Pr 25:16 eat so much as is s· for thee, lest
Isa 40:16 And Lebanon is not s· to burn, nor
16 the beasts thereof s· for a burnt
M't 6:34 S· unto the day is the evil thereof.
Lu 14:28 cost, whether he have s· to finish it?
Joh 6: 7 pennyworth of bread is not s· for
2Co 2: 6 S· to such...is this punishment,
16 And who is s· for these things?
3: 5 Not that we are s· of ourselves to
12: 9 unto me, My grace is s· for thee:

sufficiently
2Ch 30: 3 had not sanctified themselves s·,
Isa 23:18 eat s·, and for durable clothing.

suit See also SUITS.
J'g 17:10 a s· of apparel, and thy victuals.
2Sa 15: 4 that every man which has any s·
Job 11:19 many shall make s· unto thee.

suits
Isa 3:22 The changeable s· of apparel, and the

Sukkiims (*suk'-ke-ims*)
2Ch 12: 3 the Lubims, the S·, and the

sum
Ex 21:30 be laid on him a s· of money,
30:12 takest the s· of the children of
38:21 This is the s· of the tabernacle,
Nu 1: 2 Take ye the s· of the congregation
49 Levi, neither take the s· of them
4: 2 Take the s· of the sons of Kohath
22 Take...the s· of the sons of Gershon,
26: 2 Take the s· of all the congregation
4 Take the s· of the people, from twenty
31:26 Take the s· of the prey that was
49 have taken the s· of the men of war
2Sa 24: 9 the s· of the number of the people
2Ki 22: 4 that he may s· the silver which is
1Ch 21: 5 the s· of the number of the people
Es 4: 7 the s· of the money that Haman
Ps 139:17 God! how great is the s· of them!
Eze 28:12 Thou sealest up the s·, full of
Da 7: 1 and told the s· of the matters.
Ac 7:16 Abraham bought for a s· of money
22:28 a great s· obtained I this freedom.
Heb 8: 1 we have spoken this is the s·:

summer
Ge 8:22 cold and heat, and s· and winter,
J'g 3:20 and he was sitting in a s· parlour,
24 covereth his feet in his s· chamber.
2Sa 16: 1 and an hundred of s· fruits, and a
2 s· fruit for the young men to eat;
Ps 32: 4 is turned into the drought of s·.
74:17 thou hast made s· and winter.
Pr 6: 8 Provideth her meat in the s·, and
10: 5 that gathereth in s· is a wise son:
26: 1 As snow in s·, and as rain in
30:25 they prepare their meat in the s·;
Isa 16: 9 for the shouting for thy s· fruits
18: 6 and the fowls shall s· upon them,
28: 4 as the hasty fruit before the s·;
Jer 8:20 The harvest is past, the s· is ended,
40:10 gather ye wine, and s· fruits, and
12 gathered wine and s· fruits very
48:32 spoiler is fallen upon thy s· fruits
Da 2:35 the chaff of the s· threshingfloors;
Am 3:15 winter house with the s· house;
8: 1 me: and behold a basket of s· fruit.
2 And I said, A basket of s· fruit.
Mic 7: 1 they have gathered the s· fruits,
Zec 14: 8 sea: in s· and in winter shall it be.
M't 24:32 leaves, ye know that s· is nigh:
M'r 13:28 leaves, ye know that s· is near:
Lu 21:30 selves that s· is now nigh at hand.

sumptuously See also PRESUMPTUOUSLY.
Lu 16:19 fine linen, and fared s· every day:

sun See also SUNRISING.
Ge 15:12 And when the s· was going down,
17 when the s· went down, and it was
19:23 The s· was risen upon the earth
28:11 all night, because the s· was set;
32:31 as he passed over Penuel the s· rose
37: 9 the s· and the moon and the eleven
Ex 16:21 when the s· waxed hot, it melted.
17:12 until the going down of the s·.
22: 3 If the s· be risen upon him, there
26 unto him by that the s· goeth down:
Le 22: 7 And when the s· is down, he shall be
Nu 2: 3 toward the rising of the s· shall they
25: 4 up before the Lord against the s·,
De 4:19 and when thou seest the s·, and the
11:30 the way where the s· goeth down,
16: 6 at the going down of the s·, at the
17: 3 either the s·, or moon, or any of the
23:11 when the s· is down, he shall come
24:13 again when the s· goeth down,
15 neither shall the s· go down upon it;
33:14 fruits brought forth by the s·,
Jos 1: 4 sea toward the going down of the s·,
8:29 and as soon as the s· was down,
10:12 S·, stand thou still upon Gibeon;
13 And the s· stood still, and the moon
13 s· stood still in the midst of heaven,
27 the time of the going down of the s·,
12: 1 Jordan toward the rising of the s·,
J'g 5:31 as the s· when he goeth forth in his
8:13 from battle before the s· was up,
9:33 as soon as the s· is up, thou shalt
14:18 day before the s· went down,
19:14 and the s· went down upon them
1Sa 11: 9 by that time the s· be hot, ye shall
2Sa 2:24 the s· went down when they were
3:35 or ought else, till the s· be down.
12:11 with thy wives in the sight of this s·.
12 before all Israel, and before the s·.
23: 4 of the morning, when the s· riseth,
1Ki 22:36 host about the going down of the s·,
2Ki 3:22 and the s· shone upon the water,
23: 5 burned incense unto Baal, to the s·,
11 kings of Judah had given to the s·,
11 and burned the chariots of the s·
2Ch 18:34 time of the s· going down he died.
Ne 7: 3 be opened until the s· be hot;
Job 8:16 He is green before the s·, and his
9: 7 Which commandeth the s·, and it
30:28 I went mourning without the s·:
31:26 If I beheld the s· when it shined,
Ps 19: 4 hath he set a tabernacle for the s·,
50: 1 the earth from the rising of the s·
58: 8 that they may not see the s·.
72: 5 as long as the s· and moon endure,
17 be continued as long as the s·:
74:16 hast prepared the light and the s·.
84:11 For the Lord God is a s· and shield:
89:36 and his throne as the s· before me.
104:19 the s· knoweth his going down.
22 The s· ariseth, they gather
113: 3 From the rising of the s· unto the
121: 6 The s· shall not smite thee by day,
136: 8 The s· to rule by day: for his mercy
148: 3 Praise ye him, s· and moon: praise
Ec 1: 3 labour...he taketh under the s·?
5 The s· also ariseth, and the s· goeth
9 there is no new thing under the s·.
14 works that are done under the s·;
2:11 and there was no profit under the s·.
17 work that is wrought under the s·
18 labour...I had taken under the s·:
19 shewed myself wise under the s·.
20 labour which I took under the s·.
22 he hath laboured under the s·?
3:16 under the s· the place of judgment,
4: 1 the oppressions...done under the s·:
3 evil work that is done under the s·.
7 and I saw vanity under the s·.
15 the living which walk under the s·,
5:13 sore evil...I have seen under the s·,
18 labour that he taketh under the s·
6: 1 evil which I have seen under the s·,
5 Moreover he hath not seen the s·,
12 shall be after him under the s·?
7:11 is profit to them that see the s·.
8: 9 work that is done under the s·:
15 hath no better thing under the s·,
15 which God giveth him under the s·.
17 the work that is done under the s·:
9: 3 things that are done under the s·,
6 any thing that is done under the s·.

Ec 9: 9 he hath given thee under the s·.
9 labour...thou takest under the s·.
11 I returned, and saw under the s·,
13 wisdom have I seen...under the s·,
10: 5 evil which I have seen under the s·,
11: 7 it is for the eyes to behold the s·:
12: 2 While the s·, or the light, or the
Ca 1: 6 because the s· hath looked upon me:
6:10 fair as the moon, clear as the s·,
Isa 13:10 s· shall be darkened in his going
24:23 confounded, and the s· ashamed,
30:26 moon shall be as the light of the s·,
26 light of the s· shall be sevenfold,
38: 8 is gone down in the s· dial of Ahaz,
8 So the s· returned ten degrees, by
41:25 from the rising of the s· shall he
45: 6 may know from the rising of the s·,
49:10 shall the heat nor s· smite them:
59:19 his glory from the rising of the s·.
60:19 The s· shall be no more thy light by
20 Thy s· shall no more go down;
Jer 8: 2 they shall spread them before the s·,
15: 9 her s· is gone down while it was yet
31:35 giveth the s· for a light by day,
Eze 8:16 they worshipped the s· toward the
32: 7 I will cover the s· with a cloud, and
Da 6:14 laboured till...going down of the s·
Joel 2:10 the s· and the moon shall be dark,
31 s· shall be turned into darkness,
3:15 s· and the moon shall be darkened,
Am 8: 9 cause the s· to go down at noon,
Jon 4: 8 came to pass, when the s· did arise,
8 the s· beat upon the head of Jonah,
Mic 3: 6 and the s· shall go down over the
Na 3:17 when the s· ariseth they flee away,
Hab 3:11 The s· and moon stood still in their
Mal 1:11 from the rising of the s· even unto
4: 2 the *S*· of righteousness arise with
M't 5:45 for he maketh his s· to rise on the
13: 6 And when the s· was up, they were
43 the righteous shine forth as the s·
17: 2 his face did shine as the s·, and his
24:29 days shall the s· be darkened,
M'r 1:32 when the s· did set, they brought
4: 6 But when the s· was up, it was
13:24 the s· shall be darkened, and the
16: 2 the sepulchre at the rising of the s·.
Lu 4:40 Now when the s· was setting, all they
21:25 And there shall be signs in the s·,
23:45 And the s· was darkened, and the
Ac 2:20 s· shall be turned into darkness,
13:11 blind, not seeing the s· for a season.
26:13 above the brightness of the s·,
27:20 when neither s· nor stars in many
1Co 15:41 There is one glory of the s·, and
Eph 4:26 not the s· go down upon your wrath:
Jas 1:11 For the s· is no sooner risen with a
Re 1:16 as the s· shineth in his strength.
6:12 the s· became black as sackcloth of
7:16 neither shall the s· light on them,
8:12 the third part of the s· was smitten,
9: 2 the s· and the air were darkened by
10: 1 and his face was as it were the s·,
12: 1 a woman clothed with the s·, and
16: 8 poured out his vial upon the s·;
19:17 I saw an angel standing in the s·;
21:23 And the city had no need of the s·,
22: 5 no candle, neither light of the s·;

sunder^ See also ASUNDER; SUNDERED.
Ps 46: 9 bow, and cutteth the spear in s·;
107:14 death, and break their bands in s·.
16 of brass, and cut the bars of iron in s·.
Isa 27: 9 as chalkstones that are beaten in s·,
Na 1:13 thee, and will burst thy bonds in s·.
Lu 12:46 he is not aware, and will cut him in s·,

sundered
Job 41:17 together, that they cannot be s·.

sundry
Heb 1: 1 at s· times and in divers manners

sung See also SANG.
Isa 26: 1 In that day shall this song be s· in
M't 26:30 when they had s· an hymn, they
M'r 14:26 when they had s· an hymn, they
Re 5: 9 they s· a new song, saying, Thou
14: 3 s· as it were a new song before the

sunk See also SANK.
1Sa 17:49 the stone s· into his forehead;
2Ki 9:24 and he s· down in his chariot.
Ps 9:15 heathen are s· down in the pit
Jer 38: 6 mire: so Jeremiah s· in the mire.
22 thy feet are s· in the mire, and they
La 2: 9 Her gates are s· into the ground;
Ac 20: 9 preaching, he s· down with sleep,

sunrising
Nu 21:11 is before Moab, toward the s·.
34:15 Jericho eastward, toward the s·.
De 4:41, 47 side Jordan toward the s·;
Jos 1:15 this side Jordan toward the s·.
13: 5 and all Lebanon, toward the s·.
19:12 Sarid eastward toward the s·
27 And turneth toward the s· to
34 upon Jordan toward the s·.
J'g 20:43 against Gibeah toward the s·.

sup See also SUPPED.
Hab 1: 9 faces shall s· up as the east wind,
Lu 17: 8 Make ready wherewith I may s·,
Re 3:20 in to him, and will s· with him,

superfluity
Jas 1:21 filthiness and s· of naughtiness,

superfluous
Le 21:18 hath a flat nose, or any thing s·,
22:23 any thing s· or lacking in his parts,
2Co 9: 1 it is s· for me to write to you:

superscription
M't 22:20 them, Whose is this image and s·?
M'r 12:16 them, Whose is this image and s·?
15:26 the s· of his accusation was written
Lu 20:24 Whose image and s· hath it? They
23:38 And a s· also was written over him

superstition
Ac 25:19 against him of their own s·, and

superstitious
Ac 17:22 that in all things ye are too s·.

supped
1Co 11:25 he took the cup, when he had s·,

supper
M'r 6:21 birthday made a s· to his lords,
Lu 14:12 When thou makest a dinner or a s·,
16 A certain man made a great s·, and
17 sent his servant at s· time to say to
24 were bidden shall taste of my s·.
22:20 Likewise also the cup after s·,
Joh 12: 2 There they made him a s·; and
13: 2 s· being ended, the devil having
4 He riseth from s·, and laid aside
21:20 also leaned on his breast at s·, and
1Co 11:20 this is not to eat the Lord's s·.
21 one taketh before other his own s·:
Re 19: 9 unto the marriage s· of the Lamb.
17 unto the s· of the great God;

supplant See also SUPPLANTED.
Jer 9: 4 for every brother will utterly s·,

supplanted
Ge 27:36 for he hath s· me these two times:

supple
Eze 16: 4 thou washed in water to s· thee;

suppliants
Zep 3:10 the rivers of Ethiopia my s·,

supplication See also SUPPLICATIONS.
1Sa 13:12 I have not made s· unto the Lord:
1Ki 8:28 prayer of thy servant, and to his s·,
30 And hearken thou to the s· of thy
33 make s· unto thee in this house:
38 prayer and s· soever be made by
45 in heaven their prayer and their s·,
47 and make s· unto thee in the land
49 their prayer and their s· in heaven
52 be open unto the s· of thy servant,
52 and unto the s· of thy people Israel,
54 all this prayer and s· unto the Lord,
59 I have made s· before the Lord,
9: 3 have heard thy prayer and thy s·,
2Ch 6:19 prayer of thy servant, and to his s·,
24 make s· before thee in this house;
29 what s· soever shall be made of
35 heavens their prayer and their s·,
33:13 and heard his s·, and brought him
Es 4: 8 the king, to make s· unto him,
Job 8: 5 and make thy s· to the Almighty;
9:15 but I would make s· to my judge.
Ps 6: 9 The Lord hath heard my s·; the
30: 8 and unto the Lord I made s·.
55: 1 and hide not thyself from my s·.
119:170 Let my s· come before thee:
142: 1 unto the Lord did I make my s·.
Isa 45:14 they shall make s· unto thee,
Jer 36: 7 present their s· before the Lord,
37:20 let my s·, I pray thee, be accepted
38:26 I presented my s· before the king,
42: 2 our s· be accepted before thee, and
9 me to present your s· before him;
Da 6:11 and making s· before his God.
9:20 presenting my s· before the Lord
Ho 12: 4 he wept, and made s· unto him:
Ac 1:14 with one accord in prayer and s·,
Eph 6:18 with all prayer and s· in the Spirit,
18 perseverance and s· for all saints;
Ph'p 4: 6 by prayer and s· with thanksgiving

supplications
2Ch 6:21 unto the s· of thy servant, and
39 their prayer and their s·, and
Job 41: 3 Will he make many s· unto thee?
Ps 28: 2 Hear the voice of my s·, when I cry
6 he hath heard the voice of my s·.
31:22 heardest the voice of my s· when I
86: 6 and attend to the voice of my s·.
116: 1 he hath heard my voice and my s·.
130: 2 be attentive to the voice of my s·.
140: 6 hear the voice of my s·, O Lord.
143: 1 prayer, O Lord, give ear to my s·:
Jer 3:21 weeping and s· of the children of
31: 9 and with s· will I lead them:
Da 9: 3 Lord God, to seek by prayer and s·,
17 prayer of thy servant, and his s·,
18 for we do not present our s· before
23 At the beginning of thy s· the
Zec 12:10 the spirit of grace and of s·: and
1Ti 2: 1 that, first of all, s·, prayers,
5: 5 continueth in s· and prayers night
Heb 5: 7 he had offered up prayers and s·

supplied
1Co 16:17 lacking on your part they have s·.
2Co 11: 9 which came from Macedonia s·:

supplieth
2Co 9:12 not only s· the want of the saints,
Eph 4:16 by that which every joint s·,

supply See also SUPPLIED; SUPPLIETH.
2Co 8:14 abundance...be a s· for their want,
14 also may be a s· for your want:
Ph'p 1:19 the s· of the Spirit of Jesus Christ,
2:30 to s· your lack of service toward
4:19 But my God shall s· all your need†

support
Ac 20:35 labouring ye ought to s· the weak,
1Th 5:14 s· the weak, be patient toward all

suppose See also SUPPOSED; SUPPOSING.
2Sa 13:32 not my lord s· that they have slain
Lu 7:43 I s· that he, to whom he forgave
12:51 *S*· ye that I am come to give peace
13: 2 *S*· ye that these Galilæans were
Joh 21:25 I s· that even the world itself
Ac 2:15 these are not drunken, as ye s·,
1Co 7:26 I s· therefore that this is good for
2Co 11: 5 I s· I was not a whit behind the
Heb 10:29 much sorer punishment, s· ye,
1Pe 5:12 a faithful brother...as I s·,

supposed
M't 20:10 s· that they should have received
M'r 6:49 sea, they s· it had been a spirit,
Lu 3:23 being (as was s·) the son of Joseph,
24:37 and s· that they had seen a spirit.
Ac 7:25 For he s· his brethren would have
21:29 whom they s·...Paul had brought
25:18 accusation of such things as I s·:
Ph'p 2:25 I s· it necessary to send to you

supposing
Lu 2:44 they, s· him...in the company,
Joh 20:15 She, s· him to be the gardener,
Ac 14:19 out of the city, s· he had been dead.
16:27 s· that the prisoners had been fled.
27:13 s· that they had obtained their
Ph'p 1:16 s· to add affliction to my bonds:
1Ti 6: 5 truth, s· that gain is godliness:

supreme
1Pe 2:13 whether it be to the king, as s·;

Sur (*sur*)
2Ki 11: 6 part shall be at the gate of *S*·;

sure See also ASSURE.
Ge 23:17 borders round about, were made s·
20 were made s· unto Abraham for a
Ex 3:19 I am s·...the king of Egypt will not
Nu 32:23 and be s· your sin will find you out.
De 12:23 be s· that thou eat not the blood:
1Sa 2:35 and I will build him a s· house;
20: 7 be s·...evil is determined by him.
25:28 certainly make my lord a s· house;
2Sa 1:10 I was s· that he could not live
23: 5 ordered in all things, and s·:
1Ki 11:38 and build thee a s· house, as I built
Ne 9:38 we make a s· covenant, and write
Job 24:22 riseth up, and no man is s· of life.
Ps 19: 7 the testimony of the Lord is s·,
93: 5 Thy testimonies are very s·:
111: 7 all his commandments are s·.
Pr 6: 3 thyself, and make s· thy friend.
11:15 and he that hateth suretiship is s·.
18 righteousness shall be a s· reward.
Isa 22:23 fasten him as a nail in a s· place;
25 nail that is fastened in the s· place
28:16 corner stone, a s· foundation:
32:18 and in s· dwellings, and in quiet
33:16 given him; his waters shall be s·.
55: 3 you, even the s· mercies of David.
Da 2:45 and the interpretation thereof s·.
4:26 thy kingdom shall be s· unto thee,
M't 27:64 sepulchre be made s· until the third
65 your way, make it as s· as ye can.
66 went, and made the sepulchre s·,
Lu 10:11 be ye s· of this, that the kingdom
Joh 6:69 are s· that thou art that Christ,
16:30 Now are we s· that thou knowest
Ac 13:34 give you the s· mercies of David.
Ro 2: 2 we are s· that the judgment of God
4:16 might be s· to all the seed;
15:29 And I am s· that, when I come
2Ti 2:19 the foundation of God standeth s·,
Heb 6:19 of the soul, both s· and stedfast,
2Pe 1:10 make your calling and election s·:
19 also a more s· word of prophecy;

surely^
Ge 2:17 thou eatest thereof thou shalt s· die.
3: 4 unto the woman, Ye shall not s· die:
9: 5 s· your blood...will I require;
18:18 Abraham shall s· become a great and
20: 7 know thou that thou shalt s· die,
11 *S*· the fear of God is not in this
26:11 or his wife shall s· be put to death.
28:16 said, *S*· the Lord is in this place;
22 me I will s· give the tenth unto thee.
29:14 *S*· thou art my bone and my flesh.
32 *S*· the Lord hath looked upon my
30:16 s· I have hired thee with my son's
31:42 s· thou hadst sent me away now
32:12 I will s· do thee good, and make thy
42:16 by the life of Pharaoh s· ye are spies.
43:10 *S*·...we had returned this second
44:28 *S*· he is torn in pieces; and I saw
46: 4 and I will also s· bring thee up again:
50:24 God will s· visit you, and bring you
25 God will s· visit you, and ye shall
Ex 2:14 and said, *S*· this thing is known.
3: 7 I have s· seen the affliction of my
16 I have s· visited you, and seen that
4:25 *S*· a bloody husband art thou to
11: 1 he shall s· thrust you out hence
13:19 of Israel, saying, God will s· visit you;
18:18 Thou wilt s· wear away, both thou,
19:12 the mount shall be s· put to death:
13 touch it, but he shall s· be stoned,
21:12 so that he die, shall be s· put to death.
15 or his mother, shall be s· put to death.
16 in his hand, he shall s· be put to death.
17 or his mother, shall s· be put to death
20 his hand; he shall be s· punished.

Ex 21:22 he shall be s' punished, according as
28 then the ox shall be s' stoned, and his
36 he shall s' pay ox for ox; and the dead
22: 6 the fire shall s' make restitution.
14 not with it, he shall s' make it good.
16 he shall s' endow her to be his wife.
19 with a beast shall s' be put to death.
23 at all unto me, I will s' hear their cry;
23: 4 shalt s' bring it back to him again.
5 help him, thou shalt s' help with him.
33 it will s' be a snare unto thee.
31:14 that defileth it shall s' be put to death:
15 day, he shall s' be put to death.
40:15 anointing shall s' be an everlasting
Le 20: 2 Molech; he shall s' be put to death:
9 or his mother shall be s' put to death:
10 the adulteress shall s' be put to death.
11 both of them shall s' be put to death;
12 both of them shall s' be put to death:
13 they shall s' be put to death; their
15 a beast, he shall s' be put to death:
16 beast: they shall s' be put to death;
27 a wizard, shall s' be put to death:
24:16 the Lord, he shall s' be put to death,
17 any man shall s' be put to death.
27:29 redeemed; but shall s' be put to death.
Nu 13:27 and s' it floweth with milk and honey;
14:23 S' they shall not see the land
35 I will s' do it unto all this evil
15:35 The man shall be s' put to death:
18:15 firstborn of man shalt thou s' redeem,
22:33 s' now also I had slain thee, and
23:23 S' there is no enchantment against
26:65 They shall s' die in the wilderness.
27: 7 thou shalt s' give them a possession of
32:11 S' none of the men that came up
35:16, 17, 18 shall s' be put to death.
21 smote him shall s' be put to death;
31 death: but he shall be s' put to death.
De 1:35 S' there shall not one of these men
4: 6 S' this great nation is a wise and
8:19 this day that ye shall s' perish.
13: 9 But thou shalt s' kill him; thine
15 s' smite the inhabitants of that city
15: 8 shalt s' lend him sufficient for his need,
10 Thou shalt s' give him, and thine
16:15 therefore thou shalt s' rejoice.
22: 4 s' help him to lift them up again.
23:21 thy God will s' require it of thee;
30:18 that ye shall s' perish, and that
31:18 And I will s' hide my face in that day
Jos 14: 9 S' the land whereon thy feet have
J'g 3:24 said, S' he covereth his feet in his
4: 9 And she said, I will s' go with thee:
6:16 S' I will be with thee, and thou
11:31 of Ammon, shall s' be the Lord's,
13:22 We shall s' die, because we have seen
15:13 hand: but s' we will not kill thee.
20:39 S' they are smitten down before
21: 5 saying, He shall s' be put to death.
Ru 1:10 S' we will return with thee unto
1Sa 9: 6 all that he saith cometh s' to pass:
14:39 Jonathan my son, he shall s' die.
44 for thou shalt s' die, Jonathan.
15:32 S' the bitterness of death is past.
16: 6 S' the Lord's anointed is before
17:25 s' to defy Israel is he come up:
20:26 he is not clean; s' he is not clean.
31 him unto me, for he shall s' die.
22:16 Thou shalt s' die, Ahimelech, thou,
22 there, that he would s' tell Saul:
24:20 well that thou shalt s' be king,
25:21 S' in vain have I kept all that this
34 s' there had not been left unto
28: 2 S' thou shalt know what thy
29: 6 S', as the Lord liveth, thou hast been
30: 8 for thou shalt s' overtake them,
2Sa 2:27 s' then in the morning the people
9: 7 s' shew the kindness for Jonathan
11:23 S' the men prevailed against us,
12: 5 hath done this thing shall s' die:
14 that is born unto thee shall s' die.
15:21 s' in what place my lord the king
18: 2 I will s' go forth with you myself also.
20:18 They shall s' ask counsel at Abel:
24:24 will s' buy it of thee at a price:
1Ki 2:37 for certain that thou shalt s' die:
42 any whither, that thou shalt s' die?
8:13 I have s' built thee an house to
11: 2 for s' they will turn away your heart
11 I will s' rend the kingdom from thee,
13:32 of Samaria, shall s' come to pass.
18:15 I will s' shew myself unto him to
20:23, 25 s' we shall be stronger than
22:32 they said, S' it is the king of Israel.
2Ki 1: 4, 6, 16 art gone up, but shalt s' die.
3:14 s', were it not that I regard the
23 the kings are s' slain, and they have
5:11 He will s' come out to me, and stand,
8:10 shewed me that he shall s' die.
14 me that thou shouldest s' recover.
9:26 S' I have seen yesterday the blood of
18:30 The Lord will s' deliver us, and this
23:22 S' there was not holden such a
24: 3 S' at the commandment of the
Es 6:13 him, but shalt s' fall before him.
Job 8: 6 s' now he would awake for thee,
13: 3 S' I would speak to the Almighty,
10 He will s' reprove you, if ye do
14:18 And s' the mountain falling cometh
18:21 S' such are the dwellings of the
20:20 S' he shall not feel quietness in
28: 1 S' there is a vein for the silver, and
31:36 S' I would take it upon my
33: 8 S'...hast spoken in mine hearing,
34:12 Yea, s' God will not do wickedly,
Job 34:31 S' it is meet to be said unto God,
35:13 S' God will not hear vanity, neither
37:20 s' he shall be swallowed up.
40:20 S' the mountains bring him forth
Ps 23: 6 S' goodness and mercy shall
32: 6 s' in the floods of great waters
39: 6 S' every man walketh in a vain
6 s' they are disquieted in vain: he
11 like a moth: s' every man is vanity.
62: 9 S' men of low degree are vanity,
73:18 S' thou didst set them in slippery
76:10 S' the wrath of man shall praise
77:11 s' I will remember thy wonders of old.
85: 9 S' his salvation is nigh them that
91: 3 S' he shall deliver thee from the
112: 6 S' he shall not be moved for ever:
131: 2 S' I have behaved and quieted518,
132: 3 S' I will not come into...tabernacle
139:11 S' the darkness shall cover me;
19 S' thou wilt slay the wicked, O God:
Pr 1:17 S' in vain the net is spread in the
3:34 S' he scorneth the scorners: but
10: 9 that walketh uprightly walketh s':
22:16 to the rich, shall s' come to want.
23:18 For s' there is an end; and thine
30: 2 S' I am...brutish than any man,
33 S' the churning of milk bringeth
Ec 4:16 S' this also is vanity and vexation
7: 7 S' oppression maketh a wise man
8:12 s' I know it shall be well with them
10:11 S' the serpent will bite without
Isa 7: 9 s' ye shall not be established.
14:24 S' as I have thought, so shall
16: 7 ye mourn; s' they are stricken.
19:11 S' the princes of Zoan are fools,
22:14 S' this iniquity shall not be purged
17 mighty captivity, and will s' cover thee.
18 He will s' violently turn and toss thee
29:16 S' your turning of things upside
36:15 saying, The Lord will s' deliver us:
40: 7 upon it: s' the people is grass.
45:14 S' God is in thee; and there is none
49: 4 s' my judgment is with the Lord,
18 shalt s' clothe thee with them all.
53: 4 S' he hath borne our griefs, and
54:15 they shall s' gather together, but not
60: 9 S' the isles shall wait for me, and
62: 8 S' I will no more give thy corn to
63: 8 For he said, S' they are my people,
Jer 2:35 s' his anger shall turn from me.
3:20 S' as a wife treacherously
4:10 s' thou hast greatly deceived this
5: 2 Lord liveth; s' they swear falsely.
4 S' these are poor; they are foolish:
8:13 I will s' consume them, saith the
16:19 S' our fathers have inherited lies,
22: 6 S' I...make thee a wilderness,
22 s' then shalt thou be ashamed and
24: 8 s' thus saith the Lord, So will I give
26: 8 took him, saying, Thou shalt s' die.
15 ye shall s' bring innocent blood
31:18 I have s' heard Ephraim bemoaning
19 S' after...I was turned, I repented;
20 I will s' have mercy upon him, saith
32: 4 shall s' be delivered into the hand of
34: 3 not escape...but shalt s' be taken,
36:16 will s' tell the king of all these words.
37: 9 The Chaldeans shall s' depart from us:
38: 3 This city shall s' be given into the
15 thee, wilt thou not s' put me to death?
39:18 For I will s' deliver thee, and thou
44:25 We will s' perform our vows that we
25 ye will s' accomplish your vows, and
25 your vows, and s' perform your vows.
29 my words shall s' stand against
46:18 S' as Tabor is among...mountains,
49:12 but thou shalt s' drink of it.
20 S' the least of the flock shall
20 s' he...make their habitations
50:45 S' the least of the flock shall
45 s' he shall make their habitation
51:14 S' I will fill thee with men, as
56 God of recompences shall s' requite.
La 3: 3 S' against me is he turned; he
Eze 3: 6 S', had I sent thee to them,
18 say unto the wicked, Thou shalt s' die;
21 and he doth not sin, he shall s' live,
5:11 S', because thou hast defiled
17:16 s' in the place where the king
19 s' mine oath that he hath
18: 9 he is just, he shall s' live, saith the
13 he shall s' die; his blood shall be upon
17 iniquity of his father, he shall s' live.
19 and hath done them, he shall s' live.
21, 28 he shall s' live, he shall not die.
20:33 s' with a mighty hand, and
31:11 heathen; he shall s' deal with him:
33: 8 O wicked man, thou shalt s' die;
13 to the righteous, that he shall s' live;
14 unto the wicked, Thou shalt s' die;
15 he shall s' live, he shall not die.
16 is lawful and right; he shall s' live.
27 s' they that are in the wastes
34: 8 s' because my flock became a
36: 5 S' in the fire of my jealousy
7 S' the heathen that are about
38:19 S' in that day there shall be a
Ho 5: 9 made known that which shall s' be.
12:11 s' they are vanity: they sacrifice
Am 3: 7 S' the Lord God will do nothing,
5: 5 for Gilgal shall s' go into captivity,
7:11 Israel shall s' be led away captive out
17 Israel shall s' go into captivity forth
Mic 2:12 I will s' assemble, O Jacob, all of thee;
Hab 2: 3 it will s' come, it will not tarry.
Zep 2: 9 S' Moab shall be as Sodom, and
M't 26:73 S' thou also art one of them;
M'r 14:70 to Peter, S' thou art one of them:
Lu 1: 1 things which are most s' believed
4:23 will s' say unto me this proverb,
Joh 17: 8 known s' that I came out from
Heb 6:14 S' blessing I will bless thee, and
Re 22:20 things saith, S' I come quickly.

sureties
Pr 22:26 or of them that are s' for debts.

suretiship
Pr 11:15 it: and he that hateth s' is sure.

surety See also SURETIES.
Ge 15:13 Know of a s' that thy seed shall be
18:13 Shall I of a s' bear a child, which
26: 9 said, Behold, of a s' she is thy wife:
43: 9 I will be s' for him; of my hand
44:32 servant became s' for the lad unto
Job 17: 3 down now, put me in a s' with thee;
Ps 119:122 Be s' for thy servant for good: let
Pr 6: 1 My son, if thou be s' for thy friend,
11:15 He that is s' for a stranger shall
17:18 becometh s' in the presence of his
20:16 garment that is s' for a stranger:
27:13 garment that is s' for a stranger,
Ac 12:11 Now I know of a s', that the Lord
Heb 7:22 made a s' of a better testament.

surfeiting
Lu 21:34 hearts be overcharged with s',

surmisings
1Ti 6: 4 cometh envy, strife, railings, evil s',

surname See also SURNAMED.
Isa 44: 5 s' himself by the name of Israel.
M't 10: 3 whose s' was Thaddæus;
Ac 10: 5 for one Simon, whose s' is Peter:
32 hither Simon, whose s' is Peter;
11:13 call for Simon, whose s' is Peter;
12:12 of John, whose s' was Mark;
25 them John, whose s' was Mark.
15:37 them John, whose s' was Mark.

surnamed
Isa 45: 4 I have s' thee, though thou hast
M'r 3:16 And Simon he s' Peter;
17 he s' them Boanerges, which
Lu 22: 3 Satan into Judas s' Iscariot,
Ac 1:23 Barsabas, who was s' Justus, and
4:36 by the apostles was s' Barnabas,
10:18 whether Simon, which was s' Peter,
15:22 Judas s' Barsabas, and Silas, chief

surprised
Isa 33:14 fearfulness hath s' the hypocrites.
Jer 48:41 taken, and the strong holds are s',
51:41 is the praise of the whole earth s'!

Susah See HAZAR-SUSAH.

Susanchites (*su'-san-kites*)
Ezr 4: 9 the S', the Dehavites, and the

Susanna (*su-zan'-nah*)
Lu 8: 3 wife of...Herod's steward, and S',

Susi (*su'-si*)
Nu 13:11 of Manasseh, Gaddi the son of S'.

Susim See HAZAR-SUSIM.

sustain See also SUSTAINED.
1Ki 17: 9 a widow woman there to s' thee.
Ne 9:21 Yea, forty years didst thou s' them
Ps 55:22 upon the Lord, and he shall s' thee:
Pr 18:14 spirit of a man will s' his infirmity;

sustained
Ge 27:37 with corn and wine have I s' him:
Ps 3: 5 I awaked; for the Lord s' me.
Isa 59:16 and his righteousness, it s' him.

sustenance
J'g 6: 4 left no s' for Israel, neither sheep,
2Sa 19:32 and he had provided the king of s'
Ac 7:11 and our fathers found no s'.

swaddled
La 2:22 those...I have s' and brought up
Eze 16: 4 wast not salted at all, nor s' at all.

swaddling See also SWADDLINGBAND.
Lu 2: 7 and wrapped him in s' clothes,
12 find the babe wrapped in s' clothes,

swaddlingband
Job 38: 9 and thick darkness a s' for it,

swaddling-clothes See SWADDLING and CLOTHES.

swallow See also SWALLOWED; SWALLOWETH.
Nu 16:30 open her mouth, and s' them up,
34 said, Lest the earth s' us up also.
2Sa 20:19 why wilt thou s' up the inheritance
20 me, that I should s' up or destroy.
Job 7:19 me alone till I s' down my spittle?
20:18 he restore, and shall not s' it down:
Ps 21: 9 Lord shall s' them up in his wrath,
56: 1 O God: for man would s' me up;
2 Mine enemies would daily s' me up:
57: 3 reproach of him that would s' me
69:15 neither let the deep s' me up, and
84: 3 house, and the s' a nest for herself,
Pr 1:12 us s' them up alive as the grave;
26: 2 by wandering, as the s' by flying,
Ec 10:12 the lips of a fool will s' up himself.
Isa 25: 8 He will s' up death in victory; and
38:14 Like a crane or a s', so did I
Jer 8: 7 s' observe the time of their coming;
Ho 8: 7 yield, the strangers shall s' it up.
Am 8: 4 this, O ye that s' up the needy,
Ob 16 drink, and they shall s' down,
Jon 1:17 a great fish to s' up Jonah.
M't 23:24 strain at a gnat, and s' a camel.

swallowed
Ex 7:12 but Aaron's rod s' up their rods.
15:12 thy right hand, the earth s' them.
Nu 16:32 and s' them up, and their houses,
26:10 and s' them up together with Korah,
De 11: 6 s' them up, and their households,
2Sa 17:16 lest the king be s' up, and all the
Job 6: 3 sea: therefore my words are s' up.
20:15 He hath s' down riches, and he
37:20 man speak, surely he shall be s' up.
Ps 35:25 them not say, We have s' him up.
106:17 The earth opened and s' up Dathan,
124: 3 Then they had s' us up quick, when
Isa 28: 7 they are s' up of wine, they are out
49:19 that s' thee up shall be far away.
Jer 51:34 he hath s' me up like a dragon, he
44 mouth that which he hath s' up:
La 2: 2 Lord hath s' up all the habitations
5 as an enemy: he hath s' up Israel,
5 he hath s' up all her palaces: he
16 We have s' her up: certainly this is
Eze 36: 3 and s' you up on every side, that
Ho 8: 8 Israel is s' up: now shall they be
1Co 15:54 written, Death is s' up in victory.
2Co 2: 7 be s' up with overmuch sorrow.
5: 4 that mortality might be s' up of life.
Re 12:16 s' up the flood which the dragon

swalloweth
Job 5: 5 the robber s' up their substance.
39:24 He s' the ground with fierceness

swan
Le 11:18 And the s', and the pelican, and
De 14:16 owl, and the great owl, and the s',

sware^ See also SWAREST.
Ge 21:31 because there they s' both of them.
24: 7 me, and that s' unto me, saying,
9 s' to him concerning that matter.
25:33 me this day; and he s' unto him:
26: 3 oath which I s' unto Abraham thy
31 the morning, and s' one to another:
31:53 Jacob s' by the fear of his father
47:31 unto me. And he s' unto him.
50:24 the land which he s' to Abraham,
Ex 13: 5 he s' unto thy fathers to give thee,
11 he s' unto thee and to thy fathers,
33: 1 the land which I s' unto Abraham,
Nu 14:16 the land which he s' unto them,
23 land which I s' unto their fathers,
30 I s' to make you dwell therein,
32:10 kindled the same time, and he s',
11 the land which I s' unto Abraham,
De 1: 8 land which the Lord s' unto your
34 your words, and was wroth, and s',
35 land, which I s' to give unto your
2:14 the host, as the Lord s' unto them.
4:21 s' that I should not go over Jordan,
31 covenant...which he s' unto them.
6:10 land which he s' unto thy fathers,
18 which the Lord s' unto thy fathers,
23 land which he s' unto our fathers.
7:12 which he s' unto thy fathers:
13 land which he s' unto thy fathers
8: 1 the Lord s' unto your fathers.
18 his covenant which he s' unto thy
9: 5 which the Lord s' unto thy fathers,
10:11 which I s' unto their fathers to give
11: 9, 21 the Lord s' unto your fathers
26: 3 which the Lord s' unto your fathers
28:11 which the Lord s' unto thy fathers
30:20 which the Lord s' unto thy fathers,
31:20 land which I s' unto their fathers,
21 them into the land which I s'.
23 into the land which I s' unto them:
34: 4 the land which I s' unto Abraham,
Jos 1: 6 which I s' unto their fathers to give
5: 6 the Lord s' that he would not shew
6 land, which the Lord s' unto their
6:22 all that she hath, as ye s' unto her.
9:15 princes of the congregation s' unto
20 of the oath which we s' unto them.
14: 9 And Moses s' on that day, saying,
21:43 he s' to give unto their fathers;
44 to all that he s' unto their fathers:
J'g 2: 1 land which I s' unto your fathers;
1Sa 19: 6 and Saul s', As the Lord liveth, he
20: 3 And David s' moreover, and said,
24:22 And David s' unto Saul. And Saul
28:10 Saul s' to her by the Lord, saying,
2Sa 3:35 while it was yet day, David s',
19:23 not die. And the king s' unto him.
21:17 Then the men of David s' unto him,
1Ki 1:29 the king s', and said, As the Lord
30 Even as I s' unto thee by the Lord
2: 8 and I s' to him by the Lord, saying,
2Ki 25:24 Gedaliah s' to them, and to their
2Ch 15:14 s' unto the Lord with a loud voice,
Ezr 10: 5 according to this word. And they s'.
Ps 95:11 Unto whom I s' in my wrath that
132: 2 he s' unto the Lord, and vowed
Jer 38:16 So Zedekiah the king s' secretly
40: 9 son of Shaphan s' unto them and to
Eze 16: 8 I s' unto thee, and entered into a
Da 12: 7 and s' by him that liveth for ever
M'r 6:23 he s' unto her, Whatsoever thou
Lu 1:73 The oath which he s' to our father
Heb 3:11 So I s' in my wrath, They shall not
18 to whom s' he that they should not
6:13 by no greater, he s' by himself,
7:21 The Lord s' and will not repent,
Re 10: 6 s' by him that liveth for ever and

swarest
Ex 32:13 to whom thou s' by thine own self,
Nu 11:12 the land which thou s' unto their
De 26:15 as thou s' unto our fathers, a land
1Ki 1:17 thou s' by the Lord thy God unto
Ps 89:49 thou s' unto David in thy truth?

swarm See also SWARMS.
Ex 8:24 there came a grievous s' of flies
24 by reason of the s' of flies.
J'g 14: 8 was a s' of bees and honey in the

swarms
Ex 8:21 I will send s' of flies upon thee,
21 Egyptians shall be full of s' of flies,
22 that no s' of flies shall be there;
29 that the s' of flies may depart from
31 and he removed the s' of flies from

swear See also FORSWEAR; SWARE; SWEARETH; SWEARING; SWORN.
Ge 21:23 therefore s' unto me here by God
24 And Abraham said, I will s'.
24: 3 I will make thee s' by the Lord, the
37 And my master made me s', saying,
25:33 And Jacob said, S' to me this day;
47:31 And he said, S' unto me. And he
50: 5 My father made me s', saying, Lo, I
6 according as he made thee s'.
Ex 6: 8 I did s' to give it to Abraham,
Le 5: 4 Or if a soul s', pronouncing with
19:12 ye shall not s' by my name falsely,
Nu 30: 2 or s' an oath to bind his soul with
De 6:13 him, and shalt s' by his name.
10:20 thou cleave, and s' by his name.
Jos 2:12 s' unto me by the Lord, since I
17 oath which thou hast made us s'.
20 oath which thou hast made us to s'.
23: 7 nor cause to s' by them, neither
J'g 15:12 said unto them, S' unto me, that
1Sa 20:17 Jonathan caused David to s' again,
24:21 S' now...unto me by the Lord,
30:15 S' unto me by God, that thou wilt
2Sa 19: 7 for I s' by the Lord, if thou go not
1Ki 1:13 O king, s' unto thine handmaid,
51 Let king Solomon s' unto me to
2:42 I not make thee to s' by the Lord,
8:31 laid upon him to cause him to s',
2Ch 6:22 be laid upon him to make him s',
36:13 who had made him s' by God:
Ezr 10: 5 to s' that they should do according
Ne 13:25 and made them s' by God, saying,
Isa 3: 7 In that day shall he s', saying, I
19:18 and s' to the Lord of hosts; one
45:23 shall bow, every tongue shall s'.
48: 1 which s' by the name of the Lord,
65:16 earth shall s' by the God of truth;
Jer 4: 2 And thou shalt s', The Lord liveth,
5: 2 Lord liveth; surely they s' falsely.
7: 9 commit adultery, and s' falsely,
12:16 to s' by my name, The Lord liveth;
16 taught my people to s' by Baal;
22: 5 I s' by myself, saith the Lord, that
32:22 thou didst s' to their fathers to give
Hos 4:15 Beth-aven, nor s', The Lord liveth.
Am 8:14 They that s' by the sin of Samaria,
Zep 1: 5 worship and that s' by the Lord,
5 and that s' by Malcham;
M't 5:34 S' not at all; neither by heaven;
36 Neither shalt thou s' by thy head,
23:16 Whosoever shall s' by the temple,
16 shall s' by the gold of the temple,
18 Whosoever shall s' by the altar, it
20 therefore shall s' by the altar,
21 And whoso shall s' by the temple,
22 And he that shall s' by heaven,
26:74 Then began he to curse and to s',
M'r 14:71 But he began to curse and to s',
Heb 6:13 because he could s' by no greater,
16 For men verily s' by the greater:
Jas 5:12 all things, my brethren, s' not,

swearers
Mal 3: 5 and against false s', and against

sweareth
Le 6: 3 lieth concerning it, and s' falsely;
Ps 15: 4 He that s' to his own hurt, and
63:11 one that s' by him shall glory:
Ec 9: 2 he that s', as he that feareth an
Isa 65:16 he that s' in the earth shall swear
Zec 5: 3 every one that s' shall be cut off as
4 of him that s' falsely by my name:
M't 23:18 whosoever s' by the gift that is
20 s' by it, and by all things thereon.
21 s' by it, and by him that dwelleth
22 by heaven, s' by the throne of God,

swearing
Le 5: 1 soul sin, and hear the voice of s',
Jer 23:10 because of s' the land mourneth;
Ho 4: 2 By s', and lying, and killing, and
10: 4 s' falsely in making a covenant:

sweat
Ge 3:19 In the s' of thy face shalt thou eat
Eze 44:18 with any thing that causeth s'.
Lu 22:44 his s' was as it were great drops of

sweep See also SWEEPING; SWEPT.
Isa 14:23 and I will s' it with the besom of
28:17 hail shall s' away the refuge of lies,
Lu 15: 8 light a candle, and s' the house,

sweeping
Pr 28: 3 is like a s' rain that leaveth no

sweet See also SWEETER; SWEETSMELLING.
Ge 8:21 And the Lord smelled a s' savour;
Ex 15:25 waters, the waters were made s':
25: 6 anointing oil, and for s' incense,
29:18 it is a s' savour, an offering made
25 for a s' savour before the Lord:
41 for a s' savour, an offering made
30: 7 burn thereon s' incense every
23 and of s' cinnamon half so much,
Ex 30:23 of s' calamus two hundred and fifty
34 Take unto thee s' spices, stacte,
34 s' spices with pure frankincense:
31:11 and s' incense for the holy place:
35: 8 anointing oil,...for the s' incense,
15 anointing oil, and the s' incense,
28 anointing oil, and for the s' incense.
37:29 and the pure incense of s' spices,
39:38 anointing oil, and the s' incense,
40:27 And he burnt s' incense thereon; as
Le 1: 9, 13, 17 of a s' savour unto the Lord.
2: 2 by fire, of a s' savour unto the Lord:
9 by fire, of a s' savour unto the Lord.
12 burnt on the altar for a s' savour.
3: 5 by fire, of a s' savour unto the Lord.
16 made by fire for a s' savour:
4: 7 the horns of the altar of s' incense
31 for a s' savour unto the Lord;
6:15 it upon the altar for a s' savour,
21 offer for a s' savour unto the Lord.
8:21 a burnt sacrifice for a s' savour,
28 were consecrations for a sweet s':
16:12 his hands full of s' incense beaten
17: 6 fat for a s' savour unto the Lord.
23:13 fire unto the Lord for a s' savour:
18 by fire, of s' savour unto the Lord.
26:31 smell the savour of your s' odours.
Nu 4:16 for the light, and the s' incense,
15: 3 to make a s' savour unto the Lord,
7 wine, for a s' savour unto the Lord.
10, 13 fire, of a s' savour unto the Lord.
14 by fire, of a s' savour unto the Lord:
24 for a s' savour unto the Lord,
18:17 fire, for a s' savour unto the Lord.
28: 2 by fire, for a s' savour unto me,
6 in mount Sinai for a s' savour,
8 by fire, of a s' savour unto the Lord.
13 for a burnt offering of a s' savour,
24 fire, of a s' savour unto the Lord:
27 for a s' savour unto the Lord;
29: 2 for a s' savour unto the Lord;
6 for a s' savour, a sacrifice made by
8 unto the Lord for a s' savour;
13 fire, of a s' savour unto the Lord;
36 fire, of a s' savour unto the Lord:
2Sa 23: 1 and the s' psalmist of Israel, said,
2Ch 2: 4 and to burn before him s' incense,
13:11 burnt sacrifices and s' incense:
16:14 in the bed...filled with s' odours
Ezr 6:10 s' savours unto the God of heaven,
Ne 8:10 way, eat the fat, and drink the s',
Es 2:12 and six months with s' odours,
Job 20:12 wickedness be s' in his mouth,
21:33 The clods of the valley shall be s'
38:31 bind the s' influences of Pleiades,
Ps 55:14 We took s' counsel together, and
104:34 My meditation of him shall be s':
119:103 How s' are thy words unto my
141: 6 hear my words; for they are s'.
Pr 3:24 lie down, and thy sleep shall be s'.
9:17 Stolen waters are s', and bread
13:19 desire accomplished is s' to the
16:24 as an honeycomb, s' to the soul,
20:17 Bread of deceit is s' to a man; but
23: 8 vomit up, and lose thy s' words.
24:13 the honeycomb, which is s' to thy
27: 7 hungry soul every bitter thing is s'.
Ec 5:12 The sleep of a labouring man is s',
11: 7 Truly the light is s', and a pleasant
Ca 2: 3 and his fruit was s' to my taste.
14 s' is thy voice, and thy countenance
5: 5 fingers with s' smelling myrrh,
13 as a bed of spices, as s' flowers:
13 lilies, dropping s' smelling myrrh.
16 His mouth is most s': yea, he is
Isa 3:24 instead of s' smell...shall be stink;
5:20 put bitter for s', and s' for bitter!
23:16 make s' melody, sing many songs,
43:24 hast bought me no s' cane with money,
49:26 their own blood, as with s' wine:
Jer 6:20 the s' cane from a far country?
20 nor your sacrifices s' unto me.
31:26 and my sleep was s' unto me.
Eze 6:13 offer s' savour to all their idols.
16:19 set it before them for a s' savour:
20:28 there also they made their s' savour,
41 will accept you with your s' savour,
Da 2:46 an oblation and s' odours unto him.
Am 9:13 the mountains shall drop s' wine,
Mic 6:15 and s' wine, but shalt not drink
M'r 16: 1 and Salome, had bought s' spices,
2Co 2:15 are unto God a s' savour of Christ,
Ph'p 4:18 an odour of a s' smell, a sacrifice
Jas 3:11 same place s' water and bitter?
Re 10: 9 it shall be in thy mouth s' as honey.
10 and it was in my mouth s' as honey:

sweeter
J'g 14:18 What is s' than honey? and what
Ps 19:10 s'...than honey and the honeycomb.
119:103 yea, s' than honey to my mouth!

sweetly
Job 24:20 the worm shall feed s' on him; he
Ca 7: 9 that goeth down s', causing the

sweetness
J'g 9:11 Should I forsake my s', and my
14:14 and out of the strong came forth s'.
Pr 16:21 s' of the lips increaseth learning.
27: 9 so doth the s' of a man's friend by
Eze 3: 3 was in my mouth as honey for s'.

sweetsmelling See also SWEET and SMELLING.
Eph 5: 2 a sacrifice to God for a s' savour.

swell See also SWELLED; SWELLING; SWOLLEN.
Nu 5:21 thigh to rot, and thy belly to s';
22 to make thy belly to s', and thy

Nu 5:27 and her belly shall s·, and her thigh
De 8: 4 neither did thy foot s·, these forty

swelled See also SWOLLEN.
Ne 9:21 waxed not old, and their feet s· not.

swelling See also SWELLINGS.
Ps 46: 3 the mountains shake with the s·
Isa 30:13 s· out in a high wall, whose
Jer 12: 5 wilt thou do in the s· of Jordan?
49:19 up like a lion from the s· of Jordan
50:44 up like a lion from the s· of Jordan
2Pe 2:18 speak great s· words of vanity,
Jude 16 mouth speaketh great s· words,

swellings
2Co 12:20 backbitings, whisperings, s·,

swept
J'g 5:21 The river of Kishon s· them away,
Jer 46:15 Why are thy valiant men s· away?
M't 12:44 findeth it empty, s·, and garnished.
Lu 11:25 he findeth it s· and garnished.

swerved
1Ti 1: 6 From which some having s· have

swift See also SWIFTER.
De 28:49 of the earth, as s· as the eagle flieth;
1Ch 12: 8 were as s· as the roes upon the
Job 9:26 are passed away as the s· ships:
24:18 He is s· as the waters; their
Pr 6:18 feet...be s· in running to mischief,
Ec 9:11 that the race is not to the s·, nor
Isa 18: 2 Go, ye s· messengers, to a nation
19: 1 the Lord rideth upon a s· cloud,
30:16 flee: and, We will ride upon the s·;
16 shall they that pursue you be s·.
66:20 upon mules, and upon s· beasts,
Jer 2:23 thou art a s· dromedary traversing
46: 6 Let not the s· flee away, nor the
Am 2:14 the flight shall perish from the s·,
15 and he that is s· of foot shall not
Mic 1:13 bind the chariot to the s· beast:
Mal 3: 5 I will be a s· witness against the
Ro 3:15 Their feet are s· to shed blood:
Jas 1:19 let every man be s· to hear, slow
2Pe 2: 1 upon themselves s· destruction.

swifter
2Sa 1:23 they were s· than eagles, they
Job 7: 6 My days are s· than a weaver's
9:25 Now my days are s· than a post:
Jer 4:13 his horses are s· than eagles.
La 4:19 persecutors are s· than the eagles
Hab 1: 8 horses...are s· than the leopards,

swiftly
Ps 147:15 earth: his word runneth very s·.
Isa 5:26 they shall come with speed s·:
Da 9:21 being caused to fly s·, touched me
Joe 3: 4 s· and speedily will I return your

swim See also SWIMMEST; SWIMMETH.
2Ki 6: 6 it in thither; and the iron did s·.
Ps 6: 6 all the night make I my bed to s·;
Isa 25:11 spreadeth forth his hands to s·:
Eze 47: 5 waters were risen, waters to s· in,
Ac 27:42 lest any of them should s· out,
43 they which could s· should cast

swimmest
Eze 32: 6 thy blood the land wherein thou s·,

swimmeth
Isa 25:11 that s· spreadeth forth his hands

swine See also SWINE'S.
Le 11: 7 the s·, though he divide the hoof,
De 14: 8 the s·, because it divideth the hoof,
M't 7: 6 neither cast ye...pearls before s·,
8:30 them an herd of many s· feeding.
31 us to go away into the herd of s·.
32 out, they went into the herd of s·:
32 whole herd of s· ran violently down
M'r 5:11 a great herd of s· feeding.
12 Send us into the s·, that we may
13 went out, and entered into the s·:
14 they that fed the s· fled, and told
16 the devil, and also concerning the s·.
Lu 8:32 an herd of many s· feeding on the
33 of the man, and entered into the s·:
15:15 he sent him into his fields to feed s·.
16 with the husks that the s· did eat:

swine's
Pr 11:22 As a jewel of gold in a s· snout, so
Isa 65: 4 which eat s· flesh, and broth of
66: 3 oblation, as if he offered s· blood;
17 tree in the midst, eating s· flesh,

swollen See also SWELLED.
Ac 28: 6 looked when he should have s·,

swoon See also SWOONED.
La 2:11 the sucklings s· in the streets of

swooned
La 2:12 when they s· as the wounded in

sword See also SWORDS.
Ge 3:24 a flaming s· which turned every
27:40 And by thy s· shalt thou live, and
31:26 as captives taken with the s·?
34:25 brethren, took each man his s·,
26 his son with the edge of the s·,
48:22 hand of the Amorite with my s·
Ex 5: 3 us with pestilence, or with the s·.
21 to put a s· in their hand to slay us.
15: 9 I will draw my s·, my hand shall
17:13 his people with the edge of the s·.
18: 4 delivered me from the s· of Pharaoh:
22:24 hot, and I will kill you with the s·;
32:27 Put every man his s· by his side,
Le 26: 6 shall the s· go through your land.
Le 26: 7 they shall fall before you by the s·.
8 enemies...fall before you by the s·.
25 And I will bring a s· upon you, that
33 and will draw out a s· after you:
36 they shall flee, as fleeing from a s·;
37 as it were before a s·, when none
Nu 14: 3 us unto this land, to fall by the s·,
43 you, and ye shall fall by the s·:
19:16 is slain with a s· in the open fields,
20:18 I come out against thee with the s·.
21:24 smote him with the edge of the s·,
22:23 way, and his s· drawn in his hand:
29 would there were a s· in mine hand,
31 way, and his s· drawn in his hand:
31: 8 son of Beor they slew with the s·.
De 13:15 of that city with the edge of the s·,
15 cattle thereof, with...edge of the s·.
20:13 male thereof with the edge of the s·:
28:22 and with the s·, and with blasting,
32:25 The s· without, and terror within,
41 If I whet my glittering s·, and mine
42 blood, and my s· shall devour flesh;
33:29 and who is the s· of thy excellency!
Jos 5:13 him with his s· drawn in his hand:
6:21 and ass, with the edge of the s·.
8:24 were all fallen on the edge of the s·,
24 and smote it with the edge of the s·.
10:11 children of Israel slew with the s·.
28, 30, 32, 35, 37, 39 the edge of the s·,
11:10 smote the king thereof with the s·:
11 souls...therein with...edge of the s·,
12 smote them with the edge of the s·,
14 they smote with the edge of the s·,
13:22 children of Israel slay with the s·
19:47 and smote it with the edge of the s·,
24:12 not with thy s·, nor with thy bow.
J'g 1: 8 smitten it with the edge of the s·,
25 smote the city with...edge of the s·;
4:15 the edge of the s· before Barak;
16 Sisera fell upon the edge of the s·;
7:14 nothing else save the s· of Gideon
18 The s· of the Lord, and of Gideon.
20 The s· of the Lord, and of Gideon.
22 every man's s· against his fellow,
8:10 twenty thousand men that drew s·.
20 But the youth drew not his s·: for
9:54 Draw thy s·, and slay me, that men
18:27 smote them with the edge of the s·,
20: 2 thousand footmen that drew s·.
15 and six thousand men that drew s·,
17 hundred thousand men that drew s·:
25 thousand men; all these drew the s·.
35 hundred men: all these drew the s·.
37 all the city with the edge of the s·.
46 five thousand men that drew the s·;
48 smote them with the edge of the s·,
21:10 Jabesh-gilead with the edge of the s·,
1Sa 13:22 was neither s· nor spear found in
14:20 every man's s· was against his
15: 8 the people with the edge of the s·.
33 thy s· hath made women childless,
17:39 girded his s· upon his armour,
45 Thou comest to me with a s·, and
47 that the Lord saveth not with s· and
50 was no s· in the hand of David.
51 upon the Philistine, and took his s·,
18: 4 and his garments, even to his s·,
21: 8 here under thine hand spear or s·?
8 have neither brought my s· nor my
9 The s· of Goliath the Philistine,
22:10 and gave him the s· of Goliath the
13 thou hast given him bread, and a s·,
19 smote he with the edge of the s·,
19 and sheep, with the edge of the s·.
25:13 men, Gird ye on every man his s·.
13 they girded on every man his s·;
13 and David also girded on his s·:
31: 4 Draw thy s·, and thrust me through
4 Saul took a s·, and fell upon it.
5 dead, he fell likewise upon his s·,
2Sa 1:12 because they were fallen by the s·.
22 the s· of Saul returned not empty.
2:16 thrust his s· in his fellow's side;
26 said, Shall the s· devour for ever?
3:29 or that falleth on the s·, or that
11:25 for the s· devoureth one as well as
12: 9 killed Uriah the Hittite with the s·,
9 hast slain him with the s· of the
10 the s· shall never depart from thine
15:14 the city with the edge of the s·.
18: 8 more people that day than the s·
20: 8 upon it a girdle with a s· fastened
10 Amasa took no heed to the s· that
21:16 he being girded with a new s·,
23:10 and his hand clave unto the s·:
24: 9 valiant men that drew the s·;
1Ki 1:51 will not slay his servant with the s·.
2: 8 not put thee to death with the s·.
32 than he, and slew them with the s·,
3:24 And the king said, Bring me a s·.
24 they brought a s· before the king.
19: 1 slain all the prophets with the s·.
10, 14 slain thy prophets with the s·;
17 him that escapeth the s· of Hazael
17 that escapeth from the s· of Jehu
2Ki 6:22 thou hast taken captive with thy s·
8:12 men wilt thou slay with the s·, and
10:25 smote them with the edge of the s·;
11:15 that followeth her kill with the s·.
20 slew Athaliah with the s· beside the
19: 7 to fall by the s· in his own land.
37 his sons smote him with the s·:
1Ch 5:18 men able to bear buckler and s·,
10: 4 Draw thy s·, and thrust me through
4 So Saul took a s·, and fell upon it.
5 he fell likewise on the s·, and died.
1Ch 21: 5 hundred thousand men...drew s·:
5 and ten thousand men that drew s·.
12 the s· of thine enemies overtaketh
12 else three days the s· of the Lord,
16 having a drawn s· in his hand
27 put up his s· again into the sheath
30 afraid because of the s· of the angel
2Ch 20: 9 evil cometh upon us, as the s·,
21: 4 slew all his brethren with the s·,
23:14 her, let him be slain with the s·.
21 they had slain Athaliah with the s·.
29: 9 our fathers have fallen by the s·,
32:21 bowels slew him there with the s·.
36:17 slew their young men with the s· in
20 them that had escaped from the s·
Ezr 9: 7 to the s·, to captivity, and to a spoil,
Ne 4:18 every one had his s· girded by his
Es 9: 5 enemies with the stroke of the s·,
Job 1:15, 17 servants with the edge of the s·;
5:15 But he saveth the poor from the s·,
20 and in war from the power of the s·.
15:22 and he is waited for of the s·.
19:29 Be ye afraid of the s·: for wrath
29 bringeth the punishment of the s·,
20:25 the glittering s· cometh out of his
27:14 be multiplied, it is for the s·:
33:18 his life from perishing by the s·.
36:12 not, they shall perish by the s·,
39:22 neither turneth...back from the s·.
40:19 he that made him can make his s·
41:26 s· of him that layeth at him cannot
Ps 7:12 If he turn not, he will whet his s·;
17:13 from the wicked, which is thy s·:
22:20 Deliver my soul from the s·; my
37:14 The wicked have drawn out the s·,
15 s· shall enter into their own heart,
42:10 As with a s· in my bones, mine
44: 3 land in possession by their own s·,
6 bow, neither shall my s· save me.
45: 3 Gird thy s· upon thy thigh, O most
57: 4 arrows, and their tongue a sharp s·.
63:10 They shall fall by the s·: they shall
64: 3 Who whet their tongue like a s·,
76: 3 bow, the shield, and the s·, and the
78:62 his people over also unto the s·;
64 Their priests fell by the s·; and
89:43 hast also turned the edge of his s·,
144:10 his servant from the hurtful s·.
149: 6 and a twoedged s· in their hand;
Pr 5: 4 wormwood, sharp as a twoedged s·
12:18 speaketh like the piercings of a s·:
25:18 his neighbour is a maul, and a s·,
Ca 3: 8 every man...his s· upon his thigh
Isa 1:20 ye shall be devoured with the s·:
2: 4 shall not lift up s· against nation,
3:25 Thy men shall fall by the s·, and
13:15 joined unto them shall fall by the s·.
14:19 are slain, thrust through with a s·,
21:15 from the drawn s·, and from the
22: 2 slain men are not slain with the s·,
27: 1 great and strong s· shall punish
31: 8 shall the Assyrian fall with the s·,
8 and the s·, not of a mean man, shall
8 but he shall flee from the s·, and
34: 5 my s· shall be bathed in heaven:
6 s· of the Lord is filled with blood,
37: 7 him to fall by the s· in his own land.
38 his sons smote him with the s·;
41: 2 he gave them as the dust to his s·,
49: 2 made my mouth like a sharp s·;
51:19 and the famine, and the s·: by
65:12 will I number you to the s·, and
66:16 by his s· will the Lord plead with
Jer 2:30 your own s· hath devoured your
4:10 the s· reacheth unto the soul.
5:12 neither shall we see s· nor famine:
17 wherein thou trustedst, with the s·.
6:25 for the s· of the enemy and fear is
9:16 and I will send a s· after them, till I
11:22 the young men shall die by the s·;
12:12 for the s· of the Lord shall devour
14:12 but I will consume them by the s·,
13 Ye shall not see the s·, neither shall
15 S· and famine shall not be in this
15 By s· and famine shall those
16 because of the famine and the s·;
18 then behold the slain with the s·!
15: 2 such as are for the s·, to the s·;
3 the s· to slay, and the dogs to tear,
9 will I deliver to the s· before their
16: 4 they shall be consumed by the s·,
18:21 their blood by the force of the s·;
21 their young men be slain by the s·
19: 7 I will cause them to fall by the s·
20: 4 shall fall by the s· of their enemies,
4 and shall slay them with the s·.
21: 7 from the s·, and from the famine,
7 smite them with the edge of the s·;
9 in this city shall die by the s·, and
24:10 And I will send the s·, the famine,
25:16 the s· that I will send among them.
27 the s· which I will send among you.
29 for I will call for a s· upon all the
31 give them that are wicked to the s·,
26:23 who slew him with the s·, and cast
27: 8 punish, saith the Lord, with the s·,
13 die, thou and thy people, by the s·,
29:17 I will send upon them the s·, the
18 I will persecute them with the s·,
31: 2 The people which were left of the s·
32:24 because of the s·, and of the famine,
36 of the king of Babylon by the s·,
33: 4 down by the mounts, and by the s·;
34: 4 thee, Thou shalt not die by the s·:
17 to the s·, to the pestilence, and
38: 2 in this city shall die by the s·, by

Jer 39:18 and thou shalt not fall by the s'.
41: 2 the son of Shaphan with the s'.
42:16 that the s', which ye feared, shall
17 they shall die by the s', by the
22 that ye shall die by the s', by the
43:11 and such as are for the s' to the s'.
44:12, 12 by the s' and by the famine:
13 have punished Jerusalem, by the s',
18 and have been consumed by the s'
27 shall be consumed by the s' and
28 a small number that escape the s'
46:10 and the s' shall devour, and it shall
14 for the s' shall devour round about
16 our nativity, from the oppressing s'.
47: 6 O thou s' of the Lord, how long will
48: 2 Madmen; the s' shall pursue thee.
10 that keepeth back his s' from blood.
49:37 and I will send the s' after them.
50:16 for fear of the oppressing s' they
35 A s' is upon the Chaldeans, saith
36 A s' is upon the liars; and they
36 a s' is upon her mighty men; and
37 A s' is upon their horses, and upon
37 a s' is upon her treasures; and they
51:50 that have escaped the s', go away,
La 1:20 abroad the s' bereaveth, at home
2:21 my young men are fallen by the s';
4: 9 that be slain with the s' are better
5: 9 because of the s' of the wilderness.
Eze 5: 2 and I will draw out a s' after them.
12 and a third part shall fall by the s'
12 and I will draw out a s' after them.
17 and I will bring the s' upon thee.
6: 3 I, even I, will bring a s' upon you,
8 escape the s' among the nations.
11 shall fall by the s', by the famine,
12 he that is near shall fall by the s';
7:15 The s' is without, and the pestilence
15 is in the field shall die with the s';
11: 8 Ye have feared the s'; and I will
8 bring a s' upon you, saith the Lord
10 Ye shall fall by the s'; I will judge
12:14 I will draw out the s' after them.
16 leave a few men of them from the s',
14:17 Or if I bring a s' upon that land,
17 and say, S', go through the land;
21 Jerusalem, the s', and the famine,
17:21 all his bands shall fall by the s',
21: 3 draw forth my s' out of his sheath,
4 my s' go forth out of his sheath
5 drawn forth my s' out of his sheath:
9 Say, A s', a s' is sharpened, and
11 s' is sharpened, and it is furbished,
12 terrors by reason of the s' shall be
13 what if the s' contemn even the rod?
14 and let the s' be doubled the third
14 time, the s' of the slain: it is the
14 s' of the great men that are slain,
15 I have set the point of the s' against
19 s' of the king of Babylon may come:
20 the s' may come to Rabbath of the
28 say thou, The s', the s' is drawn:
23:10 daughters, and slew her with the s':
25 and thy remnant shall fall by the s':
24:21 whom ye have left shall fall by the s'.
25:13 they of Dedan shall fall by the s'.
26: 6 in the field shall be slain by the s':
8 shall slay with the s' thy daughters
11 he shall slay thy people by the s',
28:23 judged in the midst of her by the s'
29: 8 I will bring a s' upon thee, and cut
30: 4 And the s' shall come upon Egypt,
5 shall fall with them by the s'.
6 Syene shall they fall in it by the s',
17 and of Pi-beseth shall fall by the s':
21 it, to make it strong to hold the s'.
22 cause the s' to fall out of his hand.
24 Babylon, and put my s' in his hand:
25 put my s' into the hand of the king
31:17 unto them that be slain with the s';
18 with them that be slain by the s'.
32:10 I shall brandish my s' before them;
11 s' of the king of Babylon shall come
20 of them that are slain by the s':
20 she is delivered to the s': draw her
21 lie uncircumcised, slain by the s'.
22 all of them slain, fallen by the s':
23, 24 all of them slain, fallen by the s',
25 them uncircumcised, slain by the s':
26 them uncircumcised, slain by the s',
28 with them that are slain with the s'.
29 by them that were slain by the s':
30 with them that be slain by the s',
31 and all his army slain by the s',
32 with them that are slain with the s'.
33: 2 When I bring the s' upon a land, if
3 he seeth the s' come upon the land,
4 if the s' come, and take him away,
6 if the watchman see the s' come,
6 if the s' come, and take any person
26 Ye stand upon your s', ye work
27 are in the wastes shall fall by the s',
35: 5 blood...of Israel by the force of the s'
8 they fall that are slain with the s'.
38: 8 that is brought back from the s',
21 And I will call for a s' against him
21 every man's s' shall be against his
39:23 enemies: so fell they all by the s'.
Da 11:33 yet they shall fall by the s', and by
Ho 1: 7 not save them by bow, nor by s',
2:18 and I will break the bow and the s'
7:16 their princes shall fall by the s'
11: 6 And the s' shall abide on his cities,
13:16 they shall fall by the s': their
Joe 2: 8 and when they fall upon the s',
Am 1:11 did pursue his brother with the s',
4:10 young men have I slain with the s',
7: 9 the house of Jeroboam with the s'.
11 saith, Jeroboam shall die by the s',
17 thy daughters shall fall by the s',
9: 1 slay the last of them with the s':
4 thence will I command the s', and
10 sinners of my people...die by the s',
Mic 4: 3 shall not lift up a s' against nation,
5: 6 waste...land of Assyria with the s',
6:14 deliverest will I give up to the s'.
Na 2:13 the s' shall devour thy young lions:
3: 3 horseman lifteth up...the bright s'
15 the s' shall cut thee off, it shall eat
Zep 2:12 also, ye shall be slain by my s'.
Hag 2:22 every one by the s' of his brother.
Zec 9:13 made thee as the s' of a mighty man.
11:17 the s' shall be upon his arm, and
13: 7 Awake, O s', against my shepherd,
M't 10:34 I came not to send peace, but a s'.
26:51 drew his s', and struck a servant
52 Put up again thy s' into his place:
52 for all they that take the s'
52 shall perish with the s'.
M'r 14:47 one of them that stood by drew a s',
Lu 2:35 a s'...pierce through thy own soul
21:24 they shall fall by the edge of the s',
22:36 he that hath no s', let him sell his
49 Lord, shall we smite with the s'?
Joh 18:10 Simon Peter having a s' drew it,
11 Peter, Put up thy s' into the sheath:
Ac 12: *2 And he killed James...with the s'.
16:27 doors open, he drew out his s', and
Ro 8:35 or nakedness, or peril, or s'?
13: 4 for he beareth not the s' in vain:
Eph 6:17 s' of the Spirit, which is the word
Heb 4:12 and sharper than any twoedged s',
11:34 escaped the edge of the s', out of
37 tempted, were slain with the s':
Re 1:16 mouth went a sharp twoedged s':
2:12 hath the sharp s' with two edges;
16 them with the s' of my mouth.
6: 4 was given unto him a great s'.
8 to kill with s', and with hunger,
13:10 he that killeth with the s'
10 must be killed with the s'.
14 beast, which had the wound by a s',
19:15 out of his mouth goeth a sharp s',
21 the remnant were slain with the s',
21 which s' proceeded out of his mouth:

swords
1Sa 13:19 Lest the Hebrews make them s'
2Ki 3:26 seven hundred men that drew s',
Ne 4:13 after their families with their s',
Ps 55:21 than oil, yet were they drawn s'.
59: 7 their mouths: s' are in their lips:
Pr 30:14 a generation, whose teeth are as s',
Ca 3: 8 all hold s', being expert in war:
Isa 2: 4 shall beat their s' into plowshares,
21:15 For they fled from the s', from the
Eze 16:40 thrust thee through with their s'.
23:47 and dispatch them with their s';
28: 7 draw their s' against the beauty of
30:11 shall draw their s' against Egypt,
32:12 By the s' of the mighty will I cause
27 have laid their s' under their heads,
38: 4 and shields, all of them handling s':
Joe 3:10 Beat your plowshares into s', and
Mic 4: 3 shall beat their s' into plowshares,
M't 26:47 with him a great multitude with s'
55 come out as against a thief with s'
M'r 14:43 with him a great multitude with s'
48 come out, as against a thief, with s'
Lu 22:38 said, Lord, behold, here are two s'.
52 come out, as against a thief, with s'

swore See SWARE.

sworn
Ge 22:16 By myself have I s', saith the Lord,
Ex 13:19 straitly s' the children of Israel,
17:16 Lord hath s' that the
Le 6: 5 about which he hath s' falsely;
De 7: 8 keep the oath which he hath s'
13:17 thee, as he hath s' unto thy fathers;
19: 8 as he hath s' unto thy fathers,
28: 9 himself, as he hath s' unto thee,
29:13 and as he hath s' unto thy fathers,
31: 7 Lord hath s' unto their fathers to
Jos 9:18 the princes...had s' unto them by
19 We have s' unto them by the Lord
J'g 2:15 and as the Lord had s' unto them:
21: 1 the men of Israel had s' in Mizpeh,
7 seeing we have s' by the Lord that
18 for the children of Israel have s'
1Sa 3:14 I have s' unto the house of Eli,
20:42 we have s' both of us in the name of
2Sa 3: 9 as the Lord hath s' to David, even
21: 2 children of Israel had s' unto them:
2Ch 15:15 for they had s' with all their heart,
Ne 6:18 many in Judah s' unto him,
9:15 which thou hadst s' to give them.
Ps 24: 4 unto vanity, nor s' deceitfully.
89: 3 I have s' unto David my servant,
35 Once have I s' by my holiness that
102: 8 mad against me are s' against me.
110: 4 Lord hath s', and will not repent,
119:106 I have s', and I will perform it,
132:11 Lord hath s' in truth unto David;
Isa 14:24 The Lord of hosts hath s', saying,
45:23 I have s' by myself, the word is
54: 9 I have s' that the waters of Noah
9 so have I s' that I would not be
62: 8 Lord hath s' by his right hand, and
Jer 5: 7 and s' by them that are no gods:
11: 5 the oath which I have s' unto your
44:26 I have s' by my great name, saith
49:13 I have s' by myself, saith the Lord,
51:14 Lord of hosts hath s' by himself,
Eze 21:23 sight, to them that have s' oaths:
Am 4: 2 Lord God hath s' by his holiness,
6: 8 The Lord God hath s' by himself,
8: 7 hath s' by the excellency of Jacob,
Mic 7:20 which thou hast s' unto our fathers
Ac 2:30 God had s' with an oath to him,
7:17 which God had s' to Abraham, the
Heb 4: 3 As I have s' in my wrath, if they

sycamine
Lu 17: 6 ye might say unto the s' tree, Be

sycamore See SYCOMORE.

Sychar (*si'-kar*) See also SHECHEM.
Joh 4: 5 city of Samaria, which is called S',

Sychem (*si'-kem*) See also SHECHEM.
Ac 7:16 And were carried over into S',
16 sons of Emmor the father of S'.

sycomore See also SYCOMORES.
1Ki 10:27 as the s' trees that are in the vale,
1Ch 27:28 s' trees that were in the low plains
2Ch 1:15 cedar trees made he as the s' trees
9:27 cedar trees made he as the s' trees
Ps 78:47 hail, and their s' trees with frost.
Am 7:14 herdman, and a gatherer of s' fruit:
Lu 19: 4 climbed up into a s' tree to see

sycomores
Isa 9:10 the s' are cut down, but we will

sycomore-trees See SYCOMORE and TREES.

Syene (*si-e'-ne*)
Eze 29:10 from the tower of S' even unto
30: 6 from the tower of S' shall they fall

synagogue See also SYNAGOGUE'S; SYNAGOGUES.
M't 12: 9 thence, he went into their s':
13:54 country, he taught them in their s',
M'r 1:21 sabbath day he entered into the s',
23 in their s' a man with an unclean
29 when they were come out of the s',
3: 1 And he entered again into the s';
5:22 cometh one of the rulers of the s',
36 unto the ruler of the s', Be not
38 to the house of the ruler of the s',
6: 2 come, he began to teach in the s':
Lu 4:16 he went into the s' on the sabbath
20 eyes of all them that were in the s'
28 And all they in the s', when they
33 in the s' there was a man, which
38 he arose out of the s', and entered
6: 6 he entered into the s' and taught:
7: 5 nation, and he hath built us a s'.
8:41 and he was a ruler of the s': and
13:14 the ruler of the s' answered with
Joh 6:59 These things said he in the s', as
9:22 he should be put out of the s'.
12:42 lest they should be put out of the s':
18:20 I ever taught in the s', and in the
Ac 6: 9 Then there arose certain of the s',
9 is called the s' of the Libertines,
13:14 and went into the s' on the sabbath
15 the rulers of the s' sent unto them,
42 the Jews were gone out of the s',
14: 1 both together into the s' of the
17: 1 where was a s' of the Jews:
10 thither went into the s' of the Jews.
17 disputed he in the s' with the Jews,
18: 4 reasoned in the s' every sabbath,
7 whose house joined hard to the s'.
8 Crispus, the chief ruler of the s',
17 Sosthenes, the chief ruler of the s',
19 but he himself entered into the s',
26 he began to speak boldly in the s':
19: 8 And he went into the s', and spake
22:19 and beat in every s' them that
26:11 I punished them oft in every s',
Re 2: 9 and are not, but are the s' of Satan.
3: 9 I will make them of the s' of Satan.

synagogue's
M'r 5:35 came from the ruler of the s' house
Lu 8:49 one from the ruler of the s' house,

synagogues
Ps 74: 8 have burned up all the s' of God
M't 4:23 teaching in their s', and preaching
6: 2 as the hypocrites do in the s' and
5 they love to pray standing in the s'
9:35 teaching in their s', and preaching
10:17 they will scourge you in their s';
23: 6 feasts, and the chief seats in the s',
34 of them shall ye scourge in your s',
M'r 1:39 he preached in their s' throughout
12:39 And the chief seats in the s', and
13: 9 and in the s' ye shall be beaten:
Lu 4:15 And he taught in their s', being
44 he preached in the s' of Galilee.
11:43 love the uppermost seats in the s',
12:11 when they bring you unto the s',
13:10 he was teaching in one of the s'
20:46 and the highest seats in the s', and
21:12 delivering you up to the s', and into
Joh 16: 2 They shall put you out of the s':
Ac 9: 2 him letters to Damascus to the s',
20 he preached Christ in the s', that
13: 5 preached the word of God in the s'
15:21 being read in the s' every sabbath
24:12 neither in the s', nor in the city:

Syntyche (*sin'-ti-ke*)
Ph'p 4: 2 I beseech Euodias, and beseech S',

Syracuse (*sir'-a-cuse*)
Ac 28:12 landing at S', we tarried there

Syria (*sir'-e-ah*) See also ARAM; SYRIA-DAMASCUS; SYRIA-MAACHAH; SYRIAN.
J'g 10: 6 and the gods of S', and the gods of
2Sa 8: 6 put garrisons in S' of Damascus:
12 Of S', and of Moab, and of the
15: 8 vow while I abode at Geshur in S',
1Ki 10: 29 Hittites, and for the kings of S',
11: 25 Israel, and reigned over S'.
15: 18 the son of Hezion, king of S' that
19: 15 anoint Hazael to be king over S':
20: 1 Ben-hadad the king of S' gathered
20 the king of S' escaped on an horse
22 king of S' will come up against thee.
23 servants of the king of S' said unto
22: 1 without war between S' and Israel.
3 not out of the hand of the king of S'?
31 king of S' commanded his thirty
2Ki 5: 1 captain of the host of the king of S',
1 Lord had given deliverance unto S':
5 the king of S' said, Go to, go, and I
6: 8 king of S' warred against Israel,
11 the heart of the king of S' was sore
23 the bands of S' came no more into
24 Ben-hadad king of S' gathered all
7: 5 uttermost part of the camp of S',
8: 7 Ben-hadad the king of S' was sick;
9 Ben-hadad king of S' hath sent me
13 that thou shalt be king over S'.
28 the war against Hazael king of S'
29 he fought against Hazael king of S'.
9: 14 Israel, because of Hazael king of S'.
15 he fought with Hazael king of S'.)
12: 17 Then Hazael king of S' went up, and
18 and sent it to Hazael king of S':
13: 3 into the hand of Hazael king of S',
4 the king of S' oppressed them.
7 the king of S' had destroyed them,
17 the arrow of deliverance from S':
19 then hadst thou smitten S' till thou
19 now thou shalt smite S' but thrice.
22 Hazael king of S' oppressed Israel
24 So Hazael king of S' died; and
15: 37 against Judah Rezin the king of S',
16: 5 Then Rezin king of S' and Pekah
6 Rezin king of S' recovered Elath
6 recovered Elath to S', and drave the
7 me out of the hand of the king of S',
2Ch 1: 17 for the kings of S', by their means.
16: 2 and sent to Ben-hadad king of S',
7 thou hast relied on the king of S',
7 king of S' escaped out of thine hand.
18: 10 With these thou shalt push S' until
30 the king of S' had commanded the
20: 2 from beyond the sea on this side S';
22: 5 to war against Hazael king of S' at
2Ch 22: 6 he fought with Hazael king of S'.
24: 23 the host of S' came up against him:
28: 5 him into the hand of the king of S';
23 gods of the kings of S' help them,
Isa 7: 1 Rezin the king of S', and Pekah the
2 S' is confederate with Ephraim.
4 for the fierce anger of Rezin with S',
5 Because S', Ephraim, and the son
8 For the head of S' is Damascus, and
17: 3 Damascus, and the remnant of S':
Eze 16: 57 thy reproach of the daughters of S',
27: 16 S' was thy merchant by reason of
Ho 12: 12 Jacob fled into the country of S',
Am 1: 5 people of S' shall go into captivity
M't 4: 24 his fame went throughout all S':
Lu 2: 2 when Cyrenius was governor of S'.
Ac 15: 23 of the Gentiles in Antioch and S'
41 he went through S' and Cilicia,
18: 18 brethren, and sailed thence into S',
20: 3 as he was about to sail into S', he
21: 3 sailed into S', and landed at Tyre:
Gal 1: 21 I came into the regions of S' and

Syriack (*sir'-e-ak*) See also SYRIAN.
Da 2: 4 the Chaldeans to the king in S',

Syria-damascus (*sir''-e-ah-da-mas'-cus*) See also SYRIA and DAMASCUS.
1Ch 18: 6 David put garrisons in S';

Syria-maachah (*sir''-e-ah-ma'-a-kah*)
1Ch 19: 6 and out of S', and out of Zobah.

Syrian (*sir'-e-un*) See also ARAMITES; SYRIACK; SYRIANS; SYROPHENICIAN.
Ge 25: 20 of Bethuel the S' of Padan-aram,
20 the sister to Laban the S'.
28: 5 unto Laban, son of Bethuel the S',
31: 20 away unawares to Laban the S',
24 And God came to Laban the S' in a
De 26: 5 A S' ready to perish was my father,
2Ki 5: 20 master hath spared Naaman this S'.
18: 26 to thy servants in the S' language;
Ezr 4: 7 letter was written in the S' tongue,
7 and interpreted in the S' tongue.
Isa 36: 11 thy servant in the S' language;
Lu 4: 27 cleansed, saving Naaman the S'.

Syrians (*sir'-e-uns*)
2Sa 8: 5 S' of Damascus came to succour
5 David slew of the S' two and twenty
6 the S' became servants to David,
13 from smiting of the S' in the valley
10: 6 and hired the S' of Beth-rehob,
6 and the S' of Zoba, twenty thousand
8 the S' of Zoba, and of Rehob, and
9 put them in array against the S':
11 If the S' be too strong for me, then
2Sa 10: 13 him, unto the battle against the S':
14 of Ammon saw that the S' were fled,
15 the S' saw that they were smitten
16 the S' that were beyond the river:
17 S' set themselves in array against
18 And the S' fled before Israel; and
18 of seven hundred chariots of the S',
19 the S' feared to help the children of
1Ki 20: 20 S' fled; and Israel pursued them:
21 slew the S' with a great slaughter.
26 that Ben-hadad numbered the S',
27 kids; but the S' filled the country.
28 Because the S' have said, The Lord
29 the children of Israel slew of the S'
22: 11 With these shalt thou push the S',
35 up in his chariot against the S',
2Ki 5: 2 the S' had gone out by companies,
6: 9 for thither the S' are come down.
7: 4 let us fall unto the host of the S':
5 to go unto the camp of the S':
6 made...host of the S' to hear a noise
10 We came to the camp of the S', and,
12 you what the S' have done to us.
14 the king sent after the host of the S',
15 which the S' had cast away in their
16 out, and spoiled the tents of the S'.
8: 28 and the S' wounded Joram.
29 wounds which the S' had given him
9: 15 wounds which the S' had given him.
13: 5 out from under the hand of the S':
17 for thou shalt smite the S' in Aphek,
16: 6 and the S' came to Elath, and dwelt
24: 2 bands of the S', and bands of the
1Ch 18: 5 the S' of Damascus came to help
5 David slew of the S' two and twenty
6 and the S' became David's servants,
19: 10 and put them in array against the S'.
12 If the S' be too strong for me, then
14 nigh before the S' unto the battle;
15 Ammon saw that the S' were fled,
16 the S' saw that they were put to the
16 the S' that were beyond the river:
17 the battle in array against the S',
18 But the S' fled before Israel; and
18 David slew of the S' seven thousand
19 the S' help the children of Ammon
2Ch 18: 34 in his chariot against the S' until
22: 5 and the S' smote Joram.
24: 24 army of the S' came with a small
Isa 9: 12 The S' before, and the Philistines
Jer 35: 11 and for fear of the army of the S':
Am 9: 7 from Caphtor, and the S' from Kir?

Syrophenician (*sy''-ro-fe-ne'-she-un*)
M'r 7: 26 The woman was a Greek, a S' by

T.

Taanach (*ta'-a-nak*) See also TANACH.
Jos 12: 21 The king of T', one; the king of
17: 11 the inhabitants of T' and her towns,
J'g 1: 27 nor T' and her towns, nor the
5: 19 fought the kings of Canaan in T'
1Ki 4: 12 to him pertained T' and Megiddo,
1Ch 7: 29 T' and her towns, Megiddo and her

Taanath-shiloh (*ta''-a-nath-shi'-lo*)
Jos 16: 6 went about eastward unto T',

Tabbaoth (*tab'-ba-oth*)
Ezr 2: 43 of Hasupha, the children of T',
Ne 7: 46 of Hashupha, the children of T',

Tabbath (*tab'-bath*)
J'g 7: 22 border of Abel-meholah, unto T'.

Tabeal (*tab'-e-al*) See also TABEEL.
Isa 7: 6 the midst of it, even the son of T':

Tabeel (*tab'-e-el*) See also TABEAL.
Ezr 4: 7 wrote Bishlam, Mithredath, T',

taber See TABERING.

Taberah (*tab'-e-rah*)
Nu 11: 3 called the name of the place T':
De 9: 22 And at T', and at Massah, and at

tabering
Na 2: 7 of doves, t' upon their breasts.

tabernacle ^ See also TABERNACLES.
Ex 25: 9 thee, after the pattern of the t',
26: 1 shalt make the t' with ten curtains
6 the taches: and it shall be one t'.
7 hair to be a covering upon the t':
9 curtain in the forefront of the t'.
12 hang over the backside of the t'.
13 it shall hang over the sides of the t',
15 boards for the t' of shittim wood
17 make for all the boards of the t'.
18 shalt make the boards for the t',
20 second side of the t' on the north
22 And for the sides of the t' westward
23 thou make for the corners of the t'
26 the boards of the one side of the t',
27 boards of the other side of the t',
27 for the boards of the side of the t',
30 shalt rear up the t' according to the
35 the side of the t' toward the south:
27: 9 thou shalt make the court of the t':
19 vessels of the t' in all the service
21 In the t' of...congregation without
28: 43 come in unto...t' of...congregation,
29: 4 door of the t' of the congregation,
10 before the t' of the congregation:
11 door of the t' of the congregation.
30 into the t' of the congregation
Ex 29: 32 door of the t' of the congregation.
42 door of the t' of the congregation
43 the t' shall be sanctified by my glory.
44 sanctify the t' of the congregation,
30: 16 service of the t' of the congregation;
18 between the t' of the congregation
20 go into the t' of the congregation,
26 anoint the t' of the congregation
36 testimony in...t' of...congregation,
31: 7 t' of the congregation, and the ark
7 and all the furniture of the t',
33: 7 And Moses took the t', and pitched it
7 called it...T' of the congregation.
7 out unto the t' of the congregation,
8 when Moses went out unto the t',
8 Moses, until he was gone into the t'.
9 pass, as Moses entered into the t',
9 pillar...stood at the door of the t',
10 cloudy pillar stand at the t' door:
11 Joshua,...departed not out of the t'.
35: 11 The t', his tent, and his covering,
15 the door at the entering in of the t',
18 The pins of the t', and the pins of
21 work of the t' of the congregation,
36: 8 that wrought the work of the t'
13 with the taches: so it became one t'.
14 goats' hair for the tent over the t':
20 boards for the t' of shittim wood,
22 he make for all the boards of the t'.
23 And he made boards for the t';
25 And for the other side of the t',
27 And for the sides of the t' westward
28 made he for the corners of the t'
31 the boards of the one side of the t',
32 boards of the other side of the t',
32 and five bars for the boards of the t'
37 made an hanging for the t' door.
38: 8 door of the t' of the congregation.
20 And all the pins of the t', and of
21 This is the sum of the t', even of
21 even of the t' of testimony, as it was
30 door of the t' of the congregation,
31 and all the pins of the t', and all
39: 32 t' of the tent of the congregation
33 And they brought the t' unto Moses,
38 and the hanging for the t' door,
40 the vessels of the service of the t',
40: 2 t' of the tent of the congregation.
5 put the hanging of the door to the t'.
6 t' of the tent of the congregation.
9 anoint the t', and all that is therein,
12 door of the t' of the congregation,
17 month, that the t' was reared up.
18 And Moses reared up the t', and
19 spread abroad the tent over the t',
Ex 40: 21 And he brought the ark into the t',
22 upon the side of the t' northward,
24 on the side of the t' southward.
28 up the hanging at the door of the t'.
29 t' of the tent of the congregation,
33 round about the t' and the altar,
34, 35 the glory of the Lord filled the t'.
36 cloud was taken up from over the t',
38 cloud of the Lord was upon the t'
Le 1: 1 out of the t' of the congregation,
3 door of the t' of the congregation
5 door of the t' of the congregation
3: 2 door of the t' of the congregation:
8, 13 before the t' of the congregation:
4: 4 door of the t' of the congregation
5 bring it to the t' of...congregation:
7 is in the t' of the congregation;
7 door of the t' of the congregation.
14 before the t' of the congregation.
16 blood to the t' of the congregation:
18 that is in the t' of the congregation,
18 door of the t' of the congregation.
6: 16 court of the t' of the congregation
26 court of the t' of the congregation.
30 into the t' of the congregation
8: 3, 4 door of the t' of the congregation.
10 anointed the t' and all...therein,
31 door of the t' of the congregation:
35 door of the t' of the congregation
9: 5 before the t' of the congregation:
23 went into the t' of the congregation,
10: 7 door of the t' of the congregation,
9 go into the t' of the congregation,
12: 6 door of the t' of the congregation,
14: 11 door of the t' of the congregation:
23 door of the t' of the congregation,
15: 14 door of the t' of the congregation,
29 door of the t' of the congregation.
31 defile my t' that is among them.
16: 7 door of the t' of the congregation.
16 he do for the t' of the congregation,
17 no man in the t' of the congregation
20 place, and the t' of...congregation,
23 come into the t' of...congregation,
33 atonement for...t' of...congregation,
17: 4 door of the t' of the congregation,
4 the Lord before the t' of the Lord;
5, 6, 9 door of the t' of...congregation,
19: 21 door of the t' of the congregation,
24: 3 in the t' of the congregation,
26: 11 And I will set my t' among you:
Nu 1: 1 Sinai, in the t' of the congregation,
50 Levites over the t' of testimony,
50 shall bear the t', and all the vessels
50 shall encamp round about the t'.

Nu 1:51 And when the t' setteth forward,
51 and when the t' is to be pitched, the
53 round about the t' of testimony,
53 the charge of the t' of testimony.
2: 2 about the t' of the congregation
17 the t' of the congregation shall set
3: 7 before the t' of the congregation,
7 to do the service of the t'.
8 of the t' of the congregation,
8 Israel, to do the service of the t'.
23 shall pitch behind the t' westward.
25 in the t' of the congregation
25 shall be the t', and the tent,
25 door of the t' of the congregation,
26 of the court, which is by the t',
29 on the side of the t' southward.
35 on the side of the t' northward.
36 shall be the boards of the t', and
38 before the t' toward the east, even
38 before the t' of the congregation
4: 3 work in the t' of the congregation
4 Kohath in the t' of...congregation,
15 Kohath in the t' of...congregation.
16 and the oversight of all the t', and
23 work in the t' of the congregation.
25 shall bear the curtains of the t',
25 and the t' of the congregation, his
25 door of the t' of the congregation,
26 which is by the t' and by the altar
28 Gershon in the t' of...congregation:
30 work of the t' of the congregation.
31 service in the t' of...congregation;
31 the boards of the t', and the bars
33 service, in the t' of...congregation,
35 work in the t' of the congregation:
37 service in the t' of the congregation,
39 work in the t' of the congregation,
41 service in the t' of the congregation,
43 work in the t' of the congregation,
47 burden in the t' of the congregation,
5:17 dust that is in the floor of the t'
6:10, 13 door of the t' of...congregation:
18 door of the t' of the congregation,
7: 1 that Moses had fully set up the t',
3 they brought them before the t'.
5 service of the t' of...congregation;
89 gone into the t' of the congregation
8: 9 before the t' of the congregation:
15 service of the t' of the congregation:
19 Israel in the t' of the congregation,
22 service in the t' of the congregation
24 service of the t' of the congregation:
26 brethren in the t' of...congregation,
9:15 And on the day that the t' was
15 reared up the cloud covered the t',
15 at even there was upon the t' as it
17 the cloud was taken up from the t',
18 as the cloud abode upon the t'
19 the cloud tarried long upon the t'
20 cloud was a few days upon the t';
22 that the cloud tarried upon the t'.
10: 3 door of the t' of the congregation.
11 was taken up from off the t' of the
17 And the t' was taken down; and the
17 Merari set forward, bearing the t'.
21 the other did set up the t' against
11:16 them unto the t' of...congregation,
24 and set them round about the t'.
26 but went not out unto the t': and
12: 4 three unto the t' of...congregation.
5 and stood in the door of the t', and
10 the cloud departed from off the t';
14:10 appeared in the t' of...congregation
16: 9 do the service of the t' of the Lord.
18 door of the t' of the congregation
19 door of the t' of the congregation:
24 you up from about the t' of Korah,
27 they gat up from the t' of Korah,
42 toward the t' of the congregation:
43 before the t' of the congregation.
50 door of the t' of the congregation:
17: 4 them up in the t' of...congregation
7 before the Lord in the t' of witness.
8 Moses went into the t' of witness;
13 near unto the t' of the Lord shall
18: 2 minister before the t' of witness.
3 charge, and the charge of all the t':
4 charge of the t' of the congregation,
4 for all the service of the t': and a
6 service of the t' of the congregation.
21 service of the t' of the congregation.
22 come nigh the t' of...congregation,
23 service of the t' of the congregation,
31 service in the t' of the congregation.
19: 4 before the t' of the congregation
13 himself, defileth the t' of the Lord;
20: 6 door of the t' of the congregation,
25: 6 door of the t' of the congregation.
27: 2 door of the t' of the congregation,
31:30 the charge of the t' of the Lord.
47 the charge of the t' of the Lord;
54 it into the t' of the congregation,
De 31:14 yourselves in...t' of...congregation,
14 in the t' of the congregation.
15 Lord appeared in the t' in a pillar of
15 cloud stood over the door of the t'.
Jos 18: 1 set up the t' of the congregation
19:51 door of the t' of the congregation.
22:19 wherein the Lord's t' dwelleth,
29 Lord our God that is before his t'.
1Sa 2:22 door of the t' of the congregation.
2Sa 6:17 t' that David had pitched for it:
7: 6 have walked in a tent and in a t'.
1Ki 1:39 took an horn of oil out of the t',
2:28 Joab fled unto the t' of the Lord,
29 was fled unto the t' of the Lord;

1Ki 2:30 Benaiah came to the t' of the Lord,
8: 4 and the t' of the congregation, and
4 the holy vessels that were in the t',
1Ch 6:32 place of the t' of the congregation
48 of the t' of the house of God.
9:19 keepers of the gates of the t':
21 door of the t' of the congregation.
23 the house of the t', by wards.
16:39 priests, before the t' of the Lord
17: 5 to tent, and from one t' to another.
21:29 For the t' of the Lord, which Moses
23:26 they shall no more carry the t', nor
32 charge of the t' of...congregation,
2Ch 1: 3 there was the t' of the congregation
5 he put before the t' of the Lord:
6 was at the t' of the congregation,
13 before the t' of the congregation,
5: 5 and the t' of the congregation,
5 the holy vessels that were in the t'
24: 6 of Israel, for the t' of witness?
Job 5:24 know that thy t' shall be in peace;
18: 6 The light shall be dark in his t', and
14 confidence...be rooted out of his t',
15 It shall dwell in his t', because it is
19:12 me, and encamp round about my t'.
20:26 go ill with him that is left in his t'.
29: 4 the secret of God was upon my t';
31:31 If the men of my t' said not, Oh
36:29 the clouds, or the noise of his t'?
Ps 15: 1 Lord, who shall abide in thy t'?
19: 4 In them hath he set a t' for the sun,
27: 5 In the secret of his t' shall he hide
6 will I offer in his t' sacrifices of joy;
61: 4 I will abide in thy t' for ever: I will
76: 2 In Salem also is his t', and his
78:60 So that he forsook the t' of Shiloh,
67 he refused the t' of Joseph, and
132: 3 not come into the t' of my house,
Pr 14:11 the t' of the upright shall flourish.
Isa 4: 6 a t' for a shadow in the daytime
16: 5 upon it in truth in the t' of David,
33:20 a t' that shall not be taken down;
Jer 10:20 My t' is spoiled, and all my cords
La 2: 4 in the t' of the daughter of Zion:
6 he hath violently taken away his t',
Eze 37:27 My t' also shall be with them:
41: 1 which was the breadth of the t'.
Am 5:26 the t' of your Moloch and Chiun
9:11 day will I raise up the t' of David
Ac 7:43 ye took up the t' of Moloch, and
44 Our fathers had the t' of witness in
46 to find a t' for the God of Jacob.
15:16 will build again the t' of David,
2Co 5: 1 our earthly house of this t' were
4 For we that are in this t' do groan,
Heb 8: 2 and of the true t', which the Lord
5 when he was about to make the t',
9: 2 For there was a t' made; the first,
3 t' which is called the Holiest of all;
6 priests went always into the first t',
8 as the first t' was yet standing:
11 by a greater and more perfect t',
21 he sprinkled with blood both the t',
13:10 no right to eat which serve the t'.
2Pe 1:13 as long as I am in this t', to stir
14 shortly I must put off this my t',
Re 13: 6 to blaspheme his name, and his t',
15: 5 temple of the t' of the testimony
21: 3 the t' of God is with men, and he

tabernacles
Le 23:34 be the feast of t' for seven days
Nu 24: 5 tents, O Jacob, and thy t', O Israel!
De 16:13 observe the feast of t' seven days,
16 feast of weeks, and in the feast of t':
31:10 the year of release, in the feast of t'.
2Ch 8:13 feast of weeks, and in the feast of t'.
Ezr 3: 4 They kept also the feast of t', as it is
Job 11:14 let not wickedness dwell in thy t'.
12: 6 The t' of robbers prosper, and they
15:34 fire shall consume the t' of bribery.
22:23 put away iniquity far from thy t'.
Ps 43: 3 me unto thy holy hill, and to thy t'.
46: 4 place of the t' of the most High.
78:51 of their strength in the t' of Ham:
83: 6 t' of Edom, and the Ishmaelites;
84: 1 How amiable are thy t', O Lord of
118:15 is in the t' of the righteous:
132: 7 We will go into his t': we will
Da 11:45 he shall plant the t' of his palace
Ho 9: 6 them: thorns shall be in their t'.
12: 9 will yet make thee to dwell in t',
Zec 14:16 of hosts, and to keep the feast of t'.
18, 19 not up to keep the feast of t'.
Mal 2:12 the scholar, out of the t' of Jacob,
M't 17: 4 let us make here three t'; one for
M'r 9: 5 let us make three t'; one for thee,
Lu 9:33 let us make three t'; one for thee,
Joh 7: 2 the Jews' feast of t' was at hand.
Heb 11: 9 dwelling in t' with Isaac...Jacob,

Tabitha (*tab'-ith-ah*)
Ac 9:36 a certain disciple named T',
40 him to the body said, T', arise.

table See also TABLES.
Ex 25:23 also make a t' of shittim wood:
27 places of the staves to bear the t'.
28 that the t' may be borne with them.
30 thou shalt set upon the t' shewbread
26:35 thou shalt set the t' without the vail,
35 the candlestick over against the t'
35 shalt put the t' on the north side.
30:27 And the t' and all his vessels, and
31: 8 And the t' and his furniture, and the
35:13 The t', and his staves, and all his
37:10 And he made the t' of shittim wood:
Ex 37:14 places for the staves to bear the t'.
15 them with gold, to bear the t'.
16 the vessels which were upon the t',
39:36 The t', and all the vessels thereof,
40: 4 And thou shalt bring in the t', and
22 And he put the t' in the tent of the
24 over against the t', on the side of
Le 24: 6 upon the pure t' before the Lord.
Nu 3:31 charge shall be the ark, and the t',
4: 7 upon the t' of shewbread they shall
J'g 1: 7 gathered their meat under my t':
1Sa 20:29 he cometh not unto the king's t'.
34 Jonathan arose from the t' in fierce
2Sa 9: 7 and thou shalt eat bread at my t'
10 son shall eat bread alway at my t'.
11 he shall eat at my t', as one of the
13 did eat continually at the king's t';
19:28 them that did eat at thine own t'.
1Ki 2: 7 them be of those that eat at thy t':
4:27 that came unto king Solomon's t',
7:48 the altar of gold, and the t' of gold,
10: 5 the meat of his t', and the sitting
13:20 it came to pass, as they sat at the t',
18:19 hundred, which eat at Jezebel's t'.
2Ki 4:10 us set for him there a bed, and a t',
1Ch 28:16 tables of shewbread, for every t';
2Ch 9: 4 the meat of his t', and the sitting
13:11 set they in order upon the pure t';
29:18 and the shewbread t', with all the
Ne 5:17 there were at my t' an hundred and
Job 36:16 that which should be set on thy t'
Ps 23: 5 Thou preparest a t' before me in the
69:22 Let their t' become a snare before
78:19 God furnish a t' in the wilderness?
128: 3 like olive plants round about thy t'.
Pr 3: 3 them upon the t' of thine heart:
7: 3 write them upon the t' of thine heart.
9: 2 she hath also furnished her t'.
Ca 1:12 While the king sitteth at his t', my
Isa 21: 5 Prepare the t', watch in the
30: 8 Now go, write it before them in a t',
65:11 that prepare a t' for that troop,
Jer 17: 1 graven upon the t' of their heart,
Eze 23:41 bed, and a t' prepared before it,
39:20 Thus ye shall be filled at my t' with
41:22 This is the t' that is before the Lord.
44:16 and they shall come near to my t',
Da 11:27 and they shall speak lies at one t';
Mal 1: 7 The t' of the Lord is contemptible.
12 say, The t' of the Lord is polluted;
M't 15:27 which fall from their masters' t'.
M'r 7:28 yet the dogs under the t' eat of the
Lu 1:63 And he asked for a writing t', and
16:21 which fell from the rich man's t':
22:21 betrayeth me is with me on the t'.
30 ye may eat and drink at my t' in my
Joh 12: 2 of them that sat at the t' with him.
13:28 Now no man at the t' knew for what
Ro 11: 9 saith, Let their t' be made a snare,
1Co 10:21 cannot be partakers of the Lord's t',
21 and of the t' of devils.
Heb 9: 2 and the t', and the shewbread;

tables
Ex 24:12 and I will give thee t' of stone,
31:18 two t' of testimony, t' of stone,
32:15 two t' of the testimony were in his
15 t' were written on both their sides;
16 And the t' were the work of God,
16 writing of God, graven upon the t'.
19 and he cast the t' out of his hands,
34: 1 two t' of stone like unto the first:
1 I will write upon these t' the words
1 in the first t', which thou brakest.
4 two t' of stone like unto the first;
4 took in his hand the two t' of stone.
28 wrote upon the t' the words of the
29 two t' of testimony in Moses' hand,
De 4:13 he wrote them upon two t' of stone.
5:22 he wrote them in two t' of stone,
9: 9 the mount to receive the t' of stone,
9 t' of the covenant which the Lord
10 delivered unto me two t' of stone
11 Lord gave me the two t' of stone,
11 stone, even the t' of the covenant.
15 two t' of the covenant were in my
17 I took the two t', and cast them out
10: 1 two t' of stone like unto the first,
2 I will write on the t' the words that
2 in the first t' which thou brakest,
3 two t' of stone like unto the first,
3 having the two t' in mine hand.
4 he wrote on the t', according to the
5 and put the t' in the ark which I had
1Ki 8: 9 in the ark save the two t' of stone,
1Ch 28:16 gave gold for the t' of shewbread,
16 likewise silver for the t' of silver:
2Ch 4: 8 He made also ten t', and placed
19 t' whereon the shewbread was set;
5:10 nothing in the ark save the two t'
Isa 28: 8 For all t' are full of vomit and
Eze 40:39 in the porch of the gate were two t'
39 this side, and two t' on that side,
40 entry of the north gate, were two t':
40 the porch of the gate, were two t'.
41 Four t' were on this side, and four
41 and four t' on that side, by the side
41 eight t', whereupon they slew their
42 four t' were of hewn stone for the
43 and upon the t' was the flesh of the
Hab 2: 2 vision, and make it plain upon t',
M't 21:12 the t' of the moneychangers, and
M'r 7: 4 and pots, brasen vessels, and of t'.
11:15 the t' of the moneychangers,
Joh 2:15 money, and overthrew the t';
Ac 6: 2 leave the word of God, and serve t'.
2Co 3: 3 living God; not in t' of stone,

2Co 3: 3 but in fleshy t' of the heart.
Heb 9: 4 budded, and the t' of the covenant;
tablets
Ex 35:22 and earrings, and rings, and t', all
Nu 31:50 bracelets, rings, earrings, and t'.
Isa 3:20 headbands, and the t', and
Tabor (ta'-bor) See also AZNOTH-TABOR; CHISLOTH-TABOR.
Jos 19:22 And the coast reacheth to T', and
J'g 4: 6 Go and draw toward mount T', and
12 Barak...was gone up to mount T'.
14 Barak went down from mount T',
8:18 men were they whom ye slew at T'?
1Sa 10: 3 thou shalt come to the plain of T',
1Ch 6:77 her suburbs, T' with her suburbs:
Ps 89:12 T' and Hermon shall rejoice in thy
Jer 46:18 as T' is among the mountains, and
Ho 5: 1 Mizpah, and a net spread upon T'.
tabret See also TABRETS.
Ge 31:27 with songs, with t', and with harp?
1Sa 10: 5 and a t', and a pipe, and a harp,
Job 17: 6 and aforetime I was as a t'.
Isa 5:12 the t', and pipe, and wine, are in
tabrets
1Sa 18: 6 to meet king Saul, with t', with
Isa 24: 8 The mirth of t' ceaseth, the noise of
30:32 him, it shall be with t' and harps:
Jer 31: 4 shalt again be adorned with thy t',
Eze 28:13 the workmanship of thy t' and of
Tabrimon (tab'-rim-on)
1Ki 15:18 them to Ben-hadad,...son of T',
taches (tatch'-ez)
Ex 26: 6 thou shalt make fifty t' of gold,
6 the curtains together with the t':
11 thou shalt make fifty t' of brass,
11 and put the t' into the loops, and
33 shalt hang up the vail under the t',
35:11 his covering, his t', and his boards,
36:13 And he made fifty t' of gold, and
13 one unto another with the t': so
18 made fifty t' of brass to couple the
39:33 all his furniture, his t', his boards,
Tachmonite (tak'-mun-ite) See also HACHMONITE.
2Sa 23: 8 The T' that sat in the seat, chief
tackling See also TACKLINGS.
Ac 27:19 our own hands the t' of the ship.
tacklings
Isa 33:23 Thy t' are loosed; they could not
Tadmor (tad'-mor)
1Ki 9:18 Baalath, and T' in the wilderness,
2Ch 8: 4 he built T' in the wilderness, and
Tahan (ta'-han) See also TAHANITES.
Nu 26:35 T', the family of the Tahanites.
1Ch 7:25 and Telah his son, and T' his son,
Tahanites (ta'-han-ites)
Nu 26:35 of Tahan, the family of the T'.
Tahapanes (ta-hap'-a-neze) See also TAHPANHES; TAHPENES.
Jer 2:16 the children of Noph and T' have
Tahath (ta'-hath)
Nu 33:26 Makheloth, and encamped at T'.
27 they departed from T', and pitched
1Ch 6:24 T' his son, Uriel his son, Uzziah
37 The son of T', the son of Assir,
7:20 Bered his son, and T' his son,
20 Eladah his son, and T' his son,
Tahpanhes (tah'-pan-heze) See also TAHAPANES; TAHPENES; TEHAPHNEHES.
Jer 43: 7 Lord: thus came they even to T'.
8 of the Lord unto Jeremiah in T',
9 the entry of Pharaoh's house in T',
44: 1 which dwell at Migdol, and at T',
46:14 and publish in Noph and in T':
Tahpenes (tah'-pe-neze) See also TAHPANHES.
1Ki 11:19 wife, the sister of T' the queen.
20 sister of T' bare him Genubath
20 T' weaned in Pharaoh's house:
Tahrea (tah'-re-ah) See also TAREA.
1Ch 9:41 and Melech, and T', and Ahaz.
Tahtim-hodshi (tah''-tim-hod'-shi)
2Sa 24: 6 to Gilead, and to the land of T';
tail See also TAILS.
Ex 4: 4 thine hand, and take it by the t'.
De 28:13 thee the head, and not the t';
44 the head, and thou shalt be the t'.
J'g 15: 4 turned t' to t', and put a firebrand
Job 40:17 He moveth his t' like a cedar: the
Isa 9:14 cut off from Israel head and t',
15 that teacheth lies, he is the t'.
19:15 which the head or t', branch or
Re 12: 4 his t' drew the third part of the
tails
J'g 15: 4 in the midst between two t'.
Isa 7: 4 two t' of these smoking firebrands,
Re 9:10 they had t' like unto scorpions,
10 and there were stings in their t':
19 is in their mouth, and in their t':
19 their t' were like unto serpents,
take^ See also OVERTAKE; TAKEN; TAKEST; TAKETH; TAKING; TOOK; UNDERTAKE.
Ge 3:22 t' also of the tree of life, and eat,
6:21 t' thou unto thee of all food that is
7: 2 clean beast thou shalt t' to thee by
12:19 behold thy wife, t' her, and go thy
14:21 persons, and t' the goods to thyself.
23 I will not t' from a thread even to a
Ge 14:23 I will not t' any thing that is thine,
24 Mamre; let them t' their portion.
15: 9 T' me an heifer of three years old,
19:15 t' thy wife, and thy two daughters,
19 lest some evil t' me, and I die:
21:30 lambs shalt thou t' of my hand,
22: 2 T' now thy son, thine only son
23:13 t' it of me, and I will bury my dead
24: 3 shalt not t' a wife unto my son of
4 and t' a wife unto my son Isaac.
7 and thou shalt t' a wife unto my son
37 shalt not t' a wife to my son of the
38 kindred, and t' a wife unto my son.
40 thou shalt t' a wife for my son of
48 to t' my master's brother's daughter
51 Rebekah is before thee, t' her, and
27: 3 t', I pray thee, thy weapons, thy
3 the field, and t' me some venison;
46 if Jacob t' a wife of the daughters
28: 1 shalt not t' a wife of the daughters
2 t' thee a wife from thence of the
6 to t' him a wife from thence; and
6 shalt not t' a wife of the daughters
30:15 t' away my son's mandrakes also?
31:24 T' heed that thou speak not to
29 T' thou heed that thou speak not
31 t' by force thy daughters from
32 is thine with me, and t' it to thee.
50 if thou shalt t' other wives beside
33:11 T', I pray thee, my blessing that is
12 Let us t' our journey, and let us go.
34: 9 and t' our daughters unto you.
16 we will t' your daughters to us,
17 then will we t' our daughter, and
21 let us t' their daughters to us for
38:23 Let her t' it to her, lest we be
41:34 t' up the fifth part of the land of
42:33 and t' food for the famine of your
36 not, and ye will t' Benjamin away:
43:11 t' of the best fruits in the land in
12 t' double money in your hand; and
13 T' also your brother, and arise, go
18 t' us for bondmen, and our asses.
44:29 And if ye t' this also from me, and
45:18 t' your father and your households,
19 t' your wagons out of the land of
Ex 2: 9 T' this child away, and nurse it
4: 4 thine hand, and t' it by the tail.
9 shalt t' of the water of the river,
17 shalt t' this rod in thine hand,
6: 7 I will t' you to me for a people, and
7: 9 T' thy rod, and cast it before
15 serpent shalt thou t' in thine hand.
19 T' thy rod, and stretch out thine
8: 8 that he may t' away the frogs from
9: 8 T' to you handfuls of ashes of the
10:17 t' away from me this death only.
26 we t' to serve the Lord our God;
28 t' heed to thyself, see my face no
12: 3 t' to them every man a lamb,
4 t' it according to the number of the
5 ye shall t' it out from the sheep,
7 And they shall t' of the blood, and
21 t' you a lamb according to your
22 And ye shall t' a bunch of hyssop,
32 Also t' your flocks and your herds,
15:14 shall t' hold on the inhabitants of
15 trembling shall t' hold upon them;
16:16 t' ye every man for them which
33 T' a pot, and put an omer full of
17: 5 t' with thee of the elders of Israel;
5 the river, t' in thine hand, and go.
19:12 T' heed to yourselves, that ye go
20: 7 shalt not t' the name of the Lord
21:10 If he t' him another wife; her
14 thou shalt t' him from mine altar,
22:26 at all t' thy neighbour's raiment
23: 8 And thou shalt t' no gift: for the
25 t' sickness away from the midst
25: 2 his heart ye shall t' my offering.
3 offering which ye shall t' of them;
26: 5 loops may t' hold one of another.
28: 1 And t' thou unto thee Aaron thy
5 And they shall t' gold, and blue,
9 And thou shalt t' two onyx stones,
29: 1 T' one young bullock, and two
5 And thou shalt t' the garments,
7 Then shalt thou t' the anointing oil,
12 shalt t' of the blood of the bullock,
13 thou shalt t' all the fat that covereth
15 Thou shalt also t' one ram; and
16 ram, and thou shalt t' his blood,
19 And thou shalt t' the other ram;
20 kill the ram, and t' of his blood,
21 t' of the blood that is upon the altar,
22 t' of the ram the fat and the rump,
26 thou shalt t' the breast of the ram
31 shalt t' the ram of the consecration,
30:16 thou shalt t' the atonement money
23 T' thou also unto thee principal
34 T' unto thee sweet spices, stacte,
33:23 And I will t' away mine hand,
34: 9 sin, and t' us for thine inheritance.
12 T' heed to thyself, lest thou make
16 t' of their daughters unto thy sons,
35: 5 T' ye from among you an offering
40: 9 And thou shalt t' the anointing oil,
Le 2: 2 t' thereout his handful of the flour
9 shall t' from the meat offering
3: 4 and the fat...it shall he t' away.
9 shall he t' off hard by the backbone;
10, 15 and the fat...it shall he t' away.
4: 5 shall t' of the bullock's blood,
8 he shall t' off from it all the fat of
9 and the fat...it shall he t' away,
19 he shall t' all his fat from him,
Le 4:25 t' of the blood of the sin offering
30 And the priest shall t' of the blood
31 he shall t' away all the fat thereof,
34 t' of the blood of the sin offering
35 he shall t' away all the fat thereof,
5:12 the priest shall t' his handful of it,
6:10 t' up the ashes which the fire hath
15 And he shall t' of it his handful,
7: 4 and the fat...it shall he t' away:
8: 2 T' Aaron and his sons with him,
9: 2 T'...a young calf for a sin offering,
3 T' ye a kid of the goats for a sin
10:12 T' the meat offering that remaineth
14: 4 to t' for him that is to be cleansed
6 As for the living bird, he shall t' it,
10 t' two he lambs without blemish,
12 And the priest shall t' one he lamb,
14 the priest shall t' some of the blood
15 priest shall t' some of the log of oil,
21 t' one lamb for a trespass offering
24 t' the lamb of the trespass offering,
25 the priest shall t' some of the blood
40 t'...the stones in which the plague
42 And they shall t' other stones, and
42 he shall t' other morter, and shall
49 And he shall t' to cleanse the house
51 he shall t' the cedar wood, and the
15:14 he shall t' to him two turtledoves,
29 she shall t' unto her two turtles,
16: 5 And he shall t' of the congregation
7 And he shall t' the two goats, and
12 t' a censer full of burning coals of
14, 18 t' of the blood of the bullock,
18:17 shalt thou t' her son's daughter,
18 shalt thou t' a wife to her sister,
20:14 if a man t' a wife and her mother,
17 And if a man shall t' his sister, his
21 if a man shall t' his brother's wife,
21: 7 shall not t' a wife that is a whore,
7 shall they t' a woman put away from
13 he shall t' a wife in her virginity.
14 or an harlot, these shall he not t':
14 he shall t' a virgin of his own people
22: 5 a man of whom he may t' uncleanness,
23:40 t' you on the first day the boughs
24: 5 thou shalt t' fine flour, and bake
25:36 T' thou no usury of him, or
46 t' them as an inheritance for your
Nu 1: 2 T' ye the sum of...congregation
49 Levi, neither t' the sum of them
51 the Levites shall t' it down:
3:40 and t' the number of their names.
41 thou shalt t' the Levites from me
45 T' the Levites instead of all the
47 shalt even t' five shekels apiece
47 of the sanctuary shalt thou t' them:
4: 2 T' the sum of the sons of Kohath
5 they shall t' down the covering vail,
9 And they shall t' a cloth of blue,
12 t' all the instruments of ministry,
13 shall t' away the ashes from the altar,
22 T'...sum of the sons of Gershon,
5:17 And the priest shall t' holy water
17 and of the dust...the priest shall t',
25 priest shall t' the jealousy offering
26 shall t' an handful of the offering,
6:18 shall t' the hair of the head of his
19 priest shall t' the sodden shoulder
7: 5 T' it of them, that they may be to
8: 6 T' the Levites from among the
8 Then let them t' a young bullock
8 shalt thou t' for a sin offering.
10: 6 the south side shall t' their journey:
11:17 t' of the spirit which is upon thee,
16: 3 Ye t' too much upon you, seeing all
6 T' you censers, Korah, and all his
7 ye t' too much upon you, ye sons of
17 And t' every man his censer, and
37 that he t' up the censers out of the
46 T' a censer, and put fire therein
17: 2 and t' of every one of them a rod
10 quite t' away their murmurings
18:26 t' of the children of Israel the tithes
19: 4 Eleazar...shall t' of her blood
6 And the priest shall t' cedar wood,
17 t' of the ashes of the burnt heifer
18 And a clean person shall t' hyssop,
20: 8 T' the rod, and gather thou the
25 T' Aaron and Eleazar his son, and
21: 7 he t' away the serpents from us.
23:12 Must I not t' heed to speak that
25: 4 T' all the heads of the people, and
26: 2 T' the sum of all the congregation
4 T' the sum of the people, from twenty
27:18 T' thee Joshua the son of Nun,
31:26 T' the sum of the prey that was
29 T' it of their half, and give it unto
30 thou shalt t' one portion of fifty, of
34:18 ye shall t' one prince of every tribe,
35:31 t' no satisfaction for the life of a
32 t' no satisfaction for him that is fled
De 1: 7 Turn you, and t' your journey, and go
13 T' you wise men, and
40 t' your journey into the wilderness
2: 4 t' ye good heed unto yourselves
24 Rise ye up, t' your journey, and pass
4: 9 Only t' heed to thyself, and keep
15 T' ye...good heed unto yourselves;
23 T' heed unto yourselves, lest ye
34 assayed to go and t' him a nation
5:11 shalt not t' the name of the Lord
7: 3 his daughter...t' unto thy son.
15 t' away from thee all sickness,
25 silver or gold...nor t' it unto thee.
10:11 Arise, t' thy journey before the people,
11:16 T' heed to yourselves, that your

De 12:13 T' heed to thyself that thou offer
19 T' heed to thyself that thou forsake
26 and thy vows, thou shalt t', and go
30 T' heed to thyself that thou be
15:17 Then thou shalt t' an aul, and
16:19 respect persons, neither t' a gift:
20: 7 the battle, and another man t' her.
14 thereof, shalt thou t' unto thyself;
19 in making war against it to t' it,
21: 3 elders of that city...t' an heifer,
22: 6 shalt not t' the dam with the young:
7 dam go, and t' the young to thee;
13 If any man t' a wife, and go in unto
15 t' and bring forth the tokens of the
18 elders of that city shall t' that man
30 man shall not t' his father's wife,
24: 4 may not t' her again to be his wife,
6 shall t' the nether or the upper
8 T' heed in the plague of leprosy,
17 t' a widow's raiment to pledge:
25: 5 unto her, and t' her to him to wife,
7 man like not to t' his brother's wife,
8 to it, and say, I like not to t' her:
26: 2 shalt t' of the first of all the fruit of
4 t' the basket out of thine hand,
27: 9 T' heed, and hearken, O Israel;
31:26 T' this book of the law, and put
32:41 mine hand t' hold on judgment;
Jos 3: 6 T' up the ark of the covenant, and
12 t' you twelve men out of the tribes
4: 2 T' you twelve men...of the people,
3 T' you hence out of the midst of
5 t' ye up every man of you a stone
6: 6 T' up the ark of the covenant, and
18 when ye t' of the accursed thing,
7:13 t' away the accursed thing from
14 the family which the Lord shall t'
14 household which the Lord shall t'
8: 1 t' all the people of war with thee,
2 shall ye t' for a prey unto yourselves:
29 t' his carcase down from a tree,
9:11 T' victuals...for the journey,
10:42 their land...Joshua t' at one time,
11:12 all the kings of them, did Joshua t',
20: 4 shall t' him into the city unto them,
22: 5 t'...heed to do the commandment
19 and t' possession among us: but
23:11 T' good heed therefore unto your
J'g 4: 6 t' with thee ten thousand men of
5:30 the necks of them that t' the spoil?
6:20 T' the flesh and the unleavened
25 T' thy father's young bullock, even
26 t' the second bullock, and offer a
7:24 t' before them the waters unto
14: 3 to t' a wife of the uncircumcised
8 after a time he returned to t' her,
15 ye called us to t' that we have?
15: 2 sister fairer than she? t' her,
19:30 consider of it, t' advice, and speak
20:10 we will t' ten men of an hundred
Ru 2:10 thou shouldest t' knowledge of me,
19 be he that did t' knowledge of thee.
1Sa 2:16 and then t' as much as thy soul
16 now: and if not, I will t' it by force.
6: 7 t' two milch kine, on which there
8 t' the ark of the Lord, and lay it
8:11 He will t' your sons, and appoint
13 And he will t' your daughters to be
14 And he will t' your fields, and your
15 And he will t' the tenth of your seed,
16 And he will t' your menservants,
17 He will t' the tenth of your sheep:
9: 3 T' now one of the servants with
5 for the asses, and t' thought for us.
16: 2 T' an heifer with thee, and say, I
17:17 T' now for thy brethren an ephah
18 brethren fare, and t' their pledge.
46 thee, and t' thine head from thee;
19: 2 t' heed to thyself until...morning,
14 Saul sent messengers to t' David,
20 Saul sent messengers to t' David:
20:21 are on this side of thee, t' them;
21: 9 if thou wilt t' that, t' it: for there
23:23 t' knowledge of all the lurking places
26 his men round about to t' them.
24:11 yet thou huntest my soul to t' it.
25:11 Shall I then t' my bread, and my
39 Abigail, to t' her to him to wife.
40 unto thee, to t' thee to him to wife.
26:11 t' thou now the spear that is at his
2Sa 2:21 young men, and t' thee his armour.
4:11 and t' you away from the earth?
5: 6 t' away the blind and the lame,
12: 4 he spared to t' of his own flock
11 I will t' thy wives before thine eyes,
28 encamp against the city, and t' it:
28 lest I t' the city, and it be called
13:33 the king t' the thing to his heart,
15:20 return thou, and t' back thy brethren:
16: 9 me go over,...and t' off his head.
19:19 the king should t' it to his heart.
30 Yea, let him t' all, forasmuch as
20: 6 t' thou thy lord's servants, and
24:10 t' away the iniquity of thy servant;
22 t' and offer up what seemeth good
1Ki 1:33 T' with you the servants of your
2: 4 thy children t' heed to their way,
31 mayest t' away the innocent blood,
8:25 thy children t' heed to their way,
11:31 to Jeroboam, T' thee ten pieces:
34 will not t' the whole kingdom out
35 I will t' the kingdom out of his
37 I will t' thee, and thou shalt reign
14: 3 And t' with thee ten loaves, and
10 t' away the remnant of the house
16: 3 t' away the posterity of Baasha,

1Ki 18:40 them, T' the prophets of Baal;
19: 4 now, O Lord, t' away my life; for
10, 14 they seek my life, to t' it away.
20: 6 put it in their hand, and t' it away.
18 come out for peace, t' them alive:
18 be come out for war, t' them alive.
24 T' the kings away, every man out
21:15 t' possession of the vineyard of
16 the Jezreelite, to t' possession of it.
21 and will t' away thy posterity,
22: 3 t' it not out of the hand of the king
26 T' Micaiah, and carry him back
2Ki 2: 1 when the Lord would t' up Elijah
3, 5 Lord will t' away thy master
4: 1 creditor is come to t' unto him my
29 loins, and t' my staff in thine hand,
36 unto him, he said, T' up thy son.
5:15 thee, t' a blessing of thy servant.
16 And he urged him to t' it; but he
20 after him, and t' somewhat of him.
23 said, Be content, t' two talents.
6: 2 and t' thence every man a beam,
7 Therefore said he, T' it up to thee.
32 hath sent to t' away mine head?
7:13 Let some t',...five of the horses
8: 8 T' a present in thine hand, and go,
9: 1 and t' this box of oil in thine hand,
3 t' the box of oil, and pour it on his
17 T' an horseman, and send to meet
25 T' up, and cast him in the portion
26 t' and cast him into the plat of
10: 6 t' ye the heads of the men your
14 And he said, T' them alive.
12: 5 Let the priests t' it to them,
13:15 said unto him, T' bow and arrows.
18 And he said, T' the arrows. And he
18:32 Until I come and t' you...to a land
20: 7 And Isaiah said, T' a lump of figs.
18 of thy sons...shall they t' away;
1Ch 7:21 came down to t' away their cattle.
17:13 not t' my mercy away from him,
21:23 said unto David, T' it to thee, and
24 I will not t' that which is thine for
28:10 T' heed now; for the Lord hath
2Ch 6:16 t' heed to their way to walk in my
18:25 T' ye Micaiah, and carry him back
19: 6 to the judges, T' heed what ye do:
7 be upon you; t' heed and do it:
20:25 his people came to t' away the spoil
32:18 them; that they might t' the city.
33: 8 they will t' heed to do all that I
Ezr 4:22 T' heed now that ye fail not to do
5:14 Cyrus the king t' out of the temple
15 T' these vessels, go, carry them
9:12 t' their daughters unto your sons.
Ne 5: 2 therefore we t' up corn for them,
6: 7 and let us t' counsel together.
10:30 nor t' their daughters for our sons:
38 Levites, when the Levites t' tithes:
13:25 t' their daughters unto your sons,
Es 4: 4 to t' away his sackcloth from him:
6:10 and t' the apparel and the horse,
8:11 and to t' the spoil of them for a prey,
Job 7:21 and t' away mine iniquity?
9:18 He will not suffer me to t' my breath,
34 Let him t' his rod away from me,
10:20 alone, that I may t' comfort a little,
11:18 and thou shalt t' thy rest in safety.
13:14 do I t' my flesh in my teeth, and
18: 9 The gin shall t' him by the heel,
21:12 They t' the timbrel and harp, and
23:10 But he knoweth the way that I t':
24: 2 they violently t' away flocks, and
3 they t' the widow's ox for a pledge.
9 breast, and t' a pledge of the poor.
10 they t' away the sheaf from the
27:20 Terrors t' hold on him as waters,
30:17 season: and my sinews t' no rest.
31:36 I would t' it upon my shoulder,
32:22 my maker would soon t' me away.
36:17 judgment and justice t' hold on
18 he t' thee away with his stroke:
21 T' heed, regard not iniquity: for
38:13 it might t' hold of the ends of the
20 thou shouldest t' it to the bound
41: 4 thou t' him for a servant for ever?
42: 8 t' unto you now seven bullocks and
Ps 2: 2 and the rulers t' counsel together,
7: 5 persecute my soul, and t' it;
13: 2 long shall I t' counsel in my soul,
16: 4 nor t' up their names into my lips.
27:10 me, then the Lord will t' me up.
31:13 they devised to t' away my life.
35: 2 T' hold of shield and buckler, and
39: 1 I will t' heed to my ways, that I
50: 9 will t' no bullock out of thy house,
16 or thou shouldest t' my covenant
51:11 and t' not thy holy spirit from me.
52: 5 he shall t' thee away, and pluck
58: 9 t' them away as with a whirlwind,
69:20 I looked for some to t' pity, but there
24 wrathful anger t' hold of them.
71:10 that lay wait for my soul t' counsel
11 persecute and t' him; for there is
80: 9 and didst cause it to t' deep root,
81: 2 T' a psalm, and bring hither the
83:12 t'...the houses of God in possession.
89:33 will I not utterly t' from him,
102:14 thy servants t' pleasure in her stones,
24 t' me not away in the midst of my
109: 8 few; and let another t' his office.
116:13 I will t' the cup of salvation, and
119:43 t' not the word of truth utterly out
139: 9 If I t' the wings of the morning,
20 thine enemies t' thy name in vain.
Pr 2:19 t' they hold of the paths of life.

Pr 4:13 T' fast hold of instruction; let her
5: 5 to death; her steps t' hold on hell.
22 own iniquities shall t' the wicked
6:25 let her t' thee with her eyelids.
27 Can a man t' fire in his bosom, and
7:18 let us t' our fill of love until the
20:16 T' his garment that is surety for
16 t' a pledge of him for a strange
22:27 why should he t' away thy bed
25: 4 T' away the dross from the silver,
5 T' away the wicked from before
27:13 T' his garment that is surety for
13 t' a pledge of him for a strange
30: 9 and t' the name of my God in vain.
Ec 5:15 and shall t' nothing of his labour,
19 t' his portion, and to rejoice in his
7:18 that thou shouldest t' hold of this;
21 t' no heed unto all words that are
Ca 2:15 T' us the foxes, the little foxes,
7: 8 I will t' hold of the boughs thereof:
Isa 1:25 thy dross, and t' away all thy tin:
3: 1 t' away from Jerusalem and from
6 a man shall t' hold of his brother
18 Lord will t' away the bravery of
4: 1 seven women shall t' hold of one
1 thy name, to t' away our reproach.
5: 5 I will t' away the hedge thereof,
23 and t' away the righteousness of the
7: 4 unto him, T' heed, and be quiet;
8: 1 T' thee a great roll, and write in
10 T' counsel together, and it shall
10: 2 to t' away the right from the poor
6 give him a charge, to t' the spoil,
6 to t' the prey, and to tread them
13: 8 and sorrows shall t' hold of them;
14: 2 And the people shall t' them, and
2 they shall t' them captives, whose
4 shalt t' up this proverb against
16: 3 T' counsel, execute judgment;
18: 4 I will t' my rest, and I will consider
5 t' away and cut down the branches.
23:16 T' an harp, go about the city,
25: 8 the rebuke of his people...t' away
27: 5 Or let him t' hold of my strength,
6 them that come of Jacob to t' root:
9 is all the fruit to t' away his sin;
28:19 that it goeth forth it shall t' you:
30: 1 that t' counsel, but not of me;
14 a sherd to t' fire from the hearth,
14 or to t' water withal out of the pit.
33:23 spoil divided; the lame t' the prey.
36:17 Until I come and t' you away to a
37:31 of Judah shall...t' root downward,
38:21 Let them t' a lump of figs, and lay
39: 7 shalt beget, shall they t' away;
40:24 their stock shall not t' root in the
24 the whirlwind shall t' them away
44:15 for he will t' thereof, and warm
45:21 yea, let them t' counsel together:
47: 2 T' the millstones, and grind meal:
3 I will t' vengeance, and I will not
56: 4 me, and t' hold of my covenant;
57:13 all away; vanity shall t' them:
14 t' up the stumbling block out of
58: 2 they t' delight in approaching to God.
9 t' away from the midst of thee the
64: 7 up himself to t' hold of thee: for
66:21 I will also t' of them for priests
Jer 2:22 with nitre, and t' thee much sope,
3:14 and I will t' you one of a city,
4: 4 and t' away the foreskins of your
5:10 t' away her battlements; for they
7:29 and t' up a lamentation on high
9: 4 T' ye heed every one of his
10 mountains will I t' up a weeping
18 and t' up a wailing for us, that our
13: 4 T' the girdle that thou hast got,
6 t' the girdle from thence, which
21 shall not sorrows t' thee, as a
15:15 O Lord,...t' me not away in thy
19 if thou t' forth the precious from
16: 2 Thou shalt not t' thee a wife,
17:21 T' heed to yourselves, and bear
18:22 they have digged a pit to t' me,
19: 1 and t' of the ancients of the people,
20: 5 shall spoil them, and t' them,
10 and we shall t' our revenge on him.
25: 9 and t' all the families of the north,
10 will t' from them the voice of mirth,
15 T' the wine cup of this fury at my
28 if they refuse to t' the cup at thine
29: 6 T' ye wives, and beget sons and
6 and t' wives for your sons, and give
32: 3 king of Babylon, and he shall t' it;
14 T' these evidences, this evidence
24 are come unto the city to t' it;
25 field for money, and t' witnesses;
28 king of Babylon, and he shall t' it:
44 t' witnesses...land of Benjamin,
33:26 not t' any of his seed to be rulers
34:22 shall fight against it, and t' it,
36: 2 T' thee a roll of a book, and write
14 T' in thine hand the roll wherein
26 to t' Baruch the scribe and
28 T' thee again another roll, and
37: 8 fight against this city, and t' it,
38: 3 Babylon's army, which shall t' it.
10 T' from hence thirty men with
10 t' up Jeremiah the prophet out of
39:12 T' him, and look well to him, and
43: 9 T' great stones in thine hand, and
10 will send and t' Nebuchadrezzar
44:12 I will t' the remnant of Judah,
46:11 Go up into Gilead, and t' balm,
49:29 and their flocks shall they t' away:
29 they shall t' to themselves their

Jer 50:15 t' vengeance upon her; as she hath
51: 8 t' balm for her pain, if so be she
26 not t' of thee a stone for a corner,
36 cause, and t' vengeance for thee;
La 2:13 thing shall I t' to witness for thee?
Eze 4: 1 t' thee a tile, and lay it before
3 t' thou unto thee an iron pan, and
9 T' thou also unto thee wheat, and
5: 1 son of man, t' thee a sharp knife,
1 t' thee a barber's rasor, and cause
1 then t' thee balances to weigh, and
2 and thou shalt t' a third part, and
3 shalt...t' thereof a few in number,
4 Then t' of them again, and cast
10: 6 T' fire from between the wheels,
11:18 t' away all the detestable things
19 t' the stony heart out of their flesh,
14: 5 That I may t' the house of Israel
15: 3 will men t' a pin of it to hang any
16:16 And of thy garments thou didst t',
39 and shall t' thy fair jewels, and
17:22 I will also t' of the highest branch
19: 1 t' thou up a lamentation for the
21:26 the diadem, and t' off the crown:
22:16 thou shalt t' thine inheritance
23:25 t' away thy nose and thine ears;
25 t' thy sons and thy daughters;
26 and t' away thy fair jewels.
29 and shall t' away all thy labour,
24: 5 T' the choice of the flock, and
8 fury to come up to t' vengeance;
16 I t' away from thee the desire of
25 when I t' from them their strength,
26:17 shall t' up a lamentation for thee,
27: 2 t' up a lamentation for Tyrus;
32 shall t' up a lamentation for thee,
28:12 t' up a lamentation upon the king
29:19 and he shall t' her multitude,
19 t' [7997] her spoil, and t' her prey;
30: 4 they shall t' away her multitude,
32: 2 t' up a lamentation for Pharaoh
33: 2 people...t' a man of their coasts,
4 the sword come, and t' him away,
6 any person from among them,
6 shall t' away from among them,
36:24 t' you from among the heathen,
26 I will t' away the stony heart out
37:16 t' thee one stick, and write upon
16 then t' another stick, and write
19 I will t' the stick of Joseph, which
21 I will t' the children of Israel from
38:12 To t' [7997] a spoil, and to t' a prey;
13 thee, Art thou come to t' a spoil?
13 gathered thy company to t' a prey?
13 gold, to t' away cattle and goods,
13 and goods, to t' a great spoil?
39:10 shall t' no wood out of the field,
43:20 thou shalt t' of the blood thereof,
21 shalt t' the bullock also of the sin
44:22 they t' for their wives a widow,
22 t' maidens of the seed of the house
45: 9 t' away your exactions from my
18 thou shalt t' a young bullock
19 t' of the blood of the sin offering,
46:18 prince shall not t' of the people's
Da 6:23 should t' Daniel up out of the den.
7:18 most High shall t' the kingdom,
26 they shall t' away his dominion,
11:15 and t' the most fenced cities:
18 unto the isles, and shall t' many:
31 shall t' away the daily sacrifice,
Ho 1: 2 to Hosea, Go, t' unto thee a wife of
6 but I will utterly t' them away.
2: 9 and t' away my corn in the time
17 will t' away the names of Baalim
4:10 have left off to t' heed to the Lord.
11 and new wine t' away the heart.
5:14 I will t' away, and none shall
11: 4 as they that t' off the yoke on their
14: 2 T' with you words, and turn to the
2 T' away all iniquity, and receive
Am 3: 5 one t' up a snare from the earth,
4: 2 he will t' you away with hooks,
5: 1 this word which I t' up against you,
11 ye t' from him burdens of wheat:
12 they afflict the just, they t' a bribe,
23 T' thou away from me the noise of
6:10 And a man's uncle shall t' him up,
9: 2 thence shall mine hand t' them;
3 I will search and t' them out thence;
Jon 1:12 T' me up, and cast me forth into
4: 3 O Lord, t', I beseech thee, my life
Mic 2: 2 fields, and t' them by violence;
2 and houses, and t' them away: so
4 one t' up a parable against you,
6 them, that they shall not t' shame.
6:14 and thou shalt t' hold, but shalt not
Na 1: 2 will t' vengeance on his adversaries,
2: 9 T' ye the spoil of silver,
9 t' the spoil of gold: for there is none
Hab 1:10 for they shall heap dust, and t' it.
15 They t' up all of them with the
2: 6 not all these t' up a parable against
Zep 3:11 I will t' away out of the midst of
Hag 1: 8 I will t' pleasure in it, and I will be
2:23 will I t' thee, O Zerubbabel, my
Zec 1: 6 they not t' hold of your fathers?
3: 4 T' away the filthy garments from
6:10 T' of them of the captivity, even
11 Then t' silver and gold, and make
8:23 that ten men shall t' hold out of all
23 t' hold of the skirt of him that is a
9: 7 I will t' away his blood out of his
11:15 T' unto thee yet the instruments
14:21 sacrifice shall come and t' of them,
Mal 2: 3 and one shall t' you away with it.
15 Therefore t' heed to your spirit,
Mal 2:16 therefore t' heed to your spirit,
M't 1:20 fear not to t' unto thee Mary thy
2:13, 20 t' the young child and his mother,
5:40 at the law, and t' away thy coat,
6: 1 T' heed that ye do not your alms
25 T' no thought for your life, what
28 And why t' ye thought for raiment?
31 t' no thought, saying, What shall
34 T' therefore no thought for the
34 shall t' thought for the things of itself.
9: 6 t' up thy bed, and go unto thine
10:19 t' no thought how or what ye shall
11:12 and the violent t' it by force.
29 T' my yoke upon you, and learn of
15:26 not meet to t' the children's bread,
16: 5 side, they had forgotten to t' bread.
6 T' heed and beware of the leaven
24 and t' up his cross, and follow me.
17:25 do the kings of the earth t' custom
27 t' up the fish that first cometh up;
27 that t', and give unto them for me
18:10 T' heed that ye despise not one of
16 then t' with thee one or two more,
23 would t' account of his servants.
20:14 T' that thine is, and go thy way: I
22:13 him hand and foot, and t' him away,
24: 4 T' heed that no man deceive you.
17 to t' any thing out of his house:
18 the field return back to t' his clothes.
25:28 T' therefore the talent from him,
26: 4 they might t' Jesus by subtilty,
26 and said, T', eat; this is my body.
45 Sleep on now, and t' your rest:
52 they that t' the sword shall perish
55 swords and staves for to t' me?
M'r 2: 9 or to say, Arise, and t' up thy bed,
11 unto thee, Arise, and t' up thy bed,
4:24 unto them, T' heed what ye hear:
6: 8 should t' nothing for their journey,
7:27 not meet to t' the children's bread,
8:14 disciples had forgotten to t' bread,
15 T' heed, beware of the leaven of
34 deny himself, and t' up his cross,
10:21 come, t' up the cross, and follow me.
12:19 that his brother should t' his wife,
13: 5 T' heed lest any man deceive you:
9 t' heed to yourselves: for they shall
11 t' no thought beforehand what ye shall
15 to t' any thing out of his house:
16 back again for to t' up his garment.
23 But t' ye heed: behold, I have foretold
33 T' ye heed, watch and pray: for ye
14: 1 how they might t' him by craft,
22 and said, T', eat: this is my body.
36 to thee; t' away this cup from me:
41 Sleep on now, and t' your rest: it is
44 t' him, and lead him away safely.
48 swords and with staves to t' me?
15:24 them, what every man should t'.
36 Elias will come to t' him down.
16:18 They shall t' up serpents; and if
Lu 1:25 to t' away my reproach among men.
5:24 t' up thy couch, and go into thine
6: 4 and did t' and eat the shewbread,
29 thy cloke forbid not to t' thy coat also.
8:18 T' heed therefore how ye hear: for
9: 3 them, T' nothing for your journey,
23 himself, and t' up his cross daily,
10:35 and said unto him, T' care of him;
11:35 T' heed therefore that the light
12:11 t' ye no thought how or what thing
15 T' heed, and beware of covetousness:
19 t' thine ease, eat, drink, and be merry.
22 T' no thought for your life, what
26 why t' ye thought for the rest?
14: 9 with shame to t' the lowest room.
16: 6 T' thy bill, and sit down quickly,
7 him, T' thy bill, and write fourscore.
17: 3 T' heed to yourselves: If thy
31 let him not come down to t' it away:
19:24 T' from him the pound, and give it
20:20 that they might t' hold of his words,
26 they could not t' hold of his words
28 that his brother should t' his wife,
21: 8 T' heed that ye be not deceived:
34 t' heed to yourselves, lest at any
22:17 said, T' this, and divide it among
36 he that hath a purse, let him t' it,
Joh 2:16 sold doves, T' these things hence;
5: 8 him, Rise, t' up thy bed, and walk.
11 unto me, T' up thy bed, and walk.
12 unto thee, T' up thy bed, and walk?
6: 7 every one of them may t' a little.
15 would come and t' him by force,
7:30 Then they sought to t' him: but no
32 chief priests sent officers to t' him.
10:17 my life, that I might t' it again.
18 and I have power to t' it again.
39 they sought again to t' him: but he
11:39 Jesus said, T' ye away the stone.
48 t' away both our place and nation.
57 shew it, that they might t' him.
16:15 he shall t' of mine, and shall shew
17:15 shouldest t' them out of the world,
18:31 said Pilate unto them, T' ye him,
19: 6 them, T' ye him, and crucify him:
38 he might t' away the body of Jesus:
20:15 hast laid him, and I will t' him away.
Ac 1:20 and his bishoprick let another t'.
25 he may t' part of this ministry and
5:35 t' heed to yourselves what ye
12: 3 he proceeded further to t' Peter
15:14 to t' out of them a people for his
37 determined to t' with them John,
38 not good to t' him with them, who
20:13 Assos, there intending to t' in Paul:
Ac 20:26 I t' you to record this day, that
28 T' heed therefore unto yourselves, and
21:24 Them t', and purify thyself with
22:26 T' heed what thou doest: for this
23:10 t' him by force from among them,
24: 8 t' knowledge of all these things,
27:33 Paul besought them all to t' meat,
34 I pray you to t' some meat: for
Ro 11:21 t' heed lest he also spare not thee.
27 when I shall t' away their sins.
15:24 I t' my journey into Spain, I will
1Co 3:10 let every man t' heed how he buildeth
6: 7 Why do ye not rather t' wrong? Why
15 then t' the members of Christ, and
8: 9 But t' heed lest by any means this
9: 9 corn. Doth God t' care for oxen?
10:12 he standeth t' heed lest he fall.
11:24 T', eat: this is my body, which is
2Co 8: 4 t' upon us the fellowship of the
11:20 if a man t' of you, if a man exalt
12:10 I t' pleasure in infirmities, in
Ga 5:15 t' heed that ye be not consumed one
Eph 6:13 t' unto you the whole armour of
17 t' the helmet of salvation, and the
Col 4:17 T' heed to the ministry which thou
1Ti 3: 5 shall he t' care of the church of God?)
4:16 T' heed unto thyself, and unto the
2Ti 4:11 T' Mark, and bring him with thee:
Heb 3:12 T' heed, brethren, lest there be in
7: 5 t' tithes of the people according to the
10: 4 and of goats should t' away sins.
11 which can never t' away sins:
Jas 5:10 T', my brethren, the prophets, who
1Pe 2:20 your faults, ye shall t' it patiently?
20 ye t' it patiently, this is acceptable
2Pe 1:19 whereunto ye do well that ye t' heed, as
1Jo 3: 5 manifested to t' away our sins;
Re 3:11 hast, that no man t' thy crown.
5: 9 Thou art worthy to t' the book, and
6: 4 thereon to t' peace from the earth,
10: 8 Go and t' the little book which is
9 said unto me, T' it, and eat it up;
22:17 let him t' the water of life freely.
19 if any man shall t' away from the
19 God shall t' away his part out of the

taken See also OVERTAKEN; UNTAKEN.
Ge 2:22 rib,...the Lord God had t' from man,
23 because she was t' out of Man.
3:19 ground; for out of it wast thou t':
23 the ground from whence he was t'.
4:15 vengeance shall be t' on him sevenfold.
12:15 the woman was t' into Pharaoh's
19 I might have t' her to me to wife:
14:14 that his brother was t' captive,
18:27, 31 I have t' upon me to speak unto
20: 3 for the woman which thou hast t';
21:25 servants had violently t' away.
27:33 where is he that hath t' venison,
35 and hath t' away thy blessing.
36 now he hath t' away my blessing.
30:15 that thou hast t' my husband?
23 God hath t' away my reproach:
31: 1 Jacob hath t' away all that was
9 God hath t' away the cattle of your
16 which God hath t' from our father,
26 as captives t' with the sword?
34 Rachel had t' the images, and put
Ex 14:11 hast thou t' us away to die in the
25:15 ark: they shall not be t' from it.
40:36 the cloud was t' up from over the
37 if the cloud were not t' up, then
37 not till the day that it was t' up.
Le 4:10 As it was t' off from the bullock
31 fat is t' away from off the sacrifice
35 as the fat of the lamb is t' away from
6: 2 or in a thing t' away by violence,
7:34 and the heave shoulder have I t'
14:43 that he hath t' away the stones,
24: 8 being t' from the children of Israel by
Nu 3:12 I have t' the Levites from among
5:13 neither she be t' with the manner;
8:16 of Israel, have I t' them unto me.
18 And I have t' the Levites for all the
9:17 when the cloud was t' up from the
21 the cloud was t' up in the morning,
21 by night that the cloud was t' up,
22 when it was t' up, they journeyed.
10:11 the cloud was t' up from off the
17 the tabernacle was t' down; and
16:15 I have not t' one ass from them,
18: 6 I have t' your brethren the Levites
21:26 and t' all his land out of his hand,
31:26 the sum of the prey that was t',
49 servants have t' the sum of...men
53 (For the men of war had t' spoil, every
36: 3 be t' from the inheritance of our
3 t' from the lot of our inheritance.
4 shall their inheritance be t' away
De 4:20 the Lord hath t' you, and brought
20: 7 a wife, and hath not t' her?
21:10 and thou hast t' them captive,
24: 1 When a man hath t' a wife, and
5 When a man hath t' a new wife, he
5 cheer up his wife which he hath t'.
26:14 neither have I t' away ought
28:31 thine ass shall be violently t' away
Jos 7:11 have even t' of the accursed thing,
15 that is t' with the accursed thing
16 and the tribe of Judah was t':
17 man by man; and Zabdi was t':
18 Zerah, of the tribe of Judah, was t'.
8: 8 shall be, when ye have t' the city
21 that the ambush had t' the city,
10: 1 had heard how Joshua had t' Ai,
J'g 1: 8 against Jerusalem, and had t' it,
11:36 Lord hath t' vengeance for thee

J'g 14: 9 had t' the honey out of the carcase
15: 6 because he had t' his wife, and
17: 2 shekels of silver...t' from thee,
18: 24 Ye have t' away my gods which I
1Sa 4: 11 the ark of God was t'; and the two
17 are dead, and the ark of God is t'.
19 tidings that the ark of God was t',
21 because the ark of God was t', and
22 from Israel: for the ark of God is t'.
7: 14 cities which the Philistines had t'
10: 20 near, the tribe of Benjamin was t'.
21 the family of Matri was t', and Saul
21 and Saul the son of Kish was t':
12: 3 his anointed: whose ox have I t'?
3 or whose ass have I t'? or whom
4 neither hast thou t' ought of any
14: 41 And Saul and Jonathan were t':
42 my son. And Jonathan was t'.
21: 6 that was t' from before the Lord,
6 in the day when it was t' away.
30: 2 And had t' the women captives,
3 their daughters, were t' captives.
5 David's two wives were t' captives,
16 all the great spoil that they had t'
19 any thing that they had t' to them:
2Sa 12: 9 and hast t' his wife to be thy wife,
10 hast t' the wife of Uriah the Hittite
27 and have t' the city of waters.
16: 8 behold, thou art t' in thy mischief,
18: 9 t' up between the heaven and the
18 had t' and reared up...a pillar,
23: 6 they cannot be t' with hands:
1Ki 7: 8 daughter, whom he had t' to wife,
9: 9 and have t' hold upon other gods,
16 Egypt had gone up, and t' Gezer,
16: 18 when Zimri saw that the city was t',
21: 19 thou killed, and also t' possession?
22: 43 the high places were not t' away;
2Ki 2: 9 before I be t' away from thee.
10 thou see me when I am t' from thee,
16 Spirit of the Lord hath t' him up,
4: 20 when he had t' him, and brought
6: 22 thou hast t' captive with thy sword
12: 3 But...high places were not t' away:
13: 25 the cities, which he had t' out of
14: 4 the high places were not t' away:
18: 10 king of Israel, Samaria was t'.
22 altars Hezekiah hath t' away,
24: 7 king of Babylon had t' from the
1Ch 24: 6 one principal household being t'
6 for Eleazer, and one t' for Ithamar.
2Ch 15: 8 cities which he had t' from mount
17 the high places were not t' away
17: 2 which Asa his father had t'.
19: 3 hast t' away the groves out of the
20: 33 the high places were not t' away:
28: 11 have t' captive of your brethren:
18 had t' Beth-shemesh, and Ajalon,
30: 2 For the king had t' counsel, and
32: 12 Hezekiah t' away his high places
Ezr 9: 2 t' of their daughters...themselves,
10: 2 t' strange wives of the people of
10 and have t' strange wives,
14 them which have t' strange wives
17 the men that had t' strange wives
18 found that had t' strange wives:
44 All these had t' strange wives:
Ne 5: 15 had t' of them bread and wine,
6: 18 son Johanan had t' the daughter of
Es 2: 15 who had t' her for his daughter,
16 Esther was t' unto king Ahasuerus
8: 2 ring, which he had t' from Haman.
Job 1: 21 gave, and the Lord hath t' away;
16: 12 he hath also t' me by my neck, and
19: 9 and t' the crown from my head.
20: 19 hath violently t' away an house
22: 6 hast t' a pledge from thy brother
24: 24 are t' out of the way as all other,
27: 2 who hath t' away my judgment;
28: 2 Iron is t' out of the earth, and
30: 16 of affliction have t' hold upon me.
34: 5 God hath t' away my judgment.
20 and the mighty shall be t' away
Ps 9: 15 which they hid is their own foot t'.
10: 2 let them be t' in the devices that
40: 12 iniquities have t' hold upon me,
59: 12 let them even be t' in their pride:
83: 3 They have t' crafty counsel against
85: 3 Thou hast t' away all thy wrath:
119: 53 Horror hath t' hold upon me
111 testimonies have I t' as an heritage
143 and anguish have t' hold on me:
Pr 3: 26 shall keep thy foot from being t'.
4: 16 and their sleep is t' away, unless
6: 2 t' with the words of thy mouth.
7: 20 hath t' a bag of money with him,
11: 6 transgressors shall be t' in their
Ec 2: 18 labour which I had t' under the
3: 14 put to it, nor any thing t' from it:
7: 26 but the sinner shall be t' by her.
9: 12 the fishes that are t' in an evil net,
Isa 6: 6 he had t' with the tongs from off
7 thine iniquity is t' away, and thy
7: 5 have t' evil counsel against thee,
8: 4 spoil of Samaria shall be t' away
15 broken, and be snared, and be t'.
10: 27 that his burden shall be t' away
29 have t' up their lodging at Geba;
16: 10 And gladness is t' away, and joy out
17: 1 Damascus is t' away from being a
21: 3 pangs have t' hold upon me, as the
23: 8 hath t' this counsel against Tyre,
24: 18 of the pit shall be t' in the snare:
28: 13 and be broken, and snared, and t'.
33: 20 tabernacle...shall not be t' down;
36: 7 altars Hezekiah hath t' away,

Isa 41: 9 have t' from the ends of the earth,
49: 24 the prey be t' from the mighty, or
25 captives of the mighty shall be t'
51: 22 have t' out of thine hand the cup of
52: 5 my people is t' away for nought?
53: 8 He was t' from prison and from
57: 1 and merciful men are t' away, none
1 righteous is t' away from the evil to
64: 6 like the wind, have t' us away.
Jer 6: 11 husband with the wife shall be t',
24 anguish hath t' hold of us, and
8: 9 ashamed,...are dismayed and t':
21 astonishment hath t' hold on me.
12: 2 planted them, yea, they have t' root:
16: 5 t' away my peace from this people,
29: 22 And of them shall be t' up a curse
34: 3 shalt surely be t', and delivered
38: 23 shalt be t' by...the king of Babylon:
28 until the day...Jerusalem was t':
28 was there when Jerusalem was t'.
39: 5 and when they had t' him, they
40: 1 when he had t' him being bound in
10 dwell in your cities that ye have t'.
48: 1 Kiriathaim is confounded and t':
7 thy treasures, thou shalt also be t':
33 joy...is t' from the plentiful field,
41 Kerioth is t', and the strong holds
44 out of the pit shall be t' in the snare:
46 for thy sons are t' captives, and thy
49: 20 Lord, that he hath t' against Edom;
24 anguish and sorrows have t' her,
30 king of Babylon hath t' counsel
50: 2 Babylon is t', Bel is confounded,
9 from thence she shall be t': their
24 thou art also t', O Babylon, and thou
45 that he hath t' against Babylon;
51: 31 king of Babylon that his city is t'
41 How is Sheshach t'! and how is the
56 Babylon, and her mighty men are t',
La 2: 6 hath violently t' away his tabernacle,
4: 20 of the Lord, was t' in their pits,
Eze 12: 13 and he shall be t' in my snare:
15: 3 wood be t' thereof to do any work?
16: 17 Thou hast also t' thy fair jewels of
20 t' thy sons and thy daughters,
37 with whom thou hast t' pleasure,
17: 12 and hath t' the king thereof, and
13 And hath t' of the king's seed, and
13 him, and hath t' an oath of him:
13 hath also t' the mighty of the land:
20 and he shall be t' in my snare, and
18: 8 neither hath t' any increase, that
13 upon usury, and hath t' increase:
17 hath t' off his hand from the poor,
19: 4 he was t' in their pit, and they
8 net over him: he was t' in their pit.
21: 23 the iniquity, that they may be t'.
24 ye shall be t' with the hand.
22: 12 have they t' gifts to shed blood;
12 thou hast t' usury and increase,
25 have t' the treasure and precious
25: 15 t' vengeance with a despiteful heart,
27: 5 they have t' cedars from Lebanon
33: 6 he is t' away in his iniquity; but
36: 3 ye are t' up in the lips of talkers,
Da 5: 2 had t' out of the temple which
3 the golden vessels that were t' out
6: 23 So Daniel was t' up out of the den,
7: 12 they had their dominion t' away:
8: 11 the daily sacrifice was t' away,
11: 12 he hath t' away the multitude,
12: 11 the daily sacrifice shall be t' away,
Ho 4: 3 the fishes...also shall be t' away.
Joe 3: 5 ye have t' my silver and my gold,
Am 3: 4 of his den, if he have t' nothing?
5 earth, and have t' nothing at all?
12 children of Israel be t' out that
4: 10 and have t' away your horses;
6: 13 Have we not t' to us horns by our
Mic 2: 9 have ye t' away my glory for ever.
4: 9 pangs have t' thee as a woman in
Zep 3: 15 Lord hath t' away thy judgments,
Zec 14: 2 the city shall be t', and the houses
M't 4: 24 that were t' with divers diseases
9: 15 bridegroom shall be t' from them,
13: 12 from him shall be t' away even that
16: 7 It is because we have t' no bread.
21: 43 kingdom of God shall be t' from you,
24: 40, 41 one shall be t', and the other
25: 29 be t' away even that which he hath.
27: 59 And when Joseph had t' the body,
28: 12 with the elders, and had t' counsel,
M'r 2: 20 bridegroom shall be t' away from
4: 25 shall be t' even that which he hath.
6: 41 when he had t' the five loaves and
9: 36 when he had t' him in his arms, he
Lu 1: 1 as many have t' in hand to set
4: 38 mother was t' with a great fever;
5: 5 all the night, and have t' nothing:
9 of the fishes which they had t':
18 bed a man which was t' with a palsy:
35 bridegroom shall be t' away from
36 the piece that was t' out of the new
8: 18 from him shall be t' even that which
37 for they were t' with great fear:
9: 17 there was t' up of fragments that
10: 42 which shall not be t' away from her.
11: 52 have t' away the key of knowledge:
17: 34, 35 the one shall be t', and the other
36 one shall be t', and the other left.
19: 8 t' any thing...by false accusation,
26 he hath shall be t' away from him.
Joh 7: 44 some of them would have t' him;
8: 3 unto him a woman t' in adultery;
4 this woman was t' in adultery, in
13: 12 had t' his garments, and was set

Joh 19: 31 and that they might be t' away.
20: 1 and seeth the stone t' away from the
2 They have t' away the Lord out of
13 they have t' away my Lord, and I
Ac 1: 2 Until the day in which he was t' up,
9 while they beheld, he was t' up;
11 Jesus, which is t' up from you into
22 same day that he was t' up from us.
2: 23 ye have t', and by wicked hands
8: 7 and many t' with palsies, and that
33 his judgment was t' away:
33 for his life is t' from the earth.
17: 9 when they had t' security of Jason,
20: 9 the third loft, and was t' up dead.
21: 6 And when we had t' our leave one of
23: 27 This man was t' of the Jews, and
27: 17 Which when they had t' up, they
20 should be saved was then t' away.
33 fasting, having t' nothing.
40 when they had t' up the anchors,
Ro 9: 6 the word of God hath t' none effect.
1Co 5: 2 done this deed might be t' away
10: 13 There hath no temptation t' you
2Co 3: 16 the Lord, the vail shall be t' away.
1Th 2: 17 being t' from you for a short time
2Th 2: 7 let, until he be t' out of the way.
1Ti 5: 9 not a widow be t' into the number
2Ti 2: 26 who are t' captive by him at his will.
Heb 5: 1 every high priest t' from among
2Pe 2: 12 beasts, made to be t' and destroyed,
Re 5: 8 when he had t' the book, the four
11: 17 thou hast t' to thee thy great power,
19: 20 the beast was t', and with him the

taker See also PARTAKER.
Isa 24: 2 as with the t' of usury, so with the

takest See also PARTAKEST.
Ex 4: 9 the water which thou t' out of the
30: 12 thou t' the sum of the children
J'g 4: 9 the journey that thou t' shall not be.
1Ch 22: 13 if thou t' heed to fulfil the statutes
Ps 104: 29 thou t' away their breath, they die,
Ec 9: 9 labour...thou t' under the sun.
Isa 58: 3 our soul, and thou t' no knowledge?
Lu 19: 21 t' up that thou layedst not down,

taketh See also OVERTAKETH.
Ex 20: 7 guiltless that t' his name in vain.
De 5: 11 guiltless that t' his name in vain.
10: 17 not persons, nor t' reward:
24: 6 for he t' a man's life to pledge.
25: 11 hand, and t' him by the secrets:
27: 25 that t' reward to slay an innocent
32: 11 t' them, beareth them on her wings:
Jos 7: 14 tribe which the Lord t' shall come
15: 16 smiteth Kirjath-sepher, and t' it,
J'g 1: 12 smiteth Kirjath-sepher, and t' it,
1Sa 17: 26 t' away the reproach from Israel?
1Ki 14: 10 as a man t' away dung, till it be
Job 5: 5 and t' it even out of the thorns,
13 He t' the wise in their...craftiness:
9: 12 he t' away, who can hinder him?
12: 20 t' away the understanding of the
24 He t' away the heart of the chief
21: 6 and trembling t' hold on my flesh.
27: 8 gained, when God t' away his soul?
40: 24 He t' it with his eyes: his nose
Ps 15: 3 nor t' up a reproach against his
5 nor t' reward against the innocent.
118: 7 Lord t' my part with them that help
137: 9 that t' and dasheth thy little ones
147: 10 t' not pleasure in the legs of a man.
11 Lord t' pleasure in them that fear
149: 4 the Lord t' pleasure in his people:
Pr 1: 19 which t' away the life of the owners
16: 32 his spirit than he that t' a city.
17: 23 man t' a gift out of the bosom
25: 20 As he that t' away a garment in
26: 17 like one that t' a dog by the ears.
30: 28 The spider t' hold with her hands,
Ec 1: 3 labour which he t' under the sun?
2: 23 yea, his heart t' not rest in the night.
5: 18 his labour that he t' under the sun
Isa 13: 14 and as a sheep that no man t' up:
40: 15 he t' up the isles as a very little
44: 14 and t' the cypress and the oak,
51: 18 there any that t' her by the hand
56: 6 polluting it,...t' hold of my covenant;
Eze 16: 32 which t' strangers instead of her
33: 4 of the trumpet, and t' not warning;
5 that t' warning shall deliver his soul.
Am 3: 12 t' out of the mouth of the lion
M't 4: 5 devil t' him up into the holy city,
8 devil t' him up into an exceeding
9: 16 in to fill it up t' from the garment,
10: 38 And he that t' not his cross, and
12: 45 t' with himself seven other spirits
17: 1 after six days Jesus t' Peter, James,
M'r 2: 21 that filled it up t' away from the old,
4: 15 and t' away the word that was sown
5: 40 he t' the father and the mother of
9: 2 six days Jesus t' with him Peter,
18 wheresoever he t' him, he teareth
14: 33 he t' with him Peter and James and
Lu 6: 29 him that t' away thy cloke forbid
30 of him that t' away thy goods ask
8: 12 t' away the word out of their hearts,
9: 39 lo, a spirit t' him, and he suddenly
11: 22 he t' from him all his armour
26 and t' to him seven other spirits
16: 3 t' away from me the stewardship:
Joh 1: 29 which t' away the sin of the world.
10: 18 No man t' it from me, but I lay it
15: 2 me that beareth not fruit he t' away:
16: 22 and your joy no man t' from you.
21: 13 and t' bread, and giveth them,
Ro 3: 5 unrighteous who t' vengeance?

1Co 3:19 t' the wise in their own craftiness.
11:21 t' before other his own supper:
Heb 5: 4 no man t' this honour unto himself,
10: 9 He t' away the first, that he may

taking
2Ch 19: 7 respect of persons, nor t' of gifts.
Job 5: 3 I have seen the foolish t' root: but
Ps 119: 9 by t' heed thereto according to thy
Jer 50:46 At the noise of the t' of Babylon the
Eze 25:12 the house of Judah by t' vengeance,
Ho 11: 3 also to go, t' them by their arms;
M't 6:27 Which of you by t' thought can
M'r 13:34 of man is as a man t' a far journey,
Lu 4: 5 t' him up into an high mountain,
12:25 And which of you with t' thought
19:22 man, t' up that I laid not down.
Joh 11:13 he had spoken of t' of rest in sleep.
Ro 7: 8 But sin, t' occasion by the
11 For sin, t' occasion by the
2Co 2:13 t' my leave of them, I went from
11: 8 other churches, t' wages of them,
Eph 6:16 Above all, t' the shield of faith,
2Th 1: 8 t' vengeance on them that know
1Pe 5: 2 flock...t' the oversight thereof, not by
3Jo 7 forth, t' nothing of the Gentiles.

tale See also TALEBEARER; TALES.
Ex 5: 8 And the t' of the bricks, which
18 yet shall ye deliver the t' of bricks.
1Sa 18:27 they gave them in full t' to the king,
1Ch 9:28 bring them in and out by t'.
Ps 90: 9 spend our years as a t' that is told.

talebearer
Le 19:16 down as a t' among thy people:
Pr 11:13 A t' revealeth secrets: but he
18: 8 The words of a t' are as wounds,
20:19 about as a t' revealeth secrets:
26:20 there is no t', the strife ceaseth.
22 The words of a t' are as wounds,

talent See also TALENTS.
Ex 25:39 Of a t' of pure gold shall he make
37:24 Of a t' of pure gold made he it, and
38:27 hundred talents, a t' for a socket.
2Sa 12:30 a t' of gold with the precious stones
1Ki 20:39 or else thou shalt pay a t' of silver.
2Ki 5:22 give them, I pray thee, a t' of silver,
23:33 talents of silver, and a t' of gold.
1Ch 20: 2 and found it to weigh a t' of gold,
2Ch 36: 3 talents of silver and a t' of gold.
Zec 5: 7 there was lifted up a t' of lead:
M't 25:24 he which had received the one t'
25 went and hid thy t' in the earth:
28 Take therefore the t' from him, and
Re 16:21 stone about the weight of a t':

talents
Ex 38:24 offering, was twenty and nine t',
25 the silver...was an hundred t',
27 of the hundred t' of silver were cast
27 hundred sockets of the hundred t',
29 brass of the offering was seventy t',
1Ki 9:14 sent to the king sixscore t' of gold.
28 gold, four hundred and twenty t',
10:10 an hundred and twenty t' of gold,
14 threescore and six t' of gold.
16:24 of Shemer for two t' of silver,
2Ki 5: 5 and took with him ten t' of silver,
23 said, Be content, take two t'.
23 bound two t' of silver in two bags,
15:19 gave Pul a thousand t' of silver,
18:14 unto Hezekiah...three hundred t'
14 of silver and thirty t' of gold.
23:33 tribute of an hundred t' of silver,
1Ch 19: 6 Ammon sent a thousand t' of silver
22:14 an hundred thousand t' of gold,
14 a thousand thousand t' of silver;
29: 4 Even three thousand t' of gold, of
4 seven thousand t' of refined silver,
7 of gold five thousand t' and ten
7 and of silver ten thousand t',
7 and of brass eighteen thousand t',
7 one hundred thousand t' of iron.
2Ch 3: 8 gold, amounting to six hundred t'.
8:18 four hundred and fifty t' of gold,
9: 9 an hundred and twenty t' of gold,
13 and threescore and six t' of gold;
25: 6 Israel for an hundred t' of silver.
9 the hundred t' which I have given
27: 5 same year an hundred t' of silver,
36: 3 the land in an hundred t' of silver
Ezr 7:22 Unto an hundred t' of silver, and
8:26 six hundred and fifty t' of silver,
26 and silver vessels an hundred t',
26 and of gold an hundred t';
Es 3: 9 I will pay ten thousand t' of silver
M't 18:24 which owed him ten thousand t'.
25:15 And unto one he gave five t', and to
16 he that had received the five t' went
16 same, and made them other five t'.
20 And so he that had received five t'
20 came and brought other five t',
20 thou deliveredst unto me five t':
20 gained beside them five t' more.
22 He also that had received two t'
22 thou deliveredst unto me two t':
22 gained two other t' beside them.
28 give it unto him which hath ten t'.

tales
Eze 22: 9 men that carry t' to shed blood:
Lu 24:11 words seemed to them as idle t',

Talitha (*tal'-ith-ah*)
M'r 5:41 hand, and said unto her, T' cumi;

talk See also TALKED; TALKEST; TALKETH; TALKING.
Nu 11:17 come down and t' with thee there:
De 5:24 this day that God doth t' with man,
6: 7 t' of them when thou sittest in thine
1Sa 2: 3 T' no more so exceeding proudly;
2Ki 18:26 and t' not...in the Jews' language
1Ch 16: 9 t' ye of all his wondrous works.
Job 11: 2 should a man full of t' be justified?
13: 7 God? and t' deceitfully for him?
15: 3 he reason with unprofitable t'?
Ps 69:26 they t' to the grief of those whom
71:24 also shall t' of thy righteousness
77:12 all thy work, and t' of thy doings.
105: 2 t' ye of all his wondrous works.
119:27 so shall I t' of thy wondrous works:
145:11 thy kingdom, and t' of thy power;
Pr 6:22 thou awakest, it shall t' with thee.
14:23 but the t' of the lips tendeth only
24: 2 and their lips t' of mischief.
Ec 10:13 the end of his t' is mischievous
Jer 12: 1 t' with thee of thy judgments:
Eze 3:22 plain, and I will there t' with thee.
Da 10:17 the servant...t' with this my lord?
M't 22:15 they might entangle him in his t'.
Joh 14:30 Hereafter I will not t' much with

talked
Ge 4: 8 And Cain t' with Abel his brother:
17: 3 on his face: and God t' with him,
35:13 in the place where he t' with him.
14 in the place where he t' with him,
45:15 after that his brethren t' with him.
Ex 20:22 that I have t' with you from heaven.
33: 9 and the Lord t' with Moses.
34:29 his face shone while he t' with him.
31 unto him: and Moses t' with them.
De 5: 4 The Lord t' with you face to face
J'g 14: 7 went down, and t' with the woman:
1Sa 14:19 pass, while Saul t' unto the priest,
17:23 And as he t' with them, behold,
1Ki 1:22 lo, while she yet t' with the king,
2Ki 2:11 to pass, as they still went on, and t',
6:33 And while he yet t' with them,
8: 4 the king t' with Gehazi the servant
2Ch 25:16 as he t' with him, that the king said
Jer 38:25 princes hear...I have t' with thee,
Da 9:22 informed me, and t' with me, and
Zec 1: 9 And the angel that t' with me said
13 answered the angel that t' with me
19 said unto the angel that t' with me,
2: 3 angel that t' with me went forth,
4: 1 angel that t' with me came again,
4 spake to the angel that t' with me,
5 the angel that t' with me answered
5: 5 angel that t' with me went forth,
10 said I to the angel that t' with me,
6: 4 said unto the angel that t' with me.
M't 12:46 While he yet t' to the people,
M'r 6:50 And immediately t' with them,
Lu 9:30 there t' with him two men, which
24:14 they t' together of all these things
32 while he t' with us by the way,
Joh 4:27 marvelled...he t' with the woman:
Ac 10:27 as he t' with him, he went in, and
20:11 and t' a long while, even till break
26:31 aside, they t' between themselves,
Re 17: 1 t' with me, saying unto me, Come
21: 9 t' with me, saying, Come hither,
15 that t' with me had a golden reed

talkers
Eze 36: 3 ye are taken up in the lips of t',
Tit 1:10 unruly and vain t' and deceivers,

talkest
J'g 6:17 me a sign that thou t' with me.
1Ki 1:14 while thou...t' there with the king,
Joh 4:27 thou? or, Why t' thou with her?

talketh
Ps 37:30 and his tongue t' of judgment.
Joh 9:37 him, and it is he that t' with thee.

talking
Ge 17:22 And he left off t' with him, and
1Ki 18:27 either he is t', or he is pursuing,
Es 6:14 while they were yet t' with him,
Job 29: 9 The princes refrained t', and laid
Eze 33:30 people still are t' against thee
M't 17: 3 them Moses and Elias t' with him.
M'r 9: 4 Moses: and they were t' with Jesus.
Eph 5: 4 nor foolish t', nor jesting,
Re 4: 1 it were of a trumpet t' with me;

tall See also TALLER.
De 2:10 a people great, and many, and t',
21 A people great, and many, and t',
9: 2 A people great and t', the children
2Ki 19:23 will cut down the t' cedar trees
Isa 37:24 I will cut down the t' cedars thereof,

taller
De 1:28 people is greater and t' than we;

Talmai (*tal'-mahee*)
Nu 13:22 where Ahiman, Sheshai, and T',
Jos 15:14 Sheshai, and Ahiman, and T',
J'g 1:10 slew Sheshai, and Ahiman, and T'.
2Sa 3: 3 the daughter of T' king of Geshur;
13:37 But Absalom fled, and went to T',
1Ch 3: 2 the daughter of T' king of Geshur:

Talmon (*tal'-mon*)
1Ch 9:17 Shallum, and Akkub, and T',
Ezr 2:42 children of Ater, the children of T',
Ne 7:45 children of Ater, the children of T',
11:19 the porters, Akkub, T', and their
12:25 Meshullam T', Akkub, were porters

Tamah (*ta'-mah*) See also THAMAH.
Ne 7:55 of Sisera, the children of T',

Tamar (*ta'-mar*) See also BAAL-TAMAR; HAZAZON-TAMAR; THAMAR.
Ge 38: 6 his firstborn, whose name was T'.
11 Judah to T' his daughter in law,
38:11 T' went and dwelt in her father's
13 And it was told T', saying, Behold
24 T' thy daughter in law hath played
Ru 4:12 Pharez, whom T' bare unto Judah,
2Sa 13: 1 a fair sister, whose name was T';
2 that he fell sick for his sister T';
4 I love T', my brother Absalom's
5 let my sister T' come, and give me
6 let T' my sister come, and make me
7 David sent home to T', saying, Go
8 So T' went to her brother Amnon's
10 And Amnon said unto T', Bring the
10 T' took the cakes which she had
19 T' put ashes on her head, and rent
20 So T' remained desolate in her
22 because he had forced his sister T'.
32 the day that he forced his sister T'.
14:27 one daughter, whose name was T':
1Ch 2: 4 T' his daughter in law bare him
3: 9 the concubines, and T' their sister.
Eze 47:19 from T' even to the waters of strife
48:28 from T' unto the waters of strife in

tame See also TAMED.
M'r 5: 4 neither could any man t' him.
Jas 3: 8 But the tongue can no man t'; it is

tamed
Jas 3: 7 and of things in the sea, is t',
7 and hath been t' of mankind:

Tammuz (*tam'-muz*)
Eze 8:14 there sat women weeping for T'.

Tanach (*ta'-nak*) See also TAANACH.
Jos 21:25 Manasseh, T' with her suburbs,

tangle See ENTANGLE.

Tanhumeth (*tan'-hu-meth*)
2Ki 25:23 the son of T' the Netophathite,
Jer 40: 8 Kareah, and Seraiah the son of T',

tanner
Ac 9:43 days in Joppa with one Simon a t'.
10: 6 He lodgeth with one Simon a t',
32 in the house of one Simon a t' by the

tapestry
Pr 7:16 decked my bed with coverings of t',
31:22 She maketh herself coverings of t';

Taphath (*ta'-fath*)
1Ki 4:11 T'...daughter of Solomon to wife:

Tappuah (*tap'-pu-ah*) See also BETH-TAPPUAH; EN-TAPPUAH.
Jos 12:17 The king of T', one; the king of
15:34 and En-gannim, T', and Enam,
16: 8 from T' westward unto the river
17: 8 Now Manasseh had the land of T':
8 but T' on the border of Manasseh
1Ch 2:43 the sons of Hebron; Korah, and T',

Tarah (*ta'-rah*)
Nu 33:27 from Tahath, and pitched at T'.
28 they removed from T', and pitched

Taralah (*tar'-a-lah*)
Jos 18:27 And Rekem, and Irpeel, and T',

tare See also TARES.
2Sa 13:31 king arose, and t' his garments,
2Ki 2:24 t' forty and two children of them.
M'r 9:20 him, straightway the spirit t' him;
Lu 9:42 devil threw him down, and t' him.

Tarea (*ta'-re-ah*) See also TAHREA.
1Ch 8:35 and Melech, and T', and Ahaz.

tares
M't 13:25 and sowed t' among the wheat,
26 fruit, then appeared the t' also.
27 field? from whence then hath it t'?
29 Nay; lest while ye gather up the t',
30 Gather ye together first the t', and
36 us the parable of the t' of the field.
38 the t' are the children of the wicked
40 the t' are gathered and burned in the

target See also TARGETS.
1Sa 17: 6 t' of brass between his shoulders.
1Ki 10:16 shekels of gold went to one t'.
2Ch 9:15 of beaten gold went to one t'.

targets
1Ki 10:16 two hundred t' of beaten gold:
2Ch 9:15 two hundred t' of beaten gold:
14: 8 had an army of men that bare t' and

Tarpelites (*tar'-pel-ites*)
Ezr 4: 9 the Apharsathchites, the T', the

tarried
Ge 24:54 were with him, and t' all night;
28:11 certain place, and t' there all night,
31:54 bread, and t' all night in the mount.
Nu 9:19 cloud t' long upon the tabernacle
22 the cloud t' upon the tabernacle,
J'g 3:25 they t' till they were ashamed:
26 And Ehud escaped while they t',
19: 8 And they t' until afternoon, and
Ru 2: 7 that she t' a little in the house.
1Sa 13: 8 he t' seven days, according to the
14: 2 Saul t' in the uttermost part of
2Sa 11: 1 But David t' still at Jerusalem.
15:17 and t' in a place that was far off.
29 to Jerusalem: and they t' there.
20: 5 but he t' longer than the set time
2Ki 2:18 again to him, (for he t' at Jericho,)
1Ch 20: 1 Rabbah. But David t' at Jerusalem.
Ps 68:12 and she that t' at home divided the
M't 25: 5 While the bridegroom t', they all
Lu 1:21 that he t' so long in the temple.
2:43 child Jesus t' behind in Jerusalem;
Joh 3:22 and there he t' with them, and

Ac 9:43 he *t* many days in Joppa with one
15:33 after they had *t* there a space,
18:18 Paul after this *t* there yet a good
20: 5 These going before *t*...at Troas.
15 at Samos, and *t* at Trogyllium;
21: 4 disciples, we *t* there seven days:
10 And as we *t* there many days,
25: 6 he had *t* among them more than
27:33 the fourteenth day that ye have *t*
28:12 at Syracuse, we *t* there three days.

tarriest
Ac 22:16 And now why *t* thou? arise, and be

tarrieth
1Sa 30:24 his part be that *t* by the stuff;
Mic 5: 7 upon the grass, that *t* not for man,

tarry See also TARRIED; TARRIEST; TARRIETH; TARRYING.
Ge 19: 2 *t* all night, and wash your feet,
27:44 And *t* with him a few days, until
30:27 I have found favour in thine eyes, *t*
45: 9 Egypt: come down unto me, *t* not:
Ex 12:39 out of Egypt, and could not *t*,
24:14 *T* ye here for us, until we come
Le 14: 8 *t* abroad out of his tent seven days.
Nu 22:19 *t* ye also here this night, that I may
J'g 5:28 why *t* the wheels of his chariots?
6:18 I will *t* until thou come again.
19: 6 and *t* all night, and let thine
9 evening, I pray you *t* all night:
10 But the man would not *t* that night,
Ru 1:13 *t* for them till they were grown?
3:13 *T* this night, and it shall be in the
1Sa 1:23 *t* until thou have weaned him;
10: 8 seven days shalt thou *t*, till I come
14: 9 *T* until we come to you; then we
2Sa 10: 5 *T* at Jericho until your beards be
11:12 *T* here to day also, and to morrow
15:28 *t* in the plain of the wilderness,
18:14 Joab, I may not *t* thus with thee.
19: 7 there will not *t* one with thee this
2Ki 2: 2 unto Elisha, *T* here, I pray thee;
4 him, Elisha, *t* here, I pray thee;
6 unto him, *T*, I pray thee, here;
7: 9 if we *t* till the morning light, some
9: 3 open the door, and flee, and *t* not.
14:10 glory of this, and *t* at home: for
1Ch 19: 5 *T* at Jericho until your beards be
Ps 101: 7 he that telleth lies shall not *t* in
Pr 23:30 They that *t* long at the wine; they
Isa 46:13 off, and my salvation shall not *t*:
Jer 14: 8 that turneth aside to *t* for a night?
Hab 2: 3 not lie: though it *t*, wait for it;
3 it will surely come, it will not *t*.
M't 26:38 *t* ye here, and watch with me.
M'r 14:34 unto death: *t* ye here, and watch
Lu 24:29 And he went in to *t* with them.
49 but *t* ye in the city of Jerusalem,
Joh 4:40 him that he would *t* with them:
21:22, 23 If I will that he *t* till I come,
Ac 10:48 prayed they him to *t* certain days.
18:20 they desired him to *t* longer time
28:14 desired to *t* with them seven days:
1Co 11:33 together to eat, *t* one for another.
16: 7 I trust to *t* a while with you, if the
8 will *t* at Ephesus until Pentecost.
1Ti 3:15 But if I *t* long, that thou mayest
Heb 10:37 come will come, and will not *t*.

tarrying
Ps 40:17 deliverer; make no *t*, O my God.
70: 5 my deliverer; O Lord, make no *t*.

Tarshish (*tar'-shish*) See also THARSHISH.
Ge 10: 4 sons of Javan; Elishah, and *T*,
1Ch 1: 7 the sons of Javan; Elishah and *T*,
2Ch 9:21 For the king's ships went to *T*
21 came the ships of *T* bringing gold,
20:36 him to make ships to go to *T*:
37 they were not able to go to *T*.
Es 1:14 Admatha, *T*, Meres, Marsena,
Ps 48: 7 Thou breakest the ships of *T*
72:10 The kings of *T* and of the isles
Isa 2:16 And upon all the ships of *T*, and
23: 1 Howl, ye ships of *T*; for it is laid
6 Pass ye over to *T*; howl, ye
10 land as a river, O daughter of *T*:
14 Howl, ye ships of *T*: for your
60: 9 for me, and the ships of *T* first,
66:19 them unto the nations, to *T*, Pul,
Jer 10: 9 into plates is brought from *T*,
Eze 27:12 *T* was thy merchant by reason of
25 The ships of *T* did sing of thee
38:13 Dedan, and the merchants of *T*,
Jon 1: 3 But Jonah rose up to flee unto *T*
3 and he found a ship going to *T*:
3 unto it, to go with them unto *T*
4: 2 Therefore I fled before unto *T*:

Tarsus (*tar'-sus*)
Ac 9:11 Judas for one called Saul, of *T*:
30 Cæsarea, and sent him forth to *T*.
11:25 Then departed Barnabas to *T*,
21:39 I am a man which am a Jew of *T*,
22: 3 man which am a Jew, born in *T*,

Tartak (*tar'-tak*)
2Ki 17:31 the Avites made Nibhaz and *T*,

Tartan (*tar'-tan*)
2Ki 18:17 And the king of Assyria sent *T*
Isa 20: 1 year that *T* came unto Ashdod,

Taschith See AL-TASCHITH.

task See also TASKMASTERS; TASKS.
Ex 5:14 fulfilled your *t* in making brick
19 from your bricks of your daily *t*.

taskmasters
Ex 1:11 they did set over them *t*
3: 7 their cry by reason of their *t*;
5: 6 And Pharaoh commanded...the *t*
10 And the *t* of the people went out,
13 And the *t* hasted them, saying,
14 Pharaoh's *t* had set over them,

tasks
Ex 5:13 Fulfil your works, your daily *t*,

taste See also TASTED; TASTETH.
Ex 16:31 *t* of it was like wafers made with
Nu 11: 8 the *t* of it was as the *t* of fresh oil.
1Sa 14:43 I did but *t* a little honey with the
2Sa 3:35 to me, and more also, if I *t* bread,
19:35 *t* what I eat or what I drink?
Job 6: 6 there any *t* in the white of an egg?
30 my *t* discern perverse things?
12:11 and the mouth *t* his meat?
Ps 34: 8 O *t* and see that the Lord is good:
119:103 sweet are thy words unto my *t*!
Pr 24:13 honeycomb, which is sweet to thy *t*:
Ca 2: 3 and his fruit was sweet to my *t*.
Jer 48:11 therefore his *t* remained in him,
Jon 3: 7 beast, herd nor flock, *t* any thing:
M't 16:28 here, which shall not *t* of death,
M'r 9: 1 here, which shall not *t* of death,
Lu 9:27 here, which shall not *t* of death,
14:24 were bidden shall *t* of my supper.
Joh 8:52 saying, he shall never *t* of death.
Col 2:21 (Touch not; *t* not; handle not;
Heb 2: 9 should *t* death for every man.

tasted
1Sa 14:24 So none of the people *t* any food.
29 because I *t* a little of this honey.
Da 5: 2 Belshazzar, whiles he *t* the wine,
M't 27:34 had *t* thereof, he would not drink.
Joh 2: 9 *t* the water that was made wine,
Heb 6: 4 and have *t* of the heavenly gift, and
5 And have *t* the good word of God,
1Pe 2: 3 ye have *t* that the Lord is gracious.

tasteth
Job 34: 3 words, as the mouth *t* meat.

Tatnai (*tat'-nahee*)
Ezr 5: 3, 6 *T*, governor on this side the
6: 6 *T*, governor beyond the river,
13 *T*, governor on this side the river,

tattlers
1Ti 5:13 idle, but *t* also and busybodies,

taught
De 4: 5 Behold, I have *t* you statutes and
31:22 day, and *t* it the children of Israel.
J'g 8:16 them he *t* the men of Succoth.
2Ki 17:28 *t* them how they should fear the
2Ch 6:27 thou hast *t* them the good way,
17: 9 they *t* in Judah, and had the book
9 cities of Judah, and *t* the people.
23:13 and such as *t* to sing praise.
30:22 *t* the good knowledge of the Lord:
35: 3 unto the Levites that *t* all Israel,
Ne 8: 9 and the Levites that *t* the people,
Ps 71:17 thou hast *t* me from my youth:
119:102 judgments: for thou hast *t* me.
171 when thou hast *t* me thy statutes.
Pr 4: 4 He *t* me also, and said unto me,
11 I have *t* thee in the way of wisdom;
31: 1 prophecy that his mother *t* him.
Ec 12: 9 he still *t* the people knowledge;
Isa 29:13 fear toward me is *t* by the precept
40:13 being his counsellor hath *t* him?
14 *t* him in the path of judgment,
14 and *t* him knowledge, and shewed
54:13 children shall be *t* of the Lord;
Jer 2:33 hast thou also *t* the wicked ones
9: 5 have *t* their tongue to speak lies,
14 Baalim, which their fathers *t* them:
12:16 they *t* my people to swear by Baal;
13:21 thou hast *t* them to be captains,
28:16 hast *t* rebellion against the Lord.
29:32 hath *t* rebellion against the Lord.
32:33 though I *t* them, rising up early
Eze 23:48 be *t* not to do after your lewdness.
Ho 10:11 Ephraim is as an heifer that is *t*,
11: 3 I *t* Ephraim also to go, taking
Zec 13: 5 *t* me to keep cattle from my youth.
M't 5: 2 he opened his mouth, and *t* them,
7:29 he *t* them as one having
13:54 he *t* them in their synagogue,
28:15 the money, and did as they were *t*:
M'r 1:21 entered into the synagogue, and *t*.
22 for he *t* them as one that had 2258,
2:13 resorted unto him, and he *t* them.
4: 2 he *t* them many things by parables,
6:30 they had done, and what they had *t*
9:31 For he *t* his disciples, and said unto
10: 1 as he was wont, he *t* them again.
11:17 he *t*, saying unto them, Is it not
12:35 and said, while he *t* in the temple,
Lu 4:15 And he *t* in their synagogues, being
31 *t* them on the sabbath days.
5: 3 and *t* the people out of the ship.
6: 6 entered into the synagogue and *t*:
11: 1 pray, as John also *t* his disciples.
13:26 and thou hast *t* in our streets.
19:47 And he *t* daily in the temple.
20: 1 as he *t* the people in the temple,
Joh 6:45 And they shall be all *t* of God.
59 synagogue, as he *t* in Capernaum.
7:14 went up into the temple, and *t*.
28 cried Jesus in the temple as he *t*,
8: 2 and he sat down, and *t* them.
20 treasury, as he *t* in the temple:
28 as my Father hath *t* me, I speak
18:20 I ever *t* in the synagogue, and in
Ac 4: 2 grieved that they *t* the people,
5:21 temple early in the morning, and *t*.
11:26 the church, and *t* much people.
14:21 to that city, and had *t* many,
15: 1 down from Judæa *t* the brethren,
18:25 *t* diligently the things of the Lord.
20:20 you, and have *t* you publickly,
22: 3 *t* according to the perfect manner
Ga 1:12 it of man, neither was I *t* it,
6: 6 Let him that is *t* in the word
Eph 4:21 heard him, and...been *t* by him,
Col 2: 7 in the faith, as ye have been *t*,
1Th 4: 9 are *t* of God to love one another.
2Th 2:15 traditions which ye have been *t*,
Tit 1: 9 faithful word as he hath been *t*,
1Joh 2:27 no lie, and even as it hath *t* you,
Re 2:14 *t* Balac to cast a stumblingblock

taunt See also TAUNTING.
Jer 24: 9 and a proverb, a *t* and a curse,
Eze 5:15 So it shall be a reproach and a *t*,

taunting
Hab 2: 6 and a *t* proverb against him, and

taverns
Ac 28:15 far as Appii forum,...The three *t*:

taxation
2Ki 23:35 of every one according to his *t*, to

taxed
2Ki 23:35 he *t* the land to give the money
Lu 2: 1 that all the world should be *t*.
3 all went to be *t*, every one into his
5 be *t* with Mary his espoused wife,

taxes
Da 11:20 a raiser of *t* in the glory of the

taxing
Lu 2: 2 And this *t* was first made when
Ac 5:37 Judas of Galilee in the days of the *t*,

teach See also TAUGHT; TEACHER; TEACHEST; TEACHETH; TEACHING.
Ex 4:12 and *t* thee what thou shalt say.
15 and will *t* you what ye shall do.
18:20 thou shalt *t* them ordinances and
24:12 written; that thou mayest *t* them.
35:34 hath put in his heart that he may *t*,
Le 10:11 may *t* the children of Israel all the
14:57 *t* when it is unclean, and when it is
De 4: 1 the judgments, which I *t* you, for
9 but *t* them thy sons, and thy sons'
10 and that they may *t* their children.
14 me at that time to *t* you statutes
5:31 judgments, which thou shalt *t* them,
6: 1 your God commanded to *t* you,
7 shalt *t* them diligently unto thy
11:19 And ye shall *t* them your children,
17:11 of the law which they shall *t* thee,
20:18 they *t* you not to do after all their
24: 8 the priests the Levites shall *t* you:
31:19 you, and *t* it the children of Israel:
33:10 They shall *t* Jacob thy judgments,
J'g 3: 2 Israel might know, to *t* them war,
13: 8 and *t* us what we shall do unto the
1Sa 12:23 I will *t* you the good and the right
2Sa 1:18 bade them *t* the children of Judah
1Ki 8:36 that thou *t* them the good way
2Ki 17:27 *t* them the manner of the God of
2Ch 17: 7 to *t* in the cities of Judah.
Ezr 7:10 and to *t* in Israel statutes and
25 and *t* ye them that know them not.
Job 6:24 *T* me, and I will hold my tongue:
8:10 Shall not they *t* thee, and tell thee,
12: 7 the beasts, and they shall *t* thee;
8 to the earth, and it shall *t* thee:
21:22 Shall any *t* God knowledge? seeing
27:11 I will *t* you by the hand of God:
32: 7 multitude of years...*t* wisdom.
33:33 peace, and I shall *t* thee wisdom.
34:32 That which I see not *t* thou me:
37:19 *T* us what we shall say unto him;
Ps 25: 4 thy ways, O Lord; *t* me thy paths.
5 Lead me in thy truth, and *t* me:
8 will he *t* sinners in the way.
9 and the meek will he *t* his way.
12 him shall he *t* in the way that he
27:11 *T* me thy way, O Lord, and lead
32: 8 I will instruct thee and *t* thee in the
34:11 I will *t* you the fear of the Lord.
45: 4 thy right hand shall *t* thee terrible
51:13 will I *t* transgressors thy ways;
60: *title* Michtam of David, to *t*; when
86:11 *T* me thy way, O Lord; I will
90:12 *t* us to number our days, that we
105:22 pleasure; and *t* his senators wisdom.
119:12 thou, O Lord: *t* me thy statutes.
26 heardest me: *t* me thy statutes.
33 *T* me, O Lord, the way of thy
64 of thy mercy: *t* me thy statutes.
66 *T* me...judgment and knowledge;
68 and doest good; *t* me thy statutes.
108 O Lord, and *t* me thy judgments.
124 thy mercy, and *t* me thy statutes.
135 thy servant; and *t* me thy statutes.
132:12 my testimony that I shall *t* them,
143:10 *T* me to do thy will; for thou art
Pr 9: 9 *t* a just man, and he will increase
Isa 2: 3 he will *t* us of his ways, and we
28: 9 Whom shall he *t* knowledge? and
26 him to discretion, and doth *t* him.
Jer 9:20 and *t* your daughters wailing, and
31:34 *t* no more every man his neighbour,
Eze 44:23 shall *t* my people the difference
Da 1: 4 whom they might *t* the learning
Mic 3:11 and the priests thereof *t* for hire,
4: 2 and he will *t* us of his ways, and we
Hab 2:19 Arise, it shall *t*! Behold, it is laid
M't 5:19 and shall *t* men so, he shall be

M't 5:19 but whosoever shall do and t' them,
11: 1 to t' and to preach in their cities.
28:19 Go ye therefore, and t' all nations,
M'r 4: 1 began again to t' by the sea side:
6: 2 he began to t' in the synagogue:
34 he began to t' them many things.
8:31 he began to t' them, that the Son of
Lu 11: 1 said unto him, Lord, t' us to pray,
12:12 Holy Ghost shall t' you in the same
Joh 7:35 the Gentiles, and t' the Gentiles?
9:34 born in sins, and dost thou t' us?
14:26 he shall t' you all things, and bring
Ac 1: 1 that Jesus began both to do and t',
4:18 at all nor t' in the name of Jesus.
5:28 that ye should not t' in this name?
42 ceased not to t' and preach Jesus
16:21 t' customs, which are not lawful
1Co 4:17 I t' every where in every church.
11:14 Doth not even nature itself t' you,
14:19 by my voice I might t' others also,
1Ti 1: 3 some that they t' no other doctrine,
2:12 But I suffer not a woman to t', nor
3: 2 given to hospitality, apt to t';
4:11 These things command and t'.
6: 2 benefit. These things t' and exhort.
3 If any man t' otherwise, and
2Ti 2: 2 who shall be able to t' others also.
24 but be gentle unto all men, apt to t',
Tit 2: 4 t' the young women to be sober,
Heb 5:12 ye have need that one t' you again
8:11 not t' every man his neighbour,
1Jo 2:27 ye need not that any man t' you:
Re 2:20 to t' and to seduce my servants to

teacher See also TEACHERS.
1Ch 25: 8 as the great, the t' as the scholar.
Hab 2:18 the molten image, and a t' of lies,
Joh 3: 2 that thou art a t' come from God:
Ro 2:20 a t' of babes, which hast the form
1Ti 2: 7 a t' of the Gentiles in faith and
2Ti 1:11 an apostle, and a t' of the Gentiles.

teachers
Ps 119:99 understanding than all my t':
Pr 5:13 have not obeyed the voice of my t',
Isa 30:20 not thy t' be removed into a corner
20 but thine eyes shall see thy t':
43:27 t' have transgressed against me.
Ac 13: 1 at Antioch certain prophets and t';
1Co 12:28 secondarily prophets, thirdly t',
29 are all prophets? are all t'? are all
Eph 4:11 and some, pastors and t';
1Ti 1: 7 Desiring to be t' of the law;
2Ti 4: 3 shall they heap to themselves t',
Tit 2: 3 to much wine, t' of good things;
Heb 5:12 when for the time ye ought to be t',
2Pe 2: 1 there shall be false t' among you,

teachest
Ps 94:12 O Lord, and t' him out of thy law;
M't 22:16 true, and t' the way of God in truth,
M'r 12:14 men, but t' the way of God in truth:
Lu 20:21 know that thou sayest and t' rightly,
21 of any, but t' the way of God truly:
Ac 21:21 that thou t' all the Jews which are
Ro 2:21 Thou therefore which t' another,
21 t' thou not thyself? thou that

teacheth
2Sa 22:35 He t' my hands to war; so that a
Job 35:11 Who t' us more than the beasts of
36:22 by his power: who t' like him?
Ps 18:34 He t' my hands to war, so that a
94:10 he that t' man knowledge, shall not
144: 1 which t' my hands to war, and my
Pr 6:13 his feet, he t' with his fingers;
16:23 The heart of the wise t' his mouth,
Isa 9:15 prophet that t' lies, he is the tail.
48:17 thy God which t' thee to profit,
Ac 21:28 man, that t' all men every where
Ro 12: 7 or he that t', on teaching;
1Co 2:13 the words which man's wisdom t',
13 but which the Holy Ghost t';
Gal 6: 6 unto him that t' in all good things.
1Jo 2:27 as the same anointing t' you of all

teaching
2Ch 15: 3 without a t' priest, and without
Jer 32:33 them, rising up early and t' them,
M't 4:23 all Galilee, t' in their synagogues,
9:35 and villages, t' in their synagogues,
15: 9 t' for doctrines the commandments
21:23 people came unto him as he was t',
26:55 sat daily with you t' in the temple,
28:20 T' them to observe all things
M'r 6: 6 he went round about the villages, t'.
7: 7 t' for doctrines the commandments
14:49 was daily with you in the temple t',
Lu 5:17 pass on a certain day, as he was t',
13:10 he was t' in one of the synagogues
22 through the cities and villages, t',
21:37 day time he was t' in the temple;
23: 5 the people, t' throughout all Jewry,
Ac 5:25 in the temple, and t' the people.
15:35 t' and preaching the word of the
18:11 t' the word of God among them.
28:31 t' those things which concern the
Ro 12: 7 or he that teacheth, on t';
Col 1:28 and t' every man in all wisdom;
3:16 t' and admonishing one another
Tit 1:11 t' things which they ought not, for
2:12 T' us that, denying ungodliness

tear See also TARE; TEARETH; TEARS; TORN.
J'g 8: 7 I will t' your flesh with the thorns
Ps 7: 2 Lest he t' my soul like a lion,
35:15 they did t' me, and ceased not:
50:22 lest I t' you in pieces, and there be
Jer 15: 3 sword to slay, and the dogs to t',
16: 7 shall men t' themselves for them
Eze 13:20 and I will t' them from your arms,
21 Your kerchiefs also will I t', and
Ho 5:14 I, even I, will t' and go away; I will
13: 8 lion: the wild beast shall t' them.
Am 1:11 and his anger did t' perpetually,
Na 2:12 The lion did t' in pieces enough for
Zec 11:16 the fat, and t' their claws in pieces.

teareth
De 33:20 t' the arm with the crown of the
Job 16: 9 He t' me in his wrath, who hateth
18: 4 He t' himself in his anger: shall
Mic 5: 8 both treadeth down, and t' in pieces,
M'r 9:18 he taketh him, he t' him: and he
Lu 9:39 and it t' him that he foameth again,

tears
2Ki 20: 5 thy prayer, I have seen thy t':
Es 8: 3 besought him with t' to put away
Job 16:20 but mine eye poureth out t' unto God.
Ps 6: 6 to swim; I water my couch with t'.
39:12 my cry; hold not thy peace at my t'.
42: 3 My t' have been my meat day and
56: 8 put thou my t' into thy bottle: are
80: 5 feedest them with the bread of t';
5 them t' to drink in great measure.
116: 8 mine eyes from t', and my feet from
126: 5 They that sow in t' shall reap in joy.
Ec 4: 1 the t' of such as were oppressed,
Isa 16: 9 I will water thee with my t', O
25: 8 Lord God will wipe away t' from off
38: 5 heard thy prayer, I have seen thy t':
Jer 9: 1 and mine eyes a fountain of t', that
18 that our eyes may run down with t',
13:17 weep sore, and run down with t',
14:17 Let mine eyes run down with t'
31:16 weeping, and thine eyes from t':
La 1: 2 night, and her t' are on her cheeks:
2:11 Mine eyes do fail with t', my
18 let t' run down like a river day and
Eze 24:16 weep, neither shall thy t' run down.
Mal 2:13 covering...altar of the Lord with t',
M'r 9:24 and said with t', Lord, I believe;
Lu 7:38 and began to wash his feet with t',
44 she hath washed my feet with t',
Ac 20:19 humility of mind, and with many t',
31 every one night and day with t'.
2Co 2: 4 I wrote unto you with many t'; not
2Ti 1: 4 to see thee, being mindful of thy t',
Heb 5: 7 with strong crying and t' unto him
12:17 he sought it carefully with t'.
Re 7:17 and God shall wipe away all t' from
21: 4 and God shall wipe away all t' from

teats
Isa 32:12 They shall lament for the t', for
Eze 23: 3 bruised the t' of their virginity.
21 in bruising thy t' by the Egyptians

Tebah (*te'-bah*)
Ge 22:24 was Reumah, she bare also T',

Tebaliah (*teb-a-li'-ah*)
1Ch 26:11 Hilkiah the second, T' the third,

Tebeth (*te'-beth*)
Es 2:16 month, which is the month T',

tedious
Ac 24: 4 that I be not further t' unto thee,

teeth
Ge 49:12 wine, and his t' white with milk.
Nu 11:33 the flesh was yet between their t',
De 32:24 also send the t' of beasts upon them,
1Sa 2:13 a fleshhook of three t' in his hand;
Job 4:10 lions, and the t' of the young lions,
13:14 do I take my flesh in my t', and put
16: 9 he gnasheth upon me with his t';
19:20 I am escaped with the skin of my t'
29:17 and plucked the spoil out of his t'.
41:14 his t' are terrible round about.
Ps 3: 7 hast broken the t' of the ungodly.
35:16 they gnashed upon me with their t'.
37:12 and gnasheth upon him with his t'.
57: 4 whose t' are spears and arrows,
58: 6 Break their t', O God, in their
6 break out the great t' of the young
112:10 he shall gnash with his t', and
124: 6 not given us as a prey to their t'.
Pr 10:26 As vinegar to the t', and as smoke
30:14 generation, whose t' are as swords,
14 their jaw t' as knives, to devour
Ca 4: 2 Thy t' are like a flock of sheep
6: 6 Thy t' are as a flock of sheep which
Isa 41:15 threshing instrument having t':
Jer 31:29 the children's t' are set on edge.
30 grape, his t' shall be set on edge.
La 2:16 thee: they hiss and gnash the t':
3:16 broken my t' with gravel stones,
Eze 18: 2 the children's t' are set on edge?
Da 7: 5 mouth of it between the t' of it:
7 it had great iron t': it devoured
19 whose t' were of iron, and his nails
Joe 1: 6 whose t' are the t' of a lion, and
6 hath the cheek t' of a great lion.
Am 4: 6 have given you cleanness of t'
Mic 3: 5 people err, that bite with their t',
Zec 9: 7 abominations from between his t':
M't 8:12 be weeping and gnashing of t'.
13:42, 50 be wailing and gnashing of t'.
22:13 be weeping and gnashing of t'.
24:51 be weeping and gnashing of t'.
25:30 be weeping and gnashing of t'.
27:44 with him, cast the same in his t'.
M'r 9:18 foameth, and gnasheth with his t',
Lu 13:28 be weeping and gnashing of t',
Ac 7:54 they gnashed on him with their t'.
Re 9: 8 and their t' were as...of lions.
8 were as the t' of lions.

Tehaphnehes (*te-haf'-ne-heze*) See also TAHAPANES.
Eze 30:18 At T'...the day shall be darkened,

Tehinnah (*te-hin'-nah*)
1Ch 4:12 and T' the father of Ir-nahash.

teil (*teel*)
Isa 6:13 as a t' tree, and as an oak, whose

Tekel (*te'-kel*)
Da 5:25 Mene, Mene, T', Upharsin.
27 T'; Thou art weighed in the

Tekoa (*te-ko'-ah*) See also TEKOAH; TEKOITE.
1Ch 2:24 bare him Ashur the father of T'.
4: 5 Ashur the father of T' had two
2Ch 11: 6 even Beth-lehem, and Etam, and T',
20:20 went forth into the wilderness of T':
Jer 6: 1 and blow the trumpet in T', and
Am 1: 1 who was among the herdmen of T',

Tekoah (*te-ko'-ah*) See also TEKOA.
2Sa 14: 2 And Joab sent to T', and fetched
4 woman of T' spake to the king,
9 woman of T' said unto the king,

Tekoite (*te-ko'-ite*) See also TEKOITES.
2Sa 23:26 Ira the son of Ikkesh the T',
1Ch 11:28 Ira the son of Ikkesh the T',
27: 9 was Ira the son of Ikkesh the T':

Tekoites (*te-ko'-ites*)
Ne 3: 5 next unto them the T' repaired;
27 the T' repaired another piece,

Tel See TEL-ABIB; TEL-HARESHA; TEL-MELAH.

Tel-abib (*tel-a'-bib*)
Eze 3:15 to them of the captivity at T',

Telah (*te'-lah*)
1Ch 7:25 and T' his son, and Tahan his son,

Telaim (*tel'-a-im*) See also TELEM.
1Sa 15: 4 and numbered them in T',

Telassar (*te-las'-sar*) See also THELASSAR.
Isa 37:12 children of Eden which were in T'?

Telem (*te'-lem*) See also TELAIM.
Jos 15:24 Ziph, and T', and Bealoth,
Ezr 10:24 porters; Shallum, and T', and Uri.

Tel-haresha (*tel-ha-re'-shah*) See also TEL-HARSA.
Ne 7:61 Tel-melah, T', Cherub, Addon,

Tel-harsa (*tel-har'-sah*) See also TEL-HARESHA.
Ezr 2:59 Tel-melah, T', Cherub, Addan,

tell See also FORETELL; TELLEST; TELLETH; TELLING; TOLD.
Ge 12:18 not t' me that she was thy wife?
15: 5 toward heaven, and t' the stars,
21:26 neither didst thou t' me, neither
22: 2 mountains which I will t' thee of.
24:23 daughter art thou? t' me, I pray
49 and truly with my master, t' me:
49 and if not, t' me; that I may turn
26: 2 in the land which I shall t' thee of:
29:15 t' me, what shall thy wages be?
31:27 and didst not t' me, that I might
32: 5 I have sent to t' my lord, that I may
29 said, T' me, I pray thee, thy name.
37:16 t' me, I pray thee, where they feed
40: 8 to God? t' me them, I pray you.
43: 6 to t' the man whether ye had yet
22 we cannot t' who put our money
45:13 shall t' my father of all my glory
49: 1 t' you that which shall befall you
Ex 9: 1 Go in unto Pharaoh, and t' him,
10: 2 mayest t' in the ears of thy son,
14:12 this the word that we did t' thee
19: 3 and t' the children of Israel;
Le 14:35 house shall come and t' the priest,
Nu 14:14 t' it to the inhabitants of this land:
21: 1 heard t' that Israel came by the way
23: 3 he sheweth me I will t' thee.
De 17:11 judgment which they shall t' thee,
32: 7 thy elders, and they will t' thee.
Jos 7:19 t' me now what thou hast done;
J'g 14:16 my mother, and shall I t' it thee?
16: 6 T' me, I pray thee, wherein thy
10 t' me, I pray thee, wherewith thou
13 t' me wherewith thou mightest be
20: 3 T' us, how was this wickedness?
Ru 3: 4 he will t' thee what thou shalt do.
4: 4 it, then t' me, that I may know:
1Sa 6: 2 t' us wherewith we shall send it
9: 8 the man of God, to t' us our way.
18 T' me...where the seer's house is.
19 will t' thee all that is in thine heart.
10:15 T' me, I pray thee, what Samuel
14:43 T' me what thou hast done.
15:16 will t' thee what the Lord hath said
17:55 thy soul liveth, O king, I cannot t'.
19: 3 and what I see, that I will t' thee.
20: 9 thee, then would not I t' it thee?
10 to Jonathan, Who shall t' me? or
22:22 there, that he would surely t' Saul:
23:11 Israel, I beseech thee, t' thy servant.
27:11 Lest they should t' on us, saying,
2Sa 1: 4 went the matter? I pray thee, t' me.
20 T' it not in Gath, publish it not in
7: 5 Go and t' my servant David, Thus
12:18 feared to t' him that the child was
18 if we t' him that the child is dead?
22 Who can t' whether God will be
13: 4 day to day? wilt thou not t' me?
15:35 shalt t' it to Zadok and Abiathar the
17:16 send quickly, and t' David, saying,
18:21 Go t' the king what thou hast seen.
1Ki 1:20 t' them who shall sit on the throne
14: 3 he shall t' thee what shall become
7 t' Jeroboam, Thus saith the Lord
18: 8, 11 t' thy lord, Behold, Elijah is here.

1Ki 18: 12 and so when I come and t' Ahab,
14 t' thy lord, Behold, Elijah is here:
20: 9 T' my lord the king, All that thou
:: T' him, Let not him that girdeth
22: 16 t' me nothing but that which is true
18 Did I not t' thee that he would
2Ki 4: 2 t' me, what hast thou in the house?
7: 9 may go and t' the king's household.
8: 4 T' me, I pray thee, all the great
9: 12 they said, It is false; t' us now.
15 of the city to go to t' it in Jezreel.
20: 5 and t' Hezekiah the captain of my
22: 15 T' the man that sent you to me,
1Ch 17: 4 Go and t' David my servant, Thus
10 I t' thee that the Lord will build
21: 10 Go and t' David, saying, Thus
2Ch 18: 17 Did I not t' thee that he would not
34: 23 T' ye the man that sent you to me.
Job 1: 15, 16, 17, 19 escaped alone to t' thee.
8: 10 not they teach thee, and t' thee,
12: 7 of the air, and they shall t' thee:
34: 34 Let men of understanding t' me,
Ps 22: 17 I may t' all my bones: they look
26: 7 and t' of all thy wondrous works.
48: 12 about her: t' the towers thereof.
13 that ye may t' it to the generation
50: 12 I were hungry, I would not t' thee:
Pr 30: 4 is his son's name, if thou canst t'?
Ec 6: 12 for who can t' a man what shall be
8: 7 for who can t' him when it shall be?
10: 14 a man cannot t' what shall be; and
14 shall be after him, who can t' him?
20 hath wings shall t' the matter.
Ca 1: 7 T' me, O thou whom my soul loveth,
5: 8 ye t' him, that I am sick of love.
Isa 5: 5 I will t' you what I will do to my
6: 9 and t' this people, Hear ye indeed,
19: 12 let them t' thee now, and let them
42: 9 they spring forth I t' you of them.
45: 21 T' ye, and bring them near; yea,
48: 20 t' this, utter it even to the end of
Jer 15: 2 shalt t' them, Thus saith the Lord;
19: 2 the words that I shall t' thee,
23: 27 they t' every man to his neighbour,
28 hath a dream, let him t' a dream;
32 do t' them, and cause my people
28: 13 Go and t' Hananiah, saying, Thus
34: 2 Zedekiah king of Judah, and t' him,
35: 13 Go and t' the men of Judah and the
36: 16 We will surely t' the king of all
17 T' us now, How didst thou write all
48: 20 t' ye it in Arnon,...Moab is spoiled,
Eze 3: 11 and speak unto them, and t' them,
12: 23 T' them therefore, Thus saith the
17: 12 t' them, Behold, the king of Babylon
24: 19 t' us what these things are to us,
Da 2: 4 t' thy servants the dream, and we
7 the king t' his servants the dream,
9 t' me the dream, and I shall know
36 and we will t' the interpretation
4: 9 t' me the visions of my dream that I
Joe 1: 3 T' ye your children of it, and let
3 and let your children t' their children,
Jon 1: 8 T' us,...for whose cause this
3: 9 Who can t' if God will turn and
M't 8: 4 saith unto him, See thou t' no man;
10: 27 What I t' you in darkness, that
16: 20 should t' no man that he was Jesus
17: 9 T' the vision to no man, until the
18: 15 t' him his fault between thee and
17 hear them, t' it unto the church:
21: 5 T' ye the daughter of Sion, Behold,
24 ask you one thing, which if ye t' me,
24 will t' you by what authority I do
27 Jesus, and said, We cannot t'.
27 Neither t' I you by what authority
22: 4 T' them which are bidden, Behold,
17 T' us therefore, What thinkest thou?
24: 3 T' us, when shall these things be?
26: 63 t' us whether thou be the Christ,
28: 7 t' his disciples that he is risen from
9 And as they went to t' his disciples,
10 go t' my brethren that they go into
M'r 1: 30 fever, and anon they t' him of her.
5: 19 t' them how great things the Lord
7: 36 them that they should t' no man:
8: 26 town, nor t' it to any in the town.
30 that they should t' no man of him.
9: 9 t' no man what things they had
10: 32 and began to t' them what things
11: 29 will t' you by what authority I do
33 and said unto Jesus, We cannot t'.
33 them, Neither do I t' you by what
13: 4 T' us, when shall these things be?
16: 7 t' his disciples and Peter that he
Lu 4: 25 I t' you of a truth, many widows
5: 14 And he charged him to t' no man:
7: 22 t' John what things ye have seen
42 T' me...which of them will love
8: 56 should t' no man what was done.
9: 21 them to t' no man that thing;
27 I t' you of a truth, there be some
10: 24 For I t' you, that many prophets
12: 51 I t' you, Nay; but rather division:
59 I t' thee, thou shalt not depart
13: 3, 5 I t' you, Nay: but, except ye
27 I t' you, I know you not whence ye
32 Go ye, and t' that fox, Behold, I
17: 34 I t' you, in that night there shall
18: 8 I t' you that he will avenge them
14 I t' you, this man went down to his
19: 40 I t' you that, if these should hold
20: 2 T' us, by what authority doest
7 they could not t' whence it was.
8 Neither t' I you by what authority
22: 34 I t' thee, Peter, the cock shall not
Lu 22: 67 Art thou the Christ? t' us. And he
67 them, If I t' you, ye will not believe:
Joh 3: 8 but canst not t' whence it cometh,
12 if I t' you of heavenly things?
4: 25 he is come, he will t' us all things.
8: 14 but ye cannot t' whence I come,
45 And because I t' you the truth, ye
10: 24 If thou be the Christ, t' us plainly.
12: 22 again Andrew and Philip t' Jesus.
13: 19 Now I t' you before it come, that,
16: 7 Nevertheless I t' you the truth; It is
18 while? we cannot t' what he saith.
18: 34 or did others t' it thee of me?
20: 15 t' me where thou hast laid him, and
Ac 5: 8 T' me whether ye sold the land for
10: 6 t' thee what thou oughtest to do.
11: 14 Who shall t' thee words, whereby
15: 27 t' you the same things by mouth.
17: 21 either to t', or to hear some new
22: 27 him, T' me, art thou a Roman?
23: 17 he hath a certain thing to t' him.
19 him, What is that thou hast to t' me?
22 t' no man that thou hast shewed
2Co 12: 2 (whether in the body, I cannot t';
2 whether out of the body, I cannot t':
3 or out of the body, I cannot t':
Ga 4: 16 enemy, because I t' you the truth?
21 T' me, ye that desire to be under
5: 21 of the which I t' you before, as I
Ph'p 3: 18 and now t' you even weeping, that
Heb 11: 32 time would fail me to t' of Gedeon,
Re 17: 7 t' thee the mystery of the woman,

tellest
Ps 56: 8 Thou t' my wanderings: put thou

telleth
2Sa 7: 11 Also the Lord t' thee that he will
2Ki 6: 12 t' the king of Israel the words that
Ps 41: 6 when he goeth abroad, he t' it.
101: 7 he that t' lies shall not tarry in my
147: 4 He t' the number of the stars; he
Jer 33: 13 the hands of him that t' them,
Joh 12: 22 Philip cometh and t' Andrew: and

telling
J'g 7: 15 Gideon heard the t' of the dream,
2Sa 11: 19 an end of t' the matters of the war
2Ki 8: 5 as he was t' the king how he had

Tel-melah (*tel-me'-lah*)
Ezr 2: 59 were they which went up from T',
Ne 7: 61 they which went up also from T'.

Tema (*te'-mah*)
Ge 25: 15 Hadar, and T', Jetur, Naphish,
1Ch 1: 30 and Dumah, Massa, Hadad, and T',
Job 6: 19 The troops of T' looked, the
Isa 21: 14 inhabitants...of T' brought water
Jer 25: 23 Dedan, and T', and Buz, and all

Teman (*te'-man*) See also TEMANITE.
Ge 36: 11 And the sons of Eliphaz were T',
15 duke T', duke Omar, duke Zepho,
42 Duke Kenaz, duke T', duke Mibzar,
1Ch 1: 36 The sons of Eliphaz; T', and Omar,
53 Duke Kenaz, duke T', duke Mibzar,
Jer 49: 7 Is wisdom no more in T'? is counsel
20 against the inhabitants of T':
Eze 25: 13 I will make it desolate from T';
Am 1: 12 But I will send a fire upon T', which
Ob 9 And thy mighty men, O T', shall be
Hab 3: 3 God came from T', and the Holy

Temani (*te'-ma-ni*) See also TEMANITE.
Ge 36: 34 Husham of the land of T' reigned

Temanite (*te'-man-ite*) See also TEMANI; TEMANITES.
Job 2: 11 Eliphaz the T', and Bildad the
4: 1 Eliphaz the T' answered and said,
15: 1 Then answered Eliphaz the T', and
22: 1 Eliphaz the T' answered and said,
42: 7 the Lord said to Eliphaz the T', My
9 So Eliphaz the T' and Bildad the

Temanites (*te'-man-ites*)
1Ch 1: 45 Husham of the land of the T'

Temeni (*tem'-e-ni*)
1Ch 4: 6 Hepher, and T', and Haahashtari.

temper See also TEMPERED.
Eze 46: 14 hin of oil, to t' with the fine flour;

temperance
Ac 24: 25 as he reasoned of righteousness, t',
Ga 5: 23 Meekness, t': against such there is
2Pe 1: 6 And to knowledge t'; and to
6 and to t' patience; and to patience

temperate
1Co 9: 25 for the mastery is t' in all things.
Tit 1: 8 of good men, sober, just, holy, t';
2: 2 the aged men be sober, grave, t',

tempered See also UNTEMPERED.
Ex 29: 2 and cakes unleavened t' with oil,
30: 35 t' together, pure and holy:
1Co 12: 24 but God hath t' the body together,

tempest
Job 9: 17 For he breaketh me with a t', and
27: 20 t' stealeth him away in the night.
Ps 11: 6 and brimstone, and an horrible t':
55: 8 from the windy storm and t'.
83: 15 So persecute them with thy t', and
Isa 28: 2 strong one, which as a t' of hail
29: 6 and great noise, with storm and t',
30: 30 scattering, and t', and hailstones.
32: 2 the wind, and a covert from the t';
54: 11 O thou afflicted, tossed with t', and
Am 1: 14 a t' in the day of the whirlwind:
Jon 1: 4 there was a mighty t' in the sea,
Jon 1: 12 my sake this great t' is upon you.
M't 8: 24 there arose a great t' in the sea,
Ac 27: 18 being exceedingly tossed with a t',
20 and no small t' lay on us, all hope
Heb 12: 18 blackness, and darkness, and t',
2Pe 2: 17 clouds that are carried with a t';

tempestuous
Ps 50: 3 it shall be very t' round about him.
Jon 1: 11 for the sea wrought, and was t'.
13 wrought, and was t' against them.
Ac 27: 14 there arose against it a t' wind,

temple See also TEMPLES.
1Sa 1: 9 seat by a post of the t' of the Lord.
3: 3 lamp...went out in the t' of the Lord,
2Sa 22: 7 he did hear my voice out of his t',
1Ki 6: 3 the porch before the t' of the house,
5 both of the t' and of the oracle:
17 the t' before it, was forty cubits
33 for the door of the t' posts of olive
7: 21 up the pillars in the porch of the t':
50 doors of the house, to wit, of the t'.
2Ki 11: 10 that were in the t' of the Lord.
11 king, from the right corner of the t'
11 to the left corner of the t', along by
11 along by the altar and the t'.
13 she came to the people into the t'
18: 16 gold from the doors of the t' of the
23: 4 bring forth out of the t' of the Lord
24: 13 had made in the t' of the Lord,
1Ch 6: 10 office in the t' that Solomon built
10: 10 fastened his head in...t' of Dagon.
2Ch 3: 17 reared up the pillars before the t',
4: 7 set them in the t', five on the right
8 and placed them in the t', five on the
22 doors of the house of the t', were of
23: 10 hand, from the right side of the t'
10 to the left side of the t', along by
10 along by the altar and the t', by the
26: 16 went into the t' of the Lord to burn
27: 2 entered not into the t' of the Lord.
29: 16 that they found in the t' of the Lord
35: 20 when Josiah had prepared the t',
36: 7 and put them in his t' at Babylon.
Ezr 3: 6 the foundation of the t' of the Lord
10 the foundation of the t' of the Lord,
4: 1 builded the t' unto the Lord God
5: 14 out of the t' that was in Jerusalem,
14 brought them into the t' of Babylon,
14 king take out of the t' of Babylon,
15 them into the t' that is in Jerusalem,
6: 5 out of the t' which is at Jerusalem,
5 unto the t' which is at Jerusalem,
Ne 6: 10 in the house of God, within the t',
10 and let us shut the doors of the t':
11 go into the t' to save his life?
Ps 5: 7 will I worship toward thy holy t'.
11: 4 The Lord is in his holy t', the Lord's
18: 6 he heard my voice out of his t', and
27: 4 of the Lord, and to enquire in his t'.
29: 9 in his t' doth every one speak of his
48: 9 O God, in the midst of thy t'.
65: 4 of thy house, even of thy holy t'.
68: 29 Because of thy t' at Jerusalem shall
79: 1 thy holy t' have they defiled; they
138: 2 I will worship toward thy holy t',
Isa 6: 1 lifted up, and his train filled the t'.
44: 28 and to the t', Thy foundation shall
66: 6 a voice from the t', a voice of the
Jer 7: 4 words, saying, The t' of the Lord,
4 t' of the Lord, The t' of the Lord,
24: 1 were set before the t' of the Lord,
50: 28 our God, the vengeance of his t'.
51: 11 the Lord, the vengeance of his t'.
Eze 8: 16 at the door of the t' of the Lord,
16 backs toward the t' of the Lord,
41: 1 Afterward he brought me to the t',
4 breadth, twenty cubits, before the t':
15 with the inner t', and the porches of
20 trees made, and on the wall of the t'.
21 The posts of the t' were squared,
23 t' and the sanctuary had two doors.
25 made on them, on the doors of the t',
42: 8 the t' were an hundred cubits.
Da 5: 2 of the t' which was in Jerusalem;
3 out of the t' of the house of God
Am 8: 3 songs of the t' shall be howlings
Jon 2: 4 I will look again toward thy holy t'.
7 came in unto thee, into thine holy t'.
Mic 1: 2 you, the Lord from his holy t'.
Hab 2: 20 But the Lord is in his holy t': let all
Hag 2: 15 upon a stone in the t' of the Lord:
18 foundation of the Lord's t' was laid,
Zec 6: 12 he shall build the t' of the Lord:
13 he shall build the t' of the Lord;
14 for a memorial in the t' of the Lord.
15 come and build in the t' of the Lord,
8: 9 was laid, that the t' might be built.
Mal 3: 1 seek, shall suddenly come to his t',
M't 4: 5 setteth him on a pinnacle of the t',
12: 5 priests in the t' profane...sabbath,
6 this place is one greater than the t'.
21: 12 And Jesus went into the t' of God,
12 them that sold and bought in the t',
14 and the lame came to him in the t';
15 and the children crying in the t',
23 And when he was come into the t',
23: 16 Whosoever shall swear by the t',
16 shall swear by the gold of the t',
17 or the t' that sanctifieth the gold?
21 And whoso shall swear by the t',
35 slew between the t' and the altar.
24: 1 out, and departed from the t':
1 to shew him the buildings of the t'.
26: 55 daily with you teaching in the t',
61 I am able to destroy the t' of God,

M't 27: 5 down the pieces of silver in the t',
40 Thou that destroyest the t', and
51 the veil of the t' was rent in twain
M'r 11: 11 into Jerusalem, and into the t':
15 Jesus went into the t', and began to
15 them that sold and bought in the t',
16 carry any vessel through the t'.
27 as he was walking in the t', there
12: 35 and said, while he taught in the t',
13: 1 as he went out of the t', one of his
3 mount of Olives over against the t',
14: 49 daily with you in the t' teaching,
58 destroy this t'...made with hands,
15: 29 Ah, thou that destroyest the t',
38 the veil of the t' was rent in twain
Lu 1: 9 when he went into the t' of the Lord.
21 that he tarried so long in the t'.
22 that he had seen a vision in the t':
2: 27 he came by the Spirit into the t':
37 which departed not from the t', but
46 three days they found him in the t',
4: 9 and set him on a pinnacle of the t',
11: 51 between the altar and the t':
18: 10 men went up into the t' to pray;
19: 45 And he went into the t', and began
47 And he taught daily in the t'. But
20: 1 as he taught the people in the t',
21: 5 And as some spake of the t', how
37 day time he was teaching in the t';
38 in the morning to him in the t',
22: 52 chief priests, and captains of the t',
53 When I was daily with you in the t',
23: 45 veil of the t' was rent in the midst.
24: 53 And were continually in the t',
Joh 2: 14 found in the t' those that sold oxen
15 he drove them all out of the t',
19 Destroy this t', and in three days
20 six years was this t' in building,
21 But he spake of the t' of his body.
5: 14 Jesus findeth him in the t', and
7: 14 the feast Jesus went up into the t',
28 cried Jesus in the t' as he taught,
8: 2 morning he came again into the t',
20 the treasury, as he taught in the t':
59 hid himself, and went out of the t',
10: 23 Jesus walked in the t' in Solomon's
11: 56 themselves, as they stood in the t',
18: 20 in the synagogue, and in the t',
Ac 2: 46 daily with one accord in the t',
3: 1 John went up together into the t'
2 gate of the t'...is called Beautiful,
2 alms of them that entered...the t';
3 and John about to go into the t'
8 and entered with them into the t',
10 alms at the Beautiful gate of the t':
4: 1 priests, and the captain of the t',
5: 20 and speak in the t' to the people
21 into the t' early in the morning,
24 the captain of the t' and the chief
25 put in prison are standing in the t',
42 daily in the t',and in every house,
19: 27 the t' of the great goddess Diana
21: 26 with them entered into the t',
27 Asia, when they saw him in the t',
28 brought Greeks also into the t',
29 that Paul had brought into the t'.)
30 Paul, and drew him out of the t':
22: 17 while I prayed in the t', I was in a
24: 6 hath gone about to profane the t':
12 And they neither found me in the t'
18 Asia found me purified in the t',
25: 8 neither against the t', nor yet
26: 21 the Jews caught me in the t',
1Co 3: 16 ye not that ye are the t' of God,
17 If any man defile the t' of God,
17 destroy; for the t' of God is holy,
17 of God is holy, which t' ye are.
6: 19 body is the t' of the Holy Ghost
8: 10 knowledge sit at meat in the idol's
9: 13 things live of the things of the t'?
2Co 6: 16 hath the t' of God with idols?
16 for ye are the t' of the living God;
Eph 2: 21 groweth unto an holy t' in the Lord:
2Th 2: 4 he as God sitteth in the t' of God,
Re 3: 12 I make a pillar in the t' of my God,
7: 15 serve him day and night in his t':
11: 1 Rise, and measure the t' of God,
2 the court which is without the t'
19 the t' of God was opened in heaven,
19 was seen in his t' the ark of his
14: 15 another angel came out of the t',
17 another angel came out of the t'
15: 5 t' of the tabernacle of the testimony
6 the seven angels came out of the t',
8 And the t' was filled with smoke
8 no man was able to enter into the t',
16: 1 I heard a great voice out of the t'
17 great voice out of the t' of heaven,
21: 22 I saw no t' therein: for the Lord
22 and the Lamb are the t' of it.

temples
J'g 4: 21 and smote the nail into his t', and
22 lay dead, and the nail was in his t'.
5: 26 pierced and stricken through his t'.
Ca 4: 3 t' are like a piece of a pomegranate
6: 7 a piece of a pomegranate are thy t'
Ho 8: 14 his Maker, and buildeth t';
Joe 3: 5 have carried into your t' my goodly
Ac 7: 48 dwelleth not in t' made with
17: 24 dwelleth not in t' made with hands;

temporal
2Co 4: 18 the things which are seen are t';

tempt See also TEMPTED; TEMPTETH; TEMPTING.
Ge 22: 1 things, that God did t' Abraham,
Ex 17: 2 me? wherefore do ye t' the Lord?
De 6: 16 Ye shall not t' the Lord your God,
Isa 7: 12 not ask, neither will I t' the Lord.
Mal 3: 15 that t' God are even delivered.
M't 4: 7 shalt not t' the Lord thy God.
22: 18 said, Why t' ye me, ye hypocrites?
M'r 12: 15 said unto them, Why t' ye me?
Lu 4: 12 shalt not t' the Lord thy God.
20: 23 and said unto them, Why t' ye me?
Ac 5: 9 to t' the Spirit of the Lord?
15: 10 Now therefore why t' ye God, to
1Co 7: 5 t' you not for your incontinency.
10: 9 Neither let us t' Christ, as some of

temptation See also TEMPTATIONS.
Ps 95: 8 in the day of t' in the wilderness:
M't 6: 13 lead us not into t', but deliver
26: 41 and pray, that ye enter not into t':
M'r 14: 38 ye and pray, lest ye enter into t'.
Lu 4: 13 when the devil had ended all the t',
8: 13 believe, and in time of t' fall away.
11: 4 lead us not into t'; but deliver
22: 40 Pray that ye enter not into t'.
46 rise and pray, lest ye enter into t'.
1Co 10: 13 There hath no t' taken you but such
13 with the t'...make a way to escape,
Ga 4: 14 And my t' which was in my flesh ye
1Ti 6: 9 will be rich fall into t' and a snare,
Heb 3: 8 in the day of t' in the wilderness:
Jas 1: 12 is the man that endureth t':
Re 3: 10 will keep thee from the hour of t',

temptations
De 4: 34 by t', by signs, and by wonders,
7: 19 The great t' which thine eyes saw,
29: 3 The great t' which thine eyes have
Lu 22: 28 have continued with me in my t'.
Ac 20: 19 and t', which befell me by the lying
Jas 1: 2 all joy when ye fall into divers t';
1Pe 1: 6 in heaviness through manifold t':
2Pe 2: 9 how to deliver the godly out of t',

tempted
Ex 17: 7 because they t' the Lord, saying,
Nu 14: 22 and have t' me now these ten times,
De 6: 16 your God, as ye t' him in Massah.
Ps 78: 18 they t' God in their heart by asking
41 they turned back and t' God, and
56 they t' and provoked the most high
95: 9 When your fathers t' me, proved me,
106: 14 wilderness, and t' God in the desert.
M't 4: 1 wilderness to be t' of the devil.
M'r 1: 13 wilderness forty days, t' of Satan;
Lu 4: 2 Being forty days t' of the devil.
10: 25 lawyer stood up, and t' him,
1Co 10: 9 as some of them also t', and were
13 not suffer you to be t' above that ye
Ga 6: 1 thyself, lest thou also be t'.
1Th 3: 5 means the tempter have t' you,
Heb 2: 18 he himself hath suffered being t',
18 is able to succour them that are t'.
3: 9 When your fathers t' me, proved
4: 15 was in all points t' like as we are,
11: 37 they were sawn asunder, were t',
Jas 1: 13 say when he is t', I am t' of God:
13 for God cannot be t' with evil,
14 every man is t', when he is drawn

tempter
M't 4: 3 And when the t' came to him, he
1Th 3: 5 means the t' have tempted you,

tempteth
Jas 1: 13 with evil, neither t' he any man:

tempting
M't 16: 1 and t' desired him that he would
19: 3 came unto him, t' him, and saying
22: 35 asked him a question, t' him,
M'r 8: 11 of him a sign from heaven, t' him.
10: 2 a man to put away his wife? t' him.
Lu 11: 16 others, t' him, sought of him a sign
Joh 8: 6 This they said, t' him, that they

ten See also EIGHTEEN; FOURTEEN; NINETEEN; SEVENTEEN; SIXTEEN; TEN'S; TENS.
Ge 5: 14 were nine hundred and t' years:
16: 3 after Abram had dwelt t' years in
18: 32 Peradventure t' shall be found
24: 10 the servant took t' camels of the
22 hands of t' shekels weight of gold;
55 with us a few days, at the least t';
31: 7 and changed my wages t' times;
41 hast changed my wages t' times.
32: 15 their colts, forty kine, and t' bulls,
15 twenty she asses, and t' foals.
42: 3 Joseph's t' brethren went down to
45: 23 t' asses laden with the good things
23 t' she asses laden with corn and
46: 27 Into Egypt, were threescore and t'.
50: 3 mourned for him threescore and t' days.
22 Joseph lived an hundred and t'
26 being an hundred and t' years old:
Ex 15: 27 and threescore and t' palm trees:
26: 1 with t' curtains of fine twined linen,
16 T' cubits shall be the length of a
27: 12 their pillars t', and their sockets t'.
34: 28 the covenant, the t' commandments.
36: 8 t' curtains of fine twined linen,
21 The length of a board was t' cubits,
38: 12 their pillars t', and their sockets t';
Le 26: 8 you shall put t' thousand to flight:
26 t' women shall bake your bread
27: 5, 7 and for the female t' shekels.
Nu 7: 14 One spoon of t' shekels of gold,
20 One spoon of gold of t' shekels,
26, 32, 38, 44, 50, 56, 62, 68, 74, 80 One
golden spoon of t' shekels, full of
86 weighing t' shekels apiece, after the
11: 19 neither t' days, nor twenty days;
32 gathered least gathered t' homers:
Nu 14: 22 have tempted me now these t' times
29: 23 And on the fourth day t' bullocks,
33: 9 and threescore and t' palm trees;
De 4: 13 perform, even t' commandments;
10: 4 the t' commandments, which the
22 Egypt with threescore and t' persons;
32: 30 and two put t' thousand to flight,
33: 2 he came with t' thousands of saints:
17 are the t' thousands of Ephraim,
Jos 15: 57 t' cities with their villages.
17: 5 there fell t' portions to Manasseh,
21: 5 the half tribe of Manasseh, t' cities.
26 the cities were t' with their suburbs
22: 14 with him t' princes, of each chief
24: 29 being an hundred and t' years old.
J'g 1: 4 of them in Bezek t' thousand men.
7 Threescore and t' kings, having their
2: 8 being an hundred and t' years old.
3: 29 that time about t' thousand men,
4: 6 and take with thee t' thousand men
10 he went up with t' thousand men
14 and t' thousand men after him.
6: 27 Gideon took t' men of his servants,
7: 3 and there remained t' thousand.
8: 30 Gideon had threescore and t' sons
9: 2 which are threescore and t' persons,
4 him threescore and t' pieces of silver
5 being threescore and t' persons,
18 his sons, threescore and t' persons,
24 done to the threescore and t' sons of
12: 11 and he judged Israel t' years.
14 rode on threescore and t' ass colts:
17: 10 I will give thee t' shekels of silver
20: 10 we will take t' men of an hundred
10 and a thousand out of t' thousand,
34 came against Gibeah t' thousand
Ru 1: 4 they dwelled there about t' years.
4: 2 he took t' men of the elders of the
1Sa 1: 8 am not I better to thee than t' sons?
6: 19 thousand and threescore and t' men:
15: 4 and t' thousand men of Judah.
17: 17 these t' loaves, and run to the camp
18 these t' cheeses unto the captain of "
18: 7 and David his t' thousands.
8 ascribed unto David t' thousands,
21: 11 and David his t' thousands?
25: 5 And David sent out t' young men,
38 it came to pass about t' days after,
29: 5 and David his t' thousands?
2Sa 15: 16 And the king left t' women, which
18: 3 thou art worth t' thousand of us:
11 have given thee t' shekels of silver,
15 And t' young men that bare Joab's
19: 43 We have t' parts in the king, and
20: 3 and the king took the t' women his
1Ki 4: 23 T' fat oxen, and twenty oxen out of
5: 14 t' thousand a month by courses:
15 and t' thousand that bare burdens,
6: 3 t' cubits was the breadth thereof
23 cherubims...each t' cubits high.
24 part of the other were t' cubits.
25 And the other cherub was t' cubits:
26 of the one cherub was t' cubits,
7: 10 great stones, stones of t' cubits,
23 t' cubits from the one brim to the
24 t' in a cubit, compassing the sea
27 And he made t' bases of brass; four
37 this manner he made the t' bases:
38 Then made he t' lavers of brass:
38 upon every one of the t' bases one
43 t' bases, and t' lavers on the bases;
11: 31 to Jeroboam, Take thee t' pieces:
31 and will give t' tribes to thee:
35 will give it unto thee, even t' tribes.
14: 3 And take with thee t' loaves and
2Ki 5: 5 took with him t' talents of silver,
5 of gold, and t' changes of raiment.
13: 7 but fifty horsemen, and t' chariots,
7 and t' thousand footmen;
14: 7 in the valley of salt t' thousand,
15: 17 and reigned t' years in Samaria.
20: 9 the shadow go forward t' degrees,
9 degrees, or go back t' degrees?
10 the shadow to go down t' degrees:
10 shadow return backward t' degrees.
11 the shadow t' degrees backward,
24: 14 valour, even t' thousand captives,
25: 25 and t' men with him, and smote
1Ch 6: 61 tribe of Manasseh, by lot, t' cities.
21: 5 t' thousand men that drew sword:
29: 7 talents and t' thousand drams,
7 and of silver t' thousand talents,
2Ch 2: 2 t' thousand men to bear burdens,
18 t' thousand of them to be bearers of
4: 1 and t' cubits the height thereof.
2 a molten sea of t' cubits from brim
3 t' in a cubit, compassing the sea
6 He made also t' lavers, and put five
7 And he made t' candlesticks of gold
8 He made also t' tables, and placed
14: 1 his days the land was quiet t' years.
25: 11 of the children of Seir t' thousand.
12 And other t' thousand left alive did
27: 5 and t' thousand measures of wheat,
5 of wheat, and t' thousand of barley.
29: 32 was threescore and t' bullocks, an
30: 24 bullocks and t' thousand sheep:
36: 9 reigned three months and t' days in
21 to fulfil threescore and t' years.
Ezr 1: 10 a second sort four hundred and t',
8: 12 with him an hundred and t' males.
24 and t' of their brethren with them,
Ne 4: 12 they said unto us t' times, From all
5: 18 once in t' days store of all sorts of
11: 1 bring one of t' to dwell in Jerusalem
Es 3: 9 will pay t' thousand talents of silver

Es 9:10 The t' sons of Haman the son of
12 palace, and the t' sons of Haman;
13 let Haman's t' sons be hanged upon
14 and they hanged Haman's t' sons.
Job 19: 3 t' times have ye reproached me: ye
Ps 3: 6 be afraid of t' thousands of people,
33: 2 and an instrument of t' strings.
90: 10 our years are threescore years and t';
91: 7 and t' thousand at thy right hand;
92: 3 Upon an instrument of t' strings,
144: 9 instrument of t' strings will I sing
13 and t' thousands in our streets:
Ec 7:19 the wise more than t' mighty men
Ca 5:10 the chiefest among t' thousand.
Isa 5:10 t' acres of vineyard shall yield one
38: 8 dial of Ahaz, t' degrees backward.
8 So the sun returned t' degrees, by
Jer 41: 1 even t' men with him, came unto
2 and the t' men that were with him,
8 But t' men were found among them
42: 7 And it came to pass after t' days,
Eze 40:11 of the entry of the gate, t' cubits;
41: 2 breadth of the door was t' cubits;
42: 4 chambers was a walk of t' cubits
45: 1 the breadth shall be t' thousand.
3 and the breadth of t' thousand:
5 and the t' thousand of breadth,
14 cor, which is an homer of t' baths;
14 for t' baths are an homer:
48: 9 and of t' thousand in breadth.
10 the west t' thousand in breadth,
10 the east t' thousand in breadth,
13 length, and t' thousand in breadth:
13 and the breadth t' thousand.
18 shall be t' thousand eastward,
18 and t' thousand westward:
Da 1:12 Prove thy servants,...t' days;
14 matter, and proved them t' days.
15 end of t' days their countenances
20 he found them t' times better than
7: 7 before it; and it had t' horns.
10 t' thousand times t' thousand
20 the t' horns that were in his head,
24 And the t' horns out of this kingdom
24 are t' kings that shall arise:
11:12 cast down many t' thousands:
Am 5: 3 forth by an hundred shall leave t',
6: 9 there remain t' men in one house,
Mic 6: 7 with t' thousands of rivers of oil?
Hag 2:16 twenty measures, there were...t':
Zec 1:12 these threescore and t' years?
5: 2 and the breadth thereof t' cubits.
8:23 t' men shall take hold out of all
M't 18:24 owed him t' thousand talents.
20:24 the t' heard it, they were moved
25: 1 of heaven be likened unto t' virgins,
28 it unto him which hath t' talents.
M'r 10:41 when the t' heard it, they began to
Lu 14:31 able with t' thousand to meet him
15: 8 woman having t' pieces of silver,
17:12 met him t' men that were lepers,
17 said, Were there not t' cleansed?
19:13 And he called his t' servants, and
13 and delivered them t' pounds, and
16 thy pound hath gained t' pounds.
17 have thou authority over t' cities.
24 give it to him that hath t' pounds.
25 unto him, Lord, he hath t' pounds.)
Ac 23:23 and horsemen threescore and t',
25: 6 among them more than t' days,
1Co 4:15 ye have t' thousand instructers in
14:19 t' thousand words in an unknown
Jude 14 with t' thousands of his saints,
Re 2:10 ye shall have tribulation t' days:
5:11 was t' thousand times t' thousand,
12: 3 having seven heads and t' horns,
13: 1 having seven heads and t' horns,
1 and upon his horns t' crowns, and
17: 3 having seven heads and t' horns.
7 hath the seven heads and t' horns.
12 t' horns...thou sawest are t' kings,
16 the t' horns which thou sawest

tend See also ATTEND; CONTEND; EXTEND; INTEND; TENDETH.
Pr 21: 5 the diligent t' only to plenteousness;

tender See also TENDERHEARTED.
Ge 18: 7 and fetcht a calf t' and good, and
29:17 Leah was t' eyed; but Rachel was
33:13 knoweth that the children are t',
De 28:54 that the man that is t' among you,
56 The t' and delicate woman among
32: 2 as the small rain upon the t' herb, and
2Sa 23: 4 t' grass springing out of the earth
2Ki 22:19 Because thine heart was t', and
1Ch 22: 5 Solomon my son is young and t',
29: 1 Solomon...is yet young and t',
2Ch 34:27 Because thine heart was t', and
Job 14: 7 t' branch thereof will not cease.
38:27 the bud of the t' herb to spring forth?
Ps 25: 6 Remember, O Lord, thy t' mercies
40:11 Withhold not thou thy t' mercies from
51: 1 unto the multitude of thy t' mercies
69:16 to the multitude of thy t' mercies.
77: 9 he in anger shut up his t' mercies?
79: 8 let thy t' mercies speedily prevent us:
103: 4 with lovingkindness and t' mercies;
119: 77 Let thy t' mercies come unto me, that
156 Great are thy t' mercies, O Lord:
145: 9 his t' mercies are over all his works.
Pr 4: 3 t' and only beloved in the sight of
12:10 the t' mercies of the wicked are cruel.
27:25 and the t' grass sheweth itself, and
Ca 2:13 with the t' grape give a good smell.
15 vines: for our vines have t' grapes.
7:12 whether the t' grape appear,
Isa 47: 1 thou shalt no more be called t' and
53: 2 grow up before him as a t' plant,
Eze 17:22 the top of his young twigs a t' one,
Da 1: 9 Daniel into favour and t' love
4:15, 23 brass, in the t' grass of the field;
M't 24:32 When his branch is yet t', and
M'r 13:28 When her branch is yet t', and
Lu 1:78 Through the t' mercy of our God;
Jas 5:11 is very pitiful, and of t' mercy.

tender-eyed See TENDER and EYED.

tenderhearted
2Ch 13: 7 Rehoboam was young and t',
Eph 4:32 t', forgiving one another, even as

tenderness
De 28:56 ground for delicateness and t',

tendeth
Pr 10:16 The labour of the righteous t' to life:
11:19 As righteousness t' to life: so he that
24 more than is meet, but it t' to poverty.
14:23 the talk of the lips t' only to penury.
19:23 The fear of the Lord t' to life: and he

tenons
Ex 26:17 Two t' shall there be in one board,
19 under one board for his two t',
19 under another board for his two t'.
36:22 One board had two t', equally
24 under one board for his two t',
24 under another board for his two t'.

tenor
Ge 43: 7 according to the t' of these words:
Ex 34:27 for after the t' of these words I have

ten's
Ge 18:32 I will not destroy it for t' sake.

tens
Ex 18:21 rulers of fifties, and rulers of t':
25 rulers of fifties, and rulers of t'.
De 1:15 over fifties, and captains over t',

tent See also TENTMAKERS; TENTS.
Ge 9:21 and he was uncovered within his t'.
12: 8 pitched his t', having Beth-el on the
13: 3 place where his t' had been at the
12 and pitched his t' toward Sodom.
18 Then Abram removed his t', and
18: 1 he sat in the t' door in the heat of
2 he ran to meet them from the t' door,
6 Abraham hastened into the t' unto
9 wife? And he said, Behold, in the t'.
10 And Sarah heard it in the t' door,
24:67 her into his mother Sarah's t',
26:17 pitched his t' in the valley of Gerar,
25 the Lord, and pitched his t' there:
31:25 Now Jacob had pitched his t' in the
33 into Jacob's t', and into Leah's t',
33 Then went he out of Leah's t',
33 and entered into Rachel's t'.
34 And Laban searched all the t', but
33:18 and pitched his t' before the city.
19 a field, where he had spread his t',
35:21 and spread his t' beyond the tower of
Ex 18: 7 welfare; and they came into the t'.
26:11 couple the t' together, that it may be
12 remaineth of the curtains of the t',
13 in the length of the curtains of the t',
14 a covering for the t' of rams' skins
36 an hanging for the door of the t',
33: 8 and stood every man at his t' door,
10 worshipped, every man in his t' door.
35:11 The tabernacle, his t', and his
36:14 made curtains of goats' hair for the t'
18 of brass to couple the t' together,
19 a covering for the t' of rams' skins
39:32 the t' of the congregation finished:
33 the tabernacle unto Moses, the t', and
40 for the t' of the congregation,
40: 2, 6 of the t' of the congregation.
7 between the t' of the congregation
19 abroad the t' over the tabernacle,
19 and put the covering of the t' above
22 table in the t' of the congregation,
24 candlestick in...t' of...congregation,
26 altar in the t' of the congregation
29 of the t' of the congregation,
30 between the t' of the congregation
32 went into the t' of the congregation,
34 covered the t' of the congregation,
35 enter into the t' of the congregation,
Le 14: 8 tarry abroad out of his t' seven days.
Nu 3:25 shall be the tabernacle, and the t',
9:15 namely, the t' of the testimony:
11:10 every man in the door of his t':
19:14 is the law, when a man dieth in a t':
14 into the t', and all that is in the t',
18 the water, and sprinkle it upon the t',
25: 8 after the man of Israel into the t',
Jos 7:21 in the earth in the midst of my t',
22 they ran unto the t'; and, behold,
22 it was hid in his t', and the silver
23 took them out of the midst of the t',
24 and his t', and all that he had:
J'g 4:11 his t' unto the plain of Zaanaim,
17 Sisera fled away on his feet to the t'
18 he had turned in unto her into the t',
20 Stand in the door of the t', and it
21 Heber's wife took a nail of the t',
22 And when he came into her t', behold,
5:24 shall she be above women in the t'.
7: 8 rest of Israel every man unto his t',
13 host of Midian, and came unto a t',
13 overturned it, that the t' lay along.
20: 8 We will not any of us go to his t',
1Sa 4:10 and they fled every man into his t':
13: 2 people he sent every man to his t'.
1Sa 17:54 but he put his armour in his t'.
2Sa 7: 6 walked in a t' and in a tabernacle.
16:22 So they spread Absalom a t' upon
18:17 all Israel fled every one to his t'.
19: 8 Israel had fled every man to his t'.
20:22 from the city, every man to his t'.
2Ki 7: 8 they went into one t', and did eat
8 again, and entered into another t',
1Ch 15: 1 ark of God, and pitched for it a t'.
16: 1 and set it in the midst of the t' that
17: 5 but have gone from t' to t', and
2Ch 1: 4 had pitched a t' for it at Jerusalem.
25:22 and they fled every man to his t'.
Ps 78:60 the t' which he placed among men;
Isa 13:20 shall the Arabian pitch t' there;
38:12 from me as a shepherd's t':
40:22 them out as a t' to dwell in:
54: 2 Enlarge the place of thy t', and let
Jer 10:20 none to stretch forth my t' any more,
37:10 they rise up every man in his t',

tent-door See TENT and DOOR.

tenth
Ge 8: 5 continually until the t' month:
5 in the t' month, on the first day of
28:22 I will surely give the t' unto thee.
Ex 12: 3 In the t' day of this month they
16:36 an omer is the t' part of an ephah.
29:40 with the one lamb a t' deal of flour
Le 5:11 t' part of an ephah of fine flour
6:20 the t' part of an ephah of fine flour
14:10 three t' deals of fine flour for a
21 one t' deal of fine flour mingled
16:29 month, on the t' day of the month,
23:13 two t' deals of fine flour mingled
17 two wave loaves of two t' deals:
27 Also on the t' day of this seventh
24: 5 two t' deals shall be in one cake.
25: 9 the t' day of the seventh month,
27:32 the t' shall be holy unto the Lord.
Nu 5:15 the t' part of an ephah of barley
7:66 On the t' day Ahiezer the son of
15: 4 meat offering of a t' deal of flour
6 meat offering two t' deals of flour
9 offering of three t' deals of flour
18:21 children of Levi...the t' in Israel
26 Lord, even a t' part of the tithe.
28: 5 a t' part of an ephah of flour for a
9 two t' deals of flour for a meat
12 three t' deals of flour for a meat
12 and two t' deals of flour for a meat
13 a several t' deal of flour mingled
20 three t' deals shall ye offer for a
20 and two t' deals for a ram;
21 A several t' deal shalt thou offer
28 oil, three t' deals unto one bullock,
28 bullock, two t' deals unto one ram,
29 A several t' deal unto one lamb,
29: 3 oil, three t' deals for a bullock,
3 bullock, and two t' deals for a ram,
4 And one t' deal for one lamb,
7 on the t' day of this seventh month
9 oil, three t' deals to a bullock,
9 and two t' deals to one ram,
10 A several t' deal for one lamb,
14 three t' deals unto every bullock of
14 two t' deals to each ram of the two
15 a several t' deal to each lamb of
De 23: 2 even to his t' generation shall he
3 even to their t' generation shall
Jos 4:19 on the t' day of the first month,
1Sa 8:15 he will take the t' of your seed,
17 He will take the t' of your sheep:
2Ki 25: 1 year of his reign, in the t' month,
1 in the t' day of the month, that
1Ch 12:13 Jeremiah the t', Machbanai the
24:11 to Jeshuah, the t' to Shecaniah,
25:17 t' to Shimei, he, his sons, and his
27:13 The t' captain for the t' month was
Ezr 10:16 down in the first day of the t' month
Es 2:16 into his house royal in the t' month,
Isa 6:13 But yet in it shall be a t', and it
Jer 32: 1 t' year of Zedekiah king of Judah,
39: 1 t' month, came Nebuchadrezzar
52: 4 year of his reign, in the t' month,
4 in the t' day of the month, that
12 month, in the t' day of the month,
Eze 20: 1 month, the t' day of the month, that
24: 1 in the ninth year, in the t' month,
1 in the t' day of the month, the
29: 1 In the t' year, in the t' month,
33:21 in the t' month, in the fifth day of
40: 1 year, in the t' day of the month,
45:11 contain the t' part of an homer,
11 the ephah the t' part of an homer:
14 the t' part of a bath out of the cor,
Zec 8:19 and the fast of the t', shall be to
Joh 1:39 day: for it was about the t' hour.
Heb 7: 2 also Abraham gave a t' part of all;
4 Abraham gave the t' of the spoils.
Re 11:13 and the t' part of the city fell, and
21:20 a topaz; the t', a chrysoprasus;

tenth-deal See TENTH and DEAL.

ten-thousand See TEN and THOUSAND.

tentmakers
Ac 18: 3 by their occupation they were t'.

tents
Ge 4:20 the father of such as dwell in t',
9:27 and he shall dwell in the t' of Shem;
13: 5 Abram, had flocks, and herds, and t'.
25:27 was a plain man, dwelling in t'.
31:33 and into the two maidservants' t';
Ex 16:16 man for them which are in his t'.
Nu 1:52 children of Israel shall pitch their t',
9:17 the children of Israel pitched their t'

Nu 9:18 tabernacle they rested in their *t*'.
20 of the Lord they abode in their *t*'.
22 children of Israel abode in their *t*'.
23 of the Lord they rested in the *t*'.
13:19 whether in *t*', or in strong holds;
16:26 from the *t*' of these wicked men.
27 out, and stood in the door of their *t*',
24: 2 saw Israel abiding in his *t*' according
5 How goodly are thy *t*', O Jacob.
De 1:27 And ye murmured in your *t*', and
33 you out a place to pitch your *t*' in.
5:30 to them, Get you into your *t*' again.
11: 6 their households, and their *t*', and
16: 7 in the morning, and go unto thy *t*'.
33:18 going out; and, Issachar, in thy *t*'.
Jos 3:14 the people removed from their *t*',
22: 4 return ye, and get you unto your *t*',
6 away: and they went unto their *t*'.
7 sent them away also unto their *t*',
8 with much riches unto your *t*', and
J'g 6: 5 came up with their cattle and their *t*',
8:11 by the way of them that dwelt in *t*'
1Sa 17:53 Philistines, and...spoiled their *t*'.
2Sa 11:11 Israel, and Judah, abide in *t*';
20: 1 every man to his *t*', O Israel.
1Ki 8:66 went unto their *t*' joyful and glad
12:16 to your *t*', O Israel: now see to thine
16 So Israel departed unto their *t*'.
2Ki 7: 7 left their *t*', and their horses, and
10 asses tied, and the *t*' as they were.
16 and spoiled the *t*' of the Syrians.
8:21 and the people fled into their *t*'.
13: 5 children of Israel dwelt in their *t*',
14:12 and they fled every man to their *t*'.
1Ch 4:41 smote their *t*', and the habitations
5:10 they dwelt in their *t*' throughout all
2Ch 7:10 he sent the people away into their *t*',
10:16 every man to your *t*', O Israel:
16 So all Israel went to their *t*'.
14:15 They smote also the *t*' of cattle, and
31: 2 in the gates of the *t*' of the Lord.
Ezr 8:15 there abode we in *t*' three days:
Ps 69:25 and let none dwell in their *t*'.
78:55 tribes of Israel to dwell in their *t*'.
84:10 than to dwell in the *t*' of wickedness.
106:25 But murmured in their *t*', and
120: 5 that I dwell in the *t*' of Kedar!
Ca 1: 5 as the *t*' of Kedar, as the curtains of
8 thy kids beside the shepherds' *t*'.
Jer 4:20 suddenly are my *t*' spoiled, and my
6: 3 they shall pitch their *t*' against her
30:18 again the captivity of Jacob's *t*',
35: 7 but all your days ye shall dwell in *t*';
10 But we have dwelt in *t*', and have
49:29 Their *t*' and their flocks shall they
Hab 3: 7 I saw the *t*' of Cushan in affliction:
Zec 12: 7 also shall save the *t*' of Judah first,
14:15 the beasts that shall be in these *t*'.

Terah (*te'-rah*) See also THARA.
Ge 11:24 and twenty years, and begat *T*':
25 And Nahor lived after he begat *T*'
26 *T*' lived seventy years, and begat
27 these are the generations of *T*':
27 *T*' begat Abram, Nahor, and Haran;
28 Haran died before his father *T*' in
31 *T*' took Abram his son, and Lot
32 days of *T*' were two hundred and
32 five years: and *T*' died in Haran.
Jos 24: 2 even *T*', the father of Abraham,
1Ch 1:26 Serug, Nahor, *T*',

teraphim (*ter'-af-im*)
J'g 17: 5 and made an ephod, and *t*', and
18:14 is in these houses an ephod, and *t*',
17 image, and the ephod, and the *t*',
18 carved image, the ephod, and the *t*',
20 and he took the ephod, and the *t*',
Hos 3: 4 without an ephod, and without *t*':

Teresh (*te'-resh*)
Es 2:21 chamberlains, Bigthan and *T*',
6: 2 had told of Bigthana and *T*',

termed
Isa 62: 4 Thou shalt no more be *t*' Forsaken;
4 thy land any more be *t*' Desolate:

terraces
2Ch 9:11 king made of the algum trees *t*'

terrestrial
1Co 15:40 also celestial bodies, and bodies *t*':
40 and the glory of the *t*' is another.

terrible
Ex 34:10 for it is a *t*' thing that I will do
De 1:19 all that great and *t*' wilderness,
7:21 is among you, a mighty God and *t*'.
8:15 through...great and *t*' wilderness,
10:17 a great God, a mighty, and a *t*',
21 for thee these great and *t*' things,
J'g 13: 6 of an angel of God, very *t*':
2Sa 7:23 to do for you great things and *t*',
Ne 1: 5 of heaven, the great and *t*' God,
4:14 the Lord, which is great and *t*',
9:32 great, the mighty, and the *t*' God,
Job 37:22 the north: with God is *t*' majesty.
39:20 the glory of his nostrils is *t*'.
41:14 face? his teeth are *t*' round about.
Ps 45: 4 hand shall teach thee *t*' things.
47: 2 For the Lord most high is *t*'; he is
65: 5 By *t*' things in righteousness wilt
66: 3 God, How *t* art thou in thy works!
5 he is *t*' in his doing toward the
68:35 O God, thou art *t*' out of thy holy
76:12 he is *t*' to the kings of the earth.
99: 3 them praise thy great and *t*' name;
106:22 Ham, and *t*' things by the Red sea.
145: 6 speak of the might of thy *t*' acts:
Ca 6: 4 *t*' as an army with banners.
6:10 and *t*' as an army with banners?
Isa 13:11 lay low the haughtiness of the *t*'.
18: 2 to a people *t*' from their beginning
7 to a people *t*' from their beginning
21: 1 from the desert, from a *t*' land.
25: 3 the city of the *t*' nations shall fear
4 the blast of the *t*' ones is as a storm
5 the branch of the *t*' ones shall be
29: 5 multitude of the *t*' ones shall be as
20 For the *t*' one is brought to nought,
49:25 the prey of the *t*' shall be delivered:
64: 3 When thou didst *t*' things which we
Jer 15:21 thee out of the hand of the *t*'.
20:11 Lord is with me as a mighty *t*' one:
La 5:10 an oven because of the *t*' famine.
Eze 1:22 was as the colour of the *t*' crystal,
28: 7 upon thee, the *t*' of the nations:
30:11 with him, the *t*' of the nations,
31:12 the *t*' of the nations, have cut him
32:12 the *t*' of the nations, all of them:
Da 2:31 thee; and the form thereof was *t*'.
7: 7 a fourth beast, dreadful and *t*',
Joe 2:11 day of the Lord is great and very *t*';
31 the great and the *t*' day of the Lord
Hab 1: 7 They are *t*' and dreadful: their
Zep 2:11 The Lord will be *t*' unto them:
Heb 12:21 so *t*' was the sight, that Moses

terribleness
De 26: 8 and with great *t*', and with signs,
1Ch 17:21 thee a name of greatness and *t*',
Jer 49:16 Thy *t*' hath deceived thee, and the

terribly
Isa 2:19, 21 he ariseth to shake *t*' the earth.
Na 2: 3 and the fir trees shall be *t*' shaken.

terrified
De 20: 3 neither be ye *t*' because of them;
Lu 21: 9 of wars and commotions, be not *t*':
24:37 But they were *t*' and affrighted,
Ph'p 1:28 in nothing *t*' by your adversaries:

terrifiest
Job 7:14 dreams, and *t*' me through visions:

terrify See also TERRIFIED; TERRIFIEST.
Job 3: 5 let the blackness of the day *t*' it.
9:34 from me, and let not his fear *t*' me:
31:34 the contempt of families *t*' me,
2Co 10: 9 seem as if I would *t*' you by letters.

terror See also TERRORS.
Ge 35: 5 the *t*' of God was upon the cities
Le 26:16 I will even appoint over you *t*',
De 32:25 The sword without, and *t*' within,
34:12 the great *t*' which Moses shewed
Jos 2: 9 and that your *t*' is fallen upon us,
Job 31:23 destruction from God was a *t*' to
33: 7 my *t*' shall not make thee afraid,
Ps 91: 5 not be afraid for the *t*' by night;
Isa 10:33 hosts, shall lop the bough with *t*':
19:17 of Judah shall be a *t*' unto Egypt,
33:18 Thine heart shall meditate *t*'.
54:14 and from *t*'; for it shall not come
Jer 17:17 Be not a *t*' unto me: thou art my
20: 4 I will make thee a *t*' to thyself,
32:21 strong hand,...and with great *t*';
Eze 26:17 which cause their *t*' to be on all
21 I will make thee a *t*', and thou
27:36 thou shalt be a *t*', and never shalt
28:19 thou shalt be a *t*', and never shalt
32:23 which caused *t*' in the land of the
24 which caused their *t*' in the land of
25 their *t*' was caused in the land of
26 they caused their *t*' in the land of
27 the *t*' of the mighty in the land of
30 with their *t*' they are ashamed of
32 I have caused my *t*' in the land of
Ro 13: 3 rulers are not a *t*' to good works,
2Co 5:11 Knowing...the *t*' of the Lord, we
1Pe 3:14 be not afraid of their *t*', neither be

terrors
De 4:34 stretched out arm, and by great *t*',
Job 6: 4 *t*' of God do set themselves in
18:11 *T*' shall make him afraid on every
14 shall bring him to the king of *t*'.
20:25 out of his gall: *t*' are upon him.
24:17 in the *t*' of the shadow of death.
27:20 *T*' take hold on him as waters, a
30:15 *T*' are turned upon me: they
Ps 55: 4 the *t*' of death are fallen upon me.
73:19 they are utterly consumed with *t*'.
88:15 while I suffer thy *t*' I am distracted.
16 over me; thy *t*' have cut me off.
Jer 15: 8 it suddenly, and *t*' upon the city.
La 2:22 a solemn day my *t*' round about,
Eze 21:12 *t*' by reason of the sword shall be

Tertius (*tur'-she-us*)
Ro 16:22 I *T*', who wrote this epistle,

Tertullus (*tur-tul'-lus*)
Ac 24: 1 with a certain orator named *T*',
2 *T*' began to accuse him, saying,

testament
M't 26:28 For this is my blood of the new *t*',
M'r 14:24 This is my blood of the new *t*',
Lu 22:20 This cup is the new *t*' in my blood,
1Co 11:25 This cup is the new *t*' in my blood:
2Co 3: 6 us able ministers of the new *t*';
14 away in the reading of the old *t*';
Heb 7:22 Jesus made a surety of a better *t*'.
9:15 he is the mediator of the new *t*',
15 that were under the first *t*',
16 For where a *t*' is, there must also
17 For a *t*' is of force after men are
18 Whereupon neither the first *t*' was
20 This is the blood of the *t*' which
Re 11:19 seen in his temple the ark of his *t*':

testator
Heb 9:16 necessity be the death of the *t*'.
17 strength at all while the *t*' liveth.

testified See also TESTIFIEDST.
Ex 21:29 and it hath been *t*' to his owner,
De 19:18 hath *t*' falsely against his brother;
Ru 1:21 seeing the Lord hath *t*' against me,
2Sa 1:16 for thy mouth hath *t*' against thee,
2Ki 17:13 Yet the Lord *t*' against Israel, and
15 his testimonies which he *t*' against
2Ch 24:19 Lord; and they *t*' against them:
Ne 9:26 slew thy prophets which *t*' against
13:15 and I *t*' against them in the day
21 Then I *t*' against them, and said
Joh 4:39 the saying of the woman, which *t*',
44 For Jesus himself *t*', that a prophet
13:21 he was troubled in spirit, and *t*',
Ac 8:25 they had *t*' and preached the word
18: 5 *t*' to the Jews that Jesus was
23:11 as thou hast *t*' of me in Jerusalem,
28:23 and *t*' the kingdom of God,
1Co 15:15 we have *t*' of God that he raised
1Th 4: 6 also have forewarned you and *t*'.
1Ti 2: 6 ransom for all, to be *t*' in due time.
Heb 2: 6 But one in a certain place *t*',
1Pe 1:11 it *t*' beforehand the sufferings of
1Jo 5: 9 God which he hath *t*' of his Son.
3Jo 3 and *t*' of the truth that is in thee,

testifiedst
Ne 9:29 And *t*' against them, that thou
30 *t*' against them by thy spirit in thy

testifieth
Ho 7:10 the pride of Israel *t*' to his face:
Joh 3:32 hath seen and heard, that he *t*';
21:24 disciple which *t*' of these things,
Heb 7:17 For he *t*', Thou art a priest for ever
Re 22:20 He which *t*' these things saith,

testify See also TESTIFIED; TESTIFIETH; TESTIFYING.
Nu 35:30 one witness shall not *t*' against
De 8:19 I *t*' against you this day that ye
19:16 to *t*' against him that which is
31:21 this song shall *t*' against them as a
32:46 words which I *t*' among you this
Ne 9:34 thou didst *t*' against them.
Job 15: 6 yea, thine own lips *t*' against thee.
Ps 50: 7 Israel, and I will *t*' against thee:
81: 8 my people, and I will *t*' unto thee:
Isa 59:12 thee, and our sins *t*' against us:
Jer 14: 7 though our iniquities *t*' against us,
Ho 5: 5 pride of Israel doth *t*' to his face:
Am 3:13 and *t*' in the house of Jacob, saith
Mic 6: 3 I wearied thee? *t*' against me.
Lu 16:28 that he may *t*' unto them, lest
Joh 2:25 not that any should *t*' of man;
3:11 know, and *t*' that we have seen;
5:39 and they are they which *t*' of me.
7: 7 me it hateth, because I *t*' of it,
15:26 from the Father, he shall *t*' of me:
Ac 2:40 other words did he *t*' and exhort,
10:42 to *t*' that it is he which was
20:24 to *t*' the gospel of the grace of God.
26: 5 if they would *t*', that after the
Ga 5: 3 For I *t*' again to every man that is
Eph 4:17 *t*' in the Lord, that ye henceforth
1Jo 4:14 and do *t*' that the Father sent the
Re 22:16 sent mine angel to *t*' unto you
18 I *t*' unto every man that heareth

testifying
Ac 20:21 *T*' both to the Jews, and also to
Heb 11: 4 was righteous, God *t*' of his gifts:
1Pe 5:12 and *t*' that this is the true grace

testimonies
De 4:45 These are the *t*', and the statutes,
6:17 his *t*', and his statutes, which he
20 What mean the *t*', and the statutes,
1Ki 2: 3 his judgments, and his *t*', as it is
2Ki 17:15 his *t*' which he testified against
23: 3 keep his commandments and his *t*'
1Ch 29:19 keep thy commandments, thy *t*',
2Ch 34:31 keep his commandments, and his *t*',
Ne 9:34 thy commandments and thy *t*',
Ps 25:10 as keep his covenant and his *t*'.
78:56 high God, and kept not his *t*':
93: 5 Thy *t*' are very sure: holiness
99: 7 they kept his *t*', and the ordinance
119: 2 Blessed are they that keep his *t*',
14 have rejoiced in the way of thy *t*',
22 contempt; for I have kept thy *t*'.
24 Thy *t*' also are my delight and my
31 I have stuck unto thy *t*': O Lord,
36 Incline my heart unto thy *t*', and
46 I will speak of thy *t*' also before
59 and turned my feet unto thy *t*'.
79 and those that have known thy *t*'.
95 me: but I will consider thy *t*'.
99 for thy *t*' are my meditation.
111 Thy *t*' have I taken as an heritage
119 dross: therefore I love thy *t*'.
125 that I may know thy *t*'.
129 Thy *t*' are wonderful: therefore
138 Thy *t*' that thou hast commanded
144 The righteousness of thy *t*' is
146 save me, and I shall keep thy *t*'.
152 Concerning thy *t*', I have known of
157 yet do I not decline from thy *t*'.
167 My soul hath kept thy *t*'; and I
168 I have kept thy precepts and thy *t*':
Jer 44:23 nor in his statutes, nor in his *t*';

testimony See also TESTIMONIES.
Ex 16:34 so Aaron laid it up before the *T*',
25:16 thou shalt put into the ark the *t*'
21 in the ark thou shalt put the *t*'

Ex 25:22 which are upon the ark of the t',
26:33 within the vail the ark of the t':
34 mercy seat upon the ark of the t'
27:21 the vail, which is before the t',
30: 6 the vail that is by the ark of the t',
6 the mercy seat that is over the t',
26 therewith, and the ark of the t',
36 of it before the t' in the tabernacle
31: 7 the ark of the t', and the mercy seat
18 two tables of t', tables of stone,
32:15 the two tables of the t' were in his
34:29 the two tables of t' in Moses' hand,
38:21 even of the tabernacle of t', as it
39:35 The ark of the t', and the staves
40: 3 shalt put therein the ark of the t',
5 the incense before the ark of the t',
20 he took and put the t' into the ark,
21 and covered the ark of the t':
Le 16:13 the mercy seat that is upon the t',
24: 3 Without the vail of the t', in the
Nu 1:50 Levites over the tabernacle of t',
53 round about the tabernacle of t',
53 the charge of the tabernacle of t'.
4: 5 vail, and cover the ark of t' with it:
7:89 seat that was upon the ark of t',
9:15 namely, the tent of the t':
10:11 up from off the tabernacle of the t'.
17: 4 of the congregation before the t',
10 Bring Aaron's rod again before...t',
Jos 4:16 priests that bear the ark of the t',
Ru 4: 7 and this was a t' in Israel.
2Ki 11:12 upon him, and gave him the t';
2Ch 23:11 him the crown, and gave him the t',
Ps 19: 7 the t' of the Lord is sure, making
78: 5 he established a t' in Jacob, and
81: 5 he ordained in Joseph for a t',
119:88 so shall I keep the t' of thy mouth.
122: 4 unto the t' of Israel, to give thanks
132:12 and my t' that I shall teach them,
Isa 8:16 Bind up the t', seal the law among
20 To the law and to the t': if they
M't 8: 4 commanded, for a t' unto them.
10:18 a t' against them and the Gentiles.
M'r 1:44 commanded, for a t' unto them.
6:11 your feet for a t' against them.
13: 9 for my sake, for a t' against them.
Lu 5:14 commanded, for a t' unto them.
9: 5 your feet for a t' against them.
21:13 And it shall turn to you for a t'.
Joh 3:32 and no man receiveth his t'.
33 He that hath received his t' hath
5:34 But I receive not t' from man: but
8:17 law, that the t' of two men is true.
21:24 and we know that his t' is true.
Ac 13:22 to whom also he gave t', and said,
14: 3 which gave t' unto the word of his
22:18 not receive thy t' concerning me.
1Co 1: 6 Even as the t' of Christ was
2: 1 declaring unto you the t' of God.
2Co 1:12 is this, the t' of our conscience,
2Th 1:10 our t' among you was believed)
2Ti 1: 8 ashamed of the t' of our Lord,
Heb 3: 5 a t' of those things which were to be
11: 5 had this t', that he pleased God.
Re 1: 2 God, and of the t' of Jesus Christ,
9 God, and for the t' of Jesus Christ.
6: 9 God, and for the t' which they held:
11: 7 they shall have finished their t',
12:11 Lamb, and by the word of their t';
17 God, and have the t' of Jesus Christ.
15: 5 the tabernacle of the t' in heaven
19:10 brethren that have the t' of Jesus:
10 t' of Jesus is the spirit of prophecy.

tetrarch
M't 14: 1 Herod the t' heard of the fame of
Lu 3: 1 and Herod being t' of Galilee, and
1 his brother Philip t' of Ituræa and
1 and Lysanias the t' of Abilene,
19 Herod the t', being reproved by
9: 7 Herod the t' heard of all that was
Ac 13: 1 been brought up with Herod the t'.

Thaddæus (*thad-de'-us*) See also JUDE; LEBBÆUS.
M't 10: 3 Lebbæus, whose surname was T';
M'r 3:18 the son of Alphæus, and T', and

Thahash (*tha'-hash*)
Ge 22:24 Gaham, and T', and Maachah.

Thamah (*tha'-mah*) See also TAMAH.
Ezr 2:53 of Sisera, the children of T',

Thamar (*tha'-mar*) See also TAMAR.
M't 1: 3 begat Phares and Zara of T';

than
Ge 3: 1 more subtle t' any beast of the field
4:13 My punishment is greater t' I can bear.
19: 9 we deal worse with thee, t' with them.
25:23 shall be stronger t' the other people;
26:16 us; for thou art much mightier t' we.
29:19 t' that I should give her to another
30 and he loved also Rachel more t' Leah,
34:19 more honourable t' all the house of
36: 7 riches were more t' that they might
37: 3 loved Joseph more t' all his children,
4 their father loved him more t' all his
38:26 She hath been more righteous t' I;
41:40 in the throne will I be greater t' thou.
48:19 younger brother shall be greater t' he,
Ex 1: 9 of Israel are more and mightier t' we:
14:12 t' that we should die in the wilderness.
18:11 that the Lord is greater t' all gods:
30:15 poor shall not give less t' half a shekel,
36: 5 much more t' enough for the service
Le 13: 3 sight be deeper t' the skin of his flesh,
4 and in sight be not deeper t' the skin,
21 if it be not lower t' the skin, and be 4480

Le 13:25 it be in sight deeper t' the skin;
26 and it be no lower t' the other skin,
30 be in sight deeper t' the skin; and
31 it be not in sight deeper t' the skin,
32 be not in sight deeper t' the skin;
34 nor be in sight deeper t' the skin;
14:37 which in sight are lower t' the wall;
27: 8 But if he be poorer t' thy estimation,
Nu 3:46 which are more t' the Levites;
22:15 more, and more honourable t' they.
24: 7 and his king shall be higher t' Agag,
De 1:28 The people is greater and taller t' we;
4:38 thee greater and mightier t' thou art,
7: 1 nations greater and mightier t' thou;
7 ye were more in number t' any people;
17 heart, These nations are more t' I;
9: 1 nations greater and mightier t' thyself,
14 a nation mightier and greater t' they.
11:23 nations and mightier t' yourselves.
20: 1 and a people more t' thou, be not
Jos 10: 2 and because it was greater t' Ai,
11 t' they whom the children of Israel
J'g 2:19 themselves more t' their fathers,
8: 2 better t' the vintage of Abiezer?
11:25 art thou any thing better t' Balak the
14:18 went down, What is sweeter t' honey?
18 and what is stronger t' a lion? And he
15: 2 is not her younger sister fairer t' she?
3 be more blameless t' the Philistines,
16:30 more t' they which he slew in his life.
Ru 3:10 the latter end t' at the beginning,
12 howbeit there is a kinsman nearer t' I.
4:15 which is better to thee t' seven sons,
1Sa 1: 8 am not I better to thee t' ten sons?
9: 2 of Israel a goodlier person t' he:
2 he was higher t' any of the people.
10:23 he was higher t' any of the people
15:22 Behold, to obey is better t' sacrifice,
22 and to hearken t' the fat of rams.
28 of thine, that is better t' thou.
18:30 wisely t' all the servants of Saul;
24:17 to David, Thou art more righteous t' I:
27: 1 me t' that I should speedily escape
2Sa 1:23 divided: they were swifter t' eagles,
23 eagles, they were stronger t' lions.
6:22 And I will yet be more vile t' thus, and
13:14 but, being stronger t' she, forced her,
15 he hated her was greater t' the love
16 greater t' the other that thou didst
17:14 is better t' the counsel of Ahithophel.
19: 7 worse unto thee t' all the evil that
43 have also more right in David t' ye:
43 fiercer t' the words of the men of Israel.
20: 5 he tarried longer t' the set time
6 do us more harm t' did Absalom:
23:23 was more honourable t' the thirty,
1Ki 1:37 greater t' the throne of my lord king
47 name of Solomon better t' thy name,
47 make his throne greater t' thy throne.
2:32 men more righteous and better t' he,
4:31 For he was wiser t' all men,
31 t' Ethan the Ezrahite, and Heman, and
12:10 shall be thicker t' my father's loins.
19: 4 life; for I am not better t' my fathers.
20:23 therefore they were stronger t' we;
23, 25 we shall be stronger t' they.
21: 2 give thee for it a better vineyard t' it;
2Ki 5:12 better t' all the waters of Israel?
9:35 no more of her t' the skull,
21: 9 to do more evil t' did the nations
1Ch 4: 9 was more honourable t' his brethren:
11:21 he was more honourable t' the two;
24: 4 Eleazar t' of the sons of Ithamar;
2Ch 10:10 shall be thicker t' my father's loins.
21:13 house, which were better t' thyself:
25: 9 is able to give thee much more t' this.
29:34 to sanctify themselves t' the priests.
32: 7 for there be more with us t' with him:
33: 9 and to do worse t' the heathen,
Es 1:19 unto another that is better t' she.
2:17 favour in his sight more t' all the
13 the king's house, more t' all the Jews.
6: 6 delight to do honour more t' to myself?
Job 3:21 dig for it more t' for hid treasures;
4:17 Shall mortal man be more just t' God?
17 shall a man be more pure t' his maker?
6: 3 be heavier t' the sand of the sea:
7: 6 My days are swifter t' a weaver's
15 strangling, and death rather t' my life.
9:25 Now my days are swifter t' a post:
11: 6 God exacteth of thee less t' thine
9 thereof is longer t' the earth,
9 the earth, and broader t' the sea.
17 age shall be clearer t' the noonday;
15:10 aged men, much elder t' thy father.
23: 2 stroke is heavier t' my groaning.
12 his mouth more t' my necessary food.
30: 1 are younger t' I have me in derision,
8 men: they were viler t' the earth.
32: 4 spoken, because they were elder t' he.
33:12 thee, that God is greater t' man.
25 His flesh shall be fresher t' a child's:
34:19 regardeth the rich more t'...poor?
23 will not lay upon man more t' right;
35: 2 My righteousness is more t' God's?
5 the clouds which are higher t' thou.
11 Who teacheth us more t' the beasts of
11 and maketh us wiser t' the fowls of
36:21 hast thou chosen rather t' affliction.
42:12 latter end of Job more t' his beginning:
Ps 4: 7 more t' in the time that their corn and
19:10 are they t' gold, yea, t' much fine gold:
10 sweeter also t' honey and...honeycomb.
37:16 is better t' the riches of many wicked.
40: 5 they are more t' can be numbered.
12 are more t' the hairs of mine head:

Ps 52: 3 Thou lovest evil more t' good; and
3 lying rather t' to speak righteousness.
55:21 of his mouth were smoother t' butter,
21 his words were softer t' oil, yet were
63: 3 thy lovingkindness is better t' life,
69: 4 are more t' the hairs of mine head:
31 please the Lord better t' an ox or
73: 7 they have more t' heart could wish.
84:10 in thy courts is better t' a thousand.
10 t' to dwell in the tents of wickedness.
87: 2 Zion more t' all the dwellings of Jacob.
93: 4 mightier t' the noise of many waters,
4 yea, t' the mighty waves of the sea.
105:24 made them stronger t' their enemies:
118: 9 Lord t' to put confidence in princes.
119:72 unto me t' thousands of gold and
98 hast made me wiser t' mine enemies:
99 understanding t' all my teachers:
100 I understand more t' the ancients,
130: 6 Lord more t' they that watch for the
6 I say, more t' they that watch for the
139:18 they are more in number t' the sand:
142: 6 persecutors; for they are stronger t' I.
Pr 3:14 it is better t' the merchandise of silver,
14 silver, and the gain thereof t' fine gold.
15 She is more precious t' rubies: and all
5: 3 and her mouth is smoother t' oil:
8:10 and knowledge rather t' choice gold.
11 For wisdom is better t' rubies; and all
19 is better t' gold, yea, t' fine gold;
11:24 is that withholdeth more t' is meet,
12: 9 is better t' he that honoureth himself,
26 is more excellent t' his neighbour:
15:16 t' great treasure and trouble therewith.
17 is, t' a stalled ox and hatred therewith.
16: 8 t' great revenues without right.
16 much better is it to get wisdom t' gold!
16 rather to be chosen t' silver!
19 t' to divide the spoil with the proud.
32 his spirit t' he that taketh a city.
17: 1 t' an house full of sacrifices with
10 wise man t' an hundred stripes into a
12 meet a man, rather t' a fool in his folly.
18:19 is harder to be won t' a strong city:
24 friend that sticketh closer t' a brother.
19: 1 t' he that is perverse in his lips, and is
22 and a poor man is better t' a liar.
21: 3 acceptable to the Lord t' sacrifice.
9 t' with a brawling woman in a wide
19 t' with a contentious and an angry
22: 1 is rather to be chosen t' great riches,
1 loving favour rather t' silver and gold.
25: 7 t' that thou shouldest be put lower in
24 t' with a brawling woman and in a
27: 3 a fool's wrath is heavier t' them both.
5 Open rebuke is better t' secret love.
10 that is near t' a brother far off.
28: 6 t' he that is perverse in his ways,
23 favour t' he that flattereth with the
29:20 there is more hope of a fool t' of him.
30: 2 Surely I am more brutish t' any man.
Ec 1:16 wisdom t' all they that have been
2: 9 increased more t' all that were before
16 wise more t' of the fool for ever;
24 a man, t' that he should eat and drink,
25 else can hasten hereunto, more t' I?
3:22 t' that a man should rejoice in his own
4: 2 t' the living which are yet alive.
3 Yea, better is he t' both they, which
5: 1 to hear, t' to give the sacrifice of fools:
5 t' that thou shouldest vow and not pay.
8 for he that is higher t' the highest
8 and there be higher t' they.
6: 3 that an untimely birth is better t' he.
5 this hath more rest t' the other.
8 hath the wise more t' the fool?
9 sight of the eyes t' the wandering
10 with him that is mightier t' he.
7: 1 A good name is better t' precious
1 day of death t' the day of one's birth.
2 t' to go to the house of feasting:
3 Sorrow is better t' laughter: for by
5 t' for a man to hear the song of fools.
8 is the end of a thing t' the beginning
8 in spirit is better t' the proud in spirit.
10 the former days were better t' these?
19 the wise more t' mighty men which
26 I find more bitter t' death the woman,
8:15 thing under the sun, t' to eat,
9: 4 living dog is better t' a dead lion.
16 said I, Wisdom is better t' strength:
17 more t' the cry of him that ruleth
18 Wisdom is better t' weapons of war:
Ca 4:10 how much better is thy love t' wine!
10 smell of thine ointments t' all spices!
5: 9, 9 thy beloved more t' another beloved,
Isa 13:12 a man more precious t' fine gold;
12 a man t' the golden wedge of Ophir.
28:20 is shorter t' that a man can stretch
20 narrower t' that he can wrap himself
33:19 deeper speech t' thou canst perceive;
40:17 to him less t' nothing, and vanity.
52:14 visage was so marred more t' any man,
14 and his form more t' the sons of men:
54: 1 t' the children of the married wife,
55: 9 as the heavens are higher t' the earth,
9 so are my ways higher t' your ways,
9 and my thoughts t' your thoughts.
56: 5 better t' of sons and of daughters:
65: 5 near to me; for I am holier t' thou.
Jer 4:13 his horses are swifter t' eagles.
5: 3 have made their faces harder t' a rock;
7:26 neck: they did worse t' their fathers.
8: 3 death shall be chosen rather t' life by
16:12 ye have done worse t' your fathers;
20: 7 thou art stronger t' I, and hast

Jer 31: 11 hand of him that was stronger t' he.
La 4: 7 Her Nazarites were purer t' snow, they
7 they were whiter t' milk, they were
7 were more ruddy in body t' rubies,
8 Their visage is blacker t' a coal; they
9 t' they that be slain with hunger:
19 are swifter t' the eagles of the heaven:
Eze 3: 9 As an adamant harder t' flint have I
5: 6 wickedness more t' the nations,
6 statutes more t' the countries that
7 multiplied more t' the nations that
6: 14 more desolate t' the wilderness
8: 15 see greater abominations t' these.
15: 2 What is the vine tree more t' any tree,
2 or t' a branch which is among the
16: 47 wast corrupted more t' they in all thy
51 thine abominations more t' they,
52 committed more abominable t' they:
52 they are more righteous t' thou: yea,
23: 11 corrupt in her inordinate love t' she,
11 more t' her sister in her whoredoms.
28: 3 thou art wiser t' Daniel; there is no
42: 5 for the galleries were higher t' these,
5 t' the lower, and
5 t' the middlemost of the building.
6 straitened more t' the lowest and the
Da 1: 10 faces worse liking t' the children
15 fatter in flesh t' all the children
20 better t' all the magicians and
2: 30 that I have more t' any living,
3: 19 seven times more t' it was wont
7: 20 was more stout t' his fellows.
8: 3 one was higher t' the other, and
11: 2 fourth shall be far richer t' they all:
8 more years t' the king of the north.
13 multitude greater t' the former,
Ho 2: 7 then was it better with me t' now.
6: 6 of God more t' burnt offerings.
Am 6: 2 be they better t' these kingdoms?
2 or their border greater t' your border?
Jon 4: 3 for it is better for me to die t' to live.
8 said, It is better for me to die t' to live.
11 are more t' sixscore thousand persons
Mic 7: 4 upright is sharper t' a thorn hedge:
Na 3: 8 Art thou better t' populous No, that
Hab 1: 8 horses also are swifter t' the leopards,
8 are more fierce t' the evening wolves:
13 art of purer eyes t' to behold evil, and
13 the man that is more righteous t' he?
Hag 2: 9 shall be greater t' of the former,
M't 3: 11 that cometh after me is mightier t' I,
5: 37 is more t' these cometh of evil.
47 only, what do ye more t' others?
6: 25 Is not the life more t' meat, and the
25 meat, and the body t' raiment?
26 them. Are ye not much better t' they?
10: 15 day of judgment, t' for that city.
31 are of more value t' many sparrows.
37 loveth father or mother more t' me
37 loveth son or daughter more t' me
11: 9 unto you, and more t' a prophet.
11 hath not risen a greater t' John the
11 the kingdom of heaven is greater t' he.
22 at the day of judgment, t' for you.
24 in the day of judgment, t' for thee.
12: 6 place is one greater t' the temple.
12 much then is a man better t' a sheep?
41 behold, a greater t' Jonas is here.
42 behold, a greater t' Solomon is here.
45 other spirits more wicked t' himself,
45 state of that man is worse t' the first.
18: 8 t' having two hands or two feet
9 t' having two eyes to be cast into
13 t' of the ninety and nine which
19: 24 t' for a rich man to enter into the
21: 36 sent other servants more t' the first:
23: 15 more the child of hell t' yourselves.
26: 53 more t' twelve legions of angels?
27: 64 last error shall be worse t' the first:
M'r 1: 7 cometh one mightier t' I after me,
4: 31 is less t' all the seeds that be in the
32 and becometh greater t' all herbs,
6: 11 day of judgment, t' for that city.
8: 14 ship with them more t' one loaf.
9: 43 t' having two hands to go into hell,
45 t' having two feet to be cast into
47 t' having two eyes to be cast into
10: 25 t' for a rich man to enter into the
12: 31 other commandment greater t' these.
33 is more t' all whole burnt offerings
43 t' all they which have cast into the
14: 5 for more t' three hundred pence,
Lu 3: 13 no more t' that which is appointed
16 one mightier t' I cometh, the latchet
7: 26 you, and much more t' a prophet.
28 a greater prophet t' John the Baptist:
28 in the kingdom of God is greater t' he.
10: 12 day for Sodom, t' for that city.
14 Sidon at the judgment, t' for you.
11: 26 other spirits more wicked t' himself;
26 of that man is worse t' the first.
31 behold, a greater t' Solomon is here.
32 behold, a greater t' Jonas is here.
12: 7 ye are of more value t' many sparrows.
23 The life is more t' meat,
23 and the body is more t' raiment.
24 much more are ye better t' the fowls?
14: 8 a more honourable man t' thou be
15: 7 more t' over ninety and nine just
16: 8 wiser t' the children of light.
17 t' one tittle of the law to fail.
17: 2 t' that he should offend one of
18: 14 house justified rather t' the other:
25 t' for a rich man to enter into the
21: 3 widow hath cast in more t' they all:
Joh 1: 50 thou shalt see greater things t' these.
Joh 3: 19 loved darkness rather t' light,
4: 1 and baptized more disciples t' John,
12 Art thou greater t' our father Jacob,
5: 20 shew him greater works t' these, that
36 I have greater witness t' that of John:
7: 31 he do more miracles t' these which
8: 53 thou greater t' our father Abraham,
10: 29 which gave them me, is greater t' all;
12: 43 of men more t' the praise of God.
13: 16 The servant is not greater t' his lord;
16 is sent greater t' he that sent him.
14: 12 and greater works t' these shall he do;
28 Father: for my Father is greater t' I.
15: 13 Greater love hath no man t' this, that
20 The servant is not greater t' his lord.
21: 15 Jonas, lovest thou me more t' these?
Ac 4: 19 unto you more t' unto God, judge
5: 29 ought to obey God rather t' men.
15: 28 you no greater burden t' these
20: 35 is more blessed to give t' to receive.
23: 13 more t' forty which had made this
21 for him of them more t' forty men,
25: 6 among them more t' ten days,
26: 22 saying none other things t' those
27: 11 t' those things which were spoken
Ro 1: 25 the creature more t' the Creator,
3: 9 are we better t' they? No, in no wise:
8: 37 more t' conquerors through him
12: 3 more highly t' he ought to think;
13: 11 nearer t' when we believed.
1Co 1: 25 foolishness of God is wiser t' men;
25 weakness of God is stronger t' men.
3: 11 can no man lay t' that is laid,
7: 9 for it is better to marry t' to burn.
9: 15 t' that any man should make my
10: 22 to jealousy? are we stronger t' he?
14: 5 t' he that speaketh with tongues,
18 speak with tongues more t' ye all:
19 t' ten thousand words in an
15: 10 laboured more abundantly t' they all:
2Co 1: 13 t' what ye read or acknowledge;
Ga 1: 8 t' that which we have preached
9 you t' that ye have received,
4: 27 more children t' she which hath a
Eph 3: 8 who am less t' the least of all saints,
Ph'p 2: 3 esteem other better t' themselves.
1Ti 1: 4 rather t' godly edifying which is
2Ti 3: 4 pleasures more t' lovers of God;
Ph'm 21 thou wilt also do more t' I say.
Heb 1: 4 Being made so much better t' angels,
4 a more excellent name t' they.
2: 7 him a little lower t' the angels;
9 was made a little lower t' the angels
3: 3 worthy of more glory t' Moses,
3 house hath more honour t' the house.
4: 12 sharper t' any twoedged sword,
7: 26 and made higher t' the heavens;
9: 23 with better sacrifices t' these.
11: 4 a more excellent sacrifice t' Cain,
25 t' to enjoy the pleasures of sin
26 greater riches t' the treasures in
12: 24 better things t' that of Abel.
1Pe 1: 7 more precious t' of gold that perisheth,
3: 17 for well doing, t' for evil doing.
2Pe 2: 20 worse with them t' the beginning.
21 t', after they have known it, to
1Jo 3: 20 God is greater t' our heart, and
4: 4 in you, t' he that is in the world.
3Jo 4 no greater joy t' to hear that my
Re 2: 19 and the last to be more t' the first.

thank See also THANKED; THANKFUL; THANKING; THANKS; THANKWORTHY.
1Ch 16: 4 to t' and praise the Lord God of
7 first this psalm to t' the Lord
23: 30 morning to t' and praise the Lord,
29: 13 our God, we t' thee, and praise thy
2Ch 29: 31 t' offerings into the house of the
31 brought...sacrifices and t' offerings;
33: 16 peace offerings and t' offerings,
Da 2: 23 I t' thee, and praise thee, O thou
M't 11: 25 and said, I t' thee, O Father, Lord
Lu 6: 32 which love you, what t' have ye?
33 do good to you, what t' have ye?
34 ye hope to receive, what t' have ye?
10: 21 and said, I t' thee, O Father, Lord
17: 9 he t' that servant because
18: 11 God, I t' thee, that I am not as
Joh 11: 41 I t' thee that thou hast heard me.
Ro 1: 8 I t' my God through Jesus Christ
7: 25 I t' God through Jesus Christ our
1Co 1: 4 I t' my God always on your behalf,
14 I t' God that I baptized none of you,
14: 18 I t' my God, I speak with tongues
Ph'p 1: 3 t' my God upon every remembrance
1Th 2: 13 this cause also t' we God without
2Th 1: 3 We are bound to t' God always for
1Ti 1: 12 And I t' Christ Jesus our Lord,
2Ti 1: 3 I t' God, whom I serve from my "
Ph'm 4 I t' my God, making mention of

thanked
2Sa 14: 22 bowed himself, and t' the king:
Ac 28: 15 saw, he t' God, and took courage.
Ro 6: 17 But, God be t', that ye were the

thankful See also UNTHANKFUL.
Ps 100: 4 be t' unto him, and bless his name.
Ro 1: 21 him not as God, neither were t';
Col 3: 15 called in one body; and be ye t'.

thankfulness
Ac 24: 3 most noble Felix, with all t'.

thanking
2Ch 5: 13 heard in praising and t' the Lord;

thank-offerings See THANK and OFFERINGS.

thanks See also THANKSGIVING.
2Sa 22: 50 Therefore I will give t' unto thee,
1Ch 16: 8 Give t' unto the Lord, call upon his
34 O give t' unto the Lord; for he is
35 we may give t' to thy holy name,
41 by name, to give t' to the Lord,
25: 3 to give t' and to praise the Lord.
2Ch 31: 2 to minister, and to give t', and to
Ezr 3: 11 and giving t' unto the Lord;
Ne 12: 24 to praise and to give t', according
31 companies of them that gave t',
38 other company of them that gave t'
40 companies of them that gave t'
Ps 6: 5 in the grave who shall give thee t'?
18: 49 will I give t' unto thee, O Lord,
30: 4 give t' at the remembrance of his
12 I will give t' unto thee for ever.
35: 18 thee t' in the great congregation:
75: 1 Unto thee, O God, do we give t',
1 unto thee do we give t': for that
79: 13 we thy people...give thee t' for ever:
92: 1 good thing to give t' unto the Lord,
97: 12 give t' at the remembrance of his
105: 1 O give t' unto the Lord; call upon
106: 1 O give t' unto the Lord; for he is
47 to give t' unto thy holy name, and
107: 1 O give t' unto the Lord, for he is
118: 1, 29 O give t' unto the Lord; for he is
119: 62 At midnight I will rise to give t'
122: 4 give t' unto the name of the Lord.
136: 1 O give t' unto the Lord; for he is
2 O give t' unto the God of gods: for
3 O give t' to the Lord of lords: for
26 O give t' unto the God of heaven:
140: 13 the righteous shall give t' unto thy
Da 6: 10 prayed, and gave t' before his God,
M't 15: 36 and gave t', and brake them,
26: 27 And he took the cup, and gave t',
M'r 8: 6 took the seven loaves, and gave t',
14: 23 when he had given t', he gave it to
Lu 2: 38 gave t' likewise unto the Lord,
17: 16 his face at his feet, giving him t':
22: 17 And he took the cup, and gave t',
19 And he took bread, and gave t',
Joh 6: 11 when he had given t', he distributed
23 after that the Lord had given t':)
Ac 27: 35 gave t' to God in presence of them
Ro 14: 6 to the Lord, for he giveth God t';
6 he eateth not, and giveth God t'.
16: 4 unto whom not only I give t', but
1Co 10: 30 of for that for which I give t'?
11: 24 when he had given t', he brake it,
14: 16 say Amen at thy giving of t',
17 thou verily givest t' well, but the
15: 57 But t' be to God, which giveth us
2Co 1: 11 t' may be given by many on our
2: 14 Now t' be unto God, which always
8: 16 But t' be to God, which put the
9: 15 T' be unto God for his unspeakable
Eph 1: 16 Cease not to give t' for you,
5: 4 convenient: but rather giving of t'.
20 Giving t' always for all things
Col 1: 3 We give t' to God and the Father
12 Giving t' unto the Father, which
3: 17 giving t' to God and the Father by
1Th 1: 2 We give t' to God always for you
3: 9 For what t' can we render to God
5: 18 In every thing give t': for this is
2Th 2: 13 are bound to give t' alway to God
1Ti 2: 1 intercessions, and giving of t',
Heb 13: 15 of our lips giving t' to his name.
Re 4: 9 t' to him that sat on the throne,
11: 17 We give thee t', O Lord God

thanksgiving See also THANKSGIVINGS.
Le 7: 12 If he offer it for a t', then he shall
12 with the sacrifice of t' unleavened
13 bread with the sacrifice of t' of his
15 his peace offerings for t' shall be
22: 29 offer a sacrifice of t' unto the Lord,
Ne 11: 17 principal to begin the t' in prayer:
12: 8 Mattaniah, which was over the t',
46 songs of praise and t' unto God.
Ps 26: 7 may publish with the voice of t',
50: 14 Offer unto God t'; and pay thy vows
69: 30 song, and will magnify him with t'.
95: 2 us come before his presence with t',
100: 4 Enter into his gates with t', and
107: 22 them sacrifice the sacrifices of t',
116: 17 I will offer to thee the sacrifice of t',
147: 7 Sing unto the Lord with t'; sing
Isa 51: 3 gladness shall be found therein, t',
Jer 30: 19 out of them shall proceed t' and the
Am 4: 5 offer a sacrifice of t' with leaven,
Jon 2: 9 unto thee with the voice of t';
2Co 4: 15 through the t' of many redound to
9: 11 which causeth through us t' to God.
Ph'p 4: 6 by prayer and supplication with t'
Col 2: 7 taught, abounding therein with t'.
4: 2 and watch in the same with t';
1Ti 4: 3 to be received with t' of them which
4 be refused, if it be received with t':
Re 7: 12 and wisdom, and t', and honour,

thanksgivings
Ne 12: 27 both with t', and with singing,
2Co 9: 12 also by many t' unto God;

thankworthy
1Pe 2: 19 this is t', if a man for conscience

Thara (*tha'-rah*) See also TERAH.
Lu 3: 34 which was the son of T', which

Tharshish (*thar'-shish*) See also TARSHISH.
1Ki 10: 22 the king had at sea a navy of T'
22 in three years came the navy of T'.

1Ki 22:48 Jehoshaphat made ships of T' to
1Ch 7:10 Zethan, and T', and Ahishahar.

theatre
Ac 19:29 rushed with one accord into the t'.
31 not adventure himself into the t'.

Thebez (*the'-bez*)
J'g 9:50 Then went Abimelech to T', and
50 encamped against T', and took it.
2Sa 11:21 from the wall, that he died in T'?

thee-ward
1Sa 19: 4 his works have been to t' very good:

theft See also THEFTS.
Ex 22: 3 then he shall be sold for his t'.
4 If the t' be certainly found in his

thefts
M't 15:19 fornications, t', false witness,
M'r 7:22 T', covetousness, wickedness,
Re 9:21 of their fornication, nor of their t'.

theirs
Ge 15:13 a stranger in a land that is not t',
34:23 and every beast of t' be ours?
43:34 was five times so much as any of t'.
Ex 29: 9 the priest's office shall be t' for a
Le 18:10 for t' is thine own nakedness.
Nu 16:26 and touch nothing of t', lest ye be
18: 9 from the fire: every oblation of t',
9 every meat offering of t', and every
9 and every sin offering of t', and
9 every trespass offering of t', which
Jos 21:10 Levi, had: for t' was the first lot.
1Ch 6:54 the Kohathites: for t' was the lot.
2Ch 18:12 I pray thee, be like one of t', and
Jer 44:28 whose words shall stand, mine, or t'.
Eze 7:11 of their multitude, nor of any of t':
44:29 dedicated thing in Israel shall be t'.
Hab 1: 6 the dwellingplaces that are not t'.
M't 5: 3, 10 for t' is the kingdom of heaven.
1Co 1: 2 Christ our Lord, both t' and ours:
2Ti 3: 9 manifest unto...men, as t' also

Thelasar (*the-la'-sar*) See also TELASSAR.
2Ki 19:12 of Eden which were in T'?

themselves^
Ge 3: 7 together, and made t' aprons.
8 hid t' from the presence of the Lord
13:11 they separated t' the one from the
19:11 that they wearied t' to find the door.
30:40 and he put his own flocks by t',
32:16 of his servants, every drove by t';
33: 6 their children, and they bowed t':
7 children came near, and bowed t':
7 near and Rachel, and they bowed t'.
34:30 they shall gather t' together against
42: 6 and bowed down t' before him with
43:26 and bowed t' to him to the earth.
32 him by himself, and for them by t',
32 which did eat with him, by t':
Ex 5: 7 let them go and gather straw for t'.
11: 8 and bow down t' unto me, saying,
12:39 they prepared for t' any victual.
18:26 every small matter they judged t'.
19:22 sanctify t', lest the Lord break forth
26: 9 thou shalt couple five curtains by t',
9 and six curtains by t', and shalt
32: 1 the people gathered t' together unto
7 the land of Egypt, have corrupted t':
26 sons of Levi gathered t' together unto
33: 6 of Israel stripped t' of their ornaments
36:16 And he coupled five curtains by t',
16 and six curtains by t'.
Le 15:18 they shall both bathe t' in water, and
22: 2 that they separate t' from the holy
Nu 6: 2 shall separate t' to vow a vow of a
2 Nazarite, to separate t' unto the Lord:
8: 7 clothes, and so make t' clean.
10: 3 shall assemble t' to thee at the door
4 of Israel, shall gather t' unto thee.
11:32 them all abroad for t' round about
16: 3 gathered t' together against Moses
20: 2 gathered t' together against Moses
27: 3 gathered t' together against the Lord
De 7:20 that are left, and hide t' from thee,
9:12 forth out of Egypt have corrupted t';
31:14 and presented t' in the tabernacle of
20 they shall have eaten and filled t',
32: 5 They have corrupted t', their spot is
27 adversaries...behave t' strangely,
31 even our enemies t' being judges.
Jos 8:27 city Israel took for a prey unto t',
9: 2 That they gathered t' together, to
10: 5 king of Eglon, gathered t' together,
13 had avenged t' upon their enemies.
16 fled, and hid t' in a cave at Makkedah.
11:14 of Israel took for a prey unto t';
22:12 children of Israel gathered t' together
24: 1 and they presented t' before God.
J'g 2:12 about them, and bowed t' unto them,
17 other gods, and bowed t' unto them:
19 corrupted t' more than their fathers,
5: 2 when the people willingly offered t'.
9 offered t' willingly among the people.
7: 2 lest Israel vaunt t' against me, saying,
23 gathered t' together out of Naphtali,
24 men of Ephraim gathered t' together,
10:17 of Israel assembled t' together,
12: 1 men of Ephraim gathered t' together,
J'g 15: 9 in Judah, and spread t' in Lehi.
20: 2 presented t' in the assembly of the
14 of Benjamin gathered t' together out
20 men of Israel put t' in array to fight
22 the men of Israel encouraged t',
22 where they put t' in array the first
30 and put t' in array against Gibeah,
33 and put t' in array at Baal-tamar:
37 and the liers in wait drew t' along,
1Sa 2: 5 were full have hired out t' for bread;
3:13 because his sons made t' vile, and
4: 2 the Philistines put t' in array against
8: 4 elders of Israel gathered t' together,
13: 5 Philistines gathered t' together to
6 then the people did hide t' in caves,
11 Philistines gathered t' together at
14:11 discovered t' unto the garrison of the
11 out of the holes where they had hid t'.
20 that were with him assembled t',
22 which had hid t' in mount Ephraim,
21: 4 have kept t' at least from women.
22: 2 discontented, gathered t' unto him;
28: 4 the Philistines gathered t' together,
2Sa 2:25 of Benjamin gathered t' together
5:18, 22 and spread t' in the valley of
10: 8 and Maacah, were by t' in the field.
15 Israel, they gathered t' together.
17 the Syrians set t' in array against
16:14 came weary, and refreshed t' there.
22:45 Strangers shall submit t' unto me:
1Ki 8: 2 all the men of Israel assembled t'
47 they shall bethink t' in the land
18:23 let them choose one bullock for t',
28 and cut t' after their manner with
20:12 they set t' in array against the city.
2Ki 2:15 bowed t' to the ground before him.
7:12 out of the camp to hide t' in the field,
8:20 of Judah, and made a king over t'.
17:17 sold t' to do evil in the sight of the
19:29 eat this year such things as grow of t',
1Ch 11: 1 Then all Israel gathered t' to David
10 who strengthened t' with him in his
14 they set t' in the midst of that parcel,
12: 8 Gadites there separated t' unto David
13: 2 that they may gather t' unto us:
14: 9 spread t' in the valley of Rephaim.
13 spread t' abroad in the valley.
15:14 sanctified t' to bring up the ark of the
19: 6 that they had made t' odious to David,
7 gathered t' together from their cities,
9 were come were by t' in the field.
11 they set t' in array against the children
21:20 and his four sons with him hid t'.
29:24 submitted t' unto Solomon the king.
2Ch 3:13 spread t' forth twenty cubits:
5: 3 all the men of Israel assembled t'
6:37 Yet if they bethink t' in the land
7: 3 bowed t' with their faces to the
14 shall humble t', and pray, and seek
12: 6 Israel and the king humbled t';
7 the Lord saw that they humbled t',
7 They have humbled t'; therefore
13: 7 strengthened t' against Rehoboam
14:13 that they could not recover t';
15:10 gathered t' together at Jerusalem
20: 4 And Judah gathered t' together, to
25 jewels, which they stripped off for t',
26 assembled t' in the valley of Berachah;
21: 8 of Judah, and made t' a king.
29:15 their brethren, and sanctified t',
29 that were present with him bowed t',
34 the other priests had sanctified t':
34 more upright in heart to sanctify t'
30: 3 had not sanctified t' sufficiently,
3 had the people gathered t' together
11 Manasseh and of Zebulun humbled t',
15 were ashamed, and sanctified t',
18 and Zebulun, had not cleansed t',
24 great number of priests sanctified t'.
31:18 for in their set office they sanctified t'
32: 8 rested t' upon the words of Hezekiah
35:14 afterward they made ready for t',
14 the Levites prepared for t', and
Ezr 3: 1 people gathered t' together as one
6:20 brethren the priests, and for t'.
21 such as had separated t' unto them
9: 1 have not separated t' from the people
2 taken of their daughters for t',
2 mingled t' with the people of those
10: 7 that they should gather t' together
9 gathered t' together unto Jerusalem
Ne 4: 2 feeble Jews? will they fortify t'?
8: 1 people gathered t' together as one
16 and made t' booths, every one
9: 2 Israel separated t' from all strangers,
25 and delighted t' in thy great goodness.
10:28 that had separated t' from the people
11: 2 that willingly offered t' to dwell at
12:28 of the singers gathered t' together,
30 the priests and the Levites purified t',
13:22 Levites, that they should cleanse t',
Es 8:11 in every city to gather t' together,
13 that day to avenge t' on their enemies.
9: 2 Jews gathered t' together in their
15 gathered t' together on the fourteenth
16 king's provinces gathered t' together,
27 upon all such as joined t' unto them,
31 had decreed for t' and for their
Job 1: 6 came to present t' before the Lord,
2: 1 came to present t' before the Lord,
3:14 which built desolate places for t';
6: 4 terrors of God do set t' in array
16:10 have gathered t' together against me.
24: 4 the poor of the earth hide t' together.
16 had marked for t' in the daytime:
29: 8 The young men saw me, and hid t':
Job 30:14 the desolation they rolled t' upon me.
34:22 the workers of iniquity may hide t'.
41:23 they are firm in t'; they cannot be
25 by reason of breakings they purify t'.
Ps 2: 2 The kings of the earth set t', and the
3: 6 have set t' against me round about.
9:20 nations may know t' to be but men.
18:44 strangers shall submit t' unto me.
35:15 rejoiced, and gathered t' together:
15 gathered t' together against me,
26 dishonour that magnify t' against me.
37:11 delight t' in the abundance of peace.
38:16 slippeth, they magnify t' against me.
44:10 and they which hate us spoil for t'.
49: 6 boast t' in the multitude of their
56: 6 They gathered t' together, they hide
6 they hide t', they mark my steps,
57: 6 the midst whereof they are fallen t'.
59: 4 They run and prepared t' without my
64: 5 They encourage t' in an evil matter:
8 their own tongue to fall upon t':
66: 3 thine enemies submit t' unto thee.
7 nations: let not the rebellious exalt t'
80: 6 and our enemies laugh among t'.
81:15 should have submitted t' unto him:
94: 4 all the workers of iniquity boast t'?
21 They gather t' together against the
97: 7 graven images, that boast t' of idols:
104:22 sun ariseth, they gather t' together,
106:28 They joined t' also unto Baal-peor,
109:29 cover t' with their own confusion,
140: 8 his wicked device; lest they exalt t'.
Pr 23: 5 for riches certainly make t' wings;
28:28 When the wicked rise, men hide t':
Ec 3:18 might see that they t' are beasts.
11: 3 of rain, they empty t' upon the earth:
12: 3 and the strong men shall bow t', and
Isa 2: 6 please t' in the children of strangers.
3: 9 they have rewarded evil unto t'.
8:21 they shall be hungry, they shall fret t',
10:31 inhabitants of Gebim gather t' to flee.
15: 3 they shall gird t' with sackcloth:
22: 7 and the horsemen shall set t' in array
30: 2 strengthen t' in the strength of
46: 2 but t' are gone into captivity.
47:14 deliver t' from the power of the
48: 2 For they call t' of the holy city, and
2 and stay t' upon the God of Israel;
49:18 all these gather t' together, and
56: 6 that join t' to the Lord, to serve him,
59: 6 shall they cover t' with their works:
60: 4 all they gather t' together, they come
14 bow t' down at the soles of thy feet;
66:17 They that sanctify t', and purify
17 and purify t' in the gardens behind
Jer 2:24 that seek her will not weary t';
4: 2 and the nations shall bless t' in him,
5: 7 assembled t' by troops in the harlot's
22 and though the waves thereof toss t',
7:19 do they not provoke t' to the
9: 5 and weary t' to commit iniquity.
11:17 done against t' to provoke me
12:13 they have put t' to pain, but shall not
16: 6 shall men lament for them, nor cut t',
6 nor make t' bald for them:
7 Neither shall men tear t' for them in
25:14 great kings shall serve t' of them also:
27: 7 and great kings shall serve t' of him.
30: 8 shall no more serve t' of him:
21 And their nobles shall be of t', and
34:10 none should serve t' of them any
41: 5 their clothes rent, and having cut t',
49:29 they shall take to t' their curtains,
50: 9 shall set t' in array against her;
La 2:10 they have girded t' with sackcloth:
4:14 they have polluted t' with blood, so
Eze 6: 9 and they shall lothe t' for the evils
7:18 They shall also gird t' with sackcloth,
10:17 lifted up, these lifted up t' also:
22 of Chebar, their appearances and t':
14:18 but they only shall be delivered t'.
26:16 they shall clothe t' with trembling;
27:30 they shall wallow t' in the ashes:
31 shall make t' utterly bald for thee,
31:14 by the waters exalt t' for their height,
34: 2 shepherds of Israel that do feed t'!
8 the shepherds fed t', and fed not my
10 the shepherds feed t' any more;
27 hand of those that served t' of them.
37:23 defile t' any more with their idols,
43:26 it; and they shall consecrate t'.
44:18 gird t' with any thing that causeth
25 come at no dead person to defile t':
25 had no husband, they may defile t'.
45: 5 ministers of the house, have for t',
Da 2:43 shall mingle t' with the seed of men:
10: 7 upon them, so that they fled to hide t'.
11: 6 end of years they shall join t' together;
14 shall exalt t' to establish the vision;
Ho 1:11 together, and appoint t' one head,
4:14 for t' are separated with whores,
7:14 they assemble t' for corn and wine,
9: 9 They have deeply corrupted t', as in
10 and separated t' unto that shame;
10:10 they shall bind t' in their furrows.
Am 2: 8 And they lay t' down upon clothes
6: 4 and stretch t' upon their couches, and
5 invent to t' instruments of
6 anoint t' with the chief ointments:
7 that stretched t' shall be removed.
9: 3 they hide t' in the top of Carmel,
Mic 3: 4 have behaved t' ill in their doings.
Hab 1: 7 and their dignity shall proceed of t'.
8 and their horsemen shall spread t',
Zep 2: 8 and magnified t' against their border.
10 magnified t' against the people of

Zec 4:12 pipes empty the golden oil out of t'?
11: 5 slay them, and hold t' not guilty: and
12: 3 burden t' with it shall be cut in pieces,
7 do not magnify t' against Judah.
M't 9: 3 of the scribes said within t',
14: 2 works do shew forth t' in him.
15 the villages, and buy t' victuals.
16: 7 they reasoned among t', saying,
19:12 made t' eunuchs for the kingdom
21:25 And they reasoned with t', saying,
38 they said among t', This is the
23: 4 but they t' will not move them with
M'r 1:27 they questioned among t', saying,
2: 8 that they so reasoned within t',
4:17 have no root in t', and so endure
6:14 mighty works do shew forth t' in him.
30 apostles gathered t' together unto
36 into the villages, and buy t' bread:
51 they were sore amazed in t' beyond
8:16 they reasoned among t', saying,
9: 2 into an high mountain apart by t'
8 any more, save Jesus only with t',
10 they kept that saying with t',
34 way they had disputed among t',
10:26 saying among t', Who then can be
11:31 they reasoned with t', saying, If we
12: 7 those husbandmen said among t',
14: 4 some that had indignation within t',
15:31 priests mocking said among t'
16: 3 they said among t', Who shall roll
Lu 4:36 all amazed, and spake among t',
7:30 the counsel of God against t',
49 with him began to say within t',
18: 9 unto certain which trusted in t'
20: 5 they reasoned with t', saying, If we
14 they reasoned among t', saying,
20 which should feign t' just men,
22:23 they began to enquire among t',
23:12 they were at enmity between t',
24:12 beheld the linen clothes laid by t',
Joh 6:52 Jews therefore strove among t',
7:35 Then said the Jews among t',
11:55 before the passover, to purify t'.
56 spake among t', as they stood in
12:19 Pharisees therefore said among t',
16:17 said some of his disciples among t',
17:13 might have my joy fulfilled in t'.
18:18 it was cold: and they warmed t':
28 they t' went not into the judgment
19:24 They said therefore among t', Let
Ac 4:15 the council, they conferred among t',
5:36 of men, about four hundred, joined
11:26 they assembled t' with the church,
15:32 and Silas, being prophets also t',
16:37 let them come t' and fetch us out.
18: 6 when they opposed t', and blasphemed,
21:25 keep t' from things offered to idols,
23:12 and bound t' under a curse,
21 which have bound t' with an oath,
24:15 which they t' also allow, that there
26:31 gone aside, they talked between t',
27:40 they committed t' unto the sea, and
43 swim should cast t' first into the sea,
28: 4 they said among t', No doubt this
25 And when they agreed not among t',
29 had great reasoning among t'.
Ro 1:22 Professing t' to be wise, they became
24 their own bodies between t':
27 receiving in t' that recompence of
2:14 not the law, are a law unto t':
10: 3 submitted t' unto the righteousness of
13: 2 resist shall receive to t' damnation.
1Co 6: 9 nor abusers of t' with mankind,
16:15 have addicted t' to the ministry
2Co 5:15 should not henceforth live unto t',
8: 3 their power they were willing of t';
10:12 with some that commend t':
12 but they measuring t' by t',
12 and comparing t' among t',
11:13 transforming t' into the apostles of
Ga 6:13 neither they t' who are circumcised
Eph 4:19 given t' over unto lasciviousness,
Ph'p 2: 3 let each esteem other better than t'.
1Th 1: 9 For they t' shew of us what manner
1Ti 1:10 for them that defile t' with mankind,
2: 9 that women adorn t' in modest
3:13 well purchase to t' a good degree,
6:10 pierced t' through with many
19 Laying up...for t' a good foundation
2Ti 2:25 instructing those that oppose t';
26 recover t' out of the snare of the devil,
4: 3 lusts shall they heap to t' teachers,
Tit 1:12 One of t', even a prophet of their
Heb 6: 6 they crucify to t' the Son of God
9:23 the heavenly things t' with better
1Pe 1:12 that not unto t', but unto us they
3: 5 adorned t', being in subjection unto
2Pe 2: 1 and bring upon t' swift destruction.
19 t' are the servants of corruption:
Jude 7 manner, giving t' over to fornication,
10 in those things they corrupt t'.
12 with you, feeding t' without fear:
19 These be they who separate t',
Re 6:15 hid t' in the dens and in the rocks
8: 6 trumpets prepared t' to sound.

then^

Ge 3: 5 thereof, t' your eyes shall be opened,
4:26 t' began men to call upon the name
8: 9 t' he put forth his hand, and took her,
12: 6 the Canaanite was t' in the land.
13: 7 the Perizzite dwelled t' in the land.
9 the left hand, t' I will go to the right;
9 the right hand, t' I will go to the left.
11 T' Lot chose him all the plain of
16 t' shall thy seed also be numbered.
18 T' Abram removed his tent, and
Ge 17:17 T' Abraham fell upon his face, and
18:15 T' Sarah denied, saying, I laughed
26 t' I will spare all the place for their
19:15 arose, t' the angels hastened Lot,
24 T' the Lord rained upon Sodom and
20: 9 T' Abimelech called Abraham, and
21:32 t' Abimelech rose up, and Phichol the
22: 4 T' on the third day Abraham lifted up
24: 8 t' thou shalt be clear from this my
41 T' shalt thou be clear from this my
50 T' Laban and Bethuel answered and
25: 1 T' again Abraham took a wife, and
8 T' Abraham gave up the ghost, and
34 T' Jacob gave Esau bread and
26:12 T' Isaac sowed in that land, and
26 T' Abimelech went to him from Gerar,
27:41 hand; t' will I slay my brother Jacob.
45 t' I will send, and fetch thee from
28: 9 T' went Esau unto Ishmael, and took
21 in peace; t' shall the Lord be my God:
29: 1 T' Jacob went on his journey, and
8 well's mouth; t' we water the sheep.
25 wherefore t' hast thou beguiled me?
30:14 T' Rachel said to Leah, Give me, I
31: 8 wages; t' all the cattle bare speckled:
8 t' bare all the cattle ringstraked.
16 now t', whatsoever God hath said unto
17 T' Jacob rose up, and set his sons and
25 T' Laban overtook Jacob. Now Jacob
33 T' went he out of Leah's tent, and
54 T' Jacob offered sacrifice upon the
32: 7 T' Jacob was greatly afraid and
8 t' the other company which is left
18 T' thou shalt say, They be thy servant
33: 6 T' the handmaidens came near, they
10 t' receive my present at my hand:
34:16 T' will we give our daughters unto you,
17 t' will we take our daughter, and we
35: 2 T' Jacob said unto his household, and
37:28 T' there passed by Midianites
38:11 T' said Judah to Tamar his daughter
21 T' he asked the men of that place,
39: 9 how t' can I do this great wickedness,
41: 9 T' spake the chief butler unto Pharaoh,
14 T' Pharaoh sent and called Joseph,
42:25 T' Joseph commanded to fill their
34 t' shall I know that ye are no spies,
38 t' shall ye bring down my gray hairs
43: 9 thee, t' let me bear the blame for ever:
44: 8 t' should we steal out of thy lord's
11 T' they speedily took down every man
13 T' they rent their clothes, and laded
18 T' Judah came near unto him, and
26 brother be with us, t' will we go down:
32 t' I shall bear the blame to my father
45: 1 T' Joseph could not refrain himself
47: 1 T' Joseph came and told Pharaoh, and
6 t' make them rulers over my cattle.
23 T' Joseph said unto the people, Behold,
49: 4 father's bed; t' defiledst thou it:
Ex 1:16 stools; if it be a son, t' ye shall kill him:
16 but if it be a daughter, t' she shall live.
2: 7 T' said his sister to Pharaoh's
4:25 T' Zipporah took a sharp stone, and
26 t' she said, A bloody husband thou
31 t' they bowed their heads and
5:15 T' the officers of the children of Israel
6: 1 T' the Lord said unto Moses, Now
12 how t' shall Pharaoh hear me, who am
7: 9 t' thou shalt say unto Aaron, Take thy
11 T' Pharaoh also called the wise men
8: 8 T' Pharaoh called for Moses and
19 T' the magicians said unto Pharaoh,
10:16 T' Pharaoh called for Moses and
12:21 T' Moses called for all the elders of
44 him, t' shall he eat thereof.
48 t' let him come near and keep it;
13:13 redeem it, t' thou shalt break his neck:
15: 1 T' sang Moses and the children of
15 T' the dukes of Edom shall be
16: 4 T' said the Lord unto Moses, Behold,
6 t' ye shall know that the Lord hath
7 t' ye shall see the glory of the Lord;
17: 8 T' came Amalek, and fought with
18:23 t' thou shalt be able to endure, and all
19: 5 t' ye shall be a peculiar treasure unto
21: 3 t' his wife shall go out with him.
6 T' his master shall bring him unto
8 t' shall he let her be redeemed:
11 t' shall she go out free without money.
13 t' I will appoint thee a place whither
19 t' shall he that smote him be quit:
23 follow, t' thou shalt give life for life,
28 t' the ox shall be surely stoned, and
30 t' he shall give for the ransom of his
35 t' they shall sell the live ox, and divide
22: 3 t' he shall be sold for his theft.
8 t' the master of the house shall be
11 T' shall an oath of the Lord be
13 pieces, t' let him bring it for witness,
23:22 t' I will be an enemy unto thine
24: 9 T' went up Moses, and Aaron, Nadab,
29: 7 T' shalt thou take the anointing oil,
20 T' shalt thou kill the ram, and take of
34 t' thou shalt burn the remainder with
30:12 t' shall they give every man a ransom
32:24 t' I cast it into the fire, and there came
26 T' Moses stood in the gate of the
34:20 him not, t' shalt thou break his neck.
36: 1 T' wrought Bezaleel and Aholiab, and
40:34 T' a cloud covered the tent of the
37 t' they journeyed not till the day that
Le 1:14 t' he shall bring his offering of
3: 7 t' shall he offer it before the Lord.
12 t' he shall offer it before the Lord.
4: 3 t' let him bring for his sin, which he
Le 4:14 t' the congregation shall offer a young
28 t' he shall bring his offering, a kid of
5: 1 utter it, t' he shall bear his iniquity.
3 knoweth of it, t' he shall be guilty.
4 t' he shall be guilty in one of these.
7 t' he shall bring for his trespass, which
11 t' he that sinned shall bring for his
12 T' shall he bring it to the priest, and
15 t' he shall bring for his trespass unto
6: 4 T' it shall be, because he hath sinned,
7:12 t' he shall offer with the sacrifice of
10: 3 T' Moses said unto Aaron, This is it
12: 2 t' she shall be unclean seven days;
4 shall t' continue in the blood of her
5 t' she shall be unclean two weeks,
8 t' she shall bring two turtles, or two
13: 2 t' he shall be brought unto Aaron the
4 t' the priest shall shut him up that
5 t' the priest shall shut him up seven
8 t' the priest shall pronounce him
9 t' he shall be brought unto the priest;
13 T' the priest shall consider: and,
17 t' the priest shall pronounce him
21 t' the priest shall shut him up seven
22 t' the priest shall pronounce him
25 T' the priest shall look upon it: and,
26 t' the priest shall shut him up seven
27 t' the priest shall pronounce him
30 T' the priest shall see the plague:
30 t' the priest shall pronounce him
31 t' the priest shall shut up him that
34 t' the priest shall pronounce him
36 T' the priest shall look on him: and,
39 T' the priest shall look: and, behold,
43 T' the priest shall look upon it: and,
54 T' the priest shall command that they
56 t' he shall rend it out of the garment,
58 t' it shall be washed the second time,
14: 4 T' shall the priest command to take
21 t' he shall take one lamb for a trespass
36 T' the priest shall command that they
38 T' the priest shall go out of the house
40 T' the priest shall command that they
44 T' the priest shall come and look, and,
48 t' the priest shall pronounce the house
15: 8 t' he shall wash his clothes, and bathe
13 t' he shall number to himself seven
16 t' he shall wash all his flesh in water,
28 t' she shall number to herself seven
16:15 T' shall he kill the goat of the sin
17:15 until the even: t' shall he be clean.
16 his flesh; t' he shall bear his iniquity.
19:23 t' ye shall count the fruit thereof as
20: 5 T' I will set my face against that man,
22:14 t' he shall put the fifth part thereof
27 t' it shall be seven days under the dam;
23:10 t' ye shall bring a sheaf of the
19 T' ye shall sacrifice one kid of the
25: 2 t' shall the land keep a sabbath unto
9 T' shalt thou cause the trumpet of the
21 T' I will command my blessing upon
25 t' shall he redeem that which his
27 T' let him count the years of the sale
28 t' that which is sold shall remain in
29 t' he may redeem it within a whole
30 t' the house that is in the walled city
33 t' the house that was sold, and the city
35 with thee; t' thou shalt relieve him:
41 t' shall he depart from thee, both he
52 t' he shall count with him, and
54 t' he shall go out in the year of jubilee.
26: 4 T' I will give you rain in due season,
18 t' I will punish you seven times more
24 T' will I also walk contrary unto you,
28 T' I will walk contrary unto you also
34 T' shall the land enjoy...sabbaths,
34 t' shall the land rest, and enjoy her
41 if t' their uncircumcised hearts be
41 they t' accept of the punishment of
42 T' will I remember my covenant with
27: 4 t' thy estimation shall be thirty
5, 6 t' thy estimation shall be of the
7 t' thy estimation shall be fifteen
8 t' he shall present himself before the
10 t' it and the exchange thereof shall be
11 t' he shall present the beast before the
13 t' he shall add a fifth part thereof unto
14 t' the priest shall estimate it, whether
15 t' he shall add the fifth part of the
16 t' thy estimation shall be according to
18 t' the priest shall reckon unto him the
19 t' he shall add the fifth part of the
23 T' the priest shall reckon unto him the
27 t' he shall redeem it according to
27 t' it shall be sold according to thy
33 t' both it and the change thereof shall
Nu 2: 7 T' the tribe of Zebulun: and Eliab the
14 T' the tribe of Gad: and the captain of
17 T' the tabernacle of the congregation
22 T' the tribe of Benjamin: and the
29 T' the tribe of Naphtali: and the
5: 7 T' they shall confess their sin which
15 T' shall the man bring his wife unto
21 T' the priest shall charge the woman
25 T' the priest shall take the jealousy
27 t' it shall come to pass, that, if she be
28 t' she shall be free, and shall conceive
31 T' shall the man be guiltless from
6: 9 t' he shall shave his head in the day of
7:89 t' he heard the voice of one speaking
8: 8 T' let him take a young bullock with
9:17 t' after that the children of Israel
19 t' the children of Israel kept the
21 in the morning, t' they journeyed:
10: 4 t' the princes, which are heads of
5 t' the camps that lie on the east parts

Nu 10: 6 t' the camps that lie on the south side
9 t' ye shall blow an alarm with the
11:10 T' Moses heard the people weep
12: 8 wherefore t' were ye not afraid to speak
14: 5 T' Moses and Aaron fell on their faces
8 in us, t' he will bring us into this land,
13 T' the Egyptians shall hear it, (for
15 t' the nations which have heard the
45 T' the Amalekites came down, and the
15: 4 T' shall he that offereth his offering
9 T' shall he bring with a bullock a
24 T' it shall be, if ought be committed
27 t' he shall bring a she goat of the first
16: 3 wherefore t' lift ye up yourselves
29 all men; t' the Lord hath not sent me.
30 t' ye shall understand that these men
18:26 t' ye shall offer up an heave offering of
30 t' it shall be counted unto the Levites
19: 7 T' the priest shall wash his clothes,
12 t' the seventh day he shall not be
20: 1 T' came the children of Israel, even
19 drink of thy water, t' I will pay for it:
21: 1 t' he fought against Israel, and took
2 t' I will utterly destroy their cities.
17 T' Israel sang this song, Spring up,
22:31 T' the Lord opened the eyes of
27: 1 T' came the daughters of Zelophehad,
8 t' ye shall cause his inheritance to
9, 10, 11 t' ye shall give...inheritance unto
30: 4 t' all her vows shall stand, and every
7 t' her vows shall stand, and her bonds
11 t' all her vows shall stand, and every
12 t' whatsoever proceedeth out of her
14 t' he establisheth all her vows, or all
15 them; t' he shall bear her iniquity.
32:22 t' afterward ye shall return, and be
33:52 T' ye shall drive out all the inhabitants
55 t' it shall come to pass, that those
34: 3 T' your south quarter shall be from
35:11 T' ye shall appoint you cities to be
24 T' the congregation shall judge
36: 3 t' shall their inheritance be taken from
4 t' shall their inheritance be put unto
De 1:29 T' I said unto you, Dread not, neither
41 T' ye answered and said unto me, We
2: 1 T' we turned, and took our journey
32 T' Sihon came out against us, he and
3: 1 T' we turned, and went up the way to
20 t' shall ye return every man unto his
4:41 T' Moses severed three cities on
5:25 Lord our God any more, t' we shall die.
6:12 T' beware lest thou forget the Lord,
21 T' thou shalt say unto thy son, We
8:10 t' thou shalt bless the Lord thy God
14 T' thine heart be lifted up, and thou
9: 9 t' I abode in the mount forty days and
23 t' ye rebelled against...commandment
11:17 t' the Lord's wrath be kindled against
23 T' will the Lord drive out all these
12:11 T' there shall be a place which the
21 t' thou shalt kill of thy herd and of thy
13:14 T' shalt thou enquire, and make
14:25 T' shalt thou turn it into money, and
15:12 t' in the seventh year thou shalt let
17 T' thou shalt take an aul, and thrust
17: 5 T' shalt thou bring forth that man or
8 t' shalt thou arise, and get thee up
18: 7 T' he shall minister in the name of the
19: 9 t' shalt thou add three cities more for
12 T' the elders of his city shall send and
17 T' both the men, between whom the
19 T' shall ye do unto him, as he had
20:10 against it, t' proclaim peace unto it.
12 against thee, t' thou shalt besiege it:
21: 2 T' thy elders and thy judges shall
12 T' thou shalt bring her home to thine
14 t' thou shalt let her go whither she
16 T' it shall be, when he maketh his
19 T' shall his father and his mother lay
22: 2 t' thou shalt bring it unto thine own
8 t' thou shalt make a battlement for
15 T' shall the father of the damsel, and
21 T' they shall bring out the damsel to
22 t' they shall both of them die, both the
24 T' ye shall bring them both out unto
25 t' the man only that lay with her shall
29 T' the man that lay with her shall
23: 9 t' keep thee from every wicked thing.
10 t' shall he go abroad out of the camp,
24: 1 t' let him write her a bill of
7 or selleth him; t' that thief shall die;
25: 1 t' they shall justify the righteous, and
3 t' thy brother should seem vile unto
7 t' let his brother's wife go up to the
8 T' the elders of his city shall call him,
9 T' shall his brother's wife come unto
12 T' thou shalt cut off her hand, thine
26:13 T' thou shalt say before the Lord thy
28:59 T' the Lord will make thy plagues
29:20 but t' the anger of the Lord and his
25 T' men shall say, Because they have
30: 3 That t' the Lord thy God will turn thy
31:17 T' my anger shall be kindled against
20 t' will they turn unto other gods, and
32:15 t' he forsook God which made him,
33:28 Israel t' shall dwell in safety alone:
Jos 1: 8 for t' thou shalt make thy way
8 and t' thou shalt have good success.
10 T' Joshua commanded the officers of
15 t' ye shall return unto the land of your
2:15 T' she let them down by a cord
20 t' we will be quit of thine oath which
3: 3 t' ye shall remove from your place,
4: 4 T' Joshua called the twelve men,
7 T' ye shall answer them, That the
22 T' ye shall let your children know,

Jos 6:10 day I bid you shout; t' shall ye shout.
7:21 t' I coveted them, and took them; and,
8: 7 T' ye shall rise up from the ambush,
21 t' they turned again, and slew the men
30 T' Joshua built an altar unto the
10:12 T' spake Joshua to the Lord in the
22 T' said Joshua, Open the mouth of the
29 T' Joshua passed from Makkedah,
33 T' Horam king of Gezer came up
14: 6 T' the children of Judah came unto
11 as my strength was t', even so is
12 t' I shall be able to drive them out,
15: 1 This t' was the lot of the tribe of the
17:15 t' get thee up to the wood country, and
19:12 t' goeth out to Daberath, and goeth up
29 t' the coast turneth to Ramah, and to
34 And t' the coast turneth westward to
20: 5 t' they shall not deliver the slayer up
6 t' shall the slayer return, and come
21: 1 T' came near the heads of the fathers
22: 1 T' Joshua called the Reubenites,
7 unto their tents, t' he blessed them,
19 t' pass ye over unto the land of the
21 T' the children of Reuben and the
23:16 t' shall the anger of the Lord be
24: 9 T' Balak the son of Zippor, king of
20 t' he will turn and do you hurt, and
J'g 2:18 judges, t' the Lord was with the judge,
3:23 T' Ehud went forth through the porch,
4: 8 If thou wilt go with me, t' I will go:
8 wilt not go with me, t' I will not go.
21 T' Jael Heber's wife took a nail of the
5: 1 T' sang Deborah and Barak the son
8 new gods; t' was war in the gates:
11 t' shall the people of the Lord go down
13 T' he made him that remaineth
19 t' fought the kings of Canaan in
22 T' were the horsehoofs broken by
6:13 with us, why t' is all this befallen us?
17 t' shew me a sign that thou talkest
21 T' the angel of the Lord put forth the
21 T' the angel of the Lord departed out
24 T' Gideon built an altar there unto
27 T' Gideon took ten men of his
30 T' the men of the city said unto Joash,
33 T' all the Midianites and the
37 t' shall I know that thou wilt save
7: 1 T' Jerubbaal, who is Gideon, and all
11 T' went he down with Phurah his
18 t' blow ye the trumpets also on every
24 T' all the men of Ephraim gathered
8: 3 T' their anger was abated toward
7 t' I will tear your flesh with the thorns
18 T' said he unto Zebah and Zalmunna,
21 T' Zebah and Zalmunna said, Rise
22 T' the men of Israel said unto
9:12 T' said the trees unto the vine, Come
14 T' said all the trees unto the bramble,
15 you, t' come and put your trust in my
19 If ye t' have dealt truly and sincerely
19 t' rejoice ye in Abimelech, and let
23 T' God sent an evil spirit between
29 hand! T' would I remove Abimelech.
33 t' mayest thou do to them as thou
38 T' said Zebul unto him, Where is now
50 T' went Abimelech to Thebez, and
54 T' he called hastily unto the young
10:17 T' the children of Ammon were
11: 3 T' Jephthah fled from his brethren,
11 T' Jephthah went with the elders of
17 T' Israel sent messengers unto the
18 T' they went along through the
29 T' the Spirit of the Lord came upon
31 T' it shall be, that whatsoever
12: 3 t' are ye come up unto me this day,
4 T' Jephthah gathered together all the
6 T' said they unto him, Say now
6 T' they took him, and slew him at the
7 T' died Jephthah the Gileadite, and
10 T' died Ibzan, and was buried at
13: 6 T' the woman came and told her
8 T' Manoah intreated the Lord, and
21 T' Manoah knew that he was an
14: 3 T' his father and his mother said
5 T' went Samson down, and his
12 t' I will give you thirty sheets and
13 t' shall ye give me thirty sheets and
15: 6 T' the Philistines said, Who hath
9 T' the Philistines went up, and
11 T' three thousand men of Judah went
16: 1 T' went Samson to Gaza, and saw
7 t' shall I be weak, and be as another
8 T' the lords of the Philistines brought
11 t' shall I be weak, and be as another
17 t' my strength will go from me,
18 T' the lords of the Philistines came up
23 T' the lords of the Philistines
31 T' his brethren and all the house of
17:13 T' said Micah, Now know I that the
18: 7 T' the five men departed, and came
14 T' answered the five men that went
18 T' said the priest unto them, What do
19:26 T' came the woman in the dawning of
28 T' the man took her up upon an ass,
20: 1 T' all the children of Israel went out,
3 T' said the children of Israel, Tell us,
26 T' all the children of Israel, and all
21:16 T' the elders of the congregation said,
19 T' they said, Behold, there is a feast
21 t' come ye out of the vineyards,
Ru 1: 6 T' she arose with her daughters in
9 T' she kissed them; and they lifted
18 her, t' she left speaking unto her.
21 why t' call ye me Naomi, seeing the
2: 5 T' said Boaz unto his servant that
8 T' said Boaz unto Ruth, Hearest thou

Ru 2:10 T' she fell on her face, and bowed
13 T' she said, Let me find favour in thy
3: 1 T' Naomi her mother in law said unto
13 t' will I do the part of a kinsman to
18 T' said she, Sit still, my daughter,
4: 1 T' went Boaz up to the gate, and sat
4 redeem it, t' tell me, that I may know:
5 T' said Boaz, What day thou buyest
1Sa 1: 8 T' said Elkanah her husband to her,
11 t' I will give him unto the Lord all the
17 T' Eli answered and said, Go in peace:
22 be weaned, and t' I will bring him,
2:16 t' take as much as thy soul desireth;
16 t' he would answer him, Nay; but
3:10 T' Samuel answered, Speak; for thy
16 T' Eli called Samuel, and said,
6: 3 t' ye shall be healed, and it shall be
4 T' said they, What shall be the
6 t' do ye harden your hearts, as the
9 t' he hath done us this great evil:
9 t' we shall know that it is not his
7: 3 t' put away the strange gods and
4 T' the children of Israel did put away
12 T' Samuel took a stone, and set it
8: 4 T' all the elders of Israel gathered
9: 4 t' they passed through the land of
7 T' said Saul to his servant, But,
10 T' said Saul to his servant, Well said;
18 T' Saul drew near to Samuel in the
21 wherefore t' speakest thou so to me?
10: 1 T' Samuel took a vial of oil, and
2 t' thou shalt find two men by Rachel's
3 T' shalt thou go on forward from
11 t' the people said one to another,
25 T' Samuel told the people the manner
11: 1 T' Nahash the Ammonite came up,
3 t', if there be no man to save us, we
4 T' came the messengers to Gibeah of
14 T' said Samuel to the people, Come,
12: 8 t' the Lord sent Moses and Aaron,
14 t' shall both ye and also the king that
15 t' shall the hand of the Lord be
21 t' should ye go after vain things,
13: 6 t' the people did hide themselves in
14: 8 T' said Jonathan, Behold, we will
10 Come up unto us; t' we will go up:
17 T' said Saul unto the people that were
28 T' answered one of the people, and
29 T' said Jonathan, My father hath
33 T' they told Saul, saying, Behold, the
36 T' said the priest, Let us draw near
40 T' said he unto all Israel, Be ye on
43 T' Saul said to Jonathan, Tell me
46 T' Saul went up from following the
15:10 T' came the word of the Lord unto
14 What meaneth t' this bleating of the
16 T' Samuel said unto Saul, Stay, and
19 Wherefore t' didst thou not obey the
30 T' he said, I have sinned: yet honour
32 T' said Samuel, Bring ye hither to
34 T' Samuel went to Ramah; and Saul
16: 8 T' Jesse called Abinadab, and made
9 T' Jesse made Shammah to pass by.
13 T' Samuel took the horn of oil, and
18 T' answered one of the servants, and
17: 9 kill me, t' will we be your servants:
9 t' shall ye be our servants, and serve
45 T' said David to the Philistine, Thou
18: 3 T' Jonathan and David made a
30 T' the princes of the Philistines went
19: 5 wherefore t' wilt thou sin against
22 T' went he also to Ramah, and came
20: 4 T' said Jonathan unto David,
6 t' say, David earnestly asked leave of
7 t' be sure that evil is determined by
9 upon thee, t' would not I tell it thee?
10 T' said David to Jonathan, Who
12 I t' send not unto thee, and shew it
13 t' I will shew it thee, and send thee
18 T' Jonathan said to David, To
19 t' thou shalt go down quickly, and
21 t' come thou: for there is peace to
30 T' Saul's anger was kindled against
21: 1 T' came David to Nob to Ahimelech
14 T' said Achish unto his servants, Lo,
14 wherefore t' have ye brought him to
22: 5 T' David departed, and came into the
7 T' Saul said unto his servants that
9 T' answered Doeg the Edomite,
11 T' the king sent to call Ahimelech the
14 T' Ahimelech answered the king, and
15 I t' begin to enquire of God for
23: 1 T' they told David, saying, Behold,
3 how much more t' if we come to
4 T' David enquired of the Lord yet
10 T' said David, O Lord God of Israel,
12 T' said David, Will the men of Keilah
13 T' David and his men, which were
19 T' came up the Ziphites to Saul to
24: 2 T' Saul took three thousand chosen
4 T' David arose, and cut off the skirt
25:11 Shall I t' take my bread, and my
18 T' Abigail made haste, and took two
31 my lord, t' remember thine handmaid.
26: 2 T' Saul arose, and went down to the
6 T' answered David and said to
8 T' said Abishai to David, God hath
13 T' David went over to the other side,
14 T' Abner answered and said, Who art
15 wherefore t' hast thou not kept thy
21 T' said Saul, I have sinned: return,
25 T' Saul said to David, Blessed be
27: 6 T' Achish gave him Ziklag that day:
28: 7 T' said Saul unto his servants, Seek
9 wherefore t' layest thou a snare for
11 T' said the woman, Whom shall I

1Sa 28:16 T· said Samuel, Wherefore
16 Wherefore t· dost thou ask of me,
20 T· Saul fell straightway all along on
25 T· they rose up, and went away that
29: 3 T· said the princes of the Philistines,
6 T· Achish called David, and said unto
30: 4 T· David and the people that were
22 T· answered all the wicked men and
23 T· said David, Ye shall not do so, my
31: 4 T· said Saul unto his armourbearer,
2Sa 1:11 T· David took hold on his clothes,
2:15 T· there arose and went over by
20 T· Abner looked behind him, and
22 how t· should I hold up my face to
26 T· Abner called to Joab, and said,
27 surely t· in the morning the people
3: 8 T· was Abner very wroth for the
16 T· said Abner unto him, Go, return
18 Now t· do it: for the Lord hath
24 T· Joab came to the king, and said,
5: 1 T· came all the tribes of Israel to
24 that t· thou shalt bestir thyself:
24 t· shall the Lord go out before thee,
6:20 T· David returned to bless his
7:18 T· went king David in, and sat before
8: 6 T· David put garrisons in Syria of
10 T· Toi sent Joram his son unto king
9: 5 T· king David sent, and fetched him
9 T· the king called to Ziba, Saul's
11 T· said Ziba unto the king, According
10: 2 T· said David, I will shew kindness
5 your beards be grown, and t· return,
11 strong for me, t· thou shalt help me:
11 for thee, t· I will come and help thee.
14 t· fled they also before Abishai, and
11:10 why t· didst thou not go down unto
11 shall I t· go into mine house, to eat
18 T· Joab sent and told David all the
21 t· say thou, Thy servant Uriah the
25 T· David said unto the messenger,
12:18 how will he t· vex himself, if we tell
20 T· David arose from the earth, and
20 t· he came to his own house; and
21 T· said his servants unto him, What
13: 7 T· David sent home to Tamar, saying,
15 T· Amnon hated her exceedingly; so
17 T· he called his servant that
18 T· his servant brought her out, and
26 T· said Absalom, If not, I pray thee,
28 Smite Amnon; t· kill him, fear not:
29 T· all the king's sons arose, and
31 T· the king arose, and tare his
14:11 T· said she, I pray thee, let the king
12 T· the woman said, Let thine
13 Wherefore t· hast thou thought
17 T· thine handmaid said, The word of
18 T· the king answered and said unto
31 T· Joab arose, and came to Absalom
15: 2 t· Absalom called unto him, and said,
8 to Jerusalem, t· I will serve the Lord.
10 t· ye shall say, Absalom reigneth in
19 T· said the king to Ittai the Gittite,
34 t· mayest thou for me defeat the
16: 4 T· said the king to Ziba, Behold,
9 T· said Abishai the son of Zeruiah,
10 Who shall t· say, Wherefore hast thou
20 T· said Absalom to Ahithophel, Give
21 t· shall the hands of all that are with
17: 5 T· said Absalom, Call now Hushai the
13 t· shall all Israel bring ropes to that
15 T· said Hushai unto Zadok and to
22 T· David arose, and all the people that
24 T· David came to Mahanaim. And
18:14 T· said Joab, I may not tarry thus
19 T· said Ahimaaz the son of Zadok,
21 T· said Joab to Cushi, Go tell the
22 T· said Ahimaaz the son of Zadok
23 T· Ahimaaz ran by the way of the
19: 6 this day, t· it had pleased thee well.
8 T· the king arose, and sat in the gate.
12 wherefore t· are ye the last to bring
35 wherefore t· should thy servant be
40 T· the king went on to Gilgal, and
42 wherefore t· be ye angry for this
43 why t· did ye despise us, that our
20: 4 T· said the king to Amasa, Assemble
16 T· cried a wise woman out of the
17 T· she said unto him, Hear the words
18 T· she spake, saying, They were wont
22 T· the woman went unto all the
21: 1 T· there was a famine in the days of
17 T· the men of David sware unto
18 t· Sibbechai the Hushathite slew
22: 8 T· the earth shook and trembled; the
43 T· did I beat them as small as the
23:14 And David was t· in an hold, and
14 the Philistines was t· in Beth-lehem.
1Ki 1: 5 T· Adonijah the son of Haggith
13 throne? why t· doth Adonijah reign?
28 T· king David answered and said,
31 T· Bath-sheba bowed with her face to
35 T· ye shall come up after him, that he
2:12 T· sat Solomon upon the throne of
20 T· she said, I desire one small petition
23 T· king Solomon sware by the Lord,
28 T· tidings came to Joab: for Joab had
29 T· Solomon sent Benaiah the son of
3:14 did walk, t· I will lengthen thy days.
16 T· came there two women, that
23 T· said the king, The one saith, This
26 T· spake the woman whose the living
27 T· the king answered and said, Give
6:10 t· he built chambers against all the
12 t· will I perform my word with thee,
7: 7 T· he made a porch for the throne*
38 T· made he ten lavers of brass: one*

1Ki 8: 1 T· Solomon assembled the elders
12 T· spake Solomon, The Lord said
32 T· hear thou in heaven, and do, and
34, 36 T· hear thou in heaven, and
39 T· hear thou in heaven thy
45 T· hear thou in heaven their prayer
49 T· hear thou their prayer and their
9: 5 T· I will establish the throne of thy
7 T· will I cut off Israel out of the land
11 that t· king Solomon gave Hiram
24 built for her: t· did he build Millo.
11: 7 T· did Solomon build an high place
22 T· Pharaoh said unto him, But what
12: 5 for three days, t· come again to me.
7 t· they will be thy servants for ever.
18 T· king Rehoboam sent Adoram, who
25 T· Jeroboam built Shechem in mount
27 t· shall the heart of this people turn
13:15 T· he said unto him, Come home with
31 t· bury me in the sepulchre wherein
15:18 T· Asa took all the silver and the gold
22 T· king Asa made a proclamation
16: 1 T· the word of the Lord came to Jehu
21 T· were the people of Israel
18:21 follow him: but if Baal, t· follow him.
22 T· said Elijah unto the people, I, even
38 T· the fire of the Lord fell, and
19: 2 T· Jezebel sent a messenger unto
5 behold, t· an angel touched him, and
20 my mother, and t· I will follow thee.
21 T· he arose, and went after Elijah,
20: 7 T· the king of Israel called all the
14 T· he said, Who shall order the
15 T· he numbered the young men of the
33 T· he said, Go ye, bring him.
33 T· Ben-hadad came forth to him; and
34 T· said Ahab, I will send thee away
36 T· said he unto him, Because thou
37 T· he found another man, and said,
39 t· shall thy life be for his life, or else
21:10 t· carry him out, and stone him, that
13 T· they carried him forth out of the
14 T· they sent to Jezebel, saying,
22: 6 T· the king of Israel gathered the
9 T· the king of Israel called an officer,
47 There was t· no king in Edom: a
49 T· said Ahaziah the son of Ahab
2Ki 1: 1 T· Moab rebelled against Israel after
9 T· the king sent unto him a captain of
10 t· let fire come down from heaven,
3:27 T· he took his eldest son that should
4: 3 T· he said, Go, borrow thee vessels
7 T· she came and told the man of God.
14 he said, What t· is to be done for her?
20 sat on her knees till noon, and t· died.
24 T· she saddled an ass, and said to her
28 T· she said, Did I desire a son of my
29 T· he said to Gehazi, Gird up thy
35 T· he returned, and walked in the
37 T· she went in, and fell at his feet,
41 But he said, T· bring meal. And he
5:13 how much rather t·, when he saith to
14 T· went he down, and dipped himself
17 Shall there not t·, I pray thee, be
6: 8 T· the king of Syria warred against
31 T· he said, God do so and more also to
7: 1 T· Elisha said, Hear ye the word of
2 T· a lord on whose hand the king
4 t· the famine is in the city, and we
9 T· they said one to another, We do
8: 1 T· spake Elisha unto the woman,
16 Jehoshaphat being t· king of Judah,
22 T· Libnah revolted at the same
9: 3 T· take the box of oil, and pour it on
3 T· open the door, and flee, and tarry
11 T· Jehu came forth to the servants of
13 T· they hasted, and took every man
15 t· let none go forth nor escape out of
19 T· he sent out a second on horseback,
25 T· said Jehu to Bidkar his captain,
10: 4 before him: how t· shall we stand?
6 T· he wrote a letter the second time
12: 7 T· king Jehoash called for Jehoiada
17 T· Hazael king of Syria went up,
13:17 T· Elisha said, Shoot. And he shot.
19 t· hadst thou smitten Syria till thou
14: 8 T· Amaziah sent messengers to
15:16 T· Menahem smote Tiphsah, and
16: 5 T· Rezin king of Syria, and Pekah
17: 5 T· the king of Assyria came up
27 T· the king of Assyria commanded,
28 T· one of the priests whom they had
18:24 How t· wilt thou turn away the face of
26 T· said Eliakim the son of Hilkiah,
28 T· Rab-shakeh stood and cried with a
31 t· eat ye every man of his own vine,
37 T· came Eliakim the son of Hilkiah,
19:20 T· Isaiah the son of Amoz sent to
20: 2 T· he turned his face to the wall, and
14 T· came Isaiah the prophet unto king
19 T· said Hezekiah unto Isaiah, Good is
23:17 T· he said, What title is that that I see?
24: 1 t· he turned and rebelled against him.
1Ch 1:29 t· Kedar, and Adbeel, and Mibsam,
2:24 t· Abiah Hezron's wife bare him
6:32 t· they waited on their office according
9:36 And his firstborn son Abdon, t· Zur,
10: 4 T· said Saul to his armourbearer,
7 t· they forsook their cities, and fled:
11: 1 T· all Israel gathered themselves to
16 And David was t· in the hold, and
16 garrison was t· at Beth-lehem.
12: 3 The chief was Ahiezer, t· Joash, the
18 T· the spirit came upon Amasai, who
18 T· David received them, and made
14:11 T· David said, God hath broken in

1Ch 14:15 that t· thou shalt go out to battle:
15: 2 T· David said, None ought to carry
16: 7 T· on that day David delivered first
33 T· shall the trees of the wood sing
17: 2 T· Nathan said unto David, Do all
18: 6 T· David put garrisons in
19: 5 T· there went certain, and told David
5 your beards be grown, and t· return.
12 strong for me, t· thou shalt help me:
12 strong for thee, t· I will help thee.
15 city. T· Joab came to Jerusalem.
21: 3 why t· doth my lord require this
16 T· David and the elders of Israel, who
18 T· the angel of the Lord commanded
22 T· David said to Ornan, Grant me the
28 the Jebusite, t· he sacrificed there.
22: 1 T· David said, This is the house of
6 T· he called for Solomon his son, and
13 T· shalt thou prosper, if thou
26:14 T· for Zechariah his son, a wise
28: 2 T· David the king stood up upon his
11 T· David gave to Solomon his son the
29: 5 And who t· is willing to consecrate his
6 T· the chief of the fathers and princes
9 T· the people rejoiced, for that they
23 T· Solomon sat on the throne of the
2Ch 1: 2 T· Solomon spake unto all Israel, to
13 T· Solomon came from his journey to
2: 6 who am I t·, that I should build him a
11 T· Huram the king of Tyre answered
3: 1 T· Solomon began to build the house
5: 2 T· Solomon assembled the elders
11 and did not t· wait by course:
13 t· the house was filled with a cloud,
6: 1 T· said Solomon, The Lord hath
17 Now t·, O Lord God of Israel, let thy
23 T· hear thou from heaven, and do,
25 T· hear thou from the heavens, and
27 T· hear thou from heaven, and forgive
29 T· what prayer or what supplication
30 T· hear thou from heaven thy
33 T· hear thou from the heavens, even
35 T· hear thou from the heavens their
39 T· hear thou from the heavens, even
7: 4 T· the king and all the people offered
14 t· will I hear from heaven, and will
18 T· will I stablish the throne of thy
20 T· will I pluck them up by the roots
8:12 T· Solomon offered burnt offerings
17 T· went Solomon to Ezion-geber,
10:18 T· king Rehoboam sent Hadoram that
12: 5 T· came Shemaiah the prophet to
13:15 T· the men of Judah gave a shout:
14:10 T· Asa went out against him, and
16: 2 T· Asa brought out silver and gold
6 T· Asa the king took all Judah; and
10 T· Asa was wroth with the seer, and
18:16 T· he said, I did see all Israel
20 T· there came out a spirit, and stood
23 T· Zedekiah the son of Chenaanah
25 T· the king of Israel said, Take ye
27 t· hath not the Lord spoken by me.
20: 2 T· there came some that told
9 affliction, t· thou wilt hear and help.
14 T· upon Jahaziel the son of
27 T· they returned, every man of Judah
37 T· Eliezer the son of Dodavah of
21: 9 T· Jehoram went forth with his
23:11 T· they brought out the king's son,
13 T· Athaliah rent her clothes, and said,
14 T· Jehoiada the priest brought out
17 T· all the people went to the house of
24:17 T· the king hearkened unto them.
25:10 T· Amaziah separated them, to wit,
16 T· the prophet forbare, and said, I
17 T· Amaziah king of Judah took
26: 1 T· all the people of Judah took
19 T· Uzziah was wroth, and had a
28:12 T· certain of the heads of the children
15 brethren: t· they returned to Samaria.
29:12 T· the Levites arose, Mahath the son
18 T· they went in to Hezekiah the king,
20 T· Hezekiah the king rose early, and
31 T· Hezekiah answered and said, Now
30:15 T· they killed the passover on the
27 T· the priests the Levites arose and
31: 1 T· all the children of Israel returned,
9 T· Hezekiah questioned with the
11 T· Hezekiah commanded to prepare
32:18 T· they cried with a loud voice in the
33:13 T· Manasseh knew that the Lord he
34:18 T· Shaphan the scribe told the king,
29 T· the king sent and gathered
36: 1 T· the people of the land took
Ezr 1: 5 T· rose up the chief of the fathers of
3: 2 T· stood up Jeshua the son of
9 T· stood Jeshua with his sons and his
4: 2 T· they came to Zerubbabel, and to
4 T· the people of the land weakened
9 T· wrote Rehum the chancellor,
13 t· will they not pay toll, tribute, and
17 T· sent the king an answer unto
24 T· ceased the work of the house of
5: 1 T· the prophets, Haggai the prophet,
2 T· rose up Zerubbabel the son of
4 T· said we unto them after this
5 t· they returned answer by letter
9 T· asked we those elders, and said
16 T· came the same Sheshbazzar, and
6: 1 T· Darius the king made a decree,
13 T· Tatnai, governor on this side the
8:16 T· sent I for Eliezer, for Ariel, for
21 T· I proclaimed a fast there, at the
24 T· I separated twelve of the chief of
31 T· we departed from the river of
9: 4 T· were assembled unto me every one

Ezr 10: 5 *T'* arose Ezra, and made the chief
6 *T'* Ezra rose up from before the
9 *T'* all the men of Judah and
12 *T'* all the congregation answered and
Ne 2: 2 of heart. *T'* I was very sore afraid.
4 *T'* the king said unto me, For what
9 *T'* I came to the governors beyond the
14 *T'* I went on to the gate of the
15 *T'* went I up in the night by the
17 *T'* said I unto them, Ye see the
18 *T'* I told them of the hand of my God
20 *T'* answered I them, and said unto
3: 1 *T'* Eliashib the high priest rose up
4: 7 to be stopped, *t'* they were very wroth,
5: 7 *T'* I consulted with myself, and I
8 *T'* held they their peace, and found
12 *T'* said they, We will restore them, and
12 *T'* I called the priests, and took an
6: 5 *T'* sent Sanballat his servant unto me
8 *T'* I sent unto him, saying, There are
8:10 *T'* he said unto them, Go your way,
9: 4 *T'* stood up upon the stairs, of the
5 *T'* the Levites, Jeshua, and Kadmiel,
12:31 *T'* I brought up the princes of Judah
13: 9 *T'* I commanded, and they cleansed
11 *T'* contended I with the rulers, and
12 *T'* brought all Judah the tithe of the
17 *T'* I contended with the nobles of
21 *T'* I testified against them, and said
27 Shall we *t'* hearken unto you to do all
Es 1:13 *T'* the king said to the wise men,
2: 2 *T'* said the king's servants that
13 *T'* thus came every maiden unto the
18 *T'* the king made a great feast unto
19 *t'* Mordecai sat in the king's gate.
3: 3 *T'* the king's servants, which were in
5 reverence, *t'* was Haman full of wrath.
12 *T'* were the king's scribes called on
4: 4 *T'* was the queen exceedingly grieved;
5 *T'* called Esther for Hatach, one of the
13 *T'* Mordecai commanded to answer
14 *t'* shall there enlargement and
15 *T'* Esther bade them return Mordecai
5: 3 *T'* said the king unto her, What wilt
5 *T'* the king said, Cause Haman to
7 *T'* answered Esther, and said, My
9 *T'* went Haman forth that day joyful
14 *T'* said Zeresh his wife and all his
14 *t'* go thou in merrily with the king
6: 3 *T'* said the king's servants that
10 *T'* the king said to Haman, Make
11 *T'* took Haman the apparel and the
13 *T'* said his wise men and Zeresh his
7: 3 *T'* Esther the queen answered and
5 *T'* the king Ahasuerus answered and
6 *T'* Haman was afraid before the king
8 *T'* the king returned out of the palace
8 *T'* said the king, Will he force the
9 *T'* the king said, Hang him thereon.
10 *T'* was the king's wrath pacified.
8: 4 *T'* the king held out the golden
7 *T'* the king Ahasuerus said unto
9 *T'* were the king's scribes called at
9:13 *T'* said Esther, If it please the king,
29 *T'* Esther the queen, the daughter of
Job 1: 7, 9 *T'* Satan answered the Lord, and
20 *T'* Job arose, and rent his mantle, and
2: 9 *T'* said his wife unto him, Dost thou
3:13 have slept: *t'* had I been at rest,
4: 1 *T'* Eliphaz the Temanite answered
15 *T'* a spirit passed before my face; the
6:10 *T'* should I yet have comfort; yea, I
7:14 *T'* thou scarest me with dreams, and
8: 1 *T'* answered Bildad the Shuhite, and
18 *t'* it shall deny him, saying, I have not
9: 1 *T'* Job answered and said,
29 If I be wicked, why *t'* labour I in vain?
35 *T'* would I speak, and not fear him;
10:14 If I sin, *t'* thou markest me, and thou
18 Wherefore *t'* hast thou brought me
20 cease *t'*, and let me alone, that I may
11: 1 *T'* answered Zophar the Naamathite,
10 or gather together, *t'* who can hinder
11 also; will he not *t'* consider it?
15 For *t'* shalt thou lift up thy face
13:20 *t'* will I not hide myself from thee.
22 *T'* call thou, and I will answer: or let
15: 1 *T'* answered Eliphaz the Temanite,
16: 1 *T'* Job answered and said,
22 *t'* I shall go the way whence I shall
18: 1 *T'* answered Bildad the Shuhite, and
19: 1 *T'* Job answered and said,
20: 1 *T'* answered Zophar the Naamathite,
21:34 How *t'* comfort ye me in vain, seeing
22: 1 *T'* Eliphaz the Temanite answered
24 *T'* shalt thou lay up gold as dust, and
26 For *t'* shalt thou have thy delight
29 *t'* thou shalt say, There is lifting up;
23: 1 *T'* Job answered and said,
25: 1 *T'* answered Bildad the Shuhite, and
4 How *t'* can man be justified with God?
27:12 it; why *t'* are ye thus altogether vain?
28:20 Whence *t'* cometh wisdom? and where
27 *T'* did he see it, and declare it; he
29:11 the ear heard me, *t'* it blessed me;
18 *T'* I said, I shall die in my nest, and I
30:26 looked for good, *t'* evil came unto me:
31: 1 why *t'* should I think upon a maid?
8 *T'* let me sow, and let another eat;
10 *T'* let my wife grind unto another, and
14 What *t'* shall I do when God riseth up?
22 *T'* let mine arm fall from my shoulder
32: 2 *T'* was kindled the wrath of Elihu the
5 three men, *t'* his wrath was kindled.
33:16 *T'* he openeth the ears of men, and
24 *T'* he is gracious unto him, and saith,

Job 34:29 quietness, who *t'* can make trouble?
29 hideth his face, who *t'* can behold him?
36: 9 *T'* he sheweth them their work, and
18 *t'* a great ransom cannot deliver thee.
37: 8 *T'* the beasts go into dens, and
38: 1 *T'* the Lord answered Job out of the
21 thou it, because thou wast *t'* born?
40: 3 *T'* Job answered the Lord, and said,
6 *T'* answered the Lord unto Job out of
14 *T'* will I also confess unto thee that
41:10 up: who *t'* is able to stand before me?
42: 1 *T'* Job answered the Lord, and said,
11 *T'* came there unto him all his
Ps 2: 5 *T'* shall he speak unto them in his
18: 7 *T'* the earth shook and trembled; the
15 *T'* the channels of waters were seen,
42 *T'* did I beat them small as the dust
19:13 *t'* shall I be upright, and I shall be
27:10 forsake me, *t'* the Lord will take me
39: 3 burned: *t'* spake I with my tongue,
40: 7 *T'* said I, Lo, I come: in the volume
43: 4 *T'* will I go unto the altar of God,
50:18 a thief, *t'* thou consentedst with him,
51:13 *T'* will I teach transgressors thy ways;
19 *T'* shalt thou be pleased with the
19 *t'* shall they offer bullocks upon
55: 6 for *t'* would I fly away, and be at rest.
7 Lo, *t'* would I wander far off, and
12 me; *t'* I could have borne it:
12 *t'* I would have hid myself from him:
56: 9 *t'* shall mine enemies turn back:
67: 6 *T'* shall the earth yield her increase;
69: 4 *t'* I restored that which I took not
73:17 of God; *t'* understood I their end.
78:34 he slew them, *t'* they sought him: and
65 *T'* the Lord awaked as one out of
80:12 Why hast thou *t'* broken down her
89:19 *T'* thou spakest in vision to thy
32 *T'* will I visit their transgression with
96:12 *t'* shall all the trees of the wood
106:12 *T'* believed they his words; they sang
30 *T'* stood up Phinehas, and executed
107: 6, 13 *T'* they cried unto the Lord in
19, 28 *T'* they cry unto the Lord in
30 *T'* are they glad because they be quiet;
116: 4 *T'* called I upon the name of the Lord;
119: 6 *T'* shall I not be ashamed, when I
92 I should *t'* have perished in mine
124: 3 *T'* they had swallowed us up quick,
4 *T'* the waters had overwhelmed us,
5 *T'* the proud waters had gone over
126: 2 *T'* was our mouth filled with
2 *t'* said they among the heathen,
142: 3 within me, *t'* thou knewest my path.
Pr 1:28 *T'* shall they call upon me, but I
2: 5 *T'* shalt thou understand the fear
9 *T'* shalt thou understand
3:23 *T'* shalt thou walk in thy way safely,
8:30 *T'* I was by him, as one brought up
11: 2 When pride cometh, *t'* cometh shame:
15:11 how much more *t'* the hearts of the
18: 3 cometh, *t'* cometh also contempt,
20:14 he is gone his way, *t'* he boasteth.
24 how can a man *t'* understand his own
24:14 found it, *t'* there shall be a reward,
32 *T'* I saw, and considered it well: I
Ec 2:11 *T'* I looked on all the works that my
13 *T'* I saw that wisdom excelleth folly,
15 *T'* said I in my heart, As it happeneth
15 to me; and why was I *t'* more wise?
15 *T'* I said in my heart, that this also is
4: 7 *T'* I returned, and I saw vanity under
11 if two lie together, *t'* they have heat:
8:15 *T'* I commended mirth, because a man
17 *T'* I beheld all the work of God, that a
9:16 *T'* said I, Wisdom is better than
10:10 edge, *t'* must he put to more strength:
12: 7 *T'* shall the dust return to the earth
Ca 8:10 *t'* was I in his eyes as one that found
Isa 5:17 *T'* shall the lambs feed after their
6: 5 *T'* said I, Woe is me! for I am undone;
6 *T'* flew one of the seraphims unto me,
8 us? *T'* said I, Here am I; send me.
11 *T'* said I, Lord, how long? And he
7: 3 *T'* said the Lord unto Isaiah, Go forth
8: 3 *T'* said the Lord to me, Call his name
14:25 *t'* shall his yoke depart from off them,
32 shall one *t'* answer the messengers of
24:23 *T'* the moon shall be confounded, and
28:18 *t'* ye shall be trodden down by it.
30:23 *T'* shall he give the rain of thy seed,
31: 8 *T'* shall the Assyrian fall with the
32:16 *T'* judgment shall dwell in the
33:23 *t'* is the prey of a great spoil
35: 5 *T'* the eyes of the blind shall be
6 *T'* shall the lame man leap as an
36: 3 *T'* came forth unto him Eliakim,
9 How *t'* wilt thou turn away the face of
11 *T'* said Eliakim and Shebna and Joah
13 *T'* Rabshakeh stood, and cried with a
22 *T'* came Eliakim, the son of Hilkiah,
37:21 *T'* Isaiah the son of Amoz sent unto
36 *T'* the angel of the Lord went forth,
38: 2 *T'* Hezekiah turned his face toward
4 *T'* came the word of the Lord to
39: 3 *T'* came Isaiah the prophet unto king
4 *T'* said he, What have they seen in
5 *T'* said Isaiah to Hezekiah, Hear the
8 *T'* said Hezekiah to Isaiah, Good is
40:18 To whom *t'* will ye liken God? or what
25 To whom *t'* will ye liken me, or shall I
41: 1 them come near; *t'* let them speak:
44:15 *T'* shall it be for a man to burn: for he
48:18 *t'* had thy peace been as a river, and
49: 4 *T'* I said, I have laboured in vain, I
21 *T'* shalt thou say in thine heart, Who

Isa 58: 8 *T'* shall thy light break forth as
9 *T'* shalt thou call, and the Lord
10 *t'* shall thy light rise in obscurity, and
14 *T'* shalt thou delight thyself in the
60: 5 *T'* thou shalt see, and flow together,
63:11 *T'* he remembered the days of old,
66:12 *t'* shall ye suck, ye shall be borne
Jer 1: 4 *T'* the word of the Lord came unto
6 *T'* said I, Ah, Lord God! behold, I
9 *T'* the Lord put forth his hand, and
12 *T'* said the Lord unto me, Thou hast
14 *T'* the Lord said unto me, Out of the
2:21 how *t'* art thou turned into the
4: 1 of my sight, *t'* shalt thou not remove.
10 *T'* said I, Ah, Lord God! surely thou
5: 7 to the full, they *t'* committed adultery,
19 *t'* shalt thou answer them, Like as ye
7: 7 *T'* will I cause you to dwell in this
34 *T'* will I cause to cease from the cities
8: 5 Why *t'* is this people of Jerusalem
22 why *t'* is not the health of the
11: 5 *T'* answered I, and said, So be it, O
6 *T'* the Lord said unto me, Proclaim all
12 *T'* shall the cities of Judah and
15 thou doest evil, *t'* thou rejoicest.
18 *t'* thou shewedst me their doings.
12: 5 *t'* how canst thou contend with horses?
5 *t'* how wilt thou do in the swelling of
16 *t'* shall they be built in the midst of my
13: 7 *T'* I went to Euphrates, and digged,
8 *T'* the word of the Lord came unto
13 *T'* shalt thou say unto them, Thus
23 *t'* may ye also do good, that are
14:11 *T'* said the Lord unto me, Pray not
13 *T'* said I, Ah, Lord God! behold, the
14 *T'* the Lord said unto me, The
18 *t'* behold the slain with the sword!
18 *t'* behold them that are sick with
15: 1 *T'* said the Lord unto me, Though
2 *t'* thou shalt tell them, Thus saith the
19 thou return, *t'* will I bring thee again,
16:11 *T'* shalt thou say unto them, Because
17:25 *T'* shall there enter into the gates of
18: 3 *T'* I went down to the potter's house,
5 *T'* the word of the Lord came to me,
10 *t'* I will repent of the good, wherewith
18 *T'* said they, Come, and let us devise
19:10 *T'* shalt thou break the bottle in the
14 *T'* came Jeremiah from Tophet,
20: 2 *T'* Pashur smote Jeremiah the
3 *T'* said Jeremiah unto him, The Lord
9 *T'* I said, I will not mention of him,
21: 3 *T'* said Jeremiah unto them, Thus
22: 4 *t'* shall there enter in by the gates of
9 *T'* they shall answer, Because they
15 justice, and *t'* it was well with him?
16 and needy; *t'* it was well with him:
22 surely *t'* shalt thou be ashamed and
23:22 *t'* they should have turned them from
33 thou shalt *t'* say unto them, What
24: 3 *T'* said the Lord unto me, What seest
25:17 *T'* took I the cup at the Lord's hand,
28 *t'* shalt thou say unto them, Thus
26: 6 *T'* will I make this house like Shiloh,
10 *t'* they came up from the king's house
11 *T'* spake the priests and the prophets
12 *T'* spake Jeremiah unto all the
16 *T'* said the princes and all the people
17 *T'* rose up certain of the elders of the
27: 7 *t'* many nations and great kings shall
22 *t'* will I bring them up, and restore
28: 5 *T'* the prophet Jeremiah said unto the
9 *t'* shall the prophet be known, that the
10 *T'* Hananiah the prophet took the
12 *T'* the word of the Lord came unto
15 *T'* said the prophet Jeremiah unto
29:12 *T'* shall ye call upon me, and ye shall
30 *T'* came the word of the Lord unto
31:13 *T'* shall the virgin rejoice in the
36 *t'* the seed of Israel also shall cease
32: 2 For *t'* the king of Babylon's army
8 *T'* I knew that this was the word of
26 *T'* came the word of the Lord unto
33:21 *T'* may also my covenant be broken
26 *T'* will I cast away the seed of
34: 6 *T'* Jeremiah the prophet spake all
10 more, *t'* they obeyed, and let them go.
35: 3 *T'* I took Jaazaniah the son of
12 *T'* came the word of the Lord unto
36: 4 *T'* Jeremiah called Baruch the son of
10 *T'* read Baruch in the book the words
12 *T'* he went down into the king's house,
13 *T'* Michaiah declared unto them all
18 *T'* Baruch answered them, He
19 *T'* said the princes unto Baruch, Go,
27 *T'* the word of the Lord came to
32 *T'* took Jeremiah another roll, and
37: 5 *T'* Pharaoh's army was come forth out
6 *T'* came the word of the Lord unto the
12 *T'* Jeremiah went forth out of
14 *T'* said Jeremiah, It is false; I fall not
17 *T'* Zedekiah the king sent, and took
21 *T'* Zedekiah the king commanded
38: 1 *T'* Shephatiah the son of Mattan, and
5 *T'* Zedekiah the king said, Behold, he
6 *T'* took they Jeremiah, and cast him
7 king *t'* sitting in the gate of Benjamin;
10 *T'* the king commanded Ebed-melech
14 *T'* Zedekiah the king sent, and took
15 *T'* Jeremiah said unto Zedekiah, If I
17 *T'* said Jeremiah unto Zedekiah, Thus
17 *t'* thy soul shall live, and this city shall
18 *t'* shall this city be given into the hand
24 *T'* said Zedekiah unto Jeremiah, Let
26 *T'* thou shalt say unto them, I
27 *T'* came all the princes unto Jeremiah

Jer 39: 4 *t'* they fled, and went forth out of the
6 *T'* the king of Babylon slew the sons
9 *T'* Nebuzar-adan the captain of the
40: 6 *T'* went Jeremiah unto Gedaliah the
8 *T'* they came to Gedaliah to Mizpah,
15 *T'* Johanan the son of Kareah spake
41: 2 *T'* arose Ishmael the son of Nethaniah,
10 *T'* Ishmael carried away captive all
12 *T'* they took all the men, and went to
13 that were with him, *t'* they were glad.
16 *T'* took Johanan the son of Kareah,
42: 1 *T'* all the captains of the forces, and
4 *T'* Jeremiah the prophet said unto
5 *T'* they said to Jeremiah, The Lord
8 *T'* called he Johanan the son of
10 abide in this land, *t'* will I build you,
16 *T'* it shall come to pass, that the
43: 2 *T'* spake Azariah the son of Hoshaiah,
8 *T'* came the word of the Lord unto
44:15 *T'* all the men which knew that their
17 *t'* had we plenty of victuals, and were
20 *T'* Jeremiah said unto all the people,
47: 2 *t'* the men shall cry, and all the
49: 1 why *t'* doth their king inherit Gad,
2 *t'* shall Israel be heir unto them that
51:48 *T'* the heaven and the earth, and all
62 *T'* shalt thou say, O Lord, thou hast
52: 7 *T'* the city was broken up, and all
9 *T'* they took the king, and carried
11 *T'* he put out the eyes of Zedekiah;
15 *T'* Nebuzar-adan the captain of the
La 3:54 mine head; *t'* I said, I am cut off.
Eze 3: 3 *T'* did I eat it; and it was in my
12 *T'* the spirit took me up, and I heard
15 *T'* I came to them of the captivity at
23 *T'* I arose, and went forth into the
24 *T'* the spirit entered into me, and set
4:14 *T'* said I, Ah Lord God! behold, my
15 *T'* he said unto me, Lo, I have given
5: 1 *t'* take thee balances to weigh, and
4 *T'* take of them again, and cast them
6:13 *T'* shall ye know that I am the Lord,
7:26 *t'* shall they seek a vision of the
8: 2 *T'* I beheld, and lo a likeness as the
5, 8, 12 *T'* said he unto me, Son of man,
14 *T'* he brought me to the door of the
15 *T'* said he unto me, Hast thou seen
17 *T'* he said unto me, Hast thou seen
9: 6 *T'* they began at the ancient men
9 *T'* said he unto me, The iniquity of
10: 1 *T'* I looked, and, behold, in the
4 *T'* the glory of the Lord went up from
6 *t'* he went in, and stood beside the
18 *T'* the glory of the Lord departed from
11: 2 *T'* said he unto me, Son of man, these
13 *T'* fell I down upon my face, and cried
22 *T'* did the cherubims lift up their
25 *T'* I spake unto them of the captivity
12: 4 *T'* shalt thou bring forth thy stuff by
14: 1 *T'* came certain of the elders of Israel
13 *t'* will I stretch out mine hand upon it,
16: 9 *T'* washed I thee with water; yea, I
53 *t'* will I bring again the captivity of
55 *t'* thou and thy daughters shall return
61 *T'* thou shalt remember thy ways, and
18:13 shall he *t'* live? he shall not live: he
19: 5 *t'* she took another of her whelps, and
8 *T'* the nations set against him on
20: 2 *T'* came the word of the Lord unto
7 *T'* said I unto them, Cast ye away
8 *t'* I said, I will pour out my fury upon
13, 21 *t'* I said, I would pour out my fury
28 *t'* they saw every high hill, and all the
29 *T'* I said unto them, What is the high
49 *T'* said I, Ah Lord God! they say of
21: 4 Seeing *t'* that I will cut off from thee
10 glitter: should we *t'* make mirth?
22: 3 *T'* say thou, Thus saith the Lord
23:13 *T'* I saw that she was defiled, that
18 *t'* my mind was alienated from her,
39 *t'* they came the same day into my
43 *T'* said I unto her that was old in
24:11 *T'* set it empty upon the coals thereof,
20 *T'* I answered them, The word of the
26:16 *T'* all the princes of the sea shall come
28:25 *t'* shall they dwell in their land that I
32: 4 *T'* will I leave thee upon the land,
14 *T'* will I make their waters deep,
15 *t'* shall they know that I am the Lord.
33: 4 *T'* whosoever heareth the sound of the
10 away in them, how should we *t'* live?
22 *T'* the word of the Lord came unto me,
29 *T'* shall they know that I am the Lord,
33 *t'* shall they know that a prophet hath
36:25 *T'* will I sprinkle clean water upon
31 *T'* shall ye remember your own evil
36 *T'* the heathen that are left round
37: 9 *T'* said he unto me, Prophesy unto the
11 *T'* he said unto me, Son of man, these
14 *t'* shall ye know that I the Lord have
16 *t'* take another stick, and write upon
39:15 *t'* shall he set up a sign by it, till the
28 *T'* shall they know that I am the Lord
40: 6 *T'* came he unto the gate which looketh
8 *T'* measured he the porch of the gate,
13 He measured *t'* the gate from the roof
17 *T'* brought he me into the outward
19 *T'* he measured the breadth from the
41: 3 *T'* went he inward, and measured the
42: 1 *T'* he brought me forth into the utter
13 *T'* said he unto me, The north
14 *t'* shall they not go out of the holy
44: 1 *T'* he brought me back the way of the
2 *T'* said the Lord unto me; This gate
4 *T'* brought he me the way of the
46: 2 *t'* he shall go forth; but the gate shall
Eze 46:12 one shall *t'* open him the gate that
12 *t'* he shall go forth; and after his
17 *t'* it shall be his to the year of liberty;
20 *T'* said he unto me, This is the place
21 *T'* he brought me forth into the utter
24 *T'* said he unto me, These are the
47: 2 *T'* brought he me out of the way of
6 *T'* he brought me, and caused me to
8 *T'* said he unto me, These waters
Da 1:10 *t'* shall ye make me endanger my
11 *T'* said Daniel to Melzar, whom the
13 *T'* let our countenances be looked
18 *t'* the prince of the eunuchs brought
2: 2 *T'* the king commanded to call the
4 *T'* spake the Chaldeans to the king in
14 *T'* Daniel answered with counsel
15 *T'* Arioch made the thing known to
16 *T'* Daniel went in, and desired of the
17 *T'* Daniel went to his house, and
19 *T'* was the secret revealed unto
19 *T'* Daniel blessed the God of heaven.
25 *T'* Arioch brought in Daniel before
35 *T'* was the iron, the clay, the brass,
46 *T'* the king Nebuchadnezzar fell
48 *T'* the king made Daniel a great
49 *T'* Daniel requested of the king, and
3: 2 *T'* Nebuchadnezzar the king sent to
3 *T'* the princes, the governors, and
4 *T'* an herald cried aloud, To you it is
13 *T'* Nebuchadnezzar in his rage and
13 *T'* they brought these men before
19 *T'* was Nebuchadnezzar full of fury,
21 *T'* these men were bound in their
24 *T'* Nebuchadnezzar the king was
26 *T'* Nebuchadnezzar came near to
26 *T'* Shadrach, Meshach, and
28 *T'* Nebuchadnezzar spake, and said,
30 *T'* the king promoted Shadrach,
4: 7 *T'* came in the magicians, the
19 *T'* Daniel, whose name was
5: 3 *T'* they brought the golden vessels
6 *T'* the king's countenance was
8 *T'* came in all the king's wise men:
9 *T'* was king Belshazzar greatly
13 *T'* was Daniel brought in before the
17 *T'* Daniel answered and said before
24 *T'* was the part of the hand sent
29 *T'* commanded Belshazzar, and they
6: 3 *T'* this Daniel was preferred above
4 *T'* the presidents and princes
5 *T'* said these men, We shall not find
6 *T'* these presidents and princes
11 *T'* these men assembled, and found
12 *T'* they came near, and spake before
13 *T'* answered they and said before
14 *T'* the king, when he heard these
15 *T'* these men assembled unto the
16 *T'* the king commanded, and they
18 *T'* the king went to his palace, and
19 *T'* the king arose very early in the
21 *T'* said Daniel unto the king, O king,
23 *T'* was the king exceeding glad for
25 *T'* king Darius wrote unto all people,
7: 1 *t'* he wrote the dream, and told the
11 I beheld *t'* because of the voice of
19 *T'* I would know the truth of the
8: 3 *T'* I lifted up mine eyes, and saw,
13 *T'* I heard one saint speaking, and
14 *t'* shall the sanctuary be cleansed.
15 *t'*, behold, there stood before me as
10: 5 *T'* I lifted up mine eyes, and looked,
9 *t'* was I in a deep sleep on my face,
12 *T'* said he unto me, Fear not, Daniel:
16 *t'* I opened my mouth, and spake, and
18 *T'* there came again and touched me
20 *T'* said he, Knowest thou wherefore I
11:10 *t'* shall he return, and be stirred up,
19 *T'* he shall turn his face toward the
20 *T'* shall stand up in his estate a
28 *T'* shall he return into his land with
12: 5 *T'* I Daniel looked, and, behold, there
8 *t'* said I, O my Lord, what shall be the
Ho 1: 9 *T'* said God, Call his name Lo-ammi:
11 *T'* shall the children of Judah and the
2: 7 *t'* shall she say, I will go and return to
7 *t'* was it better with me than now.
3: 1 *T'* said the Lord unto me, Go yet,
5:13 *t'* went Ephraim to the Assyrian,
6: 3 *T'* shall we know, if we follow on
7: 1 *t'* the iniquity of Ephraim was
10: 3 Lord; what *t'* should a king do to us?
11: 1 Israel was a child, *t'* I loved him, and
10 *t'* the children shall tremble from the
Joe 2:18 *T'* will the Lord be jealous for his
23 Be glad *t'*, ye children of Zion, and
3:17 *t'* shall Jerusalem be holy, and there
Am 6: 2 *t'* go down to Gath of the Philistines:
10 *T'* shall he say, Hold thy tongue: for
7: 2 *t'* I said, O Lord God, forgive, I
5 *T'* said I, O Lord God, cease, I
8 *T'* said the Lord, Behold, I will set a
10 *T'* Amaziah the priest of Beth-el sent
14 *T'* answered Amos, and said to
8: 2 *T'* said the Lord unto me, The end is
Jon 1: 5 *T'* the mariners were afraid, and cried
8 *T'* said they unto him, Tell us, we
10 *T'* were the men exceedingly afraid,
11 *T'* said they unto him, What shall we
16 *T'* the men feared the Lord
2: 1 *T'* Jonah prayed unto the Lord his
4 *T'* I said, I am cast out of thy sight;
4: 4 *T'* said the Lord, Doest thou well to
10 *T'* said the Lord, thou hast had pity
Mic 3: 4 *T'* shall they cry unto the Lord,
7 *T'* shall the seers be ashamed, and
5: 3 *t'* the remnant of his brethren shall
Mic 5: 5 *t'* shall we raise against him seven
7:10 *T'* she that is mine enemy shall see it,
Hab 1:11 *T'* shall his mind change, and he
Zep 3: 9 *t'* will I turn to the people a pure
11 *t'* I will take away out of the midst
Hag 1: 3 *T'* came the word of the Lord by
12 *T'* Zerubbabel the son of Shealtiel,
13 *T'* spake Haggai the Lord's
2:13 *T'* said Haggai, If one that is
14 *T'* answered Haggai, and said, So is
Zec 1: 9 *T'* said I, O my lord, what are these?
12 *T'* the angel of the Lord answered
18 *T'* lifted I up mine eyes, and saw, and
21 *T'* said I, What come these to do?
2: 2 *T'* said I, Whither goest thou? And
3: 7 *t'* thou shalt also judge my house,
4: 5 *T'* the angel that talked with me
6 *T'* he answered and spake unto me,
11 *T'* answered I, and said unto him,
14 *T'* said he, These are the two
5: 1 *T'* I turned, and lifted up mine eyes,
3 *T'* said he unto me, This is the curse
5 *T'* the angel that talked with me went
9 *T'* lifted I up mine eyes, and looked,
10 *T'* said I to the angel that talked with
6: 4 *T'* I answered and said unto the
8 *T'* cried he upon me, and spake unto
11 *T'* take silver and gold, and make
7: 4 *T'* came the word of the Lord of hosts
11: 9 *T'* said I, I will not feed you: that that
14 *T'* I cut asunder mine other staff, even
13: 3 *t'* his father and his mother that begat
6 *T'* he shall answer, Those with which
14: 3 *T'* shall the Lord go forth, and fight
Mal 1: 6 if *t'* I be a father, where is mine
3: 4 *T'* shall the offering of Judah and
16 *T'* they that feared the Lord spake
18 *T'* shall ye return, and discern
M't 1:19 *T'* Joseph her husband,...a just
24 *T'* Joseph being raised from sleep
2: 7 *T'* Herod, when he had privily
16 *T'* Herod, when he saw that he was
17 *T'* was fulfilled that which was
3: 5 *T'* went out to him Jerusalem, and
13 *T'* cometh Jesus from Galilee to
15 righteousness. *T'* he suffered him.
4: 1 *T'* was Jesus led up of the spirit
5 *T'* the devil taketh him up into the
10 *T'* saith Jesus unto him, Get thee
11 *T'* the devil leaveth him, and,
5:24 and *t'* come and offer thy gift.
7: 5 *t'* shalt thou see clearly to cast out
11 If ye *t'*, being evil, know how to
23 *t'* will I profess unto them, I never
8:26 *T'* he arose, and rebuked the winds
9: 6 (*t'* saith he to the sick of the palsy,)
14 *T'* came to him the disciples of
15 from them, and *t'* shall they fast.
29 *T'* touched he their eyes, saying,
37 *T'* saith he unto his disciples, The
11:20 *T'* began he to upbraid the cities
12:12 How much *t'* is a man better than
13 *T'* saith he to the man, Stretch
14 *T'* the Pharisees went out,...held
22 *T'* was brought unto him one
26 how shall *t'* his kingdom stand?
28 *t'* the kingdom of God is come
29 and *t'* he will spoil his house.
38 *T'* certain of the scribes and of the
44 *T'* he saith, I will return into my
45 *T'* goeth he, and taketh with
47 *T'* one said unto him, Behold, thy
13:19 *t'* cometh the wicked one, and
26 fruit, *t'* appeared the tares also.
27 from whence *t'* hath it tares?
28 Wilt thou *t'* that we go and gather
36 *T'* Jesus sent the multitude away,
43 *T'* shall the righteous shine forth
52 *T'* said he unto them, Therefore
56 Whence *t'* hath this man all these
14:33 *T'* they that were in the ship came
15: 1 *T'* came to Jesus scribes and
12 *T'* came his disciples, and said unto
15 *T'* answered Peter and said unto
21 *T'* Jesus went thence, and
25 *T'* came she and worshipped him,
28 *T'* Jesus answered and said unto
32 *T'* Jesus called his disciples unto
16: 6 *T'* Jesus said unto them, Take
12 *T'* understood they how that he
20 *T'* charged he his disciples that
22 *T'* Peter took him, and began to
24 *T'* said Jesus unto his disciples,
27 and *t'* he shall reward every man
17: 4 *T'* answered Peter, and said unto
10 Why *t'* say the scribes that Elias
13 *T'* the disciples understood that
17 *T'* Jesus answered and said, O
19 *T'* came the disciples to Jesus
26 unto him, *T'* are the children free.
18:16 *t'* take with thee one or two more,
21 *T'* came Peter to him, and said,
27 *T'* the lord of that servant was
32 *T'* his lord, after that he had
19: 7 did Moses *t'* command to give a
13 *T'* were...brought unto him little
23 *T'* said Jesus unto his disciples,
25 saying, Who *t'* can be saved?
27 *T'* answered Peter and said unto
20:20 *T'* came to him the mother of
21: 1 Olives, *t'* sent Jesus two disciples,
25 us, Why did ye not *t'* believe him?
22: 8 *T'* saith he to his servants, The
13 *T'* said the king to the servants,
15 *T'* went the Pharisees, and took
21 *T'* saith he unto them, Render

M't 22:35 *T'* one of them, which was a
43 How *t'* doth David in spirit call
45 If David *t'* call him Lord, how is he
23: 1 *T'* spake Jesus to the multitude,
32 Fill ye up *t'* the measure of your
24: 9 *T'* shall they deliver you up to be
10 *t'* shall many be offended, and shall
14 nations; and *t'* shall the end come.
16 *T'* let them which be in Judæa flee
21 *t'* shall be great tribulation, such as
23 *T'* if any man shall say unto you,
30 *t'* shall appear the sign of the Son
30 *t'* shall all the tribes of the earth
40 *T'* shall two be in the field; the one
45 *t'* is a faithful and wise servant,
25: 1 *T'* shall the kingdom of heaven be
7 *T'* all those virgins arose, and
16 *T'* he that had received the five
24 *T'* he which had received the one
27 *t'* at my coming I should have received
31 *t'* shall he sit upon the throne of
34 *T'* shall the King say unto them on
37 *T'* shall the righteous answer him,
41 *T'* shall he say also unto them on
44 *T'* shall they also answer him,
45 *T'* shall he answer them, saying,
26: 3 *T'* assembled together the chief
14 *T'* one of the twelve, called Judas
25 *T'* Judas, which betrayed him,
31 *T'* saith Jesus unto them, All ye
36 *T'* cometh Jesus with them unto a
38 *T'* saith he unto them, My soul is
45 *T'* cometh he to his disciples, and
50 *T'* came they, and laid hands on
52 *T'* said Jesus unto him, Put up
54 But how *t'* shall the scriptures be
56 *T'* all the disciples forsook him,
65 *T'* the high priest rent his clothes,
67 *T'* did they spit in his face, and
74 *T'* began he to curse and to swear,
27: 3 *T'* Judas, which had betrayed him,
9 *T'* was fulfilled that which was
13 *T'* said Pilate unto him, Hearest
16 And they had *t'* a notable prisoner,
22 What shall I do *t'* with Jesus
25 *T'* answered all the people, and
26 *T'* released he Barabbas unto
27 *T'* the soldiers of the governor took
38 *T'* were there two thieves crucified
58 *T'* Pilate commanded the body to
28:10 *T'* said Jesus unto them, Be not
16 *T'* the eleven disciples went away
M'r 2:20 and *t'* shall they fast in those days.
3:27 man; and *t'* he will spoil his house.
31 There came *t'* his brethren and his
4:13 and how *t'* will ye know all parables?
28 first the blade, *t'* the ear, after
7: 1 *T'* came together unto him the
5 *T'* the Pharisees and scribes
10: 8 so *t'* they are no more twain, but one
21 *T'* Jesus beholding him loved
26 themselves, Who *t'* can be saved?
28 *T'* Peter began to say unto him,
11:31 say, Why *t'* did ye not believe him?
12:18 *T'* come unto him the Sadducees,
37 him Lord; and whence is he *t'* his son?
13:14 *t'* let them that be in Judæa flee to
21 *t'* if any man shall say to you, Lo,
26 *t'* shall they see the Son of man
27 And *t'* shall he send his angels, and
14:63 *T'* the high priest rent his clothes,
15:12 What will ye *t'* that I shall do unto
14 *T'* Pilate said unto them, Why,
16:19 So *t'* after the Lord had spoken
Lu 1:34 *T'* said Mary unto the angel, How
2:28 *T'* took he him up in his arms,
3: 7 *T'* said he to the multitude that
10 him, saying, What shall we do *t'*?
12 *T'* came also publicans to be
5:35 and *t'* shall they fast in those days.
36 *t'* both the new maketh a rent,
6: 9 *T'* said Jesus unto them, I will
42 *t'* shalt thou see clearly to pull out
7: 6 *T'* Jesus went with them. And
22 *T'* Jesus answering said unto
31 Whereunto *t'* shall I liken the men
8:12 *t'* cometh the devil, and taketh
19 *T'* came to him his mother and
24 *T'* he arose, and rebuked the wind
33 *T'* went the devils out of the man,
35 *T'* they went out to see what was
37 *T'* the...multitude of the country
9: 1 *T'* he called his twelve disciples
12 *t'* came the twelve, and said unto
16 *T'* he took the five loaves and the
46 *T'* there arose a reasoning among
10:37 *T'* said Jesus unto him, Go, and
11:13 If ye *t'*, being evil, know how to give
26 *T'* goeth he, and taketh to him
45 *T'* answered one of the lawyers,
12:20 *t'* whose shall those things be,
26 If ye *t'* be not able to do that thing
28 If *t'* God so clothe the grass, which
41 *T'* Peter said unto him, Lord,
42 Who *t'* is that faithful and wise
13: 7 *T'* said he unto the dresser of his
9 *t'* after that thou shalt cut it down.
15 The Lord *t'* answered him, and
18 *T'* said he, Unto what is the
23 *T'* said one unto him, Lord, are
26 *T'* shall ye begin to say, We have
14:10 *t'* shalt thou have worship in the
12 *T'* said he also to him that bade
16 *T'* said he unto him, A certain
21 *T'* the master of the house being
15: 1 *T'* drew near...all the publicans

Lu 16: 3 *T'* the steward said within himself,
7 *T'* said he to another, And how
27 *T'* he said, I pray thee, therefore,
17: 1 *T'* said he unto the disciples, It is
18:26 heard it said, Who *t'* can be saved?
28 *T'* Peter said, Lo, we have left all,
31 *T'* he took unto him the twelve,
19:15 *t'* he commanded these servants to
16 *T'* came the first, saying, Lord,
23 Wherefore *t'* gavest not thou my
20: 5 say, Why *t'* believe ye him not?
9 *T'* began he to speak to the people
13 *T'* said the lord of the vineyard,
17 What is this *t'* that is written,
27 *T'* came to him certain of the
39 *T'* certain of the scribes answering
44 calleth...Lord, how is he *t'* his son?
45 *T'* in the audience of all the
21:10 *T'* said he unto them, Nation shall
20 *t'* know that the desolation thereof is
21 *T'* let them which are in Judæa
27 *t'* shall they see the Son of man
28 *t'* look up, and lift up your heads;
22: 3 *T'* entered Satan into Judas
7 *T'* came the day of unleavened
36 *T'* said he unto them, But now,
52 *T'* Jesus said unto...chief priests,
54 *T'* took they him, and led him,
70 *T'* said they all, Art thou
70 all, Art thou *t'* the Son of God?
23: 4 *T'* said Pilate to the chief priests
9 *T'* he questioned...him in many
30 *T'* shall they begin to say to the
34 *T'* said Jesus, Father, forgive
24:12 *T'* arose Peter, and ran unto the
25 *T'* he said unto them, O fools, and
45 *T'* opened he their understanding,
Joh 1:21 him, What *t'*? Art thou Elias?
22 *T'* said they unto him, Who art
25 Why baptizest thou *t'*, if thou be
38 *T'* Jesus turned, and saw them
2:10 well drunk, *t'* that which is worse:
18 *T'* answered the Jews and said
20 *T'* said the Jews, Forty and six
3:25 *T'* there arose a question between
4: 5 *T'* cometh he to a city of Samaria,
9 *T'* saith the woman of Samaria
11 from whence *t'* hast thou that
28 The woman *t'* left her waterpot,
30 *T'* they went out of the city, and
35 four months, and *t'* cometh harvest?
45 *T'* when he was come into Galilee,
48 *T'* said Jesus unto him, Except ye
52 *T'* enquired he of them the hour
5: 4 whosoever *t'* first after...troubling
12 *T'* asked they him, What man is
19 *T'* answered Jesus and said unto
6: 5 When Jesus *t'* lifted up his eyes,
14 *T'* those men, when they had seen
21 *T'* they willingly received him into
28 *T'* said they unto him, What shall
30 What sign shewest thou *t'*, that we
32 *T'* Jesus said unto them, Verily,
34 *T'* said they unto him, Lord,
41 The Jews *t'* murmured at him,
42 how is it *t'* that he saith, I came
53 *T'* Jesus said unto them, Verily,
67 *T'* said Jesus unto the twelve, Will
68 *T'* Simon Peter answered him,
7: 6 *T'* Jesus said unto them, My time
10 *t'* went he also up unto the feast,
11 *T'* the Jews sought him at the
25 *T'* said some of them of Jerusalem,
28 *T'* cried Jesus in the temple as he
30 *T'* they sought to take him: but no
33 *T'* said Jesus unto them, Yet a
33 and *t'* I go unto him that sent me.
35 *T'* said the Jews among
45 *T'* came the officers to the chief
47 *T'* answered them the Pharisees,
8:12 *T'* spake Jesus again unto them,
19 *T'* said they unto him, Where is
21 *T'* said Jesus again unto them, I
22 *T'* said the Jews, Will he kill
25 *T'* said they unto him, Who art
28 *T'* said Jesus unto them, When ye
28 *t'* shall ye know that I am he,
31 *T'* said Jesus to those Jews which
31 *t'* are ye my disciples indeed;
41 *T'* said they to him, We be not
48 *T'* answered the Jews, and said
52 *T'* said the Jews unto him, Now
57 *T'* said the Jews unto him, Thou
59 *T'* took they up stones to cast at
9:12 *T'* said they unto him, Where is he?
15 *T'* again the Pharisees also asked
19 born blind? how *t'* doth he now see?
24 *T'* again called they the man that
26 *T'* said they to him again, What
28 *T'* they reviled him, and said,
10: 7 *T'* said Jesus unto them again,
24 *T'* came the Jews round about him,
31 *T'* the Jews took up stones again
11: 7 *T'* after that saith he to his
12 *T'* said his disciples, Lord, if he
14 *T'* said Jesus unto them plainly,
16 *T'* said Thomas, which is called
17 *T'* when Jesus came, he found that
20 *T'* Martha, as soon as she heard
21 *T'* said Martha unto Jesus, Lord,
31 The Jews *t'* which were with her in
32 *T'* when Mary was come where
36 *T'* said the Jews, Behold how he
41 *T'* they took away the stone from
45 *T'* many of the Jews which came
47 *T'* gathered the chief priests and

Joh 11:53 *T'* from that day forth they took
56 *T'* sought they for Jesus, and
12: 1 *T'* Jesus six days before the
3 *T'* took Mary a pound of ointment
4 *T'* saith one of his disciples, Judas
7 *T'* said Jesus, Let her alone:
16 *t'* remembered they that these
28 *T'* came there a voice from
35 *T'* Jesus said unto them, Yet a
13: 6 *T'* cometh he to Simon Peter: and
14 If I *t'*, your Lord and Master, have
22 *T'* the disciples looked one on
25 He *t'* lying on Jesus' breast saith
27 *T'* said Jesus unto him, That thou
30 He *t'* having received the sop went
14: 9 and how sayest thou *t'*, Shew us the
16:17 *T'* said some of his disciples
18: 3 Judas *t'*, having received a band of
6 As soon *t'* as he had said unto them,
7 *T'* asked he them again, Whom
10 *T'* Simon Peter having a sword
11 *T'* said Jesus unto Peter, Put up
12 *T'* the band and the captain and
16 *T'* went out that other disciple,
17 *T'* saith the damsel that kept the
19 The high priest *t'* asked Jesus of
27 Peter *t'* denied again: and
28 *T'* led they Jesus from Caiaphas
29 Pilate *t'* went out unto them, and
31 *T'* said Pilate unto them, Take ye
33 *T'* Pilate entered into the judgment
36 world, *t'* would my servants fight,
37 said unto him, Art thou a king *t'*?
40 *T'* cried they all again, saying,
19: 1 *T'* Pilate therefore took Jesus,
5 *T'* came Jesus forth, wearing the
10 *T'* saith Pilate unto him, Speakest
16 *T'* delivered he him therefore
20 This title *t'* read many of the Jews:
21 *T'* said the chief priests of the
23 *T'* the soldiers, when they had
27 *T'* saith he to the disciple,
32 *T'* came the soldiers, and brake
40 *T'* took they the body of Jesus,
20: 2 *T'* she runneth, and cometh to
6 *T'* cometh Simon Peter following
8 *T'* went in also that other disciple,
10 *T'* the disciples went away again
19 *T'* the same day at evening, being
20 *T'* were the disciples glad, when
21 *T'* said Jesus to them again, Peace
26 *t'* came Jesus, the doors being shut,
27 *T'* said he to Thomas, Reach
21: 5 *T'* Jesus saith unto them,
9 soon *t'* as they were come to land,
13 Jesus *t'* cometh, and taketh bread,
20 *T'* Peter, turning about, seeth the
23 *T'* went this saying abroad among
Ac 1:12 *T'* returned they unto Jerusalem
2:38 *T'* Peter said unto them, Repent,
41 *T'* they that gladly received his
3: 6 *T'* Peter said, Silver and gold have
4: 8 *T'* Peter, filled with the Holy
5: 9 *T'* Peter said unto her, How is it
10 *T'* fell she down straightway at his
17 *T'* the high priest rose up, and all
25 *T'* came one and told them, saying,
26 *T'* went the captain with the
29 *T'* Peter and the other apostles
34 *T'* stood there up one in...council,
6: 2 *T'* the twelve called the multitude
9 *T'* there arose certain of the
11 *T'* they suborned men, which said,
7: 1 *T'* said the high priest, Are these
4 *T'* came he out of the land of the
14 *T'* sent Joseph, and called his
29 *T'* fled Moses at this saying, and
32 *T'* Moses trembled, and durst not
33 *T'* said the Lord to him, Put off thy
42 *T'* God turned, and gave them up
57 *T'* they cried out with a loud voice,
8: 5 *T'* Philip went down to the city of
13 *T'* Simon himself believed also:
17 *T'* laid they their hands on them,
24 *T'* answered Simon, and said,
29 *T'* the Spirit said unto Philip, Go
35 *T'* Philip opened his mouth, and
9:13 *T'* Ananias answered, Lord, I have
19 *T'* was Saul certain days with the
25 *T'* the disciples took him by night,
31 *T'* had the churches rest
39 *T'* Peter arose and went with
10:21 *T'* Peter went down to the men
23 *T'* called he them in, and lodged
34 *T'* Peter opened his mouth, and
46 magnify God. *T'* answered Peter,
48 *T'* prayed they him to tarry
11:16 *T'* remembered I the word of the
17 Forasmuch *t'* as God gave them
18 *T'* hath God also to the Gentiles
22 *T'* tidings of these things came
25 *T'* departed Barnabas to Tarsus,
29 *T'* the disciples, every man
12: 3 (*T'* were the days of unleavened
15 even so. *T'* said they, It is his
13: 9 *T'* Saul, (who also is called Paul,)
12 *T'* the deputy, when he saw what
16 *T'* Paul stood up, and beckoning
46 *T'* Paul and Barnabas waxed bold,
14:13 *T'* the priest of Jupiter, which was
15:12 *T'* all the multitude kept silence,
22 *T'* pleased it the apostles and
16: 1 *T'* came he to Derbe and Lystra:
29 *T'* he called for a light, and
17:14 *t'* immediately the brethren sent
18 *T'* certain philosophers of the

Ac 17:22 T· Paul stood in the midst of Mars'
29 Forasmuch t· as we are the
18: 9 T· spake the Lord to Paul in the
17 T· all the Greeks took Sosthenes,
18 and t· took his leave of the brethren,
19: 3 Unto what t· were ye baptized?
4 T· said Paul, John verily baptized
13 T· certain of the vagabond Jews,
36 Seeing t· that these things cannot
21:13 T· Paul answered, What mean ye
26 T· Paul took the men, and the
33 T· the chief captain came near,
22:22 and t· lifted up their voices, and said,
27 T· the chief captain came, and
29 T· straightway they departed from
23: 3 T· said Paul unto him, God shall
5 T· said Paul, I wist not, brethren,
17 T· Paul called one of...centurions
19 T· the chief captain took him by
22 captain t· let the young man depart,
27 t· came I with an army, and rescued
31 T· the soldiers, as it was
24:10 T· Paul, after that...governor had
25: 2 T· the high priest and the chief of
10 T· said Paul, I stand at Cæsar's
12 T· Festus, when he had conferred
22 T· Agrippa said...Festus, I would
26: 1 T· Agrippa said unto Paul, Thou
1 T· Paul stretched forth the hand,
20 of Judæa, and t· to the Gentiles,
28 T· Agrippa said unto Paul,
32 T· said Agrippa unto Festus, This
27:20 be saved was t· taken away.
29 T· fearing lest we should have
32 T· the soldiers cut off the ropes of
36 T· were they all of good cheer, and
28: 1 t· they knew that the island was
Ro 3: 1 What advantage t· hath the Jew?
6 for t· how shall God judge the world?
9 What t·? are we better than they?
27 Where is boasting t·? It is
31 Do we t· make void the law through
4: 1 What shall we say t· that Abraham
9 Cometh this blessedness t· upon
10 How was it t· reckoned? when he
5: 9 Much more t·, being now justified
6: 1 What shall we say t·? Shall we
15 What t·? shall we sin, because we
18 Being t· made free from sin, ye
21 fruit had ye t· in those things
7: 3 So t· if, while her husband liveth,
7 What shall we say t·? Is the law
13 t· that which is good made death
16 If t· I do that which I would not, I
17 t· it is no more I that do it, but sin
21 I find t· a law, that, when I would
25 t· with the mind I myself serve the
8: 8 So t· they that are in...flesh cannot
17 if children, t· heirs; heirs of God,
25 t· do we with patience wait for it.
31 What shall we t· say to these
9:14 What shall we say t·? Is there
16 So t· it is not of him that willeth,
19 Thou wilt say t· unto me, Why
30 What shall we say t·? That the
10:14 t· shall they call on him in whom
17 So t· faith cometh by hearing, and
11: 1 I say t·, Hath God cast away his
5 Even so t· at this present time also
6 if by grace, t· is it no more of works:
6 it be of works, t· is it no more grace:
7 What t·? Israel hath not obtained
11 I say t·, Have they stumbled that
19 Thou wilt say t·, The branches
12: 6 Having t· gifts differing according
13: 3 thou t· not be afraid of the power?
14:12 So t· every one of us shall give an
16 Let not t· your good be evil spoken
15: 1 We t· that are strong ought to bear
1Co 3: 5 Who t· is Paul, and who is
7 So t· neither is he that planteth any
4: 5 t· shall every man have praise of
5:10 t· must ye needs go out of the world
6: 4 If t· ye have judgments of things
15 I t· take the members of Christ,
7:38 t· he that giveth her in marriage
9:18 What is my reward t·? Verily
10:19 What say I t·? that the idol is
12:28 t· gifts of healings, helps,
13:10 t· that which is in part shall be
12 a glass, darkly; but t· face to face:
12 t· shall I know even as also I am
14:15 What is it t·? I will pray with the
26 How is it t·, brethren? when ye
15: 5 seen of Cephas, t· of the twelve:
7 seen of James; t· of all the apostles.
13 of the dead, t· is Christ not risen:
14 not risen, t· is our preaching vain,
16 rise not, t· is not Christ raised:
18 T· they also which are fallen
24 T· cometh the end, when he shall
28 t· shall the Son also himself be
29 why are they t· baptized for the dead?
54 t· shall be brought to pass the
2Co 2: 2 who is he t· that maketh me glad,
3:12 Seeing t· that we have such hope,
4:12 So t· death worketh in us, but life
5:14 if one died for all, t· were all dead:
20 Now t· we are ambassadors for Christ,
6: 1 We t·, as workers together with
12:10 am weak, t· am I strong.
Ga 1:18 T· after three years I went up to
2: 1 T· fourteen years after I went up
21 the law, t· Christ is dead in vain.
3: 9 So t· they which be of faith are
19 Wherefore t· serveth the law? It
Ga 3:21 law t· against the promises of God?
29 Christ's, t· are ye Abraham's seed,
4: 7 t· an heir of God through Christ.
8 Howbeit t·, when ye knew not
15 Where is t· the blessedness ye
29 But as t· he that was born after
31 So t·, brethren, we are not
5:11 t· is the offense of the cross ceased.
16 This I say t·, Walk in the Spirit,
6: 4 t· shall he have rejoicing in
Eph 5:15 See t· that ye walk circumspectly,
Ph'p 1:18 What t·? notwithstanding, every
Col 3: 1 If ye t· be risen with Christ, seek
4 t· shall ye also appear with him in
1Th 4: 1 t· we beseech you, brethren,
17 T· we which are alive and remain
5: 3 t· sudden destruction cometh upon
2Th 2: 8 t· shall that Wicked be revealed,
1Ti 2:13 For Adam was first formed, t· Eve.
3: 2 A bishop t· must be blameless,
10 t· let them use the office of a
Heb 2:14 Forasmuch t· as the children are
4: 8 t· would he not afterward have
14 Seeing t· that we have a great
7:27 own sins, and t· for the people's:
8: 7 t· should no place have been sought
9: 1 T· verily the first covenant had
9 a figure for the time t· present,
26 For t· must he often have suffered
10: 2 For t· would they not have ceased to
7 T· said I, Lo, I come (in the
9 T· said he, Lo, I come to do thy
12: 8 t· are ye bastards, and not sons.
26 Whose voice t· shook the earth:
Jas 1:15 T· when lust hath conceived, it
2: 4 Are ye not t· partial in yourselves,
24 Ye see t· how that by works a
3:17 above is first pure, t· peaceable,
4:14 a little time, and t· vanisheth away.
1Pe 4: 1 Forasmuch t· as Christ hath
2Pe 3: 6 Whereby the world that t· was,
11 Seeing t· that all these things
1Jo 1: 5 This t· is the message which we
3:21 t· have we confidence toward God.
Re 3:16 So t· because thou art lukewarm, and
22: 9 T· saith he unto me, See thou do

thence^ See also THENCEFORTH.
Ge 2:10 from t· it was parted, and became
11: 8 Lord scattered them abroad from t·
9 t· did the Lord scatter them abroad
12: 8 removed from t· unto a mountain
18:16 And the men rose up from t·, and
22 the men turned their faces from t·,
20: 1 And Abraham journeyed from t·
26:17 And Isaac departed t·, and pitched
22 he removed from t·, and digged
23 he went up from t· to Beer-sheba.
27:45 I will send, and fetch thee from t·:
28: 2 take thee a wife from t· of the
6 to take him a wife from t·;
30:32 removing from t· all the speckled
42: 2 thither, and buy for us from t·;
26 asses with the corn, and departed t·.
49:24 (from t· is the shepherd, the stone
Nu 13:23 cut down from t· a branch with one
24 children of Israel cut down from t·.
21:12, 13 From t· they removed, and
22:41 t· he might see the utmost part of
23:13 all: and curse me them from t·.
27 mayest curse me them from t·.
De 4:29 But if from t· thou shalt seek the
6:23 he brought us out from t·, that he
10: 7 From t· they journeyed unto
19:12 his city shall send and fetch him t·,
22: 8 thine house, if any man fall from t·.
24:18 Lord thy God redeemed thee t·:
30: 4 from t· will the Lord thy God
4 thee, and from t· will he fetch thee:
Jos 6:22 and bring out t· the woman, and all
15: 4 From t· it passed toward Azmon,
14 And Caleb drove t· the three sons
15 he went up t· to the inhabitants
18:13 went over from t· toward Luz,
14 border was drawn t·, and compassed
19:13 And from t· passeth on along on
34 and goeth out from t· to Hukkok,
J'g 1:11 And from t· he went against the
20 expelled t· the three sons of Anak.
8: 8 he went up t· to Penuel, and spake
18:11 there went from t· of the family of
13 passed t· unto mount Ephraim,
19:18 from t· am I: and I went to
21:24 children of Israel departed t· at
24 went out from t· every man to his
1Sa 4: 4 might bring from t· the ark of the
10: 3 shalt thou go on forward from t·,
23 And they ran and fetched him t·:
17:49 took t· a stone, and slang it, and
22: 1 David therefore departed t·, and
3 David went t· to Mizpeh of Moab:
23:29 And David went up from t·, and
2Sa 6: 2 bring up from t· the ark of God,
14: 2 fetched t· a wise woman, and said
16: 5 t· came out a man of the family of
21:13 he brought up from t· the bones of
1Ki 1:45 they are come up from t· rejoicing,
2:36 and go not forth t· any whither.
9:28 to Ophir, and fetched from t· gold,
12:25 and went out from t·, and built
19:19 So he departed t·, and found Elisha
2Ki 2:21 shall not be from t· any more death
23 he went up from t· unto Beth-el:
25 he went from t· to mount Carmel,
25 and from t· he returned to Samaria.
6: 2 and take t· every man a beam,
7: 8 and carried t· silver, and gold,
2Ki 7: 8 carried t· also, and went and hid it.
10:15 when he was departed t·, he lighted
17:27 priests whom ye brought from t·;
33 whom they carried away from t·
23:12 brake them down from t·, and cast
24:13 he carried out t· all the treasures
1Ch 13: 6 to bring up t· the ark of God the
2Ch 8:18 and took t· four hundred and fifty
26:20 they thrust him out from t·; yea,
Ezr 6: 6 beyond the river, be ye far from t·:
Ne 1: 9 yet will I gather them from t·, and
Job 39:29 From t· she seeketh the prey, and
Isa 52:11 depart ye, go ye out from t·,
65:20 be no more t· an infant of days,
Jer 5: 6 one that goeth out t· shall be torn
13: 6 and take the girdle from t·,
36:29 cause to cease from t· man and beast?
37:12 separate himself t· in the midst of
38:11 took t· old cast clouts and old rotten
43:12 he shall go forth from t· in peace.
49:16 I will bring thee down from t·, saith
38 will destroy from t· the king and
50: 9 her; from t· she shall be taken:
Eze 11:18 all the abominations thereof from t·.
Ho 2:15 give her her vineyards from t·,
Am 6: 2 from t· go ye to Hamath the great:
9: 2 hell, t· shall mine hand take them;
2 to heaven, t· will I bring them down:
3 I will search and take them out t·;
3 t· will I command the serpent, and
4 t· will I command the sword, and it
Ob 4 t· will I bring thee down, saith the
M't 4:21 going on from t·, he saw other two
5:26 by no means come out t·, till thou
9: 9 as Jesus passed forth from t·, he saw
27 when Jesus departed t·, two blind
10:11 worthy; and there abide till ye go t·.
11: 1 he departed t· to teach and to preach
12: 9 when he was departed t·, he went
15 knew it,...withdrew himself from t·:
13:53 these parables, he departed t·.
14:13 he departed t· by ship into a desert
15:21 Jesus went t·, and departed into the
29 Jesus departed from t·, and came
19:15 his hands on them, and departed t·.
M'r 1:19 when he had gone a little farther t·,
6: 1 he went out from t·, and came into
11 when ye depart t·, shake off the
7:24 from t· he arose, and went into the
9:30 they departed t·, and passed
10: 1 And he arose from t·, and cometh
Lu 9: 4 into, there abide, and t· depart.
12:59 thou shalt not depart t·, till thou
16:26 pass to us, that would come from t·.
Joh 4:43 Now after two days he departed t·,
11:54 went t· unto a country near to the
Ac 7: 4 from t·, when his father was dead,
13: 4 and from t· they sailed to Cyprus.
14:26 And t· sailed to Antioch, from
16:12 from t· to Philippi, which is the chief
18: 7 he departed t·, and entered into a
18 sailed t· into Syria, and with him
20:15 And we sailed t·, and came the
21: 1 Rhodes, and from t· unto Patara:
27: 4 when we had launched from t·, we
12 more part advised to depart t· also,
13 loosing t·, they sailed close by Crete.
28:13 And from t· we fetched a compass,
15 And from t·, when the brethren
2Co 2:13 them, I went from t· into Macedonia.

thenceforth
Le 22:27 and t· it shall be accepted for an
2Ch 32:23 the sight of all nations from t·.
M't 5:13 it is t· good for nothing, but to be
Joh 19:12 t· Pilate sought to release

Theophilus (*the-of'-il-us*)
Lu 1: 3 thee in order, most excellent T·,
Ac 1: 1 treatise have I made, O T·, of all

there^ See also THEREABOUT; THEREAT; THEREBY; THEREFORE; THEREFROM; THEREIN; THEREOF; THEREON; THEREOUT; THEREUNTO; THEREUPON; THEREWITH.
Ge 1: 3 Let t· be light: and t· was light.
6 Let t· be a firmament in the midst
14 said, Let t· be lights in the firmament
30 upon the earth, wherein t· is life,
2: 5 t· was not a man to till the ground.
6 But t· went up a mist from the earth,
8 t· he put the man whom he had
11 land of Havilah, where t· is gold;
12 t· is bdellium and the onyx stone.
20 Adam t· was not found an help meet
4:26 to Seth, to him also t· was born a son;
6: 4 T· were giants in the earth in those
7: 9 T· went in two and two unto Noah
9:11 shall t· any more be a flood to destroy
11: 2 land of Shinar; and they dwelt t·.
7 and t· confound their language,
9 Lord did t· confound the language
31 they came unto Haran, and dwelt t·.
12: 7 t· builded he an altar unto the Lord,
8 t· he builded an altar unto the Lord,
10 And t· was a famine in the land: and
10 down into Egypt to sojourn t·;
13: 4 which he had made t· at the first:
7 t· was a strife between the herdmen
8 said unto Lot, Let t· be no strife,
18 built t· an altar unto the Lord.
14: 8 And t· went out the king of Sodom,
10 and Gomorrah fled, and fell t·;
13 And t· came one that had escaped, and
18:24 t· be fifty righteous within the city:
28 t· shall lack five of the fifty righteous:
28 If I find t· forty and five, I will
29 t· shall be forty found t·.

Ge 18:30 t' shall thirty be found t'.
30 I will not do it, if I find thirty t'.
31 t' shall be twenty found t'.
32 Peradventure ten shall be found t'.
19: 1 t' came two angels to Sodom at even;
31 is old, and t' is not a man in the earth
21:31 t' they sware both of them.
33 called t' on the name of the Lord.
22: 2 and offer him t' for a burnt offering
9 Abraham built an altar t', and laid
23:13 it of me, and I will bury my dead t'.
24:23 is t' room in thy father's house for us
33 t' was set meat before him to eat: but
25:10 t' was Abraham buried, and Sarah
24 behold, t' were twins in her womb.
26: 1 And t' was a famine in the land,
8 when he had been t' a long time,
17 in the valley of Gerar, and dwelt t'.
19 found t' a well of springing water.
25 he builded an altar t', and called
25 the Lord, and pitched his tent t':
25 and t' Isaac's servants digged a well
28 said, Let t' be now an oath betwixt us.
28:11 place, and tarried t' all night,
29: 2 t' were three flocks of sheep lying
31:14 Is t' yet any portion or inheritance for
46 and they did eat t' upon the heap.
32: 4 with Laban, and stayed t' until now:
13 And he lodged t' that same night;
24 and t' wrestled a man with him until
29 my name? And he blessed him t'.
33:20 And he erected t' an altar, and
35: 1 Arise, go up to Beth-el, and dwell t':
1 and make t' an altar unto God,
3 I will make t' an altar unto God,
7 he built t' an altar, and called the
7 because t' God appeared unto him,
16 t' was but a little way to come to
36:31 before t' reigned any king over the
37:24 pit was empty, t' was no water in it.
28 t' passed by Midianites merchantmen;
38: 2 And Judah saw t' a daughter of a
21 said, T' was no harlot in this place.
22 that t' was no harlot in this place.
39: 9 T' is none greater in this house than I;
11 and t' was none of the men of the
11 of the men of the house t' within.
20 and he was t' in the prison.
22 whatsoever they did t', he was the
40: 8 a dream, and t' is no interpreter of it.
17 t' was of all manner of bakemeats
41: 2 t' came up out of the river seven well
8 t' was none that could interpret them
12 And t' was...with us a young man,
12 was t' with us a young man, an
15 and t' is none that can interpret it:
18 t' came up out of the river seven kine,
24 t' was none that could declare it to me.
29 t' come seven years of great plenty
30 t' shall arise after them seven years of
39 t' is none so discreet and wise as thou
54 in all the land of Egypt t' was bread.
42: 1 Jacob saw that t' was corn in Egypt,
2 I have heard that t' is corn in Egypt:
16 proved, whether t' be any truth in you:
43:25 heart that they should eat bread t'.
30 into his chamber, and wept t'.
44:14 to Joseph's house; for he was yet t':
45: 1 And t' stood no man with him, while
6 and yet t' are five years, in the
6 which t' shall neither be earing nor
11 And t' will I nourish thee; for yet
11 for yet t' are five years of famine,
46: 3 will t' make of thee a great nation:
47:13 t' was no bread in all the land; for the
18 t' is not ought left in the sight of my
48: 7 yet t' was but a little way to come
7 and I buried her t' in the way of
49:31 T' they buried Abraham and Sarah
31 t' they buried Isaac and Rebekah
31 his wife; and t' I buried Leah.
50: 5 of Canaan, t' shalt thou bury me.
9 t' went up with him both chariots and
10 t' they mourned with a great and
Ex 1: 8 t' arose up a new king over Egypt,
10 when t' falleth out any war, they join
2: 1 t' went a man of the house of Levi,
12 and when he saw that t' was no man,
5: 9 t' more work be laid upon the men,
13 daily tasks, as when t' was straw.
16 T' is no straw given unto thy
18 for t' shall no straw be given you,
7:19 that t' may be blood throughout all
21 t' was blood throughout all the land
8:10 t' is none like unto the Lord our God.
15 when Pharaoh saw that t' was respite,
18 so t' were lice upon man, and upon
24 t' came a grievous swarm of flies into
31 from his people; t' remained not one.
9: 3 t' shall be a very grievous murrain.
4 t' shall nothing die of all that is the
7 t' was not one of the cattle of the
14 that t' is none like me in all the earth.
22 that t' may be hail in all the land of
24 So t' was hail, and fire mingled with
24 such as t' was none like it in all the
26 children of Israel were, was t' no hail.
28 t' be no more mighty thunderings and
29 neither shall t' be any more hail;
10:14 t' were no such locusts as they,
15 t' remained not any green thing in
19 t' remained not one locust in all the
21 that t' may be darkness over the land
22 t' was a thick darkness in all the land
26 t' shall not an hoof be left behind; for
11: 6 t' shall be a great cry throughout all

Ex 11: 6 such as t' was none like it, nor shall
12:16 day t' shall be an holy convocation,
16 day t' shall be an holy convocation,
19 Seven days shall t' be no leaven found
30 and t' was a great cry in Egypt;
30 cry in Egypt; for t' was not a house
30 house where t' was not one dead.
43 T' shall no stranger eat thereof:
13: 3 t' shall no leavened bread be eaten.
7 t' shall no leavened bread be seen with
7 neither shall t' be leaven seen with
14:11 Because t' were no graves in Egypt,
28 t' remained not so much as one of
15:25 t' he made for them a statute and
25 ordinance, and t' he proved them.
27 they encamped t' by the waters.
16:14 wilderness t' lay a small round thing,
24 neither was t' any worm therein.
26 is the sabbath, in it t' shall be none.
27 that t' went out some of the people on
17: 1 t' was no water for the people to drink.
3 the people thirsted t' for water;
6 I will stand before thee t' upon the
6 t' shall come water out of it, that the
19: 2 t' Israel camped before the mount.
13 T' shall not an hand touch it, but he
16 that t' were thunders and lightnings,
21:30 If t' be laid on him a sum of money,
22: 2 die, t' shall no blood be shed for him.
23:26 T' shall nothing cast their young, nor
24:10 and t' was under his feet as it were a
12 to me into the mount, and be t':
25:35 t' shall be a knop under two branches
26:17 Two tenons shall t' be in one board,
20 side t' shall be twenty boards:
27: 9 t' shall be hangings for the court of
11 t' shall be hangings of an hundred
28:32 t' shall be an hole in the top of it,
29:42 meet you, to speak t' unto thee.
43 t' I will meet with the children of
30:12 that t' be no plague among them,
34 of each shall t' be a like weight:
32:17 T' is a noise of war in the camp.
24 into the fire, and t' came out this calf.
28 t' fell of the people that day about
33:20 for t' shall no man see me, and live.
21 Lord said, Behold, t' is a place by me,
34: 2 present thyself t' to me in the top
5 in the cloud, and stood with him t',
28 he was t' with the Lord forty days
35: 2 day t' shall be to you an holy day,
36:30 And t' were eight boards; and their
39:23 t' was an hole in the midst of the robe,
40:30 put water t', to wash withal.
Le 6:27 when t' is sprinkled of the blood
7: 7 t' is one law for them: the priest that
8:31 t' eat it with the bread that is in
9:24 t' came a fire out from before the Lord,
10: 2 t' went out fire from the Lord, and
13:10 t' be quick raw flesh in the rising;
19 place of the boil t' be a white rising,
21 behold, t' be no white hairs therein,
24 Or if t' be any flesh, in the
24 in the skin whereof t' is a hot burning,
26 t' be no white hair in the bright spot,
30 skin; and t' be in it a yellow thin hair;
31 skin, and that t' is no black hair in it;
32 not, and t' be in it no yellow hair,
37 t' is black hair grown up therein;
42 if t' be in the bald head, or bald
14:35 t' is as it were a plague in the house:
16:17 t' shall be no man in the tabernacle
23 place, and shall leave them t':
17: 3 What man soever t' be of the house of
8, 10 man t' be of the house of Israel,
13 man t' be of the children of Israel,
20:14 that t' be no wickedness among you.
21: 1 T' shall none be defiled for the dead
22:10 T' shall no stranger eat of the holy
13 but t' shall no stranger eat thereof.
21 t' shall be no blemish therein.
23:27 seventh month t' shall be a day of
25:51 If t' be yet many years behind,
52 t' remain but few years unto the year
Nu 1: 4 you t' shall be a man of every tribe;
53 t' be no wrath upon the congregation
5:13 and t' be no witness against her,
6: 5 t' shall no rasor come upon his
8:19 t' be no plague among the children of
9: 6 t' were certain men, who were defiled
15 at even t' was upon the tabernacle as
17 t' the children of Israel pitched
11: 6 t' is nothing at all, beside this manna,
16 that they may stand t' with thee.
17 come down and talk with thee t':
26 But t' remained tw of the men in the
27 t' ran a young man, and told Moses,
31 t' went forth a wind from the Lord,
34 because t' they buried the people
12: 6 If t' be a prophet among you, I the
13:20 whether t' be wood therein, or not.
33 t' we saw the giants, the sons of
14:35 be consumed, and t' they shall die.
43 the Canaanites are t' before you,
16:35 And t' came out a fire from the Lord,
46 for t' is wrath gone out from the Lord;
18: 5 that t' be no wrath any more upon
19:18 and upon the persons that were t',
20: 1 Miriam died t', and was buried t'.
2 t' was no water for the congregation:
4 we and our cattle should die t'?
5 neither is t' any water to drink.
26 unto his people, and shall die t'.
28 and Aaron died t' in the top of the
21: 5 the wilderness? for t' is no bread,
5 neither is t' any water;

Nu 21:28 For t' is a fire gone out of Heshbon,
32 out the Amorites that were t'.
35 until t' was none left him alive:
22: 5 t' is a people come out from Egypt:
11 t' is a people come out of Egypt,
29 I would t' were a sword in mine hand,
23:23 t' is no enchantment against Jacob,
23 is t' any divination against Israel:
24:17 t' shall come a Star out of Jacob, and a
26:62 t' was no inheritance given them
64 among these t' was not a man of them
65 And t' was not left a man of them,
31: 5 t' were delivered out of the thousands
16 t' was a plague among the
49 and t' lacketh not one man of us.
32:26 shall be t' in the cities of Gilead:
33: 9 ten palm trees; and they pitched t'.
38 and died t', in the fortieth year
35: 6 t' shall be six cities for refuge,
De 1: 2 (T' are eleven days' journey from
28 seen the sons of the Anakims t'.
35 t' shall not one of these men of this
46 unto the days that ye abode t'.
2:36 t' was not one city too strong for us:
3: 4 t' was not a city which we took not
24 what God is t' in heaven or in earth,
4: 7 For what nation is t' so great, who
8 what nation is t' so great, that hath
28 t' ye shall serve gods, the work of
32 whether t' hath been any such thing
35 he is God; t' is none else beside him.
39 the earth beneath: t' is none else.
5:26 For who is t' of all flesh, that hath
29 O that t' were such a heart in them,
7:14 t' shall not be male nor female barren
24 t' shall no man be able to stand before
8:15 and drought, where t' was no water;
10: 5 t' they be, as the Lord commanded
6 t' Aaron died, and t' he was buried;
11:17 that t' be no rain, and that the land
25 T' shall no man be able to stand before
12: 5 all your tribes to put his name t',
7 t' ye shall eat before the Lord your
11 t' shall be a place which the Lord
11 to cause his name to dwell t';
14 t' thou shalt offer thy burnt
14 t' thou shalt do all that I
21 God hath chosen to put his name t'
13: 1 If t' arise among you a prophet, or a
17 t' shall cleave nought of the cursed
14:23 shall choose to place his name t',
24 God shall choose to set his name t',
26 shalt eat t' before the Lord thy God,
15: 4 when t' shall be no poor among you;
7 If t' be among you a poor man of one
9 t' be not a thought in thy wicked
21 And if t' be any blemish therein, as if
16: 2 shall choose to place his name t'.
4 t' shall be no leavened bread seen
4 neither shall t' any thing of the flesh,
6 t' thou shalt sacrifice the passover
11 hath chosen to place his name t'.
17: 2 If t' be found among you, within
3 If t' arise a matter too hard for thee in
12 to minister t' before the Lord thy
18: 7 do, which stand t' before the Lord.
10 T' shall not be found among you any
20: 5 man is t' that hath built a new house,
7 man is t' that hath betrothed a wife,
8 What man is t' that is fearful and
21: 4 the heifer's neck t' in the valley:
22:26 t' is in the damsel no sin worthy of
27 cried, and t' was none to save her.
23:10 t' be among you any man, that is not
17 T' shall be no whore of the daughters
25: 1 If t' be a controversy between men,
26: 2 shall choose to place his name t'.
5 Egypt, and sojourned t' with a few,
5 t' a nation, great, mighty, and
27: 5 t' shalt thou build an altar unto the
7 peace offerings, and shalt eat t',
28:32 and t' shall be no might in thine hand.
36 t' shalt thou serve other gods,
64 and t' thou shalt serve other gods,
65 shall give thee t' a trembling heart,
68 t' ye shall be sold unto your enemies
29:18 Lest t' should be among you man, or
18 lest t' should be among you a root that
31:26 it may be t' for a witness against
32:12 and t' was no strange god with him.
28 is t' any understanding in them.
36 is gone, and t' is none shut up, or left.
39 I, am he, and t' is no god with me:
39 neither is t' any that can deliver out
33:19 t' they shall offer sacrifices of
21 t', in a portion of the lawgiver, was
26 T' is none like unto the God of
34: 5 the servant of the Lord died t' in
10 t' arose not a prophet since in Israel
Jos 1: 5 T' shall not any man be able to stand
2: 1 house, named Rahab, and lodged t'.
2 t' came men in hither to night of the
4 T' came men unto me, but I wist not
11 neither did t' remain...more courage
16 and hide yourselves t' three days,
22 mountain, and abode t' three days,
3: 1 lodged t' before they passed over.
4 Yet t' shall be a space between you
4: 8 lodged, and laid them down t'.
9 stood: and they are t' unto this day.
5: 1 neither was t' spirit in them any more,
13 t' stood a man over against him with
7: 4 So t' went up thither of the people
13 T' is an accursed thing in the midst
8:11 t' was a valley between them and Ai.
14 wist not that t' were liers in ambush

Jos 8:17 t' was not a man left in Ai or Beth-el,
32 And he wrote t' upon the stones
35 T' was not a word of all that Moses
9:23 and t' shall none of you be freed
10: 8 t' shall not a man of them stand before
14 And t' was no day like that before it
11:11 t' was not any left to breathe: and he
19 T' was not a city that made peace
22 T' was none of the Anakims left in
22 in Gath, and in Ashod, t' remained.
13: 1 t' remaineth yet very much land to be
14:12 day how the Anakims were t',
17: 1 T' was also a lot for the tribe of
2 T' was also a lot for the rest of the
5 And t' fell ten portions to Manasseh,
15 cut down for thyself t' in the land
18: 1 tabernacle of the congregation t'.
2 t' remained among the children of
10 t' Joshua divided the land unto the
21:44 t' stood not a man of all their enemies
45 T' failed not ought of any good thing
22:10 tribe of Manasseh built t' an altar
17 t' was a plague in the congregation of
24:26 and set it up t' under an oak,
J'g 1: 7 him to Jerusalem, and t' he died.
2: 5 they sacrificed t' unto the Lord.
10 t' arose another generation after them,
3:29 of valour; and t' escaped not a man.
4:16 the sword; and t' was not a man left.
17 t' was peace between Jabin the king
20 of thee, and say, Is t' any man here?
5: 8 was t' a shield or spear seen among
11 t' shall they rehearse the righteous
14 Out of Ephraim was t' a root of them
15 t' were great thoughts of heart.
16 t' were great searchings of heart.
27 he bowed, t' he fell down dead.
6:11 t' came an angel of the Lord, and sat
21 t' rose up fire out of the rock, and
24 Then Gideon built an altar t' unto
39 and upon all the ground let t' be dew.
40 only, and t' was dew on all the ground.
7: 3 t' returned of the people twenty and
3 and t' remained ten thousand.
4 and I will try them for thee t':
13 t' was a man that told a dream unto
8:10 t' fell an hundred and twenty
9:21 and went to Beer, and dwelt t',
36 t' come people down from the top
37 t' come people down by the middle
51 t' was a strong tower within the city,
10: 1 t' arose to defend Israel Tola the son
11: 3 t' were gathered vain men to Jephthah,
12: 6 t' fell at that time of the Ephraimites,
13: 2 t' was a certain man of Zorah, of the
14: 3 t' never a woman among the daughters
8 t' was a swarm of bees and honey in
10 and Samson made t' a feast;
15:19 the jaw, and t' came water thereout;
16: 1 to Gaza, and saw t' an harlot,
9 t' were men lying in wait, abiding
12 t' were liers in wait abiding in the
17 T' hath not come a rasor upon mine
27 lords of the Philistines were t';
27 t' were upon the roof about three
17: 1 And t' was a man of mount Ephraim,
6 In those days t' was no king in Israel,
7 And t' was a young man out of
7 was a Levite, and he sojourned t'.
18: 1 In those days t' was no king in Israel:
2 house of Micah, they lodged t'.
7 t' was no magistrate in the land, that
10 where t' is no want of any thing
11 t' went from thence of the family
14 that t' is in these houses an ephod,
28 t' was no deliverer, because it was far
19: 1 days, when t' was no king in Israel,
1 t' was a certain Levite sojourning on
2 and was t' four whole months.
4 did eat and drink, and lodged t'.
7 him: therefore he lodged t' again.
10 t' were with him two asses saddled,
15 for t' was no man that took them into
16 t' came an old man from his work
18 t' is no man that receiveth me to
19 t' is both straw and provender for our
19 and t' is bread and wine also for me,
19 servants: t' is no want of any thing.
30 T' was no such deed done, nor seen
20:16 t' were seven hundred chosen men
26 wept, and sat t' before the Lord,
27 ark of the covenant of God was t'
34 t' came against Gibeah ten thousand
38 Now t' was an appointed sign between
44 t' fell of Benjamin eighteen thousand
21: 1 T' shall not any...give his daughter
2 and abode t' till even before God,
3 t' should be to day one tribe lacking
4 rose early, and built t' an altar,
5 Who is t' among all the tribes of Israel
6 T' is one tribe cut off from Israel this
8 What one is t' of the tribes of Israel
8 t' came none to the camp from
9 t' were none of the inhabitants of
9 inhabitants of Jabesh-gilead t'.
17 T' must be an inheritance for them
19 t' is a feast of the Lord in Shiloh
25 In those days t' was no king in Israel:
Ru 1: 1 that t' was a famine in the land.
2 country of Moab, and continued t'.
4 they dwelled t' about ten years.
11 are t' yet any more sons in my womb,
17 will I die, and t' will I be buried:
3: 12 t' is a kinsman nearer than I.
4: 1 to the gate, and sat him down t':
4 for t' is none to redeem it beside thee;

Ru 4:17 saying, T' is a son born to Naomi;
1Sa 1: 1 Now t' was a certain man of
3 the priests of the Lord, were t'.
11 t' shall no rasor come upon his head.
22 the Lord, and t' abide for ever.
28 And he worshipped the Lord t'.
2: 2 T' is none holy as the Lord:
2 for t' is none beside thee:
2 neither is t' any rock like our God.
27 And t' came a man of God unto Eli,
31, 32 t' shall not be an old man in thine
3: 1 in those days; t' was no open vision.
4: 4 were t' with the ark of the covenant
7 for t' hath not been such a thing
10 and t' was a very great slaughter;
10 for t' fell of Israel thirty thousand
12 t' ran a man of Benjamin out of the
16 And he said, What is t' done, my son?
17 and t' hath been also a great slaughter
5:11 t' was a deadly destruction throughout
11 the hand of God was very heavy t'.
6: 7 kine, on which t' hath come no yoke,
14 the cart came...and stood t',
14 where t' was a great stone:
7: 6 and said t', We have sinned against
14 t' was peace between Israel and the
17 to Ramah; for t' was his house;
17 and t' he judged Israel; and
17 t' he built an altar unto the Lord.
9: 1 Now t' was a man of Benjamin, whose
2 t' was not among the children of Israel
4 land of Shalim, and t' they were not:
6 now, t' is in this city a man of God,
7 t' is not a present to bring to the man
12 t' is a sacrifice of the people to day
10: 3 and t' shall meet thee three men
24 t' is none like him among all the
26 and t' went with him a band of men,
11: 3 and then, if t' be no man to save us,
13 T' shall not a man be put to death
14 Gilgal, and renew the kingdom t'.
15 t' they made Saul king before the
15 t' they sacrificed sacrifices of peace
15 t' Saul and all the men of Israel
13:19 t' was no smith found throughout all
22 that t' was neither sword nor spear
22 with Jonathan his son was t' found.
14: 4 t' was a sharp rock on the one side,
6 for t' is no restraint to the Lord to
15 And t' was trembling in the host, in
17 and his armourbearer were not t'.
20 and t' was a very great discomfiture.
25 and t' was honey upon the ground.
30 for had t' not been now a much
34 him that night, and slew them t'.
39 But t' was not a man among all the
45 t' shall not one hair of his head fall to
52 t' was sore war against the Philistines
16:11 said, T' remaineth yet the youngest,
17: 3 and t' was a valley between them.
4 And t' went out a champion out of the
23 behold, t' came up the champion,
29 have I now done? Is t' not a cause?
34 father's sheep, and t' came a lion,
46 may know that t' is a God in Israel.
50 t' was no sword in the hand of David.
18:10 and t' was a javelin in Saul's hand.
19: 8 t' was war again: and David went out,
16 in, behold, t' was an image in the bed,
20: 3 t' is but a step between me and death.
6 his city: for t' is a yearly sacrifice
6 sacrifice t' for all the family.
8 if t' be in me iniquity, slay me thyself;
12 behold, if t' be good toward David,
21 come thou: for t' is peace to thee,
29 he hath commanded me to be t':
21: 3 in mine hand, or what t' is present.
4 T' is no common bread under mine
4 mine hand, but t' is hallowed bread;
6 hallowed bread: for t' was no bread
6 was no bread t' but the shewbread,
7 of the servants of Saul was t' that day,
8 is t' not here under thine hand spear
9 it: for t' is no other save that here.
9 And David said, T' is none like that;
22: 2 t' were with him about four hundred
8 t' is none that sheweth me that my
8 and t' is none of you that is sorry
22 when Doeg the Edomite was t',
23:22 haunt is, and who hath seen him t':
27 But t' came a messenger unto Saul,
24:11 and see that t' is neither evil nor
25: 2 And t' was a man in Maon, whose
7 neither was t' ought missing unto
10 t' be many servants now a days that
13 t' went up after David about four
34 surely t' had not been left unto Nabal
26:15 t' came one of the people in to destroy
27: 1 t' is nothing better for me than that I
5 the country, that I may dwell t':
28: 7 t' is a woman that hath a familiar
10 t' shall no punishment happen to thee
20 and t' was no strength in him; for he
30:17 and t' escaped not a man of them, save
19 And t' was nothing lacking to them,
31:12 came to Jabesh, and burnt them t'.
2Sa 1:21 mountains of Gilboa, let t' be no dew,
21 neither let t' be rain, upon you, nor
21 t' the shield of the mighty is vilely
2: 4 t' they anointed David king over the
15 t' arose and went over by number
17 And t' was a very sore battle that day;
18 And t' were three sons of Zeruiah
18 were three sons of Zeruiah t',
23 and he fell down t', and died in the
30 t' lacked of David's servants nineteen

2Sa 3: 1 t' was long war between the house of
6 while t' was war between the house of
27 smote him t' under the fifth rib,
29 let t' not fail from the house of Joab
38 Know ye not that t' is a prince and a
4: 3 were sojourners t' until this day.)
5:13 t' were yet sons and daughters born to
20 David smote them t', and said, The
21 t' they left their images, and David
6: 7 and God smote him t' for his error;
7 and t' he died by the ark of God.
7:22 O Lord God: for t' is none like thee,
22 neither is t' any God beside thee,
9: 1 Is t' yet any that is left of the house of
2 t' was of the house of Saul a servant
3 Is t' not yet any of the house of Saul,
10:18 captain of their host, who died t'.
11: 8 t' followed him a mess of meat from
17 t' fell some of the people of the
12: 1 T' were two men in one city; the one
4 t' came a traveller unto the rich man,
13:16 And she said unto him, T' is no cause:
30 sons, and t' is not one of them left.
34 t' came much people by the way of the
38 to Geshur, and was t' three years.
14: 6 t' was none to part them, but the one
11 t' shall not one hair of thy son fall to
25 t' was none to be so much praised as
25 crown of his head t' was no blemish
27 unto Absalom t' were born three sons,
30 he hath barley t'; go and set it on
32 good for me to have been t' still:
32 if t' be any iniquity in me, let him kill
15: 3 t' is no man deputed of the king to
13 t' came a messenger to David, saying,
21 even t' also will thy servant be.
28 until t' come word from you to certify
29 to Jerusalem: and they tarried t'.
35 hast thou not t' with thee Zadok
36 have t' with them their two sons,
16:14 weary, and refreshed themselves t'.
17: 9 T' is a slaughter among the people
12 t' shall not be left so much as one.
13 until t' be not one small stone found
13 be not one small stone found t'.
22 by the morning light t' lacked not one
18: 7 and t' was...a great slaughter that day
7 was t' a great slaughter that day
8 the battle was t' scattered over the
11 and why didst thou not smite him t'
13 for t' is no matter hid from the king,
19: 7 t' will not tarry one with thee this
17 t' were a thousand men of Benjamin
18 And t' went over a ferry boat to carry
22 shall t' any man be put to death this
20: 1 t' happened to be...a man of Belial,
1 happened to be t' a man of Belial,
7 And t' went out after him Joab's men,
21: 1 t' was a famine in the days of David
18 t' was again a battle with the
19 t' was again a battle in Gob with the
20 And t' was yet a battle in Gath, where
22: 9 T' went up a smoke out of his nostrils,
42 They looked, but t' was none to save;
23: 9 defied the Philistines that were t'
24: 9 and t' were in Israel eight hundred
15 t' died of the people from Dan even to
25 David built t' an altar unto the
1Ki 1: 2 Let t' be sought for my lord the king a
14 thou yet talkest t' with the king,
34 anoint him t' king over Israel:
52 t' shall not an hair of him fall to the
2: 4 t' shall not fail thee (said he) a man on
33 shall t' be peace for ever from the
36 house in Jerusalem, and dwell t',
3: 2 t' was no house built unto the name
4 king went to Gibeon to sacrifice t';
12 that t' was none like thee before thee,
13 t' shall not be any among the kings
18 t' was no stranger with us in the
4:34 And t' came of all people to hear the
5: 4 that t' is neither adversary nor evil
6 for thou knowest that t' is not among
9 cause them to be discharged t',
12 t' was peace between Hiram and
6: 7 t' was neither hammer nor axe nor
18 all was cedar; t' was no stone seen.
19 to set t' the ark of the covenant of
7: 4 And t' were windows in three rows,
24 brim of it round about t' were knops
29 upon the ledges t' was a base above:
34 t' were four undersetters to the four
35 top of the base was t' a round compass
8: 8 and t' they are unto this day.
9 T' was nothing in the ark save the
9 which Moses put t' at Horeb,
21 I have set t' a place for the ark,
23 t' is no God like thee, in heaven above,
25 T' shall not fail thee a man in my
29 hast said, My name shall be t':
35 heaven is shut up, and t' is no rain,
37 If t' be in the land famine,
37 If t' be pestilence, blasting, mildew,
37 locust, or if t' be caterpillar;
37 plague, whatsoever sickness t' be;
46 (for t' is no man that sinneth not,)
56 t' hath not failed one word of all his
60 Lord is God, and that t' is none else.
64 for t' he offered burnt offerings,
9: 3 built, to put my name t' for ever;
3 mine heart shall be t' perpetually.
5 T' shall not fail thee a man upon the
10: 3 t' was not any thing hid from the king,
5 the Lord; t' was no more spirit in her.
10 t' came no more such abundance of
12 t' came no such almug trees, nor were

1Ki 10:19 t' were stays on either side on the
20 And twelve lions stood t' on the
20 t' was not the like made in any
11:16 six months did Joab remain t'
36 have chosen me to put my name t'.
12:20 t' was none that followed the house of
13: 1 t' came a man of God out of Judah by
11 t' dwelt an old prophet in Beth-el;
17 eat no bread nor drink water t',
14: 2 t' is Ahijah the prophet, which told
13 in him t' is found some good thing
21 tribes of Israel, to put his name t'.
24 t' were also Sodomites in the land:
30 t' was war between Rehoboam and
15: 6 t' was war between Rehoboam and
7 t' was war between Abijam and
16 t' was war between Asa and Baasha
19 T' is a league between me and thee,
32 t' was war between Asa and Baasha
17: 1 t' shall not be dew nor rain these
4 the ravens to feed thee t'.
7 because t' had been no rain in the land.
9 belongeth to Zidon, and dwell t':
9 a widow woman t' to sustain thee.
10 the widow woman was t' gathering
17 sore, that t' was no breath left in him.
18: 2 And t' was a sore famine in Samaria.
10 t' is no nation or kingdom, whither my
10 when they said, He is not t'; he took
26 But t' was no voice, nor any that
29 that t' was neither voice, nor any to
40 brook Kishon, and slew them t'.
41 for t' is a sound of abundance of rain,
43 and looked, and said, T' is nothing.
44 t' ariseth a little cloud out of the sea,
45 and wind, and t' was a great rain.
19: 3 to Judah, and left his servant t'.
6 t' was a cake baken on the coals,
9 thither unto a cave, and lodged t';
13 behold, t' came a voice unto him, and
20: 1 t' were thirty and two kings with him,
13 t' came a prophet unto Ahab king of
17 T' are men come out of Samaria.
28 t' came a man of God, and spake unto
30 t' a wall fell upon twenty and seven
40 as thy servant was busy here and t',
21:13 t' came in two men, children of
25 t' was none like unto Ahab, which did
22: 7 Is t' not here a prophet of the Lord
8 T' is yet one man, Micaiah the son of
21 t' came forth a spirit, and stood before
36 t' went a proclamation throughout
47 T' was then no king in Edom: a
2Ki 1: 3 it not because t' is not a God in Israel,
6 T' came a man up to meet us, and said
6 it not because t' is not a God in Israel,
10 t' came down fire from heaven, and
14 Behold, t' came fire down from heaven,
16 t' is no God in Israel to enquire of
2:11 t' appeared a chariot of fire, and
16 t' be with thy servants fifty strong
21 the waters, and cast the salt in t',
21 t' shall not be from thence any more
23 t' came forth little children out of the
24 t' came forth two she bears out of the
3: 9 t' was no water for the host, and for
11 Is t' not here a prophet of the Lord,
20 t' came water by the way of Edom, and
27 t' was great indignation against Israel:
4: 1 t' cried a certain woman of the wives
6 said unto her, T' is not a vessel more.
10 and let us set for him t' a bed, and
11 into the chamber, and lay t'.
31 but t' was neither voice, nor hearing.
38 t' was a dearth in the land; and the
40 thou man of God, t' is death in the pot.
41 eat. And t' was no harm in the pot.
42 t' came a man from Baal-shalisha, and
5: 8 know that t' is a prophet in Israel.
15 now I know that t' is no God in all the
17 Shall t' not then, I pray thee, be given
18 house of Rimmon to worship t',
22 t' be come to me from mount Ephraim
6: 2 let us make us a place t', where
10 and saved himself t', not once nor
25 t' was a great famine in Samaria:
26 t' cried a woman unto him, saying,
7: 3 And t' were four leprous men at the
4 enter into the city,...we shall die t':
5 camp of Syria, behold, t' was no man
5 of Syria, behold,...was no man t'.
10 Syrians, and, behold, t' was no man
10 was no man t'; neither voice of
9: 2 out t' Jehu the son of Jehoshaphat
10 and t' shall be none to bury her.
16 went to Jezreel; for Joram lay t'.
17 t' stood a watchman on the tower in
18 t' went one on horseback to meet him,
23 and said to Ahaziah, T' is treachery,
27 he fled to Megiddo, and died t'.
32 t' looked out to him two or three
10: 2 t' are with you chariots and horses,
8 t' came a messenger, and told him,
10 now that t' shall fall unto the earth
21 t' was not a man left that came not.
23 and look that t' be here with you none
11:16 king's house: and t' was she slain.
12:10 they saw that t' was much money they
13 Howbeit t' were not made for the house
13: 6 t' remained the grove also in Samaria.
14: 9 t' passed by a wild beast that was in
19 him to Lachish, and slew him t'.
26 t' was not any shut up, nor any left,
15:20 and stayed not t' in the land.
16: 6 to Elath, and dwelt t' to this day.
17:11 t' they burnt incense in all the high

2Ki 17:18 t' was none left but the tribe of Judah
25 the beginning of their dwelling t',
27 and let them go and dwell t', and
18:18 t' came out to them Eliakim the son
19: 3 and t' is not strength to bring forth.
32 this city, nor shoot an arrow t',
20:13 t' was nothing in his house, nor in all
15 t' is nothing among my treasures that
22: 7 t' was no reckoning made with them
23:16 spied the sepulchres that were t'
20 upon the high places that were t'
22 t' was not holden such a passover
25 like unto him was t' no king before
25 neither after him arose t' any like him.
27 which I said, My name shall be t'.
34 and he came to Egypt, and died t'.
25: 3 t' was no bread for the people of the
23 t' came to Gedaliah to Mizpah,
1Ch 3: 4 t' he reigned seven years and six
4:23 t' they dwelt with the king for his
40 for they of Ham had dwelt t' of old.
41 the habitations that were found t',
41 in their rooms: because t' was pasture
41 was pasture t' for their flocks.
43 escaped, and dwelt t' unto this day.
5:22 For t' fell down many slain, because
11:13 t' the Philistines were gathered
12: 8 of the Gadites t' separated themselves
16 t' came of the children of Benjamin
17 seeing t' is no wrong in mine hands,
19 t' fell some of Manasseh to David,
20 to Ziklag, t' fell to him of Manasseh,
22 day by day t' came to David to help
39 t' they were with David three
40 abundantly: for t' was joy in Israel.
13:10 ark: and t' he died before God.
14:11 and David smote them t'.
12 when they had left their gods t',
16:37 So he left t' before the ark of the
17:20 O Lord, t' is none like thee, neither is
20 neither is t' any God beside thee,
19: 5 Then t' went certain, and told David
20: 2 gold, and t' were precious stones in it;
4 that t' arose war at Gezer with the
5 t' was war again with the Philistines;
6 And yet again t' was war at Gath,
21:14 and t' fell of Israel seventy thousand
26 David built t' an altar unto the
28 the Jebusite, then he sacrificed t'.
22:15 Moreover t' are workmen with thee in
16 brass, and the iron, t' is no number.
24: 4 t' were more chief men found of the
4 t' were sixteen chief men of the house
26:31 t' were found among them mighty
27:24 t' fell wrath for it against Israel;
28:21 t' shall be with thee for all manner of
29:15 as a shadow, and t' is none abiding.
2Ch 1: 3 for t' was the tabernacle of the
12 neither shall t' any after thee have the
5: 9 And t' it is unto this day.
10 T' was nothing in the ark save the
6: 5, 6 that my name might be t';
14 t' is no God like thee in the heaven,
16 T' shall not fail thee a man in my
20 thou wouldest put thy name t';
26 heaven is shut up, and t' is no rain,
28 If t' be dearth in the land,
28 if t' be pestilence, if t' be blasting,
28 sore or whatsoever sickness t' be:
36 (for t' is no man which sinneth not,)
7: 7 t' he offered burnt offerings, and
13 If I shut up heaven that t' be no rain,
16 that my name may be t' for ever:
16 mine heart shall be t' perpetually.
18 T' shall not fail thee a man to be ruler
8: 2 the children of Israel to dwell t'.
9: 2 and t' was nothing hid from Solomon
4 Lord; t' was no more spirit in her.
9 neither was t' any such spice as the
11 t' were none such seen before in the
18 And t' were six steps to the throne,
19 twelve lions stood t' on the one
19 T' was not the like made in any
12:13 tribes of Israel, to put his name t'.
15 t' were wars between Rehoboam and
13: 2 And t' was war between Abijah and
7 t' are gathered unto him vain men,
8 t' are with you golden calves, which
17 t' fell down slain of Israel five hundred
14: 9 t' came out against them Zerah the
14 t' was exceeding much spoil in them.
15: 5 t' was no peace to him that went out,
19 t' was no more war unto the five and
16: 3 T' is a league between me and thee,
3 as t' was between my father and thy
18: 6 Is t' not here a prophet of the Lord
7 T' is yet one man, by whom we may
20 Then t' came out a spirit, and stood
19: 3 t' are good things found in thee,
7 for t' is no iniquity with the Lord our
20: 2 t' came some that told Jehoshaphat,
2 T' cometh a great multitude against
6 and in thine hand is t' not power and
26 t' they blessed the Lord: therefore
21:12 t' came a writing to him from Elijah
17 so that t' was never a son left him,
23:15 king's house, they slew her t'.
24:11 they saw that t' was much money,
25: 7 t' came a man of God to him, saying,
18 t' passed by a wild beast that was in
27 after him, and slew him t'.
28: 9 But a prophet of the Lord was t'.
10 but are t' not with you, even with you,
13 and t' is fierce wrath against Israel.
18 villages thereof: and they dwelt t'
30:13 And t' assembled at Jerusalem much

2Ch 30:17 t' were many in the congregation that
26 So t' was great joy in Jerusalem: for
26 Israel t' was not the like in Jerusalem.
32: 4 So t' was gathered much people
7 for t' be more with us than with him:
14 Who was t' among all the gods of
21 bowels slew him t' with the sword.
25 therefore t' was wrath upon him, and
34:13 and of the Levites t' were scribes, and
35:18 And t' was no passover like to that
36:16 his people, till t' was no remedy.
23 Who is t' among you of all his people?
Ezr 1: 3 Who is t' among you of all his people?
2:63 till t' stood up a priest with Urim and
65 of whom t' were seven thousand three
65 and t' were among them two hundred
4:20 T' have been mighty kings also over
5:17 let t' be search made in the king's
17 house, which is t' at Babylon,
6: 2 And t' was found at Achmetha, in the
12 hath caused his name to dwell t'
7: 7 t' went up some of the children of
23 should t' be wrath against the realm
8:15 t' abode we in tents three days:
15 found t' none of the sons of Levi.
21 Then I proclaimed a fast t', at the
25 all Israel t' present, had offered:
32 and abode t' three days.
9:14 t' should be no remnant nor escaping?
10: 1 t' assembled unto him out of Israel a
2 t' is hope in Israel concerning this
18 among the sons of the priests t' were
Ne 1: 3 are left of the captivity t' in the
9 though t' were of you cast out unto
9 I have chosen to set my name t'.
2:10 t' was come a man to seek the welfare
11 Jerusalem, and was t' three days.
12 neither was t' any beast with me,
14 t' was no place for the beast that was
4:10 t' is much rubbish; so that we are not
5: 1 t' was a great cry of the people and
2 t' were that said, We, our sons, and
3 Some also t' were that said, We have
4 T' were also that said, We have
17 t' were at my table an hundred and
6: 1 that t' was no breach left therein;
7 T' is a king in Judah: and now shall
8 T' are no such things done as thou
11 and who is t', that, being as I am,
18 t' were many in Judah sworn unto
7:65 till t' stood up a priest with Urim and
67 of whom t' were seven thousand three
8:17 so. And t' was very great gladness.
12:46 of old t' were chief of the singers,
13:16 T' dwelt men of Tyre also therein,
19 t' should no burden be brought in on
26 many nations was t' no king like him,
Es 1:18 Thus shall t' arise too much contempt
19 t' go a royal commandment from him,
2: 2 Let t' be fair young virgins sought for
5 in...the palace t' was a certain Jew,
3: 8 T' is a certain people scattered
12 t' was written according to all that
4: 3 t' was great mourning among the
11 t' is one law of his to put him to death.
14 t' enlargement and deliverance arise
6: 3 unto him, T' is nothing done for him.
7: 7 he saw that t' was evil determined
Job 1: 1 T' was a man in the land of Uz,
2 t' were born unto him seven sons and
6 t' was a day when the sons of God
8 that t' is none like him in the earth,
13 t' was a day when his sons and his
14 And t' came a messenger unto Job,
16, 17, 18 speaking, t' came also another,
19 t' came a great wind from the
2: 1 Again t' was a day when the sons of
3 that t' is none like him in the earth,
3: 3 was said, T' is a man child conceived.
17 T' the wicked cease from
17 and t' the weary be at rest.
18 T' the prisoners rest together; they
19 The small and great are t'; and
4:16 t' was silence, and I heard a voice,
5: 1 if t' be any that will answer thee;
4 gate, neither is t' any to deliver them.
19 in seven t' shall no evil touch thee.
6:30 Is t' iniquity in my tongue? cannot
7: 1 Is t' not an appointed time to man
9:33 Neither is t' any daysman betwixt us,
10: 7 t' is none that can deliver out of thine
11:18 thou shalt be secure, because t' is hope;
12:14 up a man, and t' can be no opening.
24 in a wilderness where t' is no way.
14: 7 For t' is hope of a tree, if it be cut
15:11 is t' any secret thing with thee?
17: 2 Are t' not mockers with me? and doth
19: 7 I cry aloud, but t' is no judgment.
29 that ye may know t' is a judgment.
20:21 T' shall none of his meat be left;
21:33 him, as t' are innumerable before him.
34 your answers t' remaineth falsehood?
22:29 then thou shalt say, T' is lifting up;
23: 7 T' the righteous might dispute
8 Behold, I go forward, but he is not t';
25: 3 Is t' any number of his armies? and
28: 1 Surely t' is a vein for the silver, and a
7 T' is a path which no fowl knoweth,
30:26 I waited for light, t' came darkness.
31: 2 what portion of God is t' from above?
32: 5 Elihu saw that t' was no answer in
8 But t' is a spirit in man: and the
12 t' was none of you that convinced Job,
33: 9 innocent; neither is t' iniquity in me.
23 If t' be a messenger with him, an
34:22 T' is no darkness, nor shadow of

Job 35:12 T' they cry, but none giveth
36:16 broad place, where t' is no straitness;
18 Because t' is wrath, beware lest he
38:26 the wilderness, wherein t' is no man;
39:30 and where the slain are, t' is she.
41:33 Upon earth t' is not his like, who is
42:11 Then came t' unto him all his
Ps 3: 2 Many t' be which say of my soul,
2 T' is no help for him in God. Selah.
4: 6 T' be many that say, Who will shew
5: 9 t' is no faithfulness in their mouth;
6: 5 For in death t' is no remembrance of
7: 2 it in pieces, while t' is none to deliver.
3 if t' be iniquity in my hands;
14: 1 hath said in his heart, T' is no God.
1 works, t' is none that doeth good.
2 if t' were any that did understand,
3 t' is none that doeth good, no, not one.
5 T' were they in great fear: for
16:11 hand t' are pleasures for evermore.
18: 8 T' went up a smoke out of his nostrils,
41 cried, but t' was none to save them:
19: 3 T' is no speech nor language, where
6 t' is nothing hid from the heat thereof.
11 in keeping of them t' is great reward.
22:11 trouble is near; for t' is none to help.
30: 9 What profit is t' in my blood, when I
32: 2 and in whose spirit t' is no guile.
33:16 T' is no king saved by the multitude
34: 9 for t' is no want to them that fear him.
36: 1 t' is no fear of God before his eyes.
12 T' are the workers of iniquity
38: 3 T' is no soundness in my flesh
3 neither is t' any rest in my bones
7 and t' is no soundness in my flesh.
45:12 the daughter of Tyre shall be t'
46: 4 T' is a river, the streams whereof
48: 6 Fear took hold upon them t', and
50:22 in pieces, and t' be none to deliver.
53: 1 hath said in his heart, T' is no God.
1 iniquity: t' is none that doeth good.
2 if t' were any that did understand,
3 t' is none that doeth good, no, not one.
5 T' were they in great fear, where
55:18 against me: for t' were many with me.
58:11 Verily t' is a reward for the righteous:
66: 6 on foot: t' did we rejoice in him.
68:27 T' is little Benjamin with their
69: 2 in deep mire, where t' is no standing:
20 some to take pity, but t' was none;
35 that they may dwell t', and have it in
71:11 him; for t' is none to deliver him.
72:16 T' shall be an handful of corn in the
73: 4 For t' are no bands in their death:
11 and is t' knowledge in the most High?
25 t' is none upon earth that I desire
74: 9 our signs: t' is no more any prophet:
9 neither is t' among us any that
75: 8 in the hand of the Lord t' is a cup,
76: 3 T' brake he the arrows of the bow,
79: 3 and t' was none to bury them.
81: 9 T' shall no strange god be in thee;
86: 8 Among the gods t' is none like unto
8 are t' any works like unto thy works.
87: 4 Ethiopia; this man was born t'.
6 people, that this man was born t'.
7 the players on instruments shall be t':
91:10 T' shall no evil befall thee, neither
92:15 and t' is no unrighteousness in him.
104:26 T' go the ships:
26 t' is that leviathan, whom thou
105:31 spake, and t' came divers sorts of flies,
37 t' was not one feeble person among
106:11 enemies: t' was not one of them left.
107:12 fell down, and t' was none to help.
36 t' he maketh the hungry to dwell,
40 in the wilderness, where t' is no way.
109:12 Let t' be none to extend mercy unto
12 let t' be any to favour his fatherless
112: 4 t' ariseth light in the darkness:
122: 5 For t' are set thrones of judgment,
130: 4 But t' is forgiveness with thee, that
7 for with the Lord t' is mercy, and with
132:17 T' will I make the horn of David
133: 3 for t' the Lord commanded the
135:17 neither is t' any breath in their
137: 1 rivers of Babylon, t' we sat down,
3 For t' they that carried us away
139: 4 For t' is not a word in my tongue, but,
8 ascend up into heaven, thou art t':
8 my bed in hell, behold, thou art t'.
10 Even t' shall thy hand lead me,
16 when as yet t' was none of them.
24 see if t' be any wicked way in me, and
142: 4 t' was no man that would know me:
144:14 that t' be no breaking in, nor going
14 t' be no complaining in our streets.
146: 3 the son of man, in whom t' is no help.
Pr 7:10 t' met him a woman with the attire of
8: 8 t' is nothing froward or perverse in
24 t' were no depths, I was brought forth;
24 t' were no fountains abounding with
27 prepared the heavens, I was t':
9:18 he knoweth not that the dead are t';
10:19 In the multitude of words t' wanteth
11:10 when the wicked perish, t' is shouting.
14 multitude of counsellers, t' is safety.
24 T' is that scattereth, and yet
24 t' is that withholdeth more than is
12:18 T' is that speaketh like the piercings
21 T' shall no evil happen to the just:
28 in the pathway thereof t' is no death.
13: 7 T' is that maketh himself rich, yet
7 t' is that maketh himself poor, yet
23 t' is that is destroyed for want of
14: 9 but among the righteous t' is favour.

Pr 14:12 T' is a way which seemeth right unto
23 In all labour t' is profit: but the talk
16:25 T' is a way that seemeth right unto a
27 and in his lips t' is as a burning fire.
17:16 is t' a price in the hand of a fool to
18:24 t' is a friend that sticketh closer than a
19:18 Chasten thy son while t' is hope, and
21 T' are many devices in a man's heart;
20:15 T' is gold, and a multitude of rubies:
21:20 T' is treasure to be desired and oil in
30 T' is no wisdom nor understanding
22:13 The slothful man saith, T' is a lion
23:18 For surely t' is an end; and thine
24: 6 in multitude of counsellers t' is safety.
14 found it, then t' shall be a reward,
20 t' shall be no reward to the evil man;
25: 4 and t' shall come forth a vessel for the
26:12 t' is more hope of a fool than of him.
13 man saith, T' is a lion in the way;
20 no wood is, t' the fire goeth out: so
20 t' is no talebearer, the strife ceaseth.
25 t' are seven abominations in his heart.
28:12 men do rejoice, t' is great glory:
29: 6 of an evil man t' is a snare:
9 he rage or laugh, t' is no rest.
18 Where t' is no vision, the people
20 t' is more hope of a fool than of him.
30:11 T' is a generation that curseth their
12 T' is a generation that are pure in
13 T' is a generation, O how lofty are
14 T' is a generation, whose teeth are as
15 T' are three things that are never
18 T' be three things which are too
24 T' be four things which are little upon
29 T' be three things which go well, yea,
31 king, against whom t' is no rising up.
Ec 1: 9 t' is no new thing under the sun.
10 Is t' any thing whereof it may be said,
11 T' is no remembrance of former
11 neither shall t' be any remembrance
2:11 and t' was no profit under the sun.
16 t' is no remembrance of the wise
21 t' is a man whose labour is in wisdom,
24 T' is nothing better for a man, than
3: 1 To every thing t' is a season, and a
12 I know that t' is no good in them, but
16 judgment, that wickedness was t';
16 righteousness, that iniquity was t'.
17 t' is a time...for every purpose and
17 is a time t' for every purpose and
22 I perceive that t' is nothing better,
4: 1 side of their oppressors t' was power;
8 T' is one alone, and...is not a second;
8 is one alone, and t' is not a second;
8 is t' no end of all his labour; neither
16 T' is no end of all the people, even of
5: 7 words t' are also divers vanities:
8 regardeth; and t' be higher than they.
11 what good is t' to the owners thereof,
13 T' is a sore evil which I have seen
14 a son, and t' is nothing in his hand.
6: 1 T' is an evil which I have seen under
11 t' be many things that increase vanity,
7:11 by it t' is profit to them that see the
15 t' is a just man that perisheth in his
15 t' is a wicked man that prolongeth his
20 For t' is not a just man upon earth,
8: 4 the word of a king is, t' is power:
6 to every purpose t' is time and
8 T' is no man that hath power over the
8 and t' is no discharge in that war;
9 t' is a time wherein one man ruleth
14 T' is a vanity which is done upon the
14 that t' be just men, unto whom it
14 again, t' be wicked men, to whom it
16 t' is that neither day nor night seeth
9: 2 t' is one event to the righteous, and
3 the sun, that t' is one event unto all:
4 is joined to all the living t' is hope:
10 for t' is no work, nor device, nor
14 T' was a little city, and few men
14 and t' came a great king against it,
15 t' was found in it a poor wise man,
10: 5 T' is an evil which I have seen under
11: 3 the tree falleth, t' it shall be.
12:12 of making many books t' is no end;
Ca 4: 4 whereon t' hang a thousand bucklers,
7 all fair, my love; t' is no spot in thee.
6: 6 t' is not one barren among them.
8 T' are threescore queens, and
7:12 bud forth: t' will I give thee my loves.
8: 5 t' thy mother brought thee forth:
5 t' she brought thee forth that bare
Isa 1: 6 unto the head t' is no soundness in it;
2: 7 is t' any end of their treasures;
7 neither is t' any end of their chariots:
3:24 instead of sweet smell t' shall be stink;
4: 6 t' shall be a tabernacle for a shadow
5: 6 but t' shall come up briers and thorns:
8 lay field to field, till t' be no place,
6:12 t' be a great forsaking in the midst
7:23 where t' were a thousand vines at a
25 t' shall not come thither the fear of
8:20 it is because t' is no light in them.
9: 7 and peace t' shall be no end,
10:14 t' was none that moved the wing, or
11: 1 t' shall come forth a rod out of the
10 in that day t' shall be a root of Jesse,
16 t' shall be an highway for the remnant
13:20 shall the Arabian pitch tent t';
20 the shepherds make their fold t'.
21 beasts of the desert shall lie t';
21 creatures; and owls shall dwell t',
21 and satyrs shall dance t'.
14:31 t' shall come from the north a smoke,
15: 6 the grass faileth, t' is no green thing.

Isa 16:10 in the vineyards t' shall be no singing,
10 neither shall t' be shouting: the
17: 9 Israel: and t' shall be desolation.
19:15 shall t' be any work for Egypt, which
19 In that day shall t' be an altar to the
23 In that day shall t' be a highway out
22:18 a large country: t' shalt thou die,
18 t' the chariots of thy glory shall be
23: 1 laid waste, so that t' is no house,
10 of Tarshish: t' is no more strength.
12 t' also shalt thou have no rest.
24:11 T' is a crying for wine in the streets;
13 t' shall be as the shaking of an olive
27:10 wilderness: t' shall the calf feed,
10 t' shall he lie down, and consume
28: 8 filthiness, so that t' is no place clean.
10 line; here a little, and t' a little:
13 line; here a little, and t' a little;
29: 2 and t' shall be heaviness and sorrow:
30:14 so that t' shall not be found in the
25 t' shall be upon every high mountain,
28 t' shall be a bridle in the jaws of the
33:21 But t' the glorious Lord will be
34:12 the kingdom, but none shall be t',
14 the screech owl also shall rest t',
15 T' shall the great owl make her
15 t' shall the vultures also be
35: 8 And an highway shall be t', and a
9 No lion shall be t', nor any
9 up thereon, it shall not be found t';
9 but the redeemed shall walk t':
37: 3 and t' is not strength to bring forth.
33 this city, nor shoot an arrow t',
39: 2 t' was nothing in his house, nor in all
4 t' is nothing among my treasures that
8 t' shall be peace and truth in my days.
40:28 t' is no searching of his understanding.
41:17 and needy seek water, and t' is none,
26 yea, t' is none that sheweth,
26 yea, t' is none that declareth,
26 t' is none that heareth your words.
28 For I beheld, and t' was no man; even
28 among them, and t' was no counseller,
43:10 before me t' was no God formed,
10 formed, neither shall t' be after me.
11 Lord; and beside me t' is no saviour.
12 t' was no strange god among you:
13 t' is none that can deliver out of my
44: 6 the last; and beside me t' is no God.
8 my witnesses. Is t' a God beside me?
8 Yea, t' is no God; I know not any.
19 neither is t' knowledge nor
20 say, Is t' not a lie in my right hand?
45: 5 I am the Lord, and t' is none else,
5 t' is no God beside me: I girded thee,
6 the west, that t' is none beside me.
6 I am the Lord, and t' is none else.
14 thee; and t' is none else, t' is no God.
18 I am the Lord; and t' is none else.
21 and t' is no God else beside me; a just
21 and a Saviour; t' is none beside me.
22 for I am God, and t' is none else.
46: 9 old: for I am God, and t' is none else;
9 I am God, and t' is none like me,
47: 1 t' is no throne, O daughter of the
14 t' shall not be a coal to warm at, nor
48:16 from the time that it was, t' am I:
22 T' is no peace, saith the Lord, unto
50: 2 when I came, was t' no man?
2 when I called, was t' none to answer?
2 t' is no water, and dieth for thirst.
51:18 T' is none to guide her among all the
18 neither is t' any that taketh her by the
52: 4 for henceforth t' shall no more come
4 aforetime into Egypt to sojourn t';
53: 2 t' is no beauty that we should desire
57:10 yet saidst thou not, T' is no hope:
21 T' is no peace, saith my God, to the
59: 8 and t' is no judgment in their goings:
11 we look for judgment, but t' is none;
15 him that t' was no judgment.
16 and he saw that t' was no man, and
16 wondered that t' was no intercessor:
63: 3 and of the people t' was none with me:
5 And I looked, and t' was none to help;
5 and I wondered that t' was none to
64: 7 t' is none that calleth upon thy name,
65: 9 it, and my servants shall dwell t'.
20 T' shall be no more thence an infant
Jer 2:10 diligently, and see if t' be such a thing.
25 T' is no hope: no; for I have loved
3: 3 and t' hath been no latter rain;
6 tree, and t' hath played the harlot.
4:25 I beheld, and, lo, t' was no man, and
5: 1 if t' be any that executeth judgment,
6:14 Peace, peace; when t' is no peace.
20 purpose cometh t' to me incense from
7: 2 house, and proclaim t' this word,
32 bury in Tophet, till t' be no place.
8:11 Peace, peace; where t' is no peace.
13 t' shall be no grapes on the vine, nor
14 cities, and let us be silent t':
22 Is t' no balm in Gilead; is t' no
22 is...no physician t'? why then is
10: 6 as t' is none like unto thee, O Lord;
7 kingdoms, t' is none like unto thee.
13 t' is a multitude of waters in the
14 falsehood, and t' is no breath in them
20 t' is none to stretch forth my tent any
11:23 t' shall be no remnant of them: for I
13: 4 and hide it t' in a hole of the rock.
6 which I commanded thee to hide t'.
14: 4 for t' was no rain in the earth, the
5 and forsook it, because t' was no grass,
6 eyes did fail, because t' was no grass.
19 smitten us, and t' is no healing for us?

Jer 14:19 looked for peace, and *t'* is no good;
22 Are *t'* any among the vanities of the
16:13 *t'* shall ye serve other gods day
19 and things wherein *t'* is no profit.
17:25 *t'* enter into the gates of this city kings
18: 2 *t'* I will cause thee to hear my
12 And they said, *T'* is no hope: but we
19: 2 proclaim *t'* the words that I shall
11 in Tophet, till *t'* be no place to bury.
20: 6 to Babylon, and *t'* thou shalt die,
6 and shalt be buried *t'*, thou, and all
22: 1 of Judah, and speak *t'* this word,
4 then shall *t'* enter in by the gates of
26 were not born; and *t'* shall ye die.
26:20 And *t'* was also a man that prophesied
27:22 *t'* shall they be until the day that
29: 6 that ye may be increased *t'*, and
30:13 *T'* is none to plead thy cause, that
31: 6 For *t'* shall be a day, that the
17 *t'* is hope in thine end, saith the Lord,
24 *t'* shall dwell in Judah itself, and in
32: 5 *t'* shall he be until I visit him,
17 and *t'* is nothing too hard for thee:
27 flesh: is *t'* any thing too hard for me?
33:10 Again *t'* shall be heard in this place,
20 that *t'* should not be day and night in
36:12 the princes sat *t'*, even Elishama
22 *t'* was a fire on the hearth burning
32 *t'* were added besides unto them many
37:10 *t'* remained but wounded men among
13 a captain of the ward was *t'*,
16 had remained *t'* many days;
17 said, Is *t'* any word from the Lord?
17 And Jeremiah said, *T'* is: for, said he,
20 Jonathan the scribe, lest I die *t'*.
38: 6 in the dungeon *t'* was no water, but
9 for *t'* is no more bread in the city.
26 to Jonathan's house, to die *t'*.
28 he was *t'* when Jerusalem was taken.
41: 1 *t'* they did eat bread together in
3 the Chaldeans that were found *t'*,
5 That *t'* came certain from Shechem,
42:14 of bread; and *t'* will we dwell:
15 into Egypt, and go to sojourn *t'*;
16 shall overtake you *t'* in the land of
16 follow close after you *t'* in Egypt;
16 in Egypt; and *t'* ye shall die.
17 faces to go into Egypt to sojourn *t'*;
43: 2 Go not into Egypt to sojourn *t'*:
44:12, 14 the land of Egypt to sojourn *t'*,
14 have a desire to return to dwell *t'*:
27 the famine, until *t'* be an end of them.
28 the land of Egypt to sojourn *t'*,
46:17 They did cry *t'*, Pharaoh king of
47: 7 sea shore? *t'* hath he appointed it.
48: 2 *T'* shall be no more praise of Moab:
38 *T'* shall be lamentation generally
49:18 the Lord, no man shall abide *t'*,
23 *t'* is sorrow on the sea; it cannot be
33 for ever: *t'* shall no man abide
33 shall no man abide *t'*, nor any
36 and *t'* shall be no nation whither the
50: 3 out of the north *t'* cometh up a nation
20 be sought for, and *t'* shall be none;
39 beasts of the islands shall dwell *t'*,
40 so shall no man abide *t'*, neither
51:16 voice, *t'* is a multitude of waters in the
17 falsehood, and *t'* is no breath in them.
52: 6 so that *t'* was no bread for the people
23 *t'* were ninety and six pomegranates
34 *t'* was a continual diet given him of
La 1:12 see if *t'* be any sorrow like unto my
17 hands, and *t'* is none to comfort her:
20 bereaveth, at home *t'* is as death.
21 that I sigh: *t'* is none to comfort me:
3:29 in the dust; if so be *t'* may be hope.
4:15 They shall no more sojourn *t'*.
5: 8 *t'* is none that doth deliver us out of
Eze 1: 3 hand of the Lord was *t'* upon him.
25 And *t'* was a voice from the firmament
2: 5 *t'* hath been a prophet among them.
10 *t'* was written therein lamentations,
3:15 sat, and remained *t'* astonished
22 hand of the Lord was *t'* upon me;
22 plain, and I will *t'* talk with thee.
23 the glory of the Lord stood *t'*, as
4:14 neither came *t'* abominable flesh into
7:11 neither shall *t'* be wailing for them.
25 shall seek peace, and *t'* shall be none.
8: 1 hand of the Lord...fell *t'* upon me.
4 glory of the God of Israel was *t'*,
11 And *t'* stood before them seventy men
14 *t'* sat women weeping for Tammuz.
10: 1 *t'* appeared over them as it were a
8 *t'* appeared in the cherubims the form
12:13 not see it, though he shall die *t'*.
24 *t'* shall be no more any vain vision nor
28 *T'* shall none of my words be prolonged
13:10 saying, Peace; and *t'* was no peace;
11 *t'* shall be an overflowing shower; and
13 and *t'* shall be an overflowing shower
16 and *t'* is no peace, saith the Lord God.
20 wherewith ye *t'* hunt the souls to
17: 7 *T'* was also another great eagle with
20 plead with him *t'* for his trespass
20:28 and they offered *t'* their sacrifices,
28 *t'* they presented the provocation
28 *t'*...they made their sweet savour,
28 poured out *t'* their drink offerings.
35 *t'* will I plead with you face to face.
40 *t'* shall all the house of Israel, all of
40 serve me: *t'* will I accept them,
40 and *t'* will I require your offerings,
43 *t'* shall ye remember your ways,
22:20 and I will leave you *t'*, and melt you.
25 *T'* is a conspiracy of her prophets in

Eze 23: 2 *t'* were two women, the daughters of
3 *t'* were their breasts pressed, and
3 *t'* they bruised the teats of their
28: 3 *t'* is no secret that they can hide from
24 *t'* shall be no more a pricking brier
29:14 they shall be *t'* a base kingdom.
30:13 *t'* shall be no more a prince of the land
18 shall break *t'* the yokes of Egypt:
32:22 Asshur is *t'* and all her company:
24 *T'* is Elam and all her multitude
26 *T'* is Meshech, Tubal, and all her
29 *T'* is Edom, her kings, and all her
30 *T'* be the princes of the north, all
34: 5 scattered, because *t'* is no shepherd:
8 because *t'* was no shepherd, neither
14 *t'* shall they lie in a good fold, and
26 season; *t'* shall be showers of blessing.
35:10 whereas the Lord was *t'*:
37: 2 *t'* were very many in the open valley;
7 *t'* was a noise, and behold a shaking,
8 but *t'* was no breath in them.
38:19 in that day *t'* shall be a great shaking
39:11 give unto Gog a place *t'* of graves
11 *t'* shall they bury Gog and all his
28 have left none of them any more *t'*.
40: 3 *t'* was a man, whose appearance
16 *t'* were narrow windows to the little
17 court, and, lo, *t'* were chambers,
25 *t'* were windows in it and in the arches
26 And *t'* were seven steps to go up to it,
27 *t'* was a gate in the inner court toward
29 *t'* were windows in it and in the arches
33 *t'* were windows therein and in the
49 *t'* were pillars by the posts, one on this
41: 7 *t'* was an enlarging, and a winding
25 *t'* were made on them, on the doors of
25 *t'* were thick planks upon the face of
26 *t'* were narrow windows and palm
42:13 *t'* shall they lay the most holy
14 *t'* they shall lay their garments
45: 2 this *t'* shall be for the sanctuary five
46:19 *t'* was a place on the two sides
21 corner of the court *t'* was a court.
22 of the court *t'* were courts joined
23 *t'* was a row of building round about
47: 2 *t'* ran out waters on the right side.
9 *t'* shall be a very great multitude of
23 *t'* shall ye give him his inheritance,
48:35 that day shall be, The Lord is *t'*.
Da 2: 9 the dream, *t'* is but one decree for you:
10 *T'* is not a man upon the earth that
10 *t'* is no king, lord, nor ruler, that
11 *t'* is none other that can shew it before
28 *t'* is a God in heaven that revealeth
41 *t'* shall be in it of the strength of the
3:12 *T'* are certain Jews whom thou hast
29 *t'* is no other God that can deliver
4:31 mouth, *t'* fell a voice from heaven,
5:11 *T'* is a man in thy kingdom, in whom
6: 4 neither was *t'* any error or fault found
7: 8 *t'* came up among them another little
8 before whom *t'* were three of the
14 And *t'* was given him dominion, and
8: 3 *t'* stood before the river a ram which
4 neither was *t'* any that could deliver
7 *t'* was no power in the ram to stand
7 *t'* was none that could deliver the ram
15 *t'* stood before me as the appearance
10: 8 and *t'* remained no strength in me:
13 I remained *t'* with the kings of
17 *t'* remained no strength in me,
17 in me, neither is *t'* breath left in me.
18 *t'* came again and touched me one
21 *t'* is none that holdeth with me in these
11: 2 *t'* shall stand up yet three kings in
14 in those times *t'* shall many stand up
15 neither shall *t'* be any strength to
12: 1 *t'* shall be a time of trouble, such as
1 such as never was since *t'* was a nation
5 *t'* stood other two, the one on this side
11 *t'* shall be a thousand two hundred and
Ho 1:10 people, *t'* it shall be said unto them,
2:15 she shall sing *t'*, as in the days of
4: 1 because *t'* is no truth, nor mercy,
9 And *t'* shall be, like people, like priest:
6: 7 *t'* have they dealt treacherously
10 *t'* is the whoredom of Ephraim,
7: 7 *t'* is none among them that calleth
9 gray hairs are here and *t'* upon him,
9:12 them, that *t'* shall not be a man left:
15 in Gilgal: for *t'* I hated them:
10: 9 the days of Gibeah: *t'* they stood:
12: 4 in Beth-el, and *t'* he spake with us;
11 Is *t'* iniquity in Gilead? surely they
13: 4 but me: for *t'* is no saviour beside me.
8 *t'* will I devour them like a lion:
Joe 2: 2 *t'* hath not been ever the like, neither
3: 2 plead with them *t'* for my people
12 *t'* will I sit to judge all the heathen
17 *t'* shall no strangers pass through her
Am 3: 6 shall *t'* be evil in a city, and the Lord
11 An adversary *t'* shall be even round
4: 7 when *t'* were yet three months to the
5: 2 her land; *t'* is none to raise her up.
6 and *t'* be none to quench it in Beth-el.
6: 9 if *t'* remain ten men in one house,
10 of the house, Is *t'* yet any with thee?
12 rock? will one plow *t'* with oxen?
7:12 and *t'* eat bread, and prophesy *t'*:
8: 3 *t'* shall be many dead bodies in every
Ob 7 thee: *t'* is none understanding in him.
17 deliverance, and *t'* shall be holiness;
18 and *t'* shall not be any remaining of
Jon 1: 4 *t'* was a mighty tempest in the sea.
4: 5 and *t'* made him a booth, and sat
Mic 3: 7 their lips; for *t'* is no answer of God.

Mic 4: 9 is *t'* no king in thee? is thy counseller
10 to Babylon; *t'* shalt thou be delivered;
10 *t'* the Lord shall redeem thee from
6:10 Are *t'* yet the treasures of wickedness
7: 1 of the vintage: *t'* is no cluster to eat:
2 and *t'* is none upright among men:
Na 1:11 *T'* is one come out of thee, that
2: 9 for *t'* is none end of the store and glory
3: 3 *t'* is a multitude of slain, and a great
3 and *t'* is none end of their corpses;
15 *T'* shall the fire devour thee; the
19 *T'* is no healing of thy bruise; thy
Hab 1: 3 and *t'* are that raise up strife and
2:19 *t'* is no breath at all in the midst of it.
3: 4 and *t'* was the hiding of his power.
17 and *t'* shall be no herd in the stalls:
Zep 1:10 *t'* shall be the noise of a cry from the
14 mighty man shall cry *t'* bitterly.
2: 5 thee, that *t'* shall be no inhabitant.
15 heart, I am, and *t'* is none beside me:
3: 6 are destroyed, so that *t'* is no man,
6 is no man, that *t'* is none inhabitant.
Hag 1: 6 ye clothe you, but *t'* is none warm;
2:14 that which they offer *t'* is unclean.
16 of twenty measures, *t'* were but ten:
16 out of the press, *t'* were but twenty.
Zec 1: 8 and behind him were *t'* red horses,
5: 7 behold, *t'* was lifted up a talent of lead:
9 and, behold, *t'* came out two women,
11 and set *t'* upon her own base.
6: 1 behold, *t'* came four chariots out from
8: 4 *T'* shall yet old men and old women
10 these days *t'* was no hire for man,
10 neither was *t'* any peace to him that
20 to pass, that *t'* shall come people,
10: 2 troubled, because *t'* was no shepherd.
11: 3 *T'* is a voice of the howling of the
12:11 that day shall *t'* be a great mourning
13: 1 that day *t'* shall be a fountain opened
14: 4 and *t'* shall be a very great valley;
9 that day shall *t'* be one Lord, and his
11 *t'* shall be no more utter destruction;
18 *t'* shall be the plague, wherewith the
20 that day shall *t'* be upon the bells of
21 in that day *t'* shall be no more the
Mal 1:10 is *t'* even among you that would shut
3:10 that *t'* may be meat in mine house,
10 *t'* shall not be room enough to receive
M't 2: 1 *t'* came wise men from the east to
13 be thou *t'* until I bring thee word:
15 And was *t'* until the death of Herod:
18 In Rama was *t'* a voice heard,
4:25 *t'* followed him great multitudes of
5:23 *t'* rememberest that thy brother
24 Leave *t'* thy gift before the altar,
6:21 is, *t'* will your heart be also.
7: 9 Or what man is *t'* of you, whom if his
13 and many *t'* be which go in thereat:
14 unto life, and few *t'* be that find it.
8: 2 *t'* came a leper and worshipped him,
5 *t'* came unto him a centurion,
12 *t'* shall be weeping and gnashing
24 *t'* arose a great tempest in the sea,
26 and the sea; and *t'* was a great calm.
28 *t'* met him two possessed with devils,
30 And *t'* was a good way off from them
10:11 and *t'* abide till ye go thence.
26 *t'* is nothing covered, that shall not be
11:11 *t'* hath not risen a greater than John
12:10 *t'* was a man which had his hand
11 What man shall *t'* be among you, that
39 *t'* shall no sign be given to it, but the
45 and they enter in and dwell *t'*:
13:42, 50 *t'* shall be wailing and gnashing
58 he did not many mighty works *t'*
14:23 evening was come, he was *t'* alone.
15:29 up into a mountain, and sat down *t'*.
16: 4 and *t'* shall no sign be given unto it,
28 *T'* be some standing here, which shall
17: 3 *t'* appeared unto them Moses and
14 *t'* came to him a certain man, kneeling
18:20 name, *t'* am I in the midst of them.
19: 2 him; and he healed them *t'*.
12 For *t'* are some eunuchs, which were
12 *t'* are some eunuchs, which were made
12 *t'* be eunuchs, which have made
13 were *t'* brought unto him...children,
17 *t'* is none good but one, that is, God:
21:17 into Bethany; and he lodged *t'*.
33 *T'* was a certain householder, which
22:11 saw *t'* a man which had not on a
13 *t'* shall be weeping and gnashing of
23 which say that *t'* is no resurrection,
25 Now *t'* were with us seven brethren:
24: 2 *T'* shall not be left here one stone
7 *t'* shall be famines, and pestilences,
22 shortened, *t'* should no flesh be saved:
23 unto you, Lo, here is Christ, or *t'*;
24 *t'* shall arise false Christs, and false
28 is, *t'* will the eagles be gathered
51 *t'* shall be weeping and gnashing of
25: 6 at midnight *t'* was a cry made,
9 lest *t'* be not enough for us and you:
25 earth: lo, *t'* thou hast that is thine.
30 *t'* shall be weeping and gnashing
26: 5 lest *t'* be an uproar among the people.
7 *T'* came unto him a woman having
13 *t'* shall also this, that this woman
71 and said unto them that were *t'*,
27:36 sitting down they watched him *t'*;
38 were *t'* two thieves crucified with him,
45 from the sixth hour *t'* was darkness
47 Some of them that stood *t'*, when
55 many women were *t'* beholding
57 *t'* came a rich man of Arimathæa,
61 *t'* was Mary Magdalene, and the

M't 28: 2 behold, *t'* was a great earthquake: for
7 *t'* shall ye see him: lo, I have told
10 Galilee, and *t'* shall they see me.
M'r 1: 5 *t'* went out unto him all the land of
7 *T'* cometh one mightier than I after
11 *t'* came a voice from heaven, saying,
13 *t'* in the wilderness forty days,
23 *t'* was in their synagogue a man with
35 into a solitary place, and *t'* prayed.
38 towns, that I may preach *t'* also:
40 *t'* came a leper to him, beseeching
2: 2 that *t'* was no room to receive them,
6 *t'* were certain of the scribes sitting
6 scribes sitting *t'*, and reasoning
15 for *t'* were many, and they followed
3: 1 and *t'* was a man...which had a
1 a man *t'* which had a withered
31 *T'* came then his brethren and his
4: 1 *t'* was gathered unto him a great
3 Behold, *t'* went out a sower to sow:
22 For *t'* is nothing hid, which shall not
36 *t'* were also with him other little
37 *t'* arose a great storm of wind, and the
39 wind ceased, and *t'* was a great calm.
5: 2 *t'* met him out of the tombs a man
11 *t'* was...nigh unto the mountains
11 was *t'* nigh unto the mountains
22 *t'* cometh one of the rulers of the
35 *t'* came from the ruler of the
6: 5 he could *t'* do no mighty work,
10 *t'* abide till ye depart...that place.
31 for *t'* were many coming and going,
7: 4 And many other things *t'* be, which
15 *T'* is nothing from without a man,
8: 12 *T'* shall no sign be given unto this
9: 1 That *t'* be some of them that stand
4 *t'* appeared unto them Elias with
7 *t'* was a cloud that overshadowed
39 for *t'* is no man which shall do a
10: 17 *t'* came one running, and kneeled to
18 *t'* is none good but one, that is, God.
29 *T'* is no man that hath left house,
11: 5 certain of them that stood *t'*
27 *t'* come to him the chief priests,
12: 18 which say *t'* is no resurrection; and
20 *t'* were seven brethren: and the first
31 *T'* is none other commandment
32 hast said the truth: for *t'* is one God;
32 one God; and *t'* is none other but he:
42 And *t'* came a certain poor widow,
13: 2 *t'* shall not be left one stone upon
8 and *t'* shall be earthquakes in divers
8 and *t'* shall be famines and troubles:
21 here is Christ; or, lo, he is *t'*;
14: 2 day, lest *t'* be an uproar of the people.
3 *t'* came a woman having an alabaster
4 And *t'* were some that had indignation
13 and *t'* shall meet you a man bearing a
15 prepared: *t'* make ready for us.
51 *t'* followed him a certain young man,
57 *t'* arose certain, and bare false witness
66 *t'* cometh one of the maids of the high
15: 7 And *t'* was one named Barabbas,
33 *t'* was darkness over the whole land
40 *T'* were also women looking on afar
16: 7 *t'* shall ye see him, as he said unto
Lu 1: 5 *T'* was in the days of Herod, the king
11 *t'* appeared unto him an angel of the
33 and of his kingdom *t'* shall be no end.
45 *t'* shall be a performance of those
61 *T'* is none of thy kindred that is
2: 1 that *t'* went out a decree from Cæsar
6 while they were *t'*, the days were
7 *t'* was no room for them in the inn.
8 *t'* were in the same country shepherds
13 And suddenly *t'* was with the angel a
25 *t'* was a man in Jerusalem, whose
36 And *t'* was one Anna, a prophetess, the
4: 14 *t'* went out a fame of him through all
17 *t'* was delivered unto him the book
33 And in the synagogue *t'* was a man,
5: 15 much the more went *t'* a fame abroad
17 that *t'* were Pharisees and doctors of
29 *t'* was a great company of publicans
6: 6 *t'* was a man whose right hand
19 for *t'* went virtue out of him, and
7: 12 behold, *t'* was a dead man carried out,
16 And *t'* came a fear on all: and they
28 *t'* is not a greater prophet than
41 *T'* was a certain creditor which had
8: 23 *t'* came down a storm of wind on the
24 and they ceased, and *t'* was a calm.
27 *t'* met him out of the city a certain
32 And *t'* was...an herd of many swine
32 *t'* an herd of many swine feeding
41 behold, *t'* came a man named Jairus,
49 *t'* cometh one from the ruler of the
9: 4 house ye enter into, *t'* abide, and
17 *t'* was taken up of fragments that
27 of a truth, *t'* be some standing here,
30 behold, *t'* talked with him two men,
34 While he thus spake, *t'* came a cloud,
35 And *t'* came a voice out of the cloud,
46 *t'* arose a reasoning among them,
10: 6 And if the son of peace be *t'*, your
31 by chance *t'* came down a certain
11: 26 they enter in, and dwell *t'*: and
29 and *t'* shall no sign be given it, but
12: 1 when *t'* were gathered together an
2 For *t'* is nothing covered, that shall
18 *t'* will I bestow all my fruits and
34 treasure is, *t'* will your heart be
52 *t'* shall be five in one house divided,
54 *T'* cometh a shower; and so it is.
55 *T'* will be heat; and it cometh to pass.
13: 1 *T'* were present at that season some
Lu 13: 11 *t'* was a woman which had a spirit of
14 *T'* are six days in which men ought
23 him, Lord, are *t'* few that be saved?
28 *T'* shall be weeping and gnashing
30 behold, *t'* are last which shall be first,
30 and *t'* are first which shall be last.
31 The same day *t'* came certain of the
14: 2 *t'* was a certain man before him
22 hast commanded, and yet *t'* is room.
25 *t'* went great multitudes with him:
15: 10 *t'* is joy in the presence of the angels
13 and *t'* wasted his substance with
14 *t'* arose a mighty famine in that land;
16: 1 *T'* was a certain rich man, which had
19 *T'* was a certain rich man, which was
20 *t'* was a...beggar named Lazarus,
26 between us and you *t'* is a great gulf
17: 12 *t'* met him ten men that were lepers,
17 Were *t'* not ten cleansed? but where
18 *T'* are not found that returned to give
21 shall they say, Lo here! or, lo *t'*!
23 shall say to you, See here; or, see *t'*:
34 night *t'* shall be two men in one bed;
18: 2 *T'* was in a city a judge, which feared
3 And *t'* was a widow in that city; and
29 *T'* is no man that hath left house, or
19: 2 behold, *t'* was a man named Zacchæus,
20: 27 which deny that *t'* is any resurrection;
29 *T'* were therefore seven brethren: and
21: 6 *t'* shall not be left one stone upon
7 what sign will *t'* be when these things
11 great signs shall *t'* be from heaven.
18 *t'* shall not an hair of your head perish.
23 *t'* shall be great distress in the land,
25 *t'* shall be signs in the sun, and in the
22: 10 into the city, *t'* shall a man meet you,
12 room furnished: *t'* make ready.
24 *t'* was also a strife among them,
43 *t'* appeared an angel unto him from
23: 27 *t'* followed him a great company of
32 *t'* were also two other, malefactors,
33 Calvary, *t'* they crucified him,
44 *t'* was a darkness over all the earth
50 behold, *t'* was a man named Joseph,
24: 18 things which are come to pass *t'*
Joh 1: 6 *T'* was a man sent from God, whose
26 *t'* standeth one among you, whom ye
46 Can *t'* any good thing come out of
2: 1 the third day *t'* was a marriage in Cana
1 and the mother of Jesus was *t'*:
6 *t'* were set...six waterpots of stone,
6 set *t'* six waterpots of stone,
12 they continued *t'* not many days.
3: 1 *T'* was a man of the Pharisees, named
22 and *t'* he tarried with them, and
23 to Salim, because *t'* was much water
23 because...was much water *t'*:
25 Then *t'* arose a question between some
4: 6 Now Jacob's well was *t'*. Jesus
7 *T'* cometh a woman of Samaria to
35 *T'* are yet four months, and then
40 them: and he abode *t'* two days.
46 And *t'* was a certain nobleman, whose
5: 1 After this *t'* was a feast of the Jews;
2 Now *t'* is at Jerusalem by the sheep
5 And a certain man was *t'*, which
32 *T'* is another that beareth witness of
45 *t'* is one that accuseth you, even Moses.
6: 3 and *t'* he sat with his disciples.
9 *T'* is a lad here, which hath five
10 Now *t'* was much grass in the place.
22 saw that *t'* was none other boat
22 saw that...was none other boat *t'*,
23 *t'* came other boats from Tiberias
24 therefore saw that Jesus was not *t'*,
64 But *t'* are some of you that believe not.
7: 4 *t'* is no man that doeth any thing in
12 *t'* was much murmuring among the
43 So *t'* was a division among the people
8: 44 the truth, because *t'* is no truth in him.
50 *t'* is one that seeketh and judgeth.
9: 16 And *t'* was a division among them.
10: 16 *t'* shall be one fold, and one shepherd.
19 *T'* was a division therefore again
40 at first baptized; and *t'* he abode.
42 And many believed on him *t'*.
11: 9 Are *t'* not twelve hours in the day?
10 stumbleth, because *t'* is no light in him.
15 for your sakes that I was not *t'*,
31 She goeth unto the grave to weep *t'*.
54 and *t'* continued with his disciples.
12: 2 *T'* they made him a supper; and
9 Jews therefore knew that he was *t'*:
20 *t'* were certain Greeks among them
26 I am, *t'* shall also my servant be:
28 Then came *t'* a voice from heaven,
13: 23 *t'* was leaning on Jesus' bosom one of
14: 3 that where I am, *t'* ye may be also.
18: 18 And the servants and officers stood *t'*,
19: 25 Now *t'* stood by the cross of Jesus his
29 Now *t'* was set a vessel full of vinegar:
34 and forthwith came *t'* out blood and
39 *t'* came also Nicodemus, which at the
41 where he was crucified *t'* was a garden:
42 *T'* laid they Jesus therefore
21: 2 *T'* were together Simon Peter, and
9 they saw a fire of coals *t'*, and fish
11 and for all *t'* were so many, yet was
25 *t'* are also many other things which
Ac 2: 2 And suddenly *t'* came a sound from
3 And *t'* appeared unto them cloven
5 *t'* were dwelling at Jerusalem Jews,
41 *t'* were added unto them about three
4: 12 Neither is *t'* salvation in any other:
12 *t'* is none other name under heaven
34 Neither was *t'* any among them that
Ac 5: 16 *T'* came also a multitude out of the
34 Then stood *t'* up one in the council,
6: 1 *t'* arose a murmuring of the Grecians
9 *t'* arose certain of the synagogue,
7: 11 *t'* came a dearth over all the land of
12 Jacob heard that *t'* was corn in Egypt,
30 *t'* appeared to him in the wilderness
8: 1 at that time *t'* was a great persecution
8 And *t'* was great joy in that city.
9 But *t'* was a certain man, called Simon,
9: 3 suddenly *t'* shined round about him a
10 *t'* was a certain disciple at Damascus,
18 *t'* fell from his eyes as it had been
33 *t'* he found a certain man named
36 Now *t'* was at Joppa a certain disciple
38 had heard that Peter was *t'*,
10: 1 *T'* was a certain man in Cæsarea
13 *t'* came a voice to him, Rise, Peter;
18 surnamed Peter, were lodged *t'*.
11: 11 immediately *t'* were three men already
28 And *t'* stood up one of them named
28 spirit that *t'* should be great dearth
12: 18 *t'* was no small stir among the soldiers,
19 from Judæa to Cæsarea, and *t'* abode.
13: 1 Now *t'* were in the church that was at
11 immediately *t'* fell on him a mist and a
25 *t'* cometh one after me, whose shoes
14: 5 And when *t'* was an assault made both
7 And *t'* they preached the gospel.
8 And *t'* sat a certain man at Lystra,
19 *t'* came thither certain Jews from
28 *t'* they abode long time with the
15: 5 *t'* rose up certain of the sect of the
7 And when *t'* had been much disputing,
33 And after they had tarried *t'* a space,
34 it pleased Silas to abide *t'* still.
16: 1 a certain disciple was *t'*, named
9 *T'* stood a man of Macedonia, and
15 come into my house, and abide *t'*.
26 suddenly *t'* was a great earthquake, so
17: 7 that *t'* is another king, one Jesus.
14 Silas and Timotheus abode *t'* still.
21 and strangers which were *t'*
18 11 And he continued *t'* a year and six
18 Paul after this tarried *t'* yet a good
19 came to Ephesus, and left them *t'*:
23 after he had spent some time *t'*, he
19: 2 heard whether *t'* be any Holy Ghost.
14 *t'* were seven sons of one Sceva, a
21 After I have been *t'*, I must also
23 same time *t'* arose no small stir about
35 what man is *t'* that knoweth not how
38 the law is open, and *t'* are deputies:
40 this day's uproar, *t'* being no cause
20: 3 *t'* abode three months. And when the
4 And *t'* accompanied him into Asia
8 And *t'* were many lights in the upper
9 *t'* sat in a window a certain young
13 Assos, *t'* intending to take in Paul:
22 things that shall befall me *t'*:
21: 3 for *t'* the ship was to unlade her
4 disciples, we tarried *t'* seven days:
10 And as we tarried *t'* many days,
10 *t'* came down from Judæa a certain
16 *T'* went with us also certain of the
20 thousands of Jews *t'* are which believe;
40 when *t'* was made a great silence, he
22: 5 were *t'* bound unto Jerusalem,
6 *t'* shone from heaven a great light
10 *t'* it shall be told thee of all things
12 report of all the Jews which dwelt *t'*,
23: 7 he had so said, *t'* arose a dissension
8 say that *t'* is no resurrection,
9 *t'* arose a great cry: and the scribes
10 when *t'* arose a great dissension, the
21 for *t'* lie in wait for him of them more
24: 11 that *t'* are yet but twelve days since
15 *t'* shall be a resurrection of the dead,
25: 5 man, if *t'* be any wickedness in him.
9 *t'* be judged of these things before
11 if *t'* be none of these things whereof
14 when they had been *t'* many days,
14 *T'* is a certain man left in bonds by
20 and *t'* be judged of these matters.
27: 6 And *t'* the centurion found a ship
12 attain to Phenice, and *t'* to winter;
14 after *t'* arose against it a tempestuous
22 *t'* shall be no loss of any man's life
23 For *t'* stood by me this night the angel
34 for *t'* shall not an hair fall from the
28: 3 the fire, *t'* came a viper out of the heat,
12 at Syracuse, we tarried *t'* three days.
18 *t'* was no cause of death in me.
23 *t'* came many to him into his lodging;
Ro 2: 11 *t'* is no respect of persons with God.
3: 1 or what profit is *t'* of circumcision?
10 *T'* is none righteous, no, not one:
11 *T'* is none that understandeth,
11 *t'* is none that seeketh after God.
12 *t'* is none that doeth good, no, not one.
18 *T'* is no fear of God before their eyes.
20 *t'* shall no flesh be justified in his
22 that believe: for *t'* is no difference:
4: 15 where no law is, *t'* is no transgression.
5: 13 sin is not imputed when *t'* is no law.
8: 1 *T'* is therefore now no condemnation
9: 14 Is *t'* unrighteousness with God? God
26 *t'* shall they be called the children
10: 12 *t'* is no difference between the Jew
11: 5 present time also *t'* is a remnant
26 *T'* shall come out of Sion the
13: 1 For *t'* is no power but of God: the
9 if *t'* be any other commandment, it is
14: 14 that *t'* is nothing unclean of itself:
15: 12 saith, *T'* shall be a root of Jesse,
1Co 1: 10 and that *t'* be no divisions among you;

1Co 1:11 that t' are contentions among you.
3: 3 for whereas t' is among you envying,
5: 1 reported...that t' is fornication
6: 5 that t' is not a wise man among you?
7 t' is utterly a fault among you,
7:34 T' is difference also between a wife
8: 4 and that t' is none other God but one.
5 For though t' be that are called gods,
5 (as t' be gods many, and lords many,)
6 But to us t' is but one God, the Father,
7 t' is not in every man that knowledge:
10:13 T' hath no temptation taken you but
11:18 I hear that t' be divisions among you;
19 t' must be also heresies among you,
12: 4 t' are diversities of gifts, but the same
5 t' are differences of administrations,
6 t' are diversities of operations, but it
25 t' should be no schism in the body;
13: 8 but whether t' be prophecies, they
8 whether t' be tongues, they shall
8 whether t' be knowledge, it shall
14:10 T' are, it may be, so many kinds of
23 t' come in those that are unlearned, or
24 t' come in one that believeth not, or
28 But if t' be no interpreter, let him
15:12 among you that t' is no resurrection
13 if t' be no resurrection of the dead,
39 but t' is one kind of flesh of men,
40 T' are also celestial bodies, and
41 T' is one glory of the sun, and
44 T' is a natural body,
44 and t' is a spiritual body.
16: 2 that t' be no gatherings when I come.
9 unto me, and t' are many adversaries.
2Co 1:17 that with me t' should be yea yea, and
3:17 Spirit of the Lord is, t' is liberty.
8:11 that as t' was a readiness to will,
11 so t' may be a performance also out of
12 For if t' be first a willing mind, it is
14 for your want: that t' may be equality:
12: 7 t' was given to me a thorn in the flesh,
20 lest t' be debates, envyings, wraths,
Ga 1: 7 but t' be some that trouble you, and
3:21 for if t' had been a law given which
28 T' is neither Jew nor Greek,
28 t' is neither bond nor free,
28 t' is neither male nor female: for ye
5:23 temperance: against such t' is no law.
Eph 4: 4 T' is one body, and one Spirit, even as
6: 9 neither is t' respect of persons with
Ph'p 2: 1 If t' be therefore any consolation in
4: 8 if t' be any virtue,...if t' be any praise,
Col 3:11 Where t' is neither Greek nor Jew,
25 done: and t' is no respect of persons.
2Th 2: 3 except t' come a falling away first,
3:11 t' are some which walk among you
1Ti 1:10 if t' be any other thing that is contrary
2: 5 For t' is one God, and one mediator
2Ti 2:20 t' are not only vessels of gold and of
4: 8 t' is laid up for me a crown of
Tit 1:10 t' are many unruly and vain talkers
3:12 for I have determined t' to winter.
Ph'm 23 T' salute thee Epaphras, my
Heb 3:12 lest t' be in any of you an evil heart of
4: 9 T' remaineth therefore a rest to the
13 Neither is t' any creature that is not
7: 8 t' he receiveth them, of whom it is
11 what further need was t' that another
12 t' is made of necessity a change also
15 of Melchisedec t' ariseth another
18 For t' is verily a disannulling of the
8: 4 t' are priests that offer gifts according
9: 2 For t' was a tabernacle made; the
16 t' must also of necessity be the death
10: 3 in those sacrifices t' is a remembrance
18 these is, t' is no more offering for sin.
26 t' remaineth no more sacrifice for sins,
11:12 sprang t' even of one, and he as good
12:16 Lest t' be any fornicator, or profane
Jas 2: 2 t' come unto your assembly a man
2 t' come in also a poor man in vile
3 and say to the poor, Stand thou t',
19 Thou believest that t' is one God;
3:16 t' is confusion and every evil work.
4:12 T' is one lawgiver, who is able to save
13 such a city, and continue t' a year,
2Pe 1:17 t' came such a voice to him from the
2: 1 t' were false prophets also among the
1 t' shall be false teachers among you,
3: 3 t' shall come in the last days scoffers,
1Jo 2:10 t' is none occasion of stumbling in
18 even now are t' many antichrists;
4:18 T' is no fear in love; but perfect love
5: 7 t' are three that bear record in heaven,
8 t' are three that bear witness in earth,
16 T' is a sin unto death: I do not say
17 is sin: and t' is a sin not unto death.
2Jo 10 t' come any unto you, and bring not
Jude 4 t' are certain men crept in unawares,
18 t' should be mockers in the last time,
Re 2:14 thou hast t' them that hold the
4: 3 t' was a rainbow round about the
5 t' were seven lamps of fire burning
6 before the throne t' was a sea of glass
6: 4 t' went out another horse that was
4 t' was given unto him a great sword.
12 and, lo, t' was a great earthquake;
7: 4 t' were sealed an hundred and forty
8: 1 t' was silence in heaven about the
3 t' was given unto him much incense,
5 and t' were voices, and thunderings,
7 t' followed hail and fire mingled with
10 and t' fell a great star from heaven,
9: 2 and t' arose a smoke out of the pit,
3 t' came out of the smoke locusts upon
10 and t' were stings in their tails:

Re 9:12 t' come two woes more hereafter.
10: 6 that t' should be time no longer:
11: 1 t' was given me a reed like unto a rod:
13 same hour was t' a great earthquake,
15 t' were great voices in heaven, saying,
19 t' was seen in his temple the ark of
19 and t' were lightnings, and voices,
12: 1 t' appeared a great wonder in heaven;
3 t' appeared another wonder in heaven;
6 should feed her t' a thousand two
7 t' was war in heaven: Michael and his
13: 5 And t' was given unto him a mouth
14: 8 And t' followed another angel, saying,
16: 2 t' fell a noisome and grievous sore
17 t' came a great voice out of the temple
18 And t' were voices, and thunders,
18 t' was a great earthquake, such as
21 t' fell upon men a great hail out of
17: 1 t' came one of the seven angels which
10 t' are seven kings: five are fallen,
20:11 and t' was found no place for them.
21: 1 passed away; and t' was no more sea.
4 t' shall be no more death, neither*
4 neither shall t' be any more pain:
9 t' came unto me one of the seven
25 at all by day: for t' shall be no night
25 shall be no night t'.
27 t' shall in no wise enter into it any
22: 2 of the river, was t' the tree of life,
3 And t' shall be no more curse: but the
5 t' shall be no night...and they need
5 shall be no night t'; and they

thereabout
Lu 24: 4 they were much perplexed t',

thereat
Ex 30:19 wash their hands and their feet t':
40:31 washed their hands and their feet t':
M't 7:13 many there be which go in t':

thereby
Le 11:43 them, that ye should be defiled t'.
Job22:21 peace: t' good shall come unto thee.
Pr 20: 1 whosoever is deceived t' is not wise.
Ec 10: 9 cleaveth wood shall be endangered t'.
Isa 33:21 oars, neither shall gallant ship pass t'.
Jer 18:16 that passeth t' shall be astonished,
19: 8 that passeth t' shall be astonished
51:43 doth any son of man pass t'.
Eze 12: 5 wall in their sight, and carry out t'.
12 dig through the wall to carry out t':
33:12 he shall not fall t' in the day that he
18 iniquity, he shall even die t'.
19 is lawful and right, he shall live t'.
Zec 9: 2 And Hamath also shall border t';
Joh 11: 4 of God might be glorified t'.
Eph 2:16 having slain the enmity t':
Heb12:11 them which are exercised t'.
15 you, and t' many be defiled;
13: 2 t' some have entertained angels
1Pe 2: 2 the word, that ye may grow t':

therefore
Ge 2:24 T' shall a man leave...father
3:23 T' the Lord God sent him forth from
4:15 T' whosoever slayeth Cain,
11: 9 T' is the name of it called
12:12 T' it shall come to pass, when the
19 t' behold thy wife, take her, and go
17: 9 Thou shalt keep my covenant t', thou
18: 5 for t' are ye come to your
12 T' Sarah laughed within herself,
19: 8 t' came they under the
22 T' the name of the city was
20: 6 t' suffered I thee not to touch
7 t' restore the man his wife; for he
8 T' Abimelech rose early in the
21:23 Now t' sware unto me here by God
24:65 t' she took a vail, and covered herself.
25:30 t' was his name called Edom.
26:33 t' the name of the city is
27: 3 t' take, I pray thee, thy weapons,
8 Now t', my son, obey my voice
28 T' God give thee of the dew of heaven.
43 Now t', my son, obey my voice; and
29:15 shouldest thou t' serve me for nought?
32 now t' my husband will love me.
33 he hath t' given me this son also:
34 t' was his name called Levi.
35 t' she called his name Judah;
30: 6 t' called she his name Dan.
15 T' he shall lie with thee to night
31:44 t' come thou, let us make a covenant,
48 T' was the name of it called
32:32 T' the children of Israel eat
33:10 for t' I have seen thy face, as
17 t' the name of the place is
34:21 t' let them dwell in the land, and
37:20 Come now t', and let us slay him,
38:29 thee: t' his name was called Pharez.
41:33 t' let Pharaoh look out a man discreet
42:21 t' is this distress come upon
22 t', behold,...his blood is required.
44:30 Now t' when I come to thy servant my
33 t', I pray thee, let thy servant abide
45: 5 Now t' be not grieved, nor angry with
47: 4 t', we pray thee, let thy servants dwell
50: 5 t' let me go up, I pray thee, and bury
21 Now t' fear ye not: I will nourish you,
Ex 1:11 T' they did set over them taskmasters
20 T' God dealt well with the midwives:
3: 9 Now t', behold, the cry of the children
10 Come now t', and I will send thee
4:12 Now t' go, and I will be with thy
5: 8 t' they cry, saying, Let us go
17 t' ye say, Let us go and do
18 Go t' now, and work; for there shall

Ex 9:19 Send t' now, and gather thy cattle,
10:17 Now t' forgive, I pray thee, my sin
12:17 t' shall ye observe this day in your
13:10 Thou shalt t' keep this ordinance in
15 t' I sacrifice to the Lord all
15:23 t' the name of it was called
16:29 t' he giveth you on the sixth
19: 5 Now t', if ye will obey my voice
31:14 Ye shall keep the sabbath t'; for it is
32:10 t' let me alone, that my wrath may
34 T' now go, lead the people unto the
33: 5 t' now put off thy ornaments from
13 Now t', I pray thee, if I have found
Le 8:35 T' shall ye abide at the door of the
9: 8 Aaron t' went unto the altar, and
11:44 ye shall t' sanctify yourselves, and ye
45 God: ye shall t' be holy, for I am holy.
13:52 He shall t' burn that garment,
16: 4 t' shall he wash his flesh in water,
17:12 T' I said unto the children of
14 t' I said unto the children of Israel,
18: 5 Ye shall t' keep my statutes, and my
25 t' I do visit the iniquity thereof upon
26 Ye shall t' keep my statutes and my
30 T' shall ye keep mine ordinance, that
19: 8 T' every one that eateth it shall bear
37 T' shall ye observe all my statutes,
20: 7 Sanctify yourselves t', and be ye holy:
22 Ye shall t' keep all my statutes, and
23 these things, and t' I abhorred them.
25 Ye shall t' put difference between
21: 6 they do offer: t' they shall be holy.
8 Thou shalt sanctify him t'; for he
22: 9 They shall t' keep mine ordinance,
9 for it, and die t', if they profane it:
31 T' shall ye keep my commandments.
25:17 Ye shall not t' oppress one another;
Nu 3:12 Israel: t' the Levites shall be mine;
11:18 t' the Lord will give you flesh, and ye
14:16 t' he hath slain them in the
43 Lord, t' the Lord will not be with you.
16:38 before the Lord, t' they are hallowed:
18: 7 T' thou and thy sons with thee shall
24 t' I have said unto them,
30 T' thou shalt say unto them, When ye
20:12 t' ye shall not bring this
21: 7 T' the people came to Moses, and
22: 5 He sent messengers t' unto Balaam
6 Come now t', I pray thee, curse me
17 come t', I pray thee, curse me this
19 Now t', I pray you, tarry ye also here
34 now t', if I displease thee, I will get
24:11 T' now flee thou to thy place: I
14 come t', and I will advertise thee
27: 4 Give unto us t' a possession among
31:17 t' kill every male among the little
50 t' brought an oblation for the Lord,
35:34 Defile not t' the land which ye shall
De 2: 4 take ye good heed unto yourselves t':
4: 1 Now t' hearken, O Israel, unto the
6 Keep t' and do them; for this is your
15 Take ye t' good heed unto yourselves;
37 t' he chose their seed after them, and
39 Know t' this day, and consider it in
40 Thou shalt keep t' his statutes, and
5:15 t' the Lord...commanded
25 t' why should we die? for this great
32 Ye shall observe to do t' as the Lord
6: 3 Hear t', O Israel, and observe to do it;
7: 9 Know t' that the Lord thy God, he is
11 shalt t' keep the commandments,
8: 6 T' thou shalt keep the
9: 3 Understand t' this day, that the Lord
6 Understand t', that the Lord thy God
26 I prayed t' unto the Lord, and said,
10:16 Circumcise t' the foreskin of your
19 Love ye t' the stranger: for ye were
11: 1 T' thou shalt love the Lord thy God,
8 T' shall ye keep all the
18 T' shall ye lay up these my words in
14: 7 hoof; t' they are unclean unto you.
15:11 t' I command thee, saying,
15 t' I command thee this thing to
16: 2 Thou shalt t' sacrifice the passover
15 hands, t' thou shalt surely rejoice.
18: 2 T' shall they have no inheritance
23:14 before thee; t' shall thy camp be holy:
24:18, 22 t' I command thee to do
25:19 T' it shall be, when the Lord thy God
26:16 thou shalt t' keep and do them with
27: 4 T' it shall be when ye be gone over
10 shalt t' obey the voice of the Lord
28:48 T' shalt thou serve thine enemies
29: 9 Keep t' the words of this covenant,
30:19 t' choose life, that both thou and thy
31:19 Now t' write ye this song for you, and
22 Moses t' wrote this song the same
Jos 1: 2 now t' arise, go over this Jordan,
2:12 Now t', I pray you, swear unto me by
3:12 Now t' take you twelve men out of the
4:17 Joshua t' commanded the priests,
7:12 T' the children of Israel could not
14 In the morning t' ye shall be brought
8: 6 the first: t' we will flee before them.
9 Joshua t' sent them forth: and they
9: 6 now t' make ye a league with us.
11 t' now make ye a league with us.
19 Israel: now t' we may not touch them.
23 Now t' ye are cursed, and there shall
24 t' we were sore afraid of our lives
10: 5 T' the five kings of the Amorites, the
9 Joshua t' came unto them suddenly,
13: 7 t' divide this land for an inheritance
14: 4 t' they gave no part unto the Levites
12 Now t' give me this mountain, whereof
14 Hebron t' became the inheritance of

Jos 17: 1 of war, t' he had Gilead and Bashan.
4 T' according to the commandment of
18: 6 shall t' describe the land into seven
19: 9 t' the children of Simeon had their
47 t' the children of Dan went up to
22: 4 t' now return ye, and get you unto
26 T' we said, Let us now prepare to
28 T' said we, that it shall be, when they
23: 6 Be ye t' very courageous to keep and
11 Take good heed t' unto your selves,
15 T' it shall come to pass, that as all
24: 10 t' he blessed you still: so I delivered
14 Now t' fear the Lord, and serve him in
18 t' will we also serve the Lord; for he
23 t' put away, said he, the strange gods
27 it shall be t' a witness unto you, lest
J'g 2: 23 T' the Lord left those nations,
3: 8 T' the anger of the Lord was hot
25 t' they took a key, and opened them:
6: 32 T' on that day he called him
7: 3 t' go to, proclaim in the ears of the
8: 7 T' when the Lord hath delivered
9: 16 Now t', if ye have done truly and
32 Now t' up by night, thou and the
11: 8 T' we turn again to thee now,
13 t' restore those lands again peaceably.
26 why t' did ye not recover them within
13: 4 t' beware, I pray thee, and drink not
14: 2 now t' get her for me to wife.
15: 2 her; t' I gave her to thy companion:
16: 12 Delilah t' took new ropes, and bound
17: 3 now t' I will restore it unto thee.
18: 14 now t' consider what ye have to do.
19: 7 urged him: t' he lodged there again.
20: 13 Now t' deliver us the men, the
42 T' they turned their backs before the
21: 20 T' they commanded the children of
Ru 3: 3 Wash thyself t', and anoint thee, and
9 spread t' thy skirt over thine
4: 8 T' the kinsman said unto Boaz, Buy
1Sa 1: 7 her; t' she wept, and did not eat.
13 t' Eli thought she had been drunken.
28 T' also I have lent him to the Lord; as
3: 9 T' Eli said unto Samuel, Go, lie down:
14 t' I have sworn unto the house of Eli.
5: 5 T' neither the priests of
8 They sent t' and gathered all the
10 T' they sent the ark of God to Ekron.
6: 7 Now t' make a new cart, and take two
8: 9 Now t' hearken unto their voice:
9: 13 Now t' get you up; for about this time
10: 12 T' it became a proverb, Is
19 t' present yourselves before the Lord
22 T' they enquired of the Lord further,
11: 10 T' the men of Jabesh said, To
12: 7 Now t' stand still, that I may reason
13 Now t' behold the king whom ye have
16 Now t' stand and see this great
13: 12 T' said I, The Philistines will come
12 I forced myself t', and offered a burnt
14: 41 T' Saul said unto the Lord God of
15: 1 now t' hearken thou unto the voice of
25 Now t', I pray thee, pardon my sin,
17: 51 T' David ran, and stood upon the
18: 13 T' Saul removed him from him, and
22 thee: now t' be the king's son in law.
19: 2 now t', I pray thee, take heed to
20: 8 T' thou shalt deal kindly with thy
29 T' he cometh not unto the
21: 3 Now t' what is under thine hand? give
22: 1 David t' departed thence, and escaped
23: 2 T' David enquired of the Lord,
20 Now t', O king, come down according
23 See t', and take knowledge of all the
28 t' they called that place
24: 15 The Lord t' be judge, and judge
21 Swear now t' unto me by the Lord,
25: 17 t' know and consider what thou wilt
26 Now t', my lord, as the Lord liveth,
26: 4 David t' sent out spies, and
8 now t' let me smite him, I pray thee,
19 Now t', I pray thee, let my lord the
20 Now t', let not my blood fall to the
27: 12 him; t' he shall be my servant for ever.
28: 2 T' will I make thee keeper of mine
15 t' I have called thee, that thou mayest
18 t' hath the Lord done this
22 Now t', I pray thee, hearken thou also
31: 4 T' Saul took a sword, and fell upon it.
2Sa 2: 7 T' now let your hands be
4: 11 shall I not t' now require his blood
5: 20 T' he called the name of that
6: 21 Israel: t' will I play before the Lord.
23 T' Michal the daughter of Saul had
7: 8 Now t' so shalt thou say unto my
27 t' hath thy servant found in his heart
29 T' now let it please thee to bless the
9: 10 Thou t', and thy sons, and thy
12: 10 Now t' the sword shall never depart
16 David t' besought God for the child;
19 t' David said unto his servants, Is the
28 Now t' gather the rest of the people
13: 13 Now t', I pray thee, speak unto the
33 t' let not my lord the king take the
14: 15 t' that I am come to speak of this
17 t' the Lord thy God will be with thee.
21 t', bring the young man Absalom
26 was heavy on him, t' he polled it:)
29 T' Absalom sent for Joab, to have
30 T' he said unto his servants, See,
32 now t' let me see the king's face; and
15: 29 Zadok t' and Abiathar carried the ark
35 t' it shall be, that what thing soever
17: 11 T' I counsel that all Israel be
16 Now t' send quickly, and tell David,
18: 3 t' now it is better that thou succour us

2Sa 19: 7 Now t' arise, go forth, and speak
10 t' why speak ye not a word of bringing
20 t', behold, I am come the first this day
23 T' the king said unto Shimei, Thou
27 God: do t' what is good in thine eyes.
28 What right t' have I yet to cry any
22: 25 T' the Lord hath recompensed me
50 T' I will give thanks unto
23: 17 of their lives? t' he would not drink it.
19 of three? t' he was their captain:
1Ki 1: 12 now t' come, let me, I pray thee, give
2: 2 be thou strong t', and show thyself a
6 Do t' according to thy wisdom, and let
9 Now t' hold him not guiltless: for
19 Bath-sheba t' went unto king
24 Now t', as the Lord liveth, which hath
33 Their blood shall t' return upon the
44 t' the Lord shall return thy wickedness
3: 9 Give t' thy servant an understanding
5: 6 Now t' command thou that they hew
8: 25 T' now, Lord God of Israel, keep
61 your heart t' be perfect with the Lord
9: 9 t' hath the Lord brought upon
10: 9 t' made he thee king, to do judgment
11: 40 Solomon sought t' to kill Jeroboam.
12: 4 now t' make thou the grievous service
18 t' king Rehoboam made speed to get
24 They hearkened t' to the word of the
13: 26 t' the Lord hath delivered him unto
14: 10 T', behold, I will bring evil upon the
12 Arise thou t', get thee to thine own
18: 19 Now t' send, and gather to me all
23 Let them t' give us two bullocks; and
20: 23 t' they were stronger than we;
28 t' will I deliver all this great multitude
42 t' thy life shall go for his life, and thy
22: 19 Hear thou t' the word of the Lord:
23 Now t', behold, the Lord hath put a
2Ki 1: 4 Now t' thus saith the Lord, Thou
6 t' thou shalt not come down from
14 t' let my life now be precious in thy
16 t' thou shalt not come down off that
2: 17 They sent t' fifty men; and they
3: 23 another: now t', Moab, to the spoil.
4: 33 He went in t', and shut the door upon
5: 15 now t', I pray thee, take a blessing of
27 leprosy t' of Naaman shall cleave unto
6: 7 T' said he, Take it up to thee. And he
11 T' the heart of the king of Syria was
14 T' sent he thither horses, and
7: 4 Now t' come, and let us fall unto the
9 now t' come, that we may go and tell
12 t' are they gone out of the camp to
14 They took t' two chariot horses; and
9: 26 Now t' take and cast him into the plat
10: 19 Now t' call unto me all the prophets of
12: 7 now t' receive no more money of your
14: 11 T' Jehoash king of Israel went up;
15: 16 they opened not to him, t' he smote it;
17: 4 t' the king of Assyria shut him up, and
18 T' the Lord was very angry with
25 t' the Lord sent lions among them,
26 t' he hath sent lions among them, and
18: 23 Now t', I pray thee, give pledges to my
19: 18 stone: t' they have destroyed them.
19 Now t', O Lord our God, I beseech thee,
26 T' their inhabitants were of small
28 t' I will put my hook in thy nose, and
32 T' thus saith the Lord concerning
21: 12 T' thus saith the Lord God of
22: 17 t' my wrath shall be kindled against
20 Behold t', I will gather thee unto
1Ch 10: 14 t' he slew him, and turned the
11: 3 T' came all the elders of Israel to the
7 t' they called it the city of
19 brought it. T' he would not drink it.
14: 11 t' they called the name of
14 T' David inquired again of God; and
16 David t' did as God commanded him:
17: 7 t' thus shalt thou say unto my servant
23 T' now, Lord, let the thing that thou
25 t' thy servant hath found in
27 Now t' let it please thee to bless the
21: 7 with this thing; t' he smote Israel.
12 t' advise thyself what word I shall
22: 5 I will t' now make preparation for it.
16 Arise t', and be doing, and the Lord be
19 arise t', and build ye the sanctuary
23: 11 t' they were in one reckoning,
24: 2 t' Eleazar and Ithamar executed the
28: 8 Now t', in the sight of all Israel the
29: 13 Now t', our God, we thank thee, and
2Ch 2: 7 Send me now t' a man cunning to
15 Now t' the wheat, and the barley, the
6: 10 The Lord t' hath performed his word
16 Now t', O Lord God of Israel, keep
19 Have respect t' to the prayer of thy
21 Hearken t' unto the supplications of
41 Now t' arise, O Lord God, into thy
7: 22 t' hath he brought all this
9: 8 t' made he thee king over them, to do
10: 4 now t' ease thou somewhat the
12: 5 t' have I also left you in the hand of
7 t' I will not destroy them, but I will
14: 7 T' he saith unto Judah, Let us build
15: 7 Be ye strong t', and let not your hands
16: 7 t' is the host of the king of
9 t'...henceforth thou shalt have wars.
17: 5 T' the Lord stablished the kingdom in
18: 5 T' the king of Israel gathered
12 let thy word t', I pray thee, be like one
16 them return t' every man to his house
18 T' hear the word of the Lord;
22 Now t', behold, the Lord hath put a
31 T' they compassed about him to fight:
33 t' he said to his chariot man, Turn

2Ch 19: 2 t' is wrath come upon thee from
20: 26 t' the name of the same place
28: 11 Now hear me t', and deliver the
23 t' will I sacrifice to them, that they
30: 7 who t' gave them up to desolation, as
17 t' the Levites had the charge of the
32: 15 Now t' let not Hezekiah deceive you,
25 t' there was wrath upon him, and
34: 25 t' my wrath shall be poured out upon
35: 14 t' the Levites prepared for themselves,
24 His servants t' took him out of that
36: 17 T' he brought upon them the king of
Ezr 2: 62 t' were they, as polluted, put from the
4: 14 t' have we sent and certified
5: 17 Now t', if it seem good to the king, let
6: 6 Now t', Tatnai, governor beyond the
9: 12 t' give not your daughters unto their
10: 3 t' let us make a covenant with our God
11 Now t' make confession unto the Lord
Ne 2: 20 t' we his servants will arise and build:
4: 13 T' set I in the lower places behind the
20 In what place t' ye hear the sound of
5: 2 t' we take up corn for them, that we
6: 7 Come now t', and let us take counsel
9 Now t', O God, strengthen my hands.
13 T' was he hired, that I should be
7: 64 t' were they, as polluted, put from the
9: 27 T' thou deliveredst them into the
28 t' leftest thou them in the hand of
30 t' gavest thou them into the hand of
32 Now t', our God, the great, the mighty,
13: 8 t' I cast forth all the household stuff
28 Horonite: t' I chased him from me.
Es 1: 12 t' was the king very wroth, and his
2: 23 t' they were both hanged on a tree:
3: 8 t' it is not for the king's profit to suffer
9: 19 T' the Jews of the villages,
26 T' for all the words of this
Job 5: 17 t' despise not thou the chastening of
6: 3 t' my words are swallowed up.
28 Now t' be content, look upon me; for
7: 11 T' I will not refrain my mouth; I
9: 22 This is one thing, t' I said it,
10: 15 confusion; t' see thou mine affliction;
11: 6 Know t' that God exacteth of thee less
17: 4 t' shalt thou not exalt them.
20: 2 T' do my thoughts cause me to
21 t' shall no man look for his
21: 14 T' they say unto God, Depart from
22: 10 T' snares are round about
23: 15 T' am I troubled at his
32: 10 T' I said, Hearken to me; I also
34: 10 T' hearken unto me, ye men of
25 T' he knoweth their works, and he
33 and not I: t' speak what thou knowest.
35: 14 is before him; t' trust thou in him.
16 T' doth Job open his mouth in vain;
37: 24 Men do t' fear him: he respecteth
42: 3 t' have I uttered that I understood
8 T' take unto you now seven bullocks
Ps 1: 5 T' the ungodly shall not
2: 10 Be wise now t', O ye kings: be
7: 7 for their sakes t' return thou on high.
16: 9 T' my heart is glad, and my glory
18: 24 T' hath the Lord recompensed me
49 T' will I give thanks unto
21: 12 T' shalt thou make them turn their
25: 8 t' will he teach sinners in the
26: 1 also in the Lord; t' I shall not slide.
27: 6 t' will I offer in his tabernacle
28: 7 t' my heart greatly rejoiceth; and
31: 3 t' for thy name's sake lead me, and
36: 7 t' the children of men put their trust
40: 12 of mine head: t' my heart faileth me.
42: 6 t' will I remember thee from
45: 2 t' God hath blessed thee
7 t' God, thy God, hath anointed
17 t' shall the people praise thee
46: 2 T' will not we fear, though the
55: 19 have no changes, t' they fear not God.
59: 5 Thou t', O Lord God of hosts, the God
63: 7 t' in the shadow of thy wings will I
73: 6 T' pride compasseth them about as a
10 T' his people return hither: and
78: 21 T' the Lord heard this, and was
33 T' their days did he consume in
91: 14 his love upon me, t' will I deliver him:
106: 23 T' he said that he would destroy them,
26 T' he lifted up his hand against them,
40 T' was the wrath of the Lord kindled
107: 12 T' he brought down their heart with
110: 7 t' shall he lift up the head.
116: 2 t' will I call upon him as long as I live.
10 I believed, t' have I spoken: I was
118: 7 t' shall I see my desire upon them that
119: 104 t' I hate every false way.
119 dross: t' I love thy testimonies.
127 T' I love thy commandments
128 T' I esteem all thy precepts
129 t' doth my soul keep them.
140 is very pure: t' thy servant loveth it.
139: 19 depart from me t', ye bloody men.
143: 4 T' is my spirit overwhelmed within
Pr 1: 31 T' shall they eat of the fruit of their
4: 7 is the principal thing; t' get wisdom:
5: 7 Hear me now t', O ye children, and
6: 15 T' shall his calamity come
34 t' he will not spare in the day of
7: 15 T' came I forth to meet thee,
24 Hearken unto me now t', O ye
8: 32 Now t' hearken unto me, O ye
17: 11 t' a cruel messenger shall be sent
14 t' leave off contention, before it be
20: 4 t' shall he beg in harvest, and have
19 t' meddle not with him that flattereth
Ec 2: 1 thee with mirth, t' enjoy pleasure:

Ec 2:17 T· I hated life; because the work
20 T· I went about to cause my heart to
5: 2 earth: t· let thy words be few.
8: 6 t· the misery of man is great upon
11 t· the heart of the sons of men
11:10 T· remove sorrow from thy heart, and
Ca 1: 3 t· do the virgins love thee.
Isa 1:24 T· saith the Lord, the Lord of hosts,
2: 6 T· thou hast forsaken thy people the
9 humbleth himself: t· forgive them not.
3:17 T· the Lord will smite with a scab the
5:13 T· my people are gone into
14 T· hell hath enlarged herself, and
24 T· as the fire devoureth the stubble,
25 T· is the anger of the Lord
7:14 T· the Lord himself shall give you
8: 7 Now t·, behold, the Lord bringeth
9:11 T· the Lord shall set up the
14 T· the Lord will cut off from Israel
17 T· the Lord shall have no joy
10:16 T· shall the Lord, the Lord of hosts,
24 T· thus saith the Lord God of hosts,
12: 3 T· with joy shall ye draw water out of
13: 7 T· shall all hands be faint,
13 T· I will shake the heavens,
15: 4 t· the armed soldiers of Moab
7 T· the abundance they have
16: 7 T· shall Moab howl for Moab, every
9 T· I will bewail with the
17:10 t· shalt thou plant pleasant
21: 3 T· are my loins filled with
22: 4 T· said I, Look away fromme;
24: 6 T· hath the curse devoured the
6 t· the inhabitants of the earth
25: 3 T· shall the strong people
26:14 t· hast thou visited and destroyed
27: 9 t· shall the iniquity of Jacob be
11 t· he that made them will not
28:16 T· thus saith the Lord God, Behold,
22 Now t· be ye not mockers, lest your
29:14 T·, behold, I will proceed to do a
22 T· thus saith the Lord, who
30: 3 T· shall the strength of Pharaoh be
7 t· have I cried concerning this,
13 T· this iniquity shall be to you as a
16 upon horses; t· shall ye flee:
16 t· shall they that pursue you be
18 t· will the Lord wait, that he may
18 unto you, and t· will he be exalted,
36: 8 Now t· give pledges, I pray thee, to
37:19 stone: t· they have destroyed them.
20 Now t·, O Lord our God, save us from
27 T· their inhabitants were of small
29 t· will I put my hook in thy nose, and
33 T· thus saith the Lord concerning
38:20 t· we will sing my songs to the stringed
42:25 T· he hath poured upon him the fury
43: 4 t· will I give men for thee, and people
12 t· ye are my witnesses, saith the Lord,
28 T· I have profaned the princes of the
47: 8 T· hear now this, thou that art given
11 T· shall evil come upon thee; thou
50: 7 t· shall I not be confounded:
7 t· have I set my face like a
51:11 T· the redeemed of the Lord shall
21 T· hear now this, thou afflicted,
52: 5 Now t·, what have I here, saith the
6 T· my people shall know my
6 t· they shall know in that day that I
53:12 T· will I divide him a portion with
57:10 t· thou wast not grieved.
59: 9 T· is judgment far from us,
16 t· his arm brought salvation unto
60:11 T· thy gates shall be open continually;
61: 7 t· in their land they shall possess
63: 5 t· mine own arm brought salvation
10 t· he was turned to be their enemy,
65: 7 t· will I measure their former work
12 T· will I number you to the sword,
13 T· thus saith the Lord God,
Jer 1:17 Thou t· gird up thy loins, and arise,
2:19 know t· and see that it is an evil thing
33 t· hast thou also taught the wicked
3: 3 T· the showers have been withholden,
5: 4 T· I said, Surely these are poor; they
27 t· they are become great, and
6:11 T· I am full of the fury of the Lord: I
15 t· they shall fall among them that
18 T· hear, ye nations, and know, O
21 T· thus saith the Lord, Behold, I
7:14 T· will I do unto this house, which is
16 T· pray not thou for this people,
20 T· thus saith the Lord God;
27 T· thou shalt speak all these words
32 T·, behold, the days come, saith
8:10 T· will I give their wives unto
12 t· shall they fall among them that
9: 7, 15 T· thus saith the Lord of hosts,
10:21 t· they shall not prosper, and
11: 8 t· I will bring upon them all the words
11 T· thus saith the Lord, Behold, I
14 T· pray not thou for this people,
21 T· thus saith the Lord of the men
22 T· thus saith the Lord of hosts,
12: 8 against me: t· have I hated it.
13:12 T· thou shalt speak unto them this
24 T· will I scatter them as the stubble
26 T· will I discover thy skirts upon thy
14:10 t· the Lord doth not accept them;
15 T· thus saith the Lord concerning
17 T· thou shalt say this word unto
22 t· we will wait upon thee: for thou
15: 6 t· will I stretch out my hand against
19 T· thus saith the Lord, If thou
16:13 T· will I cast you out of this land into
14 T·, behold, the days come, saith

Jer 16:21 T·, behold, I will this once cause
18:11 Now t· go to, speak to the men of
13 T· thus saith the Lord; Ask ye
21 T· deliver up their children to the
19: 6 T·, behold, the days come, saith
20:11 t· my persecutors shall
22:18 T· thus saith the Lord concerning
23: 2 T· thus saith the Lord God of
7 T·, behold, the days come, saith
15 T· thus saith the Lord of hosts
30 T·, behold, I am against the
32 t· they shall not profit this people at
38 T· thus saith the Lord; Because
39 T·, behold, I, even I, will utterly
25: 8 T· thus saith the Lord of hosts;
27 T· thou shalt say unto them, Thus
30 T· prophesy thou against them all
26:13 T· now amend your ways and your
27: 9 T· hearken not ye to your prophet,
14 T· hearken not unto the words of the
28:16 T· thus saith the Lord; Behold, I
29:20 Hear ye t· the word of the Lord, all ye
27 Now t· why hast thou not reproved
28 t· he sent unto us in Babylon,
32 T· thus saith the Lord; Behold, I
30:10 T· fear thou not, O my servant Jacob,
16 T· all they that devour thee shall
31: 3 t· with lovingkindness have I
12 T· they shall come and sing in the
20 t· my bowels are troubled for
32:23 t· thou hast caused all this evil to
28 T· thus saith the Lord;
36 And now t· thus saith the Lord, the
34:12 T· the word of the Lord came to
17 T· thus saith the Lord; Ye have
35:17 T· thus saith the Lord God of hosts,
19 T· thus saith the Lord of hosts,
36: 6 T· go thou, and read in the roll, which
14 T· all the princes sent Jehudi the son
30 T· thus saith the Lord of
37:20 T· hear now, I pray thee, O my lord
38: 4 T· the princes said unto the king, We
40: 3 voice, t· this thing is come upon you.
42:15 now t· hear the word of the Lord,
22 t· know certainly that ye shall die
44: 7 T· now thus saith the Lord, the God
11 T· thus saith the Lord of hosts,
22 t· is your land a desolation, and an
26 T· hear ye the word of the Lord,
48:11 t· his taste remained in him,
12 T·, behold, the days come, saith
31 T· will I howl for Moab, and
36 T· mine heart shall sound for
49: 2 T·, behold, the days come, saith
20 T· hear the counsel of the Lord,
26 T· her young men shall fall in her
50:18 T· thus saith the Lord of hosts, in
30 T· shall her young men fall in the
39 T· the wild beasts of the desert
45 T· hear ye the counsel of the Lord,
51: 7 wine; t· the nations are mad.
36 T· thus saith the Lord; Behold, I
47 T·, behold, the days come, that I
La 1: 8 sinned; t· she is removed:
9 end; t· she came down wonderfully:
2: 8 t· he made the rampart and the wall
3:21 to my mind, t· have I hope.
24 my soul; t· will I hope in him.
Eze 3:17 t· hear the word at my mouth, and
4: 7 T· thou shalt set thy face toward the
5: 7, 8 T· thus saith the Lord God;
10 T· the fathers shall eat the sons in
11 t· will I also diminish thee; neither
7:20 t· have I set it far from them.
8:18 T· will I also deal in fury: mine eye
11: 4 T· prophesy against them,
7 T· thus saith the Lord God; Your
16, 17 T· say, Thus saith the Lord God;
12: 3 T·, thou son of man, prepare thee
23 Tell them t·, Thus saith the Lord
28 T· say unto them, Thus saith the
13: 8 T· thus saith the Lord God;
8 t·, behold, I am against you, saith
13 T· thus saith the Lord God; I will
23 T· ye shall see no more vanity,
14: 4 T· speak unto them, and say unto
6 T· say unto the house of Israel,
15: 6 T· thus saith the Lord God; As the
16:27 t· I have stretched out my hand
34 given unto thee, t· thou art contrary.
37 t· I will gather all thy lovers, with
43 t· I also will recompense thy way upon
50 t· I took them away as I saw good.
17:19 T· thus saith the Lord God; As I
18:30 T· I will judge you, O house of
20:27 T·, son of man, speak unto the
21: 4 t· shall my sword go forth out of his
6 Sigh t·, thou son of man, with the
12 my people: smite t· upon thy thigh.
14 Thou t·, son of man, prophesy, and
24 T· thus saith the Lord God;
22: 4 t· have I made thee a reproach
13 t· I have smitten mine hand at thy
19 T· thus saith the Lord God;
19 t· I will gather you into the midst
31 T· have I poured out mine indignation
23:22 T·, O Aholibah, thus saith the
31 t· will I give her cup into thine hand.
35 T· thus saith the Lord God;
35 t· bear thou also thy lewdness and thy
24: 9 T· thus saith the Lord God; Woe
25: 4 t· I will deliver thee to the men of
7 t· I will stretch out mine hand
9 T·, behold, I will open the side of
13, 16 T· thus saith the Lord God; I
26: 3 T· thus saith the Lord God;

Eze 28: 6 T· thus saith the Lord God;
7 t· I will bring strangers upon thee,
16 t· I will cast thee as profane out of the
18 t· will I bring forth a fire from the
29: 8 T· thus saith the Lord God;
10 t· I am against thee, and against
19 T· thus saith the Lord God;
30:22 T· thus saith the Lord God;
31: 5 T· his height was exalted above
10 T· thus saith the Lord God;
11 I have t· delivered him into the hand
32: 3 I will t· spread out my net over thee
33: 7 t· thou shalt hear the word at my
10 T·, O thou son of man, speak unto the
12 T·, thou son of man, say unto the
34: 7 T·, ye shepherds, hear the word of
9 T·, O ye shepherds, hear the word
20 T· thus saith the Lord God unto
22 T· will I save my flock, and they shall
35: 6, 11 T·, as I live, saith the Lord God,
36: 3 T· prophesy and say, Thus saith
4 T·, ye mountains of Israel, hear
5 T· thus saith the Lord God; Surely
6 Prophesy t· concerning the land of
7 T· thus saith the Lord God; I have
14 T· thou shalt devour men no more,
22 T· say unto the house of Israel,
37:12 T· prophesy and say unto them,
38:14 T·, son of man, prophesy and say
39: 1 T·, thou son of man, prophesy
23 t· hid I my face from them, and gave
25 T· thus saith the Lord God; Now
41: 7 t· the breadth of the house
42: 6 t· the building was straitened
44: 2 hath entered in by it, t· it shall be shut.
12 t· have I lifted up mine hand
Da 1: 8 t· he requested of the prince of the
19 Azariah: t· stood they before the king.
2: 6 t· shew me the dream, and the
9 t· tell me the dream, and I shall
10 t· there is no king, lord,
24 T· Daniel went in unto
3: 7 T· at that time, when all
19 t· he spake, and commanded that they
22 T· because the king's
29 T· I make a decree, That every
4: 6 T· made I a decree to bring in all the
8: 8 T· the he goat waxed very great: and
9:11 t· the curse is poured upon us, and the
14 T· hath the Lord watched upon the
17 Now t·, O our God, hear the prayer of
23 t· understand the matter, and consider
25 Know t· and understand, that from the
10: 8 T· I was left alone, and saw this great
11:30 t· he shall be grieved, and return, and
44 t· he shall go forth with great fury to
Ho 2: 2 let her t· put away her whoredoms out
6 T·, behold, I will hedge up thy
9 T· will I return, and take away my
14 T·, behold, I will allure her, and
4: 3 T· shall the land mourn, and
5 T· shalt thou fall in the day, and the
7 t· will I change their glory into shame.
13 t· your daughters...commit
14 t· the people that doth not understand
5: 5 t· shall Israel and Ephraim fall in
10 t· I will pour out my wrath upon them
12 T· will I be unto Ephraim as a moth,
6: 5 T· have I hewed them by the
8: 6 workman made it; t· it is not God:
9: 9 t· he will remember their iniquity, he
10:14 T· shall a tumult arise among thy
12: 6 T· turn thou to thy God: keep mercy
14 t· shall he leave his blood upon him,
13: 3 T· they shall be as the morning
6 t· have they forgotten me.
7 T· I will be unto them as a lion: as a
Joe 2:12 T· also now, saith the Lord, turn
Am 2:14 T· the flight shall perish from the
3: 2 t· I will punish you for all
11 T· thus saith the Lord God; An
4:12 T· thus will I do unto thee, O
5:11 Forasmuch t· as your treading is
13 T· the prudent shall keep silence
16 T· the Lord, the God of hosts, the
27 T· will I cause you to go into captivity
6: 7 T· now shall they go captive with
8 t· will I deliver up the city with all
7:16 Now t· hear thou the word of the Lord:
17 T· thus saith the Lord; Thy wife
Jon 4: 2 T· I fled...unto Tarshish:
3 T· now, O Lord, take, I beseech thee,
Mic 1: 6 T· I will make Samaria as an heap of
8 T· I will wail and howl, I will go
14 T· shalt thou give presents to
2: 3 T· thus saith the Lord; Behold,
5 T· thou shalt have none that shall
3: 6 T· night shall be unto you, that ye
12 T· shall Zion for your sake be
5: 3 T· will he give them up, until the
6:13 T· also will I make thee sick in
16 t· ye shall bear the reproach of my
7: 7 T· I will look unto the Lord; I will
Hab 1: 4 T· the law is slacked, and
4 righteous; t· wrong judgment
15 t· they rejoice and are glad.
16 T· they sacrifice unto their net,
17 Shall they t· empty their net, and
Zep 1:13 T· their goods shall become a booty,
2: 9 T· as I live, saith the Lord of
3: 8 T· wait ye upon me, saith the Lord,
Hag 1: 5 Now t· thus saith the Lord of hosts;
10 T· the heaven over you is
Zec 1: 3 T· say thou unto them, Thus saith the
16 T· thus saith the Lord; I am
7:12 t· came a great wrath from the Lord

Zec 7:13 T' it is come to pass, that as he cried,
8:19 feasts: t' love the truth and peace.
10: 2 t' they went their way as a
Mal 2: 9 T' have I also made you contemptible
15 T' take heed to your spirit, and let
16 t' take heed to your spirit, that ye deal
3: 6 t' ye sons of Jacob are not consumed.
M't 3: 8 Bring forth t' fruits meet for
10 t' every tree which bringeth not
5:19 Whosoever t' shall break one of
23 T' if thou bring thy gift to the
48 Be ye t' perfect, even as your Father
6: 2 T' when thou doest thine alms, do
8 Be not ye t' like unto them: for
9 After this manner t' pray ye: Our
22 if t' thine eye be single, thy whole
23 If t' the light that is in thee be
25 T' I say unto you, Take no
31 T' take no thought, saying, What
34 Take t' no thought for the morrow.
7:12 T' all things whatsoever ye would
24 T' whosoever heareth these sayings
9:38 Pray ye t' the Lord of the harvest,
10:16 be ye t' wise as serpents, and
26 Fear them not t': for there is
31 Fear ye not t', ye are of more value
32 Whosoever t' shall confess me before
12:27 t' they shall be your judges.
13:13 T' speak I to them in parables:
18 Hear ye t' the parable of the sower.
40 As t' the tares are gathered and
52 T' every scribe which is
14: 2 t' mighty works do shew forth
18: 4 Whosoever t' shall humble himself
23 T' is the kingdom of heaven
26 The servant t' fell down, and
19: 6 What t' God hath joined together,
27 thee; what shall we have t'?
21:40 When the lord t' of the vineyard
43 T' say I unto you, The
22: 9 Go ye t' into the highways, and as
17 Tell us t', What thinkest thou? Is it
21 Render t' unto Cæsar the things
28 T' in the resurrection whose wife
23: 3 t' whatsoever they bid you observe,
14 t' ye shall receive the greater
20 Whoso t' shall swear by the altar,
24:15 ye t' shall see the abomination
42 Watch t': for ye know not what
44 T' be ye also ready: for in
25:13 Watch t', for ye know neither the
27 Thou oughtest t' to have put my
28 Take t' the talent from him, and
27:17 T' when they were gathered
64 Command t' that the sepulchre be
28:19 Go ye t', and teach all nations,
M'r 1:38 there also: for t' came I forth.
2:28 T' the Son of man is Lord also of
6:14 t' mighty works do shew forth
19 T' Herodias had a quarrel against
8:38 Whosoever t' shall be ashamed of
10: 9 What t' God hath joined together,
11:24 T' I say unto you, What
12: 6 Having yet t' one son, his
9 What shall t' the lord of the
23 In the resurrection t', when they
24 Do ye not t' err, because ye
27 the living: ye t' do greatly err.
37 David t' himself calleth him Lord;
13:35 Watch ye t': for ye know not when
Lu 1:35 t' also that holy thing which shall
3: 8 Bring forth t' fruits worthy of
9 every tree t' which bringeth not
4: 7 If thou t' wilt worship me, all shall
43 cities also: for t' am I sent.
6:36 Be ye t' merciful, as your Father
7:42 Tell me t', which of them will love
8:18 Take heed t' how ye hear: for
10: 2 T' said he unto them, The harvest
2 pray ye t' the Lord of the harvest,
40 alone? bid her t' that she help me.
11:19 t' shall they be your judges.
34 t' when thine eye is single, thy
35 Take heed t' that the light which is
36 If thy whole body t' be full of light,
49 T' also said the wisdom of God, I
12: 3 T' whatsoever ye have spoken
7 Fear not t': ye are of more value
22 T' I say unto you, Take no
40 Be ye t' ready also: for the Son of
13:14 in them t' come and be healed, and
14:20 a wife, and t' I cannot come.
15:28 t' came his father out, and
16:11 If t' ye have not been faithful in
27 I pray thee t', father, that thou
19:12 He said t', a certain nobleman
20:15 What t' shall the lord of the
25 Render t' unto Cæsar the things
29 There were t' seven brethren: and
33 T' in the resurrection whose wife
44 David t' calleth him Lord, how is he
21: 8 near: go ye not t' after them.
14 Settle it t' in your hearts, not
36 Watch ye t', and pray always, that
23:16 I will t' chastise him, and release
20 Pilate t', willing to release Jesus,
22 I will t' chastise him, and let him
Joh 1:31 t' am I come baptizing with
2:22 When t' he was risen from the
3:29 voice: this my joy t' is fulfilled.
4: 1 When t' the Lord knew how the
6 Jesus t', being wearied with his
33 T' said the disciples one to
5:10 Jews t' said unto him that was
16 And t' did the Jews persecute
18 T' the Jews sought the more to
Joh 6:13 T' they gathered them together,
15 When Jesus t' perceived that they
24 When the people t' saw that Jesus
30 They said t' unto him, What sign
43 Jesus t' answered and said unto
45 Every man t' that hath heard, and
52 Jews t' strove among themselves,
60 Many t' of his disciples, when they
65 T' said I unto you, that no
7: 3 His brethren t' said unto him
22 Moses t' gave unto you
40 Many of the people t', when they
8:13 The Pharisees t' said unto him,
24 I said t' unto you, that ye shall die
36 If the Son t' shall make you free, ye
47 ye t' hear them not, because
9: 7 He went his way t', and washed,
8 The neighbours t', and they which
10 T' said they unto him, How were
16 T' said some of the Pharisees, This
23 T' said his parents, He is of
41 We see; t' your sin remaineth.
10:17 T' doth my Father love me,
19 was a division t' again among the
39 T' they sought again to take him:
11: 3 T' his sisters sent unto him,
6 he had heard t' that he was sick,
33 When Jesus t' saw her weeping,
38 Jesus t' again groaning in himself
54 Jesus t' walked no more openly
12: 9 the Jews t' knew that he was there:
17 people t' that was with him when
19 The Pharisees t' said among
21 The same came t' to Philip, which
29 The people t', that stood by, and
39 T' they could not believe,
50 I speak t', even as the Father,
13:11 t' said he, Ye are not all clean.
24 Simon Peter t' beckoned to him,
31 T', when he was gone out, Jesus
15:19 world, t' the world hateth you.
16:15 t' said I, that he shall take of
18 They said t', What is this that he
22 And ye now t' have sorrow: but I
18: 4 Jesus t', knowing all things that
8 if t' ye seek me, let these go their
25 They said t' unto him, Art not thou
31 The Jews t' said unto him, It is not
37 Pilate t' said unto him, Art thou a
39 will ye t' that I release unto you
19: 1 Then Pilate t' took Jesus, and
4 Pilate t' went forth again, and
6 the chief priests t' and officers saw
8 When Pilate t' heard that saying,
11 t' he that delivered me unto
13 When Pilate t' heard that saying,
16 Then delivered he him t' unto them
24 They said t' among themselves, Let
24 These things t' the soldiers did.
26 When Jesus t' saw his mother, and
30 When Jesus t' had received the
31 The Jews t', because it was the
38 He came t', and took the body of
42 There laid they Jesus t' because of
20: 3 Peter t' went forth, and that other
25 other disciples t' said unto him,
21: 6 They cast t', and now they were not
7 T' that disciple whom Jesus loved
Ac 1: 6 When they t' were come together,
2:26 T' did my heart rejoice, and
30 T' being a prophet, and knowing
33 T' being by the right hand of God
36 T' let all the house of Israel know
3:19 Repent ye t', and be converted,
8: 4 T' they that were scattered abroad
22 Repent t' of this thy wickedness,
10:20 Arise t', and get thee down, and go
29 T' came I unto you without
29 I ask t' for what intent ye have
32 Send t' to Joppa, and call hither
33 Immediately t' I sent to thee; and
33 t' are we all here present before
12: 5 Peter t' was kept in prison: but
13:38 Be it known unto you t', men and
40 Beware t', lest that come upon you,
14: 3 Long time t' abode they speaking
15: 2 When t' Paul and Barnabas had no
10 Now t' why tempt ye God, to put a
27 We have sent t' Judas and Silas,
16:11 T' loosing from Troas, we came
36 go: now t' depart, and go in peace.
17:12 T' many of them believed; also of
17 T' disputed he in the synagogue
20 know t' what these things mean.
23 Whom t' ye ignorantly worship,
19:32 Some t' cried one thing, and some
20:11 When he t' was come up again,
28 Take heed t' unto yourselves, and to
31 T' watch, and remember, that by
21:22 What is it t'? the multitude must
23 Do t' this that we say to thee: We
23:15 Now t' ye with the council signify
25: 5 Let them t', said he, which among
17 T', when they were come hither,
26:22 Having t' obtained help of God, I
28:20 For this cause t' have I called for
28 Be it known t' unto you, that the
Ro 2: 1 T' thou art inexcusable, O man,
21 Thou t' which teachest another,
26 T' if the uncircumcision keep the
3:20 T' by the deeds of the law there
28 T' we conclude that a man is
4:16 T' it is of faith, that it might
22 t' it was imputed to him for
5: 1 T' being justified by faith, we
18 T' as by the offence of one
Ro 6: 4 T' we are buried with him by
12 Let not sin t' reign in your mortal
8: 1 There is t' now no condemnation
12 T', brethren, we are debtors,
9:18 T' hath he mercy on whom he
11:22 Behold t' the goodness...of God:
12: 1 I beseech you t', brethren, by the
20 T' if thine enemy hunger, feed
13: 2 Whosoever t' resisteth the power,
7 Render t' to all their dues:
10 t' love is the fulfilling of the law.
12 us t' cast off the works of darkness,
14: 8 whether we live t', or die, we are
13 Let us not t' judge one another any
19 Let us t' follow after the things
15:17 t' whereof I may glory through
28 When t' I have performed this,
16:19 I am glad t' on your behalf: but yet
1Co 3:21 T' let no man glory in men. For
4: 5 T' judge nothing before the time,
5: 7 Purge out t' the old leaven, that
8 T' let us keep the feast, not with
13 T' put away from among yourselves
6: 7 Now t' there is utterly a fault
20 t' glorify God in your body, and in
7: 8 I say t' to the unmarried and
26 I suppose t' that this is good for
8: 4 As concerning t' the eating of those
9:26 I t' so run, not as uncertainly; so
10:31 Whether t' ye eat, or drink, or
11:20 ye come together t' into one place,
12:15, 16 is it t' not of the body?
14:11 T' if I know not the meaning of
23 If t' the whole church be come
15:11 T' whether it were I or they, so we
58 T', my beloved brethren, be ye
16:11 Let no man t' despise him: but
18 t' acknowledge ye them that are
2Co 1:17 When I t' was thus minded, did I
4: 1 T' seeing we have this
13 I believed, and t' have I spoken,
13 we also believe, and t' speak;
5: 6 T' we are always confident,
11 Knowing t' the terror of the Lord,
17 T' if any man be in Christ, he is a
7: 1 Having t' these promises, dearly
13 T' we were comforted in your
16 I rejoice t' that I have confidence in
8: 7 T', as ye abound in every thing,
11 Now t' perform the doing of it;
9: 5 T' I thought it necessary to exhort
11:15 T' it is no great thing if his
12: 9 gladly t' will I rather glory in my
10 T' I take pleasure in infirmities,
13:10 T' I write these things being
Ga 2:17 is t' Christ the minister of sin?
3: 5 He t' that ministereth to you the
7 Know ye t' that they which are of
4:16 Am I t' become your enemy,
5: 1 Stand fast t' in the liberty
6:10 As we have t' opportunity, let
Eph 2:19 Now t' ye are no more strangers
4: 1 I t', the prisoner of the Lord,
17 This I say t', and testify in the
5: 1 Be ye t' followers of God, as dear
7 Be not ye t' partakers with them.
24 T' as the church is subject unto
6:14 Stand t', having your loins girt
Ph'p 2: 1 If there be t' any consolation in
23 Him t' I hope to send presently,
28 I sent him t' the more carefully,
29 Receive him t' in the Lord with all
3:15 Let us t', as many as be perfect, be
4: 1 T', my brethren dearly beloved
Col 2: 6 As ye have t' received Christ
16 Let no man t' judge you in meat,
3: 5 Mortify t' your members which are
12 Put on t', as the elect of God, holy
1Th 3: 7 T', brethren, we were
4: 8 He t' that despiseth, despiseth not
5: 6 T' let us not sleep, as do
2Th 2:15 T', brethren, stand fast, and
1Ti 2: 1 I exhort t', that, first of all,
8 I will t' that men pray every where,
4:10 t' we both labour and suffer
5:14 t' that the younger women marry,
2Ti 1: 8 Be not thou t' ashamed of the
2: 1 Thou t', my son, be strong in the
3 Thou t' endure hardness, as a good
10 T' I endure all things for the elect's
21 If a man t' purge himself from
4: 1 I charge thee t' before God, and
Ph'm 12 thou t' receive him, that is, mine own
15 he t' departed for a season,
17 If thou count me t' a partner,
Heb 1: 9 t' God, even thy God, hath
2: 1 T' we ought to give the more
4: 1 Let us t' fear, lest, a promise
6 Seeing t' it remaineth that some
9 remaineth t' a rest unto the people
11 labour t' to enter into that rest,
16 Let us t' come boldly unto the
6: 1 T' leaving the principles of the
7:11 If t' perfection were by the
9:23 It was t' necessary that the
10:19 Having t', brethren, boldness to
35 Cast not away t' your confidence,
11:12 T' sprang there even of one, and
13:13 Let us go forth t' unto him without
15 By him t' let us offer the sacrifice
Jas 4: 4 whosoever t' will be a friend of the
7 Submit yourselves t' to God.
17 T' to him that knoweth to do good,
5: 7 Be patient t', brethren, unto the
1Pe 2: 7 Unto you t' which believe he is
4: 7 be ye t' sober, and watch unto

1Pe 5: 6 Humble yourselves t' under the
2Pe 3:17 Ye t', beloved, seeing ye know
1Jo 2:24 Let that t' abide in you, which ye
3: 1 t' the world knoweth us not,
4: 5 t' speak they of the world, and
3Jo 8 We t' ought to receive such, that
Jude 5 I will t' put you in remembrance,
Re 2: 5 Remember t' from whence thou
3: 3 Remember t' how thou hast
3 If t' thou shalt not watch, I will
19 chasten: be zealous t', and repent.
7:15 T' are they before the throne
12:12 T' rejoice, ye heavens, and ye
18: 8 T' shall her plagues come in one

therefrom
Jos 23: 6 ye turn not aside t' to the right hand
2Ki 3: 3 made Israel to sin; he departed not t'.
13: 2 made Israel to sin; he departed not t'.

therein See also THEREINTO.
Ge 9: 7 in the earth, and multiply t'.
18:24 for the fifty righteous that are t'?
23:11 and the cave that is t', I give it thee;
17 field, and the cave was t', and all the
20 And the field, and the cave that is t',
34:10 be before you; dwell and trade ye t',
10 and get you possessions t'.
21 dwell in the land, and trade t';
47:27 they had possessions t', and grew, and
49:32 of the cave that is t' was from the
Ex 2: 3 and with pitch, and put the child t';
5: 9 the men, that they may labour t';
16:24 stink, neither was there any worm t'.
33 and put an omer full of manna t',
21:33 cover it, and an ox or an ass fall t';
29:29 his sons' after him, to be anointed t'.
30:18 altar, and thou shalt put water t'.
31:14 for whosoever doeth any work t', that
35: 2 doeth work t' shall be put to death.
40: 3 put t' the ark of the testimony,
7 the altar, and shall put water t'.
9 the tabernacle, and all that is t',
Le 6: 3 these that a man doeth, sinning t':
7 that he hath done in trespassing t'.
8:10 the tabernacle and all that was t',
10: 1 them his censer, and put fire t',
13:21 and, behold, there be no white hairs t',
37 that there is black hair grown up t';
18: 4 and keep mine ordinances, to walk t':
30 and that ye defile not yourselves t':
20:22 land, whither I bring you to dwell t',
22:21 accepted; there shall be no blemish t'.
23: 3 convocation; ye shall do no work t':
7, 8 ye shall do no servile work t'.
21 you: ye shall do no servile work t':
25 Ye shall do no servile work t': but ye
35, 36 ye shall do no servile work t'.
25:19 eat your fill, and dwell t' in safety.
26:32 your enemies which dwell t' shall be
Nu 4:16 all the tabernacle, and of all that t' is,
13:18 and the people that dwelleth t',
20 fat or lean, whether there be wood t',
14:30 which I sware to make you dwell t',
16: 7 And put fire t', and put incense in
46 and put fire t' from off the altar,
28:18 shall do no manner of servile work t':
29: 7 your souls: ye shall not do any work t':
35 ye shall do no servile work t':
32:40 the son of Manasseh; and he dwelt t'.
33:53 inhabitants of the land, and dwell t':
35:33 be cleansed of the blood that is shed t',
De 2:10 The Emims dwelt t' in times past, a
20 of giants: giants dwelt t' in old time;
7:25 it unto thee, lest thou be snared t':
8:12 hast built goodly houses, and dwelt t';
10:14 God, the earth also, with all that t' is.
11:31 and ye shall possess it, and dwell t'.
13:15 destroying it utterly, and all that is t',
15:21 And if there be any blemish t', as if it
16: 8 thy God: thou shalt do no work t'.
17:14 and shalt possess it, and shalt dwell t',
19 he shall read t' all the days of his life:
20:11 the people that is found t' shall be
26: 1 and possessest it, and dwellest t';
28:30 an house, and thou shalt not dwell t':
29:23 nor beareth, nor any grass groweth t',
Jos 1: 8 thou shalt meditate t' day and night,
8 do according to all that is written t':
6:17 even it, and all that are t', to the Lord:
24 the city with fire, and all that was t':
10:28 them, and all the souls that were t';
30 sword, and all the souls that were t';
32 sword, and all the souls that were t',
35 souls that were t' he utterly destroyed
37 thereof, and all the souls that were t';
37 utterly, and all the souls that were t'.
39 destroyed all the souls that were t';
11:11 they smote all the souls that were t'
19:47 and dwelt t', and called Leshem, Dan,
50 and he built the city, and dwelt t'.
21:43 and they possessed it, and dwelt t'.
J'g 2:22 keep the way of the Lord to walk t',
8:25 did cast t' every man the earrings
9:45 and slew the people that was t', and
16:30 and upon all the people that were t'.
18: 7 and saw the people that were t',
28 And they built a city, and dwelt t'.
1Sa 30: 2 the women captives, that were t':
2Sa 12:31 brought forth the people that were t',
1Ki 8:16 house, that my name might be t';
11:24 they went to Damascus, and dwelt t',
12:25 in mount Ephraim, and dwelt t';
2Ki 2:20 me a new cruse, and put salt t'.
12: 9 put t' all the money that was brought
13: 6 who made Israel sin, but walked t':
11 who made Israel sin: but he walked t'.

2Ki 15:16 smote Tiphsah, and all that were t',
16 the women t' that were with child he
1Ch 16:32 let the fields rejoice, and all that is t'.
21:22 I may build an altar t' unto the Lord:
2Ch 2: 3 cedars to build him an house to dwell t',
5:10 the two tables which Moses put t' at
20: 8 And they dwelt t', and have built thee
8 built thee a sanctuary t' for thy name,
Ezr 4:19 and sedition have been made t'.
6: 2 and t' was a record thus written:
Ne 6: 1 and that there was no breach left t';
7: 4 but the people were few t', and the
5 up at the first, and found written t',
8: 3 And he read t' before the street that
9: 6 earth, and all things that are t',
6 the seas, and all that is t', and thou
13: 1 and t' was found written, that the
16 There dwelt men of Tyre also t', which
Job 3: 7 be solitary, let no joyful voice come t'.
20:18 be, and he shall not rejoice t'.
Ps 24: 1 the world, and they that dwell t'.
37:29 the land, and dwell t' for ever.
68:10 Thy congregation hath dwelt t': thou,
69:34 seas, and every thing that moveth t'.
36 they that love his name shall dwell t'.
96:12 Let the field be joyful, and all that is t':
98: 7 the world, and they that dwell t'.
104:26 whom thou hast made to play t'.
107:34 the wickedness of them that dwell t'.
111: 2 out of all them that have pleasure t'.
119:35 thy commandments; for t' do I delight.
146: 6 and earth, the sea, and all that t' is:
Pr 15: 4 but perverseness t' is a breach in the
22:14 abhorred of the Lord shall fall t'.
26:27 Whoso diggeth a pit shall fall t': and
Ec 2:21 yet to a man that hath not laboured t'
Isa 5: 2 of it, and also made a winepress t':
7: 6 it, and let us make a breach t' for us,
24: 6 and they that dwell t' are desolate:
33:24 the people that dwell t' shall be
34: 1 the earth hear, and all that is t';
17 to generation shall they dwell t'.
35: 8 men, though fools, shall not err t'.
42: 5 upon it, and spirit to them that walk t':
10 down to the sea, and all that is t';
44:23 mountains, O forest, and every tree t':
51: 3 joy and gladness shall be found t',
6 and they that dwell t' shall die in like
59: 8 whosoever goeth t' shall not know
Jer 4:29 forsaken, and not a man dwell t'.
6:16 where is the good way, and walk t',
16 But they said, We will not walk t'.
8:16 in it; the city, and those that dwell t'.
9:13 obeyed my voice, neither walked t';
12: 4 the wickedness of them that dwell t'?
17:24 the sabbath day, to do no work t';
23:12 they shall be driven on, and fall t':
27:11 Lord; and they shall till it, and dwell t'.
36: 2 write t' all the words that I have
29 Why hast thou written t', saying,
32 who wrote t' from the mouth of
44: 2 a desolation, and no man dwelleth t',
47: 2 overflow the land, and all that is t';
2 the city, and them that dwell t':
48: 9 desolate, without any to dwell t'.
50: 3 land desolate, and none shall dwell t':
39 dwell there, and the owls shall dwell t':
40 neither shall any son of man dwell t'.
51:48 all that is t', shall sing for Babylon:
Eze 2: 9 me; and, lo, a roll of a book was t';
10 there was written t' lamentations,
7:20 and of their detestable things t':
12:19 may be desolate from all that is t',
19 the violence of all them that dwell t'.
14:22 t' shall be left a remnant that shall be
20:47 south to the north shall be burned t'.
24: 5 let them seethe the bones of it t'.
6 to the pot whose scum is t', and whose
28:26 And they shall dwell safely t', and
30:12 the land waste, and all that is t',
32:15 I shall smite all them that dwell t',
37:25 and they shall dwell t', even they,
40:33 and there were windows t' and in the
42:14 When the priests enter t', then shall
44:14 and for all that shall be done t'.
Da 5: 2 and his concubines, might drink t'.
Ho 4: 3 one that dwelleth t' shall languish,
14: 9 but the transgressors shall fall t'.
Am 6: 8 up the city with all that is t'.
8: 8 and every one mourn that dwelleth t'?
9: 5 melt, and all that dwell t' shall mourn:
Mic 1: 2 hearken, O earth, and all that t' is:
7:13 desolate because of them that dwell t',
Na 1: 5 yea, the world, and all that dwell t'.
Hab 2: 8, 17 of the city, and of all that dwell t'.
18 the maker of his work trusteth t',
Zec 2: 4 the multitude of men and cattle t':
6: 6 black horses which are t' go forth into
13: 8 two parts t' shall be cut off and die;
8 and die; but the third shall be left t'.
14:21 come and take of them, and seethe t':
M't 23:21 by it, and by him that dwelleth t'.
M'r 10:15 child, he shall not enter t'.
13:15 down into the house, neither enter t',
Lu 10: 9 And heal the sick that are t',
18:17 child shall in no wise enter t'.
19:45 to cast out them that sold t',
Joh 12: 6 the bag, and bare what was put t'.
Ac 1:20 and let no man dwell t':
14:15 sea, and all things that are t':
17:24 made the world and all things t',
27: 6 sailing into Italy; and he put us t'.
Ro 1:17 t' is the righteousness of God
6: 2 dead to sin, live any longer t'?
1Co 7:24 he is called, t' abide with God.
Eph 6:20 that t' I may speak boldly, as I

Ph'p 1:18 and I t' do rejoice, yea, and will
Col 2: 7 abounding t'...thanksgiving.
Heb 4: 6 that some must enter t',
10: 8 not, neither hadst pleasure t':
13: 9 that have been occupied t'.
Jas 1:25 law of liberty, and continueth t',
2Pe 2:20 they are again entangled t', and
3:10 the works that are t' shall be
Re 1: 3 things which are written t':
10: 6, 6 and the things that t' are,
6 and the things which are t',
11: 1 altar, and them that worship t'.
13:12 earth and them which dwell t'
21:22 And I saw no temple t': for the

thereinto
Lu 21:21 are in the countries enter t'.

thereof^
Ge 2:19 living creature, that was the name t'.
21 ribs, and closed up the flesh instead t.;
3: 5 doth know that in the day ye eat t',
6 she took of the fruit t', and did eat,
4: 4 firstlings of his flock and of the fat t'.
6:16 of the ark shalt thou set in the side t';
9: 4 with the life t', which is the blood t',
40:10 the clusters t' brought forth ripe
18 and said, This is the interpretation t':
41: 8 of Egypt, and all the wise men t':
47:21 of Egypt even to the other end t'.
Ex 3:20 which I will do in the midst t':
5: 8 ye shall not diminish ought t':
9:18 been in Egypt since the foundation t'
10:26 t' must we take to serve the Lord our
12: 9 his legs, and with the purtenance t'.
43 there shall no stranger eat t':
44 circumcised him, then shall he eat t'.
45 and an hired servant shall not eat t'.
46 neither shall ye break a bone t'.
48 no uncircumcised person shall eat t'.
16:31 of Israel called the name t' Manna:
19:18 the smoke t' ascended as the smoke of
22:11 and the owner of it shall accept t', and
12 make restitution unto the owner t'.
14 or die, the owner t' being not with it,
15 if the owner t' be with it, he shall not
23:10 land, and shalt gather in the fruits t':
25: 9 the pattern of all the instruments t',
10 and a half shall be the length t',
10 and a cubit and a half the breadth t',
10 and a cubit and a half the height t'.
12 it, and put them in the four corners t';
17 and a half shall be the length t',
17 and a cubit and a half the breadth t'.
19 the cherubims on the two ends t'.
23 two cubits shall be the length t',
23 and a cubit the breadth t',
23 and a cubit and a half the height t'.
25 make a golden crown to the border t'
26 corners that are on the four feet t'.
29 shalt make the dishes t', and spoons t',
29 and covers t', and bowls t', to cover
37 thou shalt make the seven lamps t':
37 and they shall light the lamps t', that
38 the tongs t', and the snuffdishes t',
26:30 to the fashion t' which was shewed
27: 1 and the height t' shall be three cubits.
2 horns of it upon the four corners t':
3 vessels t' thou shalt make of brass.
4 four brasen rings in...four corners t'.
10 the twenty pillars t' and their twenty
19 of the tabernacle in all the service t',
19 and all the pins t', and all the pins of
28: 7 It shall have the two shoulderpieces t'
7 joined at the two edges t'; and so it
8 of the same, according to the work t';
16 doubled; a span shall be the length t',
16 and a span shall be the breadth t'.
26 of the breastplate in the border t',
27 underneath, toward the forepart t',
27 over against the other coupling t',
28 bind the breastplate by the rings t'
32 hole in the top of it, in the midst t':
33 of scarlet, round about the hem t';
29:33 but a stranger shall not eat t', because
41 according to the drink offering t', for a
30: 2 A cubit shall be the length t',
2 a cubit the breadth t'; foursquare
2 and two cubits shall be the height t':
2 the horns t' shall be of the same.
3 overlay it with pure gold, the top t',
3 and the sides t' round about, and the
3 and the horns t'; and thou shalt make
4 the crown of it, by the two corners t',
37 according to the composition t':
35:12 The ark, and the staves t', with the
36:29 coupled together at the head t', to one
37: 6 two cubits and a half was the length t',
6 one cubit and a half the breadth t'.
8 he the cherubims on the two ends t'.
10 wood: two cubits was the length t',
10 and a cubit the breadth t', and a cubit
10 and a cubit and a half the height t':
12 made a crown of gold for the border t'
13 four corners that were in...four feet t'.
18 six branches going out of the sides t';
18 the candlestick out of the one side t',
18 candlestick out of the other side t':
24 gold made he it, and all the vessels t'.
25 height of it; horns t' were of the same
26 top of it, and the sides t' round about,
27 rings of gold for it under the crown t'
27 corners of it, upon the two sides t',
38: 1 wood: five cubits was the length t',
1 and five cubits the breadth t', it was
1 and three cubits the height t':
2 he made the horns t' on the four

Ex 38: 2 the horns t' were of the same: and he
3 all the vessels t' made he of brass.
4 of network under the compass t'
39: 5 of the same, according to the work t';
9 double: a span was the length t',
9 a span the breadth t', being doubled.
20 it, over against the other coupling t',
35 ark of the testimony, and the staves t',
36 The table, and all the vessels t', and
37 pure candlestick, with the lamps t',
37 be set in order, and all the vessels t',
40: 4 the candlestick, and light the lamps t'.
9 shalt hallow it, and all the vessels t':
18 his sockets, and set up the boards t',
18 and put in the bars t', and reared up
Le 1: 15 the blood t' shall be wrung out at the
17 he shall cleave it with the wings t',
2: 2 of the flour t', and of the oil t',
2 with all the frankincense t'; and the
9 from the meat offering a memorial t',
16 beaten corn t', and part of the oil t',
16 with all the frankincense t': it is an
3: 8 Aaron's sons shall sprinkle the blood t'
9 the fat t', and the whole rump, it shall
13 Aaron shall sprinkle the blood t' upon
14 And he shall offer t' his offering, even
4: 30 the priest shall take of the blood t'
30 and shall pour out all the blood t' at
31 he shall take away all the fat t', as the
34 and shall pour out all the blood t' at
35 he shall take away all the fat t', as the
5: 12 his handful of it, even a memorial t',
6: 15 of the meat offering, and of the oil t',
16 remainder t' shall Aaron and his sons
20 it in the morning, and half t' at night.
27 shall touch the flesh t' shall be holy:
27 when there is sprinkled of the blood t'
29 males among the priests shall eat t':
7: 2 the blood t' shall he sprinkle round
3 And he shall offer of it all the fat t';
6 male among the priests shall eat t':
19 the flesh, all that be clean shall eat t'.
8: 11 he sprinkled t' upon the altar seven
9: 13 him, with the pieces t', and the head:
17 took a handful t', and burnt it upon
11: 39 he that toucheth the carcase t' shall
13: 4 and the hair t' be not turned white;
18 which, even in the skin t', was a boil,
14: 45 and the timber t', and all the morter
17: 13 he shall even pour out the blood t',
14 the blood of it is for the life t':
14 for the life of all flesh is the blood t':
18: 25 I do visit the iniquity t' upon it,
19: 23 count the fruit t' as uncircumcised:
24 all the fruit t' shall be holy to praise
25 fifth year shall ye eat of the fruit t',
25 it may yield unto you the increase t':
22: 13 but there shall no stranger eat t'.
14 he shall put the fifth part t' unto it,
24 neither shall ye make any offering t'
23: 10 and shall reap the harvest t', then ye
13 And the meat offering t' shall be two
13 drink offering t' shall be of wine,
24: 5 fine flour, and bake twelve cakes t':
25: 3 vineyard, and gather in the fruit t';
7 land, shall all the increase t' be meat.
10 all the land unto all the inhabitants t':
12 eat the increase t' out of the field.
16 years thou shalt increase the price t',
27 let him count the years of the sale t',
27: 10 it and the exchange t' shall be holy.
13 add a fifth part t' unto thy estimation.
16 shall be according to the seed t':
21 the possession t' shall be the priest's.
31 he shall add thereto the fifth part t'.
33 it and the change t' shall be holy;
Nu 1: 50 testimony, and over all the vessels t',
50 the tabernacle, and all the vessels t';
2: 6, 8, 11 and those that were numbered t',
3: 25 the covering t', and the hanging for
26 the cords of it for all the service t'.
31 the hanging, and all the service t'.
36 and the bars t', and the pillars t',
36 the sockets t', and all the vessels t',
4: 6 of blue, and shall put in the staves t'.
9 snuffdishes, and all the oil vessels t',
10 they shall put it and all the vessels t'
11 skins, and shall put to the staves t':
14 shall put upon it all the vessels t',
16 in the sanctuary, and in the vessels t'.
31 of the tabernacle, and the bars t',
31 and the pillars t', and sockets t',
5: 7 his trespass with the principal t',
7 add unto it the fifth part t', and give
26 of the offering, even the memorial t',
7: 1 sanctified it, and all...instruments t',
1 both the altar and all the vessels t',
8: 3 he lighted the lamps t' over against
4 unto the shaft t', unto the flowers t',
25 shall cease waiting upon the service t',
9: 3 and according to all the ceremonies t',
14 and according to the manner t', so
11: 7 the colour t' as the colour of bdellium.
13: 32 land that eateth up the inhabitants t';
18: 28 shall give t' the Lord's heave offering
29 offering of the Lord, of all the best t',
29 even the hallowed part t' out of it.
30 ye have heaved the best t' from it,
21: 25 in Heshbon, and in all the villages t'.
32 Jaazer, and they took the villages t',
26: 56 shall the possession t' be divided
28: 7 drink offering t' shall be the fourth
8 and as the drink offering t', thou shalt
9 with oil, and the drink offering t':
29: 19 and the meat offering t', and their
32: 33 with the cities t' in the coasts, even

Nu 32: 41 went and took the small towns t',
42 and took Kenath, and the villages t',
34: 2 the land of Canaan with the coasts t':)
4 and the going forth t' shall be from
12 shall be your land with the coasts t'
De 3: 11 nine cubits was the length t', and
12 half mount Gilead, and the cities t',
17 plain also, and Jordan, and the coast t',
9: 21 and I cast the dust t' into the brook
12: 15 the unclean and the clean may eat t',
13: 15 all that is therein, and the cattle t',
16 of it into the midst of the street t',
16 city, and all the spoil t' every whit,
15: 23 Only thou shalt not eat the blood t';
20: 13 smite every male t' with the edge of
14 is in the city, even all the spoil t',
19 thou shalt not destroy the trees t' by
26: 14 I have not eaten t' in my mourning,
14 neither have I taken away ought t' for
14 use, nor given ought t' for the dead:
28: 30 and shalt not gather the grapes t'.
31 thine eyes, and thou shalt not eat t':
29: 23 that the whole land t' is brimstone,
33: 16 things of the earth and fulness t',
Jos 6: 2 thine hand Jericho, and the king t',
26 he shall lay the foundation t' in his
7: 14 come according to the families t';
8: 2 only the spoil t', and the cattle t',
9: 1 and Hivite, and the Jebusite, heard t';
10: 2 Ai, and all the men t' were mighty.
28 and the king t' he utterly destroyed,
30 the king t', into the hand of Israel;
30 but did unto the king t' as he did unto
37 and the king t', and all the cities t',
39 and the king t', and all the cities t';
39 so he did to Debir, and to the king t';
11: 10 and smote the king t' with the sword:
13: 23 Reuben was Jordan, and the border t'.
23 families, the cities and the villages t'.
15: 7 and the goings out t' were at En-rogel:
12 was to the great sea, and the coast t'.
47 and the great sea, and the border t'.
16: 3 and the goings out t' are at the sea.
8 and the goings out t' were at the sea.
18: 12, 14 and the goings out t' were at
20 by the coasts t' round about,
19: 14 outgoings t' are in the valley of
29 the outgoings t' are at the sea from
33 and the outgoings t' were at Jordan:
21: 2 in, with the suburbs t' for our cattle.
11 with the suburbs t' round about it.
12 fields of the city, and the villages t',
22: 7 unto the other half t' gave Joshua
23: 14 you, and not one thing hath failed t'.
J'g 1: 18 Judah took Gaza with the coast t',
18 and Askelon with the coast t',
18 and Ekron with the coast t'.
26 a city, and called the name t' Luz:
26 which is the name t' unto this day.
3: 2 least such as before knew nothing t';
5: 23 curse ye bitterly the inhabitants t';
7: 15 the dream, and the interpretation t',
8: 14 princes of Succoth, and the elders t',
27 And Gideon made an ephod t', and
14: 9 he took t' in his hands, and went on
15: 19 he called the name t' En-hakkore,
17: 4 who made t' a graven image and a
1Sa 5: 6 even Ashdod and the coasts t'.
6: 8 offering, in a coffer by the side t';
7: 14 the coasts t' did Israel deliver out of
17: 51 sword, and drew it out of the sheath t',
20: 20 I will shoot three arrows on the side t',
28: 24 it, and did bake unleavened bread t':
2Sa 20: 8 upon his loins in the sheath t';
1Ki 2: 32 my father David not knowing t', to
3: 27 in no wise slay it: she is the mother t'.
6: 2 the length t' was threescore cubits,
2 and the breadth t' twenty cubits,
2 and the height t' thirty cubits.
3 twenty cubits was the length t',
3 and ten cubits was the breadth t'
20 and twenty cubits in the height t': and
38 finished throughout all the parts t',
7: 2 the length t' was an hundred cubits,
2 and the breadth t' fifty cubits,
2 and the height t' thirty cubits,
6 pillars; the length t' was fifty cubits,
6 and the breadth t' thirty cubits: and
21 pillar, and called the name t' Jachin:
21 pillar, and called the name t' Boaz.
26 brim t' was wrought like the brim of a
27 base, and four cubits the breadth t',
30 the four corners t' had undersetters:
31 the mouth t' was round after the work
35 on the top of the base the ledges t'
35 and the borders t' were of the same.
36 For on the plates of the ledges t', and
36 and on the borders t', he graved
8: 7 covered the ark and the staves t'
13: 26 him back from the way heard t',
15: 21 when Baasha heard t', that he left off
22 stones of Ramah, and the timber t',
16: 34 he laid the foundation t' in Abiram his
34 and set up the gates t' in his youngest
17: 13 but make me t' a little cake first,
2Ki 2: 12 chariot of Israel, and the horsemen t'.
3: 25 in Kir-haraseth left they the stones t';
4: 39 gathered t' wild gourds his lap full,
40 in the pot. And they could not eat t'.
42 and full ears of corn in the husk t'.
43 They shall eat, and shall leave t'.
44 them, and they did eat, and left t',
7: 2, 19 thine eyes, but shalt not eat t'.
13: 14 chariot of Israel, and the horsemen t'.
15: 16 therein, and the coasts t' from Tirzah:
16: 10 according to all the workmanship t'.

2Ki 17: 24 Samaria, and dwelt in the cities t'.
18: 8 unto Gaza, and the borders t', from
19: 23 will cut down the tall cedar trees t',
23 and the choice fir trees t': and I will
29 plant vineyards, and eat the fruits t'.
22: 16 place, and upon the inhabitants t',
19 place, and against the inhabitants t',
23: 6 and cast the powder t' upon the graves
1Ch 2: 23 the towns t', even threescore cities.
6: 55 and the suburbs t' round about it.
56 and the villages t', they gave to Caleb
7: 28 Beth-el and the towns t', and eastward
28 westward Gezer, with the towns t';
28 Shechem also and the towns t',
28 unto Gaza and the towns t':
8: 12 built Ono, and Lod, with the towns t':
9: 27 opening t' every morning pertained to
16: 32 Let the sea roar, and the fulness t':
21: 27 up his sword again into the sheath t'.
23: 26 nor any vessels of it for the service t'.
28: 11 the houses t', and of the treasuries t',
11 and of the upper chambers t',
11 and of the inner parlours t', and of the
15 candlestick, and for the lamps t':
15 candlestick, and also for the lamps t',
2Ch 3: 7 the beams, the posts, and the walls t',
7 and the doors t', with gold:
8 and the breadth t' twenty cubits:
4: 1 of brass, twenty cubits the length t',
1 and twenty cubits the breadth t',
1 and ten cubits the height t'.
2 compass, and five cubits the height t':
22 inner doors t' for the most holy place,
5: 8 covered the ark and the staves t'
13: 11 candlestick of gold with the lamps t',
19 from him, Beth-el with the towns t',
19 and Jeshanah with the towns t',
19 and Ephrain with the towns t'.
16: 6 stones of Ramah, and the timber t',
28: 18 and Shocho with the villages t',
18 and Timnah with the villages t',
18 Gimzo also and the villages t': they
29: 18 burnt offering, with all the vessels t',
18 table, with all the vessels t'.
32: 1 things, and the establishment t',
34: 24 place, and upon the inhabitants t',
27 place, and against the inhabitants t',
36: 19 and burnt all the palaces t' with fire,
19 and destroyed all the goodly vessels t'.
Ezr 4: 12 and have set up the walls t', and
16 builded again, and the walls t' set up,
6: 3 let the foundations t' be strongly laid;
3 the height t' threescore cubits,
3 and the breadth t' threescore cubits;
9: 9 to repair the desolations t', and to
10: 14 elders of every city, and the judges t',
Ne 1: 3 and the gates t' are burned with fire.
2: 3 the gates t' are consumed with fire?
13 the gates t' were consumed with fire.
17 and the gates t' are burned with fire:
3: 3 the beams t', and set up the doors t',
3 the locks t', and the bars t'.
6 the beams t', and set up the doors t',
6 and the locks t', and the bars t'.
13 they built it, and set up the doors t',
13 the locks t', and the bars t', and a
14 he built it, and set up the doors t',
14 the locks t', and the bars t'.
15 and covered it, and set up the doors t',
15 the locks t', and the bars t', and the
4: 6 was joined together unto the half t':
6: 16 that when all our enemies heard t',
9: 36 to eat the fruit t' and the good t',
11: 25 at Kirjath-arba, and in the villages t',
25 and at Dibon, and in the villages t',
25 at Jekabzeel, and in the villages t',
27 at Beer-sheba, and in the villages t',
28 and at Mekonah, and in the villages t',
30 at Lachish, and the fields t',
30 at Azekah, and in the villages t'.
13: 14 house of my God, and for the offices t'.
Es 1: 22 province according to the writing t',
2: 22 Esther certified the king t' in
3: 12 province according to the writing t',
8: 9 on the three and twentieth day t';
9 province according to the writing t',
9: 18 together on the thirteenth day t',
18 and on the fourteenth t'; and on
Job 3: 9 the stars of the twilight t' be dark;
4: 12 to me, and mine ear received a little t'.
16 but I could not discern the form t':
9: 6 her place, and the pillars t' trembled.
24 he covereth the faces of the judges t';
11: 9 The measure t' is longer than the
14: 7 the tender branch t' will not cease.
8 the root t' wax old in the earth,
8 and the stock t' die in the ground;
15: 29 he prolong the perfection t' upon the
24: 2 take away the flocks, and feed t'.
13 the light; they know not the ways t',
13 nor abide in the paths t'.
26: 5 the waters, and the inhabitants t'.
28: 13 Man knoweth not the price t'; neither
15 shall silver be weighed for the price t'.
22 heard the fame t' with our ears.
23 God understandeth the way t',
23 and he knoweth the place t'.
31: 17 and the fatherless hath not eaten t';
38 that the furrows likewise t' complain;
39 If I have eaten the fruits t' without
39 the owners t' to lose their life:
36: 27 down rain according to the vapour t':
33 The noise t' sheweth concerning it,
38: 5 Who hath laid the measures t', if
6 are the foundations t' fastened?
6 or who laid the corner stone t';

Job 38: 9 I made the cloud the garment t'.
19 as for darkness, where is the place t'.
20 thou shouldest take it to the bound t'.
20 know the paths to the house t'?
33 thou set the dominion t' in the earth?
Ps 19: 6 there is nothing hid from the heat t'.
24: 1 earth is the Lord's, and the fulness t';
34: 2 the humble shall hear t', and be glad.
46: 3 Though the waters t' roar and be
3 mountains shake with the swelling t'.
48: 12 go round about her: tell the towers t'.
50: 1 of the sun unto the going down t'.
12 the world is mine, and the fulness t'.
55: 10 they go about it upon the walls t':
11 Wickedness is in the midst t': deceit
60: 2 heal the breaches t'; for it shaketh.
65: 10 waterest the ridges t' abundantly:
10 thou settlest the furrows t': thou
10 thou blessest the springing t'.
71: 15 days; for I know not the numbers t'.
72: 16 the fruit t' shall shake like Lebanon:
74: 6 they break down the carved work t' at
75: 3 all the inhabitants t' are dissolved:
8 but the dregs t', all the wicked of the
80: 10 the boughs t' were like the goodly
89: 9 when the waves t' arise, thou stillest
11 for the world and the fulness t', thou
96: 11 let the sea roar, and the fulness t'.
97: 1 let the multitude of isles be glad t'.
98: 7 Let the sea roar, and the fulness t';
102: 14 in her stones, and favour the dust t'.
103: 16 and the place t' shall know it no more.
107: 25 wind, which lifteth up the waves t'.
29 a calm, so that the waves t' are still.
137: 2 harps upon the willows in the midst t'.
7 it, rase it, even to the foundation t'.
Pr 1: 19 taketh away the life of the owners t'.
3: 14 silver, and the gain t' than fine gold.
12: 28 in the pathway t' there is no death.
14: 12 but the end t' are the ways of death.
16: 25 but the end t' are the ways of death.
33 the whole disposing t' is of the Lord.
18: 21 they that love it shall eat the fruit t'.
20: 21 but the end t' shall not be blessed.
21: 22 down the strength of the confidence t'.
24: 31 and nettles had covered the face t',
31 the stone wall t' was broken down.
25: 8 know not what to do in the end t',
27: 18 the fig tree shall eat the fruit t':
28: 2 of a land many are the princes t':
2 knowledge the state t' shall be
Ec 5: 11 what good is there to the owners t',
13 riches kept for the owners t' to their
19 and hath given him power to eat t',
6: 2 God giveth him not power to eat t',
7: 8 end of a thing than the beginning t':
Ca 1: 12 spikenard sendeth forth the smell t'.
3: 10 He made the pillars t' of silver,
10 the bottom t' of gold, the covering of
10 midst t' being paved with love, for the
4: 16 that the spices t' may flow out.
7: 8 tree, I will take hold of the boughs t':
8: 6 the coals t' are coals of fire, which
11 every one for the fruit t' was to bring
12 and those that keep the fruit t' two
Isa 3: 14 of his people, and the princes t':
4: 4 blood of Jerusalem from the midst t'
5: 2 it, and gathered out the stones t',
5 I will take away the hedge t', and
5 and break down the wall t', and it
30 light is darkened in the heavens t'.
6: 13 holy seed shall be the substance t'.
13: 9 shall destroy the sinners t' out of it.
10 of heaven and the constellations t'
14: 17 wilderness, and destroyed the cities t';
15: 8 of Moab; the howling t' unto Eglaim,
8 and the howling t' unto Beer-elim.
16: 8 broken down the principal plants t',
17: 6 in the outmost fruitful branches t',
19: 3 of Egypt shall fail in the midst t';
3 and I will destroy the counsel t': and
10 shall be broken in the purposes t',
13 they that are the stay of the tribes t'.
14 a perverse spirit in the midst t':
14 caused Egypt to err in every work t',
17 one that maketh mention t' shall
19 a pillar at the border t' to the Lord.
21: 2 all the sighing t' have I made to cease.
22: 11 have not looked unto the maker t',
23: 11 city to destroy the strong holds t'.
13 wilderness: they set up the towers t',
13 they raised up the palaces t'; and he
24: 1 scattereth abroad the inhabitants t'.
5 is defiled under the inhabitants t';
20 transgression t' shall be heavy upon
27: 10 down, and consume the branches t'.
11 When the boughs t' are withered,
28: 25 When he hath made plain the face t',
30: 27 his anger, and the burden t' is heavy:
33 the pile t' is fire and much wood;
31: 4 for mount Zion, and for the hill t'.
33: 20 not one of the stakes t' shall ever be
20 shall any of the cords t' be broken.
34: 9 streams t' shall be turned into pitch,
9 and the dust t' into brimstone, and
9 land t' shall become burning pitch.
10 the smoke t' shall go up for ever:
12 call the nobles t' to the kingdom,
13 and brambles in the fortresses t':
37: 24 and I will cut down the tall cedars t',
24 and the choice fir trees t': and I will
30 plant vineyards, and eat the fruit t'.
40: 6 and all the godliness t' is as the flower
16 beasts t' sufficient for a burnt offering.
22 inhabitants t' are as grasshoppers;
41: 9 called thee from the chief men t', and
Isa 42: 10 the isles, and the inhabitants t'.
11 wilderness and the cities t' lift up
44: 15 for he will take t', and warm himself;
16 He burneth part t' in the fire; with
16 with part t' he eateth flesh; he
17 And the residue t' he maketh a god,
19 I have baked bread upon the coals t';
19 I make the residue t' an abomination?
26 I will raise up the decayed places t':
48: 19 of thy bowels like the gravel t';
62: 1 the righteousness t' go forth as
1 and the salvation t' as a lamp that
Jer 1: 13 and the face t' is toward the north.
15 against all the walls t' round about,
18 the princes t', against the priests t',
2: 7 to eat the fruit t' and the goodness t';
4: 26 and all the cities t' were broken down
5: 1 know, and seek in the broad places t'.
22 though the waves t' toss themselves,
31 and what will ye do in the end t'?
6: 24 We have heard the fame t': our hands
11: 19 us destroy the tree with the fruit t',
14: 2 mourneth, and the gates t' languish;
8 the saviour t' in time of trouble, why
17: 27 then will I kindle a fire in the gates t',
19: 8 and hiss because of all the plagues t'.
12 the Lord, and to the inhabitants t',
20: 5 of this city, and all the labours t',
5 and all the precious things t', and all
21: 14 I will kindle a fire in the forest t', and
23: 14 and the inhabitants t' as Gomorrah.
25: 9 and against the inhabitants t', and
18 and the kings t', and the princes t', to
26: 15 this city, and upon the inhabitants t':
29: 7 in the peace t' shall ye have peace.
30: 18 shall remain after the manner t'.
31: 23 the land of Judah and in the cities t'.
24 itself, and in all the cities t' together,
35 the sea when the waves t' roar;
33: 2 Thus saith the Lord the maker t',
12 and in all the cities t', shall be a
34: 1 Jerusalem, against all the cities t',
18 twain, and passed between the parts t',
46: 8 destroy the city and the inhabitants t'.
22 voice t' shall go like a serpent; for
48: 9 the cities t' shall be desolate, without
38 of Moab, and in the streets t':
49: 13 the cities t' shall be perpetual wastes.
17 and shall hiss at all the plagues t'.
18 Gomorrah and the neighbour cities t',
21 the noise t' was heard in the Red sea.
32 bring their calamity from all sides t',
50: 29 it round about; let none t' escape:
40 Gomorrah and the neighbour cities t',
51: 28 the captains t', and all the rulers t',
42 with the multitude of the waves t'.
52: 21 and the thickness t' was four fingers:
La 2: 2 polluted the kingdom and the princes t'.
4: 11 it hath devoured the foundations t'.
Eze 1: 4 and out of the midst t' as the colour of
5 out of the midst t' came the likeness
4: 9 in one vessel, and make thee bread t',
9 and ninety days shalt thou eat t'.
5: 3 shalt also take t' a few in number,
4 for t' shall a fire come forth into all the
7: 12 for wrath is upon all the multitude t'.
13 is touching the whole multitude t',
14 my wrath is upon all the multitude t'.
9: 4 that be done in the midst t'.
10: 7 and took t', and put it into the hands
11: 6 have filled the streets t' with the slain.
9 I will bring you out of the midst t', and
11 shall ye be the flesh in the midst t';
18 take away all the detestable things t'
18 all the abominations t' from thence.
13: 14 the foundation t' shall be discovered,
14 ye shall be consumed in the midst t':
14: 13 and will break the staff of the bread t',
15: 3 Shall wood be taken t' to do any work?
17: 6 him, and the roots t' were under him:
9 shall he not pull up the roots t',
9 and cut off the fruit t', that it wither?
9 people to pluck it up by the roots t'.
12 taken the king t', and the princes t',
23 in the shadow of the branches t' shall
19: 7 land was desolate, and the fulness t',
20: 29 the name t' is called Bamah unto this
22: 21 and ye shall be melted in the midst t'.
22 so shall ye be melted in the midst t';
25 of her prophets in the midst t',
25 made her many widows in the midst t'.
27 Her princes in the midst t' are like
23: 34 and thou shalt break the sherds t', and
24: 4 Gather the pieces t' into it, even every
11 Then set it empty upon the coals t',
27: 9 wise men t' were in thee thy calkers:
31: 15 and I restrained the floods t', and the
32: 7 heaven, and make the stars t' dark;
12 all the multitude t' shall be destroyed.
13 I will destroy also all the beasts t'
38: 13 Tarshish, with all the young lions t',
40: 6 the east, and went up the stairs t',
9 and the posts t', two cubits; and the
20 the length t', and the breadth t'.
21 little chambers t' were three on this
21 the posts t' and the arches t' were after
21 the length t' was fifty cubits, and the
22 and the arches t' were before them.
24 measured the posts t' and the arches t'
25 in it and in the arches t' round about,
26 it, and the arches t' were before them:
26 on that side, upon the posts t'.
29 the little chambers t', and the posts t',
29 and the arches t', according to these
29 in it and in the arches t' round about:
31 arches t' were toward the utter court;
Eze 40: 31 and palm trees were upon the posts t':
33 the little chambers t', and the posts t',
33 and the arches t', were according to
33 and in the arches t' round about:
34 the arches t' were toward the outward
34 and palm trees were upon the posts t'
36 The little chambers t', the posts t',
36 and the arches t', and the windows
37 posts t' were toward the utter court;
37 and palm trees were upon the posts t',
38 the entries t' were by the posts of the
41: 2 and he measured the length t', forty
4 he measured the length t', twenty
12 about, and the length t' ninety cubits.
13 and the building, with the walls t',
15 and the galleries t' on the one side and
22 high, and the length t' two cubits;
22 and the corners t', and the length t',
22 and the walls t', were of wood:
42: 7 chambers, the length t' was fifty cubits.
43: 11 form of the house, and the fashion t',
11 and the goings out t',
11 and the comings in t',
11 and all the forms t',
11 and all the ordinances t',
11 and all the forms t',
11 and all the laws t': and write it in
11 that they may keep the whole form t',
11 and all the ordinances t', and do them.
12 the whole limit t' round about shall
13 the breadth a cubit, and the border t'
13 by the edge t' round about shall be a
16 broad, square in the four squares t'.
17 fourteen broad in the four squares t';
17 the bottom t' shall be a cubit about;
20 And thou shalt take of the blood t', and
44: 5 house of the Lord, and all the laws t';
14 of the house, for all the service t',
45: 1 This shall be holy in all the borders t'
2 cubits round about for the suburbs t'.
11 measure t' shall be after the homer.
46: 8 and he shall go forth by the way t'.
16 the inheritance t' shall be his sons';
47: 11 But the miry places t', and
11 the marishes t' shall not be healed;
12 And by the river upon the bank t',
12 neither shall the fruit t' be consumed:
12 and the fruit t' shall be for meat,
12 and the leaf t' for medicine.
48: 10 sanctuary...shall be in the midst t'.
15 and the city shall be in the midst t'.
16 And these shall be the measures t';
18 and the increase t' shall be for food
21 sanctuary...shall be in the midst t'.
Da 1: 5 at the end t' they might stand before
2: 5 the dream, with the interpretation t',
6 the dream, and the interpretation t',
6 the dream, and the interpretation t'.
9 ye can shew me the interpretation t'.
26 I have seen, and the interpretation t'?
31 thee; and the form t' was terrible.
36 and we will tell the interpretation t'
45 certain, and the interpretation t' sure.
3: 1 cubits, and the breadth t' six cubits:
4: 7 known unto me the interpretation t'.
9 I have seen, and the interpretation t'.
10 the earth, and the height t' was great.
11 and the height t' reached unto heaven,
11 the sight t' to the end of all the earth:
12 The leaves t' were fair, and the
12 and the fruit t' much, and in it was
12 of the heaven dwelt in the boughs t',
18 declare the interpretation t',
19 or the interpretation t', trouble thee.
19 the interpretation t' to thine enemies.
20 and the sight t' to all the earth;
21 and the fruit t' much, and in it was
23 yet leave the stump of the roots t' in
5: 7 and shew me the interpretation t',
8 known to the king the interpretation t'.
15 known unto me the interpretation t':
16 known to me the interpretation t',
7: 4 I beheld till the wings t' were plucked,
9: 26 and the end t' shall be with a flood,
Ho 2: 9 and take away my corn in the time t',
9 and my wine in the season t',
4: 13 elms, because the shadow t' is good:
8: 14 and it shall devour the palaces t'.
9: 4 all that eat t' shall be polluted:
10: 5 for the people t' shall mourn over it,
5 and the priests t' that rejoiced on it,
5 for the glory t', because it is departed
14: 7 the scent t' shall be as the wine of
Joe 1: 7 away; the branches t' are made white.
Am 1: 3, 6 not turn away the punishment t';
7 which shall devour the palaces t':
9 will not turn away the punishment t';
10 which shall devour the palaces t'.
11, 13 not turn away the punishment t';
14 and it shall devour the palaces t', with
2: 1 will not turn away the punishment t';
3 will cut off the judge from the midst t',
3 will slay all the princes t' with him,
4, 6 not turn away the punishment t';
3: 9 the great tumults in the midst t',
9 and the oppressed in the midst t'.
8: 10 son, and the end t' as a bitter day.
9: 11 is fallen, and close up the breaches t';
14 plant vineyards, and drink the wine t';
Jon 1: 3 so he paid the fare t', and went down
Mic 1: 6 pour down the stones t' into the valley,
6 and I will discover the foundations t'.
7 the graven images t' shall be beaten
7 and all the hires t' shall be burned*
7 and all the idols t' will I lay desolate:
3: 11 The heads t' judge for reward,

Mic 3:11 and the priests t' teach for hire,
11 and the prophets t' divine for money:
5: 6 the land of Nimrod in the entrances t':
6:12 For the rich men t' are full of violence,
12 the inhabitants t' have spoken lies,
16 and the inhabitants t' an hissing:
Na 1: 8 will make an utter end of the place t',
2: 5 they shall make haste to the wall t',
Hab 2:18 that the maker t' hath graven it;
Zep 1:13 vineyards, but not drink the wine t'.
3: 5 The just Lord is in the midst t'; he
Zec 2: 2 to see what is the breadth t',
2 and what is the length t'.
3: 9 I will engrave the graving t', saith
4: 2 lamps, which are upon the top t':
3 and the other upon the left side t'.
7 forth the headstone t' with shoutings,
11 candlestick and upon the left side t'?
5: 2 roll; the length t' is twenty cubits,
2 and the breadth t' ten cubits.
4 it with the timber t' and the stones t'.
8 weight of lead upon the mouth t'.
7: 7 and the cities t' round about her, when
8: 5 boys and girls playing in the streets t'.
9: 1 and Damascus shall be the rest t':
14: 4 of Olives shall cleave in the midst t'
Mal 1:12 and the fruit t', even his meat, is
M't 2:16 in Bethlehem, and in all the coasts t',
6:34 Sufficient unto the day is the evil t'.
12:36 they shall give account t' in
13:32 come and lodge in the branches t'.
44 for joy t' goeth and selleth all that he
14:13 and when the people had heard t', they
21:43 a nation bringing forth the fruits t'
22: 7 But when the king heard t', he was
27:34 and when he had tasted t', he would
M'r 6:16 But when Herod heard t', he said, It is
Lu 19:33 owners t' said unto them, Why loose
21:20 know that the desolation t' is nigh.
22:16 I will not any more eat t', until
Joh 3: 8 thou hearest the sound t', but canst
4:12 the well, and drank t' himself,
6:50 a man may eat t', and not die.
7: 7 of it, that the works t' are evil.
Ac 15:16 I will build again the ruins t', and I
Ro 6:12 that ye should obey it in the lusts t'.
13:14 for the flesh, to fulfil the lusts t'.
1Co 9: 7 and eateth not of the fruit t'?
23 that I might be partaker t' with you.
10:26 earth is the Lord's, and the fulness t':
28 earth is the Lord's, and the fulness t':
2Ti 3: 5 godliness, but denying the power t':
Heb 7:18 weakness and unprofitableness t'.
Jas 1:11 the grass, and the flower t' falleth,
1Pe 1:24 and the flower t' falleth away:
5: 2 is among you, taking the oversight t'
1Jo 2:17 world passeth away, and the lust t':
Re 5: 2 the book, and to loose the seals t'?
5 book, and to loose the seven seals t'.
9 the book, and to open the seals t':
16:12 water t' was dried up, that the way
21 for the plague t' was exceeding great.
21:15 city, and the gates t', and the wall t'.
17 he measured the wall t', an hundred
23 lighten it, and the Lamb is the light t'.

thereon See also THEREUPON.
Ge 35:14 and he poured a drink offering t',
14 and he poured oil t'.
Ex 17:12 and put it under him, and he sat t';
20:24 shalt sacrifice t' thy burnt offerings,
26 thy nakedness be not discovered t'.
30: 7 Aaron shall burn t' sweet incense
9 Ye shall offer no strange incense t',
9 shall ye pour drink offering t'.
40:27 And he burnt sweet incense t'; as
35 because the cloud abode t', and the
Le 2: 1 oil upon it, and put frankincense t':
6 part it in pieces, and pour oil t':
15 put oil upon it, lay frankincense t':
5:11 shall he put any frankincense t':
6:12 he shall burn t' the fat of the peace
10: 1 put fire therein, and put incense t',
11:38 and any part of their carcase fall t',
Nu 4: 6 put t' the covering of badgers' skins,
7 put t' the dishes, and the spoons,
7 and the continual bread shall be t':
13 altar, and spread a purple cloth t':
5:15 oil upon it, nor put frankincense t';
9:22 upon the tabernacle, remaining t',
16:18 put fire in them, and laid incense t',
De 27: 6 thou shalt offer burnt offerings t'
Jos 8:29 and raise t' a great heap of stones,
31 they offered t' burnt offerings unto
22:23 or if to offer t' burnt offering or
23 or if to offer peace offerings t', let
2Sa 17:19 mouth, and spread ground corn t';
19:26 saddle me an ass, that I may ride t',
1Ki 6:35 carved t' cherubims and palm trees
13:13 him the ass: and he rode t',
2Ki 16:12 to the altar, and offered t'.
1Ch 12:17 the God of our fathers look t', and
15:15 their shoulders with the staves t',
2Ch 3: 5 and set t' palm trees and chains.
14 linen, and wrought cherubims t'.
33:16 and sacrificed t' peace offerings and
Ezr 3: 2 to offer burnt offerings t', as it is
3 they offered burnt offerings t' unto
6:11 being set up, let him be hanged t';
Es 5:14 that Mordecai may be hanged t':
7: 9 Then the king said, Hang him t'.
Isa 30:12 and perverseness, and stay t':
35: 9 nor any ravenous beast shall go up t'.
Eze 15: 3 a pin of it to hang any vessel t'?
40:39 to slay t' the burnt offering and the
43:18 make it, to offer burnt offerings t',
18 and to sprinkle blood t'.

Zec 4: 2 and his seven lamps t', and seven
M't 21: 7 clothes, and they set him t'.
19 found nothing t', but leaves
23:20 by it, and by all things t'.
22 God, and by him that sitteth t'.
M'r 11:13 he might find any thing t':
14:72 And when he thought t', he wept.
Lu 13: 6 he came and sought fruit t',
19:35 upon the colt, and they set Jesus
Joh 12:14 had found a young ass, sat t';
21: 9 coals there, and fish laid t', and
1Co 3:10 foundation, and another buildeth t'.
Re 5: 3 to open the book, neither to look t'.
4 to read the book, neither to look t'.
6: 4 was given to him that sat t'
21:12 and names written t', which are the

thereout
Le 2: 2 he shall take t' his handful of the
J'g 15:19 in the jaw, and there came water t';

thereto
Ex 25:24 make t' a crown of gold round about.
29:41 shalt do t' according to the meat
30:38 shall make like unto that, to smell t'
Le 5:16 and shall add the fifth part t',
6: 5 and shall add the fifth part more t',
18:23 stand before a beast to lie down t':
20:16 unto any beast, and lie down t',
27:27 and shall add a fifth part of it t':
31 shall add t' the fifth part thereof.
Nu 3:36 vessels thereof, and all that serveth t',
19:17 running water shall be put t' in a
De 12:32 thou shalt not add t', nor diminish
J'g 11:17 king of Edom would not hearken t'.
1Ch 22:14 prepared; and thou mayest add t'.
2Ch 10:14 your yoke heavy, but I will add t':
21:11 fornication, and compelled Judah t'.
Ps 119: 9 taking heed t' according to thy word.
Isa 44:15 a graven image, and falleth down t'.
M'r 14:70 a Galilæan, and thy speech agreeth t'.
Ga 3:15 no man disannulleth, or addeth t'.

thereunto
Ex 32: 8 worshipped it, and have sacrificed t',
36:36 he made t' four pillars of shittim
37:11 made t' a crown of gold round about.
12 he made t' a border of an handbreadth
De 1: 7 and unto all the places nigh t', in the
Eph 6:18 and watching t' with all
1Th 3: 3 that we are appointed t'.
Heb 10: 1 make the comers t' perfect.
1Pe 3: 9 knowing that ye are t' called,

thereupon
Ex 31: 7 and the mercy seat that is t',
Eze 16:16 colours, and playedst the harlot t':
Zep 2: 7 the house of Judah; they shall feed t':
1Co 3:10 man take heed how he buildeth t'.
14 work abide which he hath built t',

therewith
Ex 22: 6 corn, or the field, be consumed t';
30:26 the tabernacle of the congregation t',
38:30 t' he made the sockets to the door
Lev 7: 7 that maketh atonement t' shall have it.
8: 7 of the ephod, and bound it unto him t'.
15:32 goeth from him, and is defiled t';
18:23 lie with any beast to defile thyself t':
22: 8 he shall not eat to defile himself t':
De 16: 3 shalt thou eat unleavened bread t',
23:13 thou shalt dig t', and shalt turn back
J'g 15:15 took it, and slew a thousand men t'.
16:12 took new ropes, and bound him t',
1Sa 12: 3 any bribe to blind mine eyes t'? and
17:51 and slew him, and cut off his head t'.
31: 4 thy sword, and thrust me through t';
2Sa 20:10 so he smote him t' in the fifth rib, and
2Ki 5: 6 I have t' sent Naaman my servant to
12:14 and repaired t' the house of the Lord.
1Ch 10: 4 thy sword, and thrust me through t';
23: 5 which I made, said David, to praise t'.
2Ch 16: 6 and he built t' Geba and Mizpah.
Pr 15:16 than great treasure and trouble t'.
17 love is, than a stalled ox and hatred t'.
17: 1 is a dry morsel, and quietness t',
25:16 thee, lest thou be filled t', and vomit it.
Ec 1:13 to the sons of man to be exercised t'.
2: 6 pools of water, to water t' the wood
10: 9 removeth stones shall be hurt t';
Isa 10:15 itself against him that heweth t'?
Eze 4:15 thou shalt prepare thy bread t'.
Joe 2:19 and oil, and ye shall be satisfied t':
Ph'p 4:11 whatsoever state I am, t' to be content.
1Ti 6: 8 and raiment let us be t' content.
Jas 3: 9 T' bless we God, even the
9 t' curse we men, which are
3Jo 10 not content t', neither doth

these A
Ge 2: 4 T' are the generations of the
6: 9 T' are the generations of Noah:
9:19 T' are three sons of Noah: and of
10: 1 t' are the generations of the sons
5 By t' were the isles of the Gentiles
20 T' are the sons of Ham, after their
29 all t' were the sons of Joktan.
31 T' are the sons of Shem, after their
32 T' are the families of the sons of
32 by t' were the nations divided in
11:10 T' are the generations of Shem:
27 t' are the generations of Terah:
14: 2 That t' made war with Bera king
3 All t' were joined together in the
13 t' were confederate with Abram.
15: 1 After t' things the word of the
10 he took unto him all t', and divided
19: 8 only unto t' men do nothing; for
20: 8 and told all t' things in their ears.
25: 4 All t' were the children of Keturah.

Ge 25: 7 And t' are the days of the years of
12 Now t' are the generations of
13 And t' are the names of the sons of
16 T' are the sons of Ishmael, and
16 t' are their names, by their towns,
17 And t' are the years of the life of
19 And t' are the generations of Isaac.
26: 3 thy seed, I will give all t' countries,
4 give unto thy seed all t' countries;
27:36 hath supplanted me t' two times:
42 t' words of Esau her elder son
46 as t' which are of the daughters
29:13 And he told Laban all t' things.
31:43 T' daughters are my daughters,
43 and t' children are my children,
43 and t' cattle are my cattle, and all that
32:17 thou? and whose are t' before thee?
33: 8 T' are to find grace in the sight of my
34:21 T' men are peaceable with us;
35:26 t' are the sons of Jacob, which were
36: 1 Now t' are the generations of Esau,
5 t' are the sons of Esau, which were
9 And t' are the generations of Esau
10 T' are the names of Esau's sons;
12 t' were the sons of Adah Esau's
13 t' are the sons of Reuel; Nahath,
13 t' were the sons of Bashemath
14 t' were the sons of Aholibamah, the
15 T' were the dukes of the sons of
16 t' are the dukes that came of
16 of Edom; t' were the sons of Adah.
17 t' are the sons of Reuel Esau's son;
17 t' are the dukes that came of Reuel
17 t' are the sons of Bashemath Esau's
18 t' are the sons of Aholibamah
18 t' were the dukes that came of
19 T' are the sons of Esau, who is
19 Edom, and t' are their dukes.
20 T' are the sons of Seir the Horite,
21 t' are the dukes of the Horites, the
23 And the children of Shobal were t';
24 t' are the children of Zibeon; both
25 And the children of Anah were t';
26 And t' are the children of Dishon;
27 The children of Ezer are t'; Bilhan,
28 The children of Dishan are t'; Uz,
29 T' are the dukes that came of the
30 T' are the dukes that came of Hori,
31 t' are the kings that reigned in the
40 t' are the names of the dukes that
43 t' be the dukes of Edom, according
37: 2 T' are the generations of Jacob.
38:25 man, whose t' are, am I with child:
25 whose are t', the signet, and
39: 7 it came to pass after t' things, that
17 unto him according to t' words,
40: 1 And it came to pass after t' things,
42:36 away: all t' things are against me.
43: 7 according to the tenor of t' words:
16 Bring t' men home, and slay, and
16 for t' men shall dine with me at noon.
44: 6 he spake unto them t' same words.
7 Wherefore saith my lord t' words?
45: 6 t' two years hath the famine been
46: 8 t' are the names of the children of
15 T' be the sons of Leah, which she
18 T' are the sons of Zilpah, whom
18 t' she bare unto Jacob, even
22 T' are the sons of Rachel, which
25 T' are the sons of Bilhah, which
25 and she bare t' unto Jacob: all the
48: 1 And it came to pass after t' things,
8 Joseph's sons, and said, Who are t'?
49:28 All t' are the twelve tribes of Israel:
Ex 1: 1 t' are the names of the children of
4: 9 will not believe also t' two signs,
6:14 T' be the heads of their father's
14 Carmi: t' be the families of Reuben.
15 t' are the families of Simeon.
16 t' are the names of the sons of Levi
19 t' are the families of Levi according
24 t' are the families of the Korhites.
25 t' are the heads...of the Levites
26 T' are that Aaron and Moses, to
27 T' are they which spake to
10: 1 might shew t' my signs before him:
11: 8 all t' thy servants shall come down
10 Moses and Aaron did all t' wonders
14:20 them, but it gave light by night to t':
15:26 will put none of t' diseases upon thee,
19: 7 laid before their faces all t' words
20: 1 And God spake all t' words, saying,
21: 1 Now t' are the judgments which
11 if he do not t' three unto her, then
24: 8 with you concerning all t' words.
25:39 shall he make it, with all t' vessels.
28: 4 t' are the garments which they shall
30:34 t' sweet spices with...frankincense:
32: 4, 8 T' be thy gods, O Israel, which
33: 4 the people heard t' evil tidings, they
34: 1 I will write upon t' tables the words
27 unto Moses, Write thou t' words:
27 for after the tenor of t' words I have
35: 1 T' are the words which the Lord
Le 2: 8 is made of t' things unto the Lord:
5: 4 then he shall be guilty in one of t'.
5 shall be guilty in one of t' things,
13 sin that he hath sinned in one of t',
17 commit any of t' things which are
6: 3 any of all t' that a man doeth, sinning
11: 2 T' are the beasts which ye shall
4 t' shall ye not eat of them that
9 T' shall ye eat of all that are in
13 t' are they which ye shall have in
21 Yet t' may ye eat of every
22 Even t' of them ye may eat; the

Le 11:24 And for *t*· ye shall be unclean:
29 *T*· also shall be unclean unto you
31 *T*· are unclean to you among all
16: 4 *t*· are holy garments; therefore
18:24 ye yourselves in any of *t*· things:
24 for in all *t*· the nations are defiled
26 not commit any of *t*· abominations;
27 all *t*· abominations have the men
29 commit any of *t*· abominations,
30 any one of *t*· abominable customs,
20:23 for they committed all *t*· things,
21:14 or an harlot, *t*· shall he not take:
22:22 ye shall not offer *t*· unto the Lord,
25 the bread of your God of any of *t*·;
23: 2 convocations, even *t*· are my feasts.
4, 37 *T*· are the feasts of the Lord,
25:54 he be not redeemed in *t*· years, then
26:14 will not do all *t*· commandments;
23 not be reformed by me by *t*· things,
46 *T*· are the statutes and judgments
27:34 *T*· are the commandments, which
Nu 1: 5 *t*· are the names of the men that
16 *T*· were the renowned of the
17 And Moses and Aaron took *t*· men
44 *T*· are those that were numbered,
2: 9 their armies. *T*· shall first set forth.
32 *T*· are those which were numbered
3: 1 *T*· also are the generations of
2 *t*· are the names of the sons of
3 *T*· are the names of the sons of
17 *t*· were the sons of Levi by their
18 *t*· are the names of the sons of
20 *T*· are the families of the Levites
21 *t*· are the families of...Gershonites.
27 *t*· are the families of...Kohathites.
33 *t*· are the families of Merari.
35 *t*· shall pitch on the side of the
4:15 *T*· things are the burden of the
37 *T*· were they that were numbered
41 *T*· are they that were numbered of
45 *T*· be those that were numbered of
5:23 priest shall write *t*· curses in a book,
13: 4 *t*· were their names: of the tribe of
16 *T*· are the names of the men which
14:22 tempted me now *t*· ten times, and
39 Moses told *t*· sayings unto all the
15:13 shall do *t*· things after this manner,
22 not observed all *t*· commandments,
16:14 thou put out the eyes of *t*· men?
26 from the tents of *t*· wicked men,
28 hath sent me to do all *t*· works;
29 If *t*· men die the common death of
30 that *t*· men have provoked the Lord.
31 an end of speaking all *t*· words,
38 censers of *t*· sinners against their
21:25 And Israel took all *t*· cities: and
22: 9 said, What men are *t*· with thee?
28 hast smitten me *t*· three times?
32 smitten thine ass *t*· three times?
33 and turned from me *t*· three times:
24:10 blessed them *t*· three times.
26: 7, 14, 18 *T*· are the families of the
22 *T*· are the families of Judah
25 *T*· are the families of Issachar
27 *T*· are the families of the
30 *T*· are the sons of Gilead: of Jeezer,
34 *T*· are the families of Manasseh,
35 *T*· are the sons of Ephraim after
36 And *t*· are the sons of Shuthelah:
37 *T*· are the families of the sons of
37 *T*· are the sons of Joseph after their
41 *T*· are the sons of Benjamin after
42 *T*· are the sons of Dan after their
42 *T*· are the families of Dan after
47 *T*· are the families of the sons of
50 *T*· are the families of Naphtali
51 *T*· were the numbered of the
53 Unto *t*· the land shall be divided for
57 *t*· are they that were numbered of
58 *T*· are the families of the Levites:
63 *T*· are they that were numbered by
64 But among *t*· there was not a man
27: 1 *t*· are the names of his daughters;
28:23 offer *t*· beside the burnt offering
29:39 *T*· things ye shall do unto the Lord
30:16 *T*· are the statutes, which the Lord
31:16 *t*· caused the children of Israel,
33: 1 *T*· are the journeys of the children
2 *t*· are their journeys according to
34:17 *T*· are the names of the men which
19 And the names of the men are *t*·: Of
29 *T*· are they whom the Lord
35:13 *t*· cities which ye shall give six cities
15 *T*· six cities shall be a refuge, both
24 blood according to *t*· judgments:
29 So *t*· things shall be for a statute of
36:13 *T*· are the commandments and the
De 1: 1 *T*· be the words which Moses spake
35 shall not one of *t*· men of this evil
2: 7 *t*· forty years the Lord thy God
3: 5 *t*· cities were fenced with high
21 God hath done unto *t*· two kings:
4: 6 which shall hear all *t*· statutes, and
30 all *t*· things are come upon thee,
42 fleeing unto one of *t*· cities he might
45 *T*· are the testimonies, and the
5:22 *T*· words the Lord spake unto all
6: 1 Now *t*· are the commandments,
24 commanded us to do all *t*· statutes,
25 to do all *t*· commandments before
7:12 if ye hearken to *t*· judgments, and
17 heart, *T*· nations are more than I;
8: 2 thy God led thee *t*· forty years in
4 did thy foot swell, *t*· forty years.
9: 4, 5 for the wickedness of *t*· nations
10:21 for thee *t*· great and terrible things,

De 11:18 ye lay up *t*· my words in your heart
22 keep all *t*· commandments which
23 the Lord drive out all *t*· nations
12: 1 *T*· are the statutes and judgments,
28 hear all *t*· words which I command
30 How did *t*· nations serve their gods?
14: 4 *T*· are the beasts which ye shall
7 *t*· ye shall not eat of them that
9 *T*· ye shall eat of all that are in
12 *t*· are they of which ye shall not eat:
15: 5 to do all *t*· commandments which
16:12 shalt observe and do *t*· statutes.
17:19 the words of this law and *t*· statutes,
18:12 that do *t*· things are an abomination
12 because of *t*· abominations the
14 For *t*· nations, which thou shalt
19: 9 keep all *t*· commandments to do
9 cities more for thee, beside *t*· three:
11 die, and fleeth into one of *t*· cities:
20:15 not of the cities of *t*· nations.
16 But of the cities of *t*· people, which
22:17 *t*· are the tokens of my daughter's
23:18 even both *t*· are abomination unto the
25: 3 beat him above *t*· with many stripes,
26:16 commanded thee to do *t*· statutes
27: 4 that ye shall set up *t*· stones, which I
12 *T*· shall stand upon mount Gerizim
13 *t*· shall stand upon mount Ebal to
28: 2 all *t*· blessings shall come on thee,
15, 45 all *t*· curses shall come upon thee,
65 among *t*· nations shalt thou find no
29: 1 *T*· are the words of the covenant,
18 and serve the gods of *t*· nations;
30: 1 all *t*· things are come upon thee,
7 all *t*· curses upon thine enemies,
31: 1 and spake *t*· words unto all Israel.
3 destroy *t*· nations from before thee,
17 Are not *t*· evils come upon us,
28 I may speak *t*· words in their ears,
32:45 an end of speaking all *t*· words
Jos 2:11 And as soon as we heard *t*· things, our
4: 6 saying, What mean ye by *t*· stones?
7 *t*· stones shall be for a memorial
21 come, saying, What mean *t*· stones?
9:13 *t*· bottles of wine, which we filled,
13 *t*· our garments and our shoes are
10:16 But *t*· five kings fled, and hid
24 your feet upon the necks of *t*· kings.
42 *t*· kings and their land did Joshua
11: 5 when all *t*· kings were met together,
14 And all the spoil of *t*· cities, and the
12: 1 Now *t*· are the kings of the land,
7 *t*· are the kings of the country which
13:12 *t*· did Moses smite, and cast them out.
32 *T*· are the countries which Moses
14: 1 And *t*· are the countries which the
10 as he said, *t*· forty and five years,
17: 2 *t*· were the male children of
3 *t*· are the names of his daughters,
9 *t*· cities of Ephraim are among the
19: 8 the villages...round about *t*· cities
16, 31, 48 *t*· cities with their villages.
51 *T*· are the inheritances, which
20: 9 *T*· were the cities appointed for all
21: 3 the Lord, *t*· cities and their suburbs.
8 unto the Levites *t*· cities with their
9 *t*· cities which are here mentioned
42 *T*· cities were every one with their
42 about them: thus were all *t*· cities.
22: 3 not left your brethren *t*· many days
23: 3 done unto all *t*· nations because of
4 you by lot *t*· nations that remain,
7 That ye come not among *t*· nations,
7 *t*· that remain among you; neither
12 unto the remnant of *t*· nations,
12 even *t*· that remain among you, and
13 no more drive out any of *t*· nations
24:26 Joshua wrote *t*· words in the book
29 And it came to pass after *t*· things,
J'g 2: 4 the angel of the Lord spake *t*· words
3: 1 Now *t*· are the nations which the
9: 3 all the men of Shechem all *t*· words:
13:23 he have shewed us all *t*· things,
23 have told us such things as *t*·.
16:15 hast mocked me *t*· three times,
18:14 that there is in *t*· houses an ephod,
18 And *t*· went into Micah's house, and
19:13 draw near to one of *t*· places to lodge
20:17 sword: all *t*· were men of war.
25 men; all *t*· drew the sword.
35 hundred men: all *t*· drew the sword.
44 men: all *t*· were men of valour.
46 sword: all *t*· were men of valour.
Ru 3:17 *T*· six measures of barley gave he
4:18 *t*· are the generations of Pharez:
1Sa 4: 8 out of the hand of *t*· mighty Gods?
8 *t*· are the Gods that smote the
6:17 *t*· are the golden emerods which
10: 7 when *t*· signs are come unto thee,
14: 6 the garrison of *t*· uncircumcised:
8 Behold, we will pass over unto *t*· men,
49 names of his two daughters were *t*·;
16:10 Jesse, The Lord hath not chosen *t*·.
17:17 *t*· ten loaves, and run to the camp
18 And carry *t*· ten cheeses unto the
39 said unto Saul, I cannot go with *t*·;
18:26 his servants told David *t*· words,
21: 5 been kept from us about *t*· three days,
12 David laid up *t*· words in his heart,
23: 2 Shall I go and smite *t*· Philistines?
24: 7 stayed his servants with *t*· words, and
16 made an end of speaking *t*· words
29: 3 What do *t*· Hebrews here?
3 been with me *t*· days, or *t*· years,
4 not be with the heads of *t*· men?
31: 4 *t*· uncircumcised come and thrust

2Sa 3: 5 *T*· were born to David in Hebron.
39 *t*· men the sons of Zeruiah be too
5:14 *t*· be the names of those that were
7:17 According to all *t*· words, and
21 hast thou done all *t*· great things,
13:21 king David heard of all *t*· things,
14:19 he put all *t*· words in the mouth of
16: 2 unto Ziba, What meanest thou by *t*·?
21:22 *T*· four were born to the giant in
23: 1 Now *t*· be the last words of David.
8 *T*· be the names of the mighty men
17 *T*· [428] things did *t*· [*]...mighty men.
22 *T*· things did Benaiah the son of
24:17 but *t*· sheep, what have they done?
23 All *t*· things did Araunah, as a king,
1Ki 4: 2 *t*· were the princes which he had;
8 And *t*· are their names: The son of
7: 9 All *t*· were of costly stones, according
45 all *t*· vessels, which Hiram made
8:59 And let *t*· my words, wherewith I
9:13 What cities are *t*· which thou hast
23 *T*· were the chief of the officers that
10: 8 happy are *t*· thy servants, which
10 abundance of spices as *t*· which
11: 2 Solomon clave unto *t*· in love.
17: 1 shall not be dew nor rain *t*· years,
17 And it came to pass after *t*· things,
18:36 have done all *t*· things at thy word.
20:19 So *t*· young men of the princes of
21: 1 And it came to pass after *t*· things,
22:11 With *t*· shalt thou push the Syrians,
17 the Lord said, *T*· have no master:
23 the mouth of all *t*· thy prophets,
2Ki 1: 7 to meet you, and told you *t*· words?
13 and the life of *t*· fifty thy servants,
2:21 the Lord, I have healed *t*· waters;
3:10, 13 called *t*· three kings together,
6:20 Lord, open the eyes of *t*· men, that
7: 8 And when *t*· lepers came to the
10: 9 and slew him: but who slew all *t*·?
17:41 So *t*· nations feared the Lord, and
18:27 and to thee, to speak *t*· words?
20:14 said unto him, What said *t*· men?
21:11 of Judah hath done *t*· abominations,
23:16 proclaimed, who proclaimed *t*· words,
17 and proclaimed *t*· things that thou
25:16 the brass of all *t*· vessels was without
17 like unto *t*· had the second pillar
20 captain of the guard took *t*·, and
1Ch 1:23 All *t*· were the sons of Joktan.
29 *T*· are their generations: The
31 *T*· are the sons of Ishmael.
33 All *t*· are the sons of Keturah.
43 *t*· are the kings that reigned in the
54 Iram. *T*· are the dukes of Edom.
2: 1 *T*· are the sons of Israel; Reuben,
18 her sons are *t*·; Jesher, and Shobab,
23 *t*· belonged to the sons of Machir
33 Zaza. *T*· were the sons of Jerahmeel.
50 *T*· were the sons of Caleb the son of
55 *T*· are the Kenites that came of
3: 1 Now *t*· were the sons of David,
4 *T*· six were born unto him in Hebron;
5 And *t*· were born unto him in
9 *T*· were all the sons of David, beside
4: 2 *T*· are the families of the
3 And *t*· were of the father of Etam;
4 *T*· are the sons of Hur, the
6 *T*· were the sons of Naarah.
12 Ir-nahash. *T*· are the men of Rechah.
18 And *t*· are the sons of Bithiah the
22 And *t*· are ancient things.
23 *T*· were the potters, and those
31 *T*· were their cities unto the reign
33 *T*· were their habitations, and
38 *T*· mentioned by their names were
41 *t*· written by name came in the days
5:14 *T*· are the children of Abihail the
17 *t*· were reckoned by genealogies in the
24 *t*· were the heads of the house of
6:17 And *t*· be the names of the sons of
19 *t*· are the families of the Levites
31 *t*· are they whom David set over the
33 *t*· are they that waited with their
50 *t*· are the sons of Aaron; Eleazar his
54 Now *t*· are their dwelling places
64 to the Levites *t*· cities with their
65 *t*· cities, which are called by their
7: 8 All *t*· are the sons of Becher.
11 All *t*· the sons of Jediael, by the
17 *T*· were the sons of Gilead, the son
29 In *t*· dwelt the children of Joseph
33 *T*· are the children of Japhlet.
40 All *t*· were the children of Asher,
8: 6 And *t*· are the sons of Ehud:
6 *t*· are the heads of the fathers
10 *T*· were his sons, heads of the
28 *T*· were heads of the fathers, by
28 chief men. *T*· dwelt in Jerusalem.
32 *t*· also dwelt with their brethren
38 sons, whose names are *t*·, Azrikam,
38 Hanan. All *t*· were the sons of Azel.
40 fifty. All *t*· are the sons of Benjamin.
9: 9 *t*· men were chief of the fathers in
22 *t*· which were chosen to be porters in
22 *T*· were reckoned by their
26 *t*· Levites, the four chief porters,
33 And *t*· are the singers, chief of the
34 *T*· chief fathers of the Levites were
34 generations; *t*· dwelt at Jerusalem.
44 had six sons, whose names are *t*·,
44 Hanan: *t*· were the sons of Azel.
10: 4 lest *t*· uncircumcised come and
11:10 *T*· also are the chief of the mighty
19 shall I drink the blood of *t*· men that
19 *T*· things did...three mightiest.

1Ch 11: 19 things did t' three mightiest.
24 T' things did Benaiah the son of
12: 1 t' are they that came to David to
14 T' were of the sons of Gad, captains
15 T' are they that went over
23 t' are the numbers of the bands
38 t' men of war, that could keep rank,
14: 4 Now t' are the names of his children
17: 15 According to all t' words, and
19 in making known all t' great things.
18: 11 that he brought from all t' nations;
20: 8 T' were born unto the giant in
21: 17 but as for t' sheep, what have they
23: 9 T' were the chief of the fathers of
10 T' four were the sons of Shimei.
24 T' were the sons of Levi after the
24: 1 t' are the divisions of the sons of
19 T' were the orderings of them in
20 the rest of the sons of Levi were t':
30 T' were the sons of the Levites
31 T' likewise cast lots over against
25: 5 All t' were the sons of Heman the
6 All t' were under the hands of their
26: 8 All t' of the sons of Obed-edom:
12 Among t' were the divisions of the
19 T' are the divisions of the porters
27: 22 T' were the princes of the tribes of
31 t' were the rulers of the substance
29: 17 I have willingly offered all t' things:
19 and to do all t' things, and to build
2Ch 3: 3 t' are the things wherein Solomon
13 The wings of t' cherubims spread
4: 18 Solomon made all t' vessels in great
5: 5 t' did the priests and Levites bring
8: 10 t' were the chief of king Solomon's
9: 7 men, and happy are t' thy servants,
14: 7 Let us build t' cities, and make
8 all t' were mighty men of valour.
15: 8 when Asa heard t' words, and the
17: 14 And t' are the numbers of them
19 T' waited on the king, beside those
18: 10 With t' thou shalt push Syria until
16 the Lord said, T' have no master;
22 in the mouth of t' thy prophets,
21: 2 all t' were the sons of Jehoshaphat
24: 26 t' are they that conspired against
29: 32 t' were for a burnt offering to the
32: 1 After t' things, and the
35: 7 t' were of the king's substance.
36: 18 princes; all t' he brought to Babylon.
Ezr 1: 11 t' did Sheshbazzar bring up with them
2: 1 t' are the children of the province
59 t' were they which went up from
62 T' sought their register among
4: 21 to cause t' men to cease,
5: 9 house, and to make up t' walls?
11 that was builded t' many years ago,
15 Take t' vessels, go, carry them into
6: 8 ye shall do to the elders of t' Jews
8 expences be given unto t' men,
7: 1 Now after t' things, in the reign of
8: 1 T' are now the chief of their fathers
13 whose names are t', Eliphelet, Jeiel,
9: 1 Now when t' were done, the princes
14 with the people of t' abominations?
10: 44 All t' had taken strange wives: and
Ne 1: 4 came to pass, when I heard t' words,
10 Now t' are thy servants and thy
4: 2 and said, What do t' feeble Jews?
5: 6 when I heard their cry and t' words.
6: 6 be their king, according to t' words.
7 to the king according to t' words.
14 according to t' their works,
16 heathen...about us saw t' things,
7: 6 T' are the children of the province,
61 t' were they which went up also from
64 T' sought their register among
10: 8 Shemaiah: t' were the priests.
11: 3 t' are the chief of the province that
7 t' are the sons of Benjamin; Sallu
12: 1 t' are the priests and the Levites
7 T' were the chief of the priests and
26 T' were in the days of Joiakim the
Es 1: 5 And when t' days were expired, the
2: 1 After t' things, when the wrath of
3: 1 After t' things did king Ahasuerus
4: 11 in unto the king t' thirty days.
9: 20 And Mordecai wrote t' things, and
26 Wherefore they called t' days Purim
27 that they would keep t' two days
28 that t' days should be remembered
28 and that t' days of Purim should not
31 To confirm t' days of Purim in their
32 confirmed t' matters of Purim;
Job 8: 2 How long wilt thou speak t' things?
10: 13 And t' things hast thou hid in thine
12: 3 who knoweth not such things as t'?
9 knoweth not in all t' that the hand
19: 3 T' ten times have ye reproached
26: 14 Lo, t' are parts of his ways: but
32: 1 t' three men ceased to answer Job,
5 answer in the mouth of t' three men.
33: 29 t' things worketh God oftentimes
42: 7 Lord had spoken t' words unto Job,
Ps 15: 5 He that doeth t' things shall never
42: 4 When I remember t' things, I pour
50: 21 T' things hast thou done, and I
57: 1 refuge, until t' calamities be overpast.
73: 12 t' are the ungodly, who prosper in
104: 27 T' wait all upon thee; that thou
107: 24 T' see the works of the Lord, and
43 is wise, and will observe t' things,
Pr 6: 16 T' six things doth the Lord hate:
24: 23 T' things also belong to the wise.
25: 1 T' are also proverbs of Solomon,
Ec 7: 10 the former days were better than t'?

Ec 11: 9 that for all t' things God will bring
12: 12 by t', my son, be admonished: of
Isa 7: 4 two tails of t' smoking firebrands,
34: 16 no one of t' shall fail, none shall
36: 12 and to thee to speak t' words?
20 they among all the gods of t' lands,
38: 16 O Lord, by t' things men live,
16 in all t' things is the life of my spirit:
39: 3 said unto him, What said t' men?
40: 26 behold who hath created t' things,
42: 16 T' things will I do unto them, and
44: 21 Remember t', O Jacob and Israel;
45: 7 evil: I the Lord do all t' things.
47: 7 didst not lay t' things to thy heart,
9 But t' two things shall come to thee
13 save thee from t' things that shall
48: 14 them hath declared t' things?
49: 12 Behold, t' shall come from far: and,
12 t' from the north and from the west;
12 west; and t' from the land of Sinim.
18 all t' gather themselves together, an
21 Who hath begotten me t', seeing I
21 fro? and who hath brought up t'?
21 left alone; t', where had they been?
51: 19 T' two things are come unto thee;
57: 6 Should I receive comfort in t'?
60: 8 Who are t' that fly as a cloud, and as
64: 12 thou refrain thyself for t' things,
65: 5 T' are a smoke in my nose, a fire
Jer 2: 34 it by secret search, but upon all t'.
3: 7 said after she had done all t' things,
12 Go and proclaim t' words toward
4: 18 have procured t' things unto thee;
5: 4 I said, Surely t' are poor; they are
5 t' have altogether broken the yoke,
9 Shall I not visit for t' things? saith
19 Lord our God all t' things unto us?
25 have turned away t' things,
29 Shall I not visit for t' things? saith
7: 2 that enter in at t' gates to worship
4 The temple of the Lord, are t'.
10 delivered to do all t' abominations?
13 because ye have done all t' works,
27 shalt speak all t' words unto them;
9: 9 Shall I not visit them for t' things?
24 for in t' things I delight, saith the
26 for all t' nations are uncircumcised,
10: 11 earth, and from under t' heavens.
11: 6 Proclaim all t' words in the cities of
13: 22 Wherefore come t' things upon me?
14: 22 for thou hast made all t' things.
16: 10 shalt shew this people all t' words,
17: 20 Jerusalem, that enter in by t' gates:
20: 1 that Jeremiah prophesied t' things.
22: 2 thy people that enter in by t' gates:
5 if ye will not hear t' words, I swear
23: 21 I have not sent t' prophets, yet they
24: 5 Like t' good figs, so will I
25: 9 against all t' nations round about,
11 t' nations shall serve the king of
30 thou against them all t' words,
26: 7 heard Jeremiah speaking t' words in
10 the princes of Judah heard t' things,
15 to speak all t' words in your ears.
27: 6 now have I given all t' lands into the
12 of Judah according to all t' words,
28: 14 iron upon the neck of all t' nations,
29: 1 Now t' are the words of the letter
30: 4 t' are the words that the Lord spake
15 I have done t' things unto thee.
31: 21 of Israel, turn again to t' thy cities.
32: 14 Take t' evidences, this evidence of
34: 6 spake all t' words unto Zedekiah
7 t' defenced cities remained of the
36: 16 surely tell the king of all t' words.
17 thou write all t' words at his mouth?
18 He pronounced all t' words unto me
24 his servants that heard all t' words.
38: 9 t' men have done evil in all that they
12 Put now t' old cast clouts and rotten
16 hand of t' men that seek thy life.
24 Let no man know of t' words, and
27 told them according to all t' words
43: 1 sent him to them, even all t' words,
10 set his throne upon t' stones that I
51: 60 all t' words that are written against
61 shalt see, and shalt read all t' words;
52: 20 the brass of all t' vessels was without
22 the pomegranates were like unto t'.
La 1: 16 For t' things I weep; mine eye, mine
4: 9 for t' pine away, stricken through
5: 17 for t' things our eyes are dim.
Eze 1: 21 When those went, t' went; and when
21 when those stood, t' stood; and when
8: 15 see greater abominations than t'.
10: 17 When they stood, t' stood; and when
17 were lifted up, t' lifted up themselves
11: 2 t' are the men that devise mischief,
14: 3 t' men have set up their idols in
14 Though t' three men, Noah, Daniel,
16, 18 Though t' three men were in it,
16: 5 to do any of t' unto thee, to have
20 t' hast thou sacrificed unto them to be
30 seeing thou doest all t' things, the
43 but hast fretted me in all t' things;
17: 12 Know ye not what t' things mean?
18 and hath done all t' things, he shall
18: 10 doeth the like to any one of t' things,
13 he hath done all t' abominations; he
23: 10 T' discovered her nakedness:
30 I will do t' things unto thee,
24: 19 not tell us what t' things are to us,
27: 21 goats: in t' were they thy merchants.
24 T' were thy merchants in all sorts
30: 17 t' cities shall go into captivity.
35: 10 T' two nations and t' two countries

Eze 36: 20 T' are the people of the Lord, and
37: 3 me, Son of man, can t' bones live?
4 Prophesy upon t' bones, and say
5 saith the Lord God unto t' bones;
9 breathe upon t' slain, that they may
11 man, t' bones are the whole house of
18 shew us what thou meanest by t'?
40: 24 thereof according to t' measures.
28 south gate according to t' measures;
29 thereof, according to t' measures:
32 the gate according to t' measures.
33 were according to t' measures:
35 it according to t' measures;
46 t' are the sons of Zadok among the
42: 5 the galleries were higher than t',
9 under t' chambers was the entry
43: 13 t' are the measures of the altar after
18 T' are the ordinances of the altar in
27 when t' days are expired, it shall
46: 22 t' four corners were of one measure.
24 T' are the places of them that boil,
47: 8 T' waters issue out toward the east
9 because t' waters shall come thither:
48: 1 Now t' are the names of the tribes.
1 for t' are his sides east and west; a
16 t' shall be the measures thereof;
29 and t' are their portions, saith the
30 t' are the goings out of the city on
Da 1: 6 among t' were of the children of
17 As for t' four children, God gave
2: 28 of thy head upon thy bed, are t';
40 as iron that breaketh all t', shall it
44 in the days of t' kings shall the
44 and consume all t' kingdoms,
3: 12 t' men, O king, have not regarded
13 they brought t' men before the king.
21 t' men were bound in their coats,
23 t' three men, Shadrach, Meshach,
27 saw t' men, upon whose bodies the
6: 2 And over t' three presidents; of
5 Then said t' men, We shall not find
6 Then t' presidents and princes
11 Then t' men assembled, and found
14 when he heard t' words, was sore
15 t' men assembled unto the king,
7: 17 T' great beasts, which are four, are
10: 21 that holdeth with me in t' things,
11: 6 he that strengthened her in t' times.
27 both t' kings' hearts shall be to do
41 t' shall escape out of his hand, even
12: 6 shall it be to the end of t' wonders?
7 all t' things shall be finished.
8 what shall be the end of t' things?
Ho 2: 12 T' are my rewards that my lovers
14: 9 and he shall understand t' things?
Am 6: 2 be they better than t' kingdoms? or
Mic 2: 7 Lord straitened? are t' his doings?
Hab 2: 6 Shall not all t' take up a parable
Hag 2: 13 by a dead body touch any of t',
Zec 1: 9 Then said I, O my lord, what are t'?
9 unto me, I will shew thee what t' be.
10 T' are they whom the Lord hath
12 had indignation t' threescore and
19 that talked with me, What be t'?
19 T' are the horns which have
21 Then said I, What come t' to do?
21 saying, T' are the horns which have
21 but t' are come to fray them, to cast
3: 7 to walk among t' that stand by.
4: 4 me, saying, What are t', my lord?
5 me, Knowest thou not what t' be?
11 What are t' two olive trees upon the
12 What be t' two olive branches which
13 said, Knowest thou not what t' be?
14 T' are the two anointed ones, that
5: 10 me, Whither do t' bear the ephah?
6: 4 with me, What are t', my lord?
5 T' are the four spirits of the
8 t' that go toward the north country
7: 3 as I have done t' so many years?
8: 6 remnant of this people in t' days,
9 ye that hear in t' days t' words by
10 before t' days there was no hire
12 this people to possess all t' things.
15 have I thought in t' days to do well
16 T' are the things that ye shall do;
17 for all t' are things that I hate,
13: 6 What are t' wounds in thine hands?
14: 15 the beasts that shall be in t' tents,
M't 1: 20 But while he thought on t' things,
2: 3 Herod the king had heard t' things,
3: 9 God is able of t' stones to raise up
4: 3 command that t' stones be made
9 him, All t' things will I give thee,
5: 19 one of t' least commandments,
37 whatsoever is more than t' cometh
6: 29 glory was not arrayed like one of t'.
32 all t' things do the Gentiles seek:)
32 that ye have need of all t' things.
33 t' things shall be added unto you.
7: 24 whosoever heareth t' sayings of
26 every one that heareth t' sayings of
28 when Jesus had ended t' sayings,
9: 18 While he spake t' things unto them,
10: 2 names of the twelve apostles are t';
5 T' twelve Jesus sent forth, and
42 unto one of t' little ones a cup of
11: 25 hast hid t' things from the wise
13: 34 All t' things spake Jesus unto the
51 Have ye understood all t' things?
53 when Jesus...finished t' parables,
54 this wisdom, and t' mighty works?
56 then hath this man all t' things?
15: 20 T' are the things which defile a
18: 6 shall offend one of t' little ones
10 ye despise not one of t' little ones;

M't 18:14 one of t' little ones should perish.
19: 1 when Jesus had finished t' sayings,
20 All t' things have I kept from my
20:12 T' last have wrought but one
21 Grant that t' my two sons may sit,
21:16 unto him, Hearest thou what t' say?
23 authority doest thou t' things?
24, 27 by what authority I do t' things.
22:22 had heard t' words, they marvelled,
40 On t' two commandments hang all
23:23 t' ought ye to have done, and not
36 All t' things shall come upon this
24: 2 unto them, See ye not all t' things?
3 Tell us, when shall t' things be?
6 for all t' things must come to pass,
8 All t' are the beginning of sorrows.
33 ye, when ye shall see all t' things,
34 pass, till all t' things be fulfilled.
25:40 one of the least of t' my brethren,
45 ye did it not to one of the least of t',
46 t' shall go away into everlasting
26: 1 Jesus had finished all t' sayings,
62 what is it which t' witness against
M'r 2: 8 reason ye t' things in your hearts?
4:11 all t' things are done in parables:
15 And t' are they by the way side,
16 t' are they likewise which are sown
18 t' are they which are sown among
20 t' are they which are sown on good
6: 2 whence hath this man t' things?
7:23 t' evil things come from within,
8: 4 can a man satisfy t' men with
9:42 offend one of t' little ones that
10:20 t' have I observed from my youth.
11:28 what authority doest thou t' things?
28 thee this authority to do t' things?
29, 33 by what authority I do t' things.
12:31 commandment greater than t'.
40 t' shall receive greater damnation.
13: 2 Seest thou t' great buildings?
4 Tell us, when shall t' things be?
4 when all t' things shall be fulfilled?
8 t' are the beginnings of sorrows.
29 ye shall see t' things come to pass,
30 not pass, till all t' things be done.
14:60 what is it which t' witness against
16:17 t' signs shall follow them that
Lu 1:19 and to shew thee t' glad tidings.
20 that t' things shall be performed,
65 all t' sayings were noised abroad
2:19 But Mary kept all t' things, and
51 his mother kept all t' sayings in
3: 8 God is able of t' stones to raise up
4:28 when they heard t' things, were
5:27 And after t' things he went forth,
7: 9 When Jesus heard t' things, he
18 John shewed him of all t' things.
8: 8 And when he had said t' things, he
13 and t' have no root, which for a
21 are t' which hear the word of God,
9:28 an eight days after t' sayings,
44 Let t' sayings sink down into your
10: 1 After t' things the Lord appointed
21 hast hid t' things from the wise
36 Which now of t' three, thinkest
11:27 as he spake t' things, a certain
42 t' ought ye to have done, and not to
53 as he said t' things unto them, the
12:27 was not arrayed like one of t'.
30 all t' things do the nations of the
30 that ye have need of t' things.
31 t' things shall be added unto you.
13: 2 Suppose ye that t' Galilæans were
7 t' three years I come seeking fruit on
16 hath bound, lo, t' eighteen years,
17 when he had said t' things, all his
14: 6 not answer him again to t' things.
15 sat at meat with him heard t' things,
21 came, and shewed his lord t' things.
15:26 and asked what t' things meant.
29 Lo, t' many years do I serve thee,
16:14 Pharisees...heard all t' things:
17: 2 should offend one of t' little ones.
18:21 All t' have I kept from my youth
22 Now when Jesus heard t' things,
34 they understood none of t' things:
19:11 And as they heard t' things, he
15 he commanded t' servants to be
40 that, if t' should hold their peace,
20: 2 authority doest thou t' things?
8 by what authority I do t' things.
16 come and destroy t' husbandmen,
21: 4 all t' have of their abundance cast
6 As for t' things which ye behold,
7 Master, but when shall t' things be?
7 when t' things shall come to pass?
9 t' things must first come to pass;
12 But before all t', they shall lay
22 For t' be the days of vengeance,
28 when t' things begin to come to
31 when ye see t' things come to pass,
36 worthy to escape all t' things
23:31 if they do t' things in a green tree,
49 stood afar off, beholding t' things.
24: 9 told all t' things unto the eleven,
10 told t' things unto the apostles.
14 they talked together of all t' things
17 of communications are t' that ye
18 are come to pass there in t' days?
21 day since t' things were done.
26 Christ to have suffered t' things,
44 T' are the words which I spake
48 And ye are witnesses of t' things.
Joh 1:28 T' things were done in Bethabara
50 shalt see greater things than t'.
2:16 sold doves, Take t' things hence;
Joh 2:18 seeing that thou doest t' things?
3: 2 for no man can do t' miracles that
9 unto him, How can t' things be?
10 Israel, and knowest not t' things?
22 After t' things came Jesus and his
5: 3 In t' lay a great multitude of
16 had done t' things on the sabbath
19 t' also doeth the Son likewise.
20 shew him greater works than t',
34 t' things I say, that ye might be
6: 1 After t' things Jesus went over the
5 we buy bread, that t' may eat?
59 T' things said he in the synagogue,
7: 1 t' things Jesus walked in Galilee:
4 If thou do t' things, shew thyself to
9 When he had said t' words unto
31 will he do more miracles than t'
8:20 T' words spake Jesus in the
28 hath taught me, I speak t' things.
30 As he spake t' words, many
9:22 T' words spake his parents,
40 were with him heard t' words,
10:19 among the Jews for t' sayings.
21 T' are not the words of him that
11:11 T' things said he: and after that he
12:16 T' things understood not his
16 that t' things were written of him,
16 they had done t' things unto him.
36 T' things spake Jesus, and
41 T' things said Esaias, when he saw
13:17 If ye know t' things, happy are ye
14:12 greater works than t' shall he do;
25 T' things have I spoken unto you,
15:11 T' things have I spoken unto you,
17 T' things I command you, that ye
21 all t' things will they do unto you
16: 1 T' things have I spoken unto you,
3 And t' things will they do unto you,
4 t' things have I told you, that when
4 t' things I said not unto you at the
6 I have said t' things unto you,
25 T' things have I spoken unto you
33 T' things I have spoken unto you,
17: 1 T' words spake Jesus, and lifted up
11 but t' are in the world, and I come
13 and t' things I speak in the world,
20 Neither pray I for t' alone, but for
25 t' have known that thou hast sent
18: 1 When Jesus had spoken t' words,
8 ye seek me, let t' go their way:
19:24 T' things therefore the soldiers
36 For t' things were done, that the
20:18 he had spoken t' things unto her.
31 But t' are written, that ye might
21: 1 After t' things Jesus shewed
15 lovest thou me more than t'?
24 which testifieth of t' things,
24 and wrote t' things: and we know
Ac 1: 9 And when he had spoken t' things,
14 T' all continued with one accord
21 t' men which have companied
24 whether of t' two thou hast chosen,
2: 7 not all t' which speak Galilæans?
13 said, T' men are full of new wine.
15 For t' are not drunken, as ye
22 Ye men of Israel, hear t' words;
3:24 have likewise foretold of t' days.
4:16 What shall we do to t' men? for
5: 5 And Ananias hearing t' words fell
5 on all them that heard t' things.
11 upon as many as heard t' things.
24 the chief priests heard t' things,
32 we are his witnesses of t' things;
35 intend to do as touching t' men.
36 before t' days rose up Theudas,
38 Refrain from t' men, and let them
7: 1 the high priest, Are t' things so?
50 not my hand made all t' things?
54 they heard t' things, they were cut
8:24 that none of t' things which ye have
10: 8 when he had declared all t' things
44 While Peter yet spake t' words,
47 that t' should not be baptized,
11:12 t' six brethren accompanied me,
18 When they heard t' things, they
22 Then tidings of t' things came unto
27 in t' days came prophets from
12:17 Go shew t' things unto James, and
13:42 Gentiles besought that t' words
14:15 saying, Sirs, why do ye t' things?
15 turn from t' vanities unto the
18 t' sayings scarce restrained they
15:17 the Lord, who doeth all t' things.
28 burden than t' necessary things;
16:17 T' men are the servants of the most
20 T' men, being Jews, do exceedingly
38 serjeants told t' words unto the
17: 6 T'...have turned the world upside
7 t' all do contrary to the decrees of
8 the city, when they heard t' things.
11 T' were more noble than those in
20 know...what t' things mean.
18: 1 After t' things Paul departed from
19:21 After t' things were ended, Paul
28 And when they heard t' sayings, they
36 that t' things cannot be spoken
37 For ye have brought hither t' men,
20: 5 T' going before tarried for us at
24 But none of t' things move me,
34 t' hands have ministered unto my
21:12 And when we heard t' things, both
38 before t' days madest an uproar,
23:22 thou hast shewed t' things to me.
24: 8 take knowledge of all t' things,
9 saying that t' things were so.
20 Or else let t' same here say, if they
Ac 24:22 And when Felix heard t' things,
25: 9 be judged of t' things before me?
11 if there be none of t' things
11 whereof t' accuse me, no man may
20 and there be judged of t' matters.
26:16 of t' things which thou hast seen,
21 For t' causes the Jews caught me
26 For the king knoweth of t' things,
26 that none of t' things are hidden
29 such as I am, except t' bonds.
27:31 Except t' abide in the ship, ye
28:29 And when he had said t' words,
Ro 2:14 t', having not the law, are a law
8:31 What shall we then say to t' things?
37 in all t' things we are more than
9: 8 t' are not the children of God:
11:24 how much more shall t', which be
31 so have t' also now not believed,
14:18 he that in t' things serveth Christ
15:23 having no more place in t' parts,
23 having a great desire t' many years
1Co 4: 6 And t' things, brethren, I have in
14 I write not t' things to shame you,
9: 8 Say I t' things as a man? or saith
15 But I have used none of t' things:
15 neither have I written t' things,
10: 6 Now t' things were our examples,
11 Now all t' things happened unto
12:11 But all t' worketh that one and the
23 upon t' we bestow more abundant
13:13 faith, hope, charity, t' three;
13 but the greater of t' is charity.
2Co 2:16 And who is sufficient for t' things?
7: 1 Having therefore t' promises,
13:10 I write t' things being absent,
Ga 2: 6 But of t' who seemed to be somewhat,
4:24 for t' are the two covenants, one
5:17 t' are contrary the one to the
19 of the flesh are manifest, which are t';
Eph 5: 6 of t' things cometh the wrath of
Ph'p 4: 8 be any praise, think on t' things.
Col 3:14 above all t' things put on charity,
4:11 T' only are my fellowworkers unto
1Th 3: 3 should be moved by t' afflictions:
4:18 comfort one another with t' words.
2Th 2: 5 yet with you, I told you t' things?
1Ti 3:10 And let t' also first be proved;
14 T' things write I unto thee,
4: 6 in remembrance of t' things,
11 T' things command and teach.
15 Meditate upon t' things; give
5: 7 And t' things give in charge, that
21 that thou observe t' things without
6: 2 T' things teach and exhort.
11 thou, O man of God, flee t' things;
2Ti 1:12 which cause I also suffer t' things:
2:14 Of t' things put them in
21 therefore purge himself from t',
3: 8 so do t' also resist the truth:
Tit 2:15 T' things speak, and exhort, and
3: 8 t' things I will that thou affirm
8 T' things are good and profitable
Heb 1: 2 in t' last days spoken unto us by
7:13 he of whom t' things are spoken
9: 6 t' things were thus ordained,
23 should be purified with t';
23 with better sacrifices than t'.
10:18 Now where remission of t' is, there
11:13 T' all died in faith, not having
39 And t' all, having obtained a good
Jas 3:10 t' things ought not so to be.
1Pe 1:20 manifest in t' last times for you,
2Pe 1: 4 that by t' ye might be partakers of
8 For if t' things be in you, and
9 he that lacketh t' things is blind,
10 for if ye do t' things, ye shall never
12 in remembrance of t' things,
15 t' things always in remembrance.
2:12 But t', as natural brute beasts,
17 T' are wells without water, clouds
3:11 all t' things shall be dissolved,
16 speaking in them of t' things;
1Jo 1: 4 And t' things write we unto you,
2: 1 t' things write I unto you, that ye
26 T' things have I written unto you
5: 7 Holy Ghost: and t' three are one.
8 blood: and t' three agree in one.
13 T' things have I written unto you
Jude 8 Likewise also t' filthy dreamers
10 But t' speak evil of those things
12 T' are spots in your feasts of
14 prophesied of t', saying, Behold,
16 T' are murmurers, complainers,
19 T' be they who separate
Re 2: 1 T' things saith he that holdeth
8 T' things saith the first and the
12 T' things saith he which hath the
18 T' things saith the Son of God,
3: 1 T' things saith he that hath the
7 T' things saith he that is holy, he
14 T' things saith the Amen, the
7: 1 after t' things I saw four angels
13 What are t' which are arrayed in
14 T' are they which came out of
9:18 By t' three was the third part of
20 were not killed by t' plagues yet
11: 4 T' are the two olive trees, and the
6 T' have power to shut heaven, that
10 t' two prophets tormented them
14: 4 T' are they which were not defiled
4 T' are they which follow the Lamb
4 T' were redeemed from among
16: 9 which hath power over t' plagues:
17:13 T' have one mind, and shall give
14 T' shall make war with the Lamb,
16 t' shall hate the whore, and shall

Re 18: 1 after *t'* things I saw another angel
15 The merchants of *t'* things, which
19: 1 after *t'* things I heard a great
9 *T'* are the true sayings of God.
20 *T'* both were cast alive into a lake
21: 5 for *t'* words are true and faithful.
22: 6 *T'* sayings are faithful and true:
8 I John saw *t'* things, and heard
8 angel which shewed me *t'* things.
16 angel to testify unto you *t'* things
18 any man shall add unto *t'* things,
20 He which testifieth *t'* things saith,

Thessalonians^ (*thes-sa-lo'-ne-uns*)
Ac 20: 4 and of the *T'*. Aristarchus and
1Th 1: 1 unto the church of the *T'* which
subscr. The first epistle unto the *T'* was
2Th 1: 1 unto the church of the *T'* in God
subscr. The second epistle to the *T'* was

Thessalonica (*thes-sa-lo-ni'-cah*) See also THESSALONIANS.
Ac 17: 1 they came to *T'*, where was a
11 were more noble than those in *T'*,
13 the Jews of *T'* had knowledge
27: 2 Aristarchus, a Macedonian of *T'*,
Ph'p 4: 16 For even in *T'* ye sent once and
2Ti 4: 10 world, and is departed into *T'*;

Theudas (*thew'-das*)
Ac 5: 36 For before these days rose up *T'*,

thick See also THICKER.
Ex 10: 22 there was a *t'* darkness in all the
19: 9 Lo, I come unto thee in a *t'* cloud,
16 and a *t'* cloud upon the mount,
20: 21 Moses drew near unto the *t'* darkness
Le 23: 40 and the boughs of *t'* trees, and
De 4: 11 darkness, clouds, and *t'* darkness.
5: 22 the cloud, and of the *t'* darkness,
32: 15 art waxen fat, thou art grown *t'*,
2Sa 18: 9 under the *t'* boughs of a great oak,
22: 12 waters, and *t'* clouds of the skies.
1Ki 7: 6 and the *t'* beam were before them.
26 And it was an hand breadth *t'*,
8: 12 he would dwell in the *t'* darkness.
2Ki 8: 15 he took a *t'* cloth, and dipped it in
2Ch 6: 1 he would dwell in the *t'* darkness.
Ne 8: 15 and branches of *t'* trees, to make
Job 15: 26 upon the *t'* bosses of his bucklers:
22: 14 *T'* clouds are a covering to him,
26: 8 up the waters in his *t'* clouds;
37: 11 by watering he wearieth the *t'* cloud:
38: 9 *t'* darkness a swaddlingband for it,
Ps 18: 11 dark waters and *t'* clouds of the
12 before his *t'* clouds passed,
74: 5 lifted up axes upon the *t'* trees.
Isa 44: 22 blotted out, as a *t'* cloud, thy
Eze 6: 13 green tree, and under every *t'* oak,
8: 11 and a *t'* cloud of incense went up.
19: 11 was exalted among the *t'* branches,
20: 28 high hill, and all the *t'* trees,
31: 3 his top was among the *t'* boughs.
10 up his top among the *t'* boughs,
14 up their top among the *t'* boughs,
41: 12 of the building was five cubits *t'*
25 *t'* planks upon the face of the
26 of the house, and *t'* planks.
Joe 2: 2 day of clouds and of *t'* darkness,
Hab 2: 6 that ladeth himself with *t'* clay!
Zep 1: 15 a day of clouds and *t'* darkness,
Lu 11: 29 the people were gathered *t'* together,

thicker
1Ki 12: 10 finger shall be *t'* than my father's
2Ch 10: 10 finger shall be *t'* than my father's

thicket See also THICKETS.
Ge 22: 13 a ram caught in a *t'* by his horns:
Jer 4: 7 The lion is come up from his *t'*,

thickets
1Sa 13: 6 hide themselves in caves, and in *t'*,
Isa 9: 18 shall kindle in the *t'* of the forests,
10: 34 shall cut down the *t'* of the forest
Jer 4: 29 they shall go into the *t'*, and climb

thickness
2Ch 4: 5 the *t'* of it was an handbreadth,
Jer 52: 21 and the *t'* thereof was four fingers:
Eze 41: 9 The *t'* of the wall, which was for
42: 10 chambers were in the *t'* of the wall

thief See also THIEVES.
Ex 22: 2 If a *t'* be found breaking up, and
7 if a *t'* be found, let him pay double.
8 If the *t'* be not found, then the
De 24: 7 selleth him; then that *t'* shall die;
Job 24: 14 needy, and in the night is as a *t'*.
30: 5 (they cried after them as after a *t'*;)
Ps 50: 18 When thou sawest a *t'*, then thou
Pr 6: 30 Men do not despise a *t'*, if he steal
29: 24 Whoso is partner with a *t'* hateth
Jer 2: 26 As the *t'* is ashamed when he is
Ho 7: 1 the *t'* cometh in, and the troop of
Joe 2: 9 enter in at the windows like a *t'*.
Zec 5: 4 shall enter into the house of the *t'*,
M't 24: 43 in what watch the *t'* would come,
26: 55 Are ye come out as against a *t'*
M'r 14: 48 Are ye come out, as against a *t'*,
Lu 12: 33 where no *t'* approacheth, neither
39 what hour the *t'* would come,
22: 52 Be ye come out, as against a *t'*,
Joh 10: 1 way, the same is a *t'* and a robber.
10 The *t'* cometh not, but for to steal,
12: 6 but because he was a *t'*, and had a
1Th 5: 2 Lord so cometh as a *t'* in the night.
4 day should overtake you as a *t'*.
1Pe 4: 15 you suffer as a murderer, or as a *t'*,
2Pe 3: 10 Lord will come as a *t'* in the night;

Re 3: 3 watch, I will come on thee as a *t'*,
16: 15 Behold, I come as a *t'*. Blessed is

thieves
Isa 1: 23 rebellious, and companions of *t'*:
Jer 48: 27 unto thee? was he found among *t'*?
49: 9 if *t'* by night, they will destroy till
Ob 5 If *t'* came to thee, if robbers by
M't 6: 19 where *t'* break through and steal:
20 where *t'* do not break through nor
21: 13 but ye have made it a den of *t'*.
27: 38 there two *t'* crucified with him;
44 The *t'* also, which were crucified
M'r 11: 17 but ye have made it a den of *t'*.
15: 27 And with him they crucify two *t'*;
Lu 10: 30 to Jericho, and fell among *t'*,
36 unto him that fell among the *t'*?
19: 46 but ye have made it a den of *t'*.
Joh 10: 8 that ever came before me are *t'*
1Co 6: 10 Nor *t'*, nor covetous, nor drunkards,

thigh See also THIGHS.
Ge 24: 2 pray thee, thy hand under my *t'*:
9 his hand under the *t'* of Abraham
32: 25 he touched the hollow of his *t'*;
25 hollow of Jacob's *t'* was out of joint,
31 him, and he halted upon his *t'*.
32 which is upon the hollow of the *t'*,
32 touched the hollow of Jacob's *t'* in
47: 29 I pray thee, thy hand under my *t'*,
Nu 5: 21 the Lord doth make thy *t'* to rot,
22 thy belly to swell, and thy *t'* to rot:
27 shall swell, and her *t'* shall rot:
J'g 3: 16 under his raiment upon his right *t'*
21 took the dagger from his right *t'*,
15: 8 And he smote them hip and *t'* with
Ps 45: 3 Gird thy sword upon thy *t'*, O most
Ca 3: 8 man hath his sword upon his *t'*
Isa 47: 2 bare the leg, uncover the *t'*,
Jer 31: 19 instructed, I smote upon my *t'*:
Eze 21: 12 smite therefore upon thy *t'*.
24: 4 good piece, the *t'*, and the shoulder:
Re 19: 16 and on his *t'* a name written,

thighs
Ex 28: 42 the loins even unto the *t'* they
Ca 7: 1 the joints of thy *t'* are like jewels,
Da 2: 32 silver, his belly and his *t'* of brass,

Thimnathah (*thim'-nath-ah*) See also TIMNAH.
Jos 19: 43 And Elon, and *T'*, and Ekron,

thin
Ge 41: 6 seven *t'* ears and blasted with the
7 And the seven *t'* ears devoured the
23 behold, seven ears, withered, *t'*,
24 the *t'* ears devoured the seven good
27 the seven *t'* and ill favoured kine
Ex 39: 3 they did beat the gold into *t'* plates,
Le 13: 30 and there be in it a yellow *t'* hair;
1Ki 7: 29 certain additions made of *t'* work.
Isa 17: 4 the glory of Jacob shall be made *t'*,

thine^ See also THY.
Ge 13: 14 Lift up now *t'* eyes, and look from the
14: 20 delivered *t'* enemies into thy hand.
23 that I will not take any thing that is *t'*,
15: 4 him, saying, This shall not be *t'* heir;
4 out of *t'* own bowels shall be *t'* heir.
20: 7 surely die, thou, and all that are *t'*.
21: 18 up the lad, and hold him in *t'* hand;
22: 2 Take now thy son, *t'* only son Isaac,
12 Lay not *t'* hand upon the lad, neither
12 withheld thy son, *t'* only son from me.
16 hast not withheld thy son, *t'* only son:
30: 27 if I have found favour in *t'* eyes, tarry:
31: 12 he said, Lift up now *t'* eyes, and see,
32 discern thou what is *t'* with me,
38: 18 and thy staff that is in *t'* hand.
40: 13 days shall Pharaoh lift up *t'* head,
44: 18 not *t'* anger burn against thy servant:
46: 4 shall put his hand upon *t'* eyes.
47: 19 Wherefore shall we die before *t'* eyes,
48: 6 thou begettest after them, shall be *t'*,
49: 8 shall be in the neck of *t'* enemies;
Ex 4: 4 Put forth *t'* hand, and take it by the
6 him, Put now *t'* hand into thy bosom.
7 Put *t'* hand into thy bosom again.
17 And thou shalt take this rod in *t'* hand,
21 Pharaoh, which I have put in *t'* hand:
5: 16 but the fault is in *t'* own people.
7: 15 to a serpent shalt thou take in *t'* hand.
19 stretch out *t'* hand upon the waters of
8: 3 shall go up and come into *t'* house,
3 and upon thy people, and into *t'* ovens,
5 Stretch forth *t'* hand with thy rod over
9: 14 send all my plagues upon *t'* heart,
22 Stretch forth *t'* hand toward heaven,
10: 12 Stretch out *t'* hand over the land of
21 Stretch out *t'* hand toward heaven,
13: 9 be for a sign unto thee upon *t'* hand,
9 and for a memorial between *t'* eyes,
16 it shall be for a token upon *t'* hand,
16 and for frontlets between *t'* eyes:
14: 16 and stretch out *t'* hand over the sea,
26 Stretch out *t'* hand over the sea, that
15: 7 in the greatness of *t'* excellency thou
16 by the greatness of *t'* arm they shall
17 them in the mountain of *t'* inheritance,
17: 5 thou smotest the river, take in *t'* hand,
20: 24 offerings, thy sheep, and *t'* oxen:
22: 30 Likewise shalt thou do with *t'* oxen,
23: 1 put not *t'* hand with the wicked to be
4 meet *t'* enemy's ox or his ass going
12 that *t'* ox and *t'* ass may rest, and the
22 I will be an enemy unto *t'* enemies,
22 and an adversary unto *t'* adversaries.
27 I will make all *t'* enemies turn their
32: 13 to whom thou swarest by *t'* own self,
34: 9 our sin, and take us for *t'* inheritance.

Le 2: 13 all *t'* offerings thou shalt offer salt.
10: 15 it shall be *t'*, and thy sons' with thee,
18: 10 for theirs is *t'* own nakedness.
19: 17 shalt not hate thy brother in *t'* heart:
27: 23 he shall give *t'* estimation in that day,
27 redeem it according to *t'* estimation,
Nu 5: 20 have lain with thee beside *t'* husband:
10: 35 Lord, and let *t'* enemies be scattered;
18: 9 shall be *t'* of the most holy things,
11 And this is *t'*; the heave offering of
13 shall bring unto the Lord, shall be *t'*;
13 every one that is clean in *t'* house
14 thing devoted in Israel shall be *t'*.
15 it be of men or beasts, shall be *t'*:
16 redeem, according to *t'* estimation,
18 And the flesh of them shall be *t'*,
18 breast and as the right shoulder are *t'*.
20 I am thy part and *t'* inheritance
22: 30 Am not I *t'* ass, upon which thou hast
30 ridden ever since I was *t'* unto this
32 thou smitten *t'* ass these three times?
27: 18 is the spirit, and lay *t'* hand upon him;
20 shalt put some of *t'* honour upon him,
De 2: 24 I have given into *t'* hand Sihon the
3: 21 *T'* eyes have seen all that the Lord
27 Pisgah, and lift up *t'* eyes westward,
27 eastward, and behold it with *t'* eyes:
4: 9 the things which *t'* eyes have seen,
19 lest thou lift up *t'* eyes unto heaven,
39 consider it in *t'* heart, that the Lord
6: 5 the Lord thy God with all *t'* heart,
6 thee this day, shall be in *t'* heart:
7 of them when thou sittest in *t'* house,
8 bind them for a sign upon *t'* hand,
8 shall be as frontlets between *t'* eyes.
19 To cast out all *t'* enemies from before
7: 16 *t'* eye shall have no pity upon them:
17 say in *t'* heart, These nations are
19 great temptations which *t'* eyes saw,
24 shall deliver their kings into *t'* hand,
26 bring an abomination into *t'* house,
8: 2 thee, to know what was in *t'* heart,
5 Thou shalt also consider in *t'* heart,
14 Then *t'* heart be lifted up, and thou
17 And thou say in *t'* heart, My power
9: 4 Speak not thou in *t'* heart, after that
5 or for the uprightness of *t'* heart, dost
29 are thy people and *t'* inheritance,
10: 21 things, which *t'* eyes have seen.
11: 14 in thy corn, and thy wine, and *t'* oil.
20 them upon the door posts of *t'* house,
12: 17 offerings, or heave offering of *t'* hand:
18 in all that thou puttest *t'* hands unto.
13: 6 thy friend, which is as *t'* own soul,
9 *t'* hand shall be first upon him to
14: 23 of thy corn, of thy wine, and of *t'* oil,
25 and bind up the money in *t'* hand,
26 shalt rejoice, thou, and *t'* household,
28 bring forth all the tithe of *t'* increase
29 bless thee in all the work of *t'* hand
15: 3 but that which is *t'* with thy brother
3 with thy brother *t'* hand shall release;
7 thee, thou shalt not harden *t'* heart,
7 nor shut *t'* hand from thy poor brother:
8 thou shalt open *t'* hand wide unto
9 *t'* eye be evil against thy poor brother,
10 *t'* heart shall not be grieved when thou
10 in all that thou puttest *t'* hand unto.
11 open *t'* hand wide unto thy brother,
16 because he loveth thee and *t'* house,
16: 10 tribute of a freewill offering of *t'* hand,
15 God shall bless thee in all *t'* increase,
15 and in all the works of *t'* hands,
18: 21 say in *t'* heart, How shall we know the
19: 13 *T'* eye shall not pity him, but thou
14 of old time have set in *t'* inheritance,
21 *t'* eye shall not pity; but life shall go.
20: 1 goest out to battle against *t'* enemies,
13 thy God hath delivered it into *t'* hands,
14 thou shalt eat the spoil of *t'* enemies,
21: 10 goest forth to war against *t'* enemies,
10 God hath delivered them into *t'* hands,
12 thou shalt bring her home to *t'* house;
13 shall remain in *t'* house, and bewail
22: 2 thou shalt bring it unto *t'* own house,
8 thou bring not blood upon *t'* house,
23: 9 host goeth forth against *t'* enemies,
14 and to give up *t'* enemies before thee;
20 thee in all that thou settest *t'* hand to
24 eat grapes thy fill at *t'* own pleasure;
25 mayest pluck the ears with *t'* hand;
24: 19 cuttest down *t'* harvest in thy field,
19 bless thee in all the work of *t'* hands.
20 When thou beatest *t'* olive tree, thou
25: 12 off her hand, *t'* eye shall not pity her.
14 have in *t'* house divers measures,
19 given thee rest from all *t'* enemies
26: 4 shall take the basket out of *t'* hand,
11 given unto thee, and unto *t'* house,
12 all the tithes of *t'* increase the third
16 keep and do them with all *t'* heart,
28: 7 The Lord shall cause *t'* enemies that
8 in all that thou settest *t'* hand unto;
12 and to bless all the work of *t'* hand:
20 in all that thou settest *t'* hand unto
25 thee to be smitten before *t'* enemies:
31 *T'* ox shall be slain before *t'* eyes, and
31 *t'* ass shall be violently taken away
31 sheep shall be given unto *t'* enemies,
32 *t'* eyes shall look, and fail with
32 there shall be no might in *t'* hand.
34 shalt be mad for the sight of *t'* eyes
40 oil; for *t'* olive shall cast his fruit.
48 shalt thou serve *t'* enemies which
53 thou shalt eat the fruit of *t'* own body,
53 *t'* enemies shall distress thee:

De 28: 55 t' enemies shall distress thee in all
57 t' enemy shall distress thee in thy
67 fear of t' heart wherewith thou shalt
67 for the sight of t' eyes which thou
29: 3 temptations which t' eyes have seen,
30: 2 with all t' heart, and with all thy soul;
4 If any of t' be driven out unto the
6 thy God will circumcise t' heart,
6 the Lord thy God with all t' heart,
7 put all these curses upon t' enemies,
9 plenteous in every work of t' hand,
10 the Lord thy God with all t' heart,
17 But if t' heart turn away, so that thou
33: 10 whole burnt sacrifice upon t' altar.
29 t' enemies shall be found liars unto
34: 4 caused thee to see it with t' eyes,
Jos 2: 3 thee, which are entered into t' house:
17 We will be blameless of this t' oath
20 then we will be quit of t' oath which
6: 2 I have given into t' hand Jericho,
7: 13 canst not stand before t' enemies,
8: 18 Ai; for I will give it into t' hand.
9: 25 And now, behold, we are in t' hand:
10: 8 I have delivered them into t' hand;
14: 9 have trodden shall be t' inheritance,
17: 18 But the mountain shall be t'; for it is
18 and the outgoings of it shall be t':
J'g 4: 7 and I will deliver him into t' hand.
9 thou takest shall not be for t' honour;
14 hath delivered Sisera into t' hand:
5: 31 So let all t' enemies perish, O Lord:
6: 39 Let not t' anger be hot against me,
7: 7 deliver the Midianites into t' hand:
9 for I have delivered it into t' hand.
11 shall t' hands be strengthened
8: 6 Zebah and Zalmunna now in t' hand,
6 we should give bread unto t' army?
15 Zebah and Zalmunna now in t' hand,
9: 29 to Abimelech, Increase t' army, and
11: 36 vengeance for thee of t' enemies,
12: 1 burn t' house upon thee with fire.
16: 15 thee, when t' heart is not with me?
18: 19 lay t' hand upon thy mouth, and go
19: 5 Comfort t' heart with a morsel of
6 all night, and let t' heart be merry.
8 said, Comfort t' heart, I pray thee.
9 here, that t' heart may be merry;
22 forth the man that came into t' house,
20: 28 I will deliver them into t' hand.
Ru 2: 9 Let t' eyes be on the field that they do
10 Why have I found grace in t' eyes,
11 in law since the death of t' husband:
13 spoken friendly unto t' handmaid,
13 not like unto one of t' handmaidens.
3: 9 answered, I am Ruth t' handmaid:
9 therefore thy skirt over t' handmaid;
4: 11 that is come into t' house like Rachel
15 thy life, and a nourisher of t' old age:
1Sa 1: 11 look on the affliction of t' handmaid,
11 me, and not forget t' handmaid,
11 wilt give unto t' handmaid a man
16 Count not t' handmaid for a daughter
18 Let t' handmaid find grace in thy
2: 31 days come, that I will cut off t' arm,
31 shall not be an old man in t' house.
32 not be an old man in t' house for ever.
33 the man of t', whom I shall not cut
33 consume t' eyes, and to grieve t' heart:
33 all the increase of t' house shall die
36 every one that is left in t' house shall
9: 19 and will tell thee all that is in t' heart.
20 for t' asses that were lost three days
14: 7 unto him, Do all that is in t' heart:
19 unto the priest, Withdraw t' hand.
15: 17 When thou wast little in t' own sight,
28 and hath given it to a neighbour of t',
16: 1 fill t' horn with oil, and go, I will send
17: 28 pride, and the naughtiness of t' heart;
46 thee, and take t' head from thee;
20: 3 that I have found grace in t' eyes;
29 if I have found favour in t' eyes, let
30 the son of Jesse to t' own confusion,
21: 3 Now therefore what is under t' hand?
8 is there not here under t' hand spear
22: 14 bidding, and is honourable in t' house?
23: 4 deliver the Philistines into t' hand.
24: 4 I will deliver t' enemy into t' hand,
10 this day t' eyes have seen how that the
15 cause, and deliver me out of t' hand.
18 Lord had delivered me into t' hand,
20 Israel shall be established in t' hand.
25: 6 both to thee, and peace be to t' house,
8 the young men find favour in t' eyes:
8 whatsoever cometh to t' hand unto
24 and let t' handmaid, I pray thee,
24 speak in t' audience, and hear the
24 and hear the words of t' handmaid.
25 I t' handmaid saw not the young men
26 avenging thyself with t' own hand,
26 now let t' enemies, and they that
27 now this blessing which t' handmaid
28 forgive the trespass of t' handmaid:
29 and the souls of t' enemies, them shall
31 my lord, then remember t' handmaid.
35 unto her, Go up in peace to t' house;
41 let t' handmaid be a servant to wash
26: 8 hath delivered t' enemy into t' hand
21 my soul was precious in t' eyes this
27: 5 If I have now found grace in t' eyes,
28: 16 from thee, and is become t' enemy?
17 hath rent the kingdom out of t' hand,
21 t' handmaid hath obeyed thy voice,
22 also unto the voice of t' handmaid,
2Sa 1: 14 not afraid to stretch forth t' hand to
16 thou wast slain in t' high places.
3: 21 reign over all that t' heart desireth.
2Sa 4: 8 Ish-bosheth the son of Saul t' enemy,
5: 19 deliver the Philistines into t' hand.
7: 3 the king, Go, do all that is in t' heart;
9 have cut off all t' enemies out of thy
11 thee to rest from all t' enemies.
16 t' house and thy kingdom shall be
21 according to t' own heart, hast thou
11: 10 didst thou not go down unto t' house?
12: 10 shall never depart from t' house;
11 evil against thee out of t' own house,
11 I will take thy wives before t' eyes,
13: 10 chamber, that I may eat of t' hand.
14: 7 family is risen against t' handmaid,
8 Go to t' house, and I will give charge
12 Let t' handmaid, I pray thee, speak
17 Then t' handmaid said, The word of
19 words in the mouth of t' handmaid:
16: 4 t' are all that pertained unto
17: 11 thou go to battle in t' own person.
19: 6 In that thou lovest t' enemies, and
27 do therefore what is good in t' eyes.
28 them that did eat at t' own table.
20: 17 him, Hear the words of t' handmaid.
22: 28 t' eyes are upon the haughty, that
24: 13 flee three months before t' enemies,
16 people, It is enough: stay now t' hand.
17 let t' hand, I pray thee, be against me,
1Ki 1: 12 that thou mayest save t' own life, and
13 O king, swear unto t' handmaid,
17 by the Lord thy God unto t' handmaid,
53 said unto him, Go to t' house.
2: 26 thee to Anathoth, unto t' own fields;
37 thy blood shall be upon t' own head.
44 wickedness which t' heart is privy to,
44 thy wickedness upon t' own head;
3: 11 nor hast asked the life of t' enemies;
20 beside me, while t' handmaid slept,
26 it be neither mine nor t', but divide it.
8: 18 it was in t' heart to build an house
18 thou didst well that it was in t' heart.
24 and hast fulfilled it with t' hand,
29 That t' eyes may be open toward this
31 the oath come before t' altar in this
51 they be thy people, and t' inheritance,
52 That t' eyes may be open unto the
53 of the earth, to be t' inheritance,
11: 22 thou seekest to go to t' own country?
12: 16 now see to t' own house, David.
13: 8 If thou wilt give me half t' house, I
18 Bring him back with thee into t' house,
14: 12 therefore, get thee to t' own house:
17: 11 thee, a morsel of bread in t' hand.
19: 10, 14 thrown down t' altars, and slain thy
20: 4 thy saying, I am t', and all that I have.
6 they shall search t' house, and the
6 that whatsoever is pleasant in t' eyes,
13 I will deliver it into t' hand this day;
28 all this great multitude into t' hand,
21: 7 eat bread, and let t' heart be merry:
19 shall dogs lick thy blood, even t'.
22 And will make t' house like the house
22: 34 Turn t' hand, and carry me out of the
2Ki 4: 2 T' handmaid hath not any thing in
16 of God, do not lie unto t' handmaid.
29 and take my staff in t' hand, and go
7: 2, 19 thou shalt see it with t' eyes, but
8: 1 Arise, and go thou and t' household,
8 Take a present in t' hand, and go,
9: 1 and take this box of oil in t' hand,
10: 5 do thou that which is good in t' eyes.
15 Is t' heart right, as my heart is with
13: 16 of Israel, Put t' hand upon the bow.
14: 10 and t' heart hath lifted thee up:
19: 16 Lord, bow down t' ear, and hear:
16 open, Lord, t' eyes, and see: and hear
22 voice, and lifted up t' eyes on high?
20: 1 Set t' house in order; for thou shalt
15 said, What have they seen in t' house?
17 days come, that all that is in t' house,
22: 19 Because t' heart was tender, and thou
20 t' eyes shall not see all the evil which
1Ch 4: 10 and that t' hand might be with me,
12: 18 T' are we, David, and on thy side,
18 unto thee, and peace be to t' helpers;
14: 10 for I will deliver them into t' hand.
17: 2 unto David, Do all that is in t' heart;
8 cut off all t' enemies from before thee,
10 Moreover I will subdue all t' enemies.
17 was a small thing in t' eyes, O God;
19 according to t' own heart, hast thou
22 Israel didst thou make t' own people
21: 12 sword of t' enemies overtaketh thee;
15 It is enough, stay now t' hand.
17 let t' hand, I pray thee, O Lord my
24 not take that which is t' for the Lord,
29: 11 T', O Lord, is the greatness, and the
11 is in the heaven and in the earth is t';
11 t' is the kingdom, O Lord, and thou
12 and in t' hand is power and might;
12 and in t' hand it is to make great, and
14 and of t' own have we given thee.
16 build thee an house for t' holy name
16 cometh of t' hand, and is all t' own.
2Ch 1: 11 Because this was in t' heart, and thou
11 or honour, nor the life of t' enemies,
6: 8 as it was in t' heart to build an house
8 didst well in that it was in t' heart:
15 and hast fulfilled it with t' hand, as it
20 That t' eyes may be open upon this
22 the oath come before t' altar in this
40 Now, my God, let,...t' eyes be open,
40 let t' ears be attent unto the prayer
42 turn not away the face of t' anointed:
9: 5 I heard in mine own land of t' acts,
10: 16 and now, David, see to t' own house.
16: 7 king of Syria escaped out of t' hand.
2Ch 16: 8 Lord, he delivered them into t' hand.
18: 33 Turn t' hand, that thou mayest carry
19: 3 hast prepared t' heart to seek God.
20: 6 in t' hand is there not power and
25: 15 their own people out of t' hand?
19 and t' heart lifteth thee up to boast:
19 why shouldest thou meddle to t' hurt,
26: 18 neither shall it be for t' honour from
34: 27 Because t' heart was tender, and thou
28 neither shall t' eyes see all the evil
Ezr 7: 14 law of thy God which is in t' hand;
25 wisdom of thy God, that is in t' hand,
Ne 1: 6 Let t' ear now be attentive, and
6 and t' eyes open, that thou mayest
11 let now t' ear be attentive to the prayer
6: 8 thou feignest them out of t' own heart.
Job 1: 11 But put forth t' hand now, and touch
12 upon himself put not forth t' hand.
2: 5 But put forth t' hand now, and touch
6 he is in t' hand; but save his life.
9 Dost thou still retain t' integrity?
5: 25 t' offspring as the grass of the earth.
7: 8 t' eyes are upon me, and I am not.
17 thou shouldest set t' heart upon him?
10: 3 shouldest despise the work of t' hands,
7 none that can deliver out of t' hand.
8 T' hands have made me and
13 these things hast thou hid in t' heart:
17 increasest t' indignation upon me;
11: 4 is pure, and I am clean in t' eyes.
6 of thee less than t' iniquity deserveth.
13 If thou prepare t' heart, and stretch
13 and stretch out t' hands toward him;
14 If iniquity be in t' hand, put it far
17 And t' age shall be clearer than the
13: 21 Withdraw t' hand far from me: and
24 thy face, and holdest me for t' enemy?
14: 3 thou open t' eyes upon such an one,
15 have a desire to the work of t' hands.
15: 5 For thy mouth uttereth t' iniquity,
6 T' own mouth condemneth thee, and
6 yea, t' own lips testify against thee.
12 Why doth t' heart carry thee away?
22: 5 great? and t' iniquities infinite?
22 and lay up his words in t' heart.
30 delivered by the pureness of t' hands.
35: 7 him? or what receiveth he of t' hand?
40: 14 that t' own right hand can save thee.
41: 8 Lay t' hand upon him, remember the
Ps 2: 8 thee the heathen for t' inheritance,
6: 1 O Lord, rebuke me not in t' anger,
7: 6 Arise, O Lord, in t' anger, lift up
8: 2 strength because of t' enemies,
10: 12 O God, lift up t' hand: forget not the
17 heart, thou wilt cause t' ear to hear:
16: 10 wilt thou suffer t' Holy One to see
17: 2 let t' eyes behold the things that are
6 incline t' ear unto me, and hear my
20: 4 Grant thee according to t' own heart,
21: 8 T' hand shall find out all t' enemies:
9 as a fiery oven in the time of t' anger:
12 make ready t' arrows upon thy strings
13 thou exalted, Lord, in t' own strength:
26: 6 so will I compass t' altar, O Lord:
8 the place where t' honour dwelleth.
27: 14 and he shall strengthen t' heart:
28: 9 thy people, and bless t' inheritance:
31: 2 Bow down t' ear to me; deliver me
5 Into t' hand I commit my spirit: thou
22 haste, I am cut off from before t' eyes:
37: 4 he shall give thee the desire of t' heart.
38: 2 For t' arrows stick fast in me, and thy
3 in my flesh because of t' anger;
39: 10 I am consumed by the blow of t' hand.
44: 3 t' arm,...the light of thy countenance,
45: 5 T' arrows are sharp in the heart of the
10 and consider, and incline t' ear;
10 forget also t' own people, and thy
50: 20 thou slanderest t' own mother's son.
21 and set them in order before t' eyes.
51: 19 shall they offer bullocks upon t' altar.
56: 7 in t' anger cast down the people, O
66: 3 shall t' enemies submit themselves
68: 9 thou didst confirm t' inheritance,
23 be dipped in the blood of t' enemies,
69: 9 the zeal of t' house hath eaten me up;
24 Pour out t' indignation upon them,
71: 2 incline t' ear unto me, and save me.
16 of thy righteousness, even of t' only.
74: 1 why doth t' anger smoke against the
2 rod of t' inheritance, which thou hast
4 T' enemies roar in the midst of thy
16 The day is t', the night also is t': thou
22 Arise, O God, plead t' own cause:
23 Forget not the voice of t' enemies: the
77: 15 hast with t' arm redeemed thy people,
17 a sound: t' arrows also went abroad.
79: 1 heathen are come into t' inheritance;
83: 2 For, lo, t' enemies make a tumult:
84: 3 she may lay her young, even t' altars,
9 and look upon the face of t' anointed.
85: 3 thyself from the fierceness of t' anger.
4 and cause t' anger toward us to cease.
5 wilt thou draw out t' anger to all
86: 1 Bow down t' ear, O Lord, hear me: for
16 and save the son of t' handmaid.
88: 2 before thee: incline t' ear unto my cry;
89: 10 hast scattered t' enemies with thy
11 the heavens are t', the earth also is t':
38 thou hast been wroth with t' anointed.
51 Wherewith t' enemies...reproached, O
51 reproached the footsteps of t' anointed.
90: 7 For we are consumed by t' anger, and
11 Who knoweth the power of t' anger?
91: 8 Only with t' eyes shalt thou behold
92: 9 For, lo, t' enemies, O Lord, for, lo,

Ps 92: 9 *t'* enemies shall perish; all the
93: 5 holiness becometh *t'* house, O Lord,
94: 5 people, O Lord, and afflict *t'* heritage.
102: 2 am in trouble; incline *t'* ear unto me:
10 Because of *t'* indignation and thy
103: 3 Who forgiveth all *t'* iniquities; who
104: 28 thou openest *t'* hand, they are filled
106: 5 that I may glory with *t'* inheritance.
110: 1 until I make *t'* enemies thy footstool.
2 rule thou in the midst of *t'* enemies.
116: 16 servant, and the son of *t'* handmaid:
119: 91 this day according to *t'* ordinances:
94 I am *t'*, save me; for I have sought
173 Let *t'* hand help me; for I have chosen
128: 2 thou shalt eat the labour of *t'* hands:
3 a fruitful vine by the side of *t'* house:
130: 2 let *t'* ears be attentive to the voice of
132: 10 turn not away the face of *t'* anointed.
138: 7 thou shalt stretch forth *t'* hand against
8 forsake not the works of *t'* own hands.
139: 5 and before, and laid *t'* hand upon me.
16 *T'* eyes did see my substance, yet
20 and *t'* enemies take thy name in vain.
144: 6 shoot out *t'* arrows, and destroy them.
7 Send *t'* hand from above; rid me, and
145: 16 Thou openest *t'* hand, and satisfiest
Pr 2: 2 that thou incline *t'* ear unto wisdom,
2 and apply *t'* heart to understanding;
10 When wisdom entereth into *t'* heart,
3: 1 let *t'* heart keep my commandments:
3 write them upon the table of *t'* heart:
5 Trust in the Lord with all *t'* heart;
5 lean not unto *t'* own understanding.
7 Be not wise in *t'* own eyes: fear the
9 with the firstfruits of all *t'* increase:
21 son, let not them depart from *t'* eyes:
27 it is in the power of *t'* hand to do it.
4: 4 unto me, Let *t'* heart retain my words:
9 give to *t'* head an ornament of grace:
20 words; incline *t'* ear unto my sayings.
21 Let them not depart from *t'* eyes;
21 keep them in the midst of *t'* heart.
25 Let *t'* eyes look right on, and let
25 let *t'* eyelids look straight before thee.
5: 1 and bow *t'* ear to my understanding:
9 Lest thou give *t'* honour unto others,
15 Drink waters out of *t'* own cistern, and
15 and running waters out of *t'* own well.
17 Let them be only *t'* own, and not
6: 4 Give not sleep to *t'* eyes, nor slumber
4 eyes, nor slumber to *t'* eyelids.
21 Bind them continually upon *t'* heart,
25 Lust not after her beauty in *t'* heart;
7: 2 live; and my law as the apple of *t'* eye.
3 write them upon the table of *t'* heart.
25 Let not *t'* heart decline to her ways, go
20: 13 open *t'* eyes, and thou shalt be satisfied
22: 17 Bow down *t'* ear, and hear the words
17 and apply *t'* heart unto my knowledge.
23: 4 to be rich: cease from *t'* own wisdom.
5 thou set *t'* eyes upon that which is not?
12 Apply *t'* heart unto instruction, and
12 and *t'* ears to the words of knowledge.
15 if *t'* heart be wise, my heart shall
17 Let not *t'* heart envy sinners: but be
18 and *t'* expectation shall not be cut off.
19 be wise, and guide *t'* heart in the way.
26 My son, give me *t'* heart, and let
26 heart, and let *t'* eyes observe my ways.
33 *T'* eyes shall behold strange women,
33 *t'* heart shall utter perverse things.
24: 17 Rejoice not when *t'* enemy falleth, and
17 let not *t'* heart be glad when he
27 field; and afterwards build *t'* house.
25: 7 of the prince whom *t'* eyes have seen.
10 shame, and *t'* infamy turn not away.
21 If *t'* enemy be hungry, give him bread
27: 2 praise thee, and not *t'* own month;
2 a stranger, and not *t'* own lips.
10 *T'* own friend, and thy father's friend,
30: 32 evil, lay *t'* hand upon thy mouth.
Ec 5: 2 not *t'* heart be hasty to utter any thing
6 and destroy the work of *t'* hands?
7: 18 also from this withdraw not *t'* hand:
22 oftentimes also *t'* own heart knoweth
11: 6 in the evening withhold not *t'* hand:
9 and walk in the ways of *t'* heart, and
9 and in the sight of *t'* eyes: but know
Ca 4: 9 ravished my heart with one of *t'* eyes,
10 smell of *t'* ointments than all spices!
6: 5 Turn away *t'* eyes from me, for they
7: 4 *t'* eyes like the fishpools in Heshbon,
5 *T'* head upon thee is like Carmel, and
5 and the hair of *t'* head like purple;
8: 6 Set me as a seal upon *t'* heart, as a seal
6 as a seal upon *t'* arm; for love is
Isa 6: 7 *t'* iniquity is taken away, and thy sin
12: 1 *t'* anger is turned away, and thou
14: 13 For thou hast said in *t'* heart, I will
26: 11 fire of *t'* enemies shall devour them.
30: 20 but *t'* eyes shall see thy teachers:
21 *t'* ears shall hear a word behind thee,
33: 17 *T'* eyes shall see the king in...beauty:
18 *T'* heart shall meditate terror. Where
20 *t'* eyes shall see Jerusalem a quiet
37: 17 Incline *t'* ear, O Lord, and hear; open
17 hear; open *t'* eyes, O Lord, and see:
23 thy voice, and lifted up *t'* eyes on high?
38: 1 Set *t'* house in order: for thou shalt
39: 4 he, What have they seen in *t'* house?
6 days come, that all that is in *t'* house,
42: 6 will hold *t'* hand, and will keep thee,
43: 24 hast wearied me with *t'* iniquities.
44: 3 and my blessing upon *t'* offspring:
45: 14 over unto thee, and they shall be *t'*:
47: 6 and given them into *t'* hand:

Isa 47: 8 that sayest in *t'* heart, I am, and none
9 great abundance of *t'* enchantments.
10 and thou hast said in *t'* heart, I am,
12 Stand now with *t'* enchantments, and
48: 8 that time that *t'* ear was not opened:
49: 18 Lift up *t'* eyes round about, and
20 the other, shall say again in *t'* ears,
21 Then shalt thou say in *t'* heart, Who
51: 22 have taken out of *t'* hand the cup of
54: 2 forth the curtains of *t'* habitations:
5 For thy Maker is *t'* husband; the Lord
57: 10 thou hast found the life of *t'* hand;
58: 7 thou hide not thyself from *t'* own flesh?
8 *t'* health shall spring forth speedily:
13 honour him, not doing *t'* own ways,
13 nor finding *t'* own pleasure, nor
13 pleasure, nor speaking *t'* own words:
60: 4 Lift up *t'* eyes round about, and see:
5 *t'* heart shall fear, and be enlarged;
17 peace, and *t'* exactors righteousness.
20 the Lord shall be *t'* everlasting light,
62: 8 thy corn to be meat for *t'* enemies;
63: 2 Wherefore art thou red in *t'* apparel,
17 sake, the tribes of *t'* inheritance.
19 We art *t'*: thou never barest rule
64: 2 thy name known to *t'* adversaries,
Jer 2: 2 of thy youth, the love of *t'* espousals,
19 *T'* own wickedness shall correct thee,
22 yet *t'* iniquity is marked before me,
37 from him, and *t'* hands upon *t'* head:
3: 2 Lift up *t'* eyes unto the high places,
13 Only acknowledge *t'* iniquity, that
4: 1 put away *t'* abominations out of my
14 wash *t'* heart from wickedness,
18 because it reacheth unto *t'* heart.
5: 3 Lord, are not *t'* eyes upon the truth?
17 shall eat up *t'* harvest, and thy bread,
17 shall eat up thy flocks and *t'* herds:
6: 9 turn back *t'* hand as a grapegatherer
7: 29 Cut off *t'* hair, O Jerusalem, and cast
9: 6 *T'* habitation is in the midst of
10: 24 not in *t'* anger, lest thou bring me to
13: 22 And if thou say in *t'* heart, Wherefore
22 For the greatness of *t'* iniquity are thy
27 I have seen *t'* adulteries, and thy
27 and *t'* abominations on the hills in
15: 14 to pass with *t'* enemies into a land
17: 4 discontinue from *t'* heritage that I
4 I will cause thee to serve *t'* enemies in
18: 23 thus with them in the time of *t'* anger.
20: 4 enemies, and *t'* eyes shall behold it:
6 Pashur, and all that dwell in *t'* house
22: 17 But *t'* eyes and *t'* heart are not but for
25: 28 refuse to take the cup at *t'* hand to
28: 7 now this word that I speak in *t'* ears,
30: 14 one, for the multitude of *t'* iniquity;
15 Why criest thou for *t'* affliction? thy
15 for the multitude of *t'* iniquity:
16 all *t'* adversaries, every one of them,
31: 16 from weeping, and *t'* eyes from tears:
17 And there is hope in *t'* end, saith the
21 set *t'* heart toward the highway, even
32: 7 Hanameel the son of Shallum *t'* uncle
7 the right of redemption is *t'* to buy it.
8 for the right of inheritance is *t'*, and
8 the redemption is *t'*; buy it for thyself.
19 for *t'* eyes are open upon all the ways
34: 3 *t'* eyes shall behold the eyes of the
36: 14 Take in *t'* hand the roll wherein thou
38: 12 rotten rags under *t'* armholes under
17 fire; and thou shalt live, and *t'* house:
40: 4 the chains which were upon *t'* hand.
42: 2 few of many, as *t'* eyes do behold us:)
43: 9 Take great stones in *t'* hand, and
49: 16 and the pride of *t'* heart, O thou that
51: 13 abundant in treasures, *t'* end is come,
La 2: 14 they have not discovered *t'* iniquity,
16 *t'* enemies have opened their mouth
17 caused *t'* enemy to rejoice over thee,
17 set up the horn of *t'* adversaries.
18 rest; let not the apple of *t'* eye cease.
19 pour out *t'* heart like water before
21 hast slain them in the day of *t'* anger;
3: 56 hide not *t'* ear at my breathing, at my
4: 22 The punishment of *t'* iniquity is
22 he will visit *t'* iniquity, O daughter of
Eze 3: 10 speak unto thee receive in *t'* heart,
10 heart, and hear with *t'* ears.
18, 20 his blood will I require at *t'* hand.
24 me, Go, shut thyself within *t'* house.
4: 7 and *t'* arm shall be uncovered,
5: 1 and cause it to pass upon *t'* head and
9 like, because of all *t'* abominations.
11 and with all *t'* abominations, therefore
6: 11 Smite with *t'* hand, and stamp with
7: 3 upon thee all *t'* abominations.
4 *t'* abominations shall be in the midst
8 thee for all *t'* abominations.
9 thy ways and *t'* abominations that are
8: 5 lift up *t'* eyes now the way toward the
10: 2 fill *t'* hands with coals of fire between
16: 6 saw thee polluted in *t'* own blood, I
7 are fashioned, and *t'* hair is grown,
12 thy forehead, and earrings in *t'* ears,
12 and a beautiful crown upon *t'* head.
15 But thou didst trust in *t'* own beauty,
22 *t'* abominations and thy whoredoms
27 and have diminished *t'* ordinary food,
30 How weak is *t'* heart, saith the Lord
31 buildest *t'* eminent place in the head
31 makest *t'* high place in every street;
39 shall throw down *t'* eminent place,
41 they shall burn *t'* houses with fire, and
43 will recompense thy way upon *t'* head,
43 lewdness above all *t'* abominations.
46 *t'* elder sister is Samaria, she and her

Eze 16: 51 multiplied *t'* abominations more than
51 thy sisters in all *t'* abominations
52 bear *t'* own shame for thy sins that
54 That thou mayest bear *t'* own shame,
58 thy lewdness and *t'* abominations,
61 thy sisters, *t'* elder and thy younger:
21: 14 prophesy, and smite *t'* hands together,
22: 4 and hast defiled thyself in *t'* idols
14 Can *t'* heart endure, or can
14 can *t'* hands be strong, in the days
16 shalt take *t'* inheritance in thyself
23: 25 shall take away thy nose and *t'* ears;
27 shalt not lift up *t'* eyes unto them,
31 will I give her cup into *t'* hand.
34 thereof, and pluck off *t'* own breasts:
24: 16 the desire of *t'* eyes with a stroke:
17 bind the tire of *t'* head upon thee,
26 to cause thee to hear it with *t'* ears?
25: 6 Because thou hast clapped *t'* hands,
27: 6 of Bashan have they made *t'* oars;
10 of Lud and of Phut were in *t'* army,
11 The men of Arvad with *t'* army were
15 isles were the merchandise of *t'* hand:
28: 2 Because *t'* heart is lifted up, and thou
2 thou set *t'* heart as the heart of God:
4 thy wisdom and with *t'* understanding
5 *t'* heart is lifted up because of thy
6 hast set *t'* heart as the heart of God;
17 *T'* heart was lifted up because of thy
18 by the multitude of *t'* iniquities, by
33: 8 but his blood will I require at *t'* hand.
35: 11 I will even do according to *t'* anger,
11 according to *t'* envy which thou hast
37: 17 and they shall become one in *t'* hand.
20 shall be in *t'* hand before their eyes.
38: 4 will bring thee forth, and all *t'* army,
12 turn *t'* hand upon the desolate places
39: 3 *t'* arrows to fall out of thy right hand.
40: 4 me, Son of man, behold with *t'* eyes,
4 eyes, and hear with *t'* ears,
4 set *t'* heart upon all that I shall shew
44: 5 mark well, and behold with *t'* eyes,
5 hear with *t'* ears all that I say unto
30 cause the blessing to rest in *t'* house.
Da 2: 38 the heaven hath he given into *t'* hand,
3: 17 and he will deliver us out of *t'* hand, O
4: 19 interpretation thereof to *t'* enemies.
27 *t'* iniquities by shewing mercy to the
5: 22 hast not humbled *t'* heart, though
9: 16 *t'* anger and thy fury be turned away
18 O my God, incline *t'* ear, and hear;
18 open *t'* eyes, and behold our
19 defer not, for *t'* own sake, O my God:
10: 12 thou didst set *t'* heart to understand,
Ho 9: 7 mad, for the multitude of *t'* iniquity,
13: 9 thyself; but in me is *t'* help.
14: 1 for thou hast fallen by *t'* iniquity.
Joe 2: 17 and give not *t'* heritage to reproach,
Ob 3 The pride of *t'* heart hath deceived
15 reward shall return upon *t'* own head.
Jon 1: 8 What is *t'* occupation? and whence
2: 7 came in unto thee, into *t'* holy temple.
Mic 4: 10 thee from the hand of *t'* enemies.
13 of Zion: for I will make *t'* horn iron,
5: 9 *T'* hand shall be lifted up upon
9 shall be lifted up upon *t'* adversaries,
9 and all *t'* enemies shall be cut off.
12 will cut off witchcrafts out of *t'* hand;
13 more worship the work of *t'* hands.
7: 14 the flock of *t'* heritage, which dwell
Na 3: 13 be set wide open unto *t'* enemies:
Hab 3: 8 was *t'* anger against the rivers? was
8 that thou didst ride upon *t'* horses
11 at the light of *t'* arrows they went,
13 even for salvation with *t'* anointed;
15 walk through the sea with *t'* horses,
Zep 3: 15 judgments, he hath cast out *t'* enemy:
16 and to Zion, Let not *t'* hands be slack.
Zec 3: 4 I have caused *t'* iniquity to pass from
5: 5 Lift up now *t'* eyes, and see what is
13: 6 What are these wounds in *t'* hands?
M't 5: 25 Agree with *t'* adversary quickly,
33 perform unto the Lord *t'* oaths:
43 thy neighbour, and hate *t'* enemy.
6: 2 Therefore when thou doest *t'* alms,
4 That *t'* alms may be in secret:
13 *t'* is the kingdom, and the power,
17 when thou fastest, anoint *t'* head,
22 if therefore *t'* eye be single, thy
23 But if *t'* eye be evil, thy whole body
7: 3 not the beam that is in *t'* own eye?
4 me pull out the mote out of *t'* eye;
4 behold, a beam is in *t'* own eye?
5 cast out the beam out of *t'* own eye;
9: 6 up thy bed, and go unto *t'* house.
12: 13 to the man, Stretch forth *t'* hand.
18: 9 if *t'* eye offend thee, pluck it out,
20: 14 Take that *t'* is, and go thy way: I
15 Is *t'* eye evil, because I am good?
22: 44 till I make *t'* enemies thy footstool?
25: 25 lo, there thou hast that is *t'*.
M'r 2: 11 bed, and go thy way into *t'* house.
3: 5 the man, Stretch forth *t'* hand.
9: 47 if *t'* eye offend thee, pluck it out:
12: 36 till I make *t'* enemies thy footstool.
Lu 4: 7 wilt worship me, all shall be *t'*.
5: 24 up thy couch, and go into *t'* house.
33 Pharisees; but *t'* eat and drink?
6: 41 not the beam that is in *t'* own eye?
42 pull out the mote that is in *t'* eye,
42 not the beam that is in *t'* own eye?
42 out first the beam out of *t'* own eye,
7: 44 I entered into *t'* house, thou gavest
8: 39 Return to *t'* own house, and shew
11: 34 therefore when *t'* eye is single, thy
34 but when *t'* eye is evil, thy body also

Lu 12:19 take t' ease, eat, drink, and be merry.
58 When thou goest with t' adversary
13:12 thou art loosed from t' infirmity.
15:31 with me, and all that I have is t'.
19:22 Out of t' own mouth will I judge
42 but now they are hid from t' eyes.
43 that t' enemies shall cast a trench
20:43 I make t' enemies thy footstool.
22:42 not my will, but t', be done.
Joh 2:17 zeal of t' house hath eaten me up.
8:10 where are those t' accusers?
9:10 unto him, How were t' eyes opened?
17 of him, that he hath opened t' eyes?
26 he to thee? how opened he t' eyes?
17: 5 glorify thou me with t' own self
6 t' they were, and thou gavest them
9 thou hast given me; for they are t'.
10 And all mine are t', and
10 and t' are mine; and I am
11 keep through t' own name those
18:35 T' own nation and the chief
Ac 2:27 wilt thou suffer t' Holy One to see
4:30 By stretching forth t' hand to heal:
5: 3 Satan filled t' heart to lie to the
4 it remained, was it not t' own?
4 was it not in t' own power?
4 conceived this thing in t' heart?
8:22 the thought of t' heart may be
37 If thou believest with all t' heart,
10: 4 t' alms are come up for a memorial
31 t' alms are had in remembrance
13:35 shalt not suffer t' Holy One to see
23:35 when t' accusers are also come.
Ro 10: 6 Say not in t' heart, Who shall
9 shalt believe in t' heart that God
11: 3 and digged down t' altars;
12:20 Therefore if t' enemy hunger, feed
1Co 10:29 I say, not t' own, but of the other:
1Ti 5:23 sake and t' often infirmities.
Ph'm 19 unto me even t' own self besides.
Heb 1:10 heavens are the works of t' hands:
13 I make t' enemies thy footstool?
Re 3:18 and anoint t' eyes with eyesalve,

thing^ See also ANYTHING; NOTHING; SOMETHING; THINGS.
Ge 1:24 and creeping t', and beast of the earth
25 every t' that creepeth upon the earth
26 over every creeping t' that creepeth
28 every living t' that moveth upon the
30 every t' that creepeth upon the earth,
31 God saw every t' that he had made,
6: 7 man, and beast, and the creeping t',
17 every t' that is in the earth shall die.
19 And of every living t' of all flesh, two
20 every creeping t' of the earth after his
7: 8 every t' that creepeth upon the earth,
14, 21 every creeping t' that creepeth
8: 1 and every living t', and all the cattle
17 Bring forth with thee every living t'
17 every creeping t' that creepeth upon
19 Every beast, every creeping t', and
9: 3 Every moving t' that liveth shall be
18:14 Is any t' too hard for the Lord?
19:21 thee concerning this t' also,
20:10 thou, that thou hast done this t'?
21:11 And the t' was very grievous in
26 I wot not who hath done this t':
22:16 for because thou hast done this t',
24:50 The t' proceedeth from the Lord:
30:31 Thou shalt not give me any t':
31 if thou wilt do this t' for me, I will
34: 7 which t' ought not to be done.
14 We cannot do this t', to give our
19 man deferred not to do the t',
38:10 the t' which he did displeased the
39: 9 hath he kept back any t' from me
23 looked not to any t' that was under
41:28 This is the t' which I have spoken
32 because the t' is established by God,
37 t' was good in the eyes of Pharaoh,
44: 7 should do according to this t':
Ex 1:18 Why have ye done this t', and have
2:14 and said, Surely this t' is known.
15 Now when Pharaoh heard this t',
9: 5 the Lord shall do this t' in the land.
6 the Lord did that t' on the morrow,
10:15 remained not any green t' in the trees,
12:24 observe this t' for an ordinance
16:14 there lay a small round t', as small as
16, 32 This is the t' which the Lord
18:11 in the t' wherein they dealt proudly
14 t' that thou doest to the people?
17 The t' that thou doest is not good.
18 for this t' is too heavy for thee;
23 If thou shalt do this t', and God
20: 4 or any likeness of any t' that is in
17 ass, nor any t' that is thy neighbour's.
22: 9 raiment, or for any manner of lost t',
15 if it be an hired t', it came for his
29: 1 this is the t' that thou shalt do
33:17 this t' also that thou hast spoken:
34:10 is a terrible t' that I will do with thee.
35: 4 the t' which the Lord commanded,
Le 2: 3, 10 it is a t' most holy of the offerings
4:13 the t' be hid from the eyes of the
5: 2 Or if a soul touch any unclean t',
5 confess that he hath sinned in that t':
16 harm that he hath done in the holy t',
6: 2 or in a t' taken away by violence, or
4 the t' which he hath deceitfully gotten,
4 to keep, or the lost t' which he found,
7 forgiven him for any t' of all that he
7:19 flesh that toucheth any unclean t'
21 soul that shall touch any unclean t',
21 beast, or any abominable unclean t',
Le 8: 5 the t' which the Lord commanded
9: 6 the t' which the Lord commanded
11:10 living t' which is in the waters,
21 may ye eat of every flying creeping t'
35 every t' whereupon any part of their
41 every creeping t' that creepeth upon
43 abominable with any creeping t' that
44 creeping t' that creepeth upon the
12: 4 she shall touch no hallowed t', nor
13:48 a skin, or in any t' made of skin;
49 or in the woof, or in any t' of skin;
52 linen, or any t' of skin, wherein the
53 or in the woof, or in any t' of skin;
54 wash the t' wherein the plague is,
57 or in the woof, or in any t' of skin;
58 woof, or whatsoever t' of skin it be,
59 warp, or woof, or any t' of skins,
15: 4 and every t', whereon he sitteth,
6 he that sitteth on any t' whereon
10 toucheth any t' that was under him
20 And every t' that she lieth upon in
20 every t' also that she sitteth upon
22 toucheth any t' that she sat upon
23 or on any t' whereon she sitteth,
17: 2 This is the t' which the Lord hath
19: 8 hath profaned the hallowed t' of the
26 Ye shall not eat any t' with the blood:
20:17 it is a wicked t'; and they shall be cut
21 his brother's wife, it is an unclean t':
25 any manner of living t' that creepeth
21:18 hath a flat nose, or any t' superfluous,
22: 4 whoso toucheth any t' that is unclean
5 whosoever toucheth any creeping t',
10 shall no stranger eat of the holy t':
10 servant, shall not eat of the holy t'.
14 if a man eat of the holy t' unwittingly,
14 give it unto the priest with the holy t'.
23 lamb that hath any t' superfluous or
23:37 offerings, every t' upon his day:
27:23 that day, as a holy t' unto the Lord.
28 no devoted t', that a man shall devote
28 every devoted t' is most holy unto the
Nu 4:15 but they shall not touch any holy t',
16: 9 Seemeth it but a small t' unto you,
13 it a small t' that thou hast brought us
30 But if the Lord make a new t', and the
17:13 cometh any t' near unto the tabernacle
18: 7 office for every t' of the altar,
14 t' devoted in Israel shall be thine.
15 t' that openeth the matrix in all flesh,
20:19 without doing any t' else, go
22:38 now any power at all to say any t'?
30: 1 t'...the Lord hath commanded.
31:23 Every t' that may abide the fire,
32:20 If ye will do this t', if ye will go
35:22 him any t' without laying of wait,
36: 6 t' which the Lord doth command
De 1:14 t' which thou hast spoken is good
32 this t' ye did not believe the Lord
4:18 The likeness of any t' that creepeth on
23, 25 image, or the likeness of any t',
32 there hath been any such t' as this
32 been any such...as this great t' is,
5: 8 likeness of any t' that is in heaven
21 or any t' that is thy neighbour's.
7:26 house, lest thou be a cursed t' like it:
26 utterly abhor it; for it is a cursed t'.
8: 9 thou shalt not lack any t' in it;
12:32 What t' soever I command you,
13:14 if it be truth, and the t' certain,
17 of the cursed t' to thine hand:
14: 3 Thou shalt not eat any abominable t'.
19 every creeping t' that flieth is unclean
21 not eat of any t' that dieth of itself:
15:10 for this t' the Lord thy God shall
15 I command thee this t' to day.
16: 4 shall there any t' of the flesh,
17: 4 it be true, and the t' certain,
5 have committed that wicked t',
18:22 if the t' follow not, nor come to pass,
22 t' which the Lord hath not spoken,
22: 3 and with all lost t' of thy brother's,
20 But if this t' be true, and the tokens
23: 9 keep thee from every wicked t'.
14 that he see no unclean t' in thee,
19 usury of any t' that is lent upon
24:10 dost lend thy brother any t',
18, 22 I command thee to do this t'.
26:11 thou shalt rejoice in every good t'
31:13 children, which have not known any t',
32:47 For it is not a vain t' for you;
47 through this t' you shall prolong
Jos 4:10 until every t' was finished that the
6:18 keep yourselves from the accursed t',
18 accursed, when ye take the accursed t',
7: 1 a trespass in the accursed t':
1 of Judah, took of the accursed t':
11 have even taken of the accursed t',
13 is an accursed t' in the midst of thee,
13 away the cursed t' from among you.
15 he that is taken with the accursed t'
9:24 of you, and have done this t'.
14: 6 knowest the t' that the Lord said
21:45 failed not ought of any good t' which
22:20 commit a trespass in the accursed t',
24 rather done it for fear of this t',
33 the t' pleased the children of Israel;
23:14 not one t' hath failed of all the good
14 and not one t' hath failed thereof.
J'g 6:29 another, Who hath done this t'?
29 the son of Joash hath done this t'.
8:27 which t' became a snare unto Gideon,
11:25 art thou any t' better than Balak
37 father, Let this t' be done for me:
13: 4 drink, and eat not any unclean t':
7 drink, neither eat any unclean t':
J'g 13:14 not eat of any t' that cometh from the
14 strong drink, nor eat any unclean t':
18: 7 put them to shame in any t';
10 where there is no want of any t'
19:19 servants: there is no want of any t'.
24 unto this man do not so vile a t'.
20: 9 the t' which we will do to Gibeah;
21:11 And this is the t' that ye shall do,
Ru 3:18 he have finished the t' this day.
1Sa 3:11 Behold, I will do a t' in Israel, at
17 the t' that the Lord hath said unto
17 if thou hide any t' from me of all
4: 7 hath not been such a t' heretofore.
8: 6 But the t' displeased Samuel,
12:16 stand and see this great t',
14:12 up to us, and we will shew you a t'.
15: 9 every t' that was vile and refuse,
18:20 told Saul, and the t' pleased him.
23 a light t' to be the king's son in law,
20: 2 my father hide this t' from me?
26 Saul spake not any t' that day:
39 But the lad knew not any t': only
21: 2 man know any t' of the business
22:15 impute any t' unto his servant,
24: 6 should do this t' unto my master,
25:15 hurt, neither missed we any t',
26:16 t' is not good that thou hast done.
28:10 happen to thee for this t'.
18 hath the Lord done this t' unto thee
30:19 any t' that they had taken to them:
2Sa 2: 6 because ye have done this t'.
3:13 but one t' I require of thee, that is,
7:19 yet a small t' in thy sight, O Lord
11:11 soul liveth, I will not do this t'.
25 Let not this t' displease thee, for
27 But the t' that David had done
12: 5 the man that hath done this t' shall
6 fourfold, because he did this t',
12 I will do this t' before all Israel,
21 What t' is this that thou hast done?
13: 2 hard for him to do any t' to her.
12 for no such t' ought to be done in
20 thy brother; regard not this t'.
33 the king take the t' to his heart,
14:13 thought such a t' against the people of
13 speak this t' as one that is faulty.
15 speak of this t' unto my lord the
18 thee, the t' that I shall ask thee.
20 hath thy servant Joab done this t':
21 Behold now, I have done this t':
15:11 simplicity, and they knew not any t'.
35 that what t' soever thou shalt hear
36 send unto me every t' that ye can
17:19 thereon; and the t' was not known.
24: 3 my lord the king delight in this t'?
1Ki 1:27 Is this t' done by my lord the king,
3:10 that Solomon had asked this t'.
11 Because thou hast asked this t',
10: 3 was not any t' hid from the king,
11:10 commanded him concerning this t',
12:24 to his house; for this t' is from me.
30 And this t' became a sin: for the
13:33 After this t' Jeroboam returned not
34 this t' became sin unto the house of
14: 5 wife of Jeroboam cometh to ask a t'
13 there is found some good t' toward
15: 5 turned not aside from any t' that he
16:31 had been a light t' for him to walk in
20: 9 I will do: but this t' I may not do.
24 And do this t', Take the kings away,
33 whether any t' would come from him,
2Ki 2:10 And he said, Thou hast asked a hard t':
3:18 but a light t' in the sight of the Lord:
4: 2 Thine handmaid hath not any t' in the
5:13 had bid thee do some great t',
18 this t' the Lord pardon thy servant,
18 Lord pardon thy servant in this t'.
6:11 Syria was sore troubled for this t';
7: 2 windows in heaven, might this t' be?
19 in heaven, might such a t' be?
8: 9 even of every good t' of Damascus,
13 that he should do this great t'?
11: 5 This is the t' that ye shall do; A
17:12 unto them, Ye shall not do this t'.
20: 9 will do the t' that he hath spoken:
10 is a light t' for the shadow to go down
1Ch 2: 7 who transgressed in the t' accursed.
11:19 forbid it me, that I should do this t':
13: 4 t' was right in the eyes of all the
17:17 yet this was a small t' in thine eyes,
23 let the t' that thou hast spoken
21: 3 why then doth my lord require this t'?
7 God was displeased with this t';
8 greatly, because I have done this t':
26:28 and whosoever had dedicated any t',
2Ch 9:20 any t' accounted of in the days of
11: 4 house: for this t' is done of me.
16:10 in a rage with him because of this t'.
23: 4 This is the t' that ye shall do; A
19 unclean in any t' should enter in.
29:36 people: for the t' was done suddenly.
30: 4 the t' pleased the king and all the
Ezr 7:27 such a t' as this in the king's heart,
9: 3 when I heard this t', I rent my
10: 2 is hope in Israel concerning this t'.
13 that have transgressed in this t'.
Ne 2:19 What is this t' that ye do? will ye
13:17 What evil t' is this that ye do, and
Es 2: 4 And the t' pleased the king; and he
22 the t' was known to Mordecai, who
5:14 And the t' pleased Haman; and he
6:13 friends every t' that had befallen him.
8: 5 the t' seem right before the king,
Job 3:25 the t' which I greatly feared is come
4:12 a t' was secretly brought to me,
6: 8 God would grant me the t' that I long

Job 9:22 This is one t', therefore I said it, He
12:10 hand is the soul of every living t',
13:28 And he, as a rotten t', consumeth, as a
14: 4 can bring a clean t' out of an unclean?
15:11 is there any secret t' with thee?
22:28 Thou shalt also decree a t', and it
23:14 he performeth the t' that is appointed
26: 3 plentifully declared the t' as it is?
28:10 and his eye seeth every precious t'.
11 the t' that is hid bringeth he forth to
33:32 [*In most editions*] If thou hast any t' to
39: 8 and he searcheth after every green t'.
42: 2 I know that thou canst do every t',
7 not spoken of me the t' that is right,
8 not spoken of me the t' which is right,
Ps 2: 1 and the people imagine a vain t'?
27: 4 One t' have I desired of the Lord, that
33:17 An horse is a vain t' for safety:
34:10 the Lord shall not want any good t'.
38:20 because I follow the t' that good is.
69:34 seas, and every t' that moveth therein.
84:11 no good t' will he withhold from them
89:34 nor alter the t' that is gone out of my
92: 1 It is a good t' to give thanks unto the
101: 3 set no wicked t' before mine eyes:
141: 4 Incline not my heart to any evil t',
145:16 satisfiest the desire of every living t'.
150: 6 t' that hath breath praise the Lord.
Pr 4: 7 Wisdom is the principal t'; therefore
18:22 Whoso findeth a wife findeth a good t',
22:18 For it is a pleasant t' if thou keep
25: 2 is the glory of God to conceal a t':
27: 7 the hungry soul every bitter t' is sweet.
Ec 1: 9 The t' that hath been, it is that which
9 and there is no new t' under the sun.
10 Is there any t' whereof it may be
3: 1 To every t' there is a season, and a
11 He hath made every t' beautiful in his
14 be put to it, nor any t' taken from it:
19 beasts; even one t' befalleth them:
5: 2 thine heart be hasty to utter any t'
6: 5 not seen the sun, nor known any t':
7: 8 end of a t' than the beginning
8: 1 knoweth the interpretation of a t'?
3 stand not in an evil t'; for he doeth
5 commandment shall feel no evil t':
15 a man hath no better t' under the sun,
9: 5 but the dead know not any t',
6 any more a portion forever in any t'
11: 7 A pleasant t' it is for the eyes to
12:14 with every secret t', whether it be good,
Isa 7:13 Is it a small t' for you to weary men,
15: 6 the grass faileth, there is no green t'.
17:13 like a rolling t' before the whirlwind.
19: 7 every t' sown by the brooks, shall
29:16 the t' framed say of him that framed it,
21 turn aside the just for a t' of nought.
38: 7 will do this t' that he hath spoken;
40:15 he taketh up the isles as a very little t'.
41:12 be as nothing, and as a t' of nought.
43:19 Behold, I will do a new t'; now it shall
49: 6 a light t' that thou shouldest be my
52:11 out from thence, touch no unclean t';
55:11 prosper in the t' whereto I sent it.
64: 6 But we are all as an unclean t', and
66: 8 Who hath heard such a t'? who hath
Jer 2:10 diligently, and see if there be such a t'.
19 see that it is an evil t' and bitter,
5:30 horrible t' is committed in the land:
7:23 But this t' commanded I them,
11:13 ye set up altars to that shameful t',
14:14 a t' of nought, and the deceit of their
18:13 of Israel hath done a very horrible t'.
22: 4 if ye do this t' indeed, then shall
23:14 prophets of Jerusalem an horrible t':
31:22 Lord hath created a new t' in the earth,
32:27 is there any t' too hard for me?
33:14 I will perform that good t' which I
38: 5 he that can do any t' against you.
14 unto Jeremiah, I will ask thee a t';
40: 3 therefore this t' is come upon you.
16 Kareah, Thou shalt not do this t':
42: 3 walk, and the t' that we may do.
4 that whatsoever t' the Lord shall
21 nor any t' for the which he hath sent
44: 4 not this abominable t' that I hate.
17 do whatsoever t' goeth forth out of
La 2:13 What t' shall I take to witness for thee?
13 what t' shall I liken to thee, O
Eze 8:17 Is it a light t' to the house of Judah
14: 9 deceived when he hath spoken a t',
16:47 but, as if that were a very little t',
34:18 a small t' unto you to have eaten up
44:18 with any t' that causeth sweat.
29 every dedicated t' in Israel shall be
31 shall not eat of any t' that is dead of
47: 9 every t' that liveth, which moveth,
9 every t' shall live whither the river
48:12 shall be unto them a t' most holy
Da 2: 5 Chaldeans, The t' is gone from me:
8 ye see the t' is gone from me.
11 is a rare t' that the king requireth,
15 Then Arioch made the t' known to
17 made the t' known to Hananiah,
3:29 which speak any t' amiss against the
4:33 The same hour was the t' fulfilled
5:15 shew the interpretation of the t':
26 This is the interpretation of the t':
6:12 answered and said, The t' is true,
10: 1 a t' was revealed unto Daniel,
1 and the t' was true, but the time
1 was long: and he understood the t',
Ho 6:10 seen an horrible t' in the house of
8: 3 Israel hath cast off the t' that is good
12 but they were counted as a strange t'
Am 6:13 Ye which rejoice in a t' of nought,

Jon 3: 7 beast, herd nor flock, taste any t':
Mal 1:14 sacrificeth unto the Lord a corrupt t':
M't 8:33 and told every t', and what was
18:19 agree on earth as touching any t'
19:16 Good Master, what good t' shall I do,
20:20 him, and desiring a certain t' of him.
21:24 I also will ask you one t', which if
24:17 to take any t' out of his house:
M'r 1:27 themselves, saying, What t' is this?
4:22 neither was any t' kept secret, but
5:32 about to see her that had done this t'.
7:18 whatsoever t' from without entereth
9:22 but if thou canst do any t', have
10:21 and said unto him, One t' thou lackest:
11:13 haply he might find any t' thereon:
13:15 to take any t' out of his house:
16: 8 neither said they any t' to any man;
18 and if they drink any deadly t', it shall
Lu 1:35 also that holy t' which shall be born
2:15 see this t' which is come to pass,
6: 9 unto them, I will ask you one t';
8:17 neither any t' hid, that shall not be
9:21 them to tell no man that t';
10:42 But one t' is needful: and Mary
12:11 how or what t' ye shall answer,
26 not able to do that t' which is least,
18:22 unto him, Yet lackest thou one t':
19: 8 have taken any t' from any man by
20: 3 them, I will also ask you one t';
22:23 of them it was that should do this t'.
35 and scrip, and shoes, lacked ye any t'?
Joh 1: 3 was not any t' made that was made.
46 any good t' come out of Nazareth?
5:14 more, lest a worse t' come unto thee.
7: 4 is no man that doeth any t' in secret,
9:25 one t' I know, that, whereas I was
30 Why herein is a marvellous t', that ye
14:14 If ye shall ask any t' in my name,
18:34 Sayest thou this t' of thyself, or did
Ac 5: 4 conceived this t' in thine heart?
10:14 never eaten any t' that is common
28 unlawful t' for a man that is a Jew to
12:12 And when he had considered the t', he
17:21 either to tell, or to hear some new t'.)
25 as though he needed any t', seeing
19:32 Some therefore cried one t', and some
39 any t' concerning other matters,
21:25 concluded that they observe no such t',
34 And some cried one t', some another,
23:17 for he hath a certain t' to tell him.
25: 8 Cæsar, have I offended any t' at all.
11 committed any t' worthy of death,
26 no certain t' to write unto my lord.
26: 8 be thought a t' incredible with you,
10 Which t' I also did in Jerusalem:
26 this t' was not done in a corner.
Ro 7:18 is, in my flesh,) dwelleth no good t':
8:33 Who shall lay any t' to the charge of
9:20 Shall the t' formed say to him that
13: 6 attending continually upon this very t'.
8 Owe no man any t', but to love one
14:14 that esteemeth any t' to be unclean,
21 nor any t' whereby thy brother
22 condemneth not himself in that t'
1Co 1: 5 in every t' ye are enriched by him,
10 that ye all speak the same t', and that
2: 2 not to know any t' among you,
3: 7 neither is he that planteth any t',
4: 3 very small t' that I should be judged
8: 2 man think that he knoweth any t',
7 hour eat it as a t' offered unto an idol;
9:11 is it a great t' if we shall reap your
17 For if I do this t' willingly, I have a
10:19 say I then? that the idol is any t',
19 offered in sacrifice to idols is any t'?
14:30 If any t' be revealed to another that
35 And if they will learn any t', let
2Co 2:10 To whom ye forgive any t', I forgive
10 for if I forgave any t', to whom I
3: 5 to think any t' as of ourselves;
5: 5 wrought us for the selfsame t' is God,
6: 3 Giving no offence in any t', that
17 Lord, and touch not the unclean t';
7:11 For behold this selfsame t', that ye
14 For if I have boasted any t' to him of
8: 7 Therefore, as ye abound in every t', in
9:11 in every t' to all bountifulness,
10: 5 every high t' that exalteth itself
11:15 it is no great t' if his ministers
12: 8 For this t' I besought the Lord thrice,
Ga 4:18 affected always in a good t',
5: 6 circumcision availeth any t', nor
6:15 neither circumcision availeth any t',
Eph 4:28 with his hands the t' which is good,
5:24 be to their own husbands in every t'.
27 spot, or wrinkle, or any such t';
6: 8 whatsoever good t' any man doeth,
Ph'p 1: 6 Being confident of this very t', that
3:13 but this one t' I do, forgetting
15 if in any t' ye be otherwise minded,
16 the same rule, let us mind the same t'
4: 6 in every t' by prayer and supplication
1Th 1: 8 that we need not to speak any t'.
5:18 In every t' give thanks: for this is the
2Th 1: 6 righteous t' with God to recompense
1Ti 1:10 and if there be any other t' that is
2Ti 1:14 good t' which was committed unto
Tit 2: 8 having no evil t' to say of you.
Ph'm 6 by the acknowledging of every good t'
Heb10:29 an unholy t', and hath done despite
31 It is a fearful t' to fall into the hands
11:40 God having provided some better t'
13: 9 it is a good t' that the heart be
Jas 1: 7 he shall receive any t' of the Lord.
1Pe 4:12 some strange t' happened unto you:
2Pe 3: 8 be not ignorant of this one t'.

1Jo 2: 8 which t' is true in him and in you:
5:14 if we ask any t' according to his will,
Re 2:15 of the Nicolaitanes, which t' I hate.
9: 4 neither any green t', neither any tree;
21:27 enter into it any t' that defileth.

things^ See also THINGS'.

Ge 7:23 and the creeping t', and the fowl of the
9: 3 the green herb have I given you all t'
15: 1 After these t' the word of the Lord
20: 8 and told all these t' in their ears:
22: 1, 20 And it came to pass after these t',
24:28 of her mother's house these t'.
53 brother and to her mother precious t'.
66 servant told Isaac all t' that he
29:13 And he told Laban all these t'.
39: 7 And it came to pass after these t',
40: 1 And it came to pass after these t',
42:36 away: all these t' are against me.
45:23 ten asses laden with the good t' of
48: 1 And it came to pass after these t',
Ex 10: 2 what t' I have wrought in Egypt, and
12:36 unto them such t' as they required.
23:13 And in all t' that I have said unto you
25:22 of all t' which I will give thee in
28:38 may bear the iniquity of the holy t',
29:33 eat those t' wherewith the atonement
35 all t' which I have commanded thee:
40: 4 order the t' that are to be set in order
Le 2: 8 offering that is made of these t' unto
4: 2 t' which ought not to be done,
13, 22 t' which should not be done,
27 t' which ought not to be done,
5: 2 or the carcase of unclean creeping t',
5 he shall be guilty in one of these t',
15 ignorance, in the holy t' of the Lord;
17 commit any of these t' which are
8:36 Aaron and his sons did all the t'
10:19 Lord; and such t' have befallen me:
11:23 But all other flying creeping t', which
29 unto you among the creeping t'
42 hath more feet among all creeping t'
14:11 that is to be made clean, and those t',
15:10 and he that beareth any of those t'
27 whosoever toucheth those t' shall be
18:24 not ye yourselves in any of these t':
20:23 for they committed all these t', and
22: 2 from the holy t' of the children of
2 name in those t' which they hallow
3 that goeth unto the holy t', which the
4 he shall not eat of the holy t', until he
6 and shall not eat of the holy t', unless
7 and shall afterward eat of the holy t';
12 not eat of an offering of the holy t'.
15 And they shall not profane the holy t'
16 trespass, when they eat their holy t':
26:23 will not be reformed by me by these t',
Nu 1:50 and over all t' that belong to it:
4: 4 congregation, about the most holy t':
15 t' are the burden of the sons of Kohath
19 they approach unto the most holy t':
20 in to see when the holy t' are covered,
5: 9 And every offering of all the holy t' of
10 every man's hallowed t' shall be his:
15:13 shall do these t' after this manner, in
18: 8 hallowed t' of the children of Israel;
9 This shall be thine of the most holy t',
19 All the heave offerings of the holy t',
32 neither shall ye pollute the holy t' of
29:39 These t' ye shall do unto the Lord
31:20 of goats' hair, and all t' made of wood.
35:29 So these t' shall be for a statute of
De 1:18 at that time all the t' which ye
4: 7 God is in all t' that we call upon him
9 the t' which thine eyes have seen,
30 and all these t' are come upon thee,
6:11 And houses full of all good t', which
10:21 for thee these great and terrible t',
12: 8 do after all the t' that we do here this
26 Only thy holy t' which thou hast, and
18:12 For all that do these t' are an
25:16 For all that do such t', and all that do
26:13 I have brought away the hallowed t'
28:47 of heart, for the abundance of all t';
48 in nakedness, and in want of all t':
57 for she shall eat them for want of all t'
29:29 secret t' belong unto the Lord our
29 t' which are revealed belong unto us
30: 1 all these t' are come upon thee,
32:35 the t' that shall come upon them make
33:13 for the precious t' of heaven, for the
14 for the precious t' put forth by the moon,
15 chief t' of the ancient mountains,
15 for the precious t' of the lasting hills,
16 And for the precious t' of the earth
Jos 1:17 as we hearkened unto Moses in all t',
2:11 And as soon as we had heard these t',
23 and told him all t' that befell them:
11: 1 king of Hazor had heard those t',
23:14 thing hath failed of all the good t'
15 as all good t' are come upon you,
15 the Lord bring upon you all evil t',
24:29 And it came to pass after these t',
J'g 13:23 would he have shewed us all these t',
23 time have told us such t' as these.
18:27 took the t' which Micah had made,
Ru 4: 7 changing, for to confirm all t';
1Sa 2:23 unto them, Why do ye such t'?
3:12 against Eli all t' which I have spoken
17 hide any thing from me of all the t'
12:21 for then should ye go after vain t',
24 consider how great t' he hath done for
15:21 the chief of the t' which should
19: 7 Jonathan shewed him all those t'.
25:37 and his wife had told him these t',
26:25 David: thou shalt both do great t',
2Sa 7:21 hast thou done all these great t', to

2Sa 7:23 and to do for you great t' and terrible,
11:18 told David all the t' concerning
12: 8 have given unto thee such and such t'.
13:21 king David heard of all these t',
14:20 to know all t' that are in the earth.
23: 5 covenant, ordered in all t' and sure:
17 These t' did these three mighty men.
22 These t' did Benaiah the son of
24:12 saith the Lord, I offer thee three t';
23 all these t' did Araunah, as a king
1Ki 4:33 fowl, and of creeping t', and of fishes.
5: 8 considered the t' which thou sentest
7:51 the t' which David his father had
15:15 brought in the t' which his father had
15 the t' which himself had dedicated,
17:17 And it came to pass after these t',
18:36 I have done all these t' that thy
21: 1 And it came to pass after these t',
26 according to all t' as did the Amorites,
2Ki 8: 4 the great t' that Elisha hath done.
11: 9 according to all t' that Jehoiada the
12: 4 All the money of the dedicated t' that
18 all the hallowed t' that Jehoshaphat,
18 and his own hallowed t', and all the
14: 3 according to all t' as Joash his father
17: 9 did secretly those t' that were not
11 wrought wicked t' to provoke the
19:29 shall eat this year such t' as grow of
20:13 them all the house of his precious t',
15 All the t' that are in mine house have
23:17 proclaimed these t' that thou hast
25:15 and such t' as were of gold, in gold,
1Ch 4:22 And these are ancient t'.
9:31 set office over the t' that were made in
11:19 These t' did these three mightiest.
24 These t' did Benaiah the son of
17:19 in making known all these great t'.
21:10 saith the Lord, I offer thee three t':
23:13 he should sanctify the most holy t', he
28 and in the purifying of all holy t', and
26:20 over the treasures of the dedicated t'.
26 all the treasures of the dedicated t',
28:12 of the treasuries of the dedicated t':
14 gave of gold by weight for t' of gold,
29: 2 God the gold for t' to be made of gold,
2 and the silver for t' of silver,
2 and the brass for t' of brass,
2 the iron for t' of iron,
2 and wood for t' of wood;
5 The gold for t' of gold,
5 and the silver for t' of silver,
14 for all t' come of thee, and of thine
17 I have willingly offered all these t':
19 and to do all these t', and to build the
2Ch 3: 3 t' wherein Solomon was instructed
4: 6 such t' as they offered for the burnt
5: 1 all the t' that David his father had
12:12 and also in Judah t' went well.
15:18 of God the t' that his father had
19: 3 there are good t' found in thee, in
21: 3 silver, and of gold, and of precious t',
23: 8 according to all t' that Jehoiada the
24: 7 the dedicated t' of the house of the
29:33 consecrated t' were six hundred oxen
31: 5 the tithe of all t' brought they in
6 of holy t' which were consecrated
12 tithes and the dedicated t' faithfully:
14 of the Lord, and the most holy t'.
32: 1 After these t', and the
Ezr 1: 6 with beasts, and with precious t',
2:63 should not eat of the most holy t',
7: 1 Now after these t', in the reign of
9: 1 Now when these t' were done, the
Ne 6: 8 are no such t' done as thou sayest,
16 that were about us saw these t',
7:65 should not eat of the most holy t',
9: 6 the earth, and all t' that are therein,
10:33 for the set feasts, and for the holy t',
12:47 sanctified holy t' unto the Levites;
13:26 Solomon king of Israel sin by these t'?
Es 2: 1 After these t', when the wrath of
3 let their t' for purification be given
9 gave her her t' for purification,
9 with such t' as belonged to her, and
12 with other t' for the purifying of the
3: 1 After these t' did king Ahasuerus
5:11 all the t' wherein the king had
9:20 And Mordecai wrote these t',
Job 5: 9 doeth great t' and unsearchable;
9 marvellous t' without number:
6: 7 The t' that my soul refused to touch
30 cannot my taste discern perverse t'?
8: 2 How long wilt thou speak these t'?
9:10 Which doeth great t' past finding out;
10:13 these t' hast thou hid in thine heart:
12: 3 yea, who knoweth not such t' as these?
22 discovereth deep t' out of darkness,
13:20 Only do not two t' unto me: then will I
26 For thou writest bitter t' against me,
14:19 thou washest away the t' which grow
16: 2 I have heard many such t': miserable
22:18 Yet he filled their houses with good t':
23:14 me: and many such t' are with him.
26: 5 Dead t' are formed from under the
33:29 these t' worketh God oftentimes with
37: 5 great t' doeth he, which we cannot
41:30 sharp pointed t' upon the mire.
34 He beholdeth all high t': he is a king
42: 3 t' too wonderful for me, which I knew
Ps 8: 6 thou hast put all t' under his feet:
12: 3 the tongue that speaketh proud t':
15: 5 He that doeth these t' shall never be
17: 2 thine eyes behold the t' that are equal.
31:18 which speak grievous t' proudly and
35:11 laid to my charge t' that I knew not.
38:12 seek my hurt speak mischievous t',

Ps 42: 4 When I remember these t', I pour out
45: 1 I speak of the t' which I have made
4 right hand shall teach thee terrible t'.
50:21 These t' hast thou done, and I kept
57: 2 God that performeth all t' for me.
60: 3 Thou hast shewed thy people hard t':
65: 5 By terrible t' in righteousness wilt
71:19 is very high, who hast done great t':
72:18 of Israel, who only doeth wondrous t'.
78:12 Marvellous t' did he in the sight of
86:10 thou art great, and doest wondrous t':
87: 3 Glorious t' are spoken of thee, O city
94: 4 long shall they utter and speak hard t'?
98: 1 song; for he hath done marvellous t':
103: 5 Who satisfieth thy mouth with good t';
104:25 wherein are t' creeping innumerable,
106:21 which had done great t' in Egypt;
22 Ham, and terrible t' by the Red sea.
107:43 is wise, and will observe these t',
113: 6 to behold the t' that are in heaven,
119:18 may behold wondrous t' out of thy law.
128 thy precepts concerning all t' to be
126: 2 The Lord hath done great t' for them.
3 The Lord hath done great t' for us;
131: 1 great matters, or in t' too high for me.
148:10 all cattle; creeping t', and flying fowl:
Pr 2:12 the man that speaketh froward t';
3:15 and all the t' thou canst desire are not
6:16 These six t' doth the Lord hate: yea,
8: 6 for I will speak of excellent t'; and
6 opening of my lips shall be right t'.
11 all the t' that may be desired are not
15:28 of the wicked poureth out evil t'.
16: 4 The Lord hath made all t' for himself:
30 shutteth his eyes to devise froward t':
22:20 Have not I written to thee excellent t'
23:16 rejoice, when thy lips speak right t'.
33 and thine heart shall utter perverse t'.
24:23 These t' also belong to the wise. It is
26:10 The great God that formed all t' both
28: 5 that seek the Lord understand all t'.
10 the upright shall have good t' in
30: 7 Two t' have I required of thee; deny
15 are three t' that are never satisfied,
15 yea, four t' say not, It is enough:
18 be three t' which are too wonderful
21 For three t' the earth is disquieted,
24 There be four t' which are little upon
29 There be three t' which go well, yea,
Ec 1: 8 All t' are full of labour: man
11 is no remembrance of former t';
11 be any remembrance of t' that are
13 out by wisdom concerning all t' that
6:11 be many t' that increase vanity,
7:15 All t' have I seen in the days of my
25 seek out wisdom, and the reason of t',
9: 2 All t' come alike to all: there is one
3 is an evil among all t' that are done
10:19 merry: but money answereth all t'.
11: 9 that for all these t' God will bring thee
Isa 12: 5 Lord; for he hath done excellent t':
25: 1 for thou hast done wonderful t'; thy
6 make unto all people a feast of fat t',
6 of fat t' full of marrow, of wines on
29:16 Surely your turning of t' upside down
30:10 Prophesy not unto us right t',
10 speak unto us smooth t', prophesy
32: 8 But the liberal deviseth liberal t';
8 and by liberal t' shall he stand.
34: 1 world, and all t' that come forth of it.
38:16 O Lord, by these t' men live,
16 in all these t' is the life of my spirit:
39: 2 them the house of his precious t',
40:26 and behold who hath created these t',
41:22 let them shew the former t', what they
22 of them; or declare us t' for to come.
23 Shew the t' that are to come hereafter,
42: 9 Behold, the former t' are come to pass,
9 and new t' do I declare: before they
16 them, and crooked t' straight.
16 These t' will I do unto them, and
20 Seeing many t', but thou observest
43: 9 declare this, and shew us former t'?
18 Remember ye not the former t',
18 neither consider the t' of old.
44: 7 and the t' that are coming, and shall
9 and their delectable t' shall not profit;
24 I am the Lord that maketh all t';
45: 7 create evil: I the Lord do all these t'.
11 Ask me of t' to come concerning my
19 I declare t' that are right.
46: 9 Remember the former t' of old: for I
10 from ancient times the t' that are not
47: 7 thou didst not lay these t' to thy heart,
9 these two t' shall come to thee in a
13 save thee from these t' that shall come
48: 3 I have declared the former t' from the
6 I have shewed thee new t' from this
6 even hidden t', and thou didst not
14 among them hath declared these t'?
51:19 These two t' are come unto thee; who
56: 4 choose the t' that please me, and take
61:11 garden causeth the t' that are sown
64: 3 terrible t' which we looked not for,
11 and all our pleasant t' are laid waste.
12 refrain thyself for these t', O Lord?
65: 4 of abominable t' is in their vessels;
66: 2 For all those t' hath mine hand made,
2 and all those t' have been, saith the
8 such a thing? who hath seen such t'?
Jer 2: 8 and walked after t' that do not profit.
3: 5 thou hast spoken and done evil t' as
7 said after she had done all these t',
4:18 have procured these t' unto thee;
5: 9 Shall I not visit for these t'? saith the
19 doeth the Lord our God all these t'

Jer 5:25 iniquities have turned away these t',
25 your sins have withholden good t
29 Shall I not visit for these t'? saith the
8:13 t' that I have given them shall pass
9: 9 Shall I not visit them for these t'?
24 in these t' I delight, saith the Lord.
10:16 for he is the former of all t'; and Israel
13:22 Wherefore come these t' upon me?
14:22 thee: for thou hast made all these t'.
16:18 of their detestable and abominable t'.
19 and t' wherein there is no profit.
17: 9 The heart is deceitful above all t', and
18:13 the heathen, who hath heard such t':
20: 1 that Jeremiah prophesied these t'.
5 and all the precious t' thereof, and all
21:14 it shall devour all t' round about it.
26:10 princes of Judah heard these t',
30:15 I have done these t' unto thee.
31: 5 and shall eat them as common t'.
33: 3 and shew thee great and mighty t',
42: 5 according to all t' for the which
44:18 we have wanted all t', and have been
45: 5 And seekest thou great t' for thyself?
51:19 them; for he is the former of all t':
La 1: 7 all her pleasant t' that she had in the
10 out his hand upon all her pleasant t':
11 have given their pleasant t' for meat
16 For these t' I weep; mine eye, mine
2:14 prophets have seen vain and foolish t'
5:17 is faint; for these t' our eyes are dim.
Eze 5:11 sanctuary with all thy detestable t',
7:20 and of their detestable t' therein:
8:10 and behold every form of creeping t',
11: 5 for I know the t' that come into your
18 take away all the detestable t' thereof
21 after the heart of their detestable t'
25 all the t' that the Lord had shewed
16:16 the like t' shall not come, neither shall
30 seeing thou doest all these t', the work
43 but hast fretted me in all these t';
17:12 Know ye not what these t' mean?
15 shall he escape that doeth such t'? or
18 and hath done all these t', he shall not
18:10 doeth the like to any one of these t',
20:40 your oblations, with all your holy t'.
22: 8 Thou hast despised mine holy t', and
25 taken the treasure and precious t';
26 law, and have profaned mine holy t':
23:30 I will do these t' unto thee, because
24:19 thou not tell us what these t' are to us,
27:24 were thy merchants in all sorts of t',
37:23 their idols, nor with their detestable t',
38:10 time shall t' come into thy mind,
20 and all creeping t' that creep upon the
42:13 the Lord shall eat the most holy t':
13 there shall they lay the most holy t',
14 to those t' which are for the people.
44: 8 not kept the charge of mine holy t':
13 nor to come near to any of my holy t',
30 the first of all the firstfruits of all t',
Da 2:10 that asked such t' at any magician,
22 He revealeth the deep and secret t':
40 breaketh in pieces and subdueth all t':
7: 8 man, and a mouth speaking great t'.
16 know the interpretation of the t'.
20 and a mouth that spake very great t',
10:21 none that holdeth with me in these t',
11:36 marvellous t' against the God of gods,
38 with precious stones, and pleasant t'.
43 and over all the precious t' of Egypt:
12: 7 people, all these t' shall be finished.
8 Lord, what shall be the end of these t'?
Ho 2:18 and with the creeping t' of the ground:
8:12 written to him the great t' of my law,
9: 3 they shall eat unclean t' in Assyria.
14: 9 and he shall understand t' things?
Joe 2:20 up, because he hath done great t'.
21 rejoice: for the Lord will do great t'.
3: 5 your temples my goodly pleasant t':
Ob 6 How are the t' of Esau searched out!
6 how are his hidden t' sought up!
Mic 7:15 will I shew unto him marvellous t'.
Hab 1:14 as the creeping t', that have no ruler
Zep 1: 2 utterly consume all t' from off the
Zec 4:10 who hath despised the day of small t'?
8:12 of this people to possess all these t'.
16 These are the t' that ye shall do;
17 for all these are t' that I hate, saith
M't 1:20 But while he thought on these t',
2: 3 Herod the king had heard these t',
4: 9 All these t' will I give thee, if thou
6: 8 knoweth what t' ye have need of,
32 all these t' do the Gentiles seek:)
32 that ye have need of all these t'.
33 all these t' shall be added unto you.
34 take thought for the t' of itself.
7:11 is in heaven give good t' to them that
12 Therefore all t' whatsoever ye would
9:18 While he spake these t' unto them,
11: 4 shew John again those t' which ye do
25 hast hid these t' from the wise and
27 All t' are delivered unto me of my
12:34 can ye, being evil, speak good t'?
35 of the heart bringeth forth good t':
35 the evil treasure bringeth forth evil t'.
13: 3 he spake many t' unto them in
17 desired to see those t' which ye see,
17 and to hear those t' which ye hear,
34 All these t' spake Jesus unto the
35 I will utter t' which have been kept
41 out of his kingdom all t' that offend,
51 Have ye understood all these t'?
52 out of his treasure t' new and old.
56 then hath this man all these t'?
15:18 those t' which proceed out of the
20 These are the t' which defile a man:

M't 16:21 and suffer many t' of the elders and
23 savourest not the t' that be of God,
17:11 shall first come, and restore all t'
19:20 All these t' have I kept from my
26 But with God all t' are possible.
21:15 saw the wonderful t' that he did,
22 all t', whatsoever ye shall ask in
23 authority doest thou these t'?
24, 27 by what authority I do these t'.
22: 4 all t' are ready: come unto the
21 Cæsar the t' which are Cæsar's;
21 unto God the t' that are God's.
23:20 sweareth by it, and by all t' thereon.
36 All these t' shall come upon this
24: 2 unto them, See ye not all these t'?
3 Tell us, when shall these t' be?
6 for all these t' must come to pass,
33 ye, when ye shall see all these t',
34 not pass, till all these t' be fulfilled.
25:21 thou hast been faithful over a few t',
21 I will make thee ruler over many t':
23 thou hast been faithful over a few t',
23 I will make thee ruler over many t':
27:13 many t' they witness against thee?
19 I have suffered many t' this day in
54 and those t' that were done,
28:11 priests all the t' that were done.
20 to observe all t' whatsoever I have
M'r 1:44 those t' which Moses commanded,
2: 8 Why reason ye these t' in your
3: 8 they had heard what great t' he did,
4: 2 taught them many t' by parables,
11 all these t' are done in parables:
19 lusts of other t' entering in, choke
34 he expounded all t' to his disciples.
5:19 tell them how great t' the Lord hath
20 great t' Jesus had done for him:
26 And had suffered many t' of many
6: 2 whence hath this man these t'?
20 he did many t', and heard him gladly.
30 unto Jesus, and told him all t',
34 and he began to teach them many t'.
7: 4 many other t' there be, which they
8 and many other such like t' ye do.
13 and many such like t' do ye.
15 but the t' which come out of him,
23 All these evil t' come from within,
37 saying, He hath done all t' well: he
8:31 the Son of man must suffer many t',
33 savourest not the t' that be of God,
33 of God, but the t' that be of men.
9: 9 tell no man what t' they had seen,
12 cometh first, and restoreth all t';
12 of man, that he must suffer many t',
23 t' are possible to him that believeth.
10:27 for with God all t' are possible.
32 tell them what t' should happen
11:11 had looked round about upon all t',
23 those t' which he saith shall come
24 What t' soever ye desire, when ye
28 what authority doest thou these t'?
28 thee this authority to do these t'?
29, 33 by what authority I do these t'.
12:17 to Cæsar the t' that are Cæsar's,
17 and to God the t' that are God's.
13: 4 Tell us, when shall these t' be?
4 when all these t' shall be fulfilled?
7 for such t' must needs be; but the
23 behold, I have foretold you all t'.
29 shall see these t' come to pass,
30 not pass, till all these t' be done.
14:36 Father, all t' are possible unto thee;
15: 3 priests accused him of many t':
4 how many t' they witness against
Lu 1: 1 in order a declaration of those t'
3 had perfect understanding of all t'
4 know the certainty of those t',
20 until the day that these t' shall be
45 of those t' which were told her
49 mighty hath done to me great t';
53 hath filled the hungry with good t';
2:18 wondered at those t' which were told
19 But Mary kept all these t', and
20 praising God for all the t' that they
33 marvelled at those t' which were
39 had performed all t' according to the
3:18 other t' in his exhortation preached
4:28 when they heard these t', were filled
5:26 We have seen strange t' to day.
27 And after these t' he went forth,
6:46 Lord, and do not the t' which I say?
7: 9 Jesus heard these t', he marvelled
18 John shewed him of all these t'.
22 tell John what t' ye have seen and
8: 8 when he had said these t', he cried,
39 how great t' God hath done unto
39 how great t' Jesus had done unto
9: 9 who is this, of whom I hear such t'?
22 Son of man must suffer many t',
36 any of those t' which they had seen.
43 they wondered every one at all t'
10: 1 After these t' the Lord appointed
7 and drinking such t' as they give:
8 eat such t' as are set before you:
21 hid these t' from the wise and
22 All t' are delivered to me of my
23 eyes which see the t' that ye see:
24 desired to see those t' which ye see,
24 and to hear those t' which ye hear,
41 careful and troubled about many t':
11:27 as he spake these t', a certain
41 give alms of such t' as ye have;
41 behold, all t' are clean unto you.
53 as he said these t' unto them,
53 to provoke him to speak of many t':
12:15 of the t' which he possesseth.

Lu 12:20 then whose shall those t' be, which
30 these t' do the nations of the world
30 that ye have need of these t'.
31 all these t' shall be added unto
48 and did commit t' worthy of stripes,
13: 2 because they suffered such t'?
17 And when he had said these t',
17 glorious t' that were done by him.
14: 6 not answer him again to these t'.
15 sat at meat with him heard these t',
17 Come; for all t' are now ready.
21 came, and shewed his lord these t'.
15:26 and asked what these t' meant.
16:14 were covetous, heard all these t':
25 thy lifetime receivedst thy good t',
25 and likewise Lazarus evil t': but now
17: 9 he did the t' that were commanded
10 he shall have done all those t' which
25 But first must he suffer many t',
18:22 Now when Jesus heard these t',
27 t' which are impossible with men are
31 t' that are written by the prophets
34 they understood none of these t':
34 neither knew they the t' which were
19:11 as they heard these t', he added
42 the t' which belong unto thy peace!
20: 2 authority doest thou these t'?
8 by what authority I do these t'.
25 Cæsar the t' which be Cæsar's,
25 and unto God the t' which be God's.
21: 6 As for these t' which ye behold,
7 Master, but when shall these t' be?
7 when these t' shall come to pass?
9 for these t' must first come to pass;
22 t' which are written may be fulfilled.
26 looking after those t' which are
28 when these t' begin to come to pass,
31 when ye see these t' come to pass,
36 these t' that shall come to pass,
22:37 the t' concerning me have an end.
65 many other t' blasphemously spake
23: 8 because he had heard many t' of him;
14 touching those t' whereof ye accuse
31 if they do these t' in a green tree,
48 beholding the t' which were done,
49 stood afar off, beholding these t'.
24: 9 and told all these t' unto the eleven,
10 which told these t' unto the apostles.
14 they talked together of all these t'
18 hast not known the t' which are come
19 And he said unto them, What t'? And
21 third day since these t' were done.
26 not Christ to have suffered these t',
27 scriptures the t' concerning himself.
35 they told what t' were done in the way,
44 that all t' must be fulfilled, which
48 And ye are witnesses of these t'.
Joh 1: 3 All t' were made by him; and without
28 These t' were done in Bethabara
50 thou shalt see greater t' than these.
2:16 Take these t' hence; make not
18 us, seeing that thou doest these t'?
3: 9 unto him, How can these t' be?
10 Israel, and knowest not these t'?
12 If I have told you earthly t', and ye
12 ye believe if I tell you of heavenly t'?
22 After these t' came Jesus and his
35 and hath given all t' into his hand.
4:25 when he is come, he will tell us all t'.
29 which told me all t' that ever I did:
45 seen all t' that he did at Jerusalem
5:16 done these t' on the sabbath day.
19 for what t' soever he doeth, these also
20 sheweth him all t' that himself doeth:
34 these t' I say, that ye might be saved.
6: 1 After these t' Jesus went over the
59 These t' said he in the synagogue,
7: 1 After these t' Jesus walked in
4 If thou do these t', shew thyself to
32 that the people murmured such t'
8:26 I have many t' to say and to judge of
26 world those t' which I have heard of
28 hath taught me, I speak these t'.
29 I do always those t' that please him.
10: 6 they understood not what t' they were
41 but all t' that John spake of this man
11:11 These t' said he: and after that he
45 and had seen the t' which Jesus did,
46 and told them what t' Jesus had done.
12:16 These t' understood not his disciples
16 they that these t' were written of him,
16 they had done these t' unto him.
36 These t' spake Jesus, and departed,
41 These t' said Esaias, when he saw
13: 3 Father had given all t' into his hands,
17 If ye know these t', happy are ye
29 Buy those t' that we have need of
14:25 These t' have I spoken unto you,
26 he shall teach you all t', and bring all
26 and bring all t' to your remembrance,
15:11 These t' have I spoken unto you,
15 all t' that I have heard of my Father
17 These t' I command you, that ye
21 But all these t' will they do unto
16: 1 These t' have I spoken unto you,
3 And these t' will they do unto you,
4 But these t' have I told you, that
4 these t' I said not unto you at the
6 I have said these t' unto you,
12 I have yet many t' to say unto you,
13 and he will shew you t' to come.
15 All t' that the Father hath are mine:
25 These t' have I spoken unto you
30 are we sure that thou knowest all t',
33 These t' have I spoken unto you,
17: 7 that all t' whatsoever thou hast given

Joh 17:13 and these t' I speak in the world, that
18: 4 knowing all t' should come upon him,
19:24 these t' therefore the soldiers did.
28 that all t' were now accomplished,
36 For these t' were done, that the
20:18 he had spoken these t' unto her.
21: 1 After these t' Jesus shewed himself
17 unto him, Lord, thou knowest all t';
24 disciple which testifieth of these t',
24 and wrote these t': and we know
25 also many other t' which Jesus did,
Ac 1: 3 t' pertaining to the kingdom of God:
9 And when he had spoken these t',
2:44 together, and had all t' common;
3:18 But those t', which God before had
21 the times of restitution of all t', which
22 shall ye hear in all t' whatsoever he
4:20 speak the t' which we have seen and
25 rage, and the people imagine vain t'?
32 ought of the t' which he possessed
32 his own; but they had all t' common.
34 the prices of the t' that were sold,
5: 5 on all them that heard these t'.
11 and upon as many as heard these t'.
24 the chief priests heard these t',
32 we are his witnesses of these t';
7: 1 the high priest, Are these t' so?
50 Hath not my hand made all these t'?
54 When they heard these t', they were
8: 6 gave heed unto those t' which Philip
12 Philip preaching the t' concerning
24 none of these t' which ye have spoken
9:16 shew him how great t' he must suffer
10: 8 had declared all these t' unto them,
12 beasts, and creeping t', and fowls
33 to hear all t' that are commanded thee
39 we are witnesses of all t' which he did
11: 6 beasts, and creeping t', and fowls
18 When they heard these t', they held
22 Then tidings of these t' came unto
12:17 said, Go shew these t' unto James,
13:39 that believe are justified from all t',
45 those t' which were spoken by Paul,
14:15 Sirs, why do ye these t'? We also
15 and the sea, and all t' that are therein:
15: 4 and they declared all t' that God had
17 the Lord, who doeth all these t'.
20 fornication, and from t' strangled,
27 also tell you the same t' by mouth.
28 burden than these necessary t';
29 and from blood, and from t' strangled,
16:14 unto the t' which were spoken of Paul.
17: 8 the city, when they heard these t'.
11 daily, whether those t' were so.
20 bringest certain strange t' to our ears:
20 know therefore what these t' mean.
22 that in all t' ye are too superstitious.
24 that made the world and all t' therein,
25 giveth to all life, and breath, and all t';
18: 1 After these t' Paul departed from
17 And Gallio cared for none of those t'.
25 taught diligently the t' of the Lord,
19: 8 the t' concerning the kingdom of God.
21 After these t' were ended, Paul
36 these t' cannot be spoken against,
20:22 not knowing the t' that shall befall me
24 But none of these t' move me,
30 shall men arise, speaking perverse t',
35 I have shewed you all t', how that so
21:12 And when we heard these t', both
19 particularly what t' God had wrought
24 and all may know that those t',
25 themselves from t' offered to idols,
22:10 told thee of all t' which are appointed
23:22 thou hast shewed these t' to me.
24: 8 take knowledge of all these t',
9 saying that these t' were so.
13 they prove the t' whereof they now
14 all t' which are written in the law
22 when Felix heard these t', having
25: 9 be judged of these t' before me?
11 none of these t' whereof these accuse
18 accusation of such t' as I supposed:
26: 2 touching all the t' whereof I am
9 many t' contrary to the name of Jesus
16 both of these t' which thou hast seen,
16 of those t' in the which I will appear
22 saying none other t' than those which
26 For the king knoweth of these t',
26 that none of these t' are hidden
27:11 those t' which were spoken by Paul.
28:10 us with such t' as were necessary.
24 And some believed the t' which were
31 teaching those t' which concern the
Ro 1:20 invisible t' of him from the creation
20 understood by the t' that are made,
23 fourfooted beasts, and creeping t'.
28 do those t' which are not convenient;
30 inventors of evil t', disobedient to
32 which commit such t' are worthy of
2: 1 thou that judgest doest the same t'.
2 against them which commit such t'.
3 that judgest them which do such t',
14 nature the t' contained in the law,
18 approvest the t' that are more
3:19 that what t' soever the law saith,
4:17 those t' which be not as though they
6:21 What fruit had ye then in those t'
21 for the end of those t' is death.
8: 5 the flesh do mind the t' of the flesh;
5 after the Spirit the t' of the Spirit.
28 we know that all t' work together for
31 What shall we then say to these t'?
32 not with him also freely give us all t'?
37 in all these t' we are more than
38 nor t' present, nor t' to come.

Ro 10: 5 man which doeth those *t* shall live
15 and bring glad tidings of good *t*!
11: 36 through him, and to him, are all *t*:
12: 16 Mind not high *t*, but condescend to
17 Provide *t* honest in the sight of all
14: 2 one believeth that he may eat all *t*:
18 For he that in these *t* serveth Christ
19 after the *t* which make for peace,
19 *t* wherewith one may edify another.
20 All *t* indeed are pure; but it is evil
15: 4 For whatsoever *t* were written
17 in those *t* which pertain to God.
18 not dare to speak of any of those *t*
27 made partakers of their spiritual *t*,
27 to minister unto them in carnal *t*.
1Co 1: 27 hath chosen the foolish *t* of the world
27 hath chosen the weak *t* of the world
27 to confound the *t* which are mighty;
28 And base *t* of the world, and
28 and *t* which are despised, hath God
28 God chosen, yea, and *t* which are not,
28 are not, to bring to nought *t* that are:
2: 9 *t* which God hath prepared for them
10 searcheth all *t*, yea, the deep *t* of God.
11 For what man knoweth the *t* of a man,
11 even so the *t* of God knoweth no man,
12 know the *t* that are freely given to us
13 Which *t* also we speak, not in the
13 comparing spiritual *t* with spiritual.
14 natural man receiveth not the *t* of
15 But he that is spiritual judgeth all *t*,
3: 21 glory in men. For all *t* are yours;
22 or death, or *t* present, or *t* to come;
4: 5 to light the hidden *t* of darkness,
6 these *t*, brethren, I have in a figure
13 the offscouring of all *t* unto this day.
14 I write not these *t* to shame you,
6: 3 much more *t* that pertain to this life?
4 judgments of *t* pertaining to this life,
12 All *t* are lawful unto me, but all
12 unto me, but all *t* are not expedient:
12 all *t* are lawful for me, but I will not
7: 1 concerning the *t* whereof ye wrote
32 is unmarried careth for the *t* that
33 married careth for the *t* that are of
34 woman careth for the *t* of the Lord,
34 married careth for the *t* of the world,
8: 1 Now as touching *t* offered unto idols,
4 the eating of those *t* that are offered
6 God, the Father, of whom are all *t*,
6 Lord Jesus Christ, by whom are all *t*,
10 eat those *t* which are offered to idols;
9: 8 Say I these *t* as a man? or saith not
11 If we have sown unto you spiritual *t*,
11 thing if we shall reap your carnal *t*?
12 but suffer all *t*, lest we should hinder
13 they which minister about holy *t*
13 live of the *t* of the temple? and they
15 But I have used none of these *t*:
15 neither have I written these *t*,
22 I am made all *t* to all men, that I
25 for the mastery is temperate in all *t*.
10: 6 Now these *t* were our examples,
6 intent we should not lust after evil *t*,
11 all these *t* happened unto them
20 that the *t* which the Gentiles sacrifice,
23 All *t* are lawful for me, but all
23 but all *t* are not expedient:
23 all *t* are lawful for me, but all
23 are lawful for me, but all *t* edify not.
33 Even as I please all men in all *t*, not
11: 2 that ye remember me in all *t*,
12 also by the woman; but all *t* of God.
13: 7 Beareth all *t*, believeth all *t*,
7 hopeth all *t*, endureth all *t*.
11 became a man, I put away childish *t*.
14: 7 And even *t* without life giving sound,
26 Let all *t* be done unto edifying.
37 acknowledge that the *t* that I write
40 all *t* be done decently and in order.
15: 27 For he hath put all *t* under his feet.
27 he saith all *t* are put under him,
27 which did put all *t* under him.
28 when all *t* shall be subdued unto him,
28 unto him that put all *t* under him,
16: 14 Let all your *t* be done with charity.
2Co 1: 13 For we write none other *t* unto you,
17 or the *t* that I purpose, do I purpose
2: 9 you, whether ye be obedient in all *t*.
16 And who is sufficient for these *t*?
4: 2 have renounced the hidden *t* of
15 For all *t* are for your sakes, that the
18 we look not at the *t* which are seen,
18 but at the *t* which are not seen:
18 for the *t* which are seen are temporal;
18 the *t* which are not seen are eternal.
5: 10 every one may receive the *t* done in
17 new creature: old *t* are passed away;
17 behold, all *t* are become new.
18 all *t* are of God, who hath reconciled
6: 4 in all *t* approving ourselves as the
10 nothing, and yet possessing all *t*.
7: 11 In all *t* ye have approved yourselves
14 but as we spake all *t* to you in truth,
16 I have confidence in you in all *t*.
8: 21 Providing for honest *t*, not only in the
22 oftentimes proved diligent in many *t*,
9: 8 always having all sufficiency in all *t*,
10: 7 on *t* after the outward appearance?
13 not boast of *t* without our measure,
15 boasting of *t* without our measure,
16 line of *t* made ready to our hand.
11: 6 made manifest among you in all *t*.
9 all *t* I have kept myself from being
28 Beside those *t* that are without, that
30 glory of the *t* which concern mine
2Co 12: 19 we do all *t*, dearly beloved, for your
13: 10 I write these *t* being absent, lest
Ga 1: 20 Now the *t* which I write unto you,
2: 18 For if I build again the *t* which I
3: 4 Have ye suffered so many *t* in vain?
10 that continueth not in all *t* which are
4: 24 Which *t* are an allegory: for these are
5: 17 that ye cannot do the *t* that ye would.
21 which do such *t* shall not inherit the
6: 6 him that teacheth in all good *t*.
Eph 1: 10 together in one all *t* in Christ,
11 who worketh all *t* after the counsel
22 And hath put all *t* under his feet, and
22 be the head over all *t* to the church,
3: 9 who created all *t* by Jesus Christ:
4: 10 all heavens, that he might fill all *t*.)
15 may grow up into him in all *t*, which
5: 6 because of these *t* cometh the
12 those *t* which are done of them in
13 But all *t* that are reproved are made
20 Giving thanks always for all *t* unto
6: 9 ye masters, do the same *t* unto them,
21 Lord, shall make known to you all *t*:
Ph'p 1: 10 ye may approve *t* that are excellent;
12 the *t* which happened unto me have
2: 4 Look not every man on his own *t*,
4 but every man also on the *t* of others.
10 knee should bow, of *t* in heaven,
10 and *t* in earth, and *t* under the earth;
14 Do all *t* without murmurings and
21 not the *t* which are Jesus Christ's.
3: 1 To write the same *t* to you, to me
7 But what *t* were gain to me, those I
8 and I count all *t* but loss for the
8 whom I have suffered the loss of all *t*,
13 forgetting those *t* which are behind,
13 reaching forth unto those *t* which
19 is in their shame, who mind earthly *t*.
21 he is able even to subdue all *t* unto
4: 8 brethren, whatsoever *t* are true,
8 whatsoever *t* are honest,
8 whatsoever *t* are just,
8 whatsoever *t* are pure,
8 whatsoever *t* are lovely,
8 whatsoever *t* are of good report; if
8 there be any praise, think on these *t*.
9 Those *t*, which ye have both learned,
12 in all *t* I am instructed both to be
13 I can do all *t* through Christ which
18 the *t* which were sent from you, an
Col 1: 16 For by him were all *t* created, that are
16 all *t* were created by him, and for
17 before all *t*, and by him all *t* consist.
18 that in all *t* he might have the
20 him to reconcile all *t* unto himself;
20 they be *t* in earth, or *t* in heaven.
2: 17 Which are a shadow of *t* to come;
18 intruding into those *t* which he hath
23 *t* have indeed a shew of wisdom
3: 1 Christ, seek those *t* which are above,
2 Set your affection on *t* above,
2 not on *t* on the earth.
14 And above all these *t* put on charity,
20 Children, obey your parents in all *t*:
22 obey in all *t* your masters according
4: 9 shall make known unto you all *t*
1Th 2: 14 have suffered like *t* of your own
5: 21 Prove all *t*; hold fast that which is
2Th 2: 5 yet with you, I told you these *t*?
3: 4 will do the *t* which we command you.
1Ti 3: 11 not slanderers sober, faithful in all *t*.
14 These *t* write I unto thee, hoping
4: 6 brethren in remembrance of these *t*,
8 but godliness is profitable unto all *t*,
11 These *t* command and teach.
15 Meditate upon these *t*; give thyself
5: 7 And these *t* give in charge, that
13 speaking *t* which they ought not.
21 observe these *t* without preferring
6: 2 benefit. These *t* teach and exhort.
11 thou, O man of God, flee these *t*;
13 sight of God, who quickeneth all *t*,
17 who giveth us richly all *t* to enjoy;
2Ti 1: 12 which cause I also suffer these *t*:
18 how many *t* he ministered unto me at
2: 2 *t* that thou hast heard of me among
7 Lord give thee understanding in all *t*.
10 I endure all *t* for the elect's sake,
14 these *t* put them in remembrance,
3: 14 in the *t* which thou hast learned
4: 5 But watch thou in all *t*, endure
Tit 1: 5 set in order the *t* that are wanting,
11 teaching *t* which they ought not, for
15 Unto the pure all *t* are pure: but unto
2: 1 *t* which become sound doctrine:
3 too much wine, teachers of good *t*;
7 In all *t* shewing thyself a pattern of
9 and to please them well in all *t*;
10 doctrine of God our Saviour in all *t*.
15 These *t* speak, and exhort, and
3: 8 *t* I will that thou affirm constantly,
8 *t* are good and profitable unto
Heb 1: 2 whom he hath appointed heir of all *t*,
3 and upholding all *t* by the word of his
2: 1 earnestly to the *t* which we have
8 put all *t* in subjection under his feet.
8 we see not yet all *t* put under him.
10 it became him, for whom are all *t*,
10 and by whom are all *t*, in bringing
17 in all *t* it behoved him to be made like
17 high priest in *t* pertaining to God,
3: 4 man; but he that built all *t* is God.
5 those *t* which were to be spoken after;
4: 13 *t* are naked and opened unto the eyes
5: 1 for men in *t* pertaining to God,
8 learned he obedience by the *t* which
Heb 5: 11 Of whom we have many *t* to say, and
6: 9 we are persuaded better *t* of you,
9 and *t* that accompany salvation,
18 That by two immutable *t*, in
7: 13 he of whom these *t* are spoken
8: 1 *t* which we have spoken this is the
5 example and shadow of heavenly *t*,
5 make all *t* according to the pattern
9: 6 Now when these *t* were thus
11 being come a high priest of good *t*
22 all *t* are by the law purged with blood
23 the patterns of *t* in the heavens
23 the heavenly *t* themselves with better
10: 1 having a shadow of good *t* to come,
1 and not the very image of the *t*,
11: 1 faith is the substance of *t* hoped
1 for, the evidence of *t* not seen.
3 so that *t* which are seen were not
3 were not made of *t* which do appear.
7 being warned of God of *t* not seen as
14 they that say such *t* declare plainly
20 Jacob and Esau concerning *t* to come.
12: 24 speaketh better *t* than that of Abel.
27 removing of those *t* that are shaken,
27 that are shaken, as of *t* that are made,
27 those *t* which cannot be shaken may
13: 5 and be content with such *t* as ye have:
18 in all *t* willing to live honestly.
Jas 2: 16 ye give them not those *t* which are
3: 2 For in many *t* we offend all. If any
5 little member, and boasteth great *t*.
7 and of serpents, and of *t* in the sea, is
10 these *t* ought not so to be.
5: 12 But above all *t*, my brethren, swear
1Pe 1: 12 unto us they did minister the *t*,
12 which *t* the angels desire to look into.
18 were not redeemed with corruptible *t*,
4: 7 But the end of all *t* is at hand: be ye
8 And above all *t* have fervent charity
11 that God in all *t* may be glorified
2Pe 1: 3 given unto us all *t* that pertain unto
8 For if these *t* be in you, and
9 he that lacketh these *t* is blind,
10 for if ye do these *t*, ye shall never
12 always in remembrance of these *t*,
15 these *t* always in remembrance.
2: 12 speak evil of the *t* that they
3: 4 *t* continue as they were from the
11 that all these *t* shall be dissolved,
14 seeing that ye look for such *t*,
16 speaking in them of these *t*;
16 are some *t* hard to be understood,
17 seeing ye know these *t* before,
1Jo 1: 4 And these *t* write we unto you,
2: 1 children, these *t* write I unto you,
15 neither the *t* that are in the world.
20 from the Holy One, and ye know all *t*.
26 These *t* have I written unto you
27 same anointing teacheth you of all *t*,
3: 20 than our heart, and knoweth all *t*.
22 and do those *t* that are pleasing in his
5: 13 These *t* have I written unto you
2Jo 8 not those *t* which we have wrought,
12 Having many *t* to write unto you,
3Jo 2 above all *t* that thou mayest prosper
13 I had many *t* to write, but I will not
Jude 10 speak evil of those *t* which they know
10 in those *t* they corrupt themselves.
Re 1: 1 servants *t* which must shortly come
2 Christ, and of all *t* that he saw.
3 keep those *t* which are written
19 Write the *t* which thou hast seen, and
19 thou hast seen, and the *t* which are,
19 and the *t* which shall be hereafter;
2: 1 These *t* saith he that holdeth the
8 These *t* saith the first and the last,
10 Fear none of those *t* which thou shalt
12 These *t* saith he which hath the sharp
14 But I have a few *t* against thee,
14 to eat *t* sacrificed unto idols, and to
18 These *t* saith the Son of God, who
20 I have a few *t* against thee,
20 and to eat *t* sacrificed unto idols.
3: 1 These *t* saith he that hath the seven
2 and strengthen the *t* which remain,
7 These *t* saith he that is holy, he that
14 These *t* saith the Amen, the faithful
4: 1 shew these *t* which must be hereafter.
11 for thou hast created all *t*, and for
7: 1 after these *t* I saw four angels
10: 4 *t* which the seven thunders uttered,
6 heaven, and the *t* that therein are,
6 the earth, and the *t* that therein are,
6 the sea, and the *t* which are therein,
13: 5 a mouth speaking great *t* and
18: 1 And after these *t* I saw another
14 and all *t* which were dainty and
15 The merchants of these *t*, which
19: 1 after these *t* I heard a great voice
20: 12 *t* which were written in the books,
21: 4 for the former *t* are passed away.
5 said, Behold, I make all *t* new.
7 that overcometh shall inherit all *t*;
22: 6 the *t* which must shortly be done.
8 And I John saw these *t*, and
8 angel which shewed me these *t*.
16 testify unto you these *t* in the
18 If any man shall add unto these *t*,
19 the *t* which are written in this book.
20 He which testifieth these *t* saith,

things'
Col 3: 6 For which *t* sake the wrath of God

think See also BETHINK; THINKEST; THINKETH; THINKING; THOUGHT.
Ge 40: 14 *t* on me when it shall be well

Nu 36: 6 them marry to whom they t' best;
2Sa 13: 33 t' that all the king's sons are dead:
2Ch 13: 8 And now ye t' to withstand the
Ne 5: 19 T' upon me, my God, for good,
6: 6 that thou and the Jews t' to rebel:
14 My God, t' thou upon Tobiah and
Es 4: 13 T' not with thyself that thou shalt
Job 31: 1 why then should I t' upon a maid?
41: 32 one would t' the deep to be hoary.
Ec 8: 17 though a wise man t' to know it,
Isa 10: 7 so, neither doth his heart t' so;
Jer 23: 27 Which t' to cause my people to
29: 11 the thoughts that I t' toward you,
Eze 38: 10 and thou shalt t' an evil thought:
Da 7: 25 and t' to change times and laws:
Jon 1: 6 if so be that God will t' upon us,
Zec 11: 12 If ye t' good, give me my price;
M't 3: 9 t' not to say within yourselves,
5: 17 T' not that I am come to destroy
6: 7 they t' that they shall be heard for
9: 4 Wherefore t' ye evil in your hearts?
10: 34 T' not that I am come to send
18: 12 How t' ye? if a man have an
21: 28 what t' ye? A certain man had
22: 42 Saying, What t' ye of Christ? whose
24: 44 in such an hour as ye t' not the Son
26: 66 What t' ye? They answered and
M'r 14: 64 heard the blasphemy: what t' ye?
Lu 12: 40 cometh at an hour when ye t' not.
13: 4 t' ye that they were sinners above
Joh 5: 39 in them ye t' ye have eternal life:
45 Do not t' that I will accuse you to
11: 56 What t' ye, that he will not come to
16: 2 will t' that he doeth God service.
Ac 13: 25 Whom t' ye that I am? I am not
17: 29 not to t' that the Godhead is like
26: 2 I t' myself happy, king Agrippa,
Ro 12: 3 not to t' of himself more highly
3 more highly than he ought to t';
3 but to t' soberly, according as God
1Co 4: 6 not to t' of men above that which is
9 For I t' that God hath set forth us
7: 36 if any man t' that he behaveth
40 I t' also that I have the Spirit of
8: 2 if any man t' that he knoweth any
12: 23 which we t' to be less honourable,
14: 37 If any man t' himself to be a
2Co 3: 5 to t' any thing as of ourselves;
10: 2 I t' to be bold against some, which
2 which t' of us as if we walked
7 let him of himself t' this again,
11 Let such an one t' this, that, such
11: 16 say again, Let no man t' me a fool;
12: 6 man should t' of me above that
19 t' ye that we excuse ourselves unto
Ga 6: 3 if a man t' himself to be something,
Eph 3: 20 above all that we ask or t',
Ph'p 1: 7 is meet for me to t' this of you all,
4: 8 be any praise, t' on these things.
Jas 1: 7 that man t' that he shall receive
4: 5 Do ye t' that the scripture saith in
1Pe 4: 4 t' it strange that ye run not with them
12 t' it not strange concerning the fiery
2Pe 1: 13 Yea, I t' it meet, as long as I am in

thinkest
2Sa 10: 3 T' thou that David doth honour
1Ch 19: 3 T' thou that David doth honour
Job 35: 2 T' thou this to be right, that thou
M't 17: 25 him, saying, What t' thou, Simon?
22: 17 Tell us therefore, What t' thou?
26: 53 T' thou that I cannot now pray to
Lu 10: 36 Which now of these three, t' thou,
Ac 28: 22 desire to hear of thee what thou t':
Ro 2: 3 And t' thou this, O man, that

thinketh
2Sa 18: 27 Me t' the running of the foremost
Ps 40: 17 needy; yet the Lord t' upon me:
Pr 23: 7 For as he t' in his heart, so is he:
1Co 10: 12 let him that t' he standeth take
13: 5 is not easily provoked, t' no evil;
Ph'p 3: 4 If any other man t' that he hath

thinking
2Sa 4: 10 t'...have brought good tidings,
5: 6 t', David cannot come in hither.

third
Ge 1: 13 and the morning were the t' day.
2: 14 name of the t' river is Hiddekel:
6: 16 and t' stories shalt thou make it.
22: 4 t' day Abraham lifted up his eyes,
31: 22 told Laban on the t' day that Jacob
32: 19 he the second, and the t', and all
34: 25 came to pass on the t' day, when
40: 20 came to pass the t' day, which was
42: 18 Joseph said unto them the t' day,
50: 23 children of the t' generation:
Ex 19: 1 In the t' month, when the children
11 And be ready against the t' day:
11 t' day the Lord will come down in
15 Be ready against the t' day: come
16 it came to pass on the t' day in the
20: 5 unto the t' and fourth generation
28: 19 the t' row a ligure, an agate, and
34: 7 unto the t' and to the fourth
39: 12 the t' row, a ligure, an agate, and
Le 7: 17 flesh of the sacrifice on the t' day
18 be eaten at all on the t' day,
19: 6 if ought remain until the t' day, it
7 if it be eaten at all on the t' day, it
Nu 2: 24 they shall go forward in the t' rank.
7: 24 On the t' day Eliab the son of Helon,
14: 18 unto the t' and fourth generation
15: 6 mingled with the t' part of an hin
7 offer the t' part of an hin of wine,
19: 12 purify himself with it on the t' day,
Nu 19: 12 if he purify not himself the t' day,
19 upon the unclean on the t' day,
28: 14 and the t' part of an hin unto a ram,
29: 20 on the t' day eleven bullocks, two
31: 19 and your captives on the t' day,
De 5: 9 unto the t' and fourth generation
23: 8 of the Lord in their t' generation.
26: 12 tithes of thine increase the t' year,
Jos 9: 17 came unto their cities on the t' day.
19: 10 the t' lot came up for the children
J'g 20: 30 children of Benjamin on the t' day,
1Sa 3: 8 called Samuel again the t' time.
17: 13 Abinadab, and the t' Shammah.
19: 21 sent messengers again the t' time,
20: 5 myself in the field unto the t' day
12 to morrow any time, or the t' day,
30: 1 were come to Ziklag on the t' day,
2Sa 1: 2 It came even to pass on the t' day,
3: 3 the t', Absalom the son of Maacah
18: 2 David sent forth a t' part of the
2 a t' part under the hand of Abishai
2 t' part under the hand of Ittai the
1Ki 3: 18 the t' day after that I was delivered,
6: 6 the t' was seven cubits broad: for
8 and out of the middle into the t'.
12: 12 came to Rehoboam the t' day,
12 saying, Come to me again the t' day.
15: 28 Even in the t' year of Asa king of
33 t' year of Asa king of Judah began
18: 1 Lord came to Elijah in the t' year,
34 And he said, Do it the t' time.
34 And they did it the t' time.
22: 2 it came to pass in the t' year, that
2Ki 1: 13 sent again a captain of the t' fifty
13 And the t' captain of fifty went up,
11: 5 A t' part of you that enter in on the
6 a t' part shall be at the gate of Sur;
6 a t' part at the gate behind the
18: 1 to pass in the t' year of Hoshea
19: 29 in the t' year sow ye, and reap, and
20: 5 t' day thou shalt go up unto the
8 the house of the Lord the t' day?
1Ch 2: 13 the second, and Shimma the t',
3: 2 t', Absalom the son of Maachah the
15 t' Zedekiah, the fourth Shallum.
8: 1 the second, and Aharah the t',
39 the second, and Eliphelet the t'.
12: 9 Obadiah the second, Eliab the t',
23: 19 Jahaziel the t', and Jekameam the
24: 8 t' to Harim, the fourth to Seorim,
23 Jehaziel the t', Jekameam the
25: 10 t' to Zaccur, he, his sons, and his
26: 2 Zebadiah the t', Jathniel the fourth,
4 Joah the t', and Sacar the fourth,
11 Tebaliah the t', Zechariah
27: 5 t' captain of the host for the
5 t' month was Benaiah the son of
2Ch 10: 12 came to Rehoboam on the t' day,
12 Come again to me on the t' day.
15: 10 at Jerusalem in the t' month, in
17: 7 in the t' year of his reign he sent
23: 4 A t' part of you entering on the
5 t' part shall be at the king's house;
5 t' part at the gate of the foundation:
27: 5 both the second year, and the t'.
31: 7 t' month they began to lay the
Ezr 6: 15 house was finished on the t' day
Ne 10: 32 t' part of a shekel for the service
Es 1: 3 In the t' year of his reign, he made
5: 1 Now it came to pass on the t' day,
8: 9 called at that time in the t' month,
Job 42: 14 the name of the t', Keren-happuch.
Isa 19: 24 shall Israel be the t' with Egypt
37: 30 in the t' year sow ye, and reap, and
Jer 38: 14 t' entry that is in the house of the
Eze 5: 2 Thou shalt burn with fire a t' part
2 thou shalt take a t' part, and smite
2 a t' part thou shalt scatter in the
12 A t' part of thee shall die with the
12 a t' part shall fall by the sword
12 I will scatter a t' part into all the
10: 14 and the t' the face of a lion, and the
21: 14 let the sword be doubled the t' time,
31: 1 the eleventh year, in the t' month,
46: 14 the t' part of an hin of oil, to temper
Da 1: 1 t' year of the reign of Jehoiakim
2: 39 and another t' kingdom of brass,
5: 7 shall be the t' ruler in the kingdom.
16, 29 be the t' ruler in the kingdom.
8: 1 In the t' year of the reign of king
10: 1 the t' year of Cyrus king of Persia
Ho 6: 2 t' day he will raise us up, and we
Zec 6: 3 And in the t' chariot white horses;
13: 8 die; but the t' shall be left therein.
9 bring the t' part through the fire,
M't 16: 21 and be raised again the t' day.
17: 23 and the t' day he shall be raised
20: 3 And he went out about the t' hour,
19 and the t' day he shall rise again.
22: 26 also, and the t', unto the seventh.
26: 44 and prayed the t' time, saying the
27: 64 be made sure until the t' day,
M'r 9: 31 he is killed, he shall rise the t' day.
10: 34 and the t' day he shall rise again.
12: 21 he any seed: and the t' likewise.
14: 41 he cometh the t' time, and saith
15: 25 And it was the t' hour, and they
Lu 9: 22 be slain, and be raised the t' day.
12: 38 watch, or come in the t' watch,
13: 32 and the t' day I shall be perfected.
18: 33 and the t' day he shall rise again.
20: 12 And again he sent a t': and they
31 And the t' took her; and in like
23: 22 And he said unto them the t' time,
24: 7 crucified, and the t' day rise again.
21 to day is the t' day since these
Lu 24: 46 to rise from the dead the t' day:
Joh 2: 1 the t' day there was a marriage
21: 14 t' time that Jesus shewed himself
17 He saith unto him the t' time,
17 he said unto him the t' time,
Ac 2: 15 it is but the t' hour of the day.
10: 40 Him God raised up the t' day, and
20: 9 and fell down from the t' loft,
23: 23 at the t' hour of the night;
27: 19 And the t' day we cast out with
1Co 15: 4 he rose again the t' day according
2Co 12: 2 an one caught up to the t' heaven.
14 t' time I am ready to come to you;
13: 1 is the t' time I am coming to you.
Re 4: 7 and the t' beast had a face as a man,
6: 5 when he had opened the t' seal,
5 I heard the t' beast say, Come and
8: 7 the t' part of trees was burnt up,
8 the t' part of the sea became blood;
9 the t' part of the creatures which
9 t' part of the ships were destroyed.
10 And the t' angel sounded, and there
10 fell upon the t' part of the rivers,
11 the t' part of the waters became
12 the t' part of the sun was smitten,
12 and the t' part of the moon, and the
12 moon, and the t' part of the stars;
12 t' part of them was darkened, and
12 the day shone not for a t' part of it,
9: 15 year, for to slay the t' part of men.
18 three was the t' part of men killed,
11: 14 behold, the t' woe cometh quickly.
12: 4 tail drew the t' part of the stars of
14: 9 And the t' angel followed them,
16: 4 t' angel poured out his vial upon
21: 19 the t', a chalcedony; the fourth, an

thirdly
1Co 12: 28 secondarily prophets, t' teachers,

thirst See also ATHIRST; THIRSTED; THIRSTETH.
Ex 17: 3 our children and our cattle with t'?
De 28: 48 hunger, and in t', and in nakedness,
29: 19 heart, to add drunkenness to t':
J'g 15: 18 and now shall I die for t', and fall
2Ch 32: 11 yourselves to die by famine and...t',
Ne 9: 15 for them out of the rock for their t',
20 and gavest them water for their t'.
Job 24: 11 their winepresses, and suffer t'.
Ps 69: 21 in my t' they gave me vinegar to
104: 11 the wild asses quench their t'.
Isa 5: 13 their multitude dried up with t'.
41: 17 and their tongue faileth for t',
49: 10 They shall not hunger nor t';
50: 2 there is no water, and dieth for t'.
Jer 2: 25 unshod, and thy throat from t':
48: 18 down from thy glory, and sit in t';
La 4: 4 to the roof of his mouth for t':
Ho 2: 3 like a dry land, and slay her with t'.
Am 8: 11 famine of bread, nor a t' for water,
13 virgins and young men faint for t'.
M't 5: 6 hunger and t' after righteousness:
Joh 4: 13 drinketh...this water shall t' again:
14 that I shall give him shall never t';
15 give me this water, that I t' not,
6: 35 that believeth on me shall never t'.
7: 37 If any man t', let him come unto
19: 28 might be fulfilled, saith, I t'.
Ro 12: 20 feed him; if he t', give him drink:
1Co 4: 11 both hunger, and t', and are naked,
2Co 11: 27 watchings often, in hunger and t',
Re 7: 16 no more, neither t' any more;

thirsted
Ex 17: 3 And the people t' there for water;
Isa 48: 21 And they t' not when he led them

thirsteth
Ps 42: 2 My soul t' for God, for the living
63: 1 my soul t' for thee, my flesh longeth
143: 6 my soul t' after thee, as a thirsty
Isa 55: 1 Ho, every one that t', come ye to

thirsty See also BLOODTHIRSTY.
J'g 4: 19 a little water to drink; for I am t'.
2Sa 17: 29 is hungry, and weary, and t',
Ps 63: 1 longeth for thee in a dry and t' land,
107: 5 Hungry and t', their soul fainted
143: 6 soul thirsteth after thee, as a t' land
Pr 25: 21 and if he be t', give him water to
25 As cold waters to a t' soul, so is good
Isa 21: 14 brought water to him that was t',
29: 8 or as when a t' man dreameth, and,
32: 6 will cause the drink of the t' to fail.
35: 7 and the t' land springs of water:
44: 3 pour water upon him that is t',
65: 13 shall drink, but ye shall be t':
Eze 19: 13 wilderness, in a dry and t' ground.
M't 25: 35 I was t', and ye gave me drink:
37 fed thee? or t', and gave thee drink?
42 I was t', and ye gave me no drink:

thirteen
Ge 17: 25 his son was t' years old,
Nu 3: 43 hundred and threescore and t'.
46 hundred and threescore and t' of
29: 13 t' young bullocks, two rams,
14 every bullock of the t' bullocks,
Jos 19: 6 t' cities and their villages:
21: 4 the tribe of Benjamin, t' cities.
6 Manasseh in Bashan, t' cities.
19 t' cities with their suburbs.
33 t' cities with their suburbs.
1Ki 7: 1 building his own house t' years,
1Ch 6: 60 their families were t' cities.
62 Manasseh in Bashan, t' cities.
26: 11 and brethren of Hosah were t'.
Eze 40: 11 length of the gate, t' cubits.

thirteenth
Ge 14: 4 in the t' year they rebelled.
1Ch 24:13 t' to Huppah, the fourteenth
25:20 The t' to Shubael, he, his sons,
Es 3:12 scribes called on the t' day
13 upon the t' day of the twelfth
8:12 upon the t' day of the twelfth
9: 1 Adar, on the t' day of the same,
17 the t' day of the month Adar;
18 together on the t' day thereof,
Jer 1: 2 in the t' year of his reign.
25: 3 the t' year of Josiah the son of

thirtieth
2Ki 15:13 in the nine and t' year of Uzziah
17 In the nine and t' year of Azariah
25:27 seven and t' year of the captivity of
2Ch 15:19 five and t' year of the reign of Asa.
16: 1 six and t' year of the reign of Asa
Ne 5:14 two and t' year of Artaxerxes the
13: 6 the two and t' year of Artaxerxes
Jer 52:31 seven and t' year of the captivity of
Eze 1: 1 Now it came to pass in the t' year,

thirty See also THIRTYFOLD.
Ge 5: 3 And Adam lived an hundred and t'
5 were nine hundred and t' years:
16 Jared eight hundred and t' years,
6:15 cubits, and the height of it t' cubits.
11:12 Arphaxad lived five and t' years,
14 And Salah lived t' years, and begat
16 And Eber lived four and t' years,
17 Peleg four hundred and t' years,
18 And Peleg lived t' years, and begat
20 And Reu lived two and t' years, and
22 And Serug lived t' years, and begat
18:30 there shall t' be found there.
30 I will not do it, if I find t' there.
25:17 an hundred and t' and seven years:
32:15 T' milch camels with their colts,
41:46 And Joseph was t' years old when
46:15 his daughters were t' and three.
47: 9 are an hundred and t' years:
Ex 6:16 were an hundred t' and seven years.
18 were an hundred t' and three years.
20 an hundred and t' and seven years.
12:40 was four hundred and t' years.
41 end of the four hundred and t' years,
21:32 their masters t' shekels of silver,
26: 8 of one curtain shall be t' cubits,
36:15 length of one curtain was t' cubits,
38:24 and seven hundred and t' shekels,
Le 12: 4 of her purifying three and t' days;
27: 4 thy estimation shall be t' shekels.
Nu 1:35 were t' and two thousand and two
37 were t' and five thousand and four
2:21 were t' and two thousand and two
23 were t' and five thousand and four
4: 3, 23, 30, 35, 39 t' years old and upward
40 thousand and six hundred and t'.
43, 47 From t' years old and upward
7:13, 19, 25, 31, 37, 43, 49, 55, 61, 67, 73,
79, 85 an hundred and t' shekels,
20:29 they mourned for Aaron t' days,
26: 7 thousand and seven hundred and t'.
37 them, t' and two thousand and five
51 a thousand seven hundred and t'.
31:35 t' and two thousand persons in all,
36 seven and t' thousand and five
38 beeves were t' and six thousand;
39 the asses were t' thousand and five
40 the Lord's tribute was t' and two
43 hundred thousand and t' thousand
44 And t' and six thousand beeves,
45 t' thousand asses and five hundred,
De 2:14 brook Zered, was t' and eight years;
34: 8 Moses in the plains of Moab t' days:
Jos 7: 5 smote of them about t' and six men:
8: 3 and Joshua chose out t' thousand
12:24 one: all the kings t' and one.
J'g 10: 4 had t' sons that rode on t' ass colts,
4 and they had t' cities, which are
12: 9 he had t' sons, and t' daughters,
9 took in t' daughters from abroad
14 he had forty sons and t' nephews,
14:11 they brought t' companions to be
12 t' sheets and t' change of garments:
13 t' sheets and t' change of garments.
19 slew t' men of them, and took their
20:31 in the field, about t' men of Israel.
39 and kill of the men of Israel about t'
1Sa 4:10 fell of Israel t' thousand footmen.
9:22 which were about t' persons.
11: 8 and the men of Judah t' thousand.
13: 5 t' thousand chariots, and six
2Sa 5: 4 David was t' years old when he
5 he reigned t' and three years over
6: 1 chosen men of Israel, t' thousand.
23:13 And three of the t' chief went down,
23 He was more honourable than the t',
24 brother of Joab was one of the t';
39 the Hittite: t' and seven in all.
1Ki 2:11 t' and three years reigned he in
4:22 day was t' measures of fine flour,
5:13 and the levy was t' thousand men.
6: 2 and the height thereof t' cubits.
7: 2 and the height thereof t' cubits,
6 and the breadth thereof t' cubits:
23 and a line of t' cubits did compass it
16:23 the t' and first year of Asa king of
29 the t' and eighth year of Asa king
20: 1 there were t' and two kings with
15 they were two hundred and t' two:
16 t' and two kings that helped him.
22:31 t' and two captains that had rule
42 Jehoshaphat was t' and five years
2Ki 8:17 T' and two years old was he when
13:10 t' and seventh year of Joash king
15: 8 t' and eighth year of Azariah king
18:14 of silver and t' talents of gold.
22: 1 and he reigned t' and one years in
1Ch 3: 4 he reigned t' and three years.
7: 4 for war, six and t' thousand men:
7 and two thousand and t' and four.
11:15 Now three of the t' captains went
25 he was honourable among the t',
42 of the Reubenites, and t' with him,
12: 4 man among the t', and over the t';
34 and spear t' and seven thousand.
15: 7 and his brethren an hundred and t':
19: 7 hired t' and two thousand chariots,
23: 3 the age of t' years and upward:
3 by man, was t' and eight thousand.
27: 6 among the t', and above the t':
29:27 t' and three years reigned he in
2Ch 3:15 two pillars of t' and five cubits high,
4: 2 a line of t' cubits did compass it
16:12 Asa in the t' and ninth year of his
20:31 he was t' and five years old when he
21: 5 Jehoram was t' and two years old
20 T' and two years old was he when
24:15 an hundred and t' years old was he
34: 1 in Jerusalem one and t' years.
35: 7 to the number of t' thousand, and
Ezr 1: 9 t' chargers of gold, a thousand
10 T' basons of gold, silver basons of
2:35 thousand and six hundred and t'.
42 in all an hundred t' and nine.
65 three hundred t' and seven:
66 were seven hundred t' and six;
67 camels, four hundred t' and five;
Ne 7:38 three thousand nine hundred and t'.
45 of Shobai, an hundred t' and eight.
67 three hundred t' and seven:
68 horses, seven hundred t' and six:
69 camels, four hundred t' and five:
70 hundred and t' priests' garments.
Es 4:11 come in unto the king these t' days.
Jer 38:10 Take from hence t' men with thee,
52:29 eight hundred t' and two persons:
Eze 40:17 t' chambers were upon the
41: 6 one over another, and t' in order;
46:22 of forty cubits long and t' broad:
Da 6: 7 of any God or man for t' days,
12 of any God or man within t' days,
12:12 hundred and five and t' days.
Zec 11:12 for my price t' pieces of silver.
13 and I took the t' pieces of silver,
M't 13:23 hundredfold, some sixty, some t'.
26:15 with him for t' pieces of silver.
27: 3 brought again the t' pieces of silver
9 they took the t' pieces of silver, the
M'r 4: 8 forth, some t', and some sixty, and
Lu 3:23 began to be about t' years of age,
Joh 5: 5 had an infirmity t' and eight years.
6:19 about five and twenty or t' furlongs,
Ga 3:17 four hundred and t' years after,

thirtyfold
M't 13: 8 some sixtyfold, some t'.
M'r 4:20 forth fruit, some t', some sixty,

thirty-thousand See THIRTY and THOUSAND.

this^ See also THESE.
Ge 2:23 T' is now bone of my bones, and
3:13 What is t' that thou hast done?
14 Because thou hast done t', thou
4:14 thou hast driven me out t' day from
5: 1 T' is the book of the generations
29 T' same shall comfort us
6:15 t' is the fashion which thou shalt
7: 1 before me in t' generation.
9:12 T' is the token of the covenant
11: 6 t' they begin to do: and now
12: 7 Unto thy seed will I give t' land:
12 that they shall say, T' is his wife:
18 What is t' that thou hast done
15: 2 house is t' Eliezer of Damascus?
4 saying, T' shall not be thine heir;
7 to give thee t' land to inherit it.
18 Unto thy seed have I given t' land,
17:10 T' is my covenant, which ye shall
21 at t' set time in the next year.
18:25 from thee to do after t' manner,
32 and I will speak yet but t' once:
19: 5 men which came in to thee t' night?
9 T' one fellow came in to sojourn,
12 city, bring them out of t' place:
13 For we will destroy t' place,
14 said, Up, get you out of t' place;
14 for the Lord will destroy t' city.
20 now, t' city is near to flee unto,
21 accepted thee concerning t' thing
21 that I will not overthrow t' city,
34 make him drink wine t' night also;
37 father of the Moabites unto t' day.
38 the children of Ammon unto t' day.
20: 5 of my hands have I done t'.
6 thou didst t' in the integrity of thy
10 that thou hast done t' thing?
11 the fear of God is not in t' place;
13 T' is thy kindness which thou
21:10 Cast out t' bondwoman and her
10 the son of t' bondwoman shall not
26 I wot not who hath done t' thing:
24:58 unto her, Wilt thou go with t' man?
65 What man is t' that walketh in
25:31 said, Sell me t' day thy birthright.
32 what profit shall t' birthright do
33 And Jacob said, Swear to me t' day;
26: 3 Sojourn in t' land, and I will be
10 What is t' thou hast done unto us?
11 He that toucheth t' man or his
33 the city is Beer-sheba unto t' day.
Ge 28:15 will bring thee again into t' land;
16 Surely the Lord is in t' place; and
17 and said, How dreadful is t' place!
17 t' is none other but the house of
17 God, and t' is the gate of heaven.
20 will keep me in t' way that I go,
22 t' stone, which I have set for a
29:25 What is t' thou hast done unto me?
27 we will give thee t' also for the
33 therefore given me t' son also:
34 t' time will my husband be joined
30:31 if thou wilt do t' thing for me, I
31: 1 father's hath he gotten all t' glory.
13 arise, get thee out from t' land,
38 T' twenty years have I been with
43 what can I do t' day unto these my
48 T' heap is a witness between me
48 witness between me and thee t' day.
51 said to Jacob, Behold t' heap,
51 behold t' pillar, which I have
52 T' heap be witness, and
52 t' pillar be witness, that I will not
52 will not pass over t' heap to thee,
52 t' heap [2088] and t' pillar unto
32: 2 them, he said, T' is God's host:
10 my staff I passed over t' Jordan;
19 On t' manner shall ye speak unto
32 hollow of the thigh, unto t' day:
33: 8 What meanest thou by all t' drove
34: 4 saying, Get me t' damsel to wife.
14 We cannot do t' thing, to give our
15 in t' will we consent unto you:
35:17 thou shalt have t' son also.
20 pillar of Rachel's grave unto t' day.
36:24 t' was that Anah that found the
37: 6 t' dream which I have dreamed:
10 t' dream that thou hast dreamed?
19 Behold, t' dreamer cometh.
22 cast him into t' pit that is in the
32 and said, T' have we found:
38:21 There was no harlot in t' place.
22 that there was no harlot in t' place.
23 behold, I sent t' kid, and thou
28 thread, saying, T' came out first.
39: 9 is none greater in t' house than I:
9 can I do t' great wickedness, and
11 And it came to pass about t' time,
19 t' manner did thy servant to me;
40:12 T' is the interpretation of it:
14 and bring me out of t' house:
18 T' is the interpretation thereof:
41: 9 I do remember my faults t' day:
24 and I told t' unto the magicians;
34 Let Pharaoh do t', and let him
38 Can we find such a one as t' is,
39 as God hath shewed thee all t',
42:13 youngest is t' day with our father,
18 T' do, and live; for I fear God:
21 is t' distress come upon us.
28 What is t' that God hath done
32 youngest is t' day with our father
43:10 we had returned t' second time.
11 If it must be so now, do t';
29 Is t' your younger brother, of
44: 5 Is not t' it in which my lord
7 should do according to t' thing:
29 And if ye take t' also from me,
45:17 Say unto thy brethren, T' do ye;
19 Now thou art commanded, t' do ye;
23 his father he sent after t' manner;
47:23 I have bought you t' day and your
26 the land of Egypt unto t' day,
48: 4 will give t' land to thy seed after
9 God hath given me in t' place.
18 for t' is the firstborn; put thy
49:28 t' is it that their father spake
50:11 T' is a grievous mourning to the
20 as it is t' day, to save much people
24 bring you out of t' land unto the
Ex 1:18 Why have ye done t' thing, and
2: 6 T' is one of the Hebrews' children.
9 Take t' child away, and nurse it
12 he looked t' way and that way,
14 and said, Surely t' thing is known.
15 when Pharaoh heard t' thing,
3: 3 turn aside, and see t' great sight,
15 unto you: t' is my name for ever,
15 and t' is my memorial unto all
4:17 shalt take t' rod in thine hand,
5:22 thou so evil entreated t' people?
23 he hath done evil to t' people;
7:17 In t' thou shalt know that I am
23 did he set his heart to t' also.
8:19 Pharaoh, T' is the finger of God:
23 to morrow shall t' sign be.
32 hardened his heart at t' time also,
9: 5 the Lord shall do t' thing in the
14 For I will at t' time send all my
16 for t' cause have I raised thee up,
18 to morrow about t' time I will cause
27 unto them, I have sinned t' time:
10: 6 were upon the earth unto t' day.
7 How long shall t' man be a snare
17 I pray thee, my sin only t' once,
17 take away from me t' death only.
12: 2 T' month shall be unto you the
3 In the tenth day of t' month they
12 through the land of Egypt t' night,
14 t' day shall be unto you for a
17 in t' selfsame day have I brought
24 observe t' thing for an ordinance
26 you, What mean ye by t' service?
42 t' is that night of the Lord to be
13: 3 Remember t' day, in which ye
3 brought you out from t' place:
4 T' day came ye out in the month

Ex 13: 5 shalt keep t' service in t' month.
8 T' is done because of that which
10 keep t' ordinance in his season
14 time to come, saying, What is t'?
14: 5 Why have we done t', that we have
12 Is not t' the word that we did tell
15: 1 the children of Israel t' song unto
16: 3 us forth into t' wilderness,
3 to kill t' whole assembly with
15 T' is the bread which the Lord
16 T' is the thing which the Lord
23 T' is that which the Lord hath
32 T' is the thing which the Lord
17: 3 Wherefore is t' that thou hast
4 What shall I do unto t' people?
14 Write t' for a memorial in a book,
18: 14 What is t' thing that thou doest
18 and t' people that is with thee:
18 for t' thing is too heavy for thee;
23 If thou shalt do t' thing, and God
23 all t' people shall also go to their
21: 31 according to t' judgment shall it be
25: 3 t' is the offering which ye shall
26: 13 on t' side and on that side,
28: 17 carbuncle: t' shall be the first row.
29: 1 t' is the thing that thou shalt do
38 t' is that which thou shalt offer
42 T' shall be a continual burnt
30: 13 T' they shall give, every one that
31 T' shall be an holy anointing oil
32: 1 for as for t' Moses, the man that
9 unto Moses, I have seen t' people,
12 repent of t' evil against thy people.
13 all t' land that I have spoken of
21 What did t' people unto thee, that
23 for as for t' Moses, the man that
24 the fire, and there came out t' calf.
29 bestow upon you a blessing t' day.
31 t' people have sinned a great sin,
33: 12 sayest unto me, Bring up t' people:
17 I will do t' thing also that thou
34: 11 that which I command thee t' day:
35: 4 T' is the thing which the Lord
37: 8 One cherub on the end on t' side,
38: 15 on t' hand and that hand, were
21 T' is the sum of the tabernacle,
39: 10 and a carbuncle: t' was the first row.
Le 4: 20 a sin offering, so shall he do with t':
6: 9 T' is the law of the burnt offering:
14 t' is the law of the meat offering:
20 T' is the offering of Aaron and of
25 T' is the law of the sin offering:
7: 1 t' is the law of the trespass
11 t' is the law of the sacrifice of peace
35 T' is the portion of the anointing
37 T' is the law of the burnt offering,
8: 5 T' is the thing which the Lord
34 As he hath done t' day, so the Lord
9: 6 T' is the thing which the Lord
10: 3 T' is it that the Lord spake,
19 t' day have they offered their sin
11: 46 T' is the law of the beasts, and of
12: 7 T' is the law for her that hath born
13: 59 T' is the law of the plague of
14: 2 T' shall be the law of the leper in
32 T' is the law of him in whom is the
54 T' is the law for all manner of
57 it is clean: t' is the law of leprosy.
15: 3 t' shall be his uncleanness in his
32 T' is the law of him that hath an
16: 29 t' shall be a statute for ever unto you:
34 t' shall be an everlasting statute
17: 2 T' is the thing which the Lord
7 T' shall be a statute for ever unto
23: 27 the tenth day of t' seventh month
34 fifteenth day of t' seventh month
24: 10 t' son of the Israelitish woman and a
25: 13 In the year of t' jubile ye shall
26: 18 if ye will not yet for all t' hearken
27 if ye will not for all t' hearken
Nu 4: 4 T' shall be the service of the sons
24, 28 T' is the service of the families
31 And t' is the charge of their burden,
33 T' is the service of the families of
5: 19 free from t' bitter water that causeth
22 t' water that causeth the curse shall
29 T' is the law of jealousies, when
30 shall execute upon her all t' law.
31 t' woman shall bear her iniquity.
6: 13 And t' is the law of the Nazarite,
20 t' is holy for the priest, with the
21 T' is the law of the Nazarite who
23 On t' wise ye shall bless the
7: 17 t' was the offering of Nahshon the
23 t' was the offering of Nathaneel the
29 t' was the offering of Eliab the son
35 t' was the offering of Elizur the son
41 t' was the offering of Shelumiel the
47 t' was the offering of Eliasaph the
53 t' was the offering of Elishama the
59 t' was the offering of Gamaliel the
65 t' was the offering of Abidan the
71 t' was the offering of Ahiezer the
77 t' was the offering of Pagiel the son
83 t' was the offering of Ahira the son
84, 88 T' was the dedication of the
8: 4 t' work of the candlestick was of
24 T' is it that belongeth unto the
9: 3 In the fourteenth day of t' month,
11: 6 is nothing at all, beside t' manna,
11 burden of all t' people upon me?
12 Have I conceived all t' people?
13 have flesh to give unto all t' people?
14 not able to bear all t' people alone,
31 it were a day's journey on t' side,
13: 17 Get you up t' way southward, and
Nu 13: 27 and honey; and t' is the fruit of it.
14: 2 God we had died in t' wilderness!
3 the Lord brought us unto t' land,
8 then he will bring us into t' land,
11 long will t' people provoke me?
13 (for thou broughtest up t' people in
14 tell it to the inhabitants of t' land:
14 thou Lord art among t' people,
15 shalt kill all t' people as one man,
16 was not able to bring t' people into
19 Pardon,...the iniquity of t' people
19 and as thou hast forgiven t' people,
27 I bear with t' evil congregation,
29 carcases...fall in t' wilderness;
32 they shall fall in t' wilderness.
35 do it unto all t' evil congregation,
35 in t' wilderness they shall be
15: 13 shall do these things after t' manner
16: 6 T' do; Take you censers, Korah,
21 from among t' congregation,
45 you up from among t' congregation,
18: 9 T' shall be thine of the most holy
11 t' is thine; the heave offering of
27 And t' your heave offering shall be
19: 2 T' is the ordinance of the law
14 T' is the law, when a man dieth in
20: 4 of the Lord into t' wilderness,
5 to bring us in unto t' evil place?
10 we fetch you water out of t' rock?
12 ye shall not bring t' congregation
13 T' is the water of Meribah;
21: 2 deliver t' people into my hand,
5 and our soul loatheth t' light bread.
17 Then Israel sang t' song, Spring
22: 1 plains of Moab on t' side Jordan
4 Now shall t' company lick up all that
6 I pray thee, curse me t' people;
8 Lodge here t' night, and I will bring
17 I pray thee, curse me t' people.
19 tarry ye also here t' night, that I may
24 a wall being on t' side, and a wall
30 ever since I was thine unto t' day?
23: 23 according to t' time it shall be said of
24: 14 t' people shall do to thy people
23 Alas, who shall live when God doeth t'!
26: 9 T' is that Dathan and Abiram,
27: 12 Get thee up into t' mount Abarim,
28: 10 T' is the burnt offering of every
14 t' is the burnt offering of every
17 the fifteenth day of t' month is the
24 After t' manner ye shall offer daily,
29: 7 day of t' seventh month an holy
30: 1 T' is the thing which the Lord hath
31: 21 T' is the ordinance of the law
32: 5 t' land be given unto thy servants
15 and ye shall destroy all t' people.
19 is fallen to us on t' side Jordan
20 If ye will do t' thing, if ye will go
22 t' land shall be your possession
32 inheritance on t' side Jordan may
34: 2 (t' is the land that shall fall unto
6 t' shall be your west border.
7 And t' shall be your north border:
9 t' shall be your north border.
12 t' shall be your land with the
13 T' is the land...ye shall inherit by
15 inheritance on t' side Jordan near
35: 5 t' shall be to them the suburbs of
14 give three cities on t' side Jordan,
36: 6 T' is the thing which the Lord
De 1: 1 unto all Israel on t' side Jordan
5 On t' side Jordan, in the land of
5 began Moses to declare t' law,
6 dwelt long enough in t' mount:
10 ye are t' day as the stars of heaven
32 Yet in t' thing ye did not believe
35 of these men of t' evil generation
2: 3 have compassed t' mountain long
7 walking through t'...wilderness:
18 through Ar, the coast of Moab, t' day:
22 in their stead even unto t' day:
25 T' day will I begin to put the dread
30 into thy hand, as appeareth t' day.
3: 8 land that was on t' side Jordan,
12 t' land, which we possessed at
14 Bashan-havoth-jair, unto t' day.
18 your God hath given you t' land
26 no more unto me of t' matter.
27 thou shalt not go over t' Jordan.
28 he shall go over before t' people,
4: 4 God are alive every one of you t' day.
6 for t' is your wisdom and your
6 Surely t' great nation is a wise
8 so righteous as all t' law, which
8 law, which I set before you t' day?
20 of inheritance, as ye are t' day.
22 But I must die in t' land, I must
26 earth to witness against you t' day,
32 any such thing as t' great thing
38 for an inheritance, as it is t' day.
39 Know therefore t' day, and consider it
40 which I command thee t' day, that
41 three cities on t' side Jordan
44 t' is the law which Moses set
46 On t' side Jordan, in the valley
47 which were on t' side Jordan
49 plain on t' side Jordan eastward,
5: 1 which I speak in your ears t' day,
3 Lord made not t' covenant with
3 who are all of us here alive t' day.
24 seen t' day that God doth talk
25 for t' great fire will consume us:
28 the voice of the words of t' people,
6: 6 words, which I command thee t' day,
24 preserve us alive, as it is at t' day.
7: 11 which I command thee t' day,
De 8: 1 which I command thee t' day shall ye
11 which I command thee t' day:
17 hand hath gotten me t' wealth.
18 unto thy fathers, as it is t' day.
19 I testify against you t' day that ye
9: 1 Thou art to pass over Jordan t' day,
3 Understand therefore t' day, that the
4 brought me in to possess t' land:
6 God giveth thee not t' good land
7 until ye came unto t' place, ye
13 me, saying, I have seen t' people,
27 unto the stubbornness of t' people,
10: 8 to bless in his name, unto t' day.
13 I command thee t' day for thy good?
15 above all people, as it is t' day.
11: 2 And know ye t' day: for I speak not
4 hath destroyed them unto t' day;
8, 13 which I command you t' day,
26 I set before you t' day a blessing and
27 God, which I command you t' day:
28 the way which I command you t' day,
32 which I set before you t' day.
12: 8 all the things that we do here t' day,
13: 11 such wickedness as t' is among
18 which I command thee t' day,
15: 2 t' is the manner of the release:
5 which I command thee t' day.
10 t' thing the Lord thy God shall
15 I command thee t' thing to day.
17: 18 him a copy of t' law in a book
19 to keep all the words of t' law and
18: 3 t' shall be the priest's due from
16 neither let me see t' great fire
19: 4 t' is the case of the slayer, which
9 I command thee t' day, to love the
20: 3 ye approach t' day unto battle against
21: 7 Our hands have not shed t' blood,
20 T' our son is stubborn and
22: 14 I took t' woman, and when I came
16 my daughter unto t' man to wife,
20 But if t' thing be true, and the
26 slayeth him, even so is t' matter:
24: 18, 22 I command thee to do t' thing.
26: 3 I profess t' day unto the Lord thy God,
9 he hath brought us into t' place,
9 given us t' land, even a land that
16 T' day the Lord thy God hath
17 the Lord t' day to be thy God,
18 Lord hath avouched thee t' day to be
27: 1 which I command you t' day.
3 upon them all the words of t' law,
4 which I command you t' day, in
8 the stones all the words of t' law
9 t' day thou art become the people
10 which I command thee t' day.
26 not all the words of t' law to do
28: 1, 13 which I command thee t' day,
14 words which I command thee t' day,
15 which I command thee t' day;
58 to do all the words of t' law that
58 that are written in t' book, that
58 fear t' glorious and fearful name,
61 not written in the book of t' law,
29: 4 see, and ears to hear, unto t' day.
7 when ye came unto t' place, Sihon
9 therefore the words of t' covenant,
10 stand t' day all of you before the Lord
12 Lord thy God maketh with thee t' day:
14 do I make t' covenant and t' oath;
15 him that standeth here with us t' day
15 him that is not here with us t' day:
18 heart turneth...t' day from the Lord
19 he heareth the words of t' curse,
20 curses that are written in t' book
21 are written in t' book of the law:
24 the Lord done thus unto t' land?
24 the heat of t' great anger?
27 Lord was kindled against t' land,
27 curses that are written in t' book:
28 into another land, as it is t' day.
29 may do all the words of t' law.
30: 2 to all that I command thee t' day,
8 which I command thee t' day.
10 are written in t' book of the law,
11 For t' commandment which I
11 which I command thee t' day, it is
15 set before thee t' day life and good,
16 that I command thee t' day to love
18 I denounce unto you t' day, that ye
19 earth to record t' day against you,
31: 2 hundred and twenty years old t' day;
2 Thou shalt not go over t' Jordan.
7 thou must go with t' people unto
9 Moses wrote t' law, and delivered
11 read t' law before all Israel in their
12 to do all the words of t' law:
16 t' people will rise up, and go a
19 therefore write ye t' song for you,
19 t' song may be a witness for me
21 t' song shall testify against them
22 Moses therefore wrote t' song the
24 writing the words of t' law in a
26 Take t' book of the law, and put
27 while I am yet alive with you t' day,
30 of Israel the words of t' song,
32: 27 and the Lord hath not done all t'.
29 were wise, that they understood t',
34 Is not t' laid up in store with me,
44 words of t' song in the ears of the
46 which I testify among you t' day,
46 to do, all the words of t' law.
47 through t' thing ye shall prolong
49 thee up into t' mountain Abarim,
33: 1 t' is the blessing, wherewith Moses
7 t' is the blessing of Judah: and he
34: 4 T' is the land which I sware unto

De 34: 6 of his sepulchre unto *t'* day.
Jos 1: 2 therefore arise, go over *t'* Jordan,
2 thou, and all *t'* people, unto the
4 *t'* Lebanon even unto the great
6 unto *t'* people shalt thou divide for
8 *T'* book of the law shall not depart
11 days ye shall pass over *t'* Jordan,
13 rest, and hath given you *t'* land.
14 Moses gave you on *t'* side Jordan;
15 servant gave you on *t'* side Jordan
2:14 if ye utter not *t'* our business.
17 will be blameless of *t'* thine oath
18 shalt bind *t'* line of scarlet thread
20 And if thou utter *t'* our business,
3: 4 ye have not passed *t'* way heretofore.
7 *T'* day will I begin to magnify
4: 3 place, where ye shall lodge *t'* night.
6 That *t'* may be a sign among you,
9 and they are there unto *t'* day.
22 Israel came over *t'* Jordan on dry
5: 4 *t'* is the cause why Joshua did
9 *T'* day have I rolled away the
9 place is called Gilgal unto *t'* day.
6:25 dwelleth in Israel even unto *t'* day;
26 that riseth up and buildeth *t'* city
7: 7 all brought *t'* people over Jordan,
25 the Lord shall trouble thee *t'* day.
26 a great heap of stones unto *t'* day.
26 The valley of Achor, unto *t'* day.
8:20 had no power to flee *t'* way or that
22 some on *t'* side, and some on that
28 ever, even a desolation unto *t'* day.
29 stones, that remaineth unto *t'* day.
33 stood on *t'* side the ark and on that
9: 1 which were on *t'* side Jordan,
12 *T'* our bread we took hot for our
20 *T'* we will do to them; we will
24 of you, and have done *t'* thing.
27 altar of the Lord, even unto *t'* day.
10:13 Is not *t'* written in the book of
27 which remain until *t'* very day.
11: 6 for to morrow about *t'* time will I
12: 7 Israel smote on *t'* side Jordan on
13: 2 *T'* is the land that yet remaineth:
7 divide *t'* land for an inheritance
13 among the Israelites until *t'* day.
23 *T'* was the inheritance of the
28 *T'* is the inheritance of the children
29 *t'* was the possession of the half tribe
14:10 Lord spake *t'* word unto Moses,
10 I am *t'* day fourscore and five years
11 I am as strong *t'* day as I was in the
12 therefore give me *t'* mountain,
14 Jephunneh the Kenezite...*t'* day,
15: 1 *T'* then was the lot of the tribe of the
4 sea: *t'* shall be your south coast.
12 *T'* is the coast of the children of
20 *T'* is the inheritance of the tribe
63 Judah at Jerusalem unto *t'* day.
16: 8 *T'* is the inheritance of the tribe
10 the Ephraimites unto *t'* day,
18:14 Judah: *t'* was the west quarter.
19 of Jordan: *t'* was the south coast.
20 *T'* was the inheritance of the
28 *T'* is the inheritance of the children
19: 8 *T'* is the inheritance of the tribe of
16 *T'* is the inheritance of the children
23, 31, 39, 48 *T'* is the inheritance of
22: 3 these many days unto *t'* day,
7 their brethren on *t'* side Jordan
16 What trespass is *t'* that ye have
16 turn away *t'* day from following the
16 ye might rebel *t'* day against the
17 we are not cleansed until *t'* day,
18 turn away *t'* day from following the
22 the Lord, (save us not *t'* day,)
24 rather done it for fear of *t'* thing,
29 turn *t'* day from following the Lord, to
31 *T'* day we perceive that the Lord is
31 not committed *t'* trespass against
23: 8 God, as ye have done unto *t'* day.
9 to stand before you unto *t'* day.
13 perish from off *t'* good land which
14 *t'* day I am going the way of all the
15 destroyed you from off *t'* good land
24:15 choose you *t'* day whom ye will serve:
27 *t'* stone shall be a witness unto
J'g 1:21 Benjamin in Jerusalem unto *t'* day.
26 is the name thereof unto *t'* day.
2: 2 with the inhabitants of *t'* land;
2 my voice: why have ye done *t'*?
20 that *t'* people hath transgressed
4:14 *t'* is the day in which the Lord hath
6:13 us, why then is all *t'* befallen us?
14 Go in *t'* thy might, and thou shalt
20 cakes, and lay them upon *t'* rock,
24 *t'* day it is yet in Ophrah of the
26 thy God upon the top of *t'* rock,
29 to another, Who hath done *t'* thing?
29 the son of Joash hath done *t'* thing.
39 me, and I will speak but *t'* once:
39 thee, but *t'* once with the fleece;
7: 4 *T'* shall go with thee, the same
4 *T'* shall not go with thee, the same
14 *T'* is nothing else save the sword
8: 9 in peace, I will break down *t'* tower.
9:18 up against my father's house *t'* day,
19 and with his house *t'* day,
29 to God *t'* people were under my
38 *t'* the people...thou hast despised?
10: 4 are called Havoth-jair unto *t'* day,
15 us only, we pray thee, *t'* day.
11:27 *t'* day between the children of Israel
37 Let *t'* thing be done for me:
12: 3 then are ye come up unto me *t'* day,
13:23 as at *t'* time have told us such things

J'g 15: 6 Philistines said, Who hath done *t'*?
7 Though ye have done *t'*, yet will
11 what is *t'* that thou hast done unto
18 hast given *t'* great deliverance into
19 which is in Lehi unto *t'* day.
16:18 Come up *t'* once, for he hath
28 I pray thee, only *t'* once, O God,
18: 3 and what makest thou in *t'* place?
12 place Mahaneh-dan unto *t'* day:
24 and what is *t'* that ye say unto me,
19:11 let us turn in into *t'* city of the
23 seeing that *t'* man is come into
23 into mine house, do not *t'* folly.
24 unto *t'* man do not so vile a thing.
30 of the land of Egypt unto *t'* day:
20: 3 Tell us, how was *t'* wickedness?
9 *t'* shall be the thing that we will do
12 wickedness is *t'* that is done among
16 Among all *t'* people there were
21: 3 why is *t'* come to pass in Israel,
6 one tribe cut off from Israel *t'* day.
11 And *t'* is the thing that ye shall do,
22 ye did not give unto them at *t'* time,
Ru 1:19 them, and they said, Is *t'* Naomi?
2: 5 the reapers, Whose damsel is *t'*?
3:13 Tarry *t'* night, and it shall be in the
18 he have finished the thing *t'* day.
4: 7 *t'* was the manner in former time
7 and *t'* was the testimony in Israel.
9 Ye are witnesses *t'* day, that I have
10 of his place: ye are witnesses *t'* day.
12 shall give thee of *t'* young woman.
1Sa 1: 3 *t'* man went up out of his city
27 For *t'* child I prayed; and the
2:20 give thee seed of *t'* woman for the
23 your evil dealings by all *t'* people.
34 And *t'* shall be a sign unto thee,
4: 6 meaneth the noise of *t'* great shout
14 meaneth the noise of *t'* tumult?
5: 5 of Dagon in Ashdod unto *t'* day.
6: 9 then he hath done us *t'* great evil:
18 stone remaineth unto *t'* day in the
20 to stand before *t'* holy Lord God?
8: 8 up out of Egypt even unto *t'* day,
11 *T'* will be the manner of the king
9: 6 there is in *t'* city a man of God,
13 up; for about *t'* time ye shall find him.
16 To morrow about *t'* time I will send
17 *t'* same shall reign over my people.
24 for unto *t'* time hath it been kept for
10:11 What is *t'* that is come unto the
19 And ye have *t'* day rejected your God,
27 said, How shall *t'* man save us?
11: 2 On *t'* condition will I make a
13 not a man be put to death *t'* day:
12: 2 you from my childhood unto *t'* day.
5 and his anointed is witness *t'* day,
16 stand and see *t'* great thing,
19 have added unto all our sins *t'* evil,
20 ye have done all *t'* wickedness:
14:10 and *t'* shall be a sign unto us.
28 the man that eateth any food *t'* day.
29 because I tasted a little of *t'* honey.
33 roll a great stone unto me *t'* day.
38 wherein *t'* sin hath been *t'* day.
45 hath wrought *t'* great salvation in
45 he hath wrought with God *t'* day.
15:14 What meaneth then *t'* bleating of
16 the Lord hath said to me *t'* night.
28 kingdom of Israel from thee *t'* day,
16: 8, 9 Neither hath the Lord chosen *t'*.
12 Arise, anoint him: for *t'* is he.
17:10 defy the armies of Israel *t'* day;
17 an ephah of *t'* parched corn,
25 Have ye seen *t'* man that is come
26 the man that killeth *t'* Philistine,
26 who is *t'* uncircumcised Philistine,
27 answered him after *t'* manner,
32 will go and fight with *t'* Philistine.
33 not able to go against *t'* Philistine
36 *t'* uncircumcised Philistine shall be
37 me out of the hand of *t'* Philistine.
46 *T'* day will the Lord deliver thee
46 the Philistines *t'* day unto the fowls
47 *t'* assembly shall know that the
55 host, Abner, whose son is *t'* youth?
18:21 Thou shalt *t'* day be my son in law in
24 saying, On *t'* manner spake David.
20: 2 should my father hide *t'* thing
3 Let not Jonathan know *t'*, lest he
21 the arrows are on *t'* side of thee,
21: 5 it were sanctified *t'* day in the vessel.
11 not *t'* David the king of the land?
15 have brought *t'* fellow to play the
15 shall *t'* fellow come into my house?
22: 8, 13 me, to lie in wait, as at *t'* day?
15 thy servant knew nothing of all *t'*,
23:26 And Saul went on *t'* side of the
24: 6 should do *t'* thing unto my master,
16 said, Is *t'* thy voice, my son David?
18 thou hast shewed *t'* day how that thou
19 thou hast done unto me *t'* day.
25:21 have I kept all that *t'* fellow hath
24 my lord, upon me let *t'* iniquity be:
25 regard *t'* man of Belial, even
27 *t'* blessing which thine handmaid
31 That *t'* shall be no grief unto thee,
32 which sent thee *t'* day to meet me:
33 hast kept me *t'* day from coming to
26: 8 enemy into thine hand *t'* day:
16 *T'* thing is not good that thou
17 said, Is *t'* thy voice, my son David?
19 driven me out *t'* day from abiding
21 was precious in thine eyes *t'* day:
24 much set by *t'* day in mine eyes,
27: 6 the kings of Judah unto *t'* day.

1Sa 28:10 happen to thee for *t'* thing.
18 Lord done *t'* thing unto thee *t'* day.
29: 3 Is not *t'* David, the servant of Saul
3 since he fell unto me unto *t'* day?
4 Make *t'* fellow return, that he may
5 Is not *t'* David, of whom they sang
6 of thy coming unto me unto *t'* day:
8 I have been with thee unto *t'* day,
30: 8 Shall I pursue after *t'* troop? shall I
15 thou bring me down to *t'* company?
15 will bring thee down to *t'* company.
20 cattle, and said, *T'* is David's spoil.
24 will hearken unto you in *t'* matter?
25 an ordinance for Israel unto *t'* day.
2Sa 1:17 David lamented with *t'*
2: 1 And it came to pass after *t'*, that
5 *t'* kindness unto your Lord,
6 I also will requite you *t'* kindness,
6 because ye have done *t'* thing.
3: 8 shew kindness *t'* day unto the house
8 with a fault concerning *t'* woman?
38 great man fallen *t'* day in Israel?
39 I am *t'* day weak, though anointed
4: 3 were sojourners there until *t'* day.)
8 my lord the king *t'* day of Saul,
6: 8 of the place Perez-uzzah to *t'* day.
7: 6 even to *t'* day, but have walked in a
17 and according to all *t'* vision, so did
19 *t'* was yet a small thing in thy
19 And is *t'* the manner of man, O
27 found in his heart to pray *t'* prayer
28 promised *t'* goodness unto thy
8: 1 And after *t'* it came to pass, that
10: 1 And it came to pass after *t'*, that
11: 3 Is not *t'* Bath-sheba, the daughter
11 soul liveth, I will not do *t'* thing.
25 Let not *t'* thing displease thee, for
12: 5 hath done *t'* thing shall surely die:
6 because he did *t'* thing, and
11 thy wives in the sight of *t'* sun.
12 I will do *t'* thing before all Israel,
14 because by *t'* deed thou hast given
21 What thing is *t'* that thou hast
13: 1 And it came to pass after *t'*, that
12 in Israel: do not thou *t'* folly.
16 *t'* evil in sending me away is
17 Put now *t'* woman out from me,
20 is thy brother; regard not *t'* thing.
32 *t'* hath been determined from the day
14: 3 and speak on *t'* manner unto him.
13 for the king doth speak *t'* thing as
15 come to speak of *t'* thing unto my
19 hand of Joab with thee in all *t'*?
20 To fetch about *t'* form of speech hath
20 thy servant Joab done *t'* thing:
21 Behold now, I have done *t'* thing:
15: 1 And it came to pass after *t'*, that
6 on *t'* manner did Absalom to all
20 should I *t'* day make thee go up and
16: 9 Why should *t'* dead dog curse my
11 more now may *t'* Benjamite do it?
12 me good for his cursing *t'* day.
17 Is *t'* thy kindness to thy friend?
18 but whom the Lord, and *t'* people,
17: 1 arise and pursue after David *t'* night:
6 hath spoken after *t'* manner:
7 hath given is not good at *t'* time.
16 Lodge not *t'* night in the plains of the
18:18 it is called unto *t'* day, Absalom's
20 Thou shalt not bear tidings *t'* day,
20 *t'* day thou shalt bear no tidings,
31 Lord hath avenged thee *t'* day of all
19: 5 hast shamed *t'* day the faces of all thy
5 which *t'* day have saved thy life,
6 thou hast declared *t'* day, that thou
6 *t'* day I perceive, that if Absalom had
6 we had died *t'* day, then it had pleased
7 will not tarry one with thee *t'* night:
14 that they sent *t'* word unto the king,
20 I am come the first *t'* day of all the
21 not Shimei be put to death for *t'*,
22 ye should *t'* day be adversaries unto
22 man be put to death *t'* day in Israel?
22 that I am *t'* day king over Israel?
35 I am *t'* day fourscore years old: and
42 then be ye angry for *t'* matter?
21:18 it came to pass after *t'*, that there
22: 1 unto the Lord the words of *t'* song
23: 5 for *t'* is all my salvation, and all my
17 me, O Lord, that I should do *t'*:
17 *t'* the blood of the men that went in
24: 3 lord the king delight in *t'* thing?
1Ki 1:25 For he is gone down *t'* day, and hath
27 *t'* thing done by my lord the king,
30 even so will I certainly do *t'* day.
41 Wherefore is *t'* noise of the city being
45 *T'* is the noise that ye have heard.
48 given one to sit on my throne *t'* day,
2:23 spoken *t'* word against his own
24 Adonijah shall be put to death *t'* day.
26 not at *t'* time put thee to death:
3: 6 hast kept for him *t'* great kindness,
6 to sit on his throne, as it is *t'* day.
9 to judge *t'* thy so great a people?
10 that Solomon had asked *t'* thing.
11 Because thou hast asked *t'* thing,
17 lord, I and *t'* woman dwell in one
18 that *t'* woman was delivered also:
19 *t'* woman's child died in the night;
22 *t'* said, No; but the dead is thy son,
23 one saith, *T'* is my son that liveth,
4:24 all the region on *t'* side the river,
24 all the kings on *t'* side the river:
5: 7 Blessed be the Lord *t'* day, which hath
7 a wise son over *t'* great people.
6:12 Concerning *t'* house which thou art

1Ki 7: 8 taken to wife, like unto t' porch.
28 of the bases was on t' manner:
37 After t' manner he made the ten
8: 8 and there they are unto t' day.
24 it with thine hand, as it is t' day.
27 less t' house that I have builded?
29 eyes may be open toward t' house
29 servant shall make toward t' place.
30 they shall pray toward t' place:
31 come before thine altar in t' house:
33 supplication unto thee in t' house:
35 if they pray toward t' place, and
38 forth his hands toward t' house:
42 come and pray toward t' house;
43 that they may know that t' house,
54 an end of praying all t' prayer
61 his commandments, as at t' day.
9: 3 have hallowed t' house, which thou
7 t' house, which I have hallowed for
8 And at t' house, which is high,
8 the Lord done thus unto t' land,
9 Lord brought upon them all t' evil.
13 the land of Cabul unto t' day.
15 t' is the reason of the levy which
21 tribute of bondservice unto t' day.
10: 12 trees, nor were seen unto t' day.
11: 10 had commanded him concerning t'
11 Forasmuch as t' is done of thee,
27 And t' was the cause that he lifted
39 will for t' afflict the seed of David,
12: 6 that I may answer t' people?
7 be a servant unto t' people t' day,
9 ye that we may answer t' people,
10 shalt thou speak unto t' people
19 the house of David unto t' day.
24 his house; for t' thing is from me.
27 If t' people go up to do sacrifice in
27 the heart of t' people turn again
30 And t' thing became a sin: for the
13: 3 T' is the sign which the Lord hath
8 bread nor drink water in t' place:
16 drink water with thee in t' place:
33 After t' thing Jeroboam returned
34 t' thing became sin unto the house
14: 2 that I should be king over t' people.
15 root up Israel out of t' good land,
17: 21 let t' child's soul come into him
24 by t' I know that thou art a man of
18: 36 be known t' day that thou art God
37 that t' people may know that thou
19: 2 of them by to morrow about t' time.
20: 6 unto thee to morrow about t' time,
7 see how t' man seeketh mischief:
9 will do: but t' thing I may not do.
12 when Ben-hadad heard t' message,
13 thou seen all t' great multitude?
13 deliver it into thine hand t' day;
24 And do t' thing, Take the kings
28 deliver all t' great multitude into
34 I will send thee away with t' covenant.
39 unto me, and said, Keep t' man:
22: 20 And one said on t' manner, and
27 Put t' fellow in the prison, and
2Ki 1: 2 whether I shall recover of t' disease.
2: 19 the situation of t' city is pleasant,
22 the waters were healed unto t' day,
3: 16 Lord, Make t' valley full of ditches.
18 t' is but a light thing in the sight
23 they said, T' is blood: the kings
4: 9 that t' is an holy man of God,
12 his servant, Call t' Shunammite.
13 been careful for us with all t' care;
16 About t' season, according to the
36 and said, Call t' Shunammite.
43 I set t' before an hundred men?
5: 6 when t' letter is come unto thee,
7 that t' man doth send unto me to
18 In t' thing the Lord pardon thy
18 Lord pardon thy servant in t' thing.
20 hath spared Naaman t' Syrian,
6: 11 was sore troubled for t' thing:
18 Smite t' people, I pray thee, with
19 said unto them, T' is not the way,
19 neither is t' the city: follow me,
24 And it came to pass after t', that
28 T' woman said unto me, Give thy
31 Shaphat shall stand on him t' day.
33 said, Behold, t' evil is of the Lord;
7: 1 To morrow about t' time shall a
2 in heaven, might t' thing be?
9 t' day is a day of good tidings, and
18 to morrow about t' time in the gate of
8: 5 My lord, O king, t' is the woman,
5 and t' is her son, whom Elisha
8, 9 Shall I recover of t' disease?
13 that he should do t' great thing?
9: 1 and take t' box of oil in thine hand,
11 came t' mad fellow to thee?
25 the Lord laid t' burden upon him;
26 and I will requite thee in t' plat,
27 Ahaziah the king of Judah saw t',
34 Go, see now t' cursed woman, and
36 T' is the word of the Lord, which
37 they shall not say, T' is Jezebel.
10: 2 as soon as t' letter cometh to you,
6 to me to Jezreel by to morrow t' time.
27 it a draught house unto t' day.
11: 5 T' is the thing that ye shall do;
14: 7 the name of it Joktheel unto t' day.
10 up: glory of t', and tarry at home:
15: 12 T' was the word of the Lord
16: 6 Elath, and dwelt there unto t' day.
17: 12 unto them, Ye shall not do t' thing.
23 own land to Assyria unto t' day.
34 t' day they do after the former
41 their fathers, so do they unto t' day.

2Ki 18: 19 What confidence is t' wherein thou
21 upon the staff of t' bruised reed,
22 before t' altar in Jerusalem?
25 Lord against t' place to destroy it?
25 Go up against t' land, and destroy
30 t' city shall not be delivered into
19: 3 T' day is a day of trouble, and of
21 T' is the word that the Lord hath
29 And t' shall be a sign unto thee, Ye
29 shall eat t' year such things as grow of
31 of the Lord of hosts shall do t'.
33 and shall not come into t' city,
34 For I will defend t' city, to save it,
20: 6 I will deliver thee and t' city out of
6 defend t' city for mine own sake,
9 T' sign shalt thou have of the
17 have laid up in store unto t' day,
21: 7 In t' house, and in Jerusalem,
15 forth out of Egypt, even unto t' day.
22: 13 concerning the words of t' book
13 hearkened unto the words of t' book,
16 I will bring evil upon t' place, and
17 shall be kindled against t' place,
19 what I spake against t' place,
20 which I will bring upon t' place.
23: 3 perform the words of t' covenant
3 that were written in t' book.
21 written in the book of t' covenant.
23 wherein t' passover was holden to
27 and will cast off t' city Jerusalem
24: 3 of the Lord came t' upon Judah,
1Ch 4: 43 and dwelt there unto t' day.
5: 26 and to the river Gozan, unto t' day.
11: 11 t' is the number of the mighty men
19 it me, that I should do t' thing:
13: 11 place is called Perez-uzza to t' day.
16: 7 first t' psalm to thank the Lord
17: 5 I brought up Israel unto t' day;
15 according to all t' vision, so did
17 t' was a small thing in thine eyes,
19 hast thou done all t' greatness,
26 hast promised t' goodness unto thy
18: 1 Now after t' it came to pass, that
19: 1 Now it came to pass after t', that
20: 4 And it came to pass after t', that
21: 3 then doth my lord require t' thing?
7 God was displeased with t' thing;
8 because I have done t' thing:
22 me the place of t' threshingfloor,
22: 1 T' is the house of the Lord God,
1 t' is the altar of the burnt offering
27: 6 T' is that Benaiah, who was
28: 7 and my judgments, as at t' day.
8 that ye may possess t' good land, and
19 All t', said David, the Lord made me
19 me, even all the works of t' pattern.
29: 5 consecrate his service t' day unto the
14 to offer so willingly after t' sort?
16 all t' store that we have prepared
18 keep t' for ever in the imagination
2Ch 1: 10 out and come in before t' people:
10 for who can judge t' thy people,
11 Because t' was in thine heart, and
2: 4 T' is an ordinance for ever to Israel.
5: 9 And there it is unto t' day.
6: 18 how much less t' house which I
20 eyes may be open upon t' house
20 thy servant prayeth toward t' place.
21 they shall make toward t' place:
22 come before thine altar in t' house;
24 supplication before thee in t' house;
26 yet if they pray toward t' place, and
29 spread forth his hands in t' house:
32 if they come and pray in t' house;
33 know that t' house which I have
34 pray unto thee toward t' city
40 prayer that is made in t' place.
7: 12 chosen t' place to myself for an
15 prayer that is made in t' place.
16 I chosen and sanctified t' house,
20 t' house, which I have sanctified
21 And t' house, which is high, shall
21 the Lord done thus unto t' land,
21 land, and unto t' house?
22 he brought all t' evil upon them.
8: 8 make to pay tribute until t' day.
10: 6 me to return answer to t' people?
7 If thou be kind to t' people, and
9 we may return answer to t' people,
19 the house of David unto t' day.
11: 4 house: for t' thing is done of me.
14: 11 name we go against t' multitude.
16: 10 rage with him because of t' thing.
18: 19 one spake saying after t' manner,
26 Put t' fellow in the prison, and
19: 10 t' do, and ye shall not trespass.
20: 1 It came to pass after t' also, that
2 from beyond the sea on t' side Syria;
7 out the inhabitants of t' land
9 we stand before t' house, and in
9 (for thy name is in t' house,) and
12 might against t' great company
15 by reason of t' great multitude;
17 shall not need to fight in t' battle:
26 valley of Berachah, unto t' day.
35 after t' did Jehoshaphat king of
21: 10 the hand of Judah unto t' day.
18 after all t' the Lord smote him in
23: 4 T' is the thing that ye shall do;
24: 4 And it came to pass after t', that
18 Jerusalem for t' their trespass.
25: 9 to give thee much more than t'.
16 because thou hast done t', and
28: 22 the Lord: t' is that king Ahaz.
29: 9 our wives are in captivity for t'.
28 t' continued until the burnt offering

2Ch 30: 9 shall come again unto t' land:
31: 1 Now when all t' was finished, all
10 that which is left is t' great store.
32: 9 t' did Sennacherib king of Assyria
15 nor persuade you on t' manner,
20 for t' cause Hezekiah the king,
30 T' same Hezekiah also stopped
33: 7 In t' house, and in Jerusalem,
14 after t' he built a wall without
34: 21 after all that is written in t' book.
24 I will bring evil upon t' place, and
25 shall be poured out upon t' place,
27 heardest his words against t' place,
28 evil that I will bring upon t' place,
31 which are written in t' book.
35: 19 of Josiah was t' passover kept.
20 After all t', when Josiah had
21 I come not against thee t' day, but
25 in their lamentations to t' day,
Ezr 1: 9 t' is the number of them: thirty
3: 12 foundation of t' house was laid
4: 8 to Artaxerxes the king in t' sort:
10 rest that are on t' side the river,
11 T' is the copy of the letter that
11 servants the men on t' side the
13 if t' city be builded, and the walls
15 that t' city is a rebellious city,
15 which cause was t' city destroyed.
16 if t' city be builded again, and the
16 by t' means thou shalt have no
16 have no portion on t' side the river
19 that t' city of old time hath made
21 that t' city be not builded, until
22 heed now that ye fail not to do t':
5: 3 governor on t' side the river,
3 commanded you to build t' house,
3 and to make up t' wall?
4 we unto them after t' manner,
4 of the men that make t' building?
5 by letter concerning t' matter.
6 governor on t' side the river,
6 which were on t' side the river,
8 and t' work goeth fast on, and
9 commanded you to build t' house,
12 Chaldean, who destroyed t' house,
13 a decree to build t' house of God.
17 king to build t' house of God at
17 to us concerning t' matter.
6: 7 work of t' house of God alone;
7 of the Jews build t' house of God
8 for the building of t' house of God:
11 that whosoever shall alter t' word,
11 his house be made a dunghill for t'.
12 to alter and to destroy t' house of
13 governor on t' side the river,
15 t' house was finished on the third
16 dedication of t' house of God with
17 the dedication of t' house of God
7: 6 T' Ezra went up from Babylon;
11 t' is the copy of the letter that
17 speedily with t' money bullocks,
24 or ministers of t' house of God,
27 a thing as t' in the king's heart,
8: 1 t' is the genealogy of them that
23 and besought our God for t':
35 t' was a burnt offering unto the Lord.
36 governors on t' side the river:
9: 2 hath been chief in t' trespass.
3 And when I heard t' thing, I rent
7 in a great trespass unto t' day;
7 confusion of face, as it is t' day.
10 God, what shall we say after t'?
13 given us such deliverance as t';
15 remain yet escaped, as it is t' day:
15 stand before thee because of t'.
10: 2 hope in Israel concerning t' thing.
4 t' matter belongeth unto thee: we
5 should do according to t' word.
9 God, trembling because of t' matter,
13 neither is t' a work of one day or two:
13 that have transgressed in t' thing.
14 wrath of our God for t' matter be
15 were employed about t' matter:
Ne 1: 11 I pray thee, thy servant t' day,
11 him mercy in the sight of t' man.
2: 2 t' is nothing else but sorrow of
18 their hands for t' good work.
19 What is t' thing that ye do? will
3: 7 the governor on t' side the river.
5: 10 pray you, let us leave off t' usury.
11 to them, even t' day, their lands,
12 should do according to t' promise.
13 that performeth not t' promise,
13 people did according to t' promise.
16 continued in the work of t' wall,
18 for all t' required not I the bread
18 bondage was heavy upon t' people.
19 all that I have done for t' people.
6: 4 unto me four times after t' sort;
12 pronounced t' prophecy against me:
16 t' work was wrought of our God.
7: 7 men of the people of Israel was t':
8: 9 T' day is holy unto the Lord your
10 for t' day is holy unto our Lord:
9: 1 twenty and fourth day of t' month
10 get thee a name, as it is t' day.
18 T' is thy God that brought thee up
32 of the kings of Assyria unto t' day.
36 Behold, we are servants t' day, and
38 because of all t' we make a sure
13: 4 And before t', Eliashib the priest,
6 all t' time was not I at Jerusalem:
14 me, O my God, concerning t', and
17 What evil thing is t' that ye do,
18 our God bring all t' evil upon us,
18 upon us, and upon t' city? yet ye

Ne 13:22 me, O my God, concerning t' also,
27 unto you to do all t' great evil,
Es 1: 1 (t' is Ahasuerus which reigned,
17 For t' deed of the queen shall come
18 of Persia and Media say t' day
4:14 holdest thy peace at t' time,
14 the kingdom for such a time as t'?
15 them return Mordecai t' answer,
5: 4 Haman come t' day unto the banquet
13 Yet all t' availeth me nothing,
6: 3 hath been done to Mordecai for t'?
9 let t' apparel and horse be delivered
7: 6 and enemy is t' wicked Haman.
9: 4 t' man Mordecai waxed greater and
13 also according unto t' day's decree,
21 To stablish t' among them, that they
26 had seen concerning t' matter,
29 confirm t' second letter of Purim.
Job 1: 3 so that t' man was the greatest
22 In all t' Job sinned not, nor
2:10 In all t' did not Job sin with his
11 heard of all t' evil that was come
3: 1 After t' opened Job his mouth,
4: 6 Is not t' thy fear, thy confidence, thy
5:27 Lo t', we have searched it, so it is;
8:19 t' is the joy of his way, and out of
9:22 T' is one thing, therefore I said it,
10:13 heart: I know that t' is with thee.
12: 9 hand of the Lord hath wrought t'?
13: 1 Lo, mine eye hath seen all t', mine ear
17: 8 men shall be astonied at t', and
18:21 t' is the place of him that knoweth
19:26 my skin worms destroy t' body,
20: 4 Knowest thou not t' of old, since
29 T' is the portion of a wicked man
21: 2 and let t' be your consolations.
27:13 T' is the portion of a wicked man
31:11 For t' is an heinous crime; yea, it
28 T' also were an iniquity to be
33:12 Behold, in t' thou art not just: I
34:16 thou hast understanding, hear t':
35: 2 Thinkest thou t' to be right, that
36:21 t' hast thou chosen rather than
37: 1 At t' also my heart trembleth,
14 Hearken unto t', O Job: stand still,
38: 2 Who is t' that darkeneth counsel
42:16 After t' lived Job an hundred and
Ps 2: 7 my Son; t' day have I begotten thee.
7: 3 O Lord my God, if I have done t';
11: 6 t' shall be the portion of their cup.
12: 7 preserve them from t' generation
17:14 which have their portion in t' life,
18: *title* the words of t' song in the day
22:31 shall be born, that he hath done t'.
24: 6 T' is the generation of them that
8 Who is t' King of glory? The Lord
10 Who is t' King of glory? The Lord
27: 3 me, in t' will I be confident.
32: 6 t' shall every one that is godly pray
34: 6 T' poor man cried, and the Lord
35:22 T' thou hast seen, O Lord: keep not
41:11 t' I know that thou favourest me,
44:17 t' is come upon us; yet have we
21 Shall not God search t' out? for he
48:14 For t' God is our God for ever and
49: 1 Hear t', all ye people; give ear, all
13 T' their way is their folly: yet
50:22 Now consider t', ye that forget
51: 4 I sinned, and done t' evil in thy sight:
52: 7 t' is the man that made not God his
56: 9 back: t' I know; for God is for me.
62:11 twice have I heard t'; that power
68:16 t' is the hill which God desireth to
69:31 T' also shall please the Lord better
32 The humble shall see t', and be glad:
71:18 thy strength unto t' generation,
73:16 When I thought to know t', it was
74: 2 t' mount Zion, wherein thou hast
18 Remember t', that the enemy
77:10 And I said, T' is my infirmity:
78:21 Therefore the Lord heard t', and was
32 For all t' they sinned still, and
54 even to t' mountain, which his
59 When God heard t', he was wroth, and
80:14 and behold, and visit t' vine;
81: 4 t' was a statute for Israel, and a
5 T' he ordained in Joseph for a
87: 4 Ethiopia; t' man was born there.
5 T' and that man was born in her:
6 that t' man was born there.
92: 6 neither doth a fool understand t'.
95:10 long was I grieved with t' generation,
102:18 T' shall be written for the
104:25 So is t' great and wide sea, wherein
109:20 Let t' be the reward of mine
27 they may know that t' is thy hand;
113: 2 name of the Lord from t' time forth
115:18 will bless the Lord from t' time forth
118:20 T' gate of the Lord, into which
23 T' is the Lord's doing; it is
24 T' is the day which the Lord hath
119:91 continue t' day according to thine
121: 8 and thy coming in from t' time forth,
149: 9 t' honour have all his saints.
Pr 6: 3 Do t' now, my son, and deliver
7:14 me; t' day have I payed my vows.
22:19 I have made known to thee t' day,
Ec 1:10 it may be said, See, t' is new?
13 t' sore travail hath God given to
17 I perceived that t' also is vexation
2: 1 and, behold, t' also is vanity.
10 and t' was my portion of all my
15 in my heart, that t' also is vanity.
19 under the sun. T' is also vanity.
21 T' also is vanity and a great evil.
23 the night. T' is also vanity.
Ec 2:24 T' also I saw, that it was from the
26 T' also is vanity and vexation of
4: 4 that for t' a man is envied of his
4 T' is also vanity and vexation of
8 T' is also vanity, yea, it is a sore
16 t' also is vanity and vexation of
5:10 with increase: t' is also vanity.
16 t' also is a sore evil, that in all
19 in his labour; t' is the gift of God.
6: 2 it: t' is vanity, and it is an evil
5 t' hath more rest than the other.
9 t' is also vanity and vexation of
12 what is good for man in t' life,
7: 6 of the fool: t' also is vanity.
10 not enquire wisely concerning t'?
18 that thou shouldest take hold of t';
18 from t' withdraw not thine hand:
23 All t' have I proved by wisdom:
27 Behold, t' have I found, saith the
29 t' only have I found, that God hath
8: 9 All t' have I seen, and applied my
10 they had so done: t' is also vanity.
14 I said that t' also is vanity.
9: 1 For all t' I consider in my heart
1 even to declare all t', that the
3 T' is an evil among all things that
9 that is thy portion in t' life, and
13 T' wisdom have I seen also under
11: 6 shall prosper, either t' or that,
12:13 for t' is the whole duty of man.
Ca 3: 6 Who is t' that cometh out of the
5:16 T' is my beloved, and t' is my
7: 7 T' thy stature is like to a palm
8: 5 Who is t' that cometh up from the
Isa 1:12 who hath required t' at your hand,
3: 6 and let t' ruin be under thy hand:
5:25 For all t' his anger is not turned
6: 7 said, Lo, t' hath touched thy lips;
9 And he said, Go, and tell t' people,
10 Make the heart of t' people fat, and
8: 6 as t' people refuseth the waters of
11 not walk in the way of t' people,
12 them to whom t' people shall say,
20 they speak not according to t' word,
9: 7 the Lord of hosts will perform t'.
12 For all t' his anger is not turned
16 the leaders of t' people cause them
17, 21 all t' his anger is not turned
10: 4 For all t' his anger is not turned
12: 5 things: t' is known in all the earth.
14: 4 take up t' proverb against the
16 Is t' the man that made the earth
26 T' is the purpose that is purposed
26 t' is the hand that is stretched out
28 king Ahaz died was t' burden.
16:13 T' is the word that the Lord hath
17:14 T' is the portion of them that spoil
20: 6 inhabitant of t' isle shall say in that
22:14 t' iniquity shall not be purged from
15 Go, get thee unto t' treasurer, even
23: 7 Is t' your joyous city, whose
8 hath taken t' counsel against Tyre,
13 t' people was not, till the Assyrian
24: 3 for the Lord hath spoken t' word.
25: 6 And in t' mountain shall the Lord
7 he will destroy in t' mountain the
9 in that day, Lo, t' is our God;
9 t' is the Lord; we have waited for
10 in t' mountain shall the hand of the
26: 1 In that day shall t' song be sung
27: 9 By t' therefore shall the iniquity
9 t' is all the fruit to take away his
28:11 tongue will he speak to t' people.
12 T' is the rest wherewith ye may
12 to rest: and t' is the refreshing:
14 that rule t' people...in Jerusalem.
29 T' also cometh forth from the Lord
29:11, 12 saying, Read t', I pray thee:
14 marvellous work among t' people,
30: 7 have I cried concerning t', Their
9 That t' is a rebellious people,
12 Because ye despise t' word, and
13 t' iniquity shall be to you as a
21 T' is the way, walk ye in it, when
36: 4 What confidence is t' wherein thou
6 in the staff of t' broken reed,
7 Ye shall worship before t' altar?
10 Lord against t' land to destroy it?
10 unto me, Go up against t' land, and
15 t' city shall not be delivered into
37: 3 T' day is a day of trouble, and of
22 T' is the word which the Lord hath
30 And t' shall be a sign unto thee,
30 eat t' year such as groweth of itself;
32 of the Lord of hosts shall do t'.
33 He shall not come into t' city, nor
34 and shall not come into t' city, saith
35 For I will defend t' city to save it
38: 6 I will deliver thee and t' city out of
6 of Assyria: and I will defend t' city.
7 t' shall be a sign unto thee from
7 Lord will do t' thing that he hath
19 he shall praise thee, as I do t' day:
39: 6 have laid up in store until t' day,
41:20 the hand of the Lord hath done t',
42:22 t' is a people robbed and spoiled;
23 Who among you will give ear to t'?
43: 9 who among them can declare t',
21 T' people have I formed for
45:21 declared t' from ancient time?
46: 8 Remember t', and shew yourselves
47: 8 Therefore hear now t', thou that art
48: 1 Hear ye t', O house of Jacob, which
6 Thou hast heard, see all t'; and will
6 shewed thee new things from t' time,
16 Come ye near unto me, hear ye t';
Isa 48:20 tell t', utter it even to the end of the
50:11 T' shall ye have of mine hand; ye
51:21 hear now t', thou afflicted, and
54: 9 t' is as the waters of Noah unto me:
17 T' is the heritage of the servants of
56: 2 Blessed is the man that doeth t',
12 and to morrow shall be as t' day,
58: 4 ye shall not fast as ye do t' day, to
5 wilt thou call t' a fast, and an
6 Is not t' the fast that I have chosen?
59:21 me, t' is my covenant with them,
63: 1 Who is t' that cometh from Edom,
1 t' that is glorious in his apparel,
66: 2 but to t' man will I look, even to
14 And when ye see t', your heart shall
Jer 1:10 t' day set thee over the nations
18 have made thee t' day a defenced city,
2:12 Be astonished, O ye heavens, at t',
17 thou not procured t' unto thyself,
3: 4 thou not from t' time cry unto me,
10 yet for all t' her treacherous sister
25 from our youth even unto t' day,
4: 8 For t' gird you with sackcloth,
10 hast greatly deceived t' people and
11 time shall it be said to t' people
18 t' is thy wickedness, because it is
28 For t' shall the earth mourn, and
5: 7 How shall I pardon thee for t'? thy
9 be avenged on such a nation as t'?
14 Because ye speak t' word, behold, I
14 t' people wood, and it shall devour
20 Declare t' in the house of Jacob,
21 Hear now t', O foolish people, and
23 But t' people hath a revolting and
6: 6 t' is the city to be visited; she is
19 I will bring evil upon t' people,
21 stumblingblocks before t' people,
7: 2 house, and proclaim there t' word,
3 I will cause you to dwell in t' place.
6 shed not innocent blood in t' place,
7 will I cause you to dwell in t' place,
10 and stand before me in t' house,
11 Is t' house, which is called by my
14 Therefore will I do unto t' house,
16 pray not thou for t' people, neither
20 shall be poured out upon t' place,
23 But t' thing commanded I them,
25 out of the land of Egypt unto t' day
28 T' is a nation that obeyeth not the
33 carcases of t' people shall be meat
8: 3 them that remain of t' evil family,
5 then is t' people of Jerusalem
9: 9 be avenged on such a nation as t'?
12 wise man, that may understand t'?
15 even t' people, with wormwood,
24 let him that glorieth glory in t',
10:18 inhabitants of the land at t' once,
19 Truly t' is a grief, and I must bear.
11: 2 Hear ye the words of t' covenant,
3 not the words of t' covenant,
5 with milk and honey, as it is t' day.
6 Hear ye the words of t' covenant,
7 even unto t' day, rising early and
8 them all the words of t' covenant,
14 pray not thou for t' people, neither
13: 9 After t' manner will I mar the pride of
10 T' evil people, which refuse to
10 shall even be as t' girdle, which is
12 thou shalt speak unto them t' word;
13 I will fill all the inhabitants of t' land,
25 T' is thy lot, the portion of thy
14:10 Thus saith the Lord unto t' people,
11 Pray not for t' people for their good.
13 give you assured peace in t' place.
15 and famine shall not be in t' land;
17 thou shalt say t' word unto them;
15: 1 mind could not be toward t' people:
20 unto t' people a fenced brasen wall:
16: 2 have sons or daughters in t' place.
3 daughters that are born in t' place,
3 fathers that begat them in t' land;
5 away my peace from t' people,
6 and the small shall die in t' land:
9 cease out of t' place in your eyes,
10 shew t' people all these words,
10 Lord pronounced all t' great evil
13 I cast you out of t' land into a land
21 I will t' once cause them to know,
17:24 burden through the gates of t' city
25 enter into the gates of t' city kings
25 and t' city shall remain for ever.
18: 6 cannot I do with you as t' potter?
19: 3 I will bring evil upon t' place,
4 me, and have estranged t' place,
4 t' place with the blood of innocents;
6 t' place shall no more be called
7 of Judah and Jerusalem in t' place;
8 And I will make t' city desolate,
11 Even so will I break t' people and
11 t' city, as one breaketh a potter's
12 Thus will I do unto t' place, saith
12 and even make t' city as Tophet:
20: 5 deliver all the strength of t' city,
21: 4 them into the midst of t' city,
6 will smite the inhabitants of t' city,
7 such as are left in t' city from the
8 And unto t' people thou shalt say,
9 abideth in t' city shall die by the
10 set my face against t' city for evil,
22: 1 of Judah, and speak there t' word,
3 shed innocent blood in t' place.
4 if ye do t' thing indeed, then shall
4 enter in by the gates of t' house
5 t' house shall become a desolation.
8 many nations shall pass by t' city,
8 Lord done thus unto t' great city?

Jer 22:11 which went forth out of *t'* place;
12 and shall see *t'* land no more.
16 was not *t'* to know me? saith the
21 *T'* hath been thy manner from
28 Is *t'* man Coniah a despised broken
30 Write ye *t'* man childless, a man
23: 6 *t'* is his name whereby he shall be
26 shall *t'* be in the heart of the prophets
32 shall not profit *t'* people at all,
33 when *t'* people, or the prophet, or a
38 Because ye say *t'* word, The burden
24: 5 whom I have sent out of *t'* place into
6 I will bring them again to *t'* land:
8 residue...that remain in *t'* land,
25: 3 even unto *t'* day, that is the three
9 will bring them against *t'* land,
11 *t'* whole land shall be a desolation,
13 even all that is written in *t'* book,
15 Take the wine cup of *t'* fury at my
18 and a curse; as it is *t'* day;
26: 1 Judah came *t'* word from the Lord,
6 will I make *t'* house like Shiloh,
6 *t'* city a curse to all the nations
9 *T'* house shall be like Shiloh,
9 *t'* city shall be desolate without an
11 *T'* man is worthy to die; for he
11 he hath prophesied against *t'* city,
12 me to prophesy against *t'* house
12 and against *t'* city all the words
15 upon yourselves, and upon *t'* city,
16 *T'* man is not worthy to die: for
20 against *t'* city and against *t'* land
27: 1 came *t'* word unto Jeremiah from
16 to the priests and to all *t'* people,
17 should *t'* city be laid waste?
19 of the vessels that remain in *t'* city,
22 up, and restore them to *t'* place.
28: 3 will I bring again into *t'* place all
3 Babylon took away from *t'* place,
4 And I will bring again to *t'* place
6 captive, from Babylon into *t'* place.
7 hear thou now *t'* word that I speak
15 makest *t'* people to trust in a lie.
16 *t'* year thou shalt die, because thou
29: 10 causing you to return to *t'* place.
16 the people that dwelleth in *t'* city,
28 saying, *T'* captivity is long:
32 a man to dwell among *t'* people;
30: 17 *T'* is Zion, whom no man seeketh
21 who is *t'*...engaged his heart
31: 23 they shall use *t'* speech in the land
26 Upon *t'* I awaked, and beheld;
33 *t'* shall be the covenant that I will
32: 3 will give *t'* city into the hand of the
8 that *t'* was the word of the Lord.
14 *t'* evidence of the purchase, both
14 and *t'* evidence which is open;
15 be possessed again in *t'* land.
20 land of Egypt, even unto *t'* day,
20 made thee a name, as at *t'* day;
22 And hast given them *t'* land,
23 all *t'* evil to come upon them:
28 give *t'* city into the hand of the
29 Chaldeans, that fight against *t'* city,
29 shall come and set fire on *t'* city,
31 For *t'* city hath been to me as a
31 that they built it even unto *t'* day;
35 they should do *t'* abomination,
36 concerning *t'* city, whereof ye say;
41 will plant them in *t'* land assuredly
42 as I have brought all *t'* great evil
42 evil upon *t'* people, so will I bring
43 fields shall be bought in *t'* land,
33: 4 concerning the houses of *t'* city,
5 I have hid my face from *t'* city.
10 there shall be heard in *t'* place,
12 Again in *t'* place, which is desolate
16 *t'* is the name wherewith she shall
24 not what *t'* people have spoken,
34: 2 give *t'* city into the hand of the
8 *T'* is the word that came unto
22 cause them to return to *t'* city;
35: 14 for unto *t'* day they drink none,
16 *t'* people hath not hearkened unto
36: 1 *t'* word came unto Jeremiah from
2 days of Josiah, even unto *t'* day.
7 hath pronounced against *t'* people.
29 Thou hast burned *t'* roll, saying,
29 certainly come and destroy *t'* land,
37: 8 and fight against *t'* city, and take it,
10 his tent, and burn *t'* city with fire.
18 thy servants, or against *t'* people,
19 against you, nor against *t'* land?
38: 2 He that remaineth in *t'* city shall
3 *T'* city shall surely be given into
4 thee, let *t'* man be put to death:
4 men of war that remain in *t'* city,
4 for *t'* man seeketh not the welfare
4 welfare of *t'* people, but the hurt.
16 Lord liveth, that made us *t'* soul,
17 *t'* city shall not be burned with fire;
18 *t'* city be given into the hand of the
21 *t'* is the word that the Lord hath
23 *t'* city to be burned with fire.
39: 16 bring my words upon *t'* city for evil,
40: 2 thy God hath pronounced *t'* evil
2 evil upon *t'* place.
3 *t'* thing is come upon you.
4 I loose thee *t'* day from the chains
16 Thou shalt not do *t'* thing: for
42: 2 thy God, even for all *t'* remnant;
10 If ye will still abide in *t'* land, then
13 say, We will not dwell in *t'* land,
18 and ye shall see *t'* place no more.
19 that I have admonished you *t'* day.
21 now I have *t'* day declared it to you;

Jer 44: 2 *t'* day they are a desolation, and
4 do not *t'* abominable thing that
6 wasted and desolate, as at *t'* day.
7 Wherefore commit ye *t'* great evil
10 are not humbled even unto *t'* day,
22 without an inhabitant, as at *t'* day.
23 therefore *t'* evil is happened unto
23 happened unto you, as at *t'* day.
29 And *t'* shall be a sign unto you,
29 that I will punish you in *t'* place,
45: 4 I will pluck up, even *t'* whole land.
46: 7 Who is *t'* that cometh up as a
10 *t'* is the day of the Lord God of
50: 17 and last *t'* Nebuchadrezzar king of
25 *t'* is the work of the Lord God of
51: 6 for *t'* is the time of the Lord's
59 And *t'* Seraiah was a quiet prince.
62 thou hast spoken against *t'* place,
63 made an end of reading *t'* book,
52: 28 *T'* is the people...Nebuchadrezzar
La 2:15 Is *t'* the city that men call The
16 *t'* is the day that we looked for;
20 to whom thou hast done *t'*.
3:21 *T'* I recall to my mind, therefore
5: 17 For *t'* our heart is faint; for these
Eze **1:** 5 *t'* was their appearance; they had
23 had two, which covered on *t'* side,
28 *T'* was the appearance of the
2: 3 against me, even unto *t'* very day.
3: 1 eat *t'* roll, and go speak unto the
3 fill thy bowels with *t'* roll that I
4: 3 *T'* shall be a sign to the house of
5: 5 *T'* is Jerusalem: I have set it in
6: 10 that I would do *t'* evil unto them.
8: 5 *t'* image of jealousy in the entry.
15, 17 Hast thou seen *t'*, O son of man?
10: 15, 20 *T'* is the living creature that I
11: 2 and give wicked counsel in *t'* city:
3 *t'* city is the caldron, and we be
6 multiplied your slain in *t'* city,
7 flesh, and *t'* city is the caldron:
11 *T'* city shall not be your caldron,
15 unto us is *t'* land given in
12: 10 *T'* burden concerneth the prince
23 I will make *t'* proverb to cease, and
16: 20 *t'* of thy whoredoms a small matter.
43 shalt not commit *t'* lewdness above all
44 shall use *t'* proverb against thee,
49 *t'* was the iniquity of thy sister
17: 7 *t'* vine did bend her roots toward
18: 2 use *t'* proverb concerning the land
3 more to use *t'* proverb in Israel.
19: 14 *T'* is a lamentation, and shall be
20: 27 in *t'* your fathers have blasphemed
29 is called Bamah unto *t'* day.
31 with all your idols, even unto *t'* day:
21: 11 *t'* sword is sharpened, and it is
26 *t'* shall not be the same: exalt him
23: 11 And when her sister Aholibah saw *t'*,
38 *t'* they have done unto me: they
24: 2 of the day, even of *t'* same day:
2 against Jerusalem *t'* same day.
24 and when *t'* cometh, ye shall know
31: 18 *T'* is Pharaoh and all his
32: 16 *T'* is the lamentation wherewith
33: 33 And when *t'* cometh to pass, (lo, it will
36: 22 I do not *t'* for your sakes, O house of
32 Not for your sakes do I *t'*, saith the
35 *T'* land that was desolate is
39: 8 *t'* is the day whereof I have
40: 10 eastward were three on *t'* side,
10 one measure on *t'* side and on that
12 chambers was one cubit on *t'* side,
12 were six cubits on *t'* side,
21 three on *t'* side and three on that
26 it had palm trees, one on *t'* side,
34, 37 on *t'* side, and on that side:
39 the gate were two tables on *t'* side,
41 Four tables were on *t'* side, and
45 *T'* chamber, whose prospect is
48 five cubits on *t'* side, and five
48 the gate was three cubits on *t'* side,
49 one on *t'* side, and another on that
41: 4 me, *T'* is the most holy place.
22 *T'* is the table that is before the
43: 12 *T'* is the law of the house; Upon
12 Behold, *t'* is the law of the house.
13 *t'* shall be the higher place of the
44: 2 *T'* gate shall be shut, it shall not
45: 1 *T'* shall be holy in all the borders
2 Of *t'* there shall be for the
3 of *t'* measure shalt thou measure
13 *T'* is the oblation that ye shall offer;
16 *t'* oblation for the prince in Israel.
46: 3 worship at the door of *t'* gate
20 *T'* is the place where the priests
47: 6 unto me, Son of man, hast thou seen *t'*?
12 on *t'* side and on that side, shall
13 *T'* shall be the border, whereby ye
14 *t'* land shall fall unto you for
15 *t'* shall be the border of the land
17 of Hamath. And *t'* is the north side.
18 the east sea. And *t'* is the east side.
19 And *t'* is the south side southward.
20 Hamath. *T'* is the west side.
21 So shall ye divide *t'* land unto
48: 10 the priests, shall be *t'* holy oblation;
12 *t'* oblation of the land that is offered
29 *T'* is the land which ye shall
Da 1:14 he consented to them in *t'* matter,
2:12 For *t'* cause the king was angry
18 God of heaven concerning *t'* secret;
30 *t'* secret is not revealed to me for
31 *T'* great image, whose brightness
32 *T'* image's head was of fine gold,
36 *T'* is the dream; and we will tell

Da 2:38 them all. Thou art *t'* head of gold.
47 thou couldest reveal *t'* secret.
3:16 careful to answer thee in *t'* matter.
29 God that can deliver after *t'* sort.
4: 17 *T'* matter is by the decree of the
18 *t'* dream I king Nebuchadnezzar
24 *T'* is the interpretation, O king,
24 *t'* is the decree of the most High,
28 *t'* came upon the king Nebuchadnezzar.
30 and said, Is not *t'* great Babylon,
5: 7 Whosoever shall read *t'* writing,
15 that they should read *t'* writing, and
22 heart, though thou knewest all *t'*;
24 him; and *t'* writing was written.
25 *t'* is the writing that was written,
26 *T'* is the interpretation of the
6: 3 *t'* Daniel was preferred above the
5 find any occasion against *t'* Daniel,
28 *t'* Daniel prospered in the reign of
7: 6 After *t'* I beheld, and lo another,
7 After *t'* I saw in the night visions,
8 in *t'* horn were eyes like the eyes
16 and asked him the truth of all *t'*.
24 horns out of *t'* kingdom are ten kings
8: 16 *t'* man to understand the vision.
9: 7 us confusion of faces, as at *t'* day;
13 Moses, all *t'* evil is come upon us:
15 hast gotten thee renown, as at *t'* day;
10: 8 was left alone, and saw *t'* great vision,
11 he had spoken *t'* word unto me,
17 how can the servant of *t'* my lord
17 talk with *t'* my lord? for as for me,
11: 18 *t'* shall he turn his face unto the isles,
12: 5 on *t'* side of the bank of the river,
Ho 5: 1 Hear ye *t'*, O priests; and hearken,
7:10 their God, nor seek him for all *t'*.
16 *t'* shall be their derision in the
Joe 1: 2 Hear *t'*, ye old men, and give ear,
2 Hath *t'* been in your days, or even
3: 9 Proclaim ye *t'* among the Gentiles;
Am 3: 1 Hear *t'* word that the Lord hath
4: 1 Hear *t'* word, ye kine of Bashan,
5 *t'* liketh you, O ye children of
12 because I will do *t'* unto thee,
5: 1 Hear ye *t'* word which I take up
7: 3 The Lord repented for *t'*: It shall
6 The Lord repented for *t'*:
6 *T'* also shall not be, saith the
8: 4 Hear *t'*, O ye that swallow up the
8 Shall not the land tremble for *t'*,
9:12 name, saith the Lord that doeth *t'*.
Ob 20 captivity of *t'* host of the children
Jon 1: 7 for whose cause *t'* evil is upon us.
8 for whose cause *t'* evil is upon us;
10 unto him, Why hast thou done *t'*?
14 let us not perish for *t'* man's life,
4: 2 thee, O Lord, was not *t'* my saying,
Mic 1: 5 transgression of Jacob is all *t'*,
2: 3 against *t'* family do I devise an evil,
3 ye go haughtily: for *t'* time is evil.
10 depart; for *t'* is not your rest:
11 even be the prophet of *t'* people.
3: 9 Hear *t'*, I pray you, ye heads of the
5: 5 And *t'* man shall be the peace,
Hab 1:11 imputing *t'* his power unto his
Zep 2:10 *T'* shall they have for their pride,
15 *T'* is the rejoicing city that dwelt
Hag 1: 2 *T'* people say, The time is not
4 houses, and *t'* house lie waste?
2: 3 that saw *t'* house in her first glory?
7 and I will fill *t'* house with glory,
9 The glory of *t'* latter house shall be
9 and in *t'* place will I give peace,
14 So is *t'* people, and so is *t'* nation
15 consider from *t'* day and upward,
18 Consider now from *t'* day and
19 fourth: from *t'* day will I bless you.
Zec 2: 4 Run, speak to *t'* young man,
3: 2 is not *t'* a brand plucked out of
4: 6 *T'* is the word of the Lord unto
9 have laid the foundation of *t'* house;
5: 3 *T'* is the curse that goeth forth
3 shall be cut off as on *t'* side
5 see what is *t'* that goeth forth.
6 *T'* is an ephah that goeth forth.
6 *T'* is their resemblance through
7 *t'* is a woman that sitteth in the
8 And he said, *T'* is wickedness.
6:15 And *t'* shall come to pass, if ye
8: 6 remnant of *t'* people in these days,
11 not be unto the residue of *t'* people
12 remnant of *t'* people to possess all
14:12 *t'* shall be the plague wherewith
15 shall be in these tents, as *t'* plague.
19 *T'*...be the punishment of Egypt,
Mal 1: 9 *t'* hath been your means: will he
13 should I accept *t'* of your hand?
2: 1 *t'* commandment is for you.
4 sent *t'* commandment unto you,
12 Lord will cut off the man that doeth *t'*,
13 *t'* have ye done again, covering the
3: 9 have robbed me, even *t'* whole nation.
4: 3 your feet in the day that I shall do *t'*,
M't 1:18 of Jesus Christ was on *t'* wise:
22 Now all *t'* was done, that it might
3: 3 *t'* is he that was spoken of by the
17 *T'* is my beloved Son, in whom I
6: 9 After *t'* manner therefore pray ye:
11 Give us *t'* day our daily bread.
7:12 for *t'* is the law and the prophets.
8: 9 I say to *t'* man, Go, and he goeth;
9 my servant, Do *t'*, and he doeth it.
27 What manner of man is *t'*, that
9: 3 themselves, *T'* man blasphemeth.
28 Believe ye that I am able to do *t'*?
10: 23 when they persecute you in *t'* city,

M't 11:10 For *t'* is he, of whom it is written,
16 shall I liken *t'* generation?
23 would have remained until *t'* day.
12: 6 in *t'* place is one greater than the
7 But if ye had known what *t'* meaneth,
23 said, Is not *t'* the son of David?
24 *T'* fellow doth not cast out devils.
32 neither in *t'* world, neither in the
41 in judgment with *t'* generation,
42 in the judgment with *t'* generation,
45 be also unto *t'* wicked generation.
13: 15 *t'* people's heart is waxed gross,
19 *T'* is he which received seed by
22 and the care of *t'* world, and the
28 unto them, An enemy hath done *t'*.
40 shall it be in the end of *t'* world.
54 hath *t'* [5129] man *t'* wisdom, and
55 Is not *t'* the carpenter's son? is not
56 then hath *t'* man all these things?
14: 2 *T'* is John the Baptist; he is risen
15 *T'* is a desert place, and the time
15: 8 *T'* people draweth nigh unto me
11 out of the mouth, *t'* defileth a man.
12 offended, after they heard *t'* saying?
15 him, Declare unto us *t'* parable.
16: 18 upon *t'* rock I will build my church;
22 Lord: *t'* shall not be unto thee.
17: 5 *T'* is my beloved Son, in whom I
20 ye shall say unto *t'* mountain,
21 Howbeit *t'* kind goeth not out by
18: 4 humble himself as *t'* little child,
19: 5 *t'* cause shall a man leave father
11 All men cannot receive *t'* saying,
26 With men *t'* is impossible; but
20: 14 I will give unto *t'* last, even as unto
21: 4 All *t'* was done, that it might be
10 city was moved, saying, Who is *t'*?
11 *T'* is Jesus the prophet of Nazareth
21 only do *t'* which is done to the fig
21 if ye shall say unto *t'* mountain,
23 and who gave thee *t'* authority?
38 among themselves, *T'* is the heir;
42 *t'* is the Lord's doing, and it is
44 whosoever shall fall on *t'* stone
22: 20 unto them, Whose is *t'* image and
33 And when the multitude heard *t'*,
38 *T'* is the first and great
23: 36 shall come upon *t'* generation.
24: 14 *t'* gospel of the kingdom shall be
21 beginning of the world to *t'* time,
34 *T'* generation shall not pass, till
43 But know *t'*, that if the goodman
26: 8 To what purpose is *t'* waste?
9 *t'* ointment might have been sold
12 poured *t'* ointment on my body,
13 *t'* gospel shall be preached in the
13 the whole world, there shall also *t'*,
13 that *t'* woman hath done, be told
26 and said, Take, eat; *t'* is my body.
28 *t'* is my blood of the new testament,
29 not drink henceforth of *t'* fruit of
31 offended because of me *t'* night:
34 That *t'* night, before the cock crow,
39 possible, let *t'* cup pass from me:
42 if *t'* cup may not pass away from
56 But all *t'* was done, that the
61 *T'* fellow said, I am able to
71 *T'* fellow was also with Jesus of
27: 8 The field of blood, unto *t'* day.
19 I have suffered many things *t'* day
24 of the blood of *t'* just person:
37 *T'* Is Jesus The King Of The
47 that, said, *T'* man calleth for Elias.
54 saying, Truly *t'* was the Son of God.
28: 14 if *t'* come to the governor's ears,
15 *t'* saying is commonly reported
15 among the Jews until *t'* day.
M'r 1: 27 saying, What thing is *t'*? what
27 what new doctrine is *t'*? for with
2: 7 Why doth *t'* man thus speak
12 We never saw it on *t'* fashion.
4: 13 them, Know ye not *t'* parable?
19 And the cares of *t'* world, and the
41 What manner of man is *t'*, that even
5: 32 to see her that had done *t'* thing.
39 Why make ye *t'* ado, and weep?
6: 2 whence hath *t'* man these things?
2 what wisdom is *t'* which is given
3 Is not *t'* the carpenter, the son of
35 *T'* is a desert place, and now the
7: 6 *T'* people honoureth me with their
29 unto her, For *t'* saying go thy way;
8: 12 Why doth *t'* generation seek after
12 sign be given unto *t'* generation.
38 *t'* adulterous and sinful generation;
9: 7 *T'* is my beloved Son: hear him.
21 is it ago since *t'* came unto him?
29 *T'* kind can come forth by nothing,
10: 5 your heart he wrote you *t'* precept.
7 *t'* cause shall a man leave his father
30 an hundredfold now in *t'* time,
11: 3 man say unto you, Why do ye *t'*?
23 shall say unto *t'* mountain, Be
28 who gave thee *t'* authority to do
12: 7 among themselves, *T'* is the heir;
10 And have ye not read *t'* scripture;
11 *T'* was the Lord's doing, and it is
16 is *t'* image and superscription?
30 *t'* is the first commandment.
31 the second is like, namely *t'*,
43 *t'* poor widow hath cast more in,
13: 19 which God created unto *t'* time,
30 that *t'* generation shall not pass,
14: 4 Why was *t'* waste of the ointment
9 *t'* gospel shall be preached
9 *t'* also that she hath done shall be

M'r 14: 22 and said, Take, eat: *t'* is my body.
24 *T'* is my blood of the new testament,
27 offended because of me *t'* night:
30 I say unto thee, That *t'* day,
30 even in *t'* night, before the cock
36 thee; take away *t'* cup from me:
58 destroy *t'* temple that is made
69 that stood by, *T'* is one of them.
71 I know not *t'* man of whom ye
15: 39 Truly *t'* man was the Son of God.
Lu 1: 18 angel, Whereby shall I know *t'*?
29 manner of salutation *t'* should be.
34 How shall *t'* be, seeing I know not
36 *t'* is the sixth month with her, who
43 And whence is *t'* to me, that the
61 kindred that is called by *t'* name.
66 What manner of child shall *t'* be!
2: 2 (And *t'* taxing was first made when
11 is born *t'* day in the city of David a
12 *t'* shall be a sign unto you; ye shall
15 *t'* thing which is come to pass,
17 was told them concerning *t'* child.
34 *t'* child is set for the fall and rising
3: 20 Added yet *t'* above all, that he shut
4: 3 *t'* stone that it be made bread.
6 All *t'* power will I give thee, and
21 *T'* day is...scripture fulfilled in
21 is *t'* scripture fulfilled in your
22 they said, Is not *t'* Joseph's son?
23 will surely say unto me *t'* proverb,
36 saying, What a word is *t'*! for
5: 6 And when they had *t'* done, they
21 saying, Who is *t'* which speaketh
6: 3 Have ye not read so much as *t'*,
7: 4 worthy for whom he should do *t'*:
8 my servant, Do *t'*, and he doeth it.
17 *t'* rumour of him went forth
27 *T'* is he, of whom it is written,
31 I liken the men of *t'* generation?
39 *T'* man, if he were a prophet,
39 manner of woman *t'*...that toucheth
44 unto Simon, Seest thou *t'* woman?
45 *t'* woman since the time I came in,
46 *t'* woman hath anointed my feet
49 Who is *t'* that forgiveth sins also?
8: 9 saying, What might *t'* parable be?
11 Now the parable is *t'*: The seed is
14 and riches and pleasures of *t'* life,
25 another, What manner of man is *t'*!
9: 9 but who is *t'*, of whom I hear such
13 go and buy meat for all *t'* people.
35 *T'* is my beloved Son: hear him.
45 they understood not *t'* saying,
48 shall receive *t'* child in my name
54 his disciples James and John saw *t'*,
10: 5 first say, Peace be to *t'* house.
11 notwithstanding be ye sure of *t'*,
20 Notwithstanding in *t'* rejoice not,
28 right: *t'* do, and thou shalt live.
11: 29 to say, *T'* is an evil generation:
30 the Son of man be to *t'* generation.
31 with the men of *t'* generation,
32 the judgment with *t'* generation,
50 may be required of *t'* generation;
51 It shall be required of *t'* generation.
12: 18 And he said, *T'* will I do: I will
20 *t'* night thy soul shall be required
39 *t'* know, that if the goodman of the
41 speakest thou *t'* parable unto us,
56 is it that ye do not discern *t'* time?
13: 6 He spake also *t'* parable; A certain
7 I come seeking fruit on *t'* fig tree,
8 Lord, let it alone *t'* year also, till I
16 And ought not *t'* woman, being a
16 be loosed from *t'* bond on the
14: 9 and say to thee, Give *t'* man place;
30 *T'* man began to build, and was
15: 2 *T'* man receiveth sinners, and
3 And he spake *t'* parable unto them,
24 *t'* my son was dead, and is alive
30 as soon as *t'* thy son was come,
32 *t'* thy brother was dead, and is alive
16: 2 How is it that I hear *t'* of thee?
8 children of *t'* world are in their
24 for I am tormented in *t'* flame.
26 beside all *t'*, between us and you
28 also come into *t'* place of torment.
17: 6 might say unto *t'* sycamine tree,
18 give glory to God, save *t'* stranger.
25 and be rejected of *t'* generation.
18: 1 a parable unto them to *t'* end,*
5 because *t'* widow troubleth me, I
9 he spake *t'* parable unto certain
11 adulterers, or even as *t'* publican.
14 *t'* man went down to his house
23 And when he heard *t'*, he was very
30 manifold more in *t'* present time,
34 *t'* saying was hid from them,
19: 9 him, *T'* day is salvation come
9 is salvation come to *t'* house,
14 not have *t'* man to reign over us.
42 known,...at least in *t'* thy day,
20: 2 is he that gave thee *t'* authority?
9 he to speak to the people *t'* parable;
14 *T'* is the heir: come, let us kill
17 What is *t'* then that is written,
19 spoken *t'* parable against them.
34 The children of *t'* world marry,
21: 3 *t'* poor widow hath cast in more
23 the land, and wrath upon *t'* people.
32 *T'* generation shall not pass away,
34 and drunkenness, and cares of *t'* life,
22: 15 to eat *t'* passover with you before
17 Take *t'*, and divide it among
19 *T'* is my body which is given for
19 you: *t'* do in remembrance of me.

Lu 22: 20 *T'* cup is the new testament in my
23 them it was that should do *t'* thing.
34 the cock shall not crow *t'* day,
37 that *t'* that is written must yet be
42 be willing, remove *t'* cup from me:
53 but *t'* is your hour, and the power of
56 said, *T'* man was also with him.
59 Of a truth *t'* fellow also was with
23: 2 We found *t'* fellow perverting the
4 people, I find no fault in *t'* man.
5 beginning from Galilee to *t'* place.
14 Ye have brought *t'* man unto me,
14 have found no fault in *t'* man
18 Away with *t'* man, and release unto
38 *T'* Is The King Of The Jews.
41 *t'* man hath done nothing amiss.
47 Certainly *t'* was a righteous man.
52 *T'* man went unto Pilate, and
24: 21 and beside all *t'*, to day is the third
Joh 1: 15 *T'* was he of whom I spake, He
19 *t'* is the record of John, when the
30 *T'* is he of whom I said, After me
34 bare record that *t'* is the Son of God.
2: 11 *T'* beginning of miracles did Jesus
12 After *t'* he went...to Capernaum,
19 Destroy *t'* temple, and in three
20 Forty and six years was *t'* temple
22 that he had said *t'* unto them;
3: 19 And *t'* is the condemnation, that
29 voice: *t'* my joy therefore is fulfilled.
4: 13 drinketh of *t'* water shall thirst
15 Sir, give me *t'* water, that I thirst
20 fathers worshipped in *t'* mountain;
21 ye shall neither in *t'* mountain, nor
27 And upon *t'* came his disciples, and
29 that ever I did: is not *t'* the Christ?
42 know that *t'* is indeed the Christ,
54 *T'* is again the second miracle
5: 1 After *t'* there was a feast of the
28 Marvel not at *t'*: for the hour is
6: 6 And *t'* he said to prove him: for he
14 *T'* is of a truth that prophet that
29 *T'* is the work of God, that ye
34 Lord, evermore give us *t'* bread.
39 *t'* is the Father's will which hath
40 *t'* is the will of him that sent me,
42 Is not *t'* Jesus, the son of Joseph,
50 *T'* is the bread which cometh down
51 if any man eat of *t'* bread, he shall
52 How can *t'* man give us his flesh
58 *T'* is that bread which came down
58 he that eateth of *t'* bread shall live
60 disciples, when they heard *t'*, said,
60 *T'* is an hard saying; who can
61 unto them, Doth *t'* offend you?
7: 8 Go ye up unto *t'* feast: I go not up
8 I go not up yet unto *t'* feast; for
15 How knoweth *t'* man letters,
25 Is not *t'* he, whom they seek to kill?
26 indeed that *t'* is the very Christ?
27 we know *t'* man whence he is: but
31 these which *t'* man hath done?
36 What manner of saying is *t'* that he
39 (But *t'* spake he of the Spirit, which
40 when they heard *t'* saying,
40 said, Of a truth *t'* is the Prophet.
41 Others said, *T'* is the Christ. But
46 Never man spake like *t'* man.
49 *t'* people who knoweth not the law
8: 4 *t'* woman was taken in adultery,
6 *T'* they said, tempting him, that
23 am from above: ye are of *t'* world;
23 I am not of *t'* world.
40 heard of God: *t'* did not Abraham.
9: 2 who did sin, *t'* man, or his parents,
3 Neither hath *t'* man sinned, nor his
8 Is not *t'* he that sat and begged?
9 Some said, *T'* is he: others said,
16 *T'* man is not of God, because he
19 Is *t'* your son, who...was born blind?
20 We know that *t'* is our son, and
24 we know that *t'* man is a sinner.
29 as for *t'* fellow, we know not from
33 If *t'* man were not of God, he
39 judgment I am come into *t'* world
10: 16 sheep I have....are not of *t'* fold:
18 *T'* commandment have I received
41 John spake of *t'* man were true.
11: 4 *T'* sickness is not unto death, but
9 he seeth the light of *t'* world.
26 shall never die. Believest thou *t'*?
37 Could not *t'* man, which opened
37 even *t'* man should not have died?
39 him, Lord, by *t'* time he stinketh:
47 for *t'* man doeth many miracles.
51 And *t'* spake he not of himself: but
12: 5 *t'* ointment sold for three hundred
6 *T'* he said, not that he cared for the
7 day of my burying hath she kept *t'*.
18 *t'* cause the people also met him,
18 heard that he had done *t'* miracle.
25 he that hateth his life in *t'* world
27 say? Father, save me from *t'* hour:
27 but for *t'* cause came I unto...hour.
27 cause came I unto *t'* hour.
30 *T'* voice came not because of me,
31 Now is the judgment of *t'* world:
31 the prince of *t'* world be cast out.
33 *T'* he said, signifying what death
34 lifted up? who is *t'* Son of man?
13: 1 out of *t'* world unto the Father,
28 what intent he spake *t'* unto him.
35 *t'* shall all men know that ye are
14: 30 for the prince of *t'* world cometh,
15: 12 *T'* is my commandment, That ye
13 Greater love hath no man than *t'*,

Joh 15:25 But t' cometh to pass, that the word
16:11 the prince of t' world is judged.
17 What is t' that he saith unto us,
18 What is t' that he saith, A little
30 by t' we believe that thou camest
17: 3 t' is life eternal, that they might
18:17 also one of t' man's disciples?
29 accusation bring ye against t' man?
34 Sayest thou t' thing of thyself, or
36 My kingdom is not of t' world:
36 if my kingdom were not of t' world,
37 I am a king. To t' end was I born,
37 for t' cause came I into the world,
38 when he had said t', he went out
40 saying, Not t' man, but Barabbas.
19:12 If thou let t' man go, thou art not
20 T' title then read many of the Jews:
28 After t', Jesus knowing that all
38 And after t' Joseph of Arimathæa,
20:22 And when he had said t', he
30 which are not written in t' book:
21: 1 and on t' wise shewed he himself.
14 T' is now the third time that
19 T' spake he, signifying by what
19 when he had spoken t', he saith
21 Lord, and what shall t' man do?
23 Then went t' saying abroad
24 T' is the disciple which testifieth
Ac 1: 6 wilt thou at t' time restore again
11 t' same Jesus, which is taken up
16 t' scripture must needs have been
17 had obtained part of t' ministry.
18 Now t' man purchased a field
25 he may take part of t' ministry
2: 6 Now when t' was noised abroad, the
12 one to another, What meaneth t'?
14 t' known unto you, and hearken to
16 t' is that which was spoken by the
29 his sepulchre is with us unto t' day.
31 seeing t' before spake of...resurrection
32 T' Jesus hath God raised up,
33 he hath shed forth t', which ye
37 they heard t', they were pricked in
40 Save yourselves from t' untoward
3:12 men of Israel, why marvel ye at t'?
12 we had made t' man to walk?
16 name hath made t' man strong,
16 given him t' perfect soundness
4: 7 or by what name, have ye done t'?
9 If we t' day be examined of the
10 by him doth t' man stand here
11 T' is the stone which was set at
17 speak...to no man in t' name.
22 on whom t' miracle of healing was
5: 4 conceived t' thing in thine heart?
20 to the people all the words of t' life.
24 of them whereunto t' would grow.
28 ye should not teach in t' name?
28 to bring t' man's blood upon us.
37 After t' man rose up Judas of
38 for if t' [3778] counsel or t' work
6: 3 we may appoint over t' business.
13 T' man ceaseth not to speak
13 words against t' holy place, and
14 t' Jesus of Nazareth shall destroy
14 of Nazareth shall destroy t' place,
7: 4 he removed him into t' land,
6 And God spake on t' wise, That
7 forth, and serve me in t' place.
29 Then fled Moses at t' saying, and
35 T' Moses whom they refused,
37 T' is that Moses, which said unto
38 T' is he, that was in the church in
40 for as for t' Moses, which brought
60 Lord, lay not t' sin to their charge.
60 And when he had said t', he fell
8:10 T' man is the great power of God.
19 Give me also t' power, that on
21 neither part nor lot in t' matter:
22 Repent...of t' thy wickedness,
29 near, and join thyself to t' chariot.
32 the scripture which he read was t',
34 of whom speaketh the prophet t'?
9: 2 if he found any of t' way, whether
13 I have heard by many of t' man,
21 Is not t' he that destroyeth them
21 called on t' name in Jerusalem,
22 proving that t' is very Christ.
36 t' woman was full of good works
10:16 T' was done thrice: and the
17 what t' vision which he had seen
30 ago I was fasting until t' hour;
11:10 And t' was done three times: and
13:17 The God of t' people of Israel chose
23 t' man's seed hath God according
26 you is the word of t' salvation sent.
33 Son, t' day have I begotten thee.
34 he said on t' wise, I will give you
38 through t' man is preached unto you
48 when the Gentiles heard t', they were
15: 2 and elders about t' question.
6 for to consider of t' matter.
15 And to t' agree the words of the
16 After t' I will return, and will
23 they wrote letters by them after t'
16:18 And t' did she many days. But
36 the prison told t' saying to Paul,
17: 3 t' Jesus, whom I preach unto you,
18 said, What will t' babbler say?
19 May we know what t' new doctrine,
23 I found an altar with t' inscription,
30 times of t' ignorance God winked
32 will hear thee again of t' matter.
18:10 for I have much people in t' city.
13 T' fellow persuadeth men to
18 Paul after t' tarried there yet a good

Ac 18:21 t' feast that cometh in Jerusalem:
25 T' man was instructed in the way
19: 5 When they heard t', they were baptized
10 t' continued by the space of two
17 t' was known to all the Jews and
25 by t' craft we have our wealth.
26 t' Paul hath persuaded and turned
27 not only t' our craft is in danger to
40 in question for t' day's uproar,
40 give an account of t' concourse.
20:26 Wherefore I take you to record t'
29 For I know t', that after my
21:11 bind the man that owneth t' girdle,
23 therefore t' that we say to thee:
28 T' is the man, that teacheth all
28 people, and the law, and t' place:
28 and hath polluted t' holy place.
22: 3 in t' city at the feet of Gamaliel,
3 toward God, as ye all are t' day.
4 I persecuted t' way unto the death,
22 gave him audience unto t' word,
26 thou doest: for t' man is a Roman.
28 a great sum obtained I t' freedom.
23: 1 conscience before God until t' day.
9 saying, We find no evil in t' man:
13 which had made t' conspiracy.
17 Bring t' young man unto the chief
18 to bring t' young man unto thee,
25 he wrote a letter after t' manner:
27 T' man was taken of the Jews, and
24: 2 unto t' nation by thy providence,
5 found t' man a pestilent fellow,
10 many years a judge unto t' nation,
14 But t' I confess unto thee, that
21 Except it be for t' one voice, that I
21 called in question by you t' day.
25 Go thy way for t' time; when I
25: 5 down with me, and accuse t' man,
24 ye see t' man, about whom all the
26: 2 I shall answer for myself t' day
16 appeared unto thee for t' purpose,
22 I continue unto t' day, witnessing
26 t' thing was not done in a corner.
29 but also all that hear me t' day,
31 T' man doeth nothing worthy of
32 T' man might have been set at
27:10 I perceive that t' voyage will be
21 to have gained t' harm and loss.
23 stood by me t' night the angel of
33 T' day is the fourteenth day that
34 meat: for t' is for your health:
28: 4 No doubt t' man is a murderer,
9 So when t' was done, others also,
20 For t' cause therefore have I called
20 of Israel I am bound with t' chain.
22 for as concerning t' sect, we know
26 Go unto t' people, and say,
27 heart of t' people is waxed gross,
Ro 1:26 For t' cause God gave them up
2: 3 And thinkest thou t', O man, that
3:26 at t' time his righteousness:
4: 9 Cometh t' blessedness then upon
5: 2 into t' grace wherein we stand,
6: 6 Knowing t', that our old man is
7:24 me from the body of t' death?
8:18 sufferings of t' present time are
9: 9 For t' is the word of promise, At
9 At t' time will I come, and Sarah
10 And not only t'; but when Rebecca
17 for t' same purpose...I raised thee
10: 6 is of faith speaketh on t' wise,
11: 5 t' present time...there is a remnant
8 they should not hear;) unto t' day.
25 should be ignorant of t' mystery,
27 For t' is my covenant unto them,
12: 2 And be not conformed to t' world:
13: 6 for t' cause pay ye tribute also:
6 continually upon t' very thing.
9 For t', Thou shalt not commit
9 briefly comprehended in t' saying,
14: 9 For to t' end Christ both died, and
13 but judge t' rather, that no man
15: 9 For t' cause I will confess to thee
28 When therefore I have performed t',
28 and have sealed to them t' fruit,
16:22 I Tertius, who wrote t' epistle,
1Co 1:12 Now t' I say, that every one of you
20 where is the disputer of t' world?
20 foolish the wisdom of t' world?
2: 6 yet not the wisdom of t' world, nor
6 nor of the princes of t' world, that
8 of the princes of t' world knew:
3:12 man build upon t' foundation gold,
18 seemeth to be wise in t' world,
19 wisdom of t' world is foolishness
4:11 t' present hour we both hunger,
13 offscouring of all things unto t' day.
17 For t' cause have I sent unto you
5: 2 he that hath done t' deed might be
3 him that hath so done t' deed,
10 with the fornicators of t' world,
6: 3 more things that pertain to t' life?
4 of things pertaining to t' life,
7: 6 But I speak t' by permission, and
7 one after t' manner, and another
26 t' is good for the present distress,
29 t' I say, brethren, the time is short:
31 And they that use t' world, as not
31 for the fashion of t' world passeth
35 t' I speak for your own profit; not
8: 7 conscience of the idol unto t' hour
9 t' liberty of yours become a
9: 3 to them that do examine me is t',
10 For our sakes, no doubt, t' is written:
12 If others be partakers of t' power
12 we have not used t' power;

1Co 9:17 if I do t' thing willingly, I have a
23 t' I do for the gospel's sake, that I
10:28 T' is offered in sacrifice unto idols,
11:10 For t' cause ought the woman to
17 in t' that I declare unto you I praise
20 t' is not to eat the Lord's supper.
22 to you? shall I praise you in t'?
24 t' is my body, which is broken for
24 you: t' do in remembrance of me.
25 T' cup is the new testament in my
25 t' do ye, as oft as ye drink it, in
26 For as often as ye eat t' bread,
26 and drink t' cup, ye do shew the
27 whosoever shall eat t' bread, and
27 and drink t' cup of the Lord,
30 t' cause many are weak and sickly
14:21 lips will I speak unto t' people;
15: 6 greater part remain unto t' present,
19 If in t' life only we have hope in
34 of God: I speak t' to your shame.
50 Now t' I say, brethren, that flesh
53 For t' corruptible must put on
53 t' mortal must put on immortality.
54 t' corruptible shall have put on
54 and t' mortal shall have put on
16:12 was not at all to come at t' time;
2Co 1:12 our rejoicing is t', the testimony
15 in t' confidence I was minded to
2: 1 But I determined t' with myself,
3 And I wrote t' same unto you, lest,
6 to such a man is t' punishment,
9 For to t' end also did I write, that
3:10 glorious had no glory in t' respect,
14 until t' day remaineth the same
15 But even unto t' day, when Moses
4: 1 seeing we have t' ministry,
4 god of t' world hath blinded the
7 t' treasure in earthen vessels,
5: 1 earthly house of t' tabernacle
2 in t' we groan, earnestly desiring
4 that are in t' tabernacle do groan,
7: 3 I speak not t' to condemn you: for
11 behold t' selfsame thing, that ye
11 yourselves...be clear in t' matter.
8: 5 t' they did, not as we hoped, but first
7 that ye abound in t' grace also.
10 t' is expedient for you, who have
14 at t' time your abundance may
19 to travel with us with t' grace,
20 Avoiding t', that no man should
20 in t' abundance which is
9: 3 you should be in vain in t' behalf;
4 in t' same confident boasting.
6 But t' I say, He which soweth
12 the administration of t' service
13 the experiment of t' ministration
10: 7 let him of himself think t' again,
11 Let such an one think t', that, such
11:10 man shall stop me of t' boasting in
17 in t' confidence of boasting.
12: 8 For t' thing I besought the Lord
13 to you? forgive me t' wrong.
13: 1 T' is the third time I am coming
9 t' also we wish, even your perfection.
Ga 1: 4 deliver us from t' present evil
3: 2 T' only would I learn of you,
17 t' I say, that the covenant, that
4:25 t' Agar is mount Sinai in Arabia,
5: 8 T' persuasion cometh not of him
14 is fulfilled in one word, even in t';
16 T' I say then, Walk in the Spirit, and
6:16 many as walk according to t' rule,
Eph 1:21 not only in t' world, but also in
2: 2 according to the course of t' world,
3: 1 For t' cause I Paul, the prisoner
8 is t' grace given, that I should
14 For t' cause I bow my knees unto
4:17 T' I say therefore, and testify in
5: 5 t' ye know, that no whoremonger,
31 For t' cause shall a man leave his
32 T' is a great mystery: but I speak
6: 1 parents in the Lord: for t' is right.
12 rulers of the darkness of t' world,
Ph'p 1: 6 Being confident of t' very thing,
7 meet for me to think t' of you all,
9 t' I pray, that your love may abound
19 that t' shall turn to my salvation
22 flesh, t' is the fruit of my labour:
25 having t' confidence, I know that
2: 5 Let t' mind be in you, which was
3:13 t' one thing I do, forgetting those
15 God shall reveal even t' unto you.
Col 1: 9 For t' cause we also, since the day
27 the glory of t' mystery among the
2: 4 And t' I say, lest any man should
3:20 t' is well pleasing unto the Lord.
4:16 when t' epistle is read among you,
1Th 2:13 t' cause also thank we God without
3: 5 For t' cause, when I could no
4: 3 For t' is the will of God, even your
15 t' we say unto you by the word of
5:18 t' is the will of God in Christ Jesus
27 t' epistle be read unto all the holy
2Th 1:11 count you worthy of t' calling,
2:11 for t' cause God shall send them
3:10 t' we commanded you, that if any
14 man obey not our word by t' epistle,
1Ti 1: 9 Knowing t', that the law is not
15 T' is a faithful saying, and worthy
16 for t' cause I obtained mercy,
18 T' charge I commit unto thee,
2: 3 For t' is good and acceptable in
4: 9 T' is a faithful saying and worthy
16 in doing t' thou shalt both save
6: 7 we brought nothing into t' world,
14 That thou keep t' commandment

1Ti 6:17 them that are rich in t' world,
2Ti 1:15 T' thou knowest, that all they
2: 4 himself with the affairs of t' life;
19 standeth sure, having t' seal.
3: 1 T' know also, that in the last days
6 t' sort are they which creep into
4:10 me, having loved t' present world,
Tit 1: 5 For t' cause left I thee in Crete,
13 T' witness is true. Wherefore
2:12 and godly, in t' present world;
3: 8 T' is a faithful saying, and these
Heb 1: 5 Son, t' day have I begotten thee?
3: 3 For t' man was counted worthy of
4: 4 place of the seventh day on t' wise,
5 And in t' place again, If they shall
5: 4 man taketh t' honour unto himself,
6: 3 And t' will we do, if God permit.
7: 1 t' Melchisedec, king of Salem,
4 consider how great t' man was,
27 t' he did once, when he offered up
8: 1 which we have spoken t' is the sum:
3 t' man have somewhat...to offer.
10 t' is the covenant that I will make
9: 8 The Holy Ghost t' signifying, that
11 that is to say, not of t' building;
15 for t' cause he is the mediator of
20 T' is the blood of the testament
27 to die, but after t' the judgment:
10:12 t' man, after he had offered one
16 T' is the covenant that I will make
11: 5 his translation he had t' testimony,
12:27 t' word, Yet once more, signifieth
13:19 I beseech you the rather to do t',
Jas 1: 3 Knowing t', that the trying of your
25 t' man shall be blessed in his
26 heart, t' man's religion is vain.
27 before God and the Father is t',
2: 5 the poor of t' world rich in faith,
3:15 T' wisdom descendeth not from
4:15 we shall live, and do t', or that.
1Pe 1:25 t' is the word which by the gospel
2:19 For t' is thankworthy, if a man for
20 patiently, t' is acceptable with God.
3: 5 For after t' manner in the old time
4: 6 t' cause was the gospel preached
16 let him glorify God on t' behalf.
5:12 that t' is the true grace of God
2Pe 1: 5 beside t', giving all diligence,
13 as long as I am in t' tabernacle,
14 I must put off t' my tabernacle,
17 T' is my beloved Son, in whom I
18 t' voice which came from heaven
20 Knowing t' first, that no prophecy
3: 1 T' second epistle, beloved, I now
3 Knowing t' first, that there shall
5 t' they willingly are ignorant of,
8 be not ignorant of t' one thing,
1Jo 1: 5 T' then is the message which we
2:25 And t' is the promise that he hath
3: 3 every man that hath t' hope in him
8 For t' purpose the Son of God was
10 In t' the children of God are
11 t' is the message that ye heard
17 But whoso hath t' world's good,
23 t' is his commandment, That we
4: 3 t' is that spirit of antichrist,
9 In t' was manifested the love of
17 as he is, so are we in t' world.
21 t' commandment have we from
5: 2 By t' we know that we love the
3 t' is the love of God, that we keep
4 t' is the victory that overcometh
6 T' is he that came by water and
9 t' is the witness of God which he
11 t' is the record, that God hath
11 life, and t' life is in his Son.
14 t' is the confidence that we have in
20 T' is the true God, and eternal life.
2Jo 6 t' is love, that we walk after his
6 T' is the commandment, That, as
7 T' is a deceiver and an antichrist.
10 you, and bring not t' doctrine,
Jude 4 old ordained to t' condemnation,
5 though ye once knew t', how
Re 1: 3 that hear the words of t' prophecy,
2: 6 t' thou hast, that thou hatest the
24 as many as have not t' doctrine,
4: 1 After t' I looked, and, behold, a
7: 9 After t' I beheld, and, lo, a great
11: 5 he must in t' manner be killed.
15 kingdoms of t' world are become
20: 5 T' is the first resurrection.
14 of fire. T' is the second death.
22: 7 sayings of the prophecy of t' book.
9 which keep the sayings of t' book:
10 sayings of the prophecy of t' book:
18 words of the prophecy of t' book,
18 plagues that are written in t' book:
19 words of the book of t' prophecy,
19 which are written in t' book.

thistle See also THISTLES.
2Ki 14: 9 The t' that was in Lebanon sent
9 Lebanon, and trode down the t'.
2Ch 25:18 The t' that was in Lebanon sent
18 Lebanon, and trode down the t'.
Ho 10: 8 t' shall come up on their altars;

thistles
Ge 3:18 and t' shall it bring forth to thee;
Job 31:40 Let t' grow instead of wheat,
M't 7:16 grapes of thorns, or figs of t'?

thither^ See also THITHERWARD.
Ge 29: 3 t' were all the flocks gathered:
39: 1 which had brought him down t'.
42: 2 get you down t', and buy for us
Ex 10:26 serve the Lord, until we come t'.
26:33 bring in t' within the vail the ark
Nu 35: 6 manslayer, that he may flee t':
11 that the slayer may flee t', which
15 any person unawares may flee t'.
De 1:37 saying, Thou also shalt not go in t'.
38 before thee, he shall go in t':
39 they shall go in t', and unto them
4:42 that the slayer might flee t', which
12: 5 ye seek, and t' thou shalt come:
6 And t' ye shall bring your burnt
11 t' shall ye bring all that I command
19: 3 parts, that every slayer may flee t'.
4 of the slayer, which shall flee t',
32:52 thou shalt not go t' unto the land
34: 4 but thou shalt not go over t'.
Jos 7: 3 not all the people to labour t';
4 So there went up t' of the people
20: 3 and unwittingly may flee t':
9 person at unawares might flee t',
J'g 8:27 Israel went t' a whoring after it:
9:51 and t' fled all the men and women,
18: 3 they turned in t', and said unto
17 came in t', and took the graven
19:15 And they turned aside t', to go in
21:10 sent t' twelve thousand men of the
1Sa 2:14 unto all the Israelites that came t'.
5: 8 the ark of the God of Israel about t'.
10: 5 when thou art come t' to the city,
10 And when they came t' to the hill,
22 if the man should yet come t'.
19:23 he went t' to Naioth in Ramah:
22: 1 heard it, they went down t' to him.
30: 7 brought t' the ephod to David.
2Sa 2: 2 So David went up t', and his two
4: 6 came t' into the midst of the house,
1Ki 6: 7 made ready before it was brought t':
19: 9 And he came t' unto a cave, and
2Ki 2: 8 they were divided hither and t',
14 waters, they parted hither and t':
4: 8 by, he turned in t' to eat bread.
10 to us, that he shall turn in t'.
11 And it fell on a day, that he came t',
6: 6 cut down a stick, and cast it in t';
9 for t' the Syrians are come down.
14 Therefore sent he t' horses, and
9: 2 And when thou comest t', look out
17:27 Carry t' one of the priests whom ye
2Ch 1: 6 Solomon went up t' to the brasen
Ezr 10: 6 when he came t', he did eat no bread,
Ne 4:20 of the trumpet, resort ye t' unto us:
5:16 were gathered t' unto the work.
13: 9 t' brought I again the vessels of
Job 1:21 womb, and naked shall I return t':
6:20 they came t', and were ashamed.
Ec 1: 7 rivers come, t' they return again.
Isa 7:24 and with bows shall men come t';
25 not come t' the fears of briers and
32:20 that send forth t' the feet of the ox
55:10 from heaven, and returneth not t',
57: 7 t' wentest thou up to offer sacrifice.
Jer 22:11 He shall not return t' any more:
27 to return, t' shall they not return.
31: 8 a great company shall return t'.
40: 4 convenient for thee to go, t' go.
Eze 1:20 they went, t' was their spirit to go;
11:18 they shall come t', and they shall
40: 1 was upon me, and brought me t'.
3 And he brought me t', and, behold,
M't 2:22 Herod, he was afraid to go t':
M'r 6:33 and ran afoot t' out of all cities,
Lu 17:37 t' will the eagles be gathered
21: 2 poor widow casting in t' two mites.
Joh 7:34 and where I am, t' ye cannot come.
36 and where I am, t' ye cannot come?
11: 8 thee; and goest thou t' again?
18: 2 Jesus ofttimes resorted t' with his
3 cometh t' with lanterns and torches
Ac 8:30 Philip ran t' to him, and heard him
14:19 came t' certain Jews from Antioch
16:13 unto the women which resorted t'.
17:10 coming t' went into the synagogue
13 they came t' also, and stirred up
25: 4 he himself would depart shortly t'.

thitherward
J'g 18:15 And they turned t', and came to the
Jer 50: 5 the way to Zion with their faces t',
Ro 15:24 to be brought on my way t' by you,

Thomas (*tom'-us*) See also DIDYMUS.
M't 10: 3 T', and Matthew the publican;
M'r 3:18 T', and James the son of Alphæus,
Lu 6:15 T', James the son of Alphæus,
Joh 11:16 said T', which is called Didymus,
14: 5 T' saith unto him, Lord, we know
20:24 But T', one of the twelve, called
26 were within, and T' with them:
27 Then saith he to T', Reach hither
28 T' answered and said unto him,
29 T', because thou hast seen me,
21: 2 Peter, and T' called Didymus,
Ac 1:13 T', Bartholomew, and Matthew,

thongs
Ac 22:25 as they bound him with t', Paul

thorn See also THORNS.
Job 41: 2 or bore his jaw through with a t'?
Pr 26: 9 As a t' goeth up into the hand of a
Isa 55:13 of the t' shall come up the fir tree,
Eze 28:24 grieving t' of all that are round
Ho 10: 8 the t' and the thistle shall come up
Mic 7: 4 upright is sharper than a t' hedge:
2Co 12: 7 was given to me a t' in the flesh,

thorn-hedge See THORN and HEDGE.

thorns
Ge 3:18 T' also and thistles shall it bring
Ex 22: 6 If fire break out, and catch in t', so
Nu 33:55 in your eyes, and t' in your sides,
Jos 23:13 in your sides, and t' in your eyes,
J'g 2: 3 but they shall be as t' in your sides,
8: 7 I will tear your flesh with the t'
16 and t' of the wilderness and briers,
2Sa 23: 6 be all of them as t' thrust away,
2Ch 33:11 took Manasseh among the t',
Job 5: 5 and taketh it even out of the t',
Ps 58: 9 Before your pots can feel the t', he
118:12 they are quenched as the fire of t':
Pr 15:19 slothful man is as an hedge of t':
22: 5 T' and snares are in the way of
24:31 all grown over with t', and nettles
Ec 7: 6 as the crackling of t' under a pot,
Ca 2: 2 As the lily among t', so is my love
Isa 5: 6 there shall come up briers and t':
7:19 upon all t', and upon all bushes.
23 it shall even be for briers and t'.
24 the land shall become briers and t'.
25 thither the fear of briers and t':
9:18 it shall devour the briers and t',
10:17 shall burn and devour his t' and his
27: 4 set the briers and t' against me in
32:13 people shall come up t' and briers;
33:12 t' cut up shall they be burned in the
34:13 t' shall come up in her palaces,
Jer 4: 3 ground, and sow not among t'.
12:13 have sown wheat, but shall reap t':
Eze 2: 6 though briers and t' be with thee,
Ho 2: 6 I will hedge up thy way with t',
9: 6 t' shall be in their tabernacles.
Na 1:10 while they be folden together as t',
M't 7:16 Do men gather grapes of t', or figs
13: 7 And some fell among t';
7 and the t' sprung up, and choked them:
22 also that received seed among the t'
27:29 when they had platted a crown of t',
M'r 4: 7 And some fell among t',
7 and the t' grew up, and choked it,
18 are they which are sown among t';
15:17 platted a crown of t', and put it
Lu 6:44 of t' men do not gather figs, nor of
8: 7 And some fell among t';
7 t' sprung up with it, and choked it.
14 that which fell among t' are they,
Joh 19: 2 the soldiers platted a crown of t',
5 Jesus forth, wearing the crown of t'.
Heb 6: 8 that which beareth t' and briers is

thoroughly See also THROUGHLY.
Ex 21:19 shall cause him to be t' healed.
2Ki 11:18 his images brake they in pieces t',

those^
Ge 6: 4 were giants in the earth in t' days;
15:17 lamp that passed between t' pieces.
19:25 And he overthrew t' cities, and all
24:60 possess the gate of t' which hate them.
33: 5 and said, Who are t' with thee?
41:35 gather all the food of t' good years
42: 5 came to buy corn among t' that came:
50: 3 the days of t' which are embalmed:
Ex 2:11 And it came to pass in t' days,
4:21 thou do all t' wonders before Pharaoh,
29:33 they shall eat t' things wherewith the
35:35 and of t' that devise cunning work.
Le 11:27 all four, t' are unclean unto you:
14:11 and t' things, before the Lord,
42 and put them in the place of t' stones;
15:10 that beareth any of t' things shall
27 whosoever toucheth t' things shall be
22: 2 t' things which they hallow unto me:
Nu 1:21 T' that were numbered of them, even
22 fathers, t' that were numbered of them,
23, 25, 27, 29, 31, 33, 35, 37, 39, 41, 43 t'
that were numbered of them, even of
44 These are t' that were numbered,
45 t' that were numbered of the children
2: 4 t' that were numbered of them, were
5 t' that do pitch next unto him shall be
6, 8, 11 t' that were numbered thereof,
12 And t' which pitch by him shall be the
13 t' that were numbered of them, were
15, 19, 21, 23, 26 t' that were numbered of
27 t' that encamp by him shall be the
28, 30 t' that were numbered of them,
32 are t' which were numbered of the
3:22 T' that were numbered of them,
22 t' that were numbered of them were
34 And t' that were numbered of them,
38 But t' that encamp before the
43 t' that were numbered of them, were
46 for t' that are to be redeemed of the
4:36 t' that were numbered of them by
38 t' that were numbered of the sons of
40 Even t' that were numbered of them,
42 t' that were numbered of the families
44 t' that were numbered of them after
45 These be t' that were numbered of
46 t' that were numbered of the Levites,
48 Even t' that were numbered of them.
9: 7 And t' men said unto him, we are
14:22 t' men which have seen my glory,
37 t' men that did bring up the evil
18:16 And t' that are to be redeemed from a
25: 9 t' that died in the plague were twenty
26:18, 22, 25, 27 according to t' that were
numbered of them,
34 and t' that were numbered of them,
37, 43, 47, 54 according to t' that were
numbered of
62 t' that were numbered of them were
33:55 t' which ye let remain of them shall
De 7:22 will put out t' nations before thee
17: 9 the judge that shall be in t' days,
18: 9 the abominations of t' nations.
19: 5 he shall flee unto one of t' cities,

De 19:17 judges, which shall be in t' days;
20 And t' which remain shall hear, and
26: 3 the priest that shall be in t' days,
29: 3 the signs, and t' great miracles:
32:21 with t' which are not a people;
Jos 3:16 t' that came down toward the sea of
4:20 t' twelve stones, which they took
10:22 and bring out t' five kings unto me
23 brought forth t' five kings unto him
24 brought out t' kings unto Joshua,
11: 1 king of Hazor had heard t' things,
10 was the head of all t' kingdoms.
12 And all the cities of t' kings, and all
18 war a long time with all t' kings.
17:12 drive out the inhabitants of t' cities;
20: 4 he that doth flee unto one of t' cities
21:16 nine cities out of t' two tribes.
24:17 which did t' great signs in our sight,
J'g 2:16 of the hand of t' that spoiled them.
23 the Lord left t' nations, without
7: 8 and retained t' three hundred men:
11:13 therefore restore t' lands again
12: 5 t' Ephraimites which were escaped
17: 6 In t' days there was no king in
18: 1 In t' days there was no king in
1 in t' days the tribe of the Danites
19: 1 it came to pass in t' days, when
20:27 of God was there in t' days,
28 of Aaron, stood before it in t' days,)
21:25 In t' days there was no king in
1Sa 3: 1 the Lord was precious in t' days;
7:16 and judged Israel in all t' places.
10: 9 all t' signs came to pass that day.
11: 6 upon Saul when he heard t' tidings,
17:11 Saul and all Israel heard t' words of
28 whom hast thou left t' few sheep
18:23 Saul's servants spake t' words in
19: 7 Jonathan shewed him all t' things.
25: 9 according to all t' words in the
12 came and told them all t' sayings.
27: 8 for t' nations were of old the
28: 1 And it came to pass in t' days, that
3 had put away t' that had familiar
9 hath cut off t' that have familiar
30: 9 where t' that were left behind stayed.
20 they drave before t' other cattle,
22 of Belial, of t' that went with David,
2Sa 5:14 be the names of t' that were born unto
16:23 which he counselled in t' days,
1Ki 2: 7 let them be of t' that eat at thy table:
3: 2 name of the Lord, until t' days.
4:27 t' officers provided victual for
8: 4 t' did the priests and the Levites
9:21 upon t' did Solomon levy a tribute of
21:27 when Ahab heard t' words, that he
2Ki 4: 4 shalt pour out into all t' vessels,
6:22 wouldest thou smite t' whom thou
10:32 In t' days the Lord began to cut
15:37 In t' days the Lord began to send
17: 9 did secretly t' things that were not
18: 4 unto t' days the children of Israel
20: 1 In t' days was Hezekiah sick unto
24:15 t' carried he into captivity from
1Ch 4:23 and t' that dwelt among plants and
16:42 and cymbals for t' that should make a
2Ch 14: 6 rest, and he had no war in t' years;
15: 5 t' times there was no peace to him
17:19 t' whom the king put in the fenced
20:29 on all the kingdoms of t' countries,
32:13 the gods of the nations of t' lands
14 among all the gods of t' nations
24 In t' days Hezekiah was sick to
Ezr 1: 8 Even t' did Cyrus king of Persia bring
2: 1 t' which had been carried away, whom
3: 3 because of the people of t' countries:
5: 9 Then asked we t' elders, and said
14 t' did Cyrus the king take out of
7:19 t' deliver thou before the God of
8:35 children of t' that had been carried
9: 2 themselves with the people of t' lands:
4 transgression of t' that had been
10: 3 and of t' that trembled at the
8 congregation of t' that had been
Ne 4:17 that bare burdens, with t' that laded,
5:17 beside t' that came unto us from
6:17 in t' days the nobles of Judah sent
7: 6 of t' that had been carried away, whom
64 register among t' that were reckoned
8: 3 women, and t' that could understand;
10: 1 Now t' that sealed were, Nehemiah,
13:15 In t' days saw I in Judah some
23 In t' days also saw I Jews that had
Es 1: 2 That in t' days, when the king
2:21 In t' days, while Mordecai sat in
21 of t' which kept the door, were wroth,
3: 9 the hands of t' that have the charge
9: 5 they would unto t' that hated them.
11 the number of t' that were slain in
Job 5:11 To set up on high t' that be low; that
11 which mourn may be exalted to
21:22 seeing he judgeth t' that are high.
24:13 are of t' that rebel against the light;
19 doth the grave t' which have sinned.
27:15 T' that remain of him shall be buried
Ps 5:11 t' that put their trust in thee rejoice:
13: 4 t' that trouble me rejoice when I am
17: 7 thee from t' that rise up against them.
18:30 is a buckler to all t' that trust in him.
39 subdued under me t' that rose up
48 liftest me up above t' that rise up
21: 8 hand shall find out t' that hate thee.
37: 9 t' that wait upon the Lord, they shall
40:16 Let all t' that seek thee rejoice and be
50: 5 t' that have made a covenant with me
61: 5 the heritage of t' that fear thy name.
63: 9 But t' that seek my soul, to destroy it,
Ps 68: 6 he bringeth out t' which are bound
11 the company of t' that published it.
69: 6 let not t' that seek thee be confounded
26 they talk to the grief of t' whom thou
70: 4 Let all t' that seek thee rejoice and be
74:23 the tumult of t' that rise up against
79:11 preserve thou t' that are appointed to
92:13 T' that be planted in the house of the
102:20 to loose t' that are appointed to death;
103:18 t' that remember his commandments
106:46 of all t' that carried them captives.
109:31 him from t' that condemn his soul.
119:79 Let t' that fear thee turn unto me,
79 t' that have known thy testimonies.
132 usest to do unto t' that love thy name.
123: 4 the scorning of t' that are at ease,
125: 4 Do good, O Lord, unto t' that be good,
139:21 I grieved with t' that rise up against
140: 9 As for the head of t' that compass me
143: 3 as t' that have been long dead.
145:14 raiseth up all t' that be bowed down.
147:11 fear him, in t' that hope in his mercy.
Pr 1:12 whole, as t' that go down into the pit:
4:22 they are life unto t' that find them,
8:17 t' that seek me early shall find me.
21 may cause t' that love me to inherit
22:23 spoil the soul of t' that spoiled them.
24:11 death, and t' that are ready to be slain;
26:28 A lying tongue hateth t' that are
31: 6 and wine unto t' that be of heavy
Ec 1:11 are to come with t' that shall come
5:14 t' riches perish by evil travail:
7:28 a woman among all t' have I not
8: 8 deliver t' that are given to it.
12: 3 t' that look out of the windows be
Ca 7: 9 the lips of t' that are asleep to speak.
8:12 and t' that keep the fruit thereof two
Isa 14:19 as the raiment of t' that are slain,
27: 7 him, as he smote t' that smote him?
35: 8 not pass over it; but it shall be for t':
38: 1 In t' days was Hezekiah sick unto
40:11 gently lead t' that are with young.
56: 8 beside t' that are gathered unto him.
60:12 yea, t' nations shall be utterly wasted.
64: 5 t' that remember thee in thy ways:
5 in t' is continuance, and we shall
66: 2 all t' things hath mine hand made,
2 all t' things have been, saith the
19 t' that escape of them unto the
Jer 3:16 in t' days, saith the Lord, they
18 In t' days the house of Judah
4:12 full wind from t' places shall come
5:18 Nevertheless in t' days, saith the
8:16 it; the city, and t' that dwell therein.
14:15 and famine shall t' prophets be
21: 7 the hand of t' that seek their life:
27:11 t' will I let remain still in their own
31:29 In t' days they shall say no more,
33 After t' days, saith the Lord, I will
36 If t' ordinances depart from
33:15 In t' days, and at that time, will
16 In t' days shall Judah be saved,
38:22 t' women shall say, Thy friends
39: 9 and t' that fell away, that fell to him,
46:26 the hand of t' that seek their lives,
49: 5 hosts, from all t' that be about thee;
36 scatter them toward all t' winds;
50: 4, 20 In t' days, and in that time,
52:15 t' that fell away, that fell to the king
La 2:22 t' that I have swaddled and brought
3:62 The lips of t' that rose up against me,
Eze 1:21 When t' went, these went; and when
21 and when t' stood, these stood; and
21 when t' were lifted up from the earth,
18:11 that doeth not any of t' duties, but
22: 5 T' that be near, and t' that be far
28:26 upon all t' that despise them round
33:24 that inhabit t' wastes of the land
34:27 hand of t' that served themselves of
38:17 prophesied in t' days many years,
39:14 t' that remain on the face of the
40:25 round about, like t' windows:
42:14 approach to t' things which are for
Da 3:22 flame of the fire slew t' men that
4:37 t' that walk in pride he is able to
6:24 t' men which had accused Daniel,
10: 2 In t' days I Daniel was mourning
11: 4 up, even for others beside t'.
14 And in t' times there shall many
Joe 2:16 children, and t' that suck the breasts:
29 t' days will I pour out my spirit.
3: 1 For, behold, in t' days, and in that
Ob 14 to cut off t' of his that did escape;
14 have delivered up t' of his that did
Zep 1: 6 t' that have not sought the Lord,
9 punish all t' that leap on the
Hag 2:16 Since t' days were, when one came to
22 chariots, and t' that ride in them;
Zec 3: 4 spake unto t' that stood before him,
4:10 hand of Zerubbabel with t' seven;
7: 5 even t' seventy years, did ye at
8:23 In t' days it shall come to pass,
11:16 which shall not visit t' that be cut off,
13: 6 T' with which I was wounded in the
14: 3 forth, and fight against t' nations,
Mal 3: 5 against t' that oppress the hireling
M't 3: 1 In t' days came John the Baptist,
4:24 t'...were possessed with devils,
24 devils, and t' which were lunatick,
24 lunatick, and t' that had the palsy;
11: 4 shew John again t' things which ye
13:17 desired to see t' things which ye see,
17 and to hear t' things which ye hear,
15:18 t' things which proceed out of the
30 with them t' that were lame, blind,
16:23 be of God, but t' that be of men.
M't 21:40 will he do unto t' husbandmen?
41 miserably destroy t' wicked men,
22: 7 and destroyed t' murderers, and
10 So t' servants went out into the
24:19 to them that give suck in t' days!
22 except t' days should be shortened,
22 sake t' days shall be shortened.
29 after the tribulation of t' days
25: 7 Then all t' virgins arose, and
19 the lord of t' servants cometh,
27:54 and t' things that were done, they
M'r 1: 9 And it came to pass in t' days, that
44 cleansing t' things which Moses
2:20 then shall they fast in t' days.
6:55 about in beds t' that were sick,
7:15 t' are they that defile the man.
8: 1 In t' days the multitude being very
10:13 disciples rebuked t' that brought
11:23 shall believe that t' things which he
12: 7 But t' husbandmen said among
13:17 to them that give suck in t' days!
19 For in t' days shall be affliction,
20 the Lord had shortened t' days,
24 in t' days, after that tribulation,
Lu 1: 1 a declaration of t' things which are
4 know the certainty of t' things,
24 after t' days his wife Elisabeth
39 Mary arose in t' days, and went
45 t' things which were told her from
2: 1 it came to pass in t' days, that
18 wondered at t' things which were told
33 marvelled at t' things which were
4: 2 And in t' days he did eat nothing:
5:35 and then shall they fast in t' days.
6:12 And it came to pass in t' days, that
32 sinners also love t' that love them.
7:28 Among t' that are born of women
8:12 T' by the way side are they that
9:36 close, and told no man in t' days
36 any of t' things which they had seen.
10:24 desired to see t' things which ye see,
24 and to hear t' things which ye hear,
12:20 then whose shall t' things be, which
37 Blessed are t' servants, whom the
38 them so, blessed are t' servants.
13: 4 Or t' eighteen, upon whom the
14: 7 a parable to t' which were bidden,
24 t' men which were bidden shall
17:10 have done all t' things which are
19:27 t' mine enemies, which would not
20: 1 that on one of t' days, as he taught
21:23 to them that give suck, in t' days!
23:14 touching t' things whereof ye accuse
Joh 2:14 in the temple t' that sold oxen
6:14 Then t' men, when they had seen
8:10 where are t' thine accusers?
26 t' things which I have heard of
29 always t' things that please him.
31 said Jesus to t' Jews which believed
10:32 which of t' works do ye stone me?
13:29 Buy t' things that we have need of
17:11 name t' whom thou hast given me,
12 t' that thou gavest me I have kept,
Ac 1:15 t' days Peter stood up in the
2:18 pour out in t' days of my Spirit;
3:18 But t' things, which God before had
24 Samuel and t' that follow after,
6: 1 And in t' days, when the number
7:41 made a calf in t' days, and offered
8: 6 unto t' things which Philip spake,
9:37 to pass in t' days, that she was
13:45 spake against t' things which were
16: 3 Jews which were in t' quarters:
35 serjeants, saying, Let t' men go.
17:11 noble than t' in Thessalonica,
11 daily, whether t' things were so.
18:17 Gallio cared for none of t' things.
20: 2 when he had gone over t' parts,
21: 5 when we had accomplished t' days,
15 t' days we took up our carriages,
24 all may know that t' things, whereof
26:16 t' things in the which I will appear
22 saying none other things than t' which
27:11 t' things which were spoken by
28:31 teaching t' things which concern
Ro 1:28 t' things which are not convenient;
4:17 calleth t' things which be not as
6:13 as t' that are alive from the dead,
21 fruit had ye then in t' things which
21 for the end of t' things is death.
10: 5 man which doeth t' things shall live
15:17 in t' things which pertain to God.
18 t' things which Christ hath not
1Co 8: 4 eating of t' things that are offered
10 eat t' things which are offered to
12:22 much more t' members of the body,
23 t' members of the body, which we
14:23 there come in t' that are unlearned,
2Co 7: 6 comforteth t' that are cast down,
11:28 Beside t' things that are without,
Eph 5:12 t' things which are done in secret.
Ph'p 3: 7 me, t' I counted loss for Christ.
13 forgetting t' things...are behind,
13 reaching forth unto t' things which
4: 9 T' things, which ye have both
Col 2:18 into t' things which he hath not seen,
3: 1 Christ, seek t' things which are
1Ti 4:10 all men, specially of t' that believe.
5: 8 specially for t' of his own house,
2Ti 2:25 instructing t'...oppose themselves;
3: 3 fierce, despisers of t' that are good,
Heb 3: 5 testimony of t' things which were
5:14 t' who by reason of use have their
6: 4 it is impossible for t' who were once
7:21 t' priests were made without an
27 needeth not daily, as t' high priests,

Heb 8:10 the house of Israel after t' days.
10: 1 can never with t' sacrifices
3 in t' sacrifices...is a remembrance
16 will make with them after t' days,
12:27 removing of t' things...are shaken,
27 t' things which cannot be shaken
13:11 For the bodies of t' beasts, whose
Jas 2:16 t' things which are needful to the
2Pe 2: 6 ensample unto t' that after should
18 t' that were clean escaped from
1Jo 3:22 t' things that are pleasing in his
2Jo 8 lose not t' things we have wrought,
Jude 10 t' things which they know not:
10 t' things they corrupt themselves.
Re 1: 3 t' things...are written therein:
2:10 Fear none of t' things which thou
13 t' days wherein Antipas was my
4: 9 t' beasts give glory and honour
9: 4 t' men which have not the seal of
6 in t' days shall men seek death,
10: 4 t' things which the seven thunders
13:14 means of t' miracles which he had
20:12 t' things which were written in the

though^ See also ALTHOUGH.
Ge 31:30 t' thou wouldest needs be gone,
33:10 t' I had seen the face of God, and
40:10 and it was as t' it budded, and her
Le 5:17 t' he wist it not, yet is he guilty,
11: 7 And the swine, t' he divide the hoof,
25:35 t' he be a stranger, or a sojourner;
De 29:19 t' I walk in the imagination of
Jos 17:18 t' they have iron chariots,
18 chariots, and t' they be strong.
J'g 13:16 T' thou detain me, I will not eat
15: 3 t' I do them a displeasure.
7 T' ye have done this, yet will I be
Ru 2:13 t' I be not like unto one of thine
1Sa 14:39 t' it be in Jonathan my son,
20:20 side thereof, as t' I shot at a mark.
21: 5 t' it were sanctified this day in
2Sa 1:21 as t' he had not anointed with oil.
3:39 am this day weak, t' anointed king;
4: 6 as t' they would have fetched wheat;
18:12 T' I should receive a thousand
1Ki 2:28 t' he turned not after Absalom.
1Ch 26:10 t' he was not the firstborn, yet his
2Ch 30:19 t' he be not cleansed according to the
Ne 1: 9 t' there were of you cast out unto
6: 1 (t' at that time I had not set up
Es 9: 1 (t' it was turned to the contrary,
Job 8: 7 T' thy beginning was small, yet thy
9:15 t' I were righteous, yet would I
21 T' I were perfect, yet would I not
10:19 have been as t' I had not been;
11:12 t' man be born like a wild ass's colt.
13:15 T' he slay me, yet will I trust in him:
14: 8 T' the root thereof wax old in the
16: 6 T' I speak, my grief is not
6 and t' I forbear, what am I eased?
19:17 t' I entreated for the children's sake
26 And t' after my skin worms destroy
27 t' my reins be consumed within me.
20: 6 T' his excellency mount up to the
12 T' wickedness be sweet in his
12 mouth, t' he hide it under his tongue;
13 T' he spare it, and forsake it not; but
24:23 T' it be given him to be in safety,
27: 8 t' he hath gained, when God taketh
16 T' he heap up silver as the dust
30:24 grave, t' they cry in his destruction.
39:16 young ones, as t' they were not hers:
Ps 23: 4 t' I walk through the valley of
27: 3 T' an host should encamp against
3 t' war should rise against me, in
35:14 t' he had been my friend or brother:
37:24 T' he fall, he shall not be utterly
44:19 T' thou hast sore broken us in
46: 2 we fear, t' the earth be removed,
2 and t' the mountains be carried into
3 T' the waters thereof roar and be
3 t' the mountains shake with the
49:18 T' while he lived he blessed his
68:13 T' ye have lien among the pots,
78:23 T' he had commanded the clouds
99: 8 t' thou tookest vengeance of their
138: 6 T' the Lord be high, yet hath he
7 T' I walk in the midst of trouble,
Pr 6:35 content, t' thou givest many gifts.
11:21 T' hand join in hand, the wicked shall
16: 5 t' hand join in hand, he shall not be
27:22 T' thou shouldest bray a fool in a
28: 6 is perverse in his ways, t' he be rich.
Ec 6: 6 t' he live a thousand years twice told,
8:12 T' a sinner do evil an hundred times,
17 because t' a man labour to seek it
17 t' a wise man think to know it,
Isa 1:18 t' your sins be as scarlet, they shall
18 t' they be red like crimson, they
10:22 t' thy people Israel be as the sand
12: 1 t' thou wast angry with me, thine
30:20 And t' the Lord give you the bread
35: 8 men, t' fools, shall not err therein.
45: 4 thee, t' thou hast not known me.
5 thee, t' thou hast not known me:
49: 5 T' Israel be not gathered, yet shall I
63:16 t' Abraham be ignorant of us,
Jer 2:22 For t' thou wash thee with nitre,
4:30 T' thou clothest thyself with
30 t' thou deckest thee with ornaments
30 t' thou rentest thy face with
5: 2 t' they say, The Lord liveth; surely
22 t' the waves thereof toss themselves,
22 t' they roar, yet can they not pass over
11:11 t' they shall cry unto me, I will not
Jer 12: 6 t' they speak fair words unto thee.
14: 7 t' our iniquities testify against us,
15: 1 T' Moses and Samuel stood before
22:24 t' Coniah the son of Jehoiakim
30:11 t' I make a full end of all nations
32: 5 t' ye fight with the Chaldeans, ye
33 t' I taught them, rising up early and
37:10 For t' ye had smitten the whole
49:16 t' thou shouldest make thy nest
51: 5 t' their land was filled with sin
53 T' Babylon should mount up to
53 t' she should fortify the height of
La 3:32 But t' he cause grief, yet will he
Eze 2: 6 t' briers and thorns be with thee,
6 looks, t' they be a rebellious house.
3: 9 looks, t' they be a rebellious house.
8:18 t' they cry in mine ears with a loud
12: 3 t' they be a rebellious house.
13 shall he not see it, t' he shall die there.
14:14 T' these three men, Noah, Daniel, and
16, 18 T' these three men were in it, as I
20 T' Noah, Daniel, and Job, were in it,
26:21 t' thou be sought for, yet shalt thou
28: 2 t' thou set thine heart as the heart of
32:25 t' their terror was caused in the
26 t' they caused their terror in the
27 t' they were the terror of the mighty
Da 5:22 t' thou knewest all this;
9: 9 t' we have rebelled against him;
Ho 4:15 T' thou, Israel, play the harlot,
5: 2 t' I have been a rebuker of them all.
7:13 t' I have redeemed them, yet they
15 T' I have bound and strengthened
8:10 Yea, t' they have hired among the
9:12 T' they bring up their
16 yea, t' they bring forth, yet will I
11: 7 t' they called them to the most High,
13:15 T' he be fruitful among his
Am 5:22 T' ye offer me burnt offerings
9: 2 T' they dig into hell, thence shall
2 t' they climb up to heaven, thence
3 t' they hide themselves in the top
3 t' they be hid from my sight in the
4 t' they go into captivity before their
Ob 4 T' thou exalt thyself as the eagle,
4 t' thou set thy nest among the stars,
16 they shall be as t' they had not been.
Mic 5: 2 Beth-lehem Ephratah, t' thou be little
Na 1:12 T' they be quiet, and likewise
12 T' I have afflicted thee, I will afflict
Hab 1: 5 will not believe, t' it be told you.
2: 3 t' it tarry, wait for it; because it
Zec 9: 2 and Zidon, t' it be very wise.
10: 6 be as t' I had not cast them off:
12: 3 t' all the people of the earth be
M't 26:33 T' all men shall be offended
35 T' I should die with thee, yet will
60 t' many false witnesses came, yet found
Lu 9:53 was as t' he would go to Jerusalem.
11: 8 T' he will not rise and give him,
16:31 t' one rose from the dead.
18: 4 T' I fear not God, nor regard man;
7 him, t' he bear long with them?
24:28 as t' he would have gone further.
Joh 4: 2 (T' Jesus himself baptized not,
8: 6 on the ground, as t' he heard them not.
14 T' I bear record of myself, yet my
10:38 t' ye believe not me, believe the
11:25 t' he were dead, yet shall he live:
12:37 t' he had done so many miracles before
Ac 3:12 as t' by our own power or holiness we
13:28 t' they found no cause of death in him,
41 t' a man declare it unto you.
17:25 as t' he needed any thing, seeing he
27 t' he be not far from every one of
23:15 as t' ye would enquire something
20 as t' they would enquire somewhat of
27:30 as t' they would have cast anchors out
28: 4 whom, t' he hath escaped the sea,
17 t' I have committed nothing against
Ro 4:11 believe, t' they be not circumcised;
17 things which be not as t' they were.
7: 3 t' she be married to another man.
9: 6 Not as t' the word of God hath
27 T' the number of the children of
1Co 4:15 t' ye have ten thousand instructers
18 up, as t' I would not come to you.
5: 3 judged already, as t' I were present,
7:29 that have wives be as t' they had none;
30 they that weep, as t' they wept not;
30 that rejoice, as t' they rejoiced not;
30 they that buy, as t' they possessed not;
8: 5 t' there be that are called gods,
9:16 For t' I preach the gospel, I have
19 For t' I be free from all men, yet
13: 1 T' I speak with the tongues of
2 And t' I have the gift of prophecy,
2 t' I have all faith, so that I could
3 t' I bestow all my goods to feed
3 and t' I give my body to be burned,
2Co 4:16 t' our outward man perish, yet the
5:16 t' we have known Christ after the
20 as t' God did beseech you by us:
7: 8 t' I made you sorry with a letter,
8 I do not repent, t' I did repent:
8 sorry, t' it were but for a season.
12 Wherefore, t' I wrote unto you, I
8: 9 that, t' he was rich, yet for your sakes
10: 3 t' we walk in the flesh, we do not war
8 t' I should boast somewhat more
14 as t' we reached not unto you:
11: 6 t' I be rude in speech, yet not in
21 reproach, as t' we had been weak.
12: 6 For t' I would desire to glory, I
11 chiefest apostles, t' I be nothing.
15 t' the more abundantly I love you,
2Co 13: 4 For t' he was crucified through
7 is honest, t' we be as reprobates.
Ga 1: 8 But t' we, or an angel from heaven,
3:15 T' it be but a man's covenant, yet
4: 1 from a servant, t' he be lord of all;
Ph'p 3: 4 T' I might also have confidence in
12 Not as t' I had already attained,
Col 2: 5 t' I be absent in the flesh, yet am
20 as t' living in the world, are ye subject
Ph'm 8 t' I might be much bold in Christ to
Heb 5: 8 T' he were a Son, yet learned he
6: 9 salvation, t' we thus speak.
7: 5 t' they come out of the loins of
12:17 t' he sought it carefully with tears.
Jas 2:14 t' a man say he hath faith, and
3: 4 the ships, which t' they be so great,
1Pe 1: 6 ye greatly rejoice, t' now for a season,
7 that perisheth, t' it be tried with fire,
8 t' now ye see him not, yet believing,
4:12 t' some strange thing happened unto
2Pe 1:12 of these things, t' ye know them,
2Jo 5 not as t' I wrote a new commandment
Jude 5 in remembrance, t' ye once knew this,

thought See also THOUGHTEST; THOUGHTS.
Ge 20:11 I t', Surely the fear of God is not
38:15 saw her, he t' her to be an harlot:
48:11 I had not t' to see thy face:
50:20 as for you, ye t' evil against me;
Ex 32:14 the evil which he t' to do unto his
Nu 24:11 I t' to promote thee unto great
33:56 unto you, as I t' to do unto them.
De 15: 9 be not a t' in thy wicked heart,
19:19 as he had t' to have done unto his
J'g 15: 2 I verily t' that thou hadst utterly
20: 5 by night, and t' to have slain me:
Ru 4: 4 I t' to advertise thee, saying, Buy
1Sa 1:13 Eli t' she had been drunken.
9: 5 for the asses, and take t' for us.
18:25 Saul t' to make David fall by the
20:26 for he t', Something hath befallen
2Sa 4:10 who t' that I would have given him a
13: 2 Amnon t' it hard for him to do
14:13 hast thou t' such a thing against
19:18 and to do what he t' good.
21:16 new sword, t' to have slain David.
2Ki 5:11 I t', He will surely come out to me,
2Ch 11:22 for he t' to make him king.
32: 1 and t' to win them for himself.
Ne 6: 2 But they t' to do me mischief.
Es 3: 6 t' scorn to lay hands on Mordecai
6: 6 Now Haman t' in his heart, To
Job 12: 5 despised in the t' of him that is at
42: 2 no t' can be withholden from
Ps 48: 9 We have t' of thy lovingkindness,
49:11 Their inward t' is, that their houses
64: 6 the inward t' of every one of them,
73:16 When I t' to know this, it was too
119:59 I t' on my ways, and turned my
139: 2 thou understandest my t' afar off.
Pr 24: 9 The t' of foolishness is sin: and
30:32 or if thou hast t' evil, lay thine
Ec 10:20 not the king, no not in thy t';
Isa 14:24 Surely as I have t', so shall it come
Jer 18: 8 the evil that I t' to do unto them.
Eze 38:10 and thou shalt think an evil t':
Da 4: 2 I t' it good to shew the signs
6: 3 king t' to set him over the whole
Am 4:13 declareth unto man what is his t',
Zec 1: 6 the Lord of hosts t' to do unto us,
8:14 As I t' to punish you, when your
15 again have I t' in these days to do
Mal 3:16 Lord, and that t' upon his name.
M't 1:20 But while he t' on these things,
6:25 Take no t' for your life, what ye
27 you by taking t' can add one cubit
28 And why take ye t' for raiment?
31 take no t', saying, What shall we
34 Take...no t' for the morrow:
34 morrow shall take t' for the things
10:19 take no t' how or what ye shall
M'r 13:11 take no t' beforehand what ye
14:72 And when he t' thereon, he wept.
Lu 7: 7 neither t' I myself worthy to come
9:47 perceiving the t' of their heart,
12:11 take ye no t' how or what thing ye
17 And he t' within himself, saying,
22 Take no t' for your life, what ye
25 you with taking t' can add to his
26 is least, why take ye t' for the rest?
19:11 they t' that the kingdom of God
Joh 11:13 they t' that he had spoken of taking
13:29 some of them t', because Judas had
Ac 8:20 thou hast t' that the gift of God
22 t' of thine heart may be forgiven
10:19 While Peter t' on the vision, the
12: 9 the angel; but t' he saw a vision.
15:38 Paul t' not good to take him with
26: 8 should it be t' a thing incredible
9 I verily t' with myself, that I
1Co 13:11 as a child, I t' as a child:
2Co 9: 5 I t' it necessary to exhort the
10: 5 every t' to the obedience of Christ;
Ph'p 2: 6 t' it not robbery to be equal with
1Th 3: 1 we t' it good to be left at Athens
Heb 10:29 shall he be t' worthy, who hath

thoughtest
Ps 50:21 thou t' that I was altogether such

thoughts
Ge 6: 5 the t' of his heart was only evil
J'g 5:15 there were great t' of heart.
1Ch 28: 9 all the imaginations of the t':
29:18 of the t' of the heart of thy people,
Job 4:13 t' from the visions of the night,
17:11 broken off, even the t' of my heart.

Job 20: 2 do my t' cause me to answer,
21: 27 I know your t', and the devices
Ps 10: 4 after God: God is not in all his t'.
33: 11 t' of his heart to all generations.
40: 5 and thy t' which are to us-ward:
56: 5 all their t' are against me for evil.
92: 5 thy works! and thy t' are very deep.
94: 11 The Lord knoweth the t' of man,
19 In the multitude of my t' within
119: 113 I hate vain t': but thy law do I
139: 17 How precious...are thy t' unto me,
23 heart: try me, and know my t':
146: 4 in that very day his t' perish.
Pr 12: 5 The t' of the righteous are right:
15: 26 t' of the wicked are an abomination
16: 3 and thy t' shall be established.
21: 5 The t' of the diligent tend only to
Isa 55: 7 and the unrighteous man his t':
8 For my t' are not your t', neither
9 your ways, and my t' than your t'.
59: 7 blood: their t' are t' of iniquity;
65: 2 was not good, after their own t';
66: 18 For I know their works and their t':
Jer 4: 14 How long shall thy vain t' lodge
6: 19 people, even the fruit of their t',
23: 20 have performed the t' of his heart:
29: 11 I know the t' that I think toward
11 t' of peace, and not of evil, to
Da 2: 29 O king, thy t' came into thy mind
30 mightest know the t' of thy heart.
4: 5 t' upon my bed and the visions
19 one hour, and his t' troubled him.
5: 6 changed, and his t' troubled him,
10 let not thy t' trouble thee, nor
Mic 4: 12 they know not the t' of the Lord,
M't 9: 4 And Jesus knowing their t' said,
12: 25 Jesus knew their t', and said unto
15: 19 out of the heart proceed evil t',
M'r 7: 21 the heart of men, proceed evil t',
Lu 2: 35 t' of many hearts may be revealed.
5: 22 But when Jesus perceived their t',
6: 8 he knew their t', and said to the
11: 17 knowing their t', said unto them,
24: 38 and why do t' arise in your hearts?
Ro 2: 15 and their t' the mean while
1Co 3: 20 Lord knoweth the t' of the wise,
Heb 4: 12 a discerner of the t' and intents of
Jas 2: 4 and are become judges of evil t'?
thousand See also THOUSANDS.
Ge 20: 16 thy brother a t' pieces of silver:
Ex 12: 37 six hundred t' on foot that were
32: 28 people that day about three t' men.
38: 25 a t' seven hundred and threescore
26 six hundred t' and three t' and five
28 t' seven hundred seventy and five
29 two t' and four hundred shekels.
Le 26: 8 of you shall put ten t' to flight:
Nu 1: 21 forty and six t' and five hundred.
23 fifty and nine t' and three hundred.
25 and five t' six hundred and fifty.
27 and fourteen t' and six hundred.
29 fifty and four t' and four hundred.
31 fifty and seven t' and four hundred.
33 were forty t' and five hundred.
35 thirty and two t' and two hundred.
37 thirty and five t' and four hundred.
39 and two t' and seven hundred.
41 forty and one t' and five hundred.
43 fifty and three t' and four hundred.
46 numbered were six hundred t' and
46 three t' and five hundred and fifty.
2: 4 and fourteen t' and six hundred.
6 fifty and four t' and four hundred.
8 fifty and seven t' and four hundred.
9 were an hundred t' and fourscore t'
9 and six t' and four hundred.
11 forty and six t' and five hundred.
13 fifty and nine t' and three hundred.
15 five t' and six hundred and fifty.
16 were an hundred t' and fifty and one
16 one t' and four hundred and fifty,
19 were forty t' and five hundred.
21 thirty and two t' and two hundred.
23 thirty and five t' and four hundred.
24 were an hundred t' and eight t'
26 and two t' and seven hundred.
28 forty and one t' and five hundred.
30 fifty and three t' and four hundred.
31 camp of Dan were an hundred t'
31 fifty and seven t' and six hundred.
32 their hosts were six hundred t'
32 three t' and five hundred and fifty.
3: 22 were seven t' and five hundred.
28 were eight t' and six hundred,
34 were six t' and two hundred.
39 upward, were twenty and two t'.
43 two t' two hundred and threescore
50 t' three hundred and threescore
4: 36 two t' seven hundred and fifty.
40 two t' and six hundred and thirty.
44 were three t' and two hundred.
48 were eight t' and five hundred and
7: 85 two t' and four hundred shekels,
11: 21 I am, are six hundred t' footmen;
16: 49 were fourteen t' and seven hundred,
25: 9 the plague were twenty and four t'.
26: 7 and three t' and seven hundred and
14 twenty and two t' and two hundred.
18 of them, forty t' and five hundred.
22 and sixteen t' and five hundred.
25 and four t' and three hundred.
27 threescore t' and five hundred.
34 fifty and two t' and seven hundred.
37 thirty and two t' and five hundred.
41 forty and five t' and six hundred.
43 and four t' and four hundred.

Nu 26: 47 fifty and three t' and four hundred.
50 forty and five t' and four hundred.
51 children of Israel, six hundred t'
51 and a t' seven hundred and thirty.
62 of them were twenty and three t',
31: 4 Of every tribe a t', throughout all
5 of Israel, a t' of every tribe,
5 every tribe, twelve t', armed for war.
6 them to the war, a t' of every tribe.
32 war had caught, was six hundred t'
32 seventy t' and five t' sheep,
33 threescore and twelve t' beeves,
34 And threescore and one t' asses,
35 And thirty and two t' persons in all,
36 was in number three hundred t'
36 thirty t' and five hundred sheep:
38 the beeves were thirty and six t';
39 were thirty t' and five hundred;
40 And the persons were sixteen t';
43 congregation was three hundred t'
43 and thirty t' and seven t' and five
44 And thirty and six t' beeves,
45 And thirty t' asses and five hundred,
46 And sixteen t' persons;)
52 was sixteen t' seven hundred and
35: 4 outward a t' cubits round about.
5 city on the east side two t' cubits,
5 and on the south side two t' cubits,
5 and on the west side two t' cubits,
5 and on the north side two t' cubits;
De 1: 11 make you a t' times so many more
7: 9 commandments to a t' generations;
32: 30 How should one chase a t', and two
30 and two put ten t' to flight, except
Jos 3: 4 it, about two t' cubits by measure:
4: 13 About forty t' prepared for war
7: 3 let about two or three t' men go up
4 of the people about three t' men:
8: 3 chose out thirty t' mighty men of
12 And he took about five t' men, and
25 men and women, were twelve t',
23: 10 One man of you shall chase a t': for
J'g 1: 4 slew of them in Bezek ten t' men.
3: 29 slew...at that time about ten t' men,
4: 6 with thee ten t' men of the children
10 went up with ten t' men at his feet:
14 Tabor, and ten t' men after him.
5: 8 spear seen among forty t' in Israel?
7: 3 of the people twenty and two t';
3 and there remained ten t'.
8: 10 with them, about fifteen t' men,
10 and twenty t' men that drew sword.
26 a t' and seven hundred shekels of
9: 49 also, about a t' men and women.
12: 6 the Ephraimites forty and two t'.
15: 11 Then three t' men of Judah went to
15 took it, and slew a t' men therewith.
16 jaw of an ass have I slain a t' men.
16: 27 roof about three t' men and women,
20: 2 hundred t' footmen that drew sword.
10 of Israel, and an hundred of a t',
10 a t'...to fetch victual for the people,
10 out of ten t', to fetch victual for
15 and six t' men that drew sword,
17 four hundred t' men that drew
21 that day twenty and two t' men.
25 of Israel again eighteen t' men;
34 against Gibeah ten t' chosen men
35 twenty and five t' and an hundred
44 fell of Benjamin eighteen t' men;
45 them in the highways five t' men;
45 unto Gidom, and slew two t' men of
46 twenty and five t' men that drew the
21: 10 twelve t' men of the valiantest,
1Sa 4: 2 army in the field about four t' men.
10 there fell of Israel thirty t' footmen.
6: 19 fifty t' and threescore and ten men:
11: 8 of Israel were three hundred t',
8 and the men of Judah thirty t'.
13: 2 Saul chose him three t' men of
2 two t' were with Saul in Michmash
2 a t' were with Jonathan in Gibeah
5 to fight with Israel, thirty t' chariots,
5 six t' horsemen, and people as the
15: 4 in Telaim, two hundred t' footmen,
4 footmen, and ten t' men of Judah.
17: 5 the coat was five t' shekels of brass.
18 cheeses unto the captain of their t',
18: 13 and made him his captain over a t';
24: 2 Saul took three t' chosen men out of
25: 2 had three t' sheep, and a t' goats:
26: 2 three t' chosen men of Israel with
2Sa 6: 1 the chosen men of Israel, thirty t'.
8: 4 David took from him a t' chariots,
4 horsemen, and twenty t' footmen:
5 the Syrians two and twenty t' men.
13 valley of salt, being eighteen t' men.
10: 6 Syrians of Zoba, twenty t' footmen,
6 and of king Maacah a t' men,
6 and of Ish-tob twelve t' men.
18 the Syrians, and forty t' horsemen,
17: 1 me now choose out twelve t' men,
18: 3 but now thou art worth ten t' of us:
7 slaughter that day of twenty t' men.
12 I should receive a t' shekels of silver
19: 17 a t' men of Benjamin with him,
24: 9 Israel eight hundred t' valiant men
9 of Judah were five hundred t' men.
15 even to Beer-sheba seventy t' men.
1Ki 3: 4 t' burnt offerings did Solomon offer
4: 26 Solomon had forty t' stalls of horses
26 chariots, and twelve t' horsemen.
32 And he spake three t' proverbs:
32 And his songs were a t' and five.
5: 11 gave Hiram twenty t' measures of
13 and the levy was thirty t' men.

1Ki 5: 14 Lebanon, ten t' a month by courses:
15 and ten t' that bare burdens,
15 and fourscore t' hewers in the
16 three t' and three hundred, which
7: 26 of lilies: it contained three t' baths.
8: 63 the Lord, two and twenty t' oxen,
63 and an hundred and twenty t' sheep.
10: 26 had a t' and four hundred chariots,
26 and twelve t' horsemen, whom he
12: 21 hundred and fourscore t' chosen
19: 18 Yet I have left me seven t' in Israel,
20: 15 the children of Israel, being seven t'.
29 the Syrians an hundred t' footmen
30 upon twenty and seven t' of the men
2Ki 3: 4 king of Israel an hundred t' lambs,
4 an hundred t' rams, with the wool.
5: 5 six t' pieces of gold, and ten changes
13: 7 ten chariots, and ten t' footmen;
14: 7 of Edom in the valley of salt ten t',
15: 19 gave Pul a t' talents of silver,
18: 23 and I will deliver thee two t' horses,
19: 35 an hundred fourscore and five t':
24: 14 men of valour, even ten t' captives,
16 all the men of might, even seven t',
16 and craftsmen and smiths a t', all
1Ch 5: 18 four and forty t' seven hundred
21 their cattle; of their camels fifty t',
21 of sheep two hundred and fifty t',
21 and of asses two t',
21 and of men an hundred t'.
7: 2 two and twenty t' and six hundred.
4 for war, six and thirty t' men:
5 genealogies fourscore and seven t'.
7 twenty and two t' and thirty and
9 was twenty t' and two hundred.
11 were seventeen t' and two hundred
40 battle was twenty and six t' men.
9: 13 a t' and seven hundred and
12: 14 hundred, and the greatest over a t'.
24 were six t' and eight hundred,
25 the war, seven t' and one hundred.
26 children of Levi four t' and six
27 were three t' and seven hundred;
29 the kindred of Saul, three t':
30 of Ephraim twenty t' and eight
31 half tribe of Manasseh eighteen t',
33 war, fifty t', which could keep rank:
34 And of Naphtali a t' captains, and
34 shield and spear thirty and seven t'.
35 in war twenty and eight t' and six
36 to battle, expert in war, forty t'.
37 battle, an hundred and twenty t'.
16: 15 he commanded to a t' generations;
18: 4 David took from him a t' chariots,
4 and seven t' horsemen,
4 and twenty t' footmen: David also
5 the Syrians two and twenty t' men.
12 in the valley of salt eighteen t'.
19: 6 Ammon sent a t' talents of silver to
7 they hired thirty and two t' chariots,
18 slew of the Syrians seven t' men
18 in chariots, and forty t' footmen,
21: 5 all they of Israel were a t' t' and
5 an hundred t' men that drew sword:
5 hundred threescore and ten t' men
14 there fell of Israel seventy t' men.
22: 14 Lord an hundred t' talents of gold,
14 and a t' t' talents of silver;
23: 3 man by man, was thirty and eight t'.
4 four t' were to set forward the work
4 and six t' were officers and judges:
5 Moreover four t' were porters;
5 and four t' praised the Lord with the
26: 30 of valour, a t' and seven hundred,
32 were two t' and seven hundred chief
27: 1 course were twenty and four t'.
2 his course were twenty and four t'.
4 likewise were twenty and four t'.
5, 7, 8, 9, 10, 11, 12, 13, 14, 15
his course were twenty and four t'.
29: 4 Even three t' talents of gold, of the
4 and seven t' talents of refined silver,
7 of God of gold five t' talents
7 and ten t' drams,
7 and of silver ten t' talents, and of
7 and of brass eighteen t' talents,
7 and one hundred t' talents of iron.
21 even a t' bullocks, a t' rams,
21 a t' lambs, with their drink offerings,
2Ch 1: 6 offered a t' burnt offerings upon it.
14 had a t' and four hundred chariots,
14 and twelve t' horsemen, which he
2: 2 and ten t' men to bear burdens,
2 fourscore t' to hew in the mountain,
2 three t' and six hundred to oversee
10 twenty t' measures of beaten wheat,
10 and twenty t' measures of barley,
10 barley, and twenty t' baths of wine,
10 wine, and twenty t' baths of oil.
17 were found an hundred and fifty t'
17 and three t' and six hundred.
18 and ten t' of them to be bearers of
18 and fourscore t' to be hewers in the
18 three t' and six hundred overseers
4: 5 it received and held three t' baths.
7: 5 a sacrifice of twenty and two t' oxen,
5 and an hundred and twenty t' sheep:
9: 25 Solomon had four t' stalls for horses
25 chariots, and twelve t' horsemen;
11: 1 and fourscore t' chosen men,
12: 3 chariots, and threescore t' horsemen:
13: 3 even four hundred t' chosen men:
3 with eight hundred t' chosen men,
17 of Israel five hundred t' chosen men.
14: 8 out of Judah three hundred t';
8 bows, two hundred and fourscore t':

2Ch 14: 9 the Ethiopian with an host of a t' t',
15: 11 hundred oxen and seven t' sheep.
17: 11 seven t' and seven hundred rams,
11 seven t' and seven hundred he goats.
14 men of valour three hundred t'.
15 him two hundred and fourscore t'.
16 hundred t' mighty men of valour.
17 with bow and shield two hundred t'.
18 fourscore t' ready prepared for the
25: 5 them three hundred t' choice men,
6 hired also an hundred t' mighty men
11 smote of the children of Seir ten t'.
12 ten t' left alive did the children of
13 and smote three t' of them, and took
26: 12 valour were two t' and six hundred.
13 was an army, three hundred t' and
13 and seven t' and five hundred, that
27: 5 silver, and ten t' measures of wheat,
5 and ten t' of barley. So much did
28: 6 an hundred and twenty t' in one day,
8 of their brethren two hundred t',
29: 33 six hundred oxen and three t' sheep.
30: 24 a t' bullocks and seven t' sheep;
24 a t' bullocks and ten t' sheep:
35: 7 present, to the number of thirty t',
7 and three t' bullocks: these were of
8 two t' and six hundred small cattle,
9 offerings five t' small cattle,
Ezr 1: 9 of gold, a t' chargers of silver,
10 and ten, a t' other vessels a t'.
11 silver were five t' and four hundred.
2: 3 two t' an hundred seventy and two.
6 two t' eight hundred and twelve.
7 a t' two hundred fifty and four.
12 a t' two hundred twenty and two.
14 of Bigvai, two t' fifty and six.
31 a t' two hundred fifty and four.
35 three t' and six hundred and thirty.
37 children of Immer, a t' fifty and two.
38 a t' two hundred forty and seven.
39 of Harim, a t' and seventeen.
64 forty and two t' three hundred and
65 seven t' three hundred thirty and
67 six t' seven hundred and twenty.
69 threescore and one t' drams of gold,
69 and five t' pound of silver, and one
8: 27 basons of gold, of a t' drams;
Ne 3: 13 a t' cubits on the wall unto the dung
7: 8 two t' an hundred seventy and two.
11 two t' and eight hundred and
12 a t' two hundred fifty and four.
17 two t' three hundred twenty and
19 Bigvai, two t' threescore and seven.
34 a t' two hundred fifty and four.
38 three t' nine hundred and thirty.
40 children of Immer, a t' fifty and two.
41 a t' two hundred forty and seven.
42 of Harim, a t' and seventeen.
66 two t' three hundred and threescore,
67 were seven t' three hundred thirty
69 t' seven hundred and twenty asses.
70 to the treasure a t' drams of gold,
71 the work twenty t' drams of gold,
71 and two t' and two hundred pound
72 gave was twenty t' drams of gold,
72 and two t' pound of silver, and
Es 3: 9 I will pay ten t' talents of silver to
9: 16 slew of their foes seventy and five t',
Job 1: 3 substance also was seven t' sheep,
3 three t' camels, and five hundred
9: 3 he cannot answer him one of a t'.
33: 23 one among a t', to shew unto man
42: 12 for he had fourteen t' sheep, and six
12 sheep, and six t' camels, and a
12 and a t' yoke of oxen, and a
12 yoke of oxen, and a t' she asses.
Ps 50: 10 mine, and the cattle upon a t' hills.
60: *title* Edom in the valley of salt twelve t'.
68: 17 The chariots of God are twenty t',
84: 10 a day in thy courts is better than a t'.
90: 4 For a t' years in thy sight are but as
91: 7 A t' shall fall at thy side, and ten
7 and ten t' at thy right hand; but it
105: 8 he commanded to a t' generations.
Ec 6: 6 though he live a t' years twice told,
7: 28 one man among a t' have I found;
Ca 4: 4 whereon there hang a t' bucklers,
5: 10 ruddy, the chiefest among ten t'.
8: 11 was to bring a t' pieces of silver.
12 thou, O Solomon, must have a t',
Isa 7: 23 were a t' vines at a t' silverlings,
30: 17 One t' shall flee at the rebuke of one;
36: 8 and I will give thee two t' horses,
37: 36 a hundred and fourscore and five t':
60: 22 A little one shall become a t', and a
Jer 52: 28 three t' Jews and three and twenty:
30 were four t' and six hundred.
Eze 45: 1 length of five and twenty t' reeds,
1 and the breadth shall be ten t'.
3 the length of five and twenty t',
3 the breadth of ten t': and in it shall
5 And the five and twenty t' of length,
5 and the ten t' of breadth, shall also
6 possession of the city five t' broad,
6 and five and twenty t' long, over
47: 3 eastward, he measured a t' cubits,
4, 4 Again he measured a t', and
5 Afterward he measured a t'; and it
48: 8 five and twenty t' reeds in breadth,
9 be of five and twenty t' in length,
9 in length, and of ten t' in breadth.
10 north five and twenty t' in length,
10 toward the west ten t' in breadth,
10 toward the east ten t' in breadth,
10 south five and twenty t' in length:
13 have five and twenty t' in length,
Eze 48: 13 in length, and ten t' in breadth:
13 length shall be five and twenty t',
13 and the breadth ten t'.
15 five t', that are left in the breadth
15 over against the five and twenty t',
16 north side four t' and five hundred,
16 south side four t' and five hundred,
16 east side four t' and five hundred,
16 west side four t' and five hundred,
18 holy portion shall be ten t' eastward,
18 and ten t' westward: and it shall be
20 and twenty t' by five and twenty t':
21 the five and twenty t' of the oblation
21 over against the five and twenty t'
30 four t' and five hundred measures.
32 east side four t' and five hundred:
33 four t' and five hundred measures:
34 west side four t' and five hundred,
35 round about eighteen t' measures:
Da 5: 1 a great feast to a t' of his lords,
1 lords, and drank wine before the t'.
7: 10 t' thousands ministered unto him,
10 ten t' times ten t' stood before him:
8: 14 Unto two t' and three hundred days;
12: 11 be a t' two hundred and ninety days.
12 cometh to the t' three hundred and
Am 5: 3 city that went out by a t' shall leave
Jon 4: 11 sixscore t' persons that cannot
M't 14: 21 had eaten were about five t' men,
15: 38 they that did eat were four t' men,
16: 9 the five loaves of the five t',
10 the seven loaves of the four t',
18: 24 which owed him ten t' talents.
M'r 5: 13 (they were about two t';) and were
6: 44 the loaves were about five t' men.
8: 9 that had eaten were about four t':
19 brake the five loaves among five t',
20 And when the seven among four t',
Lu 9: 14 For they were about five t' men.
14: 31 be able with ten t' to meet him
31 cometh against him with twenty t'?
Joh 6: 10 sat down, in number about five t'.
Ac 2: 41 unto them about three t' souls.
4: 4 of the men was about five t'.
19: 19 and found it fifty t' pieces of silver.
21: 38 four t' men that were murderers?
Ro 11: 4 reserved to myself seven t' men,
1Co 4: 15 ye have ten t' instructers in Christ,
10: 8 fell in one day three and twenty t'.
14: 19 ten t' words in an unknown tongue.
2Pe 3: 8 day is with the Lord as a t' years,
8 years, and a t' years as one day.
Re 5: 11 of them was ten t' times ten t',
7: 4 forty and four t' of all the tribes
5 tribe of Juda were sealed twelve t'.
5 of Reuben were sealed twelve t'.
5 tribe of Gad were sealed twelve t'.
6 tribe of Aser were sealed twelve t'.
6 of Nepthalim were sealed twelve t'.
6 of Manasses were sealed twelve t'.
7 of Simeon were sealed twelve t'.
7 tribe of Levi were sealed twelve t'.
7 of Issachar were sealed twelve t'.
8 of Zabulon were sealed twelve t'.
8 of Joseph were sealed twelve t'.
8 of Benjamin were sealed twelve t'.
9: 16 horsemen were two hundred t' t':
11: 3 a t' two hundred and threescore
13 were slain of men seven t':
12: 6 a t' two hundred and threescore
14: 1 him an hundred forty and four t',
3 the hundred and forty and four t',
20 of a t' and six hundred furlongs.
20: 2 Satan, and bound him a t' years,
3 till the t' years should be fulfilled:
4 and reigned with Christ a t' years.
5 until the t' years were finished.
6 and shall reign with him a t' years.
7 when the t' years are expired, Satan
21: 16 with the reed, twelve t' furlongs.

thousands

Ge 24: 60 be thou the mother of t' of millions,
Ex 18: 21 to be rulers of t', and rulers of
25 rulers of t', rulers of hundreds,
20: 6 shewing mercy unto t' of them that
34: 7 Keeping mercy for t', forgiving
Nu 1: 16 their fathers, heads of t' in Israel.
10: 4 which are heads of the t' of Israel,
36 O Lord, unto the many t' of Israel.
31: 5 were delivered out of the t' of Israel,
14 the host, with the captains over t',
48 which were over t' of the host,
48 the captains of t', and captains of
52 of the captains of t', and of the
54 took the gold of the captains of t'
De 1: 15 heads over you, captains over t',
5: 10 shewing mercy unto t' of them that
33: 2 and he came with ten t' of saints:
17 and they are the ten t' of Ephraim,
17 and they are the t' of Manasseh.
Jos 22: 14 fathers among the ten t' of Israel.
21 unto the heads of the t' of Israel,
30 the t' of Israel which were with him,
1Sa 8: 12 he will appoint him captains over t',
10: 19 Lord by your tribes, and by your t'.
18: 7 Saul hath slain his t',
7 and David his ten t'.
8 have ascribed unto David ten t',
8 to me they have ascribed but t':
21: 11 Saul hath slain his t',
11 and David his ten t'?
22: 7 and make you all captains of t', and
23: 23 out throughout all the t' of Judah.
29: 2 passed on by hundreds, and by t':
5 Saul slew his t',
5 and David his ten t'?
2Sa 18: 1 and set captains of t' and captains
4 came out by hundreds and by t'.
1Ch 12: 20 captains of the t' that were of
13: 1 the captains of t' and hundreds,
15: 25 and the captains over t', went to
26: 26 the captains over t' and hundreds,
27: 1 and captains of t' and hundreds,
28: 1 and the captains over the t', and
29: 6 the captains of t' and of hundreds,
2Ch 1: 2 to the captains of t' and of hundreds,
17: 14 Of Judah, the captains of t'; Adnah
25: 5 and made them captains over t',
Ps 3: 6 not be afraid of ten t' of people,
68: 17 thousand, even t' of angels;
119: 72 unto me than t' of gold and silver.
144: 13 our sheep may bring forth t'
13 and ten t' in our streets:
Jer 32: 18 shewest lovingkindness unto t',
Da 7: 10 thousand t' ministered unto him,
11: 12 he shall cast down many ten t':
Mic 5: 2 thou be little among the t' of Judah,
6: 7 the Lord be pleased with t' of rams,
7 or with ten t' of rivers of oil? shall
Ac 21: 20 t' of Jews there are which believe;
Jude 14 cometh with ten t' of his saints,
Re 5: 11 times ten thousand, and t' of t';

thousand-thousand See THOUSAND.

thread

Ge 14: 23 take from a t' even to a shoelatchet,
38: 28 bound upon his hand a scarlet t',
30 that had the scarlet t' upon his hand:
Jos 2: 18 shalt bind this line of scarlet t'
J'g 16: 9 as a t' of tow is broken when it
12 them from off his arms like a t'.
Ca 4: 3 Thy lips are like a t' of scarlet, and

threaten See also THREATENED; THREATENING.

Ac 4: 17 let us straitly t' them, that they

threatened

Ac 4: 21 So when they had further t' them,
1Pe 2: 23 again; when he suffered, he t' not;

threatening See also THREATENINGS.

Eph 6: 9 things unto them, forbearing t':

threatenings

Ac 4: 29 And now, Lord, behold their t': and
9: 1 And Saul, yet breathing out t' and

three See also THIRTEEN; THREEFOLD; THREESCORE.

Ge 5: 22 Methuselah t' hundred years,
23 Enoch was t' hundred sixty and five
6: 10 Noah begat t' sons, Shem, Ham,
15 the ark shall be t' hundred cubits,
7: 13 the t' wives of his sons with them,
9: 19 These are the t' sons of Noah: and
28 after the flood t' hundred and fifty
11: 13 Salah four hundred and t' years,
15 Eber four hundred and t' years,
14: 14 own house, t' hundred and eighteen,
15: 9 Take me an heifer of t' years old,
9 and a she goat of t' years old, and a
9 a ram of t' years old, and a
18: 2 and, lo, t' men stood by him:
6 quickly t' measures of fine meal,
29: 2 there were t' flocks of sheep lying
34 because I have born him t' sons:
30: 36 t' days' journey betwixt himself and
38: 24 came to pass about t' months after,
40: 10 And in the vine were t' branches:
12 The t' branches are t' days:
13 within t' days shall Pharaoh lift
16 I had t' white baskets on my head:
18 thereof: The t' baskets are t' days:
19 within t' days shall Pharaoh lift
42: 17 them all together into ward t' days.
45: 22 gave t' hundred pieces of silver,
46: 15 his daughters were thirty and t'.
Ex 2: 2 goodly child, she hid him t' months.
3: 18 t' days' journey into the wilderness,
5: 3 t' days' journey into the desert, and
6: 18 an hundred thirty and t' years.
7: 7 Aaron fourscore and t' years old,
8: 27 t' days' journey into the wilderness,
10: 22 in all the land of Egypt t' days:
23 rose any from his place for t' days:
15: 22 they went t' days in the wilderness,
21: 11 And if he do not these t' unto her,
23: 14 T' times thou shalt keep a feast
17 T' times in the year all thy males
25: 32, 32 t' branches of the candlestick
33 T' bowls made like unto almonds,
33 t' bowls made like almonds in the
27: 1 the height thereof shall be t' cubits.
14, 15 pillars t', and their sockets t'
32: 28 that day about t' thousand men.
37: 18, 18 t' branches of the candlestick
19 T' bowls made after the fashion of
19 and t' bowls made like almonds in
38: 1 and t' cubits the height thereof.
14, 15 pillars t', and their sockets t'.
26 t' thousand and five hundred and
Le 12: 4 of her purifying t' and thirty days;
14: 10 t' tenth deals of fine flour for a
19: 23 t' years shall it be as uncircumcised
25: 21 it shall bring forth fruit for t' years.
27: 6 estimation...be t' shekels of silver.
Nu 1: 23 and nine thousand and t' hundred.
43 fifty and t' thousand and four
46 hundred thousand and t' thousand
2: 13 and nine thousand and t' hundred.
30 and t' thousand and four hundred.
32 hundred thousand and t' thousand
3: 50 t' hundred and threescore and five
4: 44 were t' thousand and two hundred.
10: 33 mount of the Lord t' days' journey:

Nu 10:33 before them in the t' days' journey,
12: 4 Come out ye t' unto the tabernacle
4 And they t' came out.
15: 9 offering of t' tenth deals of flour
22:28 hast smitten me these t' times?
32 smitten thine ass these t' times?
33 and turned from me these t' times:
24:10 blessed them these t' times.
26: 7 forty and t' thousand and seven
25 and four thousand and t' hundred.
47 were fifty and t' thousand and four
62 twenty and t' thousand, all males
28:12 t' tenth deals of flour for a meat
20 t' tenth deals shall ye offer for a
28 t' tenth deals unto one bullock, two
29: 3 t' tenth deals for a bullock, and
9 t' tenth deals to a bullock, and two
14 t' tenth deals unto every bullock of
31:36 t' hundred thousand and seven
43 t' hundred thousand and thirty
33: 8 t' days' journey in the wilderness
39 hundred and twenty and t' years
35:14 give t' cities on this side Jordan,
14 t' cities shall ye give in the land of
De 4:41 Moses severed t' cities on this side
14:28 the end of t' years thou shalt bring
16:16 T' times in a year shall all thy
17: 6 of two witnesses, or t' witnesses,
19: 2 separate t' cities for thee in the
3 thee to inherit, into t' parts,
7 shalt separate t' cities for thee.
9 thou add t' cities more for thee,
15 or at the mouth of t' witnesses,
Jos 1:11 within t' days ye shall pass over
2:16 and hide yourselves there t' days,
22 and abode there t' days, until the
3: 2 it came to pass after t' days, that
7: 3 about two or t' thousand men go up
4 the people about t' thousand men:
9:16 came to pass at the end of t' days
15:14 drove thence the t' sons of Anak,
17:11 and her towns, even t' countries.
18: 4 among you t' men for each tribe:
21:32 Kartan with her suburbs; t' cities.
J'g 1:20 thence the t' sons of Anak.
7: 6 their mouth, were t' hundred men:
7 By the t' hundred men that lapped
8 and retained those t' hundred men:
16 t' hundred men into t' companies,
20 the t' companies blew the trumpets,
22 the t' hundred blew the trumpets,
8: 4 t' hundred men that were with him,
9:22 had reigned t' years over Israel,
43 and divided them into t' companies,
10: 2 judged Israel twenty and t' years,
11:26 coasts of Arnon, t' hundred years?
14:14 not in t' days expound the riddle.
15: 4 went and caught t' hundred foxes,
11 t' thousand men of Judah went to
16:15 hast mocked me these t' times,
27 about t' thousand men and women,
19: 4 and he abode with him t' days:
1Sa 1:24 him up with her, with t' bullocks,
2:13 a fleshhook of t' teeth in his hand;
21 bare t' sons and two daughters.
9:20 thine asses that were lost t' days
10: 3 meet thee t' men going up to God
3 one carrying t' kids, and another
3 another carrying t' loaves of bread,
11: 8 of Israel were t' hundred thousand,
11 put the people in t' companies;
13: 2 Saul chose him t' thousand men of
17 of the Philistines in t' companies:
17:13 the t' eldest sons of Jesse went and
13 the names of his t' sons that went
14 and the t' eldest followed Saul.
20:19 when thou hast stayed t' days,
20 I will shoot t' arrows on the side
41 and bowed himself t' times:
21: 5 kept from us about these t' days,
24: 2 took t' thousand chosen men out
25: 2 he had t' thousand sheep, and a
26: 2 having t' thousand chosen men of
30:12 any water, t' days and t' nights.
13 because t' days agone I fell sick.
31: 6 So Saul died, and his t' sons, and
8 Saul and his t' sons fallen in mount
2Sa 2:18 there were t' sons of Zeruiah there,
31 so that t' hundred and threescore
5: 5 he reigned thirty and t' years over
6:11 Obed-edom the Gittite t' months:
13:38 to Geshur, and was there t' years.
14:27 Absalom there were born t' sons,
18:14 And he took t' darts in his hand,
20: 4 the men of Judah within t' days,
21: 1 famine in the days of David t' years,
16 spear weighed t' hundred shekels
23: 9 one of the t' mighty men with
13 t' of the thirty chief went down,
16 the t' mighty men brake through
17 things did these t' mighty men.
18 son of Zeruiah, was chief among t'.
18 up his spear against t' hundred,
18 them, and had the name among t'.
19 Was he not most honourable of t'?
19 he attained not unto the first t'.
22 the name among t' mighty men.
23 but he attained not to the first t'.
24:12 the Lord, I offer thee t' things;
13 wilt thou flee t' months before
13 that there be t' days' pestilence in
1Ki 2:11 thirty and t' years reigned he in
39 came to pass at the end of t' years,
4:32 And he spake t' thousand proverbs:
5:16 t' thousand and t' hundred, which
6:36 court with t' rows of hewed stone,
1Ki 7: 4 And there were windows in t' rows,
4, 5 was against light in t' ranks.
12 was with t' rows of hewed stones,
25 oxen, t' looking toward the north,
25 and t' looking toward the west,
25 and t' looking toward the south,
25 and t' looking toward the east:
27 and t' cubits the height of it.
9:25 t' times in a year did Solomon offer
10:17 t' hundred shields of beaten gold;
17 t' pound of gold went to one shield:
22 once in t' years came the navy of
11: 3 and t' hundred concubines: and
12: 5 Depart yet for t' days, then come
15: 2 T' years reigned he in Jerusalem.
17:21 himself upon the child t' times,
22: 1 they continued t' years without war
2Ki 2:17 they sought t' days, but found him
3:10, 13 called these t' kings together,
9:32 out to him two or t' eunuchs.
12: 6 the t' and twentieth year of king
13: 1 the t' and twentieth year of Joash
25 T' times did Joash beat him, and
17: 5 to Samaria, and besieged it t' years.
18:10 at the end of t' years they took it:
14 t' hundred talents of silver and
23:31 Jehoahaz was twenty and t' years
31 he reigned t' months in Jerusalem.
24: 1 became his servant t' years:
8 he reigned in Jerusalem t' months.
25:17 the height of the chapiter t' cubits;
18 and the t' keepers of the door:
1Ch 2: 3 which t' were born unto him of the
16 Abishai, and Joab, and Asahel, t'.
22 who had t' and twenty cities in the
3: 4 he reigned thirty and t' years.
23 and Hezekiah, and Azrikam, t'.
7: 6 Bela, and Becher, and Jediael, t'.
10: 6 Saul died, and his t' sons, and all
11:11 t' hundred slain by him at one time.
12 who was one of the t' mighties.
15 t' of the thirty captains went down
18 the t' brake through the host of the
19 These things did these t' mightiest.
20 of Joab, he was chief of the t':
20 up his spear against t' hundred,
20 and had a name among the t'.
21 Of the t', he was more honourable
21 he attained not to the first t'.
24 the name among the t' mighties.
25 but attained not to the first t':
12:27 t' thousand and seven hundred;
29 the kindred of Saul, t' thousand:
39 there they were with David t' days,
13:14 Obed-edom in his house t' months.
21:10 the Lord, I offer thee t' things:
12 Either t' years' famine;
12 or t' months to be destroyed before
12 else t' days the sword of the Lord,
23: 8 Jehiel, and Zetham, and Joel, t'.
9 and Haziel, and Haran, t'.
23 Mahli, and Eder, and Jeremoth, t'.
24:18 The t' and twentieth to Delaiah,
25: 5 fourteen sons and t' daughters.
30 The t' and twentieth to Mahazioth,
29: 4 Even t' thousand talents of gold,
27 thirty and t' years reigned he in
2Ch 2: 2 t' thousand and six hundred to
17 and t' thousand and six hundred.
18 and t' thousand and six hundred
4: 4 oxen, t' looking toward the north,
4 and t' looking toward the west,
4 and t' looking toward the south,
4 and t' looking toward the east: and
5 and held t' thousand baths.
6:13 t' cubits high, and had set it in the
7:10 t' and twentieth day of the seventh
8:13 solemn feasts, t' times in the year,
9:16 t' hundred shields made he of
16 t' hundred shekels of gold went to
21 every t' years once came the ships
10: 5 Come again unto me after t' days.
11:17 the son of Solomon strong, t' years:
17 for t' years they walked in the way
13: 2 He reigned t' years in Jerusalem.
14: 8 out of Judah t' hundred thousand;
9 thousand, and t' hundred chariots;
17:14 men of valour t' hundred thousand.
20:25 they were t' days in gathering of
25: 5 found them t' hundred thousand
13 and smote t' thousand of them,
26:13 t' hundred thousand and seven
29:33 oxen and t' thousand sheep.
31:16 from t' years old and upward,
35: 7 thousand, and t' thousand bullocks:
8 small cattle, and t' hundred oxen.
36: 2 was twenty and t' years old when
2 he reigned t' months in Jerusalem.
9 he reigned t' months and ten days
Ezr 2: 4 t' hundred seventy and two.
11 of Bebai, six hundred twenty and t'.
17 of Bezai, t' hundred twenty and t'.
19 two hundred twenty and t'.
21 an hundred twenty and t'.
25 seven hundred and forty and t'.
28 and Ai, two hundred twenty and t'.
32 of Harim, t' hundred and twenty.
34 Jericho, t' hundred forty and five.
35 t' thousand and six hundred and
36 nine hundred seventy and t'.
58 were t' hundred ninety and two.
64 forty and two thousand t' hundred
65 seven thousand t' hundred thirty
6: 4 With t' rows of great stones, and a
8: 5 and with him t' hundred males.
15 there abode we in tents t' days:
Ezr 8:32 Jerusalem, and abode there t' days.
10: 8 would not come within t' days,
9 unto Jerusalem within t' days.
Ne 2:11 Jerusalem, and was there t' days.
7: 9 t' hundred seventy and two.
17 two thousand t' hundred twenty
22 t' hundred twenty and eight.
23 Bezai, t' hundred twenty and four.
29 Beeroth, seven hundred forty and t'.
32 and Ai, an hundred twenty and t'.
35 of Harim, t' hundred and twenty.
36 Jericho, t' hundred forty and five.
38 t' thousand nine hundred and
39 nine hundred seventy and t'.
60 were t' hundred ninety and two.
66 thousand t' hundred and threescore,
67 t' hundred thirty and seven:
Es 4:16 neither eat nor drink t' days, night
8: 9 on the t' and twentieth day thereof:
9:15 slew t' hundred men at Shushan;
Job 1: 2 him seven sons and t' daughters.
3 and t' thousand camels, and five
4 their t' sisters to eat and to drink
17 The Chaldeans made out t' bands,
2:11 Job's t' friends heard of all this evil
32: 1 these t' men ceased to answer Job,
3 against his t' friends was his wrath
5 answer in the mouth of these t' men,
42:13 also seven sons and t' daughters.
Pr 30:15 t' things that are never satisfied,
18 t' things which are too wonderful
21 For t' things the earth is disquieted,
29 There be t' things which go well,
Isa 15: 5 Zoar, an heifer of t' years old:
16:14 Within t' years, as the years of an
17: 6 two or t' berries in the top of the
20: 3 walked naked and barefoot t' years
Jer 25: 3 that is the t' and twentieth year,
36:23 Jehudi had read t' or four leaves,
48:34 as an heifer of t' years old:
52:24 and the t' keepers of the door:
28 t' thousand Jews and t' and twenty:
30 In the t' and twentieth year of
Eze 4: 5 days, t' hundred and ninety days:
9 t' hundred and ninety days shalt
14:14 Though these t' men, Noah, Daniel,
16, 18 Though these t' men were in it,
40:10 t' on this side, and t' on that side;
10 side; they t' were of one measure:
21 t' on this side and t' on that side;
48 the gate was t' cubits on this side,
48 this side, and t' cubits on that side.
41: 6 the side chambers were t', one
16 round about on their t' stories,
22 altar of wood was t' cubits high,
42: 3 gallery against gallery in t' stories.
6 For they were in t' stories, but had
48:31 t' gates northward; one gate of
32 t' gates; and one gate of Joseph,
33 hundred measures: and t' gates;
34 five hundred, with their t' gates;
Da 1: 5 so nourishing them t' years, that at
3:23 these t' men, Shadrach, Meshach,
24 Did not we cast t' men bound into
6: 2 And over these t' presidents; of
10 upon his knees t' times a day,
13 maketh his petition t' times a day.
7: 5 it had t' ribs in the mouth of it
8 whom there were t' of the first
20 came up, and before whom t' fell;
24 first, and he shall subdue t' kings.
8:14 thousand and t' hundred days;
10: 2 Daniel was mourning t' full weeks.
3 till t' whole weeks were fulfilled.
11: 2 shall stand up yet t' kings in Persia;
12:12 thousand t' hundred and five and
Am 1: 3 For t' transgressions of Damascus,
6 For t' transgressions of Gaza, and
9 For t' transgressions of Tyrus, and
11 For t' transgressions of Edom, and
13 For t' transgressions of the children
2: 1 For t' transgressions of Moab, and
4 For t' transgressions of Judah, and
6 For t' transgressions of Israel, and
4: 4 and your tithes after t' years:
7 were yet t' months to the harvest:
8 So two or t' cities wandered unto
Jon 1:17 belly of the fish t' days and t' nights.
3: 3 great city of t' days' journey.
Zec 11: 8 T' shepherds also I cut off in one
M't 12:40 as Jonas was t' days and t' nights
40 t' days and t' nights in the heart of
13:33 and hid in t' measures of meal,
15:32 they continue with me now t' days,
17: 4 let us make here t' tabernacles;
18:16 in the mouth of two or t' witnesses
20 two or t' are gathered together in
26:61 of God, and to build it in t' days.
27:40 and buildest it in t' days, save
63 alive, After t' days I will rise again.
M'r 8: 2 have now been with me t' days,
31 killed, and after t' days rise again.
9: 5 and let us make t' tabernacles; one
14: 5 for more than t' hundred pence,
58 within t' days I will build another
15:29 temple, and buildest it in t' days,
Lu 1:56 abode with her about t' months,
2:46 after t' days they found him in the
4:25 shut up t' years and six months,
9:33 and let us make t' tabernacles; one
10:36 Which now of these t', thinkest
11: 5 unto him, Friend, lend me t' loaves;
12:52 t' against two, and two against t'.
13: 7 these t' years I come seeking fruit
21 took and hid in t' measures of meal,
Joh 2: 6 containing two or t' firkins apiece.

Joh 2:19 and in t' days I will raise it up.
20 and wilt thou rear it up in t' days?
12: 5 ointment sold for t' hundred pence,
21:11 fishes, an hundred and fifty and t':
Ac 2:41 them about t' thousand souls.
5: 7 about the space of t' hours after,
7:20 up in his father's house t' months:
9: 9 And he was t' days without sight,
10:19 unto him, Behold, t' men seek thee.
11:10 And this was done t' times: and all
11 t' men already come unto the house
17: 2 t' sabbath days reasoned with them
19: 8 boldly for the space of t' months,
20: 3 And there abode t' months. And
31 the space of t' years I ceased not
25: 1 after t' days he ascended from
28: 7 and lodged us t' days courteously.
11 And after t' months we departed in
12 Syracuse, we tarried there t' days.
15 as Appii forum, and The t' taverns:
17 after t' days Paul called the chief
1Co 10: 8 in one day t' and twenty thousand.
13:13 faith, hope, charity, these t';
14:27 let it be by two, or at the most by t',
29 Let the prophets speak two or t',
2Co 13: 1 mouth of two or t' witnesses shall
Ga 1:18 Then after t' years I went up to
1Ti 5:19 but before two or t' witnesses.
Heb10:28 mercy under two or t' witnesses:
11:23 was hid t' months of his parents,
Jas 5:17 space of t' years and six months.
1Jo 5: 7 are t' that bear record in heaven,
7 Holy Ghost: and these t' are one.
8 are t' that bear witness in earth,
8 blood: and these t' agree in one.
Re 6: 6 t' measures of barley for a penny;
8:13 of the trumpet of the t' angels,
9:18 By these t' was the third part of
11: 9 dead bodies t' days and an half,
11 after t' days and an half the Spirit
16:13 I saw t' unclean spirits like frogs
19 great city was divided into t' parts,
21:13 On the east t' gates;
13 on the north t' gates;
13 on the south t' gates;
13 and on the west t' gates.

threefold
Ec 4:12 a t' cord is not quickly broken.

three-hundred See THREE and HUNDRED.

threescore
Ge 25: 7 an hundred t' and fifteen years.
26 Isaac was t' years old when she
46:26 all the souls were t' and six;
27 came into Egypt, were t' and ten.
50: 3 mourned for him t' and ten days.
Ex 15:27 water, and t' and ten palm trees:
38:25 hundred and t' and fifteen shekels,
Le 12: 5 of her purifying t' and six days.
Nu 1:27 were t' and fourteen thousand
39 were t' and two thousand and
2: 4 were t' and fourteen thousand
26 were t' and two thousand and
3:43 two hundred and t' and thirteen.
46 two hundred and t' and thirteen
50 hundred and t' and five shekels,
26:22 t' and sixteen thousand and five
25 t' and four thousand and three
27 them, t' thousand and five hundred.
43 were t' and four thousand and
31:33 t' and twelve thousand beeves,
34 And t' and one thousand asses,
37 six hundred and t' and fifteen.
38 Lord's tribute was t' and twelve.
39 the Lord's tribute was t' and one.
33: 9 water, and t' and ten palm trees;
De 3: 4 t' cities, all the region of Argob,
10:22 Egypt with t' and ten persons;
Jos 13:30 which are in Bashan, t' cities:
J'g 1: 7 T' and ten kings, having their
8:14 thereof, even t' and seventeen men.
30 had t' and ten sons of his body
9: 2 which are t' and ten persons, reign
4 they gave him t' and ten pieces
5 Jerubbaal, being t' and ten persons,
18 slain his sons, t' and ten persons,
24 to the t' and ten sons of Jerubbaal
12:14 that rode on t' and ten ass colts:
1Sa 6:19 fifty thousand and t' and ten men:
2Sa 2:31 three hundred and t' men died.
1Ki 4:13 t' great cities with walls and
22 fine flour, and t' measures of meal,
5:15 had t' and ten thousand that bare
6: 2 the length thereof was t' cubits,
10:14 hundred t' and six talents of gold,
2Ki 25:19 and t' men of the people of the land
1Ch 2:21 whom he married when he was t'
23 the towns thereof, even t' cities.
5:18 thousand seven hundred and t',
9:13 and seven hundred and t';
16:38 with their brethren, t' and eight;
21: 5 t' and ten thousand men that drew
26: 8 were t' and two of Obed-edom.
2Ch 2: 2 t' and ten thousand men to bear
18 t' and ten thousand of them to be
3: 3 the first measure was t' cubits,
9:13 six hundred and t' and six talents
11:21 eighteen wives, and t' concubines;
21 and eight sons, and t' daughters.)
12: 3 chariots, and t' thousand horsemen:
29:32 brought, was t' and ten bullocks,
36:21 sabbath, to fulfil t' and ten years.
Ezr 2: 9 of Zaccai, seven hundred and t'.
64 two thousand three hundred and t'.
69 t' and one thousand drams of gold,
6: 3 the height thereof t' cubits, and
Ezr 6: 3 and the breadth thereof t' cubits;
8:10 him an hundred and t' males.
13 Shemaiah, and with them t' males.
Ne 7:14 of Zaccai, seven hundred and t'.
18 six hundred t' and seven.
19 Bigvai, two thousand t' and seven.
66 two thousand three hundred and t',
72 and t' and seven priests' garments.
11: 6 four hundred t' and eight valiant
Ps 90:10 of our years are t' years and ten;
Ca 3: 7 t' valiant men are about it, of the
6: 8 There are t' queens, and fourscore
Isa 7: 8 and within t' and five years shall
Jer 52:25 and t' men of the people of the land,
Eze 40:14 He made also posts of t' cubits,
Da 3: 1 gold, whose height was t' cubits,
5:31 being about t' and two years old.
9:25 weeks, and t' and two weeks:
26 And after t' and two weeks shall
Zec 1:12 indignation these t' and ten years?
Lu 24:13 from Jerusalem about t' furlongs.
Ac 7:14 his kindred, t' and fifteen souls.
23:23 and horsemen t' and ten, and
27:37 two hundred t' and sixteen souls.
1Ti 5: 9 the number under t' years old,
Re 11: 3 thousand two hundred and t' days,
12: 6 thousand two hundred and t' days.
13:18 number is Six hundred t' and six.

threescore-thousand See THREESCORE and THOUSAND.

three-taverns See THREE and TAVERNS.

three-thousand See THREE and THOUSAND.

thresh See also THRESHED; THRESHETH; THRESHING.
Isa 41:15 thou shalt t' the mountains, and
Jer 51:33 threshingfloor, it is time to t' her:
Mic 4:13 Arise and t', O daughter of Zion:
Hab 3:12 thou didst t' the heathen in anger.

threshed
J'g 6:11 Gideon t' wheat by the winepress,
Isa 28:27 fitches are not t' with a threshing
Am 1: 3 they have t' Gilead with threshing

thresheth
1Co 9:10 he that t' in hope should be partaker

threshing See also THRESHINGFLOOR; THRESHINGPLACE.
Le 26: 5 And your t' shall reach unto the
2Sa 24:22 and t' instruments and other
2Ki 13: 7 had made them like the dust by t'.
1Ch 21:20 Now Ornan was t' wheat.
23 and the t' instruments for wood,
Isa 21:10 O my t', and the corn of my floor:
28:27 not threshed with a t' instrument,
28 because he will not ever be t' it,
41:15 a new sharp t' instrument having
Am 1: 3 Gilead with t' instruments of iron:

threshingfloor See also THRESHINGFLOORS.
Ge 50:10 And they came to the t' of Atad,
Nu 15:20 as ye do the heave offering of the t',
18:27 as though it were the corn of the t',
30 Levites as the increase of the t',
Ru 3: 2 winnoweth barley to night in the t'.
2Sa 6: 6 when they came to Nachon's t',
24:18 unto the Lord in the t' of Araunah
21 David said, To buy the t' of thee,
24 David bought the t' and the oxen
1Ch 13: 9 they came unto the t' of Chidon,
21:15 angel of the Lord stood by the t'
18 unto the Lord in the t' of Ornan
21 saw David, and went out of the t',
22 Grant me the place of this t', that
28 answered him in the t' of Ornan
2Ch 3: 1 had prepared in the t' of Ornan
Jer 51:33 The daughter of Babylon is like a t',

threshingfloors
1Sa 23: 1 Keilah, and they rob the t'.
Da 2:35 like the chaff of the summer t';

threshingplace
2Sa 24:16 angel of the Lord was by the t'

threshold See also THRESHOLDS.
J'g 19:27 and her hands were upon the t'.
1Sa 5: 4 his hands were cut off upon the t';
5 tread on the t' of Dagon in Ashdod
1Ki 14:17 she came to the t' of the door,
Eze 9: 3 he was, to the t' of the house.
10: 4 and stood over the t' of the house;
18 from off the t' of the house,
40: 6 and measured the t' of the gate,
6 and the other t' of the gate, which
7 the t' of the gate by the porch of
43: 8 setting of their t' by my thresholds,
46: 2 shall worship at the t' of the gate:
47: 1 waters issued out from under the t'
Zep 1: 9 punish all those that leap on the t',

thresholds
Ne 12:25 the ward at the t' of the gates.
Eze 43: 8 setting of their threshold by my t',
Zep 2:14 desolation shall be in the t':

threw See also OVERTHREW; THREWEST.
2Sa 16:13 t' stones at him, and cast dust.
2Ki 9:33 her down. So they t' her down:
2Ch 31: 1 t' down the high places and the
M'r 12:42 widow, and she t' in two mites,
Lu 9:42 devil t' him down, and tare him.
Ac 22:23 clothes, and t' dust into the air,

threwest
Ne 9:11 persecutors thou t' into the deeps.

thrice
Ex 34:23 T' in the year shall all your
24 Lord thy God t' in the year.
2Ki 13:18 And he smote t', and stayed.
19 thou shalt smite Syria but t'.
M't 26:34, 75 crow, thou shalt deny me t'.
M'r 14:30, 72 twice, thou shalt deny me t'.
Lu 22:34 shalt t' deny that thou knowest
61 cock crow, thou shalt deny me t'.
Joh 13:38 crow, till thou hast denied me t'.
Ac 10:16 This was done t': and the vessel
2Co 11:25 T' was I beaten with rods, once
25 t' I suffered shipwreck, a night
12: 8 this thing I besought the Lord t',

throat
Ps 5: 9 their t' is an open sepulchre; they
69: 3 weary of my crying: my t' is dried:
115: 7 neither speak they through their t'.
Pr 23: 2 And put a knife to thy t', if thou
Jer 2:25 unshod, and thy t' from thirst:
M't 18:28 and took him by the t', saying,
Ro 3:13 Their t' is an open sepulchre;

throne See also THRONES.
Ge 41:40 only in the t' will I be greater
Ex 11: 5 of Pharaoh that sitteth upon his t',
12:29 of Pharaoh that sat on his t'
De 17:18 sitteth upon the t' of his kingdom,
1Sa 2: 8 make them inherit the t' of glory:
2Sa 3:10 to set up the t' of David over Israel
7:13 will stablish the t' of his kingdom
16 thy t' shall be established for ever.
14: 9 the king and his t' be guiltless.
1Ki 1:13 me, and he shall sit upon my t'?
17 me, and he shall sit upon my t'.
20 who shall sit on the t' of my lord
24 me, and he shall sit upon my t'?
27 who should sit on the t' of my lord
30 he shall sit upon my t' in my stead;
35 he may come and sit upon my t';
37 Solomon, and make his t' greater
37 than the t' of my lord king David.
46 Solomon sitteth on the t' of the
47 and make his t' greater than thy t'.
48 given one to sit on my t' this day,
2: 4 (said he) a man on the t' of Israel.
12 sat Solomon upon the t' of David
19 and sat down on his t', and caused
24 set me on the t' of David my father,
33 upon his t', shall there be peace
45 the t' of David shall be established
3: 6 hast given him a son to sit on his t',
5: 5 son, whom I will set upon thy t' in
7: 7 he made a porch for the t' where he
8:20 my father, and sit on the t' of Israel,
25 in my sight to sit on the t' of Israel;
9: 5 will establish the t' of thy kingdom
5 thee a man upon the t' of Israel.
10: 9 thee, to set thee on the t' of Israel:
18 the king made a great t' of ivory,
19 The t' had six steps, and the top of
19 the top of the t' was round behind:
16:11 reign, as soon as he sat on his t',
22:10 king of Judah sat each on his t',
19 I saw the Lord sitting on his t',
2Ki 10: 3 sons, and set him on his father's t',
30 shall sit on the t' of Israel.
11:19 And he sat on the t' of the kings.
13:13 and Jeroboam sat upon his t':
15:12 sons shall sit on the t' of Israel
25:28 set his t' above the t' of the kings
1Ch 17:12 and I will stablish his t' for ever.
14 and his t' shall be established for
22:10 establish the t' of his kingdom over
28: 5 to sit upon the t' of the kingdom of
29:23 Solomon sat on the t' of the Lord
2Ch 6:10 and am set on the t' of Israel, as
16 sight to sit upon the t' of Israel;
7:18 will I stablish the t' of thy kingdom,
9: 8 in thee to set thee on his t',
17 the king made a great t' of ivory,
18 And there were six steps to the t',
18 gold, which were fastened to the t',
18: 9 Judah sat either of them on his t',
18 I saw the Lord sitting upon his t',
23:20 king upon the t' of the kingdom.
Ne 3: 7 unto the t' of the governor on this
Es 1: 2 king Ahasuerus sat on the t' of his
5: 1 king sat upon his royal t' in the
Job 26: 9 He holdeth back the face of his t',
36: 7 with kings are they on the t'; yea,
Ps 9: 4 thou satest in the t' judging right.
7 ever: he hath prepared his t' for
11: 4 temple, the Lord's t' is in heaven:
45: 6 Thy t', O God, is for ever and ever:
47: 8 God sitteth upon the t' of his
89: 4 build up thy t' to all generations.
14 are the habitation of thy t':
29 and his t' as the days of heaven.
36 and his t' as the sun before me.
44 and cast his t' down to the ground.
93: 2 Thy t' is established of old: thou
94:20 the t' of iniquity have fellowship
97: 2 are the habitation of his t'.
103:19 hath prepared his t' in the heavens;
132:11 of thy body will I set upon thy t'.
12 also sit upon thy t' for evermore.
Pr 16:12 t' is established by righteousness.
20: 8 A king that sitteth in the t' of
28 and his t' is upholden by mercy.
25: 5 his t' shall be established in
29:14 his t' shall be established for ever.
Isa 6: 1 saw also the Lord sitting upon a t',
9: 7 upon the t' of David, and upon his
14:13 exalt my t' above the stars of God:
16: 5 in mercy shall the t' be established:
22:23 a glorious t' to his father's house.
47: 1 there is no t', O daughter of the
66: 1 The heaven is my t', and the earth

Jer 1:15 set every one his t' at the entering
3:17 call Jerusalem the t' of the Lord;
13:13 the kings that sit upon David's t',
14:21 do not disgrace the t' of thy glory:
17:12 A glorious high t' from the
25 princes sitting upon the t' of David,
22: 2 that sittest upon the t' of David,
4 kings sitting upon the t' of David,
30 sitting upon the t' of David,
29:16 that sitteth upon the t' of David,
33:17 upon the t' of the house of Israel;
21 not have a son to reign upon his t';
36:30 none to sit upon the t' of David:
43:10 will set his t' upon these stones
49:38 I will set my t' in Elam, and will
52:32 set his t' above the t' of the kings
La 5:19 t' from generation to generation.
Eze 1:26 their heads was the likeness of a t',
26 upon the likeness of the t' was the
10: 1 appearance of the likeness of a t'.
43: 7 the place of my t', and the place of
Da 5:20 he was deposed from his kingly t',
7: 9 his t' was like the fiery flame, and
Jon 3: 6 Nineveh, and he arose from his t',
Hag 2:22 I will overthrow the t' of kingdoms,
Zec 6:13 and shall sit and rule upon his t';
13 he shall be a priest upon his t':
M't 5:34 by heaven; for it is God's t':
19:28 man shall sit in the t' of his glory,
23:22 heaven, sweareth by the t' of God,
25:31 shall he sit upon the t' of his glory:
Lu 1:32 unto him the t' of his father David:
Ac 2:30 raise up Christ to sit on his t';
7:49 Heaven is my t', and earth is my
12:21 in royal apparel, sat upon his t',
Heb 1: 8 Thy t', O God, is for ever and ever:
4:16 come boldly unto the t' of grace,
8: 1 right hand of the t' of the Majesty
12: 2 at the right hand of the t' of God.
Re 1: 4 Spirits which are before his t';
3:21 will I grant to sit with me in my t',
21 set down with my Father in his t'.
4: 2 and, behold, a t' was set in heaven,
2 and one sat on the t'.
3 was a rainbow round about the t',
4 about the t' were four and twenty
5 out of the t' proceeded lightnings
5 lamps of fire burning before the t',
6 before the t' there was a sea of
6 and in the midst of the t',
6 and round about the t', were four
9 thanks to him that sat on the t',
10 down before him that sat on the t',
10 and cast their crowns before the t',
5: 1 hand of him that sat on the t' a
6 in the midst of the t' and of the
7 hand of him that sat upon the t'.
11 of many angels round about the t'
13 unto him that sitteth upon the t',
6:16 face of him that sitteth on the t',
7: 9 stood before the t', and before the
10 our God which sitteth upon the t',
11 angels stood round about the t',
11 and fell before the t' on their faces,
15 are they before the t' of God,
15 he that sitteth on the t' shall dwell
17 Lamb which is in the midst of the t'
8: 3 altar which was before the t'.
12: 5 caught up unto God, and to his t'.
14: 3 as it were a new song before the t',
5 without fault before the t' of God.
16:17 from the t', saying, It is done.
19: 4 worshipped God that sat on the t',
5 a voice came out of the t', saying,
20:11 I saw a great white t', and him that
21: 5 he that sat upon the t' said, Behold,
22: 1 proceeding out of the t' of God and
3 the t' of God and of the Lamb shall

thrones
Ps 122: 5 For there are set t' of judgment,
5 the t' of the house of David.
Isa 14: 9 raised up from their t' all the kings
Eze 26:16 sea shall come down from their t',
Da 7: 9 I beheld till the t' were cast down,
M't 19:28 ye also shall sit upon twelve t',
Lu 22:30 sit on t' judging the twelve tribes
Col 1:16 whether they be t', or dominions,
Re 20: 4 I saw t', and they sat upon them,

throng See also THRONGED; THRONGING.
M'r 3: 9 multitude, lest they should t' him.
Lu 8:45 the multitude t' thee and press

thronged
M'r 5:24 people followed him, and t' him.
Lu 8:42 But as he went the people t' him.

thronging
M'r 5:31 Thou seest the multitude t' thee,

through^ See also THROUGHOUT.
Ge 6:13 is filled with violence t' them;
12: 6 Abram passed t' the land unto the
13:17 walk t' the land in the length of it and
30:32 I will pass t' all thy flock to day,
41:36 that the land perish not t' the famine.
Ex 10:15 of the field, t' all the land of Egypt.
12:12 pass t' the land of Egypt this night,
23 will pass t' to smite the Egyptians;
13:17 God led them not t' the way of the
18 t' the way of the wilderness of the
14:16 ground t' the midst of the sea.
24 of the Egyptians t' the pillar of fire
19:13 shall surely be stoned, or shot t';
21 lest they break t' unto the Lord to
24 people break t' to come up unto the
21: 6 shall bore his ear t' with an aul;
Ex 36:33 middle bar to shoot t' the boards
Le 4: 2 If a soul shall sin t' ignorance against
13 congregation...Israel sin t' ignorance,
22 and done somewhat t' ignorance
27 the common people sin t' ignorance,
5:15 a trespass, and sin t' ignorance,
18:21 of thy seed pass t' the fire to Molech,
26: 6 neither shall the sword go t' your land.
Nu 13:32 t' which we have gone to search it,
14: 7 land, which we passed t' to search it,
15:27 And if any soul sin t' ignorance,
29 law for him that sinneth t' ignorance,
20:17 us pass, I pray thee, t' thy country:
17 country: we will not pass t' the fields,
17 or t' the vineyards, neither will we
19 any thing else, go t' on my feet.
20 And he said, Thou shalt not go t'.
21 to give Israel passage t' his border:
21:22 Let me pass t' thy land: we will not
23 not suffer Israel to pass t' his border:
24: 8 and pierce them t' with his arrows.
25: 8 the tent, and thrust both of them t',
8 Israel, and the woman t' her belly.
31:16 t' the counsel of Balaam, to commit
23 ye shall make it go t' the fire, and it
23 fire ye shall make go t' the water.
33: 8 and passed t' the midst of the sea
De 1:19 t' all that great and terrible wilderness,
2: 4 are to pass t' the coast of your brethren
7 thy walking t' this great wilderness:
8 t' the way of the plain from Elath,
18 Thou art to pass over t' Ar, the coast
27 Let me pass t' thy land: I will go
28 drink: only I will pass t' on my feet;
5:15 thee out thence t' a mighty hand
8:15 t' that great and terrible wilderness,
9:26 thou hast redeemed t' thy greatness,
15:17 and thrust it t' his ear unto the door,
18:10 son or his daughter to pass t' the fire,
29:16 t' the nations which ye passed by;
31:29 him to anger t' the work of your hands.
32:47 t' this thing ye shall prolong your days
33:11 smite t' the loins of them that rise
Jos 1:11 Pass t' the host, and command the
2:15 down by a cord t' the window:
3: 2 that the officers went t' the host;
18: 4 and they shall rise, and go t' the land,
8 Go and walk t' the land, and describe
9 the men went and passed t' the land,
12 went up t' the mountains westward;
24:17 all the people t' whom we passed:
J'g 2:22 That t' them I may prove Israel,
3:23 Then Ehud went forth t' the porch,
5: 6 and the travellers walked t' byways.
26 pierced and stricken t' his temples.
28 a window, and cried t' the lattice,
9:54 And his young man thrust him t',
11:16 t' the wilderness unto the Red sea,
17 Let me, I pray thee, pass t' thy land:
18 they went along t' the wilderness,
19 pray thee, t' thy land into my place.
20 trusted not Israel to pass t' his coast:
20:12 sent men t' all the tribe of Benjamin,
1Sa 9: 4 And he passed t' mount Ephraim, and
4 and passed t' the land of Shalisha,
4 then they passed t' the land of Shalim,
4 passed t' the land of the Benjamites,
19:12 Michal let David down t' a window:
31: 4 sword, and thrust me t' therewith;
4 uncircumcised come and thrust me t',
2Sa 2:29 men walked all that night t' the plain,
29 over Jordan, and went t' all Bithron,
4: 7 and gat them away t' the plain all
6:16 daughter looked t' a window,
12:31 and made them pass t' the brickkiln:
18:14 thrust them t' the heart of Absalom,
20:14 And he went t' all the tribes of Israel
22:13 T' the brightness before him were
30 For by thee I have run t' a troop: by
23:16 brake t' the host of the Philistines,
24: 2 Go now t' all the tribes of Israel,
8 So when they had gone t' all the land,
2Ki 1: 2 Ahaziah fell down t' a lattice in his
3: 8 The way t' the wilderness of Edom.
26 break t'...unto the king of Edom:
10:21 And Jehu sent t' all Israel: and all the
16: 3 and made his son to pass t' the fire,
17:17 and their daughters to pass t' the fire,
21: 6 And he made his son pass t' the fire,
23:10 daughter to pass t' the fire to Molech.
24:20 t' the anger of the Lord it came to
1Ch 10: 4 sword, and thrust me t' therewith;
11:18 brake t' the host of the Philistines,
2Ch 19: 4 he went out again t' the people from
23:20 they came t' the high gate into
24: 9 made a proclamation t' Judah and
30:10 t' the country of Ephraim and
32: 4 that ran t' the midst of the land,
33: 6 caused his children to pass t' the fire
Ezr 6:14 they prospered t' the prophesying of
Ne 9:11 they went t' the midst of the sea
Es 6: 9 bring him on horseback t' the street
11 brought him on horseback t' the street
Job 7:14 dreams, and terrifiest me t' visions:
14: 9 Yet t' the scent of water it will bud,
20:24 the bow of steel shall strike him t'.
22:13 know? can he judge t' the dark cloud?
24:16 In the dark they dig t' houses,
26:12 understanding he smiteth t' the proud.
29: 3 when by his light I walked t' darkness;
7 I went out to the gate t' the city,
40:24 his eyes: his nose pierceth t' snares.
41: 2 nose? or bore his jaw t' with a thorn?
Ps 8: 8 passeth t' the paths of the seas.
10: 4 wicked, t' the pride of his countenance,
18:29 For by thee I have run t' a troop; and
Ps 19: 4 Their line is gone out t' all the earth,
21: 7 t' the mercy of the most High he shall
23: 4 t' the valley of the shadow of death,
32: 3 my bones waxed old t' my roaring all
44: 5 T' thee will we push down our
5 t' thy name will we tread them under
60:12 T' God we shall do valiantly: for he it
66: 3 t' the greatness of thy power shall
6 land: they went t' the flood on foot:
12 heads; we went t' fire and t' water:
68: 7 thou didst march t' the wilderness;
73: 9 their tongue walketh t' the earth.
78:13 the sea, and caused them to pass t';
81: 5 he went out t' the land of Egypt:
84: 6 passing t' the valley of Baca make it a
92: 4 Lord, hast made me glad t' thy work:
106: 9 t' the depths, as t' the wilderness.
107:39 and brought low t' oppression,
108:13 T' God we shall do valiantly: for he it
109:24 My knees are weak t' fasting; and
110: 5 strike t' kings in the day of his wrath.
115: 7 not: neither speak they t' their throat.
119:98 Thou t' thy commandments hast
104 T' thy precepts I get understanding:
136:14 Israel to pass t' the midst of it:
16 which led his people t' the wilderness:
Pr 7: 6 of my house I looked t' my casement,
8 Passing t' the street near her corner;
23 Till a dart strike t' his liver; as a bird
11: 9 but t' knowledge shall the just be
18: 1 T' desire a man, having separated
24: 3 T' wisdom is an house builded; and
Ec 5: 3 a dream cometh t' the multitude of
10:18 t' idleness of the hands the house
18 the hands the house droppeth t'.
Ca 2: 9 shewing himself t' the lattice.
Isa 8: 8 And he shall pass t' Judah; he shall
21 And they shall pass t' it, hardly
9:19 T' the wrath of the Lord of hosts is
13:15 one that is found shall be thrust t';
14:19 are slain, thrust t' with a sword,
16: 8 they wandered t' the wilderness:
21: 1 As whirlwinds in the south pass t'; so
23:10 Pass t' thy land as a river, O daughter
27: 4 I would go t' them, I would burn
28: 7 But they also have erred t' wine, and
7 t' strong drink are out of the way;
7 have erred t' strong drink,
7 are out of the way t' strong drink;
15, 18 overflowing scourge shall pass t',
30:31 For t' the voice of the Lord shall the
34:10 none shall pass t' it for ever and ever.
43: 2 When thou passest t' the waters, I will
2 t' the rivers, they shall not overflow
2 when thou walkest t' the fire, thou
48:21 not when he led them t' the deserts:
60:15 hated, so that no man went t' thee,
62:10 Go t', go t' the gates; prepare ye
63:13 That led them t' the deep, as an horse
Jer 2: 6 of Egypt, that led us t' the wilderness,
6 t' a land of deserts and of pits,
6 t' a land of drought, and of the shadow
6 t' a land that no man passed t', and
3: 9 t' the lightness of her whoredom
5: 1 Run ye to and fro t' the streets of
9: 6 t' deceit they refuse to know me, saith
10 up, so that none can pass t' them;
12 a wilderness, that none passeth t'?
12:12 upon all high places t' the wilderness:
17:24 in no burden t' the gates of this city
32:35 their daughters to pass t' the fire unto
51: 4 that are thrust t' in her streets.
52 t' all her land the wounded shall
52: 3 t' the anger of the Lord it came to
La 3:44 that our prayer should not pass t'.
4: 9 stricken t' for want of the fruits of the
21 the cup shall also pass t' unto thee:
Eze 5:17 and blood shall pass t' thee;
6: 8 ye shall be scattered t' the countries.
9: 4 Go t' the midst of the city,
4 t' the midst of Jerusalem, and set a
5 Go ye after him t' the city, and smite:
12: 5 Dig thou t' the wall in their sight, and
7 and in the even I digged t' the wall
12 they shall dig t' the wall to carry out
14: 5 all estranged from me t' their idols.
15 noisome beasts to pass t' the land,
15 no man may pass t' because of the
17 land, and say, Sword, go t' the land;
16:14 for it was perfect t' my comeliness,
21 cause them to pass t' the fire for them?
36 discovered t' thy whoredoms with thy
40 and thrust thee t' with their swords.
20:23 and disperse them t' the countries;
26 t' the fire all that openeth the womb,
31 ye make your sons to pass t' the fire,
23:37 to pass for them t' the fire, to devour
29:11 No foot of man shall pass t' it, nor
11 foot of beast shall pass t' it, neither
12 will disperse them t' the countries.
30:23 will disperse them t' the countries.
33:28 be desolate, that none shall pass t'.
34: 6 My sheep wandered t' all the
36:19 they were dispersed t' the countries:
39:14 passing t' the land to bury with the
15 the passengers that pass t' the land,
41:19 made t' all the house round about.
46:19 he brought me t' the entry, which was
47: 3 and he brought me t' the waters;
4 and brought me t' the waters;
4 a thousand, and brought me t';
Da 8:25 And t' his policy also he shall
9: 7 t' all the countries whither thou hast
11: 2 strength t' his riches he shall stir up
10 come, and overflow, and pass t':
Joe 3:17 no strangers pass t' her any more.

Am 2:10 led you forty years t' the wilderness.
5:17 for I will pass t' thee, saith the
Jon 3: 7 proclaimed and published t' Nineveh
Mic 2:13 and have passed t' the gate, and are
5: 8 if he go t', both treadeth down,
Na 1:12 be cut down, when he shall pass t'.
15 the wicked shall no more pass t' thee;
3: 4 that selleth nations t' her whoredoms,
4 and familiar t' her witchcrafts.
Hab 1: 6 shall march t' the breadth of the land,
3:12 didst march t' the land in indignation,
14 Thou didst strike t' with his staves
15 didst walk t' the sea with thine horses,
15 horses, t' the heap of great waters.
Zec 1:10 sent to walk to and fro t' the earth.
11 have walked to and fro t' the earth,
17 My cities t' prosperity shall yet be
4:10 run to and fro t' the whole earth.
12 t' the two golden pipes empty the
5: 6 is their resemblance t' all the earth.
6: 7 might walk to and fro t' the earth:
7 hence, walk to and fro t' the earth.
7 So they walked to and fro t' the earth.
7:14 that no man passed t' nor returned:
9: 8 no oppressor shall pass t' them any
15 drink, and make a noise as t' wine;
10: 7 their heart shall rejoice as t' wine:
11 he shall pass t' the sea with affliction,
13: 3 that begat him shall thrust him t'
9 I will bring the third part t' the fire,
M't 6:19 where thieves break t' and steal:
20 thieves do not break t' nor steal:
9:34 devils t' the prince of the devils.
12: 1 on the sabbath day t' the corn;
43 he walketh t' dry places, seeking
19:24 camel to go t' the eye of a needle,
M'r 2:23 t' the corn fields on the sabbath
6:55 ran t' that whole region round
7:13 God of none effect t' your tradition,
31 t' the midst of the coast of
9:30 thence, and passed t' Galilee;
10:25 a camel to go t' the eye of a needle,
11:16 carry any vessel t' the temple.
Lu 1:78 T' the tender mercy of our God:
2:35 sword shall pierce t' thy own soul
4:14 fame of him t' all the region
30 he passing t' the midst of them
5:19 let him down t' the tiling with his
6: 1 that he went t' the corn fields;
9: 6 and went t' the towns, preaching
10:17 are subject unto us t' thy name.
11:15 casteth out devils t' Beelzebub the
18 I cast out devils t' Beelzebub.
24 he walketh t' dry places, seeking
12:39 suffered his house to be broken t'.
13:22 he went t' the cities and villages,
17: 1 woe unto him, t' whom they come!
11 he passed t' the midst of Samaria
18:25 for a camel to go t' a needle's eye,
19: 1 Jesus entered...passed t' Jericho.
Joh 1: 7 that all men t' him might believe.
3:17 the world t' him might be saved.
4: 4 And he must needs go t' Samaria.
8:59 t' the midst of them, and so passed
15: 3 Now ye are clean t' the word which
17:11 t' thine own name those whom
17 Sanctify them t' thy truth: thy
19 might be sanctified t' the truth.
20 shall believe on me t' their word;
20:31 ye might have life t' his name.
Ac 1: 2 after that he t' the Holy Ghost had
3:16 his name t' faith in his name
17 I wot that t' ignorance ye did it,
4: 2 preached t' Jesus the resurrection
8:18 that t' laying on of the apostles'
40 passing t' he preached in all the
10:43 t' his name whosoever believeth
12:10 out, and passed on t' one street;
13: 6 when they had gone t' the isle unto
38 that t' this man is preached unto
14:22 t' much tribulation enter into the
15: 3 they passed t' Phenice and Samaria,
11 we believe that t' the grace of the
41 And he went t' Syria and Cilicia,
16: 4 And as they went t' the cities, they
17: 1 when they had passed t' Amphipolis
18:27 which had believed t' grace:
19: 1 having passed t' the upper coasts
21 when he had passed t' Macedonia
20: 3 purposed to return t' Macedonia.
21: 4 who said to Paul t' the Spirit, that
Ro 1: 8 I thank my God t' Jesus Christ for
24 uncleanness t' the lusts of their
2:23 t' breaking the law dishonourest
24 blasphemed among the Gentiles t'
3: 7 abounded t' my lie unto his glory;
24 t' the redemption that is in Christ
25 a propitiation t' faith in his blood,
25 past, t' the forbearance of God;
30 faith, and uncircumcision t' faith.
31 then make void the law t' faith?
4:13 Abraham, or to his seed, t' the law,
13 but t' the righteousness of faith.
20 not at the promise of God t' unbelief;
5: 1 peace with God t' our Lord Jesus
9 shall be saved from wrath t' him.
11 in God t' our Lord Jesus Christ,
15 if t' the offence of one many be dead,
21 grace reign t' righteousness
6:11 alive unto God t' Jesus Christ our
23 God is eternal life t' Jesus Christ
7:25 I thank God t' Jesus Christ our
8: 3 do, in that it was weak t' the flesh,
13 if ye t' the Spirit do mortify the deeds
37 conquerors t' him that loved us.
11:11 rather t' their fall salvation is come

Ro 11:30 now obtained mercy t' their belief:
31 t' your mercy they also may obtain
36 and t' him, and to him, are all
12: 3 For I say, t' the grace given unto me,
15: 4 we t' patience and comfort of the
13 t' the power of the Holy Ghost.
17 I may glory t' Jesus Christ in
19 T' mighty signs and wonders, by
16:27 be glory t' Jesus Christ for ever.
1Co 1: 1 Jesus Christ t' the will of God,
4:15 I have begotten you t' the gospel.
8:11 t' thy knowledge shall the weak
10: 1 cloud, and all passed t' the sea;
13:12 For now we see t' a glass, darkly;
15:57 the victory t' our Lord Jesus Christ.
16: 5 you, when I shall pass t' Macedonia:
5 for I do pass t' Macedonia.
2Co 3: 4 such trust have we t' Christ to
4:15 t' the thanksgiving of many
8: 9 that ye t' his poverty might be rich.
9:11 causeth t' us thanksgiving to God.
10: 4 but mighty t' God to the pulling down
11: 3 beguiled Eve t' his subtilty,
33 t' a window in a basket was I let
12: 7 t' the abundance of the revelations,
13: 4 he was crucified t' weakness,
Ga 2:19 I t' the law am dead to the law,
3: 8 would justify the heathen t' faith,
14 on the Gentiles t' Jesus Christ;
14 the promise of the Spirit t' faith.
4: 7 son, then an heir of God t' Christ.
13 t' infirmity of the flesh I preached
5: 5 For we t' the Spirit wait for the hope
10 confidence in you t' the Lord,
Eph 1: 7 we have redemption t' his blood,
2: 7 toward us t' Christ Jesus.
8 For by grace are ye saved t' faith;
18 t' him we both have access by one
22 an habitation of God t' the Spirit.
4: 6 above all, and t' all, and in you all.
18 t' the ignorance that is in them,
Ph'p 1:19 to my salvation t' your prayer,
2: 3 Let nothing be done t' strife or
3: 9 that which is t' the faith of Christ,
4: 7 hearts and minds t' Christ Jesus.
13 I can do all things t' Christ which
Col 1:14 we have redemption t' his blood,
20 peace t' the blood of his cross,
22 In the body of his flesh t' death, to
2: 8 any man spoil you t' philosophy
12 ye are risen with him t' the faith of
2Th 2:13 you to salvation t' sanctification
16 consolation and good hope t' grace,
1Ti 6:10 pierced themselves t' with many
2Ti 1:10 immortality to light t' the gospel:
3:15 salvation t' faith which is in Christ
Tit 1: 3 manifested his word t' preaching,
3: 6 on us abundantly t' Jesus Christ
Ph'm 22 that t' your prayers I shall be given
Heb 2:10 their salvation perfect t' sufferings.
14 that t' death he might destroy him
15 t' fear of death were all their lifetime
3:13 hardened t' the deceitfulness of sin.
6:12 who t' faith and patience inherit
9:14 who t' the eternal Spirit offered
10:10 t' the offering of the body of Jesus
20 t' the veil, that is to say, his flesh;
11: 3 T' faith we understand that the
11 T' faith also Sara herself received
28 T' faith he kept the passover, and the
29 they passed t' the Red sea as by dry
33 Who t' faith subdued kingdoms,
39 obtained a good report t' faith,
12:20 be stoned, or thrust t' with a dart:
13:20 t' the blood of the everlasting
21 in his sight, t' Jesus Christ;
1Pe 1: 2 t' sanctification of the Spirit, unto
5 of God t' faith unto salvation
6 heaviness t' manifold temptations:
22 in obeying the truth t' the Spirit
4:11 may be glorified t' Jesus Christ,
2Pe 1: 1 faith with us t' the righteousness
2 unto you t' the knowledge of God,
3 t' the knowledge of him that hath
4 that is in the world t' lust.
2: 3 t' covetousness shall they with
18 they allure t' the lusts of the flesh,
18 t' much wantonness, those that
20 world t' the knowledge of the Lord
1Jo 4: 9 world, that we might live t' him.
Re 8:13 an angel flying t' the midst of
18: 3 rich t' the abundance of her
22:14 may enter in t' the gates into the city.

throughly See also THOROUGHLY.
Ge 11: 3 us make brick, and burn them t'.
Job 6: 2 Oh that my grief were t' weighed,
Ps 51: 2 Wash me t' from mine iniquity,
Jer 6: 9 They shall t' glean the remnant
7: 5 if ye t' amend your ways and your
5 if ye t' execute judgment between
50:34 he shall t' plead their cause, that
Eze 16: 9 I t' washed away thy blood from thee,
M't 3:12 he will t' purge his floor, and gather
Lu 3:17 he will t' purge his floor, and will
2Co 11: 6 been t' made manifest among
2Ti 3:17 t' furnished unto all good works.

throughout ^
Ge 41:29 great plenty t' all the land of Egypt:
46 and went t' all the land of Egypt.
45: 8 and a ruler t' all the land of Egypt.
Ex 5:12 abroad t' all the land of Egypt
7:19 may be blood t' all the land of Egypt,
21 was blood t' all the land of Egypt.
8:16 become lice t' all the land of Egypt.
17 became lice t' all the land of Egypt.

Ex 9: 9 upon beast, t' all the land of Egypt.
16 name may be declared t' all the earth
22 herb of the field, t' the land of Egypt.
25 hail smote t' all the land of Egypt
12:14 feast to the Lord t' your generations;
29:42 burnt offering t' your generations
30: 8 before the Lord t' your generations.
10 upon it t' your generations:
21 and to his seed t' their generations.
31 oil unto me t' your generations.
31:13 me and you t' your generations;
16 the sabbath t' their generations,
32:27 and out from gate to gate t' the camp,
34: 3 let any man be seen t' all the mount;
35: 3 kindle no fire t' your habitations
36: 6 caused it to be proclaimed t' the camp,
37:19 t' the six branches going out of the
40:15 priesthood t' their generations.
38 house of Israel, t' all their journeys.
Le 3:17 your generations t' all your dwellings,
7:36 a statute for ever t' their generations.
10: 9 a statute for ever t' your generations:
17: 7 ever unto them t' their generations.
23:14 a statute for ever t' your generations
21 all your dwellings t' your generations,
31 a statute for ever t' your generations
25: 9 the trumpet sound t' all your land.
10 proclaim liberty t' all the land unto
30 him that bought it t' his generations:
Nu 1:42 of Naphtali, t' their generations,
52 by his own standard, t' their hosts.
2: 3 camp of Judah pitch t' their armies:
9 and four hundred, t' their armies.
16 hundred and fifty, t' their armies.
24 and an hundred, t' their armies.
32 numbered of the camps t' their hosts
3:39 t' their families, all the males from a
4:22 Gershon, t' the houses of their fathers,
38 the sons of Gershon, t' their families,
40 numbered of them, t' their families,
42 of the sons of Merari, t' their families,
10: 8 ordinance for ever t' your generations.
25 of all the camps t' their hosts:
11:10 the people weep t' their families,
15:38 of their garments t' their generations,
18:23 a statute for ever t' your generations,
26: 2 and upward, t' their father's house,
28:14 every month t' the months of the year.
21 for every lamb, t' the seven lambs:
24 ye shall offer daily, t' the seven days,
29 unto one lamb, t' the seven lambs:
29: 4, 10 for one lamb, t' the seven lambs:
31: 4 a thousand, t' all the tribes of Israel,
35:29 unto you t' your generations in all
De 16:18 thy God giveth thee, t' thy tribes:
28:40 shalt have olive trees t' all thy coasts,
52 wherein thou trustedst, t' all thy land:
52 thee in all thy gates t' all thy land,
Jos 2:22 pursuers sought them t' all the way,
6:27 his fame was noised t' all the country.
16: 1 up from Jericho t' mount Beth-el,
22:14 a prince t' all the tribes of Israel;
24: 3 and led him t' all the land of Canaan,
J'g 6:35 he sent messengers t' all Manasseh;
7:22 against his fellow, even t' the host:
24 sent messengers t' all mount Ephraim,
20: 6 and sent her t' all the country of the
10 an hundred t' all the tribes of Israel,
1Sa 5:11 a deadly destruction t' all the city;
11: 7 sent them t' all the coasts of Israel
13: 3 Saul blew the trumpet t' all the land,
19 no smith found t' all the land of Israel
23:23 out t' all the thousands of Judah.
2Sa 8:14 t' all Edom put he garrisons, and all
15:10 sent spies t' all the tribes of Israel,
19: 9 were at strife t' all the tribes of Israel,
1Ki 1: 3 for a fair damsel t' all the coasts
6:38 house finished t' all the parts thereof,
15:22 made a proclamation t' all Judah;
18: 6 the land between them to pass t' it:
22:36 there went a proclamation t' the host
2Ki 17: 5 of Assyria came up t' all the land,
1Ch 5:10 in their tents t' all the east land
6:54 their dwelling places t' their castles
60 t' their families were thirteen cities.
62 the sons of Gershom t' their families
63 were given by lot, t' their families,
7:40 t' the genealogy of them that were
9:34 were chief t' their generations;
12:30 famous t' the house of their fathers.
21: 4 Joab departed, and went t' all Israel,
12 destroying t' all the coasts of Israel.
22: 5 of fame and of glory t' all countries:
26: 6 that ruled t' the house of their father:
27: 1 by month t' all the months of the year
2Ch 8: 6 and t' all the land of his dominion.
11:23 children t' all the countries of Judah
16: 9 run to and fro t' the whole earth,
17: 9 went about t' all the cities of Judah,
19 put in the fenced cities t' all Judah.
19: 5 t' all the fenced cities of Judah,
20: 3 and proclaimed a fast t' all Judah.
25: 5 fathers, t' all Judah and Benjamin:
26:14 for them t' all the host shields,
30: 5 to make proclamation t' all Israel,
6 the king and his princes t' all Israel
22 they did eat t' the feast seven days,
31:20 And thus did Hezekiah t' all Judah,
34: 7 the idols t' all the land of Israel,
36:22 a proclamation t' all his kingdom,
Ezr 1: 1 a proclamation t' all his kingdom,
10: 7 And they made proclamation t' Judah
Es 1:20 shall be published t' all his empire,
3: 6 Jews that were t' the whole kingdom
9: 2 cities t' all the provinces of the king
4 his fame went out t' all the provinces:

Es 9:28 and kept t· every generation.
Ps 72: 5 and moon endure, t· all generations.
102:24 thy years are t· all generations.
135:13 memorial, O Lord, t· all generations.
145:13 dominion endureth t· all generations.
Jer 17: 3 high places for sin, t· all thy borders.
Eze 38:21 against him t· all my mountains,
M't 4:24 And his fame went t· all Syria:
M'r 1:28 fame spread abroad t· all the region
39 in their synagogues t· all Galilee,
14: 9 be preached t· the whole world,
Lu 1:65 t· all the hill country of Judæa.
4:25 great famine was t· all the land;
7:17 of him went forth t· all Judæa,
17 and t· all the region round about.
8: 1 he went t· every city and village,
39 and published t· the whole city how
23: 5 the people, teaching t· all Jewry,
Joh 19:23 seam, woven from the top t·.
Ac 8: 1 scattered abroad t· the regions of
9:31 had the churches rest t· all Judæa
32 as Peter passed t· all quarters, he
42 And it was known t· all Joppa;
10:37 which was published t· all Judæa,
11:28 be great dearth t· all the world:
13:49 was published t· all the region.
14:24 after they had passed t· Pisidia,
16: 6 when they had gone t· Phrygia
19:26 but almost t· all Asia, this Paul
24: 5 among all the Jews t· the world,
26:20 and t· all the coast of Judæa,
Ro 1: 8 is spoken of t· the whole world.
9:17 might be declared t· all the earth.
2Co 8:18 is in the gospel t· all the churches;
Eph 3:21 church by Christ Jesus t· all ages,
1Pe 1: 1 to the strangers scattered t· Pontus,

throw See also OVERTHROW; THREW; THROWING; THROWN.
J'g 2: 2 ye shall t· down their altars:
6:25 t· down the altar of Baal that thy
2Sa 20:15 battered the wall, to t· it down.
2Ki 9:33 And he said, T· her down. So
Jer 1:10 and to destroy, and to t· down,
31:28 to t· down, and to destroy, and to
Eze 16:39 shall t· down thine eminent place,
Mic 5:11 and t· down all thy strong holds:
Mal 1: 4 They shall build, but I will t· down;

throwing
Nu 35:17 if he smite him with t· a stone,

thrown See also OVERTHROWN.
Ex 15: 1, 21 rider hath he t· into the sea.
J'g 6:32 because he hath t· down his altar.
2Sa 20:21 his head shall be t· to thee over
1Ki 19:10, 14 covenant, t· down thine altars,
Jer 31:40 nor t· down any more for ever.
33: 4 which are t· down by the mounts,
50:15 are fallen, her walls are t· down:
La 2: 2 he hath t· down in his wrath the
17 hath t· down, and hath not pitied:
Eze 29: 5 leave thee t· into the wilderness,
38:20 the mountains shall be t· down,
Na 1: 6 and the rocks are t· down by him.
M't 24: 2 another, that shall not be t· down.
M'r 13: 2 another, that shall not be t· down.
Lu 4:35 the devil had t· him in the midst,
21: 6 another, that shall not be t· down.
Re 18:21 that great city Babylon be t· down,

thrust See also THRUSTETH.
Ex 11: 1 he shall surely t· you out hence
12:39 because they were t· out of Egypt,
Nu 22:25 she t· herself unto the wall, and
25: 8 tent, and t· both of them through,
35:20 But if he t· him of hatred, or hurl
22 t· him suddenly without enmity,
De 13: 5 to t· thee out of the way which
10 to t· thee away from the Lord thy
15:17 t· it through his ear unto the door,
33:27 he shall t· out the enemy from
J'g 3:21 right thigh, and t· it into his belly:
6:38 t· the fleece together, and wringed
9:41 Zebul t· out Gaal and his brethren,
54 his young man t· him through,
11: 2 they t· out Jephthah, and said
1Sa 11: 2 I may t· out all your right eyes,
31: 4 and t· me through therewith;
4 come and t· me through,
2Sa 2:16 and t· his sword in his fellow's side;
18:14 and t· them through the heart of
23: 6 be all of them as thorns t· away,
1Ki 2:27 So Solomon t· out Abiathar from
2Ki 4:27 Gehazi came near to t· her away.
1Ch 10: 4 and t· me through therewith;
2Ch 26:20 and they t· him out from thence;
Ps 118:13 Thou hast t· sore at me that I
Isa 13:15 that is found shall be t· through:
14:19 are slain, t· through with a sword,
Jer 51: 4 that are t· through in her streets.
Eze 16:40 t· thee through with their swords.
34:21 ye have t· with side and with
46:18 to t· them out of their possession;
Joe 2: 8 Neither shall one t· another; they
Zec 13: 3 begat him shall t· him through
Lu 4:29 rose up, and t· him out of the city,
5: 3 would t· out a little from the land.
10:15 heaven, shall be t· down to hell.
13:28 of God, and you yourselves t· out.
Joh 20:25 nails, and t· my hand into his side,
27 thy hand, and t· it into my side:
Ac 7:27 his neighbour wrong t· him away,
39 not obey, but t· him from them,
16:24 t· them into the inner prison,
37 and now do they t· us out privily?
27:39 it were possible, to t· in the ship.
Heb 12:20 stoned, or t· through with a dart:

Re 14:15 T· in thy sickle, and reap: for
16 cloud t· in his sickle on the earth;
18 T· in thy sharp sickle, and gather
19 the angel t· in his sickle into the

thrusteth
Job 32:13 God t· him down, not man.

thumb See also THUMBS.
Ex 29:20 and upon the t· of their right hand,
Le 8:23 and upon the t· of his right hand,
14:14, 17, 25, 28 the t· of his right hand,

thumbs
Le 8:24 upon the t· of their right hands,
J'g 1: 6 cut off his t· and his great toes.
7 t· and their great toes cut off,

Thummim (*thum'-mim*)
Ex 28:30 of judgment the Urim and the T·;
Le 8: 8 breastplate the Urim and the T·.
De 33: 8 Let thy T· and thy Urim be with
Ezr 2:63 a priest with Urim and with T·.
Ne 7:65 up a priest with Urim and T·.

thunder See also THUNDERBOLTS; THUNDERED; THUNDERETH; THUNDERINGS; THUNDERS.
Ex 9:23 the Lord sent t· and hail, and the
29 and the t· shall cease, neither shall
1Sa 2:10 of heaven shall he t· upon them:
7:10 the Lord thundered with a great t·
12:17 Lord, and he shall send t· and rain;
18 the Lord sent t· and rain that day:
Job 26:14 but the t· of his power who can
28:26 a way for the lightning of the t·:
38:25 or a way for the lightning of t·;
39:19 hast thou clothed his neck with t·?
25 the t· of the captains, and the
40: 9 thou t· with a voice like him?
Ps 77:18 voice of thy t· was in the heaven:
81: 7 thee in the secret place of t·:
104: 7 voice of thy t· they hasted away.
Isa 29: 6 visited of the Lord of hosts with t·,
M'r 3:17 Boanerges,...The sons of t·:
Re 6: 1 I heard, as it were the noise of t·,
14: 2 waters, and as a voice of a great t·:

thunderbolts
Ps 78:48 the hail, and their flocks to hot t·.

thundered
1Sa 7:10 the Lord t· with a great thunder
2Sa 22:14 The Lord t· from heaven, and
Ps 18:13 The Lord also t· in the heavens,
Joh 12:29 and heard it, said that it t·:

thundereth
Job 37: 4 t· with the voice of his excellency;
5 God t· marvellously with his voice;
Ps 29: 3 the God of glory t·: the Lord is

thunderings
Ex 9:28 be no more mighty t· and hail;
20:18 And all the people saw the t·, and
Re 4: 5 lightnings and t· and voices:
8: 5 and there were voices, and t·, and
11:19 were lightnings, and voices, and t·,
19: 6 and as the voice of mighty t·,

thunders
Ex 9:33 t· and hail ceased, and the rain
34 and the hail and the t· were ceased,
19:16 that there were t· and lightnings,
Re 10: 3 cried, seven t· uttered their voices.
4 seven t· had uttered their voices,
4 things which the seven t· uttered,
16:18 were voices, and t·, and lightnings;

thus^A
Ge 2: 1 T· the heavens and the earth were
6:22 T· did Noah; according to all that
19:36 T· were both the daughters of Lot
20:16 with all other: t· she was reproved.
24:30 T· spake the man unto me; that
25:22 she said, If it be so, why am I t·?
34 t· Esau despised his birthright.
31: 8 If he said t·, The speckled shall
8 if he said t·, The ringstraked shall
9 T· God hath taken away the cattle of
40 T· I was; in the day the drought
41 T· have I been twenty years in
32: 4 T· shall ye speak unto my lord
4 Thy servant Jacob saith t·, I have
36: 8 T· dwelt Esau in mount Seir: Esau
37:35 T· his father wept for him.
42:25 the way: and t· did he unto them.
45: 9 T· saith thy son Joseph, God hath
Ex 3:14, 15 T· shalt thou say unto the
4:22 T· saith the Lord, Israel is my son,
5: 1 T· saith the Lord God of Israel,
10 T· saith Pharaoh, I will not give
15 dealest thou t· with thy servants?
8: 1, 20 T· saith the Lord, Let my
9: 1, 13 T· saith the Lord God of the
10: 3 T· saith the Lord God of the
11: 4 T· saith the Lord, About midnight
12:11 t· shall ye eat it; with your loins
50 T· did all the children of Israel; as
14:11 hast thou dealt t· with us, to carry
30 T· the Lord saved Israel that day out
19: 3 T· shalt thou say to the house of
20:22 T· thou shalt say unto the
26:17 t· shalt thou make for all the
24 t· shall it be for them both; they
29:35 t· shalt thou do unto Aaron, and to his
32:27 T· saith the Lord God of Israel,
36:22 t· did he make for all the boards
29 t· he did to both of them in both the
39:32 T· was all the work of the tabernacle
40:16 T· did Moses: according to all that
Le 15:31 T· shall ye separate the children of
16: 3 T· shall Aaron come into the holy

Nu 4:19 t· do unto them, that they may live,
49 t· were they numbered of him, as the
8: 7 t· shalt thou do unto them, to
14 T· shalt thou separate the Levites
26 T· shalt thou do unto the Levites
10:28 T· were the journeyings of the
11:15 if thou deal t· with me, kill me,
15:11 T· shall it be done for one bullock,
18:26 T· speak unto the Levites, and say
28 T· ye also shall offer an heave
20:14 T· saith thy brother Israel, Thou
21 T· Edom refused to give Israel
21:31 T· Israel dwelt in the land of the
22:16 T· saith Balak the son of Zippor,
23: 5 unto Balak, and t· thou shalt speak.
16 Go again unto Balak, and say t·.
32: 8 T· did your fathers, when I sent
De 7: 5 t· shall ye deal with them; ye shall
9:25 T· I fell down before the Lord forty
20:15 T· shalt thou do unto all the
29:24 the Lord done t· unto this land?
32: 6 Do ye t· requite the Lord, O
Jos 2: 4 said t·, There came men unto me,
6: 3 once. T· shalt thou do six days.
7:10 liest thou t· upon thy face?
13 for t· saith the Lord God of Israel,
20 Israel, and t· and t· have I done:
10:25 t· shall the Lord do to all your
16: 5 according to their families was t·:
21:13 T· they gave to the children of Aaron
42 them: t· were all these cities.
22:16 T· saith the whole congregation of
24: 2 T· saith the Lord God of Israel,
J'g 6: 8 T· saith the Lord God of Israel, I
8: 1 Why hast thou served us t·,
28 T· was Midian subdued before the
9:56 T· God rendered the wickedness of
11:15 T· saith Jephthah, Israel took not
33 T· the children of Ammon were
13:18 askest thou t· after my name,
18: 4 T·...dealeth Micah with me,
4 and t· dealeth Micah with me,
20:43 T· they inclosed the Benjamites
1Sa 2:27 T· saith the Lord, Did I plainly
9: 9 t· he spake, Come, and let us go to
10:18 T· saith the Lord God of Israel,
11: 9 T· shall ye say unto the men of
14: 9 If they say t· unto us, Tarry until
10 But if they say t·, Come up unto us;
15: 2 T· saith the Lord of hosts, I
18:25 T· shall ye say to David, The king
20: 7 If he say t·, It is well; thy servant
22 But if I say t· unto the young man,
25: 6 t· shall ye say to him that liveth in
26:18 doth my lord t· pursue after his
2Sa 6:22 I will yet be more vile than t·,
7: 5 T· saith the Lord, Shalt thou
8 T· saith the Lord of hosts, I took
11:25 T· shalt thou say unto Joab, Let
12: 7 T· saith the Lord God of Israel, I
11 T· saith the Lord, Behold, I will
31 t· did he unto all the cities of the
15:26 But if he t· say, I have no delight
16: 7 And t· said Shimei when he cursed,
17:15 T· and t· did Ahithophel counsel
15 and t· and t· have I counselled.
21 for t· hath Ahithophel counselled
18:14 Joab, I may not tarry t· with thee.
33 t· he said, O my son Absalom,
24:12 T· saith the Lord, I offer thee
1Ki 1:48 also t· said the king, Blessed be
2:30 T· saith the king, Come forth.
30 T· said Joab, and t· he answered
3:22 T· they spake before the king.
5:11 t· gave Solomon to Hiram year by
9: 8 the Lord done t· unto this land,
11:31 for t· saith the Lord, the God of
12:10 T· shalt thou speak unto this
10 t· shalt thou say unto them, My
24 T· saith the Lord, Ye shall not go
13: 2 O altar, altar, t· saith the Lord;
21 T· saith the Lord, Forasmuch as
14: 5 t·...shalt thou say unto her:
5 and t· shalt thou say unto her:
7 T· saith the Lord God of Israel,
16:12 T· did Zimri destroy all the house
17:14 For t· saith the Lord God of Israel,
20: 2 said unto him, T· saith Ben-hadad,
5 T· speaketh Ben-hadad, saying,
13 T· saith the Lord, Hast thou seen
14 T· saith the Lord, Even by the
28 T· saith the Lord, Because the
42 T· saith the Lord, Because thou
21:19 T· saith the Lord, Hast thou killed,
19 T· saith the Lord, In the place
22:11 T· saith the Lord, With these shalt
27 T· saith the king, Put this fellow
2Ki 1: 4 Now therefore t· saith the Lord,
6 T· saith the Lord, Is it not because
11 t· hath the king said, Come down
16 T· saith the Lord, Forasmuch as
2:21 T· saith the Lord, I have healed
3:16 T· saith the Lord, Make this valley
17 t· saith the Lord, Ye shall not see
4:43 t· saith the Lord, They shall eat.
5: 4 T· and t· said the maid that is of
7: 1 T· saith the Lord, To morrow
9: 3 T· saith the Lord, I have anointed
6 T· saith the Lord God of Israel,
12 he said, T· and t· spake he to me,
12 T· saith the Lord, I have anointed
18, 19 T· saith the king, Is it peace?
10:28 T· Jehu destroyed Baal out of
16:16 T· did Urijah the priest, according
18:19 T· saith the great king, the king
29 T· saith the king, Let not

2Ki 18:31 t' saith the king of Assyria, Make
19: 3 T' saith Hezekiah, This day is a
6 T' shall ye say to your master,
6 T' saith the Lord, Be not afraid of
10 T' shall ye speak to Hezekiah king
20 T' saith the Lord God of Israel,
32 t' saith the Lord concerning the
20: 1 T' saith the Lord, Set thine house
5 T' saith the Lord, the God of David
21:12 t' saith the Lord God of Israel,
22:15 T' saith the Lord God of Israel,
16 T' saith the Lord, Behold, I will
18 of the Lord, t' shall ye say to him,
18 T' saith the Lord God of Israel,
1Ch 15:28 T' all Israel brought up the ark of
17: 4 T' saith the Lord, Thou shalt not
7 t' shalt thou say unto my servant
7 T' saith the Lord of hosts, I took
18: 6, 13 T' the Lord preserved David
21:10 T' saith the Lord, I offer thee
11 T' saith the Lord, Choose thee
24: 4 Ithamar; and t' were they divided.
5 T' were they divided by lot, one sort
29:26 T' David the son of Jesse reigned
2Ch 4:18 T' Solomon made all these vessels
5: 1 T' all the work that Solomon made
7:11 T' Solomon finished the house of the
21 the Lord done t' unto this land,
10:10 T' shalt thou answer the people
10 t' shalt thou say unto them, My
11: 4 T' saith the Lord, Ye shall not go
12: 5 T' saith the Lord, Ye have forsaken
13:18 T' the children of Israel were brought
18:10 T' saith the Lord, With these thou
26 T' saith the king, Put this fellow
19: 9 T' shall ye do in the fear of the
20:15 T' saith the Lord unto you, Be not
21:12 T' saith the Lord God of David thy
24:11 T' they did day by day, and
20 T' saith God, Why transgress ye
22 T' Joash the king remembered not
31:20 t' did Hezekiah throughout all
32:10 T' saith Sennacherib king of
22 T' the Lord saved Hezekiah and
34:23 T' saith the Lord God of Israel,
24 T' saith the Lord, Behold, I will
26 T' saith the Lord God of Israel
36:23 T' saith Cyrus king of Persia, All
Ezr 1: 2 T' saith Cyrus king of Persia, The
5: 3 and said t' unto them, Who hath
7 unto him, wherein was written t';
9 and said unto them t', Who
11 t' they returned us answer, saying,
6: 2 therein was a record t' written:
Ne 5:13 even t' be he shaken out, and
13:18 Did not your fathers t', and did
30 T' cleansed I them from all strangers,
Es 1:18 T' shall there arise too much
2:13 t' came every maiden unto the
6: 9 T' shall it be done to the man
11 T' shall it be done unto the man
9: 5 T' the Jews smote all their enemies
Job 1: 5 hearts. T' did Job continually.
27:12 then are ye t' altogether vain?
Ps 38:14 T' I was as a man that heareth not,
63: 4 T' will I bless thee while I live:
73:15 If I say, I will speak t'; behold,
21 T' my heart was grieved, and I
106:20 T' they changed their glory into the
29 T' they provoked him to anger with
39 T' were they defiled with their own
128: 4 t' shall the man be blessed that
Isa 7: 7 T' saith the Lord God, It shall
8:11 spake t' to me with a strong hand,
10:24 t' saith the Lord God of hosts,
21: 6 t' hath the Lord said unto me, Go,
16 For t' hath the Lord said unto me,
22:15 T' saith the Lord God of hosts, Go,
24:13 When t' it shall be in the midst of
28:16 Therefore t' saith the Lord God,
29:22 t' saith the Lord, who redeemed
30:12 t' saith the Holy One of Israel,
15 t' saith the Lord God, the Holy One
31: 4 t' hath the Lord spoken unto me,
36: 4 T' saith the great king, the king of
14 T' saith the king, Let not Hezekiah
16 t' saith the king of Assyria, Make
37: 3 T' saith Hezekiah, This day is a
6 T' shall ye say unto your master,
6 T' saith the Lord, Be not afraid of
10 T' shall ye speak to Hezekiah king
21 T' saith the Lord God of Israel,
33 t' saith the Lord concerning the
38: 1 T' saith the Lord, Set thine house
5 T' saith the Lord, the God of David
42: 5 T' saith God the Lord, he that
43: 1 now t' saith the Lord that created
14 T' saith the Lord, your redeemer,
16 T' saith the Lord, which maketh a
44: 2 T' saith the Lord that made thee,
6 T' saith the Lord the King of Israel,
24 T' saith the Lord, thy redeemer,
45: 1 T' saith the Lord to his anointed,
11 T' saith the Lord, the Holy One of
14 T' saith the Lord, The labour of
18 For t' saith the Lord that created
47:15 T' shall they be unto thee with
48:17 T' saith the Lord, thy Redeemer,
49: 7 T' saith the Lord, the Redeemer of
8 T' saith the Lord, In an acceptable
22 T' saith the Lord God, Behold, I
25 t' saith the Lord, Even the captives
50: 1 T' saith the Lord, Where is the bill
51:22 T' saith thy Lord the Lord, and
52: 3 For t' saith the Lord, Ye have sold
4 t' saith the Lord God, My people

Isa 56: 1 T' saith the Lord, Keep ye
4 t' saith the Lord unto the eunuchs
57:15 For t' saith the high and lofty One
65: 8 T' saith the Lord, As the new wine
13 Therefore t' saith the Lord God,
66: 1 T' saith the Lord, The heaven is
12 For t' saith the Lord, Behold, I will
Jer 2: 2 T' saith the Lord; I remember
5 T' saith the Lord, What iniquity
4: 3 For t' saith the Lord to the men of
27 For t' hath the Lord said, The
5:13 them: t' shall it be done unto them.
14 t' saith the Lord God of hosts,
6: 6 For t' hath the Lord of hosts said,
9 T' saith the Lord of hosts, They
16 T' saith the Lord, Stand ye in the
21 Therefore t' saith the Lord, Behold,
22 T' saith the Lord, Behold, a people
7: 3 T' saith the Lord of hosts, the God
20 Therefore t' saith the Lord God;
21 T' saith the Lord of hosts, the God
8: 4 say unto them, T' saith the Lord;
9: 7, 15 t' saith the Lord of hosts,
17 T' saith the Lord of hosts, Consider
22 T' saith the Lord, Even the
23 T' saith the Lord, Let not the wise
10: 2 T' saith the Lord, Learn not the
11 T' shall ye say unto them, The
18 For t' saith the Lord, Behold, I
11: 3 T' saith the Lord God of Israel;
11 Therefore t' saith the Lord, Behold,
21 Therefore t' saith the Lord of the
22 t' saith the Lord of hosts, Behold,
12:14 T' saith the Lord against all mine
13: 1 T' saith the Lord unto me, Go and
9 T' saith the Lord, After this
12 T' saith the Lord God of Israel,
13 T' saith the Lord, Behold, I will
14:10 T' saith the Lord unto this people,
10 T' have they loved to wander,
15 t' saith the Lord concerning the
15:19 t' saith the Lord, If thou return,
16: 3 t' saith the Lord concerning the
5 T' saith the Lord, Enter not into the
9 t' saith the Lord of hosts, the God
17: 5 T' saith the Lord; Cursed be the
19 T' said the Lord unto me; Go and
21 T' saith the Lord; Take heed to
18:11 saying, T' saith the Lord; Behold,
13 Therefore t' saith the Lord; Ask ye
23 deal t' with them in the time of thine
19: 1 T' saith the Lord, Go and get a
3 T' saith the Lord of hosts, the God
11 them, T' saith the Lord of hosts;
12 T' will I do unto this place, saith
15 T' saith the Lord of hosts, the
20: 4 t' saith the Lord, Behold, I will
21: 3 them, T' shall ye say to Zedekiah:
4 T' saith the Lord God of Israel;
8 thou shalt say, T' saith the Lord;
12 house of David, t' saith the Lord;
22: 1 T' saith the Lord; Go down to the
3 T' saith the Lord; Execute ye
6 t' saith the Lord unto the king's
8 Lord done t' unto this great city?
11 For t' saith the Lord touching
18 t' saith the Lord concerning
30 T' saith the Lord, Write ye this
23: 2 t' saith the Lord God of Israel
15 Therefore t' saith the Lord of hosts
16 T' saith the Lord of hosts, Hearken
35 T' shall ye say every one to his
37 T' shalt thou say to the prophet,
38 therefore t' saith the Lord;
24: 5 T' saith the Lord, the God of
8 t' saith the Lord, So will I give
25: 8 t' saith the Lord of hosts; Because
15 t' saith the Lord God of Israel unto
27 T' saith the Lord of hosts, the God
28 T' saith the Lord of hosts; Ye shall
32 T' saith the Lord of hosts, Behold,
26: 2 T' saith the Lord; Stand in the
4 T' saith the Lord; If ye will not
18 T' saith the Lord of hosts; Zion
19 T' might we procure great evil
27: 2 T' saith the Lord to me; Make
4 T' saith the Lord of hosts, the God
4 T' shall ye say unto your masters;
16 T' saith the Lord; Hearken not to
19 For t' saith the Lord of hosts
21 t' saith the Lord of hosts, the God
28: 2 T' speaketh the Lord of hosts, the
11 T' saith the Lord; Even so will I
13 T' saith the Lord; Thou hast
14 t' saith the Lord of hosts, the God
16 t' saith the Lord; Behold, I will
29: 4 T' saith the Lord of hosts, the God
8 t' saith the Lord of hosts, the God
10 For t' saith the Lord, That after
16 that t' saith the Lord of the king
17 T' saith the Lord of hosts; Behold,
21 T' saith the Lord of hosts, the God
24 T' shalt thou also speak to Shemaiah
25 T' speaketh the Lord of hosts, the
31 T' saith the Lord concerning
32 Therefore t' saith the Lord; Behold,
30: 2 T' speaketh the Lord God of Israel,
5 t' saith the Lord; We have heard a
12 t' saith the Lord, Thy bruise is
18 T' saith the Lord; Behold, I will
31: 2 T' saith the Lord, The people
7 For t' saith the Lord; Sing with
15 T' saith the Lord; A voice was
16 T' saith the Lord; Refrain thy
18 heard Ephraim bemoaning himself t';
23 T' saith the Lord of hosts, the

Jer 31:35 T' saith the Lord, which giveth the
37 T' saith the Lord; If heaven above
32: 3 T' saith the Lord, Behold, I will
14 T' saith the Lord of hosts, the God
15 t' saith the Lord of hosts, the God
28 t' saith the Lord; Behold, I will
36 And now therefore t' saith the Lord,
42 t' saith the Lord; Like as I have
33: 2 T' saith the Lord the maker
4 For t' saith the Lord, the God of
10 T' saith the Lord; Again there
12 T' saith the Lord of hosts; Again
17 t' saith the Lord; David shall never;
20 T' saith the Lord; If ye can break
24 t' they have despised my people, that
25 T' saith the Lord; If my covenant
34: 2 T' saith the Lord, the God of Israel;
2 T' saith the Lord; Behold, I will
4 T' saith the Lord of thee, Thou
13 T' saith the Lord, the God of Israel;
17 t' saith the Lord; ye have not
35: 8 T' have we obeyed the voice of
13 T' saith the Lord of hosts, the
17 t' saith the Lord God of hosts, the
18 T' saith the Lord of hosts, the God
36:29 T' saith the Lord; Thou hast
30 t' saith the Lord of Jehoiakim king
37: 7 T' saith the Lord, the God of Israel;
7 T' shall ye say to the king of Judah,
9 T' saith the Lord; Deceive not
21 T' Jeremiah remained in the court of
38: 2 T' saith the Lord, He that
3 T' saith the Lord, This city shall
4 t' he weakeneth the hands of
17 T' saith the Lord, the God of
39:16 T' saith the Lord of hosts, the God
42: 9 T' saith the Lord, the God of Israel,
15 T' saith the Lord of hosts, the God
18 For t' saith the Lord of hosts, the
43: 7 t' came they even to Tahpanhes.
10 T' saith the Lord of hosts, the
44: 2 T' saith the Lord of hosts, the God
7 now t' saith the Lord, the God
11 t' saith the Lord of hosts, the God
25 T' saith the Lord of hosts, the God
30 T' saith the Lord; Behold, I will
45: 2 T' saith the Lord, the God of Israel,
4 T' shalt thou say unto him, The
4 Lord saith t'; Behold, that which
47: 2 T' saith the Lord; Behold, waters
48: 1 Moab t' saith the Lord of hosts,
40 t' saith the Lord; Behold, he shall
47 T' far is the judgment of Moab.
49: 1 t' saith the Lord; Hath Israel no
7 Edom, t' saith the Lord of hosts;
12 For t' saith the Lord; Behold, they
28 t' saith the Lord; Arise ye, go up to
35 T' saith the Lord of hosts; Behold,
50:18 t' saith the Lord of hosts, the God
33 T' saith the Lord of hosts; The
51: 1 T' saith the Lord; Behold, I will
4 T' the slain shall fall in the land of
33 t' saith the Lord of hosts, the God
36 t' saith the Lord; Behold, I will
58 T' saith the Lord of hosts; The
64 T' shall Babylon sink, and shall
64 T' far are the words of Jeremiah.
52:27 T' Judah was carried away captive
Eze 1:11 T' were their faces: and their wings
2: 4 unto them, T' saith the Lord God.
3:11 T' saith the Lord God; whether
27 T' saith the Lord God; He that
4:13 t' shall the children of Israel eat
5: 5 T' saith the Lord God; This is
7 t' saith the Lord God; Because ye
8 t' saith the Lord God; Behold, I,
13 T' shall mine anger be accomplished,
6: 3 T' saith the Lord God to the
11 T' saith the Lord God; Smite with
12 t' will I accomplish my fury upon
7: 2 t' saith the Lord God unto the
5 T' saith the Lord God; An evil, an
11: 5 unto me, Speak; T' saith the Lord;
5 T' have ye said, O house of Israel:
7 Therefore t' saith the Lord God;
16 T' saith the Lord God; Although I
17 T' saith the Lord God; I will even
12:10 T' saith the Lord God; This
19 T' saith the Lord God of the
23 T' saith the Lord God; I will make
28 T' saith the Lord God; There shall
13: 3 T' saith the Lord God; Woe unto
8, 13 Therefore t' saith the Lord God;
15 T' will I accomplish my wrath upon
18 T' saith the Lord God; Woe to the
20 Wherefore t' saith the Lord God;
14: 4 T' saith the Lord God; Every man
6 T' saith the Lord God; Repent, and
15: 6 Therefore t' saith the Lord God; As
16: 3 say, T' saith the Lord God unto
13 T' wast thou decked with gold and
19 and t' it was, saith the Lord God.
36 T' saith the Lord God; Because
59 For t' saith the Lord God; I will
17: 3 T' saith the Lord God; A great
9 T' saith the Lord God; Shall it
19 Therefore t' saith the Lord God; As
22 T' saith the Lord God; I will also
20: 3 T' saith the Lord God; Are ye
5 T' saith the Lord God; In the day
27 T' saith the Lord God; Yet in this
30 T' saith the Lord God; Are ye
39 t' saith the Lord God; Go ye, serve
47 T' saith the Lord God; Behold, I
21: 3 T' saith the Lord; Behold, I am
9 T' saith the Lord; Say, A sword, a

Eze 21: 24 t' saith the Lord God; Because ye
26 T' saith the Lord God; Remove the
28 T' saith the Lord God concerning
22: 3 T' saith the Lord God, The city
19 t' saith the Lord God; Because ye
28 T' saith the Lord God, when the
23: 4 T' were their names; Samaria is
7 T' she committed her whoredoms
21 T' thou calledst to remembrance the
22 t' saith the Lord God; Behold, I
27 T' will I make thy lewdness to cease
28 t' saith the Lord God; Behold, I
32 T' saith the Lord God; Thou shalt
35 Therefore t' saith the Lord God;
39 t' have they done in the midst of
46 t' saith the Lord God; I will bring
48 T' will I cause lewdness to cease out
24: 3 T' saith the Lord God; Set on a
6 Wherefore t' saith the Lord God;
9 Therefore t' saith the Lord God;
21 T' saith the Lord God; Behold, I
24 T' Ezekiel is unto you a sign according
25: 3 T' saith the Lord God; Because
6 For t' saith the Lord God; Because
8, 12 T' saith the Lord God; Because
13 t' saith the Lord God; I will also
15 T' saith the Lord God; Because the
16 t' saith the Lord God; Behold, I
26: 3 t' saith the Lord God; Behold, I am
7 For t' saith the Lord God; Behold,
15 T' saith the Lord God to Tyrus;
19 t' saith the Lord God; When I shall
27: 3 T' saith the Lord God; O Tyrus,
28: 2 T' saith the Lord God; Because
6 Therefore t' saith the Lord God;
12 T' saith the Lord God; Thou
22 T' saith the Lord God; Behold, I
25 T' saith the Lord God; When I
29: 3 T' saith the Lord God; Behold, I
8 Therefore t' saith the Lord God;
13 Yet t' saith the Lord God; At the
19 Therefore t' saith the Lord God;
30: 2 T' saith the Lord God; Howl ye,
6 T' saith the Lord; They also that
10, 13 T' saith the Lord God; I will
19 T' will I execute judgments in Egypt:
22 Therefore t' saith the Lord God;
31: 7 T' was he fair in his greatness, in the
10 Therefore t' saith the Lord God;
15 T' saith the Lord God; In the day
18 To whom art thou t' like in glory
32: 3 T' saith the Lord God; I will
11 For t' saith the Lord God; The
33: 10 T' ye speak, saying, If our
25 T' saith the Lord God; Ye eat
27 Say thou t' unto them,
27 T' saith the Lord God; As I live,
34: 2 T' saith the Lord God unto the
10 T' saith the Lord God; Behold, I
11, 17 t' saith the Lord God; Behold,
20 t' saith the Lord God unto them;
30 T' shall they know that I the Lord
35: 3 T' saith the Lord God; Behold, O
7 T' will I make mount Seir most
13 T' with your mouth ye have boasted
14 T' saith the Lord God; When the
36: 2, 3 T' saith the Lord God; Because
4 T' saith the Lord God to the
5 Therefore t' saith the Lord God;
6 T' saith the Lord God; Behold, I
7 t' saith the Lord God; I have lifted
13 T' saith the Lord God; Because
22 T' saith the Lord God; I do not
33 T' saith the Lord God; In the day
37 T' saith the Lord God; I will yet
37: 5 T' saith the Lord God unto these
12, 19, 21 T' saith the Lord God;
38: 3 T' saith the Lord God; Behold, I
10 T' saith the Lord God; It shall
14 T' saith the Lord God; In that day
17 T' saith the Lord God; Art thou he
23 T' will I magnify myself, and sanctify
39: 1 T' saith the Lord God; Behold, I
16 T' shall they cleanse the land.
17 t' saith the Lord God; Speak unto
20 T' ye shall be filled at my table with
25 t' saith the Lord God; Now will I
43: 18 t' saith the Lord God; These are
20 t' shalt thou cleanse and purge it.
44: 6 T' saith the Lord God; O ye house
9 T' saith the Lord God; No stranger,
45: 9 T' saith the Lord God; Let it
18 T' saith the Lord God; In the first
46: 1 T' saith the Lord God; The gate of
15 T' shall they prepare the lamb, and
16 T' saith the Lord God; If the
47: 13 T' saith the Lord God; This shall
Da 1: 16 T' Melzar took away the portion of
2: 24 said t' unto him; Destroy not the
25 said t' unto him; I have found a
4: 10 T' were the visions of mine head in
14 He cried aloud, and said t', Hew
6: 6 and said t' unto him, King Darius,
7: 5 they said t' unto it, Arise, devour
23 T' he said, The fourth beast shall
11: 17 upright ones with him; t' shall he do:
39 T' shall he do in the most strong holds
Ho 10: 4 t' judgment springeth up as hemlock
Am 1: 3, 6, 9, 11, 13 T' saith the Lord; For
2: 1, 4, 6 T' saith the Lord; For three
11 Is it not even t', O ye children of
3: 11 Therefore t' saith the Lord God;
12 T' saith the Lord; As the shepherd
4: 12 Therefore t' will I do unto thee, O
5: 3 t' saith the Lord God; The city that
4 t' saith the Lord unto the house of
Am 5: 16 the Lord, saith t'; Wailing shall be
7: 1, 4 T' hath the Lord God shewed
7 T' he shewed me: and, behold, the
11 For t' Amos saith, Jeroboam shall
17 t' saith the Lord; Thy wife shall
8: 1 T' hath the Lord God shewed unto
Ob 1 T' saith the Lord God concerning
Mic 2: 3 t' saith the Lord; Behold, against
3: 5 T' saith the Lord concerning the
5: 6 t' shall he deliver us from the
Na 1: 12 T' saith the Lord; Though they
12 yet t' shall they be cut down,
Zec 1: 3, 4 T' saith the Lord of hosts;
14 T' saith the Lord of hosts; I am
16 Therefore t' saith the Lord; I am
17 T' saith the Lord of hosts; My
2: 8 For t' saith the Lord of hosts; After
3: 7 T' saith the Lord of hosts; If thou
6: 12 T' speaketh the Lord of hosts,
7: 9 T' speaketh the Lord of hosts,
14 T' the land was desolate after them,
8: 2 T' saith the Lord of hosts; I was
3 T' saith the Lord; I am returned
4 T' saith the Lord of hosts; There
6 T' saith the Lord of hosts; If it be
7 T' saith the Lord of hosts; Behold,
9 T' saith the Lord of hosts; Let
14 For t' saith the Lord of hosts; As I
19 T' saith the Lord of hosts; The fast
20 T' saith the Lord of hosts; It shall
23 T' saith the Lord of hosts; In those
11: 4 T' saith the Lord my God; Feed
M't 2: 5 for t' it is written by the prophet,
3: 15 for t' it becometh us to fulfil all
15: 6 T' have ye...the commandment
26: 54 be fulfilled, that t' it must be?
M'r 2: 7 this man t' speak blasphemies?
Lu 1: 25 T' hath the Lord dealt with me in
2: 48 Son, why hast thou t' dealt with us?
9: 34 While he t' spake, there came a
11: 45 t' saying thou reproachest us also.
17: 30 Even t' shall it be in the day
18: 11 stood and prayed t' with himself,
19: 28 when he had t' spoken, he went
31 t' shall ye say unto him, Because
22: 51 answered and said, Suffer ye t' far.
23: 46 and having said t', he gave up the
24: 36 And as they t' spake, Jesus himself
40 when he had t' spoken, he shewed
46 said unto them, T' it is written,
46 t' it behoved Christ to suffer,
Joh 4: 6 with his journey, sat t' on the well:
9: 6 When he had t' spoken, he spat on
11: 43 when he t' had spoken, he cried
48 If we let him t' alone, all men will
13: 21 When Jesus had t' said, he was
18: 22 when he had t' spoken, one of the
20: 14 when she had t' said, she turned
Ac 19: 41 And when he had t' spoken, he
20: 36 when he had t' spoken, he kneeled
21: 11 T' saith the Holy Ghost, So shall
26: 24 And as he t' spake for himself,
30 when he had t' spoken, the king
27: 35 when he had t' spoken, he took
Ro 9: 20 it, Why hast thou made me t'?
1Co 14: 25 t' are the secrets of his heart made
2Co 1: 17 When I therefore was t' minded,
5: 14 because we t' judge, that if one died
Ph'p 3: 15 as many as be perfect, be t' minded:
Heb 6: 9 salvation, though we t' speak.
9: 6 when these things were t' ordained,
Re 9: 17 t' I saw the horses in the vision,
16: 5 be, because thou hast judged t'.
18: 21 T' with violence shall that great

Thyatira (*thi-a-ti'-rah*)
Ac 16: 14 a seller of purple, of the city of T',
Re 1: 11 and unto T', and unto Sardis, and
2: 18 the angel of the church in T' write;
24 you I say, and unto the rest in T',

thyine (*thi'-ine*)
Re 18: 12 silk, and scarlet, and all t' wood,

thyself ^
Ge 13: 9 separate t', I pray thee, from me: if
16: 9 and submit t' under her hands.
33: 9 brother; keep that thou hast unto t'.
Ex 9: 17 yet exaltest thou t' against my people,
10: 3 thou refuse to humble t' before me
28 take heed to t', see my face no more;
18: 14 why sittest thou t' alone, and all the
18 thou art not able to perform it t' alone.
22 so shall it be easier for t', and they
20: 5 Thou shalt not bow down t' to them,
34: 2 present t' there to me in the top of the
12 Take heed to t', lest thou make a
Le 9: 7 and make an atonement for t', and for
18: 20 neighbour's wife, to defile t' with her.
23 with any beast to defile t' therewith:
19: 18 thou shalt love thy neighbour as t':
34 you, and thou shalt love him as t';
Nu 11: 17 thee, that thou bear it not t' alone.
16: 13 thou make t' altogether a prince over
De 4: 9 Only take heed to t', and keep thy
5: 9 shalt not bow down t' unto them, nor
9: 1 nations greater and mightier than t',
12: 13 Take heed to t' that thou offer not thy
19 Take heed to t' that thou forsake not
30 Take heed to t' that thou be not
20: 14 spoil thereof, shalt thou take unto t';
22: 1 go astray, and hide t' from them:
3 do likewise: thou mayest not hide t'.
4 by the way, and hide t' from them:
12 vesture, wherewith thou coverest t'.
De 23: 13 when thou wilt ease t' abroad, thou
28: 40 thou shalt not anoint t' with the oil;
Jos 17: 15 and cut down for t' there in the land
Ru 3: 3 Wash t' therefore, and anoint thee,
3 make not t' known unto the man,
4: 6 redeem thou my right to t'; for I
1Sa 19: 2 thee, take heed to t' until the morning,
2 abide in a secret place, and hide t':
20: 8 there be in me iniquity, slay me t';
19 to the place where thou didst hide t'
25: 26 from avenging t' with thine own hand,
2Sa 5: 24 trees, that then thou shalt bestir t':
7: 24 hast confirmed to t' thy people Israel
13: 5 down on thy bed, and make t' sick:
14: 2 I pray thee, feign t' to be a mourner,
2 and anoint not t' with oil, but be as a
18: 13 and thou t' wouldest have set
13 wouldest have set t' against me.
22: 26 merciful thou wilt shew t' merciful,
26 upright man thou wilt shew t' upright.
27 With the pure thou wilt shew t' pure;
27 froward thou wilt shew t' unsavoury.
1Ki 2: 2 strong therefore, and shew t' a man;
3 and whithersoever thou turnest t':
3: 11 and hast not asked for t' long life;
11 neither hast asked riches for t', nor
11 t' understanding to discern judgment;
13: 7 Come home with me, and refresh t',
14: 2 and disguise t', that thou be not known
6 why feignest thou t' to be another?
17: 3 hide t' by the brook Cherith, that is
18: 1 year, saying, Go, shew t' unto Ahab;
20: 22 Go, strengthen t', and mark, and see
40 thy judgment be; t' hast decided it.
21: 20 sold t' to work evil in the sight of the
22: 25 go into an inner chamber to hide t'.
2Ki 22: 19 thou hast humbled t' before the Lord,
1Ch 21: 12 advise t' what word I shall bring
2Ch 1: 11 asked wisdom and knowledge for t',
18: 24 go into an inner chamber to hide t'.
20: 37 thou hast joined t' with Ahaziah,
21: 13 house, which were better than t':
34: 27 and thou didst humble t' before God,
27 and humbledst t' before me, and
Es 4: 13 Think not with t' that thou shalt
Job 8: 8 prepare t' to the search of their
10: 16 thou shewest t' marvellous upon me.
15: 8 dost thou restrain wisdom to t'?
22: 21 Acquaint now t' with him, and be
30: 21 hand thou opposest t' against me.
40: 10 Deck t' now with majesty and
10 and array t' with glory and beauty.
Ps 7: 6 lift up t' because of the rage of mine
10: 1 why hidest thou t' in times of trouble?
18: 25 merciful thou wilt shew t' merciful;
25 man thou wilt shew t' upright;
26 With the pure thou wilt shew t' pure;
26 froward thou wilt shew t' froward.
35: 23 Stir up t', and awake to my judgment,
37: 1 Fret not t' because of evildoers,
4 Delight t' also in the Lord; and he
7 fret not t' because of him who
8 fret not t' in any wise to do evil.
49: 18 thee, when thou doest well to t'.
50: 21 I was altogether such an one as t':
52: 1 Why boastest thou t' in mischief, O
55: 1 and hide not t' from my supplication.
60: 1 displeased; O turn t' to us again.
80: 15 branch that thou madest strong for t'.
17 man whom thou madest strong for t'.
85: 3 turned t' from the fierceness of thine
89: 46 long, Lord? wilt thou hide t' forever?
94: 1 whom vengeance belongeth, shew t'.
2 Lift up t', thou judge of the earth:
104: 2 Who coverest t' with light as with a
Pr 6: 3 Do this now, my son, and deliver t',
3 humble t', and make sure thy friend.
5 Deliver t' as a roe from the hand of
9: 12 thou be wise, thou shalt be wise for t':
24: 19 Fret not t' because of evil men,
27 and make it fit for t' in the field;
25: 6 Put not forth t' in the presence of the
27: 1 Boast not t' of to morrow; for thou
30: 32 hast done foolishly in lifting up t',
Ec 7: 16 over much; neither make t' over wise:
16 wise: why shouldest thou destroy t'?
22 thou t' likewise hast cursed others.
Isa 26: 20 hide t' as it were for a little moment,
33: 3 at the lifting up of t' the nations
45: 15 Verily thou art a God that hidest t',
52: 2 Shake t' from the dust; arise, and sit
2 loose t' from the bands of thy neck,
57: 8 hast discovered t' to another than me,
9 off, and didst debase t' even unto hell.
58: 7 thou hide not t' from thine own flesh?
14 Then shalt thou delight t' in the Lord;
63: 14 people, to make t' a glorious name.
64: 12 Wilt thou refrain t' for these things,
65: 5 say, Stand by t', come not near to me;
Jer 2: 17 Hast thou not procured this unto t',
4: 30 Though thou clothest t' with crimson,
30 in vain shalt thou make t' fair;
6: 26 sackcloth, and wallow t' in ashes:
17: 4 And thou, even t', shalt discontinue
20: 4 I will make thee a terror to t', and to
22: 15 because thou closest t' in cedar?
32: 8 the redemption is thine; buy it for t'.
45: 5 And seekest thou great things for t'?
46: 19 Egypt, furnish t' to go into captivity:
47: 5 their valley: how long wilt thou cut t'?
6 put up t' into thy scabbard, rest, and
La 2: 18 give t' no rest; let not the apple of
3: 44 Thou hast covered t' with a cloud,
4: 21 be drunken, and shalt make t' naked.
Eze 3: 24 me, Go, shut t' within thine house.
16: 17 thee, and madest to t' images of men,

Eze 22: 4 defiled *t'* in thine idols which thou
16 thou shalt take thine inheritance in *t'*
23: 40 for whom thou didst wash *t'*,
40 eyes, and deckedst *t'* with ornaments,
31: 10 thou hast lifted up *t'* in height, and
38: 7 and prepare for *t'*, thou, and all thy
Da 5: 17 Let thy gifts be to *t'*, and give thy
23 hast lifted up *t'* against the Lord of
10: 12 and to chasten *t'* before thy God, thy
Hos 13: 9 O Israel, thou hast destroyed *t'*; but
Ob 4 Though thou exalt *t'* as the eagle,
Mic 1: 10 house of Aphrah roll *t'* in the dust.
5: 1 Now gather *t'* in troops, O daughter
Na 3: 15 make *t'* many as the cankerworm,
15 make *t'* many as the locusts.
Zec 2: 7 Deliver *t'*, O Zion, that dwellest with
M't 4: 6 be the Son of God, cast *t'* down:
5: 33 Thou shalt not forswear *t'*, but shalt
8: 4 shew *t'* to the priest, and offer the
19: 19 Thou shalt love thy neighbour as *t'*.
22: 39 Thou shalt love thy neighbour as *t'*.
27: 40 buildest it in three days, save *t'*.
M'r 1: 44 shew *t'* to the priest, and offer for
12: 31 Thou shalt love thy neighbour as *t'*.
15: 30 Save *t'*, and come down from the
Lu 4: 9 of God, cast *t'* down from hence:
23 me this proverb, Physician, heal *t'*:
5: 14 but go, and shew *t'* to the priest,
6: 42 when thou *t'* beholdest not the beam
7: 6 unto him, Lord, trouble not *t'*: for
10: 27 thy mind; and thy neighbour as *t'*.
17: 8 and gird *t'*, and serve me, till I have
23: 37 be the king of the Jews, save *t'*.
39 If thou be Christ, save *t'* and us.
Joh 1: 22 sent us. What sayest thou of *t'*?
7: 4 these things, shew *t'* to the world.
8: 13 him, Thou bearest record of *t'*;
53 are dead: whom makest thou *t'*?
10: 33 thou, being a man, makest *t'* God.
14: 22 that thou wilt manifest *t'* unto us,
18: 34 Sayest thou this thing of *t'*, or did
21: 18 thou wast young, thou girdedst *t'*,
Ac 8: 29 Go near, and join *t'* to this chariot.
12: 8 him, Gird *t'*, and bind on thy sandals.
16: 28 Do *t'* no harm: for we are all here.
21: 24 take, and purify *t'* with them,
24 that thou *t'* also walkest orderly,
24: 8 *t'* mayest take knowledge of all
26: 1 Thou art permitted to speak for *t'*.
24 a loud voice, Paul, thou art beside *t'*;
Ro 2: 1 another, thou condemnest *t'*;
5 treasurest up unto *t'* wrath against
19 thou *t'* art a guide of the blind,
21 another, teachest thou not *t'*?
13: 9 Thou shalt love thy neighbour as *t'*.
14: 22 thou faith? have it to *t'* before God.
Ga 5: 14 Thou shalt love thy neighbour as *t'*.
6: 1 considering *t'*, lest thou also be
1Ti 3: 15 to behave *t'* in the house of God,
4: 7 exercise *t'* rather unto godliness.
15 these things; give *t'* wholly to them;
16 Take heed unto *t'*, and unto the
16 doing this thou shalt both save *t'*,
5: 22 of other men's sins: keep *t'* pure.
6: 5 godliness: from such withdraw *t'*.
2Ti 2: 15 Study to shew *t'* approved unto
Tit 2: 7 shewing *t'* a pattern of good works:
Jas 2: 8 Thou shalt love thy neighbour as *t'*,

Tiberias (*ti-be'-re-as*)
Joh 6: 1 of Galilee, which is the sea of *T'*.
23 there came other boats from *T'*
21: 1 to the disciples at the sea of *T'*;

Tiberius (*ti-be'-re-us*) See also CÆSAR.
Lu 3: 1 year of the reign of *T'* Cæsar,

Tibhath (*tib'-hath*)
1Ch 18: 8 Likewise from *T'*, and from Chun,

Tibni (*tib'-ni*)
1Ki 16: 21 the people followed *T'* the son of
22 people that followed *T'* the son of
22 so *T'* died, and Omri reigned.

Tidal (*ti'-dal*)
Ge 14: 1 of Elam, and *T'* king of nations;
9 Elam, and with *T'* king of nations,

tide See EVENINGTIDE; EVENTIDE; NOONTIDE.

tidings
Ge 29: 13 when Laban heard the *t'* of Jacob
Ex 33: 4 when the people heard these evil *t'*,
1Sa 4: 19 heard the *t'* that the ark of God
11: 4 and told the *t'* in the ears of the
5 him the *t'* of the men of Jabesh.
6 upon Saul when he heard those *t'*,
27: 11 nor woman alive, to bring *t'* to Gath,
2Sa 4: 4 five years old when the *t'* came
10 thinking to have brought good *t'*,
10 have given him a reward for his *t'*:
13: 30 that *t'* came to David, saying,
18: 19 me now run, and bear the king *t'*,
20 Thou shalt not bear *t'* this day,
20 but thou shalt bear *t'* another day:
20 but this day thou shalt bear no *t'*,
22 seeing that thou hast no *t'* ready?
25 be alone, there is *t'* in his mouth.
26 the king said, He also bringeth *t'*.
27 man, and cometh with good *t'*.
31 Cushi said, *T'*, my lord the king:
1Ki 1: 42 valiant man, and bringest good *t'*.
2: 28 Then *t'* came to Joab: for Joab
14: 6 for I am sent to thee with heavy *t'*.
2Ki 7: 9 this day is a day of good *t'*, and we
1Ch 10: 9 to carry *t'* unto their idols, and to
Ps 112: 7 He shall not be afraid of evil *t'*:
Isa 40: 9 O Zion, that bringest good *t'*, get
9 O Jerusalem, that bringest good *t'*,
Isa 41: 27 one that bringeth good *t'*.
52: 7 feet of him that bringeth good *t'*,
7 that bringeth good *t'* of good, that
61: 1 to preach good *t'* unto the meek;
Jer 20: 15 man who brought *t'* to my father,
37: 5 Jerusalem heard *t'* of them,
49: 23 Arpad: for they have heard evil *t'*:
Eze 21: 7 that thou shalt answer, For the *t'*;
Da 11: 44 But *t'* out of the east and out of the
Na 1: 15 feet of him that bringeth good *t'*,
Lu 1: 19 thee, and to shew thee these glad *t'*.
2: 10 I bring you good *t'* of great joy,
8: 1 shewing the glad *t'* of the kingdom
Ac 11: 22 *t'* of these things came unto the
13: 32 And we declare unto you glad *t'*,
21: 31 *t'* came unto the chief captain of
Ro 10: 15 and bring glad *t'* of good things!
1Th 3: 6 and brought us good *t'* of your faith

tie See also TIED.
1Sa 6: 7 no yoke, and *t'* the kine to the cart,
Pr 6: 21 and *t'* them about thy neck.

tied
Ex 39: 31 And they *t'* unto it a lace of blue,
1Sa 6: 10 milch kine, and *t'* them to the cart,
2Ki 7: 10 but horses *t'*, and asses *t'*, and the
M't 21: 2 straightway ye shall find an ass *t'*,
M'r 11: 2 ye shall find a colt *t'*, whereon
4 and found the colt *t'* by the door
Lu 19: 30 your entering ye shall find a colt *t'*,

Tiglath-pileser (*tig''-lath-pi-le'-zur*) See also TILGATH-PILNESER.
2Ki 15: 29 Israel came *T'* king of Assyria,
16: 7 So Ahaz sent messengers to *T'*
10 Ahaz went to Damascus to meet *T'*

Tikvah (*tik'-vah*) See also TIKVATH.
2Ki 22: 14 wife of Shallum the son of *T'*,
Ezr 10: 15 and Jahaziah the son of *T'* were

Tikvath (*tik'-vath*) See also TIKVAH.
2Ch 34: 22 the wife of Shallum the son of *T'*,

tile See also TILING.
Eze 4: 1 son of man, take thee a *t'*, and lay it

Tilgath-pilneser (*til''-gath-pil-ne'-zur*) See also TIGLATH-PILESER.
1Ch 5: 6 whom *T'* king of Assyria carried
26 and the spirit of *T'* king of Assyria,
2Ch 28: 20 *T'* king of Assyria came unto him,

tiling
Lu 5: 19 let him down through the *t'* with

till^ See also TILLED; TILLER; TILLEST; TILLETH; UNTIL.
Ge 2: 5 was not a man to *t'* the ground.
3: 19 *t'* thou return unto the ground;
23 to *t'* the ground from whence he
19: 22 I cannot do any thing *t'* thou be
29: 8 *t'* they roll the stone from the well's
38: 11 house, *t'* Shelah my son be grown:
17 give me a pledge, *t'* thou send it?
Ex 15: 16 *t'* thy people pass over, O Lord,
16 *t'* the people pass over, which thou
16: 19 no man leave of it *t'* the morning.
24 And they laid it up *t'* the morning,
34: 33 *t'* Moses had done speaking with them,
40: 37 *t'* the day that it was taken up.
Nu 12: 15 *t'* Miriam was brought in again.
De 17: 5 stone them with stones, *t'* they die.
28: 45 thee, *t'* thou be destroyed;
Jos 5: 6 *t'* all the people that were men of
8 in the camp, *t'* they were whole.
8: 6 *t'* we have drawn them from the
10: 20 slaughter, *t'* they were consumed,
J'g 3: 25 they tarried *t'* they were ashamed:
6: 4 *t'* thou come unto Gaza, and left no
11: 33 even *t'* thou come to Minnith,
16: 3 Samson lay *t'* midnight, and arose
19: 26 where her lord was, *t'* it was light.
21: 2 and abode there *t'* even before God,
Ru 1: 13 tarry for them *t'* they were grown?
1Sa 10: 8 shalt thou tarry, *t'* I come to thee,
16: 11 will not sit down *t'* he come hither.
22: 3 *t'* I know what God will do for me.
2Sa 3: 35 or ought else, *t'* the sun be down.
9: 10 servants, shall *t'* the land for him,
1Ki 14: 10 taketh away dung, *t'* it be all gone.
18: 28 *t'* the blood gushed out upon them.
2Ki 2: 17 they urged him *t'* he was ashamed,
4: 20 he sat on her knees *t'* noon, and
7: 9 if we tarry *t'* the morning light,
10: 17 Samaria, *t'* he had destroyed him,
21: 16 *t'* he had filled Jerusalem from one
2Ch 26: 15 helped, *t'* he was strong.
34 help them, *t'* the work was ended,
36: 16 his people, *t'* there was no remedy.
Ezr 2: 63 *t'* there stood up a priest with Urim
5: 5 *t'* the matter came to Darius:
9: 14 us *t'* thou hadst consumed us,
Ne 2: 7 me over *t'* I come into Judah;
4: 11 *t'* we come in the midst among
21 the morning *t'* the stars appeared.
7: 65 *t'* there stood up a priest with Urim
13: 19 not be opened *t'* after the sabbath:
Job 7: 19 alone *t'* I swallow down my spittle?
8: 21 *T'* he fill thy mouth with laughing,
14: 6 *t'* he shall accomplish, as an
12 *t'* the heavens be no more, they
14 will I wait, *t'* my change comes.
27: 5 *t'* I die I will not remove mine
32: 4 Elihu had waited *t'* Job had spoken,
Ps 10: 15 out his wickedness *t'* thou find none.
18: 37 turn again *t'* they were consumed.
68: 30 *t'* every one submit himself with
Pr 7: 23 *T'* a dart strike through his liver;
29: 11 a wise man keepeth it in *t'* afterwards.
Ec 2: 3 *t'* I might see what was that good
Ca 2: 7 nor awake my love, *t'* he please.
3: 5 nor awake my love, *t'* he please.
Isa 5: 8 field to field, *t'* there be no place,
11 until night, *t'* wine inflame them!
22: 14 not be purged from you *t'* ye die,
23: 13 *t'* the Assyrian founded it for them
30: 17 *t'* ye be left as a beacon upon the top
38: 13 I reckoned *t'* morning, that, as a
42: 4 *t'* he have set judgment in the
62: 7 give him no rest, *t'* he establish,
7 *t'* he make Jerusalem a praise in
Jer 7: 32 bury in Tophet, *t'* there be no place.
9: 16 them, *t'* I have consumed them.
19: 11 in Tophet, *t'* there be no place to bury.
23: 20 *t'* he have performed the thoughts
24: 10 *t'* they be consumed from off the
27: 11 they shall *t'* it, and dwell therein.
49: 37 them, *t'* I have consumed them:
52: 3 *t'* he had cast them out from his
11 in prison *t'* the day of his death.
La 3: 50 *T'* the Lord look down, and behold
Eze 4: 8 *t'* thou hast ended the days of thy
14 even *t'* now have I not eaten of that
24: 13 *t'* I have caused my fury to rest
28: 15 *t'* iniquity was found in thee.
34: 21 *t'* ye have scattered them abroad;
39: 15 *t'* the buriers have buried it in the
19 And ye shall eat fat *t'* ye be full, and
19 and drink blood *t'* ye be drunken, of
47: 20 *t'* a man come over against
Da 2: 9 before me, *t'* the time be changed:
34 sawest *t'* that a stone was cut out
4: 23 field, *t'* seven times pass over him;
25 *t'* thou know that the most High
33 *t'* his hairs were grown like eagles'
5: 21 *t'* he knew that the most high God
6: 14 laboured *t'* the going down of the
7: 4 *t'* the wings thereof were plucked,
9 *t'* the thrones were cast down,
11 beheld even *t'* the beast was slain,
10: 3 *t'* three whole weeks were fulfilled.
11: 36 *t'* the indignation be accomplished:
12: 9 and sealed *t'* the time of the end.
13 But go thou thy way *t'* the end be:
Ho 5: 15 *t'* they acknowledge their offence,
10: 12 *t'* he come and rain righteousness
Ob 5 not have stolen *t'* they had enough?
Jon 4: 5 *t'* he might see what would
Zep 3: 3 gnaw not the bones *t'* the morrow.
M't 1: 25 not *t'* she had brought forth her
2: 9 *t'* it came and stood over where the
5: 18 *T'* heaven and earth pass, one jot
18 pass from the law, *t'* all be fulfilled.
26 *t'* thou hast paid the uttermost
10: 11 and there abide *t'* ye go thence.
23 Israel, *t'* the Son of man be come.
12: 20 *t'* he send forth judgment unto
13: 33 meal, *t'* the whole was leavened.
16: 28 *t'* they see the Son of man coming
18: 21 and I forgive him? *t'* seven times?
30 prison, *t'* he should pay the debt.
34 *t'* he should pay all that was due
22: 44 *t'* I make thine enemies thy
23: 39 *t'* ye shall say, Blessed is he that
24: 34 pass, *t'* all these things be fulfilled.
M'r 6: 10 abide *t'* ye depart from that place.
9: 1 *t'* they have seen the kingdom of
9 *t'* the Son of man were risen
12: 36 *t'* I make thine enemies thy
13: 30 pass, *t'* all these things be done.
Lu 1: 80 *t'* the day of his shewing unto
9: 27 *t'* they see the kingdom of God.
12: 50 straitened *t'* it be accomplished!
59 *t'* thou hast paid the very last mite.
13: 8 *t'* I shall dig about it, and dung it:
21 meal, *t'* the whole was leavened.
15: 8 and seek diligently *t'* she find it?
17: 8 me, *t'* I have eaten and drunken;
19: 13 said unto them, Occupy *t'* I come.
20: 43 *T'* I make thine enemies thy
21: 32 not pass away, *t'* all be fulfilled.
Joh 13: 38 crow, *t'* thou hast denied me thrice.
21: 22, 23 If I will that he tarry *t'* I come,
Ac 7: 18 *T'* another king arose, which
8: 40 the cities, *t'* he came to Cæsarea.
20: 11 even *t'* break of day, so he departed.
21: 5 children, *t'* we were out of the city:
23: 12 nor drink *t'* they had killed Paul.
21 nor drink *t'* they have killed him:
25: 21 kept *t'* I might send him to Cæsar.
28: 23 prophets, from morning *t'* evening.
1Co 11: 26 the Lord's death *t'* he come.
15: 25 *t'* he hath put all enemies under
Ga 3: 19 *t'* the seed should come to whom
Eph 4: 13 *T'* we all come in the unity of the
Ph'p 1: 10 offence *t'* the day of Christ;
1Ti 4: 13 *T'* I come, give attendance to
Heb 10: 13 *t'* his enemies be made his footstool.
Re 2: 25 have already hold fast *t'* I come.
7: 3 *t'* we have sealed the servants of
15: 8 *t'* the seven plagues of the seven
20: 3 *t'* the thousand years shall be

tillage
1Ch 27: 26 the work of the field for *t'* of the
Ne 10: 37 the tithes in all the cities of our *t'*.
Pr 13: 23 Much food is in the *t'* of the poor:

tilled
Eze 36: 9 you, and ye shall be *t'* and sown:
34 And the desolate land shall be *t'*,

tiller
Ge 4: 2 but Cain was a *t'* of the ground.

tillest
Ge 4: 12 When thou *t'* the ground, it shall

tilleth
Pro 12:11 He that t' his land shall be
28:19 He that t' his land shall have plenty
Tilon (*ti'-lon*)
1Ch 4:20 and Rinnah, Ben-hanan, and T'.
Timæus (*ti-me'-us*) See also BARTIMÆUS.
M'r 10:46 blind Bartimæus, the son of T'.
timber
Ex 31: 5 and in carving of t', to work in all
Le 14:45 the stones of it, and the t' thereof,
1Ki 5: 6 that can skill to hew t' like unto the
8 thy desire concerning t' of cedar,
8 of cedar, and concerning t' of fir.
18 prepared t' and stones to build the
6:10 rested on the house with t' of cedar.
15:22 stones of Ramah, and the t' thereof,
2Ki 12:12 to buy t' and hewed stone to repair
22: 6 to buy t' and hewn stone to repair
1Ch 14: 1 and t' of cedars, with masons and
22:14 t' also and stone have I prepared;
15 and workers of stone and t', and
2Ch 2: 8 can skill to cut t' in Lebanon;
9 to prepare me t' in abundance:
10 thy servants, the hewers that cut t',
14 brass, in iron, in stone, and in t',
16: 6 stones of Ramah, and the t' thereof,
34:11 hewn stone, and t' for couplings,
Ezr 5: 8 stones, and t' is laid in the walls,
6: 4 of great stones, and a row of new t':
11 let t' be pulled down from his house,
Ne 2: 8 he may give me t' to make beams
Eze 26:12 thy stones and thy t' and thy dust
Hab 2:11 beam out of the t' shall answer it.
Zec 5: 4 the t' thereof and the stones thereof.

timbrel See also TIMBRELS.
Ex 15:20 of Aaron, took a t' in her hand;
Job 21:12 They take the t' and harp, and
Ps 81: 2 a psalm, and bring hither the t',
149: 3 sing praises unto him with the t'
150: 4 Praise him with the t' and dance:
timbrels
Ex 15:20 women went out after her with t'
J'g 11:34 came out to meet him with t' and
2Sa 6: 5 harps, and on psalteries, and on t',
1Ch 13: 8 and with psalteries, and with t',
Ps 68:25 were the damsels playing with t'.
time^ See also AFORETIME; BEFORETIME; DAYTIME; LIFETIME; MEALTIME; SOMETIME; TIMES; UNTIMELY.
Ge 4: 3 And in process of t' it came to pass,
17:21 shall bear unto thee at this set t'
18:10 thee according to the t' of life;
14 At the t' appointed I will return
14 according to the t' of life, and
21: 2 at the set t' of which God had
22 it came to pass at that t', that
22:15 out of heaven the second t',
24:11 of water at the t' of the evening,
11 the t' that women go out to draw
26: 8 when he had been there a long t',
29: 7 neither is it t' that the cattle
34 this t' will my husband be joined
30:33 answer for me in t' to come,
31:10 at the t' that the cattle conceived,
38: 1 came to pass at that t', that Judah
12 in process of t' the daughter of
27 to pass in the t' of her travail,
39: 5 from the t' that he had made him
11 it came to pass about this t', that
41: 5 he slept and dreamed the second t':
43:10 we had returned this second t'.
18 returned in our sacks at the first t'
20 we came indeed down at the first t'
47:29 the t' drew nigh that Israel must
Ex 2:23 it came to pass in process of t',
8:32 hardened his heart at this t' also,
9: 5 And the Lord appointed a set t',
14 will at this t' send all my plagues
18 to morrow about this t' I will cause
27 unto them, I have sinned this t':
13:14 thy son asketh thee in t' to come,
21:19 he shall pay for the loss of his t',
29 push with his horn in t' past,
36 hath used to push in t' past,
23:15 in the t' appointed of the month
34:18 thee, in the t' of the month Abib:
21 in earing t' and in harvest thou shalt
Le 13:58 then it shall be washed the second t'
15:25 out of the t' of her separation,
25 run beyond the t' of her separation;
18:18 besides the other in her life t'.
25:32 may the Levites redeem at any t'.
50 according to the t' of an hired servant
26: 5 vintage shall reach unto the sowing t':
Nu 10: 6 When ye blow an alarm the second t',
13:20 t' was the t' of the firstripe grapes.
20:15 we have dwelt in Egypt a long t';
22: 4 king of the Moabites at that t'.
23:23 according to this t' it shall be said
26:10 t' the fire devoured two hundred and
32:10 anger was kindled the same t',
35:26 if the slayer shall at any t' come
De 1: 9 I spake unto you at that t', saying,
16 I charged your judges at that t',
18 I commanded you at that t' all the
2:20 giants dwelt therein in old t'; and
34 And we took all his cities at that t',
3: 4 And we took all his cities at that t',
8 we took at that t' out of the hand
12 land, which we possessed at that t',
18 I commanded you at that t', saying,
21 I commanded Joshua at that t',
23 And I besought the Lord at that t',
De 4:14 the Lord commanded me at that t'
5: 5 between the Lord and you at that t',
6:20 thy son asketh thee in t' to come,
9:19 Lord hearkened unto me at that t'
20 prayed for Aaron also the same t'.
10: 1 At that t' the Lord said unto me,
8 At that t' the Lord separated the
10 according to the first t', forty days
10 Lord hearkened unto me at that t'
19: 4 whom he hated not in t' past;
6 as he hated him not in t' past.
14 which they of old t' have set in thine
20:19 thou shalt besiege a city a long t',
32:35 their foot shall slide in due t': for
Jos 2: 5 about the t' of shutting of the gate,
3:15 all his banks all the t' of harvest,)
4: 6, 21 ask their fathers in t' to come,
5: 2 At that t' the Lord said unto
2 the children of Israel the second t'.
6:16 it came to pass at the seventh t',
26 Joshua adjured them at that t',
8:14 he and all his people, at a t' appointed,
10:27 at the t' of the going down of the
42 land did Joshua take at one t',
11: 6 about this t' will I deliver them
10 And Joshua at that t' turned back,
18 Joshua made war a long t' with
21 And at that t' came Joshua, and
22:24 In t' to come your children might
27 say to our children in t' to come,
28 to our generations in t' to come,
23: 1 it came to pass a long t' after that
24: 2 the other side of the flood in old t',
J'g 3:29 slew of Moab at that t' about ten
4: 4 she judged Israel at that t'.
9: 8 The trees went forth on a t' to anoint
10:14 you in the t' of your tribulation.
11: 4 it came to pass in process of t',
26 ye not recover them within that t'?
12: 6 fell at that t' of the Ephraimites
13:23 nor would as at this t' have told us
14: 4 for at that t' the Philistines had
8 after a t' he returned to take her,
15: 1 in the t' of wheat harvest, that
18:31 all the t' that the house of God was
20:15 Benjamin were numbered at that t'
21:14 Benjamin came again at that t';
22 ye did not give unto them at this t',
24 of Israel departed thence at that t'.
Ru 4: 7 the manner in former t' in Israel
1Sa 1: 4 the t' was that Elkanah offered,
20 when the t' was come about after
3: 2 And it came to pass at that t', when
8 Lord called Samuel again the third
4:20 And about the t' of her death the
7: 2 that the t' was long; for it
9:13 for about this t' ye shall find him.
16 To morrow about this t' I will
24 unto this t' hath it been kept for
11: 9 To morrow, by that t' the sun be hot,
13: 8 according to the set t' that Samuel
14:18 the ark of God was at that t' with
21 the Philistines before that t',
18:19 came to pass at the t' when Merab
19:21 sent messengers again the third t',
20:12 my father about to morrow any t',
35 at the t' appointed with David,
26: 8 I will not smite him the second t'.
27: 7 the t' that David dwelt in the
2Sa 2:11 the t' that David was king in
5: 2 Also in t' past, when Saul was
7: 6 since the t' that I brought up the
11 as since the t' that I commanded
11: 1 at the t' when kings go forth to
14: 2 woman that had a long t' mourned
29 when he sent again the second t',
17: 7 hath given is not good at this t'.
20: 5 he tarried longer than the set t'
18 They were wont to speak in old t',
23: 8 hundred, whom he slew at one t'.
13 came to David in the harvest t' unto
20 in the midst of a pit in t' of snow:
24:15 morning even to the t' appointed:
1Ki 1: 6 had not displeased him at any t' in
2:26 will not at this t' put thee to death.
8:65 at that t' Solomon held a feast,
9: 2 appeared to Solomon the second t',
11:29 at that t' when Jeroboam went
42 And the t' that Solomon reigned in
14: 1 At that t' Abijah the son of
15:23 in the t' of his old age he was
18:29 until the t' of the offering of the
34 And he said, Do it the second t'.
34 And they did it the second t'.
34 And he said, Do it the third t'.
34 And they did it the third t'.
36 t' of the offering of the evening
44 And it came to pass at the seventh t',
19: 2 them by to morrow about this t'.
7 of the Lord came again the second t',
20: 6 unto thee to morrow about this t',
2Ki 3: 6 went out of Samaria the same t',
4:16 according to the t' of life, thou
17 unto her, according to the t' of life.
5:26 Is it a t' to receive money, and to
7: 1 To morrow about this t' shall a
18 to morrow about this t' in the gate
8:22 Libnah revolted at the same t'.
10: 6 Then he wrote a letter the second t'
6 me to Jezreel by to morrow this t'.
36 t' that Jehu reigned over Israel
16: 6 At that t' Rezin king of Syria
18:16 At that t' did Hezekiah cut off the
20:12 that t' Berodach-baladan, the son
24:10 t' the servants of Nebuchadnezzar
1Ch 9:20 was the ruler over them in t' past,
1Ch 9:25 seven days from t' to t' with them.
11: 2 And moreover in t' past, even
11 hundred slain by him at one t'.
12:22 at that t' day by day there came
17:10 since the t' that I commanded
20: 1 the t' that kings go out to battle,
4 t' Sibbechai the Hushathite slew
21:28 t' when David saw that the Lord
29:22 the son of David king the second t',
27 t' that he reigned over Israel was
2Ch 7: 8 at the same t' Solomon kept the
13:18 were brought under at that t',
15:11 offered unto the Lord the same t',
16: 7 t' Hanani the seer came to Asa
10 some of the people the same t'.
18:34 t' of the sun going down he died.
21:10 The same t' also did Libnah revolt
19 came to pass, that in process of t',
24:11 at what t' the chest was brought
25:27 after the t' that Amaziah did turn
28:16 At that t' did king Ahaz send unto
22 And in the t' of his distress did he
30: 3 they could not keep it at that t',
5 they had not done it of a long t' in
26 since the t' of Solomon the son of
35:17 kept the passover at that t',
Ezr 4:10, 11 side the river, and at such a t'.
15 sedition within the same of old t':
17 the river, Peace, and at such a t'.
19 it is found that this city of old t'
5: 3 the same t' came to them Tatnai,
16 and since that t' even until now
7:12 perfect peace, and at such a t'.
8:34 the weight was written at that t'.
10:13 many, and it is a t' of much rain,
Ne 2: 6 to send me; and I set him a t'.
4:16 it came to pass from that t' forth,
22 the same t' said I unto the people,
5:14 from the t' that I was appointed
6: 1 at that t' I had not set up the
5 fifth t' with an open letter in his
9:27 and in the t' of their trouble, when
32 since the t' of the kings of Assyria
12:44 And at that t' were some appointed
13: 6 in all this t' was not I at Jerusalem:
21 From that t' forth came they no
Es 2:19 were gathered together the second t',
4:14 holdest thy peace at this t',
14 to the kingdom for such a t' as this?
8: 9 called at that t' in the third month,
9:27 according to their appointed t'
Job 6:17 What t' they wax warm, they
7: 1 appointed t' to man upon earth?
9:19 who shall set me a t' to plead?
14:13 thou wouldest appoint me a set t',
14 days of my appointed t' will I wait,
15:32 shall be accomplished before his t',
22:16 Which were cut down out of t',
30: 3 in former t' desolate and waste.
38:23 reserved against the t' of trouble,
39: 1 thou the t' when the wild goats
2 thou the t' when they bring forth?
18 What t' she lifteth up herself on
Ps 4: 7 in the t' that their corn and their
21: 9 a fiery oven in the t' of thine anger:
27: 5 t' of trouble he shall hide me in
32: 6 pray unto thee in a t' when thou
37:19 shall not be ashamed in the evil t':
39 is their strength in the t' of trouble.
41: 1 will deliver him in t' of trouble.
56: 3 What t' I am afraid, I will trust in
69:13 thee, O Lord, in an acceptable t':
71: 9 Cast me not off in the t' of old age;
78:38 many a t' turned he his anger
81: 3 t' appointed, on our solemn feast
15 their t' should have endured for
89:47 Remember how short my t' is:
102:13 for the t' to favour her, yea,
13 her, yea, the set t', is come.
105:19 Until the t' that his word came:
113: 2 from this t' forth and for evermore.
115:18 bless the Lord from this t' forth
119:126 It is t' for thee, Lord, to work:
121: 8 and thy coming in from this t' forth,
129: 1, 2 Many a t' have they afflicted me
Pr 25:13 cold of snow in the t' of harvest,
19 an unfaithful man in t' of trouble
31:25 and she shall rejoice in t' to come.
Ec 1:10 it hath been already of old t',
3: 1 a t' to every purpose under the
2 A t' to be born, and a t' to die;
2 a t' to plant, and a t' to pluck up that
3 A t' to kill, and a t' to heal;
3 a t' to break down, and a t' to build
4 A t' to weep, and a t' to laugh;
4 a t' to mourn, and a t' to dance;
5 A t' to cast away stones, and a
5 and a t' to gather stones together;
6 a t' to embrace, and a t' to refrain
6 A t' to get, and a t' to lose;
6 a t' to keep, and a t' to cast away;
7 A t' to rend, and a t' to sew;
7 a t' to keep silence, and a t' to speak;
8 A t' to love, and a t' to hate;
8 a t' of war, and a t' of peace.
11 every thing beautiful in his t':
17 there is a t' there for every purpose
7:17 shouldest thou die before thy t'?
8: 5 man's heart discerneth both t' and
6 to every purpose there is t' and
9 a t' wherein one man ruleth over
9:11 t' and chance happeneth to them
12 For man also knoweth not his t':
12 sons of men snared in an evil t',
Ca 2:12 t' of the singing of birds is come,
Isa 11:11 shall set his hand again the second

Isa 13:22 and her *t'* is near to come, and
16:13 concerning Moab since that *t'*.
18: 7 In that *t'* shall the present be
20: 2 At the same *t'* spake the Lord by
26:17 draweth near the *t'* of her delivery,
28:19 From the *t'* that it goeth forth it
30: 8 may be for the *t'* to come for ever
33: 2 salvation also in the *t'* of trouble.
39: 1 At that *t'* Merodach-baladan, the
42:14 I have long *t'* holden my peace;
23 and hear for the *t'* to come?
44: 8 have not I told thee from that *t'*,
45:21 hath declared this from ancient *t'*?
21 who hath told it from that *t'*? have
48: 6 thee new things from this *t'*,
8 from that *t'* that thine ear was not
16 from the *t'* that it was, there am I:
49: 8 an acceptable *t'* have I heard thee,
60:22 I the Lord will hasten it in his *t'*.
Jer 1:13 Lord came unto me the second *t'*,
2:20 For of old *t'* I have broken thy yoke,
27 *t'* of their trouble they will say,
28 save thee in the *t'* of thy trouble:
3: 4 thou not from this *t'* cry unto me,
17 At that *t'* they shall call Jerusalem
4:11 At that *t'* shall it be said to this
6:15 at the *t'* that I visit them they shall
8: 1 At that *t'*, saith the Lord, they
7 crane and...swallow observe the *t'*
12 *t'* of their visitation they shall be
15 and for a *t'* of health, and behold
10:15 *t'* of their visitation they shall
11:12 at all in the *t'* of their trouble.
14 hear them in the *t'* that they cry
13: 3 Lord came unto me the second *t'*,
14: 8 the saviour thereof in *t'* of trouble,
19 and for the *t'* of healing, and behold
15:11 *t'* of evil and in the *t'* of affliction.
18:23 with them in the *t'* of thine anger.
27: 7 until the very *t'* of his land come:
30: 7 it is even the *t'* of Jacob's trouble;
31: 1 At the same *t'*, saith the Lord, will
33: 1 came unto Jeremiah the second *t'*,
15 at that *t'*, will I cause the Branch
39:10 vineyards and fields at the same *t'*.
46:17 he hath passed the *t'* appointed.
21 them, and the *t'* of their visitation.
49: 8 him, the *t'* that I will visit him.
19 and who will appoint me the *t'*? and
50: 4 and in that *t'*, saith the Lord,
16 the sickle in the *t'* of harvest:
20 and in that *t'*, saith the Lord, the
27 day is come, the *t'* of their visitation.
31 is come, the *t'* that I will visit thee.
44 and who will appoint me the *t'*? and
51: 6 is the *t'* of the Lord's vengeance;
18 *t'* of their visitation they perish.
33 threshingfloor, it is *t'* to thresh her:
33 and the *t'* of her harvest is come.
La 5:20 ever, and forsake us so long *t'*?
Eze 4:10 from *t'* to *t'* shalt thou eat it.
11 hin: from *t'* to *t'* shalt thou drink.
7: 7 the *t'* is come, the day of trouble
12 The *t'* is come, tne day draweth
16: 8 behold, thy *t'* was the *t'* of love;
57 as the *t'* of thy reproach of the
21:14 the sword be doubled the third *t'*,
22: 3 midst of it, that her *t'* may come,
26:20 with the people of old *t'*, and
27:34 the *t'* when thou shalt be broken
30: 3 it shall be the *t'* of the heathen.
35: 5 sword in the *t'* of their calamity,
5 in the *t'* that their iniquity had an
38:10 same *t'* shall things come into thy
17 of whom I have spoken in old *t'*
18 come to pass at the same *t'* when
Da 2: 8 certainty that ye would gain the *t'*,
9 before me, till the *t'* be changed:
16 king that he would give him *t'*,
3: 5 at what *t'* ye hear the sound of
7 at that *t'*, when all the people
8 at that *t'* certain Chaldeans came
15 at what *t'* ye hear the sound of
4:36 the same *t'* my reason returned
7:12 prolonged for a season and *t'*.
22 *t'* came that the saints possessed
25 given into his hand until a *t'* and
25 and times and the dividing of *t'*.
8:17 at the *t'* of the end shall be the
19 the *t'* appointed the end shall be.
23 And in the latter *t'* of their kingdom,
9:21 about the *t'* of the evening
10: 1 true, but the *t'* appointed was long:
11:24 the strong holds, even for a *t'*.
27 end shall be at the *t'* appointed.
29 At the *t'* appointed he shall return,
35 white, even to the *t'* of the end:
35 because it is yet for a *t'* appointed.
40 at the *t'* of the end shall the king
12: 1 at that *t'* shall Michael stand up,
1 and there shall be a *t'* of trouble,
1 was a nation even to that same *t'*:
1 that *t'* thy people shall be delivered,
4 the book, even to the *t'* of the end:
7 be for a *t'*, times, and an half;
9 and sealed till the *t'* of the end.
11 the *t'* that the daily sacrifice shall
Ho 2: 9 away my corn in the *t'* thereof,
9:10 in the fig tree at her first *t'*:
10:12 for it is *t'* to seek the Lord, till he
Joe 3: 1 in that *t'*, when I shall bring again
Am 5:13 shall keep silence in that *t'*;
13 for it is an evil *t'*.
Jon 3: 1 Lord came unto Jonah the second *t'*,
Mic 2: 3 go haughtily: for this *t'* is evil.
3: 4 hide his face from them at that *t'*.

Mic 5: 3 the *t'* that she which travaileth
Na 1: 9 shall not rise up the second *t'*.
Hab 2: 3 vision is yet for an appointed *t'*,
Zep 1:12 it shall come to pass at that *t'*,
3:19 at that *t'* I will undo all that afflict
20 At that *t'* will I bring you again,
20 even in the *t'* that I gather you: for
Hag 1: 2 people say, The *t'* is not come,
2 the *t'* that the Lord's house should
4 Is it *t'* for you, O ye, to dwell in
Zec 10: 1 rain in the *t'* of the latter rain;
14: 7 that at evening *t'* it shall be light.
Mal 3:11 your vine cast her fruit before the *t'*
M't 1:11 about the *t'* they were carried
2: 7 of them diligently what *t'* the star
16 according to the *t'* which he had
4: 6 lest at any *t'* thou dash thy foot
17 that *t'* Jesus began to preach,
5:21 that it was said by them of old *t'*,
25 lest at any *t'* the adversary deliver
27 that it was said by them of old *t'*,
33 it hath been said by them of old *t'*,
8:29 hither to torment us before the *t'*?
11:25 At that *t'* Jesus answered and said,
12: 1 that *t'* Jesus went on the sabbath
13:15 lest at any *t'* they should see with
30 in the *t'* of harvest I will say to the
14: 1 At that *t'* Herod the tetrarch heard
15 place, and the *t'* is now past;
16:21 From that *t'* forth began Jesus to
18: 1 At the same *t'* came the disciples
21:34 when the *t'* of the fruit drew near,
24:21 beginning of the world to this *t'*,
25:19 After a long *t'* the lord of those
26:16 from that *t'* he sought opportunity
18 The Master saith, My *t'* is at hand;
42 He went away again the second *t'*,
44 away again, and prayed the third *t'*,
M'r 1:15 The *t'* is fulfilled, and the kingdom
4:12 lest at any *t'* they...be converted,
17 and so endure but for a *t'*:
6:35 and now the *t'* is far passed:
10:30 an hundredfold now in this *t'*,
11:13 for the *t'* of figs was not yet.
13:19 which God created unto this *t'*,
33 for ye know not when the *t'* is.
14:41 he cometh the third *t'*, and saith unto
72 And the second *t'* the cock crew.
Lu 1:10 were praying without at the *t'* of
57 Now Elisabeth's full *t'* came that
4: 5 of the world in a moment of *t'*.
11 lest at any *t'* thou dash thy foot
27 were in Israel in the *t'* of Eliseus
7:45 woman since the *t'* I came in hath
8:13 and in *t'* of temptation fall away.
27 man, which had devils long *t'*, and
9:51 the *t'* was come that he should be
12:56 is it that ye do not discern this *t'*?
13:35 until the *t'* come when ye shall say,
14:17 sent his servant at supper *t'* to say
15:29 neither transgressed I at any *t'* thy
16:16 *t'* the kingdom of God is preached,
18:30 manifold more in this present *t'*,
19:44 knewest not the *t'* of thy visitation.
20: 9 into a far country for a long *t'*.
21: 8 Christ; and the *t'* draweth near:
34 at any *t'*...hearts be overcharged
37 in the day *t'* he was teaching in
23: 7 also was at Jerusalem at that *t'*.
22 And he said unto them the third *t'*,
Joh 1:18 No man hath seen God at any *t'*;
3: 4 second *t'* into his mother's womb,
5: 6 had been now a long *t'* in that case,
37 neither heard his voice at any *t'*,
6:66 From that *t'* many of his disciples
7: 6 unto them, My *t'* is not yet come:
6 come: but your *t'* is alway ready.
8 feast; for my *t'* is not yet full come.
11:39 him, Lord, by this *t'* he stinketh:
14: 9 Have I been so long *t'* with you,
16: 2 yea, the *t'* cometh, that whosoever
4 when the *t'* shall come, ye may
25 the *t'* cometh, when I shall no more
21:14 now the third *t'* that Jesus shewed
16 saith to him again the second *t'*,
17 He saith unto him the third *t'*, Simon,
17 said unto him the third *t'*, Lovest thou
Ac 1: 6 thou at this *t'* restore again the
21 have companied with us all the *t'*
7:13 And at the second *t'* Joseph was made
17 the *t'* of the promise drew nigh,
20 In which *t'* Moses was born, and
8: 1 And at that *t'* there was a great
11 of long *t'* he had bewitched them
10:15 spake unto him again the second *t'*,
11: 8 hath at any *t'* entered into my mouth.
12: 1 Now about that *t'* Herod the king
13:18 about the *t'* of forty years suffered
14: 3 Long *t'*...abode they speaking
28 abode long *t'* with the disciples.
15:21 Moses of old *t'* hath in every city
17:21 spent their *t'* in nothing else, but
18:20 him to tarry longer *t'* with them,
23 after he had spent some *t'* there, he
19:23 same *t'* there arose no small stir
20:16 he would not spend the *t'* in Asia:
24:25 answered, Go thy way for this *t'*;
27: 9 when much *t'* was spent, and when
Ro 3:26 I say, at this *t'* his righteousness:
5: 6 in due *t'* Christ died for...ungodly.
8:18 sufferings of this present *t'* are not
9: 9 At this *t'* will I come, and Sarah
11: 5 at this present *t'* also there is a
13:11 And that, knowing the *t'*, that now
11 it is high *t'* to awake out of sleep:
1Co 4: 5 judge nothing before the *t'*, until

1Co 7: 5 except it be with consent for a *t'*,
29 this I say, brethren, the *t'* is short:
9: 7 warfare any *t'* at his own charges?
15: 8 me also, as of one born out of due *t'*.
16:12 was not at all to come at this *t'*;
12 when he shall have convenient *t'*.
2Co 6: 2 I have heard thee in a *t'* accepted,
2 now is the accepted *t'*; behold, now
8:14 this *t'* your abundance may be a
12:14 the third *t'* I am ready to come to you;
13: 1 This is the third *t'* I am coming to you.
2 as if I were present, the second *t'*;
Ga 1:13 heard of my conversation in *t'* past
4: 2 until...*t'* appointed of the father.
4 the fulness of the *t'* was come,
5:21 as I have also told you in *t'* past,
Eph 2: 2 in *t'* past ye walked according to
11 that ye being in *t'* past Gentiles
12 at that *t'* ye were without Christ,
5:16 Redeeming the *t'*, because the days
Col 3: 7 the which ye also walked some *t'*,
4: 5 that are without, redeeming the *t'*.
1Th 2: 5 neither at any *t'* used we flattering
17 from you for a short *t'* in presence,
2Th 2: 6 that he might be revealed in his *t'*.
1Ti 2: 6 for all, to be testified in due *t'*.
6:19 foundation against the *t'* to come,
2Ti 4: 3 the *t'* will come when they will not
6 the *t'* of my departure is at hand.
subscr. brought before Nero the second *t'*.
Ph'm 11 in *t'* past was to thee unprofitable,
Heb 1: 1 spake in *t'* past unto the fathers
5, 13 of the angels said he at any *t'*,
2: 1 at any *t'* we should let them slip.
4: 7 David, To day, after so long a *t'*;
16 and find grace to help in *t'* of need.
5:12 for the *t'* ye ought to be teachers,
9: 9 a figure for the *t'* then present, in
10 on them until the *t'* of reformation.
28 shall he appear the second *t'* without
11:32 *t'* would fail me to tell of Gideon,
Jas 4:14 that appeareth for a little *t'*, and then
1Pe 1: 5 ready to be revealed in the last *t'*.
11 or what manner of *t'* the Spirit of
17 *t'* of your sojourning here in fear:
2:10 Which in *t'* past were not a people,
3: 5 in the old *t'* the holy women also,
4: 2 should live the rest of his *t'* in the
3 *t'* past of our life may suffice us to
17 the *t'* is come that judgment must
5: 6 that he may exalt you in due *t'*:
2Pe 1:21 prophecy came not in old *t'* by the
2: 3 whose judgment now of a long *t'*
13 count it pleasure to riot in the day *t'*.
1Jo 2:18 Little children, it is the last *t'*:
18 whereby we know...it is the last *t'*.
4:12 No man hath seen God at any *t'*.
Jude 18 should be mockers in the last *t'*,
Re 1: 3 therein: for the *t'* is at hand.
10: 6 that there should be *t'* no longer:
11:18 is come, and the *t'* of the dead,
12:12 knoweth that he hath but a short *t'*.
14 where she is nourished for a *t'*,
14 and half a *t'*, from the face of the
14:15 for the *t'* is come for thee to reap;
22:10 of this book: for the *t'* is at hand.

times See also BETIMES; OFTENTIMES; OFTTIMES; SOMETIMES.
Ge 27:36 hath supplanted me these two *t'*:
31: 7 me, and changed my wages ten *t'*;
41 thou hast changed my wages ten *t'*.
33: 3 himself to the ground seven *t'*,
43:34 five *t'* so much as any of theirs.
Ex 23:14 Three *t'* thou shalt keep a feast unto
17 Three *t'* in the year all thy males
Le 4: 6 and sprinkle of the blood seven *t'*
17 sprinkle it seven *t'* before the Lord,
8:11 thereof upon the altar seven *t'*,
14: 7 cleansed from the leprosy seven *t'*,
16 of the oil with his finger seven *t'*
27 oil that is in his left hand seven *t'*
51 and sprinkle the house seven *t'*:
16: 2 not at all *t'* into the holy place
14 the blood with his finger seven *t'*.
19 upon it with his finger seven *t'*,
19:26 ye use enchantment, nor observe *t'*.
25: 8 unto thee, seven *t'* seven years;
26:18 punish you seven *t'* more for your
21 bring seven *t'* more plagues upon
24 punish you yet seven *t'* for your
28 chastise you seven *t'* for your sins.
Nu 14:22 have tempted me now these ten *t'*,
19: 4 of the congregation seven *t'*.
22:28 thou hast smitten me these three *t'*?
32 these thou smitten thine ass three *t'*?
33 and turned from me these three *t'*:
24: 1 he went not, as at other *t'*, to seek
10 altogether blessed them these three *t'*.
De 1:11 you a thousand *t'* so many more
2:10 The Emims dwelt therein in *t'* past,
4:42 and hated him not in *t'* past;
16:16 Three *t'* in a year shall all they
18:10 divination, or an observer of *t'*,
14 hearkened unto observers of *t'*, and
Jos 6: 4 ye shall compass the city seven *t'*,
15 after the same manner seven *t'*:
15 they compassed the city seven *t'*.
J'g 13:25 began to move him at *t'* in the camp
16:15 hast mocked me these three *t'*,
20 I will go out as at other *t'* before,
20:30 against Gibeah, as at other *t'*,
31 the people, and kill, as at other *t'*,
1Sa 3:10 and called as other *t'*, Samuel,
18:10 with his hand, as at other *t'*:
19: 7 in his presence, as in *t'* past.
20:25 sat upon his seat, as at other *t'*,

1Sa 20: 41 ground,...bowed himself three t':
2Sa 3: 17 ye sought for David in t' past
1Ki 8: 59 cause of his people Israel at all t',
9: 25 three t' in a year did Solomon
17: 21 himself upon the child three t',
18: 43 And he said, Go again seven t'.
22: 16 How many t' shall I adjure thee
2Ki 4: 35 and the child sneezed seven t', and
5: 10 Go and wash in Jordan seven t',
14 dipped himself seven t' in Jordan,
13: 19 shouldest have smitten five or six t';
25 Three t' did Joash beat him, and
19: 25 of ancient t' that I have formed it?
21: 6 fire, and observed t', and used
1Ch 12: 32 men that had understanding of the t',
21: 3 his people an hundred t' so many
29: 30 and the t' that went over him, and
2Ch 8: 13 three t' in the year, even in the
15: 5 in those t' there was no peace to him
18: 15 How many t' shall I adjure thee
33: 6 also he observed t', and used
Ezr 10: 14 in our cities come at appointed t',
Ne 4: 12 they said unto us ten t', From all
6: 4 they sent unto me four t' after
9: 28 many t' didst thou deliver them
10: 34 at t' appointed year by year, to
13: 31 the wood offering, at t' appointed,
Es 1: 13 to the wise men, which knew the t',
9: 31 of Purim in their t' appointed,
Job 19: 3 ten t' have ye reproached me:
24: 1 seeing t' are not hidden from the
Ps 9: 9 oppressed, a refuge in t' of trouble.
10: 1 hidest thou thyself in t' of trouble?
12: 6 in a furnace of earth, purified seven t'.
31: 15 My t' are in thy hand: deliver me
34: 1 I will bless the Lord at all t': his
44: 1 in their days, in the t' of old.
62: 8 Trust in him at all t'; ye people,
77: 5 days of old, the years of ancient t'.
106: 3 that doeth righteousness at all t'.
43 Many t' did he deliver them; but
119: 20 hath unto thy judgments at all t'.
164 Seven t' a day do I praise thee because
Pr 5: 19 her breasts satisfy thee at all t';
17: 17 A friend loveth at all t', and a
24: 16 For a just man falleth seven t', and
Ec 8: 12 a sinner do evil an hundred t',
Isa 14: 31 shall be alone in his appointed t'.
33: 6 shall be the stability of thy t',
37: 26 ancient t', that I have formed it?
46: 10 from ancient t' the things that are not
Jer 8: 7 heaven knoweth her appointed t';
Eze 12: 27 he prophesieth of the t' that are far
Da 1: 20 he found them ten t' better than all
2: 21 changeth the t' and the seasons:
3: 19 heat the furnace one seven t' more
4: 16 and let seven t' pass over him.
23 field, till seven t' pass over him;
25, 32 and seven t' shall pass over thee,
6: 10 upon his knees three t' a day,
13 maketh his petition three t' a day.
7: 10 ten thousand t' ten thousand stood
25 and think to change t' and laws:
25 a time and t' and the dividing of
9: 25 and the wall, even in troublous t'.
11: 6 he that strengtheneth her in these t'.
14 in those t' there shall many stand
12: 7 shall be for a time, t', and an half;
M't 16: 3 can ye not discern...signs of the t'?
18: 21 me, and I forgive him till seven t'?
22 I say not unto thee, Until seven t':
22 but, Until seventy t' seven.
Lu 17: 4 trespass against thee seven t' in a
4 seven t' in a day turn again to thee,
21: 24 the t' of the Gentiles be fulfilled.
Ac 1: 7 you to know the t' or the seasons,
3: 19 when the t' of refreshing shall
21 until the t' of restitution of all
11: 10 And this was done three t': and
14: 16 Who in t' past suffered all nations
17: 26 determined...t' before appointed,
30 the t' of this ignorance God winked
Ro 11: 30 in t' past have not believed God,
2Co 11: 24 five t' received I forty stripes save
Ga 1: 23 he which persecuted us in t' past
4: 10 observe days, and months, and t',
Eph 1: 10 the dispensation of the fulness of t'
2: 3 our conversation in t' past in the
1Th 5: 1 of the t' and the seasons, brethren,
1Ti 4: 1 latter t' some shall depart from
6: 15 Which in his t' he shall shew, who
2Ti 3: 1 the last days perilous t' shall come.
Tit 1: 3 hath in due t' manifested his word
Heb 1: 1 who at sundry t' and in divers
1Pe 1: 20 manifest in these last t' for you,
Re 5: 11 was ten thousand t' ten thousand,
12: 14 for a time, and t', and half a time,

Timna (*tim'-nah*) See also TIMNATH.
Ge 36: 12 T' was concubine to Eliphaz
22 Hemam; and Lotan's sister was T'.
1Ch 1: 36 Gatam, Kenaz, and T', and Amalek.
39 Homam: and T' was Lotan's sister.

Timnah (*tim'-nah*) See also TIMNA; TIMNATH; TIMNITE.
Ge 36: 40 duke T', duke Alvah, duke
Jos 15: 10 and passed on to T':
57 Gibeah, and T'; ten cities with
1Ch 1: 51 the dukes of Edom were; duke T',
2Ch 28: 18 and T' with the villages thereof,

Timnath (*tim'-nath*) See also THIMNATHAH; TIMNAH; TIMNATH-HERES.
Ge 38: 12 up unto his sheepshearers to T',
13 father in law goeth up to T' to
14 place, which is by the way to T';
J'g 14: 1 Samson went down to T', and
1, 2 a woman in T' of the daughters
5 his father and his mother, to T',
5 and came to the vineyards of T':

Timnath-heres (*tim''-nath-he'-rez*) See also TIMNATH-SERAH.
J'g 2: 9 border of his inheritance in T',

Timnath-serah (*tim''-nath-se'-rah*) See also TIMNATH-HERES.
Jos 19: 50 asked, even T' in mount Ephraim:
24: 30 border of his inheritance in T',

Timnite (*tim'-nite*)
J'g 15: 6 Samson, the son in law of the T',

Timon (*ti'-mon*)
Ac 6: 5 T', and Parmenas, and Nicolas a

Timotheus (*tim-o'-the-us*) See also TIMOTHY.
Ac 16: 1 disciple was there, named T',
17: 14 but Silas and T' abode there still.
15 a commandment unto Silas and T'
18: 5 when Silas and T' were come from
19: 22 ministered unto him, T' and
20: 4 and Gaius of Derbe, and T';
Ro 16: 21 T' my workfellow, and Lucius,
1Co 4: 17 this cause have I sent unto you T',
16: 10 if T' come, see that he may be with
subscr. Fortunatus, and Achaicus, and T'.
2Co 1: 19 even by me and Silvanus and T',
Ph'p 1: 1 Paul and T', the servants of Jesus
2: 19 Jesus to send T' shortly unto you,
Col 1: 1 the will of God, and T' our brother,
1Th 1: 1 Silvanus, and T', unto the church
3: 2 sent T', our brother, and minister
6 But now when T' came from you
2Th 1: 1 Silvanus, and T', unto the church
2Ti *subscr.* The second epistle unto T',

Timothy (*tim'-o-thy*) See also TIMOTHEUS.
2Co 1: 1 T' our brother, unto the church
1Ti 1: 2 Unto T', my own son in the faith:
18 charge I commit unto thee, son T',
6: 20 O T', keep that which is committed
subscr. The first to T' was written from
2Ti 1: 2 To T', my dearly beloved son:
Ph'm 1 and T' our brother, unto Philemon
Heb 13: 23 our brother T' is set at liberty;
subscr. to the Hebrews from Italy by T'.

tin
Nu 31: 22 the brass, the iron, the t', and the
Isa 1: 25 away thy dross, take away all thy t':
Eze 22: 18 all they are brass, and t', and iron,
20 brass, and iron, and lead, and t',
27: 12 with silver, iron, t', and lead, they

tingle
1Sa 3: 11 every one that heareth it shall t'.
2Ki 21: 12 heareth of it, both his ears shall t'.
Jer 19: 3 whosoever heareth, his ears shall t'.

tinkling
Isa 3: 16 and making a t' with their feet:
18 of their t' ornaments about their feet;
1Co 13: 1 as sounding brass, or a t' cymbal.

tip
Ex 29: 20 the t' of the right ear of Aaron,
20 the t' of the right ear of his sons,
Le 8: 23 it upon the t' of Aaron's right ear,
24 blood upon the t' of their right ear,
14: 14 put it upon the t' of the right ear
17 put upon the t' of the right ear
25 put it upon the t' of the right ear
28 upon the t' of the right ear of him
Lu 16: 24 may dip the t' of his finger in water,

Tiphsah (*tif'-sah*)
1Ki 4: 24 T' even to Azzah, over all the
2Ki 15: 16 Then Menahem smote T', and all

Tiras (*ti'-ras*)
Ge 10: 2 and Tubal, and Meshech, and T'.
1Ch 1: 5 and Tubal, and Meshech, and T'.

Tirathites (*ti'-rath-ites*)
1Ch 2: 55 the T', the Shimeathites, and

tire See also ATTIRE; RETIRE; TIRED; TIRES.
Eze 24: 17 the t' of thine head upon thee, and

tired See also RETIRED.
2Ki 9: 30 painted her face, and t' her head,

tires
Isa 3: 18 and their round t' like the moon,
Eze 24: 23 your t' shall be upon your heads,

Tirhakah (*tur-ha'-kah*)
2Ki 19: 9 heard say of T' king of Ethiopia,
Isa 37: 9 say concerning T' king of Ethiopia,

Tirhanah (*tur-ha'-nah*)
1Ch 2: 48 concubine, bare Sheber, and T'.

Tiria (*tir'-e-ah*)
1Ch 4: 16 Jehaleleel; Ziph, and Ziphah, T',

Tirshatha (*tur'-sha-thah*)
Ezr 2: 63 the T' said unto them, that they
Ne 7: 65 the T' said unto them, that they
70 The T' gave to the treasure a
8: 9 And Nehemiah, which is the T',
10: 1 sealed were, Nehemiah, the T',

Tirzah (*tur'-zah*)
Nu 26: 33 Noah, Hoglah, Milcah, and T'.
27: 1 and Hoglah, and Milcah, and T'.
36: 11 For Mahlah, T', and Hoglah, and
Jos 12: 24 The king of T', one: all the kings
17: 3 and Noah, Hoglah, Milcah, and T'.
1Ki 14: 17 and departed, and came to T':
15: 21 building of Ramah, and dwelt in T'.
33 Ahijah to reign over all Israel in T',
16: 6 his fathers, and was buried in T':
1Ki 16: 8 Baasha to reign over Israel in T',
9 as he was in T', drinking himself
9 of Arza steward of his house in T'.
15 did Zimri reign seven days in T'.
17 with him, and they besieged T'.
23 years: six years reigned he in T'.
2Ki 15: 14 the son of Gadi went up from T',
16 and the coasts thereof from T':
Ca 6: 4 art beautiful, O my love, as T',

Tishbite (*tish'-bite*)
1Ki 17: 1 And Elijah the T', who was of
21: 17, 28 the Lord came to Elijah the T',
2Ki 1: 3 of the Lord said to Elijah the T',
8 And he said, It is Elijah the T'.
9: 36 spake by his servant Elijah the T',

tithe See also TITHES; TITHING.
Le 27: 30 all the t' of the land, whether of
32 concerning the t' of the herd, or of
Nu 18: 26 Lord, even a tenth part of the t'.
De 12: 17 within thy gates the t' of thy corn,
14: 22 truly t' all the increase of thy seed,
23 t' of thy corn, of thy wine, and of
28 forth all the t' of thine increase
2Ch 31: 5 the t' of all things brought they in
6 brought in the t' of oxen and sheep,
6 the t' of holy things which were
Ne 10: 38 the Levites shall bring up the t' of
13: 12 brought all Judah the t' of the corn
M't 23: 23 for ye pay t' of mint and anise
Lu 11: 42 ye t' mint and rue and all manner

tithes
Ge 14: 20 hand. And he gave him t' of all.
Le 27: 31 will at all redeem ought of his t',
Nu 18: 24 But the t' of the children of Israel,
26 the t' which I have given you from
28 offering unto the Lord of all your t',
De 12: 6 your t', and heave offerings of your
11 your t', and the heave offering of
26: 12 the t' of thine increase the third
2Ch 31: 12 brought in the offerings and the t'
Ne 10: 37 the t' of our ground unto the
37 have the t' in all the cities of our
38 Levites, when the Levites take t':
38 bring up the tithe of the t' unto
12: 44 for the firstfruits, and for the t',
13: 5 the vessels, and the t' of the corn,
Am 4: 4 and your t' after three years:
Mal 3: 8 robbed thee? In t' and offerings.
10 ye all the t' into the storehouse,
Lu 18: 12 week, I give t' of all that I possess.
Heb 7: 5 to take t' of the people according to
6 from them received t' of Abraham,
8 And here men that die receive t';
9 receiveth t', payed t' in Abraham.

tithing
De 26: 12 made an end of t' all the tithes
12 third year, which is the year of t',

title See also TITLES.
2Ki 23: 17 said, What t' is that that I see?
Joh 19: 19 And Pilate wrote a t', and put it
20 This t' then read many of the Jews:

titles
Job 32: 21 let me give flattering t' unto man.
22 For I know not to give flattering t';

tittle
M't 5: 18 one t' shall in no wise pass from
Lu 16: 17 pass, than one t' of the law to fail.

Titus (*ti'-tus*)
2Co 2: 13 I found not T' my brother:
7: 6 comforted us by the coming of T';
13 the more joyed we for the joy of T',
14 boasting, which I made before T',
8: 6 Insomuch that we desired T', that
16 care into the heart of T' for you.
23 Whether any do enquire of T', he
12: 18 I desired T', and with him I sent
18 brother. Did T' make a gain of you?
subscr. of Macedonia, by T' and Lucas.
Ga 2: 1 and took T' with me also.
3 But neither T', who was with me,
2Ti 4: 10 to Galatia, T' unto Dalmatia.
Tit 1: 4 To T', mine own son after the
subscr. written to T', ordained the first

Tizite (*ti'-zite*)
1Ch 11: 45 and Joha his brother, the T',

Toah (*to'-ah*) See also NAHATH; TOHU.
1Ch 6: 34 the son of Eliel, the son of T',

Tob (*tob*) See also ISH-TOB; TOB-ADONIJAH.
J'g 11: 3 and dwelt in the land of T':
5 Jephthah out of the land of T':

Tob-adonijah (*tob''-ad-o-ni'-jah*)
2Ch 17: 8 and Tobijah, and T', Levites;

Tobiah (*to-bi'-ah*) See also TOBIJAH.
Ezr 2: 60 of Delaiah, the children of T',
Ne 2: 10, 19 Horonite, and T' the servant,
4: 3 Now T' the Ammonite was by him,
7 pass, that when Sanballat, and T',
6: 1 to pass, when Sanballat, and T',
12 for T' and Sanballat had hired him.
14 think thou upon T' and Sanballat
17 Judah sent many letters unto T',
17 the letters of T' came unto them.
19 T' sent letters to put me in fear.
7: 62 the children of T', the children of
13: 4 of our God, was allied unto T':
7 the evil that Eliashib did for T',
8 forth all the household stuff of T'

Tobijah (*to-bi'-jah*) See also TOBIAH.
2Ch 17: 8 and T', and Tob-adonijah, Levites;
Zec 6: 10 even of Heldai, of T', and of
14 shall be to Helem, and to T',

Tochen (*to'-ken*)
1Ch 4: 32 and T', and Ashan, five cities:

to-day See DAY.

toe See also TOES.
Ex 29: 20 upon the great t' of their right foot,
Le 8: 23 upon the great t' of his right foot.
14: 14 upon the great t' of his right foot:
17 upon the great t' of his right foot,
25 upon the great t' of his right foot:
28 upon the great t' of his right foot,

toes
Le 8: 24 the great t' of their right feet:
J'g 1: 6 off his thumbs and his great t'.
7 thumbs and...great t' cut off,
2Sa 21: 20 fingers, and on every foot six t',
1Ch 20: 6 whose fingers and t' were four and
Da 2: 41 whereas thou sawest the feet and t',
42 And as the t' of the feet were part of

Togarmah (*to-gar'-mah*)
Ge 10: 3 Ashkenaz, and Riphath, and T'.
1Ch 1: 6 Ashchenaz, and Riphath, and T'.
Eze 27: 14 the house of T' traded in thy fairs
38: 6 house of T' of the north quarters,

together See also ALTOGETHER.
Ge 1: 9 heaven be gathered t' unto one place,
10 gathering t' of the waters called he
3: 7 and they sewed fig leaves t', and
13: 6 them, that they might dwell t':
6 so that they could not dwell t'.
14: 3 were joined t' in the vale of Siddim,
22: 6 and they went both of them t'.
8 so they went both of them t'.
19 rose up and went t' to Beer-sheba;
25: 22 children struggled t' within her;
29: 7 the cattle should be gathered t':
8 until all the flocks be gathered t',
22 Laban gathered t' all the men of
34: 30 gather themselves t' against me,
36: 7 than that they might dwell t';
42: 17 put them all t' into ward three days.
49: 1 and said, Gather yourselves t',
2 Gather yourselves t', and hear, ye
Ex 2: 13 two men of the Hebrews strove t':
3: 16 and gather the elders of Israel t',
4: 29 and gathered t' all the elders of the
8: 14 they gathered them t' upon heaps:
15: 8 the waters were gathered t',
19: 8 And all the people answered t',
21: 18 And if men strive t', and one smite
26: 3 five curtains shall be coupled t'
6 and couple the curtains t' with the
11 and couple the tent t', that it may be
24 they shall be coupled t' beneath,
24 and they shall be coupled t' above
28: 7 and so it shall be joined t'.
30: 35 art of the apothecary, tempered t',
32: 1 gathered themselves t' unto Aaron,
26 gathered themselves t' unto him.
35: 1 of the children of Israel t',
36: 18 taches of brass to couple the tent t',
29 coupled t' at the head thereof,
39: 4 shoulderpieces for it, to couple it t':
4 by the two edges was it coupled t'.
Le 8: 3 gather thou all the congregation t'
4 and the assembly was gathered t'
24: 10 a man of Israel strove t' in the camp;
26: 25 ye are gathered t' within your cities,
Nu 1: 18 assembled all the congregation t'
8: 9 gather...the children of Israel t':
10: 7 congregation is to be gathered t',
11: 22 the fish of the sea be gathered t' for
14: 35 that are gathered t' against me:
16: 3 And they gathered themselves t'
11 all thy company are gathered t'
20: 2 and they gathered themselves t'
8 and gather thou the assembly t',
10 Aaron gathered the congregation t'
21: 16 unto Moses, Gather the people t',
23 but Sihon gathered all his people t',
26: 10 and swallowed them up t' with Korah,
27: 3 gathered themselves t' against
De 4: 10 unto me, Gather me the people t',
22: 10 plough with an ox and an ass t'.
11 sorts, as of woollen and linen t'.
25: 5 If brethren dwell t', and one of
11 men strive t' one with another,
31: 12 Gather the people t', men, and
33: 5 tribes of Israel were gathered t'.
17 he shall push the people t' to the
Jos 8: 16 people that were in Ai were called t'
9: 2 That they gathered themselves t',
10: 5 gathered themselves t', and went
6 mountains are gathered t' against us.
11: 5 when all these kings were met t',
5 came and pitched t' at the waters
17: 10 they met t' in Asher on the north,
18: 1 of Israel assembled t' at Shiloh,
22: 12 gathered themselves t' at Shiloh,
J'g 4: 13 Sisera gathered t' all his chariots,
6: 33 of the east were gathered t',
38 and thrust the fleece t', and wringed
7: 23 of Israel gathered themselves t'
24 of Ephraim gathered themselves t',
9: 6 the men of Shechem gathered t',
47 of Shechem were gathered t'.
10: 17 children of Ammon were gathered t',
17 of Israel assembled themselves t',
11: 20 but Sihon gathered all his people t',
12: 1 Ephraim gathered themselves t',
4 Jephthah gathered t' all the men
J'g 16: 23 Philistines gathered them t' for to
18: 22 to Micah's house were gathered t',
19: 6 did eat and drink both of them t':
29 and divided her, t' with her bones
20: 1 was gathered t' as one man,
11 the city, knit t' as one man.
14 of Benjamin gathered themselves t'
1Sa 5: 11 gathered t' all the lords of the
7: 6 And they gathered t' to Mizpeh,
7 Israel were gathered t' to Mizpeh,
8: 4 of Israel gathered themselves t',
10: 17 Samuel called the people t' unto
11: 11 that two of them were not left t'.
13: 4 people were called t' after Saul to
5 Philistines gathered...t' to fight
11 Philistines gathered themselves t'
15: 4 And Saul gathered the people t',
17: 1 Philistines gathered t' their armies
1 and were gathered t' at Shochoh,
2 men of Israel were gathered t',
10 give me a man, that we may fight t'.
23: 8 Saul called all the people t' to war,
25: 1 all the Israelites were gathered t',
28: 1 Philistines gathered their armies t'
4 Philistines gathered themselves t',
4 and Saul gathered all Israel t', and
23 But his servants, t' with the woman,
29: 1 the Philistines gathered t' all their
31: 6 and all his men, that same day t'.
2Sa 2: 13 and met t' by the pool of Gibeon:
16 fellow's side; so they fell down t':
25 Benjamin gathered themselves t'
30 he had gathered all the people t',
6: 1 David gathered t' all the chosen men
10: 15 they gathered themselves t'.
17 told David, he gathered all Israel t',
12: 3 it grew up t' with him, and with
28 gather the rest of the people t',
29 David gathered all the people t',
14: 6 and they two strove t' in the field,
16 would destroy me and my son t'
20: 14 they were gathered t', and went also
21: 9 they fell all seven t', and were put
23: 9 were there gathered t' to battle,
11 Philistines were gathered t' into a
1Ki 3: 18 we were t'; there was no stranger
5: 12 and they two made a league t'.
10: 26 And Solomon gathered t' chariots
11: 1 t' with the daughter of Pharaoh,
18: 20 and gathered the prophets t' unto
20: 1 of Syria gathered all his host t':
22: 6 of Israel gathered the prophets t',
2Ki 2: 8 took his mantle, and wrapped it t',
3: 10, 13 hath called these three kings t',
9: 25 I and thou rode t' after Ahab his
10: 18 Jehu gathered all the people t',
1Ch 10: 6 Saul...and all his house died t'.
11: 13 Philistines were gathered t' to
13: 5 So David gathered all Israel t',
15: 3 And David gathered all Israel t'
16: 35 and gather us t', and deliver us
19: 7 of Ammon gathered themselves t'
22: 2 David commanded to gather t' the
23: 2 he gathered t' all the princes of
2Ch 12: 5 that were gathered t' to Jerusalem
15: 10 they gathered...t' at Jerusalem
18: 5 of Israel gathered t' of prophets
20: 4 And Judah gathered themselves t',
24: 5 he gathered t' the priests and the
25: 5 Amaziah gathered Judah t', and
28: 24 Ahaz gathered t' the vessels of the
29: 4 and gathered them t' into the east
30: 3 the people gathered themselves t'
32: 4 was gathered much people t',
6 gathered them t'...in the street
34: 17 they have gathered t' the money
29 sent and gathered t' all the elders
Ezr 2: 64 whole congregation t' was forty
3: 1 gathered themselves t' as one man
9 and his sons, the sons of Judah, t',
11 they sang t' by course in praising
4: 3 we ourselves t' will build unto the
6: 20 and the Levites were purified t',
7: 28 gathered t' out of Israel chief men
8: 15 I gathered them t' to the river that
10: 7 should gather...t' unto Jerusalem;
9 Benjamin gathered themselves t'
Ne 4: 6 all the wall was joined t' unto the
8 conspired all of them t' to come
6: 2 Come, let us meet t' in some one of
7 therefore, and let us take counsel t'.
10 Let us meet t' in the house of God,
7: 5 mine heart to gather t' the nobles,
66 whole congregation t' was forty
8: 1 gathered themselves t' as one man
13 were gathered t' the chief of the
12: 28 the singers gathered themselves t',
13: 11 And I gathered them t', and set
Es 2: 3 gather t' all the fair young virgins
8 many maidens were gathered t'
19 virgins were gathered t' the second
4: 16 Go, gather t' all the Jews that are
8: 11 every city to gather themselves t',
9: 2 The Jews gathered themselves t'
15 in Shushan gathered themselves t'
16 provinces gathered themselves t'
18 that were at Shushan assembled t'
Job 2: 11 they had made an appointment t'
3: 18 There the prisoners rest t'; they
6: 2 my calamity laid in the balances t'!
9: 32 and we should come t' in judgment.
10: 8 have made me and fashioned me t'
11: 10 cut off, and shut up, or gather t',
16: 10 gathered themselves t' against me.
17: 16 pit, when our rest t' is in the dust.
19: 12 His troops come t', and raise up
Job 24: 4 the poor of the earth hide...t'.
30: 7 the nettles they were gathered t'.
34: 15 All flesh shall perish t', and man
38: 7 When the morning stars sang t',
38 and the clods cleave fast t'?
40: 13 Hide them in the dust t'; and bind
17 sinews of his stones are wrapped t'.
41: 15 pride, shut up t' as with a close seal.
17 they stick t', that they cannot be
23 flakes of his flesh are joined t':
Ps 2: 2 and the rulers take counsel t',
14: 3 aside, they are all t' become filthy:
31: 13 they took counsel t' against me,
33: 7 He gathereth the waters of the sea t'
34: 3 me, and let us exalt his name t'.
35: 15 and gathered themselves t':
15 the abjects gathered themselves t'
26 and brought to confusion t'
37: 38 transgressors shall be destroyed t':
40: 14 be ashamed and confounded t'
41: 7 All that hate me whisper t' against
47: 9 The princes...are gathered t',
48: 4 were assembled, they passed by t'.
49: 2 Both low and high, rich and poor, t'.
50: 5 Gather my saints t' unto me;
55: 14 We took sweet counsel t', and
56: 6 They gather themselves t', they hide
71: 10 wait for my soul take counsel t',
74: 8 hearts, Let us destroy them t':
83: 5 have consulted t' with one consent:
85: 10 Mercy and truth are met t';
88: 17 they compassed me about t'.
94: 21 They gather themselves t' against
98: 8 hands: let the hills be joyful t'
102: 22 When the people are gathered t',
104: 22 ariseth, they gather themselves t',
122: 3 as a city that is compact t':
133: 1 is for brethren to dwell t' in unity!
140: 2 are they gathered t' for war.
147: 2 gathered t' the outcasts of Israel.
Pr 22: 2 The rich and poor meet t': the Lord is
29: 13 poor and the deceitful man meet t':
Ec 3: 5 and a time to gather stones t';
4: 11 if two lie t', then they have heat:
Isa 1: 18 Come now, and let us reason t', saith
28 and of the sinners shall be t', and
31 spark, and they shall both burn t',
8: 10 Take counsel t', and it shall come to
9: 11 him, and join his enemies t';
21 they t' shall be against Judah.
11: 6 the young lion and the fatling t';
7 their young ones shall lie down t':
12 gather t' the dispersed of Judah
14 shall spoil them of the east t':
13: 4 kingdoms of nations gathered t':
18: 6 They shall be left t' unto the fowls
22: 3 All thy rulers are fled t', they are
3 that are found in thee are bound t',
9 gathered t' the waters of the lower
24: 22 And they shall be gathered t', as
25: 11 and he shall bring down their pride t'
26: 19 t' with my dead body shall they arise.
27: 4 them, I would burn them t'.
31: 3 fall down, and they shall fail t'.
34: 4 the heavens shall be rolled t' as
40: 5 and all flesh shall see it t':
41: 1 let us come near t' to judgment.
19 and the pine, and the box tree t':
20 and consider, and understand t',
23 may be dismayed, and behold it t'.
43: 9 Let all the nations be gathered t',
17 they shall lie down t', they shall not
26 me in remembrance: let us plead t':
44: 11 let them all be gathered t', let
11 and they shall be ashamed t'.
45: 8 let righteousness spring up t'; I
16 go to confusion t' that are makers
20 draw near t', ye that are escaped of
21 near; yea, let them take counsel t':
46: 2 They stoop, they bow down t';
48: 13 call unto them, they stand up t'.
49: 18 all these gather themselves t', and
50: 8 contend with me? let us stand t':
52: 8 with the voice t' shall they sing:
9 Break forth into joy, sing t', ye
54: 15 they shall surely gather t', but
15 whosoever shall gather t' against
60: 4 all they gather themselves t', they
5 Then thou shalt see, and flow t',
7 shall be gathered t' unto thee,
13 tree, the pine tree, and the box t',
62: 9 that have brought it t' shall drink
65: 7 the iniquities of your fathers t',
25 The wolf and the lamb shall feed t',
66: 17 the mouse, shall be consumed t',
Jer 3: 18 they shall come t' out of the land of
4: 5 cry, gather t', and say, Assemble
6: 11 the assembly of young men t':
12 with their fields and wives t':
21 the sons t' shall fall upon them;
13: 14 even the fathers and the sons t',
31: 8 her that travaileth with child t':
12 shall flow t' to the goodness of the
13 dance, both young men and old t':
24 and in all the cities thereof t',
41: 1 they did eat bread t' in Mizpah.
46: 12 mighty, and they are fallen both t'.
21 turned back, and are fled away t':
48: 7 with his priests and his princes t'.
49: 3 and his priests and his princes t'.
14 Gather ye t', and come against
50: 4 they and the children of Judah t',
29 Call t' the archers against
33 of Judah were oppressed t':
51: 27 call t' against her the kingdoms of
38 They shall roar t' like lions: they

Jer 51: 44 nations shall not flow *t* any more
La 2: 8 to lament; they languished *t*.
Eze 21: 14 prophesy, and smite thine hands *t*,
17 I will also smite mine hands *t*, and I
29: 5 thou shalt not be brought *t*, nor
37: 7 bones came *t*, bone to his bone.
Da 2: 35 and the gold, broken to pieces *t*,
3: 2 king sent to gather *t* the princes,
3 gathered *t* unto the dedication of
27 counsellers, being gathered *t*,
6: 6 presidents and princes assembled *t*
7 have consulted *t* to establish
11: 6 they shall join themselves *t*;
Ho 1: 11 children of Israel be gathered *t*,
11: 8 me, my repentings are kindled *t*.
Joe 3: 11 gather yourselves *t* round about:
Am 1: 15 captivity, he and his princes *t*,
3: 3 Can two walk *t*, except they be
Mic 2: 12 them *t* as the sheep of Bozrah,
Na 1: 10 while they be folden *t* as thorns,†‡
2: 10 melteth, and the knees smite *t*,
Zep 2: 1 Gather yourselves *t*, yea,
1 yea, gather *t*, O nation not desired:
Zec 10: 4 bow, out of him every oppressor *t*.
12: 3 people of the earth be gathered *t*
14: 14 round about shall be gathered *t*,
M't 1: 18 before they came *t*, she was found
2: 4 priests and scribes of the people *t*,
13: 2 great multitudes were gathered *t*
30 Let both grow *t* until the harvest:
30 Gather ye *t* first the tares, and
18: 20 three are gathered *t* in my name,
19: 6 What therefore God hath joined *t*,
22: 10 gathered *t* all as many as they
34 they were gathered *t*.
41 the Pharisees were gathered *t*,
23: 37 I have gathered thy children *t*,
24: 28 will the eagles be gathered *t*.
31 gather *t* his elect from the four
26: 3 Then assembled *t* the chief priests,
27: 17 when they were gathered *t*,
62 and Pharisees came *t* unto Pilate,
M'r 1: 33 city was gathered *t* at the door.
2: 2 many were gathered *t*,
15 and sinners sat also *t* with Jesus
3: 20 the multitude cometh *t* again,
6: 30 apostles gathered themselves *t*
33 them, and came *t* unto him.
7: 1 came *t* unto him the Pharisees,
9: 25 that the people came running *t*,
10: 9 What therefore God hath joined *t*,
12: 28 having heard them reasoning *t*,
13: 27 gather *t* his elect from the four
14: 56 him, but their witness agreed not *t*.
59 neither so did their witness agree *t*.
15: 16 and they call *t* the whole band.
Lu 5: 15 great multitudes came *t* to hear,
6: 38 measure, pressed down, and shaken *t*,
8: 4 much people were gathered *t*,
9: 1 he called his twelve disciples *t*,
11: 29 the people were gathered thick *t*,
12: 1 were gathered *t* an innumerable
13: 11 was bowed *t*, and could in no wise
34 I have gathered thy children *t*,
15: 6 he calleth *t* his friends and
9 her friends and her neighbours *t*,
13 the younger son gathered all *t*,
17: 35 women...be grinding *t*;
37 will the eagles be gathered *t*.
22: 55 were set down *t*, Peter sat down
66 priests and the scribes came *t*,
23: 12 Herod were made friends *t*:
13 he had called *t* the chief priests
48 all the people that came *t* to that
24: 14 they talked *t* of all these
15 they communed *t* and reasoned,
33 and found the eleven gathered *t*,
Joh 4: 36 he that reapeth may rejoice *t*.
6: 13 Therefore they gathered them *t*,
11: 52 gather *t* in one the children of God
53 they took counsel *t* for to put
20: 4 So they ran both *t*: and the
7 but wrapped *t* in a place by itself.
21: 2 There were *t* Simon Peter, and
Ac 1: 4 being assembled *t* with them,
6 When they therefore were come *t*,
15 of names *t* were about an
2: 6 abroad, the multitude came *t*,
44 all that believed were *t*,
3: 1 Peter and John went up *t*
11 all the people ran *t* unto
4: 6 were gathered *t* at Jerusalem.
26 rulers were gathered *t*
27 people of Israel, were gathered *t*,
31 where they were assembled *t*;
5: 9 it that ye have agreed *t* to tempt
21 him, and called the council *t*,
10: 24 called *t* his kinsmen and near
27 and found many that were come *t*.
12: 12 many were gathered *t* praying.
13: 44 came almost the whole city *t* to
14: 1 they went both *t* into the
27 and had gathered the church *t*,
15: 6 And the apostles and elders came *t*
30 they had gathered the multitude *t*,
16: 22 multitude rose up *t* against them:
19: 19 arts brought their books *t*,
25 he called *t* with the workmen
32 not wherefore they were come *t*.
20: 7 disciples came *t* to break bread,
8 where they were gathered *t*.
21: 22 multitude must needs come *t*:
30 was moved, and the people ran *t*:
23: 12 certain of the Jews banded *t*,
28: 17 Paul called the chief of the Jews *t*:
17 and when they were come *t*, he

Ro 1: 12 I may be comforted *t* with you
3: 12 they are *t* become unprofitable;
6: 5 planted *t* in the likeness of his
8: 17 that we may be also glorified *t*.
22 groaneth and travaileth in pain *t*
28 that all things work *t* for good
15: 30 strive *t* with me in your prayers
1Co 1: 10 that ye be perfectly joined *t* in the
3: 9 For we are labourers *t* with God:
5: 4 when ye are gathered *t*, and my
7: 5 come *t* again, that Satan
11: 17 that ye come *t* not for the better,
18 when ye come *t* in the church, I
20 When ye come *t* therefore into one
33 when ye come *t* to eat, tarry one
34 ye come not *t* unto condemnation.
12: 24 but God hath tempered the body *t*,
14: 23 whole church be come *t* into one
26 when ye come *t*, every one of you
2Co 1: 11 Ye also helping *t* by prayer for us,
6: 1 We then, as workers *t* with him,
14 Be ye not unequally yoked *t* with
Eph 1: 10 might gather *t* in one all things
2: 5 hath quickened us *t* with Christ,
6 And hath raised us up *t*,
6 made us sit *t* in heavenly places
21 all the building fitly framed *t*
22 In whom ye also are builded *t* for
4: 16 the whole body fitly joined *t* and
Ph'p 1: 27 one mind striving *t* for the faith
3: 17 Brethren, be followers *t* of me,
Col 2: 2 be comforted, being knit *t* in love,
13 hath he quickened *t* with him,
19 ministered, and knit *t*,
1Th 4: 17 remain shall be caught up *t* with
5: 10 sleep, we should live *t* with him.
11 Wherefore comfort yourselves *t*,
2Th 2: 1 and by our gathering *t* unto him,
Heb 10: 25 the assembling of ourselves *t*,
Jas 5: 3 Ye have heaped treasure *t* for the
1Pe 3: 7 being heirs *t* of the grace of life;
5: 13 is at Babylon, elected *t* with you,
Re 6: 14 as a scroll when it is rolled *t*;
16: 16 he gathered them *t* into a place
19: 17 Come and gather yourselves *t* unto
19 armies, gathered *t* to make war
20: 8 Magog, to gather them *t* to battle:

Tohu (*to'-hu*) See also NAHATH; TOAH.
1Sa 1: 1 the son of Elihu, the son of *T*,

Toi (*to'-i*) See also TOU.
2Sa 8: 9 When *T* king of Hamath heard
10 *T* sent Joram his son unto king
10 for Hadadezer had wars with *T*.

toil See also TOILED; TOILING.
Ge 5: 29 our work and *t* of our hands,
41: 51 hath made me forget all my *t*,
M't 6: 28 they *t* not, neither do they spin:
Lu 12: 27 grow: they *t* not, they spin not;

toiled
Lu 5: 5 Master, we have *t* all the night,

toiling
M'r 6: 48 And he saw them *t* in rowing; for

token See also TOKENS.
Ge 9: 12 This is the *t* of the covenant which
13 *t* of a covenant between me and
17 This is the *t* of the covenant, which
17: 11 *t* of the covenant betwixt me and
Ex 3: 12 this shall be a *t* unto thee, that I
12: 13 the blood shall be to you for a *t*
13: 16 shall be for a *t* upon thine hand,
Nu 17: 10 be kept for a *t* against the rebels;
Jos 2: 12 father's house, and give me a true *t*:
Ps 86: 17 Shew me a *t* for good; that they
M'r 14: 44 betrayed him had given them a *t*,
Ph'p 1: 28 to them an evident *t* of perdition,
2Th 1: 5 a manifest *t* of the righteous
3: 17 which is the *t* in every epistle:

tokens
De 22: 15 forth the *t* of the damsel's virginity
17 are the *t* of my daughter's virginity.
20 *t* of virginity be not found for the
Job 21: 29 way? and do ye not know their *t*,
Ps 65: 8 uttermost parts are afraid at thy *t*:
135: 9 sent *t* and wonders into the midst
Isa 44: 25 That frustrateth the *t* of the liars,

Tola (*to'-lah*) See also TOLAITES.
Ge 46: 13 sons of Issachar; *T*, and Phuvah,
Nu 26: 23 of *T*, the family of the Tolaites:
J'g 10: 1 defend Israel *T* the son of Puah,
1Ch 7: 1 sons of Issachar were, *T*, and
2 sons of *T*; Uzzi, and Rephaiah,
2 their father's house, to wit, of *T*:

Tolad (*to'-lad*) See also EL-TOLAD.
1Ch 4: 29 Bilhah, and at Ezem, and at *T*,

Tolaites (*to'-lah-ites*)
Nu 26: 23 of Tola, the family of the *T*:

told See also FORETOLD.
Ge 3: 11 Who *t* thee that thou wast naked?
9: 22 and *t* his two brethren without.
14: 13 escaped, and *t* Abram the Hebrew;
20: 8 *t* all these things in their ears:
22: 3 the place of which God had *t* him.
9 the place which God had *t* him of;
20 that it was *t* Abraham, saying,
24: 28 *t* them of her mother's house these
33 eat, until I have *t* mine errand.
66 servant *t* Isaac all things that he
26: 32 and *t* him concerning the well
27: 42 her elder son were *t* to Rebekah:
29: 12 Jacob *t* Rachel that he was her
12 and she ran and *t* her father.
13 And he *t* Laban all these things.

Ge 31: 20 in that he *t* him not that he fled.
22 *t* Laban on the third day that
37: 5 a dream, and he *t* it his brethren:
9 dream, and *t* it his brethren, and
10 And he *t* it to his father, and to
38: 13 was *t* Tamar, saying, Behold, thy
24 that it was *t* Judah, saying,
40: 9 chief butler *t* his dream to Joseph,
41: 8 and Pharaoh *t* them his dream;
12 we *t* him, and he interpreted to us
24 and I *t* this unto the magicians;
42: 29 *t* him all that befell unto them;
43: 7 we *t* him according to the tenor
44: 24 we *t* him the words of my lord.
45: 26 *t* him, saying, Joseph is yet alive,
27 *t* him all the words of Joseph,
47: 1 Joseph came and *t* Pharaoh, and
48: 1 that one *t* Joseph, Behold, thy
2 one *t* Jacob, and said, Behold,
Ex 4: 28 Moses *t* Aaron all the words of
5: 1 Aaron went in, and *t* Pharaoh,
14: 5 it was *t* the king of Egypt that the
16: 22 congregation came and *t* Moses.
18: 8 Moses *t* his father in law all that
19: 9 Moses *t* the words of the people
24: 3 Moses came and *t* the people all
Le 21: 24 Moses *t* it unto Aaron, and to his
Nu 11: 24 *t* the people the words of the Lord,
27 ran a young man, and *t* Moses,
13: 27 *t* him, and said, We came unto
14: 39 Moses *t* these sayings unto all
23: 26 said unto Balak, *T* not I thee,
29: 40 *t* the children of Israel according
De 17: 4 And it be *t* thee, and thou hast
Jos 2: 2 And it was *t* the king of Jericho,
23 *t* him all things that befell them:
9: 24 it was certainly *t* thy servants,
10: 17 it was *t* Joshua, saying, The five
J'g 6: 13 miracles which our fathers *t* us
7: 13 there was a man that *t* a dream
9: 7 And when they *t* it to Jotham,
25 by them: and it was *t* Abimelech.
42 the field; and they *t* Abimelech.
47 it was *t* Abimelech, that all the men
13: 6 woman came and *t* her husband,
6 was, neither *t* he me his name:
23 at this time have *t* us such things
14: 2 and *t* his father and his mother,
6 he *t* not his father or his mother
9 he *t* not them that he had taken
16 my people, and hast not *t* it me.
16 I have not *t* it my father nor my
17 on the seventh day, that he *t* her,
17 she *t* the riddle to the children of
16: 2 it was *t* the Gazites, saying, Samson
10, 13 hast mocked me, and *t* me lies:
15 hast not *t* me wherein thy great
17 That he *t* her all his heart, and
18 saw that he had *t* her all his heart,
Ru 3: 16 she *t* her all that the man had done
1Sa 3: 13 *t* him that I will judge his house
18 Samuel *t* him every whit, and hid
4: 13 man came into the city, and *t* it,
14 man came in hastily, and *t* Eli.
8: 10 Samuel *t* all the words of the Lord
9: 15 Lord had *t* Samuel in his ear a
10: 16 He *t* us plainly that the asses
16 Samuel spake, he *t* him not.
25 Samuel *t* the people the manner
11: 4 *t* the tidings in the ears of the
5 *t* him the tidings of the men of
14: 1 side. But he *t* not his father.
33 Then they *t* Saul, saying, Behold,
43 Jonathan *t* him, and said, I did but
15: 12 it was *t* Samuel, saying, Saul came
18: 20 they *t* Saul, and the thing pleased
24 the servants of Saul *t* him, saying,
26 his servants *t* David these words,
19: 2 and Jonathan *t* David, saying,
11 Michal David's wife *t* him, saying,
18 and *t* him all that Saul had done to
19 *t* Saul, saying, Behold, David is at
21 when it was *t* Saul, he sent other
23: 1 they *t* David, saying, Behold, the
7 it was *t* Saul that David was come
13 was *t* Saul that David was escaped
22 *t* me that he dealeth very subtilly.
25 they *t* David: wherefore he came
24: 1 that it was *t* him, saying, Behold,
25: 12 came and *t* him all those sayings.
14 one of the young men *t* Abigail,
19 But she *t* not her husband Nabal.
36 she *t* him nothing, less or more,
37 his wife had *t* him these things,
27: 4 *t* Saul that David was fled to Gath:
2Sa 1: 5 unto the young man that *t* him,
6 the young man that *t* him said, As
13 said unto the young man that *t* him,
2: 4 And they *t* David, saying, That the
3: 23 they *t* Joab, saying, Abner the son
4: 10 When one *t* me, saying, Behold,
6: 12 And it was *t* king David, saying,
10: 5 When they *t* it unto David, he sent
17 was *t* David, he gathered all Israel
11: 5 conceived, and sent and *t* David,
10 when they had *t* David, saying,
18 Then Joab sent and *t* David all the
14: 33 Joab came to the king, and *t* him:
15: 31 And one *t* David, saying, Ahithophel
17: 17 and a wench went and *t* them;
17 and they went and *t* king David.
18 a lad saw them, and *t* Absalom:
21 went and *t* king David, and said
18: 10 a certain man saw it, and *t* Joab,
11 Joab said unto the man that *t* him,
25 watchman cried, and *t* the king.

2Sa 19: 1 And it was *t'* Joab, Behold, the king
8 they *t'* unto all the people, saying,
21: 11 it was *t'* David what Rizpah the
24: 13 So Gad came to David, and *t'* him,
1Ki 1: 23 they *t'* the king, saying, Behold
51 And it was *t'* Solomon, saying,
2: 29 *t'* king Solomon that Joab was fled
39 And they *t'* Shimei, saying, Behold,
41 it was *t'* Solomon that Shimei had
8: 5 that could not be *t'* nor numbered
10: 3 Solomon *t'* her all her questions:
3 from the king, which he *t'* her not.
7 and, behold, the half was not *t'* me:
13: 11 his sons came and *t'* him all the
11 them they *t'* also to their father.
25 and *t'* it in the city where the old
14: 2 which *t'* me that I should be king
18: 13 Was it not *t'* my lord what I did
16 went to meet Ahab, and *t'* him:
19: 1 Ahab *t'* Jezebel all that Elijah had
20: 17 Ben-hadad sent out, and they *t'* him,
2Ki 1: 7 meet you, and *t'* you these words?
4: 7 she came and *t'* the man of God.
27 hid it from me, and hath not *t'* me.
31 and *t'* him, saying, The child is not
5: 4 one went in, and *t'* his lord, saying,
6: 10 man of God *t'* him and warned him
13 was *t'* him, saying, Behold, he is
7: 10 they *t'* them, saying, We came to
11 they *t'* it to the king's house within.
15 messengers returned,...*t'* the king.
8: 6 king asked the woman, she *t'* him.
7 *t'* him, saying, The man of God is
14 He *t'* me that thou shouldest surely
9: 18 the watchman *t'*, saying, The
20 watchman *t'*, saying, He came even
36 they came again, and *t'* him.
10: 8 there came a messenger, and *t'* him,
12: 10 *t'* the money that was found in
11 they gave the money, being *t'*,
18: 37 *t'* him the words of Rab-shakeh.
23: 17 the men of the city *t'* him, It is the
1Ch 17: 25 hast *t'* thy servant that thou wilt
19: 5 *t'* David how the men were served.
17 it was *t'* David; and he gathered
2Ch 2: 2 Solomon *t'* out threescore and ten
5: 6 which could not be *t'* nor numbered
9: 2 Solomon *t'* her all her questions:
2 from Solomon which he *t'* her not.
6 of thy wisdom was not *t'* me:
20: 2 came some that *t'* Jehoshaphat,
34: 18 Then Shaphan the scribe *t'* the king,
Ezr 8: 17 I *t'* them what they should
Ne 2: 12 neither *t'* I any man what my God
16 neither had I as yet *t'* it to the Jews,
18 I *t'* them of the hand of my God
Es 2: 22 who *t'* it unto Esther the queen;
3: 4 that they *t'* Haman, to see whether
4 he had *t'* them that he was a Jew.
4: 4 chamberlains came and *t'* it her.
7 And Mordecai *t'* him of all that had
9 And Hatach came and *t'* Esther the
12 they *t'* to Mordecai Esther's words.
5: 11 Haman *t'* them of the glory of his
6: 2 that Mordecai had *t'* of Bigthana
13 Haman *t'* Zeresh his wife and all
8: 1 Esther had *t'* what he was unto
Job 15: 18 wise men have *t'* from their fathers,
37: 20 Shall it be *t'* him that I speak? if a
Ps 44: 1 our fathers have *t'* us, what work
52: *title* the Edomite came and *t'* Saul,
78: 3 known, and our fathers have *t'* us.
90: 9 we spend our years as a tale that is *t'*.
Ec 6: 6 he live a thousand years twice *t'*,
Isa 7: 2 And it was *t'* the house of David,
36: 22 *t'* him the words of Rabshakeh.
40: 21 not been *t'* you from the beginning?
44: 8 have not I *t'* thee from that time,
45: 21 who hath *t'* it from that time?
52: 15 that which had not been *t'* them
Jer 36: 20 and *t'* all the words in the ears of
38: 27 he *t'* them according to all these
Da 4: 7 and I *t'* the dream before them;
8 before him I *t'* the dream, saying,
7: 1 and *t'* the sum of the matters.
16 So he *t'* me, and made me know the
8: 26 the vision...which was *t'* is true:
Jon 1: 10 the Lord, because he had *t'* them.
Hab 1: 5 not believe, though it be *t'* you.
Zec 10: 2 a lie, and have *t'* false dreams;
M't 8: 33 into the city, and *t'* every thing,
12: 48 and said unto him that *t'* him,
14: 12 buried it, and went and *t'* Jesus.
18: 31 *t'* unto their lord all that was done.
24: 25 Behold, I have *t'* you before.
26: 13 done, be *t'* for a memorial of her.
28: 7 shall ye see him: lo, I have *t'* you.
M'r 5: 14 *t'* it in the city, and in the country.
16 they that saw it *t'* them how it
33 him, and *t'* him all the truth.
6: 30 *t'* him all things, both what they
9: 12 he answered and *t'* them, Elias
16: 10 *t'* them that had been with him,
13 they went and *t'* it unto the residue:
Lu 1: 45 which were *t'* her from the Lord.
2: 17 was *t'* them concerning this child.
18 were *t'* them by the shepherds.
20 and seen, as it was *t'* unto them.
8: 20 it was *t'* him by certain which said,
34 went and *t'* it in the city and in the
36 which saw it *t'* them by what means
9: 10 *t'* him all that they had done.
36 and *t'* no man in those days any of
13: 1 some that *t'* him of the Galilæans,
18: 37 they *t'* him, that Jesus of Nazareth
24: 9 *t'* all these things unto the eleven,

Lu 24: 10 *t'* these things unto the apostles.
35 *t'* what things were done in the
Joh 3: 12 If I have *t'* you earthly things, and
4: 29 *t'* me all things that ever I did:
39 He *t'* me all that ever I did.
51 and *t'* him, saying, Thy son liveth.
5: 15 and *t'* the Jews that it was Jesus,
8: 40 a man that hath *t'* you the truth,
9: 27 I have *t'* you already, and ye did
10: 25 them, I *t'* you, and ye believed not:
11: 46 and *t'* them what things Jesus had
14: 2 it were not so, I would have *t'* you.
29 have *t'* you before it come to pass,
16: 4 But these things have I *t'* you,
4 remember that I *t'* you of them.
18: 8 I have *t'* you that I am he:
20: 18 *t'* the disciples that she had seen
Ac 5: 22 the prison, they returned, and *t'*
25 Then came one and *t'* them, saying,
9: 6 be *t'* thee what thou must do.
12: 14 *t'* how Peter stood before the gate.
16: 36 keeper of the prison *t'* this saying
38 serjeants *t'* these words unto the
22: 10 it shall be *t'* thee of all things
26 he went and *t'* the chief captain,
23: 16 entered into the castle, and *t'* Paul.
30 it was *t'* me how that the Jews
27: 25 it shall be even as it was *t'* me.
2Co 7: 7 when he *t'* us your earnest desire,
13: 2 I *t'* you before, and foretell you,
Ga 5: 21 as I have also *t'* you in time past,
Ph'p 3: 18 walk of whom I have *t'* you often,
1Th 3: 4 we *t'* you before that we should
2Th 2: 5 with you, I *t'* you these things?
Jude 18 that they *t'* you there should be

tolerable
M't 10: 15 It shall be more *t'* for the land of
11: 22 It shall be more *t'* for Tyre and
24 it shall be more *t'* for the land of
M'r 6: 11 It shall be more *t'* for Sodom and
Lu 10: 12 it shall be more *t'* in that day for
14 it shall be more *t'* for Tyre and

toll
Ezr 4: 13 then will they not pay *t'*, tribute,
20 *t'*, tribute, and custom, was paid
7: 24 it shall not be lawful to impose *t'*,

tomb See also TOMBS.
Job 21: 32 grave, and shall remain in the *t'*.
M't 27: 60 laid it in his own new *t'*, which he
M'r 6: 29 up his corpse, and laid it in a *t'*.

tombs
M't 8: 28 with devils, coming out of the *t'*,
23: 29 ye build the *t'* of the prophets,
M'r 5: 2 there met him out of the *t'* a man
3 had his dwelling among the *t'*; and
5 and in the *t'*, crying, and cutting
Lu 8: 27 abode in any house, but in the *t'*.

to-morrow See MORROW.

tongs
Ex 25: 38 *t'* thereof, and the snuffdishes
Nu 4: 9 and his *t'*, and his snuffdishes,
1Ki 7: 49 and the lamps, and the *t'* of gold,
2Ch 4: 21 the lamps, and the *t'*, made he of
Isa 6: 6 which he had taken with the *t'*
44: 12 smith with the *t'* both worketh in

tongue See also DOUBLETONGUED; TONGUES.
Ge 10: 5 every one after his *t'*, after their
Ex 4: 10 slow of speech, and of a slow *t'*.
11: 7 Israel shall not a dog move his *t'*,
De 28: 49 whose *t'* thou shalt not understand;
Jos 10: 21 none moved his *t'* against any of
J'g 7: 5 lappeth of the water with his *t'*,
2Sa 23: 2 by me, and his word was in my *t'*.
Ezr 4: 7 letter was written in the Syrian *t'*,
7 and interpreted in the Syrian *t'*.
7: 4 bondwomen, I had held my *t'*,
Job 5: 21 be hid from the scourge of the *t'*:
6: 24 Teach me, and I will hold my *t'*:
30 Is there iniquity in my *t'*? cannot
13: 19 if I hold my *t'*, I shall give up the
15: 5 thou choosest the *t'* of the crafty.
20: 12 though he hide it under his *t'*;
16 asps: the viper's *t'* shall slay him.
27: 4 wickedness, nor my *t'* utter deceit.
29: 10 their *t'* cleaved to the roof of their
33: 2 my *t'* hath spoken in my mouth.
41: 1 or his *t'* with a cord which thou
Ps 5: 9 sepulchre; they flatter with their *t'*.
10: 7 under his *t'* is mischief and vanity.
12: 3 the *t'* that speaketh proud things:
4 said, With our *t'* will we prevail:
15: 3 He that backbiteth not with his *t'*,
22: 15 my *t'* cleaveth to my jaws; and thou
34: 13 Keep thy *t'* from evil, and thy lips
35: 28 And my *t'* shall speak of thy
37: 30 and his *t'* talketh of judgment.
39: 1 my ways, that I sin not with my *t'*:
3 burned: then spake I with my *t'*,
45: 1 my *t'* is the pen of a ready writer.
50: 19 to evil, and thy *t'* frameth deceit.
51: 14 my *t'* shall sing aloud of thy
52: 2 Thy *t'* deviseth mischiefs; like a
4 words, O thou deceitful *t'*.
57: 4 arrows, and their *t'* a sharp sword.
64: 3 Who whet their *t'* like a sword, and
8 shall make their own *t'* to fall upon
66: 17 and he was extolled with my *t'*.
68: 23 and the *t'* of thy dogs in the same.
71: 24 My *t'* also shall talk of thy
73: 9 their *t'* walketh through the earth.
109: 2 spoken against me with a lying *t'*.
119: 172 My *t'* shall speak of thy word: for
120: 2 lying lips, and from a deceitful *t'*.
3 be done unto thee, thou false *t'*?
126: 2 laughter, and our *t'* with singing:

Ps 137: 6 let my *t'* cleave to the roof of my
139: 4 For there is not a word in my *t'*,
Pr 6: 17 A proud look, a lying *t'*, and hands
24 of the *t'* of a strange woman.
10: 20 *t'* of the just is as choice silver:
31 but the froward *t'* shall be cut out.
12: 18 but the *t'* of the wise is health.
19 but a lying *t'* is but for a moment.
15: 2 The *t'* of the wise useth knowledge
4 A wholesome *t'* is a tree of life: but
16: 1 answer of the *t'*, is from the Lord.
17: 4 a liar giveth ear to a naughty *t'*.
20 a perverse *t'* falleth into mischief.
18: 21 and life are in the power of the *t'*:
21: 6 lying *t'* is a vanity tossed to and fro
23 keepeth his mouth and his *t'*
25: 15 and a soft *t'* breaketh the bone.
23 angry countenance a backbiting *t'*.
26: 28 A lying *t'* hateth those that are
28: 23 than he that flattereth with the *t'*.
31: 26 and in her *t'* is the law of kindness.
Ca 4: 11 honey and milk are under thy *t'*;
Isa 3: 8 their *t'* and their doings are against
11: 15 destroy the *t'* of the Egyptian sea;
28: 11 and another *t'* will he speak to this
30: 27 and his *t'* as a devouring fire:
32: 4 the *t'* of the stammerers shall be
33: 19 of a stammering *t'*, that thou canst
35: 6 hart, and the *t'* of the dumb sing:
41: 17 none, and their *t'* faileth for thirst,
45: 23 knee shall bow, every *t'* shall swear.
50: 4 hath given me the *t'* of the learned,
54: 17 every *t'* that shall rise against thee
57: 4 a wide mouth, and draw out the *t'*?
59: 3 your *t'* hath muttered perverseness.
Jer 9: 5 have taught their *t'* to speak lies,
8 Their *t'* is as an arrow shot out; it
18: 18 and let us smite him with the *t'*,
La 4: 4 *t'* of the sucking child cleaveth to
Eze 3: 26 make thy *t'* cleave to the roof of thy
Da 1: 4 and the *t'* of the Chaldeans.
Ho 7: 16 by the sword for the rage of their *t'*:
Am 6: 10 Then shall he say, Hold thy *t'*:
Mic 6: 12 their *t'* is deceitful in their mouth.
Hab 1: 13 holdest thy *t'* when the wicked
Zep 3: 13 shall a deceitful *t'* be found in
Zec 14: 12 their *t'* shall consume away in their
M'r 7: 33 and he spit, and touched his *t'*;
35 and the string of his *t'* was loosed,
Lu 1: 64 and his *t'* loosed, and he spake, and
16: 24 his finger in water, and cool my *t'*;
Joh 5: 2 called in the Hebrew *t'* Bethesda,
Ac 1: 19 field is called in their proper *t'*,
2: 8 hear we every man in our own *t'*,
26 heart rejoice, and my *t'* was glad;
21: 40 spake unto them in the Hebrew *t'*,
22: 2 he spake in the Hebrew *t'* to them,
26: 14 and saying in the Hebrew *t'*, Saul,
Ro 14: 11 and every *t'* shall confess to God.
1Co 14: 2 he that speaketh in an unknown *t'*
4 He that speaketh in an unknown *t'*
9 except ye utter by the *t'* words
13 him that speaketh in an unknown *t'*
14 For if I pray in an unknown *t'*, my
19 thousand words in an unknown *t'*.
26 a psalm, hath a doctrine, hath a *t'*,
27 If any man speak in an unknown *t'*,
Ph'p 2: 11 every *t'* should confess that Jesus
Jas 1: 26 be religious, and bridleth not his *t'*,
3: 5 Even so the *t'* is a little member,
6 the *t'* is a fire, a world of iniquity:
6 so is the *t'* among our members,
8 But the *t'* can no man tame; it is
1Pe 3: 10 let him refrain his *t'* from evil,
1Jo 3: 18 let us not love in word, neither in *t'*;
Re 5: 9 out of every kindred, and *t'*, and
9: 11 name in the Hebrew *t'* is Abaddon,
11 the Greek *t'* hath his name Apollyon.
14: 6 every nation, and kindred, and *t'*,
16: 16 in the Hebrew *t'* Armageddon.

tongues
Ge 10: 20, 31 their families, after their *t'*,
Ps 31: 20 in a pavilion from the strife of *t'*.
55: 9 Destroy, O Lord, and divide their *t'*:
78: 36 they lied unto him with their *t'*.
140: 3 sharpened their *t'* like a serpent:
Isa 66: 18 that I will gather all nations and *t'*;
Jer 9: 3 they bend their *t'* like their bow for
23: 31 that use their *t'*, and say, He saith.
M'r 16: 17 they shall speak with new *t'*;
Ac 2: 3 there appeared unto them cloven *t'*
4 began to speak with other *t'*, as the
11 we do hear them speak in our *t'* the
10: 46 For they heard them speak with *t'*,
19: 6 they spake with *t'*, and prophesied.
Ro 3: 13 with their *t'* they have used deceit;
1Co 12: 10 spirits; to another divers kinds of *t'*;
10 to another the interpretation of *t'*:
28 governments, diversities of *t'*.
30 do all speak with *t'*? do all
13: 1 Though I speak with the *t'* of men
8 fail; whether there be *t'*, they shall
14: 5 I would that ye all spake with *t'*,
5 than he that speaketh with *t'*,
6 if I come unto you speaking with *t'*,
18 I speak with *t'* more than ye all:
21 With men of other *t'* and other lips
22 Wherefore *t'* are for a sign, not to
23 and all speak with *t'*, and there
39 and forbid not to speak with *t'*.
Re 7: 9 kindreds, and people, and *t'*, stood
10: 11 many peoples, and nations, and *t'*,
11: 9 of the people and kindreds and *t'*
13: 7 all kindreds, and *t'*, and nations.
16: 10 and they gnawed their *t'* for pain,
17: 15 and multitudes, and nations, and *t'*.

too^A
Ge 18:14 Is any thing *t'* hard for the Lord?
Ex 12: 4 the household be *t'* little for the lamb,
18:18 for this thing is *t'* heavy for thee;
36: 7 the work to make it, and *t'* much.
Nu 11:14 alone, because it is *t'* heavy for me.
16: 3 Ye take *t'* much upon you, seeing
7 ye take *t'* much upon you, ye sons
22: 6 people; for they are *t'* mighty for me:
De 1:17 the cause that is *t'* hard for you, bring
2:36 was not one city *t'* strong for us:
12:21 his name there be *t'* far from thee,
14:24 And if the way be *t'* long for thee, so
24 or if the place be *t'* far from thee,
17: 8 arise a matter *t'* hard for thee in
Jos 17:15 mount Ephraim be *t'* narrow for thee.
19: 9 of Judah was *t'* much for them:
47 of Dan went out *t'* little for them:
22:17 Is the iniquity of Peor *t'* little for us,
J'g 18:26 saw that they were *t'* strong for him,
Ru 1:12 for I am *t'* old to have an husband.
2Sa 3:39 sons of Zeruiah be *t'* hard for me:
10:11 If the Syrians be *t'* strong for me,
11 children of Ammon be *t'* strong for
12: 8 and if that had been *t'* little, I would
22:18 me: for they were *t'* strong for me.
1Ki 1:36 Lord God of my lord the king say so *t'*.
8:64 *t'* little to receive the burnt offerings,
12:28 It is *t'* much for you to go up to
19: 7 because the journey is *t'* great for thee.
2Ki 3:26 saw that the battle was *t'* sore for him,
6: 1 we dwell with thee is *t'* strait for us.
1Ch 19:12 If the Syrians be *t'* strong for me,
12 children of Ammon be *t'* strong for
2Ch 29:34 But the priests were *t'* few, so that they
Es 1:18 shall there arise *t'* much contempt
Job 42: 3 things *t'* wonderful for me, which I
Ps 18:17 me: for they were *t'* strong for me.
35:10 from him that is *t'* strong for him,
38: 4 heavy burden they are *t'* heavy for me.
73:16 to know this, it was *t'* painful for me;
131: 1 matters, or in things *t'* high for me.
139: 6 Such knowledge is *t'* wonderful for me;
Pr 24: 7 Wisdom is *t'* high for a fool: he
30:18 three things which are *t'* wonderful
Isa 49:20 ears, The place is *t'* strait for me:
Jer 32:17 and there is nothing *t'* hard for thee:
27 flesh: is there any thing *t'* hard for me?
Ac 17:22 all things ye are *t'* superstitious.
took See also OVERTOOK; TOOKEST; UNDERTOOK.
Ge 2:15 And the Lord God *t'* the man, and
21 and he *t'* one of his ribs, and
3: 6 she *t'* of the fruit thereof, and did
4:19 And Lamech *t'* unto him two wives:
5:24 and he was not; for God *t'* him.
6: 2 they *t'* them wives of all which they
8: 9 he put forth his hand, and *t'* her,
20 *t'* of every clean beast, and of every
9:23 Shem and Japheth *t'* a garment,
11:29 Abram and Nahor *t'* them wives:
31 Terah *t'* Abram his son, and Lot
12: 5 Abram *t'* Sarai his wife, and Lot
14:11 And they *t'* all the goods of Sodom
12 they *t'* Lot, Abram's brother's son,
15:10 And he *t'* unto him all these, and
16: 3 Abram's wife *t'* Hagar her maid
17:23 And Abraham *t'* Ishmael his son,
18: 8 he *t'* butter, and milk, and the calf
20: 2 king of Gerar sent, and *t'* Sarah.
14 And Abimelech *t'* sheep, and oxen,
21:14 and *t'* bread, and a bottle of water,
21 mother *t'* him a wife out of the land
27 And Abraham *t'* sheep and oxen,
22: 3 *t'* two of his young men with him,
6 Abraham *t'* the wood of the burnt
6 he *t'* the fire in his hand, and a
10 and *t'* the knife to slay his son.
13 and Abraham went and *t'* the ram,
24: 7 which *t'* me from my father's house,
10 the servant *t'* ten camels of the
22 that the man *t'* a golden earring of
61 the servant *t'* Rebekah, and went
65 therefore she *t'* a vail, and covered
67 and *t'* Rebekah, and she became
25: 1 Then again Abraham *t'* a wife, and
20 old when he *t'* Rebekah to wife,
26 and his hand *t'* hold on Esau's heel;
26:34 old when he *t'* to wife Judith the
27:15 Rebekah *t'* goodly raiment of her
36 he *t'* away my birthright; and,
28: 9 and *t'* unto the wives which he had
11 and he *t'* of the stones of that place,
18 *t'* the stone that he had put for his
29:23 that he *t'* Leah his daughter, and
30: 9 she *t'* Zilpah her maid, and gave
37 Jacob *t'* him rods of green poplar,
31:23 And he *t'* his brethren with him,
45 And Jacob *t'* a stone, and set it up
46 they *t'* stones, and made an heap:
32:13 *t'* of that which came to his hand
22 that night, and *t'* his two wives,
23 And he *t'* them, and sent them over
33:11 And he urged him, and he *t'* it.
34: 2 he *t'* her, and lay with her, and
25 *t'* each man his sword, and came
26 *t'* Dinah out of Shechem's house,
28 They *t'* their sheep, and their oxen,
29 and their wives *t'* they captive,
36: 2 Esau *t'* his wives of the daughters
6 And Esau *t'* his wives, and his sons,
37:24 they *t'* him, and cast him into a pit:
31 they *t'* Joseph's coat, and killed a
38: 2 and he *t'* her, and went in unto her.
6 Judah *t'* a wife for Er his firstborn,
28 the midwife *t'* and bound upon his
39:20 And Joseph's master *t'* him, and
Ge 40:11 I *t'* the grapes, and pressed them
41:42 Pharaoh *t'* off his ring from his
42:24 and *t'* from them Simeon, and
30 and *t'* us for spies of the country.
43:15 And the men *t'* that present, and
15 they *t'* double money in their hand,
34 he *t'* and sent messes unto them
44:11 *t'* down every man his sack to the
46: 1 Israel *t'* his journey with all that
6 And they *t'* their cattle, and their
47: 2 And he *t'* some of his brethren,
48: 1 and he *t'* with him his two sons,
13 And Joseph *t'* them both, Ephraim
22 I *t'* out of the hand of the Amorite
50:25 Joseph *t'* an oath of the children
Ex 2: 1 and *t'* to wife a daughter of Levi.
3 she *t'* for him an ark of bulrushes,
9 the woman *t'* the child, and nursed
4: 6 when he *t'* it out, behold, his hand
20 Moses *t'* his wife and his sons,
20 Moses *t'* the rod of God in his hand.
25 Then Zipporah *t'* a sharp stone,
6:20 Amram *t'* him Jochebed his father's
23 Aaron *t'* him Elisheba, daughter of
25 Eleazar...*t'* him one of the daughters
9:10 And they *t'* ashes of the furnace,
10:19 wind, which *t'* away the locusts,
12:34 the people *t'* their dough before it
13:19 Moses *t'* the bones of Joseph with
20 they *t'* their journey from Succoth,
22 *t'* not away the pillar of the cloud
14: 6 and *t'* his people with him:
7 he *t'* six hundred chosen chariots
25 And *t'* off their chariot wheels,
15:20 Miriam...*t'* a timbrel in her hand:
16: 1 And they *t'* their journey from Elim,
17:12 they *t'* a stone, and put it under
18: 2 Moses' father in law, *t'* Zipporah,
12 *t'* a burnt offering and sacrifices for
24: 6 Moses *t'* half of the blood, and put
7 And he *t'* the book of the covenant,
8 Moses *t'* the blood, and sprinkled it
32:20 he *t'* the calf which they had made,
33: 7 And Moses *t'* the tabernacle, and
34: 4 and *t'* in his hand the two tables of
34 *t'* the vail off, until he came out.
40:20 he *t'* and put the testimony into
Le 6: 4 that which he *t'* violently away,
8:10 And Moses *t'* the anointing oil,
15 Moses *t'* the blood, and put it upon
16 And he *t'* all the fat that was upon
23 Moses *t'* of the blood of it, and put
25 he *t'* the fat, and the rump, and all
26 he *t'* one unleavened cake, and a
28 Moses *t'* them from off their hands,
29 Moses *t'* the breast, and waved it
30 And Moses *t'* of the anointing oil,
9:15 and *t'* the goat, which was the sin
17 offering, and *t'* an handful thereof,
10: 1 *t'* either of them his censer, and
Nu 1:17 And Moses and Aaron *t'* these men
3:49 Moses *t'* the redemption money of
50 Of the firstborn...*t'* he the money;
7: 6 Moses *t'* the wagons and the oxen,
10:12 children of Israel *t'* their journeys
13 they first *t'* their journey according
11:25 *t'* of the spirit that was upon him,
16: 1 of Peleth, sons of Reuben, *t'* men:
18 And they *t'* every man his censer,
39 Eleazar...*t'* the brasen censers,
47 And Aaron *t'* as Moses commanded,
17: 9 looked, and *t'* every man his rod.
20: 9 Moses *t'* the rod from before the
21: 1 and *t'* some of them prisoners.
25 And Israel *t'* all these cities: and
32 and they *t'* the villages thereof,
22:41 morning, that Balak *t'* Balaam,
23: 7 And he *t'* up his parable, and said,
11 I *t'* thee to curse mine enemies,
18 And he *t'* up his parable, and said,
24: 3, 15, 20 he *t'* up his parable, and said,
21 and *t'* up his parable, and said,
23 And he *t'* up his parable, and said,
25: 7 and *t'* a javelin in his hand;
27:22 and he *t'* Joshua, and set him
31: 9 *t'* all the women of Midian captives,
9 and *t'* the spoil of all their cattle,
11 *t'* all the spoil, and all the prey,
27 them that *t'* the war upon them,
47 Moses *t'* one portion of fifty, both
51, 54 Moses and Eleazar...*t'* the gold
32:39 Manasseh went to Gilead, and *t'* it,
41 and *t'* the small towns thereof,
42 And Nobah went and *t'* Kenath,
33:12 they *t'* their journey out of the
De 1:15 So I *t'* the chief of your tribes,
23 and I *t'* twelve men of you, one of
25 And they *t'* of the fruit of the land
2: 1 *t'* our journey into the wilderness
34 we *t'* all his cities at that time,
35 cattle we *t'* for a prey unto ourselves,
35 the spoil of the cities which we *t'*.
3: 4 we *t'* all his cities at that time,
4 was not a city which we *t'* not
7 cities, we *t'* for a prey to ourselves.
8 we *t'* at that time out of the hand
14 son of Manasseh *t'* all the country
9:17 I *t'* the two tables, and cast them
21 I *t'* your sin, the calf which ye had
10: 6 children of Israel *t'* their journey
22:14 I *t'* this woman, and when I came
24: 3 die, which *t'* her to be his wife;
29: 8 we *t'* their land, and gave it for an
Jos 2: 4 woman *t'* the two men, and hid
3: 6 they *t'* up the ark of the covenant,
4: 8 *t'* up twelve stones out of the midst
Jos 4:20 stones, which they *t'* out of Jordan,
6:12 priests *t'* up the ark of the Lord.
20 before him, and they *t'* the city.
7: 1 of Judah, *t'* of the accursed thing:
17 he *t'* the family of the Zarhites:
21 then I coveted them, and *t'* them;
23 *t'* them out of the midst of the tent,
24 Joshua, and all Israel...*t'* Achan
8:12 he *t'* about five thousand men,
19 entered into the city, and *t'* it,
23 And the king of Ai they *t'* alive,
27 Israel *t'* for a prey unto themselves.
9: 4 *t'* old sacks upon their asses, and
12 bread we *t'* hot for our provision
14 men *t'* of their victuals, and asked
10:27 they *t'* them down off the trees,
28 Joshua *t'* Makkedah, and smote it
32 *t'* it on the second day, and smote it
35 they *t'* it on that day, and smote it
37 they *t'* it, and smote it with the
39 And he *t'* it, and the king thereof,
11:10 time turned back, and *t'* Hazor,
14 Israel *t'* for a prey unto themselves;
16 So Joshua *t'* all that land, the
17 all their kings he *t'*, and smote
19 Gibeon: all other they *t'* in battle.
23 So Joshua *t'* the whole land,
15:17 Kenaz, the brother of Caleb, *t'* it:
16: 4 and Ephraim, *t'* their inheritance.
19:47 to fight against Leshem, and *t'* it,
24: 3 I *t'* your father Abraham from
26 *t'* a great stone, and set it up there
J'g 1:13 Caleb's younger brother, *t'* it:
18 Judah *t'* Gaza with the coast
3: 6 *t'* their daughters to be their wives,
21 *t'* the dagger from his right thigh,
25 therefore they *t'* a key, and opened
28 *t'* the fords of Jordan toward Moab,
4:21 Jael Heber's wife *t'* a nail of the
21 *t'* an hammer in her hand, and
5:19 Megiddo; they *t'* no gain of money.
6:27 Gideon *t'* ten men of his servants,
7: 8 people *t'* victuals in their hand,
24 *t'* the waters unto Beth-barah
25 *t'* two princes of the Midianites,
8:12 *t'* the two kings of Midian, Zebah
16 And he *t'* the elders of the city,
21 *t'* away the ornaments that were
9:43 he *t'* the people, and divided them
45 he *t'* the city, and slew the people
48 Abimelech *t'* an axe in his hand,
48 a bough from the trees, and *t'* it,
50 encamped against Thebez, and *t'* it.
11:13 Israel *t'* away my land, when they
15 Israel *t'* not away the land of Moab,
12: 5 the Gileadites *t'* the passages of
6 Then they *t'* him, and slew him at
9 *t'* in thirty daughters from abroad
13:19 So Manoah *t'* a kid with a meat
14: 9 And he *t'* thereof in his hands, and
19 men of them, and *t'* their spoil,
15: 4 *t'* firebrands, and turned tail to
15 and put forth his hand, and *t'* it,
16: 3 *t'* the doors of the gate of the city,
12 Delilah therefore *t'* new ropes,
21 the Philistines *t'* him, and put out
29 Samson *t'* hold of the two middle
31 and *t'* him, and brought him up,
17: 2 behold, the silver is with me; I *t'* it.
4 his mother *t'* two hundred shekels
18:17 in thither, and *t'* the graven image,
20 he *t'* the ephod, and the teraphim,
27 *t'* the things which Micah had made,
19: 1 who *t'* to him a concubine out of
15 no man that *t'* them into his house
25 the man *t'* his concubine, and
28 the man *t'* her up upon an ass,
29 he *t'* a knife, and laid hold on his
20: 6 And I *t'* my concubine, and cut her
21:23 *t'* them wives, according to their
Ru 1: 4 *t'* them wives of the women of Moab;
2:18 she *t'* it up, and went into the city:
4: 2 he *t'* ten men of the elders of the
13 So Boaz *t'* Ruth, and she was his
16 Naomi *t'* the child, and laid it in
1Sa 1:24 him, she *t'* him up with her,
2:14 brought up...priest *t'* for himself.
5: 1 the Philistines *t'* the ark of God,
2 Philistines *t'* the ark of God, they
3 they *t'* Dagon, and set him in his
6:10 *t'* two milch kine, and tied them
12 the kine *t'* the straight way to the
15 the Levites *t'* down the ark of the
7: 9 And Samuel *t'* a sucking lamb,
12 Then Samuel *t'* a stone, and set it
8: 3 aside after lucre, and *t'* bribes,
9:22 Samuel *t'* Saul and his servant,
24 And the cook *t'* up the shoulder,
10: 1 Then Samuel *t'* a vial of oil, and
11: 7 And he *t'* a yoke of oxen, and hewed
14:32 *t'* sheep, and oxen, and calves, and
47 Saul *t'* the kingdom over Israel,
52 valiant man, he *t'* him unto him.
15: 8 *t'* Agag the king of the Amalekites
21 But the people *t'* of the spoil,
16:13 Then Samuel *t'* the horn of oil,
20 Jesse *t'* an ass laden with bread,
23 that David *t'* an harp, and played
17:20 and went, as Jesse had
34 bear, and *t'* a lamb out of the flock:
40 And he *t'* his staff in his hand,
49 and *t'* thence a stone, and slang it,
51 *t'* his sword, and drew it out of the
54 David *t'* the head of the Philistine,
57 Abner *t'* him, and brought him
18: 2 Saul *t'* him that day, and would

1Sa 19:13 Michal t' an image, and laid it in
24: 2 Saul t' three thousand chosen men
25:18 haste, and t' two hundred loaves,
43 David also t' Ahinoam of Jezreel;
26:12 David t' the spear and the cruse of
27: 9 t' away the sheep, and the oxen,
28:24 and t' flour, and kneaded it, and did
30:20 David t' all the flocks and the herds,
31: 4 Therefore Saul t' a sword, and fell
12 t' the body of Saul and the bodies
13 they t' their bones, and buried them
2Sa 1:10 I t' the crown that was upon his
11 Then David t' hold on his clothes,
2: 8 t' Ish-bosheth the son of Saul,
32 they t' up Asahel, and buried him
3:15 and t' her from her husband, even
27 Joab t' him aside in the gate to speak
36 And all the people t' notice of it,
4: 4 and his nurse t' him up, and fled:
7 beheaded him, and t' his head,
10 I t' hold of him, and slew him in
12 they t' the head of Ish-bosheth,
5: 7 David t' the strong hold of Zion:
13 David t' him more concubines and
6: 6 to the ark of God, and t' hold of it;
7: 8 I t' thee from the sheepcote, from
15 as I t' it from Saul, whom I put
8: 1 David t' Metheg-ammah out of
4 And David t' from him a thousand
7 David t' the shields of gold that
8 king David t' exceeding much brass.
10: 4 Hanun t' David's servants,
11: 4 David sent messengers, and t' her;
12: 4 but t' the poor man's lamb, and
26 of Ammon, and t' the royal city.
29 and fought against it, and t' it.
30 he t' their king's crown from off
13: 8 And she t' flour, and kneaded it,
9 she t' a pan, and poured out before
10 Tamar t' the cakes which she had
11 he t' hold of her, and said unto
15: 5 forth his hand, and t' him, and
17:19 woman t' and spread a covering
18:14 And he t' three darts in his hand,
17 And they t' Absalom, and cast him
20: 3 the king t' the ten women his
9 Joab t' Amasa by the beard with
10 Amasa t' no heed to the sword that
21: 8 the king t' the two sons of Rizpah
10 the daughter of Aiah t' sackcloth,
12 David went and t' the bones of Saul
22:17 He sent from above, he t' me; he
23:16 and t' it, and brought it to David:
1Ki 1:39 the priest t' an horn of oil out of
3: 1 and t' Pharaoh's daughter, and
20 and t' my son from beside me,
4:15 he also t' Basmath the daughter of
8: 3 and the priests t' up the ark.
11:18 and they t' men with them out of
12:28 Whereupon the king t' counsel,
13:29 the prophet t' up the carcase of
14:26 he t' away the treasures of the
26 king's house; he even t' away all:
26 he t' away all the shields of gold
15:12 he t' away the sodomites out of
18 Then Asa t' all the silver and the
22 they t' away the stones of Ramah,
16:31 he t' to wife Jezebel the daughter
17:19 And he t' him out of her bosom,
23 Elijah t' the child, and brought him
18: 4 Obadiah t' an hundred prophets,
10 he t' an oath of the kingdom and
26 they t' the bullock which was
31 Elijah t' twelve stones, according
40 they t' them: and Elijah brought
19:21 t' a yoke of oxen, and slew them,
20:34 which my father t' from thy father
41 t' the ashes away from his face;
22:46 father Asa, he t' out of the land.
2Ki 2: 8 Elijah t' his mantle, and wrapped
12 and he t' hold of his own clothes, and
13 He t' up also the mantle of Elijah
14 he t' the mantle of Elijah that fell
3:26 he t' with him seven hundred men
27 t' his eldest son that should have
4:37 and t' up her son, and went out.
5: 5 t' with him ten talents of silver,
24 he t' them from their hand, and
6: 7 And he put out his hand, and t' it.
8 t' counsel with his servants,
7:14 t' therefore two chariot horses;
8: 9 him, and t' a present with him,
15 that he t' a thick cloth, and dipped
9:13 t' every man his garment, and put
10: 7 they t' the king's sons, and slew
14 And they t' them alive, and slew
15 he t' him up to him into the chariot.
31 But Jehu t' no heed to walk in the law
11: 2 t' Joash the son of Ahaziah, and
4 t' an oath of them in the house of
9 t' every man his men that were to
19 And he t' the rulers over hundreds,
12: 9 But Jehoiada the priest t' a chest,
17 fought against Gath, and t' it:
18 Jehoash...t' all the hallowed
13:15 he t' unto him bow and arrows.
18 Take the arrows. And he t' them.
25 Jehoash...t' again out of the hand
14: 7 t' Selah by war, and called the
13 king of Israel t' Amaziah king of
14 And he t' all the gold and silver,
21 all the people of Judah t' Azariah,
15:29 king of Assyria, and t' Ijon,
16: 8 Ahaz t' the silver and gold that was
9 up against Damascus, and t' it,
17 t' down the sea from off the brasen
2Ki 17: 6 the king of Assyria t' Samaria,
18:10 at the end of three years they t' it:
13 cities of Judah, and t' them.
20: 7 And they t' and laid it on the boil,
23:11 t' away the horses that the kings
16 t' the bones out of the sepulchres,
19 Josiah t' away, and did to them
30 the people of the land t' Jehoahaz
34 Jehoiakim, and t' Jehoahaz away:
24:12 the king of Babylon t' him in the
25: 6 So they t' the king, and brought
14 they ministered, t' they away.
15 the captain of the guard t' away.
18 the captain of the guard t' Seraiah
19 And out of the city he t' an officer
20 captain of the guard t' these,
1Ch 2:19 Caleb t' unto him Ephrath, which
23 And he t' Geshur, and Aram, with
4:18 of Pharaoh, which Mered t'.
5:21 they t' away their cattle; of their
7:15 And Machir t' to wife the sister of
10: 4 So Saul t' a sword, and fell upon it.
9 they t' his head, and his armour,
12 and t' away the body of Saul, and
11: 5 David t' the castle of Zion, which
18 and t' it, and brought it to David:
14: 3 David t' more wives at Jerusalem:
17: 7 I t' thee from the sheepcote, even
13 him, as I t' it from him that was
18: 1 t' Gath and her towns out of the
4 And David t' from him a thousand
7 And David t' the shields of gold
19: 4 Hanun t' David's servants, and
20: 2 David t' the crown of their king
23:22 brethren the sons of Kish t' them.
27:23 David t' not the number of them
2Ch 5: 4 and the Levites t' up the ark.
8:18 t' thence four hundred and fifty
10: 6 Rehoboam t' counsel with the old
8 t' counsel with the young men that
11:18 Rehoboam t' him Mahalath the
20 t' Maachah...daughter of Absalom;
21 (for he t' eighteen wives, and
12: 4 And he t' the fenced cities which
9 t' away the treasures of the house
9 of the king's house; he t' all:
13:19 Jeroboam, and t' cities from him,
14: 3 t' away the altars of the strange
5 he t' away out of all the cities of
15: 8 he t' courage, and put away the
16: 6 Then Asa the king t' all Judah;
17: 6 t' away the high places and groves
22:11 king, t' Joash the son of Ahaziah,
23: 1 t' the captains of hundreds, Azariah
8 t' every man his men that were to
20 he t' the captains of hundreds, and
24: 3 Jehoiada t' for him two wives;
11 and emptied the chest, and t' it,
25:13 of them, and t' much spoil.
17 Amaziah king of Judah t' advice,
23 the king of Israel t' Amaziah king
24 he t' all the gold and the silver, and
26: 1 all the people of Judah t' Uzziah,
28: 8 t' also away much spoil from them,
15 t' the captives, and with the spoil
21 Ahaz t' away a portion out of the
29:16 And the Levites t' it, to carry it out
30:14 and t' away the altars that were in
14 the altars for incense t' they away,
23 whole assembly t' counsel to keep
32: 3 He t' counsel with his princes and
33:11 t' Manasseh among the thorns,
15 And he t' away the strange gods,
34:33 Josiah t' away all the abominations
35:24 His servants therefore t' him out
36: 1 the people of the land t' Jehoahaz
4 And Necho t' Jehoahaz his brother,
Ezr 2:61 which t' a wife of the daughters
5:14 Nebuchadnezzar t' out of the
6: 5 Nebuchadnezzar t' forth out of the
8:30 So t' the priests and the Levites
Ne 2: 1 and I t' up the wine, and gave it
4: 1 and t' great indignation, and mocked
5:12 the priests, and t' an oath of them,
7:63 t' one of the daughters of Barzillai
9:25 And they t' strong cities, and a fat
Es 2: 7 dead, t' for his own daughter.
3:10 the king t' his ring from his hand,
6:11 Then t' Haman the apparel and
8: 2 And the king t' off his ring, which
9:27 Jews ordained, and t' upon them,
Job 1:15 fell upon them, and t' them away;
2: 8 And he t' him a potsherd to scrape
Ps 18:16 He sent from above, he t' me, he
22: 9 art he that t' me out of the womb:
31:13 while they t' counsel together
48: 6 Fear t' hold upon them there, and
55:14 We t' sweet counsel together, and
56: *title* the Philistines t' him in Gath.
69: 4 restored that which I t' not away.
71: 6 t' me out of my mother's bowels:
78:70 and t' him from the sheepfolds:
Pr 12:27 not that which he t' in hunting:
Ec 2:20 to despair of all the labour which I t'
Ca 5: 7 walls t' away my veil from me.
Isa 8: 2 I t' unto me faithful witnesses to
20: 1 fought against Ashdod, and t' it;
36: 1 cities of Judah, and t' them.
40:14 With whom t' he counsel, and who
Jer 13: 7 t' the girdle from the place where
25:17 t' I the cup at the Lord's hand, and
26: 8 prophets and all the people t' him,
27:20 Which Nebuchadnezzar...t' not,
28: 3 king of Babylon t' away from this
10 Hananiah the prophet t' the yoke
31:32 I t' them by the hand to bring
Jer 32:10 and sealed it, and t' witnesses,
11 I t' the evidence of the purchase,
35: 3 Then I t' Jaazaniah the son of
36:14 Baruch...t' the roll in his hand,
21 he t' it out of Elishama the scribe's
32 Then t' Jeremiah another roll, and
37:13 and he t' Jeremiah the prophet,
14 so Irijah t' Jeremiah, and brought
17 the king sent, and t' him out:
38: 6 Then t' they Jeremiah, and cast
11 Ebed-melech t' the men with him,
11 t' thence old cast clouts and old
13 and t' him up out of the dungeon:
14 t' Jeremiah the prophet unto him
39:14 and t' Jeremiah out of the court
40: 2 captain of the guard t' Jeremiah,
41:12 Then they t' all the men, and went
16 Then t' Johanan the son of Kareah,
43: 5 t' all the remnant of Judah, that
50:33 all that t' them captives held them
43 anguish t' hold of him, and pangs
52: 9 Then they t' the king, and carried
18 they ministered, t' they away.
19 t' the captain of the guard away.
24 the captain of the guard t' Seraiah
25 He t' also out of the city an eunuch,
26 the captain of the guard t' them,
La 5:13 They t' the young men to grind,
Eze 3:12 Then the spirit t' me up, and I
14 spirit lifted me up, and t' me away,
8: 3 and t' me by a lock of mine head;
10: 7 and t' thereof, and put it into the
7 linen: who t' it, and went out.
11:24 Afterwards the spirit t' me up,
16:50 I t' them away as I saw good.
17: 3 t' the highest branch of the cedar:
5 He t' also of the seed of the land,
19: 5 then she t' another of her whelps,
23:10 they t' her sons and her daughters,
13 was defiled, that they t' both one way,
29: 7 they t' hold of thee by thy hand,
33: 5 of the trumpet, and t' not warning;
43: 5 So the spirit t' me up, and brought
Da 1:16 Melzar t' away the portion of their
3:22 those men that t' up Shadrach,
5:20 and they t' his glory from him:
31 And Darius...t' the kingdom,
Ho 1: 3 t' Gomer the daughter of Diblaim;
12: 3 t' his brother by the heel in the womb,
13:11 and t' him away in my wrath.
Am 7:15 And the Lord t' me as I followed the
Jon 1:15 So they t' up Jonah, and cast him
Zec 11: 7 I t' unto me two staves; the one I
10 I t' my staff, even Beauty, and cut
13 And I t' the thirty pieces of silver,
M't 1:24 him, and t' unto him his wife:
2:14 he t' the young child and his
21 and t' the young child and his
8:17 saying, Himself t' our infirmities,
9:25 he went in, and t' her by the hand,
13:31 mustard seed, which a man t',
33 like unto leaven, which a woman t',
14:12 disciples came, and t' up the body,
19 and t' the five loaves, and the two
20 they t' up of the fragments that
15:36 he t' the seven loaves and the
37 they t' up of the broken meat that
39 t' ship,...came into the coasts
16: 9, 10 and how many baskets ye t' up?
22 Then Peter t' him, and began to
18:28 and t' him by the throat, saying,
20:17 t' the twelve disciples apart in the
21:35 the husbandmen t' his servants,
46 because they t' him for a prophet.
22: 6 And the remnant t' his servants,
15 t' counsel how they might entangle
24:39 flood came, and t' them all away;
25: 1 ten virgins, which t' their lamps,
3 foolish t' their lamps, and t' no oil
4 the wise t' oil in their vessels with
15 and straightway t' his journey.
35 I was a stranger, and ye t' me in:
38 we thee a stranger, and t' thee in?
43 a stranger, and ye t' me not in:
26:26 Jesus t' bread, and blessed it, and
27 And he t' the cup, and gave thanks,
37 And he t' with him Peter and the
50 laid hands on Jesus, and t' him.
27: 1 and elders of the people t' counsel
6 chief priests t' the silver pieces,
7 they t' counsel, and bought with
9 they t' the thirty pieces of silver,
24 he t' water, and washed his hands
27 t' Jesus into the common hall,
30 t' the reed, and smote him on the
31 they t' the robe off from him, and
48 and t' a spunge, and filled it with
28:15 So they t' the money, and did as
M'r 1:31 he came and t' her by the hand,
2:12 he arose, t' up the bed, and went
3: 6 t' counsel with the Herodians
4:36 t' him even as he was in the ship.
5:41 And he t' the damsel by the hand,
6:29 they came and t' up his corpse, and
43 they t' up twelve baskets full of the
7:33 he t' him aside from the multitude,
8: 6 he t' the seven loaves, and gave
8 they t' up of the broken meat that
19, 20 baskets full of fragments t' ye
23 he t' the blind man by the hand,
32 Peter t' him, and began to rebuke
9:27 But Jesus t' him by the hand, and
36 he t' a child, and set him in the
10:16 he t' them up in his arms, put his
32 he t' again the twelve, and began
12: 8 they t' him, and killed him, and

M'r 12:20 the first t' a wife, and dying left no
21 And the second t' her, and died,
14:22 Jesus t' bread, and blessed, and
23 he t' the cup, and when he had
46 their hands on him, and t' him.
49 temple teaching, and ye t' me not:
15:20 they t' off the purple from him,
46 t' him down, and wrapped him in
Lu 2:28 Then t' he him up in his arms,
5:25 and t' up that whereon he lay, and
8:54 t' her by the hand, and called,
9:10 And he t' them, and went aside
16 Then he t' the five loaves and the
28 he t' Peter and John and James,
47 t' a child, and set him by him,
10:34 him to an inn, and t' care of him.
35 he t' out two pence, and gave them
13:19 of mustard seed, which a man t',
21 is like leaven, which a woman t'
14: 4 he t' him, and healed him, and let
15:13 t' his journey into a far country,
18:31 Then he t' unto him the twelve,
20:29 the first t' a wife, and died without
30 And the second t' her to wife, and
31 And the third t' her, and in like
22:17 he t' the cup, and gave thanks,
19 And he t' bread, and gave thanks,
54 Then t' they him, and led him,
23:53 And he t' it down, and wrapped it
24:30 he t' bread, and blessed it, and
43 he t' it, and did eat before them.
Joh 5: 9 was made whole, and t' up his bed,
6:11 And Jesus t' the loaves; and when
24 they also t' shipping, and
8:59 t' they up stones to cast at him:
10:31 the Jews t' up stones again to stone
11:41 t' away the stone from the place
53 they t' counsel together for to put
12: 3 Then t' Mary a pound of ointment
13 T' branches of palm trees, and
13: 4 and t' a towel, and girded himself.
18:12 and officers of the Jews t' Jesus,
19: 1 Pilate therefore t' Jesus, and
16 they t' Jesus, and led him away.
23 t' his garments, and made four
27 disciple t' her unto his own home.
38 therefore, and t' the body of Jesus.
40 Then t' they the body of Jesus.
Ac 1:16 was guide to them that t' Jesus.
3: 7 And he t' him by the right hand,
4:13 they t' knowledge of them, that
5:33 heart, and t' counsel to slay them.
7:21 Pharaoh's daughter t' him up, and
43 ye t' up the tabernacle of Moloch,
9:23 the Jews t' counsel to kill him:
25 Then the disciples t' him by night,
27 But Barnabas t' him, and brought
10:26 Peter t' him up, saying, Stand up;
12:25 and t' with them John, whose
13:29 they t' him down from the tree,
15:39 Barnabas t' Mark, and sailed unto
16: 3 t' and circumcised him because of
33 he t' them the same hour of the
17: 5 t' unto them certain lewd fellows
19 they t' him, and brought him unto
18:17 Then all the Greeks t' Sosthenes,
18 and then t' his leave of the brethren,
26 t' him unto them, and expounded
19:13 t' upon them to call over them
20:14 we t' him in, and came to Mitylene.
21: 6 we t' ship; and they returned
11 t' Paul's girdle, and bound his own
15 those days we t' up our carriages,
26 Then Paul t' the men, and the
30 they t' Paul, and drew him out of
32 Who immediately t' soldiers and
33 captain came near, and t' him,
23:18 So he t' him, and brought him to
19 chief captain t' him by the hand,
31 as it was commanded them, t' Paul,
24: 6 whom we t', and would have
7 t' him away out of our hands,
27:35 t' bread, and gave thanks to God
36 cheer, and they also t' some meat.
28:15 he thanked God, and t' courage.
1Co 11:23 in which he was betrayed t' bread:
25 the same manner also he t' the cup,
Ga 2: 1 and t' Titus with me also.
Ph'p 2: 7 t' upon him the form of a servant,
Col 2:14 and t' it out of the way, nailing
Heb 2:14 himself likewise t' part of the
16 he t' not on him the nature of
16 he t' on him the seed of Abraham.
8: 9 when I t' them by the hand to lead
9:19 he t' the blood of calves and of
10:34 t' joyfully the spoiling of your
Re 5: 7 t' the book out of the right hand
8: 5 the angel t' the censer, and filled it
10:10 I t' the little book out of the
18:21 a mighty angel t' up a stone like a

tookest
Ps 99: 8 though thou t' vengeance of their
Eze 16:18 And t' thy broidered garments,

tool
Ex 20:25 if thou lift up thy t' upon it, thou
32: 4 and fashioned it with a graving t',
De 27: 5 shalt not lift up any iron t' upon them.
1Ki 6: 7 any t' of iron heard in the house.

tooth See also TEETH; TOOTH'S.
Ex 21:24 Eye for eye, t' for t', hand for
27 if he smite out his manservant's t',
27 or his maidservant's t'; he shall let
Le 24:20 for breach, eye for eye, t' for t':
De 19:21 t' for t', hand for hand, foot for foot.
Pr 25:19 time of trouble is like a broken t',
M't 5:38 An eye for an eye, and a t' for a t':

tooth's
Ex 21:27 shall let him go free for his t' sake.

top See also HOUSETOP; TOPS.
Ge 11: 4 whose t' may reach unto heaven;
28:12 and the t' of it reached to heaven:
18 and poured oil upon the t' of it.
Ex 17: 9 I will stand on the t' of the hill
10 Hur went up to the t' of the hill.
19:20 mount Sinai, on the t' of the mount:
20 Lord called Moses up to the t' of
24:17 like...fire on the t' of the mount
28:32 there shall be an hole in the t' of it,
30: 3 gold, the t' thereof, and the sides
34: 2 there to me in the t' of the mount.
37:26 both the t' of it, and the sides
Nu 14:40 up into the t' of the mountain,
44 presumed to go up unto the hill t':
20:28 died there in the t' of the mount:
21:20 to the t' of Pisgah, which looketh
23: 9 from the t' of the rocks I see him,
14 field of Zophim, to the t' of Pisgah,
28 brought Balaam unto the t' of Peor,
De 3:27 Get thee up into the t' of Pisgah,
28:35 of thy foot unto the t' of thy head.
33:16 and upon the t' of the head of him
34: 1 to the t' of Pisgah, that is over
Jos 15: 8 went up to the t' of the mountain
9 was drawn from the t' of the hill
J'g 6:26 an altar...upon the t' of this rock,
9: 7 stood in the t' of mount Gerizim,
25 for him in the t' of the mountains,
36 down from the t' of the mountains.
51 gat them up to the t' of the tower.
15: 8 dwelt in the t' of the rock Etam.
11 went to the t' of the rock Etam,
16: 3 carried them up to the t' of an hill
1Sa 9:25 with Saul upon the t' of the house.
26 called Saul to the t' of the house,
26:13 stood on the t' of an hill afar off:
2Sa 2:25 troop, and stood on the t' of an hill.
15:32 was come to the t' of the mount,
16: 1 was a little past the t' of the hill,
22 a tent upon the t' of the house;
1Ki 7:17 were upon the t' of the pillars;
18 the chapiters that were upon the t',
19 that were upon the t' of the pillars
22 the t' of the pillars was lily work:
35 in the t' of the base was there a
35 and on the t' of the base the ledges
41 were on the t' of the two pillars;
41 were upon the t' of the pillars;
10:19 and the t' of the throne was round
18:42 Elijah went up to the t' of Carmel;
2Ki 1: 9 behold, he sat on the t' of an hill.
9:13 under him on the t' of the stairs,
23:12 t' of the upper chamber of Ahaz,
2Ch 3:15 that was on the t' of each of them
4:12 were on the t' of the two pillars,
12 which were on the t' of the pillars;
25:12 brought them unto the t' of the rock,
12 cast...down from the t' of the rock,
Es 5: 2 and touched the t' of the sceptre.
Ps 72:16 upon the t' of the mountains;
102: 7 sparrow alone upon the house t'.
Pr 8: 2 standeth in the t' of high places,
23:34 he that lieth upon the t' of a mast.
Ca 4: 8 Lebanon: look from the t' of Amana,
8 from the t' of Shenir and Hermon,
Isa 2: 2 established in the t' of...mountains,
17: 6 in the t' of the uppermost bough,
30:17 a beacon upon the t' of a mountain,
42:11 shout from the t' of the mountains.
La 2:19 for hunger in the t' of every street.
4: 1 poured out in the t' of every street.
Eze 17: 4 cropped off the t' of his young twigs,
22 off from the t' of his young twigs
24: 7 she set it upon the t' of a rock;
8 set her blood upon the t' of a rock,
26: 4 and make her like the t' of a rock.
14 will make thee like the t' of a rock:
31: 3 his t' was among the thick boughs.
10 up his t' among the thick boughs,
14 up their t' among the thick boughs,
43:12 Upon the t' of the mountain the
Am 1: 2 and the t' of Carmel shall wither.
9: 3 hide themselves in the t' of Carmel,
Mic 4: 1 in the t' of the mountains,
Na 3:10 in pieces at the t' of all the streets:
Zec 4: 2 with a bowl upon the t' of it, and
2 which are upon the t' thereof:
M't 27:51 in twain from the t' to the bottom;
M'r 15:38 in twain from the t' to the bottom.
Joh 19:23 seam, woven from the t' throughout.
Heb 11:21 leaning upon the t' of his staff.

topaz
Ex 28:17 first row shall be a sardius, a t',
39:10 first row was a sardius, a t', and
Job 28:19 t' of Ethiopia shall not equal it,
Eze 28:13 sardius, t', and the diamond,
Re 21:20 the eighth, beryl; the ninth, a t';

Tophel (*to'-fel*)
De 1: 1 between Paran, and T', and

Tophet (*to'-fet*) See also TOPHETH.
Isa 30:33 T' is ordained of old; yea, for the
Jer 7:31 have built the high places of T',
32 that it shall no more be called T',
32 for they shall bury in T', till there
19: 6 place shall no more be called T',
11 and they shall bury them in T',
12 and even make this city as T':
13 shall be defiled as the place of T',
14 Then came Jeremiah from T',

Topheth (*to'-feth*) See also TOPHET.
2Ki 23:10 And he defiled T', which is in the

tops See also HOUSETOPS.
Ge 8: 5 were the t' of the mountains seen.
2Sa 5:24 going in the t' of the mulberry trees,
1Ki 7:16 to set upon the t' of the pillars:
2Ki 19:26 herb, as the grass on the house t',
1Ch 14:15 in the t' of the mulberry trees,
Job 24:24 cut off as the t' of the ears of corn.
Isa 2:21 into the t' of the ragged rocks,
15: 3 on the t' of their houses, and in
Eze 6:13 in all the t' of the mountains, and
Ho 4:13 upon the t' of the mountains,
Joe 2: 5 chariots on the t' of mountains shall

torch See also TORCHES.
Zec 12: 6 and like a t' of fire in a sheaf;

torches
Na 2: 3 chariots shall be with flaming t'
4 they shall seem like t', they shall
Joh 18: 3 with lanterns and t' and weapons.

tore See TARE.

torment See also TORMENTED; TORMENTS.
M't 8:29 art thou come hither to t' us before
M'r 5: 7 thee by God, that thou t' me not.
Lu 8:28 high? I beseech thee, t' me not.
16:28 they also come into this place of t'.
1Jo 4:18 out fear, because fear hath t'.
Re 9: 5 their t' was as the t' of a scorpion,
14:11 the smoke of their t' ascendeth up
18: 7 so much t' and sorrow give her:
10 Standing afar off for...fear of her t',
15 stand afar off for the fear of her t',

tormented
M't 8: 6 home sick of the palsy, grievously t'.
Lu 16:24 tongue; for I am t' in this flame.
25 he is comforted, and thou art t'.
Heb 11:37 being destitute, afflicted, t';
Re 9: 5 that they should be t' five months:
11:10 these two prophets t' them that
14:10 he shall be t' with fire and brimstone
20:10 shall be t' day and night for ever

tormentors
M't 18:34 wroth, and delivered him to the t',

torments
M't 4:24 taken with divers diseases and t',
Lu 16:23 hell he lift up his eyes, being in t',

torn
Ge 31:39 That which was t' of beasts I
44:28 Surely he is t' in pieces; and I
Ex 22:13 If it be t' in pieces, then let him
13 not make good that which was t'.
31 ye eat any flesh that is t' of beasts
Le 7:24 fat of that which is t' with beasts,
17:15 or that which was t' with beasts,
22: 8 dieth of itself, or is t' with beasts,
1Ki 13:26 unto the lion, which hath t' him,
28 eaten the carcase, nor t' the ass.
Isa 5:25 carcases were t' in the midst of
Jer 5: 6 out thence shall be t' in pieces:
Eze 4:14 dieth of itself, or is t' in pieces;
44:31 any thing that is dead of itself, or t',
Ho 6: 1 for he hath t', and he will heal us;
Mal 1:13 and ye brought that which was t',
M'r 1:26 the unclean spirit had t' him,

tortoise
Le 11:29 mouse, and the t' after his kind,

tortured
Heb 11:35 and others were t', not accepting

toss See also TOSSED; TOSSINGS.
Isa 22:18 violently turn and t' thee like a
Jer 5:22 the waves thereof t' themselves,

tossed
Ps 109:23 I am t' up and down as the locust.
Pr 21: 6 a vanity t' to and fro of them that
Isa 54:11 O thou afflicted, t' with tempest, and
M't 14:24 the midst of the sea, t' with waves:
Ac 27:18 exceedingly t' with a tempest,
Eph 4:14 t' to and fro, and carried about
Jas 1: 6 sea driven with the wind and t'.

tossings
Job 7: 4 I am full of t' to and fro unto the

tottering
Ps 62: 3 wall shall ye be, and as a t' fence.

Tou (*to'-u*) See also TOI.
1Ch 18: 9 T' king of Hamath heard how
10 (for Hadarezer had war with T';)

touch See also TOUCHED; TOUCHETH; TOUCHING.
Ge 3: 3 it, neither shall ye t' it, lest ye die.
20: 6 suffered I thee not to t' her.
Ex 19:12 the mount, or t' the border of it:
13 There shall not an hand t' it, but he
Le 5: 2 Or if a soul t' any unclean thing,
3 Or if he t' the uncleanness of man,
6:27 t' the flesh thereof shall be holy:
7:21 soul that shall t' any unclean thing,
11: 8 and their carcase ye shall not t';
31 whosoever doth t' them, when they
12: 4 she shall t' no hallowed thing, nor
Nu 4:15 but they shall not t' any holy thing,
16:26 t' nothing of theirs, lest ye be
De 14: 8 flesh, nor t' their dead carcase.
Jos 9:19 now therefore we may not t' them.
Ru 2: 9 men that they shall not t' thee?
2Sa 14:10 and he shall not t' thee any more.
18:12 that none t' the young man Absalom.
23: 7 man that shall t' them must be
1Ch 16:22 T' not mine anointed, and do my
Job 1:11 and t' all that he hath, and he will

Job 2: 5 and t' his bone and his flesh, and he
5: 19 in seven there shall no evil t' thee.
6: 7 things that my soul refused to t' are
Ps 105: 15 T' not mine anointed, and do my
144: 5 t' the mountains, and they shall
Isa 52: 11 from thence, t' no unclean thing;
Jer 12: 14 that t' the inheritance which I have
La 4: 14 men could not t' their garments.
15 it is unclean; depart, depart, t' not:
Hag 2: 12 and with his skirt do t' bread, or
13 by a dead body t' any of these,
M't 9: 21 If I may but t' his garment, I shall
14: 36 might only t' the hem of his garment:
M'r 3: 10 they pressed upon him for to t' him,
5: 28 If I may t' but his clothes, I shall be
6: 56 t' if it were but the border of his
8: 22 him, and besought him to t' him.
10: 13 to him, that he should t' them:
Lu 6: 19 whole multitude sought to t' him:
11: 46 t' not the burdens with one of your
18: 15 also infants, that he would t' them;
Joh 20: 17 Jesus saith unto her, T' me not;
1Co 7: 1 is good for a man not to t' a woman.
2Co 6: 17 t' not the unclean thing; and I will
Col 2: 21 (T' not; taste not; handle not;
Heb 11: 28 destroyed the firstborn shall t'
12: 20 And if so much as a beast t' the

touched
Ge 26: 29 us no hurt, as we have not t' thee,
32: 25 him, he t' the hollow of his thigh;
32 he t' the hollow of Jacob's thigh
Le 22: 6 The soul which hath t' any such
Nu 19: 18 and upon him that t' a bone, or one
31: 19 and whosoever hath t' any slain,
J'g 6: 21 t' the flesh and...unleavened cakes;
1Sa 10: 26 of men, whose hearts God had t'.
1Ki 6: 27 the wing of the one t' the one wall,
27 the other cherub t' the other wall;
27 their wings t' one another in the
19: 5 then an angel t' him, and said unto
7 and t' him, and said, Arise and eat;
2Ki 13: 21 let down, and t' the bones of Elisha,
Es 5: 2 near, and t' the top of the sceptre.
Job 19: 21 for the hand of God hath t' me.
Isa 6: 7 and said, Lo, this hath t' thy lips;
Jer 1: 9 forth his hand, and t' my mouth.
Eze 3: 13 creatures that t' one another,
Da 8: 5 earth, and t' not the ground:
18 but he t' me, and set me upright.
9: 21 t' me about the time of the evening
10: 10 an hand t' me, which set me upon
16 of the sons of men t' my lips:
18 t' me one like the appearance of a
M't 8: 3 put forth his hand, and t' him,
15 he t' her hand, and the fever left her:
9: 20 and t' the hem of his garment:
29 Then t' he their eyes, saying,
14: 36 many as t' were made perfectly
17: 7 Jesus came and t' them, and said,
20: 34 on them, and t' their eyes:
M'r 1: 41 put forth his hand, and t' him, and
5: 27 the press behind, and t' his garment
30 press, and said, Who t' my clothes?
31 thee, and sayest thou, Who t' me?
6: 56 as many as t' him were made whole.
7: 33 ears, and he spit, and t' his tongue;
Lu 5: 13 he put forth his hand, and t' him,
7: 14 And he came and t' the bier: and
8: 44 and t' the border of his garment:
45 And Jesus said, Who t' me? When
45 thee, and sayest thou, Who t' me?
46 Jesus said, Somebody hath t' me:
47 people for what cause she had t' him,
22: 51 And he t' his ear, and healed him.
Ac 27: 3 And the next day we t' at Sidon.
Heb 4: 15 t' with...feeling of our infirmities;
12: 18 unto the mount that might be t',

toucheth
Ge 26: 11 He that t' this man or his wife
Ex 19: 12 whosoever t' the mount shall be
29: 37 whatsoever t' the altar shall be holy.
30: 29 whatsoever t' them shall be holy.
Le 6: 18 every one that t' them shall be holy.
7: 19 the flesh that t' any unclean thing
11: 24 whosoever t' the carcase of them
26 one that t' them shall be unclean.
27 whoso t' their carcase shall be
36 which t' their carcase shall be
39 he that t' the carcase thereof shall
15: 5 whosoever t' his bed shall wash his
7 And he that t' the flesh of him that
10 whosoever t' any thing that was
11 whomsoever he t' that hath the
12 that he t' which hath the issue,
19 whosoever t' her shall be unclean
21 whosoever t' her bed shall wash his
22 whosoever t' any thing that she
23 when he t' it, he shall be unclean
27 whosoever t' these things shall be
22: 4 whoso t' any thing that is unclean
5 Or whosoever t' any creeping thing,
Nu 19: 11 He that t' the dead body of any man
13 Whosoever t' the dead body of any
16 And whosoever t' one that is slain
21 he that t' the water of separation
22 unclean person t' shall be unclean;
22 the soul that t' it shall be unclean
J'g 16: 9 of tow is broken when it t' the fire.
Job 4: 5 it t' thee, and thou art troubled.
Ps 104: 32 he t' the hills, and they smoke.
Pr 6: 29 t' her shall not be innocent.
Eze 17: 10 wither, when the east wind t' it?
Ho 4: 2 they break out, and blood t' blood.
Am 9: 5 God of hosts is he that t' the land,
Zec 2: 8 he that t' you t' the apple of his eye.

Lu 7: 39 manner of woman this is...t' him:
1Jo 5: 18 and that wicked one t' him not.

touching^
Ge 27: 42 Behold, thy brother Esau, as t' thee,
Nu 8: 26 do unto the Levites t' their charge.
1Sa 20: 23 And as t' the matter which thou and I
2Ki 22: 18 As t' the words which thou hast heard;
Ezr 7: 24 that t' any of the priests and Levites,
Job 37: 23 T' the Almighty, we cannot find him
Ps 45: 1 things which I have made t' the king:
Isa 5: 1 a song of my beloved t' his vineyard.
Jer 1: 16 them t' all their wickedness,
21: 11 And t' the house of the king of Judah,
22: 11 For thus saith the Lord t' Shallum
Eze 7: 13 the vision is t' the whole multitude
M't 18: 19 shall agree on earth as t' any thing
22: 31 as t' the resurrection of the dead,
M'r 12: 26 And as t' the dead, that they rise:
Lu 23: 14 no fault in this man t' those things
Ac 5: 35 ye intend to do as t' these men.
21: 25 As t' the Gentiles which believe,
24: 21 T' the resurrection of the dead I
26: 2 t'...the things whereof I am accused
Ro 11: 28 but as t' the election, they are
1Co 8: 1 as t' things offered unto idols,
16: 12 As t' our brother Apollos, I greatly
2Co 9: 1 as t' the ministering to the saints,
Ph'p 3: 5 Hebrews; as t' the law, a Pharisee;
6 t' the righteousness which is in the
Col 4: 10 Barnabas, (t' whom ye received
1Th 4: 9 t' brotherly love ye need not that
2Th 3: 4 have confidence in the Lord t' you,

tow
J'g 16: 9 as a thread of t' is broken when it
Isa 1: 31 the strong shall be as t', and the
43: 17 extinct, they are quenched as t'.

toward^ See also UNTOWARD.
Ge 13: 12 and pitched his tent t' Sodom.
18: 16 thence, and looked t' Sodom:
19: 1 himself with his face t' the ground;
28 And he looked t' Sodom and
28 and t' all the land of the plain,
25: 18 Egypt, as thou goest t' Assyria:
28: 10 from Beer-sheba, and went t' Haran.
30: 40 of the flocks t' the ringstraked,
31: 2 behold, it was not t' him as before.
5 that it is not t' me as before;
21 and set his face t' the mount Gilead.
48: 13 in his right hand t' Israel's left hand,
13 in his left hand t' Israel's right hand,
Ex 16: 10 that they looked t' the wilderness,
25: 20 t' the mercy seat shall the faces of
28: 27 t' the forepart thereof, over
34: 8 and bowed his head t' the earth,
36: 25 which is t' the north corner,
39: 20 underneath, t' the forepart of it,
Le 9: 22 lifted up his hand t' the people,
13: 41 the part of his head t' his face,
Nu 2: 3 on the east side t' the rising of the
3: 38 before the tabernacle t' the east,
16: 42 they looked t' the tabernacle of the
21: 11 which is before Moab, t' the sunrising.
20 which looketh t' Jeshimon.
23: 28 that looketh t' Jeshimon.
24: 1 he set his face t' the wilderness.
32: 14 fierce anger of the Lord t' Israel.
34: 15 Jericho eastward, t' the sunrising.
De 4: 41, 47 this side Jordan t' the sunrising;
28: 54 his eye shall be evil t' his brother,
54 and t' the wife of his bosom,
54 t' the remnant of his children which
56 be evil t' the husband of her bosom,
56 and t' her son, and t' her daughter,
57 t' her young one that cometh out
57 t' her children which she shall bear:
Jos 1: 4 sea t' the going down of the sun,
15 on this side Jordan t' the sunrising.
3: 16 came down t' the sea of the plain,
8: 18 the spear that is in thy hand t' Ai;
18 that he had in his hand t' the city,
12: 1 side Jordan t' the rising of the sun,
13: 5 and all Lebanon, t' the sunrising,
15: 4 From thence it passed t' Azmon, and
7 the border went up t' Debir from the
7 so northward, looking t' Gilgal,
7 passed t' the waters of En-shemesh,
21 t' the coast of Edom southward
16: 6 went out t' the sea to Michmethah
18: 13 border went over from thence t' Luz,
17 and went forth t' Geliloth,
18 passed along t' the side over
19: 11 And their border went up t' the sea,
12 from Sarid eastward t' the sunrising
18 And their border was t' Jezreel,
27 t' the sunrising to Beth-dagon,
27 t' the north side of Beth-emek,
34 Judah upon Jordan t' the sunrising.
J'g 3: 28 and took the fords of Jordan t' Moab,
4: 6 saying, Go and draw t' mount Tabor,
5: 9 My heart is t' the governors of Israel,
11 acts t' the inhabitants of his villages
8: 3 Then their anger was abated t' him,
13: 20 went up t' heaven from off the altar,
19: 9 now the day draweth t' evening,
18 t' the side of mount Ephraim;
20: 43 over against Gibeah t' the sunrising.
45 turned and fled t' the wilderness
1Sa 13: 18 the valley of Zeboim t' the wilderness.
17: 30 he turned from him t' another,
48 David hasted, and ran t' the army
20: 12 if there be good t' David, and I
41 arose out of a place t' the south,
2Sa 14: 1 the king's heart was t' Absalom.
15: 23 t' the way of the wilderness.

2Sa 24: 20 his servants coming on t' him:
1Ki 7: 9 on the outside t' the great court.
25 oxen, three looking t' the north,
25 north, and three looking t' the west,
25 west, and three looking t' the south,
25 south, and three looking t' the east:
8: 22 and spread forth his hands t' heaven:
29 eyes may be opened t' this house
29 t' the place of which thou hast said,
29 thy servant shall make t' this place.
30 when they shall pray t' this place:
35 if they pray t' this place, and confess
38 spread forth his hands t' this house:
42 shall come and pray t' this house;
44 Lord t' the city which thou hast
44 and t' the house that I have built
48 and pray unto thee t' their land,
14: 13 some good thing t' the Lord God
18: 43 Go up now, look t' the sea.
2Ki 3: 14 I would not look t' thee, nor see
25: 4 king went the way t' the plain.
1Ch 9: 24 t' the east, west, north, and south.
12: 15 both t' the east, and t' the west.
26: 17 a day, and t' Asuppim two and two.
2Ch 4: 4 oxen, three looking t' the north,
4 north, and three looking t' the west,
4 west, and three looking t' the south,
4 south, and three looking t' the east:
6: 13 and spread forth his hands t' heaven.
20 thy servant prayeth t' this place.
21 which they shall make t' this place:
26 if they pray t' this place, and confess
34 they pray unto thee t' this city
38 and pray t' their land, which thou
38 t' the city which thou hast chosen,
38 and t' the house which I have built
16: 9 them whose heart is perfect t' him.
20: 24 Judah came t' the watch tower
24: 16 done good in Israel, both t' God,
16 and t' his house.
31: 14 the Levite, the porter t' the east,
Ezr 3: 11 mercy endureth for ever t' Israel.
Ne 3: 26 against the water gate t' the east,
12: 31 hand upon the wall t' the dung gate:
Es 1: 13 manner t' all that knew law and
8: 4 held out the golden sceptre t' Esther.
Job 2: 12 dust upon their heads t' heaven.
11: 13 stretch out thine hands t' him;
39: 26 and stretch her wings t' the south?
Ps 5: 7 will I worship t' thy holy temple.
25: 15 Mine eyes are ever t' the Lord; for
28: 2 lift up my hands t' thy holy oracle.
66: 5 his doing t' the children of men.
85: 4 cause thine anger t' us to cease.
86: 13 For great is thy mercy t' me: and
103: 11 is his mercy t' them that fear him.
116: 12 the Lord for all his benefits t' me?
117: 2 merciful kindness is great t' us:
138: 2 I will worship t' thy holy temple.
Pr 14: 35 The king's favour is t' a wise servant:
23: 5 they fly away as an eagle t' heaven.
Ec 1: 6 The wind goeth t' the south, and
11: 3 and if the tree fall t' the south, or
3 t' the north, in the place where the
Ca 7: 4 Lebanon which looketh t' Damascus.
10 beloved's, and his desire is t' me.
Isa 7: 1 went up t' Jerusalem to war against
11: 14 of the Philistines t' the west;
29: 13 fear t' me is taught by the precept
38: 2 turned his face t' the wall,
49: 23 to thee with their face t' the earth,
63: 7 great goodness t' the house of Israel,
15 bowels and of thy mercies t' me?
66: 14 shall be known t' his servants,
14 and his indignation t' his enemies.
Jer 1: 13 the face thereof is t' the north.
3: 12 proclaim these words t' the north,
4: 6 Set up the standard t' Zion: retire,
11 t' the daughter of my people,
12: 3 me, and tried mine heart t' thee:
15: 1 mind could not be t' this people:
29: 10 perform my good word t' you,
11 the thoughts that I think t' you,
31: 21 set thine heart t' the highway, even
40 corner of the horse gate t' the east,
46: 6 t' the north by the river Euphrates.
49: 36 will scatter them t' all those winds;
La 2: 19 lift up thy hands t' him for the
Eze 1: 23 straight, the one t' the other:
4: 7 thy face t' the siege of Jerusalem,
6: 2 thy face t' the mountains of Israel,
14 than the wilderness t' Diblath,
8: 3 inner gate that looketh t' the north;
5 thine eyes now the way t' the north.
5 up mine eyes the way t' the north,
14 house which was t' the north;
16 backs t' the temple of the Lord,
16 Lord, and their faces t' the east;
16 they worshipped the sun t' the east.
9: 2 higher gate, which lieth t' the north,
12: 14 scatter t' every wind all that are
16: 42 So will I make my fury t' thee to rest,
17: 6 whose branches turned t' him,
7 vine did bend her roots t' him,
7 and shot forth her branches t' him,
21 shall be scattered t' all winds:
20: 46 of man, set thy face t' the south,
46 and drop thy word t' the south,
21: 2 man, set thy face t' Jerusalem,
2 drop thy word t' the holy places,
24: 23 iniquities, and mourn one t' another.
33: 25 and lift up your eyes t' your idols,
40: 6 the gate which looketh t' the east,
20 court that looked t' the north,
22 of the gate that looketh t' the east;
23 the gate t' the north, and t' the east;

Eze 40: 24 that he brought me *t'* the south,
24 behold a gate *t'* the south: and he
27 gate in the inner court *t'* the south:
27 from gate to gate *t'* the south
31 arches...were *t'* the utter court;
32 into the inner court *t'* the east:
34 arches...were *t'* the outward court:
37 posts thereof were *t'* the utter court;
44 their prospect was *t'* the south:
44 having the prospect *t'* the north.
45 whose prospect is *t'* the south,
46 whose prospect is *t'* the north is
41: 11 were *t'* the place that was left,
11 one door *t'* the north,
11 and another door *t'* the south:
12 at the end *t'* the west was seventy
14 and of the separate place *t'* the east,
19 face of a man was *t'* the palm tree
19 face of a young lion *t'* the palm tree
42: 1 utter court, the way *t'* the north:
1 before the building *t'* the north.
4 cubit; and their doors *t'* the north.
7 *t'* the utter court on the forepart
10 the wall of the court *t'* the east,
11 chambers which were *t'* the north,
12 chambers that were *t'* the south
12 directly before the wall *t'* the east.
15 he brought me forth *t'* the gate
15 whose prospect is *t'* the east, and
43: 1 the gate that looketh *t'* the east:
4 gate whose prospect is *t'* the east.
17 and his stairs shall look *t'* the east.
44: 1 sanctuary which looketh *t'* the east;
46: 1 inner court that looketh *t'* the east
12 him the gate that looketh *t'* the east,
19 priests, which looked *t'* the north:
47: 1 of the house stood *t'* the east,
8 waters issue out *t'* the east country,
15 border of the land *t'* the north side,
48: 10 *t'* the north five and twenty thousand
10 *t'* the west ten thousand in breadth,
10 *t'* the east ten thousand in breadth,
10 *t'* the south five and twenty thousand
17 *t'* the north two hundred and fifty,
17 *t'* the south two hundred and fifty,
17 *t'* the east two hundred and fifty,
17 *t'* the west two hundred and fifty.
21 the oblation *t'* the east border,
21 and twenty thousand *t'* the west
28 and to the river *t'* the great sea.
Da 4: 2 the high God hath wrought *t'* me.
6: 10 open in his chamber *t'* Jerusalem,
8: 8 ones *t* the four winds of heaven.
9 exceeding great, *t'* the south,
9 *t'* the east, and *t'* the pleasant land.
18 deep sleep on my face *t'* the ground:
10: 9 my face, and my face *t'* the ground.
15 unto me, I set my face *t'* the ground,
11: 4 be divided *t'* the four winds of heaven;
19 his face *t'* the fort of his own land:
29 shall return, and come *t'* the south;
Ho 3: 1 the Lord *t'* the children of Israel,
5: 1 for judgment is *t'* you, because ye
Joe 2: 20 with his face *t'* the east sea, and
20 his hinder part *t'* the utmost sea,
Jon 2: 4 will look again *t'* thy holy temple.
Zec 6: 6 grisled go forth *t'* the south country.
8 these that go *t'* the north country
9: 1 tribes of Israel, shall be *t'* the Lord.
14: 4 thereof *t'* the east and *t'* the west,
4 mountain shall remove *t'* the north,
4 the north, and half of it *t'* the south.
8 half of them *t'* the former sea,
8 and half of them *t'* the hinder sea:
M't 12: 49 forth his hand *t'* his disciples,
14: 14 moved with compassion *t'* them,
28: 1 to dawn *t'* the first day of the week,
M'r 6: 34 moved with compassion *t'* them,
Lu 2: 14 on earth peace, good will *t'* men.
12: 21 himself, and is not rich *t'* God.
13: 22 and journeying *t'* Jerusalem.
24: 29 for it is *t'* evening, and the day is
Joh 6: 17 went over the sea *t'* Capernaum.
Ac 1: 10 looked stedfastly *t'* heaven as he
8: 26 go *t'* the south unto the way that
20: 21 to the Greeks, repentance *t'* God,
21 and faith *t'* our Lord Jesus Christ.
22: 3 and was zealous *t'* God, as ye all are
24: 15 And have hope *t'* God, which they
16 conscience void of offence *t'* God,
16 and *t'* men.
27: 12 *t'* the south west and north west.
40 to the wind, and made *t'* shore.
28: 14 days: and so we went *t'* Rome.
Ro 1: 27 burned in their lust one *t'* another;
5: 8 God commendeth his love *t'* us,
11: 22 *t'* thee, goodness, if thou continue
12: 16 of the same mind one *t'* another.
15: 5 be likeminded one *t'* another
1Co 7: 36 himself uncomely *t'* his virgin,
2Co 1: 16 be brought on my way *t'* Judæa.
18 word *t'* you was not yea and nay.
2: 8 would confirm your love *t'* him.
7: 4 is my boldness of speech *t'* you,
7 your fervent mind *t'* me;
15 affection is more abundant *t'* you,
9: 8 to make all grace abound *t'* you;
10: 1 but being absent am bold *t'* you:
13: 4 him by the power of God *t'* you.
Gal 2: 8 was mighty in me *t'* the Gentiles:
Eph 1: 8 hath abounded *t'* us in all wisdom
2: 7 in his kindness *t'* us through
Ph'p 2: 30 supply your lack of service *t'* me.
3: 14 I press *t'* the mark for the prize
Col 4: 5 Walk in wisdom *t'* them that are
1Th 3: 12 abound in love one *t'* another,

1Th 3: 12 *t'* all men, even as we do *t'* you:
4: 10 indeed ye do it *t'* all the brethren
12 ye may walk honestly *t'* them that
5: 14 the weak, be patient *t'* all men.
2Th 1: 3 of you all *t'* each other aboundeth
Tit 3: 4 God our Saviour *t'* man appeared,
Ph'm 5 thou hast *t'* the Lord Jesus,
5 and *t'* all saints;
Heb 6: 1 dead works, and of faith *t'* God.
10 which ye have shewed *t'* his name,
1Pe 2: 19 for conscience *t'* God endure grief,
3: 21 of a good conscience *t'* God,)
1Jo 3: 21 then have we confidence *t'* God.
4: 9 manifested the love of God *t'* us,

towel
Joh 13: 4 and took a *t'*, and girded himself.
5 wipe them with the *t'* wherewith

tower See also TOWERS; WATCHTOWER.
Ge 11: 4 to, let us build us a city and a *t'*,
5 down to see the city and the *t'*,
35: 21 his tent beyond the *t'* of Edar.
J'g 8: 9 peace, I will break down this *t'*.
17 he beat down the *t'* of Penuel,
9: 46 men of the *t'* of Shechem heard
47 men of the *t'* of Shechem were
49 men of the *t'* of Shechem died also,
51 there was a strong *t'* within the city
51 gat them up to the top of the *t'*.
52 And Abimelech came unto the *t'*,
52 went hard unto the door of the *t'* to
2Sa 22: 3 my high *t'*, and my refuge, my
51 He is the *t'* of salvation for his
2Ki 5: 24 when he came to the *t'*, he took
9: 17 there stood a watchman on the *t'*
17: 9 from the *t'* of the watchmen to the
18: 8 from the *t'* of the watchmen to the
2Ch 20: 24 Judah came toward the watch *t'* in
Ne 3: 1 even unto the *t'* of Meah they
1 sanctified it, unto the *t'* of Hananeel.
11 piece, and the *t'* of the furnaces.
25 *t'* which lieth out from the king's
26 the east, and the *t'* that lieth out.
27 against the great *t'* that lieth out,
12: 38 from beyond the *t'* of the furnaces
39 fish gate, and the *t'* of Hananeel,
39 and the *t'* of Meah, even unto the
Ps 18: 2 of my salvation, and my high *t'*.
61: 3 and a strong *t'* from the enemy.
144: 2 my high *t'*, and my deliverer;
Pr 18: 10 name of the Lord is a strong *t'*:
Ca 4: 4 Thy neck is like the *t'* of David
7: 4 Thy neck is as a *t'* of ivory; thine
4 thy nose is as the *t'* of Lebanon
Isa 2: 15 And upon every high *t'*, and upon
5: 2 and built a *t'* in the midst of it,
Jer 6: 27 I have set thee for a *t'* and a
31: 38 from the *t'* of Hananeel unto the
Eze 29: 10 from the *t'* of Syene even unto the
30: 6 from the *t'* of Syene shall they fall
Mic 4: 8 And thou, O *t'* of the flock, the
Hab 2: 1 my watch, and set me upon the *t'*
Zec 14: 10 and from the *t'* of Hananeel unto
M't 21: 33 a winepress in it, and built a *t'*,
M'r 12: 1 place for the winefat, and built a *t'*
Lu 13: 4 upon whom the *t'* in Siloam fell,
14: 28 which of you, intending to build a *t'*

towers
2Ch 14: 7 make about them walls, and *t'*,
26: 9 Uzziah built *t'* in Jerusalem at the
10 Also he built *t'* in the desert, and
15 be on the *t'* and upon the bulwarks,
27: 4 the forests he built castles and *t'*.
32: 5 broken, and raised it up to the *t'*,
Ps 48: 12 about her: tell the *t'* thereof.
Ca 8: 10 I am a wall, and my breasts like *t'*:
Isa 23: 13 they set up the *t'* thereof, they
30: 25 great slaughter, when the *t'* fall.
32: 14 the forts and *t'* shall be for dens
33: 18 where is he that counted the *t'*?
Eze 26: 4 of Tyrus, and break down her *t'*:
9 his axes he shall break down thy *t'*
27: 11 the Gammadims were in thy *t'*:
Zep 1: 16 cities, and against the high *t'*.
3: 6 the nations: their *t'* are desolate

to-wit See WIT.

town See also TOWNCLERK; TOWNS.
Jos 2: 15 for her house was upon the *t'* wall
1Sa 16: 4 the elders of the *t'* trembled at his
23: 7 entering into a *t'* that hath gates
27: 5 a place in some *t'* in the country,
Hab 2: 12 him that buildeth a *t'* with blood
M't 10: 11 city or *t'* ye shall enter,
M'r 8: 23 the hand, and led him out of the *t'*
26 saying, Neither go into the *t'*, nor
26 nor tell it to any in the *t'*.
Lu 5: 17 were come out of every *t'* of Galilee
Joh 7: 42 out of the *t'* of Bethlehem, where
11: 1 the *t'* of Mary and her sister Martha
30 Jesus was not yet come into the *t'*

townclerk
Ac 19: 35 And when the *t'* had appeased the

towns
Ge 25: 16 these are their names, by their *t'*
Nu 32: 41 Jair...went and took the small *t'*
De 3: 5 beside unwalled *t'* a great many
Jos 13: 30 *t'* of Jair, which are in Bashan,
15: 45 Ekron, with her *t'* and her villages:
47 Ashdod with her *t'* and her villages,
47 Gaza with her *t'* and her villages,
17: 11 in Asher Beth-shean and her *t'*,
11 and Ibleam and her *t'*,
11 the inhabitants of Dor and her *t'*,
11 inhabitants of En-dor and her *t'*,
11 inhabitants of Taanach and her *t'*,

Jos 17: 11 inhabitants of Megiddo and her *t'*
16 who are of Beth-shean and her *t'*
J'g 1: 27 of Beth-shean and her *t'*,
27 nor Taanach and her *t'*,
27 the inhabitants of Dor and her *t'*,
27 inhabitants of Ibleam and her *t'*,
27 inhabitants of Megiddo and her *t'*:
11: 26 Israel dwelt in Heshbon and her *t'*
26 and in Aroer and her *t'*, and in all
1Ki 4: 13 to him pertained the *t'* of Jair the
1Ch 2: 23 and Aram, with the *t'* of Jair,
23 with Kenath, and the *t'* thereof,
5: 16 in her *t'*, and in all the suburbs of
7: 28 were, Beth-el and the *t'* thereof,
28 westward Gezer, with the *t'* thereof
28 Shechem also and the *t'* thereof,
28 unto Gaza and the *t'* thereof:
29 Manasseh, Beth-shean and her *t'*
29 Taanach and her *t'*,
29 Megiddo and her *t'*,
29 Dor and her *t'*.
8: 12 Ono, and Lod, with the *t'* thereof:
18: 1 Gath and her *t'* out of the hand of
2Ch 13: 19 him, Beth-el with the *t'* thereof,
19 and Jeshanah with the *t'* thereof,
19 and Ephrain with the *t'* thereof.
Es 9: 19 that dwelt in the unwalled *t'*,
Jer 19: 15 upon this city and upon all her *t'*
Zec 2: 4 inhabited as *t'* without walls for
M'r 1: 38 Let us go into the next *t'*, that I
8: 27 into the *t'* of Cæsarea Philippi:
Lu 9: 6 went through the *t'*, preaching the
12 they may go into the *t'* and country

Trachonitis (*trak-o-ni'-tis*)
Lu 3: 1 of Ituræa and of the region of *T'*.

trade See also TRADED; TRADING.
Ge 34: 10 dwell and *t'* ye therein, and get
21 dwell in the land, and *t'* therein;
46: 32 for their *t'* hath been to feed cattle;
34 Thy servants' *t'* hath been about
Re 18: 17 sailors, and as many as *t'* by sea,

traded
Eze 27: 12 tin, and lead, they *t'* in thy fairs.
13 they *t'* the persons of men and
14 house of Togarmah *t'* in thy fairs
17 *t'* in thy market wheat of Minnith,
M't 25: 16 talents went and *t'* with the same.

trading
Lu 19: 15 much every man had gained by *t'*.

tradition See also TRADITIONS.
M't 15: 2 transgress the *t'* of the elders?
3 commandment of God by your *t'*?
6 of God of none effect by your *t'*.
M'r 7: 3 eat not, holding the *t'* of the elders.
5 according to the *t'* of the elders,
8 ye hold the *t'* of men, as the
9 that ye may keep your own *t'*.
13 God of none effect through your *t'*,
Col 2: 8 vain deceit, after the *t'* of men,
2Th 3: 6 not after the *t'* which he received
1Pe 1: 18 received by *t'* from your fathers;

traditions
Ga 1: 14 zealous of the *t'* of my fathers.
2Th 2: 15 hold the *t'*...ye have been taught,

traffick
Ge 42: 34 brother, and ye shall *t'* in the land.
1Ki 10: 15 of the *t'* of the spice merchants,
Eze 17: 4 and carried it into a land of *t'*;
28: 5 by thy *t'* hast thou increased thy
18 iniquities, by the iniquity of thy *t'*;

traffickers
Isa 23: 8 *t'* are the honourable of the earth?

train See also TRAINED.
1Ki 10: 2 to Jerusalem with a very great *t'*,
Pr 22: 6 *T'* up a child in the way he should
Isa 6: 1 up, and his *t'* filled the temple.

trained
Ge 14: 14 captive, he armed his *t'* servants,

traitor See also TRAITORS.
Lu 6: 16 Iscariot, which was also the *t'*.

traitors
2Ti 3: 4 *T'*, heady, highminded, lovers of

trample
Ps 91: 13 dragon shalt thou *t'* under feet.
Isa 63: 3 anger, and *t'* them in my fury;
M't 7: 6 lest they *t'* them under their feet,

trance
Nu 24: 4, 16 into a *t'*, but having his eyes open:
Ac 10: 10 they made ready, he fell into a *t'*,
11: 5 and in a *t'* I saw a vision, A certain
22: 17 prayed in the temple, I was in a *t'*;

tranquillity
Da 4: 27 it may be a lengthening of thy *t'*.

transferred
1Co 4: 6 I have in a figure *t'* to myself and

transfigured
M't 17: 2 And was *t'* before them: and his
M'r 9: 2 and he was *t'* before them.

transformed
Ro 12: 2 ye *t'* by the renewing of your mind,
2Co 11: 14 Satan himself is *t'* into an angel
15 *t'* as...ministers of righteousness;

transforming
2Co 11: 13 *t'* themselves into the apostles of

transgress See also TRANSGRESSED; TRANGRESSEST; TRANSGRESSETH; TRANSGRESSING.
Nu 14: 41 do ye *t'* the commandment of the
1Sa 2: 24 ye make the Lord's people to *t'*.

2Ch 24:20 Why t' ye the commandments of
Ne 1: 8 If ye t', I will scatter you abroad
13:27 to t' against our God in marrying
Ps 17: 3 that my mouth shall not t'.
25: 3 ashamed which t' without cause.
Pr 28:21 a piece of bread that man will t'.
Jer 2:20 and thou saidst, I will not t';
Eze 20:38 and them that t' against me:
Am 4: 4 Come to Beth-el, and t'; at Gilgal
M't 15: 2 thy disciples t' the tradition of the
3 do ye also t' the commandment
Ro 2:27 and circumcision dost t' the law?

transgressed
De 26:13 I have not t' thy commandments,
Jos 7:11 and they have also t' my covenant
15 because he hath t' the covenant of
23:16 When ye have t' the covenant of the
J'g 2:20 this people hath t' my covenant
1Sa 14:33 he said, Ye have t': roll a great
15:24 for I have t' the commandment of
1Ki 8:50 wherein they have t' against thee,
2Ki 18:12 their God, but t' his covenant,
1Ch 2: 7 Israel, who t' in...thing accursed.
5:25 t' against the God of their fathers,
2Ch 12: 2 they had t' against the Lord,
26:16 for he t' against the Lord his God,
28:19 naked, and t' sore against the Lord.
36:14 people, t' very much after all the
Ezr 10:10 Ye have t', and have taken strange
13 many that have t' in this thing.
Isa 24: 5 because they have t' the laws,
43:27 thy teachers have t' against me.
66:24 the men that have t' against me:
Jer 2: 8 the pastors also t' against me, and
29 ye all have t' against me, saith the
3:13 hast t' against the Lord thy God,
33: 8 whereby they have t' against me.
34:18 the men that have t' my covenant,
La 3:42 We have t' and have rebelled:
Eze 2: 3 their fathers have t' against me,
18:31 transgressions, whereby ye have t':
Da 9:11 Yea, all Israel have t' thy law,
Ho 6: 7 they like men have t' the covenant:
7:13 because they have t' against me:
8: 1 because they have t' my covenant,
Zep 3:11 wherein thou hast t' against me:
Lu 15:29 neither t' I at any time thy

transgressest
Es 3: 3 Mordecai, Why t' thou the king's

transgresseth
Pr 16:10 his mouth t' not in judgment.
Hab 2: 5 Yea also, because he t' by wine,
1Jo 3: 4 Whosoever committeth sin t'
2Jo 9 Whosoever t', and abideth not in

transgressing
De 17: 2 Lord thy God, in t' his covenant,
Isa 59:13 In t' and lying against the Lord,

transgression See also TRANSGRESSIONS.
Ex 34: 7 forgiving iniquity and t' and sin,
Nu 14:18 forgiving iniquity and t', and by no
Jos 22:22 or if in t' against the Lord, (save
1Sa 24:11 is neither evil nor t' in mine hand,
1Ch 9: 1 carried away to Babylon for their t'
10:13 So Saul died for his t' which he
2Ch 29:19 in his reign did cast away in his t'
Ezr 9: 4 the t' of those that had been
10: 6 he mourned because of the t' of
Job 7:21 why dost thou not pardon my t',
8: 4 he have cast them away for their t';
13:23 make me to know my t' and my sin.
14:17 My t' is sealed up in a bag, and
33: 9 I am clean without t', I am
34: 6 my wound is incurable without t'.
Ps 19:13 shall be innocent from the great t'.
32: 1 Blessed is he whose t' is forgiven,
36: 1 The t' of the wicked saith within
59: 3 not for my t' nor for my sin, O Lord.
89:32 will I visit their t' with the rod,
107:17 Fools because of their t', and
Pr 12:13 The wicked is snared by the t' of
17: 9 He that covereth a t' seeketh love;
19 He loveth t' that loveth strife: and
19:11 and it is his glory to pass over a t'.
28: 2 For the t' of a land many are the
24 his mother, and saith, It is no t';
29: 6 t' of an evil man there is a snare:
16 are multiplied, t' increaseth:
22 and a furious man aboundeth in t'.
Isa 24:20 t' thereof shall be heavy upon it;
53: 8 for the t' of my people was he
57: 4 are ye not children of t', a seed of
58: 1 and shew my people their t', and
59:20 them that turn from t' in Jacob,
Eze 33:12 not deliver him in the day of his t':
Da 8:12 the daily sacrifice by reason of t',
13 sacrifice, and the t' of desolation,
9:24 to finish the t', and to make an end
Am 4: 4 at Gilgal multiply t'; and bring
Mic 1: 5 For the t' of Jacob is all this, and
5 What is the t' of Jacob? is it not
3: 8 to declare unto Jacob his t', and to
6: 7 shall I give my firstborn for my t',
7:18 passeth by the t' of the remnant of
Ac 1:25 from which Judas by t' fell, that
Ro 4:15 for where no law is, there is no t'.
5:14 after the similitude of Adam's t',
1Ti 2:14 woman being deceived was in the t'.
Heb 2: 2 every t' and disobedience received
1Jo 3: 4 the law: for sin is the t' of the law.

transgressions
Ex 23:21 not; for he will not pardon your t':
Le 16:16 because of their t' in all their sins:
21 and all their t' in all their sins,
Jos 24:19 not forgive your t' nor your sins.
1Ki 8:50 all their t' wherein they have
Job 31:33 If I covered my t' as Adam, by
35: 6 if thy t' be multiplied, what doest
36: 9 their t' that they have exceeded.
Ps 5:10 out in the multitude of their t';
25: 7 not the sins of my youth, nor my t':
32: 5 I will confess my t' unto the Lord;
39: 8 Deliver me from all my t': make
51: 1 thy tender mercies blot out my t'.
3 For I acknowledge my t': and my
65: 3 as for our t', thou shalt purge them
103:12 hath he removed our t' from us.
Isa 43:25 blotteth out thy t' for mine own
44:22 blotted out, as a thick cloud, thy t',
50: 1 your t' is your mother put away.
53: 5 But he was wounded for our t', he
59:12 our t' are multiplied before thee,
12 for our t' are with us; and as for
Jer 5: 6 because their t' are many, and their
La 1: 5 her for the multitude of her t':
14 yoke of my t' is bound by his hand:
22 hast done unto me for all my t':
Eze 14:11 polluted any more with all their t';
18:22 All his t' that he hath committed,
28 away from all his t' that he hath
30 turn yourselves from all your t';
31 Cast away from you all your t',
21:24 in that your t' are discovered, so
33:10 If our t' and our sins be upon us,
37:23 things, nor with any of their t':
39:24 according to their t' have I done
Am 1: 3 For three t' of Damascus, and for
6 For three t' of Gaza, and for four,
9 For three t' of Tyrus, and for four,
11 For three t' of Edom, and for four,
13 For three t' of the children of
2: 1 For three t' of Moab, and for four,
4 For three t' of Judah, and for four,
6 For three t' of Israel, and for four,
3:14 shall visit the t' of Israel upon him
5:12 your manifold t' and your mighty
Mic 1:13 the t' of Israel were found in thee.
Ga 3:19 It was added because of t', till the
Heb 9:15 the t' that were under the first

transgressor See also TRANSGRESSORS.
Pr 21:18 and the t' for the upright.
22:12 overthroweth the words of the t'.
Isa 48: 8 wast called a t' from the womb.
Ga 2:18 I destroyed, I make myself a t'.
Jas 2:11 kill, thou art become a t' of the law.

transgressors
Ps 37:38 But the t' shall be destroyed
51:13 Then will I teach t' thy ways; and
59: 5 be not merciful to any wicked t'.
119:158 I beheld the t', and was grieved;
Pr 2:22 and the t' shall be rooted out of it.
11: 3 the perverseness of t' shall destroy
6 t' shall be taken in their own
13: 2 the soul of the t' shall eat violence.
15 favour: but the way of t' is hard.
23:28 and increaseth the t' among men.
26:10 the fool, and rewardeth t'.
Isa 1:28 the destruction of the t' and of the
46: 8 men: bring it again to mind, O ye t'
53:12 and he was numbered with the t';
12 and made intercession for the t'.
Da 8:23 when the t' are come to the full,
Ho 14: 9 them: but the t' shall fall therein.
M'r 15:28 And he was numbered with the t'.
Lu 22:37 And he was reckoned among the t':
Jas 2: 9 and are convinced of the law as t'.

translate See also TRANSLATED.
2Sa 3:10 To t' the kingdom from the house

translated
Col 1:13 hath t' us into the kingdom of his
Heb 11: 5 By faith Enoch was t' that he
5 not found, because God had t' him:

translation
Heb 11: 5 for before his t' he had this

transparent
Re 21:21 was pure gold, as it were t' glass.

trap See also TRAPS.
Job 18:10 and a t' for him in the way.
Ps 69:22 for their welfare, let it become a t'
Jer 5:26 they set a t', they catch men.
Ro 11: 9 table he made a snare, and a t',

traps
Jos 23:13 shall be snares and t' unto you.

travail See also TRAVAILED; TRAVAILEST; TRAVAILETH; TRAVAILING; TRAVEL.
Ge 38:27 came to pass in the time of her t',
Ex 18: 8 all the t' that had come upon them
Ps 48: 6 and pain, as of a woman in t'.
Ec 1:13 this sore t' hath God given to the
2:23 days are sorrows, and his t' grief;
26 to the sinner he giveth t', to gather
3:10 I have seen the t', which God hath
4: 4 I considered all t', and every right
6 hands full with t' and vexation of
8 is also vanity, yea, it is a sore t'.
5:14 But those riches perish by evil t':
Isa 23: 4 I t' not, nor bring forth children,
53:11 He shall see of the t' of his soul,
54: 1 thou that didst not t' with child:
Jer 4:31 heard a voice as of a woman in t',
6:24 us, and pain, as of a woman in t'.
13:21 sorrows take thee, as a woman in t'?
22:23 thee, the pain as of a woman in t'!
30: 6 whether a man doth t' with child?
6 on his loins, as a woman in t',
49:24 have taken her, as a woman in t'.
50:43 him, and pangs as of a woman in t'.
Mic 4: 9 have taken thee as a woman in t'.
10 of Zion, like a woman in t':
Joh 16:21 A woman...in t' hath sorrow,
Ga 4:19 I t' in birth again until Christ be
1Th 2: 9 brethren, our labour and t':
5: 3 as t' upon a woman with child;
2Th 3: 8 wrought with labour and t' night

travailed
Ge 35:16 Rachel t', and she had hard labour,
38:28 it came to pass, when she t', that
1Sa 4:19 dead, she bowed herself and t';
Isa 66: 7 Before she t', she brought forth;
8 for as soon as Zion t', she brought

travailest
Ga 4:27 forth and cry, thou that t' not:

travaileth
Job 15:20 wicked man t' with pain all his
Ps 7:14 he t' with iniquity, and hath
Isa 13: 8 be in pain as a woman that t':
21: 3 as the pangs of a woman that t':
Jer 31: 8 and her that t' with child together:
Mic 5: 3 she which t' hath brought forth:
Ro 8:22 and t' in pain together until now.

travailing
Isa 42:14 now will I cry like a t' woman: I
Ho 13:13 The sorrows of a t' woman shall
Re 12: 2 being with child cried, t' in birth,

travel See also TRAVAIL; TRAVELLED; TRAVELLETH; TRAVELLING.
Nu 20:14 all the t' that hath befallen us:
La 3: 5 compassed me with gall and t'.
Ac 19:29 Macedonia, Paul's companions in t',
2Co 8:19 chosen of the churches to t' with us

travelled
Ac 11:19 Stephen t' as far as Phenice, and

traveller See also TRAVELLERS.
2Sa 12: 4 there came a t' unto the rich man,
Job 31:32 but I opened my doors to the t'.

travellers
J'g 5: 6 the t' walked through byways.

travelleth
Pr 6:11 thy poverty come as one that t',
24:34 thy poverty come as one that t';

travelling
Isa 21:13 O ye t' companies of Dedanim.
63: 1 t' in the greatness of his strength?
M't 25:14 is as a man t' into a far country,

traversing
Jer 2:23 art a swift dromedary t' her ways;

treacherous
Isa 21: 2 t' dealer dealeth treacherously,
24:16 t' dealers have dealt treacherously;
16 the t' dealers have dealt very
Jer 3: 7 And her t' sister Judah saw it.
8 yet her t' sister Judah feared not,
10 her t' sister Judah hath not
11 herself more than t' Judah.
9: 2 adulterers, an assembly of t' men.
Zep 3: 4 prophets are light and t' persons:

treacherously
J'g 9:23 Shechem dealt t' with Abimelech:
Isa 21: 2 the treacherous dealer dealeth t',
24:16 treacherous dealers have dealt t';
16 dealers have dealt very t'.
33: 1 wast not spoiled; and dealest t',
1 and they dealt not t' with thee!
1 thou shalt make an end to deal t',
1 they shall deal t' with thee.
48: 8 that thou wouldest deal very t',
Jer 3:20 as a wife t' departeth from her
20 so have ye dealt t' with me,
5:11 have dealt very t' against me,
12: 1 are all they happy that deal very t'?
6 even they have dealt t' with thee;
La 1: 2 her friends have dealt t' with her,
Ho 5: 7 have dealt t' against the Lord:
6: 7 there have they dealt t' against me.
Hab 1:13 lookest thou upon them that deal t',
Mal 2:10 we deal t' every man against his
11 Judah hath dealt t', and an
14 against whom thou hast dealt t':
15 deal t' against the wife of his youth.
16 to your spirit, that ye deal not t'.

treachery
2Ki 9:23 Ahaziah, There is t', O Ahaziah.

tread See also TREADER; TREADETH; TREADING; TRODDEN; TRODE.
De 11:24 the soles of your feet shall t' shall
25 upon all the land...ye shall t' upon,
33:29 thou shalt t' upon their high places.
Jos 1: 3 the sole of your feet shall t' upon,
1Sa 5: 5 t' on the threshold of Dagon in
Job 24:11 t' their winepresses, and suffer
40:12 t' down the wicked in their place.
Ps 7: 5 let him t' down my life upon the
44: 5 will we t' them under that rise up
60:12 it is that shall t' down our enemies.
91:13 shalt t' upon the lion and adder:
108:13 it is that shall t' down our enemies.
Isa 1:12 this at your hand, to t' my courts?
10: 6 t' them down like the mire of
14:25 my mountains t' him under foot:
16:10 treaders shall t' out no wine in
26: 6 The foot shall t' it down, even the
63: 3 for I will t' them in mine anger,
6 I will t' down the people in mine
Jer 25:30 shout, as they that t' the grapes,
48:33 none shall t' with shouting: their
Eze 26:11 shall he t' down all thy streets:
34:18 ye must t' down with your feet the
Da 7:23 shall t' it down, and break it in

Ho 10:11 and loveth to *t'* out the corn:
Mic 1: 3 *t'* upon the high places of the
5: 5 and when he shall *t'* in our palaces,
6:15 thou shalt *t'* the olives, but thou
Na 3:14 go into clay, and *t'* the morter,
Zec 10: 5 which *t'* down their enemies in the
Mal 4: 3 And ye shall *t'* down the wicked;
Lu 10:19 you power to *t'* on serpents and
Re 11: 2 holy city shall they *t'* under foot

treader See also TREADERS.
Am 9:13 the *t'* of grapes him that soweth

treaders
Isa 16:10 the *t'* shall tread out no wine in

treadeth
De 25: 4 the ox when he *t'* out the corn.
Job 9: 8 and *t'* upon the waves of the sea.
Isa 41:25 morter, and as the potter *t'* clay.
63: 2 like him that *t'* in the winefat?
Am 4:13 *t'* upon the high places of the earth.
Mic 5: 6 and when he *t'* within our borders.
8 *t'* down, and teareth in pieces,
1Co 9: 9 of the ox that *t'* out the corn.
1Ti 5:18 muzzle the ox that *t'* out the corn.
Re 19:15 and he *t'* the winepress of the

treading
Ne 13:15 *t'* wine presses on the sabbath,
Isa 7:25 and for the *t'* of lesser cattle.
22: 5 is a day of trouble, and of *t'* down,
Am 5:11 as your *t'* is upon the poor,

treason
1Ki 16:20 and his *t'* that he wrought,
2Ki 11:14 rent her clothes, and cried, *T'*, *T'*.
2Ch 23:13 rent their clothes, and said, *T'*, *T'*.

treasure See also TREASURED; TREASURES; TREASUREST.
Ge 43:23 hath given you *t'* in your sacks:
Ex 1:11 they built for Pharaoh *t'* cities,
19: 5 then ye shall be a peculiar *t'* unto me
De 28:12 shall open unto thee his good *t'*,
1Ch 29: 8 to the *t'* of the house of the Lord,
Ezr 2:69 their ability unto the *t'* of the work
5:17 be search made in the king's *t'*
7:20 it out of the king's *t'* house.
Ne 7:70 gave to the *t'* a thousand drams of
71 gave to the *t'* of the work twenty
10:38 to the chambers, into the *t'* house.
Ps 17:14 whose belly thou fillest with thy hid *t'*
135: 4 himself, and Israel for his peculiar *t'*
Pr 15: 6 house of the righteous is much *t'*:
16 Lord than great *t'* and trouble
21:20 There is *t'* to be desired and oil in
Ec 2: 8 the peculiar *t'* of kings and of the
Isa 33: 6 the fear of the Lord is his *t'*.
Eze 22:25 they have taken the *t'* and
Da 1: 2 vessels into the *t'* house of his god.
Ho 13:15 spoil the *t'* of all pleasant vessels.
M't 6:21 where your *t'* is, there will your
12:35 good *t'* of the heart bringeth forth
35 evil *t'* bringeth forth evil things.
13:44 heaven is like unto *t'* hid in a field;
52 out of his *t'* things new and old.
19:21 and thou shalt have *t'* in heaven:
M'r 10:21 and thou shalt have *t'* in heaven:
Lu 6:45 good *t'* of his heart bringeth forth
45 evil *t'* of his heart bringeth forth
12:21 he that layeth up *t'* for himself,
33 *t'* in the heavens that faileth not,
34 where your *t'* is, there will your
18:22 and thou shalt have *t'* in heaven:
Ac 8:27 who had the charge of all her *t'*,
2Co 4: 7 we have this *t'* in earthen vessels,
Jas 5: 3 heaped *t'* together for the last

treasure-cities See TREASURE and CITIES.

treasured
Isa 23:18 it shall not be *t'* nor laid up; for

treasure-house See TREASURE and HOUSE.

treasurer See also TREASURERS.
Ezr 1: 8 by the hand of Mithredath the *t'*,
Isa 22:15 get thee unto this *t'*, even unto

treasurers
Ezr 7:21 the *t'* which are beyond the river,
Ne 13:13 And I made *t'* over the treasuries,
Da 3: 2, 3 judges, the *t'*, the counsellers,

treasures
De 32:34 me, and sealed up among my *t'*?
33:19 the seas, and of *t'* hid in the sand.
1Ki 7:51 he put among the *t'* of the house of
14:26 he took away the *t'* of the house of
26 Lord, and the *t'* of the king's house
15:18 in the *t'* of the house of the Lord,
18 and the *t'* of the king's house, and
2Ki 12:18 in the *t'* of the house of the Lord,
14:14 and in the *t'* in the king's house,
16: 8 and in the *t'* in the king's house,
18:15 and in the *t'* of the king's house.
20:13 and all that was found in his *t'*:
15 among my *t'* that I have not shewed
24:13 all the *t'* of the house of the Lord,
13 and the *t'* of the king's house, and
1Ch 26:20 Ahijah was over the *t'* of the house
20 over the *t'* of the dedicated things.
22 were over the *t'* of the house of the
24 the son of Moses, was ruler of the *t'*
26 were over all the *t'* of the dedicated
27:25 over the king's *t'* was Azmaveth the
2Ch 5: 1 among the *t'* of the house of God.
8:15 any matter, or concerning the *t'*.
12: 9 took away the *t'* of the house of the
9 and the *t'* of the king's house: he
16: 2 gold out of the *t'* of the house of the
25:24 and the *t'* of the king's house, the
36:18 and the *t'* of the house of the Lord,
2Ch 36:18 and the *t'* of the king, and of his
Ezr 6: 1 the *t'* were laid up in Babylon.
Ne 12:44 over the chambers for the *t'*,
Job 3:21 and dig for it more than for hid *t'*:
38:22 entered into the *t'* of the snow?
22 or hast thou seen the *t'* of the hail,
Pr 2: 4 and searchest for her as for hid *t'*;
8:21 substance; and I will fill their *t'*.
10: 2 *T'* of wickedness profit nothing: but
21: 6 The getting of *t'* by a lying tongue
Isa 2: 7 neither is there any end of their *t'*;
10:13 people, and have robbed their *t'*,
30: 6 their *t'* upon the bunches of camels,
39: 2 and all that was found in his *t'*:
4 there is nothing among my *t'* that I
45: 3 I will give thee the *t'* of darkness,
Jer 10:13 bringeth forth the wind out of his *t'*.
15:13 Thy substance and thy *t'* will I give
17: 3 substance and all thy *t'* to the spoil,
20: 5 and all the *t'* of the kings of Judah
41: 8 we have *t'* in the field, of wheat,
48: 7 trusted in thy works and in thy *t'*,
49: 4 that trusted in her *t'*, saying, Who
50:37 a sword is upon her *t'*; and they
51:13 abundant in *t'*, thine end is come,
16 bringeth forth the wind out of his *t'*.
Eze 28: 4 gotten gold and silver into thy *t'*:
Da 11:43 have power over the *t'* of gold and
Mic 6:10 Are there yet the *t'* of wickedness
M't 2:11 and when they had opened their *t'*,
6:19 not up for yourselves *t'* upon earth,
20 lay up for yourselves *t'* in heaven,
Col 2: 3 whom are hid all the *t'* of wisdom
Heb 11:26 greater riches than the *t'* in Egypt:

treasurest
Ro 2: 5 *t'* up unto thyself wrath against

treasuries
1Ch 9:26 and *t'* of the house of God.
28:11 thereof, and of the *t'* thereof,
12 about, of the *t'* of the house of God,
12 of the *t'* of the dedicated things:
2Ch 32:27 and he made himself *t'* for silver,
Ne 13:12 the new wine and the oil unto the *t'*.
13 And I made treasurers over the *t'*,
Es 3: 9 to bring it into the king's *t'*.
4: 7 had promised to pay to the king's *t'*
Ps 135: 7 he bringeth the wind out of his *t'*.

treasury See also TREASURIES.
Jos 6:19 shall come into the *t'* of the Lord.
24 into the *t'* of the house of the Lord.
Jer 38:11 the house of the king under the *t'*,
M't 27: 6 lawful for to put them into the *t'*,
M'r 12:41 And Jesus sat over against the *t'*,
41 the people cast money into the *t'*:
43 all they which have cast into the *t'*:
Lu 21: 1 men casting their gifts into the *t'*.
Joh 8:20 These words spake Jesus in the *t'*,

treat See ENTREAT; INTREAT.

treatise
Ac 1: 1 The former *t'* have I made, O

tree See also TREES.
Ge 1:11 the fruit *t'* yielding fruit after his
12 *t'* yielding fruit, whose seed was in
29 face of all the earth, and every *t'*,
29 is the fruit of a *t'* yielding seed;
2: 9 grow every *t'* that is pleasant to the
9 the *t'* of life also in the midst of the
9 *t'* of knowledge of good and evil.
16 every *t'* of the garden thou mayest
17 of the *t'* of the knowledge of good
3: 1 Ye shall not eat of every *t'* of the
3 of the fruit of the *t'* which is in the
6 woman saw that the *t'* was good
6 a *t'* to be desired to make one wise,
11 Hast thou eaten of the *t'*, whereof I
12 she gave me of the *t'*, and I did eat.
17 and hast eaten of the *t'*, of which I
22 take also of the *t'* of life, and eat,
24 way, to keep the way of the *t'* of life.
18: 4 and rest yourselves under the *t'*:
8 and he stood by them under the *t'*,
30:37 and of the hazel and chesnut *t'*;
40:19 thee, and shall hang thee on a *t'*;
Ex 9:25 field, and brake every *t'* of the field.
10: 5 shall eat every *t'* which groweth for
15:25 the Lord shewed him a *t'*, which
Le 27:30 or of the fruit of the *t'*, is the Lord's:
Nu 6: 4 eat nothing...made of the vine *t'*,
De 12: 2 the hills, and under every green *t'*:
19: 5 with the axe to cut down the *t'*,
20:19 (for the *t'* of the field is man's life
21:22 death, and thou hang him on a *t'*:
23 not remain all night upon the *t'*,
22: 6 be before thee in the way in any *t'*,
24:20 When thou beatest thine olive *t'*, thou
Jos 8:29 the king of Ai he hanged on a *t'*
29 take his carcase down from the *t'*,
J'g 4: 5 And she dwelt under the palm *t'* of
9: 8 they said unto the olive *t'*, Reign thou
9 But the olive *t'* said unto them, Should
10 And the trees said to the fig *t'*,
11 But the fig *t'* said unto them,
1Sa 14: 2 Gibeah under a pomegranate *t'*
22: 6 Saul abode in Gibeah under a *t'* in
31:13 buried them under a *t'* at Jabesh,
1Ki 4:25 under his vine and under his fig *t'*,
33 the cedar *t'* that is in Lebanon
6:23 he made two cherubims of olive *t'*,
31 the oracle he made doors of olive *t'*:
32 The two doors also were of olive *t'*;
33 door of the temple posts of olive *t'*,
34 And the two doors were of fir *t'*:
14:23 high hill, and under every green *t'*.
19: 4 and sat down under a juniper *t'*:
1Ki 19: 5 he lay and slept under a juniper *t'*
2Ki 3:19 and shall fell every good *t'*, and
16: 4 hills, and under every green *t'*.
17:10 hills, and under every green *t'*:
18:31 vine, and every one of his fig *t'*,
2Ch 3: 5 greater house he cieled with fir *t'*,
28: 4 hills, and under every green *t'*.
Es 2:23 they were both hanged on a *t'*:
Job 14: 7 For there is hope of a *t'*, if it be cut
19:10 hope hath he removed like a *t'*.
24:20 wickedness shall be broken as a *t'*.
Ps 1: 3 be like a *t'* planted by the rivers
37:35 himself like a green bay *t'*.
52: 8 like a green olive *t'* in the house of God:
92:12 shall flourish like the palm *t'*:
Pr 3:18 She is a *t'* of life to them that lay
11:30 fruit of the righteous is a *t'* of life;
13:12 the desire cometh, it is a *t'* of life.
15: 4 A wholesome tongue is a *t'* of life:
27:18 Whoso keepeth the fig *t'* shall eat
Ec 11: 3 and if the *t'* fall toward the south,
3 the place where the *t'* falleth, there
12: 5 and the almond *t'* shall flourish,
Ca 2: 3 As the apple *t'* among the trees of
13 The fig *t'* putteth forth her green
7: 7 thy stature is like to a palm *t'*,
8 I will go up to the palm *t'*, I will
8: 5 raised thee up under the apple *t'*:
Isa 6:13 as a teil *t'*, and as an oak, whose
17: 6 as the shaking of an olive *t'*, two or
24:13 be as the shaking of an olive *t'*, and
34: 4 as a falling fig from the fig *t'*.
36:16 his vine, and every one of his fig *t'*,
40:20 chooseth a *t'* that will not rot;
41:19 wilderness the cedar, the shittah *t'*
19 and the myrtle, and the oil *t'*;
19 I will set in the desert the fir *t'*,
19 the pine, and the box *t'* together:
44:19 I fall down to the stock of a *t'*?
23 O forest, and every *t'* therein:
55:13 the thorn shall come up the fir *t'*,
13 brier shall come up the myrtle *t'*:
56: 3 eunuch say, Behold, I am a dry *t'*.
57: 5 with idols under every green *t'*,
60:13 shall come unto thee, the fir *t'*,
13 the pine *t'*, and the box together,
65:22 as the days of a *t'* are the days of
66:17 gardens behind one *t'* in the midst,
Jer 1:11 said, I see a rod of an almond *t'*.
2:20 and under every green *t'* thou
3: 6 mountain and under every green *t'*,
13 the strangers under every green *t'*,
8:13 nor figs on the fig *t'*, and the leaf
10: 3 one cutteth a *t'* out of the forest,
5 They are upright as the palm *t'*,
11:16 A green olive *t'*, fair, and of goodly
19 Let us destroy the *t'* with the fruit
17: 8 be as a *t'* planted by the waters,
Eze 6:13 under every green *t'*, and under
15: 2 What is the vine *t'* more than any *t'*,
6 As the vine *t'* among the trees of
17: 5 waters, and set it as a willow *t'*.
24 Lord have brought down the high *t'*,
24 have exalted the low *t'*, have
24 have dried up the green *t'*, and have
24 and have made the dry *t'* to flourish:
20:47 green *t'* in thee, and every dry *t'*:
21:10 the rod of my son, as every *t'*.
31: 8 nor any *t'* in the garden of God was
34:27 *t'* of the field shall yield her fruit,
36:30 I will multiply the fruit of the *t'*,
41:18 a palm *t'* was between a cherub
19 toward the palm *t'* on the one side,
19 toward the palm *t'* on the other side:
Da 4:10 a *t'* in the midst of the earth,
11 The *t'* grew, and was strong, and
14 Hew down the *t'*, and cut off his
20 The *t'* that thou sawest, which grew,
23 Hew the *t'* down, and destroy it; yet
26 leave the stump of the *t'* roots;
Ho 9:10 as the firstripe in the fig *t'* at her
14: 6 and his beauty shall be as the olive *t'*
8 I am like a green fir *t'*. From me
Joe 1: 7 vine waste, and barked my fig *t'*:
12 dried up, and the fig *t'* languisheth;
12 the pomegranate *t'*, the palm *t'*
12 the apple *t'*, even all the trees of
2:22 spring, for the *t'* beareth her fruit,
22 the fig *t'* and the vine do yield
Mic 4: 4 under his vine and under his fig *t'*;
Hab 3:17 the fig *t'* shall not blossom,
Hag 2:19 and the fig *t'*, and the pomegranate,
19 the olive *t'*, hath not brought forth:
Zec 3:10 under the vine and under the fig *t'*.
11: 2 Howl, fir *t'*; for the cedar is fallen;
M't 3:10 every *t'* which bringeth not forth
7:17 good *t'* bringeth forth good fruit;
17 corrupt *t'* bringeth forth evil fruit.
18 good *t'* cannot bring forth evil fruit,
18 a corrupt *t'* bring forth good fruit.
19 every *t'* that bringeth not forth
12:33 Either make the *t'* good, and his
33 or else make the *t'* corrupt, and his
33 for the *t'* is known by his fruit.
13:32 among herbs, and becometh a *t'*,
21:19 when he saw a fig *t'* in the way, he
19 presently the fig *t'* withered away.
20 How soon is the fig *t'* withered
21 do this which is done to the fig *t'*,
24:32 Now learn a parable of the fig *t'*;
M'r 11:13 seeing a fig *t'* afar off having leaves,
20 the fig *t'* dried up from the roots.
21 fig *t'*...thou cursedst is withered
13:28 Now learn a parable of the fig *t'*;
Lu 3: 9 every *t'* therefore which bringeth
6:43 good *t'* bringeth not forth corrupt

Lu 6:43 corrupt t' bring forth good fruit.
44 every t' is known by his own fruit.
13: 6 certain man had a fig t' planted
7 come seeking fruit on this fig t',
19 it grew, and waxed a great t';
17: 6 ye might say unto this sycamine t',
19: 4 climbed up into a sycomore t' to
21:29 Behold the fig t', and all the trees;
23:31 they do these things in a green t',
Joh 1:48 when thou wast under the fig t', I
50 thee, I saw thee under the fig t',
Ac 5:30 whom ye slew and hanged on a t'.
10:39 whom they slew and hanged on a t':
13:29 they took him down from the t',
Ro 11:17 and thou, being a wild olive t',
17 of the root and fatness of the olive t'
24 cut out of the olive t' which is wild
24 to nature into a good olive t':
24 be graffed into their own olive t'?
Ga 3:13 is every one that hangeth on a t':
Jas 3:12 Can the fig t', my brethren, bear
1Pe 2:24 our sins in his own body on the t',
Re 2: 7 will I give to eat of the t' of life,
6:13 a fig t' casteth her untimely figs,
7: 1 nor on the sea, nor on any t'.
9: 4 any green thing, neither any t';
22: 2 the river, was there the t' of life,
2 leaves of the t' were for the healing
14 may have right to the t' of life, and

trees See also AXLETREES.
Ge 3: 2 We may eat of the fruit of the t'
8 God amongst the t' of the garden.
23:17 all the t' that were in the field, that
Ex 10:15 all the fruit of the t' which the hail
15 not any green thing in the t',
15:27 and threescore and ten palm t':
Le 19:23 planted all manner of t' for food,
23:40 first day the boughs of goodly t',
40 branches of palm t',
40 and the boughs of thick t', and
26: 4 t' of the field shall yield their fruit.
20 neither shall the t' of the land yield
Nu 24: 6 t' of lign aloes which the Lord hath
6 as cedar t' beside the waters.
33: 9 and threescore and ten palm t';
De 6:11 vineyards and olive t', which thou
8: 8 and barley, and vines, and fig t',
16:21 plant thee a grove of any t' near
20:19 thou shalt not destroy the t'
20 the t' which thou knowest that they
20 they be not t' for meat, thou shalt
28:40 shalt have olive t' throughout all thy
42 All thy t' and fruit of thy land
34: 3 of Jericho, the city of palm t', unto
Jos 10:26 them, and hanged them on five t':
26 hanging upon the t' until...evening.
27 and they took them down off the t',
J'g 1:16 went up out of the city of palm t'
3:13 and possessed the city of palm t'.
9: 8 t' went forth on a time to anoint
9 and go to be promoted over the t'?
10 And the t' said to the fig tree, Come
11 and go to be promoted over the t'?
12 Then said the t' unto the vine,
13 and go to be promoted over the t'?
14 said all the t' unto the bramble,
15 And the bramble said unto the t',
48 and cut down a bough from the t',
2Sa 5:11 and cedar t', and carpenters, and
23 over against the mulberry t'.
24 in the tops of the mulberry t',
1Ki 4:33 he spake of t', from the cedar
5: 6 hew me cedar t' out of Lebanon;
10 Hiram gave Solomon cedar t'
10 fir t' according to all his desire.
6:29 figures of cherubims and palm t'
32 carvings of cherubims and palm t'
32 cherubims, and upon the palm t',
35 thereon cherubims and palm t'
7:36 cherubims, lions, and palm t',
9:11 furnished Solomon with cedar t'
11 and fir t', and with gold, according
10:11 Ophir great plenty of almug t',
12 king made of the almug t' pillars
12 there came no such almug t', nor
27 sycomore t' that are in the vale,
2Ki 3:25 water, and felled all the good t':
19:23 cut down the tall cedar t' thereof,
23 and the choice fir t' thereof: and
1Ch 14:14 them over against the mulberry t'.
15 in the tops of the mulberry t',
16:33 Then shall the t' of the wood sing
22: 4 Also cedar t' in abundance: for
27:28 the olive t' and the sycomore t'
2Ch 1:15 as stones, and cedar t' made he as
15 the sycomore t' that are in the vale
2: 8 also cedar t', [6086] fir t', and almug t'
3: 5 set thereon palm t' and chains.
9:10 algum t' and precious stones.
11 king made of the algum t' terraces
27 cedar t' made he as the sycomore
27 made he as the sycomore t' that
28:15 to Jericho, the city of palm t',
Ezr 3: 7 to bring cedar t' from Lebanon to
Ne 8:15 and branches of thick t', to make
9:25 and fruit t' in abundance:
10:35 the firstfruits of all fruit of all t',
37 and the fruit of all manner of t', of
Job 40:21 He lieth under the shady t', in the
22 The shady t' cover him with their
Ps 74: 5 lifted up axes upon the thick t'.
78:47 and their sycomore t' with frost.
96:12 shall all the t' of the wood rejoice
104:16 The t' of the Lord are full of sap;
17 the stork, the fir t' are her house.
105:33 their vines also and their fig t';

Ps 105:33 and brake the t' of their coasts.
148: 9 hills; fruitful t', and all cedars:
Ec 2: 5 I planted t' in them of all kind of
6 the wood that bringeth forth t':
Ca 2: 3 tree among the t' of the wood,
4:14 with all t' of frankincense;
Isa 7: 2 as the t' of the wood are moved
10:19 the rest of the t' of his forest shall
14: 8 Yea, the fir t' rejoice at thee, and
37:24 and the choice fir t' thereof:
44:14 among the t' of the forest:
55:12 all the t' of the field shall clap their
61: 3 might be called t' of righteousness;
Jer 5:17 eat up thy vines and thy fig t':
6: 6 Hew ye down t', and cast a mount
7:20 upon the t' of the field, and upon
17: 2 their groves by the green t' upon
Eze 15: 2 a branch which is among the t' of
6 vine tree among the t' of the forest,
17:24 t' of the field shall know that I the
20:28 every high hill, and all the thick t',
27: 5 thy ship boards of fir t' of Senir:
31: 4 rivers unto all the t' of the field.
5 above all the t' of the field,
8 the fir t' were not like his boughs,
8 and the chesnut t' were not like his
9 so that all the t' of Eden, that
14 that none of all the t' by the waters
14 neither their t' stand up in their
15 all the t' of the field fainted for
16 all the t' of Eden, the choice and
18 in greatness among the t' of Eden?
18 brought down with the t' of Eden
40:16 and upon each post were palm t'.
22 their arches, and their palm t',
26 it had palm t', one on this side, and
31, 34, 37 palm t' were upon the posts
41:18 made with cherubims and palm t',
20 were cherubims and palm t' made,
25 the temple, cherubims and palm t',
26 windows and palm t' on the one
47: 7 were very many t' on the one side
12 shall grow all t' for meat, whose
Ho 2:12 I will destroy her vines and her fig t',
Joe 1:12 even all the t' of the field, are
19 hath burned all the t' of the field.
Am 4: 9 your vineyards and your fig t'
Na 2: 3 the fir t' shall be terribly shaken.
3:12 strong holds shall be like fig t'
Zec 1: 8 he stood among the myrtle t' that
10 that stood among the myrtle t'
11 that stood among the myrtle t',
4: 3 two olive t' by it, one upon the right
11 What are these two olive t' upon the
M't 3:10 ax is laid unto the root of the t':
21: 8 cut down branches from the t', and
M'r 8:24 and said, I see men as t', walking
11: 8 cut down branches off the t', and
Lu 3: 9 axe is laid unto the root of the t':
21:29 Behold the fig tree, and all the t';
Joh 12:13 Took branches of palm t', and
Jude 12 t' whose fruit withereth, without
Re 7: 3 earth, neither the sea, nor the t',
8: 7 the third part of t' was burnt up,
11: 4 These are the two olive t', and the two

tremble See also TREMBLED; TREMBLETH; TREMBLING.
De 2:25 and shall t', and be in anguish
20: 3 faint, fear not, and do not t',
Ezr 10: 3 those that t' at the commandment
Job 9: 6 place, and the pillars thereof t'.
26:11 The pillars of heaven t' and are
Ps 60: 2 Thou hast made the earth to t';
99: 1 Lord reigneth; let the people t':
114: 7 T', thou earth, at the presence of
Ec 12: 3 the keepers of the house shall t',
Isa 5:25 the hills did t', and their carcases
14:16 the man that made the earth to t',
32:11 T', ye women that are at ease; be
64: 2 nations may t' at thy presence!
66: 5 of the Lord, ye that t' at his word;
Jer 5:22 will ye not t' at my presence,
10:10 at his wrath the earth shall t',
33: 9 they shall fear and t' for all the
51:29 the land shall t' and sorrow: for
Eze 26:16 shall t' at every moment, and be
18 Now shall the isles t' in the day of
32:10 they shall t' at every moment,
Da 6:26 men t' and fear before the God of
Ho 11:10 children shall t' from the west.
11 shall t' as a bird out of Egypt, and
Joe 2: 1 all the inhabitants of the land t':
10 before them; the heavens shall t':
Am 8: 8 Shall not the land t' for this, and
Hab 3: 7 curtains of the land of Midian did t'
Jas 2:19 the devils also believe, and t'.

trembled
Ge 27:33 And Isaac t' very exceedingly,
Ex 19:16 the people that was in the camp t'.
J'g 5: 4 earth t', and the heavens dropped,
1Sa 4:13 his heart t' for the ark of God.
14:15 and the spoilers, they also t',
16: 4 elders of the town t' at his coming,
28: 5 was afraid, and his heart greatly t'
2Sa 22: 8 Then the earth shook and t'; the
Ezr 9: 4 every one that t' at the words of
Ps 18: 7 Then the earth shook and t'; the
77:18 the world: the earth t' and shook.
97: 4 the world: the earth saw, and t'.
Jer 4:24 the mountains, and, lo, they t',
8:16 the whole land t' at the sound of
Da 5:19 t' and feared before him:
Hab 3:10 mountains saw thee, and they t':
16 When I heard, my belly t'; my
16 I t' in myself, that I might rest in

M'r 16: 8 for they t' and were amazed:
Ac 7:32 Then Moses t', and durst not
24:25 Felix t', and answered, Go thy

trembleth
Job 37: 1 At this also my heart t', and is
Ps 104:32 He looketh on the earth, and it t':
119:120 My flesh t' for fear of thee; and
Isa 66: 2 contrite spirit, and t' at my word.

trembling
Ex 15:15 t' shall take hold upon them;
De 28:65 shall give thee there a t' heart,
1Sa 13: 7 and all the people followed him t'
14:15 And there was t' in the host, in
15 quaked: so it was a very great t'.
Ezr 10: 9 t' because of this matter, and for
Job 4:14 Fear came upon me, and t', which
21: 6 and t' taketh hold on my flesh.
Ps 2:11 Lord with fear, and rejoice with t'
55: 5 Fearfulness and t' are come upon
Isa 51:17 drunken the dregs of the cup of t',
22 out of thine hand the cup of t',
Jer 30: 5 We have heard a voice of t', of
Eze 12:18 drink thy water with t' and with
26:16 shall clothe themselves with t';
Da 10:11 this word unto me, I stood t'.
Ho 13: 1 When Ephraim spake t', he
Zec 12: 2 I will make Jerusalem a cup of t'
M'r 5:33 But the woman fearing and t',
Lu 8:47 she came t', and falling down
Ac 9: 6 he t' and astonished said, Lord,
16:29 and sprang in, and came t',
1Co 2: 3 and in fear, and in much t'.
2Co 7:15 with fear and t' ye received him.
Eph 6: 5 with fear and t', in singleness of
Ph'p 2:12 your own salvation with fear and t'

trench
1Sa 17:20 he came to the t', as the host was
26: 5 Saul lay in the t', and the people
7 Saul lay sleeping within the t', and
2Sa 20:15 the city, and it stood in the t':
1Ki 18:32 and he made a t' about the altar,
35 and he filled the t' also with water.
38 up the water that was in the t'.
Lu 19:43 enemies shall cast a t' about thee,

trespass See also TRESPASSED; TRESPASSES; TRESPASSING.
Ge 31:36 What is my t'? what is my sin, that
50:17 the t' of thy brethren, and their
17 forgive the t' of thy servants of the
Ex 22: 9 For all manner of t', whether it be
Le 5: 6 he shall bring his t' offering unto
7 then he shall bring for his t', which
15 If a soul commit a t', and sin
15 shall bring for his t' unto the Lord
15 of the sanctuary, for a t' offering:
16 him with the ram of the t' offering,
18 for a t' offering, unto the priest:
19 It is a t' offering: he hath certainly
6: 2 and commit a t' against the Lord,
5 in the day of his t' offering.
6 bring his t' offering unto the Lord,
6 for a t' offering, unto the priest:
17 sin offering, and as the t' offering.
7: 1 this is the law of the t' offering:
2 shall they kill the t' offering:
5 unto the Lord: it is a t' offering.
7 sin offering is, so is the t' offering:
37 and of the t' offering, and of the
14:12 lamb, and offer him for a t' offering,
13 is the priest's, so is the t' offering:
14 some of the blood of the t' offering,
17 upon the blood of the t' offering:
21 take one lamb for a t' offering to be
24 take the lamb of the t' offering,
25 shall kill the lamb of the t' offering,
25 some of the blood of the t' offering,
28 place of the blood of the t' offering:
19:21 bring his t' offering unto the Lord,
21 even a ram for a t' offering.
22 the ram of the t' offering before the
22:16 them to bear the iniquity of t',
26:40 with their t' which they trespassed
Nu 5: 6 commit, to do a t' against the Lord,
7 shall recompense his t' with the
8 kinsman to recompense the t' unto,
8 t' be recompensed unto the Lord,
12 and commit a t' against him,
27 have done t' against her husband,
6:12 of the first year for a t' offering:
18: 9 every t' offering of theirs, which
31:16 to commit t' against the Lord in
Jos 7: 1 children of Israel committed a t' in
22:16 What t' is this...ye have committed
20 Achan the son of Zerah commit a t'
31 have not committed this t' against
1Sa 6: 3 any wise return him a t' offering:
4 What shall be the t' offering which
8 ye return him for a t' offering.
17 for a t' offering unto the Lord;
25:28 forgive the t' of thine handmaid:
1Ki 8:31 any man t' against his neighbour,
2Ki 12:16 t' money and sin money was not
1Ch 21: 3 will he be a cause of t' to Israel?
2Ch 19:10 warn them that they t' not against
10 this do, and ye shall not t'.
24:18 and Jerusalem for this their t'.
28:13 add more to our sins and to our t':
13 our t' is great, and there is fierce
22 he t' yet more against the Lord:
33:19 all his sins, and his t', and the
Ezr 9: 2 rulers hath been chief in this t'.
6 t' is grown up unto the heavens.
7 we been in a great t' unto this day;
13 our evil deeds, and for our great t'

Ezr 10: 10 wives, to increase the t' of Israel.
19 a ram of the flock for their t'.
Eze 15: 8 because they have committed a t',
17: 20 will plead with him there for his t'
18: 24 in his t' that he hath trespassed,
20: 27 have committed a t' against me.
40: 39 the sin offering and the t' offering,
42: 13 the sin offering, and the t' offering;
44: 29 the sin offering, and the t' offering;
46: 20 the priests shall boil the t' offering
Da 9: 7 their t' that they have trespassed
M't 18: 15 if thy brother shall t' against thee,
Lu 17: 3 If thy brother t' against thee, rebuke
4 if he t' against thee seven times in

trespassed
Le 5: 19 certainly t' against the Lord.
26: 40 trespass which they t' against me,
Nu 5: 7 unto him against whom he hath t'.
De 32: 51 Because ye t' against me among
2Ch 26: 18 the sanctuary; for thou hast t';
29: 6 For our fathers have t', and done
30: 7 t' against the Lord God of their
33: 23 but Amon t' more and more.
Ezr 10: 2 We have t' against our God, and
Eze 17: 20 that he hath t' against me.
18: 24 in his trespass that he hath t',
39: 23 because they t' against me,
26 whereby they have t' against me,
Da 9: 7 that they have t' against thee.
Ho 8: 1 my covenant, and t' against my law.

trespasses
Ezr 9: 15 we are before thee in our t': for
Ps 68: 21 as one as goeth on still in his t'.
Eze 39: 26 and all their t' whereby they have
M't 6: 14 For if ye forgive men their t', your
15 But if ye forgive not men their t',
15 will your Father forgive your t'.
18: 35 not every one his brother their t'.
M'r 11: 25 heaven may forgive you your t'.
26 which is in heaven forgive your t'.
2Co 5: 19 not imputing their t' unto them;
Eph 2: 1 who were dead in t' and sins;
Col 2: 13 him, having forgiven you all t';

trespassing
Le 6: 7 all that he hath done in t' therein.
Eze 14: 13 land sinneth against me by t'

trespass-money See TRESPASS and MONEY.

trespass-offering See TRESPASS and OFFERING.

trial
Job 9: 23 laugh at the t' of the innocent.
Eze 21: 13 Because it is a t', and what if the
2Co 8: 2 How that in a great t' of affliction
Heb 11: 36 others had t' of cruel mockings
1Pe 1: 7 That the t' of your faith, being
4: 12 the fiery t' which is to try you,

tribe See also TRIBES.
Ex 31: 2 the son of Hur, of the t' of Judah:
6 son of Ahisamach, of the t' of Dan:
35: 30 the son of Hur, of the t' of Judah;
34 son of Ahisamach, of the t' of Dan.
38: 22 the son of Hur, of the t' of Judah,
23 son of Ahisamach, of the t' of Dan,
Le 24: 11 daughter of Dibri, of the t' of Dan:
Nu 1: 4 there shall be a man of every t';
5 of the t' of Reuben; Elizur the son of
21 of them, even of the t' of Reuben,
23 of them, even of the t' of Simeon,
25 of them, even of the t' of Gad,
27 of them, even of the t' of Judah,
29 of them, even of the t' of Issachar,
31 of them, even of the t' of Zebulun,
33 of them, even of the t' of Ephraim,
35 of them, even of the t' of Manasseh,
37 of them, even of the t' of Benjamin,
39 of them, even of the t' of Dan,
41 of them, even of the t' of Asher,
43 of them, even of the t' of Naphtali,
47 Levites after the t' of their fathers
49 shalt not number the t' of Levi,
2: 5 unto him shall be the t' of Issachar:
7 Then the t' of Zebulun: and Eliab
12 by him shall be the t' of Simeon:
14 Then the t' of Gad: and the captain
20 by him shall be the t' of Manasseh:
22 Then the t' of Benjamin: and the
27 by him shall be the t' of Asher:
29 Then the t' of Naphtali: and the
3: 6 Bring the t' of Levi near, and
4: 18 Cut ye not off the t' of the families
7: 12 of Amminadab, of the t' of Judah:
10: 15 of the t' of the children of Issachar
16 of the t' of the children of Zebulun
19 of the t' of the children of Simeon
20 host of the t' of the children of Gad
23 the t' of the children of Manasseh
24 the t' of the children of Benjamin
26 of the t' of the children of Asher
27 of the t' of the children of Naphtali
13: 2 of every t' of their fathers shall ye
4 of the t' of Reuben, Shammua the
5 Of the t' of Simeon, Shaphat the
6 Of the t' of Judah, Caleb the son of
7 Of the t' of Issachar, Igal the son
8 Of the t' of Ephraim, Oshea the son
9 Of the t' of Benjamin, Palti the son
10 Of the t' of Zebulun, Gaddiel the
11 Of the t' of Joseph, namely, of the
11 of the t' of Manasseh, Gaddi the
12 Of the t' of Dan, Ammiel the son of
13 Of the t' of Asher, Sethur the son of
14 Of the t' of Naphtali, Nahbi the son
15 Of the t' of Gad, Geuel the son of
18: 2 thy brethren also of the t' of Levi,
2 t' of thy father, bring thou with

Nu 31: 4 Of every t' a thousand,
5 a thousand of every t', twelve
6 to the war, a thousand of every t',
32: 33 and unto half the t' of Manasseh
34: 13 the nine tribes, and to the half t':
14 the t' of the children of Reuben
14 and the t' of the children of Gad
14 and half the t' of Manasseh have
15 and the half t' have received their
18 shall take one prince of every t',
19 Of the t' of Judah, Caleb the son of
20 of the t' of the children of Simeon,
21 Of the t' of Benjamin, Elidad the
22 of the t' of the children of Dan,
23 the t' of the children of Manasseh,
24 the t' of the children of Ephraim,
25 the t' of the children of Zebulun,
26 the t' of the children of Issachar,
27 of the t' of the children of Asher,
28 the t' of the children of Naphtali,
36: 3 be put to the inheritance of the t'
4 be put unto the inheritance of the t'
4 inheritance of the t' of our fathers.
5 t' of the sons of Joseph hath said
6 t' of their father shall they marry.
7 of Israel remove from t' to t':
7 inheritance of the t' of his fathers.
8 in any t' of the children of Israel,
8 of the family of the t' of her father,
9 remove from one t' to another t';
12 the t' of the family of their father.
De 1: 23 twelve men of you, one of a t':
3: 13 gave I unto the half t' of Manasseh;
10: 8 the Lord separated the t' of Levi,
18: 1 all the t' of Levi, shall have no part
29: 8 and to the half t' of Manasseh.
18 man, or woman, or family, or t',
Jos 1: 12 to half the t' of Manasseh, spake
3: 12 of Israel, out of every t' a man.
4: 2 of the people, out of every t' a man,
4 of Israel, out of every t' a man:
12 half the t' of Manasseh, passed over
7: 1 for Achan,...of the t' of Judah,
14 that the t' which the Lord taketh
16 and the t' of Judah was taken:
18 and Achan,...of the t' of Judah,
12: 6 and the half t' of Manasseh.
13: 7 tribes, and the half t' of Manasseh,
14 unto the t' of Levi he gave none
15 the t' of the children of Reuben
24 gave inheritance unto the t' of Gad,
29 unto the half t' of Manasseh:
29 half t' of the children of Manasseh
33 unto the t' of Levi Moses gave not
14: 2 the nine tribes, and for the half t'.
3 an half t' on the other side Jordan:
15: 1, 20, 21 the t' of the children of Judah
16: 8 of the t' of the children of Ephraim
17: 1 also a lot for the t' of Manasseh;
18: 4 among you three men for each t':
7 and half the t' of Manasseh, have
11, 21 t' of the children of Benjamin
19: 1 for the t' of the children of Simeon
8 of the t' of the children of Simeon
23 of the t' of the children of Issachar
24 for the t' of the children of Asher
31 of the t' of the children of Asher
39 of the t' of the children of Naphtali
40 out for the t' of the children of Dan
48 of the t' of the children of Dan
20: 8 the plain out of the t' of Reuben,
8 in Gilead out of the t' of Gad,
8 Bashan out of the t' of Manasseh.
21: 4 had by lot out of the t' of Judah,
4 and out of the t' of Simeon,
4 and out of the t' of Benjamin,
5 of the families of the t' of Ephraim,
5 and out of the t' of Dan,
5 out of the half t' of Manasseh, ten
6 of the families of the t' of Issachar,
6 and out of the t' of Asher,
6 and out of the t' of Naphtali,
6 the half t' of Manasseh in Bashan,
7 families had out of the t' of Reuben,
7 and out of the t' of Gad,
7 and out of the t' of Zebulun, twelve
9 of the t' of the children of Judah,
9 of the t' of the children of Simeon,
17 out of the t' of Benjamin, Gibeon
20 their lot out of the t' of Ephraim.
23 And out of the t' of Dan, Eltekeh
25 of the half t' of Manasseh, Tanach
27 the other half t' of Manasseh, they
28 out of the t' of Issachar, Kishon
30 And out of the t' of Asher, Mishal
32 out of the t' of Naphtali, Kedesh
34 out of the t' of Zebulun, Jokneam
36 out of the t' of Reuben, Bezer with
38 And out of the t' of Gad, Ramoth
22: 1 and the half t' of Manasseh,
7 the one half of the t' of Manasseh
9 the half t' of Manasseh returned,
10 the half t' of Manasseh built there
11 the half t' of Manasseh have built
13, 15 and to the half t' of Manasseh,
21 the half t' of Manasseh answered,
J'g 18: 1 the t' of the Danites sought them
19 be a priest unto a t' and a family in
30 sons were priests to the t' of Dan
20: 12 men through all the t' of Benjamin.
21: 3 be to day one t' lacking in Israel?
6 There is one t' cut off from Israel
17 a t' be not destroyed out of Israel.
24 every man to his t' and to his family,
1Sa 9: 21 the families of the t' of Benjamin?
10: 20 near, the t' of Benjamin was taken.

1Sa 10: 21 caused the t' of Benjamin to come
1Ki 7: 14 widow's son of the t' of Naphtali,
11: 13 but will give one t' to thy son
32 have one t' for my servant David's
36 And unto his son will I give one t',
12: 20 of David, but the t' of Judah only.
21 of Judah, with the t' of Benjamin,
2Ki 17: 18 none left but the t' of Judah only.
1Ch 5: 18 Gadites, and half the t' of Manasseh,
23 children of the half t' of Manasseh
26 Gadites, and the half t' of Manasseh,
6: 60 And out of the t' of Benjamin;
61 were left of the family of that t',
61 were cities given out of the half t',
61 out of the half t' of Manasseh, by lot,
62 families out of the t' of Issachar,
62 and out of the t' of Asher,
62 and out of the t' of Naphtali,
62 out of the t' of Manasseh in Bashan,
63 families, out of the t' of Reuben,
63 and out of the t' of Gad,
63 and out of the t' of Zebulun, twelve
65 of the t' of the children of Judah,
65 of the t' of the children of Simeon,
65 the t' of the children of Benjamin,
66 coasts out of the t' of Ephraim.
70 of the half t' of Manasseh: Aner
71 family of the half t' of Manasseh,
72 And out of the t' of Issachar;
74 And out of the t' of Asher; Mashal
76 And out of the t' of Naphtali;
77 were given out of the t' of Zebulun,
78 given them out of the t' of Reuben,
80 And out of the t' of Gad; Ramoth
12: 31 of the half t' of Manasseh eighteen
37 and of the half t' of Manasseh,
23: 14 sons were named of the t' of Levi.
26: 32 Gadites, and the half t' of Manasseh,
27: 20 of the half t' of Manasseh, Joel the
21 Of the half t' of Manasseh in Gilead,
Ps 78: 67 and chose not the t' of Ephraim:
68 But chose the t' of Judah, the
Eze 47: 23 in what t' the stranger sojourneth,
Lu 2: 36 of Phanuel, of the t' of Aser:
Ac 13: 21 Saul...a man of the t' of Benjamin,
Ro 11: 1 of Abraham, of the t' of Benjamin.
Ph'p 3: 5 of Israel, of the t' of Benjamin,
Heb 7: 13 spoken pertaineth to another t',
14 of which t' Moses spake nothing
Re 5: 5 the Lion of the t' of Juda, the Root
7: 5 Of the t' of Juda were sealed twelve
5 Of the t' of Reuben were sealed
5 Of the t' of Gad were sealed twelve
6 Of the t' of Aser were sealed twelve
6 Of the t' of Nepthalim were sealed
6 Of the t' of Manasses were sealed
7 Of the t' of Simeon were sealed
7 Of the t' of Levi were sealed twelve
7 Of the t' of Issachar were sealed
8 Of the t' of Zabulon were sealed
8 Of the t' of Joseph were sealed
8 Of the t' of Benjamin were sealed

tribes
Ge 49: 16 people, as one of the t' of Israel.
28 All these are the twelve t' of Israel:
Ex 24: 4 according to the twelve t' of Israel.
28: 21 they be according to the twelve t'.
39: 14 name, according to the twelve t'.
Nu 1: 16 princes of the t' of their fathers,
7: 2 who were the princes of the t',
24: 2 in his tents according to their t';
26: 55 names of the t' of their fathers
30: 1 spake unto the heads of the t'
31: 4 throughout all the t' of Israel,
32: 28 and the chief fathers of the t' of
33: 54 according to the t' of your fathers
34: 13 commanded to give unto the nine t',
15 two t' and the half tribe...received
36: 3 to any of the sons of the other t'
9 every one of the t' of the children
De 1: 13 and known among your t',
15 So I took the chief of your t', wise
15 tens, and officers among your t'.
5: 23 even all the heads of your t', and
12: 5 God shall choose out of all your t'
14 Lord shall choose in one of thy t',
16: 18 God giveth thee, throughout thy t':
18: 5 hath chosen him out of all thy t',
29: 10 captains of your t', your elders,
21 unto evil out of all the t' of Israel,
31: 28 unto me all the elders of your t',
33: 5 t' of Israel were gathered together.
Jos 3: 12 twelve men out of the t' of Israel,
4: 5 according to the number of the t'
8 according unto the number of the t'
7: 14 be brought according to your t':
16 and brought Israel by their t';
11: 23 to their divisions by their t'.
12: 7 Joshua gave unto the t' of Israel
13: 7 for an inheritance unto the nine t',
14: 1 heads of the fathers of the t' of
2 for the nine t', and for the half
3 had given the inheritance of two t'
4 the children of Joseph were two t'.
18: 2 And there remained...seven t',
19: 51 heads of the fathers of the t' of
21: 1 heads of the fathers of the t' of
16 nine cities out of those two t'.
22: 14 throughout all the t' of Israel;
23: 4 to be an inheritance for your t',
24: 1 Joshua gathered all the t' of Israel
J'g 18: 1 not fallen unto them among the t'
20: 2 people, even of all the t' of Israel,
10 throughout all the t' of Israel,
12 t' of Israel sent men through all
21: 5 is there among all the t' of Israel

J'g 21: 8 What one is there of the t' of Israel
15 made a breach in the t' of Israel.
1Sa 2: 28 choose him out of all the t' of Israel
9: 21 of the smallest of the t' of Israel?
10: 19 before the Lord by your t',
20 all the t' of Israel to come near,
15: 17 made the head of the t' of Israel,
2Sa 5: 1 came all the t' of Israel to David
7: 7 I a word with any of the t' of Israel,
15: 2 servant is of one of the t' of Israel.
10 spies throughout all the t' of Israel,
19: 9 strife throughout all the t' of Israel,
20: 14 he went through all the t' of Israel
24: 2 Go now through all the t' of Israel,
1Ki 8: 1 Israel, and all the heads of the t',
16 no city out of all the t' of Israel
11: 31 and will give ten t' to thee:
32 chosen out of all the t' of Israel:)
35 will give it unto thee, even ten t'.
14: 21 did choose out of all the t' of Israel,
18: 31 of the t' of the sons of Jacob,
2Ki 21: 7 I have chosen out of all t' of Israel,
1Ch 27: 16 Furthermore over the t' of Israel:
22 were the princes of the t' of Israel.
28: 1 princes of Israel,...princes of the t',
29: 6 and princes of the t' of Israel,
2Ch 5: 2 Israel, and all the heads of the t',
6: 5 no city among all the t' of Israel
11: 16 out of all the t' of Israel such as set
12: 13 chosen out of all the t' of Israel,
33: 7 chosen before all the t' of Israel,
Ezr 6: 17 to the number of the t' of Israel.
Ps 78: 55 t' of Israel to dwell in their tents.
105: 37 one feeble person among their t'.
122: 4 the t' go up, the t' of the Lord,
Isa 19: 13 that are the stay of the t' thereof.
49: 6 servant to raise up the t' of Jacob,
63: 17 sake, the t' of thine inheritance.
Eze 37: 19 and the t' of Israel his fellows,
45: 8 house of Israel according to their t'.
47: 13 according to the twelve t' of Israel:
21 you according to the t' of Israel.
22 with you among the t' of Israel.
48: 1 Now these are the names of the t'.
19 serve it out of all the t' of Israel.
23 As for the rest of the t', from the
29 divide by lot unto the t' of Israel
31 after the names of the t' of Israel:
Ho 5: 9 among the t' of Israel have I made
Hab 3: 9 according to the oaths of the t',
Zec 9: 1 of man, as of all the t' of Israel,
M't 19: 28 judging the twelve t' of Israel.
24: 30 shall all the t' of the earth mourn,
Lu 22: 30 judging the twelve t' of Israel.
Ac 26: 7 Unto which promise our twelve t',
Jas 1: 1 the twelve t' which are scattered
Re 7: 4 all the t' of the children of Israel.
21: 12 are the names of the twelve t' of

tribulation See also TRIBULATIONS.
De 4: 30 When thou art in t', and all these
J'g 10: 14 deliver you in the time of your t'.
1Sa 26: 24 and let him deliver me out of all t'.
M't 13: 21 for when t' or persecution ariseth
24: 21 For then shall be great t', such as
29 after the t' of those days shall the
M'r 13: 24 after that t', the sun...be darkened,
Joh 16: 33 In the world ye shall have t': but
Ac 14: 22 through much t' enter into the
Ro 2: 9 T' and anguish upon every soul of
5: 3 knowing that t' worketh patience;
8: 35 shall t', or distress, or persecution,
12: 12 Rejoicing in hope; patient in t';
2Co 1: 4 Who comforteth us in all our t',
7: 4 I am exceeding joyful in all our t'.
1Th 3: 4 before that we should suffer t';
2Th 1: 6 t' to them that trouble you;
Re 1: 9 your brother, and companion in t',
2: 9 thy works, and t', and poverty,
10 and ye shall have t' ten days:
22 adultery with her into great t',
7: 14 they which came out of great t',

tribulations
1Sa 10: 19 of all your adversities and your t';
Ro 5: 3 only so, but we glory in t' also;
Eph 3: 13 that ye faint not at my t' for you,
2Th 1: 4 persecutions and t' that ye endure:

tributaries
De 20: 11 found therein shall be t' unto thee,
J'g 1: 30 dwelt among them, and became t'.
33 Beth-anath became t' unto them.
35 prevailed, so that they became t'.

tributary See also TRIBUTARIES.
La 1: 1 provinces, how is she become t'!

tribute See also DISTRIBUTE.
Ge 49: 15 and became a servant unto t'.
Nu 31: 28 levy a t' unto the Lord of the men
37 the Lord's t' of the sheep was six
38 the Lord's t' was threescore and
39 which the Lord's t' was threescore
40 the Lord's t' was thirty and two
41 Moses gave the t', which was the
De 16: 10 a t' of a freewill offering of thine
Jos 16: 10 unto this day, and serve under t'.
17: 13 that they put the Canaanites to t';
J'g 1: 28 that they put the Canaanites to t',
2Sa 20: 24 And Adoram was over the t': and
1Ki 4: 6 the son of Abda was over the t'.
9: 21 Solomon levy a t' of bondservice
12: 18 sent Adoram, who was over the t';
2Ki 23: 33 put the land to a t' of an hundred
2Ch 8: 8 make to pay t' until this day.
10: 18 sent Hadoram that was over the t';
17: 11 brought...presents, and t' silver;
Ezr 4: 13 then will they not pay toll, t', and
4: 20 t', and custom, was paid unto them.
6: 8 even of the t' beyond the river,
7: 24 lawful to impose toll, t', or custom,
Ne 5: 4 borrowed money for the king's t',
Es 10: 1 Ahasuerus laid a t' upon the land,
Pr 12: 24 but the slothful shall be under t'.
M't 17: 24 they that receive t' money came
24 said, Doth not your master pay t'?
25 of the earth take custom or t'?
22: 17 Is it lawful to give t' unto Cæsar,
19 Shew me the t' money. And they
M'r 12: 14 Is it lawful to give t' to Cæsar, or
Lu 20: 22 lawful for us to give t' unto Cæsar,
23: 2 and forbidding to give t' to Cæsar,
Ro 13: 6 For for this cause pay ye t' also:
7 t' to whom t' is due; custom to

trickleth
La 3: 49 Mine eye t' down, and ceaseth

tried
De 21: 5 controversy and every stroke be t':
2Sa 22: 31 perfect; the word of the Lord is t':
Job 23: 10 when he hath t' me, I shall come
34: 36 is that Job may be t' unto the end,
Ps 12: 6 as silver t' in a furnace of earth,
17: 3 thou hast t' me, and shalt find
18: 30 perfect: the word of the Lord is t':
66: 10 thou hast t' us, as silver is t'.
105: 19 came: the word of the Lord t' him.
Isa 28: 16 a stone, and a t' stone, a precious
Jer 12: 3 me, and t' mine heart toward thee:
Da 12: 10 purified, and made white, and t';
Zec 13: 9 and will try them as gold is t':
Heb 11: 17 when he was t', offered up Isaac:
Jas 1: 12 for when he is t', he shall receive
1Pe 1: 7 though it be t' with fire, might be
Re 2: 2 thou hast t' them which say they
10 you into prison, that ye may be t';
3: 18 to buy of me gold t' in the fire,

triest
1Ch 29: 17 my God, that thou t' the heart, and
Jer 11: 20 that t' the reins and the heart,
20: 12 that t' the righteous, and seest the

trieth
Job 34: 3 For the ear t' words, as the mouth
Ps 7: 9 for the righteous God t' the hearts
11: 5 The Lord t' the righteous: but the
Pr 17: 3 for gold: but the Lord t' the hearts.
1Th 2: 4 but God, which t' our hearts.

trimmed
2Sa 19: 24 dressed his feet, nor t' his beard,
M't 25: 7 virgins arose, and t' their lamps.

trimmest
Jer 2: 33 Why t' thou thy way to seek love?

triumph See also TRIUMPHED; TRIUMPHING.
2Sa 1: 20 daughters of the uncircumcised t'.
Ps 25: 2 let not mine enemies t' over me.
41: 11 mine enemy doth not t' over me.
47: 1 unto God with the voice of t'.
60: 8 Philistia, t' thou because of me.
92: 4 I will t' in the works of thy hands.
94: 3 how long shall the wicked t'?
106: 47 holy name, and to t' in thy praise.
108: 9 my shoes; over Philistia will I t'.
2Co 2: 14 always causeth us to t' in Christ,

triumphed
Ex 15: 1 the Lord, for he hath t' gloriously:
21 the Lord, for he hath t' gloriously;

triumphing
Job 20: 5 That the t' of the wicked is short,
Col 2: 15 of them openly, t' over them in it.

Troas (*tro'-as*)
Ac 16: 8 passing by Mysia came down to T'.
11 Therefore loosing from T', we
20: 5 going before tarried for us at T'.
6 came unto them to T' in five days;
2Co 2: 12 I came to T' to preach Christ's
2Ti 4: 13 cloke that I left at T' with Carpus,

trod See TRODDEN; TRODE.

trodden
De 1: 36 give the land that he hath t' upon,
Jos 14: 9 land whereon thy feet have t' shall
J'g 5: 21 soul, thou hast t' down strength.
Job 22: 15 old way which wicked men have t'?
28: 8 The lion's whelps have not t' it, nor
Ps 119: 118 hast t' down all them that err
Isa 5: 5 thereof, and it shall be t' down:
14: 19 the pit; as a carcase t' under feet.
18: 2 a nation meted out and t' down,
7 nation meted out and t' under foot,
25: 10 Moab shall be t' down under him,
10 straw is t' down for the dunghill.
28: 3 of Ephraim, shall be t' under feet;
18 then ye shall be t' down by it.
63: 3 I have t' the winepress alone; and
18 our adversaries have t' down thy
Jer 12: 10 they have t' my portion under foot,
La 1: 15 hath t' under foot all my mighty
15 the Lord hath t' the virgin, the
Eze 34: 19 which ye have t' with your feet;
Da 8: 13 and the host to be t' under foot?
Mic 7: 10 shall she be t' down as the mire of
M't 5: 13 out, and to be t' under foot of men.
Lu 8: 5 it was t' down, and the fowls of the
21: 24 Jerusalem shall be t' down of the
Heb 10: 29 who hath t' under foot the Son of
Re 14: 20 winepress was t' without the city,

trode
J'g 9: 27 their vineyards, and t' the grapes,
20: 43 and t' them down with ease over
2Ki 7: 17, 20 people t' upon him in the gate,
9: 33 horses: and he t' her under foot.
14: 9 in Lebanon, and t' down the thistle.
2Ch 25: 18 in Lebanon, and t' down the thistle.
Lu 12: 1 that they t' one upon another,

Trogyllium (*tro-jil'-le-um*)
Ac 20: 15 at Samos, and tarried at T';

troop See also TROOPS.
Ge 30: 11 And Leah said, A t' cometh: and
49: 19 Gad, a t' shall overcome him: but
1Sa 30: 8 Shall I pursue after this t'? shall I
2Sa 2: 25 after Abner, and became one t',
3: 22 and Joab came from pursuing a t',
22: 30 by thee I have run through a t': by
23: 11 were gathered together into a t',
13 the t' of the Philistines pitched in
Ps 18: 29 by thee I have run through a t';
Isa 65: 11 that prepare a table for that t',
Jer 18: 22 bring a t' suddenly upon them:
Hos 7: 1 the t' of robbers spoileth without,
Am 9: 6 and hath founded his t' in the earth;

troops
Job 6: 19 The t' of Tema looked, the
19: 12 His t' come together, and raise up
Jer 5: 7 assembled themselves by t' in the
Hos 6: 9 as t' of robbers wait for a man,
Mic 5: 1 Now gather thyself in t',
1 O daughter of t': he hath laid
Hab 3: 16 he will invade them with his t'.

Trophimus (*trof'-im-us*)
Ac 20: 4 and of Asia, Tychicus and T'.
21: 29 before with him in the city T' an
2Ti 4: 20 but T' have I left at Miletum sick.

troth See BETROTH.

trouble See also TROUBLED; TROUBLES; TROUBLEST; TROUBLETH; TROUBLING.
Jos 6: 18 camp of Israel a curse, and t' it.
7: 25 us? the Lord shall t' thee this day.
J'g 11: 35 thou art one of them that t' me:
2Ki 19: 3 This day is a day of t', and of
1Ch 22: 14 in my t' I have prepared for the
2Ch 15: 4 they in their t' did turn unto the
29: 8 and he hath delivered them to t',
32: 18 to affright them, and to t' them;
Ne 9: 27 and in the time of their t', when
32 let not all the t' seem little before
Job 3: 26 neither was I quiet; yet t' came.
5: 6 doth t' spring out of the ground;
7 Yet man is born unto t', as the
14: 1 is of few days, and full of t'.
15: 24 T' and anguish shall make him
27: 9 his cry when t' cometh upon him?
30: 25 weep for him that was in t'?
34: 29 quietness, who then can make t'?
38: 23 reserved against the time of t',
Ps 3: 1 how are they increased that t' me!
9: 9 oppressed, a refuge in times of t'.
13 consider my t' which I suffer of
10: 1 hidest thou thyself in times of t'?
13: 4 those that t' me rejoice when I am
20: 1 Lord hear thee in the day of t';
22: 11 Be not far from me; for t' is near;
27: 5 in the time of t' he shall hide me
31: 7 for thou hast considered my t';
9 upon me, O Lord, for I am in t':
32: 7 thou shalt preserve me from t';
37: 39 is their strength in the time of t'.
41: 1 Lord will deliver him in time of t'.
46: 1 strength, a very present help in t'.
50: 15 And call upon me in the day of t':
54: 7 he hath delivered me out of all t':
59: 16 and refuge in the day of my t'.
60: 11 Give us help from t': for vain is
66: 14 hath spoken, when I was in t'.
69: 17 from thy servant; for I am in t':
73: 5 They are not in t' as other men;
77: 2 day of my t' I sought the Lord:
78: 33 in vanity, and their years in t'.
49 wrath, and indignation, and t',
81: 7 Thou calledst in t', and I delivered
86: 7 day of my t' I will call upon thee:
91: 15 I will be with him in t'; I will deliver
102: 2 me in the day when I am in t';
107: 6, 13 cried unto the Lord in their t',
19 they cry unto the Lord in their t',
26 their soul is melted because of t'.
28 they cry unto the Lord in their t',
108: 12 Give us help from t': for vain is the
116: 3 upon me: I found t' and sorrow.
119: 143 T' and anguish have taken hold
138: 7 Though I walk in the midst of t',
142: 2 him; I shewed before him my t'.
143: 11 sake bring my soul out of t'.
Pr 11: 8 The righteous is delivered out of t',
12: 13 but the just shall come out of t'.
15: 6 in the revenues of the wicked is t'.
16 great treasure and t' therewith.
25: 19 in an unfaithful man in time of t'
Isa 1: 14 they are a t' unto me; I am weary
8: 22 behold t' and darkness, dimness
17: 14 And behold at eveningtide t';
22: 5 For it is a day of t', and of
26: 16 Lord, in t' have they visited thee,
30: 6 Into the land of t' and anguish,
33: 2 our salvation also in the time of t'.
37: 3 This day is a day of t', and of
46: 7 answer, nor save him out of his t'.
65: 23 in vain, nor bring forth for t';
Jer 2: 27 in the time of their t' they will say,
28 can save thee in the time of thy t':
8: 15 a time of health, and behold t'!
11: 12 them at all in the time of their t'.
14 that they cry unto me for their t'.
14: 8 the saviour thereof in time of t',
19 the time of healing, and behold t'!
30: 7 it is even the time of Jacob's t';
51: 2 for in the day of t' they shall be

La 1:21 mine enemies have heard of my t':
Eze 7: 7 is come, the day of t' is near,
32:13 neither shall the foot of man t' them
13 nor the hoofs of beasts t' them.
Da 4:19 the interpretation thereof, t' thee.
5:10 let not thy thoughts t' thee, nor let
11:44 and out of the north shall t' him:
12: 1 and there shall be a time of t',
Na 1: 7 good, a strong hold in the day of t';
Hab 3:16 that I might rest in the day of t':
Zep 1:15 of wrath, a day of t' and distress,
M't 26:10 them, Why t' ye the woman?
M'r 14: 6 said, Let her alone; why t' ye her?
Lu 7: 6 unto him, Lord, t' not thyself:
8:49 is dead; t' not the Master.
11: 7 shall answer and say, T' me not:
Ac 15:19 sentence is, that we t' not them,
16:20 Jews, do exceedingly t' our city,
20:10 T' not yourselves; for his life is
1Co 7:28 such shall have t' in the flesh:
2Co 1: 4 comfort them which are in any t',
8 our t' which came to us in Asia,
Ga 1: 7 but there be some that t' you, and
5:12 were even cut off which t' you.
6:17 henceforth let no man t' me:
2Th 1: 6 tribulation to them that t' you;
2Ti 2: 9 Wherein I suffer t', as an evil doer,
Heb12:15 of bitterness springing up t' you,

troubled See also TROUBLEDST.
Ge 34:30 Ye have t' me to make me to stink
41: 8 the morning that his spirit was t';
45: 3 for they were t' at his presence.
Ex 14:24 and t' the host of the Egyptians,
Jos 7:25 Joshua said, Why hast thou t' us?
1Sa 14:29 My father hath t' the land: see,
16:14 evil spirit from the Lord t' him.
28:21 Saul, and saw that he was sore t',
2Sa 4: 1 feeble, and all the Israelites were t'.
1Ki 18:18 he answered, I have not t' Israel;
2Ki 6:11 king of Syria was sore t' for this
Ezr 4: 4 Judah, and t' them in building,
Job 4: 5 it toucheth thee, and thou art t'.
21: 4 why should not my spirit be t'?
23:15 Therefore am I t' at his presence:
34:20 the people shall be t' at midnight,
Ps 30: 7 didst hide thy face, and I was t'.
38: 6 I am t'; I am bowed down greatly;
46: 3 the waters thereof roar and be t',
48: 5 they were t', and hasted away.
77: 3 I remembered God, and was t':
4 I am so t' that I cannot speak.
16 afraid: the depths also were t'.
83:17 Let them be confounded and t' for
90: 7 anger, and by thy wrath are we t'.
104:29 Thou hidest thy face, they are t':
Pr 25:26 the wicked is as a t' fountain,
Isa 32:10 Many days and years shall ye be t',
11 are at ease; be t', ye careless ones:
57:20 But the wicked are like the t' sea,
Jer 31:20 my bowels are t' for him; I will
La 1:20 my bowels are t'; mine heart is
2:11 my bowels are t', my liver is poured
Eze 7:27 of the people of the land shall be t':
26:18 isles that are in the sea shall be t'
27:35 afraid, they shall be t' in their
Da 2: 1 wherewith his spirit was t', and
3 my spirit was t' to know the dream.
4: 5 and the visions of my head t' me.
19 one hour, and his thoughts t' him.
5: 6 his thoughts t' him, so that the
9 Then was king Belshazzar greatly t',
7:15 and the visions of my head t' me.
28 Daniel, my cogitations much t' me,
Zec 10: 2 they were t', because there was no
M't 2: 3 had heard these things, he was t',
14:26 they were t', saying, It is a spirit;
24: 6 see that ye be not t': for all these
M'r 6:50 For they all saw him, and were t'.
13: 7 and rumours of wars, be ye not t':
Lu 1:12 when Zacharias saw him, he was t',
29 she was t' at his saying, and cast
10:41 careful and t' about many things:
24:38 Why are ye t'? and why do
Joh 5: 4 into the pool, and t' the water:
7 have no man, when the water is t',
11:33 groaned in the spirit,...was t',
12:27 Now is my soul t'; and what shall
13:21 he was t' in spirit, and testified,
14: 1 Let not your heart be t': ye believe
27 Let not your heart be t', neither let
Ac 15:24 out from us have t' you with words,
17: 8 they t' the people and the rulers of
2Co 4: 8 We are t' on every side, yet not
7: 5 rest, but we were t' on every side;
2Th 1: 7 And to you who are t' rest with us,
2: 2 or be t', neither by spirit, nor by
1Pe 3:14 afraid of their terror, neither be t';

troubledst
Eze 32: 2 and t' the waters with thy feet,

troubler
1Ch 2: 7 Achar, the t' of Israel, who

troubles
De 31:17 evils and t' shall befall them;
21 evils and t' are befallen them,
Job 5:19 He shall deliver thee in six t': yea,
Ps 25:17 The t' of my heart are enlarged: O
22 Israel, O God, out of all his t'.
34: 6 him, and saved him out of all his t'.
17 delivereth them out of all their t'.
71:20 hast shewed me great and sore t',
88: 3 For my soul is full of t': and my
Pr 21:23 tongue keepeth his soul from t'.
Isa 65:16 because the former t' are forgotten,
M'r 13: 8 and there shall be famines and t':

troublest
M'r 5:35 dead: why t' thou the Master any

troubleth
1Sa 16:15 an evil spirit from God t' thee.
1Ki 18:17 him, Art thou he that t' Israel?
Job 22:10 about thee, and sudden fear t' thee;
23:16 heart soft, and the Almighty t' me:
Pr 11:17 he that is cruel t' his own flesh.
29 that t' his own house shall inherit
15:27 is greedy of gain t' his own house;
Da 4: 9 is in thee, and no secret t' thee,
Lu 18: 5 yet because this widow t' me,
Ga 5:10 but he that t' you shall bear his

troubling
Job 3:17 There the wicked cease from t';
Joh 5: 4 the t' of the water stepped in was

troublous
Da 9:25 and the wall, even in t' times.

trough See also TROUGHS.
Ge 24:20 emptied her pitcher into the t',

troughs See also KNEADINGTROUGHS.
Ge 30:38 watering t' when the flocks came
Ex 2:16 filled the t' to water their father's

trow
Lu 17: 9 were commanded him? I t' not.

trucebreakers
2Ti 3: 3 Without natural affection, t', false

true
Ge 42:11 we are t' men, thy servants are no
19 If ye be t' men, let one of your
31 We are t' men; we are no spies:
33 shall I know that ye are t' men;
34 are no spies, but that ye are t' men:
De 17: 4 it be t', and the thing certain,
22:20 But if this thing be t', and the tokens
Jos 2:12 house, and give me a t' token:
Ru 3:12 it is t' that I am thy near kinsman:
2Sa 7:28 art that God, and thy words be t',
1Ki 10: 6 It was a t' report that I heard in
22:16 tell me nothing but that which is t'
2Ch 9: 5 It was a t' report which I heard in
15: 3 Israel hath been without the t' God,
Ne 9:13 them right judgments, and t' laws,
Ps 19: 9 the judgments of the Lord are t'
119:160 Thy word is t' from the beginning:
Pr 14:25 A t' witness delivereth souls: but a
Jer 10:10 But the Lord is the t' God, he is the
42: 5 Lord be a t' and faithful witness
Eze 18: 8 hath executed t' judgment between
Da 3:14 Is it t', O Shadrach, Meshach, and
24 said unto the king, T', O king.
6:12 The thing is t', according to the
8:26 the morning which was told is t':
10: 1 and the thing was t', but the time
Zec 7: 9 Execute t' judgment, and shew
M't 22:16 Master, we know that thou art t',
M'r 12:14 Master, we know that thou art t',
Lu 16:11 commit to your trust the t' riches?
Joh 1: 9 That was the t' Light, which lighteth
3:33 hath set to his seal that God is t'.
4:23 when the t' worshippers shall
37 herein is that saying t', One soweth,
5:31 of myself, my witness is not t'.
32 which he witnesseth of me is t'.
6:32 my Father giveth you the t' bread
7:18 glory that sent him, the same is t',
28 but he that sent me is t', whom ye
8:13 of thyself; thy record is not t'.
14 record of myself, yet my record is t':
16 yet if I judge, my judgment is t':
17 that the testimony of two men is t'.
26 he that sent me is t'; and I speak to
10:41 that John spake of this man were t'.
15: 1 I am the t' vine, and my Father is
17: 3 might know thee the only t' God,
19:35 it bear record, and his record is t':
35 he knoweth that he saith t', that ye
21:24 and we know that his testimony is t'.
Ac 12: 9 that it was t' which was done by the
Ro 3: 4 let God be t', but every man a liar;
2Co 1:18 But as God is t', our word toward
6: 8 report: as deceivers, and yet t';
Eph 4:24 righteousness and t' holiness.
Ph'p 4: 3 I intreat thee also, t' yokefellow,
8 brethren, whatsoever things are t',
1Th 1: 9 idols to serve the living and t' God;
1Ti 3: 1 This is a t' saying, If a man desire
Tit 1:13 This witness is t'. Wherefore
Heb 8: 2 sanctuary, and of the t' tabernacle,
9:24 which are the figures of the t';
10:22 Let us draw near with a t' heart in
1Pe 5:12 that this is the t' grace of God
2Pe 2:22 them according to the t' proverb,
1Jo 2: 8 which thing is t' in him and in you:
8 past, and the t' light now shineth.
5:20 that we may know him that is t',
20 and we are in him that is t', even in
20 This is the t' God, and eternal life.
3Jo 12 and ye know that our record is t'.
Re 3: 7 saith he that is holy, he that is t',
14 the faithful and t' witness, the
6:10 How long, O Lord, holy and t',
15: 3 just and t' are thy ways, thou King
16: 7 t' and righteous are thy judgments.
19: 2 t' and righteous are his judgments:
9 me, These are the t' sayings of God.
11 him was called Faithful and T',
21: 5 for these words are t' and faithful.
22: 6 These sayings are faithful and t':

trulyA
Ge 24:49 deal kindly and t' with my master,
47:29 and deal kindly and t' with me;
48:19 but t' his younger brother shall be
Nu 14:21 But as t' as I live, all the earth
28 As t' as I live, saith the Lord, as ye
De 14:22 Thou shalt t' tithe all the increase
Jos 2:14 will deal kindly and t' with thee.
24 T' the Lord hath delivered into
J'g 9:16 if ye have done t' and sincerely, in
19 ye then have dealt t' and sincerely
1Sa 20: 3 but t' as the Lord liveth, and as thy
Job 36: 4 For t' my words shall not be false:
Ps 62: 1 T' my soul waiteth upon God:
73: 1 T' God is good to Israel, even to
116:16 O Lord, t' I am thy servant:
Pr 12:22 they that deal t' are his delight.
Ec 11: 7 T' the light is sweet, and a pleasant
Jer 3:23 T' in vain is salvation hoped for
23 t' in the Lord...is the salvation of
10:19 but I said, T' this is a grief, and I
28: 9 that the Lord hath t' sent him.
Eze 18: 9 hath kept my judgments, to deal t'
Mic 3: 8 t' I am full of power by the spirit
M't 9:37 The harvest t' is plenteous, but
17:11 Elias t' shall first come, and
27:54 saying, T' this was the Son of God.
M'r 14:38 The spirit t' is ready, but the flesh
15:39 T' this man was the Son of God.
Lu 10: 2 The harvest t' is great, but the
11:48 T' ye bear witness that ye allow
20:21 teachest the way of God t':
22:22 t' the Son of man goeth, as it was
Joh 4:18 thy husband: in that saidst thou t'.
20:30 many other signs t' did Jesus
Ac 1: 5 For John t' baptized with water;
3:22 For Moses t' said unto the fathers,
5:23 The prison t' found we shut with
2Co 12:12 T' the signs of an apostle were
Heb 7:23 they t' were many priests, because
11:15 And t', if they had been mindful of
1Jo 1: 3 t' our fellowship is with...Father,

trump See also TRUMPET.
1Co 15:52 twinkling of an eye, at the last t':
1Th 4:16 archangel, and with the t' of God:

trumpet See also TRUMP; TRUMPETS.
Ex 19:13 when the t' soundeth long, they
16 the voice of the t' exceeding loud;
19 the voice of the t' sounded long,
20:18 lightnings, and the noise of the t',
Le 25: 9 cause the t' of the jubile to sound
9 make the t' sound throughout all
Nu 10: 4 And if they blow but with one t', then
Jos 6: 5 when ye hear the sound of the t',
20 people heard the sound of the t',
J'g 3:27 that he blew a t' in the mountain
6:34 upon Gideon, and he blew a t';
7:16 he put a t' in every man's hand,
18 When I blow with a t', I and all
1Sa 13: 3 Saul blew the t' throughout all the
2Sa 2:28 So Joab blew a t', and all the people
6:15 and with the sound of the t'.
15:10 soon as ye hear the sound of the t',
18:16 Joab blew the t', and the people
20: 1 blew a t', and said, We have no part
22 he blew a t', and they retired from
1Ki 1:34 blow ye with the t', and say, God
39 they blew the t'; and all the people
41 when Joab heard the sound of the t',
Ne 4:18 he that sounded the t' was by me.
20 place...ye hear the sound of the t',
Job 39:24 he that it is the sound of the t'.
Ps 47: 5 the Lord with the sound of a t'.
81: 3 Blow up the t' in the new moon, in
150: 3 Praise him with the sound of the t':
Isa 18: 3 and when he bloweth a t', hear ye.
27:13 that the great t' shall be blown,
58: 1 spare not, lift up thy voice like a t',
Jer 4: 5 and say, Blow ye the t' in the land:
19 heard, O my soul, the sound of the t',
21 and hear the sound of the t'?
6: 1 and blow the t' in Tekoa, and set up
17 Hearken to the sound of the t'.
42:14 war, nor hear the sound of the t',
51:27 blow the t' among the nations,
Eze 7:14 They have blown the t', even to
33: 3 blow the t', and warn the people;
4 heareth the sound of the t',
5 He heard the sound of the t', and
6 if the watchman...blow not the t',
Ho 5: 8 in Gibeah, and the t' in Ramah:
8: 1 Set the t' to thy mouth. He shall
Joe 2: 1 Blow ye the t' in Zion, and sound
15 Blow the t' in Zion, sanctify a fast,
Am 2: 2 and with the sound of the t':
3: 6 Shall a t' be blown in the city, and
Zep 1:16 A day of t' and alarm against the
Zec 9:14 and the Lord God shall blow the t',
M't 6: 2 alms, do not sound a t' before thee,
24:31 angels with a great sound of a t',
1Co 14: 8 if the t' give an uncertain sound,
15:52 for the t' shall sound, and the dead
Heb12:19 And the sound of a t', and the voice
Re 1:10 behind me a great voice, as of a t',
4: 1 as it were of a t' talking with me;
8:13 voices of the t' of the three angels,
9:14 to the sixth angel which had the t',

trumpeters
2Ki 11:14 the princes and the t' by the king,
2Ch 5:13 as the t' and singers were as one,
29:28 singers sang, and the t' sounded:
Re 18:22 musicians, and of pipers, and t',

trumpets
Le 23:24 a sabbath a memorial of blowing of t',
Nu 10: 2 Make thee two t' of silver; of a
8 the priests, shall blow with the t';
9 ye shall blow an alarm with the t';
10 blow with the t' over your burnt
29: 1 it is a day of blowing the t' unto you.

Nu 31: 6 and the t' to blow in his hand.
Jos 6: 4 shall bear before the ark seven t'
4 the priests shall blow with the t'.
6 priests bear seven t' of rams' horns
8 seven priests bearing the seven t'
8 the Lord, and blew with the t':
9 the priests that blew with the t',
9 going on, and blowing with the t'.
13 And seven priests bearing seven t'
13 continually, and blew with the t':
13 going on, and blowing with the t'.
16 when the priests blew with the t',
20 when the priests blew with the t':
J'g 7: 8 victuals in their hand, and their t':
18 blow ye the t' also on every side of
19 and they blew the t', and brake the
20 the three companies blew the t',
20 the t' in their right hands to blow
22 And the three hundred blew the t',
2Ki 9: 13 blew with t', saying, Jehu is king.
11: 14 of the land rejoiced, and blew with t':
12: 13 snuffers, basons, t', any vessels of
1Ch 13: 8 and with cymbals, and with t'.
15: 24 did blow with the t' before the ark
28 sound of the cornet, and with t',
16: 6 priests with t' continually before
42 with t' and cymbals for those that
2Ch 5: 12 twenty priests sounding with t':)
13 they lifted up their voice with the t'
7: 6 the priests sounded t' before them,
13: 12 his priests with sounding t' to cry
14 and the priests sounded with the t'.
15: 14 with shouting, and with t', and with
20: 28 harps and t' unto the house of the
23: 13 the princes and the t' by the king:
13 land rejoiced, and sounded with t',
29: 26 of David, and the priests with the t'.
27 the song...began also with the t',
Ezr 3: 10 the priests in their apparel with t',
Ne 12: 35 certain of the priests' sons with t';
41 Zechariah, and Hananiah, with t':
Job 39: 25 He saith among the t', Ha, ha; and
Ps 98: 6 With t' and sound of cornet make
Re 8: 2 and to them were given seven t'.
6 the seven t' prepared themselves to

trust See also TRUSTED; TRUSTEST; TRUSTETH; TRUSTING.
J'g 9: 15 and put your t' in my shadow:
Ru 2: 12 whose wings thou art come to t'.
2Sa 22: 3 God of my rock; in him will I t':
31 a buckler to all them that t' in him.
2Ki 18: 20 Now on whom dost thou t', that
21 of Egypt unto all that t' on him.
22 me, We t' in the Lord our God:
24 put thy t' on Egypt for chariots and
30 Hezekiah make you t' in the Lord,
1Ch 5: 20 because they put their t' in him.
Job 4: 18 he put no t' in his servants; and his
8: 14 whose t' shall be a spider's web.
13: 15 he slay me, yet will I t' in him:
15: 15 he putteth no t' in his saints; yea,
31 not him that is deceived t' in vanity:
35: 14 him; therefore t' thou in him.
39: 11 Wilt thou t' him, because his
Ps 2: 12 all they that put their t' in him.
4: 5 and put your t' in the Lord.
5: 11 that put their t' in thee rejoice:
7: 1 my God, in thee do I put my t':
9: 10 thy name will put their t' in thee:
11: 1 In the Lord put I my t': how say
16: 1 O God: for in thee do I put my t'.
17: 7 them which put their t' in thee
18: 2 God, my strength, in whom I will t';
30 buckler to all those that t' in him.
20: 7 Some t' in chariots, and some in
25: 2 O my God, I t' in thee: let me
20 ashamed; for I put my t' in thee.
31: 1 In thee, O Lord, do I put my t'; let
6 lying vanities: but I t' in the Lord.
19 wrought for them that t' in thee
34: 22 none of them that t' in him shall
36: 7 children of men put their t' under
37: 3 T' in the Lord, and do good; so
5 t' also in him; and he shall bring it
40 save them, because they t' in him.
40: 3 it, and fear, and shall t' in the Lord.
4 man that maketh the Lord his t',
44: 6 For I will not t' in my bow, neither
49: 6 They that t' in their wealth, and
52: 8 I t' in the mercy of God for ever and
55: 23 half their days; but I will t' in thee.
56: 3 time I am afraid, I will t' in thee.
4 his word, in God I have put my t';
11 In God have I put my t': I will not
61: 4 I will t' in the covert of thy wings.
62: 8 T' in him at all times; ye people,
10 T' not in oppression, and become
64: 10 in the Lord, and shall t' in him;
71: 1 In thee, O Lord, do I put my t': let
5 thou art my t' from my youth.
73: 28 I have put my t' in the Lord God,
91: 2 fortress: my God; in him will I t'.
4 and under his wings shalt thou t':
115: 9 O Israel, t' thou in the Lord: he is
10 O house of Aaron, t' in the Lord:
11 Ye that fear the Lord, t' in the Lord:
118: 8, 9 It is better to t' in the Lord than
119: 42 reproacheth me: for I t' in thy word.
125: 1 They that t' in the Lord shall be as
141: 8 in thee is my t'; leave not my soul
143: 8 in thee do I t': cause me to know
144: 2 my shield, and he in whom I t';
146: 3 Put not your t' in princes, nor in
Pr 3: 5 T' in the Lord with all thine heart;
22: 19 That thy t' may be in the Lord, I
28: 25 he that putteth his t' in the Lord
Pr 29: 25 whoso putteth his t' in the Lord shall
30: 5 unto them that put their t' in him.
31: 11 her husband doth safely t' in her,
Isa 12: 2 I will t', and not be afraid: for
14: 32 the poor of his people shall t' in it.
26: 4 T' ye in the Lord for ever: for in
30: 2 and to t' in the shadow of Egypt!
3 the t' in the shadow of Egypt your
12 t' in oppression and perverseness,
31: 1 and t' in chariots, because they are
36: 5 now on whom dost thou t', that thou
6 king of Egypt to all that t' in him.
7 to me, We t' in the Lord our God:
9 put thy t' on Egypt for chariots and
15 Hezekiah make you t' in the Lord,
42: 17 ashamed, that t' in graven images,
50: 10 let him t' in the name of the Lord,
51: 5 me, and on mine arm shall they t'.
57: 13 he that putteth his t' in me shall
59: 4 they t' in vanity, and speak lies;
Jer 7: 4 T' ye not in lying words,...The temple
8 ye t' in lying words, that cannot
14 wherein ye t', and unto the place
9: 4 and t' ye not in any brother:
28: 15 thou makest this people to t' in a lie.
29: 31 and he caused you to t' in a lie:
39: 18 thou hast put thy t' in me, saith the
46: 25 Pharaoh, and all them that t' in him:
49: 11 alive; and let thy widows t' in me.
Eze 16: 15 thou didst t' in thine own beauty,
33: 13 if he t' to his own righteousness,
Ho 10: 13 because thou didst t' in thy way,
Am 6: 1 and t' in the mountain of Samaria,
Mic 7: 5 T' ye not in a friend, put ye not
Na 1: 7 he knoweth them that t' in him.
Zep 3: 12 shall t' in the name of the Lord.
M't 12: 21 in his name shall the Gentiles t'.
M'r 10: 24 for them that t' in riches to enter
Lu 16: 11 commit to your t' the true riches?
Joh 5: 45 you, even Moses, in whom ye t'.
Ro 15: 12 in him shall the Gentiles t'.
24 for I t' to see you in my journey,
1Co 16: 7 but I t' to tarry a while with you,
2Co 1: 9 that we should not t' in ourselves,
10 in whom we t' that he will yet
13 I t' ye shall acknowledge even to
3: 4 such t' have we through Christ to
5: 11 I t' also are made manifest in
10: 7 If any man t' to himself that he
13: 6 I t' that ye shall know that we are
Ph'p 2: 19 But I t' in the Lord Jesus to send
24 I t' in the Lord that I also myself
3: 4 whereof he might t' in the flesh,
1Th 2: 4 to be put in t' with the gospel,
1Ti 1: 11 which was committed to my t'.
4: 10 because we t' in the living God,
6: 17 nor t' in uncertain riches, but in
20 that which is committed to thy t',
Ph'm 22 for I t' that through your prayers
Heb 2: 13 again, I will put my t' in him.
13: 18 we t' we have a good conscience,
2Jo 12 but I t' to come unto you, and
3Jo 14 But I t' I shall shortly see thee,

trusted See also TRUSTEDST.
De 32: 37 gods, their rock in whom they t',
J'g 11: 20 Sihon t' not Israel to pass through
20: 36 they t' unto the liers in wait which
2Ki 18: 5 He t' in the Lord God of Israel; so
Ps 13: 5 But I have t' in thy mercy; my
22: 4 Our fathers t' in thee: they t', and
5 they t' in thee, and were not
8 He t' on the Lord that he would
26: 1 I have t' also in the Lord; therefore
28: 7 my heart t' in him, and I am helped:
31: 14 But I t' in thee, O Lord: I said,
33: 21 because we have t' in his holy name.
41: 9 own familiar friend, in whom I t',
52: 7 but t' in the abundance of his riches,
78: 22 in God, and t' not in his salvation:
Isa 47: 10 For thou hast t' in thy wickedness:
Jer 13: 25 forgotten me, and t' in falsehood.
48: 7 because thou hast t' in thy works
49: 4 that t' in her treasures, saying,
Da 3: 28 his servants that t' in him, and
Zep 3: 2 she t' not in the Lord; she drew
M't 27: 43 He t' in God; let him deliver him
Lu 11: 22 him all his armour wherein he t',
18: 9 unto certain which t' in themselves
24: 21 we t' that it had been he which
Eph 1: 12 of his glory, who first t' in Christ.
13 In whom ye also t', after that ye
1Pe 3: 5 holy women also, who t' in God,

trustedst
De 28: 52 walls come down, wherein thou t',
Jer 5: 17 thy fenced cities, wherein thou t',
12: 5 the land of peace, wherein thou t',

trustest
2Ki 18: 19 confidence is this wherein thou t'?
21 thou t' upon the staff of this bruised
19: 10 God in whom thou t' deceive thee,
Isa 36: 4 confidence is this wherein thou t'?
6 thou t' in the staff of this broken
37: 10 Let not thy God, in whom thou t',

trusteth
Job 40: 23 he t' that he can draw up Jordan
Ps 21: 7 For the king t' in the Lord, and
32: 10 but he that t' in the Lord, mercy
34: 8 blessed is the man that t' in him.
57: 1 for my soul t' in thee: yea, in the
84: 12 blessed is the man that t' in thee.
86: 2 save thy servant that t' in thee.
115: 8 so is every one that t' in them.
135: 18 so is every one that t' in them.
Pr 11: 28 He that t' in his riches shall fall:
16: 20 whoso t' in the Lord, happy is he.
Pr 28: 26 He that t' in his own heart is a fool:
Isa 26: 3 on thee: because he t' in thee.
Jer 17: 5 Cursed be the man that t' in man,
7 Blessed is the man that t' in...Lord,
Hab 2: 18 the maker of his work t' therein,
1Ti 5: 5 indeed, and desolate, t' in God,

trusting
Ps 112: 7 his heart is fixed, t' in the Lord.

trusty
Job 12: 20 removeth away the speech of the t',

truth See also TRUTH'S.
Ge 24: 27 my master of his mercy and his t':
32: 10 of all the t', which thou hast shewed
42: 16 whether there be any t' in you:
Ex 18: 21 such as fear God, men of t', hating
34: 6 and abundant in goodness and t',
De 13: 14 and, behold, if it be t', and the thing
32: 4 a God of t' and without iniquity,
Jos 24: 14 serve him in sincerity and in t':
J'g 9: 15 If in t' ye anoint me king over you,
1Sa 12: 24 serve him in t' with all your heart:
21: 5 Of a t' women have been kept
2Sa 2: 6 shew kindness and t' unto you:
15: 20 mercy and t' be with thee.
1Ki 2: 4 walk before me in t' with all their
3: 6 as he walked before thee in t',
17: 24 word of the Lord in thy mouth is t'.
2Ki 19: 17 Of a t', Lord, the kings of Assyria
20: 3 how I have walked before thee in t'
19 good, if peace and t' be in my days?
2Ch 18: 15 that thou say nothing but the t'
31: 20 and right and t' before the Lord
Es 9: 30 with words of peace and t',
Job 9: 2 I know it is so of a t': but how
Ps 15: 2 and speaketh the t' in his heart.
25: 5 Lead me in thy t', and teach me:
10 paths of the Lord are mercy and t'
26: 3 eyes: and I have walked in thy t'.
30: 9 praise thee? shall it declare thy t'?
31: 5 hast redeemed me, O Lord God of t'.
33: 4 and all his works are done in t'.
40: 10 thy t' from the great congregation.
11 and thy t' continually preserve me.
43: 3 O send out thy light and thy t': let
45: 4 because of t' and meekness and
51: 6 thou desirest t' in the inward parts:
54: 5 mine enemies: cut them off in thy t'.
57: 3 send forth his mercy and his t'.
10 heavens, and thy t' unto the clouds.
60: 4 be displayed because of the t'.
61: 7 O prepare mercy and t', which may
69: 13 hear me, in the t' of thy salvation.
71: 22 thee with the psaltery, even thy t',
85: 10 Mercy and t' are met together:
11 T' shall spring out of the earth;
86: 11 way, O Lord; I will walk in thy t':
15 and plenteous in mercy and t'.
89: 14 mercy and t' shall go before thy face.
49 thou swarest unto David in thy t'?
91: 4 his t'...be thy shield and buckler.
96: 13 and the people with his t'.
98: 3 remembered his mercy and his t'
100: 5 his t' endureth to all generations.
108: 4 and thy t' reacheth unto the clouds.
111: 8 and are done in t' and uprightness.
117: 2 the t' of the Lord endureth for ever.
119: 30 I have chosen the way of t': thy
43 take not the word of t' utterly out
142 righteousness, and thy law is the t'.
151 and all thy commandments are t'.
132: 11 Lord hath sworn in t' unto David;
138: 2 thy lovingkindness and for thy t':
145: 18 him, to all that call upon him in t'.
146: 6 therein is: which keepeth t' for ever:
Pr 3: 3 Let not mercy and t' forsake thee:
8: 7 For my mouth shall speak t'; and
12: 17 He that speaketh t' sheweth forth
19 The lip of t' shall be established
14: 22 t' shall be to them that devise good.
16: 6 By mercy and t' iniquity is purged:
20: 28 Mercy and t' preserve the king: and
22: 21 the certainty of the words of t';
21 mightest answer the words of t'
23: 23 Buy the t', and sell it not; also
Ec 12: 10 was upright, even words of t'.
Isa 5: 9 Of a t' many houses shall be
10: 20 Lord, the Holy One of Israel, in t'.
16: 5 sit upon it in t' in the tabernacle
25: 1 of old are faithfulness and t'.
26: 2 which keepeth the t' may enter in.
37: 18 Of a t', Lord, the kings of Assyria
38: 3 walked before thee in t' and with a
18 into the pit cannot hope for thy t'.
19 children shall make known thy t'.
39: 8 shall be peace and t' in my days.
42: 3 shall bring forth judgment unto t'.
43: 9 or let them hear, and say, It is t'.
48: 1 but not in t', nor in righteousness.
59: 4 for justice, nor any pleadeth for t':
14 for t' is fallen in the street, and
15 t' faileth; and he that departeth
61: 8 I will direct their work in t', and I
65: 16 shall bless himself in the God of t';
16 earth shall swear by the God of t';
Jer 4: 2 The Lord liveth, in t', in judgment,
5: 1 judgment, that seeketh the t';
3 Lord, are not thine eyes upon the t'?
7: 28 t' is perished, and is cut off from
9: 3 not valiant for the t' upon the earth;
5 and will not speak the t':
26: 15 for of a t' the Lord hath sent me
33: 6 them the abundance of peace and t'.
Da 2: 47 Of a t' it is, that your God is a God
4: 37 whose works are t', and his ways
7: 16 and asked him the t' of all this.

Da 7:19 know the t' of the fourth beast,
8:12 it cast down the t' to the ground;
9:13 iniquities, and understand thy t'.
10:21 which is noted in the scripture of t':
11: 2 And now will I shew thee the t'.
Ho 4: 1 because there is no t', nor mercy,
Mic 7:20 Thou wilt perform the t' to Jacob,
Zec 8: 3 Jerusalem shall be called a city of t';
8 God, in t' and in righteousness.
16 Speak ye every man the t' to his
16 execute the judgment of t' and
19 therefore love the t' and peace.
Mal 2: 6 The law of t' was in his mouth, and
M't 14:33 Of a t' thou art the Son of God.
15:27 she said, T', Lord: yet the dogs
22:16 and teachest the way of God in t',
M'r 5:33 before him, and told him all the t'.
12:14 but teachest the way of God in t':
32 Well, Master, thou hast said the t':
Lu 4:25 I tell you of a t', many widows were
9:27 But I tell you of a t', there be some
12:44 Of a t' I say unto you, that he will
21: 3 Of a t' I say unto you, that this poor
22:59 Of a t' this fellow also was with
Joh 1:14 of the Father,) full of grace and t'.
17 grace and t' came by Jesus Christ.
3:21 he that doeth t' cometh to the light,
4:23 the Father in spirit and in t':
24 must worship him in spirit and in t'.
5:33 and he bare witness unto the t'.
6:14 This is of a t' that prophet that
7:40 said, Of a t' this is the Prophet.
8:32 And ye shall know the t', and the
32 and the t' shall make you free.
40 a man that hath told you the t',
44 beginning, and abode not in the t',
44 because there is no t' in him.
45 because I tell you the t', ye believe
46 And if I say the t', why do ye not
14: 6 I am the way, the t', and the life:
17 Even the Spirit of t'; whom the
15:26 the Father, even the Spirit of t',
16: 7 Nevertheless I tell you the t'; It is
13 when he, the Spirit of t', is come, he
13 he will guide you into all t': for he
17:17 Sanctify them through thy t':
17 thy word is t'.
19 might be sanctified through the t'.
18:37 I should bear witness unto the t'.
37 Every one that is of the t' heareth
38 Pilate saith unto him, What is t'?
Ac 4:27 of a t' against thy holy child Jesus,
10:34 Of a t' I perceive that God is no
26:25 forth the words of t' and soberness.
Ro 1:18 who hold the t' in unrighteousness;
25 Who changed the t' of God into a lie,
2: 2 judgment of God is according to t'
8 contentious, and do not obey the t',
20 knowledge and of the t' in the law.
3: 7 if the t' of God hath more abounded
9: 1 I say the t' in Christ, I lie not, my
15: 8 the circumcision for the t' of God,
1Co 5: 8 unleavened bread of sincerity and t'.
13: 6 in iniquity, but rejoiceth in the t';
14:25 report that God is in you of a t'.
2Co 4: 2 but by manifestation of the t'
6: 7 By the word of t', by the power of
7:14 as we spake all things to you in t',
14 I made before Titus, is found a t'.
11:10 As the t' of Christ is in me, no man
12: 6 not be a fool; for I will say the t':
13: 8 nothing against the t', but for the t'.
Ga 2: 5 the t' of the gospel might continue
14 according to the t' of the gospel,
3: 1 you, that ye should not obey the t',
4:16 enemy, because I tell you the t'?
5: 7 you that ye should not obey the t'?
Eph 1:13 after that ye heard the word of t',
4:15 speaking the t' in love, may grow
21 taught by him, as the t' is in Jesus:
25 speak every man t' with his
5: 9 goodness and righteousness and t';)
6:14 having your loins girt about with t',
Ph'p 1:18 whether in pretence, or in t', Christ
Col 1: 5 in the word of the t' of the gospel;
6 and knew the grace of God in t':
1Th 2:13 but as it is in t', the word of God,
2Th 2:10 they received not the love of the t',
12 be damned who believed not the t',
13 of the Spirit and belief of the t':
1Ti 2: 4 come unto the knowledge of the t'.
7 (I speak the t' in Christ, and lie not;)
3:15 God, the pillar and ground of the t'.
4: 3 them which believe and know the t'.
6: 5 corrupt minds,...destitute of the t'.
2Ti 2:15 rightly dividing the word of t'.
18 Who concerning the t' have erred,
25 to the acknowledging of the t';
3: 7 to come to the knowledge of the t'.
8 Moses, so do these also resist the t':
4: 4 turn away their ears from the t',
Tit 1: 1 of the t' which is after godliness;
14 of men, that turn from the t'.
Heb10:26 received the knowledge of the t',
Jas 1:18 will begat he us with the word of t',
3:14 glory not, and lie not against the t'.
5:19 if any of you do err from the t', and
1Pe 1:22 purified your souls in obeying the t'
2Pe 1:12 and be established in the present t'.
2: 2 the way of t' shall be evil spoken of.
1Jo 1: 6 darkness, we lie, and do not the t':
8 ourselves, and the t' is not in us.
2: 4 is a liar, and the t' is not in him.
21 unto you because ye know not the t',
21 know it, and that no lie is of the t'.
27 of all things, and is t', and is no lie,
1Jo 3:18 in tongue; but in deed and in t'.
19 we know that we are of the t', and
4: 6 Hereby know we the spirit of t', and
5: 6 witness, because the Spirit is t'.
2Jo 1 her children, whom I love in the t';
1 also all they that have known the t';
3 Son of the Father, in t' and love.
4 I found of thy children walking in t',
3Jo 1 Gaius, whom I love in the t'.
3 and testified of the t' that is in thee,
3 even as thou walkest in the t'.
4 to hear that my children walk in t'.
8 we might be fellowhelpers to the t'.
12 report of all men, and of the t' itself:

truth's
Ps 115: 1 for thy mercy, and for thy t' sake.
2Jo 2 For the t' sake, that dwelleth in us,

try See also TRIED; TRIEST; TRIETH; TRYING.
J'g 7: 4 and I will t' them for thee there:
2Ch 32:31 God left him, to t' him, that he
Job 7:18 morning, and t' him every moment?
12:11 Doth not the ear t' words? and the
Ps 11: 4 his eyelids t' the children of men.
26: 2 me; t' my reins and my heart.
139:23 t' me, and know my thoughts:
Jer 6:27 thou mayest know and t' their way.
9: 7 I will melt them, and t' them;
17:10 Lord search the heart, I t' the reins.
La 3:40 Let us search and t' our ways,
Da 11:35 fall, to t' them, and to purge, and
Zec 13: 9 and will t' them as gold is tried:
1Co 3:13 the fire shall t' every man's work
1Pe 4:12 fiery trial which is to t' you,
1Jo 4: 1 t' the spirits whether they are of
Re 3:10 t' them that dwell upon the earth.

trying
Jas 1: 3 t' of your faith worketh patience.

Tryphena (*tri-fe'-nah*)
Ro 16:12 Salute T' and Tryphosa, who

Tryphosa (*tri-fo'-sah*)
Ro 16:12 Salute Tryphena and T', who

Tubal (*tu'-bal*) See also TUBAL-CAIN.
Ge 10: 2 and T', and Meshech, and Tiras.
1Ch 1: 5 and T', and Meshech, and Tiras.
Isa 66:19 to T', and Javan, to isles afar off,
Eze 27:13 T', and Meshech, they were thy
32:26 There is Meshech, T', and all her
38: 2 chief prince of Meshech and T',
3 chief prince of Meshech and T':
39: 1 chief prince of Meshech and T':

Tubal-cain (*tu'-bal-cain*)
Ge 4:22 And Zillah, she also bare T', an
22 and the sister of T' was Naamah.

tumbled
J'g 7:13 bread t' into the host of Midian,

tumult See also TUMULTS.
1Sa 4:14 What meaneth the noise of this t'?
2Sa 18:29 I saw a great t', but I knew not
2Ki 19:28 against me and thy t' is come up
Ps 65: 7 waves, and the t' of the people.
74:23 the t' of those that rise up against
83: 2 For, lo, thine enemies make a t':
Isa 33: 3 the noise of the t' the people fled;
37:29 thy t', is come up into mine ears,
Jer 11:16 with the noise of a great t' he hath
Ho 10:14 shall a t' arise among thy people,
Am 2: 2 and Moab shall die with t', with
Zec 14:13 a great t' from the Lord shall be
M't 27:24 but that rather a t' was made, he
M'r 5:38 and seeth the t', and them that
Ac 21:34 not know the certainty for the t',
24:18 neither with multitude, nor with t'.

tumults
Am 3: 9 the great t' in the midst thereof,
2Co 6: 5 in imprisonments, in t', in labours,
12:20 strifes,...whisperings, swellings, t':

tumultuous
Isa 13: 4 a t' noise of the kingdoms of
22: 2 that art full of stirs, a t' city, a
Jer 48:45 of the head of the t' ones.

turn See also OVERTURN; RETURN; TURNED; TURNEST; TURNETH; TURNING.
Ge 19: 2 my lords, t' in, I pray you, into
24:49 that I may t' to the right hand, or
27:44 until thy brother's fury t' away:
45 Until thy brother's anger t' away
Ex 3: 3 I will now t' aside, and see this
14: 2 that they t' and encamp before
23:27 thine enemies t' their backs unto thee.
32:12 T' from thy fierce wrath, and
Le 13:16 Or if the raw flesh t' again, and be
19: 4 T' ye not unto idols, nor make to
Nu 14:25 To morrow t' you, and get you
20:17 will not t' to the right hand nor
21:22 we will not t' into the fields, or into
22:23 Balaam smote the ass, to t' her
26 was no way to t' either to the right
32:15 if ye t' away from after him, he
34: 4 your border shall t' from the south
De 1: 7 T' you, and take your journey,
40 t' you, and take your journey into
2: 3 long enough: t' you northward.
27 I will neither t' unto the right nor
4:30 if thou t' to the Lord thy God,
5:32 ye shall not t' aside to the right
7: 4 will t' away thy son from following
11:16 ye t' aside, and serve other gods,
28 t' aside out of the way which I
13: 5 spoken to t' you away from the
17 Lord may t' from the fierceness of
14:25 Then shalt thou t' it into money,
16: 7 and thou shalt t' in the morning,
De 17:17 himself, that his heart t' not away:
20 and that he t' not aside from the
23:13 shalt t' back and cover that which
14 in thee, and t' away from thee.
30: 3 Lord thy God will t' thy captivity,
10 t' unto the Lord thy God with all
17 But if thine heart t' away, as that
31:20 then will they t' unto other gods,
29 t' aside from the way I have
Jos 1: 7 t' not from it to the right hand or to
22:16, 18 t' away this day from following
23 altar to t' from following the Lord,
29 t' this day from following the Lord,
23: 6 that ye t' not aside therefrom to
24:20 then he will t' and do you hurt,
J'g 4:18 T' in, my lord, t' in to me; fear
11: 8 Therefore we t' again to thee now,
19:11 t' into this city of the Jebusites,
12 will not t' aside hither into the city
20: 8 will we any of us t' into his house.
Ru 1:11 And Naomi said, T' again, my
12 T' again, my daughter, go your
4: 1 such a one! t' aside, sit down here.
1Sa 12:20 t' not aside from following the Lord,
21 t' ye not aside: for then should ye
14: 7 t' thee; behold, I am with thee
15:25 pardon my sin,...t' again with me,
30 and t' again with me, that I may
22:17 T', and slay the priests of the
18 T' thou, and fall upon the priests.
2Sa 2:21 T' thee aside to thy right hand or
21 not t' aside from following of him.
22 T' thee aside from following me:
23 Howbeit he refused to t' aside:
14:19 none can t' to the right hand or to the
24 Let him t' to his own house, and
15:31 t' the...of Ahithophel into foolishness.
18:30 unto him, T' aside, and stand
19:37 servant, I pray thee, t' back again,
1Ki 8:33 shall t' again to thee, and confess
35 thy name, and t' from their sin,
9: 6 shall at all t' from following me,
11: 2 they will t' away your heart after
12:27 heart of this people t' again unto
13: 9 nor t' again by the same way that
17 nor t' again to go by the way that
17: 3 thee hence, and t' thee eastward,
22:34 T' thine hand, and carry me out
2Ki 1: 6 Go, t' again unto the king that
4:10 to us, that he shall t' in thither.
9:18, 19 with peace? t' thee behind me.
17:13 T' ye from your evil ways, and
18:24 then wilt thou t' away the face of
19:28 I will t' thee back by the way by
20: 5 T' again, and tell Hezekiah the
1Ch 12:23 t' the kingdom of Saul to him,
14:10 up after them; t' away from them,
2Ch 6:26 thy name, and t' from their sin,
37 t' and pray unto thee in the land of
42 t' not away...face of thine anointed:
7:14 face, and t' from thy wicked ways;
19 But if ye t' away, and forsake my
15: 4 they in their trouble did t' unto the
18:33 T' thine hand, that thou mayest
25:27 that Amaziah did t' away from
29:10 that his fierce wrath may t' away
30: 6 t' again unto the Lord God of
8 fierceness of his wrath may t' away
9 if ye t' again unto the Lord, your
9 not t' away his face from you,
35:22 Josiah would not t' his face from
Ne 1: 9 But if ye t' unto me, and keep my
4: 4 t' their reproach upon their own
9:26 against them to t' them to thee,
Es 2:12 when every maid's t' was come to
15 Now when the t' of Esther, the
Job 5: 1 to which of the saints wilt thou t'?
14: 6 T' from him, that he may rest, till
23:13 in one mind, and who can t' him?
24: 4 They t' the needy out of the way:
34:15 and man shall t' again unto dust.
Ps 4: 2 long will ye t' my glory into shame?
7:12 If he t' not, he will whet his
18:37 I t' again till they were consumed.
21:12 shalt thou make them t' their back.
22:27 remember and t' unto the Lord:
25:16 T' thee unto me, and have mercy
40: 4 proud, nor such as t' aside to lies.
44:10 us to t' back from the enemy:
56: 9 thee, then shall mine eyes t' back:
60: 1 displeased; O t' thyself to us again.
69:16 t' unto me according to the
80: 3 T' us again, O God, and cause thy
7 T' us again, O God of hosts, and
19 T' us again, O Lord God of hosts,
85: 4 T' us, O God of our salvation, and
8 but let them not t' again to folly.
86:16 O t' unto me, and have mercy
101: 3 hate...work of them that t' aside;
104: 9 that they t' not again to cover the
106:23 to t' away his wrath, lest he should
119:37 T' away mine eyes from
39 T' away my reproach which I fear:
79 those that fear thee t' unto me,
125: 5 As for such as t' aside unto their
126: 4 T' again our captivity, O Lord, as
132:10 t' not away the face of thine
11 he will not t' from it; Of the fruit
Pr 1:23 T' you at my reproof: behold, I
4:15 by it, t' from it, and pass away.
27 T' not to the right hand nor to
9: 4, 16 is simple, let him t' in hither:
24:18 he t' away his wrath from him.
25:10 and thine infamy t' not away.
29: 8 but wise men t' away wrath.
Ec 3:20 the dust, and all t' to dust again.

Ca 2:17 t', my beloved, and be thou like a
6: 5 T' away thine eyes from me, for
Isa 1:25 And I will t' my hand upon thee,
10: 2 t' aside the needy from judgment,
13:14 every man t' to his own people,
14:27 out, and who shall t' it back?
19: 6 they shall t' the rivers far away;
22:18 surely violently t' and toss thee
23:17 Tyre, and she shall t' to her hire,
28: 6 them that t' the battle to the gate.
29:21 and t' aside the just for a thing of
30:11 of the way, t' aside out of the path,
21 ye in it, when ye t' to the right hand,
21 and when ye t' to the left.
31: 6 T' ye unto him from whom the
36: 9 wilt thou t' away the face of one
37:29 t' thee back by the way by which
58:13 t' away thy foot from the sabbath,
59:20 t' from transgression in Jacob,
Jer 2:24 in her occasion who can t' her way?
35 surely his anger shall t' from me.
3: 7 these things, T' thou unto me.
14 T', O backsliding children, saith
19 and shalt not t' away from me.
4:28 repent, neither will I t' back from it.
6: 9 t' back thine hand as a
8: 4 shall he t' away, and not return?
13:16 he t' it into the shadow of death,
18: 8 t' from their evil, I will repent of
20 to t' away thy wrath from them.
21: 4 I will t' back the weapons of war
25: 5 T' ye again now every one from
26: 3 and t' every man from his evil way,
29:14 and I will t' away your captivity,
31:13 I will t' their mourning into joy,
18 t' thou me, and I shall be turned;
21 t' again, O virgin of Israel, t'
32:40 that I will not t' away from them,
44: 5 ear to t' from their wickedness,
49: 8 Flee ye, t' back, dwell deep, O
50:16 shall t' every one to his people,
La 2:14 iniquity, to t' away thy captivity;
3:35 To t' aside the right of a man
40 ways, and t' again to the Lord.
5:21 T' thou us unto thee, O Lord, and
Eze 3:19 he t' not from his wickedness, nor
20 righteous man doth t' from his
4: 8 shalt not t' thee from one side to
7:22 My face will I t' also from them,
8: 6 t' thee yet again, and thou shalt
13 T' thee yet again, and thou shalt
15 t' thee yet again, and thou shalt
14: 6 and t' yourselves from your idols;
6 and t' away your face from all your
18:21 the wicked will t' from all his sins
30 and t' yourselves from all your
32 wherefore t' yourselves, and live
33: 9 the wicked of his way to t' from it;
9 if he do not t' from his way, he
11 but that the wicked t' from his way
11 t' ye, t' ye from your evil ways; for
14 if he t' from his sin, and do that
19 the wicked t' from his wickedness,
36: 9 am for you, and I will t' unto you,
38: 4 I will t' thee back, and put hooks
12 to t' thine hand upon the desolate
39: 2 I will t' thee back, and leave but
Da 9:13 we might t' from our iniquities,
11:18 shall he t' his face unto the isles,
18 he shall cause it to t' upon him.
19 shall t' his face toward the fort of
12: 3 they that t' many to righteousness, as
Ho 5: 4 their doings to t' unto their God:
12: 6 Therefore t' thou to thy God: keep
14: 2 you words, and t' to the Lord:
Joe 2:12 t' ye even to me with all your heart,
13 and t' unto the Lord your God:
Am 1: 3, 6 will not t' away the punishment
8 I will t' mine hand against Ekron:
9, 11, 13 not t' away the punishment
2: 1, 4, 6 not t' away the punishment
7 and t' aside the way of the meek:
5: 7 Ye who t' judgment to wormwood,
12 they t' aside the poor in the gate
8:10 will t' your feasts into mourning,
Jon 3: 8 let them t' every one from his evil
9 can tell if God will t' and repent,
9 and t' away from his fierce anger,
Mic 7:19 He will t' again, he will have
Zep 2: 7 them, and t' away their captivity.
3: 9 t' to the people a pure language,
20 when I t' back your captivity
Zec 1: 3 T' ye unto me, saith the Lord of
3 I will t' unto you, saith the Lord of
4 T' ye now from your evil ways,
9:12 T' you to the strong hold, ye
10: 9 with their children, and t' again.
13: 7 t' mine hand upon the little ones.
Mal 2: 6 did t' many away from iniquity.
3: 5 that t' aside the stranger from his
4: 6 t' the heart of the fathers to the
M't 5:39 cheek, t' to him the other also.
42 borrow of thee t' not thou away.
7: 6 feet, and t' again and rend you.
M'r 13:16 is in the field not t' back again
Lu 1:16 Israel shall he t' to the Lord their
17 to t' the hearts of the fathers to the
10: 6 it: if not, it shall t' to you again.
17: 4 and seven times in a day t' again
21:13 it shall t' to you for a testimony.
Ac 13: 8 t' away the deputy from the faith.
46 life, lo, we t' to the Gentiles.
14:15 ye should t' from these vanities
26:18 to t' them from darkness to light,
20 they should repent and t' to God,
Ro 11:26 t' away ungodliness from Jacob:
2Co 3:16 when it shall t' to the Lord,
Ga 4: 9 how t' ye again to the weak and
Ph'p 1:19 that this shall t' to my salvation
2Ti 3: 5 power thereof: from such t' away.
4: 4 they shall t' away their ears from
Tit 1:14 of men, that t' from the truth.
Heb 12:25 we t' away from him that speaketh
Jas 3: 3 and we t' about their whole body.
2Pe 2:21 to t' from the holy commandment
Re 11: 6 over waters to t' them to blood,

turned See also OVERTURNED; RETURNED.
Ge 3:24 flaming sword which t' every way,
18:22 men t' their faces from thence,
19: 3 they t' in unto him, and entered
38: 1 and t' in to a certain Adullamite,
16 And he t' unto her by the way,
42:24 he t' himself about from them,
Ex 3: 4 Lord saw that he t' aside to see,
4: 7 it was t' again as his other flesh.
7:15 the rod which was t' to a serpent
17 river, and they shall be t' to blood.
20 were in the river were t' to blood.
23 And Pharaoh t' and went into his
10: 6 he t' himself, and went out from
19 Lord t' a mighty strong west wind,
14: 5 servants was t' against the people,
32: 8 They have t' aside quickly out of
15 Moses t', and went down from the
33:11 And he t' again into the camp:
Le 13: 3 the hair in the plague is t' white,
4 the hair thereof be not t' white;
10 skin, and it have t' the hair white,
13 hath the plague: it is all t' white:
17 if the plague be t' into white;
20 and the hair thereof be t' white;
25 hair in the bright spot be t' white,
Nu 14:43 ye are t' away from the Lord,
20:21 wherefore Israel t' away from him.
21:33 they t' and went up by the way of
22:23 the ass t' aside out of the way,
33 and the ass saw me, and t' from me
33 unless she had t' from me, surely
25: 4 anger of the Lord may be t' away
11 hath t' my wrath away from the
33: 7 and t' again unto Pi-hahiroth,
De 1:24 t' and went up into the mountain,
2: 1 Then we t', and took our journey
8 we t' and passed by the way of the
3: 1 Then we t', and went up the way
9:12 are quickly t' aside out of the way
15 t' and came down from the mount,
16 t' aside quickly out of the way
10: 5 t' myself and came down from the
23: 5 the Lord thy God t' the curse into
31:18 that they are t' unto other gods.
Jos 7:12 t' their backs before their enemies,
26 the Lord t' from the fierceness of
8:20 fled to the wilderness t' back
21 they t' again, and slew the men of
11:10 And Joshua at that time t' back,
19:12 And t' from Sarid eastward toward
J'g 2:17 they t' quickly out of the way
3:19 himself t' again from the quarries
4:18 And when he had t' in unto her
8:33 that the children of Israel t' again,
14: 8 he t' aside to see the carcase of
15: 4 t' tail to tail, and put a firebrand
18: 3 they t' in thither, and said unto
15 they t' thitherward, and came to
21 So they t' and departed, and put
23 they t' their faces, and said unto
26 t' and went back unto his house.
19:15 they t' aside thither, to go in and
20:41 when the men of Israel t' again,
42 they t' their backs before the men
45 t' and fled toward the wilderness
47 six hundred men t' and fled to the
48 the men of Israel t' again upon
Ru 3: 8 man was afraid, and t' himself:
4: 1 And he t' aside, and sat down.
1Sa 6:12 t' not aside to the right hand or to
8: 3 but t' aside after lucre, and took
10: 6 and shalt be t' into another man.
9 that when he had t' his back to go
13:17 one company t' unto the way that
18 And another company t' the way to
18 another company t' to the way of
14:21 they also t' to be with the Israelites
47 whithersoever he t' himself, he
15:11 he is t' back from following me,
27 as Samuel t' about to go away, he
31 So Samuel t' again after Saul; and
17:30 he t' from him toward another,
22:18 Doeg the Edomite t', and he fell
25:12 David's young men t' their way,
2Sa 1:22 the bow of Jonathan t' not back,
2:19 going he t' not to the right hand
18:30 And he t' aside, and stood still.
19: 2 victory that day was t' into mourning
22:38 and t' not again until I had
1Ki 2:15 howbeit the kingdom is t' about,
28 for Joab had t' after Adonijah,
28 though he t' not after Absalom.
8:14 And the king t' his face about, and
10:13 t' and went to her own country,
11: 3 and his wives t' away his heart.
4 wives t' away his heart after other
9 heart was t' from the Lord God of
15: 5 t' not aside from any thing that he
18:37 thou hast t' their heart back again.
20:39 a man t' aside, and brought a man
21: 4 upon his bed, and t' away his face,
22:32 they t' aside to fight against him:
33 they t' back from pursuing him.
43 he t' not aside from it, doing that
2Ki 1: 5 the messengers t' back unto him,
2Ki 1: 5 them, Why are ye now t' back?
2:24 he t' back, and looked on them,
4: 8 by, he t' in thither to eat bread.
11 he t' into the chamber, and lay
5:12 So he t' and went away in a rage.
26 man t' again from his chariot
9:23 And Joram t' his hands, and fled,
15:20 So the king of Assyria t' back, and
16:18 t' he from the house of the Lord
20: 2 Then he t' his face to the wall, and
22: 2 t' not aside to the right hand or to
23:16 as Josiah t' himself, he spied the
25 that t' to the Lord with all his
26 Lord t' not from the fierceness of
34 t' his name to Jehoiakim, and took
24: 1 he t' and rebelled against him.
1Ch 10:14 t' the kingdom unto David the son
21:20 Ornan t' back, and saw the angel;
2Ch 6: 3 the king t' his face, and blessed
9:12 she t', and went away to her own
12:12 the wrath of the Lord t' from him,
18:32 they t' back...from pursuing him.
20:10 they t' from them, and destroyed
29: 6 have t' away their faces from the
6 of the Lord, and t' their backs.
36: 4 and t' his name to Jehoiakim.
Ezr 6:22 t' the heart of the king of Assyria
10:14 God for this matter be t' from us.
Ne 2:15 and viewed the wall, and t' back,
9:35 t' they from their wicked works.
13: 2 God t' the curse into a blessing.
Es 9: 1 (though it was t' to the contrary,
22 month which was t' unto them from
Job 6:18 paths of their way are t' aside;
16:11 t' me over into the hands of the
19:19 whom I loved are t' against me.
20:14 Yet his meat in his bowels is t', it is
28: 5 and under it is t' up as it were fire.
30:15 Terrors are t' upon me: they pursue
31 My harp also is t' to mourning, and
31: 7 If my step hath t' out of the way,
34:27 Because they t' back from him,
37:12 is t' round about by his counsels:
38:14 It is t' as clay to the seal; and they
41:22 sorrow is t' into joy before him.
28 are t' with him into stubble.
42:10 the Lord t' the captivity of Job,
Ps 9: 3 When mine enemies are t' back,
17 The wicked shall be t' into hell,
30:11 hast t' for me my mourning into
32: 4 my moisture is t' into the drought
35: 4 let them be t' back and brought
44:18 Our heart is not t' back, neither
66: 6 He t' the sea into dry land: they
20 which hath not t' away my prayer,
70: 2 let them be t' backward, and put
3 Let them be t' back for a reward
78: 9 bows, t' back in the day of battle.
38 many a time t' he his anger away,
41 Yea, they t' back and tempted God,
44 And had t' their rivers into blood:
57 But t' back, and dealt unfaithfully
57 were t' aside like a deceitful bow.
81:14 and t' my hand against their
85: 3 hast t' thyself from the fierceness
89:43 hast also t' the edge of his sword,
105:25 He t' their heart to hate his people,
29 He t' their waters into blood, and
114: 8 t' the rock into a standing water,
119:59 t' my feet unto thy testimonies.
126: 1 the Lord t' again the captivity of
129: 5 and t' back that hate Zion.
Ec 2:12 t' myself to behold wisdom, and
Ca 6: 1 whither is thy beloved t' aside?
Isa 5:25 all this his anger is not t' away,
9:12, 17, 21 his anger is not t' away, but
10: 4 For all this his anger is not t' away.
12: 1 with me, thine anger is t' away,
21: 4 my pleasure hath he t' into fear
28:27 neither is a cart wheel t' about
29:17 Lebanon...t' into a fruitful field,
34: 9 streams...shall be t' into pitch,
38: 2 Hezekiah t' his face toward the
42:17 They shall be t' back, they shall
44:20 a deceived heart hath t' him aside,
50: 5 rebellious, neither t' away back.
53: 6 have t' every one to his own way;
59:14 judgment is t' away backward,
63:10 he was t' to be their enemy,
Jer 2:21 art thou t' into the degenerate plant
27 they have t' their back unto me,
3:10 sister Judah hath not t' unto me
4: 8 anger of the Lord is not t' back
5:25 Your iniquities have t' away these
6:12 houses shall be t' unto others,
8: 6 every one t' to his course, as the
11:10 They are t' back to the iniquities of
23:22 have t' them from their evil way,
30: 6 and all faces are t' into paleness?
31:18 turn thou me, and I shall be t';
19 after that I was t', I repented;
32:33 they have t' unto me the back, and
34:11 But afterward they t', and caused
15 ye were now t', and had done right
16 But ye t' and polluted my name,
38:22 mire, and they are t' away back.
46: 5 them dismayed and t' away back?
21 they also are t' back, and are fled
48:39 hath Moab t' the back with shame!
50: 6 t' them away on the mountains:
La 1:13 net for my feet, he hath t' me back:
20 mine heart is t' within me; for I
3: 3 Surely against me is he t';
11 He hath t' aside my ways, and
5: 2 Our inheritance is t' to strangers,
15 our dance is t' into mourning.

La 5:21 thee, O Lord, and we shall be *t*;
Eze 1: 9 they *t* not when they went;
12, 17 and they *t* not when they went.
10:11 they *t* not as they went, but to the
11 followed it; they *t* not as they went.
16 same wheels also *t* not from beside
17: 6 whose branches *t* toward him,
26: 2 she is *t* unto me: I shall be
42:19 He *t* about to the west side, and
Da 9:16 anger and thy fury be *t* away
10: 8 my comeliness was *t* in me into
16 vision my sorrows are *t* upon me,
Ho 7: 8 people; Ephraim is a cake not *t*.
11: 8 mine heart is *t* within me, my
14: 4 mine anger is *t* away from him.
Joe 2:31 The sun shall be *t* into darkness,
Am 6:12 for ye have *t* judgment into gall,
Jon 3:10 that they *t* from their evil way;
Na 2: 2 *t* away the excellency of Jacob,
Hab 2:16 Lord's right hand shall be *t* unto
Zep 1: 6 that are *t* back from the Lord;
Hag 2:17 yet ye *t* not to me, saith the Lord.
Zec 5: 1 Then I *t*, and lifted up mine eyes,
6: 1 And I *t*, and lifted up mine eyes,
14:10 All the land shall be *t* as a plain
M't 2:22 *t* aside into the parts of Galilee:
9:22 But Jesus *t* him about, and when
16:23 But he *t*, and said unto Peter, Get
M'r 5:30 *t* him about in the press, and said,
8:33 when he had *t* about and looked on
Lu 2:45 they *t* back again to Jerusalem,
7: 9 *t* him about, and said unto the
44 he *t* to the woman, and said unto
9:55 But he *t*, and rebuked them, and
10:23 And he *t* him unto his disciples,
14:25 him: and he *t*, and said unto them,
17:15 *t* back, and with a loud voice
22:61 Lord *t*, and looked upon Peter.
Joh 1:38 Then Jesus *t*, and saw them
16:20 your sorrow shall be *t* into joy.
20:14 she *t* herself back, and saw Jesus
16 She *t* herself, and saith unto him,
Ac 2:20 The sun shall be *t* into darkness,
7:39 hearts *t* back again into Egypt,
42 Then God *t*, and gave them up to
9:35 Saron saw him, and *t* to the Lord.
11:21 believed, and *t* unto the Lord.
15:19 among the Gentiles are *t* to God:
16:18 grieved, *t* and said to the spirit,
17: 6 that have *t* the word upside down
19:26 and *t* away much people,
1Th 1: 9 and how ye *t* to God from idols to
1Ti 1: 6 have *t* aside unto vain jangling;
5:15 are already *t* aside after Satan.
2Ti 1:15 are in Asia be *t* away from me;
4: 4 truth, and shall be *t* unto fables.
Heb11:34 *t* to flight the armies of the aliens.
12:13 which is lame be *t* out of the way;
Jas 3: 4 *t* about with a very small helm,
4: 9 let...laughter be *t* to mourning,
2Pe 2:22 dog is *t* to his own vomit again;
Re 1:12 I *t* to see the voice that spake with
12 And being *t*, I saw seven golden

turnest
1Ki 2: 3 and whithersoever thou *t* thyself:
Job 15:13 thou *t* thy spirit against God,
Ps 90: 3 Thou *t* man to destruction; and

turneth See also OVERTURNETH; RETURNETH.
Le 20: 6 the soul that *t* after such as have
De 29:18 whose heart *t* away this day from
Jos 7: 8 Israel *t* their backs before their
19:27 And *t* toward the sunrising to
29 And then the coast *t* to Ramah,
29 Tyre; and the coast *t* to Hosah;
34 And then the coast *t* westward to
Job 39:22 neither *t* he back from the sword.
Ps 107:33 He *t* rivers into a wilderness, and
35 He *t* the wilderness into a standing
146: 9 the way of the wicked he *t* upside
Pr 15: 1 A soft answer *t* away wrath: but
17: 8 whithersoever it *t*, it prospereth.
21: 1 he *t* it whithersoever he will.
26:14 As the door *t* upon his hinges, so
28: 9 that *t* away his ear from hearing
30:30 beasts, and *t* not away for any;
Ec 1: 6 south, and *t* about unto the north;
Ca 1: 7 should I be as one that *t* aside
Isa 9:13 the people *t* not unto him that
24: 1 it waste, and *t* it upside down,
44:25 that *t* wise men backward, and
Jer 14: 8 as a wayfaring man that *t* aside
49:24 feeble, and *t* herself to flee, and
La 1: 8 yea, she sigheth, and *t* backward.
3: 3 *t* his hand against me all the day.
Eze 18:24, 26 *t* away from his righteousness,
27 man *t* away from his wickedness
28 *t* away from all his transgressions
33:12 day that he *t* from his wickedness;
18 righteous *t* from his righteousness,
Am 5: 8 and *t* the shadow of death into

turning See also RETURNING.
2Ki 21:13 wiping it, and *t* it upside down.
2Ch 26: 9 gate, and at the *t* of the wall,
36:13 heart from *t* unto the Lord God
Ne 3:19 the armoury at the *t* of the wall.
20 from the *t* of the wall unto the door
24 of Azariah unto the *t* of the wall,
25 over against the *t* of the wall,
Pr 1:32 the *t* away of the simple shall slay
Isa 29:16 your *t* of things upside down
Eze 41:24 two leaves apiece, two *t* leaves;
Mic 2: 4 *t* away he hath divided our fields
Lu 23:28 But Jesus *t* unto them said,
Joh 21:20 Peter, *t* about, seeth the disciple
Ac 3:26 in *t* away every one of you from
Ac 9:40 *t* him to the body said, Tabitha,
Jas 1:17 variableness, neither shadow of *t*.
2Pe 2: 6 *t* the cities of Sodom...into ashes
Jude 4 *t* the grace of our God into

turtle See also TURTLEDOVE; TURTLES.
Ca 2:12 the voice of the *t* is heard in our
Jer 8: 7 and the *t* and the crane and the

turtledove See also TURTLEDOVES.
Ge 15: 9 old, and a *t*, and a young pigeon.
Le 12: 6 pigeon, or a *t*, for a sin offering,
Ps 74:19 O deliver not the soul of thy *t* unto

turtledoves
Le 1:14 he shall bring his offering of *t*,
5: 7 two *t*, or two young pigeons, unto
11 But if he be not able to bring two *t*,
14:22 And two *t*, or two young pigeons,
30 And he shall offer the one of the *t*,
15:14 day he shall take to him two *t*,
Lu 2:24 A pair of *t*, or two young pigeons.

turtles
Le 12: 8 lamb, then she shall bring two *t*,
15:29 day she shall take unto her two *t*,
Nu 6:10 eighth day he shall bring two *t*,

tutors
Ga 4: 2 But is under *t* and governors

twain See also TWO.
1Sa 18:21 my son in law in the one of the *t*.
2Ki 4:33 and shut the door upon them *t*,
Isa 6: 2 wings; with *t* he covered his face,
2 and with *t* he covered his feet,
2 and with *t* he did fly.
Jer 34:18 when they cut the calf in *t*, and
Eze 21:19 both *t* shall come forth out of one
M't 5:41 thee to go a mile, go with him *t*.
19: 5 wife: and they *t* shall be one flesh?
6 Wherefore they are no more *t*, but
21:31 Whether of them *t* did the will of
27:21 Whether of the *t* will ye that I
51 the veil of the temple was rent in *t*
M'r 10: 8 And they *t* shall be one flesh: so
8 so then they are no more *t*, but one
15:38 the veil of the temple was rent in *t*
Eph 2:15 make in himself of *t* one new man,

twelfth
Nu 7:78 On the *t* day Ahira the son of
1Ki 19:19 before him, and he with the *t*:
2Ki 8:25 In the *t* year of Joram the son
17: 1 In the *t* year of Ahaz king of
25:27 in the *t* month, on the seven
1Ch 24:12 to Eliashib, the *t* to Jakim,
25:19 The *t* to Hashabiah, he, his
27:15 The *t* captain for the *t* month
2Ch 34: 3 and in the *t* year he began to
Ezr 8:31 the *t* day of the first month,
Es 3: 7 the *t* year of king Ahasuerus,
7 to the *t* month, that is, the
13 thirteenth day of the *t* month,
8:12 thirteenth day of the *t* month,
9: 1 Now in the *t* month, that is,
Jer 52:31 in the *t* month, in the five and
Eze 29: 1 in the *t* day of the month, the
32: 1 it came to pass in the *t* year,
1 *t* month, in the first day of the
17 came to pass also in the *t* year,
33:21 it came to pass in the *t* year of
Re 21:20 a jacinth; the *t*, an amethyst.

twelve
Ge 5: 8 nine hundred and *t* years:
14: 4 *T* years they served
17:20 *t* princes shall he beget, and I
25:16 *t* princes according to their
35:22 Now the sons of Jacob were *t*:
42:13 Thy servants are *t* brethren,
32 We be *t* brethren, sons of our
49:28 these are the *t* tribes of Israel:
Ex 15:27 where were *t* wells of water,
24: 4 under the hill, and *t* pillars,
4 according to the *t* tribes of
28:21 of the children of Israel, *t*,
21 be according to the *t* tribes.
39:14 of the children of Israel, *t*,
14 according to the *t* tribes.
Le 24: 5 and bake *t* cakes thereof:
Nu 1:44 princes of Israel, being *t* men:
7: 3 covered wagons, and *t* oxen;
84 of Israel: *t* chargers of silver,
84 *t* silver bowls, *t* spoons of gold:
86 The golden spoons were *t*, full
87 were *t* bullocks, the rams *t*,
87 the lambs of the first year *t*,
87 of the goats for sin offering *t*.
17: 2 house of their fathers *t* rods:
6 fathers' houses, even *t* rods:
29:17 ye shall offer *t* young bullocks,
31: 5 *t* thousand armed for war.
33 And threescore and *t* thousand
38 Lord's tribute was threescore and *t*.
33: 9 were *t* fountains of water,
De 1:23 and I took *t* men of you, one of
Jos 3:12 take you *t* men out of the
4: 2 Take you *t* men out of the
3 *t* stones, and ye shall carry
4 Then Joshua called the *t* men,
8 *t* stones out of the midst of
9 Joshua set up *t* stones in the
20 And those *t* stones, which they
8:25 and women, were *t* thousand,
18:24 *t* cities with their villages:
19:15 *t* cities with their villages.
21: 7 the tribe of Zebulun, *t* cities.
40 were by their lot *t* cities.
J'g 19:29 with her bones, into *t* pieces,
21:10 sent thither *t* thousand men of
2Sa 2:15 by number *t* of Benjamin,
15 and *t* of the servants of David.
10: 6 of Ish-tob *t* thousand men.
17: 1 me now choose out *t* thousand
1Ki 4: 7 had *t* officers over all Israel,
26 and *t* thousand horsemen.
7:15 a line of *t* cubits did compass
25 It stood upon *t* oxen, three
44 sea, and *t* oxen under the sea;
10:20 *t* lions stood there on the one
26 *t* thousand horsemen, whom
11:30 on him, and rent it in *t* pieces:
16:23 to reign over Israel, *t* years:
18:31 And Elijah took *t* stones,
19:19 plowing with *t* yoke of oxen
2Ki 3: 1 of Judah, and reigned *t* years.
21: 1 Manasseh was *t* years old when
1Ch 6:63 the tribe of Zebulun, *t* cities.
9:22 gates were two hundred and *t*.
15:10 brethren an hundred and *t*.
25: 9 his brethren and sons were *t*:
10, 11, 12, 13, 14, 15, 16, 17, 18, 19, 20,
21, 22, 23, 24, 25, 26, 27, 28, 29, 30
sons, and his brethren, were *t*:
31 sons, and his brethren, were *t*.
2Ch 1:14 and *t* thousand horsemen,
4: 4 It stood upon *t* oxen, three
15 One sea, and *t* oxen under it.
9:19 *t* lions stood there on the one
25 and *t* thousand horsemen;
12: 3 With *t* hundred chariots, and
33: 1 Manasseh was *t* years old
Ezr 2: 6 thousand eight hundred and *t*.
18 of Jorah, an hundred and *t*.
6:17 *t* he goats, according to the
8:24 I separated *t* of the chief
35 *t* bullocks for all Israel, ninety
35 *t* he goats for a sin offering:
Ne 5:14 *t* years, I and my brethren
7:24 of Hariph, an hundred and *t*.
Es 2:12 that she had been *t* months,
Ps 60: *title* the valley of salt *t* thousand.
Jer 52:20 and *t* brasen bulls that were
21 a fillet of *t* cubits did compass
Eze 43:16 altar shall be *t* cubits long,
16 *t* broad, square in the four
47:13 to the *t* tribes of Israel:
Da 4:29 end of *t* months he walked in
M't 9:20 with an issue of blood *t* years,
10: 1 called unto him his *t* disciples,
2 the names of the *t* apostles are
5 These *t* Jesus sent forth, and
11: 1 of commanding his *t* disciples,
14:20 that remained *t* baskets full.
19:28 ye also shall sit upon *t* thrones,
28 judging the *t* tribes of Israel.
20:17 took the *t* disciples apart in the
26:14 Then one of the *t*, called Judas
20 was come, he sat down with the *t*.
47 lo, Judas, one of the *t*, came, and
53 me more than *t* legions of angels?
M'r 3:14 he ordained *t*, that they should be
4:10 that were about him with the *t*
5:25 had an issue of blood *t* years,
42 for she was of the age of *t* years.
6: 7 And he called unto him the *t*, and
43 they took up *t* baskets full of the
8:19 ye up? They say unto him, *T*.
9:35 And he sat down, and called the *t*,
10:32 he took again the *t*, and began to
11:11 went out unto Bethany with the *t*.
14:10 Judas Iscariot, one of the *t*, went
17 evening he cometh with the *t*.
20 It is one of the *t*, that dippeth
43 spake, cometh Judas, one of the *t*,
Lu 2:42 when he was *t* years old, they
6:13 of them he chose *t*, whom also he
8: 1 of God: and the *t* were with him,
42 daughter, about *t* years of age,
43 having an issue of blood *t* years,
9: 1 he called his *t* disciples together,
12 then came the *t*, and said unto
17 that remained to them *t* baskets.
18:31 Then he took unto him the *t*, and
22: 3 being of the number of the *t*.
14 and the *t* apostles with him.
30 judging the *t* tribes of Israel.
47 one of the *t*, went before them,
Joh 6:13 filled *t* baskets with the fragments
67 Then said Jesus unto the *t*, Will ye
70 Have not I chosen you *t*, and one
71 betray him, being one of the *t*.
11: 9 Are there not *t* hours in the day?
20:24 But Thomas, one of the *t*, called
Ac 6: 2 Then the *t* called the multitude of
7: 8 and Jacob begat the *t* patriarchs.
19: 7 And all the men were about *t*.
24:11 yet but *t* days since I went up to
26: 7 Unto which promise our *t* tribes,
1Co 15: 5 seen of Cephas, then of the *t*:
Jas 1: 1 to the *t* tribes which are scattered
Re 7: 5 of Juda were sealed *t* thousand.
5 of Reuben were sealed *t* thousand.
5 of Gad were sealed *t* thousand.
6 of Aser were sealed *t* thousand.
6 of Nepthalim were sealed *t* thousand.
6 of Manasses were sealed *t* thousand.
7 of Simeon were sealed *t* thousand.
7 of Levi were sealed *t* thousand.
7 of Issachar were sealed *t* thousand.
8 of Zabulon were sealed *t* thousand.
8 of Joseph were sealed *t* thousand.
8 Benjamin were sealed *t* thousand.
12: 1 upon her head a crown of *t* stars:
21:12 great and high, and had *t* gates,
12 at the gates *t* angels, and names

Re 21:12 of the t' tribes of the children of
14 wall of the city had t' foundations,
14 the names of the t' apostles of the
16 with the reed, t' thousand furlongs.
21 the t' gates were t' pearls; every
22: 2 life, which bare t' manner of fruits,

twelve-hundred See TWELVE and HUNDRED.

twelve-thousand See TWELVE and THOUSAND.

twentieth

Ge 8:14 the seven and t' day of the month,
Ex 12:18 the one and t' day of the month at
Nu 10:11 on the t' day of the second month,
1Ki 15: 9 t' year of Jeroboam king of Israel
2Ki 12: 6 three and t' year of king Jehoash
13: 1 In the three and t' year of Joash the
15:30 t' year of Jotham the son of Uzziah.
25:27 the seven and t' day of the month,
1Ch 24:16 to Pethahiah, the t' to Jehezekel,
17 The one and t' to Jachin, the two
17 to Jachin, the two and t' to Gamul,
18 The three and t' to Delaiah, the
18 the four and t' to Maaziah.
25:27 The t' to Eliathah, he, his sons,
28 The one and t' to Hothir, he, his
29 The two and t' to Giddalti, he, his
30 The three and t' to Mahazioth, he,
31 The four and t' to Romamti-ezer,
2Ch 7:10 and t' day of the seventh month
Ezr 10: 9 on the t' day of the month;
Ne 1: 1 the month Chisleu, in the t' year,
2: 1 in the t' year of Artaxerxes the
5:14 from the t' year even unto the two
Es 8: 9 on the three and t' day thereof;
Jer 25: 3 day, that is the three and t' year,
52:30 and t' year of Nebuchadrezzar
31 in the five and t' day of the month,
Eze 29:17 to pass in the seven and t' year,
40: 1 five and t' year of our captivity,
Da 10: 4 four and t' day of the first month,
Hag 1:15 and t' day of the sixth month,
2: 1 in the one and t' day of the month,
10, 18 and t' day of the ninth month,
20 four and t' day of the ninth month,
Zec 1: 7 and t' day of the eleventh month,

twenty See also TWENTY'S.

Ge 6: 3 shall be an hundred and t' years.
11:24 And Nahor lived nine and t' years,
18:31 there shall be t' found there.
23: 1 hundred and seven and t' years old:
31:38 t' years have I been with thee; thy
41 have I been t' years in thy house; I
32:14 hundred she goats, and t' he goats,
14 two hundred ewes, and t' rams,
15 bulls, t' she asses, and ten foals.
37:28 Ishmeelites for t' pieces of silver:
Ex 26: 2 curtain shall be eight and t' cubits,
18 t' boards on the south side
19 of silver under the t' boards;
20 north side there shall be t' boards:
27:10 And the t' pillars thereof and their
10 their t' sockets shall be of brass;
11 his t' pillars and their t' sockets of
16 shall be an hanging of t' cubits,
30:13 (a shekel is t' gerahs:) an half
14 from t' years old and above, shall
36: 9 one curtain was t' and eight cubits,
23 t' boards for the south side
24 he made under the t' boards; two
25 north corner, he made t' boards,
38:10 Their pillars were t',
10 and their brasen sockets t';
11 their pillars were t',
11 and their sockets of brass t';
18 t' cubits was the length, and the
24 the offering, was t' and nine talents,
26 from t' years old and upward,
Le 27: 3 male from t' years old even unto
5 years old even unto t' years old,
5 shall be of the male t' shekels,
25 t' gerahs shall be the shekel.
Nu 1: 3 From t' years old and upward, all
18, 20, 22, 24, 26, 28, 30, 32, 34, 36, 38, 40,
42, 45 from t' years old and upward,
3:39 upward, were t' and two thousand.
43 t' and two thousand two hundred
47 them: (the shekel is t' gerahs:)
7:86 was an hundred and t' shekels.
88 were t' and four bullocks, the
8:24 t' and five years old and upward
11:19 days, neither ten days, nor t' days;
14:29 from t' years old and upward,
18:16 the sanctuary, which is t' gerahs.
25: 9 plague were t' and four thousand.
26: 2 from t' years old and upward,
4 from t' years old and upward;
14 t' and two thousand and two
62 of them were t' and three thousand,
32:11 from t' years old and upward,
33:39 an hundred and t' and three years
De 31: 2 I am an hundred and t' years old
34: 7 hundred and t' years old when he
Jos 15:32 all the cities are t' and nine, with
19:30 t' and two cities with their villages.
J'g 4: 3 t' years he mightily oppressed the
7: 3 of the people t' and two thousand;
8:10 hundred and t' thousand men that
10: 2 he judged Israel t' and three years,
3 and judged Israel t' and two years.
11:33 come to Minneth, even t' cities,
15:20 the days of the Philistines t' years.
16:31 And he judged Israel t' years.
20:15 t' and six thousand men that drew
21 that day t' and two thousand men.
35 t' and five thousand and an hundred
J'g 20:46 t' and five thousand men that drew
1Sa 7: 2 time was long; for it was t' years:
14:14 was about t' men, within as it were
2Sa 3:20 to David to Hebron, and t' men
8: 4 and t' thousand footmen:
5 Syrians two and t' thousand men.
9:10 had fifteen sons and t' servants.
10: 6 of Zoba, t' thousand footmen,
18: 7 slaughter that day of t' thousand
19:17 sons and his t' servants with him;
21:20 six toes, four and t' in number;
24: 8 end of nine months and t' days.
1Ki 4:23 and t' oxen out of the pastures,
5:11 gave Hiram t' thousand measures
11 and t' measures of pure oil:
6: 2 and the breadth thereof t' cubits,
3 t' cubits was the length thereof,
16 he built t' cubits on the sides of
20 forepart was t' cubits in length,
20 and t' cubits in breadth,
20 t' cubits in the height thereof: and
8:63 Lord, two and t' thousand oxen,
63 an hundred and t' thousand sheep.
9:10 came to pass at the end of t' years,
11 king Solomon gave Hiram t' cities
28 gold, four hundred and t' talents,
10:10 an hundred and t' talents of gold,
14:20 reigned were two and t' years:
15:33 Israel in Tirzah, t' and four years.
16: 8 the t' and sixth year of Asa king of
10, 15 t' and seventh year of Asa king
29 Israel in Samaria t' and two years.
20:30 there a wall fell upon t' and seven
22:42 and he reigned t' and five years in
2Ki 4:42 of the firstfruits, t' loaves of barley,
8:26 Two and t' years old was Ahaziah
10:36 in Samaria was t' and eight years.
14: 2 He was t' and five years old when
2 t' and nine years in Jerusalem.
15: 1 t' and seventh year of Jeroboam
27 in Samaria, and reigned t' years.
33 Five and t' years old was he when
16: 2 T' years old was Ahaz when he
18: 2 T' and five years old was he when
2 he reigned t' and nine years in
21:19 Amon was t' and two years old
23:31 Jehoahaz was t' and three years
36 Jehoiakim was t' and five years
24:18 Zedekiah was t' and one years old
1Ch 2:22 and t' cities in the land of Gilead.
7: 2 and t' thousand and six hundred.
7 t' and two thousand and thirty and
9 was t' thousand and two hundred.
40 was t' and six thousand men.
12:28 father's house t' and two captains.
30 of Ephraim t' thousand and eight
35 war t' and eight thousand and six
37 battle, an hundred and t' thousand.
15: 5 his brethren an hundred and t':
6 his brethren two hundred and t':
18: 4 and t' thousand footmen:
5 Syrians two and t' thousand men.
20: 6 fingers and toes were four and t',
23: 4 t' and four thousand were to set
24 from the age of t' years and upward.
27 were numbered from t' years old
27: 1, 2 course were t' and four thousand.
4 course...were t' and four thousand.
5, 7, 8, 9, 10, 11, 12, 13, 14, 15 course
were t' and four thousand.
23 them from t' years old and under:
2Ch 2:10 t' thousand measures of...wheat,
10 t' thousand measures of barley,
10 and t' thousand baths of wine,
10 and t' thousand baths of oil.
3: 3 cubits, and the breadth t' cubits.
4 the breadth of the house, t' cubits,
4 the height was an hundred and t':
8 the breadth of the house, t' cubits,
8 and the breadth thereof t' cubits:
11 the cherubims were t' cubits long:
13 spread themselves forth t' cubits:
4: 1 brass, t' cubits the length thereof,
1 t' cubits the breadth thereof, and
5:12 an hundred and t' priests sounding
7: 5 of t' and two thousand oxen, and
5 an hundred and t' thousand sheep:
8: 1 came to pass at the end of t' years,
9: 9 an hundred and t' talents of gold,
11:21 and begat t' and eight sons, and
13:21 and begat t' and two sons, and
20:31 and he reigned t' and five years in
25: 1 Amaziah was t' and five years old
1 he reigned t' and nine years in
5 them from t' years old and above,
27: 1 Jotham was t' and five years old
8 He was five and t' years old when
28: 1 Ahaz was t' years old when he
6 an hundred and t' thousand in one
29: 1 when he was five and t' years old,
1 nine and t' years in Jerusalem.
31:17 Levites...t' years old and upward,
33:21 Amon was two and t' years old
36: 2 Jehoahaz was t' and three years
5 Jehoiakim was t' and five years
11 Zedekiah was one and t' years old
Ezr 1: 9 of silver, nine and t' knives,
2:11 of Bebai, six hundred t' and three.
12 thousand two hundred t' and two.
17 Bezai, three hundred t' and three.
19 Hashum, two hundred t' and three.
21 Beth-lehem, an hundred t' and three.
23 Anathoth, an hundred t' and eight.
26 and Gaba, six hundred t' and one.
27 Michmas, an hundred t' and two.
28 and Ai, two hundred t' and three.
Ezr 2:32 of Harim, three hundred and t'.
33 and Ono, seven hundred t' and five.
41 of Asaph, an hundred t' and eight.
67 six thousand seven hundred and t'.
3: 8 Levites,...t' years old and upward,
8:11 and with him t' and eight males.
19 his brethren and their sons, t';
20 two hundred and t' Nethinims:
27 t' basons of gold, of a thousand
Ne 6:15 was finished in the t' and fifth day
7:16 of Bebai, six hundred t' and eight.
17 two thousand three hundred t' and
22 Hashum, three hundred t' and eight.
23 Bezai, three hundred t' and four.
27 Anathoth, an hundred t' and eight.
30 and Gaba, six hundred t' and one.
31 an hundred and t' and two.
32 and Ai, an hundred t' and three.
35 of Harim, three hundred and t'.
37 and Ono, seven hundred t' and one.
69 seven hundred and t' asses.
71 work t' thousand drams of gold,
72 was t' thousand drams of gold,
9: 1 t' and fourth day of this month
11: 8 Sallai, nine hundred t' and eight.
12 were eight hundred t' and two:
14 valour, an hundred t' and eight:
Es 1: 1 and seven and t' provinces:)
8: 9 an hundred t' and seven provinces,
9:30 hundred t' and seven provinces of
Ps 68:17 chariots of God are t' thousand,
Jer 52: 1 Zedekiah was one and t' years old
28 thousand Jews and three and t':
Eze 4:10 shall be by weight, t' shekels a day:
8:16 were about five and t' men, with
11: 1 door of the gate five and t' men;
40:13 the breadth was five and t' cubits,
21, 25 the breadth five and t' cubits.
29 long, and five and t' cubits broad.
30 about were five and t' cubits long,
33 long, and five and t' cubits broad.
36 and the breadth five and t' cubits.
49 length of the porch was t' cubits,
41: 2 cubits, and the breadth, t' cubits.
4 the length thereof, t' cubits;
4 the breadth, t' cubits, before the
10 of t' cubits round about the house
42: 3 the t' cubits which were for the
45: 1 length of five and t' thousand reeds,
3 the length of five and t' thousand,
5 the five and t' thousand of length,
5 for a possession for t' chambers.
6 and five and t' thousand long, over
12 And the shekel shall be t' gerahs:
12 t' shekels, five and t' shekels,
48: 8 of five and t' thousand reeds in
9 of five and t' thousand in length,
10 the north five and t' thousand
10 the south five and t' thousand
13 have five and t' thousand in length,
13 length shall be five and t' thousand,
15 against the five and t' thousand,
20 shall be five and t' thousand
20 by five and t' thousand:
21, 21 against the five and t' thousand
Da 6: 1 an hundred and t' princes,
10:13 withstood me one and t' days:
Hag 2:16 one came to an heap of t' measures,
16 out of the press, there were but t'.
Zec 5: 2 the length thereof is t' cubits, and
Lu 14:31 against him with t' thousand?
Joh 6:19 about five and t' or thirty furlongs,
Ac 1:15 were about an hundred and t',)
27:28 sounded, and found it t' fathoms:
1Co 10: 8 in one day three and t' thousand.
Re 4: 4 the throne were four and t' seats:
4 I saw four and t' elders sitting,
10 The four and t' elders fall down
5: 8 the four and t' elders fell down
14 the four and t' elders fell down
11:16 four and t' elders, which sat before
19: 4 the four and t' elders and the four

twenty's

Ge 18:31 I will not destroy it for t' sake.

twenty-thousand See TWENTY and THOUSAND.

twice

Ge 41:32 was doubled unto Pharaoh t';
Ex 16: 5 t' as much as they gather daily.
22 they gathered t' as much bread,
Nu 20:11 with his rod he smote the rock t':
1Sa 18:11 avoided out of his presence t'.
1Ki 11: 9 which had appeared unto him t',
2Ki 6:10 saved himself...not once nor t'.
Ne 13:20 without Jerusalem once or t'.
Job 33:14 For God speaketh once, yea t', yet
40: 5 Once have I spoken;...yea, t': but I
42:10 gave Job t' as much as he had
Ps 62:11 t' have I heard this; that power
Ec 6: 6 he live a thousand years t' told,
M'r 14:30 before the cock crow t', thou shalt
72 Before the cock crow t', thou shalt
Lu 18:12 I fast t' in the week, I give tithes of
Jude 12 without fruit, t' dead, plucked up

twigs

Eze 17: 4 cropped off the top of his young t',
22 off from the top of his young t' a

twilight

1Sa 30:17 David smote them from the t'
2Ki 7: 5 they rose up in the t', to go unto
7 they arose and fled in the t', and
Job 3: 9 the stars of the t' thereof be dark;
24:15 of the adulterer waiteth for the t',
Pr 7: 9 In the t', in the evening, in the
Eze 12: 6 and carry it forth in the t':

Eze 12: 7 I brought it forth in the *t'*, and I
12 bear upon his shoulder in the *t'*,

twined
Ex 26: 1 with ten curtains of fine *t'* linen,
31 and fine *t'* linen of cunning work:
36 and scarlet, and fine *t'* linen,
27: 9 shall be hangings...of fine *t'* linen
16 and scarlet, and fine *t'* linen,
18 height five cubits of fine *t'* linen,
28: 6 of scarlet, and fine *t'* linen, with
8 and scarlet, and fine *t'* linen.
15 of scarlet, of fine *t'* linen, shalt thou
36: 8 made ten curtains of fine *t'* linen,
35 and scarlet, and fine *t'* linen:
37 and scarlet, and fine *t'* linen, of
38: 9 of the court were of fine *t'* linen,
16 round about were of fine *t'* linen.
18 and scarlet, and fine *t'* linen:
39: 2 and scarlet, and fine *t'* linen.
5 and scarlet, and fine *t'* linen;
8 and scarlet, and fine *t'* linen.
24 purple, and scarlet, and *t'* linen.
28 and linen breeches of fine *t'* linen,
29 And a girdle of fine *t'* linen, and blue,

twinkling
1Co 15: 52 In a moment, in the *t'* of an eye,

twins
Ge 25: 24 behold, there were *t'* in her womb.
38: 27 that, behold, *t'* were in her womb.
Ca 4: 2 whereof every one bear *t'*, and
5 like two young roes that are *t'*,
6: 6 whereof every one beareth *t'*, and
7: 3 like two young roes that are *t'*.

two^ See also TWAIN; TWOEDGED; TWOFOLD.
Ge 1: 16 And God made *t'* great lights;
4: 19 Lamech took unto him *t'* wives:
5: 18 lived an hundred sixty and *t'* years,
20 nine hundred sixty and *t'* years:
26 seven hundred eighty and *t'* years,
28 an hundred eighty and *t'* years,
6: 19 *t'* of every sort shalt thou bring
20 *t'* of every sort shall come unto
7: 2 of beasts that are not clean by *t'*,
9 There went in *t'* and *t'* unto Noah
15 into the ark, *t'* and *t'* of all flesh,
9: 22 and told his *t'* brethren without.
10: 25 And unto Eber were born *t'* sons:
11: 20 And Reu lived *t'* and thirty years,
19: 1 And there came *t'* angels to Sodom
8 I have *t'* daughters which have not
15 take thy wife, and thy *t'* daughters,
16 upon the hand of his *t'* daughters;
30 and his *t'* daughters with him;
30 in a cave, he and his *t'* daughters.
22: 3 took *t'* of his young men with him,
24: 22 and *t'* bracelets for her hands of ten
25: 23 her, *T'* nations are in thy womb,
23 and *t'* manner of people shall be
27: 9 fetch me from thence *t'* good kids
36 hath supplanted me these *t'* times:
29: 16 Laban had *t'* daughters: the name
31: 33 into the *t'* maidservants' tents;
41 fourteen years for thy *t'* daughters,
32: 7 herds, and the camels, into *t'* bands;
10 and now I am become *t'* bands.
14 *T'* hundred she goats, and twenty he
14 *t'* hundred ewes, and twenty rams,
22 that night, and took his *t'* wives,
22 and his *t'* womenservants, and
33: 1 Rachel, and unto the *t'* handmaids.
34: 25 that *t'* of the sons of Jacob, Simeon
40: 2 was wroth against *t'* of his officers,
41: 1 to pass at the end of *t'* full years, that
50 And unto Joseph were born *t'* sons
42: 37 Slay my *t'* sons, if I bring him not
44: 27 know that my wife bare me *t'* sons:
45: 6 these *t'* years hath the famine been in
46: 27 born him in Egypt, were *t'* souls:
48: 1 and he took with him his *t'* sons,
5 thy *t'* sons, Ephraim and Manasseh,
49: 14 couching down between *t'* burdens:
Ex 2: 13 *t'* men of the Hebrews strove
4: 9 will not believe also these *t'* signs,
12: 7 and strike it on the *t'* side posts
22 and the *t'* side posts with the blood
23 the lintel, and on the *t'* side posts,
16: 22 much bread, *t'* omers for one man:
29 on the sixth day the bread of *t'* days;
18: 3 her *t'* sons; of which the name of
6 thy wife, and her *t'* sons with her.
21: 21 if he continue a day or *t'*, he shall not
25: 10 *t'* cubits and a half shall be the length
12 *t'* rings shall be in the one side of
12 and *t'* rings in the other side of it.
17 *t'* cubits and a half shall be the length
18 shalt make *t'* cherubims of gold,
18 in the *t'* ends of the mercy seat.
19 cherubims on the *t'* ends thereof.
22 from between the *t'* cherubims
23 *t'* cubits shall be the length thereof,
35, 35, 35 a knop under *t'* branches of
26: 17 *T'* tenons shall there be in one
19 boards; *t'* sockets under one board
19 under one board for his *t'* tenons,
19 and *t'* sockets under another board
19 another board for his *t'* tenons.
21 silver; *t'* sockets under one board,
21 and *t'* sockets under another board.
23 *t'* boards shalt thou make for the
23 of the tabernacle in the *t'* sides.
24 they shall be for the *t'* corners.
25 *t'* sockets under one board,
25 and *t'* sockets under another board.
27 tabernacle, for the *t'* sides westward.

Ex 27: 7 be upon the *t'* sides of the altar,
28: 7 It shall have the *t'* shoulderpieces
7 joined at the *t'* edges thereof;
9 And thou shalt take *t'* onyx stones,
11 engrave the *t'* stones with the
12 the *t'* stones upon the shoulders of
12 upon his *t'* shoulders for a
14 *t'* chains of pure gold at the ends;
23 the breastplate *t'* rings of gold,
23 put the *t'* rings on the *t'* ends of the
24 put the *t'* wreathen chains of gold
24 the *t'* rings which are on the ends
25 *t'* ends of the *t'* wreathen chains
25 thou shalt fasten in the *t'* ouches,
26 thou shalt make *t'* rings of gold,
26 put them upon the *t'* ends of the
27 *t'* other rings of gold thou shalt
27 them on the *t'* sides of the ephod
29: 1 and *t'* rams without blemish,
3 with the bullock and the *t'* rams.
13, 22 the *t'* kidneys, and the fat that
38 *t'* lambs of the first year day by day
30: 2 *t'* cubits shall be the height thereof:
4 *t'* golden rings shalt thou make to
4 of it, by the *t'* corners thereof,
4 upon the *t'* sides of it shalt thou
23 even *t'* hundred and fifty shekels,
23 calamus *t'* hundred and fifty shekels,
31: 18 *t'* tables of testimony, tables of
32: 15 the *t'* tables of the testimony were
34: 1 Hew thee *t'* tables of stone like
4 he hewed *t'* tables of stone like
4 in his hand the *t'* tables of stone.
29 with the *t'* tables of testimony in
36: 22 One board had *t'* tenons, equally
24 boards; *t'* sockets under one board
24 under one board for his *t'* tenons,
24 *t'* sockets under another board for
24 another board for his *t'* tenons.
26 silver; *t'* sockets under one board,
26 and *t'* sockets under another board.
28 *t'* boards made he for the corners of
28 of the tabernacle in the *t'* sides.
30 under every board *t'* sockets.
37: 1 *t'* cubits and a half was the length of
3 even *t'* rings upon the one side of
3 *t'* rings upon the other side of it.
6 *t'* cubits and a half was the length
7 And he made *t'* cherubims of gold,
7 on the *t'* ends of the mercy seat;
8 the cherubims on the *t'* ends
10 *t'* cubits was the length thereof,
21, 21, 21 a knop under *t'* branches of
25 and *t'* cubits was the height of it;
27 And he made *t'* rings of gold for it
27 crown thereof, by the *t'* corners of
27 upon the *t'* sides thereof, to be
38: 29 *t'* thousand and four hundred shekels.
39: 4 by the *t'* edges was it coupled
16 *t'* ouches of gold, and *t'* gold rings;
16 put the *t'* rings in the *t'* ends of the
17 they put the *t'* wreathen chains of
17 in the *t'* rings on the ends of the
18 *t'* ends of the *t'* wreathen chains
18 they fastened in the *t'* ouches,
19 And they made *t'* rings of gold,
19 on the *t'* ends of the breastplate,
20 they made *t'* other golden rings,
20 them on the *t'* sides of the ephod
Le 3: 4, 10, 15 the *t'* kidneys, and the fat
4: 9 the *t'* kidneys, and the fat that is
5: 7, 11 *t'* turtledoves, or *t'* young pigeons,
7: 4 the *t'* kidneys, and the fat that is
8: 2 *t'* rams, and a basket of unleavened
16 and the *t'* kidneys, and their fat,
25 and the *t'* kidneys, and their fat,
12: 5 she shall be unclean *t'* weeks, as in
8 *t'* turtles, or *t'* young pigeons;
14: 4 cleansed *t'* birds alive and clean,
10 he shall take *t'* he lambs without
22 *t'* turtledoves, or *t'* young pigeons,
49 take to cleanse the house *t'* birds,
15: 14 *t'* turtledoves, or *t'* young pigeons,
29 her *t'* turtles, or *t'* young pigeons,
16: 1 after the death of the *t'* sons of
5 *t'* kids of the goats for a sin
7 And he shall take the *t'* goats, and
8 shall cast lots upon the *t'* goats;
23: 13 *t'* tenth deals of fine floor mingled
17 *t'* wave loaves of *t'* tenth deals:
18 one young bullock, and *t'* rams:
19 *t'* lambs of the first year for a
20 before the Lord, with the *t'* lambs:
24: 5 *t'* tenth deals shall be in one cake.
6 And thou shalt set them in *t'* rows,
Nu 1: 35 were thirty and *t'* thousand
35 thousand and *t'* hundred.
39 *t'* thousand and seven hundred.
2: 21 were thirty and *t'* thousand
21 thousand and *t'* hundred.
26 *t'* thousand and seven hundred.
3: 34 were six thousand and *t'* hundred.
39 were twenty and *t'* thousand.
43 were twenty and *t'* thousand
43 *t'* hundred and threescore and
46 be redeemed of the *t'* hundred and
4: 36 were *t'* thousand seven hundred and
40 were *t'* thousand and six hundred and
44 were three thousand and *t'* hundred.
6: 10 *t'* turtles, or *t'* young pigeons,
7: 3 a wagon for *t'* of the princes, and
7 *T'* wagons and four oxen he gave
17, 23, 29, 35, 41, 47, 53, 59, 65, 71, 77,
83 offerings, *t'* oxen, five rams,
85 silver vessels weighed *t'* thousand and
89 from between the *t'* cherubims:

Nu 9: 22 Or whether it were *t'* days, or a
10: 2 Make thee *t'* trumpets of silver; of
11: 19 shall not eat one day, nor *t'* days,
26 there remained *t'* of the men in
31 it were *t'* cubits high upon the face of
13: 23 bare it between *t'* upon a staff;
15: 6 offering *t'* tenth deals of flour
16: 2 *t'* hundred and fifty princes of the
17 *t'* hundred and fifty censers;
35 the *t'* hundred and fifty men that
22: 22 and his *t'* servants were with him.
26: 10 devoured *t'* hundred and fifty men:
14 twenty and *t'* thousand and
14 thousand and *t'* hundred.
34 *t'* thousand and seven hundred.
37 and *t'* thousand and five hundred.
28: 3, 9 *t'* lambs of the first year without
9 *t'* tenth deals of flour for a meat
11 *t'* young bullocks, and one ram,
12 *t'* tenth deals of flour for a meat
19 *t'* young bullocks, and one ram, and
20 and *t'* tenth deals for a ram;
27 *t'* young bullocks, one ram, seven
28 *t'* tenth deals unto one ram,
29: 3 and *t'* tenth deals for a ram,
9 and *t'* tenth deals to one ram,
13 *t'* rams, and fourteen lambs of the
14 *t'* tenth deals to each ram of the
14 deals to each ram of the *t'* rams,
17 twelve young bullocks, *t'* rams,
20 third day eleven bullocks, *t'* rams,
23 fourth day ten bullocks, *t'* rams,
26 the fifth day nine bullocks, *t'* rams,
29 sixth day eight bullocks, *t'* rams,
32 day seven bullocks, *t'* rams,
31: 35 and *t'* thousand persons in all,
40 tribute was thirty and *t'* persons.
34: 15 The *t'* tribes and the half tribe have
35: 5 on the east side *t'* thousand cubits,
5 the south side *t'* thousand cubits,
5 on the west side *t'* thousand cubits,
5 the north side *t'* thousand cubits;
6 ye shall add forty and *t'* cities.
De 3: 8 out of the hand of the *t'* kings
21 God hath done unto these *t'* kings:
4: 13 wrote them upon *t'* tables of stone.
47 Bashan, *t'* kings of the Amorites,
5: 22 he wrote them in *t'* tables of stone,
9: 10 delivered unto me *t'* tables of stone
11 Lord gave me the *t'* tables of stone,
15 and the *t'* tables of the covenant
15 were in my *t'* hands.
17 I took the *t'* tables, and cast them
17 cast them out of my *t'* hands, and
10: 1 Hew the *t'* tables of stone like unto
3 hewed *t'* tables of stone like unto
3 having the *t'* tables in mine hand.
14: 6 and cleaveth the cleft into *t'* claws,
17: 6 At the mouth of *t'* witnesses, or
19: 15 at the mouth of *t'* witnesses, or at
21: 15 If a man have *t'* wives, one beloved,
32: 30 and *t'* put ten thousand to flight,
Jos 2: 1 sent out of Shittim *t'* men to spy
4 And the woman took the *t'* men,
10 unto the *t'* kings of the Amorites,
23 So the *t'* men returned, and
3: 4 *t'* thousand cubits by measure:
6: 22 the *t'* men that had spied out the
7: 3 let about *t'* or three thousand men go
9: 10 to the *t'* kings of the Amorites,
14: 3 given the inheritance of *t'* tribes
4 children of Joseph were *t'* tribes,
15: 60 *t'* cities with their villages.
19: 30 twenty and *t'* cities with their
21: 16 nine cities out of those *t'* tribes.
25, 27 with her suburbs; *t'* cities.
24: 12 even the *t'* kings of the Amorites;
J'g 3: 16 him a dagger which had *t'* edges,
5: 30 prey; to every man a damsel or *t'*;
7: 3 the people twenty and *t'* thousand;
25 took *t'* princes of the Midianites,
8: 12 and took the *t'* kings of Midian,
9: 44 *t'* other companies ran upon all the
10: 3 judged Israel twenty and *t'* years.
11: 37 let me alone *t'* months, that I may
38 and he sent her away for *t'* months:
39 came to pass at the end of *t'* months,
12: 6 Ephraimites forty and *t'* thousand.
15: 4 put a firebrand...between *t'* tails.
13 they bound him with *t'* new cords,
16: 3 the gate of the city, and the *t'* posts,
28 of the Philistines for my *t'* eyes,
29 Samson took hold of the *t'* middle
17: 4 took *t'* hundred shekels of silver,
19: 10 were with him *t'* asses saddled,
20: 21 day twenty and *t'* thousand men.
45 and slew *t'* thousand men of them.
Ru 1: 1 he, and his wife, and his *t'* sons.
2 the name of his *t'* sons Mahlon and
3 and she was left, and her *t'* sons.
5 the woman was left of her *t'* sons
7 her *t'* daughters in law with her;
8 said unto her *t'* daughters in law,
19 So they *t'* went until they came to
4: 11 *t'* did build the house of Israel:
1Sa 1: 2 he had *t'* wives; the name of the
3 And the *t'* sons of Eli, Hophni and
2: 21 bare three sons and *t'* daughters.
34 that shall come upon thy *t'* sons,
4: 4, 11 the *t'* sons of Eli, Hophni and
17 and thy *t'* sons also, Hophni and
6: 7 take *t'* milch kine, on which there
10 took *t'* milch kine, and tied them
10: 2 thou shalt find *t'* men by Rachel's
4 and give thee *t'* loaves of bread;
11: 11 *t'* of them were not left together.

1Sa 13: 1 when he had reigned t' years over
2 t' thousand were with Saul in
14: 49 names of his t' daughters were
15: 4 t' hundred thousand footmen, and
18: 27 slew of the Philistines t' hundred men;
23: 18 they t' made a covenant before
25: 13 and t' hundred abode by the stuff.
18 haste, and took t' hundred loaves,
18 t' bottles of wine, and five sheep
18 t' hundred cakes of figs, and laid them
27: 3 David with his t' wives, Ahinoam
28: 8 and he went, and t' men with him,
30: 5 And David's t' wives were taken
10 t' hundred abode behind, which were
12 of figs, and t' clusters of raisins:
18 and David rescued his t' wives.
21 David came to the t' hundred men,
2Sa 1: 1 David...abode t' days in Ziklag;
2: 2 up thither, and his t' wives also,
10 over Israel, and reigned t' years.
4: 2 Saul's son had t' men that were
8: 2 even with t' lines measured he to
5 the Syrians t' and twenty thousand
12: 1 There were t' men in one city; the
13: 23 it came to pass after t' full years,
14: 6 And thy handmaid had t' sons,
6 and they t' strove together in the
28 dwelt t' full years in Jerusalem,
15: 11 with Absalom went t' hundred men
27 peace, and your t' sons with you,
36 have there with them their t' sons,
16: 1 upon them t' hundred loaves of bread,
18: 24 David sat between the t' gates:
21: 8 the king took the t' sons of Rizpah
23: 20 he slew t' lionlike men of Moab:
1Ki 2: 5 what he did to the t' captains of
32 fell upon t' men more righteous
39 t' of the servants of Shimei ran
3: 16 Then came there t' women, that
18 the house, save we t' in the house.
25 said, Divide the living child in t',
5: 12 and they t' made a league together.
14 Lebanon, and t' months at home:
6: 23 the oracle he made t' cherubims
32 The t' doors also were of olive tree;
34 And the t' doors were of fir tree:
34 the t' leaves of the one door were
34 the t' leaves of the other door were
7: 15 For he cast t' pillars of brass, of
16 made t' chapiters of molten brass,
18 t' rows round about upon the one
20 the chapiters upon the t' pillars
20 the pomegranates were t' hundred in
24 the knops were cast in t' rows,
26 it contained t' thousand baths.
41 The t' pillars, and the
41 the t' bowls of the chapiters that
41 were on top of the t' pillars;
41 t' networks, to cover the t' bowls
42 pomegranates for the t' networks,
42 t' rows of pomegranates for one
42 cover the t' bowls of the chapiters
8: 7 spread forth their t' wings over
9 the ark save the t' tables of stone,
63 t' and twenty thousand oxen, and
9: 10 Solomon had built the t' houses,
10: 16 king Solomon made t' hundred targets
19 and t' lions stood beside the stays.
11: 29 and they t' were alone in the field:
12: 28 counsel, and made t' calves of gold,
14: 20 reigned were t' and twenty years:
15: 25 and reigned over Israel t' years.
16: 8 to reign over Israel in Tirzah, t' years.
21 of Israel divided into t' parts:
24 of Shemer for t' talents of silver,
29 in Samaria twenty and t' years.
17: 12 I am gathering t' sticks, that I
18: 21 long halt ye between t' opinions?
23 them therefore give us t' bullocks;
32 would contain t' measures of seed.
20: 1 were thirty and t' kings with him,
15 and they were t' hundred
15 hundred and thirty t':
16 the thirty and t' kings that helped
27 them the t' little flocks of kids;
21: 10 set t' men, sons of Belial, before
13 there came in t' men, children of
22: 31 his thirty and t' captains that had
51 and reigned t' years over Israel.
2Ki 1: 14 burnt up the t' captains of the
2: 6 leave thee. And they t' went on.
7 off: and they t' stood by Jordan.
8 they t' went over on dry ground.
12 clothes, and rent them in t' pieces.
24 forth t' she bears out of the wood,
24 tare forty and t' children of them.
4: 1 come to take unto him my t' sons
5: 17 servant t' mules' burden of earth?
22 mount Ephraim t' young men of
22 silver, and t' changes of garments.
23 said, Be content, take t' talents.
23 bound t' talents of silver in t' bags,
23 with t' changes of garments, and
23 laid them upon t' of his servants;
7: 1 t' measures of barley for a shekel, in
14 took therefore t' chariot horses;
16 and t' measures of barley for a shekel,
18 T' measures of barley for a shekel,
8: 17 Thirty and t' years old was he
26 T' and twenty years old was
9: 32 out to him t' or three eunuchs.
10: 4 t' kings stood not before him:
8 Lay ye them in t' heaps at the
14 t' and forty men; neither left he
11: 7 t' parts of all you that go forth on
15: 2 t' and fifty years in Jerusalem.
2Ki 15: 27 In the t' and fiftieth year of Azariah
17: 16 them molten images, even t' calves,
18: 23 deliver thee t' thousand horses,
21: 5 t' courts of the house of the Lord.
19 Amon was twenty and t' years old
19 he reigned t' years in Jerusalem.
23: 12 made in the t' courts of the house
25: 16 The t' pillars, one sea, and the
1Ch 1: 19 And unto Eber were born t' sons:
4: 5 the father of Tekoa had t' wives,
5: 21 of sheep t' hundred and fifty thousand,
21 of asses t' thousand, and of men an
7: 2 t' and twenty thousand and six
7 twenty and t' thousand and thirty
9 was twenty thousand and t' hundred.
11 thousand and t' hundred soldiers,
9: 22 the gates were t' hundred and twelve.
11: 21 was more honourable than the t';
22 he slew t' lionlike men of Moab:
12: 28 house twenty and t' captains.
32 the heads of them were t' hundred;
15: 6 his brethren t' hundred and twenty:
8 the chief, and his brethren t' hundred:
18: 5 Syrians t' and twenty thousand
19: 7 thirty and t' thousand chariots,
24: 17 the t' and twentieth to Gamul,
25: 7 was t' hundred fourscore and eight.
29 The t' and twentieth to Giddalti,
26: 8 were threescore...t' of Obed-edom.
17 day, and toward Asuppim t' and t'.
18 the causeway, and t' at Parbar.
32 t' thousand and seven hundred chief
2Ch 3: 10 made t' cherubims of image work,
15 he made before the house t' pillars
4: 3 T' rows of oxen were cast, when it
12 the t' pillars, and the pommels, and
12 which were on the top of the t' pillars.
12 t' wreaths to cover the t' pommels
13 pomegranates on the t' wreaths;
13 t' rows of pomegranates on each
13 to cover the t' pommels of the
5: 10 nothing in the ark save the t' tables
7: 5 of twenty and t' thousand oxen,
8: 10 even t' hundred and fifty, that bare
9: 15 king Solomon made t' hundred targets
18 and t' lions standing by the stays:
13: 21 and begat twenty and t' sons, and
14: 8 drew bows, t' hundred and fourscore
17: 15 with him t' hundred and fourscore
16 t' hundred thousand mighty men of
17 bow and shield t' hundred thousand.
21: 5 Jehoram was thirty and t' years
19 after the end of t' years, his bowels
20 Thirty and t' years old was he when
22: 2 Forty and t' years old was Ahaziah
24: 3 And Jehoiada took for him t' wives;
26: 3 and he reigned fifty and t' years in
12 men of valour were t' thousand and six
28: 8 brethren t' hundred thousand,
29: 32 rams, and t' hundred lambs:
33: 5 t' courts of the house of the Lord.
21 Amon was t' and twenty years old
21 and reigned t' years in Jerusalem.
35: 8 t' thousand and six hundred small
Ezr 2: 3 of Parosh, t' thousand an hundred
3 thousand an hundred seventy...t'.
6 t' thousand eight hundred and twelve
7 a thousand t' hundred fifty and four
10 of Bani, six hundred forty and t'.
12 a thousand t' hundred twenty
12 hundred twenty and t'.
14 Bigvai, t' thousand fifty and six.
19 Hashum, t' hundred twenty and three.
24 children of Azmaveth, forty and t'.
27 Michmas, an hundred twenty and t'.
28 and Ai, t' hundred twenty and three.
29 The children of Nebo, fifty and t'.
31 a thousand t' hundred fifty and four.
37 of Immer, a thousand fifty and t'.
38 thousand t' hundred forty and seven.
58 were three hundred ninety and t'.
60 of Nekoda, six hundred fifty and t'.
64 and t' thousand three hundred and
65 among them t' hundred singing men
66 their mules, t' hundred forty and five;
6: 17 t' hundred rams, four hundred lambs;
8: 4 and with him t' hundred males.
9 him t' hundred and eighteen males.
20 t' hundred and twenty Nethinims:
27 and t' vessels of fine copper,
10: 13 is this a work of one day or t':
Ne 5: 14 t' and thirtieth year of Artaxerxes
6: 15 the month Elul, in fifty and t' days.
7: 8 t' thousand an hundred seventy...t'.
9 three hundred seventy and t'.
10 of Arah, six hundred fifty and t'.
11 t' thousand and eight hundred and
12 a thousand t' hundred fifty and four.
17 of Azgad, t' thousand three
17 three hundred twenty and t'.
19 t' thousand threescore and seven.
28 of Beth-azmaveth, forty and t'.
31 an hundred and twenty and t'.
33 men of the other Nebo, fifty and t'.
34 a thousand t' hundred fifty and four.
40 of Immer, a thousand fifty and t'.
41 a thousand t' hundred forty and seven.
60 were three hundred ninety and t'.
62 of Nekoda, six hundred forty and t'.
66 together was forty and t' thousand
67 t' hundred forty and five singing men
68 their mules, t' hundred forty and five:
71 drams of gold, and t' thousand
71 and t' hundred pound of silver.
72 gold, and t' thousand pound of silver,
11: 12 were eight hundred twenty and t':
Ne 11: 13 the fathers, t' hundred forty and
13 the fathers,...hundred forty and t':
18 were t' hundred fourscore and four.
19 were an hundred seventy and t'.
12: 31 t' great companies of them that
40 stood the t' companies of them that
13: 6 t' and thirtieth year of Artaxerxes
Es 2: 21 t' of the king's chamberlains,
6: 2 t' of the king's chamberlains, the
9: 27 keep these t' days according to
Job 13: 20 Only do not t' things unto me: then
42: 7 thee and against thy t' friends:
Pr 30: 7 T' things have I required of thee;
15 The horseleach hath t' daughters,
Ec 4: 9 T' are better than one; because
11 Again, if t' lie together, then they
12 against him, t' shall withstand him;
Ca 4: 5 Thy t' breasts are like t' young roes
6: 13 As it were the company of t' armies.
7: 3 Thy t' breasts are like t' young
8: 12 that keep the fruit thereof t' hundred.
Isa 7: 4 for the t' tails of these smoking
21 nourish a young cow, and t' sheep;
17: 6 t' or three berries in the top of the
22: 11 also a ditch between the t' walls for
36: 8 I will give thee t' thousand horses, if
45: 1 to open before him the t' leaved gates;
47: 9 these t' things shall come to thee
51: 19 These t' things are come unto thee;
Jer 2: 13 my people have committed t' evils;
3: 14 you one of a city, and t' of a family,
24: 1 t' baskets of figs were set before the
28: 3 Within t' full years will I bring again
11 within the space of t' full years.
33: 24 t' families...the Lord hath chosen,
52: 20 The t' pillars, one sea, and twelve
29 eight hundred thirty and t' persons:
Eze 1: 11 t' wings of every one were joined
11 and t' covered their bodies.
23, 23 every one had t', which covered
21: 19 son of man, appoint thee t' ways,
21 the way, at the head of the t' ways,
23: 2 there were t' women, the daughters
35: 10 hast said, These t' nations and
10 these t' countries shall be mine,
37: 22 they shall be no more t' nations,
22 they be divided into t' kingdoms
40: 9 and the posts thereof, t' cubits;
39 porch of the gate were t' tables on
39 this side, and t' tables on that side,
40 of the north gate, were t' tables;
40 porch of the gate, were t' tables.
41: 3 the post of the door, t' cubits;
18 and every cherub had t' faces;
22 and the length thereof t' cubits;
23 and the sanctuary had t' doors.
24 And the doors had t' leaves apiece,
24 leaves apiece, t' turning leaves;
24 t' leaves for the one door,
24 and t' leaves for the other door.
43: 14 to the lower settle shall be t' cubits,
45: 15 out of the flock, out of t' hundred,
46: 19 was a place on the t' sides westward.
47: 13 Israel: Joseph shall have t' portions.
48: 17 toward the north t' hundred and fifty,
17 toward the south t' hundred and fifty,
17 toward the east t' hundred and fifty,
17 toward the west t' hundred and fifty.
Da 5: 31 about threescore and t' years old.
8: 3 the river a ram which had t' horns:
3 the t' horns were high; but one was
6 came to the ram that had t' horns,
7 the ram, and brake his t' horns:
14 t' thousand and three hundred days;
20 ram...thou sawest having t' horns
9: 25 and threescore and t' weeks:
26 after threescore and t' weeks shall
12: 5 there stood other t', the one on this
11 thousand t' hundred and ninety days.
Ho 6: 2 After t' days will he revive us: in the
10: 10 themselves in their t' furrows.
Am 1: 1 Israel, t' years before the earthquake.
3: 3 Can t' walk together, except they
12 out of the mouth of the lion t' legs,
4: 8 So t' or three cities wandered unto
Zec 4: 3 t' olive trees by it, one upon the
11 What are these t' olive trees upon
12 What be these t' olive branches
12 through the t' golden pipes empty
14 These are the t' anointed ones,
5: 9 behold, there came out t' women,
6: 1 out from between t' mountains;
11: 7 And I took unto me t' staves; the
13: 8 t' parts therein shall be cut off and
M't 2: 16 from t' years old and under,
4: 18 saw t' brethren, Simon called
21 thence, he saw other t' brethren,
6: 24 No man can serve t' masters: for
8: 28 met him t' possessed with devils,
9: 27 t' blind men followed him, crying,
10: 10 neither t' coats, neither shoes, nor
29 t' sparrows sold for a farthing?
11: 2 Christ, he sent t' of his disciples,
14: 17 here but five loaves, and t' fishes.
19 the five loaves, and the t' fishes,
18: 8 having t' hands or t' feet to be cast
9 having t' eyes to be cast into hell
16 then take with thee one or t' more,
16 the mouth of t' or three witnesses
19 if t' of you shall agree on earth as
20 For where t' or three are gathered
20: 21 Grant that...my t' sons may sit,
24 indignation against the t' brethren.
30 t' blind men sitting by the way side,
21: 1 Olives, then sent Jesus t' disciples,
28 A certain man had t' sons; and he

M't 22:40 On these t' commandments hang
24:40 Then shall t' be in the field; the
41 T' women shall be grinding at the
25:15 he gave five talents, to another t',
17 likewise, he that had received t',
17 he also gained the other t'.
22 that had received t' talents came
22 thou deliveredst unto me t' talents:
22 I have gained t' other talents
26: 2 that after t' days is the feast of the
37 Peter and the t' sons of Zebedee,
60 At the last came t' false witnesses,
27:38 the t' thieves crucified with him,
M'r 5:13 (they were about t' thousand;)
6: 7 to send them forth by t' and t';
9 sandals; and not put on t' coats.
37 t' hundred pennyworth of bread,
38 knew, they say, Five, and t' fishes.
41 the five loaves and the t' fishes,
41 t' fishes divided he among them all.
9:43 than having t' hands to go into hell,
45 having t' feet to be cast into hell,
47 having t' eyes to be cast into hell
11: 1 he sendeth forth t' of his disciples,
4 in a place where t' ways met;
12:42 widow, and she threw in t' mites,
14: 1 After t' days was the feast of the
13 he sendeth forth t' of his disciples,
15:27 with him they crucify t' thieves;
16:12 in another form unto t' of them,
Lu 2:24 turtledoves, or t' young pigeons.
3:11 He that hath t' coats, let him impart
5: 2 saw t' ships standing by the lake:
7:19 calling unto him t' of his disciples
41 creditor which had t' debtors:
9: 3 neither have t' coats apiece.
13 more but five loaves and t' fishes;
16 took the five loaves and the t' fishes,
30 there talked with him t' men,
32 the t' men that stood with him.
10: 1 seventy others, and sent them t'
1 and sent them...t' before his face
35 he departed, he took out t' pence,
12: 6 five sparrows sold for t' farthings,
52 three against t', and t' against
15:11 he said, A certain man had t' sons:
16:13 No servant can serve t' masters:
17:34 there shall be t' men in one bed;
35 T' women shall be grinding
36 T' men shall be in the field; the
18:10 T' men went up into the temple to
19:29 Olives, he sent t' of his disciples,
21: 2 widow casting in thither t' mites.
22:38 Lord, behold, here are t' swords.
23:32 there were also t' other, malefactors,
24: 4 t' men stood by them in shining
13 t' of them went that same day to a
Joh 1:35 John stood, and t' of his disciples;
37 the t' disciples heard him speak,
40 One of the t' which heard John
2: 6 containing t' or three firkins apiece.
4:40 them: and he abode there t' days.
43 after t' days he departed thence,
6: 7 T' hundred pennyworth of bread
9 barley loaves, and t' small fishes:
8:17 that the testimony of t' men is true.

Joh 11: 6 he abode t' days still in the same
19:18 crucified him, and t' other with him,
20:12 And seeth t' angels in white sitting,
21: 2 and t' other of his disciples.
8 but as it were t' hundred cubits.)
Ac 1:10 t' men stood by them in white
23 they appointed t', Joseph called
24 of these t' thou hast chosen,
7:29 of Madian, where he begat t' sons.
9:38 they sent unto him t' men, desiring
10: 7 called t' of his household servants,
12: 6 was sleeping between t' soldiers,
6 bound with t' chains: and the
19:10 continued by the space of t' years;
22 he sent into Macedonia t' of them
34 the space of t' hours cried out,
21:33 him to be bound with t' chains;
23:23 he called unto him t' centurions,
23 Make ready t' hundred soldiers to
23 spearmen t' hundred, at the third
24:27 after t' years Porcius Festus came
27:37 t' hundred threescore and sixteen
41 into a place where t' seas met,
28:30 Paul dwelt t' whole years in his
1Co 6:16 for t', saith he, shall be one flesh.
14:27 let it be by t', or at the most by
29 Let the prophets speak t' or three,
2Co 13: 1 the mouth of t' or three witnesses
Ga 4:22 Abraham had t' sons, the one by a
24 for these are the t' covenants; the
Eph 5:31 wife, and they t' shall be one flesh.
Ph'p 1:23 For I am in a strait betwixt t',
1Ti 5:19 but before t' or three witnesses.
Heb 6:18 That by t' immutable things, in
10:28 mercy under t' or three witnesses:
Re 2:12 the sharp sword with t' edges;
9:12 there come t' woes more hereafter.
16 t' hundred thousand thousand:
11: 2 under foot forty and t' months.
3 give power unto my t' witnesses,
3 t' hundred and threescore days,
4 These are the t' olive trees, and
4 the t' candlesticks standing before
10 these t' prophets tormented them
12: 6 thousand t' hundred and threescore
14 given t' wings of a great eagle,
13: 5 to continue forty and t' months.
11 and he had t' horns like a lamb,

twoedged
Ps 149: 6 and a t' sword in their hand;
Pr 5: 4 wormwood, sharp as a t' sword.
Heb 4:12 and sharper than any t' sword,
Re 1:16 of his mouth went a sharp t' sword:

twofold
M't 23:15 make him t' more the child of hell

two-hundred See TWO and HUNDRED.

two-leaved See TWO and LEAVED.

two-thousand See TWO and THOUSAND.

Tychicus (*tik'-ik-us*)
Ac 20: 4 and of Asia, T' and Trophimus.
Eph 6:21 T', a beloved brother and faithful
subscr. Rome unto the Ephesians by T'.
Col 4: 7 All my state shall T' declare unto
subscr. from Rome to the Colossians by T'

2Ti 4:12 And T' have I sent to Ephesus.
Tit 3:12 send Artemas unto thee, or T',

Tyrannus (*ti-ran'-nus*)
Ac 19: 9 daily in the school of one T'.

Tyre (*tire*) See also TYRUS.
Jos 19:29 Ramah, and to the strong city T',
2Sa 5:11 Hiram king of T' sent messengers
24: 7 And came to the strong hold of T',
1Ki 5: 1 Hiram king of T' sent his servants
7:13 sent and fetched Hiram out of T'.
14 and his father was a man of T',
9:11 king of T' had furnished Solomon
12 Hiram came out from T' to see the
1Ch 14: 1 Hiram king of T' sent messengers
22: 4 they of T' brought much cedar
2Ch 2: 3 sent to Huram the king of T',
11 the king of T' answered in writing,
14 his father was a man of T', skilful
Ezr 3: 7 to them of T', to bring cedar trees
Ne 13:16 There dwelt men of T' also therein,
Ps 45:12 daughter of T' shall be there with
83: 7 with the inhabitants of T';
87: 4 Philistia, and T', with Ethiopia;
Isa 23: 1 The burden of T'. Howl, ye ships
5 be sorely pained at the report of T'.
8 hath taken this counsel against T',
15 T' shall be forgotten seventy years,
15 years shall T' sing as an harlot.
17 years, that the Lord will visit T',
Joe 3: 4 ye to do with me, O T', and Zidon,
M't 11:21 had been done in T' and Sidon,
22 be more tolerable for T' and Sidon
15:21 into the coasts of T' and Sidon.
M'r 3: 8 they about T' and Sidon, a great
7:24 into the borders of T' and Sidon,
31 departing from the coasts of T' and
Lu 6:17 from the sea coast of T' and Sidon,
10:13 works had been done in T' and
14 be more tolerable for T' and Sidon
Ac 12:20 highly displeased with them of T'
21: 3 sailed into Syria, and landed at T':
7 we had finished our course from T',

Tyrus (*ti'-rus*) See also TYRE.
Jer 25:22 And all the kings of T', and all the
27: 3 to the king of T', and to the king
47: 4 and to cut off from T' and Zidon
Eze 26: 2 T' hath said against Jerusalem,
3 I am against thee, O, T', and will
4 they shall destroy the walls of T',
7 will bring upon T' Nebuchadrezzar
15 Thus saith the Lord God to T';
27: 2 man, take up a lamentation for T',
3 say unto T', O thou that art situate
3 O T', thou hast said, I am of perfect
8 thy wise men, O T', that were in
32 saying, What city is like T', like
28: 2 of man, say unto the prince of T',
12 a lamentation upon the king of T
29:18 to serve a great service against T':
18 he no wages, nor his army, for T',
Ho 9:13 Ephraim, as I saw T', is planted in
Am 1: 9 For three transgressions of T', and
10 I will send a fire on the wall of T',
Zec 9: 2 T', and Zidon, though it be very
3 T' did build herself a strong hold.

U.

Ucal (*u'-cal*)
Pr 30: 1 Ithiel, even unto Ithiel and U'.

Uel (*u'-el*)
Ezr 10:34 of Bani: Maadai, Amram, and U',

Ulai (*u'-lahee*)
Da 8: 2 vision, and I was by the river of U'.
16 man's voice between the banks of U',

Ulam (*u'-lam*)
1Ch 7:16 and his sons were U' and Rakem.
17 And the sons of U'; Bedan. These
8:39 his brother were, U' his firstborn,
40 the sons of U' were mighty men of

Ulla (*ul'-lah*)
1Ch 7:39 And the sons of U'; Arah, and

Ummah (*um'-mah*)
Jos 19:30 U' also, and Aphek, and Rehob:

unaccustomed
Jer 31:18 as a bullock u' to the yoke:

unadvisedly
Ps 106:33 so that he spake u' with his lips.

unawares
Ge 31:20 Jacob stole away u' to Laban
26 thou hast stolen away u' to me,
Nu 35:11 which killeth any person at u'.
15 that killeth any person u' may flee
De 4:42 should kill his neighbour u',
Jos 20: 3 slayer that killeth any person u'
9 killeth any person at u' might flee
Ps 35: 8 destruction come upon him at u';
Lu 21:34 and so that day come upon you u'.
Ga 2: 4 of false brethren u' brought in,
Heb 13: 2 some have entertained angels u'.
Jude 4 there are certain men crept in u',

unbelief
M't 13:58 works there because of their u'.
17:20 said unto them, Because of your u':
M'r 6: 6 he marvelled because of their u'.
9:24 Lord, I believe; help thou mine u'.
16:14 upbraided them with their u' and
Ro 3: 3 shall their u' make the faith of God

Ro 4:20 at the promise of God through u';
11:20 because of u' they were broken off,
23 also, if they abide not still in u',
30 obtained mercy through their u':
32 God hath concluded them all in u',
1Ti 1:13 because I did it ignorantly in u'.
Heb 3:12 be in any of you an evil heart of u',
19 they could not enter in because of u
4: 6 entered not in because of u':
11 fall after the same example of u'.

unbelievers
Lu 12:46 him his portion with the u'.
1Co 6: 6 with brother, and that before the u
14:23 in those that are unlearned, or u',
2Co 6:14 unequally yoked together with u':

unbelieving
Ac 14: 2 the u' Jews stirred up the Gentiles,
1Co 7:14 the u' husband is sanctified by the
14 u' wife is sanctified by the husband
15 But if the u' depart, let him depart.
Tit 1:15 are defiled and u' is nothing pure;
Re 21: 8 But the fearful, and u', and the

unblameable
Col 1:22 to present you holy and u' and
1Th 3:13 stablish your hearts u' in holiness

unblameably
1Th 2:10 justly and u' we behaved ourselves

uncertain
1Co 14: 8 For if the trumpet gave an u' sound,
1Ti 6:17 nor trust in u' riches, but in the

uncertainly
1Co. 9:26 I therefore so run, not as u'; so fight

unchangeable
Heb 7:24 ever, hath an u' priesthood.

uncircumcised
Ge 17:14 And the u' man child whose flesh
34:14 give our sister to one that is u';
Ex 6:12 hear me, who am of u' lips?
30 I am of u' lips, and how shall
12:48 for no u' person shall eat thereof.

Le 19:23 shall count the fruit thereof as u':
23 three years shall it be as u' unto
26:41 if then their u' hearts be humbled,
Jos 5: 7 for they were u', because
J'g 14: 3 to take a wife of the u' Philistines?
15:18 and fall into the hand of the u'?
1Sa 14: 6 over unto the garrison of these u':
17:26 who is this u' Philistine, that he
36 this u' Philistine shall be as one of
31: 4 lest these u' come and thrust me
2Sa 1:20 the daughters of the u' triumph.
1Ch 10: 4 lest these u' come and abuse me.
Isa 52: 1 into thee the u' and the unclean.
Jer 6:10 ear is u', and they cannot hearken:
9:25 which are circumcised with the u',
26 for all these nations are u', and
26 house of Israel are u' in the heart.
Eze 28:10 Thou shalt die the deaths of the u'
31:18 thou shalt lie in the midst of the u'
32:19 down, and be thou laid with the u'.
21 they lie u', slain by the sword.
24 are gone down u' into the nether
25 All of them u', slain by the sword:
26 all of them u', slain by the sword,
27 the mighty that are fallen of the u',
28 be broken in the midst of the u',
29 they shall lie with the u', and with
30 and they lie u' with them that be
32 shall be laid in the midst of the u'
44: 7 u' in heart, and u' in flesh, to be
9 stranger, u' in heart, nor u' in flesh,
Ac 7:51 Ye stiffnecked and u' in heart and
11: 3 Thou wentest in to men u',
Ro 4:11 which he had yet being u':
12 which he had being yet u'.
1Co 7:18 let him not become u'.

uncircumcision
Ro 2:25 law, thy circumcision is made u'.
26 if the u' keep the righteousness
26 shall not his u' be counted for
27 And shall not u' which is by nature,
3:30 by faith, and u' through faith.
4: 9 or upon the u' also? for we say that
10 he was in circumcision, or in u'?

Ro 4:10 Not in circumcision, but in *u*.
1Co 7:18 Is any called in *u*? let him not be
19 is nothing, and *u* is nothing,
Ga 2: 7 gospel of the *u* was committed unto
5: 6 availeth any thing, nor *u*; but faith
6:15 availeth any thing, nor *u*, but a
Eph 2:11 who are called *U* by that which
Col 2:13 your sins and the *u* of your flesh,
3:11 Greek nor Jew, circumcision nor *u*,

uncle See also UNCLE'S.
Le 10: 4 the sons of Uzziel the *u* of Aaron,
25:49 Either his *u*, or his uncle's son,
1Sa 10:14 Saul's *u* said unto him and to his
15 Saul's *u* said, Tell me, I pray thee,
16 Saul said unto his *u*, He told us
14:50 Abner, the son of Ner, Saul's *u*.
1Ch 27:32 David's *u* was a counseller,
Es 2:15 of Abihail the *u* of Mordecai,
Jer 32: 7 Hanameel...thine *u* shall come
Am 6:10 And a man's *u* shall take him up,

unclean
Le 5: 2 Or if a soul touch any *u* thing,
2 whether it be a carcase of an *u* beast,
2 a carcase of *u* cattle, or the carcase
2 or the carcase of *u* creeping things,
2 he also shall be *u*, and guilty.
7:19 flesh that toucheth any *u* thing
21 soul that shall touch any *u* thing,
21 of man, or any *u* beast,
21 or any abominable *u* thing, and
10:10 unholy, and between *u* and clean;
11: 4, 5, 6 not the hoof; he is *u* unto you.
7 not the cud; he is *u* to you.
8 ye not touch; they are *u* to you.
24 And for these ye shall be *u*:
24 of them shall be *u* until the even.
25 his clothes, and be *u* until the even.
26 cheweth the cud, are *u* unto you:
26 that toucheth them shall be *u*.
27 on all four, those are *u* unto you:
27 carcase shall be *u* until the even.
28 clothes, and be *u* until the even:
28 the even: they are *u* unto you:
29 shall be *u* unto you among the
31 are *u* to you among all that creep:
31 be dead, shall be *u* until the even.
32 are dead, doth fall, it shall be *u*;
32 and it shall be *u* until the even;
33 whatsoever is in it shall be *u*;
34 such water cometh shall be *u*:
34 in every such vessel shall be *u*.
35 their carcase falleth shall be *u*;
35 are *u*, and shall be *u* unto you.
36 toucheth their carcase shall be *u*.
38 thereon, it shall be *u* unto you.
39 thereof shall be *u* until the even.
40 clothes, and be *u* until the even:
40 clothes, and be *u* until the even.
43 ye make yourselves *u* with them,
47 a difference between the *u* and
12: 2 then she shall be *u* seven days;
2 for her infirmity shall she be *u*.
5 then she shall be *u* two weeks,
13: 3 on him, and pronounce him *u*.
8 the priest shall pronounce him *u*:
11 the priest shall pronounce him *u*,
11 shall not shut him up: for he is *u*.
14 appeareth in him, he shall be *u*.
15 flesh, and pronounce him to be *u*:
15 for the raw flesh is *u*: it is a
20, 22, 25, 27, 30 pronounce him *u*:
36 not seek for yellow hair; he is *u*.
44 He is a leprous man, he is *u*:
44 shall pronounce him utterly *u*;
45 upper lip, and shall cry, *U*, *u*.
46 him he shall be defiled; he is *u*:
51 plague is a fretting leprosy; it is *u*.
55 the plague be not spread; it is *u*:
59 it clean, or to pronounce it *u*.
14:36 that is in the house be not made *u*:
40 shall cast them into an *u* place
41 without the city into an *u* place:
44 leprosy in the house: it is *u*.
45 out of the city into an *u* place.
46 shut up shall be *u* until the even.
57 To teach when it is *u*, and when
15: 2 flesh, because of his issue he is *u*.
4 he lieth that hath the issue, is *u*:
4 whereon he sitteth, shall be *u*.
5, 6, 7, 8 and be *u* until the even.
9 that hath the issue shall be *u*.
10 him shall be *u* until the even:
10, 11, 16, 17, 18 be *u* until the even.
19 toucheth her shall be *u* until the
20 upon in her separation shall be *u*:
20 also that she sitteth upon shall be *u*.
21, 22 and be *u* until the even.
23 it, he shall be *u* until the even.
24 him, he shall be *u* seven days;
24 bed whereon he lieth shall be *u*.
25 of her separation: she shall be *u*.
26 she sitteth upon shall be *u*,
27 toucheth those things shall be *u*,
27 in water, and be *u* until the even.
33 him that lieth with her that is *u*.
17:15 in water, and be *u* until the even:
20:21 brother's wife, it is an *u* thing:
25 between clean beasts and *u*,
25 and between *u* fowls and clean:
25 I have separated from you as *u*.
22: 4 toucheth any thing that is *u* by
5 whereby he may be made *u*, or a
6 hath touched any such shall be *u*
27:11 if it be any *u* beast, of which they
27 if it be of an *u* beast, then he shall
Nu 6: 7 not make himself *u* for his father,
9:10 be *u* by reason of a dead body,
18:15 the firstling of *u* beasts shalt
19: 7 priest shall be *u* until the even.
8 and shall be *u* until the even.
10 clothes, and be *u* until the even:
11 any man shall be *u* seven days.
13 upon him, he shall be *u*;
14 in the tent, shall be *u* seven days.
15 no covering bound upon it, is *u*.
16 or a grave, shall be *u* seven days.
17 for an *u* person they shall take of
19 shall sprinkle upon the *u* on the
20 But the man that shall be *u*, and
20 sprinkled upon him; he is *u*.
21 separation shall be *u* until even.
22 whatsoever the *u* person toucheth
22 person toucheth shall be *u*;
22 toucheth it shall be *u* until even.
De 12:15 *u* and the clean may eat thereof,
22 the *u* and the clean shall eat of
14: 7 therefore they are *u* unto you.
8 not the cud, it is *u* unto you:
10 ye may not eat; it is *u* unto you.
19 creeping thing that flieth is *u* unto
15:22 *u* and the clean person shall eat
23:14 that he see no *u* thing in thee,
26:14 away ought thereof for any *u* use,
Jos 22:19 if the land of your possession be *u*,
J'g 13: 4 drink, and eat not any *u* thing:
7 drink, neither eat any *u* thing:
14 strong drink, nor eat any *u* thing:
2Ch 23:19 none which was *u* in any thing
Ezr 9:11 an *u* land with the filthiness of
Job 14: 4 bring a clean thing out of an *u*?
36:14 and their life is among the *u*.
Ec 9: 2 and to the clean, and to the *u*;
Isa 6: 5 because I am a man of *u* lips, and
5 in the midst of a people of *u* lips:
35: 8 the *u* shall not pass over it; but it
52: 1 thee the uncircumcised and the *u*.
11 out from thence, touch no *u* thing;
64: 6 But we are all as an *u* thing, and
La 4:15 unto them, Depart ye; it is *u*;
Eze 22:26 between the *u* and the clean,
44:23 between the *u* and the clean.
Hos 9: 3 they shall eat *u* things in Assyria.
Hag 2:13 If one that is *u* by a dead body
13 touch any of these, shall it be *u*?
13 answered and said, It shall be *u*.
14 that which they offer there is *u*.
Zec 13: 2 *u* spirit to pass out of the land.
M't 10: 1 gave them power against *u* spirits,
12:43 the *u* spirit is gone out of a man,
M'r 1:23 synagogue a man with an *u* spirit;
26 And when the *u* spirit had torn him,
27 commandeth he even the *u* spirits,
3:11 *u* spirits, when they saw him, fell
30 they said, He hath an *u* spirit.
5: 2 of the tombs a man with an *u* spirit,
8 Come out of the man, thou *u* spirit.
13 the *u* spirits went out, and entered
6: 7 gave them power over *u* spirits;
7:25 young daughter had an *u* spirit,
Lu 4:33 which had a spirit of an *u* devil,
36 power he commandeth the *u* spirits,
6:18 that were vexed with *u* spirits:
8:29 commanded the *u* spirit to come
9:42 Jesus rebuked the *u* spirit, and
11:24 the *u* spirit is gone out of a man,
Ac 5:16 which were vexed with *u* spirits:
8: 7 For *u* spirits, crying with loud voice,
10:14 any thing that is common or *u*.
28 not call any man common or *u*.
11: 8 nothing common or *u* hath at any
Ro 14:14 that there is nothing *u* of itself:
14 any thing to be *u*, to him it is *u*.
1Co 7:14 else were your children *u*; but
2Co 6:17 Lord, and touch not the *u* thing;
Eph 5: 5 nor *u* person, nor covetous man,
Heb 9:13 of an heifer sprinkling the *u*,
Re 16:13 I saw three *u* spirits like frogs
18: 2 a cage of every *u* and hateful bird.

uncleanness See also UNCLEANNESSES.
Le 5: 3 Or if he touch the *u* of man,
3 whatsoever *u* it be that a man
7:20 the Lord, having his *u* upon him,
21 as the *u* of man, or any unclean
14:19 that is to be cleansed from his *u*;
15: 3 And this shall be his *u* in his issue:
3 stopped from his issue, it is his *u*.
25 all the days of the issue of her *u*
26 unclean, as the *u* of her separation.
30 the Lord for the issue of her *u*.
31 the children of Israel from their *u*;
31 they die not in their *u*, when they
16:16 of the *u* of the children of Israel,
16 among them in the midst of their *u*.
19 from the *u* of the children of Israel.
18:19 as she is put apart for her *u*.
22: 3 having his *u* upon him, that soul
5 or a man of whom he may take *u*,
5 whatsoever *u* he hath;
Nu 5:19 if thou hast not gone aside to *u*.
19:13 be unclean; his *u* is yet upon him.
De 23:10 reason of *u* that chanceth him by
24: 1 he hath found some *u* in her:
2Sa 11: 4 for she was purified from her *u*:
2Ch 29:16 out all the *u* that they found
Ezr 9:11 from end to another with their *u*.
Eze 36:17 me as the *u* of a removed woman.
39:24 According to their *u* and according
Zec 13: 1 of Jerusalem for sin and for *u*.
M't 23:27 of dead men's bones, and of all *u*.
Ro 1:24 God also gave them up to *u* through
6:19 yielded your members servants to *u*
2Co 12:21 and have not repented of the *u* and
Ga 5:19 are these; Adultery, fornication, *u*,
Eph 4:19 to work all *u* with greediness.
5: 3 But fornication, and all *u*, or
Col 3: 5 upon the earth; fornication, *u*,
1Th 2: 3 not of deceit, nor of *u*, nor in guile:
4: 7 For God hath not called us unto *u*,
2Pe 2:10 after the flesh in the lust of *u*,

uncleannesses
Eze 36:29 will also save you from all your *u*:

uncle's
Le 20:20 if a man shall lie with his *u* wife,
20 hath uncovered his *u* nakedness:
25:49 Either his uncle, or his *u* son, may
Es 2: 7 that is, Esther his *u* daughter:
Jer 32: 8 Hanameel mine *u* son came to me
9 the field of Hanameel my *u* son,
12 the sight of Hanameel mine *u* son,

unclothed
2Co 5: 4 not for that we would be *u*, but

uncomely
1Co 7:36 behaveth himself *u* toward a virgin,
12:23 our *u* parts have more abundant

uncondemned
Ac 16:37 They have beaten us openly *u*,
22:25 a man that is a Roman, and *u*?

uncorruptible See also INCORRUPTIBLE.
Ro 1:23 changed the glory of the *u* God

uncorruptness
Tit 2: 7 in doctrine shewing *u*, gravity,

uncover See also UNCOVERED; UNCOVERETH.
Le 10: 6 *U* not your heads, neither rend
18: 6 kin to him, to *u* their nakedness:
7 of thy mother, shalt thou not *u*:
7 thou shalt not *u* her nakedness.
8 thy father's wife shalt thou not *u*:
9, 10 nakedness thou shalt not *u*.
11 thou shalt not *u* her nakedness.
12 not *u* the nakedness of thy father's
13 *u* the nakedness of thy mother's
14 not *u* the nakedness of thy father's
15 *u* the nakedness of thy daughter
15 thou shalt not *u* her nakedness.
16 *u* the nakedness of thy brother's
17 not *u* the nakedness of a woman
17 daughter, to *u* her nakedness;
18 to vex her, to *u* her nakedness,
19 unto a woman to *u* her nakedness,
20:18 her sickness, and shall *u* her
19 *u* the nakedness of thy mother's
21:10 shall not *u* his head, nor rend his
Nu 5:18 Lord, and *u* the woman's head,
Ru 3: 4 and *u* his feet, and lay thee down;
Isa 47: 2 and grind meal: *u* thy locks,
2 make bare the leg, *u* the thigh,
Zep 2:14 for he shall *u* the cedar work.

uncovered
Ge 9:21 and he was *u* within his tent.
Le 20:11 wife hath *u* his father's nakedness:
17 he hath *u* his sister's nakedness:
18 and she hath *u* the fountain of her
20 he hath *u* his uncle's nakedness:
21 he hath *u* his brother's nakedness:
Ru 3: 7 and *u* his feet, and laid her down.
2Sa 6:20 who *u* himself to day in the eyes of
Isa 20: 4 foot, even with their buttocks *u*,
22: 6 horsemen, and Kir *u* the shield.
47: 3 Thy nakedness shall be *u*, yea,
Jer 49:10 bare, I have *u* his secret places,
Eze 4: 7 thine arm shall be *u*, and thou
Hab 2:16 also, and let thy foreskin be *u*:
M'r 2: 4 they *u* the roof where he was:
1Co 11: 5 or prophesieth with her head *u*
13 that a woman pray unto God *u*?

uncovereth
Le 20:19 sister; for he *u* his near kin:
De 27:20 because he *u* his father's skirt:
2Sa 6:20 fellows shamelessly *u* himself!

unction
1Jo 2:20 ye have an *u* from the Holy One,

undefiled
Ps 119: 1 Blessed are the *u* in the way,
Ca 5: 2 sister, my love, my dove, my *u*:
6: 9 My dove, my *u* is but one; she is
Heb 7:26 who is holy, harmless, *u*, separate
13: 4 is honourable in all, and the bed *u*:
Jas 1:27 Pure religion and *u* before God
1Pe 1: 4 an inheritance incorruptible, and *u*,

under^A See also UNDERGIRDING; UNDERNEATH; UNDERSETTERS; UNDERSTAND; UNDERTAKE.
Ge 1: 7 which were *u* the firmament
9 waters *u* the heaven be gathered
6:17 the breath of life, from *u* heaven;
7:19 hills, that were *u* the whole heaven,
16: 9 and submit thyself *u* her hands.
18: 4 and rest yourselves *u* the tree:
8 and he stood by them *u* the tree,
19: 8 came they *u* the shadow of my roof.
21:15 cast the child *u* one of the shrubs.
35: 4 Jacob hid them *u* the oak which
8 buried beneath Beth-el *u* an oak:
39:23 to any thing that was *u* his hand;
41:35 lay up corn *u* the hand of Pharaoh,
47:29 I pray thee, thy hand *u* my thigh,
49:25 blessings of the deep that lieth *u*,
Ex 6: 6, 7 out from *u* the burdens of the
17:12 they took a stone, and put it *u* him,
14 of Amalek from *u* heaven.
18:10 from *u* the hand of the Egyptians.

Ex 20: 4 or that is in the water u' the earth:
21: 20 with a rod, and he die u' his hand;
23: 5 hateth thee lying u' his burden,
24: 4 and builded an altar u' the hill,
10 and there was u' his feet as it were
25: 35, 35, 35 u' two branches of the same,
26: 19 of silver u' the twenty boards;
19 two sockets u' one board for his
19 two sockets u' another board for
21 of silver; two sockets u' one board,
21 and two sockets u' another board.
25 two sockets u' one board, and two
25 and two sockets u' another board.
33 hang up the vail u' the taches,
30: 4 thou make to it u' the crown of it,
36: 24 he made u' the twenty boards;
24 two sockets u' one board for his
24 two sockets u' another board for
26 two sockets u' one board, and two
26 and two sockets u' another board.
30 silver, u' every board two sockets.
37: 21, 21, 21 u' two branches of the same,
27 of gold for it u' the crown thereof,
38: 4 grate of network u' the compass
Le 15: 10 any thing that was u' him shall be
22: 27 it shall be seven days u' the dam;
27: 32 of whatsoever passeth u' the rod,
Nu 3: 36 u' the custody and charge of the sons
4: 28, 33 u' the hand of Ithamar the son of
6: 18 in the fire which is u' the sacrifice
7: 8 u' the hand of Ithamar the son of
16: 31 clave asunder that was u' them:
22: 27 the Lord, she fell down u' Balaam:
31: 49 men of war which are u' our charge,
33: 1 u' the hand of Moses and Aaron.
De 2: 25 that are u' the whole heaven.
3: 17 sea, u' Ashdoth-pisgah eastward.
4: 11 near and stood u' the mountain;
19 all nations u' the whole heaven.
49 the plain, u' the springs of Pisgah.
7: 24 destroy their name from u' heaven:
9: 14 out their name from u' heaven:
12: 2 the hills, and u' every green tree:
25: 19 of Amalek from u' heaven;
28: 23 earth that is u' thee shall be iron.
29: 20 blot out his name from u' heaven.
Jos 7: 21 of my tent, and the silver u' it.
22 hid in his tent, and the silver u' it.
11: 3 to the Hivite u' Hermon in the land
17 of Lebanon u' mount Hermon:
12: 3 from the south, u' Ashdoth-pisgah:
13: 5 from Baal-gad u' mount Hermon
16: 10 unto this day, and serve u' tribute.
24: 26 and set it up there u' an oak,
J'g 1: 7 gathered their meat u' my table:
3: 16 he did gird it u' his raiment upon
30 that day u' the hand of Israel.
4: 5 dwelt u' the palm tree of Deborah
6: 11 sat u' an oak which was in Ophrah,
19 brought it out unto him u' the oak,
9: 29 to God this people were u' my hand!
Ru 2: 12 u' whose wings thou art come to
1Sa 7: 11 them, until they came u' Beth-car.
14: 2 u' a pomegranate tree which is in
21: 3 therefore what is u' thine hand?
4 is no common bread u' mine hand,
8 here u' thine hand spear or sword?
22: 6 abode in Gibeah u' a tree in Ramah,
31: 13 buried them u' a tree at Jabesh,
2Sa 2: 23 spear smote him u' the fifth rib,
3: 27 and smote him there u' the fifth rib,
4: 6 they smote him u' the fifth rib:
12: 31 were therein, and put them u' saws,
31 u' harrows of iron, and u' axes of iron,
18: 2 part of the people u' the hand of Joab,
2 third part u' the hand of Abishai the
2 third part u' the hand of Ittai the
9 the mule went u' the thick boughs
9 the mule that was u' him went away.
22: 10 and darkness was u' his feet.
37 Thou hast enlarged my steps u' me;
39 yea, they are fallen u' my feet.
40 me hast thou subdued u' me.
48 bringeth down the people u' me,
1Ki 4: 25 man u' his vine and u' his fig tree,
5: 3 put them u' the soles of his feet.
7: 24 u' the brim of it round about there
30 u' the laver were undersetters
32 u' the borders were four wheels;
44 sea, and twelve oxen u' the sea;
8: 6 u' the wings of the cherubims.
13: 14 and found him sitting u' an oak:
14: 23 high hill, and u' every green tree.
18: 23, 23 lay it on wood, and put no fire u':
25 of your gods, but put no fire u'.
19: 4 and sat down u' a juniper tree:
5 he lay and slept u' a juniper tree,
2Ki 8: 20, 22 Edom revolted from u' the hand
9: 13 it u' him on the top of the stairs,
33 the horses: and he trode her u' foot.
13: 5 they went out from u' the hand of
14: 27 the name of Israel from u' heaven:
16: 4 the hills, and u' every green tree.
17 off the brasen oxen that were u' it,
17: 7 from u' the hand of Pharaoh king
10 high hill, and u' every green tree:
1Ch 10: 12 their bones u' the oak in Jabesh,
17: 1 the ark...remaineth u' curtains.
24: 19 their manner, u' Aaron their father,
25: 2 the sons of Asaph u' the hands of
3 six, u' the hands of their father
6 were u' the hands of their father
26: 28 it was u' the hand of Shelomith,
27: 23 from twenty years old and u':
2Ch 4: 3 u' it was the similitude of oxen,
15 One sea, and twelve oxen u' it.

2Ch 5: 7 even u' the wings of the cherubims:
13: 18 Israel were brought u' at that time,
21: 8 revolted from u' the dominion of
10 revolted from u' the hand of Judah
10 did Libnah revolt from u' his hand;
26: 11 u' the hand of Hananiah, one of
13 And u' their hand was an army,
28: 4 the hills, and u' every green tree.
10 to keep u' the children of Judah
31: 13 overseers u' the hand of Cononiah
Ne 2: 14 the beast that was u' me to pass.
8: 17 made booths, and sat u' the booths:
Job 9: 13 proud helpers do stoop u' him.
20: 12 though he hide it u' his tongue;
26: 5 are formed from u' the waters,
8 and the cloud is not rent u' them.
28: 5 u' it is turned up as it were fire.
24 and seeth u' the whole heaven;
30: 7 u' the nettles they were gathered
37: 3 He directeth it u' the whole heaven,
40: 21 He lieth u' the shady trees, in the
41: 11 whatsover is u' the whole heaven is
30 Sharp stones are u' him: he
Ps 8: 6 thou hast put all things u' his feet:
10: 7 u' his tongue is mischief and
17: 8 hide me u' the shadow of thy wings,
18: 9 and darkness was u' his feet.
36 Thou hast enlarged my steps u' me,
38 to rise: they are fallen u' my feet.
39 subdued u' me those that rose up
36: 7 their trust u' the shadow of thy wings.
44: 5 we tread them u' that rise up against
45: 5 whereby the people fall u' thee.
47: 3 He shall subdue the people u' us,
3 and the nations u' our feet.
91: 1 shall abide u' the shadow of the
4 and u' his wings shalt thou trust:
13 dragon shalt thou trample u' feet.
106: 42 into subjection u' their hand.
140: 3 adders' poison is u' their lips.
144: 2 who subdueth my people u' me.
Pr 12: 24 but the slothful shall be u' tribute.
22: 27 take away thy bed from u' thee?
Ec 1: 3 labour which he taketh u' the sun?
9 there is no new thing u' the sun.
13 all things that are done u' heaven:
14 the works that are done u' the sun;
2: 3 they should do u' the heaven all the
11 and there was no profit u' the sun.
17 work that is wrought u' the sun is
18 which I had taken u' the sun:
19 shewed myself wise u' the sun.
20 the labour which I took u' the sun.
22 he hath laboured u' the sun?
3: 16 u' the sun the place of judgment,
4: 1 that are done u' the sun:
3 evil work that is done u' the sun.
7 and I saw vanity u' the sun.
15 the living which walk u' the sun,
5: 13 evil which I have seen u' the sun,
18 labour that he taketh u' the sun
6: 1 evil which I have seen u' the sun,
12 what shall be after him u' the sun?
7: 6 the crackling of thorns u' the pot,
8: 9 every work that is done u' the sun:
15 hath no better thing u' the sun,
15 which God giveth him u' the sun.
17 the work that is done u' the sun:
9: 3 all things that are done u' the sun,
6 any thing that is done u' the sun.
9 he hath given thee u' the sun, all
9 labour...thou takest u' the sun.
11 and saw u' the sun, that the race is
13 wisdom have I seen also u' the sun,
10: 5 evil which I have seen u' the sun,
Ca 2: 3 I sat down u' his shadow with great
6 His left hand is u' my head, and
4: 11 honey and milk are u' thy tongue;
8: 3 His left hand should be u' my head,
5 I raised thee up u' the apple tree:
Isa 3: 6 and let this ruin be u' thy hand:
10: 4 shall bow down u' the prisoners,
4 they shall fall u' the slain. For all
16 and u' his glory he shall kindle a
14: 11 the worm is spread u' thee, and
19 pit; as a carcase trodden u' feet.
25 my mountains tread him u' foot:
18: 7 meted out and trodden u' foot,
24: 5 also is defiled u' the inhabitants
25: 10 Moab shall be trodden down u' him,
28: 3 of Ephraim, shall be trodden u' feet:
15 u' falsehood have we hid ourselves:
34: 15 and hatch, and gather u' her shadow:
57: 5 with idols u' every green tree,
5 valleys u' the clifts of the rocks?
58: 5 spread sackcloth and ashes u' him?
Jer 2: 20 high hill and u' every green tree
3: 6 and u' every green tree, and
13 the strangers u' every green tree,
10: 11 earth, and from u' these heavens.
12: 10 have trodden my portion u' foot,
27: 8 will not put their neck u' the yoke
11 that bring their neck u' the yoke
12 your necks u' the yoke of the king
33: 13 pass again u' the hands of him
38: 11 of the king u' the treasury,
12 rags u' thine armholes u' the cords.
48: 45 fled stood u' the shadow of Heshbon
52: 20 bulls that were u' the bases,
La 1: 15 trodden u' foot all my mighty men
3: 34 crush u' his feet all the prisoners
66 them in anger from u' the heavens
4: 20 U his shadow we shall live among
5: 5 Our necks are u' persecution: we
13 and the children fell u' the wood.
Eze 1: 8 the hands of a man u' their wings

Eze 1: 23 u' the firmament were their wings
6: 13 mountains, and u' every green tree,
13 u' every thick oak, the place where
10: 2 even u' the cherub, and fill
8 of a man's hand u' their wings.
20 creature that I saw u' the God of
21 hands of a man was u' their wings.
17: 6 and the roots thereof were u' him:
23 u' it shall dwell all fowl of every
20: 37 I will cause you to pass u' the rod,
24: 5 and burn also the bones u' it, and
31: 6 u' his branches did all the beasts
6 and u' his shadow dwelt all great
17 that dwelt u' his shadow in the midst
32: 27 laid their swords u' their heads,
42: 9 u' these chambers was the entry
46: 23 with boiling places u' the rows
47: 1 issued out from u' the threshold
1 the waters came down from u'
Da 4: 12 beasts of...field had shadow u' it,
14 let the beasts get away from u' it,
21 u' which the beasts of the field
7: 27 the kingdom u' the whole heaven,
8: 13 and the host to be trodden u' foot?
9: 12 for u' the whole heaven hath not
Ho 4: 12 gone a whoring from u' their God.
13 u' oaks and poplars and elms,
14: 7 They that dwell u' his shadow shall
Joe 1: 17 The seed is rotten u' their clods,
Am 2: 13 I am pressed u' you, as a cart is
Ob 7 bread have laid a wound u' thee:
Jon 4: 5 booth, and sat u' it in the shadow,
Mic 1: 4 mountains shall be molten u' him,
4: 4 man u' his vine and u' his fig tree;
Zec 3: 10 u' the vine and u' the fig tree.
Mal 4: 3 be ashes u' the soles of your feet
M't 2: 16 from two years old and u',
5: 13 and to be trodden u' foot of men.
15 a candle, and put it u' a bushel,
7: 6 they trample them u' their feet,
8: 8 thou shouldest come u' my roof:
9 For I am a man u' authority,
9 having soldiers u' me: and I say
23: 37 her chickens u' her wings, and
M'r 4: 21 to be put u' a bushel, or u' a bed?
32 air may lodge u' the shadow of it.
6: 11 shake off the dust u' your feet for
7: 28 yet the dogs u' the table eat of the
Lu 7: 6 thou shouldest enter u' my roof:
8 I also am a man set u' authority,
8 having u' me soldiers, and I say
8: 16 a vessel, or putteth it u' a bed;
11: 33 neither u' a bushel, but on a
13: 34 gather her brood u' her wings,
17: 24 out of the one part u' heaven,
24 unto the other part u' heaven;
Joh 1: 48 when thou wast u' the fig tree, I
50 thee, I saw thee u' the fig tree,
Ac 2: 5 out of every nation u' heaven.
4: 12 none other name u' heaven given
8: 27 of a great authority u' Candace queen
23: 12 and bound themselves u' a curse,
14 bound ourselves u' a great curse,
27: 4 we sailed u' Cyprus, because the
7 we sailed u' Crete, over against
16 running u' a certain island which
30 u' colour as though they would have
Ro 3: 9 Gentiles, that they are all u' sin;
13 the poison of asps is u' their lips:
19 saith to them who are u' the law:
6: 14 ye are not u' the law, but u' grace.
15 we are not u' the law, but u' grace?
7: 14 but I am carnal, sold u' sin.
16: 20 bruise Satan u' your feet shortly.
1Co 6: 12 not be brought u' the power of any.
7: 15 sister is not u' bondage in such cases:
9: 20 that are u' the law, as u' the law,
20 gain them that are u' the law;
21 to God, but u' the law to Christ,)
27 I keep u' my body, and bring it
10: 1 all our fathers were u' the cloud,
14: 34 commanded to be u' obedience,
15: 25, 27 hath put all enemies u' his feet.
27 he saith all things are put u' him,
27 which did put all things u' him.
28 unto him that put all things u' him,
2Co 11: 32 the governor u' Aretas the king
Ga 3: 10 works of the law are u' the curse:
22 hath concluded all u' sin, that
23 faith came, we were kept u' the law,
25 we are no longer u' a schoolmaster.
4: 2 is u' tutors and governors until the
3 u' the elements of the world;
4 made of a woman, made u' the law,
5 redeem them that were u' the law,
21 ye that desire to be u' the law, do ye
5: 18 of the Spirit, ye are not u' the law.
Eph 1: 22 And hath put all things u' his feet,
Ph'p 2: 10 in earth, and things u' the earth,
Col 1: 23 every creature which is u' heaven;
1Ti 5: 9 number u' threescore years old,
6: 1 servants as are u' the yoke count
Heb 2: 8 all things in subjection u' his feet.
8 he put all in subjection u' him,
8 left nothing that is not put u' him.
8 see not yet all things put u' him.
7: 11 u' it the people received the law,)
9: 15 the transgressions that were u' the
10: 28 mercy u' two or three witnesses:
29 trodden u' foot the Son of God,
Jas 2: 3 there, or sit here u' my footstool:
1Pe 5: 6 u' the mighty hand of God,
Jude 6 in everlasting chains u' darkness
Re 5: 3 nor in earth, neither u' the earth,
13 and on the earth, and u' the earth,
6: 9 I saw u' the altar the souls of them

Re 11: 2 shall they tread *u·* foot forty and two
12: 1 the sun, and the moon *u·* her feet,

undergirding
Ac 27:17 up, they used helps, *u·* the ship;

underneath
Ex 28:27 on the two sides of the ephod *u·*.
39:20 on the two sides of the ephod *u·*,
De 33:27 *u·* are the everlasting arms:

undersetters
1Ki 7:30 the four corners thereof had *u·*:
30 under the laver were *u·* molten,
34 were four *u·* to the four corners
34 the *u·* were of the very base itself.

understand See also UNDERSTANDEST; UNDERSTANDETH; UNDERSTANDING; UNDERSTOOD.
Ge 11: 7 may not *u·* one another's speech.
41:15 canst *u·* a dream to interpret it:
Nu 16:30 *u·* that these men have provoked
De 9: 3 *U·* therefore this day, that the Lord
6 *U·* therefore, that the Lord thy
28:49 whose tongue thou shalt not *u·*;
2Ki 18:26 the Syrian language; for we *u·* it:
1Ch 28:19 Lord made me *u·* in writing by his
Ne 8: 3 women, and those that could *u·*;
7 caused the people to *u·* the law:
8 and caused them to *u·* the reading.
13 even to *u·* the words of the law.
Job 6:24 me to *u·* wherein I have erred.
23: 5 and *u·* what he would say unto me.
26:14 thunder of his power who can *u·*?
32: 9 neither do the aged *u·* judgment.
36:29 any *u·* the spreadings of the clouds,
Ps 14: 2 see if there were any that did *u·*,
19:12 Who can *u·* his errors? cleanse
53: 2 see if there were any that did *u·*,
82: 5 They knew not, neither will they *u·*;
92: 6 not; neither doth a fool *u·* this.
94: 8 *U·*, ye brutish among the people:
107:43 *u·* the lovingkindness of the Lord.
119:27 to *u·* the way of thy precepts:
100 I *u·* more than the ancients, because
Pr 1: 6 To *u·* a proverb, and the
2: 5 shalt thou *u·* the fear of the Lord,
9 Then shalt thou *u·* righteousness,
8: 5 O ye simple, *u·* wisdom: and, ye
14: 8 of the prudent is to *u·* his way:
19:25 and he will *u·* knowledge.
20:24 how can a man then *u·* his own way?
28: 5 Evil men *u·* not judgment: but they
5 they that seek the Lord *u·* all things.
29:19 for though he *u·* he will not answer.
Isa 6: 9 people, Hear ye indeed, but *u·* not;
10 and *u·* with the heart, and convert,
28: 9 whom shall he make to *u·* doctrine?
19 be a vexation only to *u·* the report.
32: 4 also of the rash shall *u·* knowledge,
33:19 tongue, that thou canst not *u·*.
36:11 the Syrian language; for we *u·* it:
41:20 and consider, and *u·* together,
43:10 believe me, and *u·* that I am he:
44:18 their hearts, that they cannot *u·*.
56:11 they are shepherds that cannot *u·*:
Jer 9:12 is the wise man, that may *u·* this?
Eze 3: 6 whose words thou canst not *u·*.
Da 8:16 make this man to *u·* the vision.
17 he said unto me, *U·*, O son of man:
9:13 our iniquities, and *u·* thy truth.
23 therefore *u·* the matter, and
25 Know therefore and *u·*, that from
10:11 *u·* the words that I speak unto thee,
12 that thou didst set thine heart to *u·*,
14 make thee *u·* what shall befall thy
11:33 they that *u·* among the people
12:10 and none of the wicked shall *u·*;
10 but the wise shall *u·*.
Ho 4:14 people that doth not *u·* shall fall.
14: 9 is wise, and he shall *u·* these things?
Mic 4:12 Lord, neither *u·* they his counsel:
M't 13:13 they hear not, neither do they *u·*.
14 ye shall hear, and shall not *u·*;
15 and should *u·* with their heart, and
15:10 and said unto them, Hear, and *u·*:
17 Do not ye yet *u·*, that whatsoever
16: 9 Do ye not yet *u·*, neither remember
11 How is it that ye do not *u·* that I
24:15 place, (whoso readeth, let him *u·*:)
M'r 4:12 hearing they may hear, and not *u·*;
7:14 unto me every one of you, and *u·*:
8:17 perceive ye not yet, neither *u·*? have
21 them, How is it that ye do not *u·*?
13:14 (let him that readeth *u·*,) then let
14:68 not, neither *u·* I what thou sayest.
Lu 8:10 see, and hearing they might not *u·*.
24:45 that they might *u·* the scriptures,
Joh 8:43 Why do ye not *u·* my speech? even
12:40 nor *u·* with their heart, and be
Ac 24:11 Because that thou mayest *u·*, that
28:26 ye shall hear, and shall not *u·*;
27 *u·* with their heart, and should be
Ro 15:21 they that have not heard shall *u·*.
1Co 12: 3 Wherefore I give you to *u·*, that no
13: 2 of prophecy, and *u·* all mysteries.
Eph 3: 4 *u·* my knowledge in mystery of
Ph'p 1:12 I would ye should *u·*, brethren,
Heb11: 3 Through faith we *u·* that the
2Pe 2:12 speak evil of things that they *u·* not;

understandest
Job 15: 9 what *u·* thou, which is not in us?
Ps 139: 2 thou *u·* my thought afar off.
Jer 5:15 not, neither *u·* what they say.
Ac 8:30 said, *U·* thou what thou readest?

understandeth
1Ch 28: 9 and *u·* all the imaginations of the
Job 28:23 God *u·* the way thereof, and he
Ps 49:20 Man that is in honour, and *u·* not,
Pr 8: 9 They are all plain to him that *u·*,
14: 6 knowledge is easy unto him that *u·*.
Jer 9:24 that he *u·* and knoweth me, that I
M't 13:19 word of the kingdom, and *u·* it not,
23 he that heareth the word, and *u·* it;
Ro 3:11 There is none that *u·*, there is none
1Co 14: 2 for no man *u·* him; howbeit in the
16 seeing he *u·* not what thou sayest?

understanding
Ex 31: 3 of God, in wisdom, and in *u·*,
35:31 spirit of God, in wisdom, in *u·*,
36: 1 whom the Lord put wisdom and *u·*
De 1:13 Take you wise men, and *u·*, and
4: 6 your *u·* in the sight of the nations,
6 nation is a wise and *u·* people.
32:28 neither is there any *u·* in them.
1Sa 25: 3 and she was a woman of good *u·*,
1Ki 3: 9 Give...thy servant an *u·* heart
11 asked for thyself *u·* to discern
12 given thee a wise and an *u·* heart;
4:29 God gave Solomon wisdom and *u·*
7:14 he was filled with wisdom, and *u·*,
1Ch 12:32 were men that had *u·* of the times,
22:12 the Lord give thee wisdom and *u·*,
2Ch 2:12 son, endued with prudence and *u·*,
13 a cunning man, endued with *u·*,
26: 5 who had *u·* in the visions of God:
Ezr 8:16 and for Elnathan, men of *u·*.
18 us they brought us a man of *u·*,
Ne 8: 2 and all that could hear with *u·*,
10:28 having knowledge, and having *u·*;
Job 12: 3 But I have *u·* as well as you; I am
12 wisdom; and in length of days *u·*.
13 strength, he hath counsel and *u·*.
20 taketh away the *u·* of the aged.
17: 4 thou hast hid their heart from *u·*:
20: 3 of my *u·* causeth me to answer.
26:12 by his *u·* he smiteth through the
28:12, 20 and where is the place of *u·*?
28 and to depart from evil is *u·*.
32: 8 of the Almighty giveth them *u·*.
34:10 hearken unto me, ye men of *u·*:
16 If now thou hast *u·*, hear this:
34 Let men of *u·* tell me, and let a
38: 4 the earth? declare, if thou hast *u·*.
36 or who hath given *u·* to the heart?
39:17 neither hath he imparted to her *u·*.
Ps 32: 9 or as the mule, which have no *u·*:
47: 7 the earth: sing ye praises with *u·*.
49: 3 of my heart shall be of *u·*.
111:10 a good *u·* have all they that do his
119:34 Give me *u·*, and I shall keep thy
73 give me *u·*, that I may learn thy
99 more *u·* than all my teachers:
104 Through thy precepts I get *u·*:
125 give me *u·*, that I may know thy
130 light; it giveth *u·* unto the simple.
144 give me *u·*, and I shall live.
169 give me *u·* according to thy word.
147: 5 of great power: his *u·* is infinite.
Pr 1: 2 to perceive the words of *u·*;
5 a man of *u·* shall attain unto wise
2: 2 and apply thine heart to *u·*;
3 and liftest up thy voice for *u·*;
6 mouth cometh knowledge and *u·*.
11 preserve thee, *u·* shall keep thee:
3: 4 good *u·* in the sight of God and
5 and lean not unto thine own *u·*.
13 and the man that getteth *u·*.
19 earth; by *u·* hath he established the
4: 1 of a father, and attend to know *u·*.
5 Get wisdom, get *u·*: forget it not;
7 and with all thy getting get *u·*.
5: 1 and bow thine ear to my *u·*:
6:32 adultery with a woman lacketh *u·*:
7: 4 sister; and call *u·* thy kinswoman
7 youths, a young man void of *u·*,
8: 1 cry? and *u·* put forth her voice?
5 and, ye fools, be ye of an *u·* heart.
14 wisdom: I am *u·*; I have strength.
9: 4 as for him that wanteth *u·*, she
6 live; and go in the way of *u·*.
10 and the knowledge of the holy is *u·*.
16 as for him that wanteth *u·*, she
10:13 In the lips of him that hath *u·*
13 the back of him that is void of *u·*.
23 but a man of *u·* hath wisdom.
11:12 but a man of *u·* holdeth his peace.
12:11 vain persons is void of *u·*.
13:15 Good *u·* giveth favour: but the
14:29 is slow to wrath is of great *u·*:
33 in the heart of him that hath *u·*:
15:14 that hath *u·* seeketh knowledge:
21 a man of *u·* walketh uprightly.
32 he that heareth reproof getteth *u·*.
16:16 *u·* rather to be chosen than silver!
22 *U·* is a wellspring of life unto
17:18 A man void of *u·* striketh hands,
24 is before him that hath *u·*; but the
27 and a man of *u·* is of an excellent
28 his lips is esteemed a man of *u·*.
18: 2 A fool hath no delight in *u·*, but
19: 8 he that keepeth *u·* shall find good.
25 and reprove one that hath *u·*, and
20: 5 but a man of *u·* will draw it out.
21:16 wandereth out of the way of *u·*
30 no wisdom nor *u·* nor counsel
23:23 wisdom, and instruction, and *u·*.
24: 3 and by *u·* it is established:
30 vineyard of the man void of *u·*;
28: 2 by a man of *u·* and knowledge the
11 the poor that hath *u·* searcheth him
16 The prince that wanteth *u·* is also
30: 2 man, and have not the *u·* of a man.
Ec 9:11 nor yet riches to men of *u·*, nor yet
Isa 11: 2 spirit of wisdom and *u·*, the spirit
3 shall make him of quick *u·* in the
27:11 on fire: for it is a people of no *u·*:
29:14 *u·* of their prudent men shall be hid.
16 him that framed it, He had no *u·*?
24 erred in spirit shall come to *u·*,
40:14 and shewed to him the way of *u·*?
28 there is no searching of his *u·*.
44:19 is there knowledge nor *u·* to say, I
Jer 3:15 feed you with knowledge and *u·*.
4:22 children, and they have none *u·*:
5:21 O foolish people, and without *u·*;
51:15 stretched out the heaven by his *u·*.
Eze 28: 4 with thine *u·* thou hast gotten thee
Da 1: 4 in knowledge, and *u·* science,
17 Daniel had *u·* in all visions and
20 in all matters of wisdom and *u·*,
2:21 knowledge to them that know *u·*:
4:34 mine *u·* returned unto me, and I
5:11 father light and *u·* and wisdom,
12 and *u·*, interpreting of dreams,
14 *u·* and excellent wisdom is found in
8:23 *u·* dark sentences, shall stand up.
9:22 come forth to give thee skill and *u·*.
10: 1 the thing, and had *u·* of the vision.
11:35 And some of them of *u·* shall fall,
Ho 13: 2 idols according to their own *u·*,
Ob 7 under thee: there is none *u·* in him.
8 and *u·* out of the mount of Esau?
M't 15:16 said, Are ye also yet without *u·*?
M'r 7:18 them, Are ye so without *u·* also?
12:33 all the heart, and with all the *u·*,
Lu 1: 3 having had perfect *u·* of all things
2:47 him were astonished at his *u·*
24:45 Then opened he their *u·*, that they
Ro 1:31 Without *u·*, covenantbreakers,
1Co 1:19 to nothing the *u·* of the prudent.
14:14 prayeth, but my *u·* is unfruitful.
15 and I will pray with the *u·* also:
15 and I will sing with the *u·* also.
19 rather speak five words with my *u·*,
20 Brethren, be not children in *u·*:
20 be ye children, but in *u·* be men.
Eph 1:18 eyes of your *u·* being enlightened;
4:18 Having the *u·* darkened, being
5:17 *u·* what the will of the Lord is.
Ph'p 4: 7 peace of God, which passeth all *u·*,
Col 1: 9 in all wisdom and spiritual *u·*;
2: 2 riches of the full assurance of *u·*,
1Ti 1: 7 *u·* neither what they say, nor
2Ti 2: 7 Lord give thee *u·* in all things.
1Jo 5:20 is come, and hath given us an *u·*,
Re 13:18 him that hath *u·* count the number

understood
Ge 42:23 knew not that Joseph *u·* them;
De 32:29 they were wise, that they *u·* this,
1Sa 4: 6 they *u·* that the ark of the Lord
26: 4 *u·* that Saul was come in very deed.
2Sa 3:37 all the people and all Israel *u·* that
Ne 8:12 *u·* the words that were declared
13: 7 *u·* of the evil that Eliashib did for
Job 13: 1 this, mine ear hath heard and *u·* it.
42: 3 have I uttered that I *u·* not;
Ps 73:17 of God; then *u·* I their end.
81: 5 I heard a language that I *u·* not.
106: 7 Our fathers *u·* not thy wonders in
Isa 40:21 ye not *u·* from the foundations of
44:18 They have not known nor *u·*: for he
Da 8:27 at the vision, but none *u·* it.
9: 2 I Daniel *u·* by books the number of
10: 1 and he *u·* the thing, and had
12: 8 And I heard, but I *u·* not: then said
M't 13:51 them, Have ye *u·* all these things?
16:12 Then *u·* they how that he bade
17:13 the disciples *u·* that he spake unto
26:10 When Jesus *u·* it, he said unto
M'r 9:32 But they *u·* not that saying, and
Lu 2:50 *u·* not the saying which he spake
9:45 they *u·* not this saying, and it was
18:34 And they *u·* none of these things:
Joh 8:27 *u·* not that he spake to them of
10: 6 *u·* not what things they were which
12:16 These things *u·* not his disciples at
Ac 7:25 his brethren would have *u·* how
25 deliver them: but they *u·* not.
23:27 having *u·* that he was a Roman.
34 when he *u·* that he was of Cilicia;
Ro 1:20 *u·* by the things that are made,
1Co 13:11 I *u·* as a child, I thought as a child:
14: 9 by the tongue words easy to be *u·*,
2Pe 3:16 are some things hard to be *u·*,

undertake See also UNDERTOOK.
Isa 38:14 Lord, I am oppressed; *u·* for me.

undertook
Es 9:23 Jews *u·* to do as they had begun,

undo See also UNDONE.
Isa 58: 6 to *u·* the heavy burdens, and to let
Zep 3:19 that time I will *u·* all that afflict

undone
Nu 21:29 thou art *u·*, O people of Chemosh:
Jos 11:15 he left nothing *u·* of all that the
Isa 6: 5 Woe is me! for I am *u·*; because
M't 23:23 done, and not to leave the other *u·*.
Lu 11:42 done, and not to leave the other *u·*.

undressed
Le 25: 5 gather the grapes of thy vine *u·*:
11 the grapes in it of thy vine *u·*.

unequal
Eze 18:25, 29 are not your ways *u·*?

unequally
2Co 6:14 not *u·* yoked together with

unfaithful
Pr 25:19 Confidence in an *u*' man in time of

unfaithfully
Ps 78:57 and dealt *u*' like their fathers:

unfeigned
2Co 6: 6 by the Holy Ghost, by love *u*',
1Ti 1: 5 of a good conscience, and of faith *u*':
2Ti 1: 5 the *u*' faith that is in thee, which
1Pe 1:22 Spirit unto *u*' love of the brethren,

unfruitful
M't 13:22 the word, and he becometh *u*'.
M'r 4:19 choke the word, and it becometh *u*'.
1Co 14:14 but my understanding is *u*'.
Eph 5:11 with the *u*' works of darkness,
Tit 3:14 necessary uses, that they be not *u*'.
2Pe 1: 8 nor *u*' in the knowledge of our Lord

ungirded
Ge 24:32 he *u*' his camels, and gave straw

ungodliness
Ro 1:18 revealed from heaven against all *u*'
11:26 and shall turn away *u*' from Jacob:
2Ti 2:16 for they will increase unto more *u*'.
Tit 2:12 denying *u*' and worldly lusts, we

ungodly
2Sa 22: 5 floods of *u*' men made me afraid;
2Ch 19: 2 Shouldest thou help the *u*', and
Job 16:11 God hath delivered me to the *u*',
34:18 wicked? and to princes, Ye are *u*'?
Ps 1: 1 walketh not in the counsel of the *u*',
4 The *u*' are not so: but are like the
5 *u*' shall not stand in the judgment
6 but the way of the *u*' shall perish.
3: 7 hast broken the teeth of the *u*'.
18: 4 floods of *u*' men made me afraid.
43: 1 cause against an *u*' nation:
73:12 these are the *u*', who prosper in
Pr 16:27 An *u*' man diggeth up evil: and in
19:28 An *u*' witness scorneth judgment:
Ro 4: 5 on him that justifieth the *u*', his
5: 6 in due time Christ died for the *u*'.
1Ti 1: 9 for the *u*' and for sinners, for
1Pe 4:18 where shall the *u*' and the sinner
2Pe 2: 5 in the flood upon the world of the *u*'
6 unto those that after should live *u*';
3: 7 judgment and perdition of *u*' men.
Jude 4 *u*' men, turning the grace of our God
15 to convince all that are *u*' among
15 all their *u*' deeds which they have
15 which they have *u*' committed,
15 speeches which *u*' sinners have
18 walk after their own *u*' lusts.

unholy
Le 10:10 difference between holy and *u*',
1Ti 1: 9 for *u*' and profane, for murderers of
2Ti 3: 2 to parents, unthankful, *u*',
Heb10:29 he was sanctified, an *u*' thing,

unicorn See also UNICORNS.
Nu 23:22 as it were the strength of an *u*'.
24: 8 as it were the strength of an *u*':
Job 39: 9 Will the *u*' be willing to serve thee,
10 Canst thou bind the *u*' with his
Ps 29: 6 Lebanon and Sirion like a young *u*
92:10 thou exalt like the horn of an *u*':

unicorns
De 33:17 his horns are like the horns of *u*':
Ps 22:21 heard me from the horns of the *u*'.
Isa 34: 7 the *u*' shall come down with them,

unite See also UNITED.
Ps 86:11 *u*' my heart to fear thy name.

united
Ge 49: 6 mine honour, be not thou *u*':

unity
Ps 133: 1 brethren to dwell together in *u*'!
Eph 4: 3 to keep the *u*' of the Spirit in the
13 we all come in the *u*' of the faith,

unjust
Ps 43: 1 me from the deceitful and *u*' man.
Pr 11: 7 and the hope of *u*' men perisheth.
28: 8 *u*' gain increaseth his substance,
29:27 An *u*' man is an abomination to
Zep 3: 5 not; but the *u*' knoweth no shame.
M't 5:45 rain on the just and on the *u*'.
Lu 16: 8 the lord commended the *u*' steward
10 is *u*' in the least is *u*' also in much.
18: 6 said, Hear what the *u*' judge saith.
11 as other men are, extortioners, *u*',
Ac 24:15 of the dead, both of the just and *u*'.
1Co 6: 1 go to law before the *u*', and not
1Pe 3:18 suffered for sins, the just for the *u*
2Pe 2: 9 to reserve the *u*' unto the day of
Re 22:11 He that is *u*', let him be *u*' still:

unjustly
Ps 82: 2 How long will ye judge *u*', and
Isa 26:10 of uprightness will he deal *u*',

unknown^
Ac 17:23 this inscription, To The *U*' God.
1Co 14: 2 he that speaketh in an *u*' tongue
4 in an *u*' tongue edifieth himself;
14 if I pray in an *u*' tongue, my spirit
19 ten thousand words in an *u*' tongue.
27 If any man speak in an *u*' tongue, let
2Co 6: 9 As *u*', and yet well known; as dying,
Gal 1:22 was *u*' by face unto the churches of

unlade
Ac 21: 3 the ship was to *u*' her burden.

unlawful
Ac 10:28 an *u*' thing for a man that is a Jew
2Pe 2: 8 day to day with their *u*' deeds:)

unlearned
Ac 4:13 that they were *u*' and ignorant men.
1Co 14:16 the *u*' say Amen at thy giving of
23 there come in those that are *u*',
24 one that believeth not, or one *u*',
2Ti 2:23 foolish and *u*' questions avoid,
2Pe 3:16 that are *u*' and unstable wrest,

unleavened
Ge 19: 3 did bake *u*' bread, and they did
Ex 12: 8 night, roast with fire, and *u*' bread;
15 Seven days shall ye eat *u*' bread;
17 shall observe the feast of *u*' bread;
18 ye shall eat *u*' bread, until the one
20 habitations shall ye eat *u*' bread.
39 they baked *u*' cakes of the dough
13: 6 Seven days thou shalt eat *u*' bread,
7 *U*' bread shall be eaten seven
23:15 shalt keep the feast of *u*' bread:
15 (thou shalt eat *u*' bread seven days,
29: 2 *u*' bread, and cakes *u*' tempered
2 and wafers *u*' anointed with oil:
23 out of the basket of the *u*' bread
34:18 feast of *u*' bread shalt thou keep.
18 Seven days thou shalt eat *u*' bread,
Le 2: 4 *u*' cakes of fine flour mingled with
4 oil, or *u*' wafers anointed with oil.
5 a pan, it shall be of fine flour *u*',
6:16 with *u*' bread shall it be eaten in
7:12 *u*' cakes mingled with oil,
12 and *u*' wafers anointed with oil,
8: 2 rams, and a basket of *u*' bread;
26 And out of the basket of *u*' bread,
26 he took one *u*' cake, and a cake of
23: 6 the feast of *u*' bread unto the Lord:
6 seven days ye must eat *u*' bread.
Nu 6:15 and a basket of *u*' bread, cakes of
15 wafers of *u*' bread anointed with
17 Lord, with the basket of *u*' bread:
19 and one *u*' cake out of the basket,
19 one *u*' wafer, and shall put them
9:11 eat it with *u*' bread and bitter
28:17 seven days shall *u*' bread be eaten.
De 16: 3 seven days shalt thou eat *u*' bread
8 Six days thou shalt eat *u*' bread:
16 in the feast of *u*' bread, and in the
Jos 5:11 *u*' cakes, and parched corn in the
J'g 6:19 and *u*' cakes of an ephah of flour:
20 Take the flesh and the *u*' cakes,
21 touched the flesh and the *u*' cakes;
21 the flesh and the *u*' cakes.
1Sa 28:24 kneaded it, and did bake *u*' bread
2Ki 23: 9 did eat of the *u*' bread among their
1Ch 23:29 for the *u*' cakes, and for that which
2Ch 8:13 year, even in the feast of *u*' bread,
30:13 people to keep the feast of *u*' bread
21 the feast of *u*' bread seven days
35:17 the feast of *u*' bread seven days.
Ezr 6:22 the feast of *u*' bread seven days
Eze 45:21 seven days; *u*' bread shall be eaten.
M't 26:17 first day of the feast of *u*' bread
M'r 14: 1 of the passover, and of *u*' bread:
12 the first day of *u*' bread, when they
Lu 22: 1 Now the feast of *u*' bread drew nigh,
7 Then came the day of *u*' bread,
Ac 12: 3 (Then were the days of *u*' bread.)
20: 6 Philippi after the days of *u*' bread,
1Co 5: 7 ye may be a new lump, as ye are *u*'.
8 the *u*' bread of sincerity and truth.

unless
Le 22: 6 *u*' he wash his flesh with
Nu 22:33 *u*' she had turned from me, surely
2Sa 2:27 *u*' thou hadst spoken, surely
Ps 27:13 *u*' I had believed to see the
94:17 *U*' the Lord had been my help, my
119:92 *U*' thy law had been my delights, I
Pr 4:16 *u*' they cause some to fall.
1Co 15: 2 *u*' ye have believed in vain.

unloose See also LOOSE.
M'r 1: 7 not worthy to stoop down and *u*'.
Lu 3:16 whose shoes I am not worthy to *u*':
Joh 1:27 shoe's latchet I am not worthy to *u*'.

unmarried
1Co 7: 8 say therefore to the *u*' and widows,
11 and if she depart, let her remain *u*',
32 He that is *u*' careth for the things
34 The *u*' woman careth for the things

unmerciful
Ro 1:31 natural affection, implacable, *u*':

unmindful
De 32:18 Rock that begat thee thou art *u*',

unmoveable
Ac 27:41 stuck fast, and remained *u*',
1Co 15:58 brethren, be ye stedfast, *u*',

Unni (*un'-ni*)
1Ch 15:18 and Jehiel, and *U*', Eliab, and
20 and Jehiel, and *U*', and Eliab, and
Ne 12: 9 Also Bakbukiah and *U*', their

unoccupied
J'g 5: 6 the highways were *u*', and the

unperfect
Ps 139:16 did see my substance, yet being *u*';

unprepared
2Co 9: 4 come with me, and find you *u*',

unprofitable
Job 15: 3 Should he reason with *u*' talk? or
M't 25:30 cast ye the *u*' servant into outer
Lu 17:10 you, say, We are *u*' servants:
Ro 3:12 way, they are together become *u*';
Tit 3: 9 the law; for they are *u*' and vain.
Ph'm 11 Which in time past was to thee *u*',
Heb13:17 with grief: for that is *u*' for you.

unprofitableness
Heb 7:18 for the weakness and *u*' thereof.

unpunished
Pr 11:21 hand, the wicked shall not be *u*':
16: 5 join in hand, he shall not be *u*'.
17: 5 is glad at calamities shall not be *u*'.
19: 5, 9 A false witness shall not be *u*',
Jer 25:29 name, and should ye be utterly *u*'?
29 Ye shall not be *u*': for I will call for
30:11 will not leave thee altogether *u*'.
46:28 yet will I not leave thee wholly *u*'.
49:12 thou he that shall altogether go *u*'?
12 thou shalt not go *u*', but thou shalt

unquenchable
M't 3:12 will burn up the chaff with *u*' fire.
Lu 3:17 the chaff he will burn with fire *u*'.

unreasonable
Ac 25:27 seemeth to me *u*' to send a prisoner,
2Th 3: 2 delivered from *u*' and wicked men:

unrebukeable
1Ti 6:14 commandment without spot, *u*',

unreproveable
Col 1:22 unblameable and *u*' in his sight:

unrighteous
Ex 23: 1 the wicked to be an *u*' witness.
Job 27: 7 riseth up against me as the *u*'.
Ps 71: 4 the hand of the *u*' and cruel man.
Isa 10: 1 unto them that decree *u*' decrees,
55: 7 way, and the *u*' man his thoughts:
Lu 16:11 not been faithful in the *u*' mammon,
Ro 3: 5 Is God *u*' who taketh vengeance?
1Co 6: 9 *u*' shall not inherit the kingdom of
Heb 6:10 God is not *u*' to forget your work

unrighteousness
Le 19:15 Ye shall do no *u*' in judgment:
35 Ye shall do no *u*' in judgment, in
Ps 92:15 my rock, and there is no *u*' in him.
Jer 22:13 that buildeth his house by *u*',
Lu 16: 9 friends of the mammon of *u*';
Joh 7:18 the same is true, and no *u*' is in him.
Ro 1:18 all ungodliness and *u*' of men,
18 of men, who hold the truth in *u*';
29 Being filled with all *u*', fornication,
2: 8 but obey *u*', indignation and wrath,
3: 5 if our *u*' commend the righteousness
6:13 as instruments of *u*' unto sin:
9:14 we say then? Is there *u*' with God?
2Co 6:14 hath righteousness with *u*'?
2Th 2:10 deceivableness of *u*' in them that
12 not the truth, but had pleasure in *u*'.
Heb 8:12 For I will be merciful to their *u*',
2Pe 2:13 And shall receive the reward of *u*',
15 Bosor, who loved the wages of *u*';
1Jo 1: 9 sins, and to cleanse us from all *u*'.
5:17 All *u*' is sin: and there is a sin not

unrighteously
De 25:16 all that do *u*', are an abomination

unripe
Job 15:33 shake off his *u*' grape as the vine,

unruly
1Th 5:14 brethren, warn them that are *u*',
Tit 1: 6 children not accused of riot or *u*'.
10 there are many *u*' and vain talkers
Jas 3: 8 it is an *u*' evil, full of deadly poison.

unsatiable
Eze 16:28 because thou wast *u*'; yea,

unsavoury
2Sa 22:27 froward thou wilt shew thyself *u*'.
Job 6: 6 Can that which is *u*' be eaten

unsearchable
Job 5: 9 doeth great things and *u*';
Ps 145: 3 praised; and his greatness is *u*'.
Pr 25: 3 and the heart of kings is *u*'.
Ro 11:33 how *u*' are his judgments, and his
Eph 3: 8 Gentiles the *u*' riches of Christ;

unseemly
Ro 1:27 with men working that which is *u*',
1Co 13: 5 Doth not behave itself *u*', seeketh not

unshod
Jer 2:25 Withhold thy foot from being *u*',

unskilful
Heb 5:13 every one that useth milk is *u*' in

unspeakable
2Co 9:15 Thanks be unto God for his *u*' gift.
12: 4 into paradise, and heard *u*' words,
1Pe 1: 8 with joy *u*' and full of glory:

unspotted
Jas 1:27 to keep himself *u*' from the world.

unstable
Ge 49: 4 *U*' as water, thou shalt not excel;
Jas 1: 8 A double minded man is *u*' in all
2Pe 2:14 cease from sin; beguiling *u*' souls:
3:16 that are unlearned and *u*' wrest,

unstopped
Isa 35: 5 and the ears of the deaf shall be *u*'.

untaken
2Co 3:14 remaineth the same vail *u*'

untempered
Eze 13:10 others daubed it with *u*' morter:
11 them which daub it with *u*' morter,
14 that ye have daubed with *u*' morter,
15 that have daubed it with *u*' morter,
22:28 have daubed them with *u*' morter,

unthankful
Lu 6:35 is kind unto the *u*' and to the evil.
2Ti 3: 2 disobedient to parents, *u*', unholy,

until[A] See also TILL.
Ge 8: 5 continually *u'* the tenth month:
7 *u'* the waters were dried up from
26: 13 and grew *u'* he became very great:
27: 44 *u'* thy brother's fury turn
45 *U'* thy brother's anger turn
28: 15 *u'* I have done that which I
29: 8 *u'* all the flocks be gathered
32: 4 Laban, and stayed there *u'* now:
24 with him *u'* the breaking of the day.
33: 3 *u'* he came near to his brother.
14 *u'* I come unto my lord unto Seir.
34: 5 held his peace *u'* they were come.
39: 16 by her, *u'* his lord came home.
41: 49 very much, *u'* he left numbering;
46: 34 cattle from our youth even *u'* now,
49: 10 his feet, *u'* Shiloh come;
Ex 9: 18 foundation thereof even *u'* now.
10: 26 serve the Lord, *u'* we come thither.
12: 6 keep it up *u'* the fourteenth day of
10 nothing of it remain *u'*...morning;
10 which remaineth of it *u'*...morning
15 the first day *u'* the seventh day,
18 *u'* the one and twentieth day of the
22 door of his house *u'* the morning.
16: 20 of them left of it *u'* the morning,
23 for you to be kept *u'* the morning.
35 *u'* they came to a land inhabited;
35 *u'* they came unto the borders of
17: 12 *u'* the going down of the sun.
23: 18 sacrifice remain *u'* the morning.
30 *u'* thou be increased, and inherit
24: 14 for us, *u'* we come again unto you:
33: 8 *u'* he was gone into the tabernacle.
34: 34 he took the vail off, *u'* he came out.
35 *u'* he went in to speak with him.
Le 7: 15 not leave any of it *u'* the morning.
8: 33 *u'* the days of your consecration be
11: 24 them shall be unclean *u'* the even.
25 clothes, and be unclean *u'* the even.
27 shall be unclean *u'* the even.
28 clothes, and be unclean *u'* the even:
31 dead, shall be unclean *u'* the even.
32 and it shall be unclean *u'* the even;
39 shall be unclean *u'* the even.
40 clothes, and be unclean *u'* the even:
40 clothes, and be unclean *u'* the even.
12: 4 *u'* the days of her purifying be
14: 46 up shall be unclean *u'* the even.
15: 5, 6, 7 and be unclean *u'* the even.
10 him shall be unclean *u'* the even:
10, 16, 17, 18, 19, 21, 22, 23, 27 be
unclean *u'* the even.
16: 17 *u'* he come out, and have made an
17: 15 water, and be unclean *u'* the even:
19: 6 if ought remain *u'* the third day, it
13 with thee all night *u'* the morning.
22: 4 of the holy things, *u'* he be clean.
6 any such shall be unclean *u'* even,
30 leave none of it *u'* the morrow:
23: 14 *u'* the selfsame day that ye have
25: 22 eat...of old fruit *u'* the ninth year;
22 *u'* her fruits come in ye shall
28 bought it *u'* the year of jubile:
Nu 4: 3 and upward even *u'* fifty years old,
23 and upward *u'* fifty years old shalt
6: 5 *u'* the days be fulfilled, in the
9: 15 appearance of fire, *u'* the morning.
11: 20 *u'* it come out at your nostrils, and
14: 19 people, from Egypt even *u'* now.
33 *u'* your carcases be wasted in the
19: 7 priest shall be unclean *u'* the even.
8 and shall be unclean *u'* the even.
10 clothes, and be unclean *u'* the even:
21 separation shall be unclean *u'* even.
22 toucheth it shall be unclean *u'* even.
20: 17 *u'* we have passed thy borders.
21: 22 way, *u'* we be past thy borders.
35 *u'* there was none left him alive:
23: 24 not lie down *u'* he eat of the prey,
24: 22 *u'* Asshur shall carry thee away
32: 13 *u'* all the generation, that had
17 *u'* we have brought them unto
18 *u'* the children of Israel have
21 *u'* he hath driven out his enemies
35: 12 *u'* he stand before the congregation
28 *u'* the death of the high priest:
32 land, *u'* the death of the priest.
De 1: 31 went, *u'* ye came into this place.
2: 14 *u'* we were come over the brook
14 *u'* all the generation of the men of
15 the host, *u'* they were consumed.
29 *u'* I shall pass over Jordan into the
3: 3 we smote him *u'* none was left
20 *U'* the Lord have given rest unto
7: 20 *u'* they that are left, and hide
23 destruction, *u'* they be destroyed.
24 thee, *u'* thou have destroyed them.
9: 7 *u'* ye came unto this place, ye have
21 even *u'* it was as small as dust:
11: 5 *u'* ye came into this place;
16: 4 remain all night *u'* the morning.
22: 2 thee *u'* thy brother seek after it,
28: 20 for to do, *u'* thou be destroyed,
20 and *u'* thou perish quickly;
21 *u'* he have consumed thee from off
22 shall pursue thee *u'* thou perish.
24 upon thee, *u'* thou be destroyed.
48 neck, *u'* he have destroyed thee.
51 of thy land, *u'* thou be destroyed:
51 sheep, *u'* he have destroyed thee.
52 *u'* thy high and fenced walls come
61 upon thee, *u'* thou be destroyed.
31: 24 in a book, *u'* they were finished,
30 of this song, *u'* they were ended.
Jos 1: 15 *U'* the Lord have given your
Jos 2: 16 days, *u'* the pursuers be returned:
22 *u'* the pursuers were returned:
3: 17 *u'* all the people were passed clean
4: 10 *u'* every thing was finished that
23 *u'* ye were passed over, as the Lord
23 before us, *u'* we were gone over:
5: 1 of Israel, *u'* we were passed over,
6: 10 mouth, *u'* the day I bid you shout;
7: 6 the ark of the Lord *u'* the eventide,
13 *u'* ye take away the accursed thing
8: 24 the sword, *u'* they were consumed,
26 *u'* he had utterly destroyed all the
29 he hanged on a tree *u'* eventide:
10: 13 *u'* the people had avenged
26 upon the trees *u'* the evening.
27 which remain *u'* this very day.
33 *u'* he had left him none remaining.
11: 8 *u'* they left them none remaining.
14 *u'* they had destroyed them,
13: 13 among the Israelites *u'* this day.
20: 6 *u'* he stand before the congregation
6 *u'* the death of the high priest that
9 *u'* he stood before the congregation.
22: 17 we are not cleansed *u'* this day,
23: 13 *u'* ye perish from off this good land
15 *u'* he have destroyed you from off
J'g 4: 24 *u'* they had destroyed Jabin king
5: 7 in Israel, *u'* that I Deborah arose,
6: 18 *u'* I come unto thee, and bring
13: 15 *u'* we shall have made ready a kid
18: 30 *u'* the day of the captivity of the
19: 8 they tarried *u'* afternoon, and they
25 her all the night *u'* the morning:
20: 23 and wept before the Lord *u'* even,
Ru 1: 19 went *u'* they came to Beth-lehem.
2: 7 even from the morning *u'* now,
17 she gleaned in the field *u'* even,
21 *u'* they have ended all my
3: 3 *u'* he shall have done eating and
13 liveth: lie down *u'* the morning.
14 she lay at his feet *u'* the morning:
18 *u'* thou know how the matter
18 *u'* he have finished the thing
1Sa 1: 22 not go up *u'* the child be weaned,
23 tarry *u'* thou have weaned him;
23 her son suck *u'* she weaned him.
3: 15 And Samuel lay *u'* the morning,
7: 11 *u'* they came under Beth-car.
9: 13 the people will not eat *u'* he come,
11: 11 Ammonites *u'* the heat of the day:
14: 9 Tarry *u'* we come to you; then we
24 that eateth any food *u'* evening,
36 spoil them *u'* the morning light,
15: 7 Havilah *u'* thou comest to Shur,
18 against them *u'* they be consumed.
35 to see Saul *u'* the day of his death:
17: 52 *u'* thou come to the valley,
19: 2 heed to thyself *u'* the morning,
23 *u'* he came to Naioth in Ramah.
20: 41 with another, *u'* David exceeded.
25: 36 less or more, *u'* the morning light.
30: 4 *u'* they had no more power to
2Sa 1: 12 and fasted *u'* even, for Saul, and
4: 3 were sojourners there *u'* this day.)
5: 25 from Geba *u'* thou come to Gazer.
10: 5 Jericho *u'* your beards be grown,
15: 24 *u'* all the people had done passing
28 *u'* there come word from you to
17: 13 *u'* there be not one small stone
19: 7 befell thee from thy youth *u'* now.
24 king departed *u'* the day he came
21: 10 *u'* water dropped upon them out of
22: 38 not again *u'* I had consumed them.
23: 10 *u'* his hand was weary,
1Ki 3: 1 *u'* he had made an end of building
2 name of the Lord, *u'* those days.
5: 3 *u'* the Lord put them under the
6: 22 *u'* he had finished all the house:
10: 7 *u'* I came, and mine eyes had seen
11: 16 *u'* he had cut off every male in
40 in Egypt *u'* the death of Solomon.
15: 29 breathed, *u'* he had destroyed him,
17: 14 *u'* the day that the Lord sendeth
18: 26 Baal from morning even *u'* noon,
29 *u'* the time of the offering of the
22: 11 *u'* thou have consumed them.
27 of affliction, *u'* I come in peace.
2Ki 6: 25 *u'* an ass's head was sold for
7: 3 another, Why sit we here *u'* we die?
8: 6 that she left the land, even *u'* now.
11 stedfastly, *u'* he was ashamed:
10: 8 in of the gate *u'* the morning.
11 *u'* he left him none remaining.
17: 20 *u'* he had cast them out of his
23 *U'* the Lord removed Israel out of
18: 32 *U'* I come and take you away to a
24: 20 *u'* he had cast them out from his
1Ch 5: 22 in their steads *u'* the captivity.
6: 32 *u'* Solomon had built the house of
12: 22 *u'* it was a great host, like the host
19: 5 at Jericho *u'* your beards be grown,
28: 20 *u'* thou hast finished all the work
2Ch 8: 8 make to pay tribute *u'* this day.
16 of the Lord, and *u'* it was finished.
9: 6 *u'* I came, and mine eyes had seen
16: 12 *u'* his disease was exceeding great:
18: 10 push Syria *u'* they be consumed.
26 of affliction, *u'* I return in peace.
34 against the Syrians *u'* the even:
21: 15 *u'* thy bowels fall out by reason of
24: 10 the chest, *u'* they had made an end.
29: 28 *u'* the burnt offering was finished.
34 *u'* the other priests had sanctified
35: 14 burnt offerings and the fat *u'* night;
36: 16 *u'* the wrath of the Lord arose
20 *u'* the reign of the kingdom of
2Ch 36: 21 *u'* the land had enjoyed her
Ezr 4: 5 even *u'* the reign of Darius king of
21 *u'* another commandment shall be
5: 16 *u'* now hath it been in building,
8: 29 *u'* ye weigh them before the chief
9: 4 astonied *u'* the evening sacrifice.
10: 14 *u'* the fierce wrath of our God for
Ne 7: 3 be opened *u'* the sun be hot;
8: 3 gate from the morning *u'* midday,
12: 23 *u'* the days of Johanan the son of
Job 14: 13 me secret, *u'* thy wrath be past,
26: 10 *u'* the day and night come to an
Ps 36: 2 *u'* his iniquity be found to be hateful.
57: 1 *u'* these calamities be overpast.
71: 18 *u'* I have shewed thy strength unto
94: 13 *u'* the pit be digged for the wicked.
104: 23 and to his labour *u'* the evening.
105: 19 *U'* the time that his word came:
110: 1 *u'* I make thine enemies thy
112: 8 *u'* he see his desire upon his
123: 2 *u'* that he have mercy upon us.
132: 5 *U'* I find out a place for the Lord,
Pr 7: 18 take our fill of love *u'* the morning:
Ca 2: 17 *U'* the day break, and the shadows
3: 4 *u'* I had brought him into my
4: 6 *U'* the day break, and the shadows
8: 4 nor awake my love, *u'* he please.
Isa 5: 11 that continue *u'* night, till wine
6: 11 *U'* the cities be wasted without
26: 20 *u'* the indignation be overpast.
32: 15 *U'* the spirit be poured upon us
36: 17 *U'* I come and take you away to a
39: 6 have laid up in store *u'* this day,
62: 1 *u'* the righteousness...go forth as
Jer 23: 20 not return, *u'* he have executed,
27: 7 *u'* the very time of his land come:
8 *u'* I have consumed them by his
22 they be *u'* the day that I visit them,
30: 24 shall not return, *u'* he have done it,
24 *u'* he hath performed the intents of
32: 5 and there shall he be *u'* I visit him,
36: 23 *u'* all the roll was consumed in the
37: 21 *u'* all the bread in the city were
38: 28 *u'* the day that Jerusalem was
44: 27 famine, *u'* there be an end of them.
52: 34 a portion *u'* the day of his death,
Eze 21: 27 more, *u'* he come whose right it is;
33: 22 *u'* he came to me in the morning;
46: 2 shall not be shut *u'* the evening.
Da 4: 32 *u'* thou know that the most High
7: 22 *U'* the Ancient of days came, and
25 *u'* a time...times and the dividing
9: 27 desolate,...*u'* the consummation,
Ho 7: 4 the dough, *u'* it be leavened.
Mic 5: 3 *u'* the time...she which travaileth
7: 9 *u'* he plead my cause, and execute
Zep 3: 8 *u'* the day that I rise up to the prey:
M't 1: 17 *u'* the carrying away into Babylon
2: 13 be thou there *u'* I bring thee word:
15 was there *u'* the death of Herod:
11: 12 days of John the Baptist *u'* now
13 and the law prophesied *u'* John.
23 would have remained *u'* this day.
13: 30 both grow together *u'* the harvest:
17: 9 *u'* the Son of man be risen again
18: 22 say not unto thee, *U'* seven times:
22 times: but, *U'* seventy times seven.
24: 38 *u'* the day that Noe entered into
39 And knew not *u'* the flood came,
26: 29 *u'* that day when I drink it new
27: 64 be made sure *u'* the third day,
28: 15 among the Jews *u'* this day.
M'r 14: 25 *u'* that day that I drink it new
15: 33 the whole land *u'* the ninth hour.
Lu 1: 20 *u'* the day that these things shall be
13: 35 *u'* the time...when ye shall say,
15: 4 after that which is lost, *u'* he find it?
16: 16 and the prophets were *u'* John:
17: 27 *u'* the day that Noe entered into
21: 24 *u'* the times of the Gentiles be
22: 16 *u'* it be fulfilled in the kingdom of
18 *u'* the kingdom of God shall come.
23: 44 over all the earth *u'* the ninth hour.
24: 49 *u'* ye be endued with power from
Joh 2: 10 hast kept the good wine *u'* now.
9: 18 *u'* they called the parents of him
Ac 1: 2 *U'* the day in which he was taken
2: 35 *U'* I make thy foes thy footstool.
3: 21 *u'* the times of restitution of all
10: 30 ago I was fasting *u'* this hour;
13: 20 fifty years, *u'* Samuel the prophet.
20: 7 continued his speech *u'* midnight.
21: 26 *u'*...an offering should be offered
23: 1 conscience before God *u'* this day.
14 eat nothing *u'* we have slain Paul.
Ro 5: 13 (For *u'* the law sin was in the world:
8: 22 travaileth in pain together *u'* now.
11: 25 *u'* the fulness of the Gentiles
1Co 4: 5 *u'* the Lord come, who both will
16: 8 will tarry at Ephesus *u'* Pentecost.
2Co 3: 14 *u'* this day remaineth the same vail
Ga 4: 2 *u'* the time appointed of the father.
19 again *u'* Christ be formed in you,
Eph 1: 14 *u'*...redemption of the purchased
Ph'p 1: 5 gospel from the first day *u'* now;
6 it *u'* the day of Jesus Christ:
2Th 2: 7 let, *u'* he be taken out of the way.
1Ti 6: 14 *u'* the appearing of our Lord
Heb 1: 13 *u'* I make thine enemies thy
9: 10 them *u'* the time of reformation.
Jas 5: 7 *u'* he receive the early and latter
2Pe 1: 19 *u'* the day dawn, and the day star
1Jo 2: 9 brother, is in darkness even *u'* now.
Re 6: 11 *u'* their fellowservants also and
17: 17 *u'* the words of God...be fulfilled.
20: 5 *u'*...thousand years were finished.

untimely
Job 3:16 a hidden *u'* birth I had not been;
Ps 58: 8 like the *u'* birth of a woman, that
Ec 6: 3 that an *u'* birth is better than he.
Re 6:13 as a fig tree casteth her *u'* figs.

untoward
Ac 2:40 from this *u'* generation.

unwalled
De 3: 5 beside *u'* towns a great many.
Es 9:19 villages, that dwelt in the *u'* towns,
Eze 38:11 will go up to the land of *u'* villages;

unwashen
M't 15:20 to eat with *u'* hands defileth not a
M'r 7: 2 defiled, that is...with *u'*, hands,
5 elders, but eat bread with *u'* hands?

unweighed
1Ki 7:47 And Solomon left all the vessels *u'*,

unwise
De 32: 6 O foolish people and *u'*?
Ho 13:13 he is an *u'* son; for he should
Ro 1:14 both to the wise, and to the *u'*.
Eph 5:17 Wherefore be ye not *u'*, but

unwittingly
Le 22:14 if a man eat of the holy thing *u'*,
Jos 20: 3 any person unawares and *u'*
5 he smote his neighbour *u'*,

unworthily
1Co 11:27 and drink this cup of the Lord, *u'*,
29 For he that eateth and drinketh *u'*,

unworthy
Ac 13:46 *u'* of everlasting life,
1Co 6: 2 *u'* to judge the smallest matters?

upbraid See also UPBRAIDED; UPBRAIDETH.
J'g 8:15 with whom ye did *u'* me, saying,
M't 11:20 Then began he to *u'* the cities

upbraided
M'r 16:14 and *u'* them with their unbelief

upbraideth
Jas 1: 5 to all men liberally, and *u'* not;

Upharsin (*u-far'-sin*) See also PERES.
Da 5:25 written, Mene, Mene, Tekel, *U'*.

Uphaz (*u'-faz*)
Jer 10: 9 Tarshish, and gold from *U'*, the
Da 10: 5 were girded with fine gold of *U'*:

upheld
Isa 63: 5 unto me; and my fury, it *u'* me.

uphold See also UPHELD; UPHOLDEN; UPHOLDEST; UPHOLDETH; UPHOLDING.
Ps 51:12 and *u'* me with thy free spirit.
54: 4 Lord is with them that *u'* my soul.
119:116 *U'* me according unto thy word,
Pr 29:23 but honour shall *u'* the humble in
Isa 41:10 I will *u'* thee with the right hand of
42: 1 Behold my servant, whom I *u'*;
63: 5 I wondered...there was none to *u'*:
Eze 30: 6 They also that *u'* Egypt shall fall;

upholden
Job 4: 4 Thy words have *u'* him that was
Pr 20:28 and his throne is *u'* by mercy.

upholdest
Ps 41:12 me, thou *u'* me in mine integrity,

upholdeth
Ps 37:17 but the Lord *u'* the righteous.
24 for the Lord *u'* him with his hand.
63: 8 after thee: thy right hand *u'* me.
145:14 Lord *u'* all that fall, and raiseth

upholding
Heb 1: 3 *u'* all things by the word of his

upper See also UPPERMOST.
Ex 12: 7 on the *u'* door post of the houses,
Le 13:45 shall put a covering upon his *u'* lip,
De 24: 6 the nether or the *u'* millstone to
Jos 15:19 And he gave her the *u'* springs,
16: 5 unto Beth-horon the *u'*;
J'g 1:15 Caleb gave her the *u'* springs and
2Ki 1: 2 a lattice in his *u'* chamber that
18:17 stood by the conduit of the *u'* pool,
23:12 the top of the *u'* chamber of Ahaz,
1Ch 7:24 Beth-horon the nether, and the *u'*,
28:11 and of the *u'* chambers thereof,
2Ch 3: 9 he overlaid the *u'* chambers with
8: 5 Also he built Beth-horon the *u'*,
32:30 also stopped the *u'* watercourse of
Isa 7: 3 end of the conduit of the *u'* pool
36: 2 stood by the conduit of the *u'* pool
Eze 42: 5 Now the *u'* chambers were shorter:
Zep 2:14 shall lodge in the *u'* lintels of it;
M'r 14:15 shew you a large *u'* room furnished
Lu 22:12 shew you a large *u'* room furnished
Ac 1:13 they went up into an *u'* room,
9:37 they laid her in an *u'* chamber.
39 brought him into the *u'* chamber:
19: 1 having passed through the *u'* coasts
20: 8 many lights in the *u'* chamber,

uppermost
Ge 40:17 *u'* basket there was of all manner
Isa 17: 6 berries in the top of the *u'* bough,
Isa 17: 9 a forsaken bough, and an *u'* branch,
M't 23: 6 love the *u'* rooms at feasts, and
M'r 12:39 and the *u'* rooms at feasts:
Lu 11:43 love the *u'* seats in...synagogues,

upright
Ge 37: 7 lo, my sheaf arose, and also stood *u'*;
Ex 15: 8 the floods stood *u'* as an heap,
Le 26:13 of your yoke, and made you go *u'*.
1Sa 29: 6 thou hast been *u'*, and thy going
2Sa 22:24 was also *u'* before him, and have
26 merciful, and with the *u'* man
26 thou wilt shew thyself *u'*.
2Ch 29:34 the Levites were more *u'* in heart
Job 1: 1 and that man was perfect and *u'*,
8 a perfect and an *u'* man, one that
2: 3 a perfect and an *u'* man, one that
8: 6 If thou wert pure and *u'*; surely
12: 4 just *u'* man is laughed to scorn.
17: 8 *U'* men shall be astonied at this,
Ps 7:10 God, which saveth the *u'* in heart.
11: 2 may privily shoot at the *u'* in heart.
7 his countenance doth behold the *u'*.
18:23 I was also *u'* before him, and I
25 thyself merciful; with an *u'* man
25 thou wilt shew thyself *u'*;
19:13 then shall I be *u'*, and I shall be
20: 8 fallen: but we are risen, and stand *u'*.
25: 8 Good and *u'* is the Lord: therefore
32:11 for joy, all ye that are *u'* in heart.
33: 1 for praise is comely for the *u'*.
36:10 thy righteousness to the *u'* in heart.
37:14 slay such as be of *u'* conversation.
18 Lord knoweth the days of the *u'*:
37 perfect man, and behold the *u'*:
49:14 *u'* shall have dominion over them
64:10 and all the *u'* in heart shall glory.
92:15 To shew that the Lord is *u'*: he is
94:15 all the *u'* in heart shall follow it.
97:11 and gladness for the *u'* in heart.
111: 1 heart, in the assembly of the *u'*,
112: 2 generation of the *u'* shall be blessed.
4 Unto the *u'* there ariseth light in
119:137 O Lord, and *u'* are thy judgments.
125: 4 to them that are *u'* in their hearts.
140:13 the *u'* shall dwell in thy presence.
Pr 2:21 For the *u'* shall dwell in the land,
10:29 of the Lord is strength to the *u'*:
11: 3 The integrity of the *u'* shall guide
6 righteousness of the *u'* shall deliver
11 By the blessing of the *u'* the city is
20 are *u'* in their way are his delight.
12: 6 mouth of the *u'* shall deliver them
13: 6 keepeth him that is *u'* in the way:
14:11 tabernacle of the *u'* shall flourish.
15: 8 the prayer of the *u'* is his delight.
16:17 The highway of the *u'* is to depart
21:18 and the transgressor for the *u'*.
29 as for the *u'*, he directeth his way.
28:10 the *u'* shall have good things in
29:10 The bloodthirsty hate the *u'*: but
27 is *u'* in the way is abomination to
Ec 7:29 found, that God had made man *u'*:
12:10 that which was written was *u'*,
Ca 1: 4 more than wine: the *u'* love thee.
Isa 26: 7 thou, most *u'*, dost weigh the path
Jer 10: 5 They are *u'* as the palm tree, but
Da 8:18 but he touched me, and set me *u'*.
10:11 I speak unto thee, and stand *u'*:
11:17 kingdom, and *u'* ones with him;
Mic 7: 2 and there is none *u'* among men:
4 *u'* is sharper than a thorn hedge:
Hab 2: 4 which is lifted up is not *u'* in him:
Ac 14:10 a loud voice, Stand *u'* on thy feet.

uprightly
Ps 15: 2 He that walketh *u'*, and worketh
58: 1 do ye judge *u'*, O ye sons of men?
75: 2 the congregation I will judge *u'*.
84:11 withhold from them that walk *u'*.
Pr 2: 7 is a buckler to them that walk *u'*.
10: 9 He that walketh *u'* walketh surely:
15:21 man of understanding walketh *u'*.
28:18 Whoso walketh *u'* shall be saved:
Isa 33:15 righteously, and speaketh *u'*;
Am 5:10 they abhor him that speaketh *u'*.
Mic 2: 7 do good to him that walketh *u'*?
Ga 2:14 they walked not *u'* according to

uprightness
De 9: 5 or for the *u'* of thine heart, dost
1Ki 3: 6 and in *u'* of heart with thee;
9: 4 in integrity of heart, and in *u'*,
1Ch 29:17 the heart, and hast pleasure in *u'*
17 *u'* of mine heart I have willingly
Job 4: 6 thy hope, and the *u'* of thy ways?
33: 3 shall be of the *u'* of my heart:
23 thousand, to shew unto man his *u'*:
Ps 9: 8 judgment to the people in *u'*.
25:21 Let integrity and *u'* preserve me;
111: 8 ever, and are done in truth and *u'*.
119: 7 I will praise thee with *u'* of heart,
143:10 good; lead me into the land of *u'*.
Pr 2:13 Who leave the paths of *u'*, to walk
14: 2 He that walketh in his *u'* feareth
28: 6 is the poor that walketh in his *u'*,
Isa 26: 7 The way of the just is *u'*: thou,
10 land of *u'* will he deal unjustly,
57: 2 beds, each one walking in his *u'*.

uprising
Ps 139: 2 my downsitting and mine *u'*,

uproar
1Ki 1:41 noise of the city being in an *u'*?
M't 26: 5 there be an *u'* among the people.
M'r 14: 2 lest there be an *u'* of the people.
Ac 17: 5 and set all the city on an *u'*,
Ac 19:40 called in question for this day's *u'*,
20: 1 And after the *u'* was ceased, Paul
21:31 that all Jerusalem was in an *u'*.
38 before these days madest an *u'*,

upside
2Ki 21:13 wiping it, and turning it *u'*
Ps 146: 9 way of the wicked he turneth *u'* down.
Isa 24: 1 waste, and turneth it *u'* down,
29:16 your turning of things *u'* down shall
Ac 17: 6 that have turned the world *u'* down

upward
Ge 7:20 Fifteen cubits *u'* did the waters
Ex 38:26 from twenty years old and *u'*,
Nu 1: 3 From twenty years old and *u'*, all
18, 20, 22, 24, 26, 28, 30, 32, 34, 36, 38, 40,
42, 45 from twenty years old and *u'*,
3:15 every male from a month old and *u*
22, 28, 34, 39, 40, 43 a month old and *u'*,
4: 3, 23, 30, 35, 39, 43, 47 years old and *u'*
8:24 twenty and five years old and *u'*
14:29 from twenty years old and *u'*,
26: 2 from twenty years old and *u'*,
4 from twenty years old and *u'*;
62 all males from a month old and *u'*:
32:11 from twenty years old and *u'*,
J'g 1:36 to Akrabbim, from the rock, and *u'*.
1Sa 9: 2 from his shoulders and *u'* he was
10:23 people from his shoulders and *u'*.
2Ki 3:21 were able to put an armour, and *u'*,
19:30 root downward, and bear fruit *u'*.
1Ch 23: 3 the age of thirty years and *u'*:
24 the age of twenty years and *u'*.
2Ch 31:16 males, from three years old and *u'*,
17 from twenty years old and *u'*,
Ezr 3: 8 from twenty years old and *u'*,
Job 5: 7 unto trouble, as the sparks fly *u'*.
Ec 3:21 the spirit of man that goeth *u'*,
Isa 8:21 king and their God, and look *u'*.
37:31 root downward, and bear fruit *u'*:
38:14 mine eyes fail with looking *u'*:
Eze 1:11 their wings were stretched *u'*;
27 the appearance of his loins even *u'*,
8: 2 from his loins even *u'*, as the
41: 7 a winding about still *u'* to the side
7 went still *u'* round about the
7 breadth of the house was still *u'*,
43:15 altar and *u'* shall be four horns.
Hag 2:15 you, consider from this day and *u'*,
18 Consider now from this day and *u'*,

Ur (*ur*)
Ge 11:28 his nativity, in *U'* of the Chaldees.
31 with them from *U'* of the Chaldees,
15: 7 thee out of *U'* of the Chaldees,
1Ch 11:35 the Hararite, Eliphal the son of *U'*,
Ne 9: 7 him forth out of *U'* of the Chaldees,

Urbane (*ur'-bane*)
Ro 16: 9 Salute *U'*, our helper in Christ,

urge See also URGED.
Lu 11:53 the Pharisees began to *u'* him

urged
Ge 33:11 and he *u'* him, and he took it.
J'g 16:16 daily with her words, and *u'* him,
19: 7 depart, his father in law *u'* him:
2Ki 2:17 they *u'* him till he was ashamed,
5:16 And he *u'* him to take it; but he
23 he *u'* him, and bound two talents

urgent
Ex 12:33 the Egyptians were *u'* upon the
Da 3:22 the king's commandment was *u'*,

Uri (*u'-ri*)
Ex 31: 2 by name Bezaleel the son of *U'*,
35:30 by name Bezaleel the son of *U'*,
38:22 And Bezaleel the son of *U'*, the son
1Ki 4:19 Geber the son of *U'* was in the
1Ch 2:20 And Hur begat *U'*, and *U'* begat
2Ch 1: 5 that Bezaleel the son of *U'*, the son
Ezr 10:24 Shallum, and Telem, and *U'*.

Uriah (*u-ri'-ah*) See also URIAH'S; URIAS; URIJAH.
2Sa 11: 3 Eliam, the wife of *U'* the Hittite?
6 saying, Send me *U'* the Hittite.
6 And Joab sent *U'* to David.
7 And when *U'* was come unto him,
8 And David said to *U'*, Go down to
8 And *U'* departed out of the king's
9 *U'* slept at the door of the king's
10 *U'* went not down unto his house,
10 David said unto *U'*, Camest thou
11 *U'* said unto David, The ark, and
12 David said to *U'*, Tarry here to day
12 So *U'* abode in Jerusalem that day,
14 Joab, and sent it by the hand of *U'*.
15 Set ye *U'* in the forefront of the
16 he assigned *U'* unto a place where
17 David; and *U'* the Hittite died also.
21 Thy servant *U'* the Hittite is dead
24 thy servant *U'* the Hittite is dead
26 the wife of *U'* heard that *U'* her
12: 9 killed *U'* the Hittite with the sword,
10 taken the wife of *U'* the Hittite to
23:39 *U'* the Hittite: thirty and seven in
1Ki 15: 5 in the matter of *U'* the Hittite.
1Ch 11:41 *U'* the Hittite, Zabad the son of
Ezr 8:33 the hand of Meremoth the son of *U'*
Isa 8: 2 witnesses to record, *U'* the priest,

Uriah's (*u-ri'-ahz*)
2Sa 12:15 Lord struck the child that *U'* wife

Urias (*u-ri'-as*) See also URIAH.
M't 1: 6 her that had been the wife of *U'*;

Uriel (*u'-re-el*)
1Ch 6:24 Tahath his son, *U'* his son, Uzziah
15: 5 the sons of Kohath; *U'* the chief,

1Ch 15: 11 and for the Levites, for U'. Asaiah,
2Ch 13: 2 the daughter of U' of Gibeah.

Urijah (u-ri'-jah) See also URIAH.
2Ki 16: 10 Ahaz sent to U' the priest the
11 And U' the priest built an altar
11 U' the priest made it against king
15 Ahaz commanded U' the priest,
16 Thus did U' the priest, according to
Ne 3: 4 repaired Meremoth the son of U',
21 repaired Meremoth the son of U'
8: 4 and Anaiah, and U', and Hilkiah,
Jer 26: 20 U' the son of Shemaiah of
21 when U' heard it, he was afraid,
23 they fetched forth U' out of Egypt,

Urim (u'-rim)
Ex 28: 30 the breastplate of judgment the U'
Le 8: 8 he put in the breastplate the U'
Nu 27: 21 judgment of U' before the Lord:
De 33: 8 thy Thummim and thy U' be with
1Sa 28: 6 neither by dreams, nor by U', nor
Ezr 2: 63 till there stood up a priest with U'
Ne 7: 65 till there stood up a priest with U'

use See also ABUSE; USED; USES; USEST; USETH; USING.
Le 7: 24 may be used in any other u':
19: 26 neither shall ye u' enchantment,
Nu 10: 2 mayest u' them for the calling of the
15: 39 after which ye u' to go a whoring:
De 26: 14 ought thereof for any unclean u',
2Sa 1: 18 children of Judah the u' of the bow:
1Ch 12: 2 u' both the right hand and the
28: 15 to the u' of every candlestick.
Jer 23: 31 that u' their tongues, and say, He
31: 23 shall u' this speech in the land of
46: 11 in vain shalt thou u' many medicines:
Eze 12: 23 more u' it as a proverb in Israel;
16: 44 shall u' this proverb against thee,
18: 2 u' this proverb concerning the
3 more to u' this proverb in Israel.
21: 21 of the two ways, to u' divination:
M't 5: 44 them which despitefully u' you,
6: 7 when ye pray, u' not vain repetitions,
Lu 6: 28 them which despitefully u' you,
Ac 14: 5 to u' them despitefully, and to
Ro 1: 26 did change the natural u' into that
27 leaving...natural u' of the woman,
1Co 7: 21 mayest be made free, u' it rather.
31 they that u' this world, as not
2Co 1: 17 thus minded, did I u' lightness?
3: 12 we u' great plainness of speech:
13: 10 being present I...u' sharpness,
Ga 5: 13 u' not liberty for an occasion to the
Eph 4: 29 is good to the u' of edifying,
1Ti 1: 8 is good, if a man u' it lawfully;
3: 10 then let them u' the office of a deacon,
5: 23 u' a little wine for thy stomach's
2Ti 2: 21 and meet for the master's u',
Heb 5: 14 those who by reason of u' have
1Pe 4: 9 U' hospitality one to another

used See also ABUSED; MISUSED.
Ex 21: 36 the ox hath u' to push in time past,
Le 7: 24 may be u' in any other use:
J'g 14: 10 a beast, for so u' the young men to do.
20 whom he had u' as his friend.
2Ki 17: 17 u' divination and enchantments.
21: 6 times, and u' enchantments,
2Ch 33: 6 times, and u' enchantments,
6 and u' witchcraft, and dealt with a
Jer 2: 24 A wild ass u' to the wilderness,
Eze 22: 29 people of the land have u' oppression,
35: 11 envy which thou hast u' out of thy
Ho 12: 10 multiplied visions, and u' similitudes,
M'r 2: 18 and of the Pharisees u' to fast:
Ac 8: 9 in the same city u' sorcery,
19: 19 of them also which u' curious arts
27: 17 they u' helps, undergirding the ship;
Ro 3: 13 their tongues they have u' deceit;
1Co 9: 12 we have not u' this power;
15 But I have u' none of these things:
1Th 2: 5 time u' we flattering words,
1Ti 3: 13 that have u' the office of a deacon
Heb 10: 33 companions of them that were so u'.

uses
Tit 3: 14 good works for necessary u',

usest
Ps 119: 132 as thou u' to do unto those that

useth
De 18: 10 or that u' divination, or an observer
Es 6: 8 be brought which the king u' to wear,
Pr 15: 2 of the wise u' knowledge aright:
18: 23 The poor u' intreaties; but the
Jer 22: 13 that u' his neighbour's service
Eze 16: 44 every one that u' proverbs shall
Heb 5: 13 For one that u' milk is unskilful

using See also ABUSING.
Col 2: 22 Which all are to perish with the u';)
1Pe 2: 16 not u' your liberty for a cloke of

usurer
Ex 22: 25 thou shalt not be to him as an u',

usurp
1Ti 2: 12 nor to u' authority over the man,

usury
Ex 22: 25 shalt thou lay upon him u'.
Le 25: 36 Take thou no u' of him, or increase:
37 not give him thy money upon u',
De 23: 19 not lend upon u' to thy brother;
19 u' of money, u' of victuals,
19 u' of any thing that is lent upon
19 any thing that is lent upon u':
23: 20 a stranger thou mayest lend upon u';
De 23: 20 thou shalt not lend upon u':
Ne 5: 7 Ye exact u', every one of his
10 I pray you, let us leave off this u'.
Ps 15: 5 putteth not out his money to u',
Pr 28: 8 He that by u' and unjust gain
Isa 24: 2 as with the taker of u', so with
2 so with the giver of u' to him.
Jer 15: 10 I have neither lent on u', nor men
10 nor men have lent to me on u';
Eze 18: 8 thou hath not given forth upon u',
13 Hath given forth upon u', and hath
17 hath not received u' nor increase,
22: 12 thou hast taken u' and increase,
M't 25: 27 have received mine own with u'.
Lu 19: 23 have required mine own with u'?

us-ward
Ps 40: 5 and thy thoughts which are to u':
Eph 1: 19 his power to u' who believed,
2Pe 3: 9 but is longsuffering to u', not

Uthai (u'-thahee)
1Ch 9: 4 U' the son of Ammihud, the son
Ezr 8: 14 U', and Zabbud, and with them

utmost See also OUTMOST; UTTERMOST.
Ge 49: 26 the u' bound of the everlasting hills:
Nu 22: 36 Arnon, which is in the u' coast.
41 might see the u' part of the people.
23: 13 shalt see but the u' part of them,
De 34: 2 the land of Judah, unto the u' sea.
Jer 9: 26 and all that are in the u' corners,
25: 23 and all that are in the u' corners,
49: 32 them that are in the u' corners;
50: 26 against her from the u' border,
Joe 2: 20 his hinder part toward the u' sea,
Lu 11: 31 from the u' parts of the earth to

utter See also OUTER; UTTERED; UTTERETH; UTTERING; UTTERMOST.
Le 5: 1 if he do not u' it, then he shall
Jos 2: 14 yours, if ye u' not this our business.
20 And if thou u' this our business,
J'g 5: 12 Deborah: awake, awake, u' a song:
1Ki 20: 42 I appointed to u' destruction,
Job 8: 10 and u' words out of their heart?
15: 2 a wise man u' vain knowledge,
27: 4 nor my tongue u' deceit.
33: 3 lips shall u' knowledge clearly.
Ps 78: 2 I will u' dark sayings of old:
94: 4 long shall they u' and speak hard
106: 2 Who can u' the mighty acts of the
119: 171 My lips shall u' praise, when
145: 7 shall abundantly u' the memory
Pr 14: 5 but a false witness will u' lies.
23: 33 heart shall u' perverse things.
Ec 1: 8 are full of labour; man cannot u' it:
5: 2 hasty to u' any thing before God:
Isa 32: 6 and to u' error against the Lord,
48: 20 u' it even to the end of the earth;
Jer 1: 16 I will u' my judgments against
25: 30 u' his voice from his holy
Eze 24: 3 u' a parable unto the rebellious
40: 31, 37 were toward the u' court;
42: 1 brought me forth into the u' court,
3 pavement...was for the u' court,
7 toward the u' court on the forepart
8 chambers that were in the u' court
9 goeth into them from the u' court.
14 of the holy place into the u' court,
44: 19 they go forth into the u' court,
19 even into the u' court of the people,
46: 20 bear them not out into the u' court,
21 brought me forth into the u' court.
47: 2 u' gate by the way that looketh
Joe 2: 11 Lord shall u' his voice before his
3: 16 and u' his voice from Jerusalem;
Am 1: 2 and u' his voice from Jerusalem;
Na 1: 8 he will make an u' end of...place
9 he will make an u' end: affliction
Zec 14: 11 shall be no more u' destruction;
M't 13: 35 u' things which have been kept
1Co 14: 9 except ye u' by the tongue words
2Co 12: 4 it is not lawful for a man to u'.

utterance
Ac 2: 4 tongues, as the Spirit gave them u'.
1Co 1: 5 ye are enriched by him, in all u',
2Co 8: 7 in faith, and u', and knowledge,
Eph 6: 19 that u' may be given unto me, that
Col 4: 3 would open unto us a door of u',

uttered
Nu 30: 6 vowed, or u' ought out of her lips,
8 that which she u' with her lips,
J'g 11: 11 Jephthah u' all his words before
2Sa 22: 14 and the most High u' his voice.
Ne 6: 19 me, and u' my words to him.
Job 26: 4 To whom hast thou u' words? and
42: 3 have I u' that I understood not;
Ps 46: 6 he u' his voice, the earth melted.
66: 14 Which my lips have u', and my
Jer 48: 34 Jahaz, have they u' their voice,
51: 55 waters, a noise of their voice is u':
Hab 3: 10 the deep u' his voice, and lifted up
Ro 8: 26 with groanings which cannot be u'.
Heb 5: 11 things to say, and hard to be u',
Re 10: 3 seven thunders u' their voices.
4 seven thunders had u' their voices,
4 which the seven thunders u',

uttereth
Job 15: 5 For thy mouth u' thine iniquity,
Ps 19: 2 Day unto day u' speech, and night
Pr 1: 20 she u' her voice in the streets:
21 the city she u' her words, saying,
10: 18 and he that u' a slander, is a fool.
29: 11 A fool u' all his mind: but a wise
Jer 10: 13 When he u' his voice, there is a
51: 16 When he u' his voice, there is a
Mic 7: 3 he u' his mischievous desire:

uttering
Isa 59: 13 conceiving and u' from the heart

utterly ^
Ex 17: 14 I will u' put out the remembrance of
22: 17 father u' refuse to give her unto him,
20 only, he shall be u' destroyed.
23: 24 but thou shalt u' overthrow them,
Le 13: 44 priest...pronounce him u' unclean;
26: 44 I abhor them, to destroy them u',
Nu 15: 31 that soul shall be u' cut off;
21: 2 then I will u' destroy their cities.
3 they u' destroyed them and their
30: 12 husband hath u' made them void
De 2: 34 and u' destroyed the men, and the
3: 6 And we u' destroyed them, as we
6 u' destroying the men, women,
4: 26 ye shall soon u' perish from off the
26 upon it, but shall u' be destroyed.
7: 2 smite them, and u' destroy them;
26 but thou shalt u' detest it, and thou
26 and thou shalt u' abhor it; for it is a
12: 2 Ye shall u' destroy all the places,
13: 15 destroying it u', and all that is
20: 17 But thou shalt u' destroy them;
31: 29 death ye will u' corrupt yourselves,
Jos 2: 10 and Og, whom ye u' destroyed.
6: 21 they u' destroyed all that was in
8: 26 until he had u' destroyed all the
10: 1 taken Ai, and had u' destroyed it;
28 the king thereof he u' destroyed,
35 therein he u' destroyed that day,
37 destroyed it u', and all the souls
39 and u' destroyed all the souls that
40 but u' destroyed all that breathed,
11: 11 of the sword, u' destroying them:
12 he u' destroyed them, as Moses
20 that he might destroy them u',
21 destroyed them u' with their cities.
17: 13 tribute; but did not u' drive them out.
J'g 1: 17 Zephath, and u' destroyed it.
28 and did not u' drive them out.
15: 2 thought that thou hadst u' hated her;
21: 11 Ye shall u' destroy every male,
1Sa 15: 3 and u' destroy all that they have,
8 u' destroyed all the people with the
9 good, and would not u' destroy them:
9 and refuse, that they destroyed u'.
15 and the rest we have u' destroyed.
18 Go and u' destroy the sinners the
20 have u' destroyed the Amalekites.
21 which should have been u' destroyed,
27: 12 his people Israel u' to abhor him;
2Sa 17: 10 is as the heart of a lion, shall u' melt:
23: 7 they shall be u' burned with fire in the
1Ki 9: 21 also were not able u' to destroy,
2Ki 19: 11 to all lands, by destroying them u':
1Ch 4: 41 destroyed them u' unto this day,
2Ch 20: 23 Seir, u' to slay and destroy them:
31: 1 until they had u' destroyed them
32: 14 nations that my fathers u' destroyed,
Ne 9: 31 thou didst not u' consume them,
Ps 37: 24 fall, he shall not be u' cast down:
73: 19 they are u' consumed with terrors.
89: 33 my lovingkindness will I not u' take
119: 8 thy statutes: O forsake me not u'.
43 word of truth u' out of my mouth;
Ca 8: 7 for love, it would u' be contemned.
Isa 2: 18 And the idols be shall u' abolish.
6: 11 man, and the land be u' desolate,
11: 15 shall u' destroy the tongue of the
24: 3 shall be u' emptied, and u' spoiled:
19 The earth is u' broken down, the
34: 2 he hath u' destroyed them, he
37: 11 all lands by destroying them u';
40: 30 and the young men shall u' fall:
56: 3 u' separated me from his people:
60: 12 yea, those nations shall be u' wasted.
Jer 9: 4 for every brother will u' supplant,
12: 17 I will u' pluck up and destroy that
14: 19 Hast thou u' rejected Judah? hath
23: 39 behold, I, even I, will u' forget you,
25: 9 about, and will u' destroy them,
29 and should ye be u' unpunished?
50: 21 waste and u' destroy after them,
26 up as heaps, and destroy her u':
51: 3 men; destroy ye u' all her host.
58 walls of Babylon shall be u' broken.
La 5: 22 But thou hast u' rejected us; thou
Eze 9: 6 Slay u' old and young, both maids,
17: 10 shall it not u' wither, when the east
27: 31 make themselves u' bald for thee,
29: 10 of Egypt u' waste and desolate,
Da 11: 44 destroy, and u' to make away many.
Ho 1: 6 Israel; but I will u' take them away.
10: 15 shall the king of Israel u' be cut off.
Am 9: 8 I will not u' destroy the house of
Na 1: 15 through thee; he is u' cut off.
Zep 1: 2 will u' consume all things from off
Zec 11: 17 his right eye shall be u' darkened.
1Co 6: 7 there is u' a fault among you,
2Pe 2: 12 and shall u' perish in their own
Re 18: 8 she shall be u' burned with fire:

uttermost See also UTMOST.
Ex 26: 4 in the u' edge of another curtain,
36: 11 in the u' side of another curtain,
17 upon the u' edge of the curtain
Nu 11: 1 were in the u' parts of the camp.
20: 16 a city in the u' of thy border:
De 11: 24 unto the u' sea shall your coast be
Jos 15: 1 was the u' part of the south coast.
5 of the sea at the u' part of Jordan:
21 the u' cities of the tribe of the
1Sa 14: 2 tarried in the u' part of Gibeah
1Ki 6: 24 from the u' part of the one wing
24 wing unto the u' part of the other

2Ki 7: 5 the *u'* part of the camp of Syria,
8 came to the *u'* part of the camp,
Ne 1: 9 out unto the *u'* part of the heaven,
Ps 2: 8 and the *u'* parts of the earth for thy
65: 8 that dwell in the *u'* parts are afraid
139: 9 dwell in the *u'* parts of the sea;
Isa 7:18 the *u'* part of the rivers of Egypt,
24:16 From the *u'* part of the earth have
M't 5:26 till thou hast paid the *u'* farthing.
12:42 from the *u'* parts of the earth
M'r 13:27 from the *u'* part of the earth
27 to the *u'* part of heaven.
Ac 1: 8 unto the *u'* part of the earth.
24:22 I will know the *u'* of your matter.
1Th 2:16 wrath is come upon them to the *u'*.
Heb 7:25 able also to save them to the *u'*

Uz (*uz*)
Ge 10:23 children of Aram; *U'*, and Hul,
36:28 children of Dishan are these; *U'*,
1Ch 1:17 Aram, and *U'*, and Hul, and Gether,
42 The sons of Dishan; *U'*, and Aran.
Job 1: 1 There was a man in the land of *U'*,
Jer 25:20 and all the kings of the land of *U'*,
La 4:21 that dwellest in the land of *U'*;

Uzai (*u'-zahee*)
Ne 3:25 Palal the son of *U'*, over against

Uzal (*u'-zal*)
Ge 10:27 Hadoram, and *U'*, and Diklah,
1Ch 1:21 Hadoram also, and *U'*, and Diklah,

Uzza (*uz'-zah*) See also UZZAH.
2Ki 21:18 own house, in the garden of *U'*:
26 his sepulchre in the garden of *U'*:
1Ch 6:29 son, Shimei his son, *U'* his son,
8: 7 he removed them, and begat *U'*,
13: 7 and *U'* and Ahio drave the cart.
9 *U'* put forth his hand to hold the
1Ch 13:10 the Lord was kindled against *U'*,
11 Lord had made a breach upon *U'*:
Ezr 2:49 The children of *U'*, the children of
Ne 7:51 the children of *U'*, the children of

Uzzah (*uz'-zah*) See also PEREZ-UZZAH; UZZA.
2Sa 6: 3 *U'* and Ahio, the sons of Abinadab,
6 *U'* put forth his hand to the ark of
7 the Lord was kindled against *U'*;
8 Lord had made a breach upon *U'*:

Uzzen-sherah (*uz''-zen-she'-rah*)
1Ch 7:24 built Beth-horon...and *U'*.)

Uzzi (*uz'-zi*)
1Ch 6: 5 Bukki, and Bukki begat *U'*,
6 *U'* begat Zerahiah, and Zerahiah
51 Bukki his son, *U'* his son, Zerahiah
7: 2 sons of Tola; *U'*, and Rephaiah,
3 And the sons of *U'*; Izrahiah:
7 sons of Bela; Ezbon, and *U'*, and
9: 8 and Elah the son of *U'*, the son of
Ezr 7: 4 Zerahiah, the son of *U'*, the son of
Ne 11:22 was *U'* the son of Bani, the son
12:19 Joiarib, Mattenai; of Jedaiah, *U'*;
42 Eleazar, and *U'*, and Jehohanan,

Uzzia (*uz-zi'-ah*)
1Ch 11:44 *U'* the Ashterathite, Shama and

Uzziah (*uz-zi'-ah*) See also OZIAS.
2Ki 15:13 the nine and thirtieth year of *U'*
30 year of Jotham the son of *U'*.
32 Jotham the son of *U'*...to reign.
34 to all that his father *U'* had done.
1Ch 6:24 Uriel his son, *U'* his son, and
27:25 was Jehonathan the son of *U'*:
2Ch 26: 1 all the people of Judah took *U'*,
3 Sixteen years old was *U'* when he
8 the Ammonites gave gifts to *U'*:
9 *U'* built towers in Jerusalem at
2Ch 26:11 *U'* had an host of fighting men,
14 *U'* prepared for them...shields,
18 And they withstood *U'* the king,
18 It appertaineth not unto thee, *U'*,
19 *U'* was wroth, and had a censer in
21 *U'* the king was a leper unto the
22 Now the rest of the acts of *U'*, first
23 So *U'* slept with his fathers, and
27: 2 according to all his father *U'* did:
Ezr 10:21 and Shemaiah, and Jehiel, and *U'*.
Ne 11: 4 of Judah; Athaiah the son of *U'*,
Isa 1: 1 in the days of *U'*, Jotham, Ahaz,
6: 1 In the year that king *U'* died I saw
7: 1 the son of Jotham, the son of *U'*,
Ho 1: 1 in the days of *U'*, Jotham, Ahaz,
Am 1: 1 in the days of *U'* king of Judah,
Zec 14: 5 the earthquake in the days of *U'*

Uzziel (*uz-zi'-el*) See also UZZIELITES.
Ex 6:18 and Izhar, and Hebron, and *U'*:
22 And the sons of *U'*; Mishael, and
Le 10: 4 the sons of *U'* the uncle of Aaron,
Nu 3:19 and Izehar, Hebron, and *U'*.
30 shall be Elizaphan the son of *U'*.
1Ch 4:42 Rephaiah, and *U'*, the sons of Ishi.
6: 2 Amram, Izhar, and Hebron, and *U'*.
18 and Izhar, and Hebron, and *U'*.
7: 7 Ezbon, and Uzzi, and *U'*, and
15:10 Of the sons of *U'*; Amminadab
23:12 Amram, Izhar, Hebron, and *U'*,
20 Of the sons of *U'*; Micah the first,
24:24 Of the sons of *U'*; Michah:
25: 4 Bukkiah, Mattaniah, *U'*, Shebuel,
2Ch 29:14 of Jeduthun; Shemaiah, and *U'*.
Ne 3: 8 Next unto him repaired *U'* the son

Uzzielites (*uz-zi'-el-ites*)
Nu 3:27 and the family of the *U'*:
1Ch 26:23 the Hebronites, and the *U'*:

V.

vagabond See also VAGABONDS.
Ge 4:12 a *v'* shalt thou be in the earth.
14 a fugitive and a *v'* in the earth;
Ac 19:13 Then certain of the *v'* Jews,

vagabonds
Ps 109:10 Let his children be continually *v'*,

vail See also VAILS; VEIL.
Ge 24:65 therefore she took a *v'*, and
38:14 and covered her with a *v'*, and
19 laid by her *v'* from her, and put on
Ex 26:31 And thou shalt make a *v'* of blue,
33 thou shalt hang up the *v'* under
33 bring in thither within the *v'* the
33 *v'* shall divide unto you between
35 shalt set the table without the *v'*,
27:21 of the congregation without the *v'*,
30: 6 the *v'* that is by the ark of the
34:33 them, he put a *v'* on his face.
34 took the *v'* off, until he came out.
35 Moses put the *v'* upon his face
35:12 seat, and the *v'* of the covering,
36:35 he made a *v'* of blue, and purple,
38:27 sanctuary,...the sockets of the *v'*;
39:34 skins, and the *v'* of the covering,
40: 3 and cover the ark with the *v'*.
21 and set up the *v'* of the covering,
22 northward, without the *v'*.
26 of the congregation before the *v'*:
Le 4: 6 before the *v'* of the sanctuary,
17 before the Lord, even before the *v'*.
16: 2 holy place within the *v'* before the
12 small, and bring it within the *v'*:
15 and bring his blood within the *v'*,
21:23 Only he shall not go in unto the *v'*,
24: 3 Without the *v'* of the testimony, in
Nu 4: 5 shall take down the covering *v'*,
18: 7 of the altar, and within the *v'*,
Ru 3:15 Bring the *v'* that thou hast upon
2Ch 3:14 And he made the *v'* of blue, and
Isa 25: 7 *v'* that is spread over all nations.
2Co 3:13 which put a *v'* over his face, that
14 the same *v'* untaken away in the
14 which *v'* is done away in Christ.
15 read, the *v'* is upon their heart.
16 Lord, the *v'* shall be taken away.

vails
Isa 3:23 linen, and the hoods, and the *v'*.

vain See also VAINGLORY.
Ex 5: 9 let them not regard *v'* words.
20: 7 name of the Lord thy God in *v'*;
7 guiltless that taketh his name in *v'*.
Le 26:16 ye shall sow your seed in *v'*, for
20 your strength shall be spent in *v'*:
De 5:11 name of the Lord thy God in *v'*:
11 guiltless that taketh his name in *v'*.
32:47 For it is not a *v'* thing for you;
J'g 9: 4 Abimelech hired *v'* and light
11: 3 were gathered *v'* men to Jephthah,
1Sa 12:21 then should ye go after *v'* things,
21 profit nor deliver; for they are *v'*.
25:21 in *v'* have I kept all that this
2Sa 6:20 one of the *v'* fellows shamelessly
2Ki 17:15 became *v'*, and went after the
18:20 sayest, (but they are but *v'* words,)
2Ch 13: 7 are gathered unto him *v'* men,
Job 9:29 wicked, why then labour I in *v'*?
11:11 For he knoweth *v'* men: he seeth
12 For *v'* man would be wise, though
15: 2 a wise man utter *v'* knowledge, and
16: 3 Shall *v'* words have an end? or
21:34 How then comfort ye me in *v'*,
Job 27:12 then are ye thus altogether *v'*?
35:16 doth Job open his mouth in *v'*;
39:16 her labour is in *v'* without fear;
41: 9 the hope of him is in *v'*: shall not
Ps 2: 1 and the people imagine a *v'* thing?
26: 4 I have not sat with *v'* persons,
33:17 An horse is a *v'* thing for safety:
39: 6 every man walketh in a *v'* shew:
6 surely they are disquieted in *v'*:
60:11 trouble: for *v'* is the help of man.
62:10 and become not *v'* in robbery:
73:13 I have cleansed my heart in *v'*,
89:47 hast thou made all men in *v'*?
108:12 trouble: for *v'* is the help of man.
119:113 I hate *v'* thoughts: but thy law do I
127: 1 they labour in *v'* that build it:
1 the watchman waketh but in *v'*.
2 It is *v'* for you to rise up early, to
139:20 thine enemies take thy name in *v'*.
Pr 1:17 Surely in *v'* the net is spread in
12:11 he that followeth *v'* persons is
28:19 he that followeth after *v'* persons
30: 9 and take the name of my God in *v'*.
31:30 is deceitful, and beauty is *v'*: but
Ec 6:12 all the days of his *v'* life which he
Isa 1:13 Bring no more *v'* oblations;
30: 7 For the Egyptians shall help in *v'*,
36: 5 thou, (but they are but *v'* words)
45:18 he created it not in *v'*, he formed
19 Seek ye me in *v'*: I the Lord speak
49: 4 Then I said, I have laboured in *v'*,
4 strength for nought, and in *v'*:
65:23 They shall not labour in *v'*, nor
Jer 2: 5 after vanity, and are become *v'*?
30 *v'* have I smitten your children;
3:23 Truly in *v'* is salvation hoped for
4:14 thy *v'* thoughts lodge within thee?
30 in *v'* shalt thou make thyself fair;
6:29 the fire; the founder melteth in *v'*:
8: 8 us? Lo, certainly in *v'* made he it;
8 it; the pen of the scribes is in *v'*.
10: 3 customs of the people are in *v'*:
23:16 unto you: they make you *v'*:
46:11 in *v'* shalt thou use many
50: 9 man; none shall return in *v'*.
51:58 and the people shall labour in *v'*,
La 2:14 have seen *v'* and foolish things
4:17 eyes as yet failed for our *v'* help:
Eze 6:10 said in *v'* that I would do this evil
12:24 shall be no more any *v'* vision
13: 7 Have ye not seen a *v'* vision, and
Zec 10: 2 false dreams; they comfort in *v'*:
Mal 3:14 have said, It is *v'* to serve God:
M't 6: 7 when ye pray, use not *v'* repetitions,
15: 9 But in *v'* they do worship me,
M'r 7: 7 Howbeit in *v'* they do worship me,
Ac 4:25 and the people imagine *v'* things?
Ro 1:21 became *v'* in their imaginations,
13: 4 for he beareth not the sword in *v'*:
1Co 3:20 of the wise, that they are *v'*.
15: 2 you, unless ye have believed in *v'*.
10 bestowed upon me was not in *v'*;
14 risen, then is our preaching *v'*,
14 and your faith is also *v'*.
17 be not raised, your faith is *v'*;
58 your labour is not in *v'* in the Lord.
2Co 6: 1 receive not the grace of God in *v'*.
9: 3 boasting of you should be in *v'*
Ga 2: 2 I should run, or had run, in *v'*.
21 the law, then Christ is dead in *v'*.
3: 4 many things in *v'*? if it be yet in *v'*.
4:11 bestowed upon you labour in *v'*.
Ga 5:26 Let us not be desirous of *v'* glory,
Eph 5: 6 man deceive you with *v'* words:
Ph'p 2:16 not run in *v'*, neither laboured in *v'*.
Col 2: 8 through philosophy and *v'* deceit,
1Th 2: 1 in unto you, that it was not in *v'*:
3: 5 you, and our labour be in *v'*.
1Ti 1: 6 have turned aside unto *v'* jangling;
6:20 avoiding profane and *v'* babblings,
2Ti 2:16 shun profane and *v'* babblings: for
Tit 1:10 unruly and *v'* talkers and deceivers,
3: 9 for they are unprofitable and *v'*.
Jas 1:26 own heart, this man's religion is *v'*.
2:20 O *v'* man, that faith without works
4: 5 think that the scripture saith in *v'*,
1Pe 1:18 your *v'* conversation received by

vainglory See also VAIN and GLORY.
Ph'p 2: 3 be done through strife or *v'*;

vainly
Col 2:18 *v'* puffed up by his fleshly mind,

Vajezatha (*va-jez'-a-thah*)
Es 9: 9 and Arisai, and Aridai, and *V'*,

vale See also VALLEY.
Ge 14: 3 together in the *v'* of Siddim,
8 with them in the *v'* of Siddim;
10 *v'* of Siddim was full of slimepits;
37:14 sent him out of the *v'* of Hebron,
De 1: 7 in the hills, and in the *v'*, and in
Jos 10:40 of the south, and of the *v'*, and of
1Ki 10:27 sycomore trees that are in the *v'*,
2Ch 1:15 sycomore trees that are in the *v'*
Jer 33:13 in the cities of the *v'*, and in the

valiant See also VALIANTEST.
1Sa 14:52 any strong man, or any *v'* man,
16:18 a mighty *v'* man, and a man of war,
18:17 only be thou *v'* for me, and
26:15 said to Abner, Art not thou a *v'* man?
31:12 All the *v'* men arose, and went all
2Sa 2: 7 strengthened, and be ye *v'*:
11:16 where he knew that *v'* men were.
13:28 be courageous, and be *v'*.
17:10 he also that is *v'*, whose heart
10 and they be with him are *v'* men.
23:20 of Jehoiada, the son of a *v'* man,
24: 9 eight hundred thousand *v'* men
1Ki 1:42 Come in; for thou art a *v'* man,
1Ch 5:18 tribe of Manasseh, of *v'* men,
7: 2 were *v'* men of might in their
5 of Issachar were *v'* men of might,
10:12 They arose, all the *v'* men, and
11:22 the son of a *v'* man of Kabzeel,
26 Also the *v'* of the armies were,
28: 1 all the *v'* men, unto Jerusalem.
2Ch 13: 3 with an army of *v'* men of war,
26:17 of the Lord, that were *v'* men:
28: 6 day, which were all *v'* men;
Ne 11: 6 threescore and eight *v'* men.
Ca 3: 7 threescore *v'* men are about it,
7 are about it, of the *v'* of Israel.
Isa 10:13 the inhabitants like a *v'* man:
33: 7 their *v'* ones shall cry without:
Jer 9: 3 they are not *v'* for the truth upon
46:15 Why are thy *v'* men swept away?
Na 2: 3 red, the *v'* men are in scarlet:
Heb 11:34 waxed *v'* in fight, turned to flight

valiantest
J'g 21:10 thousand men of the *v'*,

valiantly
Nu 24:18 enemies; and Israel shall do *v'*.
1Ch 19:13 and let us behave ourselves *v'*

Ps 60: 12 Through God we shall do v': for
108: 13 Through God we shall do v': for he
118: 15, 16 right hand of the Lord doeth v'.

valley See also VALE; VALLEYS.
Ge 14: 17 at the v' of Shaveh, which is the
26: 17 pitched his tent in the v' of Gerar,
19 Isaac's servants digged in the v',
Nu 14: 25 the Canaanites dwelt in the v'.)
21: 12 and pitched in the v' of Zared.
20 from Bamoth in the v', that is in
32: 9 they went up unto the v' of Eshcol,
De 1: 24 and came unto the v' of Eshcol,
3: 16 unto the river Arnon half the v',
29 So we abode in the v' over against
4: 46 in the v' over against Beth-peor, in
21: 4 down the heifer unto a rough v',
4 off the heifer's neck there in the v':
6 heifer that is beheaded in the v':
34: 3 and the plain of the v' of Jericho,
6 he buried him in a v' in the land of
Jos 7: 24 brought them unto the v' of Achor.
26 place was called, The v' of Achor,
8: 11 was a v' between them and Ai.
13 that night into the midst of the v'.
10: 12 and thou, Moon, in the v' of Ajalon.
11: 2 the v', and in the borders of Dor
8 unto the v' of Mizpeh eastward;
16 all the land of Goshen, and the v',
16 of Israel, and the v' of the same;
17 Baal-gad in the v' of Lebanon
12: 7 from Baal-gad in the v' of Lebanon
13: 19 in the mount of the v',
27 And in the v', Beth-aram, and
15: 7 toward Debir from the v' of Achor,
8 up by the v' of the son of Hinnom
8 before the v' of Hinnom westward,
8 of the v' of the giants northward:
33 in the v', Eshtaol, and Zoreah,
17: 16 the land of the v' have chariots of
16 they who are of the v' of Jezreel.
18: 16 before the v' of the son of Hinnom,
16 the v' of the giants on the north,
16 descended to the v' of Hinnom, to
21 Beth-hoglah, and the v' of Keziz,
19: 14 are in the v' of Jiphthah-el:
27 to the v' of Jiphthah-el toward the
J'g 1: 9 and in the south, and in the v'.
19 drive out the inhabitants of the v',
34 suffer them to come down to the v':
5: 15 he was sent on foot into the v'.
6: 33 and pitched in the v' of Jezreel.
7: 1 them, by the hill of Moreh, in the v'.
8 Midian was beneath him in the v'.
12 of the east lay along in the v' like
16: 4 loved a woman in the v' of Sorek,
18: 28 in the v' that lieth by Beth-rehob.
1Sa 6: 13 their wheat harvest in the v':
13: 18 that looketh to the v' of Zeboim
15: 5 of Amalek, and laid wait in the v'.
17: 2 and pitched by the v' of Elah,
3 and there was a v' between them.
19 of Israel, were in the v' of Elah,
52 until thou come to the v', and to
21: 9 thou slewest in the v' of Elah,
31: 7 were on the other side of the v',
2Sa 5: 18, 22 themselves in the v' of Rephaim.
8: 13 of the Syrians in the v' of salt,
23: 13 pitched in the v' of Rephaim.
2Ki 2: 16 some mountain, or into some v'.
3: 16 Lord, Make this v' full of ditches.
17 yet that v' shall be filled with water.
14: 7 He slew of Edom in the v' of salt
23: 10 in the v' of the children of Hinnom,
1Ch 4: 14 the father of the v' of Charashim;
39 even unto the east side of the v',
10: 7 men of Israel that were in the v'
11: 15 encamped in the v' of Rephaim.
14: 9 themselves in the v' of Rephaim.
13 spread themselves abroad in the v'.
18: 12 of the Edomites in the v' of salt
2Ch 14: 10 in array in the v' of Zephathah
20: 26 themselves in the v' of Berachah;
26 was called, The v' of Berachah,
25: 11 went to the v' of salt, and smote of
26: 9 at the v' gate, and at the turning of
28: 3 in the v' of the son of Hinnom,
33: 6 fire in the v' of the son of Hinnom:
14 west side of Gihon, in the v', even
35: 22 came to fight in the v' of Megiddo.
Ne 2: 13 out by night by the gate of the v',
15 and entered by the gate of the v',
3: 13 The v' gate repaired Hanun, and
11: 30 Beer-sheba unto the v' of Hinnom.
35 Lod, and Ono, the v' of craftsmen.
Job 21: 33 The clods of the v' shall be sweet
39: 21 He paweth in the v', and rejoiceth
Ps 23: 4 through the v' of the shadow of
60: *title* smote of Edom in the v' of salt·
6 and mete out the v' of Succoth.
84: 6 Who passing through the v' of Baca
108: 7 and mete out the v' of Succoth.
Pr 30: 17 ravens of the v' shall pick it out,
Ca 6: 11 of nuts to see the fruits of the v',
Isa 17: 5 ears in the v' of Rephaim.
22: 1 The burden of the v' of vision.
5 God of hosts in the v' of vision,
28: 4 which is on the head of the fat v',
21 be wroth as in the v' of Gibeon,
40: 4 Every v' shall be exalted, and
63: 14 As a beast goeth down into the v',
65: 10 v' of Achor a place for the herds to
Jer 2: 23 see thy way in the v', know what
7: 31 is in the v' of the son of Hinnom,
32 nor the v' of the son of Hinnom,
32 but the v' of slaughter: for they
Jer 19: 2 unto the v' of the son of Hinnom,
6 nor The v' of the son of Hinnom,
6 but The v' of slaughter.
21: 13 O inhabitant of the v', and rock of
31: 40 the whole v' of the dead bodies, and
32: 35 are in the v' of the son of Hinnom,
44 in the cities of the v', and in the
47: 5 off with the remnant of their v':
48: 8 v' also shall perish, and the plain
49: 4 thy flowing v', O backsliding
Eze 37: 1 midst of the v' which was full of
2 were very many in the open v';
39: 11 v' of the passengers on the east of
11 shall call it The v' of Hamon-gog.
15 buried it in the v' of Hamon-gog.
Ho 1: 5 bow of Israel in the v' of Jezreel.
2: 15 the v' of Achor for a door of hope:
Joe 3: 2 down into the v' of Jehoshaphat,
12 come up to the v' of Jehoshaphat:
14 multitudes in the v' of decision:
14 Lord is near in the v' of decision.
18 and shall water the v' of Shittim.
Mic 1: 6 the stones thereof into the v',
Zec 12: 11 in the v' of Megiddon.
14: 4 and there shall be a very great v';
5 shall flee to the v' of the mountains;
5 the v' of the mountains shall reach
Lu 3: 5 Every v' shall be filled, and every

valleys
Nu 24: 6 As the v' are they spread forth, as
De 8: 7 and depths that spring out of v'
11: 11 possess it, is a land of hills and v',
Jos 9: 1 Jordan, in the hills, and in the v',
12: 8 In the mountains, and in the v',
1Ki 20: 28 hills, but he is not God of the v',
1Ch 12: 15 they put to flight all them of the v',
27: 29 over the herds that were in the v'
Job 30: 6 To dwell in the cliffs of the v', in
39: 10 or will he harrow the v' after thee?
Ps 65: 13 v' also are covered over with corn;
104: 8 they go down by the v' unto the
10 He sendeth the springs into the v',
Ca 2: 1 of Sharon, and the lily of the v'.
Isa 7: 19 rest all of them in the desolate v',
22: 7 choicest v' shall be full of chariots,
28: 1 head of the fat v' of them that are
41: 18 fountains in the midst of the v':
57: 5 slaying the children in the v'
Jer 49: 4 Wherefore gloriest thou in the v'
Eze 6: 3 hills, to the rivers, and to the v';
7: 16 the mountains like doves of the v',
31: 12 in all the v' his branches are fallen,
32: 5 and fill the v' with thy height.
35: 8 in thy hills, and in thy v', and in all
36: 4, 6 hills, to the rivers, and to the v',
Mic 1: 4 the v' shall be cleft, as wax before

valour
Jos 1: 14 all the mighty men of v', and
6: 2 thereof, and the mighty men of v'.
8: 3 thirty thousand mighty men of v',
10: 7 him, and all the mighty men of v'.
J'g 3: 29 men, all lusty, and all men of v';
6: 12 with thee, thou mighty man of v'.
11: 1 Jephthah...was a mighty man of v',
18: 2 men from their coasts, men of v',
20: 44 men; all these were men of v'.
46 the sword; all these were men of v'.
1Ki 11: 28 Jeroboam was a mighty man of v':
2Ki 5: 1 he was also a mighty man in v', but
24: 14 and all the mighty men of v',
1Ch 5: 24 mighty men of v', famous men, and
7: 7 of their fathers, mighty men of v';
9, 11 their fathers, mighty men of v',
40 choice and mighty men of v', chief
8: 40 of Ulam were mighty men of v',
12: 21 for they were all mighty men of v',
25 mighty men of v' for the war,
28 Zadok, a young man mighty of v',
30 eight hundred, mighty men of v',
26: 6 for they were mighty men of v'.
30 and his brethren, men of v',
31 among them mighty men of v' at
32 his brethren, men of v', were two
2Ch 13: 3 men, being mighty men of v'.
14: 8 all these were mighty men of v'.
17: 13 the men of war, mighty men of v',
14 with him mighty men of v' three
16 thousand mighty men of v'.
17 Eliada a mighty man of v', and
25: 6 mighty men of v' out of Israel
26: 12 fathers of the mighty men of v'
32: 21 cut off all the mighty men of v',
Ne 11: 14 their brethren, mighty men of v',

value See also VALUED; VALUEST.
Le 27: 8 priest, and the priest shall v' him;
8 that vowed shall the priest v' him.
12 And the priest shall v' it, whether
Job 13: 4 lies, ye are all physicians of no v'.
M't 10: 31 of more v' than many sparrows.
27: 9 of the children of Israel did v';
Lu 12: 7 of more v' than many sparrows.

valued
Le 27: 16 barley seed shall be v' at fifty shekels
Job 28: 16 be v' with the gold of Ophir,
19 neither shall it be v' with pure gold.
M't 27: 9 the price of him that was v',

valuest
Le 27: 12 as thou v' it, who art the priest, so

Vaniah (*va-ni'-ah*)
Ezr 10: 36 V', Meremoth, Eliashib,

vanish See also VANISHED; VANISHETH.
Job 6: 17 time they wax warm, they v':
Isa 51: 6 heavens shall v' away like smoke,
1Co 13: 8 be knowledge, it shall v' away.
Heb 8: 13 waxeth old is ready to v' away.

vanished
Jer 49: 7 the prudent? is their wisdom v'?
Lu 24: 31 and he v' out of their sight.

vanisheth
Job 7: 9 As the cloud is consumed and v'
Jas 4: 14 for a little time, and then v' away.

vanities
De 32: 21 me to anger with their v':
1Ki 16: 13, 26 of Israel to anger with their v'.
Ps 31: 6 hated them that regard lying v':
Ec 1: 2 Vanity of v', saith the Preacher,
2 Preacher, vanity of v'; all is vanity.
5: 7 words there are also divers v':
12: 8 Vanity of v', saith the preacher; all
Jer 8: 19 images, and with strange v'?
10: 8 the stock is a doctrine of v'.
14: 22 any among the v' of the Gentiles
Jon 2: 8 that observe lying v' forsake their
Ac 14: 15 from these v' unto the living God,

vanity See also VANITIES.
2Ki 17: 15 they followed v', and became vain,
Job 7: 3 I made to possess months of v',
16 let me alone; for my days are v'.
15: 31 him that is deceived trust in v':
31 for v' shall be his recompence.
35 mischief, and bring forth v',
31: 5 If I have walked with v', or if my
35: 13 Surely God will not hear v', neither
Ps 4: 2 how long will ye love v', and seek
10: 7 under his tongue is mischief and v'.
12: 2 They speak v' every one with his
24: 4 hath not lifted up his soul unto v',
39: 5 at his best state is altogether v'.
11 a moth: surely every man is v'.
41: 6 come to see me, he speaketh v':
62: 9 Surely men of low degree are v',
9 they are altogether lighter than v'.
78: 33 their days did he consume in v',
94: 11 thoughts of man, that they are v'.
119: 37 mine eyes from beholding v';
144: 4 Man is like to v': his days are as
8 Whose mouth speaketh v', and
11 children, whose mouth speaketh v',
Pr 13: 11 Wealth gotten by v' shall be
21: 6 treasures by a lying tongue is a v'
22: 8 that soweth iniquity shall reap v':
30: 8 Remove far from me v' and lies:
Ec 1: 2 V' of vanities, saith the Preacher,
2 saith the Preacher, v' of vanities;
2 saith the Preacher,...all is v'.
14 all is v' and vexation of spirit.
2: 1 and, behold, this also is v'.
11 all was v' and vexation of spirit,
15 in my heart, that this also is v'.
17 for all is v' and vexation of spirit.
19 under the sun. This is also v'.
21 This also is v' and a great evil.
23 rest in the night. This is also v'.
26 also is v' and vexation of spirit.
3: 19 above a beast: for all is v'.
4: 4 is also v' and vexation of spirit.
7 and I saw v' under the sun.
8 This is also v', yea, it is a sore
16 also is v' and vexation of spirit.
5: 10 with increase: this is also v'.
6: 2 this is v', and it is an evil disease.
4 For he cometh in with v', and
9 is also v' and vexation of spirit.
11 be many things that increase v',
7: 6 laughter of the fool: this is also v'.
15 have I seen in the days of my v':
8: 10 they had so done: this is also v'.
14 There is a v' which is done upon
14 I said that this also is v'.
9: 9 all the days of the life of thy v',
9 the sun, all the days of thy v':
11: 8 be many. All that cometh is v'.
10 for childhood and youth are v'.
12: 8 V' of vanities, saith the preacher;
8 saith the preacher; all is v'.
Isa 5: 18 draw iniquity with cords of v',
30: 28 sift the nations with the sieve of v':
40: 17 to him less than nothing, and v'.
23 the judges of the earth as v'.
41: 29 they are all v'; their works are
44: 9 a graven image are all of them v',
57: 13 all away; v' shall take them:
58: 9 of the finger, and speaking v';
59: 4 they trust in v', and speak lies;
Jer 2: 5 me, and have walked after v',
10: 15 They are v', and the work of errors:
16: 19 our fathers have inherited lies, v',
18: 15 they have burned incense to v',
51: 18 They are v', the work of errors:
Eze 13: 6 They have seen v' and lying
8 Because ye have spoken v', and
9 be upon the prophets that see v',
23 ye shall see no more v', nor divine
21: 29 Whiles they see v' unto thee,
22: 28 seeing v', and divining lies unto
Ho 12: 11 in Gilead? surely they are v':
Hab 2: 13 weary themselves for very v'?
Zec 10: 2 For the idols have spoken v', and
Ro 8: 20 creature was made subject to v',
Eph 4: 17 walk, in the v' of their mind,
2Pe 2: 18 speak great swelling words of v',

vantage See ADVANTAGE.

vapour See also VAPOURS.
Job 36: 27 rain according to the v' thereof:
33 the cattle also concerning the v'.

Ac 2:19 blood, and fire, and *v*· of smoke:
Jas 4:14 a *v*·, that appeareth for a little time.

vapours
Ps 135: 7 He causeth the *v*· to ascend from
148: 8 Fire, and hail; snow, and *v*·;
Jer 10:13 he causeth the *v*· to ascend from
51:16 he causeth the *v*· to ascend from

variableness
Jas 1:17 with whom is no *v*·, neither

variance
M't 10:35 a man at *v*· against his father,
Ga 5:20 *v*·, emulations, wrath, strife,

Vashni (*vash'-ni*)
1Ch 6:28 sons of Samuel; the firstborn *V*·,

Vashti (*vash'-ti*)
Es 1: 9 *V*· the queen made a feast for the
11 bring *V*· the queen before the king
12 the queen *V*· refused to come at the
15 unto the queen *V*· according to law,
16 *V*· the queen hath not done wrong
17 commanded *V*· the queen to be
19 That *V*· come no more before king
2: 1 he remembered *V*·, and what she
4 the king be queen instead of *V*·.
17 and made her queen instead of *V*·.

vaunt See also VAUNTETH.
J'g 7: 2 lest Israel *v*· themselves against

vaunteth
1Co 13: 4 charity *v*· not itself, is not puffed

vehement
Ca 8: 6 of fire, which hath a most *v*· flame.
Jon 4: 8 that God prepared a *v*· east wind;
2Co 7:11 yea, what fear, yea, what *v*· desire,

vehemently
M'r 14:31 But he spake the more *v*·, If I
Lu 6:48 stream beat *v*· upon that house,
49 which the stream did beat *v*·,
11:53 Pharisees began to urge him *v*·,
23:10 scribes stood and *v*· accused him.

veil See also VAIL.
Ca 5: 7 the keepers...took away my *v*·
M't 27:51 *v*· of the temple was rent in twain
M'r 15:38 *v*· of the temple was rent in twain
Lu 23:45 *v*· of the temple was rent in twain
Heb 6:19 entereth into that within the *v*·;
9: 3 after the second *v*·, the tabernacle
10:20 consecrated for us, through the *v*·,

vein
Job 28: 1 Surely there is a *v*· for the silver,

venge See AVENGE; REVENGE.

vengeance
Ge 4:15 *v*· shall be taken on him sevenfold.
De 32:35 To me belongeth *v*·, and
41 I will render *v*· to mine enemies,
43 will render *v*· to his adversaries,
J'g 11:36 the Lord hath taken *v*· for thee of
Ps 58:10 shall rejoice when he seeth the *v*·:
94: 1 Lord God, to whom *v*· belongeth;
1 O God, to whom *v*· belongeth, shew
99: 8 thou tookest *v*· of their inventions.
149: 7 To execute *v*· upon the heathen,
Pr 6:34 he will not spare in the day of *v*·.
Isa 34: 8 For it is the day of the Lord's *v*·,
35: 4 your God will come with *v*·, even
47: 3 I will take *v*·, and I will not meet
59:17 he put on the garments of *v*· for
61: 2 Lord, and the day of *v*· of our God;
63: 4 For the day of *v*· is in mine heart,
Jer 11:20 heart, let me see thy *v*· on them:
20:12 heart, let me see thy *v*· on them:
46:10 a day of *v*·, that he may avenge him
50:15 for it is the *v*· of the Lord:
15 take *v*· upon her; as she hath
28 declare in Zion the *v*· of the Lord
28 Lord our God, the *v*· of his temple.
51: 6 for this is the time of the Lord's *v*·;
11 *v*· of the Lord, the *v*· of his temple.
36 thy cause, and take *v*· for thee;
La 3:60 Thou hast seen all their *v*· and all
Eze 24: 8 cause fury to come up to take *v*·;
25:12 the house of Judah by taking *v*·,
14 I will lay my *v*· upon Edom by the
14 they shall know my *v*·, saith the
15 taken *v*· with a despiteful heart,
17 great *v*· upon them with furious
17 when I shall lay my *v*· upon them.
Mic 5:15 execute *v*· in anger and fury upon
Na 1: 2 will take *v*· on his adversaries,
Lu 21:22 For these be the days of *v*·, that
Ac 28: 4 the sea, yet *v*· suffereth not to live.
Ro 3: 5 Is God unrighteous who taketh *v*·?
12:19 *V*· is mine; I will repay, saith the
2Th 1: 8 In flaming fire taking *v*· on them
Heb10:30 *V*· belongeth unto me, I will
Jude 7 suffering the *v*· of eternal fire.

venison
Ge 25:28 Esau, because he did eat of his *v*·:
27: 3 to the field, and take me some *v*·;
5 went to the field to hunt for *v*·,
7 Bring me *v*·, and make me savoury
19 sit and eat of my *v*·, that thy soul
25 to me, and I will eat of my son's *v*·,
31 father arise, and eat of his son's *v*·,
33 where is he that hath taken *v*·, and

venom
De 32:33 dragons, and the cruel *v*· of asps.

venomous
Ac 28: 4 saw the *v*· beast hang on his hand,

vent See also INVENT; PREVENT.
Job 32:19 belly is as wine which hath no *v*·;

venture See also ADVENTURE.
1Ki 22:34 a certain man drew a bow at a *v*·,
2Ch 18:33 a certain man drew a bow at a *v*·,

verified
Ge 42:20 so shall your words be *v*·, and ye
1Ki 8:26 let thy word, I pray thee, be *v*·,
2Ch 6:17 God of Israel, let thy word be *v*·,

verily^
Ge 42:21 We are *v*· guilty concerning our
Ex 31:13 *V*· my sabbaths ye shall keep: for
J'g 15: 2 I *v*· thought that thou hadst utterly
1Ki 1:43 *V*· our lord king David hath made
2Ki 4:14 *V*· she hath no child, and her
1Ch 21:24 I will *v*· buy it for the full price:
Job 19:13 acquaintance are *v*· estranged
Ps 37: 3 the land, and *v*· thou shalt be fed.
39: 5 *v*· every man at his best state is
58:11 *V*· there is a reward for the
11 *v*· he is a God that judgeth in the
66:19 But *v*· God hath heard me; he hath
Isa 45:15 *V*· thou art a God that hidest
Jer 15:11 *V*· it shall be well with thy
11 *v*· I will cause the enemy to entreat
M't 5:18 For *v*· I say unto you, Till heaven
26 *V*· I say unto thee, Thou shalt by
6: 2, 5, 16 *V*· I say unto you, They have
8:10 *V*· I say unto you, I have not found
10:15 *V*· I say unto you, It shall be more
23 for *v*· I say unto you, Ye shall not
42 *v*· I say unto you, he shall in no wise
11:11 *V*· I say unto you, Among them that
13:17 For *v*· I say unto you, That many
16:28 *V*· I say unto you, There be some
17:20 for *v*· I say unto you, If ye have faith
18: 3 *V*· I say unto you, Except ye be
13 *v*· I say unto you, he rejoiceth more
18 *V*· I say unto you, Whatsoever ye
19:23 *V*· I say unto you, That a rich man
28 *V*· I say unto you, That ye which
21:21 *V*· I say unto you, If ye have faith,
31 *V*· I say unto you, That the
23:36 *V*· I say unto you, All these things
24: 2 *v*· I say unto you, There shall not be
34 *V*· I say unto you, This generation
47 *V*· I say unto you, That he shall
25:12 *V*· I say unto you, I know you not.
40, 45 *V*· I say unto you, Inasmuch as
26:13 *V*· I say unto you, Wheresoever this
21 *V*· I say unto you, that one of you
34 *V*· I say unto thee, That this night,
M'r 3:28 *V*· I say unto you, All sins shall be
6:11 *V*· I say unto you, It shall be more
8:12 *v*· I say unto you, There shall no
9: 1 *V*· I say unto you, That there be
12 Elias *v*· cometh first, and restoreth
41 *v*· I say unto you, he shall not lose
10:15 *V*· I say unto you, Whosoever shall
29 *V*· I say unto you, There is no man
11:23 *v*· I say unto you, That whosoever
12:43 *V*· I say unto you, That this poor
13:30 *V*· I say unto you, that this
14: 9 *V*· I say unto you, Wheresoever this
18 *V*· I say unto you, One of you which
25 *V*· I say unto you, I will drink no
30 *V*· I say unto thee, That this day,
Lu 4:24 *V*· I say unto you, No prophet is
11:51 *v*· I say unto you, It shall be
12:37 *v*· I say unto you, that he shall gird
13:35 and *v*· I say unto you, Ye shall not
18:17 *V*· I say unto you, Whosoever shall
29 *V*· I say unto you, There is no man
21:32 *V*· I say unto you, This generation
23:43 *V*· I say unto thee, To day shalt
Joh 1:51 *V*·, *v*·, I say unto you, Hereafter ye
3: 3, 5 *V*·, *v*·, I say unto thee, Except a
11 *V*·, *v*·, I say unto thee, We speak
5:19 *V*·, *v*·, I say unto you, The Son can
24 *V*·, *v*·, I say unto you, He that
25 *V*·, *v*·, I say unto you, The hour is
6:26 *V*·, *v*·, I say unto you, Ye seek me,
32 *V*·, *v*·, I say unto you, Moses gave
47 *V*·, *v*·, I say unto you, He that
53 *V*·, *v*·, I say unto you, Except ye eat
8:34 *V*·, *v*·, I say unto you, Whosoever
51 *V*·, *v*·, I say unto you, If a man keep
58 *V*·, *v*·, I say unto you, Before
10: 1 *V*·, *v*·, I say unto you, He that
7 *V*·, *v*·, I say unto you, I am the door
12:24 *V*·, *v*·, I say unto you, Except a corn
13:16 *V*·, *v*·, I say unto you, The servant is
20 *V*·, *v*·, I say unto you, He that
21 *V*·, *v*·, I say unto you, that one of
38 *V*·, *v*·, I say unto thee, The cock shall
14:12 *V*·, *v*·, I say unto you, He that
16:20 *V*·, *v*·, I say unto you, That ye shall
23 *V*·, *v*·, I say unto you, Whatsoever
21:18 *V*·, *v*·, I say unto thee, When thou
Ac 16:37 nay *v*·; but let them come
19: 4 John *v*· baptized with the baptism
22: 3 I am *v*· a man which am a Jew, born
26: 9 I *v*· thought with myself, that
Ro 2:25 For circumcision *v*· profiteth, if
10:18 Yes *v*·, their sound went into all
15:27 It hath pleased them *v*·; and their
1Co 5: 3 For I *v*·, as absent in body, but
9:18 *V*· that, when I preach the gospel, I
14:17 For thou *v*· givest thanks well,
Ga 3:21 *v*· righteousness should have been
1Th 3: 4 For *v*·, when we were with you, we
Heb 2:16 *v*· he took not on him the nature of
3: 5 Moses *v*· was faithful in all his
6:16 For men *v*· swear by the greater:
7: 5 *v*· they that are of the sons of Levi,
18 For there is *v*· a disannulling of the
9: 1 Then *v*· the first covenant had also
Heb12:10 For they *v*· for a few days chastened
1Pe 1:20 Who *v*· was foreordained before the
1Jo 2: 5 him *v*· is the love of God perfected:

verity
Ps 111: 7 The works of his hands are *v*· and
1Ti 2: 7 of the Gentiles in faith and *v*·.

vermilion
Jer 22:14 with cedar, and painted with *v*·.
Eze 23:14 of the Chaldeans pourtrayed with *v*·,

very^
Ge 1:31 made, and, behold, it was *v*· good.
4: 5 And Cain was *v*· wroth, and his
12:14 the woman that she was *v*· fair.
13: 2 And Abram was *v*· rich in cattle, in
18:20 because their sin is *v*· grievous;
21:11 thing was *v*· grievous in Abraham's
24:16 the damsel was *v*· fair to look upon,
26:13 and grew until he became *v*· great:
27:21 whether thou be my *v*· son Esau or
24 he said, Art thou my *v*· son Esau?
33 Isaac trembled *v*· exceedingly,
34: 7 they were *v*· wroth, because he
41:19 and *v*· ill favoured and leanfleshed,
31 following; for it shall be *v*· grievous.
49 *v*· much, until he left numbering;
47:13 for the famine was *v*· sore, so that
50: 9 and it was a *v*· great company.
10 a great and *v*· sore lamentation:
Ex 1:20 multiplied, and waxed *v*· mighty.
8:28 only ye shall not go *v*· far away:
9: 3 shall be a *v*· grievous murrain.
16 And in *v*· deed for this cause have I
18 cause it to rain a *v*· grievous hail,
24 and fire...with the hail, *v*· grievous,
10:14 *v*· grievous were they; before them
11: 3 Moses was *v*· great in the land of
12:38 and herds, even *v*· much cattle.
30:36 thou shalt beat some of it *v*· small,
Nu 6: 9 any man die *v*· suddenly by him,
11:33 the people with a *v*· great plague.
12: 3 the man Moses was *v*· meek, above
13:28 the cities are walled, and *v*· great:
16:15 Moses was *v*· wroth, and said unto
22:17 promote thee unto *v*· great honour,
32: 1 had a *v*· great multitude of cattle:
De 9:20 the Lord was *v*· angry with Aaron
21 stamped it, and ground it *v*· small,
20:15 the cities which are *v*· far off from
27: 8 all the words of this law *v*· plainly.
28:43 shall get up above thee *v*· high;
43 and thou shalt come down *v*· low.
54 tender among you, and *v*· delicate,
30:14 But the word is *v*· nigh unto thee,
32:20 they are a *v*· froward generation,
Jos 1: 7 be thou strong and *v*· courageous,
3:16 an heap *v*· far from the city Adam,
8: 4 go not *v*· far from the city, but be ye
9: 9 From a *v*· far country thy servants
13 by reason of the *v*· long journey.
22 We are *v*· far from you; when ye
10:20 them with a *v*· great slaughter,
27 which remain until this *v*· day.
11: 4 with horses and chariots *v*· many.
13: 1 there remaineth yet *v*· much land
22: 8 your tents, and with *v*· much cattle,
8 iron, and with *v*· much raiment:
23: 6 Be ye therefore *v*· courageous to
J'g 3:17 Moab: and Eglon was a *v*· fat man.
11:33 vineyards, with a *v*· great slaughter.
35 thou hast brought me *v*· low, and
13: 6 of an angel of God, *v*· terrible:
18: 9 the land, and, behold, it is *v*· good:
Ru 1:20 hath dealt *v*· bitterly with me.
1Sa 2:17 sin of the young men was *v*· great
22 Now Eli was *v*· old, and heard all
4:10 and there was a *v*· great slaughter;
5: 9 the city with a *v*· great destruction:
11 hand of God was *v*· heavy there.
14:15 so it was a *v*· great trembling.
20 there was a *v*· great discomfiture.
31 and the people were *v*· faint.
18: 8 And Saul was *v*· wroth, and the
15 that he behaved himself *v*· wisely,
19: 4 have been to thee-ward *v*· good:
20: 7 but if he be *v*· wroth, then be sure
23:22 is told me that he dealeth *v*· subtilly.
25: 2 and the man was *v*· great, and he
15 But the men were *v*· good unto us,
34 For in *v*· deed, as the Lord God of
36 him, for he was *v*· drunken:
26: 4 that Saul was come in *v*· deed.
2Sa 1:26 *v*· pleasant hast thou been unto
2:17 there was a *v*· sore battle that day;
3: 8 Then was Abner *v*· wroth for the
11: 2 the woman was *v*· beautiful to look
12:15 bare unto David, and it was *v*· sick.
13: 3 and Jonadab was a *v*· subtil man.
21 of all these things, he was *v*· wroth
36 and all his servants wept *v*· sore.
18:17 a *v*· great heap of stones upon him:
19:32 Now Barzillai was a *v*· aged man,
32 for he was a *v*· great man.
24:10 for I have done *v*· foolishly.
1Ki 1: 4 And the damsel was *v*· fair, and
6 and he also was a *v*· goodly man;
15 and the king was *v*· old; and
7:34 undersetters were of the *v*· base
10: 2 to Jerusalem with a *v*· great train,
2 and *v*· much gold, and precious
10 and of spices *v*· great store, and
19:10, 14 I have been *v*· jealous for the Lord
21:26 he did *v*· abominably in following
2Ki 14:26 of Israel, that it was *v*· bitter:
17:18 the Lord was *v*· angry with Israel,

2Ki 21:16 shed innocent blood *v·* much,
1Ch 9:13 *v·* able men for the work of the
18: 8 brought David *v·* much brass,
21: 8 servant: for I have done *v·* foolishly.
13 Lord; for *v·* great are his mercies:
23:17 sons of Rehabiah were *v·* many.
2Ch 6:18 God in *v·* deed dwell with men on
7: 8 with him, a *v·* great congregation,
9: 1 with a *v·* great company, and
14:13 they carried away *v·* much spoil.
16: 8 host, with *v·* many chariots and
14 they made a *v·* great burning 5704,
20:35 king of Israel, who did *v·* wickedly:
24:24 Lord delivered a *v·* great host
30:13 month, a *v·* great congregation.
32:29 had given him substance *v·* much.
33:14 and raised it up a *v·* great height,
36:14 transgressed *v·* much after all the
Ezr 10: 1 a *v·* great congregation of men
1 children: for the people wept *v·* sore.
Ne 1: 7 We have dealt *v·* corruptly against
2: 2 heart. Then I was *v·* sore afraid,
4: 7 stopped, then they were *v·* wroth,
5: 6 I was *v·* angry when I heard their
8:17 And there was *v·* great gladness.
Es 1:12 therefore was the king *v·* wroth,
Job 1: 3 asses, and a *v·* great household;
2:13 saw that his grief was *v·* great.
15:10 the grayheaded and *v·* aged men,
32: 6 said, I am young, and ye are *v·* old:
Ps 5: 9 their inward part is *v·* wickedness;
35: 8 into that *v·* destruction let him fall.
46: 1 a *v·* present help in trouble.
50: 3 *v·* tempestuous round about him.
71:19 righteousness...O God, is *v·* high,
79: 8 us: for we are brought *v·* low.
89: 2 shalt thou establish in the *v·* heavens.
92: 5 and thy thoughts are *v·* deep.
93: 5 Thy testimonies are *v·* sure:
104: 1 O Lord my God, thou art *v·* great;
105:12 but a few men in number; yea, *v·* few,
119:107 I am afflicted *v·* much:
138 are righteous and *v·* faithful.
140 Thy word is *v·* pure: therefore
142: 6 my cry; for I am brought *v·* low:
147:15 earth: his word runneth *v·* swiftly.
Pr 17: 9 a matter separateth *v·* friends.
27:15 continual dropping in a *v·* rainy
Isa 1: 9 left unto us a *v·* small remnant,
5: 1 hath a vineyard in a *v·* fruitful hill:
10:25 For yet a *v·* little while, and the
16: 6 the pride of Moab; he is *v·* proud:
14 the remnant shall be *v·* small and
24:16 dealers have dealt *v·* treacherously.
29:17 Is it not yet a *v·* little while, and
31: 1 because they are *v·* strong;
33:17 behold the land that is *v·* far off.
40:15 up the isles as a *v·* little thing.
47: 6 hast thou *v·* heavily laid thy yoke.
48: 8 thou wouldest deal *v·* treacherously,
52:13 and extolled, and be *v·* high.
64: 9 Be not wroth *v·* sore, O Lord,
12 thy peace, and afflict us *v·* sore?
Jer 2:12 be ye *v·* desolate, saith the Lord.
4:19 I am pained at my *v·* heart; my
5:11 dealt *v·* treacherously against me,
12: 1 happy that deal *v·* treacherously?
14:17 breach, with a *v·* grievous blow.
18:13 Israel hath done a *v·* horrible thing.
20:15 born unto thee; making him *v·* glad.
24: 2 One basket had *v·* good figs, even
2 other basket had *v·* naughty figs,
3 I said, Figs; the good figs, *v·* good;
3 and the evil, *v·* evil, that cannot be
27: 7 until the *v·* time of his land come:
40:12 wine and summer fruits *v·* much.
46:20 Egypt is like a *v·* fair heifer, but
La 5:22 thou art *v·* wroth against us.
Eze 2: 3 against me, even unto this *v·* day.
16:47 as if that were a *v·* little thing,
27:25 made *v·* glorious in the midst of
33:32 art unto them as a *v·* lovely song
37: 2 were *v·* many in the open valley;
2 valley; and, lo, they were *v·* dry.
40: 2 set me upon a *v·* high mountain,
47: 7 were *v·* many trees on the one side
9 shall be a *v·* great multitude of fish.
Da 2:12 the king was angry and *v·* furious.
7:20 mouth that spake *v·* great things,
8: 8 the he goat waxed *v·* great:
11:25 a *v·* great and mighty army;
Joe 2:11 army: for his camp is *v·* great:
11 of the Lord is great and *v·* terrible;
Am 5:20 *v·* dark, and no brightness in it?
Jon 4: 1 exceedingly, and he was *v·* angry.
Hab 2:13 people shall labour in the *v·* fire,
13 weary themselves for *v·* vanity?
Zec 1:15 I am *v·* sore displeased with the
8: 4 his staff in his hand for *v·* age.
9: 2 and Zidon, though it be *v·* wise.
5 shall see it, and be *v·* sorrowful,
14: 4 and there shall be a *v·* great valley,
M't 10:30 But the *v·* hairs of your head are
15:28 made whole from that *v·* hour.
17:18 child was cured from that *v·* hour.
18:31 was done, they were *v·* sorry,
21: 8 a *v·* great multitude spread their
24:24 they shall deceive the *v·* elect.
26: 7 box of *v·* precious ointment,
37 began to be sorrowful and *v·* heavy.
M'r 8: 1 the multitude being *v·* great, and
14: 3 ointment of spikenard *v·* precious;
33 be sore amazed, and to be *v·* heavy,
16: 2 *v·* early in the morning the first
4 rolled away: for it was *v·* great.
Lu 1: 3 of all things from the *v·* first,
Lu 9: 5 shake off the *v·* dust from your
10:11 Even the *v·* dust of your city, which
12: 7 But even the *v·* hairs of your head
59 till thou hast paid the *v·* last mite.
18:23 heard this, he was *v·* sorrowful:
23 sorrowful: for he was *v·* rich.
24 saw that he was *v·* sorrowful,
19:17 thou hast been faithful in a *v·* little,
48 were *v·* attentive to hear him.
24: 1 *v·* early in the morning, they came
Joh 7:26 indeed that this is the *v·* Christ?
8: 4 was taken in adultery, in the *v·* act.
12: 3 ointment of spikenard, *v·* costly,
14:11 else believe me for the *v·* works' sake.
Ac 9:22 proving that this is *v·* Christ.
24: 2 that *v·* worthy deeds are done unto
25:10 no wrong, as thou *v·* well knowest.
Ro 10:20 Esaias is *v·* bold, and saith, I was
13: 6 continually upon this *v·* thing.
1Co 4: 3 it is a *v·* small thing that I should
2Co 9: 2 your zeal hath provoked *v·* many.
11: 5 behind the *v·* chiefest apostles.
12:11 I behind the *v·* chiefest apostles,
15 I will *v·* gladly spend and be spent
Ph'p 1: 6 Being confident of this *v·* thing, that
1Th 5:13 to esteem them *v·* highly in love
23 the *v·* God of peace sanctify you
2Ti 1:17 he sought me out *v·* diligently,
18 at Ephesus, thou knowest *v·* well.
Heb 10: 1 and not the *v·* image of the things,
Jas 3: 4 turned about with a *v·* small helm,
5:11 that the Lord is *v·* pitiful, and of

vessel See also VESSELS.
Le 6:28 earthen *v·* wherein it is sodden
11:32 whether it be any *v·* of wood, or
32 whatsoever *v·* it be, wherein any
33 every earthen *v·*, whereinto any of
34 in every such *v·* shall be unclean.
14: 5 the birds be killed in an earthen *v·*
50 an earthen *v·* over running water:
15:12 And the *v·* of earth, that he toucheth
12 every *v·* of wood shall be rinsed in
Nu 5:17 take holy water in an earthen *v·*;
19:15 And every open *v·*, which hath no
17 water shall be put thereto in a *v·*:
De 23:24 but thou shalt not put any in thy *v·*.
1Sa 21: 5 were sanctified this day in the *v·*.
1Ki 17:10 I pray thee, a little water in a *v·*,
2Ki 4: 6 unto her son, Bring me yet a *v·*.
6 unto her, There is not a *v·* more.
Ps 2: 9 them in pieces like a potter's *v·*.
31:12 out of mind: I am like a broken *v·*.
Pr 25: 4 shall come forth a *v·* for the finer.
Isa 30:14 it as the breaking of the potters' *v·*
66:20 bring an offering in a clean *v·* into
Jer 18: 4 And the *v·* that he made of clay was
18 so he made it again another *v·*, as
19:11 as one breaketh a potter's *v·*, that
22:28 is he a *v·* wherein is no pleasure?
25:34 and ye shall fall like a pleasant *v·*.
32:14 and put them in an earthen *v·*, that
48:11 hath not been emptied from *v·* to *v·*,
38 have broken Moab like a *v·* wherein
51:34 he hath made me an empty *v·*, he
Eze 4: 9 and fitches, and put them in one *v·*,
15: 3 a pin of it to hang any *v·* thereon?
Hos 8: 8 as a *v·* wherein is no pleasure.
M'r 11:16 carry any *v·* through the temple.
Lu 8:16 a candle, covereth it with a *v·*,
Joh 19:29 there was set a *v·* full of vinegar:
Ac 9:15 he is a chosen *v·* unto me, to bear
10:11 a certain *v·* descending unto him,
16 the *v·* was received up again into
11: 5 saw a vision, A certain *v·* descend,
Ro 9:21 lump to make one *v·* unto honour,
1Th 4: 4 to possess his *v·* in sanctification
2Ti 2:21 he shall be a *v·* unto honour,
1Pe 3: 7 unto the wife, as unto the weaker *v·*,

vessels
Ge 43:11 best fruits in the land in your *v·*,
Ex 7:19 both in *v·* of wood, and in *v·* of stone.
25:39 shall he make it, with all these *v·*.
27: 3 *v·* thereof thou shalt make of brass.
19 All the *v·* of the tabernacle in all
30:27 And the table and all his *v·*,
27 and the candlestick and his *v·*,
28 And the altar...with all his *v·*,
35:13 and his staves, and all his *v·*, and
16 grate, his staves, and all his *v·*,
37:16 he made the *v·* which were upon
24 pure gold made he it, and all the *v·*
38: 3 And he made all the *v·* of the altar,
3 all the *v·* thereof made he of brass.
30 for it, and all the *v·* of the altar,
39:36 The table, and all the *v·* thereof,
37 all the *v·* thereof, and the oil for
39 brass, his staves, and all his *v·*,
40 and all the *v·* of the service of the
40: 9 hallow it, and all the *v·* thereof:
10 all his *v·*, and sanctify the altar:
Le 8:11 anointed the altar and all his *v·*,
Nu 1:50 over all the *v·* thereof, and over all
50 tabernacle, and all the *v·* thereof;
3:31 the *v·* of the sanctuary wherewith
36 all the *v·* thereof, and all that
4: 9 all the oil *v·* thereof, wherewith
10 put it and all the *v·* thereof within
14 shall put upon it all the *v·* thereof,
14 the basons, all the *v·* of the altar;
15 and all the *v·* of the sanctuary,
16 sanctuary, and in the *v·* thereof.
7: 1 the altar and all the *v·* thereof,
85 the silver *v·* weighed two thousand
18: 3 come nigh the *v·* of the sanctuary
19:18 and upon all the *v·*, and upon the
Jos 6:19 and gold, and *v·* of brass and iron,
24 and the *v·* of brass and of iron,
Ru 2: 9 go unto the *v·*, and drink of that
1Sa 9: 7 for the bread is spent in our *v·*,
21: 5 the *v·* of the young men are holy,
2Sa 8:10 brought with him *v·* of silver,
10 and *v·* of gold, and *v·* of brass:
17:28 beds, and basons, and earthen *v·*,
1Ki 7:45 all these *v·*, which Hiram made
47 Solomon left all the *v·* unweighed,
48 Solomon made all the *v·* that
51 silver, and the gold, and the *v·*,
8: 4 holy *v·* that were in the tabernacle,
10:21 Solomon's drinking *v·* were of gold,
21 all the *v·* of the house of the forest
25 present, *v·* of silver, and *v·* of gold,
15:15 the Lord, silver, and gold, and *v·*.
2Ki 4: 3 Go, borrow thee *v·* abroad of all
3 even empty *v·*; borrow not a few.
4 and shalt pour out into all those *v·*,
5 who brought the *v·* to her; and she
6 to pass, when the *v·* were full,
7:15 way was full of garments and *v·*,
12:13 any *v·* of gold, or *v·* of silver, of the
14:14 all the *v·* that were found in the
23: 4 all the *v·* that were made for Baal,
24:13 cut in pieces all the *v·* of gold
25:14 all the *v·* of brass wherewith they
16 all these *v·* was without weight.
1Ch 9:28 the charge of the ministering *v·*,
29 were appointed to oversee the *v·*,
18: 8 and the pillars, and the *v·* of brass.
10 all manner of *v·* of gold and silver
22:19 the holy *v·* of God, into the house
23:26 any *v·* of it for the service thereof.
28:13 for all the *v·* of service in the house
2Ch 4:18 Solomon made all these *v·* in great
19 Solomon made all the *v·* that were
5: 5 holy *v·* that were in the tabernacle,
9:20 the drinking *v·* of king Solomon
20 all the *v·* of the house of the forest
24 *v·* of silver, and *v·* of gold, and
15:18 dedicated, silver, and gold, and *v·*.
24:14 made *v·* for the house of the Lord,
14 even *v·* to minister, and to offer
14 spoons, and *v·* of gold and silver.
25:24 all the *v·* that were found in the
28:24 together the *v·* of the house of God,
24 cut in pieces the *v·* of the house of
29:18 offering, with all the *v·* thereof,
18 table, with all the *v·* thereof,
19 Moreover all the *v·*, which king
36: 7 Nebuchadnezzar also carried...*v·* of
10 goodly *v·* of the house of the Lord,
18 all the *v·* of the house of God,
19 destroyed all the goodly *v·* thereof.
Ezr 1: 6 their hands with *v·* of silver, with
7 Cyrus...brought forth the *v·* of
10 and ten, and other *v·* a thousand.
11 All the *v·* of gold and of silver were
5:14 the *v·* also of gold and silver of the
15 Take these *v·*, go, carry them into
6: 5 golden and silver *v·* of the house
7:19 The *v·* also that are given thee for
8:25 silver, and the gold, and the *v·*,
26 and silver *v·* an hundred talents,
27 two *v·* of fine copper, precious as
28 *v·* are holy also; and the silver
30 the silver, and the gold, and the *v·*,
33 and the *v·* weighed in the house
Ne 10:39 where are the *v·* of the sanctuary,
13: 5 the frankincense, and the *v·*, and
9 I again the *v·* of the house of God,
Es 1: 7 they gave them drink in *v·* of gold,
7 *v·* being diverse one from another,)
Isa 18: 2 *v·* of bulrushes upon the waters,
22:24 the issue, all *v·* of small quantity,
24 the *v·* of cups, even to all the *v·* of
52:11 clean, that bear the *v·* of the Lord.
65: 4 abominable things is in their *v·*;
Jer 14: 3 they returned with their *v·* empty;
27:16 *v·* of the Lord's house shall now
18 *v·* which are left in the house of
19 concerning the residue of the *v·*
21 concerning the *v·* that remain in
28: 3 bring again into this place all the *v·*
6 to bring again the *v·* of the Lord's
40:10 and put them in your *v·*, and dwell
48:12 and shall empty his *v·*, and break
49:29 and all their *v·*, and their camels;
52:18 all the *v·* of brass wherewith they
20 the brass of all these *v·* was without
Eze 27:13 the persons of men and *v·* of brass
Da 1: 2 part of the *v·* of the house of God:
2 he brought the *v·* into the treasure
5: 2 to bring the golden and silver *v·*
3 Then they brought the golden *v·*
23 have brought the *v·* of his house
11: 8 precious *v·* of silver and of gold;
Ho 13:15 spoil the treasure of all pleasant *v·*.
Hag 2:16 to draw out fifty *v·* out of the press,
M't 13:48 gathered the good into *v·*, but cast
25: 4 wise took oil in their *v·* with their
M'r 7: 4 cups, and pots, and brazen *v·*, and
Ro 9:22 *v·* of wrath fitted to destruction:
23 of his glory on the *v·* of mercy,
2Co 4: 7 have this treasure in earthen *v·*,
2Ti 2:20 are not only *v·* of gold and of silver,
Heb 9:21 and all the *v·* of the ministry.
Re 2:27 as the *v·* of a potter shall they be
18:12 wood, and all manner *v·* of ivory,
12 manner *v·* of most precious wood,

vestments
2Ki 10:22 forth *v·* for all the worshippers
22 And he brought them forth *v·*.

vestry
2Ki 10: 22 unto him that was over the *v*'.

vesture See also VESTURES.
De 22: 12 upon the four quarters of thy *v*'.
Ps 22: 18 them, and cast lots upon my *v*'.
102: 26 as a *v*' shalt thou change them,
M't 27: 35 and upon my *v*' did they cast lots.
Joh 19: 24 and for my *v*' they did cast lots.
Heb 1: 12 as a *v*' shalt thou fold them up,
Re 19: 13 clothed with a *v*' dipped in blood:
16 on his *v*' and on his thigh a name

vestures
Ge 41: 42 arrayed him in *v*' of fine linen,

vex See also VEXED.
Ex 22: 21 Thou shalt neither *v*' a stranger,
Le 18: 18 take a wife to her sister, to *v*' her,
19: 33 in your land, ye shall not *v*' him.
Nu 25: 17 *V*' the Midianites, and smite
18 For they *v*' you with their wiles,
33: 55 shall *v*' you in the land wherein
2Sa 12: 18 how will he then *v*' himself,
2Ch 15: 6 God did *v*' them with all adversity
Job 19: 2 How long will ye *v*' my soul, and
Ps 2: 5 and *v*' them in his sore displeasure
Isa 7: 6 us go up against Judah, and *v*' it,
11: 13 and Judah shall not *v*' Ephraim.
Eze 32: 9 I will also *v*' the hearts of many
Hab 2: 7 and awake that shall *v*' thee,
Ac 12: 1 hands to *v*' certain of the church.

vexation See also VEXATIONS.
De 28: 20 shall send upon thee cursing, *v*',
Ec 1: 14 all is vanity and *v*' of spirit.
17 that this also is *v*' of spirit.
2: 11 all was vanity and *v*' of spirit,
17 for all is vanity and *v*' of spirit.
22 labour, and of the *v*' of his heart,
26 also is vanity and *v*' of spirit.
4: 4 This is also vanity and *v*' of spirit.
6 full with travail and *v*' of spirit.
16 this also is vanity and *v*' of spirit.
6: 9 this is also vanity and *v*' of spirit.
Isa 9: 1 shall not be such as was in her *v*',
28: 19 shall be a *v*' only to understand
65: 14 and shall howl for *v*' of spirit.

vexations
2Ch 15: 5 but great *v*' were upon all the

vexed
Nu 20: 15 Egyptians *v*' us, and our fathers:
J'g 2: 18 that oppressed them and *v*' them.
10: 8 they *v*' and oppressed the children
16: 16 so that his soul was *v*' unto death:
1Sa 14: 47 he turned himself, he *v*' them.
2Sa 13: 2 Amnon was so *v*', that he fell sick
2Ki 4: 27 for her soul is *v*' within her:
Ne 9: 27 of their enemies, who *v*' them:
Job 27: 2 Almighty, who hath *v*' my soul;
Ps 6: 2 heal me; for my bones are *v*'.
3 My soul is also sore *v*': but thou
10 enemies be ashamed and sore *v*':
Isa 63: 10 rebelled, and *v*' his holy Spirit:
Eze 22: 5 which art infamous and much *v*'.
7 in thee have they *v*' the fatherless
29 and have *v*' the poor and needy:
M't 15: 22 is grievously *v*' with a devil.
17: 15 for he is lunatick, and sore *v*':
Lu 6: 18 that were *v*' with unclean spirits:
Ac 5: 16 which were *v*' with unclean spirits:
2Pe 2: 7 *v*' with the filthy conversation of
8 *v*' his righteous soul from day to

vial See also VIALS.
1Sa 10: 1 Then Samuel took a *v*' of oil, and
Re 16: 2 poured out his *v*' upon the earth;
3 poured out his *v*' upon the sea;
4 poured out his *v*' upon the rivers
8 poured out his *v*' upon the sun;
10 poured out his *v*' upon the seat
12 out his *v*' upon the great river
17 poured out his *v*' into the air;

vials
Re 5: 8 and golden *v*' full of odours, which
15: 7 seven golden *v*' full of the wrath of
16: 1 pour out the *v*' of the wrath of God
17: 1 angels which had the seven *v*',
21: 9 the seven *v*' full of the seven last

victory
2Sa 19: 2 the *v*' that day was turned into
23: 10 the Lord wrought a great *v*' that
12 and the Lord wrought a great *v*'.
1Ch 29: 11 and the glory, and the *v*', and the
Ps 98: 1 holy arm, hath gotten him the *v*'.
Isa 25: 8 He will swallow up death in *v*';
M't 12: 20 he send forth judgment unto *v*'.
1Co 15: 54 Death is swallowed up in *v*'.
55 thy sting? O grave, where is thy *v*'?
57 *v*' through our Lord Jesus Christ.
1Jo 5: 4 the *v*' that overcometh the world,
Re 15: 2 had gotten the *v*' over the beast,

victual See also VICTUALS.
Ex 12: 39 prepared for themselves any *v*'.
J'g 20: 10 to fetch *v*' for the people, that they
1Ki 4: 27 those officers provided *v*' for king
2Ch 11: 11 captains in them, and store of *v*',
23 he gave them *v*' in abundance.

victuals
Ge 14: 11 and Gomorrah, and all their *v*',
Le 25: 37 nor lend him thy *v*' for increase.
De 23: 19 usury of money, usury of *v*', usury
Jos 1: 11 people, saying, Prepare you *v*';
9: 11 Take *v*' with you for the journey,
14 And the men took up their *v*', and
J'g 7: 8 the people took *v*' in their hand,
17: 10 and a suit of apparel, and thy *v*'.
1Sa 22: 10 and gave him *v*', and gave him
1Ki 4: 7 provided *v*' for the king and his
11: 18 appointed him *v*', and gave him
Ne 10: 31 ware or any *v*' on the sabbath day
13: 15 in the day wherein they sold *v*'.
Jer 40: 5 captain of the guard gave him *v*'
44: 17 for then had we plenty of *v*', and
M't 14: 15 villages, and buy themselves *v*'.
Lu 9: 12 about, and lodge, and get *v*':

view See also VIEWED.
Jos 2: 1 Go *v*' the land, even Jericho.
7: 2 saying, Go up and *v*' the country.
2Ki 2: 7 went, and stood to *v*' afar off:
15 prophets...were to *v*' at Jericho

viewed
Jos 7: 2 And the men went up and *v*' Ai.
Ezr 8: 15 and I *v*' the people, and the priests,
Ne 2: 13 and *v*' the walls of Jerusalem,
15 night by the brook, and *v*' the wall,

vigilant
1Ti 3: 2 husband of one wife, *v*', sober, of
1Pe 5: 8 Be sober, be *v*'; because your

vile See also REVILE; VILER; VILEST.
De 25: 3 thy brother should seem *v*' unto
J'g 19: 24 this man do not so *v*' a thing.
1Sa 3: 13 his sons made themselves *v*', and
15: 9 but every thing that was *v*' and
2Sa 6: 22 I will yet be more *v*' than thus,
Job 18: 3 and reputed *v*' in your sight?
40: 4 I am *v*'; what shall I answer thee?
Ps 15: 4 eyes a *v*' person is contemned;
Isa 32: 5 The *v*' person shall be no more
6 the *v*' person will speak villany,
Jer 15: 19 forth the precious from the *v*',
29: 17 will make them like *v*' figs, that
La 1: 11 and consider; for I am become *v*'.
Da 11: 21 estate shall stand up a *v*' person,
Na 1: 14 make thy grave; for thou art *v*'.
3: 6 filth upon thee, and make thee *v*',
Ro 1: 26 gave them up unto *v*' affections:
Ph'p 3: 21 Who shall change our *v*' body,
Jas 2: 2 in also a poor man in *v*' raiment:

vilely
2Sa 1: 21 of the mighty is *v*' cast away,

viler
Job 30: 8 men: they were *v*' than the earth.

vilest
Ps 12: 8 when the *v*' men are exalted.

village See also VILLAGES.
M't 21: 2 Go into the *v*' over against you,
M'r 11: 2 Go your way into the *v*' over against
Lu 8: 1 went throughout every city and *v*',
9: 52 entered into a *v*' of the Samaritans,
56 them. And they went to another *v*'.
10: 38 that he entered into a certain *v*':
17: 12 And as he entered into a certain *v*',
19: 30 Go ye into the *v*' over against you;
24: 13 same day to a *v*' called Emmaus,
28 And they drew nigh unto the *v*',

villages
Ex 8: 13 out of the *v*', and out of the fields.
Le 25: 31 houses of the *v*' which have no wall
Nu 21: 25 Heshbon, and in all the *v*' thereof.
32 they took the *v*' thereof, and drove
32: 42 took Kenath, and the *v*' thereof,
Jos 13: 23 the cities and the *v*' thereof.
28 families, the cities, and their *v*'.
15: 32 are twenty and nine, with their *v*'.
36 fourteen cities with their *v*':
41 sixteen cities with their *v*'.
44 Mareshah; nine cities with their *v*'.
45 Ekron, with her towns and her *v*':
46 that lay near Ashdod, with their *v*':
47 Ashdod with her towns and her *v*',
47 Gaza with her towns and her *v*',
51 Giloh; eleven cities with their *v*'.
54 and Zior; nine cities with their *v*'.
57 Timnah; ten cities with their *v*'.
59 Eltekon: six cities with their *v*'.
60 Ribbah; two cities with their *v*'.
62 En-gedi; six cities with their *v*'.
16: 9 all the cities with their *v*'.
18: 24 Gaba; twelve cities with their *v*':
28 fourteen cities with their *v*'.
19: 6 thirteen cities and their *v*':
7 Ashan; four cities and their *v*':
8 all the *v*' that were round about
15 twelve cities with their *v*'.
16 families, these cities with their *v*'.
22 Jordan: sixteen cities with their *v*'.
23 families, the cities and their *v*'.
30 twenty and two cities with their *v*'.
31 families, these cities with their *v*'.
38 nineteen cities with their *v*'.
39 families, the cities and their *v*'.
48 families, these cities with their *v*'.
21: 12 fields of the city, and the *v*' thereof,
J'g 5: 7 The inhabitants of the *v*' ceased,
11 the inhabitants of his *v*' in Israel:
1Sa 6: 18 of fenced cities, and of country *v*',
1Ch 4: 32 And their *v*' were, Etam, and Ain,
33 all their *v*' that were round about
6: 56 fields of the city, and the *v*' thereof,
9: 16 dwelt in the *v*' of the Netophathites.
22 by their genealogy in their *v*',
25 brethren, which were in their *v*',
27: 25 and the cities, and in the *v*', and
2Ch 28: 18 and Shocho with the *v*' thereof,
18 and Timnah with the *v*' thereof,
18 Gimzo also and the *v*' thereof: and
Ne 6: 2 together in some one of the *v*'
11: 25 And for the *v*', with their fields,
25 Kirjath-arba, and in the *v*' thereof,
25 at Dibon, and in the *v*' thereof,
25 at Jekabzeel, and in the *v*' thereof,
27 Beer-sheba, and in the *v*' thereof,
28 at Mekonah, and in the *v*' thereof,
30 and in their *v*', at Lachish,
30 at Azekah, and in the *v*' thereof.
31 Aija, and Beth-el, and in their *v*',
12: 28 and from the *v*' of Netophathi;
29 for the singers had builded them *v*'
Es 9: 19 Therefore the Jews of the *v*', that
Ps 10: 8 in the lurking places of the *v*':
Ca 7: 11 the field; let us lodge in the *v*'.
Isa 42: 11 the *v*' that Kedar doth inhabit:
Eze 38: 11 go up to the land of unwalled *v*';
Hab 3: 14 with his staves the head of his *v*':
M't 9: 35 went about all the cities and *v*',
14: 15 that they may go into the *v*', and
M'r 6: 6 And he went round about the *v*',
36 and into the *v*', and buy themselves
56 he entered, into the *v*', or cities, or
Lu 13: 22 he went through the cities and *v*',
Ac 8: 25 preached the gospel in many *v*'

villany
Isa 32: 6 For the vile person will speak *v*',
Jer 29: 23 they have committed *v*' in Israel,

vine See also VINEDRESSERS; VINES; VINEYARD.
Ge 40: 9 dream, behold, a *v*' was before me;
10 And in the *v*' were three branches:
49: 11 Binding his foal unto the *v*', and
11 his ass's colt unto the choice *v*':
Le 25: 5 the grapes of thy *v*' undressed:
11 the grapes in it of thy *v*' undressed.
Nu 6: 4 eat nothing...made of the *v*' tree,
De 32: 32 For their *v*' is of the *v*' of Sodom,
J'g 9: 12 Then said the trees unto the *v*',
13 the *v*' said unto them, Should I
13: 14 of any thing that cometh of the *v*',
1Ki 4: 25 every man under his *v*' and under
2Ki 4: 39 to gather herbs, and found a wild *v*',
18: 31 eat ye every man of his own *v*', and
2Ch 26: 10 and *v*' dressers in the mountains,
Job 15: 33 off his unripe grape as the *v*', and
Ps 80: 8 hast brought a *v*' out of Egypt:
14 and behold, and visit this *v*';
128: 3 Thy wife shall be as a fruitful *v*' by
Ca 6: 11 to see whether the *v*' flourished,
7: 8 breasts shall be as clusters of the *v*',
12 let us see if the *v*' flourish, whether
Isa 5: 2 and planted it with the choicest *v*',
16: 8 languish, and the *v*' of Sibmah:
9 weeping of Jazer the *v*' of Sibmah:
24: 7 wine mourneth, the *v*' languisheth,
32: 12 pleasant fields, for the fruitful *v*'.
34: 4 as the leaf falleth off from the *v*',
36: 16 and eat ye every one of his *v*', and
Jer 2: 21 Yet I had planted thee a noble *v*',
21 degenerate plant of a strange *v*'
6: 9 glean the remnant of Israel as a *v*':
8: 13 there shall be no grapes on the *v*',
48: 32 O *v*' of Sibmah, I will weep for thee
Eze 15: 2 What is the *v*' tree more than any
6 As the *v*' tree among the trees of
17: 6 a spreading *v*' of low stature,
6 so it became a *v*', and brought forth
7 this *v*' did bend her roots toward
8 fruit, that it might be a goodly *v*'.
19: 10 Thy mother is like a *v*' in thy blood,
Ho 10: 1 Israel is an empty *v*', he bringeth
14: 7 as the corn, and grow as the *v*':
Joe 1: 7 He hath laid my *v*' waste, and
12 The *v*' is dried up, and the fig tree
2: 22 and the *v*' do yield their strength.
Mic 4: 4 sit every man under his *v*' and
Na 2: 2 out, and marred their *v*' branches.
Hag 2: 19 as yet the *v*', and the fig tree, and
Zec 3: 10 man his neighbour under the *v*'
8: 12 the *v*' shall give her fruit, and the
Mal 3: 11 neither shall your *v*' cast her fruit
M't 26: 29 henceforth of this fruit of the *v*',
M'r 14: 25 drink no more of the fruit of the *v*',
Lu 22: 18 I will not drink of the fruit of the *v*',
Joh 15: 1 I am the true *v*', and my Father is
4 of itself, except it abide in the *v*';
5 I am the *v*', ye are the branches: He
Jas 3: 12 bear olive berries? either a *v*', figs?
Re 14: 18 gather the clusters of the *v*' of
19 and gathered the *v*' of the earth,

vinedressers See also VINE and DRESSERS.
2Ki 25: 12 the land to be *v*' and husbandmen.
Isa 61: 5 shall be your plowmen and your *v*'.
Jer 52: 16 the land for *v*' and for husbandmen.
Joe 1: 11 howl, O ye *v*', for the wheat and for

vinegar
Nu 6: 3 no *v*' of wine, or *v*' of strong drink,
Ru 2: 14 bread, and dip thy morsel in the *v*'.
Ps 69: 21 my thirst they gave me *v*' to drink.
Pr 10: 26 As *v*' to the teeth, and as smoke to
25: 20 and as *v*' upon nitre, so is he that
M't 27: 34 *v*' to drink mingled with gall:
48 took a spunge, and filled it with *v*',
M'r 15: 36 ran and filled a spunge full of *v*',
Lu 23: 36 coming to him, and offering him *v*',
Joh 19: 29 there was set a vessel full of *v*':
29 and they filled a spunge with *v*',
30 When Jesus...had received the *v*',

vines
Nu 20: 5 place of seed, or of figs, or of *v*',
De 8: 8 A land of wheat, and barley, and *v*',
Ps 78: 47 He destroyed their *v*' with hail,
105: 33 He smote their *v*' also and their fig
Ca 2: 13 the *v*' with the tender grape give a
15 the little foxes, that spoil the *v*':

Ca 2:15 for our v' have tender grapes.
Isa 7:23 were a thousand v' at a thousand
Jer 5:17 they shall eat up thy v' and thy fig
31: 5 yet plant v' upon the mountains
Ho 2:12 destroy her v' and her fig trees,
Hab 3:17 neither shall fruit be in the v';

vineyard See also VINEYARDS.
Ge 9:20 husbandman, and he planted a v':
Ex 22: 5 shall cause a field or v' to be eaten,
5 of the best of his own v', shall he
23:11 manner thou shalt deal with thy v'.
Le 19:10 And thou shalt not glean thy v',
10 thou gather every grape of thy v';
25: 3 six years thou shalt prune thy v',
4 sow thy field, nor prune thy v'.
De 20: 6 man is he that hath planted a v',
22: 9 Thou shalt not sow thy v' with
9 and the fruit of thy v', be defiled.
23:24 thou comest into thy neighbour's v',
24:21 thou gatherest the grapes of thy v',
28:30 thou shalt plant a v', and shalt not
1Ki 21: 1 that Naboth the Jezreelite had a v',
2 Give me thy v', that I may have it
2 give thee for it a better v' than it;
6 Give me thy v' for money; or else,
6 I will give thee another v' for it:
6 I will not give thee my v'.
7 I will give thee the v' of Naboth
15 take possession of the v' of Naboth
16 up to go down to the v' of Naboth
18 behold, he is in the v' of Naboth,
Ps 80:15 the v' which thy right hand hath
Pr 24:30 and by the v' of the man void of
31:16 fruit of her hands she planteth a v'.
Ca 1: 6 but mine own v' have I not kept.
8:11 Solomon had a v' at Baal-hamon;
11 he let out the v' unto keepers;
12 My v', which is mine, is before me:
Isa 1: 8 of Zion is left as a cottage in a v',
3:14 ye have eaten up the v'; the spoil
5: 1 song of my beloved touching his v'.
1 hath a v' in a very fruitful hill:
3 I pray you, betwixt me and my v'.
4 have been done more to my v',
5 tell you what I will do to my v':
7 v' of the Lord of hosts is the house
10 ten acres of v' shall yield one bath,
27: 2 sing ye unto her, A v' of red wine.
Jer 12:10 Many pastors have destroyed my v',
35: 7 house, nor sow seed, nor plant v',
9 neither have we v', nor field, nor
Mic 1: 6 the field, and as plantings of a v':
M't 20: 1 to hire labourers into his v'.
2 a day, he sent them into his v'.
4 unto them; Go ye also into the v',
7 unto them, Go ye also into the v';
8 the lord of the v' saith unto his
21:28 said, Son, go work to day in my v'.
33 householder, which planted a v',
39 cast him out of the v', and slew him.
40 the lord therefore of the v' cometh,
41 and will let out his v' unto other
M'r 12: 1 A certain man planted a v', and set
2 husbandmen of the fruit of the v'.
8 him, and cast him out of the v'.
9 shall therefore the lord of the v' do?
9 and will give the v' unto others.
Lu 13: 6 man had a fig tree planted in his v';
7 said he unto the dresser of his v',
20: 9 A certain man planted a v', and let
10 give him of the fruit of the v':
13 Then said the lord of the v', What
15 So they cast him out of the v', and
15 shall the lord of the v' do unto
16 and shall give the v' to others.
1Co 9: 7 who planteth a v', and eateth not of

vineyards
Nu 16:14 us inheritance of fields and v':
20:17 the fields, or through the v',
21:22 turn into the fields, or into the v';
22:24 the Lord stood in a path of the v',
De 6:11 v' and olive trees, which thou
28:39 Thou shalt plant v', and dress
Jos 24:13 v' and oliveyards which ye planted
J'g 9:27 and gathered their v', and trode the
11:33 cities, and unto the plain of the v',
14: 5 and came to the v' of Timnath:
15: 5 corn, with the v' and olives.
21:20 saying, Go and lie in wait in the v';
21 then come ye out of the v', and
1Sa 8:14 will take your fields, and your v',
15 tenth of your seed, and of your v',
22: 7 give every one of you fields and v',
2Ki 5:26 garments, and oliveyards, and v',
18:32 and wine, a land of bread and v',
19:29 year sow ye, and reap, and plant v',
1Ch 27:27 the v' was Shimei the Ramathite:
27 over the increase of the v' for the
Ne 5: 3 We have mortgaged our lands, v',
4 and that upon our lands and v'.
5 other men have our lands and v'.
11 even this day, their lands, their v',
9:25 wells digged, v', and oliveyards,
Job 24:18 he beholdeth not the way of the v'.
Ps 107:37 And sow the fields, and plant v',
Ec 2: 4 me houses; I planted me v':
Ca 1: 6 they made me the keeper of the v';
14 of camphire in the v' of En-gedi.
7:12 Let us get up early to the v'; let us
Isa 16:10 in the v' there shall be no singing,
36:17 and wine, a land of bread and v'.
37:30 plant v', and eat the fruit thereof.
65:21 they shall plant v', and eat the fruit
Jer 32:15 and v' shall be possessed again in
39:10 gave them v' and fields at the same
Eze 28:26 shall build houses, and plant v';
Ho 2:15 I will give her her v' from thence,
Am 4: 9 when your gardens and your v' and
5:11 ye have planted pleasant v', but ye
17 And in all v' shall be wailing: for I
9:14 and they shall plant v', and drink
Zep 1:13 they shall plant v', but not drink

vintage
Le 26: 5 threshing shall reach unto the v',
5 the v' shall reach unto the sowing
J'g 8: 2 better than the v' of Abi-ezer?
Job 24: 6 they gather the v' of the wicked.
Isa 16:10 I have made their v' shouting to cease.
24:13 grapes when the v' is done.
32:10 for the v' shall fail, the gathering
Jer 48:32 summer fruits and upon thy v'.
Mic 7: 1 as the grapegleanings of the v':
Zec 11: 2 the forest of the v' is come down.

viol See also VIOLS.
Isa 5:12 And the harp, and the v', the
Am 6: 5 That chant to the sound of the v',

violated
Eze 22:26 Her priests have v' my law, and

violence
Ge 6:11 and the earth was filled with v'.
13 the earth is filled with v' through
Le 6: 2 or in a thing taken away by v', or
2Sa 22: 3 saviour; thou savest me from v'.
Ps 11: 5 him that loveth v' his soul hateth.
55: 9 I have seen v' and strife in the city.
58: 2 ye weigh the v' of your hands in
72:14 their soul from deceit and v':
73: 6 v' covereth them as a garment.
Pr 4:17 and drink the wine of v'.
10: 6, 11 but v' covereth the mouth of the
13: 2 of the transgressors shall eat v'.
28:17 A man that doeth v' to the blood
Isa 53: 9 because he had done no v',
59: 6 and the act of v' is in their hands.
60:18 V' shall no more be heard in thy
Jer 6: 7 v' and spoil is heard in her; before
20: 8 I cried out, I cried v' and spoil;
22: 3 no wrong, do no v' to the stranger,
17 for oppression, and for v', to do it.
51:35 The v' done to me and to my flesh
46 come a rumour, and v' in the land,
Eze 7:11 V' is risen up into a rod of
23 crimes, and the city is full of v'.
8:17 they have filled the land with v',
12:19 of the v' of all them that dwell
18: 7 hath spoiled none by v', hath
12 hath spoiled by v', hath not
16 neither hath spoiled by v', but
18 spoiled his brother by v', and did
28:16 filled the midst of thee with v',
45: 9 remove v' and spoil, and execute
Joe 3:19 v' against the children of Judah,
Am 3:10 who store up v' and robbery in
6: 3 cause the seat of v' to come near;
Ob 10 thy v' against thy brother Jacob
Jon 3: 8 from the v' that is in their hands.
Mic 2: 2 covet fields, and take them by v';
6:12 rich men thereof are full of v',
Hab 1: 2 even cry out unto thee of v', and
3 for spoiling and v' are before me:
9 They shall come all for v': their
2: 8 for the v' of the land, of the city,
17 the v' of Lebanon shall cover thee,
17 for the v' of the land, of the city,
Zep 1: 9 fill their masters' houses with v'
3: 4 they have done v' to the law.
Mal 2:16 one covereth v' with his garment,
M't 11:12 kingdom of heaven suffereth v',
Lu 3:14 Do v' to no man, neither accuse
Ac 5:26 and brought them without v':
21:35 the soldiers for the v' of the people.
24: 7 with great v' took him away out of
27:41 broken with the v' of the waves.
Heb 11:34 Quenched the v' of fire, escaped
Re 18:21 v' shall that great city Babylon be

violent
2Sa 22:49 delivered me from the v' man.
Ps 7:16 v' dealing shall come down upon
18:48 hast delivered me from the v' man.
86:14 the assemblies of v' men have
140: 1, 4 preserve me from the v' man;
11 evil shall hunt the v' man to
Pr 16:29 A v' man enticeth his neighbor, and
Ec 5: 8 v' perverting of judgment and
M't 11:12 and the v' take it by force.

violently
Ge 21:25 servants had v' taken away.
Le 6: 4 restore that which he took v'
De 28:31 thine ass shall be v' taken away
Job 20:19 he hath v' taken away an house
24: 2 they v' take away flocks, and feed
Isa 22:18 v' turn and toss thee like a ball
La 2: 6 v' taken away his tabernacle,
M't 8:32 of swine ran v' down a steep place
M'r 5:13 the herd ran v' down a steep place
Lu 8:33 the herd ran v' down a steep place

viols
Isa 14:11 the grave, and the noise of thy v':
Am 5:23 will not hear the melody of thy v'.

viper See also VIPER'S; VIPERS.
Isa 30: 6 the v' and fiery flying serpent,
59: 5 is crushed breaketh out into a v'.
Ac 28: 3 there came a v' out of the heat,

viper's
Job 20:16 asps: the v' tongue shall slay him.

vipers
M't 3: 7 O generation of v', who hath
12:34 O generation of v', how can ye,
23:33 ye generation of v', how can ye
Lu 3: 7 O generation of v', who hath

virgin See also VIRGIN'S; VIRGINS.
Ge 24:16 was very fair to look upon, a v',
43 v' cometh forth to draw water,
Le 21: 3 for his sister a v', that is nigh
14 he shall take a v' of his own people
De 22:19 an evil name upon a v' of Israel:
23 damsel that is a v' be betrothed
28 If a man find a damsel that is a v',
32:25 both the young man and the v', the
2Sa 13: 2 for she was a v'; and Amnon
1Ki 1: 2 for my lord the king a young v':
2Ki 19:21 The v' the daughter of Zion hath
Isa 7:14 Behold, a v' shall conceive, and
23:12 O thou oppressed v', daughter of
37:22 The v', the daughter of Zion, hath
47: 1 O v' daughter of Babylon, sit on
62: 5 For as a young man marrieth a v',
Jer 14:17 v' daughter of my people is broken
18:13 the v' of Israel hath done a very
31: 4 thou shalt be built, O v' of Israel:
13 shall the v' rejoice in the dance,
21 O v' of Israel, turn again to these
46:11 balm, O v', the daughter of Egypt:
La 1:15 the Lord hath trodden the v', the
2:13 thee, O v' daughter of Zion?
Joe 1: 8 Lament like a v' girded with
Am 5: 2 The v' of Israel is fallen; she shall
M't 1:23 Behold, a v' shall be with child,
Lu 1:27 To a v' espoused to a man whose
1Co 7:28 if a v' marry, she hath not sinned.
34 also between a wife and a v'.
36 himself uncomely toward his v',
37 his heart that he will keep his v',
2Co 11: 2 you as a chaste v' to Christ.

virginity
Le 21:13 he shall take a wife in her v'.
De 22:15 forth the tokens of the damsel's v'
17 are the tokens of my daughter's v'.
20 tokens of v' be not found for the
J'g 11:37 bewail my v', I and my fellows.
38 and bewailed her v' upon the
Eze 23: 3 they bruised the teats of their v'.
8 they bruised the breasts of her v',
Lu 2:36 husband seven years from her v';

virgin's
Lu 1:27 and the v' name was Mary.

virgins
Ex 22:17 according to the dowry of v'.
J'g 21:12 four hundred young v', that had
2Sa 13:18 the king's daughters that were v'
Es 2: 2 Let there be fair young v' sought
3 together all the fair young v' unto
17 in his sight more than all the v';
19 the v' were gathered together
Ps 45:14 the v' her companions that follow
Ca 1: 3 therefore do the v' love thee.
6: 8 and v' without number.
Isa 23: 4 up young men, nor bring up v'.
La 1: 4 priests sigh, her v' are afflicted,
18 my v' and my young men are
2:10 the v' of Jerusalem hang down
21 my v' and my young men are
Am 8:13 the fair v' and young men faint for
M't 25: 1 of heaven be likened unto ten v',
7 all those v' arose, and trimmed
11 Afterward came also the other v',
Ac 21: 9 same man had four daughters, v',
1Co 7:25 Now concerning v' I have no
Re 14: 4 with women; for they are v'.

virtue
M'r 5:30 that v' had gone out of him,
Lu 6:19 for there went v' out of him, and
8:46 perceive that v' has gone out of me.
Ph'p 4: 8 there be any v', and if there be any
2Pe 1: 3 that hath called us to glory and v':
5 diligence, add to your faith v';
5 and to v' knowledge:

virtuous
Ru 3:11 know that thou art a v' woman.
Pr 12: 4 A v' woman is a crown to her
31:10 Who can find a v' woman? for her

virtuously
Pr 31:29 Many daughters have done v', but

visage
Isa 52:14 his v' was so marred more than
La 4: 8 Their v' is blacker than a coal;
Da 3:19 the form of his v' was changed

visible See also INVISIBLE.
Col 1:16 that are in earth, v' and invisible,

vision See also DIVISION; VISIONS.
Ge 15: 1 Lord came unto Abram in a v',
Nu 12: 6 myself known unto him in a v',
24: 4, 16 saw the v' of the Almighty,
1Sa 3: 1 those days; there was no open v'.
15 Samuel feared to shew Eli the v'.
2Sa 7:17 according to all this v', so did
1Ch 17:15 according to all this v', so did
2Ch 32:32 they are written in the v' of Isaiah
Job 20: 8 chased away as a v' of the night.
33:15 in a v' of the night, when deep
Ps 89:19 thou spakest in v' to thy holy one,
Pr 29:18 Where there is no v', the people
Isa 1: 1 The v' of Isaiah the son of Amoz,
21: 2 grievous v' is declared unto me;
22: 1 The burden of the valley of v'.
5 God of hosts in the valley of v',

Isa 28: 7 they err in v', they stumble in
29: 7 shall be as a dream of a night v'.
11 the v' of all is become unto you as
Jer 14: 14 they prophesy unto you a false v'
23: 16 they speak a v' of their own heart,
La 2: 9 also find no v' from the Lord.
Eze 7: 13 v' is touching the whole multitude
26 shall they seek a v' of the prophet;
8: 4 to the v' that I saw in the plain.
11: 24 brought me in a v' by the Spirit of
24 the v' that I had seen went up from
12: 22 prolonged, and every v' faileth?
23 at hand, and the effect of every v'.
24 be no more any vain v' nor flattering
27 The v' that he seeth is for many
13: 7 Have ye not seen a vain v', and
43: 3 appearance of the v' which I saw,
3 according to the v' that I saw when
3 were like the v' that I saw by the
Da 2: 19 revealed unto Daniel in a night v'.
7: 2 and said, I saw in my v' by night,
8: 1 Belshazzar a v' appeared unto me,
2 I saw in a v'; and it came to pass,
2 I saw in a v', and I was by the river
13 shall be the v' concerning the
15 even I Daniel, had seen the v', and
16 this man to understand the v'.
17 the time of the end shall be the v'.
26 v' of the evening and the morning
26 wherefore shut thou up the v'; for
27 I was astonished at the v', but
9: 21 whom I had seen in the v' at the
23 the matter, and consider the v'.
24 and to seal up the v' and prophecy,
10: 1 and had understanding of the v'.
7 And I Daniel alone saw the v': for
7 that were with me saw not the v';
8 left alone, and saw this great v',
14 for yet the v' is for many days.
16 by the v' my sorrows are turned
11: 14 themselves to establish the v';
Ob 1 The v' of Obadiah. Thus saith the
Mic 3: 6 you, that ye shall not have a v';
Na 1: 1 The book of the v' of Nahum the
Hab 2: 2 Write the v', and make it plain
3 the v' is yet for an appointed time,
Zec 13: 4 be ashamed every one of his v',
M't 17: 9 Tell the v' to no man, until the
Lu 1: 22 he had seen a v' in the temple:
24: 23 they had also seen a v' of angels,
Ac 9: 10 and to him said the Lord in a v',
12 seen in a v' a man named Ananias
10: 3 He saw in a v' evidently about the
17 what this v' which he had seen
19 While Peter thought on the v', the
11: 5 and in a trance I saw a v', a certain
12: 9 angel; but thought he saw a v'.
16: 9 a v' appeared to Paul in the night;
10 And after he had seen the v',
18: 9 Lord to Paul in the night by a v',
26: 19 disobedient unto the heavenly v':
Re 9: 17 I saw the horses in the v', and

visions See also DIVISIONS.
Ge 46: 2 unto Israel in the v' of the night,
2Ch 9: 29 v' of Iddo the seer against
26: 5 understanding in the v' of God:
Job 4: 13 thoughts from the v' of the night,
7: 14 and terrifiest me through v':
Eze 1: 1 were opened, and I saw v' of God.
8: 3 brought me in the v' of God to
13: 16 which see v' of peace for her, and
40: 2 In the v' of God brought he me
43: 3 and the v' were like the vision
Da 1: 17 understanding in all v' and
2: 28 v' of thy head upon thy bed, are
4: 5 and the v' of my head trouble me.
9 tell me the v' of my dream that I
10 Thus were the v' of mine head in
13 I saw in the v' of my head upon my
7: 1 and v' of his head upon his bed:
7 After this I saw in the night v',
13 I saw in the night v', and, behold,
15 and the v' of my head troubled me.
Ho 12: 10 I have multiplied v', and used
Joe 2: 28 your young men shall see v':
Ac 2: 17 and your young men shall see v',
2Co 12: 1 I will come to v' and revelations

visit See also VISITED; VISITEST; VISITETH; VISITING.
Ge 50: 24 God will surely v' you, and bring
25 God will surely v' you, and ye shall
Ex 13: 19 God will surely v' you; and ye shall
32: 34 the day when I v' I will v' their sin
Le 18: 25 I do v' the iniquity thereof upon it,
Job 5: 24 and thou shalt v' thy habitation,
7: 18 thou shouldest v' him every
Ps 59: 5 Israel, awake to v' all the heathen:
80: 14 heaven, and behold, and v' this
89: 32 Then will I v' their transgression
106: 4 people: O v' me with thy salvation;
Isa 23: 17 that the Lord will v' Tyre, and she
Jer 3: 16 it; neither shall they v' it;
5: 9, 29 Shall I not v' for these things?
6: 15 time that I v' them they shall be
9: 9 Shall I not v' them for these things?
14: 10 their iniquity, and v' their sins.
15: 15 and v' me, and revenge me of my
23: 2 v' upon you the evil of your doings,
27: 22 they be until the day that I v' them,
29: 10 at Babylon I will v' you,
32: 5 and there shall he be until I v' him,
49: 8 him, the time that I will v' him.
50: 31 is come, the time that I will v' thee.
La 4: 22 he will v' thine iniquity, O daughter
Ho 2: 13 will v' upon her the days of Baalim,
8: 13 their iniquity, and v' their sins:
9: 9 their iniquity, he will v' their sins.
Am 3: 14 shall v' the transgressions of Israel
14 I will also v' the altars of Beth-el:
Zep 2: 7 the Lord their God shall v' them,
Zec 11: 16 shall not v' those that be cut off,
Ac 7: 23 to v' his brethren the children of
15: 14 God at the first did v' the Gentiles,
36 Let us go again and v' our brethren
Jas 1: 27 To v' the fatherless and widows in

visitation
Nu 16: 29 visited after the v' of all men;
Job 10: 12 thy v' hath preserved my spirit.
Isa 10: 3 And what will ye do in the day of v',
Jer 8: 12 the time of their v' they shall be
10: 15 time of their v' they shall perish.
11: 23 Anathoth, even the year of their v'.
23: 12 them, even the year of their v',
46: 21 upon them, and the time of their v'.
48: 44 upon Moab, the year of their v',
50: 27 day is come, the time of their v'.
51: 18 time of their v' they shall perish.
Ho 9: 7 The days of v' are come, the days
Mic 7: 4 of thy watchmen and thy v' cometh;
Lu 19: 44 knewest not the time of thy v'.
1Pe 2: 12 behold, glorify God in the day of v'.

visited
Ge 21: 1 the Lord v' Sarah as he had said,
Ex 3: 16 I have surely v' you, and seen that
4: 31 Lord had v' the children of Israel,
Nu 16: 29 if they be v' after the visitation of
J'g 15: 1 that Samson v' his wife with a kid;
Ru 1: 6 the Lord had v' his people in giving
1Sa 2: 21 And the Lord v' Hannah, so that she
Job 35: 15 it is not so, he hath v' in his anger;
Ps 17: 3 thou hast v' me in the night; thou
Pr 19: 23 he shall not be v' with evil.
Isa 24: 22 after many days shall they be v'.
26: 14 hast thou v' and destroyed them,
16 Lord, in trouble have they v' thee,
29: 6 Thou shalt be v' of the Lord of
Jer 6: 6 Jerusalem: this is the city to be v';
23: 2 them away, and have not v' them:
Eze 38: 8 After many days thou shalt be v':
Zec 10: 3 the Lord of hosts hath v' his flock
M't 25: 36 I was sick, and ye v' me: I was in
43 and in prison, and ye v' me not.
Lu 1: 68 hath v' and redeemed his people,
78 dayspring from on high hath v' us,
7: 16 and, That God hath v' his people.

visitest
Ps 8: 4 the son of man, that thou v' him?
65: 9 Thou v' the earth, and waterest it:
Heb 2: 6 the son of man, that thou v' him?

visiteth
Job 31: 14 when he v', what shall I answer

visiting
Ex 20: 5 v' the iniquity of the fathers upon
34: 7 v' the iniquity of the fathers upon
Nu 14: 18 v' the iniquity of the fathers upon
De 5: 9 v' the iniquity of the fathers upon

vocation See also CONVOCATION.
Eph 4: 1 walk worthy of the v' wherewith

voice See also VOICES.
Ge 3: 8 they heard the v' of the Lord God
10 I heard thy v' in the garden, and
17 hearkened unto the v' of thy wife,
4: 10 v' of thy brother's blood crieth unto
23 wives, Adah and Zillah, hear my v';
16: 2 hearkened to the v' of Sarai.
21: 12 unto thee, hearken unto her v';
16 over against him, and lift up her v',
17 And God heard the v' of the lad;
17 God hath heard the v' of the lad
22: 18 because thou hast obeyed my v'.
26: 5 that Abraham obeyed my v', and
27: 8 obey my v' according to that which
13 only obey my v', and go fetch me
22 The v' is Jacob's v', but the hands
38 And Esau lifted up his v', and wept.
43 Now therefore, my son, obey my v';
29: 11 and lifted up his v', and wept.
30: 6 me, and hath also heard my v',
39: 14 with me, and I cried with a loud v':
15 he heard that I lifted up my v' and
18 as I lifted up my v' and cried, that
Ex 3: 18 they shall hearken to thy v': and
4: 1 me, nor hearken unto my v':
8 hearken to the v' of the first sign,
8 will believe the v' of the latter sign.
9 signs, neither hearken unto thy v',
5: 2 should obey his v' to let Israel go?
15: 26 hearken to the v' of the Lord thy
18: 19 Hearken now unto my v', I will
24 to the v' of his father in law,
19: 5 if ye will obey my v' indeed, and
16 v' of the trumpet exceeding loud;
19 the v' of the trumpet sounded long,
19 and God answered him by a v'.
23: 21 Beware of him, and obey his v',
22 if thou shalt indeed obey his v',
24: 3 all the people answered with one v',
32: 18 v' of them that shout for mastery,
18 the v' of them that cry for being
Le 5: 1 hear the v' of swearing, and is a
Nu 7: 89 he heard the v' of one speaking
14: 1 the congregation lifted up their v',
22 and have not hearkened to my v';
20: 16 he heard our v', and sent an angel,
21: 3 Lord hearkened to the v' of Israel,
De 1: 34 Lord heard the v' of your words,
45 Lord would not hearken to your v',
4: 12 ye heard the v' of the words, but
12 no similitude; only ye heard a v'.
4: 30 and shalt be obedient unto his v';
33 v' of God speaking out of the midst
36 he made thee to hear his v', that
5: 22 the thick darkness, with a great v':
23 ye heard the v' out of the midst of
24 we have heard his v' out of the
25 if we hear the v' of the Lord our
26 hath heard the v' of the living God
28 Lord heard the v' of your words,
28 I have heard the v' of the words of
8: 20 obedient unto the v' of the Lord
9: 23 him not, nor hearkened to his v'.
13: 4 commandments, and obey his v',
18 shalt hearken to the v' of the Lord
15: 5 hearken to the v' of the Lord thy
18: 16 not hear again the v' of the Lord
21: 18 will not obey the v' of his father,
18 or the v' of his mother, and that,
20 rebellious, he will not obey our v';
26: 7 Lord heard our v', and looked on
14 hearkened to the v' of the Lord my
17 and to hearken unto his v':
27: 10 obey the v' of the Lord thy God,
14 all the men of Israel with a loud v',
28: 1 hearken...unto the v' of the Lord
2 hearken unto the v' of the Lord thy
15 not hearken unto the v' of the Lord
45 not unto the v' of the Lord thy
62 not obey the v' of the Lord thy God.
30: 2 obey his v' according to all that I
8 return and obey the v' of the Lord,
10 hearken unto the v' of the Lord thy
20 that thou mayest obey his v', and
33: 7 said, Hear, Lord, the v' of Judah,
Jos 5: 6 they obeyed not the v' of the Lord:
6: 10 nor make any noise with your v',
10: 14 hearkened unto the v' of a man:
22: 2 have obeyed my v' in all that I
24: 24 we serve, and his v' will we obey.
J'g 2: 2 but ye have not obeyed my v': why
4 that the people lifted up their v',
20 have not hearkened unto my v';
6: 10 but ye have not obeyed my v'.
9: 7 lifted up his v', and cried, and said
13: 9 God hearkened to the v' of Manoah;
18: 3 knew the v' of the young man the
25 Let not thy v' be heard among us,
20: 13 hearken to the v' of their brethren
Ru 1: 9 they lifted up their v', and wept.
14 they lifted up their v', and wept
1Sa 1: 13 moved, but her v' was not heard:
2: 25 not unto the v' of their father,
8: 7 Hearken unto the v' of the people in
9 therefore hearken unto their v':
19 refused to obey the v' of Samuel;
22 Hearken unto their v', and make
12: 1 have hearkened unto your v' in all
14 serve him, and obey his v', and not
15 ye will not obey the v' of the Lord,
15: 1 the v' of the words of the Lord.
19 thou not obey the v' of the Lord,
20 I have obeyed the v' of the Lord,
22 as in obeying the v' of the Lord?
24 the people, and obeyed their v'.
19: 6 hearkened unto the v' of Jonathan:
24: 16 said, Is this thy v', my son David?
16 And Saul lifted up his v', and wept.
25: 35 I have hearkened to thy v', and
26: 17 And Saul knew David's v', and said,
17 Is this thy v', my son David? And
17 David said, It is my v', my lord,
28: 12 Samuel, she cried with a loud v':
18 obeyedst not the v' of the Lord,
21 thine handmaid hath obeyed thy v',
22 unto the v' of thine handmaid,
23 and he hearkened unto their v'.
30: 4 him lifted up their v' and wept,
2Sa 3: 32 the king lifted up his v', and wept
12: 18 he would not hearken unto our v':
13: 14 he would not hearken unto her v':
36 and lifted up their v' and wept:
15: 23 all the country wept with a loud v',
19: 4 the king cried with a loud v', O my
35 any more the v' of singing men
22: 7 he did hear my v' out of his temple,
14 and the most High uttered his v'.
1Ki 8: 55 congregation of Israel with a loud v',
17: 22 the Lord heard the v' of Elijah; and
18: 26 But there was no v', nor any that
29 that there was neither v', nor any
19: 12 and after the fire a still small v'.
13 there came a v' unto him, and said,
20: 25 he hearkened unto their v', and did
36 hast not obeyed the v' of the Lord,
2Ki 4: 31 there was neither v', nor hearing.
7: 10 no man there, neither v' of man,
10: 6 and if ye will hearken unto my v',
18: 12 they obeyed not the v' of the Lord
28 a loud v' in the Jews' language,
19: 22 whom hast thou exalted thy v',
1Ch 15: 16 by lifting up the v' with joy.
2Ch 5: 13 lifted up their v' with the trumpets
15: 14 sware unto the Lord with a loud v',
20: 19 of Israel with a loud v' on high.
30: 27 and their v' was heard, and their
32: 18 with a loud v' in the Jews' speech
Ezr 3: 12 their eyes, wept with a loud v';
10: 12 answered and said with a loud v',
Ne 9: 4 cried with a loud v' unto the Lord
Job 2: 12 they lifted up their v', and wept;
3: 7 solitary, let no joyful v' come therein.
18 hear not the v' of the oppressor.
4: 10 the lion, and the v' of the fierce lion,
16 there was silence, and I heard a v',
9: 16 that he had hearkened unto my v',
30: 31 organ into the v' of them that weep.

Job 33: 8 I have heard the *v'* of thy words,
34: 16 hearken to the *v'* of my words.
37: 2 Hear attentively the noise of his *v'*,
4 After it a *v'* roareth: he thundereth
4 with the *v'* of his excellency;
4 not stay them when his *v'* is heard.
5 marvellously with his *v'*; great
38: 34 thou lift up thy *v'* to the clouds,
40: 9 thou thunder with a *v'* like him?
Ps 3: 4 I cried unto the Lord with my *v'*,
5: 2 Hearken unto the *v'* of my cry, my
3 My *v'* shalt thou hear in the
6: 8 hath heard the *v'* of my weeping.
18: 6 he heard my *v'* out of his temple,
13 and the Highest gave his *v'*;
19: 3 where their *v'* is not heard.
26: 7 with the *v'* of thanksgiving,
27: 7 O Lord, when I cry with my *v'*:
28: 2 Hear the *v'* of my supplications,
6 heard the *v'* of my supplications.
29: 3 *v'* of the Lord is upon the waters:
4 The *v'* of the Lord is powerful; the
4 the *v'* of the Lord is full of majesty.
5 *v'* of the Lord breaketh the cedars;
7 *v'* of the Lord divideth the flames
8 The *v'* of the Lord shaketh the
9 *v'* of the Lord maketh the hinds to
31: 22 heardest the *v'* of my supplications
42: 4 with the *v'* of joy and praise, with a
44: 16 For the *v'* of him that reproacheth
46: 6 he uttered his *v'*, the earth melted.
47: 1 unto God with the *v'* of triumph.
55: 3 Because of the *v'* of the enemy,
17 cry aloud: and he shall hear my *v'*.
58: 5 not hearken to the *v'* of charmers,
64: 1 Hear my *v'*, O God, in my prayer:
66: 8 the *v'* of his praise to be heard:
19 attended to the *v'* of my prayer.
68: 33 lo, he doth send out his *v'*,
33 and that a mighty *v'*.
74: 23 Forget not the *v'* of thine enemies:
77: 1 I cried unto God with my *v'*, even
1 unto God with my *v'*; and he gave
18 The *v'* of thy thunder was in the
81: 11 people would not hearken to my *v'*;
86: 6 attend to the *v'* of my supplications.
93: 3 the floods have lifted up their *v'*;
95: 7 hand. To day if ye will hear his *v'*,
98: 5 the harp, and the *v'* of a psalm.
102: 5 By reason of the *v'* of my groaning
103: 20 hearkening unto the *v'* of his word.
104: 7 at the *v'* of thy thunder they hasted
106: 25 not unto the *v'* of the Lord.
116: 1 Lord, because he hath heard my *v'*
118: 15 The *v'* of rejoicing and salvation is
119: 149 Hear my *v'* according unto thy
130: 2 Lord, hear my *v'*: let thine ears
2 thine ears be attentive to the *v'* of
141: 1 give ear unto my *v'*, when I cry
142: 1 I cried unto the Lord with my *v'*;
1 with my *v'* unto the Lord did I
Pr 1: 20 she uttereth her *v'* in the streets:
2: 3 liftest up thy *v'* for understanding;
5: 13 not obeyed the *v'* of my teachers,
8: 1 understanding put forth her *v'*?
4 and my *v'* is to the sons of man.
27: 14 blesseth his friend with a loud *v'*,
Ec 5: 3 a fool's *v'* is known by multitude of
6 should God be angry at thy *v'*,
10: 20 a bird of the air shall carry the *v'*,
12: 4 he shall rise up at the *v'* of the bird,
Ca 2: 8 The *v'* of my beloved! behold, he
12 the *v'* of the turtle is heard in our
14 me hear thy *v'*; for sweet is thy *v'*,
5: 2 *v'* of my beloved that knocketh,
8: 13 the companions hearken to thy *v'*:
Isa 6: 4 moved at the *v'* of him that cried,
8 Also I heard the *v'* of the Lord,
10: 30 Lift up thy *v'*, O daughter of
13: 2 exalt the *v'* unto them, shake the
15: 4 their *v'* shall be heard even unto
24: 14 They shall lift up their *v'*, they shall
28: 23 Give ye ear, and hear my *v'*;
29: 4 thy *v'* shall be, as of one that hath a
30: 19 unto thee at the *v'* of thy cry;
30 cause his glorious *v'* to be heard,
31 through the *v'* of the Lord shall the
31: 4 he will not be afraid of their *v'*, nor
32: 9 hear my *v'*, ye careless daughters;
36: 13 cried with a loud *v'* in the Jews'
37: 23 whom hast thou exalted thy *v'*,
40: 3 The *v'* of him that crieth in the
6 The *v'* said, Cry. And he said,
9 tidings, lift up thy *v'* with strength;
42: 2 nor cause his *v'* to be heard in the
11 and the cities thereof lift up their *v'*
48: 20 with a *v'* of singing declare ye, tell
50: 10 that obeyeth the *v'* of his servant,
51: 3 thanksgiving, and the *v'* of melody.
52: 8 Thy watchmen shall lift up the *v'*;
8 with the *v'* together shall they sing:
58: 1 not, lift up thy *v'* like a trumpet,
4 make your *v'* to be heard on high.
65: 19 the *v'* of weeping shall be no more
19 heard in her, nor the *v'* of crying.
66: 6 A *v'* of noise from the city,
6 a *v'* from the temple,
6 a *v'* of the Lord that rendereth
Jer 3: 13 and ye have not obeyed my *v'*, saith
21 A *v'* was heard upon the high
25 have not obeyed the *v'* of the Lord
4: 15 For a *v'* declareth from Dan, and
16 give out their *v'* against the cities
31 heard a *v'* as of a woman in travail,
31 the *v'* of the daughter of Zion, that
6: 23 their *v'* roareth like the sea; and

Jer 7: 23 Obey my *v'*, and I will be your God,
28 that obeyeth not the *v'* of the Lord
34 the *v'* of mirth,...the *v'* of gladness,
34 the *v'* of the bridegroom, and
34 the *v'* of the bride: for the land
8: 19 the *v'* of the cry of the daughter of
9: 10 can men hear the *v'* of the cattle;
13 and have not obeyed my *v'*, neither
19 a *v'* of wailing is heard out of Zion,
10: 13 When he uttereth his *v'*, there is a
11: 4 iron furnace, saying, Obey my *v'*,
7 and protesting, saying, Obey my *v'*.
16: 9 the *v'* of mirth,...the *v'* of gladness,
9 the *v'* of the bridegroom, and
9 and the *v'* of the bride.
18: 10 that it obey not my *v'*, then I will
19 hearken to the *v'* of them that
22: 20 and lift up thy *v'* in Bashan, and cry
21 that thou obeyedst not my *v'*.
25: 10 the *v'* of mirth,...the *v'* of gladness,
10 the *v'* of the bridegroom, and
10 and the *v'* of the bride, the sound
30 high, and utter his *v'* from his holy
36 A *v'* of the cry of the shepherds, and
26: 13 obey the *v'* of the Lord your God;
30: 5 We have heard a *v'* of trembling, of
19 the *v'* of them that make merry:
31: 15 A *v'* was heard in Ramah,
16 Refrain thy *v'* from weeping, and
32: 23 but they obeyed not thy *v'*, neither
33: 11 The *v'* of joy, and the *v'* of gladness,
11 the *v'* of the bridegroom, and
11 and the *v'* of the bride, the
11 *v'* of them that shall say, Praise the
35: 8 we obeyed the *v'* of Jonadab the
38: 20 I beseech thee, the *v'* of the Lord,
40: 3 Lord, and have not obeyed his *v'*,
42: 6 we will obey the *v'* of the Lord our
6 when we obey the *v'* of the Lord our
13 neither obey the *v'* of the Lord your
21 have not obeyed the *v'* of the Lord
43: 4 obeyed not the *v'* of the Lord, to
7 they obeyed not the *v'* of the Lord:
44: 23 have not obeyed the *v'* of the Lord,
46: 22 *v'* thereof shall go like a serpent;
48: 3 A *v'* of crying shall be from
34 Jahaz, have they uttered their *v'*,
50: 28 *v'* of them that flee and escape out
42 their *v'* shall roar like the sea, and
51: 16 When he uttereth his *v'*, there is a
55 destroyed out of her the great *v'*;
55 a noise of their *v'* is uttered:
La 3: 56 Thou hast heard my *v'*: hide not
Eze 1: 24 waters, as the *v'* of the Almighty,
24 the *v'* of speech, as the noise of
25 a *v'* from the firmament that was
28 and I heard a *v'* of one that spake.
3: 12 behind me a *v'* of a great rushing,
8: 18 they cry in mine ears with a loud *v'*,
9: 1 also in mine ears with a loud *v'*,
10: 5 as the *v'* of the Almighty God when
11: 13 cried with a loud *v'*, and said, Ah
19: 9 that his *v'* should no more be heard
21: 22 to lift up the *v'* with shouting, to
23: 42 a *v'* of a multitude being at ease
27: 30 cause their *v'* to be heard against
33: 32 song of one that hath a pleasant *v'*,
43: 2 and his *v'* was like a noise of many
Da 4: 31 there fell a *v'* from heaven, saying,
6: 20 he cried with a lamentable *v'* unto
7: 11 the *v'* of the great words which the
8: 16 I heard a man's *v'* between the
9: 10 have we obeyed the *v'* of the Lord
11 that they might not obey thy *v'*;
14 he doeth: for we obeyed not his *v'*.
10: 6 and the *v'* of his words like the
6 like the *v'* of a multitude.
9 Yet heard I the *v'* of his words:
9 when I heard the *v'* of his words,
Joe 2: 11 shall utter his *v'* before his army:
3: 16 and utter his *v'* from Jerusalem;
Am 1: 2 and utter his *v'* from Jerusalem;
Jon 2: 2 cried I, and thou heardest my *v'*.
9 thee with the *v'* of thanksgiving;
Mic 6: 1 and let the hills hear thy *v'*.
9 The Lord's *v'* crieth unto the city,
Na 2: 7 lead her as with the *v'* of doves,
13 *v'* of thy messengers shall no more
Hab 3: 10 the deep uttered his *v'*, and lifted
16 my lips quivered at the *v'*:
Zep 1: 14 even the *v'* of the day of the Lord:
2: 14 their *v'* shall sing in the windows;
3: 2 She obeyed not the *v'*; she received
Hag 1: 12 obeyed the *v'* of the Lord their God,
Zec 6: 15 diligently obey the *v'* of the Lord
11: 3 *v'* of the howling of the shepherds;
3 a *v'* of the roaring of young lions;
M't 2: 18 In Rama was there a *v'* heard,
3: 3 *v'* of one crying in the wilderness,
17 And lo a *v'* from heaven, saying,
12: 19 any man hear his *v'* in the streets.
17: 5 and behold a *v'* out of the cloud,
27: 46 Jesus cried with a loud *v'*, saying,
50 he had cried again with a loud *v'*,
M'r 1: 3 *v'* of one crying in the wilderness,
11 And there came a *v'* from heaven,
26 cried with a loud *v'*, he came out of
5: 7 cried with a loud *v'*, and said, What
9: 7 a *v'* came out of the cloud, saying,
15: 34 hour Jesus cried with a loud *v'*,
37 Jesus cried with a loud *v'*, and gave
Lu 1: 42 And she spake out with a loud *v'*,
44 *v'* of thy salutation sounded in mine
3: 4 *v'* of one crying in the wilderness,
22 a *v'* came from heaven, which said,
4: 33 devil, and cried out with a loud *v'*,

Lu 8: 28 with a loud *v'* said, What have I to
9: 35 there came a *v'* out of the cloud,
36 when the *v'* was past, Jesus was
11: 27 certain woman...lifted up her *v'*,
17: 15 and with a loud *v'* glorified God,
19: 37 praise God with a loud *v'* for all the
23: 46 when Jesus had cried with a loud *v'*,
Joh 1: 23 *v'* of one crying in the wilderness,
3: 29 because of the bridegroom's *v'*:
5: 25 shall hear the *v'* of the Son of God:
28 are in the graves shall hear his *v'*,
37 Ye have neither heard his *v'* at any
10: 3 openeth; and the sheep hear his *v'*:
4 follow him: for they know his *v'*.
5 they know not the *v'* of strangers.
16 and they shall hear my *v'*; and
27 My sheep hear my *v'*, and I know
11: 43 he cried with a loud *v'*, Lazarus,
12: 28 Then came there a *v'* from heaven,
30 This *v'* came not because of me,
18: 37 that is of the truth heareth my *v'*.
Ac 2: 14 lifted up his *v'*, and said unto them,
4: 24 they lifted up their *v'* to God with
7: 31 the *v'* of the Lord came unto him,
57 Then they cried out with a loud *v'*,
60 cried with a loud *v'*, Lord, lay not
8: 7 spirits, crying with loud *v'*, came
9: 4 and heard a *v'* saying unto him,
7 hearing a *v'*, but seeing no man.
10: 13 there came a *v'* to him, Rise, Peter;
15 the *v'* spake unto him again the
11: 7 And I heard a *v'* saying unto me,
9 But the *v'* answered me again from
12: 14 And when she knew Peter's *v'*, she
22 is the *v'* of a god, and not of a man.
14: 10 Said with a loud *v'*, Stand upright
16: 28 Paul cried with a loud *v'*, saying,
19: 34 one *v'* about the space of two hours
22: 7 heard a *v'* saying unto me, Saul,
9 heard not the *v'* of him that spake
14 shouldest hear the *v'* of his mouth.
24: 21 Except it be for this one *v'*, that I
26: 10 death, I gave my *v'* against them.
14 I heard a *v'* speaking unto me, and
24 Festus said with a loud *v'*, Paul,
1Co 14: 11 if I know not the meaning of the *v'*,
19 that by my *v'* I might teach others
Ga 4: 20 you now, and to change my *v'*;
1Th 4: 16 with the *v'* of the archangel, and
Heb 3: 7 saith, To day if ye will hear his *v'*,
15 said, To day if ye will hear his *v'*,
4: 7 said, To day if ye will hear his *v'*,
12: 19 of a trumpet, and the *v'* of words;
19 which *v'* they that heard intreated
26 Whose *v'* then shook the earth:
2Pe 1: 17 came such a *v'* to him from the
18 this *v'* which came from heaven we
2: 16 dumb ass speaking with man's *v'*
Re 1: 10 and heard behind me a great *v'*, as
12 I turned to see the *v'* that spake
15 his *v'* as the sound of many waters.
3: 20 if any man hear my *v'*, and open
4: 1 the first *v'* which I heard was as it
5: 2 angel proclaiming with a loud *v'*,
11 I heard the *v'* of many angels round
12 Saying with a loud *v'*, Worthy is the
6: 6 I heard a *v'* in the midst of the four
7 I heard the *v'* of the fourth beast
10 And they cried with a loud *v'*,
7: 2 he cried with a loud *v'* to the four
10 And cried with a loud *v'*, saying,
8: 13 saying with a loud *v'*, Woe, woe,
9: 13 I heard a *v'* from the four horns of
10: 3 cried with a loud *v'*, as when a lion
4 I heard a *v'* from heaven saying
7 days of the *v'* of the seventh angel,
8 *v'* which I heard from heaven spake
11: 12 they heard a great *v'* from heaven
12: 10 I heard a loud *v'* saying in heaven,
14: 2 And I heard a *v'* from heaven, as
2 as the *v'* of many waters, and
2 and as the *v'* of a great thunder:
2 heard the *v'* of harpers harping
7 Saying with a loud *v'*, Fear God,
9 them, saying with a loud *v'*,
13 I heard a *v'* from heaven saying
15 loud *v'* to him that sat on the cloud,
16: 1 a great *v'* out of the temple saying
17 a great *v'* out of the temple of
18: 2 he cried mightily with a strong *v'*,
4 I heard another *v'* from heaven,
22 the *v'* of harpers, and musicians,
23 the *v'* of the bridegroom and of the
19: 1 I heard a great *v'* of much people
5 And a *v'* came out of the throne,
6 it were the *v'* of a great multitude,
6 and as the *v'* of many waters,
6 as the *v'* of mighty thunderings,
17 and he cried with a loud *v'*, saying
21: 3 a great *v'* out of heaven saying,

voices
J'g 21: 2 lifted up their *v'*, and wept sore;
1Sa 11: 4 people lifted up their *v'*, and wept.
Lu 17: 13 And they lifted up their *v'*, and
23: 23 And they were instant with loud *v'*,
23 *v'* of them and of the chief priests
Ac 13: 27 nor yet the *v'* of the prophets which
14: 11 they lifted up their *v'*, saying in the
22: 22 and then lifted up their *v'*, and said,
1Co 14: 10 so many kinds of *v'* in the world,
Re 4: 5 lightnings and thunderings and *v'*:
8: 5 and there were *v'*, and thunderings,
13 of the other *v'* of the trumpet of
10: 3 seven thunders uttered their *v'*.
4 seven thunders had uttered their *v'*,
11: 15 and there were great *v'* in heaven,

Re 11:19 lightnings, and v', and thunderings,
16:18 there were v', and thunders, and

void See also AVOID.
Ge 1: 2 the earth was without form, and v';
Nu 30:12 made them v' on the day he heard
12 her husband hath made them v';
13 or her husband may make it v'.
15 make them v' after that he hath
De 32:28 For they are a nation v' of counsel,
1Ki 22:10 in a v' place in the entrance of the
2Ch 18: 9 sat in a v' place at the entering in
Ps 89:39 made v'...covenant of thy servant.
119:126 for they have made v' thy law.
Pr 7: 7 a young man v' of understanding,
10:13 of him that is v' of understanding.
11:12 He that is v' of wisdom despiseth
12:11 vain persons is v' of understanding.
17:18 A man v' of understanding striketh
24:30 of the man v' of understanding;
Isa 55:11 it shall not return unto me v', but
Jer 4:23 and, lo, it was without form, and v';
19: 7 make v' the counsel of Judah and
Na 2:10 She is empty, and v', and waste:
Ac 24:16 conscience v' of offence toward God,
Ro 3:31 make v' the law through faith?
4:14 faith is made v', and the promise
1Co 9:15 man should make my glorying v'.

volume
Ps 40: 7 in the v' of the book it is written
Heb10: 7 (in the v' of the book it is written

voluntarily
Eze 46:12 peace offerings v' unto the Lord,

voluntary
Le 1: 3 offer it of his own v' will at the
7:16 offering be a vow, or a v' offering,
Eze 46:12 shalt prepare a v' burnt offering
Col 2:18 you of your reward in a v' humility

vomit See also VOMITED; VOMITETH.
Job 20:15 and he shall v' them up again:
Pr 23: 8 thou hast eaten shalt thou v' up,
25:16 thou be filled therewith, and v' it.
26:11 a dog returneth to his v', so a fool
Isa 19:14 drunken man staggereth in his v'.
28: 8 For all tables are full of v' and
Jer 48:26 Moab also shall wallow in his v', and
2Pe 2:22 dog is turned to his own v' again;

vomited
Jon 2:10 it v' out Jonah upon the dry land.

vomiteth
Le 18:25 land itself v' out her inhabitants.

Vophsi (*vof'-si*)
Nu 13:14 of Naphtali, Nahbi the son of V'.

vouch See AVOUCH.

vow See also VOWED; VOWEST; VOWETH; VOWS.
Ge 28:20 Jacob vowed a v', saying, If God
31:13 where thou vowedst a v' unto me:
Le 7:16 the sacrifice of his offering be a v',
22:21 unto the Lord to accomplish his v',
23 for a v' it shall not be accepted.
27: 2 a man shall make a singular v', the
Nu 6: 2 shall separate themselves to v' a
2 v' of a Nazarite, to separate
5 the days of the v' of his separation
21 according to the v' which he vowed,
15: 3, 8 a sacrifice in performing a v', or
21: 2 Israel vowed a v' unto the Lord,
30: 2 If a man v'...unto the Lord,
2 v' unto the Lord, or swear
3 a woman also v'...unto the Lord,
3 v' unto the Lord, and bind
4 her father hear her v', and her bond
8 shall make her v' which she vowed,
9 But every v' of a widow, and of her
13 Every v', and every binding oath to
De 12:11 vows which ye v' unto the Lord:
23:18 of the Lord thy God for any v':
21 thou shalt v'... unto the Lord
21 v' unto the Lord thy God,
22 But if thou shalt forbear to v', it
J'g 11:30 Jephthah vowed a v' unto the Lord,
39 according to his v' which he had
1Sa 1:11 And she vowed a v', and said,
21 Lord the yearly sacrifice, and his v'.
2Sa 15: 7 pray thee, let me go and pay my v',
8 servant vowed a v' while I abode
Ps 65: 1 unto thee shall the v' be performed.
76:11 V', and pay unto the Lord your
Ec 5: 4 When thou vowest a v' unto God,
5 is it that thou shouldest not v',
5 that thou shouldest v' and not pay.
Isa 19:21 yea, they shall v'...unto the Lord,
21 a v' unto the Lord, and perform it.
Ac 18:18 head in Cenchrea: for he had a v'.
21:23 four men which have a v' on them;

vowed See also VOWEDST.
Ge 28:20 And Jacob v' a vow, saying, If God
Le 27: 8 according to his ability that v' shall
Nu 6:21 law of the Nazarite who hath v', and
21 according to the vow which he v',
21: 2 And Israel v' a vow unto the Lord,
30: 6 at all an husband, when she v',
8 shall make her vow which she v',
10 if she v' in her husband's house,
De 23:23 as thou hast v' unto the Lord thy
J'g 11:30 Jephthah v' a vow unto the Lord,
39 to his vow which he had v':
1Sa 1:11 And she v' a vow, and said, O Lord,
2Sa 15: 7 I have v' unto the Lord, in Hebron
8 thy servant v' a vow while I abode
Ps 132: 2 v' unto the mighty God of Jacob;
Ec 5: 4 pay that which thou hast v'.
Jer 44:25 perform our vows that we have v',
Jon 2: 9 I will pay that that I have v'.

vowedst
Ge 31:13 and where thou v' a vow unto me:

vowest
De 12:17 nor any of thy vows which thou v',
Ec 5: 4 When thou v' a vow unto God, defer

voweth
Mal 1:14 and v', and sacrificeth unto the

vows
Le 22:18 offer his oblation for all his v',
23:38 beside all your v', and beside all
Nu 29:39 beside your v', and your freewill
30: 4 then all her v' shall stand, and
5 not any of her v', or of her bonds
7 then her v' shall stand, and her
11 then all her v' shall stand, and
12 out of her lips concerning her v',
14 then he establisheth all her v', or
De 12: 6 your v', and your freewill offerings,
11 all your choice v' which ye vow
17 nor any of thy v' which thou
26 and thy v', thou shalt take, and go
Job 22:27 thee, and thou shalt pay thy v'.
Ps 22:25 I will pay my v' before them that
50:14 and pay thy v' unto the most High:
56:12 Thy v' are upon me, O God: I will
61: 5 For thou, O God, hast heard my v':
8 that I may daily perform my v'.
66:13 offerings: I will pay thee my v',
116:14, 18 I will pay my v' unto the Lord
Pr 7:14 me; this day have I payed my v'.
20:25 holy, and after v' to make enquiry.
31: 2 womb? and what, the son of my v'?
Jer 44:25 we will surely perform our v' that we
25 ye will surely accomplish your v',
25 and surely perform your v'.
Jon 1:16 sacrifice unto the Lord, and made v'.
Na 1:15 thy solemn feasts, perform thy v':

voyage
Ac 27:10 I perceive that this v' will be with

vulture See also VULTURE'S; VULTURES.
Le 11:14 the v', and the kite after his kind;
De 14:13 the kite, and the v' after his kind,

vulture's
Job 28: 7 which the v' eye hath not seen:

vultures
Isa 34:15 the v' also be gathered, every

W.

wafer See also WAFERS.
Ex 29:23 and one w' out of the basket of
Le 8:26 a cake of oiled bread, and one w',
Nu 6:19 the basket, and one unleavened w',

wafers
Ex 16:31 of it was like w' made with honey.
29: 2 w' unleavened anointed with oil:
Le 2: 4 unleavened w' anointed with oil.
7:12 unleavened w' anointed with oil,
Nu 6:15 w' of unleavened bread anointed

wag See also WAGGING.
Jer 18:16 be astonished, and w' his head.
La 2:15 w' their head at the daughter of
Zep 2:15 her shall hiss, and w' his hand.

wages
Ge 29:15 tell me, what shall thy w' be?
30:28 Appoint me thy w', and I will give
31: 7 and changed my w' ten times;
8 The speckled shall be thy w':
41 hast changed my w' ten times.
Ex 2: 9 me, and I will give thee thy w'.
Le 19:13 w' of him that is hired shall not
Jer 22:13 neighbour's service without w',
Eze 29:18 yet had he no w', nor his army, for
19 and it shall be the w' for his army.
Hag 1: 6 and he that earneth w' earneth
6 earneth w' to put it into a bag
Mal 3: 5 that oppress the hireling in his w',
Lu 3:14 and be content with your w'.
Joh 4:36 And he that reapeth receiveth w',
Ro 6:23 For the w' of sin is death; but the
2Co 11: 8 other churches, taking w' of them,
2Pe 2:15 loved the w' of unrighteousness;

wagging
M't 27:39 by reviled him, w' their heads,
M'r 15:29 by railed on him, w' their heads,

wagon See also WAGONS.
Nu 7: 3 a w' for two of the princes, and for

wagons
Ge 45:19 take you w' out of the land of
21 Joseph gave them w', according to
27 when he saw the w' which Joseph
46: 5 in the w' which Pharaoh had sent
Nu 7: 3 before the Lord, six covered w',
6 Moses took the w' and the oxen,
7 Two w' and four oxen he gave unto
8 four w' and eight oxen he gave
Eze 23:24 against thee with chariots, w',

wail See also BEWAILED; WAILED; WAILING.
Eze 32:18 w' for the multitude of Egypt,
Mic 1: 8 Therefore I will w' and howl, I
Re 1: 7 kindreds of the earth shall w'

wailed
M'r 5:38 and them that wept and w' greatly.

wailing
Es 4: 3 and fasting, and weeping, and w';
Jer 9:10 will I take up a weeping and w',
18 haste, and take up a w' for us,
19 a voice of w' is heard out of Zion,
20 and teach your daughters w',
Eze 7:11 neither shall there be w' for them.
27:31 bitterness of heart and bitter w'.
32 in their w' they shall take up a
Am 5:16 W' shall be in all streets; and
16 as are skilful of lamentation to w'.
17 And in all vineyards shall be w':
Mic 1: 8 I will make a w' like the dragons,
M't 13:42, 50 be w' and gnashing of teeth.
Re 18:15 of her torment, weeping and w',
19 cried, weeping and w', saying,

wait See also AWAIT; WAITED; WAITETH; WAITING.
Ex 21:13 if a man lie not in w', but God
Nu 3:10 shall w' on their priest's office:
8:24 in to w' upon the service of the
35:20 or hurl at him by laying of w',
22 him any thing without laying of w',
De 19:11 and lie in w' for him, and rise up
Jos 8: 4 ye shall lie in w' against the city,
13 liers in w' on the west of the city,
J'g 9:25 set liers in w' for him in the top of
32 with thee, and lie in w' in the field:
34 and they laid w' against Shechem
35 were with him, from lying in w'.
43 laid w' in the field, and looked,
16: 2 laid w' for him all night in the gate
9 Now there were men lying in w',
12 there were liers in w' abiding in
20:29 Israel set liers in w' round about
33 liers in w' of Israel came forth
36 they trusted unto the liers in w'
37 liers in w' hasted, and rushed upon
37 liers in w' drew themselves along,
38 men of Israel and the liers in w',
21:20 Go and lie in w' in the vineyards;
1Sa 15: 2 how he laid w' for him in the way,
5 Amalek, and laid w' in the valley.
22: 8 my servant against me, to lie in w',
13 should rise against me, to lie in w',
2Ki 6:33 I w' for the Lord any longer?
1Ch 23:28 was to w' on the sons of Aaron
2Ch 5:11 and did not then w' by course:
13:10 the Levites w' upon their business:
Ezr 8:31 and of such as lay in w' by the way.
Job 14:14 of my appointed time will I w',
Job 17:13 If I w', the grave is mine house:
31: 9 if I have laid w' at my neighbour's
38:40 and abide in the covert to lie in w'?
Ps 10: 9 He lieth in w' secretly as a lion in
9 he lieth in w' to catch the poor: he
25: 3 none that w' on thee be ashamed:
5 on thee do I w' all the day.
21 preserve me; for I w' on thee.
27:14 W' on the Lord: be of good
14 thine heart: w', I say, on the Lord.
37: 7 Lord, and w' patiently for him:
9 but those that w' upon the Lord,
34 W' on the Lord, and keep his way,
39: 7 And now, Lord, what w' I for?
52: 9 and I will w' on thy name; for it is
56: 6 steps, when they w' for my soul.
59: 3 For, lo, they lie in w' for my soul:
9 his strength will I w' upon thee:
62: 5 My soul, w' thou only upon God;
69: 3 eyes fail while I w' for my God.
6 Let not them that w' on thee,
71:10 and they that lay w' for my soul
104:27 These w' all upon thee; that thou
123: 2 so our eyes w' upon the Lord our
130: 5 I w' for the Lord, my soul doth w',
145:15 The eyes of all w' upon thee; and
Pr 1:11 let us lay w' for blood, let us lurk
18 And they lay w' for their own blood;
7:12 and lieth in w' at every corner.)
12: 6 the wicked are to lie in w' for blood:
20:22 w' on the Lord, and he shall save
23:28 She also lieth in w' as for a prey,
24:15 Lay not w', O wicked man, against
Isa 8:17 And I will w' upon the Lord, that
30:18 therefore will the Lord w', that he
18 blessed are all they that w' for him.
40:31 they that w' upon the Lord shall
42: 4 and the isles shall w' for his law.
49:23 not be ashamed that w' for me.
51: 5 the isles shall w' upon me, and on
59: 9 w' for light, but behold obscurity;
60: 9 Surely the isles shall w' for me,
Jer 5:26 they lay w', as he that setteth
9: 8 but in heart he layeth his w'.
14:22 therefore we will w' upon thee: for
La 3:10 was unto me as a bear lying in w',
25 Lord is good unto them that w'
26 quietly w' for the salvation of the
4:19 laid w' for us in the wilderness.
Ho 6: 9 as troops of robbers w' for a man,
7: 6 like an oven, whiles they lie in w':
12: 6 and w' on thy God continually.
Mic 7: 2 they all lie in w' for blood; they
7 w' for the God of my salvation:

Hab 2: 3 though it tarry, w' for it; because
Zep 3: 8 Therefore w' ye upon me, saith the
M'r 3: 9 a small ship should w' on him
Lu 11:54 Laying w' for him, and seeking to
12:36 like...men that w' for their lord,
Ac 1: 4 w' for the promise of the Father,
20: 3 the Jews laid w' for him,
19 by the lying in w' of the Jews:
23:16 son heard of their lying in w',
21 for there lie in w' for him of them
30 the Jews laid w' for the man,
25: 3 laying w' in the way to kill
Ro 8:25 then do we with patience w' for it.
12: 7 let us w' on our ministering:
1Co 9:13 they which w' at the altar are
Gal 5: 5 w' for the hope of righteousness by
Eph 4:14 whereby they lie in w' to deceive;
1Th 1:10 And to w' for his Son from heaven,

waited
Ge 49:18 I have w' for thy salvation, O Lord.
1Ki 20:38 and w' for the king by the way,
2Ki 5: 2 and she w' on Naaman's wife.
1Ch 6:32 and then they w' on their office
33 they that w' with their children.
9:18 w' in the king's gate eastward:
2Ch 7: 6 the priests w' on their offices: the
17:19 These w' on the king, beside those
35:15 and the porters w' at every gate;
Ne 12:44 priests and for the Levites that w'.
Job 6:19 the companies of Sheba w' for them.
15:22 and he is w' for of the sword.
29:21 Unto me men gave ear, and w',
23 And they w' for me as for the rain;
30:26 when I w' for light, there came
32: 4 Elihu had w' till Job had spoken,
11 Behold, I w' for your words; I
16 When I had w', (for they spake not,
Ps 40: 1 I w' patiently for the Lord; and he
106:13 they w' not for his counsel:
119:95 wicked have w' for me to destroy
Isa 25: 9 we have w' for him, and he will
9 we have w' for him, we will be glad
26: 8 O Lord, have we w' for thee;
33: 2 we have w' for thee: be thou their
Eze 19: 5 when she saw that she had w',
Mic 1:12 of Maroth w' carefully for good:
Zec 11:11 poor of the flock that w' upon me
M'r 15:43 also w' for the kingdom of God,
Lu 1:21 And the people w' for Zacharias,
23:51 himself w' for the kingdom of God.
Ac 10: 7 them that w' on him continually;
24 And Cornelius w' for them, and
17:16 while Paul w' for them at Athens,
1Pe 3:20 of God w' in the days of Noah,

waiteth
Job 24:15 the adulterer w' for the twilight,
Ps 33:20 Our soul w' for the Lord: he is
62: 1 Truly my soul w' upon God: from
65: 1 Praise w' for thee, O God, in Sion:
130: 6 My soul w' for the Lord more than
Pr 27:18 he that w' on his master shall be
Isa 64: 4 prepared for him that w' for him.
Da 12:12 Blessed is he that w', and cometh to
Mic 5: 7 man, nor w' for the sons of men.
Ro 8:19 w' for the manifestation of the
Jas 5: 7 husbandman w' for the precious

waiting
Nu 8:25 cease w' upon the service thereof,
Pr 8:34 gates, w' at the posts of my doors.
Lu 2:25 w' for the consolation of Israel:
8:40 him: for they were all w' for him.
Joh 5: 3 w' for the moving of the water.
Ro 8:23 w' for the adoption, to wit, the
1Co 1: 7 w' for the coming of our Lord Jesus
2Th 3: 5 and into the patient w' for Christ.

wake See also AWAKE; WAKED; WAKENED; WAKENETH; WAKETH; WAKING.
Jer 51:39, 57 a perpetual sleep, and not w',
Joe 3: 9 w' up the mighty men, let all the
1Th 5:10 whether we w' or sleep, we should

waked
Zec 4: 1 with me came again, and w' me,

wakened
Joe 3:12 Let the heathen be w', and come
Zec 4: 1 a man that is w' out of his sleep,

wakeneth
Isa 50: 4 he w' morning by morning,
4 w' mine ear to hear as the learned.

waketh
Ps 127: 1 the watchman w' but in vain.
Ca 5: 2 I sleep, but my heart w': it is the

waking
Ps 77: 4 Thou holdest mine eyes w': I am

walk See also WALKED; WALKEST; WALKETH; WALKING.
Ge 13:17 Arise, w' through the land in the
17: 1 w' before me, and be thou perfect.
24:40 The Lord, before whom I w', will
48:15 fathers Abraham and Isaac did w',
Ex 16: 4 whether they will w' in my law, or
18:20 the way wherein they must w',
21:19 and w' abroad upon his staff,
Le 18: 3 shall ye w' in their ordinances.
4 mine ordinances, to w' therein:
20:23 ye shall not w' in the manners of
26: 3 If ye w' in my statutes, and keep
12 I will w' among you, and will be
21 ye w' contrary unto me, and will
23 but will w' contrary unto me;
24 will I also w' contrary unto you,
27 unto me, but w' contrary unto me;
28 Then I will w' contrary unto you

De 5:33 Ye shall w' in all the ways which
8: 6 to w' in his ways, and to fear him.
19 w' after other gods, and serve
10:12 to w' in all his ways, and to love
11:22 to w' in all his ways, and to cleave
13: 4 Ye shall w' after the Lord your God,
5 thy God commanded thee to w' in.
19: 9 thy God, and to w' ever in his ways;
26:17 be thy God, and to w' in his ways,
28: 9 Lord thy God, and w' in his ways.
29:19 I w' in the imagination of mine
30:16 Lord thy God, to w' in his ways,
Jos 18: 8 Go and w' through the land, and
22: 5 God, and to w' in all his ways,
J'g 2:22 the way of the Lord to w' therein,
5:10 in judgment, and w' by the way.
1Sa 2:30 should w' before me for ever:
35 he shall w' before mine anointed
8: 5 and thy sons w' not in thy ways:
1Ki 2: 3 to w' in his ways, to keep his
4 to w' before me in truth with all
3:14 if thou wilt w' in my ways, to keep
14 as thy father David did w',
6:12 if thou wilt w' in my statutes,
12 my commandments to w' in them;
8:23 thy servants that w' before thee
25 w' before me as thou hast walked
36 good way wherein they should w',
58 unto him, to w' in all his ways,
61 Lord our God, to w' in his statutes,
9: 4 if thou wilt w' before me, as David
11:38 wilt w' in my ways, and do that
16:31 a light thing for him to w' in the
2Ki 10:31 no heed to w' in the law of the Lord
23: 3 the Lord, to w' after the Lord,
2Ch 6:14 that w' before thee with all their
16 heed to their way to w' in my law,
27 good way, wherein they should w';
31 to w' in thy ways, so long as they
7:17 for thee, if thou wilt w' before me,
34:31 the Lord, and to w' after the Lord,
Ne 5: 9 ye not to w' in the fear of our God
10:29 into an oath, to w' in God's law,
Ps 12: 8 The wicked w' on every side,
23: 4 though I w' through the valley
26:11 for me, I will w' in mine integrity:
48:12 W' about Zion, and go round
56:13 I may w' before God in the light
78:10 God, and refused to w' in his law;
82: 5 they w' on in darkness:
84:11 from them that w' uprightly.
86:11 O Lord; I will w' in thy truth:
89:15 they shall w', O Lord, in the light
30 and w' not in my judgments;
101: 2 I will w' within my house with a
115: 7 feet have they, but they w' not:
116: 9 I will w' before the Lord in the
119: 1 who w' in the law of the Lord.
3 no iniquity: they w' in his ways.
45 I will w' at liberty: for I seek thy
138: 7 I w' in the midst of trouble, thou
143: 8 know the way wherein I should w';
Pr 1:15 w' not thou in the way with them;
2: 7 buckler to them that w' uprightly.
13 to w' in the ways of darkness;
20 thou mayest w' in the way of good
3:23 shalt thou w' in thy way safely,
Ec 4:15 the living which w' under the sun,
6: 8 knoweth to w' before the living?
11: 9 and w' in the ways of thine heart,
Isa 2: 3 ways, and we will w' in his paths:
5 let us w' in the light of the Lord.
3:16 w' with stretched forth necks and
8:11 not w' in the way of this people,
30: 2 That w' to go down into Egypt,
21 This is the way, w' ye in it, when
35: 9 but the redeemed shall w' there:
40:31 and they shall w', and not faint.
42: 5 and spirit to them that w' therein:
24 for they would not w' in his ways,
50:11 w' in the light of your fire, and in
59: 9 brightness, but we w' in darkness.
Jer 3:17 neither shall they w' any more
18 shall w' with the house of Israel,
6:16 is the good way, and w' therein,
16 they said, We will not w' therein.
25 into the field, nor w' by the way;
7: 6 w' after other gods to your hurt:
9 w' after other gods whom ye know
23 w' ye in all the ways that I have
9: 4 neighbour will w' with slanders.
13:10 which w' in the imagination of
10 and w' after other gods, to serve
16:12 w' every one after the imagination
18:12 we will w' after our own devices,
15 to w' in paths, in a way not cast
23:14 commit adultery, and w' in lies:
26: 4 hearken to me, to w' in my law,
31: 9 cause them to w' by the rivers of
42: 3 us the way wherein we may w'.
La 5:18 is desolate, the foxes w' upon it.
Eze 11:20 That they may w' in my statutes,
20:18 W' ye not in the statutes of your
19 w' in my statutes, and keep my
33:15 w' in the statutes of life, without
36:12 I will cause men to w' upon you,
27 cause you to w' in my statutes,
37:24 they shall also w' in my judgments,
42: 4 chambers was a w' of ten cubits
Da 4:37 those that w' in pride he is able to
9:10 to w' in his laws, which he set
Ho 11:10 They shall w' after the Lord: he
14: 9 right, and the just shall w' in them:
Joe 2: 8 they shall w' every one in his path:
Am 3: 3 Can two w' together, except they
Mic 4: 2 ways, and we will w' in his paths:

Mic 4: 5 will w' every one in the name of his
5 will w' in the name of the Lord our
6: 8 and to w' humbly with thy God?
16 Ahab, and ye w' in their counsels:
Na 2: 5 they shall stumble in their w';
Hab 3:15 didst w' through the sea with
19 me to w' upon mine high places.
Zep 1:17 that they shall w' like blind men,
Zec 1:10 to w' to and fro through the earth.
3: 7 If thou wilt w' in my ways, and if
7 to w' among these that stand by.
6: 7 w' to and fro through the earth:
7 w' to and fro through the earth.
10:12 shall w' up and down in his name,
M't 9: 5 thee; or to say, Arise, and w'?
11: 5 and the lame w', the lepers are
15:31 the lame to w', and the blind to see:
M'r 2: 9 Arise, and take up thy bed, and w'?
7: 5 Why w' not thy disciples according
Lu 5:23 thee; or to say, Rise up and w'?
7:22 how that the blind see, the lame w',
11:44 the men that w' over them are not
13:33 I must w' to day, and to morrow,
20:46 which desire to w' in long robes,
24:17 ye have one to another, as ye w',
Joh 5: 8 him, Rise, take up thy bed, and w'.
11 unto me, Take up thy bed, and w'.
12 thee, Take up thy bed, and w'?
7: 1 for he would not w' in Jewry,
8:12 me shall not w' in darkness,
11: 9 If any man w' in the day, he
10 But if a man w' in the night, he
12:35 W' while ye have the light, lest
Ac 3: 6 Christ of Nazareth rise up and w'.
12 we had made this man to w'?
14:16 all nations to w' in their own ways.
21:21 neither to w' after the customs.
Ro 4:12 also w' in the steps of that faith
6: 4 should w' in newness of life.
8: 1 who w' not after the flesh, but
4 who w' not after the flesh, but
13:13 Let us w' honestly, as in the day;
1Co 3: 3 are ye not carnal, and w' as men?
7:17 called every one, so let him w'.
2Co 5: 7 (For we w' by faith, not by sight:)
6:16 dwell in them, and w' in them;
10: 3 For though we w' in the flesh, we
Ga 5:16 W' in the Spirit, and ye shall not
25 Spirit, let us also w' in the Spirit.
6:16 many as w' according to this rule,
Eph 2:10 that we should w' in them.
4: 1 that ye w' worthy of the vocation
17 w' not as other Gentiles w',
5: 2 w' in love, as Christ also hath loved
8 in the Lord: w' as children of light:
15 See then that ye w' circumspectly,
Ph'p 3:16 let us w' by the same rule, let us
17 mark them which w' so as ye have
18 (For many w', of whom I have told
Col 1:10 That ye might w' worthy of the
2: 6 Jesus the Lord, so w' ye in him:
4: 5 W' in wisdom toward them that
1Th 2:12 That ye would w' worthy of God,
4: 1 ye ought to w' and to please God,
12 w' honestly toward them that are
2Th 3:11 which w' among you disorderly,
2Pe 2:10 them that w' after the flesh in the
1Jo 1: 6 with him, and w' in darkness,
7 But if we w' in the light, as he is in
2: 6 in him ought himself also so to w',
2Jo 6 we w' after his commandments.
6 the beginning, ye should w' in it.
3Jo 4 hear that my children w' in truth.
Jude 18 w' after their own ungodly lusts.
Re 3: 4 they shall w' with me in white:
9:20 neither can see, nor hear, nor w':
16:15 lest he w' naked, and they see his
21:24 are saved shall w' in the light of it:

walked See also WALKEDST.
Ge 5:22 Enoch w' with God after he begat
24 Enoch w' with God: and he was
6: 9 generations, and Noah w' with God.
Ex 2: 5 her maidens w' along by the river's
14:29 children of Israel w' upon dry land
Le 26:40 they have w' contrary unto me;
41 I also have w' contrary unto them,
Jos 5: 6 w' forty years in the wilderness,
J'g 2:17 the way which their fathers w' in,
5: 6 the travellers w' through byways.
11:16 w' through the wilderness unto the
1Sa 8: 3 And his sons w' not in his ways,
12: 2 I have w' before you from my
2Sa 2:29 and his men w' all that night
7: 6 w' in a tent and in a tabernacle.
7 I have w' with all the children of
11: 2 and w' upon the roof of the king's
1Ki 3: 6 as he w' before thee in truth, and
8:25 me as thou hast w' before me.
9: 4 as David thy father w', in integrity
11:33 have not w' in my ways, to do that
15: 3 And he w' in all the sins of his
26 and w' in the way of his father, and
34 and w' in the way of Jeroboam, and
16: 2 hast w' in the way of Jeroboam,
26 he w' in all the way of Jeroboam
22:43 And he w' in all the ways of Asa his
52 and w' in the way of his father, and
2Ki 4:35 and w' in the house to and fro;
8:18 he w' in the way of the kings of
27 he w' in the way of the house of
13: 6 made Israel sin: but he w' therein.
11 made Israel sin: but he w' therein.
16: 3 But he w' in the way of the kings
17: 8 w' in the statutes of the heathen,
19 w' in the statutes of Israel which
22 children of Israel w' in all the sins

2Ki 20: 3 w' before thee in truth and with a
21: 21 And he w' in all the way that his
21 in all the way that his father w' in,
22 and w' not in the way of the Lord.
22: 2 and w' in all the way of David his
1Ch 17: 6 I have w' with all Israel,
8 thee whithersoever thou hast w',
2Ch 6: 16 law, as thou hast w' before me.
7: 17 before me, as David thy father w',
11: 17 they w' in the way of David and
17: 3 he w' in the first ways of his father
4 w' in his commandments, and not
20: 32 And he w' in the way of Asa his
21: 6 And he w' in the way of the kings
12 thou hast not w' in the ways of
13 hast w' in the way of the kings of
22: 3 also w' in the ways of the house of
5 He w' also after their counsel, and
28: 2 he w' in the ways of the kings of
34: 2 w' in the ways of David his father,
Es 2: 11 Mordecai w' every day before the
Job 29: 3 his light I w' through darkness;
31: 5 If I have w' with vanity, or if my
7 and mine heart w' after mine eyes,
38: 16 thou w' in the search of the depth?
Ps 26: 1 for I have w' in mine integrity:
3 eyes: and I have w' in thy truth.
55: 14 and w' unto the house of God in
81: 12 they w' in their own counsels.
13 and Israel had w' in my ways!
142: 3 In the way wherein I w' have they
Isa 9: 2 people that w' in darkness have
20: 3 my servant Isaiah hath w' naked
38: 3 how I have w' before thee in truth
Jer 2: 5 and have w' after vanity, and are
8 w' after things that do not profit.
7: 24 but w' in the counsels and in the
8: 2 and after whom they have w', and
9: 13 obeyed my voice, neither w' therein;
14 w' after the imagination of their
11: 8 w' every one in the imagination of
16: 11 have w' after other gods, and have
32: 23 thy voice, neither w' in thy law;
44: 10 have they feared, nor w' in my law,
23 of the Lord, nor w' in his law, nor
Eze 5: 6 statutes, they have not w' in them.
7 and have not w' in my statutes,
11: 12 for ye have not w' in my statutes,
16: 47 hast thou not w' after their ways,
18: 9 Hath w' in my statutes, and hath
17 judgments, hath w' in my statutes;
20: 13 they w' not in my statutes, and
16 and w' not in my statutes, but
21 they w' not in my statutes, neither
23: 31 hast w' in the way of thy sister;
28: 14 hast w' up and down in the midst
Da 4: 29 w' in the palace of the kingdom
Ho 5: 11 he...w' after the commandment.
Am 2: 4 the which their fathers have w':
Na 2: 11 even the old lion, w', and the lion's
Zec 1: 11 We have w' to and fro through the
6: 7 w' to and fro through the earth.
Mal 2: 6 he w' with me in peace and equity
3: 14 w' mournfully before the Lord
M't 14: 29 he w' on the water, to go to Jesus.
M'r 1: 16 Now as he w' by the sea of Galilee,
5: 42 the damsel arose, and w', for she
16: 12 form unto two of them, as they w',
Joh 1: 36 looking upon Jesus as he w', he
5: 9 whole, and took up his bed, and w':
6: 66 back, and w' no more with him.
7: 1 these things Jesus w' in Galilee:
10: 23 Jesus w' in the temple in Solomon's
11: 54 w' no more openly among the
Ac 3: 8 he leaping up stood, and w', and
14: 8 mother's womb, who never had w':
10 on thy feet. And he leaped and w'.
2Co 10: 2 as if we w' according to the flesh.
12: 18 you? w' we not in the same spirit?
18 spirit? w' we not in the same steps?
Ga 2: 14 they w' not uprightly according to
Eph 2: 2 in time past ye w' according to the
Col 3: 7 In the which ye also w' some time,
1Pe 4: 3 we w' in lasciviousness, lusts,
1Jo 2: 6 also so to walk, even as he w'.

walkedst
Joh 21: 18 and w' whither thou wouldest:

walkest
De 6: 7 and when thou w' by the way,
11: 19 and when thou w' by the way,
1Ki 2: 42 out, and w' abroad any whither,
Isa 43: 2 when thou w' through the fire,
Ac 21: 24 w' orderly, and keepest the law.
Ro 14: 15 meat, now w' thou not charitably.
3Jo 3 thee, even as thou w' in the truth.

walketh
Ge 24: 65 man is this that w' in the field to
De 23: 14 Lord thy God w' in the midst of
1Sa 12: 2 behold, the king w' before you:
Job 18: 8 own feet, and he w' upon a snare.
22: 14 and he w' in the circuit of heaven.
34: 8 iniquity, and w' with wicked men.
Ps 1: 1 that w' not in the counsel of the
15: 2 He that w' uprightly, and worketh
39: 6 Surely every man w' in a vain shew:
73: 9 and their tongue w' through the
91: 6 the pestilence that w' in darkness;
101: 6 he that w' in a perfect way, he shall
104: 3 who w' upon the wings of the wind:
128: 1 the Lord; that w' in his ways.
Pr 6: 12 man, w' with a froward mouth.
10: 9 that w' [1980] uprightly w' surely:
13: 20 He that w' with wise men shall be
14: 2 He that w' in his uprightness
15: 21 of understanding w' uprightly.
Pr 19: 1 the poor that w' in his integrity,
20: 7 The just man w' in his integrity:
28: 6 poor that w' in his uprightness,
18 Whoso w' uprightly shall be saved:
26 but whoso w' wisely, he shall be
Ec 2: 14 but the fool w' in darkness: and I
10: 3 when he that is a fool w' by the way,
Isa 33: 15 He that w' righteously, and
50: 10 that w' in darkness, and hath no
65: 2 w' in a way that was not good,
Jer 10: 23 in man that w' to direct his steps.
23: 17 one that w' after the imagination
Eze 11: 21 whose heart w' after the heart of
Mic 2: 7 do good to him that w' uprightly?
M't 12: 43 he w' through dry places, seeking
Lu 11: 24 he w' through dry places, seeking
Joh 12: 35 he that w' in darkness knoweth
2Th 3: 6 every brother that w' disorderly,
1Pe 5: 8 w' about, seeking whom he may
1Jo 2: 11 w' in darkness, and knoweth not
Re 2: 1 who w' in the midst of the seven

walking
Ge 3: 8 of the Lord God w' in the garden
De 2: 7 he knoweth thy w' through this
1Ki 3: 3 w' in the statutes of David his
16: 19 in w' in the way of Jeroboam, and
Job 1: 7 and from w' up and down in it.
2: 2 and from w' up and down in it.
31: 26 or the moon w' in brightness;
Ec 10: 7 and princes w' as servants upon the
Isa 3: 16 w' and mincing as they go, and
20: 2 he did so, w' naked and barefoot.
57: 2 each one w' in his uprightness.
Jer 6: 28 revolters, w' with slanders:
Da 3: 25 loose, w' in the midst of the fire,
Mic 2: 11 man w' in the spirit and falsehood
M't 4: 18 Jesus, w' by the sea of Galilee,
14: 25 went unto them, w' on the sea.
26 the disciples saw him w' on the sea,
M'r 6: 48 cometh unto them, w' upon the sea,
49 when they saw him w' upon the sea,
8: 24 up, and said, I see men as trees, w'.
11: 27 and as he was w' in the temple,
Lu 1: 6 w' in all the commandments and
Joh 6: 19 they see Jesus w' on the sea, and
Ac 3: 8 into the temple, w', and leaping,
9 saw him w' and praising God:
9: 31 w' in the fear of the Lord, and in
2Co 4: 2 not w' in craftiness, nor handling
2Pe 3: 3 scoffers, w' after their own lusts,
2Jo 4 found of thy children w' in truth,
Jude 16 w' after their own lusts;

wall See also WALLED; WALLS.
Ge 49: 6 selfwill they digged down a w'.
22 whose branches run over the w':
Ex 14: 22, 29 waters were a w' unto them
Le 14: 37 in sight are lower than the w';
25: 31 which have no w' round about
Nu 22: 24 vineyards, a w' being on this side,
24 this side, and a w' on that side.
25 she thrust herself unto the w',
25 Balaam's foot against the w':
35: 4 shall reach from the w' of the city
Jos 2: 15 her house was upon the town w',
15 and she dwelt upon the w'.
6: 5 w' of the city shall fall down flat,
20 shout, that the w' fell down flat,
1Sa 18: 11 I will smite David even to the w'
19: 10 to smite David even to the w' with
10 he smote the javelin into the w':
20: 25 times, even upon a seat by the w':
25: 16 w' unto us both by night and day,
22, 34 that pisseth against the w'.
31: 10 his body to the w' of Beth-shan.
12 his sons from the w' of Beth-shan,
2Sa 11: 20 that they would shoot from the w'?
21 a millstone upon him from the w',
21 Thebez? why went ye nigh the w'?
24 shooters shot from off the w' upon
18: 24 the roof over the gate unto the w',
20: 15 were with Joab battered the w',
21 shall be thrown to thee over the w'.
22: 30 by my God have I leaped over a w'.
1Ki 3: 1 the w' of Jerusalem round about.
4: 33 that springeth out of the w':
6: 5 And against the w' of the house he
6 in the w' of the house he made
27 of the one touched the one w',
27 other cherub touched the other w';
31 side posts were a fifth part of the w'.
33 of olive tree, a fourth part of the w'.
9: 15 Millo, and the w' of Jerusalem,
14: 10 him that pisseth against the w',
16: 11 not one that pisseth against a w',
20: 30 w' fell upon twenty and seven
21: 21 him that pisseth against the w',
23 eat Jezebel by the w' of Jezreel.
2Ki 3: 27 for a burnt offering upon the w'.
4: 10 chamber, I pray thee, on the w';
6: 26 Israel was passing by upon the w',
30 he passed by upon the w', and the
9: 8 him that pisseth against the w',
33 her blood was sprinkled on the w',
14: 13 brake down the w' of Jerusalem
18: 26 of the people that are on the w'.
27 me to the men which sit on the w',
20: 2 Then he turned his face to the w',
2Ch 3: 11, 12 reaching to the w' of the house:
25: 23 brake down the w' of Jerusalem
26: 6 and brake down the w' of Gath,
6 w' of Jabneh, and the w' of Ashdod,
9 turning of the w', and fortified them.
27: 3 on the w' of Ophel he built much.
32: 5 built up all the w' that was broken,
5 the towers, and another w' without,
2Ch 32: 18 of Jerusalem that were on the w',
33: 14 built a w' without the city of David,
36: 19 brake down the w' of Jerusalem,
Ezr 5: 3 this house, and to make up this w'?
9: 9 a w' in Judah and in Jerusalem.
Ne 1: 3 w' of Jerusalem also is broken
2: 8 and for the w' of the city, and for
15 by the brook, and viewed the w',
17 let us build up the w' of Jerusalem,
3: 8 Jerusalem unto the broad w'.
13 a thousand cubits on the w' unto
15 w' of the pool of Siloah by the king's
19 the armoury at the turning of the w'.
20 turning of the w' unto the door of the
24 of Azariah unto the turning of the w',
25 over against the turning of the w',
27 out, even unto the w' of Ophel.
4: 1 heard that we builded the w',
3 even break down their stone w'.
6 So built we the w'; and all the
6 all the w' was joined together unto
10 that we are not able to build the w'.
13 I in the lower places behind the w',
15 we returned all of us to the w',
17 They which builded on the w', and
19 we are separated upon the w', one
5: 16 I continued in the work of this w',
6: 1 heard that I had builded the w',
6 which cause thou buildest the w',
15 w' was finished in the twenty and
7: 1 when the w' was built, and I had
12: 27 dedication of the w' of Jerusalem
30 people, and the gates, and the w'.
31 the princes of Judah upon the w',
31 right hand upon the w' toward the
37 at the going up of the w', above the
38 the half of the people upon the w',
38 furnaces even unto the broad w';
13: 21 them, Why lodge ye about the w'?
Ps 18: 29 by my God have I leaped over a w'.
62: 3 as a bowing w' shall ye be, and as
Pr 18: 11 as an high w' in his own conceit.
24: 31 the stone w' thereof was broken
Ca 2: 9 he standeth behind our w', he
8: 9 If she be a w', we will build upon
10 I am a w', and my breasts like
Isa 2: 15 high tower, upon every fenced w',
5: 5 break down the w' thereof, and it
22: 10 ye broken down to fortify the w'.
25: 4 ones is as a storm against the w'.
30: 13 swelling out in a high w', whose
36: 11 of the people that are on the w'.
12 me to the men that sit upon the w',
38: 2 turned his face toward the w',
59: 10 We grope for the w' like the blind,
Jer 15: 20 this people a fenced brasen w':
49: 27 kindle a fire in the w' of Damascus,
51: 44 yea, the w' of Babylon shall fall.
La 2: 8 to destroy the w' of the daughter
8 the rampart and the w' to lament;
18 O w' of the daughter of Zion, let
Eze 4: 3 set it for a w' of iron between thee
8: 7 I looked, behold a hole in the w'.
8 me, Son of man, dig now in the w':
8 when I had digged in the w',
10 pourtrayed upon the w' round
12: 5 Dig thou through the w' in their
7 I digged through the w' with mine
12 shall dig through the w' to carry
13: 10 one built up a w', and, lo, others
12 when the w' was fallen, shall it not
14 will I break down the w' that ye
15 accomplish my wrath upon the w',
15 The w' is no more, neither they
23: 14 saw men pourtrayed upon the w',
38: 20 every w' shall fall to the ground.
40: 5 a w' on the outside of the house
41: 5 he measured the w' of the house,
6 they entered into the w' which
6 not hold in the w' of the house.
9 The thickness of the w', which was
12 w' of the building was five cubits
17 all the w' round about within and
20 made, and on the w' of the temple.
42: 7 And the w' that was without over
10 thickness of the w' of the court
12 the way directly before the w'
20 it had a w' round about, five
43: 8 and the w' between me and them,
Da 5: 5 upon the plaister of the w' of the
9: 25 shall be built again, and the w',
Ho 2: 6 and make a w', that she shall not
Joe 2: 7 climb the w' like men of war;
9 they shall run upon the w', they
Am 1: 7 will send a fire on the w' of Gaza,
10 will send a fire on the w' of Tyrus,
14 kindle a fire in the w' of Rabbah,
5: 19 and leaned his hand on the w',
7: 7 upon a w' made by a plumbline,
Na 2: 5 make haste to the w' thereof, and
3: 8 sea, and her w' was from the sea?
Hab 2: 11 the stone shall cry out of the w',
Zec 2: 5 will be unto her a w' of fire round
Ac 9: 25 let down by the w' in a basket.
23: 3 shall smite thee, thou whited w':
2Co 11: 33 a basket was I let down by the w',
Eph 2: 14 broken down the middle w' of
Re 21: 12 And had a w' great and high, and
14 the w' of the city had twelve
15 gates thereof, and the w' thereof.
17 And he measured the w' thereof,
18 building of the w'...was of jasper:
19 foundations of the w' of the city

walled See also UNWALLED.
Le 25: 29 sell a dwelling house in a w' city,
30 w' city shall be established for ever

Nu 13:28 and the cities are w', and very
De 1:28 are great and w' up to heaven;

wallow See also WALLOWED; WALLOWING.
Jer 6:26 sackcloth, and w' thyself in ashes:
25:34 w' yourselves in the ashes, ye
48:26 Moab also shall w' in his vomit,
Eze 27:30 shall w' themselves in the ashes:

wallowed
2Sa 20:12 Amasa w' in blood in the midst of
M'r 9:20 on the ground and w' foaming.

wallowing
2Pe 2:22 was washed to her w' in the mire.

walls
Le 14:37 plague be in the w' of the house
39 plague be spread in the w' of the
De 3:5 cities were fenced with high w',
28:52 thy high and fenced w' come down,
1Ki 4:13 great cities with w' and brasen
6:5 against the w' of the house round
6 be fastened in the w' of the house.
15 he built the w' of the house within
15 the house, and the w' of the ceiling:
16 and the w' with boards of cedar:
29 he carved all the w' of the house
2Ki 25:4 way of the gate between two w',
10 brake down the w' of Jerusalem
1Ch 29:4 to overlay the w' of the houses
2Ch 3:7 the w' thereof, and the doors
7 and graved cherubims on the w'.
8:5 fenced cities, with w', gates, and
14:7 make about them w', and towers,
Ezr 4:12 and have set up the w' thereof,
13 be builded, and the w' set up again,
16 again, and the w' thereof set up,
5:8 and timber is laid in the w', and
9 house, and to make up these w'?
Ne 2:13 and viewed the w' of Jerusalem,
4:7 the w' of Jerusalem were made up,
Job 24:11 Which make oil within their w',
Ps 51:18 build thou the w' of Jerusalem.
55:10 go about it upon the w' thereof:
122:7 Peace be within thy w', and
Pr 25:28 is broken down, and without w'.
Ca 5:7 keepers of the w' took away my veil
Isa 22:5 breaking down the w', and of
11 also a ditch between the two w'
25:12 fortress of the high fort of thy w'
26:1 salvation will God appoint for w'
49:16 thy w' are continually before me.
56:5 within my w' a place and a name
60:10 of strangers shall build up thy w',
18 thou shalt call thy w' Salvation,
62:6 I have set watchmen upon thy w',
Jer 1:15 all the w' thereof round about,
18 brasen w' against the whole land,
5:10 Go ye up upon her w', and destroy;
21:4 which besiege you without the w',
39:4 by the gate betwixt the two w':
8 brake down the w' of Jerusalem.
50:15 are fallen, her w' are thrown down:
51:12 standard upon the w' of Babylon,
58 broad w' of Babylon shall be utterly
52:7 way of the gate between the two w',
14 brake down all the w' of Jerusalem
La 2:7 of the enemy the w' of her palaces;
Eze 26:4 they shall destroy the w' of Tyrus,
9 set engines of war against thy w',
10 thy w' shall shake at the noise of
12 they shall break down thy w', and
27:11 thine army were upon thy w' round
11 hanged their shields upon thy w'
33:30 are talking against thee by the w'
38:11 all of them dwelling without w',
41:13 the building, with the w' thereof,
22 and the w' thereof, were of wood:
25 like as were made upon the w';
Mic 7:11 the day that thy w' are to be built,
Zec 2:4 inhabited as towns without w'
Heb11:30 By faith the w' of Jericho fell

wander See also WANDERED; WANDEREST; WANDERETH; WANDERING.
Ge 20:13 me to w' from my father's house,
Nu 14:33 children shall w' in the wilderness
32:13 he made them w' in the wilderness
De 27:18 he that maketh the blind to w' out
Job 12:24 causeth them to w' in a wilderness
38:41 unto God, they w' for lack of meat.
Ps 55:7 then would I w' far off, and remain
59:15 them w' up and down for meat,
107:40 them to w' in the wilderness,
119:10 not w' from thy commandments.
Isa 47:15 shall w' every one to his quarter;
Jer 14:10 Thus have they loved to w', they
48:12 that shall cause him to w', and
Am 8:12 And they shall w' from sea to sea,

wandered
Ge 21:14 and w' in the wilderness of
Jos 14:10 of Israel w' in the wilderness:
Ps 107:4 They w' in the wilderness in a
Isa 16:8 they w' through the wilderness:
La 4:14 They have w' as blind men in the
15 when they fled away and w', they
Eze 34:6 My sheep w' through all the
Am 4:8 or three cities w' unto one city,
Heb11:37 they w' about in sheepskins and
38 they w' in deserts, and in

wanderers
Jer 48:12 that I will send unto him w', that
Ho 9:17 shall be w' among the nations.

wanderest
Jer 2:20 under every green tree thou w',

wandereth
Job 15:23 He w' abroad for bread, saying,
Pr 21:16 The man that w' out of the way of
27:8 As a bird that w' from her nest, so
8 so is a man that w' from his place.
Isa 16:3 outcasts; bewray not him that w'.
Jer 49:5 none shall gather up him that w'.

wandering See also WANDERINGS.
Ge 37:15 behold, he was w' in the field:
Pr 26:2 As the bird by w', as the swallow
Ec 6:9 the eyes than the w' of the desire:
Isa 16:2 as a w' bird cast out of the nest,
1Ti 5:13 w' about from house to house;
Jude 13 w' stars, to whom is reserved the

wanderings
Ps 56:8 Thou tellest my w': put thou my

want See also WANTED; WANTETH; WANTING; WANTS.
De 28:48 nakedness, and in w' of all things:
57 shall eat them for w' of all things
J'g 18:10 a place where there is no w' of
19:19 there is no w' of any thing.
Job 24:8 embrace...rock for w' of a shelter.
30:3 For w' and famine they were
31:19 seen any perish for w' of clothing,
Ps 23:1 is my shepherd; I shall not w'.
34:9 is no w' to them that fear him.
10 Lord shall not w' any good thing.
Pr 6:11 and thy w' as an armed man.
10:21 but fools die for w' of wisdom.
13:23 is destroyed for w' of judgment.
25 the belly of the wicked shall w'.
14:28 but in the w' of people is the
21:5 every one that is hasty only to w'.
22:16 to the rich, shall surely come to w'.
24:34 and thy w' as an armed man.
Isa 34:16 shall fail, none shall w' her mate:
Jer 33:17 never w' a man to sit upon the
18 Levites w' a man before me to offer
35:19 not w' a man to stand before me for
La 4:9 for w' of the fruits of the field.
Eze 4:17 they may w' bread and water, and
Am 4:6 and w' of bread in all your places:
M'r 12:44 she of her w' did cast in all that
Lu 15:14 land; and he began to be in w'.
2Co 8:14 may be a supply for their w',
14 also may be a supply for your w':
9:12 only supplieth the w' of the saints,
Ph'p 4:11 Not that I speak in respect of w':

wanted
Jer 44:18 we have w' all things, and have
Joh 2:3 when they w' wine, the mother of
2Co 11:9 I was present with you, and w', I

wanteth
De 15:8 for his need, in that which he w'.
Pr 9:4 for him that w' understanding,
16 as for him that w' understanding,
10:19 of words there w' not sin: but
28:16 The prince that w' understanding
Ec 6:2 so that he w' nothing for his soul
Ca 7:2 round goblet, which w' not liquor:

wanting
2Ki 10:19 and all his priests; let none be w':
19 whosoever shall be w', he shall not
Pr 19:7 with words, yet they are w' to him.
Ec 1:15 which is w' cannot be numbered.
Da 5:27 in the balances, and art found w'.
Tit 1:5 set in order the things that are w',
3:13 that nothing be w' unto them.
Jas 1:4 be perfect and entire, w' nothing.

wanton
Isa 3:16 stretched forth necks and w' eyes,
1Ti 5:11 begun to wax w' against Christ,
Jas 5:5 pleasure on the earth, and been w';

wantonness
Ro 13:13 not in chambering and w', not in
2Pe 2:18 through much w', those that were

wants
J'g 19:20 let all thy w' lie upon me; only
Ph'p 2:25 and he that ministered to my w'.

war See also WARFARE; WARRED; WARRETH; WARRING; WARS.
Ge 14:2 these made w' with Bera king of
Ex 1:10 when there falleth out any w',
13:17 the people repent when they see w',
15:3 The Lord is a man of w': the Lord
17:16 the Lord will have w' with Amalek
32:17 There is a noise of w' in the camp.
Nu 1:3 able to go forth to w' in Israel:
20, 22, 24, 26, 28, 30, 32, 34, 36, 38, 40, 42
all that were able to go forth to w';
45 were able to go forth to w' in Israel;
10:9 if ye go to w' in your land against
26:2 that are able to go to w' in Israel.
31:3 some of yourselves unto the w',
4 of Israel, shall ye send to the w'.
5 twelve thousand armed for w'.
6 And Moses sent them to the w', a
6 of Eleazer the priest, to the w',
21 men of w' which went to the battle,
27 them that took the w' upon them,
28 the men of w' which went out to
32 which the men of w' had caught,
36 of them that went out to w',
49 men of w' which are under our
53 the men of w' had taken spoil,
32:6 Shall your brethren go to w', and
20 go armed before the Lord to w',
27 over, every man armed for w',
De 1:41 on every man his weapons of w',
2:14 generation of the men of w' were
De 2:16 all the men of w' were consumed
3:18 all that are meet for the w'.
4:34 signs, and by wonders, and by w',
20:12 but will make w' against thee, then
19 in making w' against it to take it,
20 the city that maketh w' with thee,
21:10 When thou goest forth to w'
24:5 new wife, he shall not go out to w',
Jos 4:13 forty thousand prepared for w'
5:4 even all the men of w', died in the
6 all the people that were men of w',
6:3 compass the city, all ye men of w',
8:1 take all the people of w' with thee,
3 arose, and all the people of w', to
11 even the people of w' that were
10:5 Gibeon, and made w' against it.
7 and all the people of w' with him,
24 captains of the men of w' which
11:7 and all the people of w' with him,
18 Joshua made w' a long time with
23 And the land rested from w'.
14:11 even so is my strength now, for w',
15 And the land had rest from w'.
17:1 he was a man of w', therefore he
22:12 to go up to w' against them.
J'g 3:2 might know, to teach them w',
10 judged Israel, and went out to w':
5:8 gods; then was w' in the gates:
11:4, 5 the children of Ammon made w'
27 doest me wrong to w' against me:
18:11 appointed with weapons of w'.
16 appointed with their weapons of w',
17 were appointed with weapons of w'.
20:17 sword: all these were men of w'.
21:22 not to each man his wife in the w':
1Sa 8:12 and to make his instruments of w',
14:52 was sore w' against the Philistines
16:18 and a man of w', and prudent in
17:33 and he a man of w' from his youth.
18:5 Saul set him over the men of w',
19:8 there was w' again: and David
23:8 called all the people together to w',
28:15 Philistines make w' against me,
2Sa 1:27 and the weapons of w' perished!
3:1 long w' between the house of Saul
6 was w' between the house of Saul
11:7 did, and how the w' prospered.
18 all the things concerning the w';
19 end of telling the matters of the w'
17:8 thy father is a man of w', and will
21:15 Philistines had yet w' again with
22:35 He teacheth my hands to w'; so
1Ki 2:5 and shed the blood of w' in peace,
5 put the blood of w' upon his girdle
9:22 but they were men of w', and his
14:30 there was w' between Rehoboam
15:6 there was w' between Rehoboam
7 there was w' between Abijam and
16, 32 there was w' between Asa and
20:18 or whether they be come out for w',
22:1 continued three years without w'
2Ki 8:28 to the w' against Hazael king of
13:25 hand of Jehoahaz his father by w'.
14:7 took Selah by w', and called the
16:5 Israel came up to Jerusalem to w':
18:20 counsel and strength for the w'.
24:16 that were strong and apt for w',
25:4 men of w' fled by night by the way
19 that was set over the men of w',
1Ch 5:10 in the days of Saul they made w'
18 to shoot with bow, and skilful in w'.
18 threescore, that went out to the w'.
19 they made w' with the Hagarites,
22 slain, because the w' was of God.
7:4 were bands of soldiers for w', six
11 fit to go out for w' and battle.
40 of them that were apt to the w' and
12:1 the mighty men, helpers of the w'.
8 and men of w' fit for the battle,
23 that were ready armed to the w',
24 hundred, ready armed to the w'.
25 mighty men of valour for the w',
33 forth to battle, expert in w',
33 with all instruments of w', fifty
35 of the Danites expert in w' twenty
36 battle, expert in w', forty thousand.
37 all manner of instruments of w'
38 All these men of w', that could
18:10 (for Hadarezer had w' with Tou;)*
20:4 there arose w' at Gezer with the
5 And there was w' again with the
6 yet again there was w' at Gath,
28:3 thou hast been a man of w', and
2Ch 6:34 If thy people go out to w' against
8:9 they were men of w', and chief of
13:2 w' between Abijah and Jeroboam.
3 with an army of valiant men of w',
14:6 and he had no w' in those years;
15:19 And there was no more w' unto the
17:10 made no w' against Jehoshaphat.
13 and the men of w', mighty men of
18 ready prepared for the w'.
18:3 and we will be with thee in the w'.
22:5 son of Ahab king of Israel to w'
25:5 choice men, able to go forth to w',
26:11 men, that went out to w' by bands,
13 that made w' with mighty power,
28:12 them that came from the w',
32:6 And he set captains of w' over the
33:14 and put captains of w' in all the
35:21 the house wherewith I have w':
Job 5:20 in w' from the power of the sword.
10:17 changes and w' are against me.
38:23 against the day of battle and w'?
Ps 18:34 He teacheth my hands to w', so
27:3 though w' should rise against me,

Ps 55:21 butter, but *w* was in his heart:
68:30 thou the people that delight in *w*.
120: 7 but when I speak, they are for *w*.
140: 2 are they gathered together for *w*.
144: 1 teacheth my hands to *w*,
Pr 20:18 and with good advice make *w*.
24: 6 counsel thou shalt make thy *w*:
Ec 3: 8 a time of *w*, and a time of peace.
8: 8 there is no discharge in that *w*;
9:18 is better than weapons of *w*: but
Ca 3: 8 hold swords, being expert in *w*:
Isa 2: 4 neither shall they learn *w* any
3: 2 mighty man, and the man of *w*,
25 sword, and thy mighty in the *w*.
7: 1 toward Jerusalem to *w* against it,
21:15 and from the grievousness of *w*.
36: 5 I have counsel and strength for *w*:
37: 9 come forth to make *w* with thee.
41:12 they that *w* against thee shall be
42:13 stir up jealousy like a man of *w*:
Jer 4:19 of the trumpet, the alarm of *w*.
6: 4 Prepare ye *w* against her; arise,
23 set in array as men for *w* against
21: 2 king of Babylon maketh *w*
4 I will turn back the weapons of *w*
28: 8 of *w*, and of evil, and of pestilence.
38: 4 the hands of the men of *w* that
39: 4 saw them, and all the men of *w*,
41: 3 found there, and the men of *w*.
16 even mighty men of *w*, and the
42:14 Egypt, where we shall see no *w*,
48:14 mighty and strong men for the *w*?
49: 2 cause an alarm of *w* to be heard in
26 all the men of *w* shall be cut off in
50:30 all her men of *w* shall be cut off in
51:20 my battle axe and weapons of *w*:
32 and the men of *w* are affrighted.
52: 7 all the men of *w* fled, and went
25 had the charge of the men of *w*;
Eze 17:17 company make for him in the *w*,
26: 9 engines of *w* against thy walls,
27:10 in thine army, thy men of *w*:
27 all thy men of *w*, that are in thee,
32:27 to hell with their weapons of *w*:
39:20 mighty men, and with all men of *w*,
Da 7:21 horn made *w* with the saints,
9:26 unto the end of the *w* desolations
Joe 2: 7 shall climb the wall like men of *w*;
3: 9 Prepare *w*, wake up the mighty
9 let all the men of *w* draw near;
Mic 2: 8 by securely as men averse from *w*.
3: 5 they even prepare *w* against him.
4: 3 neither shall they learn *w* any
Lu 14:31 to make *w* against another king,
23:11 Herod with his men of *w* set him
2Co 10: 3 flesh, we do not *w* after the flesh:
1Ti 1:18 them mightest *w* a good warfare;
Jas 4: 1 lusts that *w* in your members?
2 ye fight and *w*, yet ye have not,
1Pe 2:11 lusts, which *w* against the soul;
Re 11: 7 pit shall make *w* against them,
12: 7 there was *w* in heaven: Michael
17 went to make *w* with the remnant
13: 4 who is able to make *w* with him?
7 him to make *w* with the saints,
17:14 These...make *w* with the Lamb,
19:11 he doth judge and make *w*.
19 to make *w* against him that sat

ward See also BACKWARD; DOWNWARD; EASTWARD; FORWARD; FROWARD; GOD-WARD; INWARD; NORTHWARD; ONWARD; OUTWARD; REREWARD; REWARD; SEATWARD; SOUTHWARD; THEEWARD; THITHERWARD; TOWARD; UPWARD; USWARD; WARDROBE; WARDS; WESTWARD; YOUWARD.
Ge 40: 3 he put them in *w* in the house of
4 and they continued a season in *w*.
7 with him in the *w* of his lord's
41:10 put me in *w* in the captain of the
42:17 he put them altogether into *w*
Le 24:12 they put him in *w*, that the mind
Nu 15:34 they put him in *w*, because it was
2Sa 20: 3 put them in *w*, and fed them,
1Ch 12:29 kept the *w* of the house of Saul.
25: 8 And they cast lots, *w* against
8 against *w*, as well the small as the
26:16 of the going up, *w* against *w*.
Ne 12:24 the man of God, *w* over against *w*.
25 porters keeping the *w* at the
45 porters kept the *w* of their God,
45 and the *w* of the purification,
Isa 21: 8 I am set in my *w* whole nights:
Jer 37:13 a captain of the *w* was there,
Eze 19: 9 they put him in *w* in chains,
Ac 12:10 past the first and the second *w*,

wardrobe
2Ki 22:14 son of Harhas, keeper of the *w*;
2Ch 34:22 son of Hasrah, keeper of the *w*;

wards See also INWARDS; REWARDS.
1Ch 9:23 house of the tabernacle, by *w*.
26:12 having *w* one against another,
Ne 13:30 appointed the *w* of the priests and

ware See also AWARE; BEWARE; WARES.
Ne 10:31 the people of the land bring *w* or
13:16 brought fish, and all manner of *w*,
20 sellers of all kind of *w* lodged
Lu 8:27 devils long time, and *w* no clothes,
Ac 14: 6 They were *w* of it, and fled unto
2Ti 4:15 Of whom be thou *w* also; for he

wares See also UNAWARES.
Jer 10:17 Gather up thy *w* out of the land,
Eze 27:16, 18 of the *w* of thy making:
33 thy *w* went forth out of the seas,
Jon 1: 5 forth the *w* that were in the ship

warfare
1Sa 28: 1 their armies together for *w*,
Isa 40: 2 her, that her *w* is accomplished,
1Co 9: 7 Who goeth a *w* any time at his
2Co 10: 4 weapons of our *w* are not carnal,
1Ti 1:18 by them mightest war a good *w*;

warm See also LUKEWARM; WARMED; WARMETH; WARMING.
2Ki 4:34 the flesh of the child waxed *w*.
Job 6:17 What time they wax *w*, they
37:17 How thy garments are *w*, when
Ec 4:11 but how can one be *w* alone?
Isa 44:15 will take thereof, and *w* himself;
16 Aha, I am *w*, I have seen the fire:
47:14 there shall not be a coal to *w* at,
Hag 1: 6 clothe you, but there is none *w*;

warmed
Job 31:20 he were not *w* with the fleece of
M'r 14:54 and *w* himself at the fire.
Joh 18:18 was cold: and they *w* themselves:
18 stood with them, and *w* himself.
25 Simon Peter stood and *w* himself.
Jas 2:16 in peace, be ye *w* and filled;

warmeth
Job 39:14 the earth, and *w* them in dust,
Isa 44:16 yea, he *w* himself, and saith, Aha,

warming
M'r 14:67 when she saw Peter *w* himself,

warn See also WARNED; WARNING.
2Ch 19:10 *w* them that they trespass not
Eze 3:18 nor speakest to *w* the wicked
19 Yet if thou *w* the wicked, and he
21 if thou *w* the righteous man, that
33: 3 the trumpet, and *w* the people;
7 my mouth, and *w* them from me.
8 dost not speak to *w* the wicked
9 if thou *w* the wicked of his way to
Ac 20:31 I ceased not to *w* every one night
1Co 4:14 but as my beloved sons I *w* you.
1Th 5:14 *w* them that are unruly, comfort

warned
2Ki 6:10 of God told him and *w* him of,
Ps 19:11 by them is thy servant *w*: and in
Eze 3:21 shall surely live, because he is *w*;
33: 6 trumpet, and the people be not *w*;
M't 2:12 being *w* of God in a dream that
22 being *w* of God in a dream, he
3: 7 *w* you to flee from the wrath to
Lu 3: 7 *w* you to flee from the wrath to
Ac 10:22 *w* from God by an holy angel to
Heb 11: 7 being *w* of God of things not seen

warning
Jer 6:10 whom shall I speak, and give *w*,
Eze 3:17 mouth, and give them *w* from me.
18 givest him not *w*, nor speakest
20 because thou hast not given him *w*,
33: 4 of the trumpet, and taketh not *w*;
5 of the trumpet, and took not *w*;
5 taketh *w* shall deliver his soul.
Col 1:28 *w* every man, and teaching every

warp
Le 13:48 Whether it be in the *w*, or woof;
49, 51 either in the *w*, or in the woof,
52 whether the *w* or woof, in woolen
53 either in the *w*, or in the woof, or
56 or out of the *w*, or out of the woof:
57 either in the *w*, or in the woof, or
58 the garment, either *w*, or woof, or
59 either in the *w*, or woof, or any

warred
Nu 31: 7 they *w* against the Midianites,
42 Moses divided from the men that *w*,
Jos 24: 9 Moab, arose and *w* against Israel,
1Ki 14:19 the acts of Jeroboam, how he *w*,
20: 1 Samaria, and *w* against it.
22:45 that he shewed, and how he *w*,
2Ki 6: 8 the king of Syria *w* against Israel,
14:28 how he *w*, and how he recovered
2Ch 26: 6 and *w* against the Philistines,

warreth
2Ti 2: 4 No man that *w* entangleth himself

warring
2Ki 19: 8 king of Assyria *w* against Libnah:
Isa 37: 8 king of Assyria *w* against Libnah:
Ro 7:23 *w* against the law of my mind,

warrior See also WARRIORS.
Isa 9: 5 battle of the *w* is with confused

warriors
1Ki 12:21 chosen men, which were *w*,
2Ch 11: 1 chosen men, which were *w*,

wars
Nu 21:14 in the book of the *w* of the Lord,
J'g 3: 1 had not known all the *w* of Canaan;
2Sa 8:10 for Hadadezer had *w* with Toi.
1Ki 5: 3 the *w* which were about him on
1Ch 22: 8 abundantly, and hast made great *w*:
2Ch 12:15 there were *w* between Rehoboam
16: 9 henceforth thou shalt have *w*.
27: 7 the acts of Jotham, and all his *w*,
Ps 46: 9 maketh *w* to cease unto the end of
M't 24: 6 shall hear of *w* and rumours of *w*:
M'r 13: 7 shall hear of *w* and rumours of *w*,
Lu 21: 9 ye shall hear of *w* and commotions,
Jas 4: 1 whence come *w* and fightings

wash See also UNWASHEN; WASHED; WASHEST; WASHING; WASHPOT.
Ge 18: 4 *w* your feet, and rest yourselves
19: 2 tarry all night, and *w* your feet,
24:32 water to *w* his feet, and the men's
Ex 2: 5 daughter of Pharaoh came...to *w*
19:10 and let them *w* their clothes,
29: 4 and shalt *w* them with water.
17 and *w* the inwards of him, and his
30:18 his foot also of brass, to *w* withal:
19 and his sons shall *w* their hands
20 they shall *w* with water, that they
21 they shall *w* their hands and their
40:12 and *w* them with water.
30 and put water there, to *w* withal.
Le 1: 9 and his legs shall he *w* in water:
13 But he shall *w* the inwards and
6:27 thou shalt *w* that whereon it was
9:14 he did *w* the inwards and the
11:25, 28 of them shall *w* his clothes,
40, 40 carcase of it shall *w* his clothes,
13: 6, 34 and he shall *w* his clothes, and
54 *w* the thing wherein the plague is,
58 of skin it be, which thou shalt *w*,
14: 8 to be cleansed shall *w* his clothes,
8 and *w* himself in water, that he
9 and he shall *w* his clothes, also
9 also he shall *w* his flesh in water,
47 in the house shall *w* his clothes;
47 in the house shall *w* his clothes.
15: 5 toucheth...bed shall *w* his clothes,
6, 7 hath the issue shall *w* his clothes,
8 he shall *w* his clothes, and bathe
10 of those things shall *w* his clothes,
11 he shall *w* his clothes, and bathe
13 *w* his clothes, and bathe his flesh
16 he shall *w* all his flesh in water,
21 her bed shall *w* his clothes,
22 she sat upon shall *w* his clothes,
27 and shall *w* his clothes, and bathe
16: 4 shall he *w* his flesh in water, and
24 *w* his flesh with water in the holy
26 the scapegoat shall *w* his clothes,
28 burneth them shall *w* his clothes,
17:15 he shall both *w* his clothes, and
16 if he *w* them not, nor bathe his
22: 6 unless he *w* his flesh with water.
Nu 8: 7 and let them *w* their clothes,
19: 7 Then the priest shall *w* his clothes,
8 that burneth her shall *w* his clothes
10 of the heifer shall *w* his clothes,
19 purify himself, and *w* his clothes,
21 of separation shall *w* his clothes;
31:24 *w* your clothes on the seventh day,
De 21: 6 *w* their hands over the heifer
23:11 on, he shall *w* himself with water:
Ru 3: 3 *W* thyself therefore, and anoint
1Sa 25:41 to *w* the feet of the servants of my
2Sa 11: 8 down to thy house, and *w* thy feet.
2Ki 5:10 Go and *w* in Jordan seven times,
12 may I not *w* in them, and be clean?
13 he saith to thee, *W*, and be clean?
2Ch 4: 6 and five on the left, to *w* in them:
6 the sea was for the priests to *w* in.
Job 9:30 If I *w* myself with snow water, and
Ps 26: 6 I will *w* mine hands in innocency:
51: 2 *W* me throughly from mine
7 *w* me, and I shall be whiter than
58:10 *w* his feet in the blood of the
Isa 1:16 *W* you, make you clean; put away
Jer 2:22 though thou *w* thee with nitre,
4:14 *w* thine heart from wickedness,
Eze 23:40 for whom thou didst *w* thyself,
M't 6:17 anoint thine head, and *w* thy face;
15: 2 *w* not their hands when they eat
M'r 7: 3 except they *w* their hands oft, eat
4 except they *w*, they eat not.
Lu 7:38 began to *w* his feet with tears,
Joh 9: 7 him, Go, *w* in the pool of Siloam,
11 Go to the pool of Siloam, and *w*:
13: 5 and began to *w* the disciples' feet,
6 him, Lord, dost thou *w* my feet?
8 him, Thou shalt never *w* my feet.
8 If I *w* thee not, thou hast no part
10 needeth not save to *w* his feet,
14 also ought to *w* one another's feet.
Ac 22:16 be baptized, and *w* away thy sins,

washed See also UNWASHEN.
Ge 43:24 water, and they *w* their feet;
31 And he *w* his face, and went out,
49:11 he *w* his garments in wine, and
Ex 19:14 people; and they *w* their clothes.
40:31 Aaron and his sons *w* their hands
32 came near unto the altar, they *w*;
Le 8: 6 his sons, and *w* them with water.
21 he *w* the inwards and the legs in
13:55 the plague, after that it is *w*:
58 it shall be *w* the second time, and
15:17 shall be *w* with water, and be
Nu 8:21 purified, and they *w* their clothes;
J'g 19:21 they *w* their feet, and did eat and
2Sa 12:20 David arose from the earth, and *w*,
19:24 his beard, nor *w* his clothes,
1Ki 22:38 one *w* the chariot in the pool of
38 his blood; and they *w* his armour;
2Ch 4: 6 burnt offering they *w* in them;
Job 29: 6 When I *w* my steps with butter,
Ps 73:13 and *w* my hands in innocency.
Pr 30:12 yet is not *w* from their filthiness.
Ca 5: 3 I have *w* my feet; how shall I
12 rivers of waters, *w* with milk, and
Isa 4: 4 Lord shall have *w* away the filth
Eze 16: 4 thou *w* in water to supple thee;
9 Then *w* I thee with water; yea,
9 I throughly *w* away thy blood
40:38 where they *w* the burnt offering.
M't 27:24 *w* his hands before the multitude,
Lu 7:44 she hath *w* my feet with tears,
11:38 he had not first *w* before dinner.
Joh 9: 7 and *w*, and came seeing.

Joh 9:11 I went and w', and I received sight.
15 mine eyes, and I w', and do see.
13:10 He that is w' needeth not save to
12 So after he had w' their feet, and
14 and Master, have w' your feet;
Ac 9:37 whom when they had w', they laid
16:33 of the night, and w' their stripes;
1Co 6:11 but ye are w', but ye are sanctified,
1Ti 5:10 if she have w' the saints' feet, if
Heb10:22 and our bodies w' with pure water.
2Pe 2:22 sow that was w' to her wallowing
Re 1: 5 w' us from our sins in his own
7:14 and have w' their robes, and made

washest
Job 14:19 thou w' away the things which

washing See also WASHINGS.
Le 13:56 somewhat dark after the w' of it;
2Sa 11: 2 roof he saw a woman w' herself;
Ne 4:23 that every one put them off for w'.
Ca 4: 2 which came up from the w';
6: 6 of sheep which go up from the w',
M'r 7: 4 received to hold, as the w' of cups,
8 of men, as the w' of pots and cups:
Lu 5: 2 of them, and were w' their nets.
Eph 5:26 cleanse it with the w' of water by
Tit 3: 5 by the w' of regeneration, and

washings
Heb 9:10 in meats and drinks, and divers w'.

washpot
Ps 60: 8 Moab is my w'; over Edom
108: 9 Moab is my w'; over Edom

wast See also WERT.
Ge 3:11 Who told thee that thou w' naked?
19 ground; for out of it w' thou taken:
33:10 of God, and thou w' pleased with me.
40:13 manner when thou w' his butler.
De 5:15 w' a servant in the land of Egypt,
15:15 that thou w' a bondman in the land
16:12 that thou w' a bondman in Egypt:
23: 7 thou w' a stranger in his land.
24:18 remember that thou w' a bondman
22 thou w' a bondman in the land of
25:18 thee, when thou w' faint and weary;
28:60 of Egypt, which thou w' afraid of;
1Sa 15:17 When thou w' little in thine own sight,
17 w' thou not made the head of the
2Sa 1:14 How w' thou not afraid to stretch
25 thou w' slain in thine high places.
5: 2 thou w' he that leddest out and
1Ch 11: 2 thou w' he that leddest out and
Job 15: 7 or w' thou made before the hills?
38: 4 Where w' thou when I laid the
21 thou it, because thou w' then born?
Ps 99: 8 thou w' a God that forgavest them,
114: 5 Jordan, that thou w' driven back?
Isa 12: 1 though thou w' angry with me, thine
14: 3 wherein thou w' made to serve,
33: 1 spoilest, and thou w' not spoiled;
43: 4 Since thou w' precious in my sight,
48: 8 and w' called a transgressor from the
54: 6 of youth, when thou w' refused,
57:10 hand; therefore thou w' not grieved.
Jer 2:36 as thou w' ashamed of Assyria.
50:24 O Babylon, and thou w' not aware:
Eze 16: 4 day thou w' born thy navel was not
4 neither w' thou washed in water to
5 thou w' cast out in the open field,
5 person, in the day that thou w' born.
6, 6 thee when thou w' in thy blood,
7 whereas thou w' naked and bare.
13 Thus w' thou decked with gold and
13 thou w' exceeding beautiful, and thou
22 when thou w' naked and bare,
22 and w' polluted in thy blood.
28 Assyrians, because thou w' unsatiable;
29 yet thou w' not satisfied herewith.
47 thou w' corrupted more than they
21:30 in the place where thou w' created,
24:13 thou w' not purged, thou shalt not
26:17 that w' inhabited of seafaring men,
17 which w' strong in the sea, she and
27:25 thou w' replenished, and made very
28: 3 thee in the day that thou w' created.
14 thou w' upon the holy mountain
15 Thou w' perfect in thy ways from the
15 from the day that thou w' created,
Ob 1:11 even thou w' as one of them.
M't 26:69 Thou also w' with Jesus of Galilee.
M'r 14:67 thou also w' with Jesus of Nazareth.
Joh 1:48 when thou w' under the fig tree,
9:34 Thou w' altogether born in sins, and
21:18 When thou w' young, thou girdedst
Re 5: 9 for thou w' slain, and hast redeemed
11:17 God Almighty, which art, and w', and shalt
16: 5 Lord, which art, and w', and shalt

waste See also WASTED; WASTES; WASTETH; WASTING.
Le 26:31 And I will make your cities w',
33 be desolate, and your cities w'.
Nu 21:30 we have laid them w' even unto
De 32:10 and in the w' howling wilderness;
1Ki 17:14 The barrel of meal shall not w',
2Ki 19:25 to lay w' fenced cities into ruinous
1Ch 17: 9 of wickedness w' them any more,
Ne 2: 3 of my fathers' sepulchres, lieth w',
17 how Jerusalem lieth w', and the
Job 30: 3 in former time desolate and w'.
38:27 satisfy the desolate and w' ground;
Ps 79: 7 and laid w' his dwelling place.
80:13 boar out of the wood doth w' it,
Isa 5: 6 I will lay it w': it shall not be
17 w' places of the fat ones shall
15: 1 in the night Ar of Moab is laid w',

Isa 15: 1 the night Kir of Moab is laid w',
23: 1 for it is laid w', so that there is no
14 for your strength is laid w'.
24: 1 and maketh it w', and turneth it
33: 8 The highways lie w', the
34:10 to generation it shall lie w';
37:18 Assyria have laid w' all the nations,
26 be to lay w' defenced cities into
42:15 I will make w' mountains and
49:17 they that made thee w' shall go
19 thy w' and thy desolate places,
51: 3 he will comfort all her w' places;
52: 9 ye w' places of Jerusalem:
58:12 thee shall build the old w' places:
61: 4 they shall repair the w' cities, the
64:11 our pleasant things are laid w'.
Jer 2:15 yelled, and they made his land w':
4: 7 and thy cities shall be laid w',
27:17 should this city be laid w'?
46:19 Noph shall be w' and desolate
49:13 a reproach, a w', and a curse;
50:21 w' and utterly destroy after them,
Eze 5:14 Moreover I will make thee w',
6: 6 dwellingplaces...shall be laid w',
6 your altars may be laid w' and
12:20 are inhabited shall be laid w',
19: 7 palaces, and he laid w' their cities;
26: 2 be replenished, now she is laid w':
29: 9 of Egypt shall be desolate and w';
10 of Egypt utterly w' and desolate,
12 among the cities that are laid w'
30:12 I will make the land w', and all
35: 4 I will lay thy cities w', and thou
36:35 the w' and desolate and ruined
38 so shall the w' cities be filled with
38: 8 which have been always w':
Joe 1: 7 He hath laid my vine w', and
Am 7: 9 of Israel shall be laid w';
9:14 and they shall build the w' cities,
Mic 5: 6 shall w' the land of Assyria with
Na 2:10 She is empty, and void, and w':
3: 7 thee, and say, Nineveh is laid w':
Zep 3: 6 I made their streets w', that none
Hag 1: 4 houses, and this house lie w'?
9 Because of mine house that is w',
Mal 1: 3 mountains and his inheritance w'
M't 26: 8 To what purpose is this w'?
M'r 14: 4 Why was this w' of the ointment

wasted
Nu 14:33 carcases be w' in the wilderness.
24:22 the Kenite shall be w', until
De 2:14 the men of war were w' out from
1Ki 17:16 And the barrel of meal w' not,
1Ch 20: 1 w' the country of the children of
Ps 137: 3 they that w' us required of us
Isa 6:11 cities be w' without inhabitant,
19: 5 the river shall be w' and dried up.
60:12 those nations shall be utterly w'.
Jer 44: 6 and they are w' and desolate, as
Eze 30: 7 the midst of the cities that are w'.
Joe 1:10 The field is w', the land mourneth;
10 land mourneth; for the corn is w':
Lu 15:13 there w' his substance with riotous
16: 1 unto him that he had w' his goods.
Ga 1:13 the church of God, and w' it:

wasteness
Zep 1:15 a day of w' and desolation, a day

waster
Pr 18: 9 brother to him that is a great w'.
Isa 54:16 I have created the w' to destroy.

wastes
Isa 61: 4 And they shall build the old w',
Jer 49:13 cities thereof shall be perpetual w'.
Eze 33:24 those w' of the land of Israel
27 they that are in the w' shall fall by
36: 4 to the desolate w', and to the cities
10 and the w' shall be builded:
33 cities, and the w' shall be builded.

wasteth
Job 14:10 But man dieth, and w' away:
Ps 91: 6 destruction that w' at noonday.
Pr 19:26 He that w' his father, and

wasting
Isa 59: 7 w' and destruction are in their
60:18 w' nor destruction within thy

watch See also WATCHED; WATCHES; WATCHETH; WATCHFUL; WATCHING; WATCHMAN; WATCHTOWER.
Ge 31:49 the Lord w' between me and thee,
Ex 14:24 in the morning w' the Lord looked
J'g 7:19 in the beginning of the middle w';
19 they had but newly set the w':
1Sa 11:11 midst of the host in the morning w'
19:11 unto David's house, to w' him,
2Sa 13:34 the young man that kept the w'
2Ki 11: 5 keepers of the w' of the king's
6 shall ye keep the w' of the house,
7 they shall keep the w' of the house
2Ch 20:24 Judah came toward the w' tower
23: 6 shall keep the w' of the Lord.
Ezr 8:29 W' ye, and keep them, until ye
Ne 4: 9 set a w' against them day and
7: 3 of Jerusalem, every one in his w',
Job 7:12 that thou settest a w' over me?
14:16 dost thou not w' over my sin?
Ps 90: 4 it is past, and as a w' in the night.
102: 7 I w', and am as a sparrow alone
130: 6 than they that w' for the morning:
6 than they that w' for the morning.
141: 3 Set a w', O Lord, before my mouth;
Isa 21: 5 the table, w' in the watchtower,
29:20 all that w' for iniquity are cut off:
Jer 5: 6 a leopard shall w' over their cities:

Jer 31:28 so will I w' over them, to build, and
44:27 I will w' over them for evil, and not
51:12 make the w' strong, set up the
Na 2: 1 w' the way, make thy loins strong,
Hab 2: 1 I will stand upon my w', and set
1 will w' to see what he will say
M't 14:25 fourth w' of the night Jesus went
24:42 W' therefore: for ye know not
43 in what w' the thief would come,
25:13 W' therefore, for ye know neither
26:38 tarry ye here, and w' with me.
40 could ye not w' with me one hour?
41 W' and pray, that ye enter not into
27:65 Ye have a w': go your way, make
66 sealing the stone, and setting a w'.
28:11 some of the w' came into the city,
M'r 6:48 about the fourth w' of the night
13:33 Take ye heed, w' and pray: for ye
34 and commanded the porter to w'.
35 W' ye therefore: for ye know not
37 I say unto you I say unto all, W'.
14:34 unto death: tarry ye here, and w'.
37 couldest not thou w' one hour?
38 W' ye and pray, lest ye enter into
Lu 2: 8 keeping w' over their flock by
12:38 if he shall come in the second w',
38 or come in the third w', and find
21:36 W' ye therefore, and pray always,
Ac 20:31 Therefore w', and remember, that
1Co 16:13 W' ye, stand fast in the faith, quit
Col 4: 2 w' in the same with thanksgiving;
1Th 5: 6 others; but let us w' and be sober.
2Ti 4: 5 But w' thou in all things, endure
Heb13:17 they w' for your souls, as they that
1Pe 4: 7 sober, and w' unto prayer.
Re 3: 3 If therefore thou shalt not w', I

watched
Ps 59: *title* and they w' the house to kill him.
Jer 20:10 All my familiars w' for my halting,
31:28 that like as I have w' over them,
La 4:17 w' for a nation that could not save
Da 9:14 hath the Lord w' upon the evil,
M't 24:43 he would have w', and would not
27:36 sitting down they w' him there;
M'r 3: 2 they w' him, whether he would
Lu 6: 7 the scribes and Pharisees w' him,
12:39 he would have w', and not have
14: 1 the sabbath day, that they w' him.
20:20 they w' him, and sent forth spies,
Ac 9:24 they w' the gates day and night to

watcher See also WATCHERS.
Da 4:13 a w' and an holy one came down
23 the king saw a w' and an holy one

watchers
Jer 4:16 that w' come from a far country,
Da 4:17 matter is by the decree of the w',

watches
Ne 7: 3 w' of the inhabitants of Jerusalem.
12: 9 were over against them in the w'.
Ps 63: 6 meditate on thee in the night w'.
119:148 Mine eyes prevent the night w',
La 2:19 beginning of the w' pour out thine

watcheth
Ps 37:32 The wicked w' the righteous, and
Eze 7: 6 the end is come: it w' for thee;
Re 16:15 Blessed is he that w', and keepeth

watchful
Re 3: 2 Be w', and strengthen the things

watching See also WATCHINGS.
1Sa 4:13 sat upon a seat by the wayside w':
Pr 8:34 heareth me, w' daily at my gates,
La 4:17 in our w' we have watched for a
M't 27:54 they that were with him, w' Jesus,
Lu 12:37 lord when he cometh shall find w':
Eph 6:18 and w' thereunto with all

watchings
2Co 6: 5 in tumults, in labours, in w', in
11:27 painfulness, in w' often, in hunger

watchman See also WATCHMAN'S; WATCHMEN.
2Sa 18:24 the w' went up to the roof over the
25 And the w' cried, and told the king.
26 the w' saw another man running:
26 and the w' called unto the porter,
27 And the w' said, Me thinketh the
2Ki 9:17 there stood a w' on the tower in
18 the w' told, saying, The messenger
20 And the w' told, saying, He came
Ps 127: 1 city, the w' waketh but in vain.
Isa 21: 6 set a w', let him declare what he
11, 11 W', what of the night?
12 The w' said, The morning cometh,
Eze 3:17 thee a w' unto the house of Israel:
33: 2 coasts, and set him for their w':
6 But if the w' see the sword come,
7 thee a w' unto the house of Israel;
Ho 9: 8 w' of Ephraim was with my God:

watchman's
Eze 33: 6 blood will I require at the w' hand.

watchmen
1Sa 14:16 w' of Saul in Gibeah of Benjamin
2Ki 17: 9 from the tower of the w' to the
18: 8 from the tower of the w' to the
Ca 3: 3 The w' that go about the city
5: 7 The w' that went about the city
Isa 52: 8 Thy w' shall lift up the voice;
56:10 His w' are blind: they are all
62: 6 I have set w' upon thy walls, O
Jer 6:17 I set w' over you, saying, Hearken
31: 6 the w' upon the mount Ephraim
51:12 the watch strong, set up the w',
Mic 7: 4 the day of thy w' and thy visitation

watchtower See also WATCH and TOWER.
Isa 21: 5 the table, watch in the *w*. eat,
8 I stand continually upon the *w*. in
water See also WATERCOURSE; WATERED; WATEREST; WATERETH; WATERFLOOD; WATERING; WATERPOT; WATERS; WATERSPOUTS; WATERSPRINGS.
Ge 2:10 went out of Eden to *w*. the garden;
16: 7 found her by a fountain of *w*. in
18: 4 Let a little *w*., I pray you, be
21:14 and took bread, and a bottle of *w*.,
15 And the *w*. was spent in the bottle,
19 her eyes, and she saw a well of *w*.,
19 went, and filled the bottle with *w*.,
25 Abimelech because of a well of *w*.,
24:11 by a well of *w*. at the time of the
11 time that women go out to draw *w*.
13 I stand here by the well of *w*.;
13 of the city come out to draw *w*.;
17 thee, drink a little *w*. of thy pitcher.
32 and *w*. to wash his feet, and the
43 I stand by the well of *w*.; and it
43 virgin cometh forth to draw *w*.,
43 a little *w*. of thy pitcher to drink;
26:18 Isaac digged again the wells of *w*.,
19 found there a well of springing *w*.
20 herdmen, saying, The *w*. is ours:
32 said unto him, We have found *w*.
29: 7 *w*. ye the sheep, and go and feed
8 mouth; then we *w*. the sheep.
37:24 was empty, there was no *w*. in it.
43:24 and gave them *w*., and they washed
49: 4 Unstable as *w*., thou shalt not excel;
Ex 2:10 Because I drew him out of the *w*.
16 and they came and drew *w*., and filled
16 troughs to *w*. their father's flock.
19 and also drew *w*. enough for us,
4: 9 shalt take of the *w*. of the river,
9 the *w*. which thou takest out of the
7:15 lo, he goeth out unto the *w*.; and
18 lothe to drink of the *w*. of the river.
19 upon all their pools of *w*., that they
21 not drink of the *w*. of the river;
24 digged round about the river for *w*.
24 for they could not drink of the *w*. of
8:20 lo, he cometh forth to the *w*.; and
12: 9 nor sodden at all with *w*., but roast
15:22 in the wilderness, and found no *w*.
27 where were twelve wells of *w*.,
17: 1 was no *w*. for the people to drink.
2 said, Give us *w*. that we may drink.
3 the people thirsted there for *w*.;
6 there shall come *w*. out of it, that
20: 4 that is in the *w*. under the earth:
23:25 shall bless thy bread, and thy *w*.;
29: 4 and shalt wash them with *w*.
30:18 and thou shalt put *w*. therein.
20 they shall wash with *w*., that they
32:20 powder, and strawed it upon the *w*.
34:28 did neither eat bread, nor drink *w*.
40: 7 the altar, and shalt put *w*. therein.
12 and wash them with *w*.
30 and put *w*. there, to wash withal.
Le 1: 9 and his legs shall he wash in *w*.:
13 the inwards and the legs with *w*.:
6:28 be both scoured, and rinsed in *w*.
8: 6 his sons, and wash them with *w*.
21 the inwards and the legs in *w*.;
11:32 is done, it must be put into *w*., and
34 on which such *w*. cometh shall be
36 wherein there is plenty of *w*., shall
38 But if any *w*. be put upon the seed,
14: 5 an earthen vessel over running *w*.:
6 was killed over the running *w*.:
8 and wash himself in *w*., that he
9 he shall wash his flesh in *w*., and
50 an earthen vessel over running *w*.:
51 in the running *w*., and sprinkle the
52 with the running *w*., and with the
15: 5, 6, 7, 8, 10 and bathe himself in *w*.,
11 hath not rinsed his hands in *w*.,
11 his clothes, and bathe himself in *w*.,
12 vessel of wood shall be rinsed in *w*.
13 and bathe his flesh in running *w*.,
16 he shall wash all his flesh in *w*.,
17 shall be washed with *w*., and be
18 shall both bathe themselves in *w*.,
21, 22, 27 and bathe himself in *w*.,
16: 4 shall he wash his flesh in *w*., and so
24 shall wash his flesh with *w*. in the
26, 28 and bathe his flesh in *w*.,
17:15 and bathe himself in *w*., and be
22: 6 unless he wash his flesh with *w*.
Nu 5:17 And the priest shall take holy *w*. in
17 shall take, and put it into the *w*.:
18 bitter *w*. that causeth the curse:
19 be thou free from this bitter *w*.
22 And this *w*. that causeth the curse
23 blot them out with the bitter *w*.:
24 the woman to drink the bitter *w*.
24 the *w*. that causeth the curse shall
26 cause the woman to drink the *w*.
27 he hath made her to drink the *w*.,
27 the *w*. that causeth the curse shall
8: 7 Sprinkle *w*. of purifying upon
19: 7 and he shall bathe his flesh in *w*.,
8 her shall wash his clothes in *w*.,
8 bathe his flesh in *w*., and shall be
9 of Israel for a *w*. of separation:
13 the *w*. of separation was not
17 running *w*. shall be put thereto in
18 take hyssop, and dip it in the *w*.,
19 clothes, and bathe himself in *w*.,
20 the *w*. of separation hath not been
21 that sprinkleth the *w*. of separation
21 that toucheth the *w*. of separation

Nu 20: 2 was no *w*. for the congregation:
5 neither is there any *w*. to drink.
8 it shall give forth his *w*., and thou
8 forth to them *w*. out of the rock:
10 we fetch you *w*. out of this rock?
11 and the *w*. came out abundantly,
13 This is the *w*. of Meribah; because
17 will we drink of the *w*. of the wells:
19 if I and my cattle drink of thy *w*.,
24 my word at the *w*. of Meribah.
21: 5 is no bread, neither is there any *w*.;
16 together, and I will give them *w*.
24: 7 pour the *w*. out of his buckets, and
27:14 sanctify me at the *w*. before their
14 is the *w*. of Meribah in Kadesh in
31:23 purified with the *w*. of separation:
23 ye shall make go through the *w*.
33: 9 Elim were twelve fountains of *w*.,
14 was no *w*. for the people to drink.
De 2: 6 also buy *w*. of them for money,
28 and give me *w*. for money, that I
8: 7 good land, a land of brooks and *w*.,
15 drought, where there was no *w*.;
15 forth *w*. out of the rock of flint;
9: 9 neither did eat bread nor drink *w*.:
18 did neither eat bread, nor drink *w*.,
11: 4 he made the *w*. of the Red sea to
11 drinketh *w*. of the rain of heaven:
12:16, 24 pour it upon the earth as *w*.
15:23 shalt pour it upon the ground as *w*.
23: 4 met you not with bread and with *w*.
11 on, he shall wash himself with *w*.:
29:11 wood unto the drawer of thy *w*.:
Jos 2:10 dried up the *w*. of the Red sea for
3: 8 to the brink of the *w*. of Jordan,
15 were dipped in the brim of the *w*.,
7: 5 people melted, and became as *w*.
9:21 and drawers of *w*. unto all the
23 and drawers of *w*. for the house of
27 drawers of *w*. for the congregation,
15: 9 the fountain of the *w*. of Nephtoah,
19 land; give me also springs of *w*.
16: 1 unto the *w*. of Jericho on the east,
J'g 1:15 land; give me also springs of *w*.
4:19 Give me,...a little *w*. to drink;
5: 4 the clouds also dropped *w*.
11 of archers in the places of drawing *w*.
25 He asked *w*., and she gave him
6:38 out of the fleece, a bowl full of *w*.
7: 4 bring them down unto the *w*., and
5 down the people unto the *w*.:
5 Every one that lappeth of the *w*.
6 down upon their knees to drink *w*.
15:19 jaw, and there came *w*. thereout;
1Sa 7: 6 drew *w*., and poured it out before
9:11 maidens going out to draw *w*.,
25:11 I then take my bread, and my *w*.,
26:11 and the cruse of *w*., and let us go.
12 the cruse of *w*. from Saul's bolster;
16 cruse of *w*. that was at his bolster.
30:11 eat; and they made him drink *w*.;
12 eaten no bread, nor drunk any *w*.,
2Sa 14:14 and are as *w*. spilt on the ground,
17:20 They be gone over the brook of *w*.
21 Arise, and pass quickly over the *w*.:
21:10 until *w*. dropped upon them out of
23:15 of the *w*. of the well of Beth-lehem,
16 and drew *w*. out of the well of
1Ki 13: 8 bread nor drink *w*. in this place:
9 Eat no bread, nor drink *w*., nor
16 will I eat bread nor drink *w*. with
17 eat no bread nor drink *w*. there,
18 he may eat bread and drink *w*.
19 bread in his house, and drank *w*.
22 hast eaten bread and drunk *w*. in
22 Eat no bread, and drink no *w*.;
14:15 Israel, as a reed is shaken in the *w*.,
17:10 I pray thee, a little *w*. in a vessel,
18: 4 and fed them with bread and *w*.)
5 unto all fountains of *w*., and unto
13 and fed them with bread and *w*.?
33 Fill four barrels with *w*., and pour
35 the *w*. ran round about the altar;
35 he filled the trench also with *w*.
38 up the *w*. that was in the trench.
19: 6 coals, and a cruse of *w*. at his head.
22:27 affliction and with *w*. of affliction.
2Ki 2:19 the *w*. is naught, and the ground
3: 9 there was no *w*. for the host, and
11 poured *w*. on the hands of Elijah.
17 that valley shall be filled with *w*.,
19 good tree, and stop all wells of *w*.,
20 there came *w*. by the way of Edom,
20 and the country was filled with *w*.
22 and the sun shone upon the *w*.,
22 the Moabites saw the *w*. on the
25 they stopped all the wells of *w*.,
6: 5 beam the axe head fell into the *w*.:
22 set bread and *w*. before them, that
8:15 a thick cloth, and dipped it in *w*.,
20:20 and brought *w*. into the city, are
1Ch 11:17 of the *w*. of the well of Beth-lehem,
18 drew *w*. out of...well of Beth-lehem,
2Ch 18:26 affliction and with *w*. of affliction,
32: 4 Assyria come, and find much *w*.?
Ezr 10: 6 he did eat no bread, nor drink *w*.:
Ne 3:26 against the *w*. gate toward the east,
8: 1 street that was before the *w*. gate;
3 street that was before the *w*. gate
16 and in the street of the *w*. gate,
9:15 forth *w*. for them out of the rock
20 and gavest them *w*. for their thirst.
12:37 even unto the *w*. gate eastward.
13: 2 of Israel with bread and with *w*.,
Job 8:11 can the flag grow without *w*.?
9:30 I wash myself with snow *w*.,

Job 14: 9 through the scent of *w*. it will bud,
15:16 which drinketh iniquity like *w*.?
22: 7 not given *w*. to the weary to drink,
34: 7 who drinketh up scorning like *w*.?
36:27 he maketh small the drops of *w*.:
Ps 1: 3 a tree planted by the rivers of *w*.,
6: 6 I *w*. my couch with my tears.
22:14 I am poured out like *w*., and all
42: 1 hart panteth after the *w*. brooks,
63: 1 and thirsty land, where no *w*. is;
65: 9 the river of God, which is full of *w*.:
66:12 went through fire and through *w*.:
72: 6 as showers that *w*. the earth.
77:17 The clouds poured out *w*.: the
79: 3 Their blood have they shed like *w*.
88:17 came round about me daily like *w*.;
107:35 the wilderness into a standing *w*.,
109:18 let it come into his bowels like *w*.,
114: 8 turned the rock into a standing *w*.,
Pr 8:24 no fountains abounding with *w*.
17:14 is as when one letteth out *w*.:
20: 5 the heart of man is like deep *w*.;
21: 1 of the Lord, as the rivers of *w*.:
25:21 he be thirsty, give him *w*. to drink:
27:19 As in *w*. face answereth to face, so
30:16 the earth that is not filled with *w*.;
Ec 2: 6 I made me pools of *w*.,
6 to *w*. therewith the wood that
Isa 1:22 dross, thy wine mixed with *w*.:
30 and as a garden that hath no *w*.
3: 1 bread, and the whole stay of *w*.,
12: 3 draw *w*. out of the wells of salvation.
14:23 for the bittern, and pools of *w*.:
16: 9 I will *w*. thee with my tears, O
21:14 brought *w*. to him that was thirsty,
22:11 two walls for the *w*. of the old pool:
27: 3 I will *w*. it every moment: lest
30:14 or to take *w*. withal out of the pit.
20 adversity, and the *w*. of affliction,
32: 2 as rivers of *w*. in a dry place, as
35: 7 and the thirsty land springs of *w*.:
37:25 I have digged, and drunk *w*.; and
41:17 When the poor and needy seek *w*.,
18 make the wilderness a pool of *w*.,
18 and the dry land springs of *w*.
44: 3 pour *w*. upon him that is thirsty,
4 as willows by the *w*. courses.
12 he drinketh no *w*., and is faint.
49:10 by the springs of *w*. shall he guide
50: 2 stinketh, because there is no *w*.,
58:11 like a spring of *w*., whose waters
63:12 dividing the *w*. before them, to
Jer 2:13 broken cisterns, that can hold no *w*.
8:14 and given us *w*. of gall to drink,
9:15 and give them *w*. of gall to drink.
13: 1 thy loins, and put it not in *w*.
14: 3 came to the pits, and found no *w*.:
23:15 and make them drink the *w*. of gall:
38: 6 in the dungeon there was no *w*.,
La 1:16 mine eye runneth down with *w*.,
2:19 pour out thine heart like *w*. before
3:48 eye runneth down with rivers of *w*.
5: 4 We have drunken our *w*. for money;
Eze 4:11 shalt drink also *w*. by measure,
16 and they shall drink *w*. by measure,
17 That they may want bread and *w*.,
7:17 and all knees shall be weak as *w*.
12:18 drink thy *w*. with trembling and
19 drink their *w*. with astonishment,
16: 4 neither wast thou washed in *w*. to
9 Then washed I thee with *w*.; yea,
17: 7 he might *w*. it by the furrows of
21: 7 and all knees shall be weak as *w*.:
24: 3 set it on, and also pour *w*. into it:
26:12 and thy dust in the midst of the *w*.
31:14 in their height, all that drink *w*.:
16 of Lebanon, all that drink *w*.,
32: 6 also *w*. with thy blood the land
36:25 will I sprinkle clean *w*. upon you,
Da 1:12 us pulse to eat, and *w*. to drink.
Ho 2: 5 that give me my bread and my *w*.,
5:10 my wrath upon them that like *w*.
10: 7 is cut off as the foam upon the *w*.
Joe 3:18 and shall *w*. the valley of Shittim.
Am 4: 8 unto one city, to drink *w*.;
8:11 famine of bread, not a thirst for *w*.,
Jon 3: 7 let them not feed, nor drink *w*.:
Na 2: 8 Nineveh is of old like a pool of *w*.:
Hab 3:10 overflowing of the *w*. passed by:
Zec 9:11 out of the pit wherein is no *w*.
M't 3:11 I indeed baptize you with *w*. unto
16 went up straightway out of the *w*.:
10:42 these little ones a cup of cold *w*.
14:28 bid me come unto thee on the *w*.
29 he walked on the *w*., to go to Jesus.
17:15 into the fire, and oft into the *w*.
27:24 he took *w*., and washed his hands
M'r 1: 8 I indeed have baptized you with *w*.:
10 coming up out of the *w*., he saw
9:41 you a cup of *w*. to drink in my name,
14:13 you a man bearing a pitcher of *w*.:
Lu 3:16 all, I indeed baptize you with *w*.;
7:44 thou gavest me no *w*. for my feet:
8:23 they were filled with *w*., and were in
24 wind and the raging of the *w*.:
25 commandeth even the winds and *w*.,
16:24 may dip the tip of his finger in *w*.,
22:10 meet you, bearing a pitcher of *w*.;
Joh 1:26 them, saying, I baptize with *w*.:
31 am I come baptizing with *w*.
33 he that sent me to baptize with *w*.,
2: 7 them, Fill the waterpots with *w*.
9 tasted the *w*. that was made wine,
9 servants which drew the *w*. knew;)
3: 5 Except a man be born of *w*. and of
23 because there was much *w*. there:

Joh 4: 7 a woman of Samaria to draw w':
10 he would have given thee living w'.
11 then hast thou that living w'?
13 Whosoever drinketh of this w' shall
14 whosoever drinketh of the w' that I
14 w' that I shall give him shall be in
14 him a well of w' springing up into
15 Sir, give me this w', that I thirst
46 Galilee, where he made the w' wine.
5: 3 waiting for the moving of the w'.
4 into the pool, and troubled the w':
4 first after the troubling of the w'
7 when the w' is troubled, to put me
7:38 belly shall flow rivers of living w'.
13: 5 that he poureth w' into a bason,
19:34 came there out blood and w'.
Ac 1: 5 For John truly baptized with w';
8:36 way, they came unto a certain w':
36 See, here is w'; what doth hinder
38 they went down both into the w',
39 they were come up out of the w',
10:47 Can any man forbid w', that these
11:16 said, John indeed baptized with w';
Eph 5:26 the washing of w' by the word,
1Ti 5:23 Drink no longer w', but use a little
Heb 9:19 of calves and of goats, with w', and
10:22 our bodies washed with pure w'.
Jas 3:11 at the same place sweet w' and bitter?
12 both yield salt w' and fresh.
1Pe 3:20 is, eight souls were saved by w'.
2Pe 2:17 These are wells without w', clouds
3: 5 standing out of the w' and in the w':
6 being overflowed with w', perished:
1Jo 5: 6 is he that came by w' and blood,
6 not by w' only, but by w' and blood.
8 earth, the spirit, and the w', and
Jude 12 clouds they are without w', carried
Re 12:15 out of his mouth w' as a flood
16:12 and the w' thereof was dried up,
21: 6 the fountain of the w' of life freely.
22: 1 shewed me a pure river of w' of life,
17 will, let him take the w' of life freely.

water-brooks See WATER and BROOKS.

watercourse See also WATER and COURSES.
2Ch 32:30 the upper w' of Gihon,
Job 38:25 w' for the overflowing of waters,

watered See also WATEREDST.
Ge 2: 6 w' the whole face of the ground.
13:10 that it was well w' every where,
29: 2 out of that well they w' the flocks:
3 the well's mouth, and w' the sheep,
10 w' the flock of Laban his mother's
Ex 2:17 helped them, and w' their flock.
19 enough for us, and w' the flock.
Pr 11:25 watereth shall be w' also himself.
Isa 58:11 and thou shalt be like a w' garden,
Jer 31:12 their soul shall be as a w' garden;
1Co 3: 6 I have planted, Apollos w'; but

wateredst
De 11:10 w' it with thy foot, as a garden of

waterest
Ps 65: 9 Thou visitest the earth, and w' it:
10 Thou w' the ridges thereof

watereth
Ps 104:13 He w' the hills from his chambers:
Pr 11:25 he that w' shall be watered also
Isa 55:10 w' the earth, and maketh it bring
1Co 3: 7 any thing, neither he that w';
8 planteth and he that w' are one:

waterflood
Ps 69:15 Let not the w' overflow me,

watering
Ge 30:38 in the gutters in the w' troughs
Job 37:11 by w' he wearieth the thick cloud:
Lu 13:15 stall, and lead him away to w'?

waterpot See also WATERPOTS.
Joh 4:28 The woman then left her w', and

waterpots
Joh 2: 6 were set there six w' of stone,
7 unto them, Fill the w' with water.

waters
Ge 1: 2 moved upon the face of the w'.
6 firmament in the midst of the w',
6 and let it divide the w' from the w'.
7 divided the w' which were under
7 from the w' which were above the
9 Let the w' under the heaven be
10 together of the w' called he Seas:
20 Let the w' bring forth abundantly
21 the w' brought forth abundantly,
22 multiply, and fill the w' in the seas,
6:17 bring a flood of w' upon the earth,
7: 6 the flood of w' was upon the earth.
7 ark, because of the w' of the flood.
10 that the w' of the flood were upon
17 the w' increased, and bare up the
18 w' prevailed, and were increased
18 ark went upon the face of the w'.
19 w' prevailed exceedingly upon the
20 cubits upward did the w' prevail;
24 the w' prevailed upon the earth
8: 1 the earth, and the w' asswaged;
3 the w' returned from off the earth
3 and fifty days the w' were abated.
5 the w' decreased continually until
7 until the w' were dried up from off
8 to see if the w' were abated from
9 the w' were on the face of the whole
11 Noah knew that the w' were abated
13 w' were dried up from off the earth
9:11 off any more by the w' of a flood;

Ge 9:15 the w' shall no more become a flood
Ex 7:17 upon the w' which are in the river,
19 thine hand upon the w' of Egypt,
20 smote the w' that were in the river,
20 all the w'...in the river were turned
8: 6 out his hand over the w' of Egypt;
14:21 dry land, and the w' were divided.
22 the w' were a wall unto them on
26 w' may come...upon the Egyptians,
28 the w' returned, and covered the
29 the w' were a wall unto them on
15: 8 the w' were gathered together,
10 they sank as lead in the mighty w'.
19 brought again the w' of the sea
23 could not drink of the w' of Marah,
25 which when he had cast into the w',
25 the w' were made sweet:
27 and they encamped there by the w'.
Le 11: 9 shall ye eat of all that are in the w':
9 hath fins and scales in the w', in
10 of all that move in the w', and of
10 any living thing which is in the w',
12 hath no fins nor scales in the w',
46 living creature...moveth in the w',
Nu 21:22 will not drink of the w' of the well:
24: 6 and as cedar trees beside the w'.
7 and his seed shall be in many w',
De 4:18 that is in the w' beneath the earth:
5: 8 that is in the w' beneath the earth:
10: 7 to Jotbath, a land of rivers of w'.
14: 9 shall eat of all that are in the w':
32:51 Israel at the w' of Meribah-Kadesh,
33: 8 didst strive at the w' of Meribah;
Jos 3: 8 shall rest in the w' of the Jordan,
13 w' of the Jordan shall be cut off
13 from the w' that come down from
16 the w' which came down from above
4: 7 the w' of Jordan were cut off before
7 the w' of Jordan were cut off:
18 the w' of Jordan returned unto
23 God dried up the w' of Jordan from
5: 1 Lord had dried up the w' of Jordan
11: 5 pitched together at the w' of Merom,
7 against them by the w' of Merom
15: 7 toward the w' of En-shemesh,
18:15 out to the well of w' of Nephtoah:
J'g 5:19 in Taanach by the w' of Megiddo;
7:24 them the w' unto Beth-barah
24 took the w' unto Beth-barah and
2Sa 5:20 before me, as the breach of w'.
12:27 and have taken the city of w'.
22:12 dark w', and thick clouds of the
17 he drew me out of many w';
2Ki 2: 8 smote the w', and they were divided
14 and smote the w', and said, Where
14 when he also had smitten the w',
21 forth unto the spring of the w',
21 the Lord, I have healed these w';
22 the w' were healed unto this day,
5:12 better than all the w' of Israel?
18:31 ye every one the w' of his cistern:
19:24 have digged and drunk strange w',
1Ch 14:11 hand like the breaking forth of w':
2Ch 32: 3 men to stop the w' of the fountains
Ne 9:11 as a stone into the mighty w'.
Job 3:24 are poured out like the w'.
5:10 and sendeth w' upon the fields:
11:16 remember it as w' that pass away:
12:15 Behold, he withholdeth the w',
14:11 As the w' fail from the sea, and the
19 The w' wear the stones: thou
22:11 and abundance of w' cover thee.
24:18 He is swift as the w'; their portion
19 and heat consume the snow w': so
26: 5 are formed from under the w',
8 He bindeth up the w' in his thick
10 compassed the w' with bounds,
27:20 Terrors take hold on him as w',
28: 4 even the w' forgotten of the foot:
25 he weigheth the w' by measure.
29:19 My root was spread out by the w',
30:14 upon me as a wide breaking in of w':
37:10 breadth of the w' is straitened.
38:25 for the overflowing of w',
30 The w' are hid as with a stone,
34 abundance of w' may cover thee?
Ps 18:11 round about him were dark w' and
15 Then the channels of w' were seen,
16 me, he drew me out of many w'.
23: 2 he leadeth me beside the still w'.
29: 3 voice of the Lord is upon the w':
3 the Lord is upon many w'.
32: 6 surely in the floods of great w' they
33: 7 He gathereth the w' of the sea
46: 3 Though the w' thereof roar and be
58: 7 Let them melt away as w' which
69: 1 the w' are come in unto my soul.
2 I am come into deep w', where
14 hate me, and out of the deep w'.
73:10 and w' of a full cup are wrung out
74:13 the heads of the dragons in the w'.
77:16 w' saw thee, O God, the w' saw thee;
19 sea, and thy path in the great w',
78:13 he made the w' to stand as an heap
16 caused w' to run down like rivers.
20 the rock, that the w' gushed out,
81: 7 I proved thee at the w' of Meribah.
93: 4 mightier than the noise of many w',
104: 3 beams of his chambers in the w':
6 the w' stood above the mountains.
105:29 He turned their w' into blood, and
41 the rock, and the w' gushed out;
106:11 And the w' covered their enemies:
32 angered him also at the w' of strife,
107:23 ships, that do business in great w';
114: 8 the flint into a fountain of w'.

Ps 119:136 Rivers of w' run down mine eyes,
124: 4 Then the w' had overwhelmed us,
5 proud w' had gone over our soul.
136: 6 stretched...the earth above the w':
144: 7 and deliver me out of great w',
147:18 his wind to blow, and the w' flow.
148: 4 ye w' that be above the heavens.
Pr 5:15 Drink w' out of thine own cistern,
15 running w' out of thine own well.
16 and rivers of w' in the streets.
8:29 that the w' should not pass his
9:17 Stolen w' are sweet, and bread
18: 4 of a man's mouth are as deep w',
25:25 As cold w' to a thirsty soul, so is
30: 4 hath bound the w' in a garment?
Ec 11: 1 Cast thy bread upon the w': for
Ca 4:15 a well of living w', and streams
5:12 eyes of doves by the rivers of w',
8: 7 Many w' cannot quench love,
Isa 8: 6 the w' of Shiloah that go softly,
7 up upon them the w' of the river,
11: 9 the Lord, as the w' cover the sea.
15: 6 the w' of Nimrim shall be desolate:
9 w' of Dimon shall be full of blood:
17:12 like the rushing of mighty w'!
13 rush like the rushing of many w':
18: 2 in vessels of bulrushes upon the w',
19: 5 And the w' shall fail from the sea,
8 they that spread nets upon the w'
22: 9 gathered...the w' of the lower pool.
23: 3 And by great w' the seed of Sihor,
28: 2 a flood of mighty w' overflowing,
17 w' shall overflow the hiding place.
30:25 high hill, rivers and streams of w'
32:20 Blessed...ye that sow beside all w',
33:16 be given him; his w' shall be sure.
35: 6 the wilderness shall w' break out,
36:16 every one the w' of his own cistern;
40:12 measured the w' in the hollow of
43: 2 When thou passest through the w',
16 sea, and a path in the mighty w';
20 because I give w' in the wilderness,
48: 1 come forth out of the w' of Judah,
21 caused the w' to flow out of the rock
21 rock also, and the w' gushed out.
51:10 the sea, the w' of the great deep;
54: 9 this is as the w' of Noah unto me:
9 the w' of Noah should no more go
55: 1 that thirsteth, come ye to the w',
57:20 whose w' cast up mire and dirt.
58:11 spring of water, whose w' fail not.
64: 2 the fire causeth the w' to boil,
Jer 2:13 forsaken...the fountain of living w',
18 of Egypt, to drink the w' of Sihor?
18 to drink the w' of the river?
6: 7 As a fountain casteth out her w',
9: 1 Oh that my head were w', and mine
18 and our eyelids gush out with w'.
10:13 is a multitude of w' in the heavens,
14: 3 have sent their little ones to the w':
15:18 me as a liar, and as w' that fail?
17: 8 shall be as a tree planted by the w',
13 the Lord, the fountain of living w'.
18:14 the cold flowing w' that come from
31: 9 them to walk by the rivers of w'
41:12 by the great w' that are in Gibeon.
46: 7 whose w' are moved as the rivers?
8 his w' are moved like the rivers;
47: 2 w' rise up out of the north, and
48:34 for the w' also of Nimrim shall be
50:38 A drought is upon her w'; and they
51:13 O thou that dwellest upon many w',
16 is a multitude of w' in the heavens;
55 her waves do roar like great w',
La 3:54 W' flowed over mine head; then I
Eze 1:24 wings, like the noise of great w',
17: 5 he placed it by great w', and set it
8 planted in a good soil by great w',
19:10 in thy blood, planted by the w':
10 of branches by reason of many w'.
26:19 thee, and great w' shall cover thee;
27:26 have brought thee into great w':
34 by the seas in the depths of the w',
31: 4 The w' made him great, the deep
5 because of the multitude of w',
7 for his root was by great w'.
14 none of all the trees by the w' exalt
15 and the great w' were stayed:
32: 2 troubledst the w' with thy feet, and
13 thereof from beside the great w';
14 Then will I make their w' deep, and
34:18 and to have drunk of the deep w',
43: 2 voice was like a noise of many w':
47: 1 w' issued out from under the
1 the w' came down from under from
2 there ran out w' on the right side.
3 and he brought me through the w';
3 the w' were to the ancles.
4 and brought me through the w';
4 the w' were to the knees.
4 through; the w' were to the loins.
5 for the w' were risen, w' to swim in,
8 These w' issue out toward the east
8 the sea, the w' shall be healed.
9 these w' shall come thither:
12 their w' they issued out of the
19 even to the w' of strife in Kadesh,
48:28 unto the w' of strife in Kadesh,
Da 12: 6, 7 was upon the w' of the river,
Joe 1:20 for the rivers of w' are dried up,
3:18 rivers of Judah shall flow with w',
Am 5: 8 that calleth for the w' of the sea,
24 But let judgment run down as w',
9: 6 he that calleth for the w' of the sea,
Jon 2: 5 The w' compassed me about, even
Mic 1: 4 as the w' that are poured down a

Na 3: 8 that had the w' round about it,
14 Draw thee w' for the siege, fortify
Hab 2:14 of the Lord, as the w' cover the sea.
3:15 through the heap of great w'.
Zec 14: 8 w' shall go out from Jerusalem;
M't 8:32 the sea, and perished in the w'.
M'r 9:22 him into the fire, and into the w'.
2Co 11:26 in perils of w', in perils of robbers,
Re 1:15 his voice as the sound of many w'.
7:17 them unto living fountains of w':
8:10 and upon the fountains of w';
11 and the third part of the w' became
11 and many men died of the w',
11: 6 have power over w' to turn them to
14: 2 heaven, as the voice of many w'.
7 the sea, and the fountains of w'.
16: 4 upon...rivers and fountains of w';
5 I heard the angel of the w' say,
17: 1 whore that sitteth upon many w':
15 The w' which thou sawest, where
19: 6 and as the voice of many w',

waterspouts
Ps 42: 7 unto deep at the noise of thy w':

watersprings
Ps 107:33 and the w' into dry ground;
35 and dry ground into w'.

wave See also WAVED; WAVES.
Ex 29:24 shalt w' them...before the Lord.
24 for a w' offering before the Lord.
26 and w' it...before the Lord:
26 for a w' offering before the Lord:
27 the breast of the w' offering,
Le 7:30 for a w' offering before the Lord.
34 w' breast and the heave shoulder
8:27 for a w' offering before the Lord.
29 it for a w' offering before the Lord:
9:21 for a w' offering before the Lord;
10:14 w' breast and heave shoulder shall
15 w' breast shall they bring with the
15 the fat, to w' it...before the Lord;
15 for a w' offering before the Lord;
14:12 and w' them...before the Lord:
12 for a w' offering before the Lord:
24 shall w' them...before the Lord:
24 for a w' offering before the Lord:
23:11 w' the sheaf before the Lord,
11 after...sabbath the priest shall w' it.
12 when ye w' the sheaf an he lamb
15 the sheaf of the w' offering;
17 two w' loaves of two tenth deals:
20 priest shall w' them with the bread
20 for a w' offering before the Lord,
Nu 5:25 w' the offering before the Lord,
6:20 And the priest shall w' them for a
20 for a w' offering before the Lord:
20 the w' breast and heave shoulder:
18:11 the w' offerings of the children of
18 w' breast and as the right shoulder
Jas 1: 6 is like a w' of the sea driven with

waved
Ex 29:27 of the heave offering, which is w',
Le 7:30 the breast may be w' for a wave
8:27 w' them for a wave offering before
29 w' it for a wave offering before the
9:21 Aaron w' for a wave offering before
14:21 for a trespass offering to be w',

wave-loaf See WAVE and LOAF.

wave-offering See WAVE and OFFERING.

wavereth
Jas 1: 6 he that w' is like a wave of the sea

wavering
Heb10:23 profession of our faith without w':
Jas 1: 6 let him ask in faith, nothing w'.

waves
2Sa 22: 5 the w' of death compassed me,
Job 9: 8 treadeth upon the w' of the sea.
38:11 here shall thy proud w' be stayed?
Ps 42: 7 all thy w' and thy billows are gone
65: 7 of the seas, the noise of their w',
88: 7 hast afflicted me with all thy w'.
89: 9 when the w' thereof arise, thou
93: 3 voice; the floods lift up their w'.
4 yea, than the mighty w' of the sea.
107:25 which lifteth up the w' thereof.
29 so that the w' thereof are still.
Isa 48:18 righteousness as the w' of the sea:
51:15 divided the sea, whose w' roared:
Jer 5:22 the w' thereof toss themselves, yet
31:35 the sea when the w' thereof roar;
51:42 with the multitude of the w'
55 her w' do roar like great waters,
Eze 26: 3 the sea causeth his w' to come up.
Jon 2: 3 billows and thy w' passed over me.
Zec 10:11 and shall smite the w' in the sea,
M't 8:24 the ship was covered with the w':
14:24 midst of the sea, tossed with w':
M'r 4:37 the w' beat into the ship, so that it
Lu 21:25 the sea and the w' roaring;
Ac 27:41 broken with the violence of the w'.
Jude 13 Raging w' of the sea, foaming out

wax See also WAXED; WAXEN; WAXETH; WAXING.
Ex 22:24 And my wrath shall w' hot, and I
32:10 that my wrath may w' hot against
11 why doth thy wrath w' hot against
22 not the anger of my lord w' hot:
Le 25:47 if a sojourner or stranger w' rich
47 that dwelleth by him w' poor,
1Sa 3: 2 his eyes began to w' dim, that he
Job 6:17 What time they w' warm, they
14: 8 Though the root thereof w' old in
Ps 22:14 my heart is like w'; it is melted in
68: 2 as w' melteth before the fire, so let
97: 5 The hills melted like w' at the
102:26 all of them shall w' old like a garment;
Isa 17: 4 the fatness of his flesh shall w' lean.
29:22 neither shall his face now w' pale.
50: 9 they all shall w' old as a garment;
51: 6 earth shall w' old like a garment,
Jer 6:24 our hands w' feeble: anguish hath
Mic 1: 4 shall be cleft, as w' before the fire,
M't 24:12 the love of many shall w' cold.
Lu 12:33 yourselves bags which w' not old,
1Ti 5:11 to w' wanton against Christ,*
2Ti 3:13 and seducers shall w' worse and
Heb 1:11 all shall w' old as doth a garment;

waxed See also WAXEN.
Ge 18:12 After I am w' old shall I have
26:13 And the man w' great, and went
41:56 the famine w' sore in the land of
Ex 1: 7 multiplied and w' exceeding mighty;
20 people multiplied, and w' very mighty.
16:21 when the sun w' hot, it melted.
19:19 long, and w' louder and louder,
32:19 Moses' anger w' hot, and he cast
Nu 11:23 Is the Lord's hand w' short? thou
De 8: 4 Thy raiment w' not old upon thee,
32:15 But Jeshurun w' fat, and kicked:
Jos 23: 1 Joshua w' old and stricken in age.
1Sa 2: 5 hath many children is w' feeble.
2Sa 3: 1 David w' stronger and stronger,
1 the house of Saul w' weaker and
21:15 Philistines: and David w' faint.
2Ki 4:34 and the flesh of the child w' warm.
1Ch 11: 9 So David w' greater and greater:
2Ch 13:21 Abijah w' mighty, and married
17:12 And Jehoshaphat w' great
24:15 Jehoiada w' old, and was full of
Ne 9:21 their clothes w' not old, and their
Es 9: 4 Mordecai w' greater and greater.
Ps 32: 3 bones w' old through my roaring
Jer 49:24 Damascus is w' feeble, and
50:43 of them, and his hands w' feeble:
Da 8: 8 Therefore the he goat w' very great:
9 horn, which w' exceeding great,
10 And it w' great, even to the host of
M't 13:15 For this people's heart is w' gross,
Lu 1:80 child grew, and w' strong in spirit,
2:40 child grew, and w' strong in spirit,
13:19 and it grew, and w' a great tree;
Ac 13:46 Then Paul and Barnabas w' bold,
28:27 the heart of this people is w' gross,
Heb 11:34 made strong, w' valiant in fight,
Re 18: 3 merchants of the earth are w' rich

waxen See also WAXED.
Ge 19:13 the cry of them is w' great before
Le 25:25 If thy brother be w' poor, and
35 And if thy brother be w' poor, and
39 that dwelleth by thee be w' poor,
De 29: 5 clothes are not w' old upon you,
5 thy shoe is not w' old upon thy foot.
31:20 and filled themselves, and w' fat;
32:15 thou art w' fat, thou art grown
Jos 17:13 children of Israel were w' strong,
Jer 5:27 are become great, and w' rich.
28 They are w' fat, they shine: yea,
Eze 16: 7 thou hast increased and w' great,

waxeth
Ps 6: 7 it w' old because of all mine
Heb 8:13 and w' old is ready to vanish

waxing
Ph'p 1:14 w' confident by my bonds, are

way^ See also ALWAY; AWAY; CAUSEWAY; HIGHWAY; PATHWAY; STRAIGHTWAY; WAYFARING; WAYMARKS; WAYS; WAYSIDE.
Ge 3:24 sword which turned every w',
24 to keep the w' of the tree of life.
6:12 for all flesh had corrupted his w'
12:19 thy wife, take her, and go thy w'.
14:11 their victuals, and went their w'.
16: 7 by the fountain in the w' to Shur.
18:16 them to bring them on the w'.
19 they shall keep the w' of the Lord,
33 And the Lord went his w', as soon
21:16 over against him a good w' off,
24:27 I being in the w', the Lord led me
40 with thee, and prosper thy w';
42 thou do prosper my w' which I go:
48 had led me in the right w' to take
56 the Lord hath prospered my w';
61 took Rebekah, and went his w'.
62 Isaac came from the w' of the well
25:34 and rose up, and went his w':
28:20 will keep me in this w' that I go,
32: 1 And Jacob went on his w', and the
33:16 that day on his w' unto Seir.
35: 3 with me in the w' which I went.
16 but a little w' to come to Ephrath.
19 was buried in the w' to Ephrath,
38:14 which is by the w' to Timnath;
16 And he turned unto her by the w',
21 that was openly by the w' side?
42:25 to give them provision for the w':
38 if mischief befall him by the w' in
45:21 gave them provision for the w'.
23 and meat for his father by the w'.
24 See that ye fall not out by the w'.
48: 7 in the land of Canaan in the w',
7 a little w' to come unto Ephrath:
7 buried her...in the w' of Ephrath;
49:17 Dan shall be a serpent by the w', an
Ex 2:12 he looked this w' and that w',
4:24 came to pass by the w' in the inn,
5:20 and Aaron, who stood in the w',
13:17 w' of the land of the Philistines,
Ex 13:18 w' of the wilderness of the Red sea:
21 of a cloud, to lead them the w';
18: 8 had come upon them by the w',
20 the w' wherein they must walk,
27 he went his w' unto his own land.
23:20 to keep thee in the w', and to
32: 8 out of the w' which I commanded
33: 3 lest I consume thee in the w'.
13 shew me now thy w', that I may
Nu 13:17 Get you up this w' southward, and
14:25 wilderness by...w' of the Red sea.
20:17 we will go by the king's high w',
19 unto him, We will go by the high w':
21: 1 Israel came by the w' of the spies;
4 Hor by the w' of the Red sea,
4 much discouraged because of the w'.
22 will go along by the king's high w',
33 and went up by the w' of Bashan:
22:22 stood in the w' for an adversary
23 angel of the Lord standing in the w',
23 the ass turned aside out of the w',
23 the ass, to turn her into the w'.
26 no w' to turn either to the right
31 angel of the Lord standing in the w',
32 because thy w' is perverse before,
34 not that thou stoodest in the w'
24:25 place: and Balak also went his w'.
De 1: 2 Horeb by the w' of mount Seir
19 w' of the mountain of the Amorites,
22 again by the w' we must go up,
31 in all the w' that ye went, until ye
33 Who went in the w' before you, to
33 shew you by what w' ye should go,
40 wilderness by the w' of the Red sea.
2: 1 wilderness by the w' of the Red sea,
8 the w' of the plain from Elath,
8 by the w' of the wilderness of Moab.
27 I will go along by the high w', I
3: 1 and went up the w' to Bashan:
6: 7 when thou walkest by the w', and
8: 2 w' which the Lord thy God led thee
9:12 quickly turned aside out of the w'
16 turned aside quickly out of the w'
11:19 when thou walkest by the w', when
28 but turn aside out of the w' which I
30 the w' where the sun goeth down,
13: 5 to thrust thee out of the w' which
14:24 And if the w' be long for thee, so
17:16 henceforth return no more that w'.
19: 3 Thou shalt prepare thee a w', and
6 because the w' is long, and slay
22: 4 ass or his ox fall down by the w',
6 chance to be before thee in the w'
23: 4 bread and with water in the w',
24: 9 God did unto Miriam by the w',
25:17 Amalek did unto thee by the w',
18 How he met thee by the w', and
27:18 the blind to wander out of the w'.
28: 7 shall come out against thee one w',
25 shalt go out one w' against them,
68 the w' whereof I spake unto thee,
31:29 and turn aside from the w' which I
Jos 1: 8 thou shalt make thy w' prosperous,
2: 7 the w' to Jordan unto the fords:
16 and afterward may ye go your w'.
22 sought them throughout all the w',
3: 4 know the w' by which ye must go:
4 have not passed this w' heretofore.
5: 4 died in the wilderness by the w',
5 in the wilderness by the w' as they
7 not circumcised them by the w'.
8:15 fled by the w' of the wilderness.
20 no power to flee this w' or that w':
10:10 w' that goeth up to Beth-horon,
12: 3 the east, the w' to Beth-jeshimoth;
23:14 I am going the w' of all the earth:
24:17 us in all the w' wherein we went,
J'g 2:17 w' which their fathers walked in,
19 doings, nor from their stubborn w'.
22 they will keep the w' of the Lord
5:10 in judgment, and walk by the w'.
8:11 w' of them that dwelt in tents
9:25 that came along that w' by them:
18: 5 w' which we go shall be prosperous.
6 the Lord is your w' wherein ye go.
22 a good w' from the house of Micah,
26 the children of Dan went their w':
19: 5 of bread, and afterward go your w'.
9 morrow get you early on your w',
14 they passed on and went their w';
27 house, and went out to go his w':
20:42 unto the w' of the wilderness;
Ru 1: 7 on the w' to return unto...Judah.
1Sa 1:18 woman went her w', and did eat,
6: 9 goeth up by the w' of his own coast
12 the kine took the straight w'
12 to the w' of Beth-shemesh,
9: 6 shew us our w' that we should go.
8 to the man of God, to tell us our w'.
12:23 teach you the good and the right w':
13:17 unto the w' that leadeth to Ophrah,
18 turned the w' to Beth-horon:
18 turned to the w' of the border that
15: 2 how he laid wait for him in the w',
20 gone the w' which the Lord sent
17:52 fell down by the w' to Shaaraim,
20:22 arrows are beyond thee; go thy w'.
24: 3 came to the sheepcotes by the w',
7 out of the cave, and went on his w'.
25:12 David's young men turned their w',
26: 3 which is before Jeshimon, by the w'.
25 So David went on his w', and Saul
28:22 strength, when thou goest on thy w'.
30: 2 them away, and went on their w'.
2Sa 2:24 the w' of the wilderness of Gibeon.
13:30 to pass, while they were in the w',

2Sa 13: 34 much people by the *w*· of the hill
15: 2 and stood beside the *w*· of the gate:
23 toward the *w*· of the wilderness.
16: 13 David and his men went by the *w*·,
18: 23 Ahimaaz ran by the *w*· of the plain,
19: 36 servant will go a little *w*· over Jordan
22: 31 As for God, his *w*· is perfect;
33 and he maketh my *w*· perfect.
1Ki 1: 49 rose up, and went every man his *w*·.
2: 2 I go the *w*· of all the earth: be thou
4 If thy children take heed to their *w*·,
8: 25 thy children take heed to their *w*·,
32 to bring his *w*· upon his head;
36 good *w*· wherein they should walk,
11: 29 the Shilonite found him in the *w*·;
13: 9 by the same *w*· that thou camest.
10 went another *w*·, and returned not
10 by the *w*· that he came to Beth-el.
12 said unto them, What *w*· went he?
12 seen what *w*· the man of God went,
17 to go by the *w*· that thou camest.
24 a lion met him by the *w*·, and slew
24 and his carcase was cast in the *w*·,
25 and saw the carcase cast in the *w*·,
26 that brought him back from the *w*·
28 and found his carcase cast in the *w*·,
33 returned not from his evil *w*·,
15: 26 and walked in the *w*· of his father,
34 and walked in the *w*· of Jeroboam,
16: 2 hast walked in the *w*· of Jeroboam,
19 in walking in the *w*· of Jeroboam,
26 he walked in all the *w*· of Jeroboam
18: 6 Ahab went one *w*· by himself,
6 and Obadiah went another *w*· by
7 And as Obadiah was in the *w*·,
19: 15 return on thy *w*· to the wilderness
20: 38 and waited for the king by the *w*·,
22: 24 Which *w*· went the Spirit of
52 and walked in the *w*· of his father,
52 and in the *w*· of his mother,
52 and in the *w*· of Jeroboam the son
2Ki 2: 23 and as he was going up by the *w*·,
3: 8 he said, Which *w*· shall we go up?
8 The *w*· through the wilderness of
20 there came water by the *w*· of Edom,
5: 19 So he departed from him a little *w*·.
6: 19 This is not the *w*·, neither is this
7: 15 all the *w*· was full of garments
8: 18 in the *w*· of the kings of Israel,
27 in the *w*· of the house of Ahab,
9: 27 fled by the *w*· of the garden house.
10: 12 at the shearing house in the *w*·,
11: 16 *w*· by the which the horses came
19 by the *w*· of the gate of the guard
16: 3 in the *w*· of the kings of Israel,
19: 28 by the *w*· by which thou camest.
33 By the *w*· that he came, by the same
21: 21 walked in all the *w*· that his father
22 walked not in the *w*· of the Lord.
22: 2 and walked in all the *w*· of David
25: 4 *w*· of the gate between two walls,
4 king went the *w*· toward the plain.
2Ch 6: 16 thy children take heed to their *w*·
23 recompensing his *w*· upon his own
27 thou hast taught them the good *w*·,
34 by the *w*· that thou shalt send them,
11: 17 they walked in the *w*· of David and
18: 23 Which *w*· went the Spirit of the
20: 32 he walked in the *w*· of Asa his
21: 6, 13 in the *w*· of the kings of Israel,
Ezr 8: 21 to seek of him a right *w*· for us,
22 us against the enemy in the *w*·:
31 and of such as lay in wait by the *w*·.
Ne 9: 12 to give them light in the *w*· wherein
19 them by day, to lead them in the *w*·;
19 and the *w*· wherein they should go.
Es 4: 17 So Mordecai went his *w*·, and did
Job 3: 23 given to a man whose *w*· is hid,
6: 18 The paths of their *w*· are turned
8: 19 Behold, this is the joy of his *w*·,
12: 24 a wilderness where there is no *w*·.
16: 22 go the *w*· whence I shall not return.
17: 9 righteous...shall hold on his *w*·,
18: 10 and a trap for him in the *w*·.
19: 8 He hath fenced up my *w*· that I
12 and raise up their *w*· against me,
21: 29 not asked them that go by the *w*·?
31 Who shall declare his *w*· to his face?
22: 15 Hast thou marked the old *w*· which
23: 10 he knoweth the *w*· that I take:
11 his *w*· have I kept, and not
24: 4 They turn the needy out of the *w*·:
18 not the *w*· of the vineyards.
24 are taken out of the *w*· as all other,
28: 23 God understandeth the *w*· thereof,
26 *w*· for the lightning of the thunder:
29: 25 I chose out their *w*·, and sat chief,
31: 7 my step hath turned out of the *w*·,
36: 23 Who hath enjoined him his *w*·?
38: 19 is the *w*· where light dwelleth?
24 By what *w*· is the light parted,
25 a *w*· for the lightning of thunder;
Ps 1: 1 nor standeth in the *w*· of sinners,
6 knoweth the *w*· of the righteous:
6 the *w*· of the ungodly shall perish.
2: 12 angry, and ye perish from the *w*·,
5: 8 make thy *w*· straight before my face.
18: 30 As for God, his *w*· is perfect:
32 strength, and maketh my *w*· perfect.
25: 8 will he teach sinners in the *w*·.
9 and the meek will he teach his *w*·.
12 teach in the *w*· that he shall choose.
27: 11 Teach me thy *w*·, O Lord, and lead
32: 8 thee in the *w*· which thou shalt go:
35: 3 and stop the *w*· against them that
6 Let their *w*· be dark and slippery:
Ps 36: 4 himself in a *w*· that is not good;
37: 5 Commit thy *w*· unto the Lord;
7 of him who prospereth in his *w*·,
23 Lord: and he delighteth in his *w*·.
34 Wait on the Lord, and keep his *w*·,
44: 18 our steps declined from thy *w*·;
49: 13 This their *w*· is their folly: yet
67: 2 thy *w*· may be known upon earth,
77: 13 Thy *w*·, O God, is in the sanctuary:
19 Thy *w*· is in the sea, and thy path
78: 50 He made a *w*· to his anger;
80: 12 they which pass by the *w*· do pluck
85: 13 shall set us in the *w*· of his steps.
86: 11 Teach me thy *w*·, O Lord; I will
89: 41 All that pass by the *w*· spoil him:
101: 2 behave myself wisely in a perfect *w*·.
6 he that walketh in a perfect *w*·, he
102: 23 He weakened my strength in the *w*·;
107: 4 in the wilderness in a solitary *w*·;
7 he led them forth by the right *w*·,
40 the wilderness, where there is no *w*·.
110: 7 shall drink of the brook in the *w*·:
119: 1 Blessed are the undefiled in the *w*·,
9 shall a young man cleanse his *w*·?
14 rejoiced in...*w*· of thy testimonies.
27 to understand the *w*· of thy precepts:
29 Remove from me the *w*· of lying:
30 I have chosen the *w*· of truth: thy
32 run the *w*· of thy commandments,
33 Teach me,...the *w*· of thy statutes;
37 and quicken thou me in thy *w*·.
101 my feet from every evil *w*·,
104 therefore I hate every false *w*·.
128 be right; and I hate every false *w*·.
139: 24 if there be any wicked *w*· in me,
24 and lead me in the *w*· everlasting.
142: 3 In the *w*· wherein I walked have
143: 8 cause me to know the *w*· wherein
146: 9 *w*· of the wicked he turneth upside
Pr 1: 15 walk not thou in the *w*· with them;
31 eat of the fruit of their own *w*·,
2: 8 and preserveth the *w*· of his saints.
12 deliver thee from the *w*· of the evil
20 mayest walk in the *w*· of good men,
3: 23 shalt thou walk in thy *w*· safely,
4: 11 taught thee in the *w*· of wisdom;
14 go not in the *w*· of evil men.
19 *w*· of the wicked is as darkness:
5: 8 Remove thy *w*· far from her, and
6: 23 of instruction are the *w*· of life:
7: 8 and he went the *w*· to her house,
27 Her house is the *w*· to hell, going
8: 2 by the *w*· in the places of the paths.
13 the evil *w*·, and the froward mouth,
20 I lead in the *w*· of righteousness, in
22 me in the beginning of his *w*·,
9: 6 and go in the *w*· of understanding.
10: 17 He is in the *w*· of life that keepeth
29 The *w*· of the Lord is strength to
11: 5 of the perfect shall direct his *w*·:
20 upright in their *w*· are his delight.
12: 15 The *w*· of a fool is right in his own
26 the *w*· of the wicked seduceth them.
28 In the *w*· of righteousness is life;
13: 6 him that is upright in the *w*·:
15 but the *w*· of transgressors is hard.
14: 8 the prudent is to understand his *w*·:
12 a *w*· which seemeth right unto a
15: 9 *w*· of the wicked is an abomination
10 unto him that forsaketh the *w*·:
19 The *w*· of the slothful man is
19 the *w*· of the righteous man is
24 The *w*· of life is above to the wise,
16: 9 A man's heart deviseth his *w*·: but
17 keepeth his *w*· preserveth his soul.
25 *w*· that seemeth right unto a man,
29 him into the *w*· that is not good.
31 be found in the *w*· of righteousness.
19: 3 foolishness of man perverteth his *w*·:
20: 14 but when he is gone his *w*·, then he
24 man then understand his own *w*·?
21: 2 Every *w*· of a man is right in his
8 *w*· of man is froward and strange:
16 man that wandereth out of the *w*· of
29 for the upright, he directeth his *w*·.
22: 5 snares are in the *w*· of the froward:
6 Train up a child in the *w*· he should
23: 19 and guide thine heart in the *w*·.
26: 13 man saith, There is a lion in the *w*·;
28: 10 righteous to go astray in an evil *w*·,
29: 27 and he that is upright in the *w*· is
30: 19 The *w*· of an eagle in the air; the
19 *w*· of a serpent upon a rock; the
19 *w*· of a ship in the midst of the sea;
19 and the *w*· of a man with a maid.
20 Such is the *w*· of an adulterous
Ec 9: 7 Go thy *w*·, eat thy bread with joy,
10: 3 he that is a fool walketh by the *w*·,
11: 5 not what is the *w*· of the spirit,
12: 5 high, and fears shall be in the *w*·,
Isa 3: 12 err, and destroy the *w*· of thy paths.
8: 11 not walk in the *w*· of this people,
9: 1 afflict her by the *w*· of the sea,
15: 5 *w*· of Horonaim they shall raise up
26: 7 The *w*· of the just is uprightness:
8 in the *w*· of thy judgments, O Lord,
28: 7 strong drink are out of the *w*·;
7 of the *w*· through strong drink;
30: 11 Get you out of the *w*·, turn
21 This is the *w*·, walk ye in it,
35: 8 an highway shall be there, and a *w*·,
8 shall be called The *w*· of holiness;
37: 29 the *w*· by which thou camest.
34 By the *w*· that he came, by the
40: 3 Prepare ye the *w*· of the Lord,
14 to him the *w*· of understanding?
Isa 40: 27 My *w*· is hid from the Lord, and my
41: 3 *w*· that he had not gone with his
42: 16 blind by a *w*· that they knew not;
43: 16 which maketh a *w*· in the sea, and
19 even make a *w*· in the wilderness,
48: 15 he shall make his *w*· prosperous.
17 by the *w*· that thou shouldest go.
49: 11 I will make all my mountains a *w*·,
51: 10 a *w*· for the ransomed to pass over?
53: 6 turned every one to his own *w*·;
55: 7 Let the wicked forsake his *w*·, and
56: 11 they all look to their own *w*·, every
57: 10 wearied in the greatness of thy *w*·;
14 ye up, cast ye up, prepare the *w*·,
14 block out of the *w*· of my people.
17 on frowardly in the *w*· of his heart.
59: 8 The *w*· of peace they knew not; and
62: 10 prepare ye the *w*· of the people;
65: 2 walketh in a *w*· that was not good,
Jer 2: 17 God, when he led thee by the *w*·?
18 hast thou to do in the *w*· of Egypt,
18 hast thou to do in the *w*· of Assyria,
23 see thy *w*· in the valley, know what
33 trimmest thou thy *w*· to seek love?
36 about so much to change thy *w*·?
3: 21 for they have perverted their *w*·,
4: 7 of the Gentiles is on his *w*·;
18 Thy *w*· and thy doings have
5: 4 they know not the *w*· of the Lord,
5 they have known the *w*· of the Lord,
6: 16 the old paths, where is the good *w*·,
25 into the field, nor walk by the *w*·;
27 thou mayest know and try their *w*·.
10: 2 Learn not the *w*· of the heathen,
23 that the *w*· of man is not in himself:
12: 1 doth the *w*· of the wicked prosper?
18: 11 ye now every one from his evil *w*·,
15 walk in paths, in a *w*· not cast up;
21: 8 the *w*· of life, and the *w*· of death.
23: 12 their *w*· shall be unto them as
22 have turned them from their evil *w*·,
25: 5 now every one from his evil *w*·,
35 shepherds shall have no *w*· to flee,
26: 3 turn every man from his evil *w*·,
28: 11 the prophet Jeremiah went his *w*·.
31: 9 the rivers of waters in a straight *w*·,
21 even the *w*· which thou wentest:
32: 39 give them one heart, and one *w*·,
35: 15 ye now every man from his evil *w*·,
36: 3 return every man from his evil *w*·;
7 return every one from his evil *w*·:
39: 4 by the *w*· of the king's garden, by
4 and he went out the *w*· of the plain.
42: 3 God may shew us the *w*· wherein
48: 19 of Aroer, stand by the *w*·, and espy:
50: 5 They shall ask the *w*· to Zion with
52: 7 *w*· of the gate between the...walls,
7 they went by the *w*· of the plain.
Eze 3: 18 the wicked from his wicked *w*·,
19 nor from his wicked *w*·, he shall die
7: 27 I will do unto them after their *w*·,
8: 5 eyes now the *w*· toward the north.
5 mine eyes the *w*· toward the north,
9: 2 from the *w*· of the higher gate,
10 I will recompense their *w*· upon
11: 21 I will recompense their *w*· upon
13: 22 not return from his wicked *w*·,
14: 22 shall see their *w*· and their doings:
16: 25 high place at every head of the *w*·,
27 which are ashamed of thy lewd *w*·.
31 place in the head of every *w*·,
43 I also will recompense thy *w*· upon
18: 25 say, The *w*· of the Lord is not equal.
25 Is not my *w*· equal? are not your
29 The *w*· of the Lord is not equal.
21: 16 Go thee one *w*· or other, either on
19 it at the head of the *w*· to the city.
20 Appoint a *w*·, that the sword may
21 stood at the parting of the *w*·,
22: 31 their own *w*· have I recompensed
23: 13 defiled, that they took both one *w*·,
31 hast walked in the *w*· of thy sister;
33: 8 to warn the wicked from his *w*·,
9 warn the wicked of his *w*· to turn
9 if he do not turn from his *w*·, he
11 that the wicked turn from his *w*·
17 The *w*· of the Lord is not equal:
17 as for them, their *w*· is not equal.
20 The *w*· of the Lord is not equal.
36: 17 defiled it by their own *w*· and by
17 their *w*· was before me as the
19 according to their *w*· and according
42: 1 court, the *w*· toward the north:
4 breadth inward, a *w*· of one cubit;
11 And the *w*· before them was like the
12 was a door in the head of the *w*·,
12 even the *w*· directly before the wall
43: 2 Israel came from the *w*· of the east:
4 into the house by the *w*· of the gate
44: 1 brought me back the *w*· of the gate
3 enter by the *w*· of the porch of that
3 shall go out by the *w*· of the same.
4 he me the *w*· of the north gate
46: 2 shall enter by the *w*· of the porch
8 by the *w*· of the porch of that gate,
8 he shall go forth by the *w*· thereof.
9 in by the *w*· of the north gate
9 out by the *w*· of the south gate;
9 entereth by the *w*· of the south gate
9 forth by the *w*· of the north gate:
9 not return by the *w*· of the gate
47: 2 out of the *w*· of the gate northward,
2 and led me about the *w*· without
2 by the *w*· that looketh eastward;
15 the *w*· of Hethlon, as men go to
48: 1 to the coast of the *w*· of Hethlon,

Da 12: 9 And he said, Go thy w', Daniel: for
Ho 2: 6 I will hedge up thy w' with thorns,
6: 9 of priests murder in the w' by
10:13 because thou didst trust in thy w',
13: 7 as a leopard by the w' will I observe
Am 2: 7 and turn aside the w' of the meek:
Jon 3: 8 turn every one from his evil w',
10 that they turned from their evil w';
Na 1: 3 Lord hath his w' in the whirlwind
2: 1 watch the w', make thy loins strong,
Zec 10: 2 they went their w' as a flock, they
Mal 2: 8 But ye are departed out of the w';
3: 1 he shall prepare the w' before me:
M't 2:12 into their own country another w'.
3: 3 Prepare ye the w' of the Lord,
4:15 by the w' of the sea, beyond Jordan,
5:24 gift before the altar, and go thy w';
25 whiles thou art in the w' with him;
7:13 and broad is the w', that leadeth to
14 and narrow is the w', which leadeth
8: 4 but go thy w', shew thyself to the
13 said unto the centurion, Go thy w';
28 no man might pass by that w'.
30 a good w' off from them an herd
10: 5 Go not into the w' of the Gentiles,
11:10 shall prepare thy w' before thee.
13: 4 some seeds fell by the w' side,
19 which received seed by the w' side.
25 sowed tares...and went his w'.
15:32 fasting, lest they faint in the w'.
20: 4 will give you. And they went their w'.
14 Take that thine is, and go thy w':
17 twelve disciples apart in the w',
30 blind men sitting by the w' side,
21: 8 spread their garments in the w';
8 trees, and strawed them in the w'.
19 when he saw a fig tree in the w',
32 came...in the w' of righteousness,
22:16 and teachest the w' of God in truth,
22 and left him, and went their w'.
27:65 go your w', make it as sure as ye can.
M'r 1: 2 shall prepare thy w' before thee.
3 Prepare ye the w' of the Lord,
44 but go thy w', shew thyself to the
2:11 bed, and go thy w' into thine house.
4: 4 he sowed, some fell by the w' side,
15 And these are they by the w' side,
7:29 unto her, For this saying go thy w';
8: 3 houses, they will faint by the w':
27 by the w' he asked his disciples,
9:33 it that ye disputed...by the w'?
34 by the w' they had disputed among
10:17 when he was gone forth into the w',
21 go thy w', sell whatsoever thou hast,
32 in the w' going up to Jerusalem;
52 Go thy w'; thy faith hath made thee
52 and followed Jesus in the w'.
11: 2 Go your w' into the village over
4 they went their w', and found the colt
8 spread their garments in the w':
8 trees, and strawed them in the w'.
12:12 and they left him, and went their w'.
14 teachest the w' of God in truth:
16: 7 But go your w', tell his disciples and
Lu 1:79 guide our feet into the w' of peace.
3: 4 Prepare ye the w' of the Lord,
4:30 through the midst of them went his w',
5:19 find by what w' they might bring him
7:22 Go your w', and tell John what things
27 shall prepare thy w' before thee.
8: 5 he sowed, some fell by the w' side;
12 by the w' side are they that hear;
39 And he went his w', and published
9:57 as they went in the w', a certain
10: 4 and salute no man by the w'.
31 came down a certain priest that w':
12:58 as thou art in the w', give diligence
14:32 the other is yet a great w' off,
15:20 when he was yet a great w' off,
17:19 Arise, go thy w': thy faith hath made
18:35 blind man sat by the w' side
19: 4 to see him: for he was to pass that w'.
32 And they that were sent went their w',
36 they spread their clothes in the w'.
20:21 but teachest the w' of God truly:
22: 4 he went his w', and communed with
24:32 while he talked with us by the w',
35 what things were done in the w',
Joh 1:23 Make straight the w' of the Lord,
4:28 and went her w' into the city,
50 unto him, Go thy w'; thy son liveth.
50 spoken unto him, and he went his w'.
8:21 I go my w', and ye shall seek me,
9: 7 He went his w' therefore, and washed,
10: 1 but climbeth up some other w',
11:28 when she had so said, she went her w',
14: 4 I go ye know, and the w' ye know.
5 and how can we know the w'?
6 I am the w', the truth, and the life:
16: 5 now I go my w' to him that sent me;
18: 8 ye seek me, let these go their w':
Ac 8:26 w' that goeth...from Jerusalem
36 as they went on their w', they came
39 and he went on his w' rejoicing.
9: 2 that if he found any of this w',
15 Go thy w': for he is a chosen
17 Ananias went his w', and entered into
17 that appeared unto thee in the w'
27 how he had seen the Lord in the w',
15: 3 brought on their w' by the church,
16:17 shew unto us the w' of salvation.
18:25 instructed in the w' of the Lord;
26 him the w' of God more perfectly.
19: 9 but spake evil of that w' before the
23 arose no small stir about that w'.
21: 5 we departed and went our w';

Ac 21: 5 and they all brought us on our w',
22: 4 persecuted this w' unto the death,
24:14 after the w' which they call heresy,
22 more perfect knowledge of that w',
25 answered, Go thy w' for this time;
25: 3 laying wait in the w' to kill him.
26:13 I saw in the w' a light from heaven,
Ro 3: 2 Much every w': chiefly, because
12 They are all gone out of the w', they
17 w' of peace have they not known:
14:13 an occasion to fall in his brother's w'.
15:24 be brought on my w' thitherward
1Co 10:13 temptation...make a w' to escape,
12:31 I unto you a more excellent w'.
16: 7 I will not see you now by the w';
2Co 1:16 brought on my w' toward Judæa.
Ph'p 1:18 every w', whether in pretence, or
Col 2:14 took it out of the w', nailing it to
1Th 3:11 Christ, direct our w' unto you.
2Th 2: 7 until he be taken out of the w'.
Heb 5: 2 on them that are out of the w';
9: 8 the w' into the holiest of all was
10:20 By a new and living w', which he
12:13 is lame be turned out of the w';
Jas 1:24 beholdeth himself, and goeth his w',
2:25 had sent them out another w'?
5:20 the sinner from the error of his w'
2Pe 2: 2 w' of truth shall be evil spoken of.
15 Which have forsaken the right w',
15 following the w' of Balaam the son
21 known the w' of righteousness,
3: 1 minds by w' of remembrance:
Jude 11 they have gone in the w' of Cain,
Re 16:12 the w' of the kings of the east

wayfaring
J'g 19:17 he saw a w' man in the street of
2Sa 12: 4 the w' man that was come unto him;
Isa 33: 8 lie waste, the w' man ceaseth:
35: 8 the w' men, though fools,
Jer 9: 2 a lodging place of w' men;
14: 8 as a w' man that turneth aside to

waymarks
Jer 31:21 Set thee up w', make thee high

ways See also ALWAYS; HIGHWAYS.
Ge 19: 2 rise up early, and go on your w'.
Le 20: 4 people...do any w' hide their eyes
26:22 your high w' shall be desolate.
Nu 30:15 if he shall any w' make them void
De 5:33 walk in all the w' which the Lord
8: 6 to walk in his w', and to fear him.
10:12 to walk in all his w', and to love
11:22 to walk in all his w', and to cleave
19: 9 thy God, and to walk ever in his w';
26:17 to walk in his w', and to keep his
28: 7 way, and flee before thee seven w'.
9 Lord thy God, and walk in his w'.
25 and flee seven w' before them:
29 thou shalt not prosper in thy w':
30:16 to walk in his w', and to keep his
32: 4 for all his w' are judgment:
Jos 22: 5 to walk in all his w', and to keep
1Sa 8: 3 And his sons walked not in his w',
5 and thy sons walk not in thy w':
18:14 behaved...wisely in all his w';
2Sa 22:22 For I have kept the w' of the Lord,
1Ki 2: 3 God, to walk in his w', to keep his
3:14 And if thou wilt walk in my w', to
8:39 to every man according to his w',
58 to walk in all his w', and to keep
11:33 and have not walked in my w', to do
38 and wilt walk in my w', and do that
22:43 he walked in all the w' of Asa his
2Ki 17:13 Turn ye from your evil w', and
2Ch 6:30 every man according unto all his w',
31 to walk in thy w', so long as they
7:14 and turn from their wicked w';
13:22 acts of Abijah, and his w', and his
17: 3 in the first w' of his father David,
6 was lifted up in the w' of the Lord:
21:12 walked in the w' of Jehoshaphat
12 nor in the w' of Asa king of Judah,
22: 3 in the w' of the house of Ahab:
27: 6 prepared his w' before the Lord
7 acts of Jotham,...and his w',
28: 2 in the w' of the kings of Israel,
26 the rest of his acts and of all his w',
32:13 any w' able to deliver their lands
34: 2 and walked in the w' of David his
Job 4: 6 and the uprightness of thy w'?
13:15 maintain mine own w' before him.
21:14 desire not the knowledge of thy w'.
22: 3 that thou makest thy w' perfect?
28 the light shall shine upon thy w'.
24:13 they know not the w' thereof, nor
23 yet his eyes are upon their w'.
26:14 these are parts of his w': but how
30:12 me the w' of their destruction.
31: 4 Doth not he see my w', and count
34:11 man to find according to his w'.
21 his eyes are upon the w' of man,
27 would not consider any of his w':
40:19 He is the chief of the w' of God:
Ps 10: 5 His w' are always grievous;
18:21 For I have kept the w' of the Lord,
25: 4 Shew me thy w', O Lord; teach me
39: 1 I said, I will take heed to my w',
51:13 will I teach transgressors thy w';
81:13 and Israel had walked in my w'!
84: 5 in whose heart are the w' of them.
91:11 thee, to keep thee in all thy w'.
95:10 and they have not known my w':
103: 7 He made known his w' unto Moses,
119: 3 do no iniquity: they walk in his w'.
5 O that my w' were directed to keep

Ps 119:15 and have respect unto thy w'.
26 I have declared my w', and thou
59 I thought on my w', and turned my
168 for all my w' are before thee.
125: 5 as turn aside unto their crooked w',
128: 1 the Lord; that walketh in his w'.
138: 5 shall sing in the w' of the Lord:
139: 3 and art acquainted with all my w'.
145:17 The Lord is righteous in all his w',
Pr 1:19 the w' of every one that is greedy of
2:13 to walk in the w' of darkness;
15 Whose w' are crooked, and they
3: 6 In all thy w' acknowledge him,
17 Her w' are w' of pleasantness, and
31 and choose none of his w'.
4:26 and let all thy w' be established.
5: 6 path of life, her w' are moveable,
21 the w' of man are before the eyes
6: 6 consider her w', and be wise:
7:25 not thine heart decline to her w',
8:32 blessed are they that keep my w'.
9:15 passengers...go right on their w':
10: 9 he that perverteth his w' shall be
14: 2 but he that is perverse in his w'
12 the end thereof are the w' of death.
14 shall be filled with his own w':
16: 2 All the w' of a man are clean in his
7 When a man's w' please the Lord,
25 the end thereof are the w' of death.
17:23 to pervert the w' of judgment.
19:16 that despiseth his w' shall die.
22:25 Lest thou learn his w', and get a
23:26 and let thine eyes observe my w'.
28: 6 than he that is perverse in his w',
18 that is perverse in his w' shall fall
31: 3 nor thy w' to that which destroyeth
27 well to the w' of her household,
Ec 11: 9 and walk in the w' of thine heart,
Ca 3: 2 in the broad w' I will seek him
Isa 2: 3 and he will teach us of his w', and
42:24 for they would not walk in his w',
45:13 and I will direct all his w':
49: 9 They shall feed in the w', and their
55: 8 neither are your w' my w', saith
9 so are my w' higher than your w',
57:18 I have seen his w', and will heal
58: 2 daily, and delight to know my w',
13 not doing thine own w', nor finding
63:17 thou made us to err from thy w',
64: 5 that remember thee in thy w':
66: 3 they have chosen their own w', and
Jer 2:23 swift dromedary traversing her w';
33 also taught the wicked ones thy w'.
3: 2 In the w' hast thou sat for them, as
13 scattered thy w' to the strangers
6:16 Stand ye in the w', and see, and ask
7: 3 Amend your w' and your doings,
5 amend your w' and your doings;
23 walk ye in all the w' that I have
12:16 diligently learn the w' of my people,
15: 7 since they return not from their w'.
16:17 For mine eyes are upon all their w':
17:10 give every man according to his w',
18:11 and make your w' and your doings
15 caused them to stumble in their w'
23:12 as slippery w' in the darkness:
26:13 amend your w' and your doings,
32:19 upon all the w' of the sons of men:
19 give every one according to his w',
La 1: 4 The w' of Zion do mourn, because
3: 9 inclosed my w' with hewn stone,
11 He hath turned aside my w', and
40 Let us search and try our w', and
Eze 7: 3 will judge thee according to thy w',
4 will recompense thy w' upon thee,
8 will judge thee according to thy w',
9 recompense thee according to thy w'
14:23 ye see their w' and their doings:
16:47 hast thou not walked after their w',
47 more than they in all thy w'.
61 Then thou shalt remember thy w',
18:23 that he should return from his w',
25 equal? are not your w' unequal?
29 of Israel, are not my w' equal?
29 are not your w' unequal?
30 every one according to his w',
20:43 there shall ye remember your w',
44 not according to your wicked w',
21:19 son of man, appoint thee two w',
21 at the head of the two w', to use
24:14 according to thy w', and according
28:15 Thou wast perfect in thy w' from
33:11 turn ye, turn ye from your evil w';
20 will judge you every one after his w'.
36:31 ye remember your own evil w',
32 and confounded for your own w',
Da 4:37 are truth, and his w' judgment:
5:23 whose are all thy w', hast thou not
Ho 4: 9 I will punish them for their w',
9: 8 is a snare of a fowler in all his w',
12: 2 punish Jacob according to his w';
14: 9 for the w' of the Lord are right, and
Joe 2: 7 shall march every one on his w', and
Mic 4: 2 he will teach us of his w', and we
Na 2: 4 against another in the broad w':
Hab 3: 6 did bow: his w' are everlasting.
Hag 1: 5,7 Lord of hosts; Consider your w'.
Zec 1: 4 Turn ye now from your evil w',
6 to do unto us, according to our w',
3: 7 If thou wilt walk in my w', and if
Mal 2: 9 as ye have not kept my w', but
M't 8:33 fled, and went their w' into the city,
22: 5 made light of it, and went their w',
M'r 11: 4 in a place where two w' met;
Lu 1:76 face of the Lord to prepare his w';
3: 5 the rough w' shall be made smooth

Lu 10: 3 Go your w·: behold, I send you forth
10 go your w· out into the streets of
Joh 11: 46 them went their w· to the Pharisees,
Ac 2: 28 made known to me the w· of life;
13: 10 not cease to pervert the right w· of
14: 16 all nations to walk in their own w·.
Ro 3: 16 and misery are in their w·:
11: 33 and his w· past finding out!
1Co 4: 17 of my w· which be in Christ,
Heb 3: 10 and they have not known my w·.
Jas 1: 8 man is unstable in all his w·.
11 the rich man fade away in his w·.
2Pe 2: 2 shall follow their pernicious w·;
Re 15: 3 just and true are thy w·, thou King
16: 1 Go your w·, and pour out the vials of

wayside See also WAY and SIDE.
1Sa 4: 13 Eli sat upon a seat by the w·
Ps 140: 5 have spread a net by the w·;

weak See also WEAKER.
Nu 13: 18 whether they be strong or w·,
J'g 16: 7, 11 then shall I be w·, and be as
17 I shall become w·, and be like any
2Sa 3: 39 And I am this day w·, though
17: 2 while he is weary and w· handed,
2Ch 15: 7 and let not your hands be w·:
Job 4: 3 hast strengthened the w· hands.
Ps 6: 2 upon me, O Lord; for I am w·:
109: 24 My knees are w· through fasting;
Isa 14: 10 Art thou also become w· as we?
35: 3 Strengthen ye the w· hands, and
Eze 7: 17 all knees shall be w· as water.
16: 30 How w· is thine heart, saith the
21: 7 all knees shall be w· as water:
Joe 3: 10 let the w· say, I am strong.
M't 26: 41 is willing, but the flesh is w·.
M'r 14: 38 truly is ready, but the flesh is w·.
Ac 20: 35 ye ought to support the w·,
Ro 4: 19 being not w· in faith, he considered
8: 3 in that it was w· through the flesh,
14: 1 Him that is w· in the faith receive
2 another, who is w·, eateth herbs.
21 or is offended, or is made w·.
15: 1 to bear the infirmities of the w·,
1Co 1: 27 chosen the w· things of the world
4: 10 we are w·, but ye are strong;
8: 7 their conscience being w· is defiled.
9 stumblingblock to them that are w·.
10 the conscience of him which is w·
11 shall the w· brother perish,
12 and wound their w· conscience,
9: 22 To the w· became I as w·,
22 that I might gain the w·: I am
11: 30 many are w· and sickly among you,
2Co 10: 10 but his bodily presence is w·, and
11: 21 as though we had been w·.
29 Who is w·, and I am not w·? who is
12: 10 for when I am w·, then am I strong.
13: 3 which to you-ward is not w·, but is
4 For we also are w· in him, but we
9 when we are w·, and ye are strong:
Ga 4: 9 to the w· and beggarly elements,
1Th 5: 14 support the w·, be patient toward

weaken See also WEAKENED; WEAKENETH.
Isa 14: 12 which didst w· the nations!

weakened
Ezr 4: 4 w· the hands of...people of Judah,
Ne 6: 9 hands shall be w· from the work,
Ps 102: 23 He w· my strength in the way; he

weakeneth
Job 12: 21 w· the strength of the mighty.
Jer 38: 4 he w· the hands of the men of war

weaker
2Sa 3: 1 house of Saul waxed w· and w·.
1Pe 3: 7 the wife, as unto the w· vessel,

weak-handed See WEAK and HANDED.

weakness
1Co 1: 25 w· of God is stronger than men.
2: 3 I was with you in w·, and in fear,
15: 43 it is sown in w·; it is raised in power:
2Co 12: 9 my strength is made perfect in w·.
13: 4 though he was crucified through w·,
Heb 7: 18 for the w· and unprofitableness
11: 34 out of w· were made strong,

wealth See also COMMONWEALTH.
Ge 34: 29 their w·, and all their little ones,
De 8: 17 mine hand hath gotten me this w·.
18 he that giveth thee power to get w·,
Ru 2: 1 a mighty man of w·, of the family
1Sa 2: 32 the w· which God shall give Israel:
2Ki 15: 20 even of all the mighty men of w·,
2Ch 1: 11 not asked riches, w·, or honour,
12 I will give thee riches, and w·, and
Ezr 9: 12 nor seek their peace or their w·
Es 10: 3 seeking the w· of his people, and
Job 21: 13 They spend their days in w·, and in
31: 25 rejoiced because my w· was great,
Ps 44: 12 not increase thy w· by their price.
49: 6 They that trust in their w·, and
10 perish, and leave their w· to others.
112: 3 W· and riches...be in his house:
Pr 5: 10 strangers be filled with thy w·;
10: 15 rich man's w· is his strong city:
13: 11 W· gotten by vanity shall be
22 the w· of the sinner is laid up for
18: 11 rich man's w· is his strong city,
19: 4 W· maketh many friends; but the
Ec 5: 19 God hath given riches and w·,
6: 2 to whom God hath given riches, w·,
Zec 14: 14 w· of all the heathen round about
Ac 19: 25 that by this craft we have our w·.
1Co 10: 24 his own, but every one another's w·.

wealthy
Ps 66: 12 broughtest us out into a w· place.
Jer 49: 31 get you up unto the w· nation,

weaned
Ge 21: 8 And the child grew, and was w·:
8 the same day that Isaac was w·.
1Sa 1: 22 will not go up until the child be w·,
23 tarry until thou have w· him;
23 gave her son suck until she w· him.
24 And when she had w· him, she
1Ki 11: 20 Tahpenes w· in Pharaoh's house:
Ps 131: 2 as a child that is w· of his mother:
2 my soul is even as a w· child.
Isa 11: 8 w· child shall put his hand on the
28: 9 them that are w· from the milk,
Ho 1: 8 Now when she had w· Lo-ruhamah,

weapon See also WEAPONS.
Nu 35: 18 smite him with an hand w· of
De 23: 13 shalt have a paddle upon thy w·;
2Ch 23: 10 man having his w· in his hand,
Ne 4: 17 and with the other hand held a w·.
Job 20: 24 He shall flee from the iron w·, and
Isa 54: 17 No w· that is formed against thee
Eze 9: 1 with his destroying w· in his hand.
2 man a slaughter w· in his hand;

weapons
Ge 27: 3 therefore take, I pray thee, thy w·,
De 1: 41 girded on every man his w· of war,
J'g 18: 11 six hundred men appointed with w·
16 men appointed with their w· of war,
17 that were appointed with w· of war.
1Sa 21: 8 my sword nor my w· with me,
2Sa 1: 27 fallen, and the w· of war perished!
2Ki 11: 8 every man with his w· in his hand:
11 every man with his w· in his hand,
2Ch 23: 7 every man with his w· in his hand;
Ec 9: 18 Wisdom is better than w· of war:
Isa 13: 5 and the w· of his indignation, to
Jer 21: 4 I will turn back the w· of war that
22: 7 against thee, every one with his w·:
50: 25 forth the w· of his indignation:
51: 20 art my battle axe and w· of war:
Eze 32: 27 down to hell with their w· of war:
39: 9 shall set on fire and burn the w·,
10 for they shall burn the w· with fire:
Joh 18: 3 with lanterns and torches and w·.
2Co 10: 4 w· of our warfare are not carnal,

wear See also WARE; WEARETH; WEARING.
Ex 18: 18 Thou wilt surely w· away, both
De 22: 5 woman shall not w· that which
11 not w· a garment of divers sorts,
1Sa 2: 28 incense, to w· an ephod before me?
22: 18 persons that did w· a linen ephod.
Es 6: 8 brought which the king useth to w·,
Job 14: 19 The waters w· the stones: thou
Isa 4: 1 bread, and w· our own apparel:
Da 7: 25 w· out the saints of the most High,
Zec 13: 4 w· a rough garment to deceive:
M't 11: 8 they that w· soft clothing are in
Lu 9: 12 when the day began to w· away,

weareth
Jas 2: 3 to him that w· the gay clothing,

wearied
Ge 19: 11 w· themselves to find the door.
Isa 43: 23 offering, nor w· thee with incense.
24 hast w· me with thine iniquities.
47: 13 Thou art w· in the multitude of
57: 10 w· in the greatness of thy way:
Jer 4: 31 soul is w· because of murderers.
12: 5 and they have w· thee, then how
5 thou trustedst, they w· thee,
Eze 24: 12 She hath w· herself with lies, and
Mic 6: 3 wherein have I w· thee? testify
Mal 2: 17 w· the Lord with your words.
17 ye say, Wherein have we w· him?
Joh 4: 6 being w· with his journey, sat
Heb 12: 3 ye be w· and faint in your minds.

wearieth
Job 37: 11 by watering he w· the thick cloud:
Ec 10: 15 the foolish w· every one of them,

weariness
Ec 12: 12 much study is a w· of the flesh.
Mal 1: 13 said also, Behold, what a w· is it!
2Co 11: 27 In w· and painfulness, in

wearing
1Sa 14: 3 priest in Shiloh, w· an ephod.
Joh 19: 5 Jesus forth, w· the crown of thorns,
1Pe 3: 3 plaiting the hair, and of w· of gold,

wearisome
Job 7: 3 and w· nights are appointed to me.

weary See also WEARIED; WEARIETH; WEARISOME.
Ge 27: 46 I am w· of my life because of the
De 25: 18 when thou wast faint and w·;
J'g 4: 21 for he was fast asleep and w·.
8: 15 bread unto thy men that are w·?
2Sa 16: 14 that were with him, came w·,
17: 2 upon him while he is w· and weak
29 The people is hungry, and w·,
23: 10 Philistines until his hand was w·,
Job 3: 17 and there the w· be at rest.
10: 1 My soul is w· of my life; I will
16: 7 But now he hath made me w·:
22: 7 not given water to the w· to drink,
Ps 6: 6 I am w· with my groaning; all the
68: 9 thine inheritance, when it was w·.
69: 3 I am w· of my crying: my throat
Pr 3: 11 neither be w· of his correction:
25: 17 lest he be w· of thee, and so hate
Isa 1: 14 unto me; I am w· to bear them.
5: 27 None shall be w· nor stumble

Isa 7: 13 a small thing for you to w· men,
13 but will ye w· my God also?
16: 12 that Moab is w· on the high place,
28: 12 ye may cause the w· to rest;
32: 2 shadow of a great rock in a w· land.
40: 28 earth, fainteth not, neither is w·?
30 the youths shall faint and be w·,
31 they shall run, and not be w·; and
43: 22 thou hast been w· of me, O Israel.
46: 1 they are a burden to the w· beast.
50: 4 word in season to him that is w·:
Jer 2: 24 all they that seek her will not w·
6: 11 the Lord; I am w· with holding in:
9: 5 w· themselves to commit iniquity.
15: 6 thee, I am w· with repenting.
20: 9 I was w· with forbearing, and I
31: 25 For I have satiated the w· soul,
51: 58 in the fire, and they shall be w·.
64 upon her: and they shall be w·.
Hab 2: 13 the people shall w· themselves for
Lu 18: 5 her continual coming she w· me.
Ga 6: 9 And let us not be w· in well doing:
2Th 3: 13 brethren, be not w· in well doing.

weasel
Le 11: 29 the w·, and the mouse, and the

weather
Job 37: 22 Fair w· cometh out of the north:
Pr 25: 20 taketh away a garment in cold w·,
M't 16: 2 evening, ye say, It will be fair w·:
3 morning, It will be foul w· to day:

weave See also WEAVEST; WOVE; WOVEN.
Isa 19: 9 and they that w· networks, shall be
59: 5 eggs, and w· the spider's web:

weaver See also WEAVER'S.
Ex 35: 35 and in fine linen, and of the w·,
Isa 38: 12 I have cut off like a w· my life: he

weaver's
1Sa 17: 7 of his spear was like a w· beam;
2Sa 21: 19 of whose spear was like a w· beam.
1Ch 11: 23 hand was a spear like a w· beam;
20: 5 spear staff was like a w· beam.
Job 7: 6 days are swifter than a w· shuttle,

weavest
J'g 16: 13 If thou w· the seven locks of my

web See also WEBS.
J'g 16: 13 locks of my head with the w·.
14 pin of the beam, and with the w·.
Job 8: 14 whose trust shall be a spider's w·.
Isa 59: 5 eggs, and weave the spider's w·:

webs
Isa 59: 6 w· shall not become garments,

wed See WEDDING; WEDLOCK.

wedding
M't 22: 3 them that were bidden to the w·:
8 The w· is ready, but they which
10 the w· was furnished with guests.
11 which had not on a w· garment:
12 in hither not having a w· garment?
Lu 12: 36 when he will return from the w·;
14: 8 thou art bidden of any man to a w·,

wedge
Jos 7: 21 w· of gold of fifty shekels weight,
24 the w· of gold, and his sons, and his
Isa 13: 12 a man than the golden w· of Ophir.

wedlock
Eze 16: 38 as women that break w· and shed

weeds
Jon 2: 5 w· were wrapped about my head.

week See also WEEKS.
Ge 29: 27 Fulfil her w·, and we will give thee
28 Jacob did so, and fulfilled her w·:
Da 9: 27 the covenant with many for one w·:
27 and in the midst of the w· he shall
M't 28: 1 toward the first day of the w·,
M'r 16: 2 the morning the first day of the w·,
9 risen early the first day of the w·,
Lu 18: 12 I fast twice in the w·, I give tithes
24: 1 Now upon the first day of the w·,
Joh 20: 1 the first day of the w· cometh Mary
19 being the first day of the w·, when
Ac 20: 7 And upon the first day of the w·,
1Co 16: 2 Upon the first day of the w· let every

weeks
Ex 34: 22 thou shalt observe the feast of w·,
Le 12: 5 then she shall be unclean two w·,
Nu 28: 26 after your w· be out, ye shall have
De 16: 9 Seven w· shalt thou number unto
9 begin to number the seven w· from
10 keep the feast of w· unto the Lord
16 in the feast of w·, and in the feast
2Ch 8: 13 in the feast of w·, and in the feast
Jer 5: 24 us the appointed w· of the harvest.
Da 9: 24 Seventy w· are determined upon
25 the Prince shall be seven w·,
25 and threescore and two w·: the
26 threescore and two w· shall Messiah
10: 2 Daniel was mourning three full w·.
3 till three whole w· were fulfilled.

weep See also WEEPEST; WEEPETH; WEEPING; WEPT.
Ge 23: 2 mourn for Sarah, and to w· for her.
43: 30 and he sought where to w·; and he
Nu 11: 10 people w· throughout their families,
13 for they w· unto me, saying, Give
1Sa 11: 5 What aileth the people that they w·?
30: 4 until they had no more power to w·.
2Sa 1: 24 daughters of Israel, w· over Saul,
12: 21 thou didst fast and w· for the child,
2Ch 34: 27 rend thy clothes, and w· before me;
Ne 8: 9 Lord your God; mourn not, nor w·.

Job 27:15 death: and his widows shall not w'.
30:25 Did not I w' for him that was in
31 organ into the voice of them that w'.
Ec 3: 4 A time to w', and a time to laugh;
Isa 15: 2 to Dibon, the high places, to w':
22: 4 I will w' bitterly, labour not to
30:19 thou shalt w' no more: he will be
33: 7 the ambassadors of peace shall w'
Jer 9: 1 that I might w' day and night for
13:17 my soul shall w' in secret places for
17 and mine eye shall w' sore, and
22:10 W' ye not for the dead, neither
10 w' sore for him that goeth away:
48:32 will w' for thee with the weeping of
La 1:16 For these things I w'; mine eye,
Eze 24:16 neither shalt thou mourn nor w',
23 ye shall not mourn nor w'; but ye
27:31 shall w' for thee with bitterness
Joe 1: 5 Awake, ye drunkards, and w'; and
2:17 w' between the porch and the altar,
Mic 1:10 ye it not at Gath, w' ye not at all;
Zec 7: 3 Should I w' in the fifth month,
M'r 5:39 Why make ye this ado, and w'?
Lu 6:21 Blessed are ye that w' now: for ye
25 now! for ye shall mourn and w'.
7:13 on her, and said unto her, W' not.
8:52 he said, W' not; she is not dead,
23:28 Daughters of Jerusalem, w' not for
28 but w' for yourselves, and for your
Joh 11:31 She goeth unto the grave to w'
16:20 you, That ye shall w' and lament,
Ac 21:13 What mean ye to w' and to break
Ro 12:15 rejoice, and w' with them that w'.
1Co 7:30 they that w', as though they wept
Jas 4: 9 Be afflicted, and mourn, and w':
5: 1 w' and howl for your miseries that
Re 5: 5 W' not: behold, the Lion of the tribe
18:11 merchants of the earth shall w'

weepest
1Sa 1: 8 to her, Hannah, why w' thou?
Joh 20:13,15 unto her, Woman, why w' thou?

weepeth
2Sa 19: 1 w' and mourneth for Absalom.
2Ki 8:12 And Hazael said, Why w' my lord?
Ps 126: 6 He that goeth forth and w', bearing
La 1: 2 She w' sore in the night, and her

weeping
Nu 25: 6 were w' before the door of the
De 34: 8 days of w' and mourning for Moses
2Sa 3:16 husband went with her along w'
15:30 they went up, w' as they went up.
Ezr 3:13 the noise of the w' of the people:
10: 1 w' and casting himself down
Es 4: 3 and fasting, and w', and wailing;
Job 16:16 My face is foul with w', and on my
Ps 6: 8 Lord hath heard the voice of my w'.
30: 5 w' may endure for a night, but joy
102: 9 and mingled my drink with w',
Isa 15: 3 one shall howl, w' abundantly.
5 Luhith with w' shall they go it up;
16: 9 I will bewail with the w' of Jazer
22:12 did the Lord God of hosts call to w',
65:19 voice of w' shall be no more heard
Jer 3:21 w' and supplications of the
9:10 will I take up a w' and wailing,
31: 9 They shall come with w', and with
15 Ramah, lamentation, and bitter w';
15 Rahel w' for her children refused
16 Refrain thy voice from w', and
41: 6 them, w' all along as he went:
48: 5 Luhith continual w' shall go up;
32 weep for thee with the w' of Jazer:
50: 4 of Judah together, going and w':
Eze 8:14 there sat women w' for Tammuz.
Joe 2:12 fasting, and with w', and with
Mal 2:13 with tears, with w', and with crying
M't 2:18 lamentation, and w', and great
18 Rachel w' for her children, and
8:12 shall be w' and gnashing of teeth.
22:13 shall be w' and gnashing of teeth.
24:51 shall be w' and gnashing of teeth.
25:30 shall be w' and gnashing of teeth.
Lu 7:38 stood at his feet behind him w',
13:28 shall be w' and gnashing of teeth,
Joh 11:33 When Jesus therefore saw her w',
33 Jews also w' which came with her,
20:11 stood without at the sepulchre w':
Ac 9:39 and all the widows stood by him w',
Ph'p 3:18 often, and now tell you even w',
Re 18:15 fear of her torment, w' and wailing,
19 w' and wailing, saying, Alas, alas

weigh See also WEIGHED; WEIGHETH; WEIGHING.
1Ch 20: 2 and found it to w' a talent of gold,
Ezr 8:29 ye w' them before the chief of the
Ps 58: 2 ye w' the violence of your hands
Isa 26: 7 dost w' the path of the just.
46: 6 w' silver in the balance, and hire
Eze 5: 1 then take thee balances to w', and

weighed See also UNWEIGHED.
Ge 23:16 Abraham w' to Ephron the silver,
Nu 7:85 all the silver vessels w' two thousand
1Sa 2: 3 and by him actions are w'.
17: 7 spear's head w' six hundred shekels of
2Sa 14:26 he w' the hair of his head at two
21:16 spear w' three hundred shekels
Ezr 8:25 And w' unto them the silver, and
26 I even w' unto their hand six
33 the vessels w' in the house of our
Job 6: 2 that my grief were throughly w',
28:15 silver be w' for the price thereof.
31: 6 Let me be w' in an even balance,
Isa 40:12 and w' the mountains in scales,
Jer 32: 9 w' him the money, even seventeen
Jer 32:10 w' him the money in the balances.
Da 5:27 Thou art w' in the balances, and
Zec 11:12 they w' for my price thirty pieces

weigheth
Job 28:25 he w' the waters by measure.
Pr 16: 2 eyes; but the Lord w' the spirits.

weighing
Nu 7:85 charges of silver w' an hundred and
86 full of incense, w' ten shekels apiece,

weight See also WEIGHTS.
Ge 24:22 golden earring of half a shekel w',
22 her hands of ten shekels w' of gold;
43:21 of his sack, our money in full w':
Ex 30:34 of each shall there be a like w':
Le 19:35 in meteyard, in w', or in measure.
26:26 deliver you your bread again by w':
Nu 7:13, 19, 25 w' whereof was an hundred
31 charger of the w' of an hundred
37 w' whereof was an hundred and
43 charger of the w' of an hundred
49 w' whereof was an hundred and
55 charger of the w' of an hundred
61, 67, 73, 79 w' whereof was an
De 25:15 shalt have a perfect and just w', a
Jos 7:21 wedge of gold of fifty shekels w',
J'g 8:26 w' of the golden earrings that he
1Sa 17: 5 w' of the coat was five thousand
2Sa 12:30 the w' thereof was a talent of gold
14:26 hundred shekels after the king's w'.
21:16 the w' of whose spear weighed
16 hundred shekels of brass in w',
1Ki 7:47 neither was the w' of the brass
10:14 Now the w' of gold that came to
2Ki 25:16 of all these vessels was without w'.
1Ch 21:25 six hundred shekels of gold by w'.
22: 3 brass in abundance without w';
14 and of brass and iron without w';
28:14 of gold by w' for things of gold, for
14 for all instruments of silver by w',
15 Even the w' for the candlesticks of
15 of gold, by w' for every candlestick,
15 for the candlesticks of silver by w',
16 by w' he gave gold for the tables of
17 he gave gold by w' for every bason;
17 silver by w' for every bason of
18 altar of incense refined gold by w';
2Ch 3: 9 And the w' of the nails was fifty
4:18 for the w' of the brass could not be
9:13 Now the w' of gold that came to
Ezr 8:30 and the Levites the w' of the silver,
34 By number and by w' of every one:
34 and all the w' was written at that
Job 28:25 To make the w' for the winds; and
Pr 11: 1 Lord: but a just w' is his delight.
16:11 A just w' and balance are the
Jer 52:20 all these vessels was without w'.
Eze 4:10 thou shalt eat shall be by w',
16 and they shall eat bread by w',
Zec 5: 8 he cast the w' of lead upon the
Joh 19:39 aloes, about an hundred pound w'.
2Co 4:17 exceeding and eternal w' of glory;
Heb 12: 1 let us lay aside every w', and the
Re 16:21 every stone about the w' of a talent:

weightier
M't 23:23 omitted the w' matters of the law,

weights^
Le 19:36 Just balances, just w', a just
Pr 16:11 all the w' of the bag are his work.
20:10 Divers w', and divers measures,
23 Divers w' are an abomination unto
Mic 6:11 and with the bag of deceitful w'?

weighty See also WEIGHTIER.
Pr 27: 3 A stone is heavy, and the sand w';
2Co 10:10 his letters, say they, are w' and

welfare
Ge 43:27 he asked them of their w', and
Ex 18: 7 they asked each other of their w';
1Ch 18:10 to king David, to enquire of his w',
Ne 2:10 the w' of the children of Israel.
Job 30:15 my w' passeth away as a cloud.
Ps 69:22 should have been for their w',
Jer 38: 4 seeketh not the w' of this people,

well^ See also FAREWELL; WELFARE; WELL-BELOVED; WELLFAVOURED; WELLPLEASING; WELL'S; WELLS; WELLSPRING.
Ge 4: 7 If thou doest w', shalt thou not be
7 if thou doest not w', sin lieth at the
12:13 it may be w' with me for thy sake;
16 And he entreated Abram w' for her
13:10 of Jordan, that it was w' watered
16:14 the w' was called Beer-lahai-roi;
18:11 were old and w' stricken in age;
21:19 her eyes, and she saw a w' of water;
25 Abimelech because of a w' of water,
30 unto me, that I have digged this w'.
24: 1 was old, and w' stricken in age:
11 by a w' of water at the time of the
13 I stand here by the w' of water;
16 she went down to the w', and filled
20 and ran again unto the w' to draw
29 ran out unto the man, unto the w'.
30 he stood by the camels at the w'.
42 And I came this day unto the w',
43 Behold, I stand by the w' of water;
45 she went down unto the w', and
25:11 Isaac dwelt by the w' Lahai-roi.
26:19 and found there a w' of springing
20 he called the name of the w' Esek;
21 they digged another w', and strove
22 digged another w'; and for that they
25 there Isaac's servants digged a w'.
32 told him concerning the w' which
Ge 29: 2 looked, and behold a w' in the field,
2 for out of that w' they watered the
6 And he said unto them, Is he w'?
6 And they said, He is w': and,
17 was beautiful and w' favoured.
32: 9 and I will deal w' with thee:
37:14 see whether it be w' with thy
14 w' with the flocks; and bring me
39: 6 a goodly person, and w' favoured.
40:14 think on me when it shall be w'
41: 2 the river seven w' favoured kine
4 the seven w' favoured and fat kine.
18 kine, fatfleshed and w' favoured;
43:27 Is your father w', the old man of
45:16 and it pleased Pharaoh w', and his
49:22 even a fruitful bough by a w';
Ex 1:20 God dealt w' with the midwives:
2:15 Midian: and he sat down by a w'.
4:14 brother? I know that he can speak w'.
10:29 Thou hast spoken w', I will see thy
Le 24:16 as w' the stranger, as he that is born
22 w' for the stranger, as for one of your
Nu 11:18 for it was w' with us in Egypt:
13:30 it; for we are w' able to overcome it.
21:16 the w' whereof the Lord spake unto
17 Spring up, O w'; sing ye unto it:
18 The princes digged the w', the
22 not drink of the waters of the w':
36: 5 of the sons of Joseph hath said w'.
De 1:17 shall hear the small as w' as the great;
23 And the saying pleased me w':
3:20 unto your brethren, as w' as unto you,
4:40 that it may go w' with thee, and
5:14 maidservant may rest as w' as thou.
16 that it may go w' with thee, in the
28 w' said all that they have spoken.
29 that it might be w' with them, and
33 and that it may be w' with you,
6: 3, 18 that it may be w' with thee, and
7:18 shalt w' remember what the Lord thy
12:25, 28 that it may go w' with thee,
15:16 house, because he is w' with thee;
18:17 They have w' spoken that which
19:13 Israel, that it may go w' with thee.
20: 8 his brethren's heart faint as w' as his
22: 7 that it may be w' with thee, and
Jos 8:33 of the Lord, as w' the stranger,
18:15 to the w' of waters of Nephtoah:
J'g 7: 1 and pitched beside the w' of Harod:
9:16 if ye have dealt w' with Jerubbaal
14: 3 for me; for she pleaseth me w'.
7 and she pleased Samson w'.
Ru 3: 1 thee, that it may be w' with thee?
13 thee the part of a kinsman, w';
1Sa 9:10 said Saul to his servant, W' said;
16:16 with his hand, and thou shalt be w'.
17 me now that a man can play w',
23 so Saul was refreshed, and was w',
18:26 it pleased David w' to be the
19:22 came to a great w' that is in Sechu:
20: 7 If he say thus, It is w'; thy servant
24:18 that thou hast dealt w' with me:
19 enemy, will he let him go w' away?
20 I know w'...thou shalt surely be king,
25:31 shall have dealt w' with my lord,
2Sa 3:13 he said, W'; I will make a league
26 him again from the w' of Sirah:
6:19 Israel, as w' to the women as men,
11:25 devoureth one as w' as another:
17: 4 the saying pleased Absalom w',
18 which had a w' in his court;
21 that they came up out of the w', and
18:28 and said unto the king, All is w'.
19: 6 then it had pleased thee w'.
23:15 the water of the w' of Beth-lehem,
16 water out of the w' of Beth-lehem,
1Ki 2:18 W'; I will speak for thee unto the
8:18 thou didst w' that it was in thine
18:24 answered and said, It is w' spoken.
2Ki 4:23 And she said, It shall be w'.
26 and say unto her, Is it w' with thee?
26 is it w' with thy husband?
26 is it w' with the child?
26 And she answered, It is w'.
5:21 to meet him, and said, Is all w'?
22 And he said, All is w'. My master
7: 9 said one to another, We do not w':
9: 11 and one said unto him, Is all w'?
10:30 thou hast done w' in executing
25:24 and it shall be w' with you.
1Ch 11:17 the water of the w' of Beth-lehem,
18 water out of the w' of Beth-lehem,
25: 8 ward, as w' the small as the great.
26:13 cast lots, as w' the small as the great.
2Ch 6: 8 thou didst w' in that it was in
12:12 and also in Judah things went w'.
31:15 as w' to the great as to the small:
Ne 2:13 even before the dragon w', and to
Job 12: 3 I have understanding as w' as you:
33:31 Mark w', O Job, hearken unto me:
Ps 48:13 Mark ye w' her bulwarks,
49:18 when thou doest w' to thyself.
73: 2 gone; my steps had w' nigh slipped.
78:29 So they did eat, and were w' filled:
84: 6 the valley of Baca make it a w';
87: 7 As w' the singers as the players on
119:65 Thou hast dealt w' with thy
128: 2 be, and it shall be w' with thee.
139:14 and that my soul knoweth right w'.
Pr 5:15 running waters out of thine own w'.
10:11 of a righteous man is a w' of life:
11:10 When it goeth w' with the
13:10 but with the w' advised is wisdom.
14:15 the prudent man looketh w' to his
27:23 flocks, and look w' to thy herds.
30:29 There be three things which go w',

Pr 31:27 She looketh w' to the ways of her
Ec 8:12 be w' with them that fear God,
13 it shall not be w' with the wicked,
Ca 4:15 of gardens, a w' of living waters,
Isa 1:17 Learn to do w'; seek judgment,
3:10 that it shall be w' with him:
24 instead of w' set hair baldness:
25: 6 of wines on the lees w' refined.
33:23 not w' strengthen their mast,
42:21 w' pleased for his righteousness'
Jer 1:12 Lord unto me, Thou hast w' seen:
7:23 you, that it may be w' unto you.
15:11 Verily it shall be w' with thy
11 to entreat thee w' in the time of evil
22:15 and then it was w' with him?
16 needy; then it was w' with him:
38:20 so it shall be w' unto thee, and thy
39:12 Take him, and look w' to him,
40: 4 and I will look w' unto thee:
9 and it shall be w' with you.
42: 6 that it may be w' with us, when we
44:17 we plenty of victuals, and were w',
Eze 24: 5 under it, and make it boil w',
10 consume the flesh, and spice it w',
33:32 and can play w' on an instrument:
44: 5 Son of man, mark w', and
5 mark w' the entering in of the
47:14 shall inherit it, one as w' as another:
Da 1: 4 was no blemish, but w' favoured,
3:15 the image which I have made; w':
Jon 4: 4 Lord, Doest thou w' to be angry?
9 thou w' to be angry for the gourd?
9 he said, I do w' to be angry, even
Zec 8:15 I thought in these days to do w'
M't 3:17 Son, in whom I am w' pleased.
12:12 is lawful to do w' on the sabbath
18 in whom my soul is w' pleased:
15: 7 w' did Esaias prophesy of you,
17: 5 Son, in whom I am w' pleased;
25:21 W' done, thou good and faithful
23 him, W' done, good and faithful
M'r 1:11 Son, in whom I am w' pleased.
7: 6 W' hath Esaias prophesied of
9 Full w' ye reject the commandment
37 He hath done all things w':
12:28 that he had answered them w',
32 W', Master, thou hast said the
Lu 1: 7 were now w' stricken in years.
18 and my wife w' stricken in years.
3:22 Son; in thee I am w' pleased.
6:26 all men shall speak w' of you!
19:17 unto him, W', thou good servant:
20:39 said, Master, thou hast w' said.
Joh 2:10 and when men have w' drunk,
4: 6 Now Jacob's w' was there. Jesus
6 his journey, sat thus on the w':
11 to draw with, and the w' is deep:
12 father Jacob, which gave us the w',
14 a w' of water springing up into
17 Thou hast w' said, I have no
8:48 Say we not w' that thou art a
11:12 Lord, if he sleep, he shall do w'.
13:13 Master and Lord: and ye say w';
18:23 but if w', why smitest thou me?
Ac 10:33 thou hast w' done that thou art
47 the Holy Ghost as w' as we?
15:29 ye shall do w'. Fare ye w'.
16: 2 was w' reported of by the brethren
25:10 wrong, as thou very w' knowest.
28:25 W' spake the Holy Ghost by
Ro 2: 7 by patient continuance in w' doing
11:20 W'; because of unbelief they
1Co 7:37 he will keep his virgin, doeth w'.
38 giveth her in marriage doeth w';
9: 5 a wife, as w' as other apostles,
10: 5 of them God was not w' pleased:
14:17 For thou verily givest thanks w',
2Co 6: 9 As unknown, and yet w' known;
11: 4 ye might w' bear with him.
Gal 4:17 zealously affect you, but not w';
5: 7 Ye did run w'; who did hinder you
6: 9 let us not be weary in w' doing:
Eph 6: 3 That it may be w' with thee, and
Ph'p 4:14 Notwithstanding ye have w' done,
Col 3:20 this is w' pleasing unto the Lord.
2Th 3:13 be not weary in w' doing.
1Ti 3: 4 One that ruleth w' his own house,
12 children and their own houses w'.
13 used the office of a deacon w'
5:10 W' reported of for good works; if
17 the elders that rule w' be counted
2Ti 1:18 me at Ephesus, thou knowest very w'.
Tit 2: 9 please them w' in all things;
Heb 4: 2 preached, as w' as unto them:
13:16 such sacrifices God is w' pleased.
Jas 2: 8 thy neighbour as thyself, ye do w':
19 there is one God; thou doest w':
1Pe 2:14 for the praise of them that do w'.
15 that with w' doing ye may put to
20 when ye do w', and suffer for it, ye
3: 6 ye are, as long as ye do w', and
17 ye suffer for w' doing, than for evil
4:19 of their souls to him in w' doing,
2Pe 1:17 Son, in whom I am w' pleased.
19 ye do w' that ye take heed, as unto
3Jo 6 after a godly sort, thou shalt do w':

wellbeloved
Ca 1:13 A bundle of myrrh is my w' unto
Isa 5: 1 Now will I sing to my w' a song of
1 My w' hath a vineyard in a very
M'r 12: 6 yet therefore one son, his w', he
Ro 16: 5 Salute my w' Epænetus, who is the
3Jo 1 The elder unto the w' Gaius, whom

well-doing See WELL and DOING.

wellfavoured See also WELL and FAVOURED.
Na 3: 4 whoredoms of the w' harlot,

well-nigh See WELL and NIGH.

wellpleasing See also WELL and PLEASING.
Ph'p 4:18 a sacrifice acceptable, w' to God.
Heb 13:21 you that which is w' in his sight,

well's
Ge 29: 2 great stone was upon the w' mouth.
3 rolled the stone from the w' mouth,
3 the stone again upon the w' mouth
8 roll the stone from the w' mouth;
10 rolled the stone from the w' mouth,
2Sa 17:19 a covering over the w' mouth,

wells
Ge 26:15 the w' which his father's servants
18 Isaac digged again the w' of water,
Ex 15:27 where were twelve w' of water,
Nu 20:17 we drink of the water of the w':
De 6:11 w' digged, which thou diggest not,
2Ki 3:19 and stop all w' of water, and mar
25 they stopped all the w' of water,
2Ch 26:10 the desert, and digged many w':
Ne 9:25 w' digged, vineyards, and
Isa 12: 3 water out of the w' of salvation.
2Pe 2:17 These are w' without water,

wellspring
Pr 16:22 Understanding is a w' of life unto
18: 4 and the w' of wisdom as a flowing

wen
Le 22:22 maimed, or having a w', or scurvy,

wench
2Sa 17:17 and a w' went and told them;

went^ See also OUTWENT; WENTEST.
Ge 2: 6 there w' up a mist from the earth,
10 a river w' out of Eden to water
4:16 Cain w' out from the presence of
7: 7 And Noah w' in, and his sons, and
9 There w' in two and two unto Noah
15 they w' in unto Noah into the ark,
16 they that w' in, w' in male and
18 the ark w' upon the face of the
8: 7 a raven, which w' forth to and fro,
18 Noah w' forth, and his sons, and
19 their kinds, w' forth out of the ark.
9:18 of Noah, that w' forth of the ark,
23 and w' backward, and covered the
10:11 Out of that land w' forth Asshur,
11:31 they w' forth with him from Ur
12: 4 unto him; and Lot w' with him;
5 they w' forth to go into the land of
10 and Abram w' down into Egypt to
13: 1 Abram w' up out of Egypt, he, and
3 he w' on his journeys from the
5 which w' with Abram, had flocks,
14: 8 there w' out the king of Sodom,
11 their victuals, and w' their way.
17 king of Sodom w' out to meet him
24 of the men which w' with me,
15:17 when the sun w' down, and it was
16: 4 And he w' in unto Hagar, and she
17:22 and God w' up from Abraham.
18:16 Abraham w' with them to bring
22 thence, and w' toward Sodom:
33 And the Lord w' his way, as soon as
19: 6 Lot w' out at the door unto them,
14 Lot w' out, and spake unto his sons
28 the smoke of the country w' up as
30 Lot w' up out of Zoar, and dwelt
33 and the firstborn w' in, and lay
21:16 And she w', and sat her down over
19 and she w', and filled the bottle
22: 3 w' unto the place of which God had
6 and they w' both of them together.
8 so they w' both of them together.
13 Abraham w' and took the ram, and
19 and w' together to Beer-sheba.
23:10 all that w' in at the gate of his city,
18 all that w' in at the gate of his city.
24:10 he arose, and w' to Mesopotamia,
16 and she w' down to the well, and
45 and she w' down unto the well, and
61 took Rebekah, and w' his way.
63 Isaac w'...to meditate in the field
25:22 And she w' to enquire of the Lord.
34 drink, and rose up, and w' his way:
26: 1 Isaac w' unto Abimelech king of
13 man waxed great, and w' forward,
23 w' up from thence to Beer-sheba.
26 Abimelech w' to him from Gerar,
27: 5 Esau w' to the field to hunt for
14 And he w', and fetched, and brought
22 Jacob w' near...Isaac his father;
28: 5 he w' to Padan-aram unto Laban,
9 Then w' Esau unto Ishmael, and
10 Jacob w' out from Beer-sheba,
10 and w' toward Haran.
29: 1 Then Jacob w' on his journey,
10 that Jacob w' near, and rolled the
23 her to him; and he w' in unto her.
30 And he w' in also unto Rachel, and
30: 4 to wife: and Jacob w' in unto her.
14 Reuben w' in the days of wheat
16 and Leah w' out to meet him,
31:19 And Laban w' to shear his sheep:
33 And Laban w' into Jacob's tent,
33 Then w' he out of Leah's tent, and
32: 1 And Jacob w' on his way, and the
21 So w' the present over before him:
34: 1 w' out to see the daughters of the
6 w' out unto Jacob to commune
24 that w' out of the gate of his city;
24 that w' out of the gate of his city.
Ge 34:26 out of Shechem's house, and w' out.
35: 3 with me in the way which I w'.
13 God w' up from him in the place
22 Reuben w' and lay with Bilhah
36: 6 w' into the country from the face
37:12 brethren w' to feed their father's
17 And Joseph w' after his brethren,
38: 1 Judah w' down from his brethren,
2 he took her, and w' in unto her.
9 he w' in unto his brother's wife,
11 Tamar w' and dwelt in her father's
12 w' up unto his sheepshearers to
19 she arose, and w' away, and laid
39:11 Joseph w' into the house to do his
41:45 Joseph w' out over all the land of
46 Joseph w' out from the presence of
46 and w' throughout all the land of
42: 3 ten brethren w' down to buy corn
43:15 w' down to Egypt, and stood before
31 he washed his face, and w' out,
44:28 And the one w' out from me, and
45:25 And they w' up out of Egypt, and
46:29 w' up to meet Israel his father, to
47:10 and w' out from before Pharaoh.
49: 4 thou it: he w' up to my couch.
50: 7 Joseph w' up to bury his father:
7 w' up all the servants of Pharaoh,
9 there w' up with him both chariots
14 w' up with him to bury his father,
18 his brethren also w' and fell down
Ex 2: 1 w' a man of the house of Levi,
8 w' and called the child's mother.
11 he w' out unto his brethren, and
13 And when he w' out the second day,
4:18 Moses w' and returned to Jethro
27 he w', and met him in the mount
29 Moses and Aaron w' and gathered
5: 1 Moses and Aaron w' in, and told
10 taskmasters of the people w' out,
7:10 and Aaron w' in unto Pharaoh,
23 turned and w' into his house,
8:12 and Aaron w' out from Pharaoh:
30 And Moses w' out from Pharaoh,
9:33 w' out of the city from Pharaoh,
10: 6 himself, and w' out from Pharaoh.
14 the locusts w' up over all the land
18 And he w' out from Pharaoh,
11: 8 he w' out from Pharaoh in a great
12:28 And the children of Israel w' away,
38 multitude w' up also with them;
41 w' out from the land of Egypt.
13:18 w' up harnessed out of the land
21 Lord w' before them by day in a
14: 8 Israel w' out with an high hand.
19 God, which w' before the camp of
19 removed and w' behind them;
19 cloud w' from before their face,
22 children of Israel w' into the midst
23 w' in after them to the midst of
15:19 Pharaoh w' in with his chariots
19 Israel w' on dry land in the midst
20 w' out after her with timbrels,
22 w' out into the wilderness of Shur;
22 w' three days in the wilderness,
16:27 w' out some of the people on the
17:10 Hur w' up to the top of the hill.
18: 7 Moses w' out to meet his father in
27 he w' his way into his own land.
19: 3 Moses w' up unto God, and the
14 Moses w' down from the mount
20 top of the mount; and Moses w' up.
25 So Moses w' down unto the people,
24: 9 They w' up Moses, and Aaron,
13 Moses w' up into the mount of God.
15 Moses w' up into the mount, and a
18 w' into the midst of the cloud,
32:15 and w' down from the mount,
33: 7 w' out unto the tabernacle
8 Moses w' out unto the tabernacle,
34: 4 and w' up unto mount Sinai,
34 w' in before the Lord to speak
35 until he w' in to speak with him.
38:26 every one that w' to be numbered,
40:32 When they w' into the tent of the
36 the children of Israel w' onward
Le 9: 8 Aaron therefore w' unto the altar,
23 and Aaron w' into the tabernacle
10: 2 there w' out fire from the Lord,
5 So they w' near, and carried them
16:23 on when he w' into the holy place,
24:10 w' out among the children of
Nu 8:22 after that w' the Levites in to do
10:14 place w' the standard of the camp
33 the covenant of the Lord w' before
34 day, when they w' out of the camp.
11: 8 the people w' about, and gathered
24 Moses w' out, and told the people
26 but w' not out unto the tabernacle:
31 w' forth a wind from the Lord,
13:21 So they w' up, and searched the
26 And they w' and came to Moses,
31 the men that w' up with him said,
14:24 into the land whereinto he w';
38 men that w' to search the land,
16:25 Moses rose up and w' unto Dathan
33 w' down alive into the pit, and the
17: 8 w' into the tabernacle of witness;
20: 6 Moses and Aaron w' from the
15 our fathers w' down into Egypt,
27 they w' up into mount Hor in the
21:16 And from thence they w' to Beer:
18 the wilderness they w' to Mattanah:
23 and w' out against Israel into the
33 and w' up by the way of Bashan:
33 the king of Bashan w' out against
22:14 rose up, and they w' unto Balak,

Nu 22:21 and *w'* with the princes of Moab.
22 anger was kindled because he *w'*:
23 of the way, and *w'* into the field:
26 the angel of the Lord *w'* further,
32 I *w'* out to withstand thee,
35 *w'* with the princes of Balak.
36 he *w'* out to meet him unto a city
39 And Balaam *w'* with Balak, and
23: 3 thee. And he *w'* to an high place.
24: 1 he *w'* not, as at other times, to
25 and *w'* and returned to his place:
25 place: and Balak also *w'* his way.
25: 8 he *w'* after the man of Israel into
26: 4 *w'* forth out of the land of Egypt.
31:13 *w'* forth to meet them without the
21 men of war which *w'* to the battle,
27 upon them, who *w'* out to battle,
28 men of war which *w'* out to battle:
36 portion of them that *w'* out to war,
32: 9 *w'* up unto the valley of Eshcol,
39 the son of Manasseh *w'* to Gilead,
41 Jair...*w'* and took the small towns
42 Nobah *w'* and took Kenath, and the
33: 1 *w'* forth out of the land of Egypt
3 Israel *w'* out with an high hand
8 *w'* three days' journey in the
23 And they *w'* from Kehelathah, and
29 And they *w'* from Mithcah, and
33 And they *w'* from Hor-hagidgad,
38 the priest *w'* up into mount Hor
De 1:19 we *w'* through all that great and
24 and *w'* up into the mountain,
31 in all the way that ye *w'*, until ye
33 Who *w'* in the way before you, to
43 *w'* presumptuously up into the
2:13 And we *w'* over the brook Zered.
3: 1 and *w'* up the way to Bashan:
5: 5 fire, and *w'* not up into the mount;)
10: 3 *w'* up into the mount, having the two
22 Thy fathers *w'* down into Egypt
26: 5 he *w'* down into Egypt, and
29:26 For they *w'* and served other gods,
31: 1 Moses *w'* and spake these words
14 And Moses and Joshua *w'*, and
33: 2 from his right hand *w'* a fiery law
34: 1 *w'* up from the plains of Moab
Jos 2: 1 they *w'*, and came into an harlot's
5 it was dark, that the men *w'* out:
5 whither the men *w'* I wot not:
22 And they *w'*, and came unto the
3: 2 the officers *w'* through the host;
6 ark...and *w'* before the people.
5:13 and Joshua *w'* unto him, and said
6: 1 none *w'* out, and none came in.
9 armed men *w'* before the priests
13 ark of the Lord *w'* on continually,
13 and the armed men *w'* before them;
20 that the people *w'* up into the city,
23 young men that were spies *w'* in,
7: 2 And the men *w'* up and viewed Ai.
4 So there *w'* up thither of the people
8: 9 and they *w'* to lie in ambush, and
10 numbered the people, and *w'* up,
11 of war that were with him, *w'* up,
13 Joshua *w'* that night into the
14 of the city *w'* out against Israel
17 Beth-el, and *w'* not out after Israel:
9: 4 *w'* and made as if they had been
6 they *w'* to Joshua unto the camp
10: 5 and *w'* up, they and all their hosts,
9 and *w'* up from Gilgal all night.
24 men of war which *w'* with him,
36 And Joshua *w'* up from Eglon,
11: 4 they *w'* out, they and all their
14: 8 my brethren that *w'* up with me
15: 3 And it *w'* out to the south side to
3 to Hezron, and *w'* up to Adar,
4 *w'* out unto the river of Egypt;
6 the border *w'* up to Beth-hogla,
6 border *w'* up to the stone of Bohan
7 the border *w'* up toward Debir
8 border *w'* up by the valley of the
8 *w'* up to the top of the mountain
9 and *w'* out to the cities of mount
10 and *w'* down to Beth-shemesh,
11 *w'* out unto the side of Ekron
11 Baalah, and *w'* out unto Jabneel;
15 he *w'* up thence to the inhabitants
16: 6 the border *w'* out toward the sea
6 border *w'* about eastward unto
7 *w'* down from Janohah to Ataroth,
7 to Jericho, and *w'* out at Jordan.
8 The border *w'* out from Tappuah
17: 7 border *w'* along on the right hand
18: 8 and the men arose, and *w'* away:
8 Joshua charged them that *w'*
9 *w'* and passed through the land,
12 border *w'* up to the side of Jericho
12 and *w'* up through the mountains
13 *w'* over from thence toward Luz,
15 and the border *w'* out on the west,
15 and *w'* out to the well of waters of
17 north, and *w'* forth to En-shemesh,
17 *w'* forth toward Geliloth, which is
18 and *w'* down unto Arabah:
19:11 their border *w'* up toward the sea,
47 coast of the children of Dan *w'* out
47 children of Dan *w'* up to fight
22: 6 away: and they *w'* unto their tents.
24: 4 his children *w'* down into Egypt.
11 ye *w'* over Jordan, and came unto
17 us in all the way wherein we *w'*,
J'g 1: 3 thy lot. So Simeon *w'* with him.
4 And Judah *w'* up; and the Lord
9 children of Judah *w'* down to fight
10 Judah *w'* against the Canaanites

J'g 1:11 *w'* against...inhabitants of Debir:
16 *w'* up out of the city of palm trees
16 *w'* and dwelt among the people.
17 Judah *w'* with Simeon his brother,
22 they also *w'* up against Beth-el:
26 *w'* into the land of the Hittites,
2: 6 *w'* every man unto his inheritance
15 Whithersoever they *w'* out, the
17 they *w'* a whoring after other gods,
3:10 judged Israel, and *w'* out to war:
13 Amalek, and *w'* and smote Israel,
19 that stood by him *w'* out from him.
22 the haft also *w'* in after the blade;
23 Ehud *w'* forth through the porch,
27 *w'* down with him from the mount,
28 they *w'* down after him, and took
4: 9 and *w'* with Barak to Kedesh.
10 *w'* up with the ten thousand men
10 and Deborah *w'* up with him.
14 So Barak *w'* down from mount
18 Jael *w'* out to meet Sisera, and said
21 *w'* softly unto him, and smote the
6:19 Gideon *w'* in, and made ready a kid,
33 gathered together, and *w'* over,
7:11 Then *w'* he down with Phurah,
8: 8 And he *w'* up thence to Penuel,
11 And Gideon *w'* up by the way of
27 Israel *w'* thither a whoring after it:
29 *w'* and dwelt in his own house.
33 and *w'* a whoring after Baalim,
9: 1 son of Jerubbaal *w'* to Shechem
5 he *w'* unto his father's house at
6 *w'*, and made Abimelech king,
7 he *w'* and stood in the top of mount
8 The trees *w'* forth on a time to
21 ran away, and fled, and *w'* to Beer,
26 brethren, and *w'* over to Shechem:
27 And they *w'* out into the fields,
27 and *w'* into the house of their god,
35 And Gaal the son of Ebed *w'* out,
39 And Gaal *w'* out before the men
42 the people *w'* out into the field;
50 Then *w'* Abimelech to Thebez,
52 *w'* hard unto the door of the tower
11: 3 Jephthah, and *w'* out with him.
5 of Gilead *w'* to fetch Jephthah out
11 Then Jephthah *w'* with the elders
18 *w'* along through the wilderness,
38 she *w'* with her companions, and
40 the daughters of Israel *w'* yearly
12: 1 together, and *w'* northward,
13:11 And Manoah...*w'* after his wife,
20 the flame *w'* up toward heaven
14: 1 And Samson *w'* down to Timnath,
5 Then *w'* Samson down, and his
7 And he *w'* down, and talked with
9 in his hands, and *w'* on eating,
10 So his father *w'* down unto the
18 day before the sun *w'* down,
19 and he *w'* down to Ashkelon,
19 and he *w'* up to his father's house.
15: 4 Samson *w'* and caught three
8 he *w'* down and dwelt in the top of
9 Then the Philistines *w'* up, and
11 of Judah *w'* to the top of the rock
16: 1 Then *w'* Samson to Gaza, and
1 an harlot, and *w'* in unto her.
3 posts, and *w'* away with them,
14 *w'* away with the pin of the beam,
19 him, and his strength *w'* from him.
17:10 thy victuals. So the Levite *w'* in.
18:11 *w'* from thence of the family of
12 And they *w'* up, and pitched in
14 men that *w'* to spy out the country
17 And the five men that *w'* to spy
17 to spy out the land *w'* up,
18 And these *w'* into Micah's house,
20 and *w'* in the midst of the people.
26 the children of Dan *w'* their way:
26 and *w'* back unto his house.
19: 2 *w'* away from him unto her
3 husband arose, and *w'* after her,
14 they passed on and *w'* their way;
14 the sun *w'* down upon them when
15 when he *w'* in, he sat him down
18 I *w'* to Beth-lehem-judah, but I
23 master of the house, *w'* out unto
27 house, and *w'* out to go his way:
20: 1 all the children of Israel *w'* out,
18 and *w'* up to the house of God,
20 the men of Israel *w'* out to battle
23 children of Israel *w'* up and wept
25 Benjamin *w'* forth against them
26 *w'* up, and came unto the house
30 children of Israel *w'* up against
31 the children of Benjamin *w'* out
21:23 they *w'* and returned unto their
24 *w'* out from thence every man to
Ru 1: 1 *w'* to sojourn in the country of
7 Wherefore she *w'* forth out of the
7 *w'* on the way to return unto the
19 So they two *w'* until they came to
21 I *w'* out full, and the Lord hath
2: 3 she *w'*, and came, and gleaned in
18 took it up, and *w'* into the city:
3: 6 And she *w'* down unto the floor,
7 he *w'* to lie down at the end of the
15 it on her: and she *w'* into the city.
4: 1 Then *w'* Boaz up to the gate, and
13 and when he *w'* in unto her, the
1Sa 1: 3 And this man *w'* up out of his city
7 *w'* up to the house of the Lord,
18 So the woman *w'* her way, and did
21 *w'* up to offer unto the Lord the
22 But Hannah *w'* not up; for she
2:11 Elkanah *w'* to Ramah to his house,

1Sa 2:20 And they *w'* unto their own home.
3: 3 ere the lamp of God *w'* out in the
5 again. And he *w'* and lay down.
6 And Samuel arose and *w'* to Eli,
8 he arose and *w'* to Eli, and said,
9 So Samuel *w'* and lay down in his
4: 1 Now Israel *w'* out against the
5:12 cry of the city *w'* up to heaven.
6:12 *w'* along the highway, lowing as
12 the highway, lowing as they *w'*,
12 the Philistines *w'* after them unto
7: 7 Philistines *w'* up against Israel.
11 men of Israel *w'* out of Mizpeh,
16 he *w'* from year to year in circuit
9: 9 when a man *w'* to enquire of God,
10 *w'* unto the city where the man of
11 as they *w'* up the hill to the city,
14 And they *w'* up into the city: and
26 they *w'* out both of them, he and
10:14 and to his servant, Whither *w'* ye?
26 Saul also *w'* home to Gibeah; and
26 there *w'* with him a band of men,
11:15 And all the people *w'* to Gilgal;
13: 7 And some of the Hebrews *w'* over
10 Saul *w'* out to meet him, that he
20 all the Israelites *w'* down to the
23 Philistines *w'* out to the passage
14:16 *w'* on beating down one another.
19 the Philistines *w'* on and increased:
21 *w'* up with them into the camp
46 Then Saul *w'* up from following
46 Philistines *w'* to their own place.
15:34 Then Samuel *w'* to Ramah; and
34 Saul *w'* up to his house to Gibeah
16:13 Samuel rose up, and *w'* to Ramah.
17: 4 *w'* out a champion out of the camp
7 one bearing a shield *w'* before
12 man *w'* among men for an old man
13 sons of Jesse *w'* and followed
13 three sons that *w'* to the battle
15 David *w'* and returned from Saul
20 *w'*, as Jesse had commanded him;
35 I *w'* out after him, and smote him,
41 that bare the shield *w'* before him.
18: 5 David *w'* out whithersoever Saul
13 he *w'* out and came in before the
16 he *w'* out and came in before them.
27 Wherefore David arose and *w'*, he
30 princes of the Philistines *w'* forth:
30 came to pass, after they *w'* forth,
19: 8 David *w'* out, and fought with the
12 and he *w'*, and fled, and escaped.
18 he and Samuel *w'* and dwelt in
22 Then *w'* he also to Ramah, and
23 he *w'* thither to Naioth in Ramah:
23 and he *w'* on, and prophesied,
20:11 *w'* out both of them into the field.
35 Jonathan *w'* out into the field at
42 and Jonathan *w'* into the city.
21:10 and *w'* to Achish the king of Gath.
22: 1 it, they *w'* down thither to him.
3 And David *w'* thence to Mizpeh of
23: 5 David and his men *w'* to Keilah,
13 *w'* whithersoever they could go.
16 and *w'* to David into the wood,
18 and Jonathan *w'* to his house.
24 arose, and *w'* to Ziph before Saul:
25 Saul...and his men *w'* to seek him.
26 Saul *w'* on this side of the mountain,
28 and *w'* against the Philistines:
29 And David *w'* up from thence,
24: 2 *w'* to seek David and his men
3 and Saul *w'* in to cover his feet:
7 of the cave, and *w'* on his way.
8 afterward, and *w'* out of the cave,
22 And Saul *w'* home; but David
25: 1 *w'* down to the wilderness of
12 turned their way, and *w'* again,
13 there *w'* up after David about
42 damsels of hers that *w'* after her;
42 she *w'* after the messengers of
26: 2 *w'* down to the wilderness of Ziph,
13 David *w'* over to the other side,
25 So David *w'* on his way, and Saul
27: 8 And David and his men *w'* up, and
28: 8 and he *w'*, and two men with him,
25 rose up, and *w'* away that night.
29:11 the Philistines *w'* up to Jezreel.
30: 2 them away, and *w'* on their way.
9 David *w'*, he and the six hundred
21 and they *w'* forth to meet David,
22 of those that *w'* with David,
22 Because they *w'* not with us, we
31: 3 And the battle *w'* sore against Saul,
12 men arose, and *w'* all night, and
2Sa 1: 4 said unto him, How *w'* the matter?
2: 2 David *w'* up thither, and his two
12 *w'* out from Mahanaim to Gibeon.
13 servants of David, *w'* out, and met
15 and *w'* over by number twelve of
24 sun *w'* down when they were come
29 *w'* through all Bithron, and they
32 And Joab and his men *w'* all night,
3:16 her husband *w'* with her along
19 Abner *w'* also to speak in the ears
21 Abner away; and he *w'* in peace.
4: 5 *w'*, and came about the heat of the
5: 6 king and his men *w'* to Jerusalem
10 David *w'* on, and grew great, and
17 of it, and *w'* down to the hold.
6: 2 arose, and *w'* with all the people
4 God: and Ahio *w'* before the ark.
12 David *w'* and brought up the ark
7:18 Then *w'* king David in, and sat
23 God *w'* to redeem for a people to
8: 3 as he *w'* to recover his border at

2Sa 8: 6, 14 David whithersoever he *w*.
10: 16 the host of Hadarezer *w* before them.
11: 9 and *w* not down to his house.
10 Uriah *w* not down unto his house,
13 even he *w* out to lie on his bed
13 but *w* not down to his house.
17 And the men of the city *w* out,
21 why *w* ye nigh the wall? then say
22 So the messenger *w*, and came
12: 16 David fasted, and *w* in, and lay
17 of his house arose, and *w* to him,
24 *w* in unto her, and lay with her:
29 *w* to Rabbah, and fought against it,
13: 8 So Tamar *w* to her brother
9 they *w* out every man from him.
19 on her head, and *w* on crying.
37 Absalom fled, and *w* to Talmai,
38 So Absalom fled, and *w* to Geshur,
14: 23 So Joab arose and *w* to Geshur,
15: 9 So he arose, and *w* to Hebron.
11 with Absalom *w* two hundred
11 and they *w* in their simplicity, and
16, 17 And the king *w* forth, and all
24 and Abiather *w* up, until all the
30 David *w* up by the ascent of mount
30 wept as he *w* up, and had his head
30 head covered, and he *w* barefoot:
30 man his head, and they *w* up,
30 weeping as they *w* up.
16: 13 David and his men *w* by the way,
13 Shimei *w* along on the hill's side
13 and cursed as he *w*, and threw
22 Absalom *w* in unto his father's
17: 17 and a wench *w* and told them:
17 and they *w* and told king David.
18 they *w* both of them away quickly,
18 his court; whither they *w* down.
21 well, and *w* and told king David,
25 that *w* in to Abigail the daughter
18: 6 people *w* out into the field against
9 mule *w* under the thick boughs
9 mule that was under him *w* away.
24 the watchman *w* up to the roof
33 *w* up to the chamber over the
33 as he *w*, thus he said, O my son
19: 17 *w* over Jordan before the king.
18 there *w* over a ferry boat to carry
19 the king *w* out of Jerusalem,
31 and *w* over Jordan with the king,
39 all the people *w* over Jordan.
40 Then the king *w* on to Gilgal,
40 and Chimham *w* on with him: and
20: 2 So every man of Israel *w* up from
3 them, but *w* not in unto them.
5 So Amasa *w* to assemble the men
7 there *w* out after him Joab's men,
7 they *w* out of Jerusalem, to pursue
8 in Gibeon, Amasa *w* before them.
8 and as he *w* forth it fell out.
13 all the people *w* on after Joab, to
14 *w* through all the tribes of Israel
14 together, and *w* also after him.
22 woman *w* unto all the people in her
21: 12 David *w* and took the bones of
15 David *w* down, and his servants
22: 9 There *w* up a smoke out of his
23: 13 three of the thirty chief *w* down,
17 that *w* in jeopardy of their lives?
20 he *w* down also and slew a lion
21 but he *w* down to him with a staff,
24: 4 captains of the host *w* out from
7 they *w* out to the south of Judah,
19 *w* up as the LORD commanded.
20 and Araunah *w* out, and bowed
1Ki 1: 15 Bath-sheba *w* in unto the king
38 and the Pelethites, *w* down, and
49 up, and *w* every man his way.
50 *w*, and caught hold of the horns of
2: 8 the day when I *w* to Mahanaim:
19 Bath-sheba therefore *w* unto king
34 the son of Jehoiada *w* up, and
40 *w* to Gath to Achish to seek his
40 and Shimei *w*, and brought his
46 which *w* out, and fell upon him,
3: 4 the king *w* to Gibeon to sacrifice
6: 8 they *w* up with winding stairs
8: 66 *w* unto their tents joyful and glad
10: 5 *w* up unto the house of the LORD;
13 turned and *w* to her own country,
16 shekels of gold *w* to one target.
17 three pound of gold *w* to one
29 And a chariot...*w* out of Egypt.
11: 5 Solomon *w* after Ashtoreth the
6 *w* not fully after the LORD, as did
24 they *w* to Damascus, and dwelt
29 Jeroboam *w* out of Jerusalem,
12: 1 And Rehoboam *w* to Shechem:
25 and *w* out from thence, and built
30 people *w* to worship before the
13: 10 So he *w* another way, and returned
12 said unto them, What way *w* he?
12 seen what way the man of God *w*,
14 And *w* after the man of God,
19 he *w* back with him, and did eat
28 he *w* and found his carcase cast
14: 4 *w* to Shiloh, and came to the
28 king *w* into the house of the LORD,
15: 17 king of Israel *w* up against Judah,
16: 10 Zimri *w* in and smote him, and
17 And Omri *w* up from Gibbethon,
18 he *w* into the palace of the king's
31 and *w* and served Baal, and
17: 5 So he *w* and did according unto
5 *w* and dwelt by the brook Cherith,
10 So he arose and *w* to Zarephath.
15 she *w* and did according to the

1Ki 18: 2 Elijah *w* to shew himself unto
6 Ahab *w* one way by himself, and
6 and Obadiah *w* another way by
16 So Obadiah *w* to meet Ahab, and
16 and Ahab *w* to meet Elijah.
42 Ahab *w* up to eat and to drink.
42 Elijah *w* up to the top of Carmel;
43 he *w* up, and looked, and said,
45 And Ahab rode, and *w* to Jezreel.
19: 3 that, he arose, and *w* for his life,
4 he himself *w* a day's journey into
8 *w* in the strength of that meat
13 his face in his mantle, and *w* out,
21 *w* after Elijah, and ministered
20: 1 he *w* up and besieged Samaria,
16 And they *w* out at noon. But
17 of the provinces *w* out first;
21 king of Israel *w* out, and smote
26 *w* up to Aphek, to fight against
27 all present, and *w* against them:
39 Thy servant *w* out into the midst
43 the king of Israel *w* to his house
21: 27 lay in sackcloth, and *w* softly.
22: 24 the son of Chenaanah *w* near,
24 Which way *w* the Spirit of the
29 of Judah *w* up to Ramoth-gilead.
30 himself, and *w* into the battle.
36 And there *w* a proclamation
48 but they *w* not; for the ships
2Ki 1: 9 And he *w* up to him: and, behold,
13 the third captain of fifty *w* up,
15 *w* down with him unto the king.
2: 1 Elijah *w* with Elisha from Gilgal.
2 thee. So they *w* down to Beth-el.
6 leave thee. And they two *w* on.
7 of the sons of the prophets *w*,
8 they two *w* over on dry ground.
11 it came to pass, as they still *w* on,
11 Elijah *w* up by a whirlwind into
13 *w* back, and stood by the bank of
14 and thither: and Elisha *w* over.
21 he *w* forth unto the spring of the
23 he *w* up from thence unto Beth-el:
25 *w* from thence to mount Carmel,
3: 6 king Jehoram *w* out of Samaria
7 he *w* and sent to Jehoshaphat
9 So the king of Israel *w*, and the
12 the king of Edom *w* down to him.
24 *w* forward smiting the Moabites,
25 howbeit the slingers *w* about it,
4: 5 So she *w* from him, and shut the
18 that he *w* out to his father to the
21 And she *w* up, and laid him on
21 the door upon him, and *w* out.
25 *w* and came unto the man of God
31 he *w* again to meet him, and told
33 He *w* in therefore, and shut the
34 And he *w* up, and lay upon the
35 *w* up, and stretched himself upon
37 Then she *w* in, and fell at his feet,
37 and took up her son, and *w* out.
39 *w* out into the field to gather herbs,
5: 4 And one *w* in, and told his lord,
11 Naaman was wroth, and *w* away,
12 So he turned and *w* away in a rage.
14 Then *w* he down, and dipped
25 But he *w* in, and stood before his
25 said, Thy servant *w* no whither.
26 *W* not mine heart with thee, when
27 *w* out from his presence a leper
6: 4 So he *w* with them. And when
23 away, and they *w* to their master.
24 and *w* up, and besieged Samaria.
7: 8 they *w* into one tent, and did eat
8 and raiment, and *w* and hid it;
15 they *w* after them unto Jordan:
16 the people *w* out, and spoiled the
8: 2 and she *w* with her household,
3 she *w* forth to cry unto the king
9 So Hazael *w* to meet him, and
21 So Joram *w* over to Zair, and all
28 he *w* with Joram the son of Ahab
29 king Joram *w* back to be healed
29 of Judah *w* down to see Joram
9: 4 the prophet, *w* to Ramoth-gilead.
6 he arose, and *w* into the house;
16 in a chariot, and *w* to Jezreel;
18 So there *w* one on horseback to
21 Ahaziah king of Judah *w* out,
21 they *w* out against Jehu, and met
24 and the arrow *w* out at his heart,
35 And they *w* to bury her: but they
10: 9 he *w* out, and stood, and said to
23 Jehu *w*, and Jehonadab the son of
24 when they *w* in to offer sacrifices
25 *w* to the city of the house of Baal.
11: 16 she *w* by the way by the which the
18 people of the land *w* into the house
12: 17 Then Hazael king of Syria *w* up,
18 and he *w* away from Jerusalem.
13: 5 they *w* out from under the hand
14: 11 Jehoash king of Israel *w* up; and
15: 14 the son of Gadi *w* up from Tirzah,
16: 9 Assyria *w* up against Damascus,
10 king Ahaz *w* to Damascus to
17: 5 *w* up to Samaria, and besieged it
15 *w* after...heathen that were round
18: 7 he prospered whithersoever he *w*
17 they *w* up and came to Jerusalem.
19: 1 and *w* into the house of the LORD.
14 *w* up into the house of the LORD,
35 that the angel of the LORD *w* out,
36 and *w* and returned, and dwelt at
22: 14 *w* unto Huldah the prophetess,
23: 2 king *w* up into the house of the
29 king of Egypt *w* up against the

2Ki 23: 29 and king Josiah *w* against him;
24: 12 *w* out to the king of Babylon,
25: 4 king *w* the way toward the plain.
1Ch 2: 21 Hezron *w* in to the daughter of
4: 39 they *w* to the entrance of Gedor,
42 hundred men, *w* to mount Seir,
5: 18 threescore, that *w* out to the war.
25 *w* a whoring after the gods of the
6: 15 And Jehozadak *w* into captivity,
7: 23 And when he *w* in to his wife, she
23 because it *w* evil with his house.
10: 3 And the battle *w* sore against Saul,
11: 4 and all Israel *w* to Jerusalem,
6 Joab the son of Zeruiah *w* first up,
15 captains *w* down to the rock to
22 he *w* down and slew a lion in a pit
23 he *w* down to him with a staff, and
12: 15 These are they that *w* over Jordan
17 And David *w* out to meet them,
20 As he *w* to Ziklag, there fell to
33 Zebulun, such as *w* forth to battle,
36 of Asher, such as *w* forth to battle,
13: 6 And David *w* up, and all Israel, to
14: 8 the Philistines *w* up to seek David.
8 of it, and *w* out against them.
17 the fame of David *w* out into all
15: 25 *w* to bring up the ark of the
16: 20 when they *w* from nation to nation,
17: 21 whom God *w* to redeem to be his
18: 3 as he *w* to stablish his dominion
6, 13 David whithersoever he *w*.
19: 5 Then there *w* certain, and told
16 host of Hadarezer *w* before them.
21: 4 and *w* throughout all Israel, and
19 David *w* up at the saying of Gad,
21 and *w* out of the threshingfloor,
27: 1 in and *w* out month by month
29: 30 and the times that *w* over him,
2Ch 1: 3 *w* to the high place that was at
6 *w* up thither to the brasen altar
8: 3 Solomon *w* to Hamath-zobah,
17 Then *w* Solomon to Ezion-geber,
18 *w* with the servants of Solomon
9: 4 *w* up into the house of the LORD;
12 and *w* away to her own land,
15 shekels of...gold *w* to one target.
16 shekels of gold *w* to one shield.
21 the king's ships *w* to Tarshish
10: 1 And Rehoboam *w* to Shechem:
16 So all Israel *w* to their tents.
12: 12 and also in Judah things *w* well.
14: 10 Then Asa *w* out against him, and
15: 2 And he *w* out to meet Asa, and
5 was no peace to him that *w* out,
17: 9 *w* about throughout all the cities
18: 2 certain years he *w* down to Ahab
12 messenger that *w* to call Micaiah
23 Which way *w* the Spirit of the
28 of Judah *w* up to Ramoth-gilead.
29 himself; and they *w* to the battle.
19: 2 the seer *w* out to meet him,
4 *w* out again through the people
20: 20 and *w* forth into the wilderness of
20 and as they *w* forth, Jehoshaphat
21 as they *w* out before the army, and
21: 9 Jehoram *w* forth with his princes,
22: 5 *w* with Jehoram the son of Ahab
6 *w* down to see Jehoram the son
7 he *w* out with Jehoram against
23: 2 And they *w* about in Judah, and
17 the people *w* to the house of Baal,
25: 11 people, and *w* to the valley of salt,
21 So Joash the king of Israel *w* up;
26: 6 he *w* forth and warred against the
11 men, that *w* out to war by bands,
16 *w* into the temple of the LORD to
17 Azariah the priest *w* in after him,
28: 9 *w* out before the host that came
29: 16 the priests *w* into the inner part of
18 they *w* in to Hezekiah the king,
20 *w* up to the house of the LORD.
30: 6 posts *w* with the letters from the
31: 1 *w* out to the cities of Judah,
34: 22 *w* to Huldah the prophetess, the
30 *w* up into the house of the LORD,
35: 20 and Josiah *w* out against him.
Ezr 2: 1 that *w* up out of the captivity,
59 they which *w* up from Tel-melah,
4: 23 *w* up in haste to Jerusalem unto
5: 8 we *w* into the provinces of Judea,
7: 6 This Ezra *w* up from Babylon;
7 there *w* up some of the children of
8: 1 that *w* up with me from Babylon,
10: 6 *w* into the chamber of Johanan
Ne 2: 13 I *w* out by night by the gate of
14 I *w* on to the gate of the fountain,
15 *w* I up in the night by the brook,
16 the rulers knew not whither I *w*,
7: 6 that *w* up out of the captivity,
61 which *w* up also from Tel-melah,
8: 12 all the people *w* their way to eat,
16 the people *w* forth, and brought
9: 11 *w* through the midst of the sea on
24 So the children *w* in and possessed
12: 1 Levites that *w* up with Zerubbabel
31 one *w* on the right hand upon the
32 after them *w* Hoshaiah, and half
37 they *w* up by the stairs of the city
38 gave thanks *w* over against them,
Es 2: 14 In the evening she *w*, and on the
3: 15 The posts *w* out, being hastened
4: 1 *w* out into the midst of the city,
6 Hatach *w* forth to Mordecai unto
17 So Mordecai *w* his way, and did
5: 9 Then *w* Haman forth that day
7: 7 his wrath *w* into the palace gardens:

Es 7: 8 word w' out of the king's mouth,
8:14 upon mules and camels w' out,
15 Mordecai w' out from the presence
9: 4 his fame w' out throughout all the
Job 1: 4 sons w' and feasted in their houses,
12 Satan w' forth from the presence
2: 7 So w' Satan forth from the presence
18:20 they that w' before were affrighted.
29: 7 When I w' out to the gate through
30:28 I w' mourning without the sun: I
31:34 and w' not out of the door?
42: 9 Zophar the Naamathite w',
Ps 18: 8 w' up a smoke out of his nostrils,
42: 4 I w' with them to the house of
66: 6 they w' through the flood on foot:
12 we w' through fire and through
68:25 The singers w' before, the
73:17 Until I w' into the sanctuary of
77:17 thine arrows also w' abroad.
81: 5 when he w' out through the land
105:13 w' from one nation to another,
106:32 it w' ill with Moses for their sakes:
39 w' a whoring with their own
114: 1 When Israel w' out of Egypt, the
119:67 Before I was afflicted I w' astray:
133: 2 that w' down to the skirts of his
Pr 7: 8 and he w' the way to her house,
24:30 I w' by the field of the slothful,
Ec 2:20 I w' about to cause my heart to
Ca 5: 7 watchmen that w' about the city
6:11 I w' down into the garden of nuts
Isa 7: 1 w' up toward Jerusalem to war
8: 3 I w' unto the prophetess; and she
37: 1 and w' into the house of the Lord.
14 Hezekiah w' up unto the house of
36 the angel of the Lord w' forth,
37 departed, and w' and returned,
48: 3 they w' forth out of my mouth,
51:23 the street, to them that w' over.
52: 4 My people w' down aforetime into
57:17 he w' on frowardly in the way of
60:15 so that no man w' through thee,
Jer 3: 8 but w' and played the harlot also.
7:24 and w' backward, and not forward.
11:10 they w' after other gods to serve
13: 5 So I w', and hid it by Euphrates,
7 Then I w' to Euphrates, and
18: 3 I w' down to the potter's house,
22:11 which w' forth out of this place;
26:21 afraid, and fled, and w' into Egypt;
28: 4 of Judah, that w' into Babylon,
11 prophet Jeremiah w' his way.
31: 2 when I w' to cause him to rest.
36:12 he w' down into the king's house,
20 they w' in to the king into the
37: 4 in and w' out among the people:
12 Jeremiah w' forth out of Jerusalem
38: 8 w' forth out of the king's house,
11 w' into the house of the king under
39: 4 w' forth out of the city by night,
4 and he w' out the way of the plain.
40: 6 Then w' Jeremiah unto Gedaliah
41: 6 Ishmael...w' forth from Mizpah
6 them, weeping all along as he w':
12 w' to fight with Ishmael the son
14 and w' unto Johanan the son of
15 men, and w' to the Ammonites.
44: 3 in that they w' to burn incense,
51:59 when he w' with Zedekiah the
52: 7 w' forth out of the city by night by
7 and they w' by the way of the plain.
Eze 1: 9 they turned not when they w';
9 they w' every one straight forward.
12 they w' every one straight forward:
12 the spirit was to go, they w';
12 and they turned not when they w'.
13 it w' up and down among the
13 out of the fire w' forth lightning.
17 When they w', they w' upon their
17 and they turned not when they w'.
19 living creatures w', the wheels w'
20 the spirit was to go, they w',
21 When those w', these w'; and when
24 when they w', I heard the noise
3:14 I w' in bitterness, in the heat of my
23 and w' forth into the plain:
8:10 So I w' in and saw; and behold
11 a thick cloud of incense w' up.
9: 2 they w' in, and stood beside the
7 they w' forth, and slew in the city.
10: 2 the city. And he w' in in my sight.
3 of the house, when the man w' in;
4 glory of the Lord w' up from the
6 then he w' in, and stood beside the
7 linen: who took it, and w' out.
11 When they w', they w' upon their
11 they turned not as they w', but to
11 it; they turned not as they w'.
16 the cherubims w', the wheels w' by
19 when they w' out, the wheels also
22 w' every one straight forward.
11:23 glory of the Lord w' up from the
24 vision that I had seen w' up from
16:14 thy renown w' forth among the
19: 6 he w' up and down among the
20:16 for their heart w' after their idols.
23:44 Yet they w' in unto her, as they go
44 so w' they in unto Aholah and unto
24:12 scum w' not forth out of her:
25: 3 of Judah, when they w' into captivity;
27:33 thy wares w' forth out of the seas,
31:15 day when he w' down to the grave
17 They also w' down into hell with
36:20 whither they w', they profaned my
21 among the heathen, whither they w'.
22 among the heathen, whither ye w'.

Eze 39:23 w' into captivity for their iniquity:
40: 6 and w' up the stairs thereof, and
22 they w' up unto it by seven steps;
49 the steps whereby they w' up to it:
41: 3 Then w' he inward, and measured
7 winding...of the house w' still upward
44:10 far from me, when Israel w' astray,
10 which w' astray away from me after
15 children of Israel w' astray from me,
47: 3 line in his hand w' forth eastward,
48:11 my charge, which w' not astray
11 the children of Israel w' astray,
11 as the Levites w' astray.
Da 2:13 decree w' forth that the wise men
16 Then Daniel w' in, and desired of
17 Then Daniel w' to his house, and
24 Daniel w' in unto Arioch, whom
24 he w' and said thus unto him;
6:10 was signed, he w' into his house;
18 Then the king w' to his palace,
18 him: and his sleep w' from him.
19 w' in haste unto the den of lions.
Ho 1: 3 So he w' and took Gomer the
2:13 she w' after her lovers, and forgat
5:13 then w' Ephraim to the Assyrian,
9:10 but they w' to Baal-peor, and
11: 2 called them, so they w' from them:
Am 5: 3 city that w' out by a thousand
3 that which w' forth by an hundred
19 or w' into the house, and leaned his
Jon 1: 3 the Lord, and w' down to Joppa;
3 fare thereof, and w' down into it,
2: 6 I w' down to the bottoms of the
3: 3 arose, and w' unto Nineveh,
4: 5 So Jonah w' out of the city, and
Na 3:10 carried away, she w' into captivity:
Hab 3: 5 Before him w' the pestilence, and
5 burning coals w' forth at his feet.
11 the light of thine arrows they w',
Zec 2: 3 angel that talked with me w' forth,
3 another angel w' out to meet him,
5: 5 angel that talked with me w' forth,
6: 7 And the bay w' forth, and sought to
8:10 peace to him that w' out or came in
10: 2 they w' their way as a flock, they
M't 2: 9 saw in the east, w' before them,
3: 5 Then w' out to him Jerusalem,
16 w' up straightway out of the water:
4:23 And Jesus w' about all Galilee,
24 his fame w' throughout all Syria:
5: 1 he w' up into a mountain:
8:32 out, they w' into the herd of swine:
33 fled, and w' their ways into the city,
9:25 he w' in, and took her by the hand,
26 fame...w' abroad into all that land.
32 As they w' out, behold, they
35 Jesus w' about all the cities and
11: 7 What w' ye out into the wilderness
8 what w' ye out for to see? A man
9 But what w' ye out for to see? A
12: 1 Jesus w' on the sabbath through
9 thence, he w' into their synagogue:
14 Then the Pharisees w' out, and
13: 1 same day w' Jesus out of the house,
2 so that he w' into a ship, and sat;
3 Behold, a sower w' forth to sow;
25 among the wheat, and w' his way.
36 away, and w' into the house:
46 w' and sold all that he had, and
14:12 buried it, and w' and told Jesus.
14 Jesus w' forth, and saw a great
23 he w' up into a mountain apart to
25 of the night Jesus w' unto them,
15:21 Then Jesus w' thence, and
29 and w' up into a mountain, and sat
18:13 and nine which w' not astray.
28 But the same servant w' out, and
30 but w' and cast him into prison,
19:22 that saying, he w' away sorrowful:
20: 1 which w' out early in the morning
3 And he w' out about the third hour,
4 give you. And they w' their way.
5 Again he w' out about the sixth
6 about the eleventh hour he w' out,
21: 6 And the disciples w', and did as
9 the multitudes that w' before,
12 Jesus w' into the temple of God,
17 and w' out of the city into Bethany;
29 but afterward he repented, and w'.
30 and said, I go, sir: and w' not.
33 and w' into a far country:
22: 5 made light of it, and w' their ways,
10 servants w' out into the highways,
15 Then w' the Pharisees, and took
22 and left him, and w' their way.
24: 1 Jesus w' out, and departed from
25: 1 w' forth to meet the bridegroom.
10 And while they w' to buy, the
10 were ready w' in with him to the
16 five talents w' and traded with the
18 one w' and digged in the earth, and
25 w' and hid thy talent in the earth:
26:14 Iscariot, w' unto the chief priests,
30 w' out into the mount of Olives.
39 he w' a little farther, and fell on
42 He w' away again the second time,
44 And he left them, and w' away again,
58 the high priest's palace, and w' in,
75 And he w' out, and wept bitterly.
27: 5 and w' and hanged himself.
53 w' into the holy city, and appeared
58 He w' to Pilate, and begged the
66 So they w', and made the sepulchre
28: 9 as they w' to tell his disciples,
16 disciples w' away into Galilee,
M'r 1: 5 w' out unto him all the land of

M'r 1:20 hired servants, and w' after him.
21 And they w' into Capernaum; and
35 he w' out, and departed into a
45 he w' out, and began to publish it
2:12 bed, and w' forth before them all;
13 he w' forth again by the sea side;
23 he w' through the corn fields on
23 as they w', to pluck the ears of
26 How he w' into the house of God
3: 6 And the Pharisees w' forth, and
19 him: and they w' into an house.
21 it, they w' out to lay hold on him:
4: 3 Behold, there w' out a sower to sow:
5:13 And the unclean spirits w' out,
14 they w' out to see what it was that
24 Jesus w' with him; and much
6: 1 he w' out from thence, and came
6 he w' round about the villages,
12 they w' out, and preached that
24 she w' forth, and said unto her
27 he w' and beheaded him in the
51 he w' up unto them into the ship;
7:24 w' into the borders of Tyre and
8:27 Jesus w' out, and his disciples,
10:22 that saying, and w' away grieved:
32 and Jesus w' before them: and
46 w' out of Jericho with his disciples
11: 4 they w' their way, and found the
9 they that w' before, and they that
11 he w' out unto Bethany with the
15 and Jesus w' into the temple, and
19 was come, he w' out of the city.
12: 1 and w' into a far country.
12 and they left him, and w' their way.
13: 1 And as he w' out of the temple,
14:10 twelve, w' unto the chief priests,
16 his disciples w' forth, and came
26 w' out into the mount of Olives.
35 he w' forward a little, and fell on
39 again he w' away, and prayed, and
68 And he w' out into the porch; and
15:43 and w' in boldly unto Pilate, and
16: 8 they w' out quickly, and fled from
10 she w' and told them that had
12 walked, and w' into the country.
13 w' and told it unto the residue:
20 And they w' forth, and preached
Lu 1: 9 he w' into the temple of the Lord.
39 w' into the hill country with haste,
2: 1 there w' out a decree from Cæsar
3 all w' to be taxed, every one into
4 And Joseph also w' up from Galilee,
41 his parents w' to Jerusalem every
42 they w' up to Jerusalem after the
44 the company, w' a day's journey;
51 he w' down with them, and came
4:14 there w' out a fame of him through
16 he w' into the synagogue on the
30 the midst of them w' his way,
37 fame of him w' out into every place
42 he departed and w' into a desert
5:15 the more w' there a fame abroad
19 they w' upon the housetop, and let
27 And after these things he w' forth,
6: 1 that he w' through the corn fields;
4 How he w' into the house of God,
12 he w' out into a mountain to pray,
19 for there w' virtue out of him, and
7: 6 Then Jesus w' with them. And
11 that he w' into a city called Nain,
11 many of his disciples w' with him,
17 rumour of him w' forth throughout
24 What w' ye out into the wilderness
25, 26 But what w' ye out for to see?
36 he w' into the Pharisee's house,
8: 1 that he w' throughout every city
2 out of whom w' seven devils,
5 A sower w' out to sow his seed: and
22 w' into a ship with his disciples:
27 And when he w' forth to land,
33 Then w' the devils out of the man,
34 w' and told it in the city and in the
35 they w' out to see what was done;
37 and he w' up into the ship, and
39 And he w' his way, and published
42 as he w' the people thronged him.
9: 6 and w' through the towns,
10 w' aside privately into a desert
28 and w' up into a mountain to pray.
52 they w', and entered into a village
56 And they w' to another village.
57 as they w' in the way, a certain man
10:30 man w' down from Jerusalem to
34 And w' to him, and bound up his
38 as they w', that he entered into a
11:37 he w' in, and sat down to meat.
13:22 w' through the cities and villages,
14: 1 as he w' into the house of one of
25 w' great multitudes with him: and
15:15 w' and joined himself to a citizen
16:30 if one w' unto them from the dead,
17:11 as he w' to Jerusalem, that he
14 as they w', they were cleansed.
29 day that Lot w' out of Sodom it
18:10 Two men w' up into the temple to
14 this man w' down to his house
39 they which w' before rebuked him,
19:12 nobleman w' into a far country to
28 he w' before, ascending up to
32 they that were sent w' their way,
36 as he w', they spread their clothes
45 he w' into the temple, and began
20: 9 w' into a far country for a long time.
21:37 at night he w' out, and abode in the
22: 4 he w' his way, and communed with
13 they w', and found as he had said

Lu 22: 39 w', as he was wont, to the mount
47 one of the twelve, w' before them,
62 Peter w' out, and wept bitterly.
23: 52 This man w' unto Pilate, and
24: 13 two of them w' that same day to a
15 drew near, and w' with them.
24 were with us w' to the sepulchre,
28 unto the village, whither they w':
29 And he w' in to tarry with them.
Joh 2: 12 this he w' down to Capernaum,
13 and Jesus w' up to Jerusalem,
4: 28 w' her way into the city, and saith
30 Then they w' out of the city, and
43 departed thence, and w' into Galilee.
45 for they also w' unto the feast.
47 he w' unto him, and besought him
50 unto him, and he w' his way.
5: 1 and Jesus w' up to Jerusalem.
4 For an angel w' down at a certain
6: 1 Jesus w' over the sea of Galilee,
3 And Jesus w' up into a mountain,
16 disciples w' down unto the sea,
17 w' over...sea toward Capernaum.
21 was at the land whither they w'.
22 Jesus w' not with his disciples
66 time many of his disciples w' back,
7: 10 then w' he also up unto the feast,
14 feast Jesus w' up into the temple,
53 every man w' unto his own house.
8: 1 Jesus w' unto the mount of Olives.
9 w' out one by one, beginning at
59 himself, and w' out of the temple,
9: 7 He w' his way therefore, and
11 I w' and washed, and I received
10: 40 w' away again beyond Jordan into
11: 20 was coming, w' and met him:
28 she had so said, she w' her way,
31 she rose up hastily and w' out,
46 some of them w' their ways to the
54 w' thence unto a country near to
55 many w' out of the country up to
12: 11 of him many of the Jews w' away,
13 trees, and w' forth to meet him,
13: 3 come from God, and w' to God;
30 having received the sop w'...out:
18: 1 w' forth with his disciples over the
4 w' forth, and said unto them,
6 they w' backward, and fell to the
15 w' in with Jesus into the palace of
16 Then w' out that other disciple,
28 w' not into the judgment hall,
29 Pilate then w' out unto them, and
38 he w' out again unto the Jews,
19: 4 Pilate therefore w' forth again, and
9 w' again into the judgment hall,
17 w' forth into a place called the
20: 3 Peter therefore w' forth, and that
5 clothes lying; yet w' he not in.
6 w' into the sepulchre, and seeth
8 Then w' in also that other disciple,
10 disciples w' away again unto their
21: 3 They w' forth, and entered into a
11 Simon Peter w' up, and drew the
23 Then w' this saying abroad among
Ac 1: 10 toward heaven as he w' up,
13 they w' up into an upper room,
21 Lord Jesus w' in and out
3: 1 Now Peter and John w'...together
4: 23 they w' to their own company,
5: 26 w' the captain with the officers,
7: 15 So Jacob w' down into Egypt, and
8: 4 w' every where preaching the
5 Then Philip w' down to the city of
27 And he arose and w': and, behold,
36 And as they w' on their way, they
38 they w' down both into the water,
39 and he w' on his way rejoicing.
9: 1 the Lord, w' unto the high priest,
17 Ananias w' his way, and entered
29 but they w' about to slay him.
39 Peter arose and w' with them.
10: 9 as they w' on their journey, and
9 Peter w' up upon the housetop to
21 Then Peter w' down to the men
23 morrow Peter w' away with them,
27 he w' in, and found many that
38 who w' about doing good, and
12: 9 And he w' out, and followed him;
10 they w' out, and passed on through
17 and w' into another place.
19 And he w' down from Judæa to
13: 11 he w' about seeking some to lead
14 and w' into the synagogue on the
14: 1 w' both together into the synagogue
25 Perga, they w' down into Attalia:
15: 24 certain which w' out from us have
38 and w' not with them to the work.
41 he w' through Syria and Cilicia,
16: 4 as they w' through the cities, they
13 on the sabbath we w' out of the
16 as we w' to prayer, a certain
40 And they w' out of the prison, and
17: 2 his manner was, w' in unto them,
10 w' into the synagogue of the Jews.
18: 22 church, he w' down to Antioch.
23 w' over all the country of Galatia
19: 8 And he w' into the synagogue,
12 the evil spirits w' out of them.
20: 10 Paul w' down, and fell on him, and
13 we w' before to ship, and sailed
21: 2 we w' aboard, and set forth.
5 we departed and w' our way' and
15 carriages, and w' up to Jerusalem.
16 There w' with us also certain of
18 Paul w' in with us unto James;
31 And as they w' about to kill him,
Ac 22: 5 w' to Damascus, to bring them
26 he w' and told the chief captain,
23: 16 he w' and entered into the castle,
19 and w' with him aside privately,
24: 11 days since I w' up to Jerusalem
25: 6 days, he w' down unto Cæsarea;
26: 12 as I w' to Damascus with authority
21 temple, and w' about to kill me.
28: 14 days: and so we w' toward Rome.
Ro 10: 18 their sound w' into all the earth,
2Co 2: 13 I w' from thence into Macedonia.
8: 17 of his own accord he w' unto you.
Ga 1: 17 Neither w' I up to Jerusalem to
17 but I w' into Arabia, and returned
18 Then after three years I w' up to
2: 1 I w' up again to Jerusalem with
2 And I w' up by revelation, and
1Ti 1: 3 when I w' into Macedonia,
18 to the prophecies which w' before
Heb 9: 6 the priests w' always into the
7 into the second w' the high priest
11: 8 obeyed; and he w' out,
8 not knowing whither he w'.
1Pe 3: 19 he w' and preached unto the
1Jo 2: 19 They w' out from us, but they were
19 they w' out, that they might be made
3Jo 7 for his name's sake they w' forth,
Re 1: 16 his mouth w' a sharp twoedged
6: 2 he w' forth conquering, and to
4 there w' out another horse that
10: 9 I w' unto the angel, and said unto
12: 17 w' to make war with the remnant of
16: 2 the first w', and poured out his vial
20: 9 they w' upon the breadth of the

wentest
Ge 49: 4 thou w' up to thy father's bed;
J'g 5: 4 Lord, when thou w' out of Seir,
8: 1 when thou w' to fight with the
1Sa 10: 2 asses which thou w' to seek are
2Sa 7: 9 with thee whithersoever thou w',
16: 17 why w' thou not with thy friend?
19: 25 Wherefore w' not thou with me,
Ps 68: 7 thou w' forth before thy people,
Isa 57: 7 even thither w' thou up to offer
9 thou w' to the king with ointment,
Jer 2: 2 thou w' after me in the wilderness,
31: 21 even the way which thou w':
Hab 3: 13 Thou w' forth for the salvation of
Ac 11: 3 Thou w' in to men uncircumcised,

wept
Ge 21: 16 and lift up her voice, and w'.
27: 38 Esau lifted up his voice, and w'.
29: 11 and lifted up his voice, and w'.
33: 4 neck, and kissed him: and they w'.
37: 35 Thus his father w' for him.
42: 24 himself about from them, and w';
43: 30 into his chamber, and w' there.
45: 2 And he w' aloud:
14 brother Benjamin's neck, and w';
14 and Benjamin w' upon his neck.
15 his brethren, and w' upon them:
46: 29 and w' on his neck a good while.
50: 1 and w' upon him, and kissed him.
17 Joseph w' when they spake unto
Ex 2: 6 child: and, behold, the babe w'.
Nu 11: 4 children of Israel also w' again,
18 ye have w' in the ears of the Lord,
20 and have w' before him, saying,
14: 1 cried; and the people w' that night.
De 1: 45 returned and w' before the Lord;
34: 8 the children of Israel w' for Moses
J'g 2: 4 people lifted up their voice, and w'.
14: 16 And Samson's wife w' before him,
17 she w' before him the seven days,
20: 23 and w' before the Lord until even,
26 came unto the house of God, and w',
21: 2 lifted up their voices, and w' sore;
Ru 1: 9 they lifted up their voice, and w'.
14 lifted up their voice, and w' again:
1Sa 1: 7 therefore she w', and did not eat.
10 prayed unto the Lord, and w' sore.
11: 4 people lifted up their voices, and w'.
20: 41 w' one with another, until David
24: 16 Saul lifted up his voice, and w'.
30: 4 him lifted up their voice and w',
2Sa 1: 12 they mourned, and w', and fasted
3: 32 and w' at the grave of Abner;
32 of Abner; and all the people w'.
34 all the people w' again over him.
12: 22 child was yet alive, I fasted and w':
13: 36 and lifted up their voice and w':
36 and all his servants w' very sore.
15: 23 all the country w' with a loud voice,
30 mount Olivet, and w' as he went up,
18: 33 the chamber over the gate, and w':
2Ki 8: 11 ashamed: and the man of God w'.
13: 14 and w' over his face, and said, O my
20: 3 thy sight. And Hezekiah w' sore.
22: 19 rent thy clothes, and w' before me;
Ezr 3: 12 their eyes, w' with a loud voice;
10: 1 for the people w' very sore.
Ne 1: 4 words, that I sat down and w',
8: 9 For all the people w', when they
Job 2: 12 they lifted up their voice, and w';
Ps 69: 10 When I w', and chastened my soul
137: 1 we w', when we remembered Zion.
Isa 38: 3 thy sight. And Hezekiah w' sore.
Ho 12: 4 he w', and made supplication unto
M't 26: 75 And he went out, and w' bitterly.
M'r 5: 38 them that w' and wailed greatly.
14: 72 when he thought thereon, he w'.
16: 10 with him, as they mourned and w'.
Lu 7: 32 to you, and ye have not w'.
8: 52 all w', and bewailed her: but he
19: 41 he beheld the city, and w' over it,
Lu 22: 62 Peter went out, and w' bitterly.
Joh 11: 35 Jesus w'.
20: 11 and as she w', she stooped down,
Ac 20: 37 And they all w' sore, and fell on
1Co 7: 30 that weep, as though they w' not;
Re 5: 4 And I w' much, because no man

wert See also WAST.
Job 8: 6 If thou w' pure and upright; surely
Ca 8: 1 O that thou w' as my brother, that
Ro 11: 17 olive tree, w' graffed in among them,
24 For if thou w' cut out of the olive tree
24 and w' graffed contrary to nature into
Re 3: 15 nor hot: I would thou w' cold or hot.

west See also WESTERN; WESTWARD.
Ge 12: 8 having Beth-el on the w', and Hai
28: 14 thou shalt spread abroad to the w',
Ex 10: 19 turned a mighty strong w' wind,
27: 12 the w' side shall be hangings of fifty
38: 12 the w' side were hangings of fifty
Nu 2: 18 On the w' side shall be the standard
34: 6 this shall be your w' border.
35: 5 on the w' side two thousand cubits,
De 33: 23 possess thou the w' and the south.
Jos 8: 9 Beth-el and Ai, on the w' side of Ai:
12 and Ai, on the w' side of the city.
13 liers in wait on the w' of the city,
11: 2 in the borders of Dor on the w',
3 on the east and on the w',
12: 7 on this side Jordan on the w',
15: 12 the w' border was to the great sea,
18: 14 of Judah: this was the w' quarter.
15 and the border went out on the w',
19: 34 reacheth to Asher on the w' side,
1Ki 7: 25 and three looking toward the w',
1Ch 9: 24 toward the east, w', north, and
12: 15 the east, and toward the w'.
2Ch 4: 4 and three looking toward the w',
32: 30 to the w' side of the city of David.
33: 14 on the w' side of Gihon, in the
Ps 75: 6 from the east, nor from the w',
103: 12 As far as the east is from the w',
107: 3 from the east, and from the w',
Isa 11: 14 of the Philistines toward the w';
43: 5 east, and gather thee from the w';
45: 6 and from the w', that there is none
49: 12 and from the w'; and these from
59: 19 the name of the Lord from the w',
Eze 41: 12 end toward the w' was seventy
42: 19 He turned about to the w' side,
45: 7 city, from the w' side westward,
7 from the w' border unto the east
47: 20 w' side also shall be the great sea
20 Hamath. This is the w' side.
48: 1 for these are his sides east and w';
2 from the east side unto the w' side,
3 the east side even unto the w' side,
4, 5 the east side unto the w' side,
6 the east side even unto the w' side,
7, 8 the east side unto the w' side,
8 from the east side unto the w' side:
10 and toward the w' ten thousand in
16 the w' side four thousand and five
17 toward the w' two hundred and
21 and twenty thousand toward the w'
23, 24, 25, 26, 27 east side unto the w'
34 At the w' side four thousand and
Da 8: 5 an he goat came from the w' on
Ho 11: 10 children shall tremble from the w'.
Zec 8: 7 and from the w' country;
14: 4 toward the east and toward the w',
M't 8: 11 shall come from the east and w',
24: 27 east, and shineth even unto the w';
Lu 12: 54 ye see a cloud rise out of the w',
13: 29 from the east, and from the w',
Ac 27: 12 toward the south w' and north
12 toward the south...and north w'.
Re 21: 13 gates; and on the w' three gates.

western
Nu 34: 6 And as for the w' border, ye shall

westward
Ge 13: 14 southward, and eastward, and w':
Ex 26: 22 for the sides of the tabernacle w'
27 the tabernacle, for the two sides w'.
36: 27 for the sides of the tabernacle w'
32 of the tabernacle for the sides w'.
Nu 3: 23 pitch behind the tabernacle w'.
De 3: 27 of Pisgah, and lift up thine eyes w',
Jos 5: 1 were on the side of Jordan w', and
15: 8 before the valley of Hinnom w',
10 from Baalah w' unto mount Seir,
16: 3 down w' to the coast of Japhleti,
8 Tappuah w' unto the river Kanah;
18: 12 went up through the mountains w';
19: 26 and reacheth to Carmel w', and to
34 coast turneth w' to Aznoth-tabor,
22: 7 brethren on this side Jordan w'.
23: 4 even unto the great sea w'.
1Ch 7: 28 and w' Gezer, with the towns
26: 16 and Hosah the lot came forth w',
18 At Parbar w', four at the causeway,
30 of Israel on this side Jordan w'
Eze 45: 7 of the city, from the west side w',
46: 19 was a place on the two sides w'.
48: 18 eastward, and ten thousand w':
21 and w' over against the five and
Da 8: 4 I saw the ram pushing w', and

west-wind See WEST and WIND.

wet
Job 24: 8 They are w' with the showers of
Da 4: 15, 23 be w' with the dew of heaven,
25 w' thee with the dew of heaven,

Da 4:33 and his body was *w·* with the dew
5:21 and his body was *w·* with the dew

whale See also WHALE'S; WHALES.
Job 7:12 Am I a sea, or a *w·*, that thou
Eze 32: 2 and thou art as a *w·* in the seas:

whale's
M't 12:40 and three nights in the *w·* belly;

whales
Ge 1:21 And God created great *w·*, and

what^ See also SOMEWHAT; WHATSOEVER.
Ge 2:19 to see *w·* he would call them:
3:13 *W·* is this that thou hast done?
4:10 And he said, *W·* hast thou done?
9:24 *w·* his younger son had done
12:18 *W·* is this that thou hast done
15: 2 Lord God, *w·* wilt thou give me,
20: 9 him, *W·* hast thou done unto us?
9 and *w·* have I offended thee, that
10 *W·* sawest thou, that thou hast
21:17 unto her, *W·* aileth thee, Hagar?
24:65 *W·* man is this that walketh in
25:32 *w·* profit shall this birthright do
26:10 *W·* is this thou hast done unto us?
27:37 and *w·* shall I do now unto thee,
46 land, *w·* good shall my life do me?
29:15 tell me, *w·* shall thy wages be?
25 *W·* is this thou hast done unto me?
30:31 And he said, *W·* shall I give thee?
31:26 *W·* hast thou done, that thou hast
36 *W·* is my trespass? *w·* is my sin,
43 *w·* can I do this day unto these my
32:27 he said unto him, *W·* is thy name?
33: 8 *W·* meanest thou by all this drove
15 And he said, *W·* needeth it? let
34:11 *w·* ye shall say unto me I will give.
37:10 *W·* is this dream that thou hast
15 him, saying, *W·* seekest thou?
20 see *w·* will become of his dreams.
26 *W·* profit is it if we slay our brother,
38:16 And she said, *W·* wilt thou give me,
18 said, *W·* pledge shall I give thee?
39: 8 not *w·* is with me in the house,
41:25 Pharaoh *w·* he is about to do.
28 *W·* God is about to do he sheweth
55 unto Joseph; *w·* he saith to you, do.
42:28 *W·* is this that God hath done
44:15 *W·* deed is this that ye have done?
16 *W·* shall we say unto my lord?
16 *w·* shall we speak? or how shall we
46:33 shall say, *W·* is your occupation?
47: 3 brethren, *W·* is your occupation?
Ex 3:13 shall say to me, *W·* is his name?
13 *w·* shall I say unto them?
4: 2 unto him, *W·* is that in thine hand?
12 and teach thee *w·* thou shalt say.
15 will teach you *w·* ye shall do.
10: 2 *w·* things I have wrought in
26 with *w·* we must serve the Lord,
12:26 you, *W·* mean ye by this service?
13:14 in time to come, saying, *W·* is this?
15:24 Moses, saying, *W·* shall we drink?
16: 7 *w·* are we, that ye murmur against
8 *w·* are we? your murmurings are
15 manna: for they wist not *w·* it was.
17: 4 *W·* shall I do unto this people?
18:14 *W·* is this thing that thou doest to
19: 4 seen *w·* I did unto the Egyptians,
23:11 *w·* they leave the beasts of the field
32: 1 we wot not *w·* is become of him.
21 *W·* did this people unto thee, that
23 we wot not *w·* is become of him.
Le 15: 9 *w·* saddle soever he rideth upon
17: 3 *W·* man soever there be of...Israel,
22: 4 *W·* man soever of the seed of Aaron
25:20 *W·* shall we eat the seventh year?
Nu 9: 8 hear *w·* the Lord will command
10:32 that *w·* goodness the Lord shall do
13:18 And see the land, *w·* it is; and the
19 *w·* the land is that they dwell in,
19 *w·* cities they be that they dwell in,
20 *w·* the land is, whether it be fat or
15:34 declared *w·* should be done to him.
16:11 and *w·* is Aaron, that ye murmur
21:14 *W·* he did in the Red sea, and in
22: 9 *W·* men are these with thee?
19 may know *w·* the Lord will say
28 *W·* have I done unto thee, that
23:11 *W·* hast thou done unto me?
17 him, *W·* hath the Lord spoken?
23 of Israel, *W·* hath God wrought!
24:13 *w·* the Lord saith, that will I speak?
14 *w·* this people shall do to thy people
26:10 *w·* time the fire devoured two hundred
31:50 *w·* every man hath gotten, of
De 1:22 again by *w·* way must we go up,
22 and into *w·* cities we shall come.
33 shew you by *w·* way ye should go,
3:24 for *w·* God is there in heaven or
4: 3 eyes have seen *w·* the Lord did
7 For *w·* nation is there so great,
8 And *w·* nation is there so great,
6:20 *W·* mean the testimonies, and
7:18 remember *w·* the Lord thy God
8: 2 to know *w·* was in thine heart,
10:12 *w·* doth the Lord thy God require
11: 4 *w·* he did unto the army of Egypt,
5 *w·* he did unto you in the wilderness,
6 *w·* he did unto Dathan and Abiram,
12:32 *W·* thing soever I command you,
20: 5 *W·* man is there that hath built a
6 *w·* man is he that hath planted a
7 *w·* man is there that hath betrothed
8 *W·* man is there that is fearful
24: 9 *w·* the Lord...did unto Miriam

De 25:17 *w·* Amalek did unto thee
29:24 *w·* meaneth the heat of this great
32:20 I will see *w·* their end shall be:
Jos 2:10 *w·* ye did unto the two kings of the
4: 6 *W·* mean ye by these stones?
21 saying, *W·* mean these stones?
5:14 *W·* saith my lord unto his servant?
7: 8 O Lord, *w·* shall I say, when Israel
9 *w·* wilt thou do unto thy great
19 tell me now *w·* thou hast done;
9: 3 Gibeon heard *w·* Joshua had
15:18 said unto her, *w·* wouldest thou?
22:16 *W·* trespass is this that ye have
24 *W·* have ye to do with the Lord
24: 7 seen *w·* I have done in Egypt:
J'g 1:14 Caleb said unto her, *W·* wilt thou?
7:11 And thou shalt hear *w·* they say;
8: 2 *W·* have I done now in comparison
3 *w·* was I able to do in comparison
18 *W·* manner of men were they
9:48 *W·* ye have seen me do, make
10:18 *W·* man is he that will begin to
11:12 *W·* hast thou to do with me, that
13: 8 teach us *w·* we shall do unto the
17 *W·* is thy name, that when thy
14: 6 or his mother *w·* he had done.
18 down, *W·* is sweeter than honey?
18 *w·* is stronger than a lion? And he
15:11 *w·* is this that thou hast done unto
16: 5 *w·* means we may prevail against
18: 3 and *w·* makest thou in this place?
3 and *w·* hast thou here?
8 said unto them, *W·* say ye?
14 therefore consider *w·* ye have to do.
18 the priest unto them, *W·* do ye?
23 *W·* aileth thee, that thou comest
24 gone away: and *w·* have I more?
24 *w·* is this that ye say unto me,
24 ye say unto me, *W·* aileth thee?
19:24 them *w·* seemeth good unto you:
20:12 *W·* wickedness is this that is done
21: 8 *W·* one is there of the tribes of
Ru 2:18 in law saw *w·* she had gleaned:
3: 4 he will tell thee *w·* thou shalt do.
4: 5 *W·* day thou buyest the field
1Sa 1:23 Do *w·* seemeth thee good; tarry
3:17 *W·* is the thing that the Lord
18 let him do *w·* seemeth him good.
4: 6, 14 *W·* meaneth the noise of this
16 he said, *W·* is there done, my son?
5: 8 *W·* shall we do with the ark of the
6: 2 *W·* shall we do to the ark of the
4 *W·* shall be the trespass offering
9: 7 we go, *w·* shall we bring the man?
7 to the man of God: *w·* have we?
10: 2 saying, *W·* shall I do for my son?
8 shew thee *w·* thou shalt do.
11 *W·* is this that is come unto the
15 thee, *w·* Samuel said unto you.
11: 5 *W·* aileth the people that they
13:11 Samuel said, *W·* hast thou done?
14:40 Saul, Do *w·* seemeth good unto thee.
43 Tell me *w·* thou hast done.
15:14 *W·* meaneth then this bleating of
16 tell thee *w·* the Lord hath said
16: 3 will shew thee *w·* thou shalt do:
17:26 *W·* shall be done to the man that
29 David said, *W·* have I now done?
18: 8 *w·* can he have more but the kingdom?
18 and *w·* is my life, or my father's
19: 3 and *w·* I see, that I will tell thee.
20: 1 Jonathan, *W·* have I done?
1 *w·* is mine iniquity?
1 *w·* is my sin before thy father, that
10 or *w·* if thy father answer thee
32 shall he be slain? *w·* hath he done?
21: 2 and *w·* I have commanded thee:
3 *w·* is under thine hand? give
3 in mine hand, or *w·* there is present.
22: 3 till I know *w·* God will do for me.
25:17 and consider *w·* thou wilt do;
26:18 his servant? *w·* have I done? for
18 or *w·* evil is in mine hand?
28: 2 know *w·* thy servant can do.
9 thou knowest *w·* Saul hath done,
13 Be not afraid: for *w·* sawest thou?
14 said unto her, *W·* form is he of?
15 make known unto me *w·* I shall do.
29: 3 *W·* do these Hebrews here? And
8 unto Achish, But *w·* have I done?
8 *w·* hast thou found in thy servant
2Sa 3:24 king, and said, *W·* hast thou done?
7:18 and *w·* is my house, that thou
20 *w·* can David say more unto thee?
23 *w·* one nation in the earth is like
9: 8 *W·* is thy servant, that thou
12:21 *W·* thing is this that thou hast
14: 5 said unto her, *W·* aileth thee?
15: 2 and said, Of *w·* city art thou?
21 surely in *w·* place my lord the king
35 *w·* thing soever thou shalt hear
16: 2 Ziba, *W·* meanest thou by these?
10 *W·* have I to do with you, ye sons
17: 5 let us hear likewise *w·* he saith.
18: 4 *W·* seemeth you best I will do.
21 Go tell the king *w·* thou hast seen.
29 tumult, but I knew not *w·* it was.
19:18 and to do *w·* he thought good.
22 *W·* have I to do with you, ye sons
27 do therefore *w·* is good in thine eyes.
28 *W·* right therefore have I yet to
35 can thy servant taste *w·* I eat
35 I eat or *w·* I drink? can I hear
37 *w·* shall seem good unto thee.
21: 3 Gibeonites, *W·* shall I do for you?
4 *W·* ye shall say, that will I do for

2Sa 21:11 was told David *w·* Rizpah the
24:13 *w·* answer I shall return to him
17 these sheep, *w·* have they done?
22 offer up *w·* seemeth good unto him:
1Ki 1:16 the king said, *W·* wouldest thou?
2: 5 *w·* Joab the son of Zeruiah did
5 *w·* he did to the two captains of the
9 knowest *w·* thou oughtest to do
3: 5 God said, Ask *w·* I shall give thee.
8:38 *W·* prayer and supplication
9:13 *W·* cities are these which thou
11:22 But *w·* hast thou lacked with me,
12: 9 *W·* counsel give ye that we may
16 *W·* portion have we in David?
13:12 unto them, *W·* way went he?
12 seen *w·* way the man of God went,
14: 3 thee *w·* shall become of the child.
14 of Jeroboam that day: but *w·*?
16: 5 acts of Baasha, and *w·* he did,
17:18 *W·* have I to do with thee, O thou
18: 9 *W·* have I sinned, that thou
13 *w·* I did when Jezebel slew the
19: 9, 13 *W·* doest thou here, Elijah?
20 again: for *w·* have I done to thee?
20:22 mark, and see *w·* thou doest:
22:14 *w·* the Lord saith unto me,3588,
2Ki 1: 7 *W·* manner of man was he which
2: 9 Elisha, Ask *w·* I shall do for thee.
3:13 Israel, *W·* have I to do with thee?
4: 2 unto her, *W·* shall I do for thee?
2 tell me, *w·* hast thou in the house?
13 this care; *w·* is to be done for thee?
14 said, *W·* then is to be done for her?
43 *W·*, should I set this before an
6:28 said unto her, *W·* aileth thee?
33 *w·* should I wait for the Lord any
7:12 shew you *w·* the Syrians have
8:13 But *w·*, is thy servant a dog, that
14 to him, *W·* said Elisha to thee?
9:18, 19 *W·* hast thou to do with peace?
22 *W·* peace, so long as the
18:19 *W·* confidence is this wherein thou
19:11 heard *w·* the kings of Assyria
20: 8 *W·* shall be the sign that the Lord
14 *W·* said these men? and from
15 *W·* have they seen in thine house?
22:19 heardest *w·* I spake against this
1Ch 12:32 to know *w·* Israel ought to do;
17:16 Lord God, and *w·* is mine house,
18 *W·* can David speak more to thee
21 *w·* one nation in the earth is like
21:12 *w·* word I shall bring again to
29:14 who am I, and *w·* is my people,
2Ch 1: 7 him, Ask *w·* I shall give thee.
6:29 Then *w·* prayer or...supplication
29 *w·* supplication soever shall be
10: 6 *W·* counsel give ye me to return
9 *W·* advice give ye that we may
16 *W·* portion have we in David?
18:13 liveth, even *w·* my God saith,
19: 6 the judges, Take heed *w·* ye do:
10 *w·* cause soever shall come to you
20:12 us; neither know we *w·* to do:
24:11 *w·* time the chest was brought unto
25: 9 *w·* shall we do for the hundred
32:13 Know ye not *w·* I and my fathers
35:21 *W·* have I to do with thee, thou
Ezr 5: 4 *W·* are the names of the men that
6: 8 *w·* ye shall do to the elders
8:17 *w·* they should say unto Iddo,
9:10 God, *w·* shall we say after this?
Ne 2: 4 For *w·* dost thou make request?
12 *w·* my God had put in my heart
16 not whither I went, or *w·* I did;
19 *W·* is this thing that ye do? will ye
4: 2 *W·* do these feeble Jews? will they
20 In *w·* place therefore ye hear the
13:17 *W·* evil thing is this that ye do,
Es 1:15 *W·* shall we do unto the queen
2: 1 Vashti, and *w·* she had done,
1 and *w·* was decreed against her.
11 did, and *w·* should become of her.
15 but *w·* Hegai...appointed.
4: 5 to Mordecai, to know *w·* it was,
5: 3 her, *W·* wilt thou, queen Esther?
3 and *w·* is thy request? it shall be
6 *W·* is thy petition? and it shall be
6 and *w·* is thy request? even to
6: 3 *W·* honour and dignity hath been
6 *W·* shall be done unto the man
7: 2 *W·* is thy petition, queen Esther?
2 *w·* is thy request? and it shall be
8: 1 Esther had told *w·* he was unto her.
9: 5 did *w·* they would unto those that
12 *w·* have they done in the rest of
12 now *w·* is thy petition? and it shall
12 *w·* is thy request further? and it
Job 2:10 *W·*? shall we receive good at the
6:11 *W·* is my strength, that I should
11 *w·* is mine end, that I should
17 *W·* time they wax warm, they vanish:
25 *w·* doth your arguing reprove?
7:17 *W·* is man, that thou shouldest
20 *w·* shall I do unto thee, O thou
9:12 will say unto him, *W·* doest thou?
11: 8 high as heaven; *w·* canst thou do?
8 than hell; *w·* canst thou know?
13: 2 *W·* ye know, the same do I know also:
13 speak, and let come on me *w·* will.
15: 9 *W·* knowest thou, that we know
9 *w·* understandest thou, which is not
12 and *w·* do thy eyes wink at,
14 *W·* is man, that he should be
16: 3 or *w·* emboldeneth thee that thou
6 though I forbear, *w·* am I eased?
21:15 *W·* is the Almighty, that we

Job 21:15 *w*· profit should we have, if we pray
21 *w*· pleasure hath he in his house
31 shall repay him *w*· he hath done?
22:17 *w*· can the Almighty do for them?
23: 5 understand *w*· he would say unto
13 and *w*· his soul desireth, even that he
27: 8 *w*· is the hope of the hypocrite,
31: 2 *w*· portion of God is there from
2 *w*· inheritance of the Almighty from
14 *W*· then shall I do when God
14 visiteth, *w*· shall I answer him?
32:11 whilst ye searched out *w*· to say.
34: 4 know among ourselves *w*· is good.
7 *W*· man is like Job, who drinketh
33 therefore speak *w*· thou knowest.
35: 3 *W*· advantage will it be unto thee?
3 and, *W*· profit shall I have, if I be
6 *w*· doest thou against him? or if
6 multiplied, *w*· doest thou unto him?
7 be righteous, *w*· givest thou him?
7 or *w*· receiveth he of thine hand?
37:19 Teach us *w*· we shall say unto him;
38:24 By *w*· way is the light parted,
39:18 *W*· time she lifted up herself on high,
40: 4 I am vile; *w*· shall I answer thee?
Ps 8: 4 *W*· is man, that thou art mindful
11: 3 destroyed, *w*· can the righteous do?
25:12 *W*· man is he that feareth the
30: 9 *W*· profit is there in my blood,
34:12 *W*· man is he that desireth life,
39: 4 the measure of my days, *w*· it is;
7 Lord, *w*· wait I for? my hope is in
44: 1 us, *w*· work thou didst in their days,
46: 8 *w*· desolations he hath made in the
50:16 *W*· hast thou to do to declare my
56: 3 *W*· time I am afraid, I will trust in
4 I will not fear *w*· flesh can do
11 not be afraid *w*· man can do unto
66:16 and I will declare *w*· he hath done
85: 8 hear *w*· God the Lord will speak:
89:48 *W*· man is he that liveth, and
114: 5 *W*· ailed thee, O thou sea, that
116:12 *W*· shall I render unto the Lord
118: 6 not fear: *w*· can man do unto me?
120: 3 *W*· shall be given unto thee?
3 *w*· shall be done unto thee, thou
144: 3 Lord, *w*· is man, that thou takest
Pr 4:19 they know not at *w*· they stumble.
10:32 the righteous know *w*· is acceptable:
23: 1 diligently *w*· is before thee:
25: 8 thou know not *w*· to do in the end
27: 1 knowest not *w*· a day may bring
30: 4 *w*· is his name, and *w*· is his son's
31: 2 *W*·, my son? and
2 and *w*·, the son of my womb?
2 and *w*·, the son of my vows?
Ec 1: 3 *W*· profit hath a man of all his
2: 2 mad: and of mirth, *W*· doeth it?
3 I might see *w*· was that good for
12 *w*· can the man do that cometh
22 For *w*· hath man of all his labour,
3: 9 *W*· profit hath he that worketh in
22 him to see *w*· shall be after him?
5:11 and *w*· good is there to the owners
16 and *w*· profit hath he that hath
6: 8 *w*· hath the wise more than the
8 *w*· hath the poor, that knoweth to
11 vanity, *w*· is man the better?
12 who knoweth *w*· is good for man in
12 can tell a man *w*· shall be after him
7:10 *W*· is the cause that the former
8: 4 may say unto him, *W*· doest thou?
10:14 a man cannot tell *w*· shall be;
14 *w*· shall be after him, who can tell
11: 2 not *w*· evil shall be upon the earth.
5 not *w*· is the way of the spirit,
Ca 5: 9 *W*· is thy beloved more than
9 *w*· is thy beloved more than
6:13 *W*· will ye see in the Shulamite?
8: 8 *w*· shall we do for our sister in the
Isa 1:11 To *w*· purpose is the multitude of
3:15 *W*· mean ye that ye beat my people
5: 4 *W*· could have been done more to
5 you *w*· I will do to my vineyard:
10: 3 And *w*· will ye do in the day of
19:12 *w*· the Lord of hosts hath purposed
21: 6 let him declare *w*· he seeth.
11 Seir, Watchman, *w*· of the night?
11 night? Watchman, *w*· of the night?
22: 1 *W*· aileth thee now, that thou art
16 *W*· hast thou here? and whom
33:13 ye that are far off, *w*· I have done;
37:11 *w*· the kings of Assyria have done
38:15 *W*· shall I say? he hath both
22 *W*· is the sign that I shall go up
39: 3 *W*· said these men? and from
4 *W*· have they seen in thine house?
40: 6 *W*· shall I cry? All flesh is grass,
18 *w*· likeness will ye compare unto
41:22 and shew us *w*· shall happen:
22 the former things, *w*· they be,
45: 9 fashioneth it, *W*· makest thou?
10 unto his father, *W*· begettest thou?
10 *W*· hast thou brought forth?
52: 5 *w*· have I here, saith the Lord,
64: 4 *w*· he hath prepared for him that
Jer 1:11 saying, Jeremiah, *w*· seest thou?
13 second time, saying, *W*· seest thou?
2: 5 *W*· iniquity have your fathers
18, 18 *w*· hast thou to do in the way of
23 valley, know *w*· thou hast done:
4:30 thou art spoiled, *w*· wilt thou do?
5:15 neither understandest *w*· they say.
31 *w*· will ye do in the end thereof?
6:18 O congregation, *w*· is among
20 To *w*· purpose cometh there to

Jer 7:12 and see *w*· I did to it for the
17 thou not *w*· they do in the cities
8: 6 saying, *W*· have I done?
9 Lord; and *w*· wisdom is in them?
9:12 for *w*· the land perisheth and is
11:15 *W*· hath my beloved to do in mine
13:21 *W*· wilt thou say when he shall
16:10 *w*· is our iniquity? or *w*· is our sin
18: 7 At *w*· instant I shall speak concerning
9 And at *w*· instant I shall speak
23:25 heard *w*· the prophets said,
28 *W*· is the chaff to the wheat? saith
33 *W*· is the burden of the Lord?
33 then say unto them, *W*· burden?
35 *W*· hath the Lord answered?
35 and, *W*· hath the Lord spoken?
37 *W*· hath the Lord answered thee?
37 and, *W*· hath the Lord spoken?
24: 3 *W*· seest thou, Jeremiah? And I
32:24 *w*· thou hast spoken is come to
33:24 not *w*· this people have spoken,
37:18 *W*· have I offended against thee,
38:25 Declare unto us now *w*· thou hast
25 also *w*· the king said unto thee:
48:19 escapeth, and say, *W*· is done?
La 2:13 *W*· thing shall I take to witness for
13 *w*· thing shall I liken to thee,
13 *w*· shall I equal to thee, that I may
5: 1 O Lord, *w*· is come upon us:
Eze 2: 8 man, hear *w*· I say unto thee;
8: 6 Son of man, seest thou *w*· they do?
12 *w*· the ancients of the house of
12: 9 said unto thee, *W*· doest thou?
22 *w*· is that proverb that ye have
15: 2 *W*· is the vine tree more than any
17:12 know ye not *w*· these things mean?
18: 2 *W*· mean ye, that ye use this
19: 2 *W*· is thy mother? A lioness: she
21:13 *w*· if the sword condemn even the
24:19 tell us *w*· these things are to us,
27:32 *W*· city is like Tyrus, like the
33:30 hear *w*· is the word that cometh
37:18 shew *w*· thou meanest by these?
47:23 in *w*· tribe the stranger sojourneth,
Da 2:22 he knoweth *w*· is in the darkness,
23 me now *w*· we desired of thee:
28 *w*· shall be in the latter days.
29 *w*· should come to pass hereafter:
29 known to thee *w*· shall come to pass.
45 *w*· shall come to pass hereafter:
3: 5, 15 *w*· time ye hear the sound of the
4:35 or say unto him, *W*· doest thou?
8:19 know *w*· shall be in the last end
10:14 *w*· shall befall thy people in the
12: 8 *w*· shall be the end of these
Ho 6: 4 Ephraim, *w*· shall I do unto thee?
4 O Judah, *w*· shall I do unto thee?
9: 5 *W*· will ye do in the solemn day,
14 them, O Lord: *w*· wilt thou give?
10: 3 *w*· then should a king do to us?
14: 8 *W*· have I to do any more with
Joe 3: 4 *w*· have ye to do with me, O Tyre,
Am 4:13 unto man *w*· is his thought, that
5:18 of the Lord! to *w*· end is it for you?
7: 8 said unto me, Amos, *w*· seest thou?
Jon 1: 6 him, *W*· meanest thou, O sleeper?
8 *W*· is thine occupation? and
8 comest thou? *w*· is thy country?
8 and of *w*· people art thou?
11 *W*· shall we do unto thee, that the
4: 5 see *w*· would become of the city.
Mic 1: 5 *W*· is the transgression of Jacob?
5 *w*· are the high places of Judah?
6: 1 Hear ye now *w*· the Lord saith;
3 people, *w*· have I done unto thee?
5 *w*· Balak king of Moab consulted,
5 *w*· Balaam...son of Beor answered
8 shewed thee, O man, *w*· is good;
8 *w*· doth the Lord require of thee,
Na 1: 9 *W*· do ye imagine against the
Hab 2: 1 and will watch to see *w*· he will say
1 and *w*· I shall answer when I am
18 *W*· profiteth the graven image that
Zec 1: 9 Then said I, O my lord, *w*· are these?
9 me, I will shew thee *w*· these be.
19 that talked with me, *W*· be these?
21 Then said I, *W*· come these to do?
2: 2 to see *w*· is the breadth thereof,
2 and *w*· is the length thereof.
4: 2 And said unto me, *W*· seest thou?
4 me, saying, *W*· are these, my lord?
5 me, Knowest thou not *w*· these be?
11 *W*· are these two olive trees upon
12 *W*· be these two olive branches
13 Knowest thou not *w*· these be? And
5: 2 *W*· seest thou? And I answered,
5 and see *w*· is this that goeth forth.
6 And I said, *W*· is it? And he said,
6: 4 with me, *W*· are these, my lord?
13: 6 him, *W*· are these wounds in thine
Mal 1:13 also, Behold, *w*· a weariness is it!
3:13 say, *W*· have we spoken so much
14 *w*· profit is it that we have kept
M't 2: 7 diligently *w*· time...star appeared.
5:46 which love you, *w*· reward have ye?
47 only, *w*· do ye more than others?
6: 3 know *w*· thy right hand doeth:
8 Father knoweth *w*· things ye have
25 *w*· ye shall eat, or *w*· ye shall drink;
25 for your body, *w*· ye shall put on.
31 saying, *W*· shall we eat? or,
31 or, *W*· shall we drink? or,
7: 2 with *w*· judgment ye judge, ye shall
9 *w*· man is there of you, whom if
8:27 saying, *W*· manner of man is this,
29 *W*· have we to do with thee, Jesus,

M't 8:33 *w*· was befallen to the possessed
9:13 go ye and learn *w*· that meaneth,
10:19 thought how or *w*· ye shall speak:
19 that same hour *w*· ye shall speak.
27 *W*· I tell you in darkness, that
27 *w*· ye hear in the ear, that preach ye
11: 7 *W*· went ye out in the wilderness
8 But *w*· went ye out for to see? A
9 But *w*· went ye out for to see? A
12: 3 Have ye not read *w*· David did,
7 if ye had known *w*· this meaneth,
11 *W*· man shall there be among you,
16:26 For *w*· is a man profited, if he shall
26 *w*· shall a man give in exchange for
17:25 *W*· thinkest thou, Simon? of whom
18:31 his fellowservants saw *w*· was
19: 6 *W*· therefore God hath joined
16 *w*· good thing shall I do, that I
20 from my youth up: *w*· lack I yet?
27 thee; *w*· shall we have therefore?
20:15 me to do *w*· I will with mine own?
21 he said unto her, *W*· wilt thou?
22 and said, Ye know not *w*· ye ask.
32 *W*· will ye that I shall do unto you?
21:16 Hearest thou *w*· these say? and
23 By *w*· authority doest thou these
24, 27 by *w*· authority I do these things.
28 But *w*· think ye? A certain man
40 cometh, *w*· will he do unto those
22:17 us therefore, *W*· thinkest thou?
42 *W*· think ye of Christ? whose son is
24: 3 *w*· shall be the sign of thy coming,
42 for ye know not *w*· hour your Lord
43 known in *w*· watch the thief would
26: 8 To *w*· purpose is this waste?
15 *W*· will ye give me, and I will
40 *W*·, could ye not watch with me
62 *w*· is it which these witness
65 *w*· further need have we of
66 *W*· think ye? They answered and
70 saying, I know not *w*· thou sayest.
27: 4 *W*· is that to us? see thou to that.
22 *W*· shall I do then with Jesus
23 said, Why, *w*· evil hath he done?
M'r 1:24 *w*· have we to do with thee, thou
27 amazed,...saying, *W*· thing is this?
27 *w*· new doctrine is this?
2:25 Have ye never read *w*· David did,
3: 8 had heard *w*· great things he did,
4:24 with *w*· measure ye mete, it shall
30 *w*· comparison shall we compare
41 *W*· manner of man is this, that
5: 7 *W*· have I to do with thee, Jesus,
9 he asked him, *W*· is thy name?
14 out to see *w*· it was that was done.
33 knowing *w*· was done in her, came
6: 2 *w*· wisdom is this which is given
10 In *w*· place soever ye enter into
24 unto her mother, *W*· shall I ask?
30 *w*· they had done, and *w*· they had
8:36 For *w*· shall it profit a man, if he
37 Or *w*· shall a man give in exchange
9: 6 For he wist not *w*· to say; for they
9 tell no man *w*· things they had
10 *w*· the rising from the dead should
16 scribes, *W*· question ye with them?
33 *W*· was it that ye disputed among
10: 3 *W*· did Moses command you?
9 *W*· therefore God hath joined
17 *w*· shall I do that I may inherit
32 *w*· things should happen unto him,
36 *W*· would ye that I should do for
38 unto them, Ye know not *w*· ye ask:
51 *W*· wilt thou that I should do unto
11: 5 them, *W*· do ye, loosing the colt?
24 *W*· things soever ye desire, when
28 By *w*· authority doest thou these
29, 33 *w*· authority I do these things.
12: 9 *W*· shall therefore the lord of the
13: 1 Master, see *w*· manner of stones
1 stones and *w*· buildings are here!
4 *w*· shall be the sign when all these
11 beforehand *w*· ye shall speak,
37 And *w*· I say unto you I say unto
14: 8 She hath done *w*· she could: she is
36 not *w*· I will, but *w*· thou wilt.
40 neither wist they *w*· to answer him,
60 *w*· is it which these witness thee
63 *W*· need we any further witnesses?
64 heard the blasphemy: *w*· think ye?
68 understand I *w*· thou sayest.
15:12 *W*· will ye then that I shall do unto
14 them, Why, *w*· evil hath he done?
24 them, *w*· every man should take.
Lu 1:29 mind *w*· manner of salutation this
66 *W*· manner of child shall this
3:10 him, saying, *W*· shall we do then?
12 unto him, Master, *w*· shall we do?
14 of him, saying, And *w*· shall we do?
4:34 *w*· have we to do with thee, thou
36 saying, *W*· a word is this! for with
5:19 by *w*· way they might bring him
22 *W*· reason ye in your hearts?
6: 3 *W*· David did, when himself was an
11 another *w*· they might do to Jesus.
32 which love you, *w*· thank have ye?
33 do good to you, *w*· thank have ye?
34 hope to receive, *w*· thank have ye?
7:22 tell John *w*· things ye have seen
24 John, *W*· went ye out into the
25, 26 But *w*· went ye out for to see? A
31 generation?...to *w*· are they like?
39 and *w*· manner of woman this is
8: 9 saying, *W*· might this parable be?
25 *W*· manner of man is this!
28 *W*· have I to do with thee, Jesus,

Lu 8:30 asked him, saying, *W·* is thy name?
34 they that fed them saw *w·* was done,
35 they went out to see *w·* was done;
36 by *w·* means he that was possessed
47 for *w·* cause she had touched him,
56 they should tell no man *w·* was done.
9:25 For *w·* is a man advantaged, if he
33 for Elias: not knowing *w·* he said.
55 Ye know not *w·* manner of spirit
10:25 *w·* shall I do to inherit eternal life?
26 *W·* is written in the law? how
12:11 how or *w·* thing ye shall answer,
11 ye shall answer, or *w·* ye shall say:
12 the same hour *w·* ye ought to say.
17 *W·* shall I do, because I have no
22 for your life, *w·* ye shall eat;
22 for the body, *w·* ye shall put on.
29 And seek not ye *w·* ye shall eat, or
29 ye shall eat, or *w·* ye shall drink,
39 *w·* hour the thief would come,
49 *w·* will I, if it be already kindled?
57 yourselves judge ye not *w·* is right?
13:18 *w·* is the kingdom of God like?
14:31 Or *w·* king, going to make war
15: 4 *W·* man of you, having an hundred
8 Either *w·* woman having ten pieces
26 and asked *w·* these things meant.
16: 3 *W·* shall I do? for my lord taketh
4 I am resolved *w·* to do, that, when
18: 6 Hear *w·* the unjust judge saith.
18 *w·* shall I do to inherit eternal life?
36 passed by, he asked *w·* it meant.
41 *W·* wilt thou that I shall do unto
19:48 could not find *w·* they might do:
20: 2 by *w·* authority doest thou these
8 by *w·* authority I do these things.
13 *W·* shall I do? I will send my
15 *W·* therefore shall the lord of the
17 *W·* is this then that is written,
21: 7 *w·* sign will there be when these
14 meditate before *w·* ye shall answer:
22:49 about him saw *w·* would follow,
60 Man, I know not *w·* thou sayest.
71 *W·* need we any further witness?
23:22 Why, *w·* evil hath he done? I have
31 tree, *w·* shall be done in the dry?
34 them: for they know not *w·* they do.
47 the centurion saw *w·* was done,
24:17 *W·* manner of communications
19 he said unto them, *W·* things?
35 they told *w·* things were done in the
Joh 1:21 him, *W·* then? Art thou Elias?
22 sent us. *W·* sayest thou of thyself?
38 and saith unto them, *W·* seek ye?
2: 4 Woman, *w·* have I to do with thee?
18 *W·* sign shewest thou unto us,
25 man: for he knew *w·* was in man.
3:32 *w·* he hath seen and heard, that he
4:22 Ye worship ye know not *w·*: we
22 we know *w·* we worship: for
27 *W·* seekest thou? or, Why talkest
5:12 *W·* man is that which said unto
19 but *w·* he seeth the Father do:
19 for *w·* things soever he doeth, these
6: 6 he himself knew *w·* he would do.
9 but *w·* are they among so many?
28 *W·* shall we do, that we might work
30 *W·* sign shewest thou then, that
30 believe thee? *w·* dost thou work?
62 *W·* and if ye shall see the Son of man
7:36 *W·* manner of saying is this that
51 it hear him, and know *w·* he doeth?
8: 5 be stoned: but *w·* sayest thou?
9:17 *W·* sayest thou of him, that he hath
21 But by *w·* means he now seeth, we
26 to him again, *W·* did he to thee?
10: 6 understood not *w·* things they were
11:46 told...*w·* things Jesus had done.
47 *W·* do we? for this man doeth
56 *W·* think ye, that he will not come
12: 6 the bag, and bare *w·* was...therein.
27 *w·* shall I say? Father, save me
33 signifying *w·* death he should die.
49 *w·* I should say, and *w·* I should
13: 7 *W·* I do thou knowest not now;
12 Know ye *w·* I have done to you?
28 knew for *w·* intent he spake this
15: 7 ye shall ask *w·* ye will, and it shall
15 knoweth not *w·* his lord doeth:
16:17 *W·* is this that he saith unto us,
18 therefore, *W·* is this that he saith,
18 we cannot tell *w·* he saith.
18:21 me, *w·* I have said unto them:
21 behold, they know *w·* I said.
29 *W·* accusation bring ye against
32 signifying *w·* death he should die.
35 thee unto me: *w·* hast thou done?
38 Pilate saith unto him, *W·* is truth?
19:22 *W·* I have written I have written.
21:19 by *w·* death he should glorify God.
21 Lord, and *w·* shall this man do?
22, 23 till I come, *w·* is that to thee?
Ac 2:12 one to another, *W·* meaneth this?
37 Men and brethren, *w·* shall we do?
4: 7 By *w·* power, or by *w·* name,
9 by *w·* means he is made whole;
16 *W·* shall we do to these men? for
5: 7 his wife, not knowing *w·* was done,
35 *w·* ye intend to do as touching
7:40 we wot not *w·* is become of him.
49 *w·* house will ye build me? saith
49 or, *w·* is the place of my rest?
8:30 Understandest...*w·* thou readest?
36 *w·* doth hinder me to be baptized?
9: 6 Lord, *w·* wilt thou have me to do?
6 it shall be told thee *w·* thou must do.

Ac 10: 4 was afraid, and said, *W·* is it, Lord?
6 tell thee *w·* thou oughtest to do.
15 *W·* God hath cleansed, that call not
17 *W·* this vision which he had seen
21 *w·* is the cause wherefore ye are
29 for *w·* intent ye have sent for me?
11: 9 *W·* God hath cleansed, that call
17 *w·* was I, that I could withstand
12:18 soldiers, *w·*...become of Peter.
13:12 deputy, when he saw *w·* was done,
14:11 the people saw *w·* Paul had done,
15:12 declaring *w·* miracles and wonders
16:30 Sirs, *w·* must I do to be saved?
17:18 some said, *W·* will this babbler say?
19 we know not *w·* this new doctrine,
20 therefore *w·* these things mean.
19: 3 Unto *w·* then were ye baptized?
35 *w·* man is there that knoweth not
20:18 after *w·* manner I have been with
21:13 *W·* mean ye to weep and to break
19 *w·* things God had wrought among
22 *W·* is it therefore? the multitude
33 who he was, and *w·* he had done.
22:10 And I said, *W·* shall I do, Lord?
15 men of *w·* thou hast seen and heard.
26 saying, Take heed *w·* thou doest:
23:19 *W·* is that thou hast to tell me?
30 thee *w·* they had against him.
34 he asked of *w·* province he was.
28:22 to hear of thee *w·* thou thinkest:
Ro 3: 1 *W·* advantage then hath the Jew?
1 *w·* profit is there of circumcision?
3 For *w·* if some did not believe?
5 *w·* shall we say? Is God
9 *W·* then? are we better than they?
19 *w·* things soever the law saith,
27 By *w·* law? of works? Nay: but
4: 1 *W·* shall we say then that
3 *w·* saith the scripture? Abraham
21 *w·* he had promised, he was able
6: 1 *W·* shall we say then? Shall we
15 *W·* then? shall we sin, because we
21 *W·* fruit had ye then in those
7: 7 *W·* shall we say then? Is the law
15 not; for *w·* I would, that do I not;
15 do I not; but *w·* I hate, that do I.
8: 3 *w·* the law could not do, in that it
24 for *w·* a man seeth, why doth he yet
26 know not *w·* we should pray for
27 knoweth *w·* is the mind of the Spirit,
31 *W·* shall we then say to these
9:14 *W·* shall we say then? Is there
22 *W·* if God, willing to shew his wrath,
30 *W·* shall we say then? That the
10: 8 But *w·* saith it? The word is nigh
11: 2 *w·* the scripture saith of Elias?
4 But *w·* saith the answer of God
7 *W·* then? Israel hath not obtained
15 *w·* shall the receiving of them be,
12: 2 that ye may prove *w·* is that good,
1Co 2:11 *w·* man knoweth the things of a
3:13 every man's work of *w·* sort it is.
4: 7 *w·* hast thou that thou didst not
21 *W·* will ye? shall I come unto you
5:12 For *w·* have I to do to judge them
6:16 *W·*? know ye not that he which is
19 *W·*? know ye not that your body is
7:16 For *w·* knowest thou, O wife,
36 him do *w·* he will, he sinneth not:
9:18 *W·* is my reward then? Verily that
10:15 as to wise men; judge ye *w·* I say.
19 *W·* say I then? that the idol is any
11:22 *W·*? have ye not houses to eat...in?
22 *W·* shall I say to you? shall I
14: 6 *w·* shall I profit you, except I shall
7 it be known *w·* is piped or harped?
9 how shall it be known *w·* is spoken?
15 *W·* is it then? I will pray with the
16 understandeth not *w·* thou sayest?
36 *W·*? came the word of God out
15: 2 keep in memory *w·* I preached
10 by the grace of God I am *w·* I am:
29 Else *w·* shall they do which are
32 *w·* advantageth it me, if the dead
35 and with *w·* body do they come?
2Co 6:14 *w·* fellowship hath righteousness
14 *w·* communion hath light with
15 *w·* concord hath Christ with Belial?
15 *w·* part hath he that believeth with
16 *w·* agreement hath the temple of
7:11 *w·* carefulness it wrought in you,
11 in you, yea, *w·* clearing of yourselves,
11 of yourselves, yea, *w·* indignation,
11 yea, *w·* fear, yea, *w·* vehement desire,
11 desire, yea, *w·* zeal, yea, *w·* revenge!
12:13 *w·* is it wherein ye were inferior
Ga 4:30 Nevertheless *w·* saith the scripture?
Eph 1:18 know *w·* is the hope of his calling,
18 *w·* the riches of the glory of his
19 *w·* is the exceeding greatness of
3: 9 *w·* is the fellowship of the mystery,
18 with all saints *w·* is the breadth,
4: 9 *w·* is it but that he also descended
5:10 Proving *w·* is acceptable unto the
17 *w·* the will of the Lord is.
Ph'p 1:18 *W·* then? notwithstanding, every
22 yet *w·* I shall choose I wot not.
3: 7 But *w·* things were gain to me,
Col 1:27 *w·* is the riches of the glory of
2: 1 knew *w·* great conflict I have for
1Th 1: 5 know *w·* manner of men we were
9 *w·* manner of entering in we had
2:19 For *w·* is our hope, or joy, or
3: 9 For *w·* thanks can we render to
4: 2 know *w·* commandments we gave
2Th 2: 6 *w·* withholdeth that he might be

1Ti 1: 7 understanding neither *w·* they say,
2Ti 2: 7 Consider *w·* I say; and the Lord give
3:11 Lystra; *w·* persecutions I endured:
Heb 2: 6 *W·* is man, that thou art mindful
7:11 *w·* further need was there that
11:32 *w·* shall I more say? for the time
12: 7 for *w·* son is he whom the father
13: 6 not fear *w·* man shall do unto me.
Jas 1:24 forgetteth *w·* manner of man he
2:14 *W·* doth it profit, my brethren,
16 to the body; *w·* doth it profit?
4:14 not *w·* shall be on the morrow.
14 For *w·* is your life? It is even a
1Pe 1:11 Searching *w·*, or...manner of
11 or *w·* manner of time the Spirit
2:20 For *w·* glory is it, if, when ye be
4:17 *w·* shall the end be of them that
2Pe 3:11 *w·* manner of persons ought ye to
1Jo 3: 1 *w·* manner of love the Father hath
2 not yet appear *w·* we shall be:
Jude 10 but *w·* they know naturally, as
Re 1:11 *W·* thou seest, write in a book
2: 7, 11, 17, 29 hear *w·* the Spirit saith
3: 3 shalt not know *w·* hour I will come
6, 13, 22 hear *w·* the Spirit saith
7:13 *W·* are these which are arrayed in
18:18 *W·* city is like unto this great city!

whatsoever
Ge 2:19 *w·* Adam called every living
8:19 and *w·* creepeth upon the earth,
19:12 and *w·* thou hast in the city,
31:16 *w·* God hath said unto thee, do.
39:22 *w·* they did there, he was the
Ex 13: 2 firstborn, *w·* openeth the womb
21:30 ransom...*w·* is laid upon him.
29:37 *w·* toucheth the altar shall be holy.
30:29 *w·* toucheth them shall be holy.
Le 5: 3 *w·* uncleanness it be that a man
4 *w·*...a man shall pronounce
6:27 *W·* shall touch the flesh thereof
7:27 *W·* soul it be that eateth any
11: 3 *W·* parteth the hoof, and is
9 *w·* hath fins and scales in the
12 *W·* hath no fins nor scales in the
27 *w·* goeth upon his paws, among all
32 upon *w·* any of them, when they
32 *w·* vessel it be, wherein any work is
33 *w·* is in it shall be unclean;
42 *W·* goeth upon the belly,
42 and *w·* goeth upon all fours,
42 or *w·* hath more feet among all
13:58 *w·* thing of skin it be, which thou
15:26 *w·* she sitteth upon shall be
17: 8 *W·* man there be of the house of
10 *w·* man there be of the house of
13 *w·* man there be of the children
21:18 *w·* man he be that hath a blemish,
22: 5 *w·* uncleanness he hath;
18 *W·* he be of the house of Israel,
20 *w·* hath a blemish, that shall ye
23:29 *w·* soul it be that shall not be
30 *w·* soul it be that doeth any work in
27:32 even of *w·* passeth under the rod,
Nu 5:10 *w·* any man giveth the priest, it
18:13 and *w·* is first ripe in the land,
19:22 *w·* the unclean person toucheth
22:17 I will do *w·* thou sayest unto
23: 3 *w·* he sheweth me I will tell
30:12 then *w·* proceeded out of her lips
De 2:37 *w·* the Lord our God forbad us.
12: 8 man *w·* is right in his own eyes.
15 *w·* thy soul lusteth after, according
20 eat flesh, *w·* thy soul lusteth after.
21 thy gates *w·* thy soul lusteth after.
14:10 *w·* hath not fins and scales ye
26 money for *w·* thy soul lusteth
26 or for *w·* thy soul desireth:
J'g 10:15 us *w·* seemeth good unto thee;
11:31 *w·* cometh forth of the doors of my
1Sa 14:36 Do *w·* seemeth good unto thee.
20: 4 *W·* thy soul desireth, I will even
25: 8 *w·* cometh to thine hand unto
2Sa 3:36 as *w·* the king did pleased all
15:15 ready to do *w·* my lord the king
19:38 *w·* thou shalt require of me,
1Ki 8:37 *w·* plague, *w·* sickness there be;
10:13 Sheba all her desire, *w·* she asked,
20: 6 that *w·* is pleasant in thine eyes,
2Ch 6:28 *w·* sore or *w·* sickness there be:
9:12 Sheba all her desire, *w·* she asked,
Ezr 7:18 *w·* shall seem good to thee,
20 And *w·* more shall be needful for the
21 *w·* Ezra the priest, the scribe
23 *W·* is commanded by the God
Es 2:13 *w·* she desired was given
Job 37:12 do *w·* he commandeth them
41:11 *w·* is under the whole heaven is mine.
Ps 1: 3 and *w·* he doeth shall prosper.
8: 8 *w·* passeth through the paths of the
115: 3 hath done *w·* he hath pleased.
135: 6 *W·* the Lord pleased, that did
Ec 2:10 *w·* my eyes desireth I kept not
3:14 *w·* God doeth, it shall be for
8: 3 for he doeth *w·* pleaseth him.
9:10 *W·* thy hand findeth to do, do it
Jer 1: 7 *w·* I command thee thou shalt
42: 4 that *w·* thing the Lord shall
44:17 *w·* thing goeth forth out of our
M't 5:37 *w·* is more than these cometh of evil.
7:12 *w·* ye would that men should
10:11 into *w·* city or town ye...enter,
14: 7 to give her *w·* she would ask.
15: 5 by *w·* thou mightest be profited
17 *w·* entereth in at the mouth goeth
16:19 *w·* thou shalt bind on earth
19 *w·* thou shalt loose on earth shall

M't 17:12 have done unto him w' they listed.
18:18 W' ye shall bind on earth
18 w' ye shall loose on earth shall
20: 4 and w' is right I will give you.
7 w' is right that shall ye receive.
21:22 w' ye shall ask in prayer,
23: 3 w' they bid you observe,
28:20 things w' I have commanded you:
M'r 6:22 Ask of me w' thou wilt, and I
23 W' thou shalt ask of me, I will
7:11 by w' thou mightest be profited by
18 w' thing from without entereth
9:13 have done unto him w' they listed,
10:21 sell w' thou hast, and give to the
35 do for us w' we shall desire.
11:23 pass; he shall have w' he saith.
13:11 w' shall be given you in that
Lu 4:23 w' we have heard done in
9: 4 w' house ye enter into, there
10: 5 And into w' house ye enter, first
8, 10 into w' city ye enter, and they
35 w' thou spendest more, when I
12: 3 w' ye have spoken in darkness
Joh 2: 5 W' he saith unto you, do it.
5: 4 made whole of w' disease he had.
11:22 w' thou wilt ask of God, God
12:50 w' I speak therefore, even as the
14:13 w' ye shall ask in my name,
26 remembrance, w' I have said unto
15:14 friends, if ye do w' I command
16 w' ye shall ask of the Father
16:13 w' he shall hear, that shall he
23 W' ye shall ask the Father in
17: 7 w' thou hast given me are of thee.
Ac 3:22 in all things w' he shall say
4:28 to do w' thy hand and thy counsel
Ro 14:23 faith: for w' is not of faith is sin.
15: 4 w' things were written aforetime
16: 2 ye assist her in w' business she
1Co 10:25 W' is sold in the shambles, that
27 w' is set before you, eat, asking
31 w' ye do, do all to the glory of God.
Ga 2: 6 (w' they were, it maketh no
6: 7 w' a man soweth, that shall he
Eph 5:13 w' doth make manifest is light.
6: 8 w' good thing any man
Ph'p 4: 8 brethren, w' things are true,
8 w' things are honest,
8 w' things are just,
8 w' things are pure,
8 w' things are lovely,
8 w' things are of good report;
11 w' state I am, therewith to be
Col 3:17 w' ye do in word or deed,
23 w' ye do, do it heartily, as
1Jo 3:22 w' we ask, we receive of him,
5: 4 w' is born of God overcometh the
15 w' we ask, we know that we
3Jo 5 w' thou doest to the brethren,
Re 18:22 craftsman, of w' craft he be, shall
21:27 w' worketh abomination, or maketh

wheat See also WHEATEN.
Ge 30:14 went in the days of w' harvest,
Ex 9:32 the w' and the rie were not smitten
34:22 the firstfruits of w' harvest, and the
Nu 18:12 best of the wine, and of the w',
De 8: 8 A land of w', and barley, and
32:14 with the fat of kidneys of w';
J'g 6:11 his son Gideon threshed w' by the
15: 1 after, in the time of w' harvest,
Ru 2:23 barley harvest and of w' harvest;
1Sa 6:13 were reaping their w' harvest in
12:17 Is it not w' harvest to day? I will
2Sa 4: 6 they would have fetched w';
17:28 vessels, and w', and barley, and
1Ki 5:11 twenty thousand measures of w'
1Ch 21:20 Now Ornan was threshing w'.
23 and the w' for the meat offering;
2Ch 2:10 thousand measures of beaten w',
15 the w', and the barley, the oil, and
27: 5 and ten thousand measures of w',
Ezr 6: 9 w', salt, wine, and oil, according
7:22 and to an hundred measures of w',
Job 31:40 Let thistles grow instead of w',
Ps 81:16 them also with the finest of the w':
147:14 filleth thee with the finest of the w'.
Pr 27:22 bray a fool in a mortar among w'
Ca 7: 2 an heap of w' set about with lilies.
Isa 28:25 cast in the principal w' and the
Jer 12:13 They have sown w', but shall reap
23:28 What is the chaff to the w'? saith
31:12 for w', and for wine, and for oil,
41: 8 in the field, of w', and of barley,
Eze 4: 9 Take thou also unto thee w', and
27:17 traded in thy market w' of Minnith,
45:13 part of an ephah of an homer of w',
Joe 1:11 for the w' and for the barley;
2:24 the floors shall be full of w', and
Am 5:11 ye take from him burdens of w':
8: 5 sabbath, that we may set forth w',
6 yea, and sell the refuse of the w'?
M't 3:12 and gather his w' into the garner;
13:25 and sowed tares among the w',
29 ye root up also the w' with them.
30 but gather the w' into my barn.
Lu 3:17 will gather the w' into his garner;
16: 7 said, An hundred measures of w'.
22:31 you, that he may sift you as w':
Joh 12:24 a corn of w' fall into the ground
Ac 27:38 and cast out the w' into the sea.
1Co 15:37 it may chance of w', or of some
Re 6: 6 A measure of w' for a penny, and
18:13 and oil, and fine flour, and w',

wheaten
Ex 29: 2 of w' flour shalt thou make them.

wheel See also WHEELS.
1Ki 7:32 height of a w' was a cubit and half
33 was like the work of a chariot w':
Ps 83:13 God, make them like a w'; as the
Pr 20:26 and bringeth the w' over them.
Ec 12: 6 or the w' broken at the cistern.
Isa 28:27 neither is a cart w' turned about
28 break it with the w' of his cart,
Eze 1:15 behold one w' upon the earth by
16 it were a w' in the middle of a w'.
10: 9 cherubim, one w' by one cherub,
9 another w' by another cherub:
10 a w' had been in the midst of a w'.
13 unto them in my hearing, O w'.

wheels
Ex 14:25 took off their chariot w', that they
J'g 5:28 why tarry the w' of his chariots?
1Ki 7:30 And every base had four brasen w',
32 under the borders were four w';
32 axletrees of the w' were joined to
33 work of the w' was like the work of
Isa 5:28 and their w' like a whirlwind:
Jer 18: 3 he wrought a work on the w'.
47: 3 and at the rumbling of his w', the
Eze 1:16 appearance of the w' and their
19 creatures went, the w' went by them:
19 the earth, the w' were lifted up.
20 the w' were lifted up over against
20 of the living creature was in the w'.
21 w' were lifted up over against them:
21 of the living creature was in the w'.
3:13 noise of the w' over against them,
10: 2 Go in between the w', even under
6 Take fire from between the w',
6 went in, and stood beside the w'.
9 the four w' by the cherubims,
9 appearance of the w' was as the
12 the w' were full of eyes round about,
12 even the w' that they four had.
13 As for the w', it was cried unto
16 cherubims went, the w' went by
16 the same w' also turned not from
19 out, the w' also were beside them,
11:22 wings, and the w' beside them; and
23:24 with chariots, wagons, and w',
26:10 of the horsemen, and of the w',
Da 7: 9 flame, and his w' as burning fire.
Na 3: 2 the noise of the rattling of the w',

whelm See OVERWHELM.

whelp See also WHELPS.
Ge 49: 9 Judah is a lion's w': from the
De 33:22 Dan is a lion's w': he shall leap
Na 2:11 the lion's w', and none made them

whelps
2Sa 17: 8 as a bear robbed of her w' in the field:
Job 4:11 the stout lion's w' are scattered
28: 8 The lion's w' have not trodden it,
Pr 17:12 Let a bear robbed of her w' meet a
Jer 51:38 lions: they shall yell as lions' w'.
Eze 19: 2 she nourished her w' among
3 she brought one of her w': it
5 she took another of her w', and
Ho 13: 8 as a bear that is bereaved of her w',
Na 2:12 tear in pieces enough for his w',

when^ See also WHENSOEVER.
Ge 2: 4 of the earth w' they were created,
3: 6 w' the woman saw that the tree was
4: 8 w' they were in the field, that Cain
12 W' thou tillest the ground, it
5: 2 Adam, in the day w' they were created.
6: 1 w' men began to multiply on the
4 w' the sons of God came in unto
7: 6 w' the flood of waters was upon the
9:14 w' I bring a cloud over the earth, that
12: 4 years old w' he departed out of Haran.
11 w' he was come near to enter into
12 w' the Egyptians shall see thee,
14 w' Abram was come into Egypt, the
14:14 w' Abram heard that his brother
15:11 w' the fowls came down upon the
12 And w' the sun was going down,
17 w' the sun went down, and it was
16: 4, 5 w' she saw that she had conceived,
6 w' Sarai dealt hardly with her, she
16 w' Hagar bare Ishmael to Abram.
17: 1 w' Abram was ninety years old
24, 25 w' he was circumcised in the flesh
18: 2 w' he saw them, he ran to meet
19:15 And w' the morning arose, then
17 w' they had brought them forth
23 the earth w' Lot entered into Zoar.
29 w' God destroyed the cities of the
29 w' he overthrew the cities in the
33, 35 w' she lay down, nor w' she arose.
20:13 w' God caused me to wander from
21: 5 w' his son Isaac was born unto him.
24:36 a son to my master w' she was old.
52 w' Abraham's servant heard their
64 w' she saw Isaac, she lighted off the
25:20 years old w' he took Rebekah to wife,
24 w' her days to be delivered were
26 threescore years old w' she bare them.
26: 8 w' he had been there a long time,
27:34 w' Esau heard the words of his father,
40 w' thou shalt have the dominion,
28: 6 W' Esau saw that Isaac had blessed
29:10 w' Jacob saw Rachel the daughter
13 w' Laban heard the tidings of Jacob
31 w' the Lord saw that Leah was hated,
30: 1 w' Rachel saw that she bare Jacob no
9 W' Leah saw that she had left
25 w' Rachel had born Joseph, that
30 w' shall I provide for mine own
Ge 30:33 w' it shall come for my hire before
38 troughs w' the flocks came to drink,
38 conceive w' they came to drink.
42 w' the cattle were feeble, he put them
31:49 w' we are absent one from another.
32: 2 w' Jacob saw them, he said, This
17 W' Esau my brother meeteth
19 speak unto Esau, w' ye find him.
25 And w' he saw that he prevailed not
33:18 Canaan, w' he came from Padan-aram;
34: 2 And w' Shechem the son of Hamor
7 came out of the field w' they heard it:
25 w' they were sore, that two of the sons
35: 1 w' thou fleddest from the face of Esau
7 w' he fled from the face of his
9 w' he came out of Padan-aram, and
17 w' she was in hard labour, that the
22 w' Israel dwelt in that land, that
37: 4 w' his brethren saw that their father
18 w' they saw him afar off, even before
23 w' Joseph was come unto his
38: 5 he was at Chezib, w' she bare him.
9 w' he went in unto his brother's
15 W' Judah saw her, he thought her to
25 W' she was brought forth, she
28 w' she travailed, that the one put out
39:13 w' she saw that he had left his
15 w' he heard that I had lifted up my
19 w' his master heard the words of his
40:13 manner w' thou wast his butler.
14 on me w' it shall be well with thee,
16 W' the chief baker saw that the
41:21 And w' they had eaten them up,
46 years old w' he stood before Pharaoh
55 w' all the land of Egypt was famished,
42: 1 w' Jacob saw that there was corn in
21 w' he besought us, and we would not
35 w' both they and their father saw the
43: 2 w' they had eaten up the corn
21 w' we came to the inn, that we
26 w' Joseph came home, they brought
44: 4 And w' they were gone out of the city,
4 w' thou dost overtake them, say unto
24 w' we came up unto thy servant
30 w' I came to thy servant my father,
31 w' he seeth that the lad is not with us,
45:27 w' he saw the wagons that Joseph had
46:33 w' Pharaoh shall call you, and
47:15 w' money failed in the land of Egypt,
18 W' the year was ended, they came
48: 7 w' I came from Padan, Rachel died by
7 w' yet there was but a little way
17 w' Joseph saw that his father laid his
49:33 w' Jacob had made an end of
50: 4 w' the days of his mourning were past,
11 And w' the inhabitants of the land,
15 w' Joseph's brethren saw that their
17 Joseph wept w' they spake unto him.
Ex 1:10 that, w' there falleth out any war,
16 W' ye do the office of a midwife to the
2: 5 w' she saw the ark among the flags,
6 w' she had opened it, she saw the
11 w' Moses was grown, that he went out
12 and w' he saw that there was no man,
13 and w' he went out the second day,
15 Now w' Pharaoh heard this thing,
18 And w' they came to Reuel their father,
3: 4 w' the Lord saw that he turned aside
12 W' thou hast brought forth the
13 w' I came unto the children of Israel,
4: 6 w' he took it out, behold, his hand was
14 w' he seeth thee, he will be glad in his
21 W' thou goest to return into Egypt,
31 w' they heard that the Lord had
5:13 daily tasks, as w' they were straw.
6:28 day w' the Lord spake unto Moses in
7: 5 w' I stretch forth mine hand upon
7 years old, w' they spake unto Pharaoh.
9 W' Pharaoh shall speak unto you,
8: 9 w' shall I intreat for thee, and for
15 w' Pharaoh saw that there was respite,
9:34 w' Pharaoh saw that the rain and the
10:13 and w' it was morning, the east wind
11: 1 w' he shall let you go, he shall surely
12:13 w' I see the blood, I will pass over
13 you, w' I smite the land of Egypt.
23 w' he seeth the blood upon the lintel,
25 w' ye be come to the land which
26 w' your children shall say unto you,
27 w' he smote the Egyptians, and
44 w' thou hast circumcised him, then
13: 5 w' the Lord shall bring thee into
8 unto me w' I came forth out of Egypt.
11 w' the Lord shall bring thee into
14 w' thy son asketh thee in time to
15 w' Pharaoh would hardly let us go,
17 pass, w' Pharaoh had let the people go,
17 the people repent w' they see war,
14:10 w' Pharaoh drew nigh, the children of
18 w' I have gotten me honour upon
27 his strength w' the morning appeared;
15:23 w' they came to Marah, they could not
25 w' he had cast into the waters, the
16: 3 of Egypt, w' we sat by the flesh pots,
3 and w' we did eat bread to the full;
8 w' the Lord shall give you in the flesh
14 w' the dew that lay was gone up,
15 And w' the children of Israel saw it,
18 And w' they did mete it with an omer,
21 and w' the sun waxed hot, it melted.
32 w' I brought you forth from the land
17:11 pass, w' Moses held up his hand,
11 and w' he let down his hand,
18:14 w' Moses' father in law saw all that he
16 W' they have a matter, they come
19: 1 w' the children of Israel were gone

Ex 19: 9 people may hear *w'* I speak with thee,
13 *w'* the trumpet soundeth long, they
19 And *w'* the voice of the trumpet
20: 18 *w'* the people saw it, they removed,
22: 27 *w'* he crieth unto me, that I will
23: 16 *w'* thou hast gathered in thy labours
28: 29 *w'* he goeth in unto the holy place,
30 heart, *w'* he goeth in before the Lord:
35 *w'* he goeth in unto the holy place
35 and *w'* he cometh out, that he die not.
43 *w'* they come in unto the tabernacle
43 or *w'* they come near unto the altar to
29: 30 *w'* he cometh into the tabernacle of
36 *w'* thou hast made an atonement for
30: 7 *w'* he dresseth the lamps, he shall
8 *w'* Aaron lighteth the lamps at even,
12 *W'* thou takest the sum of the
12 the Lord, *w'* thou numberest them;
12 them, *w'* thou numberest them.
15 *w'* they give an offering unto the Lord,
20 *W'* they go into the tabernacle of the
20 or *w'* they come near to the altar to
31: 18 *w'* he made an end of communing
32: 1 *w'* the people saw that Moses delayed
5 *w'* Aaron saw it, he built an altar
17 *w'* Joshua heard the noise of the
25 *w'* Moses saw that the people were
34 nevertheless in the day *w'* I visit I
33: 4 *w'* the people heard these evil tidings,
8 *w'* Moses went out unto the tabernacle,
34: 24 *w'* thou shalt go up to appear before
29 *w'* Moses came down from mount
29 *w'* he came down from the mount,
30 *w'* Aaron and all the children of Israel
34 *w'* Moses went in before the Lord to
40: 32 *W'* they went into the tent of the
32 *w'* they came near unto the altar, they
36 *w'* the cloud was taken up from over
Le 2: 1 *w'* any will offer a meat offering unto
8 and *w'* it is presented unto the priest,
4: 14 *W'* the sin, which they have sinned
22 *W'* a ruler hath sinned, and done
5: 3, 4 *w'* he knoweth of it, then he shall be
5 *w'* he shall be guilty in one of
6: 20 the Lord in the day *w'* he is anointed;
21 *w'* it is baken, thou shalt bring it in:
27 *w'* there is sprinkled of the blood
7: 35 *w'* he presented them to minister unto
9: 24 *w'* all the people saw, they shouted,
10: 9 *w'* ye go into the tabernacle of the
20 *w'* Moses heard that, he was content.
11: 31 doth touch them, *w'* they be dead,
12: 6 *w'* the days of her purifying are
13: 2 *W'* a man shall have in the skin of
3 *w'* the hair in the plague is turned
9 *W'* the plague of leprosy is in a
14 *w'* raw flesh appeareth in him, he
20 And if, *w'* the priest seeth it, behold,
14: 34 *W'* ye be come into the land of
57 To teach *w'* it is unclean, and
57 and *w'* it is clean: this is the law of
15: 2 *W'* any man hath a running issue
13 *w'* he that hath an issue is cleansed
31 *w'* they defile my tabernacle that is
16: 1 *w'* they offered before the Lord, and
17 *w'* he goeth in to make an atonement
20 *w'* he hath made the end of reconciling
23 put on *w'* he went into the holy place,
18: 28 spue not you out also, *w'* ye defile it,
19: 9 *w'* ye reap the harvest of your land,
23 And *w'* ye shall come into the land,
20: 4 *w'* he giveth of his seed unto Molech,
22: 7 *w'* the sun is down, he shall be clean,
16 trespass, *w'* they eat their holy things:
27 *W'* a bullock, or a sheep, or a goat, is
29 And *w'* ye will offer a sacrifice of
23: 10 *W'* ye be come into the land which
12 offer that day *w'* ye wave the sheaf
22 *w'* ye reap the harvest of your land,
39 *w'* ye have gathered in the fruit of the
43 *w'* I brought them out of the land of
24: 16 *w'* he blasphemeth the name of the
25: 2 *W'* ye come into the land which I
26: 17 ye shall flee *w'* none pursueth you.
25 *w'* ye are gathered together within
26 And *w'* I have broken the staff of your
35 in your sabbaths, *w'* ye dwelt upon it.
36 and they shall fall *w'* none pursueth.
37 before a sword, *w'* none pursueth:
44 *w'* they be in the land of their enemies,
27: 2 *W'* a man shall make a singular
14 *w'* a man shall sanctify his house
21 the field, *w'* it goeth out in the jubile,
Nu 3: 4 *w'* they offered strange fire before the
4: 5 *w'* the camp setteth forward, Aaron
15 *w'* Aaron and his sons have made an
19 *w'* they approach unto the most holy
20 to see *w'* the holy things are covered,
5: 6 *W'* a man or a woman shall
21 *w'* the Lord doth make thy thigh to
27 And *w'* he hath made her to drink the
29 *w'* a wife goeth aside to another
30 Or *w'* the spirit of jealousy cometh
6: 2 *W'* either man or woman shall
7 brother, or for his sister, *w'* they die:
13 *w'* the days of his separation are
7: 84 altar, in the day *w'* it was anointed,
89 And *w'* Moses was gone into the
8: 2 *W'* thou lightest the lamps, the seven
19 *w'* the children of Israel come nigh
9: 17 *w'* the cloud was taken up from
20 *w'* the cloud was a few days upon
21 *w'* the cloud abode from even unto
22 but *w'* it was taken, they journeyed.
10: 3 But *w'* they shall blow with them,
5 *W'* ye blow an alarm, then the camps
Nu 10: 6 *W'* ye blow an alarm the second time,
7 *w'* the congregation is to be gathered
28 to their armies, *w'* they set forward.*
34 by day, *w'* they went out of the camp.
35 came to pass, *w'* the ark set forward,
36 *w'* it rested, he said, Return, O Lord,
11: 1 And *w'* the people complained, it
2 and *w'* Moses prayed unto the Lord,
9 And *w'* the dew fell upon the camp
25 that, *w'* the spirit rested upon them,
12: 12 *w'* he cometh out of his mother's
15: 2 *W'* ye be come into the land of
8 *w'* thou preparest a bullock for a
18 *W'* ye come into the land whither I
19 *w'* ye eat of the bread of the land, ye
28 *w'* he sinneth by ignorance before the
16: 4 And *w'* Moses heard it, he fell upon his
42 *w'* the congregation was gathered
18: 26 *W'* ye take of the children of
30 *W'* ye have heaved the best thereof
32 *w'* ye have heaved from it the best of
19: 14 the law, *w'* a man dieth in a tent:
20: 3 we had died *w'* our brethren died
16 *w'* we cried unto the Lord, he heard
29 And *w'* all the congregation saw that
21: 1 And *w'* king Arad the Canaanite,
8 bitten, *w'* he looketh upon it, shall live.
9 *w'* he beheld the serpent of brass, he
22: 25, 27 And *w'* the ass saw the angel of
36 And *w'* Balak heard that Balaam was
23: 17 *w'* he came to him, behold, he stood
24: 1 And *w'* Balaam saw that it pleased
20 *w'* he looked upon Amalek, he took
23 Alas, who shall live *w'* God doeth this!
25: 7 And *w'* Phinehas, the son of Eleazar,
26: 9 *w'* they strove against the Lord:
10 with Korah, *w'* that company died,
61 *w'* they offered strange fire before the
64 *w'* they numbered the children of
27: 13 *w'* thou hast seen it, thou also shalt
28: 26 *w'* ye bring a new meat offering unto
30: 6 had at all a husband, *w'* she vowed,
32: 1 *w'* they saw the land of Jazer, and the
8 *w'* I sent them from Kadesh-barnea
9 For *w'* they went up unto the valley of
33: 39 years old *w'* he died in mount Hor.
51 *W'* ye are passed over Jordan
34: 2 them, *W'* ye come into the land of
35: 10 *W'* ye be come over Jordan unto
19 *w'* he meeteth him, he shall slay him.
21 slay the murderer, *w'* he meeteth him.
36: 4 And *w'* the jubile of the children of
De 1: 19 *w'* we departed from Horeb, we went
41 *w'* ye had girded on every man his
2: 8 *w'* we passed by from our brethren
12 *w'* they had destroyed them from
16 *w'* all the men of war were
19 *w'* thou comest nigh over against the
22 *w'* he destroyed the Horims from
4: 10 *w'* the Lord said unto me, Gather me
19 *w'* thou seest the sun, and the moon,
25 *W'* thou shalt beget children, and
30 *W'* thou art in tribulation, and all
5: 23 *w'* ye heard the voice out of the midst
28 of your words, *w'* ye spake unto me;
6: 7 of them *w'* thou sittest in thine house,
7 and *w'* thou walkest by the way,
7 and *w'* thou liest down,
7 and *w'* thou risest up.
10 *w'* the Lord thy God shall have
11 *w'* thou shalt have eaten and be full;
20 *w'* thy son asketh thee in time to
7: 1 *W'* the Lord thy God shall bring
2 *w'* the Lord thy God shall deliver
8: 10 *W'* thou hast eaten and art full, then
12 Lest *w'* thou hast eaten and art full,
13 *w'* thy herds and thy flocks multiply,
9: 9 *W'* I was gone up into the mount to
23 Likewise *w'* the Lord sent you from
11: 19 of them *w'* thou sittest in thine house,
19 and *w'* thou walkest by the way,
19 *w'* thou liest down, and *w'* thou risest
29 *w'* the Lord thy God hath brought
12: 10 But *w'* ye go over Jordan, and dwell
10 *w'* he giveth you rest from all your
20 *W'* the Lord thy God shall enlarge
25 *w'* thou shalt do that which is right
28 *w'* thou doest that which is good
29 *W'* the Lord thy God shall cut off
13: 18 *W'* thou shalt hearken to the voice
14: 24 *w'* the Lord thy God hath blessed
15: 4 *w'* there shall be no poor among
10 shall not be grieved *w'* thou givest
13 And *w'* thou sendest him out free
18 *w'* thou sendest him away free from
16: 3 *w'* thou camest forth out of the land
17: 14 *W'* thou art come unto the land
18 *w'* he sitteth upon the throne of his
18: 9 *W'* thou art come into the land
22 *W'* the prophet speaketh in the
19: 1 *W'* the Lord thy God hath cut off
5 As *w'* a man goeth into the wood
20: 1 *W'* thou goest out to battle
2 *w'* ye are come nigh unto the battle,
9 *w'* the officers have made an end of
10 *W'* thou comest nigh unto a city
13 *w'* the Lord thy God hath delivered it
19 *W'* thou shalt besiege a city a
21: 9 *w'* thou shalt do that which is right
10 *W'* thou goest forth to war against
16 *w'* he maketh his sons to inherit
18 *w'* they have chastened him, will not
22: 8 *W'* thou buildest a new house,
14 *w'* I came to her, I found her not a
26 for as *w'* a man riseth against his
23: 4 way, *w'* ye came forth out of Egypt;
De 23: 9 *W'* the host goeth forth against
11 *w'* evening cometh on, he shall wash
11 *w'* the sun is down, he shall come into
13 *w'* thou wilt ease thyself abroad, thou
21 *W'* thou shalt vow a vow unto the
24 *W'* thou comest into thy
25 *W'* thou comest into the standing
24: 1 *W'* a man hath taken a wife, and
2 *w'* she is departed out of his house,
5 *W'* a man hath taken a new wife,
10 *W'* thou dost lend thy brother any
13 pledge again *w'* the sun goeth down,
19 *W'* thou cuttest down thine
20 *W'* thou beatest thine olive tree,
21 *W'* thou gatherest the grapes of
25: 4 the ox *w'* he treadeth out the corn.
11 *W'* men strive together one with
17 *w'* ye were come forth out of Egypt;
18 thee, *w'* thou wast faint and weary;
19 *w'* the Lord thy God hath given thee
26: 1 *w'* thou art come in unto the land
7 *W'* we cried unto the Lord God of our
12 *W'* thou hast made an end of
27: 2 *w'* ye shall pass over Jordan unto
3 this law, *w'* thou art passed over,
4 it shall be *w'* ye be gone over Jordan,
12 people, *w'* ye are come over Jordan;
28: 6 Blessed shalt thou be *w'* thou comest
6 blessed shalt thou be *w'* thou goest
19 Cursed shalt thou be *w'* thou comest
19 cursed shalt thou be *w'* thou goest out.
29: 7 *w'* ye came unto this place, Sihon the
19 *w'* he heareth the words of this curse,
22 *w'* they see the plagues of that land,
25 *w'* he brought them forth out of the
30: 1 *w'* all these things are come upon
31: 11 *W'* all Israel is come to appear before
20 *w'* I shall have brought them into
21 *w'* many evils and troubles are
24 *w'* Moses had made an end of writing
32: 8 *W'* the most High divided to the
8 *w'* he separated the sons of Adam, he
19 And *w'* the Lord saw it, he abhorred
36 *w'* he seeth that their power is
33: 5 *w'* the heads of the people and the
34: 7 and twenty years old *w'* he died:
Jos 2: 5 *w'* it was dark, that the men went out:
10 sea for you, *w'* ye came out of Egypt;
14 *w'* the Lord hath given us the land,
18 *w'* we come into the land, thou shalt
3: 3 *W'* ye see the ark of the covenant of
8 *W'* ye are come to the brink of the
14 *w'* the people removed from their
4: 1 *w'* all the people were clean passed
6 *w'* your children ask their fathers
7 *w'* it passed over Jordan, the waters of
11 *w'* all the people were clean passed
18 *w'* the priests that bare the ark of the
21 *W'* your children shall ask their
5: 1 *w'* all the kings of the Amorites,
8 *w'* they had done circumcising all
13 to pass, *w'* Joshua was by Jericho,
6: 5 *w'* they make a long blast with the
5 *w'* ye hear the sound of the trumpet,
8 *w'* Joshua had spoken unto the people,
16 *w'* the priests blew with the trumpets,
18 *w'* ye take of the accursed thing, and
20 shouted *w'* the priests blew with the
20 *w'* the people heard the sound of the
7: 8 *w'* Israel turneth their backs
21 *W'* I saw among the spoils a goodly
8: 5 *w'* they come out against us, as at
8 shall be, *w'* ye have taken the city,
13 *w'* they had set the people, even all
14 *w'* the king of Ai saw it, that they
20 *w'* the men of Ai looked behind them,
21 *w'* Joshua and all Israel saw that the
24 *w'* Israel had made an end of slaying
24 *w'* they were all fallen on the edge of
9: 1 *w'* all the kings which were on this
3 *w'* the inhabitants of Gibeon heard
22 far from you; *w'* ye dwell among us?
10: 12 in the day *w'* the Lord delivered up
20 *w'* Joshua and the children of Israel
24 *w'* they brought out those kings unto
11: 1 *w'* Jabin king of Hazor had heard
5 *w'* all these kings were met together,
14: 7 *w'* Moses the servant of the Lord sent
17: 13 *w'* the children of Israel were
19: 49 *W'* they had made an end of dividing
20: 4 *w'* he that doth flee unto one of those
22: 7 *w'* Joshua sent them away also
10 *w'* they came unto the borders of
12 *w'* the children of Israel heard of it,
28 *w'* they should so say to us or to
30 *w'* Phinehas the priest, and the princes
23: 16 *W'* ye have transgressed the covenant
24: 7 And *w'* they cried unto the Lord,
J'g 1: 14 it came to pass, *w'* she came to him,
25 *w'* he shewed them the entrance into
28 *w'* Israel was strong, that they put the
2: 4 *w'* the angel of the Lord spake these
6 And *w'* Joshua had let the people go,
18 *w'* the Lord raised them up judges,
19 *w'* the judge was dead, that they
21 nations which Joshua left *w'* he died:
3: 9, 15 *w'* the children of Israel cried unto
18 *w'* he had made an end to offer the
24 *W'* he was gone out, his servants came;
24 *w'* they saw that, behold, the doors of
27 pass, *w'* he was come, that he blew a
4: 1 sight of the Lord, *w'* Ehud was dead.
18 *w'* he had turned in unto her into the
20 *w'* any man doth come and enquire
22 And *w'* he came into her tent, behold,
5: 2 *w'* the people willingly offered

J'g 5: 4 Lord, w' thou wentest out of Seir,
4 w' thou marchedst out of the field of
26 w' she had pierced and stricken
31 the sun w' he goeth forth in his might.
6: 3 And so it was, w' Israel had sown,
7 w' the children of Israel cried unto
22 w' Gideon perceived that he was an
28 w' the men of the city arose early in
29 w' they enquired and asked, they said,
7:13 And w' Gideon was come, behold,
15 w' Gideon heard the telling of the
17 w' I come to the outside of the camp,
18 W' I blow with a trumpet, I and all
8: 1 w' thou wentest to fight with the
3 toward him, w' he had said that.
7 w' the Lord hath delivered Zeba and
9 W' I come again in peace, I will break
12 And w' Zeba and Zalmunna fled,
9: 7 And w' they told it to Jotham, he went
22 W' Abimelech had reigned three years
30 w' Zebul the ruler of the city heard
33 W' he and the people that is with him
36 And w' Gaal saw the people, he said to
46 And w' all the men of the tower of
55 And w' the men of Israel saw that
11: 5 w' the children of Ammon made
7 unto me now w' ye are in distress?
13 w' they came up out of Egypt, from
16 But w' Israel came up from Egypt, and
31 w' I return in peace from the children
35 to pass, w' he saw her, that he rent his
12: 2 w' I called you, ye delivered me not
3 And w' I saw that ye delivered me not,
5 w' those Ephraimites which were
13:17 w' thy sayings come to pass we
20 w' the flame went up toward heaven
14:11 w' they saw him, that they brought
15: 5 And w' he had set the brands on fire,
14 w' he came unto Lehi, the Philistines
17 w' he had made an end of speaking,
19 w' he had drunk, his spirit came again,
16: 2 w' it is day, we shall kill him.
9 of tow is broken w' it toucheth the fire.
15 thee, w' thine heart is not with me?
16 w' she pressed him daily with her
18 w' Delilah saw that he had told her all
24 w' the people saw him, they praised
25 pass, w' their hearts were merry,
17: 3 w' he had restored the eleven hundred
18: 2 who w' they came to mount Ephraim,
3 W' they were by the house of Micah,
10 W' ye go, ye shall come unto a people
22 w' they were a good way from the
26 w' Micah saw that they were too strong
19: 1 days, w' there was no king in Israel,
3 w' the father of the damsel saw him,
5 w' they arose early in the morning,
7 And w' the man rose up to depart, his
9 And w' the man rose up to depart,
11 w' they were by Jebus, the day was far
14 upon them w' they were by Gibeah,
15 w' he went in, he sat him down in a
17 w' he had lifted up his eyes, he saw a
25 w' the day began to spring, they let
29 w' he was come into his house, he
20:10 w' they come to Gibeah of Benjamin,
39 w' the men of Israel retired in the
40 w' the flame began to arise up out of
41 w' the men of Israel turned again,
21:22 w' their fathers or their brethren
Ru 1: 1 pass in the days w' the judges ruled,
18 W' she saw that she was stedfastly
19 w' they were come to Beth-lehem, that
2: 9 w' thou art athirst, go unto the
15 w' she was risen up to glean, Boaz
3: 4 be, w' he lieth down, that thou shalt
7 And w' Boaz had eaten and drunk,
15 And w' she held it, he measured six
16 And w' she came to her mother in law,
4:13 w' he went in unto her, the Lord gave
1Sa 1: 4 w' the time was that Elkanah offered,
7 w' she went up to the house of
20 w' the time was come about after
24 w' she had weaned him, she took
2:13 that, w' any man offered sacrifice,
19 w' she came up with her husband to
27 w' they were in Egypt in Pharaoh's
3: 2 w' Eli was laid down in his place,
12 w' I begin, I will also make an end.
4: 2 w' they joined battle, Israel was
3 w' the people were come into the
3 w' it cometh among us, it may save us
5 w' the ark of the covenant of the
6 w' the Philistines heard the noise of
13 w' he came, lo, Eli sat upon a seat by
13 w' the man came into the city, and
14 w' Eli heard the noise of the crying, he
18 w' he made mention of the ark of God,
19 w' she heard the tidings that the ark
5: 2 W' the Philistines took the ark of
3 w' they of Ashdod arose early on the
4 w' they arose early on the morrow
7 w' the men of Ashdod saw that it was
6: 6 w' he had wrought wonderfully
16 w' the five lords of the Philistines had
7: 7 And w' the Philistines heard that the
7 w' the children of Israel heard it, they
8: 1 w' Samuel was old, that he made
6 w' they said, Give us a king to
9: 5 w' they were come to the land of Zuph,
9 w' a man went to enquire of God,
14 and w' they were come into the city,
17 w' Samuel saw Saul, the Lord said
25 w' they were come down from the
10: 2 W' thou art departed from me to day,
5 w' thou art come thither to the city,

1Sa 10: 7 w' these signs are come unto thee,
9 w' he had turned his back to go from
10 And w' they came thither to the hill,
11 w' all that knew him beforetime saw
13 And w' he had made an end of
14 w' we saw that they were no where,
20 w' Samuel had caused all the tribes
21 W' he had caused the tribe of
21 w' they sought him, he could not be
23 w' he stood among the people, he was
11: 6 upon Saul w' he heard those tidings,
8 w' he numbered them in Bezek, the
12: 8 W' Jacob was come into Egypt,
9 w' they forgat the Lord their God, he
12 w' ye saw that Nahash the king of the
12 w' the Lord your God was your king.
13: 1 and w' he had reigned two years over
6 W' the men of Israel saw that they
14:17 And w' they had numbered, behold,
22 w' they heard that the Philistines fled,
26 And w' the people were come into the
27 not w' his father charged the people
52 w' Saul saw any strong man, or any
15: 2 in the way, w' he came up from Egypt.
6 Israel, w' they came up out of Egypt.
12 w' Samuel rose early to meet Saul
17 W' thou wast little in thine own
16: 6 w' they were come, that he looked on
16 w' the evil spirit from God is upon
23 w' thy evil spirit from God was upon
17:11 w' Saul and all Israel heard those
24 w' they saw the man, fled from him,
28 heard w' he spake unto the men;
31 w' the words were heard which David
35 w' he arose against me, I caught him
42 w' the Philistine looked about, and
48 w' the Philistine arose, and came
51 w' the Philistines saw their champion
55 w' Saul saw David go forth against
18: 1 w' he had made an end of speaking
6 w' David was returned from the
15 Wherefore w' Saul saw that he behaved
19 w' Merab Saul's daughter should have
26 w' his servants told David these words,
19:14 w' Saul sent messengers to take David,
16 And w' the messengers were come in,
20 and w' they saw the company of the
21 w' it was told Saul, he sent other
20:12 w' I have sounded my father about3588
15 w' the Lord hath cut off the enemies
19 And w' thou hast stayed three days,
19 hide thyself w' the business was in
24 w' the new moon was come, the king
37 w' the lad was come to the place of the
21: 6 in the day w' it was taken away.
22: 1 w' his brethren and all his father's
6 W' Saul heard that David was
17 because they knew w' he fled,
22 w' Doeg the Edomite was there,
23: 6 w' Abiathar the son of Ahimelech fled
25 w' Saul heard that, he pursued after
24: 1 w' Saul was returned from following
8 w' Saul looked behind him, David
16 w' David had made an end of speaking
18 as w' the Lord had delivered me
25: 9 And w' David's young men came, they
15 with them, w' we were in the fields:
23 w' Abigail saw David, she hasted,
30 w' the Lord shall have done to my
31 w' the Lord shall have dealt well with
37 w' the wine was gone out of Nabal,
39 w' David heard that Nabal was dead,
40 w' the servants of David were come
26:20 as w' one doth hunt a partridge in
28: 5 w' Saul saw the host of the Philistines,
6 And w' Saul enquired of the Lord,
12 w' the woman saw Samuel, she cried
22 strength, w' thou goest on thy way.
30: 1 w' David and his men were come to
12 w' he had eaten, his spirit came again
16 w' he had brought him down, behold,
21 w' David came near to the people, he
26 w' David came to Ziklag, he sent of
31: 5 w' his armourbearer saw that Saul
7 w' the men of Israel that were on the
8 w' the Philistines came to strip the
11 w' the inhabitants of Jabesh-gilead
2Sa 1: 1 w' David was returned from the
2 w' he came to David, that he fell to the
7 w' he looked behind him, he saw me,
2:10 old w' he began to reign over Israel,
24 down w' they were come to the hill of
30 w' he had gathered all the people
3:13 w' thou comest to see my face.
23 W' Joab and all the host that was
26 w' Joab was come out from David, he
27 w' Abner was returned to Hebron,
28 afterward w' David heard it, he said,
35 w' all the people came to cause David
4: 1 w' Saul's son heard...Abner was dead
4 w' the tidings came of Saul and
7 For w' they came into the house, he
10 W' one told me, saying, Behold, Saul
11 W' wicked men have slain a
5: 2 w' Saul was king over us, thou wast
17 w' the Philistines heard that they had
23 w' David enquired of the Lord, he
24 w' thou hearest the sound of a going
6: 6 And w' they came to Nachon's
13 w' they that bare the ark of the
7: 1 w' the king sat in his house, and
12 w' thy days be fulfilled, and thou
8: 5 w' the Syrians of Damascus came to
9 W' Toi king of Hamath heard that
13 w' he returned from smiting of the
9: 2 w' they had called him unto David,

2Sa 9: 6 Now w' Mephibosheth, the son of
10: 5 W' they told it unto David, he sent to
6 w' the children of Ammon saw that
7 w' David heard of it, he sent Joab, and
9 W' Joab saw that the front of the
14 w' the children of Ammon saw that
15 w' the Syrians saw that they were
17 w' it was told David, he gathered all
19 w' all the kings that were servants to
11: 1 time w' the kings go forth to battle,
7 w' Uriah was come unto him, David
10 w' they had told David, saying, Uriah
16 w' Joab observed the city, that he
19 W' thou hast made an end of telling
20 so nigh unto the city w' ye did fight?
26 w' the wife of Uriah heard that Uriah
27 w' the mourning was past, David sent
12:19 w' David saw that his servants
20 w' he required, they set bread before
21 w' the child was dead, thou didst
13: 5 w' thy father cometh to see thee, say
6 and w' the king was come to see him,
11 w' she had brought them unto him to
21 But w' king David heard of all these
28 ye now w' Ammon's heart is merry
28 and w' I say unto you, Smite Ammon;
14: 4 w' the woman of Tekoah spake to the
26 w' he polled his head, (for it was at
29 w' he sent again the second time, he
33 w' he had called for Absalom, he came
15: 2 w' any man that had a controversy
5 w' any man came nigh to him to do
32 w' David was come to the top of the
16: 1 w' David was a little past the top of
5 And w' king David came to Bahurim,
7 thus said Shimei w' he cursed, Come
16 w' Hushai the Archite, David's
17: 6 And w' Hushai was come to Absalom,
9 w' some of them be overthrown at the
20 w' Absalom's servants came to the
20 w' they had sought and could not find
23 w' Ahithophel saw that his counsel
27 w' David was come to Mahanaim,
18: 5 w' the king gave all the captains
29 W' Joab sent the king's servant, and
19: 3 steal away w' they flee in battle.
25 w' he was come to Jerusalem to
39 w' the king was come over, the king
20: 8 W' they were at the great stone
12 w' the man saw that all the people
13 W' he was removed out of the
17 w' he was come near unto her, the
21:12 w' the Philistines had slain Saul
21 w' he defied Israel, Jonathan the son
22: 5 W' the waves of death compassed
23: 4 of the morning, w' the sun riseth,
9 w' they defied the Philistines that
24: 8 So w' they had gone through all the
11 w' David was up in the morning, the
16 w' the angel stretched out his hand
17 w' he saw the angel that smote the
1Ki 1:21 w' my lord the king shall sleep with
23 w' he was come in before the king, he
41 And w' Joab heard the sound of the
2: 7 to me w' I fled because of Absalom
8 in the day w' I went to Mahanaim:
3:21 w' I rose in the morning to give my
21 but w' I had considered it in the
5: 7 w' Hiram heard...words of Solomon,
6: 7 w' it was in building, was built of
7:24 were cast in two rows, w' it was cast.
8: 9 w' the Lord made a covenant with
9 w' they came out of the land of Egypt.
10 w' the priests were come out of the
21 w' he brought them out of the land of
30 w' they shall pray toward this
30 and w' thou hearest, forgive.
33 W' thy people Israel be smitten down
35 W' heaven is shut up, and there is no
35 there sin, w' thou afflictest them:
42 w' he shall come and pray toward this
53 w' thou broughtest our fathers out of
54 w' Solomon had made an end of
9: 1 w' Solomon had finished the building
10 w' Solomon had built the two houses,
10: 1 w' the queen of Sheba heard of the
2 and w' she was come to Solomon, she
4 w' the queen of Sheba had seen all
11: 4 w' Solomon was old, that his
15 w' David was in Edom, and Joab the
21 w' Hadad heard in Egypt that David
24 a band, w' David slew them of Zobah:
29 w' Jeroboam went out of Jerusalem,
12: 2 w' Jeroboam the son of Nebat, who
16 So w' all Israel saw that the king
20 w' all Israel heard that Jeroboam was
21 w' Rehoboam was come to Jerusalem,
13: 4 w' king Jeroboam heard the saying of
24 w' he was gone, a lion met him by the
26 w' the prophet that brought him back
31 W' I am dead, then bury me in the
14: 5 it shall be, w' she cometh in, that she
6 w' Ahijah heard the sound of her feet,
12 and w' thy feet enter into the city, the
17 w' she came to the threshold of the
21 one years old w' he began to reign,
28 w' the king went into the house
15:21 it came to pass, w' Baasha heard
29 w' he reigned, that he smote all the
16:11 w' he began to reign, as soon as he sat
18 w' Zimri saw that the city was taken,
17:10 w' he came to the gate of the city,
18: 4 w' Jezebel cut off the prophets of
10 and w' they said, He is not there;
12 and so w' I come and tell Ahab,
13 w' Jezebel slew the prophets of the

1Ki 18: 17 w' Ahab saw Elijah, that Ahab said
29 w' midday was past, and they
39 w' all the people saw it, they fell on
19: 3 w' he saw that, he arose, and went for
13 w' Elijah heard it, that he wrapped
15 w' thou comest, anoint Hazael to be
20: 12 w' Ben-hadad heard this message,
21: 15 w' Jezebel heard that Naboth was
27 to pass, w' Ahab heard those words,
22: 25 w' thou shalt go into an inner
32, 33 w' the captains of the chariots
42 five years old w' he began to reign;
2Ki 1: 5 w' the messengers turned back unto
2: 1 w' the Lord would take up Elijah into
9 came to pass, w' they were gone over,
10 thou see me w' I am taken from thee,
14 w' he also had smitten the waters,
15 w' the sons of the prophets which
17 w' they urged him till he was ashamed,
18 w' they came again to him, (for he
3: 5 it came to pass, w' Ahab was dead,
15 came to pass, w' the minstrel played,
20 w' the meat offering was offered,
21 w' all the Moabites heard that the
24 w' they came to the camp of Israel,
26 w' the king of Moab saw that the
4: 4 w' thou art come in, thou shalt shut
6 came to pass, w' the vessels were full,
10 and it shall be, w' he cometh to us,
12 w' he had called her, she stood before
15 w' he had called her, she stood in the
18 w' the child was grown, it fell on a
20 w' he had taken him, and brought
25 w' the man of God saw her afar off,
27 w' she came to the man of God to the
32 w' Elisha was come into the house,
36 w' she was come in unto him, he said,
5: 6 Now w' this letter is come unto thee,
7 w' the king of Israel had read the
8 w' Elisha the man of God had heard
13 w' he saith to thee, Wash, and be
18 w' my master goeth into the house
18 w' I bow down myself in the house of
21 w' Naaman saw him running after
24 w' he came to the tower, he took them
26 w' the man turned again from his
6: 4 w' they came to Jordan, they cut down
15 w' the servant of the man of God was
18 w' they came down to him, Elisha
20 w' they were come into Samaria,
21 w' he saw them, My father, shall I
23 w' they had eaten and drunk, he sent
30 w' the king heard the words of the
32 w' the messenger cometh, shut the
7: 5 w' they were come to the uttermost
12 W' they come out of the city, we
17 who spake w' the king came down to
8: 6 w' the king asked the woman, she
17 old was he w' he began to reign;
26 old was Ahaziah w' he began to reign;
29 w' he fought against Hazael king of
9: 2 w' thou comest thither, look out there
5 w' he came, behold, the captains of
15 w' he fought with Hazael king of
22 w' Joram saw Jehu, that he said, Is it
25 w' I and thou rode together after
27 w' Ahaziah the king of Judah saw
30 And w' Jehu was come to Jezreel,
34 w' he was come in, he did eat and
10: 7 pass, w' the letter came to them, that
15 w' he was departed thence, he lighted
17 w' he came to Samaria, he slew all that
11: 1 w' Athaliah the mother of Ahaziah
13 w' Athaliah heard the noise of the
14 w' she looked, behold, the king stood
21 was Jehoash w' he began to reign.
12: 10 w' they saw that there was much
13: 21 and w' the man was let down, and
14: 2 five years old w' he began to reign,
15: 2, 33 old was he w' he began to reign,
16: 2 old was Ahaz w' he began to reign,
12 And w' the king was come from
18: 2 old was he w' he began to reign;
17 w' they were come up, they came and
18 w' they had called to the king, there
32 w' he persuadeth you, saying, The
19: 1 to pass, w' king Hezekiah heard it,
9 w' he heard say of Tirhakah king of
35 w' they arose early in the morning,
21: 1 years old w' he began to reign,
19 two years old w' he began to reign,
22: 1 eight years old w' he began to reign,
11 w' the king had heard the words of
19 w' thou heardest what I spake against
23: 29 him at Megiddo, w' he had seen him.
31 three years old w' he began to reign;
36 five years old w' he began to reign;
24: 8 years old w' he began to reign, and
18 one years old w' he began to reign.
25: 23 w' all the captains of the armies, they
1Ch 1: 44 w' Bela was dead, Jobab the son of
45 And w' Jobab was dead, Husham of
46 w' Husham was dead, Hadad the son
47 w' Hadad was dead, Samlah of
48 w' Samlah was dead, Shaul of
49 w' Shaul was dead, Baal-hanan the
50 w' Baal-hanan was dead, Hadad
2: 19 w' Azubah was dead, Caleb took unto
21 w' he was threescore years old;
5: 7 w' the genealogy of their generations
6: 15 w' the Lord carried away Judah and
10: 5 w' his armourbearer saw that Saul
7 w' all the men of Israel that were in
8 w' the Philistines came to strip the
9 w' they had stripped him, they took
11 w' all Jabesh-gilead heard all that the

1Ch 11: 2 time past, even w' Saul was king,
12: 15 w' it had overflown all his banks;
19 w' he came with the Philistines
13: 9 w' they came unto the threshingfloor
14: 8 w' the Philistines heard that David
12 And w' they had left their gods there,
15 w' thou shalt hear a sound of going
15: 26 w' God helped the Levites that bare
16: 2 w' David had made an end of offering
19 W' ye were but few, even a few, and
20 w' they went from nation to nation,
17: 11 w' thy days be expired that thou
18: 5 w' the Syrians of Damascus came
9 w' Tou king of Hamath heard how
19: 6 w' the children of Ammon saw that
8 w' David heard of it, he sent Joab,
10 Now w' Joab saw that the battle was
15 w' the children of Ammon saw that
16 w' the Syrians saw that they were
17 w' David had put the battle in array
19 w' the servants of Hadarezer saw that
20: 7 w' he defied Israel, Jonathan the son
21: 28 that time w' David saw that the Lord
23: 1 w' David was old and full of days, he
2Ch 4: 3 of oxen were cast, w' it was cast.
5: 10 w' the Lord made a covenant with
10 of Israel, w' they came out of Egypt.
11 w' the priests were come out of the
13 w' they lifted up their voice with the
6: 21 heaven; and w' thou hearest, forgive.
26 W' the heaven is shut up, and there
26 sin, w' thou dost afflict them,
27 w' thou hast taught them the good
29 w' every one shall know his own
7: 1 w' Solomon had made an end of
3 w' all the children of Israel saw how
6 w' David praised by their ministry;
9: 1 w' the queen of Sheba heard of the
1 w' she was come to Solomon, she
3 w' the queen of Sheba had seen the
10: 2 w' Jeroboam the son of Nebat, who
16 w' all Israel saw that the king would
11: 1 w' Rehoboam was come to Jerusalem,
12: 1 w' Rehoboam had established the
7 w' the Lord saw that they humbled
11 w' the king entered into the house
12 w' he humbled himself, the wrath of
13 forty years old w' he began to reign,
13: 7 w' Rehoboam was young and
14 w' Judah looked back, behold, the
15: 4 w' they in their trouble did turn
8 w' Asa heard these words, and the
9 w' they saw that the Lord his God was
16: 5 w' Baasha heard it, that he left off
18: 14 w' he was come to the king, the king
24 w' thou shalt go into an inner
31, 32 w' the captains of the chariots
19: 8 w' they returned to Jerusalem.
20: 9 w' evil cometh upon us, as the sword,
10 w' they came out of the land of Egypt,
21 w' he had consulted with the people,
22 w' they began to sing and to
23 w' they had made an end of the
24 w' Judah came toward the watch
25 w' Jehoshaphat and his people came
29 w' they had heard that the Lord
31 and five years w' he began to reign,
21: 4 w' Jehoram was risen up to the
5 two years old w' he began to reign,
20 old was he w' he began to reign,
22: 2 was Ahaziah w' he began to reign,
6 w' he fought with Hazael king of
7 w' he was come, he went out with
8 w' Jehu was executing judgment
9 w' they had slain him, they buried
10 w' Athaliah the mother of Ahaziah
23: 7 w' he cometh in, and w' he goeth out.
12 w' Athaliah heard the noise of the
15 w' she was come to the entering of
24: 1 seven years old w' he began to reign,
14 w' they had finished it, they brought
15 and was full of days w' he died;
15 thirty years old was he w' he died.
22 w' he died, he said, The Lord look
25 w' they were departed from him, (for
25: 1 five years old w' he began to reign,
3 w' the kingdom was established to
26: 3 old was Uzziah w' he began to reign,
16 w' he was strong, his heart was lifted
27: 1 five years old w' he began to reign,
8 twenty years old w' he began to reign,
28: 1 twenty years old w' he began to reign,
29: 1 to reign w' he was five and twenty
22 w' they had killed the rams, they
27 w' the burnt offering began, the
29 w' they had made an end of offering,
31: 1 w' all this was finished, all Israel that
8 w' Hezekiah and the princes came
32: 2 w' Hezekiah saw that Sennacherib
21 w' he was come into the house of his
33: 1 twelve years old w' he began to reign,
12 w' he was in affliction, he besought
21 twenty years old w' he began to reign,
34: 1 eight years old w' he began to reign,
7 w' he had broken down the altars and
8 w' he had purged the land, and the
9 w' they came to Hilkiah the high
14 w' they brought out the money that
19 w' the king had heard the word of the
27 w' thou heardest his words against
35: 20 w' Josiah had prepared the temple,
36: 2 three years old w' he began to reign,
5 five years old w' he began to reign,
9 eight years old w' he began to reign,
10 w' the year was expired, king
11 twenty years old w' he began to reign,

Ezr 2: 68 w' they came to the house of the Lord
3: 1 w' the seventh month was come, and
10 w' the builders laid the foundation of
11 w' they praised the Lord, because the
4: 1 w' the adversaries of Judah and
23 Now w' the copy of king
10: 1 w' Ezra had prayed, and w' he had
6 w' he came thither, he did eat no
Ne 1: 4 w' I heard these words, that I sat
2: 3 w' the city, the place of my fathers'
6 be? and w' wilt thou return?
10 W' Sanballat the Horonite, and
19 w' Sanballat the Horonite, and Tobiah
4: 1 w' Sanballat heard that we builded
7 w' Sanballat, and Tobiah, and the
12 w' the Jews which dwelt by them
15 w' our enemies heard that it was
5: 6 w' I heard their cry and these
6: 1 w' Sanballat, and Tobiah, and
16 w' all our enemies heard thereof
7: 1 w' the wall was built, and I had set
73 w' the seventh month came, the
8: 5 w' he opened it, all the people stood
9 w' they heard the words of the law.
9: 18 w' they had made them a molten
27 w' they cried unto thee, thou heardest
28 w' they returned, and cried unto thee,
10: 38 the Levites, w' the Levites take tithes:
13: 3 w' they had heard the law, that they
19 w' the gates of Jerusalem began to
Es 1: 2 w' the king Ahasuerus sat on the
4 W' he shewed the riches of his
5 w' these days were expired, the king
10 w' the heart of the king was merry
17 in their eyes, w' it shall be reported,
20 w' the king's decree, which he shall
2: 1 w' the wrath of king Ahasuerus was
7 w' her father and mother were dead,
8 w' the king's commandment and his
8 and w' many maidens were gathered
12 w' every maid's turn was come to
15 w' the turn of Esther, the daughter of
19 w' the virgins were gathered together
20 as w' she was brought up with him.
23 w' inquisition was made of the matter,
3: 4 w' they spake daily unto him, and he
5 w' Haman saw that Mordecai bowed
4: 1 W' Mordecai perceived all that was
5: 2 w' the king saw Esther the queen
9 w' Haman saw Mordecai in the king's
10 w' he came home, he sent and called
9: 1 w' the king's commandment and
25 w' Esther came before the king, he
Job 1: 5 w' the days of their feasting were
6 was a day w' the sons of God came
13 w' his sons and his daughters were
2: 1 was a day w' the sons of God came
11 Now w' Job's three friends heard of
12 w' they lifted up their eyes afar off,
3: 11 the ghost w' I came out of the belly?
22 glad, w' they can find the grave?
4: 13 night, w' deep sleep falleth upon men,
5: 21 afraid of destruction w' it cometh.
6: 5 the wild ass bray w' he hath grass?
17 w' it is hot, they are consumed out of
7: 4 W' I lie down, I say,
4 W' shall I arise, and the night
13 W' I say, My bed shall comfort
11: 3 w' thou mockest, shall no man make
16: 22 W' a few years are come, then I
17: 16 w' our rest together is in the dust.
20: 23 W' he is about to fill his belly, God
21: 6 Even w' I remember I am afraid,
21 w' the number of his months is cut off
22: 29 W' men are cast down, then thou
23: 10 w' he hath tried me, I shall come forth
15 w' I consider, I am afraid of him.
27: 8 w' God taketh away his soul?
9 cry w' trouble cometh upon him?
28: 26 W' he made a decree for the rain, and
29: 2 as in the days w' God preserved me;
3 W' his candle shined upon my head,
3 w' by his light I walked through
4 w' the secret of God was upon my
5 W' the Almighty was yet with
5 w' my children were about me;
6 W' I washed my steps with butter,
7 W' I went out to the gate through the
7 w' I prepared my seat in the street!
11 W' the ear heard me, then it
11 w' the eye saw me, it gave witness to
30: 26 W' I looked for good, then evil
26 w' I waited for light, there came
31: 13 w' they contended with me;
14 shall I do w' God riseth up? and
14 w' he visiteth, what shall I answer
21 w' I saw my help in the gate:
26 If I beheld the sun w' it shined, or
29 lifted up myself w' evil found him:
32: 5 W' Elihu saw there was no answer in
16 W' I had waited, (for they spake not,
33: 15 night, w' deep sleep falleth upon men,
34: 29 W' he giveth quietness, who then can
29 w' he hideth his face, who then can
36: 13 they cry not w' he bindeth them.
20 w' people are cut off in their place.
37: 4 stay them w' his voice is heard.
15 Dost thou know w' God disposed
38: 4 wast thou w' I laid the foundations
7 W' the morning stars sang together,
8 the sea with doors, w' it brake forth,
9 W' I made the cloud the garment
38 W' the dust groweth into hardness,
40 W' they couch in their dens, and
41 w' his young ones cry unto God,
39: 1 w' the wild goats of the rock bring

Job 39: 1 thou mark *w'* the hinds do calve?
2 thou the time *w'* they bring forth?
41: 25 *W'* he riseth up himself, the mighty
42: 10 of Job, *w'* he prayed for his friends:
Ps 2: 12 *w'* his wrath is kindled but a little.
3: *title* *w'* he fled from Absalom his son.
4: 1 Hear me *w'* I call, O God of my
1 hast enlarged me *w'* I was in distress;
3 the Lord will hear *w'* I call unto him.
8: 3 *W'* I consider thy heavens, the
9: 3 *W'* mine enemies are turned back
12 *W'* he maketh inquisition for
10: 9 poor, *w'* he draweth him into his net.
12: 8 side, *w'* the vilest men are exalted.
13: 4 trouble me rejoice *w'* I am moved.
14: 7 *w'* the Lord bringeth back the
17: 15 satisfied, *w'* I awake, with thy likeness.
20: 9 Lord: let the king hear us *w'* we call.
21: 12 *w'* thou shalt make ready thine arrows
22: 9 *w'* I was upon my mother's breasts.
24 but *w'* he cried unto me, he heard.
27: 2 *W'* the wicked, even mine enemies
7 *w'* I cry with my voice: have mercy
8 *W'* thou saidst, Seek ye my face; my
10 *W'* my father and my mother
28: 2 my supplications, *w'* I cry unto thee,
2 *w'* I lift up my hands toward thy holy
30: 9 in my blood, *w'* I go down to the pit?
31: 22 my supplications *w'* I cried unto thee.
32: 3 *W'* I kept silence, my bones
6 in a time *w'* thou mayest be found:
34: *title* *w'* he changed his behaviour before
35: 13 *w'* they were sick, my clothing was
37: 33 nor condemn him *w'* he is judged.
34 *w'* the wicked are cut off, thou shalt
38: 16 *w'* my foot slippeth, they magnify
39: 11 *W'* thou with rebukes dost correct
41: 5 me, *W'* shall he die, and his name
6 *w'* he goeth abroad, he telleth it.
42: 2 *w'* shall I come and appear before
4 *W'* I remember these things, I pour
49: 5 *w'* the iniquity of my heels shall
16 Be not thou afraid *w'* one is made
16 rich, *w'* the glory of his house is
17 *w'* he dieth he shall carry nothing
18 thee, *w'* thou doest well to thyself.
50: 18 *W'* thou sawest a thief, then thou
51: *title* *w'* Nathan the prophet came unto
4 mightest be justified *w'* thou speakest,
4 speakest, and be clear *w'* thou judgest.
52: *title* *w'* Doeg the Edomite came and told
53: 6 *W'* God bringeth back the captivity of
54: *title* *w'* the Ziphims came and said to
56: *title* *w'* the Philistines took him in Gath.
6 my steps, *w'* they wait for my soul.
9 *W'* I cry unto thee, then shall mine
57: *title* *w'* he fled from Saul in the cave.
58: 7 *w'* he bendeth his bow to shoot his
10 rejoice *w'* he seeth the vengeance:
59: *title* *w'* Saul sent, and they watched the
60: *title* *w'* he strove with Aram-naharaim
title *w'* Joab returned, and smote of Edom
61: 2 thee, *w'* my heart is overwhelmed:
63: 6 *W'* I remember thee upon my bed,
65: 9 corn, *w'* thou hast so provided for it.
66: 14 hath spoken, *w'* I was in trouble.
68: 7 God, *w'* thou wentest forth before thy
7 *w'* thou didst march through the
9 thine inheritance, *w'* it was weary.
14 *W'* the Almighty scattered kings in
69: 10 *W'* I wept, and chastened my soul
71: 9 forsake me not *w'* my strength faileth.
18 also *w'* I am old and grayheaded,
23 greatly rejoice *w'* I sing unto thee;
72: 12 shall deliver the needy *w'* he crieth;
73: 3 *w'* I saw the prosperity of the wicked.
16 *w'* I thought to know this, it was too
20 a dream *w'* one awaketh; so, O Lord,
20 *w'* thou awakest, thou shalt despise
75: 2 *W'* I shall receive the congregation
76: 7 in thy sight *w'* once thou art angry?
9 *W'* God arose to judgment, to save all
78: 34 *W'* he slew them, then they sought
42 *w'* he delivered them from the
59 *W'* God heard this, he was wroth, and
81: 5 *w'* he went out through the land of
87: 6 count, *w'* he writeth up the people,
89: 9 *w'* the waves thereof arise, thou stillest
90: 4 are but as yesterday *w'* it is past,
92: 7 *W'* the wicked spring as the grass,
7 and *w'* all the workers of iniquity do
94: 8 and ye fools, *w'* will ye be wise?
18 *W'* I said, My foot slippeth; thy
95: 9 *W'* your fathers tempted me,
101: 2 O *w'* wilt thou come unto me? I
102: *title* *w'* he is overwhelmed, and
2 me in the day *w'* I am in trouble;
2 the day *w'* I call answer me speedily.
16 *W'* the Lord shall build up Zion,
22 *W'* the people are gathered together,
105: 12 *W'* they were but a few men in
13 *W'* they went from one nation to
38 Egypt was glad *w'* they departed: for
106: 44 their affliction, *w'* he heard their cry:
109: 7 *W'* he shall be judged, let him be
23 gone like the shadow *w'* it declineth:
25 *w'* they looked upon me they shaked
28 *w'* they arise, let them be ashamed;
114: 1 *W'* Israel went out of Egypt, the
119: 6 *w'* I have respect unto all thy
7 *w'* I shall have learned thy righteous
32 *w'* thou shalt enlarge my heart.
74 fear thee will be glad *w'* they see me:
82 saying, *W'* wilt thou comfort me?
84 *w'* wilt thou execute judgment on
171 *w'* thou hast taught me thy

Ps 120: 7 but *w'* I speak, they are for war.
122: 1 I was glad *w'* they said unto me, Let
124: 2 our side, *w'* men rose up against us:
3 *w'* their wrath was kindled against
126: 1 *W'* the Lord turned again the
137: 1 yea, we wept, *w'* we remembered Zion.
138: 3 the day *w'* I cried thou answeredst me,
4 *w'* they hear the words of thy
139: 15 *w'* I was made in secret, and
16 *w'* as yet there was none of them.
18 *w'* I awake, I am still with thee.
141: 1 ear unto my voice, *w'* I cry unto thee.
6 *W'* their judges are overthrown in
7 as *w'* one cutteth and cleaveth wood
142: *title* A Prayer *w'* he was in the cave.
3 *W'* my spirit was overwhelmed
Pr 1: 26 I will mock *w'* your fear cometh;
27 *W'* your fear cometh as desolation,
27 *w'* distress and anguish cometh upon
2: 10 *W'* wisdom entereth into thine
3: 24 *W'* thou liest down, thou shalt not
25 of the wicked, *w'* it cometh.
27 *w'* it is in the power of thine hand to
28 will give; *w'* thou hast it by thee.
4: 8 honour, *w'* thou dost embrace her.
12 *W'* thou goest, thy steps shall not be
12 *w'* thou runnest, thou shalt not
5: 11 *w'* thy flesh and thy body are
6: 3 *w'* thou art come into the hand of
9 *w'* wilt thou arise out of thy sleep?
22 *W'* thou goest, it shall lead thee;
22 *w'* thou sleepest, it shall keep thee;
22 *w'* thou awakest, it shall talk with
30 satisfy his soul *w'* he is hungry;
8: 24 *W'* there were no depths, I was
24 *w'* there were no fountains abounding
27 *W'* he prepared the heavens, I was
27 *w'* he set a compass upon the face of
28 *W'* he established the clouds above:
28 *w'* he strengthened the fountains of
29 *W'* he gave to the sea his decree that
29 *w'* he appointed the fountains of the
11: 2 *W'* pride cometh, then cometh shame:
7 *W'* a wicked man dieth, his
10 *W'* it goeth well with the righteous,
10 *w'* the wicked perish, there is shouting.
13: 12 *w'* the desire cometh, it is a tree of
14: 7 *w'* thou perceivest not in him the lips
16: 7 *W'* a man's ways please the Lord, he
17: 14 strife is as *w'* one letteth out water:
28 *w'* he holdeth his peace, is counted
18: 3 *W'* the wicked cometh, then cometh
20: 14 but *w'* he is gone his way, then he
21: 11 *W'* the scorner is punished, the
11 *w'* the wise is instructed, he receiveth
27 *w'* he bringeth it with a wicked
22: 6 and *w'* he is old, he will not depart
23: 1 *W'* thou sittest to eat with a ruler,
16 rejoice, *w'* thy lips speak right things.
22 not thy mother *w'* she is old.
31 not thou upon the wine *w'* it is red,
31 *w'* it giveth his colour in the cup,
31 in the cup, *w'* it moveth itself aright.
35 *w'* shall I awake? I will seek it
24: 14 *w'* thou hast found it, then there
17 Rejoice not *w'* thine enemy falleth,
17 thine heart be glad *w'* he stumbleth:
25: 8 *w'* thy neighbour hath put thee to
26: 25 *W'* he speaketh fair, believe him
28: 1 The wicked flee *w'* no man pursueth:
12 *W'* righteous men do rejoice, there is
28 *W'* the wicked rise, men hide
28 *w'* they perish, the righteous increase.
29: 2 *W'* the righteous are in authority, the
2 *w'* the wicked beareth rule, the people
16 *W'* the wicked are multiplied,
30: 22 For a servant *w'* he reigneth; and
22 and a fool *w'* he is filled with meat;
23 odious woman *w'* she is married;
31: 23 *w'* he sitteth among the elders of the
Ec 4: 10 woe to him that is alone *w'* he falleth:
5: 1 Keep thy foot *w'* thou goest to the
4 *W'* thou vowest a vow unto God,
11 *W'* goods increase, they are increased
8: 7 can tell him *w'* it shall be?
16 *W'* I applied mine heart to know
9: 12 time, *w'* it falleth suddenly upon them.
10: 3 *w'* he that is a fool walketh by the
16 to thee, O land, *w'* thy king is a child,
17 land, *w'* thy king is the son of nobles,
12: 1 *w'* thou shalt say, I have no
3 day *w'* the keepers of the house shall
4 *w'* the sound of the grinding is low,
5 *w'* they shall be afraid of that which
Ca 5: 6 my soul failed *w'* he spake: I sought
8: 1 *w'* I should find thee without, I would
8 in the day *w'* she shall be spoken for?
Isa 1: 12 *W'* ye come to appear before me,
15 *w'* ye spread forth your hands, I will
15 *w'* ye make many prayers, I will
2: 19, 21 *w'* he ariseth to shake terribly the
3: 6 *W'* a man shall take hold of his
4: 4 *W'* the Lord shall have washed
5: 4 *w'* I looked that it should bring forth
6: 13 in them, *w'* they cast their leaves:
8: 19 *w'* they shall say unto you, Seek
21 *w'* they shall be hungry, they shall
9: 1 *w'* at the first he lightly afflicted
3 men rejoice *w'* they divide the spoil.
10: 12 *w'* the Lord hath performed his
18 be as *w'* a standardbearer fainteth.
13: 19 be as *w'* God overthrew Sodom and
16: 12 *w'* it is seen that Moab is weary on
17: 5 be as *w'* the harvestman gathereth the
18: 3 *w'* he lifteth up an ensign on the
3 and *w'* he bloweth a trumpet, hear ye.

Isa 20: 1 (*w'* Sargon the king of Assyria sent
24: 13 *W'* thus it shall be in the midst of
13 grapes *w'* the vintage is done.
23 *w'* the Lord of hosts shall reign in
25: 4 *w'* the blast of the terrible ones is
26: 9 *w'* thy judgments are in the earth,
11 *w'* thy hand is lifted up, they will not
16 *w'* thy chastening was upon them.
27: 8 In measure, *w'* it shooteth forth, thou
9 *w'* he maketh all the stones of the
11 *W'* the boughs thereof are withered,
28: 4 which *w'* he that looketh upon it seeth,
15, 18 *w'* the overflowing scourge
25 *W'* he hath made plain the face
29: 8 *w'* an hungry man dreameth, and,
8 as *w'* a thirsty man dreameth, and,
23 *w'* he seeth his children, the work
30: 19 *w'* he shall hear it, he will answer
21 in it, *w'* ye turn to the right hand,
21 hand, and *w'* ye turn to the left.
25 the great slaughter, *w'* the towers fall.
29 the night *w'* a holy solemnity is kept;
29 *w'* one goeth with a pipe to come into
31: 3 *W'* the Lord shall stretch out his
4 *w'* a multitude of shepherds is
32: 7 even *w'* the needy speaketh right.
19 *W'* it shall hail, coming down on the
33: 1 *w'* thou shalt cease to spoil, thou shalt
1 *w'* thou shalt make an end to deal
37: 1 *w'* king Hezekiah heard it, that he
9 And *w'* he heard it, he sent messengers
36 *w'* they arose early in the morning,
38: 9 *w'* he had been sick, and was
41: 17 *W'* the poor and needy seek water,
28 no counseller, that, *w'* I ask of them,
43: 2 *W'* thou passest through the
12 *w'* there was no strange god among
48: 7 the day *w'* thou heardest them not;
13 *w'* I call unto them, they stand up
21 thirsted not *w'* he led them through
50: 2 *w'* I came, was there no man?
2 *w'* I called, was there none to answer?
52: 8 *w'* the Lord shall bring again Zion.
53: 2 and *w'* we shall see him, there is no
10 *w'* thou shalt make his soul an
54: 6 youth, *w'* thou wast refused, saith
57: 13 *W'* thou criest, let thy companies
20 troubled sea, *w'* it cannot rest,
58: 7 *w'* thou seest the naked, that thou
59: 19 *W'* the enemy shall come in like a
64: 2 *w'* the melting fire burneth, the fire
3 *W'* thou didst terrible things which
65: 12 because *w'* I called, ye did not answer;
12 *w'* I spake, ye did not hear; but did
66: 4 because *w'* I called, none did answer;
4 *w'* I spake, they did not hear: but
14 *w'* ye see this, your heart shall rejoice,
Jer 2: 2 *w'* thou wentest after me in the
7 *w'* ye entered, ye defiled my land, and
17 God, *w'* he led thee by the way?
20 *w'* upon every high hill and under
26 thief is ashamed *w'* he is found,
3: 8 *w'* for all the causes whereby
16 *w'* ye be multiplied and increased
4: 30 *w'* thou art spoiled, what wilt thou do?
5: 7 *w'* I had fed them to the full, they then
19 *w'* ye shall say, Wherefore doeth
6: 14 Peace, peace; *w'* there is no peace.
15 ashamed *w'* they had committed
8: 11 Peace, peace; *w'* there is no peace.
12 ashamed *w'* they had committed
18 *W'* I would comfort myself against
10: 13 *W'* he uttereth his voice, there is a
11: 15 *w'* thou doest evil, then thou
12: 1 thou, O Lord, *w'* I plead with thee:
13: 21 thou say *w'* he shall punish thee?
27 be made clean? *w'* shall it once be?
14: 12 *W'* they fast, I will not hear their
12 *w'* they offer burnt offering and an
16: 10 *w'* thou shalt show this people all
17: 6 and shall not see *w'* good cometh;
8 and shall not see *w'* heat cometh,
18: 22 *w'* thou shalt bring a troop
21: 1 *w'* king Zedekiah sent unto him
22: 23 thou be *w'* pangs come upon thee,
23: 33 *w'* this people, or the prophet, or a
25: 12 *w'* seventy years are accomplished,
26: 8 *w'* Jeremiah had made an end of
10 *W'* the princes of Judah heard these
21 *W'* Jehoiakim the king, with all his
21 *w'* Urijah heard it, he was afraid, and
27: 20 *w'* he carried away captive Jeconiah
28: 9 *w'* the word of the prophet shall come
29: 13 *w'* ye shall search for me with all
31: 2 Israel, *w'* I went to cause him to rest.
23 *w'* I shall bring again their captivity;
35 the sea *w'* the waves thereof roar;
32: 16 *w'* I had delivered the evidence of
34: 1 *w'* Nebuchadnezzar king of Babylon,
7 *W'* the king of Babylon's army fought
10 *w'* all the princes, and all the people,
14 *w'* he hath served thee six years, thou
18 *w'* they cut the calf in twain, and
35: 11 *w'* Nebuchadrezzar king of Babylon
36: 11 *W'* Michaiah the son of Gemariah, the
13 *w'* Baruch read the book in the ears of
16 *w'* they had heard all the words, they
23 *w'* Jehudi had read three or four
37: 5 *w'* the Chaldeans that besieged
11 *w'* the army of the Chaldeans was
13 *w'* he was in the gate of Benjamin, a
16 *W'* Jeremiah was entered into
38: 7 *w'* Ebed-melech the Ethiopian, one of
28 was there *w'* Jerusalem was taken.
39: 4 *w'* Zedekiah the king of Judah saw
5 *w'* they had taken him, they brought

Jer 40: 1 w' he had taken him being bound in
7 Now w' all the captains of the forces
11 w' all the Jews that were in Moab,
41: 7 w' they came into the midst of the
11 But w' Johanan the son of Kareah,
13 that w' all the people which were with
42: 6 w' we obey the voice of the Lord
18 you, w' ye shall enter into Egypt:
20 w' ye sent me unto the Lord your
43: 1 w' Jeremiah had made an end of
11 w' he cometh, he shall smite the land
44: 19 w' we burned incense to the
45: 1 w' he had written these words in a
51: 16 W' he uttereth his voice, there is a
55 w' her waves do roar like great waters,
59 w' he went with Zedekiah the king of
61 W' thou comest to Babylon, and shalt
63 w' thou hast made an end of reading
52: 1 twenty years old w' he began to reign,
La 1: 7 w' her people fell into the hand of the
2: 12 w' they swooned as the wounded in
12 w' their soul was poured out into their
3: 8 w' I cry and shout, he shutteth
37 pass, w' the Lord commanded it not?
4: 15 w' they fled away and wandered,
Eze 1: 9 another; they turned not w' they went;
12 and they turned not w' they went.
17 W' they went, they went upon their
17 and they turned not w' they went.
19 w' the living creatures went, the
19 w' the living creatures were lifted up
21 W' those went, these went; and
21 w' those stood, these stood; and
21 w' those were lifted up from the earth,
24 w' they went, I heard the noise of
24 w' they stood, they let down their
25 w' they stood, and had let down their
28 w' I saw it, I fell upon my face, and
2: 2 into me w' he spake unto me,
9 w' I looked, behold, an hand was sent
3: 18 W' I say unto the wicked, Thou shalt
20 W' a righteous man doth turn from
27 w' I speak with thee, I will open thy
4: 6 And w' thou hast accomplished them,
5: 2 w' the days of the siege are fulfilled:
13 w' I have accomplished my fury in
15 w' I shall execute judgments in thee in
16 W' I shall send upon them the evil
6: 8 w' ye shall be scattered through the
13 w' their slain men shall be among
8: 7 w' I looked, behold a hole in the wall.
8 w' I had digged in the wall, behold a
10: 3 of the house, w' the man went in;
5 the Almighty God w' he speaketh.
6 that w' he had commanded the man
9 w' I looked, behold the four wheels
11 W' they went, they went upon their
16 w' the cherubims went, the wheels
16 w' the cherubims lifted up their wings
17 W' they stood, these stood; and
17 w' they were lifted up, these lifted up
19 w' they went out, the wheels also were
11: 13 w' I prophesied, that Pelatiah the son
12: 15 w' I shall scatter them among the
13: 12 Lo, w' the wall is fallen, shall it not
14: 9 w' he hath spoken a thing,
13 w' the land sinneth against me by
21 w' I send my four sore judgments
23 w' ye see their ways and their doings:
15: 5 w' it was whole, it was meet for no
5 w' the fire hath devoured it, and
7 w' I set my face against them.
16: 6 w' I passed by thee, and saw thee
6 thee w' thou wast in thy blood, Live;
6 thee w' thou wast in thy blood, Live.
8 w' I passed by thee, and looked upon
22 w' thou wast naked and bare, and
53 W' I shall bring again their captivity,
55 W' thy sisters, Sodom and her
61 w' thou shalt receive thy sisters, thine
63 w' I am pacified toward thee for all
17: 10 wither, w' the east wind toucheth it?
18 w', lo, he had given his hand, and
18: 19 W' the son hath done that which is
24 w' the righteous turneth away from
26 W' a righteous man turneth away
27 w' the wicked man turneth away
19: 5 w' she saw that she had waited, and
20: 5 In the day w' I chose Israel, and
5 w' I lifted up mine hand unto them,
28 w' I had brought them into the land,
31 For w' ye offer your gifts,
31 w' ye make your sons to pass through
41 w' I bring you out from the people,
42 w' I shall bring you into the land of
21: 7 w' they say unto thee, Wherefore
25 w' iniquity shall have an end,
29 w' their iniquity shall have an end.
22: 28 God, w' the Lord hath not spoken.
23: 5 played the harlot w' she was mine;
14 w' she saw men pourtrayed upon the
39 w' they had slain their children to
24: 24 w' this cometh ye shall know that I
25 w' I take from them their strength,
25: 3 w' it was profaned; and against
3 land of Israel, w' it was desolate;
3 Judah, w' they went into captivity;
17 w' I shall lay my vengeance upon
26: 10 w' he shall enter into thy gates, as
15 w' the wounded cry, w' the slaughter
19 W' I shall make thee a desolate city,
19 w' I shall bring up the deep upon
20 W' I shall bring thee down with
27: 33 W' thy wares went forth out of the
34 time w' thou shalt be broken by the
28: 22 w' I shall have executed judgments in

Eze 28: 25 W' I shall have gathered the house of
26 w' I have executed judgments upon
29: 7 W' they took hold of thee by thy hand,
7 and w' they leaned upon thee, thou
30: 4 w' the slain shall fall in Egypt, and
8 Lord, w' I have set a fire in Egypt,
8 w' all her helpers shall be destroyed.
18 w' I shall break there the yokes of
25 w' I shall put my sword into the hand
31: 5 multitude of waters, w' he shot forth.
15 the day w' he went down to the grave
16 w' I cast him down to hell with them
32: 7 w' I shall put thee out, I will cover
9 w' I shall bring thy destruction
10 w' I shall brandish my sword before
15 W' I shall make the land of Egypt
15 w' I shall smite all them that dwell
33: 2 W' I bring the sword upon a
3 w' he seeth the sword come upon the
8 W' I say unto the wicked, O wicked
13 W' I shall say to the righteous, that
14 w' I say unto the wicked, Thou shalt
18 W' the righteous turneth from his
29 w' I have laid the land most desolate,
33 w' this cometh to pass, (lo, it will
34: 5 of the field, w' they were scattered.
27 w' I have broken the bands of their
35: 11 among them, w' I have judged thee.
14 W' the whole earth rejoiceth, I will
36: 17 w' the house of Israel dwelt in their
20 And w' they entered unto the heathen,
20 w' they said to them, These are the
23 w' I shall be sanctified in you before
37: 8 w' I beheld, lo, the sinews and the
13 w' I have opened your graves, O my
18 w' the children of thy people shall
28 w' my sanctuary shall be in the midst
38: 14 day w' my people of Israel dwelleth
16 w' I shall be sanctified in thee, O Gog,
18 w' Gog shall come against the
39: 15 w' any seeth a man's bone, then shall
26 w' they dwelt safely in their land, and
27 W' I have brought them again from
42: 14 W' the priests enter therein, then
15 w' he had made an end of measuring
43: 3 I saw w' I came to destroy the city:
18 in the day w' they shall make it,
23 W' thou hast made an end of
27 w' these days are expired, it shall be,
44: 7 w' ye offer my bread, the fat and the
10 far from me, w' Israel went astray,
15 w' the children of Israel went astray
17 w' they enter in at the gates of the
19 w' they go forth into the utter court,
21 w' they enter into the inner court.
45: 1 w' ye shall divide by lot the land for
46: 8 w' the prince shall enter, he shall go
9 w' the people of the land shall come
10 in the midst of them, w' they go in,
10 and w' they go forth, shall go forth.
47: 3 w' the man that had the line in his
7 w' I had returned, behold, at the bank
48: 11 w' the children of Israel went astray,
Da 3: 7 w' all the people heard the sound
5: 20 w' his heart was lifted up, and his
6: 10 w' Daniel knew that the writing was
14 king, w' he heard these words,
20 w' he came to the den, he cried with
8: 2 pass, w' I saw, that I was at Shushan
8 w' he was strong, the great horn was
15 w' I, even I Daniel, had seen the
17 w' he came, I was afraid, and fell
23 w' the transgressors are come to the
10: 9 And w' I heard the voice of his words,
11 w' he had spoken this word unto me,
15 w' he had spoken such words unto
19 w' he had spoken unto me, I was
20 w' I am gone forth, lo, the prince of
11: 4 w' he shall stand up, his kingdom
12 w' he hath taken away the multitude,
34 w' they shall fall, they shall be holpen
12: 7 w' he held up his right hand and his
7 and w' he shall have accomplished to
Ho 1: 8 w' she had weaned Lo-ruhamah, she
2: 15 day w' she came up out of the land of
4: 14 your daughters w' they commit
14 spouses w' they commit adultery:
5: 13 W' Ephraim saw his sickness, and
6: 11 w' I returned the captivity of my
7: 1 W' I would have healed Israel, then
12 W' they shall go, I will spread my
14 w' they howled upon their beds:
9: 12 also to them w' I depart from them!
10: 10 w' they shall bind themselves in their
11: 1 W' Israel was a child, then I
10 w' he shall roar, then the children
13: 1 W' Ephraim spake trembling, he
1 but w' he offended in Baal, he died.
Joe 2: 8 w' they fall upon the sword, they
3: 1 w' I shall bring again the captivity
Am 3: 4 roar in the forest, w' he hath no prey?
4: 7 w' there were yet three months to the
9 w' your gardens and your vineyards
7: 2 w' they had made an end of eating
8: 5 W' will the new moon be gone,
Jon 2: 7 W' my soul fainted within me I
4: 2 w' I was yet in my country?
7 w' the morning rose the next day,
8 it came to pass, w' the sun did arise,
Mic 2: 1 w' the morning is light, they practise
5: 5 w' the Assyrian shall come into
5 w' he shall tread in our palaces,
6 w' he cometh into our land,
6 w' he treadeth within our borders.
7: 1 w' they have gathered the summer
8 enemy: w' I fall, I shall arise'

Mic 7: 8 w' I sit in darkness, the Lord shall be
Na 3: 17 w' the sun ariseth they flee away, and
Hab 1: 13 w' the wicked devoureth the man that
2: 1 I shall answer w' I am reproved.
3: 16 W' I heard, my belly trembled; my
16 w' he cometh up unto the people, he
Zep 3: 20 w' I turn back your captivity before
Hag 1: 9 w' ye brought it home, I did blow upon
2: 5 with you w' ye came out of Egypt,
16 w' one came to an heap of twenty
16 w' one came to the pressfat for to
Zec 7: 2 W' they had sent unto the house of
5 W' ye fasted and mourned in the
6 w' ye did eat, and w' ye did drink,
7 w' Jerusalem was inhabited and in
7 w' men inhabited the south and the
8: 14 w' your fathers provoked me to wrath,
9: 1 w' the eyes of man, as of all the
13 W' I have bent Judah for me, filled
12: 2 w' they shall be in the siege both
13: 3 that w' any shall yet prophesy,
3 thrust him through w' he prophesieth.
4 of his vision, w' he hath prophesied;
14: 3 w' he fought in the day of battle.
Mal 2: 17 w' ye say, Every one that doeth evil is
3: 2 and who shall stand w' he appeareth?
17 that day w' I make up my jewels;
M't 1: 18 W' as his mother Mary was espoused
2: 1 w' Jesus was born in Bethlehem of
3 W' Herod the king had heard these
4 And w' he had gathered all the chief
7 w' he had privily called the wise men,
8 w' ye have found him, bring me
9 W' they had heard the king, they
10 W' they saw the star, they rejoiced
11 w' they were come into the house, they
11 w' they had opened their treasures,
13 w' they were departed, behold, the
14 W' he arose, he took the young child
16 Herod, w' he saw that he was mocked
19 w' Herod was dead, behold, an angel
22 w' he heard that Archelaus did reign
3: 7 w' he saw many of the Pharisees and
16 Jesus, w' he was baptized, went up
4: 2 w' he had fasted forty days and forty
3 w' the tempter came to him, he said,
12 w' Jesus had heard that John was
5: 1 w' he was set, his disciples came unto
11 w' men shall revile you, and
6: 2 w' thou doest thine alms, do not
3 But w' thou doest alms, let not thy left
5 w' thou prayest, thou shalt not
6 thou, w' thou prayest, enter into
6 w' thou hast shut thy door, pray to
7 w' ye pray, use not vain repetitions,
16 w' ye fast, be not, as the hypocrites,
17 w' thou fastest, anoint thine head,
7: 28 w' Jesus had ended these sayings,
8: 1 W' he was come down from the
5 w' Jesus was entered into Capernaum,
10 W' Jesus heard it, he marvelled, and
14 w' Jesus was come into Peter's house,
16 W' the even was come, they brought
18 Now w' Jesus saw great multitudes
23 w' he was entered into a ship, his
28 w' he was come to the other side into
32 w' they were come out, they went into
34 w' they saw him, they besought him
9: 8 But w' the multitudes saw it, they
11 w' the Pharisees saw it, they said
12 w' Jesus heard that, he said unto
15 w' the bridegroom shall be taken
22 w' he saw her, he said, Daughter, be
23 w' Jesus came into the ruler's house,
25 w' the people were put forth,
27 w' Jesus departed thence, two blind
28 w' he was come into the house, the
31 But they, w' they were departed,
33 w' the devil was cast out, the dumb
36 w' he saw the multitudes, he was
10: 1 w' he had called unto him his twelve
12 w' ye come into an house, salute it.
14 w' ye depart out of that house or city,
19 w' they deliver you up, take no
23 w' they persecute you in this city,
11: 1 w' Jesus had made an end of
2 w' John had heard in the prison the
12: 2 w' the Pharisees saw it, they said
3 David did, w' he was an hungred,
9 w' he was departed thence, he went
15 But w' Jesus knew it, he withdrew
24 w' the Pharisees heard it, they said,
43 W' the unclean spirit is gone out
44 w' he is come, he findeth it empty,
13: 4 w' he sowed, some seeds fell
6 And w' the sun was up, they were
19 W' any one heareth the word of the
21 w' tribulation or persecution ariseth
26 But w' the blade was sprung up,
32 w' it is grown, it is the greatest
44 the which w' a man hath found, he
46 w' he hath found one pearl of great
48 w' it was full, they drew to shore,
53 that w' Jesus had finished these
54 w' he was come into his own country,
14: 5 w' he would have put him to death, he
6 w' Herod's birthday was kept, they
13 W' Jesus heard of it, he departed
13 w' the people had heard thereof, they
15 w' it was evening, his disciples came
23 w' he had sent the multitudes away,
23 w' the evening was come, he was
26 w' the disciples saw him walking on
29 w' Peter was come down out of the
30 w' he saw the wind boisterous, he was
32 w' they were come into the ship, the

M't 14: 34 w' they were gone over, they came
35 w' the men of that place had
15: 2 their hands w' they eat bread.
31 w' they saw the dumb to speak,
16: 2 W' it is evening, ye say, it will be fair
5 w' his disciples were come to the
8 Which w' Jesus perceived, he said
13 W' Jesus came into the coasts of
17: 6 w' the disciples heard it, they fell on
8 w' they had lifted up their eyes, they
14 w' they were come to the multitude,
24 w' they were come to Capernaum,
25 w' he was come into the house,
27 w' thou hast opened his mouth, thou
18: 24 w' he had begun to reckon, one was
31 w' his fellowservants saw what was
19: 1 that w' Jesus had finished these
22 w' the young man heard that saying,
25 W' his disciples heard it, they were
28 w' the Son of man shall sit in the
20: 2 w' he had agreed with the labourers
8 So w' even was come, the lord of the
9 w' they came that were hired about
10 But w' the first came, they supposed
11 And w' they had received it, they
24 w' the ten heard it, they were moved
30 w' they heard that Jesus passed by,
21: 1 And w' they drew nigh unto
10 w' he was come into Jerusalem, all
15 w' the chief priests and scribes saw
19 w' he saw a fig tree in the way, he
20 And w' the disciples saw it, they
23 And w' he was come into the temple,
32 and ye, w' ye had seen it, repented not
34 w' the time of the fruit drew near,
38 But w' the husbandmen saw the son,
40 W' the lord therefore of the
45 w' the chief priests and Pharisees had
46 w' they sought to lay hands on him,
22: 7 But w' the king heard thereof, he was
11 w' the king came in to see the guests,
22 W' they had heard these words, they
25 the first, w' he had married a wife,
33 And w' the multitude heard this, they
34 w' the Pharisees had heard that he
23: 15 w' he is made, ye make him
24: 3 Tell us, w' shall these things be?
15 W' ye therefore shall see the
32 W' his branch is yet tender, and
33 w' ye shall see all these things,
46 w' he cometh shall find so doing.
50 come in a day w' he looketh not for
25: 31 W' the Son of man shall come in
37 w' saw we thee an hungred, and
38 W' saw we thee a stranger, and
39 Or w' saw we thee sick, or in
44 w' saw we thee an hungred, or
26: 1 w' Jesus had finished all these
6 w' Jesus was in Bethany, in the house
8 But w' his disciples saw it, they had
10 W' Jesus understood it, he said unto
20 Now w' the even was come, he sat
29 until that day w' I drink it new
30 And w' they had sung an hymn, they
71 w' he was gone out into the porch,
27: 1 W' the morning was come, all the
2 w' they had bound him, they led him
3 w' he saw that he was condemned,
12 w' he was accused of the chief
17 w' they were gathered together,
19 W' he was set down on the judgment
24 W' Pilate saw that he could prevail
26 and w' he had scourged Jesus, he
29 w' they had platted a crown of thorns,
33 w' they were come unto a place called
34 w' he had tasted thereof, he would not
47 w' they heard that, said, This man
50 w' he had cried again with a loud
54 w' the centurion, and they that were
57 W' the even was come, there came a
59 w' Joseph had taken the body, he
28: 12 And w' they were assembled with the
17 w' they saw him, they worshipped
M'r 1: 19 And w' he had gone a little farther
26 w' the unclean spirit had torn him,
29 w' they were come out of the
32 w' the sun did set, they brought
37 w' they had found him, they said unto
2: 4 w' they could not come nigh unto him
4 w' they had broken it up, they let
5 W' Jesus saw their faith, he said
8 immediately w' Jesus perceived in his
16 w' the scribes and Pharisees saw him
17 W' Jesus heard it, he saith unto
20 w' the bridegroom shall be taken
25 w' he had need, and was an
3: 5 w' he had looked round about on
8 w' they had heard what great things
11 unclean spirits, w' they saw him,
21 w' his friends heard of it, they went
4: 6 w' the sun was up, it was scorched;
10 w' he was alone, they that were
15 but w' they have heard, Satan
16 w' they have heard the word,
17 w' affliction or persecution ariseth for
29 w' the fruit is brought forth,
31 w' it is sown in the earth, is less
32 But w' it is sown, it groweth up,
34 w' they were alone, he expounded all
35 the same day, w' the even was come,
36 w' they had sent away the multitude,
5: 2 w' he was come out of the ship,
6 w' he saw Jesus afar off, he ran and
18 w' he was come unto the ship, he that
21 w' Jesus was passed over again by
22 and w' he saw him, he fell at his feet,

M'r 5: 27 W' she heard of Jesus, came in the
39 w' he was come in, he saith unto
40 w' he had put them all out, he taketh
6: 2 And w' the sabbath day was come, he
11 w' ye depart thence, shake off the
16 w' Herod heard thereof, he said, It is
20 w' he heard him, he did many things,
21 w' a convenient day was come, that
22 w' the daughter of the said Herodias
29 w' his disciples heard of it, they came
34 And Jesus, w' he came out, saw much
35 And w' the day was now far spent, his
38 w' they knew, they say, Five, and two
41 w' he had taken the five loaves and
46 And w' he had sent them away, he
47 w' even was come, the ship was in the
49 w' they saw him walking upon the
53 w' they had passed over, they came
54 w' they were come out of the ship,
7: 2 w' they saw some of his disciples eat
4 w' they come from the market, except
14 w' he had called all the people unto
17 w' he was entered into the house
30 w' she was come to her house, she
8: 17 w' Jesus knew it, he saith unto
19 W' I brake the five loaves among
20 w' the seven among four thousand,
23 w' he had spit on his eyes, and put his
33 w' he had turned about and looked
34 w' he had called the people unto him
38 w' he cometh in the glory of his
9: 8 w' they had looked round about, they
14 w' he came to his disciples, he saw a
15 all the people, w' they beheld him,
20 w' he saw him, straightway the spirit
25 W' Jesus saw the people came
28 w' he was come into the house, his
36 w' he had taken him in his arms, he
10: 14 But w' Jesus saw it, he was much
17 w' he was gone forth into the way,
41 w' the ten heard it, they began to be
47 w' he heard that it was Jesus of
11: 1 w' they came nigh to Jerusalem,
11 w' he had looked round about upon all
12 w' they were come from Bethany,
13 w' he came to it, he found nothing but
19 w' even was come he went out of
24 things soever ye desire, w' ye pray,
25 w' ye stand praying, forgive, if ye
12: 14 w' they were come, they say unto him,
23 therefore, w' they shall rise,
25 For w' they shall rise from the dead,
34 And w' Jesus saw that he answered
13: 4 Tell us, w' shall these things be?
4 sign w' all these things shall be
7 And w' ye shall hear of wars and
11 w' they shall lead you, and deliver
14 w' ye shall see the abomination of
28 W' her branch is yet tender, and
29 w' ye shall see these things come to
33 for ye know not w' the time is.
35 w' the master of the house cometh,
14: 11 And w' they heard it, they were glad,
12 w' they killed the passover, his
23 w' he had given thanks, he gave it to
26 And w' they had sung an hymn, they
40 w' he returned, he found them asleep
67 w' she saw Peter warming himself,
72 And w' he thought thereon, he wept.
15: 15 Jesus, w' he had scourged him, to be
20 w' they had mocked him, they
24 And w' he had crucified him, they
33 w' the sixth hour was come, there was
35 w' they heard it, said, Behold, he
39 w' the centurion, which stood over
41 w' he was in Galilee, followed him,
42 now w' the even was come, because it
45 w' he knew it of the centurion, he gave
16: 1 w' the sabbath was past, Mary
4 And w' they looked, they saw that the
9 w' Jesus was risen early in the first
11 w' they had heard that he was alive,
Lu 1: 9 w' he went into the temple of the Lord.
12 w' Zacharias saw him, he was
22 w' he came out, he could not speak
29 w' she saw him, she was troubled at
41 w' Elisabeth heard the salutation
2: 2 w' Cyrenius was governor of Syria.
17 w' they had seen it, they made known
21 w' eight days were accomplished
22 w' the days of her purification
27 w' the parents brought in the
39 w' they had performed all things
42 w' he was twelve years old, they
43 w' they had fulfilled the days, as they
45 w' they found him not, they turned
48 w' they saw him, they were amazed:
3: 21 w' all the people were
4: 17 w' he had opened the book, he found
25 w' the heaven was shut up three
25 w' great famine was throughout
28 synagogue, w' they heard these
35 w' the devil had thrown him in the
40 Now w' the sun was setting, all they
42 And w' it was day, he departed and
5: 4 w' he had left speaking, he said
6 w' they had this done, they inclosed a
8 W' Simon Peter saw it, he fell down
11 w' they had brought their ships to
12 w' he was in a certain city,
19 w' they could not find by what way
20 w' he saw their faith, he said unto
22 w' Jesus perceived their thoughts,
35 w' the bridegroom shall be taken
6: 3 did, w' himself was an hungred,
13 w' it was day, he called unto him

Lu 6: 22 are ye w' men shall hate you, and
22 w' they shall separate you from
26 w' all men shall speak well of you:
42 w' thou thyself beholdest not the
48 w' the flood arose, the stream beat
7: 1 w' he had ended all his sayings in
3 w' he heard of Jesus, he sent unto him
4 w' they came to Jesus, they besought
6 w' he was now not far from the house,
9 W' Jesus heard these things, he
12 w' he came nigh to the gate of the
13 And w' the Lord saw her, he had
20 W' the men were come unto him, they
24 And w' the messengers of John were
37 w' she knew that Jesus sat at meat in
39 w' the Pharisee which had bidden
42 w' they had nothing to pay, he frankly
8: 4 And w' much people were gathered
8 w' he had said these things, he cried,
13 w' they hear, receive the word
14 w' they have heard, go forth, and are
16 No man, w' he hath lighted a candle,
27 w' he went forth to land, there met
28 W' he saw Jesus, he cried out, and
34 W' they that fed them saw what was
40 that, w' Jesus was returned,
45 W' all denied, Peter and they that
47 w' the woman saw that she was not
50 w' Jesus heard it, he answered him
51 w' he came into the house, he suffered
9: 5 w' ye go out of that city, shake off the
10 apostles, w' they were returned, told
11 the people, w' they knew it, followed
12 w' the day began to wear away, then
26 w' he shall come in his own glory,
32 and w' they were awake, they saw his
36 w' the voice was past, Jesus
37 w' they were come down from the hill,
51 w' the time was come that he
54 w' his disciples James and John saw
10: 31 w' he saw him, he passed by on the
32 a Levite, w' he was at the place, came
33 w' he saw him, he had compassion on
35 on the morrow w' he departed, he
35 w' I come again, I will repay
11: 1 w' he ceased, one of his disciples
2 W' ye pray, say, Our Father which
14 w' the devil was gone out, the dumb
21 W' a strong man armed keepeth
22 w' a stronger than he shall come
24 W' the unclean spirit is gone out
25 w' he cometh, he findeth it swept and
29 w' the people were gathered thick
33 No man, w' he hath lighted a candle,
34 w' thine eye is single, thy whole
34 w' thine eye is evil, thy body also
36 w' the bright shining of a candle
38 w' the Pharisee saw it, he marvelled
12: 1 w' they were gathered together an
11 w' they bring you...the synagogues,
36 w' he will return from the
36 that w' he cometh and knocketh,
37 lord w' he cometh shall find watching:
40 cometh at an hour w' ye think not.
43 whom his lord w' he cometh shall find
46 come in a day w' he looketh not for
46 at an hour w' he is not aware, and will
54 W' ye see a cloud rise out of the
55 w' ye see the south wind blow, ye
58 W' thou goest with thine
13: 12 w' Jesus saw her, he called her to him,
17 w' he had said these things, all his
25 W' once the master of the house is
28 w' ye shall see Abraham, and
35 until the time come w' ye shall
14: 7 w' he marked how they chose out the
8 W' thou art bidden of any man to
10 w' thou art bidden, go and sit down
10 w' he that bade thee cometh, he
12 W' thou makest a dinner or a
13 But w' thou makest a feast, call the
15 w' one of them that sat at meat with
15: 5 w' he hath found it, he layeth it on his
6 And w' he cometh home, he calleth
9 w' she hath found it, she calleth her
14 w' he had spent all, there arose a
17 w' he came to himself, he said, How
20 w' he was yet a great way off, his
16: 4 w' I am put out of the stewardship,
9 w' ye fail, they may receive you
17: 7 w' he is come from the field, Go and
10 w' ye shall have done all those
14 w' he saw them, he said unto them, Go
15 w' he saw that he was healed, turned
20 w' he was demanded of the Pharisees,
20 w' the kingdom of God should
22 w' ye shall desire to see one of the
30 the day w' the Son of man is revealed.
18: 8 w' the Son of man cometh, shall he
15 w' his disciples saw it, they rebuked
22 w' Jesus heard these things, he
23 w' he heard this, he was very
24 w' Jesus saw that he was very
40 w' he was come near, he asked him,
43 w' they saw it, gave praise unto God.
19: 5 And w' Jesus came to the place, he
7 w' they saw it, they all murmured,
15 w' he was returned, having
28 w' he had thus spoken, he went before,
29 w' he was come nigh to Bethphage
37 w' he was come nigh, even now at the
41 w' he was come near, he beheld
20: 13 will reverence him w' they see him.
14 w' the husbandmen saw him, they
16 And w' they heard it, they said, God
37 w' he calleth the Lord the God of

Lu 21: 7 *w'* shall these things be? and what
7 *w'* these things shall come to pass
9 But *w'* ye shall hear of wars and
20 *w'* ye...see Jerusalem compassed
28 *w'* these things begin to come to pass,
30 *W'* they now shoot forth, ye see
31 *w'* ye see these things come to pass,
22: 7 *w'*...passover must be killed.
10 *w'* ye are entered into the city, there
14 *w'* the hour was come, he sat
32 *w'* thou art converted, strengthen
35 *W'* I sent you without purse, and
40 *w'* he was at the place, he said unto
45 *w'* he rose up from prayer, and was
49 *W'* they which were about him saw
53 *W'* I was daily with you in the temple,
55 *w'* they had kindled a fire in the midst
64 And *w'* they had blindfolded him,
23: 6 *W'* Pilate heard of Galilee, he asked
8 *w'* Herod saw Jesus,.he was...glad:
13 *w'* he had called together the chief
33 *w'* they were come to the place,
42 *w'* thou comest into thy kingdom.
46 *w'* Jesus had cried with a loud voice,
47 *w'* the centurion saw what was done,
24: 6 unto you *w'* he was yet in Galilee,
23 *w'* they found not his body, they came,
40 *w'* he had thus spoken, he shewed
Joh 1:19 *w'* the Jews sent priests and
42 *w'* Jesus beheld him, he said, Thou
48 *w'* thou was under the fig tree, I saw
2: 3 *w'* they wanted wine, the mother of
9 *W'* the ruler of the feast had
10 *w'* men have well drunk, then that
15 *w'* he had made a scourge of small
22 *W'* therefore he was risen from
23 *w'* he was in Jerusalem at the
23 *w'* they saw the miracles which he did.
3: 4 How can a man be born *w'* he is old?
4: 1 *W'* therefore the Lord knew how
21 *w'* ye shall neither in this
23 *w'* the true worshippers shall
25 *w'* he is come, he will tell us all
40 *w'* the Samaritans were come unto
45 Then *w'* he was come into Galilee,
47 *W'* he heard that Jesus was come out
52 hour *w'* he began to amend.
54 *w'* he was come out of Judæa into
5: 6 *W'* Jesus saw him lie, and knew that
7 no man, *w'* the water is troubled,
25 *w'* the dead shall hear the voice of
6: 5 *W'* Jesus then lifted up his eyes, and
11 *w'* he had given thanks, he distributed
12 *W'* they were filled, he said unto
14 *w'* they had seen the miracle that
15 *W'* Jesus therefore perceived that they
16 *w'* even was now come, his
19 So *w'* they had rowed about five and
22 *w'* the people which stood on the other
24 *W'* the people therefore saw that
25 *w'* they had found him on the
25 him, Rabbi, *w'* camest thou hither?
60 disciples, *w'* they had heard this, said,
61 *W'* Jesus knew in himself that his
7: 9 *W'* he had said these words unto
10 *w'* his brethren were gone up, then
27 *w'* Christ cometh, no man knoweth
31 *W'* Christ cometh, will he do more
8: 3 *w'* they had set her in the midst,
7 *w'* they continued asking him, he
10 *W'* Jesus had lifted up himself, and
28 *W'* ye have lifted up the Son of
44 *W'* he speaketh a lie, he speaketh
9: 4 night cometh, *w'* no man can work.
6 *W'* he had thus spoken, he spat on
14 sabbath day *w'* Jesus made the
35 *w'* he had found him, he said unto him,
10: 4 *w'* he putteth forth his own sheep,
11: 4 *W'* Jesus heard that, he said, This
6 *W'* he had heard therefore that he
17 *w'* Jesus came, he found that he had
28 *w'* she had so said, she went her way,
31 *w'* they saw Mary, that she rose up
32 *w'* Mary was come where Jesus
33 *W'* Jesus therefore saw her
43 And *w'* he thus had spoken, he cried
12: 12 *w'* they heard that Jesus was coming
14 Jesus, *w'* he had found a young ass,
16 but *w'* Jesus was glorified, then
17 *w'* he called Lazarus out of his
41 *w'* he saw his glory, and spake of
13: 1 *w'* Jesus knew that his hour was come
19 *w'* it is come to pass, ye may
21 *W'* Jesus had thus said, he was
26 I shall give a sop, *w'* I have dipped it.
26 *w'* he had dipped the sop, he gave
31 *w'* he was gone out, Jesus said,
14: 29 *w'* it is come to pass, ye might
15: 26 *w'* the Comforter is come, whom I
16: 4 *w'* the time shall come, ye may
8 *w'* he is come, he will reprove the world
13 *w'* he, the Spirit of truth, is come,
21 *w'* she is in travail hath sorrow,
25 *w'* I shall no more speak unto you
18: 1 *W'* Jesus had spoken these words, he
22 *w'* he had thus spoken, one of the
38 *w'* he had said this, he went out again
19: 6 *W'* the chief priests therefore and
8, 13 *W'* Pilate therefore heard that
23 *w'* they had crucified Jesus, took
26 *W'* Jesus therefore saw his mother,
30 *W'* Jesus therefore had received
33 But *w'* they came to Jesus, and
20: 1 Magdalene early, *w'* it was yet dark,
14 *w'* she had thus said, she turned
19 *w'* the doors were shut where the

Joh 20: 20 And *w'* he had so said, he shewed
20 disciples glad, *w'* they saw the Lord.
22 *w'* he had said this, he breathed on
24 was not with them *w'* Jesus came.
21: 4 *w'* the morning was now come, Jesus
7 *w'* Simon Peter heard that it was the
15 *w'* they had dined, Jesus saith to
18 *W'* thou wast young, thou girdedst
18 *w'* thou shalt be old, thou shalt
19 *w'* he had spoken this, he saith unto
Ac 1: 6 *W'* they therefore were come together,
9 *w'* he had spoken these things, while
13 And *w'* they were come in, they
2: 1 *w'* the day of Pentecost was
6 Now *w'* this was noised abroad, the
37 *w'* they heard this, they were pricked
3: 12 *w'* Peter saw it, he answered unto the
13 *w'* he was determined to let him go.
19 *w'* the times of refreshing shall
4: 7 *w'* they had set them in the midst, they
13 Now *w'* they saw the boldness of Peter
15 But *w'* they had commanded to go
21 *w'* they had further threatened them,
24 *w'* they heard that, they lifted up their
31 *w'* they had prayed, the place was
5: 7 *w'* his wife, not knowing what was
21 *w'* they heard that, they entered into
22 But *w'* the officers came, and found
23 *w'* we had opened, we found no man
24 *w'* the high priest and the captain
27 *w'* they had brought them, they set
33 *W'* they heard that, they were cut to
40 *w'* they had called the apostles, and
6: 1 *w'* the number of the disciples was
6 *w'* they had prayed, they laid their
7: 2 Abraham, *w'* he was in Mesopotamia,
4 *w'* his father was dead, he removed
5 after him, *w'* as yet he had no child.
12 *w'* Jacob heard that there was corn in
17 *w'* the time of the promise drew
21 *w'* he was cast out, Pharaoh's daughter
23 *w'* he was full forty years old, it
30 *w'* forty years were expired, there
31 *W'* Moses saw it, he wondered at the
54 *W'* they heard these things, they were
60 And *w'* he had said this, he fell asleep.
8: 12 *w'* they believed Philip preaching
13 *w'* he was baptized, he continued with
14 *w'* the apostles which were at
15 Who, *w'* they were come down, prayed
18 *w'* Simon saw that through laying on
25 *w'* they had testified and preached the
39 *w'* they were come up out of...water,
9: 8 *w'* his eyes were opened, he saw no
19 *w'* he had received meat, he was
26 *w'* Saul was come to Jerusalem, he
30 *w'* the brethren knew, they brought
37 whom *w'* they had washed, they laid
39 *W'* he was come, they brought him
40 eyes: and *w'* she saw Peter, she sat up.
41 *w'* he had called the saints and widows,
10: 4 *w'* he looked on him, he was afraid,
7 *w'* the angel which spake unto
8 *w'* he had declared all these things
32 who, *w'* he cometh, shall speak unto
11: 2 *w'* Peter was come up to Jerusalem,
6 which *w'* I had fastened mine eyes,
18 *W'* they heard these things, they held
20 *w'* they were come to Antioch, spake
23 *w'* he came, and had seen the grace
26 *w'* he had found him, he brought him
12: 4 *w'* he had apprehended him, and put
6 *w'* Herod would have brought him
10 *W'* they were past the first and the
11 *w'* Peter was come to himself, he said,
12 *w'* he had considered the thing, he
14 *w'* she knew Peter's voice, she opened
16 *w'* they had opened the door, and saw
19 *w'* Herod had sought for him, and
25 *w'* they had fulfilled their ministry,
13: 3 *w'* they had fasted and prayed, and
5 *w'* they were at Salamis, they
6 *w'* they had gone through the isle
12 *w'* he saw what was done, believed,
13 *w'* Paul and his company loosed from
14 *w'* they departed from Perga, they
17 *w'* they dwelt as strangers in
19 *w'* he had destroyed seven nations in
22 *w'* he had removed him, he raised up
24 *W'* John had first preached before his
29 *w'* they had fulfilled all that was
42 *w'* the Jews were gone out of the
43 *w'* the congregation was broken up,
45 *w'* the Jews saw the multitudes, they
48 *w'* the Gentiles heard this, they were
14: 5 *w'* there was an assault made both
11 *w'* the people saw what Paul had done,
21 And *w'* they had preached the gospel
23 *w'* they had ordained them elders in
25 *w'* they had preached the word in
27 *w'* they had come, and had gathered
15: 2 *W'* therefore Paul and Barnabas had
4 *w'* they were come to Jerusalem, they
7 *w'* there had been much disputing,
30 So *w'* they were dismissed, they came
30 *w'* they had gathered the multitude
31 Which *w'* they had read, they rejoiced
16: 6 *w'* they had gone throughout Phrygia
15 *w'* she was baptized, and her
19 *w'* her masters saw that the hope of
23 *w'* they had laid many stripes upon
34 *w'* he had brought them into his
35 *w'* it was day, the magistrates sent the
38 *w'* they heard that they were Romans.
40 *w'* they had seen the brethren, they
17: 1 *w'* they had passed through

Ac 17: 6 *w'* they found them not, they drew
8 the city, *w'* they heard these things.
9 *w'* they had taken security of Jason,
13 But *w'* the Jews of Thessalonica
16 *w'* he saw the city wholly given to
32 *w'* they heard of the resurrection of
18: 5 *w'* Silas and Timotheus were come
6 *w'* they opposed themselves, and
12 *w'* Gallio was the deputy of Achaia,
14 *w'* Paul was now about to open his
20 *W'* they desired him to tarry longer
22 *w'* he had landed at Cæsarea, and
26 *w'* Aquila and Priscilla had heard,
27 *w'* he was disposed to pass into
27 *w'* he was come, helped them much
19: 5 *W'* they heard this, they were baptized
6 *w'* Paul had laid his hands upon them,
9 But *w'* divers were hardened, and
21 *w'* he had passed through Macedonia
28 And *w'* they heard these sayings, they
30 *w'* Paul would have entered in unto
34 But *w'* they knew that he was a Jew,
35 *w'* the townclerk had appeased the
41 *w'* he had thus spoken, he dismissed
20: 2 *w'* he had gone over those parts, and
3 *w'* the Jews laid wait for him, as he
7 *w'* the disciples came together to
11 *W'* he therefore was come again, and
14 And *w'* he met with us at Assos,
18 *w'* they were come to him, he said
36 *w'* he had thus spoken, he kneeled,
21: 3 Now *w'* we had discovered Cyprus, we
5 *w'* we had accomplished those
6 *w'* we had taken our leave one of
7 *w'* we had finished our course from
11 *w'* he was come unto us, he took Paul's
12 *w'* we heard these things, both we,
14 *w'* he would not be persuaded, we
17 *w'* we were come to Jerusalem, the
19 *w'* he had saluted them, he declared
20 *w'* they heard it, they glorified the
27 And *w'* the seven days were almost
27 *w'* they saw him in the temple, stirred
32 *w'* they saw the chief captain and the
34 *w'* he could not know the certainty for
35 *w'* he came upon the stairs, so it
40 *w'* he had given him licence, Paul
40 *w'* there was made a great silence, he
22: 2 *w'* they heard that he spake in the
11 *w'* I could not see for the glory of
17 *w'* I was come again to Jerusalem,
20 And *w'* the blood of thy martyr
26 *W'* the centurion heard that, he went
23: 6 *w'* Paul perceived that the one part
7 *w'* he had so said, there arose a
10 *w'* there arose a great dissension, the
12 *w'* it was day, certain of the Jews
16 *w'* Paul's sister's son heard of their
28 *w'* I would have known the cause
30 *w'* it was told me how that the Jews
33 Who, *w'* they came to Cæsarea, and
34 *w'* the governor had read the letter,
35 *w'* thine accusers are also come.
24: 2 *w'* he was called forth, Tertullus
22 *w'* Felix heard these things, having
22 *W'* Lysias the chief captain shall
24 *w'* Felix came with his wife Drusilla,
25 *w'* I have a convenient season, I will
25: 1 *w'* Festus was come into the province,
6 *w'* he had tarried among them more
7 *w'* he was come, the Jews which came
12 *w'* he had conferred with the council,
14 *w'* they had been there many
15 About whom, *w'* I was at Jerusalem,
17 *w'* they were come hither, without
18 Against whom *w'* the accusers stood
21 *w'* Paul had appealed to be reserved
23 *w'* Agrippa was come, and Bernice,
25 *w'* I found that he had committed
26: 10 *w'* they were put to death, I gave my
14 *w'* we were all fallen to the earth, I
30 *w'* he had thus spoken, the king rose
31 *w'* they were gone aside, they talked
27: 1 *w'* it was determined that we
4 *w'* we had launched from thence, we
5 *w'* we had sailed over the sea of
7 *w'* we had sailed slowly many days,
9 Now *w'* much time was spent, and
9 *w'* sailing was now dangerous,
13 *w'* the south wind blew softly,
15 *w'* the ship was caught, and could not
17 *w'* they had taken up, they used helps,
20 *w'* neither sun nor stars in many days
27 *w'* the fourteenth night was come,
28 *w'* they had gone a little further, they
35 And *w'* he had thus spoken, he took
35 *w'* he had broken it, he began to eat.
38 *w'* they had eaten enough, they
39 *w'* it was day, they knew not the
40 *w'* they had taken up the anchors, they
28: 1 *w'* they were escaped, then they knew
3 *w'* Paul had gathered a bundle of
4 And *w'* the barbarians saw the
6 they looked *w'* he should have swollen,
9 So *w'* this was done, others also,
10 *w'* we departed, they laded us with
15 *w'* the brethren heard of us, they came
15 *w'* Paul saw, he thanked God, and
16 And *w'* we came to Rome, the
17 *w'* they were come together, he said
18 Who, *w'* they had examined me,
19 *w'* the Jews spake against it, I was
23 *w'* they had appointed him a day,
29 *w'* he had said these words, the Jews
Ro 1: 21 *w'* they knew God, they glorified him
2: 14 For *w'* the Gentiles, which have

Ro 2:16 In the day *w·* God shall judge the
3: 4 overcome *w·* thou art judged.
4:10 *w·* he was in circumcision, or in
19 *w·* he was about an hundred years
5: 6 *w·* we were yet without strength, in
10 if, *w·* we were enemies, we were
13 sin is not imputed *w·* there is no law.
6:20 For *w·* ye were the servants of sin,
7: 5 For *w·* we were in the flesh, the
9 but *w·* the commandment came, sin
21 *w·* I would do good, evil is present
9:10 *w·* Rebecca also had conceived by one,
11:27 *w·* I shall take away their sins.
13:11 nearer than *w·* we believed.
15:28 *W·* therefore I have performed this,
29 *w·* I come unto you, I shall come in the
1Co 2: 1 And I, brethren, *w·* I came to you,
5: 4 *w·* ye are gathered together, and my
8:12 *w·* ye so sin against the brethren, and
9:18 *w·* I preach the gospel, I may make
27 *w·* I have preached to others, I myself
11:18 *w·* ye come together in the church, I
20 *W·* ye come together therefore into
24 *w·* he had given thanks, he brake it,
25 he took the cup, *w·* he had supped,
32 But *w·* we are judged, we are
33 *w·* ye come together to eat, tarry one
34 rest will I set in order *w·* I come.
13:10 *w·* that which is perfect is come,
11 *W·* I was child, I spake as a child,
11 *w·* I became a man, I put away
14:16 *w·* thou shalt bless with the spirit,
26 *w·* ye come together, every one of
15:24 *w·* he shall have delivered up the
24 *w·* he shall have put down all rule,
27 *w·* he saith all things are put under
28 *w·* all things shall be subdued unto
54 So *w·* this corruptible shall have
16: 2 there be no gatherings *w·* I come.
3 *w·* I come, whomsoever ye shall
5 *w·* I shall pass through Macedonia:
12 *w·* he shall have convenient time.
2Co 1:17 *W·* I therefore was thus minded, I did
2: 3 lest, *w·* I came, I should have sorrow
12 *w·* I came to Troas to preach Christ's
3:15 *w·* Moses is read, the vail is upon
16 *w·* it shall turn to the Lord,
7: 5 *w·* we were come into Macedonia, our
7 *w·* he told us your earnest desire,
10: 2 I may not be bold *w·* I am present
6 *w·* your obedience is fulfilled.
11 in word by letters *w·* we are absent,
11 we be also in deed *w·* we are present.
15 *w·* your faith is increased, that we
11: 9 And *w·* I was present with you, and
12:10 *w·* I am weak, then am I strong.
20 *w·* I come, I shall not find you such as
21 *w·* I come again, my God will humble
13: 9 For we are glad, *w·* we are weak,
Ga 1:15 But *w·* it pleased God, who
2: 7 *w·* they saw that the gospel of the
9 And *w·* James, Cephas, and John, who
11 *w·* Peter was come to Antioch, I
12 *w·* they were come, he withdrew
14 But *w·* I saw that they walked not
4: 3 so we, *w·* we were children, were in
4 But *w·* the fulness of the time was
8 *w·* ye knew not God, ye did service
18 and not only *w·* I am present
6: 3 to be something, *w·* he is nothing,
Eph 1:20 *w·* he raised him from the dead, and
2: 5 Even *w·* we were dead in sins, hath
3: 4 *w·* ye read, ye may understand my
Ph'p 2:19 good comfort, *w·* I know your state.
28 *w·* ye see him again, ye may rejoice,
4:15 *w·* I departed from Macedonia, no
Col 3: 4 *W·* Christ, who is our life, shall
7 some time, *w·* ye lived in them.
4:16 *w·* this epistle is read among you,
1Th 2: 6 *w·* we might have been burdensome,
13 *w·* ye received the word of God which
3: 1 *w·* we could no longer forbear, we
4 *w·* we were with you, we told you
5 *w·* I could no longer forbear, I sent
6 *w·* Timotheus came from you unto us,
5: 3 For *w·* they shall say, Peace and
2Th 1: 7 *w·* the Lord Jesus shall be
10 *W·* he shall come to be glorified
2: 5 *w·* I was yet with you, I told ye these
3:10 even *w·* we were with you, this we
1Ti 1: 3 *w·* I went into Macedonia, that thou
5:11 for *w·* they have begun to wax
2Ti 1: 5 *W·* I call to remembrance the
17 But *w·* he was in Rome, he sought me
4: 3 *w·* they will not endure sound
13 *w·* thou comest, bring with thee, and
Tit 3:12 *W·* I shall send Artemas unto
Heb 1: 3 *w·* he had by himself purged our sins,
6 *w·* he bringeth in the firstbegotten
3: 9 *W·* your fathers tempted me,
16 some, *w·* they had heard, did provoke:
5: 7 *w·* he had offered up prayers and
12 For *w·* for the time ye ought to be
6:13 *w·* God made promise to Abraham,
7:10 father, *w·* Melchisedec met him.
27 he did once, *w·* he offered up himself.
8: 5 of God *w·* he was about to make the
8 *w·* I will make a new covenant with
9 *w·* I took them by the hand to lead
9: 6 *w·* these things were thus ordained,
19 *w·* Moses had spoken every precept to
10: 5 *w·* he cometh into the world, he saith,
8 *w·* he said, Sacrifice and offering and
11: 8 *w·* he was called to go out into a place
11 of a child *w·* she was passed age,
17 Abraham, *w·* he was tried, offered

Heb11:21 *w·* he was a dying, blessed both the
22 By faith Joseph, *w·* he died, made
23 Moses, *w·* he was born, was hid three
24 Moses, *w·* he was come to years,
31 *w·* she had received the spies with
12: 5 nor faint *w·* thou art rebuked of him:
17 *w·* he would have inherited the
Jas 1: 2 *w·* ye fall into divers temptations;
12 *w·* he is tried, he shall receive the
13 Let no man say *w·* he is tempted,
14 *w·* he is drawn away of his own lust,
15 *w·* lust hath conceived, it bringeth
15 sin, *w·* it is finished, bringeth forth
2:21 *w·* he had offered Isaac his son upon
25 *w·* she had received the messengers,
1Pe 1:11 *w·* it testified beforehand the
2:20 *w·* ye be buffeted for your faults, ye
20 *w·* ye do well, and suffer for it, ye take
23 *w·* he was reviled, reviled not again;
23 *w·* he suffered, he threatened not; but
3:20 *w·* once the longsuffering of God
4: 3 *w·* we walked in lasciviousness, lusts,
13 *w·* his glory shall be revealed,
5: 4 *w·* the chief Shepherd shall appear,
2Pe 1:16 *w·* we made known unto you the power
17 *w·* there came such a voice to him
18 *w·* we were with him in the holy
2:18 *w·* they speak great swelling words of
1Jo 2:28 *w·* he shall appear, we may have
3: 2 *w·* he shall appear, we shall be like
5: 2 *w·* we love God, and keep his
3Jo 3 *w·* the brethren came and testified of
Jude 3 *w·* I gave all diligence to write unto
9 *w·* contending with the devil he
12 *w·* they feast with you, feeding
Re 1:17 *w·* I saw him, I fell at his feet as
4: 9 *w·* those beasts give glory and
5: 8 And *w·* he had taken the book, the
6: 1 I saw *w·* the Lamb opened one of
3 *w·* he had opened the second seal, I
5 *w·* he had opened the third seal, I
7 *w·* he had opened the fourth seal, I
9 *w·* he had opened the fifth seal, I
12 *w·* he had opened the sixth seal,
13 *w·* she is shaken of a mighty wind.
14 as a scroll *w·* it is rolled together;
8: 1 *w·* he had opened the seventh seal,
9: 5 scorpion, *w·* he striketh a man.
10: 3 a loud voice, as *w·* a lion roareth:
3 *w·* he had cried, seven thunders
4 And *w·* the seven thunders had
7 *w·* he shall begin to sound, the
11: 7 *w·* they shall have finished their
12:13 *w·* the dragon saw that he was
17: 6 *w·* I saw her, I wondered with great
8 *w·* they behold the beast that was, and
10 *w·* he cometh, he must continue a
18: 9 *w·* they shall see the smoke of their
18 *w·* they saw the smoke of her burning,
20: 7 *w·* the thousand years are expired,
22: 8 And *w·* I had heard and seen, I fell

whence^
Ge 16: 8 Sarai's maid, *w·* comest thou?
29: 4 unto them, My brethren, *w·* be ye?
42: 7 he said unto them, *W·* come ye?
Nu 11:13 *W·* should I have flesh to give unto
23:13 *w·* thou mayest see them:
De 9:28 land *w·* thou broughtest us out
11:10 Egypt, from *w·* ye came out,
Jos 2: 4 me, but I wist not *w·* they were:
9: 8 Who are ye? and from *w·* come ye?
20: 6 unto the city from *w·* he fled.
J'g 13: 6 but I asked him not *w·* he was,
17: 9 said unto him, *W·* comest thou?
19:17 goest thou? and *w·* comest thou?
1Sa 25:11 whom I know not *w·* they be?
30:13 belongest thou?...*w·* art thou?
2Sa 1: 3 unto him, From *w·* comest thou?
13 man that told him, *W·* art thou?
2Ki 5:25 him, *W·* comest thou, Gehazi?
6:27 not help thee, *w·* shall I help thee?
20:14 and from *w·* came they unto thee?
Job 1: 7 said unto Satan, *W·* comest thou?
2: 2 unto Satan, From *w·* comest
10:21 Before I go *w·* I shall not return,
16:22 go the way *w·* I shall not return.
28:20 *W·* then cometh wisdom? and
Ps 121: 1 the hills, from *w·* cometh my help.
Ec 1: 7 the place from *w·* the rivers come,
Isa 30: 6 *w·* come the young and the old lion,
39: 3 and from *w·* came they unto thee?
51: 1 look unto the rock *w·* ye are hewn,
1 the hole of the pit *w·* ye are digged.
Jer 29:14 *w·* I caused you to be carried
Jon 1: 8 and *w·* comest thou? what is thy
Na 3: 7 *w·* shall I seek comforters for thee?
M't 12:44 my house from *w·* I came out;
13:27 thy field? from *w·* hath it tares?
54 *W·* hath this man this wisdom,
56 *W·* then hath this man all these
15:33 *W·* should we have so much bread
21:25 The baptism of John, *w·* was it?
M'r 6: 2 *w·* hath this man these things?
8: 4 *w·* can a man satisfy these men
12:37 Lord; and *w·* is he then his son?
Lu 1:43 And *w·* is this to me, that the
11:24 unto my house *w·* I came out.
13:25 you, I know you not *w·* ye are:
27 tell you, I know you not *w·* ye are;
20: 7 that they could not tell *w·* it was.
Joh 1:48 unto him, *W·* knowest thou me?
2: 9 wine, and knew not *w·* it was:
3: 8 but canst not tell *w·* it cometh,
4:11 *w·* then hast thou that living water?
6: 5 *W·* shall we buy bread, that these
7:27 Howbeit we know this man *w·* he is:

Joh 7:27 cometh, no man knoweth *w·* he is.
28 know me, and ye know *w·* I am:
8:14 for I know *w·* I came, and whither
14 ye cannot tell *w·* I come, and
9:29 fellow, we know not from *w·* he is.
30 that ye know not from *w·* he is,
19: 9 saith unto Jesus, *W·* art thou?
Ac 14:26 to Antioch, from *w·* they had been
Ph'p 3:20 *w·* also we look for the Saviour,
Heb11:15 country from *w·* they came out,
19 from *w·* also he received him in a
Jas 4: 1 *w·* come wars and fightings
Re 2: 5 therefore from *w·* thou art fallen,
7:13 in white robes? and *w·* came they?

whensoever
Ge 30:41 *w·* the stronger cattle did conceive,
M'r 14: 7 *w·* ye will ye may do them good:
Ro 15:24 *W·* I take my journey into

where^ See also WHEREABOUT; WHEREAS; WHEREBY; WHEREFORE; WHEREIN; WHEREINSOEVER; WHEREINTO; WHEREOF; WHEREON; WHERESOEVER; WHERETO; WHEREUNTO; WHEREUPON; WHEREWITH; WHEREWITHAL.
Ge 2:11 of Havilah, *w·* there is gold;
3: 9 and said unto him, *W·* art thou?
4: 9 unto Cain, *W·* is Abel thy brother?
13: 3 place *w·* his tent had been at the
10 that it was well watered every *w·*,
18: 9 unto him, *W·* is Sarah thy wife?
19: 5 *W·* are the men which came in to
27 place *w·* he stood before the Lord:
20:15 before thee: dwell *w·* it pleaseth thee.
21:17 the voice of the lad *w·* he is.
27:33 *w·* is he that hath taken venison,
31:13 Bethel, *w·*...anointedst the pillar,
13 *w·* thou vowedst a vow unto me:
33:19 field, *w·* he had spread his tent,
35:13 in the place *w·* he talked with him.
15 the place *w·* God spake with him,
27 *w·* Abraham and Isaac sojourned.
37:16 I pray thee, *w·* they feed their flocks.
38:21 *W·* is the harlot, that was openly
39:20 *w·* the king's prisoners were bound:
40: 3 the place *w·* Joseph was bound.
43:30 and he sought *w·* to weep; and he
Ex 2:20 *w·* is he? why is it that ye have
5:11 ye, get you straw *w·* ye can find it:
12:13 a token upon the houses *w·* ye are:
30 a house *w·* there was not one dead.
15:27 *w·* were twelve wells of water,
18: 5 *w·* he encamped at the mount
20:21 the thick darkness *w·* God was.
24 *w·* I record my name I will come
29:42 *w·* I will meet you, to speak
30: 6 *w·* I will meet with thee.
36 *w·* I will meet with thee: it
Le 4:12 place, *w·* the ashes are poured out:
12 *w·* the ashes are poured out shall
24 in the place *w·* they kill the burnt
33 *w·* they kill the burnt offering
6:25 place *w·* the burnt offering is killed.
7: 2 place *w·* they kill the burnt offering
14:13 place *w·* he shall kill the sin offering
Nu 13:22 *w·* Ahiman, Sheshai, and Talmai,
17: 4 *w·* I will meet with you.
22:26 *w·* was no way to turn either to the
33:14 *w·* was no water for the people to
54 place *w·* his lot falleth;
De 1:31 *w·* thou hast seen how that the
8:15 drought, *w·* there was no water;
11:10 *w·* thou sowedst thy seed, and
30 by the way *w·* the sun goeth down, in
18: 6 of all Israel, *w·* he sojourned,
23:16 one of thy gates, *w·* it liketh him best:
32:37 *W·* are their gods, their rocks in
Jos 4: 3 place *w·* the priests' feet stood firm,
3 place, *w·* ye shall lodge this night.
8 unto the place *w·* they lodged,
9 in the place *w·* the feet of the priests
J'g 5:27 *w·* he bowed, there he fell down
6:13 *w·* be all his miracles which our
9:38 *W·* is now thy mouth, wherewith
17: 8 to sojourn *w·* he could find a place:
9 to sojourn *w·* I could find a place.
18:10 *w·* there is no want of any thing.
19:26 man's house *w·* her lord was,
20:22 *w·* they put themselves in array
Ru 1: 7 out of the place *w·* she was,
16 and *w·* thou lodgest, I will lodge:
17 *W·* thou diest, will I die, and there
2:19 her, *W·* hast thou gleaned to day?
19 *w·* wroughtest thou? blessed be he
3: 4 mark the place *w·* he shall lie,
1Sa 3: 3 *w·* the ark of God was, and
6:14 there, *w·* there was a great stone:
9:10 city *w·* the man of God was.
18 thee, *w·* the seer's house is.
10: 5 God, *w·* is the garrison of the
14 when we saw that they were no *w·*
14:11 out of the holes *w·* they hid
19: 3 my father in the field *w·* thou art,
22 said, *W·* are Samuel and David?
20:19 to the place *w·* thou didst hide
23:22 and see his place *w·* his haunt is,
23 lurking places *w·* he hideth
24: 3 by the way, *w·* was a cave; and Saul
26: 5 the place *w·* Saul had pitched:
5 David beheld the place *w·* Saul"
16 And now see *w·* the king's spear is,
30: 9 Besor, *w·* those that were left behind
31 places *w·* David himself and
2Sa 2:23 to the place *w·* Asahel fell down
9: 4 the king said unto him, *W·* is he?
11:16 *w·* he knew that valiant men were
15:32 the mount, *w·* he worshipped

2Sa 16: 3 said, And w· is thy master's son?
17: 12 place w· he shall be found,
20 said, W· is Ahimaaz and Jonathan?
18: 7 W· the people of Israel were slain
21: 12 w· the Philistines had hanged
19 w· Elhanan the son of Jaare-oregim,
20 w· was a man of great stature, that
23: 11 w· was a piece of ground full of
1Ki 4: 28 the place w· the officers were,
7: 7 the throne w· he might judge,
8 his house w· he dwelt had
13: 25 in the city w· the old prophet dwelt.
17: 19 him up into a loft w· he abode,
21: 19 w· dogs licked the blood of Naboth
2Ki 2: 14 said, W· is the Lord God of Elijah?
4: 8 Shunem, w· was a great woman;
6: 1 w· we dwelt with thee is too
2 a place there, w· we may dwell.
6 the man of God said, W· fell it?
13 Go and spy w· he is, that I may
18: 34 W· are the gods of Hamath, and
34 w· are the gods of Sepharvaim,
19: 13 W· is the king of Hamath, and the
23: 7 w· the women wove hangings
8 w· the priests had burned
1Ch 11: 4 is Jebus; w· the Jebusites were,
13: 2 abroad unto our brethren every w·,
20: 6 Gath, w· was a man of great stature,
2Ch 3: 1 w· the Lord appeared unto David
25: 4 of Moses, w· the Lord commanded,
36: 20 w· they were servants to him and his
Ezr 1: 4 in any place w· he sojourneth,
6: 1 w· the treasures were laid up in
3 the place w· they offered sacrifices,
Ne 10: 39 w· are the vessels of the sanctuary,
13: 5 w· aforetime they laid the meat
Es 1: 6 W· were white, green, and blue
7: 5 Who is he, and w· is he, that durst
Job 4: 7 or w· were the righteous cut off?
9: 24 thereof; if not, w·, and who is he?
10: 22 order, and w· the light is as darkness.
12: 24 in a wilderness w· there is no way.
15: 23 abroad for bread, saying, W· is it?
17: 15 w· is now my hope? as for my
20: 7 have seen him shall say, W· is he?
21: 28 say, W· is the house of the prince?
28 w· are the dwelling places of the
23: 3 Oh that I knew w· I might find him!
9 w· he doth work, but I cannot behold
28: 1 and a place for gold w· they fine it.
12 But w· shall wisdom be found?
12 and w· is...understanding?
20 w· is the place of understanding?
34: 22 w· the workers of iniquity may
35: 10 W· is God my maker, who giveth
36: 16 broad place, w· there is no straitness;
38: 4 W· wast thou when I laid the
19 W· is the way w· light dwelleth?
19 darkness, w· is the place thereof,
26 it to rain on the earth, w· no man is;
39: 30 and w· the slain are, there is she.
40: 20 w· all the beasts of the field play.
Ps 19: 3 language, w· their voice is not heard.
26: 8 the place w· thine honour dwelleth.
42: 3 say unto me, W· is thy God?
10 say daily unto me, W· is thy God?
53: 5 there in great fear, w· no fear was:
63: 1 a dry and thirsty land, w· no water is;
69: 2 in deep mire, w· there is no standing:
2 deep waters, w· the floods overflow me.
79: 10 W· is their God? let him be known
81: 5 w· I heard a language that I
84: 3 herself, w· she may lay her young,
89: 49 w· are thy former lovingkindnesses,
104: 17 W· the birds make their nests:
107: 40 the wilderness, w· there is no way.
115: 2 heathen say, W· is now their God?
Pr 11: 14 W· no counsel is, the people fall: but
14: 4 W· no oxen are, the crib is clean: but
15: 17 is a dinner of herbs w· love is,
26: 20 W· no wood is, the fire goeth out:
20 w· there is no talebearer, the strife
29: 18 W· there is no vision the people
Ec 1: 5 hasteth to his place w· he arose.
8: 4 W· the word of a king is, there is
10 in the city w· they had so done:
11: 3 place w· the tree falleth, there it shall
Ca 1: 7 w· thou feedest, w· thou makest
Isa 7: 23 w· there were a thousand vines at
10: 3 and w· will ye leave your glory?
19: 12 W· are they?...thy wise men?
12 w· are thy wise men? and let them
29: 1 to Ariel, the city w· David dwelt!
30: 32 w· the grounded staff shall pass;
33: 18 W· is the scribe? w· is the receiver?
18 w· is he that counted the towers?
35: 7 the habitation of dragons, w· each lay,
36: 19 W· are the gods of Hamath and
19 w· are the gods of Sepharvaim?
37: 13 W· is the king of Hamath, and the
49: 21 left alone; these, w· had they been?
50: 1 W· is the bill of your mother's
51: 13 and w· is the fury of the oppressor?
57: 8 lovedst their bed w· thou sawest it.
63: 11 W· is he that brought them up out
11 w· is he that put his holy Spirit
15 w· is thy zeal and thy strength, the
64: 11 house w· our fathers praised thee,
66: 1 w· is the house that ye build unto
1 and w· is the place of my rest?
Jer 2: 6 W· is the Lord that brought us up
6 through, and w· no man dwelt?
8 priests said not, W· is the Lord?
28 w· are thy gods that thou hast made
3: 2 see w· thou hast not been lien with.
6: 16 paths, w· is the good way, and walk

Jer 7: 12 w· I set my name at the first,
13: 7 from the place w· I hid it:
20 w· is the flock that was given thee,
16: 13 w· I will not shew you favour.
17: 15 W· is the word of the Lord? let it
22: 26 country, w· ye were not born;
35: 7 in the land w· ye be strangers.
36: 19 and let no man know w· ye be.
37: 19 W· are now your prophets which
38: 9 die for hunger in the place w· he
39: 5 w· he gave judgment upon him.
42: 14 of Egypt, w· we shall see no war,
52: 9 w· he gave judgment upon him.
La 2: 12 mothers, W· is corn and wine?
Eze 3: 15 of Chebar, and I sat w· they sat,
6: 13 place w· they did offer sweet
8: 3 w· was the seat of the image of
11: 16 countries w· they shall come.
17 w· ye have been scattered, and I
13: 12 W· is the daubing wherewith ye
17: 10 wither in the furrows w· it grew.
16 in the place w· the king dwelleth that
20: 38 out of the country w· they sojourn,
21: 30 in the place w· thou wast created,
34: 12 w· they have been scattered,
40: 38 w· they washed the burnt offering.
42: 13 w· the priests that approach
43: 7 w· I will dwell in the midst of
46: 20 place w· the priests shall boil
20 w· they shall bake the meat
24 w· the ministers of the house
Da 8: 17 So he came near w· I stood: and when
Ho 1: 10 the place w· it was said unto them,
13: 10 w· is any other that may save thee
Joe 2: 17 among the people, W· is their God?
Am 3: 5 upon the earth, w· no gin is for him?
Mic 7: 10 unto me, W· is the Lord thy God?
Na 2: 11 W· is the dwelling of the lions, and
11 w· the lion, even the old lion,
3: 17 place is not known w· they are.
Zep 3: 19 land w· they have been put to shame.
Zec 1: 5 Your fathers, w· are they? and
Mal 1: 6 I be a father, w· is mine honour?
6 and if I be a master, w· is my fear?
2: 17 or, W· is the God of judgment?
M't 2: 2 W· is he that is born King of the
4 of them w· Christ should be born.
9 stood over w· the young child was.
6: 19 w· moth and rust doth corrupt,
19 w· thieves break through and steal:
20 w· neither moth nor rust doth
20 w· thieves do not break through
21 w· your treasure is, there will your
8: 20 man hath not w· to lay his head.
13: 5 w· they had not much earth:
18: 20 For w· two or three are gathered
25: 24 reaping w· thou hast not sown,
24 and gathering w· thou hast not
26 knewest that I reap w· I sowed
26 and gather w· I have not strawed:
26: 17 W· wilt thou that we prepare for
57 w· the scribes and the elders were
28: 6 Come, see the place w· the Lord lay.
16 w· Jesus had appointed them.
M'r 2: 4 uncovered the roof w· he was:
4: 5 ground, w· it had not much earth;
15 the way side, w· the word is sown;
5: 40 and entereth in w· the damsel was
6: 55 were sick, w· they heard he was.
9: 44, 46 W· their worm dieth not, and
48 W· their worm dieth not, and
11: 4 without in a place w· two ways met;
13: 14 standing w· it ought not, (let him
14: 12 W· wilt thou that we go and
14 saith, W· is the guestchamber,
14 w· I shall eat the passover with my
15: 47 of Joses beheld w· he was laid.
16: 6 behold the place w· they laid him.
20 went forth, and preached every w·,
Lu 4: 16 w· he had been brought up:
17 found the place w· it was written,
8: 25 said unto them, W· is your faith?
9: 6 the gospel, and healing every w·.
58 of man hath not w· to lay his head.
10: 33 as he journeyed, came w· he was:
12: 17 no room w· to bestow my fruits?
33 w· no thief approacheth, neither
34 w· your treasure is, there will your
17: 17 ten cleansed? but w· are the nine?
37 and said unto him, W·, Lord?
22: 9 him, W· wilt thou that we prepare?
10 into the house w· he entereth in.
11 thee, W· is the guestchamber,
11 w· I shall eat the passover with
Joh 1: 28 Jordan, w· John was baptizing.
38 Master,) w· dwellest thou?
39 They came and saw w· he dwelt,
3: 8 The wind bloweth w· it listeth, and
4: 20 the place w· men ought to worship.
46 Galilee, w· he made the water wine.
6: 23 the place w· they did eat bread,
62 man ascend up w· he was before?
7: 11 at the feast, and said, W· is he?
34 w· I am, thither ye cannot come.
36 w· I am, thither ye cannot come?
42 town of Bethlehem w· David was?
8: 10 her, Woman, w· are those thine
19 said unto him, W· is thy Father?
9: 12 him, W· is he? He said, I know not.
10: 40 the place w· John at first baptized;
11: 6 days still in the same place w· he was.
30 in that place w· Martha met him.
32 when Mary was come w· Jesus was,
34 And said, W· have ye laid him?
41 the place w· the dead was laid.
57 if any man knew w· he were, he

Joh 12: 1 w· Lazarus was which had been
26 and w· I am, there shall also my
14: 3 that w· I am, there ye may be also.
17: 24 hast given me, be with me w· I am;
18: 1 w· was a garden, into the which he
19: 18 W· they crucified him, and two
20 place w· Jesus was crucified was
41 the place w· he was crucified there
20: 2 we know not w· they have laid
12 feet, w· the body of Jesus had lain.
13 I know not w· they have laid him.
15 tell me w· thou hast laid him, and I
19 w· the disciples were assembled
Ac 1: 13 w· abode both Peter, and James,
2: 2 all the house w· they were sitting.
4: 31 w· they were assembled
7: 29 of Madian, w· he begat two sons.
33 w· thou standest is holy
8: 4 went every w· preaching the word.
11: 11 come unto the house w· I was,
12: 12 w· many were together praying.
15: 36 city w· we have preached
16: 13 w· prayer was wont to be made;
17: 1 w· was a synagogue of the Jews:
30 all men every w· to repent:
20: 6 days; w· we abode seven days.
8 w· they were gathered together.
21: 28 men every w· against the people,
25: 10 seat, w· I ought to be judged:
27: 41 falling into a place w· two seas met,
28: 14 W· we found brethren, and were
22 that every w· it is spoken against.
Ro 3: 27 W· is boasting then? It is
4: 15 for w· no law is, there is no
5: 20 But w· sin abounded, grace did
9: 26 place w· it was said unto them,
15: 20 not w· Christ was named, lest I
1Co 1: 20 W· is the wise? w· is the scribe?
20 w· is the disputer of this world?
4: 17 I teach every w· in every church.
12: 17 were an eye, w· were the hearing?
17 hearing, w· were the smelling?
19 one member, w· were the body?
15: 55 O death, w· is thy sting? O grave,
55 sting? O grave, w· is thy victory?
2Co 3: 17 and w· the Spirit of the Lord is,
Ga 4: 15 W· is then the blessedness ye
Ph'p 4: 12 every w· and in all things I
Col 3: 1 w· Christ sitteth on the right
11 W· there is neither Greek nor
1Ti 2: 8 that men pray every w·,
Heb 9: 16 w· a testament is, there must also
10: 18 w· remission of these is, there is
Jas 3: 16 w· envying and strife is, there is
1Pe 4: 18 w· shall the ungodly and the
2Pe 3: 4 W· is the promise of his coming?
Re 2: 13 thy works, and w· thou dwellest,
13 dwellest, even w· Satan's seat is:
13 slain among you, w· Satan dwelleth.
11: 8 w· also our Lord was crucified.
12: 6 w· she hath a place prepared of
14 w· she is nourished for a time, and
17: 15 w· the whore sitteth, are peoples,
20: 10 w· the beast and the false prophet

whereabout
1Sa 21: 2 thing of the business w· I send thee,

whereas
Ge 31: 37 W· thou hast searched all my
De 19: 6 w· he was not worthy of death,
28: 62 w· ye were as the stars of heaven
1Sa 24: 17 good, w· I have rewarded thee evil.
2Sa 7: 6 W· I have not dwelt in any house
15: 20 W· thou camest but yesterday, should
1Ki 8: 18 W· it was in thine heart to
12: 11 w· my father did lade you with a
2Ki 13: 19 w· now thou shalt smite Syria but
2Ch 10: 11 w· my father put a heavy yoke
28: 13 w· we have offended against the
Job 22: 20 W· our substance is not cut down,
Ec 4: 14 w· also he that is born in his
Isa 37: 21 W· thou hast prayed to me
60: 15 W· thou hast been forsaken and
Jer 4: 10 w· the sword reacheth unto the soul.
Eze 13: 7 W· ye say, The Lord saith it;
16: 7 W· thou wast naked and bare.
34 w· none followeth thee to commit
35: 10 possess it; w· the Lord was there:
36: 34 w· it lay desolate in the sight
Da 2: 41 w· thou sawest the feet and toes,
43 w· thou sawest iron mixed with
4: 23 w· the king saw a watcher and an
26 w· they commanded to leave the
8: 22 w· four stood up for it, four
Mal 1: 4 W· Edom saith, We are
Joh 9: 25 that, w· I was blind, now I see.
1Co 3: 3 w· there is among you envying,
Jas 4: 14 W· ye know not what shall be on
1Pe 2: 12 w· they speak against you as
3: 16 w· they speak evil of you, as of
2Pe 2: 11 W· angels, which are greater in

whereby^
Ge 15: 8 w· shall I know that I shall inherit
44: 5 drinketh, and w· indeed he divineth?
Le 22: 5 w· he may be made unclean,
Nu 5: 8 w· an atonement shall be made for
17: 5 w· they murmur against you.
De 7: 19 w· the Lord thy God brought thee
28: 20 doings, w· thou hast forsaken me.
1Sa 20: 33 w· Jonathan knew that it was
Ps 45: 5 w· the people fall under thee.
8 w· they have made thee glad.
68: 9 w· thou didst confirm thine
Jer 3: 8 w· backsliding Israel committed
17: 19 w· the kings of Judah come in,
23: 6 is his name w· he shall be called,

Jer 33: 8 w' they have sinned against me;
8 iniquities, w' they have sinned,
8 w' they have transgressed against
Eze 18: 31 w' ye have transgressed; and
20: 25 judgments w' they should not live;
39: 26 w' they have trespassed against
40: 49 by the steps w' they went up to it:
46: 9 the way of the gate w' he came in,
47: 13 border, w' ye shall inherit the land
Zep 2: 8 w' they have reproached my people,
Lu 1: 18 W' shall I know this? for I
78 w' the dayspring from on high
Ac 4: 12 men, w' we must be saved.
11: 14 w' thou and all thy house shall
19: 40 w' we may give an account of
Ro 8: 15 w' we cry, Abba, Father.
14: 21 thing w' thy brother stumbleth,
Eph 3: 4 W', when ye read, ye may
4: 30 w' ye are sealed unto the day
Ph'p 3: 21 w' he is able even to subdue all
Heb 12: 28 grace, w' we may serve God
2Pe 1: 4 W' are given unto us...great
3: 6 W' the world that then was,
1Jo 2: 18 w' we know that it is the last time.
wherefore^ See also THEREFORE.
Ge 10: 9 w' it is said, Even as Nimrod
16: 14 W' the well was called
18: 13 W' did Sarah laugh, saying, Shall
21: 10 W' she said unto Abraham, Cast out
26: 27 unto them, W' come ye to me,
29: 25 w' then hast thou beguiled
31: 27 W' didst thou flee away secretly,
30 yet, w' hast thou stolen my gods?
32: 29 W' is it that thou dost ask after my
38: 10 the Lord: w' he slew him also.
40: 7 saying, W' look ye so sadly to day?
43: 6 W' dealt ye so ill with me, as to
44: 4 W' have ye rewarded evil for good?
7 him, W' saith my lord these words?
47: 19 W' shall we die before thine eyes,
22 w' they sold not their lands.
50: 11 w' the name of it was called
Ex 2: 13 wrong, W' smitest thou thy fellow?
5: 4 W' do ye, Moses and Aaron, let the
14 W' have ye not fulfilled your task
15 W' dealest thou thus with thy
22 w' hast thou so evil entreated this
6: 6 W' say unto the children of Israel,
14: 11 w' hast thou dealt with us,
15 W' criest thou unto me? speak
17: 2 W' the people did chide with Moses,
2 with me? w' do ye tempt the Lord?
3 W' is this that thou hast brought
20: 11 day: w' the Lord blessed the
31: 16 W' the children of Israel shall keep
32: 12 W' should the Egyptians speak,
Le 10: 17 W' have ye not eaten the sin
13: 25 w' the priest shall pronounce him
25: 18 W' ye shall do my statutes, and keep
Nu 9: 7 w' are we kept back, that we may
11: 11 W' hast thou afflicted thy servant?
12: 8 w' then were ye not afraid to speak
14: 3 W' hath the Lord brought us into
41 W' now do ye transgress the
16: 3 w' then lift ye up yourselves
20: 5 w' have ye made us to come up out
21 w' Israel turned away from him.
21: 5 W' have ye brought us up out of
14 W' it is said in the book of
27 W' they that speak in proverbs
22: 32 W' hast thou smitten thine ass
37 w' camest thou not unto me? am I
25: 12 W' say, Behold, I give unto him
32: 5 W', said they, if we have found grace
De 7: 12 W' it shall come to pass, if ye
10: 9 W' Levi hath no part nor
19: 7 W' I command thee, saying,
29: 24 W' hath the Lord done thus
Jos 5: 9 W' the name of the place is called
7: 5 w' the hearts of the people melted,
7 w' hast thou at all brought this
10 w' liest thou thus upon thy face?
26 W' the name of that place
9: 11 W' our elders and all the inhabitants
22 W' have ye beguiled us, saying,
10: 3 W' Adoni-zedec king of Jerusalem
J'g 2: 3 W' I also said, I will not drive them
10: 13 gods: w' I will deliver you no more.
11: 27 W' I have not sinned against thee,
12: 1 W' passedst thou over to fight
3 w' then are ye come up unto me
18: 12 w' they called that place
Ru 1: 7 W' she went forth out of the place
1Sa 1: 20 W' it came to pass, when the time
2: 17 W' the sin of the young men was
29 W' kick ye at my sacrifice and at
30 W' the Lord God of Israel saith,
4: 3 W' hath the Lord smitten us to
6: 5 W' ye shall make images of your
6 W' then do ye harden your hearts,
9: 21 w' then speakest thou so to me?
14: 27 W' he put forth the end of the rod
15: 19 W' then didst thou not obey the
16: 19 W' Saul sent messengers unto Jesse,
18: 15 W' when Saul saw that he behaved
21 W' Saul said to David, Thou shalt this
27 W' David arose and went, he and his
19: 5 w' then wilt thou sin against
24 W' they say, Is Saul also
20: 27 W' cometh not the son of Jesse to
31 W' now send and fetch him unto me,
32 W' shall he be slain? what hath
21: 14 w' then have ye brought him to me?
23: 25 w' he came down into a rock, and
28 W' Saul returned from pursuing after
24: 9 W' hearest thou men's words,
1Sa 24: 19 w' the Lord reward thee good for that
25: 8 W' let the young men find favour in
36 w' she told him nothing, less or more,
26: 15 w' then hast thou not kept thy
18 W' doth my lord thus pursue after
27: 6 w' Ziklag pertaineth unto the
28: 9 w' then layest thou a snare for my
16 W' then dost thou ask of me,
29: 7 W' now return, and go in peace,
10 W' now rise up early in the
2Sa 2: 16 together: w' that place was called
22 w' should I smite thee to the
23 w' Abner with the hinder end of the
3: 7 W' hast thou gone in unto my
7: 22 W' thou art great, O Lord
10: 4 W' Hanun took David's servants,
11: 20 W' approached ye so nigh unto
12: 9 W' hast thou despised the
23 now he is dead, w' should I fast?
14: 13 W' then hast thou thought such a
31 W' have thy servants set my field
32 say, W' am I come from Geshur?
15: 19 W' goest thou also with us? return
16: 10 then say, W' hast thou done so?
18: 22 W' wilt thou run, my son,
19: 12 w' then are ye the last to bring
25 W' wentest not thou with me,
35 w' then should thy servant be yet
42 W' then be ye angry for this
21: 3 W' David said unto the Gibeonites,
24: 21 W' is my lord the king come to
1Ki 1: 2 W' his servants said unto him, Let
11 W' Nathan spake unto Bath-sheba
41 W' is this noise of the city being
16: 16 w' all Israel made Omri, the captain
20: 9 W' he said unto the messengers of
22: 34 w' he said unto the driver of his
2Ki 4: 23 W' wilt thou go to him to day?
31 W' he went again to meet him, and
5: 7 w' consider, I pray you, and
8 W' hast thou rent thy clothes?
7: 7 W' they arose and fled in the twilight,
9: 11 w' came this mad fellow to thee?
36 W' they came again, and told him.
17: 26 W' they spake to the king of Assyria,
19: 4 w' lift up thy prayers for the remnant
1Ch 19: 4 W' Hanun took David's servants,
21: 4 W' Joab departed, and went
29: 10 W' David blessed the Lord before all
2Ch 5: 3 W' all the men of Israel assembled
19: 7 W' now let the fear of the Lord be
22: 4 W' he did evil in the sight of the Lord
25: 10 W' their anger was greatly kindled
15 W' the anger of the Lord was kindled
28: 5 W' the Lord his God delivered him
29: 8 W' the wrath of the Lord was upon
34 w' their brethren the Levites did help
33: 11 W' the Lord brought upon them the
Ne 2: 2 W' the king said unto me, Why is
Es 3: 6 w' Haman sought to destroy all the
9: 26 W' they called these days
Job 3: 20 W' is light given to him that is in
10: 2 w' thou contendest with me.
18 W' then hast thou brought me
13: 14 W' do I take my flesh in my
24 W' hidest thou thy face, and
18: 3 W' we are counted as beasts, and
21: 7 W' do the wicked live, become old,
32: 6 w' I was afraid, and durst not
33: 1 W', Job, I pray thee, hear my
42: 6 W' I abhor myself, and
Ps 10: 13 W' doth the wicked contemn
44: 24 W' hidest thou thy face, and
49: 5 W' should I fear in the days of evil,
79: 10 W' should the heathen say, Where
89: 47 W' hast thou made all men *5921.
115: 2 W' should the heathen say, Where
Pr 17: 16 W' is there a price in the
Ec 4: 2 W' I praised the dead which are
5: 6 w' should God be angry at thy
Isa 5: 4 w', when I looked that it should
10: 12 W' it shall come to pass, that when
16: 11 W' my bowels shall sound
24: 15 W' glorify ye the Lord in the
28: 14 W' hear the word of the Lord, ye
29: 13 W' the Lord said, Forasmuch as
30: 12 W' thus saith the Holy One of
37: 4 w' lift up thy prayer for the remnant
50: 2 W', when I came, was there no
55: 2 W' do ye spend money for that
58: 3 W' have we fasted, say they, and
3 w' have we afflicted our soul, and thou
63: 2 W' art thou red in thine apparel,
Jer 2: 9 W' I will yet plead with you,
29 W' will ye plead with me? ye all
31 w' say my people, We are lords;
5: 6 W' a lion out of the forest
14 W' thus saith the Lord God of
19 W' doeth the Lord our God
12: 1 W' doth the way of the wicked
1 w' are all they happy that deal very
13: 22 W' come these things upon me?
16: 10 W' hath the Lord pronounced
22: 8 W' hath the Lord done thus
28 w' are they cast out, he and his
23: 12 W' their way shall be unto them
27: 17 w' should this city be laid waste,
30: 6 w' do I see every man with his
32: 3 W' dost thou prophesy, and say,
37: 15 W' the princes were wroth with
40: 15 w' should he slay thee, that all the
44: 6 W' my fury and mine anger was
7 W' commit ye this great evil
46: 5 W' have I seen them dismayed
49: 4 W' gloriest thou in the valleys,
51: 52 W', behold, the days come, saith
La 3: 39 W' doth a living man complain, a
5: 20 W' dost thou forget us forever,
Eze 5: 11 W', as I live, saith the Lord God;
7: 24 W' I will bring the worst of the
13: 20 W' thus saith the Lord God;
16: 35 W', O harlot, hear the word of the
18: 32 w' turn yourselves, and live ye.
20: 10 W' I caused them to go forth out of
25 W' I gave them also statutes that
30 W' say unto the house of Israel,
21: 7 W' sighest thou? that thou
23: 9 W' I have delivered her unto the
24: 6 W' thus saith the Lord God; Woe
33: 25 W' say unto them, Thus saith the
36: 18 W' I poured my fury upon them
43: 8 w' I have consumed them in mine
Da 3: 8 W' at that time certain
4: 27 W', O king, let my counsel be
6: 9 W' king Darius signed
8: 26 w' shut thou up the vision; for it
10: 20 Knowest thou w' I come unto thee?
Joe 2: 17 w' should they say among the
Jon 1: 14 W' they cried unto the Lord, and
Hab 1: 13 w' lookest thou upon them that
Mal 2: 14 Yet ye say, W'? Because the
15 w' one? That he might seek a
M't 6: 30 W', if God so clothe the grass of
7: 20 W' by their fruits ye shall
9: 4 W' think ye evil in your
12: 12 W' it is lawful to do well on the
31 W' I say unto you, All
14: 31 faith, w' didst thou doubt?
18: 8 W' if thy hand or thy foot offend
19: 6 W' they are no more twain, but
23: 31 W' ye be witnesses unto yourselves,
34 W', behold, I send unto you
24: 26 W' if they shall say unto you,
26: 50 Friend, w' art thou come?
27: 8 W' that field was called, The field
Lu 7: 7 W' neither thought I myself
47 W' I say unto thee, Her sins,
19: 23 W' then gavest not thou my
Joh 9: 27 hear: w' would ye hear it again?
Ac 1: 21 W' of these men which have
6: 3 W', brethren, look ye out among
10: 21 is the cause w' ye are come?
13: 35 W' he saith also in another psalm,
15: 19 W' my sentence is, that we trouble
19: 32 w' they were come together.
38 W' if Demetrius, and the
20: 26 W' I take you to record this day,
22: 24 w' they cried so against him.
30 w' he was accused of the Jews,
23: 28 the cause w' they accused him,
24: 26 w' he sent for him the oftener,
25: 26 W' I have brought him forth before
26: 3 w' I beseech thee to hear me
27: 25 W', sirs, be of good cheer: for I
34 W' I pray you to take some meat:
Ro 1: 24 W' God also gave them up to
5: 12 W', as by...man sin entered
7: 4 W', my brethren, ye also are
12 W' the law is holy, and the
9: 32 W'? Because they sought it not
13: 5 W' ye must needs be subject, not
15: 7 W' receive ye one another, as
1Co 4: 16 W' I beseech you, be ye followers
8: 13 W', if meat make my brother to
10: 12 W' let him that thinketh he
14 W', my dearly beloved, flee from
11: 27 W' whosoever shall eat this bread,
33 W', my brethren, when ye come
12: 3 W' I give you to understand, that
14: 13 W' let him that speaketh in an
22 W' tongues are for a sign, not to
39 W', brethren, covet to prophesy,
2Co 2: 8 W' I beseech you that ye would
5: 9 W' we labour, that, whether
16 W' henceforth know we no man
6: 17 W' come out from among them,
7: 12 W', though I wrote unto you, I did
8: 24 W' shew ye to them, and before the
11: 11 W'? because I love you not? God
Ga 3: 19 W' then serveth the law? It was
24 W' the law was our schoolmaster
4: 7 W' thou art no more a servant,
Eph 1: 15 W' I also, after I heard of
2: 11 W' remember, that ye being in
3: 13 W' I desire that ye faint not at my
4: 8 W' he saith, When he ascended
25 W' putting away lying, speak
5: 14 W' he saith, Awake thou that
17 W' be ye not unwise, but
6: 13 W' take unto you the whole
Ph'p 2: 9 W' God also hath highly exalted
12 W', my beloved, as ye have always
Col 2: 20 W' if ye be dead with Christ from
1Th 2: 18 W' we would have come unto you,
3: 1 W' when we could no longer
4: 18 W' comfort one another with
5: 11 W' comfort yourselves together,
2Th 1: 11 W' also we pray always for
2Ti 1: 6 W' I put thee in remembrance
Tit 1: 13 W' rebuke them sharply, that
Ph'm 8 W', though I might be much bold
Heb 2: 17 W' in all things it behoved him to
3: 1 W', holy brethren, partakers of
7 W' (as the Holy Ghost saith, To
10 W' I was grieved with that
7: 25 W' he is able also to save them
8: 3 w' it is of necessity that this man
10: 5 W' when he cometh into the
11: 16 w' God is not ashamed to be called
12: 1 W' seeing we also are compassed
12 W' lift up the hands which hang
28 W' we receiving a kingdom, which

Heb13:12 W' Jesus also, that he might
Jas 1:19 W', my beloved brethren, let
21 W' lay apart all filthiness and
4: 6 W' he saith, God resisteth the
1Pe 1:13 W' gird up the loins of your mind,
2: 1 W' laying aside all malice, and
6 W' also it is contained in the
4:19 W' let them that suffer according
2Pe 1:10 W' the rather, brethren, give
12 W' I will not be negligent to put
3:14 W', beloved, seeing that ye look
1Jo 3:12 w' slew he him? Because his
3Jo 10 W', if I come, I will
Re 17: 7 W' didst thou marvel? I will tell

wherein^ See also WHEREINSOEVER; WHEREINTO.
Ge 1:30 w' there is life, I have given every
6:17 w' is the breath of life, from under
7:15 of all flesh, w' is the breath of life.
17: 8 the land w' thou art a stranger, all
21:23 the land w' thou hast sojourned.
28: 4 the land w' thou art a stranger,
36: 7 the land w' they were strangers,
37: 1 in the land w' his father was a
Ex 1:14 w' they made them serve, was with
6: 4 pilgrimage, w' they were strangers.
12: 7 of the houses, w' they shall eat it.
18:11 in the thing w' they dealt proudly
20 shew them the way w' they must walk,
22:27 w' shall he sleep? and it shall
33:16 w' shall it be known here that I
Le 4:23 w' he hath sinned, come to his
5:18 w' he erred and wist it not, and it
6:28 vessel w' it is sodden shall be
11:32 w' any work is done, it must be put
36 w' there is plenty of water, shall be
13:46 days w' the plague shall be in him
52 any thing of skin, w' the plague is:
54 wash the thing w' the plague is,
57 burn that w' the plague is with fire.
18: 3 land of Egypt, w' ye dwelt, shall ye
Nu 12:11 upon us, w' we have done foolishly,
11 foolishly, and w' we have sinned.*
19: 2 w' is no blemish, and upon which
31:10 burnt all their cities w' they dwelt,
33:55 vex you in the land w' ye dwell.
35:33 shall not pollute the land w' ye are:
34 shall inhabit, w' I dwell:
De 8: 9 A land w' thou shalt eat bread
15 wilderness, w' were fiery serpents,
12: 2 w' the nations which ye shall
7 w' the Lord thy God hath blessed
17: 1 or sheep, w' is blemish, or any
28:52 w' thou trustedst, throughout
Jos 8:24 wilderness w' they chased them,
10:27 cave w' they had been hid,
22:19 w' the Lord's tabernacle
33 land w' the children of Reuben
24:17 us in all the way w' we went, and
J'g 16: 5 see w' his great strength lieth,
6 w' thy great strength lieth, and
15 told me w' thy great strength lieth.
18: 6 the Lord is your way w' ye go.
1Sa 6:15 w' the jewels of gold were, and put
14:38 see w' this sin hath been this day.
2Sa 7: 7 all the places w' I have walked
1Ki 8:21 ark, w' is the covenant of the
36 the good way w' they should walk,
50 w' they have transgressed against
13:31 sepulchre w' the man of God is
2Ki 12: 2 w' Jehoiada the priest instructed
14: 6 w' the Lord commanded, saying,
17:29 in their cities w' they dwelt.
18:19 confidence is this w' thou trustest?
23:23 w' this passover was holden to the
2Ch 3: 3 w' Solomon was instructed for the
6:11 w' is the covenant of the Lord,
27 good way, w' they should walk;
8: 1 w' Solomon had built the house of
33:19 the places w' he built high places,
Ezr 5: 7 unto him, w' was written thus;
Ne 6: 6 W' was written, It is reported
13:15 them in the day w' they sold victuals.
Es 5:11 w' the king had promoted him,
8:11 W' the king granted the Jews
9:22 days w' the Jews rested from their
Job 3: 3 Let the day perish w' I was born, and
6:16 of the ice, and w' the snow is hid:
24 me to understand w' I have erred.
38:26 on the wilderness, w' there is no man;
Ps 74: 2 this mount Zion, w' thou hast dwelt.
90:15 to the days w' thou hast afflicted us,
15 and the years w' we have seen evil.
104:20 w' all the beasts of the forest do
25 wide sea, w' are things creeping
142: 3 In the way w' I walked have they
143: 8 to know the way w' I should walk;
Ec 2:19 all my labour w' I have laboured,
19 w' I have shewed myself wise under
22 w' he hath laboured under the sun?
3: 9 worketh in that w' he laboureth?
8: 9 is a time w' one man ruleth over
Isa 2:22 for w' is he to be accounted of?
14: 3 bondage w' thou wast made to
33:21 w' shall go no galley with oars,
36: 4 confidence is this w' thou trustest?
47:12 w' thou hast laboured from thy
65:12 did choose that w' I delighted not.
Jer 5:17 fenced cities, w' thou trustedst,
7:14 called by my name, w' ye trust, and
12: 5 the land of peace, w' thou trustedst,
16:19 vanity, and things w' there is no profit.
20:14 Cursed be the day w' I was born:
14 not the day w' my mother bare me
22:28 idol? is he a vessel w' is no pleasure?
31: 9 way, w' they shall not stumble:
36:14 roll w' thou hast read in the ears of
41: 9 pit w' Ishmael had cast all the dead
42: 3 shew us the way w' we may walk,
48:38 Moab like a vessel w' is no pleasure,
51:43 a land w' no man dwelleth,
Eze 20:34 the countries w' ye are scattered,
41 countries w' ye have been scattered;
43 doings, w' ye have been defiled;
23:19 w' she had played the harlot in the
26:10 enter into a city w' is made a breach.
32: 6 thy blood the land w' thou swimmest,
37:23 w' they have sinned, and will
42:14 their garments w' they minister;
Ho 2:13 w' she burned incense to them, and
8: 8 Gentiles as a vessel w' is no pleasure.
Jon 4:11 w' are more than sixscore thousand
Mic 6: 3 thee? and w' I have wearied thee?
Zep 3:11 w' thou hast transgressed against
Zec 9:11 prisoners out of the pit w' is no water.
Mal 1: 2 Yet ye say, W' hast thou loved us?
6 W' have we despised thy name?
7 W' have we polluted thee? In that
2:17 ye say, W' have we wearied him?
3: 7 But ye said, W' shall we return?
8 ye say, W' have we robbed thee?
M't 11:20 w' most of his mighty works
25:13 w' the Son of man cometh.
M'r 2: 4 w' the sick of the palsy lay.
Lu 1: 4 w' thou hast been instructed.
25 in the days w' he looked on me,
11:22 all his armour w' he trusted,
23:53 w' never man before was laid.
Joh 19:41 w' was never man yet laid.
Ac 2: 8 own tongue, w' we were born?
7: 4 into this land, w' ye now dwell.
10:12 W'...all manner of fourfooted
Ro 2: 1 for w' thou judgest another,
5: 2 into this grace w' we stand,
7: 6 being dead w' we were held;
1Co 7:20 same calling w' he was called,
24 w' he is called, therein abide
15: 1 have received, and w' ye stand;
2Co 11:12 that w' they glory, they may be
12:13 For what is it w' ye were inferior to
Eph 1: 6 w' he hath made us accepted
8 W' he hath abounded toward us
2: 2 W' in time past ye walked
5:18 drunk with wine, w' is excess;
Ph'p 4:10 w' ye were also careful, but
Col 2:12 w' also ye are risen with him
2Ti 2: 9 W' I suffer trouble, as an evil
Heb 6:17 W' God, willing more
9: 2 first, w' was the candlestick,
4 w' was the golden pot that had
1Pe 1: 6 W' ye greatly rejoice, though
3:20 w' few, that is, eight souls
4: 4 W' they think it strange that
5:12 true grace of God w' ye stand.
2Pe 3:12 w' the heavens being on fire
13 w' dwelleth righteousness.
Re 2:13 w' Antipas was my...martyr,
18:19 w' were made rich all that had

whereinsoever
2Co 11:21 w' any is bold, (I speak

whereinto
Le 11:33 w' any of them falleth,
Nu 14:24 into the land w' he went;
Joh 6:22 one w' his disciples...entered,

whereof^
Ge 3:11 w' I commanded thee that thou
Le 6:30 w' any of the blood is brought into
13:24 skin w' there is a hot burning, and
27: 9 w' men bring an offering unto the
Nu 5: 3 their camps, in the midst w' I dwell.
7:13, 19, 25, 37, 49, 61, 67, 73, 79 weight w'
was an hundred and thirty shekels,
21:16 well w' the Lord spake unto Moses,
De 13: 2 to pass, w' he spake unto thee,
28:27 itch w' thou canst not be healed.
68 by the way w' I spake unto thee,
Jos 20: 2 w' I spake unto you by the hand of
22: 9 w' they were possessed, according
1Sa 10:16 of the kingdom, w' Samuel spake,
13: 2 w' two thousand were with Saul in
2Sa 12:30 weight w' was a talent of gold with
2Ki 13:14 sick of this sickness w' he died.
17:12 w' the Lord had said unto them,
2Ch 3: 8 w' was according to the breadth
6:20 place w' thou hast said that thou
24:14 w' were made vessels for the house of
33: 4 w' the Lord had said, In Jerusalem
Ne 12:31 w' one went on the right hand upon
Job 6: 4 poison w' drinketh up my spirit:
Ps 46: 4 w' shall make glad the city of God,
57: 6 midst w' they are fallen themselves.
126: 3 great things for us; w' we are glad.
Ec 1:10 Is there any thing w' it may be said,
Ca 4: 2 w' every one bear twins, and none is
6: 6 w' every one beareth twins, and there
Jer 32:36 concerning this city, w' ye say, It
43 this land, w' ye say, It is desolate
42:16 and the famine, w' ye were afraid
Eze 32:15 be destitute of that w' it was full,
39: 8 this is the day w' I have spoken.
Da 9: 2 w' the word of the Lord came to
Ho 2:12 w' she hath said, These are my
Lu 23:14 those things w' ye accuse him:
Ac 2:32 raised up, w' we all are witnesses.
3:15 raised from the dead; w' we are
17:19 new doctrine, w' thou speakest, is?
31 w' he hath given assurance unto all
21:24 w' they were informed concerning
24: 8 all these things, w' we accuse him.
13 things w' they now accuse
25:11 of these things w' these accuse me,
26: 2 things w' I am accused of the Jews:
Ro 4: 2 he hath w' to glory; but not before
6:21 w' ye are now ashamed?
15:17 w' I may glory through Jesus Christ
1Co 7: 1 things w' ye wrote unto me:
2Co 9: 5 your bounty, w' ye had notice before,
Eph 3: 7 W' I was made a minister,
Ph'p 3: 4 he hath w' he might trust in the flesh,
Col 1: 5 w' ye heard before in the word of
23 w' I Paul am made a minister;
25 W' I am made a minister,
1Ti 1: 7 they say, nor w' they affirm.
6: 4 words, w' cometh envy, strife,
Heb 2: 5 world to come, w' we speak.
10:15 W' the Holy Ghost also is a witness
12: 8 chastisement, w' all are partakers,
13:10 w' they have no right to eat
1Jo 4: 3 w' ye have heard that it should

whereon^
Ge 28:13 land w' thou liest, to thee will
Ex 3: 5 place w' thou standest is holy
8:21 also the ground w' they are.
Le 6:27 wash that w' it was sprinkled
15: 6 sitteth on any thing w' he sat
17 w' is the seed of copulation,
23 or on any thing w' she sitteth,
24 all the bed w' he lieth shall be
26 bed w' she lieth all the days of
De 11:24 w' the soles of your feet shall tread
Jos 5:15 place w' thou standest is holy.
14: 9 land w' thy feet have trodden shall
1Sa 6:18 Abel, w' they set down the ark
2Ch 4:19 tables w' the shewbread was set;
32:10 W' do ye trust, that ye abide
Job 24:23 him to be in safety, w' he resteth;
Ca 4: 4 w' there hang a thousand bucklers,
Isa 36: 6 w' if a man lean, it will go
Eze 37:20 sticks w' thou writest shall be
M'r 11: 2 a colt tied, w' never man sat;
Lu 4:29 the hill w' their city was built,
5:25 and took up that w' he lay, and
19:30 a colt tied, w' never man sat:
Joh 4:38 to reap w' ye bestowed no labour:

wheresoever
Le 13:12 to his foot, w' the priest looketh;
2Ki 8: 1 and sojourn w' thou canst sojourn:
12: 5 w' any breach shall be found.
1Ch 17: 6 W' I...walked with all Israel,
Jer 40: 5 go w' it seemeth convenient
Da 2:38 w' the children of men dwell,
M't 24:28 w' the carcase is, there will
26:13 W' this gospel shall be
M'r 9:18 w' he taketh him, he teareth
14: 9 W' this gospel shall be
14 w' he shall go in, say ye to the
Lu 17:37 W' the body is, thither will the

whereto See also WHEREUNTO.
Job 30: 2 w' might the strength of their
Isa 55:11 prosper in the thing w' I sent it.
Ph'p 3:16 w' we have already attained,

whereunto
Nu 36: 3, 4 the tribe w' they are received:
De 4:26 perish from off the land w' ye go
2Ch 8:11 w' the ark of the Lord hath come.
Es 10: 2 w' the king advanced him,
Ps 71: 3 w' I may continually resort:
Jer 22:27 the land w' they desire to return,
Eze 5: 9 w' I will not do any more the like,
20:29 is the high place w' ye go?
M't 11:16 w' shall I liken this generation?
M'r 4:30 W' shall we liken the kingdom of
Lu 7:31 W' then shall I liken the men of
13:18 like? and w' shall I resemble it?
20 W' shall I liken the kingdom of
Ac 5:24 of them w' this would grow.
13: 2 for the work w' I have called them.
27: 8 nigh w' was the city of Lasea.
Ga 4: 9 w' ye desire again to be in
Col 1:29 W' I also labour, striving
2Th 2:14 W' he called you by our gospel,
1Ti 2: 7 W' I am ordained a preacher,
4: 6 doctrine, w' thou hast attained.
6:12 w' thou art also called, and
2Ti 1:11 W' I am appointed a preacher,
1Pe 2: 8 w' also they were appointed.
3:21 like figure w' even baptism doth
2Pe 1:19 w' ye do well that ye take heed, as

whereupon
Le 11:35 w' any part of their carcase
J'g 16:26 pillars w' the house standeth,
1Ki 7:48 of gold, w' the shewbread was,
12:28 W' the king took counsel, and made
2Ch 12: 6 W' the princes of Israel and the king
Job 38: 6 W' are the foundations
Eze 9: 3 from the cherub, w' he was,
23:41 w' thou hast set thine incense and
24:25 that w' they set their minds, their sons
40:41 tables, w' they slew their sacrifices,
42 w' also they laid the instruments
Am 4: 7 and the piece w' it rained not
M't 14: 7 W' he promised with an oath to
Ac 24:18 W' certain Jews from Asia
26:12 W' as I went to Damascus with
19 W', O king Agrippa, I was not
Heb 9:18 W' neither the first testament was

wherewith^ See also WHEREWITHAL.
Ge 27:41 blessing w' his father blessed him:
Ex 4:17 thine hand, w' thou shalt do signs.
16:32 may see the bread w' I have fed you
17: 5 thy rod, w' thou smotest the river,
29:33 things w' the atonement was made,
Nu 3:31 of the sanctuary w' they minister,
48 w' the odd number of them is to be
4: 9 thereof, w' they minister unto it:

Nu 4:12 w· they minister in the sanctuary,
14 w· they minister about it, even the
16:39 w· they that were burnt had offered;
25:18 w· they have beguiled you in the
30: 4 her bond w· she hath bound her soul
4 bond w· she hath bound her soul
5 bonds w· she hath bound her soul,
6 of her lips, w· she bound her soul;
7 w· she bound her soul shall stand.
8 lips, w· she bound her soul, of none
9 w· they have bound their souls,
11 w· she bound her soul shall stand.
35:17 throwing a stone, w· he may die,
18 weapon of wood, w· he may die,
23 with any stone, w· a man may die,
De 9:19 w· the Lord was wroth against you
15:14 w· the Lord thy God hath blessed
22:12 of thy vesture, w· thou coverest
28:53 w· thine enemies shall distress thee:
55 w· thine enemies shall distress thee
57 w· thine enemy shall distress thee
67 of thine heart w· thou shalt fear,
33: 1 w· Moses the man of God blessed
Jos 8:26 w· he stretched out the spear, until
J'g 6:15 my Lord, w· shall I save Israel?
9: 4 w· Abimelech hired vain and light
9 w· by me they honour God and man,
38 is now thy mouth, w· thou saidst,
16: 6 w· thou mightest be bound to
10 thee, w· thou mightest be bound.
1Sa 6: 2 tell us w· we shall send it to his
8: 8 w· they have forsaken me, and served
29: 4 for w· should he reconcile himself
2Sa 13:15 hatred w· he hated her was greater
15 than the love w· he had loved her.
21: 3 w· shall I make the atonement,
1Ki 8:59 w· I have made supplication before
15:22 thereof, w· Baasha had builded;
26 in his sin w· he made Israel to sin.
30 w· he provoked the Lord God of
34 in his sin w· he made Israel to sin.
16:26 in his sin w· he made Israel to sin,
21:22 w· thou hast provoked me to anger,
22:22 And the Lord said unto him, W·?
2Ki 13:12 w· he fought against Amaziah
21:16 his sin w· he made Judah to sin,
23:26 w· his anger was kindled against
25:14 vessels of brass w· they ministered,
1Ch 18: 8 w· Solomon made the brasen sea,
2Ch 2:17 w· David his father had numbered
16: 6 thereof, w· Baasha was building:
18:20 And the Lord said unto him, W·?
35:21 but against the house w· I have war:
Ne 9:34 w· thou didst testify against them.
Job 15: 3 with speeches w· he can do no good?
Ps 79:12 w· they have reproached thee, O
89:51 W· thine enemies have reproached,
51 w· they have reproached the
93: 1 strength, w· he hath girded himself:?
109:19 a girdle w· he is girded continually.
119:42 w· to answer him that reproacheth
129: 7 W· the mower filleth not his hand;
Ca 3:11 crown w· his mother crowned him
Isa 28:12 w· ye may cause the weary to rest;
37: 6 w· the servants of the king of
Jer 18:10 w· I said I would benefit them.
19: 9 w· their enemies, and they that seek
21: 4 w· ye fight against the king of
33:16 is the name w· she shall be called,
52:18 vessels of brass w· they ministered,
La 1:12 w· the Lord hath afflicted me in the
Eze 13:20 w· ye there hunt the souls to make
16:19 and oil, and honey, w· I fed thee,
29:20 labour w· he served against it,
32:16 lamentation w· they shall lament her:
36:18 their idols w· they had polluted it:
Da 2: 1 dreams, w· his spirit was troubled,
Mic 6: 6 W· shall I come before the Lord,
Zec 14:12 plague w· the Lord shall smite all
18 w· the Lord will smite the heathen
Mal 2: 5 to him for the fear w· he feared me,
M't 5:13 savour, w· shall it be salted?
M'r 3:28 w· soever they shall blaspheme:
9:50 saltness, w· will ye season it?
Lu 14:34 savour, w· shall it be seasoned?
17: 8 Make ready w· I may sup, and
Joh 13: 5 with the towel w· he was girded.
17:26 the love w· thou hast loved me may
Ro 14:19 things w· one may edify another.
2Co 1: 4 w· we ourselves are comforted of
7: 7 w· he was comforted in you,
10: 2 w· I think to be bold against some,
Ga 5: 1 liberty w· Christ hath made us free,
Eph 2: 4 for his great love w· he loved us,
4: 1 of the vocation w· ye are called,
6:16 w· ye shall be able to quench
1Th 3: 9 joy w· we joy for your sakes before
Heb 10:29 w· he was sanctified, an unholy

wherewithal^
M't 6:31 drink? or, W· shall we be clothed?

whet
De 32:41 If I w· my glittering sword, and
Ps 7:12 he turn not, he will w· his sword;
64: 3 Who w· their tongue like a sword,
Ec 10:10 blunt, and he do not w· the edge,

whether^
Ge 18:21 see w· they have done altogether
27:21 w· thou be my very son Esau or not.
31:39 w· stolen by day, or stolen by night.
37:14 w· it be well with thy brethren, and
32 now w· it be thy son's coat or no.
42:16 proved, w· there be any truth in you:
43: 6 the man w· ye had yet a brother?
Ex 4:18 Egypt, and see w· they be yet alive.
12:19 w· he be a stranger, or born in the
Ex 16: 4 w· they will walk in my law, or no.
19:13 w· it be beast or man, it shall not
21:31 W· he have gored a son, or have
22: 4 hand alive, w· it be ox, or ass,
8 to see w· he have put his hand
9 w· it be for ox, for ass, for sheep,
34:19 cattle, w· ox or sheep, that is male.
Le 3: 1 w· it be a male or female, he shall
5: 1 w· he hath seen or known of it:
2 w· it be a carcase of an unclean
7:26 blood, w· it be of fowl or of beast,
11:32 w· it be any vessel of wood, or
35 w· it be oven, or ranges for pots, they
13:47 w· it be a woolen garment, or a linen
48 W· it be in the warp, or woof, of
48 w· in a skin, or any thing made of
52 w· warp or woof, in woollen or in
55 w· it be bare within or without.
15: 3 w· his flesh run with his issue, or his
16:29 w· it be one of your own country, or
17:15 w· it be one of your own country, or
18: 9 w· she be born at home, or born
27:12 shall value it, w· it be good or bad:
14 estimate it, w· it be good or bad:
26 w· it be ox, or sheep: it is the
30 w· of the seed of the land, or of the
33 not search w· it be good or bad,
Nu 9:21 w· it was by day or by night that
22 Or w· it were two days, or a month,
11:23 w· my word shall come to pass unto
13:18 w· they be strong or weak, few or
19 they dwell in, w· it be good or bad;
19 w· in tents, or in strong holds;
20 what the land is, w· it be fat or lean,
20 lean, w· there be wood therein, or not.
15:30 w· he be born in the land, or a
18:15 w· it be of men or beasts, shall be
De 4:32 w· there hath been any such thing as
8: 2 w· thou wouldest keep his
13: 3 to know w· ye love the Lord with
18: 3 a sacrifice, w· it be ox or sheep;
22: 6 w· they be young ones, or eggs,
24:14 w· he be of thy brethren, or of thy
Jos 24:15 w· the gods which your fathers
J'g 2:22 w· they will keep the way of the Lord
3: 4 know w· they would hearken unto the
9: 2 W· is better for you, either that
18: 5 may know w· our way which we go
Ru 3:10 not young men, w· poor or rich.
2Sa 12:22 Who can tell w· God will be gracious
15:21 w· in death or life, even there also
1Ki 20:18 W· they be come out for peace,
18 or w· they be come out for war,
33 observe w· any thing would come
2Ki 1: 2 w· I shall recover of this disease.
2Ch 14:11 w· with many, or with them that
15:13 be put to death, w· small or great,
13 small or great, w· man or woman.
Ezr 2:59 their seed, w· they were of Israel:
5:17 w· it be so, that a decree was made
7:26 judgment...w· it be unto death, or
Ne 7:61 their seed, w· they were of Israel.
Es 3: 4 w· Mordecai's matters would stand:
4:11 w· man or woman, shall come unto
14 w· thou art come to the kingdom
Job 34:29 w· it be done against a nation, or
33 w· thou refuse, or w· thou choose;
37:13 w· for correction, or for his land,
Pr 20:11 w· his work be pure, and w· it be
Ec 2:19 w· he shall be a wise man or a fool?
5:12 is sweet, w· he eat little or much:
11: 6 knowest not w· shall prosper,
6 or w· they both shall be alike good.
12:14 things, w· it be good, or w· it be evil.
Ca 6:11 and to see w· the vine flourished,
7:12 flourish, w· the tender grape appear,
Jer 30: 6 and see w· a man doth travail with
42: 6 W· it be good, or w· it be evil, we
Eze 2: 5 w· they...hear, or w· they will forbear,
7 w· they...hear, or w· they will forbear:
3:11 w· they...hear, or w· they will forbear.
44:31 or torn, w· it be fowl or beast.
M't 9: 5 w· is easier, to say, Thy sins be
21:31 W· of them twain did the will of
23:17 for w· is greater, the gold, or the
19 w· is greater, the gift, or the altar
26:63 thou tell us w· thou be the Christ,
27:21 W· of the twain will ye that I
49 w· Elias will come to save him.
M'r 2: 9 W· it is easier to say to the sick of
3: 2 w· he would heal him on the
15:36 w· Elias will come to take him down.
44 him w· he had been any while dead.
Lu 3:15 w· he were the Christ, or not;
5:23 W· is easier, to say, Thy sins be
6: 7 w· he would heal on the sabbath
14:28 w· he have sufficient to finish it?
31 w· he be able with ten thousand to
22:27 w· is greater, he that sitteth at
23: 6 asked w· the man were a Galilæan.
Joh 7:17 of the doctrine, w· it be of God,
17 or w· I speak of myself.
9:25 W· he be a sinner or no, I know
Ac 1:24 w· of these two thou hast
4:19 W· it be right in the sight of God
5: 8 w· ye sold the land for so much?
9: 2 w· they were men or women
10:18 and asked w· Simon, which was
17:11 daily, w· those things were so.
19: 2 heard w· there be any Holy Ghost.
25:20 him w· he would go to Jerusalem,
Ro 6:16 ye obey; w· of sin unto death,
12: 6 w· prophecy, let us prophesy
14: 8 w· we live, we live unto the
8 w· we die, we die unto the
8 w· we live therefore, or die, we
1Co 1:16 I know not w· I baptized any other.
3:22 W· Paul, or Apollos, or Cephas, or
7:16 w· thou shalt save thy husband?
16 man, w· thou shalt save thy wife?
8: 5 gods, w· in heaven or in earth,
10:31 W· therefore ye eat, or drink, or
12:13 body, w· we be Jews or Gentiles,
13 w· we be bond or free; and have
26 And w· one member suffer, all the
13: 8 w· there be prophecies, they shall
8 w· there be tongues, they shall
8 w· there be knowledge, it shall
14: 7 w· pipe or harp, except they give a
15:11 Therefore w· it were I or they, so
2Co 1: 6 And w· we be afflicted, it is for your
6 w· we be comforted, it is for your
2: 9 w· ye be obedient in all things.
5: 9 w· present or absent, we may be
10 he hath done, w· it be good or bad.
13 w· we be beside ourselves, it is to
13 w· we be sober, it is for your cause.
8:23 W· any do enquire of Titus, he is
12: 2 (w· in the body, I cannot tell;
2 or w· out of the body, I cannot tell:
3 (w· in the body, or out of the body,
13: 5 yourselves, w· ye be in the faith;
Eph 6: 8 the Lord, w· he be bond or free.
Ph'p 1:18 w· in pretence, or in truth, Christ
20 body, w· it be by life, or by death.
27 w· I come and see you, or else be
Col 1:16 w· they be thrones, or dominions,
20 w· they be things in earth, or things
1Th 5:10 w· we wake or sleep, we should live
2Th 2:15 taught, w· by word, or our epistle.
1Pe 2:13 w· it be to the king, as supreme;
1Jo 4: 1 try the spirits w· they are of God:

which^ See also WHO.
Ge 1: 7 the waters w· were under the
7 waters w· were above the firmament:
21 w· the waters brought forth
29 w· is upon the face of all the earth,
29 in the w· is the fruit of a tree
2: 2 ended his work w· he had made;
2 from all his work w· he had made.
3 from all his work w· God created
11 is it w· compasseth the whole land of
14 that is it w· goeth toward the east of
22 rib, w· the Lord God had taken
3: 1 beast...w· the Lord God had made.
3 tree w· is in the midst of the garden,
17 the tree, of w· I commanded thee,
24 flaming sword w· turned every way,
4:11 earth, w· hath opened her mouth
5:29 ground w· the Lord hath cursed.
6: 2 them wives of all w· they chose.
4 became mighty men w· were of old,
15 fashion w· thou shalt make it of:
7:23 w· was upon the face of the ground,
8: 6 window of the ark w· he had made:
7 forth a raven, w· went forth to and fro
12 w· returned not again unto him any
9: 4 life thereof, w· is the blood thereof,
12 covenant w· I make between me
15 covenant, w· is between me and you
17 the covenant, w· I have established
11: 5 w· the children of men builded.
6 w· they have imagined to do. 3605,
13: 4 altar, w· he had made there at the
5 And Lot also, w· went with Abram,
15 For all the land w· thou seest, to
14: 2 and the king of Bela, w· is Zoar.
3 vale of Siddim, w· is the salt sea.
6 El-paran, w· is by the wilderness.
15 w· is on the left hand of Damascus.
17 of Shaveh, w· is the king's dale.
20 w· hath delivered thine enemies
24 that w· the young men have eaten,
24 of the men w· went with me,
16:15 son's name, w· Hagar bare, Ishmael.
17:10 is my covenant, w· ye shall keep,
12 any stranger, w· is not of thy seed.
21 w· Sarah shall bare unto thee at a
18: 8 milk, and the calf w· he had dressed,
10 the tent door, w· was behind him.
13 a surety bear a child, w· am old?
17 from Abraham that thing w· I do;
19 that w· he hath spoken of him.
21 to the cry of it, w· is come unto me;
27 Lord, w· am but dust and ashes:
19: 5 w· came in to thee this night?
8 daughters w· have not known man;
14 sons in law, w· married his daughters,
15 and thy two daughters, w· are here:
19 w· thou hast shewed unto me in
21 city for the w· thou hast spoken.
25 and that w· grew upon the ground.
29 the cities in the w· Lot dwelt.
20: 3 for the woman w· thou hast taken;
13 is thy kindness w· thou shalt show
21: 2 set time of w· God had spoken to
9 w· she had born unto Abraham,
25 well...w· Abimelech's servants had
24:48 w· had led me in the right way to
60 possess the gate of those w· hate them.
25: 7 years of Abraham's life w· he lived,
9 the Hittite, w· is before Mamre;
26: 2 in the land w· I shall tell thee of:
3 oath w· I sware unto Abraham thy
15 the wells w· his father's servants
18 w· they had digged in the days of
18 by w· his father had called them.
32 concerning the well w· they had
27:17 and the bread, w· she had prepared,
27 of a field w· the Lord hath blessed:
45 forget that w· thou hast done to him:
46 w· are of the daughters of the land,

Ge 28: 4 land...w' God gave unto Abraham.
9 and took unto the wives w' he had
15 done that w' I have spoken to thee
22 this stone, w' I have set for a pillar,
29: 27 service w' thou shalt serve with me
30: 26 knowest my service w' I have done
30 little w' thou hadst before I came,
37 white appear w' was in the rods.
38 set the rods w' he had pilled before
31: 1 of that w' was our father's hath he
10 the rams w' leaped upon the cattle
12 the rams w' leap upon the cattle are
16 riches w' God hath taken from our
18 and all his goods w' he had gotten,
18 w' he had gotten in Padan-aram,
39 w' was torn of beasts I brought not
43 their children w' they have born?
51 w' I have cast betwixt me and thee;
32: 8 other company w' is left shall escape.
9 the Lord w' saidst unto me, Return
10 w' thou hast shewed unto thy
12 the sand...w' cannot be numbered
13 took of that w' came to his hand a
32 Israel eat not of the sinew w' shrank,
32 w' is upon the hollow of the thigh,
33: 5 the children w' God hath graciously
8 thou by all this drove w' I met?
18 Shechem, w' is in the land of Canaan,
34: 1 of Leah, w' she bare unto Jacob,
7 w' things ought not to be done.
28 asses, and that w' was in the city,
28 the city, and that w' was in the field.
35: 3 was with me in the way w' I went.
4 strange gods w' were in their hand,
4 their earrings w' were in their ears;
4 under the oak w' was by Shechem.
6 Luz, w' is in the land of Canaan,
12 And the land w' I gave Abraham
19 way to Ephrath, w' is Bethlehem,
26 of Jacob, w' were born to him in
27 w' is Hebron, where Abraham and
36: 5 w' were born unto him in the land
6 w' he had got in the land of Canaan;
37: 6 you, this dream w' I have dreamed:
38: 10 thing w' he did displeased the Lord:
14 place, w' is by the way to Timnath:
39: 1 w' had brought him down thither.
6 he had, save the bread w' he did eat,
17 w' thou hast brought unto us,
19 his wife, w' she spake unto him,
23 that w' he did, the Lord made it to
40: 5 of Egypt, w' were bound in prison.
20 day, w' was Pharaoh's birthday,
41: 28 w' I have spoken unto Pharaoh:
36 w' shall be in the land of Egypt;
43 in the second chariot w' he had;
48 w' were in the land of Egypt, and
48 field, w' was round about every city,
50 sons...w' Asenath...bare unto him.
42: 9 the dreams w' he dreamed of them,
38 him by the way in the w' ye go,
43: 2 corn w' they had brought out of
26 the present w' was in their hand
32 the Egyptians w' did eat with him,
44: 5 not this it in w' my lord drinketh,
8 w' we found in our sacks' mouths,
45: 6 in...w' there shall neither be earing
27 Joseph, w' he had said unto them:
27 wagons w' Joseph had sent to carry
46: 5 wagons w' Pharaoh had sent to
6 w' they had gotten in the land of
8 children of Israel, w' came into Egypt,
15 of Leah, w' she bare unto Jacob
20 w' Asenath...bare unto him.
22 of Rachel, w' were born to Jacob:
25 Bilhah, w' Laban gave unto Rachel
26 into Egypt, w' came out of his loins,
27 Joseph, w' were born him in Egypt,
27 w' came into Egypt, were threescore
31 w' were in the land of Canaan, are
47: 14 for the corn w' they brought:
22 their portion w' Pharaoh gave them:
26 priests only, w' became not Pharaoh's
48: 5 w' were born unto thee in the land of
6 issue, w' thou begettest after them,
15 the God w' fed me all my life long
16 The angel w' redeemed me from all
22 w' I took out of the hand of the
49: 1 that w' shall befall you in the last
30 of Machpelah, w' is before Mamre,
30 w' Abraham bought with the field of
50: 3 the days of those w' are embalmed:
5 my grave w' I have digged for me
10 threshingfloor of Atad, w' is beyond
11 Abel-mizraim, w' is beyond Jordan.
13 w' Abraham bought with the field
15 us all the evil w' we did unto him.
24 land w' he sware unto Abraham,
Ex 1: 1 of Israel, w' came into Egypt;
8 over Egypt, w' knew not Joseph.
15 of w' the name of one was Shiphrah,
3: 7 of my people w' are in Egypt, and
4: 9 water w' thou takest out of the river
19 the men are dead w' sought thy life.
21 w' I have put in thine hand:
28 signs w' he had commanded him.
5: 8 bricks, w' they did make heretofore,
14 w' Pharaoh's taskmasters had set
6: 8 concerning the w' I did swear to
27 are they w' spake to Pharaoh king of
7: 17 the waters w' are in the river,
8: 3 w' shall go up and come into thine
22 of Goshen, in w' my people dwell,
9: 3 is upon the cattle w' is in the field,
19 beast w' shall be found in the field,
10: 2 signs w' I have done among them;

Ex 10: 5 eat the residue of that w' is escaped,
5 w' remaineth unto you from the hail,
5 every tree w' groweth for you out of
6 w' neither thy fathers, nor thy
15 fruit of the trees w' the hail left:
19 west wind, w' took away the locusts,
21 Egypt, even darkness w' may be felt.
12: 16 save that w' every man must eat,
19 whosoever eateth that w' is leavened,
25 the land w' the Lord will give you,
39 dough w' they brought forth out of
13: 3 day, in w' ye came out from Egypt,
5 w' he sware unto thy fathers to give
8 of that w' the Lord did unto me
12 cometh of a beast w' thou hast;
14: 13 Lord, w' he will shew to you to day:
19 w' went before the camp of Israel,
31 work w' the Lord did put upon the
15: 7 wrath w' consumed them as stubble.
13 the people w' thou hast redeemed:
16 pass over, w' thou hast purchased.
17 w' thou hast made for thee to dwell
17 Lord, w' thy hands have established.
25 w' when he had cast into the waters,
26 wilt do that w' is right in his sight,
26 diseases, w' I have brought upon the
16: 1 of Sin, w' is between Elim and Sinai,
5 shall prepare that w' they bring in;
8 w' ye murmur against him:
15 w' the Lord hath given you to eat.
16 thing w' the Lord hath commanded,
16 man for them w' are in his tents.
23 This is that w' the Lord hath said,
23 bake that w' ye will bake to day,
23 that w' remaineth over lay up for you
26 on the seventh day, w' is the sabbath,
32 the thing w' the Lord commandeth,
18: 3 w' the name of the one was Gershom;
9 w' the Lord had done to Israel,
19: 7 words w' the Lord commanded
22 priests also, w' come near to the Lord,
20: 2 w' have brought thee out of the
12 the land w' the Lord thy God giveth
21: 1 w' thou shalt set before them.
22: 9 w' another challengeth to be his,
13 shall not make good that w' was torn.
23: 16 w' thou hast sown in the field:
16 w' is in the end of the year,
20 into the place w' I have prepared.
28 thee, w' shall drive out the Hivite,
24: 3 the words w' the Lord hath said
5 of Israel, w' offered burnt offerings,
8 w' the Lord hath made with you
12 commandments w' I have written;
25: 3 offering w' ye shall take of them;
16 the testimony w' I shall give thee.
22 w' are upon the ark of the testimony,
22 of all things w' I will give thee in
40 w' was shewed thee in the mount.
26: 10 of the curtain w' coupleth the second.
13 that w' remaineth in the length of the
30 w' was shewed thee in the mount.
27: 21 the vail, w' is before the testimony,
28: 4 the garments w' they shall make;
8 girdle of the ephod, w' is upon it,
24 w' are on the ends of the breastplate.
26 w' is in the side of the ephod inward.
38 w' the children of Israel shall hallow
29: 27 w' is waved, and w' is heaved up, of
27 even of that w' is for Aaron,
27 and of that w' is for his sons:
35 things w' I have commanded thee:
38 w' thou shalt offer upon the altar;
30: 37 for the perfume w' thou shalt make,
32: 1 make us gods, w' shall go before us;
2 w' are in the ears of your wives,
3 earrings w' were in their ears,
4 w' brought thee up out of the land
7 w' thou broughtest out of the land
8 of the way w' I commanded them:
8 w' have brought up out of the land
11 w' thou hast brought forth out of the
14 of the evil w' he thought to do
20 took the calf w' they had made, and
23 Make us gods, w' shall go before us:
32 out of thy book w' thou hast written.
34 place of w' I have spoken unto thee:
35 they made the calf, w' Aaron made.
33: 1 people w' thou hast brought up out
1 the land w' I sware unto Abraham,
7 every one w' sought the Lord went out
7 w' was without the camp.
34: 1 in the first tables, w' thou brakest.
10 people among w' thou art shall see
11 that w' I commanded thee this day:
34 Israel that w' he was commanded.
35: 1 words w' the Lord hath commanded,
4 the thing w' the Lord commanded,
25 and brought that w' they had spun,
29 w' the Lord had commanded to be
36: 3 w' the children of Israel had brought
4 man from his work w' they made;
5 w' the Lord commanded to make.
12 the curtain w' was in the coupling
17 of the curtain w' coupleth the second.
25 w' is toward the north corner, he made
37: 16 the vessels w' were upon the table,
38: 8 w' assembled at the door of the
39: 19 w' was on the side of the ephod
Le 1: 8, 12 is on the fire w' is upon the altar:
2: 10 And that w' is left of the meat offering
11 w' ye shall bring unto the Lord,
3: 4 w' is by the flanks, and the caul
5 w' is upon the wood that is on the
10, 15 w' is by the flanks, and the caul
4: 2 things w' ought not to be done,

Le 4: 3 for his sin, w' he hath sinned,
7 w' is in the tabernacle of the
7 w' is at the door of the tabernacle
9 w' is by the flanks, and the caul
13 things w' should not be done,
14 sin, w' they have sinned against it,
18 of the altar w' is before the Lord,
18 w' is at the door of the tabernacle
22 things w' should not be done,
27 things w' ought not to be done,
28 Or of his sin, w' he hath sinned,
28 for his sin w' he hath sinned.
5: 6 Lord for his sin w' he hath sinned,
7 his trespass, w' he hath committed,
8 offer that w' is for the sin offering
10 him for his sin w' he hath sinned,
17 things w' are forbidden to be done
6: 2 that w' was delivered him to keep,
3 Or have found that w' was lost, and
4 restore that w' he took violently
4 thing w' he hath deceitfully gotten,
4 that w' was delivered him to keep,
4 or the lost thing w' he found,
5 that about w' he hath sworn falsely;
10 the ashes w' the fire hath consumed
15 w' is upon the meat offering, and
20 w' they shall offer unto the Lord in
7: 4 w' is by the flanks, and the caul that
8 burnt offering w' he hath offered.
11 w' he shall offer unto the Lord,
21 offerings, w' pertain unto the Lord,
24 the fat of that w' is torn with beasts,
25 of w' men offer an offering made by
36 W' the Lord commanded to be
38 W' the Lord commanded Moses in
8: 5 is the thing w' the Lord commanded
30 of the blood w' was upon the altar,
32 And that w' remaineth of the flesh and
36 w' the Lord commanded by the
9: 5 brought that w' Moses commanded
8 the sin offering, w' was for himself.
12 w' he sprinkled round about upon the
15 w' was the sin offering for the
18 offerings, w' was for the people:
18 w' he sprinkled upon the altar round
19 and that w' covereth the inwards,
24 w' when all the people saw, they
10: 1 Lord, w' he commanded them not.
6 burning w' the Lord hath kindled.
11 statutes w' the Lord hath spoken
14 w' are given out of the sacrifices of
16 sons of Aaron w' were left alive,
11: 2 These are the beasts w' ye shall eat
10 any living thing w' is in the waters,
13 they w' ye shall have in abomination
21 w' have legs above their feet, to
23 creeping things, w' have four feet,
26 of every beast w' divideth the hoof,
34 Of all meat w' may be eaten,
34 that on w' such water cometh shall
36 that w' toucheth their carcase shall be
37 any sowing seed w' is to be sown,
39 if any beast, of w' ye may eat, die;
13: 18 The flesh also, in w', even in the skin
58 of skin it be, w' thou shalt wash,
14: 32 get that w' pertaineth to his cleansing.
34 w' I give to you for a possession,
37 w' in sight are lower than the wall,
40 the stones in w' the plague is,
15: 12 that he toucheth w' hath the issue,
16: 2 the mercy seat, w' is upon the ark;
6 of the sin offering, w' is for himself,
9 the goat upon w' the Lord's lot fell,
10 on w' the lot fell to be the scapegoat,
11 of the sin offering, w' is for himself,
11 of the sin offering w' is for himself:
23 w' he put on when he went into the
17: 2 thing w' the Lord hath commanded,
5 w' they offer in the open field,
8 the strangers w' sojourn among you
13 w' hunteth and catcheth any beast‡
15 soul that eateth that w' died of itself,
15 that w' was torn with beasts, whether
18: 5 w' if a man do, he shall live in them:
27 the land done, w' were before you,
30 w' were committed before you,
19: 22 Lord for his sin, w' he hath done:
22 sin w' he hath done shall be forgiven
36 w' brought you out of the land of
20: 8 I am the Lord w' sanctify you.
23 the nation, w' I cast out before you.
24 w' have separated you from other
25 w' I have separated from you as
21: 3 virgin,...w' hath had no husband;
8 I the Lord, w' sanctify you, am holy.
22: 2 things w' they hallow unto me:
3 w' the children of Israel hallow unto
8 w' dieth of itself, or is torn with beasts,
15 Israel, w' they offer unto the Lord;
18 w' they will offer unto the Lord for a
24 offer unto the Lord that w' is bruised,
23: 2 w' ye shall proclaim to be holy
4 w' ye shall proclaim in their seasons.
10 unto the land w' I give unto you,
37 w' ye shall proclaim to be holy
38 offerings, w' ye give unto the Lord.
25: 2 come into the land w' I give you,
5 That w' groweth of its own accord
11 neither reap that w' groweth of itself
25 he redeem that w' his brother sold.
28 then that w' is sold shall remain in
31 w' have no wall round about them.
38 w' brought you forth out of the land
42 w' I brought forth out of the land of
44 thy bondmaids, w' thou shalt have,
45 with you, w' they begat in your land:

Le 26:13 w' brought you forth out of the
22 w' shall rob you of your children, and
32 enemies w' dwell therein shall be
40 trespass w' they trespassed against
46 and laws, w' the Lord made
27:11 of w' they do not offer a sacrifice
22 the Lord a field w' he hath bought,
22 w' is not of the fields of his
26 w' should be the Lord's firstling,
29 devoted, w' shall be devoted of men,
34 w' the Lord commanded Moses for
Nu 1:17 these men w' are expressed by their
44 w' Moses and Aaron numbered, and
2:12 those w' pitch by him shall be the
32 those w' were numbered of the
3: 3 the priests w' were anointed, whom
26 the court, w' is by the tabernacle,
39 w' Moses and Aaron numbered at
46 Israel, w' are more than the Levites;
4:37 w' Moses and Aaron did number
5: 7 confess their sin w' they have done:
9 Israel, w' they bring unto the priest,
18 hands, w' is the jealousy offering:
6: 5 in the w' he separateth himself
18 in the fire w' is under the sacrifice
21 according to the vow w' he vowed,
10: 4 w' are heads of the thousands of
25 w' was the rereward of all the camps
29 unto the place of w' the Lord said,
11: 5 fish, w' we did eat in Egypt freely;
12 the land w' thou swarest unto their
17 take of the spirit w' is upon thee,
20 despised the Lord w' is among you,
12: 3 men w' were upon the face of the
13: 2 w' I give unto the children of Israel:
16 w' Moses sent to spy out the land.
24 w' the children of Israel cut down
32 of the land w' they had searched
32 through w' we have gone to search
33 of Anak, w' come of the giants:
14: 6 w' were of them that searched the
7 w' we passed through to search it,
8 us; a land w' floweth with milk and
11 the signs w' I have shewed among
15 nations w' have heard the fame of
16 the land w' he sware unto them,
22 all those men w' have seen my glory,
22 w' I did in Egypt and in the
23 the land w' I sware unto their fathers,
27 congregation, w' murmur against
27 Israel, w' they murmur against me.
29 w' have murmured against me,
30 w' I sware to make you dwell
31 ones, w' ye said should be a prey,
31 know the land w' ye have despised.
34 the days in w' ye search the land,
36 w' Moses sent to search the land,
38 w' were of the men that went to
40 place w' the Lord hath promised:
45 the Canaanites w' dwell in that hill,
15: 2 habitations, w' I give unto you,
39 after w' ye use to go a whoring:
41 w' brought you out of the land of
16:11 For w' cause both thou and all thy
12 Eliab: w' said, We will not come up:
40 w' is not of the seed of Aaron, come
18: 9 theirs, w' they shall render unto me,
12 w' they shall offer unto the Lord,
13 w' they shall bring unto the Lord,
15 flesh, w' they bring unto the Lord,
16 the sanctuary, w' is twelve gerahs.
19 w' the children of Israel offer unto
21 for their service w' they serve,
24 w' they offer as an heave offering
26 the tithes w' I have given you from
28 w' ye receive of the children of
19: 2 law w' the Lord hath commanded,
2 and upon w' never came yoke.
15 w' hath no covering bound upon it,
20:12 unto the land w' I have given them.
24 unto the land w' I have given unto
21: 1 the Canaanite, w' dwelt in the south,
11 the wilderness w' is before Moab,
13 w' is in the wilderness that cometh
20 Pisgah, w' looketh toward Jeshimon.
30 Nophah, w' reacheth unto Medeba.
34 the Amorites, w' dwelt at Heshbon.
22: 5 Pethor, w' is by the river of the land
11 w' covereth the face of the earth:
20 the word w' I shall say unto thee,
30 upon w' thou hast ridden ever since
36 Moab, w' is in the border of Arnon,
36 Arnon, w' is in the utmost coast.
23:12 w' the Lord hath put in my mouth?
24: 4 said, w' heard the words of God,
4 w' saw the vision of the Almighty,
6 lign aloes w' the Lord hath planted,
12 messengers w' thou sentest unto
16 w' heard the words of God, and knew
16 w' saw the vision of the Almighty,
25:18 w' was slain in the day of the plague
26: 4 w' went forth out of the land of Egypt.
9 w' were famous in the congregation,
27:12 land w' I have given unto the
17 W' may go out before them, and
17 and w' may go in before them, and
17 and w' may lead them out, and
17 w' may bring them in; that the
17 not as sheep w' have no shepherd.
28: 3 fire w' ye shall offer unto the Lord;
6 w' was ordained in mount Sinai for a
23 w' is for a continual burnt offering.
30: 1 thing w' the Lord hath commanded.
8 shall make her vow w' she vowed,
8 and that w' she uttered with her lips,
14 or all her bonds, w' are upon her:

Nu 30:16 w' the Lord commanded Moses,
31:12 plains of Moab, w' are by Jordan
14 hundreds, w' came from the battle.
21 the men of war w' went to the battle,
21 w' the Lord commanded Moses;
28 the men of war w' went out to battle:
30 w' keep the charge of the tabernacle
32 prey w' the men of war had caught
36 w' was the portion of them that went
38, 39, 40 [*] of w' the Lord's tribute was
41 w' was the Lord's heave offering,
42 w' Moses divided from the men
47 w' kept the charge of the tabernacle
48 officers w' were over thousands
49 men of war w' are under our charge,
32: 4 country w' the Lord smote before
7 land w' the Lord hath given them?
9 land w' the Lord hath given them.
11 the land w' I sware unto Abraham,
24 w' hath proceeded out of your mouth.
38 unto the cities w' they builded.
39 the Amorite w' was in it.
33: 1 w' went forth out of the land of
4 firstborn, w' the Lord had smitten
6 w' is in the edge of the wilderness.
7 w' is before Baal-zephon:
36 wilderness of Zin, w' is Kadesh.
55 those w' ye let remain of them shall
34:17 w' shall divide the land unto you:
35: 4 w' ye shall give unto the Levites,
6 w' ye shall give unto the Levites
7 cities w' ye shall give to the Levites
8 the cities w' ye shall give shall be
8 to his inheritance w' he inheriteth.
11 w' killeth any person at unawares.
13 And of these cities w' ye shall give,
14 of Canaan, w' shall be cities of refuge.
25 w' was anointed with the holy oil.
31 a murderer, w' is guilty of death:
34 the land w' ye shall inhabit,
36: 6 thing w' the Lord doth command
13 w' the Lord commanded by the
De 1: 1 w' Moses spake unto all Israel
4 the Amorites, w' dwelt in Heshbon,
4 w' dwelt at Astaroth in Edrei:
8 the land w' the Lord sware unto
14 thing w' thou hast spoken is good
18 time all the things w' ye shall do.
19 wilderness, w' ye saw by the way
20 w' the Lord our God doth give unto
25 w' the Lord our God doth give us
30 Lord your God w' goeth before you,
35 land, w' I sware to give unto your
38 son of Nun, w' standeth before thee,
39 ones, w' ye said should be a prey,
39 w' in that day had no knowledge
44 Amorites, w' dwelt in that mountain,
2: 4 the children of Esau, w' dwelt in Seir;
8 children of Esau, w' dwelt in Seir,
11 W' also were accounted giants,
12 w' the Lord gave unto them.
14 the space in w' we came from
22 the children of Esau, w' dwelt in Seir,
23 And the Avims w' dwelt in Hazerim,
23 w' came forth out of Caphtor,
29 the children of Esau w' dwell in Seir,
29 Moabites w' dwell in Ar, did unto me;)
29 into the land w' the Lord our God
35 the spoil of the cities w' we took.
36 Aroer, w' is by the brink of the river
3: 2 the Amorites, w' dwelt at Heshbon.
4 not a city w' we took not from them,
9 (W' Hermon the Sidonians call
12 land, w' we possessed at that time,
12 w' is by the river Arnon, and half
13 w' was called the land of giants,
16 w' is the border of the children of
19 your cities w' I have given you;
20 w' the Lord your God hath given
20 possession, w' I have given you.
28 inherit the land w' thou shalt see.
4: 1 judgments, w' I teach you, for to do
2 unto the word w' I command you,
2 Lord your God w' I command you.
6 w' shall hear all these statutes, and
8 law, w' I set before you this day?
9 the things w' thine eyes have seen,
13 w' he commanded you to perform,
19 w' the Lord thy God hath divided
21 w' the Lord thy God giveth thee for
23 covenant...w' he made with you,
23 w' the Lord thy God hath forbidden
28 w' neither see, nor hear, nor eat,
31 fathers w' he sware unto them.
32 that are past, w' were before thee,
40 w' I command thee this day,
40 w' the Lord thy God giveth thee,
42 w' should kill his neighbour
44 law w' Moses set before the children
45 w' Moses spake unto the children of
47 w' were on this side Jordan toward
48 w' is by the bank of the river Arnon
5: 1 w' I speak in your ears this day,
6 God, w' brought thee out of the land
16 land w' the Lord thy God giveth
28 w' they have spoken unto thee:
31 judgments, w' thou shalt teach them,
31 them in the land w' I give them
33 w' the Lord your God...commanded
33 in the land w' ye shall possess.
6: 1 w' the Lord your God commanded
2 commandments, w' I command thee,
6 words, w' I command thee this day,
10 land w' he sware unto thy fathers,
10 goodly cities, w' thou buildedst not,
11 good things, w' thou filledst not,

De 6:11 wells digged, w' thou diggedst not,
11 olive trees, w' thou plantedst not;
12 w' brought thee forth out of the
14 the people w' are round about you;
17 w' he hath commanded thee.
18 shalt do that w' is right and good
18 w' the Lord sware unto thy fathers,
20 w' the Lord our God...commanded
23 land w' he sware unto our fathers.
7: 8 w' he had sworn unto your fathers,
9 w' keepeth covenant and mercy
11 w' I command thee this day, to do
12 land w' he sware unto thy fathers:
13 land w' he sware unto thy fathers
15 diseases of Egypt, w' thou knowest,
16 w' the Lord thy God shall deliver
19 temptations w' thine eyes saw,
8: 1 commandments w' I command thee
1 land w' the Lord sware unto your
2 way w' the Lord thy God led thee
3 with manna, w' thou knewest not,
10 good land w' he hath given thee.
11 w' I command thee this day:
14 w' brought thee forth out of the land
16 manna, w' thy fathers knew not,
18 w' he sware unto thy fathers, as it
20 nations w' the Lord destroyeth
9: 3 God, is he w' goeth over before thee;
5 w' the Lord sware unto thy fathers,
9 covenant w' the Lord made with
10 words w' the Lord spake with you
12 w' thou hast brought forth out of
16 way w' the Lord had commanded
18 your sins w' ye sinned, in doing
21 your sin, the calf w' ye had made,
23 the land w' I have given you;
26 w' thou hast redeemed through thy
26 w' thou hast brought forth out of
28 into the land w' he promised them,
29 w' thou broughtest out by thy
10: 2 in the first tables w' thou brakest,
4 w' the Lord spake unto you in the
5 the tables in the ark w' I had made;
11 w' I sware unto their fathers to
13 w' I command thee this day for
17 w' regardeth not persons, nor
21 terrible things, w' thine eyes have
11: 2 your children w' have not known,
3 acts, w' he did in the midst of Egypt
7 great acts of the Lord w' he did.
8 commandments w' I command you
9 w' the Lord sware unto your fathers
12 A land w' the Lord thy God careth
13 commandments w' I command you
21 w' the Lord sware unto your fathers
22 commandments w' I command you,
27 w' I command you this day:
28 the way w' I command you this day,
28 other gods, w' ye have not known.
30 w' dwell in the champaign over
31 w' the Lord your God giveth you,
32 judgments w' I set before you this
12: 1 w' ye shall observe to do in the land,
1 w' the Lord God of thy fathers hath
2 the nations w' ye shall possess
5 w' the Lord your God shall choose
9 w' the Lord your God giveth you.
10 w' the Lord your God giveth you
11 w' the Lord your God shall choose
11 vows w' ye vowed unto the Lord:
14 the place w' the Lord shall choose
15 Lord thy God w' he hath given thee:
17 nor any of thy vows w' thou vowest,
18 w' the Lord thy God shall choose,
21 w' the Lord thy God hath chosen
21 flock, w' the Lord hath given thee,
25 do that w' is right in the sight of the
26 Only thy holy things w' thou hast,
26 the place w' the Lord shall choose:
28 all these words w' I command thee,
28 doest that w' is good and right in
31 abomination...w' he hateth,
13: 2 other gods, w' thou hast not known,
5 w' brought you out of the land of
6 friend, w' is as thine own soul,
6 other gods, w' thou hast not known,
7 the people w' are round about you,
10 w' brought thee out of the land of
12 w' the Lord thy God hath given
13 other gods, w' ye have not known,
18 commandments w' I command thee
18 do that w' is right in the eyes of the
14: 4 are the beasts w' ye shall eat:
12 these are they of w' ye shall not eat:
23 in the place w' he shall choose to
24 w' the Lord thy God shall choose
25 w' the Lord thy God shall choose:
29 the widow, w' are within thy gates,
29 work of thine hand w' thou doest.
15: 3 that w' is thine with thy brother
4 land w' the Lord thy God giveth
5 w' I command thee this day,
7 land w' the Lord thy God giveth
8 for his need, in that w' he wanteth.
20 the place w' the Lord shall choose,
16: 2 the place w' the Lord shall choose
4 w' thou sacrificedst the first day at
5 w' the Lord thy God giveth thee:
6 w' the Lord thy God shall choose
7 place w' the Lord thy God shall
10 w' thou shalt give unto the Lord
11 w' the Lord thy God hath chosen
15 the place w' the Lord shall choose:
16 God in the place w' he shall choose;
17 Lord thy God w' he hath given thee.
18 w' the Lord thy God giveth thee,

De 16:20 That w' is altogether just shalt thou
20 land w' the Lord thy God giveth
21 thy God, w' thou shalt make thee.
22 image; w' the Lord thy God hateth.
17: 2 w' the Lord thy God giveth thee,
3 heaven, w' I have not commanded;
5 w' have committed that wicked
8 w' the Lord thy God shall choose.
10 sentence, w' they of that place
10 place w' the Lord shall choose
11 of the law w' they shall teach thee,
11 judgment w' they shall tell thee,
11 sentence w' they shall shew thee,
14 land w' the Lord thy God giveth thee,
15 over thee, w' is not thy brother.
18 out of that w' is before the priests
18: 6 the place w' the Lord shall choose;
7 do, w' stand there before the Lord.
8 that w' cometh of the sale of his
9 land w' the Lord thy God giveth
14 these nations, w' thou shalt possess,
17 spoken that w' they have spoken.
19 my words w' he shall speak in my
20 w' shall presume to speak a word in
20 w' I have not commanded him to
21 word w' the Lord hath not spoken?
22 thing w' the Lord hath not spoken,
19: 2, 3 w' the Lord thy God giveth thee to
4 the slayer, w' shall flee thither,
8 land w' he promised to give unto
9 them, w' I command thee this day,
10 land, w' the Lord thy God giveth thee
14 w' they of old time have set in thine
14 w' thou shalt inherit in the land
16 testify against him that w' is wrong;
17 judges, w' shall be in those days;
20 And those w' remain shall hear,
20: 1 w' brought thee up out of the land
14 w' the Lord thy God hath given
15 all the cities w' are very far off from
15 w' are not of the cities of these
16 w' the Lord thy God doth give thee
18 w' they have done unto their gods;
20 Only the trees w' thou knowest that
21: 1 land w' the Lord thy God giveth
2 cities w' are round about him that
3 the city w' is next unto the slain man,
3 w' had not been wrought with,
3 and w' hath not drawn in the yoke;
4 valley, w' is neither eared nor sown,
9 do that w' is right in the sight of the
16 his sons to inherit that w' he hath,
16 the hated, w' is indeed the firstborn:
18 w' will not obey the voice of his father,
23 w' the Lord thy God giveth thee
22: 3 of thy brother's, w' he hath lost,
5 wear that w' pertaineth unto a man,
9 fruit of thy seed w' thou hast sown,
28 is a virgin, w' is not betrothed,
23: 15 the servant w' is escaped from his‡
16 in that place w' he shall choose
23 That w' is gone out of thy lips thou
23 w' thou hast promised with thy
24: 3 die, w' took her to be his wife;
4 former husband, w' sent her away,
4 w' the Lord thy God giveth thee for
25: 6 the firstborn w' she beareth shall
6 in the name of his brother w' is dead,
15, 19 land w' the Lord thy God giveth
26: 1 the land w' the Lord giveth thee for
2 w' thou shalt bring of thy land
2 place w' the Lord God shall choose
3 w' the Lord sware unto our father
10 w' thou, O Lord, hast given me.
11 good thing w' the Lord hath given
12 third year, w' is the year of tithing,
13 w' thou hast commanded me:
15 and the land w' thou hast given us,
19 above all nations w' he hath made,
27: 1 commandments w' I command you
2, 3 w' the Lord thy God giveth thee,
4 stones, w' I command you this day,
10 statutes, w' I command thee this day.
28: 1 commandments w' I command you
8 land w' the Lord thy God giveth
11 w' the Lord sware unto thy fathers
13 thy God, w' I command thee this day,
14 words w' I command thee this day,
15 statutes w' I command thee this day;
33 nation w' thou knowest not eat up;
34 sight of thine eyes w' thou shalt see.
36 thy king w' thou shalt set over thee,
36 nation w' neither thou nor thy fathers‡
45 his statutes w' he commanded thee.
48 w' the Lord shall send against thee,
50 w' shall not regard the person of
51 w' also shall not leave thee either
52, 53 [*] w' the Lord thy God hath given
54 of his children w' he shall leave:
56 w' would not adventure to set the
57 her children w' she shall bear:
60 of Egypt, w' thou wast afraid of;
61 w' is not written in the book of this
64 w' neither thou nor thy fathers
67 sight of thine eyes w' thou shalt see.
29: 1 w' the Lord commanded Moses to
3 w' thine eyes have seen, the signs,
12 w' the Lord thy God maketh with
16 through...nations w' ye passed by;
17 and gold, w' were among them:)
22 w' the Lord hath laid upon it;
23 w' the Lord overthrew in his anger,
25 w' he made with them when he
29 those things w' are revealed belong
30: 1 the curse, w' I have set before thee,
5 the land w' thy fathers possessed,

De 30: 7 that hate thee, w' persecuted thee.
8 commandments w' I commanded
10 statutes w' are written in this book
11 commandment w' I command thee
20 w' the Lord sware unto thy fathers,
31: 5 w' I have commanded you.
7 land w' the Lord hath sworn unto
9 w' bare the ark of the covenant of
11 God in the place w' he shall choose,
13 children w' have not known any
18 evils w' they shall have wrought,
20 land w' I sware unto their fathers,
21 their imagination w' they go about,
21 them into the land w' I sware.
23 into the land w' I sware unto them:
25 w' bare the ark of the covenant of
29 from the way w' I have commanded
32: 15 then he forsook God w' made him,
21 jealously with that w' is not God;
21 with those w' are not a people;
38 W' did eat the fat of their
46 all the words w' I testify among you
46 w' ye shall command your children
49 Nebo, w' is in the land of Moab,
49 Canaan, w' I give unto the children
52 land w' I give the children of Israel.
34: 4 the land w' I sware unto Abraham,
11 the wonders, w' the Lord sent him
12 the great terror w' Moses shewed
Jos 1: 2 unto the land w' I do give to them,
6 w' I sware unto their fathers to give
7 w' Moses my servant commanded
11 w' the Lord your God giveth you to
13 word w' Moses the servant of the
14 in the land w' Moses gave you on this
15 w' the Lord your God giveth them:
15 w' Moses the Lord's servant gave
2: 3 w' are entered into thine house:
6 w' she had laid in order upon the
7 they w' pursued after them were
17 oath w' thou hast made us swear.
18 window w' thou didst let us down by:
20 oath w' thou hast made us to swear.
3: 4 know the way by w' ye must go:
16 the waters w' came down from above
4: 9 priests w' bare the ark of the covenant
10 priests w' bare the ark stood in the
20 stones w' they took out of Jordan,
23 sea, w' he dried up from before us.
5: 1 w' were on the side of Jordan
1 the Canaanites, w' were by the sea,
6 men of war, w' came out of Egypt,
6 land, w' the Lord sware unto their
6: 25 w' Joshua sent to spy out Jericho.
7: 2 Jericho to Ai, w' is beside Beth-aven,
11 my covenant w' I commanded them:
14 tribe w' the Lord taketh shall come
14 the family w' the Lord shall take
8: 27 Lord...w' he commanded Joshua.
31 over w' no man hath lifted up any
32 w' he wrote in the presence of the
33 w' bare the ark of the covenant of the
35 w' Joshua read not before all the
9: 1 kings w' were on this side Jordan,
10 king of Bashan, w' was at Ashtaroth.
13 And these bottles of wine w' we filled,
20 of the oath w' we sware unto them.
27 in the place w' he should choose.
10: 11 more w' died with hailstones than
20 the rest w' remained of them entered
24 of the men of war w' went with him,
27 mouth, w' remain until this very day.
32 of Israel, w' took it on the second day.
12: 1 w' the children of Israel smote,
2 w' is upon the bank of the river
2 w' is the border of the children of
4 w' was of the remnant of the giants,
7 w' Joshua and the children of
7 w' Joshua gave unto the tribes of
9 the king of Ai, w' is beside Beth-el,
13: 3 From Sihor, w' is before Egypt,
3 w' is counted to the Canaanite:
8 inheritance, w' Moses gave them,
10 Amorites, w' reigned in Heshbon,
12 w' reigned in Ashtaroth and in
21 Amorites, w' reigned in Heshbon,
21 and Reba, w' were dukes of Sihon,
30 towns of Jair, w' are in Bashan,
32 countries w' Moses did distribute
14: 1 w' the children of Israel inherited
1 w' Eleazar the priest, and Joshua
15 w' Arba was a great man among the
15: 7 w' is on the south side of the river:
8 w' is at the end of the valley of the
9 to Baalah, w' is Kirjath-jearim:
10 of mount Jearim, w' is Chesalon,
13 father of Anak, w' city is Hebron.
25 Kerioth, and Hezron, w' is Hazor,
49 and Kirjath-sannah, w' is Debir,
54 and Kirjath-arba, w' is Hebron,
60 Kirjath-baal, w' is Kirjath-jearim,
17: 5 w' were on the other side Jordan;
18: 2 tribes, w' had not yet received their
3 w' the Lord God of your fathers
7 w' Moses the servant of the Lord
13 to the side of Luz, w' is Beth-el,
14 Kirjath-baal, w' is Kirjath-jearim,
16 and w' is in the valley of the giants
17 w' is over against the going up of
28 and Jebusi, w' is Jerusalem,
19: 50 they gave him the city w' he asked,
51 w' Eleazar the priest, and Joshua
20: 7 and Kirjath-arba, w' is Hebron,
21: 4 the priest, w' were of the Levites,
9 these cities w' are mentioned by
10 W' the children of Aaron, being of

Jos 21: 11 father of Anak, w' city is Hebron,
20 Levites w' remained of the children
40 w' were remaining of the families of
43 land w' he sware to give unto their
45 good thing w' the Lord had spoken
22: 4, 5 w' Moses the servant of the Lord
9 Shiloh, w' is in the land of Canaan,
17 from w' we are not cleansed until
28 of the Lord, w' our fathers made,
30 of Israel w' were with him, heard
23: 13 w' the Lord your God hath given
14 things w' the Lord your God spake
15 w' the Lord your God promised you;
15 w' the Lord your God hath given
16 your God, w' he commanded you,
16 good land w' he hath given unto you
24: 5 according to that w' I did among
8 w' dwelt on the other side Jordan;
12 w' drave them out from before you,
13 you a land for w' ye did not labour,
13 cities w' ye built not, and ye dwell in
13 olive yards w' ye planted not do ye
14, 15 the gods w' your fathers served
17 w' did those great signs in our sight,
18 the Amorites w' dwelt in the land:
23 strange gods w' are among you,
27 words of the Lord w' he spake unto
30 w' is in mount Ephraim, on the north
31 w' had known all the works of the
32 w' the children of Israel brought up
32 parcel of ground w' Jacob bought
33 his son, w' was given him in mount
J'g 1: 16 Judah, w' lieth in the south of Arad;
26 w' is the name thereof unto this
2: 1 land w' I sware unto your fathers;
10 after them, w' knew not the Lord,
12 w' brought them out of the land of
16 w' delivered them out of the hand of
17 the way w' their fathers walked in,
20 my covenant w' I commanded their
21 nations w' Joshua left when he died:
3: 1 are the nations w' the Lord left,
4 w' he commanded their fathers by
16 made him a dagger w' had two edges,
20 w' he had made for himself alone:
31 w' slew of the Philistines six hundred
4: 2 was Sisera, w' dwelt in Harosheth
11 w' was of the children of Hobab the
11 plain of Zaanaim, w' is by Kedesh.
14 in w' the Lord hath delivered Sisera
6: 2 the dens w' are in the mountains,
8 children of Israel, w' said unto them,
11 sat under an oak w' was in Ophrah,
13 miracles w' our fathers told us of,
26 the grove w' thou shalt cut down.
8: 27 w' thing became a snare unto Gideon,
35 goodness w' he had shewed unto
9: 2 w' are threescore and ten persons,
4 and light persons, w' followed him.
13 my wine, w' cheereth God and man,
24 their brother, w' slew them;
24 w' aided him in the killing of his
56 Abimelech w' he did unto his father,
10: 4 w' are called Havoth-jair unto this
4 day, w' are in the land of Gilead.
8 land of the Amorites, w' is in Gilead.
14 unto the gods w' ye have chosen;
11: 24 possess that w' Chemosh thy god
28 words of Jephthah w' he sent him.
36 w' hath proceeded out of thy mouth;
39 to his vow w' he had vowed:
12: 5 those Ephraimites w' were escaped
13: 8 the man of God w' thou didst send
14: 19 unto them w' expounded the riddle.
15: 19 w' is in Lehi unto this day.
16: 8 green withs w' had not been dried,
24 of our country, w' slew many of us.
29 pillars upon w' the house stood,
29 and on w' it was borne up, of the one
30 So the dead w' he slew at his death
30 than they w' he slew in his life.
17: 2 from thee; about w' thou cursedst,
6 man did that w' was right in his own
18: 5 way w' we go shall be prosperous.
16 w' were of the children of Dan, stood
24 have taken away my gods w' I made,
27 took the things w' Micah had made,
27 and the priest w' he had, and came
31 Micah's graven image, w' he made,
19: 10 against Jebus, w' is Jerusalem;
14 Gibeah, w' belongeth to Benjamin.
16 even, w' was also of mount Ephraim,
19 young man w' is with thy servants:
20: 9 the thing w' we will do to Gibeah;
13 children of Belial, w' are in Gibeah,
15 w' were numbered seven hundred
18 W' of us shall go up first to the
31 of w' one goeth up to the house of
36 wait w' they had set beside Gibeah.
42 them w' came out of the cities they
46 all w' fell that day of Benjamin were
21: 12 Shiloh, w' is in the land of Canaan.
14 them wives w' they had saved alive
19 w' is on the north side of Beth-el
25 did that w' was right in his own eyes.
Ru 1: 22 her, w' returned out of the country of
2: 9 that w' the young men have drawn.
11 w' thou knewest not heretofore.
4: 3 w' was our brother Elimelech's:
11 w' two did build the house of Israel:
12 the seed w' the Lord shall give thee
14 Lord, w' hath not left thee this day
15 daughter in law w' loveth thee,
15 w' is better to thee than seven
1Sa 1: 27 me my petition w' I asked of him:
2: 20 for the loan w' is lent to the Lord.

1Sa 2:29 offering, w· I have commanded in
32 wealth w· God shall give Israel:
35 to that w· is in mine heart and in my
3:11 at w· both the ears of every one that
12 Eli all things w· I have spoken
13 for the iniquity w· he knoweth;
4: 4 w· dwelleth between the cherubims:
6: 4 offering w· we shall return to him?
7 kine, on w· there hath come no yoke,
8 w· ye return him for a trespass
17 golden emerods w· the Philistines
18 w· stone remaineth unto this day in
7:14 cities w· the Philistines had taken
8: 8 to all the works w· they have done
18 king w· ye shall have chosen you;
9:22 bidden, w· were about thirty persons.
23 Bring the portion w· I gave thee,
23 of w· I said unto thee, Set it by thee.
24 shoulder, and that w· was upon it,
24 Behold that w· is left! set it before
10: 2 asses w· thou wentest to seek are
4 w· thou shalt receive of their hands.
11:11 that they w· remained were scattered,
12: 7 w· he did to you and to your fathers.
8 w· brought forth your fathers out of
16 w· the Lord will do before your
17 w· ye have done in the sight of the
21 things, w· cannot profit nor deliver;
13: 5 as the sand w· is on the sea shore in
13 thy God, w· he commanded thee:
14 that w· the Lord commanded thee.
14: 2 pomegranate tree w· is in Migron:
4 w· Jonathan sought to go over unto
14 w· Jonathan and his armourbearer
14 land, w· a yoke of oxen might plow.
21 w· went up with them into the
22 men of Israel w· had hid themselves
30 of their enemies w· they found?
39 as the Lord liveth, w· saveth Israel,
15: 2 I remember that w· Amalek did to
14 the lowing of the oxen w· I hear?
20 gone the way w· the Lord sent me,
21 w· should have been utterly destroyed,
16: 4 Samuel did that w· the Lord spake,
16 thy servants, w· are before thee,
19 thy son, w· is with the sheep.
17: 1 at Shochoh, w· belongeth to Judah,
31 words were heard w· David spake,
40 them in a shepherd's bag w· he had,
20:23 matter w· thou and I have spoken
27 w· was the second day of the month,
36 out now the arrows w· I shoot.
37 of the arrow w· Jonathan had shot,
22: 9 w· was set over the servants of
14 as David, w· is the king's son in law,
23:13 his men, w· were about six hundred,
19 w· is on the south of Jeshimon?
24: 4 the day of w· the Lord said unto thee,
25: 7 now thy shepherds w· were with us,
27 this blessing w· thine handmaid
32 w· sent thee this day to meet me:
33 be thou, w· hast kept me this day
34 w· hath kept me back from hurting
35 hand that w· she had brought him,
44 the son of Laish, w· was of Gallim.
26: 1 Hachilah, w· is before Jeshimon?
3 Hachilah, w· is before Jeshimon,
28:21 words w· thou spakest unto me.
29: 1 by a fountain w· is in Jezreel.
3 w· hath been with me these days,
4 to his place w· thou hast appointed
30:10 w· were so faint that they could not
14 the coast w· belongeth to Judah,
17 men, w· rode upon camels, and fled.
20 w· they drave before those other
21 w· were so faint that they could
23 that w· the Lord hath given us,
27 To them w· were in Beth-el, and to
27 to them w· were in south Ramoth,
27 and to them w· were in Jattir,
28 And to them w· were in Aroer,
28 and to them w· were in Siphmoth,
28 and to them w· were in Eshtemoa,
29 to them w· were in Rachal, and to
29, 29 them w· were in the cities of the
30 to them w· were in Hormah, and to
30 and to them w· were in Chor-ashan,
30 and to them w· were in Athach,
31 to them w· were in Hebron, and to
31:11 w· the Philistines had done to Saul;
2Sa 2:15 w· pertained to Ish-bosheth the son
16 Helkath-hazzurim, w· is in Gibeon.
32 of his father, w· is in Beth-lehem.
3: 8 w· against Judah do shew kindness
14 wife Michal, w· I espoused to me
26 w· brought him again from the well
4: 8 thine enemy, w· sought thy life;
5: 6 w· spake unto David, saying, Except
6: 4 of Abinadab w· was at Gibeah,
21 Lord, w· chose me before thy father,
22 maidservants w· thou hast spoken
7:12 w· shall proceed out of thy bowels,
23 w· thou redeemest to thee from
8:11 W· also king David did dedicate unto
11 of all nations w· he subdued;
9: 3 hath yet a son, w· is lame on his feet.
10:12 Lord do that w· seemeth him good.
12: 3 w· he had bought and nourished
13:10 took the cakes w· she had made,
23 Baal-hazor, w· is beside Ephraim:
14: 7 they shall quench my coal w· is left,
13 speak this thing as one w· is faulty,
14 w· cannot be gathered up again;
15: 4 every man w· hath any suit or cause
7 w· I have vowed unto the Lord, in
16 left ten women, w· were concubines,
2Sa 15:18 six hundred men w· came after
16:11 my son w· came forth of my bowels,
21 w· he had left to keep the house;
23 w· he counselled in those days,
17:10 they w· be with him are valiant
18 Bahurim, w· had a well in his court;
25 w· Amasa was a man's son, whose
18:18 a pillar, w· is in the king's dale:
28 w· hath delivered up the men that
19: 5 w· this day have saved thy life,
16 a Benjamite, w· was of Bahurim,
19 remember that w· thy servant did
38 that w· shall seem good unto thee:
20: 5 set time w· he had appointed him.
8 the great stone w· is in Gibeon,
21:12 w· had stolen them from the street
16 w· was of the sons of the giant,
18 w· was of the sons of the giant.
22:44 a people w· I knew not shall serve me.
23:15 of Beth-lehem, w· is by the gate!
24: 2 of the host, w· was with him,
1Ki 1: 8 mighty men w· belonged to David,
9 of Zoheleth, w· is by En-rogel,
48 w· hath given one to sit on my
2: 4 word w· he spake concerning me,
8 w· cursed me with a grievous
24 liveth, w· hath established me,
27 w· he spake concerning the house of
31 the innocent blood, w· Joab shed,
44 wickedness w· thine heart is privy to,
46 w· went out, and fell upon him, that
3: 8 thy people w· thou hast chosen,
13 thee that w· thou hast not asked,
21 it was not my son, w· I did bear.
28 judgment w· the king had judged;
4: 2 These were the princes w· he had;
7 w· provided victuals for the king and
11 w· had Taphath the daughter of
12 w· is by Zartanah beneath Jezreel,
13 son of Manasseh, w· are in Gilead;
13 region of Argob, w· is in Bashan,
19 the only officer w· was in the land.
20 sand w· is by the sea in multitude,
34 earth, w· had heard of his wisdom.
5: 3 for the wars w· were about him
7 w· hath given unto David a wise son
8 things w· thou sentest to me for:
16 Solomon's officers w· were over the
16 w· ruled over the people that wrought
6: 1 month Zif, w· is the second month,
2 house w· king Solomon built for
12 this house w· thou art building,
12 w· I spake unto David thy father:
20 covered the altar w· was of cedar.
38 Bul, w· is the eighth month,
7: 8 the porch, w· was of the like work.
17 chapiters w· were upon the top of
20 the belly w· was by the network:
41 chapiters w· were upon the tops of
45 w· Hiram made to king Solomon
51 the things w· David his father had
8: 1 out of the city of David, w· is Zion.
2 w· is the seventh month.
9 w· Moses put there at Horeb,
15 w· spake with his mouth unto
21 Lord, w· he made with our fathers,
26 w· thou spakest unto thy servant
28 w· thy servant prayeth before thee
29 the place of w· thou hast said,
29 prayer w· thy servant shall make
34 w· thou gavest unto their fathers.
36 w· thou hast given unto thy people
38 w· shall know every man the plague
40 land w· thou gavest unto our fathers.
43 house w· I have builded, is called by
44 toward the city w· thou hast chosen,
48 enemies, w· led them away captive,
48 w· thou gavest unto their fathers,
48 the city w· thou hast chosen, and
48 house w· I have built for thy name:
51 w· thou broughtest forth out of
56 w· he promised by the hand of Moses
58 w· he commanded our fathers.
63 w· he offered unto the Lord, two and
9: 1 desire w· he was pleased to do,
3 this house w· thou hast built,
6 statutes w· I have set before you,
7 of the land w· I have given them;
7 w· I have hallowed for my name,
8 And at this house, w· is high,
12 cities w· Solomon had given him;
13 are these w· thou hast given me,
15 the levy w· king Solomon raised;
19 w· Solomon desired to build in
20 w· were not of the children of Israel,
23 w· bare rule over the people that
24 unto her house w· Solomon had
25 the altar w· he built unto the Lord,
26 Ezion-geber, w· is beside Eloth,
10: 3 from the king, w· he told her not.
5 by w· he went up into the house of
7 exceedeth the fame w· I heard.
8 w· stand continually before thee,
9 w· delighted in thee, to set thee on
10 w· the queen of Sheba gave to king
13 w· Solomon gave her of his royal
24 wisdom, w· God had put in his heart.
11: 2 nations concerning w· the Lord said
8 w· burnt incense and sacrificed unto
9 w· had appeared unto him twice,
10 not that w· the Lord commanded.
11 w· I have commanded thee,
13 Jerusalem's sake w· I have chosen.
18 w· gave him an house, and appointed
23 w· fled from his lord Hadadezer
32 the city w· I have chosen out of all
1Ki 11:33 to do that w· is right in mine eyes,
37 city w· I have chosen me to put my
12: 4 his heavy yoke w· he put upon us,
8 the old men, w· they had given him,
8 with him, and w· stood before him:
9 yoke w· thy father did put upon us
15 w· the Lord spake by Ahijah the
17 Israel w· dwelt in the cities of Judah,
21 chosen men, w· were warriors,
28 w· brought thee up out of the land
31 w· were not of the sons of Levi.
32 the high places w· he had made.
33 upon the altar w· he had made in
33 month w· he had devised of his own
13: 3 the sign w· the Lord hath spoken;
4 w· had cried against the altar in
4 hand, w· he put forth against him,
5 sign w· the man of God had given
11 the words w· he had spoken unto
12 God went, w· came from Judah.
21 w· the Lord thy God commanded
22 w· the Lord did say to thee, Eat no
26 the lion, w· hath torn him, and slain
26 of the Lord, w· he spake unto him.
32 For the saying w· he cried by the
32 high places w· are in the cities of
14: 2 w· told me that I should be king
8 that only w· was right in mine eyes;
15 land, w· he gave to their fathers,
18 w· he spake by the hand of his
20 the days w· Jeroboam reigned were
21 the city w· the Lord did choose out
22 their sins w· they had committed,
24 nations w· the Lord cast out before
26 shields of gold w· Solomon had made.
27 w· kept the door of the king's house.
15: 3 father, w· he had done before him:
5 w· was right in the eyes of the Lord,
11 Asa did that w· was right in the eyes
15 the things w· his father had dedicated,
15 the things w· himself had dedicated,
20 hosts w· he had against the cities
23 did, and the cities w· he had built,
27 w· belonged to the Philistines;
29 w· he spake by his servant Ahijah
30 sins of Jeroboam w· he sinned,
30 and w· he made Israel sin,
16:12 w· he spake against Baasha by
13 of Elah his son, by w· they sinned,
13 and by w· they made Israel to sin,
15 w· belonged to the Philistines.
19 his sins w· he sinned in doing evil
19 his sin, w· he did, to make Israel
24 the name of the city w· he built,
27 rest of the acts of Omri w· he did,
32 Baal, w· he had built in Samaria.
34 w· he spake by Joshua the son of
17: 9 to Zarephath, w· belongeth to Zidon,
16 of the Lord, w· he spake by Elijah.
18: 3 w· was the governor of his house.
19 four hundred, w· eat at Jezebel's table.
26 took the bullock w· was given them,
26 leaped upon the altar w· was made.
19: 3 Beer-sheba, w· belongeth to Judah,
18 knees w· have not bowed unto Baal,
18 every mouth w· hath not kissed
20:19 and the army w· followed them.
34 w· my father took from thy father,
21: 1 had a vineyard, w· was in Jezreel,
4 w· Naboth the Jezreelite had spoken
11 letters w· she had sent unto them.
15 w· he refused to give thee for
18 king of Israel, w· is in Samaria:
25 Ahab, w· did sell himself to work
22:13 of them, and speak that w· is good.
16 but that w· is true in the name of the
24 W· way went the Spirit of the
38 the word of the Lord w· he spake.
39 and the ivory house w· he made,
43 w· was right in the eyes of the Lord
46 w· remained in the days of his father
2Ki 1: 4, 6 that bed on w· thou art gone up,
7 was he w· came up to meet you,
16 off that bed on w· thou art gone up,
17 of the Lord w· Elijah had spoken.
18 of the acts of Ahaziah w· he did,
2:15 of the prophets w· were to view at
22 the saying of Elijah w· he spake.
3: 3 son of Nebat, w· made Israel to sin;
8 he said, W· way shall we go
11 w· poured water on the hands of
4: 4 and thou shalt set aside that w· is full.
9 of God w· passeth by us continually.
5:20 at his hands that w· he brought:
6:10 place w· the man of God told him
11 w· of us is for the king of Israel?
7:13 that remain, w· are left in the city,
15 w· the Syrians had cast away in
8:21 Edomites w· compassed him about,
29 w· the Syrians had given him.
9: 5 And Jehu said, Unto w· of all us?
15 w· the Syrians had given him,
19 second on horseback, w· came to them,
27 going up to Gur, w· is by Ibleam.
36 w· he spake by his servant Elijah
10: 5 do thou that w· is good in thine eyes.
6 men of the city, w· brought them up.
10 w· the Lord spake concerning the
10 that w· he spake by his servant
30 executing that w· is right in mine eyes,
31 of Jeroboam, w· made Israel to sin.
33 Aroer, w· is by the river Arnon,
11: 2 among the king's sons w· were slain:
16 by the way by the w· the horses came
12: 2 w· was right in the sight of the Lord
20 house of Millo, w· goeth down to Silla.

2Ki 13: 2 w· was evil in the sight of the Lord,
2 son of Nebat, w· made Israel to sin;
11 w· was evil in the sight of the Lord;
25 w· he had taken out of the hand of
14: 3 w· is right in the sight of the Lord,
6 unto that w· is written in the book
11 Beth-shemesh, w· belongeth to
15 of the acts of Jehoash w· he did,
21 Azariah, w· was sixteen years old,
24 w· was evil in the sight of the Lord:
25 w· he spake by the hand of his
25 prophet, w· was of Gath-hepher.
28 and Hamath, w· belonged to Judah,
15: 3 w· was right in the sight of the Lord,
9 w· was evil in the sight of the Lord:
12 the Lord w· he spake unto Jehu,
15 and his conspiracy w· he made,
18, 24, 28 that w· was evil in the sight of
34 w· was right in the sight of the Lord:
16: 2 w· was right in the sight of the Lord
7 king of Israel, w· rise up against me.
14 altar, w· was before the Lord,
19 rest of the acts of Ahaz w· he did,
17: 2 w· was evil in the sight of the Lord,
7 w· had brought them up out of the
8 kings of Israel, w· they had made.
13 law w· I commanded your fathers,
13 and w· I sent to you by my servants
15 w· he testified against them; and
19 statutes of Israel w· they made.
22 all the sins of Jeroboam w· he did;
25 among them, w· slew some of them.
26 The nations w· thou hast removed,
29 high places w· the Samaritans had
32 w· sacrificed for them in the
34 w· the Lord commanded the
37 commandment, w· he wrote for you,
18: 3 w· was right in the sight of the Lord,
6 w· the Lord commanded Moses.
9 w· was the seventh year of Hoshea
14 w· thou puttest on me will I bear.
16 w· Hezekiah king of Judah had
17 w· is in the highway of the fuller's
18 Hilkiah, w· was over the household,
21 Egypt, on w· if a man lean, it will go
27 sent me to the men w· sit on the wall,
37 Hilkiah, w· was over...household,
19: 2 Eliakim, w· was over the household,
4 words w· the Lord thy God hath
6 of the words w· thou hast heard,
6 with w· the servants of the king of
12 them w· my fathers have destroyed;
12 of Eden w· were in Thelasar?
15 w· dwellest between the cherubims,
16 w· hath sent him to reproach the
20 That w· thou hast prayed to me
28 by the way by w· thou camest.
29 year that w· springeth of the same;
20: 3 done that w· is good in thy sight.
17 that w· thy fathers have laid up in
18 w· thou shalt beget, shall they take
19 of the Lord w· thou hast spoken.
21: 2 w· was evil in the sight of the Lord,
3 high places w· Hezekiah his father
4 of the Lord, of w· the Lord said,
7 house, of w· the Lord said to David,
7 w· I have chosen out of all tribes
8 of the land w· I gave their fathers;
11 Amorites did, w· were before him,
15 done that w· was evil in my sight,
16 w· was evil in the sight of the Lord.
20 w· was evil in the sight of the Lord,
25 of the acts of Amon w· he did,
22: 2 w· was right in the sight of the Lord,
4 sum the silver w· is brought into the
4 w· the keepers of the door have
5 work w· is in the house of the Lord,
13 all that w· is written concerning us.
16 book w· the king of Judah hath
18 w· sent you to enquire of the Lord,
18 the words w· thou hast heard;
20 evil w· I will bring upon this place.
23: 2 covenant w· was found in the house of
8 w· were on a man's left hand at the
10 w· is in the valley of the children of
11 w· was in the suburbs, and burned
12 w· the kings of Judah had made,
12 the altars w· Manasseh had made
13 w· were on the right hand of the
13 w· Solomon the king of Israel had
15 high place w· Jeroboam the son of
16 Lord w· the man of God proclaimed,
17 man of God, w· came from Judah,
19 w· the kings of Israel had made to
24 w· were written in the book that
27 city Jerusalem w· I have chosen,
27 the house of w· I said, My name shall
32, 37 did that w· was evil in the sight of
24: 2 w· he spake by his servants the
4 blood; w· the Lord would not pardon
9 w· was evil in the sight of the Lord,
13 w· Solomon king of Israel had made
19 w· was evil in the sight of the Lord,
25: 4 walls, w· is by the king's garden:
8 w· is the nineteenth year of king
16 w· Solomon had made for the house
19 w· were found in the city, and the
19 w· mustered the people of the land,
1Ch 1: 46 w· smote Midian in the field of Moab,
2: 3 w· three were born unto him of the
19 unto him Ephrath, w· bare him Hur.
42 w· was the father of Ziph;
55 of the scribes w· dwelt at Jabez;
3: 1 w· were born unto him in Hebron;
4: 10 granted him that w· he requested.
11 w· was the father of Eshton.
1Ch 4: 18 daughter of Pharaoh, w· Mered
6: 61 w· were left of the family of that tribe
65 w· are called by their names.
9: 22 these w· were chosen to be porters in
25 brethren, w· were in the villages,
10: 13 w· he committed against the Lord,
13 word of the Lord, w· he kept not,
11: 4 went to Jerusalem, w· is Jebus;
5 of Zion, w· is the city of David.
12: 31 w· were expressed by name,
33 fifty thousand, w· could keep rank:
13: 2 and Levites w· are in their cities
6 Kirjath-jearim, w· belonged to
14: 4 of his children w· had in Jerusalem;
15: 3 place, w· he had prepared for it.
16: 15 the word w· he commanded to a
16 of the covenant w· he made with
40 Lord, w· he commanded Israel;
17: 11 after thee, w· shall be of thy sons;
19: 13 Lord do that w· is good in his sight.
18 seven thousand men w· fought in
20: 4 at w· time Sibbechai the
21: 19 w· he spake in the name of the
23 king do that w· is good in his eyes:
24 take that w· is thine for the Lord,
29 w· Moses made in the wilderness,
22: 13 w· the Lord charged Moses with
23: 4 Of w· twenty and four thousand
5 with the instruments w· I made,
29 and for that w· is baked in the pan,
25: 2 w· prophesied according to the order
26: 22 w· were over the treasures of the
26 W· Shelomith and his brethren
26 w· David the king, and the chief
27: 1 w· came in and went out month by
31 substance w· was king David's.
29: 3 w· I have given to the house of my
17 joy thy people, w· are present here, to
19 for the w· I have made provision.
2Ch 1: 3 w· Moses the servant of the Lord
4 to the place w· David had prepared
6 w· was at the tabernacle of the
14 w· he placed in the chariot cities,
2: 5 And the house w· I build is great:
9 house w· I am about to build shall
11 in writing, w· he sent to Solomon,
14 device w· shall be put to him,
15 wine, w· my lord hath spoken of,
3: 5 w· he overlaid with fine gold, and
4: 3 of oxen, w· did compass it round
12 chapiters w· were on the top of the two
12 w· were on the top of the pillars;
13 chapiters w· were upon the pillars.
5: 2 of the city of David, w· is Zion.
3 feast w· was in the seventh month.
6 and oxen, w· could not be told nor
10 two tables w· Moses put therein
12 Also the Levites w· were the singers,
6: 4 his hands fulfilled that w· he spake
9 thy son w· shall come forth out of thy
14 w· keepest covenant, and shewest
15 Thou w· hast kept with thy servant
15, 16 father that w· thou hast promised
17 w· thou hast spoken unto thy
18 less this house w· I have built!
19 w· thy servant prayeth before thee:
20 the prayer w· thy servant prayeth
21 w· they shall make toward this
25 w· thou gavest to them and to their
27 w· thou hast given unto thy people
31 w· thou gavest unto our fathers.
32 w· is not of thy people Israel,
33 house w· I have built is called by thy
34 this city w· thou hast chosen,
34 house w· I have built for thy name;
36 (for there is no man w· sinneth not,)
38 w· thou gavest unto their fathers,
38 toward the city w· thou hast chosen,
38 house w· I have built for thy name:
39 thy people w· have sinned against
7: 6 w· David the king had made to
7 brasen altar w· Solomon had made
14 people, w· are called by my name,
19 w· I have set before you, and shall go
20 of my land w· I have given them;
20 w· I have sanctified for my name,
21 And this house, w· is high, shall be
22 w· brought them forth out of the
8: 2 w· Huram had restored to Solomon,
4 store cities, w· he built in Hamath.
7 the Jebusites, w· were not of Israel,
12 w· he had built before the porch,
9: 2 from Solomon w· he told her not.
4 his ascent by w· he went up into the
5 a true report w· I heard in mine
7 w· stand continually before thee,
8 w· delighted in thee to set thee on
10 w· brought gold from Ophir,
12 that w· she had brought unto the
14 w· chapmen and merchants brought.
18 gold, w· were fastened to the throne,
10: 8 counsel w· the old men gave him,
9 w· have spoken to me, saying, Ease
15 w· he spake by the hand of Ahijah
11: 1 men, w· were warriors, to fight
10 w· are in Judah and in Benjamin,
15 and for the calves w· he had made.
19 W· bare him children; Jeush, and
20 w· bare him Abijah, and Attai, and
12: 4 cities w· pertained to Judah,
9 the shields of gold w· Solomon had
10 Instead of w· king Rehoboam made
13 the city w· the Lord had chosen out
13: 4 w· is in mount Ephraim, and said,
8 w· Jeroboam made you for gods.
10 the priests, w· minister unto the Lord,
2Ch 14: 2 w· was good and right in the eyes of
15: 8 cities w· he had taken from mount
11 time, of the spoil w· they had brought.
16: 14 w· he had made for himself in the
14 in the bed w· was filled with sweet
17: 2 w· Asa his father had taken.
18: 23 W· way went the Spirit of the
20: 2 in Hazazon-tamar; w· is En-gedi.
11 w· thou hast given us to inherit.
22 Seir, w· were come against Judah;
25 w· they stripped off for themselves,
32 w· was right in the sight of the Lord.
21: 6 w· was evil in the eyes of the Lord.
9 the Edomites w· compassed him in,
13 house, w· were better than thyself:
22: 6 of the wounds w· were given him
23: 9 w· were in the house of God.
19 that none w· was unclean in any thing
24: 2 w· was right in the sight of the Lord
20 the priest, w· stood above the people,
22 kindness w· Jehoiada his father
25: 2 w· was right in the sight of the Lord,
9 talents w· I have given to the army
13 of the army w· Amaziah sent back,
15 w· said unto me, Why hast thou
15 w· could not deliver their own
21 Beth-shemesh, w· belongeth...Judah.
26: 4 w· was right in the sight of the Lord,
23 burial w· belonged to the kings;
27: 2 w· was right in the sight of the Lord,
28: 1 w· was right in the sight of the Lord,
6 in one day, w· were all valiant men;
11 w· ye have taken captive of your
15 the men w· were expressed by name
23 the gods of Damascus, w· smote him:
29: 2 w· was right in the sight of the Lord,
6 w· was evil in the eyes of the Lord
19 w· king Ahaz in his reign did cast
32 w· the congregation brought,
30: 7 w· trespassed against the Lord God
8 w· he hath sanctified for ever:
16 w· they received of the hands of the
31: 6 holy things w· were consecrated unto
10 and that w· is left is this great store.
12 over w· Cononiah the Levite was ruler,
19 w· were in the fields of the suburbs of
20 that w· was good and right and truth
32: 3 fountains w· were without the city:
19 w· were the work of the hands of man.
21 w· cut off all the mighty men of valour,
33: 2 w· was evil in the sight of the Lord,
3 w· Hezekiah his father had broken
7 idol w· he had made, in the house of
7 of w· God had said to David and to
7 w· I have chosen before all the tribes
8 land w· I have appointed for your
11 w· took Manasseh among the thorns,
22 w· was evil in the sight of the Lord,
22 w· Manasseh his father had made,
34: 2 w· was right in the sight of the Lord.
9 w· the Levites that kept the door
11 houses w· the kings of Judah had
24 w· they have read before the king of
26 the words w· thou hast heard;
31 covenant w· are written in this book.
35: 3 all Israel, w· were holy unto the Lord,
3 the house w· Solomon the son of
26 w· was written in the law of the Lord,
36: 5 w· was evil in the sight of the Lord
8 and his abominations w· he did,
8 w· was found in him, behold, they are
9 w· was evil in the sight of the Lord.
12 w· was evil in the sight of the Lord
14 w· he had hallowed in Jerusalem.
23 house in Jerusalem, w· is in Judah.
Ezr 1: 2 house at Jerusalem, w· is in Judah.
3 go up to Jerusalem, w· is in Judah,
3 (he is the God,) w· is in Jerusalem.
5 of the Lord w· is in Jerusalem.
7 w· Nebuchadnezzar had brought
2: 1 of those w· had been carried away.
2 W· came with Zerubbabel:
59 were they w· went up from Tel-melah,
61 w· took a wife of the daughters of
68 of the Lord w· is at Jerusalem,
4: 2 of Assur, w· brought us up hither.
12 that the Jews w· came up from
15 time: for w· cause was this city
18 The letter w· ye sent unto us hath
20 w· have ruled over all countries
24 house of God w· is at Jerusalem.
5: 2 the house of God w· is at Jerusalem
6 w· were on this side the river,
8 w· is builded with great stones,
11 w· a great king of Israel builded and
14 w· Nebuchadnezzar took out of
16 house of God w· is at Jerusalem:
17 house, w· is there at Babylon,
6: 5 w· Nebuchadnezzar took forth out
5 unto the temple w· is at Jerusalem,
6 w· are beyond the river, be ye far
9 And that w· they have need of both
9 the priests w· are at Jerusalem,
12 house of God w· is at Jerusalem.
13 that w· Darius the king had sent,
15 w· was in the sixth year of the
18 service of God, w· is at Jerusalem;
21 w· were come again out of captivity,
7: 6 w· the Lord God of Israel had
8 w· was in the seventh year of the
13 w· are minded of their...freewill
14 law of thy God w· is in thine hand;
15 w· the king and his counsellers
16 of their God w· is in Jerusalem:
17 of your God w· is in Jerusalem.
20 w· thou shalt have occasion to

Ezr 7:21 treasurers *w·* are beyond the river,
25 *w·* may judge all the people that
27 *w·* hath put such a thing as this in
27 of the Lord *w·* is in Jerusalem:
8:25 *w·* the king, and his counsellers, and
35 *w·* were come out of captivity, offered
9:11 *W·* thou hast commanded by thy
11 land unto *w·* ye go to possess it, is
11 *w·* have filled it from one end to
10:14 all them *w·* have taken strange wives
Ne 1: 2 *w·* were left of the captivity,
6 *w·* I pray before thee now, day and
6 *w·* we have sinned against thee:
7 *w·* thou commandedst thy servant
2: 8 place *w·* appertained to the house,
13 Jerusalem, *w·* were broken down,
18 of my God *w·* was good upon me;
3:25 tower *w·* lieth out from the king's
4: 2 of the rubbish *w·* are burned?
3 Even that *w·* they build, if a fox
12 when the Jews *w·* dwelt by them came,
14 the Lord, *w·* is great and terrible,
17 They *w·* builded on the wall, and they
23 men of the guard *w·* followed me,
5: 8 Jews, *w·* were sold unto the heathen;
18 Now that *w·* was prepared for me
6: 6 *w·* cause thou buildest the wall,
7: 5 of them *w·* came up at the first,
61 they *w·* went up also from Tel-melah,
63 *w·* took one of the daughters of
72 *w·* the rest of the people gave was
8: 1 *w·* the Lord had commanded to
4 *w·* they had made for the purpose;
9 Nehemiah, *w·* is the Tirshatha,
14 law *w·* the Lord had commanded
9: 5 *w·* is exalted above all blessing and
15 *w·* thou hadst sworn to give them.
23 *w·* thou hadst promised to their
26 slew thy prophets *w·* testified
29 (*w·* if a man do, he shall live in
35 fat land *w·* thou gavest before them,
10:29 *w·* was given by Moses the servant
12: 8 *w·* was over the thanksgiving, he
37 gate, *w·* was over against them,
13: 5 *w·* was commanded to be given to the
15 *w·* they brought into Jerusalem on the
16 of Tyre also therein, *w·* brought fish,
Es 1: 1 (this is Ahasuerus *w·* reigned, from
2 *w·* was in Shushan the palace,
9 house *w·* belonged to king Ahasuerus.
13 to the wise men, *w·* knew the times,
14 and Media, *w·* saw the king's face,
14 and *w·* sat the first in the kingdom,)
18 *w·* have heard of the deed of the
20 the king's decree *w·* he shall make,
2: 4 the maiden *w·* pleaseth the king be
6 *w·* had been carried away with
9 maidens *w·* were meet to be given her,
14 chamberlain, *w·* kept the concubines:
16 tenth month, *w·* is the month Tebeth,
21 of those *w·* kept the door, were wroth,
3: 3 servants, *w·* were in the king's
13 month, *w·* is the month Adar,
4: 6 city, *w·* was before the king's gate.
16 king, *w·* is not according to the law:
6: 8 brought *w·* the king useth to wear,
8 crown royal *w·* is set upon his head:
7: 9 *w·* Haman had made for Mordecai,
8: 2 ring, *w·* he had taken from Haman,
5 *w·* he wrote to destroy the Jews
5 *w·* are in all the king's provinces:
8 writing *w·* is written in the king's
9 *w·* are from India unto Ethiopia,
11 the Jews *w·* were in every city
12 month, *w·* is the month Adar.
9:13 to the Jews *w·* are in Shushan
22 *w·* was turned unto them from
25 *w·* he devised against the Jews,
26 *w·* they had seen concerning this
26 matter, and *w·* had come unto them,
Job 3: 3 night in *w·* it was said, There is a man
14 *w·* built desolate places...themselves;
16 been; as infants *w·* never saw light.
21 *W·* long for death, but it cometh not;
22 *W·* rejoice exceedingly, and are glad,
25 thing *w·* I greatly feared is come upon
25 that *w·* I was afraid is come unto
4:14 *w·* made all my bones to shake.
19 dust, *w·* are crushed before the moth?
21 their excellency *w·* is in them go away?
5: 1 to *w·* of the saints wilt thou turn?
9 *W·* doeth great things and
11 those *w·* mourn may be exalted to
6: 6 Can that *w·* is unsavoury be eaten
16 *W·* are blackish by reason of the ice,
26 one that is desperate, *w·* are as wind?
9: 5 *W·* removeth the mountains, and
5 *w·* overturneth them in his anger.
6 *W·* shaketh the earth out of her place,
7 *W·* commandeth the sun, and it riseth
8 *W·* alone spreadeth out the heavens,
9 *W·* maketh Arcturus, Orion, and‡
10 *W·* doeth greater things past finding
11: 6 and they are double to that *w·* is!
14:19 things *w·* grow out of the dust of the
15: 9 understandest thou, *w·* is not in
14 and he *w·* is born of a woman, that he
16 man, *w·* drinketh iniquity like water?
17 and that *w·* I have seen I will declare;
18 *W·* wise men have told from their
28 and in houses *w·* no man inhabiteth,
28 *w·* are ready to become heaps.
16: 8 wrinkles, *w·* is a witness against me:
20: 7 they *w·* have seen him shall say,
9 eye also *w·* saw him shall see him no
11 *w·* shall be down with him in the dust.

Job 20:18 That *w·* he laboured for shall he
19 away an house *w·* he builded not;
20 he shall not save of that *w·* he desired.
21:27 devices *w·* ye wrongfully imagine
22:15 way *w·* wicked men have trodden?
16 *W·* were cut down out of time,
17 *W·* said unto God, Depart from us:
23: 5 the words *w·* he would answer me,
24:11 *W·* make oil within their walls, and
16 *w·* they had marked for themselves in
19 doth the grave those *w·* have sinned.
25: 6 and the son of man, *w·* is a worm?
27:11 *w·* is with the Almighty will I not
13 *w·* they shall receive of the Almighty.
28: 7 There is a path *w·* no fowl knoweth,
7 *w·* the vulture's eye hath not seen:
29:16 cause *w·* I knew not I searched out.
32:19 my belly is as wine *w·* hath no vent;
33:27 that *w·* was right, and it profited me
34: 8 *W·* goeth in company with...workers
32 That *w·* I see not teach thou me:
36:16 and that *w·* should be set on thy table
24 magnify his work, *w·* men behold.
28 *W·* the clouds do drop and distil
37: 5 doeth he, *w·* we cannot comprehend.
16 of him *w·* is perfect in knowledge?
18 *w·* is strong, and as a molten looking
21 the bright light *w·* is in the clouds:
38:23 *W·* I have reserved against the
24 *W·* scattereth the east wind upon the
39:14 *W·* leaveth her eggs in the earth,
40:15 behemoth, *w·* I made with thee;
41: 1 with a cord *w·* thou lettest down?
42: 3 too wonderful for me, *w·* I knew not.
8 spoken of me the thing *w·* is right,
Ps 1: 4 the chaff *w·* the wind driveth away.
3: 2 Many there be *w·* say of my soul,
7: *title* David, *w·* he sang unto the Lord,
10 *w·* saveth the upright in heart.
15 fallen into the ditch *w·* he made.
8: 3 the stars, *w·* thou hast ordained;
9:11 to the Lord, *w·* dwelleth in Zion:
13 trouble *w·* I suffer of them that hate
15 net *w·* they hid is their own foot
16 by the judgment *w·* he executeth:
17: 7 them *w·* put their trust in thee from
13 soul from the wicked, *w·* is thy sword:
14 From men *w·* are thy hand, O Lord,
14 *w·* have their portion in this life,
18:17 enemy, and from them *w·* hated me:
19: 5 *W·* is as a bridegroom coming out of
21:11 device, *w·* they are not able to perform.
25: 3 ashamed *w·* transgress without
28: 3 *w·* speak peace to their neighbours,
31:18 *w·* speak grievous things proudly
19 *w·* thou hast laid up for them that
19 *w·* thou hast wrought for them that
32: 8 thee in the way *w·* thou shalt go:
9 the mule, *w·* have no understanding:
35: 7 *w·* without cause they have digged
10 *w·* deliverest the poor from him that
27 *w·* hath pleasure in the prosperity of
40: 5 wonderful works *w·* thou hast done,
5 and thy thoughts *w·* are to us-ward:
41: 9 I trusted, *w·* did eat of my bread,
44:10 they *w·* hate us spoil for themselves.
45: 1 *w·* I have made touching the king:
51: 8 that the bones *w·* thou hast broken
58: 5 *W·* will not hearken to the voice of
7 away as waters *w·* run continually:
8 As a snail *w·* melteth, let every one of
59:12 for cursing and lying *w·* they speak.
60:10 not thou, O God, *w·* hadst cast us off?
10 *w·* didst not go out with our armies?
61: 7 and truth, *w·* may preserve him.
65: 6 *W·* by his strength setteth fast the
7 *W·* stilleth the noise of the seas, the
9 the river of God, *w·* is full of water:
66: 9 *W·* holdeth our soul in life, and
14 *W·* my lips have uttered, and my
20 God, *w·* hath not turned away my
68: 6 he bringeth out those *w·* are bound
16 the hill *w·* God desireth to dwell in;
28 *w·* thou hast wrought for us.
33 heavens of heavens, *w·* were of old;
69: 4 restored that *w·* I took not away.
22 *w·* should have been for their welfare,
71:20 *w·* hast shewed me great and sore
23 my soul, *w·* thou hast redeemed.
74: 2 *w·* thou hast purchased of old;
2 inheritance, *w·* thou hast redeemed;
78: 3 *W·* we have heard and known,
5 *w·* he commanded our fathers,
6 even the children *w·* should be born;
45 flies among them, *w·* devoured them;
45 and frogs, *w·* destroyed them.
54 *w·* his right hand had purchased.
60 the tent *w·* he placed among men;
68 Judah, the mount Zion *w·* he loved.
69 like the earth *w·* he hath established
79:10 the blood of thy servants *w·* is shed.
80:12 they *w·* pass by the way do pluck her?
15 vineyard *w·* thy right hand hath
81:10 God, *w·* brought thee out of the land
83:10 *W·* perished at En-dor: they became
85:12 Lord shall give that *w·* is good; and
86:17 that they *w·* hate me may see it,
89:49 *w·* thou swarest unto David in thy
90: 5 they are like the grass *w·* groweth up.
91: 9 hast made the Lord, *w·* is my refuge,
94:20 thee, *w·* frameth mischief by a law?
102:18 the people *w·* shall be created shall
104: 8 place *w·* thou hast founded for
10 the valleys, *w·* run among the hills.
12 fowls...*w·* sing among the branches.
15 and bread *w·* strengtheneth man's

Ps 104:16 of Lebanon, *w·* he hath planted;
105: 8 the word *w·* he commanded to a
9 *W·* covenant he made with
106:21 *w·* had done great things in Egypt;
36 idols: *w·* were a snare unto them.
107:25 wind, *w·* lifteth up the waves thereof.
37 *w·* may yield fruits of increase.
109:19 him as the garment *w·* covereth him,
114: 8 *W·* turned the rock into a standing
115:15 the Lord *w·* made heaven and earth.
118:20 into *w·* the righteous shall enter.
22 The stone *w·* the builders refused is
24 is the day *w·* the Lord hath made;
27 is the Lord, *w·* hath shewed us light:
119:21 *w·* do err from thy commandments.
39 Turn away my reproach *w·* I fear:
47 commandments, *w·* I have loved.
48 commandments, *w·* I have loved;
49 *w·* thou hast caused me to hope.
85 for me, *w·* are not after thy law.
165 peace have they *w·* love thy law:
121: 2 the Lord, *w·* made heaven and earth.
125: 1 as mount Zion, *w·* cannot be moved,
129: 6 *w·* withereth afore it groweth up:
8 Neither do they *w·* go by say, The
134: 1 *w·* by night stand in the house of the
135:21 of Zion, *w·* dwelleth at Jerusalem.
136:13 To him *w·* divided the Red sea into
16 To him *w·* led his people through the
17 To him *w·* smote great kings: for his
138: 8 will perfect that *w·* concerneth me:
139:16 *w·* in continuance were fashioned,
140: 2 *W·* imagine mischiefs in their
141: 5 oil, *w·* shall not break my head:
9 the snares *w·* they have laid for me,
144: 1 *w·* teacheth my hands to war,
146: 6 *W·* made heaven, and earth, the sea,
6 therein is: *w·* keepeth truth for ever:
7 *W·* executeth judgment for the
7 *w·* giveth food to the hungry.
147: 9 and to the young ravens *w·* cry.
148: 6 hath made a decree *w·* shall not pass.
Pr 1:19 *w·* taketh away the life of the owners
2:16 stranger *w·* flattereth with her words;
17 *W·* forsaketh the guide of her youth,
6: 7 *W·* having no guide, overseer, or
7: 5 stranger *w·* flattereth with her words.
9: 5 drink of the wine *w·* I have mingled.
11:22 fair woman *w·* is without discretion.
12:27 not that *w·* he took in hunting:
14:12 is a way *w·* seemeth right unto a man,
33 that *w·* is in the midst of fools is made
19:17 that *w·* he hath given will he pay him
20:25 man who devoureth that *w·* is holy,
22:28 landmark, *w·* thy fathers have set.
23: 5 set thine eyes upon that *w·* is not?
8 morsel *w·* thou hast eaten shalt thou
24:13 honeycomb, *w·* is sweet to thy taste:
25: 1 *w·* the men of Hezekiah king of
27:16 of his right hand, *w·* bewrayeth itself.
28: 3 a sweeping rain *w·* leaveth no food.
30:18 be three things *w·* are too wonderful
21 and for four *w·* it cannot bear:
24 things *w·* are little upon the earth,
29 There be three things *w·* go well, yea,
30 A lion *w·* is strongest among beasts,
31: 3 thy ways to that *w·* destroyeth kings.
Ec 1: 3 his labour *w·* he taketh under the sun?
9 that hath been, it is that *w·* shall be;
9 *w·* is done is that *w·* shall be done:
10 of old time, *w·* was before us.
15 That *w·* is crooked cannot be made
15 and that *w·* is wanting cannot be
2: 3 *w·* they should do under the heaven
12 that *w·* hath been already done.
16 seeing that *w·* now is in the days to
18 hated all my labour *w·* I had taken
20 despair of all the labour *w·* I took
3: 2 a time to pluck up that *w·* is planted;
10 *w·* God hath given to the sons of
15 That *w·* hath been is now; and that
15 that *w·* is to be hath already been;
15 and God requireth that *w·* is past.
19 For that *w·* befalleth the sons of men
4: 2 praised the dead *w·* are already dead
2 than the living *w·* are yet alive.
3 *w·* hath not yet been, who hath not
15 all the living *w·* walk under the sun,
5: 4 pay that *w·* thou hast vowed.
13 evil *w·* I have seen under the sun,
15 *w·* he may carry away in his hand.
18 Behold that *w·* I have seen: it is
18 days of his life, *w·* God giveth him:
6:12 vain life *w·* he spendeth as a shadow?
7:13 *w·* he hath made crooked?
19 ten mighty men *w·* are in the city.
24 That *w·* is far off, and exceeding
28 *W·* yet my soul seeketh, but I find
8: 7 he knoweth not that *w·* shall be:
12 that fear God, *w·* fear before him.
13 prolong his days, *w·* are as a shadow;
14 vanity *w·* is done upon the earth;
15 *w·* God giveth him under the sun.
9: 9 *w·* he hath given thee under the sun,
9 in thy labour *w·* thou takest under
10: 5 an evil *w·* I have seen under the sun,
5 error *w·* proceedeth from the ruler:
20 and that *w·* hath wings shall tell
12: 5 shall be afraid of that *w·* is high,
10 and that *w·* was written was upright,
11 *w·* are given from one shepherd.
Ca 1: 1 song of songs, *w·* is Solomon's.
3: 7 Behold his bed, *w·* is Solomon's;
4: 2 *w·* came up from the washing;
5 are twins, *w·* feed among the lilies.
6: 6 of sheep *w·* go up from the washing,

Ca 7: 2 goblet, w' wanteth not liquor:
4 Lebanon w' looketh toward Damascus.
13 and old, w' I have laid up for thee,
8: 6 w' hath a most vehement flame.
12 My vineyard, w' is mine, is before
Isa 1: 1 w' he saw concerning Judah and
29 of the oaks w' ye have desired,
2: 8 w' their own fingers have made:
20 w' they made each for himself to
3: 12 they w' lead thee cause thee to err.
5: 23 W' justify the wicked for reward,
6: 6 w' he had taken with the tongs
8: 18 of hosts, w' dwelleth in mount Zion.
10: 1 grievousness w' they have prescribed;
3 the desolation w' shall come from far?
11: 10 w' shall stand for an ensign of the
11, 16 of his people, w' shall be left,
13: 1 w' Isaiah the son of Amoz did see.
17 them, w' shall not regard silver;
14: 12 ground, w' didst weaken the nations!
15: 7 and that w' they have laid up,
17: 2 shall be for flocks, w' shall lie down,
8 that w' his fingers have made,
9 w' they left because of the children
12 w' make a noise like the noise of the
18: 1 w' is beyond the rivers of Ethiopia:
19: 15 w' the head or tail, branch or rush,
16 of hosts, w' he shaketh over it.
17 w' he hath determined against it.
21: 10 that w' I have heard of the Lord of
22: 3 together, w' have fled from far.
15 unto Shebna, w' is over the house,
26: 2 w' keepeth the truth may enter in.
27: 13 shall come w' were ready to perish
28: 1 w' are on the head of the fat
2 w' as a tempest of hail and a
4 w' is on the head of the fat valley,
4 w' when he that looketh upon it
14 this people w' is in Jerusalem.
29 hosts, w' is wonderful in counsel,
29: 11 w' men deliver to one that is
30: 10 W' say to the seers, See not; and
24 w' hath been winnowed with the
31 be beaten down, w' smote with a rod.
32 w' the Lord shall lay upon him,
31: 7 w' your own hands have made unto
36: 3 son, w' was over the house, and
37: 4 w' the Lord thy God hath heard:
12 delivered them w' my fathers have
12 of Eden w' were in Telassar?
17 w' hath sent to reproach the living
22 word w' the Lord hath spoken
29 back by the way w' thou camest.
30 year that w' springeth of the same:
38: 3 have done that w' is good in thy sight.
8 w' is gone down in the sun dial of
8 by w' degrees it was gone down.
39: 6 that w' thy fathers have laid up in
7 w' thou shalt beget, shall they take
8 of the Lord w' thou hast spoken.
42: 5 earth, and that w' cometh out of it;
43: 16 the Lord, w' maketh a way in the sea,
17 W' bringeth forth the chariot and
44: 2 thee from the womb, w' will help thee;
14 w' he strengtheneth for himself
45: 3 the Lord, w' call thee by thy name,
46: 3 w' are borne by me from the belly,
3 belly, w' are carried from the womb:
47: 11 thee suddenly, w' thou shalt not know.
48: 1 w' are called by the name of Israel,
1 w' swear by the name of the Lord,
14 w' among them hath declared
17 thy God w' teacheth thee to profit,
17 w' leadeth thee by the way that thou
49: 20 The children w' thou shalt have, after
50: 1 w' of my creditors is it to whom
51: 10 Art thou not it w' hath dried the sea,
12 son of man w' shall be made as grass;
17 w' hast drunk at the hand of the
23 w' have said to my soul, Bow down,
52: 15 w' had not been told them shall
15 that w' they had not heard shall they
55: 11 it shall accomplish that w' I please,
56: 8 Lord God w' gathereth the outcasts
11 dogs w' can never have enough,
57: 16 me, and the souls w' I have made.
59: 5 that w' is crushed breaketh out into a
61: 9 the seed w' the Lord hath blessed.
62: 2 w' the mouth of the Lord shall
6 w' shall never hold their peace day
8 for the w' thou hast laboured:
63: 7 w' he hath bestowed on them
64: 3 terrible things w' we looked not for,
65: 2 w' walketh in a way that was not
4 W' remain among the graves, and
4 w' eat swine's flesh, and broth of
7 w' have burned incense upon the
18 for ever in that w' I create:
66: 4 and chose that in w' I delighted not.
22 the new earth, w' I will make, shall
Jer 2: 11 their gods, w' are yet no gods?
11 glory for that w' did not profit.
3: 15 w' shall feed you with knowledge and
5: 17 w' thy sons and thy daughters should
21 w' have eyes, and see not;
21 w' have ears, and hear not:
22 w' have placed the sand for the
7: 10 w' is called by my name, and say,
11 w' is called by my name, become
12 unto my place w' was in Shiloh,
14 house, w' is called by my name,
14 the place w' I gave to you and to
30 the house w' I called by my name,
31 w' is in the valley of the son of
31 w' I commanded them not, neither
8: 3 w' remain in all the places whither I

Jer 8: 17 among you, w' will not be charmed,
9: 13 my law w' I set before them,
14 w' their fathers taught them:
24 the Lord w' exercise lovingkindness,
25 punish all them w' are circumcised
10: 1 word w' the Lord speaketh unto
11: 4 W' I commanded your fathers in
4 to all w' I commanded you:
5 oath w' I have sworn unto your
8 w' I commanded them to do;
10 w' refused to hear my words; and
10 w' I made with their fathers.
11 w' they shall not be able to escape;
17 w' they have done against
12: 14 w' I have caused my people Israel to
13: 4 thou hast got, w' is upon thy loins,
6 w' I commanded thee to hide there.
10 people, w' refuse to hear my words,
10 w' walk in the imagination of their
10 this girdle, w' is good for nothing.
15: 4 for that w' he did in Jerusalem.
14 into a land w' thou knowest not:
14 mine anger, w' shall burn upon you.
18 incurable, w' refuseth to be healed?
17: 4 in the land w' thou knowest not:
4 in mine anger, w' shall burn for ever.
16 that w' came out of my lips was right
19 by the w' they go out, and in all
18: 1 The word w' came to Jeremiah
14 snow of Lebanon w' cometh from the
19: 2 w' is by the entry of the east gate,
3 the w' whosoever heareth, his ears
5 w' I commanded not, nor spake it,
20: 2 w' was by the house of the Lord.
5 w' shall spoil them, and take them,
16 the cities w' the Lord overthrew,
21: 1 word w' came unto Jeremiah from
4 w' besiege you without the walls,
13 w' say, Who shall come down against
22: 6 and cities w' are not inhabited.
11 w' reigned instead of Josiah his
11 w' went forth out of this place; He
28 cast into a land w' they know not?
23: 4 over them w' shall feed them:
7 w' brought up the children of
8 w' brought up and w' led the seed of
27 W' think to cause my people to forget
27 w' they tell every man to his
40 shame, w' shall not be forgotten.
24: 2 naughty figs, w' could not be eaten,
8 as the evil figs, w' cannot be eaten,
25: 2 The w' Jeremiah the prophet spake
13 words w' I have pronounced against
13 w' Jeremiah hath prophesied
22 of the isles w' are beyond the sea,
26 w' are upon the face of the earth:
27 sword w' I will send among you.
29 on the city w' is called by my name,
26: 2 w' come to worship in the Lord's
3 evil w' I purpose to do unto them
4 in my law w' I have set before you,
19 of the evil w' he had pronounced
27: 3 the messengers w' come to Jerusalem
8 kingdom w' will not serve the
9 your sorcerers, w' speak unto you,
18 w' are left in the house of the Lord,
20 W' Nebuchadnezzar king of
28: 1 Azur the prophet, w' was of Gibeon,
6 thy words w' thou hast prophesied,
9 prophet w' prophesieth of peace,
29: 1 elders w' were carried away captives,
8 dreams w' ye caused to be dreamed.
19 w' I sent unto them by my servants
21 w' prophesy a lie unto you in my
22 of Judah w' are in Babylon,
23 w' I have not commanded them;
27 w' maketh himself a prophet to you?
31: 2 The people w' were left of the sword
21 even the way w' thou wentest:
32 w' my covenant they brake,
35 w' giveth the sun for a light by day,
35 w' divideth the sea when the waves
32: 1 w' was the eighteenth year of
2 w' was in the king of Judah's
8 w' is in the country of Benjamin:
11 both that w' was sealed according to
11 and custom, and that w' was open:
14 of the purchase, both w' is sealed,
14 and this evidence w' is open; and put
20 W' hast set signs and wonders in
22 w' thou didst swear to their fathers
32 w' they have done to provoke me to
34 w' is called by my name, to defile it.
35 w' are in the valley of the son of
35 w' I commanded them not, neither
33: 3 mighty things, w' thou knowest not.
4 w' are thrown down by the mounts,
9 w' shall hear all the good that I do
10 w' ye say shall be desolate without
12 w' is desolate without man and
14 good thing w' I have promised
24 families w' the Lord hath chosen,
34: 1 The word w' came unto Jeremiah
5 former kings w' were before thee,
8 all the people w' were at Jerusalem,
10 w' had entered into the covenant,
14 w' hath been sold unto thee;
15 the house w' is called by my name:
18 w' have not performed the words of
18 covenant w' they had made before
19 w' passed between the parts of the
21 army, w' are gone up from you.
35: 1 The word w' came unto Jeremiah
4 w' was by the chamber of the
4 w' was above the chamber of
15 in the land w' I have given to you

Jer 35: 16 father, w' he commanded them;
36: 3 evil w' I purpose to do unto them;
4 w' he had spoken unto him, upon a
6 w' thou hast written from my
21 the princes w' stood beside the king.
27 w' Baruch wrote at the mouth of
28 w' Jehoiakim the king of Judah hath
32 w' Jehoiakim king of Judah had
37: 2 Lord, w' he spake by the prophet
7 army, w' is come forth to help you,
19 prophets w' prophesied unto you,
38: 3 of Babylon's army, w' shall take it.
7 w' was in the king's house, heard
20 of the Lord, w' I speak unto thee:
39: 10 of the people, w' had nothing,
40: 1 The word w' came to Jeremiah from
1 w' were carried away captive unto
4 chains w' were upon thine hand.
7 of the forces w' were in the field,
10 Chaldeans w' will come unto us:
15 all the Jews w' are gathered unto thee
41: 13 the people w' were with Ishmael
17 of Chimham, w' is by Beth-lehem,
42: 5 for the w' the Lord thy God shall
8 of the forces w' were with him,
16 sword, w' ye feared, shall overtake
21 for the w' he hath sent me unto you.
43: 1 for w' the Lord their God had sent
9 w' is at the entry of Pharaoh's
44: 1 Jews w' dwell in the land of Egypt,
1 w' dwell at Migdol, and at Tahpanhes,
3 w' they have committed to provoke
9 w' they have committed in the land
14 w' are gone into the land of Egypt to
14 to the w' they...desire to return
15 men w' knew that their wives had
20 people w' had given him that answer,
22 of the abominations w' ye have
45: 4 that w' I have built will I break
4 that w' I have planted I will pluck
46: 1 The word...w' came to Jeremiah
2 w' was by the river Euphrates in
2 w' Nebuchadrezzar king of Babylon
49: 28 w' Nebuchadrezzar king of Babylon
31 nations,...w' have neither gates nor
31 neither gates nor bars w' dwell alone.
50: 3 w' shall make her land desolate,
51: 12 and done that w' he spake against
25 the Lord, w' destroyest all the earth:
44 mouth that w' he hath swallowed up:
59 The word w' Jeremiah the prophet
52: 2 that w' was evil in the eyes of the
7 walls, w' was by the king's garden:
12 w' was the nineteenth year of
12 guard, w' served the king of Babylon,
19 that w' was of gold in gold, and
19 and that w' was of silver in silver,
20 w' king Solomon had made in the
25 w' had...charge of the men of war;
25 person, w' were found in the city;
La 1: 12 my sorrow, w' is done unto me,
2: 3 fire, w' devoureth round about.
17 hath done that w' he had devised;
5: 18 the mountain of Zion, w' is desolate,
Eze 1: 2 w' was the fifth year of king
23 one had two, w' covered on this side,
23 one had two, w' covered on that side.
3: 20 his righteousness w' he hath done
23 glory w' I saw by the river of Chebar:
4: 10 And the meat w' thou shalt eat shall
14 I not eaten of that w' dieth of itself,
5: 9 do in thee that w' I have not done,
16 w' shall be for their destruction,
16 and w' I will send to destroy you:
6: 9 heart, w' hath departed from me,
9 eyes, w' go a whoring after their idols:
9 evils w' they have committed in all
7: 13 shall not return to that w' is sold,
13 multitude thereof, w' shall not return;
8: 3 of jealousy, w' provoketh to jealousy.
14 house w' was toward the north;
17 abominations w' they commit here?
9: 2 gate, w' lieth toward the north,
3 w' had the writer's inkhorn by his
6 men w' were before the house.
11 w' had the inkhorn by his side,
10: 22 w' I saw by the river of Chebar,
11: 1 Lord's house, w' looketh eastward:
3 W' say, It is not near; let us build
23 w' is on the east side of the city.
12: 2 w' have eyes to see, and see not;
28 word w' I have spoken shall be done.
13: 11 w' daub it with untempered morter,
16 w' prophesy concerning Jerusalem,
16 and w' see visions of peace for her,
17 w' prophesy out of their own heart;
14: 7 w' separateth himself from me,
15: 2 w' is among the trees of the forest?
6 w' I have given to the fire for fuel,
16: 14 comeliness, w' I had put upon thee,
17 of my silver, w' I had given thee,
19 My meat also w' I gave thee, fine
27 w' are ashamed of thy lewd way;
32 w' taketh strangers instead of her
36 w' thou didst give unto them;
45 w' lothed their husbands and their
51 abominations w' thou hast done.
52 also, w' hast judged thy sisters,
57 Philistines w' despise thee round
59 w' hast despised the oath in
17: 3 of feathers, w' had divers colours,
18: 5 and do that w' is lawful and right,
14 his father's sins w' he hath done,
18 w' is not good among his people,
19 the son hath done that w' is lawful
21 and do that w' is lawful and right, he

Eze 18:27 doeth that w' is lawful and right, he
19:14 w' hath devoured her fruit, so that she
20: 6 honey, w' is the glory of all lands:
11, 13 w' if a man do, he shall even live
15 into the land w' I have given them,
15 honey, w' is the glory of all lands;
21 w' if a man do, he shall even live in
28 w' I lifted up mine hand to give it to
32 that w' cometh into your mind shall
42 for the w' I lifted up mine hand
21:14 w' entereth into their privy chambers.
22: 4 in thine idols w' thou hast made;
5 w' art infamous and much vexed.
13 dishonest gain w' thou hast made,
13 thy blood w' hath been in the midst
23: 6 W' were clothed with blue, captains
24 w' shall set against thee buckler and
42 w' put bracelets upon their hands,
24:21 eyes, and that w' your soul pitieth;
27 mouth be opened to him w' is escaped,
25: 9 from his cities w' are on his frontiers,
26: 6 her daughters w' are in the field
17 w' wast strong in the sea, she and
17 w' cause their terror to be on all
27: 3 w' art a merchant for the people on
7 that w' thou spreadest forth to be thy
7 of Elishah was that w' covered thee.
27 company w' is in the midst of thee,
29: 3 w' hath said, My river is mine own,
16 Israel w' bringeth their iniquity to
30:22 the strong, and that w' was broken;
32: 9 countries w' thou hast not known.
23 w' caused terror in the land of the
24 w' are gone down uncircumcised
24 w' caused their terror in the land of
27 w' are gone down to hell with their
29 w' with their might are laid by them
30 w' are gone down with the slain;
33:14 and do that w' is lawful and right;
16 he hath done that w' is lawful and
29 all their abominations w' they have
34: 4 have ye healed that w' was sick,
4 have ye bound up that w' was broken,
4 ye brought again that w' was driven
4 have ye sought that w' was lost;
16 I will seek that w' was lost, and bring
16 bring again that w' was driven away,
16 and will bind up that w' was broken,
16 and will strengthen that w' was sick:
19 eat that w' ye have trodden with your
19 they drink that w' ye have fouled with
35:11 w' thou hast used out of thy hatred
12 blasphemies w' thou hast spoken
36: 4 w' became a prey and derision to
5 w' have appointed my land into
21 w' the house of Israel had profaned
22 w' ye have profaned among the
23 w' was profaned among the heathen,
23 w' ye have profaned in the midst of
37: 1 of the valley w' was full of bones,
19 w' is in the hand of Ephraim,
38: 8 Israel, w' have been always waste:
12 w' have gotten cattle and goods,
17 w' prophesied in those days many
39:19 of my sacrifice w' I have sacrificed
28 w' caused them to be led into
40: 2 w' was as the frame of a city on the
6 gate, w' looketh toward the east,
6 of the gate, w' was one reed broad;
6 of the gate, w' was one reed broad.
40 w' was at the porch of the gate,
44 w' was at the side of the north gate;
46 w' come near to the Lord to minister
41: 1 w' was the breadth of the tabernacle.
6 into the wall w' was of the house
9 w' was for the side chamber without
9 that w' was left was the place of the
15 separate place w' was behind it,
42: 1 w' was before the building toward
3 cubits w' were for the inner court,
3 the pavement w' was for the utter
11 chambers w' were toward the north,
13 w' are before the separate place,
14 to those things w' are for the people.
43: 3 appearance of the vision w' I saw,
19 seed of Zadok, w' approach unto me,
44: 1 sanctuary w' looketh toward the east;
10 w' went astray away from me after
13 their abominations w' they have
45: 4 w' shall come near to minister unto
14 cor, w' is an homer of ten baths;
46:19 w' was at the side of the gate,
19 priests, w' looked toward the north:
47: 8 w' being brought forth into the sea,
9 every thing that liveth, w' moveth,
14 concerning the w' I lifted up mine
16 w' is between the border of
16 w' is by the coast of Hauran.
22 w' shall beget children among you:
48: 8 be the offering w' ye shall offer
11 of Zadok; w' have kept my charge,
11 w' went not astray when the
22 the midst of that w' is the prince's,
29 This is the land w' ye shall divide
Da 1: 2 w' he carried into the land of Shinar
5 meat, and of the wine w' he drank:
8 meat, nor with the wine w' he drank:
10 the children w' are of your sort?
15 w' did eat the portion of the king's
2:14 w' was gone forth to slay the wise
26 unto me the dream w' I have seen,
27 secret w' the king hath demanded
34 w' smote the image upon his feet that
39 w' shall bear rule over all the
44 w' shall never be destroyed:
3: 2 image w' Nebuchadnezzar the king

Da 3:12 golden image w' thou hast set up.
14 the golden image w' I have set up?
15 worship the image w' I have made;
18 golden image w' thou hast set up.
29 w' speak any thing amiss against‡
4: 5 I saw a dream w' made me afraid,
20 tree that thou sawest, w' grew,
21 under w' the beasts of the field dwelt,
24 w' is come upon my lord the king:
5: 2 w' his father Nebuchadnezzar had
2 of the temple w' was in Jerusalem;
3 house of God w' was at Jerusalem;
13 Daniel, w' art of the children of the
23 w' see not, nor hear, nor know:
6: 1 w' should be over the whole kingdom;
8, 12 Medes and Persians, w' altereth
13 Daniel, w' is of the children of the
15 statute w' the king established
24 those men w' had accused Daniel,
26 that w' shall not be destroyed,
7: 6 w' had upon the back of it four
11 the great words w' the horn spake:
14 dominion, w' shall not pass away,
14 that w' shall not be destroyed.
17 These great beasts, w' are four, are
17 w' shall arise out of the earth.
19 w' was diverse from all the others,
19 w' devoured, brake in pieces, and
20 and of the other w' came up, and
23 earth, w' shall be diverse from all
8: 1 that w' appeared unto me at the first.
2 w' is in the province of Elam; and
3 the river a ram w' had two horns:
6 w' I had seen standing before the
9 horn, w' waxed exceeding great,
13 said unto that certain saint w' spake,
16 w' called, and said, Gabriel, make this
20 The ram w' thou sawest having
26 the vision...w' was told is true:
9: 1 w' was made king over the realm of
6 w' spake in thy name to our kings,
10 w' he set before us by his servants
12 his words, w' he spake against us,
14 in all his works w' he doeth: for we
18 the city w' is called by thy name:
10: 4 of the great river, w' is Hiddekel;
10 touched me, w' set me upon my knees,
21 that w' is noted in the scripture of
11: 4 to his dominion w' he ruled:
7 estate, w' shall come with an army,
16 w' by his hand shall be consumed.
24 that w' his fathers have not done,
12: 1 prince w' standeth for the children
6, 7 w' was upon the waters of the
Ho 1: 3 w' conceived, and bare him a son.
10 the sand...w' cannot be measured
2: 8 and gold, w' they prepared for Baal.
23 will say to them w' are not my people,
5: 9 made known that w' shall surely be.
Joe 1: 4 That w' the palmerworm hath left
4 and that w' the locust hath left hath
4 and that w' the cankerworm hath left
2:25 great army w' I sent among you.
Am 1: 1 w' he saw concerning Israel in the
4 w' shall devour the palaces of
7 w' shall devour the palaces thereof:
10 w' shall devour the palaces thereof.
12 w' shall devour the palaces of
2: 4 the w' their fathers have walked:
3: 1 w' I brought up from the land of
4: 1 of Bashan,...w' oppress the poor,
1 the poor, w' crush the needy,
1 w' say to their masters, Bring, and let
3 every cow at that w' is before her;
5: 1 word w' I take up against you,
3 and that w' went forth by an hundred
26 god, w' ye made for yourselves.
6: 1 w' are named chief of the nations,
13 Ye w' rejoice in a thing of nought,
13 w' say, Have we not taken to us horns
9:10 w' say, The evil shall not overtake nor
12 heathen, w' are called by my name,
15 of their land w' I have given them,
Ob 20 of Jerusalem, w' is in Sepharad,
Jon 1: 9 w' hath made the sea and the dry
4:10 for the w' thou hast not laboured,
10 w' came up in a night, and perished in
Mic 1: 1 w' he saw concerning Samaria and
2: 3 evil, from w' ye shall not remove
5: 3 time that she w' travaileth hath
6:14 and that w' thou deliverest will I
7:10 shame shall cover her w' said unto
14 w' dwell solitarily in the wood,
20 w' thou hast sworn unto our
Na 3:17 w' camp in the hedges in the cold day,
Hab 1: 1 The burden w' Habakkuk the
5 w' ye will not believe, though it
6 w' shall march through the breadth
2: 4 his soul w' is lifted up is not upright
6 him that increaseth that w' is not his!
17 spoil of beasts, w' made them afraid,
Zep 1: 1 the Lord w' came unto Zephaniah
9 w' fill their masters' houses with
2: 3 w' have wrought his judgment;
Hag 1:11 that w' the ground bringeth forth,
2:14 that w' they offer there is unclean.
Zec 1: 6 w' I commanded my servants the
7 month, w' is the month Sebat,
12 Judah, against w' thou hast had
19, 21 horns w' have scattered Judah,
21 w' lifted up their horn over the land of
2: 8 me unto the nations w' spoiled you:
4: 2 lamps, w' are upon the top thereof:
10 w' run to and fro through the whole
12 w' through the two golden pipes
6: 5 w' go forth from standing before the

Zec 6: 6 The black horses w' are therein go
10 w' are come from Babylon, and
7: 3 the priests w' were in the house
7 the words w' the Lord hath cried
12 and the words w' the Lord of hosts
8: 9 w' were in the day that the
10: 5 w' tread down their enemies in the
11:10 w' I had made with all the people.
16 w' shall not visit those that be cut off,
12: 1 Lord, w' stretcheth forth the heavens,
13: 6 Those with w' I was wounded in
14: 4 w' is before Jerusalem on the east,
7 day w' shall be known to the Lord,
16 of all the nations w' came against
Mal 1:13 and ye brought that w' was torn, and
14 w' hath in his flock a male,
2:11 holiness of the Lord w' he loved,
4: 4 w' I commanded unto him in
M't 1:20 w' is conceived in her is of the Holy
22 fulfilled w' was spoken of the Lord
23 Emmanuel, w' being interpreted
2: 9 lo, the star w' they saw in the east,
15 fulfilled w' was spoken of the
16 the time w' he had diligently
17 that w' was spoken by Jeremy
20 w' sought the young child's life.
23 w' was spoken by the prophets,
3:10 tree w' bringeth not forth good fruit
4:13 in Capernaum, w' is upon the sea
14 fulfilled w' was spoken by Esaias
16 people w' sat in darkness saw
16 w' sat in the region and shadow
24 those w' were possessed with devils,
24 and those w' were lunatick, and those
5: 6 Blessed are they w' do hunger
10 w' are persecuted for righteousness
12 the prophets w' were before you.
16 glorify your Father w' is in heaven.
44 pray for them w' despitefully use
45 the children of your Father w' is in
46 For if ye love them w' love you,
48 Father w' is in heaven is perfect.
6: 1 of your Father w' is in heaven.
4 Father w' seeth in secret himself
6 pray to thy Father w' is in secret;
6 Father w' seeth in secret shall
9 Our Father w' art in heaven,
18 unto thy Father w' is in secret:
18 and thy Father, w' seeth in secret,
27 W' of you by taking thought can
30 w' to day is, and to morrow is cast
7: 6 not that w' is holy unto the dogs,
11 w' is in heaven give good things
13 and many there be w' go in thereat:
14 narrow is the way, w' leadeth unto
15 w' come to you in sheep's
21 will of my Father w' is in heaven.
24 w' built his house upon a rock:
26 w' built his house upon the sand:
8:17 w' was spoken by Esaias the
9: 8 w' had given such power unto men.
16 that w' is put in to fill it up taketh
20 w' was diseased with an issue of
10:20 your Father w' speaketh in you.
28 And fear not them w' kill the body,
28 fear him w' is able to destroy
32, 33 before my Father w' is in heaven.
11: 4 those things w' ye do hear and
10 w' shall prepare thy way before
14 this is Elias, w' was for to come.
21 works, w' were done in you, had
23 w' art exalted unto heaven,
23 works, w' have been done in thee,
12: 2 do that w' is not lawful to do upon
4 w' was not lawful for him to eat,
4 neither for them w' were with him,
10 was a man w' had his hand withered.
17 w' was spoken by Esaias the
50 will of my Father w' is in heaven,
13:14 w' saith, By hearing ye shall hear,
17 to see those things w' ye see,
17 to hear those things w' ye hear,
19 that w' was sown in his heart.
19 is he w' received by the way side.
23 w' also beareth fruit, and bringeth
24 unto a man w' sowed good seed in his
31 w' a man took, and sowed in his
32 W' indeed is the least of all seeds;
33 w' a woman took, and hid in three
35 w' was spoken by the prophet,
35 I will utter things w' have been kept
41 that offend, and them w' do iniquity;
44 w' when a man hath found, he
48 W', when it was full, they drew to
52 w' is instructed unto the kingdom of
52 w' bringeth forth out of his
14: 9 and them w' sat with him at meat,
15: 1 Pharisees, w' were of Jerusalem,
11 Not that w' goeth into the mouth
11 but that w' cometh out of the mouth,
13 w' my heavenly Father hath not
18 w' proceed out of the mouth
20 are the things w' defile a man:
27 crumbs w' fall from their masters'
16: 8 W' when Jesus perceived, he said
17 but my Father w' is in heaven.
28 w' shall not taste of death, till
17: 5 a voice out of the cloud, w' said,
18: 6 these little ones w' believe in me,
10 face of my Father w' is in heaven.
11 is come to save that w' was lost.
12 seeketh that w' is gone astray?
13 ninety and nine w' went not astray
14 will of your Father w' is in heaven,
19 them of my Father w' is in heaven.
23 w' would take account of his

M't 18:24 *w'* owed him ten thousand talents.
28 *w'* owed him an hundred pence:
19: 4 *w'* made them at the beginning
9 marrieth her *w'* is put away doth
12 *w'* were so born from their
12 *w'* were made eunuchs of men:
12 *w'* have made themselves eunuchs
18 He saith unto him, *W'*? Jesus
28 That ye *w'* have followed me, in
20: 1 *w'* went out early in the morning
12 *w'* have borne the burden and
21: 4 *w'* was spoken by the prophet,
21 do this *w'* is done to the fig tree,
24 *w'* if ye tell me, I in like wise will
33 householder, *w'* planted a
41 *w'* shall render him the fruits in
42 The stone *w'* the builders rejected
22: 2 *w'* made a marriage for his son,
4 Tell them *w'* are bidden, Behold, I
8 they *w'* were bidden were not worthy.
11 *w'* had not on a wedding garment:
21 unto Cæsar the things *w'* are Cæsar's;
23 *w'* say that there is no resurrection,
31 *w'* was spoken unto you by God,
35 Then one of them, *w'* was a lawyer,
36 *w'* is the great commandment in
23: 9 is your Father, *w'* is in heaven.
16 unto you, ye blind guides, *w'* say,
24 blind guides, *w'* strain at a gnat,
26 first that *w'* is within the cup and
27 *w'* indeed appear beautiful
31 of them *w'* killed the prophets.
37 stonest them *w'* are sent unto thee,
24:17 Let him *w'* is on the housetop not
18 Neither let him *w'* is in the field
25: 1 ten virgins, *w'* took their lamps,
24 Then he *w'* had received the one
28 give it unto him *w'* hath ten talents.
29 be taken away even that *w'* he hath.
26:25 Then Judas, *w'* betrayed him,
28 *w'* is shed for many for the
51 one of them *w'* were with Jesus
62 is it *w'* these witness against thee?
75 word of Jesus, *w'* said unto him,
27: 3 Then Judas, *w'* had betrayed him,
9 that *w'* was spoken by Jeremy
17 or Jesus *w'* is called Christ?
22 then with Jesus *w'* is called Christ?
35 *w'* was spoken by the prophet,
44 also, *w'* were crucified with him,
52 bodies of the saints *w'* slept arose,
55 *w'* followed Jesus from Galilee,
56 Among *w'* was Mary Magdalene,
28: 5 ye seek Jesus, *w'* was crucified.
M'r 1: 2 *w'* shall prepare thy way before
44 those things *w'* Moses commanded,
2: 3 sick of the palsy, *w'* was borne of
24 sabbath day that *w'* is not lawful?
26 *w'* is not lawful to eat but for the
26 gave also to them *w'* were with him?
3: 1 a man there *w'* had a withered hand.
3 unto the man *w'* had the withered
17 Boanerges, *w'* is, The sons of
19 Judas Iscariot, *w'* also betrayed
22 the scribes *w'* came down from
34 about on them *w'* sat about him,
4:16 likewise *w'* are sown on stony ground;
18 are they *w'* are sown among thorns;
20 are they *w'* are sown on good ground;
22 hid, *w'* shall not be manifested;
31 *w'*, when it is sown in the earth,
5:25 *w'* had an issue of blood twelve years,
35 *w'* said, Thy daughter is dead:
41 *w'* is, being interpreted, Damsel,
6: 2 wisdom is this *w'* is given unto him,
26 for their sakes *w'* sat with him,
7: 1 the scribes *w'* came from Jerusalem.
4 be, *w'* they have received to hold,
13 tradition, *w'* ye have delivered:
15 but the things *w'* come out of him,
20 That *w'* cometh out of the man, that
9: 1 here, *w'* shall not taste of death,
17 thee my son, *w'* hath a dumb spirit;
39 man *w'* shall do a miracle in my
10:42 that they *w'* are accounted to rule
11:21 the fig tree *w'* thou cursedst is
23 *w'* he saith shall come to pass;
25 your Father also *w'* is in heaven
26 Father *w'* is in heaven forgive your
12:10 The stone *w'* the builders rejected
18 *w'* say there is no resurrection;
25 as the angels *w'* are in heaven.
28 *W'* is the first commandment of
38 *w'* love to go in long clothing,
40 *W'* devour widows' houses, and
42 in two mites, *w'* make a farthing.
43 they *w'* have cast into the treasury:
13:19 the creation *w'* God created unto
32 not the angels *w'* are in heaven,
14:18 One of you *w'* eateth with me
24 testament, *w'* is shed for many.
60 what is it *w'* these witness against
15: 7 *w'* lay bound with them that had
22 *w'* is, being interpreted, The place
28 scripture was fulfilled, *w'* saith,
34 *w'* is, being interpreted, My God,
39 centurion, *w'* stood over against
41 women *w'* came up with him unto
43 *w'*...waited for the kingdom
46 sepulchre *w'* was hewn out of a
16: 6 Jesus...Nazareth, *w'* was crucified:
14 *w'* had seen him after he was risen.
Lu 1: 1 things *w'* are most surely believed
2 *w'* from the beginning were
20 *w'* shall be fulfilled in their
35 holy thing *w'* shall be born of thee

Lu 1:45 things *w'* were told her from the Lord.
70 *w'* have been since the world
73 oath *w'* he sware to our father
2: 4 of David, *w'* is called Bethlehem;
10 great joy, *w'* shall be to all people.
11 a Saviour, *w'* is Christ the Lord.
15 see this thing *w'* is come to pass,
15 *w'* the Lord hath made known unto
17 *w'* was told them concerning the
18 things *w'* were told them by the
21 *w'* was so named of the angel
24 that *w'* is said in the law of the Lord,
31 *W'* thou hast prepared before the
33 those things *w'* were spoken of him.
34 and for a sign *w'* shall be spoken
37 *w'* departed not from the temple,
50 the saying *w'* he spake unto them.
3: 9 *w'* bringeth not forth good fruit is
13 more than that *w'* is appointed you.
19 all the evils *w'* Herod had done,
22 a voice came from heaven, *w'* said,
23 son of Joseph, *w'* was the son of Heli,
24 *W'* was the son of Matthat,
24 of Matthat, *w'* was the son of Levi,
24 son of Levi, *w'* was the son of Melchi,
24 of Melchi, *w'* was the son of Janna,
24 of Janna, *w'* was the son of Joseph,
25 *W'* was the son of Mattathias,
25 Mattathias, *w'* was the son of Amos,
25 son of Amos, *w'* was the son of Naum,
25 son of Naum, *w'* was the son of Esli,
25 son of Esli, *w'* was the son of Nagge,
26 *W'* was the son of Maath,
26 Maath, *w'* was the son of Mattathias,
26 Mattathias, *w'* was the son of Semei,
26 of Semei, *w'* was the son of Joseph,
26 son of Joseph, *w'* was the son of Juda,
27 *W'* was the son of Joanna,
27 of Joanna, *w'* was the son of Rhesa,
27 of Rhesa, *w'* was the son of Zorobabel,
27 Zorobabel, *w'* was the son of Salathiel,
27 of Salathiel, *w'* was the son of Neri,
28 *W'* was the son of Melchi,
28 son of Melchi, *w'* was the son of Addi,
28 son of Addi, *w'* was the son of Cosam,
28 Cosam, *w'* was the son of Elmodam,
28 son of Elmodam, *w'* was the son of Er,
29 *W'* was the son of Jose,
29 son of Jose, *w'* was the son of Eliezer,
29 of Eliezer, *w'* was the son of Jorim,
29 of Jorim, *w'* was the son of Matthat,
29 of Matthat, *w'* was the son of Levi,
30 *W'* was the son of Simeon,
30 son of Simeon, *w'* was the son of Juda,
30 son of Juda, *w'* was the son of Joseph,
30 of Joseph, *w'* was the son of Jonan,
30 of Jonan, *w'* was the son of Eliakim,
31 *W'* was the son of Melea,
31 son of Melea, *w'* was the son of Menan,
31 Menan, *w'* was the son of Mattatha,
31 Mattatha, *w'* was the son of Nathan,
31 of Nathan, *w'* was the son of David,
32 *W'* was the son of Jesse,
32 son of Jesse, *w'* was the son of Obed,
32 son of Obed, *w'* was the son of Booz,
32 of Booz, *w'* was the son of Salmon,
32 of Salmon, *w'* was the son of Naasson,
33 *W'* was the son of Aminadab,
33 *w'* was the son of Aram,
33 *w'* was the son of Esrom,
33 *w'* was the son of Phares,
33 of Phares, *w'* was the son of Juda,
34 *W'* was the son of Jacob,
34 *w'* was the son of Isaac,
34 *w'* was the son of Abraham,
34 *w'* was the son of Thara,
34 of Thara, *w'* was the son of Nachor,
35 *W'* was the son of Saruch,
35 *w'* was the son of Ragau,
35 *w'* was the son of Phalec,
35 *w'* was the son of Heber,
35 of Heber, *w'* was the son of Sala,
36 *W'* was the son of Cainan,
36 *w'* was the son of Arphaxad,
36 *w'* was the son of Sem,
36 *w'* was the son of Noe,
36 of Noe, *w'* was the son of Lamech,
37 *W'* was the son of Mathusala,
37 *w'* was the son of Enoch,
37 *w'* was the son of Jared,
37 *w'* was the son of Maleleel,
37 of Maleleel, *w'* was the son of Cainan,
38 *W'* was the son of Enos,
38 *w'* was the son of Seth,
38 *w'* was the son of Adam,
38 *w'* was the son of God.
4:22 *w'* proceeded out of his mouth.
33 man, *w'* had a spirit of an unclean
5: 3 one of the ships, *w'* was Simon's,
7 *w'* were in the other ship,
9 of fishes *w'* they had taken:
10 Zebedee, *w'* were partners with
17 *w'* were come out of every town of
18 a man *w'* was taken with a palsy:
21 is this *w'* speaketh blasphemies?
6: 2 do ye that *w'* is not lawful to do on
3 hungred, and they *w'* were with
4 *w'* it is not lawful to eat but for the
8 man *w'* had the withered hand,
16 Judas Iscariot, *w'* also was the
17 *w'* came to hear him, and to be
27 I say unto you *w'* hear, Love your
27 do good to them *w'* hate you,
28 for them *w'* despitefully use you.
32 if ye love them *w'* love you, what
33 ye do good to them *w'* do good to you,

Lu 6:45 heart bringeth forth that *w'* is good;
45 heart bringeth forth that *w'* is evil:
46 and do not the things *w'* I say?
48 is like a man *w'* built a house, and
49 against *w'* the stream did beat
7:25 they *w'* are gorgeously apparelled,
27 *w'* shall prepare thy way before
37 woman in the city, *w'* was a
39 *w'* had bidden him saw it, he
41 a certain creditor *w'* had two debtors:
42 *w'* of them will love him most?
47 Her sins, *w'* are many, are
8: 2 *w'* had been healed of evil spirits
3 *w'* ministered unto him of their
13 *w'*, when they hear, receive the
13 no root, *w'* for a while, believe,
14 that *w'* fell among thorns are they,
14 *w'*, when they have heard, go forth,
15 *w'* in an honest and good heart,
16 they *w'* enter in may see the light.
18 even that *w'* he seemeth to have.
20 was told him by certain *w'* said, Thy
21 these *w'* hear the word of God,
26 *w'* is over against Galilee.
27 man *w'* had devils long time, and
36 They also *w'* saw it told them by what
43 *w'* had spent all her living upon
9:27 *w'* shall not taste of death, till
30 men, *w'* were Moses and Elias:
31 *w'* he should accomplish at
36 of those things *w'* they had seen.
43 every one at all things *w'* Jesus did,
46 *w'* of them should be greatest.
61 farewell, *w'* are at home at my house,
10:11 dust of your city, *w'* cleaveth on
13 Sidon, *w'* have been done in you,
15 *w'* art exalted to heaven, shalt
23 eyes *w'* see the things that ye see:
24 desired to see those things *w'* ye
24 to hear those things *w'* ye hear,
30 *w'* stripped him of his raiment,
36 *W'* now of these three, thinkest
39 *w'* also sat at Jesus' feet, and heard
42 *w'* shall not be taken away from
11: 2 Our Father *w'* art in heaven,
5 *W'* of you shall have a friend, and
27 and the paps *w'* thou hast sucked.
33 *w'* come in may see the light.
35 light *w'* is in thee be not darkness.
40 he, that made that *w'* is without
40 make that *w'* is within also?
44 ye are as graves *w'* appear not,
50 prophets, *w'* was shed from the
51 *w'* perished between the altar and
12: 1 the Pharisees, *w'* is hypocrisy.
3 *w'* ye have spoken in the ear, in
5 *w'* after he hath killed hath power
15 abundance of the things *w'* he
20 things be, *w'* thou hast provided?
24 *w'* neither have storehouse nor
25 And *w'* of you with taking thought
26 be not able to do that thing *w'* is least,
28 the grass, *w'* is to day in the field,
33 yourselves bags *w'* wax not old,
47 servant, *w'* knew his lord's will,
13:11 a woman *w'* had a spirit of infirmity
14 six days in *w'* men ought to work:
19 of mustard seed, *w'* a man took,
21 leaven, *w'* a woman took and hid
30 there are last *w'* shall be first;
30 and there are first *w'* shall be last.
34 Jerusalem, *w'* killest the prophets,
14: 2 man before him *w'* had the dropsy.
5 *W'* of you shall have an ass or an
7 a parable to those *w'* were bidden,
24 men *w'* were bidden shall taste
28 *w'* of you, intending to build a
15: 4 go after that *w'* is lost, until he find it?
6 have found my sheep *w'* was lost.
7 persons *w'* need no repentance.
9 have found the piece *w'* I had lost.
30 *w'* hath devoured thy living with
16: 1 rich man, *w'* had a steward;
10 is faithful in that *w'* is least is faithful
12 faithful in that *w'* is another man's,
12 shall give you that *w'* is your own?
19 man *w'* was clothed in purple and
20 Lazarus, *w'* was laid at his gate,
21 crumbs *w'* fell from the rich
26 they *w'* would pass from hence to you
17: 7 *w'* of you, having a servant
10 those things *w'* are commanded you,
10 done that *w'* was our duty to do.
12 that were lepers, *w'* stood afar off:
31 he *w'* shall be upon the housetop,
18: 2 a judge, *w'* feared not God, neither
7 own elect, *w'* cry day and night
9 certain *w'* trusted in themselves
27 things *w'* are impossible with men are
34 knew they the things *w'* were spoken.
39 they *w'* went before rebuked him,
19: 2 *w'* was the chief among the
10 to seek and to save that *w'* was lost.
20 *w'* I have kept laid up in a napkin:
26 every one *w'* hath shall be given;
27 *w'* would not that I should reign
30 in the *w'* at your entering ye shall
42 the things *w'* belong unto thy peace!
20:17 The stone *w'* the builders rejected,
20 *w'* should feign themselves just men,
25 unto Cæsar the things *w'* be Cæsar's,
25 and unto God the things *w'* be God's.
27 *w'* deny that there is any
35 they *w'* shall be accounted worthy to
46 *w'* desire to walk in long robes,
47 *W'* devour widows' houses, and

Lu 21: 6 As for these things *w'* ye behold,
6 in the *w'* there shall not be left one
15 *w'* all your adversaries shall not be
21 them *w'* are in Judæa flee to the
21 let them *w'* are in the midst of it
22 that all things *w'* are written
26 those things *w'* are coming on the
22: 1 drew nigh, *w'* is called the Passover.
19 is my body *w'* is given for you:
20 in my blood, *w'* is shed for you.
23 *w'* of them it was that should do
24 *w'* of them should be accounted
28 *w'* have continued with me in my
49 *w'* were about him saw what would
52 the elders, *w'* were come to him,
23: 27 *w'* also bewailed and lamented
29 in the *w'* they shall say, Blessed
29 and the paps *w'* never gave suck,
33 to the place *w'* is called Calvary,
39 malefactors *w'* were hanged railed on
48 beholding the things *w'* were done,
55 *w'* came with him from Galilee,
24: 1 the spices *w'* they had prepared,
10 *w'* told these things unto the
12 himself at that *w'* was come to pass.
13 *w'* was from Jerusalem about
14 of all these things *w'* had happened.
18 known the things *w'* are come to pass
19 *w'* was a prophet mighty in deed
21 he *w'* should have redeemed Israel:
22 *w'* were early at the sepulchre;
23 angels, *w'* said that he was alive.
24 *w'* were with us went to the sepulchre,
44 the words *w'* I spake unto you,
44 *w'* were written in the law of
Joh 1: 9 *w'* lighteth every man that cometh
13 *W'* were born, not of blood, nor of
18 *w'* is in the bosom of the Father,
24 *w* were sent were of the Pharisees.
29 *w'* taketh away the sin of the
30 a man *w'* is preferred before me:
33 he *w'* baptizeth with the Holy Ghost.
38 (*w'* is to say, being interpreted,
40 One of the two *w'* heard John
41 *w'* is, being interpreted, the Christ.
42 *w'* is by interpretation, A stone.
2: 9 servants *w'* drew the water knew;
10 well drunk then that *w'* is worse:
22 and the word *w'* Jesus had said.
23 they saw the miracles *w'* he did.
3: 6 That *w'* is born of the flesh is flesh;
6 that *w'* is born of the Spirit is spirit.
13 the Son of man *w'* is in heaven.
29 *w'* standeth and heareth him,
4: 5 city of Samaria, *w'* is called Sychar,
9 of me, *w'* am a woman of Samaria?
12 Jacob, *w'* gave us the well,
25 Messias cometh, *w'* is called
29 *w'* told me all things that ever I
39 *w'* testified, He told me all that ever I
53 in the *w'* Jesus said unto him,
5: 2 *w'* is called in the Hebrew tongue
5 *w'* had an infirmity thirty and eight
12 *w'* said unto thee, Take up thy
15 Jesus, *w'* had made him whole.
23 not the Father *w'* hath sent him.
28 in the *w'* all that are in the graves
30 will of the Father *w'* hath sent me.
32 witness *w'* he witnesseth of me is
36 works *w'* the Father hath given me
37 Father himself, *w'* hath sent me, hath
39 and they are they *w'* testify of me.
44 *w'* receive honour one of another, and
6: 1 of Galilee, *w'* is the sea of Tiberias.
2 miracles *w'* he did on them that
9 lad here, *w'* hath five barley loaves,
13 *w'* remained over and above unto
22 people *w'* stood on the other side
27 not for the meat *w'* perisheth, but
27 meat *w'* endureth unto everlasting
27 *w'* the Son of man shall give unto
33 is he *w'* cometh down from heaven,
39 the Father's will *w'* hath sent me,
39 all *w'* he hath given me I should lose
40 that every one *w'* seeth the Son,
41 bread *w'* came down from heaven.
44 except the Father *w'* hath sent me
46 save he *w'* is of God, he hath seen
50 bread *w'* cometh down from heaven,
51 bread *w'* came down from heaven:
51 *w* I will give for the life of the
58 bread *w'* came down from heaven:
7: 31 than these *w'* this man hath done?
39 *w'* they that believe on him should
8: 9 And they *w'* heard it, being convicted
26 those things *w'* I have heard of him.
31 to those Jews *w'* believed on him,
38 I speak that *w'* I have seen with
38 ye do that *w'* ye have seen with
40 the truth, *w'* I have heard of God:
46 *W'* of you convinceth me of sin?
53 our father Abraham, *w'* is dead?
9: 1 a man *w'* was blind from his birth.
7 (*w'* is by interpretation, Sent.)
8 *w'* before had seen him that he was
39 world, that they *w'* see not might see;
39 that they *w'* see might be made blind.
40 Pharisees *w'* were with him heard
10: 6 things they were *w'* he spake
16 sheep I have, *w'* are not of this fold:
29 My Father, *w'* gave them me, is
32 *w'* of those works do ye stone me?
11: 2 Mary *w'* anointed the Lord with
16 said Thomas, *w'* is called Didymus,
27 God, *w'* should come into the world.
31 Jews then *w'* were with her in the

Joh 11: 33 Jews also weeping *w'* came with her.
37 *w'* opened the eyes of the blind,
42 because of the people *w'* stand by I
45 many of the Jews *w'* came to Mary,
45 the things *w'* Jesus did, believed
12: 1 where Lazarus was *w'* had been
4 Simon's son, *w'* should betray him,
21 Philip, *w'* was of Bethsaida of Galilee,
38 *w'* he spake, Lord, who hath
49 but the Father *w'* sent me, he
13: 1 loved his own *w'* were in the world,
14: 24 the word *w'* ye hear is not mine,
24 mine, but the Father's *w'* sent me.
26 the Comforter, *w'* is the Holy Ghost,
15: 3 the word *w'* I have spoken unto
24 the works *w'* none other man did,
26 *w'* proceedeth from the Father,
17: 4 the work *w'* thou gavest me to do.
5 *w'* I had with thee before the world
6 men *w'* thou gavest me out of the
8 them the words *w'* thou gavest me;
9 for them *w'* thou hast given me;
20 *w'* shall believe on me through their
22 glory *w'* thou gavest me I have
24 my glory, *w'* thou hast given me:
18: 1 a garden, into the *w'* he entered,
2 Judas also, *w'* betrayed him, knew
5 *w'* betrayed him, stood with them.
9 might be fulfilled, *w'* he spake,
9 Of them *w'* thou gavest me have I
11 cup *w'* my Father hath given me,
14 he, *w'* gave counsel to the Jews,
16 *w'* was known unto the high priest,
21 ask them *w'* heard me, what I have
22 the officers *w'* stood by struck Jesus
32 *w'* he spake signifying what death
19: 17 *w'* is called in the Hebrew Golgotha:
24 *w'* saith, They parted my raiment
32 the other *w'* was crucified with him.
39 *w'* at the first came to Jesus by
20: 8 *w'* came first to the sepulchre,
16 him, Rabboni; *w'* is to say, Master.
30 *w'* are not written in this book:
21: 10 of the fish *w'* ye have now caught.
20 *w'* also leaned on his breast at
20 Lord, *w'* is he that betrayeth thee?
24 *w'* testifieth of these things,
25 many other things *w'* Jesus did,
25 *w'*, if they should be written every
Ac 1: 2 the day in *w'* he was taken up,
4 *w'*, saith he, ye have heard of me.
7 *w'* the Father hath put in his own
11 *W'* also said, Ye men of Galilee,
11 *w'* is taken up from you, into
12 *w'* is from Jerusalem a sabbath
16 *w'* the Holy Ghost by the mouth of
16 *w'* was guide to them that took
21 these men *w'* have companied with us
24 Lord, *w'* knowest the hearts of all men.
25 *w'* Judas by transgression fell, and
2: 7 not all these *w'* speak Galilæans?
16 *w'* was spoken by the prophet Joel;
22 *w'* God did by him in the midst of
33 forth this, *w'* ye now see and hear.
3: 2 the temple *w'* is called Beautiful,
10 he *w'* sat for alms at the Beautiful
10 at that *w'* had happened unto him.
11 as the lame man *w'* was healed held
16 the faith *w'* is by him hath given him
18 *w'* God before had shewed by the
20 *w'* before was preached unto you:
21 *w'* God hath spoken by the mouth
23 soul, *w'* will not hear that
25 covenant *w'* God made with our
4: 4 many of them *w'* heard the word
11 stone *w'* was set at nought of you
11 *w'* is become the head of the corner.
14 man *w'* was healed standing with
20 the things *w'* we have seen and
21 glorified God for that *w'* was done.
24 *w'* hast made heaven, and earth,
32 things *w'* he possessed was his own;
36 (*w'* is, being interpreted, The son
5: 9 feet of them *w'* have buried thy
16 them *w'* were vexed with unclean
17 (*w'* is the sect of the Sadducees,)
6: 9 *w'* is called the synagogue of the
10 and the spirit by *w'* he spake.
11 they suborned men, *w'* said, We have
13 set up false witnesses, *w'* said, This
14 the customs *w'* Moses delivered us.
7: 3 into the land *w'* I shall shew thee.
17 *w'* God had sworn to Abraham,
18 king arose, *w'* knew not Joseph.
20 In *w'* time Moses was born, and
34 of my people *w'* is in Egypt,
35 of the angel *w'* appeared to him in
37 *w'* said unto the children of Israel,
38 angel *w'* spake to him in the mount
40 *w'* brought us out of the land of
43 figures *w'* ye made to worship
45 *W'* also our fathers that came after
52 *W'* of the prophets have not your
52 slain them *w'* shewed before of the
8: 1 the church *w'* was at Jerusalem;
6 unto those things *w'* Philip spake,
6 and seeing the miracles *w'* he did.
9 *w'* beforetime in the same city used
13 the miracles and signs *w'* were done.
14 apostles *w'* were at Jerusalem
24 of these things *w'* ye have spoken
26 Jerusalem unto Gaza, *w'* is desert.
32 of the scripture *w'* he read was this,
9: 7 men *w'* journeyed with him stood
11 into the street *w'* is called Straight,
19 the disciples *w'* were at Damascus.

Ac 9: 21 them *w'* called on this name in
22 the Jews *w'* dwelt at Damascus,
30 *W'* when the brethren knew, they
32 to the saints *w'* dwelt at Lydda.
33 *w'* had kept his bed eight years,
36 *w'* by interpretation is called
36 works and almsdeeds *w'* she did.
39 and garments *w'* Dorcas made,
10: 2 *w'* gave much alms to the people, and
7 the angel *w'* spake unto Cornelius
17 vision *w'* he had seen should mean.
17 men *w'* were sent from Cornelius
18 Simon, *w'* was surnamed Peter,
21 to the men *w'* were sent unto him
36 word *w'* God sent unto the children
37 *w'* was published throughout all
37 after the baptism *w'* John
39 things *w'* he did both in the land
42 *w'* was ordained of God to be the
44 fell on all them *w'* heard the word.
45 *w'* believed were astonished,
47 *w'* have received the Holy Ghost
11: 6 the *w'* when I had fastened mine
13 *w'* stood and said unto him, Send men
19 they *w'* were scattered abroad upon
20 *w'*, when they were come to
22 the church *w'* was in Jerusalem:
28 *w'* came to pass in the days of
29 unto the brethren *w'* dwelt in Judæa:
30 *W'* also they did, and sent it to
12: 9 true *w'* was done by the angel;
10 *w'* opened to them of his own
13: 1 *w'* had been brought up with Herod
7 *W'* was with the deputy of the
27 the prophets *w'* are read every
31 of them *w'* came up with him from
32 the promise *w'* was made unto the
39 from *w'* ye could not be justified
40 you, *w'* is spoken of in the prophets;
41 work *w'* ye shall in no wise believe,
45 those things *w'* were spoken by Paul,
14: 3 *w'* gave testimony unto the word
13 of Jupiter, *w'* was before their city,
14 *W'* when the apostles, Barnabas and
15 the living God, *w'* made heaven,
26 God for the work *w'* they fulfilled.
15: 1 certain men *w'* came down from
5 the sect of the Pharisees *w'* believed,
8 And God, *w'* knoweth the hearts,
10 *w'* neither our fathers nor we
16 of David, *w'* is fallen down;
19 *w'* from among the Gentiles are
23 brethren *w'* are of the Gentiles in
24 certain *w'* went out from us have
29 from *w'* if ye keep yourselves, ye
31 *W'* when they had read, they rejoiced
16: 1 of a certain woman, *w'* was a Jewess,
2 *W'* was well reported of by the
3 Jews *w'* were in those quarters:
4 and elders *w'* were at Jerusalem.
12 *w'* is the chief city of that part of
13 unto the women *w'* resorted thither.
14 Thyatira, *w'* worshipped God, heard
14 the things *w'* were spoken of Paul.
16 *w'* brought her masters much gain
17 God, *w'* shew unto us the way of
17: 5 But the Jews *w'* believed not, moved
12 of honourable women *w'* were
21 strangers *w'* were there, spent
31 in the *w'* he will judge the world
34 among the *w'* was Dionysius the
18: 27 much *w'* had believed through grace:
19: 4 on him *w'* should come after him,
10 they *w'* dwelt in Asia heard the word
13 to call over them *w'* had evil spirits
14 and chief of the priests, *w'* did so.
19 of them also *w'* used curious arts
24 *w'* made silver shrines for Diana,
26 no gods, *w'* are made with hands:
31 chief of Asia, *w'* were his friends, sent
35 the image *w'* fell down from Jupiter?
37 *w'* are neither robbers of churches,
38 and the craftsmen *w'* are with him,
20: 19 *w'* befell me by the lying in wait
24 *w'* I have received of the Lord
28 *w'* the Holy Ghost hath made you
28 *w'* he hath purchased with his own
32 grace, *w'* is able to build you up,
32 among all them *w'* are sanctified.
38 most of all for the words *w'* he
21: 8 evangelist, *w'* was one of the seven;
9 daughters, virgins, *w'* did prophesy.
20 of Jews there are *w'* believe; and
21 the Jews *w'* are among the Gentiles
23 four men *w'* have a vow on them;
25 As touching the Gentiles *w'* believe,
27 the Jews *w'* were of Asia, when they
38 *w'* before these days madest an
39 I am a man *w'* am a Jew of Tarsus, a
22: 1 my defence *w'* I make now unto you.
3 a man *w'* am a Jew, born in Tarsus,
5 bring them *w'* were there bound unto
10 things *w'* are appointed for thee
12 report of all the Jews *w'* dwelt there,
29 *w'* should have examined him:
23: 13 forty *w'* had made this conspiracy.
21 *w'* have bound themselves with
24: 14 after the way *w'* they call heresy,
14 all things *w'* are written in the
15 *w'* they themselves also allow,
24 his wife Drusilla, *w'* was a Jewess,
25: 5 *w'* among you are able, go down
7 Jews *w'* came down from Jerusalem
7 Paul, *w'* they could not prove.
16 *w'* is accused have the accusers face
19 and of one Jesus, *w'* was dead, whom

Ac 25:24 all men *w·* are here present with
26: 3 and questions *w·* are among the Jews:
4 *w·* was at first among mine own
5 *W·* knew me from the beginning, if
7 *w·* promise our twelve tribes,
7 *w·* hope's sake, king Agrippa, I
10 *W·* thing I also did in Jerusalem:
13 me and them *w·* journeyed with me.
16 of these things *w·* thou hast seen,
16 in the *w·* I will appear unto thee;
18 among them *w·* are sanctified by
27: 8 a place *w·* is called The fair havens;
11 those things *w·* were spoken of by
12 *w·* is an haven of Crete, and lieth
16 a certain island *w·* is called Clauda,
17 *W·* when they had taken up, they
39 into the *w·* they were minded,
43 *w·* could swim should cast themselves
28: 9 *w·* had diseases in the island,
11 *w·* had wintered in the isle,
24 some believed the things *w·* were
31 those things *w·* concern the Lord
Ro 1: 2 (*W·* he had promised afore by his
3 *w·* was made of the seed of David
19 *w·* may be known of God is manifest
26 into that *w·* is against nature:
27 men working that *w·* is unseemly,
27 recompence of their error *w·* was
28 those things *w·* are not convenient;
32 *w·* commit such things are worthy of
2: 2 against them *w·* commit such things.
3 that judgest them *w·* do such things,
14 the Gentiles, *w·* have not the law,
15 *W·* shew the work of the law
19 a light of them *w·* are in darkness,
20 *w·* hast the form of knowledge and of
21 Thou therefore *w·* teachest
27 not uncircumcision *w·* is by nature,
28 he is not a Jew, *w·* is one outwardly;
28 *w·* is outward in the flesh:
29 But he is a Jew, *w·* is one inwardly;
3:22 *w·* is by faith of Jesus Christ unto all
26 justifier of him *w·* believeth in Jesus.
30 *w·* shall justify the circumcision
4:11 of the faith *w·* he had yet being
12 that faith...*w·* he had being yet
14 For if they *w·* are of the law be heirs,
16 seed; not to that only *w·* is of the law,
16 also *w·* is of the faith of Abraham;
17 things *w·* be not as though they were.
18 according to that *w·* was spoken,
5: 5 Holy Ghost *w·* is given unto us.
15 *w·* is by one man, Jesus Christ,
17 much more they *w·* receive abundance
6:17 form of doctrine *w·* was delivered
7: 2 For the woman *w·* hath an husband is
5 sins, *w·* were by the law, did work
10 *w·* was ordained to life, I found
13 that *w·* is good made death unto me?
13 death in me by that *w·* is good;
15 For that *w·* I do I allow not: for
16 If then I do that *w·* I would not, I
18 but how to perform that *w·* is good I
19 not: but the evil *w·* I would not,
23 law of sin *w·* is in my members.
8: 1 to them *w·* are in Christ Jesus,
18 the glory *w·* shall be revealed in
23 *w·* have the firstfruits of the Spirit,
26 with groanings *w·* cannot be uttered.
9: 6 are not all Israel, *w·* are of Israel:
8 They *w·* are the children of the flesh,
23 *w·* he had afore prepared unto
25 my people, *w·* were not my people;
25 and her beloved, *w·* was not beloved.
30 *w·* followed not...righteousness,
30 the righteousness *w·* is of faith.
31 Israel, *w·* followed after the law of
10: 5 the righteousness *w·* is of the law,
5 man *w·* doeth those things shall live
6 *w·* is of faith speaketh on this wise,
11: 2 away his people *w·* he foreknew.
7 not obtained that *w·* he seeketh
14 to emulation them *w·* are my flesh,
22 on them *w·* fell, severity; but toward
24 cut out of the olive tree *w·* is wild
24 *w·* be the natural branches, be graffed
12: 1 God, *w·* is your reasonable service.
9 dissimulation. Abhor that *w·* is evil;
9 cleave to that *w·* is good.
14 Bless them *w·* persecute you: bless,
13: 3 do that *w·* is good, and thou shalt
4 But if thou do that *w·* is evil, be
14: 3 and let not him *w·* eateth not judge
19 after the things *w·* make for peace,
22 in that thing *w·* he alloweth.
15:17 in those things *w·* pertain to God.
18 those things *w·* Christ hath not
22 *w·* cause also I have been much
26 poor saints *w·* are at Jerusalem.
31 service *w·* I have for Jerusalem
16: 1 you Phebe our sister, *w·* is a servant
1 of the church *w·* is at Cenchrea:
10 Salute them *w·* are of Aristobulus'
11 of Narcissus, *w·* are in the Lord.
12 Persis, *w·* laboured much in the
14 and the brethren *w·* are with them.
15 and all the saints *w·* are with them.
17 them *w·* cause divisions and offences
17 the doctrine *w·* ye have learned;
19 have you wise unto that *w·* is good,
25 *w·* was kept secret since the world
1Co 1: 2 the church of God *w·* is at Corinth,
4 the grace of God *w·* is given you by
11 by them *w·* are of the house of Chloe,
18 unto us *w·* are saved it is the power
24 them *w·* are called, both Jews and

1Co 1:27 confound the things *w·* are mighty;
28 things *w·* are despised, hath God
28 things *w·* are not, to bring to
2: 7 *w·* God ordained before the world
8 *W·* none of the princes of this
9 things *w·* God hath prepared for
11 the spirit of man *w·* is in him?
12 world, but the spirit *w·* is of God;
13 *W·* things also we spake, not in
13 the words *w·* man's wisdom teacheth,
13 but *w·* the Holy Ghost teacheth;
3:10 to the grace of God *w·* is given
11 that is laid, *w·* is Jesus Christ.
14 man's work abide *w·* he hath built
17 of God is holy, *w·* temple ye are.
4: 6 of men above that *w·* is written,
17 of my ways *w·* be in Christ,
19 the speech of them *w·* are puffed up,
6:16 that he *w·* is joined to a harlot is one
19 of the Holy Ghost *w·* is in you,
19 *w·* ye have of God, and ye are not
20 and in your spirit, *w·* are God's.
7:13 woman *w·* hath an husband that
35 upon you, but for that *w·* is comely,
8:10 man see thee *w·* hast knowledge
10 conscience of him *w·* is weak be
10 those things *w·* are offered to idols:
9:13 they *w·* minister about holy things
13 and they *w·* wait at the altar are
14 that they *w·* preach the gospel should
24 that they *w·* run in a race run all,
10:16 The cup of blessing *w·* we bless, is
16 bread *w·* we break, is it not
18 not they *w·* eat of the sacrifices
19 or that *w·* is offered in sacrifice to
20 that the things *w·* the Gentiles
30 of for that for *w·* I give thanks?
11:19 they *w·* are approved may be made
23 of the Lord that *w·* also I delivered
23 same night in *w·* he was betrayed,
24 this is my body, *w·* is broken for
12: 6 the same God *w·* worketh all in all.
22 of the body, *w·* seem to be more feeble,
23 *w·* we think to be less honourable,
24 honour to that part *w·* lacked:
13:10 But when that *w·* is perfect is come,
10 that *w·* is in part shall be done away.
14:22 believe not, but for them *w·* believe.
15: 1 the gospel *w·* I preached unto you,
1 *w·* also ye have received, and
2 *w·* also ye are saved, if ye keep in
3 first of all that *w·* I also received,
10 his grace *w·* was bestowed upon me
10 but the grace of God *w·* was with
18 also *w·* are fallen asleep in Christ are
27 *w·* did put all things under him.
29 they do *w·* are baptized for the dead,
31 *w·* I have in Christ Jesus our Lord,
36 fool, that *w·* thou sowest is not
37 And that *w·* thou sowest, thou
46 that was not first *w·* is spiritual,
46 but that *w·* is natural; and afterward
46 and afterward that *w·* is spiritual.
57 *w·* giveth us the victory through
16:17 that *w·* was lacking on your part they
2Co 1: 1 church of God *w·* is at Corinth,
1 all the saints *w·* are in all Achaia:
4 comfort them *w·* are in any trouble,
6 *w·* is effectual in the enduring of
6 same sufferings *w·* ye also suffer:
8 our trouble *w·* came to us in Asia,
9 but in God *w·* raiseth the dead:
21 Now he *w·* stablisheth us with you in
2: 2 the same *w·* is made sorry by me?
4 ye might know the love *w·* I have
6 this punishment, *w·* was inflicted
14 *w·* always causeth us to triumph in
17 not as many, *w·* corrupt the word of
3: 7 *w·* glory was to be done away:
10 *w·* was made glorious had no glory in
11 that *w·* is done away was glorious,
11 more that *w·* remaineth is glorious.
13 as Moses, *w·* put a vail over his face,
13 to the end of that *w·* is abolished:
14 *w·* vail is done away in Christ.
4: 4 the minds of them *w·* believe not,
11 we *w·* live are alway delivered
14 he *w·* raised up the Lord Jesus shall
16 For *w·* cause we faint not; but
17 affliction, *w·* is but for a moment,
18 we look not at the things *w·* are seen,
18 but at the things *w·* are not seen:
18 the things *w·* are seen are temporal;
18 things *w·* are not seen are eternal.
5: 2 with our house *w·* is from heaven:
12 them *w·* glory in appearance,
15 they *w·* live should not henceforth
15 unto him *w·* died for them, and rose
7:14 *w·* I made before Titus, is found a
8:11 performance also...of that *w·* ye have.
16 *w·* put the same earnest care into
19 *w·* is administered by us to the
20 abundance *w·* is administered by us:
22 great confidence *w·* I have in you.
9: 2 for *w·* I boast of you to them of
6 He *w·* soweth sparingly shall reap
11 *w·* causeth...us thanksgiving
14 *w·* long after you for the exceeding
10: 2 *w·* think of us as if we walked
8 *w·* the Lord hath given us for
13 rule *w·* God hath distributed to us,
11: 4 spirit, *w·* ye have not received,
4 gospel, *w·* ye have not accepted,
9 for that *w·* was lacking to me, the
9 brethren *w·* came from Macedonia
12 from them *w·* desire occasion;

2Co 11:17 That *w·* I speak, I speak it not
28 that *w·* cometh upon me daily, the
30 glory of the things *w·* concern mine
31 Christ, *w·* is blessed for evermore,
12: 4 *w·* it is not lawful for a man to
6 above that *w·* he seeth me to be,
21 bewail many *w·* have sinned
21 and lasciviousness *w·* they have
13: 2 to them *w·* heretofore have sinned,
3 *w·* to you-ward is not weak, but
7 that ye should do that *w·* is honest,
10 the power *w·* the Lord hath given
Ga 1: 2 And all the brethren *w·* are with me,
7 *W·* is not another; but there be
8 you than that *w·* we have preached
11 the gospel *w·* was preached of me
17 to them *w·* are apostles before me;
20 Now the things *w·* I write unto
22 of Judæa *w·* were in Christ:
23 he *w·* persecuted us in times past now
23 the faith *w·* once he destroyed.
2: 2 that gospel *w·* I preach among the
2 but privately to them *w·* were of
4 liberty *w·* we have in Christ Jesus,
10 same *w·* I also was forward to do.
12 them *w·* were of the circumcision.
18 again the things *w·* I destroyed,
20 the life *w·* I now live in the flesh I
3: 7 ye therefore that they *w·* are of faith,
9 So then they *w·* be of faith are
10 *w·* are written in the book of the
16 And to thy seed, *w·* is Christ.
17 *w·* was four hundred and thirty years
21 been a law given *w·* could have
4: 8 unto them *w·* by nature are no gods.
14 my temptation *w·* was in my flesh ye
24 *W·* things are an allegory: for
24 Sinai *w·* gendereth to bondage,
24 to bondage, *w·* is Agar.
25 answereth to Jerusalem, *w·* now
26 But Jerusalem *w·* is above is free,
26 is free, *w·* is the mother of us all.
27 more children than she *w·* hath an
5: 6 but faith *w·* worketh by love.
12 were even cut off *w·* trouble you.
19 manifest, *w·* are these; Adultery,
21 of the *w·* I tell you before, as I
21 *w·* do such things shall not inherit
6: 1 *w·* are spiritual, restore such an
Eph 1: 1 to the saints *w·* are at Ephesus,
9 good pleasure *w·* he hath
10 *w·* are in heaven, and *w·* are on
14 *W·* is the earnest of our
20 *W·* he wrought in Christ, when he
21 world, but also in that *w·* is to come:
23 *W·* is his body, the fulness of him
2:10 *w·* God hath before ordained that
11 *w·* is called the Circumcision in
17 peace to you *w·* were afar off,
3: 2 of God *w·* is given me to you-ward:
5 *W·* in other ages was not made
9 *w·* from the beginning of the
11 *w·* he purposed in Christ Jesus our
13 my tribulations for you, *w·* is your
19 love of Christ, *w·* passeth knowledge,
4:15 him in all things *w·* is the head,
16 by that *w·* every joint supplieth,
22 *w·* is corrupt according to the
24 man, *w·* after God is created in
28 with his hands the thing *w·* is good,
29 *w·* is good to the use of edifying,
5: 4 nor jesting, *w·* are not convenient:
12 things *w·* are done of them in secret.
6: 2 *w·* is the first commandment with
17 of the Spirit, *w·* is the word of God:
20 *w·* I am an ambassador in bonds:
Ph'p 1: 1 in Christ Jesus *w·* are at Philippi,
6 *w·* hath begun a good work in you
11 *w·* are by Jesus Christ, unto the
12 things *w·* happened unto me have
23 to be with Christ; *w·* is far better:
28 *w·* is to them an evident token of
30 the same conflict *w·* ye saw in me,
2: 5 you, *w·* was also in Christ Jesus:
9 a name *w·* is above every name:
13 it is God *w·* worketh in you both
21 not the things *w·* are Jesus Christ's.
3: 3 *w·* worship God in the spirit, and
6 the righteousness *w·* is in the law,
9 own righteousness *w·* is of the law,
9 but that *w·* is the faith of Christ,
9 righteousness *w·* is of God by faith:
12 that for *w·* also I am apprehended
13 forgetting those things *w·* are behind,
13 unto those things *w·* are before,
17 and mark them *w·* walk so as ye have
4: 3 women *w·* laboured with me in
7 God, *w·* passeth all understanding,
9 things *w·* ye have both learned
13 through Christ *w·* strengtheneth
18 the things *w·* were sent from you,
21 The brethren *w·* are with me greet
Col 1: 2 brethren in Christ *w·* are at Colosse:
4 love *w·* ye have to all the saints,
5 For the hope *w·* is laid up for you
6 *W·* is come unto you, as it is in all
12 *w·* hath made us meet to be
23 hope of the gospel, *w·* ye have heard,
23 *w·* was preached to every creature
23 to every creature *w·* is under heaven;
24 that *w·* is behind of the afflictions of
24 his body's sake, *w·* is the church:
25 of God *w·* is given to me for you,
26 Even the mystery *w·* hath been
27 *w·* is Christ in you, the hope of
29 *w·* worketh in me mightily.

Col 2:10 *w*· is the head of all principality
14 against us, *w*· was contrary to us,
17 *W*· are a shadow of things to
18 those things *w*· he hath not seen,
19 *w*· all the body by joints and bands
22 *W*· all are to perish with the using;)
23 *W*· things have indeed a shew of
3: 1 seek those things *w*· are above,
5 members *w*· are upon the earth;
5 and covetousness, *w*· is idolatry:
6 *w*· things' sake the wrath of God
7 the *w*· ye also walked some time,
10 *w*· is renewed in knowledge after
14 *w*· is the bond of perfectness.
15 *w*· also ye are called in one body;
25 for the wrong *w*· he hath done:
4: 1 unto your servants that *w*· is just and
3 Christ, for *w*· I am also in bonds:
9 you all things *w*· are done here.
11 Jesus, *w*· is called Justus, who are
11 *w*· have been a comfort unto me.
15 the brethren *w*· are in Laodicea,
15 and the church *w*· is in his house.
17 ministry *w*· thou hast received in
1Th 1: 1 *w*· is in God the Father, and in
10 *w*· delivered us from the wrath
2: 4 but God *w*· trieth our hearts.
13 the word of God *w*· ye heard of us, ye
13 *w*· effectually worketh also in you
14 God *w*· in Judæa are in Christ:
3:10 that *w*· is lacking in your faith?
4: 5 the Gentiles *w*· knew not God:
10 brethren *w*· are in all Macedonia:
13 concerning them *w*· are asleep,
13 even as others *w*· have no hope.
14 them also *w*· sleep in Jesus will God
15 *w*· are alive and remain unto the
15 not prevent them *w*· are asleep.
17 *w*· are alive and remain shall be
5:12 know them *w*· labour among you,
15 but ever follow that *w*· is good,
21 things; hold fast that *w*· is good.
2Th 1: 5 *W*· is a manifest token of the
5 of God, for *w*· ye also suffer:
2:15 traditions *w*· ye have been taught,
16 our Father, *w*· hath loved us,
3: 4 do the things *w*· we command you.
6 the tradition *w*· he received of us.
11 there are some *w*· walk among you
17 *w*· is the token in every epistle:
1Ti 1: 1 Lord Jesus Christ, *w*· is our hope;
4 endless genealogies, *w*· minister
4 than godly edifying *w*· is in faith:
6 From *w*· some having swerved
11 *w*· was committed to my trust.
14 faith and love *w*· is in Christ
16 to them *w*· should hereafter believe
18 prophecies *w*· went before on thee,
19 *w*· some having put away
2:10 (*w*· becometh women professing
3: 7 good report of them *w*· are without
13 in the faith *w*· is in Christ Jesus.
15 *w*· is the church of the living
4: 3 *w*· God hath created to be received
3 *w*· believe and know the truth.
8 now is, and of that *w*· is to come.
14 *w*· was given thee by prophecy,
5:13 speaking things *w*· they ought not.
6: 3 to the doctrine *w*· is according to
9 *w*· drown men in destruction and
10 *w*· while some coveted after, they
15 *W*· in his times he shall shew,
16 light *w*· no man can approach unto;
20 that *w*· is committed to thy trust,
subscr. *w*· is the chiefest city of
2Ti 1: 1 of life *w*· is in Christ Jesus,
5 *w*· dwelt first in thy grandmother,
6 *w*· is in thee by the putting on of
9 *w*· was given us in Christ Jesus
12 *w*· cause I also suffer these things:
12 *w*· I have committed unto him
13 words *w*· thou hast heard of me,
13 and love *w*· is in Christ Jesus.
14 thing *w*· was committed unto thee
14 the Holy Ghost *w*· dwelleth in us.
15 *w*· are in Asia be turned away
2:10 the salvation *w*· is in Christ Jesus
3: 6 sort are they *w*· creep into houses,
11 *w*· came unto me at Antioch,
14 thou in the things *w*· thou hast
15 *w*· are able to make thee wise
15 through faith *w*· is in Christ Jesus.
4: 8 *w*· the Lord, the righteous judge,
Tit 1: 1 the truth *w*· is after godliness;
2 *w*· God, that cannot lie, promised
3 *w*· is committed unto me
11 teaching things *w*· they ought not
2: 1 things *w*· become sound doctrine:
3: 5 righteousness *w*· we have done,
6 *W*· he shed on us abundantly
8 they *w*· have believed in God might be
Ph'm 5 *w*· thou hast toward the Lord
6 good thing *w*· is in you in Christ
8 enjoin thee that *w*· is convenient,
11 *W*· in time past was to thee
Heb 1: 5 *w*· of the angels said he at any
13 to *w*· of the angels said he at any
2: 1 to the things *w*· we have heard,
3 *w*· at the first began to be spoken
11 for *w*· cause he is not ashamed
13 children *w*· God hath given me.
3: 5 things *w*· were to be spoken after;
4: 3 we *w*· have believed do enter into
15 not an high priest *w*· cannot be
5: 8 by the things *w*· he suffered;
12 *w*· be the first principles of the

Heb 6: 7 earth *w*· drinketh in the rain that
8 that *w*· beareth thorns and briers
10 *w*· ye have shewed toward his
18 in *w*· it was impossible for God
19 *W*· hope we have as an anchor of
19 *w*· entereth into that within the veil:
7: 2 of Salem, *w*· is, King of peace;
13 of *w*· no man gave attendance at
14 of *w*· tribe Moses spake nothing
19 by the *w*· we draw nigh unto God.
28 men high priests *w*· have infirmity;
28 of the oath, *w*· was since the law,
8: 1 things *w*· we have spoken this is
2 the true tabernacle, *w*· the Lord
6 *w*· was established upon better
13 Now that *w*· decayeth and waxeth old
9: 2 the shewbread; *w*· is called the
3 the tabernacle *w*· is called the
4 *W*· had the golden censer, and the
5 seat; of *w*· we cannot now speak
9 *W*· was a figure for the time then
9 in *w*· were offered both gifts and
10 *W*· stood only in meats and
15 they *w*· are called might receive the
20 testament *w*· God hath enjoined
24 *w*· are the figures of the true;
10: 1 *w*· they offered year by year
8 *w*· are offered by the law;
10 By the *w*· will we are sanctified
11 sacrifices, *w*· can never take away
20 *w*· he hath consecrated for us,
27 *w*· shall devour the adversaries.
32 in *w*·, after ye were illuminated,
35 *w*· hath great recompense of
11: 3 things *w*· are seen were not made
3 were not made of things *w*· do appear.
4 by *w*· he obtained witness that he
7 by the *w*· he condemned the world,
7 of the righteousness *w*· is by faith.
8 place *w*· he should after receive
10 looked for a city *w*· hath foundations,
12 as the sand *w*· is by the sea shore
29 *w*· the Egyptians assaying to do
12: 1 the sin *w*· doth so easily beset us, and
5 *w*· speaketh unto you as unto
9 fathers of our flesh *w*· corrected us,
11 unto them *w*· are exercised thereby.
12 lift up the hands *w*· hang down, and
13 lest that *w*· is lame be turned out of
14 *w*· no man shall see the Lord:
19 words, *w*· voice they that had heard
20 not endure that *w*· was commanded,
23 firstborn, *w*· are written in heaven,
27 those things *w*· cannot be shaken may
28 a kingdom *w*· cannot be moved,
13: 3 and them *w*· suffer adversity, as being
7 Remember them *w*· have the rule over
9 *w*· have not profited them that
10 right to eat *w*· serve the tabernacle.
21 that *w*· is wellpleasing in his sight,
Jas 1: 1 twelve tribes *w*· are scattered
12 *w*· the Lord hath promised to them
21 word, *w*· is able to save your souls.
2: 5 *w*· he hath promised to them that
7 name by the *w*· ye are called?
16 things *w*· are needful to the body;
23 was fulfilled *w*· saith, Abraham
3: 4 the ships, *w*· though they be so great,
9 *w* are made after the similitude
5: 4 *w*· is of you kept back by fraud,
4 the cries of them *w*· have reaped are
11 we count them happy *w*· endure.
20 that he *w*· converteth the sinner from
1Pe 1: 3 *w*· according to his abundant
10 Of *w*· salvation the prophets have
11 Spirit of Christ *w*· was in them did
12 *w*· are now reported unto you by
12 *w*· things the angels desire to look
15 But as he *w*· hath called you is holy,
23 of God, *w*· liveth and abideth for ever.
25 word *w*· by the gospel is preached
2: 7 therefore *w*· believe he is precious:
7 but unto them *w*· be disobedient,
7 the stone *w*· the builders disallowed,
8 to them *w*· stumble at the word,
10 *W*· in time past were not a people,
10 *w*· had not obtained mercy, but
11 lusts, *w*· war against the soul;
12 your good works, *w*· they shall behold,
3: 4 heart, in that *w*· is not corruptible,
4 *w*· is in the sight of God of great
13 if ye be followers of that *w*· is good?
19 By *w*· also he went and preached
20 *W*· sometime were disobedient, when
4:11 as of the ability *w*· God giveth:
12 the fiery trial *w*· is to try you,
5: 1 The elders *w*· are among you I exhort,
2 the flock of God *w*· is among you,
2Pe 1:18 this voice *w*· came from heaven we
2:11 *w*· are greater in power and might,
15 *W*· have forsaken the right way, and
3: 1 in both *w*· I stir up your pure
2 of the words *w*· were spoken before
7 heavens and the earth, *w*· are now,
10 *w*· the heavens shall pass away
16 in *w*· are some things hard to be
16 *w*· they that are unlearned and
1Jo 1: 1 That *w*· was from the beginning,
1 *w*· we have heard, *w*· we have seen
1 *w*· we have looked upon, and our
2 life, *w*· was with the Father, and
3 That *w*· we have seen and heard
5 message *w*· we have heard of him
2: 7 *w*· ye had from the beginning.
7 the word *w*· ye have heard
8 *w*· thing is true in him and in you:

1Jo 2:24 in you, *w*· ye have heard from the
24 If that *w*· ye have heard from the
27 *w*· ye have received of him abideth
3:24 by the Spirit *w*· he hath given us.
5: 9 God, *w*· he hath testified of his Son.
16 sin a sin *w*· is not unto death,
2Jo 2 the truth's sake, *w*· dwelleth in us,
5 *w*· we had from the beginning,
8 those things *w*· we have wrought,
3Jo 6 *W*· have borne witness of thy
10 remember his deeds *w*· he doeth,
11 Beloved, follow not that *w*· is evil,
11 but that *w*· is good. He that doeth
Jude 3 faith *w*· was once delivered unto the
6 angels *w*· kept not their first estate,
10 evil of those things *w*· they know
15 *w*· they have ungodly committed,
15 *w*· ungodly sinners have spoken
17 the words *w*· were spoken before
Re 1: 1 *w*· God gave unto him, to shew
1 things *w*· must shortly come to
3 those things *w*· are written therein:
4 the seven churches *w*· are in Asia:
4 *w*· is, and *w*· was, and *w*· is to come;
4 the seven Spirits *w*· are before
7 and they also *w*· pierced him:
8 *w*· is, and *w*· was, and *w*· is to come,
11 the seven churches *w*· are in Asia;
19 Write the things *w*· thou hast seen,
19 hast seen, and the things *w*· are,
19 the things *w*· shall be hereafter;
20 *w*· thou sawest in my right hand,
20 *w*· thou sawest are the seven
2: 2 thou canst not bear them *w*· are evil:
2 tried them *w*· say they are apostles,
6 the Nicolaitanes, *w*· I also hate.
7 *w*· is in the midst of the paradise
8 first and the last, *w*· was dead, and,
9 of them *w*· say they are Jews,
10 those things *w*· thou shalt suffer:
12 saith he *w*· hath the sharp sword
15 the Nicolaitanes, *w*· thing I hate.
17 *w*· no man knoweth saving he that
20 Jezebel, *w*· calleth herself a
23 he *w*· searcheth the reins and
24 *w*· have not known the depths of
25 that *w*· ye have already hold fast till I
3: 2 and strengthen the things *w*· remain,
4 Sardis *w*· have not defiled their
9 *w*· say they are Jews, and are not,
10 *w*· shall come upon all the world,
11 hold that fast *w*· thou hast, that
12 of my God, *w*· is new Jerusalem,
12 *w*· cometh down out of heaven from
4: 1 first voice *w*· I heard was as it
1 *w*· said, Come up hither, and I will
1 thee things *w*· must be hereafter.
5 *w*· are the seven Spirits of God.
8 *w*· was, and is, and is to come.
5: 6 *w*· are the seven Spirits of God
8 odours, *w*· are the prayers of saints.
13 And every creature *w*· is in heaven,
6: 9 and for the testimony *w*· they held:
7: 4 the number of them *w*· were sealed:
9 *w*· no man could number, of all
10 God *w*· sitteth upon the throne,
13 *w*· are arrayed in white robes?
14 These are they *w*· came out of great
17 For the Lamb *w*· is in the midst of
8: 2 the seven angels *w*· stood before
3 golden altar *w*· was before the
4 *w*· came with the prayers of the
6 seven angels *w*· had the seven
9 of the creatures *w*· are in the sea,
13 three angels *w*· are yet to sound!
9: 4 men *w*· have not the seal of God
11 *w*· is the angel of the bottomless pit,
13 the golden altar *w*· is before God,
14 sixth angel *w*· had the trumpet,
14 *w*· are bound in the great river
15 *w*· are prepared for an hour, and a
18 *w*· issued out of their mouths.
20 rest of the men *w*· were not killed
20 *w*· neither can see, nor hear, nor
10: 4 things *w*· the seven thunders
5 the angel *w*· I saw stand upon the
6 sea, and the things *w*· are therein,
8 the voice *w*· I heard from heaven
8 book *w*· is open in the hand of the
8 angel *w*· standeth upon the sea
11: 2 the court *w*· is without the temple,
8 *w*· spiritually is called Sodom and
11 fear fell upon them *w*· saw them.
16 *w*· sat before God on their seats,
17 *w*· art, and wast, and art to come;
18 destroy them *w*· destroy the earth.
12: 4 *w*· was ready to be delivered,
9 *w*· deceiveth the whole world:
10 *w*· accused them before our God
13 *w*· brought forth the man child.
16 the flood *w*· the dragon cast out
17 *w*· keep the commandments of
13: 2 beast *w*· I saw was like unto a
4 dragon *w*· gave power unto the
12 and them *w*· dwell therein to worship
14 miracles *w*· he had power to do
14 *w*· had the wound by a sword,
14: 3 *w*· were redeemed from the earth.
4 These are they *w*· are not defiled
4 are they *w*· follow the Lamb
10 *w*· is poured out without mixture
13 the dead *w*· die in the Lord from
17 out of the temple *w*· is in heaven,
18 from the altar *w*· had power over fire;
16: 2 *w*· had the mark of the beast,
2 upon them *w*· worshipped his image.

Re 16: 5 O Lord, w· art, and wast, and
9 w· hath power over these plagues:
14 w· go forth unto the kings of the
17: 1 seven angels w· had the seven
7 w· hath the seven heads and ten
9 here is the mind w· hath wisdom.
9 on w· the woman sitteth.
12 ten horns w· thou sawest are
12 w· have received no kingdom as
15 The waters w· thou sawest, where
16 ten horns w· thou sawest upon
18 woman w· thou sawest is that
18 w· reigneth over the kings of the
18: 6 in the cup w· she hath filled fill
14 things w· were dainty and goodly
15 w· were made rich by her, shall
19: 2 w· did corrupt the earth with her
9 they w· are called unto the marriage
14 And the armies w· were in heaven
20 with w· he deceived them that
21 w· sword proceeded out of his
20: 2 that old serpent, w· is the Devil,
4 w· had not worshipped the beast,
8 nations w· are in the four quarters
12 opened, w· is the book of life:
12 those things w· were written in the
13 gave up the dead w· were in it;
13 up the dead w· were in them:
21: 8 in the lake w· burneth with fire
8 brimstone: w· is the second death.
9 seven angels w· had the seven
12 w· are the names of the twelve
24 them w· are saved shall walk in the
27 w· are written in the Lamb's book of
22: 2 life, w· bare twelve manner of fruits,
8 angel w· shewed me these things.
9 w· keep the sayings of this book:
11 and he w· is filthy, let him be filthy
19 the things w· are written in this book
20 He w· testifieth these things saith,

while^ See also WHILES; WHILST.
Ge 8:22 W· the earth remaineth, seedtime
19:16 w· he lingered, the men laid hold
25: 6 from Isaac his son, w· he yet lived,
29: 9 w· he yet spake with them, Rachel
45: 1 w· Joseph made himself known unto
46:29 and wept on his neck a good w·.
Ex 33:22 w· my glory passeth by, that I will
22 thee with my hand w· I pass by:
34:29 his face shone w· he talked with him.
Le 4:27 ignorance, w· he doeth somewhat
14:46 the house all the w· that it is shut up
Nu 11:33 w· the flesh was yet between their
15:32 w· the children of Israel were in the
23:15 offering, w· I meet the Lord yonder.
De 19: 6 pursue the slayer, w· his heart is
31:27 w· I am yet alive with you this day,
Jos 14:10 w· the children of Israel wandered
J'g 3:26 And Ehud escaped w· they tarried,
11:26 W· Israel dwelt in Heshbon and her
15: 1 a w· after, in the time of the wheat
16:27 that beheld w· Samson made sport.
1Sa 2:13 came w· the flesh was in seething,
7: 2 to pass, w· the ark abode in
9:27 but stand thou still a w·, that I
14:19 w· Saul talked unto the priest,
20:14 w· yet I live shew me the kindness
22: 4 the w· that David was in the hold.
25: 7 all the w· they were in Carmel.
16 w· we were with them keeping the
27:11 the w· he dwelleth in the country
2Sa 3: 6 w· there was war between the house
35 David to eat meat w· it was yet day,
7:19 house for a great w· to come.
12:18 w· the child was yet alive, we spake
21 weep for the child, w· it was alive;
22 W· the child was yet alive, I fasted
13:30 w· they were in the way, that tidings
15: 8 vow w· I abode at Geshur in Syria,
12 from Giloh, w· he offered sacrifices.
17: 2 upon him w· he is weary and weak
18:14 w· he was yet alive in the midst of
19:32 sustenance w· he lay at Mahanaim;
24:13 thine enemies, w· they pursue thee?
1Ki 1:14 w· thou yet talkest there with the
22 lo, w· she yet talked with the king,
42 w· he yet spake, behold, Jonathan
3:20 beside me, w· thine handmaid slept,
6: 7 in the house, w· it was in building.
11: 6 Solomon his father w· he yet lived,
17: 7 after a w·, that the brook dried
18:45 the mean w·, that the heaven was
2Ki 6:33 And w· he yet talked with them,
1Ch 12: 1 Ziklag, w· he yet kept himself close
17:17 servant's house for a great w· to come.
2Ch 10: 6 Solomon his father w· he yet lived,
14: 7 bars, w· the land is yet before us;
15: 2 Lord is with you, w· ye be with him;
26:19 w· he was wroth with the priests, the
34: 3 w· he was yet young, he began to
Ne 7: 3 w· they stand by, let them shut
Es 2:21 w· Mordecai sat in the king's gate, two
6:14 w· they were yet talking with him,
Job 1:16, 17, 18 W· he was yet speaking,
20:23 shall rain it upon him w· he is eating.
24:24 They are exalted for a little w·, but
27: 3 All the w· my breath is in me,
Ps 7: 2 in pieces, w· there is none to deliver.
31:13 w· they took counsel together against
37:10 yet a little w·, and the wicked shall
39: 1 bridle, w· the wicked is before me.
3 me, w· I was musing the fire burned:
42: 3 w· they continually say unto me,
10 w· they say daily unto me, Where is
49:18 Though w· he lived he blest his soul:
63: 4 Thus will I bless thee w· I live: I will

Ps 69: 3 mine eyes fail w· I wait for my God.
78:30 w· their meat was yet in their
88:15 w· I suffer thy terrors I am distracted.
104:33 to my God w· I have my being.
146: 2 W· I live will I praise the Lord: I
2 unto my God w· I have any being.
Pr 8:26 W· as yet he had not made the
19:18 Chasten thy son w· there is hope,
31:15 She riseth also w· it is yet night,
Ec 9: 3 madness is in their heart w· they live,
12: 1 w· the evil days come not, nor the
2 W· the sun or the light or the
Ca 1:12 W· the king sitteth at his table,
Isa 10:25 For yet a very little w·, and the
28: 4 w· it is yet in his hand he eateth it
29:17 Is it not yet a very little w·, and
55: 6 Seek ye the Lord w· he may be found,
6 call ye upon him w· he is near:
63:18 have possessed it but a little w·:
65:24 w· they are yet speaking, I will
Jer 13:16 w· ye look for light, he turn it into the
15: 9 is gone down w· it was yet day:
33: 1 w· he was yet shut up in the court
39:15 w· he was shut up in the court of the
40: 5 now w· he was not yet gone back,
51:33 yet a little w·, and the time of her
La 1:19 w· they sought their meat to
Eze 9: 8 to pass, w· they were slaying them,
Da 4:31 W· the word was in the king's
Ho 1: 4 for yet a little w·, and I will avenge
Na 1:10 For w· they be folden together as
10 w· they are drunken as drunkards,
Hag 2: 6 it is a little w·, and I will shake the
Zec 14:12 away w· they stand upon their feet,
M't 1:20 But w· he thought on these things,
9:18 W· he spake these things unto them,
12:46 W· he yet talked to the people,
13:21 in himself, but dureth for a w·:
25 w· men slept his enemy came
29 Nay; lest w· ye gather up the tares,
14:22 w· he sent the multitudes away.
17: 5 W· he yet spake, behold, a bright
22 And w· they abode in Galilee, Jesus
22:41 W· the Pharisees were gathered
25: 5 W· the bridegroom tarried they all
10 w· they went to buy, the bridegroom
26:36 ye here, w· I go and pray yonder.
47 w· he yet spake, lo, Judas, one of the
73 after a w· came unto him they that
27:63 deceiver said, w· he was yet alive,
28:13 and stole him away w· we slept.
M'r 1:35 rising up a great w· before day, he
2:19 w· the bridegroom is with
5:35 W· he yet spake, there came from the
6:31 into a desert place, and rest a w·:
45 w· he sent away the people.
12:35 and said, w· he taught in the temple,
14:32 Sit ye here, w· I shall pray.
43 w· he yet spake cometh Judas, one of
15:44 whether he had been any w· dead.
Lu 1: 8 w· he executed...priest's office
2: 6 w· they were there, the days were
5:34 w· the bridegroom is with
8:13 for a w· believe, and in time of
49 W· he yet spake, there cometh one
9:34 W· he thus spake, there came a cloud,
43 w· they wondered every one at all
10:13 they had a great w· ago repented,
14:32 w· the other is yet a great way off, he
18: 4 And he would not for a w·: but
22:47 w· he yet spake, behold a multitude,
58 And after a little w· another saw him,
60 w· he yet spake, the cock crew.
24:15 w· they communed together
32 w· he talked with us by the way,
32 w· he opened to us the scriptures?
41 w· they yet believed not for joy, and
44 w· I was yet with you, that all things
51 w· he blessed them, he was
Joh 4:31 mean w· his disciples prayed him,
5: 7 but w· I am coming, another
7:33 Yet a little w· am I with you, and
9: 4 of him that sent me, w· it is day:
12:35 Yet a little w· is the light with you.
35 w· ye have the light, lest darkness
36 W· ye have light, believe in the
13:33 children, yet a little w· I am with you.
14:19 Yet a little w·, and the world seeth me
16:16 A little w·, and ye shall not see me:
16 again, a little w·, and ye shall see me.
17 A little w·, and ye shall not see me:
17 again, a little w·, and ye shall see me:
18 What is this that he saith, A little w·?
19 A little w·, and ye shall not see me:
19 again, a little w·, and ye shall see me?
17:12 W· I was with them in the world,
Ac 1: 9 w· they beheld, he was taken up;
10 w· they looked stedfastly toward
9:39 Dorcas made, w· she was with them.
10:10 but w· they made ready, he fell into a
17 w· Peter doubted in himself what
19 W· Peter thought on the vision, the
44 W· Peter yet spake these words, the
15: 7 that a good w· ago God made
17:16 w· Paul waited for them at Athens,
18:18 this tarried there yet a good w·,
19: 1 w· Apollos was at Corinth,
20:11 talked a long w·, even till break of
22:17 w· I prayed in the temple, I was in a
24:20 in me, w· I stood before the council,
25: 8 W· he answered for himself, neither
27:33 w· the day was coming on,
28: 6 but after they had looked a great w·,
Ro 2:15 their thoughts the mean w· accusing
5: 8 w· we were yet sinners, Christ died for
7: 3 So then if, w· her husband liveth, she

1Co 3: 4 For w· one saith, I am of Paul;
8:13 eat no flesh w· the world standeth,
16: 7 I trust to tarry a w· with you,
2Co 4:18 W· we look not at the things which
Ga 2:17 w· we seek to be justified by Christ,
1Ti 5: 6 in pleasure is dead w· she liveth.
6:10 which w· some coveted after, they
Heb 3:13 daily, w· it is called To day;
15 W· it is said, To day if ye will
9: 8 w· as the first tabernacle was yet
17 at all w· the testator liveth.
10:37 For yet a little w·, and he that
1Pe 3: 2 W· they behold your chaste
20 w· the ark was preparing, wherein
5:10 after that ye have suffered a w·,
2Pe 2:13 deceivings w· they feast with you;
19 W· they promise them liberty, they

whiles See also WHILE; WHILST.
Eze 21:29 W· they see vanity unto thee,
29 w· they divine a lie unto thee,
44:17 w· they minister in the gates of the
Da 5: 2 Belshazzar, w· he tasted the wine,
9:20 w· I was speaking and praying,
21 Yea, w· I was speaking in prayer,
Ho 7: 6 like an oven, w· they lie in wait:
M't 5:25 w· thou art in the way with
Ac 5: 4 W· it remained, was it not thine own?
2Co 9:13 W· by the experiment of this

whilst^ See also WHILE.
J'g 6:31 put to death w· it is yet morning:
Ne 6: 3 the work cease, w· I leave it,
Job 32:11 w· ye searched out what to say.
Ps 141:10 own nets, w· that I withal escape.
Jer 17: 2 W· their children remember their
2Co 5: 6 w· we are at home in the body, we are
7:15 w· he remembereth the obedience
Heb 10:33 w· ye were made a gazingstock both
33 w· ye became companions of them

whip See also WHIPS.
Pr 26: 3 A w· for the horse, a bridle for the
Na 3: 2 The noise of a w·, and the noise of

whips
1Ki 12:11 father hath chastised you with w·,
14 father also chastised you with w·,
2Ch 10:11, 14 my father chastised you with w·,

whirleth
Ec 1: 6 it w· about continually, and

whirlwind See also WHIRLWINDS.
2Ki 2: 1 up Elijah into heaven by a w·,
11 Elijah went up by a w· into heaven.
Job 37: 9 Out of the south cometh the w·:
38: 1 Lord answered Job out of the w·,
40: 6 the Lord unto Job out of the w·,
Ps 58: 9 shall take them away as with a w·,
Pr 1:27 your destruction cometh as a w·;
10:25 As the w· passeth, so is the wicked
Isa 5:28 flint, and their wheels like a w·:
17:13 like a rolling thing before the w·.
40:24 the w· shall take them away as
41:16 and the w· shall scatter them:
66:15 and with his chariots like a w·,
Jer 4:13 and his chariots shall be as a w·:
23:19 a w· of the Lord is gone forth in
19 forth in fury, even a grievous w·:
25:32 great w· shall be raised up from
30:23 w· of the Lord goeth forth with fury,
23 forth with fury, a continuing w·:
Eze 1: 4 a w· came out of the north, a
Da 11:40 shall come against him like a w·,
Ho 8: 7 wind, and they shall reap the w·:
13: 3 chaff that is driven with the w·
Am 1:14 a tempest in the day of the w·:
Na 1: 3 the Lord hath his way in the w·
Hab 3:14 came out as a w· to scatter me:
Zec 7:14 But I scattered them with a w·

whirlwinds
Isa 21: 1 As w· in the south pass through;
Zec 9:14 and shall go with w· of the south.

whisper See also WHISPERED; WHISPERINGS.
Ps 41: 7 All that hate me w· together
Isa 29: 4 and thy speech shall w· out of the

whispered
2Sa 12:19 David saw that his servants w·,

whisperer See also WHISPERERS.
Pr 16:28 and a w· separateth chief friends.

whisperers
Ro 1:29 debate, deceit, malignity; w·,

whisperings
2Co 12:20 w·, swellings, tumults:

whit
De 13:16 and all the spoil thereof every w·,
1Sa 3:18 And Samuel told him every w·,
Joh 7:23 I have made a man every w· whole
13:10 wash his feet, but is clean every w·:
2Co 11: 5 not a w· behind the very chiefest

white See also WHITED; WHITER.
Ge 30:35 every one that had some w· in it,
37 and pilled w· strakes in them, and
37 w· appear which was in the rods.
40:16 had three w· baskets on my head:
49:12 wine, and his teeth w· with milk.
Ex 16:31 and it was like coriander seed, w·;
Le 13: 3 the hair in the plague is turned w·,
4 If the bright spot be w· in the skin
4 the hair thereof be not turned w·;
10 if the rising be w· in the skin,
10 and it have turned the hair w·, and
13 hath the plague: it is all turned w·:
16 again, and be changed unto w·,

Le 13:17 if the plague be turned into w·;
19 place of a boil there be a w· rising,
19 or a bright spot, w·, and somewhat
20 and the hair thereof be turned w·;
21 there be no w· hairs therein, and
24 that burneth have a w· bright spot,
24 spot, somewhat reddish, or w·;
25 in the bright spot be turned w·,
26 there be no w· hair in the bright
38 bright spots, even w· bright spots;
39 skin of their flesh be darkish w·;
42 or bald forehead, a w· reddish sore;
43 rising of the sore be w· reddish in
Nu 12:10 Miriam became leprous, w· as snow:
J'g 5:10 Speak, ye that ride on w· asses,
2Ki 5:27 his presence a leper as w· as snow.
2Ch 5:12 brethren, being arrayed in w· linen,
Es 1: 6 Where were w·, green, and blue,
6 and blue, and w·, and black, marble.
8:15 king in royal apparel of blue and w·,
Job 6: 6 any taste in the w· of an egg?
Ps 68:14 in it, it was w· as snow in Salmon.
Ec 9: 8 Let thy garments be always w·;
Ca 5:10 My beloved is w· and ruddy, the
Isa 1:18 they shall be as w· as snow;
Eze 27:18 the wine of Helbon, and w· wool.
Da 7: 9 whose garment was w· as snow, and
11:35 to purge, and to make them w·,
12:10 shall be purified, and made w·, and
Joe 1: 7 the branches thereof are made w·.
Zec 1: 8 there red horses, speckled, and w·.
6: 3 And in the third chariot w· horses;
6 and the w· go forth after them;
M't 5:36 not make one hair w· or black.
17: 2 his raiment was w· as the light.
28: 3 and his raiment w· as snow:
M'r 9: 3 shining, exceeding w· as snow;
3 as no fuller on earth can w· them.
16: 5 side, clothed in a long w· garment;
Lu 9:29 his raiment was w· and glistering.
Joh 4:35 for they are w· already to harvest.
20:12 And seeth two angels in w· sitting,
Ac 1:10 two men stood by them in w·
Re 1:14 His head and his hairs were w· like
14 as w· as snow; and his eyes were as
2:17 will give him a w· stone, and in the
3: 4 and they shall walk with me in w·:
5 shall be clothed in w· raiment;
18 w· raiment, that thou mayest be
4: 4 sitting, clothed in w· raiment; and
6: 2 And I saw, and behold a w· horse:
11 w· robes were given unto every one
7: 9 clothed with w· robes, and palms
13 which are arrayed in w· robes?
14 made them w· in the blood of the
14:14 I looked, and behold a w· cloud,
15: 6 clothed in pure and w· linen,
19: 8 arrayed in fine linen, clean and w·:
11 opened and behold a w· horse;
14 followed him upon w· horses,
14 clothed in fine linen, w· and clean.
20:11 I saw a great w· throne, and him

whited
M't 23:27 for ye are like unto w· sepulchres,
Ac 23: 3 God shall smite thee, thou w· wall:

whiter
Ps 51: 7 me, and I shall be w· than snow.
La 4: 7 snow, they were w· than milk,

whither^ See also WHITHERSOEVER.
Ge 16: 8 camest thou? and w· wilt thou go?
20:13 every place w· we shall come,
28:15 thee in all places w· thou goest,
32:17 Whoso art thou? and w· goest thou?
37:30 child is not; and I, w· shall I go?
Ex 21:13 a place w· he shall flee.
34:12 inhabitants of the land w· thou
Le 18: 3 w· I bring you, shall ye not do:
20:22 w· I bring you to dwell therein,
Nu 13:27 unto the land w· thou sentest us,
15:18 into the land w· I bring you,
35:25 of his refuge, w· he was fled:
26 of his refuge, w· he was fled;
De 1:28 W· shall we go up? our brethren
3:21 unto all the kingdoms w· thou
4: 5 the land w· ye go to possess it.
14 w· ye go over to possess it.
27 w· the Lord shall lead you.
6: 1 the land w· ye go to possess it:
7: 1 land w· thou goest to possess
11: 8 the land, w· ye go to possess it;
10 w· thou goest in to possess it,
11 the land, w· ye go to possess it,
29 land w· thou goest to possess
12:29 w· thou goest to possess them,
21:14 then thou shalt let her go w· she will;
23:12 w· thou shalt go forth abroad:
20 land w· thou goest to possess
28:21 w· thou goest to possess it.
37 nations w· the Lord shall lead
63 land w· thou goest to possess
30: 1, 3 w· the Lord thy God hath
16 land w· thou goest to possess
18 w· thou passest over Jordan to
31:13 w· ye go over Jordan to possess
16 w· they go to be among them,
32:47 w· ye go over Jordan to possess
50 in the mount w· thou goest up,
Jos 2: 5 out: w· the men went I wot not:
J'g 19:17 W· goest thou? and whence comest
Ru 1:16 for w· thou goest, I will go:
1Sa 10:14 and to his servant, W· went ye?
27:10 W· have ye made a road to day?
2Sa 2: 1 And David said, W· shall I go up?
13:13 w· shall I cause my shame to go?
15:20 seeing I go w· I may, return
2Sa 17:18 in his court; w· they went down.
1Ki 2:36 and go not forth thence any w·.
42 out, and walkest abroad any w·,
8:47 the land w· they were carried
18:10 w· my lord hath not sent to
12 shall carry thee w· I know
21:18 w· he is gone down to possess
2Ki 5:25 he said, Thy servant went no w·.
2Ch 6:37 the land w· they are carried
38 w· they have carried them captives,
10: 2 w· he had fled from the presence of
Ne 2:16 And the rulers knew not w· I went,
Ps 122: 4 W· the tribes go up, the tribes of
139: 7 W· shall I go from thy spirit?
7 or w· shall I flee from thy presence?
Ec 9:10 in the grave, w· thou goest.
Ca 6: 1 W· is thy beloved gone, O thou
1 w· is thy beloved turned aside? that
Isa 20: 6 w· we flee for help to be
Jer 8: 3 places w· I have driven them,
15: 2 unto thee, W· shall we go forth?
16:15 lands w· he had driven them:
19:14 Tophet, w· the Lord had sent him
22:12 the place w· they have led him
23: 3 countries w· I have driven them,
8 countries w· I had driven them;
24: 9 all places w· I shall drive them.
29: 7 city w· I have caused you to be
14 the places w· I have driven you,
18 nations w· I have driven them:
30:11 nations w· I have driven them:
32:37 w· I have driven them in mine
40: 4 w· it seemeth good and convenient
45: 5 in all places w· thou goest.
46:28 nations w· I have driven thee:
49:36 nation w· the outcasts of Elam
Eze 1:12 w· the spirit was to go, they
4:13 Gentiles, w· I will drive them.
6: 9 nations w· they shall be carried
10:11 to the place w· the head looked
12:16 among the heathen w· they
29:13 people w· they were scattered:
36:20 unto the heathen, w· they went,
21, 22 the heathen, w· they went.
37:21 the heathen, w· they be gone,
47: 9 live w· the river cometh.
Da 9: 7 w· thou hast driven them,
Joe 3: 7 the place w· ye have sold them,
Zec 2: 2 Then said I, W· goest thou? And
5:10 me, W· do these bear the ephah?
Lu 10: 1 place, w· he himself would come.
24:28 nigh unto the village, w· they went:
Joh 3: 8 whence it cometh, and w· it goeth:
6:21 was at the land w· they went.
7:35 W· will he go, that we shall not
8:14 I know whence I came, and w· I go;
14 tell whence I come, and w· I go;
21 sins: w· I go, ye cannot come.
22 he saith, W· I go, ye cannot come.
12:35 darkness knoweth not w· he goeth.
13:33 Jews, W· I go, ye cannot come;
36 said unto him, Lord, w· goest thou?
36 W· I go, thou canst not follow me
14: 4 w· I go ye know, and the way ye
5 we know not w· thou goest; and
16: 5 of you asketh me, W· goest thou?
18:20 temple, w· the Jews always resort;
21:18 and walkedst w· thou wouldest:
18 carry thee w· thou wouldest not.
Heb 6:20 W· the forerunner is...entered,
11: 8 went out, not knowing w· he went.
1Jo 2:11 and knoweth not w· he goeth,

whithersoever
Jos 1: 7 mayest prosper w· thou goest.
9 God is with thee w· thou goest.
16 w· thou sendest us, we will 413,
J'g 2:15 W· they went out, the hand of
1Sa 14:47 w· he turned himself, he vexed
18: 5 David went out w· Saul sent him,
23:13 Keilah, and went w· they could go.
2Sa 7: 9 was with thee w· thou wentest,
8: 6, 14 preserved David w· he went.
1Ki 2: 3 w· thou turnest thyself:
8:44 w· thou shalt send them,
2Ki 18: 7 he prospered w· he went forth:
1Ch 17: 8 with thee w· thou hast walked,
18: 6, 13 preserved David w· he went.
Es 4: 3 w· the king's commandment
8:17 w· the king's commandment and his
Pr 17: 8 w· it turneth, it prospereth.
21: 1 he turneth it w· he will.
Eze 1:20 W· the spirit was to go, they
21:16 or on the left, w· thy face is set.
47: 9 w· the rivers...come,
M't 8:19 will follow thee w· thou goest.
M'r 6:56 And w· he entered, into
Lu 9:57 I will follow thee w· thou goest.
1Co 16: 6 me on my journey w· I go.
Jas 3: 4 helm, w· the governor listeth.
Re 14: 4 follow the Lamb w· he goeth.

who^ See also WHICH; WHOM; WHOSE; WHOSOEVER.
Ge 3:11 W· told thee that thou wast
14:12 brother's son, w· dwelt in Sodom,
21: 7 W· would have said unto
26 I wot not w· hath done this thing:
24:15 w· was born to Bethuel, son of
27:32 said unto him, W· art thou?
33 Isaac trembled...and said, W·?
30: 2 w· hath withheld from thee the
33: 5 and said, W· are those with thee?
35: 3 w· answered me in the day of my
36: 1 generations of Esau, w· is Edom.
19 are the sons of Esau, w· is Edom,
20 Seir, the Horite, w· inhabited the land;
Ge 36:35 w· smote Midian in the field of Moab,
42:30 The man, w· is the lord of the land,
43:22 tell w· put our money in our sacks.
48: 8 sons, and said, W· are these?
14 Ephraim's head, w· was...younger,
49: 9 old lion; w· shall rouse him up?
25 God of thy father, w· shall help thee;
25 w· shall bless thee with blessings of
Ex 2:14 W· made thee a prince and a judge
3:11 And Moses said unto God, W· am I,
4:11 him, W· hath made man's mouth?
11 or w· maketh the dumb, or deaf, or
28 words of the Lord w· had sent him,
5: 2 And Pharaoh said, W· is the Lord,
6:12 me, w· am of uncircumcised lips?
10: 8 God: but w· are they that shall go?
12:40 of Israel w· dwelt in Egypt, was
15:11 W· is like unto thee, O Lord,
11 w· is like thee, glorious in holiness,
18:10 w· hath delivered you out of the
10 w· hath delivered the people from
21: 8 w· hath betrothed her to himself,
32:26 said, W· is on the Lord's side?
Le 5: 8 w· shall offer that which is for the sin
12: 7 W· shall offer it before the Lord, and
27:12 as thou valuest it, w· art the priest,
Nu 6:21 law of the Nazarite w· hath vowed,
7: 2 w· were the princes of the tribes,
9: 6 w· were defiled by the dead body of
11: 4 said, W· shall give us flesh to eat?
18 saying, W· shall give us flesh to eat?
12: 7 so, w· is faithful in all mine house.
14:36 w· returned, and made all the
21:26 w· had fought against the former
23:10 W· can count the dust of Jacob,
24: 9 as a great lion: w· shall stir him up?
23 w· shall live when God doeth this!
25: 6 w· were weeping before the door
26: 9 w· strove against Moses and against
47 w· were fifty and three thousand and
63 w· numbered the children of Israel
27:21 w· shall ask council for him after the
31:27 war upon them, w· went out to battle,
De 1:33 W· went in the way before you, to
2:25 w· shall hear report of thee, and
4: 7 w· hath God so nigh unto them,
46 the Amorites, w· dwelt at Heshbon,
5: 3 w· are all of us here alive this day.
26 w· is there of all flesh, that hath
8:15 W· led thee through that great and
15 w· brought thee forth water out of the
16 W· fed thee in the wilderness with
9: 2 W· can stand before the children
21: 1 it be not known w· had slain him:
30:12 W· shall go up for us to heaven,
13 W· shall go over the sea for us,
33: 9 W· said unto his father and to his
26 w· rideth upon the heaven in thy help,
29 w· is like unto thee, O people
29 w· is the sword of thy excellency!
Jos 9: 8 W· are ye? and from whence
11: 8 the hand of Israel, w· smote them,
12: 2 of the Amorites, w· dwelt in Heshbon,
13:12 w· remained of the remnant of the
15:19 W· answered, Give me a blessing;
17:16 they w· are of Beth-shean and her
16 they w· are of the valley of Jezreel.
21:10 w· were of the children of Levi, had:
J'g 1: 1 W· shall go up for us against the
2: 7 w· had seen all the great works of
3: 9 up a deliverer...w· delivered them,
19 thee, O King: w· said, Keep silence.
6:29 another, W· hath done this thing?
35 w· also was gathered after him:
8:34 w· had delivered them out of the hands
9:28 Gaal...said, W· is Abimelech, and
28 w· is Shechem, that we shall
38 W· is Abimelech, that we should
11:39 w· did with her according to his vow
15: 6 said, W· hath done this?
17: 4 w· made thereof a graven image and a
5 one of his sons, w· became his priest.
7 a young man...w· was a Levite,
18: 2 w· when they came to mount
3 him, W· brought thee hither?
29 father, w· was born unto Israel:
19: 1 w· took to him a concubine out of
21: 5 W· is there among all the tribes
Ru 2: 3 w· was of the kindred of Elimelech.
20 w· hath not left off his kindness to
3: 9 And he said, W· art thou? And
16 said, W· art thou, my daughter?
1Sa 2:25 the Lord, w· shall intreat for him?
4: 8 w· shall deliver us out of the hand
6:20 W· is able to stand before this holy
10:19 w· himself saved you out of all
11:12 W· is he that said, Shall Saul
14:17 now and see w· is gone from us.
45 w· hath wrought this great
16:16 man, w· is a cunning player on an harp:
17:25 be, that the man w· killeth him,
26 for w· is this uncircumcised
18:18 David said unto Saul, W· am I?
20:10 to Jonathan, W· shall tell me?
22:14 w· is so faithful among all thy
23:22 is, and w· hath seen him there:
25:10 W· is David? and w· is the son of
26: 6 W· will go down with me to Saul to
9 for w· can stretch forth his hand
14 W· art thou that criest to the king?
15 and w· is like to thee in Israel?
30:23 w· hath preserved us, and delivered
24 w· will hearken unto you in this
2Sa 1: 8 And he said unto me, W· art thou?
4: 9 w· hath redeemed my soul out of
10 w· thought that I would have given

2Sa 6:20 w' uncovered himself to day in the
7:18 W' am I, O Lord God? and what is
10:18 the captain of their host, w' died there.
12:22 W' can tell whether God will be
16:10 W' shall then say, Wherefore hast
22: 4 the Lord, w' is worthy to be praised:
32 For w' is God, save the Lord?
32 and w' is a rock, save our God?
23: 1 and the man w' was raised up on high,
20 Benaiah...w' had done many acts,
1Ki 1:20, 27 w' shall sit on the throne of
2:24 and w' hath made me an house,
3: 9 for w' is able to judge this thy so
8:23 w' keepest covenant and mercy with
24 W' hast kept with thy servant
50 before them w' carried them captive,
9: 9 w' brought forth their fathers out
12: 2 Jeroboam...w' was yet in Egypt,
9 w' have spoken to me, saying,
18 Adoram, w' was over the tribute;
13:26 w' was disobedient unto the word of
14: 8 David, w' kept my commandments,
8 w' followed me with all his heart, to
14 w' shall cut off the house of
16 w' did sin, and w' made Israel to
17: 1 w' was of the inhabitants of Gilead,
19:19 w' was plowing with twelve yoke
20:14 he said, W' shall order the battle?
21:11 the nobles w' were the inhabitants
22:20 W' shall persuade Ahab, that he
52 of Nebat, w' made Israel to sin:
2Ki 4: 5 w' brought the vessels to her;
7:17 w' spake when the king came
9:31 Had Zimri peace, w' slew his master?
32 and said, W' is on my side? w'?
10: 9 slew him: but w' slew all these?
13 king of Judah, and said, W' are ye?"
29 of Nebat, w' made Israel to sin,
13: 6 Jeroboam, w' made Israel sin,
11 son of Nebat, w' made Israel to sin:
14:24 son of Nebat, w' made Israel to sin.
15: 9, 18, 24, 28 w' made Israel to sin.
17:36 w' brought you up out of the land of
18:35 W' are they among all the gods
23:15 son of Nebat, w' made Israel to sin,
16 w' proclaimed these words.
1Ch 2: 7 w' transgressed in the thing
22 w' had three and twenty cities in the
5: 8 w' dwelt in Aroer, even unto Nebo
10 the Hagarites, w' fell by their hand:
6:39 Asaph, w' stood on his right hand,
7:24 w' built Beth-horon the nether,
31 w' is the father of Birzavith.
8:13 w' were heads of the fathers of
13 w' drove away the inhabitants of
9: 1 w' were carried away to Babylon for
18 W' hitherto waited in the king's gate
31 w' was the firstborn of Shallum
33 w' remaining in the chambers were
11:10 w' strengthened themselves with him
12 w' was one of the three mighties.
22 Benaiah...w' had done many acts;
12:18 Amasai, w' was chief of the captains,
16:41 chosen, w' were expressed by name,
17:16 W' am I, O Lord God, and what is
19: 7 w' came and pitched before Medeba.
21:16 Israel, w' were clothed in sackcloth,
22: 9 to thee, w' shall be a man of rest;
24:28 Mahli came Eleazar, w' had no sons.
25: 1 w' should prophesy with harps,
3 Jeduthun, w' prophesied with a harp,
9 w' with his brethren and sons
27: 6 w' was mighty among the thirty,
29: 5 w' then is willing to consecrate
14 w' am I, and what is my people,
2Ch 1:10 for w' can judge this thy people,
2: 6 w' is able to build him an house,
6 w' am I then, that I should build
12 w' hath given to David the king a
6: 4 w' hath with his hands fulfilled that
8: 8 w' were left after them in the land,
10: 2 son of Nebat, w' was in Egypt,
17:16 w' willingly offered himself unto the
18:19 W' shall entice Ahab king of
19: 6 Lord, w' is with you in the judgment.
20: 7 w' didst drive out the inhabitants of
34 w' is mentioned in the book of
35 of Israel, w' did very wickedly:
22: 9 w' sought the Lord with all his
26: 1 Uzziah, w' was sixteen years old,
5 w' had understanding in the visions
28: 5 w' smote him with a great slaughter.
30: 7 w' therefore gave them up to
32: 4 together, w' stopped all the fountains,
14 W' was there among all the gods
31 w' sent unto him to enquire of the
34:26 w' sent you to enquire of the Lord,
35:21 w' is with me, that he destroy thee
36:13 w' had made him swear by God:
17 w' slew their young men with the
23 W' is there among you of all his
Ezr 1: 3 W' is there among you of all his
3:12 of the fathers, w' were ancient men,
5: 3 W' hath commanded you to
9 W' commanded you to build this
12 Chaldean, w' destroyed this house,
Ne 1:11 servants, w' desire to fear thy name:
3: 3 w' also laid the beams thereof,
6:10 of Mehetabeel, w' was shut up;
11 w' is there, that, being as I am,
7: 7 W' came with Zerubbabel, Jeshua,
9: 7 the God, w' didst choose Abram,
27 hand of their enemies, w' vexed them:
27 w' saved them out of the hand of their
32 God, w' keepest covenant and mercy,
13:26 like him, w' was beloved of his God,
Es 2: 6 W' had been carried away from
15 w' had taken her for his daughter,
22 w' told it unto Esther the queen;
4:11 the inner court, w' is not called,
14 w' knoweth whether thou art
6: 2 w' sought to lay hand on the king
4 the king said, W' is in the court?
7: 5 W' is he, and where is he, that
9 w' had spoken good for the king,
Job 3: 8 day, w' are ready to raise up their
15 gold, w' filled their houses with silver:
4: 2 but w' can withhold himself from
7 w' ever perished, being innocent?
5:10 W' giveth rain upon the earth, and
9: 4 w' hath hardened himself against
12 taketh away, w' can hinder him?
12 w' will say unto him, What doest
19 w' shall set me a time to plead?
24 thereof; if not, where, and w' is he?
11:10 together, then w' can hinder him?
12: 3 w' knoweth not such things as
4 w' calleth upon God, and he
9 W' knoweth not in all these that
13:19 W' is he that will plead with me?
14: 4 W' can bring a clean thing out of
16: 9 me in his wrath, w' hateth me:
17: 3 w' is he that will strike hands
15 as for my hope, w' shall see it?
21:31 W' shall declare his way to his
31 w' shall repay him what he hath
23:13 one mind, and w' can turn him?
24:25 so now, w' will make me a liar,
26:14 of his power w' can understand?
27: 2 w' hath taken away my judgment;
2 the Almighty, w' hath vexed my soul;
30: 4 W' cut up mallows by the bushes,
34: 7 w' drinketh up scorning like water?
13 W' hath given him a charge over
13 w' hath disposed the whole world?
29 w' then can make trouble?
29 his face, w' then can behold him?
35:10 maker, w' giveth songs in the night;
11 W' teacheth us more than the beasts
36:22 his power: w' teacheth like him?
23 W' hath enjoined him his way?
23 or w' can say, Thou hast wrought
38: 2 W' is this that darkeneth counsel
5 W' hath laid the measures thereof,
5 w' hath stretched the line upon it?
6 or w' laid the corner stone thereof,
8 Or w' shut up the sea with doors,
25 W' hath divided a watercourse
28 w' hath begotten the drops of dew?
29 of heaven, w' hath gendered it?
36 W' hath put wisdom in the inward
36 or w' hath given understanding to
37 W' can number the clouds in
37 w' can stay the bottles of heaven,
41 W' provideth for the raven his
39: 5 W' hath sent out the wild ass free?
5 w' hath loosed the bands of the
41:10 w' then is able to stand before me?
11 W' hath prevented me, that I
13 W' can discover the face of his
13 w' can come to him with his double
14 W' can open the doors of his face?
33 not his like, w' is made without fear.
42: 3 W' is he that hideth counsel
Ps 4: 6 say, W' will shew us any good?
6: 5 grave w' shall give thee thanks?
8: 1 w' hast set thy glory above the
12: 4 W' have said, With our tongue will
4 are our own: w' is lord over us?
14: 4 w' eat up my people as they eat
15: 1 w' shall abide in thy tabernacle?
1 w' shall dwell in thy holy hill?
16: 7 Lord, w' hath given me counsel:
17: 9 enemies, w' compass me about.
18: *title* w' spake unto the Lord the
3 the Lord, w' is worthy to be praised:
31 For w' is God save the Lord?
31 or w' is a rock save our God?
19:12 W' can understand his errors?
24: 3 W' shall ascend into the hill of the
3 w' shall stand in his holy place?
4 w' hath not lifted up his soul unto
8, 10 W' is this King of glory? The
34: *title* w' drove him away, and he departed.
35:10 say, Lord, w' is like unto thee,
37: 7 of him w' prospereth in his way,
7 the man w' bringeth wicked devices
42:11 w' is the health of my countenance,
43: 5 w' is the health of my countenance,
53: 4 w' eat up my people as they eat
59: 7 lips: for w', say they, doth hear?
60: 9 W' will bring me into the strong
9 city? w' will lead me into Edom?
64: 3 W' whet their tongue like a sword,
5 they say, W' shall see them?
65: 5 w' art the confidence of all the ends of
68:19 w' daily loadeth us with benefits,
71:19 high, w' hast done great things:
19 O God, w' is like unto thee!
72:18 w' only doeth wondrous things.
76: 7 w' may stand in thy sight when
77:13 w' is so great a God as our God?
78: 6 w' should arise and declare them to
83:12 W' said, Let us take to ourselves
84: 6 W' passing through the valley of
89: 6 w' in the heaven can be compared
6 w' among the sons of the mighty can
8 w' is a strong Lord like unto thee?
90:11 W' knoweth the power of thine
94:16 W' will rise up for me against the
16 w' will stand up for me against the
103: 3 W' forgiveth all thine iniquities;
Ps 103: 3 iniquities; w' healeth all thy diseases;
4 W' redeemeth thy life from
4 w' crowneth thee with lovingkindness
5 W' satisfieth thy mouth with good
104: 2 W' coverest thyself with light as with
2 w' stretchest out the heavens like a
3 W' layeth the beams of his chambers
3 w' maketh the clouds his chariot:
3 w' walketh upon the wings of the
4 W' maketh his angels spirits; his
5 W' laid the foundations of the earth,
105:17 Joseph, w' was sold for a servant:
106: 2 W' can utter the mighty acts of
2 w' can shew forth all his praise?
108:10 W' will bring me into the strong
10 city? w' will lead me into Edom?
11 not thou, O God, w' hast cast us off?
113: 5 W' is like unto the Lord our God,
5 Lord our God, w' dwelleth on high,
6 W' humbleth himself to behold the
119: 1 way, w' walk in the law of the Lord.
38 servant, w' is devoted to thy fear.
124: 1, 2 been the Lord w' was on our side,
6 w' hath not given us as a prey to their
8 the Lord, w' made heaven and earth.
130: 3 iniquities, O Lord, w' shall stand?
135: 8 W' smote the firstborn of Egypt, both
9 W' sent tokens and wonders into the
10 W' smote great nations, and slew
136: 4 To him w' alone doeth great wonders:
23 W' remembered us in our low estate:
25 W' giveth food to all flesh: for his
137: 7 w' said, Rase it, rase it, even to the
8 of Babylon, w' art to be destroyed;
140: 4 w' have purposed to overthrow my
144: 2 w' subdueth my people under me.
10 w' delivereth David his servant from
147: 8 W' covereth the heaven with clouds,
8 w' prepareth rain for the earth,
8 w' maketh grass to grow upon the
17 w' can stand before his cold?
Pr 2:13 W' leave the paths of uprightness, to
14 W' rejoice to do evil, and delight in
9:15 passengers w' go right on their ways:
18:14 a wounded spirit w' can bear?
20: 6 but a faithful man w' can find?
9 W' can say, I have made my heart
25 man w' devoureth that which is holy,
21:24 his name w' dealeth in proud wrath.
23:29 W' hath woe? w' hath sorrow?
29 w' hath contentions? w' hath
29 w' hath wounds without cause?
29 w' hath redness of eyes?
24:22 w' knoweth the ruin of them both?
26:18 As a mad man w' casteth firebrands,
27: 4 w' is able to stand before envy?
30: 4 W' hath ascended up into heaven,
4 w' hath gathered the wind in his
4 w' hath bound the waters in a
4 w' hath established all the ends of
9 thee, and say, W' is the Lord?
31:10 W' can find a virtuous woman?
Ec 2:25 w' can eat, or w' else can hasten
3:21 W' knoweth the spirit of man that
22 w' shall bring him to see what shall
4: 3 w' hath not seen the evil work
13 w' will no more be admonished.
6:12 w' knoweth what is good for man
7:13 for w' can make that straight,
24 exceeding deep, w' can find it out?
8: 1 W' is as the wise man? and
1 w' knoweth the interpretation of a
7 w' can tell him when it shall be?
10 w' had come and gone from the place
10:14 be after him, w' can tell him?
11: 5 the works of God w' maketh all.
12: 7 shall return unto God w' gave it.
Ca 3: 6 W' is this that cometh out of the
6:10 W' is she that looketh forth as the
8: 2 mother's house, w' would instruct me:
5 W' is this that cometh up from
Isa 1:12 w' hath required this at your
6: 8 shall I send, and w' will go for us?
14: 6 He w' smote the people in wrath
27 purposed, and w' shall disannul it?
27 out, and w' shall turn it back?
23: 8 W' hath taken this counsel against
24:18 w' fleeth from the noise of the fear
27: 4 w' would set the briers and thorns
29:15 W' seeth us? and w' knoweth us?
22 the Lord, w' redeemed Abraham,
33:14 W' among us shall dwell with the
14 w' among us shall dwell with
36:20 W' are they among all the gods of
37: 2 w' was over the household,
40:12 W' hath measured the waters in
13 W' hath directed the Spirit of the
14 w' instructed him, and taught him in
26 and behold w' hath created these
41: 2 W' raised up the righteous man
4 W' hath wrought and done it,
26 W' hath declared from the
42:19 W' is blind, but my servant? or
19 w' is blind as he that is perfect,
23 W' among you will give ear to
23 w' will hearken and hear for the time
24 W' gave Jacob for a spoil, and
43: 9 w' among them can declare this,
13 I will work, and w' shall let it?
44: 7 And w', as I, shall call, and shall
10 W' hath formed a god, or molten
45:21 w' hath declared this from ancient
21 w' hath told it from that time?
49:21 W' hath begotten me these,
50: 8 w' will contend with me? let us
8 w' is mine adversary? let him come

Isa 50: 9 *w'* is he that shall condemn me?
10 *W'* is among you that feareth the
51: 12 *w'* art thou, that thou shouldest be
19 thee; *w'* shall be sorry for thee?
53: 1 *W'* hath believed our report? and
8 *w'* shall declare his generation?
60: 8 *W'* are these that fly as a cloud,
63: 1 *W'* is this that cometh from Edom,
65: 16 That he *w'* blesseth himself in the
66: 8 *W'* hath heard such a thing?
8 *w'* hath seen such things? Shall
Jer 1: 16 *w'* have forsaken me, and have
2: 24 occasion *w'* can turn her away?
9: 12 *W'* is the wise man, that may
12 *w'* is he to whom the mouth of the
10: 7 *W'* should not fear thee, O king
15: 5 For *w'* shall have pity upon thee,
5 or *w'* shall bemoan thee?
5 or *w'* shall go aside to ask how thou
17: 9 desperately wicked: *w'* can know
18: 13 *w'* hath heard such things:
20: 1 *w'* was also chief governor in the
15 *w'* brought tidings to my father,
21: 13 *W'* shall come down against us?
13 *w'* shall enter into our habitations?
23: 18 *w'* hath stood in the counsel of the
18 *w'* hath marked his word, and
26: 20 *w'* prophesied against this city and
23 *w'* slew him with the sword, and cast
30: 21 *w'* is this that engaged his heart
36: 32 *w'* wrote therein from the mouth of
46: 7 *W'* is this that cometh up as a
49: 4 saying, *W'* shall come unto me?
19 and *w'* is a chosen man, that I may
19 *w'* is like me? and *w'* will appoint
19 *w'* is that shepherd that will stand
50: 44 and *w'* is a chosen man, that I may
44 *w'* is like me? and *w'* will appoint
44 *w'* is that shepherd that will stand
52: 25 *w'* mustered the people of the land;
La 2: 13 like the sea: *w'* can heal thee?
3: 37 *W'* is he that saith, and it cometh
Eze 10: 7 with linen: *w'* took it, and went out.
Da 1: 10 *w'* hath appointed your meat and
2: 23 *w'* hast given me wisdom and
3: 15 *w'* is that God that shall deliver
28 *w'* hath sent his angel, and
6: 27 *w'* hath delivered Daniel from the
Ho 3: 1 *w'* look to other gods, and love
7: 4 *w'* ceaseth from raising after he hath
14: 9 *W'* is wise, and he shall
Joe 2: 11 very terrible; and *w'* can abide it?
14 *W'* knoweth if he will return and
Am 1: 1 *w'* was among the herdmen of
3: 8 lion hath roared, *w'* will not fear?
8 hath spoken, *w'* can but prophesy?
10 *w'* store up violence and robbery in
5: 7 Ye *w'* turn judgment to wormwood,
Ob 3 *W'* shall bring me down to the
Jon 3: 9 *W'* can tell if God will turn and
Mic 5: 8 *w'*, if he go through, both treadeth
6: 9 the rod, and *w'* hath appointed it.
7: 18 *W'* is a God like unto thee, that
Na 1: 6 *W'* can stand before his
6 *w'* can abide in the fierceness of his
3: 7 is laid waste: *w'* will bemoan her?
Hab 2: 5 *w'* enlargeth his desire as hell,
Zep 3: 18 the solemn assembly, *w'* are of thee,
Hag 2: 3 *W'* is left among you that saw
Zec 4: 7 *W'* art thou, O great mountain?
10 *w'* hath despised the day of small
Mal 1: 10 *W'* is there even among you that
3: 2 But *w'* may abide the day of his
2 *w'* shall stand when he appeareth?
M't 1: 16 born Jesus, *w'* is called Christ.
3: 7 *w'* hath warned you to flee from
10: 2 first, Simon, *w'* is called Peter,
4 Judas Iscariot, *w'* also betrayed
11 enter, enquire *w'* in it is worthy;
12: 48 said unto him... *W'* is my mother?
48 and *w'* are my brethren?
13: 9, 43 *W'* hath ears to hear, let him
46 *W'*, when he had found one pearl
18: 1 *W'* is the greatest in the kingdom
19: 25 saying, *W'* then can be saved?
21: 10 city was moved, saying, *W'* is this?
23 and *w'* gave thee this authority?
24: 45 *W'* then is a faithful and wise
25: 14 *w'* called his own servants, and
26: 3 priest, *w'* was called Caiaphas,
68 Christ, *W'* is he that smote thee?
27: 57 *w'*...himself was Jesus' disciple:
M'r 1: 19 *w'* also were in the ship mending
24 I know thee *w'* thou art, the Holy
2: 7 *w'* can forgive sins but God only?
3: 33 *W'* is my mother, or my brethren?
4: 16 *w'*, when they have heard the
5: 3 *W'* had his dwelling among the
30 and said, *W'* touched my clothes?
31 and sayest thou, *W'* touched me?
9: 34 *w'* should be the greatest.
10: 26 themselves, *W'* then can be saved?
11: 28 *w'* gave thee this authority to do
13: 34 *w'* left his house, and gave authority
15: 7 *w'* had committed murder in the
21 one Simon a Cyrenian, *w'* passed by,
41 *W'* also, when he was in Galilee,
16: 3 *W'* shall roll us away the stone
Lu 1: 36 with her, *w'* was called barren.
3: 7 *w'* hath warned you to flee from
4: 34 I know thee *w'* thou art; the Holy
5: 12 *w'* seeing Jesus fell on his face,
21 saying, *W'* is this which speaketh
21 *W'* can forgive sins, but God alone?
7: 2 servant, *w'* was dear unto him,
39 *w'* and what manner of woman

Lu 7: 49 *W'* is this that forgiveth sins also?
8: 45 And Jesus said, *W'* touched me?
45 and sayest thou, *W'* touched me?
9: 9 but *w'* is this, of whom I hear such
31 *W'* appeared in glory, and spake
10: 22 no man knoweth *w'* the Son is,
22 and *w'* the Father is, but the Son,
29 Jesus, And *w'* is my neighbour?
12: 14 *w'* made me a judge or a divider
42 *W'* then is that faithful and wise
16: 11 *w'* will commit to your trust the
12 *w'* shall give you that which is your
14 the Pharisees also, *w'* were covetous,
18: 26 it said, *W'* then can be saved?
30 *W'* shall not receive manifold
19: 3 he sought to see Jesus *w'* he was;
20: 2 or *w'* is he that gave thee this
22: 64 Prophesy, *w'* is it that smote thee?
23: 7 *w'* himself also was at Jerusalem
19 (*W'* for a certain sedition made in
51 *w'* also himself waited for the
Joh 1: 19 to ask him, *W'* art thou?
22 said they unto them, *W'* art thou?
27 *w'* coming after me is preferred
4: 10 and *w'* it is that saith to thee,
5: 13 that was healed wist not *w'* it was:
6: 60 is an hard saying; *w'* can hear it?
64 *w'* they were that believed not,
64 and *w'* should betray him.
7: 20 a devil: *w'* goeth about to kill thee?
49 people *w'* knoweth not the law
8: 25 said they unto him, *W'* art thou?
9: 2 *w'* did sin, this man, or his parents,
19 son, *w'* ye say was born blind?
21 *w'* hath opened his eyes, we know
36 *W'* is he, Lord, that I might
12: 34 be lifted up? *w'* is this Son of man?
38 Lord, *w'* hath believed our report?
13: 11 he knew *w'* should betray him;
24 *w'* it should be of whom he spake.
25 saith unto him, Lord, *w'* is it?
18: 18 *w'* had made a fire of coals; for it was
21: 12 durst ask him, *W'* art thou?
Ac 1: 23 *w'* was surnamed Justus, and
3: 3 *W'* seeing Peter and John about
4: 25 *W'* by the mouth of thy servant
36 *w'* by the apostles was surnamed
5: 36 rose up Theudas,...*w'* was slain;
7: 27 *W'* made thee a ruler and a judge
35 *W'* made thee a ruler and a judge?
38 *w'* received the lively oracles to
46 *W'* found favour before God, and
53 *W'* have received the law by the
8: 15 *W'*, when they were come down,
27 *w'* had the charge of all her
33 *w'* shall declare his generation?
9: 5 And he said, *W'* art thou, Lord?
10: 32 *w'*, when he cometh, shall speak
38 *w'* went about doing good, and
41 *w'* did eat and drink with him
11: 14 *W'* shall tell thee words, whereby
17 *w'* believed on the Lord Jesus
23 *W'*, when he came, and had seen
13: 7 *w'* called for Barnabas and Saul,
9 Then Saul, (*w'* is also called Paul,)
31 *w'* are his witnesses unto the
43 *w'*, speaking to them, persuaded
14: 8 a cripple...*w'* never had walked:
9 *w'* stedfastly beholding him, and
16 *W'* in times past suffered all nations
19 *w'* persuaded the people, and,
15: 17 Lord, *w'* doeth all these things.
27 *w'* shall also tell you the same
38 *w'* departed from them from
16: 24 *W'*, having received such a
17: 10 *w'* coming thither went into the
18: 27 *w'*, when he was come, helped
19: 15 and Paul I know; but *w'* are ye?
21: 4 *w'* said to Paul through the
32 *W'* immediately took soldiers and
33 demanded *w'* he was, and what
37 *W'* said, Canst thou speak Greek?
22: 8 I answered, *W'* art thou, Lord?
23: 18 *w'* hath something to say unto thee.
33 *W'*, when they came to Cæsarea,
24: 1 *w'* informed the governor against
6 *W'* also hath gone about to
19 *W'* ought to have been here before
26: 15 And I said, *W'* art thou, Lord?
28: 7 *w'* received us, and lodged us
10 *W'* also honoured us with many
18 *W'*, when they had examined me,
Ro 1: 18 *w'* hold...truth in unrighteousness:
25 *W'* changed the truth of God into
25 the Creator, *w'* is blessed for ever.
32 *W'* knowing the judgment of God,
2: 6 *W'* will render to every man
7 To them *w'* by patient continuance
27 *w'* by the letter and circumcision
3: 5 unrighteous *w'* taketh vengeance?
19 it saith to them *w'* are under the law:
4: 12 *w'* are not of the circumcision
12 *w'* also walk in the steps of that
16 of Abraham; *w'* is father of us all,
17 God, *w'* quickeneth the dead,
18 *W'* against hope believed in hope,
25 *W'* was delivered for our offences,
5: 14 *w'* is the figure of him that is to
7: 4 to him *w'* is raised from the dead,
24 *w'* shall deliver me from the body
8: 1 *w'* walk not after the flesh, but after
4 *w'* walk not after the flesh, but after
20 *w'* hath subjected the same in hope;
28 *w'* are the called according to his
31 be for us, *w'* can be against us?
33 *W'* shall lay any thing to the

Ro 8: 34 *W'* is he that condemeth? **It is**
34 *w'* is even at the right hand of
34 *w'* also maketh intercession for **us.**
35 *W'* shall separate us from the
9: 4 *W'* are Israelites; to whom
5 *w'* is over all, God blessed for ever.
19 For *w'* hath resisted his will?
20 *w'* art thou that repliest against
10: 6 *W'* shall ascend into heaven?
7 Or, *W'* shall descend into the deep?
16 Lord, *w'* hath believed our report?
11: 4 *w'* have not bowed the knee to the
34 *w'* hath known the mind of the
34 or *w'* hath been his counsellor?
35 Or *w'* hath first given to him, and it
14: 2 another, *w'* is weak, eateth herbs.
4 *W'* art thou that judgest another
20 that man *w'* eateth with offence.
16: 4 *W'* have for my life laid down
5 *w'* is the firstfruits of Achaia unto
6 *w'* bestowed much labour on us.
7 *w'* are of note among the apostles,
7 *w'* also were in Christ before me.
12 Tryphosa, *w'* labour in the Lord.
22 I Tertius, *w'* wrote this epistle,
1Co 1: 8 *W'* shall also confirm you unto
30 *w'* of God is made unto us wisdom,
2: 16 *w'* hath known the mind of the
3: 5 *W'* then is Paul, and *w'* is Apollos,
4: 5 *w'* both will bring to light the
7 *w'* maketh thee to differ from
17 *w'* is my beloved son, and faithful
17 the Lord, *w'* shall bring you into
6: 4 to judge *w'* are least esteemed in the
9: 7 *W'* goeth a warfare any time at
7 *w'* planteth a vineyard, and eateth
7 *w'* feedeth a flock, and eateth not
10: 13 *w'* will not suffer you to be
14: 8 *w'*, shall prepare himself to the
2Co 1: 4 *W'* comforteth us in all our
10 *W'* delivered us from so great a
19 *w'* was preached among you by
22 *W'* hath also sealed us, and given
2: 2 *w'* is he then that maketh me
16 *w'* is sufficient for these things?
3: 6 *W'* also hath made us able
4: 4 *w'* is the image of God, should
6 *w'* commanded the light to shine
5: 5 *w'* also hath given unto us the
18 *w'* hath reconciled us to himself by
21 him to be sin for us, *w'* knew no sin;
8: 10 for you, *w'* have begun before,
19 *w'* was also chosen of the churches
10: 1 *w'* in presence am base among
11: 29 *W'* is weak, and I am not weak?
29 *w'* is offended, and I burn not?
Ga 1: 1 *w'* raised him from the dead;)
4 *W'* gave himself for our sins, that
15 *w'* separated me from my mother's
2: 3 neither Titus, *w'* was with me,
4 *w'* came in privily to spy out our
6 of these *w'* seemed to be somewhat,
6 for they *w'* seemed to be somewhat
9 and John, *w'* seemed to be pillars,
15 We *w'* are Jews by nature, and not
20 *w'* loved me, and gave himself for
3: 1 Galatians, *w'* hath bewitched you,
4: 23 he *w'* was of the bondwoman was born
5: 7 *w'* did hinder you that ye should
6: 10 them *w'* are of the household of faith,
13 they themselves *w'* are circumcised
Eph 1: 3 Jesus Christ, *w'* hath blessed us
11 purpose of him *w'* worketh all things
12 glory, *w'* first trusted in Christ.
19 of his power to us-ward *w'* believe,
2: 1 *w'* were dead in trespasses and sins.
4 But God, *w'* is rich in mercy, for his
11 *w'* are called Uncircumcision by
13 ye *w'* sometimes were far off are
14 our peace, *w'* hath made both
3: 8 *w'* am less than the least of all
9 *w'* created all things by Jesus
4: 6 and Father of all, *w'* is above all,
19 *W'* being past feeling have given
5: 5 covetous man, *w'* is an idolater,
Ph'p 2: 6 *W'*, being in the form of God,
20 *w'* will naturally care for your
3: 19 shame, *w'* mind earthly things.)
Col 1: 8 *W'* also declared unto us your love
13 *W'* hath delivered us from the
15 *W'* is the image of the invisible
18 *w'* is the beginning, the firstborn
24 *W'* now rejoice in my sufferings
2: 12 *w'* hath raised him from the dead.
3: 4 When Christ, *w'* is our life, shall
4: 7 *w'* is a beloved brother, and a
9 beloved brother, *w'* is one of you.
11 *w'* are of the circumcision.
12 Epaphras, *w'* is one of you, a
1Th 2: 15 *W'* both killed the Lord Jesus,
5: 8 But let us, *w'* are of the day, be sober.
10 *W'* died for us, that, whether we
24 that calleth you, *w'* also will do it.
2Th 1: 7 to you *w'* are troubled rest with us,
9 *W'* shall be punished with
2: 4 *W'* opposeth and exalteth himself
7 only he *w'* now letteth will let, until he
12 all might be damned *w'* believed
3: 3 *W'* shall stablish you, and keep
1Ti 1: 12 our Lord, *w'* hath enabled me,
13 *W'* was before a blasphemer, and
2: 4 *W'* will have all men to be saved,
6 *W'* gave himself a ransom for all,
4: 10 God, *w'* is the Saviour of all men,
5: 17 *w'* labour in the word and doctrine.
6: 13 of God, *w'* quickeneth all things,

1Ti 6:13 *w·* before Pontius Pilate witnessed
15 *w·* is the...only Potentate,
16 *W·* only hath immortality,
17 *w·* giveth us richly all things to
2Ti 1: 9 *W·* hath saved us, and called us
10 Christ, *w·* hath abolished death,
2: 2 *w·* shall be able to teach others
4 *w·* hath chosen him to be a soldier.
18 *W·* concerning the truth have
26 *w·* are taken captive by him at his
4: 1 *w·* shall judge the quick and the
Tit 1:11 *w·* subvert whole houses, teaching
2:14 *W·* gave himself for us, that he
Heb 1: 1 *W·* at sundry times and in divers
3 *W·* being the brightness of his
7 *W·* maketh his angels spirits,
14 them *w·* shall be heirs of salvation?
2: 9 *w·* was made a little lower than
11 sanctifieth and they *w·* are sanctified
15 them *w·* through fear of death
3: 2 *W·* was faithful to him that appointed
3 as he *w·* hath builded the house
5: 2 *W·* can have compassion on the
7 *W·* in the days of his flesh, when
14 *w·* by reason of use have their senses
6: 4 for those *w·* were once enlightened,
12 *w·* through faith and patience inherit
18 *w·* have fled for refuge to lay hold
7: 1 *w·* met Abraham returning from
5 Levi, *w·* receive the office of the
9 Levi also, *w·* receiveth tithes,
16 *W·* is made, not after the law of a
26 *w·* is holy, harmless, undefiled,
27 *W·* needeth not daily, as those
28 Son, *w·* is consecrated for evermore.
8: 1 *w·* is set on the right hand of the
5 *W·* serve unto the example and
9:14 *w·* through the eternal Spirit
10:29 *w·* hath trodden under foot the
39 of them *w·* draw back unto perdition;
11:11 judge him faithful *w·* had promised.
27 endured, as seeing him *w·* is invisible.
33 *W·* through faith subdued
12: 2 *w·* for the joy that was set before
16 *w·* for one morsel of meat sold his
25 *w·* refused him that spake on earth,
13: 7 *w·* have spoken unto you the word
Jas 3:13 *W·* is a wise man and endued
4:12 *w·* is able to save and to destroy:
12 destroy: *w·* art thou that judgest
5: 4 *w·* have reaped down your fields,
10 *w·* have spoken in the name of the
1Pe 1: 5 *W·* are kept by the power of God
10 *w·* prophesied of the grace that
17 *w·* without respect of persons
20 *W·* verily was foreordained before the
21 *W·* by him do believe in God, that
2: 9 *w·* hath called you out of darkness
22 *W·* did no sin, neither was guile
23 *W·*, when he was reviled, reviled
24 *W·* his own self bare our sins in
3: 5 women also, *w·* trusted in God,
13 *w·* is he that will harm you, if ye
22 *W·* is gone into heaven, and is on
4: 5 *W·* shall give account to him that
5: 1 *w·* am also an elder, and a witness
10 *w·* hath called us unto his eternal
2Pe 2: 1 *w·* privily shall bring in damnable
15 *w·* loved the wages of
18 escaped from them *w·* live in error.
1Jo 2:22 *W·* is a liar but he that denieth
3:12 as Cain, *w·* was of that wicked one,
4:21 he *w·* loveth God love his brother
5: 5 *W·* is he that overcometh the
2Jo 7 *w·* confess not that Jesus Christ
3Jo 9 *w·* loveth to have the preeminence
Jude 4 *w·* were before of old ordained to
18 *w·* should walk after their own
19 These be they *w·* separate themselves,
Re 1: 2 *W·* bare record of the word of
5 Christ, *w·* is the faithful witness,
9 John, *w·* am also your brother,
2: 1 *w·* walketh in the midst of the
13 martyr, *w·* was slain among you,
14 *w·* taught Balac to cast a
18 *w·* hath his eyes like unto a flame
4: 9 throne, *w·* liveth for ever and ever,
5: 2 *W·* is worthy to open the book,
6:17 and *w·* shall be able to stand?
12: 5 *w·* was to rule all nations with
13: 4 *W·* is like unto the beast?
4 *w·* is able to make war with him?
14:11 *w·* worship the beast and his
15: 4 *W·* shall not fear thee, O Lord,
7 God *w·* liveth for ever and ever.
18: 8 is the Lord God *w·* judgeth her.
9 *w·* have committed fornication

whole^ See also WHOLESOME.
Ge 2: 6 and watered the *w·* face of the
11 the *w·* land of Havilah,
13 the *w·* land of Ethiopia.
7:19 that were under the *w·* heaven,
8: 9 were on the face of the *w·* earth:
9:19 them was the *w·* earth overspread.
11: 1 the *w·* earth was of one language,
4 upon the face of the *w·* earth.
13: 9 Is not the *w·* land before thee?
47:28 the *w·* age of Jacob was an hundred
Ex 12: 6 *w·* assembly of the congregation
16: 2 the *w·* congregation of the children
3 to kill this *w·* assembly
10 the *w·* congregation of the children
19:18 and the *w·* mount quaked greatly.
29:18 thou shalt burn the *w·* ram
Le 3: 9 the fat thereof, and the *w·* rump,
4:12 Even the *w·* bullock shall he
Le 4:13 the *w·* congregation of Israel sin
7:14 offer one out of the *w·* oblation
8:21 and Moses burnt the *w·* ram
10: 6 the *w·* house of Israel, bewail the
25:29 may redeem it within a *w·* year
Nu 3: 7 charge of the *w·* congregation
8: 9 shalt gather the *w·* assembly
10: 2 of a *w·* piece shalt thou make
11:20 But even a *w·* month, until it
21 that they may eat a *w·* month,
14: 2 the *w·* congregation said unto
29 according to your *w·* number, from
20: 1 *w·* congregation, into the desert of
22 the *w·* congregation, journeyed
De 2:25 that are under the *w·* heaven,
4:19 all nations under the *w·* heaven.
27: 6 of the Lord thy God of *w·* stones:
29:23 the *w·* land thereof is brimstone,
33:10 *w·* burnt sacrifice upon thine
Jos 5: 8 in the camp, till they were *w·*.
8:31 an altar of *w·* stones, over which
10:13 not to go down about a *w·* day.
11:23 So Joshua took the *w·* land,
18: 1 *w·* congregation of the children of
22:12 *w·* congregation of the children of
16 the *w·* congregation of the Lord,
18 with the *w·* congregation of Israel.
J'g 19: 2 and was there four *w·* months.
21:13 *w·* congregation sent some to
2Sa 1: 9 because my life is yet *w·* in me.
3:19 good to the *w·* house of Benjamin.
6:19 among the *w·* multitude of Israel,
14: 7 *w·* family is risen against thine
1Ki 6:22 *w·* house be overlaid with gold,
22 the *w·* altar that was by the oracle
11:34 *w·* kingdom out of his hand.
2Ki 9: 8 the *w·* house of Ahab shall perish:
2Ch 6: 3 blessed the *w·* congregation of
15:15 sought him with their *w·* desire;
26:12 *w·* number of the chief of the fathers
30:23 *w·* assembly took counsel to keep
33: 8 according to the *w·* law and the
Ezr 2:64 *w·* congregation together was forty
Ne 7:66 *w·* congregation together was forty
Es 3: 6 the *w·* kingdom of Ahasuerus,
Job 5:18 woundeth, and his hands make *w·*.
28:24 and seeth under the *w·* heaven;
34:13 who hath disposed the *w·* world?
37: 3 directeth it under the *w·* heaven,
41:11 is under the *w·* heaven is mine.
Ps 9: 1 thee, O Lord, with my *w·* heart;
48: 2 joy of the *w·* earth, is mount Zion,
51:19 offering and *w·* burnt offering:
72:19 *w·* earth be filled with his glory;
97: 5 presence of the Lord of the *w·* earth.
105:16 he brake the *w·* staff of bread.
111: 1 praise the Lord with my *w·* heart,
119: 2 that seek him with the *w·* heart.
10 my *w·* heart have I sought thee:
34 shall observe it with my *w·* heart.
58 thy favour with my *w·* heart:
69 thy precepts with my *w·* heart.
145 I cried with my *w·* heart; hear me, O
Pr 1:12 *w·*, as those that go down into
16:33 the *w·* disposing thereof is of the
26:26 be shewed before the *w·* congregation.
Ec 12:13 the conclusion of the *w·* matter:
13 for this is the *w·* duty of man.
Isa 1: 5 *w·* head is sick, and the *w·* heart
3: 1 the staff, the *w·* stay of bread,
1 and the *w·* stay of water,
6: 3 the *w·* earth is full of his glory.
10:12 his *w·* work upon mount Zion
13: 5 indignation, to destroy the *w·* land.
14: 7 The *w·* earth is at rest, and is quiet:
26 is purposed upon the *w·* earth:
29 Rejoice not thou, *w·* Palestina,
31 thou, *w·* Palestina, art dissolved:
21: 8 I am set in my ward *w·* nights:
28:22 even determined upon the *w·* earth.
54: 5 God of the *w·* earth shall he be
Jer 1:18 brasen walls against the *w·* land,
4:20 cried; for the *w·* land is spoiled:
27 The *w·* land shall be desolate;
29 The *w·* city shall flee for the noise
7:15 even the *w·* seed of Ephraim.
8:16 the *w·* land trembled at the sound
12:11 the *w·* land is made desolate,
13:11 unto me the *w·* house of Israel
11 Israel and the *w·* house of Judah,
15:10 man of contention to the *w·* earth!
19:11 that cannot be made *w·* again:
24: 7 unto me with their *w·* heart.
25:11 this *w·* land shall be a desolation,
31:40 the *w·* valley of the dead bodies,
32:41 my *w·* heart and with my *w·* soul.
35: 3 the *w·* house of the Rechabites;
37:10 had smitten the *w·* army of the
45: 4 I will pluck up, even the *w·* land.
50:23 hammer of the *w·* earth cut asunder
51:41 praise of the *w·* earth surprised!
47 her *w·* land shall be confounded,
La 2:15 of beauty, The joy of the *w·* earth?
Eze 5:10 the *w·* remnant of thee will I
7:13 touching the *w·* multitude thereof,
10:12 their *w·* body, and their backs, and
15: 5 when it was *w·*, it was meet for no
32: 4 beasts of the *w·* earth with thee.
35:14 When the *w·* earth rejoiceth, I will
37:11 bones are the *w·* house of Israel:
39:25 mercy upon the *w·* house of Israel,
43:11 may keep the *w·* form thereof,
12 the *w·* limit thereof round about
45: 6 shall be for the *w·* house of Israel.
Da 2:35 mountain, and filled the *w·* earth.
48 him ruler over the *w·* province
Da 6: 1 should be over the *w·* kingdom;
3 to set him over the *w·* realm.
7:23 and shall devour the *w·* earth,
27 the kingdom under the *w·* heaven,
8: 5 west on the face of the *w·* earth,
9:12 for under the *w·* heaven hath not
10: 3 three *w·* weeks were fulfilled.
11:17 the strength of his *w·* kingdom,
Am 1: 6 away captive the *w·* captivity,
9 they delivered up the *w·* captivity
3: 1 against the *w·* family which I
Mic 4:13 unto the Lord of the *w·* earth.
Zep 1:18 *w·* land shall be devoured by the
Zec 4:10 to and fro through the *w·* earth.
14 stand by the Lord of the *w·* earth.
5: 3 forth over the face of the *w·* earth:
Mal 3: 9 robbed me, even the *w·* nation.
M't 5:29, 30 thy *w·* body should be cast into
6:22 thy *w·* body shall be full of light.
23 *w·* body shall be full of darkness.
8:32 the *w·* herd of swine ran violently
34 the *w·* city came out to meet Jesus:
9:12 that be *w·* need not a physician,
21 touch his garment, I shall be *w·*.
22 thy faith hath made thee *w·*.
22 woman was made *w·* from that
12:13 it was restored *w·*, like as the
13: 2 *w·* multitude stood on the shore.
33 of meal, till the *w·* was leavened.
14:36 as touched were made perfectly *w·*.
15:28 was made *w·* from that very hour.
31 the maimed to be *w·*, the lame to
16:26 if he shall gain the *w·* world, and
26:13 shall be preached in the *w·* world,
27:27 unto him the *w·* band of soldiers.
M'r 2:17 They that are *w·* have no need of
3: 5 hand was restored *w·* as the other.
4: 1 the *w·* multitude was by the sea
5:28 but his clothes, I shall be *w·*.
34 thy faith hath made thee *w·*;
34 peace, and be *w·* of thy plague.
6:55 ran through that *w·* region round
56 as touched him were made *w·*.
8:36 if he shall gain the *w·* world, and
10:52 way; thy faith hath made thee *w·*.
12:33 is more than all *w·* burnt offerings
14: 9 preached throughout the *w·*
15: 1 scribes and the *w·* council, and
16 and they call together the *w·* band.
33 was darkness over the *w·* land until
Lu 1:10 the *w·* multitude of the people
5:31 that are *w·* need not a physician;
6:10 hand was restored *w·* as the other.
19 *w·* multitude sought to touch him:
7:10 servant *w·* that had been sick.
8:37 the *w·* multitude of the country
39 published throughout the *w·* city
48 thy faith hath made thee *w·*; go in
50 only, and she shall be made *w·*.
9:25 if he gain the *w·* world, and lose
11:34 thy *w·* body also is full of light;
36 *w·* body therefore be full of light,
36 dark, the *w·* shall be full of light,
13:21 of meal, till the *w·* was leavened.
17:19 thy faith hath made thee *w·*.
19:37 *w·* multitude of the disciples began
21:35 dwell on the face of the *w·* earth.
23: 1 the *w·* multitude of them arose,
Joh 4:53 believed, and his *w·* house.
5: 4 *w·* of whatsoever disease he had.
6 unto him, Wilt thou be made *w·*?
9 immediately the man was made *w·*,
11 He that made me *w·*, the same said
14 him, Behold, thou art made *w·*:
15 was Jesus, which had made him *w·*.
7:23 every whit *w·* on the sabbath day?
11:50 and that the *w·* nation perish not.
Ac 4: 9 by what means he is made *w·*;
10 this man stand here before you *w·*.
6: 5 saying pleased the *w·* multitude:
9:34 Jesus Christ maketh thee *w·*:
11:26 that a *w·* year they assembled
13:44 came almost the *w·* city together
15:22 and elders, with the *w·* church,
19:29 *w·* city was filled with confusion:
28:30 two *w·* years in his own hired
Ro 1: 8 spoken of throughout the *w·* world.
8:22 that the *w·* creation groaneth
16:23 of the *w·* church, saluteth you.
1Co 5: 6 little leaven leaveneth the *w·* lump?
12:17 If the *w·* body were an eye,
17 If the *w·* were hearing,
14:23 *w·* church become together into one
Ga 5: 3 he is a debtor to do the *w·* law.
9 little leaven leaveneth the *w·* lump.
Eph 3:15 *w·* family in heaven and earth is
4:16 the *w·* body fitly joined together
6:11 Put on the *w·* armour of God, that ye
13 take unto you the *w·* armour of God,
1Th 5:23 your *w·* spirit and soul and body
Tit 1:11 who subvert *w·* houses, teaching
Jas 2:10 whosoever shall keep the *w·* law,
3: 2 able also to bridle the *w·* body.
3 and we turn about their *w·* body.
6 that it defileth the *w·* body, and
1Jo 2: 2 also for the sins of the *w·* world.
5:19 the *w·* world lieth in wickedness.
Re 12: 9 which deceiveth the *w·* world:
16:14 of the earth and of the *w·* world,

wholesome
Pr 15: 4 A *w·* tongue is a tree of life: but
1Ti 6: 3 and consent not to *w·* words, even

wholly
Le 6:22 the Lord; it shall be *w·* burnt.
23 offering...shall be *w·* burnt:

Le 19: 9 not w' reap the corners of thy field,
Nu 3: 9 they are w' given unto him out of
4: 6 spread over it a cloth w' of blue,
8: 16 For they are w' given unto me from
32: 11 they have not w' followed me:
12 they have w' followed the Lord.
De 1: 36 he hath w' followed the Lord.
Jos 14: 8 I w' followed the Lord my God.
9 hast w' followed the Lord my God.
14 that he w' followed the Lord God
J'g 17: 3 w' dedicated the silver unto the
1Sa 7: 9 a burnt offering w' unto the Lord:
1Ch 28: 21 people...w' at thy commandment.
Job 21: 23 full strength, being w' at ease and
Isa 22: 1 art w' gone up to the housetops?
Jer 2: 21 thee a noble vine, w' a right seed:
6: 6 is w' oppression in the midst of her.
13: 19 it shall be w' carried away captive.
42: 15 ye w' set your faces to enter into
46: 28 I not leave thee w' unpunished.
50: 13 but it shall be w' desolate:
Eze 11: 15 and all the house of Israel w',
Am 8: 8 and it shall rise up w' as a flood;
9: 5 and it shall rise up w' like a flood;
Ac 17: 16 he saw the city w' given to idolatry.
1Th 5: 23 very God of peace sanctify you w';
1Ti 4: 15 give thyself w' to them; that

whom^ See also WHOMSOEVER.
Ge 2: 8 he put the man w' he had formed.
3: 12 The woman w' thou gavest to be
4: 25 seed instead of Abel, w' Cain slew.
6: 7 will destroy man w' I have created
10: 14 (out of w' came Philistim,) and
15: 14 w' they shall serve, will I judge:
21: 3 him, w' Sarah bare to him, Isaac.
24: 40 before w' I walk, will send his angel
25: 12 w' Hagar the Egyptian, Sarah's
30: 26 children, for w' I have served thee,
41: 38 is, a man in w' the Spirit of God is?
43: 27 well, the old man of w' ye spake?
29 younger brother, of w' ye spake
44: 10 w' it is found shall be my servant:
16 he also with w' the cup is found.
45: 4 your brother, w' ye sold into Egypt.
46: 18 w' Laban gave to Leah his daughter,
48: 9 w' God hath given me in this place.
15 w' my fathers Abraham and Isaac
49: 8 art he w' thy brethren shall praise:
Ex 4: 13 by the hand of him w' thou wilt send.
6: 5 w' the Egyptians keep in bondage;
26 and Moses, to w' the Lord said,
14: 13 Egyptians w' ye have seen to day,
18: 9 w' he had delivered out of the land
22: 9 w' the judges shall condemn, he
23: 27 the people to w' thou shalt come,
28: 3 w' I have filled with the spirit of
32: 13 w' thou swarest by thine own self,
33: 12 know w' thou wilt send with me.
19 gracious to w' I will be gracious,
19 mercy on w' I will shew mercy.
35: 21 every one w' his spirit made willing,
23 every man, with w' was found blue,
24 with w' was found shittim wood
36: 1 in w' the Lord put wisdom
Le 6: 5 it unto him to w' it appertaineth,
13: 45 And the leper in w' the plague is,
14: 32 him in w' is the plague of leprosy,
15: 18 woman also with w' man shall lie
16: 32 And the priest, w' he shall anoint,
32 w' he shall consecrate to minister
17: 7 after w' they have gone a
22: 5 of w' he may take uncleanness,
25: 27 unto the man to w' he sold it;
55 my servants w' I brought forth
26: 45 w' I brought forth out of the
27: 24 unto him of w' it was bought,
24 w'...possession of the land...belong.
Nu 3: 3 w' he consecrated to minister in
4: 41 w' Moses and Aaron did number
45 w' Moses and Aaron numbered
46 w' Moses and Aaron and the chief of
5: 7 him against w' he hath trespassed,
11: 16 w' thou knowest to be the elders of
21 The people, among w' I am, are six
12: 1 woman w' he had married:
12 of w' the flesh is half consumed when
16: 5 even him w' he hath chosen will
7 the man w' the Lord doth choose,
17: 5 w' I shall choose, shall blossom:
22: 6 that he w' thou blessest is blessed,
6 and he w' thou cursest is cursed.
23: 8 shall I curse, w' God hath not cursed?
8 I defy, w' the Lord hath not defiled?
26: 5 of w' cometh the family of the
64 w' Moses and Aaron the priest
27: 18 of Nun, a man in w' is the spirit,
34: 29 are they w' the Lord commanded to
36: 6 Let them marry to w' they think best;
De 4: 46 w' Moses and the children of Israel
7: 19 people of w' thou art afraid.
9: 2 of the Anakims, w' thou knowest,
2 and of w' thou hast heard say,
17: 15 w' the Lord thy God shall choose:
19: 4 w' he hated not in time past;
17 between w' the controversy is,
21: 8 Israel, w' thou hast redeemed,
24: 11 man to w' thou dost lend shall bring
28: 55 flesh of his children w' he shall eat:
29: 26 them, gods w' they knew not,
26 and w' he had not given unto them:
31: 4 land of them, w' he destroyed.
32: 17 to gods w' they knew not, to new gods
17 newly up, w' your fathers feared not.
20 generation, children in w' is no faith.
37 gods, their rock in w' they trusted,

De 33: 8 one, w' thou didst prove at Massah,
8 with w' thou didst strive at the waters
34: 10 w' the Lord knew face to face,
Jos 2: 10 and Og, w' ye utterly destroyed.
4: 4 w' he had prepared of the children
5: 6 w' the Lord sware that he
7 w' he raised up in their stead,
10: 11 w' the children of Israel slew with
25 enemies against w' ye fight.
13: 8 With w' the Reubenites and the
21 w' Moses smote with the princes
24: 15 you this day w' ye will serve;
17 the people through w' we passed:
J'g 4: 22 shew thee the man w' thou seekest.
7: 4 shall be, that of w' I say unto thee,
8: 15 with w' ye did upbraid me, saying,
18 men were they w' ye slew at Tabor?
12: 9 thirty daughters, w' he sent abroad,
14: 20 w' he had used as his friend.
21: 23 them that danced, w' they caught:
Ru 2: 19 with w' she had wrought, and
19 w' I wrought to day is Boaz.
4: 1 kinsman of w' Boaz spake came by;
1 unto w' he said, Ho, such a one!
12 w' Tamar bare unto Judah, of the
1Sa 2: 33 w' I shall not cut off from mine altar,
6: 20 and to w' shall he go up from us?
9: 17 Behold the man w' I spake to thee
20 on w' is all the desire of Israel?
10: 24 See ye him w' the Lord hath
12: 3 I taken? or w' have I defrauded?
3 w' have I oppressed? or of whose
13 the king w' ye have chosen,
13 chosen, and w' ye have desired!
16: 3 unto me him w' I name unto thee.
17: 28 w' hast thou left those few sheep
45 of Israel, w' thou hast defied.
21: 9 w' thou slewest in the valley of
24: 14 After w' is the king of Israel come
14 after w' dost thou pursue? after a
25: 11 w' I know not whence they be?
25 men of my lord, w' thou didst send.
28: 8 up, w' I shall name unto thee.
11 W' shall I bring up unto thee?
29: 5 of w' they sang one to another
30: 13 unto him, To w' belongest thou?
21 w' they had made also to abide at the
2Sa 7: 7 w' I commanded to feed my people
15 Saul, w' I put away before thee.
23 w' God went to redeem for a people
14: 7 the life of his brother w' he slew;
15: 33 Unto w' David said, If thou passest
16: 18 but w' the Lord, and this people,
19 And again, w' should I serve?
17: 3 man w' thou seekest is as if all
19: 10 Absalom, w' we anointed over us,
20: 3 w' he had left to keep the house, and
21: 6 of Saul, w' the Lord did choose.
8 w' she bare unto Saul, Armoni and
8 w' she brought up for Adriel the son
23: 8 of the mighty men w' David had:
8 hundred, w' he slew at one time.
1Ki 2: 5 Amasa the son of Jether, w' he slew,
5: 5 son, w' I will set upon thy throne
7: 8 daughter, w' he had taken to wife,
9: 21 w' the children of Israel also were not
10: 26 w' he bestowed in the cities for
11: 20 w' Tahpenes weaned in Pharaoh's
34 w' I chose, because he kept my
13: 23 prophet w' he had brought back.
17: 1 of Israel liveth, before w' I stand,
20 upon the widow with w' I sojourn,
18: 15 of hosts liveth, before w' I stand,
31 unto w' the word of the Lord came,
20: 14 And Ahab said, By w'? And he
42 w' I appointed to utter destruction,
21: 25 w' Jezebel his wife stirred up.
26 the Amorites, w' the Lord cast out
22: 8 by w' we may enquire of the Lord:
2Ki 3: 14 of hosts liveth, before w' I stand,
5: 16 As the Lord liveth, before w' I stand,
6: 19 bring you to the man w' ye seek.
22 those w' thou hast taken captive
8: 5 her son, w' Elisha restored to life.
10: 24 of the men w' I have brought into
16: 3 w' the Lord cast out from before
17: 8 w' the Lord cast out from before
11 heathen w' the Lord carried away
15 w' the Lord had charged them,
27 priests w' ye brought from thence;
28 priests w' they had carried away
33 the nations w' they carried away
34 of Jacob, w' he named Israel;
35 w' the Lord had made a covenant,
18: 20 Now on w' dost thou trust, that
19: 4 w' the king of Assyria his master
10 thy God in w' thou trustest deceive
22 W' hast thou reproached and
22 against w' hast thou exalted thy
21: 2 w' the Lord cast out before the
9 the nations w' the Lord destroyed
23: 5 priests, w' the kings of Judah had
25: 22 w' Nebuchadnezzar king of
1Ch 1: 12 (of w' came the Philistines,)
2: 21 w' he married when he was
5: 6 w' Tilgath-pilneser...carried
25 w' God destroyed before them.
6: 31 they w' David set over the service
7: 14 of Manasseh; Ashriel, w' she bare:
9: 22 w' David and Samuel the seer
11: 10 of the mighty men w' David had,
11 of the mighty men w' David had;
17: 6 w' I commanded to feed my people,
21 w' God went to redeem to be his
21 w' thou hast redeemed out of
26: 32 w' king David made rulers over the

1Ch 29: 1 my son, w' alone God hath chosen,
8 w' precious stones were found
2Ch 1: 11 w' I have made thee king:
2: 7 w' David my father did provide.
8: 8 w' the children of Israel consumed
9: 25 w' he bestowed in the chariot cities,
17: 19 w' the king put in fenced cities
18: 7 by w' we may enquire of the Lord:
20: 10 w' thou wouldest not let Israel
22: 7 w' the Lord had anointed to cut off
23: 18 w' David had distributed in the
28: 3 w' the Lord had cast out before the
33: 2 w' the Lord had cast out before the
9 heathen, w' the Lord had destroyed
Ezr 2: 1 w' Nebuchadnezzar the king of
65 of w' there were seven thousand
4: 10 w' the great and noble Asnapper
5: 14 w' he had made governor;
8: 20 w' David and the princes had
10: 44 had wives by w' they had children.
Ne 1: 10 w' thou hast redeemed by thy
7: 6 w' Nebuchadnezzar the king of
67 of w' there were seven thousand
8: 10 them for w' nothing is prepared:
9: 37 kings w' thou hast set over us
Es 2: 6 w' Nebuchadnezzar the king of
7 w' Mordecai, when her father and
4: 5 w' he had appointed to attend
11 to w' the king shall hold out the
6: 6 man w' the king delighteth to honour?
6 To w' would the king delight to do
7 w' the king delighteth to honour
9 w' the king delighteth to honour,
9, 11 w' the king delighteth to honour.
13 before w' thou hast begun to fall,
Job 3: 23 is hid, and w' God hath hedged in?
5: 17 happy is the man w' God correcteth:
9: 15 W', though I were righteous, yet
15: 19 w' alone the earth was given,
19: 19 w' I loved are turned against me.
27 w' I shall see for myself, and mine
25: 3 upon w' doth not his light arise?
26: 4 To w' hast thou uttered words?
30: 2 me, in w' old age was perished?
Ps 10: 3 the covetous, w' the Lord abhorreth.
16: 3 the excellent, in w' is all my delight.
18: 2 God, my strength, in w' I will trust;
43 w' I have not known shall serve me.
27: 1 my salvation; w' shall I fear?
1 of my life; of w' shall I be afraid?
32: 2 w' the Lord imputeth not iniquity,
33: 12 people w' he hath chosen for his own
41: 9 familiar friend, in w' I trusted,
45: 16 w' thou mayest make princes in all
47: 4 excellency of Jacob w' he loved.
65: 4 Blessed is the man w' thou choosest
69: 26 him w' thou hast smitten;
26 grief of those w' thou hast wounded.
73: 25 W' have I in heaven but thee?
80: 17 w' thou madest strong for thyself.
86: 9 All nations w' thou hast made
88: 5 w' thou rememberest no more:
89: 21 With w' my hand...be established:
94: 1 God, to w' vengeance belongeth;
1 O God, to w' vengeance belongeth,
12 is the man w' thou chastenest, O
95: 11 Unto w' I sware in my wrath that
104: 26 w' thou hast made to play therein.
105: 26 and Aaron w' he had chosen.
106: 34 w' the Lord commanded them:
38 w' they sacrificed unto the idols of
107: 2 w' he hath redeemed from the hand
144: 2 my shield, and he in w' I trust;
146: 3 the son of man, in w' there is no help.
Pr 3: 12 For w' the Lord loveth he
12 a father the son in w' he delighteth.
27 not good from them to w' it is due,
25: 7 prince w' thine eyes have seen.
30: 31 against w' there is no rising up.
Ec 4: 8 For w' do I labour, and bereave
5: 19 man also to w' God hath given
6: 2 A man to w' God hath given riches,
8: 14 just men, unto w' it happeneth
14 to w' it happeneth according to the
9: 9 with the wife w' thou lovest all the
Ca 1: 7 Tell me, O thou w' my soul loveth,
3: 1 I sought him w' my soul loveth,
2 I will seek him w' my soul loveth:
3 the city found me: to w' I said,
3 Saw ye him w' my soul loveth?
Isa 6: 8 W' shall I send, and who will
8: 12 them to w' this people shall say,
18 children w' the Lord hath give me
10: 3 to w' will ye flee for help? and
19: 25 W' the Lord of hosts shall bless,
22: 16 w' hast thou here, that thou hast
23: 2 thou w' the merchants of Zidon, that
28: 9 W' shall he teach knowledge?
9 and w' shall he make to
12 To w' he said, This is the rest
31: 6 unto him from w' the children
36: 5 now on w' dost thou trust, that
37: 4 w' the king of Assyria his master
10 not thy God, in w' thou trustest,
23 W' hast thou reproached and
23 against w' hast thou exalted thy
40: 14 With w' took he counsel, and who
18 To w' then will ye liken God? or
25 To w' then will ye liken me, or
41: 8 servant, Jacob w' I have chosen,
9 Thou w' I have taken from the
42: 1 Behold my servant, w' I uphold;
1 mine elect, in w' my soul delighteth;
24 he against w' we have sinned?
43: 10 and my servant w' I have chosen:
44: 1 and Israel, w' I have chosen:

Isa 44: 2 and thou, Jesurun, w' I have chosen.
46: 5 To w' will ye liken me, and make
47: 15 thee with w' thou hast laboured,
49: 3 O Israel, in w' I will be glorified.
7 Holy One, to him w' man despiseth,
7 to him w' the nation abhorreth,
50: 1 divorcement, w' I have put away?
1 creditors is it to w' I have sold you?
51: 18 the sons w' she hath brought forth;
19 by w' shall I comfort thee?
53: 1 and to w' is the arm of the Lord
57: 4 Against w' do ye sport yourselves?
4 against w' make ye a wide mouth,
11 And of w' hast thou been afraid or
66: 13 As one w' his mother comforteth,
Jer 1: 2 to w' the word of the Lord came
6: 10 To w' shall I speak, and give
7: 9 after other gods w' ye know not;
8: 2 w' they have loved, and w' they
2 and after w' they have walked,
2 and w' they have sought, and
2 w' they have worshipped: they
9: 12 who is he to w' the mouth of the
16 w' neither they nor their fathers
11: 12 unto w' they offer incense:
14: 16 people to w' they prophesy
18: 8 against w' I have pronounced,
19: 4 w' neither they nor their fathers
20: 6 to w' thou hast prophesied
23: 9 like a man w' wine hath overcome,
24: 5 w' I have sent out of this place
25: 15 to w' I send thee, to drink it.
17 unto w' the Lord hath sent me:
26: 5 the prophets, w' I sent unto you,
27: 5 unto w' it seemed meet unto me.
29: 1 w' Nebuchadnezzar had carried
3 (w' Zedekiah king of Judah sent
4 w' I have caused to be carried away
20 w' I have sent from Jerusalem to
22 w' the king of Babylon roasted in
30: 9 king, w' I will raise up unto them.
17 is Zion, w' no man seeketh after.
33: 5 w' I have slain in mine anger and
34: 11 handmaids, w' they had let go free,
16 w' he had set at liberty at their
37: 1 w' Nebuchadrezzar king of Babylon
38: 9 w' they have cast into the
39: 17 men of w' thou art afraid.
40: 5 w' the king of Babylon hath made
41: 2 w' the king of Babylon had made
9 w' he had slain because of
10 w' Nebuzar-adan the captain of the
16 w' he had recovered from Ishmael
16 w' he had brought again from
18 w' the king of Babylon made
42: 6 Lord our God, to w' we send thee;
9 w' ye sent me to present your
11 Babylon, of w' ye are afraid;
44: 3 other gods, w' they knew not,
52: 28 people w' Nebuchadrezzar carried
La 1: 10 w' thou didst command that they
14 from w' I am not able to rise up.
2: 20 consider to w' thou hast done
4: 20 w' we said, Under his shadow we
Eze 9: 6 any man upon w' is the mark;
11: 1 among w' I saw Jaazaniah the son of
7 Your slain w' ye have laid in the
15 w' the inhabitants of Jerusalem
13: 22 sad, w' I have not made sad;
16: 20 w' thou hast borne unto me,
37 with w' thou hast taken pleasure,
20: 9 the heathen, among w' they were,
23: 7 and with all on w' she doted:
9 the Assyrians, upon w' she doted.
22 from w' thy mind is alienated,
28 the hand of them w' thou hatest,
28 from w' thy mind is alienated:
37 their sons, w' they bare unto me,
40 unto w' a messenger was sent;
40 for w' thou didst wash thyself,
24: 21 daughters w' ye have left shall fall
28: 25 people among w' they are scattered,
31: 2 W' art thou like in thy
18 To w' art thou thus like in glory
32: 19 W' doest thou pass in beauty? go
38: 17 Art thou he of w' I have spoken in
Da 1: 4 Children in w' was no blemish,
4 w' they might teach the learning
7 Unto w' the prince of the eunuchs
11 w' the prince of the eunuchs had
2: 24 w' the king had ordained to
3: 12 Jews w' thou hast set over the
17 God w' we serve is able to deliver
4: 8 in w' is the spirit of the holy gods:
5: 11 in w' is the spirit of the holy gods;
11 w' the king Nebuchadnezzar thy
12 w' the king named Belteshazzar:
13 w' the king my father brought
19 before him: w' he would he slew;
19 and w' he would he kept alive;
19 alive; and w' he would he set up;
19 up; and w' he would he put down.
6: 2 of w' Daniel was first:
16 God w' thou servest continually,
20 God, w' thou servest continually,
7: 8 before w' there were three of the
20 came up, and before w' three fell;
9: 21 w' I had seen in the vision at the
11: 21 w' they shall not give the honour
38 a god w' his fathers knew not
39 w' he shall acknowledge and
Ho 13: 10 and thy judges of w' thou saidst,
Joe 2: 32 the remnant w' the Lord shall call.
3: 2 w' they have scattered among the
Am 6: 1 to w' the house of Israel came!
7: 2, 5 by w' shall Jacob arise? for he

Na 3: 19 w' hath not thy wickedness passed
Zep 3: 18 to w' the reproach...was a burden
Zec 1: 4 w' the former prophets have
10 These are they w' the Lord hath
7: 14 all the nations w' they knew not.
12: 10 look upon me w' they...pierced,
Mal 1: 4 people against w' the Lord hath
2: 14 w' thou hast dealt treacherously:
3: 1 w' ye seek, shall suddenly come
1 of the covenant, w' ye delight in:
M't 1: 16 of Mary, of w' was born Jesus,
3: 17 Son, in w' I am well pleased.
7: 9 w' if his son ask bread, will he give
11: 10 he, of w' it is written, Behold, I
12: 18 my servant, w' I have chosen;
18 in w' my soul is well pleased:
27 w' do your children cast them out?
16: 13 W' do men say that I the Son of
15 them, But w' say ye that I am?
17: 5 Son, in w' I am well pleased;
25 w' do the kings of the earth take
18: 7 that man by w' the offence cometh!
19: 11 saying, save they to w' it is given.
20: 23 for w' it is prepared of my Father.
23: 35 w' ye slew between the temple and
24: 45 w' his lord hath made ruler over
46 w' his lord when he cometh shall
26: 24 by w' the Son of man is betrayed!
27: 9 w'...the children of Israel did value;
15 people a prisoner, w' they would.
17 W' will ye that I release unto you?
M'r 1: 11 Son, in w' I am well pleased.
3: 13 and calleth unto him w' he would:
6: 16 he said, It is John, w' I beheaded:
8: 27 them, W' do men say that I am?
29 them, But w' say ye that I am?
10: 40 to them for w' it is prepared.
13: 20 the elect's sake, w' he hath chosen,
14: 21 by w' the Son of man is betrayed!
71 I know not this man of w' ye speak.
15: 12 him w' ye call the King of the Jews?
40 among w' was Mary Magdalene,
16: 9 out of w' he had cast seven devils.
Lu 6: 13 twelve, w' also he named apostles;
14 Simon, (w' he also named Peter,)
34 to them of w' ye hope to receive,
47 I will shew you to w' he is like:
7: 27 This is he, of w' it is written,
43 that he, to w' he forgave most.
47 to w' little is given, the same loveth
8: 2 out of w' went seven devils,
35 out of w' the devils were departed,
38 out of w' the devils were departed
9: 9 is this, of w' I hear such things?
18 W' say the people that I am?
20 them, But w' say ye that I am?
10: 22 he to w' the Son will reveal him.
11: 19 by w' do your sons cast them out?
12: 5 will forewarn you w' ye shall fear:
37 w' the lord when he cometh shall
42 w' his lord shall make ruler over
43 w' his lord when he cometh shall
48 to w' men have committed much,
13: 4 upon w' the tower in Siloam fell,
16 w' Satan hath bound, lo, these
17: 1 unto him, through w' they come!
19: 15 to w' he had given the money, that
22: 22 that man by w' he is betrayed!
23: 25 into prison, w' they had desired;
Joh 1: 15 This was he of w' I spake, He that
26 one among you, w' ye know not;
30 This is he of w' I said, After me
33 Upon w' thou shalt see the Spirit
45 of W' Moses in the law, and the
47 Israelite indeed, in w' is no guile!
3: 26 to w' thou barest witness, behold,
34 For he w' God hath sent speaketh
4: 18 he w' thou now hast is not thy
5: 21 so the Son quickeneth w' he will.
38 w' he...sent, him ye believed not.
45 you, even Moses, in w' ye trust.
6: 29 ye believe on him w' he hath sent.
68 him, Lord, to w' shall we go?
7: 25 Is not this he, w' they seek to kill?
28 sent me is true, w' ye know not.
8: 53 dead: w' makest thou thyself?
54 of w' ye say, that he is your God:
10: 35 unto w' the word of God came,
36 him, w' the Father hath sanctified,
11: 3 behold, he w' thou lovest is sick.
12: 1 dead, w' he raised from the dead.
9 w' he had raised from the dead.
38 to w' hath the arm of the Lord
13: 18 I know w' I have chosen: but that
22 another, doubting of w' he spake.
23 one of his disciples, w' Jesus loved.
24 who it should be of w' he spake.
26 He it is, to w' I shall give a sop,
14: 17 w' the world cannot receive,
26 w'...Father will send in my name,
15: 26 w' I will send unto you from the
17: 3 Jesus Christ, w' thou hast sent.
11 name those w' thou hast given me,
24 w' thou hast given me, be with me
18: 4 and said unto them, W' seek ye?
7 asked he them again, W' seek ye?
19: 26 disciple standing by, w' he loved,
37 shall look on him w' they pierced.
20: 2 the other disciple, w' Jesus loved,
15 weepest thou? w' seekest thou?
21: 7 disciple w' Jesus loved saith unto
20 seeth the disciple w' Jesus loved
Ac 1: 2 unto the apostles w' he had chosen:
3 To w' also he shewed himself alive
2: 24 W' God hath raised up, having
36 same Jesus, w' ye have crucified,

Ac 3: 2 w' they laid daily at the gate of the
13 w' ye delivered up, and denied him
15 w' God hath raised from the dead;
4: 10 Christ of Nazareth, w' ye crucified,
10 w' God raised from the dead,
22 on w' this miracle of healing was
5: 25 the men w' ye put in prison are
30 w' ye slew and hanged on a tree.
32 w' God hath given to them that
36 to w' a number of men, about four
6: 6 W' they set before the apostles:
7: 7 to w' they shall be in bondage
35 This Moses w' they refused, saying,
39 To w' our fathers would not obey,
45 w' God drave out before the face
52 of w' ye have been...the betrayers
8: 10 To w' they all gave heed, from the
34 of w' speakest the prophet this?
9: 5 I am Jesus w' thou persecutest:
37 w' when they had washed, they
10: 21 said, Behold, I am he w' ye seek:
39 w' they slew and hanged on a tree:
13: 22 to w' also he gave testimony,
25 w' think ye that I am? I am not
37 But he, w' God raised again, saw
14: 23 to the Lord, on w' they believed.
15: 17 upon w' my name is called,
24 to w' we gave no...commandment:
17: 7 W' Jason hath received: and these
23 W'...ye ignorantly worship,
31 by that man w' he hath ordained;
18: 26 w' when Aquila and Priscilla had
19: 13 you by Jesus w' Paul preacheth.
16 the man in w' the evil spirit was
27 w' all Asia and...world worshippeth.
20: 25 among w' I have gone preaching
21: 16 disciple, with w' we should lodge.
29 w' they supposed that Paul had
22: 5 from w' also I received letters unto
8 of Nazareth, w' thou persecutest.
23: 29 W' I perceived to be accused of
24: 6 w' we took, and would have judged
8 w' thyself mayest take knowledge
25: 15 About w', when I was at
16 w' I answered, It is not the manner
18 w' when the accusers stood up,
19 dead, w' Paul affirmed to be alive.
24 w' all the multitude of the Jews
26 w' I have no certain thing to write
26: 15 I am Jesus w' thou persecutest.
17 Gentiles, unto w' now I send thee,
26 before w' also I speak freely:
27: 23 God, whose I am, and w' I serve,
28: 4 w', though he hath escaped the sea,
8 to w' Paul entered in, and prayed,
15 w' when Paul saw, he thanked God,
23 to w' he expounded and testified
Ro 1: 5 By w' we have received grace and
6 Among w' are ye also the called of
9 w' I serve with my spirit in the
3: 25 W' God had set forth to be a
4: 6 unto w' God imputed righteousness
8 to w' the Lord will not impute sin.
17 before him w' he believed, even
24 us also, to w' it shall be imputed,
5: 2 By w' also we have access by faith
11 by w' we have now received the
6: 16 to w' ye yield yourselves servants
16 his servants ye are to w' ye obey;
8: 30 Moreover w' he did predestinate,
30 w' he called, them he also
30 w' he justified, them he also
9: 4 to w' pertaineth the adoption, and
5 of w' as concerning the flesh
15 have mercy on w' I will have mercy,
15 on w' I will have compassion
18 he mercy on w' he will have mercy,
18 mercy, and w' he will he hardeneth.
24 Even us, w' he hath called, not of
10: 14 him in w' they have not believed?
14 in him of w' they have not heard?
11: 36 things: to w' be glory for ever.
13: 7 dues: tribute to w' tribute is due;
7 custom to w' custom;
9 fear to w' fear;
9 honour to w' honour.
14: 15 with thy meat, for w' Christ died.
15: 21 To w' he was not spoken of, they
16: 4 unto w' not only I give thanks, but
1Co 1: 9 by w' ye were called unto the
3: 5 but ministers by w' ye believed,
7: 39 to be married to w' she will;
8: 6 of w' are all things, and we in him;
6 by w' are all things, and we by
11 brother perish, for w' Christ died?
10: 11 upon w' the ends of the world are
15: 6 of w' the greater part remain unto
15 w' he raised not up, if so be that
2Co 1: 10 in w' we trust that he will yet
2: 3 from them of w' I ought to rejoice;
10 To w' ye forgive any thing, I forgive
10 forgave any thing, to w' I forgave it,
4: 4 In w' the god of this world hath
8: 22 w' we have oftentimes proved
10: 18 but w' the Lord commendeth.
11: 4 another Jesus, w' we have not
12: 17 any of them w' I sent unto you?
Ga 1: 5 To w' be glory for ever and ever.
2: 5 To w' we gave place by subjection,
3: 19 come to w' the promise was made;
4: 19 of w' I travail in birth again
6: 14 by w' the world is crucified unto
Eph 1: 7 In w' we have redemption through
11 In w' also we have obtained an
13 In w' ye also trusted, after that ye
2: 3 Among w' also we all had our

Eph 2:21 In w' all the building fitly framed
22 In w' ye also are builded together
3:12 In w' we have boldness and access
15 Of w' the whole family in heaven
4:16 w' the whole body fitly joined
6:22 W' I have sent unto you for the
Ph'p 2:15 among w' ye shine as lights in the
3: 8 for w' I have suffered the loss of
18 walk, of w' I have told you often,
Col 1:14 In w' we have redemption through
27 To w' God would make known what
28 W' we preach, warning every man,
2: 3 In w' are hid all the treasures of
11 In w' also ye are circumcised with
4: 8 W' I have sent unto you for the
10 w' ye received commandments:
1Th 1:10 w' he raised from the dead, even
2Th 2: 8 w' the Lord shall consume with the
1Ti 1:15 save sinners; of w' I am chief.
20 w' is Hymenæus and Alexander;
20 w' I have delivered unto Satan,
6:16 w' no man hath seen, nor can see:
16 to w' be honour and power
2Ti 1: 3 w' I serve from my forefathers
12 I know w' I have believed, and am
15 w' are Phygellus and Hermogenes.
2:17 of w' is Hymenæus and Philetus;
3:14 of w' thou hast learned them;
4:15 Of w' be thou ware also; for he
18 to w' be glory for ever and ever.
Ph'm 10 w' I have begotten in my bonds:
12 W' I have sent again: thou
13 W' I would have retained with me,
Heb 1: 2 w' he hath appointed heir of all
2 by w' also he made the worlds;
2:10 became him, for w' are all things,
10 and by w' are all things, in
3:17 with w' was he grieved forty years?
18 to w' sware he that they should not
4: 6 they to w' it was first preached
13 eyes of him with w' we have to do.
5:11 Of w' we have many things to say,
6: 7 meet for them by w' it is dressed,
7: 2 To w' also Abraham gave a tenth
4 w' even the patriarch Abraham
8 of w' it is witnessed that he liveth.
13 he of w' these things are spoken
11:18 Of w' it was said, That in Isaac
38 (Of w' the world was not worthy:)
12: 6 w' the Lord loveth he chasteneth,
6 and scourgeth every son w' he
7 what son is he w' the father
13:21 to w' be glory for ever and ever.
23 with w', if he come shortly, I will
Jas 1:17 lights, with w' is no variableness,
1Pe 1: 8 W' having not seen, ye love;
8 w', though now ye see him not, yet
12 Unto w' it was revealed, that not
2: 4 To w' coming, as unto a living
4:11 w' be praise and dominion for ever.
5: 8 about, seeking w' he may devour:
9 W' resist stedfast in the faith,
2Pe 1:17 Son, in w' I am well pleased.
2: 2 by reason of w' the way of truth
17 w' the mist of darkness is reserved
19 for of w' a man is overcome, of the
1Jo 4:20 not his brother w' he hath seen,
20 he love God w' he hath not seen?
2Jo 1 her children, w' I love in the truth;
3Jo 6 w' if thou bring forward on their
Jude 13 to w' is reserved the blackness of
Re 7: 2 to w' it was given to hurt the earth
17: 2 With w' the kings of the earth have
20: 8 the number of w' is as the sand of

whomsoever
Ge 31:32 With w' thou findest thy gods,
44: 9 With w' of thy servants it be found,
Le 15:11 w' he toucheth that hath the
J'g 7: 4 w' I say unto thee, This shall not go
11:24 w' the Lord our God shall drive
Da 4:17 giveth it to w' he will, and setteth
25, 32 men, and giveth it to w' he will.
5:21 appointeth over it w' he will.
M't 11:27 to w' the Son will reveal him.
21:44 but on w' it shall fall, it will
26:48 W' I shall kiss, that same is he:
M'r 14:44 W' I shall kiss, that same is he;
15: 6 one prisoner, w' they desired.
Lu 4: 6 me; and to w' I will I give it.
12:48 For unto w' much is given, of
20:18 w' it shall fall, it shall grind
Joh 13:20 receiveth w' I send receiveth
Ac 8:19 that on w' I lay hands, he may
1Co 16: 3 w' ye shall approve by your

whore See also WHOREMONGER; WHORE'S; WHORES; WHORING; WHORISH.
Le 19:29 daughter, to cause her to be a w';
21: 7 shall not take a wife that is a w',
9 profane herself by playing the w',
De 22:21 to play the w' in her father's house:
23:17 no w' of the daughters of Israel,
18 shalt not bring the hire of a w',
J'g 19: 2 And his concubine played the w'
Pr 23:27 For a w' is a deep ditch; and a
Isa 57: 3 seed of the adulterer and the w'.
Eze 16:28 hast played the w' also with the
Re 17: 1 judgment of the great w' that
15 where the w' sitteth, are peoples,
16 these shall hate the w', and shall
19: 2 for he hath judged the great w',

whoredom See also WHOREDOMS.
Ge 38:24 behold, she is with child by w'.
Le 19:29 lest the land fall to w', and the
20: 5 to commit w' with Molech, from
Nu 25: 1 people began to commit w' with
Jer 3: 9 through the lightness of her w',
13:27 the lewdness of thy w', and thine
Eze 16:17 and didst commit w' with them,
33 unto thee on every side for thy w'.
20:30 commit ye w' after their
23: 8 and poured their w' upon her.
17 and they defiled her with their w',
27 thy w' brought from the land of
43: 7 they, nor their kings, by their w',
9 Now let them put away their w',
Ho 1: 2 land hath committed great w',
4:10 they shall commit w', and shall not
11 W' and wine and new wine take
13 your daughters shall commit w',
14 daughters when they commit w',
18 have committed w' continually:
5: 3 O Ephraim, thou committest w',
6:10 there is the w' of Ephraim, Israel

whoredoms
Nu 14:33 and bear your w', until your
2Ki 9:22 as the w' of thy mother Jezebel
2Ch 21:13 to the w' of the house of Ahab,
Jer 3: 2 hast polluted the land with thy w'
Eze 16:20 Is this of thy w' a small matter,
22 thy w' thou hast not remembered
25 that past by, and multiplied thy w'
26 hast increased thy w', to provoke
34 thee from other women in thy w',
34 none followeth thee to commit w':
36 discovered through thy w' with
23: 3 And they committed w' in Egypt;
3 they committed w' in their youth:
7 she committed her w' with them,
8 left she her w' brought from Egypt:
11 and in her w' more than her sister
11 more than her sister in her w'.
14 And that she increased her w':
18 So she discovered her w', and
19 Yet she multiplied her w', in
29 of thy w' shall be discovered,
29 both thy lewdness and thy w'.
35 thou also thy lewdness and thy w'.
43 Will they now commit w' with her,
Ho 1: 2 a wife of w' and children of w':
2: 2 put away her w' out of her sight,
4 for they be the children of w'.
4:12 of w' hath caused them to ere,
5: 4 spirit of w' is in the midst of them,
Na 3: 4 the w' of the wellfavoured harlot,
4 that selleth nations through her w',

whoremonger See also WHOREMONGERS.
Eph 5: 5 we know, that no w', nor unclean

whoremongers
1Ti 1:10 For w', for them that defile
Heb 13: 4 w' and adulterers God will judge.
Re 21: 8 and w', and sorcerers, and
22:15 are dogs, and sorcerers, and w',

whore's
Jer 3: 3 thou hadst a w' forehead, thou

whores
Eze 16:33 They give gifts to all w': but thou
Ho 4:14 themselves are separated with w',

whoring
Ex 34:15 and they go a w' after their gods,
16 daughters go a w' after their gods,
16 thy sons go a w' after their gods.
Le 17: 7 after whom they have gone a w'.
20: 5 off, and all that go a w' after him,
6 wizards, to go a w' after them, I
Nu 15:39 after which ye used to go a w':
De 31:16 and go a w' after the gods of the
J'g 2:17 but they went a w' after other gods,
8:27 all Israel went thither a w' after it:
33 again, and went a w' after Baalim,
1Ch 5:25 and went a w' after the gods of the
2Ch 21:13 inhabitants of Jerusalem...go a w',
Ps 73:27 all them that go a w' from thee.
106:39 went a w' with their own inventions.
Eze 6: 9 which go a w' after their idols:
23:30 hast gone a w' after the heathen,
Ho 4:12 gone a w' from under their God.
9: 1 thou hast gone a w' from thy God,

whorish
Pr 6:26 by means of a w' woman a man is
Eze 6: 9 I am broken with their w' heart,
16:30 work of an imperious w' woman;

whose^ See also WHOSOEVER.
Ge 1:11 w' seed is in itself, upon the earth:
12 w' seed was in itself, after his kind:
7:22 in w' nostrils was the breath of life,
11: 4 tower, w' top may reach unto heaven;
16: 1 an Egyptian, w' name was Hagar.
17:14 w' flesh of his foreskin is not
24:23 W' daughter art thou? tell me, I
32:17 W' art thou? and whither goest
17 thou? and w' are these before thee?
38: 1 Adullamite, w' name was Hirah.
2 Canaanite, w' name was Shuah;
6 Er his firstborn, w' name was Tamar.
25 man, w' these are, am I with child:
25 Discern, I pray thee, w' are these,
44:17 man in w' hand the cup is found,
49:22 well; w' branches run over the wall:
Ex 34:14 the Lord, w' name is Jealous, is a
35:21 every one w' heart stirred him up,
26 the women w' heart stirred them up
29 w' heart made them willing to bring
36: 2 in w' heart the Lord had put wisdom,
2 one w' heart stirred him up to come
Le 13:40 man w' hair is fallen off his head,
14:32 w' hand is not able to get that
15:32 and of him w' seed goeth from him,
16:27 w' blood was brought in to make
Le 21:10 w' head the anointing oil was poured,
22: 4 or a man w' seed goeth from him;
24:10 woman, w' father was an Egyptian,
Nu 24: 3, 15 and the man w' eyes are open hath
De 8: 9 a land w' stones are iron, and out
9 out of w' hills thou mayest dig brass.
19: 1 w' land the Lord thy God giveth
28:49 a nation w' tongue thou shalt not
29:18 w' heart turneth away this day from
Jos 24:15 of the Amorites, in w' land ye dwell:
J'g 4: 2 the captain of w' host was Sisera,
6:10 the Amorites, in w' land ye dwell:
8:31 son, w' name he called Abimelech.
13: 2 of the Danites, w' name was Manoah;
16: 4 valley of Sorek, w' name was Delilah.
17: 1 mount Ephraim, w' name was Micah.
Ru 2: 2 him in w' sight I shall find grace.
5 the reapers, W' damsel is this?
12 under w' wings thou art come to
3: 2 kindred, with w' maidens thou wast?
1Sa 9: 1 w' name was Kish, the son of Abiel,
2 And he had a son, w' name was Saul,
10:26 of men, w' hearts God had touched.
12: 3 his anointed: w' ox have I taken?
3 or w' ass have I taken?
3 of w' hand have I received any
17: 4 w' height was six cubits and a span.
12 w' name was Jesse; and he had
55 host, Abner, w' son is this youth?
56 Enquire...w' son the stripling is.
58 W' son art thou, thou young man?
25: 2 Maon, w' possessions were in Carmel;
2Sa 3: 7 a concubine, w' name was Rizpah,
12 his behalf, saying, W' is the land?
6: 2 w' name is called by the name of
9: 2 of Saul a servant w' name was Ziba.
12 had a young son, w' name was Micha.
13: 1 had a fair sister, w' name was Tamar;
3 had a friend, w' name was Jonadab,
14:27 one daughter, w' name was Tamar:
16: 5 w' name was Shimei, the son of Gera:
8 Saul, in w' stead thou hast reigned;
17:10 w' heart is as the heart of a lion,
25 son, w' name was Ithra an Israelite,
20: 1 w' name was Sheba, the son of Bichri,
21:16 weight of w' spear weighed three
19 of w' spear was like a weaver's beam.
1Ki 3:26 woman w' the living child was unto
8:39 to his ways, w' heart thou knowest;
11:26 servant, w' mother's name was Zeruah,
2Ki 7: 2 a lord on w' hand the king leaned
17 the lord on w' hand he leaned to
8: 1, 5 w' son he had restored to life,
12:15 w' hand they delivered the money to
18:22 is it not he, w' high places and
22 and w' altars Hezekiah hath taken
1Ch 2:16 W' sisters were Zeruiah, and Abigail.
26 another wife, w' name was Atarah;
34 an Egyptian, w' name was Jarha.
7: 2 w' number was in the days of David
15 w' sister's name was Maachah;)
8:29 Gibeon; w' wife's name was Maachah:
38 Azel had six sons, w' names are these,
9:35 Jehiel, w' wife's name was Maachah:
44 Azel had six sons, w' names are these,
12: 8 w' faces were like the faces of lions,
20: 5 w' spear staff was like a weaver's beam.
6 w' fingers and toes were four and
26: 7 w' brethren were strong men, Elihu,
2Ch 6:30 ways, w' heart thou knowest;
16: 9 them w' heart is perfect toward him.
28: 9 Lord was there, w' name was Obed:
Ezr 1: 5 all them w' spirit God had raised,
5:14 unto one, w' name was Sheshbazzar,
7:15 w' habitation is in Jerusalem,
Es 2: 5 a certain Jew, w' name was Mordecai,
Job 1: 1 the land of Uz, w' name was Job;
3:23 light given to a man w' way is hid,
4:19 of clay, w' foundation is in the dust,
5: 5 W' harvest the hungry eateth up,
8:14 W' hope shall be cut off, and
14 and w' trust shall be a spider's web.
12: 6 w' hand God bringeth abundantly.
10 In w' hand is the soul of every living
22:16 w' foundation was overflown with a
26: 4 and w' spirit came from thee?
30: 1 w' fathers I would have disdained
38:29 Out of w' womb came the ice? and
39: 6 W' house I have made the
Ps 15: 4 In w' eyes a vile person is contemned;
17:14 w' belly thou fillest with thy hid
26:10 In w' hands is mischief, and their
32: 1 Blessed is he w' transgression is
1 is forgiven, w' sin is covered.
2 and in w' spirit there is no guile.
9 w' mouth must be held in with bit and
33:12 is the nation w' God is the Lord;
38:14 not, and in w' mouths are no reproofs.
57: 4 w' teeth are spears and arrows, and
78: 8 w' spirit was not stedfast with God.
83:18 that thou, w' name alone is Jehovah,
84: 5 is the man w' strength is in thee;
5 in w' heart are the ways of them.
105:18 W' feet they hurt with fetters: he was
144: 8 W' mouth speaketh vanity, and their
11 w' mouth speaketh vanity, and their
15 is that people, w' God is the Lord.
146: 5 help, w' hope is in the Lord his God:
Pr 2:15 W' ways are crooked, and they
26:26 W' hatred is covered by deceit, his
30:14 a generation, w' teeth are as swords,
Ec 7:26 w' heart is snares and nets,
Isa 1:30 shall be as an oak w' leaf fadeth,
2:22 man, w' breath is in his nostrils:
5:28 W' arrows are sharp, and all their
6:13 as an oak, w' substance is in them,

Isa 10: 10 w' graven images did excel them of
14: 2 them captives, w' captives they were;
18: 2 w' land the rivers have spoiled!
7 w' land the rivers have spoiled, the
23: 7 city, w' antiquity is of ancient days?
8 city, w' merchants are princes,
8 w' traffickers are the honourable of
26: 3 peace, w' mind is stayed on thee:
28: 1 w' glorious beauty is a fading flower,
30: 13 w' breaking cometh suddenly at an
31: 9 w' fire is in Zion, and his furnace in
36: 7 is it not he, w' high places and
7 and w' altars Hezekiah hath taken
43: 14 the Chaldeans, w' cry is in the ships.
45: 1 w' right hand I have holden,
51: 7 the people in w' heart is my law;
15 that divided the sea, w' waves roared:
57: 15 w' name is Holy; I dwell in the
20 rest, w' waters cast up mire and dirt.
58: 11 spring of water, w' waters fail not.
Jer 5: 15 nation w' language thou knowest not,
17: 5 and w' heart departed from the Lord.
7 the Lord, and w' hope the Lord is.
19: 13 upon w' roofs they have burned
22: 25 the hand of them w' face thou fearest,
32: 29 w' roofs they have offered incense
33: 5 w' wickedness I have hid my face
37: 13 w' name was Irijah, the son of
44: 28 know w' words shall stand, mine,
46: 7 w' waters are moved as the rivers?
18 king, w' name is the Lord of hosts,
48: 15 king, w' name is the Lord of hosts.
49: 12 they w' judgment was not to drink
51: 57 king, w' name is the Lord of hosts.
Eze 3: 6 w' words...canst not understand.
11: 21 w' heart walketh after the heart of
17: 6 w' branches turned toward him,
16 him king, w' oath he despised,
16 w' covenant he brake, even with
20: 9 w' sight I made myself known unto
14 in w' sight I brought them out.
22 in w' sight I brought them forth.
21: 25 w' day is come, when iniquity shall
27 more, until he come w' right it is;
29 w' day is come, when their iniquity
23: 20 w' flesh is as the flesh of asses,
20 w' issue is like the issue of horses.
24: 6 city, to the pot w' scum is therein,
6 and w' scum is not gone out of it!
32: 23 W' graves are set in the sides of
40: 3 w' appearance was like the appearance
45 w' prospect is toward the south,
46 w' prospect is toward the north
42: 15 w' prospect is toward the east,
43: 4 gate w' prospect is toward the east.
47: 12 trees for meat, w' leaf shall not fade,
Da 2: 11 gods, w' dwelling is not with flesh.
26 Daniel, w' name was Belteshazzar,
31 image, w' brightness was excellent,
3: 1 w' height was threescore cubits,
27 w' bodies the fire had no power,
4: 8 w' name was Belteshazzar,
19 Daniel, w' name was Belteshazzar,
20 w' height reached unto the heaven,
21 W' leaves were fair, and the fruit
21 upon w' branches the fowls of the
34 w' dominion is an everlasting
5: 23 the God in w' hand thy breath is,
23 and w' are all thy ways, hast thou not
7: 9 sit, w' garment was white as snow,
19 dreadful, w' teeth were of iron,
20 w' look was more stout than his
27 w' kingdom is an everlasting kingdom,
10: 1 w' name was called Belteshazzar;
5 w' loins were girded with fine gold of
Joe 1: 6 w' teeth are the teeth of a lion, and
Am 2: 9 w' height was like the height of
5: 27 Lord, w' name is The God of hosts.
Ob 3 of the rock, w' habitation is high;
Jon 1: 7 for w' cause this evil is upon us.
8 w' cause this evil is upon us;
Mic 5: 2 w' goings forth have been from of old,
Na 3: 8 w' rampart was the sea, and her
Zec 6: 12 the man w' name is The Branch;
11: 5 W' possessors slay them, and hold
M't 3: 11 w' shoes I am not worthy to bear:
12 W' fan is in his hand, and he will
10: 3 w' surname was Thaddæus;
22: 20 W' is this image and
28 W' wife shall she be of the seven?
42 think ye of Christ? w' son is he?
M'r 1: 7 latchet of w' shoes I am not worthy
7: 25 w' young daughter had an unclean
12: 16 them, W' is this image and
23 w' wife shall she be of them? for
Lu 1: 27 to a man w' name was Joseph,
2: 25 Jerusalem, w' name was Simeon;
3: 16 w' shoes I am not worthy to
17 W' fan is in his hand, and he will
6: 6 w' right hand was withered.
12: 20 w' shall those things be, which
13: 1 w' blood Pilate had mingled with
20: 24 W' image and superscription
33 w' wife of them is she?
24: 18 w' name was Cleopas, answering
Joh 1: 6 sent from God, w' name was John.
27 w' shoe's latchet I am not worthy
4: 46 w' son was sick at Capernaum.
6: 42 w' father and mother we know?
10: 12 w' own the sheep are not, seeth the
11: 2 hair, w' brother Lazarus was sick.
18: 26 his kinsman w' ear Peter cut off,
19: 24 but cast lots for it, w' it shall be:
20: 23 W' soever sins ye remit, they are
23 w' soever sins ye retain, they are
Ac 7: 58 young man's feet, w' name was Saul.
Ac 10: 5 Simon, w' surname was Peter:
6 tanner, w' house is by the sea side:
32 Simon, w' surname is Peter;
11: 13 Simon, w' surname is Peter;
12: 12 of John, w' surname was Mark;
25 them John, w' surname was Mark.
13: 25 w' shoes of his feet I am not
15: 37 them John, w' surname was Mark.
16: 14 w' heart the Lord opened, that she
18: 7 w' house joined hard to the
27: 23 God, w' I am, and whom I serve,
28: 7 of the island, w' name was Publius;
11 isle, w' sign was Castor and Pollux.
Ro 2: 29 w' praise is not of men, but of God.
3: 8 may come? w' damnation is just.
14 W' mouth is full of cursing and
4: 7 are they w' iniquities are forgiven,
7 forgiven, and w' sins are covered.
9: 5 W' are the fathers, and of whom
2Co 8: 18 w' praise is in the gospel
11: 15 w' end shall be according to their
Ga 3: 1 before w' eyes Jesus Christ hath
Ph'p 3: 19 W' end is destruction, w' God is
19 w' glory is in their shame, who
4: 3 w' names are in the book of life.
2Th 2: 9 w' coming is after the working of
Tit 1: 11 W' mouths must be stopped, who
Heb 3: 6 w' house are we, if we hold fast the
17 w' carcases fell in the wilderness?
6: 8 cursing; w' end is to be burned.
7: 6 he w' descent is not counted from
11: 10 w' builder and maker is God.
12: 26 W' voice then shook the earth: but
13: 7 w' faith follow, considering the end
11 w' blood is brought into the holy
1Pe 2: 24 by w' stripes ye were healed.
3: 3 W' adorning, let it not be that
6 w' daughters ye are, as long as ye
2Pe 2: 3 w' judgment now of a long time
Jude 12 trees w' fruit withereth, without
Re 13: 8 w' names are not written in the
12 beast, w' deadly wound was healed.
17: 8 w' names were not written in the
20: 11 from w' face the earth and the

whoso^ See also WHOSOEVER.
Ge 9: 6 W' sheddeth man's blood, by man
Le 11: 27 w' toucheth their carcase shall be
22: 4 w' toucheth any thing that is unclean
Nu 35: 30 W' killeth any person, the
De 19: 4 W' killeth...neighbour ignorantly,
2Ch 23: 14 w' followeth her, let him be slain with
Ps 50: 23 W' offereth praise glorifieth me: and
101: 5 W' privily slandereth his neighbour,
107: 43 W' is wise, and will observe these
Pr 6: 32 But w' committeth adultery with a
8: 35 For w' findeth me findeth life, and
9: 4, 16 W' is simple, let him turn in
12: 1 W' loveth instruction loveth
13: 13 W' despiseth the word shall be
16: 20 w' trusteth in the Lord, happy is he.
17: 5 W' mocketh the poor reproacheth his
13 W' rewardeth evil for good, evil shall
20: 2 W' provoketh him to anger sinneth
20 W' curseth his father or his mother,
21: 13 W' stoppeth his ears at the cry of the
23 W' keepeth his mouth and his
25: 14 W' boasteth himself of a false
26: 27 W' diggeth a pit shall fall therein:
27: 18 W' keepeth the fig tree shall eat the
28: 7 W' keepeth the law is a wise son:
10 W' causeth the righteous to go
13 w' confesseth and forsaketh them
18 W' walketh uprightly shall be saved:
24 W' robbeth his father or his mother,
26 but w' walketh wisely, he shall be
29: 3 W' loveth wisdom rejoiceth his
24 W' is partner with a thief hateth his
25 but w' putteth his trust in the Lord
Ec 7: 26 w' pleaseth God shall escape from
8: 5 W' keepeth the commandment shall
10: 8 w' breaketh an hedge, a serpent shall
9 W' removeth stones shall be hurt
Da 3: 6 w' falleth not...worshippeth
11 w' falleth not...worshippeth,
Zec 14: 17 that w' will not come up of all the
M't 18: 5 w' shall receive one such
6 w' shall offend one of these
19: 9 w' marrieth her which is put
23: 20 W' therefore shall swear by the
21 And w' shall swear by the temple,
24: 15 (w' readeth, let him understand:)
M'r 7: 10 W' curseth father or mother, let
Joh 6: 54 W' eateth my flesh, and drinketh
Jas 1: 25 w' looketh into the perfect law of
1Jo 2: 5 w' keepeth his word, in him

whosoever^ See also WHOSO.
Ge 4: 15 W' slayeth Cain, vengeance shall
Ex 19: 12 w' toucheth the mount shall be
22: 19 w' lieth with a beast shall surely
30: 33 W' compoundeth any like it,
33 or w' putteth any of it upon a
38 W' shall make like unto that, to
31: 14 for w' doeth any work therein, that
15 w' doeth any work in the sabbath
32: 24 W' hath any gold, let them break
33 W' hath sinned against me,
35: 2 w' doeth work therein shall be
5 w' is of a willing heart, let him
Le 7: 25 For w' eateth the fat of the beast,
11: 24 w' toucheth the carcase of them
25 w' beareth ought of the carcase of
31 w' doth touch them, when they be
15: 5 w' toucheth his bed shall wash
10 w' toucheth any thing that was
19 w' toucheth her shall be unclean
Le 15: 21 w' toucheth her bed shall wash
22 w' toucheth any thing that she sat
27 w' toucheth those things shall be
17: 14 w' eateth it shall be cut off.
18: 29 w' shall commit any of these
19: 20 w' lieth carnally with a woman,
20: 2 W' he be of the children of Israel,
21: 17 W' he be of thy seed in their
22: 3 W' he be of all your seed
5 w' toucheth any creeping thing,
21 w' offereth a sacrifice of peace
24: 15 W' curseth his God shall bear
Nu 5: 2 and w' is defiled by the dead:
15: 14 or w' be among you in your
17: 13 W' cometh any thing near unto
19: 13 W' toucheth the dead body of any
16 w' toucheth one that is slain
31: 19 w' hath killed any person, and
19 w' hath touched any slain, purify
De 18: 19 w' will not hearken unto my
Jos 1: 18 W' he be that doth rebel
2: 19 w' shall go out of the doors
19 w' shall be with thee in the
20: 9 w' killeth any person at unawares
J'g 7: 3 W' is fearful and afraid, let him
1Sa 11: 7 W' cometh not forth after Saul
2Sa 5: 8 W' getteth up to the gutter, and
14: 10 W' saith ought unto thee, bring him
17: 9 w' heareth it will say, There is a
1Ki 13: 33 w' would, he consecrated him,
2Ki 10: 19 w' shall be wanting, he shall
1Ch 11: 6 w' smiteth the Jebusites first shall
26: 28 and w' had dedicated any thing,
2Ch 13: 9 w' cometh to consecrate himself
15: 13 w' would not seek the Lord God
23: 7 and w' else cometh into the house, he
Ezr 1: 4 w' remaineth in any place where
6: 11 that w' shall alter this word,
7: 26 w' will not do the law of thy God,
10: 8 w' would not come within three
Es 4: 11 that w', whether man or woman,
Pr 6: 29 w' toucheth her shall not be
20: 1 w' is deceived thereby is not wise.
27: 16 W' hideth her hideth the wind, and
Isa 54: 15 w' shall gather together against
59: 8 w' goeth therein shall not know
Jer 19: 3 which w' heareth, his ears shall
Eze 33: 4 Then w' heareth the sound of the
Da 5: 7 W' shall read this writing, and
6: 7 w' shall ask a petition of any God
Joe 2: 32 w' shall call on the name of the
M't 5: 19 W' therefore shall break one
19 w' shall do and teach them,
21 w' shall kill shall be in danger
22 w' is angry with his brother
22 w' shall say to his brother,
22 but w' shall say, Thou fool,
28 w' looketh on a woman to
31 W' shall put away his wife,
32 w' shall put away his wife,
32 w' shall marry her that is
39 w' shall smite thee on thy right
41 w' shall compel thee to go a mile,
7: 24 w' heareth these sayings of
10: 14 And w' shall not receive you,
32 W' therefore shall confess
33 w' shall deny me before men,
42 w' shall give to drink unto
11: 6 w' shall not be offended in me.
12: 32 w' speaketh a word against
32 w' speaketh against the Holy
50 w' shall do the will of my
13: 12 For w' hath, to him shall be given,
12 w' hath not, from him shall be
15: 5 W' shall say to his father or
16: 25 w' will save his life shall lose
25 w' will lose his life for my
18: 4 W' therefore shall humble
19: 9 W' shall put away his wife,
20: 26 w' will be great among you,
27 w' will be chief among you,
21: 44 w' shall fall on this stone shall
23: 12 w' shall exalt himself shall be
16 W' shall swear by the temple
16 w' shall swear by the gold of
18 W' shall swear by the altar, it
18 w' sweareth by the gift that is
M'r 3: 35 w' shall do the will of God, the
6: 11 w' shall not receive you, nor
8: 34 W' will come after me, let him
35 w' will save his life shall lose
35 w' shall lose his life for my sake
38 W' therefore shall be ashamed
9: 37 W' shall receive one of such
37 w' shall receive me, receiveth
41 w' shall give you a cup of water
42 w' shall offend one of these
10: 11 W' shall put away his wife, and
15 W' shall not receive the
43 w' will be great among you,
44 w' of you will be the chiefest,
11: 23 That w' shall say unto this
Lu 6: 47 W' cometh to me, and
7: 23 w' shall not be offended in me.
8: 18 w' hath, to him shall be given;
18 w' hath not, from him shall be
9: 5 And w' will not receive you,
24 For w' will save his life shall
24 w' will lose his life for my sake,
26 w' shall be ashamed of me and
48 W' shall receive this child in
48 w' shall receive me receiveth
12: 8 W' shall confess me
10 w' shall speak a word against
14: 11 w' exalted himself shall be
27 w' doth not bear his cross, and

Lu 14:33 w' he be of you that forsaketh not
16:18 W' putteth away his wife,
18 w' marrieth her that is put
17:33 W' shall seek to save his life
33 w' shall lose his life shall
18:17 W' shall not receive the
20:18 W' shall fall upon that stone
Joh 3:15, 16 w' believeth in him should
4:13 W' drinketh of this water shall
14 But w' drinketh of the water
5: 4 w' then first after the troubling of
8:34 W' committeth sin is the
11:26 w' liveth and believeth in me
12:46 w' believeth on me should not
16: 2 w' killeth you will think that
19:12 w' maketh himself a king
Ac 2:21 w' shall call on the name of the
10:43 w' believeth in him shall
13:26 w' among you feareth God, to you
Ro 2: 1 man, w' thou art that judgest:
9:33 w' believeth on him shall not
10:11 W' believeth on him shall not
13 w' shall call upon the
13: 2 W' therefore resisteth the power,
1Co 11:27 w' shall eat this bread, and
Ga 5: 4 w' of you are justified by the law;
10 bear his judgment, w' he be.
Jas 2:10 w' shall keep the whole law, and
4: 4 w' therefore will be a friend
1Jo 2:23 W' denieth the Son, the same
3: 4 W' committeth sin
6 W' abideth in him sinneth not:
6 w' sinneth hath not seen him,
9 W' is born of God doth not
10 w' doeth not righteousness is
15 W' hateth his brother is a
4:15 W' shall confess that Jesus is
5: 1 W' believeth that Jesus is
18 w' is born of God sinneth not;
2Jo 9 W' transgresseth, and abideth
Re 14:11 w' receiveth the mark of his name.
20:15 w' was not found written in the
22:15 w' loveth and maketh a lie.
17 w' will, let him take the water of

why ^
Ge 4: 6 unto Cain, W' art thou wroth?
6 and w' is thy countenance fallen?
12:18 w' didst thou not tell me that she
19 W' saidst thou, She is my sister?
25:22 she said, If it be so, w' am I thus?
27:45 w' should I be deprived also of you
42: 1 W' do you look one upon another?
47:15 w' should we die in thy presence?
Ex 1:18 W' have ye done this thing, and
2:20 w' is it that ye have left the man?
3: 3 this great sight, w' the bush is
5:22 people? w' is it thou hast sent me?
14: 5 W' have we done this, that we
17: 2 unto them, W' chide ye with me?
18:14 w' sittest thou thyself alone, and
32:11 w' doth thy wrath wax hot against
Nu 11:20 W' came we forth out of Egypt?
20: 4 And w' have ye brought up the
27: 4 W' should the name of our father
De 5:25 Now therefore w' should we die?
Jos 7:25 W' hast thou troubled us? the
17:14 W' hast thou given me but one
J'g 2: 2 my voice: w' have ye done this?
5:16 W' abodest thou among the
17 and w' did Dan remain in ships?
28 W' is his chariot so long in
28 w' tarry the wheels of his chariot?
6:13 w' then is all this befallen us?
8: 1 W' hast thou served us thus, that
9:28 Shechem:...w' should we serve him?
11: 7 w' are ye come unto me now when
26 w' therefore did ye not recover
13:18 W' askest thou thus after my
15:10 W' are ye come up against us?
21: 3 w' is this come to pass in Israel,
Ru 1:11 w' will ye go with me? are there
21 w' then call ye me Naomi, seeing
2:10 W' have I found grace in thine
1Sa 1: 8 w' weepest thou? and w' eatest
8 w' is thy heart grieved? am I not
2:23 unto them, W' do ye such things?
6: 3 you w' his hand is not removed
17: 8 W' are ye come out to set your
28 said, W' camest thou down hither?
19:17 W' hast thou deceived me so, and
17 Let me go; w' should I kill thee?
20: 2 w' should my father hide this
8 for w' shouldest thou bring me to
21: 1 W' art thou alone, and no man
22:13 W' have ye conspired against me,
27: 5 for w' should thy servant dwell in
28:12 W' hast thou deceived me? for
15 W' hast thou disquieted me, to
2Sa 3:24 w' is it that thou hast sent him
7: 7 W' build ye not me an house of
11:10 w' then didst thou not go down
21 w' went ye nigh the wall? then say
13: 4 W' art thou, being the king's son,
26 him, W' should he go with thee?
16: 9 W' should this dead dog curse my
17 w' wentest thou not with thy
18:11 w' didst thou not smite him there
19:10 w' speak ye not a word of bringing
11 W' are ye the last to bring the king
29 W' speakest thou any more of thy
36 w' should the king recompense it
41 W' have our brethren the men of
43 w' then did ye despise us, that our
20:19 w' wilt thou swallow up the
24: 3 w' doth my lord the king delight
1Ki 1: 6 in saying, W' hast thou done so?
1Ki 1:13 w' then doth Adonijah reign?
2:22 And w' dost thou ask Abishag the
43 W' then hast thou not kept the
9: 8 W' hath the Lord done thus
14: 6 w' feignest thou thyself to be
21: 5 W' is thy spirit so sad, that thou
2Ki 1: 5 them, W' are ye now turned back?
7: 3 W' sit we here until we die?
8:12 Hazael said, W' weepeth my lord?
12: 7 W' repair ye not the breaches of
1Ch 17: 6 W' have ye not built me an house
21: 3 w' then doth my lord require this
3 w' will he be a cause of trespass to
2Ch 7:21 W' hath the Lord done thus unto
24: 6 W' hast thou not required of the
20 W' transgress ye the
25:15 W' hast thou sought after the gods
16 w' shouldest thou be smitten?
19 w' shouldest thou meddle to thine
32: 4 W' should the king of Assyria come,
Ezr 4:22 w' should damage grow to the
7:23 w' should there be wrath against
Ne 2: 2 W' is thy countenance sad,
3 w' should not my countenance be
6: 3 w' should the work cease, whilst
13:11 W' is the house of God forsaken?
21 them, W' lodge ye about the wall?
Es 3: 3 W' transgressest thou the king's
4: 5 know what it was, and w' it was.
Job 3:11 w' died I not from the womb?
11 w' did I not give up the ghost when I
12 W' did the knees prevent me?
12 or w' the breasts that I should suck?
23 W' is light given to a man whose way
7:20 w' hast thou set me as a mark
21 And w' dost thou not pardon my
9:29 be wicked, w' then labour I in vain?
15:12 W' doth thine heart carry thee
19:22 W' do ye persecute me as God,
28 W' persecute we him, seeing the
21: 4 so, w' should not my spirit be
24: 1 W', seeing times are not hidden
27:12 w' then are ye thus altogether
31: 1 w' then should I think upon a
33:13 W' dost thou strive against him?
Ps 2: 1 W' do the heathen rage, and the
10: 1 W' standest thou afar off, O Lord?
1 w' hidest thou thyself in times of
22: 1 My God, my God, w' hast thou
1 w' art thou so far from helping me,
42: 5 w' art thou disquieted in me?
9 rock, W' hast thou forgotten me?
9 w' go I mourning because of the
11 W' art thou cast down, O my soul?
11 w' art thou disquieted within me?
43: 2 strength: w' dost thou cast me off?
2 w' go I mourning because of the
5 W' art thou cast down, O my soul?
5 w' art thou disquieted within me?
44:23 Awake, w' sleepest thou, O Lord?
52: 1 W' boastest thou thyself in
68:16 W' leap ye, ye high hills? this is
74: 1 w' hast thou cast us off for ever?
1 w' doth thine anger smote against the
11 W' withdrawest thou thy hand,
80:12 W' hast thou then broken down
88:14 Lord, w' castest thou off my soul?
14 w' hidest thou thy face from me?
Pr 22:27 w' should he take away thy bed
Ec 2:15 me; and w' was I then more wise?
7:16 w' shouldest thou destroy thyself?
17 w' shouldest thou die before thy
Ca 1: 7 w' should I be as one that turneth
Isa 1: 5 W' should ye be stricken any
40:27 W' sayest thou, O Jacob, and
63:17 w' hast thou made us to err from
Jer 2:14 homeborn slave? w' is he spoiled?
33 W' trimmest thou thy way to
36 W' gaddest thou about so much
8: 5 W' then is this people of
14 W' do we sit still? assemble
19 W' have they provoked me to
22 w' then is not the health of the
14: 8 w' shouldest thou be as a stranger
9 W' shouldest thou be as a man
19 w' hast thou smitten us, and
15:18 W' is my pain perpetual, and my
26: 9 W' hast thou prophesied in the
27:13 W' will ye die, thou and thy
29:27 w' hast thou not reproved Jeremiah
30:15 W' criest thou for thine affliction?
36:29 W' hast thou written therein,
46:15 W' are thy valiant men swept
49: 1 w' then doth their king inherit
Eze 18:19 W'? doth not the son bear the
31 w' will ye die, O house of Israel?
33:11 w' will ye die, O house of Israel?
Da 1:10 for w' should he see your faces
2:15 W' is the decree so hasty
Jon 1:10 him, W' hast thou done this?
Mic 4: 9 Now w' dost thou cry out aloud?
Hab 1: 3 W' dost thou show me iniquity,
Hag 1: 9 W'? saith the Lord of hosts.
Mal 2:10 w' do we deal treacherously
M't 6:28 w' take ye thought for raiment?
7: 3 w' beholdest thou the mote that is
8:26 W' are ye fearful, O ye of little faith?
9:11 W' eateth your Master with
14 W' do we and the Pharisees fast
13:10 W' speakest thou unto them in
15: 2 W' do thy disciples transgress the
3 W' do ye also transgress the
16: 8 w' reason ye among yourselves,
17:10 W' then say the scribes that Elias
19 W' could not we cast him out?
19: 7 W' did Moses then command to
M't 19:17 W' callest thou me good? there is
20: 6 W' stand ye here all the day idle?
21:25 us, W' did ye not then believe him?
22:18 W' tempt ye me, ye hypocrites?
26:10 W' trouble ye the woman? for she
27:23 said, W', what evil hath he done?
46 my God, w' hast thou forsaken me?
M'r 2: 7 W' doth this man thus speak
8 W' reason ye these things in your
18 W' do the disciples of John and
24 w' do they on the sabbath day
4:40 W' are ye so fearful? how is it that
5:35 w' troublest thou the Master any
39 W' make ye this ado, and weep?
7: 5 W' walk not thy disciples
8:12 W' doth this generation seek
17 W' reason ye, because ye have no
9:11 W' say the scribes that Elias
28 W' could not we cast him out?
10:18 W' callest thou me good? there is
11: 3 man say unto you, W' do ye this?
31 W' then did ye not believe him?
12:15 said unto them, W' tempt ye me?
14: 4 W' was this waste of the
6 Let her alone; w' trouble ye her?
15:14 them, W', what evil hath he done?
34 my God, w' hast thou forsaken
Lu 2:48 w' hast thou thus dealt with us?
5:30 W' do ye eat and drink with
33 W' do the disciples of John fast
6: 2 W' do ye that which is not lawful
41 w' beholdest thou the mote that is
46 w' call ye me, Lord, Lord, and do
12:26 w' take ye thought for the rest?
57 w' even of yourselves judge ye not
13: 7 down; w' cumbereth it the ground?
18:19 him, W' callest thou me good?
19:31 man ask you, W' do ye loose him?
33 unto them, W' loose ye the colt?
20: 5 say, W' then believed ye him not?
23 said unto them, W' tempt ye me?
22:46 them, W' sleep ye? rise and pray,
23:22 time, W', what evil hath he done?
24: 5 W' seek ye the living among the
38 said unto them, W' are ye troubled?
38 w' do thoughts arise in...hearts?
Joh 1:25 W' baptizest thou then, if thou be
4:27 thou? or, W' talkest thou with her?
7:19 the law? W' go ye about to kill me?
45 them, W' have ye not brought him?
8:43 W' do ye not understand my
46 truth, w' do ye not believe me?
9:30 W' herein is a marvellous thing,
10:20 devil, and is mad; w' hear ye him?
12: 5 W' was not this ointment sold
13:37 Lord, w' cannot I follow thee now?
18:21 W' askest thou me? ask them
23 but if well, w' smitest thou me?
20:13, 15 her, Woman, w' weepest thou?
Ac 1:11 w' stand ye gazing up into heaven?
3:12 w' marvel ye at this? or w' look ye
4:25 W' did the heathen rage, and the
5: 3 w' hath Satan filled thine heart to
4 w' hast thou conceived this thing
7:26 w' do ye wrong one to another?
9: 4 Saul, w' persecutest thou me?
14:15 Sirs, w' do ye these things?
15:10 Now therefore w' tempt ye God, to
22: 7 Saul, Saul, w' persecutest thou me?
16 And now w' tarriest thou? arise,
26: 8 W' should it be thought a thing
14 Saul, Saul, w' persecutest thou me?
Ro 3: 7 w' yet am I also judged as a sinner?
8:24 man seeth, w' doth he yet hope for?
9:19 unto me, W' doth he yet find fault?
20 it, W' hast thou made me thus?
14:10 But w' dost thou judge thy brother?
10 w' dost thou set at nought thy
1Co 4: 7 w' dost thou glory, as if thou hadst
6: 7 W' do ye not rather take wrong?
7 w' do ye not rather suffer
10:29 w' is my liberty judged of
30 w' am I evil spoken of for that
15:29 w' are they then baptized for the
30 w' stand ye in jeopardy every hour?
Ga 2:14 w' compellest thou the Gentiles to
5:11 w' do I yet suffer persecution?
Col 2:20 w', as though living in the world,

wicked
Ge 13:13 the men of Sodom were w' and
18:23 destroy the righteous with the w'?
25 slay the righteous with the w':
25 the righteous should be as the w',
38: 7 was w' in the sight of the Lord;
Ex 9:27 and I and my people are w'.
23: 1 put not thine hand with the w' to
7 not: for I will not justify the w'.
Le 20:17 it is a w' thing; and they shall
Nu 16:26 from the tents of these w' men,
De 15: 9 be not a thought in thy w' heart,
17: 5 have committed that w' thing,
23: 9 keep thee from every w' thing.
25: 1 righteous, and condemn the w'.
2 w' man be worthy to be beaten,
1Sa 2: 9 the w' shall be silent in darkness;
24:13 proceedeth from the w':
30:22 answered all the w' men and
2Sa 3:34 as a man falleth before w' men,
4:11 w' men have slain a righteous
1Ki 8:32 thy servants, condemning the w',
2Ki 17:11 wrought w' things to provoke
2Ch 6:23 thy servants, by requiting the w',
7:14 face, and turn from their w' ways;
24: 7 sons of Athaliah, that w' woman,
Ne 9:35 turned they from their w' works.

Es 7: 6 and enemy is this *w'* Haman.
9: 25 by letters that his *w'* device,
Job 3: 17 the *w'* cease from troubling;
8: 22 of the *w'* shall come to nought.
9: 22 destroyeth the perfect and the *w'*.
24 is given into the hand of the *w'*:
29 If I be *w'*, why then labour I in
10: 3 shine upon the counsel of the *w'*?
7 Thou knowest that I am not *w'*;
15 If I be *w'*, woe unto me; and if I be
11: 20 But the eyes of the *w'* shall fail,
15: 20 The *w'* man travaileth with pain
16: 11 me over into the hands of the *w'*.
18: 5 the light of the *w'* shall be put out,
21 such are the dwellings of the *w'*,
20: 5 the triumphing of the *w'* is short,
22 hand of the *w'* shall come upon
29 This is the portion of the *w'* man
21: 7 Wherefore do the *w'* live, become
16 counsel of the *w'* is far from me.
17 oft is the candle of the *w'* put out!
28 are the dwelling places of the *w'*?
30 the *w'* is reserved to the day of
22: 15 way which *w'* men have trodden?
18 counsel of the *w'* is far from me.
24: 6 they gather the vintage of the *w'*.
27: 7 Let mine enemy be as the *w'*, and
13 the portion of a *w'* man with God,
29: 17 And I brake the jaws of the *w'*.
31: 3 Is not destruction to the *w'*? and
34: 8 and walketh with *w'* men.
18 fit to say to a king, Thou art *w'*?
26 He striketh them as *w'* men in the
36 because of his answers for *w'* men.
36: 6 preserveth not the life of the *w'*:
17 fulfilled the judgment of the *w'*:
38: 13 the *w'* might be shaken out of it?
15 from the *w'* their light is withholden,
40: 12 tread down the *w'* in their place.
Ps 7: 9 wickedness of the *w'* come to an
11 God is angry with the *w'* every day.
9: 5 thou hast destroyed the *w'*, thou
16 the *w'* is snared in the work of his
17 *w'* shall be turned into hell, and
10: 2 *w'* in his pride doth persecute the
3 *w'* boasteth of his heart's desire,
4 The *w'*, through the pride of his
13 doth the *w'* contemn God?
15 Break thou the arm of the *w'* and
11: 2 For, lo, the *w'* bend their bow, they
5 the *w'* and him that loveth violence
6 Upon the *w'* he shall rain snares,
12: 8 The *w'* walk on every side, when
17: 9 the *w'* that oppress me, from my
13 deliver my soul from the *w'*, which
22: 16 assembly of the *w'* have inclosed
26: 5 doers; and will not sit with the *w'*.
27: 2 When the *w'*, even mine enemies
28: 3 Draw me not away with the *w'*,
31: 17 let the *w'* be ashamed, and let
32: 10 Many sorrows shall be to the *w'*:
34: 21 Evil shall slay the *w'*: and they
36: 1 transgression of the *w'* saith
11 not the hand of the *w'* remove me.
37: 7 who bringeth *w'* devices to pass.
10 while, and the *w'* shall not be:
12 The *w'* plotteth against the just,
14 The *w'* have drawn out the sword,
16 better than the riches of many *w'*.
17 the arms of the *w'* shall be broken:
20 But the *w'* shall perish, and the
21 The *w'* borroweth, and payeth not
28 the seed of the *w'* shall be cut off.
32 The *w'* watcheth the righteous,
34 when the *w'* are cut off, thou shalt
35 I have seen the *w'* in great power,
38 the end of the *w'* shall be cut off.
40 shall deliver them from the *w'*, and
39: 1 bridle, while the *w'* is before me.
50: 16 But unto the *w'* God saith, What
55: 3 of the oppression of the *w'*:
58: 3 *w'* are estranged from the womb:
10 wash his feet in the blood of the *w'*.
59: 5 merciful to any *w'* transgressors.
64: 2 from the secret counsel of the *w'*;
68: 2 *w'* perish at the presence of God.
71: 4 my God, out of the hand of the *w'*,
73: 3 I saw the prosperity of the *w'*.
74: 19 unto the multitude of the *w'*:
75: 4 and to the *w'*, Lift not up the horn:
8 all the *w'* of the earth shall wring
10 horns of the *w'* also will I cut off;
82: 2 and accept the persons of the *w'*?
4 rid them out of the hand of the *w'*.
91: 8 and see the reward of the *w'*.
92: 7 When the *w'* spring as the grass,
11 my desire of the *w'* that rise up
94: 3 Lord, how long shall the *w'*, how
3 how long shall the *w'* triumph?
13 until the pit be digged for the *w'*.
97: 10 them out of the hand of the *w'*.
101: 3 set no *w'* thing before mine eyes:
4 me: I will not know a *w'* person.
8 destroy all the *w'* of the land;
8 that I may cut off all the *w'* doers
104: 35 earth, and let the *w'* be no more.
106: 18 the flame burned up the *w'*.
109: 2 the mouth of the *w'* and the mouth
6 Set thou a *w'* man over him: and
112: 10 The *w'* shall see it, and be grieved;
10 the desire of the *w'* shall perish.
119: 53 of the *w'* that forsake thy law.
61 bands of the *w'* have robbed me:
95 *w'* have waited for me to destroy
110 The *w'* have laid a snare for me:
119 puttest away all the *w'* of the earth

Ps 119: 155 Salvation is far from the *w'*: for
125: 3 the rod of the *w'* shall not rest
129: 4 cut asunder the cords of the *w'*.
139: 19 Surely thou wilt slay the *w'*, O God:
24 see if there be any *w'* way in me,
140: 4 O Lord, from the hands of the *w'*;
8 not, O Lord, the desires of the *w'*:
8 further not his *w'* device; lest
141: 4 to practise *w'* works with men
10 Let the *w'* fall into their own nets,
145: 20 him: but all the *w'* will he destroy.
146: 9 the way of the *w'* he turneth upside
147: 6 casteth the *w'* down to the ground.
Pr 2: 14 in the frowardness of the *w'*;
22 *w'* shall be cut off from the earth,
3: 25 neither of the desolation of the *w'*,
33 the Lord is in the house of the *w'*:
4: 14 Enter not into the path of the *w'*,
19 The way of the *w'* is as darkness:
5: 22 iniquity shall take the *w'* himself,
6: 12 *w'* man, walketh with a froward
18 heart that deviseth *w'* imaginations,
9: 7 he that rebuketh a *w'* man getteth
10: 3 away the substance of the *w'*.
6 covereth the mouth of the *w'*.
7 but the name of the *w'* shall rot.
11 violence covereth...mouth of the *w'*.
16 to life: the fruit of the *w'* to sin.
20 the heart of the *w'* is little worth.
24 The fear of the *w'*, it shall come
25 passeth, so is the *w'* no more:
27 years of the *w'* shall be shortened.
28 expectation of the *w'* shall perish.
30 the *w'* shall not inhabit the earth.
32 of the *w'* speaketh frowardness.
11: 5 *w'* shall fall by his own wickedness.
7 When a *w'* man dieth, his
8 and the *w'* cometh in his stead.
10 the *w'* perish, there is shouting.
11 overthrown by the mouth of the *w'*.
18 The *w'* worketh a deceitful work:
21 the *w'* shall not be unpunished:
23 the expectation of the *w'* is wrath.
31 much more the *w'* and the sinner.
12: 2 man of *w'* devices will...condemn.
5 the counsels of the *w'* are deceit.
6 words of the *w'* are to lie in wait
7 *w'* are overthrown, and are not:
10 tender mercies of the *w'* are cruel.
12 The *w'* desireth the net of evil men:
13 *w'* is snared by the transgression
21 *w'* shall be filled with mischief.
26 the way of the *w'* seduceth them.
13: 5 a *w'* man is loathsome, and cometh
9 the lamp of the *w'* shall be put out.
17 *w'* messenger falleth into mischief:
25 but the belly of the *w'* shall want.
14: 11 The house of the *w'* shall be
17 and a man of *w'* devices is hated.
19 *w'* at the gates of the righteous.
32 The *w'* is driven away in his
15: 6 in the revenues of the *w'* is trouble.
8 sacrifice of the *w'* is an abomination
9 way of the *w'* is an abomination
26 The thoughts of the *w'* are an
28 mouth of the *w'* poureth out evil
29 The Lord is far from the *w'*: but he
16: 4 yea, even the *w'* for the day of evil.
17: 4 A *w'* doer giveth heed to false lips;
15 He that justifieth the *w'*, and he
23 A *w'* man taketh a gift out of the
18: 3 When the *w'* cometh, then cometh
5 good to accept the person of the *w'*,
19: 28 mouth of the *w'* devoureth iniquity.
20: 26 A wise king scattereth the *w'*, and
21: 4 and the plowing of the *w'*, is sin.
7 The robbery of the *w'* shall destroy
10 The soul of the *w'* desireth evil:
12 considereth the house of the *w'*:
12 God overthroweth the *w'* for their
18 The *w'* shall be a ransom for the
27 sacrifice of the *w'* is abomination:
27 he bringeth it with a *w'* mind?
29 A *w'* man hardeneth his face: but
24: 15 Lay not wait, O *w'* man, against the
16 but the *w'* shall fall into mischief.
19 neither be thou envious at the *w'*;
20 candle of the *w'* shall be put out.
24 He that saith unto the *w'*, Thou art
25: 5 Take...the *w'* from before the king,
26 man falling down before the *w'*
26: 23 Burning lips and a *w'* heart are
28: 1 *w'* flee when no man pursueth:
4 that forsake the law praise the *w'*:
12 when the *w'* rise, a man is hidden.
15 is a *w'* ruler over the poor people.
28 the *w'* rise, men hide themselves:
29: 2 but when the *w'* beareth rule, the
7 the *w'* regardeth not to know it.
12 to lies, all his servants are *w'*.
16 When the *w'* are multiplied,
27 the way is abomination to the *w'*.
Ec 3: 17 judge the righteous and the *w'*:
7: 15 a *w'* man that prolongeth his life
17 Be not over much *w'*, neither be
8: 10 And so I saw the *w'* buried, who
13 it shall not be well with the *w'*,
14 according to the work of the *w'*;
14 again, there be *w'* men, to whom it
9: 2 to the righteous, and to the *w'*;
Isa 3: 11 Woe unto the *w'*! it shall be ill
5: 23 Which justify the *w'* for reward,
11: 4 of his lips shall he slay the *w'*.
13: 11 evil, and the *w'* for their iniquity;
14: 5 Lord..broken the staff of the *w'*,
26: 10 Let favour be shewed to the *w'*, yet

Isa 32: 7 he deviseth *w'* devices to destroy
48: 22 peace, saith the Lord, unto the *w'*.
53: 9 And he made his grave with the *w'*,
55: 7 Let the *w'* forsake his way, and the
57: 20 the *w'* are like the troubled sea,
21 no peace, saith my God, to the *w'*.
Jer 2: 33 also taught the *w'* ones thy ways.
5: 26 among my people are...*w'* men:
28 they overpass the deeds of the *w'*:
6: 29 for the *w'* are not plucked away.
12: 1 doth the way of the *w'* prosper?
15: 21 thee out of the hand of the *w'*,
17: 9 all things, and desperately *w'*:
23: 19 upon the head of the *w'*.
25: 31 give them that are *w'* to the sword,
30: 23 with pain upon the head of the *w'*.
Eze 3: 18 When I say unto the *w'*, Thou shalt
18 to warn the *w'* from his *w'* way,
18 *w'* man shall die in his iniquity;
19 if thou warn the *w'*, and he turn
19 wickedness, nor from his *w'* way,
7: 21 to the *w'* of the earth for a spoil;
8: 9 the *w'* abominations that they do
11: 2 and give *w'* counsel in this city:
13: 22 the hands of the *w'*, that he should
22 should not return from his *w'* way,
18: 20 wickedness of the *w'* shall be upon
21 if the *w'* will turn from all his sins
23 pleasure...that the *w'* should die?
24 abominations...the *w'* man doeth,
27 *w'* man turneth away from his
20: 44 not according to your *w'* ways,
21: 3 from thee the righteous and the *w'*.
4 from thee the righteous and the *w'*,
25 thou, profane *w'* prince of Israel,
29 of the *w'*, whose day is come, when
30: 12 the land into the hand of the *w'*:
33: 8 When I say unto the *w'*, O *w'* man,
8 speak to warn the *w'* from his way,
8 *w'* man shall die in his iniquity;
9 warn the *w'* of his way to turn from
11 no pleasure in the death of the *w'*;
11 the *w'* turn from his way and live:
12 as for the wickedness of the *w'*, he
14 when I say unto the *w'*, Thou shalt
15 If the *w'* restore the pledge, give
19 if the *w'* turn from his wickedness,
Da 12: 10 tried; but the *w'* shall do wickedly:
10 none of the *w'* shall understand;
Mic 6: 10 wickedness in the house of the *w'*,
11 them pure with the *w'* balances,
Na 1: 3 and will not at all acquit the *w'*:
11 against the Lord, a *w'* counsellor.
15 *w'* shall no more pass through thee:
Hab 1: 4 *w'* doth compass about the
13 when the *w'* devoureth the man
3: 13 the head out of the house of the *w'*,
Zep 1: 3 the stumblingblocks with the *w'*;
Mal 3: 18 between the righteous and the *w'*,
4: 3 And ye shall tread down the *w'*;
M't 12: 45 other spirits more *w'* than himself,
45 be also unto this *w'* generation.
13: 19 then cometh the *w'* one, and
38 are the children of the *w'* one;
49 sever the *w'* from among the just,
16: 4 A *w'* and adulterous generation
18: 32 O thou *w'* servant, I forgave thee
21: 41 miserably destroy those *w'* men,
25: 26 Thou *w'* and slothful servant,
Lu 11: 26 other spirits more *w'* than himself;
19: 22 will I judge thee, thou *w'* servant.
Ac 2: 23 *w'* hands have crucified and slain:
18: 14 a matter of wrong or *w'* lewdness,
1Co 5: 13 among yourselves that *w'* person.
Eph 6: 16 quench all the fiery darts of the *w'*.
Col 1: 21 enemies in your mind by *w'* works,
2Th 2: 8 then shall that *W'* be revealed,
3: 2 from unreasonable and *w'* men:
2Pe 2: 7 the filthy conversation of the *w'*:
3: 17 led away with the error of the *w'*,
1Jo 2: 13 ye have overcome the *w'* one.
14 and ye have overcome the *w'* one.
3: 12 as Cain, who was of that *w'* one,
5: 18 and that *w'* one toucheth him not.

wickedly
Ge 19: 7 I pray you, brethren, do not so *w'*.
De 9: 18 doing *w'* in the sight of the Lord,
J'g 19: 23 nay, I pray you, do not so *w'*;
1Sa 12: 25 if ye shall still do *w'*, ye shall be
2Sa 22: 22 have not *w'* departed from my God.
24: 17 have sinned, and I have done *w'*:
2Ki 21: 11 done *w'* above all...the Amorites
2Ch 6: 37 done amiss, and have dealt *w'*;
20: 35 king of Israel, who did very *w'*:
22: 3 mother was his counsellor to do *w'*.
Ne 9: 33 done right, but we have done *w'*:
Job 13: 7 Will ye speak *w'* for God? and
34: 12 Yea, surely God will not do *w'*,
Ps 18: 21 have not *w'* departed from my God.
73: 8 speak *w'* concerning oppression:
74: 3 hath done *w'* in the sanctuary.
106: 6 iniquity, we have done *w'*.
139: 20 For they speak against thee *w'*,
Da 9: 5 have done *w'*, and have rebelled,
15 we have sinned, we have done *w'*.
11: 32 such as do *w'* against the covenant
12: 10 tried; but the wicked shall do *w'*:
Mal 4: 1 all that do *w'*, shall be stubble:

wickedness
Ge 6: 5 saw that the *w'* of man was great
39: 9 then can I do this great *w'*, and sin
Le 18: 17 are her near kinswomen: it is *w'*.
19: 29 and the land became full of *w'*.
20: 14 a wife and her mother, it is *w'*:
14 that there be no *w'* among you.

De 9: 4, 5 but for the w· of these nations
27 nor to their w·, nor to their sin:
13: 11 do no more any such w· as this is
17: 2 wrought w· in the sight of the Lord
28: 20 because of the w· of thy doings,
J'g 9: 56 God rendered the w· of Abimelech,
20: 3 Israel, Tell us, how was this w·?
12 What w· is this that is done among
1Sa 12: 17 and see that your w· is great,
20 Fear not: ye have done all this w·:
24: 13 W· proceedeth from the wicked:
25: 39 hath returned the w· of Nabel
2Sa 3: 39 the doer of evil according to his w·.
7: 10 children of w· afflict them any
1Ki 1: 52 but if w· shall be found in him,
2: 44 w· which thine heart is privy to,
44 return thy w· upon thine own head:
8: 47 perversely, we...committed w·;
21: 25 which did sell himself to work w·
2Ki 21: 6 wrought much w· in the sight of
1Ch 17: 9 the children of w· waste them
Job 4: 8 that plow iniquity, and sow w·,
11: 11 he seeth w· also; will he not then
14 not w· dwell in thy tabernacles.
20: 12 Though w· be sweet in his mouth,
22: 5 Is not thy w· great? and thine
24: 20 and w· shall be broken as a tree.
27: 4 My lips shall not speak w·, nor my
34: 10 from God, that he should do w·;
35: 8 Thy w· may hurt a man as thou art;
Ps 5: 4 not a God that hath pleasure in w·:
9 their inward part is very w·; their
7: 9 Oh let the w· of the wicked come
10: 15 seek out his w· till thou find none.
28: 4 according to the w· of their
45: 7 righteousness, and hatest w·.
52: 7 strengthened himself in his w·.
55: 11 W· is in the midst thereof: deceit
15 for w· is in their dwellings, and
58: 2 Yea, in heart ye work w·; ye
84: 10 than to dwell in the tents of w·.
89: 22 him; nor the son of w· afflict him.
94: 23 shall cut them off in their own w·;
107: 34 the w· of them that dwell therein.
Pr 4: 17 For they eat the bread of w·, and
8: 7 w· is an abomination to my lips.
10: 2 Treasures of w· profit nothing:
11: 5 wicked shall fall by his own w·.
12: 3 shall not be established by w·:
13: 6 but w· overthroweth the sinner.
14: 32 wicked is driven away in his w·:
16: 12 abomination...kings to commit w·:
21: 12 the wicked for their w·.
26: 26 his w· shall be shewed before the
30: 20 and saith, I have done no w·.
Ec 3: 16 of judgment, that w· was there;
7: 15 that prolongeth his life in his w·.
25 and to know the w· of folly, even
8: 8 neither shall w· deliver those that
Isa 9: 18 For w· burneth as the fire: it shall
47: 10 For thou hast trusted in thy w·:
58: 4 and to smite with the fist of w·:
6 to loose the bands of w·, to undo
Jer 1: 16 against them touching all their w·,
2: 19 Thine own w· shall correct thee,
3: 2 thy whoredoms and with thy w·.
4: 14 wash thine heart from w·, that
18 this is thy w·, because it is bitter,
6: 7 waters, so she casteth out her w·:
7: 12 to it for the w· of my people Israel.
8: 6 no man repented him of his w·,
12: 4 the w· of them that dwell therein?
14: 16 I will pour their w· upon them.
20 We acknowledge, O Lord, our w·,
22: 22 and confounded for all thy w·.
23: 11 in my house have I found their w·,
14 that none doth return from his w·:
33: 5 for all whose w· I have hid my face
44: 3 of their w·...they have committed
5 their ear to turn from their w·,
9 ye forgotten the w· of your fathers,
9 and the w· of the kings of Judah,
9 and the w· of their wives,
9 of their wives, and your own w·,
9 and the w· of your wives, which
La 1: 22 Let all their w· come before thee;
Eze 3: 19 and he turn not from his w·, nor
5: 6 changed my judgments into w·
7: 11 is risen up into a rod of w·:
16: 23 it came to pass after all thy w·,
57 Before thy w· was discovered, as at
18: 20 the w· of the wicked shall be upon
27 wicked...turneth away from his w·
31: 11 I have driven him out for his w·.
33: 12 as for the w· of the wicked, he
12 day that he turneth from his w·;
19 But if the wicked turn from his w·,
Ho 7: 1 discovered, and the w· of Samaria:
2 hearts that I remember all their w·:
3 make the king glad with their w·,
9: 15 All their w· is in Gilgal: for there I
15 for the w· of their doings I will
10: 13 Ye have plowed w·, ye have reaped
15 unto you because of your great w·:
Joe 3: 13 fats overflow; for their w· is great.
Jon 1: 2 for their w· is come up before me.
Mic 6: 10 treasures of w· in the house of the
Na 3: 19 not thy w· passed continually?
Zec 5: 8 And he said, This is w·. And he
Mal 1: 4 shall call them, The border of w·,
3: 15 yea, they that work w· are set up;
M't 22: 18 But Jesus perceived their w·, and
M'r 7: 22 Thefts, covetousness, w·, deceit,
Lu 11: 39 part is full of ravening and w·.
Ac 8: 22 Repent therefore of this thy w·,
25: 5 man, if there be any w· in him.
Ro 1: 29 w·, covetousness, maliciousness;
1Co 5: 8 with the leaven of malice and w·;
Eph 6: 12 against spiritual w· in high places,
1Jo 5: 19 and the whole world lieth in w·.

wide
De 15: 8 open thine hand w· unto him,
11 thine hand w· unto thy brother,
1Ch 4: 40 the land was w·, and quiet,
Job 29: 23 opened their mouth w· as for the latter
30: 14 as a w· breaking in of waters:
Ps 35: 21 opened their mouth w· against
81: 10 open thy mouth w·, and I will fill
104: 25 So is this great and w· sea,
Pr 13: 3 he that openeth w· his lips shall have
21: 9 a brawling woman in a w· house.
25: 24 brawling woman and in a w· house.
Isa 57: 4 against whom make ye a w· mouth,
Jer 22: 14 I will build me a w· house and
Na 3: 13 the gates...shall be set w· open
M't 7: 13 for w· is the gate, and broad is the

wideness
Eze 41: 10 the w· of twenty cubits round

widow See also WIDOW'S; WIDOWS.
Ge 38: 11 Remain a w· at thy father's house,
Ex 22: 22 Ye shall not afflict any w·, or
Le 21: 14 A w·, or a divorced woman, or
22: 13 But if the priest's daughter be a w·,
Nu 30: 9 But every vow of a w·, and of her
De 10: 18 judgment of the fatherless and w·,
14: 29 and the fatherless, and the w·,
16: 11, 14 and the fatherless, and the w·,
24: 19 for the fatherless, and for the w·:
20, 21 for the fatherless, and for the w·.
26: 12 stranger, the fatherless, and the w·,
13 to the fatherless, and to the w·,
27: 19 of the stranger, fatherless, and w·.
2Sa 14: 5 answered, I am indeed a w· woman,
1Ki 11: 26 name was Zeruah, a w· woman,
17: 9 commanded a w· woman there to
10 the w· woman was there gathering
20 evil upon the w· with whom I
Job 24: 21 not: and doeth not good to the w·.
31: 16 caused the eyes of the w· to fail;
Ps 94: 6 They slay the w· and the stranger,
109: 9 be fatherless, and his wife a w·.
146: 9 he relieveth the fatherless and w·:
Pr 15: 25 will establish the border of the w·.
Isa 1: 17 the fatherless, plead for the w·.
23 the cause of the w· come unto them.
47: 8 I shall not sit as a w·, neither shall I
Jer 7: 6 stranger, the fatherless, and the w·,
22: 3 stranger, the fatherless, nor the w·,
La 1: 1 how is she become as a w·! she that
Eze 22: 7 they vexed the fatherless and the w·.
44: 22 shall they take for their wives a w·,
22 or a w· that had a priest before.
Zec 7: 10 And oppress not the w·, nor the
Mal 3: 5 the hireling in his wages, the w·,
M'r 12: 42 And there came a certain poor w·,
43 That this poor w· hath cast more in,
Lu 2: 37 a w· of about fourscore and four
4: 26 Sidon, unto a woman that was a w·.
7: 12 of his mother, and she was a w·:
18: 3 And there was a w· in that city;
5 Yet because this w· troubleth me, I
21: 2 w· casting in thither two mites.
3 w· hath cast in more than they all:
1Ti 5: 4 if any w· have children or nephews,
5 that is a w· indeed, and desolate,
9 not a w· be taken into the number
Re 18: 7 I sit a queen, and am no w·, and

widowhood
Ge 38: 19 and put on the garments of her w·.
2Sa 20: 3 the day of their death, living in w·.
Isa 47: 9 day, the loss of children, and w·:
54: 4 remember the reproach of thy w·

widow's
Ge 38: 14 And she put her w· garments off
De 24: 17 nor take the w· raiment to pledge:
1Ki 7: 14 was a w· son of the tribe of Naphtali,
Job 24: 3 they take the w· ox for a pledge.
29: 13 I caused the w· heart to sing for joy.

widows See also WIDOWS'.
Ex 22: 24 and your wives shall be w·, and
Job 22: 9 Thou hast sent w· away empty, and
27: 15 in death: and his w· shall not weep.
Ps 68: 5 the fatherless, and a judge of the w·,
78: 64 and their w· made no lamentation.
Isa 9: 17 mercy on their fatherless and w·:
10: 2 people, that w· may be their prey,
Jer 15: 8 Their w· are increased to me above
18: 21 bereaved of their children, and be w·;
49: 11 alive; and let thy w· trust in me.
La 5: 3 fatherless, our mothers are as w·.
Eze 22: 25 made her many w· in the midst
Lu 4: 25 many w· were in Israel in the days
Ac 6: 1 their w· were neglected in the daily
9: 39 all the w· stood by him weeping,
41 he had called the saints and w·,
1Co 7: 8 therefore to the unmarried and w·,
1Ti 5: 3 Honour w· that are w· indeed.
11 But the younger w· refuse: for
16 or woman that believeth have w·,
16 relieve them that are w· indeed.
Jas 1: 27 fatherless and w· in their affliction,

widows'
M't 23: 14 for ye devour w· houses, and for a
M'r 12: 40 Which devour w· houses, and for a
Lu 20: 47 Which devour w· houses, and for a

width See WIDENESS.

wife^ See also MIDWIFE; WIFE'S; WIVES.
Ge 2: 24 and shall cleave unto his w·:
25 both naked, the man and his w·,
3: 8 Adam and his w· hid themselves
17 hearkened unto the voice of thy w·,
21 Unto Adam also and to his w· did
4: 1 Adam knew Eve his w·; and she
17 Cain knew his w·; and she conceived,
25 Adam knew his w· again; and she
6: 18 ark, thou, and thy sons, and thy w·,
7: 7 Noah went in,...his sons, and his w·,
13 the sons of Noah, and Noah's w·, and
8: 16 Go forth of the ark, thou, and thy w·,
18 went forth, and his sons, and his w·
11: 29 the name of Abram's w· was Sarai;
29 the name of Nahor's w·, Milcah, the
31 daughter in law, his son Abram's w·;
12: 5 Abram took Sarai his w·, and Lot
11 he said unto Sarai his w·, Behold
12 that they shall say, This is his w·:
17 plagues because of Sarai Abram's w·.
18 thou not tell me that she was thy w·?
19 I might have taken her to me to w·:
19 behold thy w·, take her, and go thy
20 and they sent him away, and his w·,
13: 1 went up out of Egypt, he, and his w·,
16: 1 Abram's w· bare him no children:
3 Abram's w· took Hagar her maid
3 to her husband Abram to be his w·.
17: 15 As for Sarai thy w·, thou shalt not
19 Sarah thy w· shall bare thee a son
18: 9 unto him, Where is Sarah thy w·?
10 lo, Sarah thy w· shall have a son.
19: 15 take thy w·, and thy two daughters,
16 hand, and upon the hand of his w·,
26 his w· looked back from behind him,
20: 2 Abraham said of Sarah his w·, She
3 hast taken; for she is a man's w·.
7 therefore restore the man his w·;
12 my mother; and she became my w·.
14 and restored him Sarah his w·.
17 God healed Abimelech, and his w·,
18 because of Sarah Abraham's w·.
21: 21 him a w· out of the land of Egypt.
23: 19 Abraham buried Sarah his w· in
24: 3 thou shalt not take a w· unto my son
4 and take a w· unto my son Isaac.
7 thou shalt take a w· unto my son
15 the w· of Nahor, Abraham's brother,
36 Sarah my master's w· bare a son to
37 Thou shalt not take a w· to my son
38 kindred, and take a w· unto my son.
40 take a w· for my son of my kindred,
51 and let her be thy master's son's w·,
67 Rebekah, and she became his w·;
25: 1 Then again Abraham took a w·,
10 Abraham buried, and Sarah his w·.
20 old when he took Rebekah to w·,
21 Isaac intreated the Lord for his w·,
21 him, and Rebekah his w· conceived.
26: 7 men of the place asked him of his w·;
7 for he feared to say, She is my w·;
8 was sporting with Rebekah his w·.
9 Behold, of a surety she is thy w·:
10 might lightly have lien with thy w·,
11 He that toucheth this man or his w·
34 he took to w· Judith the daughter of
27: 46 if Jacob take a w· of the daughters
28: 1 shalt not take a w· of the daughters
2 take thee a w· from thence of the
6 to take him a w· from thence; and
6 shalt not take a w· of the daughters
9 the sister of Nebajoth, to be his w·.
29: 21 Give me my w·, for my days are
28 gave him Rachel his daughter to w·
30: 4 gave him Bilhah her handmaid to w·:
9 her maid, and gave her Jacob to w·.
34: 4 saying, Get me this damsel to w·.
8 I pray you give her him to w·.
12 me: but give me the damsel to w·.
36: 10 the son of Adah the w· of Esau,
10 son of Bashemath the w· of Esau.
12 were the sons of Adah Esau's w·.
13 the sons of Bashemath Esau's w·.
14 the daughter of Zibeon, Esau's w·:
17 the sons of Bashemath Esau's w·.
18 the sons of Aholibamah Esau's w·;
18 the daughter of Anah, Esau's w·.
38: 6 Judah took a w· for Er his firstborn,
8 Go in unto thy brother's w·, and
9 he went in unto his brother's w·,
12 daughter of Shuah Judah's w· died;
14 she was not given unto him to w·.
39: 7 his master's w· cast her eyes upon
8 and said unto his master's w·,
9 but thee, because thou art his w·:
19 his master heard the words of his w·,
41: 45 gave him to w· Asenath the daughter
44: 27 know that my w· bare me two sons:
46: 19 The sons of Rachel Jacob's w·;
49: 31 buried Abraham and Sarah his w·;
31 buried Isaac and Rebekah his w·;
Ex 4: 20 And Moses took his w· and his sons,
6: 20 Jochebed his father's sister to w·;
23 Amminadab, sister of Naashon, to w·;
25 one of the daughters of Putiel to w·;
18: 2 in law took Zipporah, Moses' w·,
5 with his sons and his w· unto Moses
6 and thy w·, and her two sons with
20: 17 shalt not covet thy neighbour's w·,
21: 3 then his w· shall go out with him.
4 If his master have given him a w·,
4 the w· and her children shall be her
5 I love my master, my w·, and my
10 If he take him another w·; her food,
22: 16 shall surely endow her to be his w·.
Le 18: 8 father's w· shalt thou not uncover:
14 thou shalt not approach to his w·:
15 she is thy son's w·; thou shalt not

Le 18:16 the nakedness of thy brother's *w*·:
18 shalt thou take a *w*· to her sister,
20 lie carnally with thy neighbour's *w*·,
20:10 adultery with another man's *w*·,
10 adultery with his neighbour's *w*·,
11 man that lieth with his father's *w*·
14 if a man take a *w*· and her mother,
20 a man shall lie with his uncle's *w*·,
21 if a man shall take his brother's *w*·.
21: 7 shall not take a *w*· that is a whore,
13 he shall take a *w*· in her virginity.
14 take a virgin of his own people to *w*·.
Nu 5:12 If any man's *w*· go aside, and commit
14, 14 and he be jealous of his *w*·, and
15 the man bring his *w*· unto the priest,
29 when a *w*· goeth aside to another
30 him, and he be jealous over his *w*·,
26:59 name of Amram's *w*· was Jochebed,
30:16 between a man and his *w*·, between
36: 8 shall be *w*· unto one of the family of
De 5:21 shalt thou desire thy neighbour's *w*·,
13: 6 or the *w*· of thy bosom, or thy friend,
20: 7 is there that hath betrothed a *w*·,
21:11 thou wouldest have her to thy *w*·;
13 her husband, and she shall be thy *w*·.
22:13 If a man take a *w*·, and go in unto
16 my daughter unto this man to *w*·,
19 and she shall be his *w*·; he may not
24 he hath humbled his neighbour's *w*·:
29 of silver, and she shall be his *w*·;
30 A man shall not take his father's *w*·,
24: 1 When a man hath taken a *w*·, and
2 she may go and be another man's *w*·.
3 die, which took her to be his *w*·;
4 may not take her again to be his *w*·,
5 When a man hath taken a new *w*·,
5 shall cheer up his *w*· which he hath
25: 5 the *w*· of the dead shall not marry
5 take her to him to *w*·, and perform
7 like not to take his brother's *w*·,
7 his brother's *w*· go up to the gate
9 his brother's *w*· come unto him
11 and the *w*· of the one draweth near
27:20 he that lieth with his father's *w*·;
28:30 Thou shalt betroth a *w*·, and another
54 and toward the *w*· of his bosom,
Jos 15:16 I give Achsah my daughter to *w*·.
17 gave him Achsah his daughter to *w*·.
J'g 1:12 I give Achsah my daughter to *w*·.
13 gave him Achsah his daughter to *w*·.
4: 4 a prophetess, the *w*· of Lapidoth,
17 to the tent of Jael the *w*· of Heber
21 Then Jael Heber's *w*· took a nail of
5:24 Jael the *w*· of Heber the Kenite be,
11: 2 Gilead's *w*· bare him sons; and his
13: 2 and his *w*· was barren, and bare not.
11 Manoah arose, and went after his *w*·,
19 and Manoah and his *w*· looked on.
20 And Manoah and his *w*· looked on it,
21 appear to Manoah and to his *w*·.
22 Manoah said unto his *w*·, We shall
23 But his *w*· said unto him, If the Lord
14: 2 now therefore get her for me to *w*·.
3 to take a *w*· of the uncircumcised
15 that they said unto Samson's *w*·,
16 And Samson's *w*· wept before him,
20 But Samson's *w*· was given to his
15: 1 Samson visited his *w*· with a kid;
1 will go in to my *w*· into the chamber.
6 because he had taken his *w*·, and
21: 1 his daughter unto Benjamin to *w*·.
18 be he that giveth a *w*· to Benjamin.
21 catch you every man his *w*· of the
22 we reserved not to each man his *w*·
Ru 1: 1 the country of Moab, he, and his *w*·,
2 and the name of his *w*· Naomi,
4: 5 the Moabitess, the *w*· of the dead,
10 Ruth the Moabitess,...*w*· of Mahlon,
10 have I purchased to be my *w*·, to
13 Boaz took Ruth, and she was his *w*·:
1Sa 1: 4 offered, he gave to Peninnah his *w*·,
19 and Elkanah knew Hannah his *w*·;
2:20 And Eli blessed Elkanah and his *w*·,
4:19 his daughter in law, Phinehas' *w*·,
14:50 the name of Saul's *w*· was Ahinoam,
18:17 Merab, her will I give thee to *w*·:
19 unto Adriel the Meholathite to *w*·.
27 gave him Michal his daughter to *w*·.
19:11 and Michal David's *w*· told him,
25: 3 and the name of his *w*· Abigail:
14 young men told Abigail, Nabal's *w*·,
37 his *w*· had told him these things,
39 with Abigail, to take her to him to *w*·.
40 unto thee, to take thee to him to *w*·.
42 of David, and became his *w*·.
44 Michal his daughter, David's *w*·, to
27: 3 Abigail the Carmelitess, Nabal's *w*·.
30: 5 Abigail...*w*· of Nabal the Carmelite.
22 save to every man his *w*· and his
2Sa 2: 2 Abigail Nabal's *w*· the Carmelite.
3: 3 Abigail...*w*· of Nabal the Carmelite;
5 Ithream, by Eglah David's *w*·.
14 Deliver me my *w*· Michal, which I
11: 3 Eliam, the *w*· of Uriah the Hittite?
11 and to drink, and to lie with my *w*·?
26 when the *w*· of Uriah heard that
27 she became his *w*·, and bare him a
12: 9 and hast taken his *w*· to be thy *w*·,
10 me, and hast taken the *w*· of Uriah
10 of Uriah the Hittite to be thy *w*·.
15 which Uriah's *w*· bare unto David,
24 David comforted Bath-sheba his *w*·,
1Ki 2:17 me Abishag the Shunammite to *w*·.
21 given to Adonijah thy brother to *w*·.
4:11, 15 the daughter of Solomon to *w*·:
7: 8 daughter, whom he had taken to *w*·,
1Ki 9:16 unto his daughter, Solomon's *w*·.
11:19 him to *w*· the sister of his own *w*·,
14: 2 And Jeroboam said to his *w*·, Arise,
2 not known to be the *w*· of Jeroboam;
4 Jeroboam's *w*· did so, and arose,
5 the *w*· of Jeroboam cometh to ask a
6 said, Come in, thou *w*· of Jeroboam;
17 Jeroboam's *w*· arose, and departed,
16:31 he took to *w*· Jezebel the daughter
21: 5 But Jezebel his *w*· came to him, and
7 Jezebel his *w*· said unto him, Dost
25 whom Jezebel his *w*· stirred up.
2Ki 5: 2 and she waited on Naaman's *w*·.
8:18 for the daughter of Ahab was his *w*·:
14: 9 Give thy daughter to my son to *w*·:
22:14 the prophetess, the *w*· of Shallum
1Ch 2:18 begat children of Azubah his *w*·,
24 Abiah Hezron's *w*· bare him Ashur
26 Jerahmeel had also another *w*·,
29 of the *w*· of Abishur was Abihail,
35 daughter to Jarha his servant to *w*·;
3: 3 the sixth, Ithream by Eglah his *w*·.
4:18 And his *w*· Jehudijah bare Jered the
19 the sons of his *w*· Hodiah the sister
7:15 And Machir took to *w*· the sister of
16 Maachah the *w*· of Machir bare a
23 And when he went in to his *w*·, she
8: 9 he begat of Hodesh his *w*·, Jobab,
2Ch 8:11 My *w*· shall not dwell in the house
11:18 of Jerimoth the son of David to *w*·,
21: 6 he had the daughter of Ahab to *w*·:
22:11 the *w*· of Jehoiada the priest,
25:18 Give thy daughter to my son to *w*·:
34:22 the prophetess, the *w*· of Shallum
Ezr 2:61 a *w*· of the daughters of Barzillai
Ne 7:63 of Barzillai the Gileadite to *w*·,
Es 5:10 for his friends, and Zeresh his *w*·.
14 Then said Zeresh his *w*· and all his
6:13 Haman told Zeresh his *w*· and all his
13 his wise men and Zeresh his *w*·
Job 2: 9 Then said his *w*· unto him, Dost
19:17 My breath is strange to my *w*·,
31:10 Then let my *w*· grind unto another,
Ps 109: 9 be fatherless, and his *w*· a widow.
128: 3 Thy *w*· shall be as a fruitful vine by
Pr 5:18 and rejoice with the *w*· of thy youth.
6:29 that goeth in to his neighbour's *w*·;
18:22 Whoso findeth a *w*· findeth a good
19:13 contentions of a *w*· are a continual
14 and a prudent *w*· is from the Lord.
Ec 9: 9 Live joyfully with the *w*· whom thou
Isa 54: 1 the children of the married *w*·,
6 and a *w*· of youth, when thou wast
Jer 3: 1 If a man put away his *w*·, and she
20 as a *w*· treacherously departeth
5: 8 one neighed after his neighbour's *w*·.
6:11 husband with the *w*· shall be taken,
16: 2 Thou shalt not take thee a *w*·,
Eze 16:32 as a *w*· that committeth adultery,
18: 6 hath defiled his neighbour's *w*·,
11 and defiled his neighbour's *w*·,
15 hath not defiled his neighbour's *w*·,
22:11 abomination with his neighbour's *w*·,
24:18 at even my *w*· died; and I did in the
33:26 defile every one his neighbour's *w*·:
Ho 1: 2 take unto thee a *w*· of whoredoms
2: 2 she is not my *w*·, neither am I her
12:12 of Syria, and Israel served for a *w*·,
12 and for a *w*· he kept sheep.
Am 7:17 Thy *w*· shall be an harlot in the city,
Mal 2:14 between thee and...*w*· of thy youth,
14 and the *w*· of thy covenant.
15 deal treacherously against the *w*· of
M't 1: 6 of her that had been the *w*· of Urias;
20 not to take unto thee Mary thy *w*·:
24 him, and took unto him his *w*·:
5:31 Whosoever shall put away his *w*·,
32 whosoever shall put away his *w*·,
14: 3 sake, his brother Philip's *w*·.
18:25 to be sold, and his *w*·, and children,
19: 3 lawful for a man to put away his *w*·
5 mother, and shall cleave to his *w*·:
9 Whosoever shall put away his *w*·,
10 case of the man be so with his *w*·,
29 or father, or mother, or *w*·, or
22:24 his brother shall marry his *w*·, and
25 first, when he had married a *w*·,
25 issue, left his *w*· unto his brother:
28 whose *w*· shall she be of the seven?
27:19 seat, his *w*· sent unto him, saying,
M'r 6:17 sake, his brother Philip's *w*·:
18 for thee to have thy brother's *w*·.
10: 2 for a man to put away his *w*·?
7 and mother, and cleave to his *w*·;
11 Whosoever shall put away his *w*·,
29 or father, or mother, or *w*·, or
12:19 die, and leave his *w*· behind him,
19 that his brother should take his *w*·,
20 the first took a *w*·, and dying left
23 rise, whose *w*· shall she be of them?
23 for the seven had her to *w*·.
Lu 1: 5 his *w*· was of the daughters of
13 *w*· Elisabeth shall bear thee a son,
18 and my *w*· well stricken in years.
24 days his *w*· Elisabeth conceived,
2: 5 taxed with Mary his espoused *w*·,
3:19 Herodias his brother Philip's *w*·,
8: 3 the *w*· of Chuza Herod's steward,
14:20 I have married a *w*·, and therefore
26 his father, and mother, and *w*·,
16:18 Whosoever putteth away his *w*·,
17:32 Remember Lot's *w*·.
18:29 or parents, or brethren, or *w*·,
20:28 any man's brother die, having a *w*·,
28 that his brother should take his *w*·,
29 the first took a *w*·, and died without
Lu 20:30 the second took her to *w*·, and he
33 whose *w*· of them is she?
33 for seven had her to *w*·.
Joh 19:25 sister, Mary the *w*· of Cleophas,
Ac 5: 1 Ananias, with Sapphira his *w*·,
2 price, his *w*· also being privy to it,
7 his *w*·, not knowing what was done,
18: 2 from Italy, with his *w*· Priscilla;
24:24 Felix came with his *w*· Drusilla,
1Co 5: 1 one should have his father's *w*·.
7: 2 let every man have his own *w*·, and
3 husband render unto the *w*· due
3 also the *w*· unto the husband.
4 *w*· hath not power of her own body,
4 power of his own body, but the *w*·.
10 Let not the *w*· depart from her
11 not the husband put away his *w*·.
12 brother hath a *w*· that believeth
14 husband is sanctified by the *w*·,
14 *w*· is sanctified by the husband:
16 For what knowest thou, O *w*·,
16 whether thou shalt save thy *w*·?
27 Art thou bound unto a *w*·? seek not
27 loosed from a *w*·? seek not a *w*·.
33 world, how he may please his *w*·.
34 is difference also between a *w*· and
39 The *w*· is bound by the law as long
9: 5 power to lead about a sister, a *w*·,
Eph 5:23 the husband is the head of the *w*·,
28 that loveth his *w*· loveth himself.
31 and shall be joined unto his *w*·,
33 so love his *w*· even as himself; and
33 the *w*· see that she reverence her
1Ti 3: 2 the husband of one *w*·, vigilant,
12 deacons be the husbands of one *w*·,
5: 9 having been the *w*· of one man,
Tit 1: 6 the husband of one *w*·, having
1Pe 3: 7 giving honour unto the *w*·, as unto
Re 19: 7 his *w*· hath made herself ready.
21: 9 shew thee the bride, the Lamb's *w*·.

wife's

Ge 3:20 And Adam called his *w*· name Eve;
20:11 they will slay me for my *w*· sake.
36:39 and his *w*· name was Mehetabel,
Le 18:11 The nakedness of thy father's *w*·
J'g 11: 2 and his *w*· sons grew up, and they
1Ch 1:50 and his *w*· name was Mehetabel,
8:29 whose *w*· name was Maachah:
9:35 whose *w*· name was Maachah:
M't 8:14 house, he saw his *w*· mother laid,
M'r 1:30 Simon's *w*· mother lay sick of a
Lu 4:38 And Simon's *w*· mother was taken

wild

Ge 16:12 And he will be a *w*· man; his hand
Le 26:22 also send *w*· beasts among you,
De 14: 5 the fallow deer, and the *w*· goat,
5 the pygarg, and the *w*· ox, and the
1Sa 17:46 and to the *w*· beasts of the earth;
24: 2 upon the rocks of the *w*· goats.
2Sa 2:18 was as light of foot as a *w*· roe.
2Ki 4:39 gather herbs, and found a *w*· vine,
39 gathered thereof *w*· gourds his lap
14: 9 a *w*· beast that was in Lebanon,
2Ch 25:18 a *w*· beast that was in Lebanon,
Job 6: 5 *w*· ass bray when he hath grass?
11:12 may be born like a *w*· ass's colt.
24: 5 as *w*· asses in the desert, go they
39: 1 *w*· goats of the rock bring forth?
5 Who hath sent out the *w*· ass free?
5 loosed the bands of the *w*· ass?
15 that the *w*· beast may break them.
Ps 50:11 the *w*· beasts of the field are mine.
80:13 *w*· beasts of the field doth devour it.
104:11 the *w*· asses quench their thirst.
18 hills are a refuge for the *w*· goats;
Isa 5: 2 and it brought forth *w*· grapes.
4 grapes, brought it forth *w*· grapes?
13:21 *w*· beasts of the desert shall lie
22 *w*· beasts of the islands shall cry
32:14 a joy of *w*· asses, a pasture of
34:14 *w*· beasts of the desert shall also
14 also meet with the *w*· beasts of the
51:20 the streets, as a *w*· bull in a net:
Jer 2:24 A *w*· ass used to the wilderness,
14: 6 *w*· asses did stand in the high
50:39 the *w*· beasts of the desert with
39 *w*· beasts of the islands shall dwell
Da 5:21 dwelling was with the *w*· asses:
Hos 8: 9 Assyria, a *w*· ass alone by himself:
13: 8 the *w*· beast shall tear them.
M't 3: 4 his meat was locusts and *w*· honey
M'r 1: 6 he did eat locusts and *w*· honey;
13 and was with the *w*· beasts;
Ac 10:12 *w*· beasts, and creeping things,
11: 6 *w*· beasts, and creeping things, and
Ro 11:17 being a *w*· olive tree, wert graffed
24 the olive tree which is *w*· by nature,

wild-ass See WILD and ASS.

wilderness

Ge 14: 6 El-paran, which is by the *w*·.
16: 7 by a fountain of water in the *w*·,
21:14 wandered in the *w*· of Beer-sheba.
20 and he grew, and dwelt in the *w*·,
21 And he dwelt in the *w*· of Paran:
36:24 that found the mules in the *w*·,
37:22 him into this pit that is in the *w*·,
Ex 3:18 three days' journey into the *w*·, that
4:27 Go into the *w*· to meet Moses.
5: 1 may hold a feast unto me in the *w*·.
7:16 that they may serve me in the *w*·:
8:27 go three days' journey into the *w*·,
28 to the Lord your God in the *w*·:
13:18 the way of the *w*· of the Red sea:
20 in Etham, in the edge of the *w*·.

Ex 14: 3 the land, the *w'* hath shut them in.
11 taken us away to die in the *w'*?
12 than that we should die in the *w'*.
15: 22 they went out into the *w'* of Shur;
22 and they went three days in the *w'*,
16: 1 of Israel came unto the *w'* of Sin,
2 against Moses and Aaron in the *w'*:
3 have brought us forth into this *w'*,
10 that they looked toward the *w'*,
14 upon the face of the *w'* there lay a
32 wherewith I have fed you in the *w'*,
17: 1 Israel journeyed from the *w'* of Sin,
18: 5 his wife unto Moses into the *w'*,
19: 1 came they into the *w'* of Sinai.
2 Sinai, and had pitched in the *w'*;
Le 7: 38 unto the Lord, in the *w'* of Sinai.
16: 10 him go for a scapegoat into the *w'*.
21 the hand of a fit man into the *w'*:
22 he shall let go the goat in the *w'*.
Nu 1: 1 spake unto Moses in the *w'* of Sinai,
19 numbered them in the *w'* of Sinai.
3: 4 before the Lord, in the *w'* of Sinai,
14 unto Moses in the *w'* of Sinai,
9: 1 unto Moses in the *w'* of Sinai,
5 month at even in the *w'* of Sinai:
10: 12 journeys out of the *w'* of Sinai;
12 cloud rested in the *w'* of Paran.
31 how we are to encamp in the *w'*,
12: 16 and pitched in the *w'* of Paran,
13: 3 sent them from the *w'* of Paran:
21 from the *w'* of Zin unto Rehob,
26 unto the *w'* of Paran, to Kadesh;
14: 2 would God we had died in this *w'*!
16 he hath slain them in the *w'*.
22 which I did in Egypt and in the *w'*,
25 into the *w'* by the way of the Red
29 Your carcases shall fall in this *w'*;
32 carcases, they shall fall in this *w'*.
33 shall wander in the *w'* forty years,
33 your carcases be wasted in the *w'*.
35 in this *w'* they shall be consumed,
15: 32 children of Israel were in the *w'*,
16: 13 to kill us in the *w'*, except thou
20: 4 of the Lord into this *w'*,
21: 5 us up out of Egypt to die in the *w'*?
11 in the *w'* which is before Moab,
13 which is in the *w'* that cometh out
18 the *w'* they went to Mattanah:
23 went out against Israel into the *w'*:
24: 1 but he set his face toward the *w'*.
26: 64 of Israel in the *w'* of Sinai.
65 They shall surely die in the *w'*.
27: 3 Our father died in the *w'*, and he
14 Meribah in Kadesh in the *w'* of Zin.
32: 13 them wander in the *w'* forty years,
15 he will yet leave them in the *w'*;
33: 6 which is in the edge of the *w'*.
8 the midst of the sea into the *w'*,
8 went three days' journey in the *w'*
11 and encamped in the *w'* of Sin.
12 their journey out of the *w'* of Sin,
15 and pitched in the *w'* of Sinai.
36 pitched in the *w'* of Zin, which is
34: 3 *w'* of Zin along by the coast of Edom,
De 1: 1 Israel on this side Jordan in the *w'*,
19 all that great and terrible *w'*,
31 And in the *w'*, where thou hast
40 take your journey into the *w'* by
2: 1 took our journey into the *w'* by the
7 thy walking through this great *w'*:
8 by the way of the *w'* of Moab.
26 I sent messengers out of the *w'* of
4: 43 Bezer in the *w'*, in the plain
8: 2 thee these forty years in the *w'*,
15 through that great and terrible *w'*,
16 Who fed thee in the *w'* with manna,
9: 7 Lord thy God to wrath in the *w'*:
28 them out to slay them in the *w'*.
11: 5 what he did unto you in the *w'*,
24 from the *w'* and Lebanon, from the
29: 5 have led you forty years in the *w'*:
32: 10 and in the waste howling *w'*;
51 Meribah-Kadesh, in the *w'* of Zin;
Jos 1: 4 From the *w'* and this Lebanon even
5: 4 of war, died in the *w'* by the way,
5 that were born in the *w'* by the way
6 Israel walked forty years in the *w'*,
8: 15 and fled by the way of the *w'*.
20 people that fled to the *w'* turned
24 in the *w'* wherein they chased them,
12: 8 in the *w'*, and in the south country;
14: 10 of Israel wandered in the *w'*:
15: 1 of Edom the *w'* of Zin southward
61 In the *w'*, Beth-arabah, Middin,
16: 1 the *w'* that goeth up from Jericho
18: 12 were at the *w'* of Beth-aven.
20: 8 assigned Bezer in the *w'* upon the
24: 7 ye dwelt in the *w'* a long season.
J'g 1: 16 of Judah into the *w'* of Judah,
8: 7 your flesh with the thorns of the *w'*
16 and thorns of the *w'* and briers,
11: 16 walked through the *w'* unto the
18 they went along through the *w'*,
22 and from the *w'* even unto Jordan.
20: 42 of Israel unto the way of the *w'*;
45 fled toward the *w'* unto the rock of
47 fled to the *w'* unto the rock
1Sa 4: 8 with all the plagues in the *w'*.
13: 18 valley of Zeboim toward the *w'*.
17: 28 thou left those few sheep in the *w'*?
23: 14 David abode in the *w'* in strong
14 in a mountain in the *w'* of Ziph.
15 David was in the *w'* of Ziph in a
24 his men were in the *w'* of Maon,
25 rock, and abode in the *w'* of Maon.
25 after David in the *w'* of Maon.

1Sa 24: 1 David is in the *w'* of En-gedi.
25: 1 and went down to the *w'* of Paran.
4 David heard in the *w'* that Nabal
14 sent messengers out of the *w'* to
21 all that this fellow hath in the *w'*,
26: 2 and went down to the *w'* of Ziph,
2 to seek David in the *w'* of Ziph.
3 But David abode in the *w'*, and he
3 Saul came after him into the *w'*.
2Sa 2: 24 by the way of the *w'* of Gibeon.
15: 23 over, toward the way of the *w'*.
28 I will tarry in the plain of the *w'*,
16: 2 as be faint in the *w'* may drink.
17: 16 this night in the plains of the *w'*,
29 and weary, and thirsty, in the *w'*.
1Ki 2: 34 buried in his own house in the *w'*.
9: 18 Baalath, and Tadmor in the *w'*,
19: 4 went a day's journey into the *w'*,
15 on thy way to the *w'* of Damascus:
2Ki 3: 8 The way through the *w'* of Edom.
1Ch 5: 9 unto the entering in of the *w'*
6: 78 Bezer in the *w'* with her suburbs,
12: 8 unto David into the hold to the *w'*
21: 29 Lord, which Moses made in the *w'*,
2Ch 1: 3 of the Lord had made in the *w'*.
8: 4 And he built Tadmor in the *w'*,
20: 16 the brook, before the *w'* of Jeruel.
20 went forth into the *w'* of Tekoa:
24 toward the watch tower in the *w'*,
24: 9 of God laid upon Israel in the *w'*.
Ne 9: 19 forsookest them not in the *w'*:
21 didst thou sustain them in the *w'*,
Job 1: 19 came a great wind from the *w'*,
12: 24 causeth them to wander in a *w'*
24: 5 the *w'* yieldeth food for them and
30: 3 fleeing into the *w'* in former time
38: 26 the *w'*, wherein there is no man;
39: 6 Whose house I have made the *w'*,
Ps 29: 8 voice of the Lord shaketh the *w'*;
8 Lord shaketh the *w'* of Kadesh.
55: 7 far off, and remain in the *w'*.
63: *title* when he was in the *w'* of Judah.
65: 12 drop upon the pastures of the *w'*:
68: 7 thou didst march through the *w'*;
72: 9 They that dwell in the *w'* shall
74: 14 to the people inhabiting the *w'*.
78: 15 He clave the rocks in the *w'*, and
17 provoking...most High in the *w'*.
19 Can God furnish a table in the *w'*?
40 oft did they provoke him in the *w'*,
52 guided them in the *w'* like a flock.
95: 8 in the day of temptation in the *w'*:
102: 6 I am like a pelican of the *w'*: I am
106: 9 the depths, as through the *w'*.
14 But lusted exceedingly in the *w'*,
26 them, to overthrow them in the *w'*:
107: 4 wandered in...*w'* in a solitary way;
33 He turneth rivers into a *w'*, and the
35 turneth the *w'* into a standing
40 causeth them to wander in the *w'*,
136: 16 led his people through the *w'*:
Pr 21: 19 It is better to dwell in the *w'*, than
Ca 3: 6 is this that cometh out of the *w'*
8: 5 is this that cometh up from the *w'*,
Isa 14: 17 That made the world a *w'*, and
16: 1 of the land from Sela to the *w'*,
8 they wandered through the *w'*:
23: 13 it for them that dwell in the *w'*:
27: 10 forsaken, and left like a *w'*:
32: 15 high, and the *w'* be a fruitful field,
16 judgment shall dwell in the *w'*,
33: 9 Sharon is like a *w'*; and Bashan
35: 1 *w'* and the solitary place...be glad
6 in the *w'* shall waters break out,
40: 3 voice of him that crieth in the *w'*,
41: 18 I will make the *w'* a pool of water,
19 I will plant in the *w'* the cedar,
42: 11 Let the *w'* and the cities thereof
43: 19 I will even make a way in the *w'*,
20 because I give waters in the *w'*,
50: 2 the sea, I make the rivers a *w'*:
51: 3 and he will make her *w'* like Eden,
63: 13 the deep, as an horse in the *w'*,
64: 10 Thy holy cities are a *w'*, Zion is a
10 Zion is a *w'*, Jerusalem a
Jer 2: 2 thou wentest after me in the *w'*,
6 Egypt, that led us through the *w'*,
24 A wild ass used to the *w'*, that
31 Have I been a *w'* unto Israel?
3: 2 for them, as the Arabian in the *w'*;
4: 11 wind of the high places in the *w'*
26 and, lo, the fruitful place was a *w'*,
9: 2 that I had in the *w'* a lodging place
10 and for the habitations of the *w'*
12 and is burned up like a *w'*,
26 corners, that dwell in the *w'*:
12: 10 my pleasant portion a desolate *w'*.
12 all high places through the *w'*:
13: 24 passeth away by the wind of the *w'*.
17: 6 the parched places in the *w'*,
22: 6 yet surely I will make thee a *w'*,
23: 10 places of the *w'* are dried up,
31: 2 of the sword found grace in the *w'*;
48: 6 and be like the heath in the *w'*.
50: 12 of the nations shall be a *w'*,
51: 43 a desolation, a dry land, and a *w'*,
La 4: 3 cruel, like the ostriches in the *w'*.
19 they laid wait for us in the *w'*.
5: 9 because of the sword of the *w'*.
Eze 6: 14 than the *w'* toward Diblath,
19: 13 And now she is planted in the *w'*,
20: 10 and brought them into the *w'*.
13 rebelled against me in the *w'*:
13 out my fury upon them in the *w'*,
15 up my hand unto them in the *w'*,
17 I make an end of them in the *w'*.

Eze 20: 18 said unto their children in the *w'*,
21 my anger against them in the *w'*.
23 mine hand unto them also in the *w'*,
35 bring you into the *w'* of the people,
36 pleaded with your fathers in the *w'*
23: 42 were brought Sabeans from the *w'*,
29: 5 will leave thee thrown into the *w'*,
34: 25 they shall dwell safely in the *w'*,
Hos 2: 3 and make her as a *w'*, and set her
14 her, and bring her into the *w'*,
9: 10 found Israel like grapes in the *w'*;
13: 5 I did know thee in the *w'*, in the land
15 Lord shall come up from the *w'*,
Joe 1: 19 devoured the pastures of the *w'*,
20 devoured the pastures of the *w'*.
2: 3 and behind them a desolate *w'*;
22 for the pastures of the *w'* do spring,
3: 19 and Edom shall be a desolate *w'*,
Am 2: 10 led you forty years through the *w'*,
5: 25 and offerings in the *w'* forty years,
6: 14 Hemath unto the river of the *w'*.
Zep 2: 13 a desolation, and dry like a *w'*.
Mal 1: 3 waste for the dragons of the *w'*.
M't 3: 1 preaching in the *w'* of Judæa,
3 The voice of one crying in the *w'*,
4: 1 Jesus led up of the spirit in the *w'*
11: 7 What went ye out into the *w'* to see?
15: 33 we have so much bread in the *w'*,
M'r 1: 3 The voice of one crying in the *w'*,
4 John did baptize in the *w'*, and
12 the spirit driveth him into the *w'*.
13 he was there in the *w'* forty days,
8: 4 men with bread here in the *w'*?
Lu 3: 2 the son of Zacharias in the *w'*.
4 The voice of one crying in the *w'*,
4: 1 was led by the Spirit into the *w'*,
5: 16 he withdrew himself into the *w'*,
7: 24 went ye out into the *w'* for to see?
8: 29 was driven of the devil into the *w'*.)
15: 4 leave the ninety and nine in the *w'*,
Joh 1: 23 the voice of one crying in the *w'*,
3: 14 lifted up the serpent in the *w'*,
6: 49 fathers did eat manna in the *w'*,
11: 54 unto a country near to the *w'*,
Ac 7: 30 in the *w'* of mount Sina an angel
36 Red sea, and in the *w'* forty years.
38 he, that was in the church in the *w'*
42 the space of forty years in the *w'*?
44 the tabernacle of witness in the *w'*,
13: 18 suffered he their manners in the *w'*.
21: 38 leddest out into the *w'* four
1Co 10: 5 for they were overthrown in the *w'*.
2Co 11: 26 in the city, in perils in the *w'*,
Heb 3: 8 in the day of temptation in the *w'*:
17 whose carcases fell in the *w'*?
Re 12: 6 And the woman fled into the *w'*,
14 that she might fly into the *w'*,
17: 3 me away in the spirit into the *w'*:

wild-goat See WILD and GOAT.

wild-ox See WILD and OX.

wiles
Nu 25: 18 For they vex you with their *w'*,
Eph 6: 11 stand against the *w'* of the devil.

wilfully
Heb10: 26 For if we sin *w'* after that we have

wilily
Jos 9: 4 They did work *w'*, and went and

will^ See also FREEWILL; SELFWILL; WILFULLY; WILLETH; WILLING; WILT; WOULD.
Ge 2: 18 I *w'* make him an help meet for him.
3: 15 I *w'* put enmity between thee and the
16 I *w'* greatly multiply thy sorrow and
6: 7 I *w'* destroy man whom I have
13 I *w'* destroy them with the earth.
18 with thee *w'* I establish my covenant;
7: 4 I *w'* cause it to rain upon the earth
4 that I have made *w'* I destroy from
8: 21 I *w'* not again curse the ground any
21 neither *w'* I again smite any more
9: 5 your blood of your lives *w'* I require;
5 hand of every beast *w'* I require it,
5 every man's brother *w'* I require the
11 I *w'* establish my covenant with you;
15 I *w'* remember my covenant, which is
16 I *w'* look upon it, that I may remember
11: 6 nothing *w'* be restrained from them,
12: 1 house, unto a land that I *w'* show thee:
2 I *w'* make of thee a great nation.
2 I *w'* bless thee, and make thy name
3 And I *w'* bless them that bless thee,
7 Unto thy seed *w'* I give this land:
12 *w'* kill me, but they *w'* save thee alive.
13: 9 left hand, then I *w'* go to the right;
9 right hand, then I *w'* go to the left.
15 to thee *w'* I give it, and to thy seed for
16 I *w'* make thy seed as the dust of the
17 breadth of it; for I *w'* give it unto thee.
14: 23 I *w'* not take from a thread even to a
23 I *w'* not take any thing that is thine,
15: 14 whom they shall serve, *w'* I judge:
16: 10 I *w'* multiply thy seed exceedingly,
12 And he *w'* be a wild man; his hand*
12 his hand *w'* be against every man, and
17: 2 I *w'* make my covenant between me
2 and *w'* multiply thee exceedingly.
6 I *w'* make thee exceeding fruitful,
6 and I *w'* make nations of thee, and
7 I *w'* establish my covenant between
8 I *w'* give unto thee, and unto thy
8 possession; and I *w'* be their God.
16 I *w'* bless her, and give thee a son
16 I *w'* bless her, and she shall be a
19 I *w'* establish my covenant with him
20 blessed him, and *w'* make him fruitful,

Ge 17:20 and w' multiply him exceedingly;
20 and I w' make him a great nation.
21 But my covenant w' I establish with
18: 5 I w' fetch a morsel of bread, and
10 said, I w' certainly return unto thee
14 At the time appointed I w' return
19 he w' command his children and his
21 I w' go down now, and see whether
21 come unto me; and if not, I w' know.
26 I w' spare all the place for their sakes.
28 forty and five, I w' not destroy it.
29 he said, I w' not do it for forty's sake.
30 not the Lord be angry, and I w' speak:
30 he said, I w' not do it, if I find thirty
31 I w' not destroy it for twenty's sake.
32 and I w' speak yet but this once:
32 said, I w' not destroy it for ten's sake.
19: 2 we w' abide in the street all night.
9 sojourn, and he w' needs be a judge:
9 w' we deal worse with thee, than with
13 For we w' destroy this place, because
14 for the Lord w' destroy this city.
21 that I w' not overthrow this city, for
32 and we w' lie with him, that we may
20:11 and they w' slay me for my wife's sake.
21: 6 that all that hear w' laugh with me.
13 of the bondwoman w' I make a nation,
18 for I w' make him a great nation.
24 And Abraham said, I w' swear.
22: 2 mountains which I w' tell thee of.
5 and I and the lad w' go yonder and
8 son, God w' provide himself a lamb
17 That in blessing I w' bless thee,
17 multiplying I w' multiply thy seed as
23:13 I w' give thee money for the field;
24: 3 I w' make thee swear by the Lord,
5 woman w' not be willing to follow
7 Unto thy seed w' I give this land;
8 woman w' not be willing to follow
14 and I w' give thy camels drink also:
19 w' draw water for thy camels also,
33 I w' not eat, until I have told mine
39 the woman w' not follow me.
40 w' send his angel with thee, and
44 and I w' also draw for thy camels:
46 and I w' give thy camels drink also:
49 if ye w' deal kindly and truly with my
57 We w' call the damsel, and enquire at
58 with this man? And she said, I w' go.
26: 3 I w' be with thee, and w' bless thee;
3 thy seed, I w' give all these countries,
3 I w' perform the oath which I sware
4 I w' make thy seed to multiply as the
4 and w' give unto thy seed all these
24 for I am with thee, and w' bless thee,
27: 9 I w' make them savoury meat for thy
12 My father peradventure w' feel me,
25 me, and I w' eat of my son's venison,
41 then w' I slay my brother Jacob.
45 then w' I send, and fetch thee from
28:13 thou liest, to thee w' I give it,
15 w' keep thee in all places whither thou
15 and w' bring thee again into this land;
15 for I w' not leave thee, until I have
20 a vow, saying, If God w' be with me,
20 and w' keep me in this way that I go,
20 w' give me bread to eat, and raiment
22 I w' surely give the tenth unto thee.
29:18 I w' serve thee seven years for Rachel
27 and we w' give thee this also for the
32 now therefore my husband w' love me.
34 this time w' my husband be joined
35 she said, Now w' I praise the Lord:
30:13 for the daughters w' call me blessed:
20 now w' my husband dwell with me,
28 me thy wages, and I w' give it.
31 I w' again feed and keep thy flock.
32 I w' pass through all thy flock to day,
31: 3 to thy kindred; and I w' be with thee.
52 I w' not pass over this heap to thee,
32: 9 and I w' deal well with thee:
11 him, lest he w' come and smite me,
12 thou saidst, I w' surely do thee good,
20 I w' appease him with the present
20 me, and afterward I w' see his face;
20 peradventure he w' accept of me.
26 said, I w' not let thee go, except thou
33:12 and let us go, and I w' go before thee.
13 them one day, all the flock w' die.
14 his servant; and I w' lead on softly,
34:11 what ye shall say unto me I w' give.
12 I w' give according as ye shall say
15 But in this w' we consent unto you:
15 If ye w' be as we be, that every male
16 Then w' we give our daughters unto
16 and we w' take your daughters to us,
16 and we w' dwell with you,
16 and we w' become one people.
17 But if ye w' not hearken unto us, to
17 then w' we take our daughter,
17 and we w' be gone.
22 herein w' the men consent unto us
23 unto them, and they w' dwell with us.
35: 3 I w' make there an altar unto God,
12 to thee I w' give it, and to thy seed
12 seed after thee w' I give the land.
37:13 come, and I w' send thee unto them.
20 and we w' say, Some evil beast hath
20 see what w' become of his dreams.
35 I w' go down into the grave unto my
38:17 I w' send thee a kid from the flock.
41:32 and God w' shortly bring it to pass.
40 the throne w' I be greater than thou.
42:34 w' I deliver you your brother, and ye
36 and ye w' take Benjamin away:
37 and I w' bring him to thee again.
Ge 43: 4 us, we w' go down and buy thee food:
5 wilt not send him, we w' not go down:
8 lad with me, and we w' arise and go;
9 I w' be surety for him; of my hand
44: 9 and we also w' be my lord's bondmen.
26 be with us, then w' we go down:
31 the lad is not with us, that he w' die:
45:11 And there w' I nourish thee; for yet
18 I w' give you the good of the land of
28 I w' go and see him before I die.
46: 3 for I w' there make of thee a great
4 I w' go down with thee into Egypt;
4 I w' also surely bring thee up again:
31 I w' go up, and shew Pharaoh, and say
47:16 I w' give you for your cattle, if money
18 We w' not hide it from my lord, how
19 and we and our land w' be servants
25 and we w' be Pharaoh's servants.
30 But I w' lie with my fathers, and thou
30 And he said, I w' do as thou hast said.
48: 4 I w' make thee fruitful, and multiply
4 and I w' make of thee a multitude of
4 w' give this land to thy seed after thee
9 thee, unto me, and I w' bless them.
49: 7 I w' divide them in Jacob, and scatter
50: 5 bury my father, and I w' come again.
15 said, Joseph w' peradventure hate us,
15 w' certainly requite all the evil which
21 I w' nourish you, and your little ones.
24 and God w' surely visit you, and bring
25 God w' surely visit you, and ye shall
Ex 2: 9 it for me, and I w' give thee thy wages.
3: 3 Moses said, I w' now turn aside, and
10 and I w' send thee unto Pharaoh, that
12 he said, Certainly I w' be with thee;
17 I w' bring you up out of the affliction
19 the king of Egypt w' not let you go,
20 And I w' stretch out my hand, and
20 which I w' do in the midst thereof:
20 and after that he w' let you go.
21 I w' give this people favour in the
4: 1 they w' not believe me, nor hearken
1 for they w' say, The Lord hath not
8 if they w' not believe thee, neither
8 w' believe the voice of the latter sign.
9 w' not believe also these two signs,
12 and I w' be with thy mouth, and
14 thee, he w' be glad in his heart.
15 and I w' be with thy mouth, and with
15 and w' teach you what ye shall do.
21 but I w' harden his heart, that he
23 behold, I w' slay thy son, even thy
5: 2 the Lord, neither w' I let Israel go.
10 Pharaoh, I w' not give you straw.
6: 1 thou see what I w' do to Pharaoh:
6 I w' bring you out from under the
6 and I w' rid you out of their bondage,
6 I w' redeem you with a stretched out
7 I w' take you to me for a people, and I
7 I w' be to you a God: and ye shall
8 And I w' bring you unto the land,
8 and I w' give it you for an heritage:
7: 3 I w' harden Pharaoh's heart, and
17 I w' smite with the rod that is in mine
8: 2 I w' smite all thy borders with frogs:
8 I w' let the people go, that they may
21 I w' send swarms of flies upon thee,
22 And I w' sever in that day the land of
23 I w' put a division between my people
26 their eyes, and w' they not stone us?
27 We w' go three day's journey into the
28 Pharaoh said, I w' let you go, that ye
29 I w' entreat the Lord that the swarms
9:14 I w' send at this time all my plagues
15 I w' stretch out my hand, that I may
18 I w' cause it to rain a very grievous
29 I w' spread abroad my hands unto the
30 I know that ye w' not yet fear the Lord
10: 4 w' I bring the locusts into thy coast:
9 We w' go with our young and with our
9 flocks and with our herds w' we go;
10 I w' let you go, and your little ones:
29 well, I w' see thy face again no more.
11: 1 Yet w' I bring one plague more upon
1 afterwards he w' let you go hence:
4 About midnight w' I go out into the
8 thee: and after that I w' go out.
12:12 I w' pass through the land of Egypt
12 w' smite all the firstborn in the land
12 gods of Egypt I w' execute judgment:
13 I w' pass over you, and the plague
23 the Lord w' pass through to smite the
23 posts, the Lord w' pass over the door,
23 w' not suffer the destroyer to come in
25 the land which the Lord w' give you,
48 and w' keep the passover to the Lord,
13:19 saying, God w' surely visit you;
14: 3 Pharaoh w' say of the children of
4 And I w' harden Pharaoh's heart, that
4 and I w' be honoured upon Pharaoh,
13 Lord, which he w' shew to you to day:
17 I w' harden the hearts of the
17 I w' get me honour upon Pharaoh,
15: 1 I w' sing unto the Lord, for he hath
2 and I w' prepare him an habitation;
2 my father's God, and I w' exalt him.
9 said, I w' pursue, I w' overtake,
9 I w' divide the spoil; my lust shall be
9 I w' draw my sword, my hand shall
26 I w' put none of these diseases upon
16: 4 I w' rain bread from heaven for you;
4 they w' walk in my law, or no.
23 bake that which ye w' bake to day,
23 to day, and seethe that ye w' seethe;
17: 6 I w' stand before thee there upon the
9 I w' stand on the top of the hill
Ex 17:14 I w' utterly put out the remembrance
16 the Lord w' have war with Amalek
18:19 I w' give thee counsel, and God shall
19: 5 if ye w' obey my voice indeed,
8 that the Lord hath spoken we w' do.
11 Lord w' come down in the sight of all
20: 7 for the Lord w' not hold him guiltless
19 Speak thou with us, and we w' hear:
24 record my name I w' come unto thee,
24 come unto thee, and I w' bless thee.
21: 5 my children; I w' not go out free:
13 I w' appoint thee a place whither he
22 woman's husband w' lay upon him;
22:23 all unto me, I w' surely hear their cry;
24 and I w' kill you with the sword;
27 he crieth unto me, that I w' hear;
23: 7 not: for I w' not justify the wicked.
21 he w' not pardon your transgressions:
22 I w' be an enemy unto thy enemies,
23 the Jebusites: and I w' cut them off.
25 I w' take sickness away from the
26 the number of thy days I w' fulfil.
27 I w' send my fear before thee, and
27 and w' destroy all the people to whom
27 and I w' make all thine enemies turn
28 And I w' send hornets before thee,
29 I w' not drive them out from before
30 I w' drive them out from before thee,
31 I w' set thy bounds from the Red sea
31 I w' deliver the inhabitants of the land
33 it w' surely be a snare unto thee.
24: 3 which the Lord hath said w' we do.
7 that the Lord hath said w' we do,
12 and I w' give thee tables of stone,
25:22 And there I w' meet with thee, and
22 I w' commune with thee from above
22 I w' give thee in commandment
29:42 I w' meet you, to speak there unto
43 I w' meet with the children of Israel,
44 And I w' sanctify the tabernacle
44 I w' sanctify also both Aaron and his
45 And I w' dwell among the children
45 of Israel, and w' be their God.
30: 6 testimony, where I w' meet with thee.
36 where I w' meet with thee:
32:10 and I w' make of thee a great nation.
13 I w' multiply your seed as the stars
13 spoken of w' I give unto your seed,
30 and now I w' go up unto the Lord;
33 me, him w' I blot out of my book.
34 I visit I w' visit their sin upon them.
33: 1 saying, Unto thy seed w' I give it:
2 And I w' send an angel before thee;
2 and I w' drive out the Canaanite
3 I w' not go up in the midst of thee;
5 I w' come up into the midst of thee
14 with thee, and I w' give thee rest.
17 I w' do this thing also that thou hast
19 I w' make all my goodness pass
19 I w' proclaim the name of the Lord
19 and w' be gracious unto whom I w' be
19 w' shew mercy to whom I w' shew
22 that I w' put thee in a clift of a rock,
22 w' cover thee with my hand while I
23 I w' take away mine hand, and thou
34: 1 I w' write upon these tables the words
7 that w' by no means clear the guilty;
10 before all thy people I w' do marvels,
10 for it is a terrible thing that I w' do
11 w' cast out the nations before thee,
Le 1: 3 offer it of his own voluntary w'
2: 1 when any w' offer a meat offering
9: 4 for to day the Lord w' appear unto
10: 3 I w' be sanctified in them that come
3 before all the people I w' be glorified.
16: 2 for I w' appear in a cloud upon the
17:10 I w' even set my face against that
10 and w' cut him off from among his
19: 5 ye shall offer it at your own w'.
20: 5 I w' set my face against that man,
6 I w' even set my face against that
6 and w' cut him off from among his
24 I w' give it unto you to possess it,
22:18 w' offer his oblation for all his vows,
18 which they w' offer unto the Lord
19 at your own w' a male without
29 And when ye w' offer a sacrifice
29 the Lord, offer it at your own w'.
32 I w' be hallowed among the children
23:30 w' I destroy from among his people.
25:21 I w' command my blessing upon you
26: 4 I w' give you rain in due season,
6 I w' give peace in the land, and ye
6 I w' rid evil beasts out of the land,
9 I w' have respect unto you, and make
11 I w' set my tabernacle among you:
12 I w' walk among you,
12 and w' be your God, and ye shall
14 But if ye w' not hearken unto me,
14 w' not do all these commandments;
15 Ye w' not do all my commandments,
16 I also w' do this unto you;
16 I w' even appoint over you terror,
17 I w' set my face against you, and ye
18 if ye w' not yet for all this hearken
18 I w' punish you seven times more for
19 I w' break the pride of your power;
19 and I w' make your heaven as iron,
21 me, and w' not hearken unto me;
21 I w' bring seven times more plagues
22 I w' also send wild beasts among
23 And if ye w' not be reformed by me
23 but w' walk contrary unto me;
24 Then w' I also walk contrary unto
24 w' punish you yet seven times for
25 And I w' bring a sword upon you,

Le 26:25 I *w'* send the pestilence among you;
27 if ye *w'* not for all this hearken unto
28 Then I *w'* walk contrary unto you
28 I, *w'* chastise you seven times for
30 I *w'* destroy your high places, and cut
31 I *w'* make your cities waste, and bring
31 I *w'* not smell the savour of your
32 I *w'* bring the land into desolation:
33 I *w'* scatter you among the heathen,
33 and *w'* draw out a sword after you:
36 I *w'* send a faintness into their hearts
42 Then *w'* I remember my covenant
42 with Abraham *w'* I remember;
42 and I *w'* remember the land.
44 I *w'* not cast them away, neither
44 neither *w'* I abhor them, to destroy
45 I *w'* for their sakes remember the
27:15 that sanctified it *w'* redeem his house,
19 the field *w'* in any wise redeem it,
20 And if he *w'* not redeem the field,
31 if a man *w'* at all redeem ought of
Nu 6:27 of Israel; and I *w'* bless them.
9: 8 and I *w'* hear what the Lord
8 Lord *w'* command concerning you.
14 *w'* keep the passover unto the Lord;
10:29 which the Lord said, I *w'* give it you:
29 thou with us, and we *w'* do thee good:
30 And he said unto him, I *w'* not go;
30 I *w'* depart to mine own land, and to
32 unto us, the same *w'* we do unto thee.
11:17 I *w'* come down and talk with thee
17 I *w'* take of the spirit which is upon
17 *w'* put it upon them; and they shall
18 therefore the Lord *w'* give you flesh,
21 I *w'* give them flesh, that they may eat
12: 6 I the Lord *w'* make myself known unto
6 and *w'* speak unto you in a dream.
8 With him *w'* I speak mouth to mouth,
14: 8 he *w'* bring us into this land, and give
11 How long *w'* this people provoke me?
11 how long *w'* it be ere they believe me,
12 I *w'* smite them with the pestilence,
12 and *w'* make of thee a greater nation
14 they *w'* tell it to the inhabitants of this
15 the fame of thee *w'* speak, saying,
24 him *w'* I bring into the land whereunto
28 spoken in mine ears, so *w'* I do to you:
31 them *w'* I bring in, and they shall
35 I *w'* surely do it unto all this evil
40 and *w'* go up unto the place which the
43 therefore the Lord *w'* not be with you.
15: 3 *w'* make an offering by fire unto the
14 and *w'* offer an offering made by fire,
16: 5 morrow the Lord *w'* show who are his,
5 *w'* cause him to come near unto him:
5 chosen *w'* he cause to come near unto
12 Eliab: which said, We *w'* not come up:
17: 4 testimony, where I *w'* meet with you.
5 I *w'* make to cease from me the
20:17 we *w'* not pass through the fields,
17 *w'* we drink of the water of the wells:
17 we *w'* go by the king's high way,
17 we *w'* not turn to the right hand nor to
19 unto him, We *w'* go by the high way:
19 of thy water, then *w'* I pay for it:
19 I *w'* only, without doing any thing else,
21: 2 then I *w'* utterly destroy their cities.
16 together, and I *w'* give them water.
22 we *w'* not turn into the fields, or into
22 *w'* not drink of the waters of the well:
22 we *w'* go along by the king's high way,
22: 8 I *w'* bring you word again, as the Lord
17 For I *w'* promote thee unto very great
17 I *w'* do whatsoever thou sayest unto
19 what the Lord *w'* say unto me more.
34 displease thee, I *w'* get me back again.
23: 3 Stand by thy burnt offering, and I *w'* go:
3 the Lord *w'* come to meet me:
3 whatever he sheweth me I *w'* tell thee.
27 I *w'* bring thee unto another place;
27 it *w'* please God that thou mayest
24:13 what the Lord saith, that *w'* I speak?
14 I *w'* advertise thee what this people
32:15 he *w'* yet again leave them in the
16 We *w'* build sheepfolds here for our
17 But we ourselves *w'* go ready armed
18 We *w'* not return unto our houses,
19 For we *w'* not inherit with them on
20 said unto them, If ye *w'* do this thing,
20 ye *w'* go armed before the Lord to war,
21 *w'* go all of you armed over Jordan
23 But if ye *w'* not do so, behold, ye have
23 and be sure your sin *w'* find you out.
25 *w'* do as my lord commandeth.
27 thy servants *w'* pass over, every man
29 Reuben *w'* pass with you over Jordan,
30 But if they *w'* not pass over with you
31 said unto thy servants, so *w'* we do.
32 *w'* pass over armed before the Lord
33:55 if ye *w'* not drive out the inhabitants
De 1:13 and I *w'* make them rulers over you.
17 you, bring it unto me, and I *w'* hear it.
22 We *w'* send men before us, and they
36 to him *w'* I give the land that he hath
39 and unto them *w'* I give it, and they
41 we *w'* go up and fight, according to all
2: 5 for I *w'* not give you of their land, no,
9 for I *w'* not give thee of their land
19 for I *w'* not give thee of the land of the
25 This day *w'* I begin to put the dread
27 land: I *w'* go along by the high way,
27 I *w'* neither turn unto the right hand
28 only I *w'* pass through on my feet;
3: 2 for I *w'* deliver him, and all his people,
4:10 I *w'* make them hear my words, that
31 he *w'* not forsake thee, neither destroy

De 5:11 Lord *w'* not hold them guiltless that
25 for this great fire *w'* consume us: if we
27 unto thee; and we *w'* hear it, and do it.
31 and I *w'* speak unto thee all the
7: 4 For they *w'* turn away thy son from
4 so *w'* the anger of the Lord be kindled
10 he *w'* not be slack to him that hateth
10 him, he *w'* repay him to his face.
13 And he *w'* love thee, and bless thee,
13 he *w'* also bless the fruit of thy womb,
15 the Lord *w'* take away from thee all
15 and *w'* put none of the evil diseases
15 *w'* lay them upon all them that hate
16 for that *w'* be a snare unto thee.
20 God *w'* send the hornet among them,
22 thy God *w'* put out those nations
9:14 I *w'* make of thee a nation mightier
10: 2 I *w'* write on the tables the words
11:14 I *w'* give you the rain of your land
15 I *w'* send grass in thy fields for thy
23 *w'* the Lord drive out all these
28 if ye *w'* not obey the commandments
12:20 I *w'* eat flesh, because thy soul
30 their gods? even so *w'* I do likewise.
15:16 I *w'* not go away from thee; because
17:12 man that *w'* do presumptuously, and
12 *w'* not hearken unto the priest that
14 I *w'* set a king over me, like as all the
18:15 God *w'* raise up unto thee a Prophet
18 I *w'* raise them up a Prophet from
18 and *w'* put my words in his mouth;
19 *w'* not hearken unto my words
19 in my name, I *w'* require it of him.
20:12 if it *w'* make no peace with thee,
12 *w'* make war against thee, then thou
21:14 shalt let her go whither she *w'*;
18 *w'* not obey the voice of his father,
18 him, *w'* not hearken unto them.
20 rebellious, he *w'* not obey our voice;
23:21 thy God *w'* surely require it of thee;
25: 7 *w'* not perform the duty of my
9 *w'* not build up his brother's house.
28: 1 thy God *w'* set thee on high above all
27 *w'* smite thee with the botch of Egypt,
55 that he *w'* not give to any of them
59 Lord *w'* make thy plagues wonderful,
60 he *w'* bring upon thee all the diseases
61 them *w'* the Lord bring upon thee,
63 so the Lord *w'* rejoice over you
29:20 The Lord *w'* not spare him, but then
30: 3 Lord thy God *w'* turn thy captivity,
3 *w'* return and gather thee from all
4 from thence *w'* the Lord thy God
4 and from thence *w'* he fetch thee:
5 thy God *w'* bring thee into the land
5 he *w'* do thee good, and multiply thee
6 the Lord...*w'* circumcise thine heart,
7 God *w'* put all these curses upon thine
9 Lord thy God *w'* make thee plenteous
9 for the Lord *w'* again rejoice over thee
31: 3 thy God, he *w'* go over before thee,
3 and he *w'* destroy these nations from
6 he *w'* not fail thee, nor forsake thee.
8 he *w'* be with thee, he *w'* not fail thee,
16 and this people *w'* rise up, and go
16 and *w'* forsake me, and break my
17 I *w'* forsake them, and I *w'* hide my
17 so that they *w'* say in that day, Are
18 I *w'* surely hide my face in that day
20 then *w'* they turn unto other gods,
23 unto them: and I *w'* be with thee.
29 after my death ye *w'* utterly corrupt
29 evil *w'* befall you in the latter days;
29 because ye *w'* do evil in the sight of
32: 1 ear, O ye heavens, and I *w'* speak;
3 I *w'* publish the name of the Lord:
7 ask thy father, and he *w'* shew thee;
7 thy elders, and they *w'* tell thee.
20 he said, I *w'* hide my face from them,
20 I *w'* see what their end shall be:
21 I *w'* move them to jealousy with those
21 I *w'* provoke them to anger with a
23 I *w'* heap mischiefs upon them;
23 I *w'* spend mine arrows upon them.
24 I *w'* also send the teeth of beasts upon
41 I *w'* render vengeance to mine
41 and *w'* reward them that hate me.
42 I *w'* make mine arrows drunk with
43 for he *w'* avenge the blood of his
43 and *w'* render vengeance to his
43 *w'* be merciful unto his land, and to
33:16 for the good *w'* of him that dwell in
34: 4 saying, I *w'* give it unto thy seed: I
Jos 1: 5 was with Moses, so I *w'* be with thee:
5 I *w'* not fail thee, nor forsake thee.
16 that thou commandest us we *w'* do,
16 thou sendest us, we *w'* go.
17 things, so *w'* we hearken unto thee:
18 and *w'* not hearken unto thy words
2:12 that ye *w'* also shew kindness unto
13 that ye *w'* save alive my father, and
14 we *w'* deal kindly and truly with thee.
17 We *w'* be blameless of this thine oath
19 upon his head, and we *w'* be guiltless:
20 then we *w'* be quit of thine oath
3: 5 the Lord *w'* do wonders among you.
7 This day *w'* I begin to magnify thee in
7 I was with Moses, so I *w'* be with thee.
10 and that he *w'* without fail drive out
7:12 neither *w'* I be with you any more,
8: 5 with me, *w'* approach unto the city:
5 the first, that we *w'* flee before them,
6 (For they *w'* come out after us) till we
6 for they *w'* say, They flee before us, as
6 first: therefore we *w'* flee before them.
7 the Lord your God *w'* deliver it into

Jos 8:18 Ai; for I *w'* give it into thy hand.
9:20 This we *w'* do to them;
20 we *w'* even let them live, lest
11: 6 about this time *w'* I deliver them up
13: 6 *w'* I drive out before the children
14:12 if so be the Lord *w'* be with me, then I
15:16 *w'* I give Achsah my daughter to wife.
18: 4 I *w'* send them, and they shall rise,
22:18 it *w'* be, seeing ye rebel to day against
18 to morrow he *w'* be wroth with the
23:13 Lord your God *w'* no more drive out
24:15 choose you this day whom ye *w'* serve;
15 and my house, we *w'* serve the Lord.
18 therefore *w'* we serve the Lord;
19 he *w'* not forgive your transgressions
20 then he *w'* turn and do you hurt, and
21 Nay; but we *w'* serve the Lord.
24 God *w'* we serve, and his voice *w'* we
J'g 1: 3 I likewise *w'* go with thee unto thy lot.
12 to him *w'* I give Achsah my daughter
24 the city, and we *w'* shew thee mercy.
2: 1 I *w'* never break my covenant with
3 I *w'* not drive them out from before
21 *w'* not henceforth drive out any from
22 they *w'* keep the way of the Lord
4: 7 And I *w'* draw unto thee to the river
7 and I *w'* deliver him into thine hand.
8 If thou wilt go with me, then I *w'* go:
8 wilt not go with me, then I *w'* not go.
9 And she said, I *w'* surely go with thee:
22 I *w'* shew thee the man whom thou
5: 3 I, even I, *w'* sing unto the Lord;
3 I *w'* sing praise to the Lord God of
6:16 Surely I *w'* be with thee, and thou
18 said, I *w'* tarry until thou come again.
31 *W'* ye plead for Baal? *w'* ye save him?
31 he that *w'* plead for him, let him be put
37 I *w'* put a fleece of wool in the floor;
39 me, and I *w'* speak but this once:
7: 4 and I *w'* try them for thee there:
7 men that lapped *w'* I save you,
8: 7 I *w'* tear your flesh with the thorns of
9 in peace, I *w'* break down this tower.
23 unto them, I *w'* not rule over you,
25 answered, We *w'* willingly give
10:13 wherefore I *w'* deliver you no more.
18 What man is he that *w'* begin to fight
11:24 from before us, them *w'* we possess.
31 I *w'* offer it up for a burnt offering.
12: 1 *w'* burn thine house upon thee with
13:16 detain me, I *w'* not eat of thy bread:
14:12 I *w'* now put forth a riddle unto you:
12 I *w'* give you thirty sheets and thirty
15: 1 I *w'* go in to my wife into the chamber.
7 done this, yet *w'* I be avenged of you,
7 avenged of you, and after...I *w'* cease.
12 ye *w'* not fall upon me yourselves.
13 but we *w'* bind thee fast, and deliver
13 hand: but surely we *w'* not kill thee.
16: 5 we *w'* give thee every one of us eleven
17 then my strength *w'* go from me,
20 I *w'* go out as at other times before,
17: 3 therefore I *w'* restore it unto thee.
10 I *w'* give thee ten shekels of silver by
19:12 We *w'* not turn aside hither into the
12 of Israel; we *w'* pass over to Gibeah.
24 them I *w'* bring out now, and humble
20: 8 We *w'* not any of us go to his tent,
8 neither *w'* we any of us turn into his
9 the thing which we *w'* do to Gibeah;
9 Gibeah; we *w'* go up by lot against it;
10 And we *w'* take ten men of an hundred
21: 7 we *w'* not give them of our daughters
22 complain, that we *w'* say unto them,
Ru 1:10 we *w'* return with thee unto thy people.
11 my daughters: why *w'* ye go with me?
16 for whither thou goest, I *w'* go: and
16 and where thou lodgest, I *w'* lodge:
17 *w'* I die, and there *w'* I be buried:
3: 4 and he *w'* tell thee what thou shalt do.
5 All that thou sayest unto me I *w'* do.
11 I *w'* do to thee all that thou requirest:
13 if he *w'* perform unto thee the
13 but if he *w'* not do the part of a
13 then *w'* I do the part of a kinsman to
18 thou know how the matter *w'* fall:
18 for the man *w'* not be in rest, until he
4: 4 thee. And he said, I *w'* redeem it.
1Sa 1:11 then I *w'* give him unto the Lord all
22 I *w'* not go up until the child be
22 and then I *w'* bring him, that he may
2: 9 He *w'* keep the feet of his saints, and
15 he *w'* not have sodden flesh of thee,
16 now: and if not, I *w'* take it by force.
30 for them that honour me I *w'* honour,
31 days come, that I *w'* cut off thine arm,
35 And I *w'* raise me up a faithful priest,
35 I *w'* build him a sure house; and he
3:11 Behold, I *w'* do a thing in Israel,
12 I *w'* perform against Eli all things
12 when I begin, I *w'* also make an end.
13 him that I *w'* judge his house for ever
6: 5 peradventure he *w'* lighten his hand
7: 3 he *w'* deliver you out of the hand of the
5 and I *w'* pray for you unto the Lord.
8 he *w'* save us out of the hand of the
8:11 This *w'* be the manner of the king that
11 *w'* take your sons, and appoint them
12 he *w'* appoint him captains over
12 *w'* set them to ear his ground, and to
13 he *w'* take your daughters to be
14 And he *w'* take your fields, and your
15 And he *w'* take the tenth of your seed,
16 And he *w'* take your menservants,
17 He *w'* take the tenth of your sheep:
18 the Lord *w'* not hear you in that day.

1Sa 8:19 Nay; but we *w'* have a king over us;
9: 8 *w'* I give to the man of God, to tell us
13 the people *w'* not eat until he come,
16 I *w'* send thee a man out of the land of
19 to day, and to morrow I *w'* let thee go,
19 *w'* tell thee all that is in thine heart.
10: 2 and they *w'* say unto thee, The asses
4 they *w'* salute thee, and give thee two
6 Spirit of the Lord *w'* come upon thee,
8 I *w'* come down unto thee, to offer
11: 1 with us, and we *w'* serve thee.
2 condition *w'* I make a covenant with
3 to save us, we *w'* come out to thee.
10 To morrow we *w'* come out unto you,
12: 3 there with? and I *w'* restore it you.
10 of our enemies, and we *w'* serve thee.
14 If ye *w'* fear the Lord, and serve him,
15 ye *w'* not obey the voice of the Lord,
16 the Lord *w'* do before your eyes.
17 I *w'* call unto the Lord, and he shall
22 the Lord *w'* not forsake his people
23 I *w'* teach you the good and the right
13:12 The Philistines *w'* come down now
14: 6 may be that the Lord *w'* work for us:
8 we *w'* pass over unto these men,
8 we *w'* discover ourselves unto them.
9 then we *w'* stand still in our place,
9 and *w'* not go up unto them.
10 Come up unto us; then we *w'* go up:
12 up to us, and we *w'* shew you a thing.
40 my son *w'* be on the other side.
15:16 I *w'* tell thee what the Lord hath said
26 unto Saul, I *w'* not return with thee:
29 also the Strength of Israel *w'* not lie
16: 1 go, I *w'* send thee to Jesse the
2 can I go? If Saul hear it, he *w'* kill me.
3 I *w'* shew thee what thou shalt do:
11 for we *w'* not sit down till he come
17: 9 kill me, then *w'* we be your servants:
25 the king *w'* enrich him with great
25 and *w'* give him his daughters,
32 thy servant *w'* go and fight with this
37 he *w'* deliver me out of the hand of
44 and I *w'* give thy flesh unto the fowls
46 This day *w'* the Lord deliver thee into
46 I *w'* smite thee, and take thine head
46 and I *w'* give the carcases of the host
47 and he *w'* give you into our hands.
18:11 I *w'* smite David...to the wall with it.
17 Merab, her *w'* I give thee to wife:
21 I *w'* give him her, that she may be a
19: 3 I *w'* go out and stand beside my father
3 I *w'* commune with my father of thee;
3 and what I see, that *w'* I tell thee.
20: 2 my father *w'* do nothing either great
2 but that he *w'* shew it me: and why
4 desireth, I *w'* even do it for thee.
13 I *w'* shew it thee, and send thee away,
18 missed, because thy seat *w'* be empty.
20 I *w'* shoot three arrows on the side
21 I *w'* send a lad, saying, Go, find out
22: 3 till I know what God *w'* do for me.
7 *w'* the son of Jesse give every one
23: 4 I *w'* deliver the Philistines into thine
11 *W'* the men of Keilah deliver me up
11 *w'* Saul come down, as thy servant
11 And the Lord said, He *w'* come down.
12 *W'* the men of Keilah deliver me and
12 the Lord said, They *w'* deliver thee up.
23 the certainty, and I *w'* go with you:
23 I *w'* search him out throughout all the
24: 4 I *w'* deliver thine enemy into thine
10 I *w'* not put forth mine hand against
19 enemy, *w'* he let him go well away?
25: 8 young men, and they *w'* shew thee.
28 *w'* certainly make my lord a sure
26: 6 Who *w'* go down with me to Saul
6 Abishai said, I *w'* go down with thee.
8 I *w'* not smite him the second time.
21 for I *w'* no more do thee harm,
27:11 and so *w'* be his manner all the while
28: 2 *w'* I make thee keeper of mine head
19 the Lord *w'* also deliver Israel with
23 he refused, and said, I *w'* not eat.
30:15 I *w'* bring thee down to this company.
22 we *w'* not give them ought of the spoil
24 who *w'* hearken unto you in this
2Sa 2: 6 I also *w'* requite you this kindness,
26 it *w'* be bitterness in the latter end?
3:13 Well; I *w'* make a league with thee:
18 I *w'* save my people Israel out of the
21 I *w'* arise and go, and *w'* gather all
5:19 I *w'* doubtless deliver the Philistines
6:21 therefore *w'* I play before the Lord.
22 I *w'* yet be more vile than thus, and
22 *w'* be base in mine own sight:
7:10 I *w'* appoint a place for my people
10 *w'* plant them, that they may dwell
11 that he *w'* make thee an house.
12 I *w'* set up thy seed after thee,
12 and I *w'* establish his kingdom.
13 and I *w'* stablish the throne of his
14 I *w'* be his father, and he shall be my
14 I *w'* chasten him with the rod of men,
27 saying, I *w'* build thee an house:
9: 7 for I *w'* surely shew thee kindness
7 *w'* restore thee all the land of Saul
10: 2 I *w'* shew kindness unto Hanun
11 thee, then *w'* I come and help thee.
11:11 soul liveth, I *w'* not do this thing.
12 and to morrow I *w'* let thee depart.
12:11 I *w'* raise up evil against thee out of
11 I *w'* take thy wives before thine eyes,
12 I *w'* do this thing before all Israel,
18 how *w'* he then vex himself, if we tell
22 whether God *w'* be gracious to me,

2Sa 13:13 for he *w'* not withhold me from thee.
14: 7 and we *w'* destroy the heir also:
8 and I *w'* give charge concerning thee.
15 said, I will now speak unto the king;
15 that the king *w'* perform the request
16 For the king *w'* hear, to deliver his
17 the Lord thy God *w'* be with thee.
15: 8 Jerusalem, then *w'* I serve the Lord.
21 even there also *w'* thy servant be.
25 he *w'* bring me again, and shew me
28 I *w'* tarry in the plain of the
34 Absalom, I *w'* be thy servant, O king;
34 so *w'* I now also be thy servant:
16:12 that the Lord *w'* look on my affliction,
12 that the Lord *w'* requite me good
18 his *w'* I be, and with him *w'* I abide.
19 presence, so *w'* I be in thy presence.
17: 1 and I *w'* arise and pursue after David
2 *w'* come upon him while he is weary
2 handed, and *w'* make him afraid:
2 flee; and I *w'* smite the king only:
3 And I *w'* bring back all the people
8 and *w'* not lodge with the people.
9 and it *w'* come to pass, when some of
9 that whosoever heareth it *w'* say,
12 and we *w'* light upon him as the dew
13 and we *w'* draw it into the river,
18: 2 I *w'* surely go forth with you myself
3 we flee away, they *w'* not care for us;
3 if half of us die, *w'* they care for us:
4 them, What seemeth you best I *w'* do.
19: 7 *w'* not tarry one with thee this night:
7 *w'* be worse unto thee than all the evil
26 I *w'* saddle me an ass, that I may ride
33 I *w'* feed thee with me in Jerusalem.
36 servant *w'* go a little way over Jordan
38 I *w'* do to him that which shall seem
38 require of me, that *w'* I do for thee.
20:21 only, and I *w'* depart from the city.
21: 4 We *w'* have no silver nor gold of Saul,
4 ye shall say, that *w'* I do for you.
6 we *w'* hang them up unto the Lord
6 And the king said, I *w'* give them.
22: 3 God of my rock; in him *w'* I trust:
4 I *w'* call on the Lord, who is worthy
29 and the Lord *w'* lighten my darkness.
50 Therefore I *w'* give thanks unto thee,
50 and I *w'* sing praises unto thy name.
24:24 I *w'* surely buy it of thee at a price:
24 neither *w'* I offer burnt offerings
1Ki 1: 5 himself, saying, I *w'* be a king:
14 I also *w'* come in after thee,
30 even so *w'* I certainly do this day.
51 that he *w'* not slay his servant with
52 If he *w'* shew himself a worthy man,
2: 8 I *w'* not put thee to death with the
17 king, (for he *w'* not say thee nay,)
18 I *w'* speak for thee unto the king.
20 mother: for I *w'* not say thee nay.
26 I *w'* not at this time put thee to death,
30 And he said, Nay; but I *w'* die here.
38 king hath said, so *w'* thy servant do.
3:14 did walk, then I *w'* lengthen thy days.
5: 5 whom I *w'* set upon thy throne in thy
6 thee *w'* I give hire for thy servants
8 I *w'* do all thy desire concerning
9 I *w'* convey them by sea in floats unto
9 *w'* cause them to be discharged there,
6:12 *w'* I perform my word with thee,
13 *w'* dwell among the children of Israel,
13 and *w'* not forsake my people Israel.
8:27 *w'* God indeed dwell on the earth?
9: 5 I *w'* establish the throne of thy
6 *w'* not keep my commandments and
7 *w'* I cut off Israel out of the land
7 my name, *w'* I cast out of my sight;
11: 2 *w'* turn away your heart after their
11 I *w'* surely rend the kingdom from
11 thee, and *w'* give it to thy servant.
12 I *w'* not do it for David thy father's
12 I *w'* rend it out of the hand of thy son.
13 I *w'* not rend away all the kingdom;
13 *w'* give one tribe to thy son for David
31 I *w'* rend the kingdom out of the hand
31 and *w'* give ten tribes to thee.
34 I *w'* not take the whole kingdom out
34 I *w'* make him prince all the days of
35 I *w'* take the kingdom out of his son's
35 *w'* give it unto thee, even ten tribes.
36 And unto his son *w'* I give one tribe,
37 I *w'* take thee, and thou shalt reign
38 I *w'* be with thee, and build thee a
38 David, and *w'* give Israel unto thee.
39 I *w'* for this afflict the seed of David,
12: 4 us, lighter, and we *w'* serve thee.
7 they *w'* be thy servants for ever.
11 heavy yoke, I *w'* add to your yoke:
11 but I *w'* chastise you with scorpions.
14 heavy, and I *w'* add to your yoke:
14 but I *w'* chastise you with scorpions.
13: 7 thyself, and I *w'* give thee a reward.
8 thine house, I *w'* not go with thee,
8, 16 neither *w'* I eat bread nor drink
14:10 I *w'* bring evil upon the house of
10 *w'* cut off from Jeroboam him that
10 *w'* take away the remnant of the
16: 3 *w'* take away the posterity of Baasha,
3 *w'* make thy house like the house
18: 1 and I *w'* send rain upon the earth.
15 I *w'* surely shew myself unto him to
23 I *w'* dress the other bullock, and lay
24 I *w'* call on the name of the Lord:
19:20 mother, and then I *w'* follow thee.
20: 6 I *w'* send my servants unto thee to
9 for to thy servants at first I *w'* do:
13 I *w'* deliver it into thine hand this day;

1Ki 20:22 king of Syria *w'* come up against thee.
25 we *w'* fight against them in the plain,
28 *w'* I deliver all this great multitude
31 peradventure he *w'* save thy life.
34 took from thy father, I *w'* restore;
34 *w'* send thee away with this covenant.
21: 2 I *w'* give thee for it a better vineyard
2 *w'* give thee the worth of it in money.
4 I *w'* not give thee the inheritance of
6 I *w'* give thee another vineyard for it:
6 I *w'* not give thee my vineyard.
7 I *w'* give thee the vineyard of Naboth
21 Behold, I *w'* bring evil upon thee,
21 and *w'* take thy posterity, and
21 and *w'* cut off from Ahab him that
22 *w'* make thine house like the house
29 I *w'* not bring the evil in his days:
29 in his son's day *w'* I bring the evil
22:14 the Lord saith to me, that *w'* I speak.
21 Lord, and said, I *w'* persuade him.
22 I *w'* go forth, and I *w'* be a lying spirit
30 I *w'* disguise myself, and enter into
2Ki 2: 2 thy soul liveth, I *w'* not leave thee.
3 Lord *w'* take away thy master from
4 as thy soul liveth, I *w'* not leave thee.
5 Lord *w'* take away thy master from
6 as thy soul liveth, I *w'* not leave thee.
3: 7 he said, I *w'* go up: I am as thou art,
18 *w'* deliver the Moabites also into your
4:30 as thy soul liveth, I *w'* not leave thee.
5: 5 I *w'* send a letter unto the king of
11 He *w'* surely come out to me, and
16 whom I stand, I *w'* receive none.
17 servant *w'* henceforth offer neither
20 I *w'* run after him, and take somewhat
6: 3 And he answered, I will go.
11 *W'* ye not shew me which of us is for
19 I *w'* bring you to the man whom ye
28 and we *w'* eat my son to morrow.
7: 4 We *w'* enter into the city, then the
9 light, some mischief *w'* come upon us:
12 I *w'* now shew you what the Syrians
9: 8 I *w'* cut off from Ahab him that
9 I *w'* make the house of Ahab like the
26 I *w'* requite thee in this plat, saith
10: 5 and *w'* do all that thou shalt bid us;
5 we *w'* not make any king: do thou
6 if ye *w'* hearken unto my voice, take
18:14 which thou puttest on me *w'* I bear.
21 *w'* go into his hand, and pierce it:
23 I *w'* deliver thee two thousand horses,
30 The Lord *w'* surely deliver us, and
32 you saying, The Lord *w'* deliver us.
19: 4 thy God *w'* hear all the words of
4 *w'* reprove the words which the Lord
7 I *w'* send a blast upon him, and he
7 I *w'* cause him to fall by the sword in
23 and *w'* cut down the tall cedar trees
23 I *w'* enter into the lodgings of his
28 I *w'* put my hook in thy nose,
28 I *w'* turn thee back by the way by
34 For I *w'* defend this city, to save it,
20: 5 thy tears: behold, I *w'* heal thee:
6 I *w'* add unto thy days fifteen years;
6 I *w'* deliver thee and this city out of
6 I *w'* defend this city for mine own
8 be the sign that the Lord *w'* heal me,
9 Lord *w'* do the thing he hath spoken:
21: 4 In Jerusalem *w'* I put my name.
7 of Israel, *w'* I put my name for ever:
8 Neither *w'* I make the feet of Israel
8 if they *w'* observe to do according to
13 I *w'* stretch over Jerusalem the line of
13 I *w'* wipe Jerusalem as a man wipeth
14 I *w'* forsake the remnant of mine
22:16 I *w'* bring evil upon this place, and
20 I *w'* gather thee unto thy fathers,
20 evil which I *w'* bring upon this place.
23:27 I *w'* remove Judah also out of my
27 *w'* cast off this city Jerusalem which
1Ch 12:19 He *w'* fall to his master Saul to the
14:10 I *w'* deliver them into thine hand.
16:18 Unto thee *w'* I give the land of Canaan,
17: 9 I *w'* ordain a place for my people
9 and *w'* plant them, and they shall
10 I *w'* subdue all thine enemies.
10 that the Lord *w'* build thee an house.
11 that I *w'* raise up thy seed after thee,
11 and I *w'* establish his kingdom.
12 and I *w'* stablish his throne for ever.
13 I *w'* be his father, and he shall be my
13 I *w'* not take my mercy away from
14 I *w'* settle him in mine house and in
19: 2 I *w'* shew kindness unto Hanun the
12 strong for thee, then I *w'* help thee.
21: 3 *w'* he be a cause of trespass to Israel?
24 I *w'* verily buy it for the full price:
24 I *w'* not take that which is thine for
22: 5 I *w'* therefore now make preparation
9 I *w'* give him rest from all his enemies
9 I *w'* give peace and quietness unto
10 be my son, and I *w'* be his father;
10 and I *w'* establish the throne of his
28: 6 to be my son, and I *w'* be his father.
7 I *w'* establish his kingdom for ever,
9 seek him, he *w'* be found of thee;
9 forsake him, he *w'* cast thee off for
20 God, even my God *w'* be with thee;
20 he *w'* not fail thee, nor forsake thee,
21 *w'* be wholly at thy commandment.
2Ch 1:12 I *w'* give thee riches, and wealth, and
2:10 I *w'* give to thy servants, the hewers
16 *w'* cut wood out of Lebanon, as much
16 *w'* bring it to thee in floats by sea
6:18 *w'* God in every deed dwell with men
7:14 ways, then *w'* I hear from heaven,

2Ch 7:14 and *w'* forgive their sin,
14 and *w'* heal their land.
18 *w'* I stablish the throne of thy
20 *w'* I pluck them up by the roots out of
20 my name, *w'* I cast out of my sight,
20 and *w'* make it to be a proverb and a
10: 4 he put upon us, and we *w'* serve thee.
11 upon you, I *w'* put more to your yoke:
11 but I *w'* chastise you with scorpions.
14 your yoke heavy, but I *w'* add thereto:
14 but I *w'* chastise you with scorpions.
12: 7 therefore I *w'* not destroy them,
7 I *w'* grant them some deliverance;
15: 2 if ye seek him, he *w'* be found of you;
2 if ye forsake him, he *w'* forsake you.
18: 3 and we *w'* be with thee in the war.
5 for God *w'* deliver it into the king's
13 what my God saith, that *w'* I speak.
20 the Lord, and said, I *w'* entice him.
21 I *w'* go out, and be a lying spirit
29 Jehoshaphat, I *w'* disguise myself,
29 and *w'* go to the battle; but put thou
20:17 them: for the Lord *w'* be with you.
21:14 a great plague *w'* the Lord smite thy
28:23 them, therefore *w'* I sacrifice to them,
30: 6 he *w'* return to the remnant of you,
9 *w'* not turn away his face from you.
33: 7 of Israel, *w'* I put my name for ever:
8 Neither *w'* I any more remove the foot
8 so that they *w'* take heed to do all that
34:24 I *w'* bring evil upon this place,
28 I *w'* gather thee to thy fathers,
28 evil that I *w'* bring upon this place.
Ezr 4: 3 together *w'* build unto the Lord God
13 then *w'* they not pay toll, tribute,
7:18 that do after the *w'* of your God.
26 And whosoever *w'* not do the law of
10: 4 we also *w'* be with thee: be of good
Ne 1: 8 I *w'* scatter you abroad among the
9 yet *w'* I gather them from thence,
9 *w'* bring them unto the place that
2:19 ye do? *w'* ye rebel against the king?
20 The God of heaven, he *w'* prosper us;
20 we his servants *w'* arise and build:
4: 2 Jews? *w'* they fortify themselves?
2 *w'* they sacrifice? *w'* they make an
2 *w'* they revive the stones out of the
12 return unto us they *w'* be upon you.
5: 8 *w'* ye even sell your brethren? or shall
12 We *w'* restore them, and *w'* require
12 of them; so *w'* we do as thou sayest.
6:10 temple: for they *w'* come to slay thee;
10 in the night *w'* they come to slay thee.
10:39 *w'* not forsake the house of our God.
13:21 ye do so again, I *w'* lay hands on you.
Es 3: 9 I *w'* pay ten thousand talents of silver
4:16 and my maidens *w'* fast likewise;
16 so *w'* I go in unto the king, which is not
5: 8 *w'* do to morrow as the king hath said.
7: 8 *W'* he force the queen also before me
Job 1:11 hath, and he *w'* curse thee to thy face.
2: 4 that a man hath *w'* he give for his life.
5 flesh, and he *w'* curse thee to thy face.
5: 1 if there be any that *w'* answer thee;
6:24 Teach me, and I *w'* hold my tongue:
7:11 Therefore I *w'* not refrain my mouth;
11 I *w'* speak in the anguish of my spirit;
11 I *w'* complain in the bitterness of my
8:20 God *w'* not cast away a perfect man,
20 neither *w'* he help the evil doers:
9: 3 If he *w'* contend with him, he cannot
12 who *w'* say unto him, What doest
13 If God *w'* not withdraw his anger,
18 *w'* not suffer me to take my breath,
23 *w'* laugh at the trial of the innocent.
27 If I say, I *w'* forget my complaint,
27 I *w'* leave off my heaviness,
10: 1 I *w'* leave my complaint upon myself;
1 I *w'* speak in the bitterness of my soul.
2 I *w'* say unto God, Do not condemn
15 righteous, yet *w'* I not lift up my head.
11:11 also; *w'* he not then consider it?
13: 7 *W'* ye speak wickedly for God?
8 *W'* ye accept his person? *w'* ye
10 He *w'* surely reprove you, if ye do
13 speak, and let come on me what *w'*.
15 Though he slay me, yet *w'* I trust him:
15 but I *w'* maintain mine own ways
19 Who is he that *w'* plead with me?
20 then *w'* I not hide myself from thee.
22 Then call thou, and I *w'* answer:
14: 7 be cut down, that it *w'* sprout again,
7 tender branch thereof *w'* not cease.
9 through the scent of water it *w'* bud,
14 days of my appointed time *w'* I wait,
15 Thou shalt call, and I *w'* answer thee:
15:17 I *w'* shew thee, hear me; and that
17 that which I have seen I *w'* declare;
17: 3 is he that *w'* strike hands with me?
18: 2 How long *w'* it be ere ye make an end
2 mark, and afterwards we *w'* speak.
19: 2 How long *w'* ye vex my soul,
5 If indeed ye *w'* magnify yourselves
22: 4 *W'* he reprove thee for fear of thee?
4 *w'* he enter with thee into judgment?
23: 6 *W'* he plead against me with his great
24:25 who *w'* make me a liar, and make my
27: 5 *w'* not remove mine integrity from me.
6 I hold fast, and *w'* not let it go:
9 *W'* God hear his cry when trouble
10 *W'* he delight himself in the Almighty?
10 *w'* he always call upon God?
11 I *w'* teach you by the hand of God:
11 with the Almighty *w'* I not conceal.
30:24 he *w'* not stretch out his hand to the
32:10 to me; I also *w'* shew mine opinion.

Job 32:14 neither *w'* I answer him with your
17 I said, I *w'* answer my part, I also
17 part, I also *w'* shew mine opinion.
20 I *w'* speak, that I may be refreshed:
20 I *w'* open my lips and answer.
33:12 I *w'* answer thee, that God is greater
26 and he *w'* be favourable unto him:
26 *w'* render...man his righteousness.
28 He *w'* deliver his soul from going
31 hold thy peace, and I *w'* speak.
34:12 Yea, surely God *w'* not do wickedly,
12 *w'* the Almighty pervert judgment.
23 For he *w'* not lay upon man more than
31 I *w'* not offend any more:
32 I have done iniquity, I *w'* do no more.
33 he *w'* recompense it, whether thou
35: 3 What advantage *w'* it be unto thee?
4 I *w'* answer thee, and thy companions
13 Surely God *w'* not hear vanity,
13 neither *w'* the Almighty regard it.
36: 2 and I *w'* shew thee that I have yet to
3 I *w'* fetch my knowledge from afar,
3 *w'* ascribe righteousness to my Maker.
19 *W'* he esteem thy riches? no, not gold,
37: 4 he *w'* not stay them when his voice is
23 in plenty of justice: he *w'* not afflict.
38: 3 for I *w'* demand of thee, and answer
39: 9 *W'* the unicorn be willing to serve
10 or *w'* he harrow the valleys after thee?
12 that he *w'* bring home thy seed,
40: 4 I *w'* lay mine hand upon my mouth.
5 have I spoken; but I *w'* not answer:
5 twice; but I *w'* proceed no further.
7 I *w'* demand of thee, and declare thou
14 Then *w'* I also confess unto thee that
41: 3 *W'* he make many supplications unto
3 *w'* he speak soft words unto thee?
4 *W'* he make a covenant with thee?
12 I *w'* not conceal his parts, nor his
42: 4 Hear, I beseech thee, and I *w'* speak:
4 I *w'* demand of thee, and declare thou
8 for him *w'* I accept: lest I deal with
Ps 2: 7 I *w'* declare the decree: the Lord hath
3: 6 I *w'* not be afraid of ten thousands of
4: 2 *w'* ye turn my glory into shame?
2 how long *w'* ye love vanity, and seek
3 the Lord *w'* hear when I call unto him.
6 that say, Who *w'* shew us any good?
8 I *w'* both lay me down in peace,
5: 2 and my God: for unto thee *w'* I pray.
3 in the morning *w'* direct my prayer
3 my prayer unto thee, and *w'* look up.
6 the Lord *w'* abhor the bloody and
7 I *w'* come unto thy house in the
7 and in thy fear *w'* I worship toward
6: 9 the Lord *w'* receive my prayer.
7:12 If he turn not, he *w'* whet his sword;
17 I *w'* praise the Lord according to his
17 *w'* sing praise to the name of the Lord
9: 1 I *w'* praise thee, O Lord, with my
1 I *w'* shew forth all thy marvellous
2 I *w'* be glad and rejoice in thee:
2 I *w'* sing praise to thy name, O thou
9 The Lord also *w'* be a refuge for the
10 thy name *w'* put their trust in thee:
14 Zion: I *w'* rejoice in thy salvation.
10: 4 countenance, *w'* not seek after God:
11 hideth his face; he *w'* never see it.
12: 4 said, With our tongue *w'* we prevail;
5 needy, now *w'* I arise, saith the Lord;
5 I *w'* set him in safety from him that
13: 6 I *w'* sing unto the Lord, because he
16: 4 offerings of blood *w'* I not offer,
7 I *w'* bless the Lord, who hath given
17:15 I *w'* behold thy face in righteousness:
18: 1 I *w'* love thee, O Lord, my strength.
2 my strength, in whom I *w'* trust;
3 I *w'* call upon the Lord, who is worthy
28 my God *w'* enlighten my darkness.
49 Therefore *w'* I give thanks unto thee,
20: 5 We *w'* rejoice in thy salvation, and in
5 name of our God we *w'* set up our
6 *w'* hear him from his holy heaven
7 *w'* remember the name of the Lord
21:13 so *w'* we sing and praise thy power.
22:22 I *w'* declare thy name unto my
22 of the congregation *w'* I praise thee.
25 I *w'* pay my vows before them that
23: 4 shadow of death, I *w'* fear no evil:
6 I *w'* dwell in the house of the Lord for
25: 8 *w'* he teach sinners in the way.
9 The meek *w'* he guide in judgment:
9 and the meek *w'* he teach his way.
14 and he *w'* shew them his covenant.
26: 4 neither *w'* I go in with dissemblers.
5 doers; and *w'* not sit with the wicked.
6 I *w'* wash mine hands in innocency:
6 so *w'* I compass thine altar, O Lord:
11 for me, I *w'* walk in mine integrity:
12 the congregations *w'* I bless the Lord.
27: 3 against me, in this *w'* I be confident.
4 of the Lord, that *w'* I seek after;
6 therefore *w'* I offer in his tabernacle
6 I *w'* sing, yea, I *w'* sing praises unto
8 unto thee, Thy face, Lord, *w'* I seek.
10 me, then the Lord *w'* take me up.
12 over unto the *w'* of mine enemies:
28: 1 Unto thee *w'* I cry, O Lord my rock;
7 and with my song *w'* I praise him.
29:11 The Lord *w'* give strength unto his
11 Lord *w'* bless his people with peace.
30: 1 I *w'* extol thee, O Lord; for thou hast
12 I *w'* give thanks unto thee for ever.
31: 7 I *w'* be glad and rejoice in thy mercy:
32: 5 I *w'* confess my transgressions unto
8 I *w'* instruct thee and teach thee in

Ps 32: 8 go: I *w'* guide thee with mine eye.
34: 1 I *w'* bless the Lord at all times: his
11 I *w'* teach you the fear of the Lord.
35:18 I *w'* give thee thanks in the great
18 I *w'* praise thee among much people.
37:33 Lord *w'* not leave him in his hand,
38:18 For I *w'* declare mine iniquity;
18 iniquity; I *w'* be sorry for my sin.
39: 1 I said, I *w'* take heed to my ways, that
1 I *w'* keep my mouth with a bridle,
40: 8 I delight to do thy *w'*, O my God:
41: 1 the Lord *w'* deliver him in time of
2 The Lord *w'* preserve him, and
2 him unto the *w'* of his enemies.
3 Lord *w'* strengthen him upon the bed
42: 6 *w'* I remember thee from the land of
8 Lord *w'* command his lovingkindness
9 I *w'* say unto God my rock, Why hast
43: 4 Then *w'* I go unto the altar of God,
4 upon the harp *w'* I praise thee, O God
44: 5 Through thee *w'* we push down our
5 through thy name *w'* we tread them
6 For I *w'* not trust in my bow, neither
45:17 *w'* make thy name to be remembered
46: 2 Therefore *w'* not we fear, though the
10 I *w'* be exalted among the heathen,
10 heathen, I *w'* be exalted in the earth.
48: 8 God *w'* establish it for ever. Selah.
14 he *w'* be our guide even unto death.
49: 4 I *w'* incline mine ear to a parable:
4 I *w'* open my dark saying upon the
15 But God *w'* redeem my soul from
18 and men *w'* praise thee, when thou
50: 7 Hear, O my people, and I *w'* speak;
7 Israel, and I *w'* testify against thee:
8 I *w'* not reprove thee for thy sacrifices
9 I *w'* take no bullock out of thy house,
13 *W'* I eat the flesh of bulls, or drink
15 *w'* deliver thee, and thou shalt glorify
21 but I *w'* reprove thee, and set them in
23 aright *w'* I shew the salvation of God.
51:13 *w'* I teach transgressors thy ways;
52: 9 I *w'* praise thee for ever, because thou
9 and I *w'* wait on thy name; for it is
54: 6 *w'* freely sacrifice unto thee:
6 I *w'* praise thy name, O Lord;
55:16 As for me, I *w'* call upon God; and the
17 at noon, *w'* I pray, and cry aloud:
23 their days; but I *w'* trust in thee.
56: 3 time I am afraid, I *w'* trust in thee.
4 In God I *w'* praise his word, in God I
4 I *w'* not fear what flesh can do unto
10 In God *w'* I praise his word:
10 in the Lord *w'* I praise his word.
11 I *w'* not be afraid what man can do
12 God: I *w'* render praises unto thee.
57: 1 of thy wings *w'* I make my refuge,
2 I *w'* cry unto God most high; unto
7 is fixed: I *w'* sing and give praise.
8 and harp: I myself *w'* awake early.
9 I *w'* praise thee, O Lord, among the
9 I *w'* sing unto thee among the nations.
58: 5 *w'* not hearken to the voice of
59: 9 of his strength *w'* I wait upon thee:
16 but I *w'* sing of thy power; yea,
16 I *w'* sing aloud of thy mercy in the
17 Unto thee, O my strength, *w'* I sing:
60: 6 I *w'* rejoice, I *w'* divide Shechem, and
8 over Edom *w'* I cast out my shoe:
9 Who *w'* bring me into the strong city?
9 city? who *w'* lead me unto Edom?
61: 2 end of the earth *w'* I cry unto thee,
4 I *w'* abide in thy tabernacle for ever:
4 I *w'* trust in the covert of thy wings.
8 So *w'* I sing praise unto thy name for
62: 3 How long *w'* ye imagine mischief
63: 1 art my God; early *w'* I seek thee:
4 Thus *w'* I bless thee while I live:
4 I *w'* lift up my hands in thy name.
7 the shadow of thy wings *w'* I rejoice.
66:13 I *w'* go into thy house with burnt
13 offerings: I *w'* pay thee my vows,
15 I *w'* offer unto thee burnt sacrifices of
15 rams; I *w'* offer bullocks with goats.
16 and I *w'* declare what he hath done
18 my heart, the Lord *w'* not hear me.
68:16 yea, the Lord *w'* dwell in it for ever.
22 said, I *w'* bring again from Bashan,
22 I *w'* bring my people again from the
69:30 I *w'* praise the name of God with a
30 *w'* magnify him with thanksgiving.
35 For God *w'* save Zion, and *w'* build
71:14 But I *w'* hope continually, and
14 and *w'* yet praise thee more and more.
16 I *w'* go in the strength of the Lord
16 I *w'*...mention of thy righteousness,
22 I *w'* also praise thee with the psaltery,
22 unto thee *w'* I sing with the harp,
73:15 If I say, I *w'* speak thus; behold, I
75: 2 the congregation I *w'* judge uprightly.
9 I *w'* declare for ever; I *w'* sing praises
10 horns of the wicked also *w'* I cut off;
77: 7 *W'* the Lord cast off for ever? and
7 *w'* he be favourable no more?
10 I *w'* remember the years of the right
11 I *w'* remember the works of the Lord:
11 I *w'* remember thy wonders of old.
12 I *w'* meditate also of all thy work,
78: 2 I *w'* open my mouth in a parable:
2 I *w'* utter dark sayings of old:
4 We *w'* not hide them from their
79:13 pasture *w'* give thee thanks for ever:
13 we *w'* shew forth thy praise to all
80:18 So *w'* not we go back from thee:
18 us, and we *w'* call upon thy name.
81: 8 people, and I *w'* testify unto thee:

Ps 81:10 open thy mouth wide, and I *w'* fill it.
82: 2 How long *w'* ye judge unjustly,
5 know not, neither *w'* they understand;
84: 4 house: they *w'* be still praising thee.
11 the Lord *w'* give grace and glory:
11 no good thing *w'* he withhold from
85: 8 I *w'* hear what God the Lord *w'* speak:
8 for he *w'* speak peace unto his people,
86: 7 day of my trouble I *w'* call upon thee:
11 way, O Lord; I *w'* walk in thy truth:
12 I *w'* praise thee, O Lord my God,
12 I *w'* glorify thy name for evermore.
87: 4 I *w'* make mention of Rahab and
89: 1 I *w'* sing of the mercies of the Lord
1 *w'* I make known thy faithfulness
4 Thy seed *w'* I establish for ever,
23 And I *w'* beat down his foes before his
25 I *w'* set his hand also in the sea,
27 Also I *w'* make him my firstborn,
28 My mercy *w'* I keep for him for
32 Then *w'* I visit their transgression
33 my lovingkindness *w'* I not utterly
34 My covenant *w'* I not break,
35 holiness that I *w'* not lie unto David.
91: 2 I *w'* say of the Lord, He is my refuge
2 my God; in him *w'* I trust.
14 upon me, therefore *w'* I deliver him:
14 I *w'* set him on high, because he hath
15 call upon me, and I *w'* answer him:
15 I *w'* be with him in trouble;
15 I *w'* deliver him, and honour him.
16 With long life *w'* I satisfy him,
92: 4 *w'* triumph in the works of thy hands.
94: 8 and ye fools, when *w'* ye be wise?
14 For the Lord *w'* not cast off his people,
14 neither *w'* he forsake his inheritance.
16 Who *w'* rise up for me against the
16 or who *w'* stand up for me against
95: 7 To day if ye *w'* hear his voice,
101: 1 I *w'* sing of mercy and judgment:
1 unto thee, O Lord, *w'* I sing.
2 I *w'* behave myself wisely in a perfect
2 I *w'* walk within my house with a
3 I *w'* set no wicked thing before mine
4 I *w'* not know a wicked person.
5 his neighbour, him *w'* I cut off:
5 and a proud heart *w'* not I suffer.
8 I *w'* early destroy all the wicked
102:17 He *w'* regard the prayer of the
103: 9 He *w'* not always chide: neither
9 neither *w'* he keep his anger for ever.
104:33 *w'* sing unto the Lord as long as I live:
33 I *w'* sing praise to my God while I have
34 be sweet: I *w'* be glad in the Lord.
105:11 Unto thee *w'* I give the land of Canaan,
107:43 is wise, and *w'* observe these things,
108: 1 I *w'* sing and give praise, even with
2 and harp: I myself *w'* awake early.
3 I *w'* praise thee, O Lord, among the
3 and I *w'* sing praises unto thee
7 I *w'* rejoice, I *w'* divide Shechem,
9 over Edom *w'* I cast out my shoe;
9 my shoe; over Philistia *w'* I triumph.
10 Who *w'* bring me into the strong city?
10 who *w'* lead me into Edom?
109:30 I *w'* greatly praise the Lord with my
30 I *w'* praise him among the multitude.
110: 4 Lord hath sworn, and *w'* not repent,
111: 1 I *w'* praise the Lord with my whole
5 *w'* ever be mindful of his covenant.
112: 5 he *w'* guide his affairs with discretion.
115:12 he *w'* bless us; he *w'* bless the house
12 he *w'* bless the house of Aaron.
13 He *w'* bless them that fear the Lord,
18 But we *w'* bless the Lord from this
116: 2 therefore *w'* I call upon him as long
9 I *w'* walk before the Lord in the land
13 I *w'* take the cup of salvation, and call
14 I *w'* pay my vows unto the Lord now
17 I *w'* offer to thee the sacrifice of
17 and *w'* call upon the name of the Lord.
18 I *w'* pay my vows unto the Lord now
118: 6 The Lord is on my side; I *w'* not fear:
10 name of the Lord *w'* I destroy them.
11, 12 name of the Lord I *w'* destroy them.
19 I *w'* go into them, and I *w'* praise the
21 I *w'* praise thee: for thou hast heard
24 made; we *w'* rejoice and be glad in it.
28 Thou art my God, and I *w'* praise thee:
28 thou art my God, I *w'* exalt thee.
119: 7 I *w'* praise thee with uprightness
8 I *w'* keep thy statutes: O forsake me
15 I *w'* meditate in thy precepts,
16 I *w'* delight myself in thy statutes:
16 statutes: I *w'* not forget thy word.
32 I *w'* run the way of...commandments,
45 And I *w'* walk at liberty: for I seek
46 I *w'* speak of thy testimonies also
46 kings, and *w'* not be ashamed.
47 And I *w'* delight myself in thy
48 My hands also *w'* I lift up unto thy
48 and I *w'* meditate in thy statutes.
62 At midnight I *w'* rise to give thanks
69 but I *w'* keep thy precepts with my
74 They that fear thee *w'* be glad when
78 but I *w'* meditate in thy precepts.
93 I *w'* never forget thy precepts:
95 but I *w'* consider thy testimonies.
106 I have sworn, and I *w'* perform it,
106 *w'* keep thy righteous judgments.
115 for I *w'* keep the commandments of
117 I *w'* have respect unto thy statutes
134 of man: so *w'* I keep thy precepts.
145 me, O Lord: I *w'* keep thy statutes.
121: 1 I *w'* lift up mine eyes unto the hills,
3 He *w'* not suffer thy foot to be moved:

Ps 121: 3 he that keepeth thee *w'* not slumber.
122: 8 I *w'* now say, Peace be within thee.
9 the Lord our God I *w'* seek thy good.
132: 3 I *w'* not come into the tabernacle
4 I *w'* not give sleep to mine eyes,
7 We *w'* go into his tabernacles:
7 we *w'* worship at his footstool.
11 unto David; he *w'* not turn from it;
11 of thy body *w'* I set upon thy throne.
12 If thy children *w'* keep my covenant
14 here *w'* I dwell; for I have desired it.
15 I *w'* abundantly bless her provision:
15 I *w'* satisfy her poor with bread.
16 I *w'* also clothe her priest with
17 There *w'* I make the home of David
18 His enemies *w'* I clothe with shame:
135:14 For the Lord *w'* judge his people,
14 *w'* repent himself concerning his
138: 1 I *w'* praise thee with my whole heart:
1 before the gods *w'* I sing praise unto
2 I *w'* worship toward thy holy temple,
8 Lord *w'* perfect that which concerneth
139:14 I *w'* praise thee; for I am fearfully
140:12 that the Lord *w'* maintain the cause
143:10 Teach me to do thy *w'*; for thou
144: 9 I *w'* sing a new song unto thee, O God
9 ten strings *w'* I sing praises unto thee.
145: 1 I *w'* extol thee, my God, O king;
1 and I *w'* bless thy name for ever and
2 Every day *w'* I bless thee; and I
2 and I *w'* praise thy name for ever and
5 I *w'* speak of the glorious honour
6 acts: and I *w'* declare thy greatness.
19 He *w'* fulfil the desire of them that
19 *w'* hear their cry, and *w'* save them.
20 but all the wicked *w'* he destroy.
146: 2 While I live *w'* I praise the Lord:
2 I *w'* sing praises unto my God while I
149: 4 *w'* beautify the meek with salvation.
Pr 1: 5 A wise man *w'* hear,
5 and *w'* increase learning;
22 ye simple ones, *w'* ye love simplicity?
23 I *w'* pour out my spirit unto you,
23 I *w'* make known my words unto you.
26 I also *w'* laugh at your calamity;
26 I *w'* mock when your fear cometh;
28 call upon me, but I *w'* not answer;
3:28 come again, and to morrow I *w'* give;
6:26 adulteress *w'* hunt for...precious life.
34 *w'* not spare in the day of vengeance.
35 He *w'* not regard any ransom;
35 neither *w'* he rest content,
7:20 *w'* come home at the day appointed.
8: 6 for I *w'* speak of excellent things;
21 and I *w'* fill their treasures.
9: 8 a wise man, and he *w'* love thee.
9 to a wise man, and he *w'* be yet wiser:
9 man, and he *w'* increase in learning.
10: 3 The Lord *w'* not suffer the soul of the
8 in heart *w'* receive commandments:
12: 2 man of wicked devices *w'* he condemn.
14: 5 A faithful witness *w'* not lie:
5 but a false witness *w'* utter lies.
15:12 neither *w'* he go unto the wise.
25 The Lord *w'* destroy the house of the
25 *w'* establish the border of the widow.
16:14 of death: but a wise man *w'* pacify it.
18:14 a man *w'* sustain his infirmity;
19: 6 *w'* intreat the favour of the prince:
17 he hath given *w'* he pay him again.
24 and *w'* not so much as bring it to his
25 a scorner, and the simple *w'* beware:
25 and he *w'* understand knowledge.
20: 3 strife: but every fool *w'* be meddling.
4 The sluggard *w'* not plow by reason of
5 man of understanding *w'* draw it out.
6 Most men *w'* proclaim every one his
22 Say not thou, I *w'* recompense evil;
21: 1 he turneth it whithersoever he *w'*.
22: 6 he is old, he *w'* not depart from it.
23 For the Lord *w'* plead their cause,
23: 9 he *w'* despise the wisdom of thy words.
35 shall I awake? I *w'* seek it yet again.
24:29 *w'* do so to him as he hath done to me:
29 I *w'* render to the man according to
26:27 rolleth a stone, it *w'* return upon him.
27:22 yet *w'* not his foolishness depart
28: 8 gather it for him that *w'* pity the poor.
21 piece of bread that man *w'* transgress.
29:19 servant *w'* not be corrected by words:
19 he understand he *w'* not answer.
31:12 She *w'* do him good and not evil all
Ec 2: 1 Go to now, I *w'* prove thee with mirth,
4:10 fall, the one *w'* lift up his fellow:
13 who *w'* no more be admonished.
5:12 abundance of the rich *w'* not suffer
7: 2 and the living *w'* lay it to his heart.
23 I *w'* be wise; but it was far from me.
10:11 Surely the serpent *w'* bite without
12 lips of a fool *w'* swallow up himself.
11: 9 God *w'* bring thee into judgment.
Ca 1: 4 Draw me, we *w'* run after thee: the
4 we *w'* be glad and rejoice in thee,
4 *w'* remember thy love more than wine:
11 We *w'* make thee borders of gold with
3: 2 I *w'* rise now, and go about the city in
2 I *w'* seek him whom my soul loveth:
4: 6 I *w'* get me to the mountain of myrrh,
6:13 What *w'* ye see in the Shulamite?
7: 8 I said, I *w'* go up to the palm tree,
8 I *w'* take hold of the boughs thereof:
12 forth: there *w'* I give thee my loves.
8: 9 wall, we *w'* build upon her a palace of
9 *w'* inclose her with boards of cedar.
Isa 1: 5 ye *w'* revolt more and more: the
15 hands, I *w'* hide mine eyes from you;

Isa 1:15 ye make many prayers, I *w'* not hear:
24 Ah, I *w'* ease me of mine adversaries,
25 I *w'* turn my hand upon thee, and
26 And I *w'* restore thy judges as at the
2: 3 and he *w'* teach us of his ways,
3 and we *w'* walk in his paths: for out
3: 4 I *w'* give children to be their princes,
7 swear, saying, I *w'* not be an healer;
14 Lord *w'* enter into judgment with the
17 the Lord *w'* smite with a scab the
17 and the Lord *w'* discover their secret
18 Lord *w'* take away the bravery of their
4: 1 We *w'* eat our own bread, and wear
5 And the Lord *w'* create upon every
5: 1 Now *w'* I sing my wellbeloved a song
5 I *w'* tell you what I *w'* do to my
5 I *w'* take away the hedge thereof, and
6 And I *w'* lay it waste: it shall not be
6 I *w'* also command the clouds that
26 And he *w'* lift up an ensign to the
26 and *w'* hiss unto them from the end of
6: 8 shall I send, and who *w'* go for us?
7: 9 If ye *w'* not believe, surely ye shall
12 I *w'* not ask, neither *w'* I tempt,
13 men, but *w'* ye weary my God also?
8:17 I *w'* wait upon the Lord, that hideth
17 house of Jacob, and I *w'* look for him.
9: 7 of the Lord of hosts *w'* perform this.
10 but we *w'* build with hewn stones:
10 but we *w'* change them into cedars.
14 the Lord *w'* cut off from Israel head
10: 3 And what *w'* ye do in the day of
3 from far? to whom *w'* ye flee for help?
3 and where *w'* ye leave your glory?
6 I *w'* send him against an hypocritical
6 of my wrath *w'* I give him a charge,
12 I *w'* punish the fruit of the stout heart
12: 1 shalt say, O Lord, I *w'* praise thee:
2 I *w'* trust, and not be afraid:
13:11 And I *w'* punish the world for their
11 I *w'* cause the arrogancy of the proud
11 and *w'* lay low the haughtiness of the
12 I *w'* make a man more precious than
13 Therefore I *w'* shake the heavens, and
17 I *w'* stir up the Medes against them,
14: 1 For the Lord *w'* have mercy on Jacob,
1 and *w'* yet choose Israel, and set
13 thine heart, I *w'* ascend into heaven,
13 I *w'* exalt my throne above the stars of
13 I *w'* sit also upon the mount of the
14 I *w'* ascend above the heights of the
14 I *w'* be like the most High.
22 For I *w'* rise up against them, saith
23 I *w'* also make it a possession for the
23 I *w'* sweep it with the besom of
25 That I *w'* break the Assyrian in my
30 I *w'* kill thy root with famine, and he
15: 9 for I *w'* bring more upon Dimon, lions
16: 9 I *w'* bewail with the weeping of Jazer
9 I *w'* water thee with my tears, O
18: 4 Lord said unto me, I *w'* take my rest,
4 and I *w'* consider in my dwelling place
19: 2 I *w'* set the Egyptians against the
3 and I *w'* destroy the counsel thereof:
4 And the Egyptians *w'* I give over into
21:12 if ye *w'* enquire, enquire ye: return,
22: 4 I *w'* weep bitterly, labour not to
17 Lord *w'* carry thee away with a
17 and *w'* surely cover thee.
18 He *w'* surely violently turn and toss
19 And I *w'* drive thee from thy station,
20 I *w'* call my servant Eliakim the son
21 I *w'* clothe him with thy robe, and
21 I *w'* commit thy government into his
22 the key...*w'* I lay upon his shoulder;
23 And I *w'* fasten him as a nail in a sure
23:17 that the Lord *w'* visit Tyre, and she
25: 1 I *w'* exalt thee, I *w'* praise thy name;
7 he *w'* destroy in this mountain the
8 He *w'* swallow up death in victory;
8 Lord God *w'* wipe away tears from off
9 waited for him, and he *w'* save us:
9 him, we *w'* be glad and rejoice in his
26: 1 salvation *w'* God appoint for walls and
9 spirit within me *w'* I seek thee early:
9 of the world *w'* learn righteousness.
10 yet *w'* he not learn righteousness:
10 of uprightness *w'* he deal unjustly,
10 *w'* not behold the majesty of the Lord.
11 thy hand is lifted up, they *w'* not see:
13 by thee only *w'* we make mention of
27: 3 keep it; I *w'* water it every moment:
3 hurt it, I *w'* keep it night and day.
11 them *w'* not have mercy on them,
11 formed them *w'* shew them no favour.
28:11 another tongue *w'* he speak to this
17 Judgment also *w'* I lay to the line, and
28 he *w'* not ever be threshing it, nor
29: 2 Yet I *w'* distress Ariel, and there shall
3 I *w'* camp against thee round about,
3 and *w'* lay siege against thee with a
3 and I *w'* raise forts against thee.
14 I *w'* proceed to do a marvellous work
30: 6 they *w'* carry their riches upon the
9 children that *w'* not hear the law of
16 said, No; for we *w'* flee upon horses;
16 We *w'* ride upon the swift; therefore;
18 And therefore *w'* the Lord wait, that
18 you, and therefore *w'* he be exalted,
19 he *w'* be very gracious unto thee at
19 he shall hear it, he *w'* answer thee.
32 and in battles of shaking *w'* he fight
31: 2 Yet he also is wise, and *w'* bring evil,
2 evil, and *w'* not call back his words:
2 but *w'* arise against the house of the
4 he *w'* not be afraid of their voice, nor

Isa 31: 5 so w' the Lord of hosts defend
5 defending also he w' deliver it; and
5 and passing over he w' preserve it.
32: 6 For the vile person w' speak villany,
6 and his heart w' work iniquity, to
6 he w' cause the drink of the thirsty to
33: 10 Now w' I arise, saith the Lord; now
10 w' I be exalted; now w' I lift up
21 Lord w' be unto us a place of broad
22 the Lord is our king; he w' save us.
35: 4 your God w' come with vengeance,
4 recompence; he w' come and save you.
36: 6 it w' go into his hand, and pierce it:
8 I w' give thee two thousand horses,
15 saying, The Lord w' surely deliver us;
18 you, saying, The Lord w' deliver us.
37: 4 Lord thy God w' hear the words of
4 and w' reprove the words which the
24 I w' cut down the tall cedars thereof,
24 I w' enter into the height of his border,
29 w' I put my hook in thy nose,
29 I w' turn thee back by the way by
38: 5 I w' add unto thy days fifteen years.
6 And I w' deliver thee and this city
6 Assyria: and I w' defend this city,
7 Lord w' do this thing that he hath
8 I w' bring again the shadow of the
12 he w' cut me off with pining sickness:
13 as a lion, so w' he break all my bones:
20 we w' sing my songs to the stringed
40: 10 the Lord God w' come with strong
18 To whom then w' ye liken God? or
18 or what likeness w' ye compare unto
20 chooseth a tree that w' not rot;
25 To whom then w' ye liken me, or shall
41: 10 I w' strengthen thee;
10 yea, I w' help thee;
10 I w' uphold thee with the right hand of
13 Lord thy God w' hold thy right hand,
13 unto thee, Fear not; I w' help thee.
14 I w' help thee, saith the Lord, and thy
15 I w' make thee a new sharp threshing
17 I the Lord w' hear them, I the God of
17 God of Israel w' not forsake them.
18 I w' open rivers in high places, and
18 I w' make the wilderness a pool of
19 I w' plant in the wilderness the cedar,
19 I w' set in the desert the fir tree, and
27 I w' give to Jerusalem one that
42: 6 w' hold thine hand, and w' keep thee,
8 my glory w' I not give to another,
14 now w' I cry like a travailing woman;
14 I w' destroy and devour at once.
15 I w' make waste mountains and hills,
15 and I w' make the rivers islands, and
15 islands, and I w' dry up the pools.
16 I w' bring the blind by a way that
16 I w' lead them in paths that they have
16 I w' make darkness light before them,
16 These things w' I do unto them, and
21 he w' magnify the law, and make it
23 Who among you w' give ear to this?
23 who w' hearken and hear for the time
43: 2 the waters, I w' be with thee;
4 therefore w' I give men for thee, and
5 I w' bring thy seed from the east,
6 I w' say to the north, Give up; and to
13 hand: I w' work, and who shall let it?
19 Behold, I w' do a new thing; now it
19 I w'...make a way in the wilderness,
25 sake, and w' not remember thy sins.
44: 2 from the womb, which w' help thee;
3 For I w' pour water upon him that
3 I w' pour my spirit upon thy seed,
15 for he w' take thereof, and warm
26 and I w' raise up the decayed places
27 Be dry, and I w' dry up thy rivers:
45: 1 and I w' loose the loins of kings,
2 I w' go before thee, and make the
2 I w' break in pieces the gates of brass,
3 w' give thee the treasures of darkness,
13 and I w' direct all his ways:
46: 4 and even to hoar hairs w' I carry you:
4 carry you: I have made, and I w' bear;
4 even I w' carry, and w' deliver you.
5 To whom w' ye liken me, and make
10 stand, and I w' do all my pleasure:
11 spoken it, I w' also bring it to pass;
11 I have purposed it, I w' also do it.
13 w' place salvation in Zion for Israel
47: 3 shall be seen: I w' take vengeance,
3 and I w' not meet thee as a man.
48: 6 see all this; and w' not ye declare it?
9 name's sake w' I defer mine anger,
9 for my praise w' I refrain for thee,
11 even for mine own sake, w' I do it:
11 I w' not give my glory unto another.
14 he w' do his pleasure on Babylon,
49: 3 O Israel, in whom I w' be glorified.
6 I w' also give thee for a light to the
8 and I w' preserve thee, and give thee
11 I w' make all my mountains a way,
13 w' have mercy upon his afflicted.
15 may forget, yet w' I not forget thee.
22 I w' lift up mine hand to the Gentiles,
25 w' contend with him that contendeth
25 with thee, and I w' save thy children.
26 And I w' feed them that oppress thee
50: 7 For the Lord God w' help me;
8 me; who w' contend with thee?
9 Behold, the Lord God w' help me;
51: 3 he w' comfort all her desolate places;
3 w' make her wilderness like Eden,
4 and I w' make my judgment to rest
23 But I w' put it into the hand of them
52: 12 for the Lord God w' go before you;

Isa 52: 12 God of Israel w' be your rereward.
53: 12 Therefore w' I divide him a portion
54: 7 with great mercies w' I gather thee.
8 everlasting kindness w' I have mercy
11 I w' lay thy stones with fair colours,
12 And I w' make thy windows of agates,
55: 3 and I w' make an everlasting covenant
7 Lord, and he w' have mercy upon him;
7 our God, for he w' abundantly pardon.
56: 5 unto them w' I give in mine house
5 I w' give them an everlasting name,
7 w' I bring to my holy mountain,
8 Yet w' I gather others to him, besides
12 Come ye, say they, I w' fetch wine,
12 we w' fill ourselves with strong drink;
57: 12 I w' declare thy righteousness,
16 For I w' not contend for ever, neither
16 neither w' I be always wroth: for the
18 have seen his ways, and w' heal him:
18 I w' lead him also, and restore
19 saith the Lord; and I w' heal him.
58: 14 and I w' cause thee to ride upon the
59: 2 his face from you, that he w' not hear.
18 he w' repay, fury to his adversaries,
18 to the islands he w' repay recompence.
60: 7 and I w' glorify the house of my glory.
12 and kingdom that w' not serve thee
13 w' make the place of my feet glorious.
15 I w' make thee an eternal excellency,
17 For brass I w' bring gold, and for iron
17 and for iron I w' bring silver, and for
17 I w' also make thy officers peace,
22 I the Lord w' hasten it in his time.
61: 8 and I w' direct their work in truth,
8 I w' make an everlasting covenant
10 I w' greatly rejoice in the Lord,
11 the Lord God w' cause righteousness
62: 1 For Zion's sake I w' not hold my peace,
1 and for Jerusalem's sake I w' not rest,
8 Surely I w' no more give thy corn to
63: 3 for I w' tread them in mine anger,
3 and I w' stain all my raiment.
6 I w' tread down the people in mine
6 I w' bring down their strength to the
7 I w' mention the lovingkindnesses
8 my people, children that w' not lie:
65: 6 I w' not...silence, but w' recompense
7 therefore w' I measure their former
8 so w' I do for my servants' sakes, that
9 I w' bring forth a seed out of Jacob,
12 w' I number you to the sword,
19 And I w' rejoice in Jerusalem,
24 that before they call, I w' answer;
24 they are yet speaking, I w' hear.
66: 2 but to this man w' I look, even to him
4 I also w' choose their delusions,
4 and w' bring their fears upon them;
12 I w' extend peace to her like a river,
13 comforteth, so w' I comfort you;
15 the Lord w' come with fire, and with
16 and by his sword w' the Lord plead
18 I w' gather all nations and tongues;
19 And I w' set a sign among them,
19 I w' send those that escape of them
21 And I w' also take of them for priests
22 and the new earth, which I w' make,
Jer 1: 12 for I w' hasten my word to perform it.
15 I w' call all the families of the
16 And I w' utter my judgments against
2: 9 Wherefore I w' yet plead with you,
9 your children's children w' I plead.
20 and thou saidst, I w' not transgress;
24 all they that seek her w' not weary
25 strangers, and after them w' I go.
27 of their trouble they w' say, Arise,
29 Wherefore w' ye plead with me? ye all
31 lords; we w' come no more unto thee?
35 Behold, I w' plead with thee, because
3: 5 W' he reserve his anger for ever?
5 w' he keep it to the end? Behold, thou
12 I w' not cause mine anger to fall upon
12 Lord, and I w' not keep anger for ever.
14 I w' take you one of a city, and two of
14 a family, and I w' bring you to Zion.
15 I w' give you pastors according to
22 and I w' heal your backslidings.
4: 6 for I w' bring evil from the north,
12 also w' I give sentence against them.
27 desolate; yet w' I not make a full end.
28 have purposed it, and w' not repent,
28 neither w' I turn back from it.
30 fair; thy lovers w' despise thee,
30 despise thee, they w' seek thy life.
5: 1 seeketh the truth; and I w' pardon it.
5 I w' get me unto the great men,
5 and w' speak unto them; for they
14 I w' make my words in thy mouth
15 w' bring a nation upon you from far,
18 I w' not make a full end with you.
22 w' ye not tremble at my presence,
31 and what w' ye do in the end thereof?
6: 11 I w' pour it out upon the children
12 for I w' stretch out my hand upon the
16 But they said, We w' not walk therein.
17 But they said, We w' not hearken.
19 I w' bring evil upon this people,
21 I w' lay stumblingblocks before this
7: 3 I w' cause you to dwell in this place.
7 w' I cause you to dwell in this place,
9 W' ye steal, murder, and commit
14 Therefore w' I do unto this house,
15 And I w' cast you out of my sight,
16 to me: for I w' not hear thee.
23 Obey my voice, and I w' be your God,
27 but they w' not hearken to thee;
27 them; but they w' not answer thee.

Jer 7: 34 w' I cause to cease from the cities
8: 10 w' I give their wives unto others,
13 I w' surely consume them, saith the
17 I w' send serpents, cockatrices,
17 which w' not be charmed, and they
9: 4 for every brother w' utterly supplant,
4 neighbour w' walk with slanders.
5 w' deceive every one his neighbour,
5 w' not speak the truth: they have
7 I w' melt them, and try them; for
10 For the mountains w' I take up a
11 I w' make Jerusalem heaps, and a
11 I w' make the cities of Judah desolate,
15 I w' feed them, even this people,
16 I w' scatter them also among the
16 I w' send a sword after them, till I
25 that I w' punish all them that are
10: 18 I w' sling out the inhabitants of the
18 w' distress them, that they may find it
11: 4 be my people, and I w' be your God:
8 I w' bring upon them all the words
11 I w' bring evil upon them, which they
11 unto me, I w' not hearken unto them
14 for I w' not hear them in the time
22 of hosts, Behold, I w' punish them:
23 for I w' bring evil upon the men of
12: 14 I w' pluck them out of their land,
15 I have plucked them out I w' return,
15 w' bring them again, every man to his
16 if they w' diligently learn the ways of
17 But if they w' not obey,
17 I w' utterly pluck up and destroy
13: 9 After this manner w' I mar the pride
13 I w' fill all the inhabitants of this
14 I w' dash them one against another,
14 I w' not pity, nor spare, nor have
17 But if ye w' not hear it, my soul shall
24 w' I scatter them as the stubble
26 w' I discover thy skirts upon thy face,
14: 10 he w' now remember their iniquity,
12 they fast, I w' not hear their cry;
12 and an oblation, I w' not accept them:
12 I w' consume them by the sword, and
13 but I w' give you assured peace in
16 I w' pour their wickedness upon them.
22 God? therefore we w' wait upon thee:
15: 3 I w' appoint over them four kinds,
4 I w' cause them to be removed into
6 therefore w' I stretch out my hand
7 I w' fan them with a fan in the gates
7 I w' bereave them of children,
7 I w' destroy my people, since they
9 residue of them w' I deliver to the
11 verily I w' cause the enemy to entreat
13 treasures w' I give to the spoil
14 I w' make thee to pass with thine
19 return, then w' I bring thee again,
20 I w' make thee unto this people as
21 I w' deliver thee out of the hand of
21 I w' redeem thee out of the hand of
16: 9 I w' cause to cease out of this place
13 w' I cast you out of this land into
13 where I w' not shew you favour.
15 I w' bring them again into their land
16 I w' send for many fishers, saith the
16 after w' I send for many hunters, and
18 first I w' recompense their iniquity
21 I w' this once cause them to know,
21 I w' cause them to know mine hand
17: 3 I w' give thy substance and all thy
4 I w' cause thee to serve thine enemies
27 But if ye w' not hearken unto me
27 then w' I kindle a fire in the gates
18: 2 and there w' I cause thee to hear my
8 I w' repent of the evil that I thought
10 then w' I repent of the good,
12 but we w' walk after our own devices,
12 we w' every one do the imagination of
14 W' a man leave the snow of Lebanon
17 I w' scatter them as with an east wind
17 I w' shew them the back, and not the
19: 3 I w' bring evil upon this place, the
7 I w' make void the counsel of Judah
7 I w' cause them to fall by the sword
7 their carcases w' I give to be meat for
8 I w' make this city desolate, and a
9 I w' cause them to eat the flesh of
11 Even so w' I break this people and
12 Thus w' I do unto this place, saith the
15 I w' bring upon this city and upon all
20: 4 I w' make thee a terror to thyself,
4 I w' give all Judah into the hand of
5 I w' deliver all the strength of this
5 w' I give into the hand of their enemies,
9 I w' not make mention of him, nor
10 Report, say they, and we w' report it.
10 Peradventure he w' be enticed, and
21: 2 if so be that the Lord w' deal with us
4 I w' turn back the weapons of war
4 I w' assemble them into the midst of
5 And I myself w' fight against you
6 I w' smite the inhabitants of this city,
7 I w' deliver Zedekiah king of Judah,
14 I w' punish you according to the fruit
14 and I w' kindle a fire in the forest
22: 5 But if ye w' not hear these words, I
6 surely I w' make thee a wilderness,
7 I w' prepare destroyers against thee,
14 I w' build me a wide house and large
21 but thou saidst, I w' not hear.
25 And I w' give thee in the hand of them
26 I w' cast thee out, and thy mother
23: 2 I w' visit upon you the evil of your
3 I w' gather the remnant of my flock
3 w' bring them again to their folds;
5 that I w' raise unto David a righteous

Jer 23:12 for I *w'* bring evil upon them, even the
15 I *w'* feed them with wormwood, and
33 I *w'* even forsake you, saith the Lord.
39 I, even I, *w'* utterly forget you,
39 and I *w'* forsake you, and the city that
40 I *w'* bring an everlasting reproach
24: 5 so *w'* I acknowledge them that are
6 I *w'* set mine eyes upon them for
6 I *w'* bring them again to this land:
6 I *w'* build them, and not pull them
6 I *w'* plant them, and not pluck them
7 I *w'* give them an heart to know me,
7 be my people, and I *w'* be their God:
8 So *w'* I give Zedekiah the king of
9 I *w'* deliver them to be removed into
10 And I *w'* send the sword, the famine,
25: 6 your hands; and I *w'* do you no hurt.
9 I *w'* send and take all the families
9 and *w'* bring them against this land,
9 and *w'* utterly destroy them, and
10 I *w'* take from them the voice of mirth,
12 that I *w'* punish the king of Babylon,
12 and *w'* make it perpetual desolations.
13 I *w'* bring upon that land all my words
14 I *w'* recompense them according to
16 sword that I *w'* send among them.
27 the sword which I *w'* send among you.
29 I *w'* call for a sword upon all the
31 nations: he *w'* plead with all flesh;
31 *w'* give them that are wicked to the
26: 3 so be they *w'* hearken, and turn every
4 If ye *w'* not hearken to me, to walk
6 *w'* I make this house like Shiloh,
6 *w'* make this city a curse to all the
13 and the Lord *w'* repent him of the evil
27: 8 *w'* not serve the same Nebuchadnezzar
8 *w'* not put their neck under the yoke
8 that nation *w'* I punish, saith the Lord,
11 those *w'* I let remain still in their own
13 Why *w'* ye die, thou and thy people,
13 that *w'* not serve the king of Babylon?
22 then *w'* I bring them up, and restore
28: 3 *w'* I bring again into this place all
4 *w'* bring again to this place Jeconiah
4 for I *w'* break the yoke of the king of
11 Even so *w'* I break the yoke of
16 I *w'* cast thee from off the face of the
29:10 be accomplished at Babylon I *w'* visit
12 unto me, and I *w'* hearken unto you.
14 And I *w'* be found of you, saith the
14 and I *w'* turn away your captivity,
14 I *w'* gather you from all the nations,
14 I *w'* bring you again into the place
17 I *w'* send upon them the sword, the
17 and *w'* make them like vile figs, that
18 I *w'* persecute them with the sword,
18 *w'* deliver them to be removed to all
21 I *w'* deliver them into the hand of
32 *w'* punish Shemaiah the Nehelamite,
32 the good that I *w'* do for my people,
30: 3 I *w'* bring again the captivity of my
3 I *w'* cause them to return to the land
8 I *w'* break his yoke from off thy neck,
8 *w'* burst thy bonds, and strangers
9 king, whom I *w'* raise up unto them.
10 I *w'* save thee from afar, and thy
11 yet *w'* I not make a full end of thee:
11 I *w'* correct thee in measure, and
11 and *w'* not leave thee altogether
16 prey upon thee *w'* I give for a prey.
17 For I *w'* restore health unto thee,
17 I *w'* heal thee of thy wounds, saith
18 *w'* bring again the captivity of Jacob's
19 I *w'* multiply them, and they shall
19 I *w'* also glorify them, and they shall
20 I *w'* punish all that oppress them.
21 and I *w'* cause him to draw near,
22 be my people, and I *w'* be your God.
31: 1 *w'* I be the God of all the families of
4 I *w'* build thee, and thou shalt be
8 I *w'* bring them from the north
9 and with supplications *w'* I lead them:
9 I *w'* cause them to walk by the rivers
10 that scattered Israel *w'* gather him,
13 for I *w'* turn their mourning into joy,
13 and *w'* comfort them, and make them
14 I *w'* satiate the soul of the priests
20 I *w'* surely have mercy upon him,
27 I *w'* sow the house of Israel and the
28 so *w'* I watch over them, to build, and
31 I *w'* make a new covenant with the
33 that I *w'* make with the house of
33 I *w'* put my law in their inward parts,
33 and *w'* be their God, and they shall be
34 for I *w'* forgive them their iniquity,
34 I *w'* remember their sin no more.
37 I *w'* also cast off all the seed of Israel
32: 3, 28 I *w'* give this city into the hand of
37 I *w'* gather them out of all countries,
37 I *w'* bring them again unto this place,
37 and I *w'* cause them to dwell safely:
38 be my people, and I *w'* be their God:
39 And I *w'* give them one heart, and
40 I *w'* make an everlasting covenant
40 that I *w'* not turn away from them,
40 but I *w'* put my fear in their hearts,
41 I *w'* rejoice over them to do them
41 I *w'* plant them in this land assuredly
42 so *w'* I bring upon them all the good
33: 3 I *w'* answer thee, and shew thee great
6 I *w'* bring it health and cure, and
6 I *w'* cure them, and *w'* reveal unto
7 And I *w'* cause the captivity of Judah
7 and *w'* build them, as at the first.
8 I *w'* cleanse them from all their
8 and I *w'* pardon all their iniquities,

Jer 33:11 I *w'* cause to return the captivity of
14 I *w'* perform that good thing which I
15 I *w'* I cause the Branch of righteousness
22 so *w'* I multiply the seed of David my
26 Then *w'* I cast away the seed of Jacob,
26 so that I *w'* not take any of his seed
26 for I *w'* cause their captivity to return,
34: 2 I *w'* give this city into the hand of
5 and they *w'* lament thee, saying, Ah
17 I *w'* make you to be removed into all
18 And I *w'* give the men that have
20 I *w'* even give them into the hand of
21 his princes *w'* I give into the hand of
22 I *w'* command, saith the Lord,
22 and I *w'* make the cities of Judah a
35: 6 But they said, We *w'* drink no wine:
13 *W'* ye not receive instruction to
17 I *w'* bring upon Judah and upon all
36: 3 house of Judah *w'* hear all the evil
7 they *w'* present their supplication
7 *w'* return every one from his evil way:
16 We *w'* surely tell the king all these
31 I *w'* punish him and his seed and his
31 and I *w'* bring upon them, and upon
38:14 unto Jeremiah, I *w'* ask thee a thing;
16 this soul, I *w'* not put thee to death,
16 neither *w'* I give thee into the hand
25 and we *w'* not put thee to death;
39:16 I *w'* bring my words upon this city
17 But I *w'* deliver thee in that day,
18 For I *w'* surely deliver thee, and thou
40: 4 and I *w'* look well unto thee: but if it
10 I *w'* dwell at Mizpah, to serve the
10 which *w'* come unto us: but ye,
15 I *w'* slay Ishmael the son of Nethaniah,
42: 4 I *w'* pray unto the Lord your God
4 answer you, I *w'* declare it unto you;
4 I *w'* keep nothing back from you.
6 we *w'* obey the voice of the Lord our
10 If ye *w'* still abide in this land, then
10 then *w'* I build you, and not pull you
10 I *w'* plant you, and not pluck you up:
12 And I *w'* shew mercies unto you,
13 say, We *w'* not dwell in this land,
14 but we *w'* go into the land of Egypt,
14 of bread; and there *w'* we dwell:
17 the evil that I *w'* bring upon them.
20 so declare unto us, and we *w'* do it.
43:12 I *w'* kindle a fire in the houses of the
44:11 I *w'* set my face against you for evil,
12 And I *w'* take the remnant of Judah,
13 For I *w'* punish them that dwell in the
16 Lord, we *w'* not hearken unto thee.
17 But we *w'* certainly do whatsoever
25 We *w'* surely perform our vows that
25 ye *w'* surely accomplish your vows,
27 Behold, I *w'* watch over them for evil,
29 that I *w'* punish you in this place,
30 I *w'* give Pharaoh-hophra king of
45: 4 which I have built, *w'* I break down,
4 which I have planted I *w'* pluck up,
5 I *w'* bring evil upon all flesh, saith
5 thy life *w'* I give unto thee for a prey
46: 8 I *w'* go up, and *w'* cover the earth;
8 I *w'* destroy the city and the
25 I *w'* punish the multitude of No, and
26 And I *w'* deliver them into the hand
27 behold, I *w'* save thee from afar off,
28 for I *w'* make a full end of all the
28 but I *w'* not make a full end of thee,
28 yet *w'* I not leave thee wholly
47: 4 for the Lord *w'* spoil the Philistines,
6 how long *w'* it be ere thou be quiet?
48:12 that I *w'* send unto him wanderers,
31 Therefore *w'* I howl for Moab, and
31 and I *w'* cry out for all Moab; mine
32 I *w'* weep for thee with the weeping
35 I *w'* cause to cease in Moab, saith
44 I *w'* bring upon it, even upon Moab,
47 *w'* I bring again the captivity of Moab
49: 2 that I *w'* cause an alarm of war to be
5 I *w'* bring fear upon thee, saith the
6 I *w'* bring again the captivity
8 I *w'* bring the calamity of Esau upon
8 him, the time that I *w'* visit him.
9 they *w'* destroy till they have enough.
11 I *w'* preserve them alive; and let thy
15 I *w'* make thee small among the
16 I *w'* bring thee down from thence,
19 I *w'* suddenly make him run away
19 and who *w'* appoint me the time?
19 who is that shepherd that *w'* stand
27 And I *w'* kindle a fire in the wall of
32 I *w'* scatter into all winds them that
32 I *w'* bring their calamity from all
35 I *w'* break the bow of Elam, the chief
36 upon Elam *w'* I bring the four winds
36 *w'* scatter them towards all those
37 For I *w'* cause Elam to be dismayed
37 I *w'* bring evil upon them, even my
37 and I *w'* send the sword after them,
38 And I *w'* set my throne in Elam, and
38 *w'* destroy from thence the king and
39 I *w'* bring again the captivity of Elam,
50: 9 I *w'* raise and cause to come up
18 I *w'* punish the king of Babylon and
19 And I *w'* bring Israel again to his
20 I *w'* pardon them whom I reserve.
31 is come, the time that I *w'* visit thee.
32 I *w'* kindle a fire in his cities, and it
42 are cruel, and *w'* not shew mercy:
44 I *w'* make them suddenly run away
44 and who *w'* appoint me the time?
44 shepherd that *w'* stand before me?
51: 1 I *w'* raise up against Babylon, and
2 And *w'* send unto Babylon fanners,

Jer 51: 6 he *w'* render unto her a recompense.
14 Surely I *w'* fill thee with men,
20 *w'* I break in pieces the nations,
20 and with thee *w'* I destroy kingdoms;
21 thee *w'* I break in pieces the horse
21 thee *w'* I break in pieces the chariot
23 I *w'* also break in pieces with thee
23 *w'* I break in pieces the husbandman
23 *w'* I break in pieces captains and
24 I *w'* render unto Babylon and to all
25 I *w'* stretch out mine hand upon thee,
25 and *w'* make thee a burnt mountain.
36 I *w'* plead thy cause, and take
36 I *w'* dry up her sea, and make her
39 In their heat I *w'* make their feasts,
39 I *w'* make them drunken, that they
40 I *w'* bring them down like lambs
44 And I *w'* punish Bel in Babylon,
44 I *w'* bring forth out of his mouth that
47 I *w'* do judgment upon the graven
52 I *w'* do judgment upon her graven
57 I *w'* make drunk her princes, and her
64 the evil that I *w'* bring upon her:
La 3:24 my soul; therefore *w'* I hope in him.
31 For the Lord *w'* not cast off for ever:
32 yet *w'* he have compassion
4:16 them; he *w'* no more regard them:
22 he *w'* no more carry thee away into
22 he *w'* visit thine iniquity, O daughter
22 of Edom; he *w'* discover thy sins.
Eze 2: 1 thy feet, and I *w'* speak unto thee.
5 whether they *w'* hear, or whether they
5 or whether they *w'* forbear, (for they
7 unto them, whether they *w'* hear,
7 or whether they *w'* forbear: for they
3: 7 house of Israel *w'* not hearken unto
7 for they *w'* not hearken unto me:
11 saith the Lord; whether they *w'* hear,
11 or whether they *w'* forbear.
18, 20 blood *w'* I require at thine hand.
22 plain, and I *w'* there talk with thee.
26 I *w'* make thy tongue cleave to the
27 with thee, I *w'* open thy mouth,
4: 8 I *w'* lay bands upon thee, and thou
13 the Gentiles, whither I *w'* drive them.
16 I *w'* break the staff of bread in
5: 2 and I *w'* draw out a sword after them.
8 *w'* execute judgments in the midst of
9 I *w'* do in thee that which I have not
9 I *w'* not do any more the like,
10 and I *w'* execute judgments in thee,
10 thee *w'* I scatter unto all the winds.
11 therefore *w'* I also diminish thee;
11 eye spare, neither *w'* I have any pity.
12 I *w'* scatter a third part into all
12 and I *w'* draw out a sword after them.
13 I *w'* cause my fury to rest upon them,
13 and I *w'* be comforted: and they shall
14 I *w'* make thee waste, and a reproach
16 which I *w'* send to destroy you:
16 I *w'* increase the famine upon you,
16 and *w'* break your staff of bread:
17 *w'* I send upon you famine and evil
17 and I *w'* bring the sword upon thee.
6: 3 I, even I, *w'* bring a sword upon you,
3 and I *w'* destroy your high places.
4 I *w'* cast down your slain men before
5 And I *w'* lay the dead carcases of the
5 I *w'* scatter your bones round about
8 Yet *w'* I leave a remnant, that ye may
12 *w'* I accomplish my fury upon them.
14 So *w'* I stretch out my hand upon
7: 3 and I *w'* send mine anger upon thee,
3 *w'* judge thee according to thy ways,
3 *w'* recompense upon thee all thine
4 not spare thee, neither *w'* I have pity:
4 *w'* recompense thy ways upon thee,
8 Now *w'* I shortly pour out my fury
8 *w'* judge thee according to thy ways,
8 *w'* recompense thee for all thine
9 not spare, neither *w'* I have pity:
9 I *w'* recompense thee according to thy
21 I *w'* give it into the hands of the
22 My face *w'* I turn also from them,
24 I *w'* bring the worst of the heathen,
24 I *w'* also make the pomp of the strong
27 I *w'* do unto them after their way,
27 to their deserts *w'* I judge them:
8:18 Therefore *w'* I also deal in fury: mine
18 not spare, neither *w'* I have pity:
18 a loud voice, yet *w'* I not hear them.
9:10 not spare, neither *w'* I have pity,
10 but I *w'* recompense their way upon
11: 7 But I *w'* bring you forth out of the
8 I *w'* bring a sword upon you, saith the
9 And I *w'* bring you out of the midst
9 and *w'* execute judgment among you.
10 I *w'* judge you in the border of Israel;
11 I *w'* judge you in the border of Israel:
16 yet *w'* I be to them as a little
17 I *w'* even gather you from the people,
17 and I *w'* give you the land of Israel.
19 And I *w'* give them one heart,
19 and I *w'* put a new spirit within you;
19 I *w'* take the stony heart out of their
19 and *w'* give them a heart of flesh:
20 be my people, and I *w'* be their God.
21 I *w'* recompense their way upon their
12: 3 it may be they *w'* consider, though
13 My net also *w'* I spread upon him,
13 I *w'* bring him to Babylon to the land
14 I *w'* scatter toward every wind all that
14 I *w'* draw out the sword after them.
16 I *w'* leave a few men of them from the
23 I *w'* make this proverb to cease,
25 I *w'* speak, and the word that I shall

Eze 12: 25 O rebellious house, *w'* I say the word,
25 and *w'* perform it, saith the Lord God.
13: 13 I *w'* even rend it with a stormy wind
14 *w'* I break down the wall that ye have
15 *w'* I accomplish my wrath upon the
15 *w'* say unto you, The wall is no more,
18 *W'* ye hunt the souls of my people,
18 *w'* ye save the souls alive that come
19 *w'* ye pollute me among my people for
20 and I *w'* tear them from your arms,
20 *w'* let the souls go, even the souls that
21 Your kerchiefs also *w'* I tear, and
23 *w'* deliver my people out of your hand:
14: 4 I the Lord *w'* answer him that cometh
7 I the Lord *w'* answer him by myself:
8 I *w'* set my face against that man,
8 *w'* make him a sign and a proverb,
8 I *w'* cut him off from the midst of my
9 I *w'* stretch out my hand upon him,
9 *w'* destroy him from the midst of my
13 *w'* I stretch out mine hand upon it,
13 and *w'* break the staff of the bread
13 and *w'* send famine upon it, and
13 and *w'* cut off man and beast from it:
15: 3 or *w'* men take a pin of it to hang any
6 fuel, so *w'* I give the inhabitants of
7 And I *w'* set my face against them;
8 And I *w'* make the land desolate,
16: 27 delivered thee unto the *w'* of them
37 therefore I *w'* gather all thy lovers,
37 I *w'* even gather them round about
37 *w'* discover thy nakedness unto them,
38 And I *w'* judge thee, as women that
38 and I *w'* give thee blood in fury and
39 I *w'* also give thee into their hand,
41 I *w'* cause thee to cease from playing
42 So *w'* I make my fury toward thee
42 and I *w'* be quiet, and *w'* be no more
43 I also *w'* recompense thy way upon
53 then *w'* I bring again the captivity
59 I *w'* even deal with thee as thou hast
60 I *w'* remember my covenant with thee
60 I *w'* establish unto thee an everlasting
61 *w'* give them unto thee for daughters,
62 I *w'* establish my covenant with thee;
17: 19 even it *w'* I recompense upon his own
20 And I *w'* spread my net upon him,
20 snare, and I *w'* bring him to Babylon,
20 and *w'* plead with him there for his
22 I *w'* also take of the highest branch
22 branch of the high cedar, and *w'* set it;
22 I *w'* crop off from the top of his young
22 and *w'* plant it upon an high mountain
23 of the height of Israel *w'* I plant it:
18: 21 if the wicked *w'* turn from all his sins
30 Therefore I *w'* judge you, O house of
31 for why *w'* ye die, O house of Israel?
20: 3 God, I *w'* not be enquired of by you.
8 I *w'* pour out my fury upon them,
31 God, I *w'* not be enquired of by you.
32 *w'* be as the heathen, as the families
33 fury poured out, *w'* I rule over you:
34 I *w'* bring you out from the people,
34 *w'* gather you out of countries wherein
35 I *w'* bring you into the wilderness
35 there *w'* I plead with you face to face.
36 so *w'* I plead with you, saith the Lord
37 I *w'* cause you to pass under the rod,
37 I *w'* bring you into the bond of the
38 I *w'* purge out from among you the
38 I *w'* bring them forth out of the
39 also, if ye *w'* not hearken unto me:
40 serve me: there *w'* I accept them,
40 there *w'* I require your offerings,
41 I *w'* accept you with your sweet
41 I *w'* be sanctified in you before the
47 I *w'* kindle a fire in thee, and it shall
21: 3 *w'* draw forth my sword out of the
3, 4 *w'* cut off from thee the righteous
17 I *w'* also smite mine hands together,
17 I *w'* cause my fury to rest: I the Lord
23 but he *w'* call to remembrance the
27 I *w'* overturn, overturn, overturn, it:
27 right it is; and I *w'* give it him.
30 I *w'* judge thee in the place where
31 I *w'* pour out mine indignation upon
31 I *w'* blow against thee in the fire of my
22: 14 the Lord have spoken it, and *w'* do it.
15 I *w'* scatter thee among the heathen,
15 *w'* consume thy filthiness out of thee.
19 I *w'* gather you into the midst of
20 so *w'* I gather you in mine anger and
20 I *w'* leave you there, and melt you.
21 I *w'* gather you, and blow upon you
23: 22 I *w'* raise up thy lovers against thee,
22 I *w'* bring them against thee on every
24 and I *w'* set judgment before them,
25 And I *w'* set my jealousy against thee,
27 Thus *w'* I make thy lewdness to cease
28 I *w'* deliver thee into the hand of them
30 I *w'* do these things unto thee,
31 *w'* I give her cup into thine hand.
43 *W'* they now commit whoredoms with
46 I *w'* bring up a company upon them,
46 and *w'* give them to be removed and
48 Thus *w'* I cause lewdness to cease
24: 9 I *w'* even make the pile for fire great.
14 and I *w'* do it; I *w'* not go back,
14 neither *w'* I spare, neither *w'* I repent;
21 Behold, I *w'* profane my sanctuary,
25: 4 I *w'* deliver thee to the men of the east
5 *w'* make Rabbah a stable for camels,
7 I *w'* stretch out mine hand upon thee,
7 and *w'* deliver thee for a spoil to the
7 and I *w'* cut thee off from the people,
7 and I *w'* cause thee to perish out of

Eze 25: 7 I *w'* destroy thee; and thou shalt
9 I *w'* open the side of Moab from the
10 and *w'* give them in possession, that
11 I *w'* execute judgments upon Moab;
13 I *w'* also stretch out mine hand upon
13 and *w'* cut off man and beast from it;
13 I *w'* make it desolate from Teman;
14 I *w'* lay my vengeance upon Edom by
16 I *w'* stretch out mine hand upon the
16 and I *w'* cut off the Cherethims, and
17 I *w'* execute great vengeance upon
26: 3 *w'* cause many nations to come up
4 I *w'* also scrape her dust from her,
7 Behold, I *w'* bring upon Tyrus
13 I *w'* cause the noise of thy songs to
14 I *w'* make thee like the top of a rock:
21 I *w'* make thee a terror, and thou shalt
28: 7 I *w'* bring strangers upon thee,
16 I *w'* cast thee as profane out of the
16 I *w'* destroy thee, O covering cherub,
17 I *w'* cast thee to the ground,
17 I *w'* lay thee before kings, that they
18 *w'* I bring forth a fire from the
18 and I *w'* bring thee to ashes upon the
22 I *w'* be glorified in the midst of thee:
23 For I *w'* send into her pestilence, and
29: 4 But I *w'* put hooks in thy jaws, and
4 I *w'* cause the fish of thy rivers to
4 I *w'* bring thee up out of the midst of
5 And I *w'* leave thee thrown into the
8 I *w'* bring a sword upon thee, and
10 I *w'* make the land of Egypt utterly
12 I *w'* make the land of Egypt desolate
12 I *w'* scatter the Egyptians among the
12 and *w'* disperse them through the
13 forty years *w'* I gather the Egyptians
14 I *w'* bring the captivity of Egypt,
14 and *w'* cause them to return into the land
15 for I *w'* diminish them, that they shall
19 I *w'* give the land of Egypt unto
21 day *w'* I cause the horn of the house
21 I *w'* give thee the opening of the
30: 10 I *w'* also make the multitude of Egypt
12 And I *w'* make the rivers dry, and sell
12 I *w'* make the land waste, and all that
13 I *w'* also destroy the idols, and I
13 I *w'* cause their images to cease out
13 I *w'* put a fear in the land of Egypt.
14 And I *w'* make Pathros desolate, and
14 desolate, and *w'* set fire in Zoan,
14 Zoan, and *w'* execute judgments in No.
15 And I *w'* pour my fury upon Sin,
15 and I *w'* cut off the multitude of No.
16 And I *w'* set fire in Egypt: Sin shall
19 *w'* I execute judgments in Egypt:
22 king of Egypt, and *w'* break his arms,
22 I *w'* cause the sword to fall out of his
23 I *w'* scatter the Egyptians among the
23 and *w'* disperse them through the
24 I *w'* strengthen the arms of the king
24 I *w'* break Pharaoh's arms, and he
25 I *w'* strengthen the arms of the king
26 I *w'* scatter the Egyptians among the
32: 3 I *w'* therefore spread out my net over
4 Then *w'* I leave thee upon the land,
4 I *w'* cast thee forth upon the open
4 *w'* cause all the fowls of the heaven to
4 I *w'* fill the beasts of the whole earth
5 I *w'* lay thy flesh upon the mountains,
6 I *w'* also water with thy blood the
7 I *w'* cover the heaven, and make the
7 I *w'* cover the sun with a cloud, and
8 lights of heaven *w'* I make dark over
9 I *w'* also vex the hearts of many
10 I *w'* make many people amazed at thee,
12 *w'* I cause thy multitude to fall,
13 I *w'* destroy also all the beasts thereof
14 Then *w'* I make their waters deep, and
33: 6 but his blood *w'* I require at the
8 his blood *w'* I require at thine hand.
11 for why *w'* ye die, O house of Israel?
20 I *w'* judge you every one after his
27 in the open field *w'* I give to the beasts
28 For I *w'* lay the land most desolate,
31 thy words, but they *w'* not do them:
33 this cometh to pass, (lo, it *w'* come,)
34: 10 I *w'* require my flock at their hand,
10 for I *w'* deliver my flock from their
11 I, *w'* both search my sheep, and seek
12 *w'* I seek out my sheep, and *w'* deliver
13 I *w'* bring them out from the people,
13 *w'* bring them to their own land, and
14 I *w'* feed them in a good pasture, and
15 I *w'* feed my flock, and
15 I *w'* cause them to lie down,
16 I *w'* seek that which was lost, and
16 *w'* bind up that which was broken,
16 *w'* strengthen that which was sick:
16 I *w'* destroy the fat and the strong;
16 I *w'* feed them with judgment.
20 even I, *w'* judge between the fat cattle
22 *w'* I save my flock, and they shall
22 I *w'* judge between cattle and cattle.
23 I *w'* set up one shepherd over them,
24 I the Lord *w'* be their God, and my
25 I *w'* make with them a covenant of
25 *w'* cause the evil beast to cease out of
26 I *w'* make them and the places round
26 I *w'* cause the shower to come down in
29 I *w'* raise up for them a plant of
35: 3 I *w'* stretch out mine hand against
3 and I *w'* make thee most desolate,
4 I *w'* lay thy cities waste, and thou
6 I *w'* prepare thee unto blood, and
7 *w'* I make mount Seir most desolate,
8 I *w'* fill his mountains with his slain

Eze 35: 9 I *w'* make thee perpetual desolations,
10 shall be mine, and we *w'* possess it;
11 I *w'* even do according to thine anger,
11 I *w'* make myself known among them,
14 rejoiceth, I *w'* make thee desolate.
15 it was desolate, so *w'* I do unto thee:
36: 9 and I *w'* turn unto you, and ye shall
10 I *w'* multiply men upon you, all the
11 And I *w'* multiply upon you man and
11 I *w'* settle you after your old estates,
11 *w'* do better unto you than at your
12 I *w'* cause men to walk upon you,
15 *w'* I cause men to hear in thee the
23 I *w'* sanctify my great name, which
24 For I *w'* take you from among the
24 and *w'* bring you into your own land.
25 *w'* I sprinkle clean water upon you,
25 from all your idols, *w'* I cleanse you.
26 A new heart also *w'* I give you,
26 and a new spirit *w'* I put within you:
26 I *w'* take away the stony heart out of
26 and I *w'* give you an heart of flesh,
27 I *w'* put my spirit within you, and
28 be my people, and I *w'* be your God.
29 I *w'* also save you from all your
29 I *w'* call for the corn, and *w'* increase
30 I *w'* multiply the fruit of the tree, and
33 I *w'* also cause you to dwell in the
36 Lord have spoken it, and I *w'* do it.
37 I *w'* yet for this be enquired of by the
37 I *w'* increase them with men like a
37: 5 I *w'* cause breath to enter into you,
6 And I *w'* lay sinews upon you, and
6 *w'* bring up flesh from you, and cover
12 I *w'* open your graves, and cause
19 I *w'* take the stick of Joseph, which is
19 *w'* put them with him, even with the
21 I *w'* take the children of Israel from
21 *w'* gather them on every side, and
22 I *w'* make them one nation in the
23 but I *w'* save them out of all their
23 have sinned, and *w'* cleanse them:
23 be my people, and I *w'* be their God.
26 I *w'* make a covenant of peace with
26 I *w'* place them, and multiply them,
26 *w'* set my sanctuary in the midst of
27 I *w'* be their God, and they shall be
38: 4 I *w'* turn thee back, and put hooks
4 I *w'* bring thee forth, and all thine
11 I *w'* go up to the land of unwalled
11 I *w'* go to them that are at rest, that
16 I *w'* bring thee against my land, that
21 And I *w'* call for a sword against him
22 I *w'* plead against him with pestilence
22 and I *w'* rain upon him, and upon his
23 *w'* I magnify myself, and sanctify
23 and I *w'* be known in the eyes of many
39: 2 I *w'* turn thee back, and leave but the
2 *w'* cause thee to come up from the
2 *w'* bring thee upon the mountain of
3 and I *w'* smite thy bow out of thy left
3 and *w'* cause thine arrows to fall out
4 I *w'* give thee unto the ravenous birds
6 I *w'* send a fire on Magog, and among
7 So *w'* I make my holy name known in
7 and I *w'* not let them pollute my holy
11 I *w'* give unto Gog a place there of
21 I *w'* set my glory among the heathen,
25 Now *w'* I bring again the captivity of
25 and *w'* be jealous for my holy name;
29 *w'* I hide my face any more from
43: 7 I *w'* dwell in the midst of the children
9 I *w'* dwell in the midst of them for
27 I *w'* accept you, saith the Lord God.
44: 14 But I *w'* make them keepers of the
Da 2: 4 and we *w'* shew the interpretation.
5 if ye *w'* not make known unto me the
7 we *w'* shew the interpretation of it.
9 if ye *w'* not make known unto me the
24 I *w'* shew unto the king the
25 *w'* make known unto the king the
36 we *w'* tell the interpretation thereof.
3: 17 he *w'* deliver us out of thine hand, O
18 king, that we *w'* not serve thy gods,
4: 17 and giveth it to whomsoever he *w'*,
25, 32 giveth it to whomsoever he *w'*.
35 to his *w'* in the army of heaven,
5: 12 and he *w'* shew the interpretation.
17 I *w'* read the writing unto the king,
21 over it whomsoever he *w'*.
6: 16 servest continually, he *w'* deliver thee.
8: 4 but he did according to his *w'*, and
19 I *w'* make thee known what shall be in
10: 20 *w'* I return to fight with the prince
21 I *w'* shew thee that which is noted in
11: 2 And now *w'* I shew thee the truth.
3 and do according to his *w'*.
16 shall do according to his own *w'*,
36 king shall do according to his *w'*;
Ho 1: 4 I *w'* avenge the blood of Jezreel upon
4 *w'* cause to cease the kingdom of the
5 I *w'* break the bow of Israel in the
6 I *w'* no more have mercy upon the
6 but I *w'* utterly take them away.
7 I *w'* have mercy upon the house
7 *w'* save them by the Lord their God,
7 *w'* not save them by bow, nor by
9 my people, and I *w'* not be your God.
2: 4 *w'* not have mercy upon her children;
5 I *w'* go after my lovers, that give me
6 I *w'* hedge up thy way with thorns,
7 *w'* go and return to my first husband;
9 *w'* I return, and take away my corn
9 *w'* recover my wool and my flax given
10 And now *w'* I discover her lewdness in
11 I *w'* also cause all her mirth to cease,

Ho 2:12 I *w'* destroy her vines and her fig
12 and I *w'* make them a forest, and
13 And I *w'* visit upon her the days of
14 I *w'* allure her, and bring her into
15 I *w'* give her her vineyards from
17 I *w'* take away the names of Baalim
18 day *w'* I make a covenant for them
18 I *w'* break the bow and the sword
18 and *w'* make them to lie down safely.
19 I *w'* betroth thee unto me for ever;
19 yea, I *w'* betroth thee unto me in
20 I *w'* even betroth thee unto me in
21 in that day, I *w'* hear, saith the Lord,
21 I *w'* hear the heavens, and they
23 I *w'* sow her unto me in the earth;
23 I *w'* have mercy upon her that had
23 I *w'* say to them which were not my
3: 3 another man: so *w'* I also be for thee.
4: 5 night, and I *w'* destroy thy mother.
6 I *w'* also reject thee, that thou shalt
6 God, I *w'* also forget thy children.
7 *w'* I change their glory into shame.
9 I *w'* punish them for their ways,
14 I *w'* not punish your daughters when
16 now the Lord *w'* feed them as a lamb
5: 4 *w'* not frame their doings to turn
10 I *w'* pour out my wrath upon them
12 *w'* I be unto Ephraim as a moth,
14 For I *w'* be unto Ephraim as a lion,
14 *w'* tear and go away; I *w'* take away,
15 I *w'* go and return to my place, till
15 their affliction they *w'* seek me early.
6: 1 he hath torn us, and he *w'* heal us;
1 hath smitten, and he *w'* bind us up.
2 After two days *w'* he revive us;
2 in the third day he *w'* raise us up,
7:12 go, I *w'* spread my net upon them;
12 I *w'* bring them down as the fowls of
12 I *w'* chastise them, as their
8: 5 how long *w'* it be ere they attain to
10 now *w'* I gather them, and they shall
13 now *w'* he remember their iniquity,
14 but I *w'* send a fire upon his cities,
9: 5 What *w'* ye do in the solemn day,
9 he *w'* remember their iniquity,
9 he *w'* visit their sins.
12 yet *w'* I bereave them, that there shall
15 I *w'* drive them out of mine house,
15 mine house, I *w'* love them no more:
16 yet *w'* I slay even the beloved fruit
17 My God *w'* cast them away, because
10:11 I *w'* make Ephraim to ride; Judah
11: 9 I *w'* not execute the fierceness of
9 I *w'* not return to destroy Ephraim:
9 and I *w'* not enter into the city.
11 I *w'* place them in their houses,
12: 2 and *w'* punish Jacob according to his
2 to his doings *w'* he recompense him.
9 of Egypt *w'* yet make thee to dwell
13: 7 Therefore I *w'* be unto them as a lion:
7 leopard by the way *w'* I observe them:
8 I *w'* meet them as a bear that is
8 and *w'* rend the caul of their heart,
8 there *w'* I devour them like a lion:
10 I *w'* be thy king: where is any
14 I *w'* ransom them from the power
14 I *w'* redeem them from death:
14 O death, I *w'* be thy plagues;
14 O grave, I *w'* be thy destruction:
14: 2 so *w'* we render the calves of our lips.
3 save us; we *w'* not ride upon horses:
3 neither *w'* we say any more to the
4 I *w'* heal their backsliding,
4 I *w'* love them freely: for mine anger
5 I *w'* be as the dew unto Israel:
Joe 1:19 O Lord, to thee *w'* I cry: for the fire
2:14 Who knoweth if he *w'* return and
18 *w'* the Lord be jealous for his land,
19 Lord *w'* answer and say unto his
19 I *w'* send you corn, and wine, and oil,
19 I *w'* no more make you a reproach
20 But I *w'* remove far off from you the
20 and *w'* drive him into a land barren
21 for the Lord *w'* do great things.
23 he *w'* cause to come down for you the
25 And I *w'* restore to you the years that
28 I *w'* pour out my Spirit upon all flesh;
29 in those days *w'* I pour out my spirit.
30 I *w'* shew wonders in the heavens
3: 2 I *w'* also gather all nations, and
2 *w'* bring them down into the valley
2 and *w'* plead with them there for my
4 *w'* ye render me a recompence?
4 speedily *w'* I return your recompence
7 I *w'* raise them out of the place
7 *w'* return your recompence upon your
8 I *w'* sell your sons and your daughters
12 there *w'* I sit to judge all the heathen
16 the Lord *w'* be the hope of his people,
21 I *w'* cleanse their blood that I have
Am 1: 2 The Lord *w'* roar from Zion, and utter
3 I *w'* not turn away the punishment
4 I *w'* send a fire into the house of
5 I *w'* break also the bar of Damascus,
6 I *w'* not turn away the punishment
7 I *w'* send a fire on the wall of Gaza,
8 And I *w'* cut off the inhabitant from
8 I *w'* turn mine hand against Ekron:
9 I *w'* not turn away the punishment
10 I *w'* send a fire on the wall of Tyrus,
11 I *w'* not turn away the punishment
12 But I *w'* send a fire upon Teman,
13 I *w'* not turn away the punishment
14 But I *w'* kindle a fire in the wall of
2: 1 I *w'* not turn away the punishment
2 But I *w'* send a fire upon Moab,

Am 2: 3 I *w'* cut off the judge from the midst
3 *w'* slay all the princes thereof with
4 I *w'* not turn away the punishment
5 But I *w'* send a fire upon Judah,
6 I *w'* not turn away the punishment
7 father *w'* go in unto the same maid,
3: 2 I *w'* punish you for all your iniquities.
4 *W'* a lion roar in the forest, when he
4 *w'* a young lion cry out of his den,
7 Surely the Lord God *w'* do nothing,
8 lion hath roared, who *w'* not fear?
14 I *w'* also visit the altars of Beth-el:
15 I *w'* smite the winter house with the
4: 2 that he *w'* take you away with hooks,
12 thus *w'* I do unto thee, O Israel:
12 because I *w'* do this unto thee,
5:15 *w'* be gracious unto the remnant of
17 *w'* pass through thee, saith the Lord.
21 and I *w'* not smell in your solemn
22 meat offerings, I *w'* not accept them:
22 neither *w'* I regard the peace offerings
23 I *w'* not hear the melody of thy viols.
27 *w'* I cause you to go into captivity
6: 8 *w'* I deliver up the city with all that
11 he *w'* smite the great house with
12 rock? *w'* one plow there with oxen?
14 I *w'* raise up against you a nation,
7: 8 I *w'* set a plumbline in the midst
8 I *w'* not again pass by them any more:
9 *w'* rise against the house of Jeroboam
8: 2 I *w'* not again pass by them any more.
5 When *w'* the new moon be gone,
7 I *w'* never forget any of their works.
9 I *w'* cause the sun to go down at noon,
9 I *w'* darken the earth in the clear day:
10 I *w'* turn your feasts into mourning,
10 I *w'* bring up sackcloth upon all loins,
10 I *w'* make it as the mourning of an
11 that I *w'* send a famine in the land.
9: 1 I *w'* slay the last of them with the
2 thence *w'* I bring them down:
3 I *w'* search and take them out thence;
3 thence *w'* I command the serpent,
4 thence *w'* I command the sword,
4 *w'* set mine eyes upon them for evil,
8 I *w'* destroy it from off the face of the
8 I *w'* not utterly destroy the house of
9 I *w'* command, and I *w'* sift the house
11 that day *w'* I raise up the tabernacle
11 and I *w'* raise up his ruins,
11 I *w'* build it as in the days of old:
14 I *w'* bring again the captivity of my
15 And I *w'* plant them upon their land,
Ob 4 thence *w'* I bring thee down, saith the
Jon 1: 6 if so be that God *w'* think upon us,
2: 4 yet I *w'* look again toward thy holy
9 I *w'* sacrifice unto thee with the voice
9 I *w'* pay that that I have vowed.
3: 9 can tell if God *w'* turn and repent,
Mic 1: 3 *w'* come down, and tread upon the
6 I *w'* make Samaria as an heap of the
6 and I *w'* pour down the stones thereof
6 I *w'* discover the foundations thereof.
7 all the idols thereof *w'* I lay desolate:
8 Therefore I *w'* wail and howl,
8 and howl, I *w'* go stripped and naked:
8 I *w'* make a wailing like the dragons,
15 Yet *w'* I bring an heir unto thee,
2:11 I *w'* prophesy unto thee of wine
12 I *w'* surely assemble, O Jacob, all of
12 I *w'* surely gather the remnant of
12 I *w'* put them together as the sheep
3: 4 the Lord, but he *w'* not hear them:
4 he *w'* even hide his face from them
11 *w'* they lean upon the Lord, and say,
4: 2 and he *w'* teach us of his ways,
2 ways, and we *w'* walk in his paths:
5 *w'* walk every one in the name of his
5 we *w'* walk in the name of the Lord
6 *w'* I assemble her that halteth,
6 and I *w'* gather her that is driven out,
7 I *w'* make her that halted a remnant,
13 for I *w'* make thine horn iron, and I
13 iron, and I *w'* make thy hoofs brass:
13 I *w'* consecrate their gain unto the
5: 3 Therefore *w'* he give them up, until
10 I *w'* cut off thy horses out of the midst
10 of thee, and I *w'* destroy thy chariots:
11 And I *w'* cut off the cities of thy land,
12 I *w'* cut off witchcrafts out of thine
13 Thy graven images also *w'* I cut off,
14 I *w'* pluck up thy groves out of the
14 of thee: so *w'* I destroy thy cities.
15 I *w'* execute vengeance in anger
6: 2 people, and he *w'* plead with Israel.
7 *W'* the Lord be pleased with
13 *w'* I make thee sick in smiting thee,
14 which thou deliverest *w'* I give up
7: 7 Therefore I *w'* look unto the Lord;
7 I *w'* wait for the God of my salvation:
7 of my salvation: My God *w'* hear me.
9 I *w'* bear the indignation of the Lord,
9 he *w'* bring me forth to the light,
15 *w'* I shew unto him marvellous things.
19 He *w'* turn again, he
19 he *w'* have compassion upon us;
19 he *w'* subdue our iniquities; and thou
Na 1: 2 Lord *w'* take vengeance on his
3 and *w'* not at all acquit the wicked:
8 he *w'* make an utter end of the place
9 *w'* make an utter end: affliction shall
12 thee, I *w'* afflict thee no more.
13 now *w'* I break his yoke from off thee,
13 and *w'* burst thy bonds in sunder.
14 gods *w'* I cut off the graven image
14 I *w'* make thy grave; for thou art vile.

Na 2:13 I *w'* burn her chariots in the smoke,
13 I *w'* cut off thy prey from the earth,
3: 5 *w'* discover thy skirts upon thy face,
5 I *w'* shew the nations thy nakedness,
6 *w'* cast abominable filth upon thee,
6 and *w'* set thee as a gazingstock.
7 is laid waste: who *w'* bemoan her?
Hab 1: 5 for I *w'* work a work in your days,
5 which ye *w'* not believe, though it be
2: 1 I *w'* stand upon my watch, and set
1 and *w'* watch to see what he *w'* say
3 it *w'* surely come, it *w'* not tarry.
3:16 he *w'* invade them with his troops.
18 Yet I *w'* rejoice in the Lord,
18 I *w'* joy in the God of my salvation.
19 and he *w'* make my feet like hind's
19 he *w'* make me to walk upon mine
Zep 1: 2 I *w'* utterly consume all things from
3 I *w'* consume man and beast;
3 I *w'* consume the fowls of the heaven,
3 I *w'* cut off man from off the land,
4 I *w'* also stretch out mine hand upon
4 and I *w'* cut off the remnant of Baal
8 that I *w'* punish the princes, and the
9 same day also *w'* I punish all those
12 I *w'* search Jerusalem with candles,
12 The Lord *w'* not do good,
12 neither *w'* he do evil.
17 And I *w'* bring distress upon men,
2: 5 Philistines, I *w'* even destroy thee,
11 The Lord *w'* be terrible unto them:
11 he *w'* famish all the gods of the earth;
13 he *w'* stretch out his hand against the
13 and *w'* make Nineveh a desolation,
3: 5 midst thereof; he *w'* not do iniquity:
9 then *w'* I turn to the people a pure
11 *w'* take away out of the midst of thee
12 I *w'* also leave in the midst of thee
17 he *w'* save, he *w'* rejoice over thee
17 he *w'* rest in his love, he *w'* joy over
18 I *w'* gather them that are sorrowful
19 time I *w'* undo all that afflict thee:
19 I *w'* save her that halteth, and gather
19 I *w'* get them praise and fame in
20 At that time *w'* I bring you again,
20 I *w'* make you a name and a praise
Hag 1: 8 house; and I *w'* take pleasure in it,
8 and I *w'* be glorified, saith the Lord.
2: 6 I *w'* shake the heavens, and the earth,
7 I *w'* shake all nations, and the desire
7 I *w'* fill this house with glory, saith
9 in this place *w'* I give peace, saith the
19 from this day *w'* I bless you.
21 I *w'* shake the heavens and the earth;
22 I *w'* overthrow the throne of
22 I *w'* destroy the strength of the
22 and I *w'* overthrow the chariots,
23 *w'* I take thee, O Zerubbabel, my
23 Lord, and *w'* make thee as a signet:
Zec 1: 3 I *w'* turn unto you, saith the Lord
9 me, I *w'* shew thee what these be.
2: 5 *w'* be unto her a wall of fire round
5 and *w'* be glory in the midst of her.
9 I *w'* shake mine hand upon them,
10, 11 and I *w'* dwell in the midst of thee.
3: 4 I *w'* clothe thee with change of
7 I *w'* give thee places to walk among
8 I *w'* bring forth my servant the
9 I *w'* engrave the graving thereof,
9 I *w'* remove the iniquity of that land
5: 4 I *w'* bring it forth, saith the Lord of
6:15 if ye *w'* diligently obey the voice of the
8: 3 *w'* dwell in the midst of Jerusalem:
7 I *w'* save my people from the east
8 And I *w'* bring them, and they shall
8 be my people, and I *w'* be their God,
11 I *w'* not be unto the residue of this
12 I *w'* cause the remnant of this people
13 so *w'* I save you, and ye shall be a
21 seek the Lord of hosts: I *w'* go also.
23 is a Jew, saying, We *w'* go with you:
9: 4 Behold, the Lord *w'* cast her out,
4 and he *w'* smite her power in the sea;
6 and I *w'* cut off the pride of the
7 And I *w'* take away his blood out of
8 And I *w'* encamp about mine house
10 I *w'* cut off the chariot from Ephraim,
12 that I *w'* render double unto thee;
10: 6 I *w'* strengthen the house of Judah,
6 and I *w'* save the house of Joseph,
6 I *w'* bring them again to place them;
6 the Lord their God, and *w'* hear them.
8 I *w'* hiss for them, and gather them;
9 I *w'* sow them among the people:
10 I *w'* bring them again also out of the
10 *w'* bring them into the land of Gilead
12 I *w'* strengthen them in the Lord;
11: 6 For I *w'* no more pity the inhabitants
6 I *w'* deliver the men every one into his
6 of their hand I *w'* not deliver them.
7 And I *w'* feed the flock of slaughter,
9 Then said I, I *w'* not feed you: that
16 I *w'* raise up a shepherd in the land,
12: 2 I *w'* make Jerusalem a cup of
3 *w'* I make Jerusalem a burdensome
4 I *w'* smite every horse with
4 I *w'* open mine eyes upon the house
4 and *w'* smite every horse of the
6 In that day *w'* I make the governors
9 I *w'* seek to destroy all the nations
10 I *w'* pour upon the house of David,
13: 2 I *w'* cut off the names of the idols
2 and also I *w'* cause the prophets and
7 I *w'* turn mine hand upon the ones.
9 And I *w'* bring the third part through
9 and *w'* refine them as silver is refined.

Zec 13: 9 and w' try them as gold is tried:
9 on my name, and I w' hear them:
9 I w' say, It is my people: and they
14: 2 For I w' gather all nations against
12 the Lord w' smite all the people
17 that whoso w' not come up of all the
18 the Lord w' smite the heathen
Mal 1: 4 we w' return and build the desolate
4 shall build, but I w' throw down;
5 The Lord w' be magnified from the
8 w' he be pleased with thee, or accept
9 God that he w' be gracious unto us:
9 w' he regard your persons? saith the
10 neither w' I accept an offering at your
2: 2 w' not hear, and...w' not lay it to heart,
2 I w' even send a curse upon you,
2 you, and I w' curse your blessings:
3 Behold, I w' corrupt your seed, and
12 The Lord w' cut off the man that
13 or receiveth it with good w' at
3: 1 Behold, I w' send my messenger,
5 I w' come near to you to judgment;
5 I w' be a swift witness against the
7 unto me, and I w' return unto you,
8 W' a man rob God? Yet ye have
10 if I w' not open you the windows of
11 I w' rebuke the devourer for your
17 I w' spare them, as a man spareth
4: 5 I w' send you Elijah the prophet
M't 2: 13 Herod w' seek the young child to
3: 12 and he w' throughly purge his floor,
12 but he w' burn up the chaff with
4: 9 All these things w' I give thee, if thou
19 me, and I w' make you fishers of men.
5: 40 if any man w' sue thee at the law,
6: 10 Thy w' be done in earth, as it is in
14 heavenly Father w' also forgive you:
15 neither w' your Father forgive your
21 is, there w' your heart be also.
24 for either he w' hate the one, and love
24 or else he w' hold to the one, and
7: 9 ask bread, w' he give him a stone?
10 ask a fish, w' he give him a serpent?
21 he that doeth the w' of my Father
22 Many w' say to me in that day, Lord,
23 And then w' I profess unto them, I
24 I w' liken him unto a wise man,
8: 3 him, saying, I w'; be thou clean.
7 unto him, I w' come and heal him.
19 I w' follow thee whithersoever thou
9: 13 I w' have mercy, and not sacrifice:
15 but the days w' come, when the
38 he w' send forth labourers into his
10: 17 they w' deliver you up to the councils,
17 and they w' scourge you in their
32 him w' I confess also before my Father
33 him w' I also deny before my Father
11: 14 And if ye w' receive it, this is
27 whomsoever the Son w' reveal him.
28 heavy laden, and I w' give you rest.
12: 7 I w' have mercy, and not sacrifice,
11 w' he not lay hold on it, and lift it
18 I w' put my spirit upon him, and he
29 man? and then he w' spoil his house.
44 I w' return into my house from
50 do the w' of my Father which is in
13: 30 of harvest I w' say to the reapers,
35 I w' open my mouth in parables;
35 I w' utter things which have been
15: 32 I w' not send them away fasting,
16: 2 It w' be fair weather: for the sky is
3 It w' be foul weather to day: for the
18 upon this rock I w' build my church;
19 And I w' give unto thee the keys of
24 If any man w' come after me, let
25 w' save his life shall lose it:
25 w' lose his life for my sake shall find
18: 14 so it is not the w' of your Father
16 But if he w' not hear thee, then take
26, 29 with me, and I w' pay thee all.
20: 4 and whatsoever is right I w' give you.
14 I w' give unto this last, even as
15 me to do what I w' with mine own?
26 whosoever w' be great among you,
27 whosoever w' be chief among you,
32 What w' ye that I shall do unto you?
21: 3 and straightway he w' send them.
24 I also w' ask you one thing, which if
24 I in like wise w' tell you by what
25 he w' say unto us, Why did ye not then
29 He answered and said, I w' not:
31 twain did the w' of his father?
37 saying, They w' reverence my son.
40 what w' he do unto those husbandmen?
41 He w' miserably destroy those wicked
41 and w' let out his vineyard unto other
44 shall fall, it w' grind him to powder.
23: 4 themselves w' not move them
24: 28 there w' the eagles be gathered
25: 21, 23 I w' make thee ruler over many
26: 15 unto them, What w' ye give me,
15 and I w' deliver him unto you?
18 I w' keep the passover at thy house
29 I w' not drink henceforth of this fruit
31 it is written, I w' smite the shepherd,
32 again, I w' go before you into Galilee.
33 of thee, yet w' I never be offended.
35 die with thee, yet w' I not deny thee.
39 nevertheless not as I w', but as
42 except I drink it, thy w' be done.
27: 17 Whom w' ye that I release unto
21 of the twain w' ye that I release
42 from the cross, and we w' believe him.
43 deliver him...if he w' have him:
49 whether Elias w' come to save him.
63 alive, After three days I w' rise again.
M't 28: 14 we w' persuade him, and secure you.
M'r 1: 41 saith unto him, I w'; be thou clean.
2: 20 But the days w' come, when the
22 spilled, and the bottles w' be marred:
3: 27 except he w' first bind the strong
27 and then he w' spoil his house.
35 whosoever shall do the w' of God,
4: 13 then w' ye know all the parables?
6: 22 thou wilt, and I w' give it thee.
23 I w' give it thee, unto the half of my
25 I w' that thou give me by and by
8: 3 houses, they w' faint by the way:
34 Whosoever w' come after me, let
35 whosoever w' save his life shall
9: 50 saltness, wherewith w' ye season it?
10: 43 whosoever w' be great among you,
44 whosoever of you w' be...chiefest,
11: 3 straightway, he w' send him hither.
26 neither w' your Father which is in
29 I w' also ask of you one question,
29 I w' tell you by what authority I do
31 he w' say, Why then did ye not believe
12: 6 saying, They w' reverence my son.
9 w' come and destroy the husbandmen,
9 w' give the vineyard unto others.
14: 7 whensoever ye w' ye may do them
15 he w' shew you a large upper room
25 I w' drink no more of the fruit of the
27 is written, I w' smite the shepherd,
28 risen, I w' go before you into Galilee.
29 all shall be offended, yet w' not I.
31 thee, I w' not deny thee in any wise.
36 nevertheless not what I w', but
58 I w' destroy this temple that is made
58 and within three days I w' build
15: 9 W' ye that I release unto you the
12 What w' ye then that I shall do
36 whether Elias w' come to take him
Lu 2: 14 peace, good w' toward men.
3: 17 and he w' throughly purge his floor,
17 w' gather the wheat into his garner;
17 but the chaff he w' burn with fire
4: 6 power w' I give thee, and the glory
6 and to whomsoever I w' I give it.
23 w' surely say unto me this proverb,
5: 5 at thy word I w' let down the net.
13 him, saying, I w': be thou clean.
35 days w' come, when the bridegroom
37 else the new wine w' burst the bottles,
6: 9 unto them, I w' ask you one thing;
47 I w' shew you to whom he is like:
7: 42 which of them w' love him most?
9: 5 And whosoever w' not receive you,
23 If any man w' come after me, let
24 whosoever w' save his life shall
24 whosoever w' lose his life for my sake,
57 I w' follow thee whithersoever thou
61 also said, Lord, I w' follow thee;
10: 22 he to whom the Son w' reveal him.
35 when I come again, I w' repay thee.
11: 2 Thy w' be done, as in heaven, so
8 Though he w' not rise and give him,
8 because of his importunity he w' rise
11 that is a father, w' he give him a stone?
11 w' he for a fish give him a serpent?
12 an egg, w' he offer him a scorpion?
24 I w' return unto my house whence I
49 I w' send them prophets and apostles,
12: 5 I w' forewarn you whom ye shall fear:
18 And he said, This w' I do:
18 I w' pull down my barns, and build
18 there w' I bestow all my fruits and
19 I w' say to my soul, Soul, thou hast
28 how much more w' he clothe you,
34 there w' your heart be also.
36 when he w' return from the wedding;
37 and w' come forth and serve them.
44 he w' make him ruler over all that he
46 lord of that servant w' come in a day
46 not aware, and w' cut him in sunder,
46 w' appoint him his portion with the
47 knew his lord's w', and prepared
47 neither did according to his w',
48 much, of him they w' ask the more.
49 what w' I, if it be already kindled?
55 wind blow, ye say, There w' be heat;
13: 24 I say unto you, w' seek to enter in,
31 hence: for Herod w' kill thee.
14: 5 w' not straightway pull him out on the
15: 18 I w' arise and go to my father,
18 w' say unto him, Father, I have sinned
16: 11 who w' commit to your trust the true
13 for either he w' hate the one, and love
13 or else he w' hold to the one, and
30 them from the dead, they w' repent.
31 neither w' they be persuaded, though
17: 1 impossible but that offences w' come:
7 w' say unto him by and by, when he is
8 And w' not rather say unto him,
22 The days w' come, when ye shall
37 thither w' the eagles be gathered
18: 5 I w' avenge her, lest by her continual
8 that he w' avenge them speedily.
19: 14 We w' not have this man to reign
22 of thine own mouth w' I judge thee,
20: 3 I w' ask you one thing; and answer
5 he w' say, Why then believed ye him
6 Of men; all the people w' stone us:
13 I w' send my beloved son: it may be
13 may be they w' reverence him when
18 shall fall, it w' grind him to powder.
21: 6 the days w' come, in the which there
7 what sign w' there be when these
15 For I w' give you a mouth and
22: 16 you, I w' not any more eat thereof,
18 I w' not drink of the fruit of the vine,
Lu 22: 42 nevertheless not my w', but thine,
67 If I tell you, ye w' not believe:
68 ye w' not answer me, nor let me go.
23: 16 I w' therefore chastise him, and
22 I w' therefore chastise him, and let
25 but he delivered Jesus to their w'.
Joh 1: 13 w' of the flesh, nor of the w' of man,
2: 19 and in three days I w' raise it up.
4: 25 he is come, he w' tell us all things.
34 is to do the w' of him that sent me,
48 signs and wonders, ye w' not believe.
5: 20 and he w' shew him greater works
21 the Son quickeneth whom he w'.
30 because I seek not mine own w',
30 w' of the Father which...sent me,
40 And ye w' not come to me, that ye
43 in his own name, him ye w' receive.
45 Do not think that I w' accuse you
6: 37 cometh to me I w' in no wise cast out.
38 heaven, not to do mine own w',
38 but the w' of him that sent me.
39 the Father's w' which hath sent me,
40 this is the w' of him that sent me,
40, 44 I w' raise him up at the last day.
51 the bread that I w' give is my flesh,
51 I w' give for the life of the world.
54 and I w' raise him up at the last day.
67 the twelve, W' ye also go away?
7: 17 If any man w'...he shall know
17 If any man...do his w', he shall
31 w' he do more miracles than these
35 Whither w' he go, that we shall not
35 w' he go unto the dispersed among
8: 22 said the Jews, W' he kill himself?
44 the lusts of your father ye w' do.
9: 27 w' ye also be his disciples?
31 and doeth his w', him he heareth.
10: 5 And a stranger w' they not follow,
5 w' flee from him: for they know not
11: 22 wilt ask of God, God w' give it thee.
48 thus alone, all men w' believe on him:
56 that he w' not come to the feast?
12: 26 serve me, him w' my Father honour.
28 glorified it, and w' glorify it again.
32 the earth, w' draw all men unto me.
13: 37 I w' lay down my life for thy sake.
14: 3 I w' come again, and receive you unto
13 that w' I do, that the Father may be
14 ask any thing in my name, I w' do it.
16 I w' pray the Father, and he shall give
18 I w' not leave you comfortless:
18 you comfortless: I w' come to you.
21 I w' love him, and w' manifest myself
23 a man love me, he w' keep my words:
23 w' love him, and we w' come unto him,
26 whom the Father w' send in my name,
30 Hereafter I w' not talk much with you:
15: 7 ye shall ask what ye w', and it
20 me, they w' also persecute you;
20 my sayings, they w' keep yours also.
21 all these things w' they do unto you
26 I w' send unto you from the Father,
16: 2 w' think that he doeth God service.
3 And these things w' they do unto you,
7 the Comforter w' not come unto you;
7 if I depart, I w' send him unto you.
8 he w' reprove the world of sin, and of
13 come, he w' guide you into all truth:
13 and he w' shew you things to come.
22 but I w' see you again, and your
23 Father in my name, he w' give it you.
26 that I w' pray the Father for you:
17: 24 Father, I w' that they also, whom
26 unto them thy name, and w' declare it:
18: 39 w' ye therefore that I release unto
20: 15 hast laid him, and I w' take him away.
25 hand into his side, I w' not believe.
21: 22, 23 If I w' that he tarry till I come,
Ac 2: 17 God, I w' pour out my Spirit upon all
18 I w' pour out in those days of my
19 I w' shew wonders in heaven above,
3: 23 soul, which w' not hear that prophet,
5: 38 be of men, it w' come to nought:
6: 4 we w' give ourselves continually to
7: 7 they shall be in bondage w' I judge,
34 now come, I w' send thee into Egypt.
43 w' carry you away beyond Babylon.
49 what house w' ye build me? saith the
9: 16 I w' shew him how great things he
13: 22 heart, which shall fulfil all my w'.
34 I w' give you the sure mercies of
36 own generation by the w' of God,
15: 16 After this I w' return, and w' build
17: 18 said, What w' this babbler say?
31 which he w' judge the world in
32 w' hear thee again of this matter.
18: 6 henceforth I w' go unto the Gentiles.
15 I w' be no judge of such matters.
21 but I w' return again unto you,
21 again unto you, if God w'.
21: 14 The w' of the Lord be done.
22 for they w' hear that thou art come.
22: 14 that thou shouldest know his w',
18 for they w' not receive thy testimony
21 I w' send thee far hence unto the
23: 14 we w' eat nothing until we have slain
21 they w' neither eat nor drink till they
35 I w' hear thee, said he, when thine
24: 22 I w' know the uttermost of your
25 convenient season, I w' call for thee.
26: 16 in the which I w' appear unto thee;
27: 10 that this voyage w' be with hurt
28: 28 the Gentiles, and that they w' hear it.
Ro 1: 10 by the w' of God to come unto you.
2: 6 Who w' render to every man according
18 knowest his w', and approvest the

Ro 4: 8 to whom the Lord w' not impute sin.
5: 7 for a righteous man w' one die:
7: 18 for to w' is present with me; but
8: 27 the saints according to the w' of God.
9: 9 At this time w' I come, and Sarah
15 I w' have mercy on whom I...have
15 mercy on whom I w' have mercy,
15 I w' have compassion on whom I
15 on whom I w' have compassion.
18 mercy on whom he w' have mercy,
18 and whom he w' he hardeneth.
19 For who hath resisted his w'?
25 I w' call them my people, which were
28 For he w' finish the work, and cut it
28 a short work w' the Lord make upon
10: 19 I w' provoke you to jealousy by them
19 by a foolish nation I w' anger you.
12: 2 acceptable, and perfect, w' of God.
19 Vengeance is mine; I w' repay, saith
15: 9 For this cause I w' confess to thee
18 I w' not dare to speak of any of those
24 journey into Spain, I w' come to you:
28 fruit, I w' come by you into Spain.
32 you with joy by the w' of God,
1Co 1: 1 Jesus Christ through the w' of God,
19 I w' destroy the wisdom of the wise,
19 w' bring to nothing the understanding
4: 5 who both w' bring to light the hidden
5 and w' make manifest the counsels
19 But I w' come to you shortly,
19 if the Lord w',
19 w' know, not the speech of them
21 What w' ye? shall I come unto you
6: 12 I w' not be brought under the power
14 w' also raise up us by his own power.
7: 36 let him do what he w', he sinneth
37 but hath power over his own w',
37 heart that he w' keep his virgin,
39 to be married to whom she w';
8: 13 I w' eat no flesh while the world
9: 17 but if against my w', a dispensation
10: 13 who w' not suffer you to be tempted
13 w' with the temptation also make a
11: 34 rest w' I set in order when I come.
12: 11 to every man severally as he w'.
14: 15 is it then? I w' pray with the spirit,
15 and I w' pray with the understanding
15 I w' sing with the spirit,
15 and I w' sing with the understanding
21 other lips w' I speak unto this people;
21 yet for all that w' they not hear me,
23 w' they not say that ye are mad?
25 down on his face he w' worship God,
35 And if they w' learn any thing,
15: 35 some man w' say, How are the dead
16: 3 them w' I send to bring your liberality
5 Now I w' come unto you, when I shall
6 And it may be that I w' abide, yea,
7 I w' not see you now by the way;
8 I w' tarry at Ephesus until Pentecost.
12 his w' was not at all to come at
12 but he w' come when he shall have
2Co 1: 1 of Jesus Christ by the w' of God,
10 we trust that he w' yet deliver us;
6: 16 I w' dwell in them, and walk in them,
16 and I w' be their God, and they shall
17 unclean thing; and I w' receive you,
18 And w' be a Father unto you, and ye
8: 5 and unto us by the w' of God.
11 as there was a readiness to w',
10: 11 such w' we be also in deed when we
13 we w' not boast of things without our
11: 12 But what I do, that I w' do, that I may
18 glory after the flesh, I w' glory also.
30 I w' glory of the things which concern
12: 1 I w' come to visions and revelations of
5 Of such an one w' I glory: yet of
5 of myself I w' not glory, but in mine
6 not be a fool; for I w' say the truth:
9 w' I rather glory in mine infirmities,
14 and I w' not be burdensome to you:
15 I w' very gladly spend and be spent
21 my God w' humble me among you,
13: 2 that, if I come again, I w' not spare:
Ga 1: 4 according to the w' of God and our
5: 10 that ye w' be none otherwise minded:
Eph 1: 1 of Jesus Christ by the w' of God,
5 to the good pleasure of his w',
9 unto us the mystery of his w',
11 after the counsel of his own w':
5: 17 but...what the w' of the Lord is.
6: 6 doing the w' of God from the heart;
7 With good w' doing service, as
Ph'p 1: 6 w' I perform it until the day of Jesus
15 strife; and some also of good w':
18 therein do rejoice, yea, and w' rejoice.
2: 13 both to w' and to do of his good
20 who w' naturally care for your state.
23 as I shall see how it w' go with me.
Col 1: 1 of Jesus Christ by the w' of God,
9 filled with the knowledge of his w'
2: 23 a shew of wisdom in w' worship,
4: 12 and complete in all the w' of God.
1Th 4: 3 w' of God, even your sanctification,
14 which sleep in Jesus w' God bring
5: 18 for this is the w' of God in Christ
24 that calleth you, who also w' do it.
2Th 2: 7 only he who now letteth w' let, until
3: 4 w' do the things which we command
1Ti 2: 4 Who w' have all men to be saved,
8 I w' therefore that men pray
5: 11 against Christ, they w' marry;
14 I w' therefore that the younger
6: 9 that w' be rich fall into temptation
2Ti 1: 1 of Jesus Christ by the w' of God,
2: 12 if we deny him, he also w' deny us:
2Ti 2: 16 w' increase unto more ungodliness.
17 their word w' eat as doth a canker:
25 if God...w' give them repentance
26 are taken captive by him at his w'.
3: 12 and all that w' live godly in Christ
4: 3 time w' come when they w' not endure
18 and w' preserve me unto his heavenly
Tit 3: 8 these things I w' that thou affirm
Ph'm 19 with mine own hand, I w' repay it:
Heb 1: 5 I w' be to him a Father, and he shall
2: 4 Ghost, according to his own w'?
12 I w' declare thy name unto my
12 the church w' I sing praise unto thee.
13 And again, I w' put my trust in him.
3: 7 saith, To day if ye w' hear his voice,
15 To day if ye w' hear his voice,
4: 7 To day if ye w' hear his voice, harden
6: 3 And this w' we do, if God permit.
14 Saying, Surely blessing I w' bless thee,
14 and multiplying I w' multiply thee.
7: 21 The Lord sware and w' not repent,
8: 8 when I w' make a new covenant
10 I w' make with the house of Israel
10 I w' put my laws into their mind,
10 and I w' be to them a God, and they
12 For I w' be merciful to their
12 iniquities w' I remember no more.
10: 7 written of me,) to do thy w', O God.
9 he, Lo, I come to do thy w', O God.
10 By the which w' we are sanctified
16 covenant that I w' make with them
16 I w' put my laws into their hearts,
16 and in their minds w' I write them;
17 and iniquities w' I remember no more.
30 me, I w' recompense, saith the Lord.
36 after ye have done the w' of God,
37 shall come w' come, and w' not tarry.
13: 4 and adulterers God w' judge.
5 I w' never leave thee, nor forsake
6 I w' not fear what man shall do unto
21 in every good work to do his w',
23 if he come shortly, I w' see you.
Jas 1: 18 Of his own w' begat he us with the
2: 18 I w' shew thee my faith by my works.
4: 4 therefore w' be a friend of the
7 Resist the devil, and he w' flee from
8 to God, and he w' draw nigh to you.
13 to morrow we w' go into such a city,
15 If the Lord w', we shall live, and
1Pe 2: 15 For so is the w' of God, that with
3: 10 For he that w' love life, and see
13 And who is he that w' harm you, if ye
17 it is better, if the w' of God be so,
4: 2 lusts of men, but to the w' of God.
3 wrought the w' of the Gentiles,
19 suffer according to the w' of God
2Pe 1: 12 I w' not be negligent to put you
15 I w' endeavour that ye may be able
21 not in old time by the w' of man:
3: 10 day of the Lord w' come as a thief
1Jo 2: 17 he that doeth the w' of God abideth
5: 14 according to his w', he heareth us:
3Jo 10 I w' remember his deeds which he
13 I w' not with ink and pen write
Jude 5 I w'...put you in remembrance,
Re 2: 5 or else I w' come unto thee quickly,
5 w' remove thy candlestick out of his
7 To him that overcometh w' I give to
10 and I w' give thee a crown of life.
16 or else I w' come unto thee quickly,
16 w' fight against them with the sword
17 To him that overcometh w' I give to
17 and w' give him a white stone, and in
22 Behold, I w' cast her into a bed, and
23 I w' kill her children with death;
23 and I w' give unto every one of you
24 I w' put upon you none other burden.
26 to whom w' I give power over the
28 And I w' give him the morning star.
3: 3 I w' come on thee as a thief, and
3 know what hour I w' come upon thee.
5 I w' not blot out his name out of the
5 but I w' confess his name before my
9 I w' make them of the synagogue of
9 I w' make them to come and worship
10 I also w' keep thee from the hour of
12 Him that overcometh w' I make a
12 I w' write upon him the name of my
12 I w' write upon him my new name.
16 I w' spue thee out of my mouth.
20 I w' come in to him, and w' sup with
21 To him that overcometh w' I grant to
4: 1 I w' shew thee things which must be
11: 3 w' give power unto my two witnesses,
5 And if any man w' hurt them,
5 and if any man w' hurt them, he
6 all plagues, as often as they w'.
17: 1 I w' shew unto thee the judgment of
7 I w' tell thee the mystery of the
17 put in their hearts to fulfil his w',
21: 3 and he w' dwell with them, and they
6 I w' give unto him that is athirst of
7 and I w' be his God, and he shall be
9 hither, I w' shew thee the bride, the
22: 17 whosoever w', let him take the

willeth
Ro 9: 16 So then it is not of him that w',

willing
Ge 24: 5 the woman will not be w' to follow
8 woman will not be w' to follow thee,
Ex 35: 5 whosoever is of a w' heart, let him
21 one whom his spirit made w',
22 as many as were w' hearted,
29 of Israel brought a w' offering
29 whose heart made them w' to
1Ch 28: 9 perfect heart and with a w' mind:
21 workmanship every w' skilful
29: 5 who then is w' to consecrate his
Job 39: 9 Will the unicorn be w' to serve thee,
Ps 110: 3 Thy people shall be w' in the day
Isa 1: 19 If ye be w' and obedient, ye shall eat
M't 1: 19 w' to make her a publick example,
26: 41 the spirit indeed is w', but the
M'r 15: 15 Pilate, w' to content the people,
Lu 10: 29 But he, w' to justify himself, said
22: 42 Father, if thou be w', remove this
23: 20 Pilate...w' to release Jesus, spake
Joh 5: 35 ye were w' for a season to rejoice
Ac 24: 27 w' to shew the Jews a pleasure,
25: 9 w' to do the Jews a pleasure,
27: 43 But the centurion, w' to save Paul,
Ro 9: 22 if God, w' to show his wrath, and
2Co 5: 8 w' rather to be absent from the
8: 3 power they were w' of themselves;
12 For if there be first a w' mind,
1Th 2: 8 were w' to have imparted unto you,
1Ti 6: 18 to distribute, w' to communicate;
Heb 6: 17 w' more abundantly to shew unto
13: 18 in all things w' to live honestly.
2Pe 3: 9 not w' that any should perish,

willingly
Ex 25: 2 every man that giveth it w' with
J'g 5: 2 the people w' offered themselves.
9 that offered themselves w' among
8: 25 answered, We will w' give them.
1Ch 29: 6 of the king's work, offered w',
9 rejoiced, for that they offered w',
9 with perfect heart they offered w'
14 should be able to offer so w' after
17 I have w' offered all these things:
17 present here, to offer w' unto thee.
2Ch 17: 16 w' offered himself unto the Lord;
35: 8 princes gave w' unto the people,
Ezr 1: 6 beside all that was w' offered.
3: 5 that w' offered a freewill offering
7: 16 offering w' for the house of their God
Ne 11: 2 that w' offered themselves to dwell at
Pr 31: 13 and worketh w' with her hands.
La 3: 33 For he doth not afflict w', nor
Ho 5: 11 because he w' walked after the
Joh 6: 21 they w' received him into the ship:
Ro 8: 20 subject to vanity, not w', but
1Co 9: 17 For if I do this thing w', I
Ph'm 14 it were of necessity, but w'.
1Pe 5: 2 thereof, not by constraint, but w';
2Pe 3: 5 For this they w' are ignorant of,

willow See also WILLOWS.
Eze 17: 5 waters, and set it as a w' tree.

willows
Le 23: 40 thick trees, and w' of the brook;
Job 40: 22 the w' of the brook compass him
Ps 137: 2 We hanged our harps upon the w'
Isa 15: 7 carry away to the brook of the w'.
44: 4 grass, as w' by the water courses.

will-worship See WILL and WORSHIP.

wilt^
Ge 13: 9 if thou w' take the left hand, then I
15: 2 what w' thou give me, seeing I go
16: 8 thou? and whither w' thou go?
18: 23 W' thou also destroy the righteous
24 w' thou also destroy and not spare
28 w' thou destroy all the city for lack of
20: 4 w' thou slay also a righteous nation?
21: 23 that thou w' not deal falsely with me,
23: 13 But if thou w' give it, I pray thee,
24: 58 unto her, W' thou go with this man?
30: 31 if thou w' do this thing for me, I will
38: 16 What w' thou give me, that thou
17 W' thou give me a pledge, till thou
43: 4 If thou w' send our brother with us,
5 But if thou w' not send him, we will
Ex 4: 13 the hand of him whom thou w' send.
8: 21 if thou w' not let my people go,
9: 2 let them go, and w' hold them still,
17 people, that thou w' not let them go?
10: 3 long w' thou refuse to humble thyself
13: 13 and if thou w' redeem it, then thou
15: 26 w' diligently hearken to the voice
26 and w' do that which is right in his
26 w' give ear to his commandments,
18: 18 Thou w' surely wear away, both thou
20: 25 And if thou w' make an altar of stone,
32: 32 now, if thou w' forgive their sin—;
33: 12 know whom thou w' send with me.
Nu 16: 14 w' thou put out the eyes of these men?
22 and w' thou be wroth with all the
21: 2 If thou w' indeed deliver this people
De 30: 17 so that thou w' not hear, but shall be
Jos 7: 9 what w' thou do unto thy great name?
J'g 1: 14 Caleb said unto her, What w' thou?
4: 8 If thou w' go with me, then I will go:
8 but if thou w' not go with me, then I
6: 36 If thou w' save Israel by mine hand,
37 thou w' save Israel by mine hand,
11: 24 W' not thou possess that which
13: 16 and if thou w' offer a burnt offering,
Ru 4: 4 If thou w' redeem it, redeem it:
4 but if thou w' not redeem it, then tell
1Sa 1: 11 thou w' indeed look on the affliction
11 but w' give unto thine handmaid a
14 How long w' thou be drunken?
14: 37 w' thou deliver them into the hand
16: 1 How long w' thou mourn for Saul,
19: 5 then w' thou sin against innocent
21: 9 if thou w' take that, take it: for there
24: 21 thou w' not cut off my seed after me,
21 that thou w' not destroy my name
25: 17 know and consider what thou w' do;
30: 15 by God; that thou w' neither kill me,

2Sa 13: 4 w' thou not tell me? And Amnon said
18:22 Wherefore w' thou run, my son,
20:19 why w' thou swallow up the
22:26 thou w' shew thyself merciful,
26 man thou w' shew thyself upright.
27 the pure thou w' shew thyself pure;
27 thou w' shew thyself unsavoury.
28 And the afflicted people thou w' save:
24:13 or w' thou flee three months before
1Ki 3:14 And if thou w' walk in my ways,
6:12 if thou w' walk in my statutes,
9: 4 And if thou w' walk before me,
4 and w' keep my statutes and my
11:38 w' hearken unto all that I command
38 and w' walk in my ways, and do that
12: 7 If thou w' be a servant unto this
7 and w' serve them, and answer them,
13: 8 If thou w' give me half thine house,
22: 4 W' thou go with me to battle to
2Ki 3: 7 w' thou go with me against Moab to
4:23 Wherefore w' thou go to him to day?
8:12 the evil that thou w' do unto the
12 their strong holds w' thou set on fire,
12 men w' thou slay with the sword,
12 and w' dash their children, and rip up
18:24 How then w' thou turn away the face
1Ch 14:10 w' thou deliver them into mine hand?
17:25 that thou w' build him an house:
2Ch 7:17 if thou w' walk before me, as David
18: 3 king of Judah, W' thou go with me
20: 9 affliction, then thou w' hear and help.
12 O our God, w' thou not judge them?
25: 8 But if thou w' go, do it, be strong for
Ne 2: 6 and when thou w' return?
Es 5: 3 unto her, What w' thou, queen Esther?
Job 4: 2 with thee, w' thou be grieved?
5: 1 to which of the saints w' thou turn?
7:19 How long w' thou not depart from me,
8: 2 How long w' thou not speak these
9:28 that thou w' not hold me innocent.
10: 9 and w' thou bring me into dust again?
14 and thou w' not acquit me from mine
13:25 W' thou break a leaf driven to and
25 and w' thou pursue the dry stubble?
14:15 w' have a desire to the work of thine
30:23 I know that thou w' bring me to death,
34:17 w' thou condemn him that is most
38:39 W' thou hunt the prey for the lion?
39:11 W' thou trust him, because his
11 or w' thou leave thy labour to him?
12 W' thou believe him, that he will
40: 8 W' thou also disannul my
8 w' thou condemn me, that thou
41: 4 w' thou take him for a servant for
5 W' thou play with him as with a bird,
5 or w' thou bind him for thy maidens?
Ps 5:12 Lord, w' thou bless the righteous;
12 with favour w' thou compass him as
10:13 in his heart, Thou w' not require it.
17 w' prepare their heart, thou w' cause
13: 1 How long w' thou forget me, O Lord?
1 long w' thou hide thy face from me?
16:10 For thou w' not leave my soul in hell;
10 w' thou suffer thine Holy One to see
11 Thou w' shew me the path of life:
17: 6 thee, for thou w' hear me, O God:
18:25 thou w' shew thyself merciful;
25 man thou w' shew thyself upright;
26 the pure thou w' shew thyself pure;
26 thou w' shew thyself froward.
27 For thou w' save the afflicted people;
27 but w' bring down high looks.
28 thou w' light my candle: the Lord my
35:17 Lord, how long w' thou look on?
38:15 thou w' hear, O Lord my God.
41: 2 thou w' not deliver him unto the will
3 w' make all his bed in his sickness.
51:17 heart, O God, thou w' not despise.
56:13 w' not thou deliver my feet from
60:10 W' not thou, O God, which hadst
61: 6 Thou w' prolong the king's life: and
65: 5 in righteousness w' thou answer us,
79: 5 Lord? w' thou be angry for ever?
80: 4 how long w' thou be angry against
81: 8 O Israel, if thou w' hearken unto me;
85: 5 W' thou be angry with us for ever?
5 w' thou draw out thine anger to all
6 W' thou not revive us again: that thy
86: 7 upon thee: for thou w' answer me.
88:10 W' thou shew wonders to the dead?
89:46 Lord? w' thou hide thyself for ever?
101: 2 O when w' thou come unto me? I will
108:11 W' not thou, O God, who hast cast
11 w' not thou, O God, go forth with our
119:82 saying, When w' thou comfort me?
84 w' thou execute judgment on them
138: 7 midst of trouble, thou w' revive me:
139:19 Surely thou w' slay the wicked, O God:
Pr 2: 1 My son, if thou w' receive my words,
5:20 why w' thou, my son, be ravished
6: 9 How long w' thou sleep, O sluggard?
9 when w' thou arise out of thy sleep?
23: 5 W' thou set thine eyes upon that
Isa 26: 3 Thou w' keep him in perfect peace,
12 Lord, thou w' ordain peace for us:
27: 8 shooteth forth, thou w' debate with it:
36: 9 How then w' thou turn away the face
38:12, 13 w' thou make an end of me.
16 so w' thou recover me, and make
58: 5 w' thou call this a fast, and an
64:12 W' thou refrain thyself for these
12 w' thou hold thy peace, and afflict us
Jer 3: 4 W' thou not from this time cry unto
4: 1 If thou w' return, O Israel, saith the
1 and if thou w' put away thine
30 thou art spoiled, what w' thou do?
Jer 12: 5 w' thou do in the swelling of Jordan?
13:21 What w' thou say when he shall
27 w' thou not be made clean?
15:18 w' thou be...unto me as a liar,
31:22 How long w' thou go about, O thou
38:15 w' thou not surely put me to death?
15 w' thou not hearken unto me?
17 If thou w' assuredly go forth unto the
18 But if thou w' not go forth to the
47: 5 valley: how long w' thou cut thyself?
La 1:21 thou w' bring the day that thou hast
Eze 9: 8 w' thou destroy all the residue of
11:13 w' thou make a full end of the
20: 4 W' thou judge them, son of man,
4 w' thou judge them? cause them to
22: 2 thou son of man, w' thou judge,
2 w' thou judge the bloody city?
23:36 w' thou judge Aholah and Aholibah?
24:19 W' thou not tell us these things are
28: 9 W' thou yet say before him that
37:18 W' thou not shew us what thou
Hos 9:14 O Lord: what w' thou give? give them
Mic 7:19 w' cast all their sins into the depths of
20 Thou w' perform the truth to Jacob,
Hab 1: 2 shall I cry, and thou w' not hear!
2 out of violence, and thou w' not save!
Zep 3: 7 I said, Surely thou w' fear me,
7 thou w' receive instruction; so their
Zec 1:12 how long w' thou not have mercy on
3: 7 If thou w' walk in my ways, and if
7 and if thou w' keep my charge,
M't 4: 9 if thou w' fall down and worship me.
8: 2 Lord, if thou w', thou canst make
13:28 W' thou then that we go and
15:28 be it unto thee even as thou w'.
17: 4 if thou w', let us make here three
19:17 but if thou w' enter into life, keep
21 If thou w' be perfect, go and sell
20:21 he said unto her, What w' thou?
26:17 Where w' thou that we prepare for
39 not as I will, but as thou w'.
M'r 1:40 If thou w', thou canst make me
6:22 Ask of me whatsoever thou w', and
10:51 What w' thou that I should do unto
14:12 Where w' thou that we go and
36 not what I will, but what thou w'.
Lu 4: 7 If thou therefore w' worship me, all
5:12 Lord, if thou w', thou canst make
9:54 w' thou that we command fire to
22: 9 Where w' thou that we prepare?
Joh 2:20 and w' thou rear it up in three days?
5: 6 him, W' thou be made whole?
11:22 whatsoever thou w' ask of God,
13:38 W' thou lay down thy life for my
14:22 that thou w' manifest thyself unto us,
Ac 1: 6 w' thou at this time restore again the
2:27 thou w' not leave my soul in hell,
27 neither w' thou suffer thine Holy One
7:28 W' thou kill me as thou diddest
9: 6 Lord, what w' thou have me to do?
13:10 w' thou not cease to pervert the
25: 9 W' thou go up to Jerusalem, and
Ro 9:19 Thou w' say then unto me, Why doth
11:19 Thou w' say then, The branches were
13: 3 W' thou then not be afraid of the
Ph'm 21 thou w' also do more than I say.
Jas 2:20 But w' thou know, O vain man,

wimples
Isa 3:22 and the w', and the crisping pins,

win See also WINNETH; WON.
2Ch 32: 1 thought to w' them for himself.
Ph'p 3: 8 but dung, that I may w' Christ.

wind See also WHIRLWIND; WINDING; WINDS; WOUND.
Ge 8: 1 God made a w' to pass over the
41: 6 blasted with the east w' sprung up
23 blasted with the east w', sprung up
27 empty ears blasted with the east w'
Ex 10:13 Lord brought an east w' upon the
13 the east w' brought the locusts.
19 turned a mighty strong west w',
14:21 sea to go back by a strong east w'
15:10 Thou didst blow with thy w', the
Nu 11:31 went forth a w' from the Lord, and
2Sa 22:11 was seen upon the wings of the w'.
1Ki 18:45 was black with clouds and w',
19:11 and strong w' rent the mountains,
11 but the Lord was not in the w':
11 and after the w' an earthquake;
2Ki 3:17 Ye shall not see w', neither shall
Job 1:19 a great w' from the wilderness,
6:26 is desperate, which are as w'?
7: 7 O remember that my life is w':
8: 2 of thy mouth be like a strong w'?
15: 2 and fill his belly with the east w'?
21:18 They are as stubble before the w',
27:21 The east w' carrieth him away, and
30:15 they pursue my soul as the w':
22 Thou liftest me up to the w'; thou
37:17 quieteth the earth by the south w'?
21 but the w' passeth, and cleanseth
38:24 scattereth the east w' upon the earth?
Ps 1: 4 chaff which the w' driveth away.
18:10 he did fly upon the wings of the w'.
42 small as the dust before the w':
35: 5 Let them be as chaff before the w':
48: 7 ships of Tarshish with an east w'.
78:26 He caused an east w' to blow in the
26 power he brought in the south w'.
39 a w' that passeth away, and
83:13 wheel; as the stubble before the w'.
103:16 For the w' passeth over it, and it is
104: 3 walketh upon the wings of the w':
107:25 and raiseth the stormy w',
135: 7 bringeth the w' out of his treasuries.
Ps 147:18 he caused his w' to blow, and the
148: 8 stormy w' fulfilling his word:
Pr 11:29 his own house shall inherit the w':
25:14 like clouds and w' without rain.
23 The north w' driveth away rain:
27:16 hideth her hideth the w', and
30: 4 hath gathered the w' in his fists?
Ec 1: 6 w' goeth toward the south, and
6 w' returneth again according to the
5:16 he that hath laboured for the w'?
11: 4 observeth the w' shall not sow;
Ca 4:16 Awake, O north w'; and come, thou
Isa 7: 2 the wood are moved with the w'.
11:15 with his mighty w' shall he shake
17:13 of the mountains before the w',
26:18 have as it were brought forth w';
27: 8 he stayeth his rough w'
8 in the day of the east w'.
32: 2 be as an hiding place from the w',
41:16 and the w' shall carry them away,
29 molten images are w' and confusion.
57:13 the w' shall carry them all away;
64: 6 iniquities, like the w', have taken
Jer 2:24 snuffeth up the w' at her pleasure;
4:11 A dry w' of the high places in the
12 w' from those places shall come
5:13 And the prophets shall become w',
10:13 forth the w' out of his treasures.
13:24 away by the w' of the wilderness.
14: 6 snuffed up the w' like dragons;
18:17 will scatter them as with an east w'
22:22 The w' shall eat up all thy pastors,
51: 1 up against me, a destroying w';
16 forth the w' out of his treasures.
Eze 5: 2 part thou shalt scatter in the w';
12:14 scatter toward every w' all that are
13:11 fall; and a stormy w' shall rend it.
13 rend it with a stormy w' in my fury;
17:10 when the east w' toucheth it?
19:12 and the east w' dried up her fruit:
27:26 the east w' hath broken thee in
37: 9 he unto me, Prophesy unto the w',
9 son of man, and say to the w',
Da 2:35 and the w' carried them away, that
Ho 4:19 The w' hath bound her up in her
8: 7 they have sown the w', and they
12: 1 Ephraim feedeth on w',
1 and followeth after the east w':
13:15 brethren, an east w' shall come,
15 the w' of the Lord shall come up
Am 4:13 mountains, and createth the w',
Jon 1: 4 sent out a great w' into the sea
4: 8 God prepared a vehement east w':
Hab 1: 9 their faces shall sup up as the east w',
Zec 5: 9 and the w' was in their wings;
M't 11: 7 to see. A reed shaken with the w'?
14:24 with waves: for the w' was contrary.
30 But when he saw the w' boisterous,
32 come into the ship, the w' ceased.
M'r 4:37 And there arose a great storm of w',
39 And he arose, and rebuked the w',
39 the w' ceased, and there was a great
41 even the w' and the sea obey him?
6:48 for the w' was contrary unto them:
51 into the ship; and the w' ceased:
Lu 7:24 to see? A reed shaken with the w'?
8:23 down a storm of w' on the lake;
24 rebuked the w' and the raging of
12:55 And when ye see the south w' blow,
Joh 3: 8 The w' bloweth where it listeth,
6:18 by reason of the great w' that blew.
Ac 2: 2 heaven as of a rushing mighty w',
27: 7 the w' not suffering us, we sailed
13 And when the south w' blew softly,
14 arose against it a tempestuous w',
15 and could not bear up into the w',
40 hoised up the mainsail to the w',
28:13 and after one day the south w' blew.
Eph 4:14 about with every w' of doctrine,
Jas 1: 6 wave of the sea driven with the w'
Re 6:13 when she is shaken of a mighty w'.
7: 1 the w' should not blow on the earth,

winding
1Ki 6: 8 and they went up with w' stairs
Eze 41: 7 a w' about still upward to the side
7 w' about of the house went still

window See also WINDOWS.
Ge 6:16 A w' shalt thou make to the ark,
8: 6 Noah opened the w' of the ark
26: 8 the Philistines looked out at a w',
Jos 2:15 down by a cord through the w':
18 bind this line of...thread in the w'
21 she bound the scarlet line in the w'.
J'g 5:28 of Sisera looked out at a w',
1Sa 19:12 let David down through a w':
2Sa 6:16 daughter looked through a w',
2Ki 9:30 her head, and looked out at a w'.
32 And he lifted up his face to the w',
13:17 And he said, Open the w' eastward.
1Ch 15:29 looking out at a w' saw king David
Pr 7: 6 at the w' of my house I looked
Ac 20: 9 sat in a w' a certain young man
2Co 11:33 through a w' in a basket was I let

windows
Ge 7:11 and the w' of heaven were opened.
8: 2 and the w' of heaven were stopped,
1Ki 6: 4 he made w' of narrow lights.
7: 4 And there were w' in three rows,
5 posts were square, with the w':
2Ki 7: 2 Lord would make w' in heaven,
19 Lord should make w' in heaven,
Ec 12: 3 that look out of the w' be darkened,
Ca 2: 9 he looketh forth at the w',
Isa 24:18 for the w' from on high are opened,
54:12 I will make thy w' of agates, and

Isa 60: 8 and as the doves to their w'?
Jer 9:21 For death is come up into our w',
22:14 chambers, and cutteth him out w':
Eze 40:16 narrow w' to the little chambers,
16 and w' were round about inward:
22 And their w', and their arches, and
25 were w' in it and in the arches
25 thereof round about, like those w':
29 were w' in it and in the arches
33 were w' therein and in the arches
36 and the w' to it round about:
41:16 The door posts, and the narrow w',
16 and from the ground up to the w',
16 and the w' were covered;
26 were narrow w' and palm trees
Da 6:10 his w' being open in his chamber
Joe 2: 9 shall enter in at the w' like a thief.
Zep 2:14 their voice shall sing in the w';
Mal 3:10 will not open you the w' of heaven,

winds See also WHIRLWINDS.
Job 28:25 To make the weight for the w';
Jer 49:32 I will scatter into all w' them that
36 upon Elam will I bring the four w'
36 scatter them toward all those w';
Eze 5:10 of thee will I scatter into all the w'.
12 scatter a third part into all the w',
17:21 shall be scattered toward all w':
37: 9 Come from the four w', O breath,
Da 7: 2 the four w' of the heaven strove
8: 8 ones toward the four w' of heaven.
11: 4 toward the four w' of heaven;
Zec 2: 6 as the four w' of the heaven,
M't 7:25, 27 the floods came, and the w' blew,
8:26 and rebuked the w' and the sea;
27 even the w' and the sea obey him!
24:31 together his elect from the four w',
M'r 13:27 together his elect from the four w',
Lu 8:25 commandeth even the w' and water,
Ac 27: 4 because the w' were contrary.
Jas 3: 4 are driven of fierce w', yet are they
Jude 12 without water, carried about of w';
Re 7: 1 holding the four w' of the earth,

windy
Ps 55: 8 my escape from the w' storm

wine See also WINEBIBBER; WINEFAT; WINEPRESS; WINES.
Ge 9:21 And he drank of the w', and was
24 Noah awoke from his w', and knew
14:18 Salem brought forth bread and w':
19:32 let us make our father drink w',
33 they made their father drink w'
34 make him drink w' this night also;
35 they made their father drink w'
27:25 he brought him w', and he drank.
28 earth, and plenty of corn and w':
37 corn and w' have I sustained him:
49:11 he washed his garments in w',
12 His eyes shall be red with w',
Ex 29:40 the fourth part of an hin of w'
Le 10: 9 Do not drink w' nor strong drink,
23:13 drink offering thereof shall be of w',
Nu 6: 3 He shall separate himself from w'
3 and shall drink no vinegar of w',
20 that the Nazarite may drink w'.
15: 5 the fourth part of an hin of w'
7 offer the third part of an hin of w',
10 a drink offering half an hin of w',
18:12 all the best of the w', and of the
28: 7 cause the strong w' to be poured
14 offerings shall be half an hin of w'
De 7:13 of thy land, thy corn, and thy w',
11:14 gather in thy corn, and thy w',
12:17 the tithe of thy corn, or of thy w',
14:23 the tithe of thy corn, of thy w',
26 for sheep, or for w', or for strong
16:13 gathered in thy corn and thy w':
18: 4 also of the corn, of thy w', and of
28:39 but shalt neither drink of the w',
51 leave thee either corn, w', or oil,
29: 6 neither have ye drunk w' or strong
32:33 Their w' is the poison of dragons,
38 and drank the w' of their drink
33:28 be upon a land of corn and w';
Jos 9: 4 and w' bottles, old, and rent, and
13 these bottles of w', which we filled,
J'g 9:13 Should I leave my w', which
13: 4 and drink not w' nor strong drink,
7 now drink no w' nor strong drink,
14 let her drink w' or strong drink,
19:19 there is bread and w' also for me,
1Sa 1:14 put away thy w' from thee.
15 drunk neither w' nor strong drink,
24 ephah of flour, and a bottle of w',
10: 3 another carrying a bottle of w':
16:20 with bread, and a bottle of w',
25:18 hundred loaves, two bottles of w',
37 when the w' was gone out of Nabal,
2Sa 6:19 piece of flesh, and a flagon of w'.
13:28 Amnon's heart is merry with w',
16: 1 summer fruits, and a bottle of w'.
2 and the w', that such as be faint
2Ki 18:32 own land, a land of corn and w',
1Ch 9:29 fine flour, and the w', and the oil,
12:40 bunches of raisins, and w', and oil,
16: 3 good piece of flesh, and a flagon of w'.
27:27 of the vineyards for the w' cellars
2Ch 2:10 and twenty thousand baths of w',
15 and the w', which my lord hath
11:11 store of victual, and of oil and w'.
31: 5 the firstfruits of corn, w', and oil,
32:28 increase of corn, and w', and oil;
Ezr 6: 9 God of heaven, wheat, salt, w',
7:22 and to an hundred baths of w',
Ne 2: 1 the king, that w' was before him:
1 and I took up the w', and gave it
5:11 the w', and the oil, that ye exact
15 had taken of them bread and w',
18 ten days store of all sorts of w':
10:37 of w' and of oil, unto the priests,
39 offering of the corn, of the new w',
13: 5 tithes of the corn, the new w',
12 the new w' and the oil unto the
15 some treading w' presses on the
15 as also w', grapes, and figs, and
Es 1: 7 and royal w' in abundance,
10 of the king was merry with w',
5: 6 unto Esther at the banquet of w',
7: 2 second day at the banquet of w',
7 arising from the banquet of w' in
8 into the place of the banquet of w';
Job 1:13, 18 and drinking w' in their eldest
32:19 belly is as w' which hath no vent;
Ps 4: 7 their corn and their w' increased.
60: 3 to drink the w' of astonishment.
75: 8 there is a cup, and the w' is red;
78:65 man that shouteth by reason of w'.
104:15 w' that maketh glad the heart of
Pr 3:10 shall burst out with new w'.
4:17 and drink the w' of violence.
9: 2 beasts; she hath mingled her w';
5 and drink of the w' which I have
20: 1 W' is a mocker, strong drink is
21:17 he that loveth w' and oil shall not
23:30 They that tarry long at the w';
30 they that go to seek mixed w'.
31 Look not thou upon the w' when
31: 4 it is not for kings to drink w';
6 and w' unto those that be of heavy
Ec 2: 3 mine heart to give myself unto w',
9: 7 drink thy w' with a merry heart;
10:19 for laughter, and w' maketh merry:
Ca 1: 2 for thy love is better than w'.
4 remember thy love more than w':
4:10 much better is thy love than w'!
5: 1 I have drunk my w' with my milk:
7: 9 like the best w' for my beloved,
8: 2 cause thee to drink of spiced w'
Isa 1:22 dross, thy w' mixed with water:
5:11 until night, till w' inflame them!
12 pipe, and w', are in their feasts:
22 them that are mighty to drink w',
16:10 tread out no w' in their presses;
22:13 eating flesh, and drinking w':
24: 7 The new w' mourneth, the vine
9 shall not drink w' with a song;
11 is a crying for w' in the streets;
27: 2 ye unto her, A vineyard of red w'.
28: 1 them that are overcome with w'!
7 they also have erred through w',
7 drink, they are swallowed up of w',
29: 9 they are drunken, but not with w';
36:17 own land, a land of corn and w',
49:26 their own blood, as with sweet w':
51:21 and drunken, but not with w':
55: 1 buy w' and milk without money
56:12 Come ye, say they, I will fetch w',
62: 8 the stranger shall not drink thy w',
65: 8 new w' is found in the cluster,
Jer 13:12 bottle shall be filled with w':
12 every bottle shall be filled with w'?
23: 9 like a man whom w' hath overcome,
25:15 Take the w' cup of this fury at my
31:12 for wheat, and for w', and for oil,
35: 2 chambers, and give them w' to drink.
5 of the Rechabites pots full of w',
5 and I said unto them, Drink ye w'.
6 they said, We will drink no w':
6 Ye shall drink no w', neither ye,
8 us, to drink no w' all our days,
14 his sons not to drink w',
40:10 gather ye w', and summer fruits,
12 gathered w' and summer fruits very
48:33 w' to fail from the winepresses:
51: 7 the nations have drunken of her w';
La 2:12 mothers, Where is corn and w'?
Eze 27:18 in the w' of Helbon, and white wool.
44:21 Neither shall any priest drink w',
Da 1: 5 meat, and of the w' which he drank:
8 nor with the w' which he drank:
16 and the w' that they should drink;
5: 1 and drank w' before the thousand.
2 Belshazzar, whiles he tasted the w',
4 They drank w', and praised the
23 concubines, have drunk w' in them;
10: 3 came flesh nor w' in my mouth,
Ho 2: 8 know that I gave her corn, and w',
9 and my w' in the season thereof,
22 shall hear the corn, and the w',
3: 1 other gods, and love flagons of w',
4:11 Whoredom and w' and new
11 and new w' take away the heart.
7: 5 made him sick with bottles of w';
14 themselves for corn and w',
9: 2 and the new w' shall fail in her.
4 They shall not offer w' offerings
14: 7 shall be as the w' of Lebanon.
Joe 1: 5 and howl, all ye drinkers of w',
5 because of the new w'; for it is cut
10 the new w' is dried up, the oil
2:19 I will send you corn, and w', and
24 fats shall overflow with w' and oil.
3: 3 sold a girl for w', that they might
18 shall drop down new w',
Am 2: 8 drink the w' of the condemned in
12 ye gave the Nazarites w' to drink;
5:11 but ye shall not drink w' of them.
6: 6 That drink w' in bowls, and anoint
9:13 the mountains shall drop sweet w',
14 plant vineyards, and drink the w'
Mic 2:11 I will prophesy unto thee of w'
6:15 anoint thee with oil; and sweet w',
Mic 6:15 but shalt not drink w'.
Hab 2: 5 because he transgresseth by w',
Zep 1:13 but not drink the w' thereof.
Hag 1:11 upon the new w', and upon the oil,
2:12 do touch bread, or pottage, or w',
Zec 9:15 and make a noise as through w';
17 cheerful, and new w' the maids.
10: 7 heart shall rejoice as through w':
M't 9:17 men put new w' into old bottles:
17 and the w' runneth out, and the
17 they put new w' into new bottles,
M'r 2:22 putteth new w' into old bottles;
22 the new w' doth burst the bottles,
22 and the w' is spilled, and the
22 but new w' must be put into new
15:23 to drink w' mingled with myrrh:
Lu 1:15 drink neither w' nor strong drink;
5:37 putteth new w' into old bottles;
37 the new w' will burst the bottles,
38 But new w' must be put into new
39 also having drunk old w' straightway
7:33 eating bread nor drinking w';
10:34 his wounds, pouring in oil and w',
Joh 2: 3 when they wanted w', the mother
3 saith unto him, They have no w'.
9 tasted the water that was made w',
10 beginning doth set forth good w';
10 hast kept the good w' until now.
4:46 where he made the water w'.
Ac 2:13 said, These men are full of new w'.
Ro 14:21 to eat flesh, nor to drink w',
Eph 5:18 And be not drunk with w', wherein
1Ti 3: 3 Not given to w', no striker, not
8: 8 not given to much w', not greedy
5:23 use a little w' for thy stomach's
Tit 1: 7 not given to w', no striker, not
2: 3 not given to much w', teachers of
1Pe 4: 3 lusts, excess of w', revellings,
Re 6: 6 thou hurt not the oil and the w'.
14: 8 drink of the w' of the wrath of her
10 drink of the w' of the wrath of God,
16:19 the cup of the w' of the fierceness
17: 2 drunk with the w' of her fornication.
18: 3 have drunk of the w' of the wrath
13 and w', and oil, and fine flour, and

winebibber See also WINEBIBBERS.
M't 11:19 and a w', a friend of publicans and
Lu 7:34 and a w', a friend of publicans and

winebibbers
Pr 23:20 Be not among w'; among

wine-cellars See WINE and CELLARS.

wine-cup See WINE and CUP.

winefat
Isa 63: 2 like him that treadeth in the w'?
M'r 12: 1 and digged a place for the w', and

wine-offerings See WINE and OFFERINGS.

winepress See also WINEPRESSES.
Nu 18:27 and as the fulness of the w'.
30 and as the increase of the w'.
De 15:14 out of thy floor, and out of thy w':
J'g 6:11 Gibeon threshed wheat by the w',
7:25 Zeeb they slew at the w' of Zeeb,
2Ki 6:27 of the barnfloor, or out of the w'?
Isa 5: 2 of it, and also made a w' therein:
63: 3 I have trodden the w' alone; and
La 1:15 the daughter of Judah, as in a w'.
Ho 9: 2 The floor and the w' shall not feed
M't 21:33 and digged a w' in it, and built a
Re 14:19 great w' of the wrath of God.
20 w' was trodden without the city,
20 and blood came out of the w', even
19:15 treadeth the w' of the fierceness

winepresses See also WINE and PRESSES.
Job 24:11 tread their w', and suffer thirst.
Jer 48:33 caused wine to fail from the w':
Zec 14:10 of Hananeel unto the king's w'.

wines
Isa 25: 6 a feast of w' on the lees, of fat
6 of w' on the lees well refined.

wing See also LAPWING; WINGED; WINGS.
1Ki 6:24 was the one w' of the cherub,
24 cubits the other w' of the cherub:
24 uttermost part of the one w' unto
27 w' of the one touched the one wall,
27 w' of the other cherub touched the
2Ch 3:11 one w' of the one cherub was five
11 other w' was likewise five cubits,
11 reaching to the w' of the other
12 one w' of the other cherub was five
12 and the other w' was five cubits
12 joining to...w' of the other cherub.
Isa 10:14 there was none that moved the w',
Eze 17:23 it shall dwell all fowl of every w';

winged See also LONGWINGED.
Ge 1:21 and every w' fowl after his kind:
De 4:17 likeness of any w' fowl that flieth in

wings
Ex 19: 4 and how I bare you on eagles' w',
25:20 cherubims...stretch forth their w'
20 the mercy seat with their w',
37: 9 the cherubims spread out their w'
9 and covered with their w' over the
Le 1:17 shall cleave it with the w' thereof,
De 32:11 her young, spreadeth abroad her w',
11 them, beareth them on her w':
Ru 2:12 under whose w' thou art come to
2Sa 22:11 was seen upon the w' of the wind.
1Ki 6:27 they stretched forth the w' of
27 their w' touched one another in the
8: 6 even under the w' of the cherubims.

1Ki 8: 7 spread forth their two *w·* over the
1Ch 28: 18 cherubims, that spread out their *w·*.
2Ch 3: 11 *w·* of the cherubims were twenty
13 The *w·* of these cherubims spread
5: 7 even under the *w·* of the cherubims:
8 cherubims spread forth their *w·*
Job 39: 13 the goodly *w·* unto the peacocks?
13 or *w·* and feathers unto the ostrich?
26 stretch her *w·* toward the south?
Ps 17: 8 hide me under the shadow of thy *w·*.
18: 10 he did fly upon the *w·* of the wind.
36: 7 trust under the shadow of thy *w·*.
55: 6 said, Oh that I had *w·* like a dove!
57: 1 in the shadow of thy *w·* will I
61: 4 I will trust in the covert of thy *w·*.
63: 7 the shadow of thy *w·* will I rejoice.
68: 13 *w·* of a dove covered with silver,
91: 4 and under his *w·* shalt thou trust:
104: 3 walketh upon the *w·* of the wind:
139: 9 If I take the *w·* of the morning, and
Pr 23: 5 for riches...make themselves *w·*;
Ec 10: 20 which hath *w·* shall tell the matter.
Isa 6: 2 the seraphims: each one had six *w·*;
8: 8 the stretching out of his *w·* shall
18: 1 Woe to the land shadowing with *w·*,
40: 31 shall mount up with *w·* as eagles;
Jer 48: 9 Give *w·* unto Moab, that it may
40 and shall spread his *w·* over Moab.
49: 22 and spread his *w·* over Bozrah: and
Eze 1: 6 faces, and every one had four *w·*.
8 the hands of a man under their *w·*.
8 four had their faces and their *w·*.
9 Their *w·* were joined one to
11 their *w·* were stretched upward;
11 two *w·* of every one were joined one to
23 firmament were their *w·* straight,
24 I heard the noise of their *w·*, like
24 they stood, they let down their *w·*.
25 stood, and had let down their *w·*.
3: 13 of the *w·* of the living creatures
10: 5 the sound of the cherubims *w·* was
8 of a man's hand under their *w·*.
12 and their hands, and their *w·*, and
16 the cherubims lifted up their *w·* to
19 the cherubims lifted up their *w·*,
21 apiece, and every one four *w·*; and
21 hands of a man was under their *w·*.
11: 22 did the cherubims lift up their *w·*,
17: 3 A great eagle with great *w·*,
7 another great eagle with great *w·*
Da 7: 4 was like a lion, and had eagle's *w·*:
4 till the *w·* thereof were plucked,
6 the back of it four *w·* of a fowl;
Ho 4: 19 wind hath bound her up in her *w·*,
Zec 5: 9 and the wind was in their *w·*; for
9 they had *w·* like the *w·* of a stork:
Mal 4: 2 arise with healing in his *w·*;
M't 23: 37 her chickens under her *w·*,
Lu 13: 34 gather her brood under her *w·*,
Re 4: 8 four beasts had each of them six *w·*
9: 9 sound of their *w·* was as the sound
12: 14 given two *w·* of a great eagle,

wink See also WINKED; WINKETH.
Job 15: 12 away? and what do thy eyes *w·* at,
Ps 35: 19 them *w·* with the eye that hate me

winked
Ac 17: 30 times of this ignorance God *w·* at;

winketh
Pr 6: 13 He *w·* with his eyes, he speaketh
10: 10 He that *w·* with the eye causeth

winneth
Pr 11: 30 life; and he that *w·* souls is wise.

winnowed
Isa 30: 24 hath been *w·* with the shovel and

winnoweth
Ru 3: 2 he *w·* barley to night in the

winter See also WINTERED; WINTERHOUSE.
Ge 8: 22 cold and heat, and summer and *w·*,
Ps 74: 17 thou hast made summer and *w·*.
Ca 2: 11 the *w·* is past, the rain is over and
Isa 18: 6 the beasts...shall *w·* upon them.
Am 3: 15 I will smite the *w·* house with the
Zec 14: 8 in summer and in *w·* shall it be.
M't 24: 20 that your flight may not be in *w·*,
M'r 13: 18 that your flight may not be in *w·*.
Joh 10: 22 of the dedication, and it was in *w·*.
Ac 27: 12 haven was not commodious to *w·* in,
12 attain to Phenice, and there to *w·*;
1Co 16: 6 I will abide, yea, and *w·* with you,
2Ti 4: 21 thy diligence to come before *w·*.
Tit 3: 12 for I have determined there to *w·*.

wintered
Ac 28: 11 which had *w·* in the isle, whose

winterhouse See also WINTER and HOUSE.
Jer 36: 22 the king sat in the *w·* in the ninth

wipe See also WIPED; WIPETH; WIPING.
2Ki 21: 13 and I will *w·* Jerusalem as a man
Ne 13: 14 *w·* not out my good deeds that I
Isa 25: 8 Lord God will *w·* away tears from
Lu 7: 38 did *w·* them with the hairs of her
10: 11 on us, we do *w·* off against you:
Joh 13: 5 and to *w·* them with the towel
Re 7: 17 God shall *w·* away all tears from
21: 4 God shall *w·* away all tears from

wiped
Pr 6: 33 his reproach shall not be *w·* away.
Lu 7: 44 *w·* them with the hairs of her head.
Joh 11: 2 and *w·* his feet with her hair,
12: 3 and *w·* his feet with her hair:

wipeth
2Ki 21: 13 Jerusalem as a man *w·* a dish,
Pr 30: 20 she eateth, and *w·* her mouth, and

wiping
2Ki 21: 13 *w·* it, and turning it upside down.

wires
Ex 39: 3 into thin plates, and cut it into *w·*,

wisdom
Ex 28: 3 I have filled with the spirit of *w·*,
31: 3 with the spirit of God, in *w·*,
6 are wise hearted I have put *w·*,
35: 26 whose heart stirred them up in *w·*
31 with the spirit of God, in *w·*,
35 hath he filled with *w·* of heart,
36: 1 in whom the Lord put *w·* and
2 in whose heart the Lord had put *w·*,
De 4: 6 is your *w·* and your understanding
34: 9 of Nun was full of the spirit of *w·*;
2Sa 14: 20 according to the *w·* of an angel of
20: 22 went unto all the people in her *w·*.
1Ki 2: 6 Do therefore according to thy *w·*,
3: 28 saw that the *w·* of God was in him,
4: 29 And God gave Solomon *w·* and
30 Solomon's *w·* excelled the *w·* of all
30 country, and all the *w·* of Egypt.
34 people to hear the *w·* of Solomon,
34 earth, which had heard of his *w·*.
5: 12 And the Lord gave Solomon *w·*,
7: 14 filled with *w·*, and understanding,
10: 4 Sheba had seen all Solomon's *w·*,
6 own land of thy acts and of thy *w·*.
7 thy *w·* and prosperity exceedeth
8 before thee, and that hear thy *w·*.
23 of the earth for riches and for *w·*.
24 sought to Solomon, to hear his *w·*,
11: 41 and his *w·*, are they not written
1Ch 22: 12 Only the Lord give thee *w·* and
2Ch 1: 10 Give me now *w·* and knowledge,
11 but hast asked *w·* and knowledge
12 *W·* and knowledge is granted unto
9: 3 Sheba had seen the *w·* of Solomon,
5 land of thine acts, and of thy *w·*:
6 greatness of thy *w·* was not told
7 before thee, and hear thy *w·*.
22 kings of the earth in riches and *w·*.
23 of Solomon, to hear his *w·*,
Ezr 7: 25 thou, Ezra, after the *w·* of thy God,
Job 4: 21 go away? they die, even without *w·*.
6: 13 and is *w·* driven quite from me?
11: 6 would shew thee the secrets of *w·*,
12: 2 people, and *w·* shall die with you.
12 With the ancient is *w·*; and in
13 With him is *w·* and strength, he
16 With him is strength and *w·*: the
13: 5 peace! and it should be your *w·*.
15: 8 dost thou restrain *w·* to thyself?
26: 3 counselled him that hath no *w·*?
28: 12 But where shall *w·* be found?
18 for the price of *w·* is above rubies.
20 Whence then cometh *w·*? and
28 the fear of the Lord, that is *w·*;
32: 7 multitude of years should teach *w·*.
13 should say, We have found out *w·*:
33: 33 peace, and I shall teach thee *w·*.
34: 35 and his words were without *w·*.
36: 5 he is mighty in strength and *w·*.
38: 36 hath put *w·* in the inward parts?
37 Who can number the clouds in *w·*?
39: 17 God hath deprived her of *w·*,
26 Doth the hawk fly by thy *w·*, and
Ps 37: 30 of the righteous speaketh *w·*,
49: 3 My mouth shall speak of *w·*; and
51: 6 thou shalt make me to know *w·*.
90: 12 we may apply our hearts unto *w·*.
104: 24 in *w·* hast thou made them all:
105: 22 and teach his senators *w·*.
111: 10 the Lord is the beginning of *w·*:
136: 5 him that by *w·* made the heavens:
Pr 1: 2 To know *w·* and instruction;
3 To receive the instruction of *w·*,
7 fools despise *w·* and instruction.
20 *W·* crieth without; she uttereth
2: 2 thou incline thine ear unto *w·*,
6 For the Lord giveth *w·*: out of his
7 He layeth up sound *w·* for the
10 *w·* entereth into thine heart, and
3: 13 Happy is the man that findeth *w·*,
19 Lord by *w·* hath founded the earth;
21 keep sound *w·* and discretion:
4: 5 Get *w·*, get understanding: forget
7 *W·* is the principal thing;
7 principal thing; therefore get *w·*:
11 have taught thee in the way of *w·*;
5: 1 My son, attend unto my *w·*, and
7: 4 Say unto *w·*, Thou art my sister;
8: 1 Doth not *w·* cry? and understanding
5 O ye simple, understand *w·*: and,
11 For *w·* is better than rubies; and
12 I *w·* dwell with prudence, and find
14 Counsel is mine, and sound *w·*:
9: 1 *W·* hath builded her house, she
10 of the Lord is the beginning of *w·*:
10: 13 hath understanding *w·* is found:
21 but fools die for want of *w·*.
23 man of understanding hath *w·*.
31 mouth of the just bringeth forth *w·*:
11: 2 shame: but with the lowly is *w·*.
12 He that is void of *w·* despiseth his
12: 8 commended according to his *w·*:
13: 10 but with the well advised is *w·*.
14: 6 A scorner seeketh *w·*, and findeth
8 *w·* of the prudent is to understand
33 *W·* resteth in the heart of him that
15: 21 joy to him that is destitute of *w·*:
33 the Lord is the instruction of *w·*;
16: 16 better is it to get *w·* than gold!
17: 16 price in the hand of a fool to get *w·*,
24 *W·* is before him that hath
Pr 18: 1 and intermeddleth with all *w·*.
4 wellspring of *w·* as a flowing
19: 8 getteth *w·* loveth his own soul:
21: 30 There is no *w·* nor understanding
23: 4 be rich: cease from thine own *w·*.
9 will despise the *w·* of thy words.
23 also *w·*, and instruction, and
24: 3 Through *w·* is an house builded;
7 *W·* is too high for a fool: he
14 knowledge of *w·* be unto thy soul:
29: 3 Whoso loveth *w·* rejoiceth his
15 The rod and reproof give *w·*: but
30: 3 I neither learned *w·*, nor have the
31: 26 She openeth her mouth with *w·*;
Ec 1: 13 search out by *w·* concerning all
16 have gotten more *w·* than all they
16 my heart had great experience of *w·*
17 And I gave my heart to know *w·*,
18 For in much *w·* is much grief:
2: 3 acquainting mine heart with *w·*;
9 also my *w·* remained with me.
12 And I turned myself to behold *w·*,
13 Then I saw that *w·* excelleth folly,
21 is a man whose labour is in *w·*,
26 a man that is good in his sight *w·*,
7: 11 *W·* is good with an inheritance:
12 For *w·* is a defence, and money is a
12 *w·* giveth life to them that have it.
19 *W·* strengtheneth the wise more
23 All this have I proved by *w·*:
25 to seek out *w·*, and the reason of
8: 1 a man's *w·* maketh his face to
16 I applied mine heart to know *w·*,
9: 10 nor device, nor knowledge, nor *w·*,
13 This *w·* have I seen also under the
15 he by his *w·* delivered the city;
16 said I, *W·* is better than strength:
16 the poor man's *w·* is despised,
18 *W·* is better than weapons of war:
10: 1 in reputation for *w·* and honour.
3 his *w·* faileth him, and he saith
10 but *w·* is profitable to direct.
Isa 10: 13 hand I have done it, and by my *w·*;
11: 2 the spirit of *w·* and understanding,
29: 14 *w·* of their wise men shall perish,
33: 6 *w·* and knowledge shall be the
47: 10 Thy *w·* and thy knowledge, it hath
Jer 8: 9 the Lord; and what *w·* is in them?
9: 23 not the wise man glory in his *w·*,
10: 12 hath established the world by his *w·*,
49: 7 Is *w·* no more in Teman? is counsel
7 the prudent? is their *w·* vanished?
51: 15 hath established the world by his *w·*,
Eze 28: 4 With thy *w·* and with thine
5 By thy great *w·* and by thy traffick
7 swords against the beauty of thy *w·*,
12 Thou sealest up the sum, full of *w·*,
17 thou hast corrupted thy *w·* by
Da 1: 4 and skilful in all *w·*, and cunning
17 and skill in all learning and *w·*:
20 matters of *w·* and understanding,
2: 14 answered with counsel and *w·* to
20 ever: for *w·* and might are his:
21 he giveth *w·* unto the wise, and
23 who hast given me *w·* and might,
30 is not revealed to me for any *w·*
5: 11 light and understanding and *w·*,
11 like the *w·* of the gods, was found
14 and excellent *w·* is found in thee.
Mic 6: 9 the man of *w·* shall see thy name:
M't 11: 19 But *w·* is justified of her children.
12: 42 earth to hear the *w·* of Solomon;
13: 54 Whence hath this man this *w·*, and
M'r 6: 2 *w·* is this which is given unto him,
Lu 1: 17 disobedient to the *w·* of the just;
2: 40 strong in spirit, filled with *w·*:
52 Jesus increased in *w·* and stature,
7: 35 *w·* is justified of all her children.
11: 31 earth to hear the *w·* of Solomon;
49 Therefore also said the *w·* of God,
21: 15 For I will give you a mouth and *w·*,
Ac 6: 3 full of the Holy Ghost and *w·*,
10 they were not able to resist the *w·*
7: 10 gave him favour and *w·* in the sight
22 in all the *w·* of the Egyptians,
Ro 11: 33 depth of the riches both of the *w·*
1Co 1: 17 not with *w·* of words, lest the cross
19 I will destroy the *w·* of the wise,
20 made foolish the *w·* of this world?
21 For after that in the *w·* of God
21 the world by *w·* knew not God,
22 sign, and the Greeks seek after *w·*:
24 the power of God, and the *w·* of God.
30 who of God is made unto us *w·*,
2: 1 with excellency of speech or of *w·*,
4 with enticing words of man's *w·*,
5 should not stand in the *w·* of men,
6 we speak *w·* among them that are
6 yet not the *w·* of this world, nor of
7 we speak the *w·* of God in a
7 even the hidden *w·*, which God
13 words which man's *w·* teacheth,
3: 19 *w·* of this world is foolishness with
12: 8 given by the Spirit the word of *w·*;
2Co 1: 12 not with fleshly *w·*, but by the grace
Eph 1: 8 hath abounded toward us in all *w·*
17 you the spirit of *w·* and revelation
3: 10 the church the manifold *w·* of God,
Col 1: 9 the knowledge of his will in all *w·*
28 and teaching every man in all *w·*;
2: 3 whom are hid all the treasures of *w·*
23 indeed a shew of *w·* in will worship,
3: 16 Christ dwell in you richly in all *w·*;
4: 5 Walk in *w·* toward them that are
Jas 1: 5 If any of you lack *w·*, let him ask
3: 13 his works with meekness of *w·*.

Jas 3:15 This *w*· descendeth not from above,
17 But the *w*· that is from above is
2Pe 3:15 according to the *w*· given unto him
Re 5:12 and *w*·, and strength, and honour,
7:12 Blessing, and glory, and *w*·, and
13:18 Here is *w*·. Let him that hath
17: 9 here is the mind which hath *w*·.

wise See also CONTRARIWISE; LIKEWISE; OTHERWISE; UNWISE; WISER.
Ge 3: 6 tree to be desired to make one *w*·,
41: 8 and all the *w*· men thereof:
33 look out a man discreet and *w*·,
39 so discreet and *w*· as thou art:
Ex 7:11 Pharaoh also called the *w*· men
22:23 If thou afflict them in any *w*·, and
23: 8 the gift blindeth the *w*·, and
28: 3 speak unto all that are *w*· hearted,
31: 6 the hearts of all that are *w*· hearted
35:10 every *w*· hearted among you shall
25 the women that were *w*· hearted
36: 1 every *w*· hearted man, in whom
2 every *w*· hearted man, in whose
4 And all the *w*· men, that wrought
8 every *w*· hearted man among them
Le 7:24 use: but ye shall in no *w*· eat of it.
19:17 thou shalt in any *w*· rebuke thy
27:19 the field will in any *w*· redeem it,
Nu 6:23 On this *w*· ye shall bless the children
De 1:13 Take you *w*· men, and
15 the chief of your tribes, *w*· men,
4: 6 is a *w*· and understanding people.
16:19 a gift doth blind the eyes of the *w*·,
17:15 shalt in any *w*· set him king over
21:23 shalt in any *w*· bury him that day;
22: 7 thou shalt in any *w*· let the dam go,
32:29 O that they were *w*·, that they
Jos 6:18 in any *w*· keep yourselves from the
23:12 if ye do in any *w*· go back, and cleave
J'g 5:29 Her *w*· ladies answered her, yea,
1Sa 6: 3 any *w*· return him a trespass offering:
2Sa 14: 2 and fetched thence a *w*· woman,
20 and my lord is *w*·, according to the
20:16 Then cried a *w*· woman out of the
1Ki 2: 9 for thou art a *w*· man, and knowest
3:12 a *w*· and an understanding heart;
26 the living child, and in no *w*· slay it.
27 the living child, and in no *w*· slay it:
5: 7 hath given unto David a *w*· son
11:22 Nothing: howbeit let me go in any *w*·.
1Ch 26:14 Zechariah his son, a *w*· counseller,
27:32 counseller, a *w*· man, and a scribe:
2Ch 2:12 given to David the king a *w*· son,
Es 1:13 Then the king said to the *w*· men,
6:13 Then said his *w*· men and Zeresh
Job 5:13 He taketh the *w*· in their own
9: 4 He is *w*· in heart, and mighty in
11:12 vain man would be *w*·, though
15: 2 a *w*· man utter vain knowledge,
18 *w*· men have told from their fathers,
17:10 cannot find one *w*· man among you.
22: 2 he that is *w*· may be profitable
32: 9 Great men are not always *w*·:
34: 2 Hear my words, O ye *w*· men;
34 and let a *w*· man hearken unto me.
37:24 not any that are *w*· of heart.
Ps 2:10 Be *w*· now therefore, O ye kings:
19: 7 is sure, making *w*· the simple.
36: 3 he hath left off to be *w*·, and to do
37: 8 fret not thyself in any *w*· to do evil.
49:10 For he seeth that *w*· men die,
94: 8 and ye fools, when will ye be *w*·?
107:43 Whoso is *w*·, and will observe
Pr 1: 5 *w*· man will hear, and will increase
5 man...shall attain unto *w*· counsels:
6 the words of the *w*·, and their dark
3: 7 Be not *w*· in thine own eyes: fear
35 The *w*· shall inherit glory: but
6: 6 consider her ways, and be *w*·:
8:33 Hear instruction, and be *w*·, and
9: 8 rebuke a *w*· man, and he will love
9 Give instruction to a *w*· man, and
12 If thou be *w*·, thou shalt be *w*· for
10: 1 A *w*· son maketh a glad father:
5 gathereth in summer is a *w*· son:
8 The *w*· in heart will receive
14 *W*· men lay up knowledge: but
19 he that refraineth his lips is *w*·.
11:29 be servant to the *w*· of heart.
30 and he that winneth souls is *w*·.
12:15 hearkeneth unto counsel is *w*·.
18 but the tongue of the *w*· is health.
13: 1 A *w*· son heareth his father's
14 law of the *w*· is a fountain of life,
20 He that walketh with *w*· men shall
20 shall be *w*·: but a companion of
14: 1 Every *w*· woman buildeth her
3 the lips of the *w*· shall preserve
16 A *w*· man feareth, and departeth
24 The crown of the *w*· is their riches:
35 favour is toward a *w*· servant:
15: 2 the *w*· useth knowledge aright:
7 lips of the *w*· disperse knowledge:
12 neither will he go unto the *w*·.
20 A *w*· son maketh a glad father: but
24 The way of life is above to the *w*·,
31 of life abideth among the *w*·.
16:14 death: but a *w*· man will pacify it.
21 *w*· in heart shall be called prudent:
23 heart of the *w*· teacheth his mouth,
17: 2 A *w*· servant shall have rule over
10 A reproof entereth more into a *w*·
28 holdeth his peace, is counted *w*·:
18:15 the ear of the *w*· seeketh knowledge.
19:20 that thou mayest be *w*· in thy
20: 1 is deceived thereby is not *w*·.
26 A *w*· king scattereth the wicked,
Pr 21:11 punished, the simple is made *w*·:
11 and when the *w*· is instructed, he
20 and oil in the dwelling of the *w*·;
22 A *w*· man scaleth the city of the
22:17 and hear the words of the *w*·, and
23:15 My son, if thine heart be *w*·, my
19 Hear thou, my son, and be *w*·, and
24 he that begetteth a *w*· child shall
24: 5 A *w*· man is strong; yea, a man of
6 by *w*· counsel thou shalt make thy
23 These things also belong to the *w*·.
25:12 a *w*· reprover upon an obedient ear.
26: 5 lest he be *w*· in his own conceit.
12 thou a man *w*· in his own conceit?
27:11 be *w*·, and make my heart glad,
28: 7 Whoso keepeth the law is a *w*· son:
11 rich man is *w*· in his own conceit;
29: 8 snare: but *w*· men turn away wrath.
9 a *w*· man contendeth with a foolish
11 but a *w*· man keepeth it in till
30:24 earth, but they are exceeding *w*·:
Ec 2:14 The *w*· man's eyes are in his head;
15 me; and why was I then more *w*·?
16 no remembrance of the *w*· more
16 how dieth the *w*· man? as the fool.
19 he shall be a *w*· man or a fool?
19 wherein I have shewed myself *w*·
4:13 Better is a poor and a *w*· child,
6: 8 hath the *w*· more than the fool?
7: 4 heart of the *w*· is in the house of
5 better to hear the rebuke of the *w*·,
7 oppression maketh a *w*· man mad;
16 neither make thyself over *w*·:
19 Wisdom strengtheneth the *w*·
23 I said, I will be *w*·; but it was far
8: 1 Who is as the *w*· man? and who
5 a *w*· man's heart discerneth both
17 though a *w*· man think to know it,
9: 1 that the righteous, and the *w*·, and
11 neither yet bread to the *w*·, nor
15 there was found in it a poor *w*· man,
17 The words of *w*· men are heard in
10: 2 A *w*· man's heart is at his right
12 of a *w*· man's mouth are gracious;
12: 9 because the preacher was *w*·, he
11 The words of the *w*· are as goads,
Isa 5:21 unto them that are *w*· in their own
19:11 the *w*· counsellers of Pharaoh is
11 I am the son of the *w*·, the son of
12 are they? where are thy *w*· men?
29:14 the wisdom of their *w*· men shall
31: 2 Yet he also is *w*·, and will bring
44:25 that turneth *w*· men backward,
Jer 4:22 they are *w*· to do evil, but to do
8: 8 We are *w*·, and the law of the Lord
9 *w*· men are ashamed, they are
9:12 Who is the *w*· man, that may
23 the *w*· man glory in his wisdom,
10: 7 among all the *w*· men of the nations,
18:18 nor counsel from the *w*·, nor the
50:35 her princes, and upon her *w*· men.
51:57 drunk her princes, and her *w*· men,
Eze 27: 8 thy *w*· men, O Tyrus, that were in
9 Gebal and the *w*· men thereof were
Da 2:12 destroy all the *w*· men of Babylon.
13 that the *w*· men should be slain;
14 to slay the *w*· men of Babylon:
18 the rest of the *w*· men of Babylon.
21 he giveth wisdom unto the *w*·, and
24 to destroy the *w*· men of Babylon:
24 Destroy not the *w*· men of Babylon:
27 hath demanded cannot the *w*· men,
48 over all the *w*· men of Babylon.
4: 6 bring in all the *w*· men of Babylon
18 *w*· men of my kingdom are not able
5: 7 and said to the *w*· men of Babylon,
8 Then came in all the king's *w*· men:
15 now the *w*· men, the astrologers,
12: 3 And they that be *w*· shall shine
10 but the *w*· shall understand.
Ho 14: 9 Who is *w*·, and he shall understand
Ob 8 destroy the *w*· men out of Edom,
Zec 9: 2 and Zidon, though it be very *w*·.
M't 1:18 of Jesus Christ was on this *w*·:
2: 1 there came *w*· men from the east
7 he had privily called the *w*· men,
16 that he was mocked of the *w*· men,
16 diligently enquired of the *w*· men.
5:18 one tittle shall in no *w*· pass from the
7:24 I will liken him unto a *w*· man,
10:16 be ye therefore *w*· as serpents, and
42 you, he shall in no *w*· lose his reward.
11:25 hast hid these things from the *w*·
21:24 I in like *w*· will tell you by what
23:34 unto you prophets, and *w*· men,
24:45 then is a faithful and *w*· servant,
25: 2 And five of them were *w*·, and five
4 But the *w*· took oil in their vessels
8 And the foolish said unto the *w*·,
9 the *w*· answered, saying, Not so;
M'r 14:31 thee, I will not deny thee in any *w*·.
Lu 10:21 hast hid these things from the *w*·
12:42 is that faithful and *w*· steward,
13:11 could in no *w*· lift up herself.
18:17 child shall in no *w*· enter therein.
Joh 6:37 cometh to me I will in no *w*· cast out.
21: 1 and on this *w*· shewed he himself.
Ac 7: 6 And God spake on this *w*·, that his
13:34 he said on this *w*·, I will give you
41 work which ye shall in no *w*· believe,
Ro 1:14 both to the *w*·, and to the unwise.
22 Professing themselves to be *w*·,
3: 9 No, in no *w*·: for we have before
10: 6 is of faith speaketh on this *w*·,
11:25 should be *w*· in your own conceits;
12:16 Be not *w*· in your own conceits.
Ro 16:19 you *w*· unto that which is good,
27 To God only *w*·, be glory through
1Co 1:19 I will destroy the wisdom of the *w*·,
20 Where is the *w*·? where is the scribe
26 not many *w*· men after the flesh,
27 of the world to confound the *w*·;
3:10 as a *w*· masterbuilder, I have laid
18 you seemeth to be *w*· in this world,
18 become a fool, that he may be *w*·.
19 He taketh the *w*· in their own
20 knoweth the thoughts of the *w*·,
4:10 sake, but ye are *w*· in Christ;
6: 5 there is not a *w*· man among you?
10:15 I speak as to *w*· men; judge ye
2Co 10:12 among themselves, are not *w*·.
11:19 seeing ye yourselves are *w*·.
Eph 5:15 not as fools, but as *w*·,
1Ti 1:17 the only *w*· God, be honour and
2Ti 3:15 to make thee *w*· unto salvation
Heb 4: 4 of the seventh day on this *w*·,
Jas 3:13 Who is a *w*· man and endued with
Jude 25 To the only *w*· God our Saviour,
Re 21:27 there shall in no *w*· enter into it any

wise-hearted See WISE and HEARTED

wisely
Ex 1:10 Come on, let us deal *w*· with them:
1Sa 18: 5 sent him, and behaved himself *w*·:
14 And David behaved himself *w*·
15 that he behaved himself very *w*·,
30 David behaved himself more *w*·
2Ch 11:23 And he dealt *w*·, and dispersed of
Ps 58: 5 charmers, charming never so *w*·.
64: 9 they shall *w*· consider of his doing.
101: 2 behave myself *w*· in a perfect way.
Pr 16:20 He that handeth a matter *w*· shall
21:12 The righteous man *w*· considereth
28:26 but whoso walketh *w*·, he shall be
Ec 7:10 for thou dost not enquire *w*·
Lu 16: 8 steward, because he had done *w*·:

wise-men See WISE and MEN.

wiser
1Ki 4:31 For he was *w*· than all men; than
Job 35:11 and maketh us *w*· than the fowls
Ps 119:98 commandments hast made me *w*·
Pr 9: 9 a wise man, and he will be yet *w*·:
26:16 sluggard is *w*· in his own conceit
Eze 28: 3 Behold, thou art *w*· than Daniel;
Lu 16: 8 *w*· than the children of light.
1Co 1:25 foolishness of God is *w*· than men;

wise-woman See WISE and WOMAN.

wish See also WISHED; WISHING.
Job 33: 6 I am according to thy *w*· in God's
Ps 40:14 and put to shame that *w*· me evil.
73: 7 have more than heart could *w*·.
Ro 9: 3 could *w*· that myself were accursed
2Co 13: 9 and this also we *w*·, even your
3Jo 2 I *w*· above all things that thou

wished
Jon 4: 8 and *w*· in himself to die, and said,
Ac 27:29 of the stern, and *w*· for the day.

wishing
Job 31:30 to sin by *w*· a curse to his soul.

wist See also WIT; WOT.
Ex 16:15 for they *w*· not what it was.
34:29 Moses *w*· not that the skin of his
Le 5:17 though he *w*· it not, yet is he guilty,
18 wherein he erred and *w*· it not,
Jos 2: 4 me, but I *w*· not whence they were:
8:14 he *w*· not that there were liers in
J'g 16:20 *w*· not that the Lord was departed
M'r 9: 6 For he *w*· not what to say; for they
14:40 neither *w*· they what to answer
Lu 2:49 *w*· ye not that I must be about my
Joh 5:13 that was healed *w*· not who it was:
Ac 12: 9 *w*· not that it was true which was
23: 5 Then said Paul, I *w*· not, brethren,

wit^ See also WIST; WIT'S; WITTINGLY; WOT.
Ge 24:21 to *w*· whether the Lord had made
Ex 2: 4 to *w*· what would be done to him.
Jos 17: 1 to *w*·, for Machir the firstborn of
1Ki 2:32 to *w*·, Abner the son of Ner, captain of
7:50 doors of the house, to *w*·, of the temple.
13:23 to *w*·, for the prophet whom he had
2Ki 10:29 to *w*·, the golden calves that were in
1Ch 7: 2 of their father's house, to *w*·, of Tola:
27: 1 to *w*·, the chief fathers and
2Ch 4:12 To *w*·, the two pillars, and the
25: 7 Israel, to *w*·, with all the children of
10 to *w*·, the army that was come
31: 3 to *w*·, for the morning and evening
Es 2:12 to *w*·, six months with oil of myrrh,
Jer 25:18 To *w*·, Jerusalem, and the cities of
34: 9 of them, to *w*·, of a Jew his brother.
Eze 13:16 To *w*·, the prophets of Israel which
Ro 8:23 to *w*·, the redemption of our body.
2Co 5:19 To *w*·, that God was in Christ,
8: 1 do you to *w*· of the grace of God

witch See also BEWITCH; WITCHCRAFT.
Ex 22:18 Thou shalt not suffer a *w*· to live.
De 18:10 of times, or an enchanter, or a *w*·,

witchcraft See also WITCHCRAFTS.
1Sa 15:23 For rebellion is as the sin of *w*·,
2Ch 33: 6 used enchantments, and used *w*·,
Ga 5:20 Idolatry, *w*·, hatred, variance,

witchcrafts
2Ki 9:22 Jezebel and her *w*· are so many?
Mic 5:12 will cut off *w*· out of thine hand;
Na 3: 4 the mistress of *w*·, that selleth
4 and families through her *w*·.

withal See also WHEREWITHAL.
Ex 25:29 and bowls thereof, to cover *w*:
30: 4 places for the staves to bear it *w*.
18 and his foot also of brass, to wash *w*:
36: 3 of the sanctuary, to make it *w*.
37:16 covers to cover *w*, of pure gold.
27 places for the staves to bear it *w*.
38: 7 the sides of the altar, to bear it *w*;
40:30 and put water there, to wash *w*.
Le 5: 3 it be that a man shall be defiled *w*,
6:30 to reconcile *w* in the holy place,
11:21 feet, to leap *w* upon the earth;
19:24 shall be holy to praise the Lord *w*.
Nu 4: 7 the bowls, and covers to cover *w*:
J'g 7:20 in their right hands to blow *w*:
1Sa 16:12 *w* of a beautiful countenance,
1Ki 19: 1 *w* how he had slain all the
1Ch 29: 4 to overlay the walls of the houses *w*:
2Ch 24:14 vessels to minister, and to offer *w*,
26:15 to shoot arrows and great stones *w*.
Es 6: 9 array the man *w* whom the king
Job 2: 8 him a potsherd to scrape himself *w*;
Ps 141:10 own nets, whilst that I *w* escape.
Pr 22:18 they shall *w* be fitted in thy lips.
Isa 30:14 or to take water *w* out of the pit.
23 that thou shalt sow the ground *w*;
M'r 10:39 I am baptized *w* shall ye be baptized:
Lu 6:38 that ye mete *w* it shall be measured
Ac 25:27 not *w* to signify the crimes laid
1Co 12: 7 is given to every man to profit *w*.
Col 4: 3 *W* praying also for us, that God
1Ti 5:13 *w* they learn to be idle, wandering
Ph'm 22 But *w* prepare me also a lodging:

withdraw See also WITHDRAWEST; WITHDRAWETH; WITHDRAWN; WITHDREW.
1Sa 14:19 unto the priest, *W* thine hand.
Job 9:13 If God will not *w* his anger, the
13:21 *W* thine hand far from me: and
33:17 he may *w* man from his purpose,
Pr 25:17 *W* thy foot from thy neighbour's
Ec 7:18 also from this *w* not thine hand:
Isa 60:20 neither shall thy moon *w* itself:
Joe 2:10 and the stars shall *w* their shining:
3:15 and the stars shall *w* their shining.
2Th 3: 6 *w* yourselves from every brother
1Ti 6: 5 godliness: from such *w* thyself.

withdrawest
Ps 74:11 Why *w* thou thy hand, even thy

withdraweth
Job 36: 7 He *w* not his eyes from the

withdrawn
De 13:13 *w* the inhabitants of their city,
Ca 5: 6 but my beloved had *w* himself,
La 2: 8 not *w* his hand from destroying:
Eze 18: 8 hath *w* his hand from iniquity,
Ho 5: 6 he hath *w* himself from them.
Lu 22:41 And he was *w* from them about a

withdrew
Ne 9:29 and *w* the shoulder, and
Eze 20:22 Nevertheless I *w* mine hand,
M't 12:15 it, he *w* himself from thence:
M'r 3: 7 Jesus *w* himself with his disciples
Lu 5:16 he *w* himself into the wilderness,
Ga 2:12 he *w* and separated himself,

wither See also WITHERED; WITHERETH.
Ps 1: 3 his leaf also shall not *w*; and
37: 2 grass, and *w* as the green herb.
Isa 19: 6 up: the reeds and flags shall *w*.
7 sown by the brooks, shall *w*,
40:24 blow upon them, and they shall *w*,
Jer 12: 4 and the herbs of every field *w*,
Eze 17: 9 cut off the fruit thereof, that it *w*?
9 *w* in all the leaves of her spring,
10 shall it not utterly *w*, when the
10 *w* in the furrows where it grew.
Am 1: 2 and the top of Carmel shall *w*.

withered^
Ge 41:23 seven ears, *w*, thin, and blasted
Ps 102: 4 heart is smitten, and *w* like grass;
Isa 15: 6 for the hay is *w* away, the grass
27:11 When the boughs thereof are *w*,
La 4: 8 it is *w*, it is become like a stick.
Eze 19:12 strong rods were broken and *w*;
Joe 1:12 all the trees of the field, are *w*:
12 joy is *w* away from the sons of men.
17 broken down; for the corn is *w*.
Am 4: 7 piece whereupon it rained not *w*.
Jon 4: 7 and it smote the gourd that it *w*.
M't 12:10 a man which had his hand *w*.
13: 6 they had no root, they *w* away.
21:19 And presently the fig tree *w* away.
20 How soon is the fig tree *w* away!
M'r 3: 1 man there which had a *w* hand.
3 the man which had the *w* hand,
4: 6 because it had no root, it *w* away.
11:21 which thou cursedst is *w* away.
Lu 6: 6 a man whose right hand was *w*.
8 man which had the *w* hand, Rise
8: 6 it *w*...because it lacked moisture.
Joh 5: 3 halt, *w*, waiting for the moving of
15: 6 cast forth as a branch, and is *w*;

withereth
Job 8:12 down, it *w* before any other herb.
Ps 90: 6 the evening it is cut down, and *w*.
129: 6 which *w* afore it groweth up:
Isa 40: 7, 8 The grass *w*, the flower fadeth:
Jas 1:11 burning heat, but it *w* the grass,
1Pe 1:24 The grass *w*, and the flower
Jude 12 trees whose fruit *w*, without fruit,

withheld See also WITHHELDEST; WITHHOLDEN.
Ge 20: 6 I also *w* thee from sinning
22:12 seeing thou hast not *w* thy son,
16 hast not *w* thy son, thine only son:
30: 2 who hath *w* from thee the fruit of
Job 31:16 If I have *w* the poor from their
Ec 2:10 I *w* not my heart from any joy;

withheldest
Ne 9:20 *w* not thy manna from their

withhold See also WITHHELD; WITHHOLDEN; WITHHOLDETH.
Ge 23: 6 shall *w* from thee his sepulchre,
2Sa 13:13 for he will not *w* me from thee.
Job 4: 2 can *w* himself from speaking?
Ps 40:11 *W* not thou thy tender mercies
84:11 good thing will he *w* from them
Pr 3:27 *W* no good from them to whom it
23:13 *W* not correction from a child:
Ec 11: 6 in the evening *w* not thine hand:
Jer 2:25 *W* thy foot from being unshod,

withholden See also WITHHELD.
1Sa 25:26 *w* thee from coming to shed
Job 22: 7 hast *w* bread from the hungry.
38:15 from the wicked their light is *w*,
42: 2 no thought can be *w* from thee.
Ps 21: 2 hast not *w* the request of his lips.
Jer 3: 3 the showers have been *w*,
5:25 your sins have *w* good things from
Eze 18:16 hath not *w* the pledge, neither
Joe 1:13 drink offering is *w* from the
Am 4: 7 also I have *w* the rain from you,

withholdeth
Job 12:15 he *w* the waters, and they dry up:
Pr 11:24 is that *w* more than is meet,
26 He that *w* corn, the people shall
2Th 2: 6 what *w* that he might be revealed

within^
Ge 6:14 pitch it *w* and without with pitch.
9:21 and he was uncovered *w* his tent.
18:12 Sarah laughed *w* herself, saying,
24 be fifty righteous *w* the city:
26 Sodom fifty righteous *w* the city,
25:22 children struggled together *w*
39:11 of the men of the house there *w*.
40:13, 19 Yet *w* three days shall Pharaoh
Ex 20:10 nor thy stranger that is *w* thy gates:
25:11 *w* and without shalt thou overlay
26:33 in thither *w* the vail of the ark of
37: 2 it with pure gold *w* and without,
Le 10:18 not brought in *w* the holy place:
13:55 whether it be bare *w* or without.
14:41 caused the house to be scraped *w*
16: 2 holy place *w* the vail before the
12 small, and bring it *w* the vail:
15 and bring his blood *w* the vail,
25:29 it *w* a whole year after it is sold;
29 *w* a full year may he redeem it.
30 redeemed *w* the space of a...year,
26:25 gathered together *w* your cities,
Nu 4:10 *w* a covering of badgers' skins,
18: 7 of the altar, and *w* the vail;
De 5:14 thy stranger that is *w* thy gates;
12:17 Thou mayest not eat *w* thy gates the
18 and the Levite that is *w* thy gates:
14:27 And the Levite that is *w* thy gates;
28 and shalt lay it up *w* thy gates:
29 the widow, which are *w* thy gates,
15: 7 of thy brethren *w* any of thy gates
22 Thou shalt eat it *w* thy gates: the
16: 5 the passover *w* any of thy gates,
11 and the Levite that is *w* thy gates
14 the widow, that are *w* thy gates.
17: 2 *w* any of thy gates which the Lord
8 matters of controversy *w* thy gates:
23:10 he shall not come *w* the camp:
24:14 that are in thy land *w* thy gates:
26:12 that they may eat *w* thy gates, and
28:43 stranger that is *w* thee shall get
31:12 thy stranger that is *w* thy gates,
32:25 The sword without, and terror *w*,
Jos 1:11 *w* three days ye shall pass over
19: 1 *w* the inheritance of the children
9 inheritance *w* the inheritance of
21:41 *w* the possession of the children
J'g 7:16 and lamps *w* the pitchers.
9:51 was a strong tower *w* the city,
11:18 came not *w* the border of Moab:
26 ye not recover them *w* that time?
14:12 declare it me *w* the seven days
15: 1 But it came to pass *w* a while after,
1Sa 13:11 camest not *w* the days appointed,
14:14 *w* as it were an half acre of land,
25:36 Nabal's heart was merry *w* him,
37 that his heart died *w* him, and
26: 7 Saul lay sleeping *w* the trench,
2Sa 7: 2 ark of God dwelleth *w* curtains.
20: 4 me the men of Judah *w* three days,
1Ki 6:15 house *w* with boards of cedar,
16 he even built them for it *w*, even
18 cedar of the house *w* was carved
19 oracle he prepared in the house *w*,
21 the house *w* with pure gold:
23 *w* the oracle he made two cherubims
27 cherubims *w* the inner house:
29 and open flowers, *w* and without.
30 overlaid with gold, *w* and without.
7: 8 had another court *w* the porch,
9 sawed with saws, *w* and without,
31 mouth of it *w* the chapiter and
2Ki 4:27 alone; for her soul is vexed *w* her:
6:30 had sackcloth *w* upon his flesh.
7:11 they told it to the king's house *w*.
11: 8 and he that cometh *w* the ranges,
2Ch 3: 4 he overlaid it *w* with pure gold.

Ezr 4:15 sedition *w* the same of old time:
10: 9 unto Jerusalem *w* three days.
Ne 4:22 his servant lodge *w* Jerusalem,
6:10 the house of God, *w* the temple,
Job 6: 4 arrows of the Almighty are *w* me,
14:22 and his soul *w* him shall mourn.
19:27 my reins be consumed *w* me.
20:13 but keep it still *w* his mouth:
14 it is the gall of asps *w* him.
24:11 Which make oil *w* their walls, and
32:18 the spirit *w* me constraineth me.
Ps 36: 1 of the wicked saith *w* my heart,
39: 3 My heart was hot *w* me, while I
40: 8 God: yea, thy law is *w* my heart.
10 hid thy righteousness *w* my heart;
42: 6 God, my soul is cast down *w* me:
11 why art thou disquieted *w* me?
43: 5 why art thou disquieted *w* me?
45:13 king's daughter is all glorious *w*:
51:10 and renew a right spirit *w* me.
55: 4 My heart is sore pained *w* me:
94:19 multitude of my thoughts *w* me
101: 2 walk *w* my house with a perfect
7 deceit shall not dwell *w* my house:
103: 1 all that is *w* me, bless his holy
109:22 and my heart is wounded *w* me.
122: 2 Our feet shall stand *w* thy gates,
7 Peace be *w* thy walls, and prosperity
7 walls, and prosperity *w* thy palaces.
8 I will now say, Peace be *w* thee.
142: 3 my spirit was overwhelmed *w* me,
143: 4 is my spirit overwhelmed *w* me;
4 my heart *w* me is desolate.
147:13 hath blessed thy children *w* thee.
Pr 22:18 thing if thou keep them *w* thee;
26:24 lips, and layeth up deceit *w* him;
Ec 9:14 was a little city, and a few men *w* it:
Ca 4: 1 thou hast doves' eyes *w* thy locks:
3 of a pomegranate *w* thy locks.
6: 7 are thy temples *w* thy locks.
Isa 7: 8 *w* threescore and five years shall
16:14 *W* three years, as the years of an
21:16 *W* a year, according to the years
26: 9 my spirit *w* me will I seek thee
56: 5 mine house and *w* my walls a place
60:18 nor destruction *w* thy borders;
63:11 he that put his holy Spirit *w* him?
Jer 4:14 thy vain thoughts lodge *w* thee?
23: 9 Mine heart *w* me is broken because
28: 3 *W* two full years will I bring
11 *w* the space of two full years.
La 1:20 mine heart is turned *w* me; for I
Eze 1:27 of fire round about *w* it,
2:10 it was written *w* and without:
3:24 Go, shut thyself *w* thine house.
7:15 the pestilence and the famine *w*:
11:19 and I will put a new spirit *w* you;
12:24 divination *w* the house of Israel.
36:26 and a new spirit will I put *w* you:
27 And I will put my spirit *w* you,
40: 7 porch of the gate *w* was one reed.
8 also the porch of the gate *w*,
16 posts *w* the gate round about,
43 *w* were hooks, an hand broad,
41: 9 of the side chambers that were *w*.
17 wall round about *w* and without,
44:17 gates of the inner court, and *w*.
Da 6:12 of any God or man *w* thirty days,
11:20 but *w* few days he shall be destroyed,
Ho 11: 8 mine heart is turned *w* me, my
Jon 2: 7 When my soul fainteth *w* me I
Mic 3: 3 pot, and as flesh *w* the caldron.
5: 6 and when he treadeth *w* our borders.
Zep 3: 3 princes *w* her are roaring lions;
Zec 12: 1 formeth the spirit of man *w* him.
M't 3: 9 think not to say *w* yourselves,
9: 3 of the scribes said *w* themselves,
21 For she said *w* herself, If I may
23:25 they are full of extortion and
26 first that which is *w* the cup and
27 are *w* full of dead men's bones,
28 but *w* ye are full of hypocrisy and
M'r 2: 8 they so reasoned *w* themselves,
7:21 from *w*, out of the heart of men,
23 All these evil things come from *w*,
14: 4 had indignation *w* themselves,
58 *w* three days I will build another
Lu 3: 8 begin not to say *w* yourselves, We
7:39 he spake *w* himself, saying, This
49 him began to say *w* themselves,
11: 7 he from *w* shall answer and say,
40 make that which is *w* also?
12:17 And he thought *w* himself, saying,
16: 3 Then the steward said *w* himself,
17:21 the kingdom of God is *w* you.
18: 4 but afterward he said *w* himself,
19:44 ground, and thy children *w* thee;
24:32 Did not our heart burn *w* us, while
Joh 20:26 days again his disciples were *w*,
Ac 5:23 had opened, we found no man *w*.
Ro 8:23 we ourselves groan *w* ourselves,
1Co 5:12 do not ye judge them that are *w*?
2Co 7: 5 were fightings, *w* were fears.
Heb 6:19 entereth into that *w* the vail;
Re 4: 8 and they were full of eyes *w*:
5: 1 on the throne a book written *w*

without^
Ge 1: 2 earth was *w* form, and void;
6:14 pitch it within and *w* with pitch.
9:22 and told his two brethren *w*.
19:16 him forth, and set him *w* the city.
24:11 camels to kneel down *w* the city by
31 wherefore standeth thou *w*? for I
37:33 Joseph is *w* doubt rent in pieces.
41:44 *w* thee shall no man lift up his
49 numbering; for it was *w* number.

Ex 12: 5 Your lamb shall be *w'* blemish,
25: 11 and *w'* shalt thou overlay it.
26: 35 thou shalt set the table *w'* the vail,
27: 21 of the congregation *w'* the vail,
29: 1 bullock and two rams *w'* blemish,
14 thou burn with fire *w'* the camp:
33: 7 and pitched it *w'* the camp,
7 which was *w'* the camp.
37: 2 it with pure gold within and *w'*,
40: 22 tabernacle northward, *w'* the vail.
Le 1: 3 let him offer a male *w'* blemish:
10 he shall bring it a male *w'* blemish.
3: 1 he shall offer it *w'* blemish before
6 female, he shall offer it *w'* blemish.
4: 3 a young bullock *w'* blemish unto
12 shall he carry forth *w'* the camp
21 forth the bullock *w'* the camp,
23 of the goats, a male *w'* blemish:
28 of the goats, a female *w'* blemish,
32 shall bring it a female *w'* blemish.
5: 15 a ram *w'* blemish out of the flocks,
18 a ram *w'* blemish out of the flock,
6: 6 a ram *w'* blemish out of the flock,
11 carry forth the ashes *w'* the camp
8: 17 he burnt with fire *w'* the camp;
9: 2 for a burnt offering, *w'* blemish,
3 both of the first year, *w'* blemish,
11 he burnt with fire *w'* the camp.
10: 12 eat it *w'* leaven beside the altar:
13: 46 *w'* the camp shall his habitation
55 whether it be bare within or *w'*,
14: 10 take two he lambs *w'* blemish,
10 lamb of the first year *w'* blemish,
40 into an unclean place *w'* the city:
41 *w'* the city into an unclean place:
16: 27 shall one carry forth *w'* the camp;
22: 19 your own will a male *w'* blemish,
23: 12 an he lamb *w'* blemish of the first
18 seven lambs *w'* blemish of the first
24: 3 *W'* the vail of the testimony, in
14 him that hath cursed *w'* the camp;
26: 43 while she lieth desolate *w'* them:
Nu 5: 3 *w'* the camp shall ye put them;
4 so, and put them out *w'* the camp:
6: 14, 14 lamb of the first year *w'* blemish
14 and one ram *w'* blemish for peace
15: 24 *w'* the knowledge of the congregation,
35 him with stones *w'* the camp.
36 brought him *w'* the camp,
19: 2 bring thee a red heifer *w'* spot,
3 may bring her forth *w'* the camp,
9 up *w'* the camp in a clean place,
20: 19 *w'* doing any thing else, go through
28: 3 two lambs of the first year *w'* spot
9 two lambs of the first year *w'* spot,
11 lambs of the first year *w'* spot;
19 they shall be unto you *w'* blemish:
31 they shall be unto you *w'* blemish)
29: 2 lambs of the first year *w'* blemish:
8 they shall be unto you *w'* blemish:
13 first year; they shall be *w'* blemish:
17 lambs of the first year *w'* spot:
20 lambs of the first year *w'* blemish;
23 lambs of the first year *w'* blemish:
26 lambs of the first year *w'* spot:
29, 32, 36 of the first year *w'* blemish:
31: 13 forth to meet them *w'* the camp.
19 ye abide *w'* the camp seven days:
35: 5 shall measure from *w'* the city on
22 thrust him suddenly *w'* enmity,
22 him any thing *w'* laying of wait,
26 time come *w'* the border of the city
27 find him *w'* the borders of the city
De 8: 9 thou shalt eat bread *w'* scarceness,
23: 12 have a place also *w'* the camp,
25: 5 shall not marry *w'* unto a stranger:
32: 4 a God of truth and *w'* iniquity,
25 The sword *w'*, and terror within
Jos 3: 10 he will *w'* fail drive out from before
6: 23 left them *w'* the camp of Israel.
J'g 2: 23 *w'* driving them out hastily;
6: 5 and their camels were *w'* number:
7: 12 and their camels were *w'* number,
11: 30 thou shalt *w'* fail deliver the children
Ru 4: 14 left thee this day *w'* a kinsman,
1Sa 19: 5 blood, to stay David *w'* a cause?
30: 8 overtake them, and *w'* fail recover all.
2Sa 23: 4 riseth, even a morning *w'* clouds;
1Ki 6: 6 for *w'* in the wall of the house he
29 and open flowers, within and *w'*.
30 overlaid with gold, within and *w'*.
7: 9 sawed with saws, within and *w'*,
8: 8 oracle, and they were not seen *w'*:
2Ki 10: 24 Jehu appointed fourscore men *w'*,
11: 15 Have her forth *w'* the ranges:
16: 18 the king's entry *w'*, turned he
18: 25 come up *w'* the Lord against
23: 4 he burned them *w'* Jerusalem in
6 *w'* Jerusalem, unto the brook
25: 16 all these vessels was *w'* weight.
1Ch 2: 30 but Seled died *w'* children.
32 and Jether died *w'* children.
21: 24 nor offer burnt offerings *w'* cost.
22: 14 and of brass and iron *w'* weight;
2Ch 5: 9 oracle; but they were not seen *w'*.
12: 3 people were *w'* number that came
15: 3 Israel hath been *w'* the true God,
3 *w'* a teaching priest, and *w'* law.
21: 20 and departed *w'* being desired.
24: 8 set it *w'* at the gate of the house
32: 3 fountains which were *w'* the city:
5 the towers, and another wall *w'*,
33: 14 built a wall *w'* the city of David,
Ezr 6: 9 it be given them day by day *w'* fail:
7: 22 salt *w'* prescribing how much.
10: 13 and we are not able to stand *w'*,
Ne 13: 20 ware lodged *w'* Jerusalem once or
Job 2: 3 him, to destroy him *w'* cause.
4: 20 perish forever *w'* any regarding it.
21 away? they die, even *w'* wisdom.
5: 9 marvellous things *w'* number:
6: 6 is unsavoury be eaten *w'* salt?
7: 6 shuttle, and are spent *w'* hope.
8: 11 Can the rush grow up *w'* mire?
11 can the flag grow *w'* water?
9: 10 yea, and wonders *w'* number.
17 multiplieth my wounds *w'* cause.
10: 22 shadow of death, *w'* any order,
11: 15 shalt thou lift up thy faces *w'* spot;
12: 25 They grope in the dark *w'* light,
24: 7 the naked to lodge *w'* clothing,
10 him to go naked *w'* clothing,
26: 2 thou helped him that is *w'* power?
30: 28 I went mourning *w'* the sun:
31: 19 clothing, or any poor *w'* covering;
39 eaten the fruits thereof *w'* money,
33: 9 I am clean *w'* transgression, I am
34: 6 is incurable *w'* transgression.
20 shall be taken away *w'* hand.
24 in pieces mighty men *w'* number,
35 Job hath spoken *w'* knowledge,
35 and his words were *w'* wisdom.
35: 16 multiplieth words *w'* knowledge.
36: 12 and they shall die *w'* knowledge.
38: 2 counsel by words *w'* knowledge?
39: 16 her labour is in vain *w'* fear;
41: 33 not his like, who is made *w'* fear.
42: 3 that hideth counsel *w'* knowledge?
Ps 7: 4 him that *w'* cause is mine enemy:)
25: 3 which transgress *w'* cause.
31: 11 that did see me *w'* fled from me.
35: 7 *w'* cause have they hid for me
7 *w'* cause they have digged for my
19 the eye that hate me *w'* a cause.
69: 4 They that hate me *w'* a cause are
105: 34 caterpillers, and that *w'* number,
109: 3 and fought against me *w'* a cause.
119: 78 perversely with me *w'* a cause:
161 have persecuted me *w'* a cause:
Pr 1: 11 privily for the innocent *w'* cause:
20 Wisdom crieth *w'*; she uttereth
3: 30 Strive not with a man *w'* cause,
5: 23 He shall die *w'* instruction; and
6: 15 shall he be broken *w'* remedy.
7: 12 Now is she *w'*, now in the streets,
11: 22 fair woman which is *w'* discretion.
15: 22 *W'* counsel purposes are
16: 8 than great revenues *w'* right.
19: 2 that the soul be *w'* knowledge,
22: 13 There is a lion *w'*, I shall be slain
23: 29 who hath wounds *w'* cause?
24: 27 Prepare thy work *w'*, and make it
28 against thy neighbour *w'* cause;
25: 14 gift is like clouds and wind *w'* rain.
28 that is broken down, and *w'* walls.
29: 1 be destroyed, and that *w'* remedy.
Ec 10: 11 serpent will bite *w'* enchantment;
Ca 6: 8 concubines, and virgins *w'* number.
8: 1 when I should find thee *w'*, I
Isa 5: 9 even great and fair, *w'* inhabitant.
14 opened her mouth *w'* measure:
6: 11 the cities be wasted *w'* inhabitant,
11 and the houses *w'* man, and the
10: 4 *W'* me they shall bow down under
33: 7 their valiant ones shall cry *w'*:
36: 10 now come up *w'* the Lord against
45: 17 confounded world *w'* end.
52: 3 ye shall be redeemed *w'* money.
4 oppressed them *w'* cause.
55: 1 and milk *w'* money and *w'* price.
Jer 2: 15 cities are burned *w'* inhabitant.
32 have forgotten me days *w'* number.
4: 23 the earth, and, lo, it was *w'* form,
5: 21 people, and *w'* understanding;
9: 11 Judah desolate, *w'* an inhabitant.
21 to cut off the children from *w'*,
21: 4 which besiege you *w'* the walls,
22: 13 his neighbour's service *w'* wages,
26: 9 shall be desolate *w'* an inhabitant?
32: 43 say, It is desolate *w'* man or beast;
33: 10 be desolate *w'* man and *w'* beast,
10 that are desolate, *w'* man,
10 and *w'* inhabitant, and *w'* beast.
12 desolate *w'* man and *w'* beast,
34: 22 Judah a desolation *w'*...inhabitant.
44: 19 offerings unto her, *w'* our men?
22 and a curse, *w'* an inhabitant,
46: 19 and desolate *w'* an inhabitant.
48: 9 desolate, *w'* any to dwell therein.
49: 31 nation, that dwelleth *w'* care,
51: 29 a desolation *w'* an inhabitant.
37 and an hissing, *w'* an inhabitant.
52: 20 of all these vessels was *w'* weight.
La 1: 6 *w'* strength before the pursuer.
3: 49 ceaseth not, *w'* any intermission,
52 me sore, like a bird, *w'* cause.
Eze 2: 10 and it was written within and *w'*:
7: 15 sword is *w'*, and the pestilence
14: 23 *w'* cause all that I have done in it,
17: 9 *w'* great power or many people to
33: 15 of life, *w'* committing iniquity;
38: 11 all of them dwelling *w'* walls,
40: 19 the forefront of the inner court *w'*,
40 at the side *w'*, as one goeth up to
44 *w'* the inner gate were the
41: 9 which was for the side chamber *w'*,
17 even unto the inner house, and *w'*,
17 wall round about within and *w'*,
25 upon the face of the porch *w'*.
42: 7 wall that was *w'* over against the
43: 21 of the house, *w'* the sanctuary.
22 offer a kid of the goats *w'* blemish
Eze 43: 23 offer a young bullock *w'* blemish,
23 a ram out of the flock *w'* blemish.
25 a ram out of the flock, *w'* blemish.
45: 18 take a young bullock *w'* blemish,
23 and seven rams *w'* blemish daily
46: 2 way of the porch of that gate *w'*,
4 shall be six lambs *w'* blemish,
4 and a ram *w'* blemish.
6 be a young bullock *w'* blemish,
6 a ram: they shall be *w'* blemish.
13 a lamb of the first year *w'* blemish:
47: 2 led me about the way *w'* unto
Da 2: 34 a stone was cut out *w'* hands,
45 out of the mountain *w'* hands,
8: 25 but he shall be broken *w'* hand.
11: 18 *w'* his own reproach he shall
Ho 3: 4 days *w'* a king, and *w'* a prince,
4 *w'* a sacrifice, and *w'* an image,
4 *w'* [369] an ephod, and *w'* [*] teraphim:
7: 1 the troop of robbers spoileth *w'*.
11 also is like a silly dove *w'* heart:
Joe 1: 6 my land, strong, and *w'* number,
Zec 2: 4 shall be inhabited as towns *w'* walls
M't 5: 22 angry with his brother *w'* a cause
10: 29 fall on the ground *w'* your Father.
12: 46 mother and his brethren stood *w'*,
47 mother and thy brethren stand *w'*,
13: 34 *w'* a parable spake he not unto
57 A prophet is not *w'* honour, save
15: 16 Are ye also yet *w'* understanding?
26: 69 Peter sat *w'* in the palace: and a
M'r 1: 45 city, but was *w'* in desert places:
3: 31 and, standing *w'*, sent unto him,
32 and thy brethren *w'* seek for thee.
4: 11 unto them that are *w'*, all these
34 *w'* a parable spake he not unto
6: 4 A prophet is not *w'* honour, but in
7: 15 There is nothing from *w'* a man,
18 Are ye so *w'* understanding also?
18 from *w'* entereth into the man,
11: 4 the colt tied by the door *w'* in a
14: 58 will build another made *w'* hands.
Lu 1: 10 praying *w'* at the time of incense.
74 enemies might serve him *w'* fear,
6: 49 a man that *w'* a foundation built
8: 20 mother and thy brethren stand *w'*,
11: 40 he that made that which is *w'*
13: 25 ye begin to stand *w'*, and to knock
20: 28 a wife, and he die *w'* children,
29 took a wife, and died *w'* children.
22: 35 When I sent you *w'* purse, and
Joh 1: 3 *w'* him was not any thing made
8: 7 He that is *w'* sin among you, let
15: 5 for *w'* me ye can do nothing.
25 law, They hated me *w'* a cause.
18: 16 But Peter stood at the door *w'*.
19: 23 now the coat was *w'* seam, woven
20: 11 Mary stood *w'* at the sepulchre
Ac 5: 23 the keepers standing *w'* before the
26 and brought them *w'* violence:
9: 9 And he was three days *w'* sight,
10: 29 came I unto you *w'* gainsaying,
12: 5 prayer was made *w'* ceasing of
14: 17 he left not himself *w'* witness,
25: 17 *w'* any delay on the morrow I
Ro 1: 9 *w'* ceasing I make mention of you
20 so that they are *w'* excuse:
31 *W'* understanding,
31 *w'* natural affection, implacable,
2: 12 For as many as have sinned *w'* law
12 shall also perish *w'* law; and as
3: 3 make the faith of God *w'* effect?
21 righteousness of God *w'* the law
28 by faith *w'* the deeds of the law.
4: 6 imputeth righteousness *w'* works,
5: 6 For when we were yet *w'* strength.
7: 8 For *w'* the law sin was dead.
9 I was alive *w'* the law once: but
10: 14 how shall they hear *w'* a preacher?
11: 29 calling of God are *w'* repentance.
12: 9 Let love be *w'* dissimulation.
1Co 4: 8 ye have reigned as kings *w'* us:
5: 12 do to judge them also that are *w'*?
13 But them that are *w'* God judgeth.
6: 18 that a man doeth is *w'* the body;
7: 32 I would have you *w'* carefulness.
35 attend upon the Lord *w'* distraction.
9: 18 the gospel of Christ *w'* charge,
21 To them that are *w'* law, as *w'* law,
21 not *w'* law to God, but under the law
21 I might gain them that are *w'* law.
11: 11 neither is the man *w'* the woman,
11 neither the woman *w'* the man, in
14: 7 even things *w'* life giving sound,
10 none of them is *w'* signification.
16: 10 that he may be with you *w'* fear:
2Co 7: 5 *w'* were fightings, within were
10: 13 boast of things *w'* our measure,
15 boasting of things *w'* our measure,
11: 28 Beside those things that are *w'*,
Eph 1: 4 and *w'* blame before him in love:
2: 12 at that time ye were *w'* Christ,
12 no hope, and *w'* God in the world:
3: 21 throughout all ages, world *w'* end.
5: 27 it should be holy and *w'* blemish.
Ph'p 1: 10 *w'* offence till the day of Christ,
14 bold to speak the word *w'* fear.
2: 14 Do all things *w'* murmurings
15 the sons of God, *w'* rebuke, in the
Col 2: 11 the circumcision made *w'* hands,
4: 5 wisdom toward them that are *w'*,
1Th 1: 3 Remembering *w'* ceasing your work
2: 13 also thank we God *w'* ceasing,
4: 12 honestly toward them that are *w'*,
5: 17 Pray *w'* ceasing.
1Ti 2: 8 hands, *w'* wrath and doubting.

1Ti 3: 7 good report of them which are *w*.;
16 *w*· controversy great is the mystery.
5: 21 *w*· preferring one before another,
6: 14 keep this commandment *w*· spot,
2Ti 1: 3 *w*· ceasing I have remembrance of
3: 3 *W*·...affection, trucebreakers,
Ph'm 14 *w*· thy mind would I do nothing;
Heb 4: 15 tempted like as we are, yet *w*· sin.
7: 3 *W*· father, [540] *w*· mother
3 *w*· descent, having neither
7 *w*· all contradiction the less is
20 not *w*· an oath he was made priest:
21 priests were made *w*· an oath;
9: 7 not *w*· blood, which he offered for
14 offered himself *w*· spot to God,
18 testament was dedicated *w*· blood.
22 and *w*· shedding of blood is no
28 second time *w*· sin unto salvation.
10: 23 profession of our faith *w*· wavering;
28 despised Moses' law died *w*· mercy
11: 6 *w*· faith it is impossible to please
40 *w*· us should not be made perfect.
12: 8 But if ye be *w*· chastisement,
14 *w*· which no man shall see the
13: 5 conversation be *w*· covetousness;
11 for sin, are burned *w*· the camp.
12 own blood, suffered *w*· the gate.
13 therefore unto him *w*· the camp,
Jas 2: 13 he shall have judgment *w*· mercy,
18 shew me thy faith *w*· thy works,
20 man, that faith *w*· works is dead?
26 as the body *w*· the spirit is dead,
26 so faith *w*· works is dead also.
3: 17 *w*· partiality, [87] and *w*· hypocrisy.
1Pe 1: 17 who *w*· respect of persons judgeth
19 lamb *w*· blemish [299] and *w*· spot:
3: 1 they also may *w*· the word be won
4: 9 one to another *w*· grudging.
2Pe 2: 17 These are wells *w*· water, clouds
3: 14 in peace, *w*· spot, and blameless.
Jude 12 you, feeding themselves *w*· fear:
12 clouds they are *w*· water, carried
12 *w*· fruit, twice dead, plucked up
Re 11: 2 court which is *w*· the temple leave
14: 5 *w*· fault before the throne of God.
10 poured out *w*· mixture into the cup
20 winepress was trodden *w*· the city,
22: 15 For *w*· are dogs, and sorcerers,

withs
J'g 16: 7 they bind me with seven green *w*·
8 brought up to her seven green *w*·
9 he brake the *w*·, as a thread of tow

withstand See also NOTWITHSTANDING; WITHSTOOD.
Nu 22: 32 I went out to *w*· thee, because thy
2Ch 13: 7 and could not *w*· them.
8 to *w*· the kingdom of the Lord
20: 6 so that none is able to *w*· thee?
Es 9: 2 and no man could *w*· them; for
Ec 4: 12 against him, two shall *w*· him;
Da 11: 15 the arms of the south shall not *w*·,
15 shall there be any strength to *w*·.
Ac 11: 17 what was I, that I could *w*· God?
Eph 6: 13 ye may be able to *w*· in the evil day,

withstood
2Ch 26: 18 And they *w*· Uzziah the king, and
Da 10: 13 of the kingdom of Persia *w*· me
Ac 13: 8 *w*· them, seeking to turn away the
Ga 2: 11 I *w*· him to the face, because he was
2Ti 3: 8 as Jannes and Jambres *w*· Moses,
4: 15 for he hath greatly *w*· our words.

witness See also EYEWITNESS; WITNESSED; WITNESSES; WITNESSETH; WITNESSING.
Ge 21: 30 that they may be a *w*· unto me,
31: 44 be for a *w*· between me and thee.
48 heap is a *w*· between me and thee
50 see, God is *w*· betwixt me and thee.
52 This heap be *w*·, and this pillar
52 and this pillar be *w*·, that I will
Ex 20: 16 shalt not bear false *w*· against thy.
22: 13 then let him bring it for *w*·, and he
23: 1 the wicked to be an unrighteous *w*·.
Le 5: 1 the voice of swearing, and is a *w*·,
Nu 5: 13 and there be no *w*· against her,
17: 7 the Lord in the tabernacle of *w*·.
8 went into the tabernacle of *w*·;
18: 2 before the tabernacle of *w*·.
35: 30 but one *w*· shall not testify against
De 4: 26 I call heaven and earth to *w*·
5: 20 shalt thou bear false *w*· against
17: 6 at the mouth of one *w*· he shall not
19: 15 One *w*· shall not rise up against a
16 a false *w*· rise up against any man
18 if the *w*· be a false *w*·, and hath
31: 19 that this song may be a *w*· for me
21 shall testify against them as a *w*·;
26 may be there for a *w*· against thee.
Jos 22: 27 But that it may be a *w*· between us,
28 but it is a *w*· between us and you.
34 be a *w*· between us that the Lord is
24: 27 this stone shall be a *w*· unto us;
27 it shall be therefore a *w*· unto you,
J'g 11: 10 The Lord be *w*· between us, if we
1Sa 12: 3 *w*· against me before the Lord,
5 The Lord is *w*· against you, and
5 and his anointed is *w*· this day,
5 And they answered, He is *w*·.
1Ki 21: 10 to bare *w*· against him, saying,
2Ch 24: 6 Israel, for the tabernacle of *w*·?
Job 16: 8 which is a *w*· against me:
8 up in me beareth *w*· to my face
19 my *w*· is in heaven, and my record
29: 11 the eye saw me, it gave *w*· to me:
Ps 89: 37 and as a faithful *w*· in heaven.

Pr 6: 19 A false *w*· that speaketh lies, and
12: 17 righteousness: but a false *w*· deceit.
14: 5 A faithful *w*· will not lie: but a false
5 lie: but a false *w*· will utter lies.
25 A true *w*· delivereth souls: but a
25 but a deceitful *w*· speaketh lies.
19: 5, 9 A false *w*· shall not be
28 An ungodly *w*· scorneth judgment:
21: 28 A false *w*· shall perish: but the
24: 28 Be not a *w*· against thy neighbour
25: 18 that beareth false *w*· against his
Isa 3: 9 countenance doth *w*· against them;
19: 20 it shall be for a sign and for a *w*·
55: 4 given him for a *w*· to the people,
Jer 29: 23 I know, and am a *w*·, saith the Lord.
42: 5 The Lord be a true and faithful *w*·
La 2: 13 thing shall I take to *w*· for thee?
Mic 1: 2 the Lord God be *w*· against you,
Mal 2: 14 the Lord hath been *w*· between
3: 5 a swift *w*· against the sorcerers,
M't 15: 19 thefts, false *w*·, blasphemies:
19: 18 steal, Thou shalt not bare false *w*·,
24: 14 preached in all the world for a *w*·
26: 59 sought false *w*· against Jesus,
62 is it which these *w*· against thee?
27: 13 many things they *w*· against thee?
M'r 10: 19 Do not bare false *w*·, Defraud not,
14: 55 sought for *w*· against Jesus
56 many bare false *w*· against him,
56 but their *w*· agreed not together.
57 and bare false *w*· against him,
59 neither so did their *w*· agree
60 is it which these *w*· against thee?
15: 4 many things they *w*· against thee.
Lu 4: 22 all bare him *w*·, and wondered at
11: 48 Truly ye bare *w*· that ye allow the
18: 20 Do not bare false *w*·, Honour thy
22: 71 What need we any further *w*·?
Joh 1: 7 The same came for a *w*·, to bear
7 to bear *w*· of the Light, that all
8 was sent to bear *w*· of that Light.
15 John bare *w*· of him, and cried,
3: 11 seen; and ye receive not our *w*·.
26 Jordan, to whom thou barest *w*·,
28 Ye yourselves bear me *w*·, that I
5: 31 If I bear *w*· of myself,
31 my *w*· is not true.
32 is another that beareth *w*· of me;
32 I know that the *w*· which he
33 and he bare *w*· unto the truth.
36 have greater *w*· than that of John:
36 works that I do, bear *w*· of me,
37 hath sent me, hath borne *w*· of me.
8: 18 I am one that bear *w*· of myself,
18 that sent me beareth *w*· of me.
10: 25 Father's name, they bear *w*· of me.
15: 27 ye also shall bear *w*·, because ye
18: 23 spoken evil, bear *w*· of the evil:
37 I should bear *w*· unto the truth.
Ac 1: 22 be a *w*· with us of his resurrection.
4: 33 the apostles *w*· of the resurrection
7: 44 tabernacle of *w*· in the wilderness,
10: 43 To him give all the prophets *w*·,
14: 17 he left not himself without *w*·,
15: 8 knoweth the hearts, bare them *w*·,
22: 5 the high priest doth bear me *w*·,
15 thou shalt be his *w*· unto all men
23: 11 must thou bear *w*· also at Rome.
26: 16 and a *w*· both of these things
Ro 1: 9 For God is my *w*·, whom I serve
2: 15 their conscience also bearing *w*·,
8: 16 itself beareth *w*· with our spirit,
9: 1 not, my conscience bearing me *w*·
13: 9 Thou shalt not bear false *w*·,
1Th 2: 5 a cloke of covetousness; God is *w*·:
Tit 1: 13 This *w*· is true. Wherefore rebuke
Heb 2: 4 God also bearing them *w*·, both
10: 15 the Holy Ghost also is a *w*· to us:
11: 4 obtained *w*· that he was righteous,
Jas 5: 3 the rust of them shall be a *w*·
1Pe 5: 1 a *w*· of the sufferings of Christ,
1Jo 1: 2 we have seen it, and bear *w*·,
5: 6 And it is the Spirit that beareth *w*·,
8 are three that bear *w*· in earth,
9 If we receive the *w*· of men,
9 the *w*· of God is greater:
9 this is the *w*· of God which he hath
10 Son of God hath the *w*· in himself:
3Jo 6 have borne *w*· of thy charity
Re 1: 5 Christ, who is the faithful *w*·,
3: 14 the faithful and the true *w*·, the
20: 4 beheaded for the *w*· of Jesus,

witnessed
1Ki 21: 13 the men of Belial *w*· against him,
Ro 3: 21 being *w*· by the law and the
1Ti 6: 13 Pontius Pilate *w*· a good confession;
Heb 7: 8 them, of whom it *w*· that he liveth.

witnesses See also EYEWITNESSES.
Nu 35: 30 be put to death by the mouth of *w*·:
De 17: 6 At the mouth of two *w*·,
6 or three *w*·, shall he that is worthy
7 The hands of the *w*· shall be first
19: 15 sinneth: at the mouth of two *w*·,
15 or at the mouth of three *w*·, shall
Jos 24: 22 Ye are *w*· against yourselves that
22 him. And they said, We are *w*·.
Ru 4: 9 Ye are *w*· this day, that I have
10 of his place: ye are *w*· this day.
11 and the elders, said, We are *w*·.
Job 10: 17 Thou renewest thy *w*· against me,
Ps 27: 12 false *w*· are risen up against me,
35: 11 False *w*· did rise up; they laid to
Isa 8: 2 took unto me faithful *w*· to record,
43: 9 let them bring forth their *w*·, that
10 Ye are my *w*·, saith the Lord, and

Isa 43: 12 ye are my *w*·, saith the Lord, that I
44: 8 declared it? ye are even my *w*·.
9 and they are their own *w*·; they
Jer 32: 10 evidence, and sealed it, and took *w*·
12 presence of the *w*· that subscribed
25 the field for money, and take *w*·;
44 take *w*· in the land of Benjamin,
M't 18: 16 in the mouth of two or three *w*·
23: 31 ye be *w*· unto yourselves, that
26: 60 though many false *w*· came, yet
60 At the last came two false *w*·,
65 what further need have we of *w*·?
M'r 14: 63 What need we any further *w*·?
Lu 24: 48 And ye are *w*· of these things.
Ac 1: 8 and ye shall be *w*· unto me both in
2: 32 raised up, whereof we all are *w*·.
3: 15 from the dead; whereof we are *w*·.
5: 32 And we are his *w*· of these things;
6: 13 And set up false *w*·, which said,
7: 58 and the *w*· laid down their clothes
10: 39 we are *w*· of all things which he did
41 but unto *w*· chosen before of God,
13: 31 who are his *w*· unto the people.
1Co 15: 15 and we are found false *w*· of God;
2Co 13: 1 In the mouth of two or three *w*·
1Th 2: 10 Ye are *w*·, and God also, how holily
1Ti 5: 19 but before two or three *w*·.
6: 12 a good profession before many *w*·.
2Ti 2: 2 hast heard of me among many *w*·,
Heb 10: 28 mercy unto two or three *w*·:
12: 1 about with so great a cloud of *w*·,
Re 11: 3 I will give power unto my two *w*·,

witnesseth
Joh 5: 32 witness which he *w*· of me is true.
Ac 20: 23 the Holy Ghost *w*· in every city,

witnessing
Ac 26: 22 *w*· both to small and great, saying

wit's
Ps 107: 27 man, and are at their *w*· end.

wittingly
Ge 48: 14 head, guiding his hands *w*·;

witty
Pr 8: 12 find out knowledge of *w*· inventions.

wives See also MIDWIVES; WIVES'.
Ge 4: 19 Lamech took unto him two *w*·: the
23 And Lamech said unto his *w*·, Adah
23 ye *w*· of Lamech, hearken unto my
6: 2 them *w*· of all which they chose.
18 wife, and thy sons' *w*· with thee.
7: 7 his sons' *w*· with him, into the ark,
13 the three *w*· of his sons with them,
8: 16 thy sons, and thy sons' *w*· with thee.
18 his wife, and his sons' *w*· with him:
11: 29 Abram and Nahor took them *w*·:
28: 9 and took unto the *w*· which he had
30: 26 Give me my *w*· and my children,
31: 17 set his sons and his *w*· upon camels;
50 take other *w*· beside my daughters,
32: 22 up that night, and took his two *w*·,
34: 21 us take their daughters to us for *w*·,
29 ones, and their *w*· took they captive,
36: 2 Esau took his *w*· of the daughters of
6 And Esau took his *w*·, and his sons,
37: 2 the sons of Zilpah, his father's *w*·:
45: 19 for your little ones, and for your *w*·,
46: 5 and their little ones, and their *w*·,
26 besides Jacob's sons' *w*·, all the souls
Ex 19: 15 the third day: come not at your *w*·.
22: 24 your *w*· shall be widows, and your
32: 2 which are in the ears of your *w*·,
Nu 14: 3 that our *w*· and our children should
16: 27 and their *w*·, and their sons, and
32: 26 Our little ones, our *w*·, our flocks,
De 3: 19 But your *w*·, and your little ones,
17: 17 Neither shall he multiply *w*· to
21: 15 If a man have two *w*·, one beloved,
29: 11 Your little ones, your *w*·, and thy
Jos 1: 14 Your *w*·, your little ones, and your
J'g 3: 6 took their daughters to be their *w*·,
8: 30 body begotten: for he had many *w*·.
21: 7 How shall we do for *w*· for them that
7 give them of our daughters to *w*·?
14 gave them *w*· which they had saved
16 How shall we do for *w*· for them that
18 not give them *w*· of our daughters:
23 and took them *w*·, according to
Ru 1: 4 them *w*· of the women of Moab;
1Sa 1: 2 And he had two *w*·; the name of the
25: 43 they were also both of them his *w*·.
27: 3 even David with his two *w*·,
30: 3 and their *w*·, and their sons, and
5 David's two *w*· were taken captives,
18 away: and David rescued his two *w*·.
2Sa 2: 2 up thither, and his two *w*· also,
5: 13 took him more concubines and *w*·
12: 8 and thy master's *w*· into thy bosom,
11 I will take thy *w*· before thine eyes,
11 he shall lie with thy *w*· in the sight
19: 5 daughters, and the lives of thy *w*·,
1Ki 11: 3 And he had seven hundred *w*·,
3 and his *w*· turned away his heart.
4 his *w*· turned away his heart after
8 did he for all his strange *w*·, which
20: 3 thy *w*· also and thy children, even
5 gold, and thy *w*·, and thy children;
7 for he sent unto me for my *w*·,
2Ki 4: 1 certain woman of the *w*· of the sons
24: 15 and the king's *w*·, and his officers,
1Ch 4: 5 the father of Tekoa had two *w*·,
7: 4 for they had many *w*· and sons.
8: 8 Hushim and Baara were his *w*·.
14: 3 And David took more *w*· at

2Ch 11: 21 of Absalom above all his w' and
21 (for he took eighteen w', and
23 And he desired many w'.
13: 21 mighty, and married fourteen w',
20: 13 ones, their w', and their children,
21: 14 and thy children, and thy w', and
17 and his sons also, and his w';
24: 3 And Jehoiada took for him two w';
29: 9 and our w' are in captivity for this.
31: 18 their w', and their sons, and their
Ezr 10: 2 have taken strange w' of the people
3 with our God to put away all the w',
10 and have taken strange w', to
11 the land, and from the strange w'.
14 have taken strange w' in our cities
17 the men that had taken strange w'
18 found that had taken strange w':
19 that they would put away their w';
44 All these had taken strange w': and
44 some of them had w' by whom they
Ne 4: 14 daughters, your w', and your houses.
5: 1 of their w' against their brethren
10: 28 their w', and their sons, and their
12: 43 w' also and the children rejoiced:
13: 23 Jews that had married w' of Ashdod,
27 our God in marrying strange w'?
Es 1: 20 w' shall give to their husbands
Isa 13: 16 be spoiled, and their w' ravished.
Jer 6: 12 with their fields and w' together:
8: 10 will I give their w' unto others,
14: 16 none to bury them, their w',
18: 21 let their w' be bereaved of their
29: 6 Take ye w', and begat sons and
6 take w' for your sons, and give your
23 adultery with their neighbours' w',
35: 8 our w', our sons, nor our daughters;
38: 23 So they shall bring out all thy w'
44: 9 and the wickedness of their w',
9 and the wickedness of your w',
15 that their w' had burned incense
25 Ye and your w' have both spoken
Eze 44: 22 shall they take for their w' a widow,
Da 5: 2 his w', and his concubines, might
3 his w', and his concubines, drank
23 thy w', and thy concubines, have
6: 24 them, their children, and their w';
Zec 12: 12 of David apart, and their w' apart;
12 of Nathan apart, and their w' apart;
13 of Levi apart, and their w' apart;
13 of Shimei apart, and their w'
14 family apart, and their w' apart.
M't 19: 8 suffered you to put away your w':
Lu 17: 27 they drank, they married w', they
Ac 21: 5 on our way, with w' and children,
1Co 7: 29 have w' be as though they had none;
Eph 5: 22 W', submit yourselves unto your
24 let the w' be to their own husbands
25 Husbands, love your w', even as
28 to love their w' as their own bodies.
Col 3: 18 W', submit yourselves unto your
19 Husbands, love your w', and be not
1Ti 3: 11 Even so must their w' be grave,
1Pe 3: 1 ye w', be in subjection to your own
1 won by the conversation of the w';

wives'
1Ti 4: 7 refuse profane and old w' fables,

wizard See also WIZARDS.
Le 20: 27 or that is a w', shall surely be put
De 18: 11 spirits, or a w', or a necromancer.

wizards
Le 19: 31 neither seek after w', to be defiled
20: 6 and after w', to go a whoring after
1Sa 28: 3 spirits, and the w', out of the land.
9 spirits, and the w', out of the land:
2Ki 21: 6 dealt with familiar spirits and w':
23: 24 with familiar spirits, and the w',
2Ch 33: 6 with a familiar spirit, and with w':
Isa 8: 19 unto w' that peep, and that mutter:
19: 3 have familiar spirits, and to the w'.

woe See also WOEFUL; WOES.
Nu 21: 29 W' to thee, Moab! thou art undone,
1Sa 4: 7 W' unto us! for there hath not
8 W' unto us! who shall deliver us
Job 10: 15 If I be wicked, w' unto me; and if I
Ps 120: 5 W' is me, that I sojourn in Mesech,
Pr 23: 29 Who hath w'? who hath sorrow?
Ec 4: 10 but w' to him that is alone when
10: 16 W' to thee, O land, when thy king
Isa 3: 9 W' unto their soul! for they have
11 W' unto the wicked! it shall be ill
5: 8 W' unto them that join house to
11 W' unto them that rise up early in
18 W' unto them that draw iniquity
20 W' unto them that call evil good,
21 W' unto them that are wise in
22 W' unto them that are mighty to
6: 5 said I, W' is me! for I am undone:
10: 1 W' unto them that decree
17: 12 W' to the multitude of many
18: 1 W' to the land shadowing with
24: 16 leanness, my leanness, w' unto me!
28: 1 W' to the crown of pride, to the
29: 1 W' to Ariel, to Ariel, the city
15 W' unto them that seek deep to
30: 1 W' to the rebellious children, saith
31: 1 W' to them that go down to Egypt
33: 1 W' to thee that spoilest, and thou
45: 9 W' unto him that striveth with his
10 W' unto him that saith unto his
Jer 4: 13 W' unto us! for we are spoiled.
31 W' is me now! for my soul is
6: 4 W' unto us! for the day goeth away,
10: 19 W' is me for my hurt! my wound
13: 27 W' unto thee, O Jerusalem! wilt
15: 10 W' is me, my mother, that thou
Jer 22: 13 W' unto him that buildeth his
23: 1 W' be unto the pastors that
45: 3 Thou didst say, W' is me now!
48: 1 W' unto Nebo! for it is spoiled:
46 W' be unto thee, O Moab! the
50: 27 w' unto them! for their day is
La 5: 16 w' unto us, that we have sinned!
Eze 2: 10 and mourning, and w'.
13: 3 W' unto the foolish prophets,
18 W' to the women that sew pillows
16: 23 (w', w' unto thee! saith the Lord
24: 6 W' to the bloody city, to the pot
9 W' to the bloody city! I will even
30: 2 God; Howl ye, W' worth the day!
34: 2 W' be to the shepherds of Israel
Ho 7: 13 W' unto them! for they have fled
9: 12 w' also to them when I depart
Am 5: 18 W' unto you that desire the day
6: 1 W' to them that are at ease in
Mic 2: 1 W' to them that devise iniquity,
7: 1 W' is me! for I am as when they
Na 3: 1 W' to the bloody city! it is all full
Hab 2: 6 W' to him that increaseth that
9 W' to him that coveteth an evil
12 W' to him that buildeth a town
15 W' unto him that giveth his
19 W' unto him that saith to the wood,
Zep 2: 5 W' unto the inhabitants of the sea
3: 1 W' to her that is filthy and
Zec 11: 17 W' to the idol shepherd that
M't 11: 21 W' unto thee, Chorazin!
21 w' unto thee, Bethsaida! for if the
18: 7 W' unto the world because of
7 but w' to that man by whom the
23: 13 w' unto you, scribes and Pharisees,
14 W' unto you, scribes and Pharisees,
15 W' unto you, scribes and Pharisees,
16 W' unto you, ye blind guides,
23, 25, 27, 29 W' unto you, scribes and
24: 19 w' unto them that are with child,
26: 24 w' unto that man by whom the Son
M'r 13: 17 w' to them that are with child, and
14: 21 w' to that man by whom the Son of
Lu 6: 24 But w' unto you that are rich!
25 W' unto you that are full! for ye
25 W' unto you that laugh now! for
26 W' unto you, when all men shall
10: 13 W' unto thee, Chorazin!
13 w' unto thee, Bethsaida! for if the
11: 42 But w' unto you, Pharisees! for ye
43 W' unto you, Pharisees! for ye
44 W' unto you, scribes and Pharisees,
46 W' unto you also, ye lawyers!
47 W' unto you! for ye build the
52 W' unto you, lawyers! for ye have
17: 1 w' unto him, through whom they
21: 23 w' unto them that are with child,
22: 22 w' unto that man by whom he is
1Co 9: 16 w' is unto me, if I preach not the
Jude 11 W' unto them! for they have gone
Re 8: 13 W', w', w', to the inhabiters of the
9: 12 One w' is past; and, behold, there
11: 14 The second w' is past; and,
14 behold, the third w' cometh quickly.
12: 12 W' to the inhabiters of the earth

woeful
Jer 17: 16 neither have I desired the w' day;

woes
Re 9: 12 there come two w' more hereafter.

wolf See also WOLVES.
Ge 49: 27 Benjamin shall ravin as a w':
Isa 11: 6 w' also shall dwell with the lamb,
65: 25 The w' and the lamb shall feed
Jer 5: 6 and a w' of the evenings shall spoil
Joh 10: 12 seeth the w' coming, and leaveth
12 and the w' catcheth them, and

wolves
Eze 22: 27 are like w' ravening the prey,
Hab 1: 8 more fierce than the evening w':
Zep 3: 3 her judges are evening w'; they
M't 7: 15 but inwardly they are ravening w'.
10: 16 forth as sheep in the midst of w':
Lu 10: 3 send you forth as lambs among w'.
Ac 20: 29 grievous w' enter in among you,

woman^A See also BONDWOMAN; FREEWOMAN; KINSWOMAN; WOMANKIND; WOMAN'S; WOMEN.
Ge 2: 22 made he a w', and brought her
23 she shall be called W', because she
3: 1 he said unto the w', Yea, hath God
2 w' said unto the serpent, We may
4 serpent said unto the w', Ye shall
6 the w' saw that the tree was good
12 The w' whom thou gavest to be
13 Lord God said unto the w', what is
13 w' said, The serpent beguiled me,
15 put enmity between thee and the w',
16 Unto the w' he said, I will greatly
12: 11 that thou art a fair w' to look upon:
14 the Egyptians beheld the w' that she
15 w' was taken into Pharaoh's house.
20: 3 for the w' which thou hast taken;
24: 5 w' will not be willing to follow me
8 if the w' will not be willing to follow
39 Peradventure the w' will not follow
44 same be the w' whom the Lord
46: 10 and Shaul the son of a Canaanitish w'.
Ex 2: 2 the w' conceived and bare a son:
9 w' took the child, and nursed it.
3: 22 But every w' shall borrow of her
6: 15 and Shaul the son of a Canaanitish w':
11: 2 every w' of her neighbour, jewels
21: 22 men strive, and hurt a w' with child,
28 If an ox gore a man or a w', that
29 that he hath killed a man or a w';
Ex 35: 29 every man and w', whose heart
36: 6 neither man nor w' make any more
Le 12: 2 If a w' have conceived seed, and
13: 29 If a man or w' have a plague upon
38 a man also or a w' have in the skin
15: 18 The w' also with whom man shall
19 And if a w' have an issue, and her
25 if a w' have an issue of her blood
33 issue, of the man, and of the w',
18: 17 not uncover the nakedness of a w'
19 not approach unto a w' to uncover
23 neither shall any w' stand before a
19: 20 whosoever lieth carnally with a w',
20: 13 as he lieth with a w', both of them
16 And if a w' approach unto any beast,
16 thou shalt kill the w', and the beast:
18 lie with a w' having her sickness,
27 or w' that hath a familiar spirit,
21: 7 neither shall they take a w' put away
24: 10 And the son of an Israelitish w',
10 and this son of the Israelitish w'
Nu 5: 6 man or w' shall commit any sin
18 shall set the w' before the Lord,
19 say unto the w', If no man have lain
21 shall charge the w' with an oath of
21 and the priest shall say unto the w',
22 And the w' shall say, Amen, amen.
24 cause the w' to drink the bitter
26 cause the w' to drink the water.
27 the w' shall be a curse among her
28 And if the w' be not defiled, but be
30 and shall set the w' before the Lord,
31 and this w' shall bear her iniquity.
6: 2 either man or w' shall separate
12: 1 Ethiopian w' whom he had married:
1 for he had married an Ethiopian w'.
25: 6 a Midianitish w' in the sight of Moses,
8 and the w' through her belly.
15 Midianitish w' that was slain was
30: 3 a w' also vow a vow unto the Lord,
31: 17 kill every w' that hath known man
De 15: 12 or an Hebrew w', be sold unto thee,
17: 2 man or w', that hath wrought
5 bring forth that man or that w',
5 gates, even that man or that w',
21: 11 among the captives a beautiful w',
22: 5 The w' shall not wear that which
14 I took this w', and when I came to
22 found lying with a w' married to an
22 both the man that lay with the w',
22 and the w': so shalt thou put away
28: 56 The tender and delicate w' among you,
29: 18 should be among you man, or w',
Jos 2: 4 w' took the two men, and hid them,
6: 21 both man and w', young and old,
22 house, and bring out thence the w',
J'g 4: 9 shall sell Sisera into the hand of a w'.
9: 53 And a certain w' cast a piece of a
54 men say not of me, A w' slew him.
11: 2 for thou art the son of a strange w'.
13: 3 of the Lord appeared unto the w',
6 the w' came and told her husband,
9 angel of God came again unto the w'
10 w' made haste, and ran, and told
11 the man that spakest unto the w'?
13 I said unto the w' let her beware.
24 And the w' bare a son, and called
14: 1 and saw a w' in Timnath of the
2 I have seen a w' in Timnath of the
3 never a w' among the daughters
7 went down, and talked with the w';
10 So his father went down unto the w':
16: 4 loved a w' in the valley of Sorek,
19: 26 came the w' in the dawning of the
27 the w' his concubine was fallen
20: 4 husband of the w' that was slain,
21: 11 and every w' that hath lain by man.
Ru 1: 5 and the w' was left of her two sons
3: 8 and, behold, a w' lay at his feet.
11 know that thou art a virtuous w'.
14 not be known that a w' came into
4: 11 The Lord make the w' that is come
12 Lord shall give thee of this young w'.
1Sa 1: 15 lord, I am a w' of a sorrowful spirit:
18 So the w' went her way, and did eat,
23 So the w' abode, and gave her son
26 I am the w' that stood by thee here,
2: 20 The Lord give thee seed of this w'
15: 3 but slay both man and w', infant and
20: 30 Thou son of the perverse rebellious w',
25: 3 she was a w' of good understanding,
27: 9 and left neither man nor w' alive,
11 And David saved neither man nor w'
28: 7 a w' that hath a familiar spirit,
7 is a w' that hath a familiar spirit
8 and they came to the w' by night:
9 the w' said unto him, Behold, thou
11 said the w', Whom shall I bring
11 when the w' saw Samuel, she cried
12 and the w' spake to Saul, saying,
13 the w' said unto Saul, I saw gods
21 the w' came unto Saul, and saw that
23 together with the w', compelled him;
24 the w' had a fat calf in the house;
2Sa 3: 8 day with a fault concerning this w'?
11: 2 roof he saw a w' washing herself;
2 w' was very beautiful to look upon.
3 David sent and enquired after the w'.
5 the w' conceived, and sent and told
21 did not a w' cast a piece of a
13: 17 put now this w' out from me, and bolt
14: 2 and fetched thence a wise w',
2 be as a w' that had a long time
4 when the w' of Tekoah spake to
5 answered, I am indeed a widow w',
8 king said unto the w', Go to thine

2Sa 14: 9 *w*· of Tekoah said unto the king,
12 the *w*· said, Let thine handmaid,
13 the *w*· said, Wherefore then hast
18 king answered and said unto the *w*·,
18 the *w*· said, Let my lord the king
19 the *w*· answered and said, As thy
27 she was a *w*· of a fair countenance.
17: 19 the *w*· took and spread a covering
20 Absalom's servants came to the *w*·
20 And the *w*· said unto them, They be
20: 16 Then cried a wise *w*· out of the city,
17 unto her, the *w*· said, Art thou Joab?
21 And the *w*· said unto Joab, Behold,
22 the *w*· went unto all the people
1Ki 3: 17 And the one *w*· said, O my lord, I
17 I and this *w*· dwell in one house;
18 that this *w*· was delivered also:
22 the other *w*· said, Nay; but the
26 Then spake the *w*· whose the living
11: 26 name was Zeruah, a widow *w*·,
14: 5 shall feign herself to be another *w*·.
17: 9 a widow *w*· there to sustain thee.
10 widow *w*· was...gathering of sticks:
17 that the son of the *w*·, the mistress
24 the *w*· said to Elijah, Now by this
2Ki 4: 1 Now there cried a certain *w*· of the
8 to Shunem, where was a great *w*·;
17 the *w*· conceived, and bare a son
6: 26 there cried a *w*· unto him, saying,
28 This *w*· said unto me, Give thy son,
30 the king heard the words of the *w*·,
8: 1 Then spake Elisha unto the *w*·,
2 And the *w*· arose, and did after the
3 the *w*· returned out of the land of
5 the *w*·, whose son he had restored
5 O king, this is the *w*·, and this is
6 when the king asked the *w*·, she
9: 34 see now this cursed *w*·, and bury her:
1Ch 16: 3 both man and *w*·, to every one a
2Ch 2: 14 son of a *w*· of the daughters of Dan,
15: 13 small or great, whether man or *w*·.
24: 7 sons of Athaliah, that wicked *w*·,
Es 4: 11 whether man or *w*·, shall come
Job 14: 1 Man that is born of a *w*· is of few
15: 14 he which is born of a *w*·, that he
25: 4 can he be clean that is born of a *w*·?
31: 9 heart have been deceived by a *w*·,
Ps 48: 6 and pain, as of a *w*· in travail.
58: 8 like the untimely birth of a *w*·,
113: 9 maketh the barren *w*· to keep house,
Pr 2: 16 deliver thee from the strange *w*·,
6: 24 To keep thee from the evil *w*·,
24 of the tongue of a strange *w*·.
26 by means of a whorish *w*· a man is
32 committeth adultery with a *w*·
7: 5 may keep thee from the strange *w*·,
10 met him a *w*· with the attire of a
9: 13 A foolish *w*· is clamorous: she is
11: 16 A gracious *w*· retaineth honour:
22 fair *w*· which is without discretion.
12: 4 A virtuous *w*· is a crown to her
14: 1 Every wise *w*· buildeth her house:
20: 16 a pledge of him for a strange *w*·.
21: 9 with a brawling *w*· in a wide house.
19 a contentious and an angry *w*·.
23: 27 and a strange *w*· is a narrow pit.
25: 24 a brawling *w*· in a wide house.
27: 13 a pledge of him for a strange *w*·.
15 and a contentious *w*· are alike.
30: 20 Such is the way of an adulterous *w*·;
23 an odious *w*· when she is married;
31: 10 Who can find a virtuous *w*·? for
30 a *w*· that feareth the Lord, she
Ec 7: 26 find more bitter than death the *w*·,
28 a *w*· among all those have I not
Isa 13: 8 be in pain as a *w*· that travaileth:
21: 3 as the pangs of a *w*· that travaileth:
26: 17 Like as a *w*· with child, that draweth
42: 14 now will I cry like a travailing *w*·;
45: 10 or to the *w*·, What hast thou
49: 15 Can a *w*· forget her sucking child,
54: 6 as a *w*· forsaken and grieved in
Jer 4: 31 heard a voice as of a *w*· in travail,
6: 2 of Zion to a comely and delicate *w*·.
24 of us, and pain, as of a *w*· in travail.
13: 21 take thee, as a *w*· in travail?
22: 23 thee, the pain as of a *w*· in travail!
30: 6 hands on his loins, as a *w*· in travail,
31: 8 lame, the *w*· with child and her that
22 earth, A *w*· shall compass a man.
44: 7 to cut off from you man and *w*·,
48: 41 be as the heart of a *w*· in her pangs.
49: 22 be as the heart of a *w*· in her pangs.
24 have taken her, as a *w*· in travail.
50: 43 him, and pangs as of a *w*· in travail.
51: 22 will I break in pieces man and *w*·;
La 1: 17 Jerusalem is as a menstruous *w*·
Eze 16: 30 work of an imperious whorish *w*·;
18: 6 hath come near to a menstruous *w*·,
23: 44 unto a *w*· that playeth the harlot:
44 unto Aholibah, the lewd *w*·.
36: 17 as the uncleanness of a removed *w*·.
Ho 3: 1 love a *w*· beloved of her friend,
13: 13 sorrows of a travailing *w*· shall come
Mic 4: 9 have taken thee as a *w*· in travail.
10 daughter of Zion, like a *w*· in travail;
Zec 5: 7 this is a *w*· that sitteth in the midst
M't 5: 28 whosoever looketh on a *w*· to lust
9: 20 a *w*·, which was diseased with an
22 the *w*· was made whole from that
13: 33 like unto leaven, which a *w*· took,
15: 22 a *w*· of Canaan came out of the
28 unto her, O *w*·, great is thy faith:
22: 27 And last of all the *w*· died also.
26: 7 him a *w*· having an alabaster box of
10 unto them, Why trouble ye the *w*·?

M't 26: 13 that this *w*· hath done, be told for
M'r 5: 25 certain *w*·, which had an issue of
33 But the *w*· fearing and trembling,
7: 25 a certain *w*·, whose young daughter
26 The *w*· was a Greek, a
10: 12 if a *w*· shall put away her husband,
12: 22 seed: last of all the *w*· died also.
14: 3 came a *w*· having an alabaster box
Lu 4: 26 unto a *w*· that was a widow.
7: 37 behold, a *w*· in the city, which was
39 what manner of *w*· this is that
44 he turned to the *w*·, and said unto
44 said unto Simon, Seest thou this *w*·?
45 this *w*· since the time I came in
46 this *w*· hath anointed my feet with
50 he said to the *w*·, Thy faith hath
8: 43 a *w*· having an issue of blood
47 the *w*· saw that she was not hid,
10: 38 a certain *w*· named Martha
11: 27 certain *w*· of the company lifted up
13: 11 there was a *w*· which had a spirit
12 *W*·, thou art loosed from thine
16 And ought not this *w*·, being a
21 which a *w*· took and hid in three
15: 8 what *w*· having ten pieces of silver,
20: 32 Last of all the *w*· died also.
22: 57 him, saying, *W*·, I know him not.
Joh 2: 4 *W*·, what have I to do with thee?
4: 7 a *w*· of Samaria to draw water:
9 saith the *w*· of Samaria unto him,
9 of me, which am a *w*· of Samaria?
11 *w*· saith unto him, Sir, Thou hast
15 The *w*· saith unto him, Sir, give
17 The *w*· answered and said, I have
19 The *w*· saith unto him, Sir, I
21 *W*·, believe me, the hour cometh,
25 The *w*· saith unto him, I know that
27 that he talked with the *w*·:
28 The *w*· then left her waterpot, and
39 on him for the saying of the *w*·,
42 said unto the *w*·, Now we believe,
8: 3 brought unto him a *w*· taken in
4 this *w*· was taken in adultery,
9 and the *w*· standing in the midst.
10 saw none but the *w*·, he said unto
10 *W*·, where are...thine accusers?
16: 21 A *w*· when she is in travail hath
19: 26 his mother, *W*·, behold thy son!
20: 13, 15 unto her, *W*·, why weepest thou?
Ac 9: 36 this *w*· was full of good works
16: 1 Timotheus, the son of a certain *w*·,
14 a certain *w*· named Lydia, a seller
17: 34 a *w*· named Damaris, and others
Ro 1: 27 leaving the natural use of the *w*·,
7: 2 *w*· which hath an husband is bound
1Co 7: 1 good for a man not to touch a *w*·.
2 every *w*· have her own husband.
13 the *w*· which hath an husband
34 *w*· careth for the things of the Lord,
11: 3 the head of the *w*· is the man;
5 *w*· that prayeth or prophesieth
6 if the *w*· be not covered, let her
6 it be a shame for a *w*· to be shorn
7 but the *w*· is the glory of the man.
8 For the man is not of the *w*·;
8 but the *w*· of the man.
9 was the man created for the *w*·;
9 but the *w*· for the man.
10 cause ought the *w*· to have power
11 neither is the man without the *w*·,
11 neither the *w*· without the man,
12 For as the *w*· is of the man, even so
12 even so is the man also by the *w*·;
13 a *w*· pray unto God uncovered?
15 if a *w*· have long hair, it is a glory
Ga 4: 4 sent forth his Son, made of a *w*·,
1Th 5: 3 as travail upon a *w*· with child;
1Ti 2: 11 Let the *w*· learn in silence with
12 I suffer not a *w*· to teach, nor to
14 but the *w*· being deceived was in
5: 16 If any man or *w*· that believeth have
Re 2: 20 thou sufferest that *w*· Jezebel,
12: 1 a *w*· clothed with the sun, and the
4 *w*· which was ready to be delivered,
6 *w*· fled into the wilderness, where
13 *w*· which brought forth the man
14 to the *w*· were given two wings
15 mouth water as a flood after the *w*·,
16 the earth helped the *w*·, and the
17 the dragon was wroth with the *w*·,
17: 3 a *w*· sit upon a scarlet coloured
4 *w*· was arrayed in purple and
6 I saw the *w*· drunken with the
7 tell thee the mystery of the *w*·,
9 mountains, on which the *w*· sitteth.
18 *w*· which thou sawest is that great

womankind
Le 18: 22 not lie with mankind, as with *w*·:

woman's
Ge 38: 20 his pledge from the *w*· hand:
Ex 21: 22 according as the *w*· husband will
Le 24: 11 Israelitish *w*· son blasphemed the
Nu 5: 18 uncover the *w*· head, and put the
25 jealousy offering out of the *w*· hand,
De 22: 5 shall a man put on a *w*· garment:
1Ki 3: 19 And this *w*· child died in the night;

womb See also WOMBS.
Ge 25: 23 Two nations are in thy *w*·, and two
24 behold, there were twins in her *w*·.
29: 31 Leah was hated, he opened her *w*·:
30: 2 from thee the fruit of the *w*·?
22 to her, and opened her *w*·.
38: 27 that, behold, twins were in her *w*·.
49: 25 of the beasts, and of the *w*·:
Ex 13: 2 whatsoever openeth the *w*· among

Nu 8: 16 instead of such as open every *w*·,
12: 12 he cometh out of his mother's *w*·.
De 7: 13 will also bless the fruit of thy *w*·,
J'g 13: 5 be a Nazarite unto God from the *w*·:
7 be a Nazarite to God from the *w*·
16: 17 unto God from my mother's *w*·:
Ru 1: 11 there yet any more sons in my *w*·,
1Sa 1: 5 but the Lord had shut up her *w*·.
6 the Lord had shut up her *w*·.
Job 1: 21 came I out of my mother's *w*·, and
3: 10 not up the doors of my mother's *w*·,
11 Why died I not from the *w*·? why
10: 18 brought me forth out of the *w*·?
19 carried from the *w*· to the grave.
24: 20 The *w*· shall forget him; the worm
31: 15 that made me in the *w*· make him?
15 did not one fashion us in the *w*·?
18 guided her from my mother's *w*·;)
38: 8 as if it had issued out of the *w*·?
29 Out of whose *w*· came the ice?
Ps 22: 9 art he that took me out of the *w*·:
10 I was cast upon thee from the *w*·:
58: 3 wicked are estranged from the *w*·:
71: 6 have I been holden up from the *w*·:
110: 3 from the *w*· of the morning:
127: 3 the fruit of the *w*· is his reward.
139: 13 hast covered me in my mother's *w*·.
Pr 30: 16 The grave; and the barren *w*·;
31: 2 son? and what, the son of my *w*·?
Ec 5: 15 As he came forth of his mother's *w*·,
11: 5 the bones do grow in the *w*· of her
Isa 13: 18 have no pity on the fruit of the *w*·;
44: 2 thee, and formed thee from the *w*·,
24 he that formed thee from the *w*·,
46: 3 which are carried from the *w*·:
48: 8 called a transgressor from the *w*·.
49: 1 Lord hath called me from the *w*·;
5 formed me from the *w*· to be his
15 compassion on the son of her *w*·?
66: 9 cause to bring forth, and shut the *w*·?
Jer 1: 5 thou camest forth out of the *w*· I
20: 17 he slew me not from the *w*·;
17 her *w*· to be always great with me.
18 I forth out of the *w*· to see labour
Eze 20: 26 the fire all that openeth the *w*·,
Ho 9: 11 from the birth, and from the *w*·,
14 give them a miscarrying *w*· and
16 even the beloved fruit of their *w*·.
12: 3 his brother by the heel in the *w*·,
M't 19: 12 so born from their mother's *w*·:
Lu 1: 15 Ghost, even from his mother's *w*·.
31 thou shalt conceive in thy *w*·, and
41 the babe leaped in her *w*·; and
42 and blessed is the fruit of thy *w*·.
44 the babe leaped in my *w*· for joy.
2: 21 before he was conceived in the *w*·.
23 Every male that openeth the *w*·
11: 27 Blessed is the *w*· that bare thee,
Joh 3: 4 second time into his mother's *w*·,
Ac 3: 2 man lame from his mother's *w*· was
14: 8 a cripple from his mother's *w*·,
Ro 4: 19 yet the deadness of Sarah's *w*·:
Ga 1: 15 me from my mother's *w*·, and

wombs
Ge 20: 18 Lord had fast closed up all the *w*·
Lu 23: 29 and the *w*· that never bare, and

women See also BONDWOMEN; KINSWOMEN; WOMEN'S; WOMENSERVANTS.
Ge 14: 16 and the *w*· also, and the people.
18: 11 with Sarah after the manner of *w*·.
31: 35 for the custom of *w*· is upon me.
33: 5 and saw the *w*· and the children;
Ex 1: 16 office of a midwife to the Hebrew *w*·,
19 *w*· are not as the Egyptian *w*·;
2: 7 call to thee a nurse of the Hebrew *w*·,
15: 20 all the *w*· went out after her with
35: 22 And they came, both men and *w*·,
25 all the *w*· that were wise hearted
26 all the *w*· whose heart stirred them
38: 8 lookingglasses of the *w*· assembling,
Le 26: 26 ten *w*· shall bake your bread in one
Nu 31: 9 took all the *w*· of Midian captives,
15 Have ye save all the *w*· alive?
18 all the *w*· children, that have not
35 of *w*· that had not known man by
De 2: 34 destroyed the men, and the *w*·, and
3: 6 utterly destroying the men, *w*·, and
20: 14 But the *w*·, and the little ones, and
31: 12 the people together, men, and *w*·,
Jos 8: 25 fell that day, both of men and *w*·,
35 congregation of Israel, with the *w*·,
J'g 5: 24 Blessed above *w*· shall Jael the wife
24 blessed shall she be above *w*· in the
9: 49 also, about a thousand men and *w*·.
51 and thither fled all the men and *w*·,
16: 27 the house was full of men and *w*·;
27 about three thousand men and *w*·,
21: 10 sword, with the *w*· and the children.
14 alive of the *w*· of Jabesh-gilead:
16 *w*· are destroyed out of Benjamin?
Ru 1: 4 took them wives of the *w*· of Moab;
4: 14 *w*· said unto Naomi, Blessed be
17 the *w*· her neighbours gave it a name,
1Sa 2: 22 how they lay with the *w*· that
4: 20 time of her death the *w*· that stood by
15: 33 thy sword hath made *w*· childless,
33 thy mother be childless among *w*·.
18: 6 *w*· came out of all cities of Israel,
7 *w*· answered one another as they
21: 4 kept themselves at least from *w*·.
5 Of a truth *w*· have been kept from us
22: 19 edge of the sword, both men and *w*·,
30: 2 had taken the *w*· captives, that were
2Sa 1: 26 wonderful, passing the love of *w*·.
6: 19 as well to the *w*· as men, to every

2Sa 15:16 the king left ten w', which were
19:35 voice of singing men and singing w'?
20: 3 and the king took the ten w' his
1Ki 3:16 Then came there two w', that were
11: 1 Solomon loved many strange w',
1 w' of the Moabites, Ammonites,
2Ki 8:12 and rip up their w' with child.
15:16 w' therein that were with child he
23: 7 the w' wove hangings for the grove.
2Ch 28: 8 thousand, w', sons, and daughters,
35:25 singing w' spake of Josiah in their
Ezr 2:65 hundred singing men and singing w'.
10: 1 great congregation of men and w'
Ne 7:67 and five singing men and singing w'.
8: 2 congregation both of men and w',
3 before the men and the w', and
13:26 him did outlandish w' cause to sin.
Es 1: 9 the queen made a feast for the w'
17 queen shall come abroad unto all w',
2: 3 the palace, to the house of the w',
3 chamberlain, keeper of the w';
8 custody of Hegai, keeper of the w'.
9 best place of the house of the w'.
12 according to the manner of the w',
12 things for the purifying of the w';)
13 house of the w' unto the king's house.
14 into the second house of the w',
15 chamberlain, the keeper of the w',
17 king loved Esther above all the w',
3:13 young and old, little children and w',
8:11 both little ones and w', and to take
Job 42:15 all the land were no w' found so fair
Ps 45: 9 were among thy honourable w':
Pr 22:14 mouth of strange w' is a deep pit:
31: 3 Give not thy strength unto w', nor
Ec 2: 8 I gat me men singers and w' singers,
Ca 1: 8 know not, O thou fairest among w',
5: 9 beloved, O thou fairest among w'?
6: 1 gone, O thou fairest among w'?
Isa 3:12 oppressors, and w' rule over them.
4: 1 seven w' shall take hold of one man,
19:16 day shall Egypt be like unto w':
27:11 the w' come, and set them on fire:
32: 9 Rise up, ye w' that are at ease; hear
11 Tremble, ye w' that are at ease; be
Jer 7:18 the w' knead their dough, to make
9:17 ye, and call for the mourning w',
17 send for cunning w', that they may
20 hear the word of the Lord, O ye w',
38:22 all the w' that are left in the king
22 and those w' shall say, Thy friends
40: 7 committed unto him men, and w',
41:16 and the w', and the children, and
43: 6 Even men, and w', and children,
44:15 and all the w' that stood by, a great
20 to the men, and to the w', and to all
24 and to all the w', Hear the word
50:37 her; and they shall become as w':
51:30 hath failed; they became as w':
La 2:20 Shall the w' eat their fruit, and
4:10 pitiful w' have sodden their own
5:11 They ravished the w' in Zion, and
Eze 8:14 there sat w' weeping for Tammuz.
9: 6 maids, and little children, and w':
13:18 Woe to the w' that sew pillows to all
16:34 from other w' in thy whoredoms,
38 judge thee, as w' that break wedlock
41 upon thee in the sight of many w':
23: 2 there were two w', the daughters
10 and she became famous among w';
44 and unto Aholibah, the lewd w'.
48 that all w' may be taught not to do
Da 11:17 shall give him the daughter of w',
37 nor the desire of w', nor regard any
Ho 13:16 their w' with child shall be ripped up.
Am 1:13 they have ripped up the w' with child
Mic 2: 9 w' of my people have ye cast out
Na 3:13 people in the midst of thee are w':
Zec 5: 9 behold, there came out two w',
8: 4 men and old w' dwell in the streets
14: 2 houses rifled, and the w' ravished;
M't 11:11 Among them that are born of w'
14:21 five thousand men, beside w' and
15:38 four thousand men, beside w' and
24:41 Two w' shall be grinding at the mill;
27:55 many w' were there beholding
28: 5 answered and said unto the w',
M'r 15:40 were also w' looking on afar off:
41 other w' which came up with him
Lu 1:28 blessed art thou among w'.
42 said, Blessed art thou among w',
7:28 Among those that are born of w'
8: 2 certain w', which had been healed
17:35 Two w' shall be grinding together;
23:27 company of people, and of w',
49 w' that followed him from Galilee,
55 the w' also, which came with him
24:10 and other w' that were with them,
22 and certain w' also of our company
24 it even so as the w' had said:
Ac 1:14 and supplication, with the w',
5:14 multitudes both of men and w'.)
8: 3 haling men and w' committed them
12 were baptized, both men and w'.
9: 2 whether they were men or w', he
13:50 the devout and honourable w',
16:13 spake unto the w' which resorted
17: 4 and of the chief w' not a few.
12 honourable w' which were Greeks,
22: 4 into prisons both men and w'.
Ro 1:26 their w' did change the natural use
1Co 14:34 w' keep silence in the churches:
35 for w' to speak in the church.
Ph'p 4: 3 help those w' which laboured with me
1Ti 2: 9 w' adorn themselves in modest
10 (which becometh w' professing
1Ti 5: 2 The elder w' as mothers; the younger
14 therefore that the younger w' marry,
2Ti 3: 6 captive silly w' laden with sins,
Tit 2: 3 The aged w' likewise, that they be
4 may teach the young w' to be sober,
Heb 11:35 W' received their dead raised to
1Pe 3: 5 in the old time the holy w' also,
Re 9: 8 they had hair as the hair of w'
14: 4 which were not defiled with w';

women's
Es 2:11 before the court of the w' house,

womenservants
Ge 20:14 and w', and gave them unto
32: 5 flocks, and menservants, and w':
22 his two w', and his eleven sons,

won
1Ch 26:27 Out of the spoils w' in battles did they
Pr 18:19 brother offended is harder to be w'
1Pe 3: 1 may without the word be w'

wonder See also WONDERED; WONDERFUL; WONDERING; WONDERS.
De 13: 1 and giveth thee a sign of a w',
2 the sign or the w' come to pass,
28:46 upon thee for a sign and for a w',
2Ch 32:31 enquire of the w' that was done
Ps 71: 7 I am as a w' unto many; but thou
Isa 20: 3 for a sign and w' upon Egypt
29: 9 Stay yourselves, and w'; cry ye
14 even a marvellous work and a w':
Jer 4: 9 and the prophets shall w'.
Hab 1: 5 and regard, and w' marvellously:
Ac 3:10 and they were filled with w' and
13:41 Behold, ye despisers, and w',
Re 12: 1 appeared a great w' in heaven;
3 appeared another w' in heaven;
17: 8 that dwell on the earth shall w',

wondered
Isa 59:16 w' that there was no intercessor:
63: 5 w' that there was none to uphold:
Zec 3: 8 thee: for they are men w' at:
M't 15:31 Insomuch that the multitude w',
M'r 6:51 beyond measure, and w'.
Lu 2:18 that heard it w' at those things
4:22 and w' at the gracious words which
8:25 they being afraid w', saying one to
9:43 they w' every one at all things
11:14 dumb spake; and the people w'.
24:41 they yet believed not for joy, and w',
Ac 7:31 Moses saw it, he w' at the sight:
8:13 and w', beholding the miracles
Re 13: 3 and all the world w' after the beast.
17: 6 her, I w' with great admiration.

wonderful
De 28:59 the Lord will make thy plagues w',
2Sa 1:26 thy love to me was w', passing the
2Ch 2: 9 am about to build shall be w' great.
Job 42: 3 things too w' for me, which I knew
Ps 40: 5 thy w' works which thou hast done,
78: 4 and his w' works that he hath done.
107: 8,15,21,31 w' works to the children of
111: 4 his w' works to be remembered:
119:129 Thy testimonies are w':
139: 6 Such knowledge is too w' for me;
Pr 30:18 be three things which are too w'
Isa 9: 6 and his name shall be called W',
25: 1 for thou hast done w' things; thy
28:29 which is w' in counsel, and
Jer 5:30 w' and horrible thing is committed
M't 7:22 name done many w' works?
21:15 saw the w' things that he did,
Ac 2:11 our tongues the w' works of God.

wonderfully
1Sa 6: 6 he had wrought w' among them,
Ps 139:14 for I am fearfully and w' made:
La 1: 9 therefore she came down w': she
Da 8:24 and he shall destroy w', and shall

wondering
Ge 24:21 the man w' at her held his peace,
Lu 24:12 w' in himself at that which was
Ac 3:11 is called Solomon's, greatly w'.

wonderously See also WONDROUSLY.
J'g 13:19 and the angel did w'; and Manaoh

wonders
Ex 3:20 smite Egypt with all my w' which
4:21 do all those w' before Pharaoh,
7: 3 and my w' in the land of Egypt.
11: 9 that my w' may be multiplied in
10 did all these w' before Pharaoh:
15:11 fearful in praises, doing w'?
De 4:34 by signs, and by w', and by war,
6:22 And the Lord shewed signs and w',
7:19 and the w', and the mighty hand,
26: 8 and with signs and with w':
34:11 the w', which the Lord sent him to
Jos 3: 5 the Lord will do w' among you.
1Ch 16:12 his w', and the judgments of his
Ne 9:10 signs and w' upon Pharaoh,
17 neither were mindful of thy w'
Job 9:10 out; yea, and w' without number.
Ps 77:11 I will remember thy w' of old.
14 Thou art the God that doest w':
78:11 his w' that he had shewed them.
43 and his w' in the field of Zoan:
88:10 Wilt thou shew w' to the dead?
12 Shall thy w' be known in the dark?
89: 5 And the heavens shall praise thy w',
96: 3 heathen, his w' among all people.
105: 5 his w', and the judgments of his
27 them, and w' in the land of Ham.
106: 7 Our fathers understood not thy w'
107:24 the Lord, and his w' in the deep.
135: 9 Who sent tokens and w' into the
Ps 136: 4 To him who alone doeth great w':
Isa 8:18 for w' in Israel from the Lord
Jer 32:20 signs and w' in the land of Egypt,
21 with signs, and with w', and with a
Da 4: 2 w' that the high God hath wrought
3 and how mighty are his w'!
6:27 he worketh signs and w' in heaven
12: 6 shall it be to the end of these w'?
Joe 2:30 And I will shew w' in the heavens
M't 24:24 And shall shew great signs and w';
M'r 13:22 rise, and shall shew signs and w',
Joh 4:48 Except ye see signs and w', ye will
Ac 2:19 And I will shew w' in heaven above,
22 you by miracles and w' and signs,
43 and many w' and signs were done
4:30 and that signs and w' may be done
5:12 were many signs and w' wrought
6: 8 did great w' and miracles among
7:36 that he had shewed w' and signs
14: 3 granted signs and w' to be done
15:12 declaring what miracles and w' God
Ro 15:19 Through mighty signs and w', by
2Co 12:12 signs, and w', and mighty deeds.
2Th 2: 9 all power and signs and lying w',
Heb 2: 4 witness, both with signs and w',
Re 13:13 And he doeth great w', so that he

wondrous
1Ch 16: 9 him, talk ye of all his w' works.
Job 37:14 and consider the w' works of God.
16 w' work of him which is perfect
Ps 26: 7 and tell of all thy w' works.
71:17 have I declared thy w' works.
72:18 of Israel, who only doeth w' things.
75: 1 name is near thy w' works declare.
78:32 and believed not for his w' works.
86:10 thou art great, and doest w' things:
105: 2 him: talk ye of all his w' works.
106:22 W' works in the land of Ham, and
119:18 behold w' things out of thy law.
27 so shall I talk of thy w' works.
145: 5 of thy majesty, and of thy w' works.
Jer 21: 2 us according to all his w' works,

wondrously See also WONDEROUSLY.
Joe 2:26 God, that hath dealt w' with you:

wont
Ex 21:29 ox were w' to push with his horn
Nu 22:30 was I ever w' to do so unto thee?
1Sa 30:31 and his men were w' to haunt.
2Sa 20:18 They were w' to speak in old time,
Da 3:19 seven times more than it was w'
M't 27:15 governor was w' to release unto
M'r 10: 1 and, as he was w', he taught them
Lu 22:39 and went, as he was w', to
Ac 16:13 where prayer was w' to be made;

wood^ See also WOODS; WORMWOOD.
Ge 6:14 Make thee an ark of gopher w';
22: 3 clave the w' for the burnt offering,
6 took the w' of the burnt offering,
7 he said, Behold the fire and the w':
9 and laid the w' in order, and bound
9 laid him on the altar upon the w'.
Ex 7:19 both in vessels of w', and in vessels
25: 5 and badgers' skins, and shittim w',
10 shall make an ark of shittim w':
13 shalt make staves of shittim w',
23 also make a table of shittim w':
28 shalt make the staves of shittim w',
26:15 for the tabernacle of shittim w'
26 thou shalt make bars of shittim w';
32 four pillars of shittim w' overlaid
27: 1 shalt make an altar of shittim w',
6 staves of shittim w', and overlay
30: 1 of shittim w' shalt thou make it.
5 shalt make the staves of shittim w',
35: 7 and badgers' skins, and shittim w',
24 with whom was found shittim w'
33 and in carving of w', to make any
36:20 for the tabernacle of shittim w',
31 and he made bars of shittim w'; five
36 thereunto four pillars of shittim w',
37: 1 made the ark of shittim w':
4 And he made staves of shittim w',
10 he made the table of shittim w':
15 he made the staves of shittim w',
25 made the incense altar of shittim w':
28 he made the staves of shittim w',
38: 1 altar of burnt offering of shittim w':
6 he made the staves of shittim w',
Le 1: 7 lay the w' in order upon the fire:
8 order upon the w' that is on the fire
12 order on the w' that is on the fire
17 upon the w' that is upon the fire:
3: 5 is upon the w' that is on the fire:
4:12 and burn him on the w' with fire:
6:12 the priest shall burn w' on it every
11:32 whether it be any vessel of w', or
14: 4 and cedar w', and scarlet, and
6 and the cedar w', and the scarlet,
49 and cedar w', and scarlet, and
51 the cedar w', and the hyssop,
52 with the cedar w', and with the
15:12 every vessel of w' shall be rinsed
Nu 13:20 whether there be w' therein,
19: 6 shall take cedar w', and hyssop,
31:20 hair, and all things made of w'.
35:18 him with an hand weapon of w',
De 4:28 work of men's hands, w' and stone,
10: 1 mount, and make thee an ark of w'.
3 And I made an ark of shittim w',
19: 5 As when a man goeth into the w'
5 with his neighbour to hew w',
28:36 thou serve other gods, w' and stone.
64 have known, even w' and stone.
29:11 hewer of thy w' unto the drawer

De 29:17 and their idols, w· and stone, silver
Jos 9:21 but let them be hewers of w· and
23, 27 hewers of w·...drawers of water
17:15 then get thee up to the w· country,
18 for it is a w·, and thou shalt cut it
J'g 6:26 sacrifice with the w· of the grove
1Sa 6:14 and they clave the w· of the cart,
14:25 all they of the land came to a w·;
26 the people were come into the w·,
23:15 in the wilderness of Ziph in a w·.
16 and went to David into the w·, and
18 and David abode in the w·, and
19 with us in strong holds in the w·,
2Sa 6: 5 of instruments made of fir w·,
18: 6 battle was in the w· of Ephraim;
8 the w· devoured more people that
17 cast him into a great pit in the w·,
24:22 instruments of the oxen for w·.
1Ki 6:15 covered them on the inside with w·,
18:23, 23 and lay it on w·, and put no fire
33 And he put the w· in order, and cut
33 in pieces, and laid him on the w·,
33 the burnt sacrifice, and on the w·.
38 the burnt sacrifice, and the w·,
2Ki 2:24 forth two she bears out of the w·,
6: 4 came to Jordan, they cut down w·.
19:18 work of men's hands, w· and stone:
1Ch 16:33 shall the trees of the w· sing out
21:23 the threshing instruments for w·,
22: 4 of Tyre brought much cedar w· to
29: 2 of iron, and w· for things of w·;
2Ch 2:16 And we will cut w· out of Lebanon,
Ne 8: 4 the scribe stood upon a pulpit of w·,
10:34 and the people, for the w· offering,
13:31 And for the w· offering, at times
Job 41:27 as straw, and brass as rotten w·.
Ps 80:13 boar out of the w· doth waste it,
83:14 As the fire burneth a w·, and as
96:12 shall all the trees of the w· rejoice.
132: 6 we found it in the fields of the w·.
Pr 26:20 Where no w· is, there the fire
21 to burning coals, and w· to fire;
Ec 2: 6 the w· that bringeth forth trees:
10: 9 and he that cleaveth w· shall be
Ca 2: 3 tree among the trees of the w·,
3: 9 a chariot of the w· of Lebanon.
Isa 7: 2 as the trees of the w· are moved
10:15 lift up itself, as if it were no w·.
30:33 pile thereof is fire and much w·;
37:19 work of men's hands, w· and stone:
45:20 set up the w· of their graven image,
60:17 for w· brass, and for stones iron:
Jer 5:14 thy mouth fire, and this people w·,
7:18 The children gather w·, and the
28:13 Thou hast broken the yokes of w·;
46:22 her with axes, as hewers of w·.
La 5: 4 for money; our w· is sold unto us.
13 and the children fell under the w·.
Eze 15: 3 w· be taken thereof to do any work?
20:32 countries, to serve w· and stone.
24:10 Heap on w·, kindle the fire,
39:10 shall take no w· out of the field,
41:16 door, cieled with w· round about,
22 altar of w· was three cubits high,
22 and the walls thereof, were of w·:
Da 5: 4 brass, of iron, of w·, and of stone.
23 gold, of brass, iron, w·, and stone,
Mic 7:14 which dwell solitarily in the w·,
Hab 2:19 him that saith to the w·, Awake;
Hag 1: 8 up to the mountain, and bring w·,
Zec 12: 6 an hearth of fire among the w·,
1Co 3:12 precious stones, w·, hay, stubble;
2Ti 2:20 silver, but also of w· and of earth;
Re 9:20 and brass, and stone, and of w·:
18:12 and scarlet, and all thyine w·,
12 manner vessels of most precious w·,

wood-offering See WOOD and OFFERING.

woods
Eze 34:25 wilderness, and sleep in the w·.

woof
Le 13:48 Whether it be in the warp, or w·;
49, 51 either in the warp, or in the w·,
52 whether warp or w·, in woollen or
53 either in the warp, or in the w·, or
56 or out of the warp, or out of the w·:
57 either in the warp, or in the w·,
58 the garment, either warp, or w·,
59 either in the warp, or w·, or any

wool
J'g 6:37 will put a fleece of w· in the floor;
2Ki 3: 4 thousand rams, with the w·.
Ps 147:16 He giveth snow like w·: he
Pr 31:13 She seeketh w·, and flax, and
Isa 1:18 like crimson, they shall be as w·.
51: 8 the worm shall eat them like w·:
Eze 27:18 the wine of Helbon, and white w·.
34: 3 fat, and ye clothe you with the w·,
44:17 and no w· shall come upon them,
Da 7: 9 hair of his head like the pure w·:
Ho 2: 5 my w· and my flax, mine oil and
9 will recover my w· and my flax
Heb 9:19 and scarlet w·, and hyssop, and
Re 1:14 and his hairs were white like w·,

woollen
Le 13:47 whether it be a w· garment, or a
48 warp, or woof; of linen, or of w·;
52 warp or woof, in w· or in linen,
59 leprosy in a garment of w· or linen,
19:19 garment mingled of linen and w·
De 22:11 sorts, as of w· and linen together.

word See also WORD'S; WORDS.
Ge 15: 1 w· of the Lord came unto Abram
4 the w· of the Lord came unto him,
30:34 it might be according to thy w·.
37:14 the flocks; and bring me w· again.
41:40 according unto thy w· shall all my
44: 2 to the w· that Joseph had spoken.
18 thee, speak a w· in my lord's ears,
Ex 8:10 he said, Be it according to thy w·:
13 did according to the w· of Moses;
31 Lord according to the w· of Moses;
9:20 He that feared the w· of the Lord
21 regarded not the w· of the Lord
12:35 did according to the w· of Moses;
14:12 the w· that we did tell thee in Egypt,
32:28 did according to the w· of Moses:
Le 10: 7 did according to the w· of Moses.
Nu 3:16, 51 according to the w· of the Lord,
4:45 according to the w· of the Lord
11:23 whether my w· shall come to pass
13:26 and brought back w· unto them,
14:20 have pardoned according to thy w·:
15:31 hath despised the w· of the Lord,
20:24 rebelled against my w· at the
22: 8 I will bring you w· again, as the
18 go beyond the w· of the Lord
20 the w· which I shall say unto thee,
35 the w· that I shall speak unto thee,
38 w· that God putteth in my mouth,
23: 5 Lord put a w· in Balaam's mouth,
16 Balaam, and put a w· in his mouth,
27:21 Lord: at his w· shall they go out,
21 and at his w· they shall come in,
30: 2 he shall not break his w·, he shall
36: 5 according to the w· of the Lord,
De 1:22 bring us w· again by what way we
25 and brought us w· again, and said,
4: 2 add unto the w· which I command
5: 5 to shew you the w· of the Lord:
8: 3 but by every w· that proceedeth out
9: 5 the w· which the Lord sware unto
18:20 presume to speak a w· in my name,
21 know the w· which the Lord hath
21: 5 by their w· shall every controversy
30:14 But the w· is very nigh unto thee,
33: 9 for they have observed thy w·, and
34: 5 according to the w· of the Lord.
Jos 1:13 Remember the w· which Moses
6:10 neither shall any w· proceed out
8:27 according unto the w· of the Lord
35 was not a w· of all that Moses
14: 7 I brought him w· again as it was
10 the Lord spake this w· unto Moses,
19:50 According to the w· of the Lord
22: 9 according to the w· of the Lord by
32 and brought them w· again.
1Sa 1:23 him; only the Lord establish his w·.
3: 1 the w· of the Lord was precious
7 neither was the w· of the Lord yet
21 in Shiloh by the w· of the Lord.
4: 1 w· of Samuel came to all Israel.
9:27 that I may shew thee the w· of God.
15:10 the w· of the Lord unto Samuel,
23, 26 hast rejected the w· of the Lord,
2Sa 3:11 could not answer Abner a w· again,
7: 4 w· of the Lord came unto Nathan,
7 spake I a w· with any of the tribes
25 the w· that thou hast spoken
14:12 speak one w· unto my lord the king.
17 The w· of my lord the king shall
15:28 until there come w· from you to
19:10 speak ye not a w· of bringing the king
14 that they sent this w· unto the king,
22:31 perfect; the w· of the Lord is tried:
23: 2 me, and his w· was in my tongue.
24: 4 king's w· prevailed against Joab,
11 the w· of the Lord came unto the
1Ki 2: 4 Lord may continue his w· which he
23 spoken this w· against his own life.
27 he might fulfil the w· of the Lord,
30 Benaiah brought the king w· again,
42 The w· that I have heard is good.
6:11 w· of the Lord came to Solomon,
12 will I perform my w· with thee,
8:20 Lord hath performed his w· that he
26 let thy w·, I pray thee, be verified,
56 hath not failed one w· of all his
12:22 the w· of God came unto Shemaiah
24 therefore to the w· of the Lord,
24 according to the w· of the Lord.
13: 1 by the w· of the Lord unto Beth-el:
2 the altar in the w· of the Lord,
5 had given by the w· of the Lord.
9 charged me by the w· of the Lord,
17 said to me by the w· of the Lord,
18 unto me by the w· of the Lord,
20 the w· of the Lord came unto the
26 disobedient unto the w· of the
26 according to the w· of the Lord,
32 he cried by the w· of the Lord
14:18 according to the w· of the Lord,
16: 1 the w· of the Lord came to Jehu
7 w· of the Lord against Baasha,
12, 34 according to the w· of the Lord,
17: 1 years, but according to my w·.
2 the w· of the Lord came unto him,
5 according unto the w· of the Lord:
8 the w· of the Lord came unto him,
16 according to the w· of the Lord,
24 the w· of the Lord in thy mouth
18: 1 w· of the Lord came to Elijah
21 the people answered him not a w·.
31 unto whom the w· of the Lord came,
36 have done all these things at my w·.
19: 9 the w· of the Lord came to him,
20: 9 departed, and brought him w· again.
35 neighbour in the w· of the Lord,
21: 4 w· which Naboth the Jazreelite had
17, 28 w· of the Lord came to Elijah
22: 5 thee, at the w· of the Lord to day.
1Ki 22:13 one mouth: let thy w·, I pray thee,
13 be like the w· of one of them, and
19 thou therefore the w· of the Lord:
38 according unto the w· of the Lord
2Ki 1:16 God in Israel to enquire of his w·?
17 according to the w· of the Lord
3:12 The w· of the Lord is with him.
4:44 according to the w· of the Lord.
6:18 according to the w· of Elisha.
7: 1 said, Hear ye the w· of the Lord;
16 according to the w· of the Lord.
9:26 according to the w· of the Lord.
36 This is the w· of the Lord, which he
10:10 earth nothing of the w· of the Lord,
14:25 according to the w· of the Lord God
15:12 This was the w· of the Lord which
18:28 Hear the w· of the great king, the
36 peace, and answered him not a w·:
19:21 the w· that the Lord hath spoken
20: 4 the w· of the Lord came to him,
16 Hezekiah, hear the w· of the Lord.
19 Good is the w· of the Lord which
22: 9 and brought the king w· again,
20 they brought the king w· again.
23:16 according to the w· of the Lord
24: 2 according to the w· of the Lord,
1Ch 10:13 even against the w· of the Lord,
11: 3, 10 according to the w· of the Lord
12:23 according to the w· of the Lord.
15:15 according to the w· of the Lord.
16:15 the w· which he commanded to a
17: 3 the w· of God came to Nathan,
6 spake I a w· to any of the judges of
21: 4 king's w· prevailed against Joab.
6 king's w· was abominable to Joab.
12 what w· I shall bring again to him
22: 8 but the w· of the Lord came to me,
2Ch 6:10 hath performed his w· that he hath
17 God of Israel, let thy w· be verified,
10:15 the Lord might perform his w·,
11: 2 w· of the Lord came to Shemaiah
12: 7 w· of the Lord came to Shemaiah,
18: 4 thee, at the w· of the Lord to day.
12 let thy w· therefore, I pray thee, be
18 Therefore hear the w· of the Lord;
30:12 the princes, by the w· of the Lord.
34:16 brought the king w· back again,
21 have not kept the w· of the Lord,
28 So they brought the king w· again.
35: 6 do according to the w· of the Lord
36:21 To fulfil the w· of the Lord by the
22 that the w· of the Lord spoken by
Ezr 1: 1 w· of the Lord by the mouth of
6:11 that whosoever shall alter this w·,
10: 5 should do according to this w·.
Ne 1: 8 w· that thou commandest thy
Es 1:21 according to the w· of Memucan:
7: 8 w· went out of the king's mouth,
Job 2:13 and none spake a w· unto him:
Ps 17: 4 w· of thy lips I have kept me from
18:30 the w· of the Lord is tried: he is a
33: 4 For the w· of the Lord is right;
6 By the w· of the Lord were the
56: 4 In God I will praise his w·, in God I
10 In God will I praise his w·:
10 in the Lord will I praise his w·.
68:11 The Lord gave the w·: great was
103:20 unto the voice of his w·.
105: 8 the w· which he commanded to a
19 Until the time that his w· came:
19 the w· of the Lord tried him.
28 they rebelled not against his w·.
106:24 land, they believed not his w·:
107:20 He sent his w·, and healed them,
119: 9 heed thereto according to thy w·.
11 Thy w· have I hid in mine heart,
16 statutes: I will not forget thy w·.
17 that I may live, and keep thy w·.
25 quicken...me according to thy w·.
28 thou me according unto thy w·.
38 Stablish thy w· unto thy servant,
41 thy salvation, according to thy w·.
42 me: for I trust in thy w·.
43 take not the w· of truth utterly out
49 Remember the w· unto thy servant,
50 for thy w· hath quickened me.
58 unto me according to thy w·.
65 O Lord, according unto thy w·.
67 astray: but now have I kept thy w·.
74 because I have hoped in thy w·.
76 to thy w· unto thy servant.
81 salvation: but I hope in thy w·.
82 Mine eyes fail for thy w·, saying,
89 Lord, thy w· is settled in heaven.
101 evil way, that I might keep thy w·.
105 Thy w· is a lamp unto my feet, and
107 O Lord, according unto thy w·.
114 and my shield: I hope in thy w·.
116 Uphold me according unto thy w·,
123 and for the w· of thy righteousness.
133 Order my steps in thy w·: and let not
140 Thy w· is very pure: therefore thy
147 and cried: I hoped in thy w·.
148 that I might meditate in thy w·.
154 quicken me according to thy w·.
158 because they kept not thy w·.
160 Thy w· is true from the beginning:
161 heart standeth in awe of thy w·.
162 I rejoice at thy w·, as one that
169 according to thy w·.
170 deliver me according to thy w·.
172 My tongue shall speak of thy w·:
130: 5 doth wait, and in his w· do I hope.
138: 2 hast magnified thy w· above all
139: 4 there is not a w· in my tongue,
147:15 earth: his w· runneth very swiftly.

Ps 147:18 He sendeth out his *w'*, and melteth
19 He sheweth his *w'* unto Jacob,
148: 8 stormy wind fulfilling his *w'*:
Pr 12:25 but a good *w'* maketh it glad.
13:13 despiseth the *w'* shall be destroyed:
14:15 The simple believeth every *w'*:
15:23 and a *w'* spoken in due season,
25:11 A *w'* fitly spoken is like apples of
30: 5 Every *w'* of God is pure: he is a
Ec 8: 4 Where the *w'* of a king is, there is
Isa 1:10 Hear the *w'* of the Lord, ye rulers
2: 1 The *w'* that Isaiah the son of Amoz
3 the *w'* of the Lord from Jerusalem.
5:24 despised the *w'* of the Holy One of
8:10 speak the *w'*, and it shall not
20 speak not according to this *w'*,
9: 8 The Lord sent a *w'* into Jacob, and
16:13 is the *w'* that the Lord hath spoken
24: 3 for the Lord hath spoken this *w'*.
28:13 the *w'* of the Lord was unto them
14 Wherefore hear the *w'* of the Lord,
29:21 make a man an offender for a *w'*,
30:12 Because ye despise this *w'*, and
21 ears shall hear a *w'* behind thee,
36:21 peace, and answered him not a *w'*:
37:22 the *w'* which the Lord hath spoken
38: 4 came the *w'* of the Lord to Isaiah,
39: 5 Hear the *w'* of the Lord of hosts:
8 Good is the *w'* of the Lord which
40: 8 *w'* of our God shall stand for ever.
41:28 I asked of them, could answer a *w'*.
44:26 confirmeth the *w'* of his servant,
45:23 the *w'* is gone out of my mouth in
50: 4 speak a *w'* in season to him that is
55:11 So shall my *w'* be that goeth forth
66: 2 spirit, and trembleth at my *w'*.
5 Hear the *w'* of the Lord, ye that
5 ye that tremble at his *w'*; Your
Jer 1: 2 To whom the *w'* of the Lord came
4, 11 the *w'* of the Lord came unto me,
12 I will hasten my *w'* to perform it.
13 the *w'* of the Lord came unto me
2: 1 the *w'* of the Lord came to me,
4 Hear ye the *w'* of the Lord, O
31 see ye the *w'* of the Lord.
5:13 wind, and the *w'* is not in them:
14 Because ye speak this *w'*, behold,
6:10 the *w'* of the Lord is unto them a
7: 1 *w'* that came to Jeremiah from the
2 house, and proclaim there this *w'*,
2 Hear ye the *w'* of the Lord, all ye
8: 9 have rejected the *w'* of the Lord;
9:20 Yet hear the *w'* of the Lord, O ye
20 ear receive the *w'* of his mouth,
10: 1 Hear ye the *w'* which the Lord
11: 1 The *w'* that came to Jeremiah
13: 2 according to the *w'* of the Lord,
3 the *w'* of the Lord came unto me
8 the *w'* of the Lord came unto me,
12 thou shalt speak unto them this *w'*;
14: 1 The *w'* of the Lord that came to
17 thou shalt say this *w'* unto them;
15:16 and thy *w'* was unto me the joy
16: 1 *w'* of the Lord came also unto me,
17:15 Where is the *w'* of the Lord? let it
20 Hear ye the *w'* of the Lord, ye
18: 1 *w'* which came to Jeremiah from
5 the *w'* of the Lord came to me,
18 wise, nor the *w'* from the prophet.
19: 3 Hear ye the *w'* of the Lord, O kings
20: 8 the *w'* of the Lord was made a
9 *w'* was in mine heart as a burning
21: 1 *w'* which came unto Jeremiah
11 say, Hear ye the *w'* of the Lord;
22: 1 of Judah, and speak there this *w'*,
2 Hear the *w'* of the Lord, O king of
29 earth, hear the *w'* of the Lord.
23:18 hath perceived and heard his *w'*?
18 who hath marked his *w'*, and heard
28 and he that hath my *w'*,
28 let him speak my *w'* faithfully.
29 Is not my *w'* like as a fire? saith the
36 every man's *w'* shall be his burden;
38 Because ye say this *w'*, the burden
24: 4 the *w'* of the Lord came unto me,
25: 1 The *w'* that came to Jeremiah
3 *w'* of the Lord hath come unto me,
26: 1 Judah came this *w'* from the Lord,
2 unto them; diminish not a *w'*:
27: 1 *w'* unto Jeremiah from the Lord,
18 if the *w'* of the Lord be with them,
28: 7 hear thou now this *w'* that I speak
9 the *w'* of the prophet shall come to
12 the *w'* of the Lord came unto
29:10 perform my good *w'* toward you,
20 Hear ye...the *w'* of the Lord,
30 the *w'* of the Lord unto Jeremiah,
30: 1 *w'* that came to Jeremiah from the
31:10 Hear the *w'* of the Lord, O ye
32: 1 The *w'* that came to Jeremiah
6 The *w'* of the Lord came unto me,
8 according to the *w'* of the Lord,
8 that this was the *w'* of the Lord.
26 the *w'* of the Lord unto Jeremiah,
33: 1, 19 the *w'* of the Lord came unto
23 the *w'* of the Lord came to
34: 1 The *w'* which came unto Jeremiah
4 Yet hear the *w'* of the Lord, O
5 for I have pronounced the *w'*,
8 *w'* that came unto Jeremiah from
12 the *w'* of the Lord came to
35: 1 *w'* which came unto Jeremiah from
12 the *w'* of the Lord unto Jeremiah,
36: 1 that this *w'* came unto Jeremiah
27 the *w'* of the Lord came to
37: 6 *w'* of the Lord unto the prophet

Jer 37:17 Is there any *w'* from the Lord?
38:21 *w'* that the Lord hath shewed me:
39:15 the *w'* of the Lord came unto
40: 1 The *w'* that came to Jeremiah from
42: 7 that the *w'* of the Lord came unto
15 therefore hear the *w'* of the Lord,
43: 8 the *w'* of the Lord unto Jeremiah
44: 1 The *w'* that came to Jeremiah
16 *w'* that thou hast spoken unto us
24 Hear the *w'* of the Lord, all Judah
26 hear ye the *w'* of the Lord, all
45: 1 The *w'* that Jeremiah the prophet
46: 1 The *w'* of the Lord which came to
13 The *w'* that the Lord spake to
47: 1 The *w'* of the Lord that came to
49:34 The *w'* of the Lord that came to
50: 1 *w'* that the Lord spake against
51:59 *w'* which Jeremiah the prophet
La 2:17 he hath fulfilled his *w'* that he had
Eze 1: 3 *w'* of the Lord came expressly
3:16 the *w'* of the Lord came unto me,
17 hear the *w'* at my mouth, and give
6: 1 the *w'* of the Lord came unto me,
3 hear the *w'* of the Lord God;
7: 1 the *w'* of the Lord came unto me,
11:14 the *w'* of the Lord came unto me,
12: 1 *w'* of the Lord also came unto me,
8 came the *w'* of the Lord unto me,
17 the *w'* of the Lord came to me,
21 the *w'* of the Lord came unto me,
25 *w'* that I shall speak shall come to
25 will I say the *w'*, and will perform
26 the *w'* of the Lord came to me,
28 *w'* which I have spoken shall be
13: 1 the *w'* of the Lord came unto me,
2 hearts, Hear ye the *w'* of the Lord;
6 that they would confirm the *w'*.
14: 2 the *w'* of the Lord came unto me,
12 The *w'* of the Lord came unto me,
15: 1 the *w'* of the Lord came unto me,
16: 1 the *w'* of the Lord came unto me,
35 O harlot, hear the *w'* of the Lord:
17: 1, 11 the *w'* of the Lord came unto me,
18: 1 The *w'* of the Lord came unto me
20: 2 came the *w'* of the Lord unto me,
45 the *w'* of the Lord came unto me,
46 and drop thy *w'* toward the south,
47 south, Hear the *w'* of the Lord;
21: 1 the *w'* of the Lord came unto me,
2 drop thy *w'* toward the holy places,
8 the *w'* of the Lord came unto me,
18 The *w'* of the Lord came unto me
22: 1, 17, 23 the *w'* of the Lord came
23: 1 *w'* of the Lord came again unto me,
24: 1, 15 the *w'* of the Lord came unto me,
20 The *w'* of the Lord came unto me,
25: 1 *w'* of the Lord came again unto me,
3 Hear the *w'* of the Lord God;
26: 1 the *w'* of the Lord came unto me,
27: 1 *w'* of the Lord came again unto me,
28: 1 *w'* of the Lord came again unto me,
11, 20 *w'* of the Lord came unto me,
29: 1, 17 *w'* of the Lord came unto me,
30: 1 *w'* of the Lord came again unto me,
20 the *w'* of the Lord came unto me,
31: 1 the *w'* of the Lord came unto me,
32: 1, 17 *w'* of the Lord came unto me,
33: 1 the *w'* of the Lord came unto me,
7 shalt hear the *w'* at my mouth,
23 the *w'* of the Lord came unto me,
30 what is the *w'* that cometh forth
34: 1 the *w'* of the Lord came unto me,
7, 9 hear the *w'* of the Lord;
35: 1 the *w'* of the Lord came unto me,
36: 1 Israel, hear the *w'* of the Lord:
4 Israel, hear the *w'* of the Lord God;
16 the *w'* of the Lord came unto me,
37: 4 dry bones, hear the *w'* of the Lord.
15 *w'* of the Lord came again unto me,
38: 1 the *w'* of the Lord came unto me,
Da 3:28 and have changed the king's *w'*,
4:17 demand by the *w'* of the holy ones:
31 the *w'* was in the king's mouth,
9: 2 *w'* of the Lord came to Jeremiah
10:11 he had spoken this *w'* unto me,
Ho 1: 1 The *w'* of the Lord that came unto
2 of the *w'* of the Lord by Hosea.
4: 1 Hear the *w'* of the Lord, ye
Joe 1: 1 *w'* of the Lord that came to Joel
2:11 he is strong that executeth his *w'*:
Am 3: 1 Hear this *w'* that the Lord hath
4: 1 Hear this *w'*, ye kine of Bashan,
5: 1 Hear ye this *w'* which I take up
7:16 hear thou the *w'* of the Lord:
16 not thy *w'* against the house of Isaac.
8:12 and fro to seek the *w'* of the Lord,
Jon 1: 1 the *w'* of the Lord came unto Jonah
3: 1 the *w'* of the Lord came unto Jonah
3 according to the *w'* of the Lord.
6 *w'* came unto the king of Nineveh,
Mic 1: 1 *w'* of the Lord that came to Micah
4: 2 the *w'* of the Lord from Jerusalem.
Hab 3: 9 the oaths of the tribes, even thy *w'*.
Zep 1: 1 *w'* of the Lord which came unto
2: 5 the *w'* of the Lord is against you;
Hag 1: 1, 3 came the *w'* of the Lord by Haggai
2: 1 the *w'* of the Lord by the prophet
5 the *w'* that I covenanted with you
10 came the *w'* of the Lord by Haggai
20 *w'* of the Lord came unto Haggai
Zec 1: 1, 7 *w'* of the Lord unto Zechariah,
4: 6 *w'* of the Lord unto Zerubbabel,
8 the *w'* of the Lord came unto me,
6: 9 the *w'* of the Lord came unto me,
7: 1 that the *w'* of the Lord came unto
4 came the *w'* of the Lord of hosts

Zec 7: 8 And the *w'* of the Lord came unto
8: 1, 18 *w'* of the Lord of hosts came to me,
9: 1 The burden of the *w'* of the Lord
11:11 knew that it was the *w'* of the Lord.
12: 1 The burden of the *w'* of the Lord
Mal 1: 1 The burden of the *w'* of the Lord
M't 2: 8 bring me *w'* again, that I may
13 thou there until I bring thee *w'*:
4: 4 by every *w'* that proceedeth out of
8: 8 but speak the *w'* only, and my
16 he cast out the spirits with his *w'*,
12:32 speaketh a *w'* against the Son of
36 every idle *w'* that men shall speak,
13:19 one heareth the *w'* of the kingdom,
20 the same is he that heareth the *w'*,
21 ariseth because of the *w'*,
22 thorns is he that heareth the *w'*;
22 choke the *w'*, and he becometh
23 ground is he that heareth the *w'*,
15:23 But he answered her not a *w'*.
18:16 every *w'* may be established.
22:46 man was able to answer him a *w'*,
26:75 remembered the *w'* of Jesus,
27:14 he answered him to never a *w'*;
28: 8 did run to bring his disciples *w'*.
M'r 2: 2 he preached the *w'* unto them.
4:14 The sower soweth the *w'*.
15 the way side, where the *w'* is sown;
15 taketh away the *w'* that was sown
16 when they have heard the *w'*,
18 thorns: such as hear the *w'*,
19 choke the *w'*, and it becometh
20 such as hear the *w'*, and receive it,
33 parables spake he the *w'* unto them,
5:36 Jesus heard the *w'* that was spoken,
7:13 Making the *w'* of God of none
14:72 the *w'* that Jesus said unto him,
16:20 and confirming the *w'* with signs
Lu 1: 2 and ministers of the *w'*;
38 be it unto me according to thy *w'*.
2:29 in peace, according to thy *w'*:
3: 2 the *w'* of God came unto John the
4: 4 alone, but by every *w'* of God.
32 for his *w'* was with power.
36 saying, What a *w'* is this! for with
5: 1 upon him to hear the *w'* of God,
5 at thy *w'* I will let down the net.
7: 7 but say in a *w'*, and my servant
8:11 is this: The seed is the *w'* of God.
12 away the *w'* out of their hearts,
13 they hear, receive the *w'* with joy;
15 heart, having heard the *w'*, keep it,
21 these which hear the *w'* of God,
10:39 sat at Jesus' feet, and heard his *w'*.
11:28 that hear the *w'* of God, and keep it.
12:10 speak a *w'* against the Son of man,
22:61 remembered the *w'* of the Lord,
24:19 mighty in deed and *w'* before God
Joh 1: 1 In the beginning was the *W'*,
1 and the *W'* was with God,
1 and the *W'* was God.
14 the *W'* was made flesh, and dwelt
2:22 and the *w'* which Jesus had said.
4:41 believed because of his own *w'*;
50 man believed the *w'* that Jesus had
5:24 He that heareth my *w'*, and
38 ye have not his *w'* abiding in you:
8:31 If ye continue in my *w'*, then are
37 because my *w'* hath no place in you.
43 even because ye cannot hear my *w'*.
10:35 unto whom the *w'* of God came,
12:48 the *w'* that I have spoken, the same
14:24 the *w'* which ye hear is not mine,
15: 3 *w'* which I have spoken unto you.
20 Remember the *w'* that I said unto
25 that the *w'* might be fulfilled that
17: 6 me; and they have kept thy *w'*.
14 I have given them thy *w'*; and the
17 through thy truth: thy *w'* is truth.
20 believe on me through their *w'*;
Ac 2:41 received his *w'* were baptized:
4: 4 them which heard the *w'* believed;
29 boldness they may speak thy *w'*,
31 spake the *w'* of God with boldness.
6: 2 that we should leave the *w'* of God,
4 and to the ministry of the *w'*.
7 And the *w'* of God increased; and
8: 4 went every where preaching the *w'*.
14 had received the *w'* of God, they
25 and preached the *w'* of the Lord,
10:36 The *w'* which God sent unto the
37 That *w'*, I say, ye know, which
44 on all them which heard the *w'*.
11: 1 had also received the *w'* of God.
16 remembered I the *w'* of the Lord,
19 preaching the *w'* to none but unto
12:24 the *w'* of God grew and multiplied.
13: 5 they preached the *w'* of God in the
7 and desired to hear the *w'* of God.
15 if ye have any *w'* of exhortation for
26 to you is the *w'* of this salvation
44 together to hear the *w'* of God.
46 It was necessary that the *w'* of God
48 and glorified the *w'* of the Lord:
49 the *w'* of the Lord was published
14: 3 which gave testimony unto the *w'*
25 they had preached the *w'* in Perga,
15: 7 should hear the *w'* of the gospel,
35 and preaching the *w'* of the Lord,
36 have preached the *w'* of the Lord,
16: 6 of the Holy Ghost to preach the *w'*
32 spake unto him the *w'* of the Lord,
17:11 received the *w'* with all readiness
13 *w'* of God was preached of Paul
18:11 teaching the *w'* of God among them.
19:10 in Asia heard the *w'* of the Lord

Ac 19:20 So mightily grew the *w'* of God and
20:32 to God, and to the *w'* of his grace,
22:22 gave him audience unto this *w'*,
28:25 after that Paul had spoken one *w'*,
Ro 9: 6 Not as though the *w'* of God hath
9 For this is the *w'* of promise, At
10: 8 *w'* is nigh thee, even in thy mouth,
8 the *w'* of faith, which we preach;
17 and hearing by the *w'* of God.
15:18 obedient, by *w'* and deed,
1Co 4:20 the kingdom of God is not in *w'*,
12: 8 given by the Spirit the *w'* of wisdom;
8 to another the *w'* of knowledge by
14:36 came the *w'* of God out from you?
2Co 1:18 our *w'* toward you was not yea and
2:17 many, which corrupt the *w'* of God:
4: 2 the *w'* of God deceitfully;
5:19 unto us the *w'* of reconciliation.
6: 7 By the *w'* of truth, by the power of
10:11 such as we are in *w'* by letters when
13: 1 shall every *w'* be established.
Ga 5:14 all the law is fulfilled in one *w'*,
6: 6 Let him that is taught in the *w'*
Eph 1:13 after that ye heard the *w'* of truth,
5:26 the washing of water by the *w'*,
6:17 the Spirit, which is the *w'* of God:
Ph'p 1:14 bold to speak the *w'* without fear.
2:16 Holding forth the *w'* of life; that I
Col 1: 5 heard before in the *w'* of the truth
25 me for you, to fulfil the *w'* of God;
3:16 Let the *w'* of Christ dwell in you
17 whatsoever ye do in *w'* or deed, do
1Th 1: 5 came not unto you in *w'* only,
6 received the *w'* in much affliction,
8 you sounded out the *w'* of the Lord
2:13 *w'* of God which ye heard of us,
13 ye received it not as the *w'* of men,
13 but as it is in truth, the *w'* of God,
4:15 say unto you by the *w'* of the Lord,
2Th 2: 2 neither by spirit, nor by *w'*,
15 whether by *w'*, or our epistle.
17 and stablish you in every good *w'*
3: 1 the *w'* of the Lord may have free
14 obey not our *w'* by this epistle,
1Ti 4: 5 is sanctified by the *w'* of God and
12 an example of the believers, in *w'*,
5:17 they who labour in the *w'* and
2Ti 2: 9 but the *w'* of God is not bound.
15 rightly dividing the *w'* of truth.
17 their *w'* will eat as doth a canker:
4: 2 Preach the *w'*; be instant in
Tit 1: 3 in due times manifested his *w'*
9 Holding fast the faithful *w'* as he
2: 5 the *w'* of God be not blasphemed.
Heb 1: 3 all things by the *w'* of his power,
2: 2 For if the *w'* spoken by angels was
4: 2 *w'* preached did not profit them,
12 For the *w'* of God is quick, and
5:13 unskilful in the *w'* of righteousness:
6: 5 have tasted the good *w'* of God,
7:28 but the *w'* of the oath, which was
11: 3 were framed by the *w'* of God,
12:19 that the *w'* should not be spoken
27 this *w'*, Yet once more, signifieth
13: 7 spoken unto you the *w'* of God:
22 suffer the *w'* of exhortation:
Jas 1:18 begat he us with the *w'* of truth,
21 with meekness the engrafted *w'*,
22 But be ye doers of the *w'*, and not
23 For if any be a hearer of the *w'*,
3: 2 If any man offend not in *w'*, the
1Pe 1:23 by the *w'* of God, which liveth and
25 *w'* of the Lord endureth for ever.
25 *w'* which by the gospel is preached
2: 2 desire the sincere milk of the *w'*,
8 to them which stumble at the *w'*,
3: 1 that, if any obey not the *w'*, they
1 also may without the *w'* be won
2Pe 1:19 also a more sure *w'* of prophecy;
3: 5 by the *w'* of God the heavens were
7 by the same *w'* are kept in store,
1Jo 1: 1 have handled, of the *W'* of life;
10 him a liar, and his *w'* is not in us.
2: 5 But whoso keepeth his *w'*, in him
7 the *w'* which ye have heard from
14 and the *w'* of God abideth in you,
3:18 children, let us not love in *w'*,
5: 7 the Father, the *W'*, and the Holy
Re 1: 2 Who bare record of the *w'* of God,
9 for the *w'* of God, and for the
3: 8 and hast kept my *w'*, and hast not
10 hast kept the *w'* of my patience,
6: 9 that were slain for the *w'* of God,
12:11 and by the *w'* of their testimony;
19:13 his name is called The *W'* of God,
20: 4 and for the *w'* of God, and which

word's
2Sa 7:21 For thy *w'* sake, and according to
M'r 4:17 persecution ariseth for...*w'* sake,

words^
Ge 24:30 when he heard the *w'* of Rebekah
52 Abraham's servant heard their *w'*,
27:34 Esau heard the *w'* of his father,
42 *w'* of Esau her elder son were told
31: 1 he heard the *w'* of Laban's sons,
34:18 And their *w'* pleased Hamor, and
37: 8 more for his dreams, and for his *w'*.
39:17 unto him according to these *w'*,
19 master heard the *w'* of his wife,
42:16 prison, that your *w'* may be proved,
20 so shall your *w'* be verified, and ye
43: 7 according to the tenor of these *w'*:
44: 6 he spake unto them these same *w'*.
7 Wherefore saith my lord these *w'*?
10 let it be according unto your *w'*:

Ge 44:24 we told him the *w'* of my lord.
45:27 they told him all the *w'* of Joseph,
49:21 hind let loose: he giveth goodly *w'*.
Ex 4:15 him, and put *w'* in his mouth:
28 told Aaron all the *w'* of the Lord
30 spake all the *w'* which the Lord
5: 9 and let them not regard vain *w'*.
19: 6 are the *w'* which thou shalt speak
7 *w'* which the Lord commanded him.
8 Moses returned the *w'* of the people
9 Moses told the *w'* of the people
20: 1 God spake all these *w'*, saying,
23: 8 perverteth the *w'* of the righteous.
24: 3 the people all the *w'* of the Lord,
3 *w'* which the Lord hath said will
4 Moses wrote all the *w'* of the Lord,
8 with you concerning all these *w'*.
34: 1 the *w'* that were in the first tables,
27 unto Moses, Write thou these *w'*:
27 after the tenor of these *w'* I have
28 the tables the *w'* of the covenant,
35: 1 are the *w'* which the Lord hath
Nu 11:24 told the people the *w'* of the Lord,
12: 6 And he said, Hear now my *w'*: If
16:31 an end of speaking all these *w'*,
22: 7 and spake unto him the *w'* of Balak.
24: 4, 16 which heard the *w'* of God,
De 1: 1 the *w'* which Moses spake unto all
34 the Lord heard the voice of your *w'*,
2:26 king of Heshbon with *w'* of peace,
4:10 and I will make them hear my *w'*,
12 ye heard the voice of the *w'*, but
36 heardest his *w'* out of the midst
5:22 *w'* the Lord spake unto all your
28 Lord heard the voice of your *w'*,
28 the voice of the *w'* of this people,
6: 6 these *w'*, which I command thee
9:10 written according to all the *w'*,
10: 2 the *w'* that were in the first tables
11:18 lay up these my *w'* in your heart
12:28 hear all these *w'* which I command
13: 3 hearken unto the *w'* of that prophet,
16:19 and pervert the *w'* of the righteous.
17:19 to keep all the *w'* of this law and
18:18 and will put my *w'* in his mouth;
19 *w'* which he shall speak in my name,
27: 3 upon them all the *w'* of this law,
8 upon the stones all the *w'* of this law
26 not all the *w'* of this law to do them.
28:14 *w'* which I command thee this day,
58 *w'* of this law that are written in
29: 1 These are the *w'* of the covenant,
9 therefore the *w'* of this covenant,
19 he heareth the *w'* of this curse,
29 we may do all the *w'* of this law.
31: 1 and spake these *w'* unto all Israel.
12 observe to do all the *w'* of this law:
24 an end of writing the *w'* of this law
28 I may speak these *w'* in their ears,
30 of Israel the *w'* of this song,
32: 1 hear, O earth, the *w'* of my mouth.
44 and spake all the *w'* of this song
45 end of speaking all these *w'* to all
46 hearts unto all the *w'* which I testify
46 observe to do, all the *w'* of this law.
33: 3 every one shall receive of thy *w'*.
Jos 1:18 and will not hearken unto thy *w'*
2:21 According unto your *w'*, so be it.
3: 9 hear the *w'* of the Lord your God.
8:34 he read all the *w'* of the law,
22:30 the *w'* that the children of Reuben
24:26 Joshua wrote these *w'* in the book
27 it hath heard all the *w'* of the Lord
J'g 2: 4 angel of the Lord spake these *w'*
9: 3 all the men of Shechem all these *w'*:
30 of the city heard the *w'* of Gaal
11:10 we do not so according to thy *w'*.
11 Jephthah uttered all his *w'* before
28 not unto the *w'* of Jephthah
13:12 said, Now let thy *w'* come to pass.
16:16 she pressed him daily with her *w'*,
1Sa 3:19 none of his *w'* fall to the ground.
8:10 Samuel told all the *w'* of the Lord
21 heard all the *w'* of the people,
15: 1 unto the voice of the *w'* of the Lord.
24 of the Lord, and thy *w'*:
17:11 heard those *w'* of the Philistine,
23 spake according to the same *w'*:
31 *w'* were heard which David spake,
18:23 Saul's servants spake those *w'* in
26 his servants told David these *w'*,
21:12 And David laid up these *w'* in his
24: 7 stayed his servants with these *w'*,
9 Wherefore hearest thou men's *w'*,
16 made an end of speaking these *w'*
25: 9 according to all those *w'* in the
24 and hear the *w'* of thine handmaid.
26:19 the king hear the *w'* of his servant.
28:20 afraid, because of the *w'* of Samuel:
21 hearkened unto the *w'* which thou
2Sa 3: 8 wroth for the *w'* of Ish-bosheth,
7:17 According to all these *w'*, and
28 and thy *w'* be true, and thou hast
14: 3 So Joab put the *w'* in her mouth.
19 *w'* in the mouth of thine handmaid:
19:43 *w'* of the men of Judah were fiercer
43 than the *w'* of the men of Israel.
20:17 Hear the *w'* of thine handmaid.
22: 1 unto the Lord the *w'* of this song
23: 1 Now these be the last *w'* of David.
1Ki 1:14 in after thee, and confirm thy *w'*.
3:12 I have done according to thy *w'*:
5: 7 Hiram heard the *w'* of Solomon,
8:59 And let these my *w'*, wherewith
10: 7 Howbeit I believed not the *w'*,
12: 7 speak good *w'* to them, that they

1Ki 13:11 *w'* which he had spoken unto the
21:27 when Ahab heard those *w'*, that he
22:13 *w'* of the prophets declare good
2Ki 1: 7 to meet you, and told you these *w'*?
6:12 the *w'* that thou speakest in thy
30 king heard the *w'* of the woman,
18:20 (but they are but vain *w'*,) I have
27 and to thee, to speak these *w'*?
37 told him the *w'* of Rab-shakeh.
19: 4 will hear all the *w'* of Rab-shakeh,
4 reprove the *w'* which the Lord thy
6 of the *w'* which thou hast heard,
16 hear the *w'* of Sennacherib, which
22:11 king had heard the *w'* of the book
13 the *w'* of this book that is found:
13 hearkened unto the *w'* of this book,
16 the *w'* of the book which the king
18 the *w'* which thou hast heard;
23: 2 the *w'* of the book of the covenant
3 to perform the *w'* of this covenant
16 who proclaimed these *w'*.
24 might perform the *w'* of the law
1Ch 17:15 According to these *w'*, and
23:27 by the last *w'* of David the Levites
25: 5 the king's seer in the *w'* of God,
2Ch 9: 6 I believed not their *w'*, until I came,
10: 7 speak good *w'* to them, they will
11: 4 they obeyed the *w'* of the Lord,
15: 8 And when Asa heard these *w'*, and
18:12 the *w'* of the prophets declare good
29:15 of the king, by the *w'* of the Lord,
30 unto the Lord with the *w'* of David,
32: 8 the *w'* of Hezekiah king of Judah.
33:18 *w'* of the seers that spake to him
34:19 king had heard the *w'* of the law,
21 the *w'* of the book that is found:
26 the *w'* which thou hast heard;
27 heardest his *w'* against this place,
30 the *w'* of the book of the covenant
31 to perform the *w'* of the covenant
35:22 hearkened not unto the *w'* of Necho
36:16 despised his *w'*, and misused his
Ezr 7:11 of the *w'* of the commandments
9: 4 trembled at the *w'* of the God of
Ne 1: 1 The *w'* of Nehemiah the son of
4 when I heard these *w'*, that I sat
2:18 king's *w'* that he had spoken unto
5: 6 when I heard their cry and these *w'*.
6: 6 be their king, according to these *w'*.
7 to the king, according to these *w'*.
19 me, and uttered my *w'* to him.
8: 9 when they heard the *w'* of the law.
12 the *w'* that were declared unto
13 to understand the *w'* of the law.
9: 8 seed, and hast performed thy *w'*;
Es 4: 9 and told Esther the *w'* of Mordecai.
12 they told to Mordecai Esther's *w'*.
9:26 for all the *w'* of this letter,
30 with *w'* of peace and truth,
Job 4: 4 Thy *w'* have upholden him that
6: 3 therefore my *w'* are swallowed up.
10 concealed the *w'* of the Holy One.
25 How forcible are right *w'*! but what
26 Do ye imagine to reprove *w'*, and
8: 2 *w'* of thy mouth be like a strong
10 and utter *w'* out of their heart?
9:14 out my *w'* to reason with him?
11: 2 the multitude of *w'* be answered?
12:11 Doth not the ear try *w'*? and the
15:13 lettest such *w'* go out of thy mouth?
16: 3 Shall vain *w'* have an end?
4 I could heap up *w'* against you,
18: 2 will it be ere ye make an end of *w'*?
19: 2 and break me in pieces with *w'*?
23 Oh that my *w'* were now written!
22:22 and lay up his *w'* in thine heart.
23: 5 *w'* which he would answer me,
12 have esteemed the *w'* of his mouth
26: 4 To whom hast thou uttered *w'*?
29:22 After my *w'* they spake not again;
31:40 The *w'* of Job are ended.
32:11 I waited for your *w'*; I gave ear
12 Job, or that answered his *w'*:
14 not directed his *w'* against me:
33: 1 and hearken to all my *w'*.
3 My *w'* shall be of the uprightness
5 me, set thy *w'* in order before me,
8 I have heard the voice of thy *w'*,
34: 2 Hear my *w'*, O ye wise men; and
3 For the ear trieth *w'*, as the mouth
16 hearken to the voice of my *w'*.
35 and his *w'* were without wisdom.
37 and multiplieth his *w'* against God.
35:16 he multiplieth *w'* with knowledge.
36: 4 For truly my *w'* shall not be false:
38: 2 counsel by *w'* without knowledge?
41: 3 will he speak soft *w'* unto thee?
42: 7 had spoken these *w'* unto Job,
Ps 5: 1 Give ear to my *w'*, O Lord, consider
7: *title* concerning the *w'* of Cush
12: 6 The *w'* of the Lord are pure *w'*:
18: *title* unto the Lord the *w'* of this song
19: 4 their *w'* to the end of the world.
14 Let the *w'* of my mouth, and the
22: 1 and from the *w'* of my roaring?
36: 3 The *w'* of his mouth are iniquity
50:17 and castest my *w'* behind thee.
52: 4 Thou lovest all devouring *w'*,
54: 2 give ear to the *w'* of my mouth.
55:21 *w'* of his mouth were smoother
21 his *w'* were softer than oil, yet were
56: 5 Every day they wrest my *w'*: all
59:12 the *w'* of their lips let them even
64: 3 shoot their arrows, even bitter *w'*:
78: 1 your ears to the *w'* of my mouth.
106:12 Then believed they his *w'*; they

Ps 107: 11 rebelled against the *w*' of God,
109: 3 me about also with *w*' of hatred;
119: 57 have said that I would keep thy *w*'.
103 sweet are thy *w*' unto my taste!
130 entrance of thy *w*' giveth light;
139 mine enemies have forgotten thy *w*'.
138: 4 they hear the *w*' of thy mouth.
141: 6 they shall hear my *w*'; for they are
Pr 1: 2 to perceive the *w*' of understanding;
6 the *w*' of the wise, and their dark
21 in the city she uttereth her *w*',
23 will make known my *w*' unto you.
2: 1 My son, if thou wilt receive my *w*',
16 which flattereth with her *w*';
4: 4 Let thine heart retain my *w*':
5 decline from the *w*' of my mouth.
20 My son, attend to my *w*'; incline
5: 7 not from the *w*' of my mouth.
6: 2 snared with the *w*' of thy mouth,
2 are taken with the *w*' of thy mouth.
7: 1 My son, keep my *w*', and lay up my
5 which flattereth with her *w*'.
24 and attend to the *w*' of my mouth.
8: 8 All the *w*' of my mouth are in
10: 19 multitude of *w*' there wanteth not
12: 6 *w*' of the wicked are to lie in wait
15: 1 but grievous *w*' stir up anger.
26 the *w*' [*] of the pure are pleasant *w*'.
16: 24 Pleasant *w*' are as an honeycomb,
17: 27 that hath knowledge spareth his *w*':
18: 4 The *w*' of the man's mouth are as
8 *w*' of a talebearer are as wounds,
19: 7 he pursueth them with *w*', yet they
27 to err from the *w*' of knowledge.
22: 12 the *w*' of the transgressor.
17 hear the *w*' of the wise, and apply
21 the certainty of the *w*' of truth;
21 mightest answer the *w*' of truth
23: 8 vomit up, and lose thy sweet *w*'.
9 will despise the wisdom of thy *w*'.
12 thine ears to the *w*' of knowledge.
26: 22 *w*' of a talebearer are as wounds,
29: 19 servant will not be corrected by *w*':
20 thou a man that is hasty in his *w*'?
30: 1 The *w*' of Agur the son of Jakeh,
6 Add thou not unto his *w*', lest he
31: 1 The *w*' of king Lemuel, the
Ec 1: 1 The *w*' of the Preacher, the son of
5: 2 earth: therefore let thy *w*' be few.
3 voice is known by multitude of *w*'.
7 and many *w*' there are also divers
7: 21 heed unto all *w*' that are spoken;
9: 16 despised, and his *w*' are not heard.
17 *w*' of wise men are heard in quiet
10: 12 The *w*' of a wise man's mouth are
13 beginning of the *w*' of his mouth
14 A fool also is full of *w*': a man
12: 10 sought to find out acceptable *w*':
10 was upright, even *w*' of truth.
11 The *w*' of the wise are as goads,
Isa 29: 11 as the *w*' of a book that is sealed,
18 the deaf hear the *w*' of the book,
31: 2 evil, and will not call back his *w*':
32: 7 to destroy the poor with lying *w*',
36: 5 thou, (but they are but vain *w*') I
12 and to thee to speak these *w*'?
13 Hear ye the *w*' of the great king,
22 and told him the *w*' of Rabshakeh.
37: 4 God will hear the *w*' of Rabshakeh,
4 will reprove the *w*' which the Lord
6 of the *w*' that thou hast heard,
17 and hear all the *w*' of Sennacherib,
41: 26 there is none that heareth your *w*'.
51: 16 I have put my *w*' in thy mouth,
58: 13 nor speaking thine own *w*':
59: 13 from the heart *w*' of falsehood.
21 *w*' which I have put in thy mouth,
Jer 1: 1 *w*' of Jeremiah the son of Hilkiah,
9 I have put my *w*' in thy mouth.
3: 12 Go and proclaim these *w*' toward
5: 14 I will make my *w*' in thy mouth fire,
6: 19 have not hearkened unto my *w*',
7: 4 Trust ye not in lying *w*', saying,
8 Behold, ye trust in lying *w*', that
27 shalt speak all these *w*' unto them;
11: 2 Hear ye the *w*' of this covenant,
3 obeyeth not the *w*' of this covenant,
6 Proclaim all these *w*' in the cities
6 Hear ye the *w*' of this covenant,
8 them all the *w*' of this covenant,
10 which refused to hear my *w*';
12: 6 though they speak fair *w*' unto thee.
13: 10 which refuse to hear my *w*', which
15: 16 Thy *w*' were found, and I did eat
16: 10 shalt shew this people all these *w*',
18: 2 I will cause thee to hear my *w*'.
18 us not give heed to any of his *w*'.
19: 2 there the *w*' that I shall tell thee,
15 that they might not hear my *w*'.
22: 5 But if ye will not hear these *w*', I
23: 9 because of the *w*' of his holiness.
16 not unto the *w*' of the prophets
22 caused my people to hear my *w*',
30 steal my *w*' every one from his
36 perverted the *w*' of the living God,
25: 8 Because ye have not heard my *w*',
13 my *w*' which I have pronounced
30 thou against them all these *w*',
26: 2 *w*' that I command thee to speak
5 hearken to the *w*' of my servants
7 Jeremiah speaking these *w*' in the
12 city all the *w*' that ye have heard.
15 to speak all these *w*' in your ears.
20 according to all the *w*' of Jeremiah:
21 and all the princes, heard his *w*',
27: 12 of Judah according to all these *w*',

Jer 27: 14 not unto the *w*' of the prophets
16 not to the *w*' of your prophets
28: 6 perform thy *w*' which thou hast
29: 1 *w*' of the letter that Jeremiah
19 they have not hearkened to my *w*',
23 have spoken lying *w*' in my name,
30: 2 all the *w*' that I have spoken unto
4 are the *w*' that the Lord spake
34: 6 spake all these *w*' unto Zedekiah
18 *w*' of the covenant which they had
35: 13 instruction to hearken to my *w*'?
14 *w*' of Jonadab the son of Rechab,
36: 2 write...all the *w*' that I have spoken
4 of Jeremiah all the *w*' of the Lord,
6 the *w*' of the Lord in the ears of the
8 in the book the *w*' of the Lord
10 in the book the *w*' of Jeremiah
11 of the book all the *w*' of the Lord,
13 them all the *w*' that he had heard,
16 when they had heard all the *w*',
16 surely tell the king of all these *w*'.
17 write all these *w*' at his mouth?
18 pronounced all these *w*' unto me
20 all the *w*' in the ears of the king.
24 servants that heard all these *w*'.
27 *w*' which Baruch wrote at the
28 the former *w*' that were in the first
32 *w*' of the book which Jehoiakim
32 besides unto them many like *w*'.
37: 2 hearken unto the *w*' of the Lord,
38: 1 the *w*' that Jeremiah had spoken
4 in speaking such *w*' unto them:
24 Let no man know of these *w*', and
27 *w*' that the king had commanded.
39: 16 bring my *w*' upon this city for evil,
42: 4 your God according to your *w*';
43: 1 the people all the *w*' of the Lord
1 him to them, even all these *w*',
44: 28 shall know whose *w*' shall stand,
29 know that my *w*' shall surely stand
45: 1 he had written these *w*' in a book
51: 60 all these *w*' that are written against
61 see, and shalt read all these *w*';
64 Thus far are the *w*' of Jeremiah.
Eze 2: 6 them, neither be afraid of their *w*',
6 be not afraid of their *w*', nor be
7 thou shalt speak my *w*' unto them,
3: 4 and speak with my *w*' unto them.
6 *w*' thou canst not understand.
10 my *w*' that I shall speak unto thee
12: 28 shall none of my *w*' be prolonged
33: 31 they hear thy *w*', but they will not
32 for they hear thy *w*', but they do
35: 13 have multiplied your *w*' against me:
Da 2: 9 corrupt *w*' to speak before me,
5: 10 by reason of the *w*' of the king and
6: 14 the king, when he heard these *w*',
7: 11 great *w*' which the horn spake:
25 great *w*' against the most High,
9: 12 And he hath confirmed his *w*',
10: 6 his *w*' like the voice of a multitude.
9 Yet heard I the voice of his *w*':
9 when I heard the voice of his *w*',
11 understand the *w*' that I speak
12 before thy God, thy *w*' were heard.
12 heard, and I am come for thy *w*'.
15 he had spoken such *w*' unto me,
12: 4 O Daniel, shut up the *w*', and seal
9 for the *w*' are closed up and sealed
Ho 6: 5 slain them by the *w*' of my mouth:
10: 4 They have spoken *w*', swearing
14: 2 Take with you *w*', and turn to the
Am 1: 1 The *w*' of Amos, who was among
7: 10 land is not able to bear all his *w*'.
8: 11 but of hearing the *w*' of the Lord:
Mic 2: 7 do not my *w*' do good to him that
Hag 1: 12 and the *w*' of Haggai the prophet,
Zec 1: 6 But my *w*' and my statutes, which
13 with good *w*' and comfortable *w*'.
7: 7 the *w*' which the Lord hath cried
12 *w*' which the Lord of hosts hath
8: 9 *w*' by the mouth of the prophets,
Mal 2: 17 wearied the Lord with your *w*'.
3: 13 Your *w*' have been stout against
M't 10: 14 nor hear your *w*', when ye depart
12: 37 by thy *w*' thou shalt be justified,
37 by thy *w*' thou shalt be condemned.
22: 22 When they had heard these *w*',
24: 35 but my *w*' shall not pass away.
26: 44 third time, saying the same *w*'.
M'r 8: 38 be ashamed of me and of my *w*'
10: 24 disciples were astonished at his *w*'.
12: 13 Herodians, to catch him in his *w*'.
13: 31 but my *w*' shall not pass away.
14: 39 prayed, and spake the same *w*'.
Lu 1: 20 because thou believest not my *w*',
3: 4 in the book of the *w*' of Esaias
4: 22 wondered at the gracious *w*' which
9: 26 be ashamed of me and of my *w*',
20: 20 they might take hold of his *w*',
26 they could not take hold of his *w*'
21: 33 but my *w*' shall not pass away.
23: 9 questioned with him in many *w*';
24: 8 And they remembered his *w*',
11 their *w*' seemed to them as idle
44 These are the *w*' which I spake
Joh 3: 34 hath sent speaketh the *w*' of God:
5: 47 how shall ye believe my *w*'?
6: 63 the *w*' that I speak unto you, they
68 go? thou hast the *w*' of eternal life.
7: 9 he had said these *w*' unto them,
8: 20 *w*' spake Jesus in the treasury,
30 As he spake these *w*', many believed
47 that is of God heareth God's *w*':
9: 22 These *w*' spake his parents, because
40 which were with him heard these *w*',

Joh 10: 21 the *w*' of him that hath a devil.
12: 47 And if any man hear my *w*', and
48 and receiveth not my *w*', hath one
14: 10 *w*' that I speak unto you I speak
23 man love me, he will keep my *w*':
15: 7 my *w*' abide in you, ye shall ask
17: 8 them the *w*' which thou gavest me;
18: 1 When Jesus had spoken these *w*', he
Ac 2: 14 unto you, and hearken to my *w*':
22 Ye men of Israel, hear these *w*';
40 with many other *w*' did he testify
5: 5 Ananias hearing these *w*' fell down,
20 to the people all the *w*' of this life.
6: 11 blasphemous *w*' against Moses,
13 blasphemous *w*' against this holy
7: 22 was mighty in *w*' and in deeds.
10: 22 his house, and to hear *w*' of thee.
44 While Peter yet spake these *w*',
11: 14 Who shall tell thee *w*', whereby
13: 42 that these *w*' might be preached
15: 15 this agree the *w*' of the prophets;
24 from us have troubled you with *w*',
32 exhorted...brethren with many *w*',
16: 38 told these *w*' unto the magistrates:
18: 15 it be a question of *w*' and names,
20: 35 remember the *w*' of the Lord Jesus,
38 of all for the *w*' which he spake,
24: 4 hear us of thy clemency a few *w*'.
26: 25 but speak forth the *w*' of truth
28: 29 And when he had said these *w*',
Ro 10: 18 *w*' unto the ends of the world.
16: 18 good *w*' and fair speeches deceive
1Co 1: 17 not with wisdom of *w*', lest the
2: 4 with enticing *w*' of man's wisdom,
13 *w*' which man's wisdom teacheth,
14: 9 tongue *w*' easy to be understood,
19 five *w*' with my understanding,
19 thousand *w*' in an unknown tongue.
2Co 12: 4 and heard unspeakable *w*', which
Eph 3: 3 mystery; (as I wrote afore in few *w*',
5: 6 no man deceive you with vain *w*':
Col 2: 4 beguile you with enticing *w*'.
1Th 2: 5 any time used we flattering *w*',
4: 18 comfort one another with these *w*'.
1Ti 4: 6 nourished up in the *w*' of faith and
6: 3 and consent not to wholesome *w*',
3 the *w*' of our Lord Jesus Christ,
4 about questions and strifes of *w*',
2Ti 1: 13 Hold fast the form of sound *w*',
2: 14 strive not about *w*' to no profit,
4: 15 he hath greatly withstood our *w*'.
Heb 12: 19 a trumpet, and the voice of *w*';
13: 22 a letter unto you in a few *w*'.
2Pe 2: 3 with feigned *w*' make merchandise
18 speak great swelling *w*' of vanity,
3: 2 of the *w*' which were spoken
3Jo 10 against us with malicious *w*':
Jude 16 mouth speaketh great swelling *w*',
17 the *w*' which were spoken before
Re 1: 3 that hear the *w*' of this prophecy,
17: 17 the *w*' of God shall be fulfilled.
21: 5 for these *w*' are true and faithful.
22: 18 *w*' of the prophecy of this book,
19 *w*' of the book of this prophecy,

wore See WARE.

work See also HANDYWORK; NETWORK; WORKETH; WORKFELLOW; WORKING; WORKMAN; WORK'S; WORKS; WROUGHT.
Ge 2: 2 the seventh day God ended his *w*'
2 on the seventh day from all his *w*'
3 in it he had rested from all his *w*'
5: 29 comfort us concerning our *w*'
Ex 5: 9 more *w*' be laid upon the men,
11 of your *w*' shall be diminished.
18 Go therefore now, and *w*'; for
12: 16 no manner of *w*' shall be done in
14: 31 saw that great *w*' which the Lord
18: 20 and the *w*' that they must do.
20: 9 thou labour, and do all thy *w*':
10 in it thou shalt not do any *w*', thou
23: 12 Six days thou shalt do thy *w*', and
24: 10 a paved *w*' of a sapphire stone,
25: 18 beaten *w*' shalt thou make them,
31 of beaten *w*' shall the candlestick
36 shall be one beaten *w*' of pure gold.
26: 1 cherubims of cunning *w*' shalt
31 fine twined linen of cunning *w*':
28: 6 fine twined linen, with cunning *w*'.
8 same, according to the *w*' thereof;
11 the *w*' of an engraver in stone, like
14 wreathen *w*' shalt thou make them,
15 of judgment with cunning *w*';
15 after the *w*' of the ephod thou shalt
22 ends of wreathen *w*' of pure gold.
32 a binding of woven *w*' round about
31: 4 to *w*' in gold, and in silver, and in
5 *w*' in all manner of workmanship.
14 whosoever doeth any *w*' therein,
15 Six days may *w*' be done; but in
15 doeth any *w*' in the sabbath day,
32: 16 the tables were the *w*' of God, and
34: 10 art shall see the *w*' of the Lord:
21 Six days thou shalt *w*', but on
35: 2 Six days shall *w*' be done, but on
2 whosoever doeth *w*' therein shall be
21 offering to the *w*' of the tabernacle
24 wood for any *w*' of the service,
29 to bring for all manner of *w*',
32 to *w*' in gold, and in silver, and in
33 make any manner of cunning *w*'.
35 wisdom of heart, to *w*' all manner
35 manner of *w*', of the engraver,
35 even of them that do any *w*',
35 of those that devise cunning *w*'.
36: 1 understanding to know how to *w*'

Ex 36: 1 all manner of w' for the service
2 up to come unto the w' to do it:
3 brought for the w' of the service
4 wrought all the w' of the sanctuary,
4 came every man from his w' which
5 enough for the service of the w',
6 man nor woman make any more w'
7 had was sufficient for all the w'
8 wrought the w' of the tabernacle
8 cherubims of cunning w' made he
35 made he it of cunning w'.
37: 17 beaten w' made he the candlestick;
22 it was one beaten w' of pure gold.
29 to the w' of the apothecary.
38: 24 gold that was occupied for the w'
24 all the w' of the holy place, even
39: 3 w' it in the blue, and in the purple,
3 in the fine linen, with cunning w'.
5 same, according to the w' thereof;
8 the breastplate of cunning w',
8 like the w' of the ephod; of gold,
15 ends, of wreathen w' of pure gold.
22 the robe of the ephod of woven w',
27 of fine linen of woven w' for Aaron,
32 was all the w' of the tabernacle
42 children of Israel made all the w'.
43 Moses did look upon all the w',
40: 33 gate. So Moses finished the w'.
Le 11: 32 wherein any w' is done, it must be
13: 51 or in any w' that is made of skin;
16: 29 and do no w' at all, whether it be
23: 3 Six days shall w' be done: but the
3 ye shall do no w' therein: it is the
7, 8 ye shall do no servile w' therein.
21 ye shall do no servile w' therein:
25 Ye shall do no servile w' therein:
28 ye shall do no w' in that same day:
30 that doeth any w' in that same day,
31 Ye shall do no manner of w': it
35, 36 ye shall do no servile w' therein.
Nu 4: 3 to do the w' in the tabernacle
23 to do the w' in the tabernacle of
30 to do the w' of the tabernacle of
35, 39, 43 for the w' in the tabernacle of
8: 4 this w' of the candlestick was of
4 flowers thereof, was beaten w':
28: 18 shall do no manner of servile w'
25 ye shall do no servile w'.
26 ye shall do no servile w':
29: 1 ye shall do no servile w':
7 ye shall not do any w' therein:
12 ye shall do no servile w', and ye
35 ye shall do no servile w' therein:
31: 20 of skins, and all w' of goats' hair,
De 4: 28 serve gods, the w' of men's hands,
5: 13 shalt labour, and do all thy w':
14 in it thou shalt not do any w', thou,
14: 29 thee in all the w' of thine hand
15: 19 shalt do no w' with the firstling
16: 8 God: thou shalt do no w' therein.
24: 19 thee in all the w' of thine hands.
27: 15 w' of the hands of the craftsman,
28: 12 to bless all the w' of thine hand:
30: 9 plenteous in every w' of thine hand,
31: 29 through the w' of your hands.
32: 4 He is the Rock, his w' is perfect:
33: 11 and accept the w' of his hands:
Jos 9: 4 They did w' wilily, and went and
J'g 19: 16 came an old man from his w' out
Ru 2: 12 The Lord recompense thy w', and
1Sa 8: 16 asses, and put them to his w'.
14: 6 be that the Lord will w' for us:
1Ki 5: 16 officers which were over the w',
16 the people that wrought in the w'.
6: 35 with gold fitted upon the carved w'.
7: 8 porch, which was of the like w'.
14 cunning to w' all works in brass.
14 Solomon, and wrought all his w'.
17 And nets of checker w',
17 and wreaths of chain w',
19 pillars were of lily w' in the porch,
22 the top of the pillars was lily w':
22 was the w' of the pillars finished.
28 the w' of the bases was on this
29 certain additions made of thin w'.
31 was round after the w' of the base,
33 And the w' of the wheels was like
33 was like the w' of a chariot wheel:
40 made an end of doing all the w'
51 ended all the w' that king Solomon
9: 23 that were over Solomon's w',
23 the people that wrought in the w'.
16: 7 to anger with the w' of his hands,
21: 20 w' evil in the sight of the Lord.
25 did sell himself to w' wickedness
2Ki 12: 11 the hands of them that did the w',
19: 18 but the w' of men's hands, wood
22: 5 the hand of the doers of the w',
5 them give it to the doers of the w',
9 the hand of them that do the w',
25: 17 and the wreathen w', and
17 second pillar with wreathen w'.
1Ch 4: 23 dwelt with the king for his w'.
6: 49 all the w' of the place most holy,
9: 13 able men for the w' of the service
19 were over the w' of the service,
33 employed in that w' day and night.
16: 37 as every day's w' required:
22: 15 men for every manner of w'.
23: 4 the w' of the house of the Lord;
24 the w' for the service of the house
28 the w' of the service of the house
27: 26 did the w' of the field for tillage
28: 13 the w' of the service of the house
20 the w' for the service of the house
29: 1 and tender, and the w' is great:

1Ch 29: 5 of w' to be made by the hands
6 with the rulers of the king's w',
2Ch 2: 7 a man cunning to w' in gold,
14 man of Tyre, skilful to w' in gold,
18 overseers to set the people a w'.
3: 10 made two cherubims of image w',
4: 5 it like the w' of the brim of a cup,
11 Huram finished the w' that he
5: 1 all the w' that Solomon made for
8: 9 make no servants for his w';
16 all the w' of Solomon was prepared
15: 7 for your w' shall be rewarded.
16: 5 of Ramah, and let his w' cease.
24: 12 such as did the w' of the service
13 and the w' was perfected by them,
29: 34 till the w' was ended, and until the
31: 21 in every w' that he began in the
32: 19 were the w' of the hands of man.
34: 12 the men did the w' faithfully:
13 of all that wrought the w' in any
Ezr 2: 69 ability unto the treasure of the w'
3: 8 to set forward the w' of the house
4: 24 ceased the w' of the house of God
5: 8 and this w' goeth fast on, and
6: 7 Let the w' of this house of God
22 in the w' of the house of God,
10: 13 is this a w' of one day or two:
Ne 2: 16 nor to the rest that did the w'.
18 their hands for this good w'.
3: 5 necks to the w' of their Lord.
4: 6 for the people had a mind to w'.
11 them, and cause the w' to cease.
15 to the wall, every one unto his w'.
16 of my servants wrought in the w',
17 one of his hands wrought in the w',
19 The w' is great and large, and we
21 So we laboured in the w': and half
5: 16 continued in the w' of this wall,
16 were gathered thither unto the w'.
6: 3 I am doing a great w', so that I
3 why should the w' cease, whilst I
9 shall be weakened from the w',
16 this w' was wrought of our God.
7: 70 of the fathers gave unto the w'.
71 gave to the treasure of the w'
10: 33 all the w' of the house of our God.
11: 12 that did the w' of the house
13: 10 and the singers, that did the w',
Job 1: 10 hast blessed the w' of his hands,
7: 2 looketh for the reward of his w':
10: 3 despise the w' of thine hands,
14: 15 a desire to the w' of thine hands.
23: 9 the left hand, where he doth w',
24: 5 desert, go they forth to their w';
34: 11 the w' of a man shall he render
19 they all are the w' of his hands.
36: 9 Then he sheweth them their w',
24 that thou magnify his w',
37: 7 that all men may know his w'.
Ps 8: 3 thy heavens, the w' of thy fingers,
9: 16 snared in the w' of his own hands.
28: 4 them after the w' of their hands,
44: 1 what w' thou didst in their days,
58: 2 Yea, in heart ye w' wickedness;
62: 12 to every man according to his w'.
64: 9 and shall declare the w' of God;
74: 6 they break down the carved w'
77: 12 I will meditate also of all thy w',
90: 16 thy w' appear unto thy servants,
17 establish thou the w' of our hands
17 w' of our hands establish thou it.
92: 4 made me glad through thy w':
95: 9 me, proved me, and saw my w'.
101: 3 I hate the w' of them that turn
102: 25 heavens are the w' of thy hands.
104: 23 Man goeth forth unto his w' and
111: 3 His w' is honourable and glorious:
115: 4 and gold, the w' of men's hands.
119: 126 It is time for thee, Lord, to w':
135: 15 and gold, the w' of men's hands.
141: 4 works with men that w' iniquity:
143: 5 I muse on the w' of thy hands.
Pr 11: 18 wicked worketh a deceitful w':
16: 11 the weights of the bag are his w'.
18: 9 He also that is slothful in his w'
20: 11 doings, whether his w' be pure,
21: 8 as for the pure, his w' is right.
24: 27 Prepare thy w' without, and make
29 to the man according to his w'.
Ec 2: 17 w' that is wrought under the sun
3: 11 find out the w' that God maketh
17 every purpose and for every w'.
4: 3 not seen the evil w' that is done
4 all travail, and every right w',
5: 6 and destroy the w' of thine hands?
7: 13 Consider the w' of God: for who
8: 9 applied my heart unto every w'
11 sentence against an evil w' is not
14 according to the w' of the wicked;
14 to the w' of the righteous:
17 Then I beheld all the w' of God,
17 cannot find out the w' that is done
9: 10 for there is no w', nor device, nor
12: 14 bring every w' into judgment,
Ca 7: 1 w' of the hands of a cunning
Isa 2: 8 worship the w' of their own hands,
5: 12 regard not the w' of the Lord,
19 make speed, and hasten his w',
10: 12 Lord hath performed his whole w'
17: 8 to the altars, the w' of his hands,
19: 9 Moreover they that w' in fine flax,
14 Egypt to err in every w' thereof,
15 shall there be any w' for Egypt,
25 and Assyria the w' of my hands,
28: 21 he may do his w', his strange w';
29: 14 marvellous w' among this people,

Isa 29: 14 a marvellous w' and a wonder:
16 the w' say of him that made it,
23 his children, the w' of mine hands,
31: 2 the help of them that w' iniquity.
32: 6 and his heart will w' iniquity, to
17 the w' of righteousness shall be
37: 19 the w' of men's hands, wood and
40: 10 with him, and his w' before him.
41: 24 nothing, and your w' of nought:
43: 13 I will w', and who shall let it?
45: 9 What makest thou? or thy w',
11 concerning the w' of my hands
49: 4 Lord, and my w' with my God.
54: 16 forth an instrument for his w';
60: 21 my planting, the w' of my hands,
61: 8 and I will direct their w' in truth,
62: 11 with him, and his w' before him.
64: 8 and we all are the w' of thine hand.
65: 7 will I measure their former w'
22 long enjoy the w' of their hands.
Jer 10: 3 w' of the hands of the workman,
9 the w' of the workman, and of
9 are all the w' of cunning men.
15 are vanity, and the w' of errors:
17: 22 neither do ye any w', but hallow
24 sabbath day, to do no w' therein;
18: 3 he wrought a w' on the wheels.
22: 13 and giveth him not for his w';
31: 16 for thy w' shall be rewarded, saith
32: 19 in counsel, and mighty in w':
30 anger with the w' of their hands,
48: 10 the w' of the Lord deceitfully,
50: 25 this is the w' of the Lord God of
29 her according to her w';
51: 10 declare in Zion the w' of the Lord
18 They are vanity, the w' of errors:
La 3: 64 according to the w' of their hands.
4: 2 the w' of the hands of the potter!
Eze 1: 16 their w' was like unto the colour
16 and their w' was as it were a wheel
15: 3 be taken thereof to do any w'?
4 is burned. It is meet for any w'?
5 was whole, it was meet for no w':
5 less shall it be meet for any w',
16: 10 thee also with broidered w',
13 linen, and silk, and broidered w';
30 the w' of an imperious whorish
27: 7 Fine linen with broidered w'
16 and broidered w', and fine linen,
24 in blue clothes, and broidered w',
33: 26 ye w' abomination, and ye defile
Da 11: 23 with him he shall w' deceitfully:
Ho 6: 8 a city of them that w' iniquity,
13: 2 all of it the w' of the craftsman:
14: 3 any more to the w' of our hands,
Mic 2: 1 and w' evil upon their beds!
5: 13 worship the w' of thine hands.
Hab 1: 5 marvellously: for I will w'
5 a w' in your days, which ye will
2: 18 maker of his w' trusteth therein,
3: 2 revive thy w' in the midst of the
Zep 2: 14 for he shall uncover the cedar w'.
Hag 1: 14 did w' in the house of the Lord
2: 4 the land, saith the Lord, and w':
14 and so is every w' of their hands;
Mal 3: 15 that w' wickedness are set up;
M't 7: 23 from me, ye that w' iniquity.
21: 28 Son, go w' to day in my vineyard.
26: 10 hath wrought a good w' upon me.
M'r 6: 5 he could there do no mighty w',
13: 34 servants, and to every man his w',
14: 6 she hath wrought a good w' on me.
Lu 13: 14 days in which men ought to w':
Joh 4: 34 that sent me, and to finish his w'.
5: 17 worketh hitherto, and I w'.
6: 28 that we might w' the works of God?
29 This is the w' of God, that ye
30 believe thee? what dost thou w'?
7: 21 I have done one w', and ye all
9: 4 I must w' the works of him that
4 night cometh, when no man can w'.
10: 33 For a good w' we stone thee not;
17: 4 finished the w' which thou gavest
Ac 5: 38 or this w' be of men, it will come
13: 2 for the w' whereunto I have called
41 for I w' [2038] a w' in your days,
41 a w' which ye shall in no wise
14: 26 for the w' which they fulfilled.
15: 38 and went not with them to the w'.
27: 16 we had much w' to come by
Ro 2: 15 shew the w' of the law written in
7: 5 did w' in our members to bring
8: 28 all things w' together for good to
9: 28 For he will finish the w', and cut
28 short w' will the Lord make upon
11: 6 otherwise w' is no more w'.
14: 20 meat destroy not the w' of God.
1Co 3: 13 man's w' shall be made manifest:
13 fire shall try every man's w'
14 If any man's w' abide which he
15 If any man's w' shall be burned, he
9: 1 are not ye my w' in the Lord?
15: 58 abounding in the w' of the Lord,
16: 10 for he worketh the w' of the Lord,
2Co 9: 8 may abound to every good w':
Ga 6: 4 But let every man prove his own w',
Eph 4: 12 for the w' of the ministry, for the
19 to w' all uncleanness with
Ph'p 1: 6 which hath begun a good w' in you
2: 12 w' out your own salvation with
30 for the w' of Christ he was nigh
Col 1: 10 being fruitful in every good w', and
1Th 1: 3 without ceasing your w' of faith,
4: 11 and to w' with your own hands,
2Th 1: 11 and the w' of faith with power:
2: 7 of iniquity doth already w':

2Th 2:17 you in every good word and *w*'.
3:10 that if any would not *w*', neither
12 that with quietness they *w*', and
1Ti 3: 1 of a bishop, he desireth a good *w*'.
5:10 diligently followed every good *w*'.
2Ti 2:21 and prepared unto every good *w*'.
4: 5 do the *w*' of an evangelist, make
18 shall deliver me from every evil *w*',
Tit 1:16 and unto every good *w*' reprobate.
3: 1 to be ready to every good *w*',
Heb 6:10 forget your *w*' and labour of love,
13:21 Make you perfect in every good *w*'
Jas 1: 4 let patience have her perfect *w*',
25 but a doer of the *w*', this man shall
3:16 is confusion and every evil *w*'.
1Pe 1:17 according to every man's *w*',
Re 22:12 man according as his *w*' shall be.

worked See WROUGHT.

worker See also WORKERS.
1Ki 7:14 was a man of Tyre, a *w*' in brass:

workers See also FELLOWWORKERS.
2Ki 23:24 Moreover the *w*' with familiar spirits,
1Ch 22:15 and *w*' of stone and timber, and
Job 31: 3 punishment to the *w*' of iniquity?
34: 8 in company with the *w*' of iniquity,
22 where the *w*' of iniquity may hide
Ps 5: 5 thou hatest all *w*' of iniquity.
6: 8 from me, all ye *w*' of iniquity;
14: 4 the *w*' of iniquity no knowledge?
28: 3 with the *w*' of iniquity, which speak
36:12 There are the *w*' of iniquity fallen:
37: 1 against the *w*' of iniquity.
53: 4 the *w*' of iniquity no knowledge?
59: 2 Deliver me from the *w*' of iniquity,
64: 2 insurrection of the *w*' of iniquity:
92: 7 all the *w*' of iniquity do flourish;
9 *w*' of iniquity shall be scattered.
94: 4 *w*' of iniquity boast themselves?
16 for me against the *w*' of iniquity?
125: 5 them forth with the *w*' of iniquity:
141: 9 and the gins of the *w*' of iniquity.
Pr 10:29 shall be to the *w*' of iniquity.
21:15 shall be to the *w*' of iniquity.
Lu 13:27 from me, all ye *w*' of iniquity.
1Co 12:29 teachers? are all *w*' of miracles?
2Co 6: 1 We then, as *w*' together with him,
11:13 are false apostles, deceitful *w*',
Ph'p 3: 2 Beware of dogs, beware of evil *w*',

worketh
Job 33:29 these things *w*' God oftentimes
Ps 15: 2 and *w*' righteousness, and speaketh
101: 7 He that *w*' deceit shall not dwell
Pr 11:18 The wicked *w*' a deceitful work:
26:28 and a flattering mouth *w*' ruin.
31:13 and *w*' willingly with her hands.
Ec 3: 9 What profit hath he that *w*' in that
Isa 44:12 with the tongs both *w*' in the coals,
12 *w*' it with the strength of his arms:
64: 5 rejoiceth and *w*' righteousness,
Da 6:27 *w*' signs and wonders in heaven
Joh 5:17 My Father *w*' hitherto, and I work.
Ac 10:35 *w*' righteousness, is accepted with
Ro 2:10 peace, to every man that *w*' good,
4: 4 to him that *w*' is the reward not
5 But to him that *w*' not, but
15 Because the law *w*' wrath: for
5: 3 knowing...tribulation *w*' patience;
13:10 Love *w*' no ill to his neighbour:
1Co 12: 6 the same God which *w*' all in all.
11 *w*' that one and the selfsame Spirit,
16:10 he *w*' the work of the Lord, as I
2Co 4:12 So then death *w*' in us, but life in
17 *w*' for us a far more exceeding
7:10 godly sorrow *w*' repentance unto
10 the sorrow of the world *w*' death.
Ga 3: 5 Spirit, and *w*' miracles among you,
5: 6 but faith which *w*' by love.
Eph 1:11 purpose of him who *w*' all things
2: 2 spirit that now *w*' in the children
3:20 to the power that *w*' in us,
Ph'p 2:13 is God which *w*' in you both to will
Col 1:29 working, which *w*' in me mightily.
1Th 2:13 which effectually *w*' also in you
Jas 1: 3 trying of your faith *w*' patience.
20 *w*' not the righteousness of God.
Re 21:27 whatsoever *w*' abomination, or

workfellow See also FELLOWWORKERS.
Ro 16:21 Timotheus my *w*', and Lucius,

working
Ps 52: 2 like a sharp rasor, *w*' deceitfully.
74:12 *w*' salvation in the midst of the
Isa 28:29 in counsel, and excellent in *w*'.
Eze 46: 1 east shall be shut the six *w*' days;
M'r 16:20 the Lord *w*' with them, and
Ro 1:27 men *w*' that which is unseemly,
7:13 *w*' death in me by that which is
1Co 4:12 labour, *w*' with our own hands:
9: 6 have not we power to forbear *w*'?
12:10 To another the *w*' of miracles;
Eph 1:19 to the *w*' of his mighty power,
3: 7 me by the effectual *w*' of his power.
4:16 to the effectual *w*' in the measure
28 *w*' with his hands the thing which
Ph'p 3:21 according to the *w*' whereby he is
Col 1:29 striving according to his *w*', which
2Th 2: 9 coming is after the *w*' of Satan
3:11 *w*' not at all, but are busybodies.
Heb 13:21 his will, *w*' in you that which is
Re 16:14 the spirits of devils, *w*' miracles,

workman See also WORKMANSHIP; WORKMEN.
Ex 35:35 engraver, and of the cunning *w*',
38:23 an engraver, and a cunning *w*',
Ca 7: 1 work of the hands of a cunning *w*',
Isa 40:19 The *w*' melteth a graven image,
20 seeketh unto him a cunning *w*' to
Jer 10: 3 the work of the hands of the *w*',
9 from Uphaz, the work of the *w*',
Ho 8: 6 the *w*' made it; therefore it is not
M't 10:10 for the *w*' is worthy of his meat.
2Ti 2:15 a *w*' that needeth not to be

workmanship
Ex 31: 3 and in all manner of *w*',
5 to work in all manner of *w*',
35:31 and in all manner of *w*';
2Ki 16:10 according to all the *w*' thereof.
1Ch 28:21 be with thee for all manner of *w*'
Eze 28:13 *w*' of thy tabrets and of thy pipes
Eph 2:10 For we are his *w*', created in

workmen See also WORKMEN'S.
2Ki 12:14 But they gave that to the *w*',
15 money to be bestowed on *w*':
1Ch 22:15 are *w*' with thee in abundance,
25: 1 number of the *w*' according
2Ch 24:13 So the *w*' wrought, and the
34:10 *w*' that had the oversight
10 *w*' that wrought in the house
17 and to the hand of the *w*'.
Ezr 3: 9 the *w*' in the house of God:
Isa 44:11 and the *w*', they are of men:
Ac 19:25 with the *w*' of like occupation,

workmen's
J'g 5:26 her right hand to the *w*' hammer;

work's
1Th 5:13 highly in love for their *w*' sake.

works See also NETWORKS.
Ex 5: 4 let the people from their *w*'?
13 Fulfil your *w*', your daily tasks,
23:24 serve them, nor do after their *w*':
31: 4 To devise cunning *w*', to work in
35:32 And to devise curious *w*', to work
Nu 16:28 hath sent me to do all these *w*';
De 2: 7 thee in all the *w*' of thy hand:
3:24 that can do according to thy *w*',
15:10 God shall bless thee in all thy *w*',
16:15 and in all the *w*' of thine hands,
Jos 24:31 had known all the *w*' of the Lord,
J'g 2: 7 seen all the great *w*' of the Lord,
10 *w*' which he had done for Israel.
1Sa 8: 8 to all the *w*' which they have done
19: 4 his *w*' have been to thee-ward
1Ki 7:14 cunning to work all *w*' in brass.
13:11 *w*' that the man of God had done
2Ki 22:17 with all the *w*' of their hands;
1Ch 16: 9 talk ye of all his wondrous *w*'.
12 Remember his marvellous *w*' that he
24 his marvellous *w*' among all nations
28:19 even all the *w*' of this pattern.
2Ch 20:37 the Lord hath broken thy *w*'.
32:30 Hezekiah prospered in all his *w*'.
34:25 with all the *w*' of their hands;
Ne 6:14 according to these their *w*',
9:35 turned they from their wicked *w*'.
Job 34:25 Therefore he knoweth their *w*',
37:14 consider the wondrous *w*' of God.
16 wondrous *w*' of him which is perfect
Ps 8: 6 dominion over the *w*' of thy hands
9: 1 shew forth all thy marvellous *w*'.
14: 1 they have done abominable *w*',
17: 4 Concerning the *w*' of men, by the
26: 7 and tell of all thy wondrous *w*'.
28: 5 regard not the *w*' of the Lord,
33: 4 and all his *w*' are done in truth.
15 alike; he considereth all their *w*'.
40: 5 wonderful *w*' which thou hast done,
46: 8 Come, behold the *w*' of the Lord,
66: 3 How terrible art thou in thy *w*'!
5 Come and see the *w*' of God: he is
71:17 have I declared thy wondrous *w*'.
73:28 God, that I may declare all thy *w*'.
75: 1 is near thy wondrous *w*' declare.
77:11 remember the *w*' of the Lord:
78: 4 wonderful *w*' that he hath done.
7 God, and not forget the *w*' of God,
11 forgat his *w*', and his wonders
32 believed not for his wondrous *w*'.
86: 8 neither are there any *w*' like unto
8 are there any...like unto thy *w*'.
92: 4 triumph in the *w*' of thy hands.
5 O Lord, how great are thy *w*'!
103:22 his *w*' in all places of his dominion:
104:13 is satisfied with the fruit of thy *w*'.
24 O Lord, how manifold are thy *w*'!
31 the Lord shall rejoice in his *w*'.
105: 2 talk ye of all his wondrous *w*'.
5 Remember his marvellous *w*' that
106:13 They soon forgat his *w*'; they
22 Wondrous *w*' in the land of Ham,
35 the heathen, and learned their *w*'.
39 they defiled with their own *w*',
107: 8, 15, 21 for his wonderful *w*' to the
22 and declare his *w*' with rejoicing.
24 These see the *w*' of the Lord, and
31 his wonderful *w*' to the children
111: 2 The *w*' of the Lord are great,
4 wonderful *w*' to be remembered:
6 his people the power of his *w*',
7 The *w*' of his hands are verity
118:17 and declare the *w*' of the Lord.
119:27 so shall I talk of thy wondrous *w*'.
138: 8 not the *w*' of thine own hands.
139:14 marvellous are thy *w*'; and that
141: 4 practise wicked *w*' with men that
143: 5 I meditate on all thy *w*'; I muse
145: 4 shall praise thy *w*' to another,
5 and of thy wondrous *w*'.
9 tender mercies are over all his *w*'.
10 All thy *w*' shall praise thee, O
Ps 145:17 all his ways, and holy in all his *w*'.
Pr 7:16 with carved *w*', with fine linen
8:22 of his way, before his *w*' of old.
16: 3 Commit thy *w*' unto the Lord,
24:12 every man according to his *w*'?
31:31 her own *w*' praise her in the gates.
Ec 1:14 have seen all the *w*' that are done
2: 4 I made me great *w*'; I builded me
11 *w*' that my hands had wrought,
3:22 man should rejoice in his own *w*';
9: 1 and their *w*', are in the hand of
7 for God now accepteth thy *w*'.
11: 5 thou knowest not the *w*' of God
Isa 26:12 hast wrought all our *w*' in us.
29:15 their *w*' are in the dark, and they
41:29 all vanity; their *w*' are nothing:
57:12 thy righteousness, and thy *w*';
59: 6 cover themselves with their *w*':
6 their *w*' are *w*' of iniquity, and the
66:18 know their *w*' and their thoughts:
Jer 1:16 the *w*' of their own hands.
7:13 because ye have done all these *w*',
21: 2 according to all his wondrous *w*',
25: 6 anger with the *w*' of your hands;
7 to anger with the *w*' of your hands
14 to the *w*' of their own hands.
44: 8 wrath with the *w*' of your hands,
48: 7 thou hast trusted in thy *w*' and in
Eze 6: 6 and your *w*' may be abolished.
Da 4:37 heaven, all whose *w*' are truth,
9:14 our God is righteous in all his *w*'
Am 8: 7 I will never forget any of their *w*'.
Jon 3:10 And God saw their *w*', that they
Mic 6:16 and all the *w*' of the house of Ahab,
M't 5:16 that they may see your good *w*',
7:22 name done many wonderful *w*'?
11: 2 in the prison the *w*' of Christ,
20 most of his mighty *w*' were done,
21 if the mighty *w*', which were done
23 if the mighty *w*', which have been
13:54 this wisdom, and these mighty *w*'?
58 he did not many mighty *w*' there
14: 2 therefore mighty *w*' do shew forth
16:27 every man according to his *w*'.
23: 3 but do not ye after their *w*':
5 *w*' they do for to be seen of men:
M'r 6: 2 even such mighty *w*' are wrought
14 mighty *w*' do shew forth...in him.
Lu 10:13 mighty *w*'. had been done in Tyre
19:37 the mighty *w*' that they had seen;
Joh 5:20 shew him greater *w*' than these,
36 *w*' which the Father hath given me
36 same *w*' that I do, bear witness
6:28 that we might work the *w*' of God?
7: 3 may see the *w*' that thou doest.
7 of it, that the *w*' thereof are evil.
8:39 ye would do the *w*' of Abraham.
9: 3 *w*' of God should be made manifest
4 work the *w*' of him that sent me,
10:25 *w*' that I do in my Father's name,
32 Many good *w*' have I shewed you
32 which of those *w*' do ye stone me?
37 If I do not the *w*' of my Father,
38 ye believe not me, believe the *w*':
14:10 dwelleth in me, he doeth the *w*'.
12 the *w*' that I do shall he do also;
12 greater *w*' than these shall he do;
15:24 the *w*' which none other man did,
Ac 2:11 tongues the wonderful *w*' of God.
7:41 in the *w*' of their own hands.
9:36 this woman was full of good *w*' and
15:18 Known unto God are all his *w*'
26:20 and do *w*' meet for repentance.
Ro 3:27 By what law? of *w*'? Nay: but by
4: 2 if Abraham were justified by *w*',
6 imputeth righteousness without *w*',
9:11 not of *w*', but of him that calleth;)
32 but as it were by the *w*' of the law.
11: 6 by grace, then is it no more of *w*':
6 But if it be of *w*', then is it no more
13: 3 rulers are not a terror to good *w*',
12 cast off the *w*' of darkness, and
2Co 11:15 end shall be according to their *w*'.
Ga 2:16 not justified by the *w*' of the law,
16 and not by the *w*' of the law:
16 by the *w*' of the law shall no flesh
3: 2 Received ye the Spirit by the *w*' of
5 doeth he it by the *w*' of the law,
10 many as are of the *w*' of the law
5:19 the *w*' of the flesh are manifest,
Eph 2: 9 Not of *w*', lest any man should
10 in Christ Jesus unto good *w*',
5:11 with the unfruitful *w*' of darkness,
Col 1:21 enemies in your mind by wicked *w*',
1Ti 2:10 godliness) with good *w*'.
5:10 Well reported of for good *w*'; if she
25 the good *w*' of some are manifest
6:18 that they be rich in good *w*', ready
2Ti 1: 9 calling, not according to our *w*',
3:17 furnished unto all good *w*'.
4:14 reward him according to his *w*':
Tit 1:16 but in *w*' they deny him, being
2: 7 thyself a pattern of good *w*':
14 peculiar people, zealous of good *w*'
3: 5 Not by *w*' of righteousness which
8 be careful to maintain good *w*'.
14 to maintain good *w*' for necessary
Heb 1:10 heavens are the *w*' of thine hands:
2: 7 set him over the *w*' of thy hands:
3: 9 me, and saw my *w*' forty years.
4: 3 the *w*' were finished from the
4 the seventh day from all his *w*'.
10 also hath ceased from his own *w*',
6: 1 of repentance from dead *w*', and of
9:14 purge your conscience from dead *w*'
10:24 provoke unto love and to good *w*':

Jas 2:14 say he hath faith, and have not w'?
17 so faith, if it hath not w', is dead,
18 say, Thou hast faith, and I have w':
18 shew me thy faith without thy w',
18 I will shew thee my faith by my w'.
20 man, that faith without w' is dead?
21 Abraham our father justified by w'
22 how faith wrought with his w',
22 and by w' was faith made perfect?
24 how that by w' a man is justified,
25 Rahab the harlot justified by w',
26 so faith without w' is dead also.
3:13 out of a good conversation his w'
1Pe 2:12 they may by your good w', which
2Pe 3:10 w' that are therein shall be burned
1Jo 3: 8 might destroy the w' of the devil.
12 Because his own w' were evil, and
Re 2: 2 I know thy w', and thy labour, and
5 and repent, and do the first w';
9 I know thy w', and tribulation, and
13 I know thy w', and where thou
19 I know thy w', and charity, and
19 faith, and thy patience, and thy w';
23 one of you according to your w'.
26 and keepeth my w' unto the end,
3: 1 I know thy w', that thou hast a name
2 for I have not found thy w' perfect
8 I know thy w': behold, I have set
15 I know thy w', that thou art neither
9:20 yet repented not of the w' of their
14:13 and their w' do follow them.
15: 3 Great and marvellous are thy w',
18: 6 her double according to her w':
20:12 in the books, according to their w'.
13 every man according to their w'.

works'
Joh 14:11 believe me for the very w' sake.

world See also WORLD'S; WORLDS.
1Sa 2: 8 and he hath set the w' upon them.
2Sa 22:16 the foundations of the w' were
1Ch 16:30 the w' also shall be stable, that it
Job 18:18 darkness, and chased out of the w'.
34:13 or who hath disposed the whole w'?
37:12 upon the face of the w' in the earth.
Ps 9: 8 shall judge the w' in righteousness,
17:14 from men of the w', which have
18:15 the foundations of the w' were
19: 4 their words to the end of the w'.
22:27 ends of the w' shall remember
24: 1 the w', and they that dwell therein.
33: 8 inhabitants of the w' stand in awe
49: 1 ear, all ye inhabitants of the w':
50:12 for the w' is mine, and the fulness
73:12 ungodly, who prosper in the w';
77:18 the lightnings lightened the w':
89:11 for the w' and the fulness thereof,
90: 2 hadst formed the earth and the w',
93: 1 the w' also is stablished, that it
96:10 the w' also shall be established that
13 judge the w' with righteousness,
97: 4 His lightnings enlightened the w':
98: 7 the w', and they that dwell therein.
9 righteousness shall he judge the w',
Pr 8:26 highest part of the dust of the w'.
Ec 3:11 he hath set the w' in their heart,
Isa 13:11 I will punish the w' for their evil,
14:17 That made the w' as a wilderness,
21 fill the face of the w' with cities.
18: 3 All ye inhabitants of the w', and
23:17 with all the kingdoms of the w'
24: 4 w' languisheth and fadeth away,
26: 9 of the w' will learn righteousness.
18 the inhabitants of the w' fallen.
27: 6 and fill the face of the w' with fruit.
34: 1 the w', and all things that come
38:11 with the inhabitants of the w'.
45:17 nor confounded w' without end.
62:11 proclaimed unto the end of the w',
64: 4 since the beginning of the w' men
Jer 10:12 established the w' by his wisdom,
25:26 and all the kingdoms of the w',
51:15 established the w' by his wisdom,
La 4:12 and all the inhabitants of the w',
Na 1: 5 the w', and all that dwell therein.
M't 4: 8 him all the kingdoms of the w',
5:14 Ye are the light of the w'. A city
12:32 forgiven him, neither in this w',
32 neither in the w' to come.
13:22 the word; and the care of this w',
35 from the foundation of the w'.
38 The field is the w'; the good seed
39 the harvest is the end of the w';
40 so shall it be in the end of this w'.
49 So shall it be at the end of the w':
16:26 if he shall gain the whole w', and
18: 7 Woe unto the w' because of
24: 3 coming, and of the end of the w'?
14 shall be preached in all the w' for
21 not since the beginning of the w'
25:34 you from the foundation of the w':
26:13 shall be preached in the whole w',
28:20 alway, even unto the end of the w'.
M'r 4:19 And the cares of this w', and the
8:36 if he shall gain the whole w', and
10:30 and in the w' to come eternal life.
14: 9 preached throughout the whole w',
16:15 Go ye into all the w', and preach
Lu 1:70 have been since the w' began:
2: 1 that all the w' should be taxed.
4: 5 unto him all the kingdoms of the w'
9:25 if he gain the whole w', and lose
11:50 shed from the foundation of the w',
12:30 do the nations of the w' seek
16: 8 the children of this w' are in their
18:30 in the w' to come life everlasting.
Lu 20:34 The children of this w' marry, and
35 accounted worthy to obtain that w',
Joh 1: 9 every man that cometh into the w'.
10 He was in the w',
10 and the w' was made by him,
10 and the w' knew him not.
29 which taketh away the sin of the w'.
3:16 For God so loved the w', that he
17 Son into the w' to condemn the w';
17 the w' through him might be saved.
19 that light is come into the w', and
4:42 the Christ, the Saviour of the w'.
6:14 that should come into the w'.
33 and giveth light unto the w'.
51 I will give for the life of the w'.
7: 4 these things, shew thyself to the w'.
7 The w' cannot hate you; but me it
8:12 saying, I am the light of the w':
23 am from above: ye are of this w';
23 I am not of this w'.
26 I speak to the w' those things which
9: 5 As long as I am in the w',
5 I am the light of the w'.
32 Since the w' began was it not heard
39 judgment I am come into this w',
10:36 sanctified, and sent into the w',
11: 9 he seeth the light of this w'.
27 God, which should come into the w'.
12:19 behold, the w' is gone after him.
25 that hateth his life in this w' shall
31 Now is the judgment of this w':
31 the prince of this w' be cast out.
46 I am come a light into the w', that
47 to judge the w', but to save the w'.
13: 1 he should depart out of this w' unto
1 loved his own which were in the w',
14:17 whom the w' cannot receive,
19 while, and the w' seeth me more;
22 unto us, and not unto the w'?
27 not as the w' giveth, give I unto you.
30 for the prince of this w' cometh,
31 w' may know that I love the Father;
15:18 If the w' hate you, ye know that it
19 of the w', the w' would love his own:
19 but because ye are not of the w',
19 I have chosen you out of the w',
19 therefore the w' hateth you.
16: 8 he will reprove the w' of sin, and of
11 the prince of this w' is judged.
20 lament, but the w' shall rejoice:
21 joy that a man is born into the w'.
28 Father, and am come into the w':
28 I leave the w', and go to the Father.
33 In the w' ye shall have tribulation:
33 cheer; I have overcome the w'.
17: 5 I had with thee before the w' was.
6 thou gavest me out of the w':
9 I pray not for the w', but for them
11 And now I am no more in the w',
11 but these are in the w', and I come
12 While I was with them in the w',
13 and these things I speak in the w',
14 word; and the w' hath hated them,
14 because they are not of the w',
14 even as I am not of the w'.
15 shouldest take them out of the w',
16 They are not of the w',
16 even as I am not of the w'.
18 As thou hast sent me into the w',
18 so have I also sent them into the w'.
21 w' may believe...thou hast sent me.
23 w' may know...thou hast sent me,
24 me before the foundation of the w'.
25 the w' hath not known thee: but I
18:20 I spake openly to the w'; I ever
36 My kingdom is not of this w':
36 if my kingdom were of this w', then
37 for this cause came I into the w',
21:25 even tho w' itself could not contain
Ac 3:21 holy prophets since the w' began.
11:28 dearth throughout all the w':
15:18 from the beginning of the w'.
17: 6 have turned the w' upside down
24 God that made the w' and all
31 will judge the w' in righteousness
19:27 all Asia and the w' worshippeth.
24: 5 all the Jews throughout the w',
Ro 1: 8 spoken of throughout the whole w'.
20 from the creation of the w' are
3: 6 then how shall God judge the w'?
19 all the w' may become guilty before
4:13 that he should be the heir of the w',
5:12 by one man sin entered into the w',
13 (For until the law sin was in the w':
10:18 words unto the ends of the w'.
11:12 of them be the riches of the w',
15 them be the reconciling of the w',
12: 2 And be not conformed to this w':
16:25 kept secret since the w' began,
1Co 1:20 where is the disputer of this w'?
20 foolish the wisdom of this w'?
21 the w' by wisdom knew not God,
27 chosen the foolish things of the w'
27 chosen the weak things of the w'
28 And base things of the w', and
2: 6 yet not the wisdom of this w',
6 nor of the princes of this w', that
7 God ordained before the w' unto
8 of the princes of this w' knew:
12 received, not the spirit of the w',
3:18 you seemeth to be wise in this w',
19 wisdom of this w' is foolishness
22 or the w', or life, or death, or
4: 9 are made a spectacle unto the w',
13 we are made as the filth of the w',
5:10 with the fornicators of this w',
1Co 5:10 must ye needs go out of the w'.
6: 2 that the saints shall judge the w'?
2 if the w' shall be judged by you,
7:31 And they that use this w', as not
31 fashion of this w' passeth away.
33 for the things that are of the w',
34 careth for the things of the w',
8: 4 that an idol is nothing in the w',
13 no flesh while the w' standeth,
10:11 whom the ends of the w' are come.
11:32 not be condemned with the w'.
14:10 so many kinds of voices in the w',
2Co 1:12 had our conversation in the w',
4: 4 the god of this w' hath blinded the
5:19 reconciling the w' unto himself,
7:10 sorrow of the w' worketh death.
Ga 1: 4 deliver us from the present evil w',
4: 3 under the elements of the w':
6:14 whom the w' is crucified unto me,
14 and I unto the w'.
Eph 1: 4 before the foundation of the w',
21 that is named, not only in this w',
2: 2 according to the course of this w',
12 hope, and without God in the w':
3: 9 the beginning of the w' hath been
21 throughout all ages, w' without end.
6:12 rulers of the darkness of this w',
Ph'p 2:15 whom ye shine as lights in the w';
Col 1: 6 come unto you, as it is in all the w';
2: 8 after the rudiments of the w', and
20 from the rudiments of the w', why,
20 as though living in the w', are ye
1Ti 1:15 came into the w' to save sinners;
3:16 believed on in the w', received up
6: 7 we brought nothing into this w',
17 them that are rich in this w',
2Ti 1: 9 Christ Jesus before the w' began,
4:10 me, having loved this present w',
Tit 1: 2 promised before the w' began;
2:12 and godly, in this present w';
Heb 1: 6 in the firstbegotten into the w',
2: 5 put in subjection the w' to come,
4: 3 from the foundation of the w'.
6: 5 and the powers of the w' to come,
9:26 since the foundation of the w':
26 but now once in the end of the w'
10: 5 when he cometh into the w', he
11: 7 by the which he condemned the w',
38 (Of whom the w' was not worthy:)
Jas 1:27 himself unspotted from the w'.
2: 5 the poor of this w' rich in faith,
3: 6 tongue is a fire, a w' of iniquity:
4: 4 the friendship of the w' is enmity
4 be a friend of the w' is the enemy
1Pe 1:20 before the foundation of the w',
5: 9 your brethren that are in the w'.
2Pe 1: 4 the corruption that is in the w'
2: 5 And spared not the old w', but
5 flood upon the w' of the ungodly;
20 escaped the pollutions of the w'
3: 6 Whereby the w' that then was,
1Jo 2: 2 also for the sins of the whole w'.
15 Love not the w', neither
15 the things that are in the w'.
15 If any man love the w', the love of
16 For all that is in the w', the lust of
16 not of the Father, but is of the w'.
17 And the w' passeth away, and the
3: 1 therefore the w' knoweth us not,
13 my brethren, if the w' hate you.
4: 1 prophets are gone out into the w'.
3 even now already is it in the w'.
4 is in you, than he that is in the w'.
5 They are of the w': therefore
5 therefore speak they of the w',
5 and the w' heareth them.
9 his only begotten Son into the w',
14 Son to be the Saviour of the w'.
17 as he is, so are we in this w'.
5: 4 born of God overcometh the w':
4 the victory that overcometh the w',
5 Who is he that overcometh the w',
19 the whole w' lieth in wickedness.
2Jo 7 deceivers are entered into the w',
Re 3:10 which shall come upon all the w',
11:15 kingdoms of this w' are become
12: 9 which deceiveth the whole w':
13: 3 the w' wondered after the beast.
8 from the foundation of the w'.
16:14 of the earth and of the whole w',
17: 8 from the foundation of the w',

worldly
Tit 2:12 denying ungodliness and w' lusts,
Heb 9: 1 service, and a w' sanctuary.

world's
1Jo 3:17 But whoso hath this w' good,

worlds
Heb 1: 2 by whom also he made the w';
11: 3 the w' were framed by the word of

worm See also CANKERWORM; PALMERWORM; WORMS; WORMWOOD.
Ex 16:24 neither was there any w' therein.
Job 17:14 to the w', Thou art my mother,
24:20 the w' shall feed sweetly on him;
25: 6 How much less man, that is a w'?
6 the son of man, which is a w'?
Ps 22: 6 But I am a w', and no man;
Isa 14:11 the w' is spread under thee, and
41:14 Fear not, thou w' Jacob, and ye
51: 8 the w' shall eat them like wool:
66:24 for their w' shall not die, neither
Jon 4: 7 But God prepared a w' when the
M'r 9:44, 46 Where their w' dieth not,
48 Where their w' dieth not,

worms
Ex 16:20 and it bred w', and stank:
De 28:39 grapes; for the w' shall eat them.
Job 7: 5 My flesh is clothed with w' and
19:26 after my skin w' shall destroy this
21:26 dust, and the w' shall cover them.
Isa 14:11 under thee, and the w' cover thee.
Mic 7:17 of their holes like w' of the earth:
Ac 12:23 he was eaten of w', and gave up

wormwood
De 29:18 a root that beareth gall and w';
Pr 5: 4 But her end is bitter as w', sharp
Jer 9:15 them, even this people, with w',
23:15 I will feed them with w', and make
La 3:15 hath made me drunken with w'.
19 my misery, the w' and the gall.
Am 5: 7 Ye who turn judgment to w', and
Re 8:11 the name of the star is called W':
11 part of the waters became w';

worse
Ge 19: 9 now will we deal w' with thee,
2Sa 19: 7 that will be w' unto thee than all
1Ki 16:25 did w' than all that were before
2Ki 14:12 Judah was put to the w' before
1Ch 19:16, 19 were put to the w' before Israel,
2Ch 6:24 thy people Israel be put to the w'
25:22 Judah was put to the w' before
33: 9 to do w' than the heathen, whom
Jer 7:26 they did w' than their fathers.
16:12 have done w' than your fathers;
Da 1:10 faces w' liking than the children
M't 9:16 garment, and the rent is made w'.
12:45 of that man is w' than the first.
27:64 last error shall be w' than the first.
M'r 2:21 the old, and the rent is made w'.
5:26 bettered, but rather grew w',
Lu 11:26 of that man is w' than the first.
Joh 2:10 well drunk, then that which is w':
5:14 lest a w' thing come unto thee.
1Co 8: 8 if we eat not, are we the w'.
11:17 not for the better, but for the w'.
1Ti 5: 8 faith, and is w' than an infidel.
2Ti 3:13 and seducers shall wax w' and w',
2Pe 2:20 the latter end is w' with them than

worship See also WORSHIPPED; WORSHIPPETH; WORSHIPPING.
Ge 22: 5 and the lad will go yonder and w',
Ex 24: 1 of Israel; and w' ye afar off.
34:14 For thou shalt w' no other god:
De 4:19 shouldest be driven to w' them,
8:19 and serve them, and w' them,
11:16 and serve other gods, and w' them;
26:10 and w' before the Lord thy God:
30:17 w' other gods, and serve them;
Jos 5:14 on his face to the earth, and did w',
1Sa 1: 3 went up out of his city yearly to w'
15:25 with me, that I may w' the Lord,
30 that I may w' the Lord thy God.
1Ki 9: 6 and serve other gods, and w' them:
12:30 the people went to w' before the one,
2Ki 5:18 the house of Rimmon to w' there,
17:36 shall ye fear, and him shall ye w',
18:22 w' before the altar in Jerusalem?
1Ch 16:29 w' the Lord in the beauty of
2Ch 7:19 and serve other gods, and w' them;
32:12 Ye shall w' before one altar, and
Ps 5: 7 will I w' toward thy holy temple.
22:27 the nations shall w' before thee.
29 fat upon earth shall eat and w':
29: 2 w' the Lord in the beauty of
45:11 he is thy Lord; and w' thou him.
66: 4 All the earth shall w' thee, and
81: 9 shalt thou w' any strange god.
86: 9 shall come and w' before thee;
95: 6 O come, let us w' and bow down:
96: 9 O w' the Lord in the beauty of
97: 7 of idols: w' him, all ye gods.
99: 5 our God, and w' at his footstool;
9 our God, and w' at his holy hill;
132: 7 we will w' at his footstool.
138: 2 I will w' toward thy holy temple,
Isa 2: 8 w' the work of their own hands,
20 made each one for himself to w',
27:13 shall w' the Lord in the holy mount
36: 7 Ye shall w' before this altar?
46: 6 a god: they fall down, yea, they w'.
49: 7 see and arise, princes also shall w',
66:23 all flesh come to w' before me,
Jer 7: 2 in at these gates to w' the Lord.
13:10 gods, to serve them, and to w' them,
25: 6 gods to serve them, and to w' them,
26: 2 come to w' in the Lord's house,
44:19 did we make her cakes to w' her,
Eze 46: 2 w' at the threshold of the gate:
3 shall w' at the door of this gate
9 by the way of the north gate to w'
Da 3: 5 fall down and w' the golden image
10 fall down and w' the golden image:
12 nor w' the golden image which thou
14 nor w' the golden image which I
15 ye fall down and w' the image
15 but if ye w' not, ye shall be cast
18 nor w' the golden image which thou
28 might not serve nor w' any god,
Mic 5:13 more w' the work of thine hands.
Zep 1: 5 them that w' the host of heaven
5 w' and that swear by the Lord,
2:11 and men shall w' him, every one
Zec 14:16 from year to year to w' the King,
17 unto Jerusalem to w' the King,
M't 2: 2 the east, and are come to w' him.
8 that I may come and w' him also.
4: 9 if thou wilt fall down and w' me.
10 Thou shalt w' the Lord thy God,
M't 15: 9 But in vain do they w' me, teaching
M'r 7: 7 Howbeit in vain do they w' me,
Lu 4: 7 If thou therefore wilt w' me,
8 Thou shalt w' the Lord thy God,
14:10 have w' in the presence of them
Joh 4:20 the place where men ought to w'.
21 yet at Jerusalem, w' the Father.
22 Ye w' ye know not what:
22 we know what we w': for salvation
23 shall w' the Father in spirit and in
23 the Father seeketh such to w' him.
24 is a Spirit: and they that w' him
24 must w' him in spirit and in truth.
12:20 that came up to w' at the feast:
Ac 7:42 them up to w' the host of heaven;
43 which ye made to w' them:
8:27 had come to Jerusalem for to w',
17:23 Whom therefore ye ignorantly w',
18:13 fellow persuadeth men to w' God
24:11 I went up to Jerusalem for to w'.
14 so w' I the God of my fathers,
1Co 14:25 down on his face he will w' God,
Ph'p 3: 3 which w' God in the spirit, and
Col 2:23 indeed a shew of wisdom in will w',
Heb 1: 6 let all the angels of God w' him.
Re 3: 9 to come and w' before thy feet,
4:10 and w' him that liveth for ever and
9:20 that they should not w' devils, and
11: 1 altar, and them that w' therein.
13: 8 dwell upon the earth shall w' him,
12 dwell therein to w' the first beast,
15 not w' the image of the beast
14: 7 and w' him that made heaven, and
9 If any man w' the beast and his
11 who w' the beast and his image,
15: 4 shall come and w' before thee;
19:10 And I fell at his feet to w' him.
10 w' God: for the testimony of Jesus
22: 8 I fell down to w' before the feet of
9 the sayings of this book: w' God.

worshipped
Ge 24:26 down his head, and w' the Lord.
48 down my head, and w' the Lord,
52 heard their words, he w' the Lord,
Ex 4:31 they bowed their heads and w'.
12:27 the people bowed the head and w'.
32: 8 them a molten calf, and have w' it.
33:10 and all the people rose up and w',
34: 8 his head toward the earth, and w'.
De 17: 3 and served other gods, and w' them,
29:26 and served other gods, and w' them,
J'g 7:15 interpretation thereof, that he w',
1Sa 1:19 w' before the Lord, and returned,
28 Lord. And he w' the Lord there.
15:31 after Saul; and Saul w' the Lord.
2Sa 12:20 into the house of the Lord, and w':
15:32 top of the mount, where he w' God,
1Ki 9: 9 upon other gods, and have w' them,
11:33 have w' Ashtoreth the goddess of
16:31 went and served Baal, and w' him.
22:53 For he served Baal, and w' him,
2Ki 17:16 and w' all the host of heaven, and
21: 3 and w' all the host of heaven, and
21 that his father served, and w' them:
1Ch 29:20 down their heads, and w' the Lord,
2Ch 7: 3 and w', and praised the Lord,
22 hold on other gods, and w' them,
29:28 And all the congregation w', and
29 him bowed themselves, and w'.
30 and they bowed their heads and w'.
33: 3 and w' all the host of heaven,
Ne 8: 6 and w' the Lord with their faces to
9: 3 and w' the Lord their God.
Job 1:20 fell down upon the ground, and w',
Ps 106:19 in Horeb, and w' the molten image.
Jer 1:16 w' the works of their own hands.
8: 2 sought, and whom they have w':
16:11 served them, and have w' them,
22: 9 w' other gods, and served them.
Eze 8:16 they w' the sun toward the east.
Da 2:46 and w' Daniel, and commanded
3: 7 fell down and w' the golden image
M't 2:11 mother, and fell down and w' him:
8: 2 there came a leper and w' him,
9:18 came a certain ruler, and w' him,
14:33 were in the ship came and w' him,
15:25 Then came she and w' him, saying,
18:26 fell down, and w' him, saying, Lord,
28: 9 held him by the feet, and w' him.
17 they w' him: but some doubted.
M'r 5: 6 Jesus afar off, he ran and w' him,
15:19 and bowing their knees w' him.
Lu 24:52 And they w' him, and returned to
Joh 4:20 Our fathers w' in this mountain;
9:38 Lord, I believe. And he w' him.
Ac 10:25 fell down at his feet, and w' him.
16:14 Thyatira, which w' God, heard us;
17:25 Neither is w' with men's hands,
18: 7 named Justus, one that w' God,
Ro 1:25 and w' and served the creature
2Th 2: 4 all that is called God, or that is w';
Heb 11:21 and w', leaning upon the top of
Re 5:14 and w' him that liveth for ever and
7:11 throne on their faces, and w' God,
11:16 fell upon their faces, and w' God,
13: 4 w' the dragon which gave power
4 and they w' the beast, saying, Who
16: 2 and upon them which w' his image.
19: 4 four beasts fell down and w' God
20 beast, and them that w' his image.
20: 4 which had not w' the beast, neither

worshipper See also WORSHIPPERS.
Joh 9:31 but if any man be a w' of God, and
Ac 19:35 a w' of the great goddess Diana,

worshippers
2Ki 10:19 he might destroy the w' of Baal.
21 all the w' of Baal came, so that
22 vestments for all the w' of Baal.
23 said unto the w' of Baal, Search,
23 the Lord, but the w' of Baal only.
Joh 4:23 true w' shall worship the Father
Heb 10: 2 the w' once purged should have

worshippeth
Ne 9: 6 and the host of heaven w' thee.
Isa 44:15 yea, he maketh a god, and w' it;
17 he falleth down unto it, and w' it,
Da 3: 6 whoso falleth not down and w'
11 And whoso falleth not down and w',
Ac 19:27 whom all Asia and the world w'.

worshipping
2Ki 19:37 w' in the house of Nisroch his god,
2Ch 20:18 fell before the Lord, w' the Lord.
Isa 37:38 w' in the house of Nisroch his god,
M't 20:20 w' him, and desiring a certain
Col 2:18 humility and w' of angels,

worst
Eze 7:24 I will bring the w' of the heathen,

worth^ See also PENNYWORTH.
Ge 23: 9 money as it is w' he shall give it
Le 27:23 unto him the w' of thy estimation,
De 15:18 been w' a double hired servant
2Sa 18: 3 thou art w' ten thousand of us:
1Ki 21: 2 give thee the w' of it in money.
Job 24:25 and make my speech nothing w'?
Pr 10:20 the heart of the wicked is little w'.
Eze 30: 2 God; Howl ye, Woe w' the day!

worthies
Na 2: 5 He shall recount his w': they shall

worthily See also UNWORTHILY.
Ru 4:11 do thou w' in Ephratah, and be

worthy See also THANKWORTHY; UNWORTHY; WORTHIES.
Ge 32:10 I am not w' of the least of all the
De 17: 6 is w' of death to be put to death;
19: 6 whereas he was not w' of death,
21:22 have committed a sin w' of death,
22:26 is in the damsel no sin w' of death:
25: 2 wicked man be w' to be beaten,
1Sa 1: 5 unto Hannah he gave a w' portion;
26:16 ye are w' to die, because ye have
2Sa 22: 4 the Lord, who is w' to be praised:
1Ki 1:52 will shew himself a w' man,
2:26 fields; for thou art w' of death:
Ps 18: 3 the Lord, who is w' to be praised:
Jer 26:11 saying, This man is w' to die;
16 This man is not w' to die: for he
M't 3:11 whose shoes I am not w' to bear:
8: 8 I am not w' that thou shouldest
10:10 for the workman is w' of his meat.
11 shall enter, enquire who in it is w';
13 if the house be w', let your peace
13 if it be not w', let your peace return
37 more than me is not w' of me:
37 more than me is not w' of me.
38 followeth after me, is not w' of me.
22: 8 which were bidden were not w'.
M'r 1: 7 shoes I am not w' to stoop down
Lu 3: 8 therefore fruits w' of repentance,
16 shoes I am not w' to unloose:
7: 4 he was w' for whom he should do
6 I am not w' that thou shouldest
7 thought I myself w' to come
10: 7 for the labourer is w' of his hire.
12:48 did commit things w' of stripes,
15:19 am no more w' to be called thy son:
21 am no more w' to be called thy son.
20:35 accounted w' to obtain that world,
21:36 accounted w' to escape all these
23:15 nothing w' of death is done unto
Joh 1:27 latchet I am not w' to unloose.
Ac 5:41 were counted w' to suffer shame
13:25 of his feet I am not w' to loose.
23:29 laid to his charge w' of death
24: 2 very w' deeds are done unto this
25:11 committed any thing w' of death,
25 had committed nothing w' of death,
26:31 nothing w' of death or of bonds.
Ro 1:32 such things are w' of death,
8:18 time are not w' to be compared
Eph 4: 1 that ye walk w' of the vocation
Col 1:10 might walk w' of the Lord unto
1Th 2:12 That ye would walk w' of God, who
2Th 1: 5 may be counted w' of the kingdom
11 count you w' of this calling,
1Ti 1:15 saying, and w' of all acceptation,
4: 9 saying and w' of all acceptation.
5:17 be counted w' of double honour,
18 The labourer is w' of his reward.
6: 1 their own masters w' of all honour,
Heb 3: 3 man was counted w' of more glory
10:29 shall he be thought w', who hath
11:38 (Of whom the world was not w':)
Jas 2: 7 they blaspheme that w' name
Re 3: 4 with me in white: for they are w'.
4:11 Thou art w', O Lord, to receive
5: 2 Who is w' to open the book, and to
4 no man was found w' to open and
9 Thou art w' to take the book, and
12 W' is the lamb that was slain to
16: 6 blood to drink; for they are w'.

wot See also WIST; WIT; WOTTETH.
Ge 21:26 I w' not who hath done this thing:
44:15 w' ye not that such a man as I can
Ex 32: 1, 23 w' not what is become of him.
Nu 22: 6 I w' that he whom thou blessest is
Jos 2: 5 whither the men went I w' not:

Ac 3:17 I w' that through ignorance ye
7:40 we w' not what is become of him.
Ro 11: 2 W' ye not what the scripture saith
Ph'p 1:22 yet what I shall choose I w' not.

wotteth
Ge 39: 8 my master w' not what is with me

would See also WOULDEST.
Ge 2:19 Adam to see what he w' call them:
21: 7 Who w' have said unto Abraham, that
30:34 I w' that it might be according
42:21 he besought us, and we w' not hear;
22 and ye w' not hear? therefore, behold,
43: 7 certainly know that he w' say, Bring
44:22 leave his father, his father w' die.
Ex 2: 4 afar off, to wit what w' be done to him.
8:32 neither w' he let the people go.
9:35 neither w' he let the children of
10:20 he w' not let the children of Israel
27 heart, and he w' not let them go.
11:10 he w' not let the children of Israel
13:15 when Pharaoh w' hardly let us go,
16: 3 W' to God we had died by
Nu 11:29 w' God that all the Lord's
29 Lord w' put his spirit upon them!
14: 2 W' God that we had died in the
2 w' God we...died in the wilderness!
20: 3 W' God that we had died when
21:23 And Sihon w' not suffer Israel to pass
22:18 If Balak w' give me his house full of
29 I w' there were a sword in mine
29 in mine hand, for now I w' kill thee.
24:13 If Balak w' give me his house full of
De 1:26 Notwithstanding ye w' not go up,
43 and ye w' not hear, but rebelled
45 Lord w' not hearken to your voice,
2:30 king of Heshbon w' not let us pass
3:26 for your sakes, and w' not hear me:
5:29 a heart in them, that they w' fear me,
7: 8 because he w' keep the oath which he
8:20 ye w' not be obedient unto the voice
9:25 the Lord had said he w' destroy you.
10:10 and the Lord w' not destroy thee.
23: 5 God w' not hearken unto Balaam;
21 it of thee; and it w' be sin in thee.
28:56 w' not adventure to set the sole of
67 say, W' God it were even!
67 say, W' God it were morning!
32:26 I said, I w' scatter them into corners,
26 I w' make the remembrance of them
29 they w' consider their latter end!
Jos 5: 6 that he w' not shew them the land,
6 unto their fathers that he w' give us,
7: 7 w' to God we had been content,
17:12 Canaanites w' dwell in that land.
24:10 But I w' not hearken unto Balaam;
J'g 1:27 Canaanites w' dwell in that land.
34 for they w' not suffer them to come
35 Amorites w' dwell in mount Heres
2:17 w' not hearken unto their judges,
3: 4 to know whether they w' hearken
8:19 saved them alive, I w' not slay you.
24 them, I w' desire a request from you,
24 w' give me every man the earrings
9:29 w' to God this people were
29 then w' I remove Abimelech. And he
11:17 the king of Edom w' not hearken
17 king of Moab: but he w' not consent:
13:23 he w' not have received a burnt
23 neither w' he have shewed us all
23 nor w' as at this time have told us
14: 6 he rent him as he w' have rent a kid,
15: 1 her father w' not suffer him to go in.
19:10 But the man w' not tarry that night,
25 the men w' not hearken to him:
20:13 of Benjamin w' not hearken to the
Ru 1:13 W' ye tarry for them till they were
13 w' ye stay for them from having
1Sa 2:16 then he w' answer him, Nay; but
25 because the Lord w' slay them.
13:13 for now w' the Lord have established
15: 9 and w' not utterly destroy them:
18: 2 and w' let him go no more home to his
20: 9 come upon thee, then w' not I tell it
22:17 servants of the king w' not put forth
22 was there, that he w' surely tell Saul:
26:23 but I w' not stretch forth mine hand
31: 4 But his armourbearer w' not; for he
2Sa 2:21 But Asahel w' not turn aside from
4: 6 though they w' have fetched wheat;
10 that I w' have given him a reward
6:10 So David w' not remove the ark of
11:20 knew ye not that they w' shoot from
12: 8 I w' moreover have given unto thee
17 but he w' not, neither did he eat
18 he w' not hearken unto our voice:
13:14 he w' not hearken unto her voice:
16 me. But he w' not hearken unto her.
25 howbeit he w' not go, but blessed
14:16 man that w' destroy me and my son
29 king; but he w' not come to him:
29 second time, he w' not come.
15: 4 unto me, and I w' do him justice!
18:11 I w' have given thee ten shekels of
12 yet w' I not put forth mine hand
33 W' God I had died for thee, O
23:15 that one w' give me drink of the water
16 nevertheless he w' not drink
17 therefore he w' not drink it. These
1Ki 8:12 he w' dwell in the thick darkness.
13:33 whosoever w', he consecrated him,
18:32 as great as w' contain two measures of
20:33 whether any thing w' come from him,
21: 4 away his face, and w' eat no bread.
22:18 w' prophesy no good concerning me,
49 the ships. But Jehoshaphat w' not.
2Ki 2: 1 when the Lord w' take up Elijah into
3:14 I w' not look toward thee, nor see
5: 3 W' God my lord were with the
3 for he w' recover him of his leprosy.
7: 2 the Lord w' make windows in heaven,
8:19 Yet the Lord w' not destroy Judah
13:23 and w' not destroy them, neither
14:11 But Amaziah w' not hear. Therefore
27 that he w' blot out the name of Israel
17:14 Notwithstanding they w' not hear,
18:12 and w' not hear them, nor do them.
24: 4 which the Lord w' not pardon.
1Ch 10: 4 But his armourbearer w' not; for he
11:17 that one w' give me drink of the water
18 but David w' not drink of it, but
19 Therefore he w' not drink it.
13: 4 congregation said that they w' do so:
19:19 neither w' the Syrians help the
27:23 he w' increase Israel like to the stars
2Ch 6: 1 that he w' dwell in the thick darkness.
10:16 saw that the king w' not hearken
12:12 that he w' not destroy him altogether:
15:13 whosoever w' not seek the Lord God of
18:17 that he w' not prophesy good unto me,
21: 7 w' not destroy the house of David,
24:19 them: but they w' not give ear.
25:20 But Amaziah w' not hear; for it came
33:10 his people: but they w' not hearken.
35:22 Josiah w' not turn his face from him,
Ezr 10: 8 w' not come within three days,
19 that they w' put away their wives;
Ne 6:11 w' go into the temple to save his life?
14 prophets, that w' have put me in fear.
9:24 they might do with them as they w'.
29 hardened their neck, and w' not hear.
30 yet w' they not give ear: therefore
10:30 we w' not give our daughters unto the
31 w' not buy it of them on the sabbath,
31 that we w' leave the seventh year,
Es 3: 4 whether Mordecai's matters w' stand:
6: 6 To whom w' the king delight to do
8:11 and province that w' assault them,
9: 5 what they w' unto those that hated
27 that they w' keep these two days
Job 5: 8 I w' seek unto God,
8 and unto God w' I commit my cause:
6: 3 it w' be heavier than the sand of the
8 that God w' grant me the thing that
9 that it w' please God to destroy me;
9 that he w' let loose his hand, and cut
10 I w' harden myself in sorrow: let
7:16 I loathe it, I w' not live alway: let me
8: 6 surely now he w' awake for thee, and
9:15 I were righteous, yet w' I not answer,
15 I w' make supplication to my judge.
16 w' I not believe that he had hearkened
21 perfect, yet w' I not know my soul:
21 I w' despise my life.
35 Then w' I speak, and not fear him;
11: 5 But oh that God w' speak, and open
6 he w' shew thee the secrets of wisdom,
12 For vain man w' be wise, though man
13: 3 Surely I w' speak to the Almighty, and
5 ye w' altogether hold your peace!
16: 5 I w' strengthen you with my mouth,
23: 4 I w' order my cause before him, and
4 I w' know the words which
5 he w' answer me, and understand
5 understand what he w' say unto me.
6 No; but he w' put strength in me.
27:22 spare: he w' fain flee out of his hand.
30: 1 whose fathers I w' have disdained to
31:12 and w' root out all mine increase.
35 Oh that one w' hear me! behold, my
35 that the Almighty w' answer me, and
36 Surely I w' take it upon my shoulder,
37 I w' declare unto him the number of
37 as a prince w' I go near unto him.
32:22 in so doing my maker w' soon take me
34:27 and w' not consider any of his ways:
36:16 Even so w' he have removed thee out
41:32 one w' think the deep to be hoary.
Ps 22: 8 on the Lord that he w' deliver him:
35:25 their hearts, Ah, so w' we have it:
40: 5 if I w' declare and speak of them,
50:12 If I were hungry, I w' not tell thee:
51:16 not sacrifice; else w' I give it: thou
55: 6 for then w' I fly away, and be at rest.
7 Lo, then w' I wander far off, and
8 I w' hasten my escape from the
12 then I w' have hid myself from him:
56: 1 O God: for man w' swallow me up;
2 Mine enemies w' daily swallow me up:
57: 3 reproach of him that w' swallow me
69: 4 w' destroy me, being mine enemies
81:11 people w' not hearken to my voice;
11 and Israel w' none of me.
106:23 he said that he w' destroy them,
107: 8, 15, 21, 31 men w' praise the Lord for
119:57 I have said that I w' keep thy words.
142: 4 there was no man that w' know me:
Pr 1:25 counsel, and w' none of my reproof:
30 They w' none of my counsel: they
Ca 3: 4 I held him, and w' not let him go,
8: 1 find thee without, I w' kiss thee;
2 I w' lead thee, and bring thee into
2 mother's house, who w' instruct me:
2 w' cause thee to drink of spiced wine
7 if a man w' give all the substance of
7 for love, it w' utterly be contemned.
Isa 27: 4 who w' set the briers and thorns
4 I w' go through them,
4 I w' burn them together.
28:12 refreshing: yet they w' not hear.
30:15 be your strength: and ye w' not.
42:24 for they w' not walk in his ways,
Isa 54: 9 that I w' not be wroth with thee,
Jer 8:18 I w' comfort myself against sorrow,
10: 7 Who w' not fear thee, O King of
13:11 for a glory: but they w' not hear.
18:10 wherewith I said I w' benefit them.
22:24 hand, yet w' I pluck thee hence;
29:19 but ye w' not hear, saith the Lord.
36:25 the king that he w' not burn the roll:
25 but he w' not hear them.
38:26 that he w' not cause me to return to
49: 9 w' they not leave some gleaning
51: 9 We w' have healed Babylon, but she
La 4:12 w' not have believed that the
Eze 3: 6 they w' have hearkened unto thee.
6:10 that I w' do this evil unto them.
13: 6 hope that they w' confirm the word.
20: 8 me, and w' not hearken unto me:
13 I w' pour out my fury upon them
15 I w' not bring into the land which I
21 I w' pour out my fury upon them,
23 I w' scatter them among the heathen,
38:17 that I w' bring thee against them?
Da 1: 8 heart that he w' not defile himself
2: 8 of certainty that ye w' gain the time,
16 of the king that he w' give him time,
16 w' shew the king the interpretation.
18 they w' desire mercies of the God of
5:19 before him: whom he w' he slew;
19 and whom he w' he kept alive;
19 and whom he w' he set up;
19 and whom he w' he put down.
7:19 I w' know the truth of the fourth
9: 2 that he w' accomplish seventy years
Ho 7: 1 When I w' have healed Israel, then
11: 7 most High, none at all w' exalt him.
Ob 5 w' they not have stolen till they had
Jon 3:10 he had said that he w' do unto them;
4: 5 see what w' become of the city.
Zec 7:13 as he cried, and they w' not hear;
13 so they cried, and I w' not hear,
Mal 1:10 that w' shut the doors for nought?
M't 2:18 children, and w' not be comforted,
5:42 him that w' borrow of thee turn not
7:12 ye w' that men should do to you,
8:34 he w' depart out of their coasts.
11:21 they w' have repented long ago in
23 it w' have remained until this day.
12: 7 ye w' not have condemned the
38 we w' see a sign from thee.
14: 5 when he w' have put him to death,
7 to give her whatsoever she w' ask.
16: 1 he w' shew them a sign from heaven.
18:23 w' take account of his servants.
30 he w' not: but went and cast him
22: 3 wedding: and they w' not come.
23:30 we w' not have been partakers with
37 w' I have gathered thy children
37 under her wings, and ye w' not!
24:43 in what watch the thief w' come,
43 come, he w' have watched, and
43 w' not have suffered his house to be
27:15 people a prisoner, whom they w'.
34 tasted thereof, he w' not drink.
M'r 3: 2 whether he w' heal on the sabbath
13 and calleth unto him whom he w':
5:10 that he w' not send them away out
6:19 and w' have killed him; but she
26 sat with him, he w' not reject her.
48 sea, and w' have passed by them.
7:24 and w' have no man know it:
26 that he w' cast forth the devil out of
9:30 he w' not that any man should
10:35 Master, we w' that thou shouldest
36 What w' ye that I should do for you?
11:16 And w' not suffer that any man should
Lu 1:62 father, how he w' have him called.
74 That he w' grant unto us, that we
5: 3 w' thrust out a little from the land.
6: 7 whether he w' heal on the sabbath
31 ye w' that men should do to you,
7: 3 that he w' come and heal his servant.
36 desired him that he w' eat with him.
39 w' have known who and what manner
8:31 he w' not command them to go out
32 that he w' suffer them to enter into
41 him that he w' come into his house:
9:53 as though he w' go to Jerusalem.
10: 1 whither he himself w' come.
2 that he w' send forth labourers
12:39 known what hour the thief w' come,
39 he w' have watched, and not have
13:34 w' I have gathered thy children
34 under her wings, and ye w' not!
15:16 he w' fain have filled his belly with
28 he was angry, and w' not go in:
16:26 which w' pass from hence to you
26 to us, that w' come from thence.
18: 4 And he w' not for a while: but
13 w' not lift up so much as his eyes
15 infants, that he w' touch them:
19:27 which w' not that I should reign
40 the stones w' immediately cry out.
22:49 were about him saw what w' follow,
24:28 as though he w' have gone further.
Joh 1:43 Jesus w' go forth into Galilee,
4:10 he w' have given thee living water.
40 him that he w' tarry with them:
47 besought him that he w' come down,
5:46 Moses, ye w' have believed me:
6: 6 he himself knew what he w' do.
11 of the fishes as much as they w'.
15 w' come and take him by force,
7: 1 for he w' not walk in Jewry,
44 some of them w' have taken him;
8:39 ye w' do the works of Abraham.
42 God were your Father, ye w' love me:

Joh 9:27 wherefore *w'* ye hear it again?
12:21 him, saying, Sir, we *w'* see Jesus.
14: 2 if it were not so, I *w'* have told you.
28 If ye loved me, ye *w'* rejoice, because
15:19 the world, the world *w'* love his own;
18:30 we *w'* not have delivered him up
36 then *w'* my servants fight, that I
Ac 2:30 he *w'* raise up Christ to sit on his
5:24 of them whereunto this *w'* grow.
7: 5 he *w'* give it to him for a possession,
25 brethren *w'* have understood that God
25 that God by his hand *w'* deliver them:
26 *w'* have set them at one again, saying,
39 To whom our fathers *w'* not obey,
8:31 that he *w'* come up and sit with him.
9:38 he *w'* not delay to come to them.
10:10 very hungry, and *w'* have eaten:
11:23 heart that *w'* cleave unto the Lord.
12: 6 Herod *w'* have brought him forth,
14:13 *w'* have done sacrifice with the
16: 3 Him *w'* Paul have to go forth with
27 sword, and *w'* have killed himself,
17:20 *w'* know therefore what these things
18:14 reason *w'* that I should bear with you:
19:30 when Paul *w'* have entered in unto
31 that he *w'* not adventure himself into
33 *w'* have made his defence unto the
20:16 he *w'* not spend the time in Asia:
21:14 And when he *w'* not be persuaded,
22:30 he *w'* have known the certainty
23:12 *w'* neither eat nor drink till they had
15 ye *w'* enquire something more
20 they *w'* enquire somewhat of him
28 when I *w'* have known the cause
24: 6 *w'* have judged according to our
25: 3 he *w'* send for him to Jerusalem,
4 that he himself *w'* depart shortly
20 him whether he *w'* go to Jerusalem,
22 I *w'* also hear the man myself.
26: 5 the beginning, if they *w'* testify,
29 I *w'* to God, that not only thou,
27:30 though they *w'* have cast anchors
28:18 examined me, *w'* have let me go,
Ro 1:13 Now I *w'* not have you ignorant,
5: 7 good man some *w'* even dare to die.
7:15 for what I *w'*, that I do not; but
16 If then I do that which I *w'* not,
19 For the good that I *w'* I do not:
19 the evil which I *w'* not, that I do.
20 Now if I do that I *w'* not, it is no
21 when I *w'* do good, evil is present
11:25 For I *w'* not, brethren, that ye
16:19 yet I *w'* have you wise unto that
1Co 2: 8 they *w'* not have crucified the Lord of
4: 8 and I *w'* to God ye did reign, that
18 up, as though I *w'* not come to you.
7: 7 I *w'* that all men were even as I
32 I *w'* have you without carefulness.
10: 1 I *w'* not that ye should be ignorant,
20 and I *w'* not that ye should have
11: 3 I *w'* have you know, that the head
31 For if we *w'* judge ourselves, we
12: 1 I *w'* not have you ignorant.
14: 5 I *w'* that ye all spake with tongues,
2Co 1: 8 For we *w'* not, brethren, have you
2: 1 that I *w'* not come again to you in
8 you that ye *w'* confirm your love
5: 4 not for that we *w'* be unclothed,
8: 4 intreaty that we *w'* receive the gift,
6 so he *w'* also finish in you the same
9: 5 that they *w'* go before unto you;
10: 9 seem as if I *w'* terrify you by letters.
11: 1 *W'* to God ye could bear with me
12: 6 For though I *w'* desire to glory,
20 I shall not find you such as I *w'*,
20 found unto you such as ye *w'* not:
Ga 1: 7 and *w'* pervert the gospel of Christ.
2:10 they *w'* that we should remember the
3: 2 This only *w'* I learn of you,
4:15 *w'* have plucked out your own eyes,
17 they *w'* exclude you, that ye
5:12 I *w'* they were even cut off which
17 cannot do the things that ye *w'*.
Eph 3:16 That he *w'* grant you, according to
Ph'p 1:12 But I *w'* ye should understand,
Col 1:27 To whom God *w'* make known
2: 1 For I *w'* that ye knew what great
4: 3 that God *w'* open unto us a door of
1Th 2: 9 we *w'* not be chargeable unto any
12 That ye *w'* walk worthy of God, who
18 we *w'* have come unto you,
4: 1 God, so ye *w'* abound more and more.
13 I *w'* not have you to be ignorant,
2Th 1:11 our God *w'* count you worthy of this
3:10 that if any *w'* not work, neither
Ph'm 13 Whom I *w'* have retained with me,
14 without thy mind *w'* I do nothing;
Heb 4: 8 then *w'* he not afterward have spoken
10: 2 For then *w'* they not have ceased to be
11:32 the time *w'* fail me to tell of Gideon,
12:17 he *w'* have inherited the blessing,
1Jo 2:19 *w'* no doubt have continued with us:
Re 3:15 hot: I *w'* thou wert cold or hot.
13:15 as many as *w'* not worship the image

wouldest
Ge 30:15 and *w'* thou take away my son's
31:30 now, though thou *w'* needs be gone,
31 thou *w'* take by force thy daughters
Ex 7:16 behold, hitherto thou *w'* not hear.
23: 5 burden, and *w'* forbear to help him,
De 8: 2 thou *w'* keep his commandments,
21:11 her, that thou *w'* have her to thy wife;
28:62 *w'* not obey the voice of the Lord thy
Jos 15:18 Caleb said unto her, What *w'* thou?
2Sa 14:11 *w'* not suffer the revengers of blood
18:13 thyself *w'* have set thyself against me.
1Ki 1:16 And the king said, What *w'* thou?
18: 9 *w'* deliver thy servant into the hand of
2Ki 4:13 *w'* thou be spoken for to the king,
5:13 great thing, *w'* thou not have done it?
6:22 *w'* thou smite those whom thou hast
1Ch 4:10 Oh that thou *w'* bless me indeed, and
10 and that thou *w'* keep me from evil,
2Ch 6:20 that thou *w'* put thy name there;
20:10 whom thou *w'* not let Israel invade,
Ezr 9:14 *w'* not thou be angry with us till thou
Ne 2: 5 that thou *w'* send me unto Judah,
Job 8: 5 If thou *w'* seek unto God betimes, and
14:13 O that thou *w'* hide me in the grave,
13 that thou *w'* keep me secret, until thy
13 that thou *w'* appoint me a set time,
Isa 48: 8 that thou *w'* deal very treacherously,
64: 1 Oh that thou *w'* rend the heavens,
1 that thou *w'* come down, that the
Lu 16:27 *w'* send him to my father's house:
Joh 4:10 *w'* have asked of him, and he would
11:40 if thou *w'* believe, thou shouldest see
21:18 and walkedst whither thou *w'*:
18 carry thee whither thou *w'* not.
Ac 23:20 thee that thou *w'* bring down Paul
24: 4 thou *w'* hear us of thy clemency
Heb10: 5 Sacrifice and offering thou *w'* not,
8 and offering for sin thou *w'* not,

wouldst See WOULDEST.

wound See also WOUNDED; WOUNDETH; WOUNDING; WOUNDS.
Ex 21:25 burning, *w'* for *w'*, stripe for stripe.
De 32:39 I make alive; I *w'*, and I heal:
1Ki 22:35 the blood ran out of the *w'* into
Job 34: 6 my *w'* is incurable without
Ps 68:21 But God shall *w'* the head of his
110: 6 he shall *w'* the heads over many
Pr 6:33 A *w'* and dishonour shall he get;
20:30 blueness of a *w'* cleanseth...evil:
Isa 30:26 and healeth the stroke of their *w'*.
Jer 10:19 me for my hurt! my *w'* is grievous:
15:18 perpetual, and my *w'* incurable,
30:12 incurable, and thy *w'* is grievous.
14 thee with the *w'* of an enemy,
Ho 5:13 sickness, and Judah saw his *w'*,
13 heal you, nor cure you of your *w'*.
Ob 7 bread have laid a *w'* under thee:
Mic 1: 9 her *w'* is incurable; for it is come
Na 3:19 of thy bruise; thy *w'* is grievous:
Joh 19:40 and *w'* it in linen clothes with the
Ac 5: 6 the young men arose, *w'* him up,
1Co 8:12 and *w'* their weak conscience, ye
Re 13: 3 and his deadly *w'* was healed:
12 beast, whose deadly *w'* was healed.
14 which had the *w'* by a sword, and

wounded See also WOUNDEDST.
De 23: 1 He that is *w'* in the stones,
J'g 9:40 many were overthrown and *w'*,
1Sa 17:52 the *w'* of the Philistines fell down
31: 3 he was sore *w'* of the archers.
2Sa 22:39 consumed them, and *w'* them.
1Ki 20:37 so that in smiting he *w'* him.
22:34 me out of the host; for I am *w'*.
2Ki 8:28 and the Syrians *w'* Joram.
1Ch 10: 3 and he was *w'* of the archers.
2Ch 18:33 out of the host; for I am sore *w'*.
35:23 Have me away; for I am sore *w'*.
Job 24:12 and the soul of the *w'* crieth out:
Ps 18:38 *w'* them that they were not able
64: 7 arrow; suddenly shall they be *w'*.
69:26 grief of those whom thou hast *w'*.
109:22 and my heart is *w'* within me.
Pr 7:26 For she hath cast down many *w'*:
18:14 but a *w'* spirit who can bear?
Ca 5: 7 me, they smote me, they *w'* me;
Isa 51: 9 cut Rahab, and *w'* the dragon?
53: 5 he was *w'* for our transgressions,
Jer 30:14 I have *w'* thee with the wound of
37:10 there remained but *w'* men among
51:52 all her land the *w'* shall groan.
La 2:12 swooned as the *w'* in the streets
Eze 26:15 sound of thy fall, when the *w'* cry,
28:23 the *w'* shall be judged in the midst
30:24 groanings of a deadly *w'* man.
Joe 2: 8 the sword, they shall not be *w'*.
Zec 13: 6 was *w'* in the house of my friends.
M'r 12: 4 and *w'* him in the head, and sent him
Lu 10:30 *w'* him, and departed, leaving
20:12 and they *w'* him also, and cast
Ac 19:16 fled out of that house naked and *w'*.
Re 13: 3 his heads as it were *w'* to death;

woundedst
Hab 3:13 thou *w'* the head out of the house

woundeth
Job 5:18 he *w'*, and his hands make whole.

wounding
Ge 4:23 for I have slain a man to my *w'*.

wounds
2Ki 8:29 to be healed in Jezreel of the *w'*
9:15 to be healed in Jezreel of the *w'*
2Ch 22: 6 healed in Jezreel because of the *w'*
Job 9:17 multiplieth my *w'* without cause.
Ps 38: 5 My *w'* stink and are corrupt
147: 3 in heart, and bindeth up their *w'*.
Pr 18: 8 words of a talebearer are as *w'*,
23:29 who hath *w'* without cause? who
26:22 words of a talebearer are as *w'*,
27: 6 Faithful are the *w'* of a friend;
Isa 1: 6 but *w'*, and bruises, and putrifying
Jer 6: 7 me continually is grief and *w'*.
30:17 and I will heal thee of thy *w'*, saith
Zec 13: 6 What are these *w'* in thine hands?
Lu 10:34 went to him, and bound up his *w'*,

wove See also WOVEN.
2Ki 23: 7 women *w'* hangings for the grove.

woven
Ex 28:32 it shall have a binding of *w'* work
39:22 the robe of the ephod of *w'* work,
27 of fine linen of *w'* work for Aaron,
Joh 19:23 seam, *w'* from the top throughout.

wrap See also WRAPPED.
Isa 28:20 than that he can *w'* himself in it.
Mic 7: 3 desire: so they *w'* it up.

wrapped
Ge 38:14 her with a vail and *w'* herself,
1Sa 21: 9 *w'* in a cloth behind the ephod:
1Ki 19:13 that he *w'* his face in his mantle,
2Ki 2: 8 his mantle, and *w'* it together,
Job 8:17 His roots are *w'* about the heap,
40:17 the sinews of his stones are *w'*
Eze 21:15 it is *w'* up for the slaughter.
Jon 2: 5 the weeds were *w'* about my head.
M't 27:59 he *w'* it in a clean linen cloth,
M'r 15:46 him down, and *w'* him in the linen,
Lu 2: 7 and *w'* him in swaddling clothes,
12 the babe *w'* in swaddling clothes,
23:53 it down, and *w'* it in linen,
Joh 20: 7 but *w'* together in a place by itself.

wrath See also WRATHFUL; WRATHS.
Ge 39:19 to me; that his *w'* was kindled.
49: 7 and their *w'*, for it was cruel:
Ex 15: 7 thou sentest forth thy *w'*, which
22:24 And my *w'* shall wax hot, and I
32:10 my *w'* may wax hot against them,
11 thy *w'* wax hot against thy people,
12 Turn from thy fierce *w'*, and repent
Le 10: 6 lest *w'* come upon all the people:
Nu 1:53 be no *w'* upon the congregation
11:33 *w'* of the Lord was kindled against
16:46 is *w'* gone out from the Lord;
18: 5 no *w'* any more upon the children
25:11 my *w'* away from the children
De 9: 7 provokedst the Lord thy God to *w'*
8 Horeb ye provoked the Lord to *w'*,
22 ye provoked the Lord to *w'*.
11:17 Lord's *w'* be kindled against you,
29:23 in his anger, and in his *w'*:
28 and in *w'*, and in great indignation,
32:27 that I feared the *w'* of the enemy,
Jos 9:20 let them live, lest *w'* be upon us,
22:20 *w'* fell on all the congregation of
1Sa 28:18 his fierce *w'* upon Amalek,
2Sa 11:20 if so be that the king's *w'* arise,
2Ki 22:13 great is the *w'* of the Lord that is
17 my *w'* shall be kindled against this
23:26 from the fierceness of his great *w'*,
1Ch 27:24 there fell *w'* for it against Israel;
2Ch 12: 7 my *w'* shall not be poured out
12 *w'* of the Lord turned from him,
19: 2 therefore is *w'* upon thee from
10 and so *w'* come upon you, and
24:18 *w'* came upon Judah and Jerusalem
28:11 fierce *w'* of the Lord is upon you.
13 there is fierce *w'* against Israel.
29: 8 *w'* of the Lord was upon Judah
10 fierce *w'* may turn away from us.
30: 8 fierceness of his *w'* may turn away
32:25 therefore there was *w'* upon him,
26 the *w'* of the Lord came not upon
34:21 great is the *w'* of the Lord that is
25 my *w'* shall be poured out upon
36:16 the *w'* of the Lord arose against
Ezr 5:12 the God of heaven unto *w'*,
7:23 there be *w'* against the realm
8:22 his power and his *w'* is against all
10:14 fierce *w'* of our God for this matter
Ne 13:18 yet ye bring more *w'* upon Israel
Es 1:18 arise too much contempt and *w'*.
2: 1 the *w'* of king Ahasuerus was
3: 5 then was Haman full of *w'*.
7: 7 in his *w'* went into the palace
10 Then was the king's *w'* pacified.
Job 5: 2 For *w'* killeth the foolish man,
14:13 me secret, until thy *w'* be past,
16: 9 He teareth me in his *w'*, who hateth
19:11 hath also kindled his *w'* against me,
29 for *w'* bringeth the punishments
20:23 cast the fury of his *w'* upon him,
28 shall flow away in the day of his *w'*.
21:20 drink of the *w'* of the Almighty.
30 be brought forth to the day of *w'*.
32: 2 kindled the *w'* of Elihu the son
2 against Job was his *w'* kindled,
3 his three friends was his *w'* kindled,
5 three men, then his *w'* was kindled.
36:13 hypocrites in heart heap up *w'*:
18 Because there is *w'*, beware lest
40:11 Cast abroad the rage of thy *w'*:
42: 7 My *w'* is kindled against thee, and
Ps 2: 5 shall he speak unto them in his *w'*,
12 when his *w'* is kindled but a little.
21: 9 shall swallow them up in his *w'*,
37: 8 Cease from anger, and forsake *w'*:
38: 1 O Lord, rebuke me not in thy *w'*:
55: 3 upon me, and in *w'* they hate me.
58: 9 both living, and in his *w'*.
59:13 Consume them in *w'*, consume
76:10 the *w'* of man shall praise thee:
10 remainder of *w'* shalt thou restrain.
78:31 The *w'* of God came upon them,
38 and did not stir up all his *w'*.
49 the fierceness of his anger, *w'*,
79: 6 Pour out thy *w'* upon the heathen
85: 3 Thou hast taken away all thy *w'*:
88: 7 Thy *w'* lieth hard upon me, and
16 Thy fierce *w'* goeth over me; thy
89:46 ever? shall thy *w'* burn like fire?

Ps 90: 7 and by thy w' are we troubled.
9 days are passed away in thy w':
11 according to thy fear, so is thy w'.
95: 11 Unto whom I sware in my w' that
102: 10 of thine indignation and thy w':
106: 23 to turn away his w', lest he should
40 the w' of the Lord kindleth against
110: 5 through kings in the day of his w'.
124: 3 their w' was kindled against us:
138: 7 against the w' of mine enemies,
Pr 11: 4 Riches profit not in the day of w':
23 expectation of the wicked is w'.
12: 16 A fool's w' is presently known:
14: 29 He that is slow to w' is of great
35 his w' is against him that causeth
15: 1 A soft answer turneth away w':
16: 14 The w' of a king is as messengers
19: 12 The king's w' is as the roaring of
19 A man of great w' shall suffer
21: 14 a reward in the bosom strong w'.
24 name, who dealeth in proud w'.
24: 18 and he turn away his w' from him.
27: 3 a fool's w' is heavier than them
4 W' is cruel, and anger is
29: 8 snare: but wise men turn away w'.
30: 33 forcing of w' bringeth forth strife.
Ec 5: 17 he hath much sorrow and w' with
Isa 9: 19 Through the w' of the Lord of
10: 6 against the people of my w' will I
13: 9 cruel both with w' and fierce anger,
13 in the w' of the Lord of hosts, and
14: 6 He who smote the people in w'
16: 6 and his pride, and his w':
54: 8 In a little w' I hid my face from
60: 10 in my w' I smote thee, but in my
Jer 7: 29 forsaken the generation of his w'.
10: 10 at his w' the earth shall tremble,
18: 20 to turn away thy w' from them.
21: 5 and in fury, and in great w'.
32: 37 and in my fury, and in great w';
44: 8 me unto w' with the works
48: 30 I know his w', saith the Lord;
50: 13 Because of the w' of the Lord it
La 2: 2 down in his w' the strong holds
3: 1 seen affliction by the rod of his w'.
Eze 7: 12, 14 w' is upon all the multitude
19 in the day of the w' of the Lord:
13: 15 accomplish my w' upon the wall,
21: 31 against thee in the fire of my w',
22: 21 blow upon you in the fire of my w',
31 them with the fire of my w':
38: 19 in the fire of my w' have I spoken,
Ho 5: 10 I will pour out my w' upon them
13: 11 and took him away in my w'.
Am 1: 11 and he kept his w' for ever:
Na 1: 2 and he reserveth w' for his enemies.
Hab 3: 2 known; in w' remember mercy.
8 was thy w' against the sea, that
Zep 1: 15 That day is a day of w', a day of
18 them in the day of the Lord's w';
Zec 7: 12 came a great w' from the Lord of
8: 14 your fathers provoked me to w',
M't 3: 7 you to flee from the w' to come?
Lu 3: 7 you to flee from the w' to come?
4: 28 these things, were filled with w',
21: 23 the land, and w' upon his people.
Joh 3: 36 but the w' of God abideth on him.
Ac 19: 28 these sayings, they were full of w',
Ro 1: 18 For the w' of God is revealed from
2: 5 heart treasurest up unto thyself w'
5 against the day of w' and
8 unrighteousness, indignation...w',
4: 15 Because the law worketh w': for
5: 9 be saved from w' through him.
9: 22 What if God, willing to shew his w',
22 vessels of w' fitted to destruction:
12: 19 but rather give place unto w':
13: 4 to execute w' upon him that doeth
5 needs be subject, not only for w',
Ga 5: 20 hatred, variance, emulations, w',
Eph 2: 3 were by nature the children of w',
4: 26 the sun go down upon your w':
31 and w', and anger, and clamour,
5: 6 things cometh the w' of God
6: 4 provoke not your children to w':
Col 3: 6 things' sake the w' of God cometh
8 anger, w', malice, blasphemy,
1Th 1: 10 delivered us from the w' to come.
2: 16 for the w' is come upon them to
5: 9 God hath not appointed us to w',
1Ti 2: 8 hands, without w' and doubting.
Heb 3: 11 So I sware in my w', They shall
4: 3 As I have sworn in my w', If they
11: 27 not fearing the w' of the king:
Jas 1: 19 hear, slow to speak, slow to w':
20 For the w' of man worketh not the
Re 6: 16 and from the w' of the Lamb:
17 the great day of his w' has come;
11: 18 were angry, and thy w' is come,
12: 12 having great w', because he
14: 8 wine of the w' of her fornication.
10 drink of the wine of the w' of God,
19 great winepress of the w' of God.
15: 1 in them is filled up the w' of God.
7 golden vials full of the w' of God,
16: 1 pour out the vials of the w' of God
19 wine of the fierceness of his w'.
18: 3 wine of the w' of her fornication,
19: 15 fierceness and w' of Almighty God

wrathful See also WROTH.
Ps 69: 24 thy w' anger take hold of them.
Pr 15: 18 A w' man stirreth up strife: but

wraths
2Co 12: 20 debates, envyings, w', strifes,

wreath See also WREATHED; WREATHS.
2Ch 4: 13 rows of pomegranates on each w',

wreathed See also WREATHEN.
La 1: 14 they are w', and come up upon

wreathen See also WREATHED.
Ex 28: 14 of w' work shalt thou make them,
14 fasten the w' chains to the ouches.
22 the ends of w' work of pure gold.
24 shalt put the two w' chains of gold
25 of the two w' chains thou shalt
39: 15 the ends, of w' work of pure gold.
17 they put the two w' chains of gold
18 of the two w' chains they fastened
2Ki 25: 17 the w' work, and pomegranates
17 had the second pillar with w' work.

wreaths
1Ki 7: 17 w' of chain work, for the chapiters
2Ch 4: 12 two w' to cover the two pommels
13 hundred pomegranates on...two w';

wreck See SHIPWRECK.

wrest
Ex 23: 2 after many to w' judgment:
6 shalt not w' the judgment of thy
De 16: 19 Thou shalt not w' judgment; thou
Ps 56: 5 Every day they w' my words:
2Pe 3: 16 are unlearned and unstable w',

wrestle See also WRESTLED; WRESTLINGS.
Eph 6: 12 For we w' not against flesh

wrestled
Ge 30: 8 have I w' with my sister, and I
32: 24 there w' a man with him until the
25 was out of joint, as he w' with him.

wrestlings
Ge 30: 8 With great w' have I wrestled

wretched
Ro 7: 24 O w' man that I am! who shall
Re 3: 17 and knowest not that thou art w',

wretchedness
Nu 11: 15 sight; and let me not see my w'.

wring See also WRINGED; WRINGING; WRUNG.
Le 1: 15 w' off his head, and burn it on the
5: 8 and w' off his head from his neck,
Ps 75: 8 of the earth shall w' them out,

wringed See also WRUNG.
J'g 6: 38 and w' the dew out of the fleece,

wringing
Pr 30: 33 the w' of the nose bringeth forth

wrinkle See also WRINKLES.
Eph 5: 27 spot, or w', or any such thing;

wrinkles
Job 16: 8 And thou hast filled me with w',

write See also WRITEST; WRITETH; WRITING; WRITTEN; WROTE.
Ex 17: 14 W' this for a memorial in a book,
34: 1 will w' upon these tables the words
27 unto Moses, W' thou these words:
Nu 5: 23 priest shall w' these curses in a
17: 2 w' thou every man's name upon
3 w' Aaron's name upon the rod of
De 6: 9 thou shalt w' them upon the posts
10: 2 I will w' on the tables the words
11: 20 shalt w' them upon the door posts
17: 18 he shall w' him a copy of this law
24: 1, 3 w' her a bill of divorcement,
27: 3 shalt w' upon them all the words
8 w' upon the stones all the words
31: 19 therefore w' ye this song for you,
2Ch 26: 22 the prophet, the son of Amoz, w'.
Ezr 5: 10 we might w' the names of the men
Ne 9: 38 make a sure covenant, and w' it;
Es 8: 8 W' ye also for the Jews, as it
Pr 3: 3 w' them upon the table of thine
7: 3 w' them upon the table of thine
Isa 8: 1 and w' in it with a man's pen
10: 1 that w' grievousness which they
19 be few, that a child may w' them.
30: 8 go, w' it before them in a table,
Jer 22: 30 W' ye this man childless, a man
30: 2 W' thee all the words that I have
31: 33 parts, and w' it in their hearts;
36: 2 w' therein all the words that I have
17 How didst thou w' all these words
28 w' in it all the former words that
Eze 24: 2 man, w' thee the name of the day,
37: 16 take thee one stick, and w' upon it,
16 take another stick, and w' upon it,
43: 11 w' it in their sight, that they may
Hab 2: 2 W' the vision, and make it plain
M'r 10: 4 to w' a bill of divorcement,
Lu 1: 3 very first, to w' unto thee in order,
16: 6 and sit down quickly, and w' fifty.
7 Take thy bill, and w' fourscore.
Joh 1: 45 in the law, and the prophets, did w',
19: 21 W' not, The King of the Jews;
Ac 15: 20 But that we w' unto them, that
25: 26 I have no certain thing to w' unto
26 had, I might have somewhat to w'.
1Co 4: 14 I w' not these things to shame you,
14: 37 that the things that I w' unto you
2Co 1: 13 we w' none other things unto you,
2: 9 For to this end also did I w', that I
9: 1 is superfluous for me to w' to you:
13: 2 I w' to them which heretofore have
10 I w' these things being absent, lest
Ga 1: 20 the things which I w' unto you,
Ph'p 3: 1 To w' the same things to you,
1Th 4: 9 ye need not that I w' unto you:
5: 1 have no need that I w' unto you.
2Th 3: 17 token in every epistle: so I w'.
1Ti 3: 14 These things w' I unto thee,
Heb 8: 10 mind, and w' them in their hearts:
10: 16 and in their minds will I w' them;
2Pe 3: 1 beloved, I now w' unto you;
1Jo 1: 4 And these things w' we unto you,
2: 1 these things w' I unto you, that ye
7 I w' no new commandment unto
8 new commandment I w' unto you,
12 I w' unto you, little children,
13 I w' unto you, fathers, because ye
13 I w' unto you, young men, because
13 I w' unto you, little children,
2Jo 12 Having many things to w' unto you,
12 I would not w' with paper and ink:
3Jo 13 I had many things to w', but I will
13 not with ink and pen w' unto thee:
Jude 3 to w' unto you of the common
3 needful for me to w' unto you,
Re 1: 11 What thou seest, w' in a book,
19 W' the things which thou hast
2: 1 angel of the church of Ephesus w';
8 angel of the church in Smyrna w';
12 of the church in Pergamos w';
18 angel of the church in Thyatira w';
3: 1 angel of the church in Sardis w';
7 of the church in Philadelphia w';
12 I will w' upon him the name of my
12 I will w' upon him my new name.
14 the church of the Laodiceans w';
10: 4 their voices, I was about to w':
4 thunders uttered, and w' them not.
14: 13 W', Blessed are the dead which die
19: 9 W', Blessed are they which are
21: 5 W': for these words are true

writer See also WRITER'S
J'g 5: 14 they that handle the pen of the w'.
Ps 45: 1 my tongue is the pen of a ready w'.

writer's
Eze 9: 2 with a w' inkhorn by his side:
3 had the w' inkhorn by his side;

writest
Job 13: 26 thou w' bitter things against me,
Eze 37: 20 sticks whereon thou w' shall be in

writeth
Ps 87: 6 count, when he w' up the people,

writing See also HANDWRITING; WRITINGS.
Ex 32: 16 the w' was the w' of God, graven
39: 30 pure gold, and wrote upon it a w',
De 10: 4 according to the first w', the ten
31: 24 an end of w' the words of this law
1Ch 28: 19 Lord made me understand in w'
2Ch 2: 11 the king of Tyre answered in w',
21: 12 came a w' to him from Elijah the
35: 4 to the w' of David king of Israel,
4 to the w' of Solomon his son.
36: 22 his kingdom, and put it also in w',
Ezr 1: 1 his kingdom, and put it also in w',
4: 7 w' of the letter was written in the
Es 1: 22 every province according to the w'
3: 12 every province according to the w'
14 copy of the w' for a commandment
4: 8 the copy of the w' of the decree
8: 8 w' which is written in the king's
9 every province according to the w'
9 to the Jews according to their w',
13 copy of the w' for a commandment
9: 27 two days according to their w',
Isa 38: 9 w' of Hezekiah king of Judah,
Eze 13: 9 in the w' of the house of Israel,
Da 5: 7 Whosoever shall read this w',
8 but they could not read the w',
15 that they should read this w',
16 now if thou canst read the w',
17 I will read the w' unto the king,
24 from him; and this w' was written.
25 And this is the w' that was written,
6: 8 the decree, and sign the w',
9 king Darius signed the w' and the
10 Daniel knew that the w' was signed,
M't 5: 31 let him give her a w' of divorcement:
19: 7 to give a w' of divorcement, and
Lu 1: 63 And he asked for a w' table, and
Joh 19: 19 And the w' was, Jesus Of Nazareth

writings
Joh 5: 47 if ye believe not his w', how shall

writing-table See WRITING and TABLE.

written
Ex 24: 12 commandments which I have w';
31: 18 stone, w' with the finger of God.
32: 15 tables were w' on both their sides;
15 and on the other were they w'.
32 out of thy book which thou hast w'.
Nu 11: 26 they were of them that were w',
De 9: 10 stone w' with the finger of God;
10 was w' according to all the words,
28: 58 this law that are w' in this book,
61 is not w' in the book of this law,
29: 20 the curses that are w' in this book
21 covenant that are w' in this book
27 the curses that are w' in this book:
30: 10 statutes which are w' in this book
Jos 1: 8 according to all that is w' therein:
8: 31 as it is w' in the book of the law of
34 all that is w' in the book of the law.
10: 13 not this w' in the book of Jasher?
23: 6 all that is w' in the book of the law
2Sa 1: 18 it is w' in the book of Jasher.)
1Ki 2: 3 as it is w' in the law of Moses,
11: 41 not w' in the book of the acts of
14: 19, 29 w' in the book of the chronicles
15: 7, 23, 31 not w' in the book of the
16: 5, 14, 20, 27 not w' in the book of the

1Ki 21: 11 as it was *w*' in the letters which
22: 39, 45 *w*' in the book of the chronicles
2Ki 1: 18 not *w*' in the book of the chronicles
8: 23 not *w*' in the book of the chronicles
10: 34 not *w*' in the book of the chronicles
12: 19 not *w*' in the book of the chronicles
13: 8, 12 *w*' in the book of the chronicles
14: 6 which is *w*' in the book of the law
15, 18, 28 not *w*' in the book of the
15: 6, 11, 15, 21, 26, 31, 36 not *w*' in the book
16: 19 not *w*' in the book of the chronicles
20: 20 not *w*' in the book of the chronicles
21: 17, 25 *w*' in the book of the chronicles
22: 13 all that which is *w*' concerning us.
23: 3 covenant that were *w*' in this book.
21 *w*' in the book of this covenant.
24 which were *w*' in the book of Hilkiah
28 not *w*' in the book of the chronicles
24: 5 not *w*' in the book of the chronicles
1Ch 4: 41 these *w*' by name came in the days
9: 1 were *w*' in the book of the kings of
16: 40 that is *w*' in the law of the Lord,
29: 29 *w*' in the book of Samuel the seer,
2Ch 9: 29 not *w*' in the book of Nathan the
12: 15 not *w*' in the book of Shemaiah the
13: 22 *w*' in the story of the prophet Iddo.
16: 11 *w*' in the book of the kings of Judah
20: 34 they are *w*' in the book of Jehu
23: 18 as it is *w*' in the law of Moses,
24: 27 are *w*' in the story of the book
25: 4 *w*' in the law in the book of Moses,
26 *w*' in the book of the kings of Judah
27: 7 *w*' in the book of the kings of Israel
28: 26 *w*' in the book of the kings of Judah
30: 5 long time in such sort as it was *w*'.
18 passover otherwise than it was *w*'.
31: 3 as it is *w*' in the law of the Lord.
32: 32 they are *w*' in the vision of Isaiah
33: 18 *w*' in the book of the kings of Israel.
19 *w*' among the sayings of the seers.
34: 21 do after all that is *w*' in this book.
24 the curses that are *w*' in the book
31 covenant which are *w*' in this book.
35: 12 as it is *w*' in the book of Moses.
25 they are *w*' in the lamentations.
26 was *w*' in the law of the Lord,
27 *w*' in the book of the kings of Israel
36: 8 *w*' in the book of the kings of Israel
Ezr 3: 2 as it is *w*' in the law of Moses
4 feast of tabernacles, as it is *w*',
4: 7 letter was *w*' in the Syrian tongue,
5: 7 was *w*' thus; Unto Darius the
6: 2 a roll, and therein was a record *w*':
18 as it is *w*' in the book of Moses.
8: 34 the weight was *w*' at that time.
Ne 6: 6 Wherein was *w*', It is reported
7: 5 at the first, and found *w*' therein,
8: 14 found *w*' in the law which the Lord
15 trees, to make booths, as it is *w*'.
10: 34 Lord our God, as it is *w*' in the law:
36 of our cattle, as it is *w*' in the law,
12: 23 *w*' in the book of the chronicles,
13: 1 and therein was found *w*', that the
Es 1: 19 *w*' among the laws of the Persians
2: 23 *w*' in the book of the chronicles
3: 9 it be *w*' that they may be destroyed:
12 *w*' according to all that Haman had
12 name of king Ahasuerus was it *w*',
6: 2 it was found *w*', that Mordecai had
8: 5 let it be *w*' to reverse the letters
8 which is *w*' in the king's name,
9 *w*' according to all that Mordecai
9: 23 as Mordecai had *w*' unto them;
32 Purim; and it was *w*' in the book.
10: 2 not *w*' in the book of the chronicles
Job 19: 23 Oh that my words were now *w*'!
31: 35 that mine adversary had *w*' a book.
Ps 40: 7 volume of the book it is *w*' of me,
69: 28 and not be *w*' with the righteous.
102: 18 be *w*' for the generation to come:
139: 16 thy book all my members were *w*',
149: 9 upon them the judgment *w*':
Pr 22: 20 not I *w*' to thee excellent things
Ec 12: 10 that which was *w*' was upright,
Isa 4: 3 one that is *w*' among the living
65: 6 it is *w*' before me: I will not keep
Jer 17: 1 sin of Judah is *w*' with a pen of
13 from me shall be *w*' in the earth,
25: 13 even all that is *w*' in this book,
36: 6 thou hast *w*' from my mouth,
29 saying, Why hast thou *w*' therein,
45: 1 when he had *w*' these words in a
51: 60 words that are *w*' against Babylon.
Eze 2: 10 and it was *w*' within and without:
10 there was *w*' therein lamentations,
13: 9 neither shall they be *w*' in the
Da 5: 24 him; and this writing was *w*'.
25 And this is the writing that was *w*',
9: 11 oath that is *w*' in the law of Moses
13 As it is *w*' in the law of Moses, all
12: 1 that shall be found *w*' in the book.
Ho 8: 12 I have *w*' to him the great things
Mal 3: 16 and a book of remembrance was *w*'
M't 2: 5 for thus it is *w*' by the prophet,
4: 4 It is *w*', Man shall not live by
6 for it is *w*', He shall give his angels
7 It is *w*' again, Thou shalt not tempt
10 for it is *w*', Thou shalt worship the
11: 10 For this is he, of whom it is *w*',
21: 13 It is *w*', My house shall be called
26: 24 Son of man goeth as it is *w*' of him:
31 it is *w*', I will smite the shepherd,
27: 37 up over his head his accusation *w*',
M'r 1: 2 As it is *w*' in the prophets, Behold,
7: 6 it is *w*', This people honoureth me
9: 12 how it is *w*' of the Son of man, that
M'r 9: 13 they listed, as it is *w*' of him.
11: 17 it not *w*', My house shall be called
14: 21 indeed goeth, as it is *w*' of him:
27 it is *w*', I will smite the shepherd,
15: 26 of his accusation was *w*' over,
Lu 2: 23 (As it is *w*' in the law of the Lord,
3: 4 As it is *w*' in the book of the words
4: 4 It is *w*', That man shall not live by
8 it is *w*', Thou shalt worship the
10 it is *w*', He shall give his angels
17 he found the place where it was *w*',
7: 27 This is he, of whom it is *w*', Behold,
10: 20 your names are *w*' in heaven.
26 What is *w*' in the law? how readest
18: 31 things that are *w*' by the prophets
19: 46 It is *w*', My house is the house of
20: 17 said, What is this then that is *w*',
21: 22 that all things...*w*' may be fulfilled.
22: 37 that is *w*' must yet be accomplished
23: 38 a superscription...was *w*' over him
24: 44 which were *w*' in the law of Moses,
46 is *w*', and thus it behoved Christ
Joh 2: 17 remembered that it was *w*',
6: 31 as it is *w*', He gave them bread
45 It is *w*' in the prophets, And they
8: 17 It is also *w*' in your law, that the
10: 34 Is it not *w*' in your law, I said, Ye
12: 14 young ass, sat thereon; as it is *w*',
16 that these things were *w*' of him,
15: 25 be fulfilled that is *w*' in their law,
19: 20 it was *w*' in Hebrew, and Greek,
22 What I have *w*' I have *w*'.
20: 30 which are not *w*' in this book:
31 these are *w*', that ye might believe
21: 25 if they should be *w*' every one, I
25 the books that should be *w*'.
Ac 1: 20 it is *w*' in the book of Psalms,
7: 42 it is *w*' in the book of the prophets,
13: 29 had fulfilled all that was *w*' of him,
33 it is also *w*' in the second psalm,
15: 15 words of the prophets; as it is *w*',
21: 25 we have *w*' and concluded that
23: 5 for it is *w*', Thou shalt not speak
24: 14 all things which are *w*' in the law
Ro 1: 17 as it is *w*', The just shall live by
2: 15 work of the law *w*' in their hearts,
24 Gentiles through you, as it is *w*'.
3: 4 but every man a liar; as it is *w*',
10 it is *w*', There is none righteous,
4: 17 As it is *w*', I have made thee a
23 it was not *w*' for his sake alone,
8: 36 As it is *w*', For thy sake we are
9: 13 As it is *w*', Jacob have I loved, but
33 As it is *w*', Behold, I lay in Sion a
10: 15 it is *w*', How beautiful are the feet
11: 8 (According as it is *w*', God hath
26 as it is *w*', There shall come out of
12: 19 for it is *w*', Vengeance is mine;
14: 11 For it is *w*', As I live, saith the
15: 3 as it is *w*', The reproaches of them
4 For whatsoever things were *w*'
4 were *w*' for our learning, that we
9 as it is *w*', For this cause I will
15 I have *w*' the more boldly unto you
21 But as it is *w*', To whom he was not
subscr. *W*' to the Romans from Corinthus,
1Co 1: 19 it is *w*', I will destroy the wisdom
31 as it is *w*', He that glorieth,
2: 9 But as it is *w*', Eye hath not seen,
3: 19 For it is *w*', He taketh the wise in
4: 6 of men above that which is *w*',
5: 11 *w*' unto you not to keep company,
9: 9 For it is *w*' in the law of Moses,
10 For our sakes, no doubt, this is *w*':
15 neither have I *w*' these things,
10: 7 as it is *w*', The people sat down to
11 they are *w*' for our admonition,
14: 21 In the law it is *w*', With men of
15: 45 so it is *w*', The first man Adam was
54 to pass the saying that is *w*',
subscr. to the Corinthians was *w*'
2Co 3: 2 Ye are our epistle *w*' in our hearts,
3 ministered by us, *w*' not with ink,
7 *w*' and engraven in stones,
4: 13 according as it is *w*', I believed,
8: 15 As it is *w*', He that had gathered
9: 9 (As it is *w*', He hath dispersed
subscr. epistle to the Corinthians was *w*'
Ga 3: 10 for it is *w*', Cursed is every one
10 which are *w*' in the book of the law
13 for it is *w*', Cursed is every one
4: 22 is *w*', that Abraham had two sons,
27 For it is *w*', Rejoice, thou barren
6: 11 large a letter I have *w*' unto you
subscr. Unto the Galatians *w*' from Rome.
Eph *subscr*. *W*' from Rome unto...Ephesians
Ph'p *subscr*. It was *w*' to the Philippians
Col *subscr*. *W*' from Rome to the Colossians
1Th *subscr*. unto the Thessalonians was *w*'
2Th *subscr*. to the Thessalonians was *w*'
1Ti *subscr*. The first to Timothy was *w*' from
2Ti *subscr*. Ephesians, was *w*' from Rome,
Tit *subscr*. *W*' to Titus, ordained the
Ph'm 19 I Paul have *w*' it with mine own
subscr. *W*' from Rome to Philemon, by
Heb 10: 7 volume of the book it is *w*' of me,)
12: 23 firstborn, which are *w*' in heaven,
13: 22 *w*' a letter unto you in few words.
subscr. *W*' to the Hebrews from Italy
1Pe 1: 16 Because it is *w*', Be ye holy;
5: 12 I have *w*' briefly, exhorting, and
2Pe 3: 15 given unto him hath *w*' unto you;
1Jo 2: 14 I have *w*' unto you, fathers,
14 I have *w*' unto you, young men,
21 I have not *w*' unto you because ye
26 These things have I *w*' unto you
1Jo 5: 13 These things have I *w*' unto you
Re 1: 3 those things which are *w*' therein:
2: 17 and in the stone a new name *w*',
5: 1 book *w*' within and on the backside,
13: 8 names are not *w*' in the book of life
14: 1 Father's name *w*' in their foreheads.
17: 5 upon her forehead was a name *w*',
8 names...not *w*' in the book of life
19: 12 had a name *w*', that no man knew,
16 and on his thigh a name *w*',
20: 12 things which were *w*' in the books,
15 was not found *w*' in the book of life
21: 12 and names *w*' thereon, which are
27 are *w*' in the Lamb's book of life.
22: 18 plagues that are *w*' in this book:
19 things which are *w*' in this book.

wrong See also WRONGED; WRONGETH; WRONGFULLY.
Ge 16: 5 unto Abram, My *w*' be upon thee:
Ex 2: 13 he said to him that did the *w*',
De 19: 16 against him that which is *w*';
J'g 11: 27 doest me *w*' to war against me:
1Ch 12: 17 there is no *w*' in mine hands,
16: 21 suffered no man to do them *w*':
Es 1: 16 the queen hath not done *w*' to the
Job 19: 7 Behold, I cry out of *w*', but I am
Ps 105: 14 suffered no man to do them *w*':
Jer 22: 3 and do no *w*', do no violence
13 and his chambers by *w*';
La 3: 59 O Lord, thou hast seen my *w*':
Hab 1: 4 *w*' judgment proceedeth.
M't 20: 13 Friend, I do thee no *w*': didst not
Ac 7: 24 And seeing one of them suffer *w*',
26 why do ye *w*' one to another?
27 he that did his neighbour *w*' thrust
18: 14 matter of *w*' or wicked lewdness,
25: 10 to the Jews have I done no *w*',
1Co 6: 7 Why do ye not rather take *w*'? why
8 Nay, ye do *w*', and defraud, and that
2Co 7: 12 for his cause that had done the *w*',
12 for his cause that suffered *w*', but
12: 13 to you? forgive me this *w*'.
Col 3: 25 But he that doeth *w*' shall receive
25 for the *w*' which he hath done:

wronged
2Co 7: 2 we have *w*' no man, we have
Ph'm 18 If he hath *w*' thee, or oweth thee

wrongeth
Pr 8: 36 against me *w*' his own soul:

wrongfully
Job 21: 27 which ye *w*' imagine against me.
Ps 35: 19 mine enemies *w*' rejoice over me:
38: 19 that hate me *w*' are multiplied.
69: 4 being mine enemies *w*', are
119: 86 they persecute me *w*'; help thou
Eze 22: 29 oppressed the stranger *w*'.
1Pe 2: 19 God endure grief, suffering *w*'.

wrote
Ex 24: 4 Moses *w*' all the words of the
34: 28 he *w*' upon the tables the words of
39: 30 pure gold, and *w*' upon it a writing,
Nu 33: 2 And Moses *w*' their goings out
De 4: 13 *w*' them upon two tables of stone.
5: 22 he *w*' them in two tables of stone,
10: 4 he *w*' on the tables, according to
31: 9 Moses *w*' this law, and delivered it
22 Moses therefore *w*' this song the
Jos 8: 32 he *w*' there upon the stones a copy
32 which he *w*' in the presence of the
24: 26 Joshua *w*' these words in the book
1Sa 10: 25 and *w*' it in a book, and laid it up
2Sa 11: 14 that David *w*' a letter to Joab, and
15 he *w*' in the letter, saying, Set ye
1Ki 21: 8 So she *w*' letters in Ahab's name,
9 And she *w*' in the letters, saying,
2Ki 10: 1 And Jehu *w*' letters, and sent to
6 Then he *w*' a letter the second time
17: 37 commandment, which he *w*' for you,
1Ch 24: 6 Levites, *w*' them before the king,
2Ch 30: 1 *w*' letters also to Ephraim and
32: 17 *w*' also letters to rail on the Lord
Ezr 4: 6 *w*' they unto him an accusation
7 days of Artaxerxes *w*' Bishlam,
8 Shimshai the scribe *w*' a letter
9 Then *w*' Rehum the chancellor, and
Es 8: 5 which he *w*' to destroy the Jews
10 *w*' in the king Ahasuerus' name,
9: 20 And Mordecai *w*' these things, and
29 Mordecai...*w*' with all authority,
Jer 36: 4 *w*' from the mouth of Jeremiah
18 I *w*' them with ink in the book.
27 *w*' at the mouth of Jeremiah,
32 *w*'...from the mouth of Jeremiah
51: 60 Jeremiah *w*' in a book all the evil
Da 5: 5 *w*' over against the candlestick
5 saw the part of the hand that *w*'.
6: 25 king Darius *w*' unto all people,
7: 1 he *w*' the dream, and told the sum
M'r 10: 5 your heart he *w*' you this precept.
12: 19 Master, Moses *w*' unto us, If a
Lu 1: 63 and *w*', saying, His name is John.
20: 28 Master, Moses *w*' unto us, If any
Joh 5: 46 have believed me: for he *w*' of me.
8: 6 with his finger *w*' on the ground,
8 down, and *w*' on the ground.
19: 19 And Pilate *w*' a title, and put it on
21: 24 these things, and *w*' these things:
Ac 15: 23 they *w*' letters by them after this
18: 27 the brethren *w*', exhorting the
23: 25 he *w*' a letter after this manner:
Ro 16: 22 I Tertius, who *w*' this epistle,
1Co 5: 9 I *w*' unto you in an epistle not to
7: 1 the things whereof ye *w*' unto me:
2Co 2: 3 And I *w*' this same unto you, lest,

2Co 2: 4 I *w*· unto you with many tears;
7:12 though I *w*· unto you, I did it not
Eph 3: 3 (as I *w*· afore in few words,
Ph'm 21 in thy obedience I *w*· unto thee,
2Jo 5 though I *w*· a new commandment
3Jo 9 I *w*· unto the church: but

wroth See also WRATHFUL.
Ge 4: 5 And Cain was very *w*, and his
6 said unto Cain, Why art thou *w*?
31:36 Jacob was *w*, and chode with
34: 7 and they were very *w*·, because he
40: 2 Pharaoh was *w*· against two of his
41:10 Pharaoh was *w*· with his servants,
Ex 16:20 and Moses was *w*· with them.
Nu 16:15 And Moses was very *w*·, and said
22 be *w*· with all the congregation?
31:14 Moses was *w*· with the officers of
De 1:34 words, and was *w*·, and sware,
3:26 the Lord was *w*· with me for your
9:19 the Lord was *w*· against you to
Jos 22:18 he will be *w*· with the whole
1Sa 18: 8 Saul was very *w*·, and the saying
20: 7 but if he be very *w*·, then be sure
29: 4 the Philistines were *w*· with him;
2Sa 3: 8 was Abner very *w*· for the words
13:21 all these things, he was very *w*·.
22: 8 and shook, because he was *w*·.
2Ki 5:11 Naaman was *w*·, and went away,
13:19 the man of God was *w*· with him,
2Ch 16:10 Then Asa was *w*· with the seer,
26:19 Then Uzziah was *w*·, and had a
19 while he was *w*· with the priests,
28: 9 of your fathers was *w*· with Judah,
Ne 4: 1 we builded the wall, he was *w*·,
7 be stopped, then they were very *w*·,
Es 1:12 therefore was the king very *w*·,
2:21 were *w*·, and sought to lay hand on
Ps 18: 7 were shaken, because he was *w*·.
78:21 the Lord heard this, and was *w*·:
59 When God heard this, he was *w*·,
62 and was *w*· with his inheritance.
89:38 hast been *w*· with thine anointed.
Isa 28:21 he shall be *w*· as in the valley of
47: 6 I was *w*· with my people, I have
54: 9 that I would not be *w*· with thee,
57:16 ever, neither will I be always *w*·:
17 of his covetousness was I *w*·,
17 I hid me, and was *w*·, and he went
64: 5 thou art *w*·; for we have sinned:
9 Be not *w*· very sore, O Lord,
Jer 37:15 the princes were *w*· with Jeremiah,
La 5:22 thou art very *w*· against us.
M't 2:16 was exceeding *w*·, and sent forth,
18:34 his lord was *w*·, and delivered
22: 7 the king heard thereof, he was *w*·:
Re 12:17 dragon was *w*· with the woman,

wrought[A] See also WROUGHTEST.
Ge 34: 7 because he had *w*· folly in Israel
Ex 10: 2 what things I have *w*· in Egypt,
27:16 twined linen, *w*· with needlework;
36: 1 Then *w*· Bezaleel and Aholiab,
4 *w*· all the work of the sanctuary,
8 *w*· the work of the tabernacle
39: 6 *w*· onyx stones inclosed in ouches
Le 20:12 they have *w*· confusion; their blood
Nu 23:23 and of Israel, What hath God *w*·!
31:51 gold of them, even all *w*· jewels.
De 13:14 abomination is *w*· among you;
17: 2 hath *w*· wickedness in the sight
4 such abomination is *w*· in Israel:
21: 3 which hath not been *w*· with,
22:21 she hath *w*· folly in Israel, to play
31:18 the evils which they shall have *w*·,
Jos 7:15 because he hath *w*· folly in Israel.
J'g 20:10 folly that they have *w*· in Israel.
Ru 2:19 in law with whom she had *w*·, and
19 with whom I *w*· to day is Boaz.
1Sa 6: 6 *w*· wonderfully among them,
11:13 Lord hath *w*· salvation in Israel.
14:45 *w*· this great salvation in Israel?
45 for he hath *w*· with God this day.
19: 5 the Lord *w*· a great salvation for all
2Sa 18:13 I should have *w*· falsehood against
23:10 Lord *w*· a great victory that day;
12 and the Lord *w*· a great victory.
1Ki 5:16 over the people that *w*· in the work.
7:14 king Solomon, and *w*· all his work.
26 was *w*· like the brim of a cup,
9:23 the people that *w*· in the work.
16:20 his treason that he *w*·, are they
25 But Omri *w*· evil in the eyes of the
2Ki 3: 2 he *w*· evil in the sight of the Lord;
12:11 that *w*· upon the house of the Lord,
17:11 *w*· wicked things to provoke the
21: 6 he *w*· much wickedness in the
1Ch 4:21 house of them that *w*· fine linen,
22: 2 set masons to hew *w*· stones to
2Ch 3:14 linen, and *w*· cherubims thereon.
21: 6 and he *w*· that which was evil in
24:12 such as *w*· iron and brass to mend
13 So the workmen *w*·, and the work
31:20 *w*· that which was good and right
33: 6 he *w*· much evil in the sight of the
34:10 workmen that *w*· in the house of
13 all that *w*· the work in any manner
Ne 4:16 half of my servants *w*· in the work,
17 one of his hands *w*· in the work,
6:16 that this work was *w*· of our God.
9:18 and had *w*· great provocations;
26 and they *w*· great provocations.
Job 12: 9 the hand of the Lord hath *w*· this?
36:23 can say, Thou hast *w*· iniquity?
Ps 31:19 thou hast *w*· for them that trust in
45:13 within: her clothing is of *w*· gold.
68:28 that which thou hast *w*· for us.
78:43 How he had *w*· his signs in Egypt,
139:15 curiously *w*· in the lowest parts of
Ec 2:11 the works that my hands had *w*·,
17 the work that is *w*· under the sun is
Isa 26:12 also hast *w*· all our works in us.
18 we have not *w*· any deliverance in
41: 4 Who hath *w*· and done it, calling
Jer 11:15 she hath *w*· lewdness with many,
18: 3 he *w*· a work on the wheels.
Eze 20: 9, 14, 22 *w*· for my name's sake,
44 *w*· with you for my name's sake,
29:20 because they *w*· for me, saith the
Da 4: 2 the high God hath *w*· toward me.
Jon 1:11 unto us, for the sea *w*·, and was
13 sea *w*·, and was tempestuous.
Zep 2: 3 which have *w*· his judgment;
M't 20:12 These last have *w*· but one hour,
26:10 she hath *w*· a good work upon me.
M'r 6: 2 mighty works are *w*· by his hands?
14: 6 she hath *w*· a good work on me.
Joh 3:21 manifest, that they are *w*· in God.
Ac 5:12 and wonders *w*· among the people;
15:12 God had *w*· among the Gentiles
18: 3 he abode with them, and *w*·:
19:11 God *w*· special miracles by the
21:19 God had *w*· among the Gentiles by
Ro 7: 8 *w*· in me all manner of
15:18 which Christ hath not *w*· by me,
2Co 5: 5 that hath *w*· us for the selfsame
7:11 what carefulness it *w*· in you, yea,
12:12 signs of an apostle were *w*· among
Ga 2: 8 (For he that *w*· effectually in
Eph 1:20 Which he *w*· in Christ, when he
2Th 3: 8 *w*· with labour and travail night
Heb 11:33 *w*· righteousness, obtained
Jas 2:22 thou how faith *w*· with his works,
1Pe 4: 3 have *w*· the will of the Gentiles,
2Jo 8 not those things which we have *w*·,
Re 19:20 the false prophet that *w*· miracles

wroughtest
Ru 2:19 to day? and where *w*· thou?

wrung See also WRINGED.
Le 1:15 the blood thereof shall be *w*· out
5: 9 rest of the blood shall be *w*· out
Ps 73:10 of a full cup are *w*· out to them.
Isa 51:17 cup of trembling, and *w*· them out.

Y.

yard See METEYARD; OLIVEYARD; VINEYARD.

yarn
1Ki 10:28 out of Egypt, and linen *y*·:
28 received the linen *y*· at a price.
2Ch 1:16 out of Egypt, and linen *y*·:
16 received the linen *y*· at a price.

yea[A] See also YES.
Ge 3: 1 *Y*·, hath God said, Ye shall
17:16 *y*·, I will bless her, and she shall be a
20: 6 *Y*·, I know that thou didst this in
27:33 him? *y*·, and he shall be blessed.
Le 25:35 *y*·, though he be a stranger, or a
Nu 10:32 *y*·, it shall be, that what goodness the
De 33: 3 *Y*·, he loved the people; all his
J'g 5:29 *y*·, she returned answer to herself,
1Sa 15:20 *Y*·, I have obeyed the voice of the
21: 5 *y*·, though it were sanctified this
24:11 *y*·, see the skirts of thy robe in my
2Sa 19:30 unto the king, *Y*·, let him take all,
22:39 *y*·, they are fallen under my feet.
2Ki 2: 3, 5 *Y*·, I know it; hold...your peace.
16: 3 *y*·, and made his son to pass
1Ch 16:21 *y*·, he reproved kings for their sakes.
Ezr 9: 2 *y*·, the hand of the princes and rulers
Ne 5:15 *y*·, even their servants bare rule
16 *Y*·, also I continued in the work
6:10 *y*·, in the night will they come to slay
9:18 *Y*·, when they had made them a
21 *Y*·, forty years didst thou sustain
Es 5:12 *Y*·, Esther the queen did let no man
Job 1:17 *y*·, and slain the servants with the
2: 4 *y*·, all that a man hath will he give
5:19 *y*·, in seven there shall no evil touch
6:10 *y*·, I would harden myself in sorrow·
27 *Y*·, ye overwhelm the fatherless,
29 *Y*·, return again, my righteousness is
10 out; *y*·, and wonders without number.
11:15 *y*·, thou shalt be stedfast, and shalt
18 *y*·, thou shalt dig about thee, and thou
19 *y*·, many shall make suit unto thee.
12: 3 *y*·, who knoweth not such things as
14:10 *y*·, man giveth up the ghost, and where
15: 4 *Y*·, thou castest off fear, and
6 *y*·, thine own lips testify against thee.
15 *y*·, the heavens are not clean in his
18: 5 *Y*·, the light of the wicked shall
19:18 *Y*·, young children despised me;
20: 8 *y*·, he shall be chased away as a
25 *y*·, the glittering sword cometh out
21: 7 old, *y*·, are mighty in power?
22:25 *Y*·, the Almighty shall be thy
25: 5 *y*·, the stars are not pure in his sight.
28:27 he prepared it, *y*·, and searched it
30: 2 *Y*·, whereto might the strength
8 of fools, *y*·, children of base men:
9 I their song, *y*·, I am their byword.
31: 8 *y*·, let my offspring be rooted out.
11 *y*·, it is an iniquity to be punished
32:12 *Y*·, I attended unto you, and, behold,
33:14 For God speaketh once, *y*· twice, yet
22 *Y*·, his soul draweth near unto the
34:12 *Y*·, surely God will not do
36: 7 *y*·, he doth establish them for ever,
40: 5 not answer: *y*·, twice; but I will
41:24 *y*·, as hard as a piece of the nether
Ps 7: 4 (*y*·, I have delivered him that without
5 *y*·, let him tread down my life upon
8: 7 *y*·, and the beasts of the field;
16: 6 *y*·, I have a goodly heritage.
18:10 *y*·, he did fly upon the wings of the
14 *Y*·, he sent out his arrows, and
48 *y*·, thou liftest me up above those
19:10 than gold, *y*·, than much fine gold:
25: 3 *Y*·, let none that wait on thee be
27: 6 *y*·, I will sing praises unto the Lord.
29: 5 *y*·, the Lord breaketh the cedars of
10 *y*·, the Lord sitteth King for ever.
31: 9 with grief, *y*·, my soul and my belly.
35:10 *y*·, the poor and the needy from him
15 *y*·, the abjects gathered themselves
21 *Y*·, they opened their mouth wide
37:10 *y*·, thou shalt diligently consider his
36 *y*·, I sought him, but he could not
40: 8 God: *y*·, thy law is within my heart.
41: 9 *Y*·, mine own familiar friend,
44:22 *Y*·, for thy sake are we killed all
57: 1 *y*·, in the shadow of thy wings will I
58: 2 *Y*·, in heart ye work wickedness;
59:16 *y*·, I will sing aloud of thy mercy
68: 3 God: *y*·, let them exceedingly rejoice.
16 *y*·, the Lord will dwell in it for ever.
18 for men: *y*·, for the rebellious also,
72:11 *Y*·, all kings shall fall down before
78:19 *Y*·, they spake against God; they
38 *y*·, many a time turned he his anger
41 *Y*·, they turned back and tempted
83:11 Zeeb: *y*·, all their princes as Zebah,
17 *y*·, let them be put to shame, and
84: 2 My soul longeth, *y*·, even fainteth
3 *Y*·, the sparrow hath found an
85:12 *Y*·, the Lord shall give that which
90:17 *y*·, the work of our hands establish
93: 4 *y*·, than the mighty waves of the sea.
94:23 *y*·, the Lord our God shall cut them
102:13 her, *y*·, the set time, is come.
26 *y*·, all of them shall wax old like a
105:12 *y*·, very few, and strangers in it.
14 *y*·, he reproved kings for their sakes;
106:24 *Y*·, they despised the pleasant land,
37 *Y*·, they sacrificed their sons and
109:30 *y*·, I will praise him among the
Ps 116: 5 righteous; *y*·, our God is merciful.
118:11 *y*·, they compassed me about:
119:34 *y*·, I shall observe it with my...heart.
103 *y*·, sweeter than honey to my mouth.
127 above gold; *y*·, above fine gold.
128: 6 *Y*·, thou shalt see thy children's
137: 1 *y*·, we wept, when we remembered
138: 5 *Y*·, they shall sing in the ways of the
139:12 *Y*·, the darkness hideth not from
144:15 *y*·, happy is that people, whose God
Pr 2: 3 *Y*·, if thou criest after knowledge,
9 and equity; *y*·, every good path.
3:24 *y*·, thou shalt lie down, and thy sleep
6:16 *y*·, seven are an abomination unto
7:26 *y*·, many strong men have been slain
8:18 *y*·, durable riches and righteousness.
19 better than gold, *y*·, than fine gold;
16: 4 *y*·, even the wicked for the day of
22:10 *y*·, strife and reproach shall cease.
23:16 *Y*·, my reins shall rejoice, when thy
34 *Y*·, thou shalt be as he that lieth
24: 5 *y*·, a man of knowledge increaseth
29:17 *y*·, he shall give delight unto thy soul.
30:15 *y*·, four things say not, It is enough:
18 for me, *y*·, four which I know not:
29 go well, *y*·, four are comely in going.
31:20 *y*·, she reacheth forth her hands to the
Ec 1:16 *y*·, my heart had great experience of
2:18 *Y*·, I hated all my labour which I had
23 *y*·, his heart taketh not rest in the
3:19 *y*·, they have all one breath; so that
4: 3 *Y*·, better is he than both they, which
8 *y*·, he hath neither child nor
8 is also vanity, *y*·, it is a sore travail.
6: 6 *Y*·, though he live a thousand years
7:18 *y*·, also from this withdraw not
8:17 *y*·, farther; though a wise man
9: 3 *y*·, also the heart of the sons of men
10: 3 *Y*·, also, when he that is a fool
12: 9 *y*·, he gave good heed, and sought out,
Ca 1:16 art fair, my beloved, *y*·, pleasant:
5: 1 *y*·, drink abundantly, O beloved.
16 most sweet: *y*·, he is altogether lovely.
6: 9 *y*·, the queens and the concubines,
8: 1 *y*·, I should not be despised.
Isa 1:15 *y*·, when ye make many prayers,
5:10 *Y*·, ten acres of vineyard shall
29 *y*·, they shall roar, and lay hold of the
14: 8 *Y*·, the fir trees rejoice at thee,
19:21 *y*·, they shall vow a vow unto the
24:16 *y*·, the treacherous dealers have dealt
26: 8 *Y*·, in the way of thy judgments,
9 *y*·, with my spirit within me will I
11 *y*·, the fire of thine enemies shall
29: 5 *y*·, it shall be at an instant suddenly.
30:33 *y*·, for the king it is prepared;
32:13 *y*·, upon all the houses of joy in

Isa 40:24 Y'. they shall not be planted;
24 y'. they shall not be sown:
24 y'. their stock shall not take root in
41:10 y'. I will help thee; y'. I will uphold
23 y'. do good, or do evil, that we may
26 y'. there is none that sheweth,
26 y'. there is none that declareth,
26 y'. there is none that heareth your
42:13 he shall cry, y'. roar; he shall
43: 7 formed him; y'. I have made him.
44: 8 y'. there is no God; I know not any.
12 y'. he is hungry, and his strength
15 y'. he kindleth it, and baketh
15 y'. he maketh a god, and
16 y'. he warmeth himself, and saith,
19 y'. also I have baked bread upon
45:21 y'. let them take counsel together:
46: 6 they fall down, y'. they worship.
7 y'. one shall cry unto him, yet can
11 y'. I have spoken it, I will also bring
47: 3 y'. thy shame shall be seen: I will
48: 8 Y'. thou heardest not; y'. thou
8 y'. from that time that thine ear
15 have spoken; y'. I have called him:
49:15 y'. they may forget, yet will I not
55: 1 y'. come, buy wine and milk without
56: 9 devour, y'. all ye beasts in the forest.
11 y'. they are greedy dogs which can
59:15 Y'. truth faileth; and he that
60:12 y'. these nations shall be utterly
66: 3 Y'. they have chosen their own
Jer 2:37 y'. thou shalt go forth from him,
5:28 y'. they overpass the deeds of the
8: 7 Y'. the stork in the heaven
12: 2 them, y'. they have taken root:
2 grow, y'. they bring forth fruit:
6 y'. they have called a multitude
14: 5 Y'. the hind also calved in
18 y'. both the prophet and the
23:11 y'. in my house have I found their
26 y'. they are prophets of the deceit of
27:21 Y'. thus saith the Lord of hosts,
31: 3 Y'. I have loved thee with an
19 was ashamed, y'. even confounded,
32:41 Y'. I will rejoice over them to do
46:16 many to fall, y'. one fell upon another:
51:44 y'. the wall of Babylon shall fall.
La 1: 8 y'. she sigheth, and turneth
Eze 6:14 desolate, y'. more desolate than the
16: 6 y'. I said unto thee when thou wast in
8 y'. I sware unto thee, and entered
9 y'. I throughly washed away thy
28 y'. thou hast played the harlot with
52 y'. be thou confounded also, and
17:10 Y'. behold, being planted, shall it
22: 2 y'. thou shalt shew her all her
21 Y'. I will gather you, and blow upon
29 y'. they have oppressed the stranger
23:36 Aholibah? y'. declare unto them
26:18 y'. the isles that are in the sea shall be
28:26 y'. they shall dwell with confidence,
32:10 Y'. I will make many people amazed
28 Y'. thou shalt be broken in the midst
34: 6 y'. my flock was scattered upon all
36:12 Y'. I will cause men to walk upon
37:27 y'. I will be their God, and they
39:13 Y'. all the people of the land shall
Da 8:11 Y'. he magnified himself even to the
9:11 Y'. all Israel have transgressed thy
21 Y'. whiles I was speaking in prayer,
10:19 be unto thee; be strong, y'. be strong.
11:22 y'. also the prince of the covenant.
24 y'. and he shall forecast his devices
26 Y'. they that feed of the portion of
Ho 2:19 y'. I will betroth thee unto me in
4: 3 y'. the fishes of the sea also shall
7: 9 y'. gray hairs are here and there
8:10 Y'. though they have hired among
9:12 y'. woe also to them when I
12: 4 Y'. he had power over the angel, and
11 y'. their altars are as heaps in the
Joe 1:16 y'. joy and gladness from the house of
18 y'. the flocks of sheep are made
2: 3 y'. and nothing shall escape them.
19 Y'. the Lord will answer and say
3: 4 Y'. and what have ye to do with
Am 8: 6 y'. and sell the refuse of the wheat!
Ob 13 y'. thou shouldest not have looked
16 y'. they shall drink, and they shall
Jon 3: 8 y'. let them turn every one from his
Mic 3: 7 y'. they shall all cover their lips;
Na 1: 5 y'. the world, and all that dwell
Hab 2: 5 Y'. also, because he transgresseth
Zep 2: 1 y'. gather together, O nation not
Hag 2:19 y'. as yet the vine, and the fig tree,
Zec 7:12 Y'. they made their hearts as an
8:22 Y'. many people and strong nations
10: 7 y'. their children shall see it, and be
14: 5 y'. ye shall flee, like as ye fled from
21 Y'. every pot in Jerusalem and in
Mal 2: 2 y'. I have cursed them already,
3:15 y'. they that work wickedness are
15 y'. they that tempt God are even
4: 1 proud, y'. and all that do wickedly,
M't 5:37 let your communication be, Y'. y';
9:28 They said unto him, Y'. Lord.
11: 9 A prophet? y'. I say unto you, and
13:51 They say unto him, Y'. Lord.
21:16 Y'; have ye never read, Out of the
26:60 y'. though many false witnesses
Lu 2:35 (Y'. a sword shall pierce through
7:26 A prophet? Y'. I say unto you,
11:28 Y' rather, blessed are they that
12: 5 hell; y'. I say unto you, Fear him.
57 Y'. and why even of yourselves judge
:22 Y'. and certain women also of our

Joh 11:27 Y'. Lord: I believe that thou art
16: 2 y'. the time cometh, that whosoever
32 the hour cometh, y'. is now come,
21:15, 16 Y'. Lord; thou knowest that I
Ac 3:16 y'. the faith which is by him hath
24 Y'. and all the prophets from
5: 8 And she said, Y'. for so much.
7:43 Y'. ye took up the tabernacle of
20:34 Y'. ye yourselves know, that these
22:27 art thou a Roman? He said, Y'.
Ro 3: 4 y'. let God be true, but every man a
31 forbid: y'. we establish the law.
14: 4 Y'. he shall be holden up: for God
15:20 Y'. so have I strived to preach the
1Co 1:28 chosen, y'. and things which are not,
2:10 things, y'. the deep things of God.
4: 3 y'. I judge not mine own self.
9:16 y'. woe is unto me, if I preach not
15:15 Y'. and we are found false witnesses
16: 6 will abide, y'. and winter with you,
2Co 1:17 that with me there should be y' y'.
18 toward you was not y' and nay.
19 not y' and nay, but in him was y'.
20 the promises of God in him are y'.
5:16 y'. though we have known Christ
7:11 y'. what clearing of yourselves,
11 y'. what indignation, y'. what fear,
11 y'. what vehement desire,
11 y'. what zeal, y'. what revenge!
13 y'. and exceedingly the more joyed we
8: 3 y'. and beyond their power they were
Ga 4:17 y'. they would exclude you, that ye
Ph'p 1:18 do rejoice, y'. and will rejoice.
2:17 Y'. and if I be offered upon the
3: 8 Y' doubtless, and I count all
2Ti 3:12 Y'. and all that will live godly in
Ph'm 20 Y'. brother, let me have joy of
Heb 11:36 y'. moreover of bonds and
Jas 2:18 Y'. a man may say, Thou hast
5:12 your y' be y'. and your nay, nay;
1Pe 5: 5 Y'. all of you be subject one to
2Pe 1:13 Y'. I think it meet, as long as I am
3Jo 12 y'. and we also bear record; and ye
Re 14:13 Y'. saith the Spirit, that they may

year See also YEAR'S; YEARS.
Ge 7:11 six hundredth y' of Noah's life,
8:13 in the six hundredth and first y'.
14: 4 in the thirteenth y' they rebelled.
5 fourteenth y' came Chedorlaomer,
17:21 thee at this set time in the next y'.
26:12 in the same y' an hundredfold:
47:17 bread for all their cattle for that y'.
18 When that y' was ended, they came
18 they came unto him the second y'.
Ex 12: 2 be the first month of the y' to you.
5 blemish, a male of the first y':
13:10 in his season from y' to y'.
23:11 the seventh y' thou shalt let it rest
14 keep a feast unto me in the y'.
16 which is in the end of the y', when
17 Three times in the y' all thy males
29 out from before thee in one y';
29:38 two lambs of the first y' day by day
30:10 upon the horns of it once in a y'
10 once in the y' shall he make
34:23 Thrice in the y' shall all your
24 the Lord thy God thrice in the y'.
40:17 in the first month in the second y'.
Le 9: 3 calf and a lamb, both of the first y'.
12: 6 shall bring a lamb of the first y'
14:10 one ewe lamb of the first y' without
16:34 of Israel for all their sins once a y'.
19:24 in the fourth y' all the fruit thereof
25 the fifth y' shall ye eat of the fruit
23:12 lamb without blemish of the first y'
18 without blemish of the first y',
19 two lambs of the first y' for a
41 unto the Lord seven days in the y'.
25: 4 the seventh y' shall be a sabbath
5 it is a y' of rest unto the land.
10 And ye shall hallow the fiftieth y'.
11 A jubile shall that fiftieth y' be
13 In the y' of this jubile ye shall
20 What shall we eat the seventh y'?
21 blessing upon you in the sixth y'.
22 ye shall sow the eight y', and eat
22 yet of old fruit until the ninth y';
28 bought it until the y' of jubile:
29 within a whole y' after it is sold;
29 within a full y' may he redeem it.
30 within the space of a full y',
33 shall go out in the y' of jubile:
40 serve thee unto the y' of jubile:
50 him that bought him from the y'
50 sold to him unto the y' of jubile
52 but few years unto the y' of jubile,
54 he shall go out in the y' of jubile,
27:17 his field from the y' of jubile,
18 even unto the y' of the jubile,
23 even unto the y' of the jubile:
24 In the y' of the jubile the field shall
Nu 1: 1 in the second y' after they were
6:12 bring a lamb of the first y' for a
14 one he lamb of the first y' without
14 one ewe lamb of the first y' without
7:15 one ram, one lamb of the first y',
17 he goats, five lambs of the first y':
21 one ram, one lamb of the first y',
23 he goats, five lambs of the first y':
27 one ram, one lamb of the first y',
29 he goats, five lambs of the first y':
33 one ram, one lamb of the first y',
35 he goats, five lambs of the first y':
39 one ram, one lamb of the first y',
41 he goats, five lambs of the first y':
45 one ram, one lamb of the first y',

Nu 7:47 he goats, five lambs of the first y':
51 one ram, one lamb of the first y',
53 he goats, five lambs of the first y':
57 one ram, one lamb of the first y',
59 he goats, five lambs of the first y':
63 one ram, one lamb of the first y',
65 he goats, five lambs of the first y':
69 one ram, one lamb of the first y',
71 he goats, five lambs of the first y':
75 one ram, one lamb of the first y',
77 he goats, five lambs of the first y':
81 one ram, one lamb of the first y',
83 he goats, five lambs of the first y':
87 the lambs of the first y' twelve,
88 the lambs of the first y' sixty.
9: 1 of the second y' after they were
22 month, or a y', that the cloud
10:11 in the second y', that the cloud
14:34 each day for a y', shall ye bear your
15:27 shall bring a she goat of the first y'
28: 3 lambs of the first y' without spot
9 lambs of the first y' without spot,
11 lambs of the first y' without spot;
14 throughout the months of the y'.
19 and seven lambs of the first y':
27 ram, seven lambs of the first y';
29: 2 seven lambs of the first y' without
8 and seven lambs of the first y';
13 and fourteen lambs of the first y';
17, 20, 23, 26, 29, 32 fourteen lambs of
the first y' without
36 seven lambs of the first y' without
33:38 the fortieth y' after the children
De 1: 3 it came to pass in the fortieth y',
11:12 from the beginning of the y'
12 even unto the end of the y'.
14:22 the field bringeth forth y' by y'.
28 tithe of thine increase the same y',
15: 9 The seventh y', the y' of release,
12 the seventh y' thou shalt let him go
20 before the Lord thy God y' by y'
16:16 Three times in a y' shall all thy
24: 5 but he shall be free at home one y',
26:12 tithes of thine increase the third y',
12 which is the y' of tithing, and hast
31:10 in the solemnity of the y' of release,
Jos 5:12 fruit of the land of Canaan that y'.
J'g 10: 8 that y' they vexed and oppressed
11:40 the Gileadite four days in a y'.
17:10 ten shekels of silver by the y',
1Sa 1: 7 And as he did so y' by y', when she
2:19 brought it to him from y' to y',
7:16 he went from y' to y' in circuit to
13: 1 Saul reigned one y'; and when he
27: 7 of the Philistines was a full y'
2Sa 11: 1 after the y' was expired, at the
21: 1 of David three years, y' after y';
1Ki 4: 7 each man his month in a y' made
5:11 gave Solomon to Hiram y' by y'.
6: 1 and eightieth y' after the children
1 in the fourth y' of Solomon's reign
37 In the fourth y' was the foundation
38 in the eleventh y', in the month
9:25 three times in a y' did Solomon
10:14 that came to Solomon in one y'
25 horses, and mules, a rate y' by y'.
14:25 in the fifth y' of king Rehoboam,
15: 1 the eighteenth y' of king Jeroboam
9 in the twentieth y' of Jeroboam
25 the second y' of Asa king of Judah,
28, 33 the third y' of Asa king of Judah
16: 8 twenty and sixth y' of Asa king
10, 15 twenty and seventh y' of Asa king
23 thirty and first y' of Asa king of
29 thirty and eighth y' of Asa king of
18: 1 Lord came to Elijah in the third y',
20:22 at the return of the y' the king
26 to pass at the return of the y',
22: 2 And it came to pass in the third y',
41 the fourth y' of Ahab king of Israel.
51 the seventeenth y' of Jehoshaphat
2Ki 1:17 in the second y' of Jehoram the son
3: 1 the eighteenth y' of Jehoshaphat
8:16 fifth y' of Joram the son of Ahab
25 twelfth y' of Joram the son of Ahab
26 he reigned one y' in Jerusalem.
9:29 the eleventh y' of Joram the son of
11: 4 the seventh y' Jehoiada sent and
12: 1 In the seventh y' of Jehu Jehoash
6 three and twentieth y' of...Jehoash
13: 1 three and twentieth y' of Joash
10 thirty and seventh y' of Joash king
20 the land at the coming in of the y'.
14: 1 second y' of Joash son of Jehoahaz
23 fifteenth y' of Amaziah the son of
15: 1 twenty and seventh y' of Jeroboam
8 thirty and eighth y' of Azariah king
13 nine and thirtieth y' of Uzziah
17 nine and thirtieth y' of Azariah
23 fiftieth y' of Azariah king of Judah
27 two and fiftieth y' of Azariah king
30 twentieth y' of Jotham the son of
32 the second y' of Pekah the son of
16: 1 seventeenth y' of Pekah the son of
17: 1 twelfth y' of Ahaz king of Judah
4 of Assyria, as he had done y' by y':
6 the ninth y' of Hoshea the king of
18: 1 to pass in the third y' of Hoshea
9 the fourth y' of king Hezekiah,
9 which was the seventh y' of Hoshea
10 even in the sixth y' of Hezekiah,
10 that is the ninth y' of Hoshea king
13 the fourteenth y' of king Hezekiah
19:29 eat this y' such things as grow
29 the second y' that which springeth
29 in the third y' sow ye, and reap,

2Ki 22: 3 in the eighteenth y' of king Josiah,
23:23 in the eighteenth y' of king Josiah,
24:12 him in the eighth y' of his reign.
25: 1 to pass in the ninth y' of his reign,
2 the eleventh y' of king Hezekiah.
8 which is the nineteenth y' of king
27 and thirtieth y' of the captivity
27 in the y' that he began to reign
1Ch 20: 1 pass, that after the y' was expired,
26:31 fortieth y' of the reign of David
27: 1 throughout all the months of the y'.
2Ch 3: 2 month, in the fourth y' of his reign.
8:13 solemn feasts, three times in the y',
9:13 that came to Solomon in one y'
24 horses, and mules, a rate y' by y'.
12: 2 in the fifth y' of king Rehoboam
13: 1 the eighteenth y' of king Jeroboam
15:10 the fifteenth y' of the reign of Asa.
19 thirtieth y' of the reign of Asa.
16: 1 and thirtieth y' of the reign of Asa
12 Asa in the thirty and ninth y' of his
13 the one and fortieth y' of his reign.
17: 7 third y' of his reign he sent to his
22: 2 he reigned one y' in Jerusalem.
23: 1 And in the seventh y' Jehoiada
24: 5 the house of your God from y' to y',
23 it came to pass at the end of the y',
27: 5 the same y' an hundred talents of
5 pay unto him, both the second y',
29: 3 He in the first y' of his reign,
34: 3 For in the eighth y' of his reign,
3 in the twelfth y' he began to purge
8 in the eighteenth y' of his reign,
35:19 In the eighteenth y' of the reign of
36:10 when the y' was expired, king
22 the first y' of Cyrus king of Persia,
Ezr 1: 1 the first y' of Cyrus king of Persia,
3: 8 in the second y' of their coming
4:24 unto the second y' of the reign
5:13 in the first y' of Cyrus the king of
6: 3 In the first y' of Cyrus the king
15 the sixth y' of the reign of Darius
7: 7 in the seventh y' of Artaxerxes
8 was in the seventh y' of the king.
Ne 1: 1 month Chisleu, in the twentieth y',
2: 1 the twentieth y' of Artaxerxes the
5:14 the twentieth y' even unto the two
14 two and thirtieth y' of Artaxerxes
10:31 we would leave the seventh y',
34 at times appointed y' by y', to burn
35 of all fruit of all trees, y' by y',
13: 6 two and thirtieth y' of Artaxerxes
Es 1: 3 In the third y' of his reign, he made
2:16 in the seventh y' of his reign.
3: 7 in the twelfth y' of king Ahasuerus,
9:27 to their appointed time every y';
Job 3: 6 be joined unto the days of the y',
Ps 65:11 crownest the y' with thy goodness;
Isa 6: 1 In the y' that king Uzziah died I
14:28 In the y' that king Ahaz died was
20: 1 y' that Tartan came unto Ashdod,
21:16 Within a y', according to the years
29: 1 add ye y' to y'; let them kill
34: 8 and the y' of recompences for the
36: 1 the fourteenth y' of king Hezekiah,
37:30 Ye shall eat this y' such as groweth
30 the second y' that which springeth
30 in the third y' sow ye, and reap,
61: 2 the acceptable y' of the Lord,
63: 4 and the y' of my redeemed is come.
Jer 1: 2 in the thirteenth y' of his reign.
3 end of the eleventh y' of Zedekiah
11:23 even the y' of their visitation.
17: 8 not be careful in the y' of drought,
23:12 even the y' of their visitation, said
25: 1 fourth y' of Jehoiakim the son of
1 was the first y' of Nebuchadrezzar
3 thirteenth y' of Josiah the son of
3 that is the three and twentieth y',
28: 1 And it came to pass the same y',
1 in the fourth y', and in the fifth
16 this y' thou shalt die, because thou
17 the prophet died the same y'
32: 1 in the tenth y' of Zedekiah king of
1 eighteenth y' of Nebuchadrezzar
36: 1 pass in the fourth y' of Jehoiakim
9 to pass in the fifth y' of Jehoiakim
39: 1 In the ninth y' of Zedekiah king of
2 And in the eleventh y' of Zedekiah,
45: 1 in the fourth y' of Jehoiakim the
46: 2 smote in the fourth y' of Jehoiakim
48:44 Moab, the y' of their visitation,
51:46 a rumour shall both come one y',
46 in another y' shall come a rumour,
59 in the fourth y' of his reign.
52: 4 to pass in the ninth y' of his reign,
5 the eleventh y' of king Zedekiah.
12 the nineteenth y' of Nebuchadrezzar
28 the seventh y' three thousand Jews
29 eighteenth y' of Nebuchadrezzar
30 and twentieth y' of Nebuchadrezzar
31 and thirtieth y' of the captivity
31 in the first y' of his reign lifted up
Eze 1: 1 it came to pass in the thirtieth y',
2 the fifth y' of king Jehoiachin's
4: 6 appointed thee each day for a y'.
8: 1 it came to pass in the sixth y',
20: 1 it came to pass in the seventh y',
24: 1 in the ninth y', in the tenth month,
26: 1 came to pass in the eleventh y',
29: 1 In the tenth y', in the tenth month,
17 pass in the seven and twentieth y',
30:20 it came to pass in the eleventh y',
31: 1 it came to pass in the eleventh y',
32: 1 it came to pass in the twelfth y',
17 came to pass also in the twelfth y',
Eze 33:21 in the twelfth y' of our captivity,
40: 1 and twentieth y' of our captivity,
1 in the beginning of the y', in the
1 fourteenth y' after that the city
46:13 of a lamb of the first y' without
17 it shall be his to the y' of liberty;
Da 1: 1 third y' of the reign of Jehoiakim
21 even unto the first y' of king Cyrus.
2: 1 in the second y' of the reign of
7: 1 In the first y' of Belshazzar king
8: 1 In the third y' of the reign of king
9: 1 In the first y' of Darius the son of
2 In the first y' of his reign I Daniel
10: 1 the third y' of Cyrus king of Persia
11: 1 I in the first y' of Darius the Mede,
Mic 6: 6 offerings, with calves of a y' old?
Hag 1: 1 the second y' of Darius the king,
15 the second y' of Darius the king.
2:10 in the second y' of Darius, came
Zec 1: 1, 7 in the second y' of Darius, came
7: 1 pass in the fourth y' of king Darius,
14:16 even go up from y' to y' to worship
Lu 2:41 parents went to Jerusalem every y'
3: 1 fifteenth y' of the reign of Tiberius
4:19 the acceptable y' of the Lord.
13: 8 Lord, let it alone this y' also, till I
Joh 11:49 being the high priest that same y',
51 but being high priest that y', he
18:13 was the high priest that same y'.
Ac 11:26 that a whole y' they assembled
18:11 he continued there a y' and six
2Co 8:10 but also to be forward a y' ago.
9: 2 Achaia was ready a y' ago;
Heb 9: 7 the high priest alone once every y',
25 into the holy place every y' with
10: 1 they offered y' by y' continually,
3 again made of sins every y'.
Jas 4:13 and continue there a y', and buy
Re 9:15 and a day, and a month, and a y',

yearly
Le 25:53 as a y' hired servant shall he be
J'g 11:40 of Israel went y' to lament
21:19 is a feast of the Lord in Shiloh y'
1Sa 1: 3 up out of his city y' to worship
21 offer unto the Lord the y' sacrifice,
2:19 husband to offer the y' sacrifice.
20: 6 there is a y' sacrifice there for all
Ne 10:32 charge ourselves y' with the third
Es 9:21 the fifteenth day of the same, y',

yearn [*some eds.* YERN] See also YEARNED.
Ge 43:30 bowels did y' upon his brother:

yearned [*some eds.* YERNED]
1Ki 3:26 for her bowels y' upon her son,

year's
Ex 34:22 feast of ingathering at the y' end.
2Sa 14:26 at every y' end that he polled it:

years
Ge 1:14 for seasons, and for days, and y':
5: 3 lived an hundred and thirty y',
4 Seth were eight hundred y':
5 were nine hundred and thirty y':
6 Seth lived an hundred and five y',
7 Enos eight hundred and seven y',
8 were nine hundred and twelve y':
9 Enos lived ninety y', and begat
10 eight hundred and fifteen y',
11 were nine hundred and five y':
12 Cainan lived seventy y', and begat
13 eight hundred and forty y', and
14 were nine hundred and ten y':
15 Mahalaleel lived sixty and five y',
16 Jared eight hundred and thirty y',
17 eight hundred ninety and five y':
18 lived an hundred sixty and two y',
19 he begat Enoch eight hundred y',
20 nine hundred sixty and two y':
21 Enoch lived sixty and five y', and
22 Methuselah three hundred y',
23 three hundred sixty and five y':
25 an hundred eighty and seven y',
26 seven hundred eighty and two y',
27 nine hundred sixty and nine y':
28 an hundred eighty and two y',
30 five hundred ninety and five y',
31 hundred seventy and seven y':
32 Noah was five hundred y' old:
6: 3 shall be an hundred and twenty y'.
7: 6 Noah was six hundred y' old when
9:28 flood three hundred and fifty y'.
29 were nine hundred and fifty y':
11:10 Shem was an hundred y' old,
10 Arphaxad two y' after the flood:
11 begat Arphaxad five hundred y',
12 Arphaxad lived five and thirty y',
13 Salah four hundred and three y',
14 Salah lived thirty y', and begat
15 Eber four hundred and three y',
16 And Eber lived four and thirty y',
17 Peleg four hundred and thirty y',
18 Peleg lived thirty y', and begat
19 begat Reu two hundred and nine y',
20 And Reu lived two and thirty y',
21 Serug two hundred and seven y',
22 Serug lived thirty y', and begat
23 he begat Nahor two hundred y',
24 Nahor lived nine and twenty y',
25 Terah an hundred and nineteen y',
26 Terah lived seventy y', and begat
32 were two hundred and five y':
12: 4 Abram was seventy and five y' old
14: 4 Twelve y' they served
15: 9 Take me an heifer of three y' old,
9 and a she goat of three y' old,
Ge 15: 9 and a ram of three y' old, and a
13 shall afflict them four hundred y';
16: 3 Abram had dwelt ten y' in the land
16 Abram was fourscore and six y' old,
17: 1 Abram was ninety y' old and nine,
17 unto him that is an hundred y' old?
17 Sarah, that is ninety y' old, bear?
24 Abraham was ninety y' old and
25 his son was thirteen y' old,
21: 5 Abraham was an hundred y' old,
23: 1 and seven and twenty y' old:
1 were the y' of the life of Sarah.
25: 7 days of the y' of Abraham's life
7 hundred threescore and fifteen y'.
8 old age, an old man, and full of y';
17 are the y' of the life of Ishmael,
17 hundred and thirty and seven y':
20 Isaac was forty y' old when he took
26 Isaac was threescore y' old when
26:34 Esau was forty y' old when he took
29:18 will serve thee seven y' for Rachel
20 Jacob served seven y' for Rachel;
27 serve with me yet seven other y'.
30 served with him yet seven other y'.
31:38 twenty y' have I been with thee;
41 have I been twenty y' in thy house;
41 I served thee fourteen y' for thy
41 six y' for thy cattle: and thou hast
35:28 were an hundred and fourscore y'.
37: 2 Joseph, being seventeen y' old, was
41: 1 to pass at the end of two full y',
26 The seven good kine are seven y';
26 the seven good ears are seven y';
27 came up after them are seven y';
27 wind shall be seven y' of famine.
29 there come seven y' of great plenty
30 after them seven y' of famine;
34 of Egypt in the seven plenteous y'.
35 food of those good y' that come,
36 against the seven y' of famine,
46 Joseph was thirty y' old when he
47 in the seven plenteous y' the earth
48 up all the food of the seven y',
50 sons before the y' of famine came,
53 And the seven y' of plenteousness,
54 seven y' of dearth began to come,
45: 6 these two y' hath the famine been
6 and yet there are five y', in which
11 for yet there are five y' of famine;
47: 9 days of the y' of my pilgrimage are
9 are an hundred and thirty y':
9 the days of the y' of my life been,
9 of the y' of the life of my fathers
28 in the land of Egypt seventeen y':
28 was an hundred forty and seven y'.
50:22 lived an hundred and ten y'.
26 being an hundred and ten y' old:
Ex 6:16 the y' of the life of Levi were an
16 an hundred thirty and seven y'.
18 the y' of the life of Kohath were an
18 an hundred thirty and three y'.
20 the y' of the life of Amram were an
20 hundred and thirty and seven y'.
7: 7 Moses was fourscore y' old,
7 Aaron fourscore and three y' old,
12:40 was four hundred and thirty y'.
41 of the four hundred and thirty y',
16:35 of Israel did eat manna forty y',
21: 2 servant, six y' he shall serve:
23:10 And six y' thou shalt sow thy land,
30:14 from twenty y' old and above, shall
38:26 from twenty y' old and upward,
Le 19:23 three y' shall it be as
25: 3 Six y' thou shalt sow thy field,
3 y' thou shalt prune thy vineyard,
8 number seven sabbaths of y' unto
8 unto thee, seven times seven y';
8 space of the seven sabbaths of y'
8 be unto thee forty and nine y'.
15 the number of y' after the jubile
15 the number of y' of the fruits
16 According to the multitude of y'
16 according to the fewness of y' thou
16 according to the number of the y'
21 shall bring forth fruit for three y'.
27 let him count the y' of the sale
50 according unto the number of y',
51 If there be yet many y' behind,
52 but few y' unto the year of jubile,
52 according unto his y' shall he give
54 if he be not redeemed in these y',
27: 3 twenty y' old even unto sixty y' old,
5 five y' old even unto twenty y' old,
6 a month old even unto five y' old,
7 if it be from sixty y' old and above;
18 according to the y' that remain,
Nu 1: 3 From twenty y' old and upward,
18, 20, 22, 24, 26, 28, 30, 32, 34, 36, 38,
40, 42, 45 from twenty y' old and
4: 3 thirty y' old...until fifty y' old,
23 thirty y' old...until fifty y' old
30 thirty y' old...unto fifty y' old
35, 39, 43, 47 thirty y' old...unto fifty y'
8:24 twenty and five y' old and upward
25 the age of fifty y' they shall cease
13:22 Hebron was built seven y' before
14:29 from twenty y' old and upward,
33 wander in the wilderness forty y',
34 even forty y', and ye shall know
26: 2 from twenty y' old and upward,
4 from twenty y' old and upward;
32:11 from twenty y' old and upward,
13 wander in the wilderness forty y',
33:39 and twenty and three y' old
De 2: 7 these forty y' the Lord thy God
14 Zered, was thirty and eight y';

De 8: 2 thy God led thee these forty y'
4 did thy foot swell, these forty y'.
14: 28 end of three y' thou shalt bring
15: 1 end of every seven y' thou shalt
12 unto thee, and serve thee six y';
18 to thee, in serving thee six y':
29: 5 And I have led you forty y' in the
31: 2 hundred and twenty y' old this day;
10 At the end of every seven y',
32: 7 the y' of many generations:
34: 7 was an hundred and twenty y' old
Jos 5: 6 children of Israel walked forty y'
13: 1 Joshua was old and stricken in y';
1 Thou art old and stricken in y',
14: 7 Forty y' old was I when Moses the
10 these forty and five y', even since
10 this day fourscore and five y' old.
24: 29 being an hundred and ten y' old.
J'g 2: 8 being an hundred and ten y' old.
3: 8 Chushan-rishathaim eight y'.
11 And the land had rest forty y'.
14 the king of Moab eighteen y'.
30 And the land had rest fourscore y'.
4: 3 twenty y' he mightily oppressed
5: 31 And the land had rest forty y'.
6: 1 into the hand of Midian seven y'.
25 the second bullock of seven y' old,
8: 28 country was in quietness forty y'
9: 22 Abimelech had reigned three y'
10: 2 judged Israel twenty and three y',
3 judged Israel twenty and two y'.
8 eighteen y', all the children of
11: 26 coasts of Arnon, three hundred y'?
12: 7 And Jephthah judged Israel six y'.
9 And he judged Israel seven y'.
11 Israel; and he judged Israel ten y'.
14 and he judged Israel eight y'.
13: 1 the hand of the Philistines forty y'.
15: 20 days of the Philistines twenty y'.
16: 31 And he judged Israel twenty y'.
Ru 1: 4 they dwelled there about ten y'.
1Sa 4: 15 Eli was ninety and eight y' old;
18 And he had judged Israel forty y'.
7: 2 time was long; for it was twenty y':
13: 1 he had reigned two y' over Israel,
29: 3 with me these days, or these y',
2Sa 2: 10 Saul's son was forty y' old when
10 over Israel, and reigned two y'.
11 Judah was seven y' and six
4: 4 He was five y' old when the tidings
5: 4 David was thirty y' old when he
4 to reign, and he reigned forty y'.
5 he reigned over Judah seven y' and
5 thirty and three y' over all Israel
13: 23 it came to pass after two full y',
38 to Geshur, and was there three y'.
14: 28 So Absalom dwelt two full y' in
15: 7 And it came to pass after forty y',
19: 32 aged man, even fourscore y' old:
35 I am this day fourscore y' old:
21: 1 famine in the days of David three y',
24: 13 Shall seven y' of famine come unto
1Ki 1: 1 David was old and stricken in y';
2: 11 reigned over Israel were forty y':
11 seven y' reigned he in Hebron,
11 thirty and three y' reigned he in
39 came to pass at the end of three y',
6: 38 So was he seven y' in building it.
7: 1 building his own house thirteen y',
9: 10 to pass at the end of twenty y',
10: 22 once in three y' came the navy of
11: 42 over all Israel was forty y'.
14: 20 reigned were two and twenty y':
21 Rehoboam was forty and one y' old
21 reigned seventeen y' in Jerusalem,
15: 2 Three y' reigned he in Jerusalem.
10 And forty and one y' reigned he in
25 and reigned over Israel two y'.
33 Israel in Tirzah, twenty and four y'.
16: 8 reign over Israel in Tirzah, two y'.
23 to reign over Israel, twelve y':
23 six y' reigned he in Tirzah.
29 in Samaria twenty and two y'.
17: 1 shall not be dew nor rain these y',
22: 1 they continued three y' without war
42 thirty and five y' old when he
42 he reigned twenty and five y' in
51 and reigned two y' over Israel.
2Ki 3: 1 of Judah, and reigned twelve y'.
8: 1 also come upon the land seven y'.
2 land of the Philistines seven y'.
17 Thirty and two y' old was he when
17 he reigned eight y' in Jerusalem.
26 Two and twenty y' old was Ahaziah
10: 36 Samaria was twenty and eight y'.
11: 3 hid in the house of the Lord six y'.
21 Seven y' old was Jehoash when he
12: 1 forty y' reigned he in Jerusalem.
13: 1 Samaria, and reigned seventeen y'.
10 Samaria, and reigned sixteen y'.
14: 2 twenty and five y' old when he
2 twenty and nine y' in Jerusalem.
17 Jehoahaz king of Israel fifteen y'.
21 which was sixteen y' old, and made
23 and reigned forty and one y'.
15: 2 Sixteen y' old was he when he
2 two and fifty y' in Jerusalem.
17 and reigned ten y' in Samaria.
23 in Samaria, and reigned two y'.
27 in Samaria, and reigned twenty y'.
33 Five and twenty y' old was he when
33 he reigned sixteen y' in Jerusalem.
16: 2 Twenty y' old was Ahaz when he
2 reigned sixteen y' in Jerusalem,
17: 1 in Samaria over Israel nine y'.
5 Samaria, and besieged it three y'.
2Ki 18: 2 Twenty and five y' old was he when
2 twenty and nine y' in Jerusalem.
10 at the end of three y' they took it:
20: 6 will add unto thy days fifteen y';
21: 1 Manasseh was twelve y' old when
1 fifty and five y' in Jerusalem.
19 Amon was twenty and two y' old
19 he reigned two y' in Jerusalem.
22: 1 Josiah was eight y' old when he
1 thirty and one y' in Jerusalem.
23: 31 Jehoahaz was twenty and three y'
36 Jehoiakim was twenty and five y'
36 reigned eleven y' in Jerusalem.
24: 1 became his servant three y':
8 Jehoiachin was eighteen y' old
18 Zedekiah was twenty and one y' old
18 he reigned eleven y' in Jerusalem.
1Ch 2: 21 when he was threescore y' old;
3: 4 reigned seven y' and six months:
4 he reigned thirty and three y'.
23: 3 the age of thirty y' and upward:
24 the age of twenty y' and upward.
27 from twenty y' old and above:
27: 23 from twenty y' old and under:
29: 27 he reigned over Israel was forty y';
27 seven y' reigned he in Hebron,
27 and thirty and three y' reigned he
2Ch 8: 1 to pass at the end of twenty y',
9: 21 every three y' once came the ships
30 Jerusalem over all Israel forty y'.
11: 17 son of Solomon strong, three y':
17 three y' they walked in the way of
12: 13 Rehoboam was one and forty y' old
13 reigned seventeen y' in Jerusalem,
13: 2 He reigned three y' in Jerusalem.
14: 1 his days the land was quiet ten y'.
6 rest, and he had no war in those y';
18: 2 after certain y' he went down to
20: 31 he was thirty and five y' old when
31 he reigned twenty and five y' in
21: 5 Jehoram was thirty and two y' old
5 he reigned eight y' in Jerusalem.
19 of time, after the end of two y',
20 Thirty and two y' old was he
20 he reigned in Jerusalem eight y',
22: 2 Forty and two y' old was Ahaziah
12 them hid in the house of God six y':
24: 1 Joash was seven y' old when he
1 he reigned forty y' in Jerusalem.
15 an hundred and thirty y' old was he
25: 1 Amaziah was twenty and five y' old
1 he reigned twenty and nine y' in
5 from twenty y' old and above,
25 Jehoahaz king of Israel fifteen y'.
26: 1 Uzziah, who was sixteen y' old,
3 Sixteen y' old was Uzziah when he
3 and he reigned fifty and two y' in
27: 1 Jotham was twenty and five y' old
1 he reigned sixteen y' in Jerusalem.
8 He was five and twenty y' old
8 reigned sixteen y' in Jerusalem.
28: 1 Ahaz was twenty y' old when he
1 he reigned sixteen y' in Jerusalem:
29: 1 when he was five and twenty y' old,
1 he reigned nine and twenty y' in
31: 16 from three y' old and upward, even
17 from twenty y' old and upward,
33: 1 Manasseh was twelve y' old when
1 and he reigned fifty and five y' in
21 Amon was two and twenty y' old
21 and reigned two y' in Jerusalem.
34: 1 Josiah was eight y' old when he
1 in Jerusalem one and thirty y'.
36: 2 Jehoahaz was twenty and three y'
5 Jehoiakim was twenty and five y'
5 he reigned eleven y' in Jerusalem:
9 Jehoiachin was eight y' old when
11 Zedekiah was one and twenty y' old
11 reigned eleven y' in Jerusalem.
21 to fulfill threescore and ten y'.
Ezr 3: 8 from twenty y' old and upward,
5: 11 was builded these many y' ago,
Ne 5: 14 twelve y', I and my brethren have
9: 21 forty y' didst thou sustain them in
30 Yet many y' didst thou forbear
Job 10: 5 of man? are thy y' as man's days,
15: 20 the number of y' is hidden to the
16: 22 When a few y' are come, then I
32: 7 and multitude of y' should teach
36: 11 and their y' in pleasures.
26 number of his y' be searched out.
42: 16 lived Job an hundred and forty y',
Ps 31: 10 with grief, and my y' with sighing:
61: 6 and his y' as many generations.
77: 5 days of old, the y' of ancient times.
10 remember the y' of the right hand
78: 33 in vanity, and their y' in trouble.
90: 4 For a thousand y' in thy sight are
9 we spend our y' as a tale that is
10 The days of our y' are threescore y'
10 of strength they be fourscore y',
15 the y' wherein we have seen evil.
95: 10 Forty y' long was I grieved with
102: 24 y' are throughout all generations.
27 same, and thy y' shall have no end.
Pr 4: 10 and the y' of thy life shall be many.
5: 9 others, and thy y' unto the cruel:
9: 11 the y' of thy life shall be increased.
10: 27 y' of the wicked shall be shortened
Ec 6: 3 hundred children, and live many y',
3 so that the days of his y' be many,
6 though he live a thousand y' twice
11: 8 But if a man live many y', and
12: 1 nor the y' draw nigh, when thou
Isa 7: 8 within threescore and five y' shall
15: 5 unto Zoar, an heifer of three y' old:
Isa 16: 14 Within three y', as the y' of an
20: 3 walked naked and barefoot three y'
21: 16 according to the y' of an hireling,
23: 15 Tyre shall be forgotten seventy y',
15 end of seventy y' shall Tyre sing
17 to pass after the end of seventy y',
32: 10 days and y' shall ye be troubled,
38: 5 I will add unto thy days fifteen y'.
10 deprived of the residue of my y'.
15 I shall go softly all my y' in the
65: 20 child shall die an hundred y' old;
20 the sinner being an hundred y' old
Jer 25: 11 the king of Babylon seventy y'.
12 when seventy y' are accomplished,
28: 3 Within two full y' will I bring
11 within the space of two full y'.
29: 10 after seventy y' be accomplished
34: 14 At the end of seven y' let ye go
14 when he hath served thee six y',
48: 34 as an heifer of three y' old:
52: 1 Zedekiah was one and twenty y'
1 he reigned eleven y' in Jerusalem.
Eze 4: 5 upon thee the y' of their iniquity,
22: 4 and art come even unto thy y':
29: 11 shall it be inhabited forty y'.
12 waste shall be desolate forty y':
13 At the end of forty y' will I gather
38: 8 in the latter y' thou shalt come
17 in those days many y' that I would
39: 9 shall burn them with fire seven y':
Da 1: 5 so nourishing them three y', that at
5: 31 about threescore and two y' old.
9: 2 by books the number of the y',
2 he would accomplish seventy y' in
11: 6 and in the end of y' they shall join
8 continue more y' than the king
13 come after certain y' with a great
Joe 2: 2 after it, even to the y' of many
25 restore to you the y' that the locust
Am 1: 1 two y' before the earthquake.
2: 10 led you forty y' through the
4: 4 and your tithes after three y':
5: 25 in the wilderness forty y',
Hab 3: 2 thy work in the midst of the y',
2 in the midst of the y' make known;
Zec 1: 12 these threescore and ten y'?
7: 3 as I have done these so many y'?
5 even those seventy y', did ye all
Mal 3: 4 the days of old, and as in former y'.
M't 2: 16 from two y' old and under,
9: 20 with an issue of blood twelve y',
M'r 5: 25 had an issue of blood twelve y',
42 for she was of the age of twelve y'.
Lu 1: 7 both were now well stricken in y'.
18 and my wife well stricken in y'.
2: 36 had lived with an husband seven y'
37 of about fourscore and four y',
42 when he was twelve y' old, they
3: 23 began to be about thirty y' of age,
4: 25 shut up three y' and six months,
8: 42 daughter, about twelve y' of age,
43 having an issue of blood twelve y',
12: 19 much goods laid up for many y';
13: 7 these three y' I come seeking fruit
11 had a spirit of infirmity eighteen y',
16 hath bound, lo, these eighteen y',
15: 29 Lo, these many y' do I serve thee,
Joh 2: 20 Forty and six y' was this temple in
5: 5 had an infirmity thirty and eight y'.
8: 57 Thou art not yet fifty y' old, and
Ac 4: 22 the man was above forty y' old,
7: 6 entreat them evil four hundred y'.
23 And when he was full forty y' old,
30 And when forty y' were expired,
36 and in the wilderness forty y'.
42 space of forty y' in the wilderness?
9: 33 which had kept his bed eight y',
13: 18 And about the time of forty y'
20 space of four hundred and fifty y',
21 Benjamin, by the space of forty y'.
19: 10 continued by the space of two y';
20: 31 the space of three y' I ceased not
24: 10 thou hast been of many y' a judge
17 after many y' I came to bring alms
27 after two y' Porcius Festus came
28: 30 Paul dwelt two whole y' in his own
Ro 4: 19 he was about an hundred y' old,
15: 23 a great desire these many y' to
2Co 12: 2 in Christ above fourteen y' ago,
Ga 1: 18 Then after three y' I went up to
2: 1 fourteen y' after I went up again
3: 17 four hundred and thirty y' after,
4: 10 and months, and times, and y'.
1Ti 5: 9 number under threescore y' old,
Heb 1: 12 the same, and thy y' shall not fail.
3: 9 me, and saw my works forty y'.
17 whom was he grieved forty y'?
11: 24 when he was come to y',
Jas 5: 17 earth by the space of three y' and
2Pe 3: 8 is with the Lord as a thousand y',
8 and a thousand y' as one day.
Re 20: 2 and bound him a thousand y',
3 the thousand y' should be fulfilled:
4 reigned with Christ a thousand y'.
5 until the thousand y' were finished.
6 shall reign with him a thousand y'.
7 when the thousand y' are expired,

years'

2Ki 8: 3 came to pass at the seven y' end,
1Ch 21: 12 Either three y' famine; or three

yell See also YELLED.

Jer 51: 38 they shall y' as lions' whelps.

yelled

Jer 2: 15 lions roared upon him, and y',

yellow
Le 13:30 and there be in it a y' thin hair;
32 and there be in it no y' hair,
36 the priest shall not seek for y' hair:
Ps 68:13 and her feathers with y' gold.
yern See YEARN.
yes See also YEA.
M't 17:25 He saith, Y'. And when he was
M'r 7:28 and said unto him, Y', Lord:
Ro 3:29 Gentiles? Y', of the Gentiles also:
10:18 Y', verily, their sound went into
yesterday
Ex 5:14 task in making brick both y'
1Sa 20:27 to meat, neither y', nor to day?
2Sa 15:20 Whereas thou camest but y',
2Ki 9:26 I have seen y' the blood of Naboth,
Job 8: 9 (For we are but of y', and know
Ps 90: 4 years in thy sight are but as y'
Joh 4:52 Y' at the seventh hour the fever
Ac 7:28 as thou didst the Egyptian y'?
Heb13: 8 Jesus Christ the same y', and to day,
yesternight
Ge 19:34 Behold, I lay y' with my father:
31:29 God of your father spake unto me y'
42 of my hands, and rebuked thee y'.
yet^
Ge 6: 3 y' his days shall be an hundred and
7: 4 y' seven days, and I will cause it
8:10, 12 And he stayed y' other seven days;
15:16 of the Amorites is not y' full.
18:22 but Abraham stood y' before the
29 And he spake unto him y' again,
32 and I will speak y' but this once:
20:12 And y' indeed she is my sister;
21:26 neither y' heard I of it, but to day.
25: 6 Isaac his son, while he y' lived,
27:30 Jacob was y' scarce gone out from
29: 7 And he said, Lo, it is y' high day,
9 And while he y' spake with them,
27 serve with me y' seven other years.
30 with him y' other seven years.
31:14 Is there y' any portion or
30 y' wherefore hast...stolen my gods?
37: 5 and they hated him y' the more.
8 And they hated him y' the more
9 And he dreamed y' another dream,
38: 5 And she y' again conceived, and
40:13, 19 Y' within three days shall
23 Y' did not the chief butler remember
43: 6 man whether ye had y' a brother?
7 saying, Is your father y' alive?
27 of whom ye spake? Is he y' alive?
28 is in good health, he is y' alive.
44: 4 gone out of the city, and not y' far off,
14 house; for he was y' there:
45: 3 am Joseph; doth my father y' live?
6 y' there are five years, in the which
11 for y' there are five years of famine;
26 told him, saying, Joseph is y' alive,
28 Joseph my son is y' alive: I will go
46:30 thy face, because thou art y' alive.
48: 7 when y' there was but a little way
Ex 4:18 and see whether they be y' alive.
5:11 y' not ought of your work shall
18 y' shall ye deliver the tale of bricks.
9:17 y' exaltest thou thyself against
30 ye will not y' fear the Lord God.
34 he sinned y' more, and hardened
10: 7 knowest thou not y' that Egypt is
11: 1 Y' will I bring one plague more
21:22 from her, and y' no mischief follow:
33:12 Y' thou hast said, I know thee by
36: 3 brought y' unto him free offerings
Le 5:17 though he wist it not, y' is he guilty,
11: 7 y' he cheweth not the cud;
21 Y' these may ye eat of every flying
13:40 his head, he is bald; y' is he clean.
41 he is forehead bald; y' is he clean.
25:22 eat y' of old fruit until the ninth year;
51 If there be y' many years behind,
26:18 ye will not y' for all this hearken
24 you y' seven times for your sins.
44 y' for all that, when they be in the
Nu 9:10 y' he shall keep the passover unto
11:33 flesh was y' between their teeth,
22:15 And Balak sent y' again princes,
20 y' the word which I shall say unto
30:16 y' in her youth in her father's house.
32:14 to augment y' the fierce anger of
15 he will y' again leave them in the
De 1:32 Y' in this thing ye did not believe the
9:29 Y' they are thy people and thine
12: 9 not as y' come to the rest
14: 8 the hoof, y' cheweth not the cud,
20: 6 vineyard, and hath not y' eaten of it?
22:17 and y' these are the tokens of my
29: 4 Y' the Lord hath not given you
31:27 while I am y' alive with you this
32:52 Y' thou shalt see the land before
Jos 3: 4 Y' there shall be a place between
13: 1 there remaineth y' very much land
2 This is the land that y' remaineth:
14:11 As y' I am as strong this day as I
17:12 Y' the children of Manasseh could
13 Y' it came to pass, when the children
18: 2 had not y' received their inheritance.
J'g 1:35 y' the hand of the house of Joseph
2:10 nor y' the works which he had
17 y' they would not hearken unto
6:24 is y' in Ophrah of the Abi-ezrites.
31 to death whilst it is y' morning:
7: 4 The people are y' too many;
8: 4 with him, faint, y' pursuing them.
20 feared, because he was y' a youth.
9: 5 y' Jotham the youngest son of
J'g 10:13 Y' ye have forsaken me, and served
15: 7 y' will I be avenged of you,
17: 4 Y' he restored the money unto his
19:19 Y' there is both straw and
20:28 Shall I y' again go out to battle
21:14 and y' so they sufficed them not.
Ru 1:11 are there y' any more sons in my
1Sa 3: 6 the Lord called y' again, Samuel.
7 Samuel did not y' know the Lord,
7 word of the Lord y' revealed unto
8: 9 y' protest solemnly unto them,
10:22 if the man should y' come thither.
12:20 y' turn not aside from following
13: 7 As for Saul, he was y' in Gilgal,
21 Y' they had a file for the mattocks,
15:30 I have sinned: y' honour me now,
16:11 There remaineth y' the youngest,
18:29 Saul was y' the more afraid of
20:14 not only while y' I live shew me
23: 4 enquired of the Lord y' again.
22 Go, I pray you, prepare y', and know
24:11 y' thou huntest my soul to take it.
25:29 Y' a man is risen to pursue thee,
2Sa 1: 9 because my life is y' whole in me.
3:35 to eat meat while it was y' day,
5:13 were y' sons and daughters born
22 the Philistines came up y' again,
6:22 I will y' be more vile than thus,
7:19 was y' a small thing in thy sight,
9: 1 there y' any that is left of the house
3 not y' any of the house of Saul,
3 Jonathan hath y' a son, which is
12:18 while the child was y' alive, we
14:14 y' doth he devise means, that his
18:12 y' would I not put forth mine hand
14 was y' alive in the midst of the oak.
22 the son of Zadok y' again
19:28 y' didst thou set thy servant among
28 What right therefore have I y' to cry
35 servant be y' a burden unto my
21:15 the Philistines had y' war again
20 there was y' a battle in Gath,
23: 5 y' he hath made with me an
1Ki 1:14 y' talkest there with the king,
22 while she y' talked with the king,
42 And while he y' spake, behold,
8:28 Y' have thou respect unto the prayer
47 Y' if they shall bethink themselves
11:17 Egypt; Hadad being y' a little child.
12: 2 Nebat, who was y' in Egypt, heard
5 Depart y' for three days, then
6 Solomon his father while he y' lived,
14: 8 y' thou hast not been as my servant
19:18 Y' I have left me seven thousand in
20: 6 Y' I will send my servants unto
32 And he said, Is he y' alive? he is
22: 8 There is y' one man, Micaiah the
43 burn incense y' in the high places.
2Ki 3:17 y' that valley shall be filled with water,
4: 6 unto her son, bring me y' a vessel.
6:33 And while he y' talked with them,
8:19 Y' the Lord would not destroy Judah
22 Y' Edom revolted from under the
13:23 them from his presence as y'.
14: 3 y' not like David his father:
4 as y' the people did sacrifice
17:13 Y' the Lord testified against Israel,
19:30 Judah shall y' again take root
1Ch 12: 1 while he y' kept himself close
14:13 the Philistines y' again spread
17:17 y' this was a small thing in thine
20: 6 y' again there was war at Gath,
26:10 y' his father made him the chief;)
29: 1 hath chosen, is y' young and tender,
2Ch 1:11 neither y' hast asked long life;
6:16 y' so that thy children take heed
26 y' if they pray toward this place, and
37 Y' if they bethink themselves in the
10: 6 Solomon his father while he y' lived,
13: 6 Y' Jeroboam the son of Nebat,
14: 7 while the land is y' before us;
16: 8 y', because thou didst rely on the
12 y' in his disease he sought not to
18: 7 There is y' one man, by whom we
20:33 as y' the people had not prepared
24:19 Y' he sent prophets to them, to bring
28:22 trespass y' more against the Lord:
30:18 y' did they eat the passover
32:15 this manner, neither y' believe him:
16 And his servants spake y' more
33:17 y' unto the Lord their God only.
34: 3 while he was y' young, he began
Ezr 3: 6 the temple of the Lord was not y' laid.
5:16 in building, and y' it is not finished.
9: 9 y' our God hath not forsaken us in
15 for we remain y' escaped, as it is this
10: 2 y' now there is hope in Israel
Ne 1: 9 y' will I gather them from thence,
2:16 neither had I as y' told it to
5: 5 Y' now our flesh is as the flesh of our
18 y' for all this required not I the bread
6: 4 Y' they sent unto me four times
9:19 Y' thou in thy manifold mercies
28 y' when they returned, and cried unto
29 y' they dealt proudly, and hearkened
30 Y' many years didst thou forbear
30 prophets: y' would they not give ear:
13:18 y' ye bring more wrath upon Israel by
26 y' among many nations was there no
Es 2:20 Esther had not y' shewed her
5:13 Y' all this availeth me nothing,
6:14 they were y' talking with him,
8: 3 Esther spake y' again before the
Job 1:16, 17, 18 While he was y' speaking,
3:26 neither was I quiet; y' trouble came.
5: 7 Y' man is born to trouble, as the
Job 6:10 Then should I y' have comfort;
8: 7 y' thy latter end should greatly
12 Whilst it is y' in his greenness,
9:15 righteous, y' would I not answer,
16 y' would I not believe that he had
21 y' would I not know my soul:
31 Y' shalt thou plunge me in the
10: 8 about; y' thou dost destroy me.
15 y' will I not lift up my head.
13:15 he slay me, y' will I trust in him:
14: 9 Y' through the scent of water it will
19:26 body, y' in my flesh shall I see God:
20: 7 Y' he shall perish for ever like his
14 Y' his meat in his bowels is turned,
21:32 Y' shall he be brought to the grave,
22:18 Y' he filled their houses with good
24:12 y' God layeth not folly to them.
23 y' his eyes are upon their ways.
29: 5 the Almighty was y' with me,
32: 3 answer, and y' had condemned Job.
33:14 yea twice, y' man perceiveth it not.
35:14 y' judgment is before him;
15 anger; y' he knoweth it not in great
36: 2 have y' to speak on God's behalf
Ps 2: 6 Y' have I set my king upon my holy
37:10 For y' a little while, and the
25 y' have I not seen the righteous
36 Y' he passed away, and, lo, he was
40:17 needy; y' the Lord thinketh upon me:
42: 5 I shall y' praise him for the help
8 Y' the Lord will command his
11 for I shall y' praise him, who is
43: 5 for I shall y' praise him, who is
44:17 y' have we not forgotten thee, neither
49:13 y' their posterity approve their
55:21 than oil, y' were they drawn swords.
68:13 y' shall ye be as the wings of a dove
71:14 will y' praise thee more and more.
78:17 sinned y' more against him
30 their meat was y' in their mouths,
56 Y' they tempted and provoked the
90:10 years, y' is their strength labour and
94: 7 Y' they say, The Lord shall not see,
107:41 Y' setteth he the poor on high from
119:51 y' have I not declined from thy law.
83 smoke; y' do I not forget thy statutes
109 my hand: y' do I not forget thy law.
110 me: y' I erred not from thy precepts
141 y' do not I forget thy precepts.
143 me: y' thy commandments are my
157 y' do not I decline from thy
129: 2 y' they have not prevailed
138: 6 y' hath he respect unto the lowly:
139:16 my substance, y' being unperfect;
16 when as y' there was none of them.
141: 5 for y' my prayer also shall be in
Pr 6:10 Y' a little sleep, a little slumber,
8:26 While as y' he had not made the
9: 9 man, and he will be y' wiser:
11:24 that scattereth, and y' increaseth;
13: 7 maketh himself rich, y' hath nothing:
7 himself poor, y' hath great riches.
19: 7 words, y' they are wanting to him.
19 him, y' thou must do it again.
23:35 awake? I will seek it y' again.
24:33 Y' a little sleep, a little slumber,
27:22 y' will not his foolishness depart from
30:12 y' is not washed from their filthiness.
25 y' they prepare...meat in the summer;
26 y' make they...houses in the rocks;
27 y' go they forth all of them by bands;
31:15 riseth also while it is y' night,
Ec 1: 7 run into the sea; y' the sea is not full;
2: 3 y' acquainting mine heart with
19 y' shall he have rule over all my
21 y' to a man that hath not laboured
4: 2 than the living which are y' alive.
3 both they, which have not y' been,
8 y' is there no end of all his labour;
6: 2 y' God giveth him not power to eat
6 twice told, y' hath he seen no good:
7 and y' the appetite is not filled.
7:28 Which y' my soul seeketh, but I
8:12 y' surely I know that it shall be
17 to seek it out, y' he shall not find it;
17 y' shall he not be able to find it.
9:11 neither y' bread to the wise,
11 y' riches to men of understanding,
11 nor y' favour to men of skill;
15 y' no man remembered that same
11: 8 y' let him remember the days of
Isa 6:13 But y' it shall be a tenth, and it
10:22 y' a remnant of them shall return:
25 For y' a very little while, and the
32 y' shall he remain at Nob that day:
14: 1 and will y' choose Israel, and set
15 Y' thou shalt be brought down to
17: 6 Y' gleaning grapes shall be left in it,
26:10 y' will he not learn righteousness:
27:10 Y' the defenced city shall be desolate,
28: 4 is y' in his hand he eateth it up.
12 refreshing: y' they would not hear.
29: 2 Y' I will distress Ariel, and there
17 Is it not y' a very little while, and
30:20 y' shall not thy teachers be removed
31: 2 Y' he also is wise, and will bring evil,
42:25 fire round about, y' he knew not;
25 burned him, y' he laid it not to heart.
44: 1 Y' now hear, O Jacob my servant;
11 y' they shall fear, and they shall be
46: 7 y' can he not answer, nor save him
10 the things that are not y' done,
49: 4 y' surely my judgment is with the
5 y' shall I be glorious in the eyes of
15 may forget, y' will I not forget thee.
53: 4 y' we did esteem him stricken,

Isa 53: 7 afflicted, y' he opened not his mouth:
10 Y' it pleased the Lord to bruise him:
56: 8 Y' will I gather others to him,
57: 10 y' saidst thou not, There is no hope:
58: 2 Y' they seek me daily, and delight to
65: 24 while they are y' speaking, I will
Jer 2: 9 Wherefore I will y' plead with you,
11 their gods, which are y' no gods?
21 Y' I had planted thee a noble vine,
22 y' thine iniquity is marked before me,
32 y' my people have forgotten me days
35 Y' thou sayest, Because I am
3: 1 y' return again to me, saith the Lord.
8 y' her treacherous sister Judah
10 And y' for all this her treacherous
4: 27 desolate; y' will I not make a full end.
5: 22 themselves, y' can they not prevail;
22 roar, y' can they not pass over it?
28 of the fatherless, y' they prosper;
7: 26 Y' they hearkened not unto me, nor
9: 20 Y' hear the word of the Lord,
11: 8 Y' they obeyed not, nor inclined their
12: 1 y' let me talk with thee of thy
14: 9 y' thou, O Lord, art in the midst of
15 not, y' they say, Sword and famine
15: 1 y' my mind could not be toward this
9 sun is gone down while it is y' day:
10 y' every one of them doth curse me.
18: 23 Y', Lord, thou knowest all their
22: 6 y' surely I will make thee a
24 hand, y' would I pluck thee hence;
23: 21 not sent these prophets, y' they ran:
21 spoken to them, y' they prophesied.
32 y' I sent them not, nor commanded
25: 7 Y' ye have not hearkened unto me,
27: 15 y' they prophesy a lie in my name;
30: 11 y' will I not make a full end of
31: 5 Thou shalt y' plant vines upon
23 As y' they shall use this speech in
39 the measuring line shall y' go forth
32: 33 y' they have not hearkened to receive
33: 1 he was y' shut up in the court
34: 4 Y' hear the word of the Lord,
36: 24 Y' they were not afraid, nor rent
37: 10 y' should they rise up every man in
40: 5 while he was not y' gone back,
44: 28 Y' a small number that escape the
46: 28 y' will I not leave thee wholly
48: 47 Y' will I bring again the captivity of
51: 33 y' a little while, and the time of
53 y' from me shall spoilers come
La 3: 32 y' will he have compassion according
4: 17 eyes as y' failed for our vain help:
Eze 2: 5 y' shall know that there hath been a
3: 19 Y' if thou warn the wicked, and he
6: 8 Y' will I leave a remnant, that ye may
7: 13 sold, although they were y' alive:
8: 6 turn thee y' again, and thou shalt
13 Turn thee y' again, and thou shalt
15 turn thee y' again, and thou shalt
18 a loud voice, y' will I not hear them.
11: 16 y' will I be to them as a little
12: 13 y' shall he not see it, though he shall
14: 22 Y', behold, therein shall be left a
15: 5 less shall it be meet y' for any work,
16: 28 and y' couldest not be satisfied.
29 and y' thou wast not satisfied
47 Y' hast thou not walked after their
18: 19 Y' say ye, Why? doth not the son
25 Y' ye say, The way of the Lord is not
29 Y' saith the house of Israel, The way
20: 15 Y' also I lifted up my hand unto
27 Y' in this your fathers have
23: 19 Y' she multiplied her whoredoms,
44 Y' they went in unto her, as they
24: 16 y' neither shalt thou mourn nor weep,
26: 21 y' shalt thou never be found again,
28: 2 y' thou art a man, and not God,
9 Wilt thou y' say before him that
29: 13 Y' thus saith the Lord God; At
18 y' had he no wages, nor his army,
31: 18 y' shalt thou be brought down with
32: 24, 25 y' have they borne their shame
33: 17 Y' the children of thy people say,
20 Y' ye say, The way of the Lord is not
36: 37 I will y' for this be enquired of by
44: 11 Y' they shall be ministers in my
Da 4: 23 y' leave the stump of the roots
5: 17 y' I will read the writing unto the
7: 12 y' their lives were prolonged for a
9: 13 y' made we not our prayer before the
10: 9 Y' heard I the voice of his words: and
14 for y' the vision is for many days:
11: 2 stand up y' three kings in Persia;
27 for y' the end shall be at the time
33 y' they shall fall by the sword, and by
35 it is y' for a time appointed.
45 y' he shall come to his end, and none
Ho 1: 4 for y' a little while, and I will
10 Y' the number of the children of
3: 1 Go y', love a woman beloved of
1 of her friend, y' an adulteress,
4: 4 Y' let no man strive, nor reprove
15 the harlot, y' let not Judah offend;
5: 13 y' could he not heal you, nor cure you
7: 9 there upon him, y' he knoweth not:
13 y' they have spoken lies against me.
15 y' do they imagine mischief against
9: 12 their children, y' will I bereave them,
16 y' will I slay even the beloved fruit of
11: 12 but Judah y' ruleth with God, and
12: 8 Y' I am become rich, I have found
9 Egypt will y' make thee to dwell
13: 4 Y' I am the Lord thy God from the
Am 2: 9 Y' destroyed I the Amorite before
9 y' I destroyed his fruit from above,

Am 4: 6 y' have ye not returned unto me, saith
7 when there was y' three months
8, 9, 10, 11 y' have ye not returned unto
6: 10 the house, Is there y' any with thee?
9: 9 y' shall not the least grain fall upon
Jon 2: 4 y' I will look again toward thy holy
6 y' hast thou brought up my life from
3: 4 Y' forty days, and Nineveh shall
4: 2 when I was y' in my country?
Mic 1: 15 Y' will I bring an heir unto thee,
3: 11 y' will they lean upon the Lord, and
5: 2 y' out of thee shall he come forth unto
6: 10 Are there y' the treasures of
Na 1: 12 many, y' thus shall they be cut down,
2: 8 of water: y' they shall flee away.
3: 10 Y' was she carried away, she
Hab 2: 3 vision is y' for an appointed time,
3: 18 Y' I will rejoice in the Lord, I will
Hag 2: 4 Y' now be strong, O Zerubbabel, saith
6 Y' once, it is a little while, and I
17 y' ye turned not to me, saith the Lord.
19 Is the seed y' in the barn? yea,
19 as y' the vine, and the fig tree,
Zec 1: 17 Cry y', saying, Thus saith the
17 through prosperity shall y' be
17 the Lord shall y' comfort Zion,
17 and shall y' choose Jerusalem.
8: 4 shall y' old men and old women
20 It shall y' come to pass, that there
11: 15 Take unto thee y' the instruments
13: 3 that when any shall y' prophesy,
Mal 1: 2 Y' ye say, Wherein hast thou loved
2 saith the Lord: y' I loved Jacob,
2: 14 Y' ye say, Wherefore? Because the
14 y' is she thy companion, and the wife
15 Y' had he the residue of the spirit.
17 Y' ye say, Wherein have we wearied
3: 8 rob God? Y' have ye robbed me.
13 Y' ye say, What have we spoken so
M't 6: 25 y' for your body, what ye shall put
26 y' your heavenly Father feedeth them.
29 y' I say unto you, That even Solomon
10: 10 coats, neither shoes, nor y' staves:
12: 46 While he y' talked to the people,
13: 21 Y' hath he not root in himself, but
15: 16 ye also y' without understanding?
17 Do ye not y' understand, that
27 y' the dogs eat of the crumbs
16: 9 Do ye not y' understand, neither
17: 5 While he y' spake, behold, a bright
19: 20 from my youth up: what lack I y'?
24: 6 come to pass, but the end is not y'.
32 When his branch is y' tender, and
26: 33 of thee, y' will I never be offended.
35 die with thee, y' will I not deny
47 And while he y' spake, lo, Judas,
60 witnesses came, y' found they none.
27: 63 said, while he was y' alive,
M'r 5: 35 While he y' spake, there came
6: 26 y' for his oath's sake, and for their
7: 28 y' the dogs under the table eat
8: 17 perceive ye not y', neither
17 have ye your heart y' hardened?
11: 13 for the time of figs was not y'.
12: 6 Having y' therefore one son, his
13: 7 be; but the end shall not be y'.
28 When her branch is y' tender, and
14: 29 all shall be offended, y' will not I.
43 while he y' spake, cometh Judas,
15: 5 But Jesus y' answered nothing;
Lu 3: 20 Added y' this above all, that he
8: 49 While he y' spake, there cometh
9: 42 And as he was y' a coming, the
11: 8 y' because of his importunity he
12: 27 y' I say unto you, that Solomon in all
14: 22 commanded, and y' there is room.
32 while the other is y' a great way off,
35 the land, nor y' for the dunghill;
15: 20 when he was y' a great way off,
29 y' thou never gavest me a kid, that I
18: 5 Y' because this widow troubleth
22 him, Y' lackest thou one thing:
19: 30 colt tied, whereon y' never man sat:
22: 37 written must y' be accomplished
47 And while he y' spake, behold a
60 while he y' spake, the cock crew.
23: 15 No, nor y' Herod: for I sent you to
24: 6 you when he was y' in Galilee,
41 while they y' believed not for joy,
44 unto you, while I was y' with you,
Joh 2: 4 thee? mine hour is not y' come.
3: 24 John was not y' cast into prison.
4: 21 mountain, nor y' at Jerusalem,
27 y' no man said, What seekest
35 There are y' four months, and
7: 6 unto them, My time is not y' come:
8 I go not up y' unto this feast;
8 for my time is not y' full come.
19 and y' none of you keepeth the law?
30 because his hour was not y' come.
33 Y' a little while am I with you,
39 the Holy Ghost was not y' given;
39 that Jesus was not y' glorified.)
8: 14 record of myself, y' my record is true:
16 y' if I judge, my judgment is true:
20 him; for his hour was not y' come.
55 Y' ye have not known him; but I
57 Thou art not y' fifty years old, and
9: 30 and y' he hath opened mine eyes.
11: 25 though he were dead, y' shall he live:
30 Jesus was not y' come into the
12: 35 Y' a little while is the light with
37 them, y' they believed not on him:
13: 33 y' a little while I am with you.
14: 9 y' hast thou not known me, Philip?
19 Y' a little while, and the world

Joh 14: 25 unto you, being y' present with you.
16: 12 I have y' many things to say unto
32 y' I am not alone, because the Father
19: 41 wherein was never man y' laid.
20: 1 when it was y' dark, unto the
5 clothes lying; y' went they not in.
9 as y' they knew not the scripture,
17 I am not y' ascended to my Father:
29 have not seen, and y' have believed.
21: 11 so many, y' was not the net broken.
23 y' Jesus said not unto him, He shall
Ac 7: 5 y' he promised that he would give
5 him, when as y' he had no child.
8: 16 as y' he was fallen upon none of
9: 1 y' breathing out threatenings and
10: 44 While Peter y' spake these words,
13: 27 nor y' the voices of the prophets
28 y' desired they Pilate that he should
18: 18 this tarried there y' a good while,
19: 37 nor y' blasphemers of your
22: 3 y' brought up in this city at the feet
24: 11 there are y' but twelve days since
25: 8 the temple, nor y' against Cæsar,
28: 4 y' vengeance suffereth not to live.
17 y' was I delivered prisoner from
Ro 3: 7 why y' am I also judged as a
4: 11 which he had y' being uncircumcised:
12 which he had being y' uncircumcised.
19 y' the deadness of Sarah's womb:
5: 6 we were y' without strength,
7 y' peradventure for a good man
8 while we were y' sinners, Christ
8: 24 man seeth, why doth he y' hope for?
9: 11 (For the children being not y' born,
19 me, Why doth he y' find fault?
11: 30 y' have now obtained mercy through
16: 19 y' I would have you wise unto that
1Co 2: 6 y' not the wisdom of this world, nor
15 y' he himself is judged of no man.
3: 2 bear it, neither y' now are ye able.
3 For ye are y' carnal: for whereas
15 shall be saved; y' so as by fire.
4: 4 y' am I not hereby justified: but he
15 Christ, y' have ye not many fathers:
5: 10 Y' not altogether with the
7: 10 y' not I, but the Lord, Let not the wife
25 y' I give my judgment, as one that
8: 2 knoweth nothing y' as he ought
9: 2 others, y' doubtless I am to you:
19 y' have I made myself servant unto
12: 20 many members, y' but one body.
31 and y' shew I unto you a more
14: 19 Y' in the church I had rather
21 y' for all that will they not hear me,
15: 10 y' not I, but the grace of God which
17 is vain; ye are y' in your sins.
2Co 1: 10 we trust that he will y' deliver us;
23 you I came not as y' unto Corinth.
4: 8 on every side, y' not distressed;
16 y' the inward man is renewed day
5: 16 y' now henceforth know we him
6: 8 good report: as deceivers, and y' true;
9 As unknown, and y' well known;
10 As sorrowful, y' alway rejoicing;
10 as poor, y' making many rich;
10 nothing, and y' possessing all things.
8: 9 y' for your sakes he became poor,
9: 3 Y' have I sent the brethren, lest
11: 6 in speech, y' not in knowledge;
16 y' as a fool receive me, that I may
12: 5 y' of myself I will not glory, but in
13: 4 y' he liveth by the power of God.
Ga 1: 10 for if I y' pleased men, I should
2: 20 y' not I, but Christ liveth in me:
3: 4 things in vain? if it be y' in vain.
15 y' if it be confirmed, no man
5: 11 if I y' preach circumcision,
11 why do I y' suffer persecution?
Eph 5: 29 no man ever y' hated his own flesh;
Ph'p 1: 9 love may abound y' more and
22 y' what I shall choose I wot not.
Col 1: 21 works, y' now hath he reconciled
2: 5 y' am I with you in the spirit,
1Th 2: 6 nor y' of others, when we might have
2Th 2: 5 when I was y' with you, I told you
3: 15 Y' count him not as an enemy, but
2Ti 2: 5 for masteries, y' is he not crowned,
13 we believe not, y' he abideth faithful:
Ph'm 9 Y' for love's sake I rather beseech
Heb 2: 8 not y' all things put under him.
4: 15 tempted like as we are, y' without sin.
5: 8 y' learned he obedience by the things
7: 10 he was y' in the loins of his father,
15 And it is y' far more evident:
9: 8 of all was not y' made manifest,
8 first tabernacle was y' standing:
25 Nor y' that he should offer himself
10: 37 For y' a little while, and he that
11: 4 by it he being dead y' speaketh.
7 of God of things not seen as y',
12: 4 Ye have not y' resisted unto blood,
26 Y' once more I shake not the
27 word, Y' once more, signifieth the
Jas 2: 10 y' offend in one point, he is guilty of
11 commit no adultery, y' if thou kill,
3: 4 y' are they turned about with a very
4: 2 y' ye have not, because ye ask not.
1Pe 1: 8 now ye see him not, y' believing,
4: 16 Y' if any man suffer as a Christian,
1Jo 3: 2 not y' appear what we shall be:
Jude 9 Y' Michael the archangel, when
Re 6: 11 should rest y' for a little season,
8: 13 angels, which are y' to sound.
9: 20 by these plagues y' repented not
17: 10 one is, and the other is not y' come;
12 have received no kingdom as y':

yield See also YIELDED; YIELDETH; YIELDING.
Ge 4:12 not henceforth y' unto thee fruits.
49:20 fat, and he shall y' royal dainties.
Le 19:25 it may y' unto you the increase
25:19 And the land shall y' her fruit,
26: 4 and the land shall y' her increase,
4 trees of the field shall y' their fruit.
20 your land shall not y' her increase,
20 the trees of the land y' their fruits.
De 11:17 and that the land y' not her fruit;
2Ch 30: 8 y' yourselves unto the Lord,
Ps 67: 6 shall the earth y' her increase;
85:12 and our land shall y' her increase.
107:37 which may y' fruits of increase.
Pr 7:21 fair speech she caused him to y',
Isa 5:10 of vineyard shall y' one bath,
10 seed of an homer shall y' an ephah.
Eze 34:27 tree of the field shall y' her fruit,
27 and the earth shall y' her increase,
36: 8 and y' your fruit to my people of
Ho 8: 7 stalk: the bud shall y' no meal:
7 if so be it y', the strangers shall
Joe 2:22 and the vine do y' their strength.
Hab 3:17 fail, and the field shall y' no meat
M'r 4: 8 and did y' fruit that sprang up
Ac 23:21 But do not thou y' unto them:
Ro 6:13 Neither y' ye your members as
13 but y' yourselves unto God, as
16 ye y' yourselves servants to obey,
19 so now y' your members servants
Jas 3:12 no fountain both y' salt water and

yielded
Ge 49:33 y' up the ghost, and was gathered
Nu 17: 8 blossoms, and y' almonds.
Da 3:28 king's word, and y' their bodies,
M't 27:50 with a loud voice, y' up the ghost.
M'r 4: 7 and choked it, and it y' no fruit.
Ac 5:10 at his feet, and y' up the ghost:
Ro 6:19 have y' your members servants
Re 22: 2 and y' her fruit every month:

yieldeth
Ne 9:37 it y' much increase unto the kings
Job 24: 5 the wilderness y' food for them and
Pr 12:12 the root of the righteous y' fruit.
Heb 12:11 afterward it y' the peaceable fruit

yielding
Ge 1:11 forth grass, the herb y' seed,
11 fruit tree y' fruit after his kind,
12 and herb y' seed after his kind,
12 and the tree y' fruit, whose seed
29 is the fruit of a tree y' seed;
Ec 10: 4 for y' pacifieth great offences.
Jer 17: 8 neither shall cease from y' fruit.

yoke See also YOKED; YOKEFELLOW; YOKES.
Ge 27:40 break his y' from off thy neck.
Le 26:13 I have broken the bands of your y',
Nu 19: 2 and upon which never came y':
De 21: 3 which hath not drawn in the y';
28:48 shall put a y' of iron upon thy neck,
1Sa 6: 7 on which there hath come no y',
11: 7 And he took a y' of oxen, and
14:14 which a y' of oxen might plow
1Ki 12: 4 Thy father made our y' grievous:
4 his heavy y' which he put upon us,
9 y' which thy father did put upon us
10 Thy father made our y' heavy, but
11 father did lade you with a heavy y',
11 I will add to your y': my father
14 My father made your y' heavy, and
14 and I will add to your y': my
19:19 plowing with twelve y' of oxen
21 took a y' of oxen, and slew them,
2Ch 10: 4 Thy father made our y' grievous:
4 his heavy y' that he put upon us,
9 y' that thy father did put upon us?
10 Thy father made our y' heavy,
11 my father put a heavy y' upon you,
11 will put more to your y': my father
14 My father made your y' heavy,
Job 1: 3 and five hundred y' of oxen,
42:12 and a thousand y' of oxen, and a
Isa 9: 4 hast broken the y' of his burden,
10:27 and his y' from off thy neck,
27 and the y' shall be destroyed
14:25 shall his y' depart from off them,
47: 6 hast thou very heavily laid thy y'.
58: 6 free, and that ye brake every y'?
9 away from the midst of thee the y',
Jer 2:20 of old time I have broken thy y',
5: 5 have altogether broken the y',
27: 8, 11, 12 the y' of the king of Babylon,
28: 2 the y' of the king of Babylon.
4 brake the y' of the king of Babylon.
10 took the y' from off the prophet
11 I break the y' of Nebuchadnezzar
12 the prophet had broken the y'
14 a y' of iron upon the neck of all
30: 8 break his y' from off thy neck,
31:18 as a bullock unaccustomed to the y':
51:23 husbandman and his y' of oxen;
La 1:14 The y' of my transgressions is
3:27 that he bear the y' in his youth.
Eze 34:27 have broken the bands of their y',
Ho 11: 4 that take off the y' on their jaws,
Na 1:13 will I break his y' from off thee,
M't 11:29 Take my y' upon you, and learn of
30 For my y' is easy, and my burden
Lu 14:19 I have bought five y' of oxen,
Ac 15:10 y' upon the neck of the disciples,
Ga 5: 1 again with the y' of bondage.
1Ti 6: 1 many servants as are under the y'

yoked
2Co 6:14 y' together with unbelievers:

yokefellow
Ph'p 4: 3 true y', help those women which

yokes
Jer 27: 2 Make thee bonds and y', and put
28:13 Thou hast broken the y' of wood;
13 shalt make for them y' of iron.
Eze 30:18 shall break there the y' of Egypt:

yonder
Ge 22: 5 lad will go y' and worship,
Nu 16:37 and scatter thou the fire y';
23:15 offering, while I meet the Lord y'.
32:19 inherit with them on y' side Jordan,
2Ki 4:25 Behold, y' is that Shunammite:
M't 17:20 Remove hence to y' place;
26:36 Sit ye here, while I go and pray y'.

young See also YOUNGER; YOUNGEST.
Ge 4:23 and a y' man to my hurt.
14:24 which the y' men have eaten,
15: 9 and a turtledove, and a y' pigeon.
18: 7 good, and gave it unto a y' man;
19: 4 the house round, both old and y',
22: 3 took two of his y' men with him,
5 Abraham said unto his y' men,
19 Abraham returned unto his y' men,
31:38 thy she goats have not cast their y',
33:13 and herds with y' are with me:
34:19 y' man deferred not to do the
41:12 there was there with us a y' man,
Ex 10: 9 go with our y' and with our old,
23:26 There shall nothing cast their y', nor
24: 5 y' men of the children of Israel,
29: 1 Take one y' bullock, and
33:11 Joshua, the son of Nun, a y' man,
Le 1:14 of turtledoves, or of y' pigeons.
4: 3 a y' bullock without blemish
14 offer a y' bullock for the sin,
5: 7 or two y' pigeons, unto the Lord;
11 two y' pigeons, then he that sinned
9: 2 a y' calf for a sin offering,
12: 6 a y' pigeon, or a turtledove,
8 two turtles, or two y' pigeons;
14:22 two y' pigeons, such as he is able
30 y' pigeons, such as he can get;
15:14 or two y' pigeons, and come before
29 or two y' pigeons, and bring them
16: 3 a y' bullock for a sin offering,
22:28 kill it and her y' both in one day.
23:18 one y' bullock, and two rams:
Nu 6:10 or two y' pigeons, to the priest,
7:15, 21, 27, 33, 39, 45, 51, 57, 63, 69, 75,
81 One y' bullock, one ram, one
8: 8 Then let them take a y' bullock"
8 y' bullock shalt thou take "
11:27 ran a y' man, and told Moses,
28 one of his y' men, answered
15:24 offer one y' bullock for a burnt
23:24 and lift up himself as a y' lion:
28:11, 19, 27 y' bullocks, ...one ram,
29: 2, 8 one y' bullock, one ram, and
13 thirteen y' bullocks, two rams,
17 shall offer twelve y' bullocks,
De 22: 6 whether they be y' ones, or eggs,
6 and the dam sitting upon the y',
6 not take the dam with the y':
7 dam go, and take the y' to thee;
28:50 old, nor shew favour to the y':
57 toward her y' one that cometh out
32:11 fluttereth over her y', spreadeth
25 shall destroy both the y' man and
Jos 6:21 both man and woman, y' and old,
23 y' men that were spies went in,
J'g 6:25 Take thy father's y' bullock, even
8:14 a y' man of the men of Succoth,
9:54 unto the y' man his armourbearer,
54 his y' man thrust him through, and
14: 5 a y' lion roared against him.
10 feast; for so used the y' men to do.
17: 7 a y' man out of Beth-lehem-judah
11 y' man was unto him as one of his
12 and the y' man became his priest,
18: 3 the voice of the y' man the Levite:
15 the house of the y' man the Levite,
19:19 y' man which is with thy servants:
21:12 four hundred y' virgins, that had
Ru 2: 9 have I not charged the y' men
9 that which the y' men have drawn.
15 Boaz commanded his y' men,
21 shalt keep fast by my y' men,
3:10 as thou followedst not y' men,
4:12 shall give thee of this y' woman.
1Sa 1:24 in Shiloh: and the child was y'.
2: , the sin of the y' men was very great
8:16 your goodliest y' men, and your
9: 2 Saul, a choice y' man, and a goodly:
11 y' maidens going out to draw
14: 1 son of Saul said unto the y' man
6 Jonathan said to the y' man that
17:58 Whose son art thou, thou y' man?
20:22 But if I say thus unto the y' man,
21: 4 if the y' men have kept themselves
5 vessels of the y' men are holy,
25: 5 And David sent out ten y' men,
5 David said unto the y' men, Get
8 Ask thy y' men, and they will shew
8 let the y' men find favour in thine
9 And when David's y' men came,
12 So David's y' men turned their way,
14 But one of the y' men told Abigail,
25 thine handmaid saw not the y' men
27 the y' men that follow my lord.
26:22 let one of the y' men come over and
30:13 he said, I am a y' man of Egypt,
1Sa 30:17 save four hundred y' men, which
2Sa 1: 5 David said unto the y' man that
6 And the y' man that told him said,
13 And David said unto the y' man
15 David called one of the y' men, and
2:14 Let the y' men now arise, and
21 lay thee hold on one of the y' men,
4:12 And David commanded his y' men,
9:12 Mephibosheth had a y' son, whose
13:32 all the y' men the king's sons;
34 the y' man that kept the watch
14:21 bring the y' man Absalom again.
16: 2 summer fruit for the y' men to eat:
18: 5 gently for my sake with the y' man,
12 none touch the y' man Absalom.
15 y' men that bare Joab's armour
29 said, Is the y' man Absalom safe?
32 Is the y' man Absalom safe? And
32 do thee hurt, be as that y' man is.
1Ki 1: 2 for my lord the king a y' virgin:
11:28 Solomon seeing the y' man that
12: 8 consulted with the y' men that
10 y' men that were grown up with
14 after the counsel of the y' men,
20:14, 15, 17, 19 y' men of the princes of
2Ki 4:22 me, I pray thee, one of the y' men,
5:22 two y' men of the sons of the
6:17 Lord opened the eyes of the y' man;
8:12 their y' men wilt thou slay with
9: 4 So the y' man, even the
4 even the y' man the prophet,
1Ch 12:28 Zadok, a y' man mighty of valour,
22: 5 Solomon my son is y' and tender,
29: 1 hath chosen, is yet y' and tender,
2Ch 10: 8 took counsel with the y' men that
10 y' men that were brought up with
14 after the advice of the y' men,
13: 7 when Rehoboam was y' and
9 himself with a y' bullock
34: 3 while he was yet y', he began to
36:17 who slew their y' men with the
17 had no compassion upon y' man or
Ezr 6: 9 both y' bullocks, and rams,
Es 2: 2 there be fair y' virgins sought
3 together all the fair y' virgins
3:13 perish, all Jews, both y' and old,
8:10 camels, and y' dromedaries:
Job 1:19 it fell upon the y' men, and they
4:10 and the teeth of the y' lions, are
19:18 Yea, y' children despised me;
29: 8 The y' men saw me, and hid
32: 6 I am y', and ye are very old;
38:39 or fill the appetite of the y' lions,
41 when his y' ones cry unto God,
39: 3 they bring forth their y' ones,
4 Their y' ones are in good liking,
16 is hardened against her y' ones,
30 Her y' ones also suck up blood:
Ps 17:12 a y' lion lurking in secret places.
29: 6 and Sirion like a y' unicorn.
34:10 The y' lions do lack, and suffer
37:25 I have been y', and now am old;
58: 6 out the great teeth of the y' lions,
78:63 The fire consumed their y' men;
71 following the ewes great with y'
84: 3 where she may lay her y', even
91:13 y' lion and the dragon shalt thou
104:21 The y' lions roar after their prey,
119: 9 shall a y' man cleanse his way?
147: 9 and to the y' ravens which cry.
148:12 Both y' men, and maidens; old
Pr 1: 4 y' man knowledge and discretion.
7: 7 a y' man void of understanding,
20:29 glory of y' men is their strength:
30:17 out, and the y' eagles shall eat it.
Ec 11: 9 Rejoice, O y' man, in thy youth;
Ca 2: 9 beloved is like a roe or a y' hart:
17 roe or a y' hart upon the mountains
4: 5 are like two y' roes that are twins,
7: 3 are like two y' roes that are twins.
8:14 be thou like to a roe or to a y' hart
Isa 5:29 lion, they shall roar like y' lions:
7:21 that a man shall nourish a y' cow,
9:17 shall have no joy in their y' men,
11: 6 and the y' lion and the fatling
7 y' ones shall lie down together:
13:18 shall dash the y' men to pieces;
20: 4 Ethiopians captives, y' and old,
23: 4 neither do I nourish up y' men,
30: 6 whence come the y' and old lion,
6 riches upon the shoulders of y' asses,
24 y' asses that ear the ground shall eat
31: 4 the y' lion roaring on his prey,
8 his y' men shall be discomfited.
40:11 gently lead those that are with y'.
30 the y' men shall utterly fall:
62: 5 For as a y' man marrieth a virgin,
Jer 2:15 The y' lions roared upon him, and
6:11 the assembly of y' men together:
9:21 and the y' men from the streets.
11:22 the y' men shall die by the sword;
15: 8 against the mother of the y' men
18:21 their y' men be slain by the sword
31:12 the y' of the flock and of the herd:
13 both y' men and old together:
48:15 his chosen y' men are gone down to
49:26 her y' men shall fall in her streets,
50:30 shall her y' men fall in the streets,
51: 3 spare ye not her y' men; destroy ye
22 will I break in pieces old and y';
22 in pieces the y' man and the maid;
La 1:15 against me to crush my y' men:
18 my y' men are gone into captivity.
2:19 him for the life of thy y' children,
21 y' and the old lie on the ground
21 virgins and my y' men are fallen

La 4: 3 they give suck to their y' ones:
4 the y' children ask bread, and no man
5:13 They took the y' men to grind, and
14 gate, the y' men from their musick,
Eze 9: 6 Slay utterly old and y', both maids,
17: 4 off the top of his y' twigs, and
22 off from the top of his y' twigs
19: 2 her whelps among y' lions.
3 it became a y' lion, and it learned
5 whelps, and made him a y' lion.
6 he became a y' lion, and learned
23: 6 all of them desirable y' men,
12 all of them desirable y' men.
23 them: all of them desirable y' men,
30:17 y' men of Aven and of Pi-beseth
31: 6 of the field bring forth their y',
32: 2 art like a y' lion of the nations,
38:13 of Tarshish, with all the y' lions
41:19 face of a y' lion toward the palm
43:19 y' bullock for a sin offering.
23 a y' bullock without blemish,
25 shall also prepare a y' bullock,
45:18 a y' bullock without blemish,
46: 6 a y' bullock without blemish,
Ho 5:14 as a y' lion to the house of Judah:
Joe 2:28 your y' men shall see visions:
Am 2:11 and of your y' men for Nazarites.
3: 4 will a y' lion cry out of his den,
4:10 your y' men have I slain with the
8:13 virgins and y' men faint for thirst.
Mic 5: 8 as a y' lion among the flocks of
Na 2:11 the feedingplace of the y' lions,
13 sword shall devour thy y' lions:
3:10 her y' children also were dashed in
Zec 2: 4 Run, speak to this y' man, saying,
9:17 shall make the y' men cheerful,
11: 3 a voice of the roaring of y' lions;
16 neither shall seek the y' one,
M't 2: 8 search diligently for the y' child;
9 stood over where the y' child was.
11 the y' child with Mary his mother,
13 take the y' child and his mother,
13 seek the y' child to destroy him.
14 he took the y' child and his mother
20 take the y' child and his mother,
20 which sought the y' child's life.
21 took the y' child and his mother,
19:20 The y' man saith unto him, All
22 the y' man heard that saying, he
M'r 7:25 y' daughter had an unclean spirit,
10:13 they brought y' children to him,
14:51 followed him a certain y' man,
51 and the y' men laid hold on him:
16: 5 saw a y' man sitting on the right
Lu 2:24 of turtledoves, or two y' pigeons.
7:14 Y' man, I say unto thee, Arise.
Joh 12:14 when he had found a y' ass, sat
21:18 When thou wast y', thou girdedst
Ac 2:17 and your y' men shall see visions,
5: 6 the y' men arose, wound him up,
10 y' men came in, and found her
7:19 they cast out their y' children,
58 their clothes at a y' man's feet,
20: 9 a certain y' man named Eutychus,
12 they brought the y' man alive,
23:17 this y' man unto the chief captain:
18 prayed me to bring this y' man
22 then let the y' man depart,
Tit 2: 4 teach the y' women to be sober,
6 Y' men likewise exhort to be
1Jo 2:13 I write unto you, y' men, because
14 written unto you, y' men, because

younger

Ge 9:24 knew what his y' son had done
19:31, 34 the firstborn said unto the y',
35 and the y' arose, and lay with him;
38 And the y', she also bare a son,
25:23 and the elder shall serve the y'.
27:15 put them upon Jacob her y' son:
42 sent and called Jacob her y' son,
29:16 and the name of the y' was Rachel.
18 years for Rachel the y' daughter.
26 to give the y' before the firstborn.
43:29 Is this your y' brother, of whom
48:14 Ephraim's head, who was the y',
19 his y' brother shall be greater
J'g 1:13 Kenaz, Caleb's y' brother, took it:
3: 9 son of Kenaz, Caleb's y' brother.
15: 2 is not her y' sister fairer than she?
1Sa 14:49 and the name of the y' Michal:
1Ch 24:31 over against their y' brethren.
Job 30: 1 y' than I have me in derision,
Eze 16:46 thy y' sister, that dwelleth at thy
61 thy sisters, thine elder and thy y':
Lu 15:12 the y' of them said to his father,
13 the y' son gathered all together,
22:26 among you, let him be as the y';
Ro 9:12 her, The elder shall serve the y'.
1Ti 5: 1 and the y' men as brethren;
2 the y' as sisters, with all purity.
11 But the y' widows refuse: for when
14 therefore that the y' women marry,
1Pe 5: 5 ye y', submit yourselves unto the

youngest

Ge 42:13 the y' is this day with our father,
15 your y' brother come hither.
20 bring your y' brother unto me;
32 the y' is this day with our father
34 bring your y' brother unto me:
43:33 and the y' according to his youth:
44: 2 cup, in the sack's mouth of the y',
12 at the eldest, and left at the y':
23 Except your y' brother come down
26 if our y' brother be with us, then
26 except our y' brother be with us.

Jos 6:26 and in his y' son shall he set up
J'g 9: 5 the y' son of Jerubbaal was left;
1Sa 16:11 said, There remaineth yet the y',
17:14 And David was the y': and the
1Ki 16:34 gates thereof in his y' son Segub,
2Ch 21:17 save Jehoahaz, the y' of his sons.
22: 1 made Ahaziah his y' son king in

your^ See also YOURS; YOURSELVES.

Ge 3: 5 thereof, then y' eyes shall be opened,
9: 2 sea; into y' hand are they delivered.
5 y' blood of y' lives will I require;
9 with you, and with y' seed after you;
17:11 circumcise the flesh of y' foreskin;
12 every man child in y' generations, he
13 my covenant shall be in y' flesh for
18: 4 you, be fetched, and wash y' feet,
5 of bread, and comfort ye y' hearts;
5 therefore are ye come to y' servant.
19: 2 I pray you, into y' servant's house,
2 and tarry all night, and wash y' feet,
2 rise up early, and go on y' ways.
8 do ye to them as is good in y' eyes:
23: 8 y' mind that I should bury my dead
31: 5 I see y' father's countenance, that it
6 my power I have served y' father.
7 And y' father hath deceived me,
9 taken away the cattle of y' father,
29 the God of y' father spake unto me
34: 8 Shechem longeth for y' daughter:
9 give y' daughters unto us, and take
11 Let me find grace in y' eyes, and what
16 we will take y' daughters, and we
35: 2 be clean, and change y' garments:
37: 7 y' sheaves stood round about,
42:15 except y' youngest brother come
16 of you, and let him fetch y' brother,
16 that y' words may be proved, whether
19 true men, let one of y' brethren
19 bound in the house of y' prison:
19 corn for the famine of y' houses:
20 bring y' youngest brother unto me;
20 so shall y' words be verified, and ye
33 one of y' brethren here with me,
33 food for the famine of y' households,
34 bring y' youngest brother unto me:
34 so will I deliver you y' brother, and
43: 3, 5 except y' brother be with you.
7 saying, Is y' father yet alive?
7 would say, Bring y' brother down?
11 best fruits in the land in y' vessels,
12 And take double money in y' hand;
12 again in the mouth of y' sacks,
12 carry it again in y' hand;
13 Take also y' brother, and arise, go
14 he may send away y' other brother,
23 y' God, and the God of y' father,
23 hath given you treasure in y' sacks:
23 I had y' money. And he brought
27 Is y' father well, the old man of whom
29 Is this y' younger brother, of whom
44:10 let it be according unto y' words:
17 get you up in peace unto y' father.
23 Except y' youngest brother come
45: 4 I am Joseph y' brother, whom ye sold
7 and to save y' lives by a great
12 y' eyes see, and the eyes of my brother
17 lade y' beasts, and go, get you unto
18 take y' father, and y' households,
19 the land of Egypt for y' little ones,
19 and for y' wives, and bring y' father,
20 Also regard not y' stuff; for the good
46:33 shall say, What is y' occupation?
47: 3 his brethren, What is y' occupation?
16 And Joseph said, Give y' cattle;
16 I will give you for y' cattle, if money
23 I have bought you this day and y' land
24 and four parts shall be y' own, for seed
24 y' food, and for them of y' households,
24 and for food for y' little ones.
48:21 you again unto the land of y' fathers.
49: 2 and hearken unto Israel y' father.
50: 4 now I have found grace in y' eyes,
21 I will nourish you, and y' little ones.
Ex 3:13 God of y' fathers hath sent me unto
15, 16 The Lord God of y' fathers,
22 upon y' sons, and upon y' daughters;
5: 4 works? get you unto y' burdens.
11 ought of y' work shall be diminished.
13 hasted them, saying, Fulfil y' works,
13 y' daily tasks, as when there was
14 have ye not fulfilled y' task
19 ought from y' bricks of y' daily task.
6: 7 shall know that I am the Lord y' God,
8:25 Go ye, sacrifice to y' God in the land.
28 ye may sacrifice to the Lord y' God
10: 8 unto them, Go, serve the Lord y' God:
10 I will let you go, and y' little ones:
16 have sinned against the Lord y' God,
17 and intreat the Lord y' God, that he
24 let y' flocks and y' herds be stayed:
24 let y' little ones also go with you.
12: 4 to his eating shall make y' count
5 Y' lamb shall be without blemish,
11 y' loins girded, y' shoes on y' feet,
11 and y' staff in y' hand;
14 the Lord throughout y' generations;
15 put away leaven out of y' houses:
17 y' armies out of the land of Egypt:
17 ye observe this day in y' generations
19 there be no leaven found in y' houses:
20 in all y' habitations shall ye eat
21 you a lamb according to y' families,
23 destroyer to come in unto y' houses to
26 when y' children shall say unto you,
32 Also take y' flocks and y' herds,
14:14 for you, and ye shall hold y' peace.

Ex 16: 7 he heareth y' murmurings against
8 y' murmurings which ye murmur
8 y' murmurings are not against us,
9 for he hath heard y' murmurings.
12 shall know that I am the Lord y' God.
16 to the number of y' persons;
32 of it to be kept for y' generations;
33 Lord, to be kept for y' generations.
19:15 the third day: come not at y' wives.
20:20 that his fear may be before y' faces,
22:24 and y' wives shall be widows,
24 and y' children fatherless.
23:21 he will not pardon y' transgressions:
25 And ye shall serve the Lord y' God,
31 inhabitants of the land into y' hand;
29:42 offerings throughout y' generations
30: 8 the Lord throughout y' generations.
10 upon it throughout y' generations:
15, 16 to make an atonement for y' souls
31 unto me throughout y' generations.
31:13 and you throughout y' generations;
32: 2 which are in the ears of y' wives,
2 of y' sons, and of y' daughters,
13 I will multiply y' seed as the stars of
13 spoken of will I give unto y' seed,
30 I shall make an atonement for y' sin.
34:23 all y' menchildren appear before the
35: 3 no fire throughout y' habitations
Le 1: 2 ye shall bring y' offering of the cattle,
3:17 a perpetual statute for y' generations
17 throughout all y' dwellings, that ye
6:18 a statute for ever in y' generations
7:26 or of beast, in any of y' dwellings.
32 of the sacrifices of y' peace offerings.
8:33 until the days of y' consecration be
10: 4 carry y' brethren from before the
6 his sons, Uncover not y' heads,
6 neither rend y' clothes; lest ye die,
6 but let y' brethren, the whole house
9 for ever throughout y' generations:
11:43 not make y' selves abominable?
44 For I am the Lord y' God: ye shall
45 of the land of Egypt, to be y' God:
14:34 a house of the land of y' possession;
16:29 ye shall afflict y' souls, and do no
29 whether it be one of y' own country,
30 ye may be clean from all y' sins
31 and ye shall afflict y' souls, by a
17:11 to make an atonement for y' souls:
15 whether it be one of y' own country,
18: 2 say unto them, I am the Lord y' God.
4 walk therein: I am the Lord y' God.
26 neither any of y' own nation, nor any
19: 2 holy: for I the Lord y' God am holy.
3 my sabbaths: I am the Lord y' God.
4 molten gods: I am the Lord y' God.
5 Lord, ye shall offer it at y' own will.
9 when ye reap the harvest of y' land,
10 and stranger: I am the Lord y' God.
25 thereof: I am the Lord y' God.
27 not round the corners of y' heads,
28 not make any cuttings in y' flesh
31 defiled by them: I am the Lord y' God.
33 stranger sojourn with thee in y' land,
34 land of Egypt: I am the Lord y' God.
36 I am the Lord y' God, which brought
20: 7 be ye holy: for I am the Lord y' God.
24 I am the Lord y' God, which have
25 shall not make y' souls abominable
22: 3 of all y' seed among y' generations,
19 Ye shall offer at y' own will a male*
24 make any offering thereof in y' land.
25 offer the bread of y' God of any of
29 unto the Lord, offer it at y' own will.
33 of the land of Egypt, to be y' God:
23: 3 of the Lord in all y' dwellings.
10 sheaf of the firstfruits of y' harvest
14 brought an offering unto y' God:
14 y' generations in all y' dwellings.
17 Ye shall bring out of y' habitations
21 statute for ever in all y' dwellings
21 throughout y' generations.
22 when ye reap the harvest of y' land,
22 the stranger: I am the Lord y' God.
27 and ye shall afflict y' souls, and offer
28 for you before the Lord y' God.
31 y' generations in all y' dwellings.
32 of rest, and ye shall afflict y' souls:
32 even, shall ye celebrate y' sabbath.
38 beside y' gifts, and beside all y' vows,
38 and beside all y' freewill offerings,
40 shall rejoice before the Lord y' God
41 a statute for ever in y' generations:
43 That y' generations may know that I
43 land of Egypt: I am the Lord y' God.
24: 3 a statute for ever in y' generations.
22 as for one of y' own country:
22 for I am the Lord y' God.
25: 9 sound throughout all y' land.
17 thy God: for I am the Lord y' God.
19 and ye shall eat y' fill, and dwell
24 And in all the land of y' possession
38 I am the Lord y' God, which brought
38 the land of Canaan, and to be y' God.
45 you, which they begat in y' land:
45 and they shall be y' possession.
46 inheritance for y' children after you,
46 they shall be y' bondmen for ever:
46 over y' brethren the children of Israel,
55 land of Egypt: I am the Lord y' God.
26: 1 set up any image of stone in y' land,
1 unto it: for I am the Lord y' God.
5 y' threshing shall reach unto the
5 and ye shall eat y' bread to the full,
5 to the full, and dwell in y' land safely
6 shall the sword go through y' land.

Le 26: 7 And ye shall chase y' enemies, and
8 and y' enemies shall fall before you
12 walk among you, and will be y' God,
13 I am the Lord y' God, which brought
13 I have broken the bands of y' yoke,
15 or if y' soul abhor my judgments, so
16 and ye shall sow y' seed in vain,
16 for y' enemies shall eat it.
17 ye shall be slain before y' enemies:
18 you seven times more for y' sins.
19 I will break the pride of y' power:
19 y' heaven...iron, and y' earth as brass:
20 And y' strength shall be spent in vain:
20 y' land shall not yield her increase,
21 plagues upon you according to y' sins.
22 of y' children, and destroy y' cattle,
22 and y' high ways shall be desolate.
24 you yet seven times for y' sins.
25 are gathered together within y' cities,
26 I have broken the staff of y' bread,
26 ten women shall bake y' bread in one
26 deliver you y' bread again by weight:
29 And ye shall eat the flesh of y' sons,
29 the flesh of y' daughters shall ye eat.
30 I will destroy y' high places,
30 and cut down y' images,
30 cast y' carcases upon the carcases
30 upon the carcases of y' idols,
31 And I will make y' cities waste,
31 bring y' sanctuaries unto desolation,
31 smell the savour of y' sweet odours.
32 and y' enemies which dwell therein
33 y' land shall be desolate, and y' cities
34 and ye be in y' enemies' land;
35 because it did not rest in y' sabbaths,
37 no power to stand before y' enemies.
38 land of y' enemies shall eat you up.
39 in their iniquity in y' enemies' lands;
Nu 9: 10 If any man of you or of y' posterity
10: 8 for ever throughout y' generations.
9 And if ye go to war in y' land against
9 remembered before the Lord y' God,
9 ye shall be saved from y' enemies.
10 of y' gladness, and in y' solemn days,
10 and in the beginnings of y' months,
10 the trumpets over y' burnt offerings,
10 the sacrifices of y' peace offerings;
10 you for a memorial before y' God:
10 I am the Lord y' God.
11: 20 until it come out at y' nostrils, and it
14: 29 Y' carcases shall fall in this
29 you, according to y' whole number,
31 But y' little ones, which ye said
32 as for you, y' carcases, they shall
33 y' children shall wander in the
33 years, and bear y' whoredoms,
33 until y' carcases be wasted
34 shall ye bear y' iniquities, even forty
42 ye be not smitten before y' enemies.
15: 2 come into the land of y' habitations,
3 offering, or in y' solemn feasts,
14 be among you in y' generations,
15 ordinance for ever in y' generations:
20 of y' dough for an heave offering:
21 Of the first of y' dough ye shall give
21 an heave offering in y' generations.
23 henceforward among y' generations;
39 after y' own heart and y' own eyes,
40 and be holy unto y' God.
41 I am the Lord y' God, which brought
41 to be y' God: I am the Lord y' God.
18: 1 bear the iniquity of y' priesthood.
6 I have taken y' brethren the Levites
7 with thee shall keep y' priest's office
7 I have given y' priest's office unto
23 for ever throughout y' generations,
26 you from them for y' inheritance,
27 y' heave offering shall be reckoned
28 offering unto the Lord of all y' tithes,
29 Out of all y' gifts ye shall offer
31 every place, ye and y' households:
31 for it is y' reward for y' service in
22: 13 Get you into y' land: for the Lord
28: 11 And in the beginning of y' months ye
26 unto the Lord, after y' weeks be out,
29: 7 and ye shall afflict y' souls: ye shall
39 Lord in y' set feasts, beside y' vows,
39 y' freewill offerings, for y' burnt
39 y' meat offerings, and for y' drink
39 offerings, and for y' peace offerings.
31: 19 both yourselves and y' captives
20 And purify all y' raiment, and all
24 wash y' clothes on the seventh day,
32: 6 Shall y' brethren go to war, and shall
8 Thus did y' fathers, when I sent
14 ye are risen up in y' fathers' stead,
22 and this land shall be y' possession
23 and be sure y' sin will find you out.
24 Build you cities for y' little ones,
24 and folds for y' sheep;
24 hath proceeded out of y' mouth.
33: 54 for an inheritance among y' families:
54 to the tribes of y' fathers ye
55 in y' eyes, and thorns in y' sides,
34: 3 Then y' south quarter shall be from
3 y' south border shall be the outmost
4 y' border shall turn from the south
6 border: this shall be y' west border.
7 And this shall be y' north border:
8 Hor ye shall point out y' border
9 this shall be y' north border.
10 ye shall point out y' east border from
12 this shall be y' land with the coasts
35: 29 y' generations in all y' dwellings.
De 1: 7 Turn you, and take y' journey, and go
8 the Lord sware unto y' fathers,

De 1: 10 The Lord y' God hath multiplied you,
11 (The Lord God of y' fathers make you
12 I myself alone bear y' cumbrance,
12 and y' burden, and y' strife?
13 and known among y' tribes, and I
15 So I took the chief of y' tribes,
15 over tens, and officers among y' tribes.
16 And I charged y' judges at that time,
16 Hear the causes between y' brethren,
26 commandment of the Lord y' God:
27 And ye murmured in y' tents, and
30 Lord y' God which goeth before you,
30 did for you in Egypt before y' eyes;
32 ye did not believe the Lord y' God,
33 you out a place to pitch y' tents in,
34 the Lord heard the voice of y' words,
35 which I sware to give unto y' fathers,
37 was angry with me for y' sakes,
39 Moreover y' little ones, which ye said
39 y' children, which in that day had no
40 take y' journey into the wilderness
42 lest ye be smitten before y' enemies.
45 Lord would not hearken to y' voice,
2: 4 pass through the coast of y' brethren
3: 18 The Lord y' God hath given you this
18 pass over armed before y' brethren
19 But y' wives, and y' little ones,
19 and y' cattle, (for I know that ye have
19 shall abide in y' cities which I have
20 Lord have given rest unto y' brethren,
20 the Lord y' God hath given them
21 all that the Lord y' God hath done
22 Lord y' God he shall fight for you.
26 Lord was wroth with me for y' sakes,
4: 1 Lord God of y' fathers giveth you.
2 commandments of the Lord y' God
3 Y' eyes have seen what the Lord did
4 that did cleave unto the Lord y' God
6 is y' wisdom and y' understanding
21 Lord was angry with me for y' sakes,
26 ye shall not prolong y' days upon it,
34 to all that the Lord y' God did
34 for you in Egypt before y' eyes?
5: 22 the Lord spake unto all y' assembly
28 the Lord heard the voice of y' words,
30 to them, Get you into y' tents again.
32 Lord y' God hath commanded you:
33 Lord y' God hath commanded you,
33 ye may prolong y' days in the land
6: 1 the Lord y' God commanded to teach
16 Ye shall not tempt the Lord y' God,
17 commandments of the Lord y' God,
7: 8 which he had sworn unto y' fathers,
14 barren among you, or among y' cattle.
8: 1 which the Lord sware unto y' fathers.
20 the Lord destroyeth before y' face,
20 unto the voice of the Lord y' God.
9: 16 had sinned against the Lord y' God,
17 hands, and brake them before y' eyes.
18 of all y' sins which ye sinned,
21 And I took y' sin, the calf which ye
28 the commandment of the Lord y' God,
10: 16 therefore the foreskin of y' heart,
17 For the Lord y' God is God of gods,
11: 2 I speak not with y' children which
2 chastisement of the Lord y' God,
7 y' eyes have seen all the great acts
9 ye may prolong y' days in the land,
9 Lord sware unto y' fathers to give
13 this day, to love the Lord y' God,
13 with all y' heart and with all y' soul,
14 I will give you the rain of y' land
16 that y' heart be not deceived, and ye
18 my words in y' heart and in y' soul,
18 bind them for a sign upon y' hand,
18 may be as frontlets between y' eyes.
19 And ye shall teach them y' children,
21 That y' days may be multiplied,
21 and the days of y' children, in the
21 Lord sware unto y' fathers to give
22 to love the Lord y' God, to walk in all
24 the soles of y' feet shall tread shall be
24 the uttermost sea shall y' coast be.
25 the Lord y' God shall lay the fear of
27, 28 commandments of the Lord y' God,
31 which the Lord y' God giveth you,
12: 4 shall not do so unto the Lord y' God.
5 y' God shall choose out of all y' tribes
6 y' burnt offerings, and y' sacrifices,
6 y' tithes, and heave offerings of y'
6 and y' vows, and y' freewill offerings,
6 firstlings of y' herds and of y' flocks,
7 ye shall eat before the Lord y' God,
7 rejoice in all that ye put y' hand unto,
7 ye and y' household, wherein the
9 which the Lord y' God giveth you.
10 which the Lord y' God giveth you
10 rest from all y' enemies round about,
11 which the Lord y' God shall choose
11 I command you; y' burnt offerings,
11 and y' sacrifices, y' tithes,
11 and the heave offering of y' hand,
11 and all y' choice vows which ye vow
12 shall rejoice before the Lord y' God,
12 ye, and y' sons, and y' daughters,
12 y' menservants, and y' maidservants,
12 the Levite that is within y' gates;
13: 3 for the Lord y' God proveth you, to
3 whether ye love the Lord y' God,
3 with all y' heart and with all y' soul.
4 Ye shall walk after the Lord y' God,
5 turn you away from the Lord y' God,
14: 1 are the children of the Lord y' God:
1 make any baldness between y' eyes
20: 3 day unto battle against y' enemies:
3 let not y' hearts faint, fear not, and

De 20: 4 y' God is he that goeth with you,
4 to fight for you against y' enemies,
18 should ye sin against the Lord y' God.
28: 68 ye shall be sold unto y' enemies
29: 2 did before y' eyes in the land of Egypt
5 y' clothes are not waxen old upon you,
6 know that I am the Lord y' God.
10 day all of you before the Lord y' God;
10 y' captains of y' tribes, y' elders,
10 y' officers, with all the men of Israel,
11 Y' little ones, y' wives, and thy
22 y' children that shall rise up after you,
30: 18 not prolong y' days upon the land,
31: 5 shall give them up before y' face, *
12 may learn, and fear the Lord y' God,
13 and learn to fear the Lord y' God,
26 of the covenant of the Lord y' God,
28 elders of y' tribes, and y' officers,
29 anger through the work of y' hands.
32: 17 up, whom y' fathers feared not.
38 and help you, and be y' protection.
46 Set y' hearts unto all the words
46 command y' children to observe
47 thing for you, because it is y' life:
47 shall prolong y' days in the land,
Jos 1: 3 the sole of y' foot shall tread upon,
4 down of the sun, shall be y' coast.
11 Lord y' God giveth you to possess
13 The Lord y' God hath given you rest,
14 Y' wives, y' little ones, and y' cattle,
14 shall pass before y' brethren armed,
15 the Lord hath given y' brethren rest,
15 which the Lord y' God giveth them:
15 unto the land of y' possession,
2: 9 and that y' terror is fallen upon us,
11 the Lord y' God, he is God in heaven
16 and afterward may ye go y' way.
21 According unto y' words, so be it.
3: 3 of the covenant of the Lord y' God,
3 then ye shall remove from y' place,
9 hear the words of the Lord y' God.
4: 5 over before the ark of the Lord y' God
6 when y' children ask their fathers
21 y' children shall ask their fathers
22 Then ye shall let y' children know,
23 the Lord y' God dried up the waters
23 as the Lord y' God did to the Red sea,
24 that ye might fear the Lord y' God for
6: 10 nor make any noise with y' voice,
10 any word proceed out of y' mouth,
7: 14 be brought according to y' tribes:
8: 7 y' God will deliver it into y' hand.
9: 11 say unto them, We are y' servants:
10: 19 ye not, but pursue after y' enemies,
19 y' God...delivered them into y' hand.
24 y' feet upon the necks of these kings.
25 shall the Lord do to all y' enemies
15: 4 the sea: this shall be y' south coast.
18: 3 Lord God of y' fathers hath given you
20: 3 shall be y' refuge from the avenger
22: 3 Ye have not left y' brethren these
3 commandment of the Lord y' God.
4 the Lord y' God hath given rest
4 hath given rest unto y' brethren,
4 return ye, and get you unto y' tents,
4 and unto the land of y' possession,
5 to love the Lord y' God, and to walk
5 with all y' heart and with all y' soul.
8 with much riches unto y' tents,
8 spoil of y' enemies with y' brethren.
19 the land of y' possession be unclean,
24 time to come y' children might speak
25 y' children make our children cease
27 y' children may not say to our
23: 3 all that the Lord y' God hath done
3 the Lord y' God is he that hath fought
4 to be an inheritance for y' tribes,
5 the Lord y' God, he shall expel them
5 and drive them from out of y' sight;
5 Lord y' God hath promised unto you.
8 But cleave unto the Lord y' God,
10 Lord y' God, he it is that fighteth for
11 heed therefore unto y' selves,
11 that ye love the Lord y' God.
13 Lord y' God will no more drive out
13 unto you, and scourges in y' sides,
13 and thorns in y' eyes, until ye perish
13 the Lord y' God hath given you.
14 in all y' hearts and in all y' souls,
14 things which the Lord y' God spake
15 the Lord y' God promised you;
15 the Lord y' God hath given you.
16 the covenant of the Lord y' God,
24: 2 Y' fathers dwelt on the other side of
3 I took y' father Abraham from the
6 I brought y' fathers out of Egypt:
6 Egyptians pursued after y' fathers
7 y' eyes have seen what I have done in
8 and I gave them into y' hand,
11 and I delivered them into y' hand.
14, 15 the gods which y' fathers served
19 forgive y' transgressions nor y' sins.
23 incline y' heart unto the Lord God
27 unto you, lest ye deny y' God.
J'g 2: 1 land which I sware unto y' fathers;
3 they shall be as thorns in y' sides,
3: 28 y' enemies the Moabites into y' hand.
6: 10 said unto you, I am the Lord y' God;
7: 15 delivered into y' hand the host of
8: 3 delivered into y' hand the princes
7 I will tear y' flesh with the thorns
9: 2 also that I am y' bone and y' flesh.
15 come and put y' trust in my shadow:
18 Shechem, because he is y' brother;
10: 14 you in the time of y' tribulation.
11: 9 them before me, shall I be y' head?

J'g 18: 6 the Lord is y' way wherein ye go.
10 for God hath given it into y' hands;
19: 5 of bread, and afterward go y' way.
9 to morrow get you early on y' way,
30 take advice, and speak y' minds.
20: 7 give here y' advice and counsel.
Ru 1:11 womb, that they may be y' husbands?
12 again, my daughters, go y' way;
13 for it grieveth me much for y' sakes
1Sa 2: 3 not arrogancy come out of y' mouth:
23 for I hear of y' evil dealings by all
6: 4 was on you all, and on y' lords.
5 ye shall make images of y' emerods,
5 images of y' mice that mar the land;
5 from off y' gods, and from off y' land.
6 then do ye harden y' hearts,
7: 3 unto the Lord with all y' hearts,
3 and prepare y' hearts unto the Lord,
8:11 He will take y' sons, and appoint
13 y' daughters to be confectionaries,
14 he will take y' fields, and y' vineyards,
14 y' oliveyards, even the best of them,
15 tenth of y' seed, and of y' vineyards,
16 y' menservants, and y' maidservants,
16 y' goodliest young men, and y' asses,
17 He will take the tenth of y' sheep:
18 cry out in that day because of y' king
10:19 And ye have this day rejected y' God,
19 all y' adversities and y' tribulations;
19 by y' tribes, and by y' thousands.
11: 2 that I may thrust out all y' right eyes,
12: 1 I have hearkened unto y' voice
6 brought y' fathers up out of the land
7 which he did to you and to y' fathers.
8 and y' fathers cried unto the Lord,
8 brought forth y' fathers out of Egypt,
11 you out of the hand of y' enemies
12 when the Lord y' God was y' king.
14 continue following the Lord y' God:
15 you, as it was against y' fathers.
16 which the Lord will do before y' eyes.
17 and see that y' wickedness is great,
20 but serve the Lord with all y' heart;
24 serve him in truth with all y' heart:
25 be consumed, both ye and y' king.
17: 8 ye come out to set y' battle in array?
9 kill me, then will we be y' servants:
26:16 because ye have not kept y' master,
2Sa 1:24 on ornaments of gold upon y' apparel.
2: 5 shewed this kindness unto y' lord,
7 now let y' hands be strengthened,
7 for y' master Saul is dead, and also
3:31 Rend y' clothes, and gird you with
4:11 require his blood of y' hand, and take
10: 5 at Jericho until y' beards be grown,
15:27 in peace, and y' two sons with you,
1Ki 1:33 take with you the servants of y' lord,
8:61 Let y' heart therefore be perfect with
9: 6 from following me, ye or y' children,
11: 2 turn away y' heart after their gods:
12:11 a heavy yoke, I will add to y' yoke:
14 My father made y' yoke heavy, and I
14 and I will add to y' yoke: my father
16 to y' tents, O Israel: now see to thine
24 nor fight against y' brethren the
18:24 And call ye on the name of y' gods,
25 call on the name of y' gods, but put
2Ki 2: 3, 5 Yea, I know it; hold ye y' peace.
3:17 both ye, and y' cattle, and y' beasts.
18 deliver the Moabites...into y' hand.
9:15 If it be y' minds, then let none go
10: 2 seeing y' master's sons are with you,
3 best and meetest of y' master's sons,
3 throne, and fight for y' master's house.
6 heads of the men y' master's sons,
24 I have brought into y' hands escape,
12: 7 no more money of y' acquaintance,
17:13 Turn ye from y' evil ways, and keep
13 law which I commanded y' fathers,
39 But the Lord y' God ye shall fear;
39 you out of the hand of all y' enemies.
18:32 you away to a land like y' own land,
19: 6 Thus shall ye say to y' master, Thus
23:21 the passover unto the Lord y' God,
1Ch 15:12 yourselves, both ye and y' brethren,
16:18 of Canaan, the lot of y' inheritance;
19: 5 at Jericho until y' beards be grown,
22:18 Is not the Lord y' God with you? and
19 Now set y' heart and y' soul to
19 seek the Lord y' God; arise
28: 8 commandments of the Lord y' God:
8 inheritance for y' children after you
29:20 Now bless the Lord y' God. And all
2Ch 10:11 upon you, I will put more to y' yoke:
14 My father made y' yoke heavy, but I
16 every man to y' tents, O Israel: and
11: 4 go up, nor fight against y' brethren:
13:12 against the Lord God of y' fathers;
15: 7 and let not y' hands be weak:
7 for y' work shall be rewarded.
18:14 they shall be delivered into y' hand.
19:10 y' brethren that dwell in their cities,
10 come upon you, and upon y' brethren:
20:20 Believe in the Lord y' God, so shall
24: 5 repair the house of y' God from year
28: 9 the Lord God of y' fathers was wroth
9 he hath delivered them into y' hand,
10 you, sins against the Lord y' God?
11 ye have taken captive of y' brethren:
29: 5 house of the Lord God of y' fathers,
8 and to hissing, as ye see with y' eyes.
30: 7 like y' fathers, and like y' brethren,
8 not stiffnecked, as y' fathers were,
8 and serve the Lord y' God, that the
9 y' brethren and y' children shall find
9 the Lord y' God is gracious and
2Ch 32:14 y' God should be able to deliver you
15 much less shall y' God deliver you
33: 8 which I have appointed for y' fathers;
35: 3 not be a burden upon y' shoulders:
3 serve now the Lord y' God, and his
4 by the houses of y' fathers,
4 after y' courses, according to the
5 families of the fathers of y' brethren
6 and prepare y' brethren, that they
Ezr 4: 2 for we seek y' God, as ye do; and we
6: 6 y' companions the Apharsachites,
7:17 altar of the house of y' God which is
18 gold, that do after the will of y' God.
8:28 unto the Lord God of y' fathers.
9:12 not y' daughters unto their sons,
12 take their daughters unto y' sons,
12 an inheritance to y' children for ever.
10:11 unto the Lord God of y' fathers,
Ne 4:14 and fight for y' brethren, y' sons, and
14 y' daughters, y' wives, and y' houses.
5: 8 and will ye even sell y' brethren?
8: 9 day is holy unto the Lord y' God;
10 Go y' way, eat the fat, and drink the
10 for the joy of the Lord is y' strength.
11 Hold y' peace, for the day is holy;
9: 5 bless the Lord y' God for ever and
13:18 Did not y' fathers thus, and did not
25 give y' daughters unto their sons,
25 take their daughters unto y' sons,
Job 6:22 a reward for me of y' substance?
25 but what doth y' arguing reprove?
27 and ye dig a pit for y' friend.
13: 5 ye would altogether hold y' peace!
5 and it should be y' wisdom.
12 Y' remembrances are like unto
12 ashes, y' bodies to bodies of clay.
13 Hold y' peace, let me alone, that I
17 and my declaration with y' ears.
16: 4 if y' souls were in my soul's stead,
5 of my lips should asswage y' grief.
18: 3 beasts, and reputed vile in y' sight?
21: 2 and let this be y' consolations.
5 and lay y' hand upon y' mouth.
27 I know y' thoughts, and the devices
34 seeing in y' answers there remaineth
32:11 Behold, I waited for y' words;
11 I gave ear to y' reasons, whilst ye
14 will I answer him with y' speeches.
42: 8 lest I deal with you after y' folly,
Ps 4: 4 with y' own heart upon y' bed,
5 and put y' trust in the Lord.
11: 1 Flee as a bird to y' mountain?
22:26 seek him: y' heart shall live for ever.
24: 7 Lift up y' heads, O ye gates; and be
9 Lift up y' heads, O ye gates; even lift
31:24 he shall strengthen y' heart, all ye
47: 1 O clap y' hands, all ye people;
58: 2 the violence of y' hands in the earth.
9 Before y' pots can feel the thorns,
62: 8 people, pour out y' heart before him:
10 increase, set not y' heart upon them.
69:32 y' heart shall live that seek God.
75: 5 Lift not up y' horn on high: speak
76:11 Vow, and pay unto the Lord y' God:
78: 1 incline y' ears to the words of my
95: 8 Harden not y' heart, as in the
9 When y' fathers tempted me, proved
105:11 of Canaan, the lot of y' inheritance:
115:14 more and more, you and y' children.
134: 2 Lift up y' hands in the sanctuary,
146: 3 Put not y' trust in princes, nor in
Pr 1:26 I also will laugh at y' calamity;
26 I will mock when y' fear cometh;
27 When y' fear cometh as desolation,
27 y' destruction cometh as a whirlwind;
Isa 1: 7 Y' country is desolate, y' cities are
7 y' land, strangers devour it in y'
11 is the multitude of y' sacrifices
12 who hath required this at y' hand,
14 Y' new moons and y' appointed feasts
15 And when ye spread forth y' hands,
15 not hear: y' hands are full of blood.
16 put away the evil of y' doings from
18 though y' sins be as scarlet, they
3:14 the spoil of the poor is in y' houses.
8:13 be y' fear, and let him be y' dread.
10: 3 and where will ye leave y' glory?
23: 7 Is this y' joyous city, whose antiquity
14 for y' strength is laid waste.
28:18 y' covenant with death shall be
18 y' agreement with hell shall not stand;
22 lest y' bands be made strong:
29:10 deep sleep, and hath closed y' eyes:
10 the prophets and y' rulers, the seers
16 Surely y' turning of things upside
30: 3 the strength of Pharaoh be y' shame,
3 in the shadow of Egypt y' confusion.
15 in confidence shall be y' strength:
31: 7 which y' own hands have made unto
32:11 and gird sackcloth upon y' loins.
33: 4 y' spoil shall be gathered like the
11 y' breath, as fire, shall devour you.
35: 4 y' God will come with vengeance,
36:17 you away to a land like y' own land,
37: 6 Thus shall ye say unto y' master,
40: 1 comfort ye my people, saith y' God.
9 the cities of Judah, Behold y' God!
26 Lift up y' eyes on high, and behold
41:21 Produce y' cause, saith the Lord;
21 bring forth y' strong reasons, saith
24 of nothing, and y' work of nought:
26 there is none that heareth y' words.
43:14 Thus saith the Lord, y' redeemer,
14 For y' sake I have sent to Babylon,
15 I am the Lord, y' Holy One,
15 the creator of Israel, y' King.
Isa 46: 1 y' carriages were heavy laden; they
4 And even to y' old age I am he;
50: 1 the bill of y' mother's divorcement,
1 y' iniquities have ye sold yourselves,
1 for y' transgressions is y' mother put
11 walk in the light of y' fire, and in
51: 2 Look unto Abraham y' father, and
6 Lift up y' eyes to the heavens, and
52:12 the God of Israel will be y' rereward.
55: 2 y' labour for that which satisfieth not?
2 let y' soul delight itself in fatness.
3 Incline y' ear, and come unto me:
3 hear, and y' soul shall live; and I
8 For my thoughts are not y' thoughts,
8 neither are y' ways my ways, saith
9 so are my ways higher than y' ways,
9 and my thoughts than y' thoughts.
58: 3 in the day of y' fast ye find pleasure,
3 and exact all y' labours.
4 to make y' voice to be heard on high.
59: 2 But y' iniquities have separated
2 y' God and y' sins have hid his face
3 For y' hands are defiled with blood,
3 and y' fingers with iniquity;
3 y' lips have spoken lies,
3 y' tongue hath muttered perverseness.
61: 5 shall stand and feed y' flocks,
5 be y' plowmen and y' vinedressers.
7 For y' shame ye shall have double;
65: 7 Y' iniquities, and the iniquities of
7 iniquities of y' fathers together,
15 ye shall leave y' name for a curse
66: 5 Y' brethren that hated you, that cast
5 but he shall appear to y' joy, and
14 ye see this, y' heart shall rejoice,
14 y' bones shall flourish like an herb:
20 And they shall bring all y' brethren
22 so shall y' seed and y' name remain.
Jer 2: 5 What iniquity...y' fathers found in me,
9 with y' children's children will I
30 In vain have I smitten y' children;
30 y' own sword...devoured y' prophets,
3:18 for an inheritance unto y' fathers.
22 and I will heal y' backslidings.
4: 3 Break up y' fallow ground, and sow
4 take away the foreskins of y' heart,
4 it, because of the evil of y' doings.
5:19 and served strange gods in y' land,
25 Y' iniquities have turned away these
25 y' sins have withholden good things
6:16 and ye shall find rest for y' souls.
20 y' burnt offerings are not acceptable,
20 nor y' sacrifices sweet unto me.
7: 3 Amend y' ways and y' doings, and I
5 amend y' ways and y' doings; if ye
6 walk after other gods to y' hurt:
7 in the land that I gave to y' fathers,
11 become a den of robbers in y' eyes?
14 which I gave to you and to y' fathers,
15 as I have cast out all y' brethren,
21 y' burnt offerings unto y' sacrifices,
22 For I spake not unto y' fathers,
23 Obey my voice, and I will be y' God,
25 Since the day that y' fathers came
9:20 let y' ear receive the word at his
20 and teach y' daughters wailing, and
11: 4 I commanded y' fathers in the day
4 be my people, and I will be y' God:
5 which I have sworn unto y' fathers,
7 I earnestly protested unto y' fathers
12:13 they shall be ashamed of y' revenues
13:16 Give glory to the Lord y' God, before
16 before y' feet stumble upon the dark
17 weep in secret places for y' pride;
18 for y' principalities shall come down,
18 even the crown of y' glory.
20 Lift up y' eyes, and behold them that
16: 9 this place in y' eyes, and in y' days,
11 Because y' fathers have forsaken me,
12 have done worse than y' fathers;
13 know not, neither ye nor y' fathers;
17: 1 and upon the horns of y' altars;
22 carry forth a burden out of y' houses
22 day, as I commanded y' fathers.
18:11 and make y' ways and y' doings good.
21: 4 weapons of war that are in y' hands,
12 it, because of the evil of y' doings.
14 according to the fruit of y' doings.
23: 2 visit upon you the evil of y' doings,
39 city that I gave you and y' fathers,
25: 4 hearkened, nor inclined y' ear to hear,
5 evil way, and the evil of y' doings,
5 unto you and to y' fathers for ever
6 to anger with the works of y' hands;
7 the works of y' hands to y' own hurt.
34 for the days of y' slaughter and
34 of y' dispersions are accomplished;
26:11 city, as ye have heard with y' ears.
13 now amend y' ways and y' doings,
13 obey the voice of the Lord y' God;
14 As for me, behold, I am in y' hand:
15 to speak all these things in y' ears.
27: 4 Thus shall ye say unto y' masters;
9 hearken not ye to y' prophets,
9 to y' diviners, nor to y' dreamers,
9 to y' enchanters, nor to y' sorcerers,
10 to remove you far from y' land;
12 Bring y' necks under the yoke of the
16 not to the words of y' prophets that
29: 6 and take wives for y' sons,
6 and give y' daughters to husbands,
8 Let not y' prophets and y' diviners
8 hearken to y' dreams which ye
13 shall search for me with all y' heart.
14 and I will turn away y' captivity, and
16 y' brethren that are not gone forth

Jer 29:21 and he shall slay them before y' eyes,
30:22 be my people, and I will be y' God.
34:13 I made a covenant with y' fathers in
14 y' fathers hearkened not unto me,
35: 6 wine, neither ye, nor y' sons for ever:
7 but all y' days ye shall dwell in tents;
15 amend y' doings, and go not after
15 I have given to you and to y' fathers:
15 but ye have not inclined y' ear, nor
18 commandment of Jonadab y' father,
37:19 now y' prophets which prophesied
38: 5 king said, Behold, he is in y' hand:
40:10 and oil, and put them in y' vessels,
10 and dwell in y' cities that ye have
42: 4 I will pray unto the Lord y' God
4 according to y' words; and it shall
9 present y' supplication before him;
12 cause you to return to y' own land.
13 obey the voice of the Lord y' God,
15 If ye wholly set y' faces to enter into
20 ye dissembled in y' hearts, when ye
20 ye sent me unto the Lord y' God,
21 obeyed the voice of the Lord y' God,
44: 3 not, neither they, ye, nor y' fathers.
7 ye this great evil against y' souls,
8 wrath with the works of y' hands,
9 forgotten the wickedness of y' fathers,
9 of their wives, and y' own wickedness,
9 and the wickedness of y' wives,
10 I set before you and before y' fathers.
21 y' fathers, y' kings, and y' princes,
22 because of the evil of y' doings, and
22 therefore is y' land a desolation, and
25 Ye and y' wives have both spoken
25 y' mouths, and fulfilled with y' hand,
25 ye will surely accomplish y' vows,
25 and surely perform y' vows.
46: 4 and stand forth with y' helmets;
48: 6 Flee, save y' lives, and be like the
50:12 Y' mother shall be sore confounded;
51:24 they have done in Zion in y' sight,
46 And lest y' heart faint, and ye fear
50 and let Jerusalem come into y' mind.
Eze 5:16 you, and will break y' staff of bread:
6: 3 you, and I will destroy y' high places.
4 And y' altars shall be desolate,
4 and y' images shall be broken: and I
4 down y' slain men before y' idols.
5 y' bones round about y' altars.
6 In all y' dwellingplaces the cities
6 that y' altars may be laid waste and
6 y' idols may be broken and cease,
6 and y' images may be cut down,
6 and y' works may be abolished.
9: 5 let not y' eye spare, neither have ye
11: 5 the things that come into y' mind,
6 have multiplied y' slain in this city,
7 Y' slain whom ye have laid in the
11 This city shall not be y' caldron,
12:11 Say, I am y' sign: like as I have done,
25 for in y' days, O rebellious house, will
13:19 by y' lying to my people that hear
19 to my people that hear y' lies?
20 Behold, I am against y' pillows,
20 and I will tear them from y' arms,
21 Y' kerchiefs also will I tear, and
21 and deliver my people out of y' hand,
21 be no more in y' hand to be hunted;
23 will deliver my people out of y' hand:
14: 6 and turn yourselves from y' idols;
6 y' faces from all y' abominations.
16:45 y' mother was an Hittite,
45 and y' father an Amorite.
55 shall return to y' former estate.
18:25 way equal? are not y' ways unequal?
29 ways equal? are not y' ways unequal?
30 yourselves from all y' transgressions;
30 so iniquity shall not be y' ruin.
31 away from you all y' transgressions,
20: 5 them, saying, I am the Lord y' God;
7 idols of Egypt: I am the Lord y' God.
18 ye not in the statutes of y' fathers,
19 I am the Lord y' God; walk in my
20 may know that I am the Lord y' God.
27 in this y' fathers have blasphemed
30 after the manner of y' fathers?
31 For when ye offer y' gifts, when ye
31 make y' sons to pass through the fire,
31 pollute yourselves with all y' idols,
32 And that which cometh into y' mind
36 Like as I pleaded with y' fathers
39 more with y' gifts, and with y' idols.
40 and there will I require y' offerings,
40 y' oblations, with all y' holy things.
41 will accept you with y' sweet savour,
42 up mine hand to give it to y' fathers.
43 And there shall ye remember y' ways,
43 and all y' doings, wherein ye have
43 shall lothe yourselves in y' own sight
43 all y' evils that ye have committed.
44 not according to y' wicked ways,
44 nor according to y' corrupt doings,
21:24 made y' iniquity to be remembered,
24 that y' transgressions are discovered,
24 that in all y' doings y' sins do appear;
23:48 be taught not to do after y' lewdness.
49 they shall recompense y' lewdness
49 and ye shall bear the sins of y' idols:
24:21 of y' strength, the desire of y' eyes,
21 and that which y' soul pitieth;
21 and y' sons and y' daughters whom
22 ye shall not cover y' lips, nor eat the
23 And y' tires shall be upon y' heads,
23 and y' shoes upon y' feet; ye shall
23 ye shall pine away for y' iniquities,
33:11 turn ye from y' evil ways; for why will
Eze 33:25 and lift up y' eyes toward y' idols, and
26 Ye stand upon y' sword, ye work
34:18 with y' feet the residue of y' pastures?
18 ye must foul the residue with y' feet?
19 which ye have trodden with y' feet;
19 which ye have fouled with y' feet.
21 pushed all the diseased with y' horns,
31 men, and I am y' God, saith the Lord
35:13 Thus with y' mouth ye have boasted
13 have multiplied y' words against me:
36: 8 ye shall shoot forth y' branches,
8 yield y' fruit to my people of Israel;
11 I will settle you after y' old estates,
11 unto you than at y' beginnings:
22 I do not this for y' sakes, O house of
24 and will bring you into y' own land.
25 all y' filthiness, and from all y' idols,
26 away the stony heart out of y' flesh,
28 in the land that I gave to y' fathers;
28 be my people, and I will be y' God.
29 save you from all y' uncleannesses:
31 shall ye remember y' own evil ways,
31 and y' doings that were not good,
31 lothe yourselves in y' own sight for
31 y' iniquities and for y' abominations.
32 Not for y' sakes do I this, saith the
32 and confounded for y' own ways,
33 cleansed you from all y' iniquities
37:12 O my people, I will open y' graves,
12 cause you to come up out of y' graves,
13 when I have opened y' graves, O my
13 and brought you up out of y' graves,
14 and I shall place you in y' own land:
25 wherein y' fathers have dwelt;
43:27 y' burnt offerings upon the altar,
27 and y' peace offerings; and I will
44: 6 it suffice you of all y' abominations,
7 because of all y' abominations.
30 every sort of y' oblations, shall be
30 unto the priest the first of y' dough,
45: 9 away y' exactions from my people,
12 fifteen shekels, shall be y' maneh.
47:14 mine hand to give it unto y' fathers:
Da 1:10 hath appointed y' meat and y' drink:
10 for why should he see y' faces worse
10 the children which are of y' sort?
2: 5 y' houses shall be made a dunghill.
47 it is, that y' God is a God of gods,
10:21 in these things, but Michael y' prince.
Ho 1: 9 my people, and I will not be y' God.
2: 1 Say ye unto y' brethren, Ammi;
1 and to y' sisters, Ruhamah.
2 Plead with y' mother, plead: for she
4:13 y' daughters shall commit
13 y' spouses shall commit adultery.
14 I will not punish y' daughters when
14 nor y' spouses when they commit
5:13 heal you, nor cure you of y' wound.
6: 4 y' goodness is as a morning cloud,
9:10 I saw y' fathers as the firstripe in the
10:12 in mercy, break up y' fallow ground:
15 you because of y' great wickedness:
Joe 1: 2 the land. Hath this been in y' days,
2 or even in the days of y' fathers?
3 Tell ye y' children of it, and let
3 let y' children tell their children,
5 wine; for it is cut off from y' mouth.
13 withholden from the house of y' God.
14 into the house of the Lord y' God,
2:12 turn ye even to me with all y' heart,
13 rend y' heart, and not y' garments,
13 and turn unto the Lord y' God: for he
14 drink offering unto the Lord y' God?
23 Zion, and rejoice in the Lord y' God:
26 praise the name of the Lord y' God,
27 and that I am the Lord y' God,
28 and y' sons and y' daughters shall
28 y' old men shall dream dreams,
28 y' young men shall see visions:
3: 4 y' recompence upon y' own head;
5 and have carried into y' temple my
7 y' recompence upon y' own head:
8 I will sell y' sons and y' daughters
10 Beat y' plowshares into swords,
10 and y' pruninghooks into spears:
17 ye know that I am the Lord y' God
Am 2:11 I raised up of y' sons for prophets,
11 and of y' young men for Nazarites.
3: 2 I will punish you for all y' iniquities.
4: 2 hooks, and y' posterity with fishhooks.
4 and bring y' sacrifices every morning,
4 and y' tithes after three years:
6 you cleanness of teeth in all y' cities,
6 and want of bread in all y' places:
9 when y' gardens and y' vineyards
9 and y' fig trees and y' olive trees
10 y' young men have I slain with the
10 and have taken away y' horses;
10 I have made the stink of y' camps
10 to come up unto y' nostrils: yet have
5:11 as y' treading is upon the poor,
12 I know y' manifold transgressions
12 y' mighty sins: they afflict the just,
21 I hate, I despise y' feast days,
21 will not smell in y' solemn assemblies.
22 burnt offerings and y' meat offerings,
22 the peace offerings of y' fat beasts.
26 borne the tabernacle of y' Moloch
26 Chiun y' images, the star of y' god,
6: 2 or their border greater than y' border?
8:10 I will turn y' feasts into mourning,
10 and all y' songs into lamentation;
Mic 2: 3 which ye shall not remove y' necks;
10 and depart; for this is not y' rest:
3:12 shall Zion for y' sake be plowed as
Hab 1: 5 for I will work a work in y' days,
Zep 3:20 turn back y' captivity before y' eyes,
Hag 1: 4 O ye, to dwell in y' cieled houses,
5 the Lord of hosts; Consider y' ways.
2: 3 is it not in y' eyes in comparison of it
17 hail in all the labours of y' hands;
Zec 1: 2 been sore displeased with y' fathers.
4 Be ye not as y' fathers, unto whom
4 turn ye now from y' evil ways,
4 and from y' evil doings: but they did
5 Y' fathers, where are they? and the
6 did they not take hold of y' fathers?
6:15 obey the voice of the Lord y' God.
7:10 evil against his brother in y' heart.
8: 9 Let y' hands be strong, ye that hear
13 fear not, but let y' hands be strong.
14 when y' fathers provoked me to wrath,
16 of truth and peace in y' gates:
17 none of you imagine evil in y' hearts
Mal 1: 5 And y' eyes shall see, and ye shall say,
9 unto us: this hath been by y' means:
9 will he regard y' persons? saith
10 will I accept an offering at y' hand.
13 should I accept this of y' hand? saith
2: 2 I will curse y' blessings: yea, I have
3 Behold I will corrupt y' seed,
3 and spread dung upon y' faces,
3 even the dung of y' solemn feasts;
13 it with good will at y' hand.
15 Therefore take heed to y' spirit, and
16 therefore take heed to y' spirit, that
17 have wearied the Lord with y' words.
3: 7 Even from the days of y' fathers
11 will rebuke the devourer for y' sakes,
11 not destroy the fruits of y' ground;
11 shall y' vine cast her fruit before the
13 Y' words have been stout against me,
4: 3 be ashes under the soles of y' feet
M't 5:12 for great is y' reward in heaven:
16 Let y' light so shine before men,
16 that they may see y' good works,
16 and glorify y' Father which is in
20 except y' righteousness exceed
37 But let y' communication be, Yea,
44 Love y' enemies, bless them that
45 ye may be the children of y' Father
47 And if ye salute y' brethren only,
48 as y' Father which is in heaven is
6: 1 that ye do not y' alms before men,
1 ye have no reward of y' Father
8 for y' Father knoweth what things
14 y' heavenly Father will also forgive
15 will y' Father forgive y' trespasses.
21 For where y' treasure is,
21 there will y' heart be also.
25 Take no thought for y' life, what ye
25 nor yet for y' body, what ye shall
26 y' heavenly Father feedeth them.
32 for y' heavenly Father knoweth
7: 6 cast ye y' pearls before swine,
11 give good gifts unto y' children,
11 how much more shall y' Father
9: 4 Wherefore think ye evil in y' hearts?
11 eateth y' Master with publicans
29 According to y' faith be it unto you.
10: 9 nor silver, nor brass in y' purses,
10 Nor script for y' journey, neither
13 worthy, let y' peace come upon it:
13 worthy, let y' peace return to you.
14 not receive you, nor hear y' words,
14 city, shake off the dust of y' feet.
20 Spirit of y' Father which speaketh
29 on the ground without y' Father.
30 hairs of y' head are all numbered.
11:29 ye shall find rest unto y' souls.
12:27 by whom do y' children cast them
27 therefore they shall be y' judges.
13:16 blessed are y' eyes, for they see:
16 and y' ears, for they hear.
15: 3 of God by y' tradition?
6 God of none effect by y' tradition.
17:20 Because of y' unbelief: for verily I
24 Doth not y' master pay tribute?
18:14 will of y' Father which is in heaven,
35 ye from y' hearts forgive not every
19: 8 because of the hardness of y' hearts
8 suffered you to put away y' wives:
20:26 among you, let him be y' minister;
27 among you, let him be y' servant:
23: 8 for one is y' Master, even Christ;
9 no man y' father upon the earth:
9 for one is y' Father, which is in
10 for one is y' Master, even Christ.
11 among you shall be y' servant.
32 up then the measure of y' fathers.
34 shall ye scourge in y' synagogues,
38 y' house is left unto you desolate.
24:20 that y' flight be not in the winter,
42 not what hour y' Lord doth come.
25: 8 Give us of y' oil; for our lamps are
26:45 Sleep on now, and take y' rest:
27:65 go y' way, make it as sure as you
M'r 2: 8 reason ye these things in y' hearts?
6:11 shake off the dust under y' feet
7: 9 that ye may keep y' own tradition.
13 of none effect through y' tradition,
8:17 have ye y' heart yet hardened?
10: 5 For the hardness of y' heart be
43 among you, shall be y' minister:
11: 2 Go y' way into the village over
25 y' Father also which is in heaven
25 may forgive you y' trespasses.
26 neither will y' Father which is in
26 is in heaven forgive y' trespasses.
13:18 that y' flight be not in the winter.
14:41 Sleep on now, and take y' rest: it is
16: 7 But go y' way, tell his disciples and

Lu 3:14 and be content with y' wages.
4:21 is this scripture fulfilled in y' ears.
5: 4 and let down y' nets for a draught.
22 What reason ye in y' hearts?
6:22 and cast out y' name as evil, for
23 y' reward is great in heaven:
24 ye have received y' consolation.
27 Love y' enemies, do good to them
35 But love ye y' enemies, and do good,
35 and y' reward shall be great, and
36 as y' Father also is merciful.
38 shall men give into y' bosom.
7:22 Go y' way, and tell John what things
8:25 unto them, Where is y' faith?
9: 3 Take nothing for y' journey,
5 shake off the very dust from y' feet
44 sayings sink down into y' ears:
10: 3 Go y' ways: behold, I send you
6 there, y' peace shall rest upon it:
10 go y' ways out into the streets of
11 Even the very dust of y' city,
20 y' names are written in heaven.
11:13 to give good gifts unto y' children:
13 more shall y' heavenly Father
19 by whom do y' sons cast them out?
19 therefore shall they be y' judges.
39 y' inward part is full of ravening
46 the burdens with one of y' fingers.
47 prophets,...y' fathers killed them.
48 ye allow the deeds of y' fathers:
12: 7 hairs of y' head are all numbered.
22 Take no thought for y' life, what ye
30 y' Father knoweth that ye have
32 for it is y' Father's good pleasure
34 For where y' treasure is,
34 there will y' heart be also.
35 Let y' loins be girded about, and
35 and y' lights burning;
13:35 y' house is left unto you desolate:
16:11 commit to y' trust the true riches?
12 give you that which is y' own?
15 but God knoweth y' hearts: for
19:30 at y' entering ye shall find a colt
21:14 Settle it therefore in y' hearts, not
15 y' adversaries shall not be able
18 shall not an hair of y' head perish.
19 In y' patience possess ye y' souls.
28 then look up, and lift up y' heads;
28 for y' redemption draweth nigh.
30 ye see and know of y' own selves
34 any time y' hearts be overcharged
22:53 but this is y' hour, and the power of
23:28 for yourselves, and for y' children.
24:38 why do thoughts arise in y' hearts?
Joh 4:35 Lift up y' eyes, and look on the
6:49 Y' fathers did eat manna in the
58 not as y' fathers did eat manna,
7: 6 but y' time is alway ready.
8:17 It is also written in y' law, that the
21 seek me, and shall die in y' sins:
24 you, that ye shall die in y' sins:
24 that I am he, ye shall die in y' sins.
38 which ye have seen with y' father.
41 Ye do the deeds of y' father. Then
42 If God were y' Father, ye would
44 Ye are of y' father the devil,
44 the lusts of y' father ye will do.
54 of whom ye say, that he is y' God:
56 Y' father Abraham rejoiced to see
9:19 Is this y' son, who ye say was born
41 We see; therefore y' sin remaineth.
10:34 Is it not written in y' law, I said,
11:15 glad for y' sakes that I was not
12:30 not because of me, but for y' sakes.
13:14 If I then, y' Lord and Master,
14 have washed y' feet; ye also ought
14: 1 Let not y' heart be troubled:
26 all things to y' remembrance,
27 Let not y' heart be troubled,
15:11 and that y' joy might be full.
16 and that y' fruit should remain:
16: 6 you, sorrow hath filled y' heart.
20 y' sorrow shall be turned into joy.
22 again, and y' heart shall rejoice,
22 and y' joy no man taketh from you.
24 receive, that y' joy may be full.
18:31 and judge him according to y' law.
19:14 unto the Jews, Behold y' King!
15 unto them, Shall I crucify y' King?
20:17 unto my Father, and y' Father;
17 and to my God, and y' God.
Ac 2:17 y' sons and y' daughters shall
17 and y' young men shall see visions
17 y' old men shall dream dreams:
39 is unto you, and to y' children,
3:17 ye did it, as did also y' rulers.
19 that y' sins may be blotted out,
22 A prophet shall the Lord y' God
22 raise up unto you of y' brethren,
5:28 filled Jerusalem with y' doctrine,
7:37 A prophet shall the Lord y' God
37 raise up unto you of y' brethren,
43 and the star of y' god Remphan,
51 Ghost: as y' fathers did, so do ye.
52 have not y' fathers persecuted?
13:41 for I work a work in y' days,
15:24 subverting y' souls, saying, Ye
17:23 passed by, and beheld y' devotions,
28 also of y' own poets have said,
18: 6 Y' blood be upon y' own heads;
15 and names, and of y' law,
19:37 yet blasphemers of y' goddess.
20:30 of y' own selves shall men arise,
24:22 know...uttermost of y' matter.
27:34 meat: for this is for y' health:
Ro 1: 8 y' faith is spoken of throughout
Ro 6:12 therefore reign in y' mortal body,
13 yield ye y' members as instruments
13 and y' members as instruments of
19 because of the infirmity of y' flesh:
19 have yielded y' members servants
19 so now yield y' members servants
22 ye have y' fruit unto holiness, and
8:11 quicken y' mortal bodies by his
11:25 be wise in y' own conceits;
28 they are enemies for y' sakes:
31 through y' mercy they also may
12: 1 y' bodies a living sacrifice,
1 which is y' reasonable service.
2 by the renewing of y' mind,
16 Be not wise in y' own conceits.
14:16 then y' good be evil spoken of:
15:24 somewhat filled with y' company.
30 together with me in y' prayers
16:19 For y' obedience is come abroad
19 I am glad therefore on y' behalf:
20 bruise Satan under y' feet shortly.
1Co 1: 4 thank my God always on y' behalf,
26 For ye see y' calling, brethren,
2: 5 That y' faith should not stand in
4: 6 myself and to Apollos for y' sakes;
5: 6 Y' glorifying is not good. Know
6: 5 I speak to y' shame. Is it so, that
8 and defraud, and that y' brethren.
15 that y' bodies are the members of
19 ye not that y' body is the temple
19 of God, and ye are not y' own?
20 therefore glorify God in y' body,
20 and in y' spirit, which are God's.
7: 5 tempt you not for y' incontinency.
14 else were y' children unclean;
35 And this I speak for y' own profit;
9:11 if we shall reap y' carnal things?
14:34 Let y' women keep silence in the
15:14 vain, and y' faith is also vain.
17 be not raised, y' faith is vain;
17 ye are yet in y' sins.
31 I protest by y' rejoicing which I
34 of God: I speak this to y' shame.
58 ye know that y' labour is not
16: 3 ye shall approve by y' letters,
3 will I send to bring y' liberality
14 y' things be done with charity.
17 that which was lacking on y' part
2Co 1: 6, 6 it is for y' consolation and
14 that we are y' rejoicing, even as ye
24 that we have dominion over y' faith,
24 are helpers of y' joy: for by faith
2: 8 would confirm y' love toward him.
10 for y' sakes forgave I it in the
4: 5 ourselves y' servants for Jesus'
15 For all things are for y' sakes,
5:11 made manifest in y' consciences.
13 we be sober, it is for y' cause.
6:12 ye are straitened in y' own bowels.
7: 7 when he told us y' earnest desire,
7 y' mourning, y' fervent mind
13 we were comforted in y' comfort:
8: 7 and in y' love to us, see that ye
8 to prove the sincerity of y' love.
9 yet for y' sakes he became poor,
14 y' abundance may be a supply for
14 also may be a supply for y' want:
19 and declaration of y' ready mind:
24 the churches, the proof of y' love,
24 and of our boasting on y' behalf.
9: 2 know the forwardness of y' mind,
2 y' zeal hath provoked very many.
5 and make up beforehand y' bounty,
10 both minister bread for y' food,
10 and multiply y' seed sown,
10 the fruits of y' righteousness;)
13 y' professed subjection unto the
13 y' liberal distribution unto them,
10: 6 when y' obedience is fulfilled.
8 and not for y' destruction, I should
15 when y' faith is increased, that we
11: 3 so y' minds should be corrupted
12:19 dearly beloved, for y' edifying.
13: 5 in the faith; prove y' own selves.
5 Know ye not y' own selves, how
9 we wish, even y' perfection.
Ga 4: 6 the Spirit of his Son into y' hearts,
15 have plucked out y' own eyes,
16 Am I therefore become y' enemy,
6:13 that they may glory in y' flesh.
18 Lord Jesus Christ be with y' spirit.
Eph 1:13 truth, the gospel of y' salvation:
15 of y' faith in the Lord Jesus,
18 eyes of y' understanding being
3:13 tribulations for you, which is y' glory.
17 that Christ may dwell in y' hearts
4: 4 are called in one hope of y' calling;
23 renewed in the spirit of y' mind;
26 the sun go down upon y' wrath:
29 proceed out of y' mouth,
5:19 melody in y' heart to the Lord;
22 yourselves unto y' own husbands;
25 Husbands, love y' wives, even as
6: 1 obey y' parents in the Lord:
4 provoke not y' children to wrath:
5 to them that are y' masters
5 in singleness of y' heart, as unto
9 that y' Master also is in heaven;
14 y' loins girt about with truth,
15 y' feet shod with the preparation
22 that he might comfort y' hearts.
Ph'p 1: 5 For y' fellowship in the gospel
9 that y' love may abound yet more
19 my salvation through y' prayer,
25 with you all for y' furtherance and
26 y' rejoicing may be more abundant
Ph'p 1:27 y' conversation be as it becometh
27 I may hear of y' affairs, that ye
28 nothing terrified by y' adversaries:
2:12 work out y' own salvation with fear
17 sacrifice and service of y' faith,
19 comfort, when I know y' state.
20 who will naturally care for y' state.
25 but y' messenger, and he that
30 to supply y' lack of service toward
4: 5 y' moderation be known unto all
6 let y' requests be made known unto
7 keep y' hearts and minds through
10 last y' care of me hath flourished
17 may abound unto y' account.
19 my God shall supply all y' need
Col 1: 4 Since we heard of y' faith in Christ
8 unto us y' love in the Spirit.
21 enemies in y' mind by wicked
2: 5 joying and beholding y' order,
5 stedfastness of y' faith in Christ.
13 And you, being dead in y' sins and
13 and the uncircumcision of y' flesh,
18 no man beguile you of y' reward
3: 2 Set y' affection on things above, not
3 y' life is hid with Christ in God.
5 Mortify therefore y' members
8 communication out of y' mouth.
15 the peace of God rule in y' hearts,
16 singing with grace in y' hearts to
18 yourselves unto y' own husbands,
19 Husbands, love y' wives, and be not
20 Children, obey y' parents in all
21 provoke not y' children to anger,
22 obey in all things y' masters
4: 1 unto y' servants that which is just
6 y' speech be alway with grace,
8 that he might know y' estate,
8 and comfort y' hearts;
1Th 1: 3 ceasing y' work of faith,
4 beloved, y' election of God.
5 we were among you for y' sake.
8 every place y' faith to God-ward
2:14 like things of y' own countrymen,
17 to see y' face with great desire.
3: 2 to comfort you concerning y' faith:
5 I sent to know y' faith, lest by
6 brought us good tidings of y' faith
7 affliction and distress by y' faith:
9 we joy for y' sakes before our God;
10 that we might see y' face, and
10 that which is lacking in y' faith?
13 the end he may stablish y' hearts
4: 3 will of God, even y' sanctification,
11 quiet, and to do y' own business,
11 and to work with y' own hands,
5:23 I pray God y' whole spirit and soul
2Th 1: 3 that y' faith groweth exceedingly,
4 of God for y' patience and faith
4 y' persecutions and tribulations
2:17 Comfort y' hearts, and stablish you
3: 5 Lord direct y' hearts into the love
Ph'm 22 for I trust that through y' prayers
25 Lord Jesus Christ be with y' spirit.
Heb 3: 8 Harden not y' hearts, as in the
9 When y' fathers tempted me,
15 hear his voice, harden not y' hearts,
4: 7 hear his voice, harden not y' hearts.
6:10 forget y' work and labour of love,
9:14 purge y' conscience from dead
10:34 joyfully the spoiling of y' goods,
35 not away therefore y' confidence,
12: 3 ye be wearied and faint in y' minds.
13 make straight paths for y' feet,
13: 5 Let y' conversation be without
17 for they watch for y' souls,
Jas 1: 3 trying of y' faith worketh patience.
21 which is able to save y' souls.
22 only, deceiving y' own selves.
2: 2 come unto y' assembly a man
3:14 envying and strife in y' hearts,
4: 1 y' lusts that war in y' members?
3 ye may consume it upon y' lusts.
8 Cleanse y' hands, ye sinners;
8 and purify y' hearts, ye double minded.
9 y' laughter be turned to mourning,
9 and y' joy to heaviness.
14 For what is y' life? It is even a
16 now ye rejoice in y' boastings:
5: 1 weep and howl for y' miseries that
2 Y' riches are corrupted, and
2 and y' garments are motheaten.
3 Y' gold and silver is cankered;
3 shall eat y' flesh as it were fire.
4 who have reaped down y' fields,
5 ye have nourished y' hearts, as in a
8 ye also patient; stablish y' hearts:
12 oath: but let y' yea be yea;
12 and y' nay, nay; lest ye fall
16 Confess y' faults one to another,
1Pe 1: 7 That the trial of y' faith, being
9 Receiving the end of y' faith,
9 even the salvation of y' souls.
13 gird up the loins of y' mind,
14 to the former lusts in y' ignorance:
17 time of y' sojourning here in fear:
18 from y' vain conversation received
18 by tradition from y' fathers;
21 y' faith and hope might be in God.
22 Seeing ye have purified y' souls in
2:12 Having y' conversation honest
12 they may by y' good works, which
16 and not using y' liberty for a cloke
18 subject to y' masters with all fear:
20 when ye be buffeted for y' faults,
25 Shepherd and Bishop of y' souls.
3: 1 in subjection to y' own husbands;

1Pe 3: 2 behold y' chaste conversation
7 that y' prayers be not hindered.
15 the Lord God in y' hearts:
16 accuse y' good conversation
4:14 of, but on y' part he is glorified.
5: 7 Casting all y' care upon him; for
8 because y' adversary the devil,
9 are accomplished in y' brethren
2Pe 1: 5 add to y' faith virtue; and to
10 give diligence to make y' calling
19 the day star arise in y' hearts:
3: 1 both which I stir up y' pure minds
17 fall from y' own stedfastness.
1Jo 1: 4 unto you, that y' joy may be full.
2:12 because y' sins are forgiven you for
2Jo 10 receive him not into y' house, neither
Jude 12 are spots in y' feasts of charity,
20 yourselves on y' most holy faith,
Re 1: 9 I John, who also am y' brother,
2:23 one of you according to y' works.
16: 1 Go y' ways, and pour out the vials of

yours See also YOURSELVES.
Ge 45:20 the good of all the land of Egypt is y'.
De 11:24 of your feet shall tread shall be y':
Jos 2:14 Our life for y', if ye utter not this our
2Ch 20:15 for the battle is not y', but God's.
Jer 5:19 strangers in a land that is not y'.
Lu 6:20 poor: for y' is the kingdom of God.
Joh 15:20 my saying, they will keep y' also.
1Co 3:21 in men: for all things are y'.
22 or things to come; all are y';
8: 9 means this liberty of y' become a
16:18 have refreshed my spirit and y':
2Co 12:14 for I seek not y', but you: for the

yourselves^ See also YOUR and SELVES.
Ge 18: 4 your feet, and rest y' under the tree:
45: 5 be not grieved, nor angry with y',
49: 1 Gather y' together, that I may tell
2 Gather y' together, and hear, ye
Ex 19:12 Take heed to y', that ye go not up
30:37 ye shall not make to y' according to
32:29 Consecrate y' to day to the Lord,
Le 11:43 neither shall ye make [y'] unclean
44 ye shall therefore sanctify y', and
44 neither shall ye defile y' with any
18:24 Defile not ye y' in any of these
30 and that ye defile not y' therein:
19: 4 idols, nor make to y' molten gods:
20: 7 Sanctify y' therefore, and be ye
Nu 11:18 Sanctify y' against to morrow, and ye
16: 3 lift ye up y' above the congregation
21 Separate y' from among this
31: 3 Arm some of y' unto the war, and
18 lying with him, keep alive for y'.
19 purify both y' and your captives on
De 2: 4 take ye good heed unto y' therefore:
4:15 ye therefore good heed unto y';
16 Lest ye corrupt y', and make you
23 Take heed unto y', lest ye forget
25 corrupt y', and make a graven image,
11:16 Take heed to y', that your heart
23 greater nations and mightier than y'.
14: 1 ye shall not cut y', nor make any
31:14 and present y' in the tabernacle of the
29 my death ye will utterly corrupt y',
Jos 2:16 and hide y' there three days, until the
3: 5 Sanctify y': for to morrow the Lord
6:18 keep y' from the accursed thing,
18 lest ye make y' accursed, when ye
7:13 say, Sanctify y' against to morrow:
8: 2 shall ye take for a prey unto y':
23: 7 serve them, nor bow y' unto them:
16 other gods, and bowed y' to them;
24:22 Ye are witnesses against y' that ye
J'g 15:12 that ye will not fall upon me y'.
1Sa 2:29 to make y' fat with the chiefest of
4: 9 Be strong, and quit y' like men,
9 to you: quit y' like men, and fight.
10:19 therefore present y' before the Lord
14:34 said, Disperse y' among the people,
16: 5 sanctify y', and come with me to
1Ki 18:25 Choose you one bullock for y',
20:12 unto his servants, Set y' in array.
2Ki 17:35 nor bow y' to them, nor serve them,
1Ch 15:12 sanctify y', both ye and your brethren,
2Ch 20:17 set y', stand ye still, and see the
29: 5 ye Levites, sanctify now y', and
31 have consecrated y' unto the Lord,
30: 8 but yield y' unto the Lord, and
32:11 to give over y' to die by famine
35: 4 And prepare y' by the houses of
6 So kill the passover, and sanctify y',
Ezr 10:11 separate y' from the people of the
Ne 13:25 daughters unto your sons, or for y'.
Job 19: 3 that ye make y' strange to me.
5 ye will magnify y' against me.
27:12 Behold, all ye y' have seen it;
42: 8 and offer up for y' a burnt offering;
Isa 8: 9 Associate y', O ye people, and ye
9, 9 gird y', and ye shall be broken in
Isa 29: 9 Stay y', and wonder; cry ye out,
45:20 Assemble y' and come; draw near
46: 8 Remember this, and shew y' men:
48:14 All ye, assemble y', and hear;
49: 9 them that are in darkness, Shew y'.
50: 1 for your iniquities have ye sold y',
11 that compass y' about with sparks:
52: 3 Ye have sold y' for nought;
57: 4 Against whom do ye sport y'?
5 Enflaming y' with idols under every
61: 6 and in their glory shall ye boast y'.
Jer 4: 4 Circumcise y' to the Lord, and take
5 Assemble y', and let us go into the
6: 1 gather y' to flee out of the midst of
8:14 assemble y', and let us enter into
13:18 to the queen, Humble y', sit down:
17:21 Take heed to y', and bear no
25:34 and wallow y' in the ashes, ye
26:15 surely bring innocent blood upon y',
37: 9 Deceive not y', saying, The
44: 8 that ye might cut y' off, and that
50:14 Put y' in array against Babylon
Eze 14: 6 and turn y' from your idols;
18:30 y' from all your transgressions;
32 wherefore turn y', and live ye.
20: 7 defile not y' with the idols of Egypt:
18 nor defile y' with their idols:
31 ye pollute y' with all your idols,
43 ye shall lothe y' in your own sight
36:31 and shall lothe y' in your own sight
39:17 of the field, Assemble y', and come;
17 gather y' on every side to my
44: 8 my charge in my sanctuary for y'.
Ho 10:12 Sow to y' in righteousness, reap
Joe 1:13 Gird y', and lament, ye priests:
3:11 Assemble y', and come, all ye
11 and gather y' together round about:
Am 3: 9 Assemble y' upon the mountains of
5:26 of your God, which ye made to y'.
Zep 2: 1 Gather y' together, yea, gather
Zec 7: 6 not ye eat for y', and drink for y'?
M't 3: 9 And think not to say within y',
6:19 up for y' treasures upon earth,
20 lay up for y' treasures in heaven,
16: 8 why reason ye among y', because
23:13 for ye neither go in y', neither suffer
15 more the child of hell than y'.
31 Wherefore ye be witnesses unto y',
25: 9 to them that sell, and buy for y'.
M'r 6:31 Come ye y' apart into a desert
9:33 ye disputed among y' by the way?
50 Have salt in y', and have peace one
13: 9 But take heed to y': for they shall
Lu 3: 8 to say within y', We have Abraham
11:46 and ye y' touch not the burdens
52 ye entered not in y', and them that
12:33 provide y' bags which wax not old,
36 And ye y' like unto men that wait
57 why even of y' judge ye not what
13:28 of God, and you y' thrust out.
16: 9 to y' friends of the mammon of
15 they which justify y' before men;
17: 3 Take heed to y': If thy brother
14 them, Go shew y' unto the priests.
21:34 And take heed to y', lest at any
22:17 Take this, and divide it among y':
23:28 weep not for me, but weep for y',
Joh 3:28 Ye y' bear me witness, that I
6:43 unto them, Murmur not among y',
16:19 enquire among y' of that I said,
Ac 2:22 midst of you, as ye y' also know:
40 y' from this untoward generation.
5:35 take heed to y' what ye intend to
13:46 y' unworthy of everlasting life,
15:29 from which if ye keep y', ye shall
20:10 Trouble not y'; for his life is in him.
28 Take heed therefore unto y', and
34 Yea, ye y' know, that these hands
Ro 6:11 also y' to be dead indeed unto sin,
13 but yield y' unto God, as those
16 whom ye yield y' servants to obey,
12:19 Dearly beloved, avenge not y',
1Co 5:13 from among y' that wicked
6: 7 not rather suffer y' to be defrauded?
7: 5 may give y' to fasting and prayer;
11:13 Judge in y': is it comely that a
16:16 That ye submit y' unto such, and
2Co 7:11 in you, yea, what clearing of y',
11 have approved y' to be clear in this
11:19 fools gladly, seeing ye y' are wise.
13: 5 Examine y', whether ye be in
Eph 2: 8 and that not of y': it is the gift of
5:19 Speaking to y' in psalms and
21 Submitting y' one to another
22 submit y' unto your own husbands,
Col 3:18 submit y' unto your own husbands,
1Th 2: 1 For y', brethren, know our entrance
3: 3 for y' know that we are appointed
4: 9 for ye y' are taught of God to love
5: 2 For y' know perfectly that the day
11 Wherefore comfort y' together,
1Th 5:13 And be at peace among y'.
15 that which is good, both among y',
2Th 3: 6 ye withdraw y' from every brother
7 For y' know how ye ought to follow
Heb 10:34 knowing in y' that ye have in
13: 3 as being y' also in the body.
17 the rule over you, and submit y':
Jas 2: 4 Are ye not then partial in y',
4: 7 Submit y' therefore to God.
10 Humble y' in the sight of the Lord,
1Pe 1:14 not fashioning y' according to the
2:13 Submit y' to every ordinance
4: 1 arm y' likewise with the same mind:
8 have fervent charity among y':
5: 5 ye younger, submit y' unto the elder.
6 Humble y' therefore under the
1Jo 5:21 Little children, keep y' from idols.
2Jo 8 Look to y', that we lose not those
Jude 20 building up y' on your most holy
21 Keep y' in the love of God, looking
Re 19:17 gather y' together unto the supper

youth See also YOUTHFUL; YOUTHS.
Ge 8:21 of man's heart is evil from his y';
43:33 the youngest according to his y':
46:34 cattle from our y' even until now,
Le 22:13 her father's house, as in her y',
Nu 30: 3 in her father's house in her y';
16 yet in her y' in her father's house.
J'g 8:20 But the y' drew not his sword:
20 feared, because he was yet a y'.
1Sa 17:33 with him: for thou art but a y',
33 and he a man of war from his y'.
42 for he was but a y', and ruddy,
55 host, Abner, whose son is this y'?
2Sa 19: 7 evil that befell thee from thy y'
1Ki 18:12 servant fear the Lord from my y'.
Job 13:26 to possess the iniquities of my y'.
20:11 bones are full of the sin of his y',
29: 4 As I was in the days of my y',
30:12 Upon my right hand rise the y';
31:18 from my y' he was brought up
33:25 shall return to the days of his y':
36:14 They die in y', and their life is
Ps 25: 7 Remember not the sins of my y',
71: 5 thou art my trust from my y'.
17 thou hast taught me from my y':
88:15 and ready to die from my y' up:
89:45 The days of his y' hast thou
103: 5 thy y' is renewed like the eagle's.
110: 3 thou hast the dew of thy y'.
127: 4 man; so are children of the y'.
129: 1 have they afflicted me from my y',
2 have they afflicted me from my y':
144:12 be as plants grown up in their y';
Pr 2:17 forsaketh the guide of her y',
5:18 rejoice with the wife of thy y'.
Ec 11: 9 Rejoice, O young man, in thy y';
9 cheer thee in the days of thy y',
10 for childhood and y' are vanity.
12: 1 thy Creator in the days of thy y',
Isa 47:12 thou hast laboured from thy y';
15 even thy merchants, from thy y':
54: 4 shalt forget the shame of thy y',
6 and a wife of y', when thou wast
Jer 2: 2 the kindness of thy y', the love
3: 4 father, thou art the guide of my y'?
24 labour of our fathers from our y';
25 from our y' even unto this day,
22:21 been thy manner from thy y',
31:19 I did bear the reproach of my y'.
32:30 done evil before me from their y':
48:11 hath been at ease from his y',
La 3:27 that he bear the yoke in his y'.
Eze 4:14 from my y' up even till now have I
16:22, 43 remembered the days of thy y',
60 with thee in the days of thy y',
23: 3 committed whoredoms in their y':
8 for in her y' they lay with her,
19 to remembrance the days of her y',
21 the lewdness of thy y',
21 Egyptians for the paps of thy y'.
Ho 2:15 sing there, as in the days of her y',
Joe 1: 8 for the husband of her y'.
Zec 13: 5 me to keep cattle from my y'.
Mal 2:14 thee and the wife of thy y',
15 against the wife of his y'.
M't 19:20 have I kept from my y' up:
M'r 10:20 these have I observed from my y'.
Lu 18:21 these have I kept from my y' up.
Ac 26: 4 My manner of life from my y',
1Ti 4:12 Let no man despise thy y'; but be

youthful
2Ti 2:22 Flee also y' lusts: but follow

youths
Pr 7: 7 I discerned among the y', a young
Isa 40:30 the y' shall faint and be weary,

you-ward
2Co 1:12 and more abundantly to y'.
13: 3 which to y' is not weak, but is
Eph 3: 2 grace...which is given me to y':

Z.

Zaanaim (*za-an-a'-im*) See also ZAANANNIM.
J'g 4:11 his tent unto the plain of Z',

Zaanan (*za'-an-an*) See also ZENAN.
Mic 1:11 inhabitant of Z' came not forth

Zaanannim (*za-an-an'-nim*) See also ZAANAIM.
Jos 19:33 from Heleph, from Allon to Z',

Zaavan (*za'-av-an*) See also ZAVAN.
Ge 36:27 of Ezer are these; Bilhan, and Z',

Zabad (*za'-bad*) See also JOSABAD; JOZACHAR.
1Ch 2:36 Nathan, and Nathan begat Z',
37 And Z' begat Ephlal, and Ephlal
7:21 And Z' his son, and Shuthelah
11:41 the Hittite, Z' the son of Ahlai,
2Ch 24:26 Z' the son of Shimeath an
Ezr 10:27 Mattaniah, and Jeremoth, and Z',
33 Mattathah, Z', Eliphelet, Jeremai,
43 Mattithiah, Z', Zebina, Jadau,

Zabbai (*zab'-bahee*) See also ZACCAI.
Ezr 10:28 Hananiah, Z', and Athlai.
Ne 3:20 Baruch the son of Z' earnestly

Zabbud (*zab'-bud*) See also ZACCUR.
Ezr 8:14 Uthai, and Z', and with them

Zabdi (*zab'-di*) See also ZACCHUR; ZICHRI.
Jos 7: 1 the son of Carmi, the son of Z',
17 man by man; and Z' was taken.

Jos 7:18 the son of Carmi, the son of Z·,
1Ch 8:19 And Jakim, and Zichri, and Z·,
27:27 wine cellars was Z· the Shiphmite:
Ne 11:17 the son of Z·, the son of Asaph,

Zabdiel (*zab'-de-el*)
1Ch 27: 2 was Jashobeam the son of Z·:
Ne 11:14 and their overseer was Z·, the son

Zabud (*za'-bud*)
1Ki 4: 5 Z· the son of Nathan was principal

Zabulon (*zab'-u-lon*) See also ZEBULUN.
M't 4:13 borders of Z· and Nephthalim:
15 The land of Z·, and the land of
Re 7: 8 Of the tribe of Z· were sealed

Zaccai (*zac'-cahee*) See also ZABBAI.
Ezr 2: 9 The children of Z·, seven hundred
Ne 7:14 The children of Z·, seven hundred

Zacchæus (*zak-ke'-us*)
Lu 19: 2 there was a man named Z·,
5 and unto him, Z·, make haste,
8 Z· stood, and said unto the Lord;

Zacchur (*zac'-cur*) See also ZACCUR.
1Ch 4:26 Hamuel his son, Z· his son,

Zaccur (*zac'-cur*) See also ZABBUD; ZABDI; ZACCHUR; ZICHRI.
Nu 13: 4 Reuben, Shammua the son of Z·.
1Ch 24:27 and Shoham, and Z·, and Ibri.
25: 2 Z·, and Joseph, and Nethaniah,
10 The third to Z·, he, his sons, and
Ne 3: 2 them builded Z· the son of Imri.
10:12 Z·, Sherebiah, Shebaniah,
12:35 the son of Michaiah, the son of Z·,
13:13 to them was Hanan the son of Z·,

Zachariah (*zak-a-ri'-ah*) See also ZECHARIAH.
2Ki 14:29 Z·, his son reigned in his stead.
15: 8 did Z· the son of Jeroboam reign
11 And the rest of the acts of Z·,
18: 2 also was Abi, the daughter of Z·.

Zacharias (*zak'-a-ri'-as*) See also ZECHARIAH.
M't 23:35 blood of Z· son of Barachias,
Lu 1: 5 a certain priest named Z·, of the
12 And when Z· saw him, he was
13 angel said unto him, Fear not, Z·:
18 And Z· said unto the angel,
21 And the people waited for Z·,
40 And entered into the house of Z·,
59 they called him Z·, after the name
67 And his father Z· was filled with
3: 2 came unto John the son of Z·
11:51 of Abel unto the blood of Z·,

Zacher (*za'-kur*) See also ZECHARIAH.
1Ch 8:31 And Gedor, and Ahio, and Z·.

Zadok (*za'-dok*) See also ZADOK'S.
2Sa 8:17 And Z· the son of Ahitub, and
15:24 And lo Z· also, and all the Levites
25 the king said unto Z·, Carry back
27 king said also unto Z· the priest,
29 Z· therefore and Abiathar carried
35 hast thou not there with thee Z·
35 thou shalt tell it to Z· and Abiathar
17:15 Then said Hushai unto Z· and to
18:19 Then said Ahimaaz the son of Z·,
22 Then said Ahimaaz the son of Z·
27 running of Ahimaaz the son of Z·.
19:11 David sent to Z· and to Abiathar
20:25 Z· and Abiathar were the priests:
1Ki 1: 8, 26 Z· the priest, and Benaiah...son
32 Call me Z· the priest, and Nathan
34 let Z· the priest, and Nathan the
38 So Z· the priest, and Nathan the
39 And Z· the priest took an horn of oil
44 hath sent with him Z· the priest,
45 And Z· the priest and Nathan the
2:35 Z· the priest did the king put in
4: 2 Azariah the son of Z· the priest,
4 Z· and Abiathar were the priests:
2Ki 15:33 was Jerusha, the daughter of Z·.
1Ch 6: 8, 12 Ahitub begat Z·, and Z· begat
53 Z· his son, Ahimaaz his son.
9:11 son of Meshullam, the son of Z·,
12:28 And Z·, a young man mighty of
15:11 David called for Z· and Abiathar
16:39 And Z· the priest, and his brethren
18:16 And Z· the son of Ahitub, and
24: 3 both Z· of the sons of Eleazar,
6 and the princes, and Z· the priest,
31 presence of David the king, and Z·,
27:17 of Kemuel: of the Aaronites, Z·:
29:22 chief governor, and Z· to be priest.
2Ch 27: 1 was Jerushah, the daughter of Z·.
31:10 chief priest of the house of Z·
Ezr 7: 2 The son of Shallum, the son of Z·,
Ne 3: 4 repaired Z· the son of Baana.
29 repaired Z· the son of Immer
10:21 Meshezabeel, Z·, Jaddua,
11:11 son of Meshullam, the son of Z·,
13:13 the priest, and Z· the scribe,
Eze 40:46 these are the sons of Z· among the
43:19 Levites that be of the seed of Z·,
44:15 the sons of Z·, that kept the charge
48:11 are sanctified of the sons of Z·;

Zadok's (*za'-doks*)
2Sa 15:36 Ahimaaz Z· son, and Jonathan

Zaham (*za'-ham*)
2Ch 11:19 Jeush, and Shamariah, and Z·.

Zair (*za'-ur*)
2Ki 8:21 So Joram went over to Z·, and all

Zalaph (*za'-laf*)
Ne 3:30 and Hanun the sixth son of Z·.

Zalmon (*zal'-mon*) See also ILAI; SALMON.
J'g 9:48 got him up to mount Z·,
2Sa 23:28 Z· the Ahohite, Maharai the

Zalmonah (*zal-mo'-nah*)
Nu 33:41 mount Hor, and pitched in Z·.
42 And they departed from Z·, and

Zalmunna (*zal-mun'-nah*)
J'g 8: 5 am pursuing after Zebah and Z·,
6 Are the hands of Zebah and Z· now
7 Lord hath delivered Zebah and Z·
10 Zebah and Z· were in Karkor,
12 And when Zebah and Z· fled, he
12 two kings of Midian, Zebah and Z·,
15 Behold Zebah and Z·, with whom
15 Are the hands of Zebah and Z· now
18 Then said he unto Zebah and Z·,
21 Zebah and Z· said, Rise thou,
21 arose, and slew Zebah and Z·,
Ps 83:11 their princes as Zebah, and as Z·:

Zamzummims (*zam-zum'-mims*) See also ZUZIMS.
De 2:20 and the Ammonites call them Z·;

Zanoah (*za-no'-ah*)
Jos 15:34 Z·, and En-gannim, Tappuah,
56 And Jezreel, and Jokdeam, and Z·,
1Ch 4:18 and Jekuthiel the father of Z·.
Ne 3:13 Hanun, and the inhabitants of Z·;
11:30 Z·, Adullam, and in their villages,

Zaphnath-paaneah (*zaf''-nath-pa-a-ne'-ah*)
Ge 41:45 called Joseph's name Z·;

Zaphon (*za'-fon*)
Jos 13:27 and Z·, the rest of the kingdom

Zara (*za'-rah*) See also ZARAH; ZERAH.
M't 1: 3 Judas begat Phares and Z· of

Zarah (*za'-rah*) See also ZARA; ZERAH.
Ge 38:30 and his name was called Z·.
46:12 and Shelah, and Pharez, and Z·:

Zareah (*za'-re-ah*) See also ZAREATHITES; ZORAH.
Ne 11:29 And at En-rimmon, and at Z·,

Zareathites (*za'-re-ath-ites*) See also ZORATHITES.
1Ch 2:53 of them came the Z·, and the

Zared (*za'-red*) See also ZERED.
Nu 21:12 and pitched in the valley of Z·.

Zarephath (*zar'-e-fath*) See also SAREPTA.
1Ki 17: 9 Arise, get thee to Z·, which
10 So he arose and went to Z·.
Ob 20 of the Canaanites, even unto Z·;

Zaretan (*zar'-e-tan*) See also ZARTANAH; ZEREDATHAH.
Jos 3:16 the city Adam, that is beside Z·:

Zareth-shahar (*za''-reth-sha'-har*)
Jos 13:19 and Z· in the mount of the valley,

Zarhites (*zar'-hites*)
Nu 26:13 Of Zerah, the family of the Z·:
20 of Zerah, the family of the Z·.
Jos 7:17 and he took the family of the Z·:
17 he brought the family of the Z·
1Ch 27:11 Sibbecai the Hushathite, of the Z·:
13 the Netophathite, of the Z·:

Zartanah (*zar'-ta-nah*) See also ZARETAN; ZARTHAN.
1Ki 4:12 which is by Z· beneath Jezreel,

Zarthan (*zar'-than*) See also ZARETAN; ZARTANAH.
1Ki 7:46 ground between Succoth and Z·.

Zatthu (*zath'-u*) See also ZATTU.
Ne 10:14 Parosh, Pahath-moab, Elam, Z·,

Zattu (*zat'-tu*) See also ZATTHU.
Ezr 2: 8 The children of Z·, nine hundred
10:27 sons of Z·; Elioenai, Eliashib,
Ne 7:13 The children of Z·, eight hundred

Zavan (*za'-van*) See also ZAAVAN.
1Ch 1:42 Ezer; Bilhan, and Z·, and Jakan.

Zaza (*za'-zah*)
1Ch 2:33 sons of Jonathan; Peleth and Z·.

zeal
2Sa 21: 2 slay them in his z· to the children
2Ki 10:16 and see my z· for the Lord.
19:31 z· of the Lord of hosts shall do this.
Ps 69: 9 z· of thine house hath eaten me up;
119:139 My z· hath consumed me, because
Isa 9: 7 The z· of the Lord of hosts will
37:32 z· of the Lord of hosts shall do this.
59:17 and was clad with z· as a cloke.
63:15 where is thy z· and thy strength,
Eze 5:13 I the Lord have spoken it in my z·,
Joh 2:17 z· of thine house hath eaten me
Ro 10: 2 record that they have a z· of God,
2Co 7:11 yea, what z·, yea, what revenge!
9: 2 your z· hath provoked very many.
Ph'p 3: 6 Concerning z·, persecuting the
Col 4:13 that he hath a great z· for you,

zealous
Nu 25:11 while he was z· for my sake
13 because he was z· for his God, and
Ac 21:20 and they are all z· of the law:
22: 3 and was z· toward God, as ye all
1Co 14:12 as ye are z· of spiritual gifts,
Ga 1:14 z· of the traditions of my fathers.
Tit 2:14 a peculiar people, z· of good works.
Re 3:19 be z· therefore, and repent.

zealously
Ga 4:17 They z· affect you, but not well;
18 good to be z· affected always in a

Zebadiah (*zeb-ad-i'-ah*)
1Ch 8:15 And Z·, and Arad, and Ader,
17 And Z·, and Meshullam, and
12: 7 and Z·, the sons of Jeroham
26: 2 Jediael the second, Z· the third,
27: 7 Joab, and Z· his son after him:
2Ch 17: 8 and Nethaniah, and Z·, and Asahel,
19:11 Z· the son of Ishmael, the ruler
Ezr 8: 8 Z· the son of Michael, and with
10:20 sons of Immer; Hanani, and Z·.

Zebah (*ze'-bah*)
J'g 8: 5 and I am pursuing after Z· and
6 Are the hands of Z· and Zalmunna
7 when the Lord hath delivered Z·
10 Now Z· and Zalmunna were in
12 And when Z· and Zalmunna fled,
12 kings of Midian, Z· and Zalmunna,
15 Behold Z· and Zalmunna, with
15 Are the hands of Z· and Zalmunna
18 said he unto Z· and Zalmunna,
21 Z· and Zalmunna said, Rise thou,
21 slew Z· and Zalmunna, and took
Ps 83:11 all their princes as Z·, and as

Zebaim (*ze-ba'-im*)
Ezr 2:57 the children of Pochereth of Z·,
Ne 7:59 the children of Pochereth of Z·,

Zebedee (*zeb'-e-dee*) See also ZEBEDEE'S.
M't 4:21 James the son of Z·, and John his
21 in a ship with Z· their father,
10: 2 James the son of Z·, and John his
26:37 him Peter and the two sons of Z·,
M'r 1:19 he saw James the son of Z·, and
20 left their father Z· in the ship
3:17 And James the son of Z·, and John
10:35 James and John, the sons of Z·,
Lu 5:10 James, and John, the sons of Z·,
Joh 21: 2 and the sons of Z·, and two other

Zebedee's (*zeb'-e-dees*)
M't 20:20 came...the mother of Z· children
27:56 and the mother of Z· children.

Zebina (*ze-bi'-nah*)
Ezr 10:43 Zabad, Z·, Jadan, and Joel.

Zeboiim (*ze-boy'-im*) See also ZEBOIM.
Ge 14: 2 Shemeber king of Z·, and the
8 king of Z·, and the king of Bela

Zeboim (*ze-bo'-im*) See also ZEBOIIM.
Ge 10:19 Gomorrah, and Admah, and Z·,
De 29:23 and Gomorrah, Admah, and Z·,
1Sa 13:18 that looketh to the valley of Z·
Ne 11:34 Hadid, Z·, Neballat,
Ho 11: 8 how shall I set thee as Z·?

Zebub See BAAL-ZEBUB.

Zebudah (*ze-bu'-dah*)
2Ki 23:36 And his mother's name was Z·,

Zebul (*ze'-bul*)
J'g 9:28 And Z· his officer? serve the men
30 when Z· the ruler of the city heard
36 he said to Z·, Behold, there come
36 And Z· said unto him, Thou seest
38 Then said Z· unto him, Where is
41 Z· thrust out Gaal and his brethren,

Zebulonite (*zeb'-u-lon-ite*) See also ZEBULUNITES.
J'g 12:11 after him Elon, a Z·, judged
12 And Elon the Z· died, and was

Zebulun (*zeb'-u-lun*) See also ZABULON; ZEBULONITE; ZEBULUNITES.
Ge 30:20 and she called his name Z·.
35:23 and Judah, and Issachar, and Z·:
46:14 sons of Z·; Sered, and Elon,
49:13 Z· shall dwell at the haven
Ex 1: 3 Issachar, Z·, and Benjamin,
Nu 1: 9 Of Z·; Eliab the son of Helon.
30 Of the children of Z·, by their
31 even of the tribe of Z·, were fifty
2: 7 Then the tribe of Z·: and Eliab
7 be captain of the children of Z·.
7:24 Helon, prince of the children of Z·,
10:16 of the children of Z· was Eliab
13:10 Of the tribe of Z·, Gaddiel the
26:26 sons of Z· after their families:
34:25 of the tribe of the children of Z·,
De 27:13 Gad, and Asher, and Z·, Dan,
33:18 of Z· he said, Rejoice, Z·, in thy
Jos 19:10 came up for the children of Z·
16 inheritance of the children of Z·
27 reacheth to Z·, and to the valley
34 reacheth to Z· on the south side,
21: 7 out of the tribe of Z·, twelve cities.
34 out of the tribe of Z·, Jokneam
J'g 1:30 Z· drive out the inhabitants
4: 6 Naphtali and of the children of Z·?
10 Barak called Z· and Naphtali to
5:14 out of Z· they that handle the pen
18 Z· and Naphtali were a people that
6:35 and unto Z·, and unto Naphtali;
12:12 in Aijalon in the country of Z·.
1Ch 2: 1 and Judah, Issachar, and Z·,
6:63 out of the tribe of Z·, twelve cities.
77 were given out of the tribe of Z·,
12:33 Of Z·, such as went forth to battle,
40 even unto Issachar and Z· and
27:19 Of Z·, Ishmaiah the son of
2Ch 30:10 and Manasseh even unto Z·:
11 and Manasseh and of Z· humbled
18 Issachar and Z·, had not cleansed
Ps 68:27 princes of Z·, and the princes of
Isa 9: 1 he lightly afflicted the land of Z·
Ezr 48:26 unto the west side, Z· a portion.
27 And by the border of Z·, from the
33 gate of Issachar, one gate of Z·.

Zebulunites (*zeb'-u-lun-ites*) See also ZEBULONITE.
Nu 26:27 These are the families of the Z'

Zechariahᴬ (*zek-a-ri'-ah*) See also ZACCUR; ZACHARIAH; ZACHARIAS; ZACHER.
1Ch 5: 7 were the chief, Jeiel, and Z',
9:21 And Z' the son of Meshelemiah
37 And Gedor, and Ahio, and Z',
15:18 Z', Ben, and Jaaziel, and
20 And Z', and Aziel, and
24 and Z', and Benaiah, and Eliezer,
16: 5 the chief, and next to him Z',
24:25 of the sons of Isshiah; Z'.
26: 2 Z' the firstborn, Jediael the
11 Tebaliah the third, Z' the fourth:
14 for Z' his son, a wise counseller,
27:21 in Gilead, Iddo the son of Z':
2Ch 17: 7 and to Obadiah, and to Z', and
20:14 Then upon Jahaziel the son of Z',
21: 2 and Jehiel, and Z', and Azariah,
24:20 Spirit of God came upon Z' the son
26: 5 he sought God in the days of Z',
29: 1 was Abijah, the daughter of Z'.
13 sons of Asaph; Z', and Mattaniah:
34:12 and Z' and Meshullam, of the sons
35: 8 Hilkiah and Z' and Jehiel,
Ezr 5: 1 prophet, and Z' the son of Iddo,
6:14 prophet and Z' the son of Iddo.
8: 3 of the sons of Pharosh; Z':
11 Z' the son of Bebai, and with him
16 for Z', and for Meshullam, chief
10:26 Mattaniah, Z', and Jehiel, and
Ne 8: 4 Hashbadana, Z', and Meshullam.
11: 4 the son of Z', the son of Amariah,
5 the son of Joiarib, the son of Z',
12 the son of Z', the son of Pashur,
12:16 Of Iddo, Z'; of Ginnethon,
35 namely, Z' the son of Jonathan,
41 Z', and Hananiah, with trumpets;
Isa 8: 2 and Z' the son of Jeberechiah.
Zec 1: 1, 7 came the word of the Lord unto Z',
7: 1 the word of the Lord came unto Z'
8 the word of the Lord came unto Z',

Zedad (*ze'-dad*)
Nu 34: 8 forth of the border shall be to Z':
Eze 47:15 way of Hethlon, as men go to Z';

Zedekiah (*zed-e-ki'-ah*) See also MATTANIAH; ZEDEKIAH'S; ZIDKIJAH.
1Ki 22:11 Z' the son of Chenaanah made
24 Z' the son of Chenaanah went near,
2Ki 24:17 stead, and changed his name to Z'.
18 Z' was twenty and one years old
20 that Z' rebelled against the king
25: 2 unto the eleventh year of king Z'.
7 slew the sons of Z' before his eyes,
7 put out the eyes of Z', and bound
1Ch 3:15 second Jehoiakim, the third Z',
16 Jeconiah his son, Z' his son.
2Ch 18:10 Z' the son of Chenaanah had made
23 Z' the son of Chenaanah came
36:10 made Z' his brother king over
11 Z' was one and twenty years old
Jer 1: 3 eleventh year of Z' the son of
21: 1 king Z' sent unto him Pashur the
3 them, Thus shall ye say to Z':
7 I will deliver Z' king of Judah,
24: 8 will I give Z' the king of Judah,
27: 3 come to Jerusalem unto Z' king of
12 I spake also to Z' king of Judah
28: 1 in the beginning of the reign of Z'
29: 3 (whom Z' king of Judah sent unto
21 and of Z' the son of Maaseiah,
22 The Lord make thee like Z' and
32: 1 the Lord in the tenth year of Z'
3 For Z' king of Judah had shut him
4 Z' king of Judah shall not escape
5 And he shall lead Z' to Babylon,
34: 2 Go and speak to Z' king of Judah,
4 of the Lord, O Z' king of Judah;
6 spake all these words unto Z' king
8 the king Z' had made a covenant
21 Z' king of Judah and his princes
36:12 and Z' the son of Hananiah,
37: 1 king Z' the son of Josiah reigned
3 Z' the king sent Jehucal the son
17 Z' the king sent, and took him out:
18 Jeremiah said unto king Z', What
21 Z' the king commanded that they
38: 5 Z' the king said, Behold, he is in
14 Then Z' the king sent, and took
15 Jeremiah said unto Z', If I declare
16 So Z' the king sware secretly unto
17 Then said Jeremiah unto Z', Thus
19 Z' the king said unto Jeremiah, I
24 said Z' unto Jeremiah, Let no man
39: 1 ninth year of Z' king of Judah,
2 And in the eleventh year of Z',
4 when Z' the king of Judah saw
5 and overtook Z' in the plains of
6 king of Babylon slew the sons of Z'
44:30 as I gave Z' king of Judah into
49:34 in the beginning of the reign of Z'
51:59 went with Z' the king of Judah
52: 1 Z' was one and twenty years old
3 that Z' rebelled against the king
5 unto the eleventh year of king Z'.
8 and overtook Z' in the plains of
10 slew the sons of Z' before his eyes:
11 Then he put out the eyes of Z';

Zedekiah's (*zed-e-ki'-ahs*)
Jer 39: 7 Moreover he put out Z' eyes,

Zeeb (*ze'-eb*)
J'g 7:25 of the Midianites, Oreb and Z';
25 Z' they slew at the winepress of Z',
J'g 7:25 heads of Oreb and Z' to Gideon
8: 3 princes of Midian, Oreb and Z':
Ps 83:11 nobles like Oreb, and like Z':

Zelah (*ze'-lah*)
Jos 18:28 Z', Eleph, and Jebusi, which is
2Sa 21:14 in the country of Benjamin in Z',

Zelek (*ze'-lek*)
2Sa 23:37 Z' the Ammonite, Nahari the
1Ch 11:39 Z' the Ammonite, Naharai the

Zelophehad (*ze-lo'-fe-had*)
Nu 26:33 Z' the son of Hepher had no sons,
33 the names of the daughters of Z'
27: 1 Then came the daughters of Z',
7 The daughters of Z' speak right:
36: 2 the inheritance of Z' our brother
6 concerning the daughters of Z',
10 Moses, so did the daughters of Z':
11 the daughters of Z', were married
Jos 17: 3 Z', the son of Hepher, the son of
1Ch 7:15 was Z': and Z' had daughters.

Zelotes (*ze-lo'-teze*) See also CANAANITE; SIMON.
Lu 6:15 of Alphæus, and Simon called Z',
Ac 1:13 Simon Z', and Judas the brother

Zelzah (*zel'-zah*)
1Sa 10: 2 in the border of Benjamin at Z';

Zemaraim (*zem-a-ra'-im*) See also ZEMARITE.
Jos 18:22 Beth-arabah, and Z', and Beth-el,
2Ch 13: 4 Abijah stood up upon mount Z',

Zemarite (*zem'-a-rite*)
Ge 10:18 and the Z', and the Hamathite:
1Ch 1:16 and the Z', and the Hamathite.

Zemira (*ze-mi'-rah*)
1Ch 7: 8 sons of Becher; Z', and Joash,

Zenan (*ze'-nan*) See also ZAANAN.
Jos 15:37 Z', and Hadashah, Migdal-gad,

Zenas (*ze'-nas*)
Tit 3:13 Bring Z' the lawyer and Apollos

Zephaniahᴬ (*zef-a-ni'-ah*)
2Ki 25:18 priest, and Z' the second priest,
1Ch 6:36 the son of Azariah, the son of Z',
Jer 21: 1 Z' the son of Maaseiah the priest,
29:25 to Z' the son of Maaseiah the priest,
29 And Z' the priest read this letter
37: 3 Z' the son of Maaseiah the priest
52:24 priest, and Z' the second priest,
Zep 1: 1 came unto Z' the son of Cushi,
Zec 6:10 the house of Josiah the son of Z';
14 Jedaiah, and to Hen the son of Z',

Zephath (*ze'-fath*) See also HORMAH.
J'g 1:17 the Canaanites that inhabited Z',

Zephathah (*zef'-a-thah*)
2Ch 14:10 in the valley of Z' at Mareshah.

Zephi (*ze'-fi*) See also ZEPHO.
1Ch 1:36 Eliphaz; Teman, and Omar, Z',

Zepho (*ze'-fo*) See also ZEPHI.
Ge 36:11 Eliphaz were Teman, Omar, Z',
15 duke Omar, duke Z', duke Kenaz,

Zephon (*ze'-fon*) See also BAAL-ZEPHON; ZEPHONITES; ZIPHION.
Nu 26:15 families: of Z', the family of the

Zephonites (*zef'-on-ites*)
Nu 26:15 of Zephon, the family of the Z':

Zer (*zur*)
Jos 19:35 the fenced cities are Ziddim, Z',

Zerah (*ze'-rah*) See also EZRAHITE; ZARAH; ZARHITES; ZOHAR.
Ge 36:13 sons of Reuel; Nahath, and Z',
17 Nahath, duke Z', duke Shammah,
33 and Jobab the son of Z' of Bozrah
Nu 26:13 Of Z', the family of the Zarhites:
20 of Z', the family of the Zarhites.
Jos 7: 1, 18 the son of Z', of the tribe of
24 took Achan the son of Z', and the
22:20 Did not Achan the son of Z'
1Ch 1:37 of Reuel; Nahath, Z', Shammah,
44 Jobab the son of Z' of Bozrah
2: 4 in law bare him Pharez and Z'.
6 sons of Z'; Zimri, and Ethan,
4:24 and Jamin, Jarib, Z', and Shaul:
6:21 Iddo his son, Z' his son, Jeaterai
41 The son of Ethni, the son of Z',
9: 6 of the sons of Z'; Jeuel and their
2Ch 14: 9 out against them Z' the Ethiopian
Ne 11:24 children of Z' the son of Judah,

Zerahiah (*zer-a-hi'-ah*)
1Ch 6: 6 Uzzi begat Z', and Z' begat
51 his son, Uzzi his son, Z' his son,
Ezr 7: 4 The son of Z', the son of Uzzi,
8: 4 Elihoenai the son of Z', and with

Zered (*ze'-red*) See also ZARED.
De 2:13 and get you over the brook Z'.
13 And we went over the brook Z'.
14 we were come over the brook Z',

Zereda (*zer'-e-dah*)
1Ki 11:26 an Ephrathite of Z', Solomon's

Zeredathah (*ze-red'-a-thah*) See also ZARTHAN; ZERERATH.
2Ch 4:17 ground between Succoth and Z'.

Zererath (*zer'-e-rath*) See also ZARTHAN; ZEREDATHAH.
J'g 7:22 host fled to Beth-shittah in Z',

Zeresh (*ze'-resh*)
Es 5:10 for his friends, and Z' his wife.
14 said Z' his wife and...his friends
Es 6:13 Haman told Z' his wife and all his
13 said his wise men and Z' his wife

Zereth (*ze'-reth*)
1Ch 4: 7 And the sons of Helah were, Z',

Zeri (*ze'-ri*) See also IZRI.
1Ch 25: 3 of Jeduthun; Gedaliah, and Z',

Zeror (*ze'-ror*)
1Sa 9: 1 the son of Abiel, the son of Z',

Zeruah (*ze-ru'-ah*)
1Ki 11:26 whose mother's name was Z',

Zerubbabel (*ze-rub'-ba-bel*) See also SHESHBAZZAR; ZOROBABEL.
1Ch 3:19 and the sons of Pedaiah were, Z',
19 and the sons of Z'; Meshullam,
Ezr 2: 2 Which came with Z': Jeshua,
3: 2 priests, and Z' the son of Shealtiel,
8 began Z' the son of Shealtiel,
4: 2 Then they came to Z', and to the
3 But Z', and Jeshua, and the rest
5: 2 rose up Z' the son of Shealtiel,
Ne 7: 7 Who came with Z', Jeshua,
12: 1 the Levites that went up with Z'
47 And all Israel in the days of Z',
Hag 1: 1 by Haggai the prophet unto Z' the
12 Then Z' the son of Shealtiel,
14 Lord stirred up the spirit of Z'
2: 2 Speak now to Z' the son of
4 Yet now be strong, O Z', saith
21 Speak to Z', governor of Judah,
23 will I take thee, O Z', my servant,
Zec 4: 6 is the word of the Lord unto Z',
7 before Z' thou shalt become a
9 The hands of Z' have laid the
10 plummet in the hand of Z' with

Zeruiah (*ze-ru-i'-ah*)
1Sa 26: 6 Abishai the son of Z', brother to
2Sa 2:13 And Joab the son of Z', and the
18 were three sons of Z' there, Joab,
3:39 the sons of Z' be too hard for me:
8:16 the son of Z' was over the host;
14: 1 the son of Z' perceived that the
16: 9 Then said Abishai the son of Z'
10 I to do with you, ye sons of Z'?
17:25 sister to Z' Joab's mother.
18: 2 the hand of Abishai the son of Z',
19:21 Abishai the son of Z' answered
22 ye sons of Z', that ye should this
21:17 the son of Z' succoured him,
23:18 son of Z', was chief among three.
37 armourbearer to Joab the son of Z'.
1Ki 1: 7 conferred with Joab the son of Z',
2: 5 also what Joab the son of Z' did
22 priest, and for Joab the son of Z'.
1Ch 2:16 Whose sisters were Z', and Abigail.
16 sons of Z'; Abishai, and Joab, and
11: 6 Joab the son of Z' went first up,
39 armourbearer to Joab the son of Z',
18:12 son of Z' slew of the Edomites
15 the son of Z' was over the host;
26:28 Joab the son of Z', had dedicated;
27:24 the son of Z' began to number,

Zetham (*ze'-tham*)
1Ch 23: 8 the chief was Jehiel, and Z', and
26:22 Z', and Joel his brother, which

Zethan (*ze'-than*)
1Ch 7:10 and Chenaanah, and Z', and

Zethar (*ze'-thar*)
Es 1:10 Bigtha, and Abagtha, Z', and

Zia (*zi'-ah*)
1Ch 5:13 and Jorai, and Jachan, and Z',

Ziba (*zi'-bah*)
2Sa 9: 2 a servant whose name was Z'.
2 king said unto him, Art thou Z'?
3 Z' said unto the king, Jonathan
4 Z' said unto the king, Behold, he
9 Then the king called to Z', Saul's
10 Now Z' had fifteen sons and
11 Then said Z' unto the king,
12 all that dwelt in the house of Z'
16: 1 Z' the servant of Mephibosheth
2 king said unto Z', What meanest
2 Z' said, The asses be for the king's
3 Z' said unto the king, Behold,
4 Then said the king to Z', Behold,
4 Z' said, I humbly beseech thee
19:17 and Z' the servant of the house
29 said, Thou and Z' divide the land.

Zibeon (*zib'-e-un*)
Ge 36: 2 the daughter of Z' the Hivite;
14 the daughter of Z', Esau's wife:
20 and Shobal, and Z', and Anah,
24 And these are the children of Z':
24 as he fed the asses of Z' his father.
29 duke Shobal, duke Z', duke Anah,
1Ch 1:38 and Shobal, and Z', and Anah,
40 the sons of Z'; Aiah, and Anah.

Zibia (*zib'-e-ah*)
1Ch 8: 9 Hodesh his wife, Jobab, and Z',

Zibiah (*zib'-e-ah*)
2Ki 12: 1 And his mother's name was Z' of
2Ch 24: 1 His mother's name also was Z' of

Zichri (*zik'-ri*) See also ZITHRI.
Ex 6:21 Korah, and Nepheg, and Z'.
1Ch 8:19 And Jakim, and Z', and Zabdi,
23 And Abdon, and Z', and Hanan,
27 and Z', the sons of Jeroham.
9:15 the son of Micah, the son of Z',
26:25 and Joram his son, and Z' his son,
27:16 was Eliezer the son of Z':
2Ch 17:16 him was Amasiah the son of Z'.

2Ch 23: 1 and Elishaphat the son of Z˙,
28: 7 And Z˙, a mighty man of Ephraim,
Ne 11: 9 the son of Z˙ was their overseer:
12:17 Of Abijah, Z˙; of Miniamin, of

Ziddim (*zid'-dim*)
Jos 19:35 And the fenced cities are Z˙, Zer,

Zidkijah (*zid-ki'-jah*) See also ZEDEKIAH.
Ne 10: 1 the son of Hachaliah, and Z˙,

Zidon (*zi'-don*) See also SIDON; ZIDONIANS.
Ge 49:13 and his border shall be unto Z˙.
Jos 11: 8 and chased them unto great Z˙,
19:28 and Kanah, even unto great Z˙;
J'g 1:31 Accho, nor the inhabitants of Z˙,
10: 6 gods of Syria, and the gods of Z˙,
18:28 because it was far from Z˙,
2Sa 24: 6 came to Dan-jaan, and about to Z˙,
1Ki 17: 9 Zarephath, which belongeth to Z˙,
1Ch 1:13 And Canaan begat Z˙ his firstborn,
Ezr 3: 7 drink, and oil, unto them of Z˙,
Isa 23: 2 thou whom the merchants of Z˙,
4 Be thou ashamed, O Z˙: for the
12 oppressed virgin, daughter of Z˙:
Jer 25:22 of Tyrus, and all the kings of Z˙,
27: 3 and to the king of Z˙, by the hand
47: 4 to cut off from Tyrus and Z˙ every
Eze 27: 8 inhabitants of Z˙ and Arvad were
28:21 Son of man, set thy face against Z˙,
22 Behold, I am against thee, O Z˙;
Joe 3: 4 ye to do with me, O Tyre, and Z˙,
Zec 9: 2 Tyrus, and Z˙, though it be very

Zidonians (*zi-do'-ne-uns*) See also SIDONIANS.
J'g 10:12 The Z˙ also, and the Amalekites,
18: 7 after the manner of the Z˙, quiet
7 and they were far from the Z˙, and
1Ki 11: 1 Ammonites, Edomites, Z˙, and
5, 33 Ashtoreth the goddess of the Z˙,
16:31 daughter of Ethbaal king of the Z˙,
2Ki 23:13 the abomination of the Z˙,
1Ch 22: 4 for the Z˙ and they of Tyre brought
Eze 32:30 north, all of them, and all the Z˙,

Zif (*zif*)
1Ki 6: 1 reign over Israel, in the month Z˙,
37 of the Lord laid, in the month Z˙:

Ziha (*zi'-hah*)
Ezr 2:43 children of Z˙, the children of
Ne 7:46 children of Z˙, the children of
11:21 and Z˙ and Gispa were over the

Ziklag (*zik'-lag*)
Jos 15:31 And Z˙, and Madmannah, and
19: 5 And Z˙, and Beth-marcaboth,
1Sa 27: 6 Then Achish gave him Z˙ that day:
6 Z˙ pertaineth unto the kings of
30: 1 and his men were come to Z˙
1 had invaded the south, and Z˙,
1 smitten Z˙, and burnt it with fire;
14 Caleb; and we burned Z˙ with fire.
26 when David came to Z˙, he sent of
2Sa 1: 1 David had abode two days in Z˙,
4:10 hold of him, and slew him in Z˙,
1Ch 4:30 Bethuel, and at Hormah, and at Z˙,
12: 1 are they that came to David to Z˙,
20 As he went to Z˙, there fell to him
Ne 11:28 And at Z˙, and at Mekonah, and

Zillah (*zil'-lah*)
Ge 4:19 and the name of the other Z˙.
22 And Z˙, she also bare Tubal-cain,
23 said unto his wives, Adah and Z˙,

Zilpah (*zil'-pah*)
Ge 29:24 gave unto his daughter Leah Z˙
30: 9 she took Z˙ her maid, and gave
10 Z˙ Leah's maid bare Jacob a son.
12 And Z˙ Leah's maid bare Jacob a
35:26 the sons of Z˙, Leah's handmaid;
37: 2 with sons of Z˙, his father's wives:
46:18 These are the sons of Z˙, whom

Zilthai (*zil'-thahee*)
1Ch 8:20 And Elienai, and Z˙, and Eliel,
12:20 and Z˙, captains of the thousands

Zimmah (*zim'-mah*)
1Ch 6:20 son, Jahath his son, Z˙ his son,
42 the son of Z˙, the son of Shimei,
2Ch 29:12 Joah the son of Z˙, and Eden

Zimran (*zim'-ran*)
Ge 25: 2 she bare him Z˙, and Jokshan,
1Ch 1:32 she bare Z˙, and Jokshan, and

Zimri (*zim'-ri*)
Nu 25:14 the Midianitish woman, was Z˙,
1Ki 16: 9 And his servant Z˙, captain of half
10 And Z˙ went in and smote him,
12 Thus did Z˙ destroy all the house
15 of Judah did Z˙ reign seven days
16 Z˙ hath conspired, and hath also
18 Z˙ saw that the city was taken,
20 the rest of the acts of Z˙, and his
2Ki 9:31 said, Had Z˙ peace, who slew his
1Ch 2: 6 sons of Zerah; Z˙, and Ethan, and
8:36 and Z˙; and Z˙ begat Moza:
9:42 and Z˙; and Z˙ begat Moza;
Jer 25:25 And all the kings of Z˙, and all the

Zin (*zin*)
Nu 13:21 the wilderness of Z˙ unto Rehob,
20: 1 congregation, into the desert of Z˙
27:14 commandment in the desert of Z˙,
14 in Kadesh in the wilderness of Z˙,
33:36 and pitched in the wilderness of Z˙,
34: 3 shall be from the wilderness of Z˙
4 of Akrabbim, and pass on to Z˙:
De 32:51 Kadesh, in the wilderness of Z˙;
Jos 15: 1 of Edom the wilderness of Z˙
3 passed along to Z˙, and ascended

Zina (*zi'-nah*) See also ZIZAH.
1Ch 23:10 sons of Shimei were, Jahath, Z˙,

Zion (*zi'-un*) See also SION; ZION'S.
2Sa 5: 7 David took the strong hold of Z˙:
1Ki 8: 1 of the city of David, which is Z˙.
2Ki 19:21 daughter of Z˙ hath despised thee,
31 they that escape out of mount Z˙:
1Ch 11: 5 David took the castle of Z˙,
2Ch 5: 2 of the city of David, which is Z˙.
Ps 2: 6 my king upon my holy hill of Z˙.
9:11 to the Lord, which dwelleth in Z˙:
14 in the gates of the daughter of Z˙:
14: 7 of Israel were come out of Z˙!
20: 2 and strengthen thee out of Z˙;
48: 2 of the whole earth, is mount Z˙,
11 Let mount Z˙ rejoice, let the
12 Walk about Z˙, and go round
50: 2 Out of Z˙ the perfection of beauty,
51:18 good in thy good pleasure unto Z˙:
53: 6 of Israel were come out of Z˙!
69:35 For God will save Z˙, and will
74: 2 this mount Z˙, wherein thou hast
76: 2 and his dwelling place in Z˙.
78:68 the mount Z˙ which he loved.
84: 7 every one of them in Z˙ appeareth
87: 2 The Lord loveth the gates of Z˙
5 And of Z˙ it shall be said, This and
97: 8 Z˙ heard, and was glad; and the
99: 2 The Lord is great in Z˙; and he is
102:13 arise, and have mercy upon Z˙:
16 when the Lord shall build up Z˙,
21 declare the name of the Lord in Z˙,
110: 2 the rod of thy strength out of Z˙:
125: 1 in the Lord shall be as mount Z˙,
126: 1 turned again the captivity of Z˙,
128: 5 The Lord shall bless thee out of Z˙:
129: 5 and turned back that hate Z˙.
132:13 For the Lord hath chosen Z˙;
133: 3 upon the mountains of Z˙:
134: 3 and earth bless thee out of Z˙.
135:21 Blessed be the Lord out of Z˙,
137: 1 we wept, when we remembered Z˙.
3 Sing us one of the songs of Z˙.
146:10 reign for ever, even thy God, O Z˙,
147:12 O Jerusalem; praise thy God, O Z˙.
149: 2 let the children of Z˙ be joyful in
Ca 3:11 Go forth, O ye daughters of Z˙, and
Isa 1: 8 daughter of Z˙ is left as a cottage
27 Z˙ shall be redeemed with
2: 3 for out of Z˙ shall go forth the law,
3:16 the daughters of Z˙ are haughty,
17 of the head of the daughters of Z˙,
4: 3 to pass, that he that is left in Z˙,
4 the filth of the daughters of Z˙,
5 every dwelling place of mount Z˙,
8:18 hosts, which dwelleth in mount Z˙.
10:12 his whole work upon mount Z˙
24 O my people that dwellest in Z˙,
32 the mount of the daughter of Z˙,
12: 6 and shout, thou inhabitant of Z˙:
14:32 That the Lord hath founded Z˙,
16: 1 the mount of the daughter of Z˙.
18: 7 of the Lord of hosts, the mount Z˙.
24:23 of hosts shall reign in mount Z˙,
28:16 I lay in Z˙ for a foundation a stone,
29: 8 be, that fight against mount Z˙.
30:19 shall dwell in Z˙ at Jerusalem:
31: 4 come down to fight for mount Z˙,
9 the Lord, whose fire is in Z˙,
33: 5 he hath filled Z˙ with judgment
14 The sinners in Z˙ are afraid;
20 Look upon Z˙, the city of our
34: 8 for the controversy of Z˙.
35:10 and come to Z˙ with songs and
37:22 daughter of Z˙, hath despised thee,
32 they that escape out of mount Z˙:
40: 9 O Z˙, that bringest good tidings,
41:27 The first shall say to Z˙, Behold,
46:13 place salvation in Z˙ for Israel my
49:14 Z˙ said, The Lord hath forsaken
51: 3 For the Lord shall comfort Z˙:
11 and come with singing unto Z˙;
16 say unto Z˙, Thou art my people.
52: 1 awake; put on thy strength, O Z˙;
2 thy neck, O captive daughter of Z˙.
7 saith unto Z˙, Thy God reigneth!
8 the Lord shall bring again Z˙.
59:20 the Redeemer shall come to Z˙,
60:14 The Z˙ of the Holy One of Israel.
61: 3 unto them that mourn in Z˙,
62:11 Say ye to the daughter of Z˙,
64:10 Z˙ is a wilderness, Jerusalem a
66: 8 for as soon as Z˙ travailed, she
Jer 3:14 family, and I will bring you to Z˙:
4: 6 Set up the standard toward Z˙:
31 the voice of the daughter of Z˙,
6: 2 have likened the daughter of Z˙ to
23 war against thee, O daughter of Z˙.
8:19 Is not the Lord in Z˙? is not her
9:19 voice of wailing is heard out of Z˙,
14:19 Judah? hath thy soul lothed Z˙?
26:18 Z˙ shall be plowed like a field, and
30:17 This is Z˙, whom no man seeketh
31: 6 let us go up to Z˙ unto the Lord
12 come and sing in the height of Z˙,
50: 5 They shall ask the way to Z˙ with
28 to declare in Z˙ the vengeance of the
51:10 to declare in Z˙ the work of the Lord
24 evil that they have done in Z˙
35 shall the inhabitant of Z˙ say;
La 1: 4 The ways of Z˙ do mourn, because
6 from the daughter of Z˙ all her
17 Z˙ spreadeth forth her hands, and
2: 1 covered the daughter of Z˙ with a
4 tabernacle of the daughter of Z˙:

La 2: 6 and sabbaths to be forgotten in Z˙,
8 the wall of the daughter of Z˙:
10 The elders of the daughter of Z˙ sit
13 thee, O virgin daughter of Z˙?
18 O wall of the daughter of Z˙, let
4: 2 The precious sons of Z˙,
11 and hath kindled a fire in Z˙,
22 is accomplished, O daughter of Z˙;
5:11 They ravished the women in Z˙,
18 Because of the mountain of Z˙,
Joe 2: 1 Blow ye the trumpet in Z˙, and
15 Blow the trumpet in Z˙, sanctify
23 Be glad then, ye children of Z˙,
32 for in mount Z˙ and in Jerusalem
3:16 Lord also shall roar out of Z˙,
17 the Lord your God dwelling in Z˙,
21 for the Lord dwelleth in Z˙.
Am 1: 2 The Lord will roar from Z˙, and
6: 1 Woe to them that are at ease in Z˙,
Ob 17 upon mount Z˙ shall be deliverance,
21 come up on mount Z˙ to judge
Mic 1:13 of the sin to the daughter of Z˙:
3:10 They build up Z˙ with blood, and
12 shall Z˙ for your sake be plowed
4: 2 for the law shall go forth of Z˙,
7 shall reign over them in mount Z˙
8 strong hold of the daughter of Z˙,
10 to bring forth, O daughter of Z˙,
11 and let our eye look upon Z˙.
13 and thresh, O daughter of Z˙:
Zep 3:14 Sing, O daughter of Z˙; shout,
16 and to Z˙, Let not thine hands be
Zec 1:14 jealous for Jerusalem and for Z˙
17 and the Lord shall yet comfort Z˙,
2: 7 Deliver thyself, O Z˙, that dwellest
10 and rejoice, O daughter of Z˙:
8: 2 jealous for Z˙ with great jealousy,
3 I am returned unto Z˙, and will
9: 9 Rejoice greatly, O daughter of Z˙;
13 and raised up thy sons, O Z˙,

Zion's (*zi'-uns*)
Isa 62: 1 For Z˙ sake will I not hold my

Zior (*zi'-or*)
Jos 15:54 which is Hebron, and Z˙; nine

Ziph (*zif*) See also ZIPHITES.
Jos 15:24 Z˙, and Telem, and Bealoth,
55 Maon, Carmel, and Z˙, and Juttah,
1Sa 23:14 mountain in the wilderness of Z˙.
15 David was in the wilderness of Z˙
24 arose, and went to Z˙ before Saul:
26: 2 went down to the wilderness of Z˙,
2 seek David in the wilderness of Z˙.
1Ch 2:42 which was the father of Z˙;
4:16 Z˙, and Ziphah, Tiria, and Asareel.
2Ch 11: 8 And Gath, and Mareshah, and Z˙,

Ziphah (*zi'-fah*)
1Ch 4:16 Ziph, and Z˙, Tiria, and Asareel.

Ziphims (*zif'-ims*) See also ZIPHITES.
Ps 54: *title* the Z˙ came and said to Saul,

Ziphion (*zif'-e-on*) See also ZEPHON.
Ge 46:16 the sons of Gad; Z˙, and Haggi,

Ziphites (*zif'-ites*) See also ZIPHIMS.
1Sa 23:19 came up the Z˙ to Saul to Gibeah,
26: 1 the Z˙ came unto Saul to Gibeah,

Ziphron (*zif'-ron*)
Nu 34: 9 And the border shall go on to Z˙,

Zippor (*zip'-por*)
Nu 22: 2 And Balak the son of Z˙ saw all
4 Balak the son of Z˙ was king of
10 Balak the son of Z˙, king of Moab,
16 Thus saith Balak the son of Z˙,
23:18 hearken unto me, thou son of Z˙:
Jos 24: 9 Balak the son of Z˙, king of Moab,
J'g 11:25 Balak the son of Z˙, king of Moab?

Zipporah (*zip-po'-rah*)
Ex 2:21 he gave Moses Z˙ his daughter.
4:25 Then Z˙ took a sharp stone, and
18: 2 father in law, took Z˙, Moses' wife,

Zithri (*zith'-ri*) See also ZICHRI.
Ex 6:22 Mishael, and Elzaphan, and Z˙.

Ziz (*ziz*)
2Ch 20:16 they come up by the cliff of Z˙;

Ziza (*zi'-zah*) See also ZIZAH.
1Ch 4:37 Z˙ the son of Shiphi, the son of
2Ch 11:20 and Attai, and Z˙, and Shelomith.

Zizah (*zi'-zah*) See also ZINA; ZIZA.
1Ch 23:11 was the chief, and Z˙ the second:

Zoan (*zo'-an*)
Nu 13:22 seven years before Z˙ in Egypt.
Ps 78:12 the land of Egypt, in the field of Z˙.
43 and his wonders in the field of Z˙:
Isa 19:11 Surely the princes of Z˙ are fools,
13 The princes of Z˙ are become fools,
30: 4 For his princes were at Z˙, and his
Eze 30:14 will set fire in Z˙, and will execute

Zoar (*zo'-ar*)
Ge 13:10 of Egypt, as thou comest unto Z˙.
14: 2 and the king of Bela, which is Z˙.
8 the king of Bela, (the same is Z˙;)
19:22 the name of the city was called Z˙.
23 earth when Lot entered into Z˙.
30 Lot went up out of Z˙, and dwelt
30 for he feared to dwell in Z˙: and
De 34: 3 the city of palm trees, unto Z˙.
Isa 15: 5 his fugitives shall flee unto Z˙,
Jer 48:34 from Z˙ even unto Horonaim,

Zoba (*zo'-bah*) See also ZOBAH.
2Sa 10: 6 and the Syrians of Z˙, twenty
8 the Syrians of Z˙, and of Rehob,

Zobah (zo'-bah) See also ARAM-ZOBAH; HAMATH-ZOBAH; ZOBA.
1Sa 14:47 and against the kings of Z·, and
2Sa 8: 3 the son of Rehob, king of Z·, as he
5 to succour Hadadezer king of Z·,
12 son of Rehob, king of Z·.
23:36 Igal the son of Nathan of Z·, Bani
1Ki 11:23 his lord Hadadezer king of Z·:
24 band, when David slew them of Z·:
1Ch 18: 3 David smote Hadarezer king of Z·
5 came to help Hadarezer king of Z·,
9 the host of Hadarezer king of Z·;
19: 6 of Syria-maachah, and out of Z·.

Zobebah (zo-be'-bah)
1Ch 4: 8 And Coz begat Anub, and Z·, and

Zohar (zo'-har) See also ZERAH; ZEROR.
Ge 23: 8 for me to Ephron the son of Z·,
25: 9 the field of Ephron the son of Z·
46:10 and Ohad, Jachin, and Z·,
Ex 6:15 and Ohad, and Jachin, and Z·.

Zoheleth (zo'-he-leth)
1Ki 1: 9 and fat cattle by the stone of Z·,

Zoheth (zo'-heth) See also BEN-ZOHETH.
1Ch 4:20 and the sons of Ishi were, Z·, and

Zophah (zo'-fah)
1Ch 7:35 Z·, and Imna, and Shelesh, and
36 sons of Z·; Suah, and Harnepher,

Zophai (zo'-fahee) See also ZUPH.
1Ch 6:26 sons of Elkanah; Z· his son, and

Zophar (zo'-far)
Job 2:11 Shuhite, and Z· the Naamathite:
11: 1 answered Z· the Naamathite, and
20: 1 answered Z· the Naamathite, and
42: 9 Z· the Naamathite went, and did

Zophim (zo'-fim) See also RAMATHAIM-ZOPHIM.
Nu 23:14 brought him into the field of Z·,

Zorah (zo'-rah) See also ZAREAH; ZORATHITES; ZOREAH; ZORITES.
Jos 19:41 coast of their inheritance was Z·,
J'g 13: 2 there was a certain man of Z·,
25 the camp of Dan between Z· and
16:31 and buried him between Z· and
18: 2 men of valour, from Z·, and from
8 came unto their brethren to Z·
11 family of the Danites, out of Z·
2Ch 11:10 And Z·, and Aijalon, and Hebron,

Zorathites (zo'-rath-ites) See also ZAREATHITES; ZORITES.
1Ch 4: 2 These are the families of the Z·.

Zoreah (zo'-re-ah) See also ZORAH.
Jos 15:33 in the valley, Eshtaol, and Z·,

Zorites (zo'-rites) See also ZAREATHITES; ZORATHITES.
1Ch 2:54 half of the Manahethites, the Z·.

Zorobabel (zo-rob'-a-bel) See also ZERUBBABEL.
M't 1:12 and Salathiel begat Z·; Salathiel;
13 And Z· begat Abiud; and Abiud
Lu 3:27 which was the son of Z·, which

Zuar (zu'-ar)
Nu 1: 8 Issachar; Nethaneel the son of Z·.
2: 5 Nethaneel the son of Z· shall be
7:18 day Nethaneel the son of Z·,
23 of Nethaneel the son of Z·.
10:15 was Nethaneel the son of Z·.

Zuph (zuf) See also RAMATHAIM-ZOPHIM.
1Sa 1: 1 the son of Z·, an Ephrathite:
9: 5 they were come to the land of Z·,
1Ch 6:35 The son of Z·, the son of Elkanah,

Zur (zur) See also BETH-ZUR.
Nu 25:15 was Cozbi, the daughter of Z·;
31: 8 namely, Evi, and Rekem, and Z·,
Jos 13:21 Midian, Evi, and Rekem, and Z·,
1Ch 8:30 his firstborn son Abdon, and Z·,
9:36 firstborn son Abdon, then Z·,

Zuriel (zu'-re-el)
Nu 3:35 of the families of Merari was Z·

Zurishaddai (zu-re-shad'-da-i)
Nu 1: 6 Simeon; Shelumiel the son of Z·.
2:12 shall be Shelumiel the son of Z·.
7:36 fifth day Shelumiel the son of Z·,
41 of Shelumiel the son of Z·.
10:19 was Shelumiel the son of Z·.

Zuzims (zu'-zims) See also ZAMZUMMIMS.
Ge 14: 5 the Z· in Ham, and the Emins in

ADDENDA.

A.

about
Ex 11: 4 A· midnight will I go out into...Egypt:
12:37 a· six hundred thousand on foot that
Re 7:11 and a· the elders and the four beasts,

above
2Ch 24:20 priest, which stood a· the people,
Es 5:11 he had advanced him a· the princes
2Co 11:23 abundant, in stripes a· measure,

according
Ge 6:22 a· to all that God command him,
7: 5 a· unto all that the Lord commanded
18:14 a· to the time of life, and Sarah shall
21 done altogether a· to the cry of it,
21:23 a· to the kindness that I have done
27:19 I have done a· as thou badest me: arise.
Ex 6:26 land of Egypt a· to their armies.
2Ch 35:12 that they might give a· to the divisions
Ps 119:170 before thee: deliver me a· to thy word.

afar
2Ki 4:25 when the man of God saw her a· off,

afflicted
Isa 54:11 O thou a·, tossed with tempest, and

after
Ge 1:26 man in our image, a· our likeness:
19:31 come in unto us a· the manner of all
Ex 25: 9 a· the pattern of the tabernacle,
1Ki 18:28 and cut themselves a· their manner
2Ch 17: 4 and not a· the doings of Israel.
Job 10: 6 iniquity, and searchest a· my sin?
42: 8 lest I deal with you a· your folly,
Ps 119:85 The proud...which are not a· thy law.
M'r 9:31 a· that he is killed, he shall rise
2Pe 2:20 For if a· they have escaped

again
Ge 24:20 ran a· unto the well to draw water,
Nu 12:15 not till Miriam was brought in a·.
2Ch 28:17 For a· the Edomites had come
Eze 11:14 A· the word of the Lord came unto me,

against
Ex 9:17 yet exaltest thou thyself a· my people,
Nu 12: 9 anger of the Lord was kindled a· them;
J'g 12: 1 over to fight a· the children of Ammon,
1Sa 5: 9 the hand of the Lord was a· the city
Ne 3:30 Meshullam...over a· his chamber.
Ps 3: 1 many are they that rise up a· me.
Pr 30:31 a· whom there is no rising up.
Eze 14: 8 And I will set my face a· that man,
30:11 shall draw their swords a· Egypt,
42: 3 was gallery a· gallery in three
Jas 5: 3 rust of them shall be a witness a· you,

age
Lu 8:42 about twelve years of a·, and she lay
Ex 1: 5 And a· the souls that came out of
3:20 and smite Egypt with a· my wonders
Ex 4:19 a· the men are dead which sought
8:16 throughout a· the land of Egypt.
9:24 none like it in a· the land of Egypt
13: 7 seen with thee in a· thy quarters.
Le 4:34 shall pour out a· the blood thereof
13:13 it is a· turned white: he is clean.
Nu 14:29 and a· that were numbered of you,
30: 2 according to a· that proceedeth out
Jos 9:19 But a· the princes said unto a· the
1Sa 13: 3 the trumpet throughout a· the land,
14:34 And a· the people brought every man
2Sa 7:17 And according to a· this vision, so
1Ch 23:28 in the purifying of a· holy things,
2Ch 10:16 So a· Israel went to their tents.
16: 4 and a· the store cities of Naphtali.
Ps 85: 5 out thine anger to a· generations?
91:11 thee, to keep thee in a· thy ways.
105: 7 his judgments are in a· the earth.
119:96 I have seen an end of a· perfection:
138: 2 thy word above a· thy name.
148: 7 the earth, ye dragons, and a· deeps:
Pr 5:19 her breasts satisfy thee at a· times:
Ec 12: 4 and a· the daughters of musick shall
Isa 21: 2 a· the sighing thereof have I made
30: 5 They were a· ashamed of a people
51:18 by the hand of a· the sons that she
65:12 shall a· bow down to the slaughter:
Jer 27: 7 And a· nations shall serve him, and
39: 1 king of Babylon and a· his army
La 3:51 heart because of a· the daughters
Eze 14: 5 they are a· estranged from me
29: 7 and madest a· their loins to be at a
35:15 Seir, and a· Idumea, even a· of it:
Zec 1:11 and, behold, a· the earth sitteth still,
2Pe 3:11 ye to be in a· holy conversation

alone
Ps 86:10 wondrous things: thou art God a·.
148:13 Lord: for his name a· is excellent;

already
Ex 1: 5 souls: for Joseph was in Egypt a·.

also
Ge 24:44 and I will a· draw for thy camels:
46 and I will give thy camels drink a·:
46 and she made the camels drink a·.
Ex 8:21 and a· the ground whereon they are.
18:23 this people shall a· go to their place
Le 26:39 a· in the iniquities of their fathers
1Ch 16:25 he a· is to be feared above all gods.
Ps 93: 1 the world a· is stablished, that it
Jer 35:15 I have sent a· unto you all my servants
38:25 death; a· what the king said unto thee:
Eze 20:12 a· I gave them my sabbaths, to be
M't 27:41 a· the chief priests mocking him,
Joh 4:45 for they a· went unto the feast.
18: 2 and Judas a·, which betrayed him,
Ac 14: 1 Jews and a· of the Greeks believed.
20:21 to the Jews, and a· to the Greeks,
Ro 1: 6 are ye a· the called of Jesus Christ:
15 preach...to you that are at Rome a·.
5: 2 By whom a· we have access by faith
8:32 shall he not with him a· freely give
11:23 and they a·, if they abide not still
31 mercy they a· may obtain mercy.
16: 7 who a· were in Christ before me.
Ph'p 2:24 that I a· myself shall come shortly.
Col 4: 1 knowing that ye a· have a Master
Tit 3: 3 we...a· were sometimes foolish,
14 let ours a· learn to maintain good
Ph'm 9 now a· a prisoner of Jesus Christ.
Jas 2:11 commit adultery, said a·, Do not kill.

altogether
Ca 5:16 is most sweet: yea, he is a· lovely.

am
Le 19:18 neighbour as thyself: I a· the Lord.
28 any marks upon you: I a· the Lord.
Ps 139:21 a· not I grieved with those that rise
Eze 6: 9 I a· broken with their whorish heart,
Jas 1:13 he is tempted, I a· tempted of God: for

among
Ex 10: 2 my signs which I have done a· them;
Nu 3:42 the firstborn a· the children of Israel.
1Sa 10:11, 12 Is Saul also a· the prophets?
22 he hath hid himself a· the stuff.
24 there is none like him a· all the people?

anger
Ps 103: 9 neither will he keep his a· for ever.

another
1Sa 18: 7 answered one a· as they played,

answereth
M'r 10:24 But Jesus a· again, and saith unto

any
Ex 1:10 when there falleth out a· war, they join
10:15 there remained not a· green thing
12:39 prepared for themselves a· victual.
22:25 If thou lend money to a· of my people
Le 7:24 may be used in a· other use:
11:32 vessel it be, wherein a· work is done,
Isa 44: 8 yea, there is no God; I know not a·.
Eze 15: 2 is the vine tree more than a· tree,
36:15 cause thy nations to fall a· more,
M't 10: 5 and into a· city of the Samaritans enter
Lu 4:40 that had a· sick with divers diseases

art
Heb 12: 5 nor faint when thou a· rebuked of him:

asked
M'r 7:17 his disciples a· him concerning the

away
Le 16:21 shall send him a· by the hand of a fit
2Sa 3:22 for he had sent him a·, and he is gone

B.

bear
Isa 54: 1 O barren, thou that didst not b·;

became
Ge 21:20 in the wilderness, and b· an archer.
1Ch 18:13 the Edomites b· David's servants.
Re 16: 3 it b· as the blood of a dead man:

because
Ge 21:31 b· there they sware both of them.
De 9:18 b· of all your sins which ye sinned,
25 b· the Lord had said he would
28 say, B· the Lord was not able to bring
28 b· he hated them, he hath brought
23: 4 b· they hired against thee Balaam
31:17 b· our God is not among us?
32:51 b· ye sanctified me not in the
1Sa 15:24 thy words: b· I feared the people,
Ne 6:18 him, b· he was the son in law of
Es 9:24 B· Haman the son of Hammedatha,
Job 8: 9 b· our days upon earth are a shadow:)
Ps 119:53 taken hold upon me b· of the wicked
Jer 39:18 b· thou hast put thy trust in me,
Eze 35: 5 B· thou hast had a perpetual
Hab 2: 8 b· thou hast spoiled many nations,
8 b· of men's blood, and for the violence

become
Pr 29:21 have him b· his son at the length.

been
Ge 46:32 their trade hath b· to feed cattle;
2Ki 20:12 he had heard that Hezekiah had b· sick.
Jer 15: 9 she hath b· ashamed and confounded:
34:14 Hebrew, which hath b· sold unto thee;
48:11 hath not b· emptied from vessel to
Eze 16:31 hast not b· as an harlot, in that
Ph'p 2:26 ye had heard that he had b· sick.

before
Ge 24:15 to pass, b· he had done speaking,
2Sa 19:28 but dead men b· my lord the king:
1Ki 1:23 he bowed himself b· the king with his
Job 2: 1 to present himself b· the Lord.
26: 6 Hell is naked b· him, and

Ps 69:19 mine adversaries are all *b'* thee.
101: 3 set no wicked thing *b'* mine eyes:
Pr 15:11 and destruction are *b'* the Lord:
Isa 40:17 all nations *b'* him are as nothing;
Jer 47: 1 *b'* that Pharaoh smote Gaza.
Eze 42: 1 which was *b'* the building toward
Da 10:16 and said unto him that stood *b'* me.
Zep 2: 2 *B'* the decree bring forth,
2 forth, *b'* the day pass as the chaff,
2 *b'* the fierce anger of the Lord
2 *b'* the day of the Lord's anger
2Ti *subscr.* Paul was brought *b'* Nero the

behold
Ge 22: 7 he said, *B'*, the fire and the wood:
13 and *b'* behind him a ram caught in
20 *B'*, Milcah, she hath also born
24:15 that, *b'*, Rebekah came out, who was
30 and, *b'*, he stood by the camels at
43 *B'*, I stand by the well of water; and
45 *b'*, Rebekah came forth with her
37:29 and, *b'*, Joseph was not in the pit;
47:23 *B'*, I have brought you this day
Ex 1: 9 *B'*, the people of the children of
2: 6 the child: and, *b'*, the babe wept.
9: 3 *B'*, the hand of the Lord is upon thy
39:43 and, *b'*, they had done it as the Lord
Le 13:43 and, *b'*, if the rising of the sore be
Nu 18: 8 *B'*, I...have given thee the charge
22: 5 *B'*, there is a people come out from
5 *b'*, they cover the face of the earth,
24:10 *b'*, thou hast altogether blessed
De 9:13 and, *b'*, it is a stiffnecked people:
1Sa 12: 3 *B'*, here I am: witness against me
15:22 *B'*, to obey is better than sacrifice,
19:19 *B'*, David is at Naioth in Ramah.
2Sa 18:10 and said, *B'*, I saw Absalom hanged
Jer 49:19 *B'*, he shall come up like a lion
50:41 *B'*, a people shall come from the
Eze 37: 7 and *b'* a shaking, and the bones
Joe 3: 1 For, *b'*, in those days, and in that
Am 6:11 For, *b'*, the Lord commandeth, and

being
Es 1: 7 (the vessels *b'* diverse one from
Eze 47: 8 which *b'* brought forth into the sea,
Ac 16:18 But Paul, *b'* grieved, turned and said

between
Ex 9: 4 the Lord shall sever *b'* the cattle of
J'g 16:31 and buried him *b'* Zorah and Eshtaol

both
Ex 7:19 *b'* in vessels of wood, and in vessels
9:25 all...in the field, *b'* man and beast;
12:12 firstborn...of Egypt, *b'* man and beast;
1Sa 6:18 five lords, *b'* of fenced cities, and of
1Ch 24: 3 distributed them, *b'* Zadok of the sons
Isa 31: 3 *b'* he that helpeth shall fall, and he
2Th 3: 4 you, that ye *b'* do and will do the

bound
J'g 16:12 new ropes, and *b'* him therewith,

bows
Eze 39: 9 bucklers, the *b'* and the arrows,

build
Ezr 5:11 and *b'* the house that was builded
Ps 127: 1 house, they labour in vain that *b'* it:

built
Jer 32:31 from the day that they *b'* it even

burned
2Ki 23:15 brake down, and *b'* the high place,

C.

call
Ps 116: 2 therefore will I *c'* upon him as long
M't 10:25 shall they *c'* them of his household.

came
Ge 35:17 it *c'* to pass, when she was in hard
18 it *c'* to pass, as her soul was in
36:30 these are the dukes that *c'* of Hori.
Le 9: 1 it *c'* to pass on the eighth day,
1Ki 19:13 And, behold, there *c'* a voice unto him,
1Ch 17: 3 that the word of God *c'* to Nathan,

can
De 1:12 How *c'* I myself alone bear your
1Ki 5: 6 not among us any that *c'* skill to hew
Isa 38:18 death *c'* not celebrate thee: they that

cannot
Le 14:21 be poor, and *c'* get so much;
Job 19: 8 fenced up my way that I *c'* pass,
Ps 88: 8 I am shut up, and I *c'* come forth.
Isa 38:18 death [*c'*] celebrate thee: they that go
Jer 5:22 perpetual decree, that it *c'* pass it:

canst
Jer 2:23 How *c'* thou say, I am not polluted, I

carcases
Le 11:26 The *c'* of every beast which divideth

caused
2Ch 34:32 And he *c'* all...to stand to it.
Jer 29:31 him not, and he *c'* you to trust in a lie:

cave
1Ki 19:13 stood in the entering in of the *c'*.

chains
Ex 28:25 two ends of the two wreathen *c'* thou

child
Ge 17:17 Shall a *c'* be born unto him that is an

come
Ge 9:14 And it shall *c'* to pass, when I bring
24:14 And let it *c'* to pass, that the damsel
Jer 12:15 it shall *c'* to pass, after that I have
16 And it shall *c'* to pass, if they will
Zec 14: 7 but it shall *c'* to pass, that at

cometh
Jer 51:54 A sound of a cry *c'* from Babylon, and

committed
Jer 29:23 and have *c'* adultery with their

concerning
Ge 12:20 commanded his men *c'* him:
1Ch 22:13 Lord charged Moses with *c'* Israel:

corn
2Ki 19:26 and as *c'* blasted before it be grown up.

D.

David
1Ch 23: 5 I made, said *D'*, to praise therewith.

day
2Ki 25: 1 month, in the tenth *d'* of the month,
Jer 39: 2 the ninth *d'* of the month, the city was

despised
Jer 22:28 Is this man Coniah a *d'* broken idol?

did
J'g 6:13 *D'* not the Lord bring us up from
11:25 or *d'* he ever fight against them,
1Sa 1: 7 her; therefore she wept, and *d'* not eat.
2Ki 23:12 of the Lord, *d'* the king beat down,
2Ch 35:18 neither *d'* all the kings of Israel keep
Jer 41: 1 and there they *d'* eat bread together in
Ac 26:10 the saints *d'* I shut up in prison,

didst
J'g 12: 1 And *d'* not call us to go with thee? we
13: 8 man of God which thou *d'* send come
1Ki 8:53 For thou *d'* separate them from among
M't 13:27 Sir, *d'* not thou sow good seed in thy

displeased
Nu 11:10 greatly; Moses also was *d'*.

do
De 17:19 and these statutes, to *d'* them:
Ps 31: 1 In thee, O Lord, *d'* I put my trust; let
34:10 young lions *d'* lack, and suffer hunger:
80:12 which pass by the way *d'* pluck her?
Jer 23:32 and *d'* tell them, and cause my people
Eze 23:30 I will *d'* these things unto thee,
M't 8:29 What have we to *d'* with thee, Jesus,
15: 9 in vain they *d'* worship me, teaching
M'r 11:33 neither *d'* I tell you by what authority
Ac 7:51 ye *d'* always resist the Holy Ghost:
Ph'm 19 albeit I *d'* not say to thee how thou

doest
2Sa 3:25 in, and to know all that thou *d'*.

doings
Eze 20:43 all your *d'*, wherein ye have been

down
Nu 34:12 the border shall go *d'* to Jordan,
M't 14:19 the multitude to sit *d'* on the grass,
Heb 10:12 sat *d'* on the right hand of God;
12: 2 sit *d'* at the right hand of the throne

drew
Ge 24:20 water, and *d'* for all his camels.

duties
Eze 18:11 And that doeth not any of those *d'*, but

dwelt
Isa 37:37 and returned, and *d'* at Nineveh.
Jer 2: 6 through, and where no man *d'*?
Re 11:10 them that *d'* on the earth.

E.

each
Le 24: 7 put pure frankincense upon *e'* row,

eat
De 15:22 and the clean person shall *e'* it alike,

edge
Eze 43:13 by the *e'* thereof round about shall

else
1Ki 20:39 or *e'* thou shalt pay a talent of silver.
21: 6 or *e'*, if it please thee, I will give thee

Elpalet (*el-pa'-let*)
1Ch 14: 5 And Ibhar, and Elishua, and *E'*,

entering
1Sa 23: 7 by *e'* into a town that hath gates
2Ki 14:25 *e'* of Hamath unto the sea of the

even
Ge 23:10 *e'* of all that went in at the gate of the
Le 20: 6 I will *e'* set my face against that soul,
De 17:12 unto the judge, *e'* that man shall die:
1Ki 14:26 he *e'* took away all: and he took away
1Ch 11: 8 city round about, *e'* from Millo
Eze 8: 6 *e'* the great abominations that the
Eph 1:10 and which are on earth; *e'* in him:

every
Ge 2:19 Adam called *e'* living creature that was
9: 2 and upon *e'* fowl of the air, upon
10 of the ark, to *e'* beast of the earth.
Ex 12:44 But *e'* man's servant that is bought
27:18 and the breadth fifty *e'* where,
Le 11:15 *E'* raven after his kind;
15: 4 *e'* thing, whereon he sitteth, shall
Nu 36: 8 *e'* daughter, that possesseth an
1Ch 28:17 silver by weight for *e'* bason of silver:
2Ch 1: 2 and to *e'* governor in all Israel,
8:14 porters also by their courses at *e'* gate:
Jer 5: 6 *e'* one that goeth out thence shall

F.

far
Ec 2:13 folly, as *f'* as light excelleth darkness.

father's
Ne 7:61 they could not shew their *f'* house,

fathers
Nu 1:42 by the house of their *f'*, according

female
De 7:14 there shall not be male or *f'* barren

findeth
Pr 14: 6 scorner seeketh wisdom, and *f'* it not:

fine
Ge 18: 6 quickly three measures of *f'* meal,

fire
Jer 32:35 their daughters to pass through the *f'*

foolishly
1Sa 13:13 Thou hast done *f'*: thou hast not

foot
2Ki 9:33 the horses: and he trode her under *f'*.

forth
1Ki 8:16 I brought *f'* my people Israel out
Heb 1:14 sent *f'* to minister for them who

forty
Ge 7:12 upon the earth *f'* days and *f'* nights.

fowl
Ge 1:28 and over the *f'* of the air, and over

free
Am 4: 5 and publish the *f'* offerings:

full
Ge 14:10 the vale of Siddim was *f'* of slimepits;

G.

gate
Re 21:21 every...*g'* was of one pearl:

glad
Ps 40:16 seek thee rejoice and be *g'* in thee:

go
Ex 9:17 that thou wilt not let them *g'*?
1Sa 12:21 for then should ye *g'* after vain things,
1Ki 12:27 and *g'* again to Rehoboam king
Jer 46:19 furnish thyself to *g'* into captivity:

God
1Ki 8:20 the name of the Lord *G'* of Israel.
Ps 140: 7 O *G'* the Lord, the strength of my

goest
M't 8:19 follow thee whithersoever thou *g'*.

good
Pr 28:10 the upright shall have *g'* things

gray [*most editions* GREY *here*]
Pr 20:29 beauty of old men is the *g'* head.

grayheaded [*most editions* GREYHEADED *here*]
Ps 71:18 Now also when I am old and *g'*, O

great
2Ch 20: 2 There cometh a *g'* multitude

greatly
Isa 61:10 I will *g'* rejoice in the Lord, my soul

grow
Job 8:11 can the flag *g'* without water?

guilty
Ex 34: 7 and that will by no means clear the *g'*;

H.

had
Ex 2: 6 And when she *h'* opened it, she saw
Nu 30: 6 And if she *h'* at all an husband,
1Sa 15:35 repented that he *h'* made Saul king
25:21 Now David *h'* said, Surely in vain have
2Sa 8: 9 that David *h'* smitten all the host of
12: 3 ewe lamb, which he *h'* bought and
21:12 when the Philistines *h'* slain Saul
1Ki 5: 1 for he *h'* heard that they *h'* anointed
6:22 until he *h'* finished all the house:
7: 8 daughter, whom he *h'* taken to wife,
Ne 10:28 all they that *h'* separated themselves
Ps 51: *title* after he *h'* gone in to Bath-sheba
Jer 41: 9 Asa the king *h'* made for fear of
52:25 which *h'* the charge of the men of
Lu 12:39 if the goodman of the house *h'* known
Ac 10:17 Cornelius *h'* made enquiry for Simon's

hand
2Sa 18:14 And he took three darts in his *h'*,
2Ki 11:11 man with his weapons in his *h'*,
23: 8 were on a man's left *h'* at the gate
Job 1:12 upon himself put not forth thine *h'*.
Isa 30:21 when ye turn to the right *h'*, and

hast
Ru 2:13 and for that thou *h'* spoken friendly
1Sa 19:17 Why *h'* thou deceived me so, and sent
1Ki 1: 6 Why *h'* thou done so? and he also was
Job 33: 8 Surely thou *h'* spoken in mine hearing,
Ps 3: 7 thou *h'* broken the teeth of the ungodly.
31: 8 And *h'* not shut me up into the hands
8 thou *h'* set my feet in a large room.
Eze 16:24 and *h'* made thee a high place in every
Da 5:23 are all thy ways, *h'* thou not glorified:
Hab 1:12 thou *h'* established them for correction.
2:10 people, and *h'* sinned against thy soul.
Joh 4:18 and he whom thou now *h'* is not thy
Ac 23:22 thou *h'* shewed these things to me.

hated
Ps 106:10 from the hand of him that *h'* them,
41 and they that *h'* them ruled over

hath
1Sa 25:21 and he *h'* requited me evil for good.
Ne 9:32 that *h'* come upon us, on our kings, on
Job 16:11 God *h'* delivered me to the ungodly,
Ps 132:13 *h'* chosen Zion; he *h'* desired it for his
Pr 30: 4 who *h'* gathered the wind in his fists?
4 who *h'* bound the waters in a garment?
4 who *h'* established all the ends of the
Ec 5: 4 to pay it; for he *h'* no pleasure in fools:
Isa 14: 4 and say, How *h'* the oppressor ceased!
Jer 48:11 and he *h'* settled on his lees,
11 and *h'* not been emptied from vessel to

11 neither *h*· he gone into captivity:
La 1: 5 for the Lord *h*· afflicted her for the
14 the Lord *h*· delivered me into their
M't 15: 13 my heavenly Father *h*· not planted,
Lu 11: 33 No man, when he *h*· lighted a candle,
Ac 24: 6 Who also *h*· gone about to profane the

have
Ge 4: 1 said, I *h*· gotten a man from the Lord.
21: 7 for I *h*· borne him a son in his old age.
26: 10 thou shouldest *h*· brought guiltiness
46: 32 and their herds, and all that they *h*·.
Nu 35: 3 the cities shall they *h*· to dwell in;
1Sa 11: 9 time the sun be hot, ye shall *h*· help.
19: 4 his works *h*· been to thee-ward
20: 3 certainly knoweth that I *h*· found grace
1Ki 1: 45 This is the noise that ye *h*· heard.
11: 36 my servant may *h*· a light alway
Ezr 4: 14 therefore *h*· we sent and certified the
Isa 14: 24 and as I *h*· purposed, so shall it stand:
43: 10 and my servant whom I *h*· chosen:
49: 21 me these, seeing I *h*· lost my children,
Jer 14: 13 the sword, neither shall ye *h*· famine;
25: 35 the shepherds shall *h*· no way to flee,
29: 7 the peace thereof shall ye *h*· peace.
30: 11 end of all nations whither I *h*· scattered
48: 4 little ones *h*· caused a cry to be heard.
Eze 23: 34 for I *h*· spoken it, saith the Lord God.
28: 26 when I *h*· executed judgments upon all
39: 29 for I *h*· poured out my spirit upon the
Ob 7 that eat thy bread *h*· laid a wound
Hag 2: 23 I *h*· chosen thee, saith the Lord of hosts.
M't 13: 17 which ye hear, and *h*· not heard them.
Ac 17: 28 certain also of your own poets *h*· said,

having
Ro 15: 23 *h*· a great desire these many years
Heb 11: 13 but *h*· seen them afar off,

hearing
M'r 4: 12 and *h*· they may hear, and not

hearkened
1Ki 20: 25 and he *h*· unto their voice, and did

henceforth
Mic 4: 7 over them in mount Zion from *h*·,

here
2Ch 18: 6 there not *h*· a prophet of the Lord
Ac 8: 36 See, *h*· is water; what doth hinder

high
1Ch 11: 23 man of great stature, five cubits *h*·;

himself
Le 15: 13 shall number to *h*· seven days for his
2Sa 18: 18 taken and reared up for *h*· a pillar,

hither
Pr 25: 7 it be said unto thee, Come up *h*·;

ho
Ru 4: 1 unto whom he said, *H*·, such a one!

holds
2Co 10: 4 to the pulling down of strong *h*·;)

horses
2Sa 8: 4 David houghed all the chariot *h*·, but

host
1Ki 22: 19 And all the *h*· of heaven standing

houses
1Ch 28: 11 and of the *h*· thereof, and of the
Ne 7: 4 therein, and the *h*· were not builded.
Pr 30: 26 yet make they their *h*· in the rocks;

how
Ex 10: 7 *H*· long shall this man be a snare
11: 7 may know *h*· that the Lord doth put a
2Sa 6: 9 *H*· shall the ark of the Lord come
Isa 14: 12 *h*· art thou cut down to the ground,
Jer 47: 5 *h*· long wilt thou cut thyself?
La 4: 2 *h*· are they esteemed as earthen
Ac 19: 35 knoweth not *h*· that the city of the

I.

if
Ex 1: 16 *i*· it be a son, then ye shall kill
16 but *i*· it be a daughter, then she
Le 5: 2 things, and *i*· it be hidden from him;
13: 58 *i*· the plague be departed from them.
Nu 19: 12 *i*· he purify not himself the third
De 30: 17 But *i*· thine heart turn away, so that
2Sa 15: 25 *i*· I shall find favour in the eyes of
2Ch 6: 26 yet *i*· they pray toward this place, and
Job 21: 15 we have, *i*· we pray unto him?
Ps 62: 10 *i*· riches increase, set not your
Pr 6: 30 do not despise a thief, *i*· he steal
30: 4 is his son's name, *i*· thou canst tell?
Ec 4: 11 Again, *i*· two lie together, then
12 And *i*· one prevail against him, two
11: 3 and *i*· the tree fall toward the south,
8 But *i*· a man live many years, and
Ca 7: 12 let us see *i*· the vine flourish,
8: 9 and *i*· she be a door, we will inclose
Isa 51: 13 as *i*· he were ready to destroy?
Jer 2: 10 and see *i*· there be such a thing.
28 *i*· they can save thee in the time of
3: 1 *I*· a man put away his wife, and
1 and *i*· thou wilt put away thine
42: 5 *i*· we do not even according to all
Eze 18: 21 But *i*· the wicked will turn from
Da 3: 18 But *i*· not, be it known unto thee,
M't 16: 26 *i*· he shall gain the whole world,
M'r 7: 16 *I*· any man have ears to hear,
8: 23 he asked him *i*· he saw ought.
Lu 14: 26 *I*· any man come to me, and hate

insomuch
Ps 106: 40 *i*· that he abhorred his own

into
Nu 4: 3 all that enter *i*· the host, to do the
Job 34: 23 that he should enter *i*· judgment with
Jer 43: 3 to deliver us *i*· the hand of the
Eze 12: 11 shall remove and go *i*· captivity.

Israel
Jer 51: 19 and *I*· is the rod of his inheritance:
Eze 18: 15 eyes to the idols of the house of *I*·,

J.

Jair
De 3: 14 *J*· the son of Manasseh took all

Judah
1Ch 6: 57 Aaron they gave the cities of *J*·,

judgments
De 30: 16 And his statutes and his *j*·, that

K.

Karnaim (*kar'-na-im*) See also ASHTEROTH.
Ge 14: 5 the Rephaims in Ashteroth *K*·,

king
1Ki 14: 25 in the fifth year of *k*· Rehoboam,

L.

laid
2Ch 24: 27 greatness of the burdens *l*· upon him,

less
Job 34: 19 How much *l*· to him that accepteth
Eze 15: 5 how much *l*· shall it be meet yet for

lest
De 1: 42 you; *l*· ye be smitten before your
Ps 91: 12 *l*· thou dash thy foot against a
Pr 30: 9 or *l*· I be poor, and steal, and take

let
Ge 1: 9 place, and *l*· the dry land appear:
Ex 22: 7 the thief be found, *l*· him pay double.
1Sa 14: 36 *L*· us draw near hither unto God.
Eze 45: 9 *L*· it suffice you, O prince of Israel:
M't 5: 16 *L*· your light so shine before men, that
6: 3 *l*· not thy left hand know what thy

lie
Re 11: 8 dead bodies shall *l*· in the street of the

like
Ex 8: 10 that there is none *l*· unto the Lord
1Sa 8: 20 That we also may be *l*· all the nations;
2Ki 5: 14 again *l*· unto the flesh of a little child,
2Ch 4: 5 of it *l*· the work of the brim of a cup,
6: 14 no God *l*· thee in the heavens, nor
30: 26 there was not the *l*· in Jerusalem.
Job 38: 3 Gird up now thy loins *l*· a man;
Ps 31: 12 out of mind: I am *l*· a broken vessel.
72: 16 city shall flourish *l*· grass of the earth.
105: 41 they ran in the dry places *l*· a river.
119: 119 all the wicked of the earth *l*· dross.
Isa 18: 4 *l*· a clear heat upon herbs, and
33: 4 *l*· the gathering of the caterpiller:
36: 17 you away to a land *l*· your own land,
Jer 48: 38 for I have broken Moab *l*· a vessel
La 4: 8 it is withered, it is become *l*· a stick.
Eze 31: 8 chestnut trees were not *l*· his branches;
Da 10: 16 one *l*· the similitude of the sons of

lo
Ex 7: 15 *l*·, he goeth out unto the water;
2Sa 24: 17 said, *L*·, I have sinned, and done
2Ki 7: 6 *L*·, the king of Israel hath hired
15 *l*·, all the way was full of garments
1Ch 17: 1 *L*·, I dwell in an house of cedars,
Eze 33: 33 cometh to pass, (*l*·, it will come,)

loft
Ac 20: 9 and fell down from the third *l*·,

long
1Sa 1: 14 How *l*· wilt thou be drunken? put
Ne 2: 6 For how *l*· shall thy journey be? and
Ps 79: 5 How *l*·, Lord? wilt thou be angry

lord (Lord)
2Ch 17: 4 But sought to the *L*· God of his father,
Ps 68: 18 that the *L*· God might dwell among

lord's (Lord's)
Le 27: 30 of the fruit of the tree, is the *L*·:

M.

made
1Ki 14: 9 hast gone and *m*· thee other gods,
1Ch 28: 2 and had *m*· ready for the building:
Joh 1: 31 he should be *m*· manifest to Israel,
Ac 8: 3 for Saul, he *m*· havock of the church.

make
Job 41: 6 the companions *m*· a banquet of him?
28 The arrow cannot *m*· him flee:
Ps 132: 17 will I *m*· the horn of David to bud:
Eze 35: 11 I will *m*· myself known among them,
Eph 5: 13 for whatsoever doth *m*· manifest

man
Ps 12: 1 Help, Lord; for the godly *m*· ceaseth;
Pr 24: 15 Lay not wait, O wicked *m*·, against
28: 17 flee to the pit; let no *m*· stay him.
Ec 8: 1 Who is as the wise *m*·? and who
Isa 28: 20 is shorter than that a *m*· can stretch
Joh 18: 40 saying, Not this *m*·, but Barabbas.
Joh 19: 12 If thou let this *m*· go, thou art not
Eph 5: 5 nor unclean person, nor covetous *m*·,

manner
2Ch 32: 15 nor persuade you on this *m*·, neither

many
Isa 61: 4 the desolations of *m*· generations.

may
Ex 31: 6 that they *m*· make all that I have
Nu 27: 20 of the children of Israel *m*· be obedient.
2Sa 18: 14 Joab, I *m*· not tarry thus with thee.
Jer 46: 10 he *m*· avenge him of his adversaries:
Eze 34: 10 that they *m*· not be meat for them.

mean
Ge 21: 29 What *m*· these seven ewe lambs which

men
Ge 4: 26 then began *m*· to call upon the name
Nu 31: 32 prey which the *m*· of war had
2Sa 19: 35 hear any more the voice of singing *m*·
1Ch 11: 22 he slew two lionlike *m*· of Moab:
12: 32 were *m*· that had understanding of
2Ch 22: 1 for the band of *m*· that came with the
Ezr 2: 65 two hundred singing *m*· and singing
7: 28 together out of Israel chief *m*· to go
Ne 13: 16 There dwelt *m*· of Tyre also therein,
Pr 7: 26 many...*m*· have been slain by her.
Ec 3: 14 that *m*· should fear before him.
Isa 35: 8 the wayfaring *m*·, though fools, shall
M't 21: 41 miserably destroy those wicked *m*·,
1Ti 5: 1 and the younger *m*· as brethren;
Heb 12: 23 the spirits of just *m*· made perfect,
Jas 1: 5 that giveth to all *m*· liberally, and

might
Ph'm 8 though I *m*· be much bold in Christ

mine
Ge 49: 6 *m*· honour, be not thou united: for in
Nu 8: 17 firstborn of the children...are *m*·,
1Ki 2: 15 knowest that the kingdom was *m*·,
Ne 7: 5 my God put into *m*· heart to gather
Ps 138: 7 against the wrath of *m*· enemies,
Pr 8: 14 counsel is *m*·, and sound wisdom: I

more
1Co 12: 22 body, which seem to be *m*· feeble, are
23 have *m*· abundant comeliness.
Ph'p 2: 28 I sent him...the *m*· carefully,

moreover
Ge 24: 25 She said *m*· unto him, We have both
Ex 3: 6 *M*· he said, I am the God of thy father,
11: 3 *M*· the man Moses was very great
1Ki 1: 47 and *m*· the king's servants came
Ne 12: 8 *M*· the Levites: Jeshua, Binnui,
Isa 8: 1 *M*· the Lord said unto me, Take thee
Eze 35: 1 *M*· the word of the Lord came unto me,

most
Ezr 2: 63 should not eat of the *m*· holy things,
Ps 82: 6 you are children of the *m*· High.

much
Ge 23: 9 for as *m*· money as it is worth he shall
De 31: 27 and how *m*· more after my death?
Ezr 7: 22 and salt without prescribing how *m*·.
Eze 15: 5 how *m*· less shall it be meet

must
Ge 24: 5 *m*· I needs bring thy son again unto
1Ch 17: 11 that thou *m*· go to be with thy fathers,
Ezr 10: 12 As thou hast said, so *m*· we do.
Isa 28: 10 For precept *m*· be upon precept,

myself
Ne 5: 7 Then I consulted with *m*·, and I

N.

name
2Sa 6: 8 called the *n*· of the place Perez-uzzah

namely
Nu 13: 11 Of the tribe of Joseph, *n*·, of the tribe

nay
Ge 19: 2 And they said, *N*·; but we will

near
Nu 33: 48 plains of Moab by Jordan *n*· Jericho.
35: 1 plains of Moab by Jordan *n*· Jericho,

needs
Ge 17: 13 thy money, must *n*· be circumcised:
24: 5 must I *n*· bring thy son again unto the

neither
Ge 3: 3 not eat of it, *n*· shall ye touch it,
8: 21 *n*· will I again smite any more every
Ex 34: 25 *n*· shall the sacrifice of the feast of
Nu 6: 3 *n*· shall he drink any liquor of
1Ki 3: 12 *n*· after thee shall any arise like
Ps 6: 1 thine anger, *n*· chasten me in thy

never
2Ch 21: 17 so that there was *n*· a son left him,

nevertheless
Eze 3: 21 *N*· if thou warn the righteous man,

night
Ps 63: 6 and meditate on thee in the *n*· watches.

no
Nu 20: 2 was *n*· water for the congregation:
Job 28: 7 is a path which *n*· fowl knoweth,
Re 22: 5 they need *n*· candle, neither light

none
Ps 139: 16 as yet there was *n*· of them.

nor
Ge 19: 35 when she lay down, *n*· when she arose.
De 10: 9 Levi hath no part *n*· inheritance with
Isa 44: 18 have not known *n*· understood:

nothing
2Ch 14: 11 said, Lord, it is *n*· with thee to help,
Ezr 4: 3 Ye have *n*· to do with us to build
Ps 17: 3 hast tried me, and shalt find *n*·;
Isa 40: 23 That bringeth the princes to *n*·;

now
Ge 24: 42 if *n*· thou do prosper my way
Ex 7: 11 *n*· the magicians of Egypt, they
10: 11 go *n*· ye that are men, and serve
1Sa 9: 6 to pass: *n*· let us go thither;

2Sa 7:29 Therefore *n*· let it please thee to
1Ki 8:26 And *n*·, O God of Israel, let thy
2Ki 13: 8 *N*· the rest of the acts of Jehoahaz,
Isa 7:13 said, Hear ye *n*·, O house of David;
37:26 *n*· have I brought it to pass, that
Jer 29:27 *N*· therefore why hast thou not
Eze 4:14 even till *n*· have I not eaten of that
Joe 2:12 Therefore also *n*·, saith the Lord,
Ac 16: 6 *N*·...they had gone throughout
Ro 6: 8 *N*· if we be dead with Christ, we
1Co 7:25 *N*· concerning virgins I have no
Jas 2:11 *N*· if thou commit no adultery, yet

O.

off
De 11:17 ye perish...from *o*· the good land
Da 4:14 shake *o*· his leaves, and scatter his
Lu 9: 5 shake *o*· the very dust from your

on
Le 14:23 bring them *o*· the eighth day for his
Nu 30: 8 husband disallowed her *o*· the day
Job 38:26 To cause it to rain *o*· the earth,
26 *o*· the wilderness, wherein there
Eze 10: 3 cherubims stood *o*· the right side of
48:21 *o*· the one side and *o*· the other of the
Lu 4:40 and he laid his hands *o*· every one
21:35 as a snare shall it come *o*· all them
1Ti 4:14 with the laying *o*· of the hands of

one
Ge 24:41 if they give not thee *o*·, thou shalt
De 21: 1 If *o*· be found slain in the land which
1Sa 26:20 as when *o*· doth hunt a partridge in
2Ki 19:22 even against the Holy *O*· of Israel.
Ne 13:28 And *o*· of the sons of Joiada, the son of
Isa 10:14 and as *o*· gathereth eggs that are left,
41:27 give to Jerusalem *o*· that bringeth
Eze 40:40 as *o*· goeth up to the entry of the north
Ro 14: 2 For *o*· believeth that he may eat all
2Co 2:16 To the *o*· we are the savour of
1Ti 3: 4 *O*· that ruleth well his own house,

one's
Ec 7: 1 day of death than the day of *o*· birth.

ones
2Ch 31:18 all their little *o*·, their wives, and their
Ps 83: 3 and consulted against thy hidden *o*·.
Jer 46: 5 and their mighty *o*· are beaten down,
Lu 17: 2 he should offend one of these little *o*·.

only
Ge 14:24 Save *o*· that which the young men
19: 8 eyes: *o*· unto these men do nothing;
24: 8 *o*· bring not my son thither again.
Ex 8: 9 they may remain in the river *o*·?
28 *o*· ye shall not go very far away:
10:17 forgive,...my sin *o*· this once, and
17 take away from me this death *o*·.
24 *o*· let your flocks and your herds
2Sa 20:21 deliver him *o*·, and I will depart
2Ch 6:30 (for thou *o*· knowest the hearts of the
Pr 5:17 Let them be *o*· thine own, and not

or
Ps 18:31 *o*· who is a rock save our God?
Jer 16: 2 sons *o*· [*some eds.* NOR] daughters in

order
Ge 22: 9 there, and laid the wood in *o*·,

other
Ge 20:16 that are with thee, and with all *o*·:
25:23 shall be stronger than the *o*· people;
Nu 24: 1 he went not, as at *o*· times, to seek for
32:38 and gave *o*· names unto the cities
Es 2:12 and with *o*· things for the purifying
Jer 12:12 the land even to the *o*· end of the land:

ought
Ge 20: 9 hast done deeds unto me that *o*· not to

over
Ex 30: 6 mercy seat that is *o*· the testimony,

own
Ge 14:14 trained servants, born in his *o*· house,
1Ki 10:13 she turned and went to her *o*· country,
2Ki 2:12 he took hold of his *o*· clothes, and rent
2Ch 24:25 his *o*· servants conspired against him
Ps 17:10 They are inclosed in their *o*· fat: with
141:10 Let the wicked fall into their *o*· nets,
Pr 5:17 Let them be only thine *o*·, and not
27:10 Thine *o*· friend, and thy father's friend,
Isa 14:18 lie in glory, every one in his *o*· house.
Jer 1:16 worshipped the works of their *o*· hands.

P.

part
Da 11:31 And arms that shall stand on his *p*·,
Re 8: 7 and the third *p*· of trees was burnt up,

parts
Eze 37:11 we are cut off for our *p*·.

pass
Ge 4: 8 and it came to *p*·, when they were in the
9:14 And it shall come to *p*·, when I bring a
12:11 And it came to *p*·, when he was come
12 Therefore it shall come to *p*·, when the
14 And it came to *p*·, that, when Abram
14: 1 it came to *p*· in the days of Amraphel
15:17 And it came to *p*·, that, when the sun
19:17 it came to *p*·, when they had brought
29 it came to *p*·, when God had destroyed
34 And it came to *p*· on the morrow, that
21:22 And it came to *p*· at that time, that
22: 1, 20 And it came to *p*· after these things,
24:14 And let it come to *p*·, that the damsel
15 And it came to *p*·, before he had done
22 And it came to *p*·, as the camels had
30 And it came to *p*·, when he saw the
43 it shall come to *p*·, that when the virgin
35:17 And it came to *p*·, when she was in
Nu 10:11 it came to *p*· on the twentieth day of
J'g 14:17 and it came to *p*· on the seventh day,
1Sa 10: 9 And all those signs came to *p*· that day.
2Sa 15: 7 And it came to *p*· after forty years, that
Jer 12:15 come to *p*·, after that I have plucked
16 shall come to *p*·, if they will diligently
Eze 20: 1 And it came to *p*· in the seventh year,
Zec 14: 7 but it shall come to *p*·, that at evening

peradventure
Ge 24: 5 *P*· the woman will not be willing to
39 *P*· the woman will not follow me
27:12 my father *p*· will feel me, and I shall

person
Nu 19:19 And the clean *p*· shall sprinkle upon
Eph 5: 5 nor unclean *p*·, nor covetous man, who

present
Lu 18:30 receive manifold more in this *p*· time,

pit
Job 6:27 and ye dig a *p*· for your friend.

place
Ex 28:29 when he goeth in unto the holy *p*·,

pray
Ge 24: 2 Put, I *p*· thee, thy hand under my
12 I *p*· thee, send me good speed this
14 Let down thy pitcher, I *p*· thee, that
17 Let me, I *p*· thee, drink a little water
23 daughter art thou? tell me, I *p*· thee:
43 Give me, I *p*· thee, a little water of
45 unto her, Let me drink, I *p*· thee.
27: 3 take, I *p*· thee, thy weapons, thy
44:18 let thy servant, I *p*· thee, speak a
48: 9 Bring them, I *p*· thee, unto me, and
1Sa 25:28 I *p*· thee, forgive the trespass of
2Sa 15:31 O Lord, I *p*· thee, turn the counsel
1Ki 20:35 Smite me, I *p*· thee. And the man
2Ki 2:16 let them go, we *p*· thee, and seek thy
6: 3 Be content, I *p*· thee, and go with
18:26 Speak, I *p*· thee, to thy servants in
Job 4: 7 Remember, I *p*· thee, whoever
Ps 119:76 Let, I *p*· thee, thy merciful kindness
Isa 29:12 saying, Read this, I *p*· thee:

provocation
Jer 32:31 For this city hath been to me as a *p*·

put
2Sa 20: 8 Joab's garment that he had *p*· on
1Ch 11:19 men that have *p*· their lives in jeopardy?

R.

ran
J'g 9:21 And Jotham *r*· away, and fled, and

rather
Jer 8: 3 And death shall be chosen *r*· than life

reach
Isa 30:28 overflowing stream, shall *r*· to the

reason
1Ki 14: 4 for his eyes were set by *r*· of his age.
Job 41:25 by *r*· of breakings...purify themselves.

remove
Eze 12:11 they shall *r*· and go into captivity.

right
Ps 139:14 and that my soul knoweth *r*· well.

ripe
Nu 18:13 And whatsoever is first *r*· in the

room
1Ki 19:16 thou anoint to be prophet in thy *r*·.
2Ch 6:10 for I am risen up in the *r*· of David

ruin
2Ch 28:23 But they were the *r*· of him, and

rule
Isa 44:13 carpenter stretcheth out his *r*·;

rulers
1Ki 9:22 captains, and *r*· of his chariots,

S.

save
2Ki 4: 2 in the house, *s*· a pot of oil.
2Ch 21:17 left him, *s*· Jehoahaz, the

say
Pr 23:35 They have stricken me, shalt thou *s*·,
M'r 12:43 Verily I *s*· unto you, That this

said
Ge 22: 5 And Abraham *s*· unto his young

sake
1Ch 17:19 Lord, for thy servant's *s*·, and
2Ch 6:32 far country for thy great name's *s*·,
Ps 6: 4 oh save me for thy mercies' *s*·.
69: 7 for thy *s*· I have borne reproach;
79: 9 away our sins, for thy name's *s*·.
Isa 45: 4 For Jacob my servant's *s*·, and
54:15 against thee shall fall for thy *s*·.
62: 1 and for Jerusalem's *s*· I will not
66: 5 that cast you out for my name's *s*·,
Eze 20:44 wrought with you for my name's *s*·,

sakes
Ps 106:32 it went ill with Moses for their *s*·:

same
Ge 23: 2 the *s*· as Hebron in the land of
19 Mamre: the *s*· is Hebron in the
24:14 lot the *s*· be she that thou hast
Ex 19: 1 *s*· day came they into...wilderness
27: 2 his horns shall be of the *s*·: and thou
Nu 4: 8 cover the *s*· with a covering of
2Ch 18: 7 always evil: the *s*· is Micaiah the
20:26 therefore the name of the *s*· place
Isa 20: 2 At the *s*· time spake the Lord
Lu 23:12 And the *s*· day Pilate and Herod

season
1Ch 21:29 offering, were at that *s*· in the

see
Eph 5:33 and the wife *s*· that she reverence her

seeing
Ge 22:12 *s*· thou hast not withheld thy son,
26:27 *s*· ye hate me, and have sent me away
Job 24: 1 *s*· times are not hidden from the
Pr 3:29 thy neighbour, *s*· he dwelleth securely

selves [*in most editions here* (YOUR)SELVES]
Le 11:43 Ye shall not make your *s*·
Jos 23:11 good heed therefore unto your *s*·,

separate
Jude 19 These be they who *s*· themselves,

served
1Ch 19: 5 how the men were *s*·. And he sent

set
1Sa 8:12 and will *s*· them to ear his ground,
1Ch 20: 2 in it; and it was *s*· upon David's head:
2Ch 4: 4 and the sea was *s*· above upon them,

shew
Eze 22: 2 yea, thou shalt *s*· her all her

should
Le 11:43 unclean with them, that he *s*· be defiled

shoulder
Ge 24:46 and let down her pitcher from her *s*·,

side
2Ch 11:12 having Judah and Benjamin on his *s*·.

since
Ex 9:24 all the land of Egypt *s*· it became a

sing
Isa 38:20 therefore we will *s*· my songs to

so
Ge 27: 1 old, and his eyes were dim, *s*· that he
Ex 8: 7 the magicians did *s*· with their
17 And they did *s*·; for Aaron stretched
18 the magicians did *s*· with their
18 *s*· there were lice upon man, and upon
26 Moses said, It is not meet *s*· to do;
32:21 that thou hast brought *s*· great a sin
Nu 22:30 was I ever wont to do *s*· unto thee?
35:29 *S*· these things shall be for a statute of
De 32:12 *S*· the Lord alone did lead him, and
Jos 10:13 *S*· the sun stood still in the midst of
1Ki 2:23 God do *s*· to me, and more also, if
21: 5 Why is thy spirit *s*· sad, that thou
22:12 prophesied *s*·, saying, Go up to
2Ki 4:36 *S*· he called her. And when she was
13: 5 a saviour, *s*· that they went out from
1Ch 17:15 all this vision, *s*· did Nathan speak
Job 21: 4 and if it were *s*·, why should not my
Ezr 4:13 and *s*· thou shalt endamage thy
Ps 68: 2 As smoke is driven away, *s*· drive them
103:15 flower of the field, *s*· he flourisheth.
119:134 the oppression of man: *s*· will I keep
Ec 11: 5 even *s*· thou knowest not the
Isa 5:24 *s*· their root shall be as rottenness,
14:24 as I have thought, *s*· shall it come
29: 8 *s*· shall the multitude of all the
31: 5 as birds flying, *s*· will the Lord of
Jer 35:11 Syrians: *s*· we dwell at Jerusalem.
48:39 *s*· shall Moab be a derision and a
Eze 3:14 *S*· the spirit lifted me up, and took me
19:14 *s*· that she hath no strong rod to be a
21:24 *s*· that in all your doings your sins do
Da 7:16 *S*· he told me, and made me know the
Ho 13: 6 to their pasture, *s*· were they filled;
Jon 1: 6 if *s*· be that God will think upon us,
Zec 4: 4 *S*· I answered and spake to the angel
M't 27:66 *S*· they went, and made the
1Pe 5:13 you; and *s*· doth Marcus my son.
Re 17: 3 *S*· he carried me away in the spirit

some
Ge 27: 3 to the field, and take me *s*· venison;
33:15 Let me...leave with thee *s*· of the folk
Le 14:25 the priest shall take *s*· of the blood of

sons
De 28:41 Thou shalt beget *s*· and daughters,

sooner
Jas 1:11 sun is no *s*· risen with a burning heat,

sort
Eze 23:42 men of the common *s*· were brought

sounded
Ex 19:19 when the voice of the trumpet *s*·

space
Ac 7:42 by the *s*· of forty years in the

spake
Nu 21:16 whereof the Lord *s*· unto Moses,

spread
M'r 6:14 (for his name was *s*· abroad:) and

stead
1Ki 14:20 Nadab his son reigned in his *s*·.
16:28 and Ahab his son reigned in his *s*·.
1Ch 29:28 Solomon his son reigned in his *s*·.
2Ch 26:23 Jotham his son reigned in his *s*·.
Ec 4:15 child that shall stand up in his *s*·.

still
Ru 3:18 Then said she, Sit s·, my daughter,
2Sa 14:32 good for me to have been there s·:
Isa 9:12 but his hand is stretched out s·.
stories
Eze 41:16 galleries round about on their three s·.
strange
Ps 144:11 me from the hand of s· children,
such
Ge 27: 9 meat for thy father, s· as he loveth:
14 savoury meat, s· as his father loved.
Ex 9:18 hail, s· as hath not been in Egypt
24 hail,...s· as there was none like it in
11: 6 cry...s· as there was none like it,
sunder
Isa 45: 2 and cut in s· the bars of iron:
surely
Ps 140:13 S· the righteous shall give thanks
Isa 45:24 S·, shall one say, in the Lord have I
Am 8: 7 S· I will never forget any of their
Mic 2:12 I will s· gather the remnant of Israel;
Zep 3: 7 I said, S· thou wilt fear me, thou

T.

tabernacle
Le 8:33 not go out of the door of the t·
take
Ge 13: 9 if thou wilt t· the left hand, then I will
Es 3:13 and to t· the spoil of them for a prey.
takest
Ps 144: 3 is man, that thou t· knowledge of him!
than
Nu 14:12 a greater nation and mightier t· they.
2Sa 18: 8 more people that day t· the sword
1Ki 16:25 did worse t· all that were before him.
33 to anger t· all the kings of Israel that
2Ki 16: 6 us are more t· they that be with them.
2Ch 20:25 more t· they could carry away: and
30:18 passover otherwise t· it was written.
Ezr 9:13 punished us less t· our iniquities
Ps 8: 5 made him a little lower t· the angels,
45: 2 Thou art fairer t· the children of men:
51: 7 wash me, and I shall be whiter t· snow.
61: 2 lead me to the rock that is higher t· I.
62: 9 they are altogether lighter t· vanity.
76: 4 excellent t· the mountains of prey.
89:27 higher t· the kings of the earth.
118: 8 trust...Lord t· to put confidence in man.
119:103 yea, sweeter t· honey to my mouth!
Pr 26:12 there is more hope of a fool t· of him.
16 is wiser in his own conceit t· seven men
Ec 4: 6 t· both the hands full with travail
9 Two are better t· one; because they
13 wise child t· an old and foolish king,
Ca 1: 2 mouth: for thy love is better t· wine.
4 will remember thy love more t· wine:
Isa 57: 8 hast discovered thyself to another t· me,
Jer 3:11 herself more t· treacherous Judah.
46:23 they are more t· the grasshoppers, and
La 4: 6 greater t· the punishment of the sin of
Lu 11:22 a stronger t· he shall come upon him,
Ac 17:11 These were more noble t· those in
1Ti 5: 8 the faith, and is worse t· an infidel.
themselves
Ge 21:28 set seven ewe lambs of the flock by t·.
29 ewe lambs which thou hast set by t·?
2Ki 17:32 and made unto t· of the lowest of
Job 39: 3 They bow t·, they bring forth their
Hab 2:13 people shall weary t· for very vanity?
2Pe 2:13 sporting t· with their own deceivings
then
Ex 9: 1 T· the Lord said unto Moses, Go in
18: 2 T· Jethro, Moses' father in law,
Nu 15:19 T· it shall be, that, when ye eat of the
30: 8 t· he shall make her vow which she
32:29 t· ye shall give them the land of Gilead
De 20:11 t· it shall be, that all the people that is
23:24 vineyard, t· thou mayest eat grapes
25 t· thou mayest pluck the ears with
2Sa 2:26 how long shall it be t·, ere thou bid the
15:33 t· thou shalt be a burden unto me:
24: 6 T· they came to Gilead, and to the
1Ki 2:43 Why t· hast thou not kept the oath of
Jer 17:27 t· will I kindle a fire in the gates
thence
Ge 24: 7 take a wife unto my son from t·.
27: 9 fetch me from t· two good kids of
Nu 21:16 And from t· they went to Beer: that
De 5:15 thy God brought thee out t· through
Jer 22:24 hand, yet would I pluck thee t·;
there
Ex 8:22 that no swarms of flies shall be t·;
Le 11:36 pit, wherein t· is plenty of water,
De 13:12 thy God hath given thee to dwell t·,
2Sa 18:25 he be alone, t· is tidings in his mouth.
24:13 or that t· be three days' pestilence in
M't 9:18 t· came a certain ruler, and worshipped
thereby
Ge 24:14 t· shall I know that thou hast shewed
therefore
Ge 23:15 me and thee? bury t· thy dead.
Jer 44:23 t· this evil is happened unto
thereof
Ge 2:17 thou eatest t· thou shalt surely die.
45:16 the fame t· was heard in Pharaoh's
Le 13:20 skin, and the hair t· be turned white;
these
Ge 22: 1 after t· things, that God did tempt
20 pass after t· things, that it was told
23 t· eight Milcah did bear to Nahor,
23: 1 t· were the years of the life of Sarah.
31:43 I do this day unto t· my daughters,
Ex 6:27 t· are that Moses and Aaron.
19: 6 T· are the words which thou shalt
De 6: 6 And t· words, which I command thee
1Sa 25:37 his wife had told him t· things, that
Ne 13:26 king of Israel sin by t· things?
Jer 45: 1 when he had written t· words in a
1Co 12: 2 carried away unto t· dumb idols,
Col 3: 8 put off all t·; anger, wrath, malice,
thine
Le 18:14 approach to his wife: she is t· aunt.
De 5:14 nor t· ox, nor t· ass, nor any of thy
7:13 and thy wine, and t· oil, the increase
11:19 when thou sittest in t· house, and
13: 8 neither shall t· eye pity him, neither
18: 4 of thy wine, and of t· oil, and the first
thing
Ge 18:17 hide from Abraham that t· which I do;
22:12 neither do thou any t· unto him: for
things
Ge 24: 1 the Lord had blessed Abraham in all t·.
this
Ge 24:41 shalt thou be clear from t· my oath,
38:29 t· breach be upon thee:
41:28 T· is the thing which I have
Ex 3:21 I will give t· people favour in the
12:25 that ye shall keep t· service.
43 Aaron, T· is the ordinance of the
16: 8 T· shall be, when the Lord shall give
Le 26:16 I also will do t· unto you; I will
Nu 28: 3 T· is the offering made by fire
De 11: 5 until ye came into t· place;
Ru 4:14 hath not left thee t· day without a
1Sa 12: 8 and made them dwell in t· place.
1Ch 26:30 on t· side Jordan westward in all
Job 20: 2 answer, and for t· I make haste.
Zep 1: 4 the remnant of Baal from t· place,
M't 11:14 t· is Elias, which was for to come.
1Ti 3: 1 T· is a true saying, If a man desire
Heb 7:21 but t· with an oath by him that
24 But t· man, because he continueth
thither
Ge 19:20 Oh, let me escape t·, (is it not a little
22 Haste thee, escape t·; for I cannot
22 do any thing till thou be come t·.
24: 6 thou bring not my son t· again.
1Sa 9: 6 now let us go t·; peradventure he
Eze 47: 9 because these waters shall come t·:
Joe 3:11 t· cause thy mighty ones to come
those
Nu 2:32 all t· that were numbered of the
13: 3 all t· men were heads of the children
De 29:29 but t· things which are revealed
Jos 20: 6 high priest that shall be in t· days:
Eze 39:10 shall spoil t· that spoiled them, and
10 rob t· that robbed them, saith
Lu 21:26 looking after t· things which are
Ph'p 4: 3 help t· women which laboured with
though
Nu 18:27 unto you, as t· it were the corn of the
Pr 29:19 words: for t· he understand he will not
Jer 46:23 the Lord, t· it cannot be searched;
through
2Ch 31:18 their daughters, t· all the congregation:
throughout
Ex 11: 6 a great cry t· all the land of Egypt,
thus
Ge 21:32 T· they made a covenant at
Ex 7:17 T· saith the Lord, In this thou
Eze 37: 9 T· saith the Lord God; Come from
Hag 1: 2 T· speaketh the Lord of hosts,
5 therefore t· saith the Lord of hosts;
7 T· saith the Lord of hosts; Consider
2: 6 For t· saith the Lord of hosts; Yet
11 T· saith the Lord of hosts; Ask now
Mal 1: 4 t· saith the Lord of hosts, They shall
13 t· ye brought an offering: should I
thyself
Ge 14:21 the persons, and take the goods to t·.
till
2Ki 13:17 Aphek, t· thou have consumed
Jer 49: 9 they will destroy t· they have enough.
time
Nu 14:14 them, by day t· in a pillar of a cloud,
Lu 12: 1 In the mean t·, when there were
together
Nu 24:10 Balaam, and he smote his hands t·:
Ec 4: 5 fool foldeth his hands t·, and eateth his
too
J'g 7: 2 people that are with thee are t· many for
4 The people are yet t· many; bring them
Isa 49:19 shall even now be t· narrow by reason
touching
Le 5:13 an atonement for him as t· his sin
toward
Ge 2:14 which goeth t· the east of Assyria.
12: 9 journeyed, going on still t· the south.
18: 2 door, and bowed himself t· the ground,
Ge 18:22 faces from thence, and went t· Sodom:
20: 1 journeyed from thence t· the south
Ex 9: 8 let Moses sprinkle it t· the heaven in
10 and Moses sprinkled it up t· heaven;
22 Stretch forth thine hand t· heaven,
23 stretched forth his rod t· heaven:
10:21 Stretch out thine hand t· heaven,
22 stretched forth his hand t· heaven;
26:35 the side of the tabernacle t· the south:
2Sa 24: 5 of the river of Gad, and t· Jazer:
Ps 98: 3 and his truth t· the house of Israel:
Eze 16:63 when I am pacified t· thee for all that
truly
Ge 4:24 t· Lamech seventy and sevenfold.
trust
2Ch 32:10 Whereon do ye t·, that ye abide in
two
Nu 31:27 And divide the prey into t· parts;
De 18: 3 the shoulder, and the t· cheeks, and
Jos 7:21 and t· hundred shekels of silver, and
2Ki 15:23 Israel in Samaria, and reigned t· years.
25: 4 the way of the gate between t· walls,
Ezr 2: 4 three hundred seventy and t·.
Jer 39: 4 by the gate betwixt the t· walls:
52: 7 way of the gate between the t· walls,

U.

under
Ge 24: 2 I pray thee, thy hand u· my thigh:
9 servant put his hand u· the thigh of
Ps 18:47 and subdueth the people u· me,
Ec 3: 1 time to every purpose u· the heaven:
unknown
1Co 14:13 that speaketh in an u· tongue pray
until
De 3:20 you, and u· they also possess the land
20:20 war with thee, u· it be subdued.
J'g 20:26 fasted that day u· even, and offered
2Ch 31: 1 u· they had utterly destroyed them
Ps 73:17 U· I went into the sanctuary of God;

V.

verily
Ps 73:13 V· I have cleansed my heart in
very
Ps 146: 4 in that v· day his thoughts perish.
Isa 30:19 he will be v· gracious unto thee at the
Da 6:19 the king arose v· early in the morning,
Ac 10:10 he became v· hungry, and would

W.

wast
Ru 3: 2 with whose maidens thou w·?
water
Ge 24:19 I will draw w· for thy camels also,
20 ran again unto the well to draw w·,
45 down unto the well, and drew w·:
way
Ne 8:10 Go your w·, eat the fat, and drink the
12 all the people went their w· to eat, and
Da 12:13 go thou thy w· till the end be: for thou
weights
De 25:13 shalt not have in thy bag divers w·,
well
Ge 24:62 from the way of the w· Lahai-roi;
J'g 20:48 sword, as w· the men of every city,
Pr 24:32 I saw, and considered it w·: I looked
Lu 13: 9 And if it bear fruit, w·: and if not, then
went
2Ki 7: 8 carried thence...and w· and hid it.
what
Ex 2: 4 afar off, to wit w· would be done to him.
33: 5 that I may know w· to do unto thee.
2Sa 16:20 counsel among you w· we shall do.
Isa 14:32 W· shall one then answer the
36: 4 W· confidence is this wherein thou
Eze 20:29 W· is the high place whereunto ye
M't 7: 2 with w· measure ye mete, it shall
2Co 1:13 than w· ye read or acknowledge;
11:12 But w· I do, that I will do, that I may
when
Ge 24:19 And w· she had done giving him drink,
30 w· he saw the earring and bracelets
43 that w· the virgin cometh forth to draw
Ex 2: 2 and w· she saw him that he was a
3 And w· she could not longer hide him,
3:21 that, w· ye go, ye shall not go empty:
12:48 And w· a stranger shall sojourn
18: 1 W· Jethro, the priest of Midian,
Le 11:32 any of them, w· they are dead, doth
Nu 1:51 And w· the tabernacle setteth forward,
51 and w· the tabernacle is to be pitched,
9:19 And w· the cloud tarried long upon the
Jos 10: 1 w· Adoni-zedec king of Jerusalem
2Sa 5: 4 David was thirty years old w· he began
11:13 And w· David had called him, he did
1Ki 21:16 w· Ahab heard that Naboth was dead,
2Ki 7: 8 w· these lepers came to the uttermost
10:24 And w· they went in to offer sacrifices
1Ch 7:23 w· he went in to his wife, she conceived,
2Ch 24:11 and w· they saw that there was much
Ezr 3:12 w· the foundation of this house was
9: 1 now w· these things were done, the
3 w· I heard this thing, I rent my
Job 37:17 warm, w· he quieteth the earth by the
Pr 28:12 w· the wicked rise, a man is hidden.
Isa 18: 5 afore the harvest, w· the bud is perfect,
43: 2 w· thou walkest through the fire,
Eze 20:44 w· I have wrought with you for my
23:11 And w· her sister Aholibah saw this,
29:16 w· they shall look after them:
Na 1:12 cut down, w· he shall pass through.
M't 28:11 Now w· they were going, behold,
Lu 4: 2 and w· they were ended, he afterward
13 w· the devil had ended all the
Joh 7:40 the people...w· they heard this saying,
Ac 14:14 Which w· the apostles, Barnabas and
23:34 w· he understood that he was of
27:30 w· they had let down the boat into the
28:25 And w· they agreed not among

Eph 4: 8 *W*' he ascended up on high, he led

whence
Ge 3:23 ground from *w*' he was taken.
24: 5 the land from *w*' thou camest?
Ne 4:12 From all places *w*' ye shall return
Isa 47:11 shalt not know from *w*' it riseth:

where
Ex 9:26 Goshen, *w*' the children...were,
27:18 cubits, and the breadth fifty every *w*'.
Nu 9:17 in the place *w*' the cloud abode,
Job 14:10 giveth up the ghost, and *w*' is he?

whereby
Eph 4:14 *w*' they lie in wait to deceive;

wherefore
Ge 21:31 *W*' he called that place
24:31 *w*' standest thou without? for I
Nu 11:11 and *w*' have I not found favour in
32: 7 And *w*' discourage ye the heart of
J'g 15:19 *w*' he called the name thereof
1Ki 11:11 *W*' the Lord said unto Solomon,
12:15 *W*' the king hearkened not unto the
1Ch 13:11 *W*' that place is called Perez-uzza to
Ec 3:22 *W*' I perceive that there is nothing
Jer 20:18 *W*' came I forth out of the womb

wherein
1Ki 2:26 afflicted in all *w*' my father was
Ne 9:12 light in the way *w*' they should go.
19 light, and the way *w*' they should go.
Eze 37:25 servant, *w*' your fathers have dwelt;
44:19 their garments *w*' they ministered,

whereof
Jos 14:12 *w*' the Lord spake in that day;

whereon
Le 15: 4 every thing, *w*' he sitteth,
Es 7: 8 upon the bed *w*' Esther was.

wherewith
Ex 3: 9 the oppression *w*' the Egyptians
J'g 16:13 tell me *w*' thou mightest be bound.
Eze 13:12 Where is the daubing *w*' ye have
40:42 instruments *w*' they slew the burnt

wherewithal
Ps 119: 9 *w*' shall a young man cleanse his

whether
Ge 24:21 to wit *w*' the Lord had made his
Le 22:28 And *w*' it be cow or ewe, ye shall not
Pr 29: 9 man, *w*' he rage or laugh, there is no

which
Ge 21:29 seven ewe lambs *w*' thou hast set
22: 2 the mountains *w*' I will tell thee of.
9 to the place *w*' God had told him of;
17 as the sand *w*' is upon the sea shore;
23: 9 *w*' he hath, *w*' is in the end of his
16 the silver, *w*' he had named in the
17 the field of Ephron, *w*' was in
17 Machpelah, *w*' was before Mamre,
17 field, and the cave *w*' was therein,
24: 7 *w*' took me from my father's house,
7 my kindred, and *w*' spake unto me,
24 the son of Milcah, *w*' she bare unto
26:35 *W*' were a grief of mind unto Isaac
27: 8 according to that *w*' I command
Ex 3:16 and seen that *w*' is done to you in
20 my wonders *w*' I will do in the
4:18 unto my brethren *w*' are in Egypt,
30 the words *w*' the Lord had spoken
6: 7 God, *w*' bringeth you out from unde'
7:15 the rod *w*' was turned to a serpent
8:12 the frogs *w*' he had brought against
12:10 and that *w*' remaineth of it until the
19: 6 These are the words *w*' thou shalt
Le 9: 6 is the thing *w*' the Lord commanded
22: 6 The soul *w*' hath touched any such
32 I am the Lord *w*' hallow you,
Nu 4:26 the court, *w*' is by the tabernacle
15:22 *w*' the Lord hath spoken unto
33:40 Canaanite, *w*' dwelt in the south
34:13 This is the land *w*' ye shall inherit
13 *w*' the Lord commanded to give
De 4:48 unto mount Sion, *w*' is Hermon.
11: 2 known, and *w*' have not seen the
17 good land *w*' the Lord giveth you.
13: 5 of the way *w*' the Lord thy God
23:13 and cover that *w*' cometh from thee:
24: 5 cheer up his wife *w*' he hath taken.
Jos 7:14 household *w*' the Lord shall take
J'g 2:10 nor yet the works *w*' he had done
2Sa 24:24 God of that *w*' doth cost me nothing.
2Ki 10:17 of the Lord, *w*' he spake to Elijah.
20:11 by *w*' it had gone down in the dial of
1Ch 12:32 *w*' were men that had understanding
23:29 in the pan, and for that *w*' is fried,
Job 35: 5 the clouds *w*' are higher than thou.
Ec 6: 1 There is an evil *w*' I have seen
10 That *w*' hath been is named already,
Isa 55: 2 spend money for that *w*' is not bread?
2 your labour for that *w*' satisfieth not?
2 eat ye that *w*' is good, and let your
59:21 words *w*' I have put in thy mouth,
65: 5 *W*' say, Stand by thyself, come not
Jer 3: 6 seen that *w*' backsliding Israel
41: 9 was it *w*' Asa the king had made for
Eze 33:19 do that *w*' is lawful and right, he shall
M't 24:16 Then let them *w*' be in Judæa flee
27:60 *w*' he had hewn out in the rock:
M'r 4:25 shall be taken even that *w*' he hath.
Lu 16:15 they *w*' justify yourselves before
15 for that *w*' is highly esteemed among
Joh 18:13 Caiaphas, *w*' was the high priest
Ac 13:22 heart, *w*' shall fulfil all my will.
16:21 *w*' are not lawful for us to receive,
26:22 *w*' the prophets and Moses did say
Ro 8:39 the love of God, *w*' is in Christ
10: 8 the word of faith, *w*' we preach;
2Co 9: 6 he *w*' soweth bountifully shall reap
Ga 3:23 faith *w*' should afterwards be revealed.
1Ti 6:21 *W*' some professing have erred
Heb 9: 7 blood, *w*' he offered for himself,
Re 22: 6 the things *w*' must shortly be done.

while
Le 26:43 *w*' she lieth desolate without them:
Nu 25:11 *w*' he was zealous for my sake among
J'g 14:17 seven days, *w*' their feast lasted:
1Ch 21:12 *w*' that the sword of thine enemies

whilst
Job 8:12 *W*' it is yet in his greenness, and not

whither
Jer 40:12 all places *w*' they were driven,
42:22 in the place *w*' ye desire to go
43: 5 nations, *w*' they had been driven,
44: 8 Egypt, *w*' ye be gone to dwell,

who
Ge 27:18 Here am I; *w*' art thou, my son?
Ex 12:27 *w*' passed over the houses of
Nu 16: 5 the Lord will shew *w*' are his,
5 and *w*' is holy; and will cause him
J'g 7: 1 Then Jerubbaal, *w*' is Gideon, and
1Sa 10:12 and said, But *w*' is their father?
2Sa 1:24 *w*' clothed you in scarlet, with other
24 *w*' put on ornaments of gold
4: 5 Ish-bosheth, *w*' lay on a bed at
1Ki 2:32 *w*' fell upon two men more
1Ch 4:22 *w*' had the dominion in Moab, and
8:12 and Shamed, *w*' built Ono, and
Ps 73:12 the ungodly, *w*' prosper in the world;
Ec 2:19 And *w*' knoweth whether he shall
6:12 for *w*' can tell a man what shall be
Mic 3: 2 *W*' hate the good, and love the evil;
2 *w*' pluck off their skin from off
3 *W*' also eat the flesh of my people,
Col 1: 7 *w*' is for you a faithful minister of
1Th 2:12 of God, *w*' hath called you unto his

whole
Ex 10:15 covered the face of the *w*' earth,
2Ch 16: 9 run to and fro through the *w*' earth,
Ps 138: 1 will praise thee with my *w*' heart:
Jer 3:10 turned unto me with her *w*' heart,

whom
Ge 24: 3 the Canaanites, among *w*' I dwell:
14 the damsel to *w*' I shall say, Let
44 woman *w*' the Lord hath appointed
47 Nahor's son, *w*' Milcah bare unto
Nu 26:59 *w*' her mother bare to Levi in
1Ch 7:21 *w*' the men of Gath that were born
Ca 3: 4 I found him *w*' my soul loveth: I held
Jer 50:20 I will pardon them *w*' I reserve.
Lu 7: 4 worthy for *w*' he should do this:
Ac 3:16 made this man strong, *w*' ye see
21 *W*' the heaven must receive until
4:27 child Jesus, *w*' thou hast anointed,
6: 3 *w*' we may appoint over this
17: 3 Jesus, *w*' I preach unto you, is
19:25 *W*' he called together with the
Ro 8:29 For *w*' he did foreknow, he also did
Eph 1:13 in *w*' also after that ye believed,
3Jo 1 Gaius, *w*' I love in the truth.

whose
Ge 24:37 Canaanites, in *w*' land I dwell:
1Ch 13: 6 cherubims, *w*' name is called on it.
Ezr 8:13 sons of Adonikam, *w*' names are these,
Ec 2:21 For there is a man *w*' labour is in
Da 4:37 all *w*' works are truth, and all his
Ac 13: 6 a Jew, *w*' name was Bar-jesus:
Re 9:11 *w*' name in the Hebrew tongue is

whoso
Pr 1:33 But *w*' hearkeneth unto me shall dwell
18:22 *W*' findeth a wife findeth a good thing,
1Jo 3:17 But *w*' hath this world's good,

whosoever
Ex 12:15 for *w*' eateth leavened bread from
2Ki 21:12 *w*' heareth of it, both his ears shall

why
2Ki 14:10 for *w*' shouldest thou meddle to
Ps 42: 5 *W*' art thou cast down, O my soul?
Pr 5:20 *w*' wilt thou, my son, be ravished

wife
Ex 2: 1 Levi, and took to *w*' a daughter of Levi.

will
Le 27:13 if he *w*' at all redeem it, then he shall
2Ch 10: 7 them, they *w*' be thy servants for ever.
Isa 37: 7 I *w*' send a blast upon him, and he shall
7 I *w*' cause him to fall by the sword in
35 For I *w*' defend this city to save it for
Jer 23: 4 And I *w*' set up shepherds over them
34 *w*' even punish that man and his house.
32:44 I *w*' cause their captivity to return,
43:10 I *w*' send and take Nebuchadrezzar
10 and *w*' set his throne upon these stones
51:22 *w*' I break in pieces man and woman.
22 *w*' I break in pieces old and young;
22 *w*' I break in pieces the young man and
M'r 1:17 *w*' make you to become fishers of men.
Ac 15:16 *w*' build again the ruins thereof, and I
16 the ruins thereof, and I *w*' set it up:
2Co 11: 9 unto you, and so *w*' I keep myself.

wilt
2Sa 5:19 *w*' thou deliver them into mine hand?
M't 7: 4 *w*' thou say to thy brother, Let me pull
Lu 18:41 What *w*' thou that I shall do unto

wit
Ne 11: 3 cities, to *w*', Israel, the priests, and the

withal
2Ki 23:26 that Manasseh had provoked him *w*'.

within
De 12:12 the Levite that is *w*' your gates;
Ezr 10: 8 would not come *w*' three days,

without
Ex 21:11 then shall she go out free *w*' money.
1Ki 22: 1 three years *w*' war between Syria and
Ps 59: 4 prepare themselves *w*' my fault:
Jer 4: 7 be laid waste, *w*' an inhabitant.
15:13 will I give to the spoil *w*' price,

woman
Nu 25:14 was slain with the Midianitish *w*'.
Pr 5: 3 For the lips of a strange *w*' drop as an
20 my son, be ravished with a strange *w*',

women
Ge 24:11 the time that *w*' go out to draw water.
Job 2:10 as one of the foolish *w*' speaketh.
Pr 23:33 Thine eyes shall behold strange *w*'.
Isa 32:10 shall ye be troubled, ye careless *w*':
Eze 23:45 after the manner of *w*' that shed blood;

wood
Ex 26:37 the hanging five pillars of shittim *w*',
Ps 141: 7 and cleaveth *w*' upon the earth.

words
Joh 17: 1 These *w*' spake Jesus, and lifted up

worth
Ge 23:15 is *w*' four hundred shekels of silver;

would
Ga 3: 8 foreseeing that God *w*' justify the
2Jo 12 I *w*' not write with paper and ink:
3Jo 10 forbiddeth them that *w*', and casteth

wrought
Ex 26:36 twined linen, *w*' with needlework.

Y.

yea
2Ch 26:20 *y*', himself hasted also to go out, because
Ps 23: 4 *y*', though I walk through the valley
35:27 *y*', let them say continually, Let the
43: 4 *y*', upon the harp will I praise thee, O
Isa 43:13 *y*', before the day was I am he; and
Ho 9:16 *y*', though they bring forth, yet will
Lu 14:26 *y*', and his own life also, he cannot
Ro 8:34 died, *y*' rather, that is risen again,

yet
Nu 19:13 his uncleanness is *y*' upon him.
2Sa 12:22 While the child was *y*' alive, I fasted
2Ch 27: 2 And the people did *y*' corruptly.
Ph'p 2:25 *Y*' I supposed it necessary to send
Re 17: 8 that was, and is not, and *y*' is.

your
Le 26:28 chastise you seven times for *y*' sins.
De 5:23 the heads of *y*' tribes, and *y*' elders:

yourselves [*so most editions in these places*]
Le 11:43 not make [*your selves*] abominable
Jos 23:11 heed therefore unto [*your selves*].